BOOKS
IN PRINT
1988–89

This edition of BOOKS IN PRINT was
prepared by R. R. Bowker's Database
Publishing Group in collaboration with the
Publication Systems Department.

Peter Simon, Vice President, Database Publishing Group
Ernest Lee, Director, Bibliographies
Albert Simmonds, Managing Editor
Basmattie Gravesande and Brian Phair, Senior Editors
John Thompson, Senior Associate Editor, Quality Control
Dereck Rousch, Associate Editor
Frank Accurso, Allan Baptiste, Domonique Fernandez,
Yvonne Holness, Malcolm MacDermott,
Myriam Nunez, Raymond Padilla, Beverly Palacio,
Joan Russell, George Tibbetts,
and Joseph Tondi, Assistant Editors.

Names & Numbers:
Brenda A. McElroy, Managing Editor
Keith L. Schiffman, Senior Editor
Rynita Anderson, Xavier Anderson and
Vincent Fiorillo, Assistant Editors.

Michael Gold, Director, Systems Development
Jack Murphy, Computer Operations Manager.

BOOKS IN PRINT

1988–89

VOLUME 6

TITLES • P–Z

R.R. BOWKER

New York

Published by R. R. Bowker a division of Reed Publishing (USA) Inc.
Copyright © 1988 by Reed Publishing (USA) Inc.
All rights reserved.

International Standard Book Numbers: Set 0-8352-2485-6
Vol. 1 0-8352-2486-4, Vol. 2 0-8352-2487-2
Vol. 3 0-8352-2488-0, Vol. 4 0-8352-2489-9
Vol. 5 0-8352-2490-2, Vol. 6 0-8352-2491-0
Vol. 7 0-8352-2492-9
International Standard Serial Number 0068-0214
Library of Congress Catalog Card Number 4-12648

Printed and bound in the United States of America

ISBN 0-8352-2485-6

9 780835 224857

BOOKS IN PRINT
1988-89
VOLUME 6
TITLES
P-Z

P

P. A. Stolypin & the Third Duma: An Appraisal of the Three Major Issues. George Tokmakoff. LC 81-40349. (Illus.). 258p. (Orig.). 1982. lib. bdg. 30.50 (ISBN 0-8191-2058-8); pap. text ed. 14.00 (ISBN 0-8191-2059-6). U Pr of Amer.

P-Adic Analysis. N. Koblitz. (London Mathematical Society Lecture Note Ser.: No. 46). 150p. 1980. pap. 17.95 (ISBN 0-521-28060-5). Cambridge U Pr.

P-Adic Numbers & Their Functions. 2nd ed. Kurt Mahler. LC 79-20103. (Cambridge Tracts in Mathematics Ser.: No. 76). 1981. 59.50 (ISBN 0-521-23102-7). Cambridge U Pr.

P-Adic Numbers, P-Adic Analysis & Zeta Functions. 2nd ed. N. Koblitz. (Graduate Tests in Mathematics Ser.: Vol. 58). (Illus.). 288p. 1984. 34.00 (ISBN 0-387-96017-1). Springer-Verlag.

P. Aelius Aristides: The Complete Works, Vol. 1. Charles Behr. viii, 538p. 1986. 100.00 (ISBN 90-04-07844-4, Pub. by E J Brill). Heinman.

P & C NMR of Transition Metal Phosphine Complexes. P. S. Pregosin & R. W. Kunz. (NMR Ser.: Vol. 16). (Illus.). 1979. 47.00 (ISBN 0-387-09163-7). Springer-Verlag.

P & I Clubs. Christopher Hill et al. 1988. write for info. (ISBN 1-850441-63-4). Lloyds London Pr.

P & L Basics for Nonfinancial Managers. Joseph P. Simini. 1989. pap. 11.95 (ISBN 0-471-61830-6). Wiley.

P. B. Wight: Architect, Contractor, & Critic, 1838-1925. Sarah B. Landau. LC 80-70799. (Illus.). 108p. 1981. pap. 14.95 (ISBN 0-86559-051-6). Art Inst Chi.

P. B. Young, Newspaperman: Race, Politics, & Journalism in the New South, 1910-62. Henry L. Suggs. LC 88-14200. (Illus.). 375p. 1988. text ed. 24.95x (ISBN 0-8139-1178-8). U Pr of Va.

P. D. James. Patricia Barney. (Mystery & Detective Ser.: No. 3). Date not set. 17.95; pap. 9.95. Starmont Hse.

P. D. James. Richard B. Gidez. (Twayne English Authors Ser.: No. 430). 184p. 1986. lib. bdg. 15.95x (ISBN 0-8057-6924-2, Twayne); (Twayne). G K Hall.

P. D. James. Norma Siebenheller. LC 81-40473. (Recognitions Ser.). 162p. 1981. 16.95x (ISBN 0-8044-2817-4). Ungar.

P. D. R. Yemen: Outpost of Socialist Development in Arabia. Helen Lackner. (Political Studies of the Middle East: No. 27). (Illus.). 232p. 1985. 32.50 (ISBN 0-86372-032-3, Pub. by Ithaca Pr UK). Humanities.

P. E. Curriculum Guide. John Ortwerth & Mel J. Nicks. (Illus.). 160p. (gr. 1-6). 1984. wkbk. 10.95 (ISBN 0-86653-262-5). Good Apple.

P. E. N. New Fiction One. Ed. by Peter Ackroyd. 246p. 1985. 14.95 (ISBN 0-7043-2453-9, Pub. by Quartet Bks). Salem Hse Pubs.

P. E. N. New Poetry, No. 1. Robert Nye. 312p. 1986. 19.95 (ISBN 0-7043-2565-9, Pub. by Quartet Bks). Salem Hse Pubs.

P. E. P. P. E. R. Dinosaurs Procedural Educational Plan for Primary Enrichment Resource Activities. Nancy L. Dehnbostel & Mary E. Hartman. (Illus.). 72p. (Orig.). 1981. pap. text ed. 5.95 (ISBN 0-914634-95-X). DOK Pubs.

P. E. P.-The Productivity Effectiveness Program. Robert Gedaliah. 1984. pap. 2.95 (ISBN 0-03-069866-9). H Holt & Co.

P. E. T. in Action. Thomas Gordon & Judith S. Sands. 1984. pap. 4.95 (ISBN 0-553-24556-2). Bantam.

P. E. T. (Parent Effectiveness Training) Thomas Gordon. 14.95 (ISBN 0-317-63115-2). McKay.

P-Functions & Boolean Matrix Factorization: A Unified Approach for Wired, Programmed & Microprogrammed Implementations of Discrete Algorithms. A. Thayse. (Lecture Notes in Computer Science Ser.: Vol. 175). xii, 248p. 1984. pap. 18.50 (ISBN 0-387-13358-5). Springer-Verlag.

P. G. T. Beauregard: Napoleon in Gray. T. Harry Williams. LC 55-7362. (Southern Biography Ser.). (Illus.). xiv, 346p. 1955. 24.95 (ISBN 0-8071-0831-6). La State U Pr.

P. G. Wodehouse: A Portrait of a Master. rev. ed. David A. Jasen. (Illus.). 352p. 1981. pap. 8.95 (ISBN 0-8264-0033-7). Continuum.

P. G. Wodehouse at Dulwich. Ed. by David Emms & Robert MacDowell. (Wodehouse Monographs: No. 5). 44p. (Orig.). Date not set. pap. 16.50 (ISBN 0-87008-104-7). Heineman.

P. G. Wodehouse Checklist. Ed. by J. Clauss. 7.95 (ISBN 0-89190-843-9, Pub. by Am Repr). Amereon Ltd.

P. G. Wodehouse: Five Complete Novels. (Avenel Readers Library). 720p. 1983. 7.98 (ISBN 0-517-40538-5, Avenel). Outlet Bk Co.

P. G. Wodehouse: Three Talks & a Few Words at a Festive Occasion. William Douglas-Home & Malcolm Muggeridge. (Wodehouse Monograph: No. 4). 48p. (Orig.). 1983. pap. 16.50 limited ed. (ISBN 0-87008-103-9). Heineman.

P. G. Wodehouse 1881-1981: Addresses Given by Frances Donaldson & Richard Usborne. Frances Donaldson & Richard Usborne. (Wodehouse Monograph: No. 2). 44p. (Orig.). 1982. pap. 14.50 (ISBN 0-87008-101-2). Heineman.

P. H. C.'s Lessons in Magic: Eighteen Sixty-Five to Eighteen Sixty-Eight. Henry Hatton & Marjie Buffum. LC 79-52207. (Illus.). Date not set. price not set (ISBN 0-934542-01-5). Abracadabra Pr.

P. H. Emerson: The Fight for Photography As a Fine Art. Nancy Newhall. LC 74-76911. (Aperture Monograph). (Illus.). 266p. pap. 20.00 (ISBN 0-912334-59-2). Aperture.

P-H Encyclopedia of World Proverbs. Wolfgang Mieder. LC 85-12345. 582p. 1986. 34.95 (ISBN 0-13-695586-X). P-H.

P-H Executive Action Report. (Information Services Ser.). Date not set. price not set ring bound l'leaf. P-H.

P. J. Andrea Balis & Robert Reiser. 160p. (gr. 3-6). 1984. 10.95 (ISBN 0-395-36006-4, 5-81180). HM.

P. J. Andrea Balis & Robert Reiser. (gr. k-6). 1987. pap. 2.95 (ISBN 0-440-46880-9, YB). Dell.

P. J. Clover, Private Eye: The Case of the Missing Mouse. Susan Meyers. (Illus.). 128p. (gr. 4-6). 1985. 11.95 (ISBN 0-525-67162-5, 01160-350). Lodestar Bks.

P. J. Clover, Private Eye: The Case of the Stolen Laundry. Susan Meyers. (Illus.). 128p. (Orig.). (gr. 3-7). 1981. Wanderer Bks.

P. J. Funnybunny in the Perfect Hiding Place. Marilyn Sadler. 1988. 1.60 (ISBN 0-307-11746-4, 11746, Pub. by Golden Bks). Western Pub.

P. J. Proudhon: A Chronology. V. Munoz. Tr. by W. Scott Johnson. (Libertarian & Anarchist Chronology Ser.). 1979. lib. bdg. 59.95 (ISBN 0-8490-3038-2). Gordon Pr.

P. Korin: Selected Works. E. V. Vinogradova. 1985. 67.00x (ISBN 0-317-61337-5, Pub. by Collets (UK)). State Mutual Bk.

P. L. Roederer: Political Thought & Practice During the French Revolution. Kenneth Margerison. LC 81-71030. (Transactions Ser.: Vol. 73, Pt. 1). (Illus.). 167p. 1983. 12.00 (ISBN 0-87169-731-9). Am Philos.

P. L. 94-142: Impact on the Schools. Roberta Weiner. LC 86-73365. 362p. (Orig.). 1985. pap. 18.00 (ISBN 0-937925-01-2). Capitol VA.

P. Lal: An Appreciation. S. Mokashi-Punekar. (Greybird Ser.). 1975. flexible bdg. 4.00 (ISBN 0-89253-790-6). Ind-US Inc.

P. M. D. Lekas. LC 84-91446. 1985. pap. 2.00 (ISBN 0-930759-05-2). D Lekas.

P. M. Friesen & His History: Understanding Mennonite Brethren Beginnings. Abraham Friesen. (Perspective on Mennonite Life & Thought Ser.: Vol. 2). 176p. (Orig.). 1979. pap. 5.95 (ISBN 0-318-18906-2). Kindred Pr.

P-M Principles & Production Processes. Ed. by H. H. Hausner & P. W. Taubenblat. (Modern Developments in Powder Metallurgy: Vol. 9). 1977. 42.50x (ISBN 0-918404-38-X). Metal Powder.

P-M Special Materials & Applications. Ed. by H. H. Hausner & P. W. Taubenblat. (Modern Developments in Powder Metallurgy: Vol. 11). 1977. 42.50x (ISBN 0-918404-40-1). Metal Powder.

P. O. W. (Vietnam Ground Zero Ser.: No. 2). Date not set. pap. 2.75 (Pub. by Worldwide). Harlequin Bks.

P. O. W. - The Uncivil Face of War. Richard Garrett. (Battle Standards Ser.). (Illus.). 240p. (Orig.). 1988. pap. 7.95 (ISBN 0-7153-9201-8, Pub. by David & Charles Pub England). Sterling.

P. Ovidi Nasonis Metamorphoseon liber I. Ovid. Ed. by A. G. Lee. LC 78-67140. pap. 42.50 (ISBN 0-317-27536-4, 2024505). Bks Demand UMI.

P. Ovidi Nasonis Metamorphoseon: Ovid's Metamorphoses, 15 bks. Ovid. Set. lib. bdg. write for info. Ayer Co Pubs.

P: Proceedings, 1980 Seminar on Harmonic Analysis. Ed. by C. Herz & R. Rigelhof. LC 81-19116. (Canadian Mathematical Society Conference: No. 1). 1982. pap. 18.00 (ISBN 0-8218-6000-3). Am Math.

P-Prolog - a Parallel Logic Programming Language. Rong Yang. 152p. 1988. 39.00 (ISBN 9971-50-508-8). World Scientific Pub.

P. R. B. Journal: William Michel Rossetti's Diary of the Pre-Raphaelite Brotherhood 1849-1853, Together with the Other Pre-Raphaelite Documents. William M. Rossetti. Ed. by William D. Fredeman. (Illus., Ed. from the original manuscript with an introduction and notes.). 1975. 49.95x (ISBN 0-19-812505-4). Oxford U Pr.

P. R. Manual. 1986. binder 56.00 (ISBN 0-317-55572-3). Am Phys Therapy Assn.

P. S. I Love You. Barbara Conklin. (Orig.). 1981. pap. 2.25 (ISBN 0-553-24460-4). Bantam.

P. S. What Do You Think of the Market. James L. Fraser. LC 66-29458. (Orig.). 1966. Repr. of 1920 ed. 5.00 (ISBN 0-87034-023-9). Fraser Pub Co.

P. S. Write Soon. Colby Rodowsky. 158p. (gr. 5 up). 1987. pap. 3.50 (ISBN 0-374-46032-9, Sunburst). FS&G.

P. S. Write Soon! All about Letters. Intro. by William F. Bolger. LC 82-600641. 64p. (Orig.). (gr. 4-8). 1982. pap. 2.50x (ISBN 0-8141-3796-2, 37962). USPS.

P. S. Your Cat Is Dead. James Kirkwood. 224p. 1973. pap. 3.95 (ISBN 0-446-30705-X). Warner Bks.

P. S. You're Not Listening. Eleanor Craig. 224p. 1973. pap. 3.50 (ISBN 0-451-13439-7, AE2194, Sig). NAL.

P-Sourcebook. Randy Hyde. 1983. 24.95 (ISBN 0-8359-5410-2, Reston). P-H.

P-Stat User's Manual. Buhler. 1985. text ed. 12.50 (ISBN 0-87150-838-9, 36G2200, Duxbury Pr). PWS Kent Pub.

P. T. Barnum Presents Jenny Lind: The American Tour of the Swedish Nightingale. W. Porter Ware & Thaddeus Lockard. LC 80-11150. xxii, 298p. 1980. 30.00 (ISBN 0-8071-0687-9). La State U Pr.

P. T. Forsyth: Per Crucem Ad Lucem. Archibald M. Hunter. LC 75-502308. 1974. pap. text ed. 5.00x (ISBN 0-8401-1146-0). A R Allenson.

P. T. Forsyth: The Man, the Preacher's Theologian & Prophet for the Twentieth Century. Donald G. Miller et al. (Pittsburgh Theological Monograph Ser.: No. 36). 1981. pap. 18.00 (ISBN 0-915138-48-4). Pickwick.

P. U. R. Analysis of Investor-Owned Electric & Gas Utilities, 1987. 6th ed. Ed. by Susan M. Johnson. (Illus.). 427p. 1987. pap. 195.00 (ISBN 0-910325-17-0). Public Util.

P. Vergilius Maro Aeneis Buch VI, Eklart von Eduard Norden. Vergilius. LC 75-41282. Repr. of 1903 ed. 30.00 (ISBN 0-404-14727-5). AMS Pr.

P. W. M. U. Cookery Book. rev. ed. 1979. pap. 4.95x (ISBN 0-85091-042-0, Pub. by Lothian). Intl Spec Bk.

P. Z. & the Snow Ghost. Ronald Tracy. 23p. 1987. 4.95 (ISBN 0-533-06903-3). Vantage.

P 0 2 Euclidean (Quantum) Field Theory. Barry Simon. (Princeton Series in Physics). 450p. 1974. 55.50x (ISBN 0-691-08143-3); pap. 15.95 (ISBN 0-691-08144-1). Princeton U Pr.

P-38 Lightning in Action. Gene Stafford. (Aircraft in Action Ser.). (Illus.). 50p. 1984. pap. 5.95 (ISBN 0-89747-024-9, 1025). Squad Sig Pubns.
P-39, P-63 in Action. 1980. pap. 5.95 (ISBN 0-89747-102-4). Squad Sig Pubns.
P-450 & Chemical Carcinogenesis. Ed. by Yusaku Tagashira & Tsuneo Omura. (GANN Monographs on Cancer Research: No. 30). 190p. 1985. 59.50x (ISBN 0-306-42123-2, Plenum Pr). Plenum Pub.
P-47 Thunderbolt in Action. Larry Davis. (Aircraft in Action Ser.). 50p. 1985. pap. 5.95 (ISBN 0-89747-161-X, 1067). Squad Sig Pubns.
P-50 Mustang in Color. Larry Davis. (Fighting Colors Ser.). (Illus.). 32p. 1984. pap. 5.95 (ISBN 0-89747-135-0, 6505). Squad Sig Pubns.
P-51 Mustang. Len Morgan. LC 63-14945. (Famous Aircraft Ser.). (Illus.). 1979. pap. 7.95 (ISBN 0-8168-5647-8, 25647, TAB-Aero). TAB Bks.
P-51 Mustang. P-51 Mustang Pilots Assoc. Staff. LC 87-51161. 144p. 1987. 45.00 (ISBN 0-938021-56-7). Turner Pub KY.
P-51 Mustang in Action. (Aircraft in Action Ser.). (Illus.). 58p. 1984. pap. 5.95 (ISBN 0-89747-114-8, 1045). Squad Sig Pubns.
P-61 Black Widow. (Illus.). 72p. 1974. pap. 7.95 (ISBN 0-87994-025-5). Aviat Pub.
P-80 Shooting Star: Evolution of a Jet Fighter. E. T. Wooldridge, Jr. LC 79-17648. (Famous Aircraft of the National Air & Space Museum Ser.: Vol. 3). (Illus.). 110p. 1979. pap. 8.95 (ISBN 0-87474-965-4, WOP8P). Smithsonian.
P-80 Shooting Star in Action. Larry Davis. (Aircraft in Action Ser.). (Illus.). 1984. pap. 5.95 (ISBN 0-89747-099-0, 1040). Squad Sig Pubns.
PA-Four Locomotive. Norman E. Anderson & C. G. Macdermot. LC 78-51249. (Illus.). 128p. 1978. 27.50 (ISBN 0-89685-035-8). Chatham Pub CA.
Pa Kua Chang, Vol. I. James Keenan. LC 84-52684. 180p. (Orig.). 1986. pap. write for info. (ISBN 0-86568-063-9, 218). Unique Pubns.
Pa Kua Chang, Vol. II. James Keenan. LC 84-52684. 180p. (Orig.). 1986. pap. write for info. (ISBN 0-86568-064-7, 219). Unique Pubns.
Pa-Kua Chang for Self-Defense. Lee Ying-Arng. 9.95x (ISBN 0-685-63771-9). Wehman.
Pa Pong: A Siamese Kitty. Phillip C. Snyder. (Illus.). 28p. (ps-1). 1981. pap. text ed. 3.95 (ISBN 0-940560-03-8). Custom Hse.
PAB Conference Report & Follow-Up. James L. Olivero & Irving S. Sato. (Brief Ser.: No. 1). 24p. 2.40 (ISBN 0-318-02112-9). NSLTIGT.
Pablo. Gordon Stowell. Tr. by S. D. de Lerin from Eng. (Libros Pescaditos Sobre Personajes Biblicos). Orig. Title: Paul: (Illus.). 24p. (gr. 1). 1981. pap. 0.60 (ISBN 0-311-38518-4, Edit Mundo). Casa Bautista.
Pablo Casals. rev. ed. Lillian Littlehales. Repr. of 1948 ed. lib. bdg. 35.00x (ISBN 0-8371-3010-7, LIPC). Greenwood.
Pablo Casals in Puerto Rico. Arturo O. Quintana. (Puerto Rico Ser.). 1979. lib. bdg. 59.95 (ISBN 0-8490-2981-3). Gordon Pr.
Pablo Cruz & the American Dream: The Experiences of an Undocumented Immigrant from Mexico. Eugene Nelson. LC 74-19157. (Illus.). 1977. text ed. 5.95 (ISBN 0-268-01525-2). U of Notre Dame Pr.
Pablo, el Lider. J. Oswald Sanders. 208p. (Span.). 1986. pap. 3.50 (ISBN 0-8297-0760-3). Life Pubs Intl.
Pablo Neruda. Marjorie Agosin. (Twayne's World Authors Ser.: 769). 176p. 1986. lib. bdg. 19.95 (ISBN 0-8057-6620-0, Twayne). G K Hall.
Pablo Neruda: All Poets the Poet. Salvatore Bizzarro. LC 78-24437. 204p. 1979. lib. bdg. 17.50 (ISBN 0-8108-1189-8). Scarecrow.
Pablo Neruda: An Annotated Bibliography. David S. Zubatsky & Hensley C. Woodbridge. LC 84-48872. 400p. 1986. lib. bdg. 50.00 (ISBN 0-8240-8732-1). Garland Pub.
Pablo Neruda: An Annotated Bibliography of Biographical & Critical Studies. Hensley C. Woodbridge & David S. Zubatsky. (Reference Library of the Humanities). 638p. 1988. lib. bdg. 80.00. Garland Pub.
Pablo Neruda: The Politics of Prophecy. Enrico M. Santi. 256p. 1982. 29.95x (ISBN 0-8014-1472-5). Cornell U Pr.
Pablo Picasso. Lepscky. LC 83-347. (Famous People Ser.). 24p. 1984. 6.95 (ISBN 0-8120-5511-X). Barron.
Pablo Picasso. Herman Nedoshivin. (Masters of World Painting Ser.). (Illus.). 1983. 30.00x (ISBN 0-317-57404-3, Pub. by Collets UK). State Mutual Bk.
Pablo Picasso. Ernest Raboff. LC 87-45156. (Art for Children Ser.). (Illus.). 32p. (gr. 1 up). 1987. 11.95i (ISBN 0-397-32224-0, Lipp Jr Bks). HarpJ.
Pablo Picasso. Ernest Raboff. LC 87-45147. (Trophy Nonfiction Art for Children Bks.). (Illus.). 32p. (gr. 1 up). 1987. pap. 5.95 (ISBN 0-06-446068-1, Trophy). HarpJ.
Pablo Picasso: A Retrospective. Ed. by William Rubin. LC 80-80107. (Illus.). 464p. 1980. 50.00 (ISBN 0-87070-528-8, 707023, Pub. by Museum Mod Art); pap. 25.00 (ISBN 0-87070-519-9, 707031, Pub. by Museum Mod Art). NYGS.
Pablo Picasso: Catalogue of the Printed Graphic Work 1904-1972, 3 Vols. Georges Bloch. 911p. 1971-79. 350.00 (ISBN 0-686-87741-1). A Wofsy Fine Arts.
Pablo Picasso: The Minotaur, An Art Play Book. Text by Daniele Giraudy. (Illus.). 32p. (gr. 2 up). 1988. 17.95 (ISBN 0-8109-1471-9). Abrams.
Pablo Picasso, Twentieth Century Genius. Patricia D. Frevert. Ed. by Ann Redpath. (People to Remember Ser.). (Illus.). 32p. (gr. 4 up). 1981. PLB 8.95 (ISBN 0-87191-800-5). Creative Ed.
Pablo's Petunias. Prieto. LC 72-190269. (Illus.). 32p. (gr. 3-5). 1972. PLB 9.95 (ISBN 0-87783-058-4); pap. 3.94 deluxe ed. (ISBN 0-87783-102-5). Oddo.
Pabna Disturbances & the Politics of Rent: 1873-1885. Kalyan Sen Gupta. LC 74-903853. 1974. 7.75x (ISBN 0-8364-0441-6). South Asia Bks.
PABX Market. Frost & Sullivan, Inc. Staff. 277p. 1986. 1750.00 (ISBN 0-86621-791-6, A1611). Frost & Sullivan.
PAC Directory, 1981-82, Book I: The Federal Candidates. Ed. by Marvin I. Weinberger et al. 984p. 1984. professional reference 95.00x (ISBN 0-88410-979-8). Ballinger Pub.
PAC Directory, 1981-82, Book II: The Federal Committees. Ed. by Marvin I. Weinberger et al. 880p. 1984. professional reference 95.00x (ISBN 0-88410-980-1). Ballinger Pub.
Pac-Finder System 34-36 Software Directory. 2nd ed. Produced by Mincron. 752p. 1984. pap. 112.25 (ISBN 0-444-00920-5). Elsevier.
PAC Power: Inside the World of Political Action Committees. Larry J. Sabato. LC 84-6068. 280p. 1984. 15.95 (ISBN 0-393-01857-1). Norton.
PAC Power: Inside the World of Political Action Committees. Larry J. Sabato. 259p. 1985. pap. 5.95 (ISBN 0-393-30257-1). Norton.
Pac-Ten Football Guide & Record Book. Thomas L. Miller. (Illus.). 192p. (Orig.). 1984. pap. 9.95 (ISBN 0-88011-228-X). Scribner.
Pac-Ten Football: The Rose Bowl Conference. John D. McCallum. (Illus.). 352p. 1982. 6.43 (ISBN 0-916076-52-0); pap. text ed. 4.00 (ISBN 0-916076-56-3). Writing.
Pacatnamu Papers, Vol. I. Ed. by Guillermo A. Cock & Christopher B. Donnan. LC 86-61112. (Illus.). 192p. (Orig.). 1986. text ed. 35.00 (ISBN 0-930741-14-5); pap. text ed. 19.00 (ISBN 0-930741-11-0). UCLA Mus Cultural Hist.
Pacatus, a Trade-Mark from Antiquity. Joseph Domjan & Evelyn A. Domjan. Ed. by Jane Emig. LC 78-73444. (Illus.). 1979. 15.00 (ISBN 0-933652-13-5). Domjan Studio.
Pacatus Panegyric to the Emperor Theodosius. C. E. Nixon. (Translated Texts for Historians - Latin Ser.). 128p. 1987. pap. text ed. 19.95 (ISBN 0-85323-076-5, Pub. by Liverpool U Pr). Humanities.
Pace-A Program for Acquiring Competence in Entrepreneurship. rev. ed. 166p. 1983. 120.00 set (ISBN 0-318-15525-7, RD240). Natl Ctr Res Voc Ed.
Pace III: A Study of Consumer Attitudes on ATMs, Debit-Credit Cards, Home Banking, Direct Deposit, Bill Paying Services, POS Services. 145.00 (ISBN 0-318-01808-X, PACE). Bank MKTG Assn.
Pace IV: Payment Attitudes Change Evaluation, Consumer Use & Attitudes. 1986. 195.00 (ISBN 0-318-20647-1). Bank Mktg Assn.
Pace of Change: Selected Articles on Politics & Society in Prerevolutionary America. Ed. by Peter C. Hoffer. (Early American History Ser.). 375p. 1987. lib. bdg. 60.00 (ISBN 0-8240-6244-2). Garland Pub.
Pace That Kills. Edgar Saltus. LC 79-93535. Repr. of 1889 ed. 17.50 (ISBN 0-404-05508-7). AMS Pr.
Pacem in Terris: Encyclical Letter "Peace on Earth". Pope John Paul XXIII. 2.95 (ISBN 0-8091-5106-5). Paulist Pr.
Pacemaker. Linda Brino. 352p. (Orig.). 1987. pap. 3.95 (ISBN 0-8439-2444-6, Leisure Bks). Leisure NY.
Pacemaker Leads: Proceedings of the International Symposium on Pacemaker Leads Leven, Belgium, September 5-7, 1984. Ed. by A. E. Aubert & H. Ector. (Progress in Biomedical Engineering Ser.: No. 2). 420p. 1985. 123.75 (ISBN 0-444-42516-0). Elsevier.
Pacemaker Therapy. Leonard S. Dreifus. LC 83-1949. (Cardiovascular Clinics Ser.: Vol. 14, No. 2). (Illus.). 287p. 1983. text ed. 45.00x (ISBN 0-8036-2901-X). Davis Co.
Pacemakers: Medical Subject Analysis with Bibliography. Judd R. Trolin. LC 87-47641. 160p. 1987. 34.50 (ISBN 0-88164-582-6); pap. 26.50 (ISBN 0-88164-583-4). ABBE Pubs Assn.
Pacemakers: Patient Care, Troubleshooting, Rhythm Analysis. Karen S. Kesten & Colleen K. Norton. 215p. (Orig.). 1985. pap. text ed. 17.00 (ISBN 0-932491-22-7). Res Appl Inc.
Pacer Story Writing Cards. 1981. 65.93 (ISBN 0-89075-084-X). Crane Pub Co.
Paces, Level 2, Bk. B. Jo M. Stanchfield et al. LC 77-83336. (Vistas Ser.). (Illus., Gr. 8). (YA) (gr. 8). 1978. pap. text ed. 8.92 (ISBN 0-395-25228-8); tchr's guide 7.28 (ISBN 0-395-25234-2); skillbk 5.08 (ISBN 0-395-25240-7); tchr's annot ed. skillbk 5.44 (ISBN 0-395-25246-6). HM.
PaceWalking: The Balanced Way to Aerobic Health. Steven Jonas & Peter Radetsky. LC 87-31857. (Illus.). 224p. 1988. pap. 9.95 (ISBN 0-517-56809-8). Crown.
Pachanga Syllabus. (Ballroom Dance Ser.). 1985. lib. bdg. 62.00 (ISBN 0-87700-840-X). Revisionist Pr.
Pachanga Syllabus. (Ballroom Dance Ser.). 1986. lib. bdg. 79.95 (ISBN 0-8490-3430-2). Gordon Pr.
Pachee Goyo: History & Legends from the Shoshone. Rupert Weeks. (Illus., Orig.). 1981. pap. 6.00 (ISBN 0-936204-16-8). Jelm Mtn.
Pachelbel's Canon: Arranged for Harp Solo, Harp Duet, & Harp & Flute or Violin. Sylvia Woods. 26p. 1986. pap. 4.95 (ISBN 0-936661-00-3). Woods Mus Bks Pub.
Pachomian Koinonia I: The Life of St. Pachomius. Tr. by Armand Veilleux. (Cistercian Studies: No. 45). 524p. (Gr.). 1981. pap. 12.95 (ISBN 0-87907-945-2). Cistercian Pubns.
Pachomian Koinonia II: Chronicles & Rules. (Cistercian Studies: No. 46). 239p. 1981. pap. 10.00 (ISBN 0-87907-946-0). Cistercian Pubns.
Pachomian Koinonia III. Instructions, Letters & Other Writings, No. 47. Armand Veilleux. (Cistercian Studies). 1983. 26.95 (ISBN 0-87907-847-2); pap. 10.00 (ISBN 0-87907-947-9). Cistercian Pubns.
Pachomius: The Making of a Community in Fourth-Century Egypt. Philip Rousseau. (Transformation of the Classical Heritage: Vol. VI). 1985. 35.00x (ISBN 0-520-05048-7). U of Cal Pr.
Pachomius: The Making of a Community in Fourth-Century Egypt, Vol. 7. Philip Rousseau. 1986. 29.00x (ISBN 0-317-38385-X). Oxford U Pr.
Pachuco. Dennis Rodriguez. 224p. (Orig.). 1980. pap. 1.95 (ISBN 0-87067-651-2, BH651). Holloway.
Pachuco: An American-Spanish Argot & Its Social Functions in Tucson, Arizona. George C. Barker. LC 50-63360. 46p. 1970. pap. 1.95x (ISBN 0-8165-0253-6). U of Ariz Pr.
Pacific. Pat Hargreaves. LC 81-50489. (Seas & Oceans Ser.). (Illus.). (gr. 4 up). 14.96 (ISBN 0-382-06581-6). Silver.
Pacific: A Forecast. Percy T. Etherton & H. Hessell Tiltman. LC 74-111754. (American Imperialism: Viewpoints of United States Foreign Policy, 1898-1941). 1970. Repr. of 1928 ed. 20.00 (ISBN 0-405-02016-3). Ayer Co Pubs.
Pacific Air Race. Robert H. Scheppler. LC 87-28847. (Illus.). 208p. 1988. 24.95 (ISBN 0-87474-832-1). Smithsonian.
Pacific Alliance: United States Foreign Economic Policy & Japanese Trade Recovery, 1947-1955. William S. Borden. LC 83-14541. 336p. 1984. text ed. 27.50x (ISBN 0-299-09550-9). U of Wis Pr.
Pacific-Asian American Research: An Annotated Bibliography. Mary L. Doi et al. LC 81-4086. (Bibliography Ser.: No.1). xvi, 269p. (Orig.). 1981. pap. 2.00 (ISBN 0-934584-11-7). Pacific-Asian.
Pacific-Asian Americans: A Selected & Annotated Bibliography of Recent Materials. Indu Vohra-Sahu. LC 83-23768. (Bibliography Ser.: No. 4). xxi, 167p. (Orig.). 1983. pap. 2.00 (ISBN 0-934584-17-6). Pacific Asian.
Pacific-Asian Issues: American & Chinese Views. Ed. by Robert A. Scalapino & Chen Qimao. LC 86-81320. (Research Papers and Policy Studies: No. 17). viii, 289p. 1986. pap. 20.00x (ISBN 0-912966-86-6). IEAS.
Pacific Atoll Populations. Ed. by Vern Carroll. LC 75-1264. (Asao Monograph Ser.: No. 3). (Illus.). 547p. 1975. text ed. 22.50x (ISBN 0-8248-0354-X, Eastwest Ctr). UH Pr.
Pacific Basin: An Annotated Bibliography. Jay Mechling. LC 84-48757. 300p. 1986. lib. bdg. 40.00 (ISBN 0-8240-8774-7). Garland Pub.
Pacific Basin & Oceania. Gerald W. Fry & Rufino Mauricio. (World Bibliography Ser.: No. 70). 468p. 1986. lib. bdg. 55.00 (ISBN 1-85109-015-0). ABC-Clio.
Pacific Basin: Concept & Challenge. Ronald A. Morse et al. LC 86-71392. (Alternatives for the 1980s Ser.). 62p. (Orig.). 1986. pap. text ed. 9.75 (ISBN 0-944237-14-2, Ctr National Policy). U Pr of Amer.
Pacific Basin Economic Cooperation. OECD Staff & Michael W. Osborne. 92p. (Orig.). 1983. pap. 9.00x (ISBN 92-64-12483-7). OECD.
Pacific Basin Economic Handbook. (Economic Handbook Ser.). 350p. 1987. 80.00x (ISBN 0-86338-139-1, Pub. by Euromonitor Pubns). Gale.
Pacific Basin, Vol. 36, No. 1. LC 86-70014. 1986. 9.95. Acad Poli Sci.
Pacific Basketmakers: A Living Tradition. Ed. by Suzi Jones. (Illus.). 80p. 1983. pap. 8.95 (ISBN 0-8248-0916-5, Consort Pac Arts). UH Pr.
Pacific Boating Almanac, 1987: Northern California & Nevada. Peter L. Griffes. LC 76-646468. (Illus.). 448p. 1988. pap. 11.95 (ISBN 0-930030-48-6). Western Marine Ent.
Pacific Boating Almanac, 1987: Pacific Northwest & Alaska. Peter L. Griffes. LC 76-646468. (Illus.). 448p. 1988. pap. 11.95 (ISBN 0-930030-49-4). Western Marine Ent.
Pacific Boating Almanac 1987: Southern California, Arizona & Baja California. Peter L. Griffes. LC 76-646468. (Illus.). 448p. 1988. pap. 11.95 (ISBN 0-930030-47-8). Western Marine Ent.
Pacific Breakthrough. Lawrence Cortesi. (Orig.). 1981. pap. 2.95 (ISBN 0-89083-814-3). Zebra.
Pacific Breakthrough. Lawrence Cortesi. 288p. 1987. pap. 3.50 (ISBN 0-8217-2051-1). Zebra.
Pacific Bridges: The New Immigration from Asia & the Pacific Islands. James T. Fawcett & Benjamin V. Carino. (Immigration Theory & Policy Ser.). 486p. 1987. 17.50; pap. 12.95. Ctr Migration.
Pacific Business Guide, 1987. World of Information Editorial Staff. (Illus.). 210p. 1987. pap. 9.95 (ISBN 0-317-55332-1, Pub. by World Info England). Hippocrene Bks.
Pacific (California, Hawaii) Thomas G. Aylesworth & Virginia L. Aylesworth. (Let's Discover the States Ser.). (Illus.). 66p. 1987. lib. bdg. 14.95x (ISBN 1-55546-564-1). Chelsea Hse.
Pacific Carrier. Ruben P. Kitchen, Jr. (Zebra World at War Ser.: No. 23). 320p. (Orig.). 1987. pap. 3.25 (ISBN 0-8217-1527-5). Zebra.
Pacific Century: Economic & Political Consequences of Asian-Pacific Dynamism. Staffan B. Linder. 168p. 1986. 18.95x (ISBN 0-8047-1294-8); pap. 7.95 (ISBN 0-8047-1305-7, SP91). Stanford U Pr.
Pacific Challenge in International Business. Ed. by W. Chan Kim & Philip K. Y. Young. LC 87-5008. (Research for Business Decisions Ser.: No. 72). 350p. 1987. 54.95 (ISBN 0-8357-1620-1). UMI Res Pr.
Pacific Charter: Our Destiny in Asia. Hallett Abend. LC 72-4478. (Essay Index Reprint Ser.). Repr. of 1943 ed. 18.00 (ISBN 0-8369-2932-2). Ayer Co Pubs.
Pacific Coast. Bayard McConnaughey & Evelyn McConnaughey. Ed. by Charles Elliott. LC 84-48673. (Audubon Society Nature Guides Ser.). (Illus.). 633p. 1985. pap. 14.95 (ISBN 0-394-73130-1). Knopf.
Pacific Coast. Rick Steber. (Old Oregon Country Ser.: Vol. 2). (Illus.). 60p. (Orig.). 1987. pap. 4.95 (ISBN 0-945134-02-9). Bonanza Pub Ltd.
Pacific Coast: A Rugged Harmony. Photos by Tim Thompson. (Illus.). 104p. 1988. 29.95 (ISBN 0-934738-43-2). Thomasson-Grant.
Pacific Coast Berry Finder. Glenn Keator. (Illus.). 1978. pap. 1.50 (ISBN 0-912550-02-3). Nature Study.
Pacific Coast Bird Finder: A Manual for Identifying 61 Common Birds of Pacific Coast. Roger J. Lederer. 1977. pap. 1.50 (ISBN 0-912550-04-X). Nature Study.
Pacific Coast Fern Finder. Glenn Keator & Ruth M. Heady. 1981. pap. 1.50 (ISBN 0-912550-13-9). Nature Study.
Pacific Coast Indians of North America. Grant Lyons. LC 83-422877. (Illus.). 96p. (gr. 3 up). 1983. PLB 9.29 (ISBN 0-671-45801-9). Messner.
Pacific Coast Inshore Fishes. rev. ed. Daniel W. Gotshall. LC 80-53027. (Illus.). 96p. 1981. ltd. ed. 22.95 (ISBN 0-930118-07-3); pap. 12.95 (ISBN 0-930118-06-5). Sea Chall.
Pacific Coast Inshore Fishes. Daniel W. Gotshall. LC 80-5327. 96p. 1981. pap. 12.95 (ISBN 0-930030-31-1). Western Marine Ent.
Pacific Coast of Mexico: From Mazatlan to Zihuatanejo. Memo Barroso. 224p. 1986. pap. 8.95 (ISBN 0-517-55860-2, Harmony). Crown.
Pacific Coast Seafaring: Photographic Collection 1850's to 1950's. Wayne Bonnett. (Illus.). 218p. 1988. 55.00 (ISBN 0-915269-07-4). Windgate Pr.
Pacific Coast Studies in Shakespeare. Ed. by Waldo F. McNeir & Thelma N. Greenfield. LC 66-9575. 1966. 7.50 (ISBN 0-87114-014-4). U of Oreg Bks.
Pacific Coast Subtidal Marine Invertebrates, a Fishwatchers' Guide. Daniel W. Gotshall & Laurence L. Laurent. LC 79-64128. 112p. 1979. pap. 13.95 (ISBN 0-930118-02-2). Sea Chall.
Pacific Coast Subtidal Marine Invertebrates. Daniel W. Gotshall & Laurence L. Laurent. LC 79-64128. (Illus.). 112p. pap. 12.95. Western Marine Ent.
Pacific Coast Tree Finder: A Manual for Identifying Pacific Coast Trees. Tom Watts. 1973. pap. 1.50 (ISBN 0-912550-06-6). Nature Study.
Pacific Coastal Wildlife Region. rev. ed. Charles Yocom & Raymond Dasmann. (American Wildlife Region Ser.: Vol. 3). (Illus.). 120p. (gr. 4 up). 1965. 11.95 (ISBN 0-911010-05-X); pap. 5.95 (ISBN 0-911010-04-1). Naturegraph.
Pacific Community. E. Gough Whitlam. (Council on East Asian Studies Ser.). 110p. 1981. text ed. 12.50x (ISBN 0-674-65070-0). Harvard U Pr.
Pacific Computer Communications '85. Ed. by K. H. Kim & K. Chon. 658p. 1986. 80.00 (ISBN 0-444-70022-6, North-Holland). Elsevier.
Pacific Crest Odyssey. David Green. LC 79-66298. (Illus.). 158p. (Orig.). 1979. pap. 8.95 (ISBN 0-911824-91-X). Wilderness Pr.
Pacific Crest Trail. William R Gray. LC 74-1565. (Special Publications Series 9: No. 4). 1975. 7.95 (ISBN 0-87044-149-3). Natl Geog.
Pacific Crest Trail: Oregon-Washington, Vol. 2. 4th ed. Jeffrey Schaffer & Andy Selters. LC 85-41030. (Illus.). 336p. 1986. pap. 19.95 (ISBN 0-89997-060-5). Wilderness Pr.
Pacific Crest Trail, Vol 1: California. 4th ed. Schaffer et al. (Illus.). 480p. 1988. pap. 19.95 (ISBN 0-89997-089-3). Wilderness Pr.
Pacific Crest Trail: Vol. 1, California. 4th ed. Jeffery P. Schaffer et al. LC 81-70345. (Illus.). 470p. (Orig.). 1982. pap. 19.95 (ISBN 0-89997-015-X). Wilderness Pr.

Pacifist. Donald Wetzel. LC 85-63552. 208p. 1986. 17.95 (ISBN 0-932966-70-5). Permanent Pr.

Pacifist in Trouble. facs. ed. William R. Inge. LC 75-152176. (Essay Index Reprint Ser). 1939. 19.00 (ISBN 0-8369-2192-5). Ayer Co Pubs.

Pacifist Program. Richard B. Gregg. 1983. pap. 2.50x (ISBN 0-686-43957-0, 005). Pendle Hill.

Pacifist's Progress: Norman Thomas & the Decline of American Socialism. Bernard K. Johnpoll. LC 87-8665. 352p. 1987. Repr. of 1970 ed. lib. bdg. 45.00x (ISBN 0-313-25895-3, JBPP). Greenwood.

Pacifying the Plains: General Alfred Terry & the Decline of the Sioux, 1866-1890. John W. Bailey. LC 78-19300. (Contributions in Military History Ser.: No. 17). 1979. lib. bdg. 35.00 (ISBN 0-313-20625-2, BAT/). Greenwood.

Pacing the Moon. Joanne M. Riley. LC 85-4159. 72p. 1985. pap. 5.95 (ISBN 0-941608-04-2). Chantry Pr.

Pacing the Void: T'ang Approaches to the Stars. Edward H. Schafer. LC 76-48362. 1978. 49.50x (ISBN 0-520-03344-2). U of Cal Pr.

Pacing Therapy: A Guide to Cardiac Pacing for Optimum Hemodynamic Benefit. Paul A Levine & Robert C. Mace. LC 83-80766. (Illus.). 272p. 1983. pap. 35.00 monograph (ISBN 0-87993-200-7). Futura Pub.

Pack. William Essex. 384p. (Orig.). 1987. pap. 3.95 (ISBN 0-8439-2532-9). Leisure NY.

Pack, Band & Colony: The World of Social Animals. Judith Kohl & Herbert Kohl. LC 82-20951. (Illus.). 114p. (gr. 6 up). 1983. 12.95 (ISBN 0-374-35694-7). FS&G.

Pack of Autolycus or Strange & Terrible News of Ghosts: Broadside Ballads of the Years 1624-1693. Ed. by Hyder E. Rollins. LC 27-4308. (Illus.). 1969. 17.50x (ISBN 0-674-65125-1). Harvard U Pr.

Pack of Labs. Tara Moore. (Illus.). 1982. special ed. 25.00 (ISBN 0-8116-2902-3). Garrard.

Pack of Wolves. Vasilii Bykov. Tr. by Lynn Solotaroff from Rus. LC 80-2456. 192p. (YA) (gr. 7 up). 1981. (Crowell Jr Bks); PLB 12.89 (ISBN 0-690-04115-2). HarpJ.

Pack Saddles & Rolling Wheels: A Century of Travel & Transportation in N. W. California & South Oregon. Don Chase & Marjory Helms. (Illus.). 1959. pap. 3.50 (ISBN 0-918634-28-8). D M Chase.

Pack up & Paint with Oils. Tom Robb. 1987. pap. 7.95 (ISBN 0-394-74972-3). Knopf.

Pack up & Paint with Watercolors. Tom Robb. 1987. pap. 7.95 (ISBN 0-394-74973-1). Knopf.

Pack up & Sketch. Tom Robb. 1987. pap. 7.95 (ISBN 0-394-74971-5). Knopf.

Pack Your Own Parachute: How to Survive Mergers, Takeovers, & Other Corporate Disasters. Paul Hirsch. LC 87-14388. 1987. pap. 9.95 (ISBN 0-201-12205-7). Addison-Wesley.

Pack 109. Mike Thaler. (Illus.). 48p. (ps-2). 1988. 9.95 (ISBN 0-525-44393-2, 0966-290). Dutton.

Package Deals: A Study of Technology Development & Transfer. Ken Marshall. (Illus.). 130p. 1983. (Pub. by Intermediate Tech England); pap. 13.50x (ISBN 0-903031-86-8). Intermediate Tech.

Package Design in Japan, Vol. 1. Japan Package Design Association. LC 85-40069. (Illus.). 300p. 80.00 (ISBN 0-87011-738-6). Kodansha.

Package Dyeing. Wira. 1977. 45.00x (ISBN 0-686-87171-5). State Mutual Bk.

Package Dyeing. Ed. by Wira Staff. 30.00x (ISBN 0-317-43625-2, Pub. by Wira Tech Group). State Mutual Bk.

Package for Miss Marshwater. Elfie Donnelly. (Illus.). (gr. 2-5). 9.95 (ISBN 0-8037-0453-4); PLB 9.89 (ISBN 0-8037-0454-2). Dial Bks Young.

Package Holiday. Jules Verne. 4.95. Assoc Bk.

Package Holiday. Jules Verne. 190p. 1977. 12.95 (ISBN 0-8464-1118-0). Beekman Pubs.

Package in Hyperspace. Janet Asimov. (Illus.). (gr. 4-7). Date not set. 13.95. Walker & Co.

Package of Love for Young & Old. Herman Anderson. 1980. 3.50 (ISBN 0-934860-12-2). Adventure Pubns.

Packaged Cogenerations Systems. Jim Clements. 350p. 1987. text ed. 48.00 (ISBN 0-88173-046-7). Fairmont Pr.

Packages Cogeneration Systems Market. 226p. 1984. 1450.00 (ISBN 0-86621-246-9, A1317). Frost & Sullivan.

Packaging Alternatives for Food Processors: Proceedings. National Food Processors Association Staff. 101p. (Orig.). 1984. pap. text ed. 25.00 (ISBN 0-937774-11-1). Food Processors.

Packaging & Transportation of Radioactive Materials-Patram 1986, Vol. I. (Proceedings Ser.). (Illus.). 634p. (Orig.). 1987. pap. text ed. 135.00 (ISBN 92-0-020087-7, ISP718 1, IAEA). UNIPUB.

Packaging & Transportation of Radioactive Materials (Patram 86) Proceedings, of a Symposium, Davos, June 16-20, 1986. (Proceedings Ser.: Vol. 2). 225p. (Orig.). 1987. pap. text ed. 165.00 (ISBN 92-0-020187-3, ISP718 2, IAEA). UNIPUB.

Packaging Challenges for the 80's: Regional Technical Conference, April 4-5, 1984, Cleveland, Ohio. Society of Plastics Engineers. pap. 44.30 (ISBN 0-317-27101-6, 2024730). Bks Demand UMI.

Packaging Design Four. (Illus.). 256p. 1988. 55.00 (ISBN 0-86636-063-8). PBC Intl Inc.

Packaging Design Three. Industrial Design Magazine Editors & Cristina Gabetti. LC 87-1745. (Illus.). 296p. 1987. 49.95 (ISBN 0-86636-019-0). PBC Intl Inc.

Packaging Design Two. Paul Schmitt & Industrial Design Magazine Editors. LC 84-25554. (Illus.). 256p. 1985. 49.95 (ISBN 0-86636-005-0). PBC Intl Inc.

Packaging Housing Mortgage Loans: Strategies for California. John Harrington. 100p. 1980. 5.95 (ISBN 0-318-13761-5); inst. 11.95 (ISBN 0-318-13762-3). NCPA Washington.

Packaging Industry. (UNIDO Guides to Information Sources: No. 27). pap. 4.00 (ISBN 92-1-106165-2, ID/194). UN.

Packaging Information Sources. Ed. by Gwendolyn Jones. LC 67-18370. (Management Information Guide Ser.: No. 10). 288p. 1967. 68.00x (ISBN 0-8103-0811-8). Gale.

Packaging Marketplace: The Practical Guide to Packaging Sources. Ed. by Joseph Hanlon. LC 78-53442. 304p. 1978. 140.00x (ISBN 0-8103-0989-0, Norback Bk). Gale.

Packaging of Power Semiconductor Devices. C. A. Neugebauer et al. (Electrocomponent Science Monographs: Vol. 7). 98p. 1986. 25.00 (ISBN 2-88124-135-2). Gordon & Breach.

Packaging: Performance Testing of Shipping Containers. 250p. 1985. pap. 34.00 (ISBN 0-8031-0463-4). ASTM.

Packaging Power: Corporate Identity & Product Recognition. Elinor Selame & Joe Selame. 1982. 10.00 (ISBN 0-8144-2274-8). AMACOM.

Packaging: Specifications, Purchasing, & Quality Control. 3rd ed. Leonard. 256p. 1986. 37.50 (ISBN 0-8247-7729-8). Dekker.

Packaging the New South. (Illus.). 112p. 3.00 (ISBN 0-317-35966-5). Southern Exposure.

Packaging the Presidency: A History & Criticism of Presidential Campaign Advertising. Kathleen H. Jamieson. LC 84-7134. (Illus.). 1984. 24.95x (ISBN 0-19-503504-6). Oxford U Pr.

Packaging the Presidency: A History & Criticism of Presidential Campaign Advertising. Kathleen H. Jamieson. (Illus.). 512p. 1988. pap. 12.95 (ISBN 0-19-505656-6). Oxford U Pr.

Packaging with Plastics. Ed. by Paul F. Bruins. LC 72-78922. 222p. 1974. 68.00 (ISBN 0-677-12200-4). Gordon & Breach.

Packaging Your Home for Profit: How to Sell Your House or Condo for More Money in Less Time. Bruce A. Percelay & Peter Arnold. 1986. pap. 12.95 (ISBN 0-316-69896-2). Little.

Packard: A History of the Motorcar and Company. Beverly R. Kimes. LC 78-71063. (Illus.). 800p. 1978. 64.50 (ISBN 0-915038-11-0, 3-AQ-0016). Auto Quarterly.

Packard Adapter for Wurlitzer Twin 2-16's & 2-12's: Complete Installation Instructions for These Record Changers. 28p. 1983. Repr. of 1940 ed. laminated spiral bdg. 9.50 (ISBN 0-913698-82-2, R-166). AMR Pub Co.

Packard, Ask the Man Who Owned One. new ed. Compiled by Otto A. Schroeder. LC 73-83510. (Illus.). 384p. 1975. 18.95 (ISBN 0-911160-63-9). Post-Era.

Packard Jukebox Manhattan Service Manual, 1948-9. 52p. 1983. Repr. of 1947 ed. 10 mil. lam. cover 24.50 (ISBN 0-913698-81-4, R-95). AMR Pub Co.

Packard Jukebox Play-Mor Model 7 Installation & Service Manual of 1946-49. 50p. 1983. Repr. of 1949 ed. 10 mil. lam. covers, spiral bound 16.50 (ISBN 0-913698-80-6, R-164). AMR Pub Co.

Packard Jukebox Remote Control Wall Box Service Manual: Including Brochure for Packard Pla-Mor Wall Box Model 30-200 of 1946. 26p. 1983. Repr. of 1946 ed. lam. cover, spiral bound 9.50 (ISBN 0-913698-83-0, R-90). AMR Pub Co.

Packard Jukebox Sales Brochures, 1946-49: Including Remote Equipment. Compiled by Frand Adams. 70p. 1984. 10 Mil laminated covers, spiral bdg. 21.50 (ISBN 0-913599-00-X, R-242). AMR Pub Co.

Packard: The Complete Story. Michael G. Scott. (Illus.). 208p. (Orig.). 1985. 24.95 (ISBN 0-8306-2108-3, 2108). TAB Bks.

Packard Truck: Ask the Man Who Owns One. John B. Montville. (Illus.). 128p. pap. cancelled (ISBN 0-89404-052-9). Aztex.

Packe of Spanish Lyes, Sent Abroard in the World. LC 77-38224. (English Experience Ser.: No. 487). 1972. Repr. of 1588 ed. 5.00 (ISBN 90-221-0487-7). Walter J Johnson.

Packer. Jack Rudman. (Career Examination Ser.: C-1647). (Cloth bdg. avail. on request). 1988. pap. 10.00 (ISBN 0-8373-1647-2). Natl Learning.

Packet for Ezra Pound. William B. Yeats. 48p. 1970. Repr. of 1929 ed. 15.00x (ISBN 0-7165-1369-2, BBA 02107, Pub. by Cuala Press Ireland). Biblio Dist.

Packet of Letters: A Selection from the Correspondence of John Henry Newman. John H. Newman. Intro. by Joyce Suggs. LC 82-4444. (Illus.). 1983. 19.95x (ISBN 0-19-826442-9). Oxford U Pr.

Packet of Poems. Selected by Jill Bennett. (Illus.). 112p. (ps-6). 1987. 10.95 (ISBN 0-19-276049-1); pap. 6.95 (ISBN 0-19-276066-1). Oxford U Pr.

Packet Radio Handbook. Jonathan L. Mayo. (Illus.). 224p. 1987. pap. 14.95 (ISBN 0-8306-2722-7, NO. 2722). TAB Bks.

Packet Radio Networks: Architectures, Protocols, Technologies & Applications. Clifford Lynch & B. Brownrigg. (Illus.). 310p. 1987. 77.50 (ISBN 0-08-035913-2). Pergamon.

Packet Switching Equipment Markets. Business Communications Staff. 295p. 1985. pap. 1750.00 (ISBN 0-89336-465-7, G-093). BCC.

Packet Switching Services & Equipment. International Resource Development Inc. Staff. 211p. 1987. 2300.00x (ISBN 0-88694-743-X). Intl Res Dev.

Packet Switching: Tomorrow's Communications Today. Roy D. Rosner. (Illus.). 371p. 1982. text ed. 37.00 (ISBN 0-534-97965-3, Lifetime Learn). Van Nos Reinhold.

Packet Switching: Tomorrow's Communications Today. Roy D. Rosner. 371p. 1982. 39.95. Van Nos Reinhold.

Packin' in on Mules & Horses. Smoke Elser & Bill Brown. LC 80-12583. (Illus.). 168p. 1980. pap. 12.95 (ISBN 0-87842-127-0). Mountain Pr.

Packing & Outfiting Field Manual. University of Wyoming. 78p. pap. 4.00 (ISBN 0-318-12508-0). Am Donkey.

Packing Industry. Institute of American Meat Packers & the School of Commerce & Administration of the University of Chicago. LC 75-22796. (America in Two Centuries Ser). (Illus.). 1976. Repr. of 1924 ed. 30.00x (ISBN 0-405-07667-3). Ayer Co Pubs.

Packing the Courts: The Conservatives' Campaign to Rewrite the Constitution. Herman Schwartz. 384p. 1988. 19.95 (ISBN 0-684-18953-4). Scribner.

Packrat Papers No. I: Tips on Equipment (& Other Stuff) for Hiker, Campers, & Those Who Travel Lightly. Ed. by Betty Mueller. (Illus.). 1977. pap. 3.95 (ISBN 0-913140-14-7). Signpost Bk Pubns.

Paco & the Lion of the North. Betty Harman & Nancy Meador. Ed. by Melissa Roberts. 112p. (gr. 4-7). 1987. 8.95 (ISBN 0-89015-598-4). Eakin Pr.

Paco y Ana Aprenden Acerca de la Amabilidad. Carol Martinez. (Paco y Ana Aprenden Ser.). (Illus.). 32p. (Orig., Span.). (gr. 2-4). 1988. pap. 1.25 (ISBN 0-311-38590-7, Edit Mundo). Casa Bautista.

Paco y Ana Aprenden Acerca de la Amistad. Carol Martinez. (Paco y Ana Aprenden Ser.). (Illus., Orig., Span.). (gr. 2-4). 1988. pap. 1.25 (ISBN 0-311-38589-3, Edit Mundo). Casa Bautista.

Paco y Ana Aprenden Acerca de la Honradez. Carol Martinez. (Paco y Ana Aprenden Ser.). (Illus.). 32p. (Orig., Span.). (gr. 2-4). 1988. pap. 1.25 (ISBN 0-311-38587-7, Edit Mundo). Casa Bautista.

Paco y Ana Aprenden Acerca de la Obediencia. Carol Martinez. (Paco y Ana Aprenden Ser.). (Illus.). 32p. (Orig., Span.). (gr. 2-4). Date not set. pap. 1.25 (ISBN 0-311-38588-5, Edit Mundo). Casa Bautista.

Paco's Story. Larry Heinemann. 224p. 1986. 15.95 (ISBN 0-374-22847-7). FS&G.

Paco's Story. Larry Heinemann. 224p. 1987. pap. 4.50 (ISBN 0-14-010085-7). Penguin.

PACs Americana: The Directory of Political Action Committees & Their Interests. 2nd ed. Ed. by Edward Roeder. 1986. 250.00 (ISBN 0-942236-01-7). Sunshine Serv.

Pact: My Friendship with Isak Dinesen. Thorkild Bjornvig. Tr. by Ingvar Schousboe & William J. Smith. (Illus.). 176p. 1987. pap. 8.95 (ISBN 0-312-00626-8). St Martin.

Pactolus Prime. Albion W. Tourgee. LC 68-57555. (Muckrakers Ser). 359p. Repr. of 1890 ed. lib. bdg. 49.00 (ISBN 0-8398-1969-2). Irvington.

Padaeng Chronicle & the Jengtung State Chronicle Translated. Sao Saimong Mangrai. LC 80-67342. (Michigan Papers on South & Southeast Asia: No. 19). (Illus.). xxiv, 301p. 1981. 26.95x (ISBN 0-89148-020-X); pap. 16.95 (ISBN 0-89148-021-8). Ctr S&SE Asian.

Padataditaka of Syamilaka. Ed. by G. H. Schokker & P. J. Worsley. LC 67-84054. 1976. Pt. 1. lib. bdg. 50.00 (ISBN 90-277-0690-5, Pub. by Reidel Holland); Pt. 2. lib. bdg. 50.00 (ISBN 90-277-0425-2); Set. lib. bdg. 79.00 (ISBN 90-277-0691-3). Kluwer Academic.

Padded Pews or Open Doors. Mark Finley. 144p. 1988. pap. 7.95 (ISBN 0-8163-0745-8). Pacific Pr Pub Assn.

Paddings & Strappings of the Foot. Ed. by Charles Kaplan & Peter Natale. LC 82-82871. (Illus.). 256p. 1982. pap. 31.00 (ISBN 0-87993-185-X). Futura Pub.

Paddington Abroad. Michael Bond. (Illus.). 128p. (gr. 2-6). 1974. pap. 0.95 (ISBN 0-440-47352-7, YB). Dell.

Paddington Abroad. Michael Bond. LC 72-2753. (Illus.). 128p. (gr. 1-5). 1972. 9.95 (ISBN 0-395-14331-4). HM.

Paddington & the Knickerbocker Rainbow. Michael Bond. LC 84-11564. (Paddington Bks.). (Illus.). 32p. (ps-1). 1985. 5.95 (ISBN 0-399-21202-7, Putnam). Putnam Pub Group.

Paddington at Large. Michael Bond. (Illus.). 128p. (gr. 3-7). 1970. pap. 2.75 (ISBN 0-440-46801-9, YB). Dell.

Paddington at Large. Michael Bond. (Illus.). (gr. 1-5). 1963. 9.95 (ISBN 0-395-06641-7). HM.

Paddington at Large see Hilarious Adventures of Paddington.

Paddington at the Airport: An Activity Board Book. Michael Bond & Karen Bond. (Illus.). 10p. (gr. 3-7). 1986. text ed. 5.95 (ISBN 0-528-82004-4). Macmillan.

Paddington at the Fair. Michael Bond. LC 85-5683. (Paddington Ser.). (Illus.). 32p. (ps-2). 1986. 5.95 (ISBN 0-399-21271-X, G&D). Putnam Pub Group.

Paddington at the Palace. Michael Bond. (Illus.). 32p. (ps-3). 1986. 5.95 (ISBN 0-399-21340-6, Putnam). Putnam Pub Group.

Paddington at the Seaside. Michael Bond. LC 77-90190. (Illus.). (ps-3). 1978. 5.95 (ISBN 0-394-83801-7, BYR); lib. bdg. 4.99 (ISBN 0-394-93801-1). Random.

Paddington at the Tower. Michael Bond. LC 77-90189. (Illus.). (ps-3). 1978. 5.95 (ISBN 0-394-83802-5, BYR); lib. bdg. 5.99 (ISBN 0-394-93802-X). Random.

Paddington at the Zoo. Michael Bond. (Paddington Bks.). (Illus.). 32p. (gr. k-2). 1985. 5.95 (ISBN 0-399-21201-9, Putnam). Putnam Pub Group.

Paddington at the Zoo. Michael Bond. (Illus.). 32p. (ps-2). pap. 4.94 (ISBN 0-317-31369-X). Putnam Pub Group.

Paddington at Work. Michael Bond. 128p. (gr. k-8). 1971. pap. 2.75 (ISBN 0-440-40797-4, YB). Dell.

Paddington at Work. Michael Bond. LC 67-20372. (Illus.). (gr. 1-5). 1967. 9.95 (ISBN 0-395-06637-9). HM.

Paddington at Work see Hilarious Adventures of Paddington.

Paddington Bear. Michael Bond. (Illus.). (ps-2). 1973. 4.95 (ISBN 0-394-82642-6, BYR); lib. bdg. 5.99 (ISBN 0-394-92642-0). Random.

Paddington Cleans Up. Michael Bond. (Illus.). 32p. (ps-3). 1986. 5.95 (ISBN 0-399-21339-2, Putnam). Putnam Pub Group.

Paddington Goes to Town. Michael Bond. 128p. (gr. 2-5). 1972. pap. 2.75 (ISBN 0-440-46793-4, YB). Dell.

Paddington Goes to Town. Michael Bond. LC 68-28043. (Illus.). (gr. 1-5). 1968. 9.95 (ISBN 0-395-06635-2). HM.

Paddington Helps Out. Michael Bond. (Illus.). 128p. (gr. 3-7). 1982. pap. 2.75 (ISBN 0-440-46802-7, YB). Dell.

Paddington Helps Out. Michael Bond. (Illus.). (gr. 4-6). 1961. 13.95 (ISBN 0-395-06639-5). HM.

Paddington Helps Out see Hilarious Adventures of Paddington.

Paddington Mails a Letter. Michael Bond & Karen Bond. (Paddington Bear Activity Bks.). (Illus.). 10p. (gr. 3-7). 1986. text ed. 5.95 (ISBN 0-528-82005-2). Macmillan.

Paddington Marches On. Michael Bond. (Illus.). (gr. 4-6). 1965. 12.95 (ISBN 0-395-06642-5). HM.

Paddington on Screen. Michael Bond. (Illus.). (gr. 2-5). 1982. 8.95 (ISBN 0-395-32950-7). HM.

Paddington on Screen. Michael Bond. (gr. k-6). 1988. pap. 2.75 (ISBN 0-440-40029-5, YB). Dell.

Paddington on Stage. Alfred Bradley & Michael Bond. LC 76-62497. (Illus.). (gr. 2-5). 1977. 9.95 (ISBN 0-395-25155-9). HM.

Paddington on Top. Michael Bond. (Illus.). 128p. (gr. 1-5). 1975. 5.95 (ISBN 0-395-21897-7). HM.

Paddington Takes the Air. Michael Bond. 128p. (gr. 2-6). 1974. pap. 0.75 (ISBN 0-440-47321-7, YB). Dell.

Paddington Takes the Air. Michael Bond. LC 78-147902. (Illus.). (gr. 3-7). 1971. 12.95 (ISBN 0-395-10909-4). HM.

Paddington Takes the Test. Michael Bond. (Illus.). (gr. 3-6). 1980. 8.95 (ISBN 0-395-29519-X). HM.

Paddington Takes the Test. Michael Bond. 128p. (gr. k-6). 1982. pap. 1.95 (ISBN 0-440-47021-8, YB). Dell.

Paddington Takes to TV. Michael Bond. (Illus.). 128p. (gr. 1-5). 1974. 9.95 (ISBN 0-395-19881-X). HM.

Paddington's Art Exhibition. Michael Bond. (Paddington Ser.). Orig. Title: Paddington's Painting Exhibition. (Illus.). 32p. (ps-2). 1986. 5.95 (ISBN 0-399-21270-1, G&D). Putnam Pub Group.

Paddington's Clock Book. Michael Bond & Karen Bond. LC 86-70397. (Paddington Bear Activity Bks.). (Illus.). 12p. (ps-2). pap. 5.95 (ISBN 0-528-82002-8). Macmillan.

Paddington's Garden. Michael Bond. (Illus.). (ps-2). 1973. (BYR). Random.

Paddington's Lucky Day. Michael Bond. LC 74-5007. (Paddington Picture Bks). (Illus.). 36p. (ps-2). 1974. (BYR); lib. bdg. 4.99 (ISBN 0-394-92919-5). Random.

Paddington's Painting Exhibition see Paddington's Art Exhibition.

Paddington's Storybook. Michael Bond. (Illus.). 160p. (gr. 1-5). 1984. 13.95 (ISBN 0-395-36667-4). HM.

Paddington's Wheel Book. Michael Bond & Karen Bond. LC 86-70396. (Paddington Bear Activity Bks.). (Illus.). 12p. (ps-2). pap. 5.95 (ISBN 0-528-82003-6). Macmillan.

Paddle-to-the-Sea. Holling C. Holling. (Illus.). (gr. 4-6). PLB 15.95 (ISBN 0-395-15082-5); pap. 5.95 (ISBN 0-395-29203-4). HM.

Paddle Washington. David F. LeRoux & Martha G. Rudersdorf. LC 84-61009. (Illus.). 163p. 1984. pap. 8.95 (ISBN 0-9613570-0-2). Neah Bay Bks.

Paddle Wheels & Pistols. Irvin Anthony. 329p. 1980. Repr. of 1929 ed. lib. bdg. 30.00 (ISBN 0-8495-0075-3). Arden Lib.

Paddleball & Racquetball. A. William Fleming & Joel A. Bloom. LC 72-90984. (Physical Activities Ser.). 1973. pap. text ed. write for info. (ISBN 0-673-16193-5). Scott F.

Paddlefish: Status, Management & Propagation. Ed. by J. G. Dillard et al. LC 86-60218. (North Central Division Special Publication Ser.: No. 7). 159p. 1986. pap. 9.00 (ISBN 0-913235-32-6). Am Fisheries Soc.

Paddler's Guide to Eastern North Carolina. Bob Benner & Tom McCloud. LC 86-31091. (Illus.). 272p. 1987. pap. 10.95 (ISBN 0-89732-041-7). Menasha Ridge.

Paddler's Guide to Quetico Provincial Park. Robert Beymer. LC 85-80675. 168p. (Orig.). 1985. pap. 7.95 (ISBN 0-933287-00-3). Fisher Co.

Paddlewheel Inboard. C. Bradford Mitchell. LC 83-50816. (Illus.). 66p. 1984. pap. 12.00 (ISBN 0-913423-06-8). Steamship Hist Soc.

Paddling Hawaii: An Insider's Guide to Exploring the Secluded Coves, Jungle Streams & Wild Coasts of the Hawaiian Islands. Audrey Sutherland. (Illus.). 240p. (Orig.). 1988. pap. 10.95 (ISBN 0-89886-180-2). Mountaineers.

Paddling My Own Canoe. Audrey Sutherland. LC 78-16374. (Illus.). 1978. (Kolowalu Bk); pap. 5.95 (ISBN 0-8248-0699-9). UH Pr.

Paddy & the Republic: Ethnicity & Nationality in Antebellum America. Dale T. Knobel. LC 85-8554. (Illus.). xx, 268p. 1986. 27.95 (ISBN 0-8195-5117-1). Wesleyan U Pr.

Paddy & the Republic: Ethnicity & Nationality in Antebellum America. Dale T. Knobel. (Illus.). xx, 252p. 1988. pap. 14.95 (ISBN 0-8195-6167-3). Wesleyan U Pr.

Paddy Camps: The Irish of Lowell, 1821-61. Brian C. Mitchell. LC 87-16724. 264p. 1988. 24.95 (ISBN 0-252-01371-9). U of Ill Pr.

Paddy Drying Manual. N. Teter. (Agricultural Services Bulletin Ser.: No. 70). 123p. (Orig.). 1987. pap. text ed. 13.50 (ISBN 92-5-102603-3, F3147, FAO). UNIPUB.

Paddy Goes Traveling. John S. Goodall. LC 82-71159. (Illus.). 32p. (ps-3). 1982. 6.95 (ISBN 0-689-50239-7, M K McElderry). Macmillan.

Paddy No More: Modern Irish Short Stories. Ed. by William Vorm. 224p. (Orig.). 1982. pap. 5.95 (ISBN 0-905473-29-9, Pub. by Wolfhound Pr Ireland). Irish Bks Media.

Paddy Quacks! Carol Thompson. (Illus.). (ps up). 1988. 4.95 (ISBN 0-448-19252-7, G&D). Putnam Pub Group.

Paddy Soils in Tropical Asia: Their Material Nature & Fertility. Keizaburo Kawaguchi & Kazutake Kyuma. (Center for Southeast Asian Studies, Kyoto University). (Illus.). 1978. text ed. 20.00x (ISBN 0-8248-0570-4); pap. text ed. 12.00x (ISBN 0-8248-0571-2). UH Pr.

Paddy Soils: Proceedings. 800p. 1981. 62.00 (ISBN 0-387-10900-5). Springer-Verlag.

Paddy the Beaver. Thornton Burgess. (Bedtime Story Bks.). 1986. Repr. lib. bdg. 15.95x (ISBN 0-89966-528-4). Buccaneer Bks.

Paddy the Cope. Patrick Gallagher. 1942. 6.95 (ISBN 0-8159-6500-1). Devin.

Paddy to the Rescue. John S. Goodall. LC 85-70231. (Illus.). 32p. (gr. k up). 1986. 8.95 (ISBN 0-689-50330-X, M K McElderry). Macmillan.

Paddy under Water. John S. Goodall. LC 83-71901. (Illus.). 32p. (ps-3). 1984. 6.95 (ISBN 0-689-50297-4, M K McElderry). Macmillan.

Paddy's Lament - Ireland 1846-1847: Prelude to Hatred. Thomas Gallagher. 1987. pap. 7.95 (ISBN 0-15-670700-4, Harv). HarBraceJ.

Paddy's Lament: Ireland 1846 to 1847; Prelude to Hatred. Thomas Gallagher. LC 81-48011. 352p. 1982. 17.95 (ISBN 0-15-170618-2). HarBraceJ.

Pade & Rational Approximation: Theory & Applications. Ed. by E. B. Saff & R. S. Varga. 1977. 56.50 (ISBN 0-12-614150-9). Acad Pr.

Pade Approximant in Theoretical Physics. Ed. by George A. Baker, Jr. & John L. Gammel. (Mathematics in Science & Engineering Ser.: Vol. 71). 1970. 95.00 (ISBN 0-12-074850-9). Acad Pr.

Pade Approximants & Their Applications. P. R. Graves-Morris. 1973. 86.00 (ISBN 0-12-295950-7). Acad Pr.

Pade Approximants for Operators: Theory & Applications. A. Cuyt. (Lecture Notes in Mathematics Ser.: Vol. 1065). ix, 138p. 1984. pap. 11.00 (ISBN 0-387-13342-9). Springer-Verlag.

Pade Approximation & Its Applications, Amsterdam 1980: Proceedings. Ed. by M. G. De Bruin & H. Van Rossum. (Lecture Notes in Mathematics Ser.: Vol. 888). 383p. 1981. pap. 22.00 (ISBN 0-387-11154-9). Springer-Verlag.

Pade Approximation & Its Application. L. Wuytack. (Lecture Notes in Mathematics: Vol. 765). 392p. 1979. pap. 25.00 (ISBN 0-387-09717-1). Springer-Verlag.

Pade Approximations & Its Applications: Bad Honnef 1983. Ed. by H. Werner & H. J. Buenger. (Lecture Notes in Mathematics: Vol. 1071). vi, 264p. (Fr. & Eng.). 1984. pap. 20.00 (ISBN 0-387-13364-X). Springer-Verlag.

Pade-Typed Approximation & General Orthogonal Polynomials. C. Brezinski. (International Series of Numerical Mathematics: No. 50). 250p. 1979. pap. 54.95 (ISBN 0-8176-1100-2). Birkhauser.

Padeia Through Laughter: Jonson's Aristophanic Appeal to Human Intelligence. Aliki L. Dick. LC 73-84787. (Studies in English Literature: No. 76). xi, 141p. (Orig.). 1974. pap. text ed. 17.60x (ISBN 90-2792-714-6). Mouton.

Paderewski Album. Wladyslaw Sokolowska. 190p. 1982. 37.00x (ISBN 0-85335-241-0, Pub. by Maclellan Sales Ltd). State Mutual Bk.

Paderewski As I Knew Him: From the Diary of Aniela Strakacz. Aniela Strakacz. LC 49-11799. (Illus.). pap. 88.00 (ISBN 0-317-09880-2, 2050667). Bks Demand UMI.

Paderewski Memoirs. Jan I. Paderewski & Mary Lawton. LC 80-21323. (Music Ser.). 1980. Repr. of 1939 ed. 45.00 (ISBN 0-306-76046-0). Da Capo.

Paderewski: The Story of a Modern Immortal. Charles J. Phillips. LC 77-17399. (Music Reprint Ser.). (Illus.). 1978. Repr. of 1934 ed. lib. bdg. 55.00 (ISBN 0-306-77534-4). Da Capo.

Padidehaye Fekr: Manifestations of Thought. 29th ed. Sadegh M. Angha. LC 87-60094. 75p. (Persian.). Date not set. 20.00; pap. 11.00. MTO Printing & Pubn Ctr.

Padju Epat: The Ma'anyan of Indonesian Borneo. Alfred B. Hudson. Ed. by George Spindler & Louise Spindler. (Case Studies in Cultural Anthropology). 144p. 1982. pap. text ed. 8.95x (ISBN 0-8290-0315-0). Irvington.

Padlock Collector. 4th ed. Franklin M. Arnall. LC 82-74067. (Illus.). 140p. 1982. pap. 8.95 (ISBN 0-914638-03-3). Collctr Clrmnt.

Padlock Collector: 100 Years of Padlocks. 5th ed. Franklin M. Arnall. LC 87-72771. (Illus.). 190p. 1988. pap. 14.95 (ISBN 0-914638-04-1). Collctr Clrmnt.

Padraic Colum. Sanford Sternlicht. (English Author Ser.). 1985. lib. bdg. 20.95 (ISBN 0-8057-6901-3, Twayne). G K Hall.

Padraic Colum: A Biographical-Critical Introduction. Zack Bowen. LC 77-83665. (Crosscurrents-Modern Critiques Ser.). 175p. 1970. 6.95x (ISBN 0-8093-0412-0). S Ill U Pr.

Padraic O'Conaire Stories. P. O. Conaire. 192p. 1982. pap. 4.95 (ISBN 0-905169-54-9, Pub. by Poolbeg Pr Ireland). Irish Bks Media.

Padraig Mac Piarais Agus Eire Lena Linn. Seamas O'Buachalla. (Illus.). 94p. (Irish.). 1979. pap. 6.50 (ISBN 0-85342-570-1, Pub. by Mercier Pr Ireland). Irish Bks Media.

Padre: An Unusual Common Man. Nigel B. Bourne. 1986. 47.00x (ISBN 0-86332-081-3, Pub. by Book Guild Ltd). State Mutual Bk.

Padre Giovanni Battista Martini, Giovanni Battista Lampugnani, Pasquale Anfossi, Luigi Boccherini, Simone Mayr, & Gaetano Donizetti. Padre G. Martini & Giovanni B. Lampugnani. Ed. by Howard Brofsky et al. (Symphony Ser.). 504p. 1983. lib. bdg. 90.00 (ISBN 0-8240-3829-0). Garland Pub.

Padre Island National Seashore--A Guide to the Geology, Natural Environments, & History of a Texas Barrier Island. B. R. Weise & W. A. White. (Illus.). 94p. 1980. 4.00 (ISBN 0-686-31762-9, GB 17). Bur Econ Geology.

Padre Martinez & Bishop Lamy. 3rd ed. Ray J. De Aragon. LC 78-70565. (History Ser.). (Illus.). 1978. pap. 7.95 (ISBN 0-932906-00-1). Pan-Am Publishing Co.

Padre Martinez & Bishop Lamy. 3rd ed. Ray J. DeAragon. (Illus.). 152p. 1978. pap. 7.95 (ISBN 0-317-67449-8). Pan-Am Publishing Co.

Padre Martini's Collection of Letters in the Civico Museo Bibliografico Musicale in Bologna: An Annotated Index. Anne Schnoebelen. LC 79-10540. (Annotated Reference Tools in Music Ser.: No. 2). 1979. lib. bdg. 80.00x (ISBN 0-918728-11-8). Pendragon NY.

Padre Miguel Hidalgo: Father of Mexican Independence. Hubert J. Miller. 77p. (Orig.). 1986. pap. text ed. write for info. (ISBN 0-938738-05-4). Pan Am Univ Las.

Padre Mio me abbandono a Te see Summoned by Love.

Padre on Horseback. Herbert E. Bolton. LC 63-13248. (Illus.). 1963. Repr. of 1962 ed. 4.95 (ISBN 0-8294-0003-6). Loyola.

Padre Pio. Dante Alimenti. (Illus.). 179p. 1987. 49.95 (ISBN 0-87973-491-4). Our Sunday Visitor.

Padre Pio. John A. Schugomcap. 1983. 9.50 (ISBN 0-8199-0864-9). Franciscan Herald.

Padre Pio see City on a Mountain - Padre Pio.

Padre Pio Profile. John A. Schug. (Orig.). 1987. pap. 6.95 (ISBN 0-932506-56-9). St Bedes Pubns.

Padre Pio: The Stigmatist. Charles M. Carty. (Illus.). 1971. pap. 4.00 (ISBN 0-89555-054-7, 115). TAN Bks Pubs.

Padre Pio: The True Story. C. Bernard Ruffin. LC 81-81525. (Illus.). 348p. (Orig.). 1982. pap. 8.95 (ISBN 0-87973-673-9, 673). Our Sunday Visitor.

Padre Porko. Robert Davis. (Illus.). 297p. (gr. 4-6). 1948. 8.95 (ISBN 0-8234-0085-9). Holiday.

Padre Varela: Biografia del Forjador de la Conciencia Cubana. 2nd ed. Antonio Hernandez-Travieso. LC 51-21483. (Coleccion Cuba y Sus Jueces Ser.). (Illus.). 460p. (Span.). 1984. pap. 14.95 (ISBN 0-89729-347-9). Ediciones.

Padres Eficaces con Entrenamiento Sistematico (PECES) Don Dinkmeyer & Gary D. McKay. (Span.). leaders manual 29.95 (ISBN 0-913476-87-0). Am Guidance.

Padres Eficaces con Entrenamiento Sistematico (PECES) Libro de los Padres. Don Dinkmeyer & Gary McKay. Tr. by Clara De Barranco from Eng. (Illus., Span.). 1981. pap. text ed. 9.95 (ISBN 0-913476-78-1). Am Guidance.

Padres Se Organizan para Mejorar las Escuelas. rev. ed. Tr. by Cesar Ramirez from Eng. 61p. (Span.). 1981. pap. 1.75x (ISBN 0-934460-16-7). NCCE.

Paduans, Medals by Giovanni Cavino. Richard H. Lawrence. (Illus.). pap. 5.00 (ISBN 0-916710-74-2). Obol Intl.

Padyacudamani of Buddhaghosacarya. Buddhaghosa. LC 78-72387. Repr. of 1921 ed. 32.50 (ISBN 0-404-17248-2). AMS Pr.

Paediatric Cardiology, 2 vols. Anderson. 1987. 295.00 (ISBN 0-443-02105-8). Churchill.

Paediatric Data Interpretation. Simon Lenton et al. 192p. 1988. pap. text ed. 19.95 (ISBN 0-407-00425-4). Butterworth.

Paediatric Diagnosis & Treatment. N. M. Jacoby. 1978. 37.50x (ISBN 0-8464-0701-9). Beekman Pubs.

Paediatric Emergencies. 2nd ed. Ed. by J. A. Black. (Illus.). 856p. 1987. text ed. 85.00 (ISBN 0-407-00280-4). Butterworth.

Paediatric Endocrinology in Clinical Practice. A. Aynsley-Green. 1984. lib. bdg. 47.50 (ISBN 0-85200-864-3, Pub. by MTP Pr England). Kluwer Academic.

Paediatric Gastroenterology. Anderson et al. 1986. 92.50 (ISBN 0-8016-0220-3). Mosby.

Paediatric Infectious Diseases in Arab Countries. 1987. 108.00 (ISBN 0-471-91120-8). Wiley.

Paediatric Nephrology. Ed. by D. Boda & S. Turi. (Contributions to Nephrology Ser.: Vol. 67). (Illus.). xii, 192p. 1988. 106.75 (ISBN 3-8055-4689-0). S Karger.

Paediatric Nephrology: Proceedings of the Sixth International Symposium of Paediatric Nephrology, Hannover, Federal Republic of Germany, 29. August to 2. September 1983. J. Brodehl & J. H. Ehrich. (Illus.). 410p. 1984. pap. 64.00 (ISBN 0-387-13598-7). Springer-Verlag.

Paediatric Neuroendocrinology. Derek Gupta et al. LC 84-26110. 256p. 1985. 48.00 (ISBN 0-8451-3012-9). A R Liss.

Paediatric Neurology. 2nd ed. Ingrid Gamstorp. (Illus.). 416p. 1985. text ed. 75.00 (ISBN 0-407-00263-4). Butterworth.

Paediatric Neurology for the Clinician. N. Gordon & W. Schutt. (Clinics in Developmental Medicine Ser.: Vols. 59 & 60). 228p. 1976. text ed. 35.50 (ISBN 0-433-12410-5, Pub. by Spastics Intl England). Lippincott.

Paediatric Nursing. 6th ed. Barbara F. Weller & Sheila Barlow. (Illus.). 424p. 1983. pap. 10.95 (ISBN 0-7216-0940-6, Bailliere-Tindall). Saunders.

Paediatric Oncology. Ed. by W. Duncan. (Recent Results in Cancer Research Ser.: Vol. 88). (Illus.). 170p. 1983. 49.00 (ISBN 0-387-12349-0). Springer-Verlag.

Paediatric Operative Dentistry. 3rd ed. Kennedy. 304p. 1986. 27.00 (ISBN 0-7236-0877-6). PSG Pub Co.

Paediatric Otolaryngology. 2nd ed. Cowan & Kerr. (Illus.). 276p. 1986. pap. 54.00 (ISBN 0-7236-0825-3). PSG Pub Co.

Paediatric Pathology. Ed. by C. L. Berry. (Illus.). 710p. 1981. 96.00 (ISBN 0-387-10507-7). Springer-Verlag.

Paediatric Priorities in the Developing World. D. Morley. 1977. 19.95 (ISBN 0-407-35113-2). Butterworth.

Paediatric Problems in General Practice. Michael Modell & Robert Boyd. (Oxford General Practice Ser.). (Illus.). 1983. pap. 23.95x (ISBN 0-19-261264-6). Oxford U Pr.

Paediatric Problems in General Practice. 2nd ed. Michael Modell & Robert Boyd. (General Practice Ser.: No. 13). (Illus.). 292p. 1989. pap. 33.95 (ISBN 0-19-261736-2). Oxford U Pr.

Paediatric Research: A Genetic Approach (Polani Festschrift) Matteo Adinolfi & F. Giannelli. (Clinics in Developmental Ser.: No. 83). 245p. 1983. text ed. 29.75 (ISBN 0-433-00111-9). Lippincott.

Paediatric Research: Report. WHO Scientific Group. Geneva, 1967. (Technical Report Ser.: No. 400). (Also avail. in French & Russian). 1968. pap. 1.20 (ISBN 92-4-120400-1). World Health.

Paediatric Respiratory Disease. Ed. by M. H. Goetz & O. B. Stur. (Progress in Respiration Research: Vol. 17). (Illus.). x, 306p. 1982. 126.75 (ISBN 3-8055-2658-X). S Karger.

Paediatric Respiratory Physiology & Clinical Aspects of Paediatric Pneumology. Ed. by R. Kraemer. (Modern Problems in Paediatrics: Vol. 21). (Illus.). xii, 248p. 1982. pap. 110.00 (ISBN 3-8055-3505-8). S Karger.

Paediatric Trauma. Ed. by E. K. Alpar & R. Owen. (Illus.). 256p. 1988. text ed. 79.50x (ISBN 0-7194-0109-7, Pub. by Castle Hse England). Sheridan Med Bks.

Paediatric Urology. Ed. by Robert H. Whitaker & John R. Woodward. (BIMR Urology Ser.: Vol. 3). 320p. 1985. text ed. 95.00 (ISBN 0-407-02360-7). Butterworth.

Paediatric Urology. 2nd ed. Innes Williams & Johnston. 564p. 1982. text ed. 145.00 (ISBN 0-407-35152-3). Butterworth.

Paediatrics. A. Evans & C. McCarthy. (Management of Common Diseases in Family Practice Ser.). 1986. lib. bdg. 24.25 (ISBN 0-317-44719-X, Pub. by MTP Pr England). Kluwer Academic.

Paediatrics & Blood Transfusion. Smith Sibinga. 1982. lib. bdg. 28.50 (ISBN 90-247-2619-0, Pub. by Martinus Nijhoff Netherlands). Kluwer Academic.

Paediatrics: Concise Medical Textbook. 2nd ed. John Apley. (Illus.). 1982. pap. text ed. 17.95 (ISBN 0-7216-0702-0, Bailliere-Tindall). Saunders.

Paediatrics Diagnosis. Girish Srivastava & Narender K. Anand. 400p. 1980. text ed. 18.95x (ISBN 0-7069-1047-8, Pub. by Vikas India). Advent NY.

Paediatrics for Nurses. A. L. Speirs. (Illus.). 244p. pap. text ed. cancelled (ISBN 0-8464-1327-2). Beekman Pubs.

Paediatrics in the Tropics: Current Review. Ed. by R. G. Hendrickse. (Illus.). 1981. text ed. 49.50x (ISBN 0-19-261291-3). Oxford U Pr.

Paediatrische Infektionskrankheiten III. Ed. by U. B. Schaad. (Paediatrische Fortbildungskurse fuer die Praxis: Vol. 58). (Illus.). xvi, 132p. 1983. pap. 32.75 (ISBN 3-8055-3680-1). S Karger.

Paediatrische Infektionskrankheiten IV. Ed. by U. B. Schaad. (Paediatrische Fortbildungskurse fuer die Praxis: Vol. 59). (Illus.). xii, 188p. 1985. pap. 26.00 (ISBN 3-8055-3954-1). S Karger.

Paedogogica Europaea, Vol. 5. Council of Europe for Cultural Cooperation Staff. 1971. 16.50 (ISBN 0-444-99978-7). Elsevier.

Paedophilia: The Radical Case. Tom O'Carroll. 288p. (Orig.). 1982. pap. 8.95 (ISBN 0-932870-24-4). Alyson Pubns.

Pagalami: Ethnopsychiatric Knowledge in Bengal. Deborah P. Bhattacharyya. (Foreign & Comparative Studies-South Asian Ser.: No. 11). (Orig.). 1986. pap. 13.00X (ISBN 0-915984-89-X). Syracuse U Foreign Comp.

Pagan Adversary. Sara Craven. (Harlequin Presents Ser.). 192p. 1983. pap. 1.95 (ISBN 0-373-10616-5). Harlequin Bks.

Pagan & Christian Anxiety: A Response to E. R. Dodds. Ed. by Robert C. Smith & John Lounibos. LC 83-27345. 248p. 1984. lib. bdg. 26.75 (ISBN 0-8191-3823-1); pap. text ed. 13.00 (ISBN 0-8191-3824-X). U Pr of Amer.

Pagan & Christian Creeds. Edward Carpenter. 59.95 (ISBN 0-8490-0794-1). Gordon Pr.

Pagan & Christian in an Age of Anxiety: Some Aspects of Religious Experience from Marcus Aurelius to Constantine. E. R. Dodds. 1970. pap. 6.95 (ISBN 0-393-00545-3, Norton Lib). Norton.

Pagan & Christian Rome. Rodolfo Lanciani. LC 67-23856. (Illus.). 1968. Repr. of 1892 ed. 27.50 (ISBN 0-405-08728-4, Blom Pubns). Ayer Co Pubs.

Pagan Babies. Gina Cascone. 1988. pap. 2.95 (ISBN 0-312-90290-5). St Martin.

Pagan Babies & Other Catholic Memories. Gina Cascone. 160p. 1983. pap. 4.95 (ISBN 0-312-59419-4). St Martin.

Pagan Background of Christianity. W. R. Halliday. 59.95 (ISBN 0-8490-0795-X). Gordon Pr.

Pagan Bible. Melvin Gorham. 296p. 1982. 8.95 (ISBN 0-914752-22-7). Sovereign Pr.

Pagan Bible. Melvin Gorham. 304p. 1986. 6.00 (ISBN 0-317-53275-8). Noontide.

Pagan Celts: The Creators of Europe. Anne Ross. LC 86-17357. (Illus.). 192p. 1986. 29.95x (ISBN 0-389-20667-9). B&N Imports.

Pagan-Christian Conflict over Miracle in the Second Century. Harold Remus. LC 83-6729. (Patristic Monograph: No. 10). xiii, 371p. 1983. pap. 11.00 (ISBN 0-915646-09-9). N Amer Patristic Soc.

Pagan Christs. John M. Robinson. 1967. 5.95 (ISBN 0-8216-0136-9, Pub. by Univ Bks). Lyle Stuart.

Pagan Divinities & Their Worship As Depicted in the Work of St. Augustine. Sr. Mary Madden. 59.95 (ISBN 0-8490-0796-8). Gordon Pr.

Pagan Enchantment. Carole Mortimer. (Harlequin Presents Ser.). 192p. 1984. pap. 1.95 (ISBN 0-373-10659-9). Harlequin Bks.

Pagan Herbal: Herbs of Welsh Witchcraft. Rhuddlwm Gawr. LC 85-73746. (Illus.). 140p. 1988. 14.95 (ISBN 0-931760-36-4, CP 10113); pap. 10.95 (ISBN 0-931760-13-5). Camelot GA.

Pagan Meditations: The Worlds of Aphrodite, Artemis, & Hestia. Ginette Paris. Tr. by Gwendolyn Moore from Fr. LC 86-6675. 204p. (Orig.). 1986. pap. 13.50 (ISBN 0-88214-330-1). Spring Pubns.

Pagan Mysteries in the Renaissance. rev. ed. Edgar Wind. (Illus.). 1969. pap. 11.95 (ISBN 0-393-00475-9, Norton Lib). Norton.

Pagan Mysteries in the Renaissance. Edgar Wind. (Illus.). 1958. 75.00x (ISBN 0-686-83672-3). Elliots Bks.

Pagan Origins of the Christ Myth. John G. Jackson. 29p. 1985. pap. 3.00 saddle-stitched (ISBN 0-911826-04-1, 5204). Am Atheist.

Pagan Papers. Kenneth Grahame. LC 72-3427. (Essay Index Reprint Ser.). Repr. of 1898 ed. 15.00 (ISBN 0-8369-2903-9). Ayer Co Pubs.

Pagan Place. Edna O'Brien. LC 84-81628. 234p. (Orig.). 1984. pap. 8.00 (ISBN 0-915308-59-2). Graywolf.

Pagan Place: A Play. Edna O'Brien. 64p. 1973. pap. 4.95 (ISBN 0-571-10316-2). Faber & Faber.

Pagan Poems see Flowers of Passion.

Pagan Prophet: William Morris. Charlotte H. Oberg. LC 77-4730. (Illus.). 189p. 1978. 16.95x (ISBN 0-8139-0714-4). U Pr of Va.

Pagan Rabbi: And Other Stories. Cynthia Ozick. 288p. 1983. pap. 6.95 (ISBN 0-525-48026-9, Obelisk). Dutton.

Pagan Races of the Malay Peninsula, 2 vols. new ed. Walter W. Skeat & Charles O. Blagden. (Illus.). 1966. 95.00x set (ISBN 0-7146-2027-0, F Cass Co). Biblio Dist.

Pagan Reality. Melvin Gorham. 201p. 1970. pap. 5.00 (ISBN 0-914752-02-2). Sovereign Pr.

Pagan Rome & the Early Christians. Stephen Benko. LC 83-48898. 192p. 1985. 20.00x (ISBN 0-253-34286-4). Ind U Pr.

Pagan Rome & the Early Christians. Stephen Benko. LC 83-48898. (Midland Books Ser.: no. 385). 192p. 1986. pap. 7.95x (ISBN 0-253-20385-6). Ind U Pr.

Pagan Symbols in Judaism see Jewish Symbols in the Greco-Roman Period.

Pagan Temptation. Thomas Molnar. 208p. (Orig.). 1987. pap. 11.95 (ISBN 0-8028-0262-1). Eerdmans.

Pagan: The Origins of Modern Burma. Michael Aung-Thwin. LC 85-14862. 288p. 1985. text ed. 25.00x (ISBN 0-8248-0960-2). UH Pr.

Paganini. Leslie Sheppard & Herbert R. Axelrod. (Illus.). 704p. 1979. 25.00 (ISBN 0-87666-618-7, Z-28). Paganiniana Pubns.

Paganini: His Life & Times. expanded ed. John Sugden. (Life & Times Ser.). (Illus.). 208p. 1980. 12.95 (ISBN 0-87666-642-X, Z-41). Paganiniana Pubns.

Paganini of Genoa. Lillian Day. LC 77-181135. 318p. 1929. Repr. 39.00 (ISBN 0-403-01536-7). Scholarly.

Paganini of Genoa. Lillian Day. 1988. Repr. of 1929 ed. lib. bdg. 49.00x. Am Biog Serv.

Paganini: The Romantic Virtuoso. Jeffrey Pulver. LC 69-11669. (Music Ser.). 1970. Repr. of 1936 ed. lib. bdg. 37.50 (ISBN 0-306-71199-0). Da Capo.

Paganism in Our Christianity. Arthur Weigall. 69.95 (ISBN 0-87968-149-7). Gordon Pr.

Paganism in Roumanian Folklore. Marcu Beza. LC 74-173102. (Illus.). 1972. Repr. of 1928 ed. lib. bdg. 14.00 (ISBN 0-405-08267-3, Blom Pubns). Ayer Co Pubs.

Paganism in Roumanian Folklore. Marcu Beza. 1976. lib. bdg. 59.95 (ISBN 0-8490-2397-1). Gordon Pr.

Paganism in the Roman Empire. Ramsay MacMullen. LC 80-54222. 384p. 1981. 32.00t (ISBN 0-300-02655-2); pap. text ed. 9.95x (ISBN 0-300-02984-5). Yale U Pr.

Pagans. Arlo Bates. LC 70-104411. 275p. Repr. of 1884 ed. lib. bdg. 29.00 (ISBN 0-8398-0153-X). Irvington.

Pagans. Arlo Bates. 1986. pap. text ed. 7.95x (ISBN 0-8290-1860-3). Irvington.

Pagans. Arthur Moore. (River of Fortune Ser.: No. 2). 400p. (Orig.). 1980. pap. 2.50 (ISBN 0-89083-608-6). Zebra.

Pagans & Christians. Robin L. Fox. 1987. 35.00 (ISBN 0-394-55495-7). Knopf.

Pagans & Christians. Robin L. Fox. LC 87-45701. 800p. 1988. pap. 16.95 (ISBN 0-06-062852-9, PL-4257, HarpR). Har-Row.

Pagans of North Borneo. Owen Rutter. LC 77-87003. (Illus.). Repr. of 1929 ed. 32.00 (ISBN 0-404-16776-4). AMS Pr.

Pagans of North Borneo. Owen Rutter. (Illus.). 296p. 1987. 32.50x (ISBN 0-19-582627-2); pap. 8.95x (ISBN 0-19-582665-5). Oxford U Pr.

Page a Day Advent & the Christmas Season, 1988. Stephanie Collins. 1988. pap. 1.95. Paulist Pr.

Page a Day for Lent, 1989. Barbara Sullivan. 1988. pap. 2.95. Paulist Pr.

Page County Marriage Bonds, Eighteen Thirty-One to Eighteen Fifty. John Vogt & T. William Kethley, Jr. (Virginia Historic Marriage Register Ser.). (Illus.). viii, 79p. (Orig.). 1983. pap. 5.50 (ISBN 0-935931-11-2). Iberian Pub.

Page County Marriage Bonds, Eighteen Thirty-One to Eighteen Fifty. John Vogt & T. William Kethley, Jr. (Virginia Historic Marriage Register Ser.). 57p. 1988. Repr. lib. bdg. 19.95x (ISBN 0-8095-8225-2). Borgo Pr.

Page County Virginia Marriages 1831-1864. Philip J. Bertrand & Joan Turpin. iii, 47p. (Orig.). 1986. pap. 8.00 (ISBN 0-917890-64-7). Heritage Bk.

Page d'Amour. Emile Zola. (Coll. Diamant). 14.95 (ISBN 0-685-23947-0). French & Eur.

Page d'Amour. Emile Zola. 384p. 1973. 4.50 (ISBN 0-686-55795-6). French & Eur.

Page Disgracie: The Text As Confession, No. 33. Mary L. Gude. LC 78-21281. (Romance Monographs Ser.). 169p. 1979. 20.00x (ISBN 84-499-2554-1). Romance.

Page Four. Sheila S. Klass. LC 86-20223. 176p. (gr. 7 up). 1986. 12.95 (ISBN 0-684-18745-0, Pub. by Scribner). Macmillan.

Page Four. Sheila S. Klass. 176p. (YA) 1988. pap. 2.95 (ISBN 0-553-26901-1, Starfire). Bantam.

Page on Wills 1965-1976: Bowe-Parker Revision, 8 vols. William J. Bowe & Douglas H. Parker. 7732p. 1983. text ed. 525.00 (ISBN 0-87084-682-5); 1986 suppl. incl.; Supp. 1987. 90.00. Anderson Pub Co.

Page One: Major Events As Presented in the New York Times, 1920-1981. Herbert J. Cohen. 16.95 (ISBN 0-405-14350-8, 19818). Ayer Co Pubs.

Page One: Major Events, Nineteen Twenty to Nineteen Seventy-Eight, As Presented in the New York Times. 14.90 (ISBN 0-405-11751-5). Ayer Co Pubs.

Page One: Major Events, Nineten-Twenty to Nineteen Eighty As Presented in the New York Times. Herbert J. Cohen. 16.95 (ISBN 0-405-13698-6). Ayer Co Pubs.

Page-Turner. David Shapiro. 1973. 4.95 (ISBN 0-87140-575-X); pap. 2.50 (ISBN 0-87140-287-4). Liveright.

Pageant. G. B. Lancaster. 408p. 1986. pap. 6.95 (ISBN 0-14-007511-9). Penguin.

Pageant. Kathryn Lasky. LC 86-12087. 228p. (YA) (gr. 7 up). 1986. 12.95 (ISBN 0-02-751720-9, Four Winds). Macmillan.

Pageant. Kathryn Lasky. (gr. k-12). 1988. pap. 3.25 (ISBN 0-440-20161-6, LFL). Dell.

Pageant-Master of the Republic. facs. ed. David L. Dowd. LC 72-75507. (Select Bibliographies Reprint Ser). 1948. 22.00 (ISBN 0-8369-5005-4). Ayer Co Pubs.

Pageant of America, 10 vols. Ed. by Ralph H. Gabriel. Incl. Vol. 1. Adventurers in the Wilderness. Clark Wissler & Constance L. Skinner (ISBN 0-911548-56-4); Vol. 2. Lure of the Frontier. Ralph H. Gabriel (ISBN 0-911548-57-2); Vol. 3. Toilers of Land & Sea. Ralph H. Gabriel (ISBN 0-911548-58-0); Vol. 4. March of Commerce. Malcolm Keir (ISBN 0-911548-59-9); Vol. 5. Epic of Industry. Malcolm Keir; Vol. 6. Winning of Freedom. William Wood & Ralph H. Gabriel; Vol. 7. In Defense of Liberty. William Wood & Ralph H. Gabriel; Vol. 8. Builders of the Republic. Frederic A. Ogg; Vol. 9. Makers of a New Nation. John S. Bassett (ISBN 0-911548-64-5); Vol. 10. American Idealism. Luther A. Weigle (ISBN 0-911548-65-3); Vol. 11. American Spirit in Letters. Stanley T. Williams (ISBN 0-911548-66-1); Vol. 12. American Spirit in Art. Frank J. Mather, Jr. et al (ISBN 0-911548-67-X); Vol. 13. American Spirit in Architecture. Talbot F. Hamlin; Vol. 14. American Stage. Oral S. Coad & Edwin Mims, Jr (ISBN 0-911548-69-6); Vol. 15. Annals of American Sport. John A. Krout (ISBN 0-911548-70-X). (Illus.). 22.95 ea. US Pubs.

Pageant of Art. Vienna I. Curtiss. LC 77-280. (Illus.). 1979. 27.50 (ISBN 0-9602742-2-7). Collectors Choice.

Pageant of Civilization: World Romance & Adventure As Told by Postage Stamps. F. B. Warren. 1978. Repr. 35.00 (ISBN 0-8492-2897-2). R West.

Pageant of Dickens. W. Walter Crotch. LC 72-3293. (Studies in Dickens, No. 52). 1972. Repr. of 1915 ed. lib. bdg. 49.95x (ISBN 0-8383-1502-X). Haskell.

Pageant of English Actors. Donald Brook. LC 71-38315. (Biography Index Reprint Ser). Repr. of 1950 ed. 18.25 (ISBN 0-8369-8116-2). Ayer Co Pubs.

Pageant of English Literature. Edward Parrott. 1973. Repr. of 1914 ed. 30.00 (ISBN 0-8274-1240-1). R West.

Pageant of Letters. facs. ed. Alfred Noyes. LC 68-22935. (Essay Index Reprint Ser). 1968. Repr. of 1940 ed. 20.00 (ISBN 0-8369-0749-3). Ayer Co Pubs.

Pageant of Medieval England. Francis G. James. LC 74-23679. 228p. (Orig.). 1974. pap. 5.95x (ISBN 0-88289-055-7). Pelican.

Pageant of Old Scandinavia. facs. ed. Ed. by Henry G. Leach. LC 68-57061. (Granger Index Reprint Ser). 1946. 19.00 (ISBN 0-8369-6025-4). Ayer Co Pubs.

Pageant of Peking. 2nd ed. Donald Mennie. 40p. 1921. 700.00x (Pub. by Han-Shan Tang Ltd). State Mutual Bk.

Pageant of Transport Through the Ages. W. H. Boulton. LC 77-81514. (Illus.). 22.00 (ISBN 0-405-08296-7, Blom Pubns). Ayer Co Pubs.

Pageant of Transport Through the Ages. W. H. Boulton. 1976. lib. bdg. 344.95 (ISBN 0-8490-2398-X). Gordon Pr.

Pageantry in the Shakespearean Theater. Ed. by David M. Bergeron. LC 83-24221. (Illus.). 251p. 1985. 26.00x (ISBN 0-8203-0716-5). U of Ga Pr.

Pageantry of the English Language. 2nd, rev. ed. W. D. Snively. LC 83-80274. (Illus.). 80p. 1983. pap. text ed. 9.95 (ISBN 0-930982-03-7). U of Evansville Pr.

Pageantry on the Shakespearean Stage. Alice V. Griffin. (Orig.). 1951. pap. 9.95x (ISBN 0-8084-0239-0). New Coll U Pr.

Pageantry on the Shakespearean Stage. Alice S. Venezky. LC 77-177560. Repr. of 1951 ed. 16.50 (ISBN 0-404-06756-5). AMS Pr.

Pageants & Entertainments of Anthony Munday: A Critical Edition. David Bergeron. (Renaissance Imagination Ser.). 162p. 1985. lib. bdg. 33.00 (ISBN 0-8240-5453-9). Garland Pub.

Pageants of Despair. Dennis Hamley. LC 74-10841. 180p. (gr. 7-10). 1974. 14.95 (ISBN 0-87599-205-6). S G Phillips.

Pagemaker: Desktop Publishing. Nathan Goldenthal. 650p. (Orig.). 1988. pap. 24.95. Weber Systems.

Pagemaker: Desktop Publishing on the IBM PC & Compatibles. Kevin Strehlo. 320p. 1987. pap. 21.95 (ISBN 0-673-18765-9). Scott F.

PageMaker: Desktop Publishing on the Macintosh. Kevin Strehlo. Date not set. pap. 21.95 (ISBN 0-673-18764-0). Scott F.

Pages & Pictures from Forgotten Children's Books. A. W. Tuer. 44.95 (ISBN 0-8490-0797-6). Gordon Pr.

Pages & Pictures from Forgotten Children's Books. Andrew W. Tuer. LC 68-31096. (Illus.). 512p. 1969. Repr. of 1899 ed. 40.00x (ISBN 0-8103-3488-7). Gale.

Pages Choisies. Antoine De Saint-Exupery. pap. 8.50 (ISBN 0-685-37085-2). French & Eur.

Pages de Prose. Paul Claudel. 428p. 1944. 14.95 (ISBN 0-686-54407-2). French & Eur.

Pages d'Italie. facsimile ed. Stendhal. 1932. 35.00 (ISBN 0-686-55076-5). French & Eur.

Pages from a Child's Documentary. Kesa Thomas. LC 79-67480. (Illus.). 1979. pap. 9.95 (ISBN 0-917986-06-7). NFS Pr.

Pages from a Cold Island. Frederick Exley. LC 74-28321. 1975. 7.95 (ISBN 0-394-49440-7). Random.

Pages from a Cold Island. Frederick Exley. 1988. pap. 6.95 (ISBN 0-394-75977-X). Random.

Pages from a Diary Written in Nineteen Hundred Thirty. William B. Yeats. 72p. 1970. Repr. of 1944 ed. 15.00x (ISBN 0-7165-1401-X, BBA 02108, Pub. by Cuala Press Ireland). Biblio Dist.

Pages from a Journal. Joyce Butler. LC 76-685. (Illus.). 171p. 1976. 4.95 (ISBN 0-89080-006-5). Rosemary Hse.

Pages from a Musician's Life. Fritz Busch. Tr. by Marjorie Strachey. LC 71-106715. (Illus.). 223p. Repr. of 1953 ed. lib. bdg. 35.00x (ISBN 0-8371-3445-5, BUML). Greenwood.

Pages from a Scrapbook of Immigrants. Morton Marcus. 144p. (Orig.). 1988. pap. 8.95 (ISBN 0-918273-47-1). Coffee Hse.

Pages from a Worker's Life. William Z. Foster. LC 72-130864. (Illus.). 1970. o. p. 7.50 (ISBN 0-7178-0297-3); pap. 3.25 (ISBN 0-7178-0149-7). Intl Pubs Co.

Pages from an Oxford Diary. Paul E. More. LC 74-159095. 1971. Repr. of 1951 ed. 18.00x (ISBN 0-8046-1638-8, Pub. by Kennikat). Assoc Faculty Pr.

Pages from Hopi History. Harry C. James. LC 73-86451. 258p. 1974. pap. 9.95 (ISBN 0-8165-0500-4). U of Ariz Pr.

Pages from the Garibaldian Epic. Ed. by Anthony P. Campanella. (Illus.). xxv, 368p. 1984. 22.50x (ISBN 92-9013-004-0). Intl Inst Garibaldian.

Pages from the Goncourt Journal. Tr. by Robert Baldick. (Lives & Letters Ser.). 464p. 1985. pap. 8.95 (ISBN 0-14-057014-4). Penguin.

Pages from the History of Novgorodian Painting. V. N. Lazarev. 1983. 74.00x (ISBN 0-317-61340-5, Pub. by Collets (UK)). State Mutual Bk.

Pages from the Past. facs. ed. Herbert A. Fisher. LC 75-90638. (Essay Index Reprint Ser). 1939. 18.00 (ISBN 0-8369-1260-8). Ayer Co Pubs.

Pages from the Virginia Story. George Bowles. (Illus.). 128p. (Orig.). 1979. pap. 8.95. Maiden Lane.

Pages from the Works of Thomas Hardy. Ruth Head. 1922. 30.00 (ISBN 0-932062-74-1). Sharon Hill.

Pages from the Works of Thomas Hardy. Ruth Head. 243p. 1984. Repr. of 1922 ed. lib. bdg. 50.00 (ISBN 0-89984-710-2). Century Bookbindery.

Pages in the Life of a Sufi. M. M. Khan. 1979. 14.95 (ISBN 11-1910-334-7, Pub. by Sufi Pub Co England). Hunter Hse.

Pages in Waiting. facsimile ed. James Milne. LC 74-93357. (Essay Index Reprint Ser). 1927. 18.00 (ISBN 0-8369-1308-6). Ayer Co Pubs.

Pages of English Prose 1390-1930. Arthur T. Quiller-Couch. 1930. 30.00 (ISBN 0-8274-3097-3). R West.

Pages of Life. Daniel S. Scott. (Illus.). 66p. 1987. 6.95 (ISBN 1-55523-047-4). Winston-Derek.

Pages of Music. Tony Johnston. (Illus.). 32p. (gr. k-3). 1988. PLB 13.95 (ISBN 0-399-21436-4, Putnam). Putnam Pub Group.

Pages of Rock History. Sean Brickell & Rich Rothschild. LC 83-1957. (Illus.). 296p. 1983. pap. 6.95 (ISBN 0-89865-304-5). Donning Co.

Pages of Stone: Geology of Western National Parks & Monuments. Halka Chronic. (Rocky Mountains & Western Great Plains Ser.: Vol. 1). (Illus.). 192p. (Orig.). 1984. pap. 14.95 (ISBN 0-89886-095-4). Mountaineers.

Pages of Stone-Geology of Western National Parks & Monuments: Sierra Nevada, Cascades & Pacific Coast, Vol. 2. Halka Chronic. (Illus.). 184p. (Orig.). 1986. pap. 14.95 (ISBN 0-89886-114-4). Mountaineers.

Pages of Stone: Geology of Western National Parks & Monuments, 3: The Desert Southwest. Halka Chronic. (Illus.). 184p. (Orig.). 1986. pap. 14.95 (ISBN 0-89886-124-1). Mountaineers.

Pages of Stone: Geology of Western National Parks & Monuments, 4: Grand Canyon & the Plateau Country. Halka Chronic. (Pages of Stone Ser.). (Illus.). 184p. (Orig.). 1988. pap. 14.95 (ISBN 0-89886-155-1). Mountaineers.

Page's Ohio Revised Code, 1953-1986: Annotated, 30 Vols. 1980. Set & updating service for a year. 950.00 (ISBN 0-686-88948-7); Ann. updating service. write for info. Anderson Pub Co.

Pages sur Crist. Blaise Pascal & Ivan Gobry. 128p. 1963. 5.95 (ISBN 0-686-54851-5). French & Eur.

Pages: The World of Books, Writers & Writing, Vol. 1. Ed. by C. E. Clark, Jr. & Matthew J. Bruccoli. LC 76-20369. (Illus.). 304p. 1976. 38.00x (ISBN 0-8103-0925-4). Gale.

Pages to Go!!! How to Start & Maintain a Successful Freelance Typing Service. Laurie Buchanan. 14.95x (ISBN 0-943102-00-6). Laurie Buchanan.

Paget's Disease of Bone. Ed. by Frederick Singer. LC 77-1303. (Topics In Bone & Mineral Disorders Ser.). (Illus.). 172p. 1977. 39.50x (ISBN 0-306-30996-3, Plenum Med Bk). Plenum Pub.

Paget's Disease of the Bone: Assessment & Management. R. C. Hamdy. 216p. 1981. 56.95 (ISBN 0-275-91344-9, C1344). Praeger.

Paginas Libres - Horas de Lucha. Manuel G. Prada. (Ayacucho Library Collection Ser.: Vol.14). (Span.). 1985. 25.00 (ISBN 0-317-56279-7, Pub. by Biblioteca Ayacucho); pap. 10.95 (ISBN 0-317-56280-0, Pub. by Biblioteca Ayacucho). Humanities.

Pagne Noir. Bernard B. Dadie. pap. 8.95 (ISBN 0-685-35935-2). French & Eur.

Pagoda Ridge & Other Stories. Gu Hua. Tr. by Gladys Yang from Chinese. 260p. 1985. pap. 5.95 (ISBN 0-8351-1335-3). China Bks.

Pagoda, Skull & Samurai. Koda Rohan. Tr. by Chieko I. Mulhern. LC 84-52723. 280p. 1985. 12.50 (ISBN 0-8048-1499-6). C E Tuttle.

Pagoda, Skull & Samurai: Three Stories by Koda Rohan. Tr. by Chieko I. Mulhern. LC 82-225992. (East Asia Papers: No. 26). 213p. 1982. 6.00 (ISBN 0-939657-26-0). Cornell East Asia Pgm.

Pagoo. Holling C. Holling. (Illus.). (gr. 3-9). 1957. PLB 10.95 (ISBN 0-395-06826-6). HM.

Pahari Folk Art. O. C. Handa. (Illus.). xviii, 84p. 1981. text ed. 25.00x (ISBN 0-86590-039-6, Pub. by Taraporevala India). Apt Bks.

Pahlavi Conjugation. Tom Jordan. LC 78-15981. 1989. pap. 12.95 (ISBN 0-87949-135-3). Ashley Bks.

Pahlavi Texts, 5 vols. E. W. West. 1974. lib. bdg. 500.00 (ISBN 0-87968-566-2). Krishna Pr.

Pahsimeroi. David V. Taggart. (Illus.). 540p. 1987. 19.95 (ISBN 0-941371-00-X). Westwind Pub ID.

Pahsimeroi: Land Beyond Words. Edson Fichter. (Illus.). 48p. 1988. pap. 12.00 (ISBN 0-937179-02-7). Blue Scarab.

PAI Career Planning Manual for Human Resource-Personnel: A Guide to the Practice & Accreditation in the Profession. Personnel Accreditation Institute Staff. 428p. 1986. pap. 24.95. Am Soc Personnel.

PAI Curriculum Guide in Human Resource Management-Personnel. Personnel Accreditation Institute Staff. 100p. 1985. pap. 56.00. Am Soc Personnel.

PAI Self-Assessment & Study Guide for Human Resource Management-Personnel. Personnel Accreditation Insititute Staff. 115p. 1986. pap. 15.00. Am Soc Personnel.

PAI Study Guide in Human Resource Management. Personnel Accreditation Institute Staff. 107p. 1986. pap. 10.00. Am Soc Personnel.

Paid Holiday & Vacation Policies. (Personnel Policies Forum Surveys Ser.: No. 115). 1976. 30.00 (ISBN 0-686-88627-5). BNA.

Paid Holiday & Vacation Policies. (Personal Policies Forum Surveys Ser.: No. 130). 1980. 30.00 (ISBN 0-317-55316-X). BNA.

Paid Holidays & Vacation Policies. (Personal Policies Forum Surveys Ser.: No. 142). 1986. 30.00 (ISBN 0-87179-968-5). BNA.

Paideia Program: An Educational Syllabus. Mortimer J. Adler. 160p. 1984. 8.95 (ISBN 0-02-500300-3); pap. 4.95 (ISBN 0-02-013040-6, Collier). Macmillan.

Paideia: The Ideals of Greek Culture, 3 vols. Werner Jaeger. Tr. by Gilbert Highet from Ger. Incl. Vol. 1. Archaic Greece; The Mind of Athens. 2nd ed. 1945 (ISBN 0-19-500399-3); Vol. 2. In Search of the Divine Center. 1943 (ISBN 0-19-500592-9); Vol. 3. The Conflict of Cultural Ideals in the Age of Plato. 1944 (ISBN 0-19-500593-7). 35.00x ea. Oxford U Pr.

Paideia, the Ideals of Greek Culture: Archaic Greece-The Mind of Athens, Vol. I. 2nd ed. Werner Jaeger. Tr. by Gilbert Highet. 544p. 1986. pap. text ed. 12.95 (ISBN 0-19-500425-6). Oxford U Pr.

Paideia, the Ideals of Greek Culture: In Search of the Divine Centre, Vol. II. Werner Jaeger. Tr. by Gilbert Highet. 460p. 1986. pap. text ed. 12.95x (ISBN 0-19-504047-3). Oxford U Pr.

Paideia, the Ideals of Greek Culture: The Conflict of Cultural ideas in the Age of Plato, Vol. III. Werner Jaeger. Tr. by Gilbert Highet. 384p. 1986. pap. text ed. 12.95x (ISBN 0-19-504048-1). Oxford U Pr.

Paiements Exterieurs et Relations Financieres Internationales. (Economies et Societes Ser.: Ser. P, No. 9). 1964. pap. 26.00 (ISBN 0-8115-0777-7). Kraus Repr.

Paint Magic. Jocasta Innes. LC 86-42519. (Illus.). 240p. 1986. pap. 19.95 (ISBN 0-394-74654-6). Pantheon.

Paint Magic. rev. ed. Jocasta Innes. 240p. 1987. 19.95 (ISBN 0-394-75434-4). Pantheon.

Paint Me a Picture--Make Me a Poem. Norbert Blei. (Illus.). 108p. 1987. pap. 5.95 (ISBN 0-933180-97-7). Spoon Riv Poetry.

Paint Now, Learn Later. Guy R. Williams. (Illus.). 10.95 (ISBN 0-87523-158-6). Emerson.

Paint on a Happy Face. Jane Roe. (Illus.). 92p. (Orig.). 1978. pap. 6.95 (ISBN 0-917119-09-6, 45-1025). Priscillas Pubns.

Paint Testing Manual: Physical & Chemical Examination of Paints, Varnishes, Lacquers & Colors. 13th ed. American Society for Testing & Materials Staff. Ed. by G. G. Sward. LC 75-186850. (ASTM Special Technical Publication Ser.: No. 500). pap. 153.00 (ISBN 0-317-20535-8, 2022835). Bks Demand UMI.

Paint the Town Red. Harold Adams. 208p. 1988. 3.95 (ISBN 0-445-40631-3). Mysterious Pr.

Paint Your Face & Other Poems. Jenny Keller. Ed. by Marquetta Herring. (Illus.). 22p. 1986. 3.50 (ISBN 0-942186-01-X). Paperbacks Plus.

Paintbox Summer. Betty Cavanna. 212p. 1981. Repr. PLB 16.95 (ISBN 0-89966-357-5). Buccaneer Bks.

Paintbox Summer. Betty Cavanna. 239p. 1981. Repr. PLB 16.95x (ISBN 0-89967-031-8). Harmony Raine.

Painted & Printed Fabrics: The History of the Manufactory at Jouy & Other Ateliers in France, 1760-1815 by Henri Clouzot: Notes on the History of Cotton Printing Especially in England & America by Frances Morris. Henri Clouzot & Frances Morris. LC 70-168418. (Metropolitan Museum of Art Publications in Reprint). (Illus.). 222p. 1972. Repr. of 1927 ed. 31.00 (ISBN 0-405-02256-5). Ayer Co Pubs.

Painted Architecture & Polychrome Monumental Sculpture in Mesoamerica. Ed. by Elizabeth H. Boone. LC 85-4514. (Illus.). 201p. 1985. 20.00x (ISBN 0-88402-142-4). Dumbarton Oaks.

Painted Bird. Jerzy Kosinski. 224p. 1983. pap. 4.50 (ISBN 0-553-26520-2). Bantam.

Painted Bird. 2nd ed. Jerzy Kosinski. LC 82-42869. 1982. Repr. 6.95 (ISBN 0-394-60433-4). Modern Lib.

Painted Canoe. Anthony Winkler. 296p. 1986. 14.95 (ISBN 0-8184-0403-5). Lyle Stuart.

Painted Cat. Elisabeth Foucart-Walter & Pierre Rosenberg. LC 88-42741. (Illus.). 224p. 1988. 50.00 (ISBN 0-8478-0995-1). Rizzoli Intl.

Painted Ceramics of the Western Mound at Awatovi. Watson Smith. LC 79-102785. (Peabody Museum Papers: Vol. 38). 1971. pap. 40.00x (ISBN 0-87365-114-6). Peabody Harvard.

Painted Churches of Romania: A Visitor's Impressions. John Fletcher. (Illus.). 52p. 1971. 22.95 (ISBN 0-88010-062-1, Pub. by Steinerbooks). Anthroposophic.

Painted Crucifixes in Croatia. Grgo Gamulin. 133p. 1983. 30.00 (ISBN 0-918660-35-1). Ragusan Pr.

Painted Crucifixes of Croatia. Grgo Gamulin. 134p. 1983. 182.00x (ISBN 0-317-61342-1, Pub. by Collets (UK)). State Mutual Bk.

Painted Delight. Stella Kramrisch. (Illus.). 240p. 1986. text ed. 52.95 (ISBN 0-8122-7954-9, Pub. by PA Mus Art). U of PA Pr.

Painted Delight: Indian Paintings from Philadelphia Collections. Stella Kramrisch. LC 85-31013. (Illus.). 195p. (Orig.). 1986. pap. 17.95 (ISBN 0-87633-064-2). Phila Mus Art.

Painted Desert, Green Shade: Essays on Contemporary Writers for Children. David Rees. LC 83-12996. 212p. 1984. pap. 13.95 (ISBN 0-87675-286-5). Horn Bk.

Painted Enamels of Limoges in the Walters Art Gallery: A Picture Book. (Illus.). 1968. pap. 4.00 (ISBN 0-911886-14-1). Walters Art.

Painted Enamels of the Renaissance in the Walters Art Gallery. Philippe Verdier. LC 68-2513. (Illus.). 1967. bds. 30.00 (ISBN 0-911886-15-X). Walters Art.

Painted Engines. James H. Russell. LC 73-101572. (Illus.). 1965. 19.95x (ISBN 0-678-06012-6). Kelley.

Painted Fans of Japan: Fifteen Noh Drama Masterpieces. Reiko Chiba. LC 62-20775. (Illus., Fr., Or Eng). 1962. 19.95 (ISBN 0-8048-0468-0). C E Tuttle.

Painted Gardens: English Watercolours, 1850-1914. Penelope Hobhouse & Christopher Wood. (Illus.). 192p. 1988. 39.95 (ISBN 0-689-11999-2). Atheneum.

Painted House. Graham Rust. LC 88-45315. (Illus.). 192p. 1988. 60.00 (ISBN 0-394-57340-4). Knopf.

Painted Illusions: A Creative Guide to Painting Murals & Trompe l'Oeil Effects. Timothy Plant. (Illus.). 1989. 22.50. Salem Hse Pubs.

Painted in Blood: Understanding Europeans. Stuart Miller. LC 86-47691. 320p. 1987. 17.95 (ISBN 0-689-11531-8). Atheneum.

Painted Inscriptions of David Jones. Nicolete Gray. (Illus.). 114p. 1981. 148.00 (ISBN 0-86092-058-5, Pub. by Gordon Fraser). State Mutual Bk.

Painted Lace & Other Pieces, (1914-1937, Vol. Five Of Unpublished Works Of Gertrude Stein In 8 Vols. facsimile ed. Gertrude Stein. LC 77-103665. (Select Bibliographies Reprint Ser). 1955. 27.50 (ISBN 0-8369-5165-4). Ayer Co Pubs.

Painted Ladies: The Art of San Francisco's Victorian Houses. Morley Baer et al. (Illus.). 1978. pap. 12.95 (ISBN 0-525-48244-X). Dutton.

Painted Message. Otto Billig & B. G. Burton-Bradley. LC 77-3293. 1978. 21.95x (ISBN 0-470-99126-7). Halsted Pr.

Painted Mountains: Two Expeditions to Kashmir. Stephen Venables. (Illus.). 231p. 1987. text ed. 22.95 (ISBN 0-89886-136-5). Mountaineers.

Painted Ponies: American Carousel Art. William Manns et al. Ed. by Dru Riley. (Illus.). 256p. 1986. 40.00 (ISBN 0-939549-01-8). Zon Intl Pub.

Painted Primitives & Dummy Board Designs. Elspeth. (Illus.). 32p. 1986. pap. 3.95 (ISBN 0-87588-285-4, 3308). Hobby Hse.

Painted Queen. Olga Hesky. 1962. 12.95 (ISBN 0-8392-1083-3). Astor-Honor.

Painted Rock of California. Myron Angel. Ed. by Lachlan P. MacDonald. LC 79-26494. (Illus.). 128p. 1979. pap. 5.95 (ISBN 0-914598-14-7). Padre Prods.

Painted Scene, & Other Stories of the Theater. facsimile ed. Henry K. Webster. LC 79-152962. (Short Story Index Reprint Ser.). (Illus.). Repr. of 1916 ed. 23.50 (ISBN 0-8369-3877-1). Ayer Co Pubs.

Painted Shadows. Richard Le Gallienne. LC 77-94738. (Short Story Index Reprint Ser.). 1904. 19.00 (ISBN 0-8369-3118-1). Ayer Co Pubs.

Painted Sky. Jeanine C. D'Hyon. 200p. 11.95 (ISBN 0-8062-2846-6). Carlton.

Painted Stone Age Pottery from the Province of Henon, China. T. J. Arne. 1925. 88.00 (ISBN 0-317-43908-1, Pub. by Han-Shan Tang Ltd). State Mutual Bk.

Painted Stone Age Pottery from the Province of Honan China. T. J. Arne. 40p. 1925. pap. 263.00x (Pub. by Han-Shan Tang Ltd). State Mutual Bk.

Painted Turtle: Woman with Guitar. Clarence Major. 1988. 14.95 (ISBN 1-55713-002-7). Sun & Moon CA.

Painted Veil. W. Somerset Maugham. LC 75-25362. (Works of W. Somerset Maugham Ser.). 1977. Repr. of 1925 ed. 20.00x (ISBN 0-405-07820-X). Ayer Co Pubs.

Painted Veil. W. Somerset Maugham. 1979. pap. 4.95 (ISBN 0-14-000872-1). Penguin.

Painted Veils. James G. Huneker. (Black & Gold Lib). 1942. 6.95 (ISBN 0-87140-913-5). Liveright.

Painted Walls of Mexico: From Prehistoric Times until Today. Emily Edwards. (Elma Dill Russell Spencer Foundation Ser.: No. 3). (Illus.). 330p. 1966. 45.00 (ISBN 0-292-73624-X). U of Tex Pr.

Painted Windows. Harold Begbie. LC 77-108696. (Essay & General Literature Index Reprint Ser). 1970. Repr. of 1922 ed. 23.50x (ISBN 0-8046-0918-7, Pub. by Kennikat). Assoc Faculty Pr.

Painted Witch. Edwin Mullins. LC 85-5774. (Illus.). 225p. (Orig.). 1985. 25.00 (ISBN 0-88184-200-1). Carroll & Graf.

Painted with Words. Mark Hornbogen. 1988. 7.95 (ISBN 0-533-07709-5). Vantage.

Painted Word. Tom Wolfe. 128p. 1976. pap. 3.50 (ISBN 0-553-25734-X). Bantam.

Painted Word. Tom Wolfe. (Illus.). 128p. 1975. 12.95 (ISBN 0-374-22878-7). FS&G.

Painter. Jack Rudman. (Career Examination Ser.: C-570). (Cloth bdg. avail. on request). pap. 14.00 (ISBN 0-8373-0570-5). Natl Learning.

Painter: A Western Odyssey. Rhett S. James. (Illus.). 125p. 1987. 30.00 (ISBN 0-937231-01-0). Western Prof.

Painter & Decorator's Book of Facts. John Snelling. (Illus.). 150p. 1973. 19.50x (ISBN 0-291-39316-0). Scholium Intl.

Painter & Poet. facs. ed. Chauncey B. Tinker. LC 73-80402. (Essay Index Reprint Ser). 1938. 22.25 (ISBN 0-8369-1052-4). Ayer Co Pubs.

Painter & the Photograph: From Delacroix to Warhol. rev. ed. Van Deren Coke. LC 75-129804. (Illus.). 338p. 1986. pap. 24.95x (ISBN 0-8263-0325-0). U of NM Pr.

Painter & the Printer: Robert Motherwell's Graphics, 1943-1980. Stephanie Terenzio. (Illus.). 248p. (Orig.). 1980. pap. 14.95 (ISBN 0-917418-65-4). Am Fed Arts.

Painter & the Wild Swans. Claude Clement. LC 86-2154. (Illus.). 32p. (gr. k up). 1986. 13.95 (ISBN 0-8037-0268-X, 01354-410). Dial Bks Young.

Painter Depicted: Painters As a Subject in Painting. Michael Levey. (Illus.). 1982. 10.95 (ISBN 0-500-55013-1). Thames Hudson.

Painter of His Dishonour (El Pintor de Su Deshonra) Pedro B. De La Calderon. Ed. by Alan K. G. Paterson. (Hispanic Classics--The Golden Age Ser.). (Span. & Eng.). 1988. text ed. 49.95 (ISBN 0-85668-346-9, Pub. by Aris & Phillips UK); pap. text ed. 16.50 (ISBN 0-85668-347-7, Pub. by Aris & Phillips UK). Humanities.

Painter of Modern Life & Other Essays. Charles Baudelaire. Ed. by Jonathan Mayne. (Illus.). 298p. 1986. 11.95 (ISBN 0-306-80279-1). Da Capo.

Painter of Our Time. John Berger. 192p. 1981. 11.95 (ISBN 0-904613-12-7); pap. 4.95 (ISBN 0-904613-13-5). Writers & Readers.

Painter of Signs. R. K. Narayan. 1983. pap. 5.95 (ISBN 0-14-006259-9). Penguin.

Painterly Approach. Mary B. McKenzie. (Illus.). 144p. 1987. 27.50 (ISBN 0-8230-3492-5). Watson-Guptill.

Painterly Figure. Klaus Kertess. LC 83-61884. (Illus.). 78p. (Orig.). 1983. pap. 8.00 catalogue (ISBN 0-943526-08-6). Parrish Art.

Painters & Personality: A Collector's View of Modern Art. facsimile ed. Sam A. Lewisohn. LC 70-152188. (Essay Index Reprint Ser). Repr. of 1937 ed. 38.50 (ISBN 0-8369-2238-7). Ayer Co Pubs.

Painters & Politics: The European Avant-Garde & Society, 1900-1925. T. Shapiro. 1976. 29.95 (ISBN 0-444-99012-7, SPN/, Pub. by Elsevier). Greenwood.

Painters & Public Life in Eighteenth-Century Paris. Thomas E. Crow. LC 85-5375. (Illus.). 292p. 1985. 45.00x (ISBN 0-300-03354-0). Yale U Pr.

Painters & Public Life in Eighteenth-Century. Thomas E. Crow. LC 85-5375. 292p. 1987. pap. 16.95x (ISBN 0-300-03764-3, Y-670). Yale U Pr.

Painters & Sculptors. facsimile ed. Kenyon Cox. LC 70-105006. (Essay Index Reprint Ser.). 1907. 27.50 (ISBN 0-8369-1458-9). Ayer Co Pubs.

Painters at the Sikh Court. Brijinder N. Goswamy. (Illus.). 135p. (Orig.). 1975. pap. 22.00x (ISBN 3-515-02097-7, Pub by Franz Steiner). Coronet Bks.

Painter's Choice: Problems in the Interpretation of Renaissance Art. Millard Meiss. (Icon Editions). (Illus.). 320p. 1977. (HarpT); pap. 9.95 (ISBN 0-06-430068-4, IN68, HarpT). Har-Row.

Painter's Craft: An Introduction to Artists' Methods & Materials. Ralph Mayer. (Penguin Handbook Ser.). (Illus.). 1979. pap. 9.95 (ISBN 0-14-046369-0). Penguin.

Painter's Guide to Studio Methods & Materials. Reed Kay. (Illus.). 352p. 1982. pap. 24.00 (ISBN 0-13-647941-3). P-H.

Painter's Handbook. William McElroy. 320p. (Orig.). 1987. pap. 21.25 (ISBN 0-934041-28-8). Craftsman.

Painter's Handbook: Experiencing Color Between Darkness & Light. Lois Schroff. (Illus.). 61p. (Orig.). 1985. pap. text ed. 9.00 (ISBN 0-9615740-0-3). Newlight Bks.

Painter's Methods & Materials. Arthur P. Laurie. (Illus.). 1967. pap. 6.50 (ISBN 0-486-21868-6). Dover.

Painter's Mind: A Study of the Relations of Structure & Space. in Painting. Romare Bearden & Carl Holty. LC 80-8527. 240p. 1981. lib. bdg. 48.00 (ISBN 0-8240-9457-3). Garland Pub.

Painter's Object. Ed. by Myfanwy Evans. LC 73-109022. (Contemporary Art Ser). (Illus.). 1971. Repr. of 1937 ed. 16.00 (ISBN 0-405-00742-6). Ayer Co Pubs.

Painters of Florence: From the Thirteenth to the Sixteenth Century. Julia Cartwright. 1979. Repr. of 1911 ed. lib. bdg. 40.00 (ISBN 0-8495-0916-5). Arden Lib.

Painters of Ireland: Sixteen Hundred to Nineteen Twenty. Anne Crookshank. (Illus.). 304p. 1979. 45.00 (ISBN 0-214-20678-5, Pub. by G Malik Bk Pubs). Eastview.

Painters of Japan 1-2. Arthur Morrison. 128p. 1911. 1120.00x (ISBN 0-317-69438-3, Pub. by Han-Shan Tang Ltd). State Mutual Bk.

Painters of the Humble Truth. H. Gerdts. (Illus.). 293p. sewn bdg. 90.00 (ISBN 0-317-54891-3). Apollo.

Painters of the Humble Truth: Masterpieces of American Still Life, 1801-1939. William H. Gerdts. LC 81-11400. (Illus.). 312p. 1982. 54.95 (ISBN 0-8262-0355-8). U of Mo Pr.

Painters of the Sea. David Cordingly. (Illus.). 1980. pap. 14.95 (ISBN 0-85331-425-X). Eastview.

Painters Painting. Emile De Antonio & Mitch Tuchman. LC 83-21526. (Illus.). 192p. 1984. 19.95 (ISBN 0-89659-418-1). Abbeville Pr.

Painter's Progress. Will H. Low. LC 75-28889. (Art Experience in Late 19th Century America Ser.: Vol. 22). (Illus.). 1976. Repr. of 1910 ed. lib. bdg. 45.00 (ISBN 0-8240-2246-7). Garland Pub.

Painter's Quest: Art as a Way of Revelation. Peter Rogers. LC 86-32128. (Illus.). 160p. (Orig.). 1987. pap. 16.95 (ISBN 0-939680-37-8). Bear & Co.

Painter's Quest: Art As a Way of Revelation. Peter Rogers. LC 88-12056. (Illus.). 160p. 1988. pap. 16.95 (ISBN 0-939680-50-5). Bear & Co.

Painter's Secret Geometry: A Study of Composition in Art. Charles Bouleau. LC 79-91815. 268p. 1980. Repr. of 1963 ed. lib. bdg. 35.00 (ISBN 0-87817-259-9). Hacker.

Painter's Trick. Piero Ventura & Marisa Ventura. LC 76-54411. (Illus.). (gr. k-2). 1977. (BYR); lib. bdg. 6.99 (ISBN 0-394-93320-6). Random.

Painter's Workshop. W. G. Constable. (Illus.). 1980. pap. 4.50 (ISBN 0-486-23836-9). Dover.

Painting. (Illus.). 32p. (gr. 6-12). 1982. pap. 1.25x (ISBN 0-8395-3372-1, 3372). BSA.

Painting a Wall. David Lan. 35p. (Orig.). 1981. pap. 3.00 (ISBN 0-86104-215-8, NO. 4133, Pub by Pluto Pr). Longwood Pub Group.

Painting & Decorating. 2nd ed. A. Fulcher et al. (Illus.). 226p. 1987. pap. text ed. 19.50x (ISBN 0-00-383206-6, Pub. by Collins England). Sheridan.

Painting & Decorating. Elizabeth Gundrey. (Orig.). 1980. pap. 8.95x (ISBN 0-8464-1036-2). Beekman Pubs.

Painting & Decorating: A Guide for Houseowner & Decorator. J. H. Goodier. pap. 40.00 (ISBN 0-317-27866-5, 2025265). Bks Demand UMI.

Painting & Decorating Encyclopedia. Ed. by William Brushwell. LC 81-13513. (Illus.). 272p. 1982. text ed. 18.00 (ISBN 0-87006-404-5). Goodheart.

Painting & Drawing Animals: Practical & Colorful Lessons on Painting Mammals, Fish, Birds, & Insects. Graeme Sims. (Illus.). 144p. 1983. 27.50 (ISBN 0-8230-3556-5). Watson-Guptill.

Painting & Drawing Boats. Moira Huntly. (Illus.). 144p. 1985. pap. 16.95 (ISBN 0-89134-161-7). North Light Bks.

Painting & Experience in Fifteenth-Century Italy. 2nd ed. Michael Baxandall. (Illus.). 176p. 1988. pap. 9.95 (ISBN 0-19-282144-X). Oxford U Pr.

Painting & Experience in Fifteenth Century Italy: A Primer in the Social History of Pictorial Style. Michael Baxandall. 1974. pap. 9.95 (ISBN 0-19-881329-5). Oxford U Pr.

Painting & Finishing Models. Ian Peacock. (Illus.). 160p. (Orig.). 1987. pap. text ed. 21.95 (ISBN 0-85242-912-6, Pub. by Argus Pubs UK). Motorbooks Intl.

Painting & Performance: Chinese Picture Recitation & Its Indian Genesis. Victor H. Mair. LC 88-21591. (Illus.). 320p. 1988. text ed. 30.00x (ISBN 0-8248-1100-3). UH Pr.

Painting & Personality: A Study of Young Children. rev. & abr. ed. Rose H. Alschuler & LaBerta W. Hattwick. LC 75-75966. (Illus.). 1969. 24.00x (ISBN 0-226-01566-1). U of Chicago Pr.

Painting & Poetry: Forms, Metaphor & the Language of Literature. Franklin R. Rogers. LC 83-46175. (Illus.). 248p. 1986. 36.50x (ISBN 0-8387-5077-X). Bucknell U Pr.

Painting & Sculpture from Antiquity to Nineteen Forty-Two. Albright-Knox Art Gallery Staff & Steven A. Nash. LC 77-79651. (Illus.). 1979. 35.00 (ISBN 0-8478-0146-2); pap. 25.00 (ISBN 0-914782-17-7). Buffalo Acad.

Painting & Sculpture from Antiquity to 1942. Steven A. Nash. LC 77-79651. (Illus.). 576p. 1979. pap. 25.00 (ISBN 0-295-96115-5). U of Wash Pr.

Painting & Sculpture in Europe: 1780-1880. Fritz Novotny. (Pelican History of Art Ser: No. 20). (Illus.). 1973. pap. 18.95x (ISBN 0-14-056120-X, Pelican). Penguin.

Painting & Sculpture in Europe 1780-1880. Fritz Novotny. (Pelican History of Art Ser: No. 20). 1961. 50.00 (ISBN 0-670-53583-4, Pelican). Viking.

Painting & Sculpture in Europe: 1880-1940. rev. ed. George H. Hamilton. (Pelican History of Art Ser: No. 29). (Illus.). 1978. pap. 18.95 (ISBN 0-14-056129-3, Pelican). Penguin.

Painting & Sculpture in Europe, 1880-1940. George H. Hamilton. (Pelican History of Art Ser.: No. 29). (Illus.). 1967. 50.00 (ISBN 0-670-53587-7, Pelican). Viking.

Painting & Sculpture in Minnesota, 1820-1914. Rena N. Coen. LC 75-27788. (Illus.). xiv, 178p. 1976. 19.50 (ISBN 0-8166-0771-0). U of Minn Pr.

Painting and Sculpture in the Museum of Modern Art, 1929-1967. Alfred H. Barr. LC 68-54923. (Illus.). 1977. 40.00 (ISBN 0-87070-540-7). Museum Mod Art.

Painting & Sculpture since Nineteen Forty: An American Renaissance. Ed. by Sam Hunter. LC 85-52251. (Illus.). 272p. 1985. 39.95 (ISBN 0-89659-649-4). Abbeville Pr.

Painting & System. Marcelin Pleynet. Tr. by Sima N. Godfrey from Fr. LC 84-209. (Illus.). 168p. 1984. lib. bdg. 17.50x (ISBN 0-226-67093-7). U of Chicago Pr.

Painting & Wallpapering. Robert C. Yeager. Ed. by Sally W. Smith. LC 82-61323. (Illus.). 96p. (Orig.). 1983. pap. 6.95 (ISBN 0-89721-015-8). Ortho.

Painting Animals in Watercolor. Sally Michel. (Illus.). 128p. 1985. 19.95 (ISBN 0-8230-3559-X). Watson-Guptill.

Painting As An Art. Richard Wollheim. (Illus.). 384p. 1987. text ed. 45.00 (ISBN 0-691-09964-2). Princeton U Pr.

Painting at Court. Michael Levey. LC 75-124528. (Wrightsman Lectures: Vol. 5). (Illus.). 1971. 45.00x (ISBN 0-8147-4950-X). NYU Pr.

Painting at Northwestern: Conger, Paschke, Valerio. Dennis Adrian et al. (Illus.). 64p. (Orig.). 1986. 30.00 (ISBN 0-941680-04-5); pap. 15.00 (ISBN 0-941680-03-7). M&L Block.

Painting at Northwestern: Conger, Paschke, Valerio. Mary & Leigh Block gallery Staff. LC 86-775. (Illus.). 64p. 1986. pap. 18.00 (ISBN 0-295-96426-X). U of Wash Pr.

Painting Better Landscapes. Margaret Kessler. (Illus.). 160p. 1987. 27.50 (ISBN 0-8230-3575-1). Watson-Guptill.

Painting Birds. Susan Rayfield. (Illus.). 144p. 1988. 27.50 (ISBN 0-8230-3560-3). Watson-Guptill.

Painting Birds. Edward J. Steinhardt. Ed. by Bill Nunn. 100p. 1988. 12.95 (ISBN 0-915637-07-3). Westphalia Pr.

Painting Birds & Animals. Patricia Monahan. (Illus.). 176p. 1987. 21.95 (ISBN 0-89134-180-3). North Light Bks.

Painting Children. Benedict Rubbra. LC 79-63839. (Start to Paint Ser.). (Illus.). 1979. pap. 3.95 (ISBN 0-8008-6203-1, Pentalic). Taplinger.

Paintings in German Museums, 2 Vols. Hans R. Schweers. 1286p. 1982. lib. bdg. 150.00 (ISBN 3-598-10308-5). K G Saur.

Paintings in Taxicabs. Richard Lyons. LC 64-64377. 160p. 1965. pap. 3.00 (ISBN 0-911042-09-1). N Dak Inst.

Paintings in the Hermitage Collection: Peinture Francaise des XV-XVII Siecles. Glickman & Krassowski. 261p. (Fr. & Rus.). 25.00 (ISBN 0-912729-24-4). Newbury Bks.

Paintings in the Kunsthistorisches Museum, Vienna, Guide. (Illus.). 68p. (Orig.). 1984. pap. text ed. 750.00 incl. microfiche (ISBN 0-85964-158-9). Chadwyck-Healey.

Paintings in the Louvre. Lawrence Gowing. LC 87-10221. (Illus.). 688p. 1987. 85.00 (ISBN 1-55670-007-5). Stewart Tabori & Chang.

Paintings in the Studiolo of Isabella d'Este at Mantua. Egon Verheyen. LC 76-164021. (College Art Association Monograph Ser.: Vol. 23). (Illus.). 122p. 1985. Repr. of 1971 ed. 30.00x (ISBN 0-271-00409-6). Pa St U Pr.

Paintings of Akbar Behkalam. Akbar Behkalam. (Illus.). 120p. (Orig.). 1987. pap. 19.95 (ISBN 0-939214-37-7). Mazda Pubs.

Paintings of Alson Skinner Clark 1876-1949. Jean Stern. LC 83-62425. (Illus.). 115p. 1983. 35.00 (ISBN 0-8227-8042-9). DeRu's Fine Art.

Paintings of Augusto Torres. Augusto Torres. Intro. by Guido Castillo. (Illus.). 176p. 1986. lib. bdg. 50.00 (ISBN 0-935748-67-9). Scala Books.

Paintings of Benjamin West. Helmut Von Erffa & Allen Staley. LC 85-22500. (Illus.). 600p. 1986. 85.00x (ISBN 0-300-03355-9). Yale U Pr.

Paintings of Carel Fabritius: Complete Edition with a Catalogue Raisonne. Christopher Brown. LC 80-69741. (Illus.). 168p. 1981. 85.00x (ISBN 0-8014-1394-X, Cornell Phaidon Books). Cornell U Pr.

Paintings of Chang Dai-Chien. National Museum of History Staff. 136p. 1974. 140.00x (ISBN 0-317-68477-9, Pub. by Han-Shan Tang Ltd). State Mutual Bk.

Paintings of Charles Bird King. Andrew J. Cosentino. LC 77-608258. (Illus.). 214p. 1978. 37.00x (ISBN 0-87474-336-2, COPK). Smithsonian.

Paintings of Cornelis Engebrechtsz. Walter S. Gibson. LC 76-23620. (Outstanding Dissertations in the Fine Arts - 16th Century). (Illus.). 1977. Repr. of 1969 ed. lib. bdg. 68.00 (ISBN 0-8240-2691-8). Garland Pub.

Paintings of Correggio. Cecil Gould. LC 75-16813. (Illus.). 501p. 1976. 125.00x (ISBN 0-8014-0973-X). Cornell U Pr.

Paintings of David Jones. Nicolette Gray. (Illus.). 120p. 1987. 60.00 (ISBN 0-85331-519-1, Pub. by Lund Humphries). Humanities.

Paintings of Domenico Veneziano, 1410-1461: A Study in Florentine Art of the Early Renaissance. Hellmut Wohl. LC 78-68140. (Illus.). 1980. 75.00x (ISBN 0-8147-9185-9). NYU Pr.

Paintings of Eugene Delacroix, 2 vols, Vols. I & II. Lee Johnson. 1981. Set. 265.00 (ISBN 0-317-68916-9). Oxford U Pr.

Paintings of Eugene Delacroix: A Critical Catalogue 1832-1863 (Moveable Pictures & Private Decorations) Lee Johnson. (Paintings of Eugene Delacroix Ser.). (Illus.). 1986. Set. 130.00x (ISBN 0-19-817378-4). Vol. III: Text, 504 p. Vol. IV: Plates, 340 p. Oxford U Pr.

Paintings of F. Grayson Sayre, 1879-1939. Ray Redfern & Barbara S. Harmon. (Illus.). 76p. 1986. pap. 35.00 (ISBN 0-939370-06-9). DeRu's Fine Art.

Paintings of Franz A. Bischoff (1864-1929) Jean Stern. Ed. by Carol E. Stern. LC 80-80157. (Illus.). 56p. 1980. lib. bdg. 25.00 (ISBN 0-8227-8028-3, Dist. by DeRu's Fine Art). Petersen Pub.

Paintings of George Caleb Bingham: A Catalogue Raisonne. E. Maurice Bloch. LC 85-29013. (Illus.). 328p. 1986. text ed. 64.00 (ISBN 0-8262-0461-9). U of Mo Pr.

Paintings of Girolamo Mazzola Bedoli. Ann R. Milstein. LC 77-94710. (Outstanding Dissertations in the Fine Arts Ser.). 1979. lib. bdg. 69.00 (ISBN 0-8240-3242-X). Garland Pub.

Paintings of Henry Miller: Paint As You Like & Die Happy. Henry Miller. LC 82-12857. (Illus.). 144p. (Orig.). 1982. text ed. 35.00 (ISBN 0-87701-280-6); pap. 18.95 (ISBN 0-87701-276-8). Chronicle Bks.

Paintings of Huang Chun-Pi. National Museum of History Staff. 132p. 1978. 126.00x (ISBN 0-317-68483-3, Pub. by Han-Shan Tang Ltd). State Mutual Bk.

Paintings of Huang Chun-pi, Vol. 1. National Museum of History Staff. 1982. 140.00x (ISBN 0-317-68485-X, Pub. by Han-Shan Tang Ltd). State Mutual Bk.

Paintings of J. M. W. Turner. rev. ed. Martin Butlin & Evelyn Joll. LC 84-40182. (Studies in British Art). (Illus.). 944p. 1984. 225.00 (ISBN 0-300-03276-5). Yale U Pr.

Paintings of J. M. W. Turner, 2 vols. rev. ed. Martin Butlin & Evelyn Joll. (Illus.). 1987. Set. pap. 60.00 (ISBN 0-318-23664-8). Yale-U-Pr.

Paintings of Jacob Ochtervelt 1634-1682: With Catalogue Raisonne. Susan D. Kuretsky. (Illus.). 245p. 1979. 48.50 (ISBN 0-8390-0240-8, Allanheld & Schram). Abner Schram Ltd.

Paintings of James McNeill Whistler, 2 vols. Andrew M. Young et al. LC 80-5214. (Studies in British Art Ser.). (Illus.). 670p. 1980. 250.00x (ISBN 0-300-02384-7). Yale U Pr.

Paintings of Joe Zucker Nineteen Sixty-Nine to Nineteen Eighty-Two. Susan Krane. LC 82-72220. (Illus.). 1982. pap. 14.00 (ISBN 0-914782-45-2). Buffalo Acad.

Paintings of Lin Gen Hwa. Lin Gen Hwa. (Illus.). 64p. 1983. pap. 5.95 (ISBN 0-934788-05-7). E W Pub Co.

Paintings of Lucas Cranach. Max J. Friedlander & Jakob Rosenberg. LC 77-18410. (Illus.). 600p. 1979. 125.00x (ISBN 0-8014-1061-4). Cornell U Pr.

Paintings of Quinten Massys: With Catalogue Raisonne. Larry Silver. LC 84-2939. (Illus.). 380p. 1984. 79.50x (Allanheld & Schram). Rowman.

Paintings of Quinten Massys: With Catalogue Raisonee. Larry Silver. (Illus.). 400p. 1984. 79.50 (ISBN 0-8390-0322-6, Allanheld & Schram). Abner Schram Ltd.

Paintings of Sam Hyde Harris (1889-1977) Jean Stern & Ruth Westphal. LC 80-83993. (Illus.). 64p. 1980. lib. bdg. 25.00 (ISBN 0-8227-8036-4, Dist. by DeRu's Fine Art). Petersen Pub.

Paintings of Samuel Palmer. Raymond Lister. (Illus.). 176p. 1985. 34.50 (ISBN 0-521-26760-9). Cambridge U Pr.

Paintings of Samuel Palmer. Raymond Lister. 178p. 1987. pap. 18.95 (ISBN 0-521-31855-6). Cambridge U Pr.

Paintings of the Babur Nama. M. S. Randhawa. 139p. 1983. 80.00. Asia Bk Corp.

Paintings of the Casa Vasari. Liana Cheney. Ed. by S. J. Freedberg. (Outstanding Dissertations in Fine Arts Ser.). (Illus.). 675p. 1985. Repr. of 1978 ed. 65.00 (ISBN 0-8240-6852-1). Garland Pub.

Paintings of the Lotus Sutra. Willa J. Tanabe. (Illus.). 340p. 65.00 (ISBN 0-8348-0217-1). Weatherhill.

Paintings of the Ming & Qing Dynasties from the Guangzhou Art Gallery. Xie Wenyong. 320p. 1986. 210.00x (ISBN 0-317-69376-X, Pub. by Han-Shan Tang Ltd). State Mutual Bk.

Paintings of the Old West by Frank C. McCarthy. Norton (R. W.) Art Gallery. LC 77-7355. (Contemporary Realists Ser.). (Illus.). 1977. pap. 5.50x (ISBN 0-913060-13-5). Norton Art.

Paintings of the 14th-15th Centuries in the Collection of the Hispanic Society of America. Elizabeth Trapier. (Illus.). 256p. 1930. 5.00 (ISBN 0-317-00625-8). Interbk Inc.

Paintings of the 19th-20th Centuries in the Collection of the Hispanic Society of America, 2 vols. Elizabeth Trapier. (Illus.). 956p. 1932. Set. 17.00 (ISBN 0-317-00623-1). Interbk Inc.

Paintings of William Blake. Raymond Lister. (Illus.). 175p. 1986. 34.50 (ISBN 0-521-30538-1). Cambridge U Pr.

Paintings of William Blake. Raymond Lister. (Illus.). 175p. 1988. 18.95 (ISBN 0-521-31557-3). Cambridge U Pr.

Paintings of Wu Ch'ang-Shih. Compiled by Chang Lee-ching. (Illus.). 16p. 1972. 455.00x (ISBN 0-317-69100-7, Pub. by Han-Shan Tang Ltd). State Mutual Bk.

Paintings of Zurbaran for the Charterhouses of las Cuevas & Jerez de la Frontera. James Hogg. (Analecta Cartusiana Ser.: No. 47-4). (Orig.). 1986. pap. 25.00 (ISBN 3-7052-0067-4, Pub by Salzburg Studies). Longwood Pub Group.

Paintings, Pastels, Drawings, Prints & Copper Plates by & Attributed to American & European Artists. rev. ed. Compiled by Burns A. Stubbs. (Occasional Papers Ser: Vol. 1, No. 2). 1967. pap. 3.50 (ISBN 0-934686-00-9). Freer.

Paints. Henry Pluckrose. Ed. by Franklin Watts Ltd. LC 87-50906. (Illus.). 32p. (gr. 1-9). 1988. 10.90 (ISBN 0-531-10471-0). Watts.

Paints & Coatings for Space. Edward C. Metzler. 100p. 1988. lib. bdg. 90.00x (ISBN 0-937041-38-6); text ed. 80.00x (ISBN 0-937041-39-4); pap. text ed. 40.00x (ISBN 0-937041-40-8). Systems Co.

Paints & Coatings Industry. 280p. 1987. pap. 750.00 (ISBN 0-318-04170-7). Busn Trend.

Paints & Surface Coatings: Theory & Practice. Ronald Lambourne. (Applied Science & Industrial Technology Ser.). 696p. 1987. 94.95 (ISBN 0-470-20809-0, Pub. by Halsted Press). Halsted Pr.

Paints, Related Coatings, & Aromatics: Volume 06.01, Paint - Tests for Formulated Products & Applied Coatings. 1340p. 1986. 74.00 (ISBN 0-8031-0881-8). ASTM.

Paints, Related Coatings, & Aromatics: Volume 06.02, Paint - Pigments, Resins & Polymers. 666p. 1986. 47.00 (ISBN 0-8031-0882-6). ASTM.

Paints, Related Coatings, & Aromatics: Volume 06.03, Paint - Fatty Oils & Acids, Solvents, Miscellaneous; Aromatic Hydrocarbons. 1186p. 1986. 67.00 (ISBN 0-8031-0883-4). ASTM.

Paiolo on Accounting. R. Gene Brown & Kenneth S. Johnston. LC 83-49104. (Accounting History & the Development of a Profession Ser.). 144p. 1984. lib. bdg. 22.00 (ISBN 0-8240-6318-X). Garland Pub.

Pair of Blue Eyes. Thomas Hardy. LC 77-81875. (Hardy New Wessex Editions). 1979. pap. 3.95 (ISBN 0-312-59466-6). St Martin.

Pair of Blue Eyes. Thomas Hardy. 448p. 1982. pap. 7.50 (ISBN 0-907746-06-3, Pub. by A Mott Ltd). Longwood Pub Group.

Pair of Blue Eyes. Thomas Hardy. Ed. by Alan Manford. (World's Classics Ser.). 1985. pap. 4.95 (ISBN 0-19-281684-5). Oxford U Pr.

Pair of Blue Eyes. Thomas Hardy. Ed. by Roger Ebbatson. 432p. 1986. pap. 4.95 (ISBN 0-14-043266-3). Penguin.

Pair of Eyes. Reese Williams. 80p. (Orig.). 1983. pap. 5.95 (ISBN 0-934378-32-0). Tanam Pr.

Pair of Hands. Doyle Schwab. Ed. by Sherri York. LC 87-50261. (Illus.). 130p. 1987. 8.95 (ISBN 1-55523-074-1). Winston-Derek.

Pair of Patient Lovers. William D. Howells. LC 78-125219. (Short Story Index Reprint Ser). 1901. 20.00 (ISBN 0-8369-3585-3). Ayer Co Pubs.

PAIR Policy & Program Management, Vol. VII. Ed. by Dale Yoder & Herbert G. Heneman, Jr. LC 74-80467. (ASPA Handbook of Personal & Industrial Relations). 182p. 1978. 12.00 (ISBN 0-87179-206-0). BNA.

Pair Trawling & Pair Seining. David Thomson. 1978. 35.00x (ISBN 0-685-63445-0). State Mutual Bk.

Pair Trawling & Pair Seining: The Technology of Two-Boat Fishing. David Thomson. (Illus.). 168p. 1978. 35.95 (ISBN 0-85238-087-9, FN73, FNB). UNIPUB.

Pair Trawling with Small Boats. (Training Ser.: No. 1). 77p. 1981. pap. 8.25 (ISBN 92-5-100627-X, F2095, FAO). UNIPUB.

PAIRallels: Narratives for Pair Work. Michael A. Rost & John Lance. (Illus.). 71p. 1984. pap. text ed. 6.95 (ISBN 0-940264-24-2); pap. text ed. 27.00 incl. 2 cassettes (ISBN 0-940264-25-0); tchr's. manual 8.00 (ISBN 0-317-17966-7). Lingual Hse Pub.

Paired Pulse Stimulation of the Heart. Ed. by Paul F. Cranefield & Brian F. Hoffman. (Illus.). 224p. 1968. 7.50x (ISBN 0-87470-009-4). Rockefeller.

Pairing. George R. Bach & Ronald M. Deutsch. 1971. pap. 3.95 (ISBN 0-380-00394-5, 65367-6). Avon.

Pairing Off. Julian Moynahan. 1979. pap. 1.75 (ISBN 0-8439-0642-1, Leisure Bks). Leisure NY.

Pairs Game. David Greenwood. 150p. (Orig.). 1982. pap. 5.95 (ISBN 0-571-11906-9). Faber & Faber.

Pais de Cuatro Pisos. Jose L. Gonzalez. LC 80-67414. (Nave y el puerto). 122p. 1981. pap. 4.95 (ISBN 0-940238-32-2). Ediciones Huracan.

PAIS Subject Headings. 319p. 1984. 55.00 (ISBN 0-318-17390-5); members 45.00 (ISBN 0-318-17391-3). Pub Aff Info.

Paisajes despues de la Batalla. Juan Goytisolo. 199p. (Span.). 1982. 12.00 (ISBN 84-85859-54-5, 2008). Ediciones Norte.

Paisano: Nuevo Mexico: Vida y Dilema. Benedicto Cuesta. 1976. pap. 4.95 (ISBN 0-913270-59-8). Sunstone Pr.

Paisanos: A Folklore Miscellany. Ed. by Francis Abernethy. 1978. 12.50 (ISBN 0-88426-054-2). Encino Pr.

Paisanos: Spanish Settlers on the Northern Frontier of New Spain. Oakah L. Jones, Jr. LC 78-58119. (Illus.). 368p. 1979. 28.95 (ISBN 0-8061-1432-0). U of Okla Pr.

Paisius Ligarides. Harry T. Hiondes. LC 70-187634. (Twayne's World Authors Ser.). 169p. 1972. text ed. 17.95 (ISBN 0-8290-1743-7). Irvington.

Paisley. Ed Maloney & Andy Pollak. (Illus.). 456p. (Orig.). 1986. pap. 12.95 (ISBN 0-905169-75-1, Pub. by Poolbeg Pr Ireland). Irish Bks Media.

Paiute. Sessions S. Wheeler. 231p. 1986. ltd. ed. 35.00 (ISBN 0-87417-119-9); pap. 8.95 (ISBN 0-87417-115-6). U of Nev Pr.

Paiute Sorcery. Beatrice B. Whiting. Repr. of 1950 ed. 19.00 (ISBN 0-384-68180-8). Johnson Repr.

Paiute: Southwest. Ed. by Frank W. Porter. (Indians of North America Ser.). (Illus.). (gr. 5 up). 1989. 16.95 (ISBN 1-55546-723-7). Chelsea Hse.

Paix Chez les Betes. Colette. 192p. 1976. 13.95 (ISBN 0-686-54601-6). French & Eur.

Paix Chez Soi. Georges Courteline. 40p. 1966. 8.95 (ISBN 0-686-54636-9). French & Eur.

Paix et Liberte, ou le Budget Republicain. Frederic Bastiat. Bd. with On the Causes of War, & the Means of Reducing Their Number. Emile L. Laveleye. LC 72-147492. (Library of War & Peace; the Political Economy of War). lib. bdg. 46.00 (ISBN 0-8240-0286-5). Garland Pub.

Pajama Story. Lin Ting. 130p. 1980. 11.95 (ISBN 0-89955-161-0, Pub. by Mei Ya China); pap. 8.95 (ISBN 0-89955-190-4, Pub. by Mei Ya China). Intl Spec Bk.

Pajamas. Livingston Taylor & Maggie Taylor. (Illus.). 32p. (ps-3). 1988. 13.95 (ISBN 0-15-200564-1, Gulliver Bks). HarBraceJ.

Pajamas Don't Matter (or: What Your Baby Really Needs) Trish Gribben. LC 79-90081. (Creative Parenting Ser.). (Illus.). 52p. 1980. pap. 5.95 (ISBN 0-915190-21-4, JP9021-4). Jalmar Pr.

Pajarito Emilio. Charles M. Schulz. 1.50 (ISBN 0-686-56190-2). French & Eur.

Pajaros Notables De Puerto Rico: Guia Para Observadores De Aves. Osvaldo Rivera Cianchini & Luis Mojica Sandoz. (Illus.). v, 101p. 1981. 7.50 (ISBN 0-8477-2324-0); pap. 9.00 (ISBN 0-8477-2325-9). U of PR Pr.

Pak-Afghanistan Relations. K. Kaur. 1986. 30.00x (ISBN 0-8364-1804-2, Pub. by Deep). South Asia Bks.

Pak Six. G. I. Basel. 192p. 1987. pap. 3.50 (ISBN 0-515-09005-0). Jove Pubns.

Pak Six, A Story of the Air-War over North Vietnam. G. I. Basel. LC 82-72150. (Illus.). 176p. (Orig.). 1982. pap. 7.95 (ISBN 0-933362-07-2). Assoc Creative Writers.

Pakistan. B. L. Johnson. LC 79-10749. 1980. text ed. 22.50x (ISBN 0-435-35484-1). Heinemann Ed.

Pakistan. (Let's Visit Places & Peoples - - Nations, Dependencies, & Sovereignties of the World Ser.). (Illus.). (gr. 5 up). 1988. 12.95 (ISBN 0-222-00907-1). Chelsea Hse.

Pakistan. S. Aleem Qureishi. (World Bibliographical Ser.: No. 10). Date not set. price not set (ISBN 0-903450-13-5). ABC-Clio.

Pakistan - The India Factor. Rajendra Sareen. 615p. 1984. 37.95. Asia Bk Corp.

Pakistan: A Country Study. 5th ed. Ed. by Richard F. Nyrop. (DA Pam 55048, Area Handbook Ser.). (Illus.). 411p. 1984. 14.00 (ISBN 0-318-21882-8, S/N 008-020-01003-1). USGPO.

Pakistan: A Nation in the Making. Shahid J. Burki. (Nations of Contemporary Asia Ser.). 128p. 1985. 28.00x (ISBN 0-86531-353-9). Westview.

Pakistan: A Pawn in the U. S. Power Game. Gaurishankar Chaudhuri. 1986. 9.00x (ISBN 0-8364-1614-7, Pub. by KL Mukhopadhyay). South Asia Bks.

Pakistan: A Travel Survival Kit. 3rd ed. Jose R. Santiago. (Illus.). 240p. (Orig.). 1987. pap. 8.95 (ISBN 0-86442-013-7). Lonely Planet.

Pakistan-American Institute of Science & Technology (PAISTECH), University of Maryland, Proceedings. Abdus Salam. Ed. by M. Yameen Zubairi. 1984. write for info. (ISBN 0-930895-03-7). Byron Daven Pubs.

Pakistan: An Annotated Bibliography on Local & Regional Development. (Country Bibliography Ser.: No. 5). 100p. 1982. pap. 8.50 (ISBN 0-686-97543-X, CRD124, UNCRD). UNIPUB.

Pakistan: An End Without a Beginning. Syed Ziaullah & Samuel Baid. 1985. 28.00x (ISBN 0-8364-1447-0, Pub. by Lancer India). South Asia Bks.

Pakistan & Asian Peace. V. Ded Chopra. 287p. 1985. 28.50 (ISBN 0-8364-1898-0, Pub. by Patriot). South Asia Bks.

Pakistan Army. Stephen P. Cohen. LC 83-6496. 230p. 1984. text ed. 35.00x (ISBN 0-520-04982-9). U of Cal Pr.

Pakistan-China Relations. P. L. Bhola. 304p. 1986. 37.50X (ISBN 0-8364-1865-4, Pub. by Manohar India). South Asia Bks.

Pakistan: Human Rights after Martial Law: Report of a Mission. Gustaf Petren et al. pap. 40.90 (2031423). Bks Demand UMI.

Pakistan: Islam, Politics, & National Solidarity. Anwar H. Syed. LC 82-12366. 218p. 1982. 35.00 (ISBN 0-275-90913-1, C0913). Praeger.

Pakistan Issue. Jung N. Yar. 1985. 29.95. Asia Bk Corp.

Pakistan: Its Ideology & Foreign Policy. Aris Hussain. 188p. 1966. 27.50x (ISBN 0-7146-2015-7, F Cass Co). Biblio Dist.

Pakistan: Its Origins & Relations with India. V. B. Kulkarni. 400p. 1988. text ed. 60.00x (ISBN 81-207-0836-9, Pub. by Sterling Pubs India). Apt Bks.

Pakistan: Its People, Its Society, Its Culture. Donald N. Wilber. LC 64-8647. (Survey of World Cultures Ser.: No. 13). pap. 125.80 (ISBN 0-317-11094-2, 2021750). Bks Demand UMI.

Pakistan: Its Politics & Bureaucracy. Mustafa Chowdhury. xi, 244p. 1988. text ed. 30.00x (ISBN 81-7045-025-X, Pub. by Associated Pub House). Advent NY.

Pakistan Literature & Society. Fahmida A. Riaz. 1986. 14.00 (ISBN 81-7050-021-4, Pub. by Abhinav India). South Asia Bks.

Pakistan or Partition of India. Bhimrao R. Ambedkar. LC 77-179171. (South & Southeast Asia Studies). Repr. of 1945 ed. 41.00 (ISBN 0-404-54801-6). AMS Pr.

Pakistan: Political Economy of a Developing State. Pandav Nayak. 1988. 48.50x (ISBN 81-7050-049-4, Pub. by Patriot). South Asia Bks.

Pakistan: Review of the Sixth Five-Year Plan. 268p. 1984. 15.00 (ISBN 0-8213-0424-0, BK 0424). World Bank.

Pakistan Society & Politics. Panda U. Nayak. 1985. 22.50x (ISBN 0-8364-1348-2, Pub. by South Asia Pubs). South Asia Bks.

Pakistan Society: Islam, Ethnicity & Leadership in South Asia. Akbar S. Ahmed. 300p. 1987. 25.00 (ISBN 0-19-577350-0). Oxford U Pr.

Pakistan: The Consolidation of a Nation. Wayne A. Wilcox. LC 63-9873. 1963. 35.00x (ISBN 0-231-02589-0). Columbia U Pr.

Pakistan: The Development of Its Laws & Constitution. Alan Gledhill. LC 80-20180. (British Commonwealth, the Development of Its Laws & Constitutions Ser.: Vol. 8). x, 263p. 1980. Repr. of 1957 ed. lib. bdg. 35.00x (ISBN 0-313-20842-5, GLPA). Greenwood.

Pakistan: The India Factor. Rajendra Sareen. 1985. 27.50x (ISBN 0-8364-1469-1, Pub. by Allied India). South Asia Bks.

Pakistan: The India Factor. Rajendra Sareen. 615p. 1984. 37.95 (ISBN 0-317-38651-4, Pub. by Allied Pubs India). Asia Bk Corp.

Palaeontographica Americana. Incl. No. 47. Revision of the Family Seraphsidae (Gastropoda: Strombacea) Peter Jung. 1974. 6.00 (ISBN 0-87710-348-8); No. 49. Comparative Morphology & Shell History of the Ordovician Strophomenacea (Brachiopoda) J. K. Pope. 1976. 6.50 (ISBN 0-87710-350-X); No. 50. Evolution & Classification of Cenozoic North American & European Lucinidae (Mollusca, Bivalvia) Sara Bretsky. 12.50 (ISBN 0-87710-351-8); No. 51. Morphology & Anatomy of Aneurophyton: A Progymnosperm from the Late Devonian of New York. B. S. Serlin & H. P. Banks. 3.75 (ISBN 0-87710-352-6). (Illus.). Set. 40.00 (ISBN 0-87710-360-7). Paleo Res.

Palaeontographica Americana, Vol. 2. Incl. No. 9. Devonian Brevicones of New York & Adjacent Areas. Rousseau H. Flower. 1938. o. p. 4.00 (ISBN 0-87710-310-0); No. 11. Notes on Giant Fasciolarias. Burnett Smith. 1940. 0.50 (ISBN 0-87710-312-7); No. 12. Titusvillidae, Paleozoic & Recent Branching Hexactinellida. Kenneth E. Caster. 1941. 2.00 (ISBN 0-87710-313-5). (Illus.). 30.00 set (ISBN 0-87710-354-2). Paleo Res.

Palaeontographica Americana, Vol. 3. Incl. No. 13. Notes on Structure & Phylogeny of Eurysiphonate Cephalopods. Rousseau H. Flower. 1941. 2.60 (ISBN 0-87710-314-3); No. 15. Two Abnormal Busycon Shells. Burnett Smith. 1943. 0.40 (ISBN 0-87710-316-X); No. 16. Fish Remains from the Middle Devonian Bone Beds of the Cincinnati Arch Region. John W. Wells. 1944. 2.25 (ISBN 0-87710-317-8); No. 17. Two Spine Rows in a Florida Busycon Contrarium. Burnett Smith. 1944. 0.40 (ISBN 0-87710-318-6); No. 18. New Jellyfish (Kirklandia Texana Caster) from the Lower Cretaceous of Texas. Kenneth E. Caster. 1945. 2.50 (ISBN 0-87710-319-4); No. 20. Some Species of Platystrophia from the Trenton of Ontario & Quebec. G. Winston Sinclair. 1946. 0.75 (ISBN 0-87710-321-6); No. 21. Observations on Gastropod Protoconchs. Burnett Smith. 1946. Pt. III. Some Protoconchs In Busycon, Fusinus, Heilprinia, Hesperisternia & Urosalpinx. o. p. 0.75 (ISBN 0-685-85237-7); No. 22. Two Marine Quaternary Localities. Burnett Smith. 1948. 1.00 (ISBN 0-87710-323-2); No. 23. Studies of Carboniferous Crinoids: Oklahoma & Nebraska, 4 pts. 2.00 (ISBN 0-87710-324-0); No. 24. Stereotoceras & Brevicoceratidae. R. H. Flower. 1950. 2.00 (ISBN 0-87710-325-9); No. 25. Pelecypod Genus Venericardia in the Paleocene & Eocene of Western North America. P. Verastegui. 1953. 8.00 (ISBN 0-87710-326-7). (Illus.). 35.00 set (ISBN 0-87710-355-0). Paleo Res.

Palaeontographica Americana, Vol. 4. Incl. No. 29. Dalmanellidae of the Cincinnatian. Donald D. Hall. 1962. 2.25 (ISBN 0-87710-330-5); No. 30. Pelecypod Genus Byssonchia in the Cincinnatian at Cincinnati, Ohio. John Pojeta, Jr. 1962. 5.00 (ISBN 0-87710-331-3); No. 32. Upper Ordovician Eurypterids of Ohio. K. E. Caster & E. N. Kjellesvig-Waering. 1964. o. p. 4.00 (ISBN 0-87710-333-X). (Illus.). 35.00 set (ISBN 0-87710-356-9). Paleo Res.

Palaeontographica Americana, Vol. 5. Incl. No. 34. Upper Tertiary Arcacea of the Mid-Atlantic Coastal Plain. S. O. Bird. 1965. 4.00 (ISBN 0-87710-335-6); No. 35. Dimyarian Pelecypods of the Mississippi Marshall Sandstone of Michigan. Egbert G. Driscoll. 1965. 4.60 (ISBN 0-87710-336-4); No. 36. North American Ambonychiidae (Pelecypoda) John Pojeta, Jr. 1977. 7.00 (ISBN 0-87710-337-2). (Illus.). 50.00 set (ISBN 0-87710-357-7). Paleo Res.

Palaeontographica Americana, Vol. 6. Incl. No. 38. Lycopsid Stems & Roots & Sphenopsid Fructifications & Stems from the Upper Freeport Coal of Southeastern Ohio. Maxine L. Abbott. 1968. 5.00 (ISBN 0-87710-339-9); No. 39. Cenozoic Evolution of the Alticostate Venericards in Gulf & East Coastal North America. William G. Heaslip. 1968. 6.50 (ISBN 0-87710-340-2); No. 40. Carboniferous Crinoids of Texas with Stratigraphic Implications. H. L. Strimple & W. T. Watkins. 1969.. (Illus.). 40.00 (ISBN 0-87710-358-5). Paleo Res.

Palaeontographica Americana, Vol. 7. Incl. No. 42. Torreites Sanchezi (Douville) from Jamaica. Peter Jung. 1970. 1.25 (ISBN 0-87710-343-7); No. 43. Cancellariid Radula & Its Interpretation. A. A. Olsson. 1970. 1.25 (ISBN 0-87710-344-5); No. 44. Ontogeny & Sexual Dimorphism of Lower Paleozoic Trilobita. Chung-Hung Hu. 1971. 12.50 (ISBN 0-87710-345-3); No. 45. Rudists of Jamaica. L. J. Chubb. 1971. 8.50 (ISBN 0-87710-346-1); No. 46. Crinoids Rom the Girardeau Limestone. J. C. Brower. 1973. 20.00 (ISBN 0-87710-347-X). (Illus.). Set. 45.00 (ISBN 0-87710-359-3). Paleo Res.

Palaeontologisches Woerterbuch. Ulrich Lehmann. (Ger.). 1977. pap. 45.00 (ISBN 3-423-03039-9, M-7577, Pub. by Dtv). French & Eur.

Palaeontology: An Introduction. E. W. Nield & V. C. Tucker. (Illus.). 250p. 1985. text ed. 29.00 (ISBN 0-08-023854-8); pap. text ed. 14.75 (ISBN 0-08-023853-X). Pergamon.

Palaeontology: An Introduction. J. Scott. (Illus.). 1973. 12.50 (ISBN 0-900707-22-4). Heinman.

Palaeontology: An Introduction. James Scott. 1978. 9.95 (ISBN 0-8008-6213-9). Taplinger.

Palaeontology: Proceedings of the 27th International Geological Congress, Vol. 2. International Geological Congress Staff. 230p. 1984. lib. bdg. 70.00x (ISBN 90-6764-011-5). Coronet Bks.

Palaeopathology of Danish Skeletons: A Comparative Study of Demography, Disease, & Injury. Pia Bennike. (Illus.). 272p. (Orig.). 1985. pap. text ed. 38.50x (Pub. by Almqvist & Wiksell). Coronet Bks.

Palaeoserology: (Blood Typing with the Fluorescent Antibody Method) I. A. Lengyel. 240p. 1975. 70.00x (ISBN 0-569-08236-6, Pub. by Collets (UK)). State Mutual Bk.

Palaeosols: Their Recognition & Interpretation. Ed. by V. P. Wright & Alfred Fischer. LC 85-43201. (Princeton Series in Geology & Paleontology). (Illus.). 290p. 1986. text ed. 42.00 (ISBN 0-691-08405-X). Princeton U Pr.

Palaeozoic Asterozoa, Pts. I-X. W. K. Spencer. Repr. of 1940 ed. Set. 120.00 (ISBN 0-384-57050-X). Johnson Repr.

Palaeozoic Plants from Central Shansi. T. G. Halle. 316p. 1927. pap. 140.00x (Pub. by Han-Shan Tang Ltd). State Mutual Bk.

Palais de la Societe des Nations, Villa les Tarrasses, & Other Buildings & Projects, 1926-1927, Vol. III. Le Corbusier. Ed. by H. Allen Brooks. LC 82-12058. (Le Corbusier Archive Ser.). 592p. 1982. lib. bdg. 240.00 (ISBN 0-8240-5052-5). Garland Pub.

Palais des Credazzi. Marina Thomas. (Collection Colombine Ser.). 192p. 1983. pap. 1.95 (ISBN 0-373-48088-1). Harlequin Bks.

Palais des Nations Unies & Other Buildings & Projects, 1946-1948. Ed. by H. Allen Brooks & Alexander Tzonis. LC 83-1578. (Le Corbusier Archive Ser.). 1983. lib. bdg. 240.00 (ISBN 0-8240-5067-3). Garland Pub.

Palais des Soviets & Other Buildings & Projects, 1930, Vol. IX. Le Corbusier. Ed. by H. Allen Brooks. LC 82-15647. (Le Corbusier Archive Ser.). 560p. 1982. lib. bdg. 240.00 (ISBN 0-8240-5058-4). Garland Pub.

Palais-Royal. Richard Sennett. 1987. 17.45 (ISBN 0-394-54538-9). Knopf.

Palanpur: The Economy of an Indian Village. C. J. Bliss & N. H. Stern. (Illus.). 1982. 39.95x (ISBN 0-19-828419-5). Oxford U Pr.

Palantla Chinantec Grammar. William R. Merrifield. 127p. 1968. microfiche (2) 4.00 (ISBN 0-88312-359-2). Summer Inst Ling.

Palaobiologie und Stammeschichte: Paleobiology & Phylogeny. Othenio Abel. Ed. by Stephen J. Gould. LC 79-8320. (History of Paleontology Ser.). (Illus., Ger.). 1980. Repr. of 1929 ed. lib. bdg. 40.00x (ISBN 0-405-12701-4). Ayer Co Pubs.

Palas of Bengal. Banerji. 1973. 13.25 (ISBN 0-89684-491-9). Orient Bk Dist.

Palatability & Flavor Use in Animal Feeds. Ed. by Hans Bickel. (Advances in Animal Physiology & Animal Nutrition: Vol. 11). (Illus.). 148p. (Orig.). 1980. pap. text ed. 34.10 (ISBN 3-490-41115-3). Parey Sci Pubs.

Palatal Diphthongization of Stem Vowels in the Old English Dialects. Clarence G. Child. 1978. Repr. of 1903 ed. lib. bdg. 20.00 (ISBN 0-8495-0839-8). Arden Lib.

Palatal Diphthongization of Stem Vowels in the Old English Dialects. Clarence G. Child. LC 73-12892. 1903. lib. bdg. 29.00 (ISBN 0-8414-3392-5). Folcroft.

Palate Pleasing Pork. Ed. by Annette Gohlke. LC 83-63080. 64p. 1983. pap. 3.95 (ISBN 0-89821-056-9). Reiman Assocs.

Palatinate-a Full Declaration of the Faith & Ceremonies Professed in the Dominions of Prince Fredericke, 5. Prince Elector Palatine. Tr. by J. Rolte. LC 79-84129. (English Experience Ser.: No. 947). 208p. 1979. Repr. of 1614 ed. lib. bdg. 20.00 (ISBN 90-221-0947-X). Walter J Johnson.

Palatine Church Visitations, 1609, Deanery of Kusel. Tr. by Ricardo W. Staudt. LC 80-68128. 136p. 1980. Repr. of 1930 ed. 12.50 (ISBN 0-8063-0908-3). Genealog Pub.

Palatine Families of New York: A Study of the German Immigrants Who Arrived in Colonial New York in 1710. Henry Z. Jones, Jr. LC 84-81704. (Illus.). xl, 1298p. 1985. 85.00 (ISBN 0-9613888-2-X). H Jones Pub.

Palatine, Hessian, Dutchman: Bd. with The Gunsmiths of York County; Journey to America; Decorated Furniture of the Schwaben Creek Valley; Earliest Records of Holy Trinity...Church, Vol. XIV. Don Yoder et al. 1980. 25.00 (ISBN 0-686-79898-8). Penn German Soc.

Palauan Reference Grammar. Lewis S. Josephs. LC 74-76377. (PALI Language Texts: Micronesia). 574p. (Orig.). 1975. pap. text ed. 15.00x (ISBN 0-8248-0331-0). UH Pr.

Palauan Social Structure. DeVerne R. Smith. 345p. 1983. 40.00 (ISBN 0-8135-0953-X). Rutgers U Pr.

Palaver: Dramatic Discussion Starters from Africa. Wole Soyinka et al. (Orig.). 1971. pap. 1.50 (ISBN 0-377-11231-3). Friendship Pr.

Palaver: West Indian Poems. Althea Romeo-Mark. 1978. pap. 1.50 (ISBN 0-917402-10-3). Downtown Poets.

Palazzi di Genova, 2 vols in 1. Peter P. Rubens. LC 68-21226. (Illus.). 1968. Repr. of 1622 ed. 60.00 (ISBN 0-405-08901-5). Ayer Co Pubs.

Palazzo da Festa in Vicenza. Erik Forssman. Tr. by Catherine Enggass from Ital. LC 75-20027. (Corpus Palladianum Ser.: Vol. 8). (Illus.). 186p. 1980. lib. bdg. 56.00x (ISBN 0-271-01202-1). Pa St U Pr.

Palazzo Incantato overo la Guerriera Amante. Luigi Rossi. Ed. by Howard M. Brown. LC 76-21077. (Italian Opera 1640-1770 Ser.). 1977. lib. bdg. 77.00 (ISBN 0-8240-2601-2). Garland Pub.

Palazzo Medici & a Ledger for the Church of San Lorenzo. Isabelle Hyman. LC 76-23631. (Outstanding Dissertations in the Fine Arts-Fifteenth Century). (Illus.). 583p. 1977. Repr. of 1968 ed. lib. bdg. 83.00 (ISBN 0-8240-2700-0). Garland Pub.

Pale Betrayer. Dorothy S. Davis. 224p. 1987. pap. 2.95 (ISBN 0-380-70132-4). Avon.

Pale Fire. Vladimir Nabokov. 1982. pap. 3.50 (ISBN 0-425-09322-0). Berkley Pub.

Pale Fire. Vladimir Nabokov. LC 79-26742. 320p. 1980. pap. 8.95 (ISBN 0-399-50458-3, Perigee). Putnam Pub Group.

Pale Gray for the Guilt. John D. MacDonald. (Large Print Books). 357p. 1986. lib. bdg. 15.95x (ISBN 0-8161-4006-5, Large Print Bks). G K Hall.

Pale Hecates Team: Examination of the Beliefs on Witchcraft & Magic Among Shakespeare's Contemporaries & His Immediate Succesors. Katherine M. Briggs. Ed. by Richard M. Dorson. LC 77-70582. (International Folklore Ser.). (Illus.). 1977. lib. bdg. 24.50x (ISBN 0-405-10083-3). Ayer Co Pubs.

Pale Horse. Agatha Christie. 224p. 1985. pap. 3.50 (ISBN 0-671-54207-9). PB.

Pale Horse, Pale Rider. Katherine A. Porter. LC 67-62420. 264p. 1962. 15.95 (ISBN 0-15-170750-2). HarBraceJ.

Pale Kings & Princes. large print ed. Robert B. Parker. 384p. 1987. 16.95 (ISBN 0-385-29555-3). Delacorte.

Pale Kings & Princes. Robert B. Parker. 1988. 14.95 (ISBN 0-671-66073-X). S&S.

Pale Kings & Princes. Robert B. Parker. 1988. pap. 4.50 (ISBN 0-440-20004-0). Dell.

Pale Kings & Princes: A Spenser Novel. Robert B. Parker. LC 86-29195. 288p. 1987. pap. 15.95 (ISBN 0-385-29538-3); ltd. ed. 75.00 (ISBN 0-385-29568-5). Delacorte.

Pale Moonlight. R. F. Willetts. 31p. 1988. 5.95 (ISBN 0-533-07436-3). Vantage.

Pale Pink. Phyllis Galembo. (Artists Bk.). (Illus.). 24p. (Orig.). 1983. pap. 6.00 (ISBN 0-89822-033-5). Visual Studies.

Pale Rider. Alan D. Foster. 1985. pap. 2.95 (ISBN 0-446-32767-0). Warner Bks.

Pale Star (Spanish Bit Saga, No. 9. Don Coldsmith. 192p. 1988. pap. 2.95 (ISBN 0-553-27604-2). Bantam.

Pale View of the Hills. Kazuo Ishiguro. 192p. 1983. pap. 4.95 (ISBN 0-14-006260-2). Penguin.

Paleface. Wyndham Lewis. 1973. lib. bdg. 75.00 (ISBN 0-87968-018-0). Gordon Pr.

Paleface. Wyndham Lewis. LC 73-95438. (English Biography Ser., No. 31). 1970. Repr. of 1929 ed. lib. bdg. 49.95 (ISBN 0-8383-0990-9). Haskell.

Paleface, the Philosophy of the Melting Pot. Wyndham Lewis. 1971. Repr. of 1929 ed. 39.00 (ISBN 0-403-01073-X). Scholarly.

Paleface's Necklace. William L. Morehead. LC 85-90297. 166p. 1986. 11.95 (ISBN 0-533-06794-4). Vantage.

Palekh. P. Kostolapov et al. 1977. 6.45 (ISBN 0-8285-0895-X, Pub. by Progress Pubs USSR). Imported Pubns.

Palekh Miniatures. Vitalii Kotov. 128p. 1985. 46.00x (ISBN 0-569-08922-0, Pub. by Collets (UK)). State Mutual Bk.

Palekh: The State Museum of Palekh Art. 320p. 1981. 90.00x (ISBN 0-317-14314-X, Pub. by Collets (UK)). State Mutual Bk.

Paleo-Hebrew Leviticus Scroll. D. N. Freedman & K. A. Mathews. (Illus.). xii, 135p. 1985. text ed. 19.95x (ISBN 0-89757-007-3). Am Sch Orient Res.

Paleo-Indian Settlement Pattern in the Hudson & Delaware River Drainages. Leonard Eisenberg. (Occasional Publications in Northeastern Anthropology: No. 4). 1978. 6.00 (ISBN 0-318-19883-5). Fund Anthrop.

Paleo-Indian Settlement Pattern in the Hudson & Delaware River Drainages. Leonard Eisenberg. (Occasional Publications in Northeastern Anthropology: No. 4). (Illus.). viii, 159p. 6.00 (ISBN 0-318-22321-X). F Pierce College.

Paleo-Indian Site in Eastern Pennsylvania: An Early Hunting Culture. John Witthoft. 40p. 1987. pap. 4.95x (ISBN 0-9615462-1-2). Persimmon NY.

Paleoalgology. Ed. by D. F. Toomey & M. H. Nitecki. (Illus.). 380p. 1985. 84.00 (ISBN 0-387-15312-8). Springer-Verlag.

Paleoanthropology: Morphology, & Paleoecology. Ed. by Russell H. Tuttle. (World Anthropology Ser.). (Illus.). xvi, 454p. 1975. 52.50 (ISBN 90-279-7699-6). Mouton.

Paleobiogeography. Ed. by C. A. Ross. LC 76-12969. (Benchmark Papers in Geology Ser.: Vol. 31). 1976. 81.00 (ISBN 0-12-787365-1). Acad Pr.

Paleobiological Study of the Late Triassic Bivalve Honotis from Japan. Hisao Ando. (Illus.). 148p. 1987. 39.50 (ISBN 0-86008-416-7, Pub. by U of Tokyo Japan). Columbia U Pr.

Paleobiology of North American Hyaenodon (Mammalia Creodonta) J. S. Mellett. Ed. by F. S. Szalay. (Contributions to Vertebrate Evolution: Vol. 1). 1977. 50.00 (ISBN 3-8055-2379-3). S Karger.

Paleobotany, 2 Vols. Taylor. 1984. Set. 101.95 (ISBN 0-442-28290-7); Vol. 1. 60.95 (ISBN 0-442-28291-5); Vol. 2. 54.95 (ISBN 0-442-28292-3). Van Nos Reinhold.

Paleobotany: An Introduction to Fossil Plant Biology. Thomas N. Taylor. (Illus.). 576p. 1981. text ed. 52.95x (ISBN 0-07-062954-4). McGraw.

Paleobotany & the Evolution of Plants. Wilson N. Stewart. LC 82-21986. 1983. 37.50 (ISBN 0-521-23315-1). Cambridge U Pr.

Paleobotany, Paleoecology, & Evolution, 2 vols. Ed. by Karl J. Niklas. LC 81-1838. 1981. Vol. 1. 56.95 (ISBN 0-275-90690-6, C06901); Vol. 2. 56.95 (ISBN 0-275-90689-2, C06892). Praeger.

Paleobotany Vol. II: Triassic Through Pliocene. Taylor. 51.95 (ISBN 0-317-64233-2). Van Nos Reinhold.

Paleoceanography. Thomas J. Schopf. LC 79-12546. (Illus.). 1980. 29.50x (ISBN 0-674-65215-0). Harvard U Pr.

Paleoceanography of the Mesozoic Alpine Tethys. Kenneth J. Hsu. LC 75-32124. (Geological Society of America, Special Paper: No. 170). pap. 20.00 (2027366). Bks Demand UMI.

Paleocene-Eocene Bathyal & Abyssal Foraminifera from the Atlantic Basin. R. C. Tjalsma & G. P. Lohmann. (Micropaleontology Special Publications Ser.: No. 4). 1982. 45.00 (ISBN 0-686-84256-1). Am Mus Natl Hist.

Paleoclimate Analysis & Modeling. A. D. Hecht. LC 84-22175. (Environmental Science & Technology Ser.). 456p. 1985. 49.95 (ISBN 0-471-86527-3). Wiley.

Paleoclimates & Economic Geology. Judith T. Parrish & Eric J. Barron. (Short Course Notes Ser.: No. 18). 162p. 1986. pap. 14.00 (ISBN 0-918985-60-9). SEPM.

Paleocology of Beringia: Symposium. Ed. by David M. Hopkins et al. LC 82-22621. 1982. 48.50 (ISBN 0-12-355860-3). Acad Pr.

Paleocurrents & Basin Analysis. 2nd ed. P. E. Potter & F. J. Pettijohn. LC 76-30293. (Illus.). 1977. 47.00 (ISBN 0-387-07952-1). Springer-Verlag.

Paleoecology & Archeology of an Acheulian Site at Caddington, England. Ed. by C. Garth Sampson. LC 67-5086. (Illus.). 168p. 1978. pap. 12.95x. SMU Press.

Paleoecology & Microfloristics of Miocene Diatomites from the Otis Basin-Juntura Region of Harney & Malheur Counties, Oregon. S. L. Van Landingham. (Illus.). 1967. pap. 24.00x (ISBN 3-7682-5426-7). Lubrecht & Cramer.

Paleoecology & Regional Paleoclimatic Implications of the Farmdalian Craigmile & Woodfordian Waubonsie Mammalian Local Faunas, Southwestern Iowa. R. Sanders Rhodes, II. (Reports of Investigations Ser.: No. 40). (Illus.). viii, 51p. (Orig.). 1984. pap. 5.00x (ISBN 0-89792-103-8). Ill St Museum.

Paleoecology Concepts & Applications. 2nd ed. Dodd. 1988. write for info. (ISBN 0-471-85711-4). Wiley.

Paleoecology, Concepts & Applications. Robert J. Dodd & Robert J. Stanton, Jr. LC 80-19623. 559p. 1981. 52.50x (ISBN 0-471-04171-8). Wiley.

Paleoecology, Constructions, Sedimentology, Diagenesis, & Association of Fossils. Ed. by Adolf Seilacher & F. Westphal. (Illus.). 276p. (Orig.). 1978. pap. text ed. 85.00x (ISBN 0-317-63385-6, Pub. by E Schweizerbartsche). Coronet Bks.

Paleoecology of Terrestial Plants: Basic Principles & Techniques. V. A. Krasilov. 210p. 1975. text ed. 47.00x (ISBN 0-7065-1488-2, Pub. by Keter Pub Jerusalem). Coronet Bks.

Paleoecology of Two Peat Deposits on the Oregon Coast. Henry P. Hansen. (Studies in Botany: No. 3). 32p. 1941. pap. 3.95x (ISBN 0-87071-013-3). Oreg St U Pr.

Paleoecology of Volcanic Soils in the Colombian Central Cordillera (Parque National Natural de los Nevados) Johannes B. Salomons. (Dissertationes Botanicae Ser.: No. 95). (Illus.). 212p. 1986. pap. 54.00x (ISBN 3-443-64007-9). Lubrecht & Cramer.

Paleoenvironmental & Tectonic Controls in Coal-Forming Basins of the United States. Ed. by Paul C. Lyons & Charles L. Rice. (Special Paper Ser.: No. 210). (Illus.). 1987. 25.00 (ISBN 0-8137-2210-1). Geol Soc.

Paleoethnobotany of the Kameda Peninsula Jomon. Gary W. Crawford. (Anthropological Papers: No. 73). (Illus.). 200p. 1983. pap. 8.00x (ISBN 0-932206-95-6). U Mich Mus Anthro.

Paleoflora of Southern Africa: Vol. 1 Molteno Formation Triassic. John M. Anderson & Heidi M. Anderson. 200p. 1984. lib. bdg. 85.00 (ISBN 90-6191-283-0, Pub. by Balkema RSA). IPS.

Paleogeographic Principles of Oil & Gas Prospecting. N. I. Markovskii. LC 75-12798. 256p. 1979. 79.95x (ISBN 0-470-57215-9). Halsted Pr.

Palestinian Dilemma: Nationalist Consciousness & University Education in Israel. Khalil Nakhleh. (Monographs: No. 10). 134p. (Orig.). 1979. pap. text ed. 6.00 (ISBN 0-937694-04-5). Assn Arab-Amer U Grads.

Palestinian Economy: Studies in Development under Prolonged Occupation. Ed. by George T. Abed. 320p. 1988. lib. bdg. 49.95 (ISBN 0-415-00471-3). Routledge Chapman & Hall.

Palestinian Entity, 1959-1974: Arab Politics & the PLO. Moshe Shemesh. 1987. 35.00 (ISBN 0-7146-3281-3, F Cass Co). Biblio Dist.

Palestinian Exodus from Galilee, 1948. Nafez Nazzal. 149p. 1978. 4.95 (ISBN 0-88728-128-1). Inst Palestine.

Palestinian Figurines in Relation to Certain Goddesses Known Through Literature. James B. Pritchard. (American Oriental Ser.: Vol. 24). 1943. 12.00 (ISBN 0-527-02698-0). Kraus Repr.

Palestinian Folk Costume. Jehan Rajab. 200p. 1988. lib. bdg. 65.00 (ISBN 0-7103-0283-5, Pub. by Kegan Paul). Routledge Chapman & Hall.

Palestinian Higher Education in the West Bank & the Gaza Strip: A Critical Assessment. Sami N. Anabtawi. 250p. 1987. text ed. 33.00 (ISBN 0-7103-0119-7, Kegan Paul). Routledge Chapman & Hall.

Palestinian Judaism & the New Testament. Martin McNamara. LC 82-84410. (Good News Studies: Vol. 4). 1983. pap. 12.95 (ISBN 0-89453-274-X). M Glazier.

Palestinian Leadership on the West Bank: The Changing Role of the Arab Mayors under Jordan & Israel. Moshe Ma'oz. (Illus.). 232p. 1984. 32.50x (ISBN 0-7146-3234-1, F Cass Co); pap. 15.00x (ISBN 0-7146-4046-8). Biblio Dist.

Palestinian Liberation Organization: People, Power & Politics. Helena Cobban. (Cambridge Middle East Library). (Illus.). 305p. 1985. pap. 9.95 (ISBN 0-521-27216-5). Cambridge U Pr.

Palestinian Messengers in America: 1849-79: A Record of Four Journeys. Baron W. Salo & Jennette M. Baron. Ed. by Moshe Davis. LC 77-70670. (America & the Holy Land Ser.). 1977. Repr. of 1943 ed. lib. bdg. 16.00x (ISBN 0-405-10226-7). Ayer Co Pubs.

Palestinian Parties & Politics that Shaped the Old Testament. Smith. Date not set. 22.95 (Pub. by SCM Pr England). Fortress.

Palestinian Press in the West Bank: The Political Dimensions. Dov Shinar & Danny Rubinstein. (West Bank Data Base Project Ser.). 83p. 1988. pap. 16.50 (ISBN 0-8133-0728-7). Westview.

Palestinian Problem & U. S. Policy: A Guide to Issues & References. Bruce R. Kuniholm & Michael Rubner. LC 85-25687. (Guides to Contemporary Issues Ser.: No. 5). 140p. 1986. lib. bdg. 18.95x (ISBN 0-941690-18-0); pap. 11.95x (ISBN 0-941690-19-9); pap. text ed. 7.75x. Regina Bks.

Palestinian Refugees in Jordan Nineteen Forty-Eight to Fifty-Seven. Avi Plascov. (Illus.). 286p. 1981. 45.00x (ISBN 0-7146-3120-5, F Cass Co). Biblio Dist.

Palestinian Self-Determination: A Study of the West Bank & Gaza Strip. Hassan B. Talal. (Illus.). 160p. 1982. 14.95 (ISBN 0-7043-2312-5, Pub. by Quartet England). Charles River Bks.

Palestinian Society & Politics. Joel S. Migdal. LC 79-84002. (Center for International Affairs at Harvard Ser.). 1980. 31.00x (ISBN 0-691-07615-4). Princeton U Pr.

Palestinian State. Mark A. Heller. 192p. 1983. text ed. 17.00x (ISBN 0-674-65221-5). Harvard U Pr.

Palestinian State: The Implications for Israel. Mark A. Heller. (Illus.). 208p. 1983. pap. 7.95 (ISBN 0-674-65222-3). Harvard U Pr.

Palestinian Uprising, Why? Ed. by Joseph Haiek. 254p. (Orig.). 1988. pap. 3.95 (ISBN 0-915652-07-2). News Circle.

Palestinian Voices: Communication & Nation Building. Dov Shinar. LC 86-20229. (Illus.). 211p. 1987. PLB 25.00 (ISBN 0-931477-41-7). Lynne Rienner.

Palestinian Wedding: A Bilingual Anthology of Contemporary Palestinian Resistance Poetry. Ed. by Abdel Elmessiri. Tr. by Abdel Elmessiri from Arabic. (Illus.). 249p. (Arabic & Eng.). 1982. 20.00 (ISBN 0-89410-095-5); pap. 10.00 (ISBN 0-89410-096-3). Three Continents.

Palestinians. Jonathan Dimbleby. 25.00 (ISBN 0-7043-2205-6, Pub. by Quartet England). Charles River Bks.

Palestinians. David Gilmour. (Issues Ser.). (Illus.). 32p. (gr. 4-9). 1986. PLB 11.90 (ISBN 0-531-17031-4, Pub. by Gloucester). Watts.

Palestinians: A Stateless Nation. Samih K. Farsoun. 200p. Date not set. 28.00 (ISBN 0-8133-0340-0). Westview.

Palestinians & Israel. Yehoshafat Harkabi. 285p. 1974. casebound 22.95x (ISBN 0-87855-172-7). Transaction Bks.

Palestinians & Their Society. Sarah Graham-Brown. (Illus.). 192p. 1981. 25.00 (ISBN 0-7043-2225-0, Pub. by Quartet England); pap. 14.95 (ISBN 0-7043-3343-0). Charles River Bks.

Palestinians: From Peasants to Revolutionaries. Rosemary Sayigh. 206p. (Orig.). 1979. (Pub. by Zed Pr England); pap. 9.25 (ISBN 0-905762-25-8, Pub. by Zed Pr England). Humanities.

Palestinians in Kuwait: The Family & the Politics of Survival. Shafeeq N. Ghabra. LC 86-10636. (Special Studies on the Middle East). 185p. 1987. 23.50 (ISBN 0-8133-7446-4). Westview.

Palestinians in Perspective: Implications for Mideast Peace & U. S. Policy. Ed. by George E. Gruen. LC 82-71810. 112p. 1982. pap. 3.50 (ISBN 0-87495-042-2). Am Jewish Comm.

Palestinians in the Arab World: Institution Building & the Search for State. Laurie A. Brand. 320p. 1988. 35.00x (ISBN 0-231-06722-4). Columbia U Pr.

Palestinians over the Green Line: Studies on the Relations Between Palestinians on Both Sides of the 1949 Armistice Line since 1967. Ed. by Alexander Scholch. (Political Studies of the Middle East: No. 22). 208p. 1983. pap. 12.50 (ISBN 0-86372-003-X, Pub. by Ithaca Pr UK). Humanities.

Palestinians: People, History, Politics. new ed. Ed. by Michael Curtis & Joseph Neyer. 278p. (Orig.). 1975. 24.95 (ISBN 0-87855-112-3). Transaction Bks.

Palestinians' Rights of Self-Determination & National Independence. M. Cherif Bassiouni. (Information Papers: No. 22). 47p. (Orig.). 1978. pap. 4.00 (ISBN 0-937694-38-X). Assn Arab-Amer U Grads.

Palestinians: Victims of Expediency. Esmond Stewart. 152p. 14.95 (ISBN 0-7043-2294-3, Pub. by Quartet Bks). Salem Hse Pubs.

Palestrina. Alberto Cametti. LC 74-24055. Repr. of 1925 ed. 32.00 (ISBN 0-404-12878-5). AMS Pr.

Palestrina. Henry Coates. LC 78-66885. (Encore Music Editions Ser.). (Illus.). 1984. Repr. of 1938 ed. 23.25 (ISBN 0-88355-732-0). Hyperion Conn.

Palette & the Flame Posters of the Spanish Civil War. 161p. 1981. 45.00x (ISBN 0-686-73054-2, Pub. by Collets (UK)). State Mutual Bk.

Palette & the Flame: Posters of the Spanish Civil War, 1936-1939. Ed. by John Tisa. LC 77-16602. 200p. 1979. 17.50 (ISBN 0-7178-0496-8). Intl Pubs Co.

Palette in the Kitchen. Constance Counter & Karl Tani. LC 74-75303. (Illus.). 1973. pap. 5.95 (ISBN 0-913270-28-8). Sunstone Pr.

Palgue: One-Two-Three. K. P. Soo. 8.95x (ISBN 0-685-41910-X). Wehman.

Palgue One, Two Three of Tae Kwon Do Hyung. Kim Pyung Soo. Ed. by John Corcoran. LC 73-85437. (Korean Arts Ser.). (Illus.). 1973. pap. text ed. 9.95 (ISBN 0-89750-008-3, 113). Ohara Pubns.

Pali Buddhist Texts. Rune E. Johansson. 160p. 1988. pap. 40.00x (ISBN 0-7007-0063-3, Pub. by Curzon Pr Ltd UK). State Mutual Bk.

Pali Buddhist Texts Explained to the Beginner. Rune Johansson. 160p. 1988. pap. 40.00x (Pub. by Curzon Pr Ltd UK). State Mutual Bk.

Pali-English Dictionary. A Budd Hahotta Mahathera. (Pali & Eng.). 39.50 (ISBN 0-87557-056-9, 056-9). Saphrograph.

Pali-English Dictionary. Ed. by T. W. Rhys & William Stede. 738p. 1925. text ed. 42.00x (ISBN 0-7100-7511-1). Routledge Chapman & Hall.

Pali Literature of Burma. Mabel H. Bode. LC 77-87008. Repr. of 1909 ed. 15.00 (ISBN 0-404-16796-9). AMS Pr.

Pali Metre: A Contribution to the History of Indian Literature. A. K. Warder. 252p. 1967. 18.50x (ISBN 0-7102-0139-7). Routledge Chapman & Hall.

Pali Reader. Dines Anderson. 130p. 1985. Repr. 39.00 (ISBN 0-932051-66-9, Pub. by Am Repr Serv). Am Biog Serv.

Pali Reader with Notes & Glossary. Dines Andersen. 1976. Repr. of 1901 ed. 39.00x (ISBN 0-403-05978-X, Regency). Scholarly.

Pali Reader with Notes & Glossary. Dines Andersen. 1988. Repr. of 1901 ed. lib. bdg. 49.00x. Am Biog Serv.

Palice of Honour. Gawin Douglas. Ed. by John G. Kinnear. LC 70-144417. (Bannatyne Club, Edinburgh. Publications: No. 17). Repr. of 1827 ed. 17.50 (ISBN 0-404-52717-5). AMS Pr.

Palice of Honour. Gawyn Douglas. Ed. by John Kinnear. Repr. of 1827 ed. 25.00 (ISBN 0-384-12440-2). Johnson Repr.

Palimpsests. Carter Scholz & Glenn Harcourt. 272p. 1984. pap. 2.95 (ISBN 0-441-65065-1). Ace Bks.

Palindromes & Anagrams. Howard W. Bergerson. 192p. (Orig.). 1973. pap. 3.50 (ISBN 0-486-20664-5). Dover.

Paling Shadows. Samir Dasgupta. (Writers Workshop Redbird Ser.). 1975. 8.00 (ISBN 0-88253-606-0); pap. text ed. 4.80 (ISBN 0-88253-605-2). Ind-US Inc.

Palio & Ponte. William Heywood. LC 68-9004. (Illus.). 1969. Repr. of 1904 ed. 20.00 (ISBN 0-87817-010-3). Hacker.

Palio: History Rites & Images of Siena's Festival. Alessandro Falassi & Guiliano Catoni. Tr. by Christopher Evans & Elizabeth Bergese. (Illus.). 369p. 1983. 65.00x (ISBN 0-8103-1643-9, Pub. by Electra Editrice). Gale.

Palis of Honoure. Garvin Douglas. LC 77-6155. (English Experience Ser.: No. 89). 80p. 1969. Repr. of 1553 ed. 25.00 (ISBN 90-221-0089-8). Walter J Johnson.

Palisades & Snedens Landing from the Beginning of History to the Turn of the Twentieth Century. Alice M. Haagensen. (Illus.). 275p. 1986. write for info. (ISBN 0-935819-01-0). Pilgrimage Pub.

Palisades of the Hudson. Arthur C. Mack. (Illus.). 64p. 1982. pap. 5.95 (ISBN 0-915850-05-2). Walking News Inc.

Palisades Project-Elyn Zimmerman: And Related Works 1972-1981. Charles F. Stuckey. LC 81-84872. (Illus.). 48p. (Orig.). 1982. pap. 4.00 (ISBN 0-943651-16-6). Hudson Riv.

Palisandriia. Sasha Sokolov. 300p. (Rus.). 1984. 27.50 (ISBN 0-88233-836-6). Ardis Pubs.

Paliser Case. Edgar Saltus. LC 70-113269. Repr. of 1919 ed. 17.50 (ISBN 0-404-05543-5). AMS Pr.

Palkhi: An Indian Pilgrimage. D. B. Mokashi. Tr. by Philip C. Engblom. LC 86-30001. 291p. 1987. 39.50x (ISBN 0-88706-461-2); pap. 12.95x (ISBN 0-88706-462-0). State U NY Pr.

Palladas & Christianity. C. M. Bowra. 1959. pap. 5.50 (ISBN 0-85672-641-9, Pub. by British Acad). Longwood Pub Group.

Palladas: Poems. Tr. by Tony Harrison. 1975. 4.75 (ISBN 0-685-78872-5, Pub. by Anvil Pr); sewn in wrappers 2.00 (ISBN 0-685-78873-3). Small Pr Dist.

Palladas: Poems. Palladas. Tr. by Tony Harrison from Gr. (Poetry in Translation Ser.). 48p. (Orig.). 1984. pap. 7.95 (ISBN 0-85646-127-X, Pub. by Anvil Pr Poetry). Longwood Pub Group.

Palladian. Elizabeth Taylor. (Virago Modern Classics Ser.). 208p. 1985. pap. 6.95 (ISBN 0-14-016113-9). Penguin.

Palladio. rev. ed. James S. Ackerman. 1974. pap. 7.95 (ISBN 0-14-020845-3, Pelican). Penguin.

Palladio & English Palladianism. Rudolf Wittkower. LC 80-52096. (Illus.). 224p. 1983. pap. 16.95f (ISBN 0-500-27296-4). Thames Hudson.

Palladio Guide. rev. ed. Caroline Constant. (Illus.). 160p. 1987. pap. 17.00 (ISBN 0-910413-10-X). Princeton Arch.

Palladio's Architecture & Its Influences: A Photographic Guide. Joseph Farber & Henry H. Reed. (Illus.). 1980. pap. 7.95 (ISBN 0-486-23922-5). Dover.

Palladio's Architecture & Its Influence: A Photographic Guide. Joseph C. Farber & Henry H. Reed. 17.00 (ISBN 0-8446-5759-X). Peter Smith.

Palladis Tamia. Francis Meres. LC 72-9751. Repr. of 1598 ed. 35.00 (ISBN 0-404-04309-7). AMS Pr.

Palladis Tamia. Francis Meres. LC 39-10093. 1978. Repr. of 1598 ed. 50.00x (ISBN 0-8201-1188-0). Schol Facsimiles.

Palladium. Alice Fulton. LC 85-31807. 128p. 1986. pap. 8.95 (ISBN 0-252-01280-1); 11.95 (ISBN 0-252-01451-0). U of Ill Pr.

Palladium Alloys. E. M. Savitskii et al. LC 69-76747. (Illus.). 215p. 1969. 37.00x (ISBN 0-911184-11-2). Primary.

Palladium Book III: Adventures on the High Seas, No. 3. Michael Kucharski. Ed. by Alex Marcinisizyn. (Fantasy Ser.). (Illus.). 168p. 1986. pap. 14.95 (ISBN 0-916211-17-7). Palladium Bks.

Palladium Book of Contemporary Weapons. Maryann Donald. Ed. by Alex Marciniszyn. (Weapons Ser.: No. 5). (Illus.). 48p. 1984. pap. 5.95 (ISBN 0-916211-01-0, 408). Palladium Bks.

Palladium Book of European Castles. Matthew Balent & Alex Marciniszyn. (Weapons Ser.: No. 7). (Illus.). 48p. (Orig.). 1985. pap. 5.95 (ISBN 0-916211-11-8). Palladium Bks.

Palladium Book of Exotic Weapons. Matthew Balent. Ed. by Alex Marciniszyn. (Weapons Ser.: No. 6). (Illus.). 48p. (Orig.). 1984. pap. 5.95 (ISBN 0-916211-06-1). Palladium Bks.

Palladium Book of Monsters & Animals. Kevin Siembieda. Ed. by Alex Marciniszyn. (Illus.). 180p. (Orig.). 1985. pap. 14.95 (ISBN 0-916211-12-6). Palladium Bks.

Palladium Book of Weapons & Armour. 4th ed. Matthew Balent. Ed. by Kevin Siembieda. (Weapon Ser.: No. 1). (Illus.). 48p. 1984. pap. 4.95 (ISBN 0-916211-07-X, 404). Palladium Bks.

Palladium Book of Weapons & Assassins. Erick Wujcik. Ed. by Paula Leasure. (Weapon Ser.: No. 3). (Illus.). 48p. 1984. pap. 5.95 (ISBN 0-916211-03-7, 406). Palladium Bks.

Palladium Book of Weapons & Castles of the Orient. Matthew Balent. Ed. by Alex Marcinisyzn. (Weapon Ser.: No. 4). (Illus.). 48p. (Orig.). 1984. pap. 5.95 (ISBN 0-916211-02-9, 407). Palladium Bks.

Palladium Books of Weapons & Castles. 3rd ed. Matthew Balent. Ed. by Robin Korona. (Weapons Ser.: No. 2). (Illus.). 48p. 1984. pap. 5.95 (ISBN 0-916211-08-8, 405). Palladium Bks.

Palladium Catalyzed Oxidation of Hydrocarbons. Patrick Henry. (Catalysis by Metal Complexes Ser.). 1979. lib. bdg. 65.00 (ISBN 90-277-0986-6, Pub. by Reidel Holland). Kluwer Academic.

Palladium of Conscience. Philip Furneaux. LC 74-122161. (Civil Liberties in American History Ser). 267p. 1974. Repr. of 1773 ed. lib. bdg. 35.00 (ISBN 0-306-71972-X). Da Capo.

Palladium Reagents in Organic Synthesis. Richard F. Heck. (Best Synthetic Methods Ser.). 1985. 115.00 (ISBN 0-12-336140-0). Acad Pr.

Palladium Role-Playing Game. rev., 3rd ed. Kevin Siembieda. Ed. by Paula Leasure. (Illus.). 274p. 1984. pap. 19.95 (ISBN 0-916211-04-5, 450). Palladium Bks.

Palladium RPG Book II: Old Ones. Kevin Siembieda. Ed. by Alex Marciniszyn. (Fantasy Adventure Ser.: No. 2). (Illus.). 210p. (Orig.). 1985. pap. 14.95 (ISBN 0-916211-09-6). Palladium Bks.

Palladius: Dialogue on the Life of St. John Chrysostom. Ed. by Robert T. Meyer. (ACW Ser.: No. 45). 1985. text ed. 16.95 (ISBN 0-8091-0358-3). Paulist Pr.

Palladius on Husbondrie. Rutilius T. Palladius. Ed. by Barton Lodge & S. J. Herrtage. (EETS, OS Ser.: No. 52, 72). Repr. of 1879 ed. 52.00 (ISBN 0-527-00047-7). Kraus Repr.

Palladius on Husbondrie, Englisht, Part. II. Ed. by S. J. Herrtage. (EETS OS Ser.: Vol. 52 & 72). pap. write for info. Kraus Repr.

Pallas Armata, or, Militarie Instructions. Thomas Kellie. LC 72-209. (English Experience Ser.: No. 331). 130p. 1971. Repr. of 1627 ed. 45.00 (ISBN 90-221-0331-5). Walter J Johnson.

Palliation in Malignant Disease. J. G. Mosley. (Illus.). 170p. 1988. text ed. 36.00 (ISBN 0-443-03690-X). Churchill.

Palliative Care: The Management of Far Advanced Illness. Ed. by Derek Doyle. LC 83-73015. 536p. 1984. 37.00 (ISBN 0-914783-02-5). Charles.

Palliative Pain & Symptom Management for Children & Adolescents. Robert A. Milch. 29p. 1985. pap. 7.95 (ISBN 0-317-61842-3). Child Hospice VA.

Pallisades Park Panorama. Fred E. Basten. LC 80-83611. (Illus.). 120p. (Orig.). 1987. pap. 11.95 (ISBN 0-317-68665-8). Graphics Calif.

Palliser's New Cottage Homes & Details. Palliser. LC 75-4887. (Architecture & Decorative Arts Ser). (Illus.). 180p. 1975. Repr. of 1887 ed. lib. bdg. 55.00 (ISBN 0-306-70744-6). Da Capo.

Palm: A Guide to Your Hidden Potential. Rita Robinson. (Illus.). 128p. 1988. Repr. lib. bdg. 24.95x (ISBN 0-8095-6133-6). Borgo Pr.

Palm: A Guide to Your Hidden Potential. Rita Robinson. 128p. (Orig.). 1988. pap. 9.95 (ISBN 0-87877-133-6). Newcastle Pub.

Palm-Aire Spa's Seven-Day Plan to Change Your Life: A Diet, Fitness & Beauty Program. Eleanor Berman. (Illus.). 224p. 1987. 19.45 (ISBN 0-13-648361-5). P-H.

Palm & the Pleiades. S. Hugh-Jones. LC 78-5533. (Studies in Social Anthropology: No. 24). (Illus.). 1979. 47.50 (ISBN 0-521-21952-3). Cambridge U Pr.

Palm & the Pleiades: Initiation & Cosmology in Northwest Amazonia. Stephen Hugh-Jones. (Cambridge Studies in Social Anthropology: No. 24). (Illus.). 332p. 1988. 15.95 (ISBN 0-521-35890-6). Cambridge U Pr.

Palm at the End of the Mind. rev. ed. Wallace Stevens. LC 84-14572. xvi, 404p. 1984. Repr. of 1971 ed. 32.50 (ISBN 0-208-02058-6, Archon). Shoe String.

Palm at the End of the Mind: Selected Poems & a Play. Wallace Stevens. Ed. by Holly Stevens. 448p. 1972. pap. 4.95 (ISBN 0-394-71768-6, Vin). Random.

Palm Beach. Pat Booth. 400p. 1985. 15.95 (ISBN 0-517-55844-0). Crown.

Palm Beach. Pat Booth. 1988. pap. 4.50 (ISBN 0-345-00738-7). Ballantine.

Palm Beach - An Irreverent Guide. Jack Owen. (Illus.). 52p. (Orig.). 1986. pap. 5.95 (ISBN 0-938673-00-9). Old Bk Shop Pubn.

Palm Beach Cook Book. Garden Club of Palm Beach Staff. 64p. 1968. pap. 2.75 (ISBN 0-913456-64-0). Interbk Inc.

Palm Beach County: An Illustrated History. Donald W. Curl. LC 86-9133. (Illus.). 224p. 1986. 24.95 (ISBN 0-89781-167-4). Windsor Pubns Inc.

Palm Beach Entertains: History & Photos of Palm Beach. The Junior League of the Palm Beaches, Inc. Ed. by Committee of the Junior League. (Illus.). 241p. 1976. 10.95 (ISBN 0-9608090-1-5). Jl Palm Beaches.

Palm Beach: Isle of Style & Splendor. Jack A. Gancarz. 96p. (Orig.). 1988. pap. 19.95 (ISBN 0-9620260-0-X). Downtown Photo Serv.

Palm Beach Long-Life Diet. E. Joan Barice & Kathleen Jonah. 224p. 1985. 14.95 (ISBN 0-671-50363-4). S&S.

Palm Beach Long Life Diet. Joan E. Barice & Kathleen Jonah. 1986. pap. 3.95 (ISBN 0-671-61211-5). PB.

Palm Beach Picture Book. Leslie Weinberg. LC 87-73016. 128p. (Orig.). 1988. pap. 9.95 (ISBN 0-914783-22-X). Charles.

Palm Beach: The Novel. Richard G. Hughes. LC 83-63232. 1984. pap. 9.95 (ISBN 0-88100-037-X). Natl Writ Pr.

Palm Beach: The Novel. Richard G. Hughes. 143p. 1984. pap. 8.95 (ISBN 0-317-11865-X). Creat Concern.

Palm Fever. Carole Marsh. (Carol Marsh Short Story Ser.). (Illus.). 48p. (gr. 4-12). 1988. pap. 7.95 (ISBN 1-55609-237-7). Gallopade Pub Group.

Palm for Mrs. Polifax. Dorothy Gilman. 192p. 1985. pap. 2.95 (ISBN 0-449-20864-8, Crest). Fawcett.

Palm Latitudes. Kate Braverman. 1988. 19.95 (ISBN 0-671-64542-0). S&S.

Palm Leaf Patterns: A New Approach to Clothing Design. Margaret Fisher. LC 76-57189. (Illus.). 20p. 1977. pap. 5.95 (ISBN 0-915572-20-6). Panjandrum.

Palm Leaves, Peanuts, & Sixty-One Other Children's Sermons. Bill Lampkin. LC 81-3497. 112p. 1981. pap. 6.50 (ISBN 0-687-30000-2). Abingdon.

Palm-of-the-Hand Stories. Yasunari Kawabata. Tr. by Lane Dunlop & J. Martin Holman. LC 87-82590. 304p. 1988. 19.95 (ISBN 0-86547-325-0). N Point Pr.

Palm Oil. F. D. Gunstone. LC 86-23426. (Critical Reports on Applied Chemistry). 100p. 1987. 59.95 (ISBN 0-471-91335-9). Wiley.

Palm Oil & Protest: An Economic History of the Ngwa Region, South-eastern Nigeria, 1800-1980. Susan M. Martin. (African Studies: No. 59). (Illus.). 226p. 1988. 42.50 (ISBN 0-521-34376-3). Cambridge U Pr.

Palm Prints of Anais Nin. Judith Hipskind. cancelled (ISBN 0-934536-08-2). Merging Media.

Palm Probabilities & Stationary Queues. F. Baccelli & P. Bremaud. (Lecture Notes in Statistics Ser.: Vol. 41). vii, 106p. 1987. pap. 15.80 (ISBN 0-387-96514-9). Springer-Verlag.

Palm Sago: A Tropical Starch from Marginal Lands. Kenneth Ruddle & Dennis Johnson. LC 77-28981. 223p. 1978. pap. text ed. 10.00x (ISBN 0-8248-0577-1, Eastwest Ctr). UH Pr.

Palm Springs a la Carte. Jack Delaney. LC 77-21834. (Illus.). 1978. pap. 3.95 (ISBN 0-88280-055-8). ETC Pubns.

Palm Springs Safari: A Guide of Palm Springs, 1977-78. Fred Hartley & Glory Hartley. pap. 2.95 (ISBN 0-686-17555-7). Hartley Ent.

Palm Sunday. Kurt Vonnegut, Jr. 1984. pap. 4.95 (ISBN 0-440-36906-1, LE). Dell.

Palm Tissue Culture: State of the Art & its Application to the Coconut: Paper Presented at the Fifth Session of the FAO Technical Working Party on Coconut Production, Protection & Processing. Manila, December 1979. A. Kovoor. (Plant Production & Protection Papers: No. 30). 76p. 1981. pap. 7.50 (ISBN 92-5-101133-8, F2271, FAO). UNIPUB.

Palm Tree of Deborah. Moses Cordovero. Tr. by Louis Jacobs from Hebrew. LC 80-54594. (Judaic Studies Library: No. SPH8). 133p. 1981. pap. 7.95 (ISBN 0-87203-097-0). Hermon.

Palm-Tree of Life: Biology, Utilization & Conservation. Ed. by Michael J. Balick. (Advances in Economic Botany Ser.: Vol. 6). 1988. pap. text ed. write for info. (ISBN 0-89327-326-0). NY Botanical.

Palm-Wine Drinkard. Amos Tutuola. 1954. pap. 3.95 (ISBN 0-394-17235-3, E328, Ever). Grove.

Palm-Wine Drinkard. Amos Tutuola. LC 83-49449. 144p. 1984. pap. 4.50 (ISBN 0-394-62168-9, B507, BC). Grove.

Palm-Wine Drinkard & His Dead Palm-Wine Tapster in the Dead's Town. Amos Tutuola. 1970. Repr. of 1953 ed. lib. bdg. 35.00x (ISBN 0-8371-4044-7, TUPD). Greenwood.

Palmas ya No Son Verdes: Analisis y Testimonios de la Tragedia Cubana. Juan E. Noya. LC 85-80134. (Coleccion Cuba y sus Jueces Ser.). (Illus.). 93p. (Orig., Span.). 1985. pap. 9.95 (ISBN 0-89729-368-1). Ediciones.

Palmer Method Cursive, Consumable. Fred D. King. (Palmer Method Easy to Teach Ser.). (Illus.). (gr. 6). 1979. wkbk. 3.96 (ISBN 0-914268-68-6, 79-6C); tchr's. ed. 5.60 (ISBN 0-914268-69-4, 79-6CTE). A N Palmer.

Palmer Method Cursive, Consumable. Fred M. King. (Palmer Method Easy to Teach Ser.). (Illus.). (gr. 4). 1979. wkbk 3.96 (ISBN 0-914268-64-3, 79-4C); tchr's. ed. 5.60 (ISBN 0-914268-65-1, 79-4CTE). A N Palmer.

Palmer Method Cursive, Consumable. Fred M. King. (Palmer Method Easy to Teach Ser.). (Illus.). (gr. 5). 1979. wkbk. 3.96 (ISBN 0-914268-66-X, 79-5C); tchr's. ed. 5.60 (ISBN 0-914268-67-8, 79-5CTE). A N Palmer.

Palmer Method Cursive, Non-Consumable. Fred M. King. (Palmer Method Easy to Teach Ser.). (gr. 8). 1979. wkbk. 4.24 (ISBN 0-914268-86-4, N79-SL2); tchr's. ed. 5.60 (ISBN 0-914268-87-2, N79-SL2TE). A N Palmer.

Palmer Method Cursive, Non-Consumable. Fred M. King. (Palmer Method Easy to Teach Ser.). (Illus.). (gr. 7). 1979. wkbk. 4.24 (ISBN 0-914268-84-8, N79-SL1); tchr's. ed. 5.60 (ISBN 0-914268-85-6, N79-SL1TE). A N Palmer.

Palmer Method Cursive, Non-Consumable. Fred M. King. (Palmer Method Easy to Teach Ser.). (Illus.). (gr. 6). 1979. wkbk. 4.24 (ISBN 0-914268-82-1, N79-6C); tchr's. ed. 5.60 (ISBN 0-914268-83-X, N79-6CTE). A N Palmer.

Palmer Method Cursive, Non-Consumable. Fred M. King. (Palmer Method Easy to Teach Ser.). (ps-8). 1979. tchr's. ed. 5.60 (ISBN 0-914268-81-3, N79-5CTE); wkbk. 4.24 (ISBN 0-914268-80-5, N79-5C). A N Palmer.

Palmer Method Cursive, Non-Consumable. Fred M. King. (Palmer Method Easy to Teach Ser.). (gr. 4). 1979. wkbk. 4.24 (ISBN 0-914268-78-3, N79-4C); tchr's. ed. 5.60 (ISBN 0-914268-79-1, N79-4CTE). A N Palmer.

Palmer Method Manuscript, Consumable. Fred M. King. (Palmer Method Easy to Teach Ser.). (Illus.). (gr. 2). 1979. wkbk. 3.96 (ISBN 0-914268-58-9, 79-2M); tchr's. ed. 5.60 (ISBN 0-914268-59-7, 79-2MTE). A N Palmer.

Palmer Method Manuscript, Consumable. Fred M. King. (Palmer Method Easy to Teach Ser.). (Illus.). (gr. 1). 1979. 3.96 (ISBN 0-914268-56-2, 79-1M); tchr's. ed. 5.60 (ISBN 0-914268-57-0, 79-1MTE). A N Palmer.

Palmer Method Manuscript, Non-Consumable. Fred M. King. (Palmer Method Easy to Teach Ser.). (Illus.). (gr. 2). 1979. wkbk. 4.24 (ISBN 0-914268-72-4, N79-2M); tchr's. ed. 5.60 (ISBN 0-914268-73-2, N79-2MTE). A N Palmer.

Palmer Method Manuscript, Non-Consumable. Fred M. King. (Palmer Method Easy to Teach Ser.). (Illus.). (gr. 1). 1979. wkbk. 4.24 (ISBN 0-914268-70-8, N79-1M); tchr's. ed. 5.60 (ISBN 0-914268-71-6, N79-1MTE). A N Palmer.

Palmer Method Transition on Cursive, Consumable. (Palmer Method Easy to Teach Ser.). (gr. 3). 1979. wkbk. 3.96 (ISBN 0-914268-62-7, 79-3TC); tchr's. ed. 5.60 (ISBN 0-914268-63-5, 79-3TC TE). A N Palmer.

Palmer Method Transition on Cursive, Non-Consumable. Fred M. King. (Palmer Method Easy to Teach Ser.). (gr. 3). 1979. wkbk. 4.24 (ISBN 0-914268-76-7, N79-3TC); tchr's. ed. 5.60 (ISBN 0-914268-77-5, N79-3TC TE). A N Palmer.

Palmer Method Transition to Cursive, Consumable. Fred M. King. (Palmer Method Easy to Teach Ser.). (Illus.). (gr. 2). 1979. wkbk. 3.96 (ISBN 0-914268-60-0, 79-2TC); tchr's. ed. 5.60 (ISBN 0-914268-61-9, 79-2TCTE). A N Palmer.

Palmer Method Transition to Cursive, Non-Consumable. Fred M. King. (Palmer Method Easy to Teach Ser.). (Illus.). (gr. 2). 1979. wkbk. 4.24 (ISBN 0-914268-74-0, N79-2TC); tchr's. ed. 5.60 (ISBN 0-914268-75-9, N79-2TCTE). A N Palmer.

Palmer Method Writing Readiness, Consumable. new ed. Fred M. King. (Illus.). (gr. k-1). 1979. wkbk. 3.96 (ISBN 0-914268-55-4, 79-WR). A N Palmer.

Palmerin Romances in Elizabethan Prose Fiction. Mary Patchell. LC 47-30744. Repr. of 1947 ed. 17.00 (ISBN 0-404-04889-7). AMS Pr.

Palmer's Cases & Materials on Trusts & Succession. 4th ed. Geaorge E. Palmer et al. LC 83-8853. (University Casebook). 894p. 1983. 27.00 (ISBN 0-88277-115-9). Foundation Pr.

Palmer's Examination Notebook. Woolf. 1975. pap. 17.95 (ISBN 0-85258-152-1). Van Nos Reinhold.

Palmer's Journal of Travels over the Rocky Mountains, 1845-46 see Early Western Travels, 1748-1846.

Palmerston. K. Bourne. (Illus.). 750p. 1982. 24.95. Macmillan.

Palmerston, Guizot & the Collapse of the Entente Cordiale. Roger Bullen. 352p. 1974. 54.50 (ISBN 0-485-13136-6, Pub. by Athlone Pr UK). Humanities.

Palmerston, Metternich & the European System: 1830-1841. C. K. Webster. LC 74-34457. (Studies in Philosophy, No. 40). 1972. Repr. of 1934 ed. lib. bdg. 35.95x (ISBN 0-8383-0135-5). Haskell.

Palmerston Papers, Gladstone & Palmerston. facsimile ed. Henry T. Palmerston. Ed. by Philip Guedalla. LC 73-157351. (Select Bibliographies Reprint Ser). Repr. of 1928 ed. 25.50 (ISBN 0-8369-5812-8). Ayer Co Pubs.

Palmerston: The Early Years, Seventeen Eighty-Four to Eighteen Forty-One. Kenneth Bourne. 1982. 24.95. Free Pr.

Palmerston's Folly: The Portsdown & Spithead Forts. A. Temple Patterson. 1980. Repr. of 1968 ed. 39.00x (ISBN 0-317-43669-4, Pub. by City of Portsmouth). State Mutual Bk.

Palmetto Country. Stetson Kennedy. (American Folkways Ser.). 1942. 9.95 (ISBN 0-317-39780-X). Brown Bk.

Palmetto Traction: Electric Railways of South Carolina. Thomas Fetters. (Illus.). 120p. (Orig.). 1978. pap. 10.00 (ISBN 0-911940-28-6). Cox.

Palmistic Dictionary. St. Germain. (Illus.). 118p. 1980. Repr. deluxe ed. 145.45 (ISBN 0-89901-017-2). Found Class Reprints.

Palmistry. Mary Anderson. (Paths to Inner Power Ser.). 1973. pap. 3.95 (ISBN 0-85030-164-5, Pub. by Thorsons UK). Weiser.

Palmistry Dictionary with Illustrations. Adrian Bartlow & Janice Baylis. LC 85-62811. (Metapsi Dictionary Ser.). (Illus.). 288p. 1986. pap. 9.95 (ISBN 0-917738-02-0). Sun Man Moon.

Palmistry Made Easy. J. S. Bright. 261p. 1975. pap. 2.95 (ISBN 0-88253-024-0). Ind-US Inc.

Palmistry Made Easy. J. S. Bright. 261p. 1983. 4.95. Asia Bk Corp.

Palmistry Made Easy. Fred Gettings. pap. 5.00 (ISBN 0-87980-114-X). Wilshire.

Palmistry Made Practical. Squire. pap. 5.00 (ISBN 0-87980-115-8). Wilshire.

Palmistry Secrets Revealed. Henry Frith. pap. 4.00 (ISBN 0-87980-116-6). Wilshire.

Palmistry-the Whole View. 2nd, rev. ed. Judith Hipskind. Ed. by Carl Weschcke. LC 83-80174. (Llewellyn's Inner Awarness Ser.). (Illus.). 236p. 1983. pap. 6.95 (ISBN 0-87542-306-X, L-306). Llewellyn Pubns.

Palmistry Workbook. Nathaniel Altman. (Illus.). 160p. (Orig.). pap. 12.95 (ISBN 0-85030-352-4, Pub. by Aquarian Pr England). Sterling.

Palms. Alec Blombery & Tony Rodd. (Illus.). 199p. 1983. 24.95 (ISBN 0-207-14848-1). Salem Hse Pubs.

Palms & Flowers of Florida. Frances W. Hall. (Illus.). pap. 1.95 (ISBN 0-8200-0408-1). Great Outdoors.

Palms & Soles in Medicine. Maurice J. Costello & Richard C. Gibbs. (Illus.). 720p. 1967. photocopy ed. 67.50x (ISBN 0-398-00351-3). C C Thomas.

Palms For the Home & Garden. Lynette Stewart. (Illus.). 72p. (Orig.). 1984. pap. 12.95 (ISBN 0-207-14270-X). Salem Hse Pubs.

Palms of British India & Ceylon. E. Blatter. (Illus.). 1978. Repr. of 1926 ed. 68.75x (ISBN 0-89955-295-1, Pub. by Intl Bk Dist). Intl Spec Bk.

Palms of South Florida. George B. Stevenson. (Illus.). 1974. pap. 7.95 (ISBN 0-916224-41-4). Banyan Bks.

Palms, Peaks & Prairies. Richard F. Fleck. 1967. 4.00 (ISBN 0-8233-0024-2). Golden Quill.

Palmway. Dennis Saleh. LC 75-42432. 46p. 1975. 3.50 (ISBN 0-87886-065-7). Greenfld Rev Pr.

Palmyra. Iain Browning. LC 79-16591. (Illus.). 223p. 1980. 18.00 (ISBN 0-8155-5054-5, Np). Noyes.

Palmyra & Zenobia. W. Wright. 432p. 1987. 320.00x (ISBN 1-85077-155-3, Pub. by Darf Pubs Ltd). State Mutual Bk.

Palmyrah Palm: Potential & Perspective. A. Kovoor. (Plant & Production Paper: No. 52). 77p. (Orig.). 1984. pap. 7.50 (ISBN 92-5-101472-8, F2556, FAO). UNIPUB.

Palmyrena: A Topographical Itinerary. Alois Musil. LC 77-87087. (American Geographical Society. Oriental Explorations & Studies: No. 4). Repr. of 1928 ed. 42.50 (ISBN 0-404-60234-7). AMS Pr.

Palo Verde Archaeological Investigations, Pts. 1 & 2. Pat H. Stein. (Research Ser.). 104p. 1981. pap. 7.50 (RS-21). Mus Northern Ariz.

Paloma. Theresa Conway. 672p. (Orig.). 1984. pap. 3.95 (ISBN 0-345-31566-9). Ballantine.

Paloma. Ed. by Frederic-Andre Engel. (Prehistoric Andean Ecologys Ser.: Vol. 1). 1980. text ed. 45.00x (ISBN 0-391-01873-6). Humanities.

Paloma. Douglas L. Heinsohn. LC 81-12683. 301p. 1987. 19.95 (ISBN 0-87949-213-9). Ashley Bks.

Palominas Pistolero & Smoke Wagon Kid. Nelson Nye. 1978. pap. 1.95 (ISBN 0-89083-418-0). Zebra.

Palomino. Elizabeth Jolley. 260p. 1987. 15.95 (ISBN 0-89255-116-X). Persea Bks.

Palomino. Elizabeth Jolley. 260p. 1987. 15.95 (ISBN 0-317-60982-3). Persea Bks.

Palomino. Elizabeth Jolley. Date not set. pap. 8.95. Persea Bks.

Palomino. Danielle Steel. 480p. 1982. pap. 4.95 (ISBN 0-440-16753-1). Dell.

Palos Verdes Peninsula: A Geologic Guide & More. Martin Reiter. 80p. 1984. pap. text ed. 10.95 (ISBN 0-8403-3408-7). Kendall-Hunt.

Palos Verdes Peninsula: Time & the Terraced Land. Augusta Finko. LC 66-18957. (Illus.). 164p. 1987. pap. 9.95 (ISBN 0-934136-37-8). Western Tanager.

Palouse Country: An Essay in Photographs. George Bedirian. LC 87-14732. (Illus.). 157p. (Orig.). 1987. pap. 21.00 (ISBN 0-943091-00-4). Whitman Cty Hist Soc.

Palouse Story. Ellis L. Boden. 206p. 1987. pap. 6.95 (ISBN 0-945536-00-3). Gem Paperbks.

Palpable God. Reynolds Price. LC 84-62310. 208p. 1985. 9.50 (ISBN 0-86547-179-7). N Point Pr.

Pals. Trish Mylet & Antoinette Sheffield. Ed. by Barry W. Burton. (Phonetic Readers for the Short Vowels Ser.: Bk. 11). (Illus.). 20p. (ps-2). 1988. pap. text ed. 5.00 (ISBN 0-945590-11-3). Sizzy Bks.

Pals: Developing Social Skills Through Language. Sharon Vaughn et al. (Illus.). 168p. (Orig.). (ps-1). 1986. pap. text ed. 139.95 (ISBN 0-88120-355-6, 1040). SRA.

PALs: Working with the Passive Activity Loss Rules. 64p. 1988. pap. 7.00 (5214). Commerce.

Palsgrave's Acolastus. Ed. by E. L. Carver. (EETS, OS Ser.: No. 202). Repr. of 1935 ed. 40.00 (ISBN 0-527-00202-X). Kraus Repr.

Paludes. Andre Gide. (Folio Ser.: No. 436). 160p. 1973. 5.95 (ISBN 0-686-56053-1). Schoenhof.

Palygorskite-Sepiolite: Occurrences, Genesis & Uses. Ed. by A. Singer & E. Galan. (Developments in Sedimentology Ser.: Vol. 37). 352p. 1984. 76.50 (ISBN 0-444-42337-0, I-145-84). Elsevier.

Palyno-Taxonomy of Selected Indian Liverworts. A. Gupta & R. Udar. (Bryophytorum Bibliotheca: 29). (Illus.). 204p. 1986. pap. 66.00x (ISBN 3-443-62003-5). Lubrecht & Cramer.

Palynological Study of the Liabeae (Asteraceae) Harold E. Robinson. LC 86-600032. (Smithsonian Contributions to Botany Ser.: No. 64). pap. 20.00 (ISBN 0-317-55528-6, 2029552). Bks Demand UMI.

Palynology, 2 Pts. Muir. 1982. Set. 99.95 (ISBN 0-317-55168-X). Van Nos Reinhold.

Palynology & Palynofacies of the Upper Tertiary in Venezuela. Maria A. Lorente. (Dissertations Botanicae Ser.: Vol. 99). (Illus.). 1986. pap. text ed. 66.00x (ISBN 3-443-64011-7). Lubrecht & Cramer.

Palynology & the Independence Shale of Iowa see Bulletins of American Paleontology.

Palynology in Oil Exploration: A Symposium. Ed. by Aureal T. Cross. LC 72-182534. (Society of Economic Paleontologists & Mineralogists, Special Publication: No. 11). pap. 52.00 (ISBN 0-317-27160-1, 2024737). Bks Demand UMI.

Palynology of Archaeological Sites. Geoffey W. Dimbleby. 1985. 58.50 (ISBN 0-12-216480-6). Acad Pr.

Palynology of the Almond Formation (Upper Cretaceous). Rock Springs Uplift, Wyoming see Bulletins of American Paleontology.

Palynology of the Eddleman Coal (Pennsylvanian) of North-Central Texas. J. F. Stone. (Report of Investigations Ser.: No. 64). (Illus.). 55p. 1969. 1.50 (ISBN 0-318-03165-5). Bur Econ Geology.

Palynology of the Robinson Site, North-Central Wisconsin. J. Gish. (No. 5). (Illus.). viii, 76p. 1976. 3.50. AZ Univ ARP.

Pam Shriver: A Season on Tour. Pam Shriver et al. (Illus.). 240p. 1986. text ed. 16.95 (ISBN 0-07-057177-5). McGraw.

Pamela, 2 Vols. Samuel Richardson. (Paper Pub. 1978, repr. from 1914). 1974. (Evman); Vol. 1. pap. 4.50x (ISBN 0-460-01683-0, Evman); Vol. 2. pap. 4.95x (ISBN 0-460-01684-9). Biblio Dist.

Pamela. Samuel Richardson. Ed. by T. C. Duncan-Eaves & B. D. Kimpel. LC 71-134860. (Orig.). 1971. pap. 6.95 (ISBN 0-395-11152-8, RivEd). HM.

Pamela. Samuel Richardson. 1958. pap. 4.95x (ISBN 0-393-00166-0, Norton Lib). Norton.

Pamela Camel. Bill Peet. LC 83-18594. (Illus.). 32p. (gr. k-3). 1984. PLB 11.95 (ISBN 0-395-35975-9, 5-93025). HM.

Pamela Camel. Bill Peet. (Illus.). (gr. 4-8). 1986. pap. 3.95 (ISBN 0-395-41670-1, Sandpiper). HM.

Pamela Deck. Rudolph L. Williams. 112p. 1987. 6.95 (ISBN 0-8062-2895-4). Carlton.

Pamela Hill: The Governess. 160p. 1985. 24.95x (ISBN 0-7090-1770-7, Pub. by R Hale Ltd UK). State Mutual Bk.

Pamela: Or Virtue Rewarded. Samuel Richardson. Ed. by Peter Sabor. (Penguin English Library). 480p. 1981. pap. 5.95 (ISBN 0-14-043140-3). Penguin.

Pamela-Shamela. S. Fieldin Richardson. 1980. pap. 5.95 (ISBN 0-452-00856-5, Mer). NAl.

Pamela, Shamela. Samuel Richardson & Henry Fielding. 1980. pap. 3.50 (ISBN 0-451-51366-5, Sig Classics). NAL.

Pamela Street: Many Waters. 192p. 1985. 24.95x (ISBN 0-7090-2139-9, Pub. by R Hale Ltd UK). State Mutual Bk.

Pamela's Daughters. Robert P. Utter & Gwendolyn B. Needham. LC 71-184236. (Illus.). xvi, 512p. 1972. Repr. of 1936 ed. 25.00x (ISBN 0-8462-1648-5). Russell.

Pamjati Igumena Fillimona. Archbishop Konstantine Zaitsev. 58p. 1954. pap. 2.00 (ISBN 0-317-29287-0). Holy Trinity.

Pamjati Posljednjago Tsarjia. Archimandrite Konstantine Zaitsev. 40p. 1968. pap. 2.00 (ISBN 0-317-29238-2). Holy Trinity.

Pamlico Sound. Hal J. Daniel, III. 12p. 1987. pap. 1.00 (ISBN 0-318-23499-8). Samisdat.

Pammelia. Musicke Miscellanie. Thomas Ravenscroft. LC 71-171788. (English Experience Ser.: No. 412). 48p. 1971. Repr. of 1609 ed. 25.00 (ISBN 90-221-0412-5). Walter J Johnson.

Pampangans: Colonial Society in a Philippine Province. John A. Larkin. LC 74-165232. (Center for South & Southeast Asia Studies, UC Berkeley: No. 11). (Illus.). 300p. 1972. 40.00x (ISBN 0-520-02076-6). U of Cal Pr.

Pampas Grass. Meredith L. Adams. 257p. (Orig.). 1985. pap. 6.95 (ISBN 0-935539-17-4). Heroica Bks.

Pamper Your Possessions. rev. ed. Veva P. Wright. 1978. 10.95 (ISBN 0-517-53617-X, Dist. by Crown); pap. 4.95 (ISBN 0-517-53524-6, Dist. by Crown). Barre.

Pamper's Parents' Handbook. Alvin N. Eden. 1987. pap. 3.95 (ISBN 0-451-14828-2, Sig). NAL.

Pamphilla to Amphilanthus. Lady Mary Wroth. Ed. by James Hogg. (Elizabethan & Renaissance Studies). 118p. (Orig.). 1977. pap. 15.00 (ISBN 3-7052-0707-5, Pub. by Salzburg Studies). Longwood Pub Group.

Pamphlet Against Anthologies. Laura Riding & Robert Graves. LC 78-120220. Repr. of 1928 ed. 17.50 (ISBN 0-404-05332-7). AMS Pr.

Pamphlet File in School, College & Public Libraries. rev. enl ed. Norma O. Ireland. (Useful Reference Ser. of Library Bks: Vol. 84). 1954. lib. bdg. 9.00x (ISBN 0-87305-084-3). Faxon.

Pamphlet Literature from Onitsha. B. Chinaka et al. 1965. Twelve works in one unit. 65.00 (ISBN 0-8115-2985-1). Kraus Repr.

Pamphlets & Leaflets by W. E. B. DuBois. W. E. B. DuBois. (Complete Published Works of W. E. B. DuBois Ser.). 353p. 1985. lib. bdg. 90.00 (ISBN 0-527-25348-0). Kraus Intl.

Pamphlets & the American Revolution. LC 76-41289. 1976. 100.00x (ISBN 0-8201-1280-1). Schol Facsimiles.

Pamphlets Libertins Contre Marie-Antoinette: D'apres des Documents Nouveaux et les Pamphlets Tires de l'Enfer de la Bibliotehque Nationale. Hector Fleischmann. 316p. (Fr.). Repr. of 1908 ed. lib. bdg. 52.50x. Coronet Bks.

Pamphlets: Nineteen Forty-Nine to Nineteen Sixty-One, 1 vol, Nos. 1-10. Tuskegee Institute, Alabama, Dept. of Records & Research. 29.00 (ISBN 0-527-91250-6). Kraus Repr.

Pamphlets of the American Revolution, 1750-1776: Vol. 1, 1750-1765. Ed. by Bernard Bailyn & Jane N. Garrett. (John Harvard Library). 1965. 35.00x (ISBN 0-674-65250-9). Harvard U Pr.

Pamphlets of Thomas Robert Malthus 1800-1817. Thomas R. Malthus. LC 77-117389. 1970. Repr. lib. bdg. 39.50x (ISBN 0-678-00646-6). Kelley.

Pamphlets on American Business Abroad: An Original Anthology. Thwaite et al. Ed. by Stuart Bruchey & Eleanor Bruchey. LC 76-5053. (American Business Abroad Ser.). (Illus.). 1976. Repr. of 1976 ed. 31.00x (ISBN 0-405-09294-6). Ayer Co Pubs.

Pamphlets on the Constitution of the U. S. Ed. by Paul L. Ford. 1971. Repr. of 1888 ed. lib. bdg. 24.00 (ISBN 0-8337-4568-9). B Franklin.

Pamphlets on the Constitution of the United States. Paul L. Ford. LC 68-22228. (American History, Politics & Law Ser). 1968. Repr. of 1888 ed. lib. bdg. 35.00 (ISBN 0-306-71144-3). Da Capo.

Pamplona: A Sociological Analysis of Migration & Urban Adaptation Patterns. James M. O'Kane. LC 81-40637. (Illus.). 174p. (Orig.). 1982. lib. bdg. 24.75 o. p. (ISBN 0-8191-1959-8); pap. text ed. 12.25 (ISBN 0-8191-1960-1). U Pr of Amer.

Pampoody & Max. Harriet Lewis. 72p. 1977. pap. 4.50 (ISBN 0-933294-01-8). Backroads.

Pamunkey Indians of Virginia. Garland Pollard. 1988. Repr. of 1894 ed. lib. bdg. 49.00x. Am Biog Serv.

Pan. Birney Dibble. 256p. (Orig.). 1987. pap. 3.50 (ISBN 0-8439-2563-9). Leisure NY.

Pan. J. Birney Dibble. 256p. 1985. pap. 2.95 (ISBN 0-8439-2238-9, Leisure Bks). Leisure NY.

Pan-Africa Biography. Ed. by Robert A. Hill. 1987. write for info. (Crossroads). African Studies Assn.

Pan-African Connection. Tony Martin. 262p. cancelled (ISBN 0-87073-712-0); pap. cancelled (ISBN 0-87073-713-9). Schenkman Bks Inc.

Pan-African Connection: From Slavery to Garvey & Beyond. Tony Martin. LC 82-19521. (New Marcus Garvey Library: No. 6). (Illus.). xii, 262p. (Orig.). 1984. text ed. 22.95 (ISBN 0-912469-10-2); pap. text ed. 7.95 (ISBN 0-912469-11-0). Majority Pr.

Pan-African Education: The Last Stage of Educational Developments. John K. Marah. (African Studies: Vol. 9). 336p. 1988. lib. bdg. 59.95x (ISBN 0-88946-186-4). E Mellen.

Pan-African Movement: A History of Pan-Africanism in America, Europe & Africa. Imanuel Geiss. LC 74-78310. 546p. 1974. 65.00 (ISBN 0-8419-0161-9, Africana); pap. 29.50 (ISBN 0-8419-0215-1). Holmes & Meier.

Pan-African Protest: West Africa & the Italo-Ethiopian Crisis, 1934-1941. S. K. Asante. LC 78-312713. (Legon History Ser.). pap. 65.00 (ISBN 0-317-27780-4, 2025231). Bks Demand UMI.

Pan-Africanism. P. Olisanwuche Esedebe. LC 82-18692. 271p. 1982. 14.95 (ISBN 0-88258-124-4); pap. 6.95 (ISBN 0-88258-125-2). Howard U Pr.

Pan-Africanism: A Short Political Guide. Colin Legum. LC 75-25492. (Illus.). 1976. Repr. of 1962 ed. lib. bdg. 27.50x (ISBN 0-8371-8420-7, LEPA). Greenwood.

Pan-Africanism & East African Integration. Joseph S. Nye, Jr. LC 65-22063. (Center for International Affairs Ser). (Illus.). 1965. 21.00x (ISBN 0-674-65300-9). Harvard U Pr.

Pan-Africanism & the Black Diaspora: A Study of Policy & Practice. Ronald Walters. Incl. Vol. I. A Study of Practice. 1982. 15.00 (ISBN 0-933184-50-6); pap. 6.95 (ISBN 0-933184-26-3); Vol. II. A Study of Policy. 1983. 15.00 (ISBN 0-933184-52-2); pap. 6.95 (ISBN 0-933184-53-0). Set (ISBN 0-933184-25-5). Flame Intl.

Pan-Africanism in Action: An Account of the UAM. Albert Tevoedjre. (Occasional Papers in International Affairs: No. 11). (Illus.). 94p. 1984. pap. text ed. 8.75 (ISBN 0-8191-4051-1). U Pr of Amer.

Pan-Africanism: New Directions in Strategy. Ed. by W. Ofuatey-Kodjoe. LC 86-20191. 472p. (Orig.). 1986. lib. bdg. 30.25 (ISBN 0-8191-5363-X); pap. text ed. 19.75 (ISBN 0-8191-5364-8). U Pr of Amer.

Pan Africanism or Neo-Colonialism: The Bankruptcy of the OAU. Elenga M'buyinga. 242p. 1982. 24.75x (ISBN 0-86232-076-3, Pub. by Zed Pr England); pap. 10.25 (ISBN 0-86232-013-5, Pub. by Zed Pr England). Humanities.

Pan Am World Guide. 26th ed. Ed. by Pan Am World Airways, Inc. Staff. 1982. text ed. 12.95 (ISBN 0-07-048433-3). McGraw.

Pan American Airways: An Airline & Its Aircraft. R. E. Davies. (Illus.). 96p. 1987. 24.95 (ISBN 0-517-56639-7, Or Press). Crown.

Pan American Exposition Supplement to Mason County Journal, Shelton Washington. Honor L. Wilhelm. (Shorey Historical Ser.). 44p. pap. 4.95 (ISBN 0-8466-0263-6, S263). Shorey.

Pan American Nuclear Technology Exchange: PRoceedings of the American Nuclear Society, Executive Conference. American Nuclear Society Staff Executive Conference. 448p. pap. 44.00 (ISBN 0-317-33003-9, 650008). Am Nuclear Soc.

Pan American Peace Plans. Charles Evans Hughes. 1929. 39.50x (ISBN 0-685-69828-9). Elliots Bks.

Pan American Poems: An Anthology. Ed. by Agnes B. Poor. 1977. lib. bdg. 59.95 (ISBN 0-8490-2400-5). Gordon Pr.

Pan American Union. John Barrett. 1977. lib. bdg. 59.95 (ISBN 0-8490-2401-3). Gordon Pr.

Pan American Visions: Woodrow Wilson in the Western Hemisphere, 1913-1921. Mark T. Gilderhus. LC 86-16024. 194p. 1986. 25.95x (ISBN 0-8165-0936-0). U of Ariz Pr.

Pan-Americanism. R. Usher. 1976. lib. bdg. 59.95 (ISBN 0-8490-2402-1). Gordon Pr.

Pan-Americanism from Monroe to the Present: A View from the Other Side. Alonso Aguilar. Tr. by Asa Zatz. LC 68-13659. 192p. 1969. pap. 4.95 (ISBN 0-85345-098-6). Monthly Rev.

Pan-Americanism: Its Beginnings. Joseph B. Lockey. LC 79-111723. (American Imperialism: Viewpoints of United States Foreign Policy, 1898-1941). 1970. Repr. of 1920 ed. 25.50 (ISBN 0-405-02034-1). Ayer Co Pubs.

Pan Americanism: Its Meaning & History. John E. Fagg. LC 81-17176. (Anvil Ser.). 218p. 1982. pap. text ed. 8.50 (ISBN 0-89874-258-7). Krieger.

Pan Am's World Guide. 9.95 (ISBN 0-685-37583-8). Pan Am Pubns.

Pan-Arabism & Arab Nationalism: The Continuing Debate. Ed. by Tawfic E. Farah. 230p. 1987. 35.00 (ISBN 0-8133-0378-8); pap. 15.95 (ISBN 0-8133-0377-X). Westview.

Pan Chao, Foremost Woman Scholar of China, First Century A. D. Nancy L. Swann. LC 68-10946. (Illus.). 1968. Repr. of 1932 ed. 8.50x (ISBN 0-8462-1085-1). Russell.

Pan con Rocio. G. Vieru. 44p. (Span.). 1983. 4.95 (ISBN 0-8285-2648-6, Pub. by Raduga Pubs USSR). Imported Pubns.

Pan-European Associations: A Directory of Multi-National Organizations in Europe. C. A. Henderson. 420p. 1983. 120.00x (ISBN 0-900246-37-5, Pub. by CBD Res Ltd.). Gale.

Pan for Gold on Your Next Vacation. Janet Ruhe-Schoen. LC 77-1378. 28p. 1985. pap. 3.50 (ISBN 0-87576-059-7). Pilot Bks.

Pan: From Lieutenant Thomas Glahn's Papers. Knut Hamsun. Tr. by James W. McFarlane from Norwegian. 192p. (Orig.). 1956. pap. 8.95 (ISBN 0-374-50016-9). FS&G.

Pan-German League, Eighteen Ninety to Nineteen Fourteen. Mildred S. Wertheimer. LC 79-159257. 1971. Repr. of 1924 ed. lib. bdg. 19.00x (ISBN 0-374-98352-6, Octagon). Hippocrene Bks.

Pan-Germanism & German Aggressiveness, 2 vols. Roland G. Usher. 317p. 1985. Set. 187.45x (ISBN 0-86722-086-4). Inst Econ Pol.

Pan-Islam. George W. Bury. LC 80-1938. Repr. of 1919 ed. 30.00 (ISBN 0-404-18956-3). AMS Pr.

Pan-Islamism. B. K. Narayan. 232p. 35.00X (ISBN 0-317-52149-7, Pub. by S Chand Mutual). State Mutual Bk.

Pan-Islamism & the Conquest of the World, 2 vols. Daniel S. Shelburne. (Illus.). 291p. 1984. Set. 187.75x (ISBN 0-86722-080-5). Inst Econ Pol.

Pan Pacific Conference of Rehabilitation International, 6th: Proceedings, Seoul, Korea, 1979. 550p. 15.00 (ISBN 0-686-94895-5). Rehab Intl.

Pan Tadeusz or the Last Foray in Lithuania. Adam Micxkiewicz. (Illus.). 600p. (Pol. & Eng.). 1986. 35.00 (ISBN 0-318-23361-4). Szwede Slavic.

Pan, the Goat-God: His Myth in Modern Times. Patricia Merivale. LC 69-12729. (Harvard Studies in Comparative Literature: No. 30). 319p. pap. 83.00 (2029996). Bks Demand UMI.

Pan Tianshou Huaji. Pan Tianshou. 1979. pap. 28.00x (ISBN 0-317-69097-3, Pub. by Han-Shan Tang Ltd). State Mutual Bk.

Pan-Turkism & Islam in Russia. Serge A. Zenkovsky. LC 60-5399. (Russian Research Center Studies: No. 36). 1960. 27.00x (ISBN 0-674-65350-5). Harvard U Pr.

Pan-Turkism in Turkey: A Study of Irredentism. Jacob M. Landau. LC 81-10914. viii, 206p. 1981. 27.50 (ISBN 0-208-01949-9, Archon). Shoe String.

Pan y Mantequilla. 3rd ed. N. Sallese & L. Fernandez. 1984. text ed. 20.75 (ISBN 0-8384-1209-2). Heinle & Heinle.

Panache Litteraire: Textes du Monde Francophone. Jean-Pierre Cauvin & Mary J. Baker. 1978. pap. text ed. 17.95 scp (ISBN 0-06-041205-4, HarpC). Har-Row.

Panada & the Bushfire. Michael Foreman. (Illus.). 32p. (gr. k-4). 1986. pap. 12.95 (ISBN 0-13-648395-X). P-H.

Panafricanist World View. Opoku Agyeman. 284p. 1984. 13.95 (ISBN 0-89697-171-6). Intl Univ Pr.

Panagia Houses at Mycenae. Ione M. Shear. (University Museum Monograph Ser.: No. 68). (Illus.). 171p. 1987. text ed. 80.00x. Univ Mus of U PA.

Panait Musoiu: A Chronology. V. Munoz. (Libertarian & Anarchist Chronology Ser.). 1980. lib. bdg. 59.95 (ISBN 0-8490-3088-9). Gordon Pr.

Panajachel: A Guatemalan Town in Thirty-Year Perspective. Robert E. Hinshaw. LC 74-17838. (Pitt Latin American Ser). 1975. 24.95x (ISBN 0-8229-3296-2). U of Pittsburgh Pr.

Panama. Ashley Carter. 1978. pap. 2.25 (ISBN 0-449-14025-3, GM). Fawcett.

Panama. Eleanor D. Langstaff. (World Bibliographical Ser.: No. 14). 184p. 1982. 28.00 (ISBN 0-903450-26-7). ABC-Clio.

Panama, 2 vols. F. Lindsay. 1976. lib. bdg. 200.00 (ISBN 0-8490-2403-X). Gordon Pr.

Panama. Thomas McGuane. LC 78-12344. 175p. 1978. 7.95 (ISBN 0-374-22942-2). FS&G.

Panama. Thomas McGuane. 1979. pap. 3.95 (ISBN 0-14-005274-7). Penguin.

Panama. Thomas McGuane. 176p. 1987. pap. 5.95 (ISBN 0-14-009908-5). Penguin.

Panama. (Let's Visit Places & Peoples - - Nations, Dependencies, & Sovereignties of the World Ser.). (Illus.). (gr. 5 up). 1988. 12.95 (ISBN 0-222-00961-6). Chelsea Hse.

Panama see American Nations Past & Present.

Panama see Statements of the Laws of the OAS Member States in Matters Affecting Business.

Panama: A Country Study. 3rd ed. Ed. by Richard F. Nyrop. LC 80-29255. (Area Handbook Ser.: DA Pam 550-46). (Illus.). 300p. 1981. 11.00 (ISBN 0-318-21883-6, S/N 008-020-00868-1). USGPO.

Panama & the Canal. W. Abbot. 1976. lib. bdg. 59.95 (ISBN 0-8490-2404-8). Gordon Pr.

Panama: Assault on Human Rights. 1988. Spanish ed. 3.00. Amnesty Intl USA.

Panama Canal: A Study in International Law & Diplomacy. Harmodio Arias. LC 79-111707. (American Imperialism: Viewpoints of United States Foreign Policy, 1898-1941). 1970. Repr. of 1911 ed. 16.00 (ISBN 0-405-02001-5). Ayer Co Pubs.

Panama Canal & Sea Power in the Pacific. Alfred T. Mahan. (Illus.). 1977. 137.75 (ISBN 0-89266-044-9). Am Classical Coll Pr.

Panama Canal & the Sea Power in the Pacific. Alfred T. Mahan. (Great Issues of History Library). (Illus.). 107p. 1983. Repr. of 1913 ed. 175.45x (ISBN 0-86722-027-9). Inst Econ Pol.

Panama Canal & the Security of the United States. Thayer A. Mahan. (Illus.). 181p. 1985. 187.50 (ISBN 0-89266-502-5). Am Classical Coll Pr.

Panama Canal: Chronology of Events & Background Documents, 2 vols. 1978. Repr. of 1977 ed. lib. bdg. 75.00 (ISBN 0-89941-192-4). W S Hein.

Panama Canal Controversy: U. S. Diplomacy & Defense Interests. Paul B. Ryan. LC 77-20643. (Publications Ser.: No. 187). (Illus.). 1977. pap. 6.95x (ISBN 0-8179-6872-5). Hoover Inst Pr.

Panama Canal: Gateway to the World. Judith St. George. 144p. (gr. 5 up). 1989. 14.95 (ISBN 0-399-21637-5, Putnam). Putnam Pub Group.

Panama Canal in American Politics: Domestic Advocacy & the Evolution of Policy. J. Michael Hogan. 264p. 1986. text ed. 24.95x (ISBN 0-8093-1277-8). S Ill U Pr.

Panama Canal: Its History, Activities & Organization. Darrell H. Smith. LC 72-3060. (Brookings Institution. Institute for Government Research. Service Monographs of the U. S. Government: No. 44). Repr. of 1927 ed. 42.50 (ISBN 0-404-57144-1). AMS Pr.

Panama Canal Negotiations. William M. Habeeb & I. William Zartman. 72p. (Orig.). 1986. pap. text ed. 8.00 (ISBN 0-941700-04-6). JH FPI SAIS.

Panama Canal: The Crisis in Historical Perspective. Walter LaFeber. 1978. 29.95x (ISBN 0-19-502360-9). Oxford U Pr.

Panama Canal: The Crisis in Historical Perspective. expanded ed. Walter LaFeber. LC 77-13270. (Illus.). 1978. pap. 8.95x (ISBN 0-19-502511-3). Oxford U Pr.

Panama Canal Treaties Swindle: Consent to Disaster. G. Russell Evans. (Constitutional Bookshelf Ser.). 350p. 1984. 16.50 (ISBN 0-930095-00-6). Signal Bks.

Panama: For Whom the Canal Tolls? (Report on the Americas: Vol. XIII, No. 5). 52p. 2.50 (ISBN 0-317-34962-7). NA Cong Lat Am.

Panama Forest & Shore. Burton Gordon. (Illus., Orig.). 1983. 15.00 (ISBN 0-910286-88-4). Boxwood.

Panama Gold see Oro de Panama.

Panama Hat Trail: A Journey from South America. Tom Miller. LC 86-868. (Illus.). 288p. 1986. 15.95 (ISBN 0-688-06395-0). Morrow.

Panama Hat Trail: A Journey to South America. Tom Miller. LC 87-45913. (Departures Ser.). (Illus.). 272p. 1988. pap. 6.95 (ISBN 0-394-75774-2, Vin). Random.

Panama in Pictures. Lerner Publications, Department of Geography Staff. (Visual Geography Ser.). (Illus.). 64p. (gr. 5 up). 1987. PLB 9.95 (ISBN 0-8225-1818-X). Lerner Pubns.

Panama in Transition: Local Reactions to Development Policies. John Bort & Mary Helms. (Monograph in Anthropology: No. 6). (Illus.). v, 195p. 1983. pap. 9.50 (ISBN 0-913134-75-9). Mus Anthro MO.

Panama 'm Tombe (My Hat Fell off) Dale M. Foreman. 300p. (Orig.). 1986. pap. text ed. 4.95 (ISBN 0-939688-19-0). Directed Media.

Panama Money in Barbados, Nineteen Hundred to Nineteen Twenty. Bonham C. Richardson. LC 85-6127. (Illus.). 308p. 1986. text ed. 24.95x (ISBN 0-87049-477-5). U of Tenn Pr.

Panama Odyssey. William J. Jorden. LC 83-22291. (Illus.). 780p. 1984. 27.50 (ISBN 0-292-76469-3). U of Tex Pr.

Panama Quadrant. Olive Brooks. 1962. 12.95x (ISBN 0-8084-0234-X). New Coll U Pr.

Panama Route. John Haskell Kemble. LC 79-139195. (American Scene Ser). (Illus.). 316p. 1972. Repr. of 1943 ed. lib. bdg. 37.50 (ISBN 0-306-70083-2). Da Capo.

Panama: Sovereignty for a Land Divided. Ed. by Diane De Graffenreid & Philip Wheaton. LC 76-53993. (Illus.). 127p. 1976. pap. 2.50 (ISBN 0-918346-01-0). EPICA.

Panama Story. Jean Niemeier. LC 68-19528. 1968. pap. 5.95 (ISBN 0-8323-0195-7). Binford-Metropolitan.

Panama: Structural Change & Growth Prospects. 384p. 1985. 20.00 (ISBN 0-8213-0580-8, BK 0580). World Bank.

Pananandata Knife Fighting. Amante P. Marinas, Sr. (Illus.). 112p. (Orig.). 1986. pap. text ed. 12.00 (ISBN 0-87364-399-2). Paladin Pr.

Panandata Yantok at Daga: Filipino Stick & Dagger. Amante P. Marinas, Sr. (Illus.). 88p. 1988. pap. text ed. 12.00 (ISBN 0-87364-447-6). Paladin Pr.

PanAngling's World Guide to Fly Fishing. Jim C. Chapralis. LC 86-62705. (Illus.). 464p. 1987. 24.95 (ISBN 0-9618193-0-8). PanAngling Pub.

Panare: Tradition & Change on the Amazonian Frontier. Paul Henley. LC 81-40432. (Illus.). 320p. 1982. text ed. 39.50t (ISBN 0-300-02504-1). Yale U Pr.

Panasonic Car Sound Fact Book & Shopper's Guide. D. Minutti. 1978. pap. 1.95 (ISBN 0-89552-025-7). DMR Pubns.

Panasonic Way: From a Chief Executive's Desk. Toshihiko Yamashita. 172p. 1988. 17.95 (ISBN 0-87011-890-0). Kodansha.

Panathenaia: Studies in Athenian Life & Thought in the Classical Age. Ed. by T. E. Gregory & Anthony Podlecki. 8.50x (ISBN 0-87291-126-8). Coronado Pr.

Pancadasi. Swami Vidyaranya. Tr. by Swami Swahananda. (Sanskrit & Eng). 9.95 (ISBN 0-87481-429-4). Vedanta Pr.

Pancadasi: A Critical Study. Shakuntala Panjani. 1985. 29.95. Asia Bk Corp.

Pancake Boy. Retold by & illus. by Lorinda B. Cauley. (Illus.). 32p. (ps-1). 1988. PLB 13.95 (ISBN 0-399-21505-0, Putnam). Putnam Pub Group.

Pancake Pie. Sven Nordqvist. LC 84-16640. (Illus.). 32p. (ps-3). 1985. 10.25 (ISBN 0-688-04141-8, Morrow Junior Books); PLB 10.88 (ISBN 0-688-04142-6, Morrow Junior Books). Morrow.

Pancake That Ran Away & Toads & Diamonds. Charles Perrault. (Upside Down Books). (Illus.). 48p. (ps-3). 1985. 4.95 (ISBN 0-88110-254-7). EDC.

Pancakes & Painted Eggs. Jean Chapman. (Teacher Resource Collections Ser.). (Illus.). (ps-6). 1982. PLB 21.27 (ISBN 0-516-08951-X). Childrens.

Pancakes at Four. Frank A. Sherman, III. 1979. 5.00 (ISBN 0-682-49427-5). Exposition-Phoenix.

Pancakes, Crackers & Pizza: A Book of Shapes. Marjorie Eberts & Margaret Gisler. LC 84-7699. (Rookie Readers Ser.). (Illus.). 32p. (ps-2). 1984. lib. bdg. 9.93 (ISBN 0-516-02063-3); pap. 2.50 (ISBN 0-516-42063-1). Childrens.

Pancakes for Breakfast. Tomie De Paola. LC 77-15523. (Illus.). (ps-2). 1978. 12.95 (ISBN 0-15-259455-8, HJ). HarBraceJ.

Pancakes for Breakfast. Tomie DePaola. LC 77-15523. (Illus.). 32p. (ps-3). 1978. pap. 5.95 (ISBN 0-15-670768-3, VoyB). HarBraceJ.

Pancakes: From Flapjacks to Crepes. Dorian L. Parker. 128p. 1988. 10.95 (ISBN 0-517-56136-0, C N Potter Bks). Crown.

Pancakes from Vinegar Hill Farm. Susan Ashby. LC 84-62909. (Illus.). 100p. 1984. 3.95 (ISBN 0-938232-26-6). Winston-Derek.

Pancakes-Waffles: The Fine Art of Pancake, Waffle, Crepe & Blintz Cooking. Carol D. Brent. LC 73-122449. 1970. 5.95 (ISBN 0-88351-007-3). Test Recipe.

Pancasila & the Search for Identity & Modernity in Indonesian Society: A Cultural & Ethical Analysis. Eka Darmaputera. x, 254p. (Orig.). 1988. pap. 45.00 (ISBN 90-04-08422-3, Pub. by E J Brill). Heinman.

Pancatantra. (Mongolia Society Special Papers: Issue II). 6.50 (ISBN 0-910980-22-5). Mongolia.

Pancatantra of Vasubhaga: A Critical Study. 145p. 1987. 19.95. Asia Bk Corp.

Pancatantra of Vishnusarman. M. R. Kale. 500p. 1986. 14.00 (ISBN 81-208-0219-5, Pub. by Motilal Banarsidass); pap. 10.50 (ISBN 81-208-0220-9, Pub. by Motilal Banarsidass). South Asia Bks.

Panchakrma Therapy in Ayurveda. Divakar Ojha & Ashok Kumar. 219p. 1979. text ed. 24.00 (ISBN 0-89744-057-9). Auromere.

Panchatantra. J. Hertel. lib. bdg. 79.95 (ISBN 0-87968-523-9). Krishna Pr.

Panchatantra. Tr. by Arthur W. Ryder. 1964. pap. 15.00x (ISBN 0-226-73249-5). U of Chicago Pr.

Panchatantra Reconstructed, 2 Vols. Ed. by F. Edgerton. (Amer Oriental Ser.). 1924. Set. 56.00 (ISBN 0-527-02677-8). Kraus Repr.

Panchayat Raj, Rural Development & the Political Economy of Village India. Norman K. Nicholson. (Occasional Paper Ser.: No. 1). 61p. (Orig.). 1973. pap. text ed. 4.99 (ISBN 0-86731-014-6). Cornell CIS RDC.

Panchayati Raj & the Weaker Sections. U. Gurumurthy. 1986. 28.50 (ISBN 81-7024-073-5, Pub. by Ashish India). South Asia Bks.

Panchikaranam. Shankara. (Sanskrit & English). pap. 1.95 (ISBN 0-87481-068-X). Vedanta Pr.

Pancho Villa & John Reed: Two Faces of Romantic Revolution. Jim Tuck. LC 84-8770. 252p. 1984. 21.95 (ISBN 0-8165-0867-4). U of Ariz Pr.

Pancho Villa at Columbus: The Raid of Nineteen-Sixteen. Haldeen Brady. (Southwestern Studies Ser.: No. 9). 1965. pap. 5.00 (ISBN 0-87404-132-5). Tex Western.

Pancho Villa: Intimate Recollections by People Who Knew Him. Ed. by Jessie Peterson & Thelma Knoles. (Illus.). 1977. 13.95 (ISBN 0-8038-5819-1). Hastings.

Pancho Villa: The Mexican Centaur. Oren Arnold. LC 76-29143. 1979. 7.50 (ISBN 0-916620-06-9). Portals Pr.

Pancratia. Ed. by Edward Kaplan. 22p. 1987. 35.00 (ISBN 0-934714-01-0); pap. 5.00 (ISBN 0-934714-02-9). Swamp Pr.

Pancreas in Cystic Fibrosis. Ed. by Claude C. Roy. 180p. 1984. pap. text ed. 37.50 (ISBN 0-88167-075-8). Raven.

Pancreatic Beta Cell Culture: Proceedings. Conference Hoechst, 5th, Kitzbuhel, 5-9 Oct. 1976. Ed. by E. Von Wasielewski & W. L. Chick. (International Congress Ser.: No. 408). 1977. 48.50 (ISBN 0-444-15262-8, Excerpta Medica). Elsevier.

Pancreatic Disease: Diagnosis & Therapy. Ed. by Thomas L. Dent. LC 81-81493. (Illus.). 576p. 1981. 79.50 (ISBN 0-8089-1376-X, 791028). Grune.

Pancreatic Transplantation. Ed. by C. C. Groth. 450p. 1987. 70.00 (ISBN 0-8089-1844-3, 791744). Grune.

Pancreatic Transplantation. C. G. Groth. 450p. 1988. 80.00 (ISBN 0-7216-2637-8). Saunders.

Pancreatic Tumors in Children. G. B. Humphrey. 1983. 58.50 (ISBN 90-247-2702-2, Pub. by Martinus Nijhoff Netherlands). Kluwer Academic.

Pancreatitis. Peter A. Banks. LC 78-11341. (Topics In Gastroenterology Ser.). (Illus.). 252p. 1979. 45.00x (ISBN 0-306-40116-9, Plenum Med Bk.). Plenum Pub.

Pancreatitis: Concepts & Classification. K. E. Gyr et al. (International Congress Ser.: Vol. 642). 1985. 148.00 (ISBN 0-444-80650-4). Elsevier.

Pancreatitis: Its Pathophysiology & Clinical Aspects. Ed. by Toshio Sato & Hidemi Yamauchi. 486p. 1986. 72.50 (ISBN 0-86008-391-8, Pub. by U of Tokyo Japan). Columbia U Pr.

Panda. Susan Bonners. LC 78-50404. (Illus.). 32p. (ps-3). 1978. pap. 6.95 (ISBN 0-385-28772-0); pap. 6.46 (ISBN 0-385-28775-5). Delacorte.

Panda. Susan Bonners. (gr. k-6). 1988. pap. 3.95 (ISBN 0-440-40110-0, YB). Dell.

Panda. Illus. by Carolyn Bracken. (Floppies Ser.). (Illus.). 6p. (ps-k). 1981. 2.50 (ISBN 0-671-42530-7, Little Simon). S&S.

Panda. Mary Hoffman. LC 84-15882. (Animals in the Wild Ser.). (Illus.). 24p. (gr. k-3). 1985. PLB 11.33 (ISBN 0-8172-2407-6). Raintree Pubs.

Panda. L. Martin. (Wildlife in Danger Ser.). (Illus.). 24p. (gr. k-5). Date not set. PLB 11.33 (ISBN 0-86592-996-3). Rourke Corp.

Panda. Nadine Saunier. (Animal Companions Ser.). (Illus.). 20p. (ps). 1988. 5.95 (ISBN 0-8120-5931-X). Barron.

Panda & the Bunyips. Michael Foreman. LC 87-9842. (Illus.). 32p. (ps-6). 1987. 10.95 (ISBN 0-8052-4041-1). Schocken.

Panda & the Enormous Cookie. Date not set. price not set. Panda Programs.

Panda & the Pet Plant. Date not set. price not set. Panda Programs.

Panda Bear Goes Visiting. Liu Qian. (Illus.). 22p. (gr. 3-4). 1982. 3.95 (ISBN 0-8351-1108-3); pap. 2.95 (ISBN 0-8351-1139-3). China Bks.

Panda Bear Is Critical. Fern Michaels. 320p. 1984. pap. 3.50 (ISBN 0-671-46420-5). PB.

Panda Climbs. LC 83-17462. (Growing up Ser.). (Illus.). 20p. (ps-1). 4.95; PLB 6.99. Sierra.

Panda Pals in Outdoor Fun. Jill Wolf. (Antioch Little Shape Bks.). (Illus.). 22p. (ps-3). 1984. 2.50 (ISBN 0-89954-276-X). Antioch Pub Co.

Panda, Panda. Tana Hoban. LC 86-3088. (Illus.). 12p. (ps). 1986. pap. 3.95 (ISBN 0-688-06564-3). Greenwillow.

Panda Puzzles. Date not set. price not set. Panda Programs.

Panda Tells about Bike Safety. Date not set. price not set. Panda Programs.

Panda Tells about Camp. Date not set. price not set. Panda Programs.

Panda Tells about Eyes. Date not set. price not set. Panda Programs.

Panda Tells about First Aid. Date not set. price not set. Panda Programs.

Panda Tells about Home Safety. Date not set. price not set. Panda Programs.

Panda Tells about Money. Date not set. price not set. Panda Programs.

Panda Tells about Moving Day. Date not set. price not set. Panda Programs.

Panda Tells about Pets. Date not set. price not set. Panda Programs.

Panda Tells about Tooth Care. Date not set. price not set. Panda Programs.

Panda Tells about Traffic Safety. Date not set. price not set. Panda Programs.

Panda Tournament Book. Date not set. price not set. Panda Programs.

Panda Visits the Dentist. Date not set. price not set. Panda Programs.

Panda Zoo. Norman A. Kirk. LC 82-22675. (Illus.). 96p. 1983. 20.00 (ISBN 0-911155-00-7); pap. 10.00 (ISBN 0-911155-01-5). West Boston.

Pandaemonium: Or the Devil's Cloyster. Richard Bovet. 1976. Repr. 18.00x (ISBN 0-7158-1136-3). Charles River Bks.

Pandaemonium: The Coming of the Machine As Seen by Contemporary Observers, 1660-1886. Humphrey Jennings. 480p. 1985. 18.95 (ISBN 0-02-916470-2). Free Pr.

Pandas. N. S. Barrett. Ed. by FS Staff. (Picture Library). (Illus.). 32p. (gr. 4-9). 1988. 10.90 (ISBN 0-531-10530-X). Watts.

Pandas. (Zoobooks). (Illus.). 20p. 1983. pap. 1.95 (ISBN 0-937934-18-6). Wildlife Educ.

Pandas see Preschool Puppet Board Books.

Pandas Take a Vacation. Betsy Maestro. (Big Little Golden Bks.). (Illus.). 24p. (gr. k-3). 1986. write for info. (ISBN 0-307-10258-0, Pub. by Golden Bks.). Western Pub.

Panda's Thumb: More Reflections in Natural History. Stephen J. Gould. (Illus.). 344p. 1982. pap. 5.95 (ISBN 0-393-30023-4). Norton.

Panda's Thumb: More Reflections in Natural History. Stephen J. Gould. (Illus.). 1980. 15.95 (ISBN 0-393-01380-4). Norton.

Pandectes of the Law of Nations. William Fulbecke. LC 79-84109. (English Experience Ser.: No.928). 192p. 1979. Repr. of 1602 ed. lib. bdg. 18.00 (ISBN 90-221-0928-3). Walter J Johnson.

Pandeleteius of Venezuela & Colombia: Curculionidae-Brachyderinae-Tanymecini. Anne T. Howden. (Memoir Ser.: No. 24). (Illus.). 310p. 1976. 25.00x (ISBN 0-686-20326-7). Am Entom Inst.

Pandelis Prevelakis & the Value of a Heritage. Andonis Decavelles. Tr. by Jean H. Woodhead from Gr. Ed. by Theofanis G. Stavrou. Bd. with Rethymno As a Style of Life. Pandelis Prevelakis. LC 81-81839. (Modern Greek History & Culture Ser.). 1981. 10.00 (ISBN 0-935476-08-3). Nostos Bks.

Pandemic Influenza Seventeen Hundred to Nineteen Hundred: A Study in Historical Epidemiology. K. David Patterson. (Illus.). 128p. 1987. 29.50x (ISBN 0-8476-7512-2). Rowman.

Pandemonium Spirit. Jake Berry. (Illus.). 28p. 1986. pap. 1.50 (ISBN 0-938309-00-5). Bomb Shelter Prop.

Pandit Govind Ballabh Pant: The Colossus Speaks. Govind B. Pant. Ed. by Bhagwan Singh & M. C. Shah. 150p. 1988. text ed. 25.00x (ISBN 81-207-0736-2, Pub. by Sterling Pubs India). Apt Bks.

Pandolfini's Endgame Course. Bruce Pandolfini. (Illus.). 288p. 1988. pap. 7.95 (ISBN 0-671-65688-0, Fireside). S&S.

Pandom Eigenvalue Problems. Ed. by Collet's Holdings, Ltd. Staff. 1985. 80.00x (ISBN 0-317-46676-3, Pub. by Collets (UK)). State Mutual Bk.

Pandora, No. 5. Jayge Carr et al. Ed. by Lois Wickstrom. (Illus.). 60p. (Orig.). 1980. pap. 2.50 (ISBN 0-916176-10-X). Sproing.

Pandora, No. 6. Jean Lorrah et al. Ed. by Lois Wickstrom. (Illus.). 60p. (Orig.). 1980. pap. 2.50 (ISBN 0-916176-11-8). Sproing.

Pandora see Aurelia.

Pandora see Daisy Miller.

Pandora see Oeuvres.

Pandora, an Original Anthology of Role-Expanding Science Fiction & Fantasy. Jayge Carr et al. Ed. by Lois Wickstrom. (Illus., Orig.). 1979. pap. 2.50 (ISBN 0-916176-08-8); Vol.1,No.3. pap. 1.50 (ISBN 0-916176-07-X). Sproing.

Pandora & the Magic Box. I. E. Clark. (Illus.). 20p. (Director's Production Script). 1968. pap. 6.00 (ISBN 0-88680-148-6). I E Clark.

Pandora Eight: Role Expanding Science Fiction & Fantasy. Jim Aikin et al. Ed. by Lois Wickstrom & Jean Lorrah. (Illus.). 64p. 1981. 2.50 (ISBN 0-916176-16-9). Sproing.

Pandora Man. Kerry Newcomb & Frank Schaefer. 1980. pap. 1.95 (ISBN 0-449-24205-6, Crest). Fawcett.

Pandora Secret: A Captain Justice Story. Anthony Forrest. 303p. 1982. 15.50 (ISBN 0-8090-7504-0). Hill & Wang.

Pandora Seven: Role Expanding Science Fiction & Fantasy. Connie Kidwell et al. Ed. by Lois Wickstrom. (Illus.). 48p. 1981. 2.25 (ISBN 0-916176-12-6). Sproing.

Pandora Stone. William Greenleaf. 224p. 1984. pap. 2.75 (ISBN 0-441-65089-9). Ace Bks.

Pandora's Bauxite: Best of Bates Selections from the Geologic Column, 1966-1985. Robert L. Bates. 90p. (Orig.). 1986. pap. 7.95 (ISBN 0-913312-84-3). Am Geol.

Pandora's Box. Parker Abell. 64p. 1987. 6.50 (ISBN 0-8062-2808-3). Carlton.

Pandora's Box. Lyvely & Farmer. (Women's Humor Ser.). (Illus.). 1973. 1.25 (ISBN 0-918440-02-5). Nanny Goat.

Pandora's Box. Mary P. Osborne. (Hello Reader Ser.). (Illus.). 32p. (Orig.). (gr. k-3). 1987. pap. 2.50 (ISBN 0-590-40767-8). Scholastic Inc.

Pandora's Box. Lisl Weil. LC 85-20128. (Illus.). 40p. (gr. 2-6). 1986. 12.95 (ISBN 0-689-31216-4, Atheneum Childrens Bks). Macmillan.

Pandora's Children. Kathryn Lance. (Orig.). 1986. pap. 3.50 (ISBN 0-445-20066-9, Pub. by Popular Library). Warner Bks.

Pandora's Daughters: The Role & Status of Women in Greek & Roman Antiquity. Eva Cantarella. Tr. by Maureen B. Fant from Ital. LC 86-7292. 256p. 1987. text ed. 30.00x (ISBN 0-8018-3193-8); pap. text ed. 9.95x (ISBN 0-8018-3385-X). Johns Hopkins.

Pandora's Genes. Kathryn Lance. 288p. 1985. pap. 2.95 (ISBN 0-317-18088-6, Pub. by Popular Lib). Warner Bks.

Pandora's Pride. May Gruber. 280p. (Orig.). 1985. pap. 9.95 (ISBN 0-8184-0374-8, Pub. by Citadel Pr). Lyle Stuart.

Pane e Lavoro: The Italian American Working Class. Ed. by George Pozzetta. 1978. 9.95 (ISBN 0-934675-11-2). Am Italian.

Panel Reviews & Relevant Papers: Symposium on the Methodology for the Survey, Monitoring & Appraisal of Fishery Resources in Lakes & Larger Rivers, Vol. 2. (European Inland Fisheries Advisory Commission (EIFAC): Technical Papers: No. 23, Supp. 1). 750p. (Eng. & Fr.). 1975. pap. 28.25 (ISBN 92-5-000326-9, F764, FAO). UNIPUB.

Panel Sawing Machinery. 1973. 39.00x (ISBN 0-317-43776-3, Pub. by F I R A). State Mutual Bk.

Panel Study of Income Dynamics: Complete Documentation for Interviewing Years 1968-1981, 2 vols. & 9 suppls. Ed. by James N. Morgan. Incl. Vol. 1. Study Design, Procedures & Available Data for 1968-1972 Interviewing Years. 392p. 1973. pap. 40.00x o.s.i (ISBN 0-87944-141-0); Vol. 2. Tape Codes & Indexes for 1968-1972 Interviewing Years. 904p. 1973. pap. 75.00x o.s.i (ISBN 0-87944-142-9); 1973 Supplement. 240p. pap. 35.00x (ISBN 0-87944-155-0); 1974 Supplement. 280p. pap. 35.00x o.s.i (ISBN 0-87944-167-4); 1975 Supplement. 298p. pap. 35.00x (ISBN 0-87944-200-X); 1976 Supplement. 516p. pap. 35.00x (ISBN 0-87944-215-8); 1977 Supplement. 354p. pap. 35.00x (ISBN 0-87944-225-5); 1978 Supplement. 416p. pap. 35.00x (ISBN 0-87944-243-3); 1979 Supplement. 512p. pap. 35.00x (ISBN 0-87944-258-1); 1980 Supplement. 590p. 1981. pap. 35.00x (ISBN 0-87944-271-9). 500p. Supplement 1981. pap. 35.00x (ISBN 0-87944-279-4). Inst Soc Res.

Panel Study of Income Dynamics: 1982 Supplement. Economic Behavior Program Staff. (Documentation for Interviewing Years: 1968-1983). 632p. 1984. pap. text ed. 40.00 (ISBN 0-87944-294-8). Inst Soc Res.

Panel Study of Income Dynamics: 1983 Supplement. Economic Behavior Program Staff & James N. Morgan. (Documentation for Interviewing Years: 1968-1983). 648p. 1985. pap. text ed. 40.00x (ISBN 0-87944-305-7). Inst Soc Res.

Panel Surveys. Kasprzyk. (Probability & Mathematical Statistics Ser.). 1987. write for info. (ISBN 0-471-62592-2). Wiley.

Panfish. Dick Sternberg & Bill Ignizio. LC 83-72749. (Hunting & Fishing Library). (Illus.). 160p. 1983. 17.95 (ISBN 0-86573-007-5). Cy De Cosse.

Panfish. Dick Sternberg & Bill Ignizio. (Hunting & Fishing Library). 1985. 16.95 (ISBN 0-13-648379-8). P-H.

Pangasinan Dictionary. Richard A. Benton. LC 75-152456. (Hawaii University Honolulu, Pacific & Asian Linguistics Ser.). pap. 82.30 (ISBN 0-317-10106-4, 2007975). Bks Demand UMI.

Pangasinan, Fifteen Seventy-Two to Eighteen Hundred. Rosario M. Cortes. 1975. Repr. of 1974 ed. newsprint 4.00x (ISBN 0-686-18692-3). Cellar.

Pangasinan Reference Grammar. Richard A. Benton. Ed. by Howard P. McKaughan. LC 72-152458. (PALI Language Texts: Philippines). Repr. of 1971 ed. 71.50 (ISBN 0-8357-9826-7, 2017213). Bks Demand UMI.

Pangur Ban. Mary Stolz. LC 87-35049. (Ursula Nordstrom Book Ser.). (Illus.). 192p. (YA) (gr. 7 up). 1988. 13.70i (ISBN 0-06-025861-6); PLB 13.89 (ISBN 0-06-025862-4). HarpJ.

Panhandle Aspect of the Chaquaqua Plateau. Robert G. Campbell. (Graduate Studies: No. 11). (Illus.). 118p. (Orig.). 1976. pap. 5.00 (ISBN 0-89672-021-7). Tex Tech Univ Pr.

Panhandle Cowboy. John R. Erickson. LC 79-24929. (Illus.). xiv, 213p. 1980. pap. 5.95 (ISBN 0-8032-6702-9, BB 777, Bison). U of Nebr Pr.

Panhandle Cowboy. write for info. (ISBN 0-9608612-3-8). Maverick Bks.

Panhandle Memories. Adelia Rosasco-Soule. Ed. by Ron Cannon. (Illus.). 143p. 1987. text ed. 12.95 (ISBN 0-944206-00-X). PanHandle Pr.

Panhandle Personalities. Claude Simpson. LC 84-50761. (Gem Bks.-Historical). (Illus.). 352p. (Orig.). 1984. pap. 14.95 (ISBN 0-89301-100-2). U of Idaho Pr.

Panhandle Pilgrimage: Illustrated Tales Tracing History in the Texas Panhandle. expanded ed. Pauline D. Robertson & R. L. Robertson. (Illus.). 400p. 1978. 23.95 (ISBN 0-942376-00-5). Paramount TX.

Panhandle Pioneer: Henry C. Hitch, His Ranch, & His Family. Donald E. Green. LC 78-21390. (Oklahoma Heritage Association Trackmaker Ser.: Vol. 7). (Illus.). 1979. 19.95 (ISBN 0-8061-1529-7). U of Okla Pr.

Panhellenica: Essays in Ancient History. Ed. by Stanley Burstein & Louis Okin. 1980. 15.00x (ISBN 0-87291-134-9). Coronado Pr.

Panic among the Philistines. Bryan F. Griffin. LC 82-60663. 259p. 1983. 12.95 (ISBN 0-89526-633-4). Regnery Gateway.

Panic among the Phillistines. Bryan F. Griffin. (Christian Activist Ser.). 259p. 1985. pap. 5.95 (ISBN 0-89526-817-5). Regnery Gateway.

Panic & Phobias. Ed. by I. Hand & H. U. Wittchen. (Illus.). 145p. 1986. 25.00 (ISBN 0-387-16513-4). Springer-Verlag.

Panic & Phobias Two. Ed. by I. Hand & H. U. Wittchen. (Illus.). 280p. 1988. 89.50 (ISBN 0-387-19088-0). Springer-Verlag.

Panic & the Runaway. Ed. by Takeshi Kaiko. Tr. by Charles Dunn. 122p. 1977. 12.50 (ISBN 0-86008-196-6, Pub. by U of Tokyo Japan). Columbia U Pr.

Panic Attack Recovery Book. Shirley Swede & Seymour Jaffe. 1987. pap. 8.95 (ISBN 0-452-25949-5, Plume). NAL.

Panic: Facing Fears, Phobias & Anxiety. Stewart Agras. LC 85-4378. 160p. 1985. pap. text ed. 12.95 (ISBN 0-7167-1731-X). W H Freeman.

Panic in Box C. John D. Carr. 272p. 1987. 3.50 (ISBN 0-88184-288-5). Carroll & Graf.

Panic in Box C. John D. Carr. 273p. 1987. pap. 3.50 (ISBN 1-55547-149-8). Critics Choice Paper.

Panic of Eighteen Sixty-Six with Its Lessons on the Currency Act. Robert Baxter. LC 73-101233. (Research & Source Works Ser.: No. 390). 1970. Repr. of 1866 ed. lib. bdg. 20.50 (ISBN 0-8337-0194-0). B Franklin.

Panic of Eighteen Thirty-Seven: Some Financial Problems of the Jacksonian Era. Reginald C. McGrane. 1965. pap. 1.95x (ISBN 0-226-55858-4, P202, Phoen). U of Chicago Pr.

Panic of Eighty-Nine. Paul Erdman. LC 86-19747. 336p. 1987. 17.95 (ISBN 0-385-23124-5). Doubleday.

Panic of Eighty-Nine. Paul Erdman. 1988. pap. 4.50 (ISBN 0-317-67137-5, Charter Bks). Berkley Pub.

Panic of 'Eighty-Nine. Paul Erdman. 1988. pap. 4.50 (ISBN 0-317-67486-2). Jove Pubns.

Panic of 1819. Murray N. Rothbard. LC 79-182706. (Columbia University Studies in the Social Sciences: No. 605). Repr. of 1962 ed. 16.50 (ISBN 0-404-51605-X). AMS Pr.

Panic of 1857. George W. Van Vleck. LC 77-182585. (Columbia University. Studies in the Social Sciences: No. 463). Repr. of 1943 ed. 12.50 (ISBN 0-404-51463-4). AMS Pr.

Panic of 1857 & the Coming of the Civil War. James L. Huston. LC 87-2705. 328p. 1987. text ed. 32.50 (ISBN 0-8071-1368-9). La State U Pr.

Panic of '89. Paul Erdman. 420p. 1988. lib. bdg. 19.95x (ISBN 0-8161-4370-6, Large Print Bks). G K Hall.

Panic on Page One. Linda Stewart. 1979. 8.95 (ISBN 0-440-07120-8). Delacorte.

Panic on Wall Street: A Classic History of America's Financial Disasters - With a Timely Exploration of the Crash of 1987. Robert Sobel. 512p. 1988. pap. 12.95 (ISBN 0-525-48404-3, Pub. by Truman Talley Bk). Dutton.

Panic or Profits: A Small Business Guide to Low-Cost Marketing. R. Joseph Desmond. Ed. by James D. Hutchinson. LC 87-61546. (Illus.). 200p. (Orig.). 1988. pap. 19.95 (ISBN 0-943423-00-7). New World Mktg.

Panic-Proof Investing: How to Profit from the Crash of '87. Gray E. Cardiff. LC 87-43149. 256p. 1988. 18.95 (ISBN 0-13-429390-8). Prentice Hall Pr.

Panini: A Survey of Research. George Cardona. (Trends in Linguistics: State-of-the-Art Reports: No. 6). 1976. pap. 42.00x (ISBN 90-2793-435-5). Mouton.

Panini: His Work & Its Traditions, Vol. 1: Background & Introduction. George Cardona. 1988. 32.00x (ISBN 81-208-0419-8, Pub. by Motilal Banarsidass). South Asia Bks.

Panini's Metalanguage. Hartmut Scharfe. LC 71-167988. (American Philosophical Society Memoirs Ser.: Vol. 89). pap. 20.00 (ISBN 0-317-27912-2, 2025132). Bks Demand UMI.

Paniolo. Joseph Brennan. 1978. pap. 2.50 (ISBN 0-914916-39-4). Topgallant.

Panj Sura: Collection of 5 Famous Prayers. 4.50 (ISBN 0-686-18594-3). Kazi Pubns.

Panjabi Language: A Descriptive Grammar. N. I. Tolstaya. (Languages of Asia & Africa Ser.). 88p. (Orig.). 1981. pap. 16.95x (ISBN 0-7100-0939-9). Routledge Chapman & Hall.

Panjabi Printed Books in the British Museum: A Supplementary Catalogue. L. D. Barnett. 132p. 1961. 30.00 (ISBN 0-7141-0624-0, Pub. by British Lib). Longwood Pub Group.

Panjandrum Number One. Ed. by Dennis Koran. (Illus.). 1972. pap. 12.00 (ISBN 0-915572-46-X). Panjandrum.

Panjandrum Poetry Journal, No. 6-7. Ed. by Dennis Koran. (Illus.). 1978. pap. 6.95 (ISBN 0-915572-34-6). Panjandrum.

Panjandrum V: An Anthology of Poetry. Ed. by Dennis Koran. (Panjandrum Poetry Journal: No. 5). (Illus.). 1977. pap. 6.95 (ISBN 0-915572-15-X). Panjandrum.

Panji. W. H. Rassers. 1983. pap. text ed. 22.00 (ISBN 90-247-6184-0, Pub. by Martinus Nijhoff Netherlands). Kluwer Academic.

Panky & William. Nancy Saxon. LC 83-2633. (Illus.). 104p. (gr. 3-7). 1983. 10.95 (ISBN 0-689-30997-X, Atheneum Childrens Bks). Macmillan.

Panky & William. Nancy Saxon. (Illus.). 104p. (gr. 4-6). 1985. pap. 2.50 (ISBN 0-590-41222-1, Apple Paperbacks). Scholastic Inc.

Panky in the Saddle. Nancy Saxon. LC 83-15910. (Illus.). 160p. (gr. 3-7). 1984. 11.95 (ISBN 0-689-31038-2, Atheneum Childrens Bks). Macmillan.

Panky in the Saddle. Nancy Saxon. (Illus.). 128p. (gr. 4-6). 1985. pap. 2.25 (ISBN 0-590-33616-9, Apple Paperbacks). Scholastic Inc.

Pannekoek & Gorter's Marxism. Intro. by D. A. Smart. 176p. 1978. pap. 5.95 (ISBN 0-904383-71-7, Pub. by Pluto Pr). Longwood Pub Group.

Pannekoek & the Workers' Councils. Serge Bricianer. Tr. by Malachy Carroll from Fr. LC 78-50978. 1978. 18.00 (ISBN 0-914386-17-4); pap. 7.50 (ISBN 0-914386-18-2). Telos Pr.

Panners' Guide to Northwest Gold. Bob Jackson. (Illus.). 50p. (Orig.). 1980. pap. 3.95 (ISBN 0-918499-04-6). Jackson Mtn.

Panning Georgia's Gold. W. Larry Otwell. LC 85-61045. (Illus.). 112p. 1985. pap. 5.95 (ISBN 0-87797-143-9). Cherokee.

Pannizzi Lectures: Bibliography & the Sociology of Texts. D. F. McKenzie. 80p. 1986. pap. 15.00 (ISBN 0-7123-0085-6, Pub. by British Lib). Longwood Pub Group.

Panofsky & the Foundations of Art History. Michael A. Holly. LC 84-45143. (Paperback Ser.). 272p. (Orig.). 1985. 27.50x (ISBN 0-8014-1614-0); pap. 7.95x (ISBN 0-8014-9896-1). Cornell U Pr.

Panogram, 1988: New York Sites, Services, Sources & Salaries for the Feature Film Producer. George Gilbert. (Illus.). 96p. (Orig.). 1988. pap. 9.00. G Gilbert Assocs.

Panorama California: Scenic Views of California. Jack Rankin. (Illus.). 112p. 1988. pap. 19.95 (ISBN 0-935180-58-3). Mutual Pub HI.

Panorama California: Scenic Views of the Golden State. Ronn Ronck & Jack Rankin. 144p. 1988. 24.95 (ISBN 0-935180-57-5). Mutual Pub HI.

Panorama de la Astronomia Moderna. rev. ed. (Serie de Fisica: No. 2). (Span.). 1976. pap. 3.50 (ISBN 0-8270-6150-1). OAS.

Panorama de la Biblia. Alfred T. Eade. Orig. Title: New Panorama Bible Study Course. 32p. 1987. pap. 4.50 (ISBN 0-311-03657-0). Casa Bautista.

Panorama de la Poesie Haitienne. Carlos Saint-Louis & Maurice A. Lubin. (Fr.). 1950. 56.00 (ISBN 0-8115-3002-7). Kraus Repr.

Panorama de las Americas. 5th ed. John A. Crow & G. D. Crow. (Span.). 1980. pap. text ed. 15.95 (ISBN 0-03-050561-5). HR&W.

Panorama del Periodismo Puertorriqueno. Jose A. Romeu. (UPREX Comunicacion Ser.: No. 67). 6.00 (ISBN 0-8477-0067-4). U of PR pr.

Panorama del Protestantismo en Cuba. Ed. by Marcos A. Ramos. 668p. (Orig., Span.). 1986. pap. 14.50 (ISBN 0-89922-241-2). Edit Caribe.

Panorama des Idees Contemporaines see Korunk Szellemi Korkepe.

Panorama Hawaii: Scenic Views of the Hawaiian Islands. Ronn Ronck. Ray J. Baker. LC 84-60785. (Illus.). 96p. 1984. 19.95x (ISBN 0-935180-10-9). Mutual Pub HI.

Panorama Historico de la Poesia en Lengua Castellana. Jesus Tome. LC 87-82693. (Huracan Academia Ser.). 336p. (Span.). 1987. pap. 9.95 (ISBN 0-940238-94-2). Ediciones Huracan.

Panorama Italiano. 4th ed. Charles Speroni & Carlo L. Golino. 304p. (Ital.). 1980. pap. text ed. 18.95 (ISBN 0-03-050601-8). HR&W.

Panorama Litteraire de l'Europe 1833-1834. Thomas R. Palfrey. LC 73-128990. (Northwestern Humanities Ser.: No. 22). (Fr). Repr. of 1950 ed. 22.00 (ISBN 0-404-50722-0). AMS Pr.

Panorama Mysli Wspolczesnych. Geotan Picon. 713p. 1960. 9.00 (ISBN 0-940962-20-9). Polish Inst Art & Sci.

Panorama of Canadian Forests. pap. 24.95 (SSC81, SSC). UNIPUB.

Panorama of Evil: Insights from the Behavioral Sciences. Leonard W. Doob. LC 77-87964. (Contributions in Philosophy Ser.: No. 10). 1978. lib. bdg. 35.00 (ISBN 0-313-20030-0, DPE/). Greenwood.

Panorama of Five Thousand Years: Korean History. rev. ed. Andrew C. Nahm. LC 81-84202. (Illus.). 125p. 1983. 19.50x (ISBN 0-930878-23-X). Hollym Intl.

Panorama of Five Thousand Years: Korean History. Andrew C. Nahm. (Illus.). 126p. 1984. 19.95 (ISBN 0-89346-248-9). Heian Intl.

Panorama of Florida. David A. Bice et al. Ed. by Alfredlene Armstrong. (Illus.). 320p. 1982. 15.95 (ISBN 0-934750-13-0); text ed. 8.99 (ISBN 0-934750-21-1). tchr's. ed. 2.99 (ISBN 0-934750-27-0); wkbk. 3.00 (ISBN 0-934750-22-X); tchrs. wkbk. 4.25 (ISBN 0-934750-23-8). Jalamap.

Panorama of German Literature from 1871-1931. Felix Bertaux. Tr. by John J. Traunstine from Fr. LC 73-132940. 1971. Repr. of 1935 ed. lib. bdg. 25.00x (ISBN 0-8154-0354-2). Cooper Sq.

Panorama of Indian Culture. P. Chopra. 183p. 1983. 11.95. Asia Bk Corp.

Panorama of Indian Culture. Prabha Chopra. (Illus.). 183p. 1983. 7.95. Asia Bk Corp.

Panorama of Indian Diplomacy. N. M. Khilnani. 314p. 1981. 27.50x (ISBN 0-940500-74-4, Pub by S Chand India). Asia Bk Corp.

Panorama of Jain Art. C. Sivaramamurti. 1984. 92.50x (ISBN 0-8364-2200-7, Pub. by Motilal Banarsidass). South Asia Bks.

Panorama of Jain Art: South India. C. Sivaramurti. (Illus.). 372p. (Orig.). 1983. 81.50 (ISBN 0-318-18465-6). Nataraj Bks.

Panorama of Judaism, 2 pts. Ed. by Leo Jung. 1974. Pt. 1, 275 pp. 9.50 (ISBN 0-900689-48-X); Pt. 2, 243 pp. 9.50 (ISBN 0-900689-49-8). Soncino Pr.

Panorama of Judaism: Part 1 see Jewish Library.

Panorama of Judaism: Part 2 see Jewish Library.

Panorama of Polish History. Collets Holdings Ltd. Staff. 180p. 1982. 44.00x (ISBN 0-317-54559-0, Pub. by Collets (UK)). State Mutual Bk.

Panorama of Pure Mathematics: As Seen by N. Bourbaki. Jean Dieudonne. Tr. by I. Macdonald. LC 80-2330. (Pure & Applied Mathematics Ser.). 1982. 39.50 (ISBN 0-12-215560-2). Acad Pr.

Panorama of Sikh Religion & Philosophy. S. C. Jain. 124p. 1985. 19.95x (ISBN 0-317-66152-3). Asia Bk Corp.

Panorama of Tennessee. David A. Bice. LC 83-80152. (Illus.). 285p. 1984. text ed. 10.95 (ISBN 0-934750-38-6); tchr's. guide 3.00 (ISBN 0-934750-39-4); skillsbk. 3.25 (ISBN 0-934750-40-8). Jalamap.

Panorama of Tennesses Skills Book Teacher's Guide. David A. Bice. (Panorama Ser.). 59p. (gr. 7). 1984. pap. text ed. 3.50 (ISBN 0-934750-41-6). Jalamap.

Panorama of the Bible. Earl P. McQuay. LC 87-72833. (Lay Action Ministry Program Ser.). 112p. (Orig.). 1988. pap. 4.95 (ISBN 0-89191-511-7, 67355). Cook.

Panorama of the Hudson: Two Hundred Photos Showing Both Sides of the River from New York to Albany. W. G. Shear. 1977. lib. bdg. 200.00 (ISBN 0-8490-2405-6). Gordon Pr.

Panorama of the Soviet Union. N. Mikhailov. 264p. 1983. 32.00x (ISBN 0-317-42792-X, Pub by Collets (UK)). State Mutual Bk.

Panorama of West Virginia. David A. Bice. LC 79-89608. 319p. (gr. 8). 1979. text ed. 12.95 (ISBN 0-934750-00-9); tchr's guide 4.00 (ISBN 0-934750-01-7); wkbk. 3.50 (ISBN 0-934750-03-3). Jalamap.

Panorama of West Virginia. David A. Bice. (Illus.). 319p. 1981. 15.95 (ISBN 0-934750-08-4); pap. 13.95 (ISBN 0-934750-15-7). Jalamap.

Panorama of West Virginia II. David A. Bice. Ed. by Harry Lynch & Alfedlene Armstrong. (Panorama Ser.). (Illus.). 311p. (gr. 7-8). 1985. text ed. 9.79 (ISBN 0-934750-66-1). Jalamap.

Panoramas for the People. Paul D. Schweizer & Barbara C. Polowy. LC 83-23670. (Illus.). 80p. pap. 5.00 (ISBN 0-915895-00-5). Munson Williams.

Panoramas of Promise: Pacific Northwest Cities & Towns on Nineteenth-Century Lithographs. John W. Reps. (Illus.). 93p. 1985. 24.95 (ISBN 0-87422-016-5); pap. 14.95 (ISBN 0-87422-017-3). Wash St U Pr.

Panoramic Dental Radiography. 2nd ed. L. R. Manson-Hing. (Illus.). 224p. 1980. 45.50x (ISBN 0-398-03976-3). C C Thomas.

Panoramic Express. Wolfgang Kunnes. (Illus.). 64p. 1988. pap. 14.50 (ISBN 3-921679-52-4, Pub. by Vlg Schweers & Wall BRD). Seven Hills Bks.

Panoramic History of Agriculture in Puerto Rico. Juana G. Garcia. (Puerto Rico Ser.). 1979. lib. bdg. 59.95 (ISBN 0-8490-2982-1). Gordon Pr.

Panoramic Hysteroscopy. Bernard Parent. 125p. 1987. 55.00 (ISBN 0-683-06751-6). Williams & Wilkins.

Panoramic Maps of Cities in the United States & Canada: A Checklist of Maps in the Collections of the Library of Congress, Geography & Map Division. 2nd, rev. ed. Ed. by John R. Hebert & Patrick E. Dempsey. LC 82-600316. (Illus.). vi, 183p. 1985. pap. 6.00 (ISBN 0-317-59989-5). Lib Congress.

Panoramic Maps of Cities in the United States & Canada: A Checklist of Maps in the Collections of the Library of Congress, Geography & Map Division. Ed. by John R. Herbert. (Illus.). 186p. 1984. pap. 16.00 (S/N 030-004-00022-1). USGPO.

Panoramic Photography of Eugene O. Goldbeck. Clyde W. Burleson & E. Jessica Hickman. (Illus.). 120p. 1986. 75.00 (ISBN 0-292-72725-9). U of Tex Pr.

Panoramic Radiology. 2nd ed. Ed. by Olaf E. Langland et al. (Illus.). 430p. 1988. price not set (ISBN 0-8121-1168-0). Lea & Febiger.

Panoramique du Cinema. L. Moussinac. 1976. lib. bdg. 99.95 (ISBN 0-8490-2406-4). Gordon Pr.

Pan's Eyes. Joel Oppenheimer. LC 74-77760. (Haystack Bks.). 64p. 1974. pap. 3.50 (ISBN 0-685-46899-2). Mulch Pr.

Pan's Garden: A Volume of Nature Stories. facsimile ed. Algernon Blackwood. LC 74-157772. (Short Story Index Reprint Ser.). (Illus.). Repr. of 1912 ed. 27.50 (ISBN 0-8369-3884-4). Ayer Co Pubs.

Panslavism. Alex Kostya. LC 81-68156. 149p. 1981. 10.00 (ISBN 0-87934-025-8). Danubian.

Panslavonic Folklore. Walter W. Strickland. LC 78-63227. (Folktale). 1980. Repr. of 1930 ed. 25.00 (ISBN 0-404-16166-9). AMS Pr.

Pantagruel. Francois Rabelais. 1964. pap. 4.50 (ISBN 0-685-11475-9, 1240). French & Eur.

Pantagruel. Francois Rabelais. (Illus.). 188p. 1974. 150.00 (ISBN 0-686-54700-4). French & Eur.

Pantagruel. Francois Rabelais. Ed. by V. L. Saulnier. 266p. 1965. 9.95 (ISBN 0-686-54701-2). French & Eur.

Pantagrueline Prognostication Pour l'An 1533: Avec les Almanachs pour les Ans 1533, 1535 et 1541. la Grande et Vraye Pronostication Nouvelle De 1544. Francois Rabelais. (Illus.). 180p. 1975. 15.00 (ISBN 0-686-54702-0). French & Eur.

Pantalette Doll. Patten Beard. LC 31-21184. (Illus.). 160p. (gr. 4 up). 1981. Repr. of 1931 ed. lib. bdg. 30.00 (ISBN 0-940070-12-X). Doll Works.

Pantaloni. Bettina. LC 57-9103. (Illus.). 32p. (gr. k-3). 1957. PLB 12.89 (ISBN 0-06-020506-7). HarpJ.

Pantarch: A Biography of Stephen Pearl Andrews. Madeleine B. Stern. (Illus.). 226p. 1968. 11.95 (ISBN 0-292-73210-4). U of Tex Pr.

Panteleimon Kulish: A Sketch of His Life & Times. George S. Luckyj. (East European Monographs: No. 127). 229p. 1983. 24.00x (ISBN 0-88033-016-3). East Eur Quarterly.

Pantera, Nineteen Seventy to Nineteen Seventy-Three. R. M. Clarke. (Brooklands Bks.). (Illus., Orig.). 1980. pap. 9.95 (ISBN 0-906589-75-4, Pub. by Brooklands Bks England). Motorbooks Intl.

Pantex Plant: Practices, Policy, & the Environmental Impact of the Final Assembly Point. Greg LeRoy. (Illus.). 35p. 1988. pap. text ed. 4.00 (ISBN 0-945210-00-0). Public Search.

Pantheism. Louise E. Cohen. LC 79-118531. 1971. Repr. of 1926 ed. 21.50x (ISBN 0-8046-1154-8, Pub. by Kennikat). Assoc Faculty Pr.

Pantheism & Christianity. John Hunt. LC 78-102573. 1970. Repr. of 1884 ed. 25.50 (ISBN 0-8046-0733-8, Pub. by Kennikat). Assoc Faculty Pr.

Pantheism & the Christian System. Arthur Schopenhauer. (Illus.). 119p. 1987. 117.50 (ISBN 0-89266-588-2). Am Classical Coll Pr.

Pantheism Is Heresy. Parker L. Johnstone. 208p. 1982. cancelled (ISBN 0-917802-05-5). Theoscience Found.

Pantheistic Monism of Ibn Al-Arabi. S. A. Husaini. 1970. 9.30x (ISBN 0-87902-164-0). Orientalia.

Pantheisticon. John Toland. Ed. by Rene Wellek. LC 75-11260. (British Philosophers & Theologians of the 17th & 18th Centuries: Vol. 59). 1977. Repr. of 1751 ed. lib. bdg. 51.00 (ISBN 0-8240-1810-9). Garland Pub.

Pantheon. Antoine Pomey. LC 75-27879. (Renaissance & the Gods Ser.: Vol. 34). (Illus.). 1976. Repr. of 1694 ed. lib. bdg. 88.00 (ISBN 0-8240-2083-9). Garland Pub.

Pantheon. Andrew Tooke. LC 75-27880. (Renaissance & the Gods Ser.: Vol. 35). (Illus.). 1976. Repr. of 1713 ed. lib. bdg. 88.00 (ISBN 0-8240-2084-7). Garland Pub.

Pantheon: An Apotheosis. Richard S. Hoehler. LC 77-84798. (Illus.). 1977. pap. 10.00 (ISBN 0-930590-01-5). R Hoehler Pub.

Pantheon: or, Ancient History of the Gods of Greece & Rome. William Godwin. Ed. by Burton Feldman & Robert D. Richardson. LC 78-60886. (Myth & Romanticism Ser.). 1984. lib. bdg. 80.00 (ISBN 0-8240-3560-7). Garland Pub.

Panther & the Lash. Langston Hughes. 1967. pap. 9.95 (ISBN 0-394-40419-X). Knopf.

Panther Book of Scottish Short Stories. Ed. by James Cambell. 240p. 1984. pap. 5.95 (ISBN 0-586-06165-7, Granada England). Academy Chi Pubs.

Panther in Action. (Armor in Action Ser.). (Illus.). 50p. 1984. pap. 5.95 (ISBN 0-89747-044-3, 2011). Squad Sig Pubns.

Panther's Feast. Robert Asprey. 318p. 1986. pap. 9.95 (ISBN 0-88184-239-7). Carroll & Graf.

Panthers in the Skins of Men. Charles Nelson. (Meadoland Ser.). 1989. pap. price not set. Lyle Stuart.

Panthers to Arrowheads: The 36th (Texas-Oklahoma) Division in World War I. 1985 ed. Lonnie J. White. (Illus.). 18.00 (ISBN 0-935978-03-8). Presidial.

Pantographia: Containing Accurate Copies of All the Known Alphabets in the World, Together with an English Explanation of the Peculiar Force or Power of Each Letter. Edmund Fry. LC 79-104956. 320p. 1983. lib. bdg. 49.95x (ISBN 0-89370-778-3). Borgo Pr.

Pantomimes for Stage & Study. T. Earl Pardoe. LC 73-173118. Repr. of 1931 ed. 22.00 (ISBN 0-405-08833-7, Pub. by Blom). Ayer Co Pubs.

Pantry Gourmet. Jane A. Doerfer. Ed. by Carol Hupping. (Illus.). 304p. 1984. 15.95 (ISBN 0-87857-506-5). Rodale Pr Inc.

Pantry Shelf Sampler Cookbook. Grace Addition. Ed. by Susan Jack. 240p. 1983. 12.95 (ISBN 0-930096-44-4). G Gannett.

Pants for Any Body. rev. & expanded ed. Pati Palmer & Susan Pletsch. LC 82-61290. 128p. (Orig.). 1982. pap. 6.95 (ISBN 0-935278-08-7). Palmer-Pletsch.

Pantun Melayu. Ed. by Richard J. Wilkinson & Richard O. Winstedt. LC 77-87058. Repr. of 1957 ed. 18.50 (ISBN 0-404-16880-9). AMS Pr.

Panty Junkyard. Mort McDonald. (Illus.). 1975. sewn in wrappers 4.25 (ISBN 0-685-79061-4). Twowindows Pr.

Pantyhose Craft Book: Making Things from Run Pantyhose & Nylons. Jean R. Laury & Joyce Aiken. LC 76-53871. (Illus.). 1977. 12.95 (ISBN 0-8008-6235-X); pap. 5.95 (ISBN 0-8008-6234-1). Taplinger.

Panychis: The Office of Christian Burial. Monks of New Skete Staff. Tr. by Laurence Mancuso from Gr. & Slavonic Church. (Liturgical Music Series II: Divine Services: Vol. I). 40p. 1987. pap. text ed. 15.00x (ISBN 0-935129-08-1). Monks of New Skete.

Panzer Armee Afrika: Tripoli to Tunis. Peter Gudgin. (Tanks Illustrated Ser.: No. 28). (Illus.). 64p. (Orig.). 1988. pap. 9.95 (ISBN 0-85368-853-2, Pub. by Arms & Armour). Sterling.

Panzer Army Africa. James Lucas. 288p. 1986. pap. 3.50 (ISBN 0-515-08513-8). Jove Pubns.

Panzer Baron: The Military Exploits of General Hasso Von Manteuffel. Donald G. Brownlow. LC 75-10245. (Illus.). 176p. 1975. 12.95 (ISBN 0-8158-0325-7); French Ed. 12.95. Chris Mass.

Panzer Battles. F. W. Von Mellenthin. 1976. pap. 4.95 (ISBN 0-345-32158-8). Ballantine.

Panzer Battles: A Study of the Employment of Armor in the Second World War. F. W. Von Mellenthin. Ed. by L. C. Turner. Tr. by H. Betzler from Ger. LC 56-5997. (Illus.). 404p. 1982. pap. 14.95 (ISBN 0-8061-1802-4). U of Okla Pr.

Panzer Colors I. Bruce Culver & Bill Murphy. (Illus.). 96p. 1984. pap. 8.95 (ISBN 0-89747-057-5, 6251). Squad Sig Pubns.

Panzer Colors II: Markings of the German Army Panzer Forces 1939-45. (Illus.). 96p. 1984. pap. 8.95 (ISBN 0-89747-069-9, 6252). Squad Sig Pubns.

Panzer Grenadiers. Heinrich Muller. 288p. (Orig.). 1980. pap. 2.50 (ISBN 0-89083-697-3). Zebra.

Panzer Leader. abr. ed. Heinz Guderian. 1976. 2.50 (ISBN 0-345-29046-1). Ballantine.

Panzer Leader. Heinz Guderian. LC 79-19897. Repr. of 1952 ed. 25.00 (ISBN 0-89201-076-2). Zenger Pub.

Panzer Leader. Heinz Guderian. (War & Warriors Ser.). (Illus.). 470p. 1988. 17.95. Noontide.

Panzergrenadiers in Action. (Weapons in Action Ser.). (Illus.). 1984. pap. 5.95 (ISBN 0-89747-096-6, 3005). Squad Sig Pubns.

Panzers in the Desert. Bruce Quarrie. (World War Two Photo Album Ser.). (Illus.). 96p. (Orig.). 1988. pap. 7.99 (ISBN 1-85260-153-1, Pub. by PSL P Stephens England). Sterling.

Paola: Journey of an Immigrant. Emma Mariane. 1987. 10.95 (ISBN 0-533-07211-5). Vantage.

Paolo Beni: A Biographical & Critical Study. P. B. Diffley. (Oxford Modern Languages & Literature Monographs Ser.). 206p. 1988. 67.00 (ISBN 0-19-815855-6). Oxford U Pr.

Paolo da Venezia. Michelangelo Muraro. LC 77-84667. (Illus.). 1970. 75.00x (ISBN 0-271-00098-8). Pa St U Pr.

Paolo Rolli & the Italian Circle in London, 1715-1744. George E. Dorris. (Studies in Italian Literature: No. 2). (Orig.). 1967. pap. text ed. 26.00x (ISBN 90-2790-329-8). Mouton.

Paolo Sarpi: Between Renaissance & Enlightenment. David Wootton. LC 82-17691. 200p. 1983. 45.50 (ISBN 0-521-23146-9). Cambridge U Pr.

Paolo Tenorista in a New Fragment of the Italian Ars Nova. facsimile ed. Nino Pirrotta. (Illus.). 83p. 1961. 16.50 (ISBN 0-934082-07-3, M61-2053, Pub. by E E Goltlieb CA). Theodore Front.

Paolo Uccello's Hunt in the Forest. Sallyann Kleibel et al. 28p. 1981. 4.50x (ISBN 0-900090-72-3, Pub. by Ashmolean Museum). State Mutual Bk.

Paolo Uccello's Hunt in the Forest. Ed. by Christopher Lloyd. (Illus.). 28p. (Orig.). 1981. pap. 7.50 (ISBN 0-317-58639-4, Pub. by Ashmolean Mus). Longwood Pub Group.

Pap Smear: Life of George N. Papanicolaou. D. Erskine Carmichael. (Illus.). 140p. 1973. photocopy ed. 12.50x (ISBN 0-398-02716-1). C C Thomas.

Papa. Sal St. John Buttaci. (Illus.). 250p. (Orig.). 1988. pap. text ed. 19.95 (ISBN 0-917398-17-3). New Worlds.

Papa: A Personal Memoir. Gregory H. Hemingway. (Illus.). 146p. 1988. pap. 8.95 (ISBN 1-55778-068-4). Paragon Hse.

Papa & Fidel. Karl Alexander. 320p. 1989. 17.95. Tor Bks.

Papa & Mama Biederbeck. Gerda B. Mantinband. LC 82-15619. (Illus.). 48p. (gr. 2-5). 1983. PLB 7.95 (ISBN 0-395-33228-1). HM.

Papa Babe's Stamp Collection. Gladys T. Turner. (Illus.). 39p. (gr. 1-8). 1983. 5.50 (ISBN 0-682-49944-7). Exposition-Phoenix.

Papa, Charly hat Gesagt. Wolf-Dietrich Zielinski. 112p. (Ger.). 1984. Lehr-und Arbeitsbuch 10.95 (ISBN 3-468-49465-3). Langenscheidt.

Papa Coke: Sixty-Five Years Selling Coca-Cola. Sanders Rowland & Bob Terrell. LC 86-9526. (Illus.). 236p. 1986. 10.95 (ISBN 0-914875-14-0). Bright Mtn Bks.

Paper Doll Portrait: Antique German Bisque Dolls. Peggy Jo Rosamond. 1985. pap. 3.95 (ISBN 0-87588-246-3, 2916). Hobby Hse.
Paper Dolls. Jim Shepard. 1988. pap. 3.95 (ISBN 0-440-20076-8). Dell.
Paper Door: Other Stories. Shiga Naoya. Tr. by Lane Dunlap from Japanese. LC 86-60992. 1987. 14.95 (ISBN 0-86547-260-2). N Point Pr.
Paper Dreams. Lorraine Bodger. LC 76-21221. (Illus.). 1977. 11.95x (ISBN 0-87663-287-8); pap. 6.95 (ISBN 0-87663-964-3). Universe.
Paper Economy. David T. Bazelon. LC 78-11587. 1979. Repr. of 1963 ed. lib. bdg. 35.00x (ISBN 0-313-21001-2, BATP). Greenwood.
Paper Engineering for Pop-Up Books & Cards. Mark Hiner. (Illus.). 72p. (Orig.). 1986. pap. 9.95 (ISBN 0-906212-49-9, Pub. by Tarquin). Parkwest Pubns.
Paper Finishing & Converting Conference: 1984, Proceedings. Technical Association of the Pulp & Paper Industry. pap. 30.30 (2024783). Bks Demand UMI.
Paper Flight: Forty-Eight Models Ready for Take-Off. Jack Botermans. Tr. by Deborah Ogle from Dutch. 1984. pap. 9.95 (ISBN 0-03-070506-1, Owl Bks). H Holt & Co.
Paper Flower Sculpture. Jeanette Westcott. (Illus.). 128p. 1986. 24.95 (ISBN 0-7137-1673-8, Pub. by Blandford Pr England). Sterling.
Paper Flowers: A Play in Six Scenes. Egon Wolff. Tr. by Margaret S. Peden. LC 76-131968. (Breakthrough Bks). 80p. 1971. 6.50x (ISBN 0-8262-0098-2); pap. 5.95 (ISBN 0-8262-0187-3). U of Mo Pr.
Paper Folding for Beginners. William D. Murray & Francis J. Rigney. (Illus.). (gr. 1 up). pap. 2.50 (ISBN 0-486-20713-7). Dover.
Paper Folding Magic. Richard Chen. 32p. 1987. 7.50 (ISBN 0-8062-2896-2). Carlton.
Paper Hero. Leon Hale. 252p. 1986. 14.95 (ISBN 0-940672-36-7). Shearer Pub.
Paper Houses. Uffe Harder. Tr. by Uffe Harder & Alexander Taylor. LC 81-15102. 30p. 1982. pap. 4.00 (ISBN 0-915306-23-9). Curbstone.
Paper Industry in Scotland. A. G. Thomson. 1974. 15.00x (ISBN 0-7073-0153-X, Pub. by Scot Acad Pr). Longwood Pub Group.
Paper Innovations: Handmade Paper & Handmade Objects of Cut, Folded & Molded Paper. LC 85-63043. (Illus.). 128p. 1986. pap. 24.95 (ISBN 0-914155-04-0). Mingei Intl Mus.
Paper Innovations: Objects of Cut, Folded or Molded Paper. Ed. by Martha Longenecker. LC 85-63043. (Illus.). 66p. 1986. pap. 24.95 (ISBN 0-295-96387-5, Pub. by Mingei Intl Museum of World Folk Art). U of Wash Pr.
Paper John. David Small. LC 86-45261. (Illus.). 32p. (ps-3). 1987. pap. 12.95 (ISBN 0-374-35738-2). FS&G.
Paper Knife. Marc Talbert. LC 88-3853. 176p. (gr. 4 up). 1988. 13.95 (ISBN 0-8037-0571-9, 01354-410). Dial Bks Young.
Paper Lion. George Plimpton. (Autographed Sports Classic Ser.). 1981. Repr. of 1965 ed. 19.95 (ISBN 0-941372-07-3). Holtzman Pr.
Paper Lion. George Plimpton. LC 88-45122. (Illus.). 384p. 1988. pap. 8.95 (ISBN 0-06-091540-4, PL 1540, PL). Har-Row.
Paper Loading Materials. Technical Association of the Pulp & Paper Industry & W. R. Willets. LC 58-1147. (TAPPI Monographs: No. 19). pap. 35.00 (ISBN 0-317-28728-1, 2020301). Bks Demand UMI.
Paper Machine Drives Seminar, 1986: Notes of Notes of TAPPI, Crown Plaza - Holiday Inn, Atlanta, GA., March 5-7, 1986. Technical Association of the Pulp & Paper Industry. pap. 34.30 (ISBN 0-317-55384-4, 2029177). Bks Demand UMI.
Paper Machine Drives: 1984 Seminar Notes. Technical Association of the Pulp & Paper Industry. pap. 28.50 (ISBN 0-317-20564-1, 2022799). Bks Demand UMI.
Paper Machine Series: The Working Piston Engine. Joel Moskowitz. 1986. pap. 9.95 (ISBN 0-671-61438-X, Fireside). S&S.
Paper Machine Series: Vol 2: The Working Piston Engine. Joel Moskowitz. 96p. pap. 7.95 (ISBN 0-671-55440-9); pap. 79.50 10 copy counter display (ISBN 0-671-93855-X). S&S.
Paper Machine Wet Press Manual. John F. Atkins. LC 79-6366. (TAPPI PRESS Books). (Illus.). 120p. 1979. 14.95 (ISBN 0-89852-042-8, 01-02 B042). TAPPI.
Paper Magic: Pop-Up Paper Craft. Masahiro Chatani. (Illus.). 92p. 1988. pap. 9.95 (ISBN 0-87040-757-0). Japan Pubns USA.
Paper-Making & Felts. 206p. 1934. 245.00x (Pub. by Han-Shan Tang Ltd). State Mutual Bk.
Paper Making in Pioneer America. Dard Hunter. LC 78-74388. (Nineteenth Century Book Arts & Printing History Ser.: Vol. 3). 1980. lib. bdg. 26.00 (ISBN 0-8240-3877-0). Garland Pub.
Paper Man. Milo Manara. Tr. by Jeff Lisle from Fr. & Span. (Illus.). 60p. (Orig.). 1986. pap. 9.95 (ISBN 0-87416-022-7). Catalan Communs.
Paper Mansions. James R. Padgett. LC 86-13628. (Illus.). 1986. 14.95 (ISBN 0-914875-12-4). Bright Mtn Bks.
Paper Mask. John Collee. 224p. 1989. 16.95 (ISBN 1-55710-026-8, Arbor Hse). Morrow.
Paper Masks & Puppets for Stories, Songs & Plays. Ron L. Feller & Marsha Y. Feller. LC 85-72952. (Illus.). 104p. (Orig.). 1986. pap. 12.95 (ISBN 0-9615873-0-X). Arts Factory.
Paper Medicine Man: John Gregory Bourke & His American West. Joseph C. Porter. LC 85-40943. (Illus.). 352p. 1986. 29.95 (ISBN 0-8061-1984-5). U of Okla Pr.
Paper Men. William Golding. 191p. 1984. 15.95 (ISBN 0-374-22980-5). FS&G.
Paper Men. William Golding. LC 84-27984. 192p. 1985. pap. 5.95 (ISBN 0-15-670800-0, Harv). HarBraceJ.
Paper Menagerie. Jerome C. Brown. (Illus.). (gr. 3-12). 1984. pap. 4.95 (ISBN 0-8224-5191-3). D S Lake Pubs.
Paper Midwife. Ingrid Johnson & Paul Johnson. 90p. 1980. pap. 6.95 (ISBN 0-908562-11-X, Pub. by Square One Pr). Intl Spec Bk.
Paper Mill Sludge Characteristics, Utilization & Disposal. (Bibliographic Ser.: No. 266). 59p. 1975. 10.00 (ISBN 0-317-34402-1). Inst Paper Chem.
Paper Money. Ken Follett. 256p. 1987. pap. 3.95 (ISBN 0-451-15002-3, Sig). NAL.
Paper Money. 2nd ed. Ken Follett. Ed. by Pat Golbitz. LC 87-7867. 216p. 1987. Repr. of 1977 ed. 15.95 (ISBN 0-688-05840-X). Morrow.
Paper Money. Adam Smith, pseud. 288p. 1981. 13.95 (ISBN 0-671-44825-0). Summit Bks.
Paper Money Bibliography. M. McKerchar. 1979. 15.00 (ISBN 0-686-51600-1, Pub. by Spink & Son England). S J Durst.
Paper Money in Maryland. Kathryn L. Behrens. LC 78-64109. (Johns Hopkins University: Studies in the Social Sciences, Forty-First: 1). Repr. of 1923 ed. 24.50 (ISBN 0-404-61224-5). AMS Pr.
Paper Money Inflation in France see Fiat Money Inflation in France.
Paper Money of Brazil. 2nd ed. Dale A. Seppa. (Illus.). 104p. 1975. pap. 5.00 (ISBN 0-916710-21-1). Obol Intl.
Paper Money of South Vietnam. Nguyen Van Phung. (Illus.). 112p. 1987. 12.95 (ISBN 0-89962-599-1). Todd & Honeywell.
Paper Money of the E.A. Wright Bank Note Company. C. Frederick Schwan. (Illus.). 36p. 1978. pap. 3.95 (ISBN 0-931960-02-9). BNR Pr.
Paper Moon. Joe D. Brown. 240p. (YA) (RL 9). 1972. pap. 2.50 (ISBN 0-451-09940-0, Sig). NAL.
Paper Movie Machines. Bud Wentz. 1975. pap. 3.95 (ISBN 0-8431-1710-9, 57-4). Troubador Pr.
Paper Napkin Poems. Leah Paransky. 62p. (Orig.). 1980. pap. 3.95 (ISBN 0-9603372-07-8). Lintel.
Paper Nautilus. Nicholas Jose. 144p. 1988. pap. 5.95 (ISBN 0-14-010019-9). Penguin.
Paper Negative. William Mortensen. (Illus.). 50p. 1988. Repr. of 1954 ed. 15.00 (ISBN 0-9619959-0-4). J Curtis.
Paper Now: Bent, Molded & Manipulated. Jane Glaubinger. 1987. pap. 17.50x (ISBN 0-910386-88-9, Pub. by Cleveland Mus Art). Ind U Pr.
Paper of the Third International Conference on Liquefied Natural Gas: Washington. 880p. 1972. form Univ. Microfilm avail. Inst Gas Tech.
Paper, Paint, & Stuff: A Calendar of Creative Art Ideas. Karen Kurtz et al. 1984. pap. 11.95 (ISBN 0-673-15989-2). Scott F.
Paper Pandas & Jumping Frogs. Florence Temko. LC 86-70960. (Illus.). 135p. (gr. 3-6). 1986. pap. 11.95 (ISBN 0-8351-1770-7). China Bks.
Paper Pandas & Jumping Frogs, with Origami Paper. Date not set. 14.95 (ISBN 0-8351-1696-4). China Bks.
Paper, Paper Everywhere. Gail Gibbons. LC 82-3109. (Illus.). 32p. (ps-3). 1983. 10.95 (ISBN 0-15-259488-4, HJ). HarBraceJ.
Paper Party. Don Freeman. (Picture Puffin Ser.). (Illus.). (gr. 1 up). 1977. pap. 3.95 (ISBN 0-14-050212-2, Puffin). Penguin.
Paper Phoenix. Mickey Friedman. 1987. pap. 2.95 (ISBN 0-345-33676-3). Ballantine.
Paper Phoenix: A Mystery of San Francisco. Mickey Friedman. 1986. 15.95 (ISBN 0-525-24407-7). Dutton.
Paper Physics Fundamentals & Papermaking Practices Seminar, 1987: Notes of TAPPI, Paper Valley Hotel, Appleton, WI, February 25-26. Technical Association of the Pulp & Paper Industry Staff. (Illus.). 184p. pap. 47.90 (2029986). Bks Demand UMI.
Paper Pile Quarterly Vol. V: April 1984-January 1985: Old Paper Collectibles, An Evolving Value Guide. Ed. by Ada Fitzsimmons. (Illus.). 96p. 1985. pap. 7.50 (ISBN 0-915195-04-6). Paper Pile.
Paper Pile Quarterly, Volume VI: April 1985-January 1986: Old Paper Collectibles, an Evolving Value Guide. Ada Fitzsimmons. (Illus.). 130p. (Orig.). 1986. pap. 8.50 (ISBN 0-915195-06-2). Paper Pile.
Paper Pleasures: The Creative Guide to Papercraft. Faith Shannon. LC 87-21047. (Illus.). 168p. 1987. 18.95 (ISBN 1-55584-105-8). Weidenfeld.
Paper Pools. David Hockney. Ed. by Nikos Stangos. (Illus.). 100p. 1980. pap. 14.95 (ISBN 0-8109-2229-0). Abrams.
Paper Pound of Seventeen Ninety-Seven to Eighteen Twelve. 2nd ed. Ed. by Edwin Cannan. 72p. 1970. Repr. of 1925 ed. 28.50x (ISBN 0-7146-1210-3, F Cass Co). Biblio Dist.
Paper Pound of Seventeen Ninety-Seven to Eighteen Twelve. 2nd ed. Ed. by Edwin Cannan. LC 67-24748. 1969. Repr. of 1925 ed. 25.00x (ISBN 0-678-00536-2). Kelley.
Paper Preservation: Nature, Extent & Recommendations. Lynn Westbrook. (Occasional Papers: No. 171). 1985. pap. 3.00 (ISBN 0-317-59025-1). U of Ill Lib Info Sci.
Paper Princess. Marion Chesney. 176p. 1987. pap. 2.95 (ISBN 0-449-21341-2). Fawcett.
Paper Projects for Creative Kids of All Ages. Jim Bottomley. 160p. (gr. 5 up). 1983. pap. 10.95 (ISBN 0-316-10349-7). Little.
Paper Prophets: A Social Critique of Accounting. Tony Tinker. LC 84-18305. 1985. 35.00 (ISBN 0-275-91758-4, C1758). Praeger.
Paper Raincoat. Sonya Dorman. (Illus.). 60p. 1979. pap. 3.50 (ISBN 0-913006-09-2). Puckerbrush.
Paper Rebellion: Development & Upheaval in Pulp & Paper Unionism. Harry E. Graham. LC 79-131059. 170p. 1970. cancelled (ISBN 0-87745-019-6). U of Iowa Pr.
Paper Recycling: A Correspondence Course. Recycling Research Division Staff. 16p. 1984. pap. text ed. 11.95 (ISBN 0-318-01188-3, Pub. by Recycling Consort). Prosperity & Profits.
Paper Recycling: Info Mapping Index. Data Notes Publishing Staff. LC 83-90731. 30p. 1983. pap. text ed. 3.95 (ISBN 0-911569-41-3, Pub. by Data Notes). Prosperity & Profits.
Paper Requirements for Printing Performance Seminar, 1984 Notes. Technical Association of the Pulp & Paper Industry. pap. 20.00 (ISBN 0-317-27229-2, 2024771). Bks Demand UMI.
Paper Rockets. Yoong Bae. (Illus.). 32p. 1980. pap. 3.95 (ISBN 0-8431-1729-X). Troubador Pr.
Paper Sculpture. rev. & enl. ed. Mary G. Johnston. LC 64-24721. (Illus.). (gr. 4-12). 1965. 8.95 (ISBN 0-87192-019-0). Davis Mass.
Paper Sculpture, No. 2. T. Taniuchi. (Illus.). 84p. 1986. pap. 14.50 (ISBN 0-318-23209-X, Pub. by Genko Sha). Bks Nippan.
Paper Shtetl: A Complete Model of an East European Jewish Town. David Grupper & David G. Klein. LC 83-42714. (Illus., Orig.). (gr. 6-12). 1984. pap. 11.95 (ISBN 0-8052-0749-X). Schocken.
Paper Snake. Ray Johnson. LC 65-15545. (Illus.). 1965. 20.00 (ISBN 0-89366-061-2). Ultramarine Pub.
Paper Song. Paul Portuges. (Illus.). 160p. 1985. pap. 9.95 (ISBN 0-915520-80-X). Ross-Erikson.
Paper Stones: A History of Electoral Socialism. Adam Przenorski & John Sprague. vi, 224p. 1988. pap. 11.95 (ISBN 0-226-68498-9). U of Chicago Pr.
Paper Stones: A History of Electoral Socialism. Adam Przeworski & John Sprague. LC 86-6984. (Illus.). vi, 224p. 1986. lib. bdg. 24.95x (ISBN 0-226-68497-0). U of Chicago Pr.
Paper Stories. Jean Stangl. LC 84-60238. (ps-3). 1984. pap. 8.95 (ISBN 0-8224-5402-5). D S Lake Pubs.
Paper Structures & Properties. Bristow & Kolseth. 360p. 1986. 110.00 (ISBN 0-8247-7560-0). Dekker.
Paper Sword of Bill Rentschler. Ed. by Bill Rentschler. LC 86-26827. 250p. 1986. 17.95 (ISBN 0-914091-98-0). Chicago Review.
Paper Talk: Charlie Russell's American West. Charles Russell. Ed. by Brian W. Dippie. LC 79-2212. (Illus.). 1979. 17.95 (ISBN 0-394-50834-3). Knopf.
Paper Tearing Bible Talks, No. 4. Arnold C. Westphal. 1970. pap. 3.95 (ISBN 0-915398-03-6). Visual Evangels.
Paper Tearing Evangels, No. 8. Arnold C. Westphal. 1975. pap. 3.95 (ISBN 0-915398-07-9). Visual Evangels.
Paper Tearing Gospel Illustrations, No. 3. Arnold C. Westphal. 1969. pap. 3.95 (ISBN 0-915398-02-8). Visual Evangels.
Paper Tearing Trick Talks, No. 1. Arnold C. Westphal. 1967. pap. 3.95 (ISBN 0-915398-00-1). Visual Evangels.
Paper Testing: Strength Properties, Vol. 1. 2nd ed. (Bibliographic Ser.: No. 139-2). 182p. 1949. 21.00 (ISBN 0-317-34403-X); Supplement 1, 1954. 8.00 (ISBN 0-317-34404-8); Supplement 2, 1960. 8.00 (ISBN 0-317-34405-6); Supplement 3, 1966. 8.00 (ISBN 0-317-34406-4); Supplement 4, 1972. 8.00 (ISBN 0-317-34407-2). Inst Paper Chem.
Paper: The Life & Death of the New York Herald Tribune. Richard Kluger. LC 86-45276. 816p. 1986. 24.95 (ISBN 0-394-50877-7). Knopf.
Paper: The Life & Death of the New York Herald Tribune. Richard Kluger. LC 87-40099. (Illus.). 816p. 1988. pap. 12.95 (ISBN 0-394-75565-0, Vin). Random.
Paper Through the Ages. Shaaron Cosner. LC 84-7760. (On My Own Bks.). (Illus.). 48p. (gr. 1-4). 1984. PLB 8.95 (ISBN 0-87614-270-6). Carolrhoda Bks.
Paper Thunderbolt. Michael Innes. 352p. 1987. pap. 3.95 (ISBN 0-14-010089-X). Penguin.
Paper Tiger: Resume Strategies That Get Your Foot in the Door. David Hizer & Arthur Rosenberg. 144p. (Orig.). 1985. pap. 5.95 (ISBN 0-937860-47-6). Adams Inc MA.
Paper Tigers: The Ideal Fictions of Jorge Luis Borges. John Sturrock. 1978. 21.95x (ISBN 0-19-815746-0). Oxford U Pr.
Paper Toy Making. Margaret W. Campbell. LC 75-2570. 96p. 1975. pap. 3.50 (ISBN 0-486-21662-4). Dover.
Paper Toys of the World. Blair Whitton. (Illus.). 1986. 24.95 (ISBN 0-87588-289-7, 3447). Hobby Hse.
Paper Trail: The Real Estate Professional's Guide to Documented Liability Protection & Marketing Success. Oliver E. Frascona. LC 87-8904. (Real Law Bks.). 1987. pap. 35.00 (ISBN 0-941937-00-3). Denver Carrington.
Paper Tricks. Florence Temko. (Illus.). 48p. (gr. 3 up). 1988. 1.95 (ISBN 0-590-41129-2). Scholastic Inc.
Paper Trip: How to Change Your Identity, 2 Vols. B. Reid. (Criminology Ser.). 1986. lib. bdg. 199.95 (ISBN 0-8490-3696-8). Gordon Pr.
Paper Tripping Overseas: New I. D. in England, Australia & New Zealand. Tony Newborn. (Illus.). 120p. (Orig.). 1985. pap. 17.95 (ISBN 0-87364-338-0). Paladin Pr.
Paper UFO's. Yoong Bae. (Illus.). 32p. (gr. 1-12). 1981. pap. 3.95 (ISBN 0-89844-080-7). Troubador Pr.
Paper Walls: America & the Refugee Crisis, 1938 to 1941. David S. Wyman. 1985. pap. 8.95 (ISBN 0-394-73659-1). Pantheon.
Paper, Wasps & Packages: The Romantic Story of Paper & Its Influence on the Course of History. Alexander Weaver. 1977. lib. bdg. 59.95 (ISBN 0-8490-2407-2). Gordon Pr.
Paper Zoo: A Collection of Animal Poems by Modern American Poets. Selected by Renee K. Weiss. LC 86-21733. (Illus.). 40p. (ps-3). 1987. 11.95 (ISBN 0-02-792750-4). Macmillan.
Paperback Books. rev. ed. Mary Steelsmith. 1985. pap. text ed. 5.00 (ISBN 0-88734-306-6). Players Pr.
Paperback Books for Young People: An Annotated Guide to Publishers & Distributors. 2nd ed. John T. Gillespie. pap. 10.00 tchr's. ed. (ISBN 0-317-06456-8). Dell.
Paperback Books for Young People: An Annotated Guide to Publishers & Distributors. 2nd ed. John T. Gillespie. LC 77-21627. pap. 57.80 (ISBN 0-317-26563-6, 2023950). Bks Demand UMI.
Paperback Books on Africa. 3rd ed. Ed. by Patricia Jones. 116p. 1977. pap. 8.00 (ISBN 0-918456-23-1). African Studies Assn.
Paperback Price Guide. 2nd ed. Kevin B. Hancer. (Illus.). 440p. 1982. pap. 9.95 (ISBN 0-517-54453-9). Overstreet.
Paperback Price Guide, No. 2. 2nd ed. Kevin B. Hancer & R. Reginald. LC 82-11790. 390p. 1982. lib. bdg. 22.95x (ISBN 0-89370-745-7); pap. 9.95x (ISBN 0-89370-899-2). Borgo Pr.
Paperback Talk. Ray Walters. (Illus.). 350p. 1985. 19.95 (ISBN 0-89733-108-7); pap. 9.95 (ISBN 0-89733-109-5). Academy Chi Pubs.
Paperbag. Richard Russell. 1979. pap. 1.75 (ISBN 0-505-51427-3, Pub. by Tower Bks). Leisure NY.
Paperboard: Boxboard, Vol. 2. Jack Weiner & Vera Pollock. LC 67-22806. (Bibliographic Ser.: No. 236, Suppl. 1). 1973. pap. 10.00 (ISBN 0-87010-022-X). Inst Paper Chem.
Paperboard: Corrugated Board, Vol.1. Jack Weiner & Vera Pollock. LC 67-22806. (Bibliographic Ser.: No. 235, Suppl 1). 1973. pap. 27.00 (ISBN 0-87010-021-1). Inst Paper Chem.
Paperbound Book in America: The History of Paperbacks & Their European Background. Frank L. Schick. LC 58-10097. pap. 70.00 (ISBN 0-317-10717-8, 2013974). Bks Demand UMI.
Paperbound Books in Print-Fall, 1988, 3 vols. Ed. by Bowker, R. R., Staff. 5700p. 1988. 139.95 (ISBN 0-8352-2456-2). Vol. 1. Vol. 2 (ISBN 0-8352-2458-9). Vol. 3 (ISBN 0-8352-2459-7). Bowker.
Paperbound Books in Print-Fall, 1989, 3 vols. Ed. by Bowker, R. R., Staff. 1989. price not set (ISBN 0-8352-2535-6). Bowker.
Paperbound Books in Print-Spring, 1989, 3 vols. Ed. by Bowker, R. R., Co. Staff. 1989. 139.95 (ISBN 0-8352-2530-5). Bowker.
Paperclip Conspiracy: The Hunt for Nazi Scientists. Tom Bower. 288p. 1988. 17.95 (ISBN 0-316-10399-3). Little.
Papercraft Projects with One Piece of Paper. Michael Grater. (Illus.). 112p. 1987. pap. 4.50 (ISBN 0-486-25504-2). Dover.
Papercrafts. Beryle Bell et al. 1984. pap. 6.95 (ISBN 0-06-464084-1, BN4084, B&N Bks). Har-Row.
Papercrafts. Judith H. Corwin. Ed. by IRosoff. (Illus.). 72p. (gr. 2-4). 1988. 11.90 (ISBN 0-531-10465-6). Watts.
Papercrafts for All Seasons. James C. Brown. (Illus.). (gr. 3-12). 1984. pap. 4.95 (ISBN 0-8224-5189-1). D S Lake Pubs.
Paperdolls. Susan B. Pfeffer. 160p. (Orig.). (gr. 7-12). 1984. pap. 2.25 (ISBN 0-440-96777-5, LFL). Dell.
Papermakers. Leonard E. Fisher. LC 65-13683. 48p. 1986. pap. 4.95 (ISBN 0-87923-608-6). Godine.
Papermakers Conference: 1984 Proceedings. Technical Association of the Pulp & Paper Industry. pap. 66.30 (ISBN 0-317-20572-2, 2022793). Bks Demand UMI.
Papermakers Conference, 1985: Proceedings of TAPPI, Marriott Hotel, Denver, CO, April 15-17. Technical Association of the Pulp & Paper Industry. pap. 87.30 (ISBN 0-317-26855-4, 2025288). Bks Demand UMI.

Papermakers Conference, 1986: Proceedings of TAPPI, Marriott Hotel, New Orleans, LA, April 14-16, 1986. Technical Association of the Pulp & Paper Industry. pap. 85.80 (ISBN 0-317-55389-5, 2029180). Bks Demand UMI.

Papermakers Conference, 1987: Proceedings of TAPPI, Hyatt Regency, Atlanta, GA, April 6-8. Technical Association of the Pulp & Paper Industry Staff. (Illus.). 352p. pap. 91.60 (2029978). Bks Demand UMI.

Papermaking. Jules Heller. (Illus.). 1978. 29.95 (ISBN 0-8230-3895-5). Watson-Guptill.

Papermaking. Dard Hunter. (Illus.). 1978. pap. 10.95 (ISBN 0-486-23619-6). Dover.

PaperMaking. Ralf Weidenmuller. (Illus.). 64p. 1984. 24.00 (ISBN 0-87930-157-0). Miller Freeman.

Papermaking Chemical Processing Aids Seminar, 1986: Notes of TAPPI, Marriott Hotel, New Orleans, LA, April 16-18, 1986. Tehnical Association of the Pulp & Paper Industry. pap. 20.00 (2029182). Bks Demand UMI.

Papermaking Fibers: A Photomicrographic Atlas. Ed. by Wilfred A. Cote. (Renewable Materials Institute Ser.). (Illus.). 200p. 1980. pap. text ed. 17.50x (ISBN 0-8156-2228-7). Syracuse U Pr.

Papermaking in America. Norman B. Wilkinson. (Industry in America Ser.). (Illus.). 1975. pap. 3.50 (ISBN 0-914650-09-2). Hagley Museum.

Papermaking in Basketry. Intro. by Lynn Stearns. LC 87-61002. (Illus.). 200p. (Orig.). 1988. pap. 19.95 (ISBN 0-942002-02-4). Press LaPlantz.

Papermaking in Britain 1488-1988: A Short History. R. L. Hills. LC 88-3322. 192p. 1988. text ed. 35.00 (ISBN 0-485-11346-5, Pub. by Athlone Pr). Humanities.

Papermaking Materials: Bast Fibers. Weiner Jack & Roth Lillian. Incl. Vol. 2. LC 50-1298. 1973. 10.00 (ISBN 0-87010-006-8); Vol. 2, Supplement 1. 243p. 1963. 13.00 (ISBN 0-317-37725-6); Vol. 2, Supplement 2. 51p. 1968. 8.00 (ISBN 0-317-37726-4); Vol. 3, Supplement 2. 81p. 1968. 8.00 (ISBN 0-317-37727-2). (Bibliographic Ser.: No. 176). Inst Paper Chem.

Paperplay Mini-Books. Incl. Vol. 1. Beauty of Irrelevant Music. Kenneth Gaburo. (Illus.). 22p. 1976. pap. 2.75 saddle-stiched (ISBN 0-939044-01-3); Vol. 2. C---IS. Kenneth Gaburo. 12p. 1976. pap. 2.75 saddle-stiched (ISBN 0-939044-02-1); Vol. 4. Extraction. Kenneth Gaburo. (Illus.). 12p. 1976. pap. 2.25 saddle-stiched (ISBN 0-939044-04-8); Vol. 7. Language, a Magical Enterprise, the Body. Barry Casselman. (Illus.). 16p. 1978. pap. 2.50 saddle-stiched (ISBN 0-939044-13-7); Vol. 8. Literal Violence. Michel Pierssens. Ed. by Lingua Press Staff. 16p. 1978. pap. 2.60 saddle-stitched (ISBN 0-939044-14-5); Vol. 3. Murmer. Kenneth Gaburo. 8p. 1976. pap. 2.25 saddle-stitched (ISBN 0-939044-03-X); Vol. 6. Music in Beckett's Play. Kenneth Gaburo. 12p. 1976. pap. 2.75 saddle-stitched (ISBN 0-939044-06-4); Musicology & Other Delights. Kenneth Gaburo. 8p. 1978. pap. 2.00 saddle-stitched (ISBN 0-939044-15-3); Vol. 9. Non-Scatological Set of Preliminary Remarks. Kenneth Gaburo. 12p. 1976. pap. 2.60 saddle-stitched (ISBN 0-939044-05-6). pap. 0.00. Lingua Pr.

Papers. Theodore Enslin. 1976. 16.00 (ISBN 0-685-79199-8). Elizabeth Pr.

Papers, 6 Vols. Mirabeau B. Lamar. Ed. by C. A. Gulick et al. LC 76-171643. Repr. of 1927 ed. Set. 280.00 (ISBN 0-404-03820-4). AMS Pr.

Papers about Goethe: Goethe & Wordsworth, Coleridge & His Contemporaries. Ed. by L. A. Willoughby. Barker Fairley. 1934. lib. bdg. 30.00 (ISBN 0-8414-9354-5). Folcroft.

Papers & Addresses. facs. ed. William P. Few. Ed. by Robert H. Woody. LC 68-20299. (Essay Index Reprint Ser). 1968. Repr. of 1951 ed. 20.00 (ISBN 0-8369-0439-7). Ayer Co Pubs.

Papers & Addresses of the Society of Colonial Wars in the State of Connecticut, Vol. 1. 1903. 3.00 (ISBN 0-940748-35-5). Conn Hist Soc.

Papers & Correspondence of William Stanley Jevons, 7 vols. William S. Jevons. LC 72-77230. 1972-81. Set. 195.00x (ISBN 0-678-07012-1); Vol. 1. 35.00x ea. (ISBN 0-678-07011-3). Vol. 2. Vol. 3 (ISBN 0-333-10253-3). Vol. 4 (ISBN 0-333-19977-4). Vol. 5 (ISBN 0-333-19978-2). Vol. 6 (ISBN 0-333-10258-4). Vol. 7 (ISBN 0-333-19979-0). Kelley.

Papers & Proceedings of Syntopican XII: Anthology. Ed. by James F. Casale et al. (Illus., Orig.). 1984. pap. 30.00 (ISBN 0-935220-11-9). Assn Info Sys.

Papers & Proceedings of the Committee on the Police Problem, City of New York. New York State Chamber of Commerce Staff. LC 79-154581. (Police in America Ser). 1971. Repr. of 1905 ed. 46.50 (ISBN 0-405-03364-8). Ayer Co Pubs.

Papers & Workshop Discussion Summaries Presented at the National Conference on the Role of the Lawyer in the 1980's. 150p. 1981. pap. 8.50 (ISBN 0-686-48074-0). Amer Bar Assn.

Papers Concerning Robertson's Colony in Texas. Compiled by Malcolm D. McLean. Incl. Vol. I, 1788-1822, The Texas Association. LC 73-78014. (Illus.). lxxi, 567p. 1980. Repr. of 1974 ed. lib. bdg. 30.00 (ISBN 0-932408-01-X); Vol. II, 1823 Through September, 1826, Leftwich's Grant. LC 75-21900. (Illus.). 687p. 1975. lib. bdg. 30.00 (ISBN 0-932408-02-8); Vol. III, October, 1826, Through April, 1830, The Nashville Colony. LC 73-78014. (Illus.). 577p. 1976. lib. bdg. 30.00 (ISBN 0-932408-03-6); Vol. IV, May Through October 10, 1830, Tenoxtitlan, Dream Capital of Texas. LC 73-78014. (Illus.). 627p. 1977. lib. bdg. 30.00 (ISBN 0-932408-04-4); Vol. V, October 11, 1830, Through March 5, 1831, The Upper Colony. LC 73-78014. (Illus.). 628p. 1978. lib. bdg. 30.00 (ISBN 0-932408-05-2); Vol. VI, March 6 Through December 5, 1831, The Campaigns Against the Tawakoni, Waco, Towash, & Comanche Indians. LC 73-78014. (Illus.). 632p. 1979. lib. bdg. 30.00 (ISBN 0-932408-06-0); Vol. VII, December 6, 1831, Through October, 1833, Those Eleven-League Grants. LC 73-78014. (Illus.). 664p. 1980. lib. bdg. 30.00 (ISBN 0-932408-07-9); Vol. VIII, November, 1833, Through September, 1834, Robertson's Colony. LC 73-78014. (Illus.). 608p. 1981. lib. bdg. 30.00 (ISBN 0-932408-08-7); Vol. IX, October, 1834, Through March 20, 1835, Sarahville de Viesca. LC 73-78014. (Illus.). 610p. 1982. lib. bdg. 30.00 (ISBN 0-932408-09-5); Vol. X, March 21 Through July 25, 1835, The Ranger Rendezvous. LC 73-78014. (Illus.). 600p. 1983. lib. bdg. 30.00 (ISBN 0-932408-10-9); Vol. XI, October 15, 1835 Through January 14, 1836: the Municipality of Milam. LC 73-78014. (Illus.). 732p. 1985. lib. bdg. 35.00 (ISBN 0-932408-12-5); Introductory Volume, Robert Leftwich's Mexico Diary & Letterbook, 1822-1824. LC 73-78014. (Illus.) 611p. 1986. lib. bdg. 35.00 (ISBN 0-932408-00-1); January 15 Through March 17 1936, Vol. XII, The Convention at Washington-on-the-Brazos. Ed. by Malcolm D. McLean. LC 73-78014. (Illus.). 792p. 1987. lib. bdg. 40.00 (ISBN 0-932408-13-3). UTA Pr.

Papers Concerning the Palaeontology of California, Arizona & Idaho. Carnegie Institution of Washington Staff. Repr. of 1934 ed. 19.00 (ISBN 0-685-02119-X). Johnson Repr.

Papers Concerning the Palaeontology of California, Nevada & Oregon. Carnegie Institution of Washington Staff. Repr. of 1935 ed. 19.00 (ISBN 0-685-02120-3). Johnson Repr.

Papers Concerning the Palaeontology of California, Oregon & the Northern Great Basin Province. Carnegie Institution of Washington Staff. Repr. of 1932 ed. 19.00 (ISBN 0-685-02121-1). Johnson Repr.

Papers Concerning the Palaeontology of the Cretaceous & Later Tertiary of Oregon, of the Pliocene of North-Western Nevada, & of the Late Miocene & Pleistocene of California. Carnegie Institution of Washington Staff. Repr. of 1928 ed. 19.00 (ISBN 0-685-02122-X). Johnson Repr.

Papers Concerning the Palaeontology of the Pleistocene of California & the Tertiary of Oregon. Carnegie Institution of Washington Staff. Repr. of 1925 ed. 19.00 (ISBN 0-685-02123-8). Johnson Repr.

Papers Connected with the Affairs of Milton & His Family. John F. Marsh. LC 74-22180. 1974. Repr. of 1851 ed. lib. bdg. 17.00 (ISBN 0-8414-5959-2). Folcroft.

Papers Contributed to the Workshop on Strategies for the Management of Fisheries & Aquaculture in Mangrove Ecosystems, Bangkok, Thailand, 23-25 June 1986 & Country Status Reports on Inland Fisheries Presented at the Third Session of the Indo-Pacific Fishery Commission Working Party of Experts in Inland Fisheries, Bangkok, Thailand, 23-25 June 1986. Ed. by R. H. Mepham & T. Petr. (FAO Fisheries Report: No. 370 Supplement). 248p. (Orig.). 1987. pap. 24.75 (ISBN 92-5-102640-8, F3172, FAO). UNIPUB.

Papers Critical & Reminiscent. William Sharp. 1912. Repr. 25.00 (ISBN 0-8274-3900-8). R West.

Papers Dedicated to Egil Amundsen: On the Occasion of his 60th Birthday March 18, 1984. Ed. by A. O. Aasen et al. (Journal: European Surgical Research: Vol. 16, Supp. 2). (Illus.). iv, 172p. 1984. pap. 34.75 (ISBN 3-8055-3889-8). S Karger.

Papers, First, Second & Third Series, 3 Vols. Central Society Of Education London Staff. LC 74-5890. (Social History of Education). 1969. Repr. of 1837 ed. 125.00x (ISBN 0-678-08456-4). Kelley.

Papers for the First Interdisciplinary Conference on Netherlandic Studies: Held at the University of Maryland 11-13 June 1982. Ed. by William H. Fletcher. LC 85-9006. 248p. (Orig.). 1985. lib. bdg. 30.25 (ISBN 0-8191-4707-9, Amer Assoc Netherlandic Studies); pap. text ed. 15.25 (ISBN 0-8191-4708-7). U Pr of Amer.

Papers for the V Congress of Southeast European Studies (Belgrade, September 1984) Ed. by Kot K. Shangriladze & Erica Townsend. 382p. 1984. pap. 18.95 (ISBN 0-89357-138-5). Slavica.

Papers from a Conference on Thai Studies in Honor of William J. Gedney. Ed. by Robert J. Bickner et al. LC 84-45446. (Michigan Papers on South & Southeast Asia: No. 25). (Illus.). 265p. 1986. 27.95 (ISBN 0-89148-030-7); pap. 16.95 (ISBN 0-89148-031-5). Ctr S&SE Asian.

Papers from a National Policy Conference on Legal Reforms in Child Sexual Abuse Cases: A Report of the American Bar Association Child Sexual Abuse Law Reform Project, National Legal Resource Center for Child Advocacy & Protection. Date not set. price not set. Amer Bar Assn.

Papers from a Viceroy's Yamen. Ku Hung-Ming. 199p. 1901. bds. 120.00x (Pub. by Han-Shan Tang Ltd). State Mutual Bk.

Papers from Eranos Yearbooks, 6 vols. Ed. by Joseph Campbell. Tr. by Ralph Manheim & R. F. Hull. Incl. Vol. 1. Spirit & Nature. (Illus.). 1954. 39.00x (ISBN 0-691-09736-4); Vol. 2. The Mysteries. 1955. pap. 12.50x (ISBN 0-691-01823-5); Vol. 3. Man & Time. LC 72-1982. (Illus.). 440p. 1957. 41.00x (ISBN 0-691-09732-1); pap. 12.50x (ISBN 0-691-01857-X); Vol. 4. Spirtual Disciplines. (Illus.). 1960. 44.50x (ISBN 0-691-09737-2); pap. 12.50x (ISBN 0-691-01863-4); Vol. 5. Man & Transformation. (Illus.). 1964. 43.50x (ISBN 0-691-09733-X); pap. 12.50x (ISBN 0-691-01834-0); Vol. 6. Mystic Vision. 1969. 51.50x (ISBN 0-691-09735-6). (Bollingen Ser.: No. 30). pap. 16.95x (ISBN 0-691-01842-1). Princeton U Pr.

Papers from the Eighth & Ninth Annual Meetings. Cara De Silva et al. (Gypsy Lore Society, North American Chapter, Publications: No. 4). (Illus.). 150p. (Orig.). 1988. pap. 19.00x (ISBN 0-9617107-3-X). Gypsy Lore Soc.

Papers from the Fifth International Conference on Historical Linguistics, Galway, April 6-10, 1981. Ed. by Anders Ahlqvist. (Current Issues in Linguistic Theory Ser.: 21). xxix, 527p. 1982. 62.00x (ISBN 90-272-3514-7). Benjamins North Am.

Papers from the Fourth & Fifth Annual Meetings. Ed. by Joanne Grumet. (Gypsy Lore Society, North American Chapter Publications: No. 2). 318p. 1985. 12.50x (ISBN 0-9617107-1-3). Gypsy Lore Soc.

Papers from the Fourth International Conference on English Historical Linguistics. Ed. by Roger Eaton et al. LC 85-22908. (Current Issues in Linguistic Theory Ser.: No. 41). xvii, 341p. 1985. 44.00x (ISBN 90-272-3531-7). Benjamins North Am.

Papers from the Fourth International Conference on Historical Linguistics, Stanford, March 26-30, 1979. Ed. by Elizabeth C. Traugott et al. (Current Issues in Linguistic Theory Ser.: No. 14). x, 437p. 1980. 54.00x (ISBN 90-272-3501-5). Benjamins North Am.

Papers from the International Conference on Music in Paris in the Eighteen Thirties (Smith College, April 1982) Sponsored by the National Endowment for the Humanities. Ed. by Peter Bloom. LC 87-2248. (La Vie Musicale en France au XIX Siecle: No. 4). (Illus.). 1987. PLB 48.00 (ISBN 0-918728-71-1). Pendragon NY.

Papers from the Second Interdisciplinary Conference on Netherlandic Studies, Georgetown University 7-9 June, 1984. Ed. by William H. Fletcher. LC 86-28221. (Illus.). 168p. (Orig.). 1987. lib. bdg. 18.75 (ISBN 0-8191-6073-3). U Pr of Amer.

Papers from the Second International Workshop on Japanese Syntax. Ed. by William J. Poser. 240p. 1988. pap. 13.95 (ISBN 0-937073-38-5). Ctr Study Language.

Papers from the Seventh International Conference on Historical Linguistics. Ed. by Anna G. Ramat et al. LC 87-8100. (Current Issues in Linguistic Theory Ser.: Vol. 48). xvi, 672p. 1987. 86.00x (ISBN 90-272-3542-2). Benjamins North Am.

Papers from the Sixth & Seventh Annual Meetings. Ed. by Joanne Grumet. (Gypsy Lore Society, North American Chapter Publication: No. 3). 203p. 1986. 12.50x (ISBN 0-9617107-2-1). Gypsy Lore Soc.

Papers from the Sixth International Conference on Historical Linguistics. Ed. by Jacek Fisiak. LC 85-13465. (Current Issues in Linguistic Theory: No. 34). xxiii, 622p. 1985. 72.00x (ISBN 90-272-3528-7). Benjamins North Am.

Papers from the Third International Conference on Historical Linguistics, Hamburg, August 22-26, 1977. Ed. by J. Peter Maher et al. (Current Issues in Linguistic Theory Ser,: 13). xvi, 434p. 1982. 50.00x (ISBN 90-272-3505-8). Benjamins North Am.

Papers from the Third Scandinavian Symposium on Syntactic Variation. Sven Jacobson. 180p. (Orig.). 1986. pap. text ed. 24.50x (ISBN 91-22-00802-0, Pub. by Almqvist & Wiksell). Coronet Bks.

Papers from the Twelfth Linguistic Symposium on Romance Languages. Ed. by Philip Baldi. (Current Issues in Linguistic Theory, (CLIT) Ser.: Vol. 26). xii, 611p. 1984. 76.00x (ISBN 90-272-3518-X). Benjamins North Am.

Papers from the West Virginia University Conference on Computer Applications in Music. Ed. by Gerald Lefkoff. (Illus.). 1967. 5.00 (ISBN 0-685-30820-0). McClain.

Papers from Twenty-First Regional Meeting of C. L. S, 2 pts. Ed. by K. Peterson et al. (Orig.). 1985. Pt. 1, 438p. pap. text ed. 9.00; Pt. 2: Parasession on Causatives & Agentivity. pap. text ed. 9.00 (ISBN 0-914203-24-X). Chicago Ling.

Papers Illustrative of the Political Condition of the Highlands of Scotland. Ed. by James M'Conechy. LC 75-175587. (Maitland Club, Glasgow. Publications: No. 64). Repr. of 1845 ed. 17.50 (ISBN 0-404-53071-0). AMS Pr.

Papers in African Prehistory. Ed. by J. D. Fage & R. A. Oliver. LC 74-77286. (Illus.). 343p. pap. 89.20 (2030592). Bks Demand UMI.

Papers in Algebra, Analysis & Statistics. Ed. by R. Lidl. LC 82-1826. (Contemporary Mathematics Ser.: Vol. 9). 400p. 1982. pap. 27.00 (ISBN 0-8218-5009-1, CONM-9). Am Math.

Papers in Caribbean Anthropology. Compiled by Sidney W. Mintz. LC 74-123185. (Yale University Publications in Anthropology Reprints Ser.: Nos. 57-64). 252p. 1970. pap. 15.00x (ISBN 0-87536-524-8). HRAFP.

Papers in Chinese Linguistics & Epigraphy. Chou Fa-kao. vii, 141p. 1986. text ed. 26.50x (ISBN 962-201-317-1, Pub. by Chinese U HK). Coronet Bks.

Papers in Cognitive-Stratificational Linguistics. Michael Bennett et al. Ed. by James E. Copeland & Philip W. Davis. (Rice University Studies: Vol. 66, No. 2). (Illus.). 208p. (Orig.). 1980. pap. 10.00x (ISBN 0-89263-245-3). Rice Univ.

Papers in Computational Linguistics. Ed. by Ferenc Papp & Gyorgy Szepe. (Janua Linguarum, Ser. Major: No. 91). 585p. text ed. 76.80x (ISBN 90-279-3285-9). Mouton.

Papers in Contrastive Linguistics. International Congress of Applied Linguistics (2nd: 1969: Cambridge) Ed. by Gerhard Nickel. LC 78-149434. pap. 32.80 (2026350). Bks Demand UMI.

Papers in Economic Prehistory: Studies. British Academy, Major Research Project in the Early History of Agriculture. Ed. by E. S. Higgs. LC 78-180019. pap. 57.30 (2026342). Bks Demand UMI.

Papers in Economics & Sociology, 1930-1960. Oskar Lange. Tr. by P. F. Knightsfield. LC 68-22080. 1970. 81.00 (ISBN 0-08-012352-X). Pergamon.

Papers in General Linguistics. J. Kramsky. (Janua Linguarum Series Minor: No. 209). 207p. (Orig.). 1976. pap. text ed. 20.80x (ISBN 90-2793-131-3). Mouton.

Papers in Greek Archaeology & History in Memory of Colin D. Gordon. Ed. by John Fossey. (McGill University Monographs in Classical Archaeology & History: No. 6). 154p. 1987. 69.00x (ISBN 90-5063-009-X, Pub. by Gieben Amsterdam). Benjamins North Am.

Papers in Korean Linguistics. Ed. by Chin-W Kim. 1979. pap. text ed. 14.50 (ISBN 0-917496-11-6). Hornbeam Pr.

Papers in Language Variation: Samla-Ads Collection. Ed. by David L. Shores & Carole P. Hines. LC 76-23162. 1977. 25.00 (ISBN 0-8173-0504-1). U of Ala Pr.

Papers in Linguistics in Honor of Leon Dostert. Ed. by William M. Austin. (Janua Linguarum, Ser. Major: No. 25). 1967. text ed. 23.20x (ISBN 90-2790-616-5). Mouton.

Papers in Linguistics & Phonetics to the Memory of Pierre Delattre. Ed. by Albert Valdman. (Janua Linguarum, Ser. Major: No. 54). (Illus.). 513p. 1972. text ed. 69.60x (ISBN 90-2792-310-8). Mouton.

Papers in Logic & Ethics. Arthur N. Prior. Ed. by P. T. Geach & A. J. Kenny. LC 76-9376. 238p. 1976. 17.50x (ISBN 0-87023-213-4). U of Mass Pr.

Papers in Mathematics. Ed. by Paul R. Meyer. (Annals of the New York Academy of Sciences: Vol. 321). (Orig.). 1979. 22.00x (ISBN 0-89766-025-0); pap. write for info. (ISBN 0-89766-026-9). NY Acad Sci.

Papers in Mayan Linguistics. Ed. by Nora C. England. (Miscellaneous Publications in Anthropology No. 6; Studies in Mayan Linguistics: No. 2). v, 310p. 1978. pap. 15.00 (ISBN 0-913134-87-2). Mus Anthro Mo.

Papers in Political Science. John S. Ambler et al. (Rice University Studies: Vol. 54, No. 3). 88p. 1968. pap. 10.00x (ISBN 0-89263-197-X). Rice Univ.

Papers in Science & Public Policy, Vol. 368, No. 1. 235p. 1981. 50.00x (ISBN 0-89766-125-7, Rosenberg Pub); pap. 50.00x (ISBN 0-89766-126-5). NY Acad Sci.

Papers in Structural & Transformational Linguistics. Z. S. Harris. LC 74-118128. (Formal Linguistics Ser: No. 1). 850p. 1970. lib. bdg. 71.00 (ISBN 90-277-0026-5, Pub. by Reidel Holland). Kluwer Academic.

Papers in the History of Linguistics: Proceedings of the Third International Conference on the History of the Language Sciences (ICHoLS III), Princeton, 19-23 August 1984. Ed. by Hans Aarsleff et al. LC 86-3528. (Studies in the History of Linguistic Science: Vol. 38). xxi, 676p. 1987. 110.00 (ISBN 90-272-4521-5). Benjamins North Am.

Papers in Theoretical Linguistics. Niels Danielsen. (Current Issues in Linguistic Theory Ser.: No. 23). 250p. Date not set. price not set (ISBN 90-272-3509-0). Benjamins North Am.

Papers in Urban & Regional Analysis. Alan G. Wilson. 261p. 1972. pap. text ed. 14.95x (ISBN 0-85086-033-4, NO. 2904, Pub. by Pion England). Routledge Chapman & Hall.

Papers in Vertebrate Paleontology Honoring Robert Warren Wilson. Ed. by Robert M. Mengel. LC 84-71697. (Special Publications: No. 9, CMNH). (Illus.). 192p. 1984. 22.50 (ISBN 0-935868-09-7). Carnegie Mus.

Papers of a Pariah. facs. ed. Robert H. Benson. LC 67-23176. (Essay Index Reprint Ser). 1907. 17.00 (ISBN 0-8369-0196-7). Ayer Co Pubs.

Papers of Admiral Sir John Fisher, Vol. II. Ed. by P. K. Kemp. 69.00x (ISBN 0-317-44200-7, Pub. by Navy Rec Soc). State Mutual Bk.

Papers of Alexander Hamilton, 20 vols, Vol. 1-17. Alexander Hamilton. Ed. by Harold C. Syrett et al. Incl. Vol. 1. 1768-1778. 1961 (ISBN 0-231-08900-7); Vol. 2. 1779-1781. 1961 (ISBN 0-231-08901-5); Vol. 3. 1782-1786. 1962 (ISBN 0-231-08902-3); Vol. 4. 1787-May, 1788. 1962 (ISBN 0-231-08903-1); Vol. 5. June, 1788-November, 1789. 1963 (ISBN 0-231-08904-X); Vol. 6. December, 1789-August, 1790. 1963 (ISBN 0-231-08905-8); Vol. 7. September, 1790-January, 1971. 1963 (ISBN 0-231-08906-6); Vol. 8. February, 1791-July, 1791. 1965 (ISBN 0-231-08907-4); Vol. 9. August, 1791-September, 1791. 1965 (ISBN 0-231-08908-2); Vol. 10. December, 1791-January, 1792. 1966 (ISBN 0-231-08909-0); Vol. 11. February-June, 1792. 1966 (ISBN 0-231-08910-4); Vol. 12. July-October, 1792. 1967 (ISBN 0-231-08911-2); Vol. 13. November, 1792-February, 1793. 1967 (ISBN 0-231-08912-0); Vol. 14. February-June, 1793. 1969 (ISBN 0-231-08913-9); Vol. 15. June, 1793-January, 1794. 1969 (ISBN 0-231-08914-7); Vol. 16. February 1794-July 1794 (ISBN 0-231-08915-5); Vol. 17. August 1794-December 1794. 65.00 (ISBN 0-231-08916-3). LC 61-15593. 65.00 ea. Columbia U Pr.

Papers of Alexander Hamilton, Vol. 23. Alexander Hamilton. Ed. by Harold C. Syrett. 624p. 1976. 70.00x (ISBN 0-231-08922-8). Columbia U Pr.

Papers of Alexander Hamilton, Vol. 24. Alexander Hamilton. Ed. by Harold C. Syrett. 664p. 1976. 70.00x (ISBN 0-231-08923-6). Columbia U Pr.

Papers of Alexander Hamilton, Vol. 25. Alexander Hamilton. Ed. by Harold C. Syrett. LC 61-15593. 70.00x (ISBN 0-231-08924-4). Columbia U Pr.

Papers of Alexander Hamilton: April 1797 to July 1798, Vol. 21. Alexander Hamilton. Ed. by Harold C. Syrett et al. 1974. 70.00x (ISBN 0-231-08920-1). Columbia U Pr.

Papers of Alexander Hamilton: August 1795 to December 1795, Vol. 19. Alexander Hamilton. Ed. by Harold C. Syrett et al. 640p. 1973. 70.00x (ISBN 0-231-08918-X). Columbia U Pr.

Papers of Alexander Hamilton: January 1796 to 1797, Vol. 20. Alexander Hamilton. Ed. by Harold C. Syrett et al. 1974. 70.00 (ISBN 0-231-08919-8). Columbia U Pr.

Papers of Alexander Hamilton: January 1795 to July 1795, Vol. 18. Alexander Hamilton. Ed. by Harold C. Syrett et al. 608p. 1973. 70.00x (ISBN 0-231-08917-1). Columbia U Pr.

Papers of Alexander Hamilton: Vol. 22, July 1798 to March 1799. Alexander Hamilton. Ed. by Harold C. Syrett et al. 640p. 1975. 70.00x (ISBN 0-231-08921-X). Columbia U Pr.

Papers of Alexander Hamilton: Vol. 26, May 1802 to July 1804, Vol. 26. Alexander Hamilton. 1978. 70.00x (ISBN 0-231-08925-2). Columbia U Pr.

Papers of Alexander Hamilton: Vol. 27, Index. Alexander Hamilton. LC 61-15593. 1981. 70.00. Columbia U Pr.

Papers of Alfred Blalock, 2 Vols. Ed. by Mark M. Ravitch. (Illus.). 1966. 155.00x (ISBN 0-8018-0544-9). Johns Hopkins.

Papers of Andrew Jackson: Guide & Index to the Microfilm Editions. Ed. by Harold D. Moser et al. LC 86-33831. 413p. 1987. 50.00x (ISBN 0-8420-4007-2). Scholarly Res Inc.

Papers of Andrew Jackson, Vol. II: Eighteen Four to Eighteen Thirteen. Harold D. Moser et al. LC 79-15078. (Andrew Jackson Ser.). 650p. 1985. 45.00x (ISBN 0-87049-441-4). U of Tenn Pr.

Papers of Andrew Jackson: 1770-1803, Vol. 1. Ed. by Sam B. Smith & Harriet C. Owsley. LC 79-15078. (Illus.). 570p. 1980. 45.00x (ISBN 0-87049-219-5). U of Tenn Pr.

Papers of Andrew Johnson, 6 vols. Andrew Johnson. Ed. by LeRoy P. Graf & Ralph W. Haskins. Incl. Vol. 1. 1822-1851. (Illus.). 752p. 1967. 45.00 (ISBN 0-87049-079-6); Vol. 2. 1852-1857. (Illus.). 608p. 1970. 45.00 (ISBN 0-87049-098-2); Vol. 3. 1858-1860. (Illus.). 796p. 1972. 45.00 (ISBN 0-87049-141-5); Vol. 4. 1860-1861. 796p. 1976. 45.00 (ISBN 0-87049-183-0); Vol. 5. 1861-1862. 752p. 1979. text ed. 45.00 (ISBN 0-87049-273-X). LC 67-25733. U of Tenn Pr.

Papers of Andrew Johnson, Vol. 7. Andrew Johnson. Ed. by Leroy P. Graf. LC 67-25733. (Papers of Andrew Johnson). (Illus.). 820p. 1986. text ed. 45.00 (ISBN 0-87049-488-0). U of Tenn Pr.

Papers of Benjamin Franklin, 18 vols. Benjamin Franklin. Incl. Vol. 1. January 6, 1706 Through December 31, 1734. Ed. by Leonard W. Labaree. (Illus.). lxxxviii, 400p. 1959 (ISBN 0-300-00650-0); Vol. 2. January 1, 1735 Through December 31, 1744. Ed. by Leonard W. Labaree. (Illus.). xxv, 471p. 1960 (ISBN 0-300-00651-9); Vol. 3. January 1, 1745 Through June 30, 1750. Ed. by Leonard W. Labaree. (Illus.). xxv, 513p. 1961 (ISBN 0-300-00652-7); Vol. 4. July 1, 1750 Through June 30, 1753. Ed. by Leonard W. Labaree. (Illus.). xxviii, 544p. 1961 (ISBN 0-300-00653-5); Vol. 5. July 1, 1753 Through March 31, 1755. Ed. by Leonard W. Labaree. (Illus.). xxvi, 575p. 1962 (ISBN 0-300-00654-3); Vol. 6. April 1, 1755 Through September 24, 1756. Ed. by Leonard W. Labaree. (Illus.). xxix, 581p. 1963 (ISBN 0-300-00655-1); Vol. 7. October 1, 1756 Through March 31, 1758. Ed. by Leonard W. Lambaree. (Illus.). xxvi, 427p. 1963 (ISBN 0-300-00657-8); Vol. 8. April 1, 1758 Through December 31, 1759. Ed. by Leonard W. Labaree. (Illus.). xxiv, 489p. 1965 (ISBN 0-300-00658-6); Vol. 9. January 1, 1760 Through December 31, 1761. Ed. by Leonard W. Labaree. (Illus.). xxvi, 429p. 1966 (ISBN 0-300-00659-4); Vol. 10. January 1, 1762 Through December 31, 1763. Ed. by Leonard W. Labaree. (Illus.). xxix, 459p. 1966 (ISBN 0-300-00660-8); Vol. 11. January 1, 1764 Through December 31, 1764. Ed. by Leonard W. Labaree. (Illus.). xxviii, 593p. 1967 (ISBN 0-300-00661-6); Vol. 12. January 1, 1765 Through December 31, 1765. Ed. by Leonard W. Labaree. (Illus.). 1968 (ISBN 0-300-01073-7); Vol. 13. January 1, 1766 Through December 31, 1766. Ed. by Leonard W. Labaree. (Illus.). 544p. 1969 (ISBN 0-300-01132-6); Vol. 14. January 1, 1767 Through December 31, 1767. Ed. by Leonard W. Labaree. (Illus.). 600p. 1970 (ISBN 0-300-01317-5); Vol. 15. January 1, 1768 Through December 31, 1768. Ed. by William B. Willcox. (Illus.). 1972 (ISBN 0-300-01469-4); Vol. 16. Papers of Benjamin Franklin: January 1 1769 Through December 31, 1769. Ed. by William B. Willcox. LC 59-12697. (Illus.) (ISBN 0-300-01570-4); Vol. 17. January 1, 1770 Through December 31, 1770. (Illus.). 1973 (ISBN 0-300-01596-8); Vol. 18. January 1, 1771 Through December 31, 1771. Ed. by William B. Willcox. LC 59-12697. 1974 (ISBN 0-300-01685-9); Vol. 19. January 1, 1792 Through December 31, 1772. 1976 (ISBN 0-300-01865-7); Vol. 20. January 1, 1773 Through December 31, 1773. 1976 (ISBN 0-300-01966-1); Vol. 21. January 1, 1774 Through March 22, 1775. 1978 (ISBN 0-300-02224-7). LC 59-12697. 60.00 ea. Yale U Pr.

Papers of Benjamin Franklin, Vol.#26. Ed. by William Wilcox. LC 59-12697. 848p. 1987. text ed. 60.00 (ISBN 0-300-03819-4). Yale U Pr.

Papers of Benjamin Franklin: January 1 1769 Through December 31, 1769 see Papers of Benjamin Franklin.

Papers of Benjamin Franklin: March 23, 1775 Through October 27, 1776; October 27, 1776-April 30, 1977, 2 Vols, Vols. 22, 23. Benjamin Franklin. Ed. by William B. Willcox. LC 59-12697. 1982, 768 60.00x (ISBN 0-300-02618-8); text ed. 60.00 1983 752pp (ISBN 0-300-02897-0). Yale U Pr.

Papers of Benjamin Franklin: May 1 Through September 30, 1777, Vol. 24. Benjamin Franklin. Ed. by William B. Willcox et al. LC 59-12697. (Illus.). 672p. 1984. text ed. 60.00x (ISBN 0-300-03162-9). Yale U Pr.

Papers of Benjamin Franklin, Vol. 27, June 1 Through October 30, 1778. Benjamin Franklin. 1988. text ed. 60.00 (ISBN 0-300-04177-2). Yale U Pr.

Papers of Captain Rufus Lincoln of Wareham, Mass. Ed. by Rufus Lincoln. LC 74-140872. (Eyewitness Accounts of the American Revolution Ser., No. 3). 1970. Repr. of 1904 ed. 20.00 (ISBN 0-405-01220-9). Ayer Co Pubs.

Papers of Charles Willson Peale Vol. 2: The Artist as Museum Keeper 1791-1810. Ed. by Lillian S. Miller. LC 87-10646. 1360p. 1988. text ed. 105.00 (ISBN 0-300-03422-9). Yale U Pr.

Papers of Chief John Ross: Volume I, 1807-1839, Volume II, 1840-1866. John Ross. Intro. by Gary E. Moulton. LC 84-21954. (Illus.). 1611p. 1985. Vol. I 824p. text ed. 95.00x set (ISBN 0-8061-1865-2). Vol. II 790p. U of Okla Pr.

Papers of Daniel Webster: Correspondence, Vol 1, 1798-1824. Daniel Webster. Ed. by Charles M. Wiltse & Harold D. Moser. LC 73-92705. (Papers of Daniel Webster: Series 1, Correspondence). (Illus.). 544p. 1974. 65.00x (ISBN 0-87451-096-1). U Pr of New Eng.

Papers of Daniel Webster: Correspondence, Vol. 2, 1825-1829. Daniel Webster. Ed. by Charles M. Wiltse & Harold D. Moser. LC 73-92705. (Papers of Daniel Webster: Series 1, Correspondence). (Illus.). 587p. 1976. 65.00x (ISBN 0-87451-120-8). U Pr of New Eng.

Papers of Daniel Webster, Correspondence, Vol. 3: 1830-1834. Daniel Webster. Ed. by Charles M. Wiltse & David G. Allen. LC 73-92705. (Papers of Daniel Webster: Series 1, Correspondence). (Illus.). 573p. 1977. 65.00x (ISBN 0-87451-131-3). U Pr of New Eng.

Papers of Daniel Webster: Correspondence, Vol. 4, 1835-1839. Daniel Webster. Ed. by Charles M. Wiltse & Harold D. Moser. LC 73-92705. (Illus.). 588p. 1980. 65.00x (ISBN 0-87451-169-0). U Pr of New Eng.

Papers of Daniel Webster: Correspondence, Vol. 5, 1840-1843. Daniel Webster. Ed. by Harold D. Moser. LC 73-92705. (Papers of Daniel Webster; Series 1, Correspondence). (Illus.). 618p. 1982. 65.00x (ISBN 0-87451-231-X). U Pr of New Eng.

Papers of Daniel Webster: Correspondence, Vol. 6, 1844-1849. Daniel Webster. Ed. by Charles M. Wiltse & Wendy B. Tilghman. LC 73-92705. (Papers of Daniel Webster: Ser. 1). (Illus.). 563p. 1984. 65.00x (ISBN 0-87451-294-8). U Pr of New Eng.

Papers of Daniel Webster, Correspondence, Vol. 7, 1850-1852, Vol. 7. Daniel Webster. Ed. by Charles M. Wiltse & Michael J. Birkner. LC 73-92705. (Papers of Daniel Webster, Series 1, Correspondence,). (Illus.). 729p. 1986. 70.00x (ISBN 0-87451-323-5). U Pr of New Eng.

Papers of Daniel Webster: Diplomatic Papers, Vol. 1, 1841-1843. Daniel Webster. Ed. by Kenneth E. Shewmaker et al. LC 73-92705. (Ser. III). (Illus.). 1004p. 1983. 85.00x (ISBN 0-87451-245-X). U Pr of New Eng.

Papers of Daniel Webster: Legal Papers, Vol. 1, The New Hampshire Practice. Daniel Webster. Ed. by Alfred S. Konefsky et al. LC 73-92705. (Papers of Daniel Webster: Series 2, Legal Papers). 611p. 1982. 65.00x (ISBN 0-87451-232-8). U Pr of New Eng.

Papers of Daniel Webster: Legal Papers, Vol. 2, The Boston Practice. Daniel Webster. Ed. by Alfred S. Konefsky & Andrew J. King. LC 73-92705. (Papers of Daniel Webster; Series 2, Legal Papers). 700p. 1983. 65.00x (ISBN 0-87451-240-9). U Pr of New Eng.

Papers of Daniel Webster: Speeches & Formal Writings, Vol. 1, 1800-1833. Daniel Webster. Ed. by Charles M. Wiltse & Alan R. Berolzheimer. LC 73-92705. (Papers of Daniel Webster, Series 4, Speeches & Formal Writings). 661p. 1986. 70.00x (ISBN 0-87451-357-X). U Pr of New Eng.

Papers of Daniel Webster: Speeches & Formal Writings, Volume 2, 1834-1852. Daniel Webster. Ed. by Charles M. Wiltse & Alan R. Berolzheimer. LC 73-92705. (Papers of Daniel Webster: Serial Speeches & Journal Writings). 718p. 1988. 75.00x (ISBN 0-87451-415-0). U Pr of New Eng.

Papers of Daniel Webster: Volume 2, the Federal Practice, 2 vols, Vol. 3. Ed. by Andrew J. King. LC 73-92705. 1136p. 1988. Set. 110.00x (ISBN 0-87451-410-X). U Pr of New Eng.

Papers of Daniel Webster: Volume 2, 1850-1852. Daniel Webster. Ed. by Kenneth E. Shewmaker & Kenneth R. Stevens. LC 73-92705. (Papers of Daniel Webster: Series 3, Diplomatic Papers). (Illus.). 854p. 1987. 85.00x (ISBN 0-87451-373-1). U Pr of New Eng.

Papers of Dwight David Eisenhower, 4 vols. Incl. Vol. 6. Occupation 1945. Ed. by Alfred D. Chandler, Jr. & Louis Galambos; Vols. 7-9. The Chief of Staff. Ed. by Louis Galambos. LC 65-27672. 1979. 95.00x (ISBN 0-8018-2061-8). Johns Hopkins.

Papers of Dwight David Eisenhower: Columbia University, 2 vols, Vols. X-XI. Ed. by Louis Galambos. LC 65-27672. 1664p. 1984. Set. 85.00x (ISBN 0-8018-2720-5). Johns Hopkins.

Papers of Dwight David Eisenhower: The War Years, 5 Vols. Ed. by Alfred D. Chandler, Jr. LC 65-27672. (Illus., Sold as set only). 1970. Set. 135.00x (ISBN 0-8018-1078-7). Johns Hopkins.

Papers of Frederick Law Olmsted, Vol. IV: Defending the Union: The Civil War & the U. S. Sanitary Commission, 1861-1863. Ed. by Jane T. Censer. LC 85-24044. 770p. 1986. text ed. 55.00x (ISBN 0-8018-3067-2). Johns Hopkins.

Papers of Frederick Law Olmsted: Vol. II: Slavery & the South, 1852-1857. Ed. by Charles E. Beveridge & Charles C. McLaughlin. LC 80-8881. (Papers of Frederick Law Olmsted). (Illus.). 528p. 1981. text ed. 45.00x (ISBN 0-8018-2242-4). Johns Hopkins.

Papers of Frederick Law Olmsted, Vol. 1: The Formative Years, 1822-1852. Ed. by Charles Capen McLaughlin. LC 76-47378. (Papers of Frederick Law Olmsted Ser). (Illus.). 448p. 1977. 45.00x (ISBN 0-8018-1798-6). Johns Hopkins.

Papers of Frederick Law Olmsted, Vol.III: Creating Central Park, 1857-1861. Charles E. Beveridge & David Schuyler. LC 82-4701. (Olsted Papers). (Illus.). 464p. 1983. text ed. 45.00x (ISBN 0-8018-2751-5). Johns Hopkins.

Papers of General Lucius D. Clay: Germany, 1945-1949, 2 vols. Lucius D. Clay. Ed. by Jean E. Smith. LC 73-16536. 570p. Vol. 1. pap. 148.20 (2056437); Vol. 2. pap. 160.00 (2056437). Bks Demand UMI.

Papers of General Nathanael Greene, December 1766 to December 1776, Vol. 1. Ed. by Richard K. Showman. 1976. 30.00 (ISBN 0-685-67666-8). RI Hist Soc.

Papers of General Nathanael Greene: January 1st, 1777 to October 16th, 1778, Vol. II. Ed. by Richard K. Showman et al. LC 76-20441. 1980. 35.00x (ISBN 0-8078-1384-2). U of NC Pr.

Papers of General Nathanael Greene, Vol.IV: 11 May 1779-31 October 1779. Ed. by Richard K. Showman et al. LC 76-20441. (Papers of General Nathanael Greene). xxxviii, 614p. 1986. 35.00x (ISBN 0-8078-1668-X). U of NC Pr.

Papers of General Nathaniel Green: Volume III, 1778-1779. Ed. by Richard K. Showman et al. LC 76-20441. xxxix, 543p. 1984. 35.00x (ISBN 0-8078-1557-8). U of NC Pr.

Papers of George Catlett Marshall, "The Soldierly Spirit", Vol. I. Ed. by Larry I. Bland & Fred L. Hadsel. LC 81-47593. (Illus.). 750p. 1981. text ed. 38.00x (ISBN 0-8018-2552-0). Johns Hopkins.

Papers of George Catlett Marshall, Vol. 2: "We Cannot Delay" July 1, 1939 - December 6, 1941. Ed. by Larry I. Bland et al. LC 81-47593. 800p. 1986. text ed. 38.00x (ISBN 0-8018-2553-9). Johns Hopkins.

Papers of George Mason, 3 vols. George Mason. Ed. by Robert A. Rutland. LC 70-97016. (Institute of Early American History & Culture Ser.). 1970. Set, vol. I-cxxvii, 483 pgs.; vol. II-xxii, 387 pgs.; vol. III-xxviii, 447 pgs. 65.00x (ISBN 0-8078-1134-3). U of NC Pr.

Papers of George Washington. George Washington. Ed. by W. W. Abbot. LC 81-16307. (Colonial Ser.: Vol. 4). 467p. 1984. text ed. 35.00x (ISBN 0-8139-1006-4). U Pr of Va.

Papers of George Washington. George Washington. Ed. by W. W. Abbot. LC 81-16307. (Colonial Ser.: Vol. 3). 488p. 1984. text ed. 35.00x (ISBN 0-8139-1003-X). U Pr of Va.

Papers of George Washington. George Washington. Ed. by W. W. Abbot & Dorothy Twohig. LC 81-16307. (Presidential Series 2, April-May 1789). 499p. 1987. text ed. 37.50x (ISBN 0-8139-1105-2). U Pr of Va.

Papers of George Washington. George Washington. Ed. by W. W. Abbot & Dorothy Twohig. LC 81-81016307. (Presidential Series 1, September 1788-March 1789). (Illus.). 477p. 1987. text ed. 37.50x (ISBN 0-8139-1103-6). U Pr of Va.

Papers of George Washington, Vols. 1 & 2. George Washington. Ed. by W. W. Abbot. LC 81-16307. (Colonial Ser. I). (Illus.). 1983. 35.00x ea. Vol. 1 (ISBN 0-8139-0912-0). Vol. 2 (ISBN 0-8139-0923-6). U Pr of Va.

Papers of George Washington: June-September 1775. George Washington. Ed. by W. W. Abbot. LC 81-16307. (Revolutionary Ser.: No. 1). 460p. 1985. text ed. 35.00x (ISBN 0-8139-1040-4). U Pr of Va.

Papers of George Washington: October 1757-August 1758. George Washington. Ed. by W. W. Abbot. LC 81-16307. (Colonial Ser.: Vol. 5). 500p. 1988. 35.00x (ISBN 0-8139-1144-3). U Pr of Va.

Papers of George Washington: Revolutionary War Series 2, September-December 1775. George Washington. Ed. by W. W. Abbot & Philander D. Chase. LC 81-16307. (Illus.). 628p. 1987. text ed. 47.50x (ISBN 0-8139-1102-8). U Pr of Va.

Papers of George Washington: Revolutionary War Series 3, January-March 1776. George Washington. Ed. by W. W. Abbot et al. LC 81-16307. 1250p. 1988. 47.50x (ISBN 0-8139-1167-2). U Pr of Va.

Papers of George Wyatt. Ed. by Royal Historical Society Staff. (Camden Fourth Ser.: No. 5). 200p. 1979. 27.00 (ISBN 0-901050-01-6, Pub. by Boydell & Brewer). Longwood Pub Group.

Papers of Governor Sir Edmund Andros, Vol. 1: 1674-1676. 1988. price not set (ISBN 0-8156-2457-3). Syracuse U Pr.

Papers of Henry Bouquet. Ed. by S. K. Stevens et al. Donald H. Kent & Autumn L. Leonard. Incl. Vol. 1. 1756-1758. 470p. 1972 (ISBN 0-911124-66-7); Vol. 2. Forbes Expedition. 736p. 1951. LC 51-9537. 15.00 ea. Pa Hist & Mus.

Papers of Henry Bouquet: January 1 to August 31, 1759, Vol. 3. 686p. 1976. 20.00 (ISBN 0-911124-86-1). Pa Hist & Mus.

Papers of Henry Bouquet: Sept 1, 1759 to August 31, 1760, Vol. 4. 759p. 1978. 20.00 (ISBN 0-911124-99-3). Pa Hist & Mus.

Papers of Henry Bouquet: September 1, 1760 to October 31, 1761, Vol. 5. 875p. 1984. 55.00 (ISBN 0-89271-030-6). Pa Hist & Mus.

Papers of Henry Clay, 9 vols. Henry Clay. Ed. by James F. Hopkins & Mary W. Hargreaves. Incl. Vol. 1. The Rising Statesman, 1797-1814. 1060p. 1959 (ISBN 0-8131-0051-8); Vol. 2. The Rising Statesman, 1815-1820. 952p. 1961. (ISBN 0-8131-0052-6); Vol. 3. Presidential Candidate, 1821-1824. 944p. 1963 (ISBN 0-8131-0053-4); Vol. 4. Secretary of State, 1825. 1004p. 1972 (ISBN 0-8131-0054-2); Vol. 5. Secretary of State, 1826. 1104p. 1973 (ISBN 0-8131-0055-0); Vol. 6. Secretary of State, 1827. 1456p. 1981 (ISBN 0-8131-0056-9); Vol. 7. Secretary of State, Jan. 1, 1828 - March 4, 1829. 792p. 1982 (ISBN 0-8131-0057-7); Vol. 8. Candidate, Compromiser, Whig, March 5, 1829 to December31, 1836. 1984 (ISBN 0-8131-0058-5); Vol. 9. Whig Leader January 1, 1837-December 31, 1843. Ed. by Robert Seager, II & Melba P. Hay. (Illus.). 976p (ISBN 0-8131-0059-3). LC 59-13605. 50.00x ea. U Pr of Ky.

Papers of Henry Clay, Vol. 2. Henry Clay. Ed. by James F. Hopkins & Mary W. M. Hargreaves. LC 59-13605. pap. 160.00 (ISBN 0-317-26735-3, 2024359). Bks Demand UMI.

Papers of the Seventh International Conference on Liquefied Natural Gas: Jakarta, Indonesia, May 15-19, 1983, 2 vols. 908p. Set. 75.00 (ISBN 0-910091-04-8). Inst Gas Tech.

Papers of the Shakespeare Society, 4 vols. in 1. (Shakespeare Society of London Publication Ser.: Vol. 11). pap. 59.00 (ISBN 0-8115-0173-6). Kraus Repr.

Papers of the Sixth International Conference on Liquefied Natural Gas: Kyoto, Japan, April 7-10, 1980, 2 Vols. 993p. Set. 60.00 (ISBN 0-910091-35-8). Inst Gas Tech.

Papers of the Texas Revolution, 10 vols. Ed. by John H. Jenkins. Set. 185.00 (ISBN 0-685-83961-3, Pub. by Presidential Press). Jenkins.

Papers of the Texas Revolution: 1835-1836, 10 Vols. Ed. by John H. Jenkins. 1973. Set. 185.00 (ISBN 0-935978-08-9). Presidial.

Papers of the University Settlement Society of New York City: Guide to a Microfilm Edition. Ed. by Eleanor M. Niermann. (Guides to Historical Resources Ser.). 1972. pap. 1.00 (ISBN 0-87020-183-2). State Hist Soc Wis.

Papers of the Women's Trade Union League & Its Principal Leaders. Ed. by Edward T. James et al. 319p. 1981. 70.00 (ISBN 0-89235-026-1). Res Pubns CT.

Papers of the Yugoslav-American Seminar on Music. Ed. by Malcolm H. Brown. 208p. 1970. 14.95 (ISBN 0-89357-007-9); pap. 9.95 (ISBN 0-89357-006-0). Slavica.

Papers of Thirteen Early Ohio Political Leaders. L. Kalette. (Illus.). 240p. 1977. pap. 9.00. Ohio Hist Soc.

Papers of Thomas Bowrey, (1669-1713) Ed. by Richard C. Temple. (Hakluyt Society Series 2: Vol. 58). (Illus.). Repr. of 1925 ed. 52.00 (ISBN 0-8115-0361-5). Kraus Repr.

Papers of Thomas Jefferson, 60 vols. Thomas Jefferson. Ed. by J. P. Boyd et al. Incl. Vol. 1. 1760-1776. 1950 (ISBN 0-691-04533-X); Vol. 2. 1777-1779. 1950 (ISBN 0-691-04534-8); Vol. 3. 1779-1780. 1951 (ISBN 0-691-04535-6); Vol. 4. 1780-1781. 1951 (ISBN 0-691-04536-4); Vol. 5. 1781. 1952 (ISBN 0-691-04537-2); Vol. 6. 1781-1784. 1952 (ISBN 0-691-04538-0); Vol. 7. 1784-1785. 1953 (ISBN 0-691-04539-9); Vol. 8. 1785. 1953 (ISBN 0-691-04540-2); Vol. 9. 1785-1786. 1954 (ISBN 0-691-04541-0); Vol. 10. 1786-1787. 1954 (ISBN 0-691-04542-9); Vol. 11. 1787. 1955 (ISBN 0-691-04543-7); Vol. 12. 1787-1788. 1955 (ISBN 0-691-04544-5); Vol. 13. Mar.-Oct. 1788. 1956 (ISBN 0-691-04545-3); Vol. 14. Oct. 1788-Mar. 1789. 1958 (ISBN 0-691-04546-1); Vol. 15. Mar.-Nov. 1789. 1958 (ISBN 0-691-04547-X); Vol. 16. Nov. 1789-Aug. 1790. 1961 (ISBN 0-691-04548-8); Vol. 17. July to Dec. 1790. 1965 (ISBN 0-691-04549-6); Vol. 18. Nov. 1790-Jan. 1791. 1971 (ISBN 0-691-04582-8); Vol. 19. Jan. 24-March 10, 1791 (ISBN 0-691-04583-6); Vol. 20. 808p. 1982. 50.00 (ISBN 0-691-04686-7). Vols. 1-20. 52.50x ea.. Princeton U Pr.

Papers of Thomas Jefferson, Vol. 21: Index, Volumes 1-20, 1760-1791. Thomas Jefferson. Ed. by Charles T. Cullen. LC 50-7486. 300p. 1982. 52.50x (ISBN 0-691-04687-5). Princeton U Pr.

Papers of Thomas Jefferson, Vol. 22: 6 August-31 December 1791. Charles T. Cullen. LC 50-7486. (Illus.). 700p. 1986. text ed. 52.50x (ISBN 0-691-04728-6). Princeton U Pr.

Papers of Thomas Jefferson: 1 January-31 May 1792, Vol. 23. Ed. by Charles T. Cullen. (Illus.). 1987. lib. bdg. 52.50 (ISBN 0-691-04739-1). Princeton U Pr.

Papers of Thomas Jordan Jarvis, Vol. 1, 1869-1882. Ed. by Wilfred B. Yearns. (Illus.). xv, 680p. 1969. 15.00x (ISBN 0-86526-045-1). NC Archives.

Papers of Thomas Ruffin, 4 Vols. Thomas Ruffin. Ed. by J. G. Hamilton. LC 74-174788. Repr. of 1920 ed. Set. 150.00 (ISBN 0-404-04630-4); 37.50 ea. Vol. 1 (ISBN 0-404-04631-2). Vol. 2 (ISBN 0-404-04632-0). Vol. 3 (ISBN 0-404-04633-9). Vol. 4 (ISBN 0-404-04634-7). AMS Pr.

Papers of Ulysses S. Grant, Vol. 11, June 1 - August 15, 1864. Ed. by Ulysses S. Grant & John Y. Simon. LC 67-10725. (Illus.). 512p. 1984. 47.50x (ISBN 0-8093-1117-8). S Ill U Pr.

Papers of Ulysses S. Grant, Vol. 12, August 16 - November 15, 1864. Ed. by Ulysses S. Grant & John Y. Simon. LC 67-10725. (Illus.). 525p. 1984. 47.50x (ISBN 0-8093-1118-6). S Ill U Pr.

Papers of Ulysses S. Grant: February 21 to April 30, 1865. Ed. by John Y. Simon & David L. Wilson. (Papers of Ulysses S. Grant: Vol. 14). (Illus.). 500p. 1985. text ed. 47.50x (ISBN 0-8093-1198-4). S Ill U Pr.

Papers of Ulysses S. Grant: November 16, 1864 to February 20, 1865. Ed. by John Y. Simon & David L. Wilson. (Papers of Ulysses S. Grant: Vol. 13). (Illus.). 512p. 1985. text ed. 47.50x (ISBN 0-8093-1197-6). S Ill U Pr.

Papers of Ulysses S. Grant: Vol. 1-1837-1861. Ed. by Ulysses S. Grant & John Y. Simon. LC 67-10725. (Illus.). 498p. 1967. 25.00x (ISBN 0-8093-0248-9). S Ill U Pr.

Papers of Ulysses S. Grant, Vol. 10: January 1 - May 31, 1864. Ed. by Ulysses S. Grant & John Y. Simon. LC 67-10725. (Illus.). 648p. 1982. 47.50x (ISBN 0-8093-0980-7). S Ill U Pr.

Papers of Ulysses S. Grant, Vol. 15: May 1-December 31, 1865. Ed. by John Y. Simon & David L. Wilson. (Illus.). 632p. 1988. text ed. 47.50x (ISBN 0-8093-1466-5). S Ill U Pr.

Papers of Ulysses S. Grant, Vol. 16: 1866. Ed. by John Y. Simon & David L. Wilson. (Illus.). 576p. 1988. text ed. 47.50x (ISBN 0-8093-1467-3). S Ill U Pr.

Papers of Ulysses S. Grant, Vol. 2: April to September, 1861. Ed. by Ulysses S. Grant & John Y. Simon. LC 67-10725. (Illus.). 437p. 1969. 25.00x (ISBN 0-8093-0366-3). S Ill U Pr.

Papers of Ulysses S. Grant, Vol. 4: January 8 to March 31, 1862. Ed. by Ulysses S. Grant & John Y. Simon. LC 67-10725. (Illus.). 558p. 1972. 25.00x (ISBN 0-8093-0507-0). S Ill U Pr.

Papers of Ulysses S. Grant, Vol. 5: April 1 to August 31, 1862. Ed. by Ulysses S. Grant & John Y. Simon. LC 67-10725. (Illus.). 488p. 1973. 32.50x (ISBN 0-8093-0636-0). S Ill U Pr.

Papers of Ulysses S. Grant, Vol. 6: September 1 to December 8, 1862. Ed. by Ulysses S. Grant & John Y. Simon. LC 67-10725. (Illus.). 516p. 1977. 35.00x (ISBN 0-8093-0694-8). S Ill U Pr.

Papers of Ulysses S. Grant, Vol. 7: December 9, 1862 to March 31, 1863. Ed. by Ulysses S. Grant & John Y. Simon. LC 67-10725. (Illus.). 612p. 1979. 40.00x (ISBN 0-8093-0880-0). S Ill U Pr.

Papers of Ulysses S. Grant, Vol. 8: April 1 to July 6, 1863. Ed. by Ulysses S. Grant & John Y. Simon. LC 67-10725. (Illus.). 634p. 1979. 40.00x (ISBN 0-8093-0884-3). S Ill U Pr.

Papers of Ulysses S. Grant, Vol. 9: July 7-December 31, 1863. Ed. by Ulysses S. Grant & John Y. Simon. LC 67-10725. (Illus.). 724p. 1982. 47.50x (ISBN 0-8093-0979-3). S Ill U Pr.

Papers of Ulysses S. Grant, Vol.3: October 1, 1861 to January 7, 1862. Ed. by Ulysses S. Grant & John Y. Simon. LC 67-10725. (Illus.). 513p. 1970. 25.00x (ISBN 0-8093-0471-6). S Ill U Pr.

Papers of Wade Hampton Frost, M.D., a Contribution to Epidemiological Method. Wade H. Frost. Ed. by Barbara G. Rosenkrantz & Kenneth F. Maxcy. LC 76-40635. (Public Health in America Ser.). (Illus.). 1977. Repr. of 1941 ed. lib. bdg. 46.50x (ISBN 0-405-09826-X). Ayer Co Pubs.

Papers of Walter Clark, 2 vols. Walter Clark. Ed. by Aubrey J. Brooks & Hugh T. Lefler. Incl. Vol. 1. xv, 607p. 1948 (ISBN 0-8078-0526-2); Vol. 2. vii, 608p. 1950 (ISBN 0-8078-0591-2). 27.50x ea. U of NC Pr.

Papers of Wilbur & Orville Wright, 2 Vols. Ed. by Marvin W. McFarland. LC 79-169428. (Literature & History of Aviation Ser.). 1971. Repr. of 1953 ed. Set. 86.00 (ISBN 0-405-03771-6); 43.00 ea. Vol. 1 (ISBN 0-405-03814-3). Vol.2 (ISBN 0-405-03815-1). Ayer Co Pubs.

Papers of William Alexander Graham, 7 vols. Ed. by J. G. Hamilton. Incl. Vol. 1, 1825-1837. xxiv, 555p. 1957. 15.00x (ISBN 0-86526-035-4); Vol. 2, 1838-1844. xviii, 552p. 1959. 15.00x (ISBN 0-86526-036-2); Vol. 3, 1845-1850. xvi, 541p. 1960. 15.00x (ISBN 0-86526-037-0); Vol. 4, 1851-1856. xxix, 701p. 1961. 15.00x (ISBN 0-86526-038-9); Vol. 5, 1857-1863. Ed. by J. G. Hamilton & Max R. Williams. xxiii, 591p. 1973. 15.00x (ISBN 0-86526-039-7); Vol. 6, 1864-1865. Ed. by Max R. Williams. 1976. 16.00x (ISBN 0-86526-040-0); Vol. 7, 1866-1868. Ed. by Max R. Williams. xxviii, 679p. 1984. 30.00x (ISBN 0-86526-212-8). Set (ISBN 0-86526-034-6). NC Archives.

Papers of William H. Seward: Guide & Index to the Microfilm Collection. Research Publications. Ed. by Janice L. Budeit. 402p. 1983. 500.00 (ISBN 0-89235-073-3). Res Pubns CT.

Papers of William Livingston, Vol. III. Ed. by Carl E. Prince. 576p. 1986. text ed. 50.00 (ISBN 0-8135-1144-5). Rutgers U Pr.

Papers of William Livingston, Vol. IV. Ed. by Carl E. Prince & Mary L. Lustig. (Illus.). 590p. 1987. text ed. 50.00 (ISBN 0-8135-1213-1). Rutgers U Pr.

Papers of William Penn: Bibliography of the Publications of William Penn, Vol. V. Ed. by Edwin Bronner & David Fraser. (Illus.). 576p. 1986. 46.25 (ISBN 0-8122-8019-9). U of Pa Pr.

Papers of William Penn: Vol. II, 1680-1684. William Penn. Ed. by Richard S. Dunn & Mary M. Dunn. LC 82-54052. 710p. 1982. 57.50x (ISBN 0-8122-7852-6). U of Pa Pr.

Papers of William Penn: 1644-1679, Vol. 1. William Penn. Ed. by Mary M. Dunn et al. 703p. 1981. 48.25 (ISBN 0-8122-7800-3). U of Pa Pr.

Papers of William Penn: 1685-1700, Vol. III. Ed. by Mary M. Dunn & Richard S. Dunn. 796p. 1986. 52.50 (ISBN 0-8122-8029-6). U of Pa Pr.

Papers of William Penn: 1701-1718, Vol. IV. Ed. by Mary M. Dunn & Richard S. Dunn. 720p. 1987. 52.50 (ISBN 0-8122-8050-4). U of Pa Pr.

Papers of Willie Person Mangum, 5 vols. Ed. by Henry T. Shanks. Incl. Vol 1, 1807-1832. xii, 613p. 1950. 15.00x (ISBN 0-86526-050-8); Vol. 2, 1833-1838. xxi, 573p. 1952. 15.00x (ISBN 0-86526-051-6); Vol. 3, 1839-1843. xxi, 521p. 1953. 15.00x (ISBN 0-86526-052-4); Vol. 4, 1844-1846. xxviii, 579p. 1955. 15.00x (ISBN 0-86526-053-2); Vol. 5, 1847-1894. xxxvii, 812p. 1956. 15.00x (ISBN 0-86526-054-0). (Illus.). Set. 15.00x ea. (ISBN 0-86526-049-4). NC Archives.

Papers of Woodrow Wilson, 30 vols, Vols. 1-7. Woodrow Wilson. Ed. by Arthur S. Link et al. Incl. Vol. 1. 1856-1880. 1966 (ISBN 0-691-04550-X); Vol. 2. 1881-1884. 1967 (ISBN 0-691-04551-8); Vol. 3. 1884-1885. 1967 (ISBN 0-691-04552-6); Vol. 4. 1885. 1968 (ISBN 0-691-04553-4); Vol. 5. 1885-1888. 1968 (ISBN 0-691-04587-9); Vol. 6. 1888-1890. 1969 (ISBN 0-691-04592-5); Vol. 7. 1890-1892. 1969 (ISBN 0-691-04596-8). 52.50x ea. Princeton U Pr.

Papers of Woodrow Wilson, 30 vols, Vols. 8-17. Woodrow Wilson. Ed. by Arthur S. Link. Incl. Vol. 8. 1892-1894. 1970 (ISBN 0-691-04599-2); Vol. 9. 1894-1896. 1970 (ISBN 0-691-04603-4); Vol. 10. 1896-1898. 1971 (ISBN 0-691-04508-9); Vol. 11. 1898-1900. 1971 (ISBN 0-691-04606-9); Vol. 12. 1900-1901. 1972 (ISBN 0-691-04612-3); Vol. 13. Contents & Index, Vols. 1-12, 1856-1900. 1977 (ISBN 0-691-04642-5); Vol. 14. 1901-1902. 1972 (ISBN 0-691-04614-X); Vol. 15. 1903-1905. 1973 (ISBN 0-691-04617-4); Vol. 16. 1905-1907. 1973 (ISBN 0-691-04620-4); Vol. 17. 1907-1908. 1974 (ISBN 0-691-04621-2). 52.50x ea. Princeton U Pr.

Papers of Woodrow Wilson, Vol. 18-33. Woodrow Wilson. Ed. by Arthur S. Link. Incl. Vol. 18. 1908-1909. 1974. 50.00 ea. (ISBN 0-691-04631-X); Vol. 19. 1909-1910. 1975. 50.00 ea. (ISBN 0-691-04633-6); Vol. 20. Jauary - July, 1910. 1975. 50.00 ea. (ISBN 0-691-04635-2); Vol. 21. July-Nov. 1910. 1976. 50.00 ea. (ISBN 0-691-04636-0); Vol. 22. 1911. 1976-1977. 50.00 ea. (ISBN 0-691-04638-7); Vol. 23. 1911-1912. 1976-1977. 50.00 ea. (ISBN 0-691-04643-3); Vol. 24. January-August, 1912. (Illus.). 1977. 50.00 ea. (ISBN 0-691-04645-X); Vol. 25. August-November, 1912. (Illus.). 1978. 50.00 ea. (ISBN 0-691-04650-6); Vol. 26. Contents & Index, Vols. 14-25, 1902-1912. 1980. 25.00 (ISBN 0-691-04664-6); Vol. 27. January-June 1913. (Illus.). 1978. 50.00 ea. (ISBN 0-691-04652-2); Vol. 28. 1913. (Illus.). 1978. 50.00 ea. (ISBN 0-691-04653-0); Vol. 29. 1913-1914. 1979. 30.00 ea. (ISBN 0-691-04659-X); Vol. 30. May - September 1914. info. 30.00 ea. (ISBN 0-691-04663-8); Vol. 31. September-December 1914. 1979. 30.00 ea. (ISBN 0-691-04666-2); Vol. 32. January - April 1915. 1979. 30.00 ea. (ISBN 0-691-04667-0); Vol. 33. April-July 1915. (Illus.). 30.00 ea. (ISBN 0-691-04668-9). LC 66-10880. 52.50x ea. Princeton U Pr.

Papers of Woodrow Wilson: August 21-November 10, 1917, Vol. 44. Woodrow Wilson. Ed. by Arthur S. Link et al. LC 66-10880. (Papers of Woodrow Wilson). (Illus.). 568p. 1984. 52.50x (ISBN 0-691-04704-9). Princeton U Pr.

Papers of Woodrow Wilson: February 8-March 16, 1919, Vol. 55. Arthur S. Link et al. Ed. by David W. Hirst & John E. Little. (Illus.). 604p. 1986. text ed. 52.50x (ISBN 0-691-04737-5). Princeton U Pr.

Papers of Woodrow Wilson: January 11-February 7, 1919, Vol. 54. Ed. by Arthur S. Link et al. (Illus.). 616p. 1986. text ed. 52.50x (ISBN 0-691-04736-7). Princeton U Pr.

Papers of Woodrow Wilson: January 16 to March 12, 1918, Vol. 46. Woodrow Wilson. Ed. by Arthur S. Linl & David W. Hirst. LC 66-10880. 664p. 1984. 52.50x (ISBN 0-691-04706-5). Princeton U Pr.

Papers of Woodrow Wilson: November 11, 1917 to January 15, 1918, Vol. 45. Woodrow Wilson. Ed. by Arthur S. Link. LC 66-10880. (Papers of Woodrow Wilson). (Illus.). 625p. 1984. 52.50x (ISBN 0-691-04705-7). Princeton U Pr.

Papers of Woodrow Wilson: November 9, 1918-January 11, 1919, Vol. 53. Ed. by Arthur S. Link & David W. Hirst. LC 66-10880. (Illus.). 736p. 1985. 52.50x (ISBN 0-691-04731-6). Princeton U Pr.

Papers of Woodrow Wilson: September 14 to November 8, 1918, Vol. 51. Ed. by Arthur S. Link. LC 66-10880. (Illus.). 648p. 1985. text ed. 52.50x (ISBN 0-691-04730-8). Princeton U Pr.

Papers of Woodrow Wilson: The Complete Press Conferences, 1913-1919, Vol. 50. Ed. by Arthur S. Link & Robert C. Hilderbrand. LC 66-10880. (Illus.). 688p. 1985. text ed. 52.50x (ISBN 0-691-04710-3). Princeton U Pr.

Papers of Woodrow Wilson: Vol. 34, July-September, 1915. Woodrow Wilson. Ed. by David W. Hirst et al. LC 66-10880. (Illus.). 1980. 52.50x (ISBN 0-691-04673-5). Princeton U Pr.

Papers of Woodrow Wilson, Vol. 36. Woodrow Wilson. Ed. by David W. Hirst et al. LC 66-10880. (Illus.). 650p. 1981. January-May, 1916. 52.50x (ISBN 0-691-04682-4); Vol. 37: May 9 - August 7, 1916. 52.50x (ISBN 0-691-04684-0). Princeton U Pr.

Papers of Woodrow Wilson, Vol. 38: August 7-November 19, 1916. Woodrow Wilson. Ed. by Arthur S. Link et al. LC 66-10880. (Illus.). 720p. 1981. 52.50x (ISBN 0-691-04689-1). Princeton U Pr.

Papers of Woodrow Wilson, Vol. 39: Content & Index to Volumes 27-38, 1913-1916. Ed. by Arthur S. Link et al. LC 66-10880. 300p. 1985. text ed. 52.50x (ISBN 0-691-04696-4). Princeton U Pr.

Papers of Woodrow Wilson, Vol. 41. Woodrow Wilson. Ed. by Arthur S. Link et al. (Papers of Woodrow Wilson Ser.). 1982. 52.50x (ISBN 0-691-04691-3). Princeton U Pr.

Papers of Woodrow Wilson, Vol. 42. Woodrow Wilson. Ed. by Arthur S. Link et al. (Papers of Woodrow Wilson Ser.). 1982. 52.50x (ISBN 0-691-04692-1). Princeton U Pr.

Papers of Woodrow Wilson, Vol. 43: June 25-August 20, 1917. Woodrow Wilson. Ed. by Arthur S. Link. LC 66-10880. (Vol. 43). (Illus.). 552p. 1983. 52.50x (ISBN 0-691-04701-4). Princeton U Pr.

Papers of Woodrow Wilson, Vol. 47: March 13-May 12, 1918. Ed. by Arthur S. Link. LC 66-10880. (Papers of Woodrow Wilson). (Illus.). 632p. 1984. text ed. 52.50x (ISBN 0-691-04707-3). Princeton U Pr.

Papers of Woodrow Wilson, Vol. 48: May 13-July 17, 1918. Ed. by Arthur S. Link. LC 66-10880. (Illus.). 585p. 1985. text ed. 52.50x (ISBN 0-691-04708-1). Princeton U Pr.

Papers of Woodrow Wilson, Vol. 49: July 18-September 18, 1918. Ed. by Arthur S. Link. LC 66-10880. (Illus.). 665p. 1985. text ed. 52.50x (ISBN 0-691-04709-X). Princeton U Pr.

Papers of Woodrow Wilson, Vol. 52: Contents & Index, Vol. 40-49, 51. Ed. by Arthur S. Link et al. 240p. 1987. text ed. 52.50x (ISBN 0-691-04744-8). Princeton U Pr.

Papers of Woodrow Wilson, Vol. 56: March 17 - April 4, 1919. Ed. by Arthur S. Link et al. (Illus.). 696p. 1987. text ed. 52.50x (ISBN 0-691-04742-1). Princeton U Pr.

Papers of Woodrow Wilson, Vol. 57: April 5 - April 22, 1919. Arthur S. Link et al. Ed. by Frederick Aandahl. (Illus.). 704p. 1987. text ed. 52.50x (ISBN 0-691-04743-X). Princeton U Pr.

Papers of Woodrow Wilson, Vol. 58: April 23 to May 9, 1919. Ed. by Arthur S. Link et al. (Illus.). 696p. 1988. text ed. 52.50 (ISBN 0-691-04748-0). Princeton U Pr.

Papers of Woodrow Wilson, Vol. 59: May 10 - May 31, 1919. Ed. by Arthur S. Link et al. (Illus.). 744p. 1988. 52.50x (ISBN 0-691-04754-5). Princeton U Pr.

Papers of Woodrow Wilson: 1915 to 1916, Vol. 35. Woodrow Wilson. Ed. by David W. Hirst et al. LC 66-10880. (Illus.). 568p. 1981. 30.00x (ISBN 0-691-04676-X). Princeton U Pr.

Papers of Zebulon Baird Vance, Vol. 1, 1843-1862. Ed. by Frontis W. Johnston. (Illus.). lxxiv, 475p. 1963. 15.00x (ISBN 0-86526-071-0). NC Archives.

Papers on Accounting History. R. H. Parker. LC 83-49443. (Accounting History & the Development of a Profession Ser.). 184p. 1984. lib. bdg. 20.00 (ISBN 0-8240-6310-4). Garland Pub.

Papers on African Literature: Given at the Seminar Series on African Art & Literature, Sheffield University, 1975. Ed. by Christopher Heywood. (Sheffield Papers on Literature & Society: 1). pap. 33.80 (2022538). Bks Demand UMI.

Papers on Central California Prehistory, No. 1. Gary S. Breschini & Trudy Haversat. (Coyote Press Archives of California Prehistory Ser.: No. 3). (Illus.). iv, 88p. (Orig.). 1984. pap. 4.95x (ISBN 1-55567-023-7). Coyote Press.

Papers on Cephalopod Paleobiology & Phylogeny. Ed. by Adolf Seilacher et al. (Illus.). 181p. (Orig.). 1983. pap. text ed. 98.50x (ISBN 0-317-63392-9, Pub. by E Schweizerbartsche). Coronet Bks.

Papers on Discourse. Joseph E. Grimes. (Publications in Linguistics & Related Fields Ser: No. 51). 389p. 1978. pap. 13.00x (ISBN 0-88312-061-5); microfiche (5) 10.00 (ISBN 0-88312-461-0). Summer Inst Ling.

Papers on Fourth International Tanker Safety Conference. INTASAFCON 4 Staff & ICS Staff. 1979. 162.00x (ISBN 0-317-61251-4, Pub Witherby & Co England). State Mutual Bk.

Papers on Fuchsian Functions. H. Poincare. Tr. by J. Stillwell from Fr. (Illus.). iv, 483p. 1985. 38.00 (ISBN 0-387-96215-8). Springer-Verlag.

Papers on Functional Sentence Perspective. International Symposium on Functional Sentence Perspective, 1st, Marienbad, Czechoslovakia. Ed. by F. Danes. (Janua Linguarum, Ser. Minor: No. 147). 222p. (Eng. & Czech.). 1974. pap. text ed. 20.80x (ISBN 90-2793-202-6). Mouton.

Papers on Godliness. Catherine Booth. (Writings of Catherine Booth Ser.). 1986. Repr. of 1890 ed. deluxe ed. 4.95 (ISBN 0-86544-032-8). Salvation Army.

Papers on Grammar, Vol. 1. Ed. by G. Calboli. 1980. pap. text ed. 24.95 (ISBN 0-905205-59-6, Pub. by F Cairns). Longwood Pub Group.

Papers on Grammar II. Ed. by G. Calboli. (Orig.). 1986. pap. text ed. 24.95 (ISBN 0-905205-60-X, Pub. by F Cairns). Longwood Pub Group.

Papers on Group Theory & Topology. M. Dehn. Tr. by J. Stillwell. (Illus.). 400p. 1987. 34.00 (ISBN 0-387-96416-9). Springer-Verlag.

Papers on Industrial Water & Industrial Waste. American Society for Testing & Materials Staff. LC 63-12705. (American Society for Testing & Materials Special Technical Publication Ser.: No. 337). pap. 20.00 (ISBN 0-317-09816-0, 2000143). Bks Demand UMI.

Papers on Inter-Racial Problems. facs. ed. Ed. by G. Spiller. LC 70-93419. (Black Heritage Library Collection). 1911. 21.00 (ISBN 0-8369-8660-1). Ayer Co Pubs.

Para Servirle. Max Novitz. (Orig.). (gr. 7-9). 1982. wkbk. 12.58 (ISBN 0-87720-523-X). AMSCO Sch.
Para: The Fall of Etan: Prelude. R. Vaughn Abrams. LC 84-24011. (Illus.). 384p. 1985. 17.95 (ISBN 0-931783-00-3). Seven Suns.
Para Todos los Panes no Estan Todos Presentes. Ricardo Cobian. Ed. by Alurista & Xelina. LC 84-60899. (Milpa Poetica). 64p. (Orig.). 1985. pap. 5.00x (ISBN 0-939558-07-6). Maize Pr.
Para-Transit: Neglected Options for Urban Mobility. Ronald F. Kirby et al. LC 74-84666. (Illus.). 1975. 9.95 (ISBN 0-87766-130-8, 87000); pap. 12.95 (ISBN 0-87766-121-9, 78000). Urban Inst.
Para una Lectura Americana del Barroco Mexicano: Sor Juana y Siguenza y Gongora. Rafael Catala. 200p. (Orig., Span.). 1987. pap. text ed. 8.95 (ISBN 0-910235-07-4). Prisma Bks.
Parabellum Automatic Pistol. 1986. lib. bdg. 79.95 (ISBN 0-8490-3482-5). Gordon Pr.
Parable a Day Keeps the Devil at Bay. Wanda Vassallo. (Orig.). 1988. pap. 5.00 (ISBN 0-915541-36-X). Star Bks Inc.
Parable of Jesus & Santa. Bobbie M. Grimes. LC 84-90331. (Illus.). 40p. (ps-5). 1984. 14.95 (ISBN 0-9613328-0-8). B & D Pub.
Parable of Pa Diggle's Son. Bruce Porter. (Illus.). 40p. (Orig.). (gr. 3 up). 1987. pap. 3.95 (ISBN 0-939925-11-7). R C Law & Co.
Parable of the Blind. Gert Hofmann. Tr. by Christopher Middleton from Ger. LC 85-24600. 160p. 1986. 14.95 (ISBN 0-88064-051-0). Fromm Intl Pub.
Parable of the Father's Heart. G. Campbell Morgan. (Morgan Library). 96p. 1981. pap. 2.95 (ISBN 0-8010-6118-0). Baker Bk.
Parable of the Tribes. Andrew B. Schmookler. LC 83-9213. 385p. 1984. 35.00x (ISBN 0-520-04874-1). U of Cal Pr.
Parable of the Tribes: The Problem of Power in Social Evolution. Andrew B. Schmookler. 1986. pap. 9.95 (ISBN 0-395-40005-8). HM.
Parable of the Wicked Tenants: An Inquiry into Parable Interpretation. Klyne Snodgrass. 150p. 1983. pap. 53.50x (Pub. by J. C. B. Mohr BRD). Coronet Bks.
Parable of Willie Juan. Brennan Manning. 1985. 2.95 (ISBN 0-87193-162-1). Dimension Bks.
Parables. Madeleine I. Boucher. LC 80-85421. (New Testament Message Ser.: Vol. 7). 12.95 (ISBN 0-89453-195-6); pap. 7.95 (ISBN 0-89453-130-1). M Glazier.
Parables, 4 vols. Nick Butterworth. LC 85-21816. (Illus.). (ps-3). 1986. 3.95 ea. Vol. 1: The House on the Rock (ISBN 0-88070-146-3). Vol. 2: The Lost Sheep (ISBN 0-88070-147-1). The Two Sons (ISBN 0-88070-145-5) (ISBN 0-88070-148-X). Multnomah.
Parables & Miracles of Jesus. G. L. LeFevre. (Bible Quiz 'n Tattletotals Ser.). 16p. (Orig.). (gr. 3-6). 1982. pap. 0.98 (ISBN 0-87239-580-4, 2807). Standard Pub.
Parables & Paradoxes: Parabeln Und Paradoxe. Franz Kafka. LC 61-14917. (Eng. & Ger.). 1961. pap. 6.95 (ISBN 0-8052-0422-9). Schocken.
Parables & Similes of the Rabbis, Agricultural & Pastoral. Asher Feldman. LC 75-23127. 1975. Repr. of 1927 ed. lib. bdg. 32.00 (ISBN 0-8414-4229-0). Folcroft.
Parables at Work. John C. Purdy. LC 84-17323. 132p. 1986. 10.95 (ISBN 0-664-21268-9); pap. 7.95 (ISBN 0-664-24640-0). Westminster John Knox.
Parables by the Sea. Pamela Reeve. LC 77-6209. (Illus.). 1976. gift ed. o.p. 5.95 (ISBN 0-930014-10-3); pap. 5.95 (ISBN 0-930014-11-1). Multnomah.
Parables for Christian Living. Douglas Beyer. 112p. 1985. pap. 5.95 (ISBN 0-8170-1074-2). Judson.
Parables for Christmas. John Killinger. 80p. (Orig.). 1985. pap. 4.25 (ISBN 0-687-30061-4). Abingdon.
Parables for Little People. Lawrence Castagnola. LC 86-62628. (Illus.). 101p. (Orig.). (gr. 4 up). 1982. pap. text ed. 7.95. Resource Pubns.
Parables for Now. Edmund Flood. 4.95 (ISBN 0-87193-186-9). Dimension Bks.
Parables for Young Teens: Twenty-Six Junior High Programs. Susan Titus. (gr. 7-9). 1986. 4.95 (ISBN 0-87403-150-8, 3412). Standard Pub.
Parables from Nature. John C. Reid. (ps-6). 1954. 4.95 (ISBN 0-8028-4025-6). Eerdmans.
Parables from the Animal Kingdom. John C. Reid. Ed. by Theresa Hayes. LC 87-32922. (Illus.). 96p. (ps-3). 1988. 5.95 (ISBN 0-87403-500-7, 14-02872). Standard Pub.
Parables from the Cross. Kenneth Rogahn & Walter Schoedel. 1981. pap. 5.95 (ISBN 0-570-03847-2, 12-2950). Concordia.
Parables in Depth. George Drew. 55p. (Orig.). 1982. pap. 6.95 (ISBN 0-940754-18-5). Ed Ministries.
Parables in Gospels. John Drury. LC 84-27652. 192p. 1985. 14.95x (ISBN 0-8245-0655-3). Crossroad NY.
Parables in Matthew's Gospel. R. K. Campbell. 1978. pap. 1.95 (ISBN 0-915374-42-0, 42-0). Rapids Christian.
Parables in Matthew's Gospel: Matthew 13. R. K. Campbell. tchr's lesson outline 3.95 (ISBN 0-88172-011-9). Believers Bkshelf.
Parables in Verse. Betty Kettlewell. 1987. 5.95 (ISBN 0-533-07190-9). Vantage.
Parables Jesus Told. Ed. by Patricia Mahany. (Classroom Activity Bks.). (Illus.). 48p. (Orig.). (ps-k). 1984. pap. 2.95 (ISBN 0-87239-714-9, 2444). Standard Pub.
Parables of Christ, Vol. 1. Gordon Lindsay. (Span.). 1.50 (ISBN 0-89985-980-1). Christ Nations.
Parables of Grace. Robert F. Capon. 1988. 14.95 (ISBN 0-8028-3648-8). Eerdmans.
Parables of Jesus. James M. Boice. 1983. pap. 6.95 (ISBN 0-8024-0163-5). Moody.
Parables of Jesus. Julianne Booth. (Arch Bks.). (gr. k-4). 1982. pap. 1.29 (ISBN 0-570-06163-6, 59-1309). Concordia.
Parables of Jesus. George A. Buttrick. (Minister's Paperback Library Ser). 274p. 1973. pap. 9.95 (ISBN 0-8010-0597-3). Baker Bk.
Parables of Jesus. Tomie DePaola. LC 86-18323. (Illus.). 32p. (gr. 1-4). 1987. PLB 14.95 (ISBN 0-8234-0636-9). Holiday.
Parables of Jesus. Herman Hendrickx. LC 86-46241. 208p. (Orig.). 1987. pap. 14.95 (ISBN 0-06-254815-8, HarpR). Har-Row.
Parables of Jesus. 2nd ed. Joachim Jeremias. LC 63-22114. (Illus.). 248p. 1972. pap. text ed. 8.95 (ISBN 0-02-360510-3, Pub. by Scribner). Macmillan.
Parables of Jesus. Simon Kistemaker. 264p. 1980. pap. 11.95 (ISBN 0-8010-5462-1). Baker Bk.
Parables of Jesus, 2 vols. Neil R. Lightfoot. (Way of Life Ser.). 1986. pap. 3.95 ea. Vol. 1, 95p; Vol. 2, 95p. Abilene Christ U.
Parables of Jesus. Geraldine Tapia. 144p. 1987. 10.95 (ISBN 0-317-53382-7). Todd & Honeywell.
Parables of Jesus, Vol. 1. Neil Lightfoot. 1986. pap. 3.95. Abilene Christ U.
Parables of Jesus: A History of Interpretation & Bibliography. Warren S. Kissinger. LC 78-23271. (American Theological Library Association (ATLA) Bibliography Ser.: No. 4). 463p. 1979. lib. bdg. 30.00 (ISBN 0-8108-1186-3). Scarecrow.
Parables of Jesus in Matthew 13. Jack D. Kingsbury. LC 76-40850. 1976. pap. text ed. 12.95 (ISBN 0-915644-08-8). Clayton Pub Hse.
Parables of Jesus: Pt. Three see Story of Jesus.
Parables of Jesus: Twenty Stories with a Message. Daniel L. Lowery. 64p. 1987. pap. 1.95 (ISBN 0-89243-266-7). Liguori Pubns.
Parables of Kierkegaard. Ed. by Thomas C. Oden. LC 78-51184. (Illus.). 1978. 18.50x (ISBN 0-691-07174-8). Princeton U Pr.
Parables of Our Lord. William Arnot. LC 80-8065. 532p. 1981. 14.95 (ISBN 0-8254-2119-5). Kregel.
Parables of Our Lord & Savior Jesus Christ. John E. Millais. 7.75 (ISBN 0-8446-5225-3). Peter Smith.
Parables of Our Lord & Savior Jesus Christ. Illus. by John E. Millais. LC 74-20328. (Illus.). 128p. 1975. pap. 3.95 (ISBN 0-486-20494-4). Dover.
Parables of Peanuts. Robert L. Short. 1978. pap. 1.95 (ISBN 0-449-23677-3, Crest). Fawcett.
Parables of the Day. Arthur Shaw. 56p. (Orig.). 1988. pap. 5.00 (ISBN 0-912395-13-3). Millers River Pub Co.
Parables of the Kingdom. Robert F. Capon. 176p. 1988. pap. 7.95 (ISBN 0-310-42671-5, 17040P). Zondervan.
Parables of the Kingdom. C. H. Dodd. 176p. 1977. pap. text ed. write for info. (ISBN 0-02-330460-X, Pub. by Scribner). Macmillan.
Parables of the Kingdom. John MacArthur, Jr. (John MacArthur's Bible Studies). (Orig.). 1985. pap. 4.95 (ISBN 0-8024-5112-8). Moody.
Parables of the Kingdom. Morris Venden. (Anchor Ser.). 79p. (Orig.). 1987. pap. 5.95 (ISBN 0-8163-0680-X). Pacific Pr Pub Assn.
Parables of Theory: Jean Ricardou's Metafiction. Lynn Higgins. LC 83-50515. 203p. 1984. pap. 13.00 (ISBN 0-917786-43-2). Summa Pubns.
Parables, Psalms, Prayers. Sean Freeman. 1985. 10.95 (ISBN 0-88347-185-X). Thomas More.
Parables: The Greatest Stories Ever Told. John White. (LifeGuide Bible Studies). (Orig.). 1988. pap. 2.95 (ISBN 0-8308-1037-4). Inter-Varsity.
Parables: Their Literary & Existential Dimension. Dan O. Via, Jr. LC 67-11910. 232p. 1974. pap. 6.95 (ISBN 0-8006-1392-9, 1-1392). Fortress.
Parables Then & Now. Archibald M. Hunter. LC 72-170113. 128p. 1972. pap. 6.95 (ISBN 0-664-24940-X). Westminster John Knox.
Parables Told by Jesus: Contemporary Approach. Wilfrid J. Harrington. LC 74-12395. 135p. (Orig.). 1974. pap. 3.95 (ISBN 0-8189-0296-5). Alba.
Parabola Rasa. D. R. Fosso. LC 84-51413. 72p. 1984. pap. 6.00 (ISBN 0-913773-14-X). S Wright.
Parabolas de Identidad: Realida Interior y Estrategia Narrativa en Tres Novelistas de Postguerra. Bernardo A. Gonzalez. 28.00 (ISBN 0-916379-31-0). Scripta.
Parabolas del Evangelio. Charles L. Neal. 144p. 1983. pap. 3.75 (ISBN 0-311-04338-0). Casa Bautista.
Parabolic Equations on an Infinite Strip. Watson. (Pure & Applied Mathematics Ser.). 256p. 1988. 89.75 (ISBN 0-8247-7999-1). Dekker.
Parabolic Subgroups of Algebraic Groups & Induction. Vella. LC 86-10942. (MEMO Ser.: No. 347). 128p. 1986. pap. text ed. 19.00 (ISBN 0-8218-2348-5). Am Math.
Paraccas Pottery of Ica a Study in Style & Time. D. Menzel. (CU PAAE Ser.). Repr. of 1964 ed. 56.00 (ISBN 0-527-01406-0). Kraus Repr.
Paracellular Pathway: Report of a Conference. Ed. by Stanley Bradley & Elizabeth F. Purcell. LC 82-81100. pap. 97.50 (2026695). Bks Demand UMI.
Paracelsus. 2nd ed. W. Pagel. (Illus.). xii, 400p. 1982. 92.75 (ISBN 3-8055-3518-X). S Karger.
Paracelsus Alchemical Catechism. Theophrastus P. Von Hohenheim. Tr. by A. E. Waite from Lat. 1983. pap. 3.95 (ISBN 0-916411-03-6, Pub. by Alchemical Pr). Holmes Pub.
Paracelsus: Life & Prophecies. 2nd ed. Franz Hartmann. LC 72-81591. 320p. 1988. pap. 12.00 (ISBN 0-89345-234-3, Steinerbooks). Garber Comm.
Paracelsus: Selected Writings. 2nd ed. Paracelsus. Ed. by J. Jacobi. Tr. by Norman Gutterman. (Bollingen Ser.: Vol. 28). (Illus.). 1958. 36.50x (ISBN 0-691-09810-7); pap. 14.95 (ISBN 0-691-01876-6). Princeton U Pr.
Paracelus: His Mystical & Medical Philosophy. Manly P. Hall. pap. 3.95 (ISBN 0-89314-808-3). Philos Res.
Paracelus: Life & Prophecies. Franz Hartmann. LC 72-81591. (Spiritual Science Library: Vol. 26). 320p. 1986. lib. bdg. 20.00 (ISBN 0-89345-034-0, Spiritual Sci Lib). Garber Comm.
Parachute. Richard Lees. (New Fiction Ser.). 304p. (Orig.). 1988. pap. 7.95 (ISBN 0-553-34510-9). Bantam.
Parachute Manual: A Technical Treatise on Aerodynamic Decelerators. 3rd, rev. ed. Dan Poynter. LC 83-13350. (Illus.). 592p. 1984. lab manual 44.95 (ISBN 0-915516-35-7). Para Pub.
Parachute Movement Activities: A Complete Parachute Movement Program for Elementary Grades & Beyond. Ron French & Michael Horvat. Ed. by Frank Alexander. (Illus.). 82p. (Orig.). tchrs ed. 8.95 (ISBN 0-915256-13-4). Front Row.
Parachute Padre: Behind German Lines with the SAS France 1944. J. Fraser McLuskey. 180p. 1986. 49.00x (Pub. by S P A Bks Ltd). State Mutual Bk.
Parachute Play. Liz Wilmes & Dick Wilmes. LC 85-71415. (Illus.). 96p. 1985. pap. 7.95 (ISBN 0-943452-03-1). Building Blocks.
Parachute Poems. Millie M. Wicklund. 1983. pap. 3.00 (ISBN 0-686-47953-X). Ghost Dance.
Parachute Rigger Question Book. Ed. by FAA Staff. (Illus.). 32p. 1986. pap. 7.95 (ISBN 0-317-68791-3). AeroGraphics.
Parachute Rigger Question Book. (FAA-T-8080 9A Ser.). (Illus.). 44p. 1988. pap. 2.25 (S/N 050-007-00778-7). USGPO.
Parachute Rigger Study Guide: Questions, Answers, Explanations & References. Deborah Blackmon & Dan Poynter. (Illus.). 72p. 1988. pap. 14.95 (ISBN 0-915516-63-2). Para Pub.
Parachute Rigging Course: A Course of Study for the FAA Rigger Certificate. 2nd, rev. ed. Dan Poynter. LC 77-71448. (Illus.). 65p. 1981. pap. 11.95 (ISBN 0-915516-14-4). Para Pub.
Parachute Songbook. 1982. pap. text ed. 3.50 (ISBN 0-9607814-0-4). AeroGraphics.
Parachutes & Kisses. Erica Jong. 352p. 1984. 16.95 (ISBN 0-453-00466-0). NAL.
Parachutes & Kisses. Erica Jong. 1985. pap. 4.95 (ISBN 0-451-13877-5, Sig). NAL.
Parachuting: Art of Freefall Relative Work. 2nd, rev. ed. Pat Works & Jan Works. (Illus.). 232p. 1988. pap. text ed. write for info. (ISBN 0-9607814-5-5). Aerographics.
Parachuting for Sport. 2nd ed. Jim Greenwood. (Modern Aircraft Ser.). 1978. 7.95 (ISBN 0-8306-9975-9, 2224H). TAB Bks.
Parachuting I-E Course. 3rd, rev. ed. Dan Poynter. LC 78-50571. (Illus.). 60p. 1978. pap. 9.95 (ISBN 0-915516-18-7). Para Pub.
Parachuting Manual for Square-Tandem Equipment. 3rd, rev. ed. Dan Poynter. LC 84-27374. (Illus.). 24p. (Orig.). 1986. pap. 2.00 (ISBN 0-915516-41-1). Para Pub.
Parachuting Manual with Log. 7th, rev. ed. Dan Poynter. LC 76-14106. (Illus.). 24p. 1984. pap. 1.50 (ISBN 0-915516-11-X); pap. 2.50 (span. ed.) 26 p. (ISBN 84-400-3931-X). Para Pub.
Parachuting: The Skydivers' Handbook. 4th ed. Dan Poynter. LC 77-83469. (Illus.). 180p. 1983. pap. 7.95 (ISBN 0-915516-16-0); pap. 11.95 span. ed. (ISBN 84-283-1386-5). Para Pub.
Parachuting's Unforgettable Jumps III. 3rd ed. Howard Gregory. (Illus.). 552p. 1987. 23.95 (ISBN 0-9607086-4-2). H Gregory.
Paraconsistent Logic: Essays on the Inconsistent. A. I. Arruda et al. Ed. by Graham Priest & Richard Routley. (Analytica Ser.). 700p. 1988. 188.50x (ISBN 3-88405-058-3). Philosophia Pr.
Paracriticisms: Seven Speculations of the Times. Ihab Hassan. LC 74-19108. 200p. 1984. pap. 8.95 (ISBN 0-252-01166-X). U of Ill Pr.
Parade. Donald Crews. LC 82-20927. (Illus.). 32p. (gr. k-3). 1983. 11.75 (ISBN 0-688-01995-1); PLB 11.88 (ISBN 0-688-01996-X). Greenwillow.
Parade. Donald Crews. (Illus.). (ps-3). 1987. 3.95 (ISBN 0-688-06520-1, Mulberry Bks). Morrow.
Parade! Tom Shachtman. LC 85-42795. (Illus.). 64p. (gr. 3-7). 1985. PLB 14.95 (ISBN 0-02-782540-X). Macmillan.
Parade: Cubism As Theater. Richard H. Axsom. LC 78-74361. (Outstanding Dissertations in the Fine Arts, Fourth Ser.). (Illus.). 1979. lib. bdg. 46.00 (ISBN 0-8240-3950-5). Garland Pub.
Parade Ground Soldiers: Military Uniforms & Headress, 1837-1910, in the Collections of the State Historical Society of Wisconsin. J. Phillip Langellier. LC 78-4681. 132p. 1978. pap. 5.00 (ISBN 0-87020-174-3). State Hist Soc Wis.
Parade of Cockeyed Creatures. George Baxt. (Library of Crime Classics). 250p. 1986. pap. 4.95 (ISBN 0-930330-47-1). Intl Polygonics.
Parade of Empty Boots. Charles A. Seltzer. 296p. 1975. Repr. of 1937 ed. lib. bdg. 18.95x (ISBN 0-88411-103-2, Pub. by Aeonian Pr). Amereon Ltd.
Parade of Ghosts. Roger Hecht. LC 75-46071. (Lightning Tree Contemporary Poets: No. 1). 1976. 12.95 (ISBN 0-89016-018-X); pap. 4.95 (ISBN 0-89016-017-1). Lightning Tree.
Parade of Gumdrop Prose. Hunce Voelcker. (Illus.). 3.00 (ISBN 0-917996-04-6). Panjandrum.
Parade of Hearts. Beecham. (Sweet Dreams Romances Ser.: No. 125). 1987. pap. 2.50 (ISBN 0-553-26527-X). Bantam.
Parade of Plays I. Ed. by L. Townsend et al. 96p. 1986. pap. 5.95 (ISBN 0-89191-322-X). Cook.
Parade of Plays II. Ed. by L. Townsend et al. 96p. 1986. pap. 5.95 (ISBN 0-89191-323-8). Cook.
Parade of Plays III. Ed. by L. Townsend et al. 96p. 1987. pap. 5.95 (ISBN 0-89191-281-9). Cook.
Parade of Saints. Mark J. Twomey. LC 82-202387. (Illus.). 176p. (gr. 5-8). 1983. 10.95 (ISBN 0-8146-1275-X). Liturgical Pr.
Parade of Soviet Holidays. Jane W. Watson. LC 73-12785. (Around the World Holidays Ser.). (Illus.). 96p. (gr. 4-7). 1974. PLB 7.12 (ISBN 0-8116-4951-2). Garrard.
Parade of Stories see Child Horizons.
Parade Pony. Illus. by Ellen Blonder. (Fast Rolling Bks.). (Illus.). (ps up). 1986. 6.95 (ISBN 0-448-09882-2, G&D). Putnam Pub Group.
Parades & Politics at Vichy: The French Officer Corps under Marshall Petain. Robert O. Paxton. LC 66-10557. pap. 123.00 (ISBN 0-317-09338-X, 2010571). Bks Demand UMI.
Parades & Power: Street Theatre in Nineteenth Century Philadelphia. Susan G. Davis. (Illus.). 248p. 1986. 32.95 (ISBN 0-87722-394-7). Temple U Pr.
Parades & Power Street Theatre in Nineteenth-Century Philadelphia. Susan G. Davis. 246p. (Orig.). 1988. pap. 10.95 (ISBN 0-520-06374-0). U of Cal Pr.
Parades & Promenades: History of Antrim, N. H. LC 76-30841. (Illus.). 1977. 15.00x (ISBN 0-914016-39-3). Phoenix Pub.
Parade's End. rev. ed. Ford Madox Ford. 1961. 18.45 (ISBN 0-394-43972-4). Knopf.
Parade's End: Consisting of "Some Do Not", "No More Parades", "A Man Could Stand up", & "The Last Post". Ford Madox Ford. LC 79-2158. 1979. pap. 9.95 (ISBN 0-394-74108-0, Vin). Random.
Parade's Gone by. Kevin Brownlow. LC 75-17302. 1976. pap. 17.95 (ISBN 0-520-03068-0). U of Cal Pr.
Paradigm & Ideology in Educational Research: The Social Function of the Intellectual. Thomas Popkewitz. 208p. 1984. 32.00x (ISBN 0-905273-98-2, Falmer Pr); pap. 15.00x (ISBN 0-905273-97-4, Falmer Pr). Taylor & Francis.
Paradigm & Parody: Images of Creativity in French Romanticism - Vigny, Hugo, Balzac, Gautier, Musset. Henry F. Majewski. 250p. 1989. text ed. price not set (ISBN 0-8139-1177-X). U Pr of Va.
Paradigm Exchange: University of Minnesota Faculty & Students in Colloquium. Ed. by Rene Jara et al. 193p. 1980. pap. text ed. 6.95 (ISBN 0-9607884-0-9). U of MN College Lib Arts.
Paradigm for Looking: Cross-Cultural Research with Visual Media. Beryl L. Bellman & Bennetta Jules-Rosette. LC 77-15284. (Modern Sociology Ser.). (Illus.). 216p. 1977. text ed. 35.00 (ISBN 0-89391-002-3). Ablex Pub.
Paradigm for Management Information Systems. Phillip Ein-Dor & Eli Segev. LC 81-1825. 304p. 1981. 44.95 (ISBN 0-275-90608-6, C0608). Praeger.
Paradigm Problem in Political Science: Perspectives from Philosophy & from Practice. Ed. by William T. Bluhm. LC 81-70433. 227p. 1982. lib. bdg. 24.75 (ISBN 0-89089-218-0); pap. 12.95 (ISBN 0-89089-219-9). Carolina Acad Pr.
Paradigm Shift: Teach the Universal Values. Robert L. Humphrey, J. D., & Associates Staff. LC 83-83386. (Illus.). 100p. 1984. pap. 7.95 (ISBN 0-915761-00-9). Life Values Pr.
Paradigms & Exercises in Syriac Grammar. 4th ed. Ed. by T. H. Robinson & L. H. Brockington. 1962. pap. 14.95x (ISBN 0-19-815458-5). Oxford U Pr.
Paradigms & Fairy Tales: An Introduction to the Science of Meanings, 2 vols. Julienne Ford. 1975. Vol. 1. pap. 8.95x (ISBN 0-7100-8248-7); Vol. 2. pap. 8.95x (ISBN 0-7100-8249-5); Set. pap. 16.95x (ISBN 0-7100-8250-9). Routledge Chapman & Hall.
Paradigms & Paradoxes: The Philosophical Challenge of the Quantum Domain. Ed. by Robert G. Colodny. LC 79-158189. (University of Pittsburgh Series in the Philosophy of Science: No. 5). pap. 121.20 (2031901). Bks Demand UMI.
Paradigms & Principal Parts for the Greek New Testament. Dale R. Bowne. LC 86-33989. 60p. (Orig.). 1987. pap. text ed. 7.75 (ISBN 0-8191-6099-7). U Pr of Amer.

Paradox of Christian Tragedy. Barbara Hunt. LC 82-50404. 155p. 1985. 18.50x (ISBN 0-87875-251-X). Whitston Pub.

Paradox of Control: Crime & the Parolee. Patrick G. Jackson. LC 83-9516. 160p. 1983. 35.00 (ISBN 0-275-91016-4, C1016). Praeger.

Paradox of Existentialist Theology: The Dialectics of a Faith-Subsumed Reason-in-Existence. Howard A. Slatte. LC 81-43508. 272p. 1982. lib. bdg. 30.50 (ISBN 0-8191-2187-8); pap. text ed. 14.00 (ISBN 0-8191-2188-6). U Pr of Amer.

Paradox of George Orwell. Richard J. Voorhees. LC 61-62508. 128p. (Orig.). 1961. pap. 3.25 (ISBN 0-911198-00-8). Purdue U Pr.

Paradox of Gissing. David Grylls. 1986. text ed. 29.95x (ISBN 0-04-800081-7). Unwin Hyman.

Paradox of History: Stendhal, Tolstoy, Pasternak & Others. rev. ed. Nicola Chiaromonte. LC 84-28102. 168p. 1985. pap. text ed. 15.95 (ISBN 0-8122-1210-X). U of Pa Pr.

Paradox of Intention: Reaching the Goal by Giving up the Attempt to Reach It. Marvin C. Shaw. LC 87-29488. (Studies in Religion). 225p. 1988. 20.95 (ISBN 1-55540-109-0, 01-00-48); pap. 13.95 (ISBN 1-55540-110-4). Scholars Pr GA.

Paradox of Man's Greatness. Stanton Coblentz. 1966. 9.00 (ISBN 0-8183-0188-0). Pub Aff Pr.

Paradox of Mass Politics. W. Russell Neuman. LC 86-288. (Illus.). 264p. 1986. text ed. 31.95x (ISBN 0-674-65455-2); pap. 13.50x (ISBN 0-674-65460-9). Harvard U Pr.

Paradox of Poverty: A Reappraisal of Economic Development Policy. Paul Steidlmeier. LC 86-26589. 344p. 1987. prof. 32.00x (ISBN 0-88730-184-3). Ballinger Pub.

Paradox of Power: The U. S. in Southwest Asia, 1973-1984. Maya Chadda. 278p. 1986. lib. bdg. 31.25 (ISBN 0-87436-454-X); pap. 18.50 (ISBN 0-87436-455-8). ABC-Clio.

Paradox of Preaching. Kring Allen. (Illus.). 104p. (Orig.). 1986. pap. 9.95 (ISBN 1-55630-018-2). Brentwood Comm.

Paradox of Privacy: Epistolary Form in Clarissa. Christina M. Gillis. LC 83-14568. (University of Florida Humanities Monographs: No. 54). viii, 167p. (Orig.). 1984. pap. 15.50x (ISBN 0-8130-0761-5). U Presses Fla.

Paradox of Professionalism: Reform & Public Service in Urban America, 1900-1940. Don S. Kirschner. LC 86-399. (Contributions in American History Ser.: No. 119). 208p. 1986. lib. bdg. 35.00 (ISBN 0-313-25345-5, KPX/). Greenwood.

Paradox of Progressive Education: The Gary Plan & Urban Schooling. Ronald Cohen & Raymond Mohl. (National University Publications,Interdisciplinary Urban Ser). 1979. 23.50x (ISBN 0-8046-9237-8, Pub. by Kennikat). Assoc Faculty Pr.

Paradox of Religion. Willard L. Sperry. LC 77-27146. (Hibbert Lectures: 1927). Repr. of 1927 ed. 20.00 (ISBN 0-404-60424-2). AMS Pr.

Paradox of Spanish Foreign Policy: Internal & External Political Structures. Benny Pollack. 240p. 1987. 27.50 (ISBN 0-312-59599-9). St Martin.

Paradox of the Employee: Variants of a Social Theme in Modern Literature. Andrew Weeks. (Germanic Studies in America: Vol. 35). 160p. 1980. 18.85 (ISBN 3-261-04757-7). P Lang Pubs.

Paradox of the Gold Watch: Planning Twenty Years Before Retirement. Daniel C. Bancroft. Ed. by Joanne Sandstrom. LC 88-90509. (Illus.). 112p. 1988. wkbk. 9.95 (ISBN 0-945211-00-7). Retirement Income Assocs.

Paradox of the Liar. Ed. by Robert L. Martin. 1979. lib. bdg. 27.00 (ISBN 0-917930-30-4); pap. text ed. 8.00 (ISBN 0-917930-10-X). Ridgeview.

Paradox of the Silicon Savior: Charting the Reformation of the High-Tech Super-State. Grant Venerable. 229p. (Orig.). 1987. pap. 12.95 (ISBN 0-943425-00-X). MVM Prodns.

Paradox of Tragedy. facs. ed. David D. Raphael. LC 77-128293. (Essay Index Reprint Ser). 1960. 15.00 (ISBN 0-8369-2021-X). Ayer Co Pubs.

Paradox Planet. Stephen Spruill. LC 87-33081. (Science Fiction Ser.). 192p. 1988. pap. 14.95 (ISBN 0-385-24486-X, Foundation Bks). Doubleday.

Paradox Politics: People, Power & Politics in Unpredictable Idaho. LC 88-90516. (Illus.). 352p. (Orig.). 1988. pap. 10.95 (ISBN 0-945648-15-4). Ridenbaugh Pr.

Paradox: Power User's Guide. Greg Salcedo & Rusel DeMaria. (Business Ser.). 500p. 1988. 23.95 (ISBN 0-07-881425-1). Osborne-McGraw.

Paradox: The Complete Reference. James Keogh. (Borland Osborne-McGraw-Hill Business Ser.). 650p. 1988. 26.95. Osborne-McGraw.

Paradox: The Pocket Reference. Edward Jones. (Borland Osborne-McGraw-Hill Business Ser.). 128p. 1988. pap. text ed. 5.95 (ISBN 0-07-881404-9). Osborne-McGraw.

Paradoxa Stoicorum see De Oratore, Bk 3.

Paradoxe sur le Comedien: Avec: Danaud, Jean-Claude. Un Ouvrage de Dames. Denis Diderot. (Illus.). 49p. 1977. 9.95 (ISBN 0-686-56020-5). French & Eur.

Paradoxe Sur le Comedien: Paris, 1902. facsimile ed. Denis Diderot. 211p. 1968. 65.00 (ISBN 0-686-56021-3). French & Eur.

Paradoxes. J. Cargile. LC 78-67299. (Cambridge Studies in Philosophy). 1979. 39.50 (ISBN 0-521-22475-6). Cambridge U Pr.

Paradoxes. John Hall. LC 56-6812. 1977. Repr. of 1650 ed. 30.00x (ISBN 0-8201-1233-X). Schol Facsimiles.

Paradoxes. R. M. Sainsbury. (Illus.). 150p. 1988. 34.50 (ISBN 0-521-33165-X); 7.95 (ISBN 0-521-33749-6). Cambridge U Pr.

Paradoxes & Problems. John Donne. Ed. by Helen Peters. (Oxford English Texts Ser.). (Illus.). 1980. 49.95x (ISBN 0-19-812753-7). Oxford U Pr.

Paradoxes & Puzzles, Historical, Judicial & Literary. John Paget. LC 75-30035. Repr. of 1874 ed. 42.50 (ISBN 0-404-14037-8). AMS Pr.

Paradoxes & Puzzles: Historical, Judicial, & Literary. John Paget. 1874. Repr. 45.00 (ISBN 0-8274-3904-0). R West.

Paradoxes in Politics: An Introduction to the Nonobvious in Political Science. Steven J. Brams. LC 75-28568. (Illus.). 1976. pap. text ed. 11.95 (ISBN 0-02-904590-8). Free Pr.

Paradoxes in Probability Theory & Mathematical Statistics. Gabor J. Szekely. 1986. lib. bdg. 59.00 (ISBN 90-277-1899-7, Pub. by Reidel Holland). Kluwer Academic.

Paradoxes in the Riddles of the Anglo-Saxons. Ed. by Sandy Sutherland. 224p. 1987. 45.00 (ISBN 0-85991-222-1, Pub. by Boydell & Brewer). Longwood Pub Group.

Paradoxes, Nouveaux Paradoxes see Paradoxes of Faith.

Paradoxes of Defence see Three Elizabethan Fencing Manuals.

Paradoxes of Defence, Wherein Is Proved the True Grounds of Fight to Be in the Short Auncient Weapons. George Silver. LC 68-27484. (English Experience Ser.: No. 8). 72p. 1968. Repr. of 1599 ed. 8.00 (ISBN 90-221-0008-1). Walter J Johnson.

Paradoxes of Democracy. Ed. by Guy Hermet & Helgio Trindade. 222p. 1988. text ed. 45.00x (ISBN 81-212-0111-X, Pub. by Gian Pubs Hse). Advent NY.

Paradoxes of Education in a Republic. Eva T. Brann. LC 78-10228. 1979. 12.95x (ISBN 0-226-07135-9). U of Chicago Pr.

Paradoxes of Faith. Henry De Lubac. Tr. by Paule Simon et al. LC 86-62928. Orig. Title: Paradoxes, Nouveaux Paradoxes. 236p. (Orig., Fr.). 1986. pap. 9.95 (ISBN 0-89870-132-5). Ignatius Pr.

Paradoxes of Freedom. Sidney Hook. 152p. 1987. pap. 5.95 (ISBN 0-87975-410-9). Prometheus Bks.

Paradoxes of Group Life: Understanding Conflict, Paralysis & Movement in Group Dynamics. Kenwyn K. Smith & David N. Berg. LC 86-33706. (Management Ser.). 1987. text ed. 26.95x (ISBN 1-55542-046-X). Jossey-Bass.

Paradoxes of Legal Science. Benjamin N. Cardozo. LC 76-104241. 142p. Repr. of 1928 ed. lib. bdg. 35.00x (ISBN 0-8371-3263-0, CALS). Greenwood.

Paradoxes of Order: Some Perspectives on the Fiction of V. S. Naipaul. Robert K. Morris. LC 74-23752. (Literary Frontiers Ser). 112p. 1975. pap. 7.95 (ISBN 0-8262-0172-5). U of Mo Pr.

Paradoxes of Play-Papers. Ed. by John W. Loy. (Association for the Anthropological Study of Play: Vol. 6). 238p. (Orig.). 1982. pap. text ed. 18.00x (ISBN 0-88011-001-5, PLOY0001). Leisure Pr.

Paradoxes of Power: The Military Establishment in the Eighties. Adam Yarmolinsky & Gregory D. Foster. LC 82-48523. (Illus.). 160p. 1983. 17.50x (ISBN 0-253-34291-0). Ind U Pr.

Paradoxes of Progress. Gunther S. Stent. LC 78-17829. (Biology Ser.). (Illus.). 231p. 1978. pap. text ed. 11.95x (ISBN 0-7167-0086-7). W H Freeman.

Paradoxes of Protest: Black Student Activism in a White University. William H. Exum. 336p. 1985. 34.95 (ISBN 0-87722-377-7). Temple U Pr.

Paradoxical Effects of Social Behavior. Ed. by A. Diekmann & P. Mitter. (Illus.). xvi, 341p. 1986. 66.00 (ISBN 0-387-91285-1). Springer-Verlag.

Paradoxical Harvest: Energy & Explanation in British History, 1870-1914. Richard N. Adams. LC 81-21631. (ASA Rose Monograph). (Illus.). 160p. 1982. 34.50 (ISBN 0-521-24637-7); pap. 10.95 o. p. (ISBN 0-521-28866-5). Cambridge U Pr.

Paradoxical Psychotherapy: Theory & Technique. Gerald R. Weeks & Luciano L'Abate. LC 81-17083. 288p. 1982. 30.00 (ISBN 0-87630-289-4). Brunner-Mazel.

Paradoxical Resolutions: American Fiction since James Joyce. Craig H. Werner. LC 81-11423. 248p. 1982. 22.95 (ISBN 0-252-00931-2). U of Ill Pr.

Paradoxical Strategies in Psychotherapy: A Comprehensive Overview & Guidebook. Leon F. Seltzer. (Personality Processes Ser.). 323p. 1986. 34.00 (ISBN 0-471-82661-8). Wiley.

Parady Anthology. Carolyn Wells. 11.25 (ISBN 0-8446-3148-5). Peter Smith.

Paraesthetics: Foucault, Lyotard, Derrida. David Carroll. 288p. 1987. 35.00 (ISBN 0-416-01721-5, A0413); pap. 12.95 (ISBN 0-416-01731-2, A0417). Routledge Chapman & Hall.

Parafin Products: Properties, Technologies, Applications. G. Mozes. (Developments in Petroleum Products Ser.: Vol. 14). 336p. 1983. 116.00 (ISBN 0-444-99712-1). Elsevier.

Paraganglia. P. Boeck. (Handbuch der Mikroskopischen Anatomie Des Menschen: Vol. 1-8). (Illus.). 400p. 1982. 134.00 (ISBN 0-387-10978-1). Springer-Verlag.

Paraganglionic Chemoreceptor System: Physiology, Pathology, & Clinical Medicine. F. G. Zak & W. Lawson. (Illus.). 576p. 1982. 189.00 (ISBN 0-387-90621-5). Springer-Verlag.

Paragon. M. Sherman. (Lecture Notes in Computer Science Ser.: Vol. 189). xi, 364p. 1985. pap. 22.50 (ISBN 0-387-15212-1). Springer-Verlag.

Paragon of Human Perfection. H. A. Omar. 85p. 1984. 21.00x (ISBN 0-7212-0566-6, Pub. by Regency Pr). State Mutual Bk.

Paragraph & Topic Sentence. Sheldon Tilkin. (Horizons II Ser.). (Illus.). 24p. (gr. 3-4). 1980. wkbk. 2.50 (ISBN 0-89403-606-8). EDC.

Paragraph Book. C. Jeriel Howard & Richard F. Tracz. (Orig.). 1982. pap. text ed. write for info. (ISBN 0-673-39270-8). Scott F.

Paragraph Composition. Wilbert J. Levy. (gr. 10-12). 1977. wkbk. 9.33 (ISBN 0-87720-957-X). AMSCO Sch.

Paragraph Development: A Guide for Students of English As a Second Language. Martin L. Arnaudet & Mary E. Barrett. (ESL Ser.). (Illus.). 160p. 1981. pap. text ed. write for info. (ISBN 0-13-648618-5). P-H.

Paragraph of Life: Killer-Your Friend? Dino Manuel. 64p. (YA) (gr. 7 up). 1981. 5.00 (ISBN 0-682-49724-X). Exposition-Phoenix.

Paragraph Patterns. Alston et al. 144p. 1987. pap. text ed. 14.95 (ISBN 0-8403-4457-0). Kendall-Hunt.

Paragraph Patterns. Barbara Auerbach & Beth Snyder. 147p. 1983. pap. text ed. 8.00 net (ISBN 0-15-567983-X, HC). HarBraceJ.

Paragraph Play. Levy. (gr. 7-9). 1985. pap. 7.83 (ISBN 0-87720-651-1). AMSCO Sch.

Paragraph Power. Wilbert J. Levy. (gr. 10-12). 1977. wkbk. 10.00 (ISBN 0-87720-334-2). AMSCO Sch.

Paragraph Power: Communicating Ideas Through Paragraphs. George M. Rooks. (Illus.). 176p. 1988. pap. text ed. 15.00 (ISBN 0-13-648585-5). P-H.

Paragraph Practice: Writing for Paragraph & Short Composition. 6th ed. Kathleen E. Sullivan. 246p. 1989. text ed. price not set (ISBN 0-02-418390-3). Macmillan.

Paragraph Practice: Writing the Paragraph & the Short Composition. 5th ed. Kathleen E. Sullivan. (Illus.). 1984. pap. text ed. write for info. (ISBN 0-02-418340-7). Macmillan.

Paragraph Production. Linda Polon. (Study Skills Ser.). 48p. (gr. 4-6). 1981. 4.95 (ISBN 0-88160-039-3, LW 224). Learning Wks.

Paragraph Structure Inference. Edward J. Crothers. LC 78-27307. 124p. 1979. 29.50 (ISBN 0-89391-016-3). Ablex Pub.

Paragraph Writing. Sandra Coats & Mary Anne Sandel. 320p. 1986. pap. text ed. write for info. (ISBN 0-13-648569-3). P-H.

Paragraphs. Vern Rutsala. LC 77-20145. (Poetry Program Ser.: Vol. 91). 1978. 17.00x; pap. 8.95. Wesleyan U Pr.

Paragraphs & Themes. 4th ed. P J. Canavan. 510p. 1983. pap. text ed. 15.50 (ISBN 0-669-05273-6); 2.00 (ISBN 0-669-05271-X). Heath.

Paragraphs on Printing. Bruce Rogers. LC 79-50699. (Illus.). 1980. pap. 6.95 (ISBN 0-486-23817-2). Dover.

Paragraphs Plus: From Ideas to Paragraphs to Essays. C. Jeriel Howard & Richard F. Tracz. (Orig.). 1988. pap. text ed. write for info. (ISBN 0-673-39727-0). Scott F.

Paraguas Amarillos. Ed. by Ivan Silen. 254p. (Span.). 1983. 8.50 (ISBN 0-910061-16-5, 1402). Ediciones Norte.

Paraguas Amarillos: Los Poetas Latinos en New York. Ed. by Ivan Silen. 254p. (Span.). 1983. pap. 10.00x. Biling Rev-Pr.

Paraguay. Rosa Q. Mesa. LC 73-180800. (Latin American Serial Documents Ser.: Vol. 9). pap. 23.30 (ISBN 0-317-10336-9, 2013551). Bks Demand UMI.

Paraguay. R. Andrew Nickson. (World Bibliographical Ser.: No. 84). 212p. 1987. lib. bdg. 45.00 (ISBN 1-85109-028-2). ABC Clio.

Paraguay. (Let's Visit Places & Peoples - - Nations, Dependencies, & Sovereignties of the World Ser.). (Illus.). (gr. 5 up). 1988. 12.95 (ISBN 0-7910-0150-4). Chelsea Hse.

Paraguay. Riordan Roett. 135p. Date not set. 26.50x (ISBN 0-86531-272-9). Westview.

Paraguay see American Nations Past & Present.

Paraguay see Statements of the Laws of the OAS Member States in Matters Affecting Business.

Paraguay: A Bibliography. David L. Jones. LC 77-83382. (Reference Library of Humanities Ser.). 523p. 1979. lib. bdg. 73.00 (ISBN 0-8240-9825-0). Garland Pub.

Paraguay: A Riverside Nation. G. Pendle. 1976. lib. bdg. 59.95 (ISBN 0-8490-2409-9). Gordon Pr.

Paraguay: An Informal History. Harris G. Warren. LC 82-15519. (Illus.). xii, 393p. 1982. Repr. of 1949 ed. lib. bdg. 48.50x (ISBN 0-313-23651-8, WARP). Greenwood.

Paraguay & the Triple Alliance: The Postwar Decade, 1869 -1878. Harris G. Warren. (Latin American Monographs: No. 44). 388p. 1978. 23.50x (ISBN 0-292-76445-6); pap. 11.50x (ISBN 0-292-76444-8). U of Tex Pr.

Paraguay, Brazil, & the Plate. Charles B. Mansfield. LC 79-128414. Repr. of 1856 ed. 32.45 (ISBN 0-404-04183-3). AMS Pr.

Paraguay in Pictures. Nathan A. Haverstock. (Visual Geography Ser.). (Illus.). 64p. (gr. 5 up). 1987. PLB 9.95 (ISBN 0-8225-1819-8). Lerner Pubns.

Paraguay: Its Cultural Heritage, Social Conditions & Educational Problems. Arthur E. Elliott. LC 70-176746. (Columbia University. Teachers College. Contributions to Education: No. 473). Repr. of 1931 ed. 22.50 (ISBN 0-404-55473-3). AMS Pr.

Paraguay: Latin America's Oldest Dictatorship under Pressure. Americas Watch Staff. 71p. 1986. 6.00 (ISBN 0-938579-23-1). Fund Free Expression.

Paraguay under Stroessner. Paul H. Lewis. LC 79-28554. xi, 256p. 1980. 26.00x (ISBN 0-8078-1437-7). U of NC Pr.

Paraguay Update. Amnesty International U. S. A. Staff. LC 86-197663. 18p. Date not set. 2.00. Amnesty Intl USA.

Paraguay: 1852 & 1968. Edward A. Hopkins & Raymond E. Crist. (Occasional Publication: No. 2). (Illus.). 64p. Repr. 3.50 (ISBN 0-318-12733-4). Am Geographical.

Paraguayan Paper Money. D. A. Seppa. (Illus.). 50p. 1973. 10.00 (ISBN 0-916710-12-2); pap. 5.00 (ISBN 0-685-64921-0). Obol Intl.

Paraguayans of To-Day. 2nd ed. William B. Parker. (Illus.). 1921. 32.00 (ISBN 0-527-69818-0). Kraus Repr.

Paraja. Gopinath Mohanty. 384p. 1987. pap. 8.95 (ISBN 0-19-562003-8). Oxford U Pr.

Parajudges: Their Role in Today's Court Systems. 78p. 1976. pap. 1.00 (ISBN 0-89656-010-4, R-027). Natl Ctr St Courts.

Parakeets. Cessa Feyerabend. (Illus.). 80p. 1984. pap. text ed. 5.95 (ISBN 0-86622-233-2, PB-119). TFH Pubns.

Parakeets. Earl Schneider & Matthew M. Vriends. (KW-036). (Illus.). 128p. 1984. Repr. of 1979 ed. 9.95 (ISBN 0-87666-749-3, KW-036). TFH Pubns.

Parakeets. Annette Wolter. (Illus.). (gr. k-12). 1982. pap. 3.95 (ISBN 0-8120-2423-0). Barron.

Parakeets of the World. Matthew M. Vriends. (Illus.). 1979. 19.95 (ISBN 0-87666-999-2, H-101). TFH Pubns.

Paralanguage & Kinesics: Nonverbal Communication with a Bibliography. Mary R. Key. LC 74-30217. 246p. 1975. 17.50 (ISBN 0-8108-0789-0). Scarecrow.

Paralation Model: Architecture-Independent Parallel Programming. Gary Sabot. (Artificial Intelligence Ser.). 230p. 1989. text ed. 25.00x (ISBN 0-262-19277-2). MIT Pr.

Paralchimie: Avec: Architruc, l'Hypothese, Nuit. 2nd ed. Robert Pinget. 212p. 1973. 9.95 (ISBN 0-686-54877-9). French & Eur.

Paralegal: A New Career. Richard Deming. LC 79-27172. 1979. 7.95 (ISBN 0-525-66655-9). Lodestar Bks.

Paralegal Aide. Jack Rudman. (Career Examination Ser.: C-2245). (Cloth bdg. avail. on request). pap. 14.00 (ISBN 0-8373-2245-6). Natl Learning.

Paralegal Careers. William R. Fry & Roy Hoopes. LC 85-20443. (Illus.). 64p. (gr. 6-12). 1986. PLB 12.95 (ISBN 0-89490-105-2). Enslow Pubs.

Paralegal Handbook: Theory, Practice & Materials. American Institute for Paralegal Studies Staff & Charles P. Nemeth. (Illus.). 608p. 1986. text ed. write for info. (ISBN 0-13-648593-6). P-H.

Paralegal Practice & Procedure: A Practical Guide for the Legal Assistant. Deborah E. Larbalestrier. LC 85-12407. 29.95 (ISBN 0-13-648726-2); pap. 14.95 (ISBN 0-13-648718-1). P-H.

Paralegal Training Manual. Deborah E. Larbalestrier. LC 81-5054. 270p. 1981. 19.95 (ISBN 0-13-648626-6, Busn). P-H.

Paralegals. (Career Blazers Guides Ser.). 192p. (Orig.). 1983. pap. 7.95 (ISBN 0-671-45870-1). Monarch Pr.

Paralegal's Encyclopedic Dictionary. Valera Grapp. 1979. 29.50 (ISBN 0-13-648675-4). P-H.

Paralegal's Guide to Computer Abbreviations & Acronyms. Mark W. Greenia. 1988. pap. 12.00 (ISBN 0-944601-08-1). Lexikon Servs.

Paralegal's Handbook of Annotated Legal Forms, Clauses & Procedures. Deborah E. Larbalestrier. 384p. 1982. 39.50 (ISBN 0-13-648642-8, Busn). P-H.

Paralegal's Litigation Handbook. Carole Bruno. LC 79-19960. 544p. 1980. 45.00 (ISBN 0-87624-425-8, Inst Busn Plan). P-H.

Paralegals: Progress & Prospects of a Satellite Occupation. Quintin Johnstone & Martin Wenglinsky. LC 85-9889. (Emerging Patterns of Work & Communications in an Information Age Ser.: No. 2). (Illus.). viii, 288p. 1985. lib. bdg. 40.95 (ISBN 0-313-24945-8, JPG/). Greenwood.

Parametric Linguistics. Louis G. Heller & James Macris. (Janua Linguarum, Ser. Minor: No. 58). (Orig.). 1967. pap. text ed. 5.60x (ISBN 0-686-22451-5). Mouton.

Parametric-Normed Spaces & Normed Massives. K. K. Golovkin. (Proceedings of the Steklov Institute of Mathematics: No. 106). 1971. 43.00 (ISBN 0-8218-3006-6, STEKLO-106). Am Math.

Parametric Optimization & Approximation. B. Brosowski. (North-Holland Mathematics Studies). 350p. 1984. write for info. (North-Holland). Elsevier.

Parametric Optimization & Approximation. Ed. by F. Brosowski & F. Deutsch. (ISNM Ser.: No. 72). 264p. 1985. text ed. 50.95 (ISBN 3-764316-71-3). Birkhauser.

Parametric Processes see Progress in Quantum Electronics.

Parametric Random Vibration. R. A. Ibrahim. LC 85-10830. (Mechanical Engineering Dynamics Ser.). 342p. 1985. 86.00 (ISBN 0-471-90830-4). Wiley.

Parametric Semi-Infinite Optimization, Vol. 22. Bruno Brosowski. (Methoden und Verfahren der Mathematischen Physik). 260p. 1981. pap. 32.95. P Lang Pubs.

Parametric Statistical Inference: Basic Theory & Modern Approaches. S. Zacks. LC 80-41715. (I.S. in Nonlinear Mathematics Series; Theory & Applications: Vol. 4). 400p. 1981. text ed. 63.00 (ISBN 0-08-026468-9). Pergamon.

Parametric Syntax: Case Studies in Semitic & Romance Languages. H. Borer. Ed. by J. Koster & H. V. Riemsdyk. (Studies in Generative Grammar: No. 13). ix, 260p. 1984. write for info. (ISBN 90-6765-024-2); pap. write for info. (ISBN 90-6765-025-0). Foris Pubns.

Parametrized Knot Theory. Stanley Ocken. LC 76-3641. (Memoirs: No. 170). 114p. 1976. pap. 16.00 (ISBN 0-8218-1870-8, MEMO-170). Am Math.

Paramilitary Plot. Don Pendleton. (Executioner Ser.). 192p. 1982. pap. 1.95 (ISBN 0-373-61045-9, Pub. by Worldwide). Harlequin Bks.

Paramount Banjos. Repr. of 1920 ed. 12.00 (ISBN 0-686-21420-X). Mih.

Paramount Doctrines of Orthodoxy-the Tricompositeness of Man, Apology of A. Makrakis & the Trial of A. Makrakis. Apostolos Makrakis. Ed. by Orthodox Christian Educational Society. Tr. by Denver Cummings from Hellenic. 904p. 1954. 15.00x (ISBN 0-938366-17-3). Orthodox Chr.

Paramount Films of Nineteen Twenty-Eight-Nineteen Twenty-Nine. Ed. by R. Gordon. 1976. lib. bdg. 70.00 (ISBN 0-8490-2410-2). Gordon Pr.

Paramount Kill. Gaylord Larsen. 208p. 1988. 16.95 (ISBN 0-525-24592-8). Dutton.

Paramount Pictures of Nineteen Thirty-One to Nineteen Thirty-Two. Ed. by R. Gordon. 1976. lib. bdg. 100.00 (ISBN 0-8490-2411-0). Gordon Pr.

Paramount Story. John D. Eames. LC 85-3745. 1985. 35.00 (ISBN 0-517-55348-1). Crown.

Parana: Social Boundaries in an Argentine City. Ruben E. Reina. LC 72-8265. (Latin American Monographs: No. 31). (Illus.). 414p. 1973. 20.00x (ISBN 0-292-76408-1). U of Tex Pr.

Paraneurons. Ed. by T. Fujita et al. (Illus.). xii, 368p. 1988. 210.90 (ISBN 0-387-70026-9). Springer-Verlag.

Paraneurons: Their Features & Functions. Ed. by T. Kanno. (International Congress Ser.: No. 552). 194p. 1981. 70.75 (ISBN 0-444-90194-9, Excerpta Medica). Elsevier.

Paranoia: A Study in Diagnosis. Yehuda Fried & Joseph Agassi. LC 76-21816. (Synthese Library Ser.: No. 102). 1976. lib. bdg. 29.00 (ISBN 9-0277-0705-7, Pub. by Reidel Holland); pap. 17.00 (ISBN 90-277-0705-7, Pub. by Reidel Holland). Kluwer Academic.

Paranoid. Sheila Oliveria. 1988. 10.95 (ISBN 0-8158-0439-3). Chris Mass.

Paranoid Foothills. Peter B. Cloud. (Illus., Orig.). 1981. pap. 2.50 (ISBN 0-942396-29-4). Blackberry ME.

Paranoid Process. William Meissner. LC 75-13537. 888p. 1978. 40.00x (ISBN 0-87668-212-3). Aronson.

Paranoid Prophet. William Backus. 128p. (Orig.). 1986. pap. 4.95 (ISBN 0-87123-874-8, 210874). Bethany Hse.

Paranoid Style in American Politics: And Other Essays. Richard Hofstadter. LC 79-12579. 1979. pap. 5.95x (ISBN 0-226-34817-2, P840, Phoen). U of Chicago Pr.

Paranormal: A Scientific Exploration of the Supernatural. Arthur J. Ellison. (Illus.). 160p. 1988. 18.95 (ISBN 0-396-08893-7). Dodd.

Paranormal & the Normal: A Historical, Philosophical & Theoretical Perspective. Morton Leeds & Gardner Murphy. LC 79-25307. 265p. 1980. lib. bdg. 20.00 (ISBN 0-8108-1278-9). Scarecrow.

Paranormal Borderlands of Science. Ed. by Kendrick Frazier. LC 80-84403. (Science & the Paranormal Ser.). 469p. 1981. pap. 16.95. Prometheus Bks.

Paranormal Foreknowledge: Problems & Perplexities. Jule Eisenbud. LC 81-2941. 312p. 1982. 39.95 (ISBN 0-89885-049-5). Human Sci Pr.

Paranormal: Mechanisms & Models, Pt. 2. Michael A. Persinger. LC 74-19227. 195p. 1974. 27.50x (ISBN 0-8422-5211-8); pap. text ed. 9.95x (ISBN 0-8422-0476-8). Irvington.

Paranormal Perception of Color. Yvonne Duplessis. LC 75-19563. (Parapsychological Monographs: No. 16). 1975. pap. 8.00 (ISBN 0-912328-27-4). Parapsych Foun.

Paranormal Phenomena, Science, & Life after Death. C. J. Ducasse. LC 79-76282. (Parapsychological Monographs No. 8). 1969. pap. 6.00 (ISBN 0-912328-12-6). Parapsych Foun.

Paranormal: The Patterns, Pt. 1. Michael A. Persinger. LC 74-19227. 248p. 1974. 29.50x (ISBN 0-8422-5212-6); pap. text ed. 10.95x (ISBN 0-8422-0477-6). Irvington.

Paraphrase & Notes on the Epistles of St. Paul, 2 vols. John Locke. (Clarendon Edition of the Works of John Locke). (Illus.). 1988. Vol. 1, 490pp. 89.00x (ISBN 0-19-824801-6); Vol. 2, 360pp. 79.00 (ISBN 0-19-824806-7). Oxford U Pr.

Paraphrase Grammars. R. M. Smaby. LC 76-13504. (Formal Linguistics Ser: No. 2). 145p. 1971. lib. bdg. 21.00 (ISBN 90-277-0178-4, Pub. by Reidel Holland). Kluwer Academic.

Paraphrases for Pilgrims. Jean Lanier. 1977. pap. 1.75 (ISBN 0-89192-187-7). Interbk Inc.

Paraphrases on Romans & Galatians. Desiderius Erasmus. Ed. by Robert D. Sider. Tr. by John B. Payne et al. (Collected Works of Erasmus Ser.: Vol. 42). 232p. 1984. 29.50x (ISBN 0-8020-2510-2). U of Toronto Pr.

Parapoems. Peter Clothier. 1974. pap. 3.95 (ISBN 0-8180-1570-5). Horizon.

Parapolitics. Raghavan Iyer. (Illus.). 17.50. Concord Grove.

Parapraxis in the Haizmann Case of Sigmund Freud. Gaston Vandendriessche. 1965. pap. 59.50x (ISBN 0-317-27533-X). Elliots Bks.

Paraprofesionales en Salud Rural en Guatemala. Forrest D. Colburn. (Special Series on Paraprofessionals: No. 8). 55p. (Span.). 1981. pap. text ed. 6.45 (ISBN 0-86731-058-8). Cornell CIS RDC.

Paraprofessional & the Professional Job Structure. Charlotte Mugnier. LC 80-12543. pap. 40.80 (ISBN 0-317-26564-4, 2023951). Bks Demand UMI.

Paraprofessional in the Treatment of Alcoholism: A New Profession. George E. Staub & Leona M. Kent. 184p. 1979. 23.00 (ISBN 0-398-02860-5). C C Thomas.

Paraprofessionals in Counseling, Guidance & Personnel Services. David G. Zimpfer. (APGA Reprint Ser.: No. 5). 280p. 1974. pap. 9.75 (ISBN 0-911547-58-4, 72097W34). Am Assn Coun Dev.

Paraprofessionals in Mental Health: Theory & Practice. Ed. by Sam Alley et al. LC 79-11115. 336p. 1979. 34.95 (ISBN 0-87705-420-7). Human Sci Pr.

Paraprofessionals in Rural Development: Issues in Field-Level Staffing for Agricultural Projects. Milton J. Esman. (Working Paper: No. 573). 72p. 1983. 3.50 (ISBN 0-8213-0180-2, WP 0573). World Bank.

Paraprofessionals in Rural Development. Milton J. Esman et al. (Special Series on Paraprofessionals: No. 1). 149p. (Orig.). 1980. pap. 9.05 (ISBN 0-86731-045-6). Cornell CIS RDC.

Paraprofessionals in the Human Services. Ed. by Stanley Robin & Morton Wagenfeld. LC 80-18011. (Community Psychology Ser.: Vol. VI). 368p. 1981. 39.95 (ISBN 0-87705-490-8). Human Sci Pr.

Paraprofessionals in Village-Level Development in Sri Lanka: The Sarvodaya Shramadana Movement. Cynthia Moore. (Special Series on Paraprofessionals: No. 4). 64p. (Orig.). 1981. pap. 6.85 (ISBN 0-86731-047-2). Cornell CIS RDC.

Parapsychology: A Programmed Course. Glenn Hawkes. (Parapsychology Ser.). 1986. 12.95 (ISBN 0-915133-19-9); pap. 7.95 (ISBN 0-915133-20-2). Grunwald & Radcliff.

Parapsychology: A Reading & Buying Guide to the Best Books in Print. Rhea A. White. (PSI Center Bibliographies Ser.). 99p. (Orig.). 1987. pap. 12.00 (ISBN 0-944446-00-0). Parapsych Sources.

Parapsychology & Anthropology: Proceedings. International Conference, London, Aug. 29-30, 1973. Ed. by Allan Angoff & Diana Barth. LC 74-82959. 17.00 (ISBN 0-912328-24-X). Parapsych Foun.

Parapsychology & Contemporary Science. A. P. Dubrov & V. N. Pushkin. LC 82-2335. 228p. 1982. 55.00x (ISBN 0-306-10973-5, Consultants). Plenum Pub.

Parapsychology & Psychology: Matches & Mismatches. Gertrude R. Schmeidler. LC 88-42505. 270p. 1988. lib. bdg. 24.95x (ISBN 0-89950-350-0). McFarland & Co.

Parapsychology & Self-Deception in Science. Ed. by R. A. McConnell. LC 81-90464. (Illus.). vii, 150p. 1983. pap. 7.00 (ISBN 0-9610232-2-8). McConnell.

Parapsychology & the Experimental Method: Proceedings of an International Conference, New York, 1981. Ed. by Betty Shapin & Lisette Coly. LC 82-61144. 120p. 1982. 16.00 (ISBN 0-912328-36-3). Parapsych Foun.

Parapsychology & the Sciences: Proceedings. International Conference, Amsterdam, Aug. 23-25, 1972. Ed. by Allan Angoff & Betty Shapin. LC 73-92492. 1974. 16.00 (ISBN 0-912328-23-1). Parapsych Foun.

Parapsychology & the Unconscious. Jule Eisenbud. 250p. 1984. 25.00 (ISBN 0-938190-07-5); pap. 12.95 (ISBN 0-938190-08-3). North Atlantic.

Parapsychology for Parents: A Bibliographic Guide. Rhea A. White. (PSI Center Bibliographies Ser.). 30p. (Orig.). 1987. pap. 6.95 (ISBN 0-944446-03-5). Parapsych Sources.

Parapsychology for Teachers & Students: A Bibliographic Guide. Rhea A. White. (PSI Center Bibliographies Ser.). 30p. (Orig.). 1987. pap. 7.05 (ISBN 0-944446-01-9). Parapsych Sources.

Parapsychology from Duke to FRNM. J. B. Rhine et al. LC 65-28963. 121p. 1965. pap. 2.75x (ISBN 0-911106-00-6). Parapsych Pr.

Parapsychology: Frontier Science of the Mind. photocopy ed. J. B. Rhine & J. G. Pratt. (Illus.). 236p. 1974. 27.25 (ISBN 0-398-01580-5). C C Thomas.

Parapsychology in Retrospect: My Search for the Unicorn. R. A. McConnell. LC 86-90590. (Illus.). 240p. (Orig.). 1987. pap. 15.00 (ISBN 0-9610232-4-4). McConnell.

Parapsychology in Retrospect: My Search for the Unicorn (Letterfile Edition) Ed. by R. A. McConnell. LC 86-90590. (Illus.). 28p. (Orig.) 1987. pap. 5.00 (ISBN 0-9610232-5-2). McConnell.

Parapsychology: Its Relation to Physics, Biology, Psychology, & Psychiatry. Ed. by Gertrude R. Schmeidler. LC 76-916. 291p. 1976. 20.00 (ISBN 0-8108-0909-5). Scarecrow.

Parapsychology, Philosophy, & Religious Concepts: Proceedings of an International Conference 1985. Ed. by Betty Shapin & Lisette Coly. LC 87-60201. (Annual International Conference Proceedings Ser.). 215p. 1987. 19.00 (ISBN 0-912328-40-1). Parapsych Foun.

Parapsychology-Science or Magic? A Psychological Perspective. James E. Alcock. (Foundations & Philosophy of Science & Technology Ser.). 300p. 1981. text ed. 50.00 (ISBN 0-08-025773-9); pap. text ed. 21.00 (ISBN 0-08-025772-0). Pergamon.

Parapsychology: Sources of Information. Rhea A. White & Laura A. Dale. LC 73-4853. 303p. 1973. 19.00 (ISBN 0-8108-0617-7). Scarecrow.

Parapsychology: Sources on Applications & Implications. Rhea A. White. (PSI Center Bibliographies Ser.). 127p. (Orig.). 1988. pap. 16.00 (ISBN 0-944446-08-6). Parapsych Sources.

Parapsychology: The Science of Psiology. Carroll B. Nash. 344p. 1986. pap. 32.75x (ISBN 0-398-05253-0). C C Thomas.

Parapsychology Today: A Geographic View; Proceedings. International Conference, France, 1971. Ed. by Allan Angoff & Betty Shapin. LC 72-94940. 1973. 16.00 (ISBN 0-912328-21-5). Parapsych Foun.

Parapsychology: When the Irrational Rejoins Science. Remy Chauvin. Tr. by Katharine M. Banham. LC 84-43225. (Illus.). 176p. (Fr.). 1985. lib. bdg. 18.95x (ISBN 0-89950-145-1). McFarland & Co.

Parapsychology's Second Century: Proceedings of An International Conference Held in London, England August 13-14, 1982. Ed. by Betty Shapin & Lisette Coly. LC 83-62083. 1983. 18.00 (ISBN 0-912328-37-1). Parapsych Foun.

Pararealities: The Nature of Our Fictions & How We Know Them. Floyd Merrell. (Purdue University Monographs in Romance Languages: No. 12). xii, 170p. 1983. 28.00x (ISBN 90-272-1722-X). Benjamins North Am.

Paras. Frank Hilton. (Illus.). 248p. 1986. 18.95 (ISBN 0-563-20099-5). Presidio Pr.

Paras: The British Parachute Regiment. James G. Shortt. (Illus.). 72p. (Orig.). 1985. pap. 9.95 (ISBN 0-85368-699-8, Pub. by Arms & Armour). Sterling.

Paraselene. Russ Thayer. 61p. 1984. pap. 6.00 (ISBN 0-318-03815-3). Latitudes Pr.

Paraside Then, & Again. Mildred Richards. 154p. (Orig.). 1985. pap. 12.95x (ISBN 0-317-39414-2). Wyndham Hall.

Parasitaster or the Fawn. John Marston. Ed. by David A. Blostein. LC 78-60170. (Revels Plays Ser.). 256p. 1979. text ed. 18.50x (ISBN 0-8018-2161-4). Johns Hopkins.

Parasite. Ramsey Campbell. 1981. pap. 2.95 (ISBN 0-671-41905-6). PB.

Parasite. Ramsey Campbell. 320p. 1989. pap. price not set. Tor Bks.

Parasite. Michel Serres. Tr. by Lawrence R. Schehr from Fr. LC 81-19277. 272p. 1982. text ed. 29.50x (ISBN 0-8018-2456-7). Johns Hopkins.

Parasite Antigens in Protection, Diagnosis & Escape. R. M. Parkhouse. (Current Topics in Microbiology & Immunology Ser.: Vol. 120). (Illus.). 310p. 1985. 59.00 (ISBN 0-387-15859-6). Springer-Verlag.

Parasite Antigens: Toward New Strategies for Vaccines. Pearson. (Immunology Ser.). 472p. 1986. 85.00 (ISBN 0-8247-7477-9). Dekker.

Parasite Life Cycles. D. D. Despommier & W. Karapelou. (Illus.). 210p. 1987. 35.00 (ISBN 0-387-96486-X). Springer-Verlag.

Parasite Lives: Papers on Parasites, Their Hosts & Their Associations to Honour J.F.A. Sprent. Ed. by Mary Cremin et al. LC 86-11334. (Illus.). 229p. (Orig.). 1988. pap. text ed. 49.50x (ISBN 0-7022-2041-8). U of Queensland Pr.

Parasites. Daphne Du Maurier. LC 72-184728. 320p. 1971. Repr. of 1950 ed. lib. bdg. 14.00x (ISBN 0-8376-0410-9). Bentley.

Parasites: A Guide to Laboratory Procedures & Identification. Lawrence R. Ash & Thomas C. Orihel. LC 86-32179. (Illus.). 328p. 1987. text ed. 38.00 (ISBN 0-89189-231-1, 45-7-013-00). Am Soc Clinical.

Parasites & Diseases of Fish Cultures in the Tropics. Z. Kabata. 310p. 1985. 66.00x (ISBN 0-85066-285-0). Taylor & Francis.

Parasites in the Immunized Host: Mechanisms of Survival. Ciba Foundation Staff. LC 75-311586. (Ciba Foundation Symposium: New Ser.: No. 25). pap. 72.00 (ISBN 0-317-29185-8, 2022154). Bks Demand UMI.

Parasites of Laboratory Animals. Robert J. Flynn. LC 77-171165. (Illus.). pap. 160.00 (ISBN 0-317-58224-0, 2056380). Bks Demand UMI.

Parasites of Man in Temperate Climates. 2nd ed. Thomas W. Cameron. LC 43-17056. pap. 56.80 (ISBN 0-317-07799-6, 2016082). Bks Demand UMI.

Parasites of North American Freshwater Fishes. Glenn L. Hoffman. LC 67-14063. 1967. 45.00x (ISBN 0-520-00565-1). U of Cal Pr.

Parasites, Pests & Predators. S. M. Gaafar et al. (World Animal Science Ser.: Vol. B2). xxi, 576p. 197.50 (ISBN 0-444-42175-0). Elsevier.

Parasites: The Inside Story. Ann L. Gittleman & J. Maxwell Desgrey. Date not set. pap. 14.95 (ISBN 0-87983-461-7). Keats.

Parasites-Their World & Ours: Proceedings of the Fifth International Congress of Parasitology, Toronto, Canada, August 7-14, 1982. Ed. by D. F. Mettrick & S. S. Desser. 465p. 1982. 99.50 (ISBN 0-444-80433-1, Biomedical Pr). Elsevier.

Parasitic & Related Diseases: Basic Mechanisms, Manifestations, & Control. Ed. by Thomas C. Cheng. LC 85-24447. (Comparative Pathobiology Ser.: Vol. 8). 176p. 1986. 45.00x (ISBN 0-306-42119-4, Plenum Pr). Plenum Pub.

Parasitic Copepoda of British Fishes. Z. Kabata. (Illus.). 670p. 1979. 67.50x (ISBN 0-903874-05-9, Pub. by Brit Mus Nat Hist England). Sabbot-Natural Hist Bks.

Parasitic Copepods from the Gulf of Mexico & Caribbean Sea. Roger F. Cressey. LC 81-9055. (Smithsonian Contributions to Zoology: No. 389). pap. 20.00 (ISBN 0-317-29739-2, 2022199). Bks Demand UMI.

Parasitic Diseases. M. Katz et al. (Illus.). 264p. 1982. 31.50 (ISBN 0-387-90689-4). Springer-Verlag.

Parasitic Diseases, Vol. 2. Mansfield. 328p. 1983. 69.75 (ISBN 0-8247-7050-1). Dekker.

Parasitic Diseases of Wild Mammals. Ed. by John W. Davis & Roy C. Anderson. LC 72-103854. (Illus.). 372p. pap. 96.80 (2029999). Bks Demand UMI.

Parasitic Fauna of Reservoir Fishes of the U. S. S. R. & Its Evolution. N. A. Izyumova. Tr. by B. R. Sharma from Rus. (Russian Translation Ser.: No. 61). 339p. 1988. text ed. 55.00 (ISBN 90-6191-906-1, Pub. by A A Balkema). Brookfield Pub Co.

Parasitic Fungi from British Guiana & Trinidad. Frank L. Stevens. (University of Illinois Biological Monographs: Vol. 8, No. 3). pap. 8.00 (ISBN 0-384-58120-X). Johnson Repr.

Parasitic Infections in the Compromised Host. Walzer & Genta. 560p. 1988. 110.00 (ISBN 0-8247-7943-6). Dekker.

Parasitic Infections of Man & Animals: A Bibliography of Articles in Chinese Medical Periodicals, 1949-64. Lai-bing Kan. LC 66-6864. pap. 33.50 (ISBN 0-317-10239-7, 2021560). Bks Demand UMI.

Parasitic Infections of Pregnancy & the Newborn. Ed. by Caroline MacLeod. (Illus.). 300p. 1988. 49.95 (ISBN 0-19-261653-6). Oxford U Pr.

Parasitic Protozoa. Julius P. Kreier & J. R. Baker. LC 87-1486. (Illus.). 224p. 1987. text ed. 50.00x (ISBN 0-04-591021-9); pap. text ed. 24.95x (ISBN 0-04-591022-7). Unwin Hyman.

Parasitic Protozoa, Vol. 1. Ed. by J. P. Kreier. 1977. 78.00 (ISBN 0-12-426001-2). Acad Pr.

Parasitic Protozoa: Gregarines, Haemogregarines, Coccida, Plasmodia, & Haemoproteids, Vol. 3. Ed. by Julius P. Kreir. LC 76-13041. 1977. 97.50 (ISBN 0-12-426003-9). Acad Pr.

Parasitic Worms. D. W. Crompton. LC 79-20223. (Wykeham Science Ser.: No. 57). 207p. 1980. pap. 18.00x (ISBN 0-8448-1342-7, Pub. by Crane Russak & Co). Taylor & Francis.

Parasitic Worms. D. W. Crompton & S. M. Joyner. 208p. 1980. pap. 18.00x (ISBN 0-85109-830-4). Taylor & Francis.

Parasitic Zoonoses: Clinical & Experimental Studies. Ed. by E. J. Soulsby. 1974. 63.00 (ISBN 0-12-655360-2). Acad Pr.

Parasitic Zoonoses: Section C, 3 vols. Ed. by Leon Jacobs. (CRC Handbook Series in Zoonoses). 1982. Volume I, 400 pp. 99.00 (ISBN 0-8493-2916-7); Volume II, 360 pp. 95.00 (ISBN 0-8493-2917-5); Volume III, 384. 99.00 (ISBN 0-8493-2918-3). CRC Pr.

Parent Involvement in Special Education. Debra Schoonover & Jack Cole. 72p. 1986. pap. text ed. 7.95x (ISBN 0-8134-2505-0). Inter Print Pubs.

Parent Involvement in the Education of Minority Language Children: A Resource Handbook. Orestes I. Crespo & Patricia Louque. 89p. 1984. 7.40 (ISBN 0-89763-104-8). Natl Clearinghse Bilingual Ed.

Parent Involvement Research: A Field in Search of Itself. Sharon L. Kagan. (IRE Report: No. 8). 21p. (Orig.). 1984. pap. 2.75x (ISBN 0-317-47202-X). Inst Responsive.

Parent Involvement Staff Handbook: A Manual for Child Development Programs. Christina M. Lundberg & Beatrice Miller. 50p. pap. 3.25 (ISBN 0-936746-05-X, P51). Day Care Coun.

Parent Letters for Early Learning. Anthony D. Fredericks & Mary F. Brigham. 1988. pap. 7.95 (ISBN 0-673-38114-5). Scott F.

Parent Manual: Handbook for a Prepared Childbirth. 3rd ed. Tamara Schuman. (Avery's Childbirth Education Ser.). (Illus.). 128p. 1983. pap. 6.00 (ISBN 0-89529-203-3). Avery Pub.

Parent of the Handicapped Child: The Study of Child-Rearing Practices. Ray H. Barsch. (Illus.). 452p. 1976. pap. 16.25x (ISBN 0-398-03559-8). C C Thomas.

Parent Partnership Training Program, 8 bks. Mary H. Moore. Incl. Bk. 1. Introductory Guide. LC 78-68013. 128p. pap. text ed. 12.90x (ISBN 0-8027-9053-4); Bk. 2. Parent's Manual. LC 78-68014. 192p. pap. text ed. 17.80x (ISBN 0-8027-9054-2); Bk. 3. Basic Communications Skills. LC 78-68015. 288p. pap. text ed. 39.10x (ISBN 0-8027-9055-0); Bk. 4. Developing Social Acceptability. LC 78-62918. 216p; Bk. 5. Developing Responsible Sexuality. LC 78-62919. 160p. pap. text ed. 24.50x (ISBN 0-8027-9057-7); Bk. 6. Light Housekeeping & In-Home Assistance. LC 78-61387. 272p; Bk. 7. Heavy Duty Cleaning & Yards & Ground Care. LC 78-62939. 240p. pap. text ed. 36.60x (ISBN 0-8027-9059-3); Bk. 8. Skills of Daily Living. LC 78-62940. 304p. (For use with K-12 handicapped). 1979. complete set o.p. 232.00; pap. text ed. Walker & Co.

Parent Power: A Common Sense Approach to Raising Your Children in the Eighties. John Rosemond. LC 81-9716. 240p. 1981. 12.95 (ISBN 0-914788-42-6). Globe Pequot.

Parent Power!: A Commonsense Approach to Raising Kids in the 80s. John K. Rosemond. 1983. pap. 3.95 (ISBN 0-671-44113-2). PB.

Parent Preferences of Young Children. Margarete Simpson. LC 79-177783. (Columbia University. Teachers College. Contributions to Education: No. 652). Repr. of 1935 ed. 22.50 (ISBN 0-404-55652-3). AMS Pr.

Parent Prerogatives: How to Handle Teacher Misbehavior & Other School Disorders. Richard Weinberg & Lynn G. Weinberg. LC 78-23718. 214p. 1979. 17.95 (ISBN 0-88229-442-3). Nelson-Hall.

Parent-Professional Partnerships in Developmental Disability Services. Ed. by James Mulick. 1983. 19.95 (ISBN 0-938550-06-3). Acad Guild.

Parent Programs & Open Houses. Susan Spaete. Ed. by Liz Wilmes & Dick Wilmes. (Illus.). 152p. (Orig.). 1987. pap. 9.95 (ISBN 0-943452-08-2). Building Blocks.

Parent Programs in Reading: Guidelines for Success. Anthony D. Fredericks & David Taylor. 85p. 1985. pap. 6.00 (ISBN 0-87207-965-1). Intl Reading.

Parent-Specific Adjustments for Assessment of Recumbent Length & Stature. Ed. by J. H. Himes et al. (Monographs in Paediatrics: Vol. 13). (Illus.). x, 90p. 1981. pap. 44.00 (ISBN 3-8055-2594-X). S Karger.

Parent-Student Instructional Grievance Committees: Helping to Professionalize Education. Don Stewart. (A Chance for Instructional Excellence Ser.: Bk. 3). (Illus.). 325p. (Orig.). 1988. 14.95 (ISBN 0-913448-16-8); pap. 10.95 (ISBN 0-913448-17-6). Slate Servs.

Parent Survival Training. Marvin Silverman & David A. Lustig. 1988. pap. 10.00 (ISBN 0-87980-419-X). Wilshire.

Parent Survival Training: A Guide for Parents of Teenagers. Paul A. Smyth & Janet Benner. LC 87-82072. 128p. (Orig.). 1988. pap. 8.95 (ISBN 0-942723-13-9). Joelle Pub.

Parent, Teacher & Physician in the Life of the Hyperactive Child: The Incoherence of the Social Environment. Stanley S. Robin & James J. Bosco. 272p. 1981. 32.75 (ISBN 0-398-04528-3). C C Thomas.

Parent-Teacher Bond: Relating, Responding, Rewarding. Kevin J. Swick & R. Eleanor Duff. 1978. pap. text ed. 10.95 (ISBN 0-8403-1847-2). Kendall-Hunt.

Parent, Teacher, Child: Working Together in Children's Learning. Dorothy Hamilton & Alex Griffiths. 192p. 1984. pap. 8.50 (ISBN 0-416-36730-5, NO. 9170). Routledge Chapman & Hall.

Parent Teacher Conferences. University of Idaho. lib. bdg. 14.00X (ISBN 0-943292-14-X, Audio-filmstrip). Foreworks.

Parent-Teacher Conferencing. Gerda Lawrence & Madeline Hunter. 103p. (Orig.). 1978. pap. 6.95x (ISBN 0-935567-08-9). TIP Pubns.

Parent-Teacher Conferencing. Caven S. Mcloughlin. (Illus.). 334p. 1987. 39.50x (ISBN 0-398-05315-4). C C Thomas.

Parent Teacher Conferencing. Joseph C. Rotter & Edward H. Robinson. (What Research Says to the Teacher Ser.). 32p. 1982. 2.50 (ISBN 0-8106-1057-4). NEA.

Parent-Teacher Conferencing. 2nd ed. Joseph C. Rotter et al. 32p. 1987. 2.95 (ISBN 0-8106-1075-2). NEA.

Parent-Teacher Guide to Helping Children Speak Better. Kirk M. Sorensen. 104p. 1982. pap. 14.25 (ISBN 0-398-04661-1). C C Thomas.

Parent-Teacher Surveys: To Improve Confidence & Morale, Vol. 6. Fredric H. Genck. (School Management Model Ser.). 50p. (Orig.). 1984. pap. 28.00 (ISBN 0-318-04006-9). Inst Pub Mgmt.

Parent-Teen Ungame Cards. 1.50 (ISBN 0-317-15778-7). Chr Marriage.

Parent, the Parish, & the Catholic School. Ed Weiss. 1986. 6.60 (ISBN 0-318-20566-1). Natl Cath Educ.

Parent Training: Foundations of Research & Practice. Ed. by Richard F. Dangel & Richard A. Polster. LC 82-15508. 576p. 1984. 40.00 (ISBN 0-89862-627-7). Guilford Pr.

Parent Tricks-of-the-Trade. Kathleen Touw. 236p. 1988. pap. 7.95 (ISBN 0-87491-839-1). Acropolis.

Parent Tricks-of-the-Trade: One Thousand & One Time & Money Saving Solutions for the First Ten Years. Kathleen Touw. LC 81-15021. (Illus.). 240p. 1981. 7.95 (ISBN 0-87491-086-2); pap. 6.95. Acropolis.

Parent Volunteer Programs in Early Childhood Education: A Practical Guide. Henry C. Brock, 3rd. LC 76-8188. 114p. 1976. 17.50 (ISBN 0-208-01566-3, Linnet). Shoe String.

Parental Alienation Syndrome & the Differentiation Between Fabricated & Genuine Child Sex Abuse. Richard A. Gardner. LC 87-27455. 314p. 1987. 20.00 (ISBN 0-933812-17-5). Creative Therapeutics.

Parental Authority: The Community & the Law. Julius Cohen & Reginald A. Robson. LC 80-153. (Illus.). xii, 301p. 1980. Repr. of 1958 ed. lib. bdg. 32.50x (ISBN 0-313-22351-3, COPR). Greenwood.

Parental Behaviour. Ed. by Wladyslaw Sluckin & Martin Herbert. 288p. 1986. text ed. 45.00 (ISBN 0-631-13487-5). Basil Blackwell.

Parental Behaviour of Rodents. Ed. by R. W. Elwood. LC 82-8625. 296p. 1983. text ed. 67.95x (ISBN 0-471-10252-0, Pub. by Wiley-Interscience). Wiley.

Parental Belief Systems: The Psychological Consequences for Children. Ed. by I. E. Sigel. LC 84-18658. 400p. 1985. text ed. 39.95x (ISBN 0-89859-448-0). L Erlbaum Assocs.

Parental Care in Mammals. Ed. by David J. Gubernick & Peter H. Klopfer. LC 80-36692. 478p. 1981. 65.00x (ISBN 0-306-40533-4, Plenum Pr). Plenum Pub.

Parental Child-Support Obligation: Research, Practice, & Social Policy. Ed. by Judith Cassetty. LC 81-48464. 320p. 1982. 36.00x (ISBN 0-669-05376-7). Lexington Bks.

Parental Choice & Educational Policy. Michael Adler et al. 228p. 1988. 32.50 (Pub. by Edinburgh U Pr Scotland). Columbia U Pr.

Parental Concerns in College Student Mental Health. Ed. by Leighton C. Whitaker. LC 87-33625. (Journal of College Student Psychotherapy Ser.: Vol. 2, Nos. 1-2). (Illus.). 210p. 1988. pap. text ed. 16.95 (ISBN 0-86656-800-X). Haworth Pr.

Parental Concerns in College Student Mental Health. Ed. by Leighton C. Whitaker. LC 87-33625. (Journal of College Student Psychotherapy Ser.: Vol. 2, Nos. 1-2). (Illus.). 210p. 1988. text ed. 29.95 (ISBN 0-86656-720-8). Haworth Pr.

Parental Death & Psychological Development. Ellen B. Berlinsky & Henry B. Biller. LC 82-48015. 176p. 1982. 25.00x (ISBN 0-669-05875-0). Lexington Bks.

Parental Encouragement & College Plans of High School Students in Korea see **Occasional Papers.**

Parental Grief: Solace & Resolution. Dennis Klass. (Death & Suicide Ser.). 248p. 1988. 26.95x (ISBN 0-8261-5930-3). Springer Pub.

Parental Income & College Opportunities. H. B. Goetsch. LC 72-176807. (Columbia University. Teachers College. Contributions to Education: No. 795). Repr. of 1940 ed. 22.50 (ISBN 0-404-55795-3). AMS Pr.

Parental Involvement in Children's Reading. Keith Topping & Sheila Wolfendale. 320p. 1985. 32.50 (ISBN 0-89397-230-4). Nichols Pub.

Parental Kidnapping: An International Resource Directory. Margaret Strickland. Ed. by Joe T. Caruso. LC 86-6748. 328p. 1986. 18.50 (ISBN 0-935834-39-7). Rainbow Books.

Parental Leave Crisis: Toward a National Policy. Ed. by Edward F. Zigler & Meryl Frank. LC 87-10724. 1988. 30.00x (ISBN 0-300-03984-0). Yale U Pr.

Parental Leave: Judicial & Legislative Trends: Current Practices in the Workplace. Mary E. Radford. write for info. Intl Found Employ.

Parental Loss Achievement. Eisenstadt et al. Tr. by Jacqueline A. Deniz. (Fr.). 1988. text ed. price not set (ISBN 0-8236-3910-X). Intl Univs Pr.

Parental Loss of a Child. Ed. by Therese A. Rando. LC 86-61549. 570p. (Orig.). 1986. pap. text ed. 19.95 (ISBN 0-87822-281-2). Res Press.

Parental Overprotection: A Risk Factor in Psychosocial Development. Gordon Parker. 352p. 1983. 49.50 (ISBN 0-8089-1557-6, 793246). Grune.

Parental Participation in Children's Development & Education. Sheila Wolfendale. LC 82-11946. (Special Aspects of Education Ser.: Vol. 3). 225p. 1983. 40.00 (ISBN 0-677-06060-2). Gordon & Breach.

Parental Reasons for Not Sending Children to School. Rajendra B. Pradhan. 56p. 1981. pap. 9.00 (ISBN 0-318-03450-6). Am-Nepal Ed.

Parental Survival. Walter E. Adams. 126p. (Orig.). 1984. pap. 6.95 (ISBN 0-937408-30-1). GMI Pubns Inc.

Parental Technology Manual. Michael Groves. 132p. 1985. pap. text ed. 29.95 (ISBN 0-935184-04-X). Interpharm.

Parentcare: A Commonsense Guide for Grown-Up Children. Lissy Jarvik & Gary Small. 1988. 19.95 (ISBN 0-517-56765-2). Crown.

Parenteral & Enteral Hyperalimentation: Proceedings of the International Symposium on Parenteral & Enteral Nutrition, Kochi, Japan 16-17, November 1984. Ed. by S. Ogoshi & H. Okada. (International Congress Ser.: No. 649). 392p. 1985. 166.50 (ISBN 0-444-80625-3, Excerpta Medica). Elsevier.

Parenteral & Enteral Nutrition for Nurses. K. Moghissi & Jennifer R. Boore. 210p. 1983. 45.00 (ISBN 0-89443-820-4). Aspen Pub.

Parenteral & Enteral Nutrition for the Hospitalized Patient. Howard Silberman & Daniel Eisenberg. (Illus.). 320p. 1982. pap. 45.00 (ISBN 0-8385-7728-8). Appleton & Lange.

Parenteral Nutrition. Ed. by F. W. Ahnefeld et al. Tr. by A. Babad from Ger. LC 75-34213. (Illus.). 200p. 1975. pap. 21.00 (ISBN 0-387-07518-6). Springer-Verlag.

Parenteral Nutrition in Acute Metabolic Illness. Ed. by H. A. Lee. 1974. 101.00 (ISBN 0-12-441750-7). Acad Pr.

Parenteral Nutrition: Proceedings. Symposium, Copenhagen, 21st, March 1975. (Nutrition & Metabolism: Vol. 20, Suppl. 1). 1977. 24.75 (ISBN 3-8055-2628-8). S Karger.

Parenteral Quality Control: Sterility, Pyrogen, Particulate & Package Integrity Testing. Michael J. Akers. (Advances in Parenteral Sciences Ser.). 256p. 1985. 59.75 (ISBN 0-8247-7357-8). Dekker.

Parenterale Ernaehrung (Forschung und Praxis) Deutsch-Skandinavisches Symposium, Kopenhagen, 1978. Ed. by N. Zoellner. (Beitraege zu Infusionstherapie und Klinische Ernaehrung: Band 1). (Illus.). 1978. pap. 11.50 (ISBN 3-8055-2963-5). S Karger.

Parenterale Ernaehrung unter besonderer Beruecksichtigung der Fettzufuhr. Ed. by J. Eckart. (Beitraege zu Infusionstherapie und Klinische Ernaehrung: Vol. 13). (Illus.). 210p. 1986. 44.75 (ISBN 3-8055-4164-3). S Karger.

Parentheses of Blood. Sony L. Tansi. Tr. by Lorraine Veach from Fr. (Ubu Repertory Theater Publications Ser.: No. 17). 74p. (Orig.). 1986. pap. text ed. 6.25 (ISBN 0-913745-19-7). Ubu Repertory.

Parenthesis in Eternity. Joel S. Goldsmith. LC 64-10368. 1963. pap. 12.95 (ISBN 0-06-063230-5, HarpR). Har-Row.

Parenthesis in Eternity: Living the Mystical Life. Joel S. Goldsmith. LC 85-45354. 1986. pap. 12.95 (ISBN 0-06-063231-3, PL 4125, PL). Har-Row.

Parenthood: A Commitment in Faith. Kathryn W. Orso. LC 75-5219. 64p. (Orig.). 1975. pap. text ed. 2.95 (ISBN 0-8192-1198-2); tchr's ed. 3.75 (ISBN 0-8192-1204-0); wkbk. 3.95 (ISBN 0-8192-1199-0). Morehouse.

Parenthood: A Psychodynamic Perspective. Ed. by Rebecca S. Cohen et al. LC 82-18370. (Guilford Psychiatry Ser.). 426p. 1984. text ed. 40.00 (ISBN 0-89862-225-5, 2225). Guilford Pr.

Parenthood after Thirty: A Guide to Personal Choice. Judith B. Cohen. LC 84-48826. 176p. 1985. pap. 10.95 (ISBN 0-669-09845-0). Lexington Bks.

Parenthood & Social Reproduction: Fostering & Occupational Roles in West Africa. Esther N. Goody. LC 80-42177. (Cambridge Studies in Social Anthropology: No. 35). 368p. 1982. 52.50 (ISBN 0-521-22721-6). Cambridge U Pr.

Parenthood Handbook. S. Lazarus. 1980. pap. write for info. (ISBN 0-201-04370-X). Addison-Wesley.

Parenthood: Its Psychology & Psychopathology. Ed. by E. James Anthony & Therese Benedek. LC 75-112005. 650p. 1970. 31.95 (ISBN 0-316-04370-2). Little.

Parenthood Without Hassles-Well, Almost. Kevin Leman. LC 78-656211. 144p. 1982. pap. 3.25 (ISBN 0-89081-304-3). Harvest Hse.

Parenthood Without Hassles...Well Almost. Kevin Leman. LC 78-65621. 141p. 1988. pap. 5.95 (ISBN 0-89081-183-0). Harvest Hse.

Parenting. Larry C. Jensen & Merrill Kingston. 464p. 1986. text ed. 25.95 (ISBN 0-03-069878-2, HoltC). HR&W.

Parenting. Thomas W. Perrin. (Issues for Children of Alcoholics Ser.). (Orig.). 1985. pap. 0.30 (ISBN 0-933825-03-X). Perrin Inc.

Parenting. Ed. by Paul F. Wilczak. LC 78-69758. (Marriage & Family Living in Depth Bk.). 1978. pap. 2.45 (ISBN 0-87029-138-6, 20220-0). Abbey.

Parenting: A Curriculum for the Single Working Mother. Barbara L. Makris & Linda Davis-Debeuneure. 22p. 1983. pap. text ed. 15.00 (ISBN 0-934966-10-9). WOW Inc.

Parenting: A Skills Training Manual. Louise F. Guerney. LC 78-70674. (Illus.). 151p. (gr. 10-12). 1980. pap. 5.95 (ISBN 0-932990-00-2). IDEALS PA.

Parenting Across the Life Span: Biosocial Dimensions. Ed. by Jane B. Lancaster et al. (Foundations of Human Behavior Ser.). (Illus.). 472p. 1987. lib. bdg. 45.95x (ISBN 0-202-30332-2). Aldine de Gruyter.

Parenting Advisor. Princeton Center for Infancy Staff. Ed. by Frank Caplan. 1978. pap. 16.95 (ISBN 0-385-14330-3, Anch). Doubleday.

Parenting Alone, Francis J. Lodato. 144p. (Orig.). 1986. pap. 7.95 (ISBN 0-941850-22-6). Liturgical Pubns.

Parenting Alone. Ed. by Patricia Roberts. 1980. pap. 4.50 (ISBN 0-8309-0297-X). Herald Hse.

Parenting & Teaching Young Children. Verna Hildebrand. Ed. by Carol Newman. (Illus.). 432p. (gr. 10-12). 1981. text ed. 27.28 (ISBN 0-07-028775-9). McGraw.

Parenting & Teaching Young Children. 2nd ed. Verna Hildebrand. 448p. 1985. text ed. 26.52 (ISBN 0-07-028778-3). McGraw.

Parenting Breakdown. (Studies in Deprivation & Disadvantage). 1988. text ed. 45.00 (ISBN 0-566-05582-1, Pub. by Gower Pub England). Gower Pub Co.

Parenting Children of Divorce. Peter Barnett et al. LC 80-11044. (Workshop Models for Family Life Education Ser.). 111p. 1980. plastic comb 14.95 (ISBN 0-87304-178-X). Family Serv.

Parenting Children with Disabilities. Peggy Miezo. 1983. 29.50x (ISBN 0-8247-1090-8). Phoenix Soc.

Parenting Education at Medford & Churchill High Schools. M. C. Jensen. 1986. 4.00. U of Oreg Bks.

Parenting for Peace & Justice. Kathleen McGinnis & James McGinnis. LC 81-3917. 143p. (Orig.). 1981. pap. 8.95 (ISBN 0-88344-376-7). Orbis Bks.

Parenting from a Distance: Your Right & Responsibilities. Jan Walker. 200p. 1987. pap. 12.95x (ISBN 0-8134-2750-9); review key 2.00 (ISBN 0-8134-2751-7). Inter Print Pubs.

Parenting Guidelines. Bill Kvols-Riedler & Kathy Kvols-Riedler. (Illus.). 40p. 1978. pap. 3.00 (ISBN 0-933450-02-8). RDIC Pubns.

Parenting Happy Healthy Children. Karen Olness. 1981. pap. 8.95 (ISBN 0-9602790-4-0). The Garden.

Parenting in an Unresponsive Society: Managing Work & Family Life. Sheila B. Kamerman. LC 80-641. 1980. 21.95 (ISBN 0-02-916730-2). Free Pr.

Parenting in Contemporary Society. Tommie J. Hamner & Pauline H. Turner. (Illus.). 416p. 1985. pap. text ed. write for info. (ISBN 0-13-648791-2). P-H.

Parenting in the Twenty-First Century. 1987. incl. six one-hour audio tapes 29.95 (ISBN 0-938308-15-7). T Jefferson Res Ctr.

Parenting Isn't for Cowards. James Dobson. 1988. write for info. Word Bks.

Parenting: Its Causes & Consequences. Ed. by L. Wladis Hoffman & R. J. Gandelman. 176p. 1982. text ed. 19.95x (ISBN 0-89859-086-8). L Erlbaum Assocs.

Parenting: Nurturing a Baby into a Well-Adjusted Teenager. Robert L. Berko. 72p. write for info. Consumer Ed Res.

Parenting Our Parents: Senior Care Options for Concerned Families. Brad Zweck. 32p. (Orig.). 1988. pap. 2.95 (ISBN 0-945485-07-7). Comm Intervention.

Parenting Skills: Workbook & Trainer's Manual. 2nd ed. Richard R. Abidin. LC 81-13314. 85p. 1982. wkbk. 188 14.95 (ISBN 0-89885-118-1); 19.95 (ISBN 0-89885-117-3); Set. 23.75 (ISBN 0-89885-119-X). Human Sci Pr.

Parenting the Adolescent. Carl Pickhardt. (Illus.). 200p. (Orig.). 1987. pap. 12.95 (ISBN 0-938934-16-3). C&M Pubns.

Parenting the Gifted: Developing the Promise. Sheila C. Perino & Joseph Perino. 214p. 1981. 34.95 (ISBN 0-8352-1354-4); pap. 14.95 (ISBN 0-8352-1408-7). Bowker.

Parenting the Handicapped Child. Miezio. LC 83-6604. (Pediatric Habilitations Ser.). 256p. 1983. 29.50. Dekker.

Parenting the Learning Disabled: A Realistic Approach. Rhoda W. Cummings & Cleborne D. Maddux. 144p. 1985. 21.75x (ISBN 0-398-05151-8). C C Thomas.

Parenting Through the College Years. Norman Giddan & Sally Vallongo. Ed. by Susan Williamson. 192p. (Orig.). 1988. pap. text ed. 9.95 (ISBN 0-913589-37-3). Williamson Pub Co.

Parenting Today: A Teaching Guide. Jerelyn Schultz et al. (Contemporary Parenting Choices Ser.: Module 3). 250p. 1984. pap. text ed. 17.95 (ISBN 0-8138-0358-6). Iowa St U Pr.

Parenting Together. Barbara J. Mesle & C. Robert Mesle. 1981. pap. 4.50 (ISBN 0-8309-0311-9). Herald Hse.

Parenting Together: Men & Women Sharing the Care of Their Children. Diane Ehrensaft. 350p. 1987. 19.95 (ISBN 0-02-909440-2). Free Pr.

Parent's Guide to String Instrument Study. Lorraine Fink. LC 77-79565. (Illus.). 1977. pap. 2.50 (ISBN 0-8497-5700-2, WS3, Pub. by Kjos West). Kjos.
Parent's Guide to Summer Camp: How to Pick the Right Summer Camp for Your Kids. Ward Akers. LC 88-60466. (Illus.). 144p. (Orig.). 1988. pap. 8.95 (ISBN 0-914457-22-5). Mustang Pub.
Parents' Guide to Teaching Kids to Play. Chet Murphy. LC 81-85622. (Illus.). 144p. (Orig.). 1983. pap. text ed. 9.95 (ISBN 0-918438-91-8). Leisure Pr.
Parents' Guide to Teenage Pregnancy. Margaret Brownley. 36p. (Orig.). 1988. pap. 2.95 (ISBN 0-945485-05-0). Comm Intervention.
Parents' Guide to Teenagers. Ed. by Leonard H. Gross. 385p. 1981. 14.95 (ISBN 0-02-545820-5). Macmillan.
Parents' Guide to the Childbearing Year. rev. ed. Peg Beals. 84p. 1980. saddle stitched 3.50 (ISBN 0-934024-04-9). Intl Childbirth.
Parent's Guide to the Delaware Valley. Cynthia Roberts. LC 88-15021. 300p. (Orig.). 1988. pap. 9.95 (ISBN 0-940159-04-X). Camino Bks.
Parents Guide to the Five U. S. Service Academies: A Firsthand Personal Account of What You Can Expect Along the Way. Helen Powers. (Illus.). 192p. 1986. pap. 12.95 (ISBN 0-8117-2192-2). Stackpole.
Parents' Guide to the Montessori Classroom. Aline D. Wolf. (Illus.). 1980. pap. 5.00x (ISBN 0-9601016-0-8). Parent-Child Pr.
Parent's Guide to the Social Studies. Daniel Roselle. 16p. 1974. pap. 1.25 (ISBN 0-87986-053-7, 491-15274). Nat Coun Soc Studies.
Parent's Guide to Video & Audio Cassettes for Children. Andrea E. Cascardi. Date not set. pap. 7.95 (ISBN 0-446-38513-1). Warner Bks.
Parent's Guide to Youth Soccer. Carolyn Mullins. LC 83-80731. (Illus.). 144p. (Orig.). 1983. pap. 8.95 (ISBN 0-88011-201-8, PMUL0201). Leisure Pr.
Parents Guide to Youth Sports. Ronald E. Smith et al. (Illus.). 208p. 1989. pap. 9.95 (ISBN 0-937359-47-5). HDL Pubs.
Parents Handbook of Childhood Allergies. Richard Garber. 208p. 1983. pap. 2.95 (ISBN 0-345-30443-8). Ballantine.
Parent's Handbook: Systematic Training for Effective Parenting (STEP) Don Dinkmeyer & Gary D. McKay. (Illus.). 120p. 1982. pap. 9.95 (ISBN 0-913476-80-3). Am Guidance.
Parent's Handbook: Systematic Training for Effective Parenting (STEP) Don Dinkmeyer & Gary D. McKay. 1982. pap. 6.95 (ISBN 0-394-71031-2). Random.
Parents Have Rights, Too! M. Donald Thomas. LC 78-63270. (Fastback Ser.: No. 120). 1978. pap. 0.90 (ISBN 0-87367-120-1). Phi Delta Kappa.
Parents Helping Students: Parents Supplement to High School Study Skills. Walter Pauk. 35p. (Orig.). 1987. pap. text ed. 2.00 (ISBN 0-9614487-3-3). Reston-Stuart Pub.
Parents in a Pressure Cooker. Jane E. Bluestein & Lynn Collins-Fantozzi. 167p. 1983. pap. 7.95 (ISBN 0-915817-02-0); wkbk. 4.95 (ISBN 0-915817-08-X). ISS Pubns.
Parents in a Pressure Cooker. rev. ed. Jane E. Bluestein & Lynn Collins-Fantozzi. (Illus.). 176p. 1985. pap. 8.95 (ISBN 0-915817-13-6). ISS Pubns.
Parents in Action. Grant B. Bitter. LC 78-58604. 1978. pap. 6.95 (ISBN 0-88200-122-1, 15672). Alexander Graham.
Parents in Contemporary America: A Sympathetic View. 4th ed. E. E. LeMasters & John Defrain. 1983. pap. 22.00x (ISBN 0-256-02679-3). Dorsey.
Parents in Control. David Rice. LC 86-80706. 208p. (Orig.). 1987. pap. 5.95 (ISBN 0-89081-505-4). Harvest Hse.
Parents in Pain. John White. LC 78-24760. 1979. pap. 7.95 (ISBN 0-87784-582-4); study guide 1.95 (ISBN 0-87784-492-5). Inter-Varsity.
Parents in Positive Control: Learn Techniques to Free Your Child from the "Adult No" for Part of Each Day. E. Robbins Kimball. LC 87-91723. (Illus.). 208p. (Orig.). 1987. pap. text ed. write for info. (ISBN 0-9619113-0-1). E R Kimball.
Parent's Journey into Magic Moments in the Kingdom of Kids. Marlee Alex & Ben Alex. 64p. 1986. 10.95 (ISBN 0-8407-6699-8). Nelson.
Parents, Kids & Sports: Making the Experience Positive. Bernie Schock. 1987. pap. 6.95 (ISBN 0-8024-6307-X). Moody.
Parents Learn Through Discussion: Principles & Practices of Parent Group Education. Aline B. Auerbach. LC 80-13749. 380p. 1980. Repr. of 1968 ed. lib. bdg. 27.50 (ISBN 0-89874-183-1). Krieger.
Parents' Manual. 2nd ed. MSA Women's Committee. LC 75-9961. 1976. pap. 4.00 (ISBN 0-89259-001-7). Am Trust Pubns.
Parents Manual. pap. 7.50 (ISBN 0-686-18465-3). Kazi Pubns.
Parents Matter: Parents' Relationships with Lesbian Daughters & Gay Sons. Ann Muller. (Illus.). 320p. 1987. pap. 9.95 (ISBN 0-930044-91-6). Naiad Pr.
Parent's Micro-Computer Handbook. Eugene Galanter. LC 82-82310. (Kids & Computer Ser.). 192p. (Orig.). 1983. 14.95 (ISBN 0-399-50876-7, G&D); pap. 7.95 (ISBN 0-399-50749-3). Putnam Pub Group.
Parents' Nutrition Book. Margaret McWilliams. LC 85-29588. 296p. 1986. pap. 16.95 (ISBN 0-471-84279-6). Wiley.
Parents of Children in Placement: Perspectives & Programs. Ed. by Paula A. Sinanoglu & Anthony N. Maluccio. 475p. 1981. 32.50 (ISBN 0-87868-205-8, 2058); pap. 21.95 (ISBN 0-87868-181-7, 1817). Child Welfare.
Parents of Oscar Wilde: Sir William & Lady Wilde. Terrence D. White. LC 79-8086. Repr. of 1967 ed. 31.00 (ISBN 0-404-18394-8). AMS Pr.
Parents of the Homosexual, Vol. 11. David K. Switzer & Shirley A. Switzer. LC 80-13748. (Christian Care Bks.). 118p. 1980. pap. 7.95 (ISBN 0-664-24327-4). Westminster John Knox.
Parents on Probation, New York Nineteen Twenty-Seven. Miriam Van Waters. Ed. by David J. Rothman & Sheila M. Rothman. (Women & Children First Ser.). 333p. 1986. lib. bdg. 40.00 (ISBN 0-8240-7679-6). Garland Pub.
Parents on Successful Parenting. John J. Evoy. LC 86-61354. 129p. (Orig.). 1987. pap. 7.95 (ISBN 0-934134-90-1). Sheed & Ward MO.
Parents on the Run. Willard Beecher & Marguerite Beecher. LC 73-83773. 238p. 1983. pap. 6.95 (ISBN 0-87516-522-2). DeVorss.
Parents on the Run. Willard Beecher & Marguerite Beecher. 238p. 1983. pap. 6.95. Beecher Found.
Parents Organizing to Improve Schools. rev. ed. National Committee for Citizens in Education. 1985. pap. 3.50 (ISBN 0-934460-21-3). NCCE.
Parents... Partners in Education. Cambodian ed. American Association of School Administrators Staff. 12p. 1987. pap. text ed. write for info. (ISBN 0-87652-116-2, 021-00197). Am Assn Sch Admin.
Parents: Partners in Education. Hmong ed. American Association of School Administrators Staff. 16p. 1987. pap. write for info. (ISBN 0-87652-117-0, 021-00198). Am Assn Sch Admin.
Parents: Partners in Education. Lao ed. American Association of School Administrators Staff. 12p. (Orig.). 1987. pap. write for info. (021-00199). Am Assn Sch Admin.
Parent's Pediatric Companion. Gil Simon & Marcia Cohen. LC 84-27302. (Illus.). 416p. 1985. 17.95 (ISBN 0-688-03791-7). Morrow.
Parent's Pediatric Companion. Gil Simon & Marcia Cohen. 378p. 1988. pap. 7.95 (ISBN 0-688-07524-X, Quill). Morrow.
Parents, Peers, & Pot II: Parents In Action. Marsha Manatt. 171p. 1983. pap. 4.50 (ISBN 0-318-11811-4, S/N 017-024-01174-6). USGPO.
Parents Perspective. Charles S. Mueller. Bd. with Teenagers' Turn. (Let's Talk Ser.). 144p. 1987. pap. 5.95 (ISBN 0-570-09061-X). Concordia.
Parents, Please Don't Sit on Your Kids: A Parent's Guide to Nonpunitive Discipline. Clare Cherry. 1985. pap. 9.95 (ISBN 0-8224-5307-X). D S Lake Pubs.
Parent's Power for Phonics. new ed. Cecil D. Alberts. (Illus.). 1978. pap. text ed. 45.00 (ISBN 0-915048-01-9). Spin-A-Test Pub.
Parents, Pregnant Teens, & the Adoption Option: Help for Families. Jeanne W. Lindsay. 160p. (Orig.). 1988. 13.95 (ISBN 0-930934-29-6); pap. 8.95 (ISBN 0-930934-28-8). Morning Glory.
Parent's Primer: What You Need to Know about Your Child's Elementary School. Elizabeth Fideler. 400p. 1987. text ed. 36.50x (ISBN 0-8290-1915-4); pap. 19.95x (ISBN 0-8290-1916-2). Irvington.
Parents, Professionals & Mentally Handicapped People. Ed. by Peter Mittler & Helen McConachie. LC 84-23751. 243p. (Orig.). 1983. pap. text ed. 14.95 (ISBN 0-914797-12-3, Co-Pub. by Croom Helm Ltd). Brookline Bks.
Parents, Professionals & Mentally Handicapped People: Approaches to Partnership. Ed. by Peter Mittler & Helen McConachie. (Illus.). 243p. 1983. 25.25 (ISBN 0-7099-1750-3, Pub. by Croom Helm Ltd). Routledge Chapman & Hall.
Parents' Record of Educational Progress: How to Insure Your Child's Success in School. Nancy Reckinger. 78p. (Orig.). 1982. pap. 10.00 (ISBN 0-943346-00-2). Ctr Ed Alternatives.
Parents Resource Book. Gail G. Velez. (Illus.). 240p. (Orig.). 1986. pap. 9.95 (ISBN 0-452-25739-5, Plume). NAL.
Parents Revolt. Kathleen Titmuss & Richard Titmuss. Ed. by F. M. Leventhal. (English Workers & the Coming of the Welfare State Ser., 1918-1945). 30.00 (ISBN 0-8240-7632-X). Garland Pub.
Parents' Rights. John W. Whitehead. LC 85-70468. 160p. 1985. pap. 7.95 (ISBN 0-89107-364-7, Crossway Bks). Good News.
Parents' Role in Campus Visits. Helene Reynolds. 11p. (Orig.). 1980. pap. 1.25 (ISBN 0-87866-166-2). Petersons Guides.
Parents: Round-the-Clock Teachers. Lawrence O. Richards. LC 87-63569. (Successful Teaching Ser.). 112p. (Orig.). 1988. pap. 4.95 (ISBN 1-55513-166-2, 60244). Cook.
Parents, Schools, & the Law. David Schimmel & Louis Fischer. 294p. 1987. 17.95 (ISBN 0-934460-29-9); pap. 10.95 (ISBN 0-934460-31-0). NCCE.
Parents' Solution Book. Lea Bramnick & Anita Simon. 320p. 1983. 14.95 (ISBN 0-531-09881-8). Watts.
Parents' Solution Book: Your Child from Five to Twelve. Lea Bramnick & Anita Simon. 1984. pap. 9.95 (ISBN 0-399-51076-1, Perigee). Putnam Pub Group.
Parents Speak Out: Then & Now. 2nd ed. Ann Turnbull & Rutherford Turnbull. 304p. 1985. pap. text ed. 16.95 (ISBN 0-675-20404-6). Merrill.
Parents Survival Guide: Baby & U. Margaret R. Spelman & Sandra L. Kosik. 1987. pap. 5.95 (ISBN 0-933803-09-5). HealthProInk.
Parent's Survival Guide: How to Cope When Your Kid Is Using Drugs. Harriet W. Hodgson. 1987. pap. 6.95 (ISBN 0-06-255424-7, HarpR). Har-Row.
Parent's Survival Guide: How to Cope When Your Kid Is Using Drugs. Harriet W. Hodgson. 66p. (Orig.). 1986. pap. 4.95 (ISBN 0-89486-390-8). Hazelden.
Parents, Take Charge! Perry L. Draper. 1982. pap. 5.95 (ISBN 0-8423-4822-0); leader's guide 2.95 (ISBN 0-8423-4823-9). Tyndale.
Parents Talk Love. Susan K. Sullivan & Matthew A. Kawaik. 1988. pap. 3.95 (ISBN 0-317-68100-1). Bantam.
Parents Talk Love: The Catholic Family Handbook on Sexuality. Susan Sullivan & Matthew Kawiak. LC 84-80361. 164p. (Orig.). 1984. pap. 7.95 (ISBN 0-8091-2639-7). Paulist Pr.
Parents: Talk with Your Children. V. Gilbert Beers. LC 87-82257. 224p. (Orig.). 1988. pap. 7.95 (ISBN 0-89081-597-6). Harvest Hse.
Parents Talking Television. Philip Simpson. 144p. 1987. lib. bdg. 35.00x (ISBN 185-178-034-3, Pub. by Comedia); pap. 11.95x (ISBN 185-178-033-5). Routledge Chapman & Hall.
Parents, Teachers & Children: Prospects for Choice in American Education. James S. Coleman et al. LC 77-89164. 336p. 1977. pap. text ed. 5.95 (ISBN 0-917616-18-9). ICS Pr.
Parents, Teenagers & Sex. Ed. by John Robson. (Illus.). 40p. (Orig.). 1982. pap. 2.50 (ISBN 0-936098-34-1). Intl Marriage.
Parents, Teens & Other Strangers. Gary Sivewright & Dan Croy. (Orig.). 1987. pap. 2.50 (ISBN 0-8341-1193-4). Beacon Hill.
Parents Terribles. Jean Cocteau. 192p. 1972. pap. 8.95 (ISBN 0-686-54546-X). French & Eur.
Parents: The Child's First Piano Teacher. Dasie Singletary. (Illus.). 48p. (gr. k-4). 1980. PLB 5.95 (ISBN 0-89962-042-6). Todd & Honeywell.
Parent's Treasure Box of Ideas for Preschoolers. Judy V. Rolfs. 96p. 1985. pap. 3.95 (ISBN 0-8423-4915-4). Tyndale.
Parent's When-Not-to Worry Book: Straight Talk About All Those Myths You've Learned from Your Parents, Friends& Even Doctors. Barry Behrstock & Richard Trubo. LC 80-7894. 256p. 1981. 13.45i (ISBN 0-690-01972-6, HarpT). Har-Row.
Parents with Careers Workbook. Ashery. 1987. pap. 6.95 (ISBN 0-317-56914-7). Acropolis.
Parents Work Is Never Done: Helping Children from 16-30 Grow Toward Psychological Well-Being. Margery Neely & James Haines. 280p. 1987. 15.95 (ISBN 0-88282-027-3). New Horizon NJ.
Parentspeak on Gifted & Talented Children. Kay Coffey et al. 61p. 8.95 (ISBN 0-318-02121-8). NSLTIGT.
Parerga & Paralipomena: Short Philosophical Essays, 2 vols. Arthur Schopenhauer. Tr. by E. F. Payne from Ger. 1201p. 1974. Vol. 1. 56.00x (ISBN 0-19-824508-4); Vol. 2. 63.00x (ISBN 0-19-824527-0); Set. 115.00x (ISBN 0-19-519813-1); Vol. 1. pap. 23.00x (ISBN 0-19-824634-X); Vol. 2. pap. 23.00x (ISBN 0-19-824635-8). Oxford U Pr.
Pares-Pares. Bienvenido M. Noriega. 238p. (Orig.). 1983. pap. 12.00x (ISBN 971-10-0064-4, Pub. by New Day Philippines). Cellar.
Pareto. Franz Borkenau. LC 78-20454. 1980. Repr. of 1936 ed. 19.00 (ISBN 0-88355-833-5). Hyperion Conn.
Pareto. Julien Freund. Ed. & tr. by Simona Draghici. LC 87-11880. 256p. (Orig.). 1988. pap. 8.95 (ISBN 0-943045-00-2). Plutarch Pr DC.
Pareto's Italian Letters. Vilfredo Pareto. (Illus.). 97p. (Fr.). 1981. Repr. of 1897 ed. 127.75 (ISBN 0-89901-371-6). Found Class Reprints.
Parfait Knight. Juliet Blyth. 1987. pap. 3.50 (ISBN 0-317-64583-8). St Martin.
Parfit Knight. Juliet Blyth. 240p. 1986. 14.95 (ISBN 0-312-59664-2). St Martin.
Parfit Knight. Juliet Blyth. 1987. pap. 3.50 (ISBN 0-312-90851-2). St Martin.
Parfum de Pluie. Jane Donnelly. (Collection Harlequin Ser.). 192p. 1983. pap. 1.95 (ISBN 0-373-49370-3). Harlequin Bks.
Pargiters; the Novel-Essay Portion of "The Years". Virginia Woolf. Ed. by Mitchell A. Leaska. LC 77-2389. (Illus.). 1977. 16.00 (ISBN 0-87104-268-1). NY Pub Lib.
Pargiters: The Novel Essay Portion of the Years. Virginia Woolf. 167p. 1985. pap. 4.95 (ISBN 0-15-671380-2). HarBraceJ.
Pari-Mutuel Examiner. Jack Rudman. (Career Examination Ser.: C-644). (Cloth bdg. avail. on request). pap. 12.00 (ISBN 0-8373-0644-2). Natl Learning.
Pariah, 3 vols. in 2. F. Anstey, pseud. LC 79-8228. Repr. of 1889 ed. Set. 84.50 (ISBN 0-404-61757-3). AMS Pr.
Pariah. Graham Masterton. (Orig.). 1984. pap. 3.50 (ISBN 0-8125-2193-5, Dist. by Warner Pub Services & Saint Martin's Press). Tor Bks.
Pariah. Collin Wilcox. (Lt. Frank Hastings Mystery Ser.). 1988. 15.95 (ISBN 0-89296-280-1). Mysterious Pr.
Pariah see Plays from the Cynical Life.
Pariah & Other Stories. Joan Williams. (Southern Writers Ser.). 1985. pap. 3.50 (ISBN 0-380-69979-6). Avon.
Pariah Syndrome: An Account of Gypsy Slavery & Persecution. Ian Hancock. (Illus.). vi, 203p. 1986. pap. 17.95 (ISBN 0-89720-079-9). Karoma.
Pariahs Stand up! The Founding of the Liberal Feminist Movement in France, 1858-1889. Patrick K. Bidelman. LC 81-4222. (Contributions in Women's Studies: No. 31). xi, 240p. 1982. lib. bdg. 35.00 (ISBN 0-313-23006-4, BPU/). Greenwood.
Parietal Cortex of Monkey & Man. J. Hyvaerinen. (Studies of Brain Function: Vol. 8). (Illus.). 210p. 1982. 44.50 (ISBN 0-387-11652-4). Springer-Verlag.
Parietal Lobes. McDonald Critchley. (Illus.). 1966. Repr. of 1953 ed. 52.95x (ISBN 0-02-843300-9). Hafner.
Parikh's Textbook of Medical Jurisprudence & Toxicology: For Classrooms & Courtrooms. C. K. Parikh. (Illus.). 1108p. 1980. 145.00 (ISBN 0-08-025522-1). Pergamon.
Pariksamukham (with Prameya-ratna-mala, by Anantavirya) Manikyanandi. Ed. & commentary by Sarat C. Ghoshal. LC 73-3845. Repr. of 1940 ed. 40.00 (ISBN 0-404-57711-3). AMS Pr.
Paris. Berlitz Editors. (Berlitz Travel Guide). 1987. pap. 6.95 (ISBN 0-02-969670-4, Berlitz). Macmillan.
Paris. Christina Carroll. 384p. 1986. pap. 3.95x (ISBN 0-441-65023-6, Pub. by Charter Bks). Ace Bks.
Paris. Photos by Rene Champollion. (Illus.). 244p. 1988. 60.00 (ISBN 0-86565-091-8). Vendome.
Paris. G. W. Edwards. 59.95 (ISBN 0-8490-0799-2). Gordon Pr.
Paris. Ronald Frame. 90p. (Orig.). 1987. pap. 7.95 (ISBN 0-571-14776-3). Faber & Faber.
Paris. Augustus J. Hare. 1976. 10.00 (ISBN 0-8495-2426-1). Arden Lib.
Paris. Photos by Francisco Hidalgo. Tr. by Roselyn Dory & Patrick O'Dowd. (Illus.). 144p. 1986. 40.00 (ISBN 0-916567-05-2). Arpel Graphic.
Paris. (Panorama Bks.). (Illus., Fr.). 3.95 (ISBN 0-685-11477-5). French & Eur.
Paris. (Badeker's City Guides Ser.). 1987. pap. 10.95 (ISBN 0-13-058066-X). P-H.
Paris. (In Your Pocket Ser.). 208p. 1987. pap. 3.95 (ISBN 0-8120-3756-1). Barron.
Paris. (Michael's Walking Guides Ser.). (Illus.). 200p. (Orig.). 1987. pap. 6.95 (ISBN 965-288-013-2). Hunter Pub NY.
Paris. (Berlitz Deluxe Guides). 1988. pap. 10.95 (ISBN 2-831-50365-5, Berlitz). Macmillan.
Paris. rev. ed. (Frommer's City Guides Ser.). (Illus.). 224p. 1988. pap. 5.95 (ISBN 0-13-047796-6). Prentice Hall Pr.
Paris. (Berlitz Deluxe Guides). (Illus.). 336p. 1988. 10.95 (ISBN 0-02-968210-X, Berlitz). Macmillan.
Paris. (Berlitz Deluxe Guide). (Illus.). 336p. 1989. 10.95 (ISBN 2-8315-0365-5, Berlitz). Macmillan.
Paris. John Russell. (Illus.). 352p. 1983. 45.00 (ISBN 0-8109-1457-3). Abrams.
Paris. Emile Zola. 586p. 1955. 8.95 (ISBN 0-686-55796-4). French & Eur.
Paris. Emile Zola. lib. bdg. 250.00 (ISBN 0-87968-236-1). Gordon Pr.
Paris see Trois Villes.
Paris: A Century of Change, Eighteen Seventy-Eight to Nineteen Seventy-Eight. Evenson. LC 78-10257. 1979. pap. 19.95x (ISBN 0-300-02667-6). Yale U Pr.
Paris: A Literary Companion. Ian Littlewood. 1988. 16.95 (ISBN 0-531-15079-8). Watts.
Paris Access. (Access Ser.). 1986. pap. 14.95. P-H.
Paris Access. Richard S. Wurman. (Access Guidebooks). (Illus.). 183p. (Orig.). 1986. pap. 14.95 (ISBN 0-671-62577-2). Access Pr.
Paris Alive, the Point of View of an American. Judith Clancy et al. Orig. Title: Paris Vivant. (Illus.). 72p. (Fr. & Eng.). 1986. pap. 10.00 (ISBN 0-912184-06-X). Synergistic Pr.
Paris & Environs. 6th ed. Ian Robertson. (Blue Guides Ser.). (Illus., Orig.). 1985. pap. 16.95 (ISBN 0-393-30073-0). Norton.
Paris & Her People under the Third Republic. E. A. Vizetelly. Repr. of 1919 ed. 29.00 (ISBN 0-527-93256-6). Kraus Repr.
Paris & Its Provinces 1792-1802. Richard Cobb. 1975. 25.00x (ISBN 0-19-212195-2). Oxford U Pr.
Paris & New York Diaries of Ned Rorem. Ned Rorem. LC 82-73718. (First in A Ser.). 432p. 1983. pap. 15.00 (ISBN 0-86547-109-6). N Point Pr.
Paris & Northern France. (Mill House All-in-One Guides). (Illus.). 416p. 1989. pap. 12.95 (ISBN 0-02-035121-6, Collier). Macmillan.
Paris & Rome: The Gallican Church & the Ultramontane Campaign 1848-1853. Austin Gough. 280p. 1986. 49.95x (ISBN 0-19-821977-6). Oxford U Pr.
Paris & Southern France. Mill House Staff. (Illus.). 416p. 1989. pap. 12.95 (ISBN 0-02-035122-4, Collier). Macmillan.

TITLE INDEX PARISH OF ST. PANCRAS

Paris & the Parisians. Fanny Trollope. 544p. 1985. pap. 5.95 (ISBN 0-87052-209-4, Pub. by Allan Sutton England). Hippocrene Bks.
Paris & the Provinces: The Politics of Local Government Reform in France. Peter A. Gourevitch. LC 79-64666. 256p. 1980. 33.00x (ISBN 0-520-03971-8). U of Cal Pr.
Paris & the Social Revolution. Alvan F. Sanborn. 1905. 35.00 (ISBN 0-686-19918-9). Quaker City.
Paris As a Financial Center. Margaret G. Myers. LC 82-48210. (Gold, Money, Inflation & Deflation Ser.). 199p. 1982. lib. bdg. 28.00 (ISBN 0-8240-5248-X). Garland Pub.
Paris As It Was. Hendon Publishing Co., Ltd. Staff. 1986. 43.00x (ISBN 0-317-54153-6, Pub. by Hendon Pub UK). State Mutual Bk.
Paris As Seen & Described by Famous Writers: Dickens, Thackeray, Etc. Ed. by Esther Singleton. Repr. of 1900 ed. 25.00 (ISBN 0-89987-016-3). Darby Bks.
Paris at Its Best. Robert S. Kane. (World at Its Best Ser.). 232p. Date not set. pap. 9.95 (ISBN 0-8442-9563-9, Passport Bks). Natl Textbk.
Paris at Night. (Panorama Bks.). (Illus., Fr.). 3.95 (ISBN 0-685-11478-3). French & Eur.
Paris Atlas, No. 011. 10th ed. 1986. pap. 8.95 (ISBN 2-06-000118-8). Michelin.
Paris Bourse & French Finance with Reference to Organized Speculation in New York. William Parker. LC 20-18734. (Columbia University Studies in the Social Sciences: No. 204). Repr. of 1920 ed. 14.50 (ISBN 0-404-51204-6). AMS Pr.
Paris by Night. Brassai. LC 87-43057. (Illus.). 96p. 1988. Repr. 24.95 (ISBN 0-394-75552-9). Pantheon.
Paris by Night. Photos by Brassai. LC 87-43053. (Illus.). 96p. 1987. 39.95 (ISBN 0-394-56327-1). Pantheon.
Paris: Center of Artistic Enlightenment. Ed. by George Mauner et al. (Papers in Art History: Vol. IV). (Illus.). 300p. (Orig.). 1988. pap. 22.00 (ISBN 0-915773-03-1). Penn St Univ Dept Art Hist.
Paris City Councillors in the Sixteenth Century: The Politics of Patrimony. B. B. Diefendorf. 1982. 39.00x (ISBN 0-691-05362-6). Princeton U Pr.
Paris Codex: Decoding an Astronomical Ephemeris. Gregory Severin. LC 80-68488. (Transactions Ser.: Vol. 71, Pt. 5). 1981. 10.00 (ISBN 0-87169-715-7). Am Philos.
Paris Commune in the Stage Valles, Grieg, Brecht, Adamov. Gerhard Fischer. (European University Studies: Series 1, German Language & Literature, Vol. 422). 242p. 1981. pap. 35.25 (ISBN 3-8204-7078-6). P Lang Pubs.
Paris Confidential. Warren Trabant & Jean Trabant. 134p. 1987. 9.95 (ISBN 0-945332-00-9). Agora Inc MD.
Paris Conservatoire & the Contest Solos for Bassoon. Kristine K. Fletcher. LC 87-45442. 160p. 1988. 17.50x (ISBN 0-253-34215-5). Ind U Pr.
Paris Convention for the Protection of Industrial Property. pap. 7.50 (ISBN 0-686-53020-9, WIPO4, WIPO). UNIPUB.
Paris During the Commune. W. Gibson. LC 75-1245. (World History Ser., No. 48). 1974. lib. bdg. 75.00x (ISBN 0-8383-1776-6). Haskell.
Paris Edition: The Autobiography of Waverly Root, 1927-1934. Waverley Root. Ed. & intro. by Samuel Abt. LC 86-62826. 224p. 1987. 16.95 (ISBN 0-86547-276-9). N Point Pr.
Paris, Eighteen Seventy to Nineteen Thiry-Five. J. Bertaut. Repr. of 1936 ed. 37.00 (ISBN 0-527-07200-1). Kraus Repr.
Paris: English Edition-Country, City & Regional Guides. (Michelin Green Guides). pap. 10.95 (ISBN 0-686-56393-X). French & Eur.
Paris et sa Banlieue: French Edition-Country & City Guides. (Michelin Green Guides). pap. 12.95 (ISBN 0-686-56409-X). French & Eur.
Paris Fashion: A Cultural History. Valerie Steele. (Illus.). 336p. 1988. 35.00 (ISBN 0-19-504465-7). Oxford U Pr.
Paris Fashions of the Eighteen Nineties: A Picture Source Book with 450 Designs, Including 24 in Full Color. Ed. by Stella Blum. (Antiques Ser.). 144p. (Orig.). 1984. pap. 7.95 (ISBN 0-486-24534-9). Dover.
Paris, France. new ed. Gertrude Stein. LC 76-131286. (Illus.). 1970. pap. 6.95 (ISBN 0-87140-231-9). Liveright.
Paris, France - Cooking with Betty Evans. Betty Evans. (Illus., Orig.). 1987. pap. 6.95 (ISBN 0-931104-20-3). Sunflower Ink.
Paris Graffiti. Photos by Joerg Huber. LC 86-50198. (Illus.). 72p. 1986. pap. 9.95 (ISBN 0-500-27440-1). Thames Hudson.
Paris Gun: The Bombardment of Paris & the Great German Offensives of 1918. Henry W. Miller. 59.95 (ISBN 0-8490-0800-X). Gordon Pr.
Paris in Color see Travel Guides in Color.
Paris in Japan. Japan Society Staff. 288p. 1987. 150.00x (Pub. by Han-Shan Tang Ltd). State Mutual Bk.
Paris in Japan: The Japanese Encounter with European Painting. Shuji Takashina & J. Thomas Rimer. LC 87-50582. (Illus.). 288p. (Orig.). 1987. pap. 20.00 (ISBN 0-936316-11-X). Wash U Gallery.
Paris in Japan: The Japanese Encounter with European Painting. Shuji Takashina et al. LC 87-50582. (Illus.). 288p. 1988. pap. 30.00 (ISBN 0-295-96700-5). U of Wash Pr.
Paris in Seventeen Eighty-Nine to Seventeen Ninety-Four, Farewell Letters of Victims of the Guillotine. John G. Alger. LC 78-113540. Repr. of 1902 ed. 49.50 (ISBN 0-404-00323-0). AMS Pr.
Paris in Splendor, 2 vols. E. A. Reynolds-Ball. 1976. Set. lib. bdg. 200.00 (ISBN 0-8490-2412-9). Gordon Pr.
Paris in the Cities. Goldstein Gallery Staff. (Illus.). 16p. (Orig.). 1986. pap. 3.00 (ISBN 0-939719-01-0). UMN Goldstein Gall.
Paris in the Fifties. Beulah Roth. 1988. 19.95. Mercury Hse Inc.
Paris in the Terror. 416p. pap. 9.95 (ISBN 0-931933-18-8). Richardson & Steirman.
Paris Is Fun: A Bilingual Guide. Lory Alder. 1969. 7.95 (ISBN 0-7207-0225-9). Transatl Arts.
Paris: Its Sites, Monuments & History. Maria H. Lansdale. 1977. lib. bdg. 59.95 (ISBN 0-8490-2413-7). Gordon Pr.
Paris Journal: Nineteen Fifty-Six - Nineteen Sixty-Five. Janet Flanner, pseud. Ed. by William Shawn. 324p. Date not set. 11.95 (ISBN 0-15-670949-X, Harv). HarBraceJ.
Paris Journal: Nineteen Forty-Four - Nineteen Fifty-Five. Janet Flanner, pseud. Ed. by William Shawn. 336p. Date not set. 11.95 (ISBN 0-15-670948-1, Harv). HarBraceJ.
Paris Journal: Vol. I, 1944-1965. Janet Flanner. Ed. by William Shawn. LC 76-45462. 624p. 1977. pap. 8.95 (ISBN 0-15-670950-3, Harv). HarBraceJ.
Paris Journal: Vol. II, 1965-1971. Janet Flanner. Ed. by William Shawn. LC 76-45462. 444p. 1977. pap. 11.95 (ISBN 0-15-670951-1, Harv). HarBraceJ.
Paris Kill. Philip Kirk. (Butler Ser.: No. 10). 240p. 1983. pap. 2.50 (ISBN 0-8439-2004-1, Leisure Bks). Leisure NY.
Paris Kill-Ground. Joseph R. Rosenberger. (Cobra Ser.: No. 2). 224p. (Orig.). 1987. pap. 2.95 (ISBN 1-55547-160-9). Critics Choice Paper.
Paris la Belle. Jacques Prevert & P. Prevert. 5.95 (ISBN 0-686-54914-7). French & Eur.
Paris Law Courts: Sketches of Men & Manners. Gerald P. Moriarty. (Illus.). viii, 293p. 1987. Repr. of 1894 ed. lib. bdg. 37.50x (ISBN 0-8377-2434-1). Rothman.
Paris Lights. Beverly Pabst. (Illus.). 40p. (Orig.). 1986. pap. 10.95 (ISBN 0-87663-504-4). Universe.
Paris-Magnum: Photographs 1935-1981. Irwin Shaw. LC 81-68200. (Illus.). 112p. 1981. 30.00 (ISBN 0-89381-085-1). Aperture.
Paris: Michelin Travel Guides. (Fr.). pap. 6.95 (ISBN 0-685-36091-1). French & Eur.
Paris, New York: Nineteen Eighty-Two to Nineteen Eighty-Four. Kazimierz Brandys. LC 87-43215. 160p. 1988. 17.95 (ISBN 0-394-54492-7). Random.
Paris Nights, No. 6. Yvonne Greene. (Kelly Blake Teen Model Ser.). 160p. (Orig.). (YA) (gr. 7-12). 1987. pap. 2.50 (ISBN 0-553-26199-1). Bantam.
Paris Nights & Other Impressions of Places & People. Arnold Bennett. (Collected Works of Arnold Bennett: Vol. 64). (Illus.). 1976. Repr. of 1913 ed. 33.00 (ISBN 0-518-19145-1, 19145). Ayer Co Pubs.
Paris Nineteen Hundred. Franco Borsi & Ezio Godoli. LC 77-77672. (Illus.). 288p. 1988. 50.00 (ISBN 0-8478-0801-7). Rizzoli Intl.
Paris: Nineteen Seventy-Nine to Nineteen Eighty-Nine. Ed. by Sabine Fachard. LC 87-28513. (Illus.). 192p. (Orig.). 1988. pap. 37.50 (ISBN 0-8478-0899-8). Rizzoli Intl.
Paris: Nineteen Twenty-Eight to Nineteen Twenty-Nine. Ed. by Wolfgang Hageney. (Illus.). 224p. (Eng., Ital., Ger., Span. & Fr.). 1986. 54.95 (ISBN 88-7070-069-0). R Silver.
Paris Nineteenth Century: Architecture & Urbanism. Francois Loyer. (Illus.). 478p. Date not set. 85.00 (ISBN 0-89659-885-3). Abbeville Pr.
Paris Notebook. C. W. Gusewelle. LC 85-18219. (Illus.). 228p. (Orig.). 1985. pap. 9.95 (ISBN 0-932845-01-0). Lowell Pr.
Paris Notebooks: Essays & Reviews. Mavis Gallant. LC 87-43212. 256p. 1988. 17.95 (ISBN 0-394-56201-1). Random.
Paris, Nouv. Arc. Frg. 13531. Ed. by Luther Dittmer. (Veroffentlichungen Mittelalterlicher Musikhandschriften-Publications of Mediaeval Musical Manuscripts Ser.: Vol. 4). (Eng. & Ger.). 1961. pap. 15.00 (ISBN 0-912024-04-6). Inst Mediaeval Mus.
Paris of the Novelists. A. B. Maurice. 59.95 (ISBN 0-8490-0801-8). Gordon Pr.
Paris Opera. Martien Kanane & Thierry Beauvert. (Illus.). 192p. 1988. 75.00 (ISBN 0-86565-092-6). Vendome.
Paris Opera: An Encyclopedia of Operas, Ballets, Composers & Performers, Genesis & Glory, 1671-1715. Spire Pitou. LC 82-21140. xii, 364p. 1983. lib. bdg. 50.95 (ISBN 0-313-21420-4, PFO/). Greenwood.
Paris Opera: An Encyclopedia of Operas, Ballets, Composers & Performers-Rococo & Romantic, 1715-1815. Spire Pitou. LC 82-21140. xviii, 619p. 1985. lib. bdg. 85.00 (ISBN 0-313-24394-8, POR/). Greenwood.
Paris, Pee Wee, & Big Dog. Rosa Guy. 1988. pap. 2.95 (ISBN 0-440-40072-4). Dell.
Paris Pendant la Reaction Thermidorienne et sous le Directoire, 5 vols. Francois V. Aulard. LC 70-161713. (Collection de documents relatifs a l'histoire de Paris pendant la Revolution francaise). Repr. of 1902 ed. Set. 422.50 (ISBN 0-404-52570-9); 84.50 ea. AMS Pr.
Paris Phaidon Cultural Guide. (Phaidon Cultural Guide Ser.). (Illus.). 1987. 17.95 (ISBN 0-13-650136-2). P-H.
Paris Psalter see Early English Manuscripts in Facsimile.
Paris Psalter & Meters of Boethius. Ed. by George P. Krapp. LC 33-2302. 239p. 1932. 30.00 (ISBN 0-231-08769-1). Columbia U Pr.
Paris Puzzle. Vincent McConnor. pap. 2.50 (ISBN 0-345-30811-5). Ballantine.
Paris Rendez-Vous: Where to Meet in Paris Hour by Hour. Alexandre Lazareff. 1988. pap. 10.95 (ISBN 0-13-650185-0). Prentice Hall Pr.
Paris Ritz. M. Boxer. (Illus.). 176p. 1988. 65.00 (ISBN 0-8050-0640-0). H Holt & Co.
Paris Salons, Cafes, Studios. Sisley Huddleston. 1973. Repr. of 1928 ed. 30.00 (ISBN 0-8274-0345-3). R West.
Paris Shopkeepers & the Politics of Resentment. Philip G. Nord. LC 85-42695. (Illus.). 480p. 1986. 47.00x (ISBN 0-691-05454-1). Princeton U Pr.
Paris sous le Consulat, 4 vols. Francois V. Aulard. LC 74-161714. (Collection de documents relatifs a l'histoire de Paris pendant la Revolution francaise). Repr. of 1909 ed. Set. 338.00 (ISBN 0-404-52580-6); 84.50 ea.; Vol. 1. (ISBN 0-404-52581-4); Vol. 2. (ISBN 0-404-52582-2); Vol. 3. 1.00 (ISBN 0-404-52583-0); Vol. 4. (ISBN 0-404-52584-9). AMS Pr.
Paris sous le Premier Empire, 3 vols. Francois V. Aulard. LC 74-161706. (Collection de documents relatifs a l'histoire de Paris pendant la Revolution francaise). Repr. of 1923 ed. Set. 253.50 (ISBN 0-404-52576-8); 84.50 ea.; Vol. 1. (ISBN 0-404-52577-6); Vol. 2. (ISBN 0-404-52578-4); Vol. 3. (ISBN 0-404-52579-2). AMS Pr.
Paris Spleen. Charles Baudelaire. Tr. by Louise Varese. LC 48-5012. 1970. pap. 4.95 (ISBN 0-8112-0007-8, NDP294). New Directions.
Paris Stage: Recent Plays. Jean Bouchaud et al. Tr. by Matthew Ward et al from Fr. 342p. (Orig.). 1988. pap. 15.95 (ISBN 0-913745-25-1). Ubu Repertory.
Paris Stage: Recent Plays. Ribes Bouchaud et al. Tr. by Ward et al. (Orig.). 1988. pap. 15.00. Ubu Repertory.
Paris Symposium on Radio Astronomy. Ed. by Ronald N. Bracewell. (Illus.). 1959. 50.00x (ISBN 0-8047-0571-2). Stanford U Pr.
Paris: The Musical Kaleidoscope 1875-1925. Elaine Brody. (Illus.). 360p. 1987. 19.95 (ISBN 0-8076-1176-X). Braziller.
Paris Trout. Pete Dexter. LC 86-29682. 352p. 1988. 17.95 (ISBN 0-394-56370-0). Random.
Paris under the Social Revolution. A. F. Sanborn. 59.95 (ISBN 0-8490-0802-6). Gordon Pr.
Paris Universite: Bibliotheque d'Arte et d'Archeologie, Catalogue General Periodiques. 95.00 (ISBN 0-317-44524-3). Kraus Repr.
Paris Vivant see Paris Alive, the Point of View of an American.
Paris Was Our Mistress: Memoirs of a Lost & Found Generation. Samuel Putnam. LC 73-93886. (Arcturus Books Paperbacks Ser.). 272p. 1970. pap. 2.45x (ISBN 0-8093-0417-1). S Ill U Pr.
Paris Was Yesterday: Nineteen Twenty-Five to Nineteen Thirty-Nine. Janet Flanner, pseud. Ed. by Irving Drutman. 1979. pap. 3.95 (ISBN 0-14-005068-X). Penguin.
Paris Was Yesterday 1925-1939. Janet Flanner. Ed. by Irving Drutman. 256p. 1988. pap. 8.95 (ISBN 0-15-670990-2). HarBraceJ.
Paris Without End: On French Art since World War I. Jed Perl. LC 87-60887. (Illus.). 192p. 1988. 19.95 (ISBN 0-86547-313-7). N Point Pr.
Paris without Regret: James Baldwin, Chester Himes, Kenny Clarke, & Donald Byrd. Ursula B. Davis. LC 86-16131. (Illus.). 141p. 1986. 14.95 (ISBN 0-87745-147-8). U of Iowa Pr.
Paris 1928. Ed. by Wolfgang Hageney. (Illus.). 96p. (Eng., Ital., Ger., Span. & Fr.). 1986. pap. 26.95 (ISBN 88-7070-092-5). R Silver.
Paris 1929. Ed. by Wolfgang Hageney. (Illus.). 96p. (Eng., Ital., Ger., Span. & Fr.). 1986. pap. 26.95 (ISBN 88-7070-093-3). R Silver.
Paris, 1985. Georgia I. Hesse. Ed. by Robert C. Fisher. (Fisher Annotated Travel Guides Ser.). 128p. 1984. 8.95 (ISBN 0-8116-0020-3). NAL.
Paris 1987-1988. (Frommer's City Guides). 224p. 5.95 (ISBN 0-671-62340-0). Prentice Hall Pr.
Parish. John Clare. Intro. by Eric Robinson. 96p. 1986. pap. 6.95 (ISBN 0-14-043242-6). Penguin.
Parish: A Place for Worship. Ed. by Mark Searle. LC 81-13655. 192p. (Orig.). 1981. pap. 5.95 (ISBN 0-8146-1236-9). Liturgical Pr.
Parish Adult Education in Five Practical Steps. Robert Y. O'Brien. 32p. 1985. pap. text ed. 1.50 (ISBN 0-89243-234-9). Liguori Pubns.
Parish & Democracy in French Canada. Maurice Roy. LC 52-1123. (University of Toronto, Duncan & John Gray Memorial Lecture Ser.). pap. 20.00 (2026546). Bks Demand UMI.
Parish & the Hill. Mary D. Curran. 250p. 1986. pap. 8.95 (ISBN 0-935312-58-7). Feminist Pr.
Parish As Learning Community. Thomas Downs. LC 78-70816. 128p. 1979. pap. 3.95 (ISBN 0-8091-2172-7). Paulist Pr.
Parish Churches of Medieval England. Colin Platt. 1981. 39.95 (ISBN 0-436-37553-2, Pub. by Secker & Warburg UK); (Pub. by Secker & Warburg UK). David & Charles.
Parish Churches: Their Architectural Development in England. Hugh Braun. 1970. 12.50 (ISBN 0-571-09045-1). Transatl Arts.
Parish Clergy in Nineteenth-Century Russia: Crisis, Reform, Counter-Reform. Gregory L. Freeze. LC 82-61361. 552p. 1983. 58.50x (ISBN 0-691-05381-2). Princeton U Pr.
Parish Clergy under the Later Stuarts: The Leicestershire Experience. John H. Pruett. LC 78-8174. 203p. 1978. 19.95 (ISBN 0-252-00662-3). U of Ill Pr.
Parish Counseling. Edgar Jackson. LC 84-45066. 221p. 1983. 25.00x (ISBN 0-87668-672-2). Aronson.
Parish Court Houses of Louisiana. new ed. Betty L. Morrison. 1978. 20.00 (ISBN 0-930676-04-1). Her Pub Co.
Parish Education in Colonial Virginia. Guy F. Wells. LC 73-177649. Repr. of 1923 ed. 22.50 (ISBN 0-404-55138-6). AMS Pr.
Parish Education in Colonial Virginia. Guy F. Wells. LC 71-89252. (American Education: Its Men, Institutions & Ideas, Ser. 1). 1969. Repr. of 1923 ed. 11.00 (ISBN 0-405-01490-2). Ayer Co Pubs.
Parish Family Life & Social Action. Joachim O'Brien. LC 77-3573. 1977. pap. 1.50 (ISBN 0-8199-0673-5). Franciscan Herald.
Parish Guide to Adult Initiation. Kenneth Boyak. LC 79-91001. 112p. (Orig.). 1980. pap. 4.95 (ISBN 0-8091-2282-0). Paulist Pr.
Parish Help Book: A Guide to Social Ministry in the Parish. Herbert Weber. LC 83-71894. 112p. 1983. pap. 3.95 (ISBN 0-87793-304-9). Ave Maria.
Parish in Transition: Proceedings of a Conference on the American Catholic Parish. Ed. by David Byers. 120p. 1986. pap. 8.95 (ISBN 1-55586-967-X). US Catholic.
Parish Institutions of Maryland. Edward Ingle. LC 78-63736. (Johns Hopkins University. Studies in Social Sciences. First Ser. 1882-1883: 6). Repr. of 1883 ed. 11.50 (ISBN 0-404-61006-4). AMS Pr.
Parish Institutions of Maryland, with Illustrations from Parish Records. E. Ingle. 1973. pap. 9.00 (ISBN 0-384-25740-2). Johnson Repr.
Parish Lines, Diocese of Southern Virginia. Charles F. Cocke. (Virginia State Library Publications: No. 22). 287p. 1979. Repr. of 1964 ed. 5.00 (ISBN 0-88490-049-5). VA State Lib.
Parish Lines, Diocese of Southwestern Virginia. Charles F. Cocke. (Virginia State Library Publications: No. 14). 196p. 1980. Repr. of 1960 ed. 5.00 (ISBN 0-686-74611-2). VA State Lib.
Parish Lines, Diocese of Virginia. Charles F. Cocke. LC 78-19035. (Virginia State Library Publications: No. 28). xv, 321p. 1978. Repr. of 1967 ed. 5.00 (ISBN 0-88490-062-2). VA State Lib.
Parish Maps of Ireland: (Depicting All Townlands in the Four Ulster Counties of Armagh, Donegal, Londonderry & Tyrone) Compiled by The Derry Youth & Community Workshop Staff & Brian Mitchell. 288p. (Orig.). 1988. pap. text ed. 19.95 (ISBN 0-933227-33-7). Closson Pr.
Parish of All Hallows, Pt. 1. Ed. by Lilian J. Redstone. LC 74-138273. (London County Council. Survey of London: No. 12). Repr. of 1929 ed. 74.50 (ISBN 0-404-51662-9). AMS Pr.
Parish of Bromley-By-Bow. Ed. by Charles R. Ashbee. LC 73-138270. (London County Council. Survey of London: No. 1). Repr. of 1900 ed. 74.50 (ISBN 0-404-51651-3). AMS Pr.
Parish of Chelsea, Pt. 1. Ed. by Walter H. Godfrey. LC 71-138271. (London County Council. Survey of London: No. 2). Repr. of 1909 ed. 74.50 (ISBN 0-404-51652-1). AMS Pr.
Parish of Chelsea, Part 4: The Royal Hospital, Chelsea. Ed. by W. H. Godfrey. LC 71-138271. (London County Council. Survey of London: No. 11). Repr. of 1927 ed. 74.50 (ISBN 0-404-51661-0). AMS Pr.
Parish of St. Margaret, Westminster. Ed. by Montagu H. Cox. LC 70-138272. (London County Council. Survey of London: No. 10). (Illus.). Repr. of 1926 ed. 74.50 (ISBN 0-404-51660-2). AMS Pr.
Parish of St. Margaret, Westminster: Neighbourhood of Whitehall, Vol. 1. Montagu H. Cox & G. Topham Forrest. LC 70-138272. (London County Council. Survey of London: No. 13). Repr. of 1930 ed. 74.50 (ISBN 0-404-51663-7). AMS Pr.
Parish of Saint Martin-in-the Fields: The Strand, Pt. 2. Ed. by George H. Gater & E. P. Wheeler. (London County Council. Survey of London: No. 18). Repr. of 1937 ed. 74.50 (ISBN 0-404-51668-8). AMS Pr.
Parish of St. Martin-in-the Fields: Trafalgar Square & Neighborhood, Pt. 3. George H. Gater & F. R. Hiorns. LC 70-37852. (London County Council. Survey of London: No. 20). Repr. of 1940 ed. 74.50 (ISBN 0-404-51670-X). AMS Pr.
Parish of St. Pancras, Pt. 1. Ed. by Percy Lovell & William Marcham. LC 76-37851. (London County Council. Survey of London: No. 17). Repr. of 1936 ed. 74.50 (ISBN 0-404-51667-X). AMS Pr.

Parish of St. Pancras, Pt. 2. Ed. by Percy Lovell & William Marcham. LC 70-37855. (London County Council. Survey of London: No. 19). Repr. of 1938 ed. 74.50 (ISBN 0-404-51669-6). AMS Pr.

Parish of St. Pancras, Part 4: King's Cross Neighbourhood. Ed. by Walter H. Godfrey. LC 76-37851. (London County Council. Survey of London: No. 24). Repr. of 1952 ed. 74.50 (ISBN 0-404-51674-2). AMS Pr.

Parish of St. Sampson. John Fenwick. 1985. 20.00x (ISBN 1-85022-018-2, Pub. by Dyllansow & Truran). State Mutual Bk.

Parish Pantry: Spizarnia Kosciol. The Catholic Daughters of the Americas Staff. Ed. by Judy H. Seikel. LC 87-72241. (Illus.). 280p. (Orig., Pol. & Eng.). 1987. pap. 7.50 (ISBN 0-9619314-0-X). CDACCK.

Parish Prayers see Prayers for Every Occasion.

Parish Priests among the Saints. facs. ed. Walter Gumbley. LC 76-148214. (Biography Index Reprint Ser.). 1947. 15.00 (ISBN 0-8369-8061-1). Ayer Co Pubs.

Parish Priests & Their People in the Middle Ages in England. Edward L. Cutts. LC 74-107457. Repr. of 1898 ed. 32.50 (ISBN 0-404-01898-X). Ams Pr.

Parish Records of Christ Episcopal Church, 1831-1863. Sharon Kraynek. 146p. (Orig.). perfect bdg. 16.00 (ISBN 0-933227-43-4). Closson Pr.

Parish Registers. 1987. 30.00x (Pub. by Birmingham Midland Soc UK). State Mutual Bk.

Parish Registers of Dymock, Gloucestershire, 1538-1790. Ed. by Irvine Gray & J. E. Gethyn-Jones. 1987. 59.00x (Pub. by Cheltenham Art Gallery & Mus UK). State Mutual Bk.

Parish Renewal at the Grassroots. David Prior. 1987. 13.95 (ISBN 0-310-38370-6, 18409). Zondervan.

Parish Secretary's Handbook. Wayne Paulson. 180p. (Orig.). 1982. pap. 14.95 (ISBN 0-8066-1898-1, 10-4868). Augsburg.

Parish Self-Study Guide. 97p. 1982. pap. 7.95 (ISBN 1-55586-842-8). US Catholic.

Parish-Side. facs. ed. Samuel H. Elliot. LC 70-76924. (American Fiction Reprint Ser). 1854. 14.00 (ISBN 0-8369-7003-9). Ayer Co Pubs.

Parish Social Ministry: A Vision & Resource. Alexandra Peeler. 194p. 1986. 14.95 (ISBN 0-318-20492-4). Catholic Charities.

Parish the Thought. Vikki Knoche. 1984. pap. 4.95 (ISBN 0-8163-0560-9). Pacific Pr Pub Assn.

Parishes & Families: A Model for Christian Formation Through Liturgy. Ed. by Gabe Huck & Virginia Sloyan. 1973. pap. 5.00 (ISBN 0-918208-11-4). Liturgical Conf.

Parisian Education of an American Surgeon: Letters of Jonathan Mason Warren (1832-1835) Russell M. Jones. LC 78-56709. (Memoirs Ser.: Vol. 128). (Illus.). 1978. pap. 10.00 (ISBN 0-87169-128-0). Am Philos.

Parisian Frolics. LC 83-83189. (Classics of the Victorian Imagination Ser.). 144p. 1984. 12.50 (ISBN 0-394-53881-1, GP 916). Grove.

Parisian Frolics. LC 83-83189. (Classics of the Victorian Imagination Ser.). 144p. 1984. pap. 5.95 (ISBN 0-394-62202-2, E933, Ever). Grove.

Parisian Order of Barristers & the French Revolution. Michael P. Fitzsimmons. LC 86-19519. (Harvard Historical Monographs: No. 74). (Illus.). 320p. 1987. text ed. 29.95x (ISBN 0-674-65464-1). Harvard U Pr.

Parisian Points of View. Ludovic Halevy. Tr. by Edith V. Matthews. LC 71-98572. (Short Story Index Reprint Ser.). 1894. 17.00 (ISBN 0-8369-3146-7). Ayer Co Pubs.

Parisian Sketches: Letters to the New York Tribune, 1875-1876. Henry James. Ed. by Edel Leon & Lind I. Dusoir. LC 78-5995. 1978. Repr. of 1957 ed. lib. bdg. 35.00x (ISBN 0-313-20448-9, JAPS). Greenwood.

Parisian Stage, 5 vols. Ed. by C. Beaumont Wicks. LC 50-2939. 1950-79. Vol. 1, 88p. pap. 6.25 (ISBN 0-8173-9502-4); Vol. 3, 287p. pap. 10.50 (ISBN 0-8173-9504-0); Vol. 5. pap. 18.50 (ISBN 0-8173-9506-7). U of Ala Pr.

Parisian Two-Part Organa: Complete Comparative Edition, 2 vols. Hans Tischler. 1400p. 1988. lib. bdg. 320.00 (ISBN 0-918728-89-4). Pendragon NY.

Parisienne. Hari Becque. (Livret). pap. 6.95 (ISBN 0-685-34881-4). French & Eur.

Parisina, 2 vols. Donizetti. Ed. by Philip Gossett & Charles Rosen. (Early Romantic Opera Ser.). Set. 198.00 (ISBN 0-8240-2924-0). Garland Pub.

Parisville Poles. Ed. by Harry Milostan. LC 77-77917. 1977. lib. bdg. 12.00 (ISBN 0-918020-03-4). Masspac Pub.

Parity, Parity, Parity. John D. Black. LC 72-2364. (FDR & the Era of the New Deal Ser.). 367p. 1972. Repr. of 1942 ed. 45.00 (ISBN 0-306-70482-X). Da Capo.

Park. Eric Hill. LC 82-60615. (Eric Hill's Baby Bear Bks.). (Illus.). 14p. (ps). 1983. pap. 2.50 (ISBN 0-394-85636-8). Random.

Park. Philippe Sollers. Tr. by A. Sheridan Smith. LC 76-90910. Orig. Title: Parc. 96p. 1969. 4.95 (ISBN 0-87376-012-3); pap. 2.25 (ISBN 0-87376-013-1). Red Dust.

Park: A Fantastic Story. John Gray. Ed. by Philip Healy. 128p. (Orig.). 1985. pap. 6.50 (ISBN 0-85635-538-0). Carcanet.

Park Administration Handbooks. 1986. Set of 3. 25.95 (ISBN 0-88314-343-7). AAHPERD.

Park & Recreation Management. Robert E. Sternloff & Roger Warren. 326p. 1984. text ed. write for info. (ISBN 0-02-417210-3). Macmillan.

Park Attendant. Jack Rudman. (Career Examination Ser.: C-1541). (Cloth bdg. avail. on request). pap. 12.00 (ISBN 0-8373-1541-7). Natl Learning.

Park Avenue. Lorayne Ashton. 368p. (Orig.). 1987. pap. 3.95 (ISBN 0-8041-0129-9, Pub. by Ivy). Ballantine.

Park Avenue Money Diet: How to Escape from the Middle Class Forever! Dan Baumgartner. Ed. by Judith M. Moretz. LC 83-50234. (Illus.). 240p. 1983. 14.95 (ISBN 0-913221-00-7). Safe Harbor Pr.

Park Bench. Fumiko Takeshita. Tr. by Ruth A. Kanagy from Japanese. (Illus.). 32p. (gr. 3-8). 1988. 11.95 (ISBN 0-916291-15-4). Kane-Miller Bk.

Park Book. Charlotte Zolotow. LC 44-9471. (Illus.). (ps-1). 1944. PLB 11.89 (ISBN 0-06-026970-7). HarpJ.

Park Book. Charlotte Zolotow. LC 44-9471. (Trophy Picture Bks.). (Illus.). 40p. (ps-3). 1986. pap. 4.95 (ISBN 0-06-443092-8, Trophy). HarpJ.

Park Builders: A History of State Parks in the Pacific Northwest. Thomas R. Cox. LC 88-5462. (Illus.). 280p. 1988. 35.00 (ISBN 0-295-96613-0); pap. 14.95 (ISBN 0-295-96620-3). U of Wash Pr.

Park Cities: A Walker's Guide & Brief History. Diane Galloway & Kathy Matthews. LC 88-42634. (Illus.). 240p. (Orig.). 1988. pap. 10.95 (ISBN 0-87074-276-0). SMU Press.

Park City. Lewis Baltz. LC 80-65768. (Illus.). 252p. 1981. 75.00. Aperture.

Park City. Lewis Baltz & Gus Blaisdell. LC 80-65768. (Illus.). 252p. 1980. 75.00. Castelli-Artspace.

Park City Trails. Raye C. Ringholz. LC 84-60807. (Illus.). 104p. 1984. pap. 6.50 (ISBN 0-915272-26-1). Wasatch Pubs.

Park Construction Coordinator. Jack Rudman. (Career Examination Ser.: C-3278). 1988. pap. 18.00 (ISBN 0-8373-3278-8). Natl Learning.

Park Engineer. Jack Rudman. (Career Examination Ser.: C-3191). (Cloth bdg. avail. on request). 1988. pap. 18.00 (ISBN 0-8373-3191-9). Natl Learning.

Park Foreman. Jack Rudman. (Career Examination Ser.: C-571). (Cloth bdg. avail. on request). pap. 14.00 (ISBN 0-8373-0571-3). Natl Learning.

Park Im. Gor'kogo. Martin C. Smith. Tr. by Aleksei Tsvetkov. 320p. (Rus.). 1985. 10.00 (ISBN 0-88233-950-8). Ardis Pubs.

Park Is Mine. Stephen Peters. 368p. 1982. pap. 2.95 (ISBN 0-446-30035-7). Warner Bks.

Park Maintenance Supervisor. Jack Rudman. (Career Examination Ser.: C-2942). (Cloth bdg. avail. on request). pap. 14.00 (ISBN 0-8373-2942-6). Natl Learning.

Park Management. Dwight R. McCurdy. LC 84-27653. 1985. 30.00x (ISBN 0-8093-1226-3); pap. 19.95x (ISBN 0-8093-1202-6). S ILL U Pr.

Park Manager. Jack Rudman. (Career Examination Ser.: C-2247). (Cloth bdg. avail. on request). pap. 14.00 (ISBN 0-8373-2247-2). Natl Learning.

Park Manager I. Jack Rudman. (Career Examination Ser.: C-383). (Cloth bdg. avail. on request). pap. 14.00 (ISBN 0-8373-0383-4). Natl Learning.

Park Manager II. Jack Rudman. (Career Examination Ser.: C-384). (Cloth bdg. avail. on request). pap. 14.00 (ISBN 0-8373-0384-2). Natl Learning.

Park Manager III. Jack Rudman. (Career Examination Ser.: C-385). (Cloth bdg. avail. on request). pap. 14.00 (ISBN 0-8373-0385-0). Natl Learning.

Park Patrolman. Jack Rudman. (Career Examination Ser.: C-1688). (Cloth bdg. avail. on request). pap. 14.00 (ISBN 0-8373-1688-X). Natl Learning.

Park Ranger. Jack Rudman. (Career Examination Ser.: C-650). (Cloth bdg. avail. on request). 1988. pap. 14.00 (ISBN 0-8373-0650-7). Natl Learning.

Park Ranger Handbook. J. W. Shiner. 300p. 1986. 24.95x (ISBN 0-910251-14-2). Venture Pub PA.

Park Row. Allen Churchill. LC 73-14193. 344p. 1973. Repr. of 1958 ed. lib. bdg. 27.50x (ISBN 0-8371-7146-6, CHPR). Greenwood.

Park Service Worker. Jack Rudman. (Career Examination Ser.: C-2468). (Cloth bdg. avail. on request). pap. 12.00 (ISBN 0-8373-2468-8). Natl Learning.

Park Slope Hipster Speaks Out, Again. Lee Houston. Ed. by Robert A. Frauenglas. 64p. (Orig.). 1985. pap. 4.95 (ISBN 0-9603950-8-3). Somrie Pr.

Park-Street Papers. facs. ed. Bliss Perry. LC 73-117826. (Essay Index Reprint Ser). 1908. 19.00 (ISBN 0-8369-2012-0). Ayer Co Pubs.

Park Superintendent. Jack Rudman. (Career Examination Ser.: C-2268). (Cloth bdg. avail. on request). 1988. pap. 14.00 (ISBN 0-8373-2268-5). Natl Learning.

Park Supervisor. Jack Rudman. (Career Examination Ser.: C-1563). (Cloth bdg. avail. on request). pap. 14.00 (ISBN 0-8373-1563-8). Natl Learning.

Park the Car. Francis H. Wise & Joyce M. Wise. (Phonetic Reader Ser: No. 12). (Illus., Dr. Wise Learn to Read Ser.). (ps-1). 1975. pap. text ed. 1.50 (ISBN 0-915766-32-9). Wise Pub.

Park Trailers, Standards for. 85p. 1982. 8.25 (ISBN 0-318-16432-9). RV Indus Assn.

Park Walks near Melbourne. Sandra Bardwell. (Illus.). 168p. 1976. pap. 8.95 (ISBN 0-9599428-4-X, Pub. by Inkata Pr Australia). Intl Spec Bk.

Park Weaves: Based on Dr. William G. Bateman's Manuscript. Ed. by Virigina I. Harvey. (Shuttle Craft Guild Monograph: No. 37). (Illus.). 96p. 1984. pap. 12.95. Shuttle Craft.

Park West Foxtrot. (Ballroom Dance Ser.). 1985. lib. bdg. 74.00 (ISBN 0-87700-803-5). Revisionist Pr.

Park West Foxtrot. (Ballroom Dance Ser.). 1986. lib. bdg. 79.95 (ISBN 0-8490-3411-6). Gordon Pr.

Parkay Margarine Cookbook. Kraft Kitchens. LC 79-54946. (Orig.). pap. 5.95 (ISBN 0-87502-074-7). Benjamin Co.

Parker Chronicle. Ed. by A. H. Smith. (Old English Ser.). 1966. pap. text ed. 9.95x (ISBN 0-89197-569-1). Irvington.

Parker Chronicle & Laws: Facsimile. rev. ed. Ed. by R. Flower & A. H. Smith. (EETS OS Ser.: Vol. 208). 1973. Repr. of 1937 ed. 42.00 (ISBN 0-8115-3384-0). Kraus Repr.

Parker Directory of Attorneys. Parker & Son Staff. LC 75-41995. 1987. 19.25 (ISBN 0-911110-18-6). Parker & Son.

Parker Family. G. T. Ridlon. LC 75-133872. (Saco Valley Settlements Ser). 1970. pap. 1.50 (ISBN 0-8048-0818-X). C E Tuttle.

Parker: Great Chief of the Comanches. Catherine T. Gonzalez. Ed. by Melissa Roberts. (Illus.). 48p. (gr. 1-5). 1987. 9.95 (ISBN 0-89015-600-X, Eakin Press). Eakin Pr.

Parker Gun. Larry L. Baer. 29.95 (ISBN 0-88227-047-8). Gun Room.

Parker Lifetime Treasury of Mystic & Occult Powers. Theodor Laurence. 1982. pap. 5.95 (ISBN 0-13-650747-6, Reward). P-H.

Parker Master Guide to Personal & Business Success. Lawrence Talbott. LC 81-3929. 240p. 1981. 17.95 (ISBN 0-13-650291-1, Parker). P-H.

Parker on the Iroquois. Arthur C. Parker. Ed. by William N. Fenton. Bd. with Code of Handsome Lake, the Seneca Prophet. 119p; Consitution of the Five Nations. 148p. 21.95x; Iroquois Uses of Maize & Other Food Plants. 158p. LC 68-31036. (Illus.). 478p. 1981. pap. 14.95x (ISBN 0-8156-0115-8). Syracuse U Pr.

Parker on Writing. Robert B. Parker. 50p. 1985. deluxe signed ed. 50.00 (ISBN 0-935716-34-3). Lord John.

Parker Ranch. Joseph Brennan. pap. 3.95 (ISBN 0-686-79501-6, PBN 5102, B&N Bks). Har-Row.

Parker Society Publications, 55 Vols. Parker Society-London. Repr. of 1841 ed. Set. 2200.00 (ISBN 0-384-44880-1). Johnson Repr.

Parker Treasury of Elementary Classroom Activities. Muriel S. Karlin. LC 81-9657. 287p. cancelled 17.95 (ISBN 0-13-650705-0, Parker). P-H.

Parker's Business Statutes & Securities Rules of Texas. 1986. 22.50 (ISBN 0-911110-40-2). Parker & Son.

Parker's History of Bedford County, Virginia. rev. ed. Lula J. Parker. Ed. & pref. by Peter Viemeister. (Indexed Edition Ser.). 160p. 1988. pap. 19.95 (ISBN 0-9608598-4-5). Hamiltons.

Parkers Town Delegate. Grace L. Hill. 10.95 (ISBN 0-89190-064-0, Pub. by Am Repr). Amereon Ltd.

Parker's Virginia Battery, CSA. Robert K. Krick. (Illus.). 408p. 1975. write for info. (ISBN 0-685-65076-6). Va Bk.

Parker's Wine Buyer's Guide. Robert M. Parker, Jr. 1987. pap. 14.95 (ISBN 0-671-63380-5, Fireside). S&S.

Parker's Wine Buyer's Guide. Robert M. Parker, Jr. 1987. 24.95 (ISBN 0-671-64349-5). S&S.

Parkia Leguminosae. H. C. Hopkins & M. F. Da Silva. (Flora Neotropica Monograph: No. 43-44). 1986. One vol. includes Dimorphandra Caesalpiniaceae. 44.75 (ISBN 0-317-11875-7). NY Botanical.

Parking Discounts & Carpool Formation in Seattle. Marie Olsson & Gerald Miller. 115p. (Orig.). 1978. pap. text ed. 6.00x (ISBN 0-87766-226-6). Urban Inst.

Parking Enforcement Agent. Jack Rudman. (Career Examination Ser.: C-572). (Cloth bdg. avail. on request). pap. 12.00 (ISBN 0-8373-0572-1). Natl Learning.

Parking Meter Attendant. Jack Rudman. (Career Examination Ser.: C-1063). (Cloth bdg. avail. on request). pap. 12.00 (ISBN 0-8373-1063-6). Natl Learning.

Parking Meter Collector. Jack Rudman. (Career Examination Ser.: C-573). (Cloth bdg. avail. on request). pap. 12.00 (ISBN 0-8373-0573-X). Natl Learning.

Parking Meter Supervisor. Jack Rudman. (Career Examination Ser.: C-2592). (Cloth bdg. avail. on request). pap. 14.00 (ISBN 0-8373-2592-7). Natl Learning.

Parking of Motors Vehicles. 2nd ed. J. Brierly. (Illus.). 347p. 1979. 61.00 (ISBN 0-85334-528-7, Pub. by Elsevier Applied Sci England). Elsevier.

Parking Principles. (Special Report). 217p. 1971. 10.00 (ISBN 0-309-01958-3); pap. 8.00 (ISBN 0-317-36096-5). Transport Res Bd.

Parking Structures. National Fire Protection Association Staff. 1985. 10.50 (88A-85). Natl Fire Prot.

Parking Structures. (Eighty-Ninety Ser.). 1973. pap. 2.00 (ISBN 0-685-58142-X, 88A). Natl Fire Prot.

Parking Structures. 64p. 1980. 13.00 (ISBN 0-317-32082-3, C-3). ACI.

Parking Violations Bureaus. Michigan Municipal League. (Technical Topics Ser.: No. 35). 1987. 2.00. MI Municipal.

Parkinson-Specific Motor & Mental Disorders. Ed. by R. G. Hassler & J. F. Christ. (Advances in Neurology Ser.: Vol. 40). (Illus.). 612p. 1984. text ed. 115.50 (ISBN 0-89004-940-8). Raven.

Parkinson: The Law Complete, Pt. II. C. Northcote Parkinson. 224p. 1983. pap. 2.95 (ISBN 0-345-30064-5). Ballantine.

Parkinson's: A Patient's View. Sidney Dorros. LC 81-14417. 240p. 1981. pap. 9.95 (ISBN 0-932020-09-7). Seven Locks Pr.

Parkinson's: A Patient's View. Sidney Dorros. 240p. 1985. pap. 3.95 (ISBN 0-446-32837-5). Warner Bks.

Parkinson's Disease. Ed. by Melvin D. Yahr & Kenneth J. Bergmann. (Advances in Neurology Ser.: Vol. 45). (Illus.). 640p. 1987. text ed. 103.50 (ISBN 0-88167-205-X). Raven.

Parkinson's Disease: A Guide for Patient & Family. 2nd ed. Roger C. Duvoisin. 220p. 1984. 27.00 (ISBN 0-89004-904-1); pap. 15.50 (ISBN 0-89004-177-6). Raven.

Parkinson's Disease & Movement Disorders. Joseph Jankovic & Eduardo Tolosa. 464p. 1988. text ed. 79.50 (ISBN 0-8067-0971-5). Urban & S.

Parkinson's Disease: Biochemistry, Clinical Pathology, & Treatment. W. Birkmayer & P. Riederer. Tr. by G. Reynolds from Ger. (Illus.). 194p. 1983. 51.00 (ISBN 0-387-81722-0). Springer-Verlag.

Parkinson's Disease: Current Progress, Problems & Management. U. K. Rinne & M. Klinger. 402p. 1980. 111.00 (ISBN 0-444-80263-0, Biomedical Pr). Elsevier.

Parkinson's Disease: The Facts. Gerald Stern & Andrew Lees. (Facts Ser.). (Illus.). 1982. 15.95x (ISBN 0-19-261293-X). Oxford U Pr.

Parkinson's Law & Other Studies in Administration. C. Northcote Parkinson. 1979. pap. 2.95 (ISBN 0-345-34785-4). Ballantine.

Parkramya Likhat (Negotiable Instruments in Hindi) 2nd ed. Avtar Singh. 110p. 1979. 23.00x (ISBN 0-317-57654-2, Pub. by Eastern Bk India). State Mutual Bk.

Parks, 2 Vols. Ed. by Lebert H. Weir. LC 71-176106. Repr. of 1928 ed. Set. 57.50 (ISBN 0-404-06900-2). AMS Pr.

Parks & Playgrounds. Linda Penn. (Young Scientist Explore Ser.). 32p. (gr. k-3). 1986. wkbk. 4.95 (ISBN 0-86653-350-8, GA 685). Good Apple.

Parks & Recreation Assistant. (Career Examination Ser.: C-3399). Date not set. pap. 14.00 (ISBN 0-8373-3399-7). Natl Learning.

Parks: Monographs. Mary Vance. (Public Administration Ser.: P 1938). 40p. 1986. 10.00 (ISBN 0-89028-878-X). Vance Biblios.

Parks of the Pacific Coast: The Complete Guide to the National & Historic Parks, California, Oregon, Washington. Doug Tatreau & Bobbe Tatreau. LC 84-48892. (Illus.). 160p. (Orig.). 1985. pap. 10.95 (ISBN 0-88742-050-8). Globe Pequot.

Parks, Preserves & Rivers: A Guide to Outdoor Adventures in Virginia's Capital Region. Louise L. Burke et al. LC 85-7255. (Illus.). 285p. 1985. 10.95x (ISBN 0-9615016-0-X). Metro Found.

Park's Quest. Katherine Paterson. LC 87-32422. 160p. (gr. 5 up). 1988. 12.95 (ISBN 0-525-67258-3, 01258-370). Lodestar Bks.

Parkside Pranks & Sunset Stunts: Growing Up with San Francisco. Mary A. Williams. Ed. by Kali Sichen. (Illus.). 83p. (gr. 4-9). 1986. pap. 7.95 (ISBN 0-916299-02-3). North Scale Co.

Parlamentsrecht des Deutschen Reiches: Im Auftrage des Deutschen Reichstages Dargestellt, Pt. 1. Julius Hatschek. xiii, 628p. (Ger.). 1973. Repr. of 1915 ed. 64.00 (ISBN 3-11-002157-9). De Gruyter.

PARLE: Parallel Architectures & Languages Europe, Vol 1: Parallel Architectures & Languages Europe. Ed. by J. W. De Bakker et al. (Lecture Notes in Computer Science Ser: Vol. 258). xii, 480p. 1987. pap. 34.60 (ISBN 0-387-17943-7). Springer-Verlag.

Parlement of Foulys. new ed. Geoffrey Chaucer. Ed. by D. S. Brewer. (Old & Middle English Texts). 168p. 1976. pap. 11.25x (ISBN 0-06-491190-X). B&N Imports.

Parlement of Paris after the Fronde, 1653-1673. Albert N. Hamscher. LC 76-6661. 1976. 29.95x (ISBN 0-8229-3325-X). U of Pittsburgh Pr.

Parlement of Paris Seventeen Seventy-Four to Seventeen Eighty-Nine. Bailey S. Stone. LC 79-27732. x, 227p. 1981. 25.00x (ISBN 0-8078-1442-3). U of NC Pr.

Parlement of Poitiers: War, Government & Politics in France, 1418-1436, No. 42. Roger G. Little. (Royal Historical Society Ser.). 251p. 1984. 38.00 (ISBN 0-901050-98-9, Pub. by Boydell & Brewer). Longwood Pub Group.

Parlement of Pratlers. John Eliot. 1928. 20.00 (ISBN 0-8274-3101-5). R West.

Parler Arabe des Juifs de Tunis: Tome 2, Etude Linguistique. David Cohen. LC 72-94452. (Janua Linguarum, Ser. Practica: No. 161). 318p. (Fr.). 1975. 44.40x (ISBN 90-2793-296-4). Mouton.

Parler Arabe du Caire. Nada Tomiche. (Recherches Mediterraneennes, Textes et Etudes Linguistiques: No. 3). 1964. pap. 22.40x (ISBN 90-2796-227-8). Mouton.

Parlers Dialectaux et Populaires dans l'Oeuvre de Guy de Maupassant. Butler. (Publ. Romanes et Franc.). 15.50 (ISBN 0-685-34943-8). French & Eur.

Parleuses. Marguerite Duras & Xaviere Gauthier. (Vol. 44). 25p. 1974. 11.95 (ISBN 0-686-55849-9). French & Eur.

Parlez sans Peur. Marlene Nusbaum & Liliane Verdier. (Fr.). text ed. 18.95 (ISBN 0-03-058577-5). HR&W.

Parliament. 2nd ed. Ivor Jennings. 1969. pap. 15.95 (ISBN 0-521-09532-8). Cambridge U Pr.

Parliament & Administration in India. Institute of Constitutional & Parliamentary Studies, New Delhi. Ed. by L. M. Singhvi. LC 72-903148. 285p. 1972. 13.50x (ISBN 0-89684-439-0). Orient Bk Dist.

Parliament & Administration: The Estimates Committee, 1964-65. Nevil Johnson. LC 67-3034. 1966. 25.00x (ISBN 0-678-06022-3). Kelley.

Parliament & Congress. Kenneth Bradshaw & David Pring. 9.95 (ISBN 0-7043-3353-8, Pub. by Quartet England). Charles River Bks.

Parliament & Health Policy: The Role of the MPs 1970-75. Stephen Ingle & Philip Tether. 180p. 1980. text ed. 34.25x (ISBN 0-566-00388-0). Gower Pub Co.

Parliament & Industry. David Judge. 200p. 1987. text ed. price not set (ISBN 0-566-05111-7). Gower Pub Co.

Parliament & Information. Dermot Englefield. 142p. 1981. 21.00x (ISBN 0-85365-570-7, Pub. by Library Assn Pub London); pap. 12.00x (ISBN 0-85365-993-1, Pub. by Library Assn Pub London). ALA.

Parliament & Library. Ed. by Gerhard Hahn & Hildebert Kirchne. 452p. (Ger., Eng. & Fr.). 1987. lib. bdg. 50.00 (ISBN 3-598-10634-3). K G Saur.

Parliament & Politics in Late Medieval England, 3 Vols. J. S. Roskell. 1985. Set. write for info.; Vol. 1, 225p. 35.00; Vol. 2, 360p. 40.00 (ISBN 0-907628-30-3); Vol. 3, 424p. 45.00. Hambledon Press.

Parliament & Public Enterprise. V. V. Ramanadham & Yash Ghai. (ICPE Monograph). 61p. 1981. pap. 10.00x (ISBN 92-9038-900-1, Pub. by Intl Ctr Pub Yugoslavia). Kumarian Pr.

Parliament & Public Enterprise in India. Laxmi Narain. 1979. text ed. 20.00x. Coronet Bks.

Parliament & Public Spending. Ann Robinson. LC 79-307097. 1978. text ed. 24.50x (ISBN 0-435-83750-8). Gower Pub Co.

Parliament & Revolution. J. R. MacDonald. LC 20-26685. Repr. of 1920 ed. 20.00 (ISBN 0-527-59300-1). Kraus Repr.

Parliament & the British Empire: Some Constitutional Controversies Concerning Imperial Legislative Jurisdiction. Robert L. Schuyler. LC 75-31133. Repr. of 1929 ed. 22.50 (ISBN 0-404-13609-5). AMS Pr.

Parliament & the Crown in the Reign of Mary Tudor. Jennifer Loach. (Oxford Historical Monographs). 280p. 1986. 39.95x (ISBN 0-19-822936-4). Oxford U Pr.

Parliament & the Ombudsman in New Zealand. Larry B. Hill. (Legislative Research Ser.: No. 8). 1973. pap. 3.50 (ISBN 0-686-18649-4). Univ OK Gov Res.

Parliament & the Press. C. J. Lloyd. 1988. 22.95 (ISBN 0-522-84372-7, Pub. by Melbourne U Pr). Intl Spec Bk.

Parliament & the Public. 2nd ed. Michael Rush. LC 85-17072. (Political Realities Ser.). 160p. 1986. pap. text ed. 9.95 (ISBN 0-582-35558-3). Longman.

Parliament at Work: A Casebook of Parliamentary Procedure. Albert Hanson & H. V. Wiseman. LC 74-29640. 358p. 1975. Repr. of 1962 ed. lib. bdg. 35.00x (ISBN 0-8371-8004-X, HAPA). Greenwood.

Parliament, Factions & Parties. Peter Loveday. 1966. 17.50x (ISBN 0-522-83659-3, Pub. by Melbourne U Pr). Intl Spec Bk.

Parliament in Elizabethan England: John Hooker's "Order & Usage". Vernon F. Snow. LC 77-23301. (Illus.). 1977. 28.50x (ISBN 0-300-02093-7). Yale U Pr.

Parliament in Perspective. David Menhennet & John Palmer. LC 67-73291. 1967. 10.95 (ISBN 0-8023-1125-3). Dufour.

Parliament in the Nineteen Eighties. Ed. by Philip Norton. 248p. 1985. 45.00x (ISBN 0-631-14056-5); pap. 19.95x (ISBN 0-631-14057-3). Basil Blackwell.

Parliament of England, 1559-1581. G. R. Elton. LC 86-12899. 1986. 42.50 (ISBN 0-521-32835-7). Cambridge U Pr.

Parliament of France. David W. Liddendale. LC 79-1633. 1980. Repr. of 1954 ed. 25.85 (ISBN 0-88355-937-4). Hyperion Conn.

Parliament of Great Britain: A Bibliography. Robert Goehlert & Fenton Martin. LC 82-47920. (Special Series in Libraries & Librarianship). 240p. 1983. 30.00x (ISBN 0-669-05700-2). Lexington Bks.

Parliament of Love. Philip Massinger. Ed. by Kathleen Marguerite. LC 82-45793. (Malone Society Reprint Ser.: No. 63). Repr. of 1928 ed. 40.00 (ISBN 0-404-63063-4). AMS Pr.

Parliament of Ravens. Laurence Millman. 32p. 1986. pap. 5.00 (ISBN 0-910477-03-5). LoonBooks.

Parliament of Sixteen Twenty-Four: Politics & Foreign Policy. Robert E. Ruigh. LC 72-135548. (Historical Studies: No. 87). (Illus.). 1971. 27.50x (ISBN 0-674-65225-8). Harvard U Pr.

Parliament, Party & the Art of Politics in Britain, 1855-1859. Angus Hawkins. LC 85-51801. 320p. 1987. text ed. 38.50x (ISBN 0-8470-1317-0). Stanford U Pr.

Parliament, Policy & Politics in the Reign of William III. Henry Horwitz. LC 76-27126. 385p. 35.00 (ISBN 0-87413-124-3). U Delaware Pr.

Parliament, the Executive & the Governor-General: A Constitutional Analysis. George Winterton. (Studies in Australian Federation). 376p. 1983. 39.00x (ISBN 0-522-84242-9, Pub. by Melbourne U Pr). Intl Spec Bk.

Parliament, the Press, & the Colonies, 1846-1880. Stanley R. Stembridge. Ed. by Peter Stansky & Leslie Hume. LC 81-48369. (Modern British History Ser.). 300p. 1982. lib. bdg. 46.00 (ISBN 0-8240-5165-3). Garland Pub.

Parliamentarians: The History of the Commonwealth Parliamentary Association 1911-1985. Ian Grey. 380p. 1986. text ed. 54.00 (ISBN 0-566-05199-0, Pub. by Gower Pub England). Gower Pub Co.

Parliamentary Control over Finance. S. Seshadri. LC 75-905958. 1975. 11.00x (ISBN 0-88386-054-6). South Asia Bks.

Parliamentary Control over Foreign Policy. A. Cassese. 216p. 1980. 32.50x (ISBN 90-286-0019-1, Pub. by Sijthoff & Noordhoff). Kluwer Academic.

Parliamentary Democracy & Socialist Politics. Barry Hindess. 200p. 1983. pap. 10.95x (ISBN 0-7100-9319-5). Routledge Chapman & Hall.

Parliamentary Democracy in Japan. Niranjan Bhuinya. 1971. 9.00 (ISBN 0-686-20282-1). Intl Bk Dist.

Parliamentary Diary of Robert Bowyer, 1606-1607. Ed. by David H. Willson. LC 72-120677. 1970. Repr. lib. bdg. 29.00x (ISBN 0-374-98636-3, Octagon). Hippocrene Bks.

Parliamentary Diary of Sir Edward Dering, 1670-73. Edward Dering. Ed. by Basil D. Henning. (Yale Historical Pubs. Miscellany Ser.: No. XVI). 1940. 59.50x (ISBN 0-685-69825-4). Elliots Bks.

Parliamentary Elections in Israel: Three Case Studies. C. Paul Bradley. LC 85-1150. 208p. (Orig.). 1985. pap. text ed. 10.00 (ISBN 0-936988-11-8, Dist. by Shoe String). Tompson Rutter Inc.

Parliamentary Franchise Reform in England from 1885 to 1918. Homer L. Morris. LC 73-78004. (Columbia University. Studies in the Social Sciences: No. 218). Repr. of 1921 ed. 18.50 (ISBN 0-404-51218-6). AMS Pr.

Parliamentary Government in Britain. Michael Rush. LC 80-25804. 260p. 1981. 39.50 (ISBN 0-8419-0680-7). Holmes & Meier.

Parliamentary Guide for Church Leaders. C. Barry McCarty. 1987. pap. 6.95 (ISBN 0-8054-3116-0). Broadman.

Parliamentary History, Vol. 4, 1985. Eveline Cruickshanks. 254p. 1986. 22.50x (ISBN 0-312-59723-1). St Martin.

Parliamentary History: A Yearbook, 3 vols. Ed. by Eveline Cruickshanks. LC 83-645281. 1984. Vol. 1, 281 p. 22.50 (ISBN 0-312-59720-7); Vol. 2, 256 p. 22.50 (ISBN 0-312-59721-5); Vol. 3, 252 p. 22.50 (ISBN 0-312-59722-3). St Martin.

Parliamentary History of England from the Norman Conquest in 1066 to the Year 1803, 36 Vols. William Cobbett. 1966. Repr. of 1820 ed. Set. 2250.00 (ISBN 0-384-09496-1); 65.00 ea. Johnson Repr.

Parliamentary History of England from the Norman Conquest in 1066 to the Year 1803, 36 Vols. Ed. by William Cobbett et al. LC 54-54297. Repr. of 1820 ed. Set. 2250.00 (ISBN 0-404-01650-2); 62.50 ea. AMS Pr.

Parliamentary Law. Franklin H. Kerfoot. 1941. 10.95 (ISBN 0-8054-7901-5). Broadman.

Parliamentary Law. Henry M. Robert. 610p. 1975. lib. bdg. 46.50 (ISBN 0-8290-0874-8). Irvington.

Parliamentary Law. Henry M. Robert. LC 75-9940. 610p. 1981. pap. 19.95 (ISBN 0-86616-006-X). Greene.

Parliamentary Law at a Glance. rev. ed. Ethel C. Utter. 60p. 1986. pap. 6.95 spiral binding (ISBN 0-8092-8891-5). Contemp Bks.

Parliamentary Law for Nonprofit Organizations. Howard L. Oleck. 160p. 1979. pap. 5.00 (ISBN 0-317-31049-6, B229). Am Law Inst.

Parliamentary Law Rules & Procedures for Conducting Conventions. Lena L. Hardcastle. LC 81-85392. 272p. 1982. 17.95 (ISBN 0-9608716-0-8). Stuart Bks.

Parliamentary Librarianship in the English-Speaking World. Philip Laundy. 166p. 1980. 41.00x (ISBN 0-85365-731-9, Pub. by Library Assn Pub London). ALA.

Parliamentary Opinion of Delegated Legislation. Chen & Chin-Mai. LC 70-76628. (Columbia University Studies in the Social Sciences: No. 394). Repr. of 1933 ed. 15.00 (ISBN 0-404-51394-8). AMS Pr.

Parliamentary Opinions: a Compilation & Revision of Opinions of the Opinions Committee, American Institute of Parliamentarians, 1958 to 1982. Virginia H. Schlotzhauer et al. LC 81-71425. viii, 199p. (Orig.). 1982. pap. 12.50 (ISBN 0-942736-00-1). Am Inst Parliamentarians.

Parliamentary Politics & the Home Rule Crisis: The British House of Commons in 1886. W. C. Lubenow. 450p. 1988. 75.00 (ISBN 0-19-822966-6). Oxford U Pr.

Parliamentary Powers of English Government Departments. John Willis. Repr. of 1933 ed. 19.00 (ISBN 0-384-68640-0). Johnson Repr.

Parliamentary Practice: An Introduction to Parliamentary Law. Henry M. Robert. 209p. 1975. 15.95 (ISBN 0-8290-0875-6). Irvington.

Parliamentary Practice: An Introduction to Parliamentary Law. Henry M. Robert. LC 75-9938. 203p. 1981. pap. 7.95 (ISBN 0-86616-008-6). Greene.

Parliamentary Privilege in the American Colonies. M. P. Clarke. LC 76-166322. (American Constitutional & Legal History Ser.). 304p. 1971. Repr. of 1943 ed. lib. bdg. 35.00 (ISBN 0-306-70237-1). Da Capo.

Parliamentary Privileges in India. Hari H. Das et al. 1985. 19.00x (ISBN 0-317-40600-0, Pub. by Ashish India). South Asia Bks.

Parliamentary Procedure: A Programmed Introduction. 2nd ed. John W. Gray & Richard Rea. 1974. pap. write for info. (ISBN 0-673-07671-7). Scott F.

Parliamentary Procedure & Practice in the Dominion of Canada. John G. Bourinot. 816p. 1971. Repr. of 1884 ed. 80.00x (ISBN 0-7165-2021-4, Pub. by Irish Academic Pr). Biblio Dist.

Parliamentary Procedure at a Glance. O. Garfield Jones. (gr. 9 up). 1971. pap. 4.95 (ISBN 0-8015-5766-6, 0481-140, Hawthorn). Dutton.

Parliamentary Procedure: Essential Principles. M. Stanley Ryan. LC 83-45012. 232p. 1985. 14.95 (ISBN 0-8453-4771-3, Cornwall Bks). Assoc Univ Prs.

Parliamentary Procedure for Practical Productive Programming. Jessie Powell & Cele Kumarich. 111p. 1983. pap. 7.95 soft cover (ISBN 0-686-40889-6). Procedures.

Parliamentary Procedure in India. 3rd ed. Ajita R. Mukherjea. 396p. 1983. 37.50x (ISBN 0-19-561133-0). Oxford U Pr.

Parliamentary Procedure Without Stress. 76p. 1976. 6.00 (ISBN 0-88210-071-8, 6207616). Natl Assn Principals.

Parliamentary Reform: Sixteen Forty to Eighteen Thirty-Two. John A. Cannon. LC 72-83588. pap. 86.80 (2026336). Bks Demand UMI.

Parliamentary Scrutiny of Government Bills. J. A. Griffith. 285p. 1974. 27.95 (ISBN 0-8464-1294-2). Beekman Pubs.

Parliamentary Selection: Social & Political Choice in Early Modern England. Mark A. Kishlansky. 272p. 1986. 37.50 (ISBN 0-521-32231-6); pap. 10.95 (ISBN 0-521-31116-0). Cambridge U Pr.

Parliamentary Socialism: A Study in the Politics of Labour. Ralph Miliband. 1972. pap. 9.95 (ISBN 0-85036-135-4, Pub. by Merlin Pr UK). Longwood Pub Group.

Parliamentary System of Israel. Samuel Sager. LC 85-12631. (Illus.). 304p. 1985. text ed. 29.95x (ISBN 0-8156-2335-6). Syracuse U Pr.

Parliamentary Taxes on Personal Property, 1290-1334. J. F. Willard. (Med. Acad. Amer. Pubns.). 1934. 36.00 (ISBN 0-527-01691-8). Kraus Repr.

Parliamentary Texts of the Later Middle Ages. Nicholas Pronay & John Taylor. 1980. 54.00x (ISBN 0-19-822368-4). Oxford U Pr.

Parliaments & Economic Affairs. Ed. by D. Coombes & S. A. Walkland. 1981. text ed. 31.00x (ISBN 0-435-83804-0). Gower Pub Co.

Parliaments & English Politics, 1621-1629. Conrad Russell. LC 78-40498. 1979. 44.95x (ISBN 0-19-822482-6); pap. 24.95x (ISBN 0-19-822691-8). Oxford U Pr.

Parliaments & Parliamentarians in Democratic Politics. Ed. by Ezra N. Suleiman. 300p. 1986. 37.50 (ISBN 0-8419-0942-3); pap. 19.95 (ISBN 0-8419-1040-5). Holmes & Meier.

Parliaments & Parties in Egypt. Jacob M. Landau. LC 79-1632. 1981. Repr. of 1954 ed. 21.75 (ISBN 0-88355-936-6). Hyperion Conn.

Parliaments & the United Nations. (United Nations Studies). 10.00 (ISBN 92-1-157065-4, E.79.XV.ST/14). UN.

Parliaments & the United Nations: Dissemination of Information to Parliamentarians. 117p. 1979. pap. 10.00 (UN79/15ST14, UNITAR). UNIPUB.

Parliaments of the World: A Comparative Study, 2 vols. Inter-Parliamentary Union Staff. LC 84-26008. 1422p. 125.00 (ISBN 0-8160-1186-9). Facts on File.

Parliamo dell'Italia. Ed. by Angela M. Jeannet. LC 84-13161. (Illus.). 366p. 1984. lib. bdg. 29.00 (ISBN 0-8191-4131-3). U Pr of Amer.

Parliamo dell'Italia. Ed. by Angela M. Jeannet. LC 84-13161. (Illus.). 366p. (Orig.). 1984. pap. text ed. 16.75 (ISBN 0-8191-4132-1). U Pr of Amer.

Parlo Italiano. L. Rapaccini. (It). 16.95 (ISBN 0-685-20245-3). Schoenhof.

Parlons de Tout: Livre Pour Cours de Conversation Francaise. Paule M. Miller. 256p. 1983. pap. 18.00 (ISBN 0-471-86847-7). Wiley.

Parlons Francais. Incl. Text 1. 1976. 8.95 (ISBN 0-8325-9662-0); Text 2. 1971. 8.95 (ISBN 0-8325-9665-5); Text 3. 1972. text ed. 8.95 (ISBN 0-8325-9669-8). 1971. Tapebook 1. 5.95 (ISBN 0-88499-070-2, Inst Mod Lang); Tapebook 2. 6.95 (ISBN 0-8325-9663-9); Reader 1. 6.95 (ISBN 0-8325-9664-7); Reader 2. 6.95 (ISBN 0-8325-9667-1); Level 1. cassettes 150.00 (ISBN 0-8325-9666-3); Level 2. cassettes 150.00 (ISBN 0-8325-9668-X). Natl Textbk.

Parlour Four & Other Stories. J. I. Stewart. 1986. 14.95 (ISBN 0-393-02292-7). Norton.

Parmana: Prehistoric Maize & Manioc Subsistence along the Orinoco & Amazon. Anna C. Roosevelt. (Studies in Archaeology). 1980. 29.95 (ISBN 0-12-595350-X). Acad Pr.

Parmenides see Republic & Other Works.

Parmenides: A Text with Translation, Commentary, & Critical Essays by Leonardo Taran. Leonardo. Taran. LC 63-23416. pap. 62.70 (ISBN 0-317-08836-X, 2015481). Bks Demand UMI.

Parmenides & Empedocles. Tr. by Stanley Lombardo. LC 81-7212. 76p. (Orig.). 1982. pap. 4.95 (ISBN 0-912516-66-6). Grey Fox.

Parmenides: Being, Bounds & Logic. Scott Austin. LC 85-29436. 204p. 1986. text ed. 21.50t (ISBN 0-300-03559-4). Yale U Pr.

Parmenides of Elea: Fragments: A Text & Translation with Introduction. Ed. by David Gallop. (Phoenix Supplementary Ser.: Vol. 18). 160p. 1984. 25.00x (ISBN 0-8020-2443-2). U of Toronto Pr.

Parmigianino: His Works in Painting. Sydney J. Freedberg. LC 72-95120. (Illus.). 1971. Repr. of 1950 ed. lib. bdg. 48.50x (ISBN 0-8371-3717-9, FRPA). Greenwood.

Parnas. Meir Bar Am. Tr. by Esther Van Handel. 1986. 9.95 (ISBN 0-87306-393-7); pap. 6.95 (ISBN 0-87306-400-3). Feldheim.

Parnasse Francais: A Book of French Poetry from A. D. 1550 to the Present Time. James Parton. 515p. 1983. Repr. of 1887 ed. lib. bdg. 65.00 (ISBN 0-89987-672-2). Darby Bks.

Parnassians Personally Encountered. Edgar Saltus. LC 75-175430. Repr. of 1923 ed. 17.50 (ISBN 0-404-05548-6). AMS Pr.

Parnassians Personally Encountered. 1st ed. Edgar E. Saltus. 1923. boxed, ltd. ed. 25.00x (ISBN 0-686-17411-9). R S Barnes.

Parnassus. 2nd ed. Ralph Waldo Emerson. 1972. Repr. of 1875 ed. lib. bdg. 24.00 (ISBN 0-8422-8043-X). Irvington.

Parnassus. Ralph Waldo Emerson. 1973. Repr. of 1874 ed. 35.00 (ISBN 0-8274-0590-1). R West.

Parnassus. 2nd ed. Ralph Waldo Emerson. 1986. pap. text ed. 8.95x (ISBN 0-8290-1862-X). Irvington.

Parnassus. facsimile ed. Ed. by Ralph Waldo Emerson. LC 73-116400. (Granger Index Reprint Ser). 1874. 25.50 (ISBN 0-8369-6141-2). Ayer Co Pubs.

Parnassus En Route: An Anthology of Poems about Places, Not People, on the European Continent. facsimile ed. Ed. by Mrs. Kenneth Horan. LC 70-38600. (Granger Index Reprint Ser.). Repr. of 1929 ed. 16.00 (ISBN 0-8369-6332-6). Ayer Co Pubs.

Parnassus in Pillory. Augustine J. Duganne. LC 76-122648. 1971. Repr. of 1851 ed. 21.00x (ISBN 0-8046-1296-X, Pub. by Kennikat). Assoc Faculty Pr.

Parnassus on the Mississippi: The Southern Review & the Baton Rouge Literary Community, 1935-1942. Thomas W. Cutrer. LC 83-24913. (Southern Literary Studies). (Illus.). 291p. 1984. text ed. 30.00 (ISBN 0-8071-1143-0). La State U Pr.

Parnell Myth & Irish Politics 1891-1956. William M. Murphy. (American University Studies IX-History: Vol 21). 216p. 1987. 32.00 (ISBN 0-8204-0351-2). P Lang Pubs.

Parochiaid & the Courts. Dale E. Twomley. (Andrews University Monographs, Studies in Education: Vol. 2). x, 165p. 1979. 3.95 (ISBN 0-943872-51-0). Andrews Univ Pr.

Parochial & Plain Sermons. John H. Newman. LC 86-62927. 1753p. (Orig.). 1987. pap. 49.00 (ISBN 0-89870-136-8). Ignatius Pr.

Parodic Sermon in European Perspective: Aspects of Liturigical Parody from the Middle Ages to the 20th Century. Sander L. Gilman. xii, 244p. (Orig.). 1974. pap. text ed. 36.50x (ISBN 3-515-01823-9, Pub. by Franz Steiner). Coronet Bks.

Parodies: An Anthology from Chaucer to Beerbohm & after. Ed. by Dwight MacDonald. (Quality Paperbacks Ser.). 600p. 1985. pap. 12.95 (ISBN 0-306-80239-2). Da Capo.

Parodies, Etc. & So Forth. W. B. Scott. Ed. by Gerald Graff & Barbara H. Monter. 150p. 1985. 24.95 (ISBN 0-8101-0673-6); pap. 9.95 (ISBN 0-8101-0674-4). Northwestern U Pr.

Parodies of the Gothic Novel. Leland C. May. Ed. by Devendra P. Varma. LC 79-8464. (Gothic Studies & Dissertations Ser.). 1980. lib. bdg. 17.00x (ISBN 0-405-12654-9). Ayer Co Pubs.

Parodies of the Works of English & American Authors, 6 Vols. Walter Hamilton. Repr. of 1884 ed. Set. cancelled (ISBN 3-487-02264-8). Adlers Foreign Bks.

Parodies of the Works of English & American Authors, Collected & Annotated, 6 Vols. Walter Hamilton. 1884-99. Repr. Set. 140.00 (ISBN 0-384-21210-7). Johnson Repr.
Parodies on Walt Whitman. Ed. by Henry S. Saunders. LC 70-119648. Repr. of 1923 ed. 16.00 (ISBN 0-404-05564-8). AMS Pr.
Parody. Christopher Stone. LC 73-13598. 1974. Repr. of 1914 ed. lib. bdg. 20.00 (ISBN 0-8414-7639-X). Folcroft.
Parody & Burlesque in the Tragicomedies of Thomas Middleton. John F. McElroy. Ed. by James Hogg. (Jacobean Drama Studies). 335p. (Orig.). 1972. pap. 15.00 (ISBN 3-7052-0318-5, Pub. by Salzburg Studies). Longwood Pub Group.
Parody Anthology. Carolyn Wells. LC 67-14060. 432p. 1968. Repr. of 1904 ed. 30.00x (ISBN 0-8103-3224-8). Gale.
Parody Anthology. Carolyn Wells. 59.95 (ISBN 0-8490-0803-4). Gordon Pr.
Parody: Critical Concepts versus Literary Practices, Aristophanes to Sterne. Joseph A. Dane. LC 87-26492. 272p. 1988. 24.50x (ISBN 0-8061-2110-6). U of Okla Pr.
Parody in Jewish Literature. Israel Davidson. LC 77-163670. (Columbia University. Oriental Studies: No. 2). Repr. of 1907 ed. 24.50 (ISBN 0-404-50492-2). AMS Pr.
Parody Murder Case. Cornelia Bonsack. 1987. 11.95 (ISBN 0-533-07279-4). Vantage.
Parody Outline of History. Donald O. Stewart. 1977. Repr. of 1921 ed. lib. bdg. 15.00 (ISBN 0-8492-2414-4). R West.
Parody Party. Ed. by Leonard Russell. LC 70-105829. 1970. Repr. of 1936 ed. 25.00x (ISBN 0-8046-0974-8, Pub. by Kennikat). Assoc Faculty Pr.
Parola E Pensiero: Introduzione Alla Lingua Italiana Moderna. 3rd ed. Vincenzo Traversa. (Illus.). 437p. 1980. text ed. 32.50 scp (ISBN 0-06-046653-7, HarpC). Har-Row.
Parole: A Bibliography. Mary Vance. 24p. 1988. pap. 6.25 (ISBN 1-55590-671-0). Vance Biblios.
Parole: A Critical Analysis. Gray Cavender. (Multidisciplinary Studies in Law & Jurisprudence). 130p. 1982. 18.50x (ISBN 0-8046-9296-3, 9296, Pub. by Kennikat). Assoc Faculty Pr.
Parole & the Community-Based Treatment of Offenders in Japan & the United States. L. Craig Parker, Jr. LC 86-50431. (Illus.). 200p. (Orig.). 1986. pap. text ed. 10.95 (ISBN 0-936285-03-6). U New Haven Pr.
Parole Chez Paul Claudel et les Negro-Africains. Leopold S. Senghor. 1973. 9.95 (ISBN 0-686-55009-9). French & Eur.
Parole: Crime Prevention or Crime Postponement? Howard R. Sacks & Charles H. Logan. LC 80-52358. 132p. 1980. pap. 9.00 (ISBN 0-939328-04-6). U Ct Law Sch Found.
Parole Crociate Per Gli Studenti. Nancy P. Goldhagen. (Illus.). 48p. (Ital.). (gr. 3 up). 1983. 6.60 (ISBN 0-8442-8021-6, Passport Bks); pap. 4.95. Natl Textbk.
Parole en Archipel. Rene Char. 168p. 1962. 8.95 (ISBN 0-686-54164-2). French & Eur.
Parole et Pensee. 5th ed. Yvone Lenard. 608p. 1987. text ed. 35.95 scp (ISBN 0-06-043925-4, HarpC). scp lab. manual & wkbk. 16.50 (ISBN 0-06-043924-6). Har-Row.
Parole: Legal Issues, Decision-Making, Research. Ed. by Charles L. Newman & William E. Amos. 430p. 1975. 15.00 (ISBN 0-87945-034-7); pap. 8.95. Fed Legal Pubn.
Parole Officer. Jack Rudman. (Career Examination Ser.: C-574). (Cloth bdg. avail. on request). pap. 12.00 (ISBN 0-8373-0574-8). Natl Learning.
Parole-Quebec, Countersign-Ticonderoga: Second New Jersey Regimental Orderly Book, 1776. Ed. by Doyen Salsig. LC 77-74398. (Illus.). 312p. 1980. 28.50 (ISBN 0-8386-1793-X). Fairleigh Dickinson.
Parole Rights, Vol. XI. Jack L. Kunsman, Jr. (Encyclopedia of Prisoner's Rights Ser.). 175p. 1983. pap. text ed. 14.50 (ISBN 0-914235-11-7). J L Kunsman.
Paroles. Jacques Prevert. (Folio Ser.: No. 762). 1957. 6.95 (ISBN 0-685-23895-4). Schoenhof.
Paroles au Choix. Francine L. Bustin. (Fr.). 1980. text ed. 15.95 (ISBN 0-03-046566-4). HR&W.
Paroles de Soie et Chien Qui Aboie. Charles M. Schulz. (Fr.). pap. 5.95 (ISBN 0-03-061652-2). H Holt & Co.
Paroles et Musique. Samuel Beckett. Bd. with Comedie; Dis Joe. (Coll. Bilingue). (Fr. & Eng.). pap. 4.50 (ISBN 0-685-37196-4). French & Eur.
Paroles et Musique see Comedies et Actes Divers.
Paroles et Pensees Lyriques. Bernice B. Feinsot. LC 55-9916. (Illus.). 127p. (Fr.). 1975. pap. 6.95x (ISBN 0-915526-01-8). B B Feinsot.
Parousia. J. Stuart Russel. pap. 12.95 (ISBN 0-8010-7725-7). Baker Bk.
Paroxisms: A Guide to the Isms. Edwin Brock. LC 74-8647. (Illus.). 96p. 1974. 5.95 (ISBN 0-8112-0549-5); pap. 2.25 (ISBN 0-8112-0554-1, NDP385). New Directions.
Parque Paquete. Arcadia Lopez & John Smith. (Illus.). 1976. pap. 86.50 teaching system (ISBN 0-913632-09-0). Am Univ Artforms.
Parramatta River Notebook. Joyce Cole. 64p. (Orig.). 1985. 5.95 (ISBN 0-949924-70-9, Pub. by Kangaroo Pr). Intl Spec Bk.
Parris Mitchell of Kings Row. Henry Bellamann & Katherine Bellamann. Ed. & intro. by Jay M. Karr. (Illus.). 1986. 18.50 (ISBN 0-9609926-3-4); pap. 9.45 (ISBN 0-9609926-4-2). Kingdom Hse.
Parrot. Vincent Serventy. (Animals in the Wild Ser.). (Illus.). 24p. (gr. k-5). 1986. PLB 11.33 (ISBN 0-8172-2705-9). Raintree Pubs.
Parrot & the Fig Tree. LC 86-24159. (Jataka Tales Ser.). (Illus.). 32p. (Orig.). (gr. k-4). 1987. PLB 9.95 (ISBN 0-89800-156-0); pap. 5.95 (ISBN 0-89800-142-0). Dharma Pub.
Parrot Cat. Nicola Bayley. LC 83-23749. (Copycats Ser.). (Illus.). 24p. (gr. k up). 1984. 3.95 (ISBN 0-394-86496-4). Knopf.
Parrot Family: Parakeets-Budgerigars-Cockatiels-Lovebirds-Lories-Macaws. Wolfgang De Grahl. LC 83-17940. (Illus.). 176p. 1985. pap. 7.95 (ISBN 0-668-06043-3). Arco.
Parrot Family: Their Training, Care, & Breeding see Parrots.
Parrot Guide. 2nd ed. Cyril H. Rogers. (Illus.). 256p. 14.95 (ISBN 0-87666-546-6, PL-2984). TFH Pubns.
Parrot Told Snake. Harry Stevens. (Viking Kestrel Board Bks.). (ps-k). 1987. 4.95 (ISBN 0-670-80530-0, Viking Kestrel). Viking.
Parrot Woman. Alice Bach. (Phreakers Ser.: No. 3). (Orig.). (gr. k-6). 1987. pap. 2.95 (ISBN 0-440-46987-2, YB). Dell.
Parrots. Althea Braithwaite. (Save Our Wildlife Bks.). (ps-6). 1988. PLB 7.95 (ISBN 0-88462-174-X); pap. 2.95 (ISBN 0-88462-175-8). Longman Crown.
Parrots. Althea Braithwaite & Carolyn Rubin. (Save Our Wildlife Ser.). (Illus.). (gr. k-3). Date not set. pap. 2.95. Longman Trade.
Parrots. Julien L. Bronson. Orig. Title: Parrot Family: Their Training, Care, & Breeding. (Illus.). 80p. 1985. pap. text ed. 5.95 (ISBN 0-86622-232-4, PB-120). TFH Pubns.
Parrots. Petra Deimer. (Pet Care Ser.). 80p. 1983. pap. 3.95 (ISBN 0-8120-2630-6). Barron.
Parrots. Matthew M. Vriends & Herbert R. Axelrod. (Illus.). 1979. 9.95 (ISBN 0-87666-995-X, KW-032). TFH Pubns.
Parrots. Wildlife Education, Ltd. Staff. (Zoobooks Ser.). (Illus.). 20p. (YA) (gr. 5 up). 1984. pap. text ed. 1.95 (ISBN 0-937934-27-5). Wildlife Educ.
Parrots & Related Birds. Henry J. Bates & Robert I. Busenbark. (Illus.). 543p. 19.95 (ISBN 0-87666-967-4, TFH H-912). TFH Pubns.
Parrot's Death & Other Poems. P. Lal. 13p. 1973. 5.00 (ISBN 0-88253-268-5); pap. 4.00 (ISBN 0-88253-806-3). Ind-US Inc.
Parrot's Egg. Alain Blondel & Shena Lamb. 167p. 1986. pap. text ed. 14.95x (ISBN 0-86975-236-7, Pub. by Ravan Pr). Ohio U Pr.
Parrots, Macaws & Cockatoos: The Art of Elizabeth Butterworth. (Illus.). 64p. 1988. pap. 18.95 (ISBN 0-8109-2378-5). Abrams.
Parrots of the World. Joseph M. Forshaw. (Illus.). 1977. Repr. of 1973 ed. 34.95 (ISBN 0-87666-959-3, PS-753). TFH Pubns.
Parrot's Perch. Michel Rio. Tr. by Leigh Hafrey from Fr. LC 85-744. 96p. 1985. 10.95 (ISBN 0-15-170964-5). HarBraceJ.
Parrots: Their Care & Breeding. Rosemary Low. (Illus.). 384p. 1986. 90.00 (ISBN 0-7137-1437-9, Pub. by Blandford Pr England). Sterling.
Parrot's Wood. Erma J. Fisk. LC 84-29462. 1985. 15.95 (ISBN 0-393-01997-7). Norton.
Parry & Hardy: EEC Law. 2nd ed. Anthony Parry & James Dinnage. 584p. 1981. lib. bdg. 55.00 (ISBN 0-379-20713-3). Oceana.
Parry's Graining & Marbling. Brian. Rhodes & John Windsor. (Illus.). 150p. 1985. pap. 22.50 (ISBN 0-00-383131-0, Pub. by Collins England). Sheridan.
Pars Distalis of the Pituitary Gland: Structure, Function & Regulation. Ed. by F. Yoshimura & A. Gorbman. 550p. 1986. 188.00 (ISBN 0-444-80709-8, Excerpta Medica). Elsevier.
Parsifal. Richard Wagner. Ed. by Nicholas John. Tr. by Andrew Porter from Ger. LC 85-52160. (The English National Opera Guide Ser.: No. 34). (Illus.). 128p. (Orig.). 1986. pap. 5.95 (ISBN 0-7145-4079-X). Riverrun NY.
Parsifal Mosaic. Robert Ludlum. 1982. 15.45 (ISBN 0-394-52111-0). Random.
Parsifal Mosaic. Robert Ludlum. 1983. pap. 4.95 (ISBN 0-553-25270-4). Bantam.
Parsifal Reception in the "Bayreuther Blaetter". Mary A. Cicora. (American University Studies: I Germanic Languages & Literatures: Vol. 55). 179p. (Orig.). 1988. text ed. 38.60 (ISBN 0-8204-0385-7). P Lang Pubs.
Parsina Saga, Bk. 3. Stephen Goldin. (Spectra Ser.). 256p. 1989. pap. 3.95 (ISBN 0-553-27711-1, Spectra). Bantam.
Parsing Guide to the Greek New Testament. Nathan E. Han. LC 77-158175. 496p. 1971. pap. 17.95 (ISBN 0-8361-1653-4). Herald Pr.
Parsing Natural Language. Ed. by M. King. 1983. 29.00 (ISBN 0-12-408280-7). Acad Pr.
Parsing Theory. S. Sippu & E. Soisalon-Soinnen. (EATCS Monographs on Theoretical Computer Science: Vol. 15). (Illus.). 290p. 1988. 59.50 (ISBN 0-387-13720-3). Springer-Verlag.
Parsing Through Customs: Essays by a Freudian Folklorist. Alan Dundes. LC 87-1675. 232p. 1987. text ed. 22.75 (ISBN 0-299-11260-8). U of Wis Pr.
Parsis. Martin Haug. 427p. 1978. Repr. of 1878 ed. 25.00 (ISBN 0-89684-157-X). Orient Bk Dist.
Parsival, or a Knight's Tale. Richard Monaco. 352p. 1984. pap. 2.95 (ISBN 0-425-07026-3). Berkley Pub.
Parsley. Ludwig Bemelmans. LC 55-7682. (Illus.). 48p. (ps-3). 1980. 14.70i (ISBN 0-06-020455-9); PLB 12.89 o.p (ISBN 0-06-020456-7). HarpJ.
Parsley Park. Mieke Tazelaar. (Illus.). 64p. (Orig.). 1983. pap. 7.95 (ISBN 0-9613792-0-0). Tazelaar.
Parson Austen's Daughter. Helen Ashton. 352p. 1982. Repr. lib. bdg. 40.00 (ISBN 0-89987-034-1). Darby Bks.
Parson Austen's Daughter. Helen Ashton. 337p. lib. bdg. 30.00 (ISBN 0-8495-0155-5). Arden Lib.
Parson in English Literature: A Galaxy of Clerical Figures Gathered from the Writers of Six Centuries. F. E. Christmas. Repr. of 1950 ed. 20.00 (ISBN 0-686-19851-4). Ridgeway Bks.
Parson of Gunbarrel Basin. Nelson Nye. 192p. 1987. pap. 2.50 (ISBN 0-441-64709-X, Pub. by Charter Bks). Ace Bks.
Parson of the Islands. Adam Wallace. LC 61-17566. (Illus.). 412p. 1978. Repr. of 1861 ed. 7.00 (ISBN 0-87033-077-2). Tidewater.
Parson Weems: A Biographical & Critical Study. Lawrence C. Wroth. LC 75-31143. Repr. of 1911 ed. 10.00 (ISBN 0-404-13615-X). AMS Pr.
Parson Weem's Life of Francis Marion. Peter Horry. LC 76-21439. 1976. 15.00 (ISBN 0-937684-04-X). Tradd St Pr.
Parson Weems of the Cherry-Tree. Harold Kellock. LC 75-107137. 224p. 1971. Repr. of 1928 ed. 35.00x (ISBN 0-8103-3785-1). Gale.
Parsons Brinckerhoff: The First Hundred Years. Benson Bobrick. (Illus.). 256p. 1985. 29.95 (ISBN 0-442-27264-2); pap. 17.95 (ISBN 0-442-27263-4). Van Nos Reinhold.
Parson's Daughter. Catherine Cookson. 1987. 19.95 (ISBN 0-671-63293-0). Summit Bks.
Parson's Daughter. Catherine Cookson. 594p. 1988. lib. bdg. 21.95x (ISBN 0-8161-4389-7, Large Print Bks). G K Hall.
Parson's Daughter. Catherine Cookson. 448p. 1988. pap. 4.50 (ISBN 0-671-64854-3). PB.
Parson's Dimly's Treasure Hunt. (Tales from Fern Hollow Ser.). (Illus.). 22p. (ps-1). 1985. 1.98 (ISBN 0-517-44572-7). Outlet Bk Co.
Parson's Diseases of the Eye. 17th ed. S. J. Miller. (Illus.). 1984. 52.00 (ISBN 0-443-02114-7). Churchill.
Parsons Family History & Record. MacCabe. 1973. Repr. of 1913 ed. 15.75 (ISBN 0-87012-170-7). McClain.
Parsons' General Theory of Action: A Summary of the Basic Theory. B. J. Bluth. LC 82-3408. (Illus.). 131p. (Orig.). 1982. pap. text ed. 9.95 (ISBN 0-937654-02-7). Natl Behavior.
Parsons on the Rose. Samuel B. Parsons. (Old Roses Ser.). 1979. text ed. 15.00 (ISBN 0-930576-13-6). E M Coleman Ent.
Parson's Pleasure. Mollie Hardwick. 208p. 1987. 14.95 (ISBN 0-312-00642-X). St Martin.
Parson's Princess. John Pellow. 1984. 20.00x (ISBN 0-906549-36-1, Pub. by J Clare Bks). State Mutual Bk.
Parson's Progress. John Pellow. 20.00x (ISBN 0-906549-18-3, Pub. by J Clare Bks). State Mutual Bk.
Parson's Son. Michael Lyne. (Illus.). signed ed 58.00 (ISBN 0-85131-176-8, NL51, Pub. by J A Allen U K). S R Smith Sporting Bks.
Part of a Man's Life. Thomas W. Higginson. LC 73-122658. 1971. Repr. of 1905 ed. 33.00x (ISBN 0-8046-1307-9, Pub. by Kennikat). Assoc Faculty Pr.
Part of a Man's Life. Thomas W. Higginson. 1973. Repr. of 1905 ed. 25.00 (ISBN 0-8274-0236-8). R West.
Part of America's Pride. Leon Knight et al. LC 84-80782. (Illus.). 60p. (Orig.). 1984. pap. 5.00 (ISBN 0-940248-20-4). Guild Pr.
Part of Cape Cod Is Missing! Noel W. Beyle. (No. 17). (Illus.). 48p. (Orig., Recipes by Lee Baldwin). 1983. pap. 0.95 (ISBN 0-912609-00-1). First Encounter.
Part of Dispatch from George Simpson, Esquire, Governor of Ruperts Land, to the Governor & Committee of the Hudson's Bay Company, London, March 1, 1829: Continued & Completed March 24 & June 5, 1829. Ed. by E. E. Rich. (Hudson's Bay Record Society Publications Ser.: Vol. 10). pap. 52.00 (ISBN 0-8115-3184-8). Kraus Repr.
Part of Fortune. Laurel Goldman. LC 86-11079. 288p. 1987. 15.95 (ISBN 1-55584-004-3). Weidenfeld.
Part of My Heart Left Here. Ed. by Mary Green. LC 85-72072. 1986. pap. 12.50 (ISBN 0-913342-53-X). Barclay Pr.
Part of My Life. Jules A. Ayer. (Illus.). 1978. pap. 7.95 (ISBN 0-19-281245-9). Oxford U Pr.
Part of My Soul Went with Him. Winnie Mandela. Ed. by Anne Benjamin & Mary Benson. LC 85-21632. (Illus.). 164p. 1985. 14.95 (ISBN 0-393-02215-3); pap. 5.95 (ISBN 0-393-30290-3). Norton.
Part of Myself: A Collection of Poems. 40p. pap. 4.00 (ISBN 0-9604794-0-6). Doris Demou.
Part of Myself: Portrait of an Epoch. Carl Zuckmayer. 435p. 1984. pap. 9.95 (ISBN 0-88184-083-1). Carroll & Graf.
Part of Nature, Part of Us: Modern American Poets. Helen Vendler. LC 79-20308. (Harvard Paperbacks Ser.). 392p. 1981. pap. 8.95 (ISBN 0-674-65476-5). Harvard U Pr.
Part of Nature, Part of Us: Modern American Poets. Helen H. Vendler. LC 79-20308. 387p. 1980. 21.00x (ISBN 0-674-65475-7). Harvard U Pr.
Part of Something Great. Jerry Aten. (gr. 4-8). 1981. 6.95 (ISBN 0-916456-97-8, GA 226). Good Apple.
Part of Speech. Joseph Brodsky. Tr. by Anthony Hecht et al from Rus. LC 80-613. 160p. 1980. 12.95 (ISBN 0-374-22987-2); pap. 7.95 (ISBN 0-374-51633-2). FS&G.
Part of the Institution & Other Stories. Ruth Suckow. LC 88-15059. (Bur Oak Bk.). 328p. (Orig.). 1988. pap. 9.95 (ISBN 0-87745-207-5). U of Iowa Pr.
Part of the Main. Edward M. Holmes. 1976. pap. 4.95 (ISBN 0-89101-031-9). U Maine Orono.
Part of the Pattern: A Personal Journey Through the World of Children's Books, 1960-1985. Elaine Moss. LC 85-30211. 224p. 1986. 11.75 (ISBN 0-688-04559-6). Greenwillow.
Part of the Solution: Portrait of a Revolutionary. Margaret Randall. LC 72-93974. 1973. pap. 2.95 (ISBN 0-8112-0471-5, NDP350). New Directions.
Part of the Story. Richard Jackson. Ed. by Robert Pack. (Grove Press Poetry Ser.). 96p. 1983. 12.50 (ISBN 0-394-53133-7, GP863). Grove.
Part of the Story. Richard Jackson. Ed. by Robert Pack. (Grove Press Poetry Ser.). 96p. 1983. pap. 5.95 (ISBN 0-394-62451-3, Ever). Grove.
Part Played by Labour in the Transition from Ape to Man. Friedrich Engels. 16p. 1972. pap. 0.75 (ISBN 0-8285-0044-4, Pub. by Progress Pubs USSR). Imported Pubns.
Part: Poems. Wendell Berry. LC 80-18268. 104p. 1980. 12.50 (ISBN 0-86547-010-3); pap. 6.95 (ISBN 0-86547-008-1). N Point Pr.
Part Taken by Women in American History. Mary S. Logan. LC 72-2613. (American Women Ser: Images & Realities). (Illus.). 956p. 1972. Repr. of 1912 ed. 54.00 (ISBN 0-405-04467-4). Ayer Co Pubs.
Part-Through Crack Fatigue Life Prediction-STP 687. Ed. by J. B. Chang. 226p. 1979. 26.25x (ISBN 0-8031-0532-0, 04-687000-30). ASTM.
Part-Time Academic Employment in the Humanities: A Sourcebook for Just Policy. Ed. by M. Elizabeth Wallace. LC 84-1124. (Options for Teaching Ser.: No. 6). 166p. 1984. 32.00x (ISBN 0-87352-306-7); pap. 17.50x (ISBN 0-87352-307-5). Modern Lang.
Part-Time & Alternative Staffing Practices. 1988. write for info. (354). BNA.
Part-Time & Summer Jobs. John H. Noble. (Illus.). 40p. (Orig., Prog. Bk.). 1984. pap. text ed. 3.39 (ISBN 0-940712-28-8). Dahlstrom & Co.
Part Time Cash for the Sportsman: Twenty-Five Ways for the Fisherman & Hunter to Earn Extra Money. Jim Capossela. LC 82-80911. 72p. 1984. pap. 5.00 (ISBN 0-942990-02-1). Northeast Sportsmans.
Part-Time Faculty: Higher Education at a Crossroads. Judith M. Gappa. Ed. by Jonathan D. Fife. LC 84-72775. (ASHE-ERIC Higher Education Report Ser.: No. 3, 1984). (Illus.). 125p. (Orig.). 1984. pap. 7.50x (ISBN 0-913317-12-8). Assn Study Higher Ed.
Part-Time Faculty in American Higher Education. David W. Leslie et al. LC 81-13773. 160p. 1982. 35.00 (ISBN 0-275-90846-1, C0846). Praeger.
Part-Time Faculty Personnel Management. George Biles. 224p. 1986. 24.95 (ISBN 0-02-903500-7). ACE.
Part-Time Faculty Personnel Management Policies. George E. Biles & Howard P. Tuckman. (Higher Education Ser.). 224p. 1986. text ed. 24.95x (2009). Macmillan.
Part-Time Family Farming. Ryohei Kada. 264p. 1980. 26.00x (ISBN 0-89955-222-6, Pub. by Japan Sci Soc Japan). Intl Spec Bk.
Part-Time Farming in the Southeast. R. H. Allen et al. LC 74-165677. (Research Monograph: Vol. 9). 1971. Repr. of 1937 ed. lib. bdg. 39.50 (ISBN 0-306-70341-6). Da Capo.
Part-Time Father. Edith Atkin & Estelle Rubin. LC 75-25146. 192p. 1976. 14.95 (ISBN 0-8149-0766-0). Vanguard.
Part Time Job Book. Arthur R. Pell. 128p. 1984. pap. 7.95 (ISBN 0-671-46270-9). Monarch Pr.
Part-Time Lady. Ann H. Workman. (Illus.). 128p. 1986. 18.95 (ISBN 0-233-97860-7, Pub. by A Deutsch England). David & Charles.
Part-Time Occupational Faculty: A Contribution to Excellence. Michael H. Parsons. 40p. 1985. 5.50. Natl Ctr Res Voc Ed.
Part-Time Professional: How to Pursue a Career on a Part-Time Basis. Diane Rothberg & Barbara Cook. LC 85-19964. 160p. 1985. pap. 8.95 (ISBN 0-87491-786-7). Acropolis.
Part-Time Types of Elementary Schools in New York City: A Comparative Study of Pupil Achievement. Frank M. Quance. LC 72-177173. (Columbia University. Teachers College. Contributions to Education: No. 249). Repr. of 1926 ed. 22.50 (ISBN 0-404-55249-8). AMS Pr.
Part Time Virgin see Virgen Insaciable.

Part-Time Workers Need Full Time Rights. Ann Sedley. 1983. 20.00x (Pub. by NCCL UK). State Mutual Bk.

Partage de Midi. Paul Claudel. (Folio Ser.: No. 245). 252p. 1949. 5.95 (ISBN 0-686-54409-9). Schoenhof.

Partakers of Divine Nature. C. Stavropoulos. 1976. pap. 4.95 (ISBN 0-937032-09-3). Light&Life Pub Co MN.

Partakers of God. Panagiotes Chrestou. (Patriarch Athenagoras Memorial Lectures Ser.). 66p. 1984. pap. 4.95 (ISBN 0-916586-67-7). Holy Cross Orthodox.

Partera: Story of a Midwife. Fran L. Buss. 1980. 14.95x (ISBN 0-472-09322-3); pap. 8.95 (ISBN 0-472-06322-7). U of Mich Pr.

Parthenia, or the Maydenhead of the First Musicke That Ever Was Printed for the Virginalls. new ed. William Byrd et al. Ed. by Kurt Stone. (Illus.). 62p. 1951. pap. 9.50x (ISBN 0-8450-6001-5). Broude.

Parthenia, or the Maydenhead of the first musicke that ever was printed for the Virginalls see Monuments of Music & Music Literature in Facsimile: Series One.

Parthenon. Alcman. Ed. by W. R. Connor. LC 78-81590. (Greek Texts Commentaries Ser.). 1979. Repr. of 1951 ed. lib. bdg. 17.00x (ISBN 0-405-11432-X). Ayer Co Pubs.

Parthenon. Susan Woodford. (Cambridge Introduction to World History Topic Bks.). (Illus.). 48p. (YA) (gr. 7 up). 1981. pap. 4.95 (ISBN 0-521-22629-5). Cambridge U Pr.

Parthenon. Susan Woodford. LC 82-25878. (Cambridge Topic Bks.). (Illus.). 52p. (gr. 5-10). 1983. PLB 8.95 (ISBN 0-8225-1228-9). Lerner Pubns.

Parthenon & Its Sculptures. John Boardman & David Finn. (Illus.). 256p. 1985. 39.95 (ISBN 0-292-76498-7). U of Tex Pr.

Parthenophil & Parthenophe: A Critical Edition. Barnabe Barnes. Ed. by Victor A. Doyno. LC 73-86185. 293p. 1971. 25.00x (ISBN 0-8093-0466-X). S Ill U Pr.

Parther in der Augusteischen Dichtung. Michael Wissemann. (European University Studies: No. 15, Vol. 24). 186p. (Ger.). 1982. 23.15 (ISBN 3-8204-5948-0). P Lang Pubs.

Parthian Art. Malcolm A. Colledge. LC 77-74919. (Illus.). 240p. 1977. 39.95x (ISBN 0-8014-1111-4). Cornell U Pr.

Parthian Period. M. A. Colledge. (Iconography of Religions XIV Ser.: No. 3). (Illus.). xiv, 47p. 1986. pap. 38.25 (ISBN 90-04-07115-6, Pub. by E J Brill). Heinman.

Parthian Shot. Lloyd Little. 1987. pap. 3.50 (ISBN 0-8041-0004-7, Pub. by Ivy). Ballantine.

Parthian Stations. Isidore Of Charax. Ed. by W. H. Schoff. 1980. 10.00 (ISBN 0-89005-058-9). Ares.

Parti-Colored Blocks for a Quilt: Poets on Poetry. Marge Piercy. 320p. 1982. pap. 8.95 (ISBN 0-472-06338-3). U of Mich Pr.

Parti Pris des Choses. Francis Ponge. (Poesie Ser.). 224p. 1966. 7.95 (ISBN 0-686-54892-2). Schoenhof.

Partial Accounts: New & Selected Poems. William Meredith. 1987. 16.45 (ISBN 0-394-55993-2); pap. 10.95 (ISBN 0-394-75191-4). Knopf.

Partial Bibliography on the Bacterial Diseases of Fish: An Annotated Bibliography for the Years 1870-1966. (Fisheries Technical Papers: No. 73). 73p. 1978. pap. 7.50 (ISBN 0-686-92817-2, F1734, FAO). UNIPUB.

Partial Denture Design: A Lingual Locking Approach. Robert A. Katsev. 220p. 1987. pap. 30.00 (ISBN 0-912791-41-1). Ishiyaku Euro.

Partial Dentures. 5th ed. Lammie. 1986. 32.95 (ISBN 0-8016-2825-3). Mosby.

Partial Dentures. Fritz Singer & Fritz Schon. (Illus.). 207p. 1973. 44.00 (ISBN 0-931386-59-4). Quint Pub Co.

Partial Differential Equations. Richard Bellman & George Adomian. 312p. 1984. PLB 49.00 (ISBN 90-277-1681-1, Pub. by Reidel Holland). Kluwer Academic.

Partial Differential Equations. Lipman Bers et al. LC 63-19664. (Lectures in Applied Mathematics Ser.: Vol. 3a). 343p. 1981. pap. 36.00 (ISBN 0-8218-0049-3, LAM-3-1). Am Math.

Partial Differential Equations. 2nd ed. George F. Carrier. 316p. 1988. write for info. (ISBN 0-12-160451-9). Acad Pr.

Partial Differential Equations. David Colton. 300p. 1988. text ed. 39.00 (ISBN 0-394-35827-9, RanC). Random.

Partial Differential Equations. Edward T. Copson. LC 74-12965. pap. 74.90 (2031635). Bks Demand UMI.

Partial Differential Equations. A. A. Dezin. LC 87-9421. (Springer Series in Soviet Mathematics). 180p. 1987. 82.00 (ISBN 0-387-16699-8). Springer-Verlag.

Partial Differential Equations. George F. Duff. LC 56-4187. (Mathematical Expositions: No. 9). pap. 64.50 (ISBN 0-317-08885-8, 2014193). Bks Demand UMI.

Partial Differential Equations. G. B. Folland. (Tata Institute Lectures on Mathematics). 160p. 1983. pap. 10.00 (ISBN 0-387-12280-X). Springer-Verlag.

Partial Differential Equations. Avner Friedman. LC 76-3513. 272p. 1976. Repr. of 1969 ed. 23.50 (ISBN 0-88275-405-X). Krieger.

Partial Differential Equations. 2nd ed. Paul R. Garabedian. LC 85-73601. (Illus.). xii, 672p. 1986. text ed. 27.50x (ISBN 0-8284-0325-2, 325). Chelsea Pub.

Partial Differential Equations. 4th ed. F. John. (Applied Mathematical Sciences Ser.: Vol. 1). (Illus.). 249p. 1981. 24.20 (ISBN 0-387-90609-6). Springer-Verlag.

Partial Differential Equations. Kenneth S. Miller. LC 87-16930. 262p. 1988. Repr. of 1953 ed. lib. bdg. 23.50 (ISBN 0-89464-234-0). Krieger.

Partial Differential Equations. O. Vejvoda. 380p. 1981. 50.00 (ISBN 0-686-30667-8, Pub. by Sijthoff & Noordhoff). Kluwer Academic.

Partial Differential Equations. W. E. Williams. (Oxford Applied Mathematics & Computing Science Ser.). (Illus.). 1980. text ed. 49.95x (ISBN 0-19-859633-2); pap. text ed. 22.50x (ISBN 0-19-859632-4). Oxford U Pr.

Partial Differential Equations. J. Wloka. (Illus.). 500p. 1987. 79.50 (ISBN 0-521-25914-2); pap. 29.95 (ISBN 0-521-27759-0). Cambridge U Pr.

Partial Differential Equations: A Basic Course. Phoolan Prasad & Renuka Ravindran. 252p. 1985. text ed. 24.95x (ISBN 0-470-20071-5). Halsted Pr.

Partial Differential Equations: An Introduction. Bernard Epstein. LC 75-11905. 284p. 1975. Repr. of 1962 ed. 22.50 (ISBN 0-88275-330-4). Krieger.

Partial Differential Equations & Continuum Mechanics. Ed. by Rudolph E. Langer. (Mathematics Research Center Pubns., No. 5). (Illus.). 414p. 1961. 17.00x (ISBN 0-299-02350-8). U of Wis Pr.

Partial Differential Equations & Continuum Mechanics. Ed. by Rudolph E. Langer. LC 61-600003. (U. S. Army. Mathematics Research Center: No. 5). pap. 103.30 (ISBN 0-317-09147-6, 2015364). Bks Demand UMI.

Partial Differential Equations & Dynamic Systems. W. E. Fitzgibbon. 300p. 1984. pap. 24.95 (ISBN 0-470-20478-8, Co-Pub. with Longman). Wiley.

Partial Differential Equations & Related Topics: Proceedings of the Ford Foundation Program, Tulane University, Jan. to May 1974. Ford Foundation Program Tulane University Staff. Ed. by J. A. Goldstein. LC 75-6604. (Lecture Notes in Mathematics Ser: Vol. 446). iv, 389p. 1975. pap. 21.00 (ISBN 0-387-07148-2). Springer-Verlag.

Partial Differential Equations for Scientists & Engineers. S. J. Farlow. 300p. (Japanese.). 1983. pap. 29.95 (ISBN 0-471-88698-X). Wiley.

Partial Differential Equations for Scientists & Engineers. Stanley J. Farlow. LC 81-12993. 402p. 1982. text ed. write for info. (ISBN 0-471-08639-8); solutions manual avail. (ISBN 0-471-09582-6). Wiley.

Partial Differential Equations for Scientists & Engineers. 3rd ed. T. Myint-U & L. Debnath. 620p. 1987. 39.95 (ISBN 0-444-01173-0, North Holland). Elsevier.

Partial Differential Equations for Scientists & Engineers. 3rd ed. G. Stephenson. (Illus.). 164p. 1985. pap. 9.95 (ISBN 0-582-44696-1). Wiley.

Partial Differential Equations for Scientists & Engineers. 3rd ed. G. Stephenson. 164p. 1986. pap. 19.95 (ISBN 0-470-20624-1, Co-Pub. with Longman). Wiley.

Partial Differential Equations in Engineering Problems. reference ed. Kenneth S. Miller. 1953. 47.00 (ISBN 0-13-650408-6). P-H.

Partial Differential Equations of Applied Mathematics. 2nd ed. Zauderer. (Pure & Applied Mathematics Ser.). 1989. price not set (ISBN 0-471-61298-7). Wiley.

Partial Differential Equations of Applied Mathematics. Erich Zauderer. LC 82-21855. (Pure & Applied Mathematics Ser.). 779p. 1983. 64.95x (ISBN 0-471-87517-1). Wiley.

Partial Differential Equations of Hyperbolic Type & Their Applications: Torino, Italy, September Second Thru the Fourteenth, Nineteen Eighty-Five. Ed. by G. Geymonat. 220p. 1987. 37.00 (ISBN 9971-50-205-4). World Scientific Pub.

Partial Differential Equations of Mathematical Physics. 2nd ed. Tyn Myint-U. 1980. 33.50. Elsevier.

Partial Differential Equations of Mathematical Physics & Integral Equations. Ronald B. Guenther & John W. Lee. (Illus.). 640p. 1988. text ed. write for info. (ISBN 0-13-651332-8). P-H.

Partial Differential Equations of Parabolic Type. Avner Friedman. LC 83-12005. 364p. 1983. Repr. of 1964 ed. text ed. 25.50 (ISBN 0-89874-660-4). Krieger.

Partial Differential Equations: Proceedings. R. A. Aleksandrjan et al. LC 76-8428. (Translations Ser.: No. 2, Vol. 105). 1976. 69.00 (ISBN 0-8218-3055-4, TRANS 2-105). Am Math.

Partial Differential Equations: Proceedings. Symposium in Pure Mathematics, Berkeley, Calif., 1971. Ed. by D. C. Spencer. LC 72-4071. (Proceedings of Symposia in Pure Mathematics: Vol. 23). 506p. 1977. Repr. of 1973 ed. 49.00 (ISBN 0-8218-1423-0, PSPUM-23). Am Math.

Partial Differential Equations: Proceedings. Symposium in Pure Mathematics, Berkeley, 1960. Ed. by C. B. Morrey, Jr. LC 50-1183. (Proceedings of Symposia in Pure Mathematics: Vol.4). 169p. 1982. pap. 30.00 (ISBN 0-8218-1404-4, PSPUM-4). Am Math.

Partial Differential Equations, Proceedings, Tianjin, 1986. Ed. by S. S. Chern. (Lecture Notes in Mathematics Ser.: Vol. 1306). vi, 294p. 1988. pap. 25.80 (ISBN 0-387-19097-X). Springer-Verlag.

Partial Differential Relations. M. Gromov. (Ergebnisse der Mathematik und ihrer Grenzgebiete: Folge 3, Vol. 9). 370p. 1986. 60.00 (ISBN 0-387-12177-3). Springer-Verlag.

Partial Glossary. William Bronk. 1974. pap. 6.00 (ISBN 0-685-40885-X). Elizabeth Pr.

Partial Hospitalization: A Current Perspective. Ed. by R. F. Luber. LC 78-31915. (Illus.). 222p. 1979. 35.00x (ISBN 0-306-40201-7, Plenum Pr). Plenum Pub.

Partial Justice: Women in State Prisons, 1800-1935. Nicole H. Rafter. LC 84-7990. (Illus.). 295p. 1985. 22.95x (ISBN 0-930350-63-4). NE U Pr.

Partial Knowledge: Philosophical Studies in Paul. Paul W. Gooch. LC 86-40589. 224p. 1987. text ed. 22.95x (ISBN 0-268-01567-8). U of Notre Dame Pr.

Partial List of Tiffany Windows. 2nd ed. Ed. by John Sweeney. 119p. 1979. pap. text ed. 8.00 (ISBN 0-914800-02-7). Tiffany.

Partial Magic: The Novel As Self-Conscious Genre. Robert Alter. LC 74-77725. 1975. 33.00x (ISBN 0-520-02755-8); pap. 7.95x (ISBN 0-520-03732-4). U of Cal Pr.

Partial Payments: Essays Arising from the Pleasures of Reading. Joseph Epstein. 1989. 18.95 (ISBN 0-393-02631-0). Norton.

Partial Portraits. Henry James. Repr. of 1888 ed. lib. bdg. 35.00x (ISBN 0-8371-2797-1, JAPA). Greenwood.

Partial Portraits. Henry James. LC 68-24939. (Studies of Henry James, No. 17). 1969. Repr. of 1911 ed. lib. bdg. 49.95x (ISBN 0-8383-0208-4). Haskell.

Partial Prestressing, from Theory to Practice: Proceedings of NATO Advanced Research Workshop on Partial Prestressing, from Theory to Practice, 2 Vols. Ed. by M. Z. Cohn. 1986. Vol. I, Survey Reports. lib. bdg. 186.50 Set (ISBN 90-247-3372-3, Pub. by Martinus Netherlands). Vol. II, Prepared Discussion. Kluwer Academic.

Partial Prestressing of Concrete Structures. Hugo Bachmann. (IBA Ser.: No. 95). 20p. 1979. pap. text ed. 9.95x (ISBN 0-8176-1150-9). Birkhauser.

Partial Progress: The Politics of Science & Technology. David Albury & Joseph Schwartz. 215p. 1982. pap. 7.50 (ISBN 0-86104-385-5, Pub. by Pluto Pr). Longwood Pub Group.

Partial Quantum Mechanics II. S. Fluegge. (Gundlehren der Mathematischen Wissenchaften Ser.: Band 178). (Illus.). xii, 287p. 1987. 77.50 (ISBN 0-317-61425-8). Springer-Verlag.

Partial Removable Prosthodontics. F. James Kratochvil. (Illus.). 304p. 1988. 32.95 (ISBN 0-7216-2382-4). Saunders.

Partial Resistance of Tomatoes Against Phytophthora Infestans, the Late Blight Fungus. new ed. L. J. Turkensteen. (Illus.). 88p. 1974. pap. 16.00 (ISBN 90-220-0497-X, PDC112, PUDOC). UNIPUB.

Partial SM T-A Operations Research. Winston. 188p. 1987. pap. write for info. (ISBN 0-87150-113-9, Duxbury Pr). PWS Kent Pub.

Partial Solutions Manual for Students to Accompany Elementary Statistics, 5th Edition. Johnson. 112p. 1988. pap. text ed. 9.00 (ISBN 0-534-91773-9, 36G0234). PWS Kent Pub.

Partial Solutions Manual T-A Precalculus. Cole. 232p. 1987. pap. 11.00 (ISBN 0-87150-147-3, Prindle). PWS Kent Pub.

Partial Solutions Manual to Accompany Applied Finite Math. Tan. 136p. 1987. pap. 9.50 (ISBN 0-87150-075-2). PWS Kent Pub.

Partial Solutions Manual to Accompany Beginning Algebra, 4th Edition, by Gobran. Gloria Langer. 352p. 1987. pap. text ed. 12.50 (ISBN 0-534-91516-7, 33L4364). PWS Kent Pub.

Partial Solutions Manual to Accompany Trigonometry. Kaufmann. 88p. 1988. pap. text ed. 8.00 (ISBN 0-534-92153-1, 33L4734). PWS Kent Pub.

Partial Solutions Manual to Accompany Precalculus. Kaufmann. 192p. 1988. pap. text ed. 10.00 (ISBN 0-534-91498-5, 33L4714). PWS Kent Pub.

Partial Student Solutions Manual to Accompany a First Course in Differential Equations with Applications. 3rd ed. Wright. 1986. pap. text ed. 11.00 (ISBN 0-87150-929-6, 33L3084, Prindle). PWS Kent Pub.

Partial Surrender: Race & Resistance in the Youth Service. Lincoln Williams. 195p. 1988. 40.00 (ISBN 1-85000-289-4, Falmer Pr); pap. 19.00 (ISBN 1-85000-290-8, Falmer Pr). Taylor & Francis.

Partial Testament: Essays on Some Moderns in the Great Tradition. Helen Lessore. (Illus.). 224p. 1987. 18.95 (ISBN 0-946590-50-8, Pub. by Tate Gall Pubns); pap. 12.95 (ISBN 0-946590-59-1). Salem Hse Pubs.

Partial Tribune Primer. Eugene Field. (Odd Books for Odd Moments: No. 9). (Illus.). iv, 140p. (Orig.). 1986. pap. 4.95 (ISBN 0-930937-39-2). Winds World Pr.

Partiality, Truth & Persistence. Tore Langholm. (CSLI Lecture Notes Ser.: No. 15). 160p. 1988. 29.95x (ISBN 0-937073-35-0); pap. 12.95x (ISBN 0-937073-34-2). Ctr Study Language.

Partially Coherent Light for the Experime. Thompson. 1988. price not set (ISBN 0-471-85999-0). Wiley.

Partially Ordered Abelian Groups with Interpolation. G. Goodearl. LC 86-7876. (Mathematical Surveys & Monographs: Vol. 20). 358p. 1986. text ed. 70.00 (ISBN 0-8218-1520-2). Am Math.

Partially Ordered Linear Topological Spaces. Isaac Namioka. LC 52-42389. (Memoirs: No. 24). 50p. 1982. pap. 16.00 (ISBN 0-8218-1224-6, MEMO-24). Am Math.

Partially Ordered Rings & Semi-Algebraic Geometry. Gregory W. Brumfiel. LC 80-469087. (London Mathematical Society Lecture Note Ser.: No. 37). (Illus.). 288p. pap. 74.90 (2030604). Bks Demand UMI.

Partially Sage: A Comic Look at Common Songs. Shari Ajemian & Sarah Newcomb. LC 83-90154. 130p. (Orig.). 1983. pap. 8.95 (ISBN 0-9611994-0-7). Rob Lynn Pub.

Partially Saturated Ocean Detection: Second Order Process Statistics, PARSAT Computer Program Manual. Efstratios Nikolaidis & Anastassios N. Perakis. (University of Michigan, Dept. of Naval Architecture & Marine Engineering Report: No. 291). pap. 20.00 (ISBN 0-317-27121-0, 2024687). Bks Demand UMI.

Partical Size Analysis 1985: Proceedings of the 5th Particle Size Analysis Conference, Univ. of Bradford, Yorkshire, U. K., September 16-19, 1985. Ed. by P. L. Lloyd. LC 86-24546. 669p. 1987. write for info. (ISBN 0-471-90832-0). Wiley.

Participant Guidebook: My Life... Right Now. Community Intervention, Inc. Staff. (Illus.). 52p. (YA) (gr. 7-12). 1988. wkbk. 2.50 (ISBN 0-9613416-9-6). Comm Intervention.

Participant Observation. Leston Havens. LC 75-42532. 192p. 1983. 20.00x (ISBN 0-87668-697-8). Aronson.

Participant Observation in Organizational Settings. Robert Bogdan. LC 72-85383. (Segregated Settings & the Problem of Change Ser.: No. 3). 106p. 1972. text ed. 10.00x (ISBN 0-8156-8080-5). Syracuse U Pr.

Participant Observer. Glenn Jacobs. 1970. o.s.i 7.95 (ISBN 0-8076-0566-2); pap. 3.95 (ISBN 0-8076-0565-4). Braziller.

Participant Perspective: A Gabriel Marcel Reader. Ed. by Thomas W. Busch. LC 87-10429. 338p. (Orig.). 1987. lib. bdg. 29.25 (ISBN 0-8191-6383-X); pap. text ed. 16.50 (ISBN 0-8191-6384-8). U Pr of Amer.

Participant Self, 2 vols. Adrian Van Kaam et al. pap. 4.95 (ISBN 0-87193-045-5). Dimension Bks.

Participant Workbook for Effective Stepparenting, 4 vols. (Workshop Models for Family Life Education Ser.). 68p. 1984. Set. 19.95 (ISBN 0-87304-209-3). Family Serv.

Participant Workbook for Parenting Children of Divorce. (Workshop Models for Family Life Education Ser.). 32p. 1983. Set of Five. 14.95 (ISBN 0-87304-203-4). Family Serv.

Participant Workbook for Stress Management Training, 5 vols. (Workshop Models for Family Life Education Ser.). 48p. 1982. Set. 17.95 (ISBN 0-87304-196-8). Family Serv.

Participant Workbook for the Coping with Depression Course. Richard Brown & Peter Lewinsohn. 54p. 1984. 2.95 (ISBN 0-916154-14-9). Castalia Pub.

Participants in American Criminal Justice: The Promise & the Performance. Clemens Baryollas & Staurt Miller. (Illus.). 416p. 1983. write for info. prof. ref. (ISBN 0-13-651349-2). P-H.

Participate in Development. Ed. by Huynh C. Tri. 371p. (Orig.). 1986. pap. text ed. 33.75 (ISBN 92-3-102180-X, U1591, UNESCO). UNIPUB.

Participating in Public Speaking. Mississippi State University Staff & Hickson. 120p. 1984. pap. 8.95 (ISBN 0-8403-3422-2). Kendall Hunt.

Participating Management & Psychology. Wilfred G. Caouette. 1988. 8.95 (ISBN 0-533-07730-3). Vantage.

Participating Reader. S. Wittig et al. 1978. pap. 12.95. P-H.

Participation. Jack H. Nagel. (Illus.). 192p. Date not set. pap. text ed. price not set (ISBN 0-13-651316-6). P-H.

Participation. Ann Richardson. (Concepts in Social Policy Ser.). 160p. 1983. pap. text ed. 8.95x (ISBN 0-7100-9469-8). Routledge Chapman & Hall.

Participation: A Platonic Inquiry. Charles P. Bigger. LC 68-21802. xvi, 224p. 1968. 27.50 (ISBN 0-8071-0326-8). La State U Pr.

Participation: A Pragmatic Agenda for the 1980s. Brad Roberts. (Significant Issues Ser. Vol. 9, No. 10). 57p. (Orig.). 1987. pap. 6.95 (ISBN 0-89206-109-X). CSI Studies.

Participation & Democratic Theory. Carole Pateman. LC 71-120193. 1970. pap. 10.95 (ISBN 0-521-29004-X). Cambridge U Pr.

Participation & Political Equality: A Seven-Nation Comparison. Sidney Verba et al. LC 87-10781. xxii, 394p. 1987. pap. text ed. 15.95 (ISBN 0-226-85298-9). U of Chicago Pr.

Participation & Tacit Knowledge in Plato, Machiavelli & Hobbes. Aryeh Botwinick. 88p. (Orig.). 1986. lib. bdg. 17.25 (ISBN 0-8191-5507-1); pap. text ed. 8.25 (ISBN 0-8191-5508-X). U Pr of Amer.

Participation & the Community see **Progress in Planning.**

Participation, Associations, Development & Change. Albert Meister. Tr. by Jack L. Ross from Fr. (Illus.). 286p. 1984. 34.95 (ISBN 0-87855-423-8). Transaction Bks.

Participation by Banks in Other Branches of the Economy: An Opinion on the Economic, Competitive & Operational Advantages & Disadvantages of Such Participation on the Basis of the Statutory Provisions of the Member States of the European Communities. Commission of the European Communities Staff & Ulrich Immenga. LC 82-133118. (Competition Approximation of Legislation: No. 25). iv, 190p. 1975. 5.20. Comm Europe Comm.

Participation by Employers & Workers Organisations in Economic & Social Planning: A General Introduction. viii, 247p. 1971. 11.20 (ISBN 92-2-100129-6). Intl Labour Office.

Participation by Families of Mentally Handicapped People in Policy Making & Planning. Alan Tyne. 1979. 22.00x (ISBN 0-317-05801-0, Pub. by Natl Inst Social Work). State Mutual Bk.

Participation de la Bretagne a la Conquete de l'Angleterre par les Normands. Etienne Dupont. LC 80-2229. Repr. of 1911 ed. 22.00 (ISBN 0-404-18758-7). AMS Pr.

Participation, Decentralization & Advocacy Planning. R. E. Kasperson & M. Breitbart. LC 74-77537. (CCG Resource Papers Ser.: No. 25). 1974. pap. text ed. 5.00 (ISBN 0-89291-072-0). Assn Am Geographers.

Participation Exemption in the Netherlands. M. J. Ellis & D. Juch. pap. 14.00 (ISBN 90-200-0501-4, Pub. by Kluwer Law Netherlands). Kluwer Academic.

Participation in America: Political Democracy & Social Equality. Sidney Verba & Norman H. Nie. LC 87-10825. xxvi, 428p. 1987. pap. text ed. 15.95 (ISBN 0-226-85296-2). U of Chicago Pr.

Participation in American Politics: The Dynamics of Agenda Building. 2nd ed. Roger W. Cobb & Charles D. Elder. LC 83-48052. 224p. 1983. pap. 7.95x (ISBN 0-8018-3086-9). Johns Hopkins.

Participation in American Presidential Nominations-1976. Austin Ranney. 1977. pap. 5.00 (ISBN 0-8447-3246-X). Am Enterprise.

Participation in Cultural Activities: Three Case Studies. (Illus.). 126p. (Orig.). 1987. pap. text ed. 13.50 (ISBN 92-3-102420-5, U1551, UNESCO). UNIPUB.

Participation in Curriculum Making As a Means of Supervision of Rural Schools. William J. Holloway. LC 77-178805. (Columbia University. Teachers College. Contributions to Education: No. 301). Repr. of 1928 ed. 22.50 (ISBN 0-404-55301-X). AMS Pr.

Participation in Development: An Evaluation of Animation Rurale in Senegal. Julie Nester-Niederman. (Graduated Student Term Paper Ser.). 19p. 1984. pap. text ed. 2.00 (ISBN 0-941934-48-9). Indiana Africa.

Participation in God: A Forgotten Strand in Anglican Tradition. A. M. Allchin. 1988. pap. 7.95 (ISBN 0-8192-1408-6). Morehouse.

Participation in Local Social Services: An Explanatory Study-Discussion Paper. Rose Deakin & Phyllis Willmot. 1979. 22.00x (ISBN 0-317-05800-2, Pub. by Natl Inst Social Work). State Mutual Bk.

Participation in Organizations: A Study of Columbia College Alumni. Alden W. Smith. LC 79-177775. (Columbia University. Teachers College. Contributions to Education: No. 935). Repr. of 1948 ed. 22.50 (ISBN 0-404-55935-2). AMS Pr.

Participation in Rural Life. Mildred B. Young. 1942. pap. 2.50x (ISBN 0-87574-019-7, 019). Pendle Hill.

Participation in Services for the Handicapped: Two Contrasting Models-Discussion Paper. Colin Low et al. 1979. 22.00x (ISBN 0-317-05799-5, Pub. by Natl Inst Social Work). State Mutual Bk.

Participation in Zambia, 1974. Peter Jambrek. LC 79-63205. 1979. write for info. codebook (ISBN 0-89138-981-4). ICPSR.

Participation of a Rural Community in the Identification of Technological Problems in Ethiopia: A Case Study from Welmera Werda: Project on Research & Development Systems in Rural Settings. Tewolde Berhan Gebre Egziabher. 61p. 1982. pap. 5.00 (ISBN 92-808-0366-2, TUNU206, UNU). UNIPUB.

Participation of People with Disabilities: International Perspectives. World Congress of Rehabilitation International. 1981. 4.50 (ISBN 0-686-94877-7). Rehab Intl.

Participation of Volunteers, Family & Community Resources in Psychosocial Programs. 1978. 6.00 (ISBN 0-938846-13-2). Ebenezer Ctr.

Participation Requirements. Theodore E. Rhodes. (Requirements for Qualification of Plans Ser.). 13p. 1978. pap. 1.50 (ISBN 0-317-31149-2, B350). Am Law Inst.

Participation Without Politics. Samuel Brittan. (Institute of Economic Affairs, Hobart Papers Ser.: No. 62). pap. 5.95 technical (ISBN 0-255-36123-8). Transatl Arts.

Participative Management. William P. Anthony. LC 77-83035. 1978. pap. text ed. write for info. (ISBN 0-201-00253-1). Addison-Wesley.

Participative Management. Fred Massarik. (Work in America Institute Studies in Productivity Ser.: No. 28). 1983. pap. 39.00 (ISBN 0-08-029509-6). Pergamon.

Participative Management. Fred Massarik. (Studies in Productivity: Highlights of the Literature Ser.: Vol. 28). 40p. 1983. pap. 39.00. Work in Amer.

Participative Management: A Practical Approach. Casimir J. Kowalski & Joseph P. Cangemi. LC 84-16627. 192p. 1985. 14.95 (ISBN 0-8022-2422-9). Philos Lib.

Participative Management: Concepts, Theory, & Implementation. Ed. by Ervin Williams. LC 76-13650. 1976. 19.95 (ISBN 0-88406-102-7). Ga St U Busn Pub.

Participative Management in Academic Libraries. Maurice P. Marchant. LC 76-8740. (Contributions in Librarianship & Information Science: No. 16). 320p. 1977. lib. bdg. 35.00 (ISBN 0-8371-8935-7, MPM/). Greenwood.

Participative Prince: Techniques for Developing Your Organization & Improving Its Performance. Daniel A. Tagliere. LC 79-83886. (Illus.). 1979. 14.95 (ISBN 0-9602516-0-X). ODS Pubns.

Participative Productivity & Quality of Work Life. Robert N. Lehrer. (Illus.). 1981. 44.00 (ISBN 0-13-651398-0). P-H.

Participative Systems At Work: Creating Quality & Employment Security. Sidney P. Rubinstein. LC 86-20044. 180p. 1987. text ed. 24.95 (ISBN 0-89885-338-9). Human Sci Pr.

Participaton in Organizational Change: The TVA Experiment. Aaron J. Nurick. LC 84-26652. 256p. 1985. 38.95 (ISBN 0-275-90149-1, C0149). Praeger.

Participatory & Self-Managed Firms: Evaluating Economic Performance. Ed. by Derek C. Jones & Jan Svejnar. LC 80-8612. (Illus.). 416p. 1982. 45.00x (ISBN 0-669-04328-1). Lexington Bks.

Participatory Approach to Urban Planning. Edmund M. Burke. LC 78-31107. 304p. 1979. text ed. 34.95 (ISBN 0-87705-393-6). Human Sci Pr.

Participatory Approaches to Agricultural Research & Development: A State-of-the-Art Paper. William F. Whyte. (Special Series on Agriculture Research & Extension: No. 1). 111p. (Orig.). 1981. pap. 8.15 (ISBN 0-86731-053-7). Cornell CIS RDC.

Participatory Communication in Nonformal Education, No. 17. John Comings. (Technical Notes Ser.). 15p. (Orig.). 1981. pap. 2.00 (ISBN 0-932288-62-6). Ctr Intl Ed U of MA.

Participatory Democracy in Zambia. Patrick E. Ollawa. 520p. 1985. 39.00x (ISBN 0-317-39410-X, Pub. by A H Stockwell England); pap. 25.00x (ISBN 0-317-39411-8, Pub. by A H Stockwell England). State Mutual Bk.

Participatory Democracy in Zambia. Patrick E. Ollawa. 520p. 1987. 60.00x (ISBN 0-317-62501-2, Pub. by A H Stockwell England); pap. 40.00x (ISBN 0-7223-1214-8). State Mutual Bk.

Participatory Democracy: Populism Revived. Joseph F. Zimmerman. LC 86-8129. 241p. 1986. lib. bdg. 38.95 (ISBN 0-275-92132-8, C2132). Praeger.

Participatory Development. Sheldon Gellar. (Special Studies in Social, Political & Economic Development). 160p. 1986. 26.50x (ISBN 0-8133-0074-6). Westview.

Participatory Economy: An Evolutionary Hypothesis & a Strategy for Development. Jaroslav Vanek. LC 77-148024. (Illus.). 208p. 1971. 35.00x (ISBN 0-8014-0639-0); pap. 10.95x 1975 ed. (ISBN 0-8014-9148-7). Cornell U Pr.

Participatory Management for Public Administrators: A Selective Bibliography. Lorna Peterson. (Public Administration Ser.: P 1834). 6p. 1985. 2.00 (ISBN 0-89028-684-1). Vance Biblios.

Participatory Management in Libraries. Donald J. Sager. LC 82-783. (Library Administration Ser.: No. 3). 216p. 1982. 14.50 (ISBN 0-8108-1530-3). Scarecrow.

Participatory Planning in Community Health Education. Preston L. Schiller et al. LC 86-51164. 210p. 1987. pap. 11.95 (ISBN 0-89914-024-6). Third Party Pub.

Participatory Pluralism: Political Participation & Influence in the United States & Sweden. Marvin E. Olsen. LC 82-2263. 324p. 1982. text ed. 25.95x (ISBN 0-88229-711-2). Nelson-Hall.

Participatory Process: Producing Photo-Literature. Bonnie Cain & John Comings. (Illus.). 40p. (Orig.). 1977. pap. 4.00 (ISBN 0-932288-45-6). Ctr Intl Ed U of MA.

Participial Substantives of the "ata" Type in the Romance Languages. Luther H. Alexander. LC 76-38481. (Columbia University Studies in Romance Philology & Literature: No. 12). Repr. of 1912 ed. 16.50 (ISBN 0-404-50612-7). AMS Pr.

Particle Acceleration & Trapping in Solar Flares. Ed. by G. Trottet & M. Pick. 1987. lib. bdg. 64.00 (ISBN 90-277-2609-4, Pub. by Reidel Holland). Kluwer Academic.

Particle Acceleration Mechanics in Astrophysics. Ed. by J. Arrons et al. LC 79-55844. (AIP Conference Proceedings: No. 56). (Illus.). 425p. lib. bdg. 22.00 (ISBN 0-88318-155-X). Am Inst Physics.

Particle Accelerator Design Computer Programs. John S. Colonias. 1974. 84.00 (ISBN 0-12-181550-1). Acad Pr.

Particle Accelerators & Their Uses, Vol. 4. Waldemar Scharf. (Accelerators & Storage Rings Ser.). 1000p. 1985. text ed. 100.00 (ISBN 3-7186-0034-X). Harwood Academic.

Particle & Fields: Proceedings of the Fourth Brazilian School of Physics Jorge Andre Swieca, Sao Paulo, Brazil 15-25 February 1987. Ed. by R. Shellard & A. da Silva. 600p. 1987. 72.00 (ISBN 9971-50-432-4, ZA0477PP). World Scientific Pub.

Particle & Nuclear Physics: Proceedings of the International Symposium, Beijing, China, September 2-7, 1985. Ed. by N. Hu & C. S. Wu. 464p. 1987. 64.00 (ISBN 9971-50-175-9, Z0319P-P). World Scientific Pub.

Particle Characterization in Technology. Ed. by John K. Beddow. Incl. Vol. I. Applications & Microanalysis. 264p. 95.00 (ISBN 0-8493-5784-5, 5784FD); Vol. II. Morphological Analysis. 288p. 115.00 (ISBN 0-8493-5785-3, 5784FD). 1984. CRC Pr.

Particle Connection: The Most Exciting Scientific Chase since DNA & the Double Helix. Christine Sutton. LC 84-10595. 352p. 1984. 16.95 (ISBN 0-671-49659-X). S&S.

Particle Diffusion in the Radiation Belts. M. Schulz & L. J. Lanzerotti. LC 73-11949. (Physics & Chemistry in Space: Vol. 7). (Illus.). ix, 250p. 1974. 55.00 (ISBN 0-387-06398-6). Springer-Verlag.

Particle Emission from Nuclei, 3 vols. Ed. by Dorin N. Poenaru & Marin S. Ivascu. 1988. 124.95. Vol. I: Nuclear Deformation Energy, 256 pgs (ISBN 0-8493-4634-7, 4634). Vol. II: Alpha, Proton, & Heavy Ion Radioactives, 272 pgs. 99.50 (ISBN 0-8493-4635-5, 4635); Vol. III: Fission & Beta-Delayed Decay Modes, 224 pgs. 99.50 (ISBN 0-8493-4636-3, 4636). CRC Pr.

Particle Explosion. Frank Close et al. LC 86-12473. (Illus.). 240p. 1987. 35.00 (ISBN 0-19-851965-6). Oxford U Pr.

Particle-Induced X-Ray Emission Analysis: Application to Analytical Problems. I. V. Mitchell & K. M. Barfoot. (Nuclear Science Applications Ser.). 63p. 1981. 20.00 (ISBN 3-7186-0085-4). Harwood Academic.

Particle Induced X-Ray Emission & Its Analytical Applications: Proceedings. Conference on Particle Induced X-Ray Emissions & Its Applications, Lund, August 23-26, 1976. Ed. by A. E. Johansson. (Nuclear Instruments & Methods Ser.: Vol. 142 Pts. 1-2). Date not set. price not set (ISBN 0-7204-0715-X, North-Holland). Elsevier.

Particle Kinematics. Eero Byckling & K. Kajantie. LC 72-8595. (Illus.). 329p. pap. 85.60 (2029796). Bks Demand UMI.

Particle of Pollen. Fredric D. Ramey. Ed. by Fredric D. Ramey. LC 82-99953. (Illus.). 73p. 1983. pap. text ed. 15.00 (ISBN 0-910889-00-7). F D Ramey.

Particle Physics. Ed. by M. Martinis et al. 400p. 1975. 37.00 (ISBN 0-444-10648-0, North-Holland). Elsevier.

Particle Physics, Vol. 2. L. B. Okun. (Contemporary Concept in Physics Ser.). 223p. 1985. text ed. 44.00 (ISBN 3-7186-0228-8); pap. 12.00 (ISBN 3-7186-0229-6). Harwood Academic.

Particle Physics: A Los Alamos Primer. Ed. by Necia G. Cooper & Geoffrey B. West. (Illus.). 208p. 1988. 49.50 (ISBN 0-521-34542-1); pap. 14.95 (ISBN 0-521-34780-7). Cambridge U Pr.

Particle Physics: An Introduction. M. Leon. 1973. 39.50 (ISBN 0-12-443850-4). Acad Pr.

Particle Physics & Introduction to Field Theory. Ed. by T. D. Lee. (Concepts in Contemporary Physics Ser.: Vol. 1). 886p. 1981. 75.00 (ISBN 3-7186-0032-3); pap. 22.00 (ISBN 3-7186-0033-1). Harwood Academic.

Particle Physics: Cargese, 1985. Ed. by Maurice Levy et al. Tr. by Jacques Weyers & Raymond Castamans. (NATO ASI Series B, Physical Sciences: Vol. 150). 447p. 1987. 79.50x (ISBN 0-306-42562-9, Plenum Pr). Plenum Pub.

Particle Physics: Cargese 1987. Ed. by M. Levy et al. LC 88-4180. (NATO ASI Series B, Physics: Vol. 173). (Illus.). 684p. 1988. 115.00x (ISBN 0-306-42835-0, Plenum Pr). Plenum Pub.

Particle Physics 1971: Proceedings of the AIP Conference, Univ. of California, Irvine, Dec., 1971, No. 6. American Institute of Physics. Ed. by M. Bander et al. LC 72-81239. 185p. 1972. 11.00 (ISBN 0-88318-105-3). Am Inst Physics.

Particle Physics 1980. Ed. by I. Andric et al. 1981. 126.50 (ISBN 0-444-86174-2). Elsevier.

Particle Searches & Discoveries: Proceedings, International Conference, Vanderbilt University, 1-3 March 1976. Ed. by R. S. Panvini. LC 76-19949. (AIP Conference Proceedings Ser.: No. 30). 1976. 18.50 (ISBN 0-88318-129-0). Am Inst Physics.

Particle Size Analysis in Estimating the Significance of Airborne Contamination. (Technical Reports Ser.: No. 179). (Illus.). 234p. 1978. pap. 37.00 (ISBN 92-0-125078-9, IDC179, IAEA). UNIPUB.

Particle Size Analysis in Industrial Hygiene. Leslie Silverman. (Atomic Energy Commission Monographs). 315p. 1971. 40.00 (ISBN 0-12-643750-5). Acad Pr.

Particle Size Analysis, 1981: Proceedings of the Fourth Particle Size Analysis Conference, Loughborough University of Technology, 21-24 September 1981. Particle Size Analysis Conference (4th: 1981: Loughborough University of Technology. Ed. by N. Stanley-Wood & T. Allen. pap. 117.80 (ISBN 0-317-30324-4, 2024805). Bks Demand UMI.

Particle Size Analysis, 1988. Lloyd. LC 88-5633. 376p. 1988. write for info. (ISBN 0-471-91997-7). Wiley.

Particle Size Classifiers. 16p. 1980. pap. 14.00 (ISBN 0-8169-0033-7, E-20). Am Inst Chem Eng.

Particle Size Distribution: Assessment & Characterization: Symposium of the 190th Meeting, Chicago, IL, September 8-13, 1985. Polymetric Materials Division Staff. Ed. by Theodore J. Provder. LC 86-32185. (ACS Symposium Ser.: No. 332). (Illus.). x, 308p. 1987. 59.95 (ISBN 0-8412-1016-0). Am Chemical.

Particle Size Measurement. 3rd ed. T. Allen. (Powder Technology Ser.). 1981. 67.00x (ISBN 0-412-15410-2, NO. 6386, Pub. by Chapman & Hall). Routledge Chapman & Hall.

Particle Sizing & Spray Analysis. Ed. by N. Chigier & G. W. Stewart. 97p. 1985. 36.00 (ISBN 0-89252-608-4, 573). SPIE.

Particle Technology. Institution of Chemical Engineers. 1982. 79.00 (ISBN 0-08-028761-1). Pergamon.

Particle Technology Research Reviews: Proceedings of the 3rd International Powder Technology & Bulk Solids Conference, Vol. 1. Ed. by A. S. Goldberg. (Powder Advisory Centre Publications Ser. (POWTECH)). 199p. 1973. 59.95 (ISBN 0-471-25734-6, Pub. by Wiley Heyden); pap. 55.95 (ISBN 0-471-25733-8). Wiley.

Particle Theory. Edward Bryant. (Orig.). 1981. pap. 2.95 (ISBN 0-671-43107-2, Timescape). PB.

Particle-Transport Simulation with the Monte Carlo Method. L. L. Carter & E. D. Cashwell. LC 75-25993. (ERDA Critical Review Ser.). 124p. 1975. pap. 11.00 (ISBN 0-87079-021-8, TID-26607); microfiche 6.50 (ISBN 0-87079-382-9, TID-26607). DOE.

Particleboard, Vol. 1: Materials. A. A. Moslemi. LC 74-2071. (Illus.). 256p. 1974. 19.95x (ISBN 0-8093-0655-7). S Ill U Pr.

Particleboard, Vol. 2: Technology. A. A. Moslemi. LC 74-2071. (Illus.). 252p. 1974. 19.95x (ISBN 0-8093-0656-5). S Ill U Pr.

Particles. Randy Blasing. LC 83-10052. 57p. (Orig.). 1983. pap. 5.00 (ISBN 0-914278-40-1). Copper Beech.

Particles: An Introduction to Particle Physics. Michael Chester. 1980. pap. 2.50 (ISBN 0-451-61899-8, ME1899, Ment). NAL.

Particles & Detectors. Ed. by K. Kleinknecht & T. D. Lee. (Tracts in Modern Physics Ser.: Vol. 108). (Illus.). 305p. 1986. 49.00 (ISBN 0-387-16265-8). Springer-Verlag.

Particles & Fields. Incl. 1971. AIP Conference, Rochester 1971. Ed. by A. C. Melissinos & P. S. Slattery. LC 71-184662. (No. 2). 323p. 1971. 13.00 (ISBN 0-88318-101-0); 1973. AIP Conference et al. Ed. by H. H. Bingham. LC 73-91923. (No. 14). 680p. 1973. 18.50 (ISBN 0-88318-113-4); 1974. AIP Conference, Williamsburg 1974. Ed. by C. A. Carlson. LC 74-27575. (No. 23). 688p. 1975. 20.50 (ISBN 0-88318-122-3); 1977. American Physical Society Division of Particles & Fields Annual Meeting, Argonne National Lab, Oct. 1977 et al. Ed. by P. A. Schreiner. LC 78-55683. (No. 43: Particles & Fields Subser. No. 13). (Illus.). 1978. 22.00 (ISBN 0-88318-142-8); 1979. Ed. by B. Margolis & D. G. Stairs. LC 80-66631. (No. 59). 452p. 1980. 23.75 (ISBN 0-88318-158-4); 1981: Testing the Standard Model (APS-DPF, Santa Cruz. Ed. by C. A. Heusch & W. T. Kirk. LC 82-71156. (No. 81). 599p. 1982. 40.25 (ISBN 0-88318-180-0); 1983: APS-DPF, Blackburg, Va. Ed. by Alexander Abashian. LC 84-70378. (No. 112). 288p. 1984. 39.75 (ISBN 0-317-37771-X). (AIP Conference Proceedings). Am Inst Physics.

Particles & Fields, APS-DPF, University of Maryland, 1982: AIP Conference Proceedings No. 98, Particles & Fields Subseries, 29th. W. E. Caswell & G. A. Snow. LC 83-70807. 413p. 1983. lib. bdg. 37.75 (ISBN 0-88318-197-5). Am Inst Physics.

Particles & Fields in the Magnetosphere: Proceedings. Summer Advanced Study Institute, University of California, Santa Barbara, California, August 4-15, 1969. Ed. by B. M. Mc Cormac. LC 78-115884. (Astrophysics & Space Science Library: No. 17). 453p. 1970. lib. bdg. 53.00 (ISBN 90-277-0131-8, Pub. by Reidel Holland). Kluwer Academic.

Partition of Cell Particles & Macromolecules. 3rd ed. Per-Ake Albertsson. 346p. 1986. 59.95 (ISBN 0-471-82820-3). Wiley.

Partitioned Africans: Ethnic Relations Across Africa's International Boundaries, 1884-1984. A. I. Asiwaju. LC 84-18002. 350p. 1985. 29.95 (ISBN 0-312-59753-3). St Martin.

Partitioning in Aqueous Two-Phase Systems: Theories, Methods, Uses & Applications to Biotechnology. Ed. by Harry Walter et al. 1986. 95.00 (ISBN 0-12-733860-8); pap. 39.95 (ISBN 0-12-733861-6). Acad Pr.

Partitions. Michael Blitz. (Illus.). 50p. (Orig.). 1982. 11.00 (ISBN 0-916258-13-0); pap. 7.50 (ISBN 0-916258-12-2). Mercury Print.

Partitions: A Bibliography of Recent Periodical Literature. Mary E. Huls. (Architecture Ser.: A 1618). 6p. 1986. 3.00 (ISBN 0-89028-908-5). Vance Biblios.

Partly Pandemonium, Partly Love. Merrill Leffler. LC 82-70051. 64p. 1982. 10.00 (ISBN 0-931848-46-6); pap. 5.25 (ISBN 0-931848-50-4). Dryad Pr.

Partly Right. Anthony Campolo. 192p. 1985. 11.95 (ISBN 0-8499-0368-8, 0368-8). Word Bks.

Partner & I. Susan Ware. LC 86-33972. 352p. 1987. 25.00x (ISBN 0-300-03820-8). Yale U Pr.

Partner & Partnership Bankruptcy. Ralph C. Anzivino. LC 86-23407. (Business Practice Library). 243p. 1987. 85.00 (ISBN 0-471-80616-1). Wiley.

Partner & Partnership Bankruptcy: 1988 Supplement. Ralph C. Anzivino. (Business Practice Library). 1988. pap. 35.00 (ISBN 0-471-63609-6). Wiley.

Partner im Satz: Handbuch fur Autoren, Herstellen, Procluktioner, Setzer. Hubert Blana et al. xi, 275p. (Ger.). 1988. lib. bdg. 42.00 (ISBN 3-598-10633-5). K G Saur.

Partner in Empire: Dwarkanath Tagore & the Age of Enterprise in Eastern India. Blair B. Kling. LC 74-27293. 1977. 40.00x (ISBN 0-520-02927-5). U of Cal Pr.

Partners. Louis Auchincloss. 1974. 6.95 (ISBN 0-395-18279-4). HM.

Partners. Marguerite Corbally. LC 77-74121. 1977. pap. text ed. 4.95x (ISBN 0-8134-1953-0). Inter Print Pubs.

Partners. Veronica Geng. LC 83-48812. (Illus.). 224p. 1984. 13.45i (ISBN 0-06-015295-8, HarpT). Har-Row.

Partners. Veronica Geng. LC 83-48812. (Illus.). 184p. 1985. pap. 6.95 (ISBN 0-06-091289-8, PL 1289, PL). Har-Row.

Partners. Grace L. Hill. 16.95 (ISBN 0-89190-071-3, Pub. by Am Repr). Amereon Ltd.

Partners, 3 bks. Michael Lewis. (Illus.). 48p. 1983. Partners 1 (Easy) pap. text ed. 3.95 (ISBN 0-317-64900-0); Partners 2 (Intermediate) pap. text ed. 3.95 (ISBN 0-317-64901-9); Partners 3 (More Demanding) pap. text ed. 3.95 (ISBN 0-317-64902-7). Alemany Pr.

Partners. John Martel. LC 87-47796. 448p. 1988. 18.95 (ISBN 0-553-05247-0). Bantam.

Partners. Carol S. Smith. (Love & Life Romance Ser.). (Orig.). 1982. pap. 1.75 (ISBN 0-345-29757-1). Ballantine.

Partners: A Guide to Working with Schools for Parents of Children with Special Instructional Needs. David L. Lillie & Patricia A. Place. 1982. pap. 9.95 (ISBN 0-673-16036-X). Scott F.

Partners: A Practical Guide to Corporate Support of the Arts. LC 81-70689. (Illus.). 112p. 1982. 10.95 (ISBN 0-317-02281-4). Alliance Arts.

Partners Across the Pacific. Winston Crawley. LC 85-29088. 1986. pap. 4.95 (ISBN 0-8054-6341-0). Broadman.

Partners Against Hunger: The Consultative Group on International Agricultural Research. Warren C. Baum. 352p. 1986. 29.95 (ISBN 0-8213-0827-0, BK 0827); pap. 10.95 (ISBN 0-8213-0829-7, BK 0829). World Bank.

Partners & Pursestrings: A History of the United States Israel Appeal. Ernest Stock. 256p. (Orig.). 1987. lib. bdg. 26.50 (ISBN 0-8191-5802-X, Pub. by Ctr Jewish Comm Studies); pap. text ed. 13.75 (ISBN 0-8191-5803-8, Pub. Ctr Jewish Comm Studies). U Pr of Amer.

Partners & Rivals: Britain's Imperial Diplomacy Concerning the United States & Japan in China, 1915-1922. Clarence B. Davis. Ed. by Stuart Bruchey. (Foreign Economic Policy of the United States Ser.). 716p. 1987. lib. bdg. 95.00 (ISBN 0-8240-8081-5). Garland Pub.

Partners & Rivals in Western Europe: Britain, France & Germany. Roger Morgan & Caroline Bray. 200p. 1985. text ed. 47.50 (ISBN 0-566-00983-8). Gower Pub Co.

Partners for Life: Making a Marriage That Lasts. Gene Getz & Elaine Getz. Ed. by Kathi Mills. 175p. (Orig.). 1988. pap. 7.95 (ISBN 0-8307-1306-9, 5419603). Regal.

Partners for Progress: UFEX 12 Conference & Exposition-Society of the Plastics Industry-Polyurethane Foam Contractors Div. 51p. 1987. pap. 20.00 (ISBN 0-87762-521-2). Technomic.

Partners in Agroeconomic Development. Douglas N. Ross. LC 77-71332. (Report Ser.: No. 711). (Illus.). 59p. 1977. pap. 15.00 (ISBN 0-8237-0146-8). Conference Bd.

Partners in Catechesis. Archdiocese of Baltimore Staff. 96p. 1984. pap. 9.95 (ISBN 0-697-02016-9). Wm C Brown.

Partners in Conflict: The United States & Latin America. Abraham F. Lowenthal. LC 86-46291. 256p. 1987. 24.50x (ISBN 0-8018-3397-3). Johns Hopkins.

Partners in Conflict: The United States & Latin America. Abraham F. Lowenthal. LC 85-46291. 256p. 1988. pap. text ed. 10.95x (ISBN 0-8018-3398-1). Johns Hopkins.

Partners in Creation. Ronald D. Petry. 126p. (Orig.). 1979. pap. 4.95 (ISBN 0-87178-688-5). Brethren.

Partners in Crime. Agatha Christie. 224p. 1971. pap. 2.50 (ISBN 0-440-16848-1). Dell.

Partners in Crime. Rolando Hinojosa. LC 84-72298. 160p. (Orig.). 1985. pap. 10.00. Arte Publico.

Partners in Design: Advising Small Business Owners & Entrepreneurs. Hamline University, Advanced Legal Education Staff. 269p. 1986. looseleaf 47.70. Hamline Law.

Partners in Design Education. Date not set. 35.00. Inst Busn Desn.

Partners in Development: An Analysis of AID-University Relations, 1950-1966. John M. Richardson, Jr. xvii, 272p. 1970. 8.50 (ISBN 0-87013-135-4). Mich St U Pr.

Partners in Dialogue: Christianity & Other World Religions. Arnulf Camps. Tr. by John Drury from Dutch. LC 82-18798. 272p. (Orig.). 1983. pap. 10.95 (ISBN 0-88344-378-3). Orbis Bks.

Partners in East-West Economic Relations: The Determinants of Choice. Ed. by Zbigniew M. Fallenbuchl & Charles H. McMillan. (Pergamon Policy Studies). (Illus.). 1980. 78.00 (ISBN 0-08-022497-0). Pergamon.

Partners in Education: How Colleges Can Work with Schools to Improve Teaching & Learning. Theodore L. Gross. LC 87-46344. (Higher Education Ser.). 225p. 1988. 22.95x (ISBN 1-55542-089-3). Jossey-Bass.

Partners in Export Trade: The/Nineteen Eighty-Seven Directory for Export Trade Contacts. 240p. (Orig.). 1987. pap. 11.00 (ISBN 0-318-23520-X, S/N 003-009-00512-4). USGPO.

Partners in Freedom & True Muslims: The Political Thought of Some Muslim Scholars in British India, 1912-1947. Peter Hardy. LC 80-13115. (Scandinavian Institute of Asian Studies, Monograph Ser.: No. 5). 63p. 1980. Repr. of 1971 ed. lib. bdg. 35.00x (ISBN 0-313-22424-2, HAPN). Greenwood.

Partners in Furs: A History of the Fur Trade in Eastern James Bay, 1600-1870. Daniel Francis & Toby Morantz. 200p. 1983. 27.50x (ISBN 0-7735-0385-4); pap. 14.95c (ISBN 0-7735-0386-2). McGill-Queens U Pr.

Partners in Health: Sexuality, Contraceptive & Reproductive Health Issues. Beverlie Conant Sloane. 1986. text ed. 4.50 (ISBN 0-675-20630-8). Merrill.

Partners in Intimacy: Living Christian Marriage Today. Challon O. Roberts & William P. Roberts. 1988. pap. 8.95. Paulist Pr.

Partners in Love. 3rd rev. ed. Eleanor Hamilton. LC 79-51018. 1981. Repr. 9.95 (ISBN 0-498-02431-8). A S Barnes.

Partners in Love: Ingredients for a Deep & Lively Marriage. Alanston B. Houghton. 1988. 16.95 (ISBN 0-8027-1005-0). Walker & Co.

Partners in Ministry. James Garlow. (Illus.). 195p. (Orig.). 1981. pap. 4.95 (ISBN 0-8341-0693-0); leader's guide 16.95. Beacon Hill.

Partners in Peacemaking: Family Workshop Models Guidebook for Leaders. Ed. by James McGinnis et al. LC 85-159853. 170p. 1984. pap. text ed. 10.75 (ISBN 0-912765-08-9). Inst Peace.

Partners in Practice. Susan Nelson. (gr. 1-6). 1988. pap. 5.95 (ISBN 0-8224-5150-6). D S Lake Pubs.

Partners in Process. Truman Esau & Beverly Burch. 156p. 1986. pap. 5.95 (ISBN 0-89693-372-5). Victor Bks.

Partners in Production: A Basis for Labor-Management Understanding a Report by the Labor Committee. Twentieth Century Fund. Labor Committee. Repr. of 1949 ed. 10.00 (ISBN 0-527-02841-X). Kraus Repr.

Partners in Progress. facs. ed. Esse V. Hathaway. LC 68-29213. (Essay Index Reprint Ser.). (Illus.). 1968. Repr. of 1935 ed. 18.00 (ISBN 0-8369-0518-0). Ayer Co Pubs.

Partners in Prosperity: Strategic Industries in the United States & Japan. Julian Gresser. LC 83-24925. 432p. 1984. text ed. 15.95 (ISBN 0-07-024671-8). McGraw.

Partners in Public Service: Government & the Nonprofit Sector in Rhode Island. Diane M. Disney et al. 164p. (Orig.). 1984. pap. text ed. 14.95x (ISBN 0-87766-344-0). Urban Inst.

Partners in Rebellion: Alabama Women in the Civil War. H. E. Sterkx. LC 74-99326. (Illus.). 238p. 1970. 22.50 (ISBN 0-8386-7614-6). Fairleigh Dickinson.

Partners in Research: The CGIAR in Latin America. Grant M. Scobie. (CGIAR Study Paper Ser.: No. 24). 60p. 1988. 6.50 (ISBN 0-8213-0991-9, BK0991). World Bank.

Partners in Revolution: The United Irishmen & France. Marianne Elliott. LC 82-50441. (Illus.). 430p. 1982. 39.00x (ISBN 0-300-02770-2). Yale U Pr.

Partners in Science: Letters of James Watt & Joseph Black. James Watt & Joseph Black. Intro. by Eric Robinson & Douglas McKie. 518p. 1969. text ed. 34.50x (ISBN 0-674-65480-3). Harvard U Pr.

Partners in Service: Toward a Biblical Theology of Christian Marriage. Elisabeth M. Tetlow & Louis M. Tetlow. LC 83-7016. 192p. (Orig.). 1983. lib. bdg. 27.50 (ISBN 0-8191-3206-3); pap. text ed. 12.00 (ISBN 0-8191-3207-1). U Pr of Amer.

Partners in the Arts: An Arts in Education Handbook. Bonnie Bernardi et al. 65p. 1983. pap. 13.95 (6300). Am Council Arts.

Partners in the Impossible. Richard W. Patt. 1984. 4.95 (ISBN 0-89536-678-9, 4854). CSS of Ohio.

Partners in the Research Enterprise: University-Corporate Relations in Science & Technology. Ed. by Thomas W. Langfitt et al. LC 83-3508. (Illus.). 224p. 1983. pap. 17.95x (ISBN 0-8122-1150-2). U of Pa Pr.

Partners: Inside America's Most Powerful Law Firms. James A. Stewart. 384p. 1983. 17.95 (ISBN 0-671-42023-2). S&S.

Partners: Inside America's Most Powerful Law Firms. James B. Stewart. LC 83-14783. 400p. (Orig.). 1984. pap. 7.95 (ISBN 0-446-38012-1). Warner Bks.

Partners: Neighborhood Revitalization Through Partnership, Pt. 1. Ranae Hanson & John McNamara. Incl. Partners: Whittier Neighborhood, a Minneapolis Case Study. pap. 15.00. LC 81-70680. (Illus.). 1981. pap. 15.00. Dayton Hudson.

Partners of the Tide. Joseph C. Lincoln. LC 72-98402. Repr. of 1905 ed. 24.95 (ISBN 0-404-03987-1). AMS Pr.

Partners on Wheels. H. R. Sheffer. Ed. by Howard Schroeder. LC 80-28428. (Teamates Ser.). (Illus.). 48p. (gr. 3 up). 1981. PLB 7.95 (ISBN 0-89686-105-8). Crestwood Hse.

Partners: Parents & Schools. Ed. by Ronald S. Brandt. LC 79-90730. 96p. 1979. pap. text ed. 4.75 (ISBN 0-87120-096-1, 611-79168). Assn Supervision.

Partners: Whittier Neighborhood, a Minneapolis Case Study see Partners: Neighborhood Revitalization Through Partnership.

Partners with Power: Social Transformation of the Large Law Firm. Robert L. Nelson. 1988. 39.95x (ISBN 0-520-05844-5). U of CaL Pr.

Partnership, A Study of the Covenant. Andrew Kuyvenhoven. 80p. 1983. pap. 2.75 (ISBN 0-933140-89-4). CRC Pubns.

Partnership Agreements: Planning, Drafting & Taxation. Lee. 1988. write for info. (ISBN 0-471-87227-X). Wiley.

Partnership Allocation Regulations: Law-Tactics-Compliance. Peter M. Fass et al. (Taxation Ser.). 1988. write for info. looseleaf. Clark Boardman.

Partnership & Profit in Medieval Islam. Abraham L. Udovitch. LC 78-104097. (Princeton Studies on the Near East). Repr. of 1970 ed. 73.50 (ISBN 0-8357-9508-X, 2014877). Bks Demand UMI.

Partnership Book. 3rd ed. Denis Clifford & Ralph Warner. 1987. pap. 18.95 (ISBN 0-87337-041-4). Nolo Pr.

Partnership Handbook. New York State Bar Association Staff. Ed. by Raymond W. Merritt & Martin Helpern. 917p. 1985. 60.00 (ISBN 0-942954-09-2). NYS Bar.

Partnership in Development. (Background Studies: No. 45). 145p. pap. 11.25 (ISBN 0-660-10668-X, SSC159, SSC). UNIPUB.

Partnership in Educational Management. Chris Day & Cyril Poster. 224p. 1988. lib. bdg. 49.95 (ISBN 0-415-00588-4). Routledge Chapman & Hall.

Partnership of Caring: A Blueprint for Social Action. Joanna Mellor et al. 1981. pap. 1.50 (ISBN 0-88156-089-8). Comm Serv Soc NY.

Partnership of Hearts. Vicki Page. (Lythway Ser.). 1987. lib. bdg. 16.50x (ISBN 0-7451-0583-1, Pub. by Chivers Pr UK). G K Hall.

Partnership of Mind & Body: Biofeedback. Larry Kettelkamp. LC 76-24818. (Illus.). (gr. 5-9). 1976. PLB 11.88 (ISBN 0-688-32088-0). Morrow.

Partnership Power: How to Profit & Reduce Taxes Investing in Real Estate Partnerships. Robert P. Gerend. 248p. 1983. perfect bdg. 18.95 (ISBN 0-8403-3161-4). Kendall-Hunt.

Partnership Tax Handbook. Prentice-Hall Editorial Staff. 176p. 1988. pap. 19.50 (ISBN 0-13-697104-0). P-H.

Partnership Tax Handbook. Prentice Hall Editorial Staff. 200p. 1989. pap. 19.75 (ISBN 0-13-705873-X, Busn). P-H.

Partnership Taxation, 2 vols. 3rd ed. Willis. 1981. text ed. 240.00 (ISBN 0-07-070623-9). McGraw.

Partnership Taxation, 4 vols. 3rd ed. Arthur B. Willis et al. (Tax & Estate Planning Ser.). 1981. 240.00. Shepards-McGraw.

Partnership Taxation: An Advanced Tax Program, 1988. Herschel M. Bloom & David W. Mills. (Tax Law & Estate Planning Ser.). 1988. 45.00 (J43612). PLI.

Partnership with China: Sino-Foreign Joint Ventures in Historical Perspective. David G. Brown. (Replica Edition Ser.). 130p. 1985. pap. 19.50x (ISBN 0-86531-891-3). Westview.

Partnership with Death. Clifton Adams. 192p. 1982. pap. 2.25 (ISBN 0-441-65203-4, Pub by Charter Bks). Ace Bks.

Partnerships Connecting School & Community. Anne Lewis. 124p. (Orig.). 1986. pap. 12.95 (ISBN 0-87652-102-2, 021-00182). Am Assn Sch Admin.

Partnerships for Improving Schools. Byrd L. Jones & Robert W. Maloy. LC 87-23774. (Contributions to the Study of Education: No. 24). 192p. 1988. lib. bdg. 35.00 (ISBN 0-313-25594-6, JPR/). Greenwood.

Partnerships, UPA, ULPA, Taxation, Securities, & Bankruptcy. 8th ed. Frwd. by Paul A. Wolkin. 897p. Date not set. pap. text ed. 50.00 (ISBN 0-8318-0166-2). Am Law Inst.

Partonopeus de Blois. Ed. by A. T. Boedtker. (EETS, ES Ser.: No. 109). (The Middle English version, 1911). Repr. of 1912 ed. 55.00 (ISBN 0-527-00312-3). Kraus Repr.

Partons in Soft-Hadronic Processes: Proceedings of the Europhysics Study Conference, Erice, Italy, March 8-14, 1981. Ed. by R. T. Van de Walle. vi, 332p. 1981. 33.00 (ISBN 9971-950-00-6). World Scientific Pub.

Partridge in a Swamp: The Journals of Viola C. White. Ed. by W. Storrs Lee. 1979. 12.95 (ISBN 0-914378-40-6). Countryman.

Partridge: Pesticides, Predation & Conservation. G. R. Potts. (Illus.). 286p. 1986. text ed. 45.00x (ISBN 0-00-383298-8, Pub. by Collins England). Sheridan.

Partridges. G. E. Robbins. (Illus.). 144p. 1985. 22.00 (ISBN 0-85115-191-4, Pub. by Boydell & Brewer). Longwood Pub Group.

Parts: A Study in Ontology. Peter Simons. (Illus.). 416p. 1987. 72.00 (ISBN 0-19-824954-3). Oxford U Pr.

Parts Added to the Mirrour for Magistrates. John Higgins & Thomas Blenerhasset. Ed. by Lily B. Campbell. LC 76-29439. Repr. of 1946 ed. 35.00 (ISBN 0-404-15319-4). AMS Pr.

Parts & Moments: Studies in Logic & Formal Ontology. Barry Smith. (Analytica). 564p. 1982. lib. bdg. 116.50 (ISBN 3-88405-012-5). Philosophia Pr.

Parts & Other Parts. Charles Stein. LC 82-5505. (Illus.). 96p. (Orig.). 1982. 4.95 (ISBN 0-930794-66-4). Station Hill Pr.

Parts Department-Inventory Management. 6th ed. Mike Nicholes. (Illus.). 505p. (Orig.). manual 150.00. Mike Nicholes.

Parts of a World: Wallace Stevens Remembered. Peter Brazeau. 1983. 19.45 (ISBN 0-394-52734-8). Random.

Parts of a World: Wallace Stevens Remembered. Peter Brazeau. LC 84-62313. 368p. 1985. 12.50 (ISBN 0-86547-190-8). N Point Pr.

Parts of Animals. Aristotle. Bd. with Movement of Animals; Progression of Animals. (Loeb Classical Library: No. 323). (Gr. & Eng.). 13.95x (ISBN 0-674-99357-8). Harvard U Pr.

Parts of Speech. Philip Lutgendorf & Shirley M. James. LC 77-730079. (Illus.). (gr. 7-9). 1976. pap. text ed. 209.00 (ISBN 0-89290-118-7, A134-SATC). Soc for Visual.

Parts of Speech. facs. ed. Brander Matthews. LC 68-54361. (Essay Index Reprint Ser). 1901. 29.25 (ISBN 0-8369-0697-7). Ayer Co Pubs.

Parts of Speech. Brander Matthews. 1901. 25.00 (ISBN 0-8274-3102-3). R West.

Parts of the Body, Level 1, Bk. 1. Judy O'Hare & Ginny Murphy. LC 84-71133. (Abuelita Espanola Ser.). (Illus.). 30p. (Orig., Span.). (ps-6). 1984. pap. 12.00x (ISBN 0-916989-01-1); pap. text ed. 12.00x. Duggan Pubns.

Parts of the Body in Older Germanic & Scandinavian. Torild W. Arnoldson. LC 71-158274. (Chicago. University. Germanic Studies: No. 2). Repr. of 1915 ed. 26.00 (ISBN 0-404-50282-2). AMS Pr.

Parts of the Body in the Later Germanic Dialects. William D. Baskett. LC 75-161725. (Chicago. University. Linguistic Studies in Germanic: No. 5). Repr. of 1920 ed. 20.00 (ISBN 0-404-50285-7). AMS Pr.

Parts of the Heart. Robin Halley. (Illus.). 59p. (Orig.). 1986. pap. 9.95 (ISBN 0-935749-09-8). Park Row Pr.

Parts Per Million Values for Estimating Quality Levels. Odeh. Ed. by Owen. (Statistics Textbooks & Monographs). 368p. 1987. 99.75 (ISBN 0-8247-7950-9). Dekker.

Parturient Hypocalcaemia Prevention in Parturient Cows Prone to Milk Fever by Dietary Measures. New ed. J. H. Westerhuis. (Agricultural Research Reports). 78p. 1974. pap. 14.00 (ISBN 90-220-0506-2, PDC63, PUDOC). UNIPUB.

Party. Jean Claverie. (It's Great to Read Ser.). 32p. (ps-1). 1986. 5.95 (ISBN 0-517-56026-7). Crown.

Party. Trevor Griffiths. 1974. pap. 4.95 (ISBN 0-571-10647-1). Faber & Faber.

Party. Christopher Pike. (Final Friends Ser.). (gr. 8 up). 1988. pap. 2.75. PB.

Party & Agricultural Crisis Management in the U. S. S. R. Cynthia S. Kaplan. LC 86-32223. (Studies in Soviet History & Society). 224p. 1987. 28.50x (ISBN 0-8014-2021-0). Cornell U Pr.

Parzival: An/Introduction. Eileen Hitchins. (Illus.). 1988. pap. 11.95 (ISBN 0-904693-05-8, Pub. by Temple Lodge Press, England). St George Bk Serv.

Parzival: Eine Auswahl mit Anmerkungen und Woerterbuch. 4th ed. Wolfram von Eschenbach. Ed. by Hermann Jantzen & Herbert Kolb. (Sammlung Goeschen 5021). 128p. 1973. pap. 5.10x (ISBN 3-11-004615-6). De Gruyter.

Parzival of Wolfram Von Eschenbach. Wolfram Von Eschenbach. LC 51-6040. (North Carolina. University. Studies in the Germanic Languages & Literatures: No. 5). Repr. of 1951 ed. 18.50 (ISBN 0-404-50905-3). AMS Pr.

Parzival: The Chalice of Ecstasy. Frater Achad. 82p. 1976. Repr. of 1923 ed. 7.00 (ISBN 0-911662-59-6). Yoga.

Parzival und der Gral in der Dichtung des Mittelalters und der Neuzeit. Wolfgang Golther. LC 74-178535. Repr. of 1925 ed. 32.50 (ISBN 0-404-56611-1). AMS Pr.

Pa's Balloon & Other Pig Tales. Arthur Geisert. LC 83-18552. (Illus.). 96p. (gr. k-3). 1984. 12.95 (ISBN 0-395-35381-5, 5-86480). HM.

Pas dans le Sable. Vercors. 288p. 1954. 3.95 (ISBN 0-686-55129-X). French & Eur.

Pas de Deux: The Art of Partnering. Anton Dolin. LC 68-17403. (Illus.). 1969. pap. 2.95 (ISBN 0-486-22038-9). Dover.

Pas de Gene: Omer Marcoux Violoneux et Sculpteur. Julien Olivier. (Oral History Ser.). (Illus.). 94p. (Fr.). (gr. 9-10). 1981. pap. 2.50x (ISBN 0-911409-06-8). Natl Mat Dev.

Pas de Trois, Fun with Ballet Words. Katherine D. Goodale. (Illus.). (Orig.). 25p. (gr. k-7). 1982. pap. 5.95 (ISBN 0-9609662-0-X). Goodale Pub.

Pas de Vacanes pour le Commissaire. Evelyn Apter. LC 82-9670. (Illus.). 40p. (Fr.). (gr. 7-12). 1982. pap. text ed. 2.25 (ISBN 0-88436-908-0, 40285); cassette 12.00 (40101). EMC.

Pas Perdus: Essai. Andre Breton. (Coll. Soleil). O.P. 11.50 (ISBN 0-685-37234-0); pap. 8.95 (ISBN 0-686-66855-3). French & Eur.

Pas Question D'Amour. Anne Hampson. (Harlequin Romantique Ser.). 192p. 1984. pap. 1.95 (ISBN 0-373-41238-X). Harlequin Bks.

Pasadena. (Shorey Historical Ser.). 22p. pap. 2.95 (ISBN 0-8466-0172-9, S172). Shorey.

Pasadena: Crown of the Valley. Ann Scheid. LC 86-4023. (Illus.). 288p. 1986. 24.95 (ISBN 0-89781-163-1). Windsor Pubns Inc.

Pasadena One Hundred Years. Ed. by Maureen R. Michelson & Michael R. Dressler. 146p. 1985. 100.00 (ISBN 0-939165-02-3). NewSage Press.

Pasadena: Resort Hotels & Paradise. Thomas D. Carpenter. (Illus.). 1984. 24.95 (ISBN 0-317-12073-5). M Sheldon Pub.

Pasaderitas Hacia el Ingles Correcto. Ida Bellegarde. Tr. by Peter Lopez. LC 77-73283. 1977. 4.45x (ISBN 0-918340-05-5). Bell Ent.

Pasadoble. Julia Fitzgerald. (Astromance Ser.: No. 1). 176p. (Orig.). 1988. pap. 2.95 (ISBN 1-55785-029-1). Bart Books.

Pasajes. 2nd ed. Mary L. Bretz et al. 1987. Grammar, 352p. text ed. write for info. (ISBN 0-394-35321-8, RanC); Cultural Reader, 256p. pap. text ed. write for info (ISBN 0-394-35322-6); Literary Reader, 256p. pap. text ed. write for info (ISBN 0-394-35323-4); write for info. lab manual (ISBN 0-394-35325-0); write for info. activities manual (ISBN 0-394-35324-2). Random.

Pasajes: Gramatica. Mary L. Bretz & Patrisha Dvorak. 1982. write for info (ISBN 0-394-32875-2, RanC); write for infos manual, 192 pp. (ISBN 0-394-32876-0); write for info (ISBN 0-394-32877-9); 9.00 (ISBN 0-394-32878-7); write for info (ISBN 0-394-33114-1); write for info (ISBN 0-394-33113-3). Random.

Pasame Otro Ladrillo. Charles R. Swindoll. 208p. 1980. 3.75 (ISBN 0-88113-315-9). Edit Betania.

Pasaporte: First Year Spanish. 2nd ed. Barbara Mujica et al. 450p. 1984. write for info. (ISBN 0-471-88348-4, FL10); pap. wkbk. avail. (ISBN 0-471-88265-8); tchr's. manual avail. (ISBN 0-471-80161-5); cassettes avail. (ISBN 0-471-80094-5). Wiley.

Pasaquina. Erin O'Shaughnessy. LC 86-6703. 232p. 1986. 16.95 (ISBN 0-933071-05-1, Dist. by W. W. Norton). Saybrook Pub Co.

Pasaquina: A Novel of El Salvador. Erin O'Shaughnessy. 232p. 1988. pap. 6.95 (ISBN 0-933071-20-5). Saybrook Pub Co.

Pasargadae: A Report on the Excavations Conducted by the British Institute of Persian Studies from 1961 to 1963. David Stronach. (Illus.). 1978. 89.00x (ISBN 0-19-813190-9). Oxford U Pr.

Pascal. G. Belford & Chung L. Liu. (Illus.). 384p. 1984. pap. text ed. 27.95 (ISBN 0-07-038138-0). McGraw.

Pascal. Dolores Etter. 600p. 1988. text ed. 25.95 (ISBN 0-8053-2533-6); instr's guide avail. (ISBN 0-8053-2534-4); tutorial disk (ISBN 0-8053-2536-0); quickbank to adopters avail. (ISBN 0-8053-2537-9). Benjamin-Cummings.

Pascal. Charles H. Goldberg et al. (Programming Language Ser.). (Illus.). 1984. pap. text ed. 23.75 (ISBN 0-87835-139-6); instr's. manual 8.00 (ISBN 0-87835-142-6). Boyd & Fraser.

Pascal. Alban Krailsheimer. (Past Masters Ser.). 1980. pap. 4.95 (ISBN 0-19-287512-4). Oxford U Pr.

Pascal. Stuart Reges. 1986. pap. text ed. write for info. (ISBN 0-673-39243-0); tchr's. manual avail. Scott F.

Pascal. James L. Richards. 1986. text ed. 18.00 (ISBN 0-12-587522-3). Acad Pr.

Pascal. Viscount St. Cyres. 1909. Repr. 25.00 (ISBN 0-8274-3103-1). R West.

Pascal. Tullock. 1898. Repr. 20.00 (ISBN 0-8274-3104-X). R West.

Pascal - SC: A Computer Language for Scientific Computation. Ed. by Gerd Bohlender & Christian Ullrich. (Perspectives in Computing Ser.). 292p. 1987. 34.00 (ISBN 0-12-111155-5). Acad Pr.

Pascal: A Considerate Approach. 2nd ed. David Price. 1984. pap. 13.95 (ISBN 0-13-652884-8). P-H.

Pascal: A Problem Solving Approach. E. B. Koffman. 1982. pap. text ed. write for info. (ISBN 0-201-10341-9). Addison-Wesley.

Pascal: Adversary & Advocate. Robert J. Nelson. LC 81-6330. 296p. 1982. text ed. 27.00x (ISBN 0-674-65615-6). Harvard U Pr.

Pascal: An Introduction to Methodical Programming. 3rd ed. William Findlay & David Watt. LC 84-25522. (Computer Software Engineering Ser.). 413p. 1985. pap. 27.95 (ISBN 0-88175-179-0, Computer Sci Pr). W H Freeman.

Pascal: An Introduction to Modern Programming. Larry J. Goldstein. 608p. 1987. pap. text ed. write for info. (ISBN 0-03-009928-5). HR&W.

Pascal: An Introduction to the Art & Science of Programming. 2nd, rev. ed. Walt Savitch. 1987. pap. 31.25 (ISBN 0-8053-8388-3); instr's guide 8.95 (ISBN 0-8053-8389-1); program listing 2-disk pkg. 15.95 (ISBN 0-318-22503-4); tutorial disk pkg. free (ISBN 0-8053-8397-2); free magnetic tape to adapters (ISBN 0-8053-8399-9). Benjamin Cummings.

Pascal & Algorithms: An Introduction to Problem Solving. Gregory F. Wetzel & William G. Bulgren. Ed. by Pamela S. Cooper & Molly Gardiner. (Computer Science Ser.). (Illus.). 512p. 1987. pap. text ed. write for info. (ISBN 0-574-18630-1, 13-1630). SRA.

Pascal & Nietzche: Etude Historique & Comparee. James R. Dionne. LC 74-3300. (Fr.). 1976. lib. bdg. 18.00 (ISBN 0-89102-032-2). B Franklin.

Pascal & Theology. Jan Miel. LC 75-93822. pap. 61.40 (2030746). Bks Demand UMI.

PASCAL Applications for the Sciences. Richard E. Crandall. LC 82-24832. (Self-Teaching Guides). 224p. 1984. pap. text ed. 16.95 (ISBN 0-471-87242-3, 1-581). Wiley.

Pascal As a Second Language. Martin V. Lines. (Illus.). 224p. 1984. pap. text ed. write for info. (ISBN 0-13-652925-9). P-H.

Pascal at Work & Play. Richard S. Forsyth. 250p. 1982. 35.00 (ISBN 0-412-23370-3, NO. 6638, Pub. by Chapman & Hall); pap. 15.95 (ISBN 0-412-23380-0, NO. 6639). Routledge Chapman & Hall.

PASCAL Compiler Validation. Ed. by Brian A. Wichmann & Z. J. Ciechanowicz. LC 82-23882. 176p. 1983. 52.50 (ISBN 0-471-90133-4). Wiley.

Pascal Database Book. Julian Ullmann. (COAMCSS Ser.). 1986. 45.00x (ISBN 0-19-859643-X); pap. 22.50x (ISBN 0-19-859642-1). Oxford U Pr.

Pascal et Descartes see Etudes Historiques et Critiques sur la Philosophie de Pascal.

Pascal et la Casuistique see Etudes Historiques et Critiques sur la Philosophie de Pascal.

Pascal: Exploring Problem Solving & Program Design. Dennis Corliss & Kathy Seagraves-Higdon. 564p. 1988. pap. text ed. 31.50 (ISBN 0-314-59360-8). West Pub.

Pascal: Exploring Problem Solving & Program Design (HC) Dennis Corliss & Kathy Seagraves-Higdon. 564p. 1988. pap. text ed. 31.50 (ISBN 0-314-59361-6). West Pub.

Pascal for BASIC Programmers. Charles Seiter & Robert Weiss. (Microbooks Popular Ser.). 224p. 1983. pap. 12.95 (ISBN 0-201-06577-0). Addison-Wesley.

Pascal for Beginners. Christopher Lampton. (Computer Literacy Skills Ser.). (Illus.). 96p. (gr. 7 up). 1984. lib. bdg. 11.90 (ISBN 0-531-04748-2). Watts.

Pascal for Beginners. Peter Lottrup. 1986. 14.95 (ISBN 0-87455-068-8); 12.95 (688BDSK); bk-disk combination for the Commodore 64 29.95 (ISBN 0-87455-069-6). Compute Pubns.

Pascal for Electrical Engineers. Attikioyzel. 1984. pap. 20.95 (ISBN 0-442-30597-4). Van Nos Reinhold.

Pascal for Electronic Engineers. 2nd ed. J. Attikiouzel. 160p. 1988. pap. text ed. 24.95 (ISBN 0-278-00072-X). Van Nos Reinhold.

Pascal for Electronics. Edward J. Pasahow. 208p. 1985. text ed. 16.95 (ISBN 0-07-048724-3). McGraw.

Pascal for Electronics & Communications. Richard Meadows & Meadows Pitman. 160p. 1986. pap. 12.95 (ISBN 0-672-22514-X). Sams.

Pascal for FORTRAN Programmers. Ronald M. Perrott & Donald H. Allison. LC 82-7253. (Computer Software Engineering Ser.). 347p. 1984. 26.95 (ISBN 0-914894-09-9, Computer Sci Pr). W H Freeman.

Pascal for Programmers. Susan Eisenbach & Christopher Sadler. (Illus.). 201p. 1981. pap. 17.50 (ISBN 0-387-10473-9). Springer-Verlag.

Pascal for Programmers. Olivier Lecarme & Jean-Louis Nebut. LC 83-16205. (Illus.). 272p. 1984. text ed. 29.95 (ISBN 0-07-036958-5). McGraw.

Pascal for Technicians. Earl Gulledge. LC 85-29192. 261p. 1986. pap. text ed. 24.95 (ISBN 0-8273-2620-3); instr's. guide 8.00 (ISBN 0-8273-2621-1). Delmar.

Pascal for the Apple. Iain MacCallum. 1983. 36.00 (ISBN 0-13-652909-7); disk incl. P-H.

Pascal for the Eighties. Sam Grier. LC 84-28518. (Computer Science Ser.). 448p. 1985. pap. text ed. 21.00 pub net (ISBN 0-534-04674-6). Brooks-Cole.

Pascal for the Humanities. Nancy M. Ide. 320p. (Orig.). 1987. pap. text ed. 26.95x (ISBN 0-8122-1242-8). U of Pa Pr.

Pascal for the IBM Personal Computer. Ted G. Lewis. LC 82-22750. 288p. 1983. pap. write for info. (ISBN 0-201-05464-7). Addison-Wesley.

Pascal for the Macintosh. Henry Ledgard & Andrew Singer. LC 84-24503. 456p. 1985. pap. text ed. 26.95 (ISBN 0-201-11772-X); solutions manual avail. (ISBN 0-201-11773-8). Addison-Wesley.

Pascal from Begin to End. Thomas C. Wilson & Joseph Shortt. LC 86-26597. 1987. pap. write for info. (ISBN 0-201-08344-2). Addison-Wesley.

Pascal Handbook. Jacques Tiberghien. LC 80-53283. (Illus.). 485p. 1981. pap. 19.95 (ISBN 0-89588-053-9, P320). SYBEX.

Pascal Implementation: The P4 Compiler, 2 Vols. Steven Pemberton & Martin Daniels. LC 81-20184. 172p. 1983. pap. 46.95x (ISBN 0-470-27386-0). Halsted Pr.

Pascal in Practice: Using the Language. L. G. Moseley et al. (Computers & Their Applications Ser.). 274p. 1987. pap. 29.95 (ISBN 0-470-20779-5). Wiley.

Pascal: Introduction to Programming & Problem Solving. Douglas W. Nance. (Illus.). 630p. (YA) (gr. 9-12). 1986. text ed. 33.00 (ISBN 0-314-93206-2). West Pub.

Pascal: Introduction to Structured Programming Using Turbo Pascal. Kenneth Morgan. 672p. 1989. pap. 24.95 (ISBN 0-675-20770-3); supplements avail. Merrill.

Pascal, les Libertins et les Jansenites see Etudes Historiques et Critiques sur la Philosophie de Pascal.

Pascal on the Macintosh. David Niguidula & Andries Van Dam. LC 86-20668. 1987. pap. 29.25 (ISBN 0-201-16588-0). Addison-Wesley.

PASCAL: Pensees. John Cruickshank. (Critical Guides to French Texts Ser.: No. 23). 79p. 1983. pap. 3.95 (ISBN 0-7293-0154-0, Pub. by Grant & Cutler). Longwood Pub Group.

Pascal Precisely. Judy Bishop. 256p. 1987. pap. text ed. 19.95x (ISBN 0-201-17525-8). Addison-Wesley.

Pascal Primer. David Fox & Mitchell Waite. LC 80-53275. 208p. 1981. pap. 17.95 (ISBN 0-672-21793-7, 21793). Sams.

Pascal Primer for the IBM PC. Michael Pardee. (Plume-Waite Computer Ser.). (Illus.). 1984. pap. 17.95 (ISBN 0-452-25496-5, Plume). NAL.

Pascal Primer for the Macintosh. Dan Shafer. 1985. pap. 19.95 (ISBN 0-452-25640-2, Plume). NAL.

Pascal: Problem Solving & Program Design. 3rd ed. Elliot B. Koffman. (Illus.). 768p. 1988. pap. text ed. price not set (ISBN 0-201-11834-3). Addison-Wesley.

PASCAL: Problem Solving & Programming with Style. William C. Jones. 1986. write for info. (ISBN 0-471-60335-X). Wiley.

Pascal: Problem Solving & Structured Program Design. Henry M. Walker. 1987. pap. text ed. write for info. (ISBN 0-673-39075-6). Scott F.

Pascal: Program Development with Ten Instruction Pascal Subset (Tips) & Standard Pascal. Michael Kennedy & Martin B. Soloman. (Illus.). 512p. 1982. text ed. write for info. (ISBN 0-13-652735-3). P-H.

Pascal Programming. Laurence Atkinson. LC 80-40126. (Computing Ser.). 428p. 1980. pap. 26.95 (ISBN 0-471-27774-6). Wiley.

Pascal Programming. Irvine H. Forkner. LC 84-17467. (Computer Science Ser.). 300p. 1985. pap. text ed. 16.00 pub net (ISBN 0-534-04215-5). Brooks-Cole.

Pascal Programming. Seymour C. Hirsch. (Illus.). 320p. 1987. pap. text ed. 26.00 (ISBN 0-8359-5438-2). P-H.

Pascal Programming. Lamie. 419p. 1987. pap. write for info. (ISBN 0-471-82308-2). Wiley.

Pascal Programming: A Beginner's Guide to Computers & Programming. Chris Hawksley. LC 82-19760. 200p. 1983. 32.50 (ISBN 0-521-25302-0); pap. 12.95 o. p. (ISBN 0-521-27292-0). Cambridge U Pr.

Pascal Programming: A Beginner's Guide to Computers & Programming. 2nd ed. Chris Hawksley. 208p. 1986. 37.50 (ISBN 0-521-33066-1); pap. 9.95 (ISBN 0-521-33714-3). Cambridge U Pr.

Pascal Programming: A Spiral Approach. Walter S. Brainerd et al. LC 82-70213. 597p. (Orig.). 1982. pap. text ed. 25.00x (ISBN 0-87835-122-1); solutions manual avail. Boyd & Fraser.

Pascal: Programming & Problem Solving. Sanford Leestma & Larry Nyhoff. 669p. 1987. pap. write for info. (ISBN 0-02-369690-7). Macmillan.

Pascal Programming for Engineers Using VPS. Susan Finger. 368p. 1983. pap. 12.95 (ISBN 0-8403-3026-X). Kendall-Hunt.

Pascal Programming for Libraries: Illustrative Examples for Information Specialists. Charles H. Davis & Gerald W. Lundeen. LC 87-32292. (Contributions in Librianship & Information Science Ser.: No. 60). 1988. write for info. (ISBN 0-313-22979-1, DPC/). Greenwood.

Pascal Programming for Libraries: Illustrative Examples for Information Specialists. Charles H. Davis et al. LC 87-32292. (Contributions in Librarianship & Information Science: No. 60). 128p. 1988. lib. bdg. 25.00 (ISBN 0-313-25259-9, DPC/). Greenwood.

Pascal: Programming for People. David Kay. 1985. 31.95 (ISBN 0-87484-717-6). Mayfield Pub.

Pascal Programming for the IBM PC & PC XT. William M. Fuori. 1984. cancelled (ISBN 0-317-06174-7, Reston). P-H.

Pascal Programming for the IBM PC: IBM DOS, Pascal & UCSD P-System Pascal. Kevin W. Bowyer & Sherryl Tomboulian. LC 83-3921. (Illus.). 352p. 1983. pap. 19.95 (ISBN 0-89303-280-8); bk. & diskette 49.95 (ISBN 0-89303-761-3); disk 30.00 (ISBN 0-89303-762-1). P-H.

Pascal Programming Structures for Motorola Microprocessors. George W. Cherry. 1981. (Reston); pap. text ed. 28.00 (ISBN 0-8359-5471-4). P-H.

Pascal Programming Structures for Motorola Microprocessors. George W. Cherry. (Motorola Series in Solid State Electronics). 384p. 1987. pap. text ed. write for info. (ISBN 0-13-652850-3). P-H.

Pascal Programming Today. Steven L. Mandell. LC 86-24610. (Illus.). 550p. (Orig.). 1986. pap. text ed. 35.50 (ISBN 0-314-33935-3); instr's. manual avail. (ISBN 0-314-97186-6). West Pub.

Pascal Programming Visual Masters. Donald D. Spencer. 112p. 1988. pap. 14.95 (ISBN 0-89218-097-8, NO. 3042). Camelot Pub.

Pascal: Programming with Style, A Brief Introduction. Richard Lamb. 208p. 1987. pap. 12.95 (ISBN 0-8053-5835-8). Benjamin-Cummings.

Pascal Programs for Scientists & Engineers. Alan R. Miller. LC 81-51128. (Scientists & Engineers Ser.: No. 1). (Illus.). 374p. 1981. pap. 17.95 (ISBN 0-89588-058-X, P340). SYBEX.

Pascal, Roy, Nineteen Hundred Four to Nineteen Eighty. A. V. Subiotto. (Memoirs of the Fellows of the British Academy Ser.). (Illus.). 16p. 1983. pap. 2.25 (ISBN 0-85672-375-4, Pub. by British Acad). Longwood Pub Group.

PASCAL-SC: A PASCAL Extenstion for Scientific Computation. Ed. by U. Kulisch et al. 1987. 224.40 (ISBN 0-471-91514-9). Wiley.

Pascal Simplified: A Guide for the First-Time User. Susan H. Gray. LC 85-14197. 144p. 1986. text ed. 22.50x (ISBN 0-8476-7428-2); pap. 9.95 (ISBN 0-8226-0394-2, Rowman & Allanheld). Rowman.

Pascal: Step-by-Step Programming. Paul M. Chirlian. 224p. 1980. pap. 15.95 (ISBN 0-916460-28-2, Matrix Pubs Inc). Weber Systems.

Pascal: Structure & Style. Richard Lamb. (Illus.). 500p. 1986. text ed. 29.95x (ISBN 0-8053-5830-7); instr's guide 6.95 (ISBN 0-8053-5831-5). Benjamin-Cummings.

Pascal Supplement for Computers & Data Processing Today. Steven L. Mandell. 150p. 1983. write for info (ISBN 0-314-77494-7). West Pub.

Pascal: Text & Reference. 2nd ed. John B. Moore. 1984. pap. text ed. 28.00 (ISBN 0-8359-5440-4, Reston). P-H.

Pascal: The Language & Its Implementation. Ed. by D. W. Barron. (Computing Ser.). 301p. 1981. 59.95x (ISBN 0-471-27835-1). Wiley.

Pascal under UNIX. J. N. Hume & R. C. Holt. 1983. (Reston); pap. text ed. 26.00 (ISBN 0-8359-5445-5). P-H.

Pascal under VPS. Finger-Correia. 176p. 1985. pap. text ed. 10.95 (ISBN 0-8403-3772-8). Kendall-Hunt.

Pascal: Understanding Programming & Problem Solving. Douglas W. Nance. (Illus.). 626p. (Orig.). 1986. pap. text ed. 33.75 (ISBN 0-314-93205-4). West Pub.

Pascal User Manual & Report. 3rd. ed. K. Jensen & N. Wirth. (Springer Study Edition). (Illus.). xvi, 266p. 1985. pap. 17.50 (ISBN 0-387-96048-1). Springer-Verlag.

Pascal with Program Design. James F. Peters. 600p. 1986. pap. text ed. 25.95 (ISBN 0-03-003282-2, HoltC). HR&W.

Pascal Wizard: A Wiley Programmer's Reference. Richard Wiener. 1987. pap. 19.95 comb binding (ISBN 0-471-85241-4). Wiley.

PASCAL 286 User's Guide for DOS. Intel Corp. 330p. 1985. pap. 22.00 (ISBN 0-917017-82-X, 122476). Intel Corp.

Pascal-86 User's Guide. rev. ed. Intel Staff. 396p. (Orig.). 1983. pap. 35.00 (ISBN 0-917017-27-7, 121539). Intel Corp.

PASCAL 86 User's Guide for DOS Systems. Intel Staff. 382p. 1985. pap. 25.00 (ISBN 0-917017-71-4, 122426). Intel Corp.

Pascalgorithms. Edwin D. Reilly & Francis D. Federighi. LC 87-80569. 700p. 1987. text ed. write for info.; IM avail. HM.

Pascalgorithms: An Introduction to Programming. Edward M. Reingold & Ruth N. Reingold. (Orig.). 1988. pap. text ed. write for info. (ISBN 0-673-39745-9). Scott F.

Pascali's Island. Barry Unsworth. 192p. 1988. pap. 5.95 (ISBN 0-14-011537-4). Penguin.

Pascalorithms. Edwin D. Reilly & Francis D. Frederighi. LC 87-80569. 1989. price not set (ISBN 0-395-35739-X). HM.

Pascal's Anguish & Joy. Charles S. MacKenzie. LC 73-77404. 272p. 1973. 12.95 (ISBN 0-8022-2117-3). Philos Lib.

Pascal's Arithmetical Triangle. A. W. Edwards. (Charles Griffin Bk.). (Illus.). 186p. 1987. 37.50 (ISBN 0-19-520546-4). Oxford U Pr.

Pascal's Philosophy of Religion. C. J. Webb. Repr. of 1929 ed. 12.00 (ISBN 0-527-94918-3). Kraus Repr.

Pascal's Triangle. V. A. Uspenskii. Tr. by Timothy McLarnan & David J. Sookne. LC 73-90941. (Popular Lectures in Mathematics Ser). 42p. 1975. pap. text ed. 3.50x (ISBN 0-226-84316-5). U of Chicago Pr.

Pascal's Unfinished Apology. Marie L. Hubert. LC 70-153272. 165p. 1973. Repr. of 1952 ed. 21.50 (ISBN 0-8046-1699-X, Pub. by Kennikat). Assoc Faculty Pr.

Pascal's Wager: A Study of Practical Reasoning in Philosophical Theology. Nicholas Rescher. LC 84-40820. 176p. 1985. text ed. 19.95 (ISBN 0-268-01556-2). U of Notre Dame Pr.

Pascha: The Resurrection of Christ. David Drillock et al. (Music Ser.). 274p. 1980. pap. 15.00 (ISBN 0-913836-50-8); 20.00 (ISBN 0-913836-65-6). St Vladimirs.

Paschal Cycle. Paul Bosch. 1979. pap. 6.75 (ISBN 0-570-03796-4, 12-2778). Concordia.

Paschal Mystery: Core Grace in the Life of the Christian. Augustine Hennessey. (Synthesis Ser.). 37p. 1977. pap. 0.75 (ISBN 0-8199-0707-3). Franciscan Herald.

Paschal Mystery in Christian Living. James Alberione. Tr. by Daughters Of St. Paul. LC 68-28102. (St. Paul Editions). (Illus.). 1968. 3.95 (ISBN 0-8198-0114-3); pap. 2.95 (ISBN 0-8198-0115-1). Dghtrs St Paul.

Paschal or Lent Fast. Peter Gunning. LC 70-168214. (Library of Anglo-Catholic Theology: No. 7). Repr. of 1845 ed. 27.50 (ISBN 0-404-52088-X). AMS Pr.

Paschal's Principles of Weight Training. John Paschal & John Dorman. (Illus.). 1979. pap. 2.95 (ISBN 0-89826-003-5). Natl Paperback.

Pascin. Gaston Diehl. (Q L P Art Ser.). (Illus.). 1968. 14.95 (ISBN 0-517-09890-3). Crown.

Pascin Catalogue Raisonne, Vol. I. Gaston Diehl & Tom Freudenheim. Compiled by Yves Hemin et al. Tr. by A. Chapman. (Illus.). 407p. (Eng. & Fr.). 1987. 125.00 (ISBN 0-8390-0382-X, Pub. by Editions Abel Rambert). Abner Schram Ltd.

Pascin: One Hundred Ten Drawings. Jules Pascin. Ed. by Alfred Werner. LC 71-154346. 1972. pap. 5.95 (ISBN 0-486-20299-2). Dover.

Pasco-Kennewick Intercity Bridge & Geometry Control for the Intercity Bridge. Prestressed Concrete Institute Staff. (PCI Journal Reprints Ser.). 36p. pap. 7.00 (ISBN 0-318-19859-2, JR205). Prestressed Concrete.

Pascua: A Yaqui Village in Arizona. Edward H. Spicer. LC 83-18312. (Illus.). 325p. 1984. pap. 9.95 (ISBN 0-8165-0845-3). U of Ariz Pr.

Pasdale Welfare. Bella Jan. 160p. 1981. 8.95 (ISBN 0-89962-207-0). Todd & Honeywell.

Pashto Newspaper Reader. MRM Staff. iv, 246p. 1984. text ed. 22.00 (ISBN 0-931745-04-7). Dunwoody Pr.

Pashukanis: Selected Writings on Marxism & Law. Ed. by Piers Beirne & Robert Sharlet. LC 79-40895. (Law, State & Society Ser.). 1980. 76.00 (ISBN 0-12-086350-2). Acad Pr.

Pasiegos: Spaniards in No Man's Land. Susan T. Freeman. LC 78-13928. (Illus.). 1979. lib. bdg. 26.00x (ISBN 0-226-26173-5). U of Chicago Pr.

Pasion del Absurdo Ensayos. Francisco J. Satue et al. LC 86-81696. (Essay Ser.). 72p. (Orig., Span.). Date not set. pap. 7.95 (ISBN 0-932367-04-6). Ed El Gato Tuerto.

Pasion por las Almas. Oswald J. Smith. Orig. Title: Passion for Souls. 208p. (Span.). 1985. pap. 4.25 (ISBN 0-8254-1672-8). Kregel.

Paslanije Svatago Ignatija Aniokhiskago I Sviatago Polykarpa Smirnskago. Repr. 2.00 (ISBN 0-317-28881-4). Holy Trinity.

Paso a Paso! Un Enfoque Communicativo, Estructual & Cultural, Workbook. Thomas A. Lathrop. 240p. 1987. pap. write for info. (ISBN 0-471-81805-4). Wiley.

Paso Adelante, Dos Pasos Atras. V. I. Lenin. 264p. (Span.). 1978. pap. 1.45 (ISBN 0-8285-1410-0, Pub. by Progress Pubs USSR). Imported Pubns.

Paso del Norte. Roe Richmond. 224p. 1982. pap. 1.95 (ISBN 0-441-20366-3). Ace Bks.

Paso Doble. Earl Atkinson. (Ballroom Dancing Ser.). 1983. lib. bdg. 79.95 (ISBN 0-87700-489-7). Revisionist Pr.

Paso Doble. Earl Atkinson. (Ballroom Dance Ser.). 1986. lib. bdg. 79.95 (ISBN 0-8490-3629-1). Gordon Pr.

Paso Doble. (Ballroom Dance Ser.). 1985. lib. bdg. 70.00 (ISBN 0-87700-784-5). Revisionist Pr.

Paso Doble. (Ballroom Dance Ser.). 1986. lib. bdg. 69.95 (ISBN 0-8490-3292-X). Gordon Pr.

Paso Doble Picador. (Ballroom Dance Ser.). 1985. lib. bdg. 51.00 (ISBN 0-87700-806-X). Revisionist Pr.

Paso Doble Picador. (Ballroom Dance Ser.). 1986. lib. bdg. 79.95 (ISBN 0-8490-3397-7). Gordon Pr.

Paso Por Aqui. Eugene M. Rhodes. LC 72-9273. (Western Frontier Library: No. 50). (Illus.). 118p. 1982. pap. 5.95 (ISBN 0-8061-1381-2). U of Okla Pr.

Pasoj Al Plena Posedo. 4th ed. Ed. by William Auld. (Esperanto.). 1974. pap. text ed. 9.80x (ISBN 8-4499-4305-1, 1052). Esperanto League North Am.

Pasolini: Selected Poems. Pier P. Pasolini. Tr. by Norman MacAfee & Luciano Martinengo. 224p. (Orig.). 1988. pap. 12.95 (ISBN 0-7145-3889-2). Riverrun NY.

Pasos Hacia la Paz Interior: Sugestiones para el Uso de Principios Armonicos para la Vida Humana. Peace Pilgrim. Tr. by Clandio Zanelli from Eng. (Peace Pilgrim Ser.). (Illus.). 64p. (Orig., Span.). 1987. pap. 3.50 (ISBN 0-943734-09-6). Ocean Tree Bks.

Pasquale Paoli: An Enlightened Hero, 1725-1807. Peter A. Thrasher. LC 70-107866. (Illus.). 352p. 1970. 35.00 (ISBN 0-208-01031-9, Archon). Shoe String.

Pasquils Mad-Cap & Mad-Cappes Message. Nicholas Breton. LC 79-25850. (English Experience Ser.: No. 200). 88p. 1969. Repr. of 1600 ed. 25.00 (ISBN 90-221-0200-9). Walter J Johnson.

Pasro: Pascal & C for Robots. 2nd ed. C. Blume et al. (Illus.). 240p. 1987. pap. 35.00 (ISBN 0-387-18093-1). Springer-Verlag.

Pass after Class. rev. ed. Fred Much. LC 86-90709. 104p. (Orig.). 1987. pap. write for info (ISBN 0-9618053-0-7). Fred Much.

Pass Controls: And the Urban African Proletariat. Doug Hindson. 121p. 1988. pap. text ed. 15.95x (ISBN 0-86975-311-8, Pub. by Ravan Pr). Ohio U Pr.

Pass It on. Robert H. Mounce. LC 78-68851. (Bible Commentary for Layman Ser.). 160p. 1979. pap. 3.95 (ISBN 0-8307-0667-4, S332108). Regal.

Pass It on: The Story of Bill Wilson & How the A. A. Message Reached the World. Alcoholics Anonymous World Services, Inc. Staff. 432p. 1984. 4.25 (ISBN 0-916856-12-7). AAWS.

Pass Me a Pine Cone. Phyllis A. Wood. LC 82-1870. (Hiway Book: A High Interest - Low Reading Level Book). 160p. (gr. 7-9). 1982. 11.95 (ISBN 0-664-32692-7). Westminster John Knox.

Pass of the North, Vol. II. C. L. Sonnichsen. LC 68-30889. 1980. 15.00 (ISBN 0-87404-066-3). Tex Western.

Pass of the North: Four Centuries on the Rio Grande, Vol. I. 4th ed. C. L. Sonnichsen. LC 68-30889. 480p. 1980. 20.00 (ISBN 0-87404-013-2). Tex Western.

Pass, Set, Crush: Volleyball Illustrated. Jeff Lucas. LC 85-13198. (Illus.). 176p. (Orig.). 1985. 24.95 (ISBN 0-9615088-0-9); pap. 19.95 (ISBN 0-9615088-1-7). Euclid Nw Pubns.

Pass, Set, Crush: Volleyball Illustrated. 2nd ed. Jeff Lucas. 167p. 1988. 19.95 (ISBN 0-317-66788-2); pap. 12.95 (ISBN 0-317-66789-0). Euclid NW Pubns.

Pass the Butler. Eric Idle. 81p. 1984. pap. 6.95 (ISBN 0-413-49990-1, NO. 9088). Heinemann Ed.

Pass the CBEST. 2nd ed. Elna M. Dimock. LC 84-13794. (Illus.). 156p. (Orig.). 1984. pap. 14.50 (ISBN 0-914763-01-6). Educ Development.

Pass the CBEST. 3rd ed. Elna M. Dimock. LC 88-16287. (Illus.). 256p. (Orig.). 1988. pap. 14.50 (ISBN 0-914763-02-4). Educ Development.

Pass the Deck. Lois Stanciak. (Writing Program Ser.). 142p. (Orig.). (gr. 9-12). 1983. text ed. 9.10 (ISBN 0-933282-14-1); pap. 6.00 (ISBN 0-933282-08-7). Stack the Deck.

Pass the Peas, Please: A Book of Manners. Dina Anastasio. LC 87-18882. (Illus.). (ps-2). 1988. 4.95 (ISBN 1-55782-021-X). Warner Bks.

Pass the Pepper Please! Healthy Meal Planning for People on Sodium Restricted Diets. Diane Reader. 1987. pap. 3.95 (ISBN 0-937721-17-4). Diabetes Ctr MN.

Pass the Plate. Pass the Plate, Inc. Staff. Ed. by Alice Underhill & Bobbie Stewart. 520p. 1981. pap. 13.95 (ISBN 0-939114-13-5). Pass the Plate.

Pass the Poetry, Please! 2nd ed. Lee B. Hopkins. LC 86-45758. 288p. 1987. 18.95i (ISBN 0-06-022602-1). HarpJ.

Pass the Poetry, Please! 2nd ed. Lee B. Hopkins. LC 86-45758. (Trophy Nonfiction Bk.). 288p. 1987. pap. 9.95 (ISBN 0-06-446062-2, Trophy). HarpJ.

Pass the Poverty Please. Patty Newman & Joyce Wenger. 1966. pap. 0.75 (ISBN 0-911956-03-4). Constructive Action.

Pass-Through Yield & Value Table for FHLMC Mortgage Participation Certificates. 5th ed. Financial Publishing Co. Staff. 284p. 1984. pap. 42.00 (ISBN 0-87600-615-2). Finan Pub.

Pass-Through Yield & Value Tables for FNMA Mortgage-Backed Securities. Financial Publishing Co. Staff. 576p. 1982. pap. 29.95 (ISBN 0-87600-657-8). Finan Pub.

Pass-Through Yield & Value Tables for GNMA Mortgage-Backed Securities. 12th ed. Financial Publishing Co. Staff. 348p. 1985. pap. 42.00 (ISBN 0-87600-715-9). Finan Pub.

Pass with Care. Cleta M. Long & Kate Long. LC 87-91319. (Illus.). 88p. (Orig.). 1987. 9.95 (ISBN 0-9619468-0-6); pap. 6.95 (ISBN 0-9619468-1-4). C M Long.

Pass Your Wastewater Operator Exams. Dan Cortinovis. LC 85-60331. 60p. (Orig.). 1985. study manual 9.95x (ISBN 0-918967-01-5). Ridgeline Pr.

Passacaglia. Robert Pinget. Tr. by Barbara Wright from Fr. LC 78-53832. (New French Writing Ser.). 1979. 6.95 (ISBN 0-87376-033-6). Red Dust.

Passacaglio & Ciaccona: From Guitar Music to Italian Keyboard Variations in the 17th Century. Richard A. Hudson. LC 81-25. (Studies in Musicology: No. 37). pap. 85.60 (ISBN 0-8357-1161-7, 2070286). Bks Demand UMI.

Passacaille. Robert Pinget. 136p. 1969. 9.95 (ISBN 0-686-54878-7). French & Eur.

Passage. W. R. Moses. LC 75-33361. (Wesleyan Poetry Program: Vol. 81). 1976. text ed. 17.00x (ISBN 0-8195-2081-0); pap. 8.95 (ISBN 0-8195-1081-5). Wesleyan U Pr.

Passage. Victor Wartofsky. (Orig.). 1980. pap. 1.95 (ISBN 0-505-51506-7, Pub. by Tower Bks). Leisure NY.

Passage: A Tragedy of the First World War. Gustav Ebelshauser. Ed. by Richard Baumgartner. (Illus.). 192p. 1984. pap. 10.95 (ISBN 0-9604770-2-0). Griffin Bks.

Passage & Possibility: A Study of Aristotle's Modal Concepts. Sarah Waterlow. 1982. 45.00x (ISBN 0-19-824656-0). Oxford U Pr.

Passage at Arms. Glen Cook. 272p. (Orig.). 1985. pap. 2.95 (ISBN 0-445-20006-5, Pub. by Popular Lib). Warner Bks.

Passage Between Rivers: A Portfolio of Photographs with a History of the Delaware & Raritan Canal. Elizabeth G. Menzies. (Illus.). 1976. pap. 9.95 (ISBN 0-8135-0832-0). Rutgers U Pr.

Passage by Night. Jack Higgins. 208p. 1987. pap. 3.50 (ISBN 0-451-15039-2, Sig). NAL.

Passage de Milan. Michel Butor. 1954. pap. 14.95 (ISBN 0-686-51944-2). French & Eur.

Passage fo Peshawar: Pakistan: Between the Hindu Kush & the Arabian Sea. Richard Reeves. pap. 7.95 (ISBN 0-671-60539-9, Touchstone Bks.). S&S.

Passage Four. Ed. by Erika Boehm & Malcolm Berd. LC 74-1564. (Passage Ser.). (Illus.). 1978. pap. 3.95 (ISBN 0-931672-03-1). Triton Coll.

Passage from Home. Isaac Rosenfeld. LC 87-40105. (Masterworks of Modern Jewish Writing Ser.). 300p. 1988. pap. 9.95 (ISBN 0-910129-75-4, Distributed by Talman Company). Wiener Pub Inc.

Passage from India: Asian Indian Immigrants in North America. Joan M. Jensen. LC 87-8316. 352p. 1988. text ed. 32.50 (ISBN 0-300-03846-1). Yale U Pr.

Passage from Russia: A Personal History. Robert N. Maupin. 432p. 13.95 (ISBN 0-8062-2799-0). Carlton.

Passage: From Sail to Steam. L. R. Beavis. Ed. by M. S. Kline. (Illus.). 224p. 1986. 32.95 (ISBN 0-295-96407-3). U of Wash Pr.

Passage into Spirit. John-Roger. 1984. pap. 8.00 (ISBN 0-914829-25-4). Mandeville LA.

Passage Makers. Michael K. Stammers. (Illus.). xx, 508p. 1980. 50.00 (Pub. by Teredo Bks England). McCartan Maritime.

Passage Makers. Michael K. Stammers. 1981. 100.00x (ISBN 0-686-75403-4). State Mutual Bk.

Passage Makers. Michael K. Stammers. 1982. 95.00x (Pub. by Teredo Bks England). State Mutual BK.

Passage of Arms. Eric Ambler. 224p. 1985. pap. 2.95 (ISBN 0-425-07137-5). Berkley Pub.

Passage of Darkness: The Ethnobiology of the Haitian Zombie. Wade Davis. LC 87-40537. (Illus.). xxi, 344p. 1988. 29.95x (ISBN 0-8078-1776-7); pap. 9.95 (ISBN 0-8078-4210-9). U of NC Pr.

Passage of Dominion: Geoffrey of Monmouth & the Periodization of Insular History in the Twelfth Century. R. William Leckie, Jr. 184p. 1981. 25.00x (ISBN 0-8020-5495-1). U of Toronto Pr.

Passage of Power: Studies in Political Succession. Robbins Burling. (Studies in Anthropology Ser.). 1974. 24.95 (ISBN 0-12-785085-6). Acad Pr.

Passage of Seasons. Emma Dally. 352p. 1984. pap. 3.50 (ISBN 0-671-44309-7). PB.

Passage of the Republic: An Interdisciplinary History of Nineteenth-Century America. William L. Barney. LC 86-80489. 429p. 1987. pap. text ed. 13.50 (ISBN 0-669-04758-9). Heath.

Passage, Port & Plantation: A History of Solomon Islands Labour Migration 1870-1914. Peter Corris. (Illus.). 201p. 1973. 22.00x (ISBN 0-522-84050-7, Pub. by Melbourne U Pr). Intl Spec Bk.

Passage Through Abortion: The Personal & Social Reality of Women's Experiences. Mary K. Zimmerman. LC 77-12742. (Praeger Special Studies). 240p. 1977. 36.95 (ISBN 0-275-90281-1, C0281). Praeger.

Passage Through Armageddon: The Russians in War & Revolution 1914-1918. W. Bruce Lincoln. 640p. 1986. 22.95 (ISBN 0-671-55709-2). S&S.

Passage Through Armageddon: The Russians in War & Revolution 1914-1918. W. Bruce Lincoln. 656p. 1987. pap. 12.95 (ISBN 0-671-64560-9, Touchstone Bks). S&S.

Passage Through El Dorado. Jonathan Kandell. 320p. (gr. 7 up). 1985. pap. 5.95 (ISBN 0-380-69959-1, Discus). Avon.

Passage Through Gehenna: A Novel. Madison Jones. LC 77-13724. 270p. 1978. 16.95 (ISBN 0-8071-0376-4). La State U Pr.

Passage Through Grief: A Pastor Comes to Terms With His Wife's Suicide. Robert Dykstra. LC 87-72513. 130p. 1988. cancelled (ISBN 0-88270-638-1). Bridge Pub.

Passage Through India. Gary Snyder. LC 83-10670. (Illus.). 130p. 1984. 12.95 (ISBN 0-912516-79-8); pap. 6.95 (ISBN 0-912516-80-1). Grey Fox.

Passage Through Menopause: Women's Life in Transition. Brenda Millette & Joellen Hawkins. 1983. pap. 12.95 (ISBN 0-8359-5461-7, Reston). P-H.

Passage Through Pakistan. Orville F. Linck. LC 59-15364. Repr. of 1959 ed. 70.80 (2027610). Bks Demand UMI.

Passage Through the Garden: Lewis & Clark & the Image of the American Northwest. John L. Allen. LC 74-14512. pap. 110.00 (ISBN 0-317-28195-X, 2022773). Bks Demand UMI.

Passage Through the Red Sea. Zofia Romanowicz. 151p. 1962. 4.00 (ISBN 0-686-30917-0). Polish Inst Art & Sci.

Passage to a Human World: The Dynamics of Creating Global Wealth. Max Singer. LC 87-82068. 360p. 1988. 21.95 (ISBN 1-55813-000-4). Hudson Inst.

Passage to America: Ralegh's Colonists Take Ship for Roanoke. Helen H. Miller. (America's 400th Anniversary Ser.). (Illus.). xiv, 84p. 1986. pap. 5.00 (ISBN 0-86526-202-0). NC Archives.

Passage to Ararat. Michael J. Arlen. 293p. 1975. 8.95 (ISBN 0-374-22989-9). FS&G.

Passage to Ararat & Exiles. Michael J. Arlen. 1982. pap. 8.95 (ISBN 0-14-006311-0). Penguin.

Passage to England. J. K. Bahl. 1986. 9.95 (ISBN 0-533-06585-2). Vantage.

Passage to ESL Literacy. Diane M. Longfield. 432p. (Orig.). 1981. pap. text ed. 18.95 instr's. guide (ISBN 0-937354-03-1); student wkbk. 6.50 (ISBN 0-937354-01-5). Delta Systems.

Passage to ESL Literacy Visuals. Diane M. Longfield. 184p. (Orig.). 1981. pap. text ed. 19.95 (ISBN 0-937354-11-2). Delta Systems.

Passage to Glory. Robin L. Smith. 400p. 1983. pap. 3.50 (ISBN 0-441-65219-0). Ace Bks.

Passage to India. E. M. Forster. 429p. 1981. Repr. lib. bdg. 19.95x (ISBN 0-89966-300-1). Buccaneer Bks.

Passage to India. E. M. Forster. LC 43-1812. (Modern Classic Ser.). 320p. 1949. 11.95 (ISBN 0-15-171141-0). HarBraceJ.

Passage to India. E. M. Forster. LC 43-1812. 322p. 1985. pap. 5.95 (ISBN 0-15-671142-7, Harv). HarBraceJ.

Passage to India. E. M. Forster. Ed. by Oliver Stallybrass. LC 78-26692. (Abinger Edition of E. M. Forster Ser.: Vol. 6). 671p. 1979. 64.50 (ISBN 0-8419-0469-3). Holmes & Meier.

Passage to India. E. M. Forster. 450p. 1981. Repr. lib. bdg. 19.95x (ISBN 0-89968-223-5). Lightyear.

Passage to India. Walt Whitman. LC 68-24946. (Studies in Whitman, No. 28). 1969. Repr. of 1871 ed. lib. bdg. 39.95x (ISBN 0-8383-0260-2). Haskell.

Passage to India: Essays in Interpretation. Ed. by John Beer. LC 85-22947. 186p. 1985. 28.50x (ISBN 0-389-20601-6); pap. 8.95x (ISBN 0-389-20602-4). B&N Imports.

Passage to India Notes. Norma Ostrander. (Orig.). 1967. pap. 3.75 (ISBN 0-8220-0985-4). Cliffs.

Passage to Paradise. Kathleen Fraser. 416p. 1987. pap. 3.95 (ISBN 0-451-40055-0, Onyx). NAL.

Passage to Peshawar: Pakistan: Between the Hindu Kush & the Arabian Sea. Richard Reeves. (Illus.). 210p. 1985. 7.95 (ISBN 0-671-50842-3). S&S.

Passage to Pontefract. Jean Plaidy. 416p. 1984. pap. 3.95 (ISBN 0-449-20265-8, Crest). Fawcett.

Passage to Power: K'ang-Hsi & His Heir Apparent, 1661-1722. Silas H. Wu. LC 79-4191. (East Asian Ser.: No. 91). (Illus.). 1979. text ed. 24.50x (ISBN 0-674-65625-3). Harvard U Pr.

Passage to Quivera. Norman Zollinger. 320p. 1989. pap. 3.95 (ISBN 0-553-27636-0). Bantam.

Passage to Tenochtitlan. Richard L. Fricker. 1985. pap. 3.00 (ISBN 0-317-60610-7). Latitudes Pr.

Passage V-VI. Ed. by Erika Boehm & Malcolm Berd. LC 74-1564. 1980. 3.95 (ISBN 0-931672-01-5). Triton Coll.

Passage VII-VIII. Ed. by Erika C. Boehn. LC 74-1564. 1982. 3.95 (ISBN 0-931672-04-X). Triton Coll.

Passage West. Ruth R. Langan. 1988. pap. 3.95 (ISBN 0-671-63980-3). PB.

"Passagenkirche" Ueber Einen Bautyp der Romanischen Baukunst in Frankreich. Volker Konerding. (Beitraege zur Kunstgeshichte, Vol. 12). 120p. (Ger.). 1976. 43.20x (ISBN 3-11-004537-0). De Gruyter.

Passagers de L'Argonaute. Sonia Daquine. (Collection Colombine). 192p. 1983. pap. 1.95 (ISBN 0-373-48081-4). Harlequin Bks.

Passages. Anderson & Louis M. Savary. (Illus.). 224p. 1972. pap. 12.95 (ISBN 0-06-067065-7, RD 51, HarpR). Har-Row.

Passages. Ann Quin. LC 76-395068. 160p. 1979. pap. 6.95 (ISBN 0-7145-0056-9, Dist by Scribner). M Boyars Pubs.

Passages. Gail Sheehy. 1977. pap. 4.95 (ISBN 0-553-24754-9). Bantam.

Passages: A Personal Journal. (Illus.). 96p. (Orig.). 1986. lib. bdg. 15.90 (ISBN 0-89471-427-9); pap. 5.95 (ISBN 0-89471-426-0). Running Pr.

Passages: A Writer's Guide. Richard Nordquist. 480p. 1986. pap. text ed. write for info. (ISBN 0-312-59770-3); instr's. manual .31 (ISBN 0-312-59771-1). St Martin.

Passages: An Intermediate-Advanced Writing Book. Len Fox. 143p. 1983. pap. text ed. 9.00 net (ISBN 0-15-568227-X, HC). HarBraceJ.

Passages from Arabia Deserta. C. M. Doughty. Ed. by Edward Garnett. (Travel Library). 336p. 1984. pap. 7.95 (ISBN 0-14-009508-X). Penguin.

Passages from Arabia Deserta. Charles M. Doughty. Ed. by Edward Garnett. 320p. 1983. Repr. of 1931 ed. lib. bdg. 45.00. Century Bookbindery.

Passages from Finnegans Wake: A Free Adaptation for the Theater. James Joyce. Ed. by Mary Manning. (Poets' Theatre Ser: No. 3). 1957. 9.95x (ISBN 0-674-65650-4). Harvard U Pr.

Passages from Friday: Poems. Charles Martin. 1983. 17.50 (ISBN 0-317-40788-0). Abattoir.

Passages from the American Notebooks. Nathaniel Hawthorne. (Illus.). 458p. 1976. Repr. of 1868 ed. deluxe ed. 59.00x (ISBN 0-317-20279-0). Scholarly.

Passages from the Diary of a Late Physician, 3 vols. in 2. Samuel Warren. LC 79-8214. (Illus.). Repr. of 1832 ed. Set. 84.50 (ISBN 0-404-62160-0). AMS Pr.

Passages from the Diary of General Patrick Gordon of Auchleuchries. Patrick Gordon. (Russia Through European Eyes Ser). 1968. Repr. of 1859 ed. lib. bdg. 39.50 (ISBN 0-306-77023-7). Da Capo.

Passages from the French & Italian Notebooks. Nathaniel Hawthorne. 574p. 1976. Repr. of 1871 ed. deluxe ed. 39.00 (ISBN 0-403-02463-3). Scholarly.

Passages from the French & Italian Notebooks of Nathaniel Hawthorne. 1982. Repr. of 1883 ed. lib. bdg. 45.00 (ISBN 0-686-98146-4). Darby Bks.

Passages from the Letter of John Butler Yeats. John B. Yeats. Ed. by Ezra Pound. 76p. 1971. Repr. of 1917 ed. 15.00x (ISBN 0-7165-1351-X, BBA 02087, Pub. by Cuala Press Ireland). Biblio Dist.

Passages from the Letters of AE to W. B. Yeats. AE. 76p. 1971. Repr. of 1936 ed. 15.00x (ISBN 0-7165-1382-X, BBA 02044, Pub. by Cuala Press Ireland). Biblio Dist.

Passages from the Letters of Auguste Comte. Auguste Comte. 59.95 (ISBN 0-8490-0804-2). Gordon Pr.

Passages from the Life of a Philosopher. Charles Babbage. LC 67-30854. 1969. Repr. of 1864 ed. 49.50x (ISBN 0-678-00479-X). Kelley.

Passages from the Prose Writings of Matthew Arnold. Ed. by William E. Buckler. 235p. 1983. Repr. of 1963 ed. lib. bdg. 35.00. Century Bookbindery.

Passages from the Prose Writings of Matthew Arnold: Selected by the Author. Ed. by William E. Buckler. LC 63-11302. (Gotham Library). 235p. (Orig.). 1963. 27.00x (ISBN 0-8147-0013-6). NYU Pr.

Passages in Modern Sculpture. Rosalind E. Krauss. (Illus.). 320p. 1981. pap. 12.50 (ISBN 0-262-61033-7). MIT Pr.

Passages in the Life of a Radical. Samuel Bamford. (Oxford Paperback Bks.). (Illus.). 1984. pap. 8.95x (ISBN 0-19-281413-3). Oxford U Pr.

Passages into the Sun: Interactive Imagery. Ellen B. Cook. Ed. by Thomas E. Roth. 100p. (Orig.). 1988. pap. 6.95. TR Pubns.

Passages of a Stream: A Chronicle of the Meramec. James P. Jackson. LC 83-16752. 152p. 1984. pap. 9.95 (ISBN 0-8262-0418-X). U of MO Pr.

Passages of a Working Life During a Half Century, 3 Vols. Charles Knight. LC 79-148807. Repr. of 1865 ed. Set. 85.00 (ISBN 0-404-07670-X). AMS Pr.

Passages of a Working Life: During Half a Century with a Prelude of Early Reminiscences, 3 vols. Charles Knight. (Development of Industrial Society Ser.). 1080p. 1971. Repr. of 1865 ed. Set. 70.00x (ISBN 0-7165-1568-7, BBA 03544, Pub. by Irish Academic Pr). Biblio Dist.

Passages of Joy. Thom Gunn. 96p. 1982. 10.00 (ISBN 0-374-22990-2); pap. 6.95 (ISBN 0-374-51796-7). FS&G.

Passages of Observation: A Guru's Guide to Salvation. Michael Friedman. Ed. by Liz Jacobsen. (Illus.). 1983. pap. 4.95 (ISBN 0-912561-00-9). Counsel & Stress.

Passages Selected from the Writings of Thomas Carlyle: With a Biographical Memoir. Thomas Ballantine. 351p. 1984. Repr. of 1855 ed. lib. bdg. 40.00 (ISBN 0-918377-07-2). Russell Pr.

Passages to the Dream Shore: Short Stories of Contemporary Hawaii. Ed. by Frank Stewart. LC 87-13594. 224p. 1987. pap. 12.95 (ISBN 0-8248-1122-4). UH Pr.

Passages Toward the Dark. Thomas McGrath. 150p. (Orig.). 1982. pap. 10.00 (ISBN 0-914742-63-9). Copper Canyon.

Passaic County (NJ) Speedy Trial Demonstration Project Evalution: Final Evaluation Report. National Center for State Courts Staff. 98p. 1981. manuscript 5.88 (NERO-085). Natl Ctr St Courts.

Passaic County (NJ) Speedy Trial Demonstration Project Evaluation: Interim Report 2. National Center for State Courts Staff. 20p. 1980. manuscript 1.20 (NERO-073). Natl Ctr St Courts.

Passaic River: Past, Present, Future. Norman F. Brydon. (Illus.). 400p. 1974. 32.00x (ISBN 0-8135-0770-7). Rutgers U Pr.

Passaic: The Story of a Struggle Against Starvation Wages & for the Right to Organize. Albert Weisbord. LC 74-22764. (Labor Movement in Fiction & Non-Fiction). Repr. of 1926 ed. 20.00 (ISBN 0-404-58517-5). AMS Pr.

Passamaquoddy Texts. John D. Prince. LC 73-3545. (American Ethnological Society. Publications: No. 10). Repr. of 1921 ed. 19.00 (ISBN 0-404-58160-9). AMS Pr.

Passbook Number F.47927. Muthoni Likimani. 240p. 1986. 35.00 (ISBN 0-275-92025-9, C2025). Praeger.

Passe-Muraille. Marcel Ayme. (Folio Ser.: No. 961). 1943. 6.95 (ISBN 0-685-11479-1). Schoenhof.

Passe-Muraille. Marcel Ayme. 1943. write for info. French & Eur.

Passel of Possums. Tony Palazzo & Robin Fox. (Illus.). (gr. k-3). 1968. PLB 8.95 (ISBN 0-87460-099-5). Lion Bks.

Passenger. Michelangelo Antonioni et al. (Illus.). 192p. (Orig.). 1986. pap. 6.95 (ISBN 0-936839-52-X). Applause Theatre Bk Pubs.

Passenger Airliners of the United States 1926-1986: A Pictorial History. Myron J. Smith, Jr. LC 86-90432. 200p. 1987. pap. 12.95 (ISBN 0-933126-83-2). Pictorial Hist.

Passenger Airliners of the United States, 1926-1986: A Pictorial History. Myron Smith, Jr. LC 86-9043. (Illus.). 1987. pap. 12.95 (ISBN 0-317-65215-X). Pictorial Hist.

Passenger & Immigration Lists Annual Supplement, 1988. Ed. by William Filby. 1988. 140.00 (ISBN 0-8103-2576-4). Gale.

Passenger & Immigration Lists Bibliography, 1538-1900. 2nd ed. Ed. by P. William Filby. LC 84-13702. 324p. 1988. 100.00x (ISBN 0-8103-2740-6). Gale.

Passenger & Immigration Lists Bibliography (1538-1900) Being a Guide to Published Lists of Arrivals in the United States & Canada. 2nd ed. Ed. by P. William Filby. 200p. 1988. 100.00x (ISBN 0-8103-1098-8). Gale.

Passenger & Immigration Lists Index: A Reference Guide to Published Lists of about 500,000 Passengers Who Arrived in America in the Seventeenth, Eighteenth & Nineteenth Centuries, 3 vols. Ed. by P. William Filby. 2438p. 1981. Set. 425.00x (ISBN 0-8103-1099-6). Gale.

Passenger & Immigration Lists Index 1982: Annual Supplement. Ed. by P. William Filby & Mary K. Meyer. 992p. 1983. 140.00x. Gale.

Passenger & Immigration Lists Index: 1983 Supplement. Ed. by P. William Filby. 1008p. 1984. 140.00x. Gale.

Passenger & Immigration Lists Index: 1984 Supplement. Ed. by P. William Filby. 648p. 1985. 140.00x (ISBN 0-8103-1791-5). Gale.

Passenger & Immigration Lists Index: 1985 Supplement. Ed. by P. William Filby. 703p. 1985. 140.00x (ISBN 0-8103-1792-3). Gale.

Passenger & Immigration Lists Index: 1986 Supplement. Ed. by P. William Filby & Mary K. Meyer. 700p. 1986. 140.00x (ISBN 0-8103-1799-0). Gale.

Passenger & Immigration Lists Index 1987: Supplement. Ed. by P. William Filby & Mary K. Meyer. 677p. 1987. 140.00x (ISBN 0-8103-2575-6). Gale.

Passenger & Immigration Lists Index: 1988 Supplement. Ed. by P. William Filby & Mary K. Meyer. 1988. 140.00x. Gale.

Passenger & Immigration Lists Index: 1982-85 Cumulation. Ed. by P. William Filby & Mary K. Meyer. 3701p. 1985. 475.00x (ISBN 0-8103-1795-8). Gale.

Passenger Arrivals at the Port of Baltimore, 1820-1834: From Customs Passenger Lists. Ed. by Michael H. Tepper. LC 82-82643. 768p. 1982. 38.50 (ISBN 0-8063-0996-2). Genealog Pub.

Passenger Car Diesels. 1982. 55.00 (ISBN 0-89883-112-1, PT24). Soc Auto Engineers.

Passenger Car Engines. 274p. 1975. 25.00 (ISBN 0-85298-425-1, MEP-07). Soc Auto Engineers.

Passenger Car Inflatable Restraint Systems: A Compedium of Published Safety Research. 1987. 75.00 (ISBN 0-89883-119-9, PT31). Soc Auto Engineers.

Passenger Car Transmissions. 1985. 22.00 (ISBN 0-89883-840-1, SP619). Soc Auto Engineers.

Passenger Cars of the Burlington 1869 to the 1930's. William L. Glick. LC 86-90543. (Illus.). 166p. 1986. 60.00 (ISBN 0-940525-00-3); pap. 39.50 (ISBN 0-940525-01-1). Quincy Hse.

Passenger Comfort, Convenience. 1986. 73.00 (ISBN 0-89883-738-3, P 174). Soc Auto Engineers.

Passenger Conveyors. J. M. Tough & C. A. O'Flaherty. 192p. 1971. 64.00 (ISBN 0-677-65360-3). Gordon & Breach.

Passenger from Scotland Yard: A Victorian Detective Novel. H. F. Wood. Ed. by E. F. Bleiler. LC 77-75266. (Illus.). 1977. pap. 5.50 (ISBN 0-486-23523-8). Dover.

Passenger Lists from Ireland. J. Dominick Hackett & Charles M. Early. LC 65-29279. 46p. 1981. pap. 5.00 (ISBN 0-8063-0166-X). Genealog Pub.

Passenger Protection Technology in Aircraft Accident Fires. Neville H. Birch. 200p. 1988. text ed. 55.00x (ISBN 0-291-39734-4, Pub. by Gower Pub England). Gower Pub Co.

Passenger Psychological Dynamics. 189p. 1968. pap. 9.00x (ISBN 0-87262-020-4). Am Soc Civil Eng.

Passenger Ship. Hannah Jacobs. (Science Seekers Series). 40p. (YA) (gr. 6-10). 1988. 13.95 (ISBN 0-241-11880-8, Pub. by Hamish Hamilton). David & Charles.

Passenger Ships of the Orient Line. Neil McCart. (Illus.). 248p. 1988. 29.95 (ISBN 0-85059-891-5, Pub. by PSL P Stephens England). Sterling.

Passenger to Frankfurt. Agatha Christie. Date not set. pap. 3.50 (ISBN 0-671-60062-1). PB.

Passenger to Frankfurt. Agatha Christie. 17.95 (ISBN 0-88411-384-1, Pub. by Aeonian Pr). Amereon Ltd.

Passenger Transport: Planning for Radical Change. J. D. Carr. 210p. 1986. text ed. 59.50 (ISBN 0-566-05183-4, Pub. by Gower Pub England). Gower Pub Co.

Passenger Travel Demand Forecasting. (Transportation Research Record Ser.). 52p. 1976. 2.80 (ISBN 0-309-02585-0). Transport Res Bd.

Passenger Travel Forecasting. (Transportation Research Record Ser.). 89p. 1979. 5.00 (ISBN 0-309-02981-3). Transport Res Bd.

Passenger Vibration in Transportation Vehicles: Presented at the Design Engineering Technical Conferenc, Chicago, Illinois, September 26-28, 1977. Design Engineering Technical Conference (1977: Chicago) Ed. by Alex Berman & Alan J. Hannibal. LC 77-82212. (AMD Ser.: Vol. 24). pap. 34.00 (ISBN 0-317-27775-8, 2015393). Bks Demand UMI.

Passengers. Daniel Besnehard. Tr. by Stephen J. Vogel. (Ubu Repertory Theater Publications Ser.: No. 11). 100p. (Orig.). 1985. pap. text ed. 6.25 (ISBN 0-913745-12-X). Ubu Repertory.

Passengers & Kings. Joe Fuoco. 128p. (Orig.). Date not set. 19.95 (ISBN 0-89754-055-7); pap. 8.95 (ISBN 0-89754-054-9). Dan River Pr.

Passengers from Ireland, Eighteen Eleven to Eighteen Seventeen. Donald M. Schlegel. LC 79-90983. 158p. 1980. 12.50 (ISBN 0-8063-0870-2). Genealog Pub.

Passengers to America: A Consolidation of Ship Passenger Lists from the New England Historical & Genealogical Register. Ed. by Michael Tepper. LC 77-72983. 554p. 1980. 20.00 (ISBN 0-8063-0767-6). Genealog Pub.

Passengers to America: A Consolidation of Ship Passenger Lists. Ed. by Michael Tepper. 554p. 1988. Repr. of 1961 ed. 25.00 (5755). Genealog Pub.

Passeport: A Beginning Reader for Communication. 2nd ed. Gilbert A. Jarvis et al. (Fr.). 1983. text ed. 14.95 (ISBN 0-03-062349-9). HR&W.

Passeport pour la France. Penrose Colyer. (Illus.). 80p. (Fr.). 1983. pap. text ed. 8.95 (ISBN 0-8219-0046-3, 40294). EMC.

Passer-by: And Other Stories. Ethel M. Dell. LC 72-5867. (Short Story Index Reprint Ser). Repr. of 1925 ed. 20.00 (ISBN 0-8369-4210-8). Ayer Co Pubs.

Passes at the Moon. Thomas Averill. 86p. 1985. pap. 5.00 (ISBN 0-939391-03-1). B Woodley Pr.

Passes for Human. Will Staple. 1977. perfect 3.00 (ISBN 0-685-50418-2, Pub by Shaman Drum Pr). Small Pr Dist.

Passin' Through. Louis L'Amour. 176p. (Orig.). 1985. pap. 2.95 (ISBN 0-553-25320-4). Bantam.

Passin' Through. Louis L'Amour. (General Ser.). 357p. 1986. lib. bdg. 14.95 (ISBN 0-8161-4067-7, Large Print Bks); pap. 10.95 (ISBN 0-8161-4068-5, Large Print Bks.). G K Hall.

Passing. Nella Larsen. LC 76-92233. (American Negro: His History & Literature, Ser. No. 3). 1970. Repr. of 1929 ed. 13.00 (ISBN 0-405-01930-0). Ayer Co Pubs.

Passing. Nella Larsen. LC 73-82056. Repr. of 1929 ed. 35.00x (ISBN 0-8371-1541-8, LAP&). Greenwood.

Passing. Ken Lucas. 1982. 15.00x (ISBN 0-903653-51-6, Pub. by New Playwrights Network). State Mutual Bk.

Passing Age. A. Kukarkin. 1979. 10.00 (ISBN 0-8285-1860-2, Pub. by Progress Pubs USSR). Imported Pubns.

Passing Ceremony. Helen Weinzweig. LC 72-95751. (Anansi Fiction Ser.: AF 24). 120p. 1973. 10.95 (Pub. by Hse Anansi Pr Canada); pap. 5.95 (ISBN 0-88784-325-5). U of Toronto Pr.

Passing Down the Farm: The OTHER Farm Crisis. Donald J. Jonovic & Wayne D. Messick. 230p. 1987. 24.95 (ISBN 0-915607-08-5). Jamieson Pr.

Passing English of the Victorian Period. J. Redding Ware. 1977. Repr. of 1905 ed. 12.50x (ISBN 0-85409-932-8). Charles River Bks.

Passing Fancies. Elizabeth Mansfield. 224p. 1987. pap. 2.50 (ISBN 0-515-09175-8). Jove Pubns.

Passing Farms, Enduring Values: California's Santa Clara Valley. Yvonne Jacobson. LC 83-29611. (Illus.). xvi, 250p. 1984. 39.50 (ISBN 0-86576-045-4). Tioga Pub Co.

Passing Freshman Chemistry: Prerequesite Skills & Concepts. T. L. Isenhour & L. G. Pedersen. 177p. (Orig.). 1981. net spiral bdg. 10.95 (ISBN 0-15-568230-X, HC); instr's. manual avail. (ISBN 0-15-568231-8). HarBraceJ.

Passing Guest: A Biography of Henry Kingsley. J. S. Mellick. LC 83-3285. 350p. 1983. 29.95x (ISBN 0-312-59777-0). St Martin.

Passing Judgments. facs. ed. George J. Nathan. LC 71-86774. (Essay Index Reprint Ser). 1935. 15.00 (ISBN 0-8369-1150-4). Ayer Co Pubs.

Passing Judgments. George J. Nathan. 1969. Repr. of 1935 ed. 17.00 (ISBN 0-384-40920-2). Johnson Repr.

Passing Judgments: The Theatre World of George Jean Nathan. George J. Nathan. LC 75-120099. 271p. 1970. 20.00 (ISBN 0-8386-7722-3). Fairleigh Dickinson.

Passing Math: Fundamentals of College Algebra. B. G. Nunley & Neal Brand. 384p. 1986. pap. text ed. 21.95 (ISBN 0-8403-4166-0). Kendall Hunt.

Passing Medical Examinations. 2nd ed. M. H. Pappworth. 144p. 1985. pap. text ed. 19.95 (ISBN 0-407-00415-7). Butterworth.

Passing of Cleverclogs. Maureen Nield. 1982. 15.00x (ISBN 0-903653-54-0, Pub. by New Playwrights Network). State Mutual Bk.

Passing of Korea. Homer B. Holbert. 33.25 (ISBN 0-8369-7141-8, 7974). Ayer Co Pubs.

Passing of Marine Griffiths. D. K. Brough. 1981. 15.00x (ISBN 0-7223-1413-2, Pub. by A H Stockwell England). State Mutual Bk.

Passing of Remoteness? Information Revolution in the Asia-Pacific. Ed. by Meheroo Jussawalla et al. 172p. 1986. text ed. 18.00x (ISBN 9971-988-45-3, Pub. by Inst Souteast Asian Stud). Gower Pub Co.

Passing of the Armies. Joshua L. Chamberlain. (Civil War Heritage Ser.: No. 4). 1985. 30.00. Pr of Morningside.

Passing of the European Age: A Study of the Transfer of Western Civilization & Its Renewal in Other Continents. Eric Fischer. 228p. 1983. Repr. of 1948 ed. lib. bdg. 45.00 (ISBN 0-89987-281-6). Darby Bks.

Passing of the Frontier. Emerson Hough. 1976. lib. bdg. 10.95x (ISBN 0-89968-046-1). Lightyear.

Passing of the Frontier. Emerson Hough. 1918. 19.50x (ISBN 0-686-83683-9). Elliots Bks.

Passing of the Frontier see Chronicles of America.

Passing of the Frontier, 1825-1850 see History of the State of Ohio.

Passing of the Gods. V. F. Calverton. 326p. 1982. Repr. of 1934 ed. lib. bdg. 35.00 (ISBN 0-89987-123-2). Darby Bks.

Passing of the Great Race, or, the Racial Basis of European History. Madison Grant. LC 74-129398. (American Immigration Collection, Ser. 2). (Illus.). 1970. Repr. of 1918 ed. 16.00 (ISBN 0-405-00577-6). Ayer Co Pubs.

Passing of the Great West: Selected Papers of George Bird Grinnell. George B. Grinnell. Ed. by John F. Reiger. LC 84-40696. (Illus.). 192p. (Orig.). 1985. pap. 7.95 (ISBN 0-8061-1925-X). U of Okla Pr.

Passing of the Idle Rich. facsimile ed. Frederick T. Martin. LC 75-1858. (Leisure Class in America Ser.). 1975. Repr. of 1911 ed. 18.00x (ISBN 0-405-06924-3). Ayer Co Pubs.

Passing of the Land. David O. Snyder. (Illus.). 260p. (Orig.). 1988. pap. 9.95 (ISBN 0-89896-310-9). Larksdale.

Passing of the Manchus. Percy H. Kent. LC 75-32316. (Studies in Chinese History & Civilization). 404p. 1977. 24.00 (ISBN 0-89093-079-1). U Pubns Amer.

Passing of the Mill Village: Revolution in a Southern Institution. Harriet L. Herring. LC 76-54298. 1977. Repr. of 1949 ed. lib. bdg. 35.00x (ISBN 0-8371-9406-7, HEPA). Greenwood.

Passing of the Phantoms: A Study of Evolutionary Psychology & Morals. Ed. by C. J. Patten. 95p. 1980. Repr. of 1924 ed. lib. bdg. 17.50 (ISBN 0-8495-4370-3). Arden Lib.

Passing of the Three-D Ranch. L. Stansberry. (American History & Americana Ser., No. 47). 1970. lib. bdg. 49.95x (ISBN 0-8383-1108-3). Haskell.

Passing of Thomas. Thomas A. Janvier. LC 79-94733. (Short Story Index Reprint Ser.). 1900. 17.00 (ISBN 0-8369-3113-0). Ayer Co Pubs.

Passing off & Misappropriation. Ed. by P. J. Kaufman. (IIC Studies). 178p. 1986. pap. 47.00 (ISBN 0-89573-485-0). VCH Pubs.

Passing on: The Social Organization of Dying. David Sudnow. (Orig.). 1967. pap. write for info. (ISBN 0-13-652719-1). P-H.

Passing on the Torch. Roger L. Dudley. Ed. by Raymond H. Woolsey. 192p. 1986. 12.95 (ISBN 0-8280-0348-3); pap. 8.95 (ISBN 0-8280-0419-6). Review & Herald.

Passing: Perspectives of Rural America. Ferrol Sams, Jr. (Illus.). 144p. 1988. 24.95 (ISBN 0-929264-03-7). Longstreet Pr Inc.

Passing Scores. 1988. 7.50 (ISBN 0-317-67892-2). Educ Testing Serv.

Passing Season. Richard Blessing. LC 82-47912. 228p. (gr. 6 up). 1982. 14.95 (ISBN 0-316-09957-0). Little.

Passing Shots. Pam Shriver et al. 1988. pap. text ed. 5.95 (ISBN 0-07-057180-5). McGraw.

Passion of Youth: An Autobiography, 1897-1922. Wilhelm Reich. Ed. by Mary B. Higgins & Chester M. Raphael. Tr. by Philip Schmitz & Jerri Tompkins. 240p. 1988. 17.95 (ISBN 0-374-22995-3). FS&G.

Passion Paths. William Grimbol. Ed. by Michael L. Sherer. LC 86-25094. (Orig.). 1987. pap. 3.95 (ISBN 0-89536-842-0, 7801). CSS of Ohio.

Passion Play. Peter Nichols. 106p. 1981. pap. 6.95 (ISBN 0-413-47800-9, NO. 3508). Heinemann Ed.

Passion Play. Charles Numrich. 1983. 4.95 (ISBN 0-89536-601-0, 1627). CSS of Ohio.

Passion Play. 3rd, rev. ed. Date not set. pap. price not set (ISBN 0-413-60040-8). Heinemann Ed.

Passion Play. Eugene Vale. 260p. 1984. 13.95 (ISBN 0-9609674-2-7); pap. 7.95 (ISBN 0-9609674-1-9). Jubilee Pr.

Passion Play. Catherine de Vinck. LC 75-26326. 68p. 1975. 8.75 (ISBN 0-911726-16-0); pap. 6.75 (ISBN 0-911726-18-7). Alleluia Pr.

Passion Play: A Season with the Purdue Boilermakers & Coach Gene Keady. Mark Montieth. 1988. 16.95 (ISBN 0-933893-73-6). Bonus Books.

Passion Rose. Mallory Burgess. 400p. (Orig.). 1987. pap. 3.95 (ISBN 0-380-75169-0). Avon.

Passion Season. Joyce Bright. LC 78-31894. 1981. 15.95 (ISBN 0-87949-144-2). Ashley Bks.

Passion Star. Mallory Burgess. 432p. 1988. pap. 3.95 (ISBN 0-380-75383-9). Avon.

Passion Stone. Harriette DeJarnette. 384p. 1984. pap. 3.50 (ISBN 0-8439-2095-5, Leisure Bks). Leisure NY.

Passionate Attachments: Fathers & Daughters in America Today. Signe Hammer. 1982. 4.95 (ISBN 0-89256-182-3). Rawson Assocs.

Passionate Attachments: Thinking about Love. Ed. by Willard Gaylin & Ethel Person. 250p. 1988. 19.95 (ISBN 0-02-911430-6). Free Pr.

Passionate Attention: An Introduction to Literary Study. Richard L. McGuire. 1973. 6.95x (ISBN 0-393-09324-7). Norton.

Passionate Centurie of Love. Thomas Watson. 1966. Repr. of 1581 ed. 18.50 (ISBN 0-8337-3696-5). B Franklin.

Passionate Doubts: Designs of Interpretation in Contemporary American Fiction. Patrick O'Donnell. LC 85-28865. 213p. 1986. 19.95x (ISBN 0-87745-138-9). U of Iowa Pr.

Passionate Enemies. Kathryn Cranmer. (Harlequin Presents Ser.). 1982. pap. 1.75. Harlequin Bks.

Passionate Escape. Mary Lyons. (Harlequin Presents Ser.). 192p. 1983. pap. 1.95 (ISBN 0-373-10625-4). Harlequin Bks.

Passionate Exiles: Madame de Stael & Madame Recamier. Maurice Levaillant. Tr. by Malcolm Barnes from Fr. LC 73-160923. (Biography Index Reprint Ser.). Repr. of 1958 ed. 21.75 (ISBN 0-8369-8086-7). Ayer Co Pubs.

Passionate Eye: The Life of William R. Valentiner. Margaret Sterne. LC 79-24961. (Illus.). 408p. 1980. 29.95x (ISBN 0-8143-1631-X). Wayne St U Pr.

Passionate God. Rosemary Haughton. LC 81-80049. 352p. 1981. pap. 9.95 (ISBN 0-8091-2383-5). Paulist Pr.

Passionate Impostor. Elizabeth Graham. (Harlequin Presents Ser.). 192p. 1982. pap. 1.75 (ISBN 0-373-10493-6). Harlequin Bks.

Passionate Intruder. Lilian Peake. (Harlequin Presents Ser.). 192p. 1983. pap. 1.95 (ISBN 0-373-10612-2). Harlequin Bks.

Passionate Investors: Winning on Wall Street Year After Year in Every Kind of Market. Madelon D. Talley. 320p. 1987. 18.95 (ISBN 0-517-56563-3). Crown.

Passionate Jade. Georgianna Bell. 1981. pap. 2.95 (ISBN 0-671-83657-9). PB.

Passionate Journey. Irving Stone. 1959. 12.95 (ISBN 0-385-17198-6). Doubleday.

Passionate Journey: A Novel in One Hundred Sixty-Five Woodcuts. Frans Masereel. (Illus.). 160p. 12.95 (ISBN 0-87286-233-X); pap. 6.95 (ISBN 0-87286-174-0). City Lights.

Passionate Journey: Poems & Drawings in the Erotic Mood. Steve Kowit & Arthur Okamura. LC 84-71153. (Illus.). 88p. 1984. 12.00 (ISBN 0-933944-08-X); pap. 7.95 (ISBN 0-933944-09-8). City Miner Bks.

Passionate Journey: The Spiritual Autobiography of Satomi Myodo. Tr. & annotations by Sallie B. King. LC 86-28057. (Illus.). 212p. (Orig.). 1987. pap. 12.95 (ISBN 0-87773-392-9). Shambhala Pubns.

Passionate Liberator: Theodore Dwight Weld & the Dilemma of Reform. Robert H. Abzug. LC 80-11819. (Illus.). 1980. 27.50x (ISBN 0-19-502771-X). Oxford U Pr.

Passionate Liberator: Theodore Dwight Weld & the Dilemma of Reform. Robert H. Abzug. 1980. pap. 8.95x (ISBN 0-19-503061-3). Oxford U Pr.

Passionate Life: Stages of Loving. Sam Keen. LC 82-48932. (Illus.). 288p. 1983. pap. 8.95 (ISBN 0-06-250469-X, CN 4095, HarpR). Har-Row.

Passionate Love of Mankind. Henry Kitt. 1988. 10.95 (ISBN 0-533-07532-7). Vantage.

Passionate Mind. Joel Kramer. 122p. 1983. pap. 7.95 (ISBN 0-938190-12-1). North Atlantic.

Passionate Necessity. Hugh Shearman. 3.50 (ISBN 0-8356-0200-1). Theos Pub Hse.

Passionate Nomad: The Diary of Isabelle Eberhardt. Isabelle Eberhardt. LC 87-42854. (Virago-Beacon Traveler Ser.). 160p. 1988. pap. 7.95 (ISBN 0-8070-7103-X, BP 779). Beacon Pr.

Passionate Opinions. John C. Holmes. LC 88-10811. (Orig.). 1988. 22.95 (ISBN 1-55728-049-5); pap. 12.95 (ISBN 1-55728-050-9). U of Ark Pr.

Passionate Perils of Publishing. Celeste West & Valerie Wheat. 76p. 1980. pap. 5.00x (ISBN 0-8389-3250-9). ALA.

Passionate Perils of Publishing. Celeste West & Valerie Wheat. LC 77-94898. (Illus.). 1978. pap. 7.00x (ISBN 0-912932-04-X). Booklegger Pr.

Passionate Pilgrim see Reverberator.

Passionate Pilgrim & Other Tales. Henry James. 496p. 1984. Repr. of 1875 ed. lib. bdg. 79.50 (ISBN 0-89984-720-X). Century Bookbindery.

Passionate Pilgrims. Allison Lockwood. LC 78-66808. (Illus.). 551p. 1981. 37.50 (ISBN 0-8453-4725-X, Cornwall Bks). Assoc Univ Prs.

Passionate Pilgrims: English Travelers to the World of the Desert Arabs. James C. Simmons. Ed. by Pat Golbitz. LC 86-28627. (Illus.). 416p. 1987. 19.95 (ISBN 0-688-06559-7). Morrow.

Passionate Pilgrims: The American Traveler in Great Britain, 1800-1914. Allison Lockwood. LC 78-66808. 650p. 1981. 37.50 (ISBN 0-8386-2272-0). Fairleigh Dickinson.

Passionate Politics: Essay 1968-1986. Charlotte Bunch. 368p. 1988. pap. 9.95 (ISBN 0-312-01804-5). St Martin.

Passionate Politics: Essays 1968-1986. Charlotte Bunch. 288p. 1987. 17.95 (ISBN 0-312-00667-5). St Martin.

Passionate Pretender. Marianne Montgomery. 288p. 1987. pap. 3.50 (ISBN 0-451-14806-1, Sig). NAL.

Passionate Prodigality. Guy Chapman. (Echoes of War Ser.). 1987. pap. 10.95 (ISBN 0-907675-42-5, Pub. by Buchan & Enright England). Seven Hills Bks.

Passionate Prodigality: Letters to Alan Bird from Richard Aldington, 1949-1962. Richard Aldington. Ed. by Miriam J. Benkovitz. LC 75-23105. (Illus.). 376p. 1975. 20.00 (ISBN 0-87104-259-2). NY Pub Lib.

Passionate Protection. Penny Jordan. (Harlequin Presents Ser.). 192p. 1983. pap. 1.95 (ISBN 0-373-10633-5). Harlequin Bks.

Passionate Prude. Elizabeth Thornton. 480p. 1988. pap. 3.95 (ISBN 0-8217-2485-1). Zebra.

Passionate Relationship. Penny Jordan. (Harlequin Presents Ser.: No. 1000). 192p. Date not set. pap. 1.95 (ISBN 0-317-63744-4). Harlequin Bks.

Passionate Sailor. Nat Philbrick. (Illus.). 1987. pap. 6.95 (ISBN 0-8092-5018-7). Contemp Bks.

Passionate Search: A Life of Charlotte Bronte. Margaret Crompton. 252p. 1982. Repr. of 1955 ed. lib. bdg. 40.00. Century Bookbindery.

Passionate Shepherdess. Maureen Duffy. 1979. pap. 2.95 (ISBN 0-380-41863-0, Discus). Avon.

Passionate Sightseer: From the Diaries 1947-1956. Bernard Berenson. LC 87-50198. (Illus.). 192p. 1988. pap. 14.95 (ISBN 0-500-27457-6). Thames Hudson.

Passionate Stranger. Flora Kidd. 1986. pap. 10.95 (ISBN 0-8161-3999-7, Large Print Bks). G K Hall.

Passionate Touch. Bonnie Drake. (Candlelight Ecstasy Ser.: No. 3). 1986. pap. 1.50 (ISBN 0-440-16776-0). Dell.

Passionate Virtuosity: The Fiction of John Barth. Charles B. Harris. LC 83-4976. 232p. 1983. 17.95 (ISBN 0-252-01037-X). U of Ill Pr.

Passionate War. Peter Wyden. 608p. 1986. pap. 12.95 (ISBN 0-671-25331-X, Touchstone Bks). S&S.

Passionate War: A Narrative History of the Spanish Civil War, 1936-1939. Peter Wyden. (Illus.). 500p. 1983. 19.95 (ISBN 0-671-25330-1). S&S.

Passionate Wisdom of Henry Miller: The Religious Dimension of His Life & Art. Dorothy Perkins. (Orig.). 1980. pap. 3.00 (ISBN 0-9604742-1-8). D J Perkins.

Passionate Witch. Grace L. Hill. 18.95 (ISBN 0-89190-433-6, Pub. by Am Repr). Amereon Ltd.

Passionate Women, Passive Men: Suicide in Yiddish Literature. Janet Hadda. LC 87-7911. (Modern Jewish Literature & Culture Ser.). 224p. 1988. 44.50 (ISBN 0-88706-595-3); pap. 14.95 (ISBN 0-88706-597-X). State U NY Pr.

Passionate Years. Caresse Crosby. LC 78-31388. (Neglected Books of the Twentieth Century). (Illus.). 1979. pap. 6.95 (ISBN 0-912946-66-0). Ecco Pr.

Passione. Albert F. Innaurato. 1981. pap. 3.50x (ISBN 0-686-76764-0). Dramatists Play.

Passionfresken Pontormos fur die Certosa del Galluzzo, 2 vols. Petra Beckers. Ed. by James Hogg. (Analecta Cartusiana Ser.: No. 121). 250p. (Orig.). 1985. pap. 50.00 (ISBN 0-317-42592-7, Pub. by Salzburg Studies). Longwood Pub Group.

Passionists of the Southwest: A Revelation of the Penitentes. Alex Darley. LC 68-57290. (Beautiful Rio Grande Classics Ser.). 134p. 1983. lib. bdg. 12.00 (ISBN 0-87380-020-6). Rio Grande.

Passions. Lillian Africano. 288p. 1985. pap. 3.50 (ISBN 0-515-08103-5). Jove Pubns.

Passions. Helen Chappell. 1987. pap. 3.95 (ISBN 0-671-64915-9). PB.

Passions. Isaac Bashevis Singer. 1980. pap. 2.95 (ISBN 0-449-24067-3, Crest). Fawcett.

Passions. Isaac Bashevis Singer. LC 75-20267. 312p. 1975. 8.95 (ISBN 0-374-22993-7). FS&G.

Passions. Robert C. Solomon. xxv, 448p. 1983. text ed. 26.95x (ISBN 0-268-01551-1); pap. text ed. 9.95x (ISBN 0-268-01552-X). U of Notre Dame Pr.

Passions. large print ed. Ellen White. 35p. 1985. pap. 6.00 (ISBN 0-914009-46-X). VHI Library.

Passions, 4 vols, Vol. 9. Charlotte Dacre. LC 73-22762. (Gothic Novels Ser.). 1974. Repr. of 1811 ed. Set. 88.00x (ISBN 0-405-06013-0). Ayer Co Pubs.

Passions & Impressions. Pablo Neruda. Tr. by Margaret S. Peden from Span. 396p. 1983. 25.00 (ISBN 0-374-22994-5); pap. 10.95 (ISBN 0-374-51811-4). FS&G.

Passions & the Homilies from Leabhar Breac. Tr. by Robert Atkinson. LC 78-72680. (Royal Irish Academy. Todd Lecture Ser.: Vol. 2). Repr. of 1887 ed. 72.50 (ISBN 0-404-60562-1). AMS Pr.

Passions & the Interests: Political Arguments for Capitalism Before Its Triumph. Albert O. Hirschman. 1977. 20.50x (ISBN 0-691-04214-4); pap. 8.95x (ISBN 0-691-00357-2). Princeton U Pr.

Passion's Betrayal. Penelope Neri. 1985. pap. 3.95 (ISBN 0-8217-1568-2). Zebra.

Passion's Blossom. Brenna McCartney. 1982. pap. 3.50 (ISBN 0-8217-1109-1). Zebra.

Passion's Bride. Jo Goodman. 528p. 1984. pap. 3.75 (ISBN 0-8217-1417-1). Zebra.

Passion's Captive. Lori Copeland. (Orig.). 1988. pap. 3.95 (ISBN 0-440-20134-9). Dell.

Passion's Child: The Extraordinary Life of Jane Digby. Margaret F. Schmidt. 5.95 (ISBN 0-7043-3202-7, Pub. by Quartet England). Charles River Bks.

Passions Dance. Lauren Fox. (Second Chance At Love Ser.: No. 266). 192p. 1985. pap. 2.25 (ISBN 0-425-08154-0). Berkley Pub.

Passion's Dark Harvest. Jessica Ward. 320p. (Orig.). 1981. pap. 3.25 (ISBN 0-8439-1001-1, Leisure Bks). Leisure NY.

Passions Dawn. Elaine Barbieri. 1985. pap. 3.95 (ISBN 0-8217-1655-7). Zebra.

Passions de l'Ame. Rene Descartes. (Idees Ser.). 1970. 6.95 (ISBN 0-686-55677-1). Schoenhof.

Passion's Dream. Casey Stuart. 1982. pap. 3.50 (ISBN 0-8217-1086-9). Zebra.

Passion's Fire. Cassie Edwards. 496p. 1986. pap. 3.95 (ISBN 0-8217-1872-X). Zebra.

Passion's Folly. Lori Copeland. (Candlelight Ecstasy Ser.: No. 498). (Orig.). 1987. pap. 2.25 (ISBN 0-440-16818-X). Dell.

Passion's Fury. Patricia Hagan. 400p. 1981. pap. 3.95 (ISBN 0-380-77727-4). Avon.

Passion's Gamble. Robin L. Hatcher. 480p. (Orig.). 1986. pap. 3.95 (ISBN 0-8439-2412-8, Leisure Bks). Leisure NY.

Passion's Glory. Anne Moore. 1983. pap. 3.50. Zebra.

Passion's Gold. Susan Sackett. 352p. (Orig.). 1987. pap. 3.95 (ISBN 0-380-75318-9). Avon.

Passion's Harvest. Marion Mallasch. 1981. pap. 2.75 (ISBN 0-89083-724-4). Zebra.

Passion's Honor. (Avon Romance Ser.). 352p. 1987. pap. 3.95 (ISBN 0-380-75097-X). Avon.

Passions of Animals. Edward P. Thompson. (Contributions to the History of Psychology Ser.: Comparative Psychology). 1980. Repr. of 1851 ed. 30.00 (ISBN 0-89093-322-7). U Pubns Amer.

Passions of Lady Meg. (Red Stripe Ser.). 1988. pap. 4.50 (ISBN 0-8216-5052-1, Univ Bks). Lyle Stuart.

Passions of Lady Meg, Bk. II. (Red Stripe Ser.). 1989. pap. 4.50 (ISBN 0-8216-5058-0, Univ Bks). Lyle Stuart.

Passions of Men: Work & Love in the Age of Stress. Mark Hunter. 320p. 1988. 19.95 (ISBN 0-399-13322-4). Putnam Pub Group.

Passions of the Human Soul, & Their Influence on Society & Civilization, 2 Vols. Francois M. Fourier. Tr. by H. Doherty. LC 67-29504. 1968. Repr. of 1851 ed. 87.50x (ISBN 0-678-00383-1). Kelley.

Passions of the Mind. Irving Stone. LC 75-139064. 1971. 19.95 (ISBN 0-385-02396-0). Doubleday.

Passions of the Mind. Irving Stone. 820p. 1972. pap. 4.95 (ISBN 0-451-13456-7, AE1580, Sig). NAL.

Passions of the Mind in General by Thomas Wright. Ed. by W. W. Newbold. 500p. 1985. lib. bdg. 76.00 (ISBN 0-8240-5458-X). Garland Pub.

Passions of the Minde in Generall: A Reprint Based on the 1604 Edition. Thomas Wright. LC 78-139807. Repr. of 1971 ed. 111.50 (ISBN 0-8357-9692-2, 2011136). Bks Demand UMI.

Passions of the Realm. Joan Balser. 1988. pap. 3.95 (ISBN 0-517-00667-7, Pageant Bks). Crown.

Passions of the Soul. Rene Descartes. Tr. by Stephen H. Voss from Fr. (Hackett Classics Ser.). 168p. 1988. lib. bdg. 17.50 (ISBN 0-87220-036-1); pap. text ed. 4.25 (ISBN 0-87220-035-3). Hackett Pub.

Passions of Uxport. Maxine Kumin. LC 75-14698. 399p. 1975. Repr. of 1968 ed. lib. bdg. 35.00x (ISBN 0-8371-8241-7, KUPU). Greenwood.

Passion's Paradise. Sonya T. Pelton. 544p. (Orig.). 1981. pap. 3.25 (ISBN 0-89083-765-1). Zebra.

Passion's Peak. Christine Carson. 448p. (Orig.). 1988. pap. 3.95 Mass Market (ISBN 0-8439-2578-7). Leisure NY.

Passion's Persuasion. Prudence Martin. 1985. pap. 2.50 (ISBN 0-8217-1631-X). Zebra.

Passion's Pleasure. Valerie Giscard. (Orig.). 1982. pap. 3.50 (ISBN 0-8217-1034-6). Zebra.

Passion's Price. Barbara Harrison. 1985. pap. 3.95 (ISBN 0-8217-1583-6). Zebra.

Passion's Promise. Danielle Steel. 1977. pap. 4.95 (ISBN 0-440-12926-5). Dell.

Passion's Rapture. Penelope Neri. (Orig.). 1982. pap. 3.50 (ISBN 0-89083-912-3). Zebra.

Passion's Reign. Karen Harper. (Orig.). 1983. pap. 3.95 (ISBN 0-8217-1177-6). Zebra.

Passion's Slave. Kay McMahon. 1983. pap. 3.50. Zebra.

Passion's Splendor. Carla Simpson. 496p. 1987. pap. 3.95 (ISBN 0-8217-2090-2). Zebra.

Passion's Storm. Betina M. Krahn. 1985. pap. 3.75 (ISBN 0-8217-1609-3). Zebra.

Passion's Surrender. Kimberly Norton. (Orig.). 1983. pap. 1.95 (ISBN 0-317-02740-9, BH214). Holloway.

Passion's Tempest. Nicole Duval. (Orig.). 1982. pap. 3.95 (ISBN 0-8217-1426-0). Zebra.

Passion's Thief. Louise MacKendrick. 1978. pap. 1.95 (ISBN 0-8439-0573-5, Leisure Bks). Leisure NY.

Passion's Torment. Victoria Pade. (Avon Romance Ser.). 432p. 1985. pap. 2.95 (ISBN 0-380-89681-8). Avon.

Passion's Treasure. Marsha Gibson. 352p. (Orig.). 1982. pap. 3.25 (ISBN 0-505-51805-8, Pub. by Tower Bks). Leisure NY.

Passion's Triumph. Mary R. Daheim. 432p. 1988. pap. 3.95 (ISBN 0-380-89850-0). Avon.

Passion's Triumph. Erica Hollis. (Superromances Ser.). 384p. 1982. pap. 2.50 (ISBN 0-373-70037-7, Pub. by Worldwide). Harlequin Bks.

Passion's Triumph. Patricia Tito. 1985. pap. 3.95 (ISBN 0-8217-1628-X). Zebra.

Passion's Vixen. Carol Finch. 480p. 1984. pap. 3.75 (ISBN 0-8217-1402-3). Zebra.

Passion's Web. Cassie Edwards. pap. 3.50 (ISBN 0-8217-1358-2). Zebra.

Passions Wild & Free. Janelle Taylor. 512p. 1988. pap. 3.95 (ISBN 0-8217-2478-9). Zebra.

Passive: A Comparative Linguistic Analysis. Anna Siewierska. LC 84-15606. 224p. 1984. 31.00 (ISBN 0-7099-3318-5, Pub. by Croom Helm Ltd). Routledge Chapman & Hall.

Passive-Aggressiveness: Theory & Practice. Ed. by Richard D. Parsons & Robert J. Wicks. LC 83-15383. 270p. 1983. 30.00 (ISBN 0-87630-344-0). Brunner-Mazel.

Passive & Active Filters: Theory & Implementations. Wai-Kai Chen. LC 85-9497. 504p. 1986. write for info. (ISBN 0-471-82352-X). Wiley.

Passive & Active Microwave Circuits. Joseph Helszajn. LC 78-5787. 274p. 1978. 49.95x (ISBN 0-471-04292-7, Pub. by Wiley-Interscience). Wiley.

Passive & Active Microwave Circuits. Joseph Helszajn. LC 78-5787. pap. 70.30 (ISBN 0-317-55585-5, 2056340). Bks Demand UMI.

Passive & Active Network Analysis & Synthesis. Aram Budak. 600p. 1974. text ed. 53.96 (ISBN 0-395-17203-9). HM.

Passive & Active Solar Heating Technology. Michael Meltzer. (Illus.). 448p. 1985. pap. text ed. 42.67 (ISBN 0-13-653114-8). P-H.

Passive & Low Energy Alternatives I: The First International PLEA Conference, Bermuda, September 13-15, 1982. Ed. by A. Bowen & R. Vagner. (Illus.). 475p. 1982. 120.00 (ISBN 0-08-029405-7). Pergamon.

Passive & Low Energy Architecture: Proceedings of the International Conference, 28 June-3 July 1983, Crete, Greece. Ed. by S. Yannas. 835p. 1983. 215.00 (ISBN 0-08-030581-4). Pergamon.

Passive & Low Energy Ecotechniques: Proceedings of the Third International PLEA Conference, Mexico City, Mexico, 6-11 August 1984. Ed. by A. Bowen. (Illus.). 1140p. 1985. 240.00 (ISBN 0-08-031644-1). Pergamon.

Passive & Voice. Ed. by Masayoshi Shibatani. (Typological Studies in Language: Vol. 16). 550p. 1988. 110.00 (ISBN 1-55619-018-2); pap. 39.00x (ISBN 1-55619-019-0). Benjamins North Am.

Passive Annual Heat Storage: Improving the Design of Earth Shelters. John N. Hait. LC 85-60066. (Illus.). 152p. (Orig.). 1983. 35.00 (ISBN 0-915207-01-X); pap. 14.95 (ISBN 0-915207-00-1). Rocky Mtn Res.

Passive Circuit Design. Vincent F. Leonard, Jr. (Engineering Design Ser.). (Illus.). 583p. 1983. pap. text ed. 17.95 (ISBN 0-87119-020-6); 9.95 (ISBN 0-87119-022-2); lab manual 10.95 (ISBN 0-87119-021-4); looseleaf with experimental pts. 49.95 (ISBN 0-87119-019-2, EE-1001). Heathkit-Zenith Ed.

Passive Cooling. Arthur Bowen et al. 1200p. 1982. pap. text ed. 150.00x (ISBN 0-89553-033-3). Am Solar Energy.

Passive Design. Anthony Tzamtzis. (Solstice: Building & Living in a Warm, Humid Climate Ser.). 43p. (Orig.). 1986. pap. 4.95 (ISBN 0-936487-00-3). Miami Dade Environ.

Passive Eighty-One: Proceedings of the National Passive Solar Conference, 6th, Portland, Oregon, 1981. National Passive Solar Conference. Ed. by John Hayes & William Kolar. LC 81-12741. 1982. pap. text ed. 150.00x (ISBN 0-89553-032-5). Am Solar Energy.

Past & Present. Thomas Carlyle. Ed. by Richard D. Altick. LC 77-70381. (Gotham Library). 294p. 1977. pap. 13.50x (ISBN 0-8147-0562-6). NYU Pr.
Past & Present. Thomas Carlyle & Edwin Mims. 363p. 1981. Repr. of 1918 ed. lib. bdg. 20.00 (ISBN 0-8495-8770-0). Arden Lib.
Past & Present. rev. ed. Lawrence Stone. 448p. 1987. lib. bdg. 49.95x (ISBN 0-7102-1253-4, Pub. by Routledge UK); pap. 16.95x (ISBN 0-7102-1193-7, Pub. by Routledge UK). Routledge Chapman & Hall.
Past & Present Condition, & the Destiny of the Colored Race. facs. ed. Henry H. Garnet. LC 77-79010. (Black Heritage Library Collection Ser). 1848. 9.00 (ISBN 0-8369-8576-1). Ayer Co Pubs.
Past & Present in Art & Taste. Francis Haskell. LC 86-24581. 264p. 1987. 37.50x (ISBN 0-300-03607-8). Yale U Pr.
Past & Present of Japanese Commerce. Yetaro Kinosita. LC 68-56663. (Columbia University. Studies in the Social Sciences: No. 41). Repr. of 1902 ed. 16.50 (ISBN 0-404-51041-8). AMS Pr.
Past & Present of Solomon Sorge. Judith Barnard. 1986. 5.95 (ISBN 0-671-61832-6). WSP.
Past & Present of Solomon Sorge. Judith Barnard. pap. 5.95 (ISBN 0-317-56808-6). PB.
Past & Present Vegetation of the Far Northwest Canada. J. C. Ritchie. 272p. 1984. 35.00x (ISBN 0-8020-2523-4). U of Toronto Pr.
Past & Repast. Betty F. Marsh. (Illus.). 88p. (Orig.). 1981. pap. 5.95 (ISBN 0-933992-16-5). Coffee Break.
Past & the Future. Alan Bullock. 48p. (Orig.). 1982. pap. text ed. 5.00 (ISBN 0-8191-5871-2, Pub. by Aspen Inst for Humanistic Studies). U Pr of Amer.
Past & the Present. Lawrence Stone. 288p. 1981. 21.95x (ISBN 0-7100-0628-4). Routledge Chapman & Hall.
Past & the Present of Political Economy. Richard T. Ely. LC 78-63743. (Johns Hopkins University. Studies in the Social Sciences. Second Ser. 1884: 3). Repr. of 1884 ed. 11.50 (ISBN 0-404-61013-7). AMS Pr.
Past & the Present of the Pike's Peak Gold Regions. Henry Villard. LC 76-87629. (American Scene Ser). (Illus.). 186p. 1972. Repr. of 1932 ed. lib. bdg. 25.00 (ISBN 0-306-71804-9). Da Capo.
Past As Prelude: New Orleans 1718-1968. Intro. by Hodding Carter. LC 68-25161. (Illus.). 1968. 10.00 (ISBN 0-911116-02-8). Pelican.
Past As Prologue I: The Underestimation of Price Increases in the Decontrol Debate: A Comparison of Oil & Natural Gas. 59p. 1982. stapled cover 10.00 (ISBN 0-318-13799-2); incl. appendix 15.00 (ISBN 0-318-13800-X). Consumer Energy Coun.
Past As Prologue II: The Economic Effects of Rising Energy Prices: A Comparison of the Oil Price Shock & Natural Gas Decontrol. 81p. 1982. stapled cover 20.00 (ISBN 0-318-13801-8). Consumer Energy Coun.
Past As Prologue: Sources & Studies in European Civilization, 2 vols. Ed. by Everett U. Crosby & Charles R. Webb, Jr. LC 70-166559. (Illus.). 1973. Vol. 1. pap. text ed. 9.95x (ISBN 0-89197-331-1); Vol. 2. pap. text ed. 9.95x (ISBN 0-89197-332-X). Set. Irvington.
Past at Present. 4th ed. Edwards E. Fish. (Illus.). 201p. 1981. 13.95 (ISBN 0-318-00996-X). H U Fish.
Past Before Us: Contemporary Historical Writing in the United States. Ed. by Michael Kammen. LC 79-25785. (Paperback Ser.). 524p. 1982. pap. 12.95x (ISBN 0-8014-9231-9). Cornell U Pr.
Past Caring. Robert Goddard. 512p. 1987. 19.95 (ISBN 0-312-00173-8). St Martin.
Past Caring. Robert Goddard. 544p. 1988. pap. 4.95 (ISBN 0-14-010600-6). Penguin.
Past Climate of Arroyo Hondo, New Mexico, Reconstructed from Tree Rings. Martin R. Rose et al. LC 80-21834. (Arroyo Hondo Archaeological Ser.: Vol. 4). (Illus.). 138p. (Orig.). 1981. pap. 10.00 (ISBN 0-933452-05-5). Schol Am Res.
Past Climates: Tree Thermometers, Commodities, & People. Leona M. Libby. (Illus.). 157p. 1983. text ed. 25.00x (ISBN 0-292-73019-5). U of Tex Pr.
Past Continuous. Yaakov Shabtai. Tr. by Dalya Bilu from Hebrew. 389p. 1985. 16.95 (ISBN 0-8276-0239-1). JPS Phila.
Past Continuous. Yaakov Shabtai. LC 88-42651. 400p. 1989. pap. 11.95 (ISBN 0-8052-0868-2). Schocken.
Past Decade in Particle Theory. Ed. by E. C. Sudarshan & Y. Ne'Eman. LC 71-181810. 832p. 1973. 195.00 (ISBN 0-677-12010-9). Gordon & Breach.
Past Due: How to Collect Money. Norman King. 174p. 19.95x (ISBN 0-87196-140-7). Facts on File.
Past Eight O'Clock. Joan Aiken. (Illus.). (gr. 2-6). 1987. 14.95 (ISBN 0-670-81636-1, Viking Kestrel). Viking.
Past Has Another Pattern: Memoirs. George W. Ball. (Illus.). 540p. 1983. pap. 9.95 (ISBN 0-393-30142-7). Norton.
Past Imperative: A Collection of Poems 1953-1964. Monika Varma. 47p. 1974. 10.00 (ISBN 0-88253-423-8). Ind-US Inc.
Past Imperfect. Joan Collins. 336p. 1985. pap. 3.95 (ISBN 0-425-07786-1). Berkley Pub.
Past Imperfect: An Autobiography. Joan Collins. LC 84-1263. 336p. 1984. 16.95 (ISBN 0-671-47360-3). S&S.
'Past' in Medieval & Modern Greek Culture. Ed. by S. Vryonis, Jr. LC 78-18624. (Byzantina kai Metabyzantina Ser.: Vol. 1). (Illus.). vii, 288p. 1978. 37.00x; pap. 27.00x (ISBN 0-89003-027-8). Undena Pubns.
Past in Pictures: A Further Collection of Photographs of the London Borough of Sutton over the Last Century. J. Broughton. 20.00x (ISBN 0-907335-03-9, Pub. by Sutton Lib & Arts). State Mutual Bk.
Past in the Present: A Thematic Study of Modern Southern Fiction. Thomas D. Young. LC 80-24074. (Southern Literary Studies). 176p. 1981. 22.50 (ISBN 0-8071-0768-9). La State U Pr.
Past in the Present: Essays on Vardis Fisher's Testament of Man. Lester Strong. 1979. lib. bdg. 69.95 (ISBN 0-87700-266-5). Revisionist Pr.
Past in the Present: History, Ecology, & Cultural Variation in Highland Madagascar. Conrad P. Kottak. (Illus.). 406p. 1980. 18.95x (ISBN 0-472-09323-1); pap. 11.95x (ISBN 0-472-06323-5). U of Mich Pr.
Past in the Present: What Is Civilisation? Arthur Mitchell. LC 77-86453. Repr. of 1880 ed. 28.00 (ISBN 0-404-16674-1). AMS Pr.
Past Is a Foreign Country. David Lowenthal. LC 85-10990. (Illus.). 516p. 1986. 29.95 (ISBN 0-521-22415-2). Cambridge U Pr.
Past is a Foreign Country. David Lowenthal. (Illus.). 489p. 1988. pap. 13.95 (ISBN 0-521-29480-0). Cambridge U Pr.
Past Is Another Country. Peter Wludyka. 448p. 1988. 18.95 (ISBN 0-671-65253-2). S&S.
Past Is Another Country: Representation, Historical Consciousness & Resistance in the Blue Ridge. Stephen W. Foster. 288p. 1988. 25.00 (ISBN 0-520-06251-5). U of Cal Pr.
Past Is Human: Ancient Mysteries Explained. Peter White. LC 75-21680. (Illus.). 165p. 1976. 9.95 (ISBN 0-8008-6265-1); pap. 4.95 (ISBN 0-8008-6266-X). Taplinger.
Past Life Therapy in Action. Dick Sutphen & Lauren L. Taylor. 100p. 1983. pap. 2.95 (ISBN 0-911842-32-2). Valley Sun.
Past Life Visions: A Christian Exploration. William DeArteaga. 256p. 1983. pap. 9.95 (ISBN 0-8164-2414-4, HarpR). Har-Row.
Past Lives & Present Problems. Manly P. Hall. pap. 2.50 (ISBN 0-89314-339-1). Philos Res.
Past Lives, Dreams & Visions. Dan Smith. 240p. 1988. pap. 7.95 (ISBN 0-935097-11-2). Unarius Pubns.
Past Lives Future Growth. Ann Druffel & Armand Marcotte. (Inner Visions Ser.). (Orig.). 1987. pap. 12.95 (ISBN 0-917086-88-0). A C S Pubns Inc.
Past Lives, Future Lives. Bruce Goldberg. 1988. pap. 3.95. Ballantine.
Past Lives, Future Lives: Accounts of Regression & Progression Through Hypnosis. Bruce Goldberg. LC 83-8748. 186p. 1983. lib. bdg. 19.95x (ISBN 0-89370-659-0). Borgo Pr.
Past Lives, Future Lives: Accounts of Regression & Progression Through Hypnosis. Bruce Goldberg. 1982. pap. 7.95 (ISBN 0-87877-059-3). Newcastle Pub.
Past Lives, Future Loves. Dick Sutphen. 1982. pap. 3.50 (ISBN 0-671-54363-6). PB.
Past Lives, Present Relationships: How Karma Affects You & Your Relationships. John Van Auken. (Illus.). 144p. 1985. pap. 8.95 (ISBN 0-917483-01-4). Innervision.
Past Lives: The Key to Your Present Relationships: Introducing the Youngs' Past Life Regression Technique. Robert Young & Loy Young. Ed. by Mignonette Pellegrin. LC 85-73214. (Illus.). 344p. (Orig.). 1985. pap. 19.95 (ISBN 0-936121-00-9). Draco Prod Pubns.
Past Master. R. A. Lafferty. 256p. 1982. pap. 2.50 (ISBN 0-441-65303-0). Ace Bks.
Past Masters, & Other Papers. facs. ed. Thomas Mann. Tr. by Helen T. Lowe-Porter. LC 68-25605. (Essay Index Reprint Ser). 1933. 15.20 (ISBN 0-8369-0674-8). Ayer Co Pubs.
Past Meets Present: Essays about Historic Interpretation & Public Audiences. Ed. by Jo Blatti. LC 86-43066. (Illus.). 192p. 1987. 19.95x (ISBN 0-87474-272-2); pap. 11.95x (ISBN 0-87474-233-1). Smithsonian.
Past Meets the Present: Essays on Oral History. Ed. by David Stricklin & Rebecca Sharpless. 164p. (Orig.). 1988. lib. bdg. 23.25 (ISBN 0-8191-6770-3); pap. text ed. 11.50 (ISBN 0-8191-6771-1). U Pr of Amer.
Past or Future Crimes: Deservedness & Dangerousness in the Sentencing of Criminals. VonHirsch. 220p. 1987. pap. 14.00 (ISBN 0-8135-1262-X). Rutgers U Pr.
Past or Future Crimes: Deservedness & Dangerousness in the Sentencing of Criminals. Andrew Von Hirsch. LC 84-29834. (Crime, Law, & Deviance Ser.). 250p. 1985. text ed. 27.50 (ISBN 0-8135-1115-1). Rutgers U Pr.
Past Perfect. (Sweet Dreams Ser.: No. 131). 192p. (Orig.). (YA) (gr. 7-12). 1987. pap. 2.50 (ISBN 0-553-26789-2). Bantam.
Past Perfect. Yaakov Shabtai. Tr. by Dalya Bilu. LC 86-40493. 1987. 18.95 (ISBN 0-670-81308-7). Viking.
Past Perspectives: Studies in Greek & Roman Historical Writing. Ed. by I. S. Moxon et al. 240p. 1986. 42.50 (ISBN 0-521-26625-4). Cambridge U Pr.
Past, Present & Future. Isaac Asimov. LC 87-2243. 374p. 1987. 19.95 (ISBN 0-87975-393-5). Prometheus Bks.
Past, Present & Future. Arthur N. Prior. 1967. 39.95x (ISBN 0-19-824311-1). Oxford U Pr.
Past, Present, & Future: A Reading-Writing Text. 2nd ed. Joan Y. Gregg & Joan Russell. 359p. 1987. pap. text ed. write for info. (ISBN 0-534-07908-3). Wadsworth Pub.
Past, Present, & Future in Prose & Poetry. B. Clark. LC 72-947. Repr. of 1867 ed. 16.25 (ISBN 0-404-00015-0). AMS Pr.
Past, Present & Future of Automotive Elastomer Applications. 48p. 1980. Seven papers. 20.00 (ISBN 0-89883-235-7, SP464). Soc Auto Engineers.
Past, Present, & Future of Biblical Theology. James D. Smart. LC 79-16943. 162p. 1979. softcover 8.95 (ISBN 0-664-24284-7). Westminster John Knox.
Past, Present, & Future of Biomedical Information. (DHHS Publication Ser.: No. NIH 88-2911). 112p. 1987. 12.00 (S/N 017-040-00506-7). USGPO.
Past, Present & Future of the Church. Fred Pruitt. 72p. pap. 0.60 (ISBN 0-686-29133-6). Faith Pub Hse.
Past, Present, & Personal: The Family & the Life Course in American History. John Demos. 288p. 1986. 19.95 (ISBN 0-19-503777-4). Oxford U Pr.
Past, Present, & Personal: The Family & the Life Course in American History. John P. Demos. 240p. 1988. pap. 8.95 (ISBN 0-19-504766-4). Oxford U Pr.
Past, Present, East & West. Sherman E. Lee. 223p. 1983. 140.00x (Pub. by Han-Shan Tang Ltd). State Mutual Bk.
Past Recaptured. Marcel Proust. Tr. by Andreas Mayor. Date Not Set. pap. 5.95 (ISBN 0-394-50649-9). Random.
Past Recaptured: Great Historians & the History of History. M. A. Fitzsimons. LC 83-1168. 239p. 1986. pap. 9.95 (ISBN 0-268-01566-X). U of Notre Dame Pr.
Past Recovered. Glenn A. May. 267p. (Orig.). 1987. pap. 11.75x (ISBN 971-10-0260-4, Pub. by New Day Philippines). Cellar.
Past Remembering. Vera K. Fish. 64p. 1984. 15.00x (ISBN 0-7212-0695-6, Pub. by Regency Pr). State Mutual Bk.
Past Ruined Ilion... A Bibliography of English & American Literature Based on Greco-Roman Mythology. Jeanetta Boswell. LC 82-5541. 333p. 1982. text ed. 25.00 (ISBN 0-8108-1549-4). Scarecrow.
Past Speaks: Sources & Problems in British History since 1688. Ed. by Walter Arnstein. 448p. 1981. pap. text ed. 11.50 (ISBN 0-669-02919-X). Heath.
Past Tense. Isobel Lambot. (Lythway Ser.). 216p. 1988. lib. bdg. 18.50 (ISBN 0-7451-0649-8, Pub. by Chivers Pr UK). G K Hall.
Past Tense of God's Word. Kenneth Hagin, Jr. 1980. pap. 0.50 mini bk. (ISBN 0-89276-706-5). Hagin Ministries.
Past Tense: The Cocteau Diaries, Vol. II. Jean Cocteau. Tr. by Richard Howard. (Illus.). 352p. 1988. 24.95 (ISBN 0-15-171291-3). HarBraceJ.
Past Tense: The Cocteau Diaries, Vol. 1. Jean Cocteau. Tr. by Richard Howard. (Illus.). 352p. 1987. 24.95 (ISBN 0-15-171289-1). HarBraceJ.
Past Tense: The Cocteau Diaries, Vol. 1. Jean Cocteau. Tr. by Richard Howard. (Illus.). 352p. 1988. pap. 7.95 (ISBN 0-15-671360-8). HarBraceJ.
Past That Poets Make. Harold Toliver. LC 80-18825. 304p. 1981. text ed. 29.50x (ISBN 0-674-65676-8). Harvard U Pr.
Past the Conemaugh Yards: Selected Poems, 1975-1985. Kathleen M. Sewalk. (Illus.). 1987. 18.95 (ISBN 0-941461-00-9); pap. 9.95 (ISBN 0-941461-01-7). Tunnel Pr.
Past, the Present, & the Future. Henry C. Carey. LC 67-18573. 1967. Repr. of 1847 ed. 45.00x (ISBN 0-678-00245-2). Kelley.
Past Three Million Years: Evolution of Climatic Variability in the North Atlantic Region. Compiled by N. J. Shackleton et al. 278p. 1988. Repr. of 1988 ed. text ed. 145.00x (ISBN 0-85403-348-3, Pub. by Royal Soc London). Scholium Intl.
Past Through Tomorrow. Robert A. Heinlein. 1988. pap. 4.95 (ISBN 0-441-65304-9). Ace Bks.
Past Times. Poul Anderson. 288p. (Orig.). 1987. pap. 2.95 (ISBN 0-8125-3081-0, Dist. by Warner Pub Services & Saint Martin's Press). Tor Bks.
Past Titan Rock: Journeys into an Appalachian Valley. Ellesa C. High. LC 83-23387. 192p. 1984. 16.00x (ISBN 0-8131-1505-1). U Pr of KY.
Past Today: Historic Places in New Zealand. Ed. by John Wilson. (Illus.). 183p. 1987. 39.95 (ISBN 0-86479-001-5, Pub. by Pacific Pubs New Zealand). Intl Spec Bk.
Past Trials & Present Tribulations: A Muslim Fundamentalist's View of the Jews. Ronald L. Nettler. LC 87-9313. (SIAS Ser.). 100p. 1987. text ed. 20.95 (ISBN 0-08-034791-6, PBL). Pergamon.
Past We Share: The Near Eastern Ancestry of Western Folk Literature. E. L. Ranelagh. (Illus.). 288p. 1981. 21.95 (ISBN 0-7043-2234-X, Pub. by Quartet England). Charles River Bks.
Past Worlds. Date not set. price not set. Hammond Inc.
Pasta. Better Homes & Gardens Editors. (Great Cooking Made Easy Ser.). 1987. 9.95 (ISBN 0-696-02198-6). BH&G.
Pasta. Time-Life Books Editors. (Good Cook Ser.). (Illus.). 176p. 1981. 16.95 (ISBN 0-8094-2891-1). Time-Life.
Pasta al Dente: Recipes from All the Regions of Italy. Alberta Nocentini. LC 86-22268. 1989. 24.95 (ISBN 0-87949-264-3). Ashley Bks.
Pasta & Cheese: The Cookbook. Henry A. Lambert. (Illus.). 213p. (Orig.). 1985. pap. 15.45. PB.
Pasta & Cheese: The Cookbook. Henry A. Lambert & James Wagenvoord. pap. 9.95 (ISBN 0-671-62778-3). PB.
Pasta & Co., the Cookbook. Pasta & Co. Staff. Ed. by Marcella Rosene. 223p. (Orig.). 1987. pap. 10.95. Pasta & Co Inc.
Pasta & Extrusion Cooked Foods: Some Technological & Nutritional Aspects. Ed. by C. Mercier & C. Cantarelli. 212p. 1986. 48.75 (ISBN 0-85334-417-5, Pub. by Elsevier Applied Sci England). Elsevier.
Pasta & Other Special Salads. Ceil Dyer. 1987. pap. 7.95 (ISBN 0-671-50880-6, Fireside). S&S.
Pasta & Pizza. Bon Appetit Magazine Editors. LC 85-9829. (Cooking with Bon Appetit Ser.). (Illus.). 144p. 1985. 12.95 (ISBN 0-89535-167-6). Knapp Pr.
Pasta & Rice Italian Style. Efrem F. Calingaert & Jacquelyn D. Serwer. 1987. pap. 3.95 (ISBN 0-451-14941-6, Plume). NAL.
Pasta Book: All You Need to Know about Pasta plus 150 of the Best Recipes from Italy. Luigi Veronelli. 188p. 1985. 16.95 (ISBN 0-312-59796-7). St Martin.
Pasta Classica: The Art of Italian Pasta Cooking. Julia Della Croce. LC 87-13515. (Illus.). 160p. 1987. 25.00 (ISBN 0-87701-414-0). Chronicle Bks.
Pasta Cook Book. Sunset Editors. LC 79-90338. (Illus.). 96p. 1980. pap. 5.95 (ISBN 0-376-02522-0, Sunset Bks). Sunset-Lane.
Pasta Cookbook. San Giorgio & Skinner Hersey. (Illus.). 64p. (Orig.). 1983. pap. 3.95 (ISBN 0-8249-3019-3). Ideals.
Pasta Cookery. Sophie Kay. 1981. pap. 2.95 (ISBN 0-440-17034-6). Dell.
Pasta Cookery. Sophie Kay. LC 79-67183. (Illus.). 1979. pap. 8.95 (ISBN 0-89586-030-9). Price Stern.
Pasta! Cooking It, Loving It. Carlo Middione. Ed. by Richard Atcheson. LC 81-70442. (Great American Cooking Schools Ser.). (Illus.). 84p. 1982. pap. 5.95 (ISBN 0-941034-12-7). I Chalmers.
Pasta! Cooking It, Loving It. Carlo Middione. LC 82-47861. (Great American Cooking Schools Ser.). (Illus.). 84p. 1982. 8.95 (ISBN 0-06-015068-8, HarpT). Har-Row.
Pasta Diet. Elisa Celli. 272p. 1985. pap. 3.95 (ISBN 0-446-32862-6). Warner Bks.
Pasta Fantasia. Janice Giampa. (Illus.). 128p. 1983. pap. 9.95 (ISBN 0-933614-22-5). Peregrine Pr Pubs.
Pasta Fresca: An Exuberant Collection of Fresh, Vivid & Uncomplicated Pasta Recipes from the Authors of Cucina Fresca. Viana La Place & Evan Kleiman. Ed. by Ann Bramson. (Illus.). 224p. 1988. 19.95 (ISBN 0-688-07763-3). Morrow.
Pasta Lover's Diet Book. June Roth. LC 83-15571. 151p. 1984. pap. 8.95 (ISBN 0-672-52803-7). Bobbs.
Pasta Market. 245p. 1986. 595.00 (ISBN 0-318-00493-3). Busn Trend.
Pasta Menus. LC 83-5107. (Great Meals in Minutes Ser.). (gr. 7 up). 1983. lib. bdg. 18.60 (ISBN 0-86706-155-3, Pub. by Time-Life). Silver.
Pasta Palace Cookbook. B. A. Emanuele. Ed. by Anthony J. Cusmano. (Orig.). 1987. pap. 5.95 (ISBN 0-943214-15-7). Media Pubns.
Pasta Palace Cookbook. 5.95 (ISBN 0-317-61577-7). Media Pubns.
Pasta Perfect. Anna Del Conte. LC 86-16546. (Illus.). 80p. 1987. pap. 9.95 (ISBN 0-385-23813-4). Doubleday.
Pasta, Please. Ed. by Annette Gohlke. LC 82-50005. 68p. 1982. pap. 3.95 (ISBN 0-89821-042-9). Reiman Assocs.
Pasta Presto: One Hundred Fast & Fabulous Pasta Sauces. Norman Kolpas. 128p. (Orig.). 1988. pap. 7.95 (ISBN 0-8092-4676-7). Contemp Bks.
Pasta Salad Book. Nina Graybill & Maxine Rapoport. LC 84-81333. (Illus.). 180p. (Orig.). 1984. pap. 9.95 (ISBN 0-918535-00-X). Farragut Pub.
Pasta Salads! Susan J. Meyer. LC 86-4215. (Specialty Cookbook Ser.). (Illus.). 146p. (Orig.). 1986. 17.95 (ISBN 0-89594-191-0); pap. 7.95 (ISBN 0-89594-190-2). Crossing Pr.
Pasta Tecnica. Pasquale Bruno, Jr. (Illus.). 128p. 1982. pap. 10.95 (ISBN 0-8092-5894-3). Contemp Bks.
Pastability. Lizzie Spender. (Cookbook Ser.). (Illus.). 153p. 1988. pap. 8.50 (ISBN 0-88001-201-3). Ecco Pr.
Paste see **Author of Beltraffio.**

Pastoral Epistles. (Erdmans Commentaries Ser.). pap. 3.95 (ISBN 0-8010-3403-5). Baker Bk.

Pastoral Epistles. Geoffrey B. Wilson. 173p. 1982. pap. 5.45 (ISBN 0-85151-335-2). Banner of Truth.

Pastoral Epistles see Practical Truth Series.

Pastoral Epistles see Word Studies in the Greek New Testament, for the English Reader.

Pastoral Epistles: Critical & Exegetical Commentary. Walter Lock. Ed. by Samuel R. Driver et al. (International Critical Commentary Ser.). 212p. 1928. 29.95 (ISBN 0-567-05033-5, Pub. by T & T Clark Ltd UK). Fortress.

Pastoral Epistles: Introduction & Commentary. Irving A. Sparks. LC 85-10925. (Orig.). 1985. pap. 6.00 (ISBN 0-942587-01-4). Papyrus Bks.

Pastoral Epistles: Timothy & Titus. J. H. Bernard. (Thornapple Commentaries Ser.). 272p. 1980. pap. 6.95 (ISBN 0-8010-0797-6). Baker Bk.

Pastoral Ethics: Professional Responsibilities of the Clergy. Gaylord Noyce. 208p. 1988. pap. 11.95 (ISBN 0-687-30338-9). Abingdon.

Pastoral Evangelism. Samuel Southard. LC 80-82196. 192p. 1981. pap. 4.50 (ISBN 0-8042-2037-9, John Knox). Westminster John Knox.

Pastoral Formation & Pastoral Field Edcation in the Catholic Seminary. 84p. 1985. pap. 4.95 (ISBN 1-55586-936-X). US Catholic.

Pastoral Health Care: Understanding the Church's Healing Ministers. Robert Patterson. LC 83-1948. 30p. 1983. pap. 1.00 (ISBN 0-87125-080-2). Cath Health.

Pastoral Jazz. Olga Broumas. 80p. (Orig.). 1983. pap. 7.00 (ISBN 0-914742-70-1). Copper Canyon.

Pastoral Letters. Ed. by Anthony T. Hanson. (Cambridge Bible Commentary on the New English Bible, New Testament Ser.). (Orig.). 1966. o. p. 17.95 (ISBN 0-521-04214-3); pap. 7.50x (ISBN 0-521-09380-5, 380). Cambridge U Pr.

Pastoral Letters of the United States Catholic Bishops: 1792-1983, 4 vols. Ed. by Hugh J. Nolan. 1890p. 1984. pap. 95.00 (ISBN 1-55586-897-5). US Catholic.

Pastoral Letters of the United States Catholic Bishops, 1975-1983, Vol. IV. Ed. by Hugh J. Nolan. 616p. 1984. pap. 24.95 (ISBN 1-55586-875-4). US Catholic.

Pastoral Letters of the United States Catholic Bishops, 1962-1974, Vol. III. Ed. by Hugh J. Nolan. 511p. 1984. pap. 24.95 (ISBN 1-55586-870-3). US Catholic.

Pastoral Letters of the United States Catholic Bishops, 1941-1961, Vol. II. Ed. by Hugh J. Nolan. 271p. 1984. pap. 24.95 (ISBN 1-55586-885-1). US Catholic.

Pastoral Letters of the United States Catholic Bishops, 1792-1940, Vol. I. Ed. by Hugh J. Nolan. 487p. 1984. pap. 24.95 (ISBN 1-55586-880-0). US Catholic.

Pastoral Life in the Power of the Spirit. Johannes Hofinger. LC 81-1439. (Illus.). 215p. 1982. pap. 6.95 (ISBN 0-8189-0427-5). Alba.

Pastoral Man in the Garden of Eden: The Maasai of the Ngorongoro Conservation Area, Tanzania. Kaj Ahrem. (Illus.). 124p. 1985. pap. text ed. 30.00x (ISBN 91-7106-232-7, Pub. by Almqvist & Wiksell). Coronet Bks.

Pastoral Marital Therapy: A Practical Primer for Ministry to Couples (Integration Book) Stephen Treat & Larry Hof. 144p. 1987. pap. 7.95 (ISBN 0-8091-2889-6). Paulist Pr.

Pastoral Medicine. Rudolf Steiner. Tr. by Gladys Hahn from Ger. 1987. 30.00 (ISBN 0-88010-250-0); pap. 20.00 (ISBN 0-88010-253-5). Anthroposophic.

Pastoral: Medieval into Renaissance. Helen Cooper. (Illus.). 279p. 1976. 41.00 (ISBN 0-85991-022-9, Pub. by Boydell & Brewer). Longwood Pub Group.

Pastoral Ministry in the AIDS Era: Focus on Families & Friends of Persons with AIDS. Louis F. Kavar. LC 88-50082. 64p. (Orig.). 1988. pap. 7.95 (ISBN 0-934104-07-7). Woodland.

Pastoral Ministry with Disabled Persons. Walter Kern. LC 84-24619. 248p. 1985. pap. 6.95 (ISBN 0-8189-0472-0). Alba.

Pastoral Mission of the Church. Ed. by Karl Rahner. LC 76-57341. (Concilium Ser.: Vol. 3). 192p. 7.95 (ISBN 0-8091-0108-4). Paulist Pr.

Pastoral Music in Practice. Funk. 1981. 5.95 (ISBN 0-9602378-3-6). Pastoral Pr.

Pastoral Nature of Healing. Wright. Date not set. 6.95 (Pub. by SCM Pr England). Fortress.

Pastoral Nature of the Ministry. Wright. Date not set. 7.50 (Pub. by SCM Pr England). Fortress.

Pastoral Novel: Studies in George Eliot, Thomas Hardy, & D. H. Lawrence. Michael Squires. LC 74-75793. pap. 60.00 (ISBN 0-317-28793-1, 2020639). Bks Demand UMI.

Pastoral Partners: Affinity & Bond Partnership among the Dassanetch of South-West Ethiopia. Uri Almagor. LC 78-4128. 258p. 1978. 49.50 (ISBN 0-8419-0384-0, Africana). Holmes & Meier.

Pastoral Pointers: Contribution by Thirteen Church of God Ministers. 1976. pap. 2.95 (ISBN 0-87148-686-5). Pathway Pr.

Pastoral Practice & the Paranormal. Bonaventure Kloppenburg. Tr. by David Smith from Span. 1979. 8.95 (ISBN 0-8199-0762-6). Franciscan Herald.

Pastoral Preaching: Timeless Truth for Changing Needs. Gary D. Stratman. 112p. (Orig.). 1983. pap. 8.75 (ISBN 0-687-30139-4). Abingdon.

Pastoral Presence & the Diocesan Priest. Paul T. Keyes. LC 78-22009. 142p. 1978. pap. 4.95 (ISBN 0-89571-004-8). Affirmation.

Pastoral Production & Society. Ed. by Equipe Ecologie et Anthropologie des Societes Pastorales Staff. LC 78-19139. (Illus.). 1979. o. p. 54.50 (ISBN 0-521-22253-2); pap. 18.95x (ISBN 0-521-29416-9). Cambridge U Pr.

Pastoral Psychology & the Gospel. W. H. Peacey. 1985. 10.00x (ISBN 0-317-62217-X, Guild of Pastoral Psych). State Mutual Bk.

Pastoral Psychotherapy: Theory & Practice. Carrol Wise. LC 84-45025. 328p. 1983. 30.00x (ISBN 0-87668-661-7). Aronson.

Pastoral Reflection see Reflexion Pastoral: El Pastor y Su Ministerio.

Pastoral Reform in Church Government. Ed. by Teodoro-J Urresti & Neophytos Edelby. LC 65-28464. (Concilium Ser.: Vol. 8). 192p. 7.95 (ISBN 0-8091-0109-2). Paulist Pr.

Pastoral Role in Caring for the Dying & Bereaved: Pragmatic & Ecumenical. Ed. by Brian P. O'Connor et al. LC 86-545. (Foundation of Thanatology Ser.: Vol. 7). 245p. 1986. lib. bdg. 40.95 (ISBN 0-275-92153-0, C2153). Praeger.

Pastoral Sermons. Ronald Knox. 1960. 12.50 (ISBN 0-8199-0823-1). Franciscan Herald.

Pastoral Societies & Resistance to Change: A Re-evaluation. Nyaga Mwaniki. (Graduate Student Paper Competition Ser.: No. 3). 40p. (Orig.). 1980. pap. text ed. 2.00 (ISBN 0-941934-32-2). Indiana Africa.

Pastoral Spirituality: A Focus for Ministry. Ben C. Johnson. 160p. 1988. pap. 12.95 (ISBN 0-664-25003-3). Westminster John Knox.

Pastoral Statement for Catholics on Biblical Fundamentalism English & Spanish. Tr. by Marina Herrera. National Conference of Catholic Bishops. 32p. (Orig., Eng & Span.). 1987. pap. 1.95 (ISBN 1-55586-161-X). US Catholic.

Pastoral Statement on the Catholic Charismatic Renewal. 48p. 1984. pap. 2.25 (ISBN 1-55586-931-9). US Catholic.

Pastoral Teaching of Paul. Edward W. Chadwick. LC 84-7123. 416p. 1984. 11.95 (ISBN 0-8254-2325-2). Kregel.

Pastoral Theologian of the Year: Seward Hiltner; Special Issue PP 29, No. 1. Liston M. Mills. LC 80-82467. 112p. 1980. pap. 12.95 (ISBN 0-89885-068-1). Human Sci Pr.

Pastoral Theology. Hills. kivar 6.95 (ISBN 0-686-12899-0). Schmul Pub Co.

Pastoral Theology: Essentials of Ministry. Thomas C. Oden. LC 82-47753. 456p. (Orig.). 1983. 16.95 (ISBN 0-06-066353-7, RD 415, HarpR). Har-Row.

Pastoral Vision of John Paul II. Ed. by Joan Bland. 1982. 7.95 (ISBN 0-8199-0839-8). Franciscan Herald.

Pastorale. Ray Buttigieg. 1978. pap. 4.99 (ISBN 0-685-63585-6). Cykx.

Pastorale Dramatique en France a la Fin du Seizieme & Au Commencement du Dix-Septieme Siecle. Jules Marsan. LC 79-159703. (Research & Source Works Ser.: No. 745). (Illus.). 1971. Repr. of 1905 ed. lib. bdg. 32.50 (ISBN 0-8337-4254-X). B Franklin.

Pastorale Stories: Stories. Susan Engberg. LC 82-4730. (Illinois Short Fiction Ser.). 168p. 1982. 11.95 (ISBN 0-252-00993-2); pap. 8.95 (ISBN 0-252-00994-0). U of Ill Pr.

Pastoralism in Crisis: The Desanetch & Their Ethiopian Lands. Claudia J. Carr. LC 77-1252. (Research Papers Ser.: No. 180). (Illus.). 1977. pap. 12.00 (ISBN 0-89065-087-X). U Chicago Comm Geo.

Pastoralism in Tropical Africa: International African Seminar, Niamey, December 1972. Ed. by Theodore Monod. (Illus.). 1975. 49.50x (ISBN 0-19-724196-4). Oxford U Pr.

Pastoralists & the Development of Pastoralism. Johan Helland. (Bergen Studies in Social Anthropology, University of Bergen, Norway: No. 20). 214p. (Orig.). 1985. pap. 10.95x (ISBN 0-936508-58-2, Pub. by Dept Soc Anthropology Norway). Barber Pr.

Pastoralists of the Andes: The Alpaca Herders of Paratia. Jorge A. Flores-Ochoa. Tr. by Ralph Bolton from Span. LC 78-31360. (Illus.). 144p. 1979. text ed. 15.00x (ISBN 0-915980-89-4). ISHI PA.

Pastoralists of the West African Savanna. Ed. by Mahdi Adamu & A. H. Kirk-Green. (International African Institute Seminar Studies). 448p. 1986. 40.00 (ISBN 0-7190-2200-2, Pub. by Manchester Univ Pr). St Martin.

Pastorals of Dorset. facsimile ed. Mary Blundell. LC 73-160931. (Short Story Index Reprint Ser.). (Illus.). Repr. of 1901 ed. 20.00 (ISBN 0-8369-3910-7). Ayer Co Pubs.

Pastores. Tr. by M. R. Cole. (AFS M Ser.). (Illus., Span.). Repr. of 1907 ed. 23.00 (ISBN 0-527-01061-8). Kraus Repr.

Pastores Tambien Lloran. Lucille Lavender. Tr. by Josie H. Smith from Eng. 136p. (Orig.). 1988. pap. 4.95. Casa Bautista.

Pastorial Perspective. Ed. by Margaret Press & Neil Brown. (Faith & Culture Ser.: No. 13). 175p. (Orig.). 1984. pap. 11.95 (ISBN 0-908224-08-7, Pub. by Catholic Inst Sydney). ANZ Religious Pubns.

Pastoring the Renewed. Robert B. Hall. 1982. pap. 4.95 (ISBN 0-686-37068-6). Episcopal Ctr.

Pastoring Youth in a New Generation. Wendell Smith. (Illus.). 132p. 1987. pap. 6.95 (ISBN 0-914936-91-3). Bible Temple.

Pastors & Masters. I. Compton-Burnett. 1952. 16.95 (ISBN 0-575-02705-3, Pub. by Gollancz England). David & Charles.

Pastors & Masters. Ivy Compton-Burnett. 96p. 1984. pap. 5.95 (ISBN 0-8052-8212-2, Pub. by Allison & Busby England). Schocken.

Pastors & People: German & Lutheran Reformed Churches in the Pennsylvania Field, 1717-1793, Vol. II, The History. Charles H. Glatfelter. LC 80-83400. (Penn. German Ser.: Vol. 15). (Illus.). 25.00 (ISBN 0-911122-44-3). Penn German Soc.

Pastors & People: German Lutheran & Reformed Churches in the Pennsylvania Field, 1717-1793. Charles H. Glatfelter. LC 80-83400. (Penn. German Ser.: Vol. 13). (Illus.). 1979. 30.00 (ISBN 0-911122-40-0). Penn German Soc.

Pastors & Pluralism in Wurttemberg, 1918-1933. David J. Diephouse. LC 87-3293. (Illus.). 400p. 1987. text ed. 49.50 (ISBN 0-691-05501-7). Princeton U Pr.

Pastors & Visionaries in Late Medieval Yorkshire. Jonathan Hughes. 320p. 1988. 57.59 (ISBN 0-85115-496-4, Pub. by Boydell & Brewer). Longwood Pub Group.

Pastors Are People Too. Ed. by David B. Biebel & Howard W. Lawrence. LC 86-3835. 205p. (Orig.). 1986. pap. 7.95 (ISBN 0-8307-1102-3, 5418654). Regal.

Pastors' Barracks. Robert Wise. 192p. 1986. pap. 11.95 (ISBN 0-89693-157-9). Victor Bks.

Pastor's Complete Model Letter Book. Stephen R. Clark & Anne Williman. 304p. 1988. 39.95 (ISBN 0-13-653312-4). P-H.

Pastor's Counseling Manual for Ministry to Those Who Must Sustain a Loved One in Crisis. Theodore W. Schroeder. 1981. pap. 2.75 (ISBN 0-570-08250-1, 12YY2922). Concordia.

Pastor's Fire-Side, 2 Vols. Jane Porter. LC 75-162887. (Bentley's Standard Novels: Nos. 18 & 19). Repr. of 1832 ed. Set. 25.00 (ISBN 0-404-54560-2); 13.00 ea. Vol. 1 (ISBN 0-404-54418-5). Vol. 2 (ISBN 0-404-54419-3). AMS Pr.

Pastors Green. John Pellow. 1984. 20.00x (ISBN 0-906549-04-3, Pub. by J Clare Bks). State Mutual Bk.

Pastor's Guidebook: A Manual for Special Occasions. Marion D. Aldridge. 1989. 9.95 (ISBN 0-8054-2318-4). Broadman.

Pastor's Guidebook: A Manual for Worship. Marion D. Aldridge. LC 83-70213. 1984. 10.95 (ISBN 0-8054-2312-5). Broadman.

Pastor's Handbook. C & MA Home Department Board Staff. 102p. 4.45 (ISBN 0-87509-118-0). Chr Pubns.

Pastor's Handbook. Jack Dunigan. (Orig.). 1985. pap. 6.95 (ISBN 0-932943-00-4). Life Lines.

Pastor's Handbook. Richard A. Hufton. 47p. (Orig.). 1984. pap. 3.00 (ISBN 0-933643-05-5). Grace World Outreach.

Pastor's Handbook, Vol. II. Wayne E. Oates. LC 79-28639. (Christian Care Bks.). 120p. 1980. pap. 7.95 (ISBN 0-664-24330-4). Westminster John Knox.

Pastor's Handbook, Vol. 1. Wayne E. Oates. LC 79-28639. (Christian Care Bks.). 120p. 1980. pap. 7.95 (ISBN 0-664-24300-2). Westminster John Knox.

Pastor's Handbook on Interpersonal Relationships. Jard DeVille. 145p. 1986. pap. 8.95 (ISBN 0-8010-2961-9). Baker Bk.

Pastors in Ministry: Guidelines for Seven Critical Issues. Ed. by William E. Hulme et al. LC 85-1213. 192p. (Orig.). 1985. pap. 10.95 (ISBN 0-8066-2159-1, 10-4898). Augsburg.

Pastor's Manual. James R. Hobbs. 1940. 8.95 (ISBN 0-8054-2301-X). Broadman.

Pastor's Primer for Premarital Guidance. Robert L. Hawkins. 1978. pap. 3.95 (ISBN 0-9607764-0-0). R L Hawkins.

Pastor's Problems. Ed. by Cyril S. Rodd. 168p. pap. 8.95 (ISBN 0-567-29117-0, Pub. by T & T Clark Ltd UK, 30-29117-1902). Fortress.

Pastor's Rib & His Flock. Phyllis E. Carter. 69p. 1988. 7.95 (ISBN 0-533-03862-6). Vantage.

Pastor's Wedding & Funeral Record. LC 68-12321. 1968. 11.95 (ISBN 0-8054-2306-0). Broadman.

Pastor's Wedding Manual. Jim Henry. LC 84-17594. 1985. 7.95 (ISBN 0-8054-2313-3). Broadman.

Pastor's Wife. Elizabeth Von Arnim. 496p. 1987. pap. 6.95 (ISBN 0-14-016177-5). Penguin.

Pastor's Wife. Sabina Wurmbrand. 1979. pap. 4.95 (ISBN 0-88264-000-3). Living Sacrifice Bks.

Pastor's Wife Today. Donna M. Sinclair. LC 80-26076. (Creative Leadership Ser.). 128p. (Orig.). 1981. pap. 7.95 (ISBN 0-687-30269-2). Abingdon.

Pastors' Wives Cookbook. Sybil DuBose. Ed. by Janine Buford. (Illus.). 1978. pap. 9.95 (ISBN 0-918544-13-0). Wimmer Bks.

Pastourelle. W. P. Jones. LC 73-3478. 244p. 1973. Repr. of 1931 ed. lib. bdg. 18.50x (ISBN 0-374-94333-8, Octagon). Hippocrene Bks.

Pastry Chef. William J. Sultan. (Illus.). 1983. 34.95 (ISBN 0-87055-422-0). AVI.

Pastrywork & Confectionery Handbook. Douglas Sutherland. (Illus.). 160p. 1985. pap. 16.95 (ISBN 0-7134-4611-0, Pub. by Batsford England). David & Charles.

Pasture & Politics: Economics, Conflict & Ritual among Shahsevan Nomads of Northwestern Iran. Richard Tapper. (Studies in Anthropology). 1979. 68.00 (ISBN 0-12-683660-4). Acad Pr.

Pasture Economy & Meadow Cultivation. I. V. Larin. 648p. 1962. text ed. 130.00x (ISBN 0-7065-0205-1, Pub. by Keter Pub Jerusalem). Coronet Bks.

Pasture for Peterkin. Agnes Sanford. pap. 3.95 (ISBN 0-910924-38-4). Macalester.

Pasture Improvement Research in Eastern & Southern Africa: Proceedings of a Workshop Held in Harare, Zimbabwe, 17-21 September 1984. Ed. by Jackson A. Kategile. (Proceeding Ser.). 508p. 1986. pap. 12.00 (ISBN 0-88936-439-7, IDRC237, IDRC). UNIPUB.

Pasture Management for Horses & Ponies. Gillian McCarthy. (Illus.). 259p. 1987. 19.95 (ISBN 0-87605-865-9). Howell Bk.

Pasture Management for Horses & Ponies. Gillian McCarthy. (Illus.). 263p. 1987. pap. 22.50x (ISBN 0-00-383330-5, Pub. by Collins England). Sheridan.

Pasture Research in Northern Australia: Its History, Achievements & Future Emphasis. A. G. Eyles et al. 222p. 1987. 75.00 (ISBN 0-643-03689-X, CSIRO Australia). State Mutual Bk.

Pastures of Heaven. John Steinbeck. (Fiction Ser.). 240p. 1982. pap. 3.95 (ISBN 0-14-004998-3). Penguin.

Pastures of Heaven. John Steinbeck. LC 83-45886. Repr. of 1932 ed. 21.50 (ISBN 0-404-20244-6, PS3537). AMS Pr.

Pat-a-Cake. Illus. by Pat Paris. (Real Mother Goose Pop-Ups Ser.). (Illus.). 12p. (gr. 2 up). 1985. 5.95 (ISBN 0-528-82603-4). Macmillan.

Pat-a-Cake. (Platt & Munk Peggy Cloth Books). (Illus.). 8p. (ps). 1978. 2.50 (ISBN 0-448-46833-6, G&D). Putnam Pub Group.

Pat Adams Paintings: A Survey 1952-1979. Ruth K. Meyer. (Illus.). 34p. (Orig.). 1980. pap. 10.00x (ISBN 0-917562-11-9). Contemp Arts.

Pat Benatar. Fissinger. (Rock 'n Pop Stars Ser.). (Illus.). 32p. (gr. 4 up). PLB 8.95. Creative Ed.

Pat Benatar: Get Nervous. Ed. by Milton Okun & Dan Fox. (Illus.). 79p. 1983. pap. 7.95 (ISBN 0-89524-179-X, 27610). Cherry Lane.

Pat Garrett: The Story of a Western Lawman. Leon C. Metz. LC 72-9261. (Illus.). 328p. 1983. pap. 10.95 (ISBN 0-8061-1838-5). U of Okla Pr.

Pat Harrison: The New Deal Years. Martha H. Swain. LC 78-7919. (Illus.). 1978. 1.00 (ISBN 0-87805-076-0). U Pr of Miss.

Pat Hobby Stories. F. Scott Fitzgerald. 1962. (ScribT); 17.50 (ISBN 0-684-16477-9). Scribner.

Pat Hobby Stories. F. Scott Fitzgerald. 192p. 1988. pap. 4.95 (ISBN 0-02-019910-4, Collier). Macmillan.

Pat Hobby Stories. Scott F. Fitzgerald. 14.95 (ISBN 0-89190-601-0, Pub. by Am Repr). Amereon Ltd.

Pat McCarran: Political Boss of Nevada. Jerome E. Edwards. LC 82-8576. (History & Political Science Ser.: No. 17). (Illus.). 237p. (Orig.). 1982. pap. 12.95x (ISBN 0-87417-071-0). U of Nev Pr.

Pat Nixon of Texas: Autobiography of a Doctor. Pat I. Nixon. Ed. & intro. by Herbert H. Lang. LC 78-65575. 248p. 1979. 13.50 (ISBN 0-89096-072-0). Tex A&M Univ Pr.

Pat Nixon: The Untold Story. Julie N. Eisenhower. 480p. 1986. 19.95 (ISBN 0-671-24424-8). S&S.

Pat Nixon: The Untold Story. Julie N. Eisenhower. 1987. pap. 4.50 (ISBN 0-8217-2300-6). Zebra.

Pat Paragraphs. Elliot Perry. Ed. by George T. Turner & Thomas E. Stanton. LC 81-68198. (Illus.). 1982. 55.00 (ISBN 0-930412-05-2). Bureau Issues.

Pat Robertson: A Biography. Neil Eskelin. 192p. (Orig.). 1987. pap. 6.95 (ISBN 0-910311-47-1). Huntington Hse Inc.

Pat Robertson: A Personal, Religious, & Political Portrait. David E. Harrell, Jr. LC 87-45176. 1988. 15.45 (ISBN 0-06-250380-4, HarpR). Har-Row.

Pat Robertson: A Warning to America. John W. Robbins. (Trinity Papers: No. 24). 175p. (Orig.). 1988. pap. 6.95 (ISBN 0-940931-24-9). Trinity Found.

Pat Robertson in Error. Walter E. Adams. 50p. (Orig.). 1983. pap. 2.95 (ISBN 0-937408-27-1). GMI Pubns Inc.

Pat Robertson: The Authorized Biography. John B. Donovan. 1987. 14.95 (ISBN 0-02-532120-X). Macmillan.

Pat Robertson: Where He Stands. Hubert Morken. 1988. pap. 8.95 (ISBN 0-317-68172-9, Power Bks). Revell.

Pat Steir: Paintings. Carter Ratcliff. (Illus.). 128p. 1986. 25.00 (ISBN 0-8109-1503-0); pap. 14.95 (ISBN 0-8109-2316-5). Abrams.

Pat the Bunny. Dorothy Kunhardt. (Golden Touch & Feel Bks.). (Illus.). (ps). 1942. 4.95 (ISBN 0-307-12000-7, Golden Bks). Western Pub.

Patents & the Federal Circuit. Robert L. Harmon. LC 87-32829. 800p. 1988. text ed. 87.00 (ISBN 0-87179-576-0, 0576). BNA.

Patents & Trademarks Style Manual: A Supplement to the United States Government Printing Office Style Manual. (Illus.). 137p. (Orig.). 1984. pap. 5.50 (ISBN 0-318-21701-5, S/N 003-004-00606-4). USGPO.

Patents (DOE) Available for Licensing: A Bibliography Covering January 1974 through December 1980. DOE Technical Information Center Staff. 284p. 1982. pap. 17.00 (ISBN 0-87079-445-0, DOE/TIC-3398); microfiche 6.50 (ISBN 0-87079-456-6, DOE/TIC-3398). DOE.

Patents (DOE) Available for Licensing: A Bibliography for the Period 1966-1974. DOE Technical Information Center Staff. 60p. 1983. pap. 9.25 (ISBN 0-87079-512-0, DOE/TIC-3398 SUPPL. 1); microfiche 6.50 (ISBN 0-87079-513-9, DOE/TIC-3398 SUPPL. 1). DOE.

Patents for Invention: Watches, Clocks & Other Timekeepers 1855-1930, 2 vols. 1330p. 1987. Set. 350.00x (Pub. by E Bruton Assocs Ltd UK). State Mutual Bk.

Patents for Inventions, 2 vols. Great Britain, Patent Office Staff. Ed. by Peter C. Bunnell & Robert A. Sobieszek. LC 76-23063. (Sources of Modern Photography Ser.). (Illus.). 1979. Repr. of 1903 ed. Set. lib. bdg. 103.00x (ISBN 0-405-09626-7); lib. bdg. 45.00x ea. Vol. 1 (ISBN 0-405-09627-5). Vol. 2 (ISBN 0-405-09628-3). Ayer Co Pubs.

Patents in Chemistry & Biotechnology. 2nd ed. Philip W. Grubb. LC 86-5306. 1986. 45.00x (ISBN 0-19-855222-X); pap. 24.95x (ISBN 0-19-855221-1). Oxford U Pr.

Patents in Perspective. Jeremy J. Phillips. 1987. pap. 89.00x (ISBN 0-906214-37-8, Pub. by ESC Ltd UK). State Mutual Bk.

Patents, Inventions & Economic Change: Data & Selected Essays. Jacob Schmookler. Ed. by Zvi Griliches & Leonid Hurwicz. LC 74-188355. (Illus.). 320p. 1972. 22.50x (ISBN 0-674-65770-5). Harvard U Pr.

Patents, Territorial Restrictions, & EEC Law: A Legal & Economic Analysis. Paul Demaret. (IIC Studies: Vol. 2). 133p. 1978. pap. 29.00 (ISBN 0-89573-016-2). VCH Pubs.

Patents Throughout the World. 2nd ed. Ed. by Alan Jacobs. LC 78-978. 1978. looseleaf 85.00 (ISBN 0-87632-125-2). Clark Boardman.

Patents Throughtout the World. 3rd ed. Ed. by Alan Jacobs. 1988. looseleaf 95.00. Clark Boardman.

Patents, Trademarks, & Related Rights: National & International Protection, 3 vols. Stephen Ladas. LC 73-89709. 1888p. 1974. text ed. 150.00x (ISBN 0-674-65775-6). Harvard U Pr.

Patents, Trademarks, Copyrights & Trade Secrets: Pennsylvania Legal Practice Course Materials. Pennsylvania Bar Institute. 86p. 1985. 25.00 (ISBN 0-318-02157-9, PLP-85). PA Bar Inst.

Pater Calendar. J. M. Kennedy. LC 73-606. 1973. lib. bdg. 17.50 (ISBN 0-8414-1531-5). Folcroft.

Pater on Style. Edmund Chandler. LC 74-3038. 1958. lib. bdg. 15.00. Folcroft.

Pater Sato-Portfolio. P. Sato. (Illus.). 104p. 1986. pap. 29.95 (ISBN 0-318-23207-3, Pub. by Genko Sha). Bks Nippan.

Pater Sato Portfolio. P. Sato. 104p. 29.95 (ISBN 4-7683-0002-2). Bks Nippan.

Paterik of the Kievan Caves Monastery. Tr. by Muriel Heppell from Rus. (Library of Early Ukrainian Literature: English Translations: Vol. 1). 200p. 1988. text ed. 25.00 (ISBN 0-916458-27-X). Harvard Ukrainian.

Paterna: The Autobiography of Cotton Mather. Cotton Mather. Ed. by Ronald A. Bosco. LC 76-10595. (Center for Editions of American Authors). 504p. 1976. lib. bdg. 75.00x (ISBN 0-8201-1273-9). Schol Facsimiles.

Paternalism. John Kleinig. LC 83-13962. (Philosophy & Society Ser.). 256p. 1984. text ed. 28.50x (ISBN 0-8476-7207-7, Rowman & Allanheld). Rowman.

Paternalism. Ed. by Rolf Sartorious. LC 83-1089. 287p. 1984. pap. 14.95x (ISBN 0-8166-1174-2). U of Minn Pr.

Paternalism & Protest: Southern Mill Workers & Organized Labor, 1875-1905. Melton McLaurin. LC 70-111261. (Contributions in Economics & Economic History, No. 3). 1971. 35.00 (ISBN 0-8371-4662-3, MPP&). Greenwood.

Paternalism & the Legal Profession. David Luban. Date not set. 1.00. IPPP.

Paternalism, Conflict, & Coproduction: Learning from Citizen Action & Citizen Participation in Western Europe. Lawrence Susskind & Michael Elliott. (Environment, Development, & Public Policy: Environmental Policy & Planning Ser.). 374p. 1983. 45.00x (ISBN 0-306-40963-1, Plenum Pr). Plenum Pub.

Paternalism in Early Victorian England. David Roberts. 1979. 40.00x (ISBN 0-8135-0868-1). Rutgers U Pr.

Paternalism in the Japanese Economy. John W. Bennett & Iwao Ishino. LC 72-3538. 307p. 1972. Repr. of 1963 ed. lib. bdg. 35.00x (ISBN 0-8371-6424-9, BEJE). Greenwood.

Paternalistic Capitalism. Andreas G. Papandreou. LC 79-187169. 192p. 1972. 10.00x (ISBN 0-8166-0631-5). U of Minn Pr.

Paternalistic Intervention: The Moral Bounds on Benevolence. Donald VanDeVeer. LC 85-43320. (Studies in Moral, Political, & Legal Philosophy). 452p. 1986. text ed. 44.50x (ISBN 0-691-07306-6). Princeton U Pr.

Paternity in Shakespeare. Arthur T. Quiller-Couch. LC 77-7883. 1932. lib. bdg. 20.50 (ISBN 0-8414-6916-4). Folcroft.

Paternoster Bible History Atlas. F. F. Bruce. 96p. 19.50 (ISBN 0-85364-312-1, Pub. by Paternoster UK). Attic Pr.

Paterson, Bks. 1-5. William Carlos Williams. LC 46-5910. 1963. pap. 7.95 (ISBN 0-8112-0233-X, NDP152). New Directions.

Paterson & Passaic County: An Illustrated History. J. Palmer Murphy & Margaret Murphy. LC 87-13262. 216p. 1987. 24.95 (ISBN 0-89781-203-4). Windsor Pubns Inc.

Paterson Pieces: Poems, Nineteen Sixty-Nine to Nineteen Seventy-Nine. William J. Higginson. (Illus.). 80p. (Orig.). 1981. pap. 4.95 (ISBN 0-89120-018-5, Old Plate). From Here.

Path. David A. Wilson. 36p. (Orig.). 1977. pap. 2.00 (ISBN 0-934852-18-9). Lorien Hse.

Path: A Career Workbook for Liberal Arts Students. Howard E. Figler. LC 79-10944. 1979. 7.75x (ISBN 0-910328-07-2). Carroll Pr.

Path Analysis: A Primer. Ching C. Li. 1975. pap. text ed. 11.95x (ISBN 0-910286-40-X). Boxwood.

Path: Autobiography of a Western Yogi. Sri Kriyananda. LC 77-72787. (Illus.). 640p. 1977. 15.00 (ISBN 0-916124-11-8); pap. 6.95 (ISBN 0-916124-12-6). Crystal Clarity.

Path Beneath the Sea. Devorah Omer. 192p. 1969. 3.50 (ISBN 0-88482-744-5). Hebrew Pub.

Path Between. Theodore Enslin. 1986. pap. 3.00 (ISBN 0-942396-37-5). Blackberry ME.

Path Between: The Poems of Emily Dickinson from Her Death until 1943. Maravene S. Loeschke. (Illus.). 300p. (Orig.). 1988. pap. 15.95 (ISBN 0-935132-11-2). C H Fairfax.

Path Between the Seas: The Creation the Panama Canal 1870-1914. David McCullough. (Illus.). 1978. pap. 13.95 (ISBN 0-671-24409-4, Touchstone Bks). S&S.

Path: Betwwen Cosmos & Created. Robert L. Peck & Thelma M. Peck. 1985. 10.00 (ISBN 0-917828-01-1). Personal Dev Ctr.

Path Breaking, an Autobiographical History of the Equal Suffrage Movement in Pacific Coast States. A. S. Duniway. LC 14-17220. Repr. of 1914 ed. 31.00 (ISBN 0-527-25700-1). Kraus Repr.

Path from Rome: An Autobiography. Anthony Kenny. 208p. 1986. pap. 9.95x (ISBN 0-19-283050-3). Oxford U Pr.

Path from the Parlor: Louisiana Women, 1879-1920. Carmen Lindig. 195p. 1986. 17.50 (ISBN 0-940984-30-X). U of SW LA Ctr LA Studies.

Path I Trod. Terence V. Powderly. LC 77-181971. Repr. of 1940 ed. 31.50 (ISBN 0-404-05098-0). AMS Pr.

Path Integral Methods in Quantum Field Theory. R. J. Rivers. (Cambridge Monographs on Mathematical Physics). 300p. 1987. 69.50 (ISBN 0-521-25979-7). Cambridge U Pr.

Path Integrals from meV to MeV. Ed. by M. C. Gutzwiller et al. 450p. 1986. 48.00 (ISBN 9971-50-066-3); pap. 30.00 (ISBN 9971-50-067-1). World Scientific Pub.

Path Is Set. Frances O'Kane. (Illus.). 200p. 1976. 6.75 (ISBN 0-522-84087-6, Pub. by Melbourne U Pr). Intl Spec Bk.

Path of a Pioneer: The Autobiography of Rabbi Leo Jung. Leo Jung. 408p. 1980. 25.00 (ISBN 0-900689-51-X). Soncino Pr.

Path of a Pioneer: The Early Days of Sun Myung Moon & the Unification Church. Ed. by Jonathan G. Gullery. (Illus.). 88p. (Orig.). 1986. pap. 3.95 (ISBN 0-910621-50-0). HSA Pubns.

Path of Action. Jack Schwarz. LC 77-2247. 1977. pap. 8.95 (ISBN 0-525-48231-8). Dutton.

Path of Awakening. Kosho Soga. Frwd. by Ruth M. Tabrah. 63p. (Orig.). 1988. pap. 6.95 (ISBN 0-938474-07-3). Buddhist Study.

Path of Bliss. S. A. Husain. pap. 1.00 (ISBN 0-686-18456-4). Kazi Pubns.

Path of Compassion: Time-honored Principles of Spiritual & Ethical Conduct. G De Purucker. LC 86-50300. 84p. 1986. pap. 4.00 (ISBN 0-911500-69-3); audio cassette 12.00 (ISBN 0-911500-60-X). Theos U Pr.

Path of Compassion: Writings on Socially Engaged Buddhism. rev. ed. 219p. 1988. pap. 14.00 (ISBN 0-938077-02-3). Parallax Pr.

Path of Darkness. Ralph Harper. 1968. 8.00 (ISBN 0-8295-0131-2). UPB.

Path of Devotion. 8th ed. Swami Paramananda. 1940. soft luxitone bdg. 3.50 (ISBN 0-911564-00-4). Vedanta Ctr.

Path of Discipleship. Beasant. 4.25 (ISBN 0-8356-7044-9). Theos Pub Hse.

Path of Dreams. facs. ed. George M. McClellan. LC 70-152925. (Black Heritage Library Collection Ser). 1916. 17.00 (ISBN 0-8369-8769-1). Ayer Co Pubs.

Path of Duty. Leonard E. Read. 120p. 1982. 3.00 (ISBN 0-910614-69-5). Foun Econ Ed.

Path of Economic Growth. A. Lowe. LC 75-38186. (Illus.). 1976. 57.50 (ISBN 0-521-20888-2). Cambridge U Pr.

Path of Empire. Carl R. Fish. 1919. 8.50x (ISBN 0-686-83685-5). Elliots Bks.

Path of Empire see No Break Here.

Path of Fire & Light: Advanced Practices of Yoga. Swami Rama. 180p. (Orig.). 1986. pap. 8.95 (ISBN 0-89389-097-9). Himalayan Pubs.

Path of God's Bondsmen from Origin to Return. Najm A. Razi. Tr. by Hamid Algar. LC 81-21780. 1983. 60.00x (ISBN 0-88206-052-X). Caravan Bks.

Path of Healing. H. K. Challoner. LC 76-3660. 175p. 1976. pap. 5.25 (ISBN 0-8356-0480-2, Quest). Theos Pub Hse.

Path of Hunters: Animal Struggle in a Meadow. Robert N. Peck. (Illus.). (gr. 4-6). 1973. Knopf.

Path of Initiation. Inayat Khan. (Sufi Message of Hazrat Inayat Khan Ser.: Vol. 10). 270p. 1979. 14.95 (ISBN 90-6325-098-3, Pub. by Servire BV Netherlands). Hunter Hse.

Path of Inland Commerce. Archer B. Hulbert. 1920. 8.50x (ISBN 0-686-83686-3). Elliots Bks.

Path of Law from 1967: Proceedings & Papers at the Harvard Law School Convocation Held on the 150th Anniversary of Its Founding. Harvard University, Law School Staff. Ed. by Arthur E. Sutherland. LC 69-71044. 1968. 9.00x (ISBN 0-674-65785-3). Harvard U Pr.

Path of Least Resistance: Principles for Creating What You Want to Create. Robert Fritz. LC 84-17512. (Illus.). 206p. 1986. Repr. of 1984 ed. 14.95 (ISBN 0-913299-34-0, Dist. by NAL). Stillpoint.

Path of Life. Cornett D. Campbell. 144p. 1986. cancelled (ISBN 0-8062-2589-0). Carlton.

Path of Light. Regina E. Lorr & Robert W. Crary. LC 83-71354. 180p. (Orig.). 1983. pap. 7.95 (ISBN 0-87516-520-6). DeVorss.

Path of Light. Santideva. LC 78-70117. Repr. of 1909 ed. 20.00 (ISBN 0-404-17374-8). AMS Pr.

Path of Love. Bhagwan Shree Rajneesh. Ed. by Ma Yoga Sudha. LC 83-181255. (Kabir Ser.). (Illus.). 350p. (Orig.). 1978. 9.95 (ISBN 0-88050-112-X); pap. 12.95 358p (ISBN 0-88050-612-1). Chidvilas Inc.

Path of No Resistance: The Story of the Worldwide Race That Led to the Revolution in Superconductivity. Bruce Schechter. 288p. 1988. 19.95 (ISBN 0-671-65785-2). S&S.

Path of Peace. Norma Warren. (Illus.). 48p. (Orig.). 1988. pap. 2.50 (ISBN 0-7459-1370-9). Lion USA.

Path of Prayer. Samuel Chadwick. 1963. pap. 2.95 (ISBN 0-87508-095-2). Chr Lit.

Path of Pregnancy. rev. ed. Bob Flaws. 113p. pap. 10.95 (ISBN 0-912111-01-1). Paradigm Pubns.

Path of Purity, 3 vols. Buddhaghosa. Tr. by Pe Maung Tin. LC 78-72389. Repr. of 1931 ed. Set. 95.00 (ISBN 0-404-17570-8). AMS Pr.

Path of Righteousness: Dhammapada-An Introductory Essay, Together with the Pali Text, English Translation with Commentary. David J. Kalupahana. LC 86-9088. 234p. (Orig., Eng. & Pali.). 1986. lib. bdg. 26.00 (ISBN 0-8191-5365-6); pap. text ed. 13.25 (ISBN 0-8191-5366-4). U Pr of Amer.

Path of Serenity & Insight. Henepola Gunaratna. 1984. 22.50x (ISBN 0-8364-1149-8). South Asia Bks.

Path of Sorrow (1832), Eonchs of Ruby (1851), Memoralia (1849), Virginalia (1853), Sons of Usna (1858, 5 vols. in 1. Thomas H. Chivers. LC 79-22103. 1979. 80.00x (ISBN 0-8201-1340-9). Schol Facsimiles.

Path of Subud. Husein Rofe. 69.95 (ISBN 0-8490-0805-0). Gordon Pr.

Path of the Bodhisattva Warrior. Glenn H. Mullin. 270p. 1988. pap. 14.95 (ISBN 0-937938-55-6). Snow Lion.

Path of the Buddha: Buddhism Interpreted by Buddhists. Kenneth W. Morgan. 1986. 24.00X (ISBN 81-208-0030-3, Pub. by Motilal Banarsidass). South Asia Bks.

Path of the Buddha: Buddhism Interpreted by Buddhists. Kenneth W. Morgan. 432p. 1986. Repr. of 1956 ed. 24.00 (ISBN 0-317-60576-3, Pub. by Motilal Banarsidass India). Orient Bk Dist.

Path of the Eclipse. Chelsea Q. Yarbro. 640p. 1989. pap. price not set. Tor Bks.

Path of the Heart: A Spiritual Guide to the Universal Quest for Joy. Beverly Lanzetta. (Patterns of World Spirituality Ser.). 108p. 1986. pap. 7.95 (ISBN 0-913757-64-0, Pub. by New Era Bks). Paragon Hse.

Path of the Just-Mesilath Yesharim. Luzzato. 1982. 12.95 (ISBN 0-87306-114-4); pap. 9.95 (ISBN 0-87306-115-2). Feldheim.

Path of the Kabbalah: An Introduction to the Living Jewish Spiritual Tradition. David Sheinkin. LC 86-18686. (Patterns of World Spirituality Ser.). 195p. 1986. pap. 9.95 (ISBN 0-913757-69-1, Pub. by New Era Bks). Paragon Hse.

Path of the Law. Oliver Holmes, Jr. pap. 1.10x (ISBN 0-686-89065-5). Michie Co.

Path of the Lonely Ones. Rosemary Dennis. LC 79-89516. (Illus.). 1979. 4.50 (ISBN 0-918482-02-X). Ageless Bks.

Path of the Ocean: Traditional Poetry of Polynesia. Ed. by Marjorie Sinclair. LC 82-8611. 239p. 1982. 17.95 (ISBN 0-8248-0804-5). UH Pr.

Path of the Paddle. Bill Mason. (Illus.). 208p. 1988. pap. 19.95 (ISBN 0-919493-38-6, Pub. by Key Porter Canada). U of Toronto Pr.

Path of the Pale Horse. Paul Fleischman. LC 82-48611. (Charlotte Zolotow Bks.). 160p. (gr. 6 up). 1983. PLB 12.89 (ISBN 0-06-021905-X). HarpJ.

Path of the Phoenix. Kendall K. McCabe. Ed. by Michael L. Sherer. (Orig.). 1986. pap. 7.25 (ISBN 0-89536-818-8, 6827). CSS of Ohio.

Path of the Righteous Gentile, Chain Clorfine: A Philosophical & Historical Presentation of the Doctrine of the Seven Laws of Noah. 142p. 1987. 10.95 (ISBN 0-87306-433-X). Feldheim.

Path of the Soul. White Eagle. 1959. 5.95 (ISBN 0-85487-020-2). DeVorss.

Path of the Storm. Douglas Reeman. 352p. 1984. pap. 3.50 (ISBN 0-515-07872-7). Jove Pubns.

Path of Thunder. Peter Abrahams. 279p. 1975. Repr. of 1948 ed. 8.95x (ISBN 0-911860-43-6). Chatham Bkseller.

Path of Transcendence. Bennett Penn. 144p. 1987. pap. text ed. 10.00 (ISBN 0-682-40332-6). Exposition-Phoenix.

Path of Virtue. Jonathon Murro. LC 79-54382. (Illus.). 487p. 1980. 14.95 (ISBN 0-917189-00-0). Colton Found.

Path of Wisdom: Biblical Investigations. Bruce Vawter. LC 85-47756. (Background Bks.: Vol. 3). 1986. pap. 12.95 (ISBN 0-89453-466-1). M Glazier.

Path Through Scripture. Mark Link. (Illus.). 288p. (YA) (gr. 9-12). 1987. pap. 10.95 (ISBN 0-89505-402-7). Tabor Pub.

Path Through Scripture. Mark Link. 328p. (YA) (gr. 9-12). 1987. 22.95 (ISBN 0-89505-403-5). Tabor Pub.

Path Through The Ashes: Inspiring Stories of the Holocaust. Nisson Wolpin. (ArtScroll Judaiscope Ser.). (Illus.). 352p. 1986. 14.95 (ISBN 0-89906-856-1); pap. 11.95 (ISBN 0-89906-857-X). Mesorah Pubns.

Path Through the Bible. John H. Piet. LC 81-2258. (Illus.). 318p. 1981. pap. 14.95 (ISBN 0-664-24369-X). Westminster John Knox.

Path to Biculturalism. Marlene Kramer & Claudia Schmalenberg. LC 77-7202. 315p. 1977. pap. 27.25 (ISBN 0-913654-30-2). Aspen Pub.

Path to Dreams Fulfilled. 115p. write for info. (ISBN 0-939509-31-8); pap. 12.00 (ISBN 0-317-58900-8). L Benton Geneal.

Path to Economic Prosperity: How to Rebuild Our Nation. J. Ray Estefania. (Victory Ser.: No. 2). 1988. 24.95 (ISBN 0-945542-01-1). Park & Park Pub.

Path to European Union: From the Marshall Plan to the Common Market. Hans A. Schmitt. LC 81-6470. xiii, 272p. 1981. Repr. of 1962 ed. lib. bdg. 35.00x (ISBN 0-313-23107-9, SCPUN). Greenwood.

Path to Excellence: Quality Assurance in Higher Education. Laurence R. Marcus et al. Ed. by Jonathan D. Fife. LC 83-146405. (ASHE-ERIC Higher Education Report Ser.: No. 1, 1983). 68p. (Orig.). 1983. pap. 7.50x (ISBN 0-913317-00-4). Assn Study Higher Educ.

Path to Illumination. Wally Richardson et al. LC 82-71211. (Illus.). 248p. (Orig.). 1982. pap. 8.95 (ISBN 0-87516-480-3). DeVorss.

Path to Light. Albert Krassner. pap. 3.00 (ISBN 0-934805-03-2). Gray Pubns WV.

Path to Mastership. John-Roger. 1982. pap. 5.00 (ISBN 0-914829-16-5). Mandeville LA.

Path to Math. Greta Erdtmann. (Gentle Revolution Ser.). (Illus.). 60p. (ps). 1981. 8.95 (ISBN 0-936676-11-6). Better Baby.

Path to Nigerian Development. Ed. by Okwudiba Nnoli. 272p. 1981. pap. 10.25 (ISBN 0-86232-021-6, Pub. by Zed Pr England). Humanities.

Path to No-Self: Life at the Center. Bernadette Roberts. LC 84-19340. 214p. (Orig.). 1985. pap. 9.95 (ISBN 0-87773-306-6, 72999-4). Shambhala Pubns.

Path to No-Self: Life at the Center. Bernadette Roberts. pap. 12.95 (ISBN 0-394-72999-4). Shambhala Pubns.

Path to Oriental Wisdom: Introductory Studies in Eastern Philosophy. George Parulski, Jr. LC 76-21011. (History & Philosophy Ser.). 1976. pap. 9.95 (ISBN 0-89750-046-6, 320). Ohara Pubns.

Path to Parnassus. Eduard C. Hargrave. 1979. 7.50 (ISBN 0-682-49381-3). Exposition-Phoenix.

Path to Parnassus. 4th ed. F. Maurice. 1956. pap. 4.00x (ISBN 0-522-83804-9, Pub. by Melbourne U Pr). Intl Spec Bk.

Path to Perfection. W. E. Sangster. Date not set. pap. 10.50 (Pub. by SCM Pr England). Fortress.

Path to Popularity Through Friends & Self-Confidence. Peggy Bud. 1986. 9.95 (ISBN 0-89824-147-2). Trillium Pr.

Path to Power: The Years of Lyndon Johnson, Vol. 1. Robert A. Caro. LC 82-47811. 1982. 29.45 (ISBN 0-394-49973-5). Knopf.

Path to Revolution: The Communist Program. Gus Hall. 1968. pap. 0.25 (ISBN 0-87898-031-8). New Outlook.

Path to Rome. Hilaire Belloc. (Travel Library). 1986. pap. 6.95 (ISBN 0-14-009530-6). Penguin.

Path to Rome. Hilaire Belloc. 267p. 1987. pap. 8.95 (ISBN 0-89526-784-5). Regnery Gateway.

Path to the Brightest Star. Sandy Brainard. (Illus.). 104p. (Orig.). 1984. pap. 6.00 (ISBN 0-942494-54-7). Coleman Pub.

Path to the Heart. rev. ed. A. Leon White. (Illus.). 188p. (Orig.). 1985. pap. 10.95 (ISBN 0-9608198-1-9). Arthurian Pr.

Path to the Nest of Spiders. Italo Calvino. LC 76-3303. (Neglected Books of the Twentieth Century Ser.). 1976. pap. 6.95 (ISBN 0-912946-31-8). Ecco Pr.

Path to the New Music. Anton Webern. Ed. by Willi Reich. Tr. by Leo Black from Ger. pap. 8.95 (ISBN 3-7024-0030-3, UE12947). Eur-Am Music.

Path to the Peak. Louise Louis. (Illus.). 176p. 1971. pap. 4.95 (ISBN 0-941242-03-X). Pen-Art.

Path to the Stars: The Story of Challenger V Astronaut Ron McNair. Dudley Clendinen. LC 86-10601. (Illus.). 160p. (gr. 5 up). 1944. PLB 3.95 (ISBN 0-394-88559-7). Knopf.

Path to Transcendence: From Philosophy to Mysticism in Saint Augustine. Paul Henry. Tr. by Francis F. Burch. (Pittsburgh Theological Monographs: No. 37). 1981. pap. 12.50 (ISBN 0-915138-49-2). Pickwick.

Path to Vietnam: Origins of the American Commitment to Southeast Asia. Andrew J. Rotter. LC 87-47603. 304p. 1987. 29.95x (ISBN 0-8014-1958-1). Cornell U Pr.

Path to Wing Chun. rev. ed. Samuel Kwok. (Illus.). 96p. 1986. pap. text ed. 12.00 (ISBN 0-87364-367-4). Paladin Pr.

Path-Way to Knowledge, Containing the First Principles of Geometrie. Robert Record. LC 74-80206. (English Experience Ser.: No. 687). 1974. Repr. of 1551 ed. 25.00 (ISBN 90-221-0687-X). Walter J Johnson.

Path-Way to Knowledge: Containing the Whole Art of Arithmeticke. John Tapp. LC 68-54667. (English Experience Ser.: No. 66). 1968. Repr. of 1613 ed. 25.00 (ISBN 90-221-0066-9). Walter J Johnson.

Path-Way to Military Practice. Barnaby Rich. LC 75-25920. (English Experience Ser.: No. 177). 88p. 1969. Repr. of 1587 ed. 11.50 (ISBN 90-221-0177-0). Walter J Johnson.

Path We Tread. Carnegie. LC 64-5203. 1988. 24.50. Lippincott.

Path with a Heart: Ericksonian Utilization with Chronic & Resistant Clients. Yvonne Dolan. LC 85-4225. 220p. 1985. 25.00 (ISBN 0-87630-389-0). Brunner-Mazel.

Pathans: 500 B.C.-A.D. 1957. Olaf Caroe. (Illus.). 1984. 39.95x (ISBN 0-19-577221-0). Oxford U Pr.

Pathar Panchali. B. Banerji. 166p. 1968. 4.95. Asia Bk Corp.

Pathbreakers from River to Ocean: Story of the Great West from Coronado to the Present. facsimile ed. Grace R. Hebard. LC 71-164604. (Select Bibliographies Reprint Ser). Repr. of 1911 ed. 32.00 (ISBN 0-8369-5888-8). Ayer Co Pubs.

Pathelin & Others Farces. Ed. by Richard Switzer. Tr. by Mirelle Guillet-Rydell. LC 84-48064. 300p. 1985. lib. bdg. 30.00 (ISBN 0-8240-8917-0). Garland Pub.

Pathetic Fallacy. Llewelyn Powys. LC 77-828. 1977. Repr. of 1930 ed. lib. bdg. 39.00 (ISBN 0-8414-6797-8). Folcroft.

Pathetic Fallacy in the Nineteenth Century. Josephine Miles. 1965. lib. bdg. 16.00x (ISBN 0-374-95662-6, Octagon). Hippocrene Bks.

Pathetic Symphony: A Biographical Novel about Tchaikovsky. Klaus Mann. LC 85-50532. (Illus.). 380p. 1985. pap. 9.95 (ISBN 0-910129-24-X, Distributed by Talman Company). Wiener Pub Inc.

Pathfinder. Cooper. (American Classics Ser.). (gr. 9-12). 1977. pap. text ed. 5.16 (ISBN 0-88343-406-7); cassettes o.p. 52.00 (ISBN 0-88343-422-9). McDougal-Littell.

Pathfinder. James Fenimore Cooper. (Airmont Classics Ser.). (gr. 6 up). 1964. pap. 2.95 (ISBN 0-8049-0035-3, CL-35). Airmont.

Pathfinder. James Fenimore Cooper. 1976. lib. bdg. 18.95 (ISBN 0-89968-159-X). Lightyear.

Pathfinder. James Fenimore Cooper. 488p. (YA) (RL 10). 1964. pap. 3.95 (ISBN 0-451-52139-0, Sig Classics). NAL.

Pathfinder. James Fenimore Cooper. Ed. by Robert J. Dixson. (American Classics Ser.: Bk. 4). (gr. 9 up). 1973. pap. text ed. 4.75 (ISBN 0-13-024548-8, 18123); cassettes 55.00 (ISBN 0-13-024704-9, 58223). Prentice ESL.

Pathfinder. James Fenimore Cooper. 419p. 1984. Repr. lib. bdg. 19.95 (ISBN 0-89966-491-1). Buccaneer Bks.

Pathfinder see Leatherstocking Tales.

Pathfinder: A Backpacker's Guide. Katherine Chaney & Don Shaw. (Illus.). 128p. (YA) (gr. 11 up). 1980. pap. 7.95 (ISBN 0-87670-060-1). Athletic Inst.

Pathfinder Area Coordinator Master Manual. Bennie Tillman & Emma L. Tillman. 300p. (Orig.). 1987. pap. 35.00 tchr's ed. (ISBN 0-936241-02-0). Cheetah Pub.

Pathfinder Field Guide. rev. ed. Lawrence Maxwell. 1980. 10.95 (ISBN 0-8280-0053-0, 16070-5); pap. 8.95 (ISBN 0-686-62242-1, 16071-3). Review & Herald.

Pathfinder: First Automobile Trip from Newport to Siletz Bay, 1912. Ed. by James E. Stembridge, Jr. (Illus.). 24p. (Orig.). 1976. pap. 1.00 (ISBN 0-911443-02-9). Lincoln Coun Hist.

Pathfinder for Norwegian Emigrants. Johan R. Reiersen. LC 81-132209. (Norwegian-American Historical Association. Travel & Description Ser.: No. 9). pap. 63.30 (ISBN 0-317-55772-6, 2029293). Bks Demand UMI.

Pathfinder: Or the Inland Sea. James Fenimore Cooper. LC 79-15598. (Writings of James Fenimore Cooper Ser.). 569p. 1981. 49.50 (ISBN 0-87395-360-6); pap. 18.95 (ISBN 0-87395-477-7). State U NY Pr.

Pathfinder Pathguide to the Nation's Capital City: Unique Self-Guided Walking Tours of Washington, D. C. & Georgetown. 2nd ed. Kristine Stevens. (Illus.). 108p. (Orig.). 1984. pap. 4.95 (ISBN 0-9613819-0-6). Pathfinder Tour Con.

Pathfinder Staff Training Manual. Bennie Tillman & Emma L. Tillman. 200p. (Orig.). 1987. pap. 25.00 tchr's. ed. (ISBN 0-936241-03-9). Cheetah Pub.

Pathfinder to the Harp. Lucile Lawrence & Carlos Salzedo. 1954. pap. 8.00 (ISBN 0-318-19430-9, 60898-907). Peer-Southern.

Pathfinder Trailblazers Group, Vol. 1: A Youth Enrichment Skill Book. Lou Gattis. (Illus.). 20p. (Orig.). (ps-5). 1986. pap. 5.00 tchr's. ed. (ISBN 0-936241-08-X). Cheetah Pub.

Pathfinders. Jeri Carroll & Candance Wells. (Famous Friends Ser.). 64p. (ps-3). 1986. wkbk. 6.95 (ISBN 0-86653-357-5). Good Apple.

Pathfinders. Geary Gravel. 240p. (Orig.). 1986. pap. 2.95 (ISBN 0-345-32339-4, Del Rey). Ballantine.

Pathfinders. David Nevin. LC 79-10967. (Epic of Flight Ser.). (gr. 9 up). 21.27 (ISBN 0-8094-3255-2, Pub. by Time-Life). Silver.

Pathfinders. David Nevin. Ed. by Time-Life Books Editors. (Epic of Flight Ser.). (Illus.). 1980. 14.95 (ISBN 0-8094-3254-4). Time-Life.

Pathfinders. Gail Sheehy. 1982. pap. 5.50 (ISBN 0-553-25601-7). Bantam.

Pathfinders: A History of the Progress of Colored Graduate Nurses. Adah H. Thoms. Ed. by Susan Reverby. LC 83-49125. (History of American Nursing Ser.). 240p. 1984. Repr. lib. bdg. 35.00 (ISBN 0-8240-6526-3). Garland Pub.

Pathfinders: A Saga of Exploration in Southern Africa. Peter Becker. LC 84-51887. 288p. 1985. 17.95 (ISBN 0-670-80126-7). Viking.

Pathfinders Guide to Understanding Computers. Ernie Philipp & Donald L. Day. 176p. 1984. pap. text ed. 14.95 (ISBN 0-8403-3297-1). Kendall Hunt.

Pathfinders of the West. Agnes C. Laut. LC 74-90651. (Essay Index Reprint Ser). 1904. 27.50 (ISBN 0-8369-1220-9). Ayer Co Pubs.

Pathfinders of the World Missionary Crusade. facs. ed. George S. Eddy. LC 76-84304. (Essay Index Reprint Ser). 1945. 20.25 (ISBN 0-8369-1127-X). Ayer Co Pubs.

Pathfinders: The Saga of Exploration in Southern Africa. Peter Becker. (Illus.). 296p. 1987. pap. 7.95 (ISBN 0-14-007478-3). Penguin.

Pathless Trail. Arthur O. Friel. (Time-Lost Ser.). 1970. pap. 0.60 (ISBN 0-87818-000-1). Centaur.

Pathless Way: John Muir & American Wilderness. Michael P. Cohen. LC 83-40260. 500p. 1984. 26.50 (ISBN 0-299-09720-X). U of Wis Pr.

Pathless Way: John Muir & American Wilderness. Michael P. Cohen. LC 83-40260. 432p. 1986. pap. 12.95 (ISBN 0-299-09724-2). U of Wis Pr.

Pathless Woods. Gloria Whelan. LC 80-8725. (Illus.). 192p. (gr. 7 up). 1981. PLB 10.89 (ISBN 0-397-31931-2). Har-Row.

Pathobiochemie: Ein Lehrbuch fur Studierende und Arzte. 2nd ed. Eckhart Buddecke. (Illus.). 477p. 1983. 23.60 (ISBN 3-11-009658-7). De Gruyter.

Pathobiologie Oraler Strukturen. H. E. Schroeder. (Illus.). x, 208p. 1983. pap. 19.50 (ISBN 3-8055-3692-5). S Karger.

Pathobiology of Cardiovascular Injury. Ed. by H. Lowell Stone & William B. Weglicki. (Developments in Cardiovascular Medicine Ser.). 1985. lib. bdg. 69.50 (ISBN 0-89838-743-4, Pub. by Martinus Nijhoff Netherlands). Kluwer Academic.

Pathobiology of Hepathic Fibrosis: Proceedings of the International Symposium on Pathobiology of Hepatic Fibrosis, Matsue, Japan, 16-17 June, 1985. Ed. by C. Hirayama & K. Kivirikko. (International Congress Ser.: No. 688). 248p. 1985. 103.75 (ISBN 0-444-80725-X, Excerpta Medica). Elsevier.

Pathobiology of Hepatic Fibrosis. Ed. by C. Hirayama & K. Kivirikko. (International Congress Ser.: No. 688). 1985. 66.75 (ISBN 0-317-47235-6). Elsevier.

Pathobiology of Invertebrate Vectors of Disease, Vol. 266. Bulla & Cheng. 1975. 64.00x (ISBN 0-89072-020-7). NY Acad Sci.

Pathobiology of Malignant Melanoma. Ed. by D. E. Elder. (Pigment Cell Ser: Vol. 8). (Illus.). viii, 224p. 1987. 116.00 (ISBN 3-8055-4348-4). S Karger.

Pathobiology of Marine Mammal Diseases, 2 Vols. Edwin B. Howard. 1983. Vol. I, 248p. 95.00 ea. (ISBN 0-8493-6311-X). Vol. II, 240p (ISBN 0-8493-6312-8). CRC Pr.

Pathobiology of Neoplasia. Ed. by A. E. Sirica. (Illus.). 572p. Date not set. 85.00x (ISBN 0-306-42950-0, Plenum Pr). Plenum Pub.

Pathobiology of Ocular Disease, Pt. A & B. Garner & Klintworth. 1982. Set. 147.50. Part A, 886p (ISBN 0-8247-1295-1). Part B., 868p (ISBN 0-8247-1393-1). Dekker.

Pathobiology of the Endothelial Cell. Ed. by Hymie Nossel & Henry J. Vogel. (P & S Biomedical Sciences Symposia Ser.). 1982. 82.50 (ISBN 0-12-521980-6). Acad Pr.

Pathochemical Markers in Major Psychoses. Ed. by H. Beckmann & P. Riederer. (Illus.). 175p. 1985. 43.00 (ISBN 0-387-13444-1). Springer-Verlag.

Pathogenesis & Immunity in Pertussis. Ed. by Alastair C. Wardlaw & Roger Parton. LC 88-125. 400p. 1988. pap. write for info. (ISBN 0-471-91820-2). Wiley.

Pathogenesis & Immunology of Treponemal Infections. Musher Schell. (Immunology Ser.). 424p. 1983. 75.00 (ISBN 0-8247-1384-2). Dekker.

Pathogenesis & Therapy of Lung Cancer. Harris. (Jung Biology in Health & Disease Ser.: Vol. 10). 1978. 110.00 (ISBN 0-8247-6611-3). Dekker.

Pathogenesis & Treatment of Diabetes Mellitus. J. K. Radder et al. 1986. lib. bdg. 56.50 (ISBN 0-89838-828-7, Pub. by Martinus Nijhoff Netherlands). Kluwer Academic.

Pathogenesis & Treatment of Immunodeficiency. S. H. Horowitz & R. Hong. (Monographs in Allergy: Vol. 10). 1977. 50.00 (ISBN 3-8055-2624-5). S Karger.

Pathogenesis & Treatment of Nephrolithiasis. Ed. by F. Linari et al. (Contributions to Nephrology Ser.: Vol. 58). x, 298p. 1987. 118.00 (ISBN 3-8055-4554-1). S Karger.

Pathogenesis of Arteriosclerosis. Ed. by Robert W. Wissler & J. C. Geer. LC 78-187919. 315p. 1972. 25.00 (ISBN 0-683-09195-6, Pub. by W & W). Krieger.

Pathogenesis of Bacterial Infections. Ed. by G. G. Jackson & H. Thomas. (Bayer Symposium: 8). (Illus.). 430p. 1985. 69.00 (ISBN 0-387-15304-7). Springer-Verlag.

Pathogenesis of Bacterial Infections in Animals. Ed. by Carlton L. Gyles & Charles O. Thoen. 228p. 1986. text ed. 20.95x (ISBN 0-8138-1343-3). Iowa St U Pr.

Pathogenesis of Colorectal Cancer. Bosil C. Morson. LC 78-1792. (Major Problems in Pathology: Vol. 10). 1978. text ed. write for info. (ISBN 0-7216-6558-6). Saunders.

Pathogenesis of Diabetes Mellitus: Proceedings of the Thirteenth Nobel Symposium. Erol Cerasi & Rolf Luft. (Illus.). 354p. (Orig.). 1970. text ed. 38.00x (Pub. by Almqvist & Wiksell). Coronet Bks.

Pathogenesis of Infectious Disease. 2nd ed. Cedric A. Mims. 1982. 31.50 (ISBN 0-12-498254-9); pap. 15.50 (ISBN 0-12-498255-7). Acad Pr.

Pathogenesis of Infectious Disease. 3rd ed. Cedric A. Mims. 352p. 1987. 39.95 (ISBN 0-12-498260-3); pap. 24.95 (ISBN 0-12-498261-1). Acad Pr.

Pathogenesis of Intestinal Infections. Ed. by M. V. Voino-Yasenetsky & T. Bakacs. 1977. cancelled 30.00 (ISBN 963-05-1131-2, Pub. by Akademiai Kaido Hungary). IPS.

Pathogenesis of Invertebrate Microbial Diseases. Ed. by Elizabeth W. Davidson. LC 81-65007. 576p. 1981. text ed. 42.50x (ISBN 0-86598-014-4, Pub. by Allanheld). Rowman.

Pathogenesis of Leprosy & Related Diseases. D. S. Ridley. 284p. 1988. price not set (ISBN 0-7236-1031-2). PSG Pub Co.

Pathogenesis of Leukemias & Lymphomas: Environmental Influences. Ed. by Ian T. Magrath et al. (Progress in Cancer Research & Therapy Ser.: Vol. 27). 430p. 1984. text ed. 104.50 (ISBN 0-89004-901-7). Raven.

Pathogenesis of Liver Diseases. Ed. by Emmanuel Farber. (International Academy of Pathology Monographs: No. 28). (Illus.). 384p. 1986. 84.50 (ISBN 0-683-03038-8). Williams & Wilkins.

Pathogenesis of Microbial Infections. American Society for Microbiology, Education & Training Board Staff. (Continuing Education Manual Ser.). 1985. 20.00 (ISBN 0-317-46546-5). Am Soc Microbio.

Pathogenesis of Myocarditis & Cardiomyopathy: Recent Experimental & Clinical Studies. Ed. by Chuichi Kawai & Walter H. Abelmann. (Cardiomyopathy Update Ser.: No. 1). 322p. 1988. 97.50x (ISBN 0-86008-419-1, Pub. by U of Tokyo Japan). Columbia U Pr.

Pathogenesis of Nervous & Mental Diseases in Children. Ed. by Ernest Harms. (Illus.). 1968. 8.50 (ISBN 0-87212-011-2). Libra.

Pathogenesis of Non-Insulin Dependent Diabetes Mellitus (Proceedings of a Karolinska Institute Nobel Conference) Ed. by Valdemar Grill & Suad Efendic. 350p. 1988. text ed. 85.00 (ISBN 0-88167-444-3). Raven.

Pathogenesis of Skin Disease. Ed. by Bruce H. Thiers & Richard L. Dobson. (Illus.). 642p. 1985. text ed. 95.00 (ISBN 0-443-08332-0). Churchill.

Pathogenesis of Stress-Induced Heart Disease. Ed. by R. E. Beamish et al. (Developments in Cardiovascular Medicine Ser.). 1985. lib. bdg. 55.00 (ISBN 0-89838-710-8, Pub. by Martinus Nijhoff Netherlands). Kluwer-Academic.

Pathogenetic Mechanisms of Disease: A Primer for the Primary Care Specialist. Richard B. Birrer. 186p. 1988. 22.50 (ISBN 0-87527-336-X). Green.

Pathogenic Anaerobic Bacteria. 3rd ed. Louis D. Smith & Betsy L. Williams. (Illus.). 348p. 1984. 43.75 (ISBN 0-398-05001-5). C C Thomas.

Pathogenic Bacteriology. Jeter. 1987. write for info. (ISBN 0-471-81783-X). Wiley.

Pathogenic Microorganisms. Ellner. Date not set. write for info. (ISBN 0-444-00824-1). Elsevier.

Pathogenic Mycoplasmas. Ciba Foundation Staff. LC 72-88563. (Ciba Foundation Symposium Ser.: No. 6). pap. 103.50 (ISBN 0-317-28318-9, 2022138). Bks Demand UMI.

Pathogenic Neisseriae: Proceedings of the Fourth International Symposium. Ed. by Gary K. Schoolnik et al. (Illus.). 647p. 1985. 52.00 (ISBN 0-914826-76-X). Am Soc Microbio.

Pathogenic Root-Infecting Fungi. S. D. Garrett. LC 72-10024. (Illus.). 1970. 52.50 (ISBN 0-521-07786-9). Cambridge U Pr.

Pathogenicity & Clinical Significance of Coagulase-Negative Staphylococci. Ed. by Gerhard Pulverer et al. 290p. 1987. lib. bdg. 103.00 (ISBN 0-89574-242-X, Pub. by Gustav Fischer Verlag). VCH Pubs.

Pathogenicity of Cationic Proteins. Ed. by P. P. Lambert et al. 396p. 1983. pap. text ed. 39.50 (ISBN 0-89004-689-1). Raven.

Pathogenicity of the Pine Wood Nematode. Ed. by Michael J. Wingfield. LC 87-71117. (Symposium Ser.). (Illus.). vi, 122p. 1987. 21.00 (ISBN 0-89054-083-7). Am Phytopathol Soc.

Pathogens & Toxins in the Marine Environment. Colwell. 1987. write for info. (ISBN 0-471-82593-X). Wiley.

Pathogens of Invertebrates: Application in Biological Control & Transmission Mechanisms. Ed. by Thomas C. Cheng. (Comparative Pathobiology Ser.: Vol. 7). 286p. 1984. 59.50x (ISBN 0-306-41700-6, Plenum Pr). Plenum Pub.

Pathogens, Parasites & Predators of Medically Important Arthropods. D. W. Jenkins. (WHO Bulletin Supplement: Vol. 30). 1964. pap. 3.60 (ISBN 92-4-168301-5). World Health.

Pathogens, Vectors & Plant Diseases: A Approach to Control. Kerry Harris & Karl Maramorosch. LC 80-4893. 1982. 44.00 (ISBN 0-12-326440-5). Acad Pr.

Pathokinesiology. pap. 5.00 (ISBN 0-912452-64-1). Am Phys Therapy Assn.

Pathologic Anatomy of Mycoses. Roger D. Baker et al. LC 25-11247. (Handbuch der Speziellen Pathologischen Anatomie: Vol. 3, Pt. 5). (Illus.). 1971. 318.60 (ISBN 0-387-05140-6). Springer-Verlag.

Pathologic Basis of Disease. 3rd ed. Stanley L. Robbins et al. (Illus.). 1461p. 1984. 68.00 (ISBN 0-7216-7597-2). Saunders.

Pathologic Basis of Disease: A Self-Assessment & Review. 2nd ed. Carolyn Compton. (Illus.). 211p. 1986. pap. 19.95 (ISBN 0-7216-2112-0). Saunders.

Pathologic Diagnosis of Fungal Infections. Francis W. Chandler & John C. Watts. (Illus.). 400p. 1987. text ed. 115.00 (ISBN 0-89189-252-4); 100 35-mm slides 100.00 (ISBN 0-89189-251-6). Am Soc Clinical.

Pathologic Mechanisms & Human Disease. Roderick A. Cawson & Alexander W. McCracken. LC 81-16834. (Illus.). 594p. 1982. pap. text ed. 37.95 (ISBN 0-8016-0939-9). Mosby.

Pathologic Physiology: Mechanisms of Disease. 7th ed. William A. Sodeman, Jr. & Thomas M. Sodeman. (Illus.). 1154p. 1985. 95.00 (ISBN 0-7216-1010-2). Saunders.

Pathologic Physiology of Dementia: With Indications for Diagnosis & Treatment. R. M. Torack. (Psychiatry Ser.: Vol. 20). (Illus.). 1978. 42.00 (ISBN 0-387-08904-7). Springer-Verlag.

Pathological Basis of Renal Disease. 2nd ed. Dunnill. 1984. 52.00 (ISBN 0-7216-0972-4, Bailliere-Tindall). Saunders.

Pathological Biometeorology see Progress in Human Biometeorology: The Effect of Weather & Climate on Man & His Living Environment, Period 1963 to 1970-75.

Pathological Conduction in Nerve Fibers, Electromyography of Sphincter Muscles, Automatic Analysis of Electrogram with Computers see New Developments in Electromyography & Clinical Neurophysiology.

Pathological Cry, Stridor & Cough in Infants. J. Hirschberg & T. Szende. 1982. cancelled 28.00 (ISBN 963-05-2820-7, Pub. by Akademiai Kaido Hungary). IPS.

Pathological Diagnosis of Acute Ischaemic Heart Disease: Report. WHO Scientific Group, Geneva, 1969. (Technical Report Ser.: No. 441). (Also avail. in French, Russian & Spanish). 1970. pap. 1.20 (ISBN 92-4-120441-9). World Health.

Pathological Effects of Oral Contraceptives. P. S. Boffa et al. LC 72-13565. (Illus.). 220p. 1973. text ed. 26.00x (ISBN 0-8422-7081-7). Irvington.

Pathological Lying, Accusation & Swindling, a Study in Forensic Psychology. William Healy & Mary T. Healy. LC 69-14932. (Criminology, Law Enforcement, & Social Problems Ser.: No. 63). 1969. Repr. of 1915 ed. 12.50x (ISBN 0-87585-063-4). Patterson Smith.

Pathological Play in Borderline-Narcissistic Personalities. Irving Steingart. 170p. 1984. text ed. 29.95 (ISBN 0-88331-172-0). Luce.

Pathological Vision: Jean Genet, Louis-Ferdinand Celine, & Tennessee Williams. Robert Hauptman. (American University Studies III: Vol. 5). 145p. (Orig.). 1983. pap. text ed. 15.25 (ISBN 0-8204-0037-8). P Lang Pubs.

Pathologies of the Modern Self: Postmodern Studies on Narcissism, Schizophrenia, & Depression. Ed. by David M. Levin. (Psychoanalytic Crosscurrents Ser.). 548p. 1988. pap. 25.00x (ISBN 0-8147-5039-7). NYU Pr.

Pathologies of the Modern Self: Studies on Narcissism, Schizophrenia, & Depression. Ed. by David M. Levin. 512p. 1986. text ed. 45.00x (ISBN 0-8147-5026-5). NYU Pr.

Pathologist. Jack Rudman. (Career Examination Ser.: C-645). (Cloth bdg. avail. on request). pap. 27.95 (ISBN 0-8373-0645-0). Natl Learning.

Pathologist & the Environment. Dante Scarpelli. (IAP Ser.: No. 26). 250p. 1985. 67.95 (ISBN 0-683-07516-0). Williams & Wilkins.

Pathologony of Tumours in Laboratory Animals: Vol. 1, Tumours of the Rat, Parts 1 & 2. Ed. by V. S. Turusov. (IARC Scientific Ser. No 5 & 6). 340p. 1987. 120.00 (ISBN 92-832-1410-2). Oxford U Pr.

Pathology. 9th ed. A. D. Fayemi. (Review Ser.). Date not set. 16.00 (ISBN 0-444-01302-4). Elsevier.

Pathology. N. K. Hall & D. L. Feeback. (Oklahoma Notes Ser.). (Illus.). xi, 223p. 1987. pap. 12.95 (ISBN 0-387-96338-3). Springer-Verlag.

Pathology. Edward B. Krumbhaar. LC 75-23692. (Clio Medica: No. 19). (Illus.). Repr. of 1937 ed. 18.50 (ISBN 0-404-58919-7). AMS Pr.

Pathology. (National Medical Series for Independent Study). 360p. 1984. pap. 19.00 (ISBN 0-471-09623-7, 1-635). Wiley.

Pathology. Emanuel Rubin et al. LC 65-8626. (Illus.). 1824p. 1988. 59.95 (ISBN 0-397-50698-8, Lippincott Medical). Lippincott.

Pathology. 4th ed. J. R. Tighe & D. R. Davies. (Illus.). 335p. 1984. pap. 15.95 (ISBN 0-7216-0978-3, Bailliere-Tindall). Saunders.

Pathology & Management of Lymphoma. Ed. by John G. Allison. (Illus.). 256p. 1984. 32.50 (ISBN 0-87993-207-4). Futura Pub.

Pathology & Pharmacology of the Eye. J. I. Rodgin. LC 82-61825. 400p. 1983. 45.00 (ISBN 0-87873-044-3). Prof Pr Bks NYC.

Pathology & Physiology of Allergic Reactions. Ed. by P. S. Norman. (Journal: International Archives of Allergy & Applied Immunology: Vol. 77, No. 1-2). (Illus.). 280p. 1985. pap. 77.50 (ISBN 3-8055-4056-6). S Karger.

Pathology & Psychology of Cognition. Ed. by Andrew Burton. LC 82-12526. (Psychology in Progress Ser.). 256p. 1982. pap. 12.85 (ISBN 0-416-30820-1, NO. 3793). Routledge Chapman & Hall.

Pathology & Recognition of Malignant Melanoma. Ed. by Martin Mihm. (IAP Monographs: No. 30). 180p. 1988. 49.50 (ISBN 0-683-06016-3). Williams & Wilkins.

Pathology Annual, Nineteen Eighty-Seven, Pt. 2. (Pathology Annual Ser.). 1987. 65.00 (ISBN 0-8385-7780-6). Appleton & Lange.

Pathology Annual, 1982, Vol. 17, Pt. 2. Sheldon C. Sommers & Paul P. Rosen. 416p. 1983. 45.00 (ISBN 0-8385-7767-9). Appleton & Lange.

Pathology Annual, 1982, Vol. 17, Pt. 1. Shedlon C. Sommers & Paul Peter Rosen. 432p. 1982. text ed. 42.50x (ISBN 0-8385-7765-2). Appleton & Lange.

Pathology Annual, 1983, 2 pts, Vol. 18. Sheldon C. Sommers & Paul P. Rosen. 1983. Pt. 1. 45.00 (ISBN 0-8385-7731-8); Pt. 2. 45.00 (ISBN 0-8385-7741-5). Appleton & Lange.

Pathology Annual, 1984, 2 Pts, Vol. 19. Sheldon C. Sommers & Paul P. Rosen. LC 66-20355. 384p. 1984. 47.50 ea. Pt. 1 (ISBN 0-8385-7750-4). Pt. 2 (ISBN 0-8385-7760-1). Appleton & Lange.

Pathology Annual, 1985, Vol. 20, Pt. 2. Ed. by Sheldon C. Sommers et al. (Pathology Ser.). 544p. 1985. 61.50 (ISBN 0-8385-7771-7). Appleton & Lange.

Pathology Annual, 1986, Vol. 21, Pt. 1. Ed. by Sheldon C. Sommers et al. (Illus.). 368p. 1985. 65.00 (ISBN 0-8385-7772-5). Appleton & Lange.

Pathology Annual, 1986, Vol. 21, Pt. 2. Ed. by Sheldon C. Sommers et al. 400p. 1986. 59.95 (ISBN 0-8385-7777-6). Appleton & Lange.

Pathology Annual 1987, Vol. 22, Pt. 1. Paul P. Rosen & Robert E. Fechner. 448p. 1986. 69.95 (ISBN 0-8385-7778-4). Appleton & Lange.

Pathology Annual, 1988, Pt. II. Paul P. Rosen & Robert E. Fechner. 1988. 65.00 (ISBN 0-8385-7789-X). Appleton & Lange.

Pathology Annual 1988, Pt. 1. Rosen & Fechner. 352p. 1988. text ed. 65.00 (ISBN 0-8385-7781-4). Appleton & Lange.

Pathology for Radiographers & Health Care Professionals. John A. Bloomfield. 150p. 1982. 20.00 (ISBN 0-8151-0946-6). Year Bk Med.

Pathology for Surgeons. Watts & Spence. 720p. 1986. 72.00 (ISBN 0-7236-0808-3). PSG Pub Co.

Pathology Illustrated. 2nd ed. Alasdair D. Govan et al. (Illus.). 890p. (Orig.). 1986. pap. text ed. 35.00 (ISBN 0-443-03547-4). Churchill.

Pathology in Gynecology & Obstetrics. 3rd ed. Claude Gompel & Steven Silverberg. LC 65-7750. (Illus.). 704p. 1985. text ed. 89.50 (ISBN 0-397-50610-4, Lippincott Medical). Lippincott.

Pathology in Health Sciences & Biology: Subject Analysis with Reference Bibliography. Norma S. Vensko. LC 85-48181. 150p. 1987. 34.50 (ISBN 0-88164-966-X); pap. 26.50 (ISBN 0-88164-967-8). ABBE Pubs Assn.

Pathology in Surgical Practice. Ed. by G. J. Hadfield et al. 500p. 1986. 89.50 (ISBN 0-683-13033-1, Pub. by E Arnold UK). Williams & Wilkins.

Pathology of a Black African Population. C. Isaacson. (Current Topics in Pathology Ser.: Vol. 72). (Illus.). 152p. 1982. 69.50 (ISBN 0-387-11381-9). Springer-Verlag.

Pathology of AIDS: Color Atlas & Textbook. Henry L. Ioachim. LC 65-10291. (Illus.). 336p. 1988. price not set (ISBN 0-397-50864-6, Lippincott Medical). Lippincott.

Pathology of Atherosclerosis. Neville Woolf. Ed. by T. Crawford. (Postgraduate Pathology Ser.). 1982. 80.00 (ISBN 0-407-00125-5). Butterworth.

Pathology of Bladder Cancer, 2 Vols. Ed. by George T. Bryan & Samuel M. Cohen. 1983. Vol. I, 148p. 73.50 (ISBN 0-8493-6225-3); Vol. II, 256p. 82.50 (ISBN 0-8493-6226-1). CRC Pr.

Pathology of Bone. P. A. Revell. (Illus.). 320p. 1985. 65.50 (ISBN 0-387-15418-3). Springer-Verlag.

Pathology of Cell Receptors & Tumor Markers. Ed. by G. Seifert & K Huebner. (Illus.). 206p. 1987. lib. bdg. 90.00 (ISBN 0-89574-249-7, Pub. by Gustav Fisher Verlag). VCH Pubs.

Pathology of Cerebrospinal Microcirculation. Ed. by J. Cervos-Navarro et al. LC 77-84125. (Advances in Neurology Ser.: Vol. 20). 632p. 1978. 100.50 (ISBN 0-89004-237-3). Raven.

Pathology of Congenital Heart Disease. Anderson & Becker. 1982. text ed. 130.00 (ISBN 0-407-00137-9). Butterworth.

Pathology of Domestic Animals, Vol. 1. 3rd ed. K. V. Jubb et al. 1985. 65.00 (ISBN 0-12-391601-1). Acad Pr.

Pathology of Domestic Aaimals, Vol. 2. 3rd ed. K. V. Jubb et al. 1985. 65.00 (ISBN 0-12-391602-X). Acad Pr.

Pathology of Domestic Animals, Vol. 3. 3rd. ed. Jubb. 1985. 65.00 (ISBN 0-12-391603-8). Acad Pr.

Pathology of Drug Induced & Toxic Diseases. R. M. Riddell. (Illus.). 736p. 1982. text ed. 83.00 (ISBN 0-443-08083-6). Churchill.

Pathology of Eating: Psychology & Treatment. Sara Gilbert. 256p. 1987. 32.50 (ISBN 0-7102-0271-7, 02717). Routledge Chapman & Hall.

Pathology of Erythroblastic Mitosis in Occupational Benzenic Erythropathy & Erythremia. E. G. Rondanelli et al. (Bibliotheca Haematologica: No. 35). (Illus.). 1970. pap. 50.75 (ISBN 3-8055-0139-0). S Karger.

Pathology of Extreme Aged, Vol. 1. Ed. by Kunio Oota & Syoichi Otsu. (Pathology of the Extreme Aged Ser.: Vol. 1). (Illus.). 200p. 1984. pap. 22.50 (ISBN 0-912791-10-1). Ishiyaku Euro.

Pathology of Fishes. Ed. by William E. Ribelin & George Migaki. LC 73-15261. (Illus.). 1016p. 1975. 75.00x (ISBN 0-299-06520-0, 652). U of Wis Pr.

Pathology of Glomerular Disease. Ed. by Seymour Rosen. LC 83-2039. (Contemporary Issues in Surgical Pathology Ser.: Vol. 1). (Illus.). 274p. 1983. text ed. 48.00 (ISBN 0-443-08198-0). Churchill.

Pathology of Granulomas. Ed. by Harry L. Ioachim. (Illus.). 552p. 1983. text ed. 96.00 (ISBN 0-89004-445-7). Raven.

Pathology of Granulomas & Neoplasms of the Nose & Paranasal Sinuses. Imrich Friedman & Dennis A. Osborn. (Illus.). 306p. 1982. 90.00 (ISBN 0-443-01410-8). Churchill.

Pathology of Heart Valve Replacement. A. G. Rose. 1987. lib. bdg. 76.50 (ISBN 0-85200-984-4, Pub. by MTP Pr England). Kluwer Academic.

Pathology of Higher Education. A. P. Srivastava. 294p. 1979. 14.95. Asia Bk Corp.

Pathology of Homicide: A Vade Mecum for Pathologist, Prosecutor & Defense Counsel. Lester Adelson. (Illus.). 992p. 1974. 74.25x (ISBN 0-398-03000-6). C C Thomas.

Pathology of Human Disease. J. B. Walter. LC 88-6855. (Illus.). 1000p. 1989. price not set (ISBN 0-8121-1151-6). Lea & Febiger.

Pathology of Human Neoplasms: An Atlas of Diagnostic Electron Microscopy & Immunohistochemistry. Ed. by Henry A. Azar. (Illus.). 656p. 1988. text ed. 99.00 (ISBN 0-88167-363-3). Raven.

Pathology of Immunoglobulins: Diagnostic & Clinical Aspects. Ed. by Stephan E. Ritzmann. LC 82-18021. (Protein Abnormalities Ser.: Vol. 2). 408p. 1982. 42.00 (ISBN 0-8451-2801-9). A R Liss.

Pathology of Incipient Neoplasia. Donald E. Henson & Jorge Albores-Saavedra. (Illus.). 463p. 1986. 68.00 (ISBN 0-7216-1144-3). Saunders.

Pathology of Infertility. Ed. by Bernard Gondos & Daniel H. Riddick. (Illus.). 352p. 1987. text ed. 93.00 (ISBN 0-86577-248-7). Thieme Med Pubs.

Pathology of Influenza. Milton C. Winternitz. (Illus.). 1920. 100.00x (ISBN 0-685-69886-6). Elliots Bks.

Pathology of Laboratory Animals, 2 vols. Ed. by K. Benirschke et al. (Illus.). 1978. Set. 420.00 (ISBN 0-387-90292-9). Springer-Verlag.

Pathology of Laboratory Animals. photocopy ed. William E. Ribelin & John R. McCoy. (Illus.). 448p. 1971. 51.25 (ISBN 0-398-02203-8). C C Thomas.

Pathology of Laboratory Mice & Rats. Ed. by P. L. Altman. (Biology Databook Ser.). 700p. 1985. 180.00 (ISBN 0-08-030077-4, Pub. by Aberdeen Scotland). Pergamon.

Pathology of Leprosy. James A. Freeman et al. LC 80-720434. 16p. 1980. pap. 55.00 (ISBN 0-89189-101-3, 15-7-011-00). Am Soc Clinical.

Pathology of Limb Ischaema. Henry Dible. LC 67-27239. (Illus.). 110p. 1967. 9.00 (ISBN 0-87527-030-1). Green.

Pathology of Mind. Henry Maudsley. Ed. by Aubrey Lewis. (Classics of Psychology & Psychiatry Ser.). 571p. 1978. pap. 29.00 (ISBN 0-86187-310-6, Pub. by Frances Pinter). Longwood Pub Group.

Pathology of Neoplasia in Children & Adolescents. Ed. by Milton Finegold. (Major Problems in Pathology Ser.). (Illus.). 481p. 1986. 63.00 (ISBN 0-7216-1337-3). Saunders.

Pathology of Neoplastic & Endocrine Induced Diseases of the Breast. Bassler & Hubner. 484p. 1987. text ed. 162.00 (ISBN 0-89574-232-2, Pub. by Gustav Fischer Verlag). VCH Pubs.

Pathology of Occupational Lung Disease. Andrew Churg. LC 87-3296. (Illus.). 416p. 1988. 68.50. Igaku-Shoin.

Pathology of Opportunistic Infections (with Pathogenetic, Diagnostic, & Clinical Correlations) Richard L. Myerowitz. (Illus.). 256p. 1983. text ed. 87.00 (ISBN 0-89004-716-2). Raven.

Pathology of Oral Manifestations of Systematic Diseases. Alvin F. Gardner. 1972. 34.95x (ISBN 0-02-845120-1). Hafner.

Pathology of Oxygen. Ed. by Anne Autor. 360p. 1982. 69.50 (ISBN 0-12-068620-1). Acad Pr.

Pathology of Oxygen Toxicity. J. Douglas Balentine. 346p. 1982. 65.50 (ISBN 0-12-077080-6). Acad Pr.

Pathology of Parasitic Diseases. Ed. by S. M. Gaafar et al. LC 72-108014. (Illus.). 408p. 1971. 15.00 (ISBN 0-911198-28-8). Purdue U Pr.

Pathology of Perinatal Brain Injury. Lucy B. Rorke. (Illus.). 160p. 1982. text ed. 28.00 (ISBN 0-89004-688-3). Raven.

Pathology of Politics: Violence, Betrayal, Corruption, Secrecy & Propaganda. Carl J. Friedrich. 1972. text ed. 49.50x (ISBN 0-8290-0343-6). Irvington.

Pathology of Power. Norman Cousins. 1987. 15.95 (ISBN 0-393-02378-8). Norton.

Pathology of Power. Norman Cousins. 1988. pap. 8.95 (ISBN 0-393-30541-4). Norton.

Pathology of Public Policy. Brian W. Hogwood & B. Guy Peters. (Illus.). 1985. 32.00x (ISBN 0-19-878011-7); pap. 11.95x (ISBN 0-19-878010-9). Oxford U Pr.

Pathology of Pulmonary Hypertension. C. A. Wagenvoort & Noeke Wagenvoort. LC 76-39782. (Wiley Ser. in Clinical Cardiology). Repr. of 1977 ed. 89.80 (ISBN 0-8357-9948-4, 2015198). Bks Demand UMI.

Pathology of Rheumatic Diseases. H. G. Fassbender. Tr. by G. Loewi from Ger. (Illus.). 360p. 1975. 61.00 (ISBN 0-387-07289-6). Springer-Verlag.

Pathology of Simian Primates, 2 pts. Ed. by R. N. Fiennes. Incl. Pt. 1. General Pathology. 132.75 (ISBN 3-8055-1307-0); Pt. 2. Infectious & Parasitic Diseases. 110.75 (ISBN 3-8055-1308-9). (Illus.). 1972. Set. 218.75 (ISBN 3-8055-1329-1). S Karger.

Pathology of Skeletal Muscle. Stirling Carpenter & George Karpati. LC 84-1849. (Illus.). 754p. 1984. 50.00 (ISBN 0-443-08068-2). Churchill.

Pathology of Soft Tissue Tumors. Steven I. Hajdu. LC 79-21735. (Illus.). 599p. 1979. text ed. 65.00 (ISBN 0-8121-0693-8). Lea & Febiger.

Pathology of the Bone Marrow. Ed. by K. Lennert & K. Hubner. (Illus.). 426p. 1984. lib. bdg. 86.00 (ISBN 0-89574-195-4, Pub. by Gustav Fischer Verlag). VCH Pubs.

Pathology of the Carotid Body & Sinus. D. Heath & P. Smith. 1985. 19.95 (ISBN 0-683-13035-8, Pub. by E Arnold UK). Williams & Wilkins.

Pathology of the Colon, Small Intestine, & Anus. Ed. by H. Thomas Norris. (Contemporary Issues in Surgical Pathology Ser.: Vol. 2). (Illus.). 338p. 1983. text ed. 55.00 (ISBN 0-443-08235-9). Churchill.

Pathology of the Ear. Harold F. Schuknecht. LC 73-92802. (Commonwealth Fund Publications Ser). (Illus.). 448p. 1974. Set of 250 Slides. 250.00x (ISBN 0-674-65786-1). Harvard U Pr.

Pathology of the Endocrine Pancreas in Diabetes. Ed. by P. J. Lefebvre & D. G. Pipeleers. 350p. 1988. 107.90 (ISBN 0-387-17836-8). Springer-Verlag.

Pathology of the Esophagus. H. T. Enterline & J. J. Thompson. (Illus.). 225p. 1984. 59.00 (ISBN 0-387-90896-X). Springer-Verlag.

Pathology of the Esophagus, Stomach & Duodenum. Henry D. Appelman. (Contemporary Issues in Surgical Pathology Ser.: Vol. 4). (Illus.). 287p. 1984. text ed. 55.00 (ISBN 0-443-08219-7). Churchill.

Pathology of the Eye. G. O. Naumann & D. J. Apple. (Illus.). xxxv, 998p. 1986. 235.00 (ISBN 0-387-96044-9). Springer-Verlag.

Pathology of the Fetus & the Infant. Edith L. Potter & John M. Craig. LC 75-16021. pap. 160.00 (2026505). Bks Demand UMI.

Pathology of the Gastro-Intestinal Tract. Ed. by B. Morson. LC 56-49162. 1976. 68.00 (ISBN 0-387-07927-0). Springer-Verlag.

Pathology of the Kidney, 3 Vols. 3rd ed. Robert H. Heptinstall. 1983. 180.00 set (ISBN 0-316-35797-9). Little.

Pathology of the Larynx. L. Michaels. (Illus.). 330p. 1984. 95.00 (ISBN 0-387-13237-6). Springer-Verlag.

Pathology of the Larynx: Atlases of the Pathology of the Head & Neck. Stacey E. Mills & Robert E. Fechner. LC 84-720142. 86p. 1985. slides 115.00 (ISBN 0-89189-187-0, 15-1-036-00). Am Soc Clinical.

Pathology of the Liver. 2nd ed. Ed. by Robert MacSween et al. (Illus.). 1987. 150.00 (ISBN 0-443-03049-9). Churchill.

Pathology of the Lung. Ed. by G. G. Pietra. (Journal: Applied Pathology: Vol. 4, No. 3, 1986). (Illus.). 96p. 1987. pap. 30.75 (ISBN 3-8055-4573-8). S Karger.

Pathology of the Lung, 2 vols. 4th ed. H. Spencer. (Illus.). 1350p. 1984. 245.00 (ISBN 0-08-030772-8). Pergamon.

Pathology of the Lung. 4th ed. Herbert Spencer. cancelled (ISBN 0-7216-8509-9). Saunders.

Pathology of the Lung. Ed. by William M. Thurlbeck. (Illus.). 850p. 1987. 180.00 (ISBN 0-86577-134-0). Thieme Med Pubs.

Pathology of the Mesothelium. Ed. by J. S. Jones. (Illus.). 1987. 150.00 (ISBN 0-387-16208-9). Springer-Verlag.

Pathology of the Myelinated Axon. Masazumi Adachi et al. LC 83-12874. (Illus.). 425p. 1985. 97.50 (ISBN 0-89640-100-6). Igaku-Shoin.

Pathology of the Nose & Paranasal Sinuses. Philip L. Barney. LC 82-720085. (Atlases of the Pathology of the Head & Neck Ser.). 1982. incl. slides 110.00 (ISBN 0-89189-082-3, 15-1-029-00). Am Soc Clinical.

Pathology of the Pancreas. A. H. Cruickshank. (Illus.). 290p. 1986. 89.00 (ISBN 0-387-16216-X). Springer-Verlag.

Pathology of the Placenta. Harold Fox. (Major Problems in Pathology Ser.: Vol. 7). (Illus.). 491p. 1978. write for info. (ISBN 0-7216-3831-7). Saunders.

Pathology of the Placenta. Ed. by Eugene V. Perrin. (Contemporary Issues in Surgical Pathology Ser.: Vol. 5). (Illus.). 216p. 1985. text ed. 50.00 (ISBN 0-443-08231-6). Churchill.

Pathology of the Salivary Glands. John G. Batsakis et al. LC 77-3537. (Atlases of the Pathology of the Head & Neck Ser.). (Illus.). 57p. 1977. slide atlas 100.00 (ISBN 0-89189-031-9, 15-1-0019-00). Am Soc Clinical.

Pathology of the Skin. Philip H. McKee. LC 65-40215. (Gower Bk.). (Illus.). 550p. 1988. price not set (ISBN 0-397-44601-2, Lippincott Medical). Lippincott.

Pathology of the Syrian Hamster. Ed. by F. Homburger. (Progress in Experimental Tumor Research: Vol. 16). 1972. 125.50 (ISBN 3-8055-1367-4). S Karger.

Pathology of the Testis & Its Adnexa. Ed. by Aleksander Talerman & Lawrence M. Roth. (Contemporary Issues in Surgical Pathology Ser.: Vol. 7). (Illus.). 263p. 1986. text ed. 55.00 (ISBN 0-443-08351-7). Churchill.

Pathology of the Uterine Cervix, Vagina, & Vulva. Fu & Reagan. 368p. 1988. price not set (ISBN 0-7216-7493-3). Saunders.

Pathology of the Vessel Wall: A Modern Appraisal. Ed. by Neville Woolf. 360p. 1983. 54.95 (ISBN 0-275-91419-4, C1419). Praeger.

Pathology of the Vulva & Vagina. Ed. by Edward J. Wilkinson. (Contemporary Issues in Surgical Pathology Ser.: Vol. 9). (Illus.). 340p. 1986. text ed. 58.00 (ISBN 0-443-08514-5). Churchill.

Pathology of Transcription & Translation. Ed. by E. Farber. (Biochemistry of Disease Ser.: Vol. 2). 192p. 1972. 49.75 (ISBN 0-8247-1180-7). Dekker.

Pathology of Tropical Food Legumes: Disease Resistance in Crop Improvement. D. J. Allen. LC 82-20301. 413p. 1984. 97.95x (ISBN 0-471-10232-6, Wiley-Interscience). Wiley.

Pathology of Tumours in Laboratory Animals, Vol. 3. Ed. by V. S. Turusov. (IARC Ser.). (Illus.). 1982. 50.00x (ISBN 0-19-723034-2). Oxford U Pr.

Pathology of Tumours in Laboratory Animals: Tumour of the Mouse, Vol. 2. Ed. by V. S. Turusov. (IARC Ser.). (Illus.). 1979. 60.00x (ISBN 0-19-723022-9). Oxford U Pr.

Pathology of Tumours in Laboratory Animals: Tumours of the Rat, Pt. 1, Vol. 1. Ed. by V. S. Turusov et al. (IARC Scientific Pub.: No. 5). 1973. 20.00 (ISBN 0-686-16790-2). World Health.

Pathology of Unusual Malignant Cutaneous Tumors. Wick. (Clinical & Biochemical Analysis Ser.). 472p. 1985. 75.00 (ISBN 0-8247-7377-2). Dekker.

Pathology of Zoo Animals: A Review of Necropsies Conducted over a Fourteen Year Period at the San Diego Zoo. Lynn A. Griner. LC 82-62698. (Illus.). 1983. 25.00 (ISBN 0-911461-11-6). Zoological Soc.

Pathology Office Assistant. (Career Examination Ser.: C-3400). Date not set. pap. 16.00 (ISBN 0-8373-3400-4). Natl Learning.

Pathology: PreTest Self-Assessment & Review. 4th ed. Ed. by Paul H. Duray. (Illus.). 216p. 1986. 14.95 (ISBN 0-07-051944-7). McGraw-Pretest.

Pathology Speciality Board Review. 5th ed. A. Olusegun Fayemi. (Speciality Board Review Ser.: Vol. 9). 1984. pap. text ed. 32.25. Med Exam.

Pathology Words & Phrases: A Quick Reference Guide. 43p. 1988. pap. 7.95 (ISBN 0-934385-09-2). Prima Vera Pubns.

Pathomechanism & Prevention of Sudden Cardiac Death Due to Coronary Insufficiency. Ed. by L. Szekers & Gy J. Papp. 350p. 1984. cancelled 28.00 (ISBN 963-05-3658-7, Pub. by Akademiai Kaido Hungary). IPS.

Pathophysiologic, Diagnostic & Therapeutic Aspects of Headache. Ed. by Mary E. Granger et al. (Pain & Headache Ser.: Vol. 4). 135p. 1976. 41.50 (ISBN 3-8055-2282-7). S Karger.

Pathophysiological Aspects of Cancer Epidemiology. Ed. by G. Mathe & P. Reizenstein. (Advances in the Biosciences Ser.: No. 50). (Illus.). 276p. 1985. 90.00 (ISBN 0-08-030780-9). Pergamon.

Pathophysiological Aspects of Cyclic Nucleotides. Ed. by Pavel Hamet & Howard Sands. (Advances in Cyclic Nucleotide Research: Vol. 12). 470p. 1980. text ed. 88.00 (ISBN 0-89004-454-6). Raven.

Pathophysiological Aspects of Sickle Cell Vaso-Occlusion. Ed. by Ronald L. Nagel. LC 87-4061. (Progress in Clinical & Biological Research Ser.: Vol. 240). 488p. 1987. 84.00 (ISBN 0-8451-5090-1, 5090). A R Liss.

Pathophysiological Effects of Endotoxins at the Cellular Level. Jeannine A. Majde & Robert J. Person. LC 81-6066. (Progress in Clinical & Biological Research Ser.: Vol. 62). 204p. 1981. 40.00 (ISBN 0-8451-0062-9). A R Liss.

Pathophysiological Phenomena in Nursing: Human Response to Illness. Virginia K. Carrieri et al. (Illus.). 436p. 1986. 43.95 (ISBN 0-7216-1083-8). Saunders.

Pathophysiological Problems in Clinical Nephrology: Proceedings of the Heidelberg Seminars in Nephrology, Heidelberg, September, 1978. Heidelberg Seminars in Nephrology Staff. Ed. by E. Ritz et al. (Contributions to Nephrology: Vol. 14). (Illus.). 1978. 58.75 (ISBN 3-8055-2910-4). S Karger.

Pathophysiology. A. A. Buehlmann et al. (Illus.). 1979. pap. 40.00 (ISBN 0-387-90370-4). Springer-Verlag.

Pathophysiology. 1988. pap. price not set (ISBN 0-471-85258-9). Wiley.

Pathophysiology. 2nd ed. Sylvia Price & Lorraine Wilson. (Illus.). 1024p. 1982. text ed. 44.95x (ISBN 0-07-050863-1). McGraw.

Pathophysiology. 3rd ed. Sylvia Price & Lorraine Wilson. 1200p. 1986. text ed. 48.95 (ISBN 0-07-050864-X). McGraw.

Pathophysiology: Adaptations & Alterations in Function. 2nd ed. Barbara Bullock & Pearl P. Rosendahl. 1988. text ed. write for info. (ISBN 0-673-39710-6). Scott F.

Pathophysiology: Adaptations & Alterations in Function. Ed. by Barbara Bullock et al. 1984. text ed. write for info. (ISBN 0-673-39386-0). Scott F.

Pathophysiology: An Introduction to the Mechanisms of Disease. 2nd ed. Bernice L. Muir. LC 87-25298. 685p. 1988. 34.95 (ISBN 0-471-83709-1). Wiley.

Pathophysiology & Management of Thromboembolic Disorders. Kenneth K. Wu. (Illus.). 456p. 1984. 42.00 (ISBN 0-88416-460-8). PSG Pub Co.

Pathophysiology & Pharmacotherapy of Myocardial Infarction. Nabil El-Sherif & Chatla V. Reddy. (Physiologic & Pharmacologic Bases of Drug Therapy Ser.). 1986. 71.50 (ISBN 0-12-238045-2). Acad Pr.

Pathophysiology & Treatment of Drowning & Near-Drowning. photocopy ed. Jerome H. Modell. (Illus.). 136p. 1971. 16.25 (ISBN 0-398-02361-1). C C Thomas.

Pathophysiology & Treatment of Inhalation Injuries. Loke. (Lung Biology in Health & Disease Ser.). 584p. 1987. 125.00 (ISBN 0-8247-7795-6). Dekker.

Pathophysiology: Concepts of Altered Health States. 2nd ed. Carol Porth. LC 64-4222. (Illus.). 1056p. 1986. 44.75 (ISBN 0-397-54481-2, Lippincott Nursing). Lippincott.

Pathophysiology for Health Practitioners. Gwen J. Stephens. (Illus.). 1980. text ed. write for info. (ISBN 0-02-417120-4). Macmillan.

Pathophysiology in Small Animal Surgery. Ed. by M. Joseph Bojrab. LC 80-25780. (Illus.). 906p. 1981. text ed. 75.00 (ISBN 0-8121-0696-2). Lea & Febiger.

Pathophysiology in the Medical Sciences. H. E. Mentz. 1982. text ed. 19.95. Butterworth.

Pathophysiology: Mechanisms & Expressions. Gary G. Ferguson. (Illus.). 1984. Pp. 400. pap. 34.95 (ISBN 0-7216-3616-0); Pp. 112. instr's. manual avail. (ISBN 0-7216-2013-2). Saunders.

Pathophysiology of Blood Disorders. Ed. by Ch. Hershko & G. Izak. (Illus.). 1979. pap. 44.00 (ISBN 3-8055-3021-8). S Karger.

Pathophysiology of Combined Injury & Trauma. R. T. Gruber et al. 1987. 59.50 (ISBN 0-12-304755-2). Acad Pr.

Pathophysiology of Combined Injury & Trauma. Richard I. Walker et al. LC 85-6128. 278p. 1985. 63.00 (ISBN 0-8391-2077-X). Aspen Pub.

Pathophysiology of Dermatologic Disease. N. A. Soter & H. P. Baden. (Illus.). 480p. 1984. text ed. 25.00 (ISBN 0-07-059746-4). McGraw.

Pathophysiology of Electrolyte & Renal Disorders. Ed. by H. David Humes. (Illus.). 707p. 1985. pap. 29.95 (ISBN 0-443-08324-X). Churchill.

Pathophysiology of Endotoxin: Handbook of Endotoxin, Vol. 2. Ed. by L. B. Hinshaw. 400p. 1985. 150.00 (ISBN 0-444-90385-2). Elsevier.

Pathophysiology of Gestational Disorders. Ed. by N. S. Assali. Incl. Vol. 1. Maternal Disorders. 1972. 77.50 (ISBN 0-12-065501-2); Vol. 2. Fetal-Placental Disorders. 1972. 68.00 (ISBN 0-12-065502-0); Vol. 3. Fetal & Neonatal Disorders. 1973. 78.00 (ISBN 0-12-065503-9). 1972. Acad Pr.

Pathophysiology of Heart Disease. Ed. by N. Dhalla et al. (Developments in Cardiovascular Medicine Ser.). 1987. lib. bdg. 69.95 (ISBN 0-89838-864-3, Pub. by Martinus Nijhoff Netherlands). Kluwer Academic.

Pathophysiology of Hypertension: Cardiovascular Aspects. Ed. by A. Zanchetti & R. C. Tarazi. (Handbook of Hypertension Ser.: No. 7). 550p. 1986. 196.50 (ISBN 0-444-90421-2). Elsevier.

Pathophysiology of Hypertension: Regulatory Mechanisms. Ed. by A. Zanchetti & R. C. Tarazi. (Handbook of Hypertension Ser.: Vol. 8). 750p. 1986. 243.25 (ISBN 0-444-90422-0). Elsevier.

Pathophysiology of Infantile Malnutrition Protein. Kerpel & Froniuis. 1984. cancelled 33.00 (ISBN 963-05-3222-0, Pub. by Akademiai Kaido Hungary). IPS.

Pathophysiology of Melanocytes. International Pigment Cell Conference, 10th, Cambridge, Mass., October 1977, Pt. 2. Ed. by S. N. Klaus. (Pigment Cell: Vol. 5). (Illus.). 1979. 92.75 (ISBN 3-8055-2973-2). S Karger.

Pathophysiology of Myocardial Perfusion. W. Schaper. 758p. 1980. 207.50 (ISBN 0-444-80048-4, Biomedical Pr). Elsevier.

Pathophysiology of Parasitic Infections. Ed. by E. J. Soulsby. 1976. 41.50 (ISBN 0-12-655365-3). Acad Pr.

Pathophysiology of Parasitic Infections. L. E. Symons. 300p. 1988. price not set (ISBN 0-12-680125-8). Acad Pr.

Pathophysiology of Plasma Protein Metabolism. Ed. by Giulian Mariant. 416p. 1985. 65.00x (ISBN 0-306-41771-5, Plenum Pr). Plenum Pub.

Pathophysiology of Puberty. Ed. by E. Cacciari & A. Prader. LC 80-40928. (Serono Symposia Ser.: No. 36). 1981. 91.50 (ISBN 0-12-154160-6). Acad Pr.

Pathophysiology of Renal Disease. (Contributions to Nephrology: Vol. 23). (Illus.). vi, 234p. 1980. pap. 65.50 (ISBN 3-8055-0943-X). S Karger.

Pathophysiology of Renal Disease. Ed. by E. Ritz & S. G. Massry. (Contributions to Nephrology: Vol. 33). (Illus.). viii, 276p. 1982. pap. 104.75 (ISBN 3-8055-3534-1). S Karger.

Pathophysiology of Renal Disease. 2nd ed. Ed. by Burton D. Rose. (Illus.). 780p. 1987. pap. text ed. 29.50 (ISBN 0-07-053629-5). McGraw.

Pathophysiology of the Reticuloendothelial System. Ed. by Burton M. Altura & Thomas M. Saba. 248p. 1981. text ed. 43.50 (ISBN 0-89004-441-4). Raven.

Pathophysiology of the Splanchnic Circulation. Ed. by Peter R. Kvietys et al. 1987. Vol. I. 2 vol. set 195.00 (ISBN 0-8493-4661-4). Vol. II, 368 pgs. CRC Pr.

Pathophysiology of the Visual System. Ed. by L. Maffei. (Documenta Ophthalmologica Proceedings Ser.: No. 30). 304p. 1981. 53.00 (ISBN 90-6193-726-4, Pub. by Junk Pubs Netherlands). Kluwer Academic.

Pathophysiology of Thermal Injury: A Practical Approach. Thomas W. Panke & Charles Mcleod. LC 79-3237. 384p. 1986. 69.50 (ISBN 0-8089-1754-4, 793237). Grune.

Pathophysiology: Principles of Disease. Martha J. Miller. (Illus.). 528p. 1983. pap. write for info. (ISBN 0-7216-6337-0). Saunders.

Pathophysiology: The Biological Principles of Disease. 2nd ed. Lloyd H. Smith, Jr. & Samuel O. Thier. (The International Textbook of Medicine Ser.: Vol. 1). (Illus.). 1372p. 1985. 105.00 (ISBN 0-7216-8411-4). Saunders.

Pathos of Distance: A Book of a Thousand & One Moments. James Hunedker. 394p. Repr. of 1916 ed. lib. bdg. 40.00 (ISBN 0-918377-50-1). Russell Pr.

Pathos of Power. Kenneth B. Clark. 188p. 1975. pap. 5.95x (ISBN 0-06-131857-4, TB1857, Torch). Har-Row.

Paths. Lawrence E. Keith. (Illus.). 1979. 5.00 (ISBN 0-932222-01-3); pap. 3.00 (ISBN 0-932222-02-1). Sunrise Tortoise.

Paths & Labyrinths: Nine Papers from a Kafka Symposium. J. P. Stern & J. J. White. (Publications of the Institute of Germanic Studies: Vol. 35). 159p. 1985. pap. text ed. 18.50x (ISBN 0-85457-124-8, Pub. by Inst Germanic UK). Humanities.

Paths & Means to Holiness. Constantine Cavarnos. 85p. (Orig.). 1986. pap. 5.00 (ISBN 0-911165-08-8). Ctr Trad Orthodox.

Paths in Dreams: Selected Prose of Ho Chi-Fang. Ho Chi-Fang. Tr. by Bonnie McDougall from Chinese. (Asian & Pacific Writing). 1977. 22.50x (ISBN 0-7022-1260-1); pap. 8.95x (ISBN 0-7022-1261-X). U of Queensland Pr.

Paths in Utopia. Martin Buber. 1988. pap. 7.95 (ISBN 0-02-084190-6, Collier). Macmillan.

Paths into American Culture: Psychology, Medicine, & Morals. John C. Burnham. 384p. 1988. 37.95 (ISBN 0-87722-505-2). Temple U Pr.

Paths Less Travelled: Dispatches from the Front Lines of Exploration. Ed. by Richard Bangs & Christian Kallen. (Illus.). 144p. 1988. 22.50 (ISBN 0-689-11819-8). Atheneum.

Paths of Armor, the Fifth Armored Division in World War II. Vic Hillery & Emerson Hurley. (Divisional Ser.: 27th). (Illus.). 358p. 1986. Repr. of 1950 ed. 25.00 (ISBN 0-89839-084-2). Battery Pr.

Paths of Attainment. Arden Rizer, Jr. 82p. 1987. pap. 18.00 (ISBN 0-939795-13-2). Amer Spirit.

Paths of Culture: A General Ethnology. Kaj Birket-Smith. Tr. by Karin Fennow. LC 64-8488. (Illus.). 550p. 1965. 27.50x (ISBN 0-299-03381-3). U of Wis Pr.

Paths of Culture: A General Ethnology. Kaj Birket-Smith. LC 64-8488. pap. 137.00 (ISBN 0-317-09286-3, 2015354). Bks Demand UMI.

Paths of Faith. 3rd ed. John A. Hutchison. (Illus.). 608p. 1980. text ed. 34.95x (ISBN 0-07-031532-9). McGraw.

Paths of Glory. Humphrey Cobb. 1980. pap. 1.65 (ISBN 0-380-01505-6, 16758, Bard). Avon.

Paths of Glory. Humphrey Cobb. LC 86-11409. 288p. 1986. pap. 11.95 (ISBN 0-8203-0884-6). U of GA Pr.

Paths of Inland Commerce see Chronicles of America.

Paths of Liberation: A Third World Spirituality. Bakole Wa Ilunga. Tr. by Matthew J. O'Connell from Fr. LC 84-5177. 240p. (Orig.). 1984. pap. 12.95 (ISBN 0-88344-401-1). Orbis Bks.

Paths of Life. Mike Giammatteo & Phil Mattox. (Illus.). 1977. 4.00 (ISBN 0-918428-10-6). Sylvan Inst.

Paths of Life: Preface to a World Religion. Charles W. Morris. LC 72-94732. 228p. 1973. pap. 2.25x (ISBN 0-226-53879-6, P541, Phoen). U of Chicago Pr.

Paths of Loneliness: The Individual Isolated in Modern Society. Margaret M. Wood. LC 53-8218. 1953. pap. 17.50x (ISBN 0-231-08503-6). Columbia U Pr.

Paths of Meditation. Ed. by Vedanta Kesari Staff. 241p. 1980. pap. 2.50 (ISBN 0-87481-501-0). Vedanta Pr.

Paths of Neighborhood Change: Race & Crime in Urban America. Richard P. Taub et al. LC 84-2488. (Illus.). 272p. 1984. lib. bdg. 25.00x (ISBN 0-226-79001-0). U of Chicago Pr.

Paths of Neighborhood Change: Race & Crime in Urban America. Richard P. Taub et al. LC 84-2488. (Illus.). xii, 264p. 1987. pap. text ed. 11.95 (ISBN 0-226-79002-9). U of Chicago Pr.

Paths of Peril. David Fickling & Perry Hinton. (Puffin Storybooks Ser.). (Illus.). 32p. (gr. 3-6). 1986. pap. 3.95 (ISBN 0-14-031898-4, Puffin). Penguin.

Paths of Resistance: Tradition & Dignity in Industrializing Missouri. David P. Thelen. 352p. 1986. text ed. 32.00x (ISBN 0-19-503667-0). Oxford U Pr.

Paths of Sociological Imagination. D. Kubat. 596p. 1971. 107.00. Gordon & Breach.

Paths of Sunshine. Florida Federation of Garden Clubs Staff. Ed. by W. Reese Harris et al. Raymond Puckett & Roy A. Mock. (Illus.). 325p. (Orig.). 1988. pap. 14.95. FL Fed Gdn Clubs.

Paths of the Law: The Pursuit of Justice in a Time of Transition, 1960-1980. Vincent A. Carrafiello. LC 83-50006. 280p. (Orig.). 1983. lib. bdg. 29.00 (ISBN 0-8191-3291-8); pap. text ed. 14.25 (ISBN 0-8191-3292-6). U Pr of Amer.

Paths of the Mound Building Indians & Great Game Animals see Historic Highways of America.

Paths of the Past: Tennessee, 1770-1970. Paul H. Bergeron. LC 79-14896. (Tennessee Three Star Books). (Illus.). 136p. 1979. pap. 3.50 (ISBN 0-87049-274-8). U of Tenn Pr.

Paths of the Perambulator. Alan D. Foster. 1985. 17.00 (ISBN 0-932096-39-5). Phantasia Pr.

Paths of Wondering. Alice S. Newton. LC 75-9424. 1975. 5.00 (ISBN 0-8233-0219-9). Golden Quill.

Paths on the Mountain. William B. Brown. (Illus.). 64p. (Orig.). 1985. pap. 4.00 (ISBN 0-913433-05-5, Everett Pr). Street Pr.

Paths That Led to War. John Mackintosh. LC 74-110915. 1970. Repr. of 1940 ed. 30.00x (ISBN 0-8046-0897-0, Pub. by Kennikat). Assoc Faculty Pr.

Paths to Authority: The Middle Class & the Industrial Labor Force in France, 1820-48. Peter N. Stearns. LC 78-16223. 238p. 1978. 19.95 (ISBN 0-252-00633-X). U of Ill Pr.

Paths to Conflict: International Dispute Initiation, 1816-1976. Zeev Maoz. LC 82-83799. 273p. 1982. pap. 31.00 softcover (ISBN 0-86531-933-2). Westview.

Paths to Educational Reform. Wm. Clark Trow. LC 71-122810. 256p. 1971. 33.95 (ISBN 0-87778-002-1). Educ Tech Pubns.

Paths to Human Perfection. Robert E. Birdsong. (Aquarian Academy Supplementary Lecture: No. 3). 1979. pap. 0.75 (ISBN 0-917108-26-4). Sirius Bks.

Paths to Knowledge of Higher Worlds. 3rd ed. Rudolf Steiner. 36p. (Ger.). 1980. pap. 2.95 (ISBN 0-919924-13-1, Pub. by Steiner Book Centre Canada). Anthroposophic.

Paths to Leadership: Power Through Feminine Dignity. Sylvia Bushell. LC 87-70893. 105p. (Orig.). 1987. pap. 8.95 (ISBN 0-943715-00-8). Aldebaran Pr.

Paths to Marriage. Bernard Murstein. (Family Studies Text Ser.). (Illus.). 160p. (Orig.). 1986. text ed. 19.95 (ISBN 0-8039-2382-1); pap. text ed. 9.95 (ISBN 0-8039-2383-X). Sage.

Paths to Mobility Checklist: Objectives for Teaching Gross Motor Skills to "Special Care" Children. J. L. Presland. 20p. 1985. 10.00x (ISBN 0-906054-48-6, Pub. by British Inst Mental). State Mutual Bk.

Paths to Mobility in "Special Care" A Guide to Teaching Gross Motor Skills to Very Handicapped Children. J. L. Presland. 1985. 59.00x (ISBN 0-906054-33-8, Pub. by British Inst Mental); pap. 39.00x (ISBN 0-906054-28-1, Pub. by British Inst Metal). State Mutual Bk.

Paths to Paradise: On the Liberation from Work. Andre Gorz. Tr. by Malcolm Imrie from Fr. 120p. (Orig.). 1985. 20.00 (ISBN 0-89608-243-1); pap. 8.00 (ISBN 0-89608-242-3). South End Pr.

Paths to Peace. Ed. by Victor H. Wallace. LC 72-134149. (Essay Index Reprint Ser). 1957. 23.00 (ISBN 0-8369-1980-7). Ayer Co Pubs.

Paths to Peace: Exploring the Feasibility of Sustainable Peace. Richard Smoke & Willis Harman. LC 87-2173. 114p. 1987. 21.50 (ISBN 0-8133-0492-X); pap. 11.95 (ISBN 0-8133-0487-3). Westview.

Paths to Peace: Major Documents Addressed to the United Nations & Its Organizations by the Popes & the Holy See. 700p. 1987. 34.95 (ISBN 0-940169-01-0). Liturgical Pubns.

Paths to Peace: The U. N. Security & Its Presidency. Ed. by Nicole Davidson & UNITAR. LC 80-20166. (Pergamon Policy Studies on International Politics). 424p. 1981. 66.00 (ISBN 0-08-026322-4). Pergamon.

Paths to Power. A. W. Tozer. 64p. pap. 2.25 (ISBN 0-87509-190-3). Chr Pubns.

Paths to Power: A Working Woman's Guide from First Job to Top Executive. Natasha Josefowitz. 1980. pap. 9.95 (ISBN 0-201-03486-7); write for info. instr's. manual (ISBN 0-201-03479-4). Addison-Wesley.

Paths to Power: Elite Mobility in Contemporary China. David M. Lampton. (Michigan Monographs in Chinese Studies Ser.: No. 55). (Illus.). 379p. (Orig.). 1986. text ed. 17.50 (ISBN 0-89264-063-4); pap. text ed. 10.00 (ISBN 0-89264-064-2). U of Mich Ctr Chinese.

Paths to Profits. Subhash Chander Grover. 146p. (Orig.). 1985. pap. 8.95 (ISBN 0-930383-04-4). Monument Pr.

Paths to Progress: Bread & Freedom in Developing Societies. William McCord & Arline McCord. LC 85-29809. 1986. 17.95 (ISBN 0-393-02307-9). Norton.

Paths to the American Past. J. R. Pole. LC 79-830. 1979. 25.00x (ISBN 0-19-502579-2). Oxford U Pr.

Paths to the Ancient Past. Tom B. Jones. LC 67-12515. 1967. pap. text ed. 11.95 (ISBN 0-02-916630-6). Free Pr.

Paths to the City: Regional Migration in 19th Century France. Leslie P. Moch. LC 83-2955. 261p. 1983. 29.95 (ISBN 0-8039-1985-9). Sage.

Paths to the Northwest: A Jesuit History of the Oregon Province. Wilfred Schoenberg. 477p. 1983. 27.50 (ISBN 0-8294-0405-8). Loyola.

Paths to the Present: Thoughts on the Contemporary Relevance of America's Past. Thomas J. Osborne & Fred R. Mabbutt. LC 84-29748. 182p. 1985. Repr. of 1974 ed. lib. bdg. 11.50 (ISBN 0-89874-842-9). Krieger.

Paths to Transformation: A Study of the General Agencies of the United Methodist Church. Kristine M. Rogers & Bruce A. Rogers. LC 81-17565. (Into Our Third Century Ser.). 96p. (Orig.). 1982. pap. 3.50 (ISBN 0-687-30094-0). Abingdon.

Paths to Writing: Developing Prose Power. Don A. Edwards. 1976. text ed. 12.50 (ISBN 0-682-48343-5, University). Exposition-Phoenix.

Pathway for Oxygen. Ewald R. Weibel. (Illus.). 320p. 1984. text ed. 32.00x (ISBN 0-674-65791-8); pap. text ed. 18.50x (ISBN 0-674-65790-X). Harvard U Pr.

Pathway Icons. Priya Mookerjee. LC 86-50885. (Illus.). 80p. (Orig.). 1987. pap. 12.95 (ISBN 0-500-27428-2). Thames Hudson.

Pathway into Number Theory. R. P. Burn. LC 81-10013. 250p. 1982. 42.50 (ISBN 0-521-24118-9); pap. 19.95 (ISBN 0-521-28534-8). Cambridge U Pr.

Pathway of Discipleship One Hundred One: Group Leader's Guide. 2nd rev. ed. Donald E. Hill. 48p. 1983. 4.00 (ISBN 0-88151-028-9). Lay Leadership.

Pathway of Discipleship One Hundred One: Home Study Guide. 2nd rev. ed. Donald E. Hill. 56p. 1983. 8.00 (ISBN 0-88151-027-0). Lay Leadership.

Pathway of Discipleship One Hundred One. 2nd rev. ed. Donald E. Hill. (Pathway of Discipleship Ser.). 184p. 1983. pap. text ed. 15.00 (ISBN 0-88151-026-2). Lay Leadership.

Pathway of Perfection. Hodson. 3.75 (ISBN 0-8356-7018-X). Theos Pub Hse.

Pathway to Energy Sufficiency: The 2050 Study. John Steinhart et al. Ed. by Sidney Hollister. LC 78-74807. (Illus.). 1979. pap. 4.95 (ISBN 0-913890-31-6). Friends of Earth.

Pathway to Personal Growth. Melvin J. Witmer. LC 84-70094. 468p. 1985. 23.95 (ISBN 0-915202-45-X). Accel Devel.

Pathway to Prayer & Pietie. Robert Hill. LC 74-28864. (English Experience Ser.: No. 744). 1975. Repr. of 1613 ed. 55.00 (ISBN 90-221-0744-2). Walter J Johnson.

Pathway to Reality. Richard B. Haldane. LC 77-27220. (Gifford Lectures: 1902-03). Repr. of 1903 ed. 22.50 (ISBN 0-404-60458-7). AMS Pr.

Pathway to Reality: Stage the Second. Richard B. Haldane. LC 77-27221. (Gifford Lectures: 1903-04). Repr. of 1904 ed. 22.50 (ISBN 0-404-60459-5). AMS Pr.

Pathway to the National Character, 1830-1861. Robert Lemelin. LC 74-80589. 1974. 19.95x (ISBN 0-8046-9087-1, Pub. by Kennikat). Assoc Faculty Pr.

Pathways. Compiled by Jo Petty. 1983. 7.95 (ISBN 0-8378-1709-9). Gibson.

Pathways: A Guide to Reading & Study Skills. Helen Gilbart. LC 81-81701. (Illus.). 400p. 1982. pap. text ed. 20.36 (ISBN 0-395-31717-7); instr's. manual 1.16 (ISBN 0-395-31718-5). HM.

Pathways: A Job Search Curriculum. Denise Bissonnette-Lamendella. 275p. (Orig.). 1987. student wkbk. 7.95 (ISBN 0-942071-05-0). M Wright & Assocs.

Pathways: A Job Search Curriculum. rev. ed. Denise Bissonnette-Lamendella. 265p. 1987. Repr. of 1986 ed. tchr's. ed. 87.95 (ISBN 0-942071-02-6). M Wright & Assocs.

Pathways: A Success Guide for a Healthy Life. 2nd ed. Donald W. Kemper et al. Ed. by Molly Mettler. (Illus.). 145p. 1986. pap. 14.65x (ISBN 0-9612690-5-7). Healthwise.

Pathways for Communication: Books & Libraries in the Information Age. D. J. Foskett. 133p. 1984. 19.50 (ISBN 0-85157-356-8, Pub. by Bingley England). ALA.

Pathways for the Poet. Viola J. Berg. LC 77-4357. (Illus.). 1977. 12.95 (ISBN 0-915134-18-7). Mott Media.

Pathways from Heroin Addiction: Recovery Without Treatment. Patrick Biernacki. (Health, Society, & Policy Ser.). 252p. 1986. 24.95 (ISBN 0-87722-410-2). Temple U Pr.

Pathways in Malacology. Ed. by S. Van Der Spoel et al. 1979. lib. bdg. 53.00 (ISBN 90-313-0319-4, Pub. by Junk Pubs Netherlands). Kluwer Academic.

Pathways in Surgical Management see Arbeitsdiagnose - Neue Wege der Chirurgischen Diagnose und Therapie.

Pathways in the Workplace: The Effect of Race & Gender on Access to Organzational Resources. Jon Miller. (ASA Rose Monographs). (Illus.). 160p. 1986. 27.95 (ISBN 0-521-32365-7). Cambridge U Pr.

Pathways of Life: Poems by Phyllis Morton. Phyllis Morton. (Illus.). 64p. 1984. 5.50 (ISBN 0-682-40173-0). Exposition-Phoenix.

Pathways of Philosophy. Manly P. Hall. 9.50 (ISBN 0-89314-516-5). Philos Res.

Pathways of Pollutants in the Atmosphere. Royal Society of London, Study Group on Pollution in the Atmosphere, 1977. (Proceedings of the Royal Society). (Illus.). 170p. 1979. 37.00x (ISBN 0-85403-107-3, Pub by Royal Soc London). Scholium Intl.

Pathways of Spiritual Living. 2nd ed. Susan A. Muto. LC 84-1564. 191p. 1988. pap. 8.95 (ISBN 0-932506-65-8). St Bedes Pubns.

Pathways of the Pulp. 4th ed. Cohen & Burns. (Illus.). 896p. 1987. 65.95 (ISBN 0-8016-1077-X). Mosby.

Pathways Through Jewish History. rev ed. Ruth Samuels. (Illus.). (gr. 7-10). 1977. pap. 9.00x (ISBN 0-87068-520-1). Ktav.

Pathways Through the Bible. rev. ed. Mortimer J. Cohen. (Illus.). 574p. 1946. 10.95 (ISBN 0-8276-0155-7, 167). JPS Phila.

Pathways Through to Space: An Experiential Journal. Franklin Merrell-Wolff. 304p. 1983. 14.95 (ISBN 0-517-52777-4); pap. 7.95 (ISBN 0-517-54961-1). Crown.

Pathways to a Southern Coast. Jim Harrison & Jerry Blackwelder. 1986. 50.00 (ISBN 0-87249-497-7). U of SC Pr.

Pathways to Employment for Adults with Developmental Disabilities. Ed. by William E. Kiernan & Jack A. Stark. LC 85-19053. 336p. 1986. text ed. 36.95 (ISBN 0-933716-57-5, 575). P H Brookes.

Pathways to Family Myths. Vimala Pillari. LC 85-29096. 200p. 1986. 25.00 (ISBN 0-87630-401-3). Brunner-Mazel.

Pathways to Fitness: Foundations, Motivation, Applications. Nolan A. Thaxton. 457p. 1987. pap. text ed. 16.50 (ISBN 0-06-046618-9, HarpC). Har-Row.

Pathways to Independence: Discovering Independence National Historical Park. Shirley Milgrim. LC 73-89767. (Illus.). 128p. 1975. 10.95 (ISBN 0-85699-101-5). Chatham Pr.

Pathways to Madness. Jules Henry. 512p. 1973. pap. 10.95 (ISBN 0-394-71882-8, Vin). Random.

Pathways to Parliament: Candidate Selection in Britain. Austin Ranney. 314p. 1965. 25.00x (ISBN 0-299-03560-3). U of Wis Pr.

Pathways to People. 2nd Rev. ed. Eileen Curns et al. 73p. 1978. 12.00 (ISBN 0-942968-00-X). Accord Il.

Pathways to People. Leonard W. Doob. LC 74-29716. (Illus.). 320p. 1975. 37.00x (ISBN 0-300-01843-6). Yale U Pr.

Pathways to Perfection. Thomas S. Monson. LC 73-886344. 328p. 1973. 10.95 (ISBN 0-87747-511-3). Deseret Bk.

Pathways to Power: Keys That Open Doors. Paul Tassell. LC 83-9576. 1983. pap. 3.95 (ISBN 0-87227-093-9). Reg Baptist.

Pathways to Power: Selecting Leaders in Pluralist Democracies. Ed. by Mattei Dogan. (New Directions in Comp & International Politics Ser.: No. 112). 256p. 1988. 25.00 (ISBN 0-8133-7596-7). Westview.

Pathways to Prosperity: Choices for Success in the Information Age. Kenneth D. Wilson & Richard Goldhurst. 160p. 1983. 35.00 (ISBN 0-275-91104-7, C1104). Praeger.

Pathways to Restoration: The Revitalization of the American Spirit. Henry Berry. LC 83-90221. 144p. (Orig.). 1983. pap. 8.95 (ISBN 0-9611846-0-4). Greenfield Pr.

Pathways to Risk Management Information Systems. Ed. by Mitchell Cole & James D. Blinn. 160p. 29.95 (ISBN 0-937802-21-2). Risk Management.

Pathways to Self Determination: Canadian Indians & the Canadian State. Ed. by Leroy Little Bear et al. 192p. (Orig.). 1984. 11.95c (ISBN 0-8020-2524-2); pap. 9.95c (ISBN 0-8020-6539-2). U of Toronto Pr.

Pathways to Serenity. Philip St. Romain. 128p. 1988. pap. text ed. 3.25 (ISBN 0-89243-289-6). Liguori Pubns.

Pathways to Solutions, Fixed Points, & Equilibria. C. B. Garcia & Willard I. Zangwill. (Computational Math Ser.). 336p. 1981. text ed. 57.00 (ISBN 0-13-653501-1). P-H.

Pathways to Suicide: A Survey of Self-Destructive Behaviors. Ronald W. Maris. LC 80-24520. (Illus.). 400p. 1981. text ed. 45.00x (ISBN 0-8018-2437-0). Johns Hopkins.

Pathways to Tax Reform. Stanley S. Surrey. LC 73-87686. 440p. 1973. text ed. 29.50x (ISBN 0-674-65789-6). Harvard U Pr.

Pathways to the Gods: The Mystery of the Andes Lines. Tony Morrison. (Illus.). 256p. 1988. pap. 8.95. Academy Chi Pubs.

Pathways to the Gods: The Stones of Kiribati. Erich Von Daniken. Tr. by Michael Heron from Ger. (Illus.). 288p. 1983. 16.95 (ISBN 0-399-12751-8, Putnam). Putnam Pub Group.

Pathways to the Information Society: Proceedings of the Sixth International Conference on Computer Communication, London, 1982. Ed. by M. B. Williams. 1018p. 1980. 61.75 (ISBN 0-444-86464-4, North Holland). Elsevier.

Pathways to the Old Northwest. xiv, 94p. 1988. 14.95 (ISBN 0-87195-014-6); pap. 6.00 (ISBN 0-87195-011-1). Ind Hist Soc.

Pathways to the Past: A Guide to the Ruins of Mezo-America. Paul R. Cheesman & Barbara W. Hutchins. LC 83-83236. 210p. 1984. pap. 8.95 (ISBN 0-88290-236-9). Horizon Utah.

Pathways to Wellness. Sherman R. Dickman. LC 87-31667. (Illus.). 561p. 1988. text ed. 34.00 (ISBN 0-87322-922-3, LDIC0922, Life Enhancement). Human Kinetics.

Patience. Beverly Fiday. LC 86-12984. (What Is It? Ser.). (Illus.). 32p. (gr. k-3). 1986. lib. bdg. 7.95 (ISBN 0-89565-358-3). Childs World.

Patience. Elaine Goley. (Learn the Value Of... Ser.). (Illus.). 32p. (gr. 1-4). 1987. PLB 106.00 10 bk. set (ISBN 0-317-60386-8); PLB 10.60 (ISBN 0-86592-379-5). Rourke Corp.

Patience. Carole MacKenthun & Paulinus Dwyer. (Fruit of the Spirit Ser.). (Illus.). 48p. (gr. 2-7). 1986. wkbk. 5.95 (ISBN 0-86653-364-8). Good Apple.

Patience. (Pocket Power Ser.). 16p. (Orig.). 1986. pap. 0.50 (ISBN 0-89486-356-8). Hazelden.

Patience: A West Midland Poem of the Fourteenth Century. Ed. by Hartley Bateson. LC 72-187860. 1912. lib. bdg. 27.00 (ISBN 0-8414-1630-3). Folcroft.

Patience & Persistence. Robert Tilton. (Orig.). 1986. mini bk. 0.75 (ISBN 0-89274-413-8). Harrison Hse.

Patience & Power: Grace for the First World. Jean-Marc Laporte. 1988. pap. 12.95 (ISBN 0-8091-2966-3). Paulist Pr.

Patience & Power: The Lives of Morrocan Village Women. Susan S. Davis. 200p. 1985. (ISBN 0-87073-503-9); pap. 11.95 (ISBN 0-87073-504-7). Schenkman Bks Inc.

Patience de Maigret. Georges Simenon. pap. 3.95 (ISBN 0-685-36570-0). French & Eur.

Patience Games: Card Games. David Parlett. (Know the Game Ser.). (Illus.). 1976. pap. 2.50 (ISBN 0-7158-0501-0). Charles River Bks.

Patience: Miracle in Progress. Sue Winget. 110p. (Orig.). 1988. pap. 5.95 (ISBN 0-89265-132-6). Randall Hse.

Patience Never Fails. Gary Jones. 45p. 1985. pap. 0.95 (ISBN 0-88144-048-5). Christian Pub.

Patience of a Saint. Andrew M. Greeley. LC 85-40921. 464p. 1986. 18.95 (ISBN 0-446-51294-X). Warner Bks.

Patience of a Saint. Andrew M. Greeley. 650p. 1988. lib. bdg. 21.95x (ISBN 0-8161-4364-1, Large Print Bks); pap. 12.95x (ISBN 0-8161-4365-X). G K Hall.

Patience of a Saint. Andrew M. Greeley. Date not set. pap. 4.95 (ISBN 0-446-34682-9). Warner Bks.

Patience of God. 4.50 (ISBN 0-8198-5821-8); 3.50. Dghtrs St Paul.

Patience of Hope. Spiros Zodhiates. (Trilogy Ser.: Vol. 1). pap. 4.95 (ISBN 0-89957-543-9). AMG Pubs.

Patience Pays Off. James R. Sherman. (Do It! Success Ser.). 72p. 1987. pap. 2.95 (ISBN 0-935538-09-7). Pathway Bks.

Patience Sparhawk & Her Times. Gertrude F. Atherton. LC 75-104407. 488p. Repr. of 1897 ed. lib. bdg. 29.50 (ISBN 0-8398-0066-5). Irvington.

Patience Sparhawk & Her Times. Gertrude F. Atherton. 1986. pap. text ed. 8.95x (ISBN 0-8290-1867-0). Irvington.

Patience Wright: American Artist & Spy in George III's London. Charles C. Sellers. LC 76-7193. 1976. 18.50x (ISBN 0-8195-5001-9). Wesleyan U Pr.

Patient Account Management. Allen B. Herkimer, Jr. LC 82-16318. 293p. 1982. 53.99 (ISBN 0-89443-835-2). Aspen Pub.

Patient Account Management Techniques. H. F. M. A. Staff. 1976. 8.50 (ISBN 0-930228-01-4, 1443). Healthcare Fin Man Assn.

Patient Administration. Intro. by Richard L. Clarke. 48p. 1987. 17.50; pap. text ed. write for info. Healthcare Fin Mgmt Assn.

Patient Administration. HFMA Staff. 40p. 1987. pap. text ed. 17.59 (ISBN 0-930228-58-8). Healthcare Fin Mgmt Assn.

Patient & Decentralised Testing. Ed. by J. P. Ashby. 1987. lib. bdg. 45.00 (ISBN 0-7462-0036-6, Pub. by MTP Pr England). Kluwer Academic.

Patient & Family Education: Teaching Programs for Managing Chronic Disease & Disability. Marcia Hanak. 272p. 1986. 22.95 (ISBN 0-8261-5441-7). Springer Pub.

Patient & the Analyst: The Basis of the Psychoanalytic Process. Joseph Sandler et al. LC 73-7023. 150p. 1973. text ed. 22.50x (ISBN 0-8236-4030-2). Intl Univs Pr.

Patient & the Plastic Surgeon. Robert M. Goldwyn. 1981. text ed. 28.00 (ISBN 0-316-31974-0). Little.

Patient As Partner: A Theory of Human Experimentation Ethics. Robert Veatch. (Medical Ethics Ser.). 1987. 27.50x (ISBN 0-253-35725-X). Ind U Pr.

Patient As Person: Exploration in Medical Ethics. Ramsey. LC 77-118737. 1970. 13.95x (ISBN 0-300-01357-4); pap. 13.95x (ISBN 0-300-01741-3, Y263). Yale U Pr.

Patient Assessment. American Dental Hygienists' Association Staff & Block Drug Company. 1980. 30.00 (ISBN 0-318-19097-4). Am Dental Hygienists.

Patient Assessment: A Handbook for Therapists. Heather Coats & Alan King. (Illus.). 1983. pap. 13.00 (ISBN 0-443-02421-9). Churchill.

Patient Assessment in Psychiatric Nursing. Philip J. Barker. 368p. 1985. pap. 18.95 (ISBN 0-7099-3254-5, Pub. by Croom Helm Ltd). Routledge Chapman & Hall.

Patient at Home: A Manual of Exercise Programs, Self-Help Devices & Home Care Products. rev. ed. Marylou R. Barnes & Carolyn Crutchfield. LC 72-185638. (Illus.). 187p. 1984. pap. text ed. 21.95. Slack Inc.

Patient at Peacock's Hall. Margery Allingham. 12.95 (ISBN 0-89190-165-5, Pub. by Am Repr). Amereon Ltd.

Patient: Biological, Psychological & Social Dimensions of Medical Practice. 2nd ed. Hoyle Leigh & Morton F. Reiser. LC 85-9265. 472p. 1985. 29.50x (ISBN 0-306-41985-8, Plenum Pr). Plenum Pub.

Patient Care Audit Criteria: Standards for Hospital Quality Assurance. Jean G. Carroll. LC 82-73622. 250p. 1983. 55.00 (ISBN 0-87094-392-8). Dow Jones-Irwin.

Patient Care Flow Chart Manual. 3rd ed. Patient Care Magazine. 608p. 1982. casebound 49.95 (ISBN 0-87489-295-3). Med Economics.

Patient Care Flowchart Manual. 4th ed. Ed. by Steven R. Alexander. 608p. 48.95 (ISBN 0-87489-430-1). Med Economics.

Patient Care Guidelines for Nurse Practioners. 3rd ed. Axalla J. Hoole et al. 1987. write for info. spiral bdg. (ISBN 0-673-39376-3). Scott F.

Patient Care Guides: Practical Information for Public Health Nurses. 2nd ed. Yvonne Harnish & Ilse Lesser. 250p. 1984. pap. text ed. 29.95 (ISBN 0-88737-127-2, 21-1968). Natl League Nurse.

Patient Care in Cardiac Surgery. 4th ed. Douglas M. Behrendt & W. Gerald Austen. 288p. 1985. pap. text ed. 25.00 (ISBN 0-316-08763-7). Little.

Patient Care in Pediatric Surgery. Lucian L. Leape. 448p. (Orig.). 1987. pap. text ed. 27.00 (ISBN 0-316-51821-2, Little Med Div). Little.

Patient Care in Radiography. 3rd ed. Ehrlich & McCloskey. (Illus.). 319p. 1989. pap. 24.95 (ISBN 0-8016-2417-7). Mosby.

Patient Care in Radiography. 2nd ed. Ruth A. Ehrlich & Ellen M. Givens. (Illus.). 190p. 1984. pap. text ed. 26.95 (ISBN 0-8016-1561-5). Mosby.

Patient Care in the Operating Room. Kaczmarowski. 1987. write for info. (ISBN 0-443-03911-9). Churchill.

Patient Care Procedures For Your Practice. Ed. by Charles E. Driscoll. Robert E. Rakel. 264p. (Orig.). 1988. pap. 25.95 (ISBN 0-87489-444-1). Med Economics.

Patient Care Services Policy Manual for the Nursing Department. Leone Douville. LC 73-88318. (Illus.). 1974. pap. 8.00 (ISBN 0-87125-011-X). Cath Health.

Patient Care Skills: Positioning, Range of Motion, Transfers, Wheelchairs & Ambulation. Scott D. Minor & Mary A. Minor. 1984. pap. text ed. 22.95 (ISBN 0-8359-5456-0). Appleton & Lange.

Patient Care Standards: Nursing Process, Diagnosis & Outcome. 4th ed. Tucker et al. 944p. 1988. pap. text ed. 29.95 (ISBN 0-8016-5133-6). Mosby.

Patient Centered Audit. Christine G. Kruse. (Illus.). 69p. (Orig.). 1983. 14.50 (ISBN 0-87527-247-9). Green.

Patient-Centered Care Manual for the Nursing Department. St. Joseph Hospital. LC 77-71736. 1977. pap. 13.00 (ISBN 0-87125-041-1). Cath Health.

Patient Charges in Short-Stay Hospitals, United States, 1968-1970. Mary Moien. LC 74-3217. (Data from the Hospital Discharge Survey Ser. 13: No. 15). 55p. 1974. pap. text ed. 1.50 (ISBN 0-8406-0001-1). Natl Ctr Health Stats.

Patient-Client-Employee Complaint Programs: An Organizational Systems Model. James T. Ziegenfuss, Jr. (Illus.). 278p. 1985. 31.50 (ISBN 0-398-05041-4). C C Thomas.

Patient Comes First: A Nurse Speaks Out. Nancy Fox. 141p. 1988. pap. 10.95 (ISBN 0-87975-479-6). Prometheus Bks.

Patient Compliance: New Light on Health Delivery Systems in Medicine & Psychotherapy. E. Lakin Phillips. 370p. Date not set. pap. price not set (ISBN 0-920887-41-4, Pub. by H Hubur Canada). Hogrefe Intl.

Patient Contact & Public Relations see Doctors' Administrative Program.

Patient Education - An Inquiry into the State of the Art. Wendy Squyres. LC 79-27556. (Springer Ser. in Health Care & Society: Vol. 4). 384p. 1980. 26.50 (ISBN 0-8261-3120-4). Springer Pub.

Patient Education: A Handbook for Teachers. Compiled by STFM. 180p. 1979. 5.00 (ISBN 0-942295-08-0). Soc Tchrs Fam Med.

Patient Education & Health Promotion in Medical Care. Wendy Squyres. 416p. 1985. text ed. 29.95 (ISBN 0-87484-553-X). Mayfield Pub.

Patient Education: Foundations of Practice. Woldum et al. 200p. 1984. 33.50 (ISBN 0-89443-562-0). Aspen Pub.

Patient Education Handbook. Margaret Chatham & Barbara Knapp. LC 81-17027. (Illus.). 192p. 1981. pap. text ed. 12.95 (ISBN 0-89303-055-4). P-H.

Patient Education: Issues, Principles & Guidelines. Ed. by Sally Rankin & Karen L. Duffy. (Illus.). 328p. 1983. pap. text ed. 17.95 (ISBN 0-397-54398-0, 64-03398, Lippincott Medical). Lippincott.

Patient Education Media Handbook, Ed. by Walter J. Carroll. 1984. 34.50x (ISBN 0-88367-475-0). Olympic Media.

Patient Education Media Handbook II, 1987. Ed. by Walter J. Carroll. 1987. 32.50x (ISBN 0-88367-477-7). Olympic Media.

Patient Education: Nurses in Partnership with Other Health Care Professionals. Ed. by Carol E. Smith. 384p. 1987. 29.50 (ISBN 0-8089-1833-8, 794144). Grune.

Patient Education Sourcebook. Ed. by Mary Rydesky & Tanya DeVaughn. 547p. 1986. 50.00 (ISBN 0-318-20441-X). Health Sci Comm.

Patient Encounters: The Experience of Disease. James H. Buchanan. 400p. 1989. 24.95 (ISBN 0-8139-1184-2). U Pr of Va.

Patient Evaluation Methods for the Health Professionals. Scott D. Minor & Mary A. Minor. 1985. pap. text ed. 18.95 (ISBN 0-8359-5484-6). Appleton & Lange.

Patient Grissell. John Phillip. LC 82-45747. (Malone Society Reprint Ser.: No. 13). Repr. of 1909 ed. 40.00 (ISBN 0-404-63013-8). AMS Pr.

Patient Grissil. Henry Chettle et al. LC 78-133653. (Tudor Facsimile Texts. Old English Plays: No. 101). Repr. of 1911 ed. 49.50 (ISBN 0-404-53401-5). AMS Pr.

Patient Has the Floor. Alistair Cooke. LC 85-45704. 224p. 1986. 16.95 (ISBN 0-394-50365-1). Knopf.

Patient Health Monitoring Instrumentation Markets. Market Intelligence Research Company Staff. 170p. 1985. pap. text ed. 595.00 (ISBN 0-317-19565-4). Market Res Co.

Patient in Cabin C. Mignon G. Eberhart. 256p. 1985. pap. 2.95 (ISBN 0-446-32505-8). Warner Bks.

Patient in Room Eighteen. Mignon G. Eberhart. 1976. Repr. of 1929 ed. lib. bdg. 18.95x (ISBN 0-88411-765-0, Pub. by Aeonian Pr). Amereon Ltd.

Patient in Surgery: A Guide for Nurses. 4th ed. George D. LeMaitre & Janet A. Finnegan. LC 79-66039. (Illus.). 523p. 1980. Soft Cover. text ed. 30.95 (ISBN 0-7216-5724-9). Saunders.

Patient in the Womb. E. Peter Volpe. LC 84-10746. (Sesquicentennial Monograph: No. 3). 151p. 1984. 14.50 (ISBN 0-86554-122-1, MUP/H110). Mercer Univ Pr.

Patient Lifting Devices in Hospitals. Frank Bell. 236p. 1984. 25.00 (ISBN 0-7099-3229-4, Pub. by Croom Helm Ltd). Routledge Chapman & Hall.

Patricide in the House Divided: A Psychological Interpretation of Lincoln & His Age. George B. Forgie. 320p. 1981. pap. 5.95 (ISBN 0-393-00035-4). Norton.

Patricios & Plebeyos: Burgueses, Hacendados, Artesanos & Obreros: Las Relaciones de Clase en el Puerto Rico de Cambio de Siglo. Angel G. Quintero-Rivera. LC 87-82379. (Nave & el Puerto Ser.). 332p. (Span.). 1988. pap. 9.95 (ISBN 0-940238-93-4). Ediciones Huracan.

Patrick & His Grandpa. Geoffrey Hayes. LC 85-62403. (Great Big Board Books Ser.). (Illus.). 14p. (ps). 1986. bds. 3.95 (ISBN 0-394-87287-8). Random.

Patrick & Ted. Geoffrey Hayes. (Illus.). 32p. (ps-3). 1986. pap. 2.95 (ISBN 0-590-40436-9). Scholastic Inc.

Patrick & Ted at the Beach. Geoffrey Hayes. LC 86-43069. (Picturebacks Ser.). (Illus.). 32p. (ps-1). 1987. lib. bdg. 5.99 (ISBN 0-394-97289-9, BYR); pap. 1.95 (ISBN 0-394-87289-4). Random.

Patrick & Ted Ride the Train: (Just Right for 4's & 5's) Geoffrey Hayes. LC 88-3084. (Just Right Bks.). (Illus.). 32p. (Orig.). (ps-k). 1988. 4.95 (ISBN 0-394-89872-9, BYR); PLB 5.99 (ISBN 0-394-99872-3, BYR). Random.

Patrick & the Great Molasses Explosion. Marjorie Stover. LC 85-6870. (Illus.). 40p. (gr. 3-6). 1985. PLB 8.95 (ISBN 0-87518-296-8, Gemstone Bks). Dillon.

Patrick & the Hungry Puppy. 22p. 1985. 5.95 (ISBN 0-8431-1084-8). Price Stern.

Patrick Branswell Bronte. Alice Law. LC 76-13012. 1976. Repr. of 1923 ed. lib. bdg. 27.20 (ISBN 0-8414-5721-2). Folcroft.

Patrick Branswell Bronte: A Complete Transcript of the Leyland Manuscripts. J. Alex Symington. 1925. lib. bdg. 25.00 (ISBN 0-8414-7995-X). Folcroft.

Patrick Campbell's Travels. Patrick Campbell. LC 78-50738. (Illus.). 96p. 1978. 12.50x (ISBN 0-8139-0858-2). U Pr of Va.

Patrick Caulfield. John McEwen. (Illus.). 126p. 1988. 75.00 (ISBN 0-85331-517-5, Pub. by Lund Humphries). Humanities.

Patrick Dennis' U. S. Revenue Cutter Vigilant-1791-1798. Florence Kern. 1976. 3.95 (ISBN 0-913377-03-1). Alised.

Patrick Duffy. Riley. 1988. pap. 3.50 (ISBN 0-312-90449-5). St Martin.

Patrick Duncan. C. J. Driver. text ed. 25.00x (ISBN 0-435-96200-0). Heinemann Ed.

Patrick Ewing. Matthew Newman. Ed. by Howard Schroeder. LC 86-16522. (Sports Close-up Ser.). (Illus.). 48p. (gr. 5-6). PLB 10.95 (ISBN 0-89686-315-8). Crestwood Hse.

Patrick Ford & His Search for America: A Case Study of Irish-American Journalism, 1870-1913. James P. Rodechko. LC 76-6362. (Irish Americans Ser). 1976. 26.50 (ISBN 0-405-09354-3). Ayer Co Pubs.

Patrick Goes to Bed. Geoffrey Hayes. LC 84-6099. (Patrick Bks.). (Illus.). 40p. (ps-1). 1985. 4.95 (ISBN 0-394-87264-9); lib. bdg. 5.99 (ISBN 0-394-97264-3). Knopf.

Patrick Henry. Diana Reische. LC 86-23363. (First Bks.). (Illus.). (gr. 4-8). 1987. lib. bdg. 10.40 (ISBN 0-531-10305-6). Watts.

Patrick Henry. Moses C. Tyler. Ed. by John T. Morse, Jr. LC 71-128936. (American Statesmen: No. 3). Repr. of 1898 ed. 24.00 (ISBN 0-404-50853-7). AMS Pr.

Patrick Henry. Moses C. Tyler. 1970. Repr. of 1898 ed. text ed. 29.00 (ISBN 0-8337-3587-X). B Franklin.

Patrick Henry. Moses C. Tyler. LC 80-18577. (American Statesmen Ser.). 460p. 1980. pap. 6.95 (ISBN 0-87754-190-6). Chelsea Hse.

Patrick Henry. Moses C. Tyler. 69.95 (ISBN 0-8490-0806-9). Gordon Pr.

Patrick Henry, Life Correspondence & Speeches, 3 Vols. William W. Henry. LC 71-108350. (Research & Source Works Ser.: No. 407). 1970. Repr. of 1891 ed. lib. bdg. 87.00 (ISBN 0-8337-1662-X). B Franklin.

Patrick Henry: Patriot & Statesman. Norine D. Campbell. (Illus.). 1969. 16.95 (ISBN 0-8159-6501-X). Devin.

Patrick Henry: Voice of American Revolution. Louis Sabin. LC 81-23068. (Illus.). 48p. (gr. 4-6). 1982. PLB 9.79 (ISBN 0-89375-764-0); pap. text ed. 1.95 (ISBN 0-89375-765-9). Troll Assocs.

Patrick Heron. Ed. by Vivien Knight. (Illus.). 128p. 1987. 75.00 (ISBN 0-85331-525-6, Pub. by Lund Humphries UK). Humanities.

Patrick Kavanagh: Complete Poems. Ed. by Peter Kavanagh. 1972. 34.50x (ISBN 0-904984-79-6); pap. 18.00. Natl Poet Foun.

Patrick Kavanaugh. Darcy O'Brien. (Irish Writers Ser.). 72p. 1975. 4.50 (ISBN 0-8387-7884-4); pap. 1.95 (ISBN 0-8387-7985-9). Bucknell U Pr.

Patrick Kavanaugh: Man & Poet. Ed. by Peter Kavanaugh. LC 85-61480. (Irish Art & Man & Poet Ser.). 500p. (Orig.). 1986. 32.00 (ISBN 0-915032-63-5); pap. 15.95 (ISBN 0-915032-64-3). Natl Poet Foun.

Patrick Matthew & Natural Selection. W. J. Dempster. 1984. 45.00 (ISBN 0-86228-065-6, Pub. by P Harris Pub). State Mutual Bk.

Patrick Moore's A-Z of Astronomy. Patrick Moore. (Illus., Orig.). 1987. pap. 13.50 (ISBN 0-393-30505-8). Norton.

Patrick N. L. Bellinger & U. S. Naval Aviation. Paolo E. Coletta. (Illus.). 478p. (Orig.). 1987. lib. bdg. 28.75 (ISBN 0-8191-6534-4). U Pr of Amer.

Patrick Pearse: The Triumph of Failure. Ruth D. Edwards. LC 78-58294. (Illus.). 1978. 14.95 (ISBN 0-8008-6267-8). Taplinger.

Patrick: Sixteen Centuries with Ireland's Patron Saint. Ed. by Alice B. Proudfoot. (Illus.). 160p. 1983. 19.95 (ISBN 0-02-599280-5). Macmillan.

Patrick Suppes. Ed. by Radu J. Bogdan. LC 78-21095. (Profiles 1 Ser.). 1979. lib. bdg. 36.00 (ISBN 9-0277-0950-5, Pub. by Reidel Holland); pap. 9.95 (ISBN 9-0277-0951-3, Pub. by Reidel Holland). Kluwer Academic.

Patrick White. May-Britt Akerholt. (Australian Playwrights Monograph Ser.: Vol. 2). 148p. 1988. pap. text ed. 19.95 (ISBN 90-6203-930-8, Pub. by Rodopi Holland). Humanities.

Patrick White. John Colmer. (Contemporary Writers Ser.). 96p. 1984. pap. 5.95 (ISBN 0-416-36790-9, NO. 4066). Routledge Chapman & Hall.

Patrick White. Geoffrey Dutton. LC 74-9788. 1962. 20.00 (ISBN 0-8414-3749-1). Folcroft.

Patrick White. Brian Kiernan. LC 80-5098. 150p. 1980. 20.00 (ISBN 0-312-59807-6). St Martin.

Patrick White. John A. Weigel. LC 83-12599. (World Authors Ser.: No. 711). 142p. 1983. lib. bdg. 18.95 (ISBN 0-8057-6558-1, Twayne). G K Hall.

Patrick White: Fiction & the Unconscious. David J. Tacey. (Illus.). 296p. 1988. 39.95 (ISBN 0-19-554867-1). Oxford U Pr.

Patrick White's Fiction: The Paradox of Fortunate Failure. Carolyn Bliss. 224p. 1986. 25.00 (ISBN 0-312-59805-X). St Martin.

Patrick's Dinosaurs. Carol Carrick. LC 83-2049. (Illus.). 32p. (gr. k-3). 1983. PLB 12.95 (ISBN 0-89919-189-4, Clarion). HM.

Patrick's Dinosaurs. Carol Carrick. LC 83-2049. (Illus.). (gr. k-3). 1985. pap. 4.95 (ISBN 0-89919-402-8, Pub. by Clarion). Ticknor & Fields.

Patrick's Dinosaurs. Donald Carrick. (Book & Cassette Favorites Ser.). (ps-3). 1987. incl. cass. 6.95 (ISBN 0-317-64570-6). HM.

Patrick's Problem. Kees Moerbeek. (Did It Happen? Bks.). (Illus.). 12p. (ps-k). 1987. 4.95 (ISBN 0-8431-1903-9). Price Stern.

Patrie! An Historical Drama in Five Acts. Victorien Sardou. LC 86-29518. 232p. 1987. Repr. of 1915 ed. lib. bdg. 29.50x (ISBN 0-86527-355-3). Fertig.

Patrimonial Foundations of the Brazilian Bureaucratic State. Fernando Uricoechea. 248p. 1980. 33.00x (ISBN 0-520-03853-3). U of Cal Pr.

Patrimonialism & Political Change in the Congo. Jean-Claude Willame. LC 79-153821. 1972. 22.50x (ISBN 0-8047-0793-6). Stanford U Pr.

Patrimonies. R. V. Cassill. 132p. 1988. pap. 10.00 (ISBN 0-935331-05-0). Ampersand RI.

Patrimony. Robert Adams. (Horseclans Ser.: No. 6). (Orig.). 1983. pap. 2.95 (ISBN 0-451-13300-5, AE3300, Sig). NAL.

Patrimony. Elsie L. Hartung. 160p. 1987. 9.95 (ISBN 0-8062-2878-4). Carlton.

Patrins: To Which Is Added an Inquirendo into the Wit & Other Good Parts of His Late Majesty King Charles the Second. Louise I. Guiney. LC 72-4750. (Essay Index Reprint Ser.). Repr. of 1897 ed. 21.00 (ISBN 0-8369-2946-2). Ayer Co Pubs.

Patriot. Pearl S. Buck. (John Day Bk.). 1963. o.s.i 8.95i (ISBN 0-381-98048-0, A60200). T Y Crowell.

Patriot, Vol. 1, No. 1. James L. Berkman. LC I-464941. (Illus., Orig.). 1984. pap. 10.00 (ISBN 0-943662-05-2). Runaway Pubns.

Patriot, Vol. 3, No. 1. James L. Berkman. (Illus., Orig.). 1986. pap. 10.00 (ISBN 0-943662-07-9). Runaway Pubns.

Patriot, Vol. 4-No. 1. James L. Berkman. (Illus., Orig.). 1987. pap. 10.00 (ISBN 0-943662-08-7). Runaway Pubns.

Patriot, Vol. 5, No. 1. James L. Berkman. (Orig.). 1988. pap. 10.00 (ISBN 0-943662-09-5). Runaway Pubns.

Patriot above Profit. Neil M. Lee. 704p. 1988. 29.95 (ISBN 0-934395-68-3). Rutledge Hill Pr.

Patriot Chiefs: A Chronicle of American Indian Resistance. Alvin M. Josephy, Jr. (Illus.). 1969. pap. 6.95 (ISBN 0-14-004219-9). Penguin.

Patriot for Me & a Sense of Detachment. John Osborne. 192p. 1983. pap. 7.95 (ISBN 0-571-13041-0). Faber & Faber.

Patriot Game. George V. Higgins. LC 81-18655. 256p. 1982. 12.45 (ISBN 0-394-51672-9). Knopf.

Patriot Game: Canada & the Canadian Question Revisited. Peter Brimelow. 320p. 1988. 26.95 (ISBN 0-8179-8681-2); pap. text ed. 16.95 (ISBN 0-8179-8682-0). Hoover Inst Pr.

Patriot Games. Tom Clancy. 416p. 1987. 19.95 (ISBN 0-399-13241-4, Putnam). Putnam Pub Group.

Patriot Games. Tom Clancy. (Large Print Bks.). 800p. 1988. lib. bdg. 21.95x (ISBN 0-8161-4382-X, Large Print Bks); pap. 13.95x (ISBN 0-8161-4383-8, Large Print Bks). G K Hall.

Patriot Games. Tom Clancy. 1988. pap. 4.95 (ISBN 0-425-10972-0). Berkley Pub.

Patriot-Heroes in England & America: Political Symbolism & Changing Values over Three Centuries. Peter Karsten. LC 78-53286. (Illus.). 268p. 1979. 32.50x (ISBN 0-299-07500-1). U of Wis Pr.

Patriot Lad of Old Cape Cod. Russell G. Carter. LC 75-5092. (Illus.). 224p. (gr. 6-8). 1975. 4.95 (ISBN 0-88492-007-0); pap. 1.95 (ISBN 0-88492-008-9). W S Sullwold.

Patriot: Nach der Originalausgabe Hamburg, 1724-26, 4 vols. Ed. by Wolfgang Martens. Incl. Vol. 1. Jahrgang 1724, Stueck 1-52. vi, 445p. 1969. 62.00 (ISBN 3-11-000360-0); Vol. 2. Jahrgang 1725, Stueck 53-104. iv, 428p. 1970. 62.00 (ISBN 3-11-000361-9); Vol. 3. Jahrgang 1726, Stueck 105-156. iv, 460p. 1970. write for info. (ISBN 3-11-002694-5); Vol. 4. Kommentarband. 132.00 (ISBN 3-11-009931-4). (Ausgaben Deutscher Literatur des Xv Bis XViii Jahrhunderts). (Ger.). De Gruyter.

Patriot or Traitor: The Case of General Mihailovich. Intro. by David Martin. (Serbian Special Project Ser.: No. 29). 507p. (Serbian.). 1981. pap. 12.50x (ISBN 0-8179-4292-0). Hoover Inst Pr.

Patriot Primer. Jan P. Pierce. 80p. 1987. pap. text ed. 2.50 (ISBN 0-932050-30-1). New Puritan.

Patriot Souvenir Edition, Eighteen Ninety-Six. Charles Bradshaw. 76p. 1976. 3.00 (ISBN 0-686-27518-7). E S Cunningham.

Patriot: The Scripturion, Vol. 2, No. 1. James L. Berkman. (Orig.). 1985. pap. text ed. 10.00 (ISBN 0-943662-06-0). Runaway Pubns.

Patriotic Addresses In. Henry W. Beecher. (Works of Henry Ward Beecher). 857p. 1985. Repr. of 1891 ed. lib. bdg. 99.00 (ISBN 0-932051-04-9, Pub. by Am Repr Serv). Am Biog Serv.

Patriotic & Historical Plays for Young People. rev. ed. Ed. by Sylvia E. Kamerman. 200p. (gr. 3-9). 1987. pap. 10.95 (ISBN 0-8238-0285-X). Plays.

Patriotic Anthology: Being Poems of American History, Written by Great American Poets. facsimile ed. LC 79-168786. (Granger Index Reprint Ser.). Repr. of 1940 ed. 10.75 (ISBN 0-8369-6306-7). Ayer Co Pubs.

Patriotic Civil War Tokens. George Fuld & Melvin Fuld. LC 81-423. (Illus.). 80p. 1981. pap. 10.00x (ISBN 0-88000-128-3). Quarterman.

Patriotic Fun. Illus. by Judith H. Corwin. LC 85-18730. (Illus.). 64p. (gr. 3 up). 1985. pap. 4.95 (ISBN 0-671-55378-X); PLB 10.29 (ISBN 0-671-50799-0). Messner.

Patriotic Gore: Studies in the Literature of the American Civil War. Edmund Wilson. 1962. 35.00x (ISBN 0-19-500666-6). Oxford U Pr.

Patriotic Gore: Studies in the Literature of the American Civil War. Edmund Wilson. LC 84-10118. 852p. 1984. pap. 13.50x (ISBN 0-930350-61-8). NE U Pr.

Patriotic Holidays & Celebrations. Valorie Grigoli. LC 85-7270. (First Bks). (Illus.). 66p. (gr. 4-7). 1985. PLB 10.40 (ISBN 0-531-10044-8). Watts.

Patriotic Murders. Agatha Christie. Ed. by Roger Cooper. 240p. 1988. pap. 3.50 (ISBN 0-425-10570-9). Berkley Pub.

Patriotic Poems of Amerikkka. 2nd ed. Todd S. Lawson. (Illus.). 64p. pap. 1.85x (ISBN 0-914024-00-0). SF Arts & Letters.

Patriotic Recitations & Readings. Ed. by Josephine Stafford. LC 79-108588. (Granger Index Reprint Ser). 1902. 14.00 (ISBN 0-8369-6116-1). Ayer Co Pubs.

Patrioticas: La Patria No Ha Muerto, No, Esta en el Viento. Jose Sanchez-Boudy. LC 86-81927. (Coleccion Espejo de Paciencia). 62p. (Orig., Span.). 1986. pap. 6.00 (ISBN 0-89729-415-7). Ediciones.

Patriotism. Nancy M. Davis et al. (Davis Teaching Units Ser.: Vol. II, No. 12). (Illus.). 34p. (Orig.). (ps-5). 1986. pap. 4.95 (ISBN 0-937103-19-5). DaNa Pubns.

Patriotism, Inc & Other Tales by Paul van Ostaijen. Ed. by E. M. Beekman. LC 79-150314. 192p. 1971. 17.50x (ISBN 0-87023-084-0); pap. 9.95x (ISBN 0-87023-097-2). U of Mass Pr.

Patriotism Limited, Eighteen Sixty-Two to Eighteen Sixty-Five: The Civil War Draft & the Bounty System. Eugene Murdock. LC 67-64665. Repr. of 1967 ed. 56.30 (ISBN 0-8357-9372-9, 2010413). Bks Demand UMI.

Patriotism on Parade: The Story of Veterans' & Hereditary Organizations in America, 1783-1900. Wallace E. Davies. LC 55-11951. (Historical Studies: No. 66). 1955. 27.50x (ISBN 0-674-65800-0). Harvard U Pr.

Patriotism, Protection & Prosperity: James Moore Swank, the American Iron & Steel Association & the Tariff, 1873-1913. Paul H. Tedesco. Ed. by Stuart Bruchey. LC 84-48315. (American Economic History Ser.). 325p. 1985. lib. bdg. 45.00 (ISBN 0-8240-6663-4). Garland Pub.

Patriots. Chet Cunningham. 720p. (Orig.). 1982. pap. 3.95 (ISBN 0-505-51835-X, Pub. by Tower Bks). Leisure NY.

Patriots. Kenneth Royce. LC 87-27612. 268p. 1968. 17.95 (ISBN 0-517-56943-4). Crown.

Patriots. Robert E. Wall. (Canadians Ser.: No. IV). 288p. 1982. pap. 3.95 (ISBN 0-7704-2172-5). Bantam.

Patriots & Liberators: Revolution in the Netherlands, 1780-1813. Simon Schama. 1977. 20.00 (ISBN 0-394-48516-5). Knopf.

Patriots & Partisans: The Merchants of Newburyport, 1764-1815. new ed. Benjamin W. Labaree. 272p. 1975. pap. 2.95 (ISBN 0-393-00786-3, Norton Lib). Norton.

Patriots in Pinstripe: Men of the National Security League. John C. Edwards. LC 81-40869. (Illus.). 248p. (Orig.). 1982. pap. text ed. 13.25 (ISBN 0-8191-2350-1). U Pr of Amer.

Patriots of Nantucket: A Romantic Comedy of the American Revolution. Oscar Mandel. LC 75-37367. 84p. 1976. pap. 4.00 (ISBN 0-914502-02-6). Spectrum Prods.

Patriots of the American Revolution. W. Edmunds Claussen. (Illus.). 202p. (Orig.). 1975. 5.00 (ISBN 0-9616068-1-9). Boyertown Hist.

Patriots off Their Pedestals. Paul Wilstach. LC 78-117862. (Essay Index Reprint Ser). 1927. 19.00 (ISBN 0-8369-1738-3). Ayer Co Pubs.

Patriots: The Men Who Started the American Revolution. A. J. Langguth. (Illus.). 624p. 1988. 22.95 (ISBN 0-671-52375-9). S&S.

Patristic Greek Lexicon Nineteen Sixty-One to Sixty-Eight. Ed. by G. W. Lampe. (Gr.). 198.00x (ISBN 0-19-864213-X). Oxford U Pr.

Patrol Administration. 2nd ed. G. Douglas Gourley. (Illus.). 400p. 1974. photocopy ed. 28.50x (ISBN 0-398-03126-6). C C Thomas.

Patrol Administration: Management by Objectives. 3rd. ed. Donald T. Shanahan. 180p. 1985. 40.95x (ISBN 0-205-08384-6, 828384, Pub. by Longwood Div); instr's. manual avail. Allyn.

Patrol Field Problems & Solutions: 476 Field Situations. John P. Kenney & Harry W. More. 194p. 1986. 27.25 (ISBN 0-398-05202-6). C C Thomas.

Patrol Leader Handbook, The Official. 208p. 1980. pap. 2.25 (ISBN 0-8395-6512-7, 6512). BSA.

Patrolling & Tracking. 104p. 1977. pap. 5.00 (ISBN 0-87364-137-X). Paladin Pr.

Patrolman Examinations-All States. Jack Rudman. (Career Examination Ser.: C-575). (Cloth bdg. avail. on request). pap. 14.00 (ISBN 0-8373-0575-6). Natl Learning.

Patrolman-Police Department. Jack Rudman. (Career Examination Ser.: C-576). (Cloth bdg. avail. on request). pap. 14.00 (ISBN 0-8373-0576-4). Natl Learning.

Patrolman-Policewoman. Jack Rudman. (Career Examination Ser.: C-1922). (Cloth bdg. avail. on request). pap. 14.00 (ISBN 0-8373-1922-6). Natl Learning.

Patrolman's Manuel (Philadelphia) 1913 see Metropolitan Police Manuals Eighteen Seventy-One to Nineteen Thirteen: Rules & Regulations for the Government of the Richmond County Police Force, of the State of New York. New York, 1871.

Patrologia Graeco Latina see Patrologiae Cursus Completus.

Patrologia Latina see Patrologiae Cursus Completus.

Patrologia Latina: Index Alphabeticus Auctorum, a Complete List of the Authors Whose Works Are Printed in the Greek Series of Migne's Patrologia. Jacques P. Migne & John B. Pearson. 48p. Repr. of 1882 ed. text ed. 20.70x (ISBN 0-576-72339-8, Pub. by Gregg Intl Pubs England). Gregg Intl.

Patrologiae Cursus Completus. Jacques P. Migne. Incl. Patrologia Latina, 221 vols. pap. write for info.; Patrologia Graeco Latina, 162 vols. pap. write for info.. 1965-71. pap. Adlers Foreign Bks.

Patrology, 4 vols. Johannes Quasten. 1514p. 1983. Set. pap. 85.00 (ISBN 0-87061-141-0); Vol. 1. pap. 15.00 (ISBN 0-87061-084-8); Vol. 2. pap. 18.00 (ISBN 0-87061-085-6); Vol. 3. pap. 21.00 (ISBN 0-87061-086-4); Vol. 4. pap. 39.95; Vol. 4 cloth ed. 48.00. Chr Classics.

Patrology: The Lives & Works of the Fathers of the Church, 3 vols. Otto Bardenhewer. pap. text ed. 37.50 (ISBN 0-317-60810-X). Eastern Orthodox.

Patrology, Vol. IV: The Golden Age of Latin Patristic Literature. Ed. by Johannes Quasten & Angelo Di Berardino. Tr. by Placid Solari. 1986. 48.00 (ISBN 0-87061-126-7); pap. 39.95 (ISBN 0-87061-127-5); Set of 4 vols. pap. 85.00. Chr Classics.

Patron Access: Issues for Online Catalogs. Walt Crawford. 258p. 1987. 36.50 (ISBN 0-8161-1850-7, Hall Library); pap. 28.50 (ISBN 0-8161-1852-3, Hall Library). G K Hall.

Patron & the Panca. Bengt-Erik Borgstrom. 184p. 1980. text ed. 17.50x (ISBN 0-7069-0997-6, Pub. by Vikas India). Advent NY.

Patron-Client State Relationships: Multilateral Crises in the Nuclear Age. Christopher C. Shoemaker. LC 83-17822. 220p. 1984. 35.00 (ISBN 0-275-91267-1, C1267). Praeger.

Patron de New-York. Barnard B. Dadie. pap. 6.50 (ISBN 0-685-35940-9). French & Eur.

Patron Happiness. Sandra McPherson. LC 82-11490. (American Poetry Ser.). 70p. 1984. 12.95 (ISBN 0-88001-021-5); pap. 6.50 (ISBN 0-88001-022-3). Ecco Pr.

Patron State: Government & the Arts in Europe, North America, & Japan. Ed. by Milton C. Cummings, Jr. & Richard S. Katz. (Illus.). 384p. 1987. 29.95 (ISBN 0-19-504364-2). Oxford U Pr.

Patronage. Maria Edgeworth. (Mothers of the Novel Reprints Ser.). 592p. 1986. pap. 8.95 (ISBN 0-86358-106-4, 81064). Routledge Chapman & Hall.

Pattern of Financial Asset Ownership: Wisconsin Individuals, 1949, Vol. 7. Thomas R. Atkinson. (National Bureau of Economic Research). 1949. 26.50x (ISBN 0-691-04155-5). Princeton U Pr.

Pattern of Freedom. Bruce L. Richmond. 266p. 1980. Repr. of 1911 ed. lib. bdg. 25.00 (ISBN 0-8492-7732-9). R West.

Pattern of God's Truth. Frank E. Gaebelein. LC 54-6908. 1968. pap. 6.95 (ISBN 0-8024-6450-5). Moody.

Pattern of God's Truth. Frank E. Gaebelein. 1985. pap. 5.95 (ISBN 0-88469-170-5). BMH Bks.

Pattern of Health. Aubrey T. Westlake. 1963. 9.95 (ISBN 0-8159-6514-1). Devin.

Pattern of Human Concerns Data, 1957-1963. Hadley Cantril. 1977. codebk. write for info. (ISBN 0-89138-115-5). ICPSR.

Pattern of Imperialism: A Study in the Theories of Power. Earle M. Winslow. LC 78-159238. xii, 278p. 1971. Repr. lib. bdg. 20.00x (ISBN 0-374-98685-1, Octagon). Hippocrene Bks.

Pattern of Imperialism: The United States, Great Britain & the Late-Industrializing World Since 1815. Tony Smith. LC 80-39676. (Illus.). 240p. 1981. 39.50 (ISBN 0-521-23619-3); pap. 14.95 (ISBN 0-521-28076-1). Cambridge U Pr.

Pattern of Land Ownership & Backwardness: A Study of Four Villages in Jaunpur District of Eastern UP. Kripa Shankar. 1986. 12.50x (ISBN 81-7024-021-2, Pub. by Ashish India). South Asia Bks.

Pattern of Life. 2nd ed. Alfred Adler. LC 81-71160. pap. 10.00x (ISBN 0-918560-28-4). A Adler Inst.

Pattern of Prayer. W. E. Sangster & Leslie Davison. 160p. (Orig.). 1988. pap. 6.95 (ISBN 0-310-51401-0, Pub. by F Asbury Pr). Zondervan.

Pattern of Responsibility. Dean Acheson. Ed. by McGeorge Bundy. LC 75-128070. 1972. Repr. of 1952 ed. 35.00x (ISBN 0-678-03560-1). Kelley.

Pattern of Rural Outmigration: A Micro Level Study. Najma Khan. (Illus.). 180p. 1986. text ed. 22.50x (ISBN 81-7018-353-7, Pub. by D K Pub Corp Delhi). Apt Bks.

Pattern of Sound in Lucretius. Rosamund E. Deutsch. Ed. by Steele Commager. LC 77-70763. (Latin Poetry Ser.). 1979. Repr. of 1939 ed. lib. bdg. 25.00 (ISBN 0-8240-2967-4). Garland Pub.

Pattern of Soviet Conduct in the Third World. Ed. by Walter Laqueur. 256p. 1983. 35.00 (ISBN 0-275-91031-8, C1031). Praeger.

Pattern of the Chinese Past: A Social & Economic Interpretation. Mark Elvin. LC 72-78869. 346p. 1973. 27.50x (ISBN 0-8047-0826-6); pap. 10.95x (ISBN 0-8047-0876-2). Stanford U Pr.

Pattern of the Iliad. John T. Sheppard. LC 68-816. (Studies in Poetry, No. 38). 1969. Repr. of 1922 ed. lib. bdg. 49.95x (ISBN 0-8383-0622-5). Haskell.

Pattern of the Past. Ed. by Ian Hodder et al. LC 79-8497. (Illus.). 424p. 1981. 67.50 (ISBN 0-521-22763-1). Cambridge U Pr.

Pattern of the Past: Can We Determine It. P Geyl et al. LC 68-23291. 126p. 1949. Repr. lib. bdg. 35.00x (ISBN 0-8371-0083-6, GEPP). Greenwood.

Pattern of the Spirit. Gerald FitzGerald. 1985. 10.00x (ISBN 0-317-62222-6, Guild of Pastoral Psych). State Mutual Bk.

Pattern of Tragicomedy in Beaumont & Fletcher. Eugene M. Waith. LC 69-15694. (Yale Studies in English Ser.: No. 120). xiv, 212p. 1969. Repr. of 1952 ed. 25.00 (ISBN 0-208-00777-6, Archon). Shoe String.

Pattern Poetry: Guide to an Unknown Literature. Dick Higgins. LC 87-10199. 304p. (Orig.). 1987. 59.50 (ISBN 0-88706-413-2); pap. 19.95 (ISBN 0-88706-414-0). State U NY Pr.

Pattern Recognition. Ed. by Bruce G. Batchelor. LC 77-12488. (Illus.). 502p. 1977. 65.00x (ISBN 0-306-31020-1, Plenum Pr). Plenum Pub.

Pattern Recognition. Michael James & Bernard Watson. LC 88-246. 1988. 29.95 (ISBN 0-471-61120-4). Wiley.

Pattern Recognition. Ed. by J. Kittler. (Lecture Notes in Computer Science Ser.: Vol. 301). vii, 668p. 1988. pap. 67.90 (ISBN 0-387-19036-8). Springer-Verlag.

Pattern Recognition & Acoustical Imaging. Ed. by Ferrari. 372p. 1987. 57.00 (ISBN 0-89252-803-6, 768). SPIE.

Pattern Recognition & Artificial Intelligence: Proceedings of a Joint Workshop held at Hyannis, Mass., June 1976. Ed. by C. H. Chen. 1976. 79.50 (ISBN 0-12-170950-7). Acad Pr.

Pattern Recognition & Image Processing. Tzay Y. Young & King-Sun Fu. (Academic Press Handbook Ser.). 1986. 89.00 (ISBN 0-12-774560-2). Acad Pr.

Pattern Recognition & Picture Processing. Bow. (Electrical Engineering & Electronics Ser.). 304p. 1984. 45.00 (ISBN 0-8247-7176-1). Dekker.

Pattern Recognition & Signal Processing, No. 29. Ed. by C. H. Chen. (NATO Advanced Study Institute Ser.). 666p. 1978. 46.00x (ISBN 90-286-0978-4, Pub. by Sijthoff & Noordhoff). Kluwer Academic.

Pattern Recognition Approach to Data Interpretation. Diane D. Wolff & Michael L. Parsons. 220p. 1983. 35.00x (ISBN 0-306-41302-7, Plenum Pr). Plenum Pub.

Pattern Recognition by Humans & Machines, Vol. 1: Speech Perception. Eileen C. Schwab & Howard C. Nusbaum. (Series in Cognition & Perception). 336p. 1986. 59.50 (ISBN 0-12-631401-2); pap. 29.95 (ISBN 0-12-631403-9). Acad Pr.

Pattern Recognition by Humans & Machines, Vol. 2: Visual Perception. Eileen C. Schwab & Howard C. Nusbaum. (Series in Cognition & Perception). 264p. 1986. 46.50 (ISBN 0-12-631402-0); pap. 23.95 (ISBN 0-12-631404-7). Acad Pr.

Pattern Recognition: Human & Mechanical. Satosi Watanabe. LC 84-7354. 156p. 1985. text ed. 49.95x (ISBN 0-471-80815-6, Pub by Wiley-Interscience). Wiley.

Pattern Recognition in Practice. Ed. by E. S. Gelsema & L. N. Kanal. 552p. 1980. 118.50 (ISBN 0-444-86115-7, North-Holland). Elsevier.

Pattern Recognition in Practice II: Proceedings of an International Workshop, Amsterdam, The Netherlands, 19-21 June, 1985. Ed. by E. S. Gelsema & L. N. Kanal. 572p. 1986. 121.00 (ISBN 0-444-87877-7, North Holland). Elsevier.

Pattern Recognition Mechanisms. Ed. by C. Chagas et al. (Experimental Brain Research Series - Supplementum 11: Suppl. 11). (Illus.). 375p. 1985. 56.00 (ISBN 0-387-15723-9). Springer-Verlag.

Pattern Recognition Problems in Geology & Paleontology. U. Bayer. (Lecture Notes in Earth Sciences: Vol. 2). vii, 229p. 1985. pap. 19.50 (ISBN 0-387-13983-4). Springer-Verlag.

Pattern Recognition Theory & Applications. Ed. by P. A. Devijver & J. Kittler. (NATO ASI Ser.: F30). xi, 543p. 1987. 100.00 (ISBN 0-387-17700-0). Springer-Verlag.

Pattern Recognition with Fuzzy Objective Function Algorithms. James C. Bezdek. LC 81-4354. (Advanced Applications in Pattern Recognition Ser.). 272p. 1981. 49.50x (ISBN 0-306-40671-3, Plenum Pr). Plenum Pub.

Pattern Sheets of Origamic Architecture. Masahiro Chatani. (Illus.). 85p. 1982. pap. 16.95 (ISBN 4-3-9527012-3, Shokokusha Tokyo). Bks Nippan.

Pattern Synthesis: Lectures in Pattern Recognition, Vol. 1. U. Grenander. LC 76-209. (Applied Mathematical Sciences: Vol. 18). 1976. pap. 29.00 (ISBN 0-387-90174-4). Springer-Verlag.

Pattern Words: Nine-Letters in Length. Sheila Carlisle. 168p. (Orig.). 1986. lib. bdg. 24.80 (ISBN 0-89412-147-2); pap. text ed. 16.80 (ISBN 0-89412-146-4). Aegean Park Pr.

Pattern Words: Three Letters to Eight Letters in Length. Sheila Carlisle. 139p. (Orig.). 1986. lib. bdg. 24.80 (ISBN 0-89412-136-7); pap. text ed. 16.80 (ISBN 0-89412-135-9). Aegean Park Pr.

Patterned Elicitation Syntax Test: PEST. Edna C. Young & Joseph J. Perachio. 45p. 1983. pap. text ed. 24.95 (ISBN 0-88450-746-7, 2082-B). Communication Skill.

Patterngrams: How to Copy Designs at Home. 2nd ed. Nancy Olson. LC 72-78471. (Illus.). 1979. pap. 10.00 (ISBN 0-87005-312-4). Fairchild.

Patterning in Shakespearean Drama: Essays in Criticism. William L. Godshalk. LC 72-94504. (De Proprietatibus Litterarum, Ser. Practica: No. 69). 199p. 1973. pap. text ed. 27.20x (ISBN 90-2792-472-4). Mouton.

Patterning of Time. Leonard W. Doob. LC 72-97346. pap. 121.50 (ISBN 0-317-10352-0, 2007547). Bks Demand UMI.

Patternless Fashions: How to Design & Make Your Own Fashions. Diehl Lewis & May Loh. LC 80-23125. (Illus.). 300p. 1987. pap. 9.95 (ISBN 0-87491-827-8). Acropolis.

Patternmaker's Guide. Ed Hamilton. (Illus.). 680p. 1976. 100.00 (ISBN 0-317-32651-1, PM7602). Am Foundrymen.

Patternmaker's Manual. 4th ed. American Foundrymen Society Staff. (Illus.). 526p. 1970. 100.00 (ISBN 0-317-32653-8, PM7000). Am Foundrymen.

Patternmaking. 108p. 1987. pap. 30.00 (ISBN 0-317-59857-0, TE8200). Am Foundrymen.

Patternmaking for Fashion Design. Helen J. Armstrong. 712p. 1986. text ed. 39.95 scp (ISBN 0-06-040332-2, HarpC). Har-Row.

Patternmaking Nineteen Five. 1982. pap. 8.95 (ISBN 0-917914-03-1). Lindsay Pubns.

Patterns. 2nd. ed. Mary L. Conclin. LC 87-80338. 369p. 1988. pap. text ed. 15.56 (ISBN 0-395-43249-9); instr's manual 2.36 (ISBN 0-395-45040-3). HM.

Patterns. Richard Dingman. (Illus.). 450p. (Orig.). 1984. pap. 32.00 (ISBN 0-9613432-0-6). Mind-Dog.

Patterns. Joan K. Hamilton. (Illus.). 1977. tchrs'. manual 5.25x (ISBN 0-8192-4078-8); parents' letters & pupils' leaflets package 5.75x (ISBN 0-8192-4077-X). Morehouse.

Patterns. Leslie Linson. 256p. 1988. 12.95 (ISBN 0-8062-3331-1). Carlton.

Patterns. Jane Verby. 400p. (Orig.). 1986. pap. 3.95 (ISBN 0-8439-2310-5, Leisure Bks). Leisure NY.

Patterns, Level 3, Bk. B. Jo M. Stanchfield. LC 77-83336. (Vistas Ser.). (Illus., Gr. 9). (YA) (gr. 9). 1978. pap. text ed. 8.92 (ISBN 0-395-25230-X); tchr's. guides 7.28 (ISBN 0-395-25231-8); skillbook 5.08; tchr's annotated skillbk 5.44 (ISBN 0-395-25248-2). HM.

Patterns & Coincidences. John G. Neihardt. LC 77-24199. 128p. 1978. 9.95 (ISBN 0-317-38044-3). U of MO Pr.

Patterns & Coincidences: A Sequel to "All Is But a Beginning". John G. Neihardt. LC 77-24199. x, 123p. 1985. 14.95 (ISBN 0-8032-3312-4). U of Nebr Pr.

Patterns & Configurations in Economic Science: A Study of Social Decision Processes. J. M. Blin. LC 72-92525. 148p. 1973. lib. bdg. 26.00 (ISBN 90-277-0302-7, Pub. by Reidel Holland). Kluwer Academic.

Patterns & Configurations in Finite Spaces. S. Vajda. (Griffin's Statistical Monographs: No. 22). 120p. 1967. pap. 17.95x (ISBN 0-85264-025-0). Lubrecht & Cramer.

Patterns & Experiments in Developmental Biology. Leland Johnson & E. Peter Volpe. 270p. 1973. write for info. wire coil (ISBN 0-697-04535-8). Wm C Brown.

Patterns & Instructions for a Child's Quiet Book. Joanne Harlow. 27p. 1977. 3.50 (ISBN 0-317-03553-3). Randall Bk Co.

Patterns & Instructions for Carving Authentic Birds. H. D. Green. (Illus.). 80p. (Orig.). 1982. pap. 3.00 (ISBN 0-486-24222-6). Dover.

Patterns & Perspectives in English Renaissance Drama. Eugene M. Waith. LC 86-40608. (Illus.). 312p. 1988. 38.50x (ISBN 0-87413-325-4). U Delaware Pr.

Patterns & Perspectives in Iowa History. Ed. by Dorothy Schwieder. LC 73-928. pap. 122.00 (ISBN 0-317-55559-6, 2029626). Bks Demand UMI.

Patterns & Processes: An Introduction to Anthropological Strategies for the Study of Sociocultural Change. Robert L. Bee. LC 73-10791. 1974. pap. text ed. 12.95 (ISBN 0-02-902090-5). Free Pr.

Patterns & Processes in the History of Life. Ed. by D. M. Raup & D. Jablonski. (Dahlem Workshop Reports: Vol. 36). (Illus.). 460p. 1986. 88.00 (ISBN 0-387-15965-7). Springer-Verlag.

Patterns & Processes of Internal Migration in Less Developed Countries: A Selected Research Bibliography. Mohammad Kamiar & J. Allan Beegle. (Public Administration Ser.: P 1928). 57p. 1986. 14.50 (ISBN 0-89028-848-8). Vance Biblios.

Patterns & Props. Bonnie Bernstein. 112p. (gr. k-3). 1984. 8.95 (ISBN 0-912107-21-9). Monday Morning Bks.

Patterns & Prospectives of the Capitalist World-Economy. 19p. 1981. pap. 5.00 (ISBN 92-808-0300-X, TUNU135, UNU). UNIPUB.

Patterns & Prospects of Development in Downtown Kearney. Ceter for Applied Urban Research Staff. 100p. (Orig.). 1982. pap. 6.00 (ISBN 1-55719-059-3). U NE Ctr Applied Urban Rsch.

Patterns & Sources of Navajo Weaving. rev. ed. W. D. Harmsen. LC 78-68721. (Illus.). 1978. write for info. Harmsen.

Patterns & Themes: A Basic English Reader. 2nd ed. Judy R. Rogers & Glenn C. Rogers. 267p. 1988. pap. text ed. write for info. (ISBN 0-534-08832-5). Wadsworth Pub.

Patterns & Themes in Indian Politics. B. Dasgupta & W. H. Morris-Jones. 364p. 1975. 16.95. Asia Bk Corp.

Patterns & Waves: Qualitative Analysis of Nonlinear Differential Equations. Ed. by T. Nishida et al. (Studies in Mathematics & Its Applications: No. 18). 692p. 1987. 150.00 (ISBN 0-444-70144-3, North Holland). Elsevier.

Patterns As Grammar see Language Teacher.

Patterns, Defects & Microstructures in Nonequilibrium Systems: Applications in Materials Science. Ed. by D. Walgraef. 1987. lib. bdg. 85.50 (ISBN 90-247-3479-7, Pub. by Martinus Nijhoff Netherlands). Kluwer Academic.

Patterns Emerge: Hippocrates to Paracelsus see Divided Legacy: A History of the Schism in Medical Thought.

Patterns for Better Living, Vol. 7. U-Bild Enterprises Staff. 112p. 1987. pap. 3.95 (ISBN 0-910495-04-1). U-Bild.

Patterns for Better Living, Vol. 8. U-Bild Enterprises Staff. 112p. Date not set. pap. 3.95 (ISBN 0-910495-05-X). U-Bild.

Patterns for Canvas Embroidery. Diana Jones. (Illus.). 96p. 1985. pap. 12.95 (ISBN 0-7134-4014-7, Pub. by Batsford England). David & Charles.

Patterns for College Writing: A Rhetorical Reader & Guide. 3rd ed. Laurie G. Kirszner & Stephen R. Mandell. LC 85-61248. 500p. 1986. pap. text ed. write for info. (ISBN 0-312-59821-1); instr's. manual avail. (ISBN 0-312-59820-3). St Martin.

Patterns for Fifty-Two Visual Lessons. Idalee W. Vonk. (Illus.). 48p. (Orig.). (gr. 3-6). 1951. pap. 4.95 (ISBN 0-87239-362-3, 2143). Standard Pub.

Patterns for Guernseys, Jerseys & Arans: Fishermans' Sweaters from the British Isles. Gladys Thompson. (Illus.). 1971. pap. 5.95 (ISBN 0-486-22703-0). Dover.

Patterns for Guernseys, Jerseys & Arans: Fisherman's Sweaters from the British Isles. 2nd & rev. ed. Gladys Thompson. (Illus.). 14.25 (ISBN 0-8446-0273-6). Peter Smith.

Patterns for Health & Safety. Marilyn Barr. (gr. 1-4). 1988. pap. 6.95 (ISBN 0-8224-5180-8). D S Lake Pubs.

Patterns for Holiday Games. 1982. 3.50 (ISBN 0-939418-48-7). Ferguson-Florissant.

Patterns for Holiday Learning Fun. Marilyn Barr. (gr. 1-4). 1988. pap. 6.95 (ISBN 0-8224-5179-4). D S Lake Pubs.

Patterns for Improvising the Touch Technique. (Illus.). 24p. 1986. pap. 8.95 (ISBN 0-937555-21-5). Kelby Pub.

Patterns for Lifelong Learning. Theodore M. Hesburgh et al. LC 73-10936. (Higher Education Ser). 1973. 22.95x (ISBN 0-87589-200-0). Jossey-Bass.

Patterns for Making Amish Dolls & Doll Clothes. Rachel T. Pellman & Jan Steffy. (Orig.). 1987. pap. 12.95 (ISBN 0-934672-47-4). Good Bks PA.

Patterns for Mature Living. Milton H. Keene. LC 76-27093. Repr. of 1976 ed. 21.30 (ISBN 0-8357-9019-3, 2016389). Bks Demand UMI.

Patterns for Pick-Ups see Build or Buy a Loom.

Patterns for Pinwheels, Pup-Ups & Puppets. Marilyn Barr. (gr. 1-4). 1988. pap. 6.95 (ISBN 0-8224-5182-4). D S Lake Pubs.

Patterns for Posters, Projects & Cards. Marilyn Barr. (gr. 1-4). 1988. pap. 6.95 (ISBN 0-8224-5181-6). D S Lake Pubs.

Patterns for Power. D. Stuart Briscoe. LC 78-68850. (Bible Commentary for Laymen Ser.). 160p. 1979. pap. 3.95 (ISBN 0-8307-0701-8, S331101). Regal.

Patterns for Practical Communications: Composition Package. Doris C. Weddington. 1977. text ed. 375.00 (ISBN 0-13-653881-9); tchr's. manual 17.00 (ISBN 0-13-653865-7). P-H.

Patterns for Practical Communications: Script Composition. Doris C. Weddington. 1977. pap. text ed. 18.75 (ISBN 0-13-653840-1). P-H.

Patterns for Practical Communications: Sentence Package. D. Weddington. 1977. text ed. 375.00 (ISBN 0-13-653790-1); script sentences wkbk. 18.75 (ISBN 0-13-653816-9). P-H.

Patterns for Prayer. Hubert Van Zeller. 128p. 1983. pap. 5.95 (ISBN 0-87243-124-X). Templegate.

Patterns for Pregnancy. Belinda Musgrave. (Illus.). 96p. 1988. 22.95 (ISBN 0-7134-5412-1, Pub. by Batsford England). David & Charles.

Patterns for Preschoolers. New York Library Association, Youth Services Section. (Illus.). 194p. 1985. 15.00 (ISBN 0-931658-11-X). NY Lib Assn.

Patterns for Quilting. Linda Macho. 80p. 1984. pap. 4.50 (ISBN 0-486-24632-9). Dover.

Patterns for Reading. Mary Hoover & Marsha Fabian. 1979. pap. 17.95 (ISBN 0-89863-022-3). Star Pub CA.

Patterns for Self-Unfoldment. Randolph Schmelig & Leddy Schmelig. 1975. 5.95 (ISBN 0-87159-127-8). Unity School.

Patterns for Soft Toys. Enid Anderson. (Illus.). 120p. 1986. 24.95 (ISBN 0-7134-4553-X, Pub. by Batsford England). David & Charles.

Patterns for Success in Managing a Business. pap. 1.95x (ISBN 0-686-02550-4). Dun.

Patterns for Tapestry Weaving: Projects & Techniques. Nancy Harvey. LC 83-19313. 168p. 1984. pap. 12.95 (ISBN 0-914718-83-5). Pacific Search.

Patterns for Teacher-Made Games. 1980. 4.00 (ISBN 0-939418-01-0). Ferguson-Florissant.

Patterns for Theatrical Costumes: Garments, Trims, & Accessories from Ancient Egypt to 1912. Katherine S. Holkeboer. (Illus.). 320p. 1984. pap. 15.95 (ISBN 0-13-654260-3). P-H.

Patterns from China: Sweater Ideas for Children. Judith Gross. 100p. 1981. 17.95 (ISBN 0-442-20399-3). Van Nos Reinhold.

Patterns from Paradise: The Art of Tahitian Quilting. Vicki Poggioli. LC 88-10010. (Illus.). 128p. (Orig.). 1988. pap. 15.95 (ISBN 1-55562-052-3). Main Street.

Patterns from the Sod. Margaret B. Bogue. Ed. by Stuart Bruchey. LC 78-56691. (Management of Public Lands Law in the U. S. Ser.). (Illus.). 1979. Repr. of 1959 ed. lib. bdg. 24.50x (ISBN 0-405-11318-8). Ayer Co Pubs.

Patterns from the Sod: Land Use & Tenure in the Grand Prairie, 1850-1900. Margaret B. Bogue. (Illinois Historical Collections Ser.: Vol. 34). 1959. 2.50 (ISBN 0-912154-14-4). Ill St Hist Lib.

Patterns in Action. Robert Schwegler. 1985. pap. text ed. write for info. (ISBN 0-673-39237-6). Scott F.

Patterns in Action. 2nd ed. Robert A. Schwegler. 1988. pap. text ed. write for info. (ISBN 0-673-39767-X). Scott F.

Patterns in Comparative Religion. Mircea Eliade. pap. 9.95 (ISBN 0-452-00728-3, Mer). NAL.

Patterns in Comparative Religion. Mircea Eliade. 17.25 (ISBN 0-8446-6226-7). Peter Smith.

Patterns in Crime. Paul J. Brantingham & Patricia Brantingham. (Illus.). 448p. 1984. text ed. write for info. (ISBN 0-02-313520-4). Macmillan.

Patterns in Criminal Homicide. Marvin Wolfgang. LC 74-34157. (Criminology, Law Enforcement, & Social Problems Ser.: No. 211). 413p. 1975. 24.00x (ISBN 0-87585-211-4). Patterson Smith.

Patterns in Crystals. Noel F. Kennon. LC 78-4531. 207p. pap. 53.90 (2030524). Bks Demand UMI.

Patterns in Education: The Unfolding of Nursing. Linda K. Amos et al. 178p. 1985. 18.95 (15-1974). Natl League Nurse.

Patterns of Love. Saffron James. 464p. 1982. 25.00x (ISBN 0-901976-71-7, Pub. by United Writers Pubns England). State Mutual Bk.

Patterns of Love & Courtesy: Essays in Memory of C. S. Lewis. Ed. by John Lawlor. 1967. 15.95x (ISBN 0-8101-0280-3). Northwestern U Pr.

Patterns of Market Behavior: Essays in Honor of Philip Taft. Ed. by Michael J. Brennan. LC 65-12932. (Studies in the Fields of General Scholarship). pap. 66.00 (ISBN 0-317-41781-9, 2025643). Bks Demand UMI.

Patterns of Mass Movements in Arab Revolutionary Progressive States. Enver M. Koury. LC 76-110953. (Studies in the Social Sciences: No. 9). (Orig.). 1970. pap. text ed. 22.00x (ISBN 90-2791-259-9). Mouton.

Patterns of Meaning. Wilbert J. Levy & Carol R. Farber. 1977. pap. text ed. 10.58 (ISBN 0-87720-956-1). AMSCO Sch.

Patterns of Minority Relations. Raymond W. Mack & Troy S. Duster. 60p. 0.75 (ISBN 0-686-74878-6). ADL.

Patterns of Modernity, 2 vols. Ed. by S. N. Eisenstadt. 252p. 30.00x ea. Vol. I: The West (ISBN 0-8147-2173-7). Vol. II: Beyond the West (ISBN 0-8147-2172-9). NYU Pr.

Patterns of Moral Complexity. Charles E. Larmore. 140p. 1987. 32.50 (ISBN 0-521-33034-3); pap. 9.95 (ISBN 0-521-33891-3). Cambridge U Pr.

Patterns of Mothering: A Study of Maternal Influence During Infancy. Sylvia Brody. LC 56-8839. 446p. (Orig.). 1970. text ed. 45.00x (ISBN 0-8236-4040-X). Intl Univs Pr.

Patterns of Muscular Activity in Selected Sport Skills: An Electromyographic Study. Marion R. Broer & Sara J. Houtz. (Illus.). 96p. 1967. photocopy ed. 15.25x (ISBN 0-398-00229-0). C C Thomas.

Patterns of Panchayati Raj in India. G. Ram Reddy. 1977. 9.50x (ISBN 0-8364-0046-1). South Asia Bks.

Patterns of Panic. Abraham M. Meerloo. LC 73-9371. 120p. 1974. Repr. of 1950 ed. lib. bdg. 18.75 (ISBN 0-8371-7009-5, MEPP). Greenwood.

Patterns of Panic. Joost A. Meerloo. LC 50-5823. pap. 30.00 (ISBN 0-317-10375-X, 2010445). Bks Demand UMI.

Patterns of Parliamentary Legislation. Rose Ven Mechelen. 104p. 1987. text ed. 35.50 (ISBN 0-566-05327-6, Pub. by Gower Pub Co England). Gower Pub Co.

Patterns of Person: Studies in Style & Form from Corneille to Laclos. Edward C. Knox. LC 82-82430. (French Forum Monographs: No. 41). 177p. (Orig.). 1983. pap. 12.95x (ISBN 0-917058-40-2). French Forum.

Patterns of Plausible Inference see Mathematics & Plausible Reasoning.

Patterns of Poetry: An Encyclopedia of Forms. Miller Williams. LC 85-23719. (Illus.). xiii, 203p. 1986. text ed. 32.50 (ISBN 0-8071-1253-4); pap. text ed. 14.95 (ISBN 0-8071-1330-1). LA State U Pr.

Patterns of Policing: A Comparative International Perspective. David H. Bayley. LC 84-24908. (Crime, Law & Deviance Ser.). 300p. 1985. text ed. 27.00 (ISBN 0-8135-1094-5). Rutgers U Pr.

Patterns of Policy: Comparative & Longitudinal Studies of Population Events. Ed. by John D. Montgomery et al. LC 77-94305. 300p. 1979. 39.95 (ISBN 0-87855-269-3). Transaction Bks.

Patterns of Political Instability. David Sanders. LC 79-21422. 1981. 27.50x (ISBN 0-312-59808-4). St Martin.

Patterns of Political Leadership: Egypt, Israel, Lebanon. R. Hrair Dekmejian. LC 74-20940. (Illus.). xi, 323p. 1975. 49.50x (ISBN 0-87395-291-X). State U NY Pr.

Patterns of Political Participation of Puerto Ricans in New York. Rosa Estades. LC 77-11625. 1978. pap. 5.00 (ISBN 0-8477-2445-X). U of PR Pr.

Patterns of Population Density in St. Louis. Henry R. Herzfeld. 1967. pap. 2.00 (ISBN 0-318-00014-8, DRA 4). Inst for Urban & Regional.

Patterns of Population Distribution: A Residential Preference Model & Its Dynamic. David J. Morgan. LC 78-18794. (Research Papers Ser: No. 176). (Illus.). 1978. pap. 12.00 (ISBN 0-89065-083-7). U Chicago Comm Geo.

Patterns of Power: Religion & Politics in America. David Chidester. 352p. 1988. pap. text ed. 22.00 (ISBN 0-13-654005-8). P-H.

Patterns of Prayer in the Psalms. Laurence Dunlop. 160p. (Orig.). 1982. pap. 9.95 (ISBN 0-8164-2377-6, HarpR). Har-Row.

Patterns of Primate Behavior. Claud A. Bramblett. (Illus.). 320p. 1985. pap. text ed. 14.95x (ISBN 0-88133-144-9). Waveland Pr.

Patterns of Problem Solving. reference ed. Mashe F. Rubinstein. LC 74-20721. (Illus.). 640p. 1975. text ed. 46.00 (ISBN 0-13-654251-4). P-H.

Patterns of Professions. Emma B. Donath. LC 84-70084. 112p. 1984. 9.00 (2299-01). Am Fed Astrologers.

Patterns of Progress. facs. ed. Horace M. Kallen. LC 68-55847. (Essay Index Reprint Ser). 1950. 14.00 (ISBN 0-8369-0582-2). Ayer Co Pubs.

Patterns of Property Tax Administration in the United States. Robert M. Clatanoff. LC 86-7240. (Research & Information Ser.: No. 5). (Illus.). 178p. 1986. 30.00 (ISBN 0-88329-145-2). IAAO.

Patterns of Prophecy. Alan Vaughan. 256p. pap. 14.50 (ISBN 0-89540-155-X, SB-155). Sun Pub.

Patterns of Protestant Church Music. Robert M. Stevenson. LC 53-8271. viii, 219p. 1953. 22.50 (ISBN 0-8223-0168-7). Duke.

Patterns of Protestant Church Music. Robert M. Stevenson. LC 53-8271. pap. 56.80 (ISBN 0-317-26858-9, 2023455). Bks Demand UMI.

Patterns of Psychopathology. Melvin Zax & George Stricker. LC 63-9238. (Case Studies of Behavioral Dysfuntion). pap. 80.00 (ISBN 0-317-28758-3, 2051678). Bks Demand UMI.

Patterns of Psychosexual Infantilism. Wilhelm Stekel. 1952. 8.95x (ISBN 0-87140-840-6). Liveright.

Patterns of Pulmonary Interstitial Disease. H. Johnson. (Illus.). 300p. Date not set. 35.00 (ISBN 0-87527-218-5). Green.

Patterns of Realism. Roy Armes. LC 82-49216. (Cinema Classics Ser.). 226p. 1985. lib. bdg. 66.00 (ISBN 0-8240-5750-3). Garland Pub.

Patterns of Redundancy: Psychological Study. Alan C. Staniland. LC 66-10067. pap. 56.00 (ISBN 0-317-10275-3, 2050797). Bks Demand UMI.

Patterns of Regional Economic Growth & Decline. Mark Perlman. 1982. pap. 5.00 (ISBN 0-8447-3502-7). Am Enterprise.

Patterns of Religious Narrative in the Canterbury Tales. Roger Ellis. LC 86-10798. 320p. 1986. 29.50x (ISBN 0-389-20649-0). B&N Imports.

Patterns of Renewal. Laurens Van Der Post. LC 62-15859. (Orig.). 1962. pap. 2.50x (ISBN 0-87574-121-5). Pendle Hill.

Patterns of Reproduction of Four Species of Vespertiliohia Bats in Paraguay. Philip Myers. (UC Publications in Zoology: Vol. 107). 1977. pap. 19.00x (ISBN 0-520-09554-5). U of Cal Pr.

Patterns of Rural-Urban Migration in India. J. P. Singh. (Illus.). xx, 275p. 1986. text ed. 37.50x (ISBN 81-210-0070-X, Pub. by Inter India Pubns N. Delhi). Apt Bks.

Patterns of Sedimentation, Diagenesis, & Hydrocarbon Accumulation in Cretaceous Rocks of the Rocky Mountains. Dudley D. Rice & Donald L. Gautier. (Short Course Notes Ser.: No. 11). 310p. 1983. pap. 25.00 (ISBN 0-918985-21-8). SEPM.

Patterns of Sexual Arousal: Psychophysiological Processes & Clinical Applications. Raymond C. Rosen & J. Gayle Beck. LC 87-19726. 404p. 1988. lib. bdg. 35.00 lib. binding (ISBN 0-89862-712-5). Guilford Pr.

Patterns of Sexual Behavior. Clellan S. Ford & Frank A. Beach. LC 80-159. (Illus.). vii, 307p. 1980. Repr. of 1951 ed. lib. bdg. 35.00x (ISBN 0-313-22355-6, FOPS). Greenwood.

Patterns of Shock: Implications for Nursing Care. 2nd ed. Katherine J. Bordicks. (Illus.). 1980. text ed. write for info. (ISBN 0-02-312450-4). Macmillan.

Patterns of Social Policy: An Introduction to Comparative Analysis. Catherine Jones. 300p. (Orig.). 1986. text ed. 32.00 (ISBN 0-422-77210-0, 9560, Pub. by Tavistock England); pap. text ed. 14.95 (ISBN 0-422-77260-7, 9561, Pub. by Tavistock England). Routledge Chapman & Hall.

Patterns of Societal Development in Iceland 1930-1980. Ingmar Einarsson. (Studia Sociologica Upsaliensia: No. 26). 152p. (Orig.). 1987. pap. text ed. 22.00x (ISBN 91-554-2015-X, Pub By Almqvist & Wiksell). Coronet Bks.

Patterns of Sound. Ian Maddieson. (Cambridge Studies in Speech Science Communication). (Illus.). 422p. 1984. 34.50 (ISBN 0-521-26536-3). Cambridge U Pr.

Patterns of Soviet Economic Decisions-Making: An Inside View of the 1965 Reform. Sergei Freidzon. Ed. by Andrew Michta. 104p. (Orig.). Date not set. pap. text ed. 42.50 (ISBN 1-55831-072-X). Delphic Associates.

Patterns of Soviet Thought: The Origins & Development of Dialectical & Historical Materialism. Richard T. De George. LC 66-17026. (Ann Arbor Paperbacks Ser.: No. AA-160). pap. 77.00 (ISBN 0-317-09962-0, 2051056). Bks Demand UMI.

Patterns of Spanish Pronunciation: A Drill Book. J. Donald Bowen & Robert P. Stockwell. LC 60-16841. (Orig.). 1960. pap. 4.50x (ISBN 0-226-06831-5). U of Chicago Pr.

Patterns of Symmetry. Ed. by Marjorie Senechal & George Fleck. LC 76-56775. (Illus.). 160p. 1977. pap. 8.95x (ISBN 0-87023-345-9). U of Mass Pr.

Patterns of Teaching: A Sourcebook for Teachers in Further Education. D. M. Yorke. (Orig.). 1981. pap. text ed. 22.50x (ISBN 0-86184-030-5). Trans Atl Phila.

Patterns of Technological Innovation. D. Sahal. 1981. write for info. (ISBN 0-201-06630-0). Addison-Wesley.

Patterns of the Fantastic: Academic Proceedings at Chicon IV. Ed. by Donald M. Hassler. LC 83-12225. (Starmont Studies in Literary Criticism: No. 2). 105p. 1983. Repr. of 1983 ed. lib. bdg. 16.95x (ISBN 0-89370-738-4). Borgo Pr.

Patterns of the Fantastic I: Academic Programming at Chicon IV. Ed. by Donald M. Hassler. LC 83-587. (Illus.). 1983. 16.95x (ISBN 0-916732-63-0); pap. 7.95x text ed. (ISBN 0-916732-62-2). Starmont Hse.

Patterns of the Fantastic II: Academic Proceedings at Constellation. Ed. by Donald M. Hassler. LC 85-10994. (Starmont Studies in Literary Criticism: No. 3). (Illus.). 90p. 1984. Repr. lib. bdg. 16.95x (ISBN 0-89370-978-6). Borgo Pr.

Patterns of the Fantastic II: Academic Programming at Constellation. Ed. by Donald M. Hassler. LC 84-2683. (Illus.). 16.95x (ISBN 0-916732-88-6); pap. text ed. 8.95x (ISBN 0-916732-87-8). Starmont Hse.

Patterns of the Hebrides. Gus Wylie. LC 81-82821. (Illus.). 96p. 1982. 24.95 (ISBN 0-8071-0991-6). La State U Pr.

Patterns of the Life-World: Essays in Honor of John Wild. Ed. by James M. Edie et al. (Studies in Phenomenology & Existential Philosophy). 1970. 26.95x (ISBN 0-8101-0311-7). Northwestern U Pr.

Patterns of the Universe. Robert Navon. xii, 116p. (Orig.). 1977. 18.00 (ISBN 0-9609866-8-5); pap. 6.95 (ISBN 0-9609866-2-6). Selene Bks.

Patterns of the Whole, Vol. 1: Healing & Quartz Crystals (A Journey with our Souls) John D. Rea. (Illus.). 376p. (Orig.). 1986. pap. 12.95 (ISBN 0-938183-01-X). Two Trees Pub.

Patterns of Thought in Rimbaud & Mallarme. John P. Houston. LC 85-80741. (French Forum Monographs: No. 63). 134p. (Orig.). 1986. pap. 12.95x (ISBN 0-917058-64-X). French Forum.

Patterns of Time in Hospital Life: A Sociological Perspective. Eviatar Zerubavel. LC 78-11385. (Illus.). 1979. lib. bdg. 13.50x (ISBN 0-226-98160-6). U of Chicago Pr.

Patterns of Time in Vergil. Sara Mack. LC 77-11704. vii, 116p. 1978. 19.50 (ISBN 0-208-01694-5, Archon). Shoe String.

Patterns of Undocumented Migration: Mexico & the U. S. Ed. by Richard C. Jones. LC 83-27233. (Illus.). 256p. 1984. 36.50x (ISBN 0-86598-130-2, Rowman & Allanheld). Rowman.

Patterns of Urban Growth in the Russian Empire during the Nineteenth Century. Thomas S. Fedor. LC 74-84783. (Research Papers Ser.: No. 163). (Illus.). 1975. pap. 12.00 (ISBN 0-89065-070-5). U Chicago Comm Geo.

Patterns of Verbal Communication in Mathematics Classes. James T. Fey. LC 74-103135. (Theory & Research in Teaching Ser.). pap. 26.00 (ISBN 0-317-41978-1, 2026011). Bks Demand UMI.

Patterns of Vertebrate Biology. E. W. Jameson, Jr. (Illus.). 480p. 1981. 36.10 (ISBN 0-387-90520-0). Springer-Verlag.

Patterns of War since the Eighteenth Century. Larry H. Addington. LC 83-48902. (Midland Bks Ser.: No. 342). (Illus.). 336p. (Orig.). 1985. 29.50x (ISBN 0-253-34305-4); pap. 10.95x (ISBN 0-253-20342-2, MB 342). Ind U Pr.

Patterns of Wealthholding in Wisconsin since 1850. Lee Soltow. (Illus.). 182p. 1972. 11.50x (ISBN 0-299-05530-2). U of Wis Pr.

Patterns of Workers' Behavior in the Business Enterprise. Lajos Hethy & Csaba Mako. 244p. 1987. 28.95 (ISBN 0-88738-177-4). Transaction Bks.

Patterns Plus: A Short Prose Reader with Agrumentation. 2nd ed. Mary Lou Conlin. LC 84-81972. 448p. 1985. pap. text ed. 16.76 (ISBN 0-395-35927-9); instr's manual 2.36 (ISBN 0-395-42466-6). HM.

Patterns: The Fertility Awareness Book. 2nd, rev ed. Barbara Kass-Annese & Hal C. Danzer. Ed. by Dana Chalberg. (Illus.). 112p. 1983. pap. 6.95. Patterns Ltd.

Patterns, Thinking, & Cognition: A Theory of Judgement. Howard Margolis. (Illus.). xii, 332p. 1987. 45.00 (ISBN 0-226-50527-8); pap. 15.95x (ISBN 0-226-50528-6). U of Chicago Pr.

Patterson & Pattersons: Fifty Years of the Patterson Function. Ed. by Jenny P. Glusker et al. Betty K. Patterson & Miram Rossi. (IUCr Chrystallographic Symposia). (Illus.). 752p. 1987. 49.95 (ISBN 0-19-855230-0). Oxford U Pr.

Patterson Family. G. T. Ridlon. LC 72-133874. (Saco Valley Settlements Ser). 1970. pap. 3.50 (ISBN 0-8048-0820-1). C E Tuttle.

Patterson-Jarratt Heritage: Sixteen Twenty-Five to Nineteen Eighty-Two. Richard Patterson. 220p. pap. text ed. 265.00x (ISBN 0-317-02246-6). R Patterson.

Patterson-Kimbro (Kimbrough) Heritage: Seventeen Forty to Nineteen Eighty-Five. Richard E. Patterson. 35p. pap. text ed. 75.00x (ISBN 0-317-46786-7). R Patterson.

Patterson-Needham Heritage: Seventeen Forty to Nineteen Seventy-Nine. Richard Patterson. 45p. pap. text ed. 95.00x (ISBN 0-317-46788-3). R Patterson.

Patterson Royal English Heritage: Four Hundred Fifty-Two to Nineteen Eighty-Two. 176p. pap. text ed. 375.00x (ISBN 0-317-46789-1). R Patterson.

Patterson-Smith Heritage: Seventeen Fifty-Two to Nineteen Eighty-Two. 170p. pap. text ed. 225.00x (ISBN 0-317-46790-5). R Patterson.

Pattersons: Missionary Publishers. Janet T. Hoffman. LC 83-71836. (Meet the Missionary Ser.). (gr. 4-6). 1984. 5.95 (ISBN 0-8054-4288-X, 4242-88). Broadman.

Patterson's Volunteers. John Smith. 352p. 1986. pap. 3.50 (ISBN 0-8217-1950-5). Zebra.

Patterson's Volunteers: A Novel. John Smith. 253p. 1985. 12.95 (ISBN 0-393-01909-8). Norton.

Pattie Round & Wally Square. Priscilla Jean. (Illus.). (gr. k-3). 1965. 8.95 (ISBN 0-8392-3048-6). Astor-Honor.

Pattie's Personal Narrative, 1824-30. Willard's Inland Trade with New Mexico, 1825, & Downfall of the Fredonia Republic. Malte-Brun's Account of Mexico see Early Western Travels, 1748-1846.

Patti's Last Sleepover, No. 9. Susan Saunders. 96p. (gr. 3-7). 1988. 2.50 (ISBN 0-590-41696-0). Scholastic Inc.

Patti's Luck. Susan Saunders. (Sleepover Friends Ser.: No. 1). 96p. (gr. 4-6). 1987. pap. 2.50 (ISBN 0-590-40641-8). Scholastic Inc.

Patti's New Look. Susan Saunders. (Sleepover Friends Ser.: No. 4). 80p. (Orig.). (gr. 4-6). 1988. pap. 2.50 (ISBN 0-590-40644-2, Apple Paperbacks). Scholastic Inc.

Patti's Pet Gorilla. Patricia R. Mauser. LC 86-20546. (Illus.). 64p. (gr. 2-4). 1987. 10.95 (ISBN 0-689-31279-2, Atheneum Childrens Bks). Macmillan.

Patton: A History of the American Main Battle Tank, Vol. I. R. P. Hunnicutt. 464p. 1984. 60.00 (ISBN 0-89141-230-1). Presidio Pr.

Patton: A Study in Command. H. Essame. LC 73-15498. 1976. 12.95 (ISBN 0-684-13671-6, ScribT); (ScribT). Scribner.

Patton & His Third Army. Brenton G. Wallace. (Combat Arms Ser.: No. 6). (Illus.). 232p. 1981. Repr. of 1946 ed. 18.50 (ISBN 0-89839-048-6). Battery Pr.

Patton & His Third Army. Brenton G. Wallace. LC 78-31806. (Illus.). 1979. Repr. of 1946 ed. lib. bdg. 38.50x (ISBN 0-8371-7755-3, WAPTA). Greenwood.

Patton on Productivity: Proven Techniques for Effective Management. John A. Patton. (Illus.). 208p. 1986. 25.50 (ISBN 0-13-654401-0). P-H.

Patton: Ordeal & Triumph. Ladislas Farago. (Illus.). 1964. 29.95 (ISBN 0-8392-1084-1). Astor-Honor.

Patton Papers, Eighteen Eighty-Five to Nineteen Forty, Vol. 1. Martin Blumensen. LC 76-156490. (Illus.). 1024p. 1972. 40.00 (ISBN 0-395-12706-8). HM.

Patton Papers, Nineteen Forty to Nineteen Forty-Five, Vol. 2. Martin Blumensen. LC 74-156490. 912p. 1974. 40.00 (ISBN 0-395-18498-3). HM.

Patton: The Man Behind the Legend. Martin Blumenson. 50p. 1987. pap. 3.95 (ISBN 0-425-09703-X). Berkley Pub.

Patton: The Man Behind the Legend-1885-1945. Martin Blumenson. LC 85-15301. (Illus.). 325p. 1985. 17.95 (ISBN 0-688-06082-X). Morrow.

Patton's Best. Nat Frankel & Larry Smith. 240p. 1988. pap. 3.50 (ISBN 0-515-08887-0). Jove Pubns.

Patton's Principles. Porter B. Williamson. LC 77-70779. (Illus.). 180p. 1984. gift ed. 16.95 (ISBN 0-918356-05-9). MSC Inc.

Patton's Principles: A Handbook for Managers Who Mean It! Porter B. Williamson. (Illus.). 1982. pap. 6.95 (ISBN 0-671-45973-2, Touchstone Bks). S&S.

Patton's Tanks. Steven J. Zaloga. (Tanks Illustrated Ser.: Vol. 11). (Illus.). 1984. pap. 9.95 (ISBN 0-85368-671-8, Arms & Armour Pr). Sterling.

Patty Cakes. Patricia Sharrigan. 96p. 1988. pap. 10.95. Pacific Pr Pub Assn.

Patty Cannon Administers Justice. R. W. Messenger. LC 60-15801. 320p. 1960. pap. 5.00 (ISBN 0-87033-079-9). Tidewater.

Patty Duke: A Bio-Bibliography. Stephen L. Eberly. LC 87-37565. (Bio-Bibliographies in the Performing Arts Ser.: No. 3). 144p. 1988. lib. bdg. 29.95 (ISBN 0-313-25675-6, EPD/). Greenwood.

Patty Hearst. Patricia C. Hearst & Alvin Moscow. 1988. pap. 4.50. Avon.

Patty! The Sports Career of Patricia Berg. James Hahn & Lynn Hahn. Ed. by Howard Schroeder. LC 80-28744. (Sports Legends Ser.). (Illus.). 48p. (Orig.). (gr. 3-5). 1981. PLB 8.95 (ISBN 0-89686-127-9). Crestwood Hse.

Patty's Industrial Hygiene & Toxicology: General Principles, Vol. 1. 3rd, rev. ed. George D. Clayton & Florence E. Clayton. LC 77-17515. 1466p. 1978. 172.00 (ISBN 0-471-16046-6). Wiley.

Pattys Industrial Hygiene & Toxicology, 4 vols. 3rd ed. G. D. Clayton & F. E. Clayton. 937p. 1981. 85.00 (ISBN 0-471-08431-X). Wiley.

Patty's Industrial Hygiene & Toxicology, Pts. A & B. 2nd ed. Lewis J. Cralley & Lester V. Cralley. 1985. 185.00 (ISBN 0-471-83459-9). Wiley.

Patty's Industrial Hygiene & Toxicology: Toxicology, Vol. 2A. 3rd, rev. ed. Ed. by George D. Clayton & Florence E. Clayton. LC 77-17515. 1420p. 1981. 162.00 (ISBN 0-471-16042-3). Wiley.

Patty's Industrial Hygiene & Toxicology: Toxicology, Vol. 2C. 3rd, rev. ed. Ed. by George D. Clayton & Florence E. Clayton. LC 77-17515. 1296p. 1982. 147.00 (ISBN 0-471-09258-4). Wiley.

Patty's Industrial Hygiene & Toxicology: Toxicology, Vol. 2B. 3rd, rev. ed. Ed. by George D. Clayton & Florence Clayton. LC 77-17515. 937p. 1981. 115.00 (ISBN 0-471-07943-X). Wiley.

Patty's Industrial Hygiene & Toxicology: Theory & Rationale of Industrial Hygiene Practice-Biological Responses, Vol. 3B. 2nd ed. Lewis J. Cralley. 753p. 1985. 100.00 (ISBN 0-471-82333-3). Wiley.

Paul Gauguin: Letters to His Wife & Friends. Paul Gauguin. Ed. by Maurice Malingue. Tr. by Henry J. Stenning. LC 83-45768. Repr. of 1949 ed. 30.00 (ISBN 0-404-20106-7). AMS Pr.

Paul Gets Lost. Nigel Snell. (Illus.). 32p. (ps-1). 1982. 7.95 (ISBN 0-241-10791-1, Pub. by Hamish Hamilton England). David & Charles.

Paul, God's Special Missionary. Bessie Dean. (Story Books to Color). 72p. (Orig.). (gr. k-5). 1980. pap. 2.95 (ISBN 0-88290-152-4). Horizon Utah.

Paul Green. Barrett H. Clark. LC 74-1164. (Studies in Drama, No. 39). 1974. lib. bdg. 29.95x (ISBN 0-8383-2016-3). Haskell.

Paul Green. Vincent Kenny. LC 79-125254. (Twayne's United States Authors Ser.). 1971. lib. bdg. 17.95 (ISBN 0-89197-880-1); pap. text ed. 9.95x (ISBN 0-8290-0007-0). Irvington.

Paul Guardino Guide to Fitness. Lois Garcia. 1985. pap. write for info. L Garcia.

Paul Hamilton Hayne. Rayburn S. Moore. Ed. by Sylvia E. Bowman. LC 73-125818. (Twayne's United States Authors Ser.). 184p. 1972. lib. bdg. 17.95 (ISBN 0-8290-1711-9). Irvington.

Paul Harvey's the Rest of the Story. Paul Aurandt. 1984. pap. 3.95 (ISBN 0-553-25962-8). Bantam.

Paul Heald: Selected Works, Nineteen Sixty to Nineteen Eighty-One. Matthew Kangas. LC 81-71891. (Illus.). 32p. (Orig.). 1982. pap. 5.95 (ISBN 0-942342-00-3). Bellevue Art.

Paul Hervieu & French Classicism. Hulet H. Cook. LC 45-37189. (Indiana University Humanities Ser.: No. 14). pap. 20.00 (ISBN 0-317-09054-2, 2055223). Bks Demand UMI.

Paul Hindemith: The Man Behind the Music. Geoffrey Skelton. (Illus.). 1977. 10.00 (ISBN 0-87597-107-5, Crescendo). Taplinger.

Paul, His Letters & Theology: An Introduction to Paul's Epistles. Stanley B. Marrow. 288p. (Orig.). 1986. pap. 9.95 (ISBN 0-8091-2744-X). Paulist Pr.

Paul: His Life & Work. Walther Loewenich. 1960. text ed. 7.50x (ISBN 0-8401-1421-4). A R Allenson.

Paul Hogan. James. 1987. pap. 3.95 (ISBN 0-312-90880-6). St Martin.

Paul Hoy Helms Library in Liberal Adult Education. Compiled by A. Charters. 1973. 4.55 (ISBN 0-686-50191-8, MSS 20). Syracuse U Cont Ed.

Paul Jenkins. Albert E. Elsen. LC 75-101622. (Contemporary Artists Ser.). (Illus.). 288p. 1973. 65.00 (ISBN 0-8109-0215-X). Abrams.

Paul Jones: Founder of the American Navy, 2 vols. facsimile ed. Augustus C. Buell. LC 70-157326. (Select Bibliographies Reprint Ser.). Repr. of 1900 ed. Set. 45.00 (ISBN 0-8369-5786-5). Ayer Co Pubs.

Paul, Judaism, & the Gentiles: A Sociological Approach. Francis Watson. (Society for New Testament Studies Monographs: No. 56). 266p. 1986. 32.50 (ISBN 0-521-32573-0). Cambridge U Pr.

Paul Kane, the Columbia Wanderer: Sketches, Paintings & Comment, 1846-1847. Ed. by Thomas Vaughan. LC 74-176250. (Illus.). 80p. 1971. pap. 3.95 (ISBN 0-87595-029-9). Oregon Hist.

Paul Keres' Best Games, Vol. 1. Egon Varnusz. (Illus.). 210p. 1987. 33.00 (ISBN 0-08-026915-X); pap. 21.00 (ISBN 0-08-032044-9). Pergamon.

Paul Keres Chess Master Class. I. Neishtadt. 182p. 1983. 24.95 (ISBN 0-08-023122-5); pap. 15.95 flexi-cover (ISBN 0-08-029719-6). Pergamon.

Paul Klee. Denys Chevalier. (Quality-Low-Price Art Ser.). 1983. 12.95 (ISBN 0-517-50302-6). Crown.

Paul Klee. Christian Geelhaar. (Pocket Art Ser.). 1982. pap. 5.95 (ISBN 0-8120-2186-X). Barron.

Paul Klee. Ed. by Carolyn Lanchner. (Illus.). 1987. 55.00 (ISBN 0-87070-403-6, Pub. by Museum Mod Art). NYGS.

Paul Klee. Ernest Raboff. LC 87-16864. (Art for Children Ser.). (Illus.). 32p. (gr. 1 up). 1988. Repr. of 1968 ed. 11.95i (ISBN 0-397-32226-7, Lipp Jr Bks). HarpJ.

Paul Klee. Ernest Raboff. LC 87-17699. (Trophy Nonfiction Art for Children). (Illus.). 32p. (gr. 1 up). 1988. pap. 5.95 (ISBN 0-06-446065-7, Trophy). HarpJ.

Paul Klee & Cubism. Jim M. Jordan. LC 83-13898. (Illus.). 233p. 1984. 64.50x (ISBN 0-691-04025-7). Princeton U Pr.

Paul Klee & Primitive Art. James S. Pierce. LC 75-23807. (Outstanding Dissertations in the Fine Arts - 20th Century). 1976. lib. bdg. 37.00 (ISBN 0-8240-2001-4). Garland Pub.

Paul Klee Art & Music. Andrew A. Kagan. LC 82-71599. (Illus.). 176p. 1983. 32.50x (ISBN 0-8014-1500-4). Cornell U Pr.

Paul Klee: Ninety Works from the Heinz Berggruen Collection. Sabine Rewald. (Illus.). 256p. 1988. 50.00 (ISBN 0-8109-1215-5). Abrams.

Paul Klee on Modern Art. Paul Klee. 64p. 1966. pap. 5.95 (ISBN 0-571-06682-8). Faber & Faber.

Paul Klee: The Formative Years. Charles W. Haxthausen. LC 79-57507. 724p. 1982. lib. bdg. 94.00 (ISBN 0-8240-3932-7). Garland Pub.

Paul Klee: The Late Years. Ed. by Serge Sabarsky. (Illus.). 96p. pap. 10.00 (ISBN 0-918825-42-3, Dist. by Kampmann & Co.). Moyer Bell Limited.

Paul Klee: Three Exhibitions: 1930, 1941, 1949. Pref. by M. Wheeler. LC 68-57298. (Museum of Modern Art Publications in Reprint Ser). (Illus.). 1970. Repr. 18.00 (ISBN 0-405-01518-6). Ayer Co Pubs.

Paul Klee, 1879-1940: In the Collection of the Solomon R. Guggenheim Museum. Louise A. Svendsen. LC 77-78148. (Illus.). 84p. 1977. pap. 12.95 (ISBN 0-295-96289-5). U of Wash Pr.

Paul Kovi's Transylvanian Feast: A Chronicle of the Most Remarkable Middle-European Cuisine. Paul Kovi. Ed. by Kim Honig. (Illus.). 1985. 15.95 (ISBN 0-517-55698-7). Crown.

Paul L. Dunbar. Tony Gentry. (Black Americans of Achievement Ser.). (Illus.). 112p. (gr. 5 up). 1989. 16.95x (ISBN 1-55546-583-8). Chelsea Hse.

Paul L. Dunbar. Tony Gentry. (Black Americans of Achievement Ser.). (Illus.). 112p. (Orig.). (YA) (gr. 7-12). 1989. pap. 9.95 (ISBN 0-7910-0223-3). Chelsea Hse.

Paul Landowski, la Main et L'Esprit: Le Main et l'Esprit. Jules Romains. 308p. 39.50 (ISBN 0-686-55328-4). French & Eur.

Paul Laurence Dunbar. Peter Revell. (United States Authors Ser.). 1979. lib. bdg. 17.95 (ISBN 0-8057-7213-8, Twayne). G K Hall.

Paul Laurence Dunbar: A Poet to Remember. Patricia McKissack. LC 84-7625. (People of Distinction Ser.). (Illus.). 112p. (gr. 4 up). 1984. lib. bdg. 14.60 (ISBN 0-516-03209-7). Childrens.

Paul Laurence Dunbar: Black Poet Laureate. Pearle H. Schultz. LC 73-22071. (Creative People Ser.). (Illus.). 144p. (gr. 4-7). 1974. PLB 7.12 (ISBN 0-8116-4516-9). Garrard.

Paul Laurence Dunbar Collection: An Inventory to the Microfilm Edition. Sara S. Fuller. 40p. 1972. 1.25 (ISBN 0-318-03199-X). Ohio Hist Soc.

Paul Lawrence Dunbar Critically Examined. V. Lawson. 59.95 (ISBN 0-8490-0808-5). Gordon Pr.

Paul Loeb's Complete Book of Dog Training. Paul Loeb. 1983. pap. 3.50 (ISBN 0-671-47297-6). PB.

Paul M. Butler: Hoosier Politician & National Political Leader. George C. Roberts. LC 87-6275. (Illus.). 210p. (Orig.). 1987. lib. bdg. 24.00 (ISBN 0-8191-6295-7); pap. text ed. 12.75 (ISBN 0-8191-6296-5). U Pr of Amer.

Paul Maas: Catalog Raisonne. A. Dasnoy. (Illus.). 277p. (Fr.). 1975. 65.00 (ISBN 0-912728-97-3). Newbury Bks.

Paul McCartney. Gelfand. (Rock 'n Pop Stars Ser.). (Illus.). 32p. (gr. 4 up). PLB 8.95 (ISBN 0-317-31142-5). Creative Ed.

Paul McCartney: In His Own Words. Paul Gambaccini. LC 76-8068. 1983. pap. 6.95 (ISBN 0-399-41008-2, Perigee). Putnam Pub Group.

Paul Mace Guide to Data Recovery. Paul Mace. (Illus.). 352p. 1988. pap. 21.95 (ISBN 0-13-654427-4). Brady Comp Bks.

Paul McLean. Malcolm McGregor. LC 85-1082. (Illus.). 217p. 1986. text ed. 25.00x (ISBN 0-7022-1885-5). U of Queensland Pr.

Paul Magriel's Met: A Discovery Tour of the Metropolitan Museum of Art. Paul Magriel & John T. Spike. Ed. by Sarah Timberman & Jason Epstein. LC 86-40522. (Illus.). 224p. 1988. pap. 9.95 (ISBN 0-394-74857-3, Vin). Random.

Paul Martin: Victorian Photographer. Roy Flukinger et al. LC 77-4764. (Illus.). 235p. 1977. 24.95 (ISBN 0-292-76436-7). U of Tex Pr.

Paul Mazursky's Tempest. Geoffrey Taylor. (Illus.). 96p. (Orig.). 1982. pap. 10.95 (ISBN 0-918432-45-6). NY Zoetrope.

Paul Meets the Masters. Lowell Dickmeyer & Martha Humphreys. LC 83-7582. (Soccer Adventure Ser.). (Illus.). 96p. (gr. 5 up). 1983. PLB 8.95 (ISBN 0-87518-250-X, Gemstone Bks). Dillon.

Paul: Mystic & Missionary. Bernard T. Smyth. LC 80-14041. 191p. (Orig.). 1980. pap. 3.98 (ISBN 0-88344-380-5). Orbis Bks.

Paul Nash. Andrew Causey. (Illus.). 1980. 105.00x (ISBN 0-19-817348-2). Oxford U Pr.

Paul Natorps Aesthetik. Inge Krebs. (Kant-Studien-Ergaenzungsheft). 1976. text ed. 34.00x (ISBN 3-11-006587-8). De Gruyter.

Paul Nizan: Committed Literature in a Conspiratorial World. W. D. Redfern. LC 78-166387. 232p. 1972. 30.50 (ISBN 0-691-06218-8). Princeton U Pr.

Paul Nizan: Communist Novelist. Michael Scriven. LC 87-32140. 192p. 1988. 35.00 (ISBN 0-312-01692-1). St Martin.

Paul of Pergula: Logica & Tractatus De Sensu Composito et Diviso. Ed. by Sr. Mary A. Brown. (Text Ser). 1961. 11.00 (ISBN 0-686-11558-9). Franciscan Inst.

Paul of Tarsus. Herold Weiss. 175p. (Orig.). 1986. pap. 9.95 (ISBN 0-943872-92-8). Andrews Univ Pr.

Paul of Venice: A Bibliographical Guide. Ed. by Alan R. Perreiah. (Bibliographies of Famous Philosophers Ser.). 140p. 1986. lib. bdg. 28.50 (ISBN 0-912632-83-6). Philos Document.

Paul of Venice, Logica Magna, Pt I, Fasc. I. Ed. by Norman Kretzmann. 344p. 1979. 64.00 (ISBN 0-85672-690-7, Pub. by British Acad). Longwood Pub Group.

Paul of Venice, Logica Magna, Part II, Fasc. 6. Ed. by Francesco Del Punta. Tr. by Marilyn M. Adams from Lat. 288p. 1978. 27.00 (ISBN 0-85672-695-8, Pub. by British Acad). Longwood Pub Group.

Paul of Venice: Logica Magna, Fascicule 7, Pt. 1. Paul of Venice. Ed. by Patricia Clarke. (Classical & Medieval Logic Texts Ser.). 1982. 135.00x (ISBN 0-19-726003-9). Oxford U Pr.

Paul of Venice: Logica Magna, Tractatus De Suppositione. Ed. by Alan Perreiah. (Text Ser). 1971. 16.00 (ISBN 0-686-11560-0). Franciscan Inst.

Paul on Trial. John MacArthur, Jr. (John MacArthur's Bible Studies). (Orig.). 1986. pap. 4.95 (ISBN 0-8024-5131-4). Moody.

Paul One. Duncan Macpherson et al. Ed. by Laurence Bright. LC 71-173033. (Scripture Discussion Ser.: Pt. 10). 224p. 1972. pap. text ed. 4.95 (ISBN 0-87946-009-1). ACTA Pubns.

Paul Ortlip: His Heritage & His Art. M. Stephen Doherty. LC 82-16686. (Illus.). 152p. 1983. 45.00 (ISBN 0-914016-91-1). Phoenix Pub.

Paul Outerbridge: A Singular Aesthetic: Photographs & Drawings 1921-1941, a Catalogue Raisonne. Ed. by Elaine Dines & Graham Howe. (Illus.). 240p. 1981. 115.00 (ISBN 0-87685-540-0). Black Sparrow.

Paul Perry's Complete Book of Triathlon. Paul Perry. (Illus.). 240p. 1983. pap. 8.95 (ISBN 0-452-25421-3, Plume). NAL.

Paul Philippe Cret: Architect & Teacher. Theo B. White. (Illus.). 158p. 1974. 25.00 (ISBN 0-87982-008-X). Art Alliance.

Paul: Portrait of a Revolutionary. Donald Coggan. 256p. (Orig.). 1985. pap. 9.95 (ISBN 0-8245-0704-5). Crossroad NY.

Paul: Rabbi & Apostle. Pinchas Lapide & Peter Stuhlmacher. Tr. by Lawrence W. Denef. LC 84-23482. 80p. (Orig.). 1984. pap. 6.95 (ISBN 0-8066-2122-2, 10-4903). Augsburg.

Paul Rand: A Designer's Art. Paul Rand. LC 85-50352. (Illus.). 239p. 1985. 45.00x (ISBN 0-300-03483-0). Yale U Pr.

Paul Rand: A Designers Art. Paul Rand. LC 85-50352. 256p. 1988. 24.95 (ISBN 0-300-04213-2). Yale U Pr.

Paul Reps: Letters to a Friend (Writings & Drawings), 1939 to 1980. Paul Reps. LC 80-52881. (Illus.). 186p. 1981. 35.00 (ISBN 0-938286-01-3); ltd. ed. 2000.00x (ISBN 0-938286-00-5). C E Tuttle.

Paul Revere. Jan Gleiter & Kathleen Thompson. (Raintree Stories Ser.). (Illus.). 32p. (gr. 2-5). 1986. PLB 15.33; pap. text ed. 9.27 (ISBN 0-8172-2648-6). Raintree Pubs.

Paul Revere. Martin Lee. LC 86-23362. (First Bks. Biographies of Great Americans). (Illus.). 96p. (gr. 4-8). 1987. lib. bdg. 10.40 (ISBN 0-531-10312-9). Watts.

Paul Revere. (Great Tales Biography Ser.). (Illus.). 32p. (gr. k-3). 1988. pap. 2.95 (ISBN 0-8249-8192-8). Ideals.

Paul Revere & Other Story Hours. Franco Pagnucci & Susan Pagnucci. (Illus.). 72p. (Orig.). (gr. k-6). 1988. Incl. sewing patterns. pap. write for info. (ISBN 0-929326-00-8). Bur Oak Pr Inc.

Paul Revere & the Boston Tea Party. (Time Traveler Ser.: No. 5). 80p. 1987. pap. 2.50 (ISBN 0-553-15529-6). Bantam.

Paul Revere & the Raiders: History Rebeats Itself! Claudia M. Doege. (Illus.). 160p. (Orig.). 1985. pap. text ed. 9.95 (ISBN 0-9615517-0-4). DIA Press.

Paul Revere & the World He Lived In. Esther Forbes. (Illus.). 528p. (gr. 4-8). 1962. pap. 9.95 (ISBN 0-395-08370-2). HM.

Paul Revere, Artisan, Businessman, & Patriot: The Man Behind the Myth. The Paul Revere Memorial Association Staff. (Artisans & the Arts). (Illus.). 192p. 1988. lib. bdg. 34.95 (ISBN 0-9619999-0-X, Dist. by Univ Pub Assocs); pap. text ed. 19.95 (ISBN 0-9619999-1-8, Dist. by Univ Pub Assocs). Paul Revere Mem Assn.

Paul Revere: Boston Patriot. Augusta Stevenson. LC 83-15731. (Childhood of Famous Americans Ser.). 1984. pap. 3.95 (ISBN 0-672-52802-9). Bobbs.

Paul Revere: Boston Patriot. Augusta Stevenson. LC 86-10743. (Macmillan Childhood of Famous Americans Ser.). (Illus.). 192p. (gr. 2-6). 1986. pap. 3.95 (ISBN 0-02-042090-0, Aladdin Bks). Macmillan.

Paul Revere, Goldsmith: Seventeen Thirty-Five to Eighteen Eighteen. rev. ed. Kathryn C. Buhler. (Illus.). 56p. 1975. pap. 1.95 (ISBN 0-87846-219-8). Mus Fine Arts Boston.

Paul Revere: Rider for Liberty. Charles P. Graves. LC 64-10938. (Garrard Discovery Ser.). (Illus.). (gr. 2-5). 1964. PLB 6.69 (ISBN 0-8116-6282-9). Garrard.

Paul Revere: Son of Liberty. Keith Brandt. LC 81-23147. (Illus.). 48p. (gr. 4-6). 1982. PLB 9.79 (ISBN 0-89375-766-7); pap. text ed. 1.95 (ISBN 0-89375-767-5). Troll Assocs.

Paul Revere's Ride. Henry Wadsworth Longfellow. LC 84-4139. (Illus.). 48p. (gr. 1 up). 1985. 13.95 (ISBN 0-688-04014-4); PLB 11.88 (ISBN 0-688-04015-2). Greenwillow.

Paul Robeson. Martin B. Duberman. LC 88-45297. (Illus.). 784p. 1989. 24.95 (ISBN 0-394-52780-1). Knopf.

Paul Robeson. Scott Ehrlich. (Black Americans of Achievement Ser.). (Illus.). 112p. (gr. 5 up). 1988. lib. bdg. 16.95x (ISBN 1-55546-608-7). Chelsea Hse.

Paul Robeson. Eloise Greenfield. LC 74-13663. (Crowell Biography Ser.). (Illus.). (gr. 1-5). 1975. PLB 12.89 (ISBN 0-690-00660-8, Crowell Jr Bks). HarpJ.

Paul Robeson. Steven Samuels. (Black Americans of Achievement Ser.). (Illus.). 112p. (Orig.). (YA) (gr. 7-12). 1989. pap. 9.95 (ISBN 0-7910-0206-3). Chelsea Hse.

Paul Robeson: Biography of a Proud Man. Joseph Nazel. (Orig.). 1980. pap. 1.95 (ISBN 0-87067-652-0, BH652). Holloway.

Paul Robeson, Citizen of the World. Shirley Graham. LC 75-152393. Repr. of 1946 ed. 35.00x (ISBN 0-8371-6055-3, GRR&). Greenwood.

Paul Robeson: Mini Play. (People of Conscience Ser.). (gr. 5 up). 1977. 6.50 (ISBN 0-89550-371-9). Stevens & Shea.

Paul Robeson Research Guide: A Selected Annotated Bibliography. Lenwood G. Davis. LC 82-11680. xxv, 879p. 1982. lib. bdg. 50.95 (ISBN 0-313-22864-7, DPR/). Greenwood.

Paul Robeson Speaks. Ed. by Philip S. Foner. (Illus.). 625p. 1982. pap. 9.95 (ISBN 0-8065-0815-9, Pub. by Citadel Pr). Lyle Stuart.

Paul Robeson: The Great Forerunner. Freedomways Associates Staff. LC 84-29747. (Illus.). 432p. 1985. pap. 10.95 (ISBN 0-7178-0625-1). Intl Pubs Co.

Paul Robeson: The Man & His Mission. Ron Ramdin. LC 88-60469. 223p. 1988. 35.00 (ISBN 0-7206-0684-5, Pub. by P Owen Ltd). Dufour.

Paul Robeson's Last Days in Philadelphia. Charlotte T. Bell. (Illus.). 48p. 1986. 6.95 (ISBN 0-8059-3026-4). Dorrance.

Paul Robin: A Chronology. V. Munoz. Tr. by W. Scott Johnson. (Libertarian & Anarchist Chronology Ser.). 1979. lib. bdg. 59.95 (ISBN 0-8490-3055-2). Gordon Pr.

Paul Rosenfeld, Voyager in the Arts. Jerome Mellquist & Lucie Wiese. 1978. Repr. of 1948 ed. lib. bdg. 19.50 (ISBN 0-374-95561-1, Octagon). Hippocrene Bks.

Paul Rudolph & Louis Kahn: A Bibliography. Charles R. Smith. LC 87-12781. (Illus.). 238p. 1987. 25.00 (ISBN 0-8108-2003-X). Scarecrow.

Paul Rudolph: Architectural Drawings. Paul Rudolph & Yukio Futagawa. (Illus.). 218p. 1981. 55.00 (ISBN 0-8038-0208-0). Architectural.

Paul Sample: Painter of the American Scene. Robert L. McCorath & Paula F. Glick. LC 87-28943. (Illus.). 112p. 1988. 30.00x (ISBN 0-944722-00-8); pap. 17.95 (ISBN 0-944722-01-6). U Pr of New Eng.

Paul Samuelson & Modern Economic Theory. Ed. by E. Carey Brown & Robert Solow. 350p. 1983. text ed. 39.95 (ISBN 0-07-059667-0). McGraw.

Paul Schalluck & the Post-War German Don Quixote: A Case History Prolegomenon to the Literature of the Federal Republic. Alan F. Keele. (Utah Studies in Literature & Linguistics: Vol. 5). 134p. 1976. pap. 18.25. P Lang Pubs.

Paul Schilder-Mind Explorer. Donald Shashkan & William L. Roller. (Illus.). 272p. 1985. 34.95 (ISBN 0-89885-144-0). Human Sci Pr.

Paul Simon for Flute & Piano. Donald Rauscher. 1979. pap. 7.95 (ISBN 0-8256-2703-6, Amsco Music). Music Sales.

Paul Simon for Recorder. Ralph Zeitlin. 1979. pap. 6.95 (ISBN 0-8256-2672-2). Music Sales.

Paul Simon for Trumpet & Piano. Donald Rauscher. 1979. pap. 6.95 (ISBN 0-8256-2704-4, Amsco Music). Music Sales.

Paul Simon: Still Crazy after All These Years. Patrick Humphries. 1988. 17.95 (ISBN 0-385-24908-X). Doubleday.

Paul, Speak for God. Charlotte Graeber. (Speak for Me Ser.). (Illus.). 24p. (gr. 1-4). 1986. 3.95 (ISBN 0-8407-6700-5). Nelson.

Paul Strand. Mark Haworth-Booth. (Masters of Photography Ser.: Vol. 1). (Illus.). 96p. 1987. 14.95 (ISBN 0-89381-077-0); pap. 9.95 (ISBN 0-89381-259-5). Aperture.

Paul Strand: Sixty Years of Photograph. Calvin Tomkins. LC 76-42103. (Illus.). 184p. 35.00 (ISBN 0-912334-81-9); pap. 19.95 (ISBN 0-912334-82-7); ltd. ed. 150.00 (ISBN 0-89381-011-8). Aperture.

Paul Strand: The Formative Years 1914-1917. Intro. by Ben Lifson. (Illus.). 1983. deluxe ed. 1500.00 portfolio of 10 in ed. ltd. to 300 boxed & numbered 1,500.00 (ISBN 0-89381-125-4). Aperture.

Paul Strand: Time in New England. Ed. by Nancy Newhall. LC 80-65763. (Illus.). 256p. 1980. 40.00 (ISBN 0-89381-060-6); ltd. ed. 175.00 (ISBN 0-89381-061-4). Aperture.

Paul Strassels' Quick & Easy Guide to Tax Mangement for 1986-1987. rev. ed. Paul Strassels. 230p. 1986. pap. cancelled (ISBN 0-87094-936-5). Dow Jones-Irwin.

Paul Temple & the Curzon Case. Francis Durbridge. 1987. 20.00x (ISBN 0-86025-224-8, Pub. by Ian Henry Pubns England). State Mutual Bk.

Paul Temple & the Curzon Case. Francis Durbridge. 1988. 30.00x (ISBN 0-86025-231-0, Pub. by Ian Henry Pubns England). State Mutual Bk.

Paul Temple & the Hardale Robbery. Francis Durbridge. 1987. 20.00x (ISBN 0-86025-223-X, Pub. by Ian Henry Pubns England). State Mutual Bk.

Paul's Revelation: The Gospel of Reconciliation. Kenneth Hagin. 1983. pap. 0.50 mini bk. (ISBN 0-89276-261-6). Hagin Ministries.

Paul's Thorn. John Ferdninand. Tr. by Dennis Balcombe from Chinese. (Illus.). 24p. pap. 2.50 (ISBN 0-941117-01-4). HIM Publish.

Paul's Thorn. Don Hughes. (Orig.). 1977. pap. 0.75 (ISBN 0-89274-047-7, HH-047). Harrison Hse.

Paul's Two-Age Construction & Apologetics. William D. Dennison. LC 85-20272. 144p. (Orig.). 1986. lib. bdg. 20.50 (ISBN 0-8191-5011-8); pap. text ed. 9.25 (ISBN 0-8191-5012-6). U Pr of Amer.

Paul's Volcano. Beatrice Gormley. LC 86-27543. (gr. 4-6). 1987. 12.95 (ISBN 0-395-43079-8). HM.

Paul's Volcano. Beatrice Gormley. 160p. 1988. pap. 2.50 (ISBN 0-380-70562-1, Camelot). Avon.

Paulus & Stalingrad. Walter Gorlitz. Tr. by R. H. Stevens. LC 74-5782. (Illus.). 301p. 1974. Repr. of 1963 ed. lib. bdg. 38.50x (ISBN 0-8371-7497-X, GOPS). Greenwood.

Paulus: The Dimensions of a Teacher. Rollo May. 1988. pap. 6.95 (ISBN 0-933071-18-3). Saybrook Pub Co.

Paulus: Tillisch As Spritual Teacher. Rollo May. (Mind Age Ser.). 1988. pap. 6.95 (ISBN 0-317-67756-X). Saybrook Pub Co.

Paumanok Rising: An Anthology of Eastern Long Island Aesthetics. Ed. by Vince Clemente & Graham Everett. LC 81-50937. (Illus.). 216p. (Orig.). 1981. pap. 7.50 (ISBN 0-935252-27-4). Street Pr.

Paumanok's Contemporary Anthology of English Literature, Vol. I: Poetry. Ed. by Dennis M. Zogbi. LC 88-61903. 126p. 1988. pap. 22.00. Paumanok Pubns.

Pauper, Brawler & Slanderer. Amos Tutuola. 176p. 1987. 15.95 (ISBN 0-571-14714-3); pap. 6.95 (ISBN 0-571-14765-8). Faber & Faber.

Pauper, the Thief & the Convict: Sketches of Some of Their Homes, Haunts & Habits. Thomas Archer. LC 84-48264. (Rise of Urban Britain Ser.). 239p. 1985. 35.00 (ISBN 0-8240-6266-3). Garland Pub.

Pauperisation de l'Agriculture en France at dans le Monde see Cahiers de l'Institut de Science Economique Appliquee.

Pauperism: Its Causes & Remedies. Henry Fawcett. LC 74-1334. 1974. Repr. of 1871 ed. lib. bdg. 35.00x (ISBN 0-678-01067-6). Kelley.

Paupers & Poor Relief in New York City & Its Rural Environs, 1700-1830. Robert E. Cray, Jr. LC 87-26693. 288p. 1988. 34.95 (ISBN 0-87722-542-7). Temple U Pr.

Paupers' Paris: How to Spend More Time in Paris Without Spending More Francs. Miles Turner. (Illus.). 256p. 1988. pap. 8.95 (ISBN 0-312-01806-1, Pub. by Thomas Dunne Bks). St Martin.

Pausanias' Guide to Ancient Greece. Christian Habicht. (Sather Classical Lectures: No. 50). 1985. 30.00 (ISBN 0-520-05398-2). U of Cal Pr.

Pause. Ada L. Snell. LC 75-23025. 1975. Repr. of 1918 ed. lib. bdg. 32.00 (ISBN 0-8414-7542-3). Folcroft.

Pause Between Acts. Mavis Cheek. 192p. 1988. 17.95 (ISBN 0-671-66730-0). S&S.

Pause for Breath. Edith Reveley. LC 82-22293. 210p. 1983. 15.95 (ISBN 0-87951-165-6). Overlook Pr.

Pause in the Light. Dorian B. Kottler. Ed. by James Perlman. LC 80-82690. 54p. (Orig.). 1980. pap. 3.00 (ISBN 0-930100-07-7). Holy Cow.

Pause on the Path. Ronald Silvers. (Illus.). 208p. 1988. 24.96 (ISBN 0-87722-559-1). Temple U Pr.

Pause Patterns in Elizabethan & Jacobean Drama: An Experiment in Prosody. Ants Oras. LC 60-62779. (University of Florida Humanities Monographs: No. 3). (Illus.). 1960. pap. 6.00x (ISBN 0-8130-0170-6). U Presses Fla.

Pauses. Sally Saunders. LC 78-51847. 1978. 5.00 (ISBN 0-8233-0272-5). Golden Quill.

Pautex & His Contemporaries: The Collection of the Museum of Clocks, Watches & Enamels in Geneva. limited ed. Fabienne X. Strum. (Illus.). 272p. (Eng. & Japanese.). 1982. 345.00 (ISBN 4-07-914250-1, Pub. by Shufunotomo Co Ltd Japan). C E Tuttle.

Pauvre Bitos, Ou, le Diner De Tetes. Jean Anouilh. (Folio Ser.: No. 301). 1973. pap. 5.95 (ISBN 0-685-11481-3). Schoenhof.

Pauvre Bitos Ou le Diner De Tetes see Pieces Grincantes.

Pauvre Christ de Bomba. Mongo Beti. (Fr.). 1956. 29.00 (ISBN 0-8115-2978-9). Kraus Repr.

Pauvrete Economique et Pauvrete Social a Byzance 4e-7e Siecles. E. Patlagean. 1977. 56.00 (ISBN 90-279-7933-2). Mouton.

Pavane. David Trinidad. 60p. (Orig.). 1988. pap. 7.95 (ISBN 0-89807-256-5). Illuminati.

Pavanne for a Fading Memory. William Pillin. LC 63-16650. 82p. 1963. 5.00 (ISBN 0-8040-0240-1, Pub. by Swallow). Ohio U Pr.

Pavannes & Divagations. Ezra Pound. LC 58-9510. 256p. 1975. pap. 9.95 (ISBN 0-8112-0575-4, NDP397). New Directions.

Pavans. Ian Krieger. (Dialogues on Dance Ser.: No. 3). 92p. 1985. pap. 6.00 (ISBN 0-941240-00-2). Ommation Pr.

Pavarotti: My Own Story. Luciano Pavarotti & William Wright. (Illus.). 352p. 1982. pap. 3.95 (ISBN 0-446-30179-5). Warner Bks.

Paved with Gold: The Romance & Reality of the London Street. 2nd ed. Augustus Mayhew. (Illus.). 408p. 1971. Repr. of 1858 ed. 25.00x (ISBN 0-7146-1412-2, BHA-01412, F Cass Co). Biblio Dist.

Paved with Good Intentions: The American Experience & Iran. Barry Rubin. (Illus.). 1980. 25.00x (ISBN 0-19-502805-8). Oxford U Pr.

Paved with Good Intentions: The American Experience in Iran. Barry Rubin. 426p. 1981. pap. 7.95 (ISBN 0-14-005964-4). Penguin.

Pavel Filonov: A Hero & His Fate: Collected Writings on Art & Revolution, 1910 - 40. Nicoletta Misler & John E. Bowlt. (Institute of Modern Russian Culture Ser.). (Illus.). 378p. 1983. 60.00x (ISBN 0-941432-05-X). Silvergirl Inc.

Pavel Florensky: A Metaphysics of Love. Robert Slesinski. LC 83-27130. 256p. 1984. pap. text ed. 12.95 (ISBN 0-88141-032-2). St Vladimirs.

Pavel Korin. N. A. Mikhailov. 102p. 1982. pap. 14.00x (ISBN 0-317-57405-1, Pub. by Collets UK). State Mutual Bk.

Pavel Tchelitchew Drawings. Ed. by Lincoln Kirstein. LC 77-116363. (Illus.). 1970. 25.00 (ISBN 0-87817-046-4). Hacker.

Pavement Analysis. P. Ullidtz. (Developments in Civil Engineering Ser.: Vol. 19). 1987. 102.00 (ISBN 0-444-42817-8). Elsevier.

Pavement & Soil Characteristics: Seven Reports. (Transportation Research Record Ser.). 81p. 1975. 3.80 (ISBN 0-309-02388-2). Transport Res Bd.

Pavement Design & Management Systems: Eight Reports. (Transportation Research Record Ser.). 73p. 1974. 3.40 (ISBN 0-309-02356-4). Transport Res Bd.

Pavement Distress, Evaluation, & Performance. (Transportation Research Record Ser.). 76p. 1979. 3.00 (ISBN 0-309-02962-7). Transport Res Bd.

Pavement Engineering. Irwin. 1989. price not set (ISBN 0-471-61174-3). Wiley.

Pavement Evaluation & Overlay Design: A Symposium & Related Papers. (Transportation Research Record Ser.). 114p. 1979. 6.20 (ISBN 0-309-02848-5). Transport Res Bd.

Pavement Evaluation Using Road Meters. (Special Report). 128p. 1973. 4.00 (ISBN 0-309-02096-4). Transport Res Bd.

Pavement Life Cycle Costing. (Promotional Ser.: No. 20). 1987. 9.00 (ISBN 0-317-58366-2). Natl Asphalt Pavement.

Pavement Maintenance & Rehabilitation - STP 881. Ed. by Bernard F. Kallas. LC 85-7550. (Illus.). 107p. 1985. pap. text ed. 20.00 (ISBN 0-8031-0424-3, 04-881000-08). ASTM.

Pavement Management Systems. Ralph C. Haas & W. Ronald Hudson. LC 81-17229. 476p. 1982. Repr. of 1978 ed. text ed. 37.50 (ISBN 0-89874-407-5). Krieger.

Pavement Performance on a Portion of Ohio's Interstate System. (Quality Improvement Program Ser.: No. 103). 18p. 1983. 10.00 (ISBN 0-317-58367-0). Natl Asphalt Pavement.

Pavement Relections. Lionel Gardner. 6.75 (ISBN 0-89253-688-8). Ind-US Inc.

Pavement Smoothness. (Information Ser.: No. 53). 1975. 4.00 (ISBN 0-317-58371-9). Natl Asphalt Pavement.

Pavement Surface Characteristics & Materials - STP 763. Ed. by C. Hayden. 131p. 1982. pap. 17.00 (ISBN 0-8031-0785-4, 04-763000-47). ASTM.

Pavement Surface Properties & Performance. (Transportation Research Record Ser.). 50p. 1977. 2.80 (ISBN 0-309-02659-8). Transport Res Bd.

Pavement Surface Properties & Vehicle Interaction: Five Reports. (Transportation Research Record Ser.). 64p. 1976. 2.80 (ISBN 0-309-02498-6). Transport Res Bd.

Pavement Surface Properties, Evaluation & Shoulders. (Transportation Research Record Ser.). 60p. 1978. 4.00 (ISBN 0-317-36097-3). Transport Res Bd.

Pavement Systems: Assessment of Load Effects, Design, & Bases. (Transportation Research Record Ser.). 88p. 1979. 5.00 (ISBN 0-309-02975-9). Transport Res Bd.

Pavements & Surfacing for Highways & Airports. Michael Sargious. (Illus.). xviii, 619p. 1975. 99.00 (ISBN 0-85334-602-X, Pub. by Elsevier Applied Sci England). Elsevier.

Pavements Management Systems (Road Transport Research) OECD. 160p. (Orig.). 1987. pap. 16.00x (ISBN 92-64-12907-3). OECD.

Paver Operations for Quality. (Information Ser.: No. 59). 1986. 8.00 (ISBN 0-317-58374-3). Natl Asphalt Pavement.

Pavia & Rome: The Lombard Monarchy & the Papacy in the Eighth Century. Jan T. Hallenbeck. LC 81-68190. (Transactions Ser.: Vol. 72, Pt. 4). 1982. 18.00 (ISBN 0-87169-724-6). Am Philos.

Pavilion. Hilda Lawrence. (Crime Ser.). 288p. 1984. pap. 3.95 (ISBN 0-14-006964-X). Penguin.

Pavilion & Other Poems. 1974. 7.50 (ISBN 0-912090-40-5); pap. 2.45 (ISBN 0-912090-41-3). Sumac Mich.

Pavillon des Temps Noureaux & Other Buildings & Projects, 1936-1937, Vol. XIII. Le Corbusier. Ed. by H. Allen Brooks. LC 82-24208. (Le Corbusier Archive Ser.). 616p. 1983. lib. bdg. 240.00 (ISBN 0-8240-5062-2). Garland Pub.

Paving Alaska'a Trails: The Work of the Alaska Road Commission. Claus M. Naske. LC 86-15850. (Illus.). 354p. (Orig.). 1986. lib. bdg. 46.75 (ISBN 0-8191-5576-4); pap. text ed. 34.75 (ISBN 0-8191-5577-2). U Pr of Amer.

Pavior Screeds. (Materials & Techniques in Building Practice: No. 1). pap. 20.00 (ISBN 0-317-08374-0, 2017713). Bks Demand UMI.

Pavlia, Portrait of a Greek Village. Antony Decaneas. (Illus.). 128p. (Orig.). 1987. 39.95 (ISBN 0-945149-00-X); pap. 22.95 (ISBN 0-945149-01-8). Panopticon Pr.

Pavlov. Ted Martin. 128p. 1988. pap. 1.95 (ISBN 0-8125-7478-8). Tor Bks.

Pavlov: A Biography. Boris P. Babkin. LC 49-11887. xiv, 366p. 1975. pap. 4.25x (ISBN 0-226-03373-2, P621, Phoen). U of Chicago Pr.

Pavlov & His School. Yuril P. Frolov. Tr. by C. P. Dutt from Rus. LC 38-901. (Psychology Ser). 1970. Repr. of 1938 ed. 23.00 (ISBN 0-384-17060-9). Johnson Repr.

Pavlova: A Collection of Memoirs. Ed. by A. H. Franks. (Quality Paperbacks Ser.). (Illus.). 144p. 1981. pap. 6.95 (ISBN 0-306-80149-3). Da Capo.

Pavlova (Eighteen Eighty-One to Nineteen Thirty-One) A Biography. Ed. by A. H. Franks. LC 79-1053. (Series in Dance). (Illus.). 144p. 1979. Repr. of 1956 ed. 25.00 (ISBN 0-306-79538-8). Da Capo.

Pavlova: Repertoire of a Legend. John Lazzarini & Roberta Lazzarini. LC 80-5560. (Illus.). 1980. 35.00 (ISBN 0-02-871970-0). Schirmer Bks.

Pavlova: Self-Portrait of a Dancer. Margot Fonteyn. LC 83-40658. (Illus.). 160p. 1984. 25.00 (ISBN 0-670-54394-2). Viking.

Pavlovian Conditioning & American Psychiatry, Vol. 5. Group for the Advancement of Psychiatry Staff. (Symposium No. 9). 1964. pap. 5.00 (ISBN 0-87318-079-8, Pub. by GAP). Brunner-Mazel.

Pavlovian Second-Order Conditioning: Studies in Associative Learning. R. A. Rescorla. 128p. 1980. text ed. 19.95x (ISBN 0-89859-485-5). L Erlbaum Assocs.

Pavlov's Pad. Ted Martin. 128p. 1988. pap. 1.95 (ISBN 0-8125-7481-8). Tor Bks.

PAVN: People's Army of Vietnam. Dougals Pike. 408p. 1986. 30.00 (ISBN 0-08-033614-0, Pub. by BDP). Pergamon.

PAVN: People's Army of Vietnam. Douglas Pike. (Illus.). 392p. 1986. 22.50 (ISBN 0-89141-243-3). Presidio Pr.

Pavologia: A Celebration of Peacocks Past. Evelyn A. Domjan. Ed. by Rose Stein & Lory Skwerer. (Illus.). 200p. 1984. 25.00 (ISBN 0-933652-17-8). Domjan Studio.

Pavor Nocturnus & Other Poems. Madeleine Hennessy. Ed. by Susan Shafarzek. (Illus., Orig.). 1979. pap. 1.95 (ISBN 0-918310-02-4). Washout.

Pawcatuck River Estuary & Little Narragansett Bay. R. Ehinger et al. 56p. 1978. free (P728). Sea Grant Pubns.

Pawn Endings. Alexander Cvetkov. Tr. by Jim Marfia from Bulgarian. 69p. 1985. pap. 5.00 (ISBN 0-931462-47-9). Chess Ent Inc.

Pawn in Frankincense. Dorothy Dunnett. 425p. 1983. Repr. lib. bdg. 21.95x (ISBN 0-89966-321-4). Buccaneer Bks.

Pawn in Frankincense. Dorothy Dunnett. 576p. 1984. pap. 3.95 (ISBN 0-446-31294-0). Warner Bks.

Pawn of Prophecy. David Eddings. (Belgariad Ser.: Bk. 1). 258p. (Orig.). 1988. pap. 3.95 (ISBN 0-345-33551-1, Del Rey). Ballantine.

Pawn Power in Chess. Hans Kmoch. (Illus.). 1978. pap. 6.95 (ISBN 0-679-14028-X, Tartan). McKay.

Pawn Structure Chess. A. Soltis. 1986. pap. 7.95 (ISBN 0-679-14475-7). McKay.

Pawn to Infinity. Ed. by Fred Saberhaben. 256p. 1982. pap. 2.50 (ISBN 0-441-65482-7). Ace Bks.

Pawnbroker. E. L. Wallant. 1979. Repr. lib. bdg. 16.95x (ISBN 0-686-92468-1). Buccaneer Bks.

Pawnbroker. Edward L. Wallant. LC 78-7101. 279p. 1978. pap. 5.95 (ISBN 0-15-671422-1, Harv). HarBraceJ.

Pawnee & Lower Loup Pottery. Roger T. Grange, Jr. (Publications in Anthropology: No. 3). 235p. 1968. pap. 6.00 (ISBN 0-686-20020-9). Nebraska Hist.

Pawnee Ghost Dance Hand Game. Alexander Lesser. LC 79-82340. (Columbia Univ. Contributions to Anthropology Ser.: Vol. 16). 1969. Repr. of 1933 ed. 37.00 (ISBN 0-404-50566-X). AMS Pr.

Pawnee Ghost Dance Hand Game: A Study of Cultural Change. Alexander Lesser. LC 79-82340. (Illus.). 368p. 1978. 22.50x (ISBN 0-299-07480-3); pap. 8.95x (ISBN 0-299-07484-6). U of Wis Pr.

Pawnee Hero Stories & Folk-Tales with Notes on the Origin, Customs & Character of the Pawnee People. George B. Grinnell. LC 61-10153. (Illus.). xiv, 417p. 1961. 35.00x (ISBN 0-8032-0896-0). U of Nebr Pr.

Pawnee Indians. George E. Hyde. LC 72-9260. (Civilization of the American Indian Ser.: Vol. 128). (Illus.). 384p. 1988. pap. 12.95 (ISBN 0-8061-2094-0). U of Okla Pr.

Pawnee Music. Frances Densmore. LC 72-1880. (Music Ser.). 160p. 1972. Repr. of 1929 ed. lib. bdg. 21.50 (ISBN 0-306-70508-7). Da Capo.

Pawnees: A Critical Bibliography. Martha R. Blaine. LC 80-8034. (Newberry Library D'Arcy McNickle Center for the History of the American Indian Bibliographical Ser.). (Illus.). 128p. 1981. pap. 4.95x (ISBN 0-253-31502-6). Ind U Pr.

Pawns & Symbols. Marjorie Nelson. (Star Trek Ser.: No. 26). 288p. (Orig.). 1985. pap. 3.95 (ISBN 0-671-66497-2). PB.

Pawns in a Triangle of Hate: The Peruvian Japanese & the United States. C. Harvey Gardiner. LC 81-51278. 232p. 1981. 27.50x (ISBN 0-295-95855-3). U of Wash Pr.

Pawns in the Game. William G. Carr. 193p. pap. 4.00 (ISBN 0-913022-34-9). Angriff Pr.

Pawns in the Game. William G. Carr. 1978. pap. 4.00x (ISBN 0-911038-29-9). Noontide.

Pawns of War. Boston Publishing Co. Staff. Ed. by Robert Manning. (Vietnam Experience Ser.: Vol. 23). (Illus.). 192p. 1987. 16.95 (ISBN 0-939526-24-7). Boston Pub Co.

Pawns of War. Boston Publishing Company Editors et al. (Vietnam Experience Ser.). (Illus.). 192p. 1987. 16.95 (ISBN 0-201-11678-2). Addison-Wesley.

Pawns of War: The Loss of the U. S. S. Langley & the U. S. S. Pecos. Dwight R. Messimer. LC 82-14415. (Illus.). 228p. 1983. 19.95 (ISBN 0-87021-515-9). Naval Inst Pr.

Pawns of Yalta: Soviet Refugees & America's Role in Their Repatriation. Mark R. Elliot. LC 81-7599. (Illus.). 300p. 1981. 24.95 (ISBN 0-252-00897-9). U of Ill Pr.

Pawnshop in China. T. S. Whelan. Ed. by Mark Elvin. (Michigan Abstracts of Chinese & Japanese Works on Chinese History Ser.: No. 6). (Orig.). 1979. pap. 5.00 (ISBN 0-89264-906-2). U of Mich Ctr Chinese.

Paws Awhile on Wineberry Acres. Sandra Mckenzie. 114p. 1986. pap. 6.67 (ISBN 0-9614476-1-3). Farr Pubs.

PAWS Keyboard Success. Ann Fidanque et al. 133p. (Orig.). (gr. k-8). 1985. pap. 20.00 (ISBN 0-924667-36-2). Intl Council Comp.

Pawtracks. Tim McNulty. LC 77-93618. (Illus.). 1978. pap. 6.00. Copper Canyon.

Pax Atomica: The Nuclear Defense Debate in West Germany During the Adenauer Era. Mark Cioc. (Illus.). 208p. 1988. 25.00 (ISBN 0-231-06590-6). Columbia U Pr.

Pax Britannica: The Climax of an Empire. James Morris. LC 79-24725. (Illus.). 544p. 1980. pap. 9.95 (ISBN 0-15-671466-3, Harv). HarBraceJ.

Pax et Sapientia: Studies in the Text & Music of Liturgical Tropes & Sequences. Ritva Jacobson. 114p. 1986. pap. text ed. 22.00x (ISBN 0-317-54527-2, Pub. by Almqvist & Wiksell). Coronet Bks.

Pax optima rerum: Friedensessais zu Grotius und Goethe, Vol. 49. Christian Gellinek. LC 84-47845. (Germanic Studies in America). 155p. (Ger.). 1984. text ed. 18.00 (ISBN 0-8204-0147-1). P Lang Pubs.

Pax: Peace. Lorenzo Marroquin. Tr. by Isaac Goldberg & W. V. Schierbrand. 1977. lib. bdg. 59.95 (ISBN 0-8490-2417-X). Gordon Pr.

Pax Romana. Peter Amey. Ed. by Malcolm Yapp et al. (World History Ser.). (Illus.). 32p. (gr. 6-11). 1980. lib. bdg. 6.95 (ISBN 0-89908-027-8); pap. text ed. 2.45 (ISBN 0-89908-002-2). Greenhaven.

Pax Romana. Paul Petit. Tr. by James Willis. 1976. 48.00x (ISBN 0-520-02171-1). U of Cal Pr.

Pax Romana & the Peace of Jesus Christ. Klaus Wengst. Tr. by John Bowden. LC 87-45320. 256p. 1987. pap. 14.95 (ISBN 0-8006-2067-4). Fortress.

Pay & Organization Development. Edward E. Lawlor, III. 230p. 1981. pap. text ed. 16.25 (ISBN 0-201-03990-7). Addison-Wesley.

Pay & Pensions for Federal Workers. Robert W. Hartman. LC 82-45980. 118p. 1983. 22.95 (ISBN 0-8157-3496-4); pap. 8.95 (ISBN 0-8157-3495-6). Brookings.

Pay & Productivity Bargaining. R. G. Searle-Barnes. LC 71-94226. (Illus.). 1969. 27.50x (ISBN 0-678-06776-7). Kelley.

Pay & Profits. Ernest H. Brown. LC 68-56546. (Illus.). 1968. 12.50x (ISBN 0-678-06753-8). Kelley.

Pay As You Exit. Katie Goldman. LC 84-23903. (gr. 6). 1985. 13.95 (ISBN 0-8037-0191-8, 01258-370). Dial Bks Young.

Pay Board's Progress: Wage Controls in Phase II. Arnold Weber & Daniel J. Mitchell. LC 77-91820. (Studies in Wage-Price Policy). pap. 118.00 (2027742). Bks Demand UMI.

Pay by Check. Janis F. Chan. (Money Matters Ser.). (Illus.). 64p. (gr. 7-12). 1981. pap. 3.95 (ISBN 0-915510-52-9). Janus Bks.

Pay Differentials: An Integration of Theories, Evidence & Policies. John Donaldson & Pamela Philby. 268p. 1985. text ed. 34.50 (ISBN 0-566-00838-6). Gower Pub Co.

Pay: Employee Compensation & Incentive Plans. Thomas H. Patten, Jr. LC 76-27155. (Illus.). 1977. text ed. 21.95 (ISBN 0-02-924920-1). Free Pr.

Pay Envelopes: Tales of the Mill, the Mine & the City Street, Vol. 1. James Oppenheim. LC 72-3288. (Short Story Index Reprint Ser). (Illus.). Repr. of 1911 ed. 16.00 (ISBN 0-8369-4158-6). Ayer Co Pubs.

PC BASIC for Beginners. Brian D. Hahn. (Illus.). 177p. (Orig.). 1988. pap. text ed. 12.95 (ISBN 0-7131-3586-7, Pub. by E Arnold UK). Routledge Chapman & Hall.

PC BASIC: Getting Started. William S. Davis. (Illus.). 1987. pap. text ed. 8.95 (ISBN 0-201-05904-5). Addison-Wesley.

PC-Bilog. Robert Mislevy & R. Darrell Bock. looseleaf binder 17.00 (ISBN 0-89498-013-0). Sci Ware.

PC CAD-CAM-CAE Software & Systems Directory. 2nd., rev ed. Ed. by Lawrence Rosenbaum & Jonathan Linden. 90p. 1986. 49.00 (ISBN 0-932007-10-4, B49). Mgmt Roundtable.

PC Care Manual: Diagnosing & Maintaining Your MS-DOS CP-M or Macintosh System. Chris Morrison & Teresa S. Stover. LC 87-26235. (Illus.). 224p. 1987. 24.95 (ISBN 0-8306-0991-1, 2991); pap. 16.95 (ISBN 0-8306-2991-2). TAB Bks.

PC COBOL. M. B. Khan. 352p. 1988. pap. text ed. write for info. (ISBN 0-697-06775-0). Instr's manual (ISBN 0-697-06983-4). Wm C Brown.

PC Compendium, Vol. 1. Chris Naylor. 340p. 1987. 25.95 (ISBN 1-85058-087-1, Pub. by Sigma Pr UK). Bk Clearing Hse.

PC Configuration Handbook: A Complete Guide to Assembling, Enhancing & Maintaining Your PC. John Woram. 1987. 19.95 (ISBN 0-553-34489-7). Bantam.

PC-DOS: A Self-Teaching Guide. 2nd ed. Ruth Ashley & Judi N. Fernandez. LC 85-9466. 246p. 1985. pap. 17.95 (ISBN 0-471-82471-2). Wiley.

PC-DOS & MS-DOS: A Ready Reference Manual. Craig A. Wood. (Illus.). 128p. 1987. pap. text ed. 8.95x (ISBN 0-201-16370-5). Addison-Wesley.

PC-DOS Customized: Create Your Own DOS Commands for the IBM-PC, XT & AT. David D. Busch. 176p. 1985. pap. 14.95 (ISBN 0-89303-753-2). Brady Comp Bks.

PC-DOS Customized: Create Your Own DOS Commands. rev. ed. David Busch. 400p. 1988. pap. 18.95. Prentice Hall Pr.

PC-DOS for Beginners. Dan Kauffmann. 150p. (Orig.). 1986. pap. text ed. 15.00x (ISBN 0-89787-415-3). Gorsuch Scarisbrick.

PC-DOS Fundamentals for Diskette-Based Operation. Peter Calingaert. (Illus.). 272p. 1986. text ed. 24.95 (ISBN 0-13-654906-3). P-H.

PC-DOS: Introduction High-Performance Computing. Peter Norton. (Illus.). 325p. 1985. pap. 18.95 (ISBN 0-89303-752-4). Brady Comp Bks.

PC-DOS, MS-DOS: User's Guide to the Most Popular Operating System for Personal Computers. Alan Boyd. 352p. (Orig.). 1985. pap. 18.95 (ISBN 0-553-34231-2). Bantam.

PC-DOS Simplified. Rod B. Southworth. 145p. 1988. pap. 22.50 (ISBN 0-87835-308-9). Boyd & Fraser.

PC-DOS Tips & Traps. Dick Andersen. 250p. (Orig.). 1985. pap. text ed. 18.95 (ISBN 0-07-881194-5). Osborne-McGraw.

PC Driven Expert Systems. LC 85-80961. 1986. 795.00 (ISBN 0-914405-09-8). Electronic Trend.

PC Economics Handbook. Dan J. Ehrlich & Joel Millonzi. 1987. write for info. (ISBN 0-395-35685-7). HM.

PC Graphics: Charts, Graphs, Games, & Art on the IBM-PC. Dick Conklin. LC 83-5797. (Professional Software Ser.). 182p. 1983. pap. text ed. 15.95 (ISBN 0-471-89207-6, 1-646, Pub. by Wiley Pr); book & program disk 40.90 (ISBN 0-471-88541-X). Wiley.

PC Hardware & Systems Implementations Reference. William J. Birnes. (Illus.). 320p. 1988. 29.95 (ISBN 0-07-005396-0). McGraw.

PC LAN Primer. The Waite Group. 240p. 1986. pap. 22.95 (ISBN 0-672-22448-8). Sams.

PC Magazine's DOS Power Tools: Techniques, Tricks, & Utilities. Paul Somerson. 1248p. 1988. pap. 39.95 incl. disk (ISBN 0-553-34526-5). Bantam.

PC-MS DOS Fundamentals. Carolyn Z. Gillay. (Information Systems Ser.). 1988. pap. text ed. 22.95 (ISBN 0-938661-09-4). Franklin Beedle.

PC MS DOS Made Easy. Tony Dowden. 1988. 14.95 (ISBN 0-87455-138-2). Compute Pubns.

PC-MS DOS Small-C Addendum to the Small-C Handbook. James E. Hendrix. 50p. 1985. documentation manual 4.95 (ISBN 0-934375-06-2). M & T Pub Inc.

PC-MS DOS 4.0 for the Hard Disk User. David D. Busch. 1988. pap. 22.95 (ISBN 0-553-34600-8). Bantam.

PC Or Not PC: Consumers Guide to Buying & Owning a Personal Computer. James M. Gardner & Annemarie Breuer. LC 84-61851. 80p. (Orig.). 1984. pap. 10.00 (ISBN 0-931671-00-0). Planet CA.

PC: Portable Standard FORTRAN 77. M. W. Clark. (Computers & Their Applications Ser.). 228p. 1986. 31.95 (ISBN 0-470-20756-6). Wiley.

PC Programming Techniques: Creative BASIC Skills for IBM Personal Computers. Alan C. Elliott. (Illus.). 176p. 1984. pap. 14.95 (ISBN 0-89303-755-9). P-H.

PC Secrets: Tips for Power Performance. James E. Kelly. 224p. (Orig.). 1985. pap. text ed. 18.95 (ISBN 0-07-881210-0). Osborne-McGraw.

PC-SIG Library Supplement (Disks 706-1000 Plus) Consumer Guide to Low Cost Software for the IBM-PC & Compatibles. PC-SIG, Inc. Staff. (Illus.). 200p. (Orig.). 1988. pap. 8.95 (ISBN 0-915835-12-6). PC Software.

PC Software Workbook. 2nd ed. O'Brien & Durham. 1988. pap. text ed. 12.95 (ISBN 0-256-06704-X). Irwin.

PC-Tax, 1988. Smith. 112p. 1987. pap. text ed. 25.00 wkbk., diskette & adopter (5272); pap. text ed. 60.00 wkbk., diskette & non-adopter (5272); wkbk. 5.00 (5271). Commerce.

PC Technical Source-Book, 1988. Chuck Philyaw & David Lippincott. Ed. by Marty Kleine. (Illus.). 76p. (Orig.). 1988. pap. 19.95 handbook (ISBN 0-929069-00-5). Industrial Computer Source.

PC to Mac & Back: A File Transfer Utility for the IBM-PC & Macintosh. Peter H. Mackie & John R. Griffin. (Illus.). 165p. incl. disk 149.95 (ISBN 0-88056-224-2). Dilithium Pr.

PC Upgrader's Manual: How to Build & Extend Your System. Gilbert Held. LC 87-33241. 1988. pap. 19.95 (ISBN 0-471-63177-9). Wiley.

PC Wizardry on Wall Street: How to Use Your IBM & Compatibles to Invest in the Stock Market. N. Douglas Adams. 224p. 1985. 21.95 (ISBN 0-13-655010-X); pap. 14.95 (ISBN 0-13-655002-9). P-H.

PC Wordperfect 5.0 Guide. Donald Richard Read. 1989. 21.95 (ISBN 0-87455-146-3). Compute Pubns.

PC Works Primer. Elna R. Tymes & Charles Prael. 1987. 21.95 (ISBN 0-553-34541-9). Bantam.

PC-Write Simplified. Howard Frazier. 1987. 16.95 (ISBN 0-87455-125-0). Compute Pubns.

PC 832 Concepts II: Required Peace Officer Training. Derald D. Hunt. LC 86-74293. 200p. 1986. pap. text ed. 12.95 (ISBN 0-942728-29-7). Custom Pub Co.

PCA Soil Primer. 1973. pap. 3.00 (ISBN 0-89312-105-3, EB007S). Portland Cement.

PCAT (Pharmacy College Admission Test) Practice Examination, No. 1. David M. Tarlow. (Practice Examination Ser.). 40p. 1987. pap. 16.95 (ISBN 0-931572-22-3). Datar Pub.

PCAT (Pharmacy College Admission Test) Practice Examination, No. 2. David M. Tarlow. (Practice Examination Ser.). 40p. 1987. pap. 16.95 (ISBN 0-931572-23-1). Datar Pub.

PCAT (Pharmacy College Admission Test) Practice Examination, No.3. David M. Tarlow. (Practice Examination Ser.). 40p. 1987. pap. 16.95 (ISBN 0-931572-24-X). Datar Pub.

PCAT (Pharmacy College Admission Test) Practice Examination, No. 4. David M. Tarlow. (Practice Examination Ser.). 40p. 1987. pap. 16.95 (ISBN 0-931572-25-8). Datar Pub.

PCAT (Pharmacy College Admission Test) Practice Examination, No. 5. David M. Tarlow. (Practice Examination Ser.). 40p. 1987. pap. 16.95 (ISBN 0-931572-26-6). Datar Pub.

PCAT Practice Examination: Annotated Master Answer Guide, No. 2. Tarlow. 1987. 4.95 (ISBN 0-931572-48-7). Datar Pub.

PCAT Practice Examination: Annotated Master Answer Guide, No. 3. Tarlow. 1987. 4.95 (ISBN 0-931572-49-5). Datar Pub.

PCAT Practice Examination: Annotated Master Answer Guide, No. 4. Tarlow. 1987. 4.95 (ISBN 0-931572-50-9). Datar Pub.

PCAT Practice Examination: Annotated Master Answer Guide, No. 5. Tarlow. 1987. 4.95 (ISBN 0-931572-51-7). Datar Pub.

PCB Compliance Guide for Electrical Equipment. Phillip L. Youngblood & Jack E. Cearley. 145p. 1988. 95.00 (ISBN 0-87179-593-0, 0593). BNA.

PCB Health Effects, 2 vols. Incl. Vol. 1. Potential Health Effects in the Human from Exposure to Polychlorinated Biphenyls (PCBs) & Related Impurities. 15.00 (ISBN 0-318-18043-X); Vol. 2. Literature Update on Potential Health Effects from Exposure to Polychlorinated Biphenlyls & Related Chlorinated Heterocycles. 15.00 (ISBN 0-318-18044-8). Set. 27.00 (ISBN 0-318-18042-1). Natl Elec Mfrs.

PCB Poisoning in Japan & Taiwan. Ed. by Masanori Kuratsune & Raymond E. Shapiro. LC 83-19645. (Progress in Clinical Biological Research Ser.: Vol. 137). 168p. 1984. 33.00 (ISBN 0-8451-0137-4, 1037). A R Liss.

PCBs & the Environment. John S. Waid. 256p. 1986. 3 vol. set 350.00. CRC Pr.

PCC-From Coast to Coast. Fred W. Schneider & Stephen P. Carlson. (Special Ser.: No. 86). (Illus.). 288p. 1983. 36.95 (ISBN 0-916374-57-2). Interurban.

PCDex: Magazine Resource Guide for Commodore 64, VIC-20 & PET-CBM Personal Computers. Ed. by Alan M. Smith. 216p. (Orig.). 1984. pap. 14.95 (ISBN 0-918391-00-8). Altacom.

PCI Architectural Precast Concrete. (Illus.). 173p. 20.00x (ISBN 0-937040-01-0, MNL-122-73). Prestressed Concrete.

PCI Design for Fire Resistance of Precast Prestressed Concrete. 88p. softcover 12.00x (ISBN 0-937040-08-8, MNL-124-82). Prestressed Concrete.

PCI Design Handbook: Precast & Prestressed Concrete. 3rd ed. 528p. 1985. write for info. (ISBN 0-318-19716-2, MNL-120-85). Prestressed Concrete.

PCI Design Handbook: Precast Prestressed Concrete. 2nd ed. 380p. 1978. 50.00x (ISBN 0-937040-12-6, MNL-120-78). Prestressed Concrete.

PCI Journal Twenty-Five Year Index: 1956-1981. 224p. 30.00 (ISBN 0-318-16189-3, JR-1-82). Prestressed Concrete.

PCI Manual for Structural Design of Architectural Precast Concrete. 448p. 50.00x (ISBN 0-937040-07-X, MNL-121-77). members 25.00. Prestressed Concrete.

PCI Manual for the Design of Hollow Core Slabs. 120p. Date not set. 42.00 (MNL-126-85). Prestressed Concrete.

PCI Membership Directory, 1988. 148p. write for info. softcover (ISBN 0-937040-13-4, SP-M); pap. 150.00 ea., first copy free, members. Prestressed Concrete.

PCjr Assembly Programming: A Gentle Introduction. Richard L. Taylor. (Illus.). 256p. 1985. 24.95 (ISBN 0-13-655036-3); pap. 14.95 (ISBN 0-13-655028-2). P-H.

PCjr Data File Programming: A Self-Teaching Guide. Jerald Brown & LeRoy Finkel. 320p. 1984. pap. 15.95 (ISBN 0-471-81580-2, Pub. by Wiley Pr). Wiley.

PCM & Digital Transmission Systems. Frank F. Owen. (Texas Instruments Electronics Ser.). (Illus.). 295p. 1982. text ed. 49.95x (ISBN 0-07-047954-2). McGraw.

PCMR Sixteenth Annual Report to the President: Citizen With Mental Retardation--Equality Under the Law. 53p. 1987. write for info. (ISBN 1-55672-026-2). US HHS.

PCP, Phencyclidine, "Angel Dust". Brent Q. Hafen & Kathryn J. Frandsen. 20p. 1.25 (ISBN 0-89486-074-7, 1942B). Hazelden.

PCP (Phencyclidine) Historical & Current Perspectives. Ed. by E. F. Domino. LC 80-81498. (Illus.). 537p. 1981. 40.00x (ISBN 0-916182-03-7). NPP Bks.

PCP: Problems & Prevention. Smith et al. 1982. pap. text ed. 17.95 (ISBN 0-8403-2809-5). Kendall-Hunt.

PCP: The Dangerous Angel. Marilyn Carroll. (Encyclopedia of Psychoactive Drugs Ser.). (Illus.). 1985. PLB 17.95 (ISBN 0-87754-753-X). Chelsea Hse.

PCPS: Achievements & Prospects. 88p. 1984. pap. 3.25 (ISBN 0-317-27356-6). Am Inst CPA.

PCPS Peer Review Manual Plus Descriptive Book. 80.00 (ISBN 0-686-90418-4, 017618). Am Inst CPA.

PC's in Personnel. Gary J. Meyer. 1985. loose leaf 76.50 (ISBN 1-55645-424-4). Busn Legal Reports.

PCT, Spin & Statistics, & All That. Raymond F. Streater & Arthur S. Wrightman. (Advanced Book Classics). 1980. 29.95 (ISBN 0-201-09410-X, Adv Bk Prog MSP). Addison-Wesley.

PDA International Conference on Liquid Borne Particle Inspection & Metrology: Conference Proceedings. Parenteral Drug Association Incorporated Staff. Ed. by Marcy Feldman. (Illus.). 662p. 1987. pap. text ed. 95.00 (ISBN 0-939459-12-4). PDA.

PDE Software-Modules, Interfaces & Systems: Proceedings of the IFIP TC 2 Working Conference Held in Soderkoping, Sweden, 22-26 August 1983. Ed. by B. Engquist & T. Smedsaas. 454p. 1984. 79.00 (ISBN 0-444-87620-0, North-Holland). Elsevier.

PDMS & Clusters: Proceedings of the International Workshop on the Physics of Small Systems, Held on the Island of Wangerooge, Germany, 1st, September 8-12, 1986. Ed. by E. R. Hilf et al. (Lecture Notes in Physics: Vol. 269). viii, 261p. 1987. 28.90 (ISBN 0-387-17209-2). Springer-Verlag.

PDP-11 Architecture Handbook. 272p. 1983. pap. 15.00 (ISBN 0-932376-37-1, EB-23657-DP). Digital Pr.

PDP-11 Structured Assembly Language Programming. Robert W. Sebesta. 352p. 1985. text ed. 34.95 (ISBN 0-8053-7005-6); instr's. guide 5.95 (ISBN 0-8053-7006-4). Benjamin Cummings.

PDP-11 Unibus: Processor Handbook. 208p. (Orig.). 1985. pap. 16.00 (ISBN 0-932376-97-5, EB-26077-DP, DEC Bks). Digital Pr.

PDQ Biochemistry. Villee. 1986. 9.95 (ISBN 0-8016-5192-1, D-5192-1). Mosby.

PDQ Embryology. Moore. 1986. 9.95 (ISBN 0-8016-3533-0). Mosby.

PDQ Statistics. Norman & Streiner. 1986. 9.95 (ISBN 0-8016-3840-2). Mosby.

PDR Drug Identification Guide. 40p. 1988. comb-bound paper 9.50 (ISBN 0-87489-491-3). Med Economics.

P.D.R. Yemen: Outpost of Socialist Development in Arabia. Helen Lackner. 219p. 1985. 30.00 (Pub. by Ithaca England). Evergreen Dist.

PDS Data: Educational Version. Harold C. Chambers & Gary Moore. (Software Learning Ser.). 300p. 1987. Incl. DiskPak. write for info. (ISBN 0-471-85469-7). Wiley.

PDS Data: Educational Version, Instruction Manual. Harold C. Chambers & Gary Moore. (Software Learning Ser.). 300p. 1987. pap. write for info. (ISBN 0-471-85470-0). Wiley.

PD's in Depth. Edith C. Trager. (Orig.). (gr. 9-12). 1982. pap. 4.95 (ISBN 0-87789-215-6, 1600); write for info. cassettes (ISBN 0-87789-216-4, 1601). ELS Educ Servs.

Pea. R. K. Makasheva. Tr. by B. R. Sharma from Rus. 275p. 1984. text ed. 29.00 (ISBN 90-6191-431-0, Pub. by A A Balkema). Brookfield Pub Co.

Pea Crop: A Basis for Improvement. P. D. Hebblethwaite et al. (Illus.). 480p. 1985. text ed. 135.00 (ISBN 0-407-00922-1). Butterworth.

Pea Patch Jig. Thacher Hurd. LC 86-2693. (Illus.). (ps-2). 1986. 11.95 (ISBN 0-517-56307-X). Crown.

Pea Pod Christmas. (Illus.). (ps-5). 1988. incl. 3 dolls 19.95 (ISBN 0-698-12012-4). Putnam Pub Group.

Pea Pod Pop-Ups. (Pea Pod Bks.). (Illus.). (ps up). 1988. 19.95 (ISBN 0-698-12000-0); 3 dolls incl. Putnam Pub Group.

Pea River Reflections: History & Legends of Coffee County, Alabama. 3rd ed. Marion B. Bronson. (Illus.). 1984. 7.95 (ISBN 0-916620-76-X). Portals Pr.

Pea Soup. Christopher Reid. LC 82-6294. 1982. pap. 11.95 (ISBN 0-19-211952-4). Oxford U Pr.

Pea Soup Andersen's Scandinavian-American Cookbook. Ulrich Riedner. Ed. by Patricia Rain. 180p. 1988. 7.95 (ISBN 0-89087-523-5). Celestial Arts.

Peabody. Earl Atkinson. (Ballroom Dance Ser.). 1986. lib. bdg. 79.95 (ISBN 0-8490-3630-5). Gordon Pr.

Peabody. (Ballroom Dance Ser.). 1985. lib. bdg. 69.00 (ISBN 0-87700-702-0). Revisionist Pr.

Peabody. William Thomas. (Illus.). 160p. Date not set. cancelled (ISBN 0-916242-51-X). Yoknapatawpha.

Peabody. Rosemary Wells. (Illus.). 32p. (ps-2). 1983. 11.95 (ISBN 0-8037-0004-0, 01160-290); PLB 11.89 (ISBN 0-8037-0005-9). Dial Bks Young.

Peabody. Rosemary Wells. LC 83-7207. (Pied Piper Bk.). (Illus.). 32p. (ps-2). 1986. pap. 3.95 (ISBN 0-8037-0211-6, 0383-120). Dial Bks Young.

Peabody Ducks. Martha L. Garrety. Created by Jean J. Garbarini. (Illus.). 32p. 1983. 8.95 (ISBN 0-9610374-0-7). Duck Tale Prods.

Peabody Homes Inert Gas System. Ed. by Lorne & MacLean Marine Staff. 1985. 95.00x (ISBN 0-317-43648-1, Pub. by Lorne & MacLean Marine). State Mutual Bk.

Peabody Law Review: Portland, Me, 1936-1941, Vols. 1-5. Bound set. 87.50x (ISBN 0-686-90011-1). Rothman.

Peabody Reading Program, Workbk. 3. Richard Woodcock & Charlotte Clark. (Peabody Rebus Reading Program Ser.). (Illus.). 112p. (ps-1). 1969. pap. text ed. cancelled (ISBN 0-913476-38-2). Am Guidance.

Peabody Rebus Program: Reader Two. Richard Woodcock & Charlotte Clark. (Peabody Rebus Reading Program Ser.). (Illus.). 72p. (gr. k-1). 1969. pap. text ed. 6.50 (ISBN 0-913476-40-4). Am Guidance.

Peabody Rebus Reading Program, Workbk. 1. Richard Woodstock et al. (Peabody Rebus Reading Program Ser.). (Illus.). 96p. (gr. k-1). 1967. pap. text ed. 6.50 (ISBN 0-913476-36-6). Am Guidance.

Peabody Rebus Reading Program, Workbk. 2. Richard Woodcock & Charlotte Clark. (Peabody Rebus Reading Program Ser.). (Illus.). 96p. (gr. k-1). 1967. pap. text ed. 6.50x (ISBN 0-913476-37-4). Am Guidance.

Peabody Rebus Reading Program: Reader One. Richard Woodcock & Charlotte Clark. (Peabody Rebus Reading Program Ser.). (Illus.). 80p. (gr. k-1). 1969. pap. text ed. 6.50x (ISBN 0-913476-39-0). Am Guidance.

Peabody Rebus Reading Program: Starter Set. Richard Woodcock & Charlotte Clark. (Peabody Rebus Reading Program Ser.). pap. text ed. 28.50 (ISBN 0-913476-42-0). Am Guidance.

Peabody Rebus Reading Program Teacher's Guide. Richard Woodstock & Charlotte Clark. (Peabody Rebus Reading Program Ser.). 72p. (gr. k-1). 1969. tchrs. ed 10.50 (ISBN 0-913476-35-8). Am Guidance.

Peabody Sister of Salem. Louise H. Tharp. (Illus.). 380p. 1988. 19.95 (ISBN 0-316-83920-5); pap. 8.95 (ISBN 0-316-83919-1). Little.

Peabody Steps. Earl Atkinson. 1983. lib. bdg. 79.95 (ISBN 0-87700-484-6). Revisionist Pr.

Peace. Aristophanes. Ed. by Alan H. Sommerstein. 225p. 1985. 49.00 (ISBN 0-86516-090-2); pap. 16.50 (ISBN 0-86516-065-1). Bolchazy Carducci.

Peace. Maurice Careme. Tr. by Helen Neumeyer. (Envelope Library). (Illus.). 8p. (Orig.). (YA) (gr. 7-9). 1982. pap. 2.50 (ISBN 0-914676-68-7). Green Tiger Pr.

Peace. Carole MacKenthun & Paulinus Dwyer. (Fruit of the Spirit Ser.). (Illus.). 48p. (gr. 2-7). 1986. wkbk. 5.95 (ISBN 0-86653-365-6). Good Apple.

Peace. Archibald Roberts. 1972. 10.00 (ISBN 0-913558-03-6). Educator Pubns.

Peace. Gene Wolfe. LC 74-15896. 264p. 1975. 15.00 (ISBN 0-06-014699-0). Ultramarine Pub.

Peace Organizations Past & Present: A Survey & Directory. Robert S. Meyer. LC 88-42515. 288p. 1988. lib. bdg. 24.95x (ISBN 0-89950-340-3). McFarland & Co.

Peace Pilgrim: Her Life & Work in Her Own Words. Peace Pilgrim. Ed. by Richard Polese et al. LC 82-18854. (Illus.). 214p. (Orig.). 1983. pap. 8.00 (ISBN 0-943734-01-0). Ocean Tree Bks.

Peace Planning for Central & Eastern Europe. Feliks Gross. 70p. 1944. 3.00 (ISBN 0-940962-21-7). Polish Inst Art & Sci.

Peace Plays. Ed. by Stephen Loew. (Theatrescripts Ser.). 144p. 1985. pap. 8.50 (ISBN 0-413-56000-7, 9050). Heinemann Ed.

Peace, Plenty, & Petroleum. Benjamin T. Brooks. LC 75-6463. (History & Politics of Oil Ser). 197p. 1976. Repr. of 1944 ed. 19.25 (ISBN 0-88355-283-3). Hyperion Conn.

Peace, Politics & Economics in Asia: The Challenge to Cooperate. Ed. by Robert A. Scalapino & Masataka Kosaka. (Illus.). 168p. 1988. text ed. 30.00 (ISBN 0-08-035961-2). Pergamon.

Peace, Politics, & the People of God. Ed. by Paul Peachey. LC 85-45490. 208p. 1986. pap. 4.95 (ISBN 0-8006-1898-X). Fortress.

Peace Porridge. Marjie Douglis. Ed. by Pete Peterson. (Illus.). 122p. (gr. 3-6). 1986. pap. 3.95 (ISBN 0-934998-22-1). Bethel Pub.

Peace Porridge, No. 1: Kids As Peacemakers. Teddy Milne. LC 86-64050. (Illus.). 295p. (gr. 3 up). 1987. pap. 10.95 (ISBN 0-938875-03-5). Pittenbruach Pr.

Peace Porridge, No. 2: Russia, to Begin With. Teddy Milne. LC 86-64052. (Illus.). 195p. (Orig.). (gr. 3 up). 1987. pap. 9.95 (ISBN 0-938875-06-X). Pittenbruach Pr.

Peace, Print & Protestantism, Fourteen Fifty to Fifteen Eighty. S. L. Davies. 1976. 24.50x (ISBN 0-8464-0706-X). Beekman Pubs.

Peace, Print & Protestantism: 1450 to 1558. C. S. Davies. (Paladin History of England Ser.). 365p. 1983. pap. 7.95 (ISBN 0-586-08266-2, Pub. by Granada England). Academy Chi Pubs.

Peace, Profits & Principles. J. Joris Voorhoeve. 1979. lib. bdg. 23.00 (ISBN 90-247-2237-3); pap. 16.50 (ISBN 90-247-2203-9). Kluwer Academic.

Peace, Prosperity & the Coming Holocaust. Dave Hunt. LC 82-84069. 224p. 1983. pap. 7.95 (ISBN 0-89081-331-0). Harvest Hse.

Peace Reader: Essential Readings on War & Justice, Non-Violence, & World Order. Ed. by Joseph Fahey & Richard Armstrong. 487p. 1987. pap. 14.95 (ISBN 0-8091-2914-0). Paulist Pr.

Peace Reform in American History. Charles DeBenedetti. LC 79-2173. 264p. 1980. 18.50x (ISBN 0-253-13095-6). Ind U Pr.

Peace Reform in American History. Charles DeBenedetti. LC 79-2173. (Midland Bks: No. 320). 264p. 1984. pap. 8.95x (ISBN 0-253-20320-1). Ind U Pr.

Peace Research: Achievements & Challenges. Ed. by Peter Wallensteen. (Special Studies in Peace, Conflict, & Conflict Resolution). 215p. 1988. pap. 19.95 (ISBN 0-8133-7474-X). Westview.

Peace Resource Book, 1988-89. Ed. by Randall Forsberg & Carl Conetta. 304p. 1988. pap. 14.95 (ISBN 0-88730-289-0). Ballinger Pub.

Peace Revolution: Ethos & Social Process. John Somerville. LC 74-5993. (Contributions in Philosophy: No. 7). 1975. lib. bdg. 35.00 (ISBN 0-8371-7532-1, SPR/). Greenwood.

Peace River Pioneers. Louise K. Frisbie. LC 74-81530. (Illus.). 1974. 9.95 (ISBN 0-912458-47-X, Pub. by E A Seemann). Imperial Pub Co.

Peace, Security & Human Dignity in Asia. Soedjatmoko. 8p. 1977. pap. text ed. 5.00 (ISBN 0-8191-5829-1, Pub. by Aspen Inst for Humanistic Studies). U Pr of Amer.

Peace, Security & the United Nations. Ed. by Hans J. Morgenthau. LC 72-10841. (Essay Index Reprint Ser.). 1973. Repr. of 1946 ed. 16.00 (ISBN 0-8369-7232-5). Ayer Co Pubs.

Peace Seekers: The Nobel Peace Prize. Nathan Aaseng. (Nobel Prize Winners Ser.). (Illus.). 80p. (gr. 5 up). 1987. PLB 9.95 (ISBN 0-8225-0654-8). Lerner Pubns.

Peace Soldiers: The Sociology of a United Nations Military Force. Charles C. Moskos, Jr. 1976. 12.50x (ISBN 0-226-54225-4). U of Chicago Pr.

Peace: Solh. Nader S. Angha. Tr. by School of Islamic Sufism. LC 87-63381. 147p. (Orig., Persian.). 1987. 32.00 (ISBN 0-910735-38-7); pap. 11.55 (ISBN 0-910735-12-3). MTO Printing & Pubn Ctr.

Peace Tax Fund & Conscientous Objection to Military Taxation. 2nd ed. Hartley S. Armen. 122p. 1986. pap. 5.00 (ISBN 0-9616313-4-1). Conscience & Military Tax.

Peace That Passes All Misunderstanding. Thomas E. Witherspoon. LC 87-50929. 144p. 1988. text ed. 5.95 (ISBN 0-87159-126-X). Unity School.

Peace That You Seek. Alan Cohen. (Illus.). 195p. (Orig.). 1985. pap. 5.95 (ISBN 0-910367-35-3, 157). A Cohen.

Peace Thinking in a Warring World. Edward L. Long, Jr. LC 83-14675. 118p. 1983. pap. 6.95 (ISBN 0-664-24503-X). Westminster John Knox.

Peace Through Economic Cooperation see My Pilgrimage for Peace.

Peace Through Education: The Contribution of the Council for Education in World Citizenship. Derek Heater. 225p. 1984. 36.00x (ISBN 1-85000-001-8, Falmer Pr). Taylor & Francis.

Peace Through Law. B. Carroll Reece. pap. 3.75 (ISBN 0-912806-21-4). Long Hse.

Peace Thru People: A Human Philosophy of Survival for the Pan-Atomic Age. W. John Weilgart. 72p. 1977. pap. 4.00 (ISBN 0-912038-17-9). Cosmic Comm.

Peace Tradition in the Catholic Church: An Annotated Bibliography. Ronald G. Musto. LC 86-31950. (Garland Reference Library of Social Science). 500p. 1987. lib. bdg. 67.00 (ISBN 0-8240-8584-1). Garland Pub.

Peace Treaty. Ruth N. Moore. LC 76-48922. (Christian Peace Shelf). (Illus.). 154p. (gr. 3-10). 1977. pap. 3.95 (ISBN 0-8361-1805-7). Herald Pr.

Peace Treaty with God. John Hendee. (Ambassadors Training Program Ser.). 16p. (Orig.). 1984. pap. 0.50 (ISBN 0-87239-814-5, 3223). Standard Pub.

Peace Truth Love: The Gospel of St. John. 80p. avail. Pocket Testament.

Peace vs. Power in the Family. Abraham A. Low. 197p. 1984. Repr. of 1967 ed. text ed. 10.95 (ISBN 0-915005-03-4). Willett Pub Co.

Peace War. Vernor Vinge. 288p. 1984. 16.95 (ISBN 0-312-94342-3); cancelled ltd. ed. (ISBN 0-312-94343-1). Bluejay Bks.

Peace War. Vernor Vinge. LC 84-14513. 286p. 1984. 16.95 (ISBN 0-317-58849-4). Ultramarine Pub.

Peace War. Vernor Vinge. 384p. pap. 3.50 (ISBN 0-671-55965-6). Baen Bks.

Peace-What Is Peace? 1985. 10.00x (ISBN 0-317-62230-7, Guild of Pastoral Psych). State Mutual Bk.

Peace Where Is It? Annie Gagiati. LC 73-91996. 1974. pap. 1.95 (ISBN 0-8198-0507-6). Dghtrs St Paul.

Peace with China? U. S. Decisions for Asia. Ed. by Earl C. Ravenal. LC 71-162433. 1971. pap. 2.95 (ISBN 0-87140-257-2). Liveright.

Peace with God. rev. ed. Billy Graham. 288p. 1985. 10.95 (ISBN 0-8499-0464-1, 0464-1); pap. text ed. 8.95 (ISBN 0-8499-2991-1, 2991-1). Word Bks.

Peace with Honor? An American Reports on Vietnam, 1973-1975. Stuart A. Herrington. (Illus.). 264p. 1983. 15.95 (ISBN 0-89141-182-8). Presidio Pr.

Peace with Justice. Dwight D. Eisenhower. LC 61-7096. 273p. 35.00x (ISBN 0-231-02472-X). Columbia U Pr.

Peace with the Apaches of New Mexico & Arizona. facsimile ed. Vincent Colyer. LC 70-165622. (Select Bibliographies Reprint Ser). Repr. of 1872 ed. 12.00 (ISBN 0-8369-5929-9). Ayer Co Pubs.

Peace with Work to Do: The Academic Study of Peace. James O'Connell & Adam Curle. LC 85-11191. 56p. (Orig.). 1985. pap. 7.95 (ISBN 0-907582-77-X, Pub. by Berg Pubs). St Martin.

Peace Within Yourself. Joseph Murphy. 300p. 1972. pap. 6.50 (ISBN 0-87516-188-X). DeVorss.

Peace Without Promise: Britain & the Peace Conferences 1919-1923. Michael Dockerill & J. Douglas Goold. LC 80-28121. 287p. 1981. 27.50 (ISBN 0-208-01909-X, Archon). Shoe String.

Peaceable Americans of 1860-1861: A Study in Public Opinion. Mary Scrugham. 1971. lib. bdg. 14.50x (ISBN 0-374-97208-7, Octagon). Hippocrene Bks.

Peaceable Classroom: Activities to Calm & Free Student Energies. Merrill Harmin & Saville Sax. 1977. pap. 5.95 (ISBN 0-86683-623-3, HarpR). Har-Row.

Peaceable Kingdom. Peter Wild. LC 83-72298. (Nightsun Bks.). 64p. (Orig.). 1984. pap. 6.95 (ISBN 0-913623-01-6, P377). Adler Pub Co.

Peaceable Kingdom: A Primer in Christian Ethics. Stanley Hauerwas. LC 83-14711. 224p. 1983. text ed. 20.95x (ISBN 0-268-01553-8, 85-15538); pap. text ed. 8.95x (ISBN 0-268-01554-6). U of Notre Dame Pr.

Peaceable Kingdom: A Year in the Life of America's Oldest Zoo. John Sedgwick. (Illus.). 352p. 1988. 19.95 (ISBN 0-688-06367-5). Morrow.

Peaceable Kingdom in Hartsdale: A Celebration of Pets & Their People. LC 82-99850. (Illus.). 192p. 1983. 20.00 (ISBN 0-9608712-0-9). Rosywick Pr.

Peaceable Kingdom: Poems by Jon Silkin. rev. 1st. ed. Jon Silkin. (Illus.). 1975. perfect bd in wrappers o.p. 10.00 (ISBN 0-685-52385-3); deluxe ed. 145.00 signed, on handmade paper (ISBN 0-685-52386-1). Heron Pr.

Peaceable Kingdom: Stability & Change in Modern Britain. Brian Harrison. 1982. 49.50x (ISBN 0-19-822603-9). Oxford U Pr.

Peaceable Kingdom: The Shaker Abecedarius. Illus. by Alice Provensen & Martin Provensen. (Picture Puffins Ser.). (Illus.). (gr. k-3). 1981. pap. 4.95 (ISBN 0-14-050370-6, Puffin). Penguin.

Peaceable Kingdom: The Shaker Abecedarius. Illus. by Alice Provensen & Martin Provensen. LC 78-125. (Illus.). 42p. (gr. k-2). 1978. lib. bdg. 13.95 (ISBN 0-670-54500-7). Viking.

Peaceable Kingdoms: New England Towns in the Eighteenth Century. Michael Zuckerman. LC 82-18365. ix, 329p. 1983. Repr. of 1970 ed. lib. bdg. 41.50 (ISBN 0-313-22634-2, ZUPK). Greenwood.

Peaceable Sex: On Aggression in Women & Men. Margarete Mitscherlich. Tr. by Craig Tomlinson from Ger. 256p. 1987. 16.95 (ISBN 0-88064-067-7). Fromm Intl Pub.

Peaceable Warrior. Marguerite Murray. LC 85-20052. 176p. (gr. 4-8). 1986. 12.95 (ISBN 0-689-31186-9, Atheneum Childrens Bks). Macmillan.

Peacebuilding. 2nd ed. Donald W. DeMott. (Illus.). 235p. 1987. pap. text ed. 14.50 (ISBN 0-317-61490-8). High Falls Pubns.

Peacebuilding: A Textbook. 2nd ed. Donald W. DeMott & Dianne K. DeMott. (Illus.). 272p. 1987. pap. text ed. 14.50 (ISBN 0-9617217-2-3). High Falls Pubns.

Peaceful Atom & the Deadly Fly. C. G. Scruggs. LC 75-28738. (Illus.). 311p. 1975. 12.95 (ISBN 0-8363-0135-8). Jenkins.

Peaceful Change. Ed. by C. A. Manning. LC 79-149540. (Library of War & Peace; the Political Economy of War). lib. bdg. 46.00 (ISBN 0-8240-0477-9). Garland Pub.

Peaceful Change & the Colonial Problem. Bryce Wood. LC 70-76639. (Columbia University. Teachers College. Contributions to Education: No. 464). Repr. of 1940 ed. 15.00 (ISBN 0-404-51464-2). AMS Pr.

Peaceful Change in Modern Society. Ed. by E. Berkeley Tompkins. LC 74-152429. (Publications Ser.: No. 101). 158p. 1971. pap. 8.95x (ISBN 0-8179-6011-2). Hoover Inst Pr.

Peaceful Change: Vol. 1 Procedures, Population, Raw Materials Colonies: Proceedings. International Studies Conference, 10th. (Library of War & Peace; the Political Economy of War). 46.00 (ISBN 0-8240-0292-X). Garland Pub.

Peaceful Change: Vol. 3 Colonial Questions & Peace: Proceedings. International Studies Conference, 10th. (Library of War & Peace; the Political Economy of War). lib. bdg. 46.00 (ISBN 0-8240-0435-3). Garland Pub.

Peaceful Coexistence: International Law in the Building of Communism. Bernard A. Ramundo. LC 67-12421. 262p. 1967. 28.50x (ISBN 0-8018-0542-2). Johns Hopkins.

Peaceful Conquest: The Industrialization of Europe, 1760-1970. Sidney Pollard. (Illus.). 1981. pap. 10.95x (ISBN 0-19-877095-2). Oxford U Pr.

Peaceful Living in a Stressful World. Ronald Hutchcraft. LC 85-10592. 228p. 1985. 11.95 (ISBN 0-8407-5470-1). Nelson.

Peaceful Living in a Stressful World: Expanded Edition with Study Guide. Ronald Hutchcraft. 1988. pap. 8.95 (ISBN 0-8407-3118-3). Nelson.

Peaceful Nuclear Explosions - 2: Their Practical Application. Incl. Peaceful Nuclear Explosions - 3: Applications, Characteristics & Effects. (Panel Proceedings Ser.). (Illus.). 488p. (Eng., Fr., Rus. & Span.). 1974. pap. 43.00 (ISBN 92-0-061074-9, ISP367). UNIPUB; Peaceful Nuclear Explosions - 4. Technical Committee, Vienna, Jan. 20-24, 1975. (Panel Proceedings Ser.). (Illus.). 479p. 1975. pap. 49.25 (ISBN 92-0-061075-7, ISP414). UNIPUB; Peaceful Nuclear Explosions - 5. (Panel Proceedings Ser.). (Illus.). 216p. 1978. pap. 24.25 (ISBN 92-0-061078-1, ISP473). UNIPUB; Peaceful Nuclear Explosions - 1: Phenomenology & Status Report, 1970. (Panel Proceedings Ser.). (Illus.). 454p. (Orig.). 1970. pap. 32.00 (ISBN 92-0-061070-6, ISP273). UNIPUB. (Panel Proceedings Ser.). (Illus.). 355p. (Orig.). 1972. pap. 28.75 (ISBN 92-0-061071-4, ISP298, IAEA). UNIPUB.

Peaceful Nuclear Explosions - 1: Phenomenology & Status Report, 1970 see Peaceful Nuclear Explosions - 2: Their Practical Application.

Peaceful Nuclear Explosions - 3: Applications, Characteristics & Effects see Peaceful Nuclear Explosions - 2: Their Practical Application.

Peaceful Nuclear Explosions - 4. Technical Committee, Vienna, Jan. 20-24, 1975 see Peaceful Nuclear Explosions - 2: Their Practical Application.

Peaceful Nuclear Explosions - 5 see Peaceful Nuclear Explosions - 2: Their Practical Application.

Peaceful Patriot. Bonnie McKeown. pap. 5.00 (ISBN 0-934538-31-X). Partnership Foundation.

Peaceful Procedures: A Master Teacher's Approach to Peaceful Classroom Management. Illus. by Pat Fellers. Kathy Gritzmacher. Ed. by Ron Marson. (Master Teacher Ser.). (Illus.). 84p. 1987. tchr's. ed. 13.95 (ISBN 0-941008-63-0). Tops Learning.

Peaceful Revolution Handbook. Al David. 120p. (Orig.). 1982. pap. 3.50 (ISBN 0-9611682-0-X). Rel Psych.

Peaceful Season: Daily Advent Meditations for Everyday Christians. Roger A. Swenson. LC 87-1047. 104p. 1987. pap. 7.95 (ISBN 0-8189-0519-0). Alba.

Peaceful Seed Living, Vols. 1 & 2. 2nd ed. Jerome F. Coniker. LC 78-66369. (Living Meditation & Prayerbook Ser.). (Illus.). 156p. 1981. pap. text ed. 3.00 ea. (ISBN 0-932406-00-9). AFC.

Peaceful Settlement of Disputes in International Law. Simone-Marie Kleckner. (Collection of Bibliographic & Research Resources Ser.). 96p. (Orig.). 1985. including other bibliographies in looseleaf 300.00; pap. text ed. 35.00 (ISBN 0-379-20905-5). Oceana.

Peaceful Storm. Charles Robertson. 1985. pap. 5.95 (ISBN 0-89221-135-0). New Leaf.

Peaceful Use of Nuclear Explosives: Some Economic Aspects. David B. Brooks & John V. Krutilla. LC 69-15904. pap. 20.00 (ISBN 0-317-26030-8, 2023788). Bks Demand UMI.

Peaceful Uses for Tuition Vouchers: Looking Back & Looking Forward. 25p. 1985. 4.00 (ISBN 0-318-22540-9, EG-85-1). Ed Comm States.

Peaceful Uses of Atomic Energy in Africa. (Proceedings Ser.). (Illus., Orig.). 1970. pap. 40.00 (ISBN 92-0-070070-5, ISP233, IAEA). UNIPUB.

Peaceful Uses of Nuclear Explosions (1969-1979, Vol. 2. (Bibliographical Ser.: No. 43). 443p. 1981. pap. 55.25 (ISBN 92-0-164080-3, ISP 21 43, IAEA). UNIPUB.

Peacefully Working to Conquer the World: Singer Sewing Machine in Foreign Markets, 1854-1920. Robert B. Davies. Ed. by Stuart Bruchey & Eleanor Bruchey. LC 76-5000. (American Business Abroad Ser.). 1976. 36.00x (ISBN 0-405-09270-9). Ayer Co Pubs.

Peacekeepers. Ben Bova. 352p. 1988. 17.95 (ISBN 0-312-93080-1). Tor Bks.

Peacekeepers. Ben Bova. 352p. 1989. pap. price not set. Tor Bks.

Peacekeepers at War: A Marine's Account of the Beirut Catastrophe. Michael Petit. (Illus.). 224p. 1986. pap. 17.95 (ISBN 0-571-12545-X). Faber & Faber.

Peacekeeper's Handbook. International Peace Academy Staff. 416p. 1984. 55.00. Pergamon.

Peacekeeper's Handbook. 439p. 1984. 50.00. Intl Peace.

Peacekeeping: Appraisals & Proposals. Ed. by Henry Wiseman. (International Peace Academy Ser.). 461p. 1983. 61.00 (ISBN 0-08-027554-0). Pergamon.

Peacekeeping in Vietnam: Canada, India, Poland, & the International Commission. Ramesh Thakur. xvi, 375p. 1984. 30.00x (ISBN 0-88864-037-4, Pub. by Univ of Alta Pr Canada). U of Nebr Pr.

Peacekeeping on Arab-Israeli Fronts: Lessons from the Sinai & Lebanon. Nathan A. Pelcovits. (SAIS Papers in International Affairs: No. 3). 150p. 1984. pap. 26.50x (ISBN 0-86531-899-9). Westview.

Peacemaker. Myron S. Augsburger. 208p. 1987. pap. 9.95 (ISBN 0-687-30353-2). Abingdon.

Peacemaker Pass. Kit Dalton. (Buckskin Ser.: No. 21). 192p. (Orig.). 1988. pap. 2.95 (ISBN 0-8439-2619-8, Pub. by Leisure Bks CT). Leisure NY.

Peacemakers: Christian Voices from the New Abolitionist Movement. Jim Wallis. LC 82-48940. 160p. (Orig.). 1983. pap. 5.95 (ISBN 0-06-069244-8, CN-4058, HarpR). Har-Row.

Peacemakers' Dilemma. Bertram Pickard. 1936. pap. 2.50x (ISBN 0-87574-016-2, 016). Pendle Hill.

Peacemakers, Eighteen Fourteen to Eighteen Fifteen. facs. ed. John G. Lockhart. LC 68-8479. (Essay Index Reprint Ser). 1968. Repr. of 1934 ed. 19.00 (ISBN 0-8369-0622-5). Ayer Co Pubs.

Peacemaker's Handbook. Christian Conciliation Service. Ed. by C. Ken Sande. 140p. (Orig.). 1978. pap. text ed. 10.00 (ISBN 0-944561-06-3). Chr Legal.

Peacemakers in the Nuclear Age. Robert Paolino. 16p. (Orig.). (gr. 7-9). 1983. student wkbk. 1.00x (ISBN 0-89622-204-7); tchr's. ed. 2.95 (ISBN 0-89622-203-9). Twenty-Third.

Peacemakers: Informing the World. Jane North. (Peacemakers Ser.). (Illus.). 128p. (gr. 7 up). Date not set. PLB cancelled (ISBN 0-87518-354-9). Dillon.

Peacemakers of Eighteen Sixty-Four. Edward C. Kirkland. LC 74-97888. Repr. of 1927 ed. 21.50 (ISBN 0-404-03706-2). AMS Pr.

Peacemakers: The Great Powers & American Independence. Richard B. Morris. LC 82-23271. 590p. 1983. text ed. 29.95X (ISBN 0-930350-35-9); pap. 10.95x (ISBN 0-930350-36-7). NE U Pr.

Peacemaking. Douglas Fisher. homily bk. 1.50 (ISBN 0-8091-9321-3); group discussion guide 1.77 (ISBN 0-8091-9326-4); participants' bks. 1.00 (ISBN 0-8091-9341-8). Paulist Pr.

Peacemaking: A Systems Approach to Conflict Management. Lynn S. Kahn. LC 87-31649. (Illus.). 280p. (Orig.). 1988. lib. bdg. 28.50 (ISBN 0-8191-6782-7); pap. text ed. 12.25 (ISBN 0-8191-6783-5). U Pr of Amer.

Peacemaking & the Community of Faith: A Handbook for Congregations. John A. Donaghy. 2.95 (ISBN 0-8091-5181-2). Paulist Pr.

Peacemaking: Family Activities for Justice & Peace. Jacqueline Haessly. LC 79-92008. 86p. 1988. pap. 7.95. Resource Pubns.

Peacemaking in the Middle East. Lester Sobel. (Checkmark Bk.). 304p. 1980. lib. bdg. 24.95x (ISBN 0-87196-267-5). Facts on File.

Peacemaking in the Renaissance. Joycelyne G. Russell. LC 86-6952. 267p. 1986. text ed. 40.95x (ISBN 0-8122-8030-X). U of Pa Pr.

Peacemaking in Your Neighborhood: Reflections of an Experiment in Community Mediation. Friends Suburban Project Staff & Jennifer E. Beer. 256p. 1986. lib. bdg. 39.95 (ISBN 0-86571-072-4); pap. 14.95 (ISBN 0-86571-071-6). New Soc Pubs.

Peacemaking Nineteen Nineteen. Harold Nicolson. 1984. 18.75 (ISBN 0-8446-6124-4). Peter Smith.

Pearl. Nancy Flynn. (La Mer Press Ser.). 24p. (Orig.). 1985. pap. 5.00 (ISBN 0-917573-02-1). CAO TIMES.

Pearl. Tr. by Israel Gollancz. LC 66-27657. (Medieval Library). (Illus.). Repr. of 1926 ed. 17.50x (ISBN 0-8154-0084-5). Cooper Sq.

Pearl. Ed. by Eric V. Gordon. 1980. Repr. of 1953 ed. 13.95x (ISBN 0-19-812675-1). Oxford U Pr.

Pearl. Helme Heine. LC 84-72404. Orig. Title: Perle. (Illus.). 32p. (ps-3). 1985. 11.95 (ISBN 0-689-50321-0, M K McElderry). Macmillan.

Pearl. Helme Heine. LC 88-3220. (Illus.). 32p. (gr. k-4). Date not set. pap. 3.95 (ISBN 0-689-71262-6, Aladdin Bks). Macmillan.

Pearl. Tabitha King. 336p. 1988. 18.95 (ISBN 0-453-00626-4). NAL.

Pearl. Charles G. Osgood. 1907. Repr. 35.50 (ISBN 0-8274-3114-7). R West.

Pearl. 1977. pap. 3.95 (ISBN 0-345-29456-4). Ballantine.

Pearl. Anne Ruck. 1986. pap. 2.95 (ISBN 9971-972-37-9). OMF Bks.

Pearl. Steinbeck. (Book Notes). 1985. pap. 2.50 (ISBN 0-8120-3534-8). Barron.

Pearl. John Steinbeck. (Illus.). 1947. 15.95 (ISBN 0-670-54575-9). Viking.

Pearl. John Steinbeck. 1986. pap. 2.50 (ISBN 0-553-26261-0). Bantam.

Pearl see Short Novels of John Steinbeck.

Pearl, a Fourteenth-Century Poem. George G. Coulton. LC 76-44809. 1976. Repr. of 1907 ed. lib. bdg. 27.00 (ISBN 0-8414-3385-2). Folcroft.

Pearl: A Middle English Poem. Sophie Jewett. 1978. Repr. of 1908 ed. lib. bdg. 27.00 (ISBN 0-8414-5404-3). Folcroft.

Pearl, a Middle English Poem. Ed. by Charles G. Osgood, Jr. LC 78-144438. Repr. of 1906 ed. 14.50 (ISBN 0-404-53614-X). AMS Pr.

Pearl: A New Verse Translation. Marie Boroff. 1977. 7.95x (ISBN 0-393-04456-4); pap. 3.95x (ISBN 0-393-09144-9). Norton.

Pearl: A Study in Spiritual Dryness. Sr. M. Madeleva. 1979. Repr. of 1925 ed. lib. bdg. 32.50 (ISBN 0-8495-3781-9). Arden Lib.

Pearl: A Study in Spiritual Dryness. Sr. M. Madeleva. LC 74-20927. 1974. lib. bdg. 27.50 (ISBN 0-8414-5963-0). Folcroft.

Pearl: A Study in Spiritual Dryness. Sr. M. Madeleva. LC 68-59311. 235p. 1968. Repr. of 1925 ed. 30.00x (ISBN 0-87753-025-4). Phaeton.

Pearl: An English Poem of the Fourteenth Century, Re-Set in Modern English. Israel Gollancz. 1918. Repr. 35.00 (ISBN 0-8274-3113-9). R West.

Pearl & Boccaccio's Olympia. Israel Gollancz. 1921. Repr. 25.00 (ISBN 0-8274-3115-5). R West.

Pearl & Hermes Reef, Hawaii, Hydrographical & Biographical Observations. P. S. Galtsoff. (BMB). pap. 10.00 (ISBN 0-527-02213-6). Kraus Repr.

Pearl & the Princes. Shirley L. Morrison. LC 84-23349. vi, 170p. 1985. 14.95 (ISBN 0-9613978-0-2); pap. 7.95 (ISBN 0-9613978-1-0). Laurel Pr.

Pearl & the Red Pony. John Steinbeck. (Fiction Ser.). 208p. 1976. pap. 3.95 (ISBN 0-14-004232-6). Penguin.

Pearl Bastard. Lillian Halegua. 2.50 (ISBN 0-7043-3828-9, Pub. by Quartet England). Charles River Bks.

Pearl Bastard. Lillian Halegua. 140p. 1985. pap. 3.95 (ISBN 0-932870-72-4). Alyson Pubns.

Pearl Beyond Price: Integration of Personality into Being--An Object Relations Approach. A. H. Almaas. LC 87-51720. (Diamond Mind Ser.: Bk. 2). 530p. (Orig.). 1988. 29.50 (ISBN 0-936713-03-8); pap. 19.50 (ISBN 0-936713-02-X). Almaas Pubns.

Pearl Buck. Ann LaFarge. (American Women of Achievement Ser.). (Illus.). 112p. (gr. 5 up). 1988. lib. bdg. 16.95x (ISBN 1-55546-645-1). Chelsea Hse.

Pearl Buck: A Woman in Conflict. Nora Stirling. LC 83-19455. (Illus.). 352p. 1983. 17.95 (ISBN 0-8329-0261-6). New Century.

Pearl Buck: Famed American Author of Oriental Stories. Celin V. Schoen. Ed. by D. Steve Rahmas. LC 70-190247. (Outstanding Personalities Ser.: No. 30). 32p. (Orig.). (gr. 7-12). 1972. lib. bdg. 3.75 incl. catalog cards (ISBN 0-87157-530-2); pap. 2.50 vinyl laminated covers (ISBN 0-87157-030-0). SamHar Pr.

Pearl Buck Reader, 2 vols. Pearl S. Buck & Reader's Digest Editors. LC 84-6784. (Illus.). 1008p. 1985. Set. 19.95 (ISBN 0-89577-196-9). RD Assn.

Pearl Cannon: Sadeq Hedayat's Greatest Works: Book One. Sadeq Hedayat. Tr. by Iraj Bashiri from Persian. LC 85-43495. (Mazda Special Bilingual Publication Ser.). 203p. (Orig.). 1986. pap. 9.95. Mazda Pubs.

Pearl Cleanness, Patience, & Sir Gawain & the Green Knight. Ed. by A. C. Cawley & J. J. Anderson. 1970. 12.95x (ISBN 0-460-00346-1, Evman); pap. 2.95x (ISBN 0-460-11346-1, Evman). Biblio Dist.

Pearl Harbor. Deborah Bachrach. (Opposing Viewpoints Sources Ser.). (Illus.). 112p. (ps-5). 1988. PLB 12.95 (ISBN 0-89908-059-6). Greenhaven.

Pearl Harbor. Nathan Harris. (Day that Made History Ser.). (Illus.). 64p. (gr. 6-8). 1987. 17.95 (ISBN 0-85219-669-5, Pub. by Batsford England). David & Charles.

Pearl Harbor. (Illus.). 34p. 1983. pap. 3.50 (ISBN 0-930492-16-1). Hawaiian Serv.

Pearl Harbor. William E. Shapiro. LC 84-7324. (Turning Points of World War II Ser.). (Illus.). 103p. (gr. 7-12). 1984. PLB 11.90 (ISBN 0-531-04865-9). Watts.

Pearl Harbor. G. C. Skipper. LC 83-6569. (World at War Ser.). (Illus.). 48p. (gr. 4-8). 1983. PLB 12.33 (ISBN 0-516-04774-4); pap. 2.95 (ISBN 0-516-44774-2). Childrens.

Pearl Harbor: A Narrative Poem. John Guenther. LC 80-83810. (Illus.). 64p. (Orig.). 1980. pap. 4.95 (ISBN 0-938266-00-4). Purchase Pr.

Pearl Harbor after a Quarter Century. Harry E. Barnes. 134p. 1980. pap. 6.00 (ISBN 0-911038-95-7). Inst Hist Rev.

Pearl Harbor after a Quarter of a Century. Harry E. Barnes. LC 75-172203. (Right Wing Individualist Tradition in America Ser). 1972. Repr. of 1968 ed. 17.00 (ISBN 0-405-00413-3). Ayer Co Pubs.

Pearl Harbor after a Quarter of a Century. Harry E. Barnes. 1981. lib. bdg. 59.95 (ISBN 0-686-73185-9). Revisionist Pr.

Pearl Harbor: Japan's Fatal Blunder. Harry Albright. 240p. 1988. 17.95 (ISBN 0-87052-507-7). Hippocrene Bks.

Pearl Harbor: Roosevelt & the Coming of the War. 3rd ed. Ed. by George M. Waller. (Problems in American Civilization Ser.). 1976. pap. text ed. 7.50 (ISBN 0-669-98376-4). Heath.

Pearl Harbor: The Continuing Controversy. Hans L. Trefousse. LC 81-14237. (Anvil Ser.). 218p. (Orig.). 1982. pap. text ed. 8.50 (ISBN 0-89874-261-7). Krieger.

Pearl Harbor: The Verdict of History. Gordon W. Prange et al. (Illus.). 864p. 1986. pap. text ed. 5.95 (ISBN 0-07-050679-5). McGraw.

Pearl Harbor: The Way It Was--December 7, 1941. Scott C. Stone. LC 77-82234. (Illus.). 1977. pap. 4.95 (ISBN 0-89610-039-1). Island Heritage.

Pearl Harbor: Warning & Decision. Roberta Wohlstetter. 1962. 35.00x (ISBN 0-8047-0597-6); pap. 11.95 (ISBN 0-8047-0598-4, SP14). Stanford U Pr.

Pearl: Hymn of the Robe of Glory. Illus. by Nonny Hogrogian. LC 79-66092. (Illus.). 1979. 7.95 (ISBN 0-89756-002-7). Two Rivers.

Pearl, Image of the Ineffable: A Study in Medieval Poetic Symbolism. Theodore Bogdanos. LC 82-42783. 184p. 1983. 22.50x (ISBN 0-271-00339-1). Pa St U Pr.

Pearl Is a Hardened Sinner. Stanley Kiesel. (Poetry Ser.). 1976. pap. 3.50 (ISBN 0-685-78484-3). Nodin Pr.

Pearl-Maiden. H. Rider Haggard. Repr. lib. bdg. 25.95x (ISBN 0-89190-708-4, Pub. by Aeonian Pr). Amereon Ltd.

Pearl Maiden. H. Rider Haggard. (Golden Age of Rome Ser.). 1978. pap. 2.50 (ISBN 0-89083-352-4). Zebra.

Pearl Makers. Mervin F. Roberts. 188p. (Orig.). 1984. pap. 6.95. Saybrook Pr.

Pearl Millet. Kenneth O. Rachie & J. V. Majmudar. LC 79-5144. (Illus.). 320p. 1980. 34.95x (ISBN 0-271-00234-4). Pa St U Pr.

Pearl Notes. Eva Fitzwater. (Orig.). 1981. pap. 3.50 (ISBN 0-8220-0994-3). Cliffs.

Pearl of Christian Counsel for the Brokenhearted. Vernard Eller. LC 82-20028. 152p. (Orig.). 1983. lib. bdg. 25.25 (ISBN 0-8191-2850-3); pap. text ed. 10.00 (ISBN 0-8191-2851-1). U Pr of Amer.

Pearl of Great Price: A History & Commentary. H. Donl Peterson. LC 87-15672. 395p. 1987. 14.95 (ISBN 0-87579-096-8). Deseret Bk.

Pearl of Great Price: The Life of Mother Maria Skobtsova 1891-1945. rev. ed. Sergei Hackel. LC 81-21356. 192p. 1982. pap. 6.95 (ISBN 0-913836-85-0). St Vladimirs.

Pearl of Orr's Island. Harriet Beecher Stowe. 1862. Repr. 14.00x (ISBN 0-403-00280-X). Scholarly.

Pearl of Orr's Island. Harriet Beecher Stowe. LC 79-18303. (Illus.). 1979. pap. 7.95 (ISBN 0-917482-18-2). Stowe-Day.

Pearl of Orr's Island: A Story of the Coast of Maine. Harriet Beecher Stowe. 437p. 1982. Repr. of 1886 ed. lib. bdg. 47.50 (ISBN 0-89984-608-4). Century Bookbindery.

Pearl Pagoda. Susannah Broome. 320p. 1982. pap. 2.95 (ISBN 0-449-24469-5, Crest). Fawcett.

Pearl Poem in Middle & Modern English. Ed. & tr. by William Vantuono. (Illus.). 140p. (Orig.). 1987. lib. bdg. 22.50 (ISBN 0-8191-5810-0); pap. text ed. 9.25 (ISBN 0-8191-5811-9). U Pr of Amer.

Pearl Poems: An Omnibus Edition. William Vantuono. LC 82-21026. 435p. 1983. lib. bdg. 75.00 (ISBN 0-8240-5450-4). Garland Pub.

Pearl Poems: An Omnibus Edition: Vol. 2: Patience & Sir Gawain & the Green Knight. William Vantuono. Ed. by Stephen Orgel. LC 82-21026. (Renaissance Imagination Ser.). 700p. 1984. lib. bdg. 80.00 (ISBN 0-8240-5451-2). Garland Pub.

Pearl-Poet. Charles Moorman. Ed. by Sylvia E. Bowman. LC 68-17243. (Twayne's English Authors Ser.). 148p. 1968. lib. bdg. 17.95 (ISBN 0-8290-1722-4). Irvington.

Pearl River in the Nineteenth Century. Laurence C. Tam. 91p. 1981. 60.00x (ISBN 0-317-68546-5, Pub. by Han-Shan Tang Ltd). State Mutual Bk.

Pearl S. Buck. Robert Cwiklik. (Great Authors Ser.). 1988. 7.95 (ISBN 0-943718-05-8). Kipling Pr.

Pearl S. Buck. rev. ed. Paul A. Doyle. (United States Authors Ser.). 1980. lib. bdg. 16.95 (ISBN 0-8057-7325-8, Twayne). G K Hall.

Pearl S. Buck's Book of Christmas. Ed. by Pearl S. Buck. 879p. 1986. lib. bdg. 19.95 (ISBN 0-8161-3975-X, Large Print Bks.). G K Hall.

Pearl Within the Shell. Dolores Dahl. LC 83-60744. (Illus.). 119p. (Orig.). 1983. pap. 7.95 (ISBN 0-9608960-1-5). Single Vision.

Pearlhanger. Jonathan Gash. 256p. 1985. 14.95 (ISBN 0-312-59970-6, J Kahn). St Martin.

Pearlhanger. Jonathan Gash. 240p. 1986. pap. 3.95 (ISBN 0-14-008468-1). Penguin.

Pearlkillers: Four Novellas. Rachel Ingalls. 1987. 15.95 (ISBN 0-671-63340-6). S&S.

Pearlkillers: Four Novellas. Rachel Ingalls. 224p. 1988. pap. 6.95 (ISBN 0-671-66240-6, Touchstone Bks). S&S.

Pearlmakers: The Tidemarsh Guide to Clams, Oysters, Mussels & Scallops. Mervin F. Roberts. (Tidemarsh Guides Ser.). 168p. 1984. pap. 6.95. Roberts M.

Pearls. Celia Brayfield. LC 87-5590. 640p. 1987. 18.95 (ISBN 0-688-06211-3). Morrow.

Pearls. C. Margaret Hall. LC 78-73516. 1979. pap. 2.25 (ISBN 0-931590-01-9). Antietam Pr.

Pearls. Shelley Smith. 160p. 1987. pap. 7.95 (ISBN 0-930044-93-2). Naiad Pr.

Pearl's Adventure. Lars Klinting. Tr. by Siv Cedering & David A. Swickar. (Illus.). 32p. (ps up). 1987. 6.95 (ISBN 91-29-56112-4, R & S Bks). FS&G.

Pearl's Adventure. Lars Klinting. Tr. by Siv Cedering & David Swickard. LC 87-45159. (Illus.). (ps-2). 1987. 6.95 (ISBN 91-29-58332-2, Pub. by R & S Bks). FS&G.

Pearls & Pepper. facsimile ed. Robert P. Utter. LC 70-152219. (Essay Index Reprint Ser). Repr. of 1924 ed. 18.00 (ISBN 0-8369-2335-9). Ayer Co Pubs.

Pearls & Pepper: (Hardy, DeFoe, Richardson) Robert P. Utter. 1924. 16.50x (ISBN 0-686-51285-5). Elliots Bks.

Pearls & Pepper: Hardy, DeFoe, Richardson. Robert P. Utter. 1924. Repr. 20.00 (ISBN 0-8274-3116-3). R West.

Pearls Are for Tears. Audrey Ellis. 352p. 1987. pap. 3.95 (ISBN 0-515-08833-1). Jove Pubns.

Pearls Before Swine. Margery Allingham. 192p. Repr. of 1945 ed. lib. bdg. 15.95x (ISBN 0-89190-196-5, Pub. by River City Pr). Amereon Ltd.

Pearls Before Swine. Ann Drysdale. 160p. 1985. 16.95 (ISBN 0-7102-0466-3). Routledge Chapman & Hall.

Pearls from My Memory Box: Very Personal Poems. 1987. 5.00. Interspace Bks.

Pearls from My Oyster. E. B. White et al. Date not set. price not set. Mainespring.

Pearls from the Prophet Ezekiel. William G. Heslop. LC 76-12081. (W. G. Heslop Bible Study Aids). 160p. 1976. pap. 4.50 (ISBN 0-8254-2832-7). Kregel.

Pearl's Holy Personal Diary, December 1970. Pearl Brians. 29p. 1988. pap. 5.00 (ISBN 1-55677-094-4). VHI Library.

Pearls in Diagnostic Radiology, Vol. 1. Harold D. Rosenbaum. (Illus.). 240p. 1980. pap. 32.50 looseleaf ed. (ISBN 0-443-08097-6). Churchill.

Pearls in the Rain. rev. ed. Ruth Seamands. 160p. 1988. pap. 5.95 (ISBN 0-917851-18-8, Bristol Bks). Forum Script.

Pearl's Kitchen. Pearl Bailey. LC 73-6624. 211p. 1973. 8.95 (ISBN 0-15-171600-5). HarBraceJ.

Pearls: Natural, Cultured & Imitation. Alexander E. Farn. (Gem Bks.). (Illus.). 180p. 1986. text ed. 29.95 (ISBN 0-408-01382-6). Butterworth.

Pearls of Consciousness. Christa F. Burka. 73p. (Orig.). 1987. pap. 5.95 (ISBN 0-914732-20-X). Bro Life Inc.

Pearls of Faith. E. Arnold. 319p. 1984. 60.00x (ISBN 0-317-39177-1, Pub. by Luzac & Co Ltd). State Mutual Bk.

Pearls of Great Price: The Wisdom of the Gospels. Gary Yamamoto. 240p. (Orig.). 1988. pap. 8.95 (ISBN 0-943173-14-0). Harbinger AZ.

Pearls of Great Price: Writings of Southeast Asians. Ed. by Gail Lando & Grace Sandness. (Illus.). 80p. 1985. pap. 6.95 (ISBN 0-931323-03-7). Mini-World Pubns.

Pearls of Love: How To Write Love Letters & Love Poems. Ara J. Movsesian. LC 84-147625. (Illus.). 294p. (Orig.). 1983. pap. 9.95 (ISBN 0-916919-00-5). Electric Pr.

Pearls of Sharah, I: Alexandra's Story. Fayrene Preston. 1989. 14.95 (ISBN 0-385-26074-1). Doubleday.

Pearls of Sharah, II: Raine's Story. Fayrene Preston. 1989. 14.95 (ISBN 0-385-26076-8, Loveswept Ser.). Doubleday.

Pearls of the Faith. A. Arnold. pap. 3.50 (ISBN 0-686-18468-8). Kazi Pubns.

Pearls of the Faith. Edwin Arnold. 368p. 1984. 250.00x (ISBN 1-85077-004-2, Pub. by Darf Pubs Ltd). State Mutual Bk.

Pearls of the Faith: Islam's Rosary. E. Arnold. pap. 3.50x (ISBN 0-87902-044-X). Orientalia.

Pearls of the Orient. Richard Manton. 1988. pap. 4.50 (ISBN 0-8216-5040-8). Blue Moon Bks.

Pearls of Wisdom: A Harvest of Gems from All Ages. Jerome Agel & Walter Glanze. LC 87-45016. 124p. 1987. pap. 7.95 (ISBN 0-06-096200-3, PL/6200, PL). Har-Row.

Pearls of Wisdom: A Prophecy of Karma, to the Earth & Her Evolutions, Vol. 23. Ed. by Elizabeth C. Prophet. LC 81-50418. 540p. 1980. 14.95 (ISBN 0-916766-41-1). Summit Univ.

Pearls of Wisdom 1965: The Mechanization Concept. Ed. by Mark Prophet & Elizabeth Prophet. LC 79-89833. 297p. 1979. 19.95 (ISBN 0-916766-48-9). Summit Univ.

Pearls of Wisdom 1968: The Master's Presence-On Consciousness, Vol. 11. Ed. by Elizabeth C. Prophet. LC 78-64502. 274p. 14.95 (ISBN 0-916766-33-0). Summit Univ.

Pearls of Wisdom 1969: Kuthumi-On Selfhood, Vol. 12. Ed. by Mark Prophet & Elizabeth Prophet. LC 79-53229. 344p. 1979. 17.95 (ISBN 0-916766-34-9). Summit Univ.

Pearls of Wisdom 1970: St. Germain-On Freedom to Create, Vol. 13. Ed. by Mark Prophet & Elizabeth C. Prophet. LC 78-60615. 258p. 15.95 (ISBN 0-916766-32-2). Summit Univ.

Pearls of Wisdom 1971: Masters of the Far East-On the Pillars of Eternity, Vol. 14. Ed. by Elizabeth C. Prophet. LC 78-60619. 246p. 14.95 (ISBN 0-916766-31-4). Summit Univ.

Pearls of Wisdom 1972: Mary the Mother-On the Temple of Understanding, Vol. 15. Ed. by Mark Prophet & Elizabeth C. Prophet. LC 75-19604. 245p. 1978. 14.95 (ISBN 0-916766-30-6). Summit Univ.

Pearls of Wisdom 1973: The Seven Chohans-On the Path of the Ascension, Vol. 16. Ed. by Elizabeth C. Prophet. LC 75-196014. 262p. 1977. 14.95 (ISBN 0-916766-28-4). Summit Univ.

Pearls of Wisdom 1974: Djwal Kul-On the Aura & the Chakras, Vol. 17. Ed. by Elizabeth C. Prophet. LC 75-19603. 264p. 1977. 13.95 (ISBN 0-916766-27-6). Summit Univ.

Pearls of Wisdom 1975: El Morya-On Discipleship East & West, Vol. 18. Ed. by Elizabeth C. Prophet. LC 79-64047. 354p. 1979. 18.95 (ISBN 0-916766-15-2). Summit Univ.

Pearls of Wisdom 1976, Vol. 19. Ed. by Elizabeth C. Prophet. LC 76-52850. 13.95 (ISBN 0-916766-24-1). Summit Univ.

Pearls of Wisdom 1977: St. Germain-On Freedom, Vol. 20. Ed. by Elizabeth C. Prophet. LC 77-91901. 280p. 1977. 15.95 (ISBN 0-916766-29-2). Summit Univ.

Pearls of Wisdom, 1978: Spoken by Elohim, Vol. 21. Ed. by Mark Prophet & Elizabeth Prophet. LC 79-66985. 513p. 1980. 14.95 (ISBN 0-916766-36-5). Summit Univ.

Pearl's Pirates. Frank Asch. LC 86-19621. (Illus.). 160p. (gr. k-3). 1987. pap. 13.95 (ISBN 0-385-29546-4). Delacorte.

Pearl's Place. Bob Graham. LC 85-47503. (Illus.). 32p. (gr. 1-5). 1985. 10.95 (ISBN 0-87226-019-4). P Bedrick Bks.

Pearl's Progress: A Novel. James Kaplan. LC 88-45440. 320p. 18.95 (ISBN 0-394-50093-8). Knopf.

Pearl's Promise. Frank Asch. LC 83-17153. (Illus.). 160p. (gr. 4-6). 1984. PLB 12.95 (ISBN 0-385-29321-6); pap. 12.95 (ISBN 0-385-29325-9). Delacorte.

Pearl's Promise. Frank Asch. 160p. (gr. 1-4). 1984. pap. 2.95 (ISBN 0-440-46863-9, YB). Dell.

Pearl's Prophetic Poetry. large print ed. Pearl Brians. 25p. 1985. pap. 4.00 (ISBN 0-914009-01-X). VHI Library.

Pearl's Song. IRma McClaurin. 91p. (Orig.). 1988. pap. 7.00 perf. bdg. (ISBN 0-916418-73-1). Lotus.

Pearls: Their Origin, Treatment & Idenification. Jean Taburiaux. LC 85-72932. 256p. 1986. 30.00 (ISBN 0-8019-7713-4). Chilton.

Pearls: Their Origin, Treatment & Identification. Jean Taburiaux. 248p. 1987. 90.00x (ISBN 0-7198-0151-6, Pub. by E Bruton Assocs Ltd UK). State Mutual Bk.

Pears from the Willow Tree. Violet D. Lannoy. LC 86-50770. 151p. (Orig.). 1989. 26.00 (ISBN 0-89410-564-7); pap. 12.00 (ISBN 0-89410-565-5). Three Continents.

Pears Round the World Quiz Book. Gyles Brandreth. (Illus.). 1979. pap. 7.95 (ISBN 0-7207-1110-X). Transatl Arts.

Pearsall Guide to Successful Dog Training. 3rd ed. Margaret Pearsall. LC 80-16840. (Illus.). 352p. 1981. 17.95 (ISBN 0-87605-759-8). Howell Bk.

Pearse & Rossa. Padraig Pearse. Ed. by Kevin T. McEneaney. (Irish Historical Pamphlet Ser.: No. 2). 15p. (Orig.). 1982. pap. 3.00 (ISBN 0-939254-04-2). At-Swim.

Peary: The Explorer & the Man. John E. Weems. (Illus.). 400p. 1988. pap. 11.95 (ISBN 0-87477-469-1). J P Tarcher.

Peasant Agriculture in Assam: A Structural Analysis. Manmohan Das. xx, 290p. 1984. 50.00x (ISBN 0-86590-322-0, Pub. by Inter-India Pubns N Delhi). Apt Bks.

Peasant & Bureaucracy in Ba'thist Syria: The Political Economy of Rural Development. Raymond Hinnebusch. (Special Study on the Middle East: No. 17). 300p. 1988. 32.00 (ISBN 0-8133-7591-6). Westview.

Peasants in Power: Alexander Stamboliski & the Bulgarian National Union, 1899-1923. J. D. Bell. 1977. 38.00x (ISBN 0-691-07584-0). Princeton U Pr.

Peasants in Revolt: A Chilean Case Study, 1965-1971. James Petras & Hugo Zemelman Merino. Tr. by Thomas Flory from Span. LC 72-1578. (Latin American Monographs: No. 28). 168p. 1972. 11.95x (ISBN 0-292-76404-9). U of Tex Pr.

Peasants in Revolt: Tenants, Landlords, Congress & the Raj in Oudh. Kapil Kumar. 1984. 22.00x (ISBN 0-8364-1221-4, Pub. by Manohar India). South Asia Bks.

Peasants in Socialist Transition: Life in a Collectivized Hungarian Village. Peter D. Bell. LC 80-25126. (Illus.). 320p. 1984. lib. bdg. 35.00x (ISBN 0-520-04157-7). U of Cal Pr.

Peasants in the Hills. Violeta Lopez-Gonzaga. 258p. 1984. (Pub. by U of Philippines Pr); pap. text ed. 10.50x (ISBN 0-8248-0902-5). UH Pr.

Peasants into Frenchmen: The Modernization of Rural France, 1870-1914. Eugen Weber. LC 75-7486. xvi, 616p. 1976. 49.50x (ISBN 0-8047-0898-3). Stanford U Pr.

Peasants, Knights & Heretics. Rodney H. Hilton. LC 76-1137. (Past & Present Publications Ser.). 320p. 1976. Cambridge U Pr.

Peasants, Landlords & Governments: Agrarian Reform in the Third World. Ed. by David Lehmann. LC 74-6091. 344p. 1974. 32.50 (ISBN 0-8419-0162-7); pap. 14.50 (ISBN 0-8419-0163-5). Holmes & Meier.

Peasants, Landlords & Merchant Capitalists: Europe & the World Economy 1500-1800. Peter Kriedte. LC 83-5141. 190p. 1984. 34.50 (ISBN 0-521-25755-7); pap. 10.95 (ISBN 0-521-27681-0). Cambridge U Pr.

Peasants of Central Russia. Stephen P. Dunn & Ethel Dunn. (Illus.). 146p. 1988. pap. text ed. 8.95x (ISBN 0-88133-317-4). Waveland Pr.

Peasants of Central Russia: Reactions to Emancipation & the Market, 1850-1900. Bob Donnorummo. Ed. by William H. McNeill & Barbara Jelavich. (Modern European History Ser.). 415p. 1987. lib. bdg. 60.00 (ISBN 0-8240-8054-8). Garland Pub.

Peasants of Costa Rica & the Rise of Agrarian Capitalism. Mitchell A. Seligson. LC 78-65015. 258p. 1980. 32.50x (ISBN 0-299-07760-8). U of Wis Pr.

Peasants of El Dorado: Conflict & Contradiction in a Peruvian Frontier Settlement. Robin Shoemaker. LC 81-9742. (Illus.). 272p. 1981. 28.50x (ISBN 0-8014-1390-7). Cornell U Pr.

Peasants of Marlhes: Economic Development & Family Organization in Nineteenth-Century France. James R. Lehning. LC 79-18707. ix, 218p. 1980. 25.00x (ISBN 0-8078-1411-3). U of NC Pr.

Peasants of the Montes: The Roots of Rural Rebellion in Spain. Michael Weisser. LC 75-43231. (Illus.). 1977. lib. bdg. 14.00x (ISBN 0-226-89158-5). U of Chicago Pr.

Peasants, Officials & Participation in Rural Tanzania: Experience with Villagization & Decentralization. Louise Fortmann. (Special Series on Rural Local Organization: No. 1). 136p. (Orig.). 1980. pap. text ed. 6.95 (ISBN 0-86731-028-6). Cornell CIS RDC.

Peasants, Politics, & Revolution: Pressures Toward Political & Social Change in the Third World. Joel S. Migdal. LC 74-2972. 368p. 1974. 38.00x (ISBN 0-691-07567-0); pap. 13.95x (ISBN 0-691-02177-5). Princeton U Pr.

Peasants, Primitives, & Proletariats: The Struggle for Identity in South America. Ed. by David L. Browman & Ronald A. Schwartz. (World Anthropology Ser.). xiv, 430p. 1980. text ed. 53.25x (ISBN 90-279-7880-8). Mouton.

Peasants, Rebels & Outcasts: The Underside of Modern Japan. Mikiso Hane. LC 81-48222. 336p. 1982. pap. 8.76 (ISBN 0-394-71040-1). Pantheon.

Peasants' Revolt. Mary Price. Ed. by Marjorie Reeves. (Then & There Ser.). (Illus.). 96p. (Orig.). (gr. 7-12). 1980. pap. text ed. 4.95 (ISBN 0-582-20164-0). Longman.

Peasants' Revolt of 1381. R. B. Dobson. 433p. 1986. (Pub. by Macmillan England); pap. text ed. 15.00x (ISBN 0-333-25505-4, Pub. by Macmillan UK). Humanities.

Peasants' Rising & the Lollards. Ed. by Edgar Powell & G. M. Trevelyan. LC 78-63202. (Heresies of the Early Christian & Medieval Era: Second Ser.). Repr. of 1899 ed. 24.00 (ISBN 0-404-16238-X). AMS Pr.

Peasants, Subsistence Ecology & Development in the Highlands of Paupa New Guinea. Lawrence C. Grossman. LC 84-42581. (Illus.). 324p. 1984. 39.00x (ISBN 0-691-09406-3). Princeton U Pr.

Peasants' War in Germany 1525-1526 see Social Side of the Reformation in Germany.

Pease Family. G. T. Ridlon. LC 76-133875. (Saco Valley Settlements Ser). 1970. pap. 1.50 (ISBN 0-8048-0821-X). C E Tuttle.

Pease Porridge Hot. Ed. by Katherine Hart. (Illus.). 1967. 10.00 (ISBN 0-88426-020-8). Encino Pr.

Peat & Water: Aspects of Water Retention & Dewatering in Peat. C. H. Fuchsman. 368p. 1986. 74.25 (ISBN 1-85166-009-7). Elsevier.

Peat As an Energy Alternative, 1st Symposium. Institute of Gas Technology Staff. 777p. 1980. 50.00 (ISBN 0-910091-36-6). Inst Gas Tech.

Peat As an Energy Alternative, 2nd Symposium. Institute of Gas Technology Staff. 800p. 1981. 75.00 (ISBN 0-910091-37-4). Inst Gas Tech.

Peat Control Strategies for the Future. National Research Council, Agricultural Board Staff. pap. 95.80 (ISBN 0-317-28680-3, 2055289). Bks Demand UMI.

Peat: Industrial Chemistry & Technology. Charles H. Fuchsman. LC 79-52791. 1980. 52.00 (ISBN 0-12-264650-9). Acad Pr.

Peat Moss & Ivy & the Birthday Present. Michael Berenstain. LC 86-611. (Picturebacks Ser.). (Illus.). 32p. (ps-2). 1986. lib. bdg. 5.99 (ISBN 0-394-97605-3, BYR); pap. 1.95 (ISBN 0-394-87605-9, BYR). Random.

Peat Moss & Ivy Meet Santa Claus. Michael Berenstain. LC 86-22029. (Picturebacks Ser.). (Illus.). 32p. (ps-1). 1987. pap. 1.95 (ISBN 0-394-88872-3, BYR). Random.

Peat Moss & Ivy's Backyard Adventure. Michael Berenstain. LC 85-43097. (Picturebacks Ser.). (Illus.). 32p. (ps-3). 1986. lib. bdg. 5.99 (ISBN 0-394-97604-5); pap. 1.95 (ISBN 0-394-87604-0). Random.

Peat Stratigraphy & Climatic Change. K. E. Barber. 242p. 1981. text ed. 53.50 (ISBN 90-6191-087-0, Pub. by A A Balkema). Brookfield Pub Co.

Peau de Chagrin. Honore De Balzac. (Coll. GF). 1960. pap. 9.95 (ISBN 0-685-11483-X, 1701). French & Eur.

Peau de Chagrin. Honore De Balzac. Ed. by Allem. (Class. Garnier). pap. 29.95 (ISBN 0-685-34091-0). French & Eur.

Peau de l'Homme. Pierre Reverdy. 220p. 1968. 9.95 (ISBN 0-686-54728-4). French & Eur.

Peau Noire, Masques Blancs. Frantz Fanon. (Coll. La Condition Humaine). 8.95 (ISBN 0-685-35936-0). French & Eur.

Peau Noire, Masques Blancs. Frantz Fanon. (Coll. Points). pap. 9.95 (ISBN 0-685-35937-9). French & Eur.

Pebble in the Sky. Isaac Asimov. LC 81-15516. 224p. 1982. Repr. of 1950 ed. 12.50x (ISBN 0-8376-0462-1). Bentley.

Pebble of Gibraltar. Ellen Corby. Date not set. 13.95 (ISBN 0-533-07623-4). Vantage.

Pebble Ring. Napoleon St. Cyr. 1966. 3.00 (ISBN 0-910380-00-7). Cider Mill.

Pebble Rings. Judy Ray. 64p. 1980. pap. 3.00 (ISBN 0-912678-42-9). Greenfld Rev Pr.

Pebble Searcher. David H. Steele. 16p. (gr. 7-10). 1986. 12.00X (ISBN 0-317-52595-6, Pub. by A H Stockwell England). State Mutual Bk.

Pebbled Shore: The Memoirs of Elizabeth Longford. Elizabeth Longford. LC 86-45465. 352p. 1986. 19.45 (ISBN 0-394-53764-5). Knopf.

Pebbles & Bamm-Bamm & with Witch Who Ran out of Jizzle. (Illus.). (gr. k-9). 1988. pap. 0.95. Scholastic Inc.

Pebbles & Sand. Louis Newman. LC 77-99935. (Illus.). 5.00 (ISBN 0-685-12169-0); pap. 3.00 (ISBN 0-912292-12-1). The Smith.

Pebbles in the Wind. Jean V. Baldner. (Illus.). 52p. (Orig.). (YA) (gr. 7 up). pap. 5.95 (ISBN 0-9615317-0-3). Baldner J V.

Pebbles of the Bloody War. Frank Omilion. 272p. 1987. 14.50 (ISBN 0-8062-3160-2). Carlton.

Pebbles on the Shore. Alfred G. Gardiner. LC 78-108700. (Essay & General Literature Index Reprint Ser.). 1970. Repr. of 1916 ed. 26.50x (ISBN 0-8046-0921-7, Pub. by Kennikat). Assoc Faculty Pr.

Pebbles to Computers: The Thread. Hans Blohm et al. (Illus.). 112p. 1987. 21.95 (ISBN 0-19-540536-6). Oxford U Pr.

Pecado Despues de la Conversion. 2nd ed. Algernon J. Pollock & Gordon H. Bennett. Tr. by Sara Bautista from Eng. (Serie Diamante). (Illus.). 36p. (Span.). 1982. pap. 0.85 (ISBN 0-942504-04-6). Overcomer Pr.

Pecadora (Seleccion de Poesias) Olga Rosado. LC 80-68759. 66p. (Orig., Span.). 1984. pap. 5.00 (ISBN 0-89729-268-5). Ediciones.

Pecados en Pandilla. Abel Perez. (Pimienta Collection Ser). (Span.). 1977. pap. 1.00 (ISBN 0-88473-261-4). Fiesta Pub.

Pecan Lovers' Cook Book. Mark Blazek. 120p. (Orig.). 1986. pap. 5.00 (ISBN 0-914846-27-2). Golden West Pub.

Pecans: From Soup to Nuts. Keith Courrege. LC 84-70931. (Illus.). 54p. 1984. pap. 5.95 (ISBN 0-9613404-0-1). Cane River.

Peccaries. Lyle K. Sowls. LC 84-8619. 251p. 1984. 29.95x (ISBN 0-8165-0822-4). U of Ariz Pr.

Peccary: With Observations on the Introduction of Pigs to the New World. R. A. Donkin. LC 84-45906. (Transactions Ser.: Vol. 75 Pt. 5). 150p. 1985. 25.00 (ISBN 0-87169-755-6). Am Philos.

Peche de l'Ange. Jacques Maritain. Ed. by De La Trinite & Journet. 248p. 1961. 19.95 (ISBN 0-686-56360-3). French & Eur.

Pecheur d'Islande. Pierre Loti, pseud. (Coll. Bleue). 21.50 (ISBN 0-685-34265-4). French & Eur.

Pecheur du Soquet see Oeuvres Completes.

Peckerneck Country. Walt Curtis. 1978. 2.50 (ISBN 0-932191-05-3). Mr Cogito Pr.

Peckham Experiment. Innes H. Pearse & Lucy H. Crocker. (Illus.). 362p. 1985. pap. 7.50 (ISBN 0-7073-0483-0, Pub. by Scot Acad Pr). Longwood Pub Group.

Peckham's Marbles. Peter De Vries. 256p. 1986. 17.95 (ISBN 0-399-13188-4, Putnam). Putnam Pub Group.

Peckham's Marbles. Peter De Vries. (Paperbacks Ser.). 256p. 1987. pap. text ed. 4.95 (ISBN 0-07-016650-1). McGraw.

Pecking Order. Mark Kennedy. LC 73-18561. Repr. of 1953 ed. 21.45 (ISBN 0-404-11374-5). AMS Pr.

Peckinpah: A Portrait in Montage. Garner Simmons. (Illus.). 308p. 1982. pap. 8.95 (ISBN 0-292-76493-6). U of Tex Pr.

Peckinpah: The Western Films. Paul Seydor. LC 79-22208. (Illus.). 324p. 1980. 19.95 (ISBN 0-252-00738-7). U of Ill Pr.

Peckinpaw's Florida Fourth of July. G. Blair Scott. (Illus.). 32p. (Orig.). (ps-5). 1985. pap. text ed. write for info. (ISBN 0-932827-14-4). Cracker Bks Pub.

Peckover Holds the Baby. Michael Kenyon. LC 87-22278. (Crime Club Ser.). 192p. 1988. 12.95 (ISBN 0-385-24324-3). Doubleday.

Peckover Holds the Baby. Michael Kenyon. 1988. pap. 3.50 (ISBN 0-380-70636-9). Avon.

Peck's Beach: A Pictorial History of Ocean City, New Jersey. Tim Cain. Ed. by Gail Travers. (Illus.). 96p. (Orig.). 1988. text ed. 23.00 (ISBN 0-945582-04-8); pap. 16.95 (ISBN 0-945582-00-5). Down the Shore Pub.

Pecos: A History of the Pioneer West, Vol. I. Alton Hughes. LC 78-61694. (Illus.). 416p. 1978. 14.95 (ISBN 0-933512-28-7). Pioneer Bk Tx.

Pecos Bill. Ariane Dewey. LC 82-9229. (Illus.). 56p. (gr. k-3). 1983. PLB 10.88 (ISBN 0-688-01412-7). Greenwillow.

Pecos Bill. As told by Brian Gleeson. LC 88-11581. (Illus.). 36p. (ps up). 1988. 14.95 (ISBN 0-88708-081-2); bk. & cass. pkg. 19.95 (ISBN 0-88708-086-3). Picture Bk Studio.

Pecos Bill. Steven Kellogg. LC 86-784. (Illus.). 32p. (ps up). 1986. 13.00 (ISBN 0-688-05871-X, Morrow Junior Books); lib. bdg. 12.88 (ISBN 0-688-05872-8, Morrow Junior Books). Morrow.

Pecos Bill. Steven Kellogg. 40p. (gr. k-3). 1987. pap. 2.95 (ISBN 0-590-41110-1). Scholastic Inc.

Pecos Bill. Nanci A. Lyman. LC 79-66319. (Illus.). 48p. (gr. 3-6). 1980. lib. bdg. 9.59 (ISBN 0-89375-308-4); pap. 1.95 (ISBN 0-89375-307-6). Troll Assocs.

Pecos Bill. Retold by Patrick McGrath. (American Folk Tales Series, Part of the First Reader Ser.). (Illus.). 24p. (gr. 6 up). 1988. 8.95 (ISBN 0-943718-15-5). Kipling Pr.

Pecos Bill & the Wonderful Clothesline Snake. Wyatt Blassingame. LC 77-17972. (American Folktales Ser.). (Illus.). (gr. 2-5). 1978. PLB 6.69 (ISBN 0-8116-4046-9). Garrard.

Pecos Bill Catches a Hidebehind. Wyatt Blassingame. LC 76-23336. (American Folktales Ser.). (Illus.). (gr. 2-5). 1977. PLB 6.69 (ISBN 0-8116-4045-0). Garrard.

Pecos Bill Finds a Horse. Kathy Darling. LC 79-12079. (American Folktales Ser.). (Illus.). (gr. 2-5). 1979. PLB 6.69 (ISBN 0-8116-4047-7). Garrard.

Pecos Bill Rides a Tornado. Wyatt Blassingame. LC 73-5894. (American Folktales Ser.). (Illus.). (gr. 2-5). 1973. PLB 6.69 (ISBN 0-8116-4038-8). Garrard.

Pecos Blood. Erie Adkins. 224p. 1987. pap. 2.50 (ISBN 0-8217-2101-1). Zebra.

Pecos Dollars. J. T. Hardin. 192p. 1984. pap. 2.50 (ISBN 0-425-07259-2). Berkley Pub.

Pecos, New Mexico: Archaeological Notes, Vol. 5. A. Kidder. LC 58-4944. 1958. 12.50 (ISBN 0-939312-06-9). Peabody Found.

Pecos to Rio Grande: Interpretations of Far West Texas by Eighteen Artists. Ron Tyler. LC 83-45105. (Joe & Betty Moore Texas Art Ser.: No. 6). (Illus.). 130p. 1983. 29.95 (ISBN 0-89096-166-2). Tex A&M Univ Pr.

Pecos Wilderness Trails for Day Walkers. Carl Overhage. LC 84-81032. 1984. pap. 3.95 (ISBN 0-88307-663-2). Gannon.

Pectic Substances in the Cell Wall & the Intercellular Cohesion of Potato Tuber Tissue During Cooking. M. J. Keijbets. (Agricultural Research Reports: No. 827). (Illus.). viii, 161p. 1975. pap. 22.00 (ISBN 90-220-0536-4, PDC64, PUDOC). UNIPUB.

Pectinesterases from the Orange Fruit: Their Purification, General Characteristics & Juice Cloud Destablizing Properties. 1979. pap. 16.00 (ISBN 90-220-0709-X, PDC147, Pudoc). UNIPUB.

Pectinesterases From the Orange Fruit: Their Purification, General Characteristics & Juice Cloud Destablizing Properties. C. Versteeg. 109p. 1979. pap. 16.00 (PDC147, Pudoc). UNIPUB.

Peculiar: A Tale of the Great Transition. Epes Sargent. LC 72-2121. (Black Heritage Library Collection Ser.). Repr. of 1863 ed. 26.50 (ISBN 0-8369-9061-7). Ayer Co Pubs.

Peculiar Characteristics of Egyptian & Assyrian Architecture. James G. Fielding. (Illus.). 147p. 1988. 137.45 (ISBN 0-86650-239-4). Gloucester Art.

Peculiar Essence of Chinese Philosophy. Roger Passarieck. (Illus.). 159p. 1982. 117.75 (ISBN 0-89266-329-4). Am Classical Coll Pr.

Peculiar Institution. Kenneth M. Stampp. 1956. 17.45 (ISBN 0-394-44015-3). Knopf.

Peculiar Institution. Kenneth M. Stampp. 1964. pap. 6.95 (ISBN 0-394-70253-0, Vin). Random.

Peculiar Kind of Politics: Canada's Overseas Ministry in the First World War. Desmond Morton. 280p. 1982. 25.00x (ISBN 0-8020-5586-9). U of Toronto Pr.

Peculiar Language: Literature as Difference from the Renaissance to James Joyce. Derek Attridge. LC 87-19060. (Paperback Ser.). 288p. 1988. 34.50x (ISBN 0-8014-2057-1); pap. 9.95x (ISBN 0-8014-9407-9). Cornell U Pr.

Peculiar Mission of a Friends School. Douglas H. Heath. LC 79-84919. 1979. pap. 2.50x (ISBN 0-87574-225-4). Pendle Hill.

Peculiar Mystical Rites of Ancient Peoples. Alexander Wilder. (Illus.). 269p. 1984. 117.85x (ISBN 0-89266-451-7). AM Classical Coll Pr.

Peculiar Paradise: A History of Blacks in Oregon, 1788-1940. Elizabeth McLagan. LC 80-52573. (Illus.). 1980. pap. 7.50 (ISBN 0-9603408-2-3). Georgian Pr.

Peculiar People. Mark Sorrell. (Illus.). 168p. 1979. text ed. 21.00 (ISBN 0-85364-263-X). Attic Pr.

Peculiar People: Iowa's Old Order Amish. Elmer Schwieder & Dorothy Schwieder. (Iowa's Heritage Collection). (Illus.). 188p. 1987. pap. 4.95 (ISBN 0-8138-0104-4). Iowa St U Pr.

Peculiar People: Slave Religion & Community Culture among the Gullah. Margaret W. Creel. (American Social Experience Ser.: No. 7). (Illus.). 416p. 1987. 40.00x (ISBN 0-8147-1404-8). NYU Pr.

Peculiar People: Slave Religion & Community-Culture among the Gullahs. Margaret W. Creel. (American Social Experience Ser.: No. 7). (Illus.). 417p. 1989. pap. 15.00 (ISBN 0-8147-1422-6). NYU Pr.

Peculiar People, the Dukhobors. Aylmer Maude. LC 72-131033. Repr. of 1904 ed. 24.50 (ISBN 0-404-04275-9). AMS Pr.

Peculiar Piece of Desert: The Story of California's Morongo Basin. Lulu R. O'Neal. LC 81-50577. (Illus.). 1981. wrappers 8.95 (ISBN 0-930704-06-1). Sagebrush Pr.

Peculiar Problem of Taxing Life Insurance Companies. Henry J. Aaron. LC 83-70788. (Studies of Government Finance). 46p. 1983. pap. 7.95 (ISBN 0-8157-0031-8). Brookings.

Peculiar Psychology of Inventors & Money Makers. F. W. Taussig. (Study of the Research Center for Economic Psychology). (Illus.). 122p. 1983. 127.75 (ISBN 0-89920-061-3). Am Inst Psych.

Peculiar Treasures: A Biblical Who's Who. Frederick Buechner. Tr. by Katherine A. Buechner. LC 78-20586. 1979. 13.95 (ISBN 0-06-061157-X, HarpR). Har-Row.

Peculiarities & Characteristics of Renaissance Architecture, 2 vols. Charles H. Moore. (Illus.). 297p. 1986. Repr. of 1909 ed. Set. 187.75. Found Class Reprints.

Peculiarities of German History: Bourgeois Society & Politics in 19th Century Germany. David Blackbourn & Geof Eley. 1984. pap. 13.95x (ISBN 0-19-873057-8). Oxford U Pr.

Pedagogia Fructifera. Findley B. Edge. Tr. by Alberto Lopez from Eng. 192p. (Span.). 1985. pap. 3.95 (ISBN 0-311-11025-8). Casa Bautista.

Pedagogia Ilustrada: El Grupo de Discusion. Using Problem Solving in Teaching & Training, Tomo 3. LeRoy Ford. (Illus.). 132p. 1986. pap. 3.95 (ISBN 0-311-11040-1). Casa Bautista.

Pedagogia Ilustrada: La Conferencia en la Ensenanza, Tomo 2. Leroy Ford. Orig. Title: Using the Lecture in Teaching & Training. (Illus.). 136p. (Span.). 1985. pap. 3.95 (ISBN 0-311-11027-4). Casa Bautista.

Pedagogia Ilustrada: Tomo I Principios Generales. Leroy Ford. Orig. Title: Primer for Teachers & Leaders. (Illus.). 144p. 1985. pap. 3.95 (ISBN 0-311-11001-0, Edit Mundo). Casa Bautista.

Pedagogical Anthropology, 3 vols. Maria Montessori. (Illus.). 517p. 1984. 227.75 (ISBN 0-89901-160-8). Found Class Reprints.

Pedagogical Discussions see For the Teaching of Mathematics.

Pedagogical Grammar of Hawaiian: Recurrent Problems. Emily A. Hawkins. 205p. 1982. pap. text ed. 6.00x (ISBN 0-8248-0812-6). UH Pr.

Pedagogical Imperative: Teaching as a Literary Genre. Yale French Studies Staff. Ed. by Barbara Johnson. (Yale French Studies Ser.: No. 63). 320p. (Orig.). 1982. pap. text ed. 13.95x (ISBN 0-300-02856-3). Yale U Pr.

Pedagogical Prognosis: Predicting the Success of Prospective Teachers. Grover T. Somers. LC 75-177758. (Columbia University. Teachers College. Contributions to Education: No. 140). Repr. of 1923 ed. 22.50 (ISBN 0-404-55140-8). AMS Pr.

Pedagogical Sketchbook. Paul Klee. (Illus.). 64p. 1968. pap. 5.95 (ISBN 0-571-08618-7). Faber & Faber.

Pedagogical Staff Development in Higher Education. R. S. Adams & D. Battersby. 107p. (Orig.). 1987. pap. text ed. 12.50 (ISBN 0-317-67233-9, UB359, UB). UNIPUB.

Pedagogie et Education: Evolution Des Ides & Des Pratiques Contemporaines. Michel Salines. (Savoir Historique: No. 3). 1972. pap. 14.40x (ISBN 90-2797-135-8). Mouton.

Pedagogie Scientifique, 3 tomes. Montessori. Set. 99.95 (ISBN 0-685-33998-X). French & Eur.

Pediatric Medicine. Mary E. Avery. (Illus.). 2000p. 1988. 75.00 (ISBN 0-683-00294-5). Williams & Wilkins.

Pediatric Nephrology. 2nd ed. Ed. by Malcolm Holliday. (Illus.). 1248p. 1987. 116.95 (ISBN 0-683-04101-0). Williams & Wilkins.

Pediatric Nephrology. Rodrigo E. Urizar & Jill A. Largent. (New Directions in Therapy Ser.). 1983. text ed. 63.75 (ISBN 0-87488-846-8). Med Exam.

Pediatric Nephrology: Proceedings, No. 3. Pediatric Nephrology, International, 5th, Symposium, 1980. Ed. by Alan B. Gruskin & Michael E. Norman. 530p. 1981. 69.50 (ISBN 90-247-2514-3, Pub. by Martinus Nijhoff Netherlands). Kluwer Academic.

Pediatric Neurologic Physical Therapy. Ed. by Suzann K. Campbell. (Clinics in Physical Therapy Ser.: Vol. 5). (Illus.). 448p. 1984. text ed. 32.00 (ISBN 0-443-08241-3). Churchill.

Pediatric Neurological Surgery. Ed. by Mark S. O'Brien. LC 78-3005. (Seminars in Neurological Surgery Ser.). 216p. 1978. 48.00 (ISBN 0-89004-178-4). Raven.

Pediatric Neurology. Marvin A. Fishman. 368p. 1986. 49.50 (ISBN 0-8089-1786-2, 791271). Grune.

Pediatric Neurology & Neuroradiology. C. Diebler & O. Dulac. (Illus.). 430p. 1987. 165.00 (ISBN 0-387-15325-X). Springer-Verlag.

Pediatric Neurology Case Studies. 2nd ed. Kenneth F. Swaiman & Stephen Ashwal. LC 84-493. (Case Study Ser.: Vol. 29). 1984. pap. text ed. 47.50 (ISBN 0-87488-071-8). Med Exam.

Pediatric Neurology for the House Officer. 2nd ed. Howard L. Weiner et al. (H.O. Ser.). (Illus.). 228p. 1982. pap. text ed. 14.95 (ISBN 0-683-08903-X). Williams & Wilkins.

Pediatric Neuropsychology. Hynd & Willis. 1987. price not set (ISBN 0-8089-1890-7). Grune.

Pediatric Neuropsychology: Surgery of the Developing Nervous System. Ed. by Robert L. McLaurin. 795p. 1982. 145.00 (ISBN 0-8089-1490-1, 792846). Grune.

Pediatric Neuroradiology. Altman & Altman. 350p. 1989. 75.00 (ISBN 0-8016-0154-1). Mosby.

Pediatric Neuroradiology. Anthony J. Raimondi. LC 74-186953. (Illus.). Repr. of 1972 ed. 160.00 (ISBN 0-8357-9552-7, 2016676). Bks Demand UMI.

Pediatric Neurosurgery. Leslie P. Ivan & H. Hugenholtz. (Illus.). 384p. 1988. 45.00 (ISBN 0-87527-352-1). Green.

Pediatric Neurosurgery. A. J. Raimondi. (Illus.). 550p. 1987. 290.00 (ISBN 0-387-96408-8). Springer-Verlag.

Pediatric Neurosurgery: Proceedings. Congress of the European Society for Pediatric Neurosurgery, 5th, Stresa, September-October 1976. Ed. by R. Villani & M. Giovanelli. (Modern Problems in Peadiatrics: Vol. 18). (Illus.). 1977. 93.50 (ISBN 3-8055-2668-7). S Karger.

Pediatric Neurosurgery: Surgery of the Developing Nervous System. 2nd ed. McLaurin et al. 848p. 1988. price not set (ISBN 0-7216-2748-X). Saunders.

Pediatric Nuclear Medicine. Ed. by Leonard M. Freeman & M. Donald Blaufox. 224p. 1975. 57.50 (ISBN 0-8089-0920-7, 7913-70). Grune.

Pediatric Nuclear Medicine. Ed. by Alton E. James et al. LC 72-97912. (Illus.). pap. 140.00 (ISBN 0-317-07923-9, 2016667). Bks Demand UMI.

Pediatric Nuclear Medicine. S. T. Treves. (Illus.). 360p. 1985. 90.00 (ISBN 0-387-96001-5). Springer-Verlag.

Pediatric Nurse & the Life-Threatened Child. Ed. by Penelope Buschman et al. (Current Thanatology Ser.). 100p. 1985. pap. 13.95 (ISBN 0-930194-39-X). Ctr Thanatology.

Pediatric Nurse Practitioner. Jack Rudman. (Certified Nurse Examination Ser.: CN-8). 25.95 (ISBN 0-8373-6158-3); pap. 13.95 (ISBN 0-8373-6108-7). Natl Learning.

Pediatric Nursing. Patricia A Lesner. LC 81-82910. (Illus.). 544p. (Orig.). 1982. pap. text ed. 25.95 (ISBN 0-8273-1932-0); instr's. guide 5.00 (ISBN 0-8273-1933-9). Delmar.

Pediatric Nursing. Janice Selekman. LC 87-18079. (Notes Ser.). 144p. 1988. pap. 9.95 (ISBN 0-87434-109-4). Springhouse Pub.

Pediatric Nursing: An Introductory Text. 5th ed. Eleanor D. Thompson. (Illus.). 624p. 1987. pap. 20.95 (ISBN 0-7216-1807-3). Saunders.

Pediatric Nursing Policies, Procedures, & Personnel. Eileen M. Sporing et al. 264p. 1984. pap. 26.95 (ISBN 0-87489-339-9). Med Economics.

Pediatric Nursing Skills Manual. Betty J. Whitson & Judith McFarlane. LC 79-27079. 304p. 1980. pap. 13.95 (ISBN 0-471-04511-X, Pub. by Wiley Med). Wiley.

Pediatric Nutrition. Ed. by G. C. Arneil & J. Metcoff. (BIMR Pediatrics Ser.: Vol. 3). 320p. 1985. text ed. 75.00 (ISBN 0-407-02310-0). Butterworth.

Pediatric Nutrition Criteria Sets. The American Dietetic Association Staff. (Orig.). 1988. pap. text ed. price not set (ISBN 0-88091-039-9). Am Dietetic Assn.

Pediatric Nutrition Handbook. 2nd ed. American Academy of Pediatrics, Committee on Nutrition Staff. LC 85-70202. 421p. 1985. pap. text ed. 20.00 (ISBN 0-910761-06-X). AM Acad Pediat.

Pediatric Nutrition in Clinical Practice. MacLean. (Illus.). 300p. 1984. write for info. Addison-Wesley.

Pediatric Nutrition in Developmental Disorders. Sushma Palmer & Shirley Ekvall. (Illus.). 640p. 1978. 71.25 (ISBN 0-398-03652-7). C C Thomas.

Pediatric Nutrition: Infant Feedings-Deficiencies-Diseases. Ed. by Fima Lifshitz. (Clinical Disorders in Pediatric Nutrition Ser.: Vol. 2). (Illus.). 648p. 1982. 75.00 (ISBN 0-8247-1430-X). Dekker.

Pediatric Nutrition: Theory & Practice. Ed. by Richard J. Grand et al. (Illus.). 1024p. 1987. text ed. 90.00 (ISBN 0-409-95111-0). Butterworth.

Pediatric Oncology. Philip Lanzkowsky. (Illus.). 576p. 1983. text ed. 55.00 (ISBN 0-07-036341-2). McGraw.

Pediatric Oncology. Ed. by C. R. Raybaud et al. (International Congress Ser.: Vol. 570). 408p. 1982. 120.75 (ISBN 0-444-90247-3, Excerpta Medica). Elsevier.

Pediatric Oncology & Hematology: Perspectives in Care. Hockenberry. 1986. 33.95 (ISBN 0-8016-2253-0). Mosby.

Pediatric Oncology One. Ed. by G. Bennett Humphrey & Louis P. Dehner. 1982. 44.50 (ISBN 90-247-2408-2, Pub. by Martinus Nijhoff Netherlands). Kluwer Academic.

Pediatric Ophthalmology, 2 vols. Ed. by Robinson D. Harley. LC 80-50561. 1983. Vol. 1. text ed. 125.00 (ISBN 0-7216-4514-3); Vol. 2. text ed. 125.00 (ISBN 0-7216-4515-1); Set. text ed. 240.00 (ISBN 0-7216-4526-7). Saunders.

Pediatric Ophthalmology. Leonard B. Nelson. (Major Problems in Clinical Pediatrics Ser.: Vol. 25). (Illus.). 288p. 1984. 48.95 (ISBN 0-7216-1191-5). Saunders.

Pediatric Ophthalmology & Strabismus. Ed. by New Orleans Academy of Ophthalmology Staff. (Transactions of the New Orleans Academy of Ophthalmology Ser.). (Illus.). 560p. 1986. text ed. 94.00 (ISBN 0-88167-164-9). Raven.

Pediatric Opthalmology. Ed. by Kenneth Wybar & David Taylor. (Illus.). 512p. 1983. 85.00 (ISBN 0-8247-1841-0). Dekker.

Pediatric Opthalmology Practice. 2nd ed. Eugene M. Helveston & Forrest D. Ellis. LC 83-8255. (Illus.). 350p. 1983. 57.00 (ISBN 0-8016-2143-7). Mosby.

Pediatric Optometry. Jerome Rosner. (Illus.). 458p. 1982. text ed. 47.95 (ISBN 0-409-95014-9). Butterworth.

Pediatric Orthopaedics, 2 Vol. Set. 2nd ed. Wood W. Lovell & Robert B. Winter. (Illus.). 1200p. 1985. text ed. 149.00 (ISBN 0-397-50706-2, Lippincott Medical). Lippincott.

Pediatric Orthopaedics. Thomas S. Renshaw. (Major Problems in Clinical Pediatric Ser.). (Illus.). 3277p. 1981. 30.95 (ISBN 0-7216-1179-6). Saunders.

Pediatric Orthopedic Radiology. M. B. Ozonoff. LC 76-54040. (Monographs in Clinical Radiology: Vol. 15). (Illus.). 1979. text ed. write for info. (ISBN 0-7216-7034-2). Saunders.

Pediatric Orthopedics, 2 vols. Mihran O. Tachdjian. LC 71-103571. (Illus.). 1972. Vol. 1. 83.95 (ISBN 0-7216-8730-X); Vol. 2. 83.95 (ISBN 0-7216-8731-8). Saunders.

Pediatric Orthopedics in Clinical Practice. Scoles. 1982. 52.50 (ISBN 0-8151-7583-3). Year Bk Med.

Pediatric Orthopedics in Clinical Practice. Scoles. 1988. 39.95 (ISBN 0-8151-7585-X). Year Bk Med.

Pediatric Orthopedics of the Lower Extremity: An Instructional Handbook. John D. McCrea. (Illus.). 360p. 1984. 42.50 (ISBN 0-87993-230-9). Futura Pub.

Pediatric Otalaryngology, 2 Vols. Ed. by Charles D. Bluestone. Sylvan F. Stool. (Illus.). 1728p. 1983. Vol. 1. 125.00 (ISBN 0-7216-1761-1); Vol. 2. 125.00 (ISBN 0-7216-1762-X); Two Vol. Set. 235.00 (ISBN 0-7216-1758-1). Saunders.

Pediatric Otolaryngology Case Studies. 2nd ed. Ed. by W. Frederick McGuirt. LC 84-492. 1984. pap. text ed. 47.50 (ISBN 0-87488-085-8). Med Exam.

Pediatric Otology. Ed. by C. Cremers & G. Hogland. (Advances in Oto-Rhino-Laryngology Ser.: Vol. 40). (Illus.). viii, 168p. 1988. 99.50 (ISBN 3-8055-4726-9). S Karger.

Pediatric Otorhinolaryngology. Ed. by B. Jazbi. (Advances in ORL: Vol. 23). (Illus.). 1978. 64.75 (ISBN 3-8055-2674-1). S Karger.

Pediatric Otorhinolaryngology. Ed. by B. Jazbi. (International Congress Ser.: Vol. 509). 288p. 1980. 82.00 (ISBN 0-444-90115-9, Excerpta Medica). Elsevier.

Pediatric Pathology. J. Thomas Stocker et al. LC 65-10648. (Illus.). 1200p. 1989. price not set (Lippincott Medical). Lippincott.

Pediatric Pathophysiology. Mohsen Ziai & A. R. Colon. 555p. 1985. text ed. 64.00 (ISBN 0-316-98755-7). Little.

Pediatric Pharmacology: Therapeutic Principles in Practice. Ed. by Sumner J. Yaffe. (Illus.). 493p. 1980. 69.50 (ISBN 0-8089-1251-8, 794942). Grune.

Pediatric Physical Diagnosis. Balu M. Athreya & Benjamin K. Silverman. 352p. 1985. 34.95 (ISBN 0-8385-7797-0). Appleton & Lange.

Pediatric Physical Therapy: An Anthology. 1981. pap. 7.00 (ISBN 0-912452-30-7). Am Phys Therapy Assn.

Pediatric Plastic Surgery. Donald Serafin & Nicholas G. Georgiade. (Illus.). 1500p. 1984. 155.00 (ISBN 0-8016-4491-7). Mosby.

Pediatric Play Program: Developing a Therapeutic Play Program for Children in Medical Settings. Pat Azarnoff & Sharon Flegal. (Illus.). 112p. 1980. spiral bdg. 14.25x (ISBN 0-398-03272-6). C C Thomas.

Pediatric Policy & Procedure Manual. Linda Black. LC 79-19681. 1980. pap. 9.50 (ISBN 0-87125-060-8). Cath Health.

Pediatric Primary Care. 3rd ed. Catherine DeAngelis. 1984. write for info. (ISBN 0-316-17783-0). Scott F.

Pediatric Procedures. 2nd ed. Walter T. Hughes & E. Stephen Buescher. (Illus.). 400p. 1980. text ed. write for info. (ISBN 0-7216-4826-6). Saunders.

Pediatric Psychiatry. Hale F. Shirley. LC 63-19147. (Commonwealth Fund Publications Ser). 1963. 52.00x (ISBN 0-674-65950-3). Harvard U Pr.

Pediatric Psychologist: Issues in Professional Development & Practice. Lizette Peterson & Cynthia Harbeck. (Health Psychology Ser.). 250p. (Orig.). 1988. pap. text ed. price not set (ISBN 0-87822-296-0). Res Press.

Pediatric Psychology: An Introduction for Pediatricians & Psychologists. John V. Lavigne & William J. Burns. 375p. 1981. 46.50 (ISBN 0-8089-1365-4, 792451). Grune.

Pediatric Psychology: Psychological Interventions & Strategies for Pediatric Problems. Micheal C. Roberts. (Psychology Practitioner Guidebooks). (Illus.). 128p. 1986. text ed. 22.50 (ISBN 0-08-032412-6, J115, PBII); pap. text ed. 12.95 (ISBN 0-08-032411-8, PBI). Pergamon.

Pediatric Psychopharmacology: A Practical Guide to Clinical Application. James White. 238p. (Orig.). 1977. pap. 17.50 (ISBN 0-683-09006-2, WW). Krieger.

Pediatric Pulmonary Disease. J. Thomas Stocker. (Aspen Seminars in Pediatric Disease Ser.). 300p. 1988. 45.00 (ISBN 0-89116-830-3). Hemisphere Pub.

Pediatric Radiographic Interpretation. Charles Dixter et al. LC 79-67303. (Exercises in Dental Radiology Ser.: Vol. 3). (Illus.). 271p. 1980. pap. write for info. (ISBN 0-7216-3095-2). Saunders.

Pediatric Radiology. 3rd ed. Alan E. Oestreich. (Medical Outline Ser.: Vol. 16). 1984. pap. text ed. 39.25. Med Exam.

Pediatric Radiology Exercises. Dox. 1986. write for info. (ISBN 0-471-84838-7). Wiley.

Pediatric Rehabilitation. Gabriella E. Molnar. (RML Ser.). (Illus.). 490p. 1985. 39.50 (ISBN 0-683-06117-8). Williams & Wilkins.

Pediatric Respiratory Disorders: Clinical Approaches. Ed. by Eliezer Nussbaum. Stanley P. Galant. 304p. 1983. 46.50 (ISBN 0-8089-1571-1, 793145). Grune.

Pediatric Respiratory Therapy: An Introductory Text. N. Balfour Slonim & Scott N. Schneider. LC 73-85533. pap. 56.00 (ISBN 0-317-29900-X, 2021838). Bks Demand UMI.

Pediatric Rheumatology for the Practitioner. J. C. Jacobs. (Comprehensive Manuals in Pediatrics). (Illus.). 556p. 1982. 65.00 (ISBN 0-387-90671-1). Springer-Verlag.

Pediatric Risk Factors for Major Chronic Disease. Christine L. Williams. 173p. 1984. 22.50. Green.

Pediatric Sonoencephalography. Abbas Mostafawy. LC 71-148261. (Illus.). 1971. 67.90 (ISBN 0-387-05216-X). Springer-Verlag.

Pediatric Spine. David S. Bradford & Robert Hensinger. (Illus.). 544p. 1985. text ed. 89.00 (ISBN 0-86577-126-X). Thieme Med Pubs.

Pediatric Sports Medicine. Ed. by Dov. B. Nudel. 442p. 1988. 55.00 (ISBN 0-89335-305-1). PMA Pub Corp.

Pediatric Sports Medicine for the Practitioner: From Physiologic Principles to Clinical Applications. O. Bar. (Comprehensive Manuals in Pediatrics). (Illus.). 350p. 1983. 45.00 (ISBN 0-387-90873-0). Springer-Verlag.

Pediatric Surgery. Thomas M. Holder & Keith W. Ashcraft. LC 78-54513. (Illus.). 1200p. 1980. text ed. write for info. (ISBN 0-7216-4737-5). Saunders.

Pediatric Surgery. 4th ed. Lewis Spitz & H. H. Nixon. (Rob & Smith's Operative Surgery Ser.). 500p. 1988. text ed. price not set (ISBN 0-407-00666-4). Butterworth.

Pediatric Surgical Oncology. Ed. by Daniel M. Hays. 352p. 1986. 64.50 (ISBN 0-8089-1782-X, 791947). Grune.

Pediatric Surgical Pathology. 2nd ed. Louis Dehner. (Illus.). 1152p. 1987. 164.50 (ISBN 0-683-02425-6). Williams & Wilkins.

Pediatric Telephone Advice. Barton D. Schmitt. 1980. 19.50 (ISBN 0-316-77386-7). Little.

Pediatric Thyroidology. Ed. by F. Delange et al. (Pediatric & Adolescent Endocrinology Ser.: Vol. 14). (Illus.). x, 412p. 1985. 183.50 (ISBN 3-8055-3968-1). S Karger.

Pediatric Trauma. Touloukian. (Illus.). 750p. 1989. 79.50 (ISBN 0-8016-5067-4). Mosby.

Pediatric Trauma. R. J. Touloukian. 646p. 1978. 100.00 (ISBN 0-471-01500-8, Pub. by Wiley Med). Wiley.

Pediatric Trauma. Ed. by Robert J. Touloukian. LC 78-7870. (Wiley Medical Publication). pap. 160.00 (ISBN 0-317-28939-X, 2055986). Bks Demand UMI.

Pediatric Trauma Care. Ed. by Martin R. Eichelberger & Geraldine L. Pratsch. 225p. 1987. 42.00 (ISBN 0-87189-881-0). Aspen Pub.

Pediatric Tumors of the Genitourinary Tract. Ed. by Bruce H. Broecker & Frederick A. Klein. LC 87-33898. 346p. 1988. 72.00 (ISBN 0-8451-4244-5, 4244). A R Liss.

Pediatric Tumors of the Genitourinary Tract. Ed. by Bruce H. Broecker & Frederick A. Klein. 1988. write for info. (ISBN 0-471-61239-1). Wiley.

Pediatric Ultrasonography. C. Keith Hayden, Jr. (Illus.). 392p. 1986. 63.95 (ISBN 0-683-03900-8). Williams & Wilkins.

Pediatric Ultrasonography. Ed. by G. Kalifa. (Illus.). 280p. 1985. 52.00 (ISBN 0-387-13085-3). Springer-Verlag.

Pediatric Upper Extremity: Diagnosis & Management. F. William Bora. (Illus.). 429p. 1986. 89.00 (ISBN 0-7216-1872-3). Saunders.

Pediatric Urology. Alan B. Retik & Jacob Cukier. (Illus.). 300p. 1987. 79.95 (ISBN 0-683-07250-1). Williams & Wilkins.

Pediatric Ward. J. M. Briley, Jr. LC 82-39991. 1986. pap. 12.95 (ISBN 0-87949-229-5). Ashley Bks.

Pediatric Work Physiology. Ed. by E. Jokl et al. (Medicine & Sport Ser.: Vol. 11). (Illus.). 1978. 52.00 (ISBN 3-8055-2866-3). S Karger.

Pediatrician's View of Marijuana. Ingrid L. Lantner. LC 82-198589. 48p. (Orig.). 1982. pap. 2.50 (ISBN 0-942348-06-0). Am Council Drug Ed.

Pediatricks. Medical Economics Company. (Illus.). 1974. pap. 9.95 (ISBN 0-87489-052-7). Med Economics.

Pediatrics. I. Booth. (Pocket Picture Guides for Nurses Ser.). 100p. 1984. text ed. 9.95 (ISBN 0-683-00922-2). Williams & Wilkins.

Pediatrics. Richard M. Heller & Lucy F. Squire. (Exercises in Diagnostic Radiology: Vol. 5). (Illus.). 162p. 1973. pap. write for info. (ISBN 0-7216-4630-1). Saunders.

Pediatrics. 2nd ed. Richard M. Heller et al. (Exercises in Diagnostic Radiology Ser.). (Illus.). 256p. 1987. pap. 20.95 (ISBN 0-7216-1569-4). Saunders.

Pediatrics. 6th ed. Hudson. (Illus.). 1104p. 1988. International ed. pap. 29.00 (ISBN 0-8016-2856-3). Mosby.

Pediatrics. Harold M. Maurer. (Illus.). 1982. text ed. 32.50 (ISBN 0-443-08084-4). Churchill.

Pediatrics. 400p. 1987. pap. 22.00 (ISBN 0-471-82346-5). Wiley.

Pediatrics. 460p. 1988. pap. write for info. (ISBN 0-471-61003-8). Wiley.

Pediatrics. 18th ed. Abraham M. Rudolph & Julien I. Hoffman. 1952p. 1987. 85.00 (ISBN 0-8385-7796-2, Dist. by Prentice-Hall). Appleton & Lange.

Pediatrics. Robert A. Wood et al. LC 65-10192. (Illus.). 500p. 1988. 29.95 (ISBN 0-397-50854-9, Lippincott Medical). Lippincott.

Pediatrics. 3rd ed. Mohsen Ziai. 868p. 1986. pap. 33.00 (ISBN 0-316-98753-0). Little.

Pediatrics: A Problem-Oriented Approach. Ed. by V. N. Mankad. (Other Medical Bks.: Vol. 22). 500p. 1986. 31.25 (ISBN 0-444-01037-8). Elsevier.

Pediatrics: An Interdisciplinary Approach. Ed. by H. M. Coles. (Illus.). 1976. text ed. 33.00x (ISBN 0-8464-0708-6). Beekman Pubs.

Pediatrics & Child Health: A Handbook for Professionals in the Third World. 2nd ed. Ed. by H. M. Coovadia & W. E. Loening. (Illus.). 544p. 1987. pap. 39.95 (ISBN 0-19-570445-2). Oxford U Pr.

Pediatrics for Parents: A Guide to Child Health. Griffith & Mofenson. (Mosby Medical Library). 1983. pap. 9.95 (ISBN 0-8016-1978-5). Mosby.

Pediatrics for Parents: A Guide to Child Health. H. Winter Griffith & Howard Mofenson. (Mosby Medical Library). 1983. pap. 9.95 (ISBN 0-452-25459-0, Plume). NAL.

Pediatrics, Neurology, & Psychiatry: Common Ground. Joel Herskowitz & N. Paul Rosman. LC 82-15280. 1982. write for info. (ISBN 0-02-354620-4). Macmillan.

Pediatrics Nursing Skills Manual. Judith M. McFarlane. 276p. (Arabic & Eng.). 1982. pap. 8.80 (ISBN 0-471-09670-9). Wiley.

Pediatrics: PreTest Self-Assessment & Review. 4th ed. Ed. by Richard K. Kravath. (Illus.). 272p. 1987. 14.95 (ISBN 0-07-051015-6). McGraw-Pretest.

Pediatrics Review. 3rd ed. Martin I. Lorin. LC 80-26732. (Illus.). 208p. 1982. pap. 17.95 (ISBN 0-668-05211-2). Appleton & Lange.

Pediatrics Update: Reviews for Physicians, 1986 Edition. Ed. by A. J. Moss. 400p. 1985. 66.75 (ISBN 0-444-00958-2). Elsevier.

Pediatrics Update: Reviews for Physicians, 1987 Edition. Ed. by A. J. Moss. (Pediatrics Update Ser.). 600p. 1986. 67.25 (ISBN 0-444-01054-8). Elsevier.

Pediatrics Update: 1979. Ed. by A. J. Moss. (Reviews for Physicians Ser.). 462p. 1979. 43.50 (ISBN 0-444-00291-X, Biomedical Pr). Elsevier.

Pediatrics Update, 1983. Ed. by A. J. Moss. (Reviews for Physicians Ser.). 410p. 1982. 71.25 (ISBN 0-444-00682-6, Biomedical Pr). Elsevier.

Peers, Politics & Power: The House of Lords, 1603-1911. Ed. by Clyve Jones & David L. Jones. 557p. 1986. 50.00 (ISBN 0-907628-78-8). Hambledon Press.

Peg Woffington. John A. Daly. LC 70-91489. (Illus.). 1888. 18.00 (ISBN 0-405-08427-7, Pub. by Blom). Ayer Co Pubs.

Pegaluis's Expositions on Thirteen Epistles of St. Paul, 3 pts. in 1 vol. A. Souter. (Texts & Studies Ser. 1: Vol. 9). pap. 83.00 (ISBN 0-8115-1712-8). Pt. 1: Introduction. Kraus Repr.

Pegando Sucio y Abajo. W. B. Murphy. (Compadre Collection, Rivera y Razoni: No. 4). 1976. pap. 0.95 (ISBN 0-88473-611-3). Fiesta Pub.

Pegasus. Eleanor A. Cox. 224p. 1981. pap. 1.95 (ISBN 0-449-50195-7, Coventry). Fawcett.

Pegasus Bridge. Stephen E. Ambrose. Date not set. pap. 3.50 (ISBN 0-317-57032-3). PB.

Pegasus Bridge: June 6, 1944. Stephen E. Ambrose. 208p. 1985. 15.95 (ISBN 0-671-52374-0). S&S.

Pegasus Bridge: June 6, 1944. Stephen E. Ambrose. (Illus.). 200p. 1988. pap. 7.95 (ISBN 0-671-67156-1, Touchstone Bks). S&S.

Pegasus: Providing Enrichment for the Gifted by Adapting Selected Units of Study. Christine L. Lewis et al. Ed. by Marjorie A. Cantor. 119p. 1980. tchr's ed. 15.00 (ISBN 0-89824-017-4). Trillium Pr.

Pegasus, the Winged Horse. new ed. Adapted by C. J. Naden. LC 80-50069. (Illus.). 32p. (gr. 4-8). 1980. PLB 10.79 (ISBN 0-89375-361-0); pap. 2.50 (ISBN 0-89375-365-3). Troll Assocs.

Peggy. North Callahan. LC 83-45139. 248p. 1983. 14.95 (ISBN 0-8453-4717-9, Cornwall Bks). Assoc Univ Prs.

Peggy. Roy J. Campbell. 187p. 1983. 10.00 (ISBN 0-682-49952-8). Exposition-Phoenix.

Peggy Alderton's Stay Young for Life! Peggy Alderton. (Illus.). 338p. 1984. 15.95 (ISBN 0-915657-00-7); pap. 7.95 (ISBN 0-915657-01-5). Books World.

Peggy & Her Boyfriend: A True Love Story. Louisa C. Culver. (Illus.). 61p. 1979. pap. 2.50 (ISBN 0-682-49251-5). Exposition-Phoenix.

Peggy & Pete: A Story of Lasting Love & Success. Louisa C. Culver. (Illus.). 224p. 1979. 7.50 (ISBN 0-682-49252-3). Exposition-Phoenix.

Peggy Fleming: Portrait of an Ice Skater. Stephanie Young. (Illus.). 96p. (Orig.). (gr. 3-7). 1984. pap. 2.25 (ISBN 0-380-85720-0, 85720, Camelot). Avon.

Peggy Guggenheim Collection. Lucy Flint. Selected by Thomas M. Messer. (Illus.). 224p. 1983. 35.00 (ISBN 0-8109-0959-6). Abrams.

Peggy Guggenheim Collection, Venice: The Solomon R. Guggenheim Foundation. Angelica Z. Rudenstine. LC 85-1307. (Illus.). 912p. 1985. 95.00 (ISBN 0-8109-0989-8). Abrams.

Peggy Hutchinson's Home Made Wine Secrets. Peggy Hutchinson. (Illus.). 129p. 1976. 13.95x (ISBN 0-572-00004-9). Trans-Atl Phila.

Peggy Nisbet Story. Peggy Nisbet. (Illus.). 160p. 1988. 19.95 (ISBN 0-87588-299-4). Hobby Hse.

Peggy Pond Church, New & Selected Poems. 3rd ed. Peggy P. Church. Ed. by Tom Trusky. LC 75-29917. (Modern & Contemporary Western Poets). 80p. (Orig.). 1976. pap. 4.50 (ISBN 0-916272-02-8). Ahsahta Pr.

Peggy Salte. Page Edwards. LC 83-6044. 216p. 1983. 12.95 (ISBN 0-7145-2795-5, Dist. by Kampmann & Co). M Boyars Pubs.

Peggy: The Wayward Guggenheim. Jacqueline B. Weld. LC 85-13162. (Illus.). 480p. 1986. 24.95 (ISBN 0-525-24380-1). Dutton.

Peggy: The Wayward Guggenheim. Jacqueline B. Weld. Ed. by DeSanti. (Illus.). 512p. 1988. pap. 12.95 (ISBN 0-525-48431-0, 01063-320). Dutton.

Peggy's Problem. Bonita Gillespie. (Illus.). 35p. (gr. 3-8). 1987. 6.95 (ISBN 1-55523-058-X). Winston-Derek.

Pegnitz Junction. Mavis Gallant. LC 84-81627. 180p. (Orig.). 1984. pap. 6.00 (ISBN 0-915308-60-6). Graywolf.

Pegs to Hang Ideas on: A Book of Quotations. Ed. by Marjorie P. Katz & Jean S. Arbeiter. LC 76-187739. 320p. (gr. 6 up). 1973. 6.95 (ISBN 0-87131-085-6). M Evans.

Pegu. Malinda Mayer. Ed. by Kendra Crossen. (Illus.). 32p. (Orig.). (gr. 3). 1987. pap. 5.00 (ISBN 0-9615163-1-3). Maji Bks.

Peguy, 2 vols. Romain Rolland. 696p. 1973. Set. 14.95 (ISBN 0-686-55263-6). French & Eur.

Peguy et les Cahiers. Charles Peguy. pap. 6.95 (ISBN 0-685-37034-8). French & Eur.

Pei Ch'i Shu Forty-Five: Biography of Yen Chih-T'ui. Albert E. Dien. (Wurzburger Sino-Japonica Ser.: Vol. 6). 184p. 1976. 24.80 (ISBN 3-261-01756-2). P Lang Pubs.

Pei Mei's Chinese Cook Book, Vol. II. Pei Mei Fu. Ed. by Nancy Murphy. (Illus.). 384p. 1974. 15.95 (ISBN 0-917056-09-4, Pub. by Pei Mei's Cook Inst Taiwan). Cheng & Tsui.

Pei Mei's Chinese Cook Book, Vol. I. Pei Mei Fu. Tr. by Nancy Murphy from Chinese. (Illus.). 398p. 1969. 15.95 (ISBN 0-917056-08-6, Pei Mei's Cook Inst Taiwan). Cheng & Tsui.

Pei Mei's Chinese Cook Book, Vol. III. Pei Mei Fu. Tr. by Nancy Murphy from Chinese. (Illus.). 378p. 1979. 15.95 (ISBN 0-917056-23-X, Pub. by Pei Mei's Cook Inst Taiwan). Cheng & Tsui.

Pei Mei's Homestyle Cooking. Pei M. Fu. (Illus.). 136p. cancelled (ISBN 0-88727-057-3, Pub. by Pei Mei's Cook Inst Taiwan). Cheng & Tsui.

PEIG: The Autobiography of Peig Sayers of the Great Blasket Island. Peig Sayers. Tr. by Bryan MacMahon from Gaelic. (Illus.). 220p. 1974. 14.95 (ISBN 0-8156-0106-9). Syracuse U Pr.

Peig: The Autobiography of Peig Sayers of the Great Blasket Island. Peig Sayers. Tr. by Bryan MacMahon from Irish. (Illus.). 212p. 1983. pap. 6.95 (ISBN 0-86167-092-2, Pub. by Educ Co of Ireland). Longwood Pub Group.

Peines et les Plaisirs De L'amour Robert Cambert see Chefs-D'oeuvres Classiques De L'opera Francais Ser.

Peintre de la Vie Londonienne Thomas Dekker (circa 1572-1632, 2 Vols. M. T. Jones-Davies. 1982. Repr. of 1958 ed. Set. lib. bdg. 150.00 (ISBN 0-8495-2800-3). Arden Lib.

Peintre-Graveur: Contenant l'histoire De la Gravare Sur Bois, Sur Metal et Au Burin Jusque Vers la Fix Du Seizieme Siecle, 6 Vols in 3. Johann D. Passavant. 1966. 99.50 (ISBN 0-8337-2682-X). B Franklin.

Peintre-Graveur Illustre, 32 vols, Vols. 1-16. Ed. by Loys Delteil. Incl. Vol. 1. J. F. Millet, Th. Rousseau, Jules Dupre, J. Barthold Jongkind. 20.00 (ISBN 0-306-78501-3); Vol. 2. Charles Meryon. 35.00 (ISBN 0-306-78502-1); Vol. 3. J. A. D. Ingres & Eugene Delacroix. 60.00 (ISBN 0-306-78503-X); Vol. 4. Anders Zorn. 45.00 (ISBN 0-306-78504-8); Vol. 5. C. Corot. 35.00 (ISBN 0-306-78505-6); Vol. 6. Rude, Barye, Carpeaux, Rodin. 20.00 (ISBN 0-306-78506-4); Vol. 7. Paul Huet. 29.50 (ISBN 0-306-78507-2); Vol. 8. Eugene Carriere. 25.00 (ISBN 0-306-78508-0); Vol. 9. Edgar Degas. 35.00 (ISBN 0-306-78509-9); Vols. 10 & 11. Toulouse-Lautrec. Set. 140.00 (ISBN 0-685-24299-4); Vol. 10. 70.00 ea. (ISBN 0-306-78510-2). Vol. 11 (ISBN 0-306-78511-0); Vol. 12. Gustave Leheutre. 35.00 (ISBN 0-306-78512-9); Vol. 13. Charles-Francois Daubigny. 40.00 (ISBN 0-306-78513-7); Francisco Goya. Vol. 14. 85.00 (ISBN 0-306-78514-5); Vol. 15. o. p. 70.00 (ISBN 0-306-78515-3); Vol. 16. Jean-Francois Raffaeli. 35.00 (ISBN 0-306-78516-1). LC 68-27720. (Graphic Art Ser). 1969. Da Capo.

Peintre-Graveur Illustre, 32 vols, Vols. 17-32. Ed. by Loys Delteil. Incl. Vol. 17. Camille Pissaro, Alfred Sisley, Auguste Renoir. 75.00 (ISBN 0-306-78517-X); Vol. 18. Theodore Gericault. 35.00 (ISBN 0-306-78518-8); Vol. 19. Henri Leys, Henri de Braekeleer, James Ensor. 65.00 (ISBN 0-306-78519-6); Vols. 20-29. Honore Daumier. Set. 650.00 (ISBN 0-306-78520-X); Vol. 30. Albert Besnard. 55.00 (ISBN 0-306-78530-7); Vol. 31. Jean Frelaut. lib. bdg. 55.00 (ISBN 0-306-78531-5); Vol. 32. Appendix. Herman J. Wechsler. 30.00 (ISBN 0-306-78532-3). LC 68-27720. (Graphic Art Ser). Da Capo.

Peintres Chinoises. Raphael Petrucci. 127p. 1920. pap. 56.00x (ISBN 0-317-69064-7, Pub. by Han-Shan Tang Ltd). State Mutual Bk.

Peinture Hollandaise Etautres Crits sur l'Art. Paul Claudel. (Illus.). 192p. 1966. 8.95 (ISBN 0-686-54413-7). French & Eur.

Peinture Sur Porcelaine see Art of Painting on Porcelain.

Peiping Municipality & the Diplomatic Quarter. Robert Duncan. LC 78-74355. (Modern Chinese Economy Ser.). 146p. 1980. lib. bdg. 20.00 (ISBN 0-8240-4271-9). Garland Pub.

Peirce: Arguments of the Philosophers Series. Christopher Hookway. 320p. 1985. 45.00x (ISBN 0-7100-9715-8). Routledge Chapman & Hall.

Peirce-Nichols House. Gerald W. Ward. LC 76-16904. (Historic House Booklet Ser.: No. 4). 1976. 2.00 (ISBN 0-88389-062-3). Essex Inst.

Peirce, Semeiotic & Pragamatism: Essays by Max H. Fisch. Ed. by Kenneth L. Ketner & Christian J. Kloesel. LC 85-42525. 408p. 1986. 45.00x (ISBN 0-253-34317-8). Ind U Pr.

Peirce's Approach to the Self: Perspectives on Human Subjectivity. Vincent M. Colapietro. Ed. by Robert C. Neville. (Philosophy Ser.). 160p. 1988. text ed. 34.50 (ISBN 0-88706-882-0); pap. text ed. 10.95 (ISBN 0-88706-883-9). State U NY Pr.

Peirce's Colonial Lists: Civil, Military & Professional Lists of Plymouth & Rhode Island Colonies. Ebenezer W. Peirce. LC 68-24684. 156p. 1968. Repr. of 1881 ed. 14.00 (ISBN 0-8063-0274-7). Genealog Pub.

Peirce's Concept of Sign. Douglas Greenlee. LC 72-94469. (Approaches to Semiotics Ser.: No. 5). 148p. 1974. pap. text ed. 15.75 (ISBN 90-2792-494-5). Mouton.

Peirce's Conception of God: A Developmental Study. Donna M. Orange. LC 84-80516. (Peirce Studies Ser.). 96p. 1984. 22.50x (ISBN 0-936842-02-4). Ind U Pr.

Peirce's Logic of Relations & Other Studies. R. M. Martin. 156p. 1980. pap. write for info. (ISBN 90-70176-17-3). Foris Pubns.

Peirce's Philosophy of Science: Critical Studies in His Theory of Induction & Scientific Method. Nicholas Rescher. LC 77-82479. 1979. pap. text ed. 4.95x (ISBN 0-268-01527-9). U of Notre Dame Pr.

Peirce's Theory of Scientific Discovery: A System of Logic Conceived As Semiotic. Richard Tursman. (Peirce Studies: No. 3). 1987. 25.00x (ISBN 0-253-34295-3). Ind U Pr.

Peire Vidal. Tr. by Paul Blackburn. LC 72-83856. (Illus.). 6.00 (ISBN 0-913142-02-6). Mulch Pr.

Peirels Eightieth Birthday Symposium: Proceedings of the Peirels 80th Birthday Symposium, Oxford, United Kingdom. Ed. by R. Dalitz & R. Stinchcombe. 400p. (Orig.). 1988. 55.00 (ISBN 9971-50-519-3); pap. 25.00 (ISBN 9971-50-520-7). World Scientific Pub.

Peirol, Troubadour of Auvergne. S. C. Aston. LC 80-2185. Repr. of 1953 ed. 35.00 (ISBN 0-404-19012-X). AMS Pr.

Pekan the Shadow. Rutherford G. Montgomery. LC 78-84779. (Illus.). (gr. 8-12). 1970. 3.95 (ISBN 0-87004-132-0). Caxton.

Peking. 2nd, rev. & enl. ed. Juliet Bredon. 523p. 1922. 525.00x (Pub. by Han-Shan Tang Ltd). State Mutual Bk.

Peking. Nigel Cameron & Brian Brake. 263p. 1965. 315.00 (ISBN 0-317-68970-3, Pub. by Han-Shan Tang Ltd). State Mutual Bk.

Peking. Felix Greene. (Illus.). 1978. 12.50 (ISBN 0-8317-6790-1, Mayflower Bks). Smith Pubs.

Peking. Anthony Grey. 560p. 1988. 19.95 (ISBN 0-316-32823-5). Little.

Peking. (Panorama Bks.). (Illus., Fr.). 3.95 (ISBN 0-685-11484-8). French & Eur.

Peking. Heinz Von Perckhammer. 1971. 735.00x (ISBN 0-317-69068-X, Pub. by Han-Shan Tang Ltd). State Mutual Bk.

Peking & the New Left: At Home & Abroad. Klaus Mehnert. LC 70-627631. (China Research Monographs: No. 4). pap. 39.00 (ISBN 0-317-08396-1, 2003419). Bks Demand UMI.

Peking Battles Cape Horn. Irving Johnson. (Illus.). 11.95 (ISBN 0-930248-01-5); pap. 5.95 (ISBN 0-930248-02-3). Sea Hist Pr.

Peking-Der Leere Thron. Ernst Cordes. 224p. 1937. 112.00x (Pub. by Han-Shan Tang Ltd). State Mutual Bk.

Peking Diary: A Year of Revolution. Derk Bodde. 1973. lib. bdg. 24.50x (ISBN 0-374-90735-8, Octagon). Hippocrene Bks.

Peking Duck. Roger L. Simon. 256p. 1986. pap. 3.50 (ISBN 0-446-30046-2). Warner Bks.

Peking: Histoire et Description. Alphonse Favier. 562p. 1897. 5250.00x (ISBN 0-317-69134-1, Pub. by Han-Shan Tang Ltd). State Mutual Bk.

Peking Kokyu Hakubutsuin Ten. Seibu Museum of Art Staff. 146p. 1982. pap. 140.00x (ISBN 0-317-68985-1, Pub. by Han-Shan Tang Ltd). State Mutual Bk.

Peking Mandate. Peter Siris. 640p. 1986. pap. 3.95 (ISBN 0-8217-1502-X). Zebra.

Peking, Moscow & Beyond: The Sino-Soviet-American Triangle. William E. Griffith. (Washington Papers: Vol. I, No. 6). 78p. (Orig.). 1973. pap. text ed. 7.95 (ISBN 0-8191-5962-X, Pub. by CSIS). U Pr of Amer.

Peking Opera. Rewi Alley. (Illus.). 103p. (Orig.). 1984. pap. 14.95 (ISBN 0-8351-1617-4). China Bks.

Peking Stories: The First Two Years under the Red Star. David Kidd. (Illus.). 224p. 1988. pap. 11.95 (ISBN 0-517-56712-1, 567121, C N Potter Bks). Crown.

Peking Story. David Kidd. (Illus.). 207p. 1988. pap. 11.95 (ISBN 0-317-70129-0, C N Potter Bks). Crown.

Peking Tample of the Eastern Peak. Anne S. Goodrich. 326p. 1964. 245.00x (ISBN 0-317-68971-1, Pub. by Han-Shan Tang Ltd). State Mutual Bk.

Peking Target. Adam Hall. LC 81-82460. 290p. Date not set. pap. 2.95 (ISBN 0-86721-188-1). Jove Pubns.

Peking to Paris. Luigi Barzini. 357p. 1986. pap. 35.00x (ISBN 0-317-69380-8, Pub. by Han-Shan Tang Ltd). State Mutual Bk.

Peking-Washington: Chinese Foreign Policy & the United States. Harold C. Hinton. (Washington Papers: Vol. IV, No. 34). 96p. (Orig.). 1976. pap. text ed. 7.95 (ISBN 0-8191-5989-1, Pub. by CSIS). U Pr of Amer.

Peking, Yeddo, San Francisco. Le Comte De Beauvoir. 360p. 1872. 140.00x (ISBN 0-317-68611-9, Pub. by Han-Shan Tang Ltd). State Mutual Bk.

Pekingese. Beverly Pisano. (Illus.). 128p. 1981. 9.95 (ISBN 0-87666-724-8, KW-095). TFH Pubns.

Pekingese Champions, 1952-1981. Jan L. Pata. (Illus.). 236p. 1987. pap. 29.95 (ISBN 0-940808-12-9). Camino E E & B.

Pekingese Champions: 1982-1986. Camino E. E. & B. Co. Staff. (Illus.). 76p. 1987. pap. 24.95 (ISBN 0-940808-57-9). Camino E E & B.

Pel among the Pueblos. Mark Hebden. 1988. 16.95 (ISBN 0-8027-5690-5). Walker & Co.

Pel & the Bombers. Mark Hebden. 1985. 13.95 (ISBN 0-8027-5608-5). Walker & Co.

Pel & the Pirates. 192p. 1987. 15.95 (ISBN 0-8027-5672-7). Walker & Co.

Pel & the Predators. Mark Hebden. LC 85-11479. 192p. 1985. 14.95 (ISBN 0-8027-5624-7). Walker & Co.

Pel & the Prowler. Mark Hebden. 208p. 1986. 15.95 (ISBN 0-8027-5658-1). Walker & Co.

Pel & the Touch of Pitch. Mark Hebden. 1988. 16.95 (ISBN 0-8027-5720-0). Walker & Co.

Pelagic & Semi Pelagic Trawling Gear. John Garner. 1978. 50.00x (ISBN 0-685-63446-9). State Mutual Bk.

Pelagic & Semi-Pelagic Trawling Gear. John Garner. (Illus.). 60p. 1979. 22.00 (ISBN 0-85238-088-7, FN74, FNB). UNIPUB.

Pelagic Tar from Bermuda & the Sargasso Sea. James N. Butler et al. LC 73-175455. (Bermuda Biological Station Special Pubn.: No. 10). (Illus.). vi, 346p. 1973. pap. 8.50 (ISBN 0-917642-10-4). Bermuda Bio.

Pelagic Tidal Constants. (Publications Scientifique Ser.). 65p. 1979. 4.50 (ISBN 0-318-14517-0). Intl Assoc Phys Sci Ocean.

Pelagie-La-Charette. Antonine Maillet. (Orig.). 1987. pap. 7.95 (ISBN 0-7145-3966-X). Riverrun NY.

Pelagius: A Historical & Theological Study. John Ferguson. LC 77-84700. Repr. of 1956 ed. 27.00 (ISBN 0-404-16107-3). AMS Pr.

Pelagius: A Reluctant Heretic. B. R. Rees. 200p. 1988. 55.00 (ISBN 0-85115-503-0, Pub. by Boydell & Brewer). Longwood Pub Group.

Pelagius & the Fifth Crusade. Joseph P. Donovan. LC 76-29822. Repr. of 1950 ed. 29.00 (ISBN 0-404-15416-6). AMS Pr.

Pelargonium Family. William J. Webb. LC 84-45556. 104p. cancelled (ISBN 0-7099-2734-7, Pub. by Croom Helm Ltd). Routledge Chapman & Hall.

Pelargoniums. David Clark. LC 87-33633. (Kew Gardening Guide Ser.). (Illus.). 128p. 1988. 19.95 (ISBN 0-88192-103-3). Timber.

Peldanos. R. L. Politzer & H. N. Urrutibeheity. LC 72-75117. Repr. of 1972 ed. text ed. 72.60 (ISBN 0-8357-9949-2, 2013629); wkbk. 36.30 (2016476). Bks Demand UMI.

Pele & Hiiaka: A Myth from Hawaii. Nathaniel B. Emerson. LC 75-35190. Repr. of 1915 ed. 29.50 (ISBN 0-404-14218-4). AMS Pr.

Pele & Hiiaka: A Myth from Hawaii. Nathaniel B. Emerson. LC 77-83040. (Illus.). 1978. 15.00 (ISBN 0-8048-1251-9). C E Tuttle.

Pele & Hi'iaka Visit the Sites at Ke'e, Ha'ena, Island of Kaua'i. Marion Kelly. (Publication in Education Ser.: No. 1). 36p. 1984. 4.50 (ISBN 0-930897-01-3). Bishop Mus.

Pele, Goddess of Hawaii's Volcanoes. Herb K. Kane. LC 87-81076. (Illus.). 64p. (Orig.). 1987. pap. 7.95 (ISBN 0-943357-00-4). Kawainui Pr.

Pele: King of Soccer. Noel Machin. (American Structural Readers Ser.: Stage 1). (Illus.). 16p. 1984. pap. text ed. 3.95 (ISBN 0-582-79883-3). Longman.

Pele, Volcano Goddess of Hawaii. L. R. McBride. (Illus.). 1968. pap. 3.95 (ISBN 0-912180-11-0). Petroglyph.

Pelecypod Genus Byssonchia in the Cincinnatian at Cincinnati, Ohio see Palaeontographica Americana.

Pelecypod Genus Venericardia in the Paleocene & Eocene of Western North America see Palaeontographica Americana.

Peleliu: 1944. Harry A. Gailey. LC 83-13394. 220p. 1983. 19.95 (ISBN 0-933852-41-X). Nautical & Aviation.

Pelerinage a la Mekke: Etude D'histoire Religieuse. Maurice Gaudefroy-Demombynes. LC 77-10690. (Studies in Islamic History: No. 7). viii, 332p. 1978. Repr. of 1923 ed. lib. bdg. 37.50x (ISBN 0-87991-456-4). Porcupine Pr.

Pelham Humfrey. Peter Dennison. LC 86-12765. (Studies of Composers: No. 21). 119p. 1987. 28.00 (ISBN 0-19-315244-4); pap. 12.95 (ISBN 0-19-315234-7). Oxford U Pr.

Pelham; or, the Adventures of a Gentleman. Edward Bulwer-Lytton. Ed. by Jerome J. McGann. LC 77-88085. xxxvi, 477p. 1972. 35.00x (ISBN 0-8032-0703-4). U of Nebr Pr.

Pelican. Siegfried Back. Ed. by John E. Rotelle. Tr. by Matthew J. O'Connell from Ger. 88p. 1987. pap. 7.95 (ISBN 0-941491-07-2). Augustinian Pr.

Pelican. Ray Ovington. LC 76-3763. (Illus.). 1977. pap. 1.95 (ISBN 0-8200-0905-9). Great Outdoors.

Pelican. Brian Wildsmith. LC 82-12431. (Illus.). 64p. (ps-2). 1983. 10.95 (ISBN 0-394-85668-6); lib. bdg. 10.99 (ISBN 0-394-95668-0). Pantheon.

Pelican & After: A Novel about Emotional Disturbance. Tom W. Lyons. LC 83-3283. 268p. 1983. 14.95 (ISBN 0-9609506-0-5). Prescott Durrell & Co.

Pelican & the Chela. Ann R. Colton & Jonathan Murro. LC 85-70766. (Illus.). 420p. 1985. 21.95 (ISBN 0-917189-04-3). Colton Found.

Pelican Economic History of Britain: Reformation to Industrial Revolution, Vol. 2. Christopher Hill. 304p. 1970. pap. 6.95 (ISBN 0-14-020897-6, Pelican). Penguin.

Pelican Economic History of Britain, Vol. 3: Industry & Empire. Eric J. Hobsbawm. (Orig.). 1970. pap. 6.95 (ISBN 0-14-020898-4, Pelican). Penguin.

Pelican Guide to Gardens of Louisiana. Joyce Y. LeBlanc. (Pelican Guide Ser.). (Illus.). 64p. 1974. pap. 2.95 (ISBN 0-88289-003-4). Pelican.

Pelican Guide to Hillsborough: Historic Orange County, North Carolina. Lucile N. Dula. LC 78-26081. (Pelican Guide Ser). (Illus.). 124p. 1979. pap. 4.95 (ISBN 0-88289-208-8). Pelican.

Penal Philosophy. Gabriel Tarde. Tr. by Rapalje Howell. LC 68-55783. (Criminology, Law Enforcement, & Social Problems Ser.: No. 16). 1968. Repr. of 1912 ed. 26.00x (ISBN 0-87585-016-2). Patterson Smith.

Penal Reform: A Comparative Study. Max Grunhut. LC 71-172568. (Criminology, Law Enforcement, & Social Problems Ser.: No. 149). 502p. 1972. Repr. of 1948 ed. 22.00x (ISBN 0-87585-149-5). Patterson Smith.

Penal Reform in England: Introductory Essays on Some Aspects of the English Criminal Policy. 2nd, rev. & enl. ed. (Cambridge Studies in Criminology: Vol. 1). pap. 24.00 (ISBN 0-8115-0415-8). Kraus Repr.

Penal Services for Offenders: Comparative Studies of England & Poland. Thelma Wilson. 112p. 1987. text ed. 38.95 (ISBN 0-566-05420-5, Pub. by Gower Pub England). Gower Pub Co.

Penal Servitude in Early Modern Spain. Ruth Pike. LC 82-70551. (Illus.). 224p. 1983. text ed. 27.50x (ISBN 0-299-09260-7). U of Wis Pr.

Penalties for Misconduct on the Job. Alfred Avins. LC 71-156375. (Legal Almanac Ser.: No. 69). 124p. 1972. lib. bdg. 6.95 (ISBN 0-379-11075-X). Oceana.

Penalty of Death: Final Report of the 1980 Chief Justice Earl Warren Conference on Advocacy in the United States. Roscoe Pound-American Trial Lawyers Foundation Staff. 121p. 1981. pap. 10.00 (ISBN 0-317-57757-3). Roscoe Pound Found.

Penalty of Eve: John Milton & Divorce. Gladys J. Willis. LC 83-49352. (American University Studies IV (English Language & Literature): Vol. 6). 164p. (Orig.). 1985. text ed. 21.55 (ISBN 0-8204-0094-7). P Lang Pubs.

Penance: A Reform Proposal. Lopresti. 1987. 2.50 (ISBN 0-912405-27-9). Pastoral Pr.

Penance & Reconciliation. Patrick J. Brennan. (Guidelines for Contemporary Catholics Ser.). (Orig.). 1986. pap. 7.95 (ISBN 0-88347-195-7). Thomas More.

Penance & Reconciliation in the Church. (Liturgy Documentary Ser.: No. 7). 96p. (Orig.). 1986. pap. 5.95 (ISBN 1-55586-104-0). US Catholic.

Penance & Reconciliation in the Mission of the Church. 68p. 1983. pap. 2.50 (ISBN 1-55586-902-5). US Catholic.

Penance for Jerry Kennedy. George V. Higgins. LC 84-48479. 336p. 1985. 16.45 (ISBN 0-394-53485-9). Knopf.

Penance for Jerry Kennedy. George V. Higgins. 320p. 1986. pap. 3.50 (ISBN 0-88184-224-9). Carroll & Graf.

Penance: God's Gift for Forgiveness. Blanche Twigg. (Illus.). 64p. 1974. pap. 2.50 (ISBN 0-912228-15-6). St Anthony Mess Pr.

Penance in the Early Church see Theological Investigations.

Penance of John Logan & Two Other Tales. facsimile ed. William Black. LC 73-106248. (Short Story Index Reprint Ser.). 1893. 18.00 (ISBN 0-8369-3284-6). Ayer Co Pubs.

Penance: The Once & Future Sacrament. Lawrence E. Mick. 95p. 1988. pap. 4.95 (ISBN 0-8146-1573-2). Liturgical Pr.

Penateuch & Haftorahs. J. H. Hertz. 1067p. 1960. 27.50. Soncino Pr.

Pencil. Don Bologness & Elaine Raphael. LC 85-32308. (Illustrator's Library). 64p. (gr. 4-9). 1986. lib. bdg. 10.90 (ISBN 0-531-10134-7). Watts.

Pencil. Paul Calle. LC 74-83836. (Illus.). 160p. 1985. pap. 16.95 (ISBN 0-89134-118-8). North Light Bks.

Pencil Drawing for the Architect. Charles I. Hobbis. (gr. 10-12). 1954. 8.95 (ISBN 0-85458-100-6); pap. 6.95 (ISBN 0-85458-101-4). Transatl Arts.

Pencil Drawing Techniques. Ed. by David Lewis. (Illus.). 144p. 1984. pap. 16.95 (ISBN 0-8230-3991-9). Watson-Guptill.

Pencil Drawings by David X: One Hundred & One Amusing, Artistic & Entertaining Drawings of Pencils. David C. Lowy. LC 79-88698. (Illus.). 1979. pap. 3.25 (ISBN 0-9602940-0-7). Lowy Pub.

Pencil Flowers. Johnny Baranski. LC 82-12057. (Kestrel Ser.). 24p. 1983. 3.00 (ISBN 0-914974-36-X). Holmgangers.

Pencil of Nature. W. H. Talbot. LC 68-25759. (Photography Ser.). (Illus.). 1969. Repr. of 1844 ed. lib. bdg. 95.00 (ISBN 0-306-71135-4). Da Capo.

Pencil, Pen, & Brush. Harvey Weiss. (Illus.). 64p. (gr. 4-6). 1974. pap. 1.95 (ISBN 0-590-02229-6). Scholastic Inc.

Pencil Play. Etienne Bruneel. 1985. 20.00x (ISBN 0-907349-71-4, Pub by Spindlewood). State Mutual Bk.

Pencil Play, Pts. C & D. Frances Clark et al. (Francis Clark Library for Piano Students). 40p. (Orig.). (gr. k-6). 1962. pap. text ed. 7.95 (ISBN 0-87487-185-9). Birch Tree Gr.

Pencil Play, Pts. A & B. Francis Clark et al. (Frances Clark Library for Piano Students). 56p. (Orig.). (gr. k-6). 1958. pap. text ed. 8.95 (ISBN 0-87487-184-0). Birch Tree Gr.

Pencil Sketching. Thomas C. Wang. (Illus.). 96p. 1977. pap. 14.95 (ISBN 0-442-29177-9). Van Nos Reinhold.

Pencil Stencil Book: Or Any Other Writing Instrument You Want to Use. Marsha Cohen. (Illus.). 15p. (gr. 2 up). 1981. plastic spiral bdg. 2.95 (ISBN 0-394-84910-8). Random.

Pencil to Write Your Name: Poems from the Nicaraguan Poetry Workshops. 10/1986 ed. Ed. & tr. by Diane Kendig. (Ohio Writers Ser.: No. 6). (Illus.). 48p. (Orig., Span. & Eng.). pap. 4.95 (ISBN 0-933087-08-X). Bottom Dog Pr.

Pencillings. facs. ed. John M. Murry. LC 70-90666. (Essay Index Reprint Ser). 1925. 19.00 (ISBN 0-8369-1229-2). Ayer Co Pubs.

Pencils & Sticks: Scripture Word-Searches for LDS Families. Joseph D. Kayne. 32p. (Orig.). 1983. pap. 3.95 (ISBN 0-88290-218-0). Horizon Utah.

Pend Oreille Profiles. Lee Taylor. 334p. 1977. 14.95 (ISBN 0-87770-185-7). Ye Galleon.

Pendant la Guerre (Juin 1940-Janv. 1946; see Discours et Messages.

Pendennis & St. Mawes: An Historical Sketch of Two Cornish Castles. S. Pasfield Oliver. 1985. 35.00x (ISBN 0-907566-90-1, Pub. by Dyllansow & Truran). State Mutual Bk.

Pender among the Residents. Forrest Reid. LC 70-131812. 1971. Repr. of 1923 ed. 39.00x (ISBN 0-403-00699-6). Scholarly.

Pender among the Residents. Forrest Reid. 1988. Repr. of 1923 ed. lib. bdg. 59.00x. Am Biog Serv.

Pender, Nebraska. Ed. by Pender Centennial Book Committee. (Illus.). 549p. 1984. 40.00 (ISBN 0-88107-021-1). Curtis Media.

Pender, Nebraska: The First Hundred Years, 1885-1985. Ed. by Pender Centennial Book Committee. (Illus.). 549p. 1985. Repr. of 1984 ed. 50.00 (ISBN 0-88107-028-9). Curtis Media.

Pendergast Machine. Lyle W. Dorsett. LC 80-11581. (Illus.). xvi, 163p. 1980. 16.50x (ISBN 0-8032-1655-6); pap. 3.95 (ISBN 0-8032-6554-9, BB 744, Bison). U of Nebr Pr.

Pendex: An Index of Pen Names & House Names in Fantastic, Thriller & Series Literature. Susannah Bates. LC 80-8486. 200p. 1981. lib. bdg. 36.00 (ISBN 0-8240-9501-4). Garland Pub.

Pending Employee Benefit Changes. Isidore Goodman. (Pension & ERISA Ser.). 24p. 1986. 2.00 (ISBN 0-317-47595-9, 5443). Commerce.

Pendle Hill: A Quaker Experiment in Education & Community. new ed. Eleanore P. Mather. 128p. 1980. 7.00 (ISBN 0-87574-954-2). Pendle-Hill.

Pendle Hill Idea. Howard Brinton. LC 50-11234. (Orig.). 1950. pap. 2.50x (ISBN 0-87574-055-3). Pendle Hill.

Pendle Hill Reader. facsimile ed. Ed. by Herrymon Maurer. LC 74-142668. (Essay Index Reprint Ser). Repr. of 1950 ed. 18.00 (ISBN 0-8369-2415-0). Ayer Co Pubs.

Pendle Witches: Third Impression. Hendon Publishing Co., Ltd. Staff. 1986. 40.25x (ISBN 0-317-56072-7, Pub. by Hendon Pub UK); pap. 23.80x (ISBN 0-317-56073-5, Pub. by Hendon Pub UK). State Mutual Bk.

Pendleton County Builder & His Houses. Ruth K. Heal. LC 84-90690. (Illus.). 77p. (Orig.). 1984. pap. 15.00 (ISBN 0-9614132-0-4). Heal.

Pendleton District & Anderson County, S. C. Wills, Estates & Legal Records, 1793 to 1857. Virginia Alexander & Colleen M. Elliott. 350p. 1979. 38.50 (ISBN 0-89308-143-4). Southern Hist Pr.

Pendleton District, S. C., Deeds, 1790 to 1806. Betty Willie. 479p. 1982. 36.50 (ISBN 0-89308-246-5). Southern Hist Pr.

Pendleton Woolen Mills. 2nd ed. (Illus.). 40p. 1987. pap. 8.50 (ISBN 0-936755-03-2, Pub. by Avanyu Pub). U of NM Pr.

Pendragon. Catherine Christian. Date not set. pap. 3.95 (ISBN 0-446-32342-X). Warner Bks.

Pendragon Calligraphic Calendar 1988: Children & Childhood. Ed. by Pamela A. Johnson. (Illus.). 128p. 1987. pap. 11.50 (ISBN 0-944022-00-6). Pendragon Gal Pubs.

Pendragon Campaign. Greg Stafford. (Illus.). 76p. 1985. pap. 10.00 incl. Pendragon roleplaying game supplement (ISBN 0-933635-21-4). Chaosium.

Pendragon: Chivalric Roleplaying in Arthur's Britain. Greg Stafford. Ed. by Yurek Chodak. (Illus.). 120p. 1985. incl. boxed roleplaying game set 20.00 (ISBN 0-933635-20-6, 2701-X). Chaosium.

Pendulum. Rotimi B. Martins. 64p. 1982. 5.95 (ISBN 0-89962-256-9). Todd & Honeywell.

Pendulum & the Toxic Cloud: The Dioxin Threat from Vietnam to Seveso. Thomas Whiteside. 1979. pap. 10.95 (ISBN 0-300-02283-2). Yale U Pr.

Pendulum of Progress: Essays in Political Science & Scientific Politics. George Young. 1931. 39.50x (ISBN 0-686-83692-8). Elliots Bks.

Pendulum, Radiesthesia & You. Phyllis Harrison. (Illus., Orig.). 1989. pap. 8.95 (ISBN 0-89407-033-9). Strawberry Hill.

Pendulum Swings. Bob Buess. 92p. (Orig.). 1974. pap. 2.50 (ISBN 0-934244-12-X, TX 391-560). Sweeter Than Honey.

Pendulum Swings. Ilona K. Szechenyi. (Illus.). 240p. 1980. 12.00 (ISBN 0-87934-024-X). Danubian.

Pendulums. (Tops Cards Ser.: No. 1). 1977. pap. 6.95 (ISBN 0-941008-01-0). Tops Learning.

Pendulums Thirty-Four. Ron Marson. LC 81-90447. (Science with Simple Things Ser: No. 34). (Illus.). 80p. 1983. pap. 13.95 tchr's ed. (ISBN 0-941008-34-7). Tops Learning.

Penelope. Jack Wikoff. 240p. (Orig.). 1983. pap. 7.95. Open Bk Pubns.

Penelope. Jack Wikoff. LC 85-2365. 240p. (Orig.). 1983. pap. 7.95 (ISBN 0-940170-10-8). Station Hill Pr.

Penelope Anne see Additional Adventures of Messrs. Box & Cox: A Continuation of the Dramatic History of Box & Cox.

Penelope Devereux. Sheila Bishop. (Inflation Fighter Ser.). 192p. 1982. pap. 1.50 (ISBN 0-8439-1094-1, Leisure Bks). Leisure NY.

Penelope Hall's Social Services of England & Wales. 10th ed. Penelope Hall. Ed. by J. B. Mays & Anthony Forder. (International Library of Sociology). 384p. (Orig.). 1983. pap. 15.95x (ISBN 0-7100-0837-6). Routledge Chapman & Hall.

Penelope the Tortoise. Sylvia A. Johnson. Tr. by Dyan Hammarberg from Fr. LC 76-3411. (Animal Friends Bks). (Illus.). 24p. (gr. k-4). 1976. PLB 5.95 (ISBN 0-87614-072-X). Carolrhoda Bks.

Penelope's Pen Pal. Linda P. Silbert & Alvin J. Silbert. (Little Twirps Understanding People Bks.). (Illus.). (gr. k-4). 1978. pap. 2.98 (ISBN 0-89544-053-9). Silbert Bress.

Penetrance & Variability in Malformation Syndromes. Ed. by James J. O'Donnell & Bryan D. Hall. LC 79-5115. (Alan R. Liss Ser.: Vol. 15, No. 5b). 1979. 50.00. March of Dimes.

Penetrance & Variability in Malformation Syndromes: Proceedings, Annual Review of Birth Defects, San Francisco, CA, 1978, Pt. B. Annual Birth Defects Conference Staff. Ed. by James J. O'Donnell & Bryan D. Hall. LC 79-5115. (Birth Defects: Original Article Ser.: Vol. XV, No. 5B). 396p. 1979. 61.00x (ISBN 0-8451-1029-2). A R Liss.

Penetrating Beam: Reflections on Light. Edith Levin. 115p. (gr. 7-12). 1978. PLB 10.97 (ISBN 0-8239-0416-4). Rosen Group.

Penetrating Craniocerebal Trauma. Arnold M. Meirowsky. (Illus.). 282p. 1984. 54.50x (ISBN 0-398-04993-9). C C Thomas.

Penetrating International Markets: Theoretical Considerations & Mexican Agriculture. David R. Mares. (Political Economy of International Change Ser.). 296p. 1987. 35.00 (ISBN 0-231-06346-6). Columbia U Pr.

Penetrating Laughter: Hakuin's Zen & Art. Kazuaki Tanahashi. LC 83-43155. (Illus.). 144p. 1987. 16.95 (ISBN 0-87951-952-5); pap. 8.95 (ISBN 0-87951-280-6). Overlook Pr.

Penetrating Poets. Gerald H. Twombly. 112p. 1982. pap. 4.95 (ISBN 0-88469-151-9). BMH Bks.

Penetrating the U. S. Auto Market: German & Japanese Strategies, 1965-1976. James Rader. LC 80-15530. (Research for Business Decisions Ser.: No. 22). pap. 54.60 (2070143). Bks Demand UMI.

Penetrating Wagner's Ring: An Anthology. Ed. by John L. DiGaetani. LC 82-25251. (Music Reprint Ser.). 453p. 1983. Repr. of 1978 ed. lib. bdg. 49.50 (ISBN 0-306-76205-6). Da Capo.

Penetration Mechanics. Anderson. 1988. write for info. (ISBN 0-471-62587-6). Wiley.

Penetration of Arabia: A Record of the Development of Western Knowledge Concerning the Arabian Peninsula. David G. Hogarth. LC 79-2863. (Illus.). 359p. 1981. Repr. of 1904 ed. 38.50 (ISBN 0-8305-0037-5). Hyperion Conn.

Penetration of Capitalism: A West African Case Study. Emile Vercruijsse. (Africa Ser.). (Illus.). 186p. 1984. bds. 26.25x (ISBN 0-86232-117-4, Pub. by Zed Pr England); pap. 10.25 (ISBN 0-86232-116-6). Humanities.

Penetration of Charged Particles Through Matter (1912-1954) Ed. by J. Thorsen. (Niels Bohr Collected Works: Vol. 8). 850p. 1988. 231.75 (ISBN 0-444-87003-2, North Holland). Elsevier.

Penetration of EC Markets by U. K. Manufacturing Industry. A. I. Millington. 200p. 1987. text ed. 35.00 (ISBN 0-566-05409-4, Pub. by Gower Pub England). Gower Pub Co.

Penetration of Money Economy in Japan & Its Effects Upon Social & Political Institutions. Matsuyo Takizawa. LC 68-54302. (Columbia University. Studies in the Social Sciences: No. 285). Repr. of 1927 ed. 16.50 (ISBN 0-404-51285-2). AMS Pr.

Penetration Testing: Proceedings of the Second European Symposium on Penetration Testing, Amsterdam, 24-27 May 1982, 2 vols. Ed. by A. Verruijt et al. 1000p. 1982. text ed. 107.00 (ISBN 90-6191-250-4, Pub. by A A Balkema). Brookfield Pub Co.

Penetration Testing, 1988: Proceedings of the First International Symposium, ISOPT-1, Orlando, 20-24 March 1988. Ed. by J. De Ruiter. 1096p. 1988. text ed. 115.00 (ISBN 90-6191-801-4, Pub. by A A Balkema). Brookfield Pub Co.

Penetrometer & Soil Exploration. G. Sanglerat. (Developments in Geotechnical Engineering Ser.: Vol. 1). 464p. 1972. 100.00 (ISBN 0-444-40976-9). Elsevier.

Penet's Square. Thomas Powell. 1976. 8.95 (ISBN 0-932052-10-X). North Country.

P'eng P'ai & the Hai-Lu-Feng Soviet. Fernando Galbiati. LC 83-40084. 496p. 1985. 45.00x (ISBN 0-8047-1219-0). Stanford U Pr.

P'eng Te-Huai: The Man & the Image. Jurgen Domes. LC 85-50942. 224p. 1986. 25.00x (ISBN 0-8047-1303-0). Stanford U Pr.

Penguin. Caroline Arnold. LC 87-31458. (Illus.). 48p. (gr. 2-7). 1988. 12.95 (ISBN 0-688-07706-4); PLB 12.88 (ISBN 0-688-07707-2). Morrow.

Penguin. Mary Hoffman. LC 84-18045. (Animals in the Wild Ser.). (Illus.). 24p. (gr. k-3). 1985. PLB 11.33 (ISBN 0-8172-2415-7). Raintree Pubs.

Penguin. Paula Hogan. LC 78-21225. (Life Cycles Clippers Ser.). (Illus.). 32p. (gr. k-3). 1984. PLB 27.99 incl. cassette (ISBN 0-8172-2231-6); cassette 14.00. Raintree Pubs.

Penguin. Paula Z. Hogan. LC 78-21225. (Life Cycles Bks.). (Illus.). 32p. (gr. k-3). 1979. PLB 14.65 (ISBN 0-8172-1257-4). Raintree Pubs.

Penguin. Angela Royston. (Animal Life Stories Ser.). (Illus.). 24p. (Orig.). (gr. 1-5). 1988. pap. 2.95 (ISBN 0-8249-8246-0). Ideals.

Penguin. Angela Royston. Ed. by JV-Warwick Press Staff. (Animal Life Stories Ser.). (Illus.). 24p. (gr. 1-3). 1988. 10.40 (ISBN 0-531-19042-0, Warwick). Watts.

Penguin. Vincent Serventy. (Animals in the Wild Ser.). (Illus.). 24p. (gr. k-3). 1986. pap. 1.95 (ISBN 0-590-40102-5). Scholastic Inc.

Penguin Adoption Handbook: A Guide to Creating Your New Family. Edmund B. Bolles. 244p. (Orig.). 1984. pap. 9.95 (ISBN 0-14-046548-0). Penguin.

Penguin Atlas of Ancient History. Colin McEvedy. 96p. Date not set. pap. 5.50 (ISBN 0-317-53194-8). Noontide.

Penguin Atlas of Ancient History. Colin McEvedy. 1986. pap. 6.95 (ISBN 0-14-051151-2). Penguin.

Penguin Atlas of Medieval History. Colin McEvedy. 96p. Date not set. pap. 5.50 (ISBN 0-317-53195-6). Noontide.

Penguin Atlas of Medieval History. Colin McEvedy. 1986. pap. 6.95 (ISBN 0-14-051152-0). Penguin.

Penguin Atlas of Modern History. Colin McEvedy. 1986. pap. 6.95 (ISBN 0-14-051153-9). Penguin.

Penguin Atlas of North American History to 1870. Colin McEvedy. 112p. 6.95 (ISBN 0-14-051128-8). Penguin.

Penguin Atlas of Recent History. Colin McEvedy. 1986. pap. 6.95 (ISBN 0-14-051154-7). Penguin.

Penguin Book of Arostic Puzzles. Albie Fiore. 128p. 1988. pap. 3.95 (ISBN 0-14-010066-0). Penguin.

Penguin Book of Bird Poetry. Intro. by Peggy Munsterberg. (Poetry Ser.). 384p. 1984. pap. 8.95 (ISBN 0-14-042278-1). Penguin.

Penguin Book of Caribbean Verse in English. Ed. by Paula Burnett. 528p. 1986. pap. 8.95 (ISBN 0-14-058511-7). Penguin.

Penguin Book of Chess Openings. W. R. Hartston. (Handbook Ser.). 192p. 1981. pap. 4.95 (ISBN 0-14-046312-7). Penguin.

Penguin Book of Christmas Carols. Ed. by Elizabeth Poston. 144p. 1987. pap. 3.95 (ISBN 0-14-008357-X). Penguin.

Penguin Book of Contemporary American Essays. Ed. by Maureen Howard. (Nonfiction Ser.). 320p. 1985. pap. 7.95 (ISBN 0-14-006618-7). Penguin.

Penguin Book of "Daily Telegraph" 50th Anniversary Crosswords. Ed. by Alan Cash. (Penguin Nonfiction Ser.). 144p. 1985. pap. 3.50 (ISBN 0-14-003988-0). Penguin.

Penguin Book of Eighteenth-Century English Verse. Ed. by Dennis Davison. (Poetry Ser.). 320p. 1973. pap. 6.95 (ISBN 0-14-042169-6). Penguin.

Penguin Book of English Christian Verse. Ed. by Peter Levi. 384p. 1988. pap. 7.95 (ISBN 0-14-058602-4). Penguin.

Penguin Book of English Pastoral Verse. Ed. by John Barrell & John Bull. 1982. pap. 7.95 (ISBN 0-14-042178-5). Penguin.

Penguin Book of German Verse. Ed. by Leonard Forster. 512p. (Ger.). (YA) (gr. 9 up). 1988. pap. 6.95 (ISBN 0-14-058546-X). Penguin.

Penguin Book of Ghost Stories. Ed. by J. A. Cuddon. (Penguin Fiction Ser.). 512p. 1985. pap. 7.95 (ISBN 0-14-006800-7). Penguin.

Penguin Book of Greek Verse. Intro. by Constantine A. Trypanis. 704p. 1988. pap. 9.95 (ISBN 0-14-058595-8). Penguin.

Penguin Book of Hebrew Verse. Ed. by T. Carmi. 448p. (Orig., Hebrew & Eng.). 1981. pap. 13.95 (ISBN 0-14-042197-1). Penguin.

Penguin Book of Homosexual Verse. Ed. by Stephen Coote. 416p. 1987. pap. 6.95 (ISBN 0-14-058551-6). Penguin.

Penguin Book of Horror Stories. Ed. by J. A. Cuddon. (Penguin Fiction Ser.). 560p. 1985. pap. 7.95 (ISBN 0-14-006799-X). Penguin.

Penguin Book of Irish Verse. Ed. by Brendan Kennelly. 470p. 1987. pap. 6.95 (ISBN 0-14-058526-5). Penguin.

Penguin Book of Japanese Verse. Tr. by Geoffrey Bownas & Anthony Thwaite. (Orig.). 1986. pap. 6.95 (ISBN 0-14-058527-3). Penguin.

Penguin Book of Jewish Short Stories. Ed. by Emanuel Litvinoff. 1979. pap. 6.95 (ISBN 0-14-004728-X). Penguin.

Penguin Book of Kites. David Pelham. (Illus.). 224p. 1976. pap. 10.95 (ISBN 0-14-004117-6). Penguin.

Penguin Book of Lieder. Tr. by S. S. Prawer. 208p. 1987. pap. 6.95 (ISBN 0-14-008123-2). Penguin.

Penguin Book of Light Verse. Ed. by Gavin Ewart. 1982. pap. 8.95 (ISBN 0-14-042270-6). Penguin.

Penguin Book of Limericks. Compiled by E. O. Parrott. (Illus.). 304p. 1987. pap. 8.95 (ISBN 0-14-007669-7). Penguin.

Penguin Book of Modern African Poetry. Ed. by Ulli Beier & Gerald Moore. 320p. 1984. pap. 6.95 (ISBN 0-14-058573-7). Penguin.

Penguin Book of Modern British Short Stories. Ed. by Malcolm Bradbury. 1988. 18.95 (ISBN 0-670-81926-3). Viking.

Penguin Book of Modern Urdu Poetry. Selected by & tr. by Mahmood Jamal. 176p. 1987. pap. 6.95 (ISBN 0-14-058512-5). Penguin.

Penguin Book of Modern Yiddish Verse. Ed. by Irving Howe et al. 752p. 1988. pap. 12.95 (ISBN 0-14-009472-5). Penguin.

Penguin Book of New Zealand Verse. Ed. by Ian Wedde & Harvey McQueen. (Poetry Ser.). 575p. 1986. pap. 9.95 (ISBN 0-14-042333-8). Penguin.

Penguin Book of Rounds. Rosemary Cass-Beggs. 1982. pap. 7.95 (ISBN 0-14-070835-9). Penguin.

Penguin Book of Russian Short Stories. Ed. by David Richards. 1981. pap. 7.95 (ISBN 0-14-004816-2). Penguin.

Penguin Book of Southern African Stories. Ed. by Stephen Gray. 336p. 1986. pap. 6.95 (ISBN 0-14-007239-X). Penguin.

Penguin Book of Spanish Verse. Ed. by J. M. Cohen. 656p. 1988. pap. 8.95 (ISBN 0-14-058570-2). Penguin.

Penguin Book of Vampire Stories. Compiled by Alan Ryan. 640p. 1988. pap. 8.95 (ISBN 0-14-010987-0). Penguin.

Penguin Book of Victorian Verse. Ed. by George MacBeth. 448p. 1986. pap. 6.95 (ISBN 0-14-042110-6). Penguin.

Penguin Book of Women Poets. Ed. by Carol Cosman et al. (Poetry Ser.). 1986. pap. 7.95 (ISBN 0-14-058533-8). Penguin.

Penguin Book of Zen Poetry. Ed. by Lucien Stryk & Takashi Ikemoto. Tr. by Lucien Stryk & Takashi Ikemoto. (Poets Ser.). 1981. pap. 6.95 (ISBN 0-14-042247-1). Penguin.

Penguin Book of Zen Poetry. Ed. by Lucien Stryk & Takashi Ikemoto. LC 77-83237. 159p. 1978. 12.95 (ISBN 0-8040-0792-6, Pub. by Swallow). Ohio U Pr.

Penguin Bronte Sisters. Emily Bronte & Charlotte Bronte. 1072p. 1984. pap. 8.95 (ISBN 0-14-009015-0). Penguin.

Penguin Companion to the Arts in the Twentieth Century. Kenneth McLeish. 608p. 1986. pap. 9.95 (ISBN 0-14-051144-X). Penguin.

Penguin Complete Saki. Intro. by Noel Coward. 960p. 1988. pap. 9.95 (ISBN 0-14-009003-7). Penguin.

Penguin Day. Victoria Winteringham. LC 81-47112. (Illus.). 32p. (gr. k-3). 1982. PLB 10.89 (ISBN 0-06-026514-0). HarpJ.

Penguin Dictionary of Archaeology. rev. ed. David Trump. (Reference Ser.). (Illus.). 1982. pap. 8.95 (ISBN 0-14-051116-4). Penguin.

Penguin Dictionary of Architecture. rev. ed. John Fleming et al. (Reference Ser.). 1966. pap. 8.95 (ISBN 0-14-051013-3). Penguin.

Penguin Dictionary of Botany. Lawrence Urdang Associates, Ltd. Ed. by Blackmore & Toothill. (Reference Ser.). 288p. 1984. pap. 8.95 (ISBN 0-14-051126-1). Penguin.

Penguin Dictionary of Building. rev. ed. John S. Scott. 384p. 1986. pap. 8.95 (ISBN 0-14-051115-6). Penguin.

Penguin Dictionary of Civil Engineering. John S. Scott. (Reference Ser.). 312p. 1984. pap. 7.95 (ISBN 0-14-051011-7). Penguin.

Penguin Dictionary of Computers. Anthony Chandor et al. (Reference Ser.). 496p. 1986. pap. 7.95 (ISBN 0-14-051127-X). Penguin.

Penguin Dictionary of Curious & Interesting Numbers. David Wells. 288p. 1987. pap. 6.95 (ISBN 0-14-008029-5). Penguin.

Penguin Dictionary of Design & Designers. Simon Jervis. (Reference Ser.). 640p. 1984. pap. 8.95 (ISBN 0-14-051089-3). Penguin.

Penguin Dictionary of English & European History 1485-1789. E. N. Williams. (Reference Ser.). 480p. 1980. pap. 8.95 (ISBN 0-14-051084-2). Penguin.

Penguin Dictionary of English Idioms. Daphne M. Gulland & David G. Hinds-Howell. 288p. 1987. pap. 6.95 (ISBN 0-14-051135-0). Penguin.

Penguin Dictionary of Human Geography. Brian Goodall. 544p. 1987. pap. 7.95 (ISBN 0-14-051095-8). Penguin.

Penguin Dictionary of Mathematics. J. Daintith & R. D. Nelson. (Reference Ser.). 304p. 1988. pap. 7.95 (ISBN 0-14-051119-9). Penguin.

Penguin Dictionary of Modern History: 1789-1945. Alan W. Palmer. 320p. 1984. pap. 7.95 (ISBN 0-14-051125-3). Penguin.

Penguin Dictionary of Modern Humorous Quotations. Ed. by Fred Metcalf. 1988. pap. 7.95 (ISBN 0-14-007568-2). Penguin.

Penguin Dictionary of Modern Quotations. rev. ed. Ed. by John M. Cohen. (Reference Ser.). 496p. 1971. pap. 7.95 (ISBN 0-14-051038-9). Penguin.

Penguin Dictionary of Physical Geography. John B. Whittow. (Reference Ser.). 608p. 1984. pap. 8.95 (ISBN 0-14-051094-X). Penguin.

Penguin Dictionary of Physics. Ed. by Valerie H. Pitt. (Reference Ser.). 1977. pap. 7.95 (ISBN 0-14-051071-0). Penguin.

Penguin Dictionary of Proverbs. Laurence Urdang Associates, Ltd. Ed. by Rosalind Ferguson & Rosalind. 256p. 1983. pap. 7.95 (ISBN 0-14-051118-0). Penguin.

Penguin Dictionary of Psychology. Arthur S. Reber. (Reference). 864p. 1986. pap. 8.95 (ISBN 0-14-051079-6). Penguin.

Penguin Dictionary of Quotations. Ed. by John M. Cohen. (Reference Ser.). (Orig.). 1960. pap. 8.95 (ISBN 0-14-051016-8). Penguin.

Penguin Dictionary of Religions. Ed. by John R. Hinnells. (Reference Ser.). 464p. 1984. pap. 7.95 (ISBN 0-14-051106-7). Penguin.

Penguin Dictionary of Saints. rev. ed. Donald Attwater. Rev. by Catherine R. John. 352p. 1984. pap. 7.95 (ISBN 0-14-051123-7). Penguin.

Penguin Dictionary of Science. 6th ed. E. B. Uvarov & Alan Isaacs. (Reference Ser.). 544p. 1986. pap. 8.95 (ISBN 0-14-051156-3). Penguin.

Penguin Dictionary of Sociology. Nicholas Abercrombie et al. (Reference Ser.). 272p. 1984. pap. 7.95 (ISBN 0-14-051108-3). Penguin.

Penguin Dictionary of Sociology. Nicholas Abercrombie et al. 336p. 1988. pap. 7.95 (ISBN 0-14-051184-9). Penguin.

Penguin Dictionary of Surnames. Basil Cottle. (Reference Ser.). 448p. 1984. pap. 7.95 (ISBN 0-14-051032-X). Penguin.

Penguin Dictionary of the Theatre. John R. Taylor. (Reference Ser.). (Orig.). 1966. pap. 6.95 (ISBN 0-14-051176-8). Penguin.

Penguin Dictionary of Troublesome Words. Bill Bryson. (Reference Ser.). 264p. 1984. pap. 7.95 (ISBN 0-14-051130-X). Penguin.

Penguin Dreams: And Stranger Things. Berke Breathed. (Illus.). 120p. 1985. pap. 6.95 (ISBN 0-316-10725-5). Little.

Penguin Edward Koren. Edward Koren. (Illus.). 128p. 1982. pap. 4.95 (ISBN 0-14-005334-4). Penguin.

Penguin Encyclopedia of Horror & the Supernatural. Ed. & frwd. by Jack Sullivan. LC 85-40558. (Illus.). 512p. 1986. 29.95 (ISBN 0-670-80902-0). Viking.

Penguin Encyclopedia of Nutrition. John Yudkin. 416p. 1986. pap. 7.95 (ISBN 0-14-008563-7). Penguin.

Penguin Family Book. Lauritz Somme & Sybille Kalas. LC 87-32830. (Illus.). (ps-12). 1988. 14.95 (ISBN 0-88708-057-X). Picture Bk Studio.

Penguin French Dictionary. Merlin Thomas & Raymond Escoffey. (Reference Ser.). 848p. 1986. pap. 6.95 (ISBN 0-14-051065-6). Penguin.

Penguin French Phrase Book. Jill Norman & Henri Orteu. 320p. (Orig.). 1988. pap. 4.95 (ISBN 0-14-009942-5). Penguin.

Penguin French Reader. Ed. by Simon Lee & David Ricks. (Orig.). (YA) (gr. 9 up). 1967. pap. 4.95 (ISBN 0-14-002656-8). Penguin.

Penguin German Phrase Book. Jill Norman & Ute Hitchin. 272p. (Orig.). 1988. pap. 4.95 (ISBN 0-14-009940-9). Penguin.

Penguin Great Novels of D. H. Lawrence. D. H. Lawrence. 1088p. 1984. pap. 9.95 (ISBN 0-14-009012-6). Penguin.

Penguin Guide to Ancient Egypt. William J. Murnane. (Illus.). 336p. 1983. pap. 12.95 (ISBN 0-14-046326-7). Penguin.

Penguin Guide to Australia 1989. (Illus.). 256p. 1988. pap. 11.95 (ISBN 0-14-019905-5). Penguin.

Penguin Guide to Canada 1989. (Illus.). 432p. 1988. pap. 12.95 (ISBN 0-14-019906-3). Penguin.

Penguin Guide to Compact Discs, Cassettes & LPs. Edward Greenfield et al. 608p. 1986. pap. 14.95 (ISBN 0-14-046754-8). Penguin.

Penguin Guide to England & Wales 1989. (Illus.). 384p. 1988. pap. 12.95 (ISBN 0-14-019901-2). Penguin.

Penguin Guide to France. Ed. by John Ardagh. LC 85-40544. (Illus.). 320p. 1985. 22.50 (ISBN 0-670-80898-9). Viking.

Penguin Guide to France 1989. (Illus.). 416p. 1988. pap. 12.95 (ISBN 0-14-019902-0). Penguin.

Penguin Guide to Ireland 1989. (Illus.). 224p. 1988. pap. 10.95 (ISBN 0-14-019904-7). Penguin.

Penguin Guide to Italy 1989. (Illus.). 448p. 1988. pap. 12.95 (ISBN 0-14-019903-9). Penguin.

Penguin Guide to Medieval Europe. Richard Barber. (Penguin Handbooks). 400p. 1984. pap. 11.95 (ISBN 0-14-046633-9). Penguin.

Penguin Guide to New York City 1989. (Illus.). 320p. 1989. pap. 11.95 (ISBN 0-14-019907-1). Penguin.

Penguin Guide to Prehistoric England & Wales. James Dyer. (Illus.). 400p. 1983. pap. 7.95 (ISBN 0-14-046351-8). Penguin.

Penguin Guide to the Caribbean 1989. (Illus.). 224p. 1988. pap. 9.95 (ISBN 0-14-019900-4). Penguin.

Penguin Guide to the Landscape of England & Wales. Paul Coones & John Patten. 400p. 1986. pap. 8.95 (ISBN 0-14-008626-9). Penguin.

Penguin-Hellenews English-Greek Dictionary. Ed. by G. Vassiliades. (Eng. & Gr.). 1978. 50.00 (ISBN 0-89241-051-5). Caratzas.

Penguin Henry Lawson. Ed. & intro. by John Barnes. 240p. 1987. pap. 6.95 (ISBN 0-14-009215-3). Penguin.

Penguin History of Canada. Kenneth McNaught. 416p. 1988. pap. 7.95 (ISBN 0-14-011033-X). Penguin.

Penguin in New York. William Rapin. LC 84-15609. (Illus.). 32p. 1984. 9.95 (ISBN 0-918273-04-8). Coffee Hse.

Penguin in the Snow. Douglas Allen. LC 87-9968. (Animal Habitats Ser.). (Illus.). 32p. (gr. 4-6). 1987. PLB 9.95 (ISBN 1-55532-270-0). Stevens Inc.

Penguin Island. Anatole France. Repr. lib. bdg. 18.95 (ISBN 0-89190-540-5). Am Repr-Rivercity Pr.

Penguin Island. Anatole France. Tr. by A. W. Evans. LC 81-80108. 1981. pap. 6.95 (ISBN 0-918172-09-8). Leetes Isl.

Penguin Island. Anatole France. LC 84-4657. 295p. 1984. 6.95 (ISBN 0-394-60516-0). Modern Lib.

Penguin Italian Phrase Book. Jill Norman & Pietro Giorgetti. 272p. 1988. pap. 4.95 (ISBN 0-14-009938-7). Penguin.

Penguin Kenneth Grahame. Kenneth Grahame. 320p. (Orig.). 1984. pap. 6.95 (ISBN 0-14-006856-2). Penguin.

Penguin London Mapguide. Michael Middleditch. (Illus.). 48p. 1988. pap. 4.95 (ISBN 0-14-046821-8). Penguin.

Penguin Map of Europe. Michael Middleditch. 1985. pap. 5.95 (ISBN 0-14-051150-4). Penguin.

Penguin Map of North America. Michael Middleditch. 1987. 4.95 (ISBN 0-317-56045-X). Penguin.

Penguin Medical Encyclopedia. Peter Wingate. (Reference Ser.). (Illus.). 1972. pap. 7.95 (ISBN 0-14-051048-6). Penguin.

Penguin New Writing. John Lehmann. 1977. Repr. of 1947 ed. 15.00 (ISBN 0-89984-214-3). Century Bookbindery.

Penguin Partners. Karen E. Little. (Illus.). (ps-1). 1981. 4.50 (ISBN 0-913545-05-8). Moonlight FL.

Penguin Persons & Peppermints. Walter P. Eaton. LC 72-93335. (Essay Index Reprint Ser). 1922. 19.00 (ISBN 0-8369-1288-8). Ayer Co Pubs.

Penguin Pete. Marcus Pfister. LC 87-1627. (Illus.). 32p. (gr. k-3). 1987. 11.95 (ISBN 0-8050-0492-0, North South Bks). H Holt & Co.

Penguin Pete's New Friends. Marcus Pfister. (Illus.). 32p. (gr. k-3). 1988. 11.95 (ISBN 0-8050-0739-3, North South Bks). H Holt & Co.

Penguin Pocket Thesaurus. Fay Carney & Maurice Waite. (Reference Ser.). 656p. (Orig.). 1985. pap. 3.50 (ISBN 0-14-051137-7). Penguin.

Penguin Pool Murder. Stuart Palmer. 224p. 1987. pap. 2.95 (ISBN 0-553-26334-X). Bantam.

Penguin Portuguese Phrase Book. Jill Norman & Antonio De Figuerdo. 288p. 1988. pap. 4.95 (ISBN 0-14-009937-9). Penguin.

Penguin Principles. David Belasic & Paul Schmidt. LC 85-15524. 1986. 5.95 (ISBN 0-89536-799-8, 6817). CSS of Ohio.

Penguin Psychology: or, The Mystery of Bridge Building. Robert Benchley. 14.95 (ISBN 0-88411-299-3, Pub. by Aeonian Pr). Amereon Ltd.

Penguin Roget's Thesaurus. rev. ed. Ed. by Sue Lloyd. (Reference Ser.). 800p. 1985. pap. 7.95 (ISBN 0-14-051155-5). Penguin.

Penguin Russian Course. J. L. Fennell. (Reference Ser). 1984. pap. 5.95 (ISBN 0-14-007053-2). Penguin.

Penguin Shorter Atlas of the Bible. Luc H. Grollenberg. Tr. by Mary F. Hedlund. (Reference Ser). (Illus.). 1978. pap. 8.95 (ISBN 0-14-051056-7). Penguin.

Penguin Spanish Phrase Book. Jill Norman & Maria V. Alvarez. 288p. 1988. pap. 4.95 (ISBN 0-14-009936-0). Penguin.

Penguin Tales from the Thousand & One Nights. Tr. by N. J. Dawood. 1973. pap. 5.95 (ISBN 0-14-044289-8). Penguin.

Penguin That Walks at Night. Pauline Reilly. (Illus.). 32p. (Orig.). 1985. pap. 5.95 (ISBN 0-86417-034-3, Pub. by Kangaroo Pr). Intl Spec Bk.

Penguin Thomas Hardy, Vol. 1. Thomas Hardy. 928p. 1984. pap. 8.95 (ISBN 0-14-009010-X). Penguin.

Penguin Thomas Hardy, Vol. 2. Thomas Hardy. 1216p. 1984. pap. 8.95 (ISBN 0-14-009011-8). Penguin.

Penguin World Omnibus of Science Fiction. Ed. by Brian Aldiss & Sam J. Lundwall. 320p. 1987. pap. 4.95 (ISBN 0-14-008067-8). Penguin.

Penguin Year. Susan Bonners. LC 79-53595. (Illus.). 48p. (ps-3). 1981. 11.95; PLB 12.95 (ISBN 0-385-28022-X). Delacorte.

Penguins. Jenny Coldrey. (Deutsch Nature's Way Ser.). (Illus.). 32p. (gr. 2-5). 1984. 9.95 (ISBN 0-233-97524-1). Andre Deutsch.

Penguins. David Hilton. (Illus.). 24p. (Orig.). 1981. pap. 3.00 (ISBN 0-912449-04-7). Floating Island.

Penguins. Sylvia A. Johnson. LC 80-28180. (Lerner Natural Science Bks.). (gr. 4-10). 1981. PLB 12.95 (ISBN 0-8225-1453-2). Lerner Pubns.

Penguins. Emilie U. Lepthien. LC 82-17911. (New True Bks.). (Illus.). 48p. (gr. k-4). 1983. PLB 12.60 (ISBN 0-516-01683-0); pap. 3.95 (ISBN 0-516-41683-9). Childrens.

Penguins. Roger T. Peterson. LC 79-10101. 1979. 40.00 (ISBN 0-395-27092-8). HM.

Penguins. Tony Soper & John Sparks. LC 67-25577. 1967. 12.50 (ISBN 0-8008-6275-9). Taplinger.

Penguins. John Sparks & Tony Soper. LC 86-29063. (Illus.). 248p. 1987. 21.95 (ISBN 0-8160-1753-0). Facts on File.

Penguins. Lynn M. Stone. (Wildlife (Habits & Habitat) Ser.). (Illus.). 48p. (gr. 4-5). 1987. PLB 10.95 (ISBN 0-89686-326-3). Crestwood Hse.

Penguins. Wildlife Education, Ltd. (Zoobooks). (Illus.). 20p. (YA) (gr. 5 up). 1983. pap. 1.95 (ISBN 0-937934-17-8). Wildlife Educ.

Penguins & Polar Bears see Books for Young Explorers.

Penguins: Animal Information Ser. 32p. (ps-1). 1986. pap. 1.25 (ISBN 0-8431-1524-6). Price Stern.

Penguins, of All People. Don Freeman. (Illus.). (gr. k-3). 1971. lib. bdg. 12.50 (ISBN 0-670-54617-8). Viking.

Penguins Paint. Valerie Tripp. LC 87-14081. (Just One More Ser.). (Illus.). 24p. (ps-2). 1987. PLB 10.60 (ISBN 0-516-01567-2); pap. 2.95 (ISBN 0-516-41567-0). Childrens.

Penguins: Past & Present, Here & There. George G. Simpson. LC 75-27211. (Illus.). pap. 8.95 08/1982 162pp (ISBN 0-300-03095-9, Y-473). Yale U Pr.

Penguin's Penguins. Dennis Traut. (Illus.). 48p. 1982. pap. 2.95 (ISBN 0-14-005987-3). Penguin.

Penhallow. Georgette Heyer. Repr. lib. bdg. 20.95x (ISBN 0-89190-646-0, Pub. by River City Pr). Amereon Ltd.

Penhallow. Georgette Heyer. 320p. 1987. pap. 3.50 (ISBN 0-425-09778-1). Berkley Pub.

Penhallow's Indian Wars. facsimile ed. Ed. by Edward Wheelock. LC 71-179534. (Select Bibliographies Reprint Ser). Repr. of 1924 ed. 20.00 (ISBN 0-8369-6663-5). Ayer Co Pubs.

Penia En Ploutos. Jacob Homelrijk. Ed. by Gregory Vlastos. LC 78-19360. (Morals & Law in Ancient Greece Ser.). 1979. Repr. of 1925 ed. lib. bdg. 14.00x (ISBN 0-405-11552-0). Ayer Co Pubs.

Penicillin Fifty Years After Fleming. 2nd ed. Ed. by James Baddiley & E. P. Abraham. (Royal Society Ser.). 378p. 1980. lib. bdg. 62.00x (ISBN 0-85403-140-5, Pub. by Royal Soc London). Scholium Intl.

Penicillin in the Treatment of Syphilis: The Experience of Three Decades. O. Idse & T. Guthe. (WHO Bulletin Supplement: Vol. 47). (Summary in French). 1972. pap. 4.80 (ISBN 92-4-068471-9). World Health.

Penicillin: Meeting the Challenge. Gladys L. Hobby. LC 84-19689. (Illus.). 319p. 1985. 35.00x (ISBN 0-300-03225-0). Yale U Pr.

Penicillium & Acremonium. Ed. by John F. Peberdy. (Biotechnology Handbooks: Vol. 1). 286p. 1987. 42.50x (ISBN 0-306-42345-6, Plenum Pr). Plenum Pub.

Peninsula. Alice H. Rice. 18.95 (ISBN 0-89190-728-9, Pub. by Am Repr). Amereon Ltd.

Peninsula Portrait: An Illustrated History of San Mateo County. Mitchell P. Postel. Ed. by Lane Powell. (Illus.). 160p. (YA) (gr. 7 up). 1988. 29.95 (ISBN 0-89781-255-7). Windsor Pubns Inc.

Peninsula Trails. 2nd ed. Jean Rusmore & Frances Spangle. (Illus.). 216p. 1988. pap. 10.95 (ISBN 0-89997-097-4). Wilderness Pr.

Peninsula y la Isla. Luis I. Larcada. LC 86-62103. (Senda de Estudios y Ensayos). (Illus.). 96p. (Orig., Span.). 1987. pap. 8.95 (ISBN 0-918454-58-1). Senda Nueva.

Peninsular Malaysia. Jin-Bee Ooi. LC 75-42166. (Geographies for Advanced Study). pap. 113.30 (2027710). Bks Demand UMI.

Peninsular Preparation: The Reform of the British Army, 1795-1809. Richard G. Glover. LC 63-25938. pap. 80.80 (ISBN 0-317-08279-5, 2051444). Bks Demand UMI.

Penitence of Adam: (A Study of the Andrius MS., No. 36. Esther C. Quinn. Tr. by Micheline Dufau. LC 79-19056. (Romance Monographs Ser.). 192p. 1980. 21.00x (ISBN 84-499-3367-6). Romance.

Penitent. Isaac Bashevis Singer. LC 83-8977. 169p. 1983. 13.95 (ISBN 0-374-23064-1). FS&G.

Penitent. Isaac Bashevis Singer. 128p. 1984. pap. 2.95 (ISBN 0-449-20612-2, Crest). Fawcett.

Penitente Elusivo: Reader 4. Kay Jarvis-Sladky. LC 81-7842. (Aventura! Ser.). (Illus., Orig., Span.). (YA) (gr. 7-12). 1982. pap. 1.95 (ISBN 0-88436-861-0, 70262). EMC.

Penitente Moradas of Abiquiu. Richard E. Ahlborn. LC 85-43242. (Illus.). 52p. 1986. pap. 3.95x (ISBN 0-87474-253-6). Smithsonian.

Penitente Self-Government: Brotherhoods & Councils 1797-1947. Thomas J. Steele & Rowena Rivera. LC 85-71320. (Illus.). 208p. (Orig.). 1985. 29.95 (ISBN 0-941270-28-9); pap. 12.95 (ISBN 0-941270-29-7). Ancient City Pr.

Penitentes. Ray J. De Aragon. (Illus.). 105p. (Orig.). 1988. pap. 5.95 (ISBN 0-932906-16-8). Pan-Am Publishing Co.

Penitentes of New Mexico. Ed. by Carlos E. Cortes. LC 73-14212. (Mexican American Ser.). (Illus.). 1974. Repr. 36.00x (ISBN 0-405-05686-9). Ayer Co Pubs.

Penitentes of the Southwest. Marta Weigle. LC 78-131971. (Illus.). 48p. 1970. pap. 2.95 (ISBN 0-941270-00-9). Ancient City Pr.

Penitential Discipline of the Primitive Church. Nathaniel Marshall. LC 74-172846. (Library of Anglo-Catholic Theology: No. 13). Repr. of 1844 ed. 27.50 (ISBN 0-404-52105-3). AMS Pr.

Penitential Rite of the Ancient Mexicans. Zelia Nuttall. (HU PMP Ser.). 1904. pap. 10.00 (ISBN 0-527-01189-4). Kraus Repr.

Penjing: The Chinese Art of Miniature Garden: The Shanghai Botanic Garden. Hu Yunhua. LC 82-823. (Illus.). 166p. 1982. 39.95 (ISBN 0-917304-70-5). Timber.

Penkovskiy Papers. Oleg Penkovskiy. 1982. pap. 3.50 (ISBN 0-345-30093-9). Ballantine.
Penmanship for Christian Writing. Daniel Strubhar. (gr. 1-4). 1981. write for info.; tchr's. ed. avail. Rod & Staff.
Penmanship of the Sixteenth, Seventeenth, & Eighteenth Centuries. Lewis F. Day. LC 78-58919. (Illus.). 1979. pap. 7.95 (ISBN 0-8008-6277-5, Pentalic). Taplinger.
Penn Central Failure & the Role of Financial Institutions. United States Congress Committee on Banking & Currency. LC 79-39322. 1972. 9.95 (ISBN 0-405-00374-9). Ayer Co Pubs.
Penn Central Power. Robert J. Yanosey. (Illus.). 248p. 1987. 45.00 (ISBN 0-9619058-0-8). Morning NJ.
Penn State: An Illustrated History. Michael Bezilla. LC 84-43057. (Illus.). 432p. 1985. 39.50 (ISBN 0-271-00392-8). Pa St U Pr.
Pennant Race. Jim Brosnan. (Penguin Sports Library). 252p. 1983. pap. 6.95 (ISBN 0-14-006755-8). Penguin.
Pennate Diatoms: A Translation of Hustedt's Die Kieselagen, Vol. 2. F. Hustedt. Tr. by Norman G. Jensen from Ger. (Illus.). 918p. 1985. Repr. of 1959 ed. lib. bdg. 150.00x (ISBN 3-7682-1416-8). Lubrecht & Cramer.
Pennaten Diatomeen Aus Dem Obereozaen Von Oamaru, Neuseeland. H. J. Schrader. (Illus.). 1969. 24.00x (ISBN 3-7682-5428-3). Lubrecht & Cramer.
Pennell Family. G. T. Ridlon. LC 70-133876. (Saco Valley Settlements Ser). 1970. pap. 2.00 (ISBN 0-8048-0822-8). C E Tuttle.
Pennell's Etchings: A Complete Catalogue. Louis A. Wuerth. (Illus.). 334p. 1986. Repr. of 1928 ed. 95.00 (ISBN 0-915346-93-1). A Wofsy Fine Arts.
Pennell's New York City Etchings: Ninety-One Prints. Joseph Pennell & Edward Bryant. (Illus.). 112p. (Orig.). 1981. pap. 6.95 (ISBN 0-486-23913-6). Dover.
Pennell's New York Etchings: Ninety Prints. Joseph Pennell. (Illus.). 16.50 (ISBN 0-8446-5801-4). Peter Smith.
Pennies for the Piper. Susan McLean. 160p. 1982. pap. 1.95 (ISBN 0-448-16920-7). Ace Bks.
Pennies for the Piper. Susan H. McLean. LC 81-4073. 132p. (gr. 5 up). 1981. 9.95 (ISBN 0-374-35791-9). FS&G.
Pennies from a Poor Box. Joseph E. Manton. 1962. 6.50 (ISBN 0-8198-0119-4). Dghtrs St Paul.
Pennies, Nickels, & Dreams. Jean Keathley. Ed. by Helen Graves. LC 88-50117. 44p. (gr. k-3). 1988. 5.95 (ISBN 1-55523-137-3). Winston-Derek.
Pennington Profile. 2nd ed. Margaret J. O'Connell. (Illus.). 452p. 1986. 25.00 (ISBN 0-9617592-1-6); deluxe ed. 50.00 (ISBN 0-9617592-0-8). Pennington Lib.
Penn's Example to the Nations: 300 Years of the Holy Experiment. Ed. by Robert G. Crist. LC 86-63552. (Illus.). 276p. (Orig.). 1987. 18.95 (ISBN 0-9618164-0-6); pap. 6.00 (ISBN 0-9618164-1-4). PA Coun Churches.
Penn's Woods: A Love Story. Bernard C. Barnick. 145p. 1980. 8.95 (ISBN 0-682-49660-X, Banner). Exposition-Phoenix.
Pennsy Power. Alvin F. Staufer & Bert Pennypacker. LC 62-20878. (Illus.). 336p. 1962. 35.00 (ISBN 0-944513-04-2). Staufer Bks.
Pennsy Power II. Alvin F. Staufer & Bert Pennypacker. LC 62-20872. (Illus.). 352p. 1968. 35.00 (ISBN 0-944513-05-0). Staufer Bks.
Pennsy Q Class. E. T. Harley. LC 82-81755. (Classic Power Ser.: No. 5). (Illus.). 88p. 1982. pap. 15.95 (ISBN 0-934088-09-8). NJ Intl Inc.
Pennsylvania. new ed. Allan Carpenter. LC 78-5089. (New Enchantment of America State Bks.). (Illus.). 96p. (gr. 4 up). 1978. PLB 15.93 (ISBN 0-516-04138-X). Childrens.
Pennsylvania. Thomas C. Cochran. (States & the Nation Ser.). (Illus.). 1978. 14.95 (ISBN 0-393-05635-X, Co-Pub by AASLH). Norton.
Pennsylvania. Robert Llewellyn. Ed. by James Patrick. (Scenic Discovery Ser.). (Illus.). 128p. 1987. 35.00 (ISBN 0-89909-129-6). Yankee Bks.
Pennsylvania. Sara Pitzer. (Off the Beaten Path Ser.). (Illus.). 1989. pap. price not set (ISBN 0-87106-622-X). Globe Pequot.
Pennsylvania. Sharon S. Shebar & Susan E. Shebar. (First Book Ser.). (Illus.). 72p. (gr. 4-9). 1987. pap. 9.90 (ISBN 0-531-10393-5). Watts.
Pennsylvania. Photos by Clyde Smith. LC 78-51218. (Belding Imprint Ser.). (Illus.). 192p. (Text by M. Cronan Minton). 1978. 29.50 (ISBN 0-912856-40-8). Gr Arts Ctr Pub.
Pennsylvania. Turner Program Services, Inc. Staff & James I. Clark. LC 85-9972. (Portrait of America Library). 48p. (gr. 4 up). 1985. PLB 15.33 (ISBN 0-86514-442-7); pap. text ed. 9.27 (ISBN 0-86514-517-2); Beta video 113.33 (ISBN 0-86514-067-7); VHS video 113.33 (ISBN 0-86514-142-8); 3/4" video 136.00 (ISBN 0-86514-217-3); tchr's guide 13.27 (ISBN 0-86514-292-0); student activity bk. 6.60 (ISBN 0-86514-367-6); index 13.27. Raintree Pubs.
Pennsylvania - Architecture & Culture: A Bibliography. E. Willard Miller & Ruby M. Miller. (Architecture Ser.: A 1508). 55p. 1985. 8.25 (ISBN 0-89028-658-2). Vance Biblios.
Pennsylvania - History & Politics: A Bibliography. E. Willard Miller & Ruby M. Miller. (Public Administration Ser.: P 1855). 71p. 1986. 17.50 (ISBN 0-89028-725-2). Vance Biblios.
Pennsylvania - Natural Resources & Economic Development: A Bibliography. E. Willard Miller & Ruby M. Miller. (Public Administration Ser.: P 1819). 66p. 1985. 9.75 (ISBN 0-89028-669-8). Vance Biblios.
Pennsylvania - Transportation: A Bibliography. E. Willard Miller & Ruby M. Miller. (Public Administration Ser.: P 1818). 25p. 1985. 3.75 (ISBN 0-89028-668-X). Vance Biblios.
Pennsylvania: A Guide to the Keystone State. Federal Writers' Project Staff. (American Guidebook Ser.). 1980. Repr. of 1940 ed. lib. bdg. 79.00x (ISBN 0-403-02187-1). Somerset Pub.
Pennsylvania: Agency. suppl. 6.00 (ISBN 0-686-90876-7). Am Law Inst.
Pennsylvania Agriculture & Country Life: 1640-1840. Stevenson W. Fletcher. LC 50-9470. 605p. 1971. 9.50 (ISBN 0-911124-33-0). Pa Hist & Mus.
Pennsylvania Album: Picture Postcards, 1900-1930. George Miller. LC 79-2707. (Illus.). 1979. 20.00x (ISBN 0-271-00243-3); pap. 12.50 (ISBN 0-271-00247-6). Pa St U Pr.
Pennsylvania & the Federal Constitution 1787-1788, 2 vols, Vol. 1. John McMaster & Frederick B. Stone. LC 74-87406. (American Constitutional & Legal History Ser). 1970. Repr. of 1888 ed. Set. lib. bdg. 79.50 (ISBN 0-306-71550-3). Da Capo.
Pennsylvania Antiwar Movement, Eighteen Sixty-One to Eighteen Sixty-Five. Arnold M. Shankman. LC 78-75186. 240p. 1980. 22.50 (ISBN 0-8386-2228-3). Fairleigh Dickinson.
Pennsylvania Appellate Practice. Pennsylvania Bar Institute. 146p. 1983. 15.00 (ISBN 0-318-02166-8, 235). PA Bar Inst.
Pennsylvania Archives: Series 1-9, 122 vols. Repr. of 1935 ed. Set. 6200.00 (ISBN 0-685-56812-1). AMS Pr.
Pennsylvania Atlas: A Thematic Atlas of the Keystone State. 2nd. ed. Paul F. Rizza & James C. Hughes. LC 83-684876. (Illus.). 127p. 1982. 16.00x (ISBN 0-933550-02-2). Ptolemy Pr.
Pennsylvania Atlas & Gazetteer. DeLorme Mapping Company Staff. (Atlas & Gazetteer Ser.). 96p. (Orig.). 1987. pap. 12.95 (ISBN 0-89933-236-6). DeLorme Map.
Pennsylvania Automotive Directory. Ed. by T. L. Spelman. 1985. 24.95 (ISBN 1-55527-028-X). Auto Contact Inc.
Pennsylvania Avenue: America's Main Street. Ted Landphair. (Illus.). 180p. 1988. 39.95 (ISBN 1-55835-000-4); pap. 29.95 (ISBN 1-55835-010-1). Am Inst Arch.
Pennsylvania Boroughs. W. P. Holcomb. 1973. pap. 9.00 (ISBN 0-384-24045-3). Johnson Repr.
Pennsylvania Boroughs. William P. Holcomb. LC 78-63761. (Johns Hopkins University. Studies in the Social Sciences. Fourth Ser. 1886: 4). Repr. of 1886 ed. 11.50 (ISBN 0-404-61029-3). AMS Pr.
Pennsylvania Butter: Tools & Processes. Elizabeth A. Powell. (Vol. I). (Illus.). 27p. 1974. pap. 3.00 (ISBN 0-910302-09-X). Bucks Co Hist.
Pennsylvania Cavalcade. Federal Writers' Project Staff. LC 76-44940. (American Guidebook Ser.). 1980. Repr. of 1942 ed. lib. bdg. 69.00x (ISBN 0-403-03821-9). Somerset Pub.
Pennsylvania Census Index 1790. Ronald V. Jackson. (Illus.). lib. bdg. 40.00 (ISBN 0-317-17064-3). Accelerated Index.
Pennsylvania Census Index 1800. Ronald V. Jackson & Gary R. Teeples. LC 77-86105. (Illus.). lib. bdg. 43.00 (ISBN 0-89593-115-X). Accelerated Index.
Pennsylvania Census Index 1810. Ronald V. Jackson. (Illus.). lib. bdg. 55.00 (ISBN 0-317-17065-1). Accelerated Index.
Pennsylvania Census Index 1820. Ronald V. Jackson & Gary R. Teeples. LC 77-86095. (Illus.). lib. bdg. 61.00 (ISBN 0-89593-117-6). Accelerated Index.
Pennsylvania Census Index 1830. Ronald V. Jackson. LC 77-86096. (Illus.). lib. bdg. 65.00 (ISBN 0-89593-118-4). Accelerated Index.
Pennsylvania Census Index 1840. Ronald V. Jackson. LC 77-86097. (Illus.). lib. bdg. 95.00 (ISBN 0-89593-119-2). Accelerated Index.
Pennsylvania Census Index 1850, 2 vols. Ronald V. Jackson. LC 77-86089. (Illus.). Set. lib. bdg. 140.00 (ISBN 0-89593-120-6). Accelerated Index.
Pennsylvania Census 1810. Ronald V. Jackson. LC 77-86094. (Illus.). lib. bdg. 48.00 (ISBN 0-89593-116-8). Accelerated Index.
Pennsylvania Child Custody: Law, Practice & Procedure - Including Using Expert Witnesses in Custody Cases. Emanuel A. Bertin. LC 82-74396. xxiv, 475p. 1983. 40.00. Bisel Co.
Pennsylvania Chronology & Factbook, Vol. 38. Robert I. Vexler. LC 78-21054. (Chronologies & Documentary Handbook of the States). 149p. 1978. 8.50 (ISBN 0-379-16163-X). Oceana.
Pennsylvania Civil Practice & Procedure. Pennsylvania Bar Institute. 254p. 1984. 25.00 (ISBN 0-318-02202-8, 258). PA Bar Inst.
Pennsylvania Civil Procedure Law & Rules, 2 vols. Gould Editorial Staff. 600p. 1983. text ed. 14.00 looseleaf (ISBN 0-87526-295-3). Gould.
Pennsylvania Clocks & Watches: Antique Timepieces & Their Makers. James W. Gibbs. LC 83-62539. (Illus.). 320p. 1984. 39.50 (ISBN 0-271-00367-7). Pa St U Pr.
Pennsylvania Coal: Resources, Technology & Utilization. Ed. by Shyamal K. Majumdar & E. Willard Miller. LC 82-62857. (Illus.). xxvi, 594p. 1983. 30.00 (ISBN 0-9606670-1-6). Penn Science.
Pennsylvania Condominium Law & Practice: Law, Practice, Checklists, Forms. Ronald B. Glazer. LC 81-68874. 1981. pap. 33.75 (ISBN 0-318-20248-4). Bisel Co.
Pennsylvania Consolidated Statutes, Constitution: 1982 Permanent Edition. Legislative Reference Bureau Staff. (Orig.). 1975. pap. 3.55 (ISBN 0-8182-0046-4). Commonweal PA.
Pennsylvania Consolidated Statutes Title: Names 1982 Special Edition. rev. ed. Legislative Reference Bureau. 29p. 1982. pap. text ed. 1.85 (ISBN 0-8182-0011-1). Commonweal PA.
Pennsylvania Consolidated Statutes, Title 18: Crime & Offence, 1982 Edition. rev. ed. Legislative Reference Bureau Staff. 302p. 1982. pap. text ed. 5.05 (ISBN 0-8182-0007-3). Commonweal PA.
Pennsylvania Consolidated Statutes, Title 13: Commercial Code, 1982 Edition. Legislative Reference Bureau Staff. 310p. 1982. pap. 5.05 (ISBN 0-8182-0006-5). Commonweal PA.
Pennsylvania Consolidated Statutes, Title 20, Decedents, Estates & Fiduciaries: 1982 Edition. Legislative Reference Bureau Staff. 278p. 1982. pap. 4.55 (ISBN 0-8182-0008-1). Commonweal PA.
Pennsylvania Consolidated Statutes, Title 24, Education: 1976 Permanent Edition. Legislative Reference Bureau Staff. (Orig.). 1976. pap. 2.55 (ISBN 0-8182-0043-X). Commonweal PA.
Pennsylvania Consolidated Statutes, Title 30, Fish: 1980 Permanent Edition. Legislatives Reference Bureau Staff. (Orig.). 1980. pap. 3.55 (ISBN 0-8182-0044-8). Commonweal PA.
Pennsylvania Consolidated Statutes, Title 42, Judiciary & Judicial Procedure: 1982 Edition. Rev. ed. Legislative Reference Bureau Staff. 554p. 1982. pap. text ed. 7.20 (ISBN 0-8182-0010-3). Commonweal PA.
Pennsylvania Consolidated Statutes, Title 71, State Government: 1975 Permanent Edition. Legislative Reference Bureau Staff. (Orig.). 1975. pap. 2.55 (ISBN 0-8182-0045-6). Commonweal PA.
Pennsylvania Consolidated Statutes: Title 75, Vehicles, 1982 Edition. rev. ed. Pennsylvania Legislative Reference Bureau Staff. 378p. 1982. pap. 5.55 (ISBN 0-8182-0013-8). Commonweal PA.
Pennsylvania Constitution of 1776. J. P. Selsam. LC 77-124925. (American Constitutional & Legal History Ser.). 1971. Repr. of 1936 ed. lib. bdg. 32.50 (ISBN 0-306-71994-0). Da Capo.
Pennsylvania Constitution of 1776: A Study in Revolutionary Democracy. J. Paul Selsam. LC 70-120664. 1970. Repr. lib. bdg. 20.50x (ISBN 0-374-97283-4, Octagon). Hippocrene Bks.
Pennsylvania Corporate Taxes. 187p. 1984. 25.00 (ISBN 0-318-03917-6, 264). PA Bar Inst.
Pennsylvania Corporation: Legal Aspects of Corporation & Operation. James F. Nasuti. (Corporation Practice Ser.: No. 30). 1982. 92.00 (ISBN 0-317-55321-6). BNA.
Pennsylvania Corporation Tax Law & Practice, 2 vols. Sherill T. Moyer. 1987. looseleaf 195.00 (ISBN 0-8322-0174-X). Banks-Baldwin.
Pennsylvania Counties: Nineteen Eighty Census Data Atlas. Pennsylvania State Data Center Staff. 91p. (Orig.). 1983. pap. 10.00 (ISBN 0-939667-03-7, PSDC80-4-83). Penn State Data Ctr.
Pennsylvania County Maps. rev. ed. Ed. by C. J. Puetz. (Illus.). 144p. Date not set. pap. 11.90 (ISBN 0-916514-13-7). Cnty Maps.
Pennsylvania Court of Common Pleas Unit Cost Procedures Manual. National Center for State Courts Staff. 135p. 1982. manuscript 8.10 (NERO-104). Natl Ctr St Courts.
Pennsylvania Court of Common Pleas Unit Cost Procedures Manual: Executive Summary. National Center for State Courts Staff. 29p. 1982. manuscript 1.74 (NERO-105). Natl Ctr St Courts.
Pennsylvania Crimes Code Annotated, Vol. 1. LC 73-93012. 869p. 69.50; Suppl. 1986. 25.00; Suppl. 1987. 27.00. Lawyers Co-Op.
Pennsylvania Criminal Law: Defendant's Mental State. J. Wesley Oler, Jr. 300p. 1986. 35.00x (ISBN 0-87215-999-X). Michie Co.
Pennsylvania Criminal Practice, 1981, 2 vols. Richard Wasserbly. LC 81-10154. 150.00. Callaghan.
Pennsylvania Culture Region: A View from the Barn. Joseph W. Glass. Ed. by Simon Bronner. LC 86-1397. (American Material Culture & Folklife Ser.). 278p. 1986. 47.95 (ISBN 0-8357-1679-1). UMI Res Pr.
Pennsylvania Dutch. Eva D. Costábel. LC 86-3334. (Illus.). 48p. (gr. 3 up). 1986. 14.95 (ISBN 0-689-31281-4, Atheneum Childrens Bks). Macmillan.
Pennsylvania Dutch. rev ed. Phebe H. Gibbons. LC 77-134378. Repr. of 1882 ed. 40.00 (ISBN 0-404-08426-5). AMS Pr.
Pennsylvania Dutch. Lucille Wallower. Ed. by Patricia L. Gump. (gr. 3-4). 1971. pap. 3.75 (ISBN 0-931992-31-1). Penns Valley.
Pennsylvania Dutch: A Dialect of South Germany with an Infusion of English. S. S. Haldeman. 1977. lib. bdg. 59.95 (ISBN 0-8490-2418-8). Gordon Pr.
Pennsylvania Dutch American Folk Art. rev. & enl. ed. Henry J. Kauffman. (Illus.). pap. 5.50 (ISBN 0-486-21205-X). Dover.
Pennsylvania Dutch American Folk Art. rev. & enl. ed. Henry J. Kauffman. (Illus.). 16.00 (ISBN 0-8446-2354-7). Peter Smith.
Pennsylvania Dutch & Their Cookery see Pennsylvania Dutch Cookbook.
Pennsylvania Dutch Cookbook. abr. ed. J. George Frederick. Orig. Title: Pennsylvania Dutch & Their Cookery. 1971. pap. 3.95 (ISBN 0-486-22676-X). Dover.
Pennsylvania Dutch Cookbook. J. George Frederick. 12.75 (ISBN 0-8446-0099-7). Peter Smith.
Pennsylvania Dutch Country: A Pictorial History. Gary R. Hovinen & Elizabeth L. Hovinen. (Illus.). 175p. (Orig.). 1986. 24.95 (ISBN 0-915133-06-7); pap. 16.95. Penn Pubs.
Pennsylvania Dutch Designs. Rebecca McKillip. (International Design Library). (Illus.). 48p. (Orig.). 1983. pap. 5.95 (ISBN 0-88045-032-0). Stemmer Hse.
Pennsylvania Dutch Folklore. (Pennsylvania Dutch Books Ser.). (Illus.). 1960. 3.00 (ISBN 0-911410-02-3). Applied Arts.
Pennsylvania Dutch Needlepoint Designs. Marcia Loeb. (Needlework Ser.). (Illus.). 137p. (Orig.). 1976. pap. 2.25 (ISBN 0-486-23299-9). Dover.
Pennsylvania Estates Practice: Pennsylvania Practice Systems Library Selection, Vol. 1. Nancy Rothkopf & Gilbert M. Cantor. LC 79-91161. 94.50; Suppl. 1986. 47.00. Lawyers Co-Op.
Pennsylvania Evidence. 280p. 1984. 35.00 (ISBN 0-318-03931-1, 280). PA Bar Inst.
Pennsylvania Evidence: Objections & Responses. Mark S. Greenberg & Anthony J. Bocchino. 146p. 1983. 20.00x (ISBN 0-87215-629-X). Michie Co.
Pennsylvania Fiduciary Guide: A Handbook for Executors & Administrators. 4th rev. ed. Ed. by M. Paul Smith et al. LC 83-72880. 463p. 1983. text ed. 42.50 (ISBN 0-318-02643-0). Bisel Co.
Pennsylvania Genealogical Research. 224p. 1986. pap. 9.00 (ISBN 0-913857-09-2). Genealog Sources.
Pennsylvania German Anthology. Ed. by Earl C. Haag. LC 86-62816. 1988. 42.50 (ISBN 0-941664-29-5). Susquehanna U Pr.
Pennsylvania German Anthology. Ed. by Earl C. Haag. LC 88-62816. 352p. (Orig.). 1988. pap. 14.95x (ISBN 0-945636-00-8). Susquehanna U Pr.
Pennsylvania German Art, Sixteen Eighty-Three to Eighteen Fifty. Ed. by Philadelphia Museum of Art & The Henry du Pont Winterthur Museum. LC 83-18267. (Chicago Visual Library: No. 43). 264p. 1984. text ed. 90.00 (ISBN 0-226-69535-2). U of Chicago Pr.
Pennsylvania German Church Records, Births, Baptisms, Marriages, Burials, Etc. LC 82-84493. (3 vols.). (Illus.). 2371p. 1983. 120.00 (ISBN 0-8063-1017-0). Genealog Pub.
Pennsylvania German Collection. Beatrice B. Garvan. LC 79-93027. (Handbooks in American Art: No. 2). (Illus.). 372p. (Orig.). 1982. pap. 14.95 (ISBN 0-87633-035-9). Phila Mus Art.
Pennsylvania German Dictionary. Marcus Lambert. LC 77-89271. (Illus.). 188p. (Ger.). pap. 15.00 (ISBN 0-916838-07-2). Schiffer.
Pennsylvania German Fraktur of the Free Library of Philadelphia: An Illustrated Catalogue, Vols. 1 & 2. Compiled by Frederick S. Weiser. (Illus.). 1976. Set. 60.00x (ISBN 0-911122-32-X, Pub. with Penn. Ger. Soc.). Phila Free Lib.
Pennsylvania German Immigrants, 1709-1786. Ed. by Don Yoder. LC 80-50502. (Illus.). 394p. 1984. 20.00 (ISBN 0-8063-0892-3). Genealog Pub.
Pennsylvania German in the Settlement of Maryland. Daniel W. Nead. LC 75-7961. (Illus.). 304p. 1980. Repr. of 1914 ed. 18.50 (ISBN 0-8063-0678-5). Genealog Pub.
Pennsylvania German Marriages: Marriages & Marriage Evidence in Pennsylvania German Churches. Donna R. Irish. LC 81-84187. 817p. 1984. 40.00 (ISBN 0-8063-0965-2). Genealog Pub.
Pennsylvania German Pioneers, 2 vols. Ralph B. Strassburger. Ed. by William J. Hinke. LC 66-23871. 1564p. 1980. Repr. of 1934 ed. Set. 60.00 (ISBN 0-8063-0323-9); Genealog Pub.
Pennsylvania German Reader & Grammar. Earl C. Haag. LC 82-80453. 320p. 1982. 20.00x (ISBN 0-271-00316-2, Keystone Bks). Pa St U Pr.
Pennsylvania German Secular Folk Songs. Albert F. Buffington. LC 74-78062. (Penn. German Ser.: Vol. 8). 1974. 15.00 (ISBN 0-911122-30-3). Penn German Soc.
Pennsylvania Germans: A Celebration of Their Arts, 1683-1850. Beatrice B. Garvan & Charles F. Hummel. LC 82-61416. (Illus.). 200p. 1982. pap. 18.95 (ISBN 0-87633-048-0). Phila Mus Art.
Pennsylvania Germans in Ontario, Canada: Bd. with Coppersmithing in Pennsylvania; & Lexical Differences Between Four Pennsylvania German Regions. Arthur D. Graeff et al. (Penn. German Folklore Ser.: Vol. 11). Repr. of 1946 ed. 25.00 (ISBN 0-911122-19-2). Penn German Soc.
Pennsylvania Grand Jury Practice. David N. Savitt. 356p. 1983. 65.00 (ISBN 0-8322-0045-X). Banks-Baldwin.

Penny Pincher's Handbook: Hundreds of Ways to Make, Save Money. Alyce W. Kingsley. LC 80-81850. (Illus.). 88p. (Orig.). 1981. pap. 9.95 (ISBN 0-937378-00-3). Poseidon Pubns.

Penny Pincher's Profit Portfolio: How to Make Dollars in Cents. Mark Laythorpe. (Illus.). 80p. 1981. pap. 19.95 (ISBN 0-939230-00-3). SNOWCO.

Penny Pincher's Supplement to the Guide-Books of Europe. Niel M. Lynch. 1978. pap. 2.95 (ISBN 0-87881-076-5). Mojave Bks.

Penny Piper of Saranac: An Episode in Stevenson's Life. Stephen Chalmers. 1973. Repr. of 1916 ed. 15.00 (ISBN 0-8274-0085-3). R West.

Penny Plain Two Pence Coloured: A History of the Juvenile Drama. Albert E. Wilson. LC 68-56476. (Illus.). 1969. Repr. 22.00 (ISBN 0-405-09080-3). Ayer Co Pubs.

Penny Pollard in Print. Robin Klein. (Illus.). 64p. (gr. 4 up). 1988. bds. 10.95 (ISBN 0-19-554638-5). Oxford U Pr.

Penny Pollard's Diary. Robin Klein. (Illus.). 56p. (ps-6). 1987. 10.95 (ISBN 0-19-554415-3); pap. 5.95 (ISBN 0-19-554649-0). Oxford U Pr.

Penny Pollard's Letters. Robin Klein. (Illus.). 64p. (ps-6). 1987. 10.95 (ISBN 0-19-554575-3). Oxford U Pr.

Penny Royal. Susan Moody. 304p. 1987. pap. 2.95 (ISBN 0-449-12867-9). Fawcett.

Penny Saved. Joan Fairman. (Illus.). (gr. 1-4). 1971. PLB 6.19 (ISBN 0-8313-0036-1). Lantern.

Penny Saved Is Impossible. Ogden Nash. 1981. 12.95 (ISBN 0-316-59832-1). Little.

Penny Saved Is Impossible. Ogden Nash. (Illus.). 132p. 1983. pap. 6.95 (ISBN 0-316-59806-2). Little.

Penny Stocks: How to Profit with Low-Priced Stocks. George Kromer & Jerome M. Wegner. 160p. 1986. pap. 7.95 (ISBN 0-89709-150-7, 30150, Liberty Hse). Tab Bks.

Penny the Medicine Maker: The Story of Penicillin. Sherrie S. Epstein. LC 60-14006. (Medical Books for Children). (Illus.). (gr. k-5). 1960. PLB 4.95 (ISBN 0-8225-0006-X). Lerner Pubns.

Penny Theatres of Victorian London. Paul Sheridan. 160p. 1981. 30.00x (ISBN 0-234-72104-9, Pub. by Dobson Bks England). State Mutual Bk.

Penny Warner's Party Book. Penny Warner. (Illus.). 144p. 1987. pap. 6.95 (ISBN 0-312-00666-7). St Martin.

Penny Whimsy. William H. Sheldon. LC 76-19190. (Illus.). 1976. Repr. 100.00x (ISBN 0-88000-136-4). Quarterman.

Penny Whistle Book. Robin Williamson. LC 76-41141. (Illus.). 64p. (Orig.). 1977. pap. 7.95 (ISBN 0-8256-0190-8, Oak). Music Sales.

Penny Whistle Children's Party Planner: Parties! Parties! Parties! Complete Step-by-Step Planning, Giving & Enjoying the Best Parties for Children of All Ages. Meredith Brokaw & Annie Gilbar. 224p. 1987. 21.95 (ISBN 1-55584-126-0); pap. 12.95 (ISBN 1-55584-090-6). Weidenfeld.

Penny Whistle Party Planner. Meredith Brokaw & Annie Gilbar. 1987. 19.95 (ISBN 0-317-56859-0); pap. 12.95 (ISBN 0-317-56860-4). Weidenfeld.

Pennypincher's Guide to Landscaping. Carol A. Boston. LC 84-17775. 192p. 1984. 17.95 (ISBN 0-13-655937-9, Busn); pap. 7.95 (ISBN 0-13-655929-8). P-H.

Penny's Poodle Puppy, Pickle. Bernard Wiseman. LC 79-26403. (Bernard Wiseman Bks.). (Illus.). 32p. (gr. k-4). 1980. PLB 6.69 (ISBN 0-8116-6080-X). Garrard.

Penny's Worth of Minced Ham: Another Look at the Great Depression. Robert J. Hastings. (Shawnee Bks). (Illus.). 104p. (Orig.). 1986. 13.95 (ISBN 0-8093-1303-0); pap. 8.95 (ISBN 0-8093-1304-9). S Ill U Pr.

Pennystock Information: Where to Find or Locate Information on Pennystock. Data Notes Research Staff. LC 83-90739. 25p. 1984. pap. text ed. 2.25 (ISBN 0-911569-60-X, Pub. by Data Notes). Prosperity & Profits.

Pennystocks. Bruce G. McWilliams. 264p. 1984. pap. 8.95 (ISBN 0-446-38010-5). Warner Bks.

Pennywhistle Primer. Peter Pickow. 1982. pap. 3.95 (Pub. by Oak). Music Sales.

Penobscot Man. Fannie Eckstorm. LC 74-128733. (Short Story Index Reprint Ser). 1904. 19.00 (ISBN 0-8369-3624-8). Ayer Co Pubs.

Penobscot: Nine Poems. Stephen Tapscott. 23p. (Orig.). 1983. pap. 4.50 (ISBN 0-913219-37-1); pap. 12.00 signed copy (ISBN 0-913219-38-X). Pym Rand Pr.

Penobscot Shamanism. Frank G. Speck. LC 20-13167. (AAA Memoirs Ser.: No. 25). 1919. pap. 28.00 (ISBN 0-527-00527-4). Kraus Repr.

Penobscot Vital Records. Donna Hoffmann. 125p. 1983. pap. 14.95 (ISBN 0-941216-13-6). Cay Bel.

Penological & Preventive Principles: London, 1889. William Tallack. LC 83-49248. (Crime & Punishment in England, 1855-1922 Ser.). 414p. 1984. lib. bdg. 45.00 (ISBN 0-8240-6214-0). Garland Pub.

Penology for Profit: A History of the Texas Prison System, 1867-1912. Donald R. Walker. LC 87-18048. (Texas A&M Southwestern Studies: No. 7). (Illus.). 218p. 1988. 24.50 (ISBN 0-89096-315-0). Tex A&M Univ Pr.

Penology: The Evolution of Corrections in America. 2nd ed. George G. Killinger et al. (Criminal Justice Ser.). (Illus.). 344p. 1979. pap. text ed. 30.00 (ISBN 0-8299-0277-5). West Pub.

Penon de las Animas. Orlando R. Lopez. (Romance Real Ser.). 192p. (Orig.). pap. 1.50 (ISBN 0-88025-007-0). Roca Pub.

Penquin Year. (Orig.). (gr. k-6). 1989. pap. price not set (ISBN 0-440-40151-8, YB). Dell.

Penrod. Booth Tarkington. Repr. lib. bdg. 21.95x (ISBN 0-88411-701-4, Pub. by Aeonian Pr). Amereon Ltd.

Penrod. Booth Tarkington. 321p. 1983. Repr. lib. bdg. 17.95x (ISBN 0-89966-178-5). Buccaneer Bks.

Penrod. Booth Tarkington. LC 85-42910. (Library of Indiana Classics: Midland Bks: No. 361). (Illus.). 320p. 1985. 15.00 (ISBN 0-253-34311-9); pap. 7.95 (ISBN 0-253-20361-9). Ind U Pr.

Penrod Again. Mary B. Christian. LC 86-21846. (Illus.). 56p. (gr. 1-4). 1987. PLB 9.95 (ISBN 0-02-718550-8). Macmillan.

Penrod & Sam. Booth Tarkington. Repr. lib. bdg. 21.95x (ISBN 0-88411-702-2, Pub. by Aeonian Pr). Amereon Ltd.

Penrod & Sam. Booth Tarkington. 1975. lib. bdg. 17.95 (ISBN 0-89966-179-3). Buccaneer Bks.

Penrod Jasber. Booth Tarkington. 321p. 1983. Repr. lib. bdg. 17.95x (ISBN 0-89966-180-7). Buccaneer Bks.

Penrod's Pants. Mary B. Christian. LC 85-11545. (Illus.). 56p. (gr. 1-4). 1986. 9.95 (ISBN 0-02-718520-6). Macmillan.

Penrose Mystery. Austin R. Freeman. 274p. 1977. Repr. lib. bdg. 13.95x (ISBN 0-89966-275-7). Buccaneer Bks.

Penross Manor. Joan W. Brown. 192p. 1986. 11.95 (ISBN 0-8499-0517-6). Word Bks.

Pens & Personalities. Joseph Ranald. 16.95x. New Coll U Pr.

Pen's Excellence. Joyce I. Whalley. LC 80-51966. (Illus.). 408p. 1982. pap. 20.00 (ISBN 0-8008-6282-1, Pentalic). Taplinger.

Pens Excellencie or the Secretaries Delight. Martin Billingsley. LC 77-6852. (English Experience Ser.: No. 849). 1977. Repr. of 1618 ed. lib. bdg. 10.50 (ISBN 90-221-0849-X). Walter J Johnson.

Pens under the Swastika. Wilhelm W. Schutz. LC 70-118415. 1971. Repr. of 1946 ed. 19.95x (ISBN 0-8046-1192-0, Pub. by Kennikat). Assoc Faculty Pr.

Pensacola Fortifications, 1698-1980: Guardians of the Gulf. James C. Coleman & Irene S. Coleman. (Illus.). 120p. 1983. pap. 7.95x (ISBN 0-939566-02-8). Pensacola Hist.

Pensacola: Spaniards to Space Age. Virginia Parks. (Illus.). 128p. 1986. 9.95 (ISBN 0-939566-04-4). Pensacola Hist.

Pensacola's Currency Issuing Banks & Their Bank Notes, 1833-1935. Philip A. Pfeiffer. Ed. by Marguerite P. Romond. LC 75-6130. (Illus.). 1975. pap. 6.50 (ISBN 0-9601038-1-3). Pfeiffer.

Pensamiento Conservador. (Ayacucho Library Collection Ser.: Vol. 31). (Span.). 1978. 35.00 (ISBN 0-317-56358-0, Pub. by Biblioteca Ayacucho); pap. 15.00 (ISBN 0-317-56359-9, Pub. by Biblioteca Ayacucho). Humanities.

Pensamiento de la Ilustracion. Ed. by J. C. Chiaramonte. (Ayacucho Library Collection Ser.: Vol. 51). (Span.). 1979. 29.95 (ISBN 0-317-56451-X, Pub. by Biblioteca Ayacucho); pap. 15.00 (ISBN 0-317-56452-8, Pub. by Biblioteca Ayacucho). Humanities.

Pensamiento en America, 2 vols. Incl. No. 1. Panorama De las Ideas En Latinoamerica. 24p. 1971; No. 2. Pensadores De America Latina. 16p. 1972 (ISBN 0-8270-5875-6); No. 3 (ISBN 0-8270-5895-0); No. 4 (ISBN 0-8270-5890-X). (Span.). pap. 1.00 ea. OAS.

Pensamiento Politico de la Emancipacion (VI) (Ayacucho Library Collection Ser.: Vol. 23). (Span.). 1977. 19.95 (ISBN 0-317-56313-0, Pub. by Biblioteca Ayacucho); pap. 9.95 (ISBN 0-317-56314-9, Pub. by Biblioteca Ayacucho). Humanities.

Pensamiento Politico de la Emancipacion (VII) (Ayacucho Library Collection Ser.: Vol. 24). (Span.). 1985. 19.95 (ISBN 0-317-56317-3, Pub. by Biblioteca Ayacucho); pap. 9.95 (ISBN 0-317-56318-1, Pub. by Biblioteca Ayacucho). Humanities.

Pensamiento Positivista Latinoamericano, Vol. VII. (Ayacucho Library Collection Ser.: Vol. 72). (Span.). 1980. 45.00 (ISBN 0-317-56577-X, Pub. by Biblioteca Ayacucho); pap. 21.50 (ISBN 0-317-56578-8, Pub. by Biblioteca Ayacucho). Humanities.

Pensamiento Positivista Latinoamericano, Vol. VI. (Ayacucho Library Collection Ser.: Vol. 71). (Span.). 1980. 40.00 (ISBN 0-317-56573-7, Pub. by Biblioteca Ayacucho); pap. 19.95 (ISBN 0-317-56574-5, Pub. by Biblioteca Ayacucho). Humanities.

Pensamientos Sobre la Cultura Intelectual y Moral. Enrique Aguilar. 1967. 7.00 (ISBN 0-686-27936-0). Franciscan Inst.

Pensando con Dios. Norman Camp. Orig. Title: Thinking with God. 128p. (Span.). 1981. pap. 3.25 (ISBN 0-8254-1100-9). Kregel.

Pensando en Su Nino. 5th ed. Ed. by Maria E. Alvarez del Real. LC 81-71533. (Illus.). 448p. (Span.). 1985. pap. 5.95x (ISBN 0-944499-09-0). Editorial Amer.

Pensar Bien y Mal. 2nd ed. Kenneth E. Hagin. (Span.). 1983. pap. 1.00 (ISBN 0-89276-104-0). Hagin Ministries.

Pensar Logico. Jose M. Lazaro. 321p. 1985. 5.00 (ISBN 0-8477-2825-0). U of PR Pr.

Pensari. Robert Katz. (Illus.). 48p. (Orig.). 1986. pap. 14.95 (ISBN 0-912938-10-2). Kepler Pr.

Pensativa. Jesus Goytortua. Ed. by Donald D. Walsh. (Orig., Span.). (gr. 10-12). 1962. pap. text ed. 15.95. P-H.

Pensee Chinoise. Granet Marcel. 614p. 1934. 40.00x (ISBN 0-317-69439-1, Pub. by Han-Shan Tang Ltd). State Mutual Bk.

Pensee Chinoise: Chinese Thought. Marcel Granet. LC 74-25753. (European Sociology Ser.). 642p. 1975. Repr. 46.50x (ISBN 0-405-06507-8). Ayer Co Pubs.

Pensee de Saint-Exupery. Christian L. Van den Berghe. (American University Studies II (Romance Languages & Literature): Vol. 24). 359p. (Fr.). 1985. text ed. 37.65 (ISBN 0-8204-0212-5). P Lang Pubs.

Pensee et le Mouvement. Henri Bergson. 39.95 (ISBN 0-685-37210-3). French & Eur.

Pensee et Structure. 2nd ed. J. L. Darbelnet. LC 68-19906. 275p. (Fr.). 1977. deluxe ed. write for info. (ISBN 0-02-327510-3, Pub. by Scribner). Macmillan.

Pensee Metaphysique de Descartes. Gouhier. 26.50 (ISBN 0-685-34225-5). French & Eur.

Pensee Politique De Platon. Jean Luccioni. Ed. by J. P. Mayer. LC 78-67365. (European Political Thought Ser.). (Fr.). 1979. Repr. of 1958 ed. lib. bdg. 25.50x (ISBN 0-405-11715-9). Ayer Co Pubs.

Pensee Religieuse et Morale De George Eliot: Essai D'interpretation. Placide-Gustave Maheu. 1973. Repr. of 1958 ed. 20.00 (ISBN 0-8274-1029-8). R West.

Pensee Sauvage. rev. ed. Claude Levi-Strauss. (Fr.). 1985. 10.00x (ISBN 2-86917-001-7). Adlers Foreign Bks.

Pensee Scientifique: Interaction. Ed. by UNESCO. (L'homme et Son Environment Sociale Ser.: No. 7). 1977. pap. 15.20x (ISBN 9-0279-7683-X). Mouton.

Pensees. Blaise Pascal. Ed. by Louis Lafuma. 1973. Repr. of 1960 ed. 14.95x (ISBN 0-460-10874-3, Evman). Biblio Dist.

Pensees. Blaise Pascal. (Univers des Lettres). pap. 5.95 (ISBN 0-685-34246-8). French & Eur.

Pensees, 2 vols. Blaise Pascal. (Folios 936 & 937). 4.50 ea. French & Eur.

Pensees. Blaise Pascal. Ed. by Desgranges. 1962. pap. 9.95 (ISBN 0-685-11485-6). French & Eur.

Pensees. Blaise Pascal. Ed. by Desgranges. (Coll. Prestige). 29.95 (ISBN 0-685-34245-X). French & Eur.

Pensees. Blaise Pascal. Tr. by A. J. Krailsheimer. (Classics Ser.). (Orig.). 1966. pap. 3.95 (ISBN 0-14-044171-9). Penguin.

Pensees. Henri Rochard. (Illus.). 1977. Repr. soft cover 5.00 (ISBN 0-686-21180-4). Maple Mont.

Pensees, 2 vols. facsimile ed. Stendhal. 1931. Set. 100.00 (ISBN 0-686-55077-3). French & Eur.

Pensees & Letters of Joseph Joubert. Joseph Joubert. 15.50 (ISBN 0-8369-6945-6, 7826). Ayer Co Pubs.

Pensees et Maximes. Charles-Augustin Sainte-Beuve. 1955. 8.95 (ISBN 0-686-55406-X). French & Eur.

Pensees of Pascal: A Study in Baroque Style. Sr. M. Julie Maggioni. LC 79-94181. (Catholic University of America Studies in Romance Languages & Literature Ser: No. 39). Repr. of 1950 ed. 25.00 (ISBN 0-404-50339-X). AMS Pr.

Pensees Philosophiques. 3rd ed. Denis Diderot. 75p. 1965. 9.95 (ISBN 0-686-56022-1). French & Eur.

Pensees sur l'interpretation de la Nature: Avec: Varloot, Jean. La Pensee de Diderot dans l'Encyclopedie. 2nd ed. Denis Diderot. 9.95 (ISBN 0-686-56023-X). French & Eur.

Penser la Bouche Pleine. Judith Schlanger. (Archontes: No. 7). 214p. (Fr.). 1976. pap. text ed. 21.60x (ISBN 90-2797-972-3). Mouton.

Penseurs de l'Islam, 5 vols. Bernard Carra de Vaux. LC 80-2197. Repr. of 1926 ed. AMS Pr.

Penshurst: The Semiotics of Place & the Poetics of History. Don E. Wayne. LC 83-40273. (Illus.). 256p. 1984. 31.50x (ISBN 0-299-09770-6). U of Wis Pr.

Pensieri. Giacomo Leopardi. Tr. by Simone Di Piero. LC 81-11745. x, 182p. 1981. 20.00x (ISBN 0-8071-0885-5). La State U Pr.

Pensieri: A Bilingual Edition. Giacomo Leopardi. Tr. by W. S. Di Piero from Ital. 1984. pap. 6.95 (ISBN 0-19-503496-1, GB768). Oxford U Pr.

Pensiero Religioso Ed Estetico Di Walter Pater. Federico Olivero. LC 76-56395. 1976. Repr. of 1939 ed. lib. bdg. 69.50 (ISBN 0-8414-6534-7). Folcroft.

Pension Administrator's Form Book. Paul C. Stein & Lewis Schier. LC 87-2299. Date not set. price not set (ISBN 0-916592-68-5). Panel Pubs.

Pension & Employee Benefits Code: ERISA--Regulations, August 3, 1987. 2808p. (Orig.). 1987. pap. 32.50 (5283). Commerce.

Pension & Employee Benefits Code: ERISA, Regulations, As of April 5, 1985. Commerce Clearing House, Inc. 2568p. 1985. 27.00 (ISBN 0-317-30621-9, 4721). Commerce.

Pension & Profit Sharing, 4 vols. in 5. Date not set. Set. price not set looseleaf. P-H.

Pension & Profit Sharing Plans. Paul R. Windmuller. Date not set. manual 15.00 (ISBN 0-318-23973-6, 6124); audiotapes 95.00 (ISBN 0-318-23974-4); videotape 500.00 (ISBN 0-318-23975-2). Natl Prac Inst.

Pension & Profit Sharing Plans, 5 vols, Vol. 19. Sheldon M. Young. 1977. looseleaf 350.00 (842); Updates 1985. 263.50; Supplement 1986. 240.00. Bender.

Pension & Profit-Sharing Plans Compliance Guide, 5 vols. Carmine V. Scudere. LC 86-70623. 1986. Bimonthly suppliments & revisions. with 1 yr service 350.00. Bender.

Pension & Profit Sharing Plans: Forms & Practice with Tax Analysis, 3 vols. 1987. write for info. (NO. 578). Bender.

Pension & Profit Sharing Plans for Small & Medium Size Businesses. Carmine V. Scudere. LC 79-92397. 1984. 150.00 (ISBN 0-916592-35-9). Panel Pubs.

Pension & Profit Sharing: Sample Plans & Workbook. Panel Publishers Staff. (Orig.). 1985. pap. 75.00 (ISBN 0-916592-58-8). Panel Pubs.

Pension & Retirement Plans: Issues & Strategies. Panel Publishers, Inc. Staff. (Orig.). 1985. pap. 45.00 (ISBN 0-317-20147-6). Panel Pubs.

Pension & Welfare Benefits in Bankruptcy. Glenn S. Gerstell & Edward R. Mackiewicz. 453p. 1988. pap. 45.00 (A4-4210). PLI.

Pension Answer Book. 3rd ed. Stephen J. Krass & Richard L. Keschner. LC 84-25510. 1984. 45.00 (ISBN 0-916592-52-9). Panel Pubs.

Pension Asset Management: The Corporate Decision. FRS Associates Staff. LC 80-69793. 285p. 1981. 8.00 (ISBN 0-910586-36-5). Finan Exec.

Pension Beaurepas see Lady Barbarina.

Pension Book Reserves in West Germany. Towers et al. LC 82-82603. 1983. 5.00. Finan Exec.

Pension Changes under Budget Act of 1987: Explanation--Law--Committee Reports. 136p. (Orig.). 1988. pap. 5.00 (5257). Commerce.

Pension Claims: Rights & Obligations. Stephen R. Bruce. 775p. 1988. 85.00 (ISBN 0-87179-550-7, 0550). BNA.

Pension Crisis. Robert J. Lynn. LC 82-48795. 192p. 1983. 25.00x (ISBN 0-669-06374-6). Lexington Bks.

Pension Disputes & Settlements, Supplement No. 3. Seymour Goldberg. LC 78-59106. pap. 82.70 (ISBN 0-8357-9482-2, 2016185). Bks Demand UMI.

Pension Fund Administration. Ed. by A. G. Shepherd. 182p. 1984. 32.95 (ISBN 0-902197-15-0, Pub. by Woodhead-Faulkner). Longwood Pub Group.

Pension Fund Investment. Ed. by A. G. Shepherd. 1987. 56.00 (ISBN 0-85941-400-0, Pub. by Woodhead-Faulkner). Longwood Pub Group.

Pension Fund Investment: The Issue of Control. Marc A. Weiss. 55p. 1978. 5.95 (ISBN 0-89788-037-4). NCPA Washington.

Pension Fund Investments in Real Estate: A Guide for Plan Sponsors & Real Estate Professionals. Natalie A. McKelvy. LC 82-25542. (Illus.). 352p. 1983. lib. bdg. 39.95 (ISBN 0-89930-035-9, MCV/, Quorum). Greenwood.

Pension Funds & British Capitalism. Richard Minns. 1981. text ed. 33.00 (ISBN 0-435-84510-1). Gower Pub Co.

Pension Funds & Economic Power. P. P. Harbrecht. (Twentieth Century Fund Ser.). Repr. of 1959 ed. 10.00 (ISBN 0-527-02820-7). Kraus Repr.

Pension Funds & Economic Renewal. Lawrence Litvak. Ed. by Michael Barker. (Studies in State Development Policy: Vol. 11). 136p. 1981. pap. 11.95 (ISBN 0-934842-10-8). CSPA.

Pension Funds & Economic Renewal. Lawrence Litvak. 136p. 1981. 14.95 (ISBN 0-318-03993-1). NCPA Washington.

Pension Funds & Economic Renewal. Lawrence Litvak. 136p. 1981. 15.95 (ISBN 0-317-57502-3). NCPA Washington.

Pension Funds & Ethical Investment: A Study of Investment Practices & Opportunities State of California Retirement Systems. Stuart A. Baldwin et al. 191p. 1985. pap. 15.00 (ISBN 0-312-94560-4, Dist. by St Martin). CEP.

Pension Funds & Ethical Investment: A Study of Investment Practices & Opportunities State of California Retirement Systems. 2nd ed. Stuart A. Baldwin et al. 191p. 1986. 25.00 (ISBN 0-312-00402-8). St Martin.

Pension Funds & Insurance Reserves: A Corporate Resource. Irving L. Finston & Robert I. Mehr. 200p. 1986. 37.50 (ISBN 0-87094-558-0). Dow Jones-Irwin.

Pension Funds & Residential Mortgage Investments. 198p. 1982. 40.00 (ISBN 0-945359-66-7). Mortgage Bankers.

Pension Funds & the Bottom Line: Managing the Corporate Pension Fund as a Financial Business. Keith P. Ambachtsheer. 200p. 1986. 35.00 (ISBN 0-87094-708-7). Dow Jones-Irwin.

Pentimento (Julia) movie ed. Lillian Hellman. (Illus.). 256p. (YA) (RL 10). 1977. pap. 3.95 (ISBN 0-451-14089-3, AE1543, Sig). NAL.

Pentjak Silat. D. Droeger. 8.95 (ISBN 0-685-38449-7). Wehman.

Pentomic Era: The United States Army Between Korea & Vietnam. A. J. Bacevich. LC 86-8536. 214p. (Orig.). 1986. pap. 3.50 (ISBN 0-318-21347-8, S/N 008-020-01075-8). USGPO.

Pentose Phosphate Pathway. Terry Wood & Bernard R. Landau. 1985. 32.50 (ISBN 0-12-762860-6). Acad Pr.

Pentoxifylline, Pharmacological & Clinical Research. Ed. by J. L. Ambrus. 20.00. PJD Pubns.

Penuel; or Face to Face with God. A. McLean & J. W. Easton. Ed. by Donald W. Dayton. (Higher Christian Life Ser.). 483p. 1985. 60.00 (ISBN 0-8240-6427-5). Garland Pub.

Penultimate Truth. Philip K. Dick. LC 83-25867. 208p. 1984. pap. 5.95 (ISBN 0-312-94356-3). Bluejay Bks.

Penultimate Words, & Other Essays. facs. ed. Leo Shestov. LC 67-22117. (Essay Index Reprint Ser). 1916. 14.00 (ISBN 0-8369-0876-7). Ayer Co Pubs.

Peonies Kana: Haiku by the Upasaka Shiki. Tr. by Harold J. Isaacson. (Bhaisajaguru Ser.). 1972. pap. 1.85 (ISBN 0-87830-547-5). Theatre Arts.

Peonies of Greece: A Taxonomic Historical Survey of the Genus Paeonia in Greece. W. T. Stearn & P. H. Davis. (Illus.). 136p. 1984. 63.00x (ISBN 0-565-00975-3, Pub by Brit Mus Nat Hist England). Sabbot-Natural Hist Bks.

Peonies, Outdoors & in. Arno Nehrling & Irene Nehrling. (Illus.). 14.75 (ISBN 0-8446-5230-X). Peter Smith.

Peony. Alice Harding. (Illus.). 253p. 1985. Repr. 27.00 (ISBN 0-947752-60-9). SagaPr.

Peony Pavilion (Mudan Ting) Tang Xianzu. Tr. by Cyril Birch. LC 79-9631. (Chinese Literature in Translation Ser.). (Illus.). 360p. 1980. 25.00x (ISBN 0-253-35723-3). Ind U Pr.

People. J. L. Angel. LC 73-139121. (Lerna Ser: Vol. 2). (Illus.). 1971. 17.50x (ISBN 0-87661-302-4). Am Sch Athens.

People. Pierre Hamp. Tr. by James Whitall. LC 74-121558. (Short Story Index Reprint Ser). 1921. 15.00 (ISBN 0-8369-3515-2). Ayer Co Pubs.

People. Victoria Ingram. (Language Arts & Crafts Ser.). 64p. (gr. k-3). 1987. 6.95 (ISBN 0-912107-62-6). Monday Morning Bks.

People. Jules Michelet. 59.95 (ISBN 0-8490-0810-7). Gordon Pr.

People. Jules Michelet. Tr. & intro. by John P. McKay. LC 72-91078. 245p. 1973. 19.50 (ISBN 0-252-00321-7); pap. 9.95 (ISBN 0-252-00331-4). U of Ill Pr.

People. Tamiko Mizushima. 45p. (Orig.). 1987. pap. 3.50 (ISBN 0-913244-68-6). Hapi Pr.

People. LC 87-16543. (Children's Encyclopedia Ser.). (Illus.). 96p. (gr. 3 up). 1987. lib. bdg. 240.00 set (ISBN 0-317-64434-3); pap. 13.27 (ISBN 0-8172-3052-1). Raintree Pubs.

People. Bruce Robertson. (North Light Drawing Workbooks Ser.). (Illus.). 64p. 1988. pap. 8.95 (ISBN 0-89134-230-3). North Light Bks.

People. Peter Spier. LC 78-19832. (Illus.). 48p. (gr. 1-3). 1980. pap. 13.95 (ISBN 0-385-13181-X); pap. 12.95 (ISBN 0-385-13182-8). Doubleday.

People. Peter Spier. LC 78-19832. (Illus.). 48p. (ps up). 1988. pap. 7.95 (ISBN 0-385-24469-X, Zephyr-BFYR). Doubleday.

People see Florentine Codex, General History of the Things of New Spain.

People -- Their Power: The Rural Electric Fact Book. rev. ed. Erma Angevine. (Illus.). 196p. 1981. pap. 3.75 (ISBN 0-686-31129-9). Natl Rural.

People among Peoples: Quaker Benevolence in Eighteenth Century America. Sydney V. James. LC 62-20248. (Center for the Study of the History of Liberty in America Ser). 1963. 27.50x (ISBN 0-674-66050-1). Harvard U Pr.

People: An International Choice. R. M. Salas. LC 76-11610. Orig. Title: Poblacion: Una Opcion Int. (Span.). 1975. 15.75 (ISBN 0-08-021952-7); pap. 9.50 (ISBN 0-08-021951-9). Pergamon.

People: An International Choice, the Multilateral Approach to Population. Rafael M. Salas. 1976. 31.00 (ISBN 0-08-021030-9); pap. 16.00 (ISBN 0-08-021029-5). Pergamon.

People & a Nation: A History of the United States. 2nd ed. Mary B. Norton et al. LC 87-80263. 656p. 1988. pap. text ed. 25.56 brief ed. (ISBN 0-395-35952-X). HM.

People & a Nation: A History of the United States. 2nd ed. Mary B. Norton et al. LC 85-60316. 1072p. 1985. Complete text. text ed. 37.96 (ISBN 0-395-35953-8); Vol. 1. 27.16; Vol. 2. text ed. 27.16; Vol. 1. study guide 12.36 (ISBN 0-395-40019-8); Vol. 2. study guide 12.36; transparencies 84.76 (ISBN 0-395-40022-8). HM.

People & a Nation: A History of the United States Since 1865, Vol. B. 2nd ed. Mary B. Norton et al. LC 87-80265. 352p. 1988. pap. text ed. 16.36 (ISBN 0-395-36933-9); study guide 11.96 (ISBN 0-395-47094-3). HM.

People & a Nation: A History of the United States to 1877, Vol. A. 2nd ed. Mary B. Norton et al. LC 87-80264. 320p. 1988. pap. text ed. 16.36 (ISBN 0-395-36932-0); write for info. instr's manual; study guide 11.96 (ISBN 0-395-46092-1). HM.

People & Animals: A Humane Education Curriculum Guide, 4 bks. rev. ed. Ed. by Kathleen Savesky & Vanessa Malcarne. 140p. 1981. pap. 7.00 ea. Level A (ISBN 0-941246-01-9). Level B (ISBN 0-941246-02-7). Level C (ISBN 0-941246-03-5). Level D (ISBN 0-941246-04-3). Set. pap. 25.00 (ISBN 0-941246-05-1). NAAHE.

People & Books. W. R. Nicoll. 15.00 (ISBN 0-8274-3118-X). R West.

People & Communication. Gordon R. Wainwright. 205p. 1981. pap. 19.95x (ISBN 0-7121-1690-7). Trans-Atl Phila.

People & Computers. Maryellen Feeman & Jeff Feeman. (Illus.). 32p. (gr. 5 up). 1984. pap. 1.98 (ISBN 0-88724-103-4, CD-9046). Carson-Dellos.

People & Computers: Computer Impacts on End Users in Organizations. James N. Danziger & Kenneth L. Kraemer. LC 85-29989. 128p. 1986. 32.50 (ISBN 0-231-06178-1). Columbia U Pr.

People & Computers: Designing the Interface; Proceedings of the First Technical Conference of the BCS Human-Computer Interaction Specialist Group, 17-20 September 1985. Ed. by P. Johnson & S. Cook. (British Computer Society Workshop Ser.). 428p. 1985. 57.50 (ISBN 0-521-32066-6). Cambridge U Pr.

People & Computers III. Ed. by D. Diaper & R. Winder. (British Computer Society Workshop Ser.). 350p. 1988. 79.50 (ISBN 0-521-35197-9). Cambridge U Pr.

People & Contexts: Social Development from Birth to Old Age. Henry S. Maas. 352p. 1984. text ed. write for info. (ISBN 0-13-655845-3). P-H.

People & Crowds: A Photographic Album for Artists & Designers. Jim Kalett. (Pictorial Archive Ser.). (Illus.). 1978. pap. 6.95 (ISBN 0-486-23696-X). Dover.

People & Crowds: A Photographic Album for Artists & Designers. Jim Kalett. 13.25 (ISBN 0-8446-5778-6). Peter Smith.

People & Cultures of Hawaii: A Psychocultural Profile. Ed. by John F. McDermott, Jr. et al. LC 80-11959. 251p. 1980. pap. 7.50 (ISBN 0-8248-0706-5). UH Pr.

People & Dog in the Sun. Ronald Wallace. LC 86-25041. (Pitt Poetry Ser.). 80p. 1986. 16.95x (ISBN 0-8229-3552-X); pap. 8.95 (ISBN 0-8229-5388-9). U of Pittsburgh Pr.

People & Economy of Southwest Virginia: A Study Prepared for the Southwest Virginia Economic Development Commission. 1986. 6.27 (ISBN 0-317-69872-9). U Va Ctr Pub Serv.

People & Folks: Gangs, Crime & the Underclass in a Rust Belt City. John Hagedorn. LC 88-9468. (Illus.). 220p. 1988. 29.95x (ISBN 0-941702-20-0); pap. 10.95 (ISBN 0-941702-21-9). Lake View Pr.

People & Food Tomorrow: The Scientific, Economic, Political, & Social Factors Affecting Food Supplies in the Last Quarter of the 20th Century. Ed. by Dorothy Hollingsworth & Elisabeth Morse. (Illus.). 173p. 1976. 43.00 (ISBN 0-85334-701-8, Pub. by Elsevier Applied Sci England). Elsevier.

People & Homes. (People of the World Ser.). (Illus.). 32p. (gr. 3-6). 1986. 10.95 (ISBN 0-86020-901-6). EDC.

People & Industries. William H. Chaloner. (Illus.). 151p. 1963. 24.00x (ISBN 0-7146-1284-7, F Cass Co). Biblio Dist.

People & Kids. Sarellen M. Wuest. 272p. (Orig.). 1986. pap. 9.95 (ISBN 0-938545-02-7). Busn Media Res.

People & Nations of Africa. Sheila Fairfield. LC 88-42922. (People & Nations Ser.). (Illus.). 64p. (gr. 4-5). 1988. PLB 12.45 (ISBN 1-55532-903-9). Stevens Inc.

People & Nations of Asia. Sheila Fairfield. LC 88-42920. (People & Nations Ser.). (Illus.). 64p. (gr. 4-5). 1988. PLB 12.45 (ISBN 1-55532-905-5). Stevens Inc.

People & Nations of Europe. Sheila Fairfield. LC 88-42919. (People & Nations Ser.). (Illus.). 64p. (gr. 4-5). 1988. PLB 12.45 (ISBN 1-55532-906-3). Stevens Inc.

People & Nations of the Americas. Sheila Fairfield. LC 88-42921. (People & Nations Ser.). (Illus.). 64p. (gr. 4-5). 1988. PLB 12.45 (ISBN 1-55532-904-7). Stevens Inc.

People & Nations of the Far East & the Pacific. Sheila Fairfield. Ed. by Rhoda Sherwood. LC 88-42918. (People & Nations Ser.). (Illus.). 64p. (gr. 4-5). 1988. PLB 12.45 (ISBN 1-55532-907-1). Stevens Inc.

People & Organizations. Andrew Kakabadse. 154p. 1982. text ed. 33.00x (ISBN 0-566-00373-2). Gower Pub Co.

People & Organizations. G. Salaman & K. Thompson. 384p. 1974. text ed. 15.95x (ISBN 0-582-48669-6). Longman.

People & Organizations: Cases in Management & Organizational Behavior. 2nd ed. John E. Dittrich & Robert A. Zawacki. 1985. pap. 20.95x (ISBN 0-256-03257-2). Business Pubns.

People & Organizations Interacting. Ed. by Aat Brakel. LC 84-5212. 258p. 1985. 41.95 (ISBN 0-471-90476-7). Wiley.

People & Other Aggravations. Judith Viorst. 112p. 1973. pap. 1.50 (ISBN 0-451-11366-7, AW1366, Sig). NAL.

People & Palces. Richard Cobb. 224p. 1987. pap. 11.95 (ISBN 0-19-283062-7). Oxford U Pr.

People & Performance: The Best of Peter Drucker on Management. Peter F. Drucker. 1977. pap. text ed. 19.50 scp (ISBN 0-06-166400-6, HarpC). Harper Row.

People & Places. Richard Cobb. 192p. 1985. 24.95x (ISBN 0-19-215881-3). Oxford U Pr.

People & Places. (Lauchbach Way to Reading Components Ser.). 64p. Date not set. 2.00 (ISBN 0-88336-924-9). New Readers.

People & Places in Colonial Venezuela. John V. Lombardi. LC 75-25433. pap. 125.00 (ISBN 0-317-27832-0, 2056043). Bks Demand UMI.

People & Places in the Bible. (Bible Reference Library). 251p. 1988. pap. 6.95 (ISBN 1-55748-030-3). Barbour & Co.

People & Places of Constantinople. Charles Newton. (Illus.). 112p. (Orig.). 1985. pap. 7.95 (ISBN 0-948107-03-0, Pub. by Victoria & Albert Mus UK). Faber & Faber.

People & Politics. 3rd ed. Herbert R. Winter et al. LC 84-19494. 593p. 1985. text ed. write for info. (ISBN 0-02-428820-9); write for info. tchr's. manual (ISBN 0-02-428830-6). Macmillan.

People & Politics in North America: Summaries of Biographical Articles in History Journals. Pamela R. Byrne & Susan K. Kinnell. (People in History Ser.). 185p. (YA) (gr. 9-12). 1988. pap. text ed. 18.00 (ISBN 0-87436-538-4). ABC Clio.

People & Politics in the Middle East. Ed. by Michael Curtis. LC 72-140617. 335p. 1971. 28.95 (ISBN 0-87855-000-3); pap. 14.95x (ISBN 0-87855-500-5). Transaction Bks.

People & Polity. Daniel J. Elazar. LC 88-17404. 720p. 1988. 59.95x (ISBN 0-8143-1843-6). Wayne St U Pr.

People & Power in Byzantium: An Introduction to Modern Byzantine Studies. Alexander Kazhdan & Giles Constable. LC 81-12640. 1982. 12.50x (ISBN 0-88402-103-3). Dumbarton Oaks.

People & Power in Sudan: The Struggle for National Stability. Bona Malwal. (Sudan Studies: No. 6). 273p. 1981. 25.00 (ISBN 0-903729-78-4, Pub. by Ithaca England). Evergreen Dist.

People & Predicaments. Milton Mazer. 332p. 1976. 21.00x (ISBN 0-674-66075-7). Harvard U Pr.

People & Productivity. 3rd ed. Sutermeister. (Management Ser). 1976. text ed. 24.95 o. p. (ISBN 0-07-062367-8); pap. text ed. 26.95 (ISBN 0-07-062371-6). McGraw.

People & Productivity in Japan. Terutomo Ozawa. (Studies in Productivity: Vol. 25). 42p. 1982. pap. 39.00 (ISBN 0-08-029506-1). Work in Amer.

People & Productivity: Keys to a Successful Harvesting Operation. 137p. (Orig.). 1985. pap. 18.00 (ISBN 0-935018-22-0). Forest Prod.

People & Productivity: The New York Stock Exchange Guide to Financial Incentives & the Quality of Work Life. Eugene Epstein & William C. Freund. LC 84-71126. 132p. 1984. 19.95 (ISBN 0-87094-510-6). Dow Jones-Irwin.

People & Programs. Tom Bassford. 240p. 1987. pap. 9.95 (ISBN 0-8010-0931-6). Baker Bk.

People & Project Management. Rob Thomsett. LC 80-51921. (Illus.). 112p. (Orig.). 1980. pap. 16.95 (ISBN 0-917072-21-9, Yourdon). P-H.

People & Protest, Eighteen Fifteen to Eighteen Eighty. Ed. by Trevor Herbert & Gareth E. Jones. (Welsh History & Its Sources Ser.). 1988. pap. text ed. 19.95 (ISBN 0-7083-0988-7, Pub. by U of Wales). Humanities.

People & Public Administration: Commentaries & Case Studies. Phillip E. Present. LC 78-70260. 1979. pap. text ed. 7.50x (ISBN 0-913530-13-1). Palisades Pub.

People & Public Places. 44p. 1984. 5.00 (ISBN 1-55516-212-6). Natl Conf State Legis.

People & Religion in North America: Summaries of Biographical Articles in History Journals. Pamela R. Byrne & Susan K. Kinnell. (People in History Ser.). 168p. (YA) (gr. 9-12). 1988. pap. text ed. 18.00 (ISBN 0-87436-542-2). ABC Clio.

People & Security: An Introduction. T. Squires. 61p. 1980. pap. 18.60 (ISBN 0-471-89417-6). Wiley.

People & Society in Scotland, Vol. I - 1760-1830: A Social History of Modern Scotland. Ed. by T. M. Devine & Rosalind Mitchinson. (People & Society of Scotland Ser.). 300p. (Orig.). 1988. pap. text ed. 35.00 (ISBN 0-85976-210-6, Pub. by John Donald Pub UK). Humanities.

People & Society in Scotland, Vol. II - 1830-1914: A Social History of Modern Scotland 1760 to the Present. Ed. by Hamish Fraser & R. J. Morris. (People & Society in Scotland Ser.). (Illus.). 300p. (Orig.). 1989. pap. 35.00 (ISBN 0-85976-211-4, Pub. by John Donald Pub UK). Humanities.

People & Society in Scotland, Volume III - 1914-Present: A Social History of Modern Scotland 1760 to the Present. Ed. by T. Duckson & J. H. Treble. (People & Society of Scotland Ser.). (Illus.). 300p. (Orig.). 1990. pap. 35.00 (ISBN 0-85976-212-2, Pub. by John Donald Pub UK). Humanities.

People & the Arts in North America. Pamela R. Byrne & Susan K. Kinnell. (People in History Ser.). 182p. (YA) (gr. 7-12). 1988. pap. text ed. 18.00 (ISBN 0-87436-541-4). ABC Clio.

People & the Court: Judicial Review in a Democracy. Charles L. Black, Jr. LC 77-8076. 238p. 1977. Repr. of 1960 ed. deluxe ed. 35.00x (ISBN 0-8371-9682-5, BLPC). Greenwood.

People & the Faith of the Bible. Andre Chouraqui. Tr. by William V. Gugli. LC 74-21237. 224p. 1975. 17.50x (ISBN 0-87023-172-3). U of Mass Pr.

People & the King: The Comunero Revolution in Colombia, 1781. John L. Phelan. LC 76-53654. (Illus.). 332p. 1978. 32.50x (ISBN 0-299-07290-8). U of Wis Pr.

People & the Party System: The Referendum & Electoral Reform in British Politics. Vernon Bogdanor. LC 81-3895. 280p. 1981. 47.50 (ISBN 0-521-24207-X); pap. 17.95 (ISBN 0-521-28525-9). Cambridge U Pr.

People & the Police. Algernon D. Black. LC 75-40991. 246p. 1976. Repr. lib. bdg. 35.00x (ISBN 0-8371-8699-4, BLPP). Greenwood.

People & the Promise. Ursula Synge. LC 74-10661. 192p. (gr. 7-10). 1974. 14.95 (ISBN 0-87599-208-0). S G Phillips.

People & the Sea, 3 Vols. P. H. Nixon. 1977. Vol. II. 2.00; Vol. III. 2.00. Sea Grant Pubns.

People & the State: An Anthropology of Planned Development. A. F. Robertson. (Cambridge Studies in Social Anthropology 52). (Illus.). 320p. 1984. 54.50 (ISBN 0-521-26549-5); pap. 19.95 (ISBN 0-521-31948-X). Cambridge U Pr.

People & the Stones. Heinz W. Sabais. Tr. by Ruth Mead & Matthew Mead. (Poetry in Translation Ser.). 72p. (Orig.). 1983. pap. 7.95 (ISBN 0-85646-110-5, Pub. by Anvil Pr Poetry). Longwood Pub Group.

People & Their Quilts. John R. Irwin. LC 83-61649. (Illus.). 214p. 1983. 45.00 (ISBN 0-916838-87-0). Schiffer.

People & Their Quilts. John R. Irwin. LC 83-61649. (Illus.). 214p. 1984. pap. 19.95 (ISBN 0-88740-024-8). Schiffer.

People & Their Religions, Part One. Thomas J. Clarke. (Literacy Volunteers of America Readers Ser.). 48p. (Orig.). 1983. pap. 1.95 (ISBN 0-8428-9609-0). Cambridge Bk.

People & Their Religions, Part Two. Thomas J. Clarke. (Literacy Volunteers of America Readers Ser.). 48p. (Orig.). 1983. pap. 1.95 (ISBN 0-8428-9610-4). Cambridge Bk.

People & Their Schools. Henry S. Commager. LC 76-23913. (Fastback Ser.: No.79). (Orig.). 1976. pap. 0.90 (ISBN 0-87367-079-5). Phi Delta Kappa.

People & Wanderings. Mark K. Gettle. 32p. 1988. 6.95 (ISBN 0-8062-3303-6). Carlton.

People & Weather. P. J. Kavanagh. 176p. (Orig.). 1986. pap. 5.95 (ISBN 0-7145-3666-0). Riverrun NY.

People Apart: Ethnicity & the Mennonite Brethren. 1987. pap. 8.95 (ISBN 0-317-62695-7). Herald Pr.

People Are Crazy Here. Rex Reed. (Illus.). 352p. 1974. pap. 7.95 (ISBN 0-440-07365-0). Delacorte.

People Are Different, People Are the Same. Marge Passamaneck. 1983. pap. 3.10 (ISBN 0-89536-615-0, 1629). CSS of Ohio.

People Are Funny. Donald R. Byrd & Stanley J. Zelinski, III. (Pictures for Practice Ser.: Bk. 1). 80p. (Orig.). 1987. pap. text ed. 6.95 (ISBN 0-582-79829-9). Longman.

People Are Our Business. Beryl Williams. LC 79-179745. (Biography Index Reprint Ser). Repr. of 1947 ed. 16.00 (ISBN 0-8369-8113-8). Ayer Co Pubs.

People Are the Funniest Animals. William H. Waddell. 320p. 1979. 8.95 (ISBN 0-8059-2507-4). Dorrance.

People As Animals see If I Were an Animal.

People Aspects of Research & Development Management: Attracting & Retaining R & D Personnel. E. M. Kipp. 116p. 1967. 55.00 (ISBN 0-677-40040-3). Gordon & Breach.

People at Play. facsimile ed. Rollin L. Hartt. LC 75-1850. (Leisure Class in America Ser.). (Illus.). 1975. Repr. of 1909 ed. 21.00x (ISBN 0-405-06917-0). Ayer Co Pubs.

People at Work. Molly Perham. LC 86-2014. (International Picture Library). (Illus.). 32p. (gr. 2 up). 1986. PLB 10.95 (ISBN 0-87518-333-6). Dillon.

People at Work see Unblocking Your Organization.

People at Work: Human Relations in Organizations. 2nd ed. Paul R. Timm & Brent D. Peterson. LC 85-20322. (Illus.). 449p. 1985. text ed. 35.50 (ISBN 0-314-93522-3). West Pub.

People at Work in China. Frances Wood. (People at Work Ser.). (gr. 6 up). 1988. 17.95 (ISBN 0-7134-5266-8, Pub. by Batsford England). David & Charles.

People at Work in India. Carol Ogle & John Ogle. (People at Work Ser.). (Illus.). 84p. (YA) (gr. 7-9). 1988. 17.95 (ISBN 0-7134-5157-2, Pub. by Batsford England). David & Charles.

People at Work in Sri Lanka. Nance L. Fyson. (People at Work Ser.). (gr. 6 up). 1988. 17.95 (ISBN 0-7134-5479-2, Pub. by Batsford England). David & Charles.

People at Work in the Middle East. Christine Osborne. (People at Work Ser.). (gr. 6 up). 1988. 17.95 (ISBN 0-7134-5571-3, Pub. by Batsford England). David & Charles.

People at Work: Nineteen Thirty to the Nineteen Eighty's. Cherry Gilchrist. (Illus.). 72p. (gr. 7-12). 1983. 17.95 (ISBN 0-7134-1366-2, Pub. by Batsford England). David & Charles.

People of Gumption & Other Stories. Fran Lehr. 90p. 7.95 (ISBN 0-935153-03-9). Stormline Pr.

People of Hamilton, Canada West: Family & Class in a Mid-Nineteenth Century City. Michael B. Katz. (Studies in Urban History). 448p. 1976. 29.50x (ISBN 0-674-66125-7). Harvard U Pr.

People of Hemso. August Strindberg. Tr. by Elspeth H. Schubert. LC 73-17625. 220p. 1974. Repr. of 1959 ed. lib. bdg. 35.00x (ISBN 0-8371-7252-7, STPH). Greenwood.

People of Hidden Sussex. Warden Swinfen & David Arscott. 168p. 1987. 30.00x (ISBN 0-9509510-1-3, Countryside Bks). State Mutual Bk.

People of Hope: The Story Behind the Modern Church. Anthony E. Gilles. (People of God Ser.: Vol. 6). (Illus.). 234p. (Orig.). 1988. pap. 7.95 (ISBN 0-86716-069-1, SBN 691). St Anthony Mess Pr.

People of Ireland. Intro. by Pat Loughrey. (Illus.). 200p. 1988. 35.00 (ISBN 0-86281-198-8, Pub. by Appletree Pr). Irish Bks Media.

People of Kauwerak: Legends of the Northern Eskimo. 2nd ed. (Alaskana Book Ser.: No. 17). 242p. 1981. pap. 9.95 (ISBN 0-935094-07-5). Alaska Pacific.

People of Lerna: Analysis of a Prehistoric Aegean Population. J. Lawrence Angel. LC 73-139121. (Illus.). 160p. 1971. 22.50x (ISBN 0-87474-098-3, ANPL). Smithsonian.

People of Longevity. Grace Halsell. Date not set. price not set (ISBN 0-394-49404-0). Random.

People of Manipur: Anthropogenetic Study of Four Manipur Population Groups. Rama Chakravartti. (Illus.). xvi, 151p. 1986. text ed. 20.00x (ISBN 81-7018-296-4, Pub. by B R Pub Corp Delhi). Apt Bks.

People of Mission: A History of General Conference Mennonite Overseas Missions. James C. Juhnke. LC 78-74809. 1979. pap. 5.95 (ISBN 0-87303-019-2). Faith & Life.

People of Murapin. Peter F. Sinnett. 208p. 1977. 75.00x (ISBN 0-317-07168-8, Pub. by FW Classey UK). State Mutual Bk.

People of Nepal. 5th ed. Dor Bahadur Bista. (Illus.). 210p. (gr. 9-12). 1986. 44.50x. Asia Bk Corp.

People of Our Neighborhood by Mary E. Wilkins. Mary E. Wilkins Freeman. LC 76-110192. (Short Story Index Reprint Ser.). 1898. 14.50 (ISBN 0-8369-3343-5). Ayer Co Pubs.

People of Our Parish. Leila H. Bugg. 20.00 (ISBN 0-405-10811-7). Ayer Co Pubs.

People of Palestine. rev. 2nd ed. Elihu Grant. LC 75-6434. (Rise of Jewish Nationalism & the Middle East Ser). 1975. Repr. of 1921 ed. 27.50 (ISBN 0-88355-321-X). Hyperion Conn.

People of Paradox: An Inquiry Concerning the Origins of American Civilization. Michael Kammen. (Illus.). 1980. pap. 9.95x (ISBN 0-19-502803-1). Oxford U Pr.

People of Paris. Daniel Roche. LC 86-24506. (Studies on the History of Society & Culture: No. 2). 300p. 1987. 37.50x (ISBN 0-520-05857-7); pap. 11.95x (ISBN 0-520-06031-8). U of Cal Pr.

People of Pascua. Edward H. Spicer. 290p. 1988. 35.00x (ISBN 0-8165-1069-5). U of Ariz Pr.

People of Penn's Woods West. Lee Gutkind. LC 84-2192. 152p. 1984. 19.95x (ISBN 0-8229-3494-9); pap. 6.95 (ISBN 0-8229-5360-9). U of Pittsburgh Pr.

People of Pern. Anne McCaffrey. 1988. price not set (Starblaze). Donning Co.

People of Plenty: Economic Abundance & the American Character. David M. Potter. LC 54-12797. 1954. 15.00x (ISBN 0-226-67632-3). U of Chicago Pr.

People of Plenty: Economic Abundance & the American Character. David M. Potter. (Walgreen Foundation Lecture Ser). 1954. pap. 8.00X (ISBN 0-226-67633-1, P28, Phoen). U of Chicago Pr.

People of Portsmouth & Some Who Came to Town. J. D. Lincoln & Rosemary Lincoln. LC 82-16543. (Illus.). 112p. 1982. pap. 13.95 (ISBN 0-914339-00-1). P E Randall Pub.

People of Rimrock: A Study of Values in Five Cultures. Ed. by Evon Z. Vogt & Ethel M. Albert. LC 66-23469. (Illus.). 1966. 24.50x (ISBN 0-674-66150-8). Harvard U Pr.

People of Roman Britain. Anthony Birley. LC 79-3604. 240p. 1980. 42.00x (ISBN 0-520-04119-4). U of Cal Pr.

People of Sale. Kenneth L. Brown. 1976. text ed. 20.00x (ISBN 0-674-66155-9). Harvard U Pr.

People of Seldwyla & Seven Legends. facs. ed. Gottfried Keller. Tr. by M. D Hottinger. LC 70-140331. (Short Story Index Reprint Ser). 1929. 16.00 (ISBN 0-8369-3723-6). Ayer Co Pubs.

People of Sonora & Yankee Capitalists. Ramon E. Ruiz. LC 87-30133. (PROFMEX Ser.). 320p. 1988. 35.00x (ISBN 0-8165-1012-1). U of Ariz Pr.

People of South Africa. Sarah G. Millin. LC 76-56107. 1976. Repr. of 1954 ed. lib. bdg. 35.00x (ISBN 0-8371-9411-3, MIPS). Greenwood.

People of South East Asia: Biological Anthropology of India, Pakistan & Nepal. Ed. by John R. Lukacs. 458p. 1984. 65.00x (ISBN 0-306-41407-4, Plenum Pr). Plenum Pub.

People of Southern Africa. R. R. Inskeep. (Peopling of Southern Africa Ser.). (Illus.). 160p. 1979. text ed. 28.50x (ISBN 0-06-493220-6). B&N Imports.

People of Taihang: An Anthology of Family Histories. Ed. by Sidney L. Greenblatt. LC 74-15389. (China Book Project). (Illus.). pap. 89.50 (ISBN 0-317-11084-5, 2021856). Bks Demand UMI.

People of That Book. Mary Willis. Ed. by Bobbie J. Van Dolson. 128p. 1981. pap. 4.95 (ISBN 0-8280-0033-6). Review & Herald.

People of the Abyss. rev. ed. Jack London. LC 80-52105. (Mind of Man Ser.). (Illus.). 240p. 1980. text ed. 30.00 (ISBN 0-934710-03-1). J Simon.

People of the Abyss. Jack London. LC 77-73613. 136p. 1977. pap. 5.95 (ISBN 0-88208-079-2). Chicago Review.

People of the Abyss. Jack London. (Illus.). 320p. 1982. pap. 7.95 (ISBN 0-932458-08-4). Star Rover.

People of the Abyss see Novels & Social Writings.

People of the Bat: Mayan Tales & Dreams from Zinacantan. Ed. by Carol Karasik. Tr. by Robert M. Laughlin from Tzotzil. LC 87-20754. (Illus.). 282p. 1988. 24.95x (ISBN 0-87474-590-X). Smithsonian.

People of the Bible & Their Prayers. Gloria A. Truitt. (Illus.). 24p. (ps-4). 1987. pap. 1.29 (ISBN 0-570-09005-9, 59-1433). Concordia.

People of the Blue Water. Flora G. Iliff. LC 84-24105. 271p. 1985. pap. 10.95 (ISBN 0-8165-0925-5). U of Ariz Pr.

People of the Book. Paul Edwards. 1987. 12.95 (ISBN 0-87243-161-4); pap. 8.95 (ISBN 0-87243-156-8). Templegate.

People of the Book: Drama, Fellowship, & Religion. Samuel C. Heilman. LC 82-13369. 264p. 1983. lib. bdg. 25.00x (ISBN 0-226-32492-3). U of Chicago Pr.

People of the Book: Drama, Fellowship, & Religion. Samuel C. Heilman. LC 82-13369. xiv, 338p. 1987. pap. text ed. 12.95 (ISBN 0-226-32493-1). U of Chicago Pr.

People of the Book: The Story Behind the Old Testament. Anthony E. Gilles. (Illus.). 178p. (Orig.). 1983. pap. text ed. 5.95 (ISBN 0-86716-026-8). St Anthony Mess Pr.

People of the Buffalo: How the Plains Indians Lived. Maria Campbell. (How They Lived Ser.). (Illus.). (YA) (gr. 5 up). pap. 6.95 (ISBN 0-317-62412-1, Pub. by Douglas & McIntyre-Grounwood). Salem Hse Pubs.

People of the Cape Verde Islands: Exploitation & Emigration. Antonio Carreira. ix, 224p. 1982. 24.50 (ISBN 0-208-01988-X, Archon). Shoe String.

People of the Chalice. Colbert S. Cartwright. Ed. by Herbert H. Lambert. 112p. (Orig.). 1987. pap. 7.95 (ISBN 0-8272-2938-0). CBP.

People of the City. Cyprian Ekwensi. (African Writers Ser.). 1963. pap. text ed. 6.00 (ISBN 0-435-90005-6). Heinemann Ed.

People of the Covenant: An Introduction to the Old Testament. 3rd ed. Henry J. Flanders, Jr. et al. (Illus.). 512p. 1988. text ed. 29.95 (ISBN 0-19-504438-X). Oxford U Pr.

People of the Creed: The Story Behind the Early Church. Anthony E. Gilles. (People Ser.: Vol. 3). (Illus., Orig.). 1985. pap. text ed. 5.95 (ISBN 0-86716-046-2). St Anthony Mess Pr.

People of the Crimson Evening: Papago Life Long Ago. Ruth Underhill. (Wild & Woolly West Ser.). (Illus.). 127p. 1982. 10.00 (ISBN 0-86541-005-4); pap. 7.00 (ISBN 0-86541-006-2). Filter.

People of the Dark. T. M. Wright. 320p. 1985. pap. 3.50 (ISBN 0-8125-2752-6, Dist. by Warner Pub Services & Saint Martin's Press). Tor Bks.

People of the Dark. T. M. Wright. 288p. 1988. pap. 3.95 (ISBN 0-8125-2768-2). Tor Bks.

People of the Deer. Farley Mowat. 304p. 1981. pap. 3.50 (ISBN 0-7704-2079-6). Bantam.

People of the Deer. Farley Mowat. 16.95 (ISBN 0-89190-818-8, PUb. by Am Repr). Amereon Ltd.

People of the Desert & Sea: Ethnobotany of the Seri Indians. Richard S. Felger & Mary B. Moser. LC 84-16357. 435p. 1985. 65.00x (ISBN 0-8165-0818-6). U of Ariz Pr.

People of the Earth. 5th ed. Brian Fagan. 1986. write for info. (ISBN 0-673-39004-7). Scott F.

People of the Earth: An Introduction to World Prehistory. 6th ed. Brian M. Fagan. 1988. pap. text ed. price not set (ISBN 0-673-39908-7). Scott F.

People of the High Country: Jackson Hole Before the Settlers. Gary A. Wright. LC 83-49508. (American University Studies XI (Anthropology & Sociology): Vol. 7). (Illus.). 191p. 1984. 20.00 (ISBN 0-8204-0103-X). P Lang Pubs.

People of the High Plateau. Carl Berman. LC 87-83386. (Illus.). 112p. 1988. 32.00 (ISBN 0-943231-04-3). Howell Pr VA.

People of the Ice: How The Inuit Lived. Heather S. Siska. (How They Lived Ser.). (Illus.). (YA) (gr. 5 up). pap. 6.95 (ISBN 0-317-62413-X, Pub. by Douglas & McIntyre-Grounwood). Salem Hse Pubs.

People of the Ice Whale: Eskimos, White Men & the Whale. David Boeri. (Illus.). 300p. 1985. pap. 6.95 (ISBN 0-15-671660-7, Harv). HarBraceJ.

People of the Lake. Richard E. Leakey & Roger Lewin. 272p. 1983. pap. 4.95 (ISBN 0-380-45575-7, Discus). Avon.

People of the Land of Flint. Richard D. Campbell. 130p. (Orig.). 1985. lib. bdg. 23.25 (ISBN 0-8191-4550-5); pap. text ed. 10.00 (ISBN 0-8191-4551-3). U Pr of Amer.

People of the Lie: The Hope for Healing Human Evil. M. Scott Peck. LC 83-13631. 269p. 1983. 15.95 (ISBN 0-671-45492-7). S&S.

People of the Lie: The Hope for Healing Human Evil. M. Scott Peck. 276p. 1985. pap. 9.95 (ISBN 0-671-52816-5, Touchstone Bks). S&S.

People of the Long Water. Peter Hoper. (Time & the Forest Trilogy Ser.: Bk. 2). 224p. 1985. pap. 14.95 (ISBN 0-86868-066-4, Pub. by J McIndoe Ltd New Zealand). Intl Spec Bk.

People of the Longhouse: How the Iroquian Tribes Lived. Jillian Ridington & Robin Ridington. (How They Lived Ser.). (Illus.). (YA) (gr. 5 up). pap. 9.95 (ISBN 0-317-62414-8, Pub. by Douglas & McIntyre-Grounwood). Salem Hse Pubs.

People of the Magic Water. Dick Brumgardt. (Illus.). 122p. 1981. 9.95 (ISBN 0-937794-11-2). Nature Trails.

People of the Magic Waters: The Cahuilla Indians of Palm Springs. John R. Brumgardt & Larry L. Bowles. (Illus.). 1981. 9.95 (ISBN 0-88280-060-4). ETC Pubns.

People of the Maldive Islands. Clarence Maloney. (Illus.). 432p. 1980. text ed. 27.95x (ISBN 0-86131-158-2, Pub. by Orient Longman Ltd India). Apt Bks.

People of the Marsh. I. Melezh. 494p. 1979. 12.75 (ISBN 0-8285-0007-X, Pub. by Progress Pubs USSR). Imported Pubns.

People of the Mesa: The Archaeology of Black Mesa, Arizona. Shirley Powell & George J. Gummerman. (Illus.). 200p. 1987. 19.95 (ISBN 0-8093-1400-2). S Ill U Pr.

People of the Middle Place: A Study of the Zuni Indians. Dorothea C. Leighton & John Adair. LC 65-28463. (Monographs Ser.). 189p. 1966. pap. 15.00x (ISBN 0-87536-320-2). HRAFP.

People of the Mirror. Richard Price. 240p. 1985. 13.95 (ISBN 0-88282-015-X). New Horizon NJ.

People of the Moonshell: A Western River Journal. Nancy M. Peterson. LC 84-15919. (Illus.). 176p. 1984. 22.95 (ISBN 0-939650-45-2); pap. 14.95 (ISBN 0-939650-42-8). R H Pub.

People of the New Testament: Arch Book Supplement. Gloria Truitt. LC 59-1311. 1983. pap. 1.29 (ISBN 0-570-06173-3). Concordia.

People of the Old Testament. Gloria Truitt. LC 59-1310. (Arch Books Supplement Ser.). (gr. k-4). 1983. pap. 1.29 (ISBN 0-570-06172-5). Concordia.

People of the Passion & Mary M: A Visit with the Magdalene. Mary Betten. LC 87-61922. (Illus.). 116p. (Orig.). 1988. pap. 7.95 (ISBN 1-55612-079-6). Sheed & Ward MO.

People of the Pilgrimage: An Expository Study of the "Pilgrim's Progress" As a Book of Character, 2 vols. J. Kerr Bain. 475p. 1981. Repr. of 1905 ed. Set. lib. bdg. 150.00. Century Bookbindery.

People of the Pit-Grave Kurgans in Eastern Hungary. Istvan Ecsedy. 148p. 1979. 66.35x (Pub. by Collets (UK)). State Mutual Bk.

People of the Plain: Class & Community in Lower Andalusia. David D. Gilmore. LC 79-20048. 1980. 31.00x (ISBN 0-231-04754-1). Columbia U Pr.

People of the Plains & Mountains: Essays in the History of the West Dedicated to Everett Dick. Ray A. Billington. LC 72-784. (Contr. in American History No. 25). (Illus.). 193p. 1973. lib. bdg. 35.00 (ISBN 0-8371-6358-7, BID/). Greenwood.

People of the Polar North. Knud Rasmussen. LC 75-167126. 586p. 1975. Repr. of 1908 ed. 34.00x. Gale.

People of the Polar North: A Record... Knud J. Rasmussen. Ed. by G. Herring. LC 74-5868. (Illus.). Repr. of 1908 ed. 56.50 (ISBN 0-404-11675-2). AMS Pr.

People of the Potteries. Henry A. Wedgwood. LC 70-108855. 1970. lib. bdg. 25.00x (ISBN 0-678-07761-4). Kelley.

People of the Resurrection. Lionel Swain. (Good News Ser.: Vol. 15). 1986. pap. 12.95 (ISBN 0-89453-434-3). M Glazier.

People of the Sacred Mountain: A History of the Northern Cheyenne Chiefs & Warrior Societies, 1830-1879, 2 vols. Peter J. Powell. LC 76-50454. (Harper & Row Native American Publishing Program). (Illus.). 1376p. 1981. Set. 124.50 (ISBN 0-06-451550-8, HarpR). Har-Row.

People of the Sacred Oak. Bill Hotchkiss. 384p. (Orig.). 1986. pap. 3.95 (ISBN 0-553-25624-6). Bantam.

People of the Saints. George Mills. (Illus.). 1967. 5.00 (ISBN 0-916537-30-7, Taylor Museum). CO Springs Fine Arts.

People of the Sea. A. G. Jamieson. 500p. 1987. 89.95 (ISBN 0-416-40540-1). Routledge Chapman & Hall.

People of the Sea. David Thomson. 222p. 1981. pap. 4.95 (ISBN 0-586-08341-3). Academy Chi Pubs.

People of the Secret. Ernest Scott. 1983. 19.95 (ISBN 0-86304-027-6, Pub. by Octagon Pr England); pap. 8.95 (ISBN 0-86304-038-1). Ins Study Human.

People of the Secret. Ernest Scott. 263p. Date not set. 10.95. Critique Pub.

People of the Shining Mountains: The Ute Indians of Colorado. Charles S. Marsh. LC 81-21032. (Illus.). 200p. (Orig.). 1982. pap. 8.95 (ISBN 0-87108-613-1). Pruett.

People of the Sierra. rev. 2nd ed. Julian Pitt-Rivers. LC 70-153710. 1971. 17.00x (ISBN 0-226-67009-0). U. of Chicago Pr.

People of the Sierra. 2nd ed. Julian Pitt-Rivers. LC 70-153710. 1972. pap. 9.00X (ISBN 0-226-67010-4, P55, Phoen). U of Chicago Pr.

People of the Small Arrow. Jack H. Driberg. LC 72-3367. (Short Story Index Reprint Ser.). (Illus.). Repr. of 1930 ed. 21.50 (ISBN 0-8369-4146-2). Ayer Co Pubs.

People of the Snow: The Story of Kitimat. John Kendrick. 160p. 1987. pap. 12.95 (ISBN 0-317-64844-6, Pub. by NC Press Ltd). U of Toronto Pr.

People of the Totem: The Indians of the Pacific Northwest. Norman Bancroft-Hunt. LC 88-4750. (Illus.). 128p. 1988. pap. 14.95 (ISBN 0-8061-2145-9). U of Okla Pr.

People of the Trail: How the Northern Forest Indians Lived. Jillian Ridington & Robin Ridington. (How They Lived Ser.). (Illus.). (YA) (gr. 5 up). pap. 6.95 (ISBN 0-317-62415-6, Pub. by Douglas & McIntyre-Grounwood). Salem Hse Pubs.

People of the Tropical Rain Forest. Ed. by Julie S. Denslow & Christine Padoch. (Illus.). 240p. 1988. 39.50x (ISBN 0-520-06295-7); pap. 19.95 (ISBN 0-520-06351-1). U of Cal Pr.

People of the Troubled Water: Years of Discovery. Nancy M. Peterson. Ed. by Eleanor H. Ayer. (Illus.). 200p. (Orig.). 1988. 24.95 (ISBN 1-55838-082-5); pap. 15.95 (ISBN 1-55838-083-3). R H Pub.

People of the Twilight. Diamond Jenness. LC 59-16100. 1959. pap. 9.95 (ISBN 0-226-39653-5, P32, Phoen). U of Chicago Pr.

People of the Ucayali: The Shipibo & Conibo of Peru. Lucille Eakin et al. LC 86-82643. (International Museum of Cultures Publication: No. 12). ix, 62p. (Orig.). 1986. pap. 9.00x (ISBN 0-88312-163-8); microfiche (2) 4.00 (ISBN 0-88312-260-X). Summer Inst Ling.

People of the Valley. Frank Waters. LC 78-137435. 201p. 1941. 10.95 (ISBN 0-8040-0242-8, Swallow); pap. 6.95 (ISBN 0-8040-0243-6). Ohio U Pr.

People of the Valley: The Concow Maidu. ltd. ed. Don Chase. (Illus.). 1973. velo-bind ltd. 3.50 (ISBN 0-918634-35-0); pap. 3.00 ltd. D M Chase.

People of the Verde Valley, Vol. 53, No. 1. 32p. 1981. 4.00 (ISBN 0-686-76170-7). Mus Northern Ariz.

People of the Way. A. J. Dueck et al. 256p. 1981. 10.95 (ISBN 0-317-64801-2); pap. 7.95. Herald Pr.

People of the Way. John A. Toews. Ed. by A. J. Dueck et al. 256p. 1981. 10.95 (ISBN 0-919797-15-6); pap. 7.95 (ISBN 0-919797-16-4). Kindred Pr.

People of the Way: The Story Behind the New Testament. Anthony E. Gilles. (Illus.). 142p. (Orig.). 1984. pap. 5.95 (ISBN 0-86716-036-5). St Anthony Mess Pr.

People of the World. Trundle. (People of the World Ser.). (gr. 4-9). 1978. (Usborne-Hayes); PLB 12.96 (ISBN 0-88110-116-8); pap. 4.95 (ISBN 0-86020-189-9). EDC.

People of the Zongo: The Transformation of Ethnic Identities in Ghana. Enid Schildkrout. LC 76-47188. (Cambridge Studies in Social Anthropology: No. 20). 1978. 39.50 (ISBN 0-521-21483-1). Cambridge U Pr.

People of Tibet. Charles A. Bell. lib. bdg. 79.95 (ISBN 0-87968-481-X). Krishna Pr.

People of Two Kingdoms. new ed. James C. Juhnke. LC 74-84697. (Mennonite Historical Ser.). (Illus.). 221p. 1975. 7.95 (ISBN 0-87303-662-X). Faith & Life.

People of Wilson County, Tennessee: 1800-1899. Thomas E. Partlow. 158p. 1983. 22.00 (ISBN 0-89308-308-9). Southern Hist Pr.

People or Monsters? And Other Stories & Reportage from China after Mao. Liu Binyan. Ed. by Perry Link. LC 82-48594. (Chinese Literature in Translation: Midland Bks: No. 313). 160p. 1983. 20.00x (ISBN 0-253-34329-1); pap. 7.95x (ISBN 0-253-20313-9). Ind U Pr.

People or Penguins: The Case for Optimal Pollution. William F. Baxter. LC 74-6102. 110p. 1974. 20.00x (ISBN 0-231-03820-8); pap. 10.00 (ISBN 0-231-03821-6). Columbia U Pr.

People-Oriented Computer Systems: The Computer in Transition. rev. ed. Edward A. Tomeski et al. LC 81-14304. 368p. 1983. 26.50 (ISBN 0-89874-385-0). Krieger.

People Painting Scrapbook. J. Everett Draper. (Illus.). 144p. 1988. 26.95 (ISBN 0-89134-252-4). North Light Bks.

People Parish: A Model of Church Where People Flourish. Gerald J. Kleba. LC 86-82035. 136p. (Orig.). 1986. pap. 4.95 (ISBN 0-87793-346-4). Ave Maria.

People, Patients & Politics. Clark R. Cahow. Ed. by Gerald N. Grob. LC 78-22554. (Historical Issues in Mental Health Ser.). (Illus.). 1979. lib. bdg. 21.00x (ISBN 0-405-11908-9). Ayer Co Pubs.

People, Pattern & Processes: An Introduction to Human Geography. Keith Chapman. LC 79-18917. 334p. 1979. 67.95x (ISBN 0-470-26719-4). Halsted Pr.

People's China & International Law, 2 vols. Jerome A. Cohen & Hungdah Chiu. LC 73-2475. (A Documentary Study). 1974. Set. 185.00x (ISBN 0-691-09229-X). Princeton U Pr.

People's Choice. 1983. 10.95 (ISBN 0-317-03676-9). North Country.

People's Choice: A History of Albany County in Art & Architecture. Allison P. Bennett. LC 80-66320. (Illus.). 145p. (Orig.). 1980. pap. 10.95 (ISBN 0-89062-124-1). Albany County.

People's Choice Cookbook. League of Women Voters of Minnesota. (Illus.). 192p. (Orig.). 1983. pap. text ed. 8.95 (ISBN 0-939816-04-0). LWV MN.

People's Choice: How the Voter Makes up His Mind in a Presidential Campaign. 3rd ed. Paul F. Lazarsfeld et al. LC 68-20443. 224p. pap. 58.30 (2030109). Bks Demand UMI.

People's Christmas. Gerald O'Collins. (Orig.). 1984. pap. 3.50 (ISBN 0-8091-2660-5). Paulist Pr.

People's Church. Bonaventure Kloppenburg. 1978. 8.95 (ISBN 0-8199-0692-1). Franciscan Herald.

People's Clearance: Highland Emigration to British North America 1770-1815. Bumsted Jack. 200p. 1981. 40.00x (ISBN 0-85224-419-3, Pub. by Edinburgh Univ England). State Mutual Bk.

People's College: Little Rock Junior College & Little Rock University, 1927-1969. Jim Lester. (Illus.). 239p. 1987. 19.95 (ISBN 0-87483-052-4). August Hse.

People's Communes & Rural Development in China. Benedict Stavis. 184p. 1974. 4.50 (ISBN 0-86731-088-X). Cornell CIS RDC.

People's Contest: The Union & Civil War 1861-1865. Phillip S. Paludan. LC 87-46161. (Illus.). 464p. 1988. 27.95 (ISBN 0-06-015903-0, HarpT). Har-Row.

People's Democratic Republic of Yemen: Politics, Economics & Society. Tareq Y. Ismael & Jacqueline S. Ismael. LC 86-15442. (Marxist Regimes Ser.). 183p. 1986. lib. bdg. 30.00 (ISBN 0-931477-96-4). Lynne Rienner.

People's Doonesbury: Notes from Underfoot. G. B. Trudeau. LC 81-80815. (Illus.). 224p. 1981. pap. 19.95 (ISBN 0-03-049166-5, Owl Bks.); pap. 12.95 (ISBN 0-03-049171-1). H Holt & Co.

People's Farm: English Radical Agrarianism, 1775-1840. Malcolm Chase. 240p. 1988. 59.00 (ISBN 0-19-820105-2). Oxford U Pr.

People's Fight. Adapted by & tr. by John Holstein. (Korean Folk Tales Ser.: No. 7). (Illus.). 36p. (Eng. & Korean.). (gr. 1-8). 1986. PLB write for info. (ISBN 0-87296-006-4, Pub. by Si-sa-yong-o-sa Korea); bilingual cassette incl. Si-sa-yong-o-sa.

People's Force: A History of the Victoria Police. Robert Haldane. 372p. 1986. 25.00 (ISBN 0-522-84306-9, Pub. by Melbourne U Pr). Intl Spec Bk.

People's Front Movement in Hungary. G. Kallai. 304p. 1979. pap. 16.25x (ISBN 0-317-53871-3, Pub. by Collets (UK)). State Mutual Bk.

People's Guide to London. Andrew Davies. (Orig.). 1985. pap. 4.95 (ISBN 0-904526-89-5, Pub. by Journeyman Pr England). Riverrun NY.

People's Guide to Mexico. rev. ed. Carl Franz. (Illus.). 576p. (Orig.). 1986. pap. 13.95 (ISBN 0-912528-56-7). John Muir.

People's Guide to Mexico. 7th ed. Carl Franz. Ed. by Lorena Havens. 600p. 1988. pap. 14.95 (ISBN 0-912528-99-0). John Muir.

People's Guide to National Defense: What Kind of Guns Are They Buying for Your Butter? Sheila Tobias et al. Ed. by Maria D. Guarnaschelli. LC 83-14004. 432p. 1984. pap. 9.45 (ISBN 0-688-02200-6, Quill NY). Morrow.

People's Guide to RV & Adventure Camping in Mexico. Carl Franz. Ed. by Lorena Havens. 356p. (Orig.). 1988. pap. 13.95 (ISBN 0-912528-91-5). John Muir.

People's Guide to Vitamins & Minerals: From A to Zinc. Dominick Bosco. 336p. 1980. pap. 11.95 (ISBN 0-8092-7139-7). Contemp Bks.

People's Guide, 1874: Directory of Henry Co., Indiana. Cline & McHaffie. 398p. 1979. 22.00 (ISBN 0-686-27818-6). Bookmark.

People's Handbook of Medical Care. Arthur Frank & Stuart Frank. LC 72-2178. 1972. 10.00 (ISBN 0-394-47925-4). Random.

People's Health: Anthropology & Medicine in a Navajo Community. John Adair et al. (Illus.). 302p. 1988. 27.50x (ISBN 0-8263-1027-3); pap. 14.95 (ISBN 0-8263-1095-8). U of NM Pr.

People's Health Eighteen Thirty-Nineteen Ten. Francis B. Smith. LC 78-13095. 436p. 1979. 47.50 (ISBN 0-8419-0448-0). Holmes & Meier.

People's Herbal. Michael Weiner. (Orig.). 1981. pap. cancelled (ISBN 0-446-97574-5). Warner Bks.

People's Herbal: A Complete Family Guide for All Ages to Safe Home Remedies. Michael A. Weiner. LC 82-80371. (Illus.). 288p. 1984. pap. 8.95 (ISBN 0-399-50756-6, G&D). Putnam Pub Group.

People's Heritage. Curtis B. Solberg & David W. Morris. 368p. 1984. pap. 21.95 (ISBN 0-8403-3243-2). Kendall-Hunt.

People's Heritage: Patterns in United States History. Curtis B. Solberg & David W. Morris. LC 74-34262. (Illus.). 292p. 1975. avail. tchr's manual (ISBN 0-471-81126-2). Wiley.

People's History & Socialist Theory. Ed. by Raphael Samuel. (History Workshop Ser.). 425p. 1981. pap. 10.95 (ISBN 0-7100-0652-7). Routledge Chapman & Hall.

People's History of Live Oak County, Texas. Ervin L. Sparkman. Ed. by Mary S. Roberts. LC 81-2937. (Illus.). 305p. 1981. 27.50 (ISBN 0-86663-402-9). Ide Hse.

People's History of the United States, 8 vols. Page Smith. 1987. Set. pap. text ed. 195.00 (ISBN 0-07-909019-2). McGraw.

People's History of the United States. Howard Zinn. 614p. 1981. pap. 9.95 (ISBN 0-06-090792-4, CN792, PL). Har-Row.

People's Idea of God. Mary Baker Eddy. 48p. Braille edition. 16.00 (ISBN 0-87952-050-7). First Church.

People's Idea of God. Mary Baker Eddy. 14p. pap. 2.00 (ISBN 0-87952-235-6). First Church.

People's Idea of God, Christian Healings No & Yes. Mary Baker Eddy. pap. 4.50 (ISBN 0-87952-042-6). First Church.

People's Instrument. Robert J. Blakely. 1971. pap. 7.00 (ISBN 0-8183-0190-2). Pub Aff Pr.

People's Law & State Law: The Bellagio Papers. Ed. by A. Allot & G. R. Woodman. viii, 354p. 1985. pap. write for info. (ISBN 90-6765-100-1). Foris Pubns.

People's Law Review. Ralph Warner. LC 80-18475. 1982. pap. 8.95 (ISBN 0-201-08306-X). Nolo Pr.

People's Lawyer. Paul Sevaried. 5.75 (ISBN 0-87018-056-8). Ross.

People's Lewiston - Auburn, Maine 1875-1975. John Rand. LC 75-7980. (Illus.). 128p. 1975. 9.95 (ISBN 0-87027-164-4); pap. 7.95 (ISBN 0-87027-165-2). Cumberland Pr.

People's Liberation Army & China's Nation-Building. Ying-mao Kau. LC 72-77203. pap. 91.80 (ISBN 0-317-08198-5, 2015408). Bks Demand UMI.

People's Medical Answer Book: Plain Answers to One Thousand One Hundred Common Questions from Thirty-Six Leading Specialists. Richard I. Pyatt. 1984. 21.95 (ISBN 0-13-656596-4); pap. 10.95 (ISBN 0-13-656588-3). P-H.

People's Medical Manual. Howard R. Lewis & Martha E. Lewis. LC 83-24003. (Illus.). 592p. 1986. flexibound 19.95 (ISBN 0-385-27649-4, Dial). Doubleday.

People's Money Pages. 1st ed. Frieda Carrol. LC 80-70419. 50p. 1981. pap. 4.95 (ISBN 0-9605246-3-0, Pub. by Biblio Pr GA). Prosperity & Profits.

People's Money Pages: Fundraising Edition. Carrol, Frieda, Research Division Staff. 50p. 1984. pap. text ed. 8.95 (ISBN 0-318-04338-6, Pub. by F. Carrol). Prosperity & Profits.

People's New Testament with Notes, 1 vol. Ed. by B. W. Johnson. 1971. 16.95 (ISBN 0-89225-141-7). Gospel Advocate.

People's Nutrition Encyclopedia. Lynne S. Hill. 352p. 1987. pap. 11.95 (ISBN 0-399-51289-6, Perigee). Putnam Pub Group.

Peoples of Africa: Cultures of Africa South of the Sahara. Ed. by James L. Gibbs, Jr. (Illus.). 594p. 1988. pap. text ed. 19.95x (ISBN 0-88133-318-2). Waveland Pr.

Peoples of Asiatic Russia. Vladimir I. Jochelson. 1928. 27.00 (ISBN 0-384-27560-5). Johnson Repr.

Peoples of Assam. B. M. Das. 98p. 1987. 16.95. Asia Bk Corp.

Peoples of Connecticut Multinational Ethnic Heritage Studies, 6 bks. Incl. Armenian Studies for Secondary Students. Frank A. Stone. 1975; Irish: In Their Homeland, In America, In Connecticut. Frank A. Stone. 1975. 6.00; Italians: In Their Homeland, In America, In Connecticut. Patricia S. Weibust. 1976. 6.50; Jews: Their Origins, In America, In Connecticut. Sally I. Gould. 1976. 8.00; Puerto Ricans: On the Island, on the Mainland, In Connecticut. Barbara Burdette-Hood. 75p. 1976; Learning About the Peoples of Connecticut. Patricia S. Weibust. 1977. tchrs. manual 2.50. Set. 30.00 (ISBN 0-685-55886-X). I N Thut World Educ Ctr.

Peoples of Connecticut: Studies of Cultural Pluralism by Connecticut High School Students. Frank A. Stone. (Peoples of Connecticut Ser.). 63p. 1981. 6.50. I N Thut World Educ Ctr.

Peoples of Europe. Herbert J. Fleure. LC 76-44717. Repr. of 1922 ed. 26.00 (ISBN 0-404-15922-2). AMS Pr.

Peoples of India. J. D. Anderson. (Illus.). xii, 118p. 1983. text ed. 15.00x (ISBN 0-86590-151-1). Apt Bks.

Peoples of Ireland: From Prehistory to Modern Times. Liam De Paor. LC 85-52221. 344p. 1986. text ed. 29.95x (ISBN 0-268-01562-7). U of Notre Dame Pr.

Peoples of Israel: Fifty-Seven Centuries of Presence. rev. & enl. ed. Herbert A. Klein. Ed. by Joseph Simon. LC 86-90358. Orig. Title: Israel - Land of the Jews. (Illus.). 240p. (ps-12). 1986. Repr. of 1972 ed. 23.50 (ISBN 0-934710-13-9). J Simon.

Peoples of North America, 53 Vols. Ed. by Fred L. Israel. (Illus.). 5472p. lib. bdg. 845.35 (ISBN 0-87754-852-8). Chelsea Hse.

Peoples of Old: Preconquest & Early Colonial Chile. Agustin Edwards. 1976. lib. bdg. 59.95 (ISBN 0-8490-2419-6). Gordon Pr.

Peoples of Philadelphia: A History of Ethnic Groups & Lower Class Life, 1790-1940. Ed. by Allen F. Davis & Mark H. Haller. LC 72-95879. 311p. 1973. 27.95 (ISBN 0-87722-053-0); pap. 8.95 (ISBN 0-87722-035-2). Temple U Pr.

Peoples of Prehistoric South Dakota. Larry J. Zimmerman. LC 84-17324. (Illus.). x, 143p. 1985. 16.50 (ISBN 0-8032-4903-9). U of Nebr Pr.

Peoples of Southeast Asia. Bruno Lasker. LC 74-161765. (Institute of Pacific Relations). Repr. of 1944 ed. 30.00 (ISBN 0-404-09029-X). AMS Pr.

Peoples of Southern Africa & Their Affinities. G. T. Nurse et al. (Research Monographs on Human Population Biology). (Illus.). 1985. 69.00x (ISBN 0-19-857541-6). Oxford U Pr.

Peoples of Southern Nigeria, 4 vols. Percy Talbot. 1976. lib. bdg. 400.00 (ISBN 0-8490-2420-X). Gordon Pr.

Peoples of the Eastern Habsburg Lands, 1526-1918. Robert A. Kann & Zdenek V. David. LC 83-21629. (History of East Central Europe Ser.: No. 6). (Illus.). 560p. 1984. 30.00x (ISBN 0-295-96095-7). U of Wash Pr.

Peoples of the Golden Triangle: Six Tribes in Thailand. Paul Lewis & Elaine Lewis. LC 84-50047. (Illus.). 1984. 35.00f (ISBN 0-500-97314-8). Thames Hudson.

Peoples of the Jos Plateau, Nigeria: Their Philosophy, Manners & Customs. Marie de Paul Neiers. (European University Studies: Series 19, Anthropology-Ethnology, Section B, Ethnology: Vol. 805). 215p. 1979. 21.35 (ISBN 3-8204-6479-4). P Lang Pubs.

Peoples of the Soviet Far East. Walter Kolarz. LC 69-12416. (Illus.). xii, 194p. 1969. Repr. of 1954 ed. 24.50 (ISBN 0-208-00701-6, Archon). Shoe String.

Peoples of the Soviet Union. Viktor Kozlov. Tr. by Pauline M. Tiffen from Rus. LC 88-637. (Second World Ser.). 274p. 1988. 37.50 (ISBN 0-253-34356-9). Ind U Pr.

Peoples of the U. S. S. R. An Ethnographic Handbook. Ronald Wixman. LC 83-18433. (Illus.). 264p. 1984. 35.00 (ISBN 0-87332-203-7). M E Sharpe.

Peoples of the World. Andrew Langley. (Topics Ser.). (Illus.). 32p. (gr. 1-6). 1986. PLB 11.90 (ISBN 0-531-18059-X, Pub. by Bookwright). Watts.

Peoples of Utah. Ed. by Helen Z. Papanikolas. LC 76-12311. (Illus.). 499p. 1981. Repr. of 1976 ed. 12.95 (ISBN 0-913738-26-3). Utah St Hist Soc.

Peoples of Zanzibar: Their Customs & Religious Beliefs. Godfrey Dale. LC 78-90112. 1969. Repr. of 1920 ed. 35.00 (ISBN 0-8371-2028-4, DAP&). Greenwood.

People's Palace: Parliament in Modern Australia. David Slomon. 194p. 1986. pap. 9.95 (ISBN 0-522-84318-2, Pub. by Melbourne U Pr). Intl Spec Bk.

People's Panel: The Grand Jury in the United States, 1634-1941. Richard D. Younger. LC 63-12993. Repr. of 1963 ed. 67.80 (2027527). Bks Demand UMI.

People's Participation in Family Planning. Vapai Panandiker & A. K. Mehra. 1987. 29.00x (ISBN 81-85024-10-3, Pub. by Uppal Pub Hse New Delhi). South Asia Bks.

People's Party Campaign Book. facsimile ed. Thomas E. Watson. Ed. by Dan C. McCurry & Richard E. Rubenstein. LC 74-30663. (American Farmers & the Rise of Agribusiness Ser.). 1975. Repr. of 1893 ed. 35.50x (ISBN 0-405-06839-5). Ayer Co Pubs.

People's Party in Texas: A Study in Third-Party Politics. Roscoe Martin. (Texas History Paperbacks: No. 7). 280p. 1970. pap. 7.95x (ISBN 0-292-70032-6). U of Tex Pr.

People's Pharmacy. Joe Graedon & Teresa Graedon. 1988. pap. 4.95 (ISBN 0-312-90499-1). St Martin.

People's Place Address Book of Amish Folk Art. 14.95 (ISBN 0-934672-49-0). Good Bks PA.

People's Poland: Patterns of Social Inequality & Conflict, No. 55. Wladyslaw Majkowski. LC 84-15689. (Contributions in Sociology Ser.). (Illus.). xvii, 234p. 1985. lib. bdg. 36.95 (ISBN 0-313-24614-9, MJP/). Greenwood.

People's President: The Electoral College in American History & the Direct Vote Alternative. rev. ed. Neal R. Peirce & Lawrence D. Longley. LC 80-24260. (Illus.). 416p. 1981. text ed. 52.00t (ISBN 0-300-02612-9); pap. 12.95x (ISBN 0-300-02704-4, Y-395). Yale U Pr.

People's Princess. S. W. Jackman. 214p. 1984. 50.00x (ISBN 0-946041-19-9, Pub. by Kensal Pr UK). State Mutual Bk.

People's Printer. Shawn Kelly. 1979. pap. 5.00 (ISBN 0-686-36545-3). Ctr Responsive Law.

People's Railway. Anthony Perles. Ed. by Jim Walker. LC 80-81311. (Interurbans Special Ser.: 69). (Illus.). 260p. 1981. 32.95 (ISBN 0-916374-42-4). Interurban.

People's Reformation: Magistrates, Clergy & Commons in Strasbourg, 1500-1598. Lorna J. Abray. LC 84-45805. 272p. 1985. 28.95x (ISBN 0-8014-1776-7). Cornell U Pr.

People's Republic of Albania. Nicholas C. Pano. LC 68-27736. (Integration & Community Building in Eastern Europe Ser: No. 4). 185p. 1968. pap. 5.95x (ISBN 0-8018-0520-1). Johns Hopkins.

People's Republic of China. Claude A. Buss. LC 63-769. 188p. (Orig.). 1962. pap. 7.50 (VN). Krieger.

People's Republic of China. Valjean McLenighan. LC 84-7025. (Enchantment of the World Ser.). (Illus.). 128p. (gr. 5-9). 1984. lib. bdg. 22.60 (ISBN 0-516-02781-6). Childrens.

People's Republic of China: A Basic Handbook. 4th ed. Steven M. Goldstein & Kathrin Sears. (Illus.). 160p. (Orig.). 1984. pap. 7.50x (ISBN 0-936876-17-4). LRIS.

People's Republic of China: A Concise Political History. Witold Rodzinski. 304p. 1988. 24.95x (ISBN 0-02-926871-0); pap. 9.95 (ISBN 0-02-926872-9). Free Pr.

People's Republic of China: A Documentary History of Revolutionary Change. Ed. by Mark Selden. 1980. pap. 15.00 (ISBN 0-85345-532-5). Monthly Rev.

People's Republic of China after Thirty Years: An Overview. Ed. by Joyce K. Kallgren. LC 79-89491. (China Research Monographs: No. 15). 122p. 1979. pap. 2.50x (ISBN 0-912966-21-1). IEAS.

People's Republic of China after Thirty Years: An Overview. Ed. by Joyce K. Kallgren. LC 79-89491. (University of California Center for Chinese Studies, China Research Monograph: No. 15). pap. 33.00 (ISBN 0-317-27740-5, 2019468). Bks Demand UMI.

People's Republic of China & the Law of Treaties. Hungdah Chiu. LC 72-173411. (Studies in East Asian Law: No. 5). 1972. 16.00x (ISBN 0-674-66175-3). Harvard U Pr.

People's Republic of China Cookbook. Nobuko Sakamoto. (Illus.). 1977. pap. 7.95 (ISBN 0-394-73380-0). Random.

People's Republic of China, International Law & Arms Control. David Salem. 325p. Maryland Studies in East Asian Law & Politics Ser., No. 3 15.00, (ISBN 0-942182-59-6); pap. 7.00, Occasional Papers-Reprints Ser. in Contemporary Asian Studies, No. 6, 1983 (ISBN 0-942182-58-8). Occasional Papers.

People's Republic of China, Nineteen Forty-Nine to Nineteen Seventy-Nine: A Documentary Survey, 5 vols. Ed. by Harold C. Hinton. LC 80-5228. 3000p. 1980. Set. lib. bdg. 400.00 (ISBN 0-8420-2166-3). Scholarly Res Inc.

People's Republic of China: Red Star of the East. rev. ed. Jane W. Watson. LC 81-910. (Illus.). 112p. (gr. 3-6). 1976. PLB 7.99 (ISBN 0-8116-6863-0). Garrard.

People's Republic of China: Social Science Reference Sources. Robert Goehlert. (Public Administration Ser.: P 2030). 18p. 1986. 5.00 (ISBN 1-55590-050-X). Vance Biblios.

People's Republic of China: Torture & Ill-Treatment of Prisoners. Amnesty International Staff. 46p. (Orig.). 1987. pap. 5.00 (ISBN 0-939994-32-1, Pub. by Amnesty Intl Pubns UK). Amnesty Intl USA.

People's Republic of China Year Book: 1986. 673p. 1986. 120.00 (ISBN 962-7167-03-7, Pub. by NCN). Taylor & Francis.

People's Republic of China, 1979-1984: A Documentary Survey, 2 vols. Ed. by Harold C. Hinton. LC 85-30391. 1986. Set. 125.00 (ISBN 0-8420-2253-8). Scholarly Res Inc.

People's Republics of Eastern Europe. Jurgen Tampke. LC 83-10920. 200p. 1983. 22.50 (ISBN 0-312-60035-6). St Martin.

People's Right to Good Health: A Guide to Consumer Health Rights & Their Enforcement. Terry Madison. 278p. 1978. 21.50 (24,849). NCLS Inc.

People's Right to Know. Harold L. Cross. LC 75-170844. Repr. of 1953 ed. 25.00 (ISBN 0-404-01859-9). AMS Pr.

People's Runnymede. R. J. Scrutton. 69.95 (ISBN 0-8490-0812-3). Gordon Pr.

People's Science: The Popular Political Economy of Exploitation & Crisis 1816-34. Noel W. Thompson. 260p. 1985. 44.50 (ISBN 0-521-25795-6). Cambridge U Pr.

Peoples Speaking to Peoples: A Report on International Mass Communication from the Commission on Freedom of the Press. Llewellyn White & Robert D. Leigh. LC 72-4685. (International Propaganda & Communications Ser.). 131p. 1972. Repr. of 1946 ed. 15.00 (ISBN 0-405-04769-X). Ayer Co Pubs.

People's Theology. Ed. by Adolf Exeler & Norbert Mette. 192p. pap. 9.95 cancelled (ISBN 0-8245-0477-1). Crossroad NY.

People's Travel Book. Compiled by Frieda Carrol. LC 80-70869. 115p. 1981. 39.95 (ISBN 0-939476-05-3, Pub. by Biblio PR GA); pap. 29.95 (ISBN 0-939476-06-1). Prosperity & Profits.

People's University: A History of Mississippi State University. John K. Bettersworth. LC 79-13648. 1980. text ed. 25.00x (ISBN 0-87805-104-X). U Pr of Miss.

People's Verdict: DCM Computer-Based Study. G. G. Mirchandani. (Illus.). 194p. 1980. text ed. 22.50x (ISBN 0-7069-1060-5, Pub. by Vikas India). Advent NY.

People's Voice: An Annotated Bibliography of American Presidential Campaign Newspapers, 1828-1984. Compiled by William Miles. LC 87-11969. (Bibliographies & Indexes in American History Ser.: No. 6). 272p. 1987. lib. bdg. 37.95 (ISBN 0-313-23976-2, MPN/). Greenwood.

People's Voice: The Orator in American Society. Barnet Baskerville. LC 79-4001. 269p. pap. 70.00 (2030048). Bks Demand UMI.

People's Wisdom. Ed. by Gabriel Z. Olowookere. LC 85-90217. 74p. 1986. 7.95 (ISBN 0-533-06704-9). Vantage.

TITLE INDEX PER CAPITA FIBRE CONSUMPTION

Peopleware: Productive Projects & Teams. Tom DeMarco & Timothy Lister. (Illus.). 160p. (Orig.). 1987. pap. 23.00 (ISBN 0-932633-05-6). Dorset Hse Pub Co.

Peoplework: Communications Dynamics for Librarians. Judith W. Powell & Robert B. LeLievre. ix, 190p. 1979. pap. 8.00x (ISBN 0-8389-0290-1, 79-18018). ALA.

Peopling of a World: Selected Articles on Immigration & Settlement Patterns in British North America. Ed. by Peter C. Hoffer. (Early American History Ser.). 412p. 1987. lib. bdg. 60.00 (ISBN 0-8240-6230-2). Garland Pub.

Peopling of America: Perspectives on Immigration. Franklin D. Scott. LC 84-71209. (AHA Pamphlets: No. 241). (Illus.). 1984. pap. text ed. 3.50 (ISBN 0-87229-006-9). Am Hist Assn.

Peopling of Ancient Egypt & the Deciphering of Metrotic Script: Proceedings of the Symposium held in Cairo, Jan. 28 - Feb. 3, 1974. (Studies & Documents Ser.: No. 1). 136p. 1978. pap. 5.25 (ISBN 92-3-101605-9, U882, UNESCO). UNIPUB.

Peopling of British North America: An Introduction. Bernard Bailyn. LC 85-82144. 160p. 1986. 16.95 (ISBN 0-394-55392-6). Knopf.

Peopling of British North America: An Introduction. Bernard Bailyn. Ed. by Peter Dimock. LC 87-45916. 192p. pap. 5.95 (ISBN 0-394-75779-3, Vin). Random.

Peopling of Hawaii. Eleanor C. Nordyke. LC 77-8842. (Illus.). 241p. 1977. pap. 5.95x (ISBN 0-8248-0511-9, Eastwest Ctr). UH Pr.

Peopling of the Earth. Geoffrey Barborka. LC 75-4243. (Illus.). 240p. 1975. 10.00 (ISBN 0-8356-0221-4). Theos Pub Hse.

Peopling of the New World. Ed. by Jonathon E. Ericson et al. LC 81-22800. (Anthropological Papers: No. 23). (Illus.). 364p. 1982. 19.95 (ISBN 0-87919-095-7). Ballena Pr.

Peopling of the Pacific Rim. Harry L. Shapiro. LC 66-84151. (Thomas Burke Memorial Lecture Ser.: No. 1). (Illus.). 1964. pap. 5.00x (ISBN 0-295-73875-8). U of Wash Pr.

Peopling of Tompkins County: A Social History. Carol Kammen. LC 85-17563. (Illus.). 250p. 1985. 19.95 (ISBN 0-932334-21-0). Heart of the Lakes.

Peopling the Argentine Pampa. Mark S. Jefferson. LC 71-123491. 1971. Repr. of 1926 ed. 24.50x (ISBN 0-8046-1378-8, Pub. by Kennikat). Assoc Faculty Pr.

Peopling the High Plains: Wyoming's European Heritage. Gordon O. Hendrickson. (Illus.). 206p. 1977. 5.95 (ISBN 0-943398-01-0). Wyoming State Press.

Peoria! Jerry Klein. (Illus.). 276p. 1985. 24.95 (ISBN 0-9615759-0-5). Visual Comm.

Peoria Directory for 1844. Simeon DeWitt Drown. 1978. Repr. of 1844 ed. 6.95x (ISBN 0-930358-02-3). Spoon River.

Peoria Way. Joe McMillan & Robert P. Olmsted. LC 83-62625. (Illus.). 136p. 1984. 29.95 (ISBN 0-934228-13-2). McMillan Pubns.

Peoria Winter: Styles & Resources in Later Life. John R. Kelly. LC 86-45421. 176p. 1987. 27.00x (ISBN 0-669-13341-8). Lexington Bks.

PEP in the Frick Elementary School: Interim Evaluation Report of the Primary Education Project 1968-1969. Margaret C. Wang et al. 52p. 1970. 1.50 (ISBN 0-318-14724-6, ED047973). Learn Res Dev.

Pep Talk: How to Analyze Political Language. Hugh Rank. LC 83-15318. (Illus.). 215p. (Orig.). 1984. pap. 11.95 (ISBN 0-943468-01-9). Counter-Prop Pr.

Pepe Botellas. Gustano A. Gardeazabal. 344p. (Span.). 1984. 11.00 (ISBN 0-317-46760-3, 3015). Ediciones Norte.

Pepito: The Little Dancing Dog. Mark Evans. LC 78-65354. (Illus.). (gr. k-4). 1979. 6.95 (ISBN 0-87592-063-2). Scroll Pr.

Pepito's Journey. 47p. 1987. pap. 4.95 (ISBN 92-1-100308-3, E.87.I.4). UN.

Pepito's Speech at the United Nations. 1986. 8.95 (ISBN 92-1-100278-8, E.85.I.7). UN.

Pepper & All the Legs. Dick Gackenbach. LC 78-5084. (Illus.). 32p. (ps-3). 1978. 7.95 (ISBN 0-395-28797-9, Clarion). HM.

Pepper & Pirates: Adventures in the Sumatra Pepper Trade of Salem. James D. Phillips. (Illus.). 141p. 1949. 15.00 (ISBN 0-88389-014-3). Essex Inst.

Pepper & Salt. Vance Havner. (Pulpit Library). 128p. 1983. pap. 4.95 (ISBN 0-8010-4276-3). Baker Bk.

Pepper: Eyewitness to a Century. Claude D. Pepper & Hays Gorey. 1987. 17.95 (ISBN 0-15-171695-1). HarBraceJ.

Pepper, Guns, & Parleys: The Dutch East India Company & China, 1662-1681. John E. Wills, Jr. LC 73-81669. (East Asian Ser.: No. 75). 288p. 1974. text ed. 18.50x (ISBN 0-674-66181-8). Harvard U Pr.

Pepper Pike: A Milan Jacovich Mystery. Les Roberts. 240p. 1988. 15.95 (ISBN 0-312-02266-2, Pub. by Thomas Dunne Bks). St Martin.

Peppercanister Poems Nineteen Seventy-Two to Nineteen Seventy-Eight. Thomas Kinsella. LC 79-63669. 159p. 1979. pap. 7.95 (ISBN 0-916390-12-8). Wake Forest.

Peppermint Gang & the Impossible Houseboat. Laurie B. Clifford. (Peppermint Gang Ser.). 192p. (Orig.). (gr. 1-3). 1985. pap. 3.50 (ISBN 0-8423-1594-2). Tyndale.

Peppermint Pig. Nina Bawden. LC 74-26922. (gr. 3-6). 1975. PLB 12.89i (ISBN 0-397-31618-6, Lipp Jr Bks). HarpJ.

Peppermint Pig. Nina Bawden. (gr. 5 up). 1988. pap. 4.95 (ISBN 0-440-40122-4, YB). Dell.

Peppermints in the Parlor. Barbara B. Wallace. LC 80-12326. 216p. (gr. 3-7). 1980. 13.95 (ISBN 0-689-30790-X, Atheneum Childrens Bks). Macmillan.

Peppermints in the Parlor. Barbara B. Wallace. LC 80-12326. 198p. (gr. 4-6). 1985. pap. 3.95 (ISBN 0-689-71048-8, Aladdin). Macmillan.

Peppernuts: Plain & Fancy. Norma J. Voth. LC 78-72160. (Illus.). 72p. 1978. pap. 3.50 (ISBN 0-8361-1877-4). Herald Pr.

Peppers: Hot & Chili. Georgeanne Brennan & Charlotte Glenn. (Aris Kitchen Edition Ser.). (Illus.). 96p. (Orig.). 1988. pap. 9.95 (ISBN 0-943186-28-5). Aris Bks Harris.

Peppers: Pickled, Sauces & Salsas. Sue J. Dremann. 54p. (Orig.). 1986. pap. 3.95. Redwood Seed.

Peppers: The Domesticated Capsicums. Jean Andrews. (Illus.). 186p. 1984. 40.00 (ISBN 0-292-76486-3). U of Tex Pr.

PepperTide. Jack Weyland. LC 82-25171. 181p. 1983. 7.95 (ISBN 0-87747-967-4). Deseret Bk.

Peppi & Poppy Search for Santa. Susie Jenkin-Pearce. (Illus.). 32p. (gr. k-3). 1988. 8.95 (ISBN 0-8120-4129-1). Barron.

Peppy Learns to Play Baseball. Pete Heller. Ed. by Thomas D. Kinsey. (Peppy Learns to Play Ser.). (Illus.). 32p. (gr. k-5). pap. 3.95 (ISBN 0-932423-00-0). Summa Pub.

Pepsinogens in Man: Clinical & Genetic Advances. Johanna Kreuning et al. LC 84-25017. (Progress in Clinical & Biological Research Ser.: Vol. 173). 318p. 1985. 58.00 (ISBN 0-8451-5023-5). A R Liss.

Peptic Ulcer & Its Drug Causation: The Role of Non-Steroidal Anti-Inflammatory Drugs. David Clinch. (Illus.). 176p. 1986. text ed. 45.00x (ISBN 0-7099-3482-3, Pub. by Croom Helm UK). Sheridan Med Bks.

Peptic Ulcer Disease. Ed. by Frank Brooks. (Contemporary Issues in Gastroenterology Ser.: Vol. 3). (Illus.). 344p. 1985. text ed. 52.00 (ISBN 0-443-08368-1). Churchill.

Peptic Ulcer Diseases: Basic & Clinical Aspects. G. F. Nelis et al. (Developments in Gastroenterology Ser.). 1985. lib. bdg. 73.00 (ISBN 0-89838-759-0, Pub. by Martinus Nijhoff Netherlands). Kluwer Academic.

Peptide & Protein Reviews, Vol. 1. (Illus.). 256p. 1983. 65.00 (ISBN 0-8247-7053-6). Dekker.

Peptide & Protein Reviews, Vol. 2. Hearn. 336p. 1983. 65.00 (ISBN 0-8247-7135-4). Dekker.

Peptide & Protein Reviews, Vol. 3. (Illus.). 240p. 1984. 65.00 (ISBN 0-8247-7241-5). Dekker.

Peptide & Protein Reviews, Vol. 4. Ed. by Milton W. Hearn. (Illus.). 256p. 1984. 65.00 (ISBN 0-8247-7292-X). Dekker.

Peptide Antibiotics. Ed. by Horst Kleinkauf & Hans Van Dohren. (Illus.). 479p. 1982. 123.00 (ISBN 3-11-008484-8). De Gruyter.

Peptide Chemistry. M. Bodanszky. (Illus.). 240p. 1988. pap. 29.95 (ISBN 0-387-18984-X). Springer-Verlag.

Peptide Hormone Receptors. Ed. by M. Y. Kalimi & J. R. Hubbard. viii, 720p. (Orig.). 1987. lib. bdg. 200.00 (ISBN 3-11-010759-7). De Gruyter.

Peptide Hormones, 2 Vols. Ed. by S. A. Berson & R. S. Yalow. LC 72-93088. (Methods in Investigative & Diagnostic Endocrinology: Vol. 2). 1200p. 1973. Set. 352.75 (ISBN 0-444-10453-4, North-Holland). Elsevier.

Peptide Hormones as Mediators in Immunology & Oncology. Ed. by R. D. Hesch & M. J. Atkinson. (Serono Symposia Publications Ser.: Vol. 19). 270p. 1985. text ed. 42.00 (ISBN 0-89004-609-3). Raven.

Peptide Hormones, Biomembranes & Cell Growth. Ed. by Liana Bolis et al. LC 84-17846. 304p. 1984. 59.50x (ISBN 0-306-41816-9, Plenum Pr). Plenum Pub.

Peptide Hormones: Effects & Mechanisms of Action. Ed. by Andrea Negro-Vilar & P. Michael Conn. 1988. Vol. I, 272p. 130.00 (ISBN 0-8493-6719-0, 6719); Vol. II, 224 pgs. 120.00 (ISBN 0-8493-6720-4, 6720); Vol. III, 224 pgs. 100.00 (ISBN 0-8493-6721-2, 6721). CRC Pr.

Peptide Hormones in Lung Cancer. Ed. by K. Havemann et al. LC 85-14879. (Recent Results in Cancer Research Ser.: Vol. 99). (Illus.). 260p. 1985. 69.00 (ISBN 0-387-15504-X). Springer-Verlag.

Peptide Synthesis. 2nd ed. Miklos O. Bodanszky et al. LC 76-16099. (Interscience Monographs on Organic Chemistry). 208p. 1976. 43.50x (ISBN 0-471-08451-4, Pub. by Wiley-Interscience). Wiley.

Peptide Transport & Hydrolysis. Symposium on Peptide Transport & Hydrolysis (1976: Ciba Foundation) LC 77-8378. (Ciba Foundation Symposium New Ser.: No. 50). pap. 98.80 (2014646). Bks Demand UMI.

Peptide Transport in Bacteria & Mammalian Cut. Ciba Foundation Staff. LC 72-76006. (Ciba Foundation Symposium Ser.: No. 4). pap. 42.50 (ISBN 0-317-28325-1, 2022136). Bks Demand UMI.

Peptidergic Mechanisms in the Cerebral Circulation. Ed. by James McCulloch & Lars Edvinsson. (Ellis Horwood Series in Biomedicine). (Illus.). 240p. 1988. lib. bdg. 115.95 (ISBN 0-89573-576-8). VCH Pubs.

Peptides, 2 vols. Ed. by Eberhard Schroder & Kraus Lubke. Incl. Vol. 1. Methods of Peptide Synthesis. 1965. 92.00 (ISBN 0-12-629801-7); Vol. 2. Synthesis, Occurrence & Action of Biologically Active Polypeptides. 1966. Acad Pr.

Peptides, Vol. 6. Ed. by Sidney Udenfriend, Jr. & Johannes Meienhofer. 1984. 104.50 (ISBN 0-12-304206-2). Acad Pr.

Peptides: Analysis, Synthesis, Biology, Vol. 5. Ed. by Erhard Gross & Johannes Meiehnhofer. (Special Methods in Peptide Synthesis Ser.: Part B). 1983. 104.50 (ISBN 0-12-304205-4). Acad Pr.

Peptides: Analysis, Synthesis, Biology, Vol. 8. Ed. by Clark W. Smith et al. 410p. 1987. 75.00 (ISBN 0-12-304208-9). Acad Pr.

Peptides: Analysis, Synthesis, Biology: Special Methods in Peptide Synthesis, Vol. 9, Pt. C. Ed. by Sidney Udenfriend & Johannes Meienhofer. 254p. 1987. 79.00 (ISBN 0-12-304209-7). Acad Pr.

Peptides: Analysis, Synthesis, Biology: Vol. I, Pt. a, Major Methods of Peptide Bond Formation. Ed. by Erhard Gross & Johannes Meienhofer. LC 78-31958. 1979. 85.50 (ISBN 0-12-304201-1). Acad Pr.

Peptides: Analysis, Synthesis, Biology, Vol. 7. Open-ended Treatise ed. Ed. by Sidney Udenfriend. 1985. 109.00 (ISBN 0-12-304207-0). Acad Pr.

Peptides: Analysis, Synthesis, Biology, Vol. 2: Special Methods in Peptide Synthesis, Pt. A. Ed. by Erhard Gross & Johannes Meienhofer. LC 78-31958. 1980. 88.50 (ISBN 0-12-304202-X). Acad Pr.

Peptides: Analysis, Synthesis, Biology: Vol. 3 Protection of Functional Groups in Peptides Synthesis. Ed. by Erhard Gross. 1981. 74.00 (ISBN 0-12-304203-8). Acad Pr.

Peptides: Analysis, Synthesis, Biology: Vol. 4, Modern Techniques of Peptide & Amino Acid Anaysis. Ed. by Erhard Gross & Johannes Meienhofer. 1981. 74.00 (ISBN 0-12-304204-6). Acad Pr.

Peptides & Neurological Disease. Ed. by P. C. Emson & M. Rossor. (Progress in Brain Research Ser.: Vol. 66). 380p. 1986. 118.00 (ISBN 0-444-80733-0). Elsevier.

Peptides & Proteases - Recent Advances: Selected Papers Presented at the 2nd International Meeting on the Molecular & Cellular Regulation of Enzyme Activity, Halle, GDR, August 17-23, 1986. R. L. Schowen & A. Barth. (Advances in the Biosciences Ser.: Vol. 67). 304p. 1987. 94.00 (ISBN 0-08-035726-1). Pergamon.

Peptides & Proteins. D. T. Elmore. LC 68-21392. (Cambridge Chemistry Texts Ser). (Illus.). 1968. 32.50 (ISBN 0-521-07107-0); pap. 9.95x o. p. (ISBN 0-521-09535-2). Cambridge U Pr.

Peptides As Immunogens. Ed. by H. Koprowski & F. Melchers. (Current Topics in Microbiology & Immunology Ser.: Vol. 130). (Illus.). 90p. 1986. 36.50 (ISBN 0-387-16892-3). Springer-Verlag.

Peptides: Chemistry & Biochemistry; Proceedings of the 1st American Peptide Symposium, Yale University, Aug. 1968. Ed. by Boris Weinstein. LC 70-107760. pap. 139.00 (ISBN 0-317-29565-9, 2021510). Bks Demand UMI.

Peptides: Chemistry-Biology-Interactions with Proteins. Ed. by Botond Penke & Angela Torok. 467p. 1988. lib. bdg. 178.00x (ISBN 0-89925-430-6). De Gruyter.

Peptides, Hormones & Behavior. Ed. by C. B. Nemeroff & A. J. Dunn. (Illus.). 944p. 1984. text ed. 150.00 (ISBN 0-88331-174-7). Luce.

Peptides: Integrators of Cell & Tissue Function. Ed. by Floyd E. Bloom. (Society of General Physiologists Ser.: Vol.35). 274p. 1980. text ed. 46.50 (ISBN 0-89004-485-6). Raven.

Peptides Nineteen Seventy-Four. Ed. by Y. Wolman. 450p. 1975. text ed. 86.00x (ISBN 0-7065-1458-0, Pub. by Keter Pub Jerusalem). Coronet Bks.

Peptides of Poisonous Amanita Mushrooms. T. Wieland. (Springer Series in Molecular Biology). (Illus.). 270p. 1986. 98.00 (ISBN 0-387-16641-6). Springer-Verlag.

Peptides of the Pars Intermedia - Symposium No. 81. CIBA Foundation Symposium. 320p. 1986. 54.95 (ISBN 0-471-91050-3). Wiley.

Peptides: Proceedings of the European Peptide Symposium, 9th, France, 1968. European Peptide Symposium Staff. Ed. by E. Bricas. 1968. 30.25 (ISBN 0-444-10156-X, North-Holland). Elsevier.

Peptides, 1982: Proceedings of the 17th European Peptide Symposium, Prague, Czechoslovakia, August 29-September 3, 1982. Ed. by K Blaha & P. Malon. (Illus.). 846p. 1982. 180.00 (ISBN 3-11-009574-2). De Gruyter.

Peptides 1984: Proceedings of the Eighteenth European Peptide Symposium. Ed. by Ulf Ragnarsson. 668p. 1984. pap. 115.00x (ISBN 91-22-00715-6, Pub. by Almqvist & Wiksell). Coronet Bks.

Pepys. Arthur Bryant. Incl. The Man in the Making 1633-1669. 352p (ISBN 0-586-06470-2); The Years of Peril 1669-1683. 384p (ISBN 0-586-06471-0); The Saviour of the Navy 1683-1689. 352p (ISBN 0-586-06472-9). 1985. pap. 8.95 ea. Academy Chi Pubs.

Pepys & Shakespeare. Sidney Lee. LC 74-22314. 1974. Repr. of 1906 ed. lib. bdg. 18.00 (ISBN 0-8414-5661-5). Folcroft.

Pepys Anthology. Samuel Pepys. Ed. by Robert Latham & Linnet Latham. 350p. 1987. 18.95 (ISBN 0-520-06354-6). U of Cal Pr.

Pepys at Table. Ed. by Christopher Driver & Michelle Berriedale-Johnson. LC 84-40346. (Illus.). 240p. 1984. 16.95 (ISBN 0-520-05386-9). U of Cal Pr.

Pepys Ballads, 5 vols. Samuel Pepys. Ed. by W. G. Day. 1987. Set. 711.00 (ISBN 0-85991-256-6, Pub. by Boydell & Brewer). Longwood Pub Group.

Pepys' Diary & the New Science. Marjorie H. Nicolson. LC 65-26012. (Illus.). 198p. 1965. 16.95x (ISBN 0-8139-0188-X). U Pr of Va.

Pepys Himself. Cecil S. Emden. LC 80-17177. xi, 146p. 1980. Repr. of 1963 ed. lib. bdg. 35.00x (ISBN 0-313-22607-5, EMPH). Greenwood.

Pepys in Love: Elizabeth's Story. Patrick Delaforce. (Illus.). 217p. 1986. 9.95 (ISBN 0-317-66029-2, Bishopsgate Pr London). Intl Spec Bk.

Pepys' Memoires of the Royal Navy. Samuel Pepys. LC 68-25260. (English Biography Ser., No. 31). 1969. Repr. of 1906 ed. lib. bdg. 39.95x (ISBN 0-8383-0228-9). Haskell.

Pepys on the Restoration Stage. Samuel Pepys. Ed. by Helen McAfee. LC 63-23195. (Illus.). 1916. 18.00 (ISBN 0-405-08848-5). Ayer Co Pubs.

Pepysian Garland: Black-Letter Broadside Ballads of the Years 1595-1639, Chiefly from the Collection of Samuel Pepys. Samuel Pepys. Ed. by Hyder E. Rollins. LC 74-176041. (Illus.). 491p. 1971. 32.50x (ISBN 0-674-66185-0). Harvard U Pr.

Pequegnat Story: The Family & the Clocks. Jane Varkaris & Costas Varkaris. 200p. 1981. pap. text ed. 20.00 (ISBN 0-8403-2655-6). Kendall-Hunt.

Pequena Enciclopedia de Hierbas (Little Herb Encyclopedia) Jack Ritchason. (Span.). Date not set. pap. 6.95 (ISBN 0-913923-00-1). Woodland UT.

Pequena Enciclopedia de la Gran Cibernetica. V. Pekelis. 423p. (Span.). 1977. 8.95 (ISBN 0-8285-1467-4, Pub. by Mir Pubs USSR). Imported Pubns.

Pequena Enciclopedia Tematica Larousse en Color, 2 vols. 1096p. 1978. Set. leatherette 150.00 (ISBN 0-686-92087-2, S-30235). French & Eur.

Pequena Gran Mujer en la China. Gladys Aylward. Orig. Title: Little Woman in China. 160p. (Span.). 1974. pap. 3.50 (ISBN 0-8254-1048-7). Kregel.

Pequeno Canto a los Mios (Poemario) Efren Rivera Ramos. LC 87-25562. 72p. 1987. pap. 5.00 (ISBN 0-8477-3236-3). U of PR Pr.

Pequeno Diccionario De Sinonimos y Sus Contrarios. 6th ed. A. J. Vinoly et al. 242p. (Span.). 1976. pap. 14.95 (ISBN 84-307-7052-6, S-12220). French & Eur.

Pequeno Diccionario De Teatro Mundial. Genoveva Dieterich. 294p. (Span.). 1976. pap. 19.95 (ISBN 84-7090-028-5, S-31395). French & Eur.

Pequeno Diccionario Espanol-Polaco, Polaco-Espanol. A. Marti & J. Marti. 707p. (Span. & Pol.). 1976. 24.95 (ISBN 0-686-92083-X, S-32367). French & Eur.

Pequeno Diccionario Kapelusz de la Lengua Espanola. 612p. (Span.). 1980. pap. 9.95 (ISBN 84-499-3146-0, S-32728). French & Eur.

Pequeno Dicionario Michaelis: Ingles-Portugues, Portugues-Ingles. 642p. (Eng. & Port.). 1980. 14.95 (ISBN 0-686-97439-5, M-9282). French & Eur.

Pequeno Larousse Illustrado. Ramon Garcia-Pelayo y Gross. 1692p. (Span.). 1988. 49.95 (ISBN 2-03-450173-X). French & Eur.

Per. see Fundamentals of Islamic Thought: God, Man & the Universe.

Per Ardua: The Rise of British Air Power 1911-1939. Hillary S. Saunders. LC 79-169436. (Literature & History of Aviation Ser). 1971. Repr. of 1945 ed. 24.50 (ISBN 0-405-03781-3). Ayer Co Pubs.

Per Capita Fibre Consumption 1967-1969: Cotton, Wool, Flax, Silk & Man-Made Fibres. Food & Agriculture Organization of the United Nations Staff. Incl. Per Capita Fibre Consumption 1970-1972: Cotton, Wool, Flax, & Man-Made Fibres. Food & Agriculture Organization of the United Nations Staff. pap. 15.00 (F1188). UNIPUB; Per Capita Fibre Consumption 1971-1973: Cotton, Wool, Flax, Silk, & Man Made Fibre. 188p. 1975. pap. 15.75 (F1189). UNIPUB; Per Capita Fibre Consumption 1973-1974: Cotton, Wool & Man-Made Fibres. 1977. pap. 8.25 (ISBN 92-5-000102-9, F1190). UNIPUB. pap. 15.00 (F1187, FAO). UNIPUB.

Per Capita Fibre Consumption 1970-1972: Cotton, Wool, Flax, & Man-Made Fibres see Per Capita Fibre Consumption 1967-1969: Cotton, Wool, Flax, Silk & Man-Made Fibres.

Per Capita Fibre Consumption 1971-1973: Cotton, Wool, Flax, Silk, & Man Made Fibre see Per Capita Fibre Consumption 1967-1969: Cotton, Wool, Flax, Silk & Man-Made Fibres.

Per Capita Fibre Consumption 1973-1974: Cotton, Wool & Man-Made Fibres see Per Capita Fibre Consumption 1967-1969: Cotton, Wool, Flax, Silk & Man-Made Fibres.

PER Handbook. rev. ed. (Illus.). 400p. 1981. 49.50 (ISBN 0-686-32574-5). PER.

Per-Immigrant & Pioneer. E. Palmer Rockswold. 1981. 13.95 (ISBN 0-934860-19-X). Adventure Pubns.

Per-Immigrant & Pioneer. Ed. by Palmer Rockswold. 1982. pap. 6.95 (ISBN 0-934860-22-X). Adventure Pubns.

Per Modo Di Dire: A First Course in Italian. Pietro Frassica & Antonio Carrara. 544p. 1981. text ed. 26.00 (ISBN 0-669-02068-0); wkbk. 12.00 (ISBN 0-669-02070-2); cassette 35.00 (ISBN 0-669-02073-7); 13 tapes-reels 60.00 (ISBN 0-669-02072-9); instr's. manual 2.00 (ISBN 0-669-02069-9); transcript 2.00 (ISBN 0-669-02074-5); demo tape 2.00 (ISBN 0-669-02075-3). Heath.

Per Olof Sundman: Writer of the North. Lars G. Warme. LC 83-26482. (Contributions to the Study of World Literature: No. 7). (Illus.). xxi, 217p. 1984. lib. bdg. 35.00 (ISBN 0-313-24346-8, WPS/). Greenwood.

Per Olov Enquist: A Critical Study. Ross Shideler. LC 83-22733. (Contributions to the Study of World Literature Ser.: No. 5). (Illus.). viii, 186p. 1984. lib. bdg. 35.00 (ISBN 0-313-24236-4, SHI/). Greenwood.

PER Questions & Answers Handbook. 1981. 12.50 (ISBN 0-686-32575-3). PER.

Per Saecula. H. McArdle & G. Suggitt. 1974. Pt. 1. pap. text ed. 4.95x (ISBN 0-582-36727-1); Pt. 2. pap. text ed. 5.25x (ISBN 0-582-36728-X); Pt. 3. pap. text ed. 4.50x (ISBN 0-05-002685-2). Longman.

Per-sist-ent Ster-e-o-types. Pat Courtney. 1988. pap. 10.00 (ISBN 0-932526-19-5). Nexus Pr.

Peradventure. Archibald T. Strong. LC 74-118416. 1971. Repr. of 1925 ed. 21.50x (ISBN 0-8046-1193-9, Pub. by Kennikat). Assoc Faculty Pr.

Perak Malay: Papers on Malay Subjects. Charles C. Brown. LC 77-87481. 128p. Repr. of 1921 ed. 24.50 (ISBN 0-404-16797-7). AMS Pr.

Peralta Country. 192p. 1987. 15.95 (ISBN 0-8027-0949-4). Walker & Co.

Peralta Country. (Illus.). 323p. 1987. Repr. lib. bdg. write for info. Thorndike Pr.

Peranakan Chinese Politics in Java, 1917-1942. rev. ed. Leo Suryadinata. (Illus.). 193p. 1981. 17.50x (ISBN 9971-69-038-1, Pub. by Singapore U Pr); pap. 12.50x (ISBN 0-686-44854-5, 82-93896). Ohio U Pr.

Perce Judd: Man of Peace. Winifred Sarre. (Illus.). 176p. 1983. pap. 10.00 (ISBN 0-8309-0377-1). Herald Hse.

Perceived Images: U. S. & Soviet Assumptions & Perceptions in Disarmament. Daniel Frei. LC 85-14207. 344p. 1986. text ed. 26.50x (ISBN 0-8476-7443-6, Rowman & Allanheld). Rowman.

Perceived Quality: How Consumers View Stores & Merchandise. Ed. by Jacob Jacoby & Jerry C. Olson. LC 83-49531. (Advances in Retailing Series of the Institute of Retail Management). 336p. 1984. 40.00x (ISBN 0-669-08272-4). Lexington Bks.

Perceived Usefulness of Financial Statements for Investors' Decisions. Lucia S. Chang & Kenneth S. Most. LC 84-25788. 127p. 1985. pap. 15.00x (ISBN 0-8130-0752-6). U Presses Fla.

Perceiving: A Philosophical Study. Roderick M. Chisholm. LC 74-7639. (Contemporary Philosophy Ser.). 214p. 1957. 27.50x (ISBN 0-8014-0077-5). Cornell U Pr.

Perceiving, Acting, & Knowing. Ed. by R. Shaw & J. Bransford. 492p. 1977. 45.00x (ISBN 0-89859-408-1). L Erlbaum Assocs.

Perceiving & Behaving. Dale G. Lake. LC 72-77891. pap. 29.00 (ISBN 0-317-41889-0, 2026038). Bks Demand UMI.

Perceiving & Remembering Faces. Ed. by G. Davies et al. LC 81-66698. 1981. 76.00 (ISBN 0-12-206220-5). Acad Pr.

Perceiving Artworks. Ed. by John Fisher. (Philosophical Monographs: 3rd Ser.). 246p. 1980. 27.95 (ISBN 0-87722-164-2). Temple U Pr.

Perceiving, Behaving, Becoming: A New Focus for Education. new ed. Arthur W. Combs. LC 44-6213. (ASCD Yearbook: 1962). 256p. 1962. 5.00 (ISBN 0-87120-050-3, 610-17278). Assn Supervision.

Perceiving India: Views from Far & Near in the Work of Nirad C. Chaudhuri, R. K. Narayan, & Ved Mehta. David S. Philip. LC 86-81404. 176p. 1986. text ed. 25.00x (ISBN 0-938719-05-X). Envoy Press.

Perceiving Ordinary Magic: Science & Intuitive Wisdom. Jeremy Hayward. LC 84-5481. (New Science Library). 323p. 1984. pap. 10.95 (ISBN 0-87773-297-3, 72704-5). Shambhala Pubns.

Perceiving Ordinary Magic: Science & Intuitive Wisdom. Jeremy W. Hayward. pap. 10.95 (ISBN 0-394-72704-5). Shambhala Pubns.

Perceiving Others: The Psychology of Interpersonal Perception. Mark Cook. 180p. 1979. pap. 9.95x (ISBN 0-416-71560-5, 2838). Routledge Chapman & Hall.

Perceiving, Sensing & Knowing: A Book of Readings from Twentieth-Century Sources in the Philosophy of Perception. Ed. by Robert J. Swartz. LC 75-3778. (Topics in Philosophy: Vol. IV). 560p. 1977. pap. 11.95x (ISBN 0-520-02986-0). U of Cal Pr.

Perceiving Similarity & Comprehending Metaphor. Ed. by Lawrence E. Marks et al. Robin J. Hammeal & Marc H. Bornstein. (CDM 215: Vol. 52, No. 1). vi, 100p. 1988. pap. 9.75x (ISBN 0-226-50611-8). U of Chicago Pr.

Perceiving Structure: How Are the Ideas Organized? Walter Pauk. (Skill at a Time Ser). 64p. (gr. 9 up). 1975. pap. text ed. 3.20x (ISBN 0-89061-030-4, ST-10). Jamestown Pubs.

Perceiving the Arts: An Introduction to the Humanities. 2nd ed. Dennis J. Sporre. (Illus.). 224p. 1985. pap. text ed. write for info. (ISBN 0-13-657040-2). P-H.

Perceiving the Author's Intent: What is the Author's Real Message? Walter Pauk. (Skill at a Time Ser). 64p. (gr. 9 up). 1975. pap. text ed. 4.00x (ISBN 0-89061-029-0, ST-9). Jamestown Pubs.

Perceiving Time: A Psychological Investigation with Men & Women. Thomas J. Cottle. LC 76-18768. 267p. 1976. 19.50 (ISBN 0-471-17530-7, JW). Krieger.

Perceiving Time: A Psychological Investigation with Men & Women. Thomas J. Cottle. LC 76-18768. pap. 70.80 (ISBN 0-8357-9950-6, 2011883). Bks Demand UMI.

Perceiving Women. Ed. by Shirley Ardener. 192p. 1982. pap. text ed. 9.95x (ISBN 0-460-12536-2, BKA 04659, Pub. by J M Dent England). Biblio Dist.

Percent. Robert Burleigh & Raymond Matlak. LC 79-730248. (Illus.). 1979. pap. 159.00 (ISBN 0-89290-096-2, A512-SATC). Soc for Visual.

Percent - Application of Percent. Allan D. Suter. (Programmed Math Ser.). (Illus.). 30p. (Orig.). (gr. 3-12). 1986. pap. text ed. 3.95 (ISBN 0-945915-24-1). Programmed Lrn.

Percent - Meaning of Percent. Allan D. Suter. (Programmed Math Ser.). (Illus.). 30p. (Orig.). (gr. 3-12). 1986. pap. text ed. 3.95 (ISBN 0-945915-22-5). Programmed Lrn.

Percent - Percent Strategies. Allan D. Suter. (Programmed Math Ser.). (Illus.). 30p. (Orig.). (gr. 3-12). 1986. pap. text ed. 3.95 (ISBN 0-945915-23-3). Programmed Lrn.

Percent - Problem Solving. Allan D. Suter. (Programmed Math Ser.). (Illus.). 30p. (Orig.). (gr. 3-12). 1986. pap. text ed. 3.95 (ISBN 0-945915-25-X). Programmed Lrn.

Percent Fat Calorie Tables. 2nd ed. Robert Stark. 48p. 1987. pap. text ed. 3.95 (ISBN 0-9618415-1-6). AZ Bariatric Phy.

Percent for Art Programs. rev. ed. (Memoranda Ser.). 7p. 1983. 1.00. Ctr for Arts Info.

Perceptanalysis. Zygmunt A. Piotrowski. LC 57-5067. (Illus.). 505p. 1985. Repr. of 1957 ed. text ed. 25.00x (ISBN 0-318-03720-3). Ex Libris PA.

Perception. Charles Bernstein et al. Ed. by Don Wellman. Tr. by David Guss. (Toward a New Poetics Ser: Vol. 2). (Illus.). 224p. 1982. pap. 6.95 (ISBN 0-942030-02-8). O ARS.

Perception. 4th ed. G. Robert Carlsen. (Themes & Writers Ser.). (Illus.). 640p. (gr. 8). 1985. text ed. 25.08 (ISBN 0-07-009805-0). McGraw.

Perception. Ed. by R. Held et al. (Handbook of Sensory Physiology: Vol. 8). (Illus.). 1978. 155.00 (ISBN 0-387-08300-6). Springer-Verlag.

Perception. 2nd ed. Julian Hochberg. LC 77-27274. (Foundations of Modern Psychology Ser.). (Illus.). 1978. pap. text ed. write for info. (ISBN 0-13-657098-4). P-H.

Perception. Henry H. Price. LC 81-13236. ix, 332p. 1982. Repr. of 1973 ed. lib. bdg. 35.00x (ISBN 0-313-23153-2, PRPT). Greenwood.

Perception. Irvin Rock. (Scientific American Library). (Illus.). 243p. 32.95 (ISBN 0-7167-5001-5). W H Freeman.

Perception. Robert Sekuler & Randy Blake. 500p. 1985. text ed. 24.00 (ISBN 0-394-32815-9, KnopfC). Knopf.

Perception: A Representative Theory. F. Jackson. LC 76-30316. 1977. 34.50 (ISBN 0-521-21550-1). Cambridge U Pr.

Perception: An Annotated Bibliography of Philosophical & Related Writings. Kathleen Emmett & Peter Machamer. LC 75-24086. (Reference Library of the Humanities: Vol. 39). 400p. 1975. lib. bdg. 26.00 (ISBN 0-8240-9966-4). Garland Pub.

Perception & Aesthetic Value. Harold N. Lee. Repr. of 1938 ed. 24.00 (ISBN 0-384-32040-6). Johnson Repr.

Perception & Cognition. John Heil. LC 82-20233. 192p. 1983. text ed. 25.00x (ISBN 0-520-04833-4). U of Cal Pr.

Perception & Cognition: Issues in the Foundations of Psychology. Ed. by C. Wade Savage. (Minnesota Studies in the Philosophy of Science: Vol. 9). 1978. 29.50x (ISBN 0-8166-0841-5). U of Minn Pr.

Perception & Communication. D. E. Broadbent. (Illus.). 352p. 1987. pap. 27.95 (ISBN 0-19-852171-5). Oxford U Pr.

Perception & Discovery: An Introduction to Scientific Inquiry. Norwood R. Hanson. Ed. by Willard C. Humphreys. LC 75-95161. (Illus.). 435p. 1969. pap. text ed. 12.00x (ISBN 0-87735-510-X). Freeman Cooper.

Perception & Evocation of Literature. Leland H. Roloff. 1973. text ed. write for info. (ISBN 0-673-07550-8). Scott F.

Perception & Experience. Ed. by R. D. Walk & H. L. Pick. LC 77-19129. (Perception & Perceptual Development Ser.: Vol. 1). (Illus.). 356p. 1978. 45.00x (ISBN 0-306-34381-9, Plenum Pr). Plenum Pub.

Perception & Expression in the Novels of Charlotte Bronte. Judith Williams. Ed. by Juliet McMaster. LC 88-6073. (Nineteenth-Century Studies). 182p. 1988. 39.95 (ISBN 0-8357-1871-9). UMI Res Pr.

Perception & Inference: An Essay on Classical Indian Theories of Knowledge. Bimal K. Matilal. 350p. 1986. 65.00x (ISBN 0-19-824625-0). Oxford U Pr.

Perception & Information. Paul J. Barber & David Legge. (Essential Psychology Ser.). 1976. pap. 4.50x (ISBN 0-416-82040-9, NO. 2615). Routledge Chapman & Hall.

Perception & Its Development: A Tribute to Eleanor J. Gibson. Ed. by A. D. Pick. 272p. 1979. text ed. 29.95x (ISBN 0-89859-409-X). L Erlbaum Assocs.

Perception & Misperception in International Politics. Robert Jervis. (Center for International Affairs at Harvard Ser.). 1976. o. p. 46.50x (ISBN 0-691-05656-0); 18.00x (ISBN 0-691-10049-7). Princeton U Pr.

Perception & Personal Identity: Proceedings. Oberlin Colloquim in Philosophy. Ed. by Norman S. Care et al. LC 68-9427. pap. 51.30 (ISBN 0-317-08114-4, 2003253). Bks Demand UMI.

Perception & Personal Identity: Proceedings of the 1967 Oberlin Colloquium in Philosophy. Ed. by Norman S. Care & Robert H. Grimm. LC 68-9427. (Oberlin Colloquia in Philosophy Ser). 1969. 20.00 (ISBN 0-8295-0145-2). UPB.

Perception & Persuasion: A New Approach to Effective Writing. Ed. by Raymond Paul & Pellegrino W. Goione. 1973. pap. text ed. 17.95 scp (ISBN 0-690-61413-6, HarpC). Har-Row.

Perception & Photography. Richard D. Zakia. LC 74-3402. (Illus.). 1979. pap. text ed. 7.95x (ISBN 0-87992-015-7). Light Impressions.

Perception & Pictorial Representation. Ed. by Calvin F. Nodine & Dennis Fisher. LC 79-4613. (Praeger Special Studies Ser.). 448p. 1979. 35.00 (ISBN 0-275-90402-4, C0402). Praeger.

Perception & Production of Fluent Speech. Ed. by Ronald A. Cole. LC 79-25481. (Illus.). 576p. 1980. text ed. 49.95x (ISBN 0-89859-019-1). L Erlbaum Assocs.

Perception & Representation. Ilona Roth & John P. Frisby. LC 85-21649. (Open Guides to Psychology Ser.). 192p. 1986. pap. 21.00x (ISBN 0-335-15328-3, Open Univ Pr). Taylor & Francis.

Perception & the Physical World. David M. Armstrong. (International Library of Philosophy & Scientific Method). 1961. text ed. 29.95x (ISBN 0-7100-3603-5). Humanities.

Perception & the Senses. Evan L. Brown & Kenneth A. Deffenbacher. (Illus.). 1979. 24.95x (ISBN 0-19-502504-0). Oxford U Pr.

Perception & Use of Streams in Suburban Areas: Effects of Water Quality & of Distance from Residence to Stream. Robert E. Coughlin et al. (Discussion Paper Ser.: No. 53). 1972. pap. 6.50 (ISBN 0-686-32220-7). Regional Sci Res Inst.

Perception & Valuation of Water Quality: A Review of Research Method & Findings. Robert E. Coughlin. (Discussion Paper Ser.: No. 80). 1975. pap. 6.50 (ISBN 0-686-32246-0). Regional Sci Res Inst.

Perception & Values in Travel Demand. (Transportation Research Record Ser.). 49p. 1976. 2.80 (ISBN 0-309-02561-3). Transport Res Bd.

Perception Barriers. Robert Frazier. 46p. 1987. pap. 5.95 (ISBN 0-917658-25-6). BPW & P.

Perception, Cognition & Development: Interactional Analyses. Ed. by Thomas J. Tighe. Bryan E. Shepp. 384p. 1983. text ed. 39.95x (ISBN 0-89859-254-2). L Erlbaum Assocs.

Perception, Consciousness, Memory: Reflections of a Biologist. G. Adam. LC 73-20153. 230p. 1980. 42.50x (ISBN 0-306-30776-6, Plenum Pr). Plenum Pub.

Perception, Decision Making & Conflict. Robert Mandel. LC 78-65350. 1978. pap. text ed. 11.50 (ISBN 0-8191-0652-6). U Pr of Amer.

Perception, Design & Practice. Benjamin Martinez & Jacqueline Block. (Illus.). 150p. 1985. pap. text ed. 19.00 (ISBN 0-13-656638-3). P-H.

Perception, Emotion & Action: A Component Approach. Irving Thalberg. LC 76-52340. 1977. 22.50x (ISBN 0-300-02129-1). Yale U Pr.

Perception: Essays in Honor of James J. Gibson. Ed. by Robert B. MacLeod & Herbert L. Pick. LC 74-1547. 317p. 1974. 44.50x (ISBN 0-8014-0835-0). Cornell U Pr.

Perception, Expression, & History: The Social Phenomenology of Maurice Merleau-Ponty. John O'Neill. 1970. 12.95x (ISBN 0-8101-0299-4). Northwestern U Pr.

Perception: From Sense to Object - The Process of Perceiving. John M. Wilding. LC 83-2887. 280p. 1984. 20.00x (ISBN 0-312-60056-9). St Martin.

Perception in Criminology. Richard L. Henshel & Robert A. Silverman. LC 74-23621. 384p. 1975. 41.50x (ISBN 0-231-03760-0). Columbia U Pr.

Perception in the Poetry of D. H. Lawrence, Vol. 109. Jillian de Vries-Mason. (European University Anglo-Saxon Language & Literature Studies: No. 14). 215p. 1982. pap. 20.95 (ISBN 3-261-05072-1). P Lang Pubs.

Perception: Its Development & Recapitulation. Estelle Breines. LC 81-81244. (Illus.). 304p. 1981. text ed. 19.00 (ISBN 0-941930-01-7). Geri-Rehab.

Perception of Asian Personality. A. Mehta. 264p. 1978. 16.95. Asia Bk Corp.

Perception of Asian Personality. Asoka Mehta. 264p. 1978. 16.95x (ISBN 0-940500-63-9). Asia Bk Corp.

Perception of Behavioral Chemicals. Ed. by D. M. Norris. 328p. 1982. 176.50 (ISBN 0-444-80347-5, Biomedical Pr). Elsevier.

Perception of Choice & Factors Affecting Industrial Water Supply Decisions in Northeastern Illinois. Shue-Tuck Wong. LC 68-56934. (Research Papers Ser.: No. 117). 93p. 1968. pap. 12.00 (ISBN 0-89065-024-1). U Chicago Comm Geo.

Perception of Complex Tastes & Smells. Ed. by B. W. Ache et al. 450p. 1988. price not set (ISBN 0-12-042990-X). Acad Pr.

Perception of Desertification. Ed. by R. L. Heathcote. 134p. 1980. pap. 22.75 (ISBN 92-808-0190-2, TUNU104, UNU). UNIPUB.

Perception of Dimensions: Drugs, Crime, & Law. Sidney Vernon. (Illus.). 100p. 1984. cancelled (ISBN 0-943150-04-3); pap. cancelled (ISBN 0-943150-05-1). Rovern Pr.

Perception of Displayed Information. Ed. by L. M. Biberman. LC 72-97695. (Optical Physics & Engineering Ser.). (Illus.). 346p. 1973. 65.00x (ISBN 0-306-30724-3, Plenum Pr). Plenum Pub.

Perception of Dotted. William Uttal. 128p. 1987. 19.95 (ISBN 0-89859-929-6). L Erlbaum Assocs.

Perception of Emotion In Self & Others. Ed. by P. Pliner et al. LC 79-12025. (Advances In the Study of Communication & Affect Ser.: Vol. 5). (Illus.). 214p. 1979. 42.50x (ISBN 0-306-40224-6, Plenum Pr). Plenum Pub.

Perception of Environment. 1987. 75.00x (Pub. by Scientific). State Mutual Bk.

Perception of Environment. T. F. Saarinen. LC 72-94261. (CCG Resource Papers Ser.: No. 5). (Illus.). 1969. pap. text ed. 5.00 (ISBN 0-89291-052-6). Assn Am Geographers.

Perception of Exertion in Physical Work. Ed. by Gunnar Borg & David Ottoson. (Wenner-Gren International Symposium Ser.: Vol. 46). 350p. 1986. text ed. 89.50x (ISBN 0-333-42306-2, Pub. by Macmillan London). Sheridan.

Perception of Form & Forms of Perception. R. M. Granovskaya et al. 224p. 1987. text ed. 39.95 (ISBN 0-89859-578-9). L Erlbaum Assocs.

Perception of Illusory Contours. Ed. by S. Petry & G. Meyer. (Illus.). 345p. 1987. 99.00 (ISBN 0-387-96518-1). Springer-Verlag.

Perception of Light & Color. Charles A. Padgham & John E. Saunders. 1975. 19.95 (ISBN 0-12-543650-5). Acad Pr.

Perception of Nonverbal Behavior in the Career Interview. Walburga von Raffler-Engel. (Pragmatics & Beyond Ser.: Vol. IV, No. 4). viii, 148p. 1983. pap. 28.00x (ISBN 90-272-2517-6). Benjamins North Am.

Perception of Number see Sociality & Sympathy.

Perception of Odors. Trygg Engen. (Series in Cognition & Perception). 1982. 27.50 (ISBN 0-12-239350-3). Acad Pr.

Perception of Other People. Franz From. Tr. by Erik Kvan & Brendan Maher. LC 76-138295. 205p. pap. 53.30 (2029828). Bks Demand UMI.

Perception of Pictures: Alberti's Window: the Projective Model of Pictorial Information, Vol. 1. Ed. by Margaret A. Hagen. LC 79-8862. (Cognition & Perception Ser.). 1980. 52.50 (ISBN 0-12-313601-6). Acad Pr.

Perception of Pictures: Durer's Devices: Beyond the Projective Model of Pictures, Vol. 2. Ed. by Margaret A. Hagen. LC 79-8862. (Cognition & Perception Ser.). 1980. 65.50 (ISBN 0-12-313602-4). Acad Pr.

Perception of Police Power: A Study in Four Cities. Anastassios D. Mylonas. (New York University Criminal Law Education & Research Center Monograph: No. 8). (Illus.). x, 131p. (Orig.). 1974. pap. text ed. 8.50x (ISBN 0-8377-0418-9). Rothman.

Perception of Poverty: Contribution to Econonmic Analysis, Vol. 156. A. J. Hagenaars. 300p. 1986. 66.00 (ISBN 0-444-87898-X, North-Holland). Elsevier.

Perception of Print: Reading Research in Experimental Psychology. Ed. by O. J. L. Tzeng & H. Singer. 384p. 1981. 39.95x (ISBN 0-89859-154-6). L Erlbaum Assocs.

Perception of Reality in the Volksmarchen of Schleswig-Holstein: A Study in Interpersonal Relationships & World View. Margarethe W. Sparing. LC 84-7321. 208p. (Orig.). 1984. lib. bdg. 26.75 (ISBN 0-8191-3987-4); pap. text ed. 13.00 (ISBN 0-8191-3988-2). U Pr of Amer.

Percutaneous & Interventional Urology & Radiology. Ed. by E. K. Lang. (Clinical Practice in Urology Ser.). (Illus.). 368p. 1986. 95.00 (ISBN 0-387-15589-9). Springer-Verlag.

Percutaneous Angiography. photocopy ed. S. Swamy et al. (Illus.). 848p. 1977. 97.00 (ISBN 0-398-03540-7). C C Thomas.

Percutaneous Collection of Arterial Blood for Laboratory Analysis: Approved Standard, Vol. 5. National Committee for Clinical Laboratory Standards. 1985. 20.00 (ISBN 0-318-19435-X, H11-A). Natl Comm Clin Lab Stds.

Percutaneous Immediate Hypersensitivity to Eight Allergens: United States, 1976-80. Peter Gergen & Paul Turkeltaub. Ed. by Mary Olmsted. LC 86-1685. (Series 11: No. 235). 116p. 1986. pap. text ed. 1.25 (ISBN 0-8406-0329-0). Natl Ctr Health Stats.

Percutaneous Immediate Hypersensitivity to Eight Allergens: United States, 1976-1980. Peter J. Gergen & Paul C. Turkeltaub. (National Health Survey Ser.: Vol. 11, No. 235). (Illus.). 80p. 1986. pap. 4.00 (ISBN 0-318-21688-4, S/N 017-022-00964-1). USGPO.

Percutaneous Surgery of Kidney Stones. K. Korth. (Techniques & Tactics Ser.). (Illus.). 95p. 1984. 44.00 (ISBN 0-387-13572-3). Springer-Verlag.

Percutaneous Transluminal Angioplasty: The Dotter Procedure. G. J. Van Andel. 180p. 1976. pap. 26.75 (ISBN 90-219-9276-0, Excerpta Medica). Elsevier.

Percutaneous Transluminal Angioplasty. Ed. by C. T. Dotter et al. (Illus.). 380p. 1983. pap. 48.00 (ISBN 0-387-12654-6). Springer-Verlag.

Percy Alexander MacMahon: Collected Papers: Combinatorics, Vol. 1. Ed. by George E. Andrews & Percy A. MacMahon. LC 77-28962. (Mathematicians of Our Time Ser.). 1978. 110.00x (ISBN 0-262-13121-8). MIT Pr.

Percy Alexander MacMahon: Collected Papers, Vol. II: Number Theory, Invariants & Applications. Ed. by George E. Andrews & Percy A. MacMahon. (Mathematicians of Our Time Ser.: No. 24). (Illus.). 904p. 1986. text ed. 95.00x (ISBN 0-262-13214-1). MIT Pr.

Percy Bysshe Shelley. Intro. by Chelsea House Staff. (Modern Critical Views Ser.). 225p. 1986. 24.50 (ISBN 0-87754-609-6). Chelsea Hse.

Percy Bysshe Shelley. Donald H. Reiman. (English Authors Ser.). 1970. lib. bdg. 13.50 (ISBN 0-8057-1488-X, Twayne). G K Hall.

Percy Bysshe Shelley: An Appreciation. Thomas R. Slicer. 82p. 1980. Repr. of 1903 ed. lib. bdg. 19.50 (ISBN 0-8414-7899-6). Folcroft.

Percy Bysshe Shelley: An Introduction to the Study of Character see Iowa University Studies in Psychology.

Percy Bysshe Shelley: Poet & Pioneer. Henry S. Salt. 1973. lib. bdg. 18.00 (ISBN 0-8414-8169-5). Folcroft.

Percy Bysshe Shelley: Poet & Pioneer. Henry S. Salt. LC 68-16285. 1968. Repr. of 1896 ed. 17.50x (ISBN 0-8046-0403-7, Pub. by Kennikat). Assoc Faculty Pr.

Percy Erskine Nobbs: Architect, Artist Craftsman-Architecte, Artiste, Atrisan. Susan Wagg. (Illus.). 114p. 1982. pap. 16.95c (ISBN 0-7735-0395-1). McGill-Queens U Pr.

Percy Grainger. John Bird. (Illus.). 360p. 1982. pap. 14.95 (ISBN 0-571-11717-1). Faber & Faber.

Percy Grainger: The Inveterate Innovator. Thomas C. Slattery. (Illus.). 12.50 (ISBN 0-686-15893-8). Instrumental Co.

Percy Grainger: The Pictorial Biography. Robert Simon. LC 83-62148. (Illus.). 150p. 1983. 27.50x (ISBN 0-87875-281-1). Whitston Pub.

Percy Lubbock Reader. Percy Lubbock. Ed. by Marjory G. Harkness. LC 57-12349. 1957. 9.95 (ISBN 0-87027-058-3). Cumberland Pr.

Percy the Parrot Strikes Out. Wayne Carley. LC 77-157998. (Garrard Venture Ser.). (Illus.). (gr. k-3). 1971. PLB 6.69 (ISBN 0-8116-6710-3); pap. 1.19 (9018). Garrard.

Percy the Parrot Yelled Quiet! Wayne Carley. LC 73-21585. (Easy Venture Ser.). (Illus.). 32p. (gr. k-2). 1974. PLB 6.69 (ISBN 0-8116-6058-3). Garrard.

Percys of Mississippi: Politics & Literature in the New South. Lewis Baker. LC 83-7916. (Southern Biography Ser.). (Illus.). 237p. 1983. 19.95 (ISBN 0-8071-1102-3). La State U Pr.

Perder Para Ganar. Evelyn Christenson. 1983. 3.75 (ISBN 0-88113-243-8). Edit Betania.

Perdido en el Museo de Historia Natural. Redro Pietri. (De Orilla a Orilla Ser.). (Illus.). 16p. 1981. pap. 3.75 (ISBN 0-940238-33-0). Ediciones Huracan.

Perdita. Isabelle Holland. 252p. (gr. 7 up). 1983. 13.95 (ISBN 0-316-37001-0). Little.

Perdita. Joan Smith. 224p. 1981. pap. 1.95 (ISBN 0-449-50173-6, Coventry). Fawcett.

Perdita's Prince. Jean Plaidy. (Georgian Saga Ser: Vol. 6). 352p. 1987. 17.95 (ISBN 0-399-13307-0, Putnam). Putnam Pub Group.

Perdition's Keepsake. Charles Behlen. Ed. by Dave Oliphant. (Illus.). 1978. pap. 5.00 (ISBN 0-933384-00-9). Prickly Pear.

Perdon de los Pecados. 2nd ed. Carlos H. Mackintosh. Ed. by Gordon H. Bennett. Tr. by Sara Bautista from Eng. (Serie Diamante). 36p. (Span.). 1982. pap. 0.85 (ISBN 0-942504-02-X). Overcomer Pr.

Perdonado. John M. Robertson. Tr. by Luis B. Lumpuy from Eng. Orig. Title: Pardoned. (Illus.). 64p. (Span.). 1985. pap. 0.95 (ISBN 0-8297-0909-6). Life Pubs Intl.

Perdonar para Ser Libre. David Augsburger. Orig. Title: Freedom of Forgiveness. 160p. (Span.). 1977. pap. 3.75 (ISBN 0-8254-1046-0). Kregel.

Perdus Dans La Foret. Mary Wibberley. (Harlequin Romantique Ser.). 192p. 1984. pap. 1.95 (ISBN 0-373-41235-5). Harlequin Bks.

Perdut. Neil Lehrman. LC 78-20558. 1979. pap. 4.50 (ISBN 0-931848-23-7); signed & numbered edition 15.00 (ISBN 0-931848-22-9). Dryad Pr.

Pere Goriot see also Old Goriot.

Pere Goriot. Balzac. (EMC Easy Readers: Series D). (YA) (gr. 7-12). 1985. pap. 4.95 (ISBN 0-88436-043-1, 40280). EMC.

Pere Goriot. Honore De Balzac. (Airmont Classics Ser.). (gr. 10 up). pap. 1.50 (ISBN 0-8049-0084-1, CL-84). Airmont.

Pere Goriot. Honore De Balzac. (Folio Ser.: No. 784). 1960. pap. 7.95 (ISBN 0-685-11486-4, 757). Schoenhof.

Pere Goriot. Honore De Balzac. Ed. by Castex. (Class. Garnier). pap. 29.95 (ISBN 0-685-34092-9). French & Eur.

Pere Goriot. Honore De Balzac. Ed. by Castex. (Coll. Prestige). 49.95 (ISBN 0-685-34093-7). French & Eur.

Pere Goriot. Honore De Balzac. Bd. with Eugenie Grandet. (Modern Library College Editions). 1950. pap. text ed. write for info (ISBN 0-394-30902-2, T2, RanC). Random.

Pere Goriot. Honore De Balzac. Tr. by Henry Reed. (Orig.). 1962. pap. 2.95 (ISBN 0-451-51976-0, CE1812, Sig Classics). NAL.

Pere Goriot. Honore De Balzac. 16.95 (ISBN 0-88411-598-4, Pub. by Aeonian Pr). Amereon Ltd.

Pere Goriot. Honore De Balzac. 1960. write for info. (757). French & Eur.

Pere Humile. Paul Claudel. 194p. 1920. 8.95 (ISBN 0-686-54414-5); pap. 3.95 (ISBN 0-686-54415-3). French & Eur.

Pere Lagrange. Marie J. Lagrange. 1985. pap. 9.95 (ISBN 0-8091-2678-8). Paulist Pr.

Pere Lamy. Paul Biver. Tr. by John O'Connor from Fr. 1973. pap. 8.00 (ISBN 0-89555-055-5). TAN Bks Pubs.

Pere Marquette Power. Arthur B. Million & Thomas W. Dixon, Jr. Ed. by Carl W. Shaver. LC 85-70004. (Illus.). 224p. (Orig.). 1984. pap. 23.95 (ISBN 0-939487-06-3). Ches & OH Hist.

Pere Marquette Railroad Company. Paul W. Ivey. LC 75-120135. (Illus.). 1978. Repr. of 1919 ed. 17.50 (ISBN 0-912382-03-1). Black Letter.

Peregrina. Judith O. Cofer. (International Poetry Chapbook Ser.). 14p. 1985. write for info. (ISBN 0-936600-06-3). Riverstone Foothills.

Peregrina. United Salvadorean Editors. 80p. 1987. pap. 5.95 (ISBN 0-933753-04-7). Canterbury.

Peregrinacion de Bayoan. rev. & annotated ed. Eugenio M. de Hostos. Ed. by Julio C. Lopez. LC 87-25566. 420p. 1988. 18.00 (ISBN 0-8477-3603-2); pap. 15.00 (ISBN 0-8477-3604-0). U of PR Pr.

Peregrinacion de Boyoan: Obras Completas, Vol. 1. Eugenio Maria De Hostos. LC 87-25566. 420p. 1988. pap. 13.00. U of PR Pr.

Peregrinaje Desde Roma. Bartholomew F. Brewer & Alfred W. Furrell. Tr. by Jose M. Vargas-Caba from Eng. (Illus.). 194p. (Span.). 1986. pap. 7.95 (ISBN 0-89084-328-7). Bob Jones Univ Pr.

Peregrinations: Adventures with the Green Parrot. Gerda W. Klein. LC 86-80966. (Illus.). 48p. (gr. 3-4). 1986. 12.95 (ISBN 0-9616699-0-X); pap. 5.95 (ISBN 0-9616699-1-8). CHB Goodyear Comm.

Peregrinations: Law, Form, Event. Jean-Francois Lyotard. (Wellek Library Lectures). 128p. 1988. 20.00x (ISBN 0-231-06670-8). Columbia U Pr.

Peregrinations of a Pariah. Flora Tristan. Ed. & tr. by Jean Hawkes. LC 86-47873. (Virago-Beacon Traveler Ser.). 320p. 1987. pap. 9.95 (ISBN 0-8070-7027-0, BP 750). Beacon Pr.

Peregrine. John Baker. LC 67-23049. 192p. 1986. pap. 10.95 (ISBN 0-89301-115-0). U of Idaho Pr.

Peregrine. William Bayer. 1988. pap. 3.50 (ISBN 0-345-00755-7). Ballantine.

Peregrine Falcon. Carl R. Green & William R. Sanford. Ed. by Howard Schroeder. LC 86-2670. (Wildlife (Habits & Habitat) Ser.). (Illus.). 48p. (gr. 4-5). 1986. PLB 10.95 (ISBN 0-89686-271-2). Crestwood Hse.

Peregrine Falcon. Derek Ratcliffe. LC 80-65963. (Illus.). 1980. 42.50 (ISBN 0-931130-05-0). Buteo.

Peregrine Falcon in Greenland: Observing an Endangered Species. James Harris. LC 78-67404. (Illus.). 256p. (Orig.). 1979. 29.00x (ISBN 0-8262-0267-5); pap. 12.95 (ISBN 0-8262-0343-4). U of Mo Pr.

Peregrinos de Aztlan. Miguel Mendez. LC 77-89977. 1978. pap. 7.00 (ISBN 0-685-87639-X). Editorial Justa.

Peregrinos de la Habana. Paul Hollander. (Biblioteca Cubana Contemporanea Ser.). 305p. (Span.). 1987. pap. 23.00 (ISBN 84-359-0502-0, Pub. by Editorial Playor). Ediciones.

Perek Shira & Zemirot. Ed. by Baruch Chait. 100p. (Orig.). 1986. text ed. 4.95 (ISBN 0-88125-095-3). Ktav.

Perekrestki Sudeb: Dve povesti. Mikhail Dyomin. LC 80-54024. 307p. (Rus.). 1983. 25.00 (ISBN 0-89830-071-1); pap. 17.00 (ISBN 0-89830-033-9). Russica Pubs.

Perelandra. C. S. Lewis. 1968. 16.95 (ISBN 0-02-570840-6); pap. 3.95 (ISBN 0-02-086950-9). Macmillan.

Perelandra see Space Trilogy.

Perelandra Garden Workbook: A Complete Guide to Gardening with Nature Intelligences. Machaelle S. Wright. LC 87-90410. (Illus.). 247p. 1987. 19.95 (ISBN 0-9617713-1-3). Perelandra Ltd.

Peremeshchennoe Litso. Zinovy Zinik. LC 84-60083. 238p. (Orig., Rus.). 1985. pap. 15.00 (ISBN 0-89830-023-1). Russica Pubs.

Perennial Adventure: A Tribute to Alice Eastwood, 1859-1943. Susanna Dakin. 48p. 1954. 2.50 (ISBN 0-940228-09-2). Calif Acad Sci.

Perennial Apprentice. George F. Bennett. (Illus.). 240p. 1985. 25.00 (ISBN 0-912608-21-8). Mid Atlantic.

Perennial Bachelor. Anne Parrish. 1976. lib. bdg. 13.95x (ISBN 0-89968-153-0). Lightyear.

Perennial Border. Phoebe A. Taylor. (Asey Mayo Cape Cod Ser.). 288p. 1986. pap. 5.95 (ISBN 0-88150-079-8, Foul Play). Countryman.

Perennial Edible Fruits of the Tropics: An Inventory. Franklin W. Martin. (Agriculture Handbook: No. 642). (Illus.). 251p. 1987. pap. 12.00 (001-000-04489-3). USGPO.

Perennial Garden: Color Harmonies Through the Season. Jeff Cox & Marilyn Cox. Ed. by Anne Halpin. (Illus.). 320p. 1985. 21.95 (ISBN 0-87857-573-1). Rodale Pr Inc.

Perennial Garden Plants. rev ed. Graham S. Thomas. (Illus.). 404p. 1982. 29.95x (ISBN 0-460-04575-X, Pub. by J M Dent England). Biblio Dist.

Perennial Gardener. Frederick McGourty. 1989. 24.95 (ISBN 0-395-45373-9). HM.

Perennial Gardens: A Practical Guide to Home Landscaping. John Williamson. LC 87-12094. (Illus.). 288p. 1988. 27.95 (ISBN 0-06-015858-1). Har-Row.

Perennial Pentecost. Frank W. Lemons. 1971. pap. 2.95 (ISBN 0-87148-679-2). Pathway Pr.

Perennial Philadelphians: The Anatomy of an American Aristocracy. facsimile ed. Nathaniel Burt. LC 75-1834. (Leisure Class in America Ser.). (Illus.). 1975. Repr. of 1963 ed. 42.00x (ISBN 0-405-06903-0). Ayer Co Pubs.

Perennial Philosophical Issues. Victor Grassian. 640p. 1984. text ed. write for info. (ISBN 0-13-656769-X). P-H.

Perennial Philosophy. Aldous Huxley. 1970. pap. 8.95 (ISBN 0-06-090191-8, CN191, PL). Har-Row.

Perennial Philosophy. Aldous L. Huxley. LC 76-167362. (Essay Index Reprint Ser.). Repr. of 1945 ed. 25.50 (ISBN 0-8369-2773-7). Ayer Co Pubs.

Perennial Promise: The New York Poetry Forum Second Anthology. Louise Louis. 44p. 1979. pap. 4.95 (ISBN 0-941242-44-7). Pen-Art.

Perennial Psychology of the Bhagavad Gita. Swami Rama. 480p. pap. 12.95 (ISBN 0-89389-090-1). Himalayan Pubs.

Perennial Question. George Grimm. Tr. by Ponisch Schoenwerth from Ger. 56p. 1979. text ed. 8.50 (ISBN 0-89684-096-4, Pub. by Motilal Banarsidass India). Orient Bk Dist.

Perennial Rebel. Bernard B. Parun. 1979. 10.00 (ISBN 0-682-49292-2). Exposition-Phoenix.

Perennial Scope of Philosophy. Karl Jaspers. Tr. by Ralph Manheim. LC 68-12525. 188p. 1968. Repr. of 1949 ed. 22.50 (ISBN 0-208-00066-6, Archon). Shoe String.

Perennial Wisdom. Elda Hartley. (Chrysalis Bk). (Illus.). 80p. (Orig.). 1986. pap. 6.95 (ISBN 0-916349-09-8). Amity Hse Inc.

Perennial Works in Sociology, 34 books. Ed. by Lewis A. Coser & Walter W. Powell. (Illus.). 1979. lib. bdg. 1064.00xset (ISBN 0-405-12081-8). Ayer Co Pubs.

Perennials. Judith Kitchen. (Poetry Ser.). 68p. (Orig.). 1986. pap. 6.95 (ISBN 0-938078-21-6). Anhinga Pr.

Perennials. Time-Life Books Editors. (Gardener's Guide Ser.). (Illus.). 144p. 1988. 12.95 (ISBN 0-8094-6604-X); lib. bdg. write for info. (ISBN 0-8094-6605-8). Time-Life.

Perennials. Alan Toogood. (Planters Encyclopedia Ser.: No. 1). (Illus.). 152p. 1988. 22.95x (ISBN 0-356-15311-8, Pub. by Mcdonald & Jone's England). Hippocrene Bks.

Perennials: A Fiftieth Anniversary Selection from the Berg Collection. Lola L. Szladits. LC 88-15211. (Illus.). vi, 94p. (Orig.). 1988. pap. 15.00 (ISBN 0-87104-401-3). NY Pub Lib.

Perennials: A Southern Celebration of Foods & Flavors. Illus. by Gwen Newman. LC 83-81825. (Illus.). vi, 426p. 1984. 14.95 (ISBN 0-9612234-0-5). Perennial Pubns.

Perennials & Their Uses. 1978. pap. 3.95 (ISBN 0-686-10621-0). Bklyn Botanic.

Perennials: How to Select, Grow & Enjoy. Frederick McGourty & Pamela Harper. LC 85-60116. 160p. 1985. pap. 9.95 (ISBN 0-89586-281-6). Price Stern.

Perennials in the Garden. Charles H. Potter. LC 59-6124. (Illus.). 1959. 17.95 (ISBN 0-87599-094-0). S G Phillips.

Perepiska A. P. Chekhova, 2 vols. Ed. by Collet's Holdings, Ltd. Staff. 448p. 1984. 95.00x (ISBN 0-317-40737-6, Pub. by Collets UK). State Mutual Bk.

Perepiska Iz Dvukh Uglov. Viacheslav Ivanov & Mikhail Gershenzon. 95p. (Rus.). 1981. pap. 2.50 (ISBN 0-88233-724-6). Ardis Pubs.

Perepiska s Sestroi. Vladimir Nabokov & Helene Sikorski. 114p. 1985. 18.50 (ISBN 0-88233-977-X). Ardis Pubs.

Perepiska, Vospominaniia, Dnevniki, 2 Vols. Druz'TA Puskina. 642p. 1984. 75.00 (Pub. by Collets UK). State Mutual Bk.

Pereskia (Cactaceae, Vol. 41. Beat E. Leuenberger. (Memoirs of the New York Botanical Garden Ser.). 1986. pap. text ed. 25.00 (ISBN 0-89327-307-4). NY Botanical.

Perestroika & Soviet National Security. Michael McGwire. LC 87-17657. 125p. 1988. pap. 8.95x (ISBN 0-8157-5553-8). Brookings.

Perestroika: From Marxism & Bolshevism to Gorbachev. Svetozar Stojanovic. 140p. 1988. 23.95 (ISBN 0-87975-488-5). Prometheus Bks.

Perestroika: How New Is Gorbachev's Thinking? Ed. by Ernest W. Lefever & Robert D. Vander Lugt. 200p. 1988. 25.95 (ISBN 0-89633-133-4); pap. 12.95 (ISBN 0-89633-134-2). Ethics & Public Policy.

Perestroika: New Thinking for Our Country & the World. Mikhail Gorbachev. 1987. 19.95 (ISBN 0-06-039085-9, C&M Bessie Bks). Har-Row.

Perestroika: New Thinking for Our Country & the World. Mikhail Gorbachev. 1988. pap. 8.95 (ISBN 0-06-091528-5, PL 1528, PL). Har-Row.

Peretses Yiesh-Vizye. Chone Shmeruk & Isaac L. Peretz. LC 78-28466. (Illus.). 362p. (Yiddish.). 1971. 10.00 (ISBN 0-914512-07-2). Yivo Inst.

Peretz. Isaac L. Peretz. Ed. & tr. by Sol Liptzin. LC 72-5689. (Biography Index Reprints - YIVO Bilingual Ser.). Repr. of 1947 ed. 21.25 (ISBN 0-8369-8137-5). Ayer Co Pubs.

Peretz Trio. 101p. 4.00 (ISBN 0-318-13630-9). Board Jewish Educ.

Perez Arson Mystery. Irwin Touster & Richard Curtis. LC 74-158729. (Casebook Mystery Ser.). (Illus.). 192p. (gr. 4-7). 1972. PLB 4.58 (ISBN 0-8037-7040-5). Dial Bks Young.

Perez de Ayala: Tigre Juan & el Curandero de su Honra. J. J. Macklin. (Critical Guides to Spanish Texts Ser.: No. 28). 100p. 1981. pap. 4.95 (ISBN 0-7293-0100-1, Pub. by Grant & Cutler). Longwood Pub Group.

Perez Galdos & the Spanish Novel of the Nineteenth Century. Leslie B. Walton. LC 77-11400. 261p. 1970. Repr. of 1927 ed. 30.00x (ISBN 0-87752-115-8). Gordian.

Perez Galdos: Dona Perfecta. J. E. Varey. (Critical Guides to Spanish Texts Ser.: No. 1). 84p. 1971. pap. 3.95 (ISBN 0-900411-22-8, Pub. by Grant & Cutler). Longwood Pub Group.

Perez Galdos: Fortunata y Jacinta. Geoffrey Ribbans. (Critical Guides to Spanish Texts Ser.: No. 21). 126p. 1977. pap. 5.50 (ISBN 0-7293-0041-2, Pub. by Grant & Cutler). Longwood Pub Group.

Perez Galdos: La de Bringas. Peter Bly. (Critical Guides to Spanish Texts Ser.: No. 30). 100p. 1981. pap. 4.95 (ISBN 0-7293-0110-9, Pub. by Grant & Cutler). Longwood Pub Group.

Perez Galdos: Miau. Eamonn Rodgers. (Critical Guides to Spanish Texts Ser.: No. 23). 74p. 1978. pap. 4.95 (ISBN 0-7293-0059-5, Pub. by Grant & Cutler). Longwood Pub Group.

Perezhyte I Peredumane: My Life & Thoughts in Retrospect. Danylo Shumuk. Ed. by Wasyl Hryshko. LC 82-84497. 536p. (Ukrainian.). 1983. 20.00 (ISBN 0-912601-00-0). Ukrainian News.

Perfect Age. F. E. Baily. 187p. 1981. Repr. of 1946 ed. lib. bdg. 30.00. Darby Bks.

Perfect Age. Dian C. Regan. 192p. 1987. pap. 2.50 (ISBN 0-380-75337-5, Flare). Avon.

Perfect Age of Man's Life. Mary Dove. (Illus.). 230p. 1987. 34.50 (ISBN 0-521-32571-4). Cambridge U Pr.

Perfect Analysis Given by a Parrot see Dragon Country: Eight Plays.

Perfect Bind. Sam Tract. 118p. (Orig.). 1984. pap. text ed. 3.50 (ISBN 0-930579-00-3). Copy Fast Ctr.

Perfect Body for You: The Eaglo Way. E. A. Gloeggler. (Illus.). 76p. (Orig.). 1987. 10.00. Eaglo Bks.

Perfect Boy. Elizabeth Reynolds. (Sweet Dreams Ser.: No. 105). 176p. (Orig.). (YA) (gr. 7-12). 1986. pap. 2.25 (ISBN 0-553-25469-3). Bantam.

Perfect C: Algebras. C. Akemann & F. Shultz. LC 85-4018. (Memoirs of the AMS Ser.: No. 326). 136p. 1985. pap. text ed. 16.00 (ISBN 0-8218-2327-2). Am Math.

Perfect Calc in Plain English. Andrew Townsend. (Software Made Simple Ser.). 224p. 1984. pap. 12.95 (ISBN 0-671-49995-5, Pub. by Computer Bks). S&S.

Perfect Christmas Picture. Fran Manushkin. LC 79-2678. (Harper I Can Read Bks.). (Illus.). 64p. (gr. k-3). 1980. 8.70i (ISBN 0-06-024068-7); PLB 9.89 (ISBN 0-06-024069-5). HarpJ.

Perfection & Perfectionism: A Dogmatic-Ethical Study of Biblical Perfection & Phenomenal Perfectionism. Hans K. LaRondelle. (Andrews University Monographs, Studies in Religion: Vol. III). vii, 364p. pap. 9.95 (ISBN 0-943872-02-2). Andrews Univ Pr.

Perfection & Progress: Two Modes of Utopian Thought. Elisabeth Hansot. 240p. 1974. pap. 9.95x (ISBN 0-262-58054-3). MIT Pr.

Perfection in the Head World. Sri Chinmoy. 55p. (Orig.). 1980. pap. 2.00 (ISBN 0-88497-492-8). Aum Pubns.

Perfection of Exile: Fourteen Contemporary Lithuanian Writers. Rimvydas Silbajoris. LC 72-108798. (Illus.). 1970. 18.95x (ISBN 0-8061-0907-6). U of Okla Pr.

Perfection of Wisdom in Eight Thousand Lines & Its Verse Summary. Tr. & pref. by Edward Conze. LC 72-76540. (Wheel Ser.: No. 1). 348p. 1973. 15.00 (ISBN 0-87704-048-6); pap. 8.95 (ISBN 0-87704-049-4). Four Seasons Foun.

Perfection of Yoga. Swami A. C. Bhaktivedanta. LC 72-76302. (Illus.). 1972. pap. 1.95 (ISBN 0-912776-36-6). Bhaktivedanta.

Perfection Salad: Women & Cooking at the Turn of the Century. Laura Shapiro. 280p. 1986. 16.95 (ISBN 0-374-23075-7). FS&G.

Perfection Salad: Women & Cooking at the Turn of the Century. Laura Shapiro. 288p. 1987. pap. 8.95 (ISBN 0-8050-0228-6). H Holt & Co.

Perfectionism. Brian. L. 20p. (Orig.). 1985. pap. 0.85 (ISBN 0-89486-259-6, 1404). Hazelden.

Perfectionism: What's Bad about Being Too Good. Miriam Adderholdt-Elliott. Ed. by Pamela Espeland. LC 86-81130. (Challenge Bks.). (Illus.). 136p. (gr. 6 up). 1987. pap. 8.95 (ISBN 0-915793-07-5). Free Spirit Pub Co.

Perfectionist. David Williamson. (Illus., Orig.). 1986. pap. 7.95 (ISBN 0-936839-44-9). Applause Theatre Bk Pubs.

Perfectionist Persuasion: The Holiness Movement & American Methodism, 1867-1936. Charles E. Jones. LC 74-13766. (ATLA Monograph: No. 5). (Illus.). 262p. 1974. 22.50 (ISBN 0-8108-0747-5). Scarecrow.

Perfectionists. Gail Godwin. (Contemporary American Fiction Ser.). 224p. 1985. pap. 6.95 (ISBN 0-14-008388-X). Penguin.

Perfectionists' How To: Bk. I, "Custom Draperies". Dolores P. Lederer. (Illus.). 100p. (Orig.). 1982. instruction manual 25.00 (ISBN 0-9608040-0-5). Lederer Enterprises.

Perfectionists' How To: Bk. II, Drapery Top Treatments. Dolores P. Lederer. (Illus.). 101p. 1983. instruction manual 25.00 (ISBN 0-9608040-1-3). Lederer Enterprises.

Perfectionists' How To: Bk. III, Window Specialties (Romans, Austrians, Balloons, Pouffs) Dolores P. Lederer. (Illus.). 112p. 1985. instruction manual 25.00 (ISBN 0-9608040-2-1). Lederer Enterprises.

Perfectionists: Radical Social Thought in the Northern States, 1815-1860. Laurence R. Veysey. LC 73-4900. (Sourcebooks in American Social Thought). Repr. of 1973 ed. 41.80 (ISBN 0-8357-9951-4, 2012576). Bks Demand UMI.

Perfectly Legal: Four Hundred Seventy-Five Foolproof Methods for Paying Less Taxes. 1987 ed. Barry R. Steiner & David W. Kennedy. 293p. 1986. 19.95 (ISBN 0-471-85073-X). Wiley.

Perfectly Legal: Three Hundred Fifty Foolproof Methods for Paying Less Taxes. 1984 ed. Barry R. Steiner & David W. Kennedy. LC 83-316716. 242p. 1984. (Pub. by Ronald Pr); pap. 7.95 (ISBN 0-471-88087-6). Wiley.

Perfectly Legal: Three Hundred Foolproof Methods for Paying Less Taxes. Barry R. Steiner & David W. Kennedy. LC 82-17501. pap. 61.50 (ISBN 0-317-07939-5, 2022495). Bks Demand UMI.

Perfectly Legal: Two Hundred & Seventy-Five Foolproof Methods for Paying Less Taxes. Barry R. Steiner & David W. Kennedy. 256p. 1982. pap. 5.95 (ISBN 0-446-37188-2). Warner Bks.

Perfidious Brethren. Bd. with Love in Its Empire: Illustrated in Seven Novels. Paul Chamberlen. (Novel in England, 1700-1775 Ser). 1973. Repr. of 1720 ed. lib. bdg. 61.00 (ISBN 0-8240-0547-3). Garland Pub.

Perfidious P. Bd. with Glorious Life & Actions of St. Whigg; Life & Adventures of Captain John Avery, the Famous English Pirate ... Now in Possession of Madagascar. (Novel in England, 1700-1775 Ser). lib. bdg. 61.00 (ISBN 0-8240-0518-X). Garland Pub.

Perfil del Aire con Otras Obras Ovidadas e Ineditas Documentos Y Epistolario. Luis Cernuda. Ed. by Derek Harris. (Serie B: Textos, XI). 204p. (Orig., Span.). 1971. pap. 14.50 (ISBN 0-900411-20-1, Pub. by Tamesis Bks Ltd). Longwood Pub Group.

Perfluorhalogenorano-Verbindungen der Haupt Gruppenelemente-Perfluorohalogenorgano-Compounds of Main Group Elements. Max Plank Society for the Advancement of Science, Gmelin Institute for Inorganic Chemistry. (Gmelin Handbuch der Anorganischen Chemie, 8th Ed., New Suppl.: Vol. 24, Pt. 3). 233p. 1975. 196.00 (ISBN 0-387-93293-3). Springer-Verlag.

Perfluorinated Ionomer Membranes. Ed. by Adi Eisenberg & Howard L. Yeager. LC 81-20570. (ACS Symposium Ser.: No. 180). 1982. 54.95 (ISBN 0-8412-0698-8). Am Chemical.

Perfluorochemical Blood Substitutes. Ed. by Naito & Ryoichi. (International Congress Ser.: Vol. 486). 1980. 123.75 (ISBN 0-444-90086-1). Elsevier.

Perforated Sovereignties & International Relations: Trans-Sovereign Contracts of Subnational Governments. Ed. by Ivo D. Duchacek et al. LC 87-36092. (Contributions in Political Science Ser.: No. 211). 256p. 1988. lib. bdg. 42.95 (ISBN 0-313-26180-6, DPD/). Greenwood.

Perforations in the "Latter-Day Pamphlets", by One of the Eighteen Millions of Bores: No. 1; Universal Suffrage; Capital Punishment--Slavery. Ed. by Elizur Wright. LC 72-3157. (Black Heritage Library Collection). Repr. of 1850 ed. 14.50 (ISBN 0-8369-9093-5). Ayer Co Pubs.

Performance. Ed. by A. Dale Timpe. (Art & Science of Business Management Ser.). 352p. 1988. 24.95x (ISBN 0-8160-1902-9). Facts on File.

Performance: A Course for Piano Study - 1C. Lynn F. Olson et al. (Music Pathways Ser.). 1974. pap. 2.50 (ISBN 0-8258-0150-8, 04915). Fischer Inc NY.

Performance Activities in Mathematics, 6 bks. Terry Shoemaker. Incl. Bk. 1 (ISBN 0-913688-10-X); Bk. 2 (ISBN 0-913688-11-8); Bk. 3 (ISBN 0-913688-12-6); Bk. 4 (ISBN 0-913688-13-4); Bk. 5 (ISBN 0-913688-14-2); Bk. 6 (ISBN 0-913688-15-0). 1974. pap. 6.64 ea. Pawnee Pub.

Performance Analysis, Modelling, & Measurement in a Hierarchically Distributed Computer System. J. Heinula. (Acta Universitatis Duluensis, Series C: Technica 34, Electronica 7). 876p. (Orig.). 1986. pap. 34.00x (ISBN 951-42-2168-0). Coronet Bks.

Performance Analysis of Local Computer Networks. Joseph L. Hammond & Peter J. O'Reilly. LC 85-13526. 1986. text ed. write for info. (ISBN 0-201-11530-1); solutions manual avail. (ISBN 0-201-11531-X). Addison-Wesley.

Performance Analysis of Multiple Access Protocols. Shuji Tasaka. (Series in Computer Systems). 300p. 1986. text ed. 25.00x (ISBN 0-262-20058-9). MIT Pr.

Performance & Credibility: Developing Excellence in Public & Nonprofit Organizations. Ed. by Joseph S. Wholey et al. Mark A. Abramson & Christopher Bellavita. LC 85-50707. 320p. 1985. 32.00x (ISBN 0-669-11037-X); pap. text ed. 16.95x (ISBN 0-669-11680-7). Lexington Bks.

Performance & Evaluation of LISP Systems. Richard P. Gabriel. (Series in Computer Systems, Research Reports & Notes). 350p. 1985. pap. text ed. 22.50x (ISBN 0-262-07093-6). MIT Pr.

Performance & Markets for Industrial Knit Fabrics. 59p. 1983. 40.00 (ISBN 0-318-01535-8, 16028). Indus Fabrics.

Performance & Perception of Notational Variants: A Study of Rhythmic Patterning in Music. Bengt Edlund. 224p. 1985. pap. text ed. 27.50x (ISBN 91-554-1675-6, Pub. by Almqvist & Wiksell). Coronet Bks.

Performance & Politics in Popular Drama: Aspects of Popular Entertainment in Theatre, Film & Television, 1800-1976. Ed. by David Bradby et al. LC 79-12036. (Illus.). 1980. 37.50 (ISBN 0-521-22755-0). Cambridge U Pr.

Performance & Politics in Popular Drama: Aspects of Popular Entertainment in Theatre, Film & Television 1800-1976. Ed. by David Bradby et al. LC 79-12036. (Illus.). 360p. 1982. pap. 14.95 (ISBN 0-521-28524-0). Cambridge U Pr.

Performance Anthology: Source Book for a Decade of California Performance Art. Ed. by Carl E. Loeffler & Darlene Tong. LC 79-55054. (Contemporary Documents: Vol. 1). (Illus.). 500p. 1980. pap. 15.95 (ISBN 0-931818-01-X). Contemporary Arts.

Performance Appraisal. 62p. 1985. pap. 12.00. Am Soc Personnel.

Performance Appraisal: A Guide to Greater Productivity. Richard F. Olson. LC 80-29274. 191p. 1981. pap. text ed. 9.95 (ISBN 0-471-09134-0). Wiley.

Performance Appraisal: A Systems Approach. Stephen J. Carroll & Craig E. Schneier. (Scott, Foresman Series in Management & Organizations). 1982. pap. text ed. write for info. (ISBN 0-673-16006-8). Scott F.

Performance Appraisal: An Investment in Human Capital. John E. Clewis & Janis Panting. 1984. 25.00 (ISBN 0-910402-73-6); 15.00. Coll & U Personnel.

Performance Appraisal & Human Development. Howard P. Smith et al. LC 76-52663. 1977. pap. text ed. write for info. (ISBN 0-201-07455-9). Addison-Wesley.

Performance Appraisal & the Manager. E. C. Keil. LC 77-79343. 1977. text ed. 19.95 (ISBN 0-86730-520-7). Lebhar Friedman.

Performance Appraisal: Assessing Human Behavior at Work. H. John Bernardin & Richard W. Beatty. LC 83-9906. (Human Resource Management Ser.). 416p. 1984. pap. text ed. 12.50 (ISBN 0-534-01398-8). PWS Kent Pub.

Performance Appraisal Bibliography of Recent Publications, 1981. Margaret C. Blasingame et al. (Special Report Ser.: No. 1). 72p. 1981. pap. 15.00 (ISBN 0-912879-50-5). Ctr Creat Leader.

Performance Appraisal: Design Manual. Ferdinand F. Fournies. (Illus.). 340p. 1983. 96.45 (ISBN 0-917472-09-8). F Fournies.

Performance Appraisal for Career Development. Clive Fletcher & Richard Williams. (Personnel Management Ser.). 1985. text ed. 29.95x (ISBN 0-09-158260-1, Pub. by Busn Bks England); pap. text ed. 15.95x (ISBN 0-09-158261-X, Pub. by Busn Bks England). Brookfield Pub Co.

Performance Appraisal for Productivity: The Nurse Manager's Handbook. Joan M. Ganong & Warren L. Ganong. LC 83-15676. 360p. 1983. 48.00 (ISBN 0-89443-945-6). Aspen Pub.

Performance Appraisal Handbook. Associated Equipment Distributors Staff. 20p. 1985. 25.00 (ISBN 0-318-19177-6). Assn Equip Distrs.

Performance Appraisal in the Public Sector: An Overview Essay & Annotated Bibliography. Toni Shaklee. 60p. 1986. pap. 4.50 (ISBN 0-317-46844-8). Univ OK Gov Res.

Performance Appraisal: Legal Aspects. Rev. ed. J. Vernon Odom & J. Keith Edwards. (Technical Report Ser.: No. 3). 20p. 1979. pap. 10.00 (ISBN 0-912879-02-5). Ctr Creat Leader.

Performance Appraisal on the Job. Judy Block. 1982. pap. 5.95 (ISBN 0-917386-52-3). Exec Ent Pubns.

Performance Appraisal on the Line. David L. DeVries et al. LC 81-10328. 160p. 1981. 29.95 (ISBN 0-471-09254-1, Pub. by Wiley-Interscience). Wiley.

Performance Appraisal on the Line. Ann Morrison et al. 162p. 1981. pap. 15.00 (ISBN 0-912879-93-9). Ctr Creat Leader.

Performance Appraisal Programs. (Personnel Policies Forum Surveys Ser.: No. 135). 59p. 1983. 30.00 (ISBN 0-87179-970-7). BNA.

Performance Appraisal: Promise & Peril. Elaine F. Gruenfeld. LC 81-3920. (Key Issues Ser.: No. 25). 72p. 1981. pap. 5.00 (ISBN 0-87546-088-7). ILR Pr.

Performance Appraisal Skills see Productive Supervisor: A Program of Practical Managerial Skills.

Performance Appraisal Source Book. Ed. by Lloyd Baird et al. (Illus.). 256p. 1982. lib. bdg. 35.00x (ISBN 0-914234-56-0). Human Res Dev.

Performance Appraisal Sourcebook. Ed. by Lloyd S. Baird et al. 272p. Date not set. 35.00. Human Res Dev Pr.

Performance Appraisal: Theory & Practice. T. V. Rao. (Aima - Vikas Management Ser.). 404p. 1985. text ed. 30.00x (ISBN 0-7069-2615-3, Pub. by Vikas India); pap. text ed. 15.95x (ISBN 0-7069-3272-2). Advent NY.

Performance Appraisal: Theory to Practice. Richard I. Henderson. (Illus.). 1984. text ed. 22.00 (ISBN 0-8359-5499-4, Reston). P-H.

Performance Appraisals in Business Industry: Keys to Effective Supervision. G. L. Morrisey. 1983. pap. write for info. (ISBN 0-201-04831-0); write for info. instrs' manual (ISBN 0-201-13982-0). Addison-Wesley.

Performance Appraisals in the Public Sector: Key to Effective Supervision. George L. Morrisey. (Illus.). 160p. 1983. pap. write for info. (ISBN 0-201-04847-7). Addison-Wesley.

Performance Approach in Determining Required Levels of Insulation in Concrete Roof Systems. (PCI Journal Reprints Ser.). 16p. pap. 6.00 (ISBN 0-686-40153-0, JR250). Prestressed Concrete.

Performance Art: From Futurism to the Present. rev. & enl ed. RoseLee Goldberg. (Illus.). 212p. 1988. pap. 12.95 (ISBN 0-8109-2371-8). Abrams.

Performance Art: Memoirs, Vol. I. Jeff Nuttall. (Orig.). 1986. pap. 6.95 (ISBN 0-7145-3788-8). Riverrun NY.

Performance Art: Scripts, Vol. II. Jeff Nuttall. (Orig.). 1986. pap. 6.95 (ISBN 0-7145-3789-6). Riverrun NY.

Performance As Political Act. Randy Martin. (Critical Perspectives in Social Theory Ser.). 288p. Date not set. lib. bdg. 39.95 (ISBN 0-89789-174-0). Bergin & Garvey.

Performance Assessment for Underground Radioactive Wastes Disposal Systems. (Safety Ser.: No. 68). 37p. 1986. pap. text ed. 9.75 (ISBN 92-0-123485-6, ISP692, IAEA). UNIPUB.

Performance Assessment in Education & Training: Alternative Techniques. Michael Priestly. LC 81-19598. (Illus.). 280p. 1982. 34.95 (ISBN 0-87778-181-8). Educ Tech Pubns.

Performance Assessment: Methods & Applications. Ed. by Ronald A. Berk. LC 86-2947. 560p. 1987. text ed. 47.50x (ISBN 0-8018-3142-3). Johns Hopkins.

Performance at Work: A Systematic Program for Analyzing Work. Richard A. Swanson & Deane Gradous. LC 85-26358. 281p. 1986. 29.95 (ISBN 0-471-83060-7). Wiley.

Performance-Based Educational Media Activities Guide. 2nd ed. Bill L. Perry. 176p. (Orig.). 1981. pap. text ed. 18.95 (ISBN 0-8403-2105-8). Kendall-Hunt.

Performance Based Placement Manual. rev. ed. Richard Pimentel et al. 52p. 1987. Repr. of 1984 ed. wkbk. 19.50 (ISBN 0-942071-01-8). M Wright & Assocs.

Performance Based Supervisory Development. Charles MacDonald. (Illus.). 224p. 1982. 35.00x (ISBN 0-914234-58-7). Human Res Dev.

Performance Based Supervisory Development. Charles Macdonald. 224p. Date not set. 35.00. Human Res Dev Pr.

Performance Benchmarks for the Comprehensive Employee Assistance Program. Donald Jones. 52p. 1983. pap. 4.95 (ISBN 0-89486-173-5). Hazelden.

Performance Budgeting System for Highway Maintenance Management. (National Cooperative Highway Research Program Report). 213p. 1972. 8.40. Transport Res Bd.

Performance by Computer Modeling or Prescription by Model Code? David R. Baker. 1986. pap. 7.50 (ISBN 0-318-22369-4, TR 86-5). Society Fire Protect.

Performance Characteristics of Hydraulic Turbines & Pumps. Ed. by W. L Swift et al. (FED Ser.: Vol. 6). 296p. 1983. pap. text ed. 40.00 (ISBN 0-317-02639-9, H00280). ASME.

Performance Contracting in Education-an Appraisal: Toward a Balanced Perspective. Ed. by Donald M. Levine. LC 72-12681. 192p. 1973. pap. 19.95 (ISBN 0-87778-046-3). Educ Tech Pubns.

Performance Control: Service & Resource Control in Complex IBM Computing Centres. T. A. Hoie. (Illus.). 252p. 1983. 63.25 (ISBN 0-444-86517-9, North Holland). Elsevier.

Performance Criteria & Incentive Systems. S. Globerson. (Advances in Industrial Engineering Ser.: No. 1). 250p. 1985. 59.95 (ISBN 0-444-42427-X). Elsevier.

Performance Data Communication Systems & Their Applications. Ed. by G. Pujolle. 432p. 1981. 76.50 (ISBN 0-444-86283-8, North-Holland). Elsevier.

Performance Data Management Program for Solar Thermal Energy Systems. O. Cobb et al. (Progress in Solar Energy Supplements SERI Ser.). 120p. pap. text ed. cancelled (ISBN 0-89553-101-1). Am Solar Energy.

Performance Dynamics & the Amsterdam Werkteater. Dunbar H. Ogden. LC 86-24927. (Illus.). 315p. Date not set. cancelled (ISBN 0-520-05814-3). U of Cal Pr.

Performance Eighty-Four: Models of Computer System Performance: Proceedings of the Anniversary Symposium of IFIP WG 7.3. on Computer Performance, 10th, Paris, France, 19-21 December, 1984. Ed. by E. Gelenbe. 560p. 1985. 118.50 (ISBN 0-444-87680-4, North-Holland). Elsevier.

Performance 'Eighty-Seven: Proceedings of the 12th IFIP WG 7.3 International Symposium on Computer Performance Modelling, Measurement & Evaluation, Brussels, Belgium, 7-9 Dec., 1987. Ed. by P. J. Courtis & G. Latrouche. 600p. 1988. 131.50 (ISBN 0-444-70347-0, North Holland). Elsevier.

Performance Eighty-Three: Proceedings of the International Symposium on Computer Performance Modelling, Measurement & Evaluation, 9th, College Park, Maryland, May 25-27, 1983. Ed. by A. K. Agrawala & S. K. Tripathi. 488p. 1984. 79.00 (ISBN 0-444-86673-6, I-467-83, North Holland). Elsevier.

Performance Evaluation: A Management Basic for Librarians. Ed. by Jonathan A. Lindsey. LC 86-42746. 232p. 1986. 35.00 (ISBN 0-89774-313-X). Oryx Pr.

Performance Evaluation: An Essential Management Tool. Ed. by Christine S. Becker. (Practical Management Ser.). 209p. 1988. pap. text ed. 21.00 (ISBN 0-87326-079-1). Intl City Mgt.

Performance Evaluation for Professional Personnel. John E. Newman & John R. Hinrichs. (Studies in Productivity: Highlights of the Literature Ser.: Vol. 14). 48p. 1980. pap. 39.00 (ISBN 0-89361-021-6). Work in Amer.

Performance Evaluation for Professional Personnel, Vol. 14. John E. Newman & John R. Hinrichs. LC 80-20739. (Studies in Productivity Highlights of the Literature). 1982. pap. 35.00. Pergamon.

Performance Evaluation of Commercial Loan Officers: State of the Art. Robert Morris Associates Staff. LC 84-1077. 64p. 1984. pap. text ed. 29.00 (ISBN 0-936742-17-8). Robt Morris Assocs.

Performance Evaluation of Educational Personnel. M. Donald Thomas. LC 79-66531. (Fastback Ser.: No. 135). 60p. (Orig.). 1979. pap. 0.90 (ISBN 0-87367-135-X). Phi Delta Kappa.

Performance Evaluation of Numerical Software. Ed. by L. Fosdick. 340p. 1979. 58.00 (ISBN 0-444-85330-8, North Holland). Elsevier.

Performance Fluorine Chemicals. Frost & Sullivan, Inc. Staff. 204p. 1986. 1950.00 (ISBN 0-86621-806-8, A1625). Frost & Sullivan.

Performance Guide for Understanding Business & Personal Law. 8th ed. G. Brown et al. 160p. 1987. pap. text ed. 7.96 (ISBN 0-07-008434-3). McGraw.

Performance Guide to Word Processing Software. W. Hession & M. Rubel. 1985. pap. text ed. 23.95 (ISBN 0-07-028451-2). McGraw.

Performance Horse: Management, Care & Training. Sarah Pilliner. LC 87-3727. 144p. 1987. 14.95 (ISBN 0-87605-867-5). Howell Bk.

Performance Improvement of Virtual Memory Systems. Edwin J. Lau. LC 82-13393. (Computer Science: Systems Programming Ser.: No. 17). pap. 59.30 (2070073). Bks Demand UMI.

Performance Limits in Communication Theory & Practice. Ed. by J. K. Skwirzynski. 1988. lib. bdg. 114.00 (ISBN 90-247-3695-1, Pub. by Martinus Nijhoff Netherlands). Kluwer Academic.

Performance Management: Basis for the System (Context of Any Management System, Bk. 4. Michael McMaster. 66p. 1984. 8.95x (ISBN 0-9605414-3-8). Precision Mod.

Performance Management: Creating a Framework (Specific Model for a Performance Management System, Bk. 2. Michael McMaster. 90p. 1984. 8.95x (ISBN 0-9605414-1-1). Precision Mod.

Performance Management: Creating a Working System (Principles & Questions to Design Your Own System, Bk. 3. Michael McMaster. 94p. 1984. 8.95x (ISBN 0-9605414-2-X). Precision Mod.

Performance Management, Creating the Conditions for Results. Michael McMasters. (Performance Management Ser.). 304p. (Orig.). 1987. 21.95 (ISBN 0-943920-69-8). Metamorphous Pr.

Performance Management: Creating the Conditions for Results (Complete System & Communication for Managing Results, 4 vols. Michael McMaster. 1984. Set. 29.95x (ISBN 0-9605414-4-6). Precision Mod.

Performance Management: Getting Results from Your Performance Planning & Appraisal System. Roger J. Plachy & Sandra J. Plachy. 320p. 1988. 59.95 (ISBN 0-8144-7705-4). AMACOM.

Performance Management: Improving Quality & Productivity Through Positive Reinforcement. Aubrey C. Daniels & Theodore A. Rosen. LC 82-61868. (Illus.). 1983. 24.95 (ISBN 0-937100-01-3). Perf Manage.

Performance Management Process: An Integrative Approach to Human Resource Management. Philip C. Grant. 352p. 1986. pap. text ed. 22.95 (ISBN 0-8403-4086-9). Kendall-Hunt.

Performance Management Sourcebook. Ed. by Craig Schneier & Lloyd Baird. 400p. 1987. pap. 39.95 (ISBN 0-87425-074-9). Human Res Dev Pr.

Performance Management: The Required Communications (Effective Communication to Make Performance Management Work, Bk. 1. Michael McMaster. 54p. 1984. 8.95x (ISBN 0-9605414-5-4). Precision Mod.

Performance: Managing for Excellence. George Manning & Kent Curtis. (Human Side of Work Ser.). 337p. 1988. pap. text ed. write for info. (ISBN 0-538-21257-8, U257). SW Pub.

Performance Measurement: A Guide for Local Elected Officials. 31p. 1980. pap. 6.00x (ISBN 0-87766-284-3, 30900). Urban Inst.

Performance Measurement & Municipalities: A Selected Bibliography. Jamie W. Coniglio. (Public Administration Ser.: P 1772). 5p. 1985. 2.00 (ISBN 0-89028-572-1). Vance Biblios.

Performance Measurement & Theory. Ed. by Frank J. Landy & Sheldon Zedeck. 416p. 1983. text ed. 45.00x (ISBN 0-89859-246-1). L Erlbaum Assocs.

Performance Measurement in Public Agencies. Ed. by Thomas J. Cook. 196p. (Orig.). 1986. pap. 8.00 (ISBN 0-918592-87-9). Policy Studies.

Performance Measurement of Computer Systems. Phillip McKerrow. (Illus.). 256p. 1988. text ed. 35.50x (ISBN 0-201-17436-7). Addison-Wesley.

Performance Measurements of Scintillation Cameras. 1983. 11.50 (ISBN 0-318-18018-9, NU 1-1980). Natl Elec Mfrs.

Performance Measures for Growing Businesses. Stahrl W. Edmunds. 200p. 1981. 25.95 (ISBN 0-442-22605-5). Van Nos Reinhold.

Performance Measures for Oklahoma Public Libraries. 115p. 1982. 10.00x; members 9.00x. ALA.

Performance Methods for Flutists. James J. Pellerite. 1968. pap. text ed. 4.95 (ISBN 0-931200-51-2). Zalo.

Performance Modelling & Prediction, 2 vols. Rees. (Infotech Computer State of the Art Reports). 448p. 1977. Set. pap. 61.00x (ISBN 0-08-028531-7). Pergamon.

Performance Models of Multiprocessor Systems. M. Ajmone Marsan et al. (Computer Systems Ser.). 300p. 1986. text ed. 35.00x (ISBN 0-262-01093-3). MIT Pr.

Performance Monitoring for Geotechnical Construction - STP 584. 204p. 1975. 14.00 (ISBN 0-8031-0533-9, 04-584000-38). ASTM.

Performance Objectives for School Principals. Jack A. Culbertson & Curtis Henson. LC 74-75367. 1974. 23.00 (ISBN 0-8211-0223-0); text ed. 20.75x 10 or more copies. McCutchan.

Performance Objectives in Education see Educational Technology Reviews Ser.

Performance of Christopher Marlowe's Dr. Faustus. N. Alexander. (Chatterton Lectures on an English Poet). 1971. pap. 5.50 (ISBN 0-85672-057-7, Pub. by British Acad). Longwood Pub Group.

Performance of Computer Communication Systems: Proceedings of the IFIP WG 7.3 TC 6 International Symposium on the Performance of Computer Communication Systems, Zurich, Switzerland, 21-23 March, 1984. Ed. by W. Bux & H. Rudin. 500p. 1985. 84.25 (ISBN 0-444-86883-6). Elsevier.

Performance of Computer Installations. Ed. by D. Ferrari. 342p. 1979. 92.00 (ISBN 0-444-85186-0, North Holland). Elsevier.

Performance of Computer Systems. Ed. by M. Arato et al. 566p. 1979. 105.25 (ISBN 0-444-85332-4). Elsevier.

Performance of Concrete in Marine Environment. 1980. 58.95 (ISBN 0-686-70072-4, SP-65). ACI.

Performance of Earth & Earth-Supported Structures: Proceedings of the Specialty Conference on June 11-14, 1972, Purdue University, Lafayette, Indiana, 3 vols. Vol. 1, Pt. 1. pap. 160.00 (ISBN 0-317-10643-0, 2019546); Vol. 1, Pt. 2. pap. 160.00 (ISBN 0-317-10644-9); Vol. 2. pap. 40.00 (ISBN 0-317-10645-7); Vol. 3. pap. 105.80 (ISBN 0-317-10646-5). Bks Demand UMI.

Performance of Literature. Pamela Miller. 212p. 1987. pap. text ed. 13.95 (ISBN 0-8403-4338-8). Kendall Hunt.

Performance of Literature in Historical Perspectives. Ed. by David W. Thompson & Wallace A. Bacon. LC 83-3470. 742p. (Orig.). 1983. lib. bdg. 45.75 (ISBN 0-8191-3146-6); pap. text ed. 29.25 (ISBN 0-8191-3147-4). U Pr of Amer.

Performance of Lubricating Oils. 2nd ed. H. H. Zuidema. LC 52-8017. (ACS Monograph: No. 143). 1959. 24.95 (ISBN 0-8412-0283-4). Am Chemical.

Performance of Macaque Monkeys on a Test of the Concept of Generalized Triangularity. G. Andrew & H. F. Harlow. LC 48-10876. (Comp Psych Monographs). pap. 40.00 (ISBN 0-527-24935-1). Kraus Repr.

Performance of Nominal Five-Eighths Inch Plywood Over Joists Spaced 24 Inches on Center, Vol. 1. (Research Report Ser.). 11p. 1981. pap. 5.50 (ISBN 0-86718-114-1). Nat Assn H Build.

Performance of Nuclear Power Reactor Components. (Proceedings Ser.). (Illus.). 678p. (Orig.). 1970. pap. 52.00 (ISBN 92-0-050170-2, ISP240, IAEA). UNIPUB.

Performance of Pavements Designed with Low-Cost Materials. (Transportation Research Record Ser.). 49p. 1980. 4.20 (ISBN 0-309-02999-6). Transport Res Bd.

Performance of Precast Prestressed Hollow Core Slab with Composite Concrete Topping. (PCI Journal Reprints Ser.). 15p. pap. 5.00 (ISBN 0-686-40052-6, JR126). Prestressed Concrete.

Performance of Prestressed Concrete on the Illinois Tollway after 25 Years of Service. (PCI Journal Reprints Ser.). 24p. pap. 6.00 (ISBN 0-318-19798-7, JR287). Prestressed Concrete.

Performance of Protective Clothing, STP 900. Ed. by Roger L. Barker & Gerard C. Coletta. LC 86-10706. (Special Technical Publications). (Illus.). 625p. 1986. text ed. 60.00 (ISBN 0-8031-0461-8, 04-900000-55). ASTM.

Performance of Public Enterprises: Concepts & Measurement. Maurice G. Marchand et al. LC 84-10124. (Studies in Mathematical & Managerial Economics: Vol. 33). 296p. 1984. 68.50 (ISBN 0-444-87551-4). Elsevier.

Performance of Rolled Asphalt Road Surfacings. (Conference Proceedings Ser.). 215p. 1980. 36.00 (ISBN 0-7277-0096-0, Pub. by T Telford UK). Am Soc Civil Eng.

Performance of Small Firms. David Storey et al. 365p. 1986. 75.00 (ISBN 0-7099-4411-X, Pub. by Croom Helm UK). Routledge Chapman & Hall.

Performance of Solar Energy Converters: Thermal Collectors & Photovoltaic Cells. Gigio Beghi. 1983. lib. bdg. 69.50 (ISBN 90-277-1545-9, Pub. by Reidel Holland). Kluwer Academic.

Performance of Test Materials in Westinghouse PDU Fluid Bed Gasifier. R. Yurkewycz & R. F. Firestone. write for info. Mater Prop coun.

Performance of the Basso Continuo in Italian Baroque Music. Tharald Borgir. Ed. by George J. Buelow. LC 86-25072. (Studies in Musicology: No. 90). 188p. 1986. 44.95 (ISBN 0-8357-1675-9); pap. write for info. (ISBN 0-8357-1912-X). UMI Res Pr.

Performance of the British Economy. Ed. by Rudi Dornbusch & Richard Layard. (Illus.). 288p. 1988. 49.95 (ISBN 0-19-877272-6). Oxford U Pr.

Performance of the U. S. Railroads since World War II. Kent T. Healy. LC 83-90465. 296p. 1985. 17.95 (ISBN 0-533-06561-5). Vantage.

Performance Planning & Appraisal: A How-to Book for Managers. Patricia King. LC 83-9831. 160p. 1984. text ed. 29.95 (ISBN 0-07-034631-3). McGraw.

Performance Planning & Appraisal: A How-to Book for Managers. Patricia King. 176p. 1988. pap. 10.95 (ISBN 0-07-034640-2). McGraw.

Performance Poems. John Dancy-Jones. (Illus.). 24p. Date not set. pap. 4.00 (ISBN 0-929170-08-3). Paper Plant.

Performance Practice & Technique in Marin Marais' "Pieces de viole". Deborah A. Teplow. Ed. by George J. Buelow. LC 85-20843. (Studies in Musicology: No. 93). 178p. 1986. 49.95 (ISBN 0-8357-1714-3). UMI Res Pr.

Performance Practice: Ethnomusicological Perspectives. Ed. by Gerard Behague. LC 83-10842. (Contributions in Intercultural & Comparative Studies: No. 12). (Illus.). vii, 262p. 1984. lib. bdg. 36.95 (ISBN 0-313-24160-0, BPE/). Greenwood.

Performance Practices in Classic Piano Music: Their Principles & Applications. Sandra P. Rosenblum. LC 87-45437. 544p. 1988. 49.50x (ISBN 0-253-34314-3). Ind U Pr.

Performance Programming Under MS-DOS. Michael J. Young. 436p. (Orig.). 1987. pap. 19.95 (ISBN 0-89588-420-8). Sybex.

Performance Requirements for Multinational Corporations: U. S. Management Response. Richard D. Robinson. 224p. 1983. 36.95 (ISBN 0-275-91066-0, C1066). Praeger.

Performance Review in Social Work Agencies. Ed. by John Tibbitt & David May. (Research Highlights in Social Work Ser.: No. 20). 144p. 1988. price not set (ISBN 1-85302-017-6, Pub. by J Kingsley Pubs UK). UNIPUB.

Performance Specification of Computer Aided Environmental Design, 2 vols. Kaiman Lee. LC 75-309149. (Illus.). 554p. 1975. 150.00x (ISBN 0-915250-15-2). Environ Design.

Performance Standards for Antimicrobial Disk Susceptibility Tests: Approved Standard, Vol. 4. 3rd ed. National Committee for Clinical Laboratory Standards. 1984. 20.00 (ISBN 0-318-19418-X, M2-A3). Natl Comm Clin Lab Stds.

Performance Standards for Antimicrobial Susceptibility Tests; Second Informational Supplement: National Committe for Clinical Laboratory Standards, Vol. 7. 1987. 20.00 (ISBN 0-318-23662-1). Natl Comm Clin Lab Stds.

Performance Standards for Laboratory Personnel. William O. Umiker & Susan M. Yohe. 1984. pap. 19.95 (ISBN 0-87489-363-1). Med Economics.

Performance Standards Made Simple! A Practical Guide for Federal Supervisors & Managers. Ralph R. Smith. (Illus.). 43p. (Orig.). 1987. pap. text ed. 6.95 (ISBN 0-936295-02-3). Fed Person Mgmt.

Performance Standards Made Simple! A Practical Guide for Federal Supervisors. 2nd ed. Ralph R. Smith. (Illus.). 70p. 1988. pap. text ed. 6.95 (ISBN 0-936295-07-4). Fed Person Mgmt.

Performance Teams: Completing the Feedback Loop - Leaders. Janis McCulloch. (Illus.). 171p. 1982. 15.00 (ISBN 0-937100-02-1). Perf Manage.

Performance Teams: Completing the Feedback Loop - Members. Janis McCulloch. (Illus.). 1982. pap. 9.95 (ISBN 0-937100-03-X). Perf Manage.

Performance Test Procedure Sodium Base Recovery Units. Technical Association of the Pulp & Paper Industry. (Technical Association of the Pulp & Paper Industry CA Report Ser.: No. 39). pap. 25.50 (ISBN 0-317-29316-8, 2022362). Bks Demand UMI.

Performance Testing: Issues Facing Vocational Education. Janet E. Spirer. 193p. 1980. 11.00 (ISBN 0-318-15529-X, RD 190). Natl Ctr Res Voc Ed.

Performance Testing of Hydraulic Fluids. Ed. by R. Tourret & E. P. Wright. 544p. 1979. 122.00 (ISBN 0-471-26059-2, Wiley Heyden). Wiley.

Performance Testing of Lubricants for Automotive Engines & Transmissions. Ed. by C. F. McCue et al. (Illus.). 811p. 1974. 73.00 (ISBN 0-85334-468-X, Pub. by Elsevier Applied Sci England). Elsevier.

Performance Testing of Lubricants: Proceedings of International Symposium on Rolling Contact Fatigue. Tourret. 1977. 88.95. Wiley.

Performance Testing of Shipping Containers - Sponsored by ASTM Committee D-10 on Packaging. American Society for Testing & Materials Staff. LC 83-641658. pap. 63.50 (ISBN 0-317-58231-3, 2056384). Bks Demand UMI.

Performance Testing of Shipping Containers. LC 83-641658. (Compilations of ASTM Standards Ser.). 250p. pap. text ed. 19.00 (ISBN 0-8031-0475-8, PCN03-410084-11). ASTM.

Performance: The Photographs of Sandy Underwood. Ed. by Ruth K. Meyer. (Illus.). 1978. pap. 5.00 (ISBN 0-917562-07-0). Contemp Arts.

Performance Tuning for the Restorer: Mopars of the 60s. Ed. by R. M. Clarke. (Illus.). 96p. (Orig.). 1988. pap. 13.95 (ISBN 1-869826-87-6, Pub. by Brooklands Bks England). Motorbooks Intl.

Performance Tuning in Theory & Practice - Four Strokes. A. Graham Bell. (Illus.). 15.95 (ISBN 0-85429-275-6, F275, Pub. by G T Foulis Ltd). Haynes Pubns.

Performance Tuning in Theory & Practice-- Two STrokes. A. Graham Bell. (Illus.). 229p. pap. 15.95 (ISBN 0-85429-329-9, F329, Pub. by G T Foulis). Haynes Pubns.

Performance under Sub-Optimal Conditions. Ed. by P. R. Davis. 104p. 1971. pap. 31.00x (ISBN 0-85066-044-0). Taylor & Francis.

Performance Windsurfing with Mike Waltze. Mike Waltze & Phil Berman. (Illus.). 1985. 15.95 (ISBN 0-393-03301-5). Norton.

Performance Without Pressure. Martin L. Seldman. 1988. 17.95 (ISBN 0-8027-1022-0); pap. 11.95 (ISBN 0-8027-7311-7). Walker & Co.

Performance Zoning. Lane H. Kendig & Susan Connor. 350p. 1980. 39.95 (ISBN 0-318-13042-4); members 37.95 (ISBN 0-318-13043-2). Am Plan Assn.

Performance, 1981: Proceedings of International Symposium on Computer Performance Modelling, Measurement. Ed. by F. J. Kylstra. 545p. 1982. 102.75 (ISBN 0-444-86330-3, North-Holland). Elsevier.

Performative Approach to Ritual. J. Tambiah. (Radcliffe-Brown Lectures in Social Anthropology). 1978. pap. 5.50 (ISBN 0-85672-197-2, Pub. by British Acad). Longwood Pub Group.

Performative Circumstances from the Avant Garde to Ramlila. Richard Schechner. 1983. pap. 16.00x (ISBN 0-8364-0963-9, Pub. by Seagull Bks India). South Asia Bks.

Performed Literature: Words & Music by Bob Dylan. Betsy Bowden. LC 81-47774. 256p. 1982. 22.50x (ISBN 0-253-34347-X). Ind U Pr.

Performer-Audience Connection: Emotion to Metaphor in Dance & Society. Judith L. Hanna. LC 83-6720. (Illus.). 283p. 1983. text ed. 25.00x (ISBN 0-292-76478-2); pap. 11.95 (ISBN 0-292-76480-4). U of Tex Pr.

Performer in Mass Media: In Media Professions & in the Community. William Hawes. 1978. pap. text ed. 12.00x (ISBN 0-8038-5825-6). Hastings.

Performers & Performances. Ed. by Jack Kamerman & Rosanne Martorella. (Illus.). 320p. 1983. 38.95 (ISBN 0-275-91020-2, C1020). Praeger.

Performers & Performances: The Social Organization of Artistic Work. Ed. by Jack B. Kamerman & Rosanne Martorella. (Illus.). 320p. 1983. text ed. 29.95x (ISBN 0-03-059743-9); pap. 18.95 (ISBN 0-89789-007-8). Bergin & Garvey.

Performers & Players. Irene M. Franck & David M. Brownstone. (Work Throughout History Ser.). (Illus.). 208p. (YA) (gr. 7 up). 1988. 16.95 (ISBN 0-8160-1448-5). Facts on File.

Performers & Their Plays. Ed. by Shirley S. Kenny & P. R. Backscheider. LC 78-66655. (Eighteenth Century English Drama Ser.). lib. bdg. 73.00 (ISBN 0-8240-3577-1). Garland Pub.

Performers as Priest & Prophet: Restoring the Intuitive in Worship Through Music & Dance. Judith Rock & Norman Mealy. LC 87-46224. (Illus.). 156p. (Orig.). 1988. pap. 13.95 (ISBN 0-06-066958-6, RD 744, HarpR). Har-Row.

Performer's Guide Through Historical Keyboard Tunings. rev., 2nd ed. Martin B. Tittle. LC 87-27095. (Illus.). 80p. 1988. lib. bdg. 12.95x (ISBN 0-942479-02-5); pap. 5.95x (ISBN 0-942479-01-7). Anderson Pr.

Performing Artist's Handbook. Janice Papolos. 219p. 1988. pap. 10.95 (ISBN 0-89879-318-1). Writers Digest.

Performing Arts & American Society. American Assembly Staff. LC 78-1404. 224p. pap. 58.30 (2029865). Bks Demand UMI.

Performing Arts Annual, 1986. Ed. by Iris Newson. (Illus.). 183p. 1986. 18.00 (ISBN 0-8444-0533-7, S/N 030-001-00115-6). USGPO.

Performing Arts Biography Master Index: A Consolidated Guide to over 270,000 Biographical Sketches of Persons Living & Dead, As They Appear in over 100 of the Principal Biographical Dictionaries Devoted to the Performing Arts. 2nd ed. Ed. by Barbara McNeil & Miranda Herbert. (Biographical Index Ser.: No. 5). 728p. 1982. 170.00x (ISBN 0-8103-1097-X). Gale.

Performing Arts Directory, 1987. Carol E. Svecz. 500p. 1986. 33.50 (ISBN 0-930036-12-3). Dance Mag Inc.

Performing Arts: Guide to the Literature. Jackson Kesler. 250p. 1989. lib. bdg. 27.50 (ISBN 0-87287-648-9). Libs Unl.

Performing Arts in American Society. Ed. by W. McNeil Lowry. LC 78-1404. (American Assembly Ser.). 1978. 10.95 (ISBN 0-13-657155-7); pap. 4.95 (ISBN 0-13-657148-4). Am Assembly.

Performing Arts in Contemporary China. Colin Mackerras. (Illus.). 220p. 1981. 30.00x (ISBN 0-7100-0778-7). Routledge Chapman & Hall.

Performing Arts Information, Nineteen Seventy-Five to Nineteen Eighty: A Bibliography of Reference Works. Paula Elliot. 1982. pap. 4.00. KSU.

Performing Arts Management & Law, 9 vols. Joseph Taubman. LC 74-189328. 1978. 495.00 set (ISBN 0-88238-055-9); 2 vols. text with 1981 suppl. 125.00 (ISBN 0-685-25465-8); 7 vols. forms 420.00. Law-Arts.

Performing Arts Management & Law. Joseph Taubman. Incl. Vol. 1. 60.00 (ISBN 0-317-40372-9); Vol. 2. 60.00 (ISBN 0-317-40373-7); Text Supplement, 1974. 20.00 (ISBN 0-317-40374-5); Text Supplement, 1977. 20.00 (ISBN 0-317-40375-3); Text Supplement, 1981, Set of 11, 12, 13, 14, 15. 20.00 (ISBN 0-317-40376-1); Vol. 1, Student Edition. write for info.; Vol. 2, Student Edition, 2 Vols., 16 & 17. 45.00 (ISBN 0-317-40377-X); Vol. 1 of Forms: Motion Pictures. 60.00 (ISBN 0-317-40378-8); Vol. 2 of Forms: Television. 60.00 (ISBN 0-317-40379-6); Vol. 3 of Forms: Theatre & Dance. 60.00 (ISBN 0-317-40380-X); Vol. 4 of Forms: Live Performance, Managers & Agents, Miscellaneous, & Book Publishing. 60.00 (ISBN 0-317-40381-8). Law Arts.

Performing Arts Management & Law. Joseph Taubman. 1974. text supplement 20.00 (ISBN 0-317-67907-4). Law Arts.

Performing Arts Management & Law. Joseph Taubman. 1981. text supplement 20.00 (ISBN 0-317-67909-0). Law Arts.

Performing Arts Management & Law, Vol. 1. Joseph Taubman. text ed. 60.00 (ISBN 0-317-67904-X). Law Arts.

Performing Arts Management & Law, Vol. 2. Joseph Taubman. text ed. 60.00 (ISBN 0-317-67906-6). Law Arts.

Performing Arts Management & Law Forms, Vols. 1 & 2: Motion Pictures & Television. Joseph Taubman. supplement 20.00 (ISBN 0-317-67922-8). Law Arts.

Performing Arts Management & Law Forms, Vol. 1: Motion Pictures. Joseph Taubman. 60.00 (ISBN 0-317-67913-9). Law Arts.

Performing Arts Management & Law Forms, Vol. 2: Television. Joseph Taubman. 60.00 (ISBN 0-317-67916-3). Law Arts.

Performing Arts Management & Law Forms, Vol. 3: Theatre & Dance. Joseph Taubman. 60.00 (ISBN 0-317-67917-1). Law Arts.

Performing Arts Management & Law Forms, Vol. 4: Live Performance, Managers, & Agents, Miscellaneous & Book Publishing. 60.00 (ISBN 0-317-67918-X). Law Arts.

Performing Arts Management & Law Forms, Vol. 5: Sound Recording & Sound. 60.00 (ISBN 0-317-67919-8). Law Arts.

Performing Arts Management & Law Forms, Vol. 6: Music Publishing. 60.00 (ISBN 0-317-67920-1). Law Arts.

Performing Arts Management & Law Forms, Vol. 7: Litigation. 60.00 (ISBN 0-317-67921-X). Law Arts.

Performing Arts Management & Law: Student Edition, 2 vols, Vols. 1 & 2. Joseph Taubman. Set. 45.00 (ISBN 0-317-67912-0); Vol. 1. write for info.; Vol. 2. write for info. Law Arts.

Performing Arts Management & Law, 1973-1980, 9 vols. Joseph Taubman. Set. 495.00 (ISBN 0-317-67903-1). Law Arts.

Performing Arts: Music & Dance. Ed. by John Blacking & Joann W. Kealiinohomoku. (World Anthropology Ser.). (Illus.). xii, 346p. 1979. text ed. 48.50 (ISBN 90-279-7870-0). Mouton.

Performing Arts Research: A Guide to Information Sources. Ed. by Marion K. Whalon. LC 75-13828. (Performing Arts Information Guide Ser.: Vol. 1). 296p. 1976. 68.00x (ISBN 0-8103-1364-2). Gale.

Performing Arts Resources, Vol. 1. Ed. by Ted Perry. LC 74-25848. 232p. 1975. 25.00 (ISBN 0-317-45815-9). Theatre Lib.

Performing Arts Resources, Vol. 2. Bowser et al. Ed. by Ted Perry. LC 75-646287. 132p. 1976. 25.00x (ISBN 0-910482-73-X). Theatre Lib.

Performing Arts Resources, Vol. 3. Ed. by Ted Perry & Robert M. Henderson. 175p. 1976. 25.00 (ISBN 0-910482-84-5); members 10.00 (ISBN 0-317-36056-6). Theatre Lib.

Performing Arts Resources, Vol. 4. Ed. by Mary C. Henderson. LC 75-646287. 116p. 1978. 25.00x (ISBN 0-932610-00-5); members 10.00. Theatre Lib.

Performing Arts Resources, Vol. 6. Ed. by Mary C. Henderson. LC 75-646287. 115p. 1980. 25.00x (ISBN 0-932610-02-1); members 10.00. Theatre Lib.

Performing Arts Resources, Vol. 10. Intro. by Barbara Cohen-Stratyner & Ginnine Cocuzza. LC 75-646287. (Performing Arts Resources Ser.). (Illus.). 85p. 1985. 25.00 (ISBN 0-932610-07-2); members 10.00. Theatre Lib.

Performing Arts Resources, Vol. 11: Scenes & Machines from the 18th Century: The Stagecraft of Jacopo Fabris & Cityoen Boullet. Jacopo Fabris & Cityoen Boullet. Ed. by Barbara Cohen-Stratyner. Tr. & intro. by C. Thomas Ault. (Performing Arts Resources Ser.). (Illus.). 146p. 1986. 25.00 (ISBN 0-932610-08-0). Theatre Lib.

Performing Arts Resources, Vol. 12: Topical Bibliographies of the American Theatre. Intro. by Barbara Cohen-Stratyner. LC 75-646287. (Performing Arts Resources Ser.). 195p. 1987. 25.00 (ISBN 0-317-64947-7). Theatre Lib.

Performing Arts Resources, Vol. 5: Recollections of O. Smith, Comedian. O. Smith. Ed. by Mary C. Henderson. LC 75-646287. (Illus.). 72p. 1979. 25.00x (ISBN 0-932610-01-3); members 10.00. Theatre Lib.

Performing Arts Resources, Vol. 7: Lazzi: The Comic Routines of Commedia Dell' Arte. Mel Gordon. Ed. by Ginnine Cocuzza & Barbara N. Cohen-Stratyner. Tr. by Claudio Vincentini. LC 75-646287. (Illus.). 82p. 1981. 25.00x (ISBN 0-932610-03-X); members 10.00. Theatre Lib.

Performing Arts Resources, Vol. 8: Stage Design: Papers from the 15th International Congress of SIBMAS. Ed. by Ginnine Cocuzza & Barbara N. Cohen-Stratyner. (Illus.). xix, 94p. 1983. 25.00 (ISBN 0-932610-04-8); members 10.00. Theatre Lib.

Performing Arts Resources, Vol. 9: An Essay on Stage Performance, A Translation of Franz Lang's Dissertatio de Actione Scenica (1727) by Alfred Siemon Golding. Franz Lang. Ed. by Ginnine Cocuzza & Barbarba N. Cohen-Stratyner. Tr. by Alfred S. Golding from Lat. LC 75-646287. (Illus.). 128p. 1984. Repr. of 1727 ed. 25.00x (ISBN 0-932610-05-6); members 10.00. Theatre Lib.

Performing Arts, the Economic Dilemma. W. J. Baumol. LC 77-16008. Repr. of 1966 ed. 56.00 (ISBN 0-527-02813-4). Kraus Repr.

Performing Arts: The Economic Dilemma. William G. Baumol & William G. Bowen. 1968. pap. 14.50x (ISBN 0-262-52011-7). MIT Pr.

Performing Arts 1876-1981: Including an International Index of Current Serial Publications. 1656p. 1981. 175.00x (ISBN 0-8352-1372-2). Bowker.

Performing Haydn's "The Creation" Reconstructing the Earliest Renditions. A. Peter Brown. LC 84-43053. (Music: Scholarship & Performance Ser.). (Illus.). 142p. 1986. 29.95x (ISBN 0-253-38820-1). Ind U Pr.

Performing Literature: An Introduction to Oral Interpretation. Beverly Long & Mary F. Hopkins. (Illus.). 550p. 1982. text ed. write for info. (ISBN 0-13-657171-9). P-H.

Performing Medieval & Renaissance Music: An Introductory Guide. Elizabeth B. Philips & John-Paul C. Jackson. 240p. 1986. pap. text ed. 24.95x (ISBN 0-02-871790-2). Schirmer Bks.

Performing Power: A New Approach for the Singer-Actor. H. Wesley Balk. LC 85-1195. xvi, 375p. 1985. 29.50x (ISBN 0-8166-1366-4); pap. 13.95 (ISBN 0-8166-1367-2). U of Minn Pr.

Performing Texts. Ed. by Michael Issacharoff & Robin F. Jones. 160p. 1987. text ed. 23.95x (ISBN 0-8122-8073-3). U of Pa Pr.

Performing Wooden Toys. William Wells. (Illus.). 96p. 1986. 20.95 (ISBN 0-7134-4721-4, Pub. by Batsford England). David & Charles.

Performing World of the Dancer. Craig Dodd. LC 81-50298. (Performing World Ser.). 114p. (gr. 7 up). 15.20 (ISBN 0-382-06590-5). Silver.

Performing World of the Musician. Christopher Headington. LC 81-50299. (Performing World Ser.). (gr. 7 up). 15.20 (ISBN 0-382-06592-1). Silver.

Performing Your Best. Tom Kubistant. LC 86-153. (Illus.). 256p. 1986. pap. 10.95 (ISBN 0-87322-900-2, LKUB0900, Pub. by Life Enhancement). Human Kinetics.

Perfume Album. 2nd ed. Jill Jessee. LC 74-13588. 194p. 1974. Repr. of 1965 ed. 12.50 (ISBN 0-88275-216-2). Krieger.

Perfume & Lace. Christine H. Cott. (Superromances). 384p. 1984. pap. 2.95 (ISBN 0-373-70098-9, Pub. by Worldwide). Harlequin Bks.

Perfume & Scent Bottle Collecting. Jean Sloan. LC 85-51092. 1986. pap. 15.95 (ISBN 0-87069-468-5). Wallace-Homestead.

Perfume, Cologne & Scent Bottles. Jacqueline North. (Illus.). 243p. 1986. 59.95 (ISBN 0-88740-072-8). Schiffer.

Perfume Industry of Myceanaean Pylos. C. Shelmerdine. (Studies in Mediterranean Archaeology: No. 34). 184p. 1985. pap. text ed. 40.00x (ISBN 9-186098-30-6, Pub. by P Astroms Pubs Sweden). Humanities.

Perfume of Eros: A Fifth Avenue Incident. Edgar Saltus. LC 75-182713. Repr. of 1905 ed. 17.50 (ISBN 0-404-05536-2). AMS Pr.

Perfume of Paradise. Jennifer Blake. 1988. pap. 7.95 (ISBN 0-449-90179-3, Columbine). Fawcett.

Perfume of the Lady in Black. Gaston Leroux. 1975. lib. bdg. 16.70x (ISBN 0-89966-138-6). Buccaneer Bks.

Perfume: The Story of a Murderer. Patrick Suskind. LC 86-45419. 288p. 1986. 16.45 (ISBN 0-394-55084-6). Knopf.

Perfume: The Story of a Murderer. Patrick Suskind. Tr. by John E. Woods. 1987. pap. 4.50 (ISBN 0-671-64370-3). PB.

Perfumed Memories. Ghulam-Sarwar Yousof. 177p. 1982. pap. 7.50 (ISBN 9-97194-712-9, Pub. by Graham Brash Singapore). Three Continents.

Perfumed Scorpion. Idries Shah. 1982. pap. 5.95 (ISBN 0-06-067254-4, CN-4036, HarpR). Har-Row.

Perfumed Scorpion. Idries Shah. 193p. 1982. 18.95 (ISBN 0-900860-62-6, Pub. by Octagon Pr England). Ins Study Human.

Perfumery Technology. 2nd ed. F. V. Wells. LC 80-42130. 449p. 1981. 142.00 (ISBN 0-470-26958-8). Halsted Pr.

Perfumery: The Psychology & Biology of Fragrance. Ed. by S. Van Toller & G. H. Dodd. (Illus.). 250p. 1988. text ed. 49.95 (ISBN 0-412-30010-9, Pub. by Chapman & Hall England). Routledge Chapman & Hall.

Perfumes & Their Production. Edward S. Maurer. LC 59-17885. pap. 82.00 (ISBN 0-317-26615-2, 2025424). Bks Demand UMI.

Perfumes, Cosmetics & Soaps. W. A. Poucher & G. M. Howard. Incl. Vol. 1. Raw Materials of Perfumery. 7th ed. LC 74-8885. 381p. 1974. 59.95x (ISBN 0-412-10640-X, NO. 6223); Vol. 2. Production, Manufacture & Application of Perfumes. 8th ed. LC 74-8883. 379p. 1974. 59.95x (ISBN 0-412-10650-7, NO. 6224); Vol. 3. Modern Cosmetics. 8th ed. LC 74-8882. 465p. 1974. 52.00x (ISBN 0-412-10660-4, NO. 6225). 1975 (Pub. by Chapman & Hall). Routledge Chapman & Hall.

Pergamon Dictionary of Perfect Spelling. 2nd ed. C. Maxwell. LC 78-40291. 335p. 1978. pap. 7.25 (ISBN 0-08-022865-8). Pergamon.

Pergamon: Gesammelte Aufsaetze. (Pergamenische Forschungen Vol. 1). (Illus.). 222p. 1972. 62.40x (ISBN 3-11-001829-2). De Gruyter.

Pergolas, Arbours, Gazebos & Follies. David Stevens. (Illus.). 128p. 1988. 29.95 (ISBN 0-7063-6555-0, Pub. by Ward Lock). David & Charles.

Pergolas, Arbours, Gazebos & Follies. David Stevens. 128p. 1987. 50.00x (ISBN 0-317-69793-5, Pub. by Ward Lock Educ Co Ltd). State Mutual Bk.

Pergolesi Studies I. Ed. by Francesco Degrada. (Pergolesi Studies). 217p. (Eng. & Ital.). 1987. lib. bdg. 36.00 (ISBN 0-918728-79-7). Pendragon NY.

Perhaps. rev. ed. Laurence Craig-Green. (Illus.). 48p. 1984. pap. 5.95 (ISBN 0-916922-12-X). Poet Tree Pr.

Perhaps God. Ralph Wright. (Illus.). 80p. 1986. 6.50 (ISBN 0-8233-0411-6). Golden Quill.

Perhaps Love. Lindsay Armstrong. (Harlequin Romances Ser.). 192p. 1983. pap. 1.75 (ISBN 0-373-02582-3). Harlequin Bks.

Perhaps Women. Sherwood Anderson. LC 76-105301. 1970. Repr. of 1931 ed. 8.95x (ISBN 0-911858-05-9). Appel.

Peri Theias Kai Hieras Proseuches see Treatise on Prayer: An Explanation of the Services of the Orthodox Church.

Peribanez. Lope De Vega. Ed. by J. M. Lloyd. (Hispanic Classics Ser.). 200p. 1988. text ed. 49.95 (ISBN 0-85668-438-4, Pub. by Aris & Phillips UK); pap. text ed. 16.50 (ISBN 0-85668-439-2, Pub. by Aris & Phillips UK). Humanities.

Pericardial Disease. Ed. by P. S. Reddy et al. (Illus.). 390p. 1982. text ed. 73.00 (ISBN 0-686-82957-3). Raven.

Pericardial Diseases. Ed. by David Spodick. LC 76-41260. (Cardiovascular Clinics Ser: Vol. 7, No. 3). (Illus.). 297p. 1976. 32.00x (ISBN 0-8036-8090-2). Davis Co.

Pericardium. Ralph Shabetai. (Clinical Cardiology Monograph). 448p. 1981. 64.50 (ISBN 0-8089-1402-2, 794015). Grune.

Pericardium in Health & Disease. Noble O. Fowler. (Illus.). 384p. 1984. 47.50 (ISBN 0-87993-229-5). Futura Pub.

Pericles. Perry S. King. (World Leaders--Past & Present Ser.). (Illus.). 112p. (gr. 5 up). 1988. lib. bdg. 16.95 (ISBN 0-87754-547-2). Chelsea Hse.

Pericles. Ed. by A. L. Rowse. LC 87-14752. (Modern Text with Introduction). 118p. (Orig.). 1987. pap. text ed. 3.45 (ISBN 0-8191-3945-9). U Pr of Amer.

Pericles. 3rd ed. William Shakespeare. Ed. by F. D. Hoeniger. (Arden Shakespeare Ser.). 1963. 37.00x (ISBN 0-416-47570-1, NO. 2486); pap. 10.95 (ISBN 0-416-27850-7, NO. 2487). Routledge Chapman & Hall.

Pericles. William Shakespeare. Ed. by Philip Edwards. 1981. pap. 3.75 (ISBN 0-14-070729-8). Penguin.

Pericles. William Shakespeare. Ed. by James McManaway. (Shakespeare Ser.). 1966. pap. 3.50 (ISBN 0-14-071438-3, Pelican). Penguin.

Pericles: An Annotated Bibliography. Nancy Michael. LC 87-17295. (Shakespeare Bibliographies Ser.: No. 13). 289p. 1987. lib. bdg. 43.00 (ISBN 0-8240-9113-2). Garland pub.

Pericles & the Golden Age of Athens. Evelyn Abbot. 1891. 25.00 (ISBN 0-8274-3926-1). R West.

Pericles & the Golden Age of Athens. Evelyn Abbott. 59.95 (ISBN 0-8490-0813-1). Gordon Pr.

Pericles & the Golden Age of Athens. Evelyn Abbott. 379p. 1982. Repr. of 1891 ed. lib. bdg. 50.00 (ISBN 0-89984-014-0). Century Bookbindery.

Pericles & the Metaphysics of Political Leadership, 2 vols. Leonard Abbott. (Illus.). 387p. 1984. 247.50 (ISBN 0-89266-477-0). Am Classical Coll Pr.

Pericles' Citizenship Law of Four Fifty-One to Four Fifty B. C. Cynthia Patterson. 25.00 (ISBN 0-405-14046-0). Ayer Co Pubs.

Pericles, Cymbeline & Two Noble Kinsmen. William Shakespeare. Ed. by Ernest Schanzer & Richard Hosely. 1986. pap. 4.95 (ISBN 0-451-52042-4, Sig Classics). NAL.

Pericopsis Elata, (Afrormosia) P. Howland. 1979. 30.00x (ISBN 0-85074-049-5, Pub. by For Lib Comm England). State Mutual Bk.

Pericyclic Reactions. G. B. Gill & M. R. Willis. 1974. pap. 17.95x (ISBN 0-412-12490-4, NO. 6125, Pub. by Chapman & Hall). Routledge Chapman & Hall.

Pericyclic Reactions. Ed. by Alan P. Marchand & Roland E. Lehr. (Organic Chemistry Series). 1977. Vol. 1. 83.00 (ISBN 0-12-470501-4); Vol. 2. 95.00 (ISBN 0-12-470502-2). Acad Pr.

Pericyclic Reactions: A Mechanistic Study. S. M. Mukherji. 1980. 16.00x (ISBN 0-8364-0637-0, Pub. by Macmillan India). South Asia Bks.

Peridineen der Plankton-Expedition der Humboldt-Stiftung I: Allgemeiner Teil. F. Schuett. (Illus.). 1978. Repr. of 1895 ed. 60.00x (ISBN 3-7682-0806-0). Lubrecht & Cramer.

Peridiniens Parasites. E. Chatton. 1975. Repr. lib. bdg. 108.00x (ISBN 3-87429-100-6). Lubrecht & Cramer.

Peridontal Disease: Recognition, Interception & Perception. S. Cripps. 1984. text ed. 82.00 (ISBN 0-86715-118-8). Quint Pub Co.

Peridontal Diseases & Dentistry: Subject Analysis Index with Research Bibliography. Virgil D. Hathawaye. LC 88-47605. 150p. 1988. 34.50 (ISBN 0-88164-356-4); pap. 26.50 (ISBN 0-88164-357-2). ABBE Pubs Assn.

Peridontal Instrumentation: A Clinical Manual. Gordon Pattison & Anna Pattison. (Illus.). 1979. text ed. 29.95 (ISBN 0-87909-604-7). Appleton & Lange.

Peridontics: In the Tradition of Gottlieb & Orban. 6th ed. Grant et al. (Illus.). 1164p. 1987. 59.95 (ISBN 0-8016-2017-1). Mosby.

Peridontology & Its Origins up to 1980. Arthur J. Held. 240p. 1988. 52.00 (ISBN 0-8176-1955-0). Birkhauser.

Perigee Visual Dictionary of Signing: An A-to-Z Guide of over 1200 Signs of American Sign Language. Rod R. Butterworth. LC 83-9728. (Illus.). 416p. (Orig.). 1984. (G&D); pap. 9.95 (ISBN 0-399-50863-5). Putnam Pub Group.

Periglacial Geomorphology. Ed. by M. J. Clark. 450p. 1987. write for info. (ISBN 0-471-90981-5). Wiley.

Periglacial Geomorphology see Glacial & Periglacial Morphology.

Periglacial Processes & Environments. A. Washburn. 1973. 35.00 (ISBN 0-312-60095-X). St Martin.

Periglacial Processes & Landforms in Britain & Ireland. Ed. by John Boardman. (Illus.). 320p. 1987. 79.50 (ISBN 0-521-33250-8). Cambridge U Pr.

Perigord: French Edition-Regions of France. (Michelin Green Guides). pap. 12.95 (ISBN 2-06-003601-1). French & Eur.

Peril & a Hope: The Scientists' Movement in America, 1945-47. rev. ed. Alice Kimball Smith. 1971. pap. 6.95x (ISBN 0-262-69026-8). MIT Pr.

Peril at Blackstone. J. H. Rhodes. (YA) (gr. 7 up). 1984. 9.95 (ISBN 0-8034-8439-9, Avalon). Bouregy.

Peril at End House. Agatha Christie. 1982. pap. 3.50 (ISBN 0-671-61120-8). PB.

Peril at End House. Agatha Christie. (Popular Author Ser.). 281p. 1988. lib. bdg. 16.95x (ISBN 0-8161-4587-3, Large Print Bks). G K Hall.

Peril at Land's End. Patricia Bird. (Orig.). 1980. pap. 1.75 (ISBN 0-8439-8008-7, Tiara Bks). Leisure NY.

Peril at Sea. Jim Gibbs. (Illus.). 224p. 1986. pap. 19.95 (ISBN 0-88740-066-3). Schiffer.

Peril at Sea & Salvage: A Guide for Masters. 2nd ed. ICS Staff & OCIMF Staff. 1982. 63.00x (ISBN 0-317-61255-7, Pub. by Witherby & Co England). State Mutual Bk.

Peril of Faith. Martin L. Bard. 155p. (Orig.). 1982. pap. 5.00 (ISBN 0-910309-05-1). Am Atheist.

Peril on the Road. Judith A. Green. (Illus.). 220p. 1985. pap. text ed. 4.80 (ISBN 0-89061-427-X). Jamestown Pubs.

Perilous Balance: Poems. Arnold S. Stein. LC 45-4997. pap. 20.00 (ISBN 0-317-29478-4, 2055918). Bks Demand UMI.

Perilous Balance: The Tragic Genius of Swift, Johnson & Sterne. Walter B. Watkins. Repr. of 1939 ed. 29.00x (ISBN 0-403-03066-8). Somerset Pub.

Perilous Bridge: Helping Clients Through Mid-Life Transitions. Naomi Golan. 256p. 1986. 23.95x (ISBN 0-02-912090-X). Free Pr.

Perilous Castle. Patricia Laye. (Orig.). 1981. pap. 1.75 (ISBN 0-8439-8027-3, Tiara Bks). Leisure NY.

Perilous Decline of Cora Sline or Don't Touch My Tutu. Eddie Cope. (Illus.). 40p. (Orig.). 1985. pap. 2.75 (ISBN 0-88680-242-3). I E Clark.

Perilous Development: Child Raising & Identity Formation. E. James Anthony & Collette Chiland. (Yearbook of the International Association of Child Psychiatry & Allied Professions Ser.). 576p. 1988. 69.95 (ISBN 0-471-84984-7). Wiley.

Perilous Dreams. Andre Norton. (Science Fiction Ser.). 1987. pap. 2.95 (ISBN 0-88677-248-6). DAW Bks.

Perilous Gard. Elizabeth M. Pope. LC 73-21648. (Illus.). 272p. (gr. 6 up). 1974. 13.95 (ISBN 0-395-18512-2). HM.

Perilous Gard, No. 2. Elizabeth M. Pope. 240p. 1984. pap. 2.25 (ISBN 0-441-65956-X). Ace Bks.

Perilous Gold. Leonard Wibberley. LC 78-7450. 144p. (gr. 5 up). 1978. 9.95 (ISBN 0-374-35824-9). FS&G.

Perilous Hunt: Symbols in Hispanic & European Balladry. Edith R. Rogers. LC 79-4010. (Studies in Romance Languages: No. 22). 192p. 1980. 17.00 (ISBN 0-8131-1396-2). U Pr of Ky.

Perilous Journey: The Mennonite Brethren in Russia. John B. Toews. (Perspectives on Mennonite Life & Thought Ser.). 94p. (Orig.). 1988. pap. 9.95 (ISBN 0-919797-78-4). Kindred Pr.

Perilous Journey to the Top. Alida Thacher. LC 79-22159. (Quest, Adventure, Survival Ser.). (Illus.). 48p. (gr. 4-9). 1982. pap. 9.27 (ISBN 0-8172-2068-2). Raintree Pubs.

Perilous Journey to the Top. Alida Thacher. LC 79-22159. (Quest, Adventure, Survival Ser.). (Illus.). 48p. (gr. 4-8). 1980. PLB 15.33 (ISBN 0-8172-1573-5). Raintree Pubs.

Perilous Kisses. Mary Lupton. 1985. 9.95 (ISBN 0-8034-8547-6, Avalon). Bouregy.

Perilous Missions: Civil Air Transport & CIA Covert Operations in Asia. William M. Leary. LC 83-3554. (Illus.). 281p. 1984. text ed. 22.50 (ISBN 0-8173-0164-X). U of Ala Pr.

Perilous Presidency. Bernard Hirschhorn. (Social Studies Student Ser.). 212p. (gr. 7-12). 1979. PLB 10.97 (ISBN 0-8239-0418-0). Rosen Group.

Perilous Progress: Managing the Hazards of Technology. Robert W. Kates & Christoph Hohenemser. (Study in Science, Technology, & Public Policy). 460p. 1985. softcover 39.50x (ISBN 0-8133-7025-6). Westview.

Perilous Quest: Image, Myth, & Prophecy in the Narratives of Victor Hugo. Richard B. Grant. LC 68-20494. pap. 67.00 (ISBN 0-317-26759-0, 2023391). Bks Demand UMI.

Perilous Sea. Ed. by Clarissa M. Silitch. LC 84-51708. (Illus.). 176p. 1985. 12.95 (ISBN 0-89909-061-3); pap. 8.95 (ISBN 0-89909-065-6). Yankee Bks.

Perilous Sky: Evolution of United States Aviation Diplomacy Toward Latin America, 1919-1931. Wesley P. Newton. LC 77-84781. (Illus.). 1978. text ed. 15.00 (ISBN 0-87024-298-9). U of Miami Pr.

Perilous Statecraft. Michael Ledeen. 320p. 1989. 19.95 (ISBN 0-684-18994-1). Scribner.

Perilous Vision of John Wyclif. Louis B. Hall. LC 82-18890. 288p. 1983. lib. bdg. 23.95X (ISBN 0-8304-1006-6). Nelson-Hall.

Perils & Prospects of Southern Black Leadership: Gordon Blaine Hancock, 1884-1970. Raymond Gavins. LC 76-44090. pap. 57.80 (ISBN 0-317-55483-2, 2052209). Bks Demand UMI.

Perils of Cultism. J. C. Da Nobrega. 1980. 6.00 (ISBN 0-682-49453-4). Exposition-Phoenix.

Perils of Democracy. Herbert Agar. LC 66-11684. (Background Ser.). 95p. 1965. 10.95 (ISBN 0-8023-1001-X). Dufour.

Perils of Flight. J. Xaudaro. LC 78-24054. (Illus.). 1979. Repr. of 1911 ed. 8.95 (ISBN 0-8317-6810-X, Mayflower Bks). Smith Pubs.

Perils of Intensive Management Training & How to Avoid them. Robert E. Kaplan. (Technical Report Ser.: No. 19). 27p. 1981. pap. 10.00 (ISBN 0-912879-17-3). Ctr Creat Leader.

Perils of Patient Government: Professionals & Patients in a Chronic-Care Hospital. Joseph W. Lella. 248p. 1986. pap. 15.00x (ISBN 0-88920-197-8, Pub. by Wilfrid Laurier Canada). Humanities.

Perils of Patriotism: John Joseph Henry & the American Attack on Quebec, 1775. J. Samuel Walker. Ed. by Joseph E. Walker. LC 75-15439. (Lancaster County During the American Revolution Ser.). (Illus.). 56p. 1975. pap. 2.00 (ISBN 0-915010-08-9). Sutter House.

Perils of Penelope. Norman Stiles & Daniel Wilcox. (Illus.). (ps-4). 1973. Random.

Perils of Personal Computing. Edward Yourdon. LC 84-52806. (Illus.). 136p. (Orig.). 1985. pap. 14.95 (ISBN 0-917072-50-2, Yourdon). P-H.

Perils of Politeness. Hagop Baronian. Tr. by Jack Antreassian from Armenian. LC 83-2524. (Illus.). 160p. (Orig.). 1983. pap. 7.50 (ISBN 0-935102-10-8). Ashod Pr.

Perils of Professionalism. Donald B. Kraybill & Phyllis P. Good. LC 82-3052. 240p. (Orig.). 1982. pap. 9.95 (ISBN 0-8361-1997-5). Herald Pr.

Perils of Prosperity: Nineteen Fourteen to Nineteen Thirty Two. William E. Leuchtenburg. LC 58-5680. (History of America Civilization Ser). pap. 8.50x (ISBN 0-226-47369-4, CHAC12). U of Chicago Pr.

Perils of Regulation: A Market-Process Approach. Israel M. Kirzner. (LEC Occasional Paper). 1979. pap. 1.00 (ISBN 0-916770-09-5). Law & Econ U Miami.

Perils of the Ocean & Wilderness: Narrative of Shipwreck & Indian Captivity. John G. Shea. (Reprints in History Ser.). Repr. of 1856 ed. lib. bdg. 39.00x (ISBN 0-697-00057-5). Irvington.

Perils or Perspective Planning: Pahang Tenggara Revisited. Benjamin Higgins. (Working Papers Ser.: No. 79-15). 27p. 1979. pap. 6.00 (ISBN 0-686-78245-3, CRD028, UNCRD). UNIPUB.

Perimenopausal & Geriatric Gynecology. Hugh R. K. Barber. 640p. 60.00 (ISBN 0-02-305880-3). Macmillan.

Perimeter of Social Repair. Ed. by W. H. Armytage & John Peel. 1978. 58.00 (ISBN 0-12-062750-7). Acad Pr.

Perimeters. Charles Levendosky. LC 78-105508. (Wesleyan Poetry Program: Vol. 49). 1970. 17.00x (ISBN 0-8195-2049-7); pap. 8.95 (ISBN 0-8195-1049-1). Wesleyan U Pr.

Perimetric Standards & Perimetric Glossary. Ed. by International Council of Ophthalmology. 135p. 45.00 (ISBN 90-6193-161-4, Pub. by Junk Pubs Netherlands). Kluwer Academic.

Perimetric Standards & Perimetric Glossary. Ed. by International Council of Opthalmology. 1979. lib. bdg. 29.00 (ISBN 90-6193-600-4, Pub. by Junk Pubs Netherlands). Kluwer Academic.

Perimetry: Principles, Technique, & Interpretation. Carl Ellenberger, Jr. 128p. 1980. text ed. 27.00 (ISBN 0-89004-504-6). Raven.

Perimetry: With & Without Automation. 2nd ed. Anderson. 1986. 65.00 (ISBN 0-8016-0208-4). Mosby.

Perinatal & Infant Brain Imaging. Rumack. 1984. 59.50 (ISBN 0-8151-7458-6). Year Bk Med.

Perinatal Anesthesia. Ed. by John Scanlon. (Contemporary Issues in Fetal & Neonatal Medicine Ser.). 300p. 1985. text ed. 35.00 (ISBN 0-86542-022-X). Blackwell Sci.

Perinatal Asphyxia. Alberto Lacoius-Petruccelli. 188p. 1987. 35.00x (ISBN 0-306-42358-8, Plenum Pr). Plenum Pub.

Perinatal Brain Damage. Pape & Wigglesworth. 1986. 35.00 (ISBN 0-8016-3787-2). Mosby.

Perinatal Brain Lesions. Ed. by Karen Pape & Jonathan Wigglesworth. (Contemporary Issues in Fetal & Neonatal Medicine Ser.: Vol. 5). (Illus.). 288p. 1988. 45.00. Blackwell Sci.

Perinatal Cardiovascular Function. Ed. by Norman Gootman & Phyllis M. Gootman. (Illus.). 408p. 1983. 75.00 (ISBN 0-8247-1671-X). Dekker.

Perinatal Care & Gestosis. Ed. by M. Suzuki & N. Furuhashi. (International Congress Ser.: No. 686). 536p. 1986. 152.00 (ISBN 0-444-80736-5, Excerpta Medica). Elsevier.

Perinatal Care Delivery Systems: Description & Evaluation in European Community Countries. Ed. by Monique Kaminski. (CEC Health Services Research Ser.: No. 1). (Illus.). 350p. 1987. 59.00 (ISBN 0-19-261610-2). Oxford U Pr.

Perinatal Coagulation. William E. Hathaway & J. Bonnar. (Monographs in Neonatology). 256p. 1978. 44.50 (ISBN 0-8089-1119-8, 791935). Grune.

Perinatal Development: A Psychobiological Perspective. Ed. by Norman A. Krasnegor et al. (Behavioral Biology Ser.). 448p. 1987. 55.00 (ISBN 0-12-445910-2); pap. 24.95 (ISBN 0-12-445911-0). Acad Pr.

Perinatal Development of the Heart & Lung. Ed. by J. Lipshitz et al. LC 86-30529. (Research in Perinatal Medicine Ser.: No. V). 1987. 50.50x (ISBN 0-916859-38-X). Perinatology.

Perinatal Endocrinology. Ed. by E. Albrecht & G. Pepe. LC 85-25821. (Research in Perinatal Medicine Ser.: IV). (Illus.). 311p. 1985. 50.50x (ISBN 0-916859-11-8). Perinatology.

Perinatal Endocrinology & Metabolism. Ed. by J. R. Girard. (Journal Biology of the Neonate: Vol. 48, No. 4, 1985). (Illus.). 76p. 1985. pap. 29.50 (ISBN 3-8055-4235-6). S Karger.

Perinatal Epidemiology. Michael B. Bracken. (Illus.). 1984. 55.00x (ISBN 0-19-503389-2). Oxford U Pr.

Perinatal Events & Brain Damage in Surviving Children. Ed. by F. Kubli et al. xviii, 336p. 1987. 73.00 (ISBN 0-387-18111-3). Springer-Verlag.

Perinatal Genetics: Diagnosis & Treatment. Ian H. Porter et al. (Birth Defects Institute Symposia Ser.). 1986. 45.00 (ISBN 0-12-562855-2). Acad Pr.

Perinatal Health Services in Europe: Searching for Better Childbirth. Ed. by J. M. Phaff. 224p. 1986. 34.50 (ISBN 0-7099-3666-4, Pub. by Croom Helm Ltd). Routledge Chapman & Hall.

Perinatal Infections. Ciba Foundation Staff. (Ciba Symposia Ser.: No. 77). 1980. 56.25 (ISBN 0-444-90158-2). Elsevier.

Perinatal Infections. Ciba Foundation Staff. LC 80-23631. (Ciba Foundation Symposium, New Ser.: 77). pap. 76.00 (ISBN 0-317-29745-7, 2022196). Bks Demand UMI.

Perinatal Medicine. Ed. by J. Clinch. 1985. lib. bdg. 73.00 (ISBN 0-85200-908-9, Pub. by MTP England). Kluwer Academic.

Perinatal Medicine. Ed. by Johan Gentz et al. LC 83-2171. 432p. 1983. 44.95 (ISBN 0-275-91431-3, C1431). Praeger.

Perinatal Medicine, 2 Vols. M. L. Rathi & S. Kumar. 1982. Vol. 1. text ed. 35.00 (ISBN 0-07-051204-3); Vol. 2. text ed. 39.50 (ISBN 0-07-051208-6). McGraw.

Perinatal Medicine: Clinical & Biochemical Aspects, Vol. 1. Ed. by Manohar Rathi & Sudhir Kumar. LC 79-28251. (Illus.). 207p. 1980. text ed. 59.95 (ISBN 0-89116-180-5). Hemisphere Pub.

Perinatal Medicine: Clinical & Biochemical Aspects, Vol. 2. Ed. by Manohar Rathi & Sudhir Kumar. LC 81-13379. (Illus.). 237p. 1982. text ed. 61.95 (ISBN 0-89116-181-3). Hemisphere Pub.

Perinatal Medicine: Clinical & Biochemical Aspects of the Evaluation, Diagnosis & Management of the Fetus & Newborn. Ed. by S. Kumar & M. Rathi. LC 78-40219. 1978. 69.00 (ISBN 0-08-021517-3). Pergamon.

Perinatal Medicine: Problems & Controversies. Ed. by G. C. Di Renzo & D. F. Hawkins. 237p. 1986. text ed. 47.00 (ISBN 8-88503-747-X). Raven.

Perinatal Medicine: Proceedings. Congress on Perinatal Medicine, 2nd European, London, 1970. Ed. by P. J. Huntingford et al. 1971. 53.50 (ISBN 3-8055-1224-4). S Karger.

Perinatal Medicine Today: Proceedings. Ed. by Bruce K. Young. LC 80-17343. (Progress in Clinical & Biological Research Ser.: Vol. 44). 244p. 1980. 31.00 (ISBN 0-8451-0044-0). A R Liss.

Perinatal-Neonatal Nursing: A Clinical Handbook. Diane Angelini et al. 449p. 1986. text ed. 37.50 (ISBN 0-86542-020-3). Blackwell Sci.

Perinatal Nephrology. Ed. by J. P. Guignard. (Journal: Biology of the Neonate Ser.: Vol. 53, No. 4, 1987). (Illus.). 80p. 1988. pap. 28.75 (ISBN 3-8055-4798-6). S Karger.

Perinatal Neurology & Neurosurgery. Ed. by Richard A. Thompson et al. LC 84-18340. 218p. 1985. text ed. 40.00 (ISBN 0-89335-216-0). PMA Pub Corp.

Perinatal Nursing: Care of the High Risk Infant. Janice Ouimette. 461p. 1986. 32.50 (ISBN 0-86720-356-0). Jones & Bartlett.

Perinatal Nutrition. Ed. by B. S. Linblad. (Bristol-Myers Nutrition Symposia Ser.: No. 6). 394p. 1988. 65.00 (ISBN 0-12-450285-7). Acad Pr.

Perinatal Parental Behavior: Nursing Research & Implications for Newborn Health. Regina P. Lederman et al. LC 81-15598. (Birth Defects: Original Article Ser.: Vol. 17, No. 6). 318p. 1981. 51.00 (ISBN 0-8451-1045-4). A R Liss.

Perinatal Pathology. Jonathan S. Wigglesworth. (Major Problems in Pathology Ser.: Vol. 15). (Illus.). 495p. 1984. 68.00 (ISBN 0-7216-9338-5). Saunders.

Perinatal Physiology. Ed. by Uwe Stave. LC 77-12596. (Illus.). 874p. 1978. 95.00x (ISBN 0-306-30999-8, Plenum Pr). Plenum Pub.

Perinatal Retinal Haemorrhages: Morphology, Aetiology & Significance. B. von Barsewisch. (Illus.). 1979. 42.00 (ISBN 0-387-09167-X). Springer-Verlag.

Perinatal Risk & Newborn Behavior. Ed. by Lewis P. Lipsitt & Tiffany M. Field. LC 82-8909. 208p. 1982. text ed. 36.50 (ISBN 0-89391-123-2). Ablex Pub.

Perinatologie. Ed. by E. Rossi. (Paediatrische Fortbildungskurse fuer die Praxis: Band 41). 200p. 1975. 52.75 (ISBN 3-8055-2115-4). S Karger.

Perinatology Case Studies. 2nd ed. Alvin Langer & Leslie Iffy. (Case Study Ser.: Vol. 32). 1985. pap. text ed. 47.50 (ISBN 0-87488-368-7). Med Exam.

Period. rev. ed. JoAnn Gardner-Loulan et al. LC 81-13125. (Illus.). 104p. (ps-5). 1981. pap. 6.00 (ISBN 0-912078-69-3). Volcano Pr.

Period & Place: Research Methods in Historical Geography. Ed. by Alan R. Baker & Mark Billinge. LC 81-12266. (Cambridge Studies in Historical Geography: No. 1). (Illus.). 375p. 1982. Cambridge U Pr.

Period Costume for Stage & Screen: Patterns for Women's Dress, 1500-1900. Jean Hunnisett. (Illus.). 176p. 1987. pap. text ed. 25.00x (ISBN 0-7135-2660-2, Pub. by Bell & Hyman). Drama Bk.

Period Details: A Sourcebook for House Restoration. Martin Miller & Judith Miller. (Illus.). 192p. 1987. 27.50 (ISBN 0-517-56514-5). Crown.

Period Growth & Withdrawal Tables for Savings Account. Ed. by Financial Publishing Co. Staff. 132p. 1986. pap. 13.25 (ISBN 0-87600-150-9). Finan Pub.

Period Houses & Their Details. Amery. 1987. pap. 39.95 (ISBN 0-85139-515-5). Van Nos Reinhold.

Period of Adjustment see Theatre of Tennessee Williams.

Period of Confinement. Moira Crone. LC 85-30013. 336p. 1986. 18.95 (ISBN 0-399-13136-1). Putnam Pub Group.

Period of Confinement. Moira Crone. LC 86-46232. 304p. 1987. pap. 6.95 (ISBN 0-06-097108-8, PL 7108, PL). Har-Row.

Period Patterns. Lucy Barton & Doris Edson. (Illus.). 1942. 9.50 (ISBN 0-87440-003-1). Baker's Plays.

Period Piece. Gwen Raverat. (Illus.). 288p. 1976. pap. 3.95 (ISBN 0-393-00822-3). Norton.

Period, Question Mark, Exclamation Mark. Barbara Gregorich. (Horizons II Ser.). (Illus.). 24p. (gr. 3-4). 1980. wkbk. 2.50 (ISBN 0-89403-592-4). EDC.

Period Style for the Theatre. 2nd ed. Russell. 1987. 40.95 (ISBN 0-205-10488-6, Pub. by Longwood Div). Allyn.

Periode Contemporaine (du XVIIIe Siecle a nos Jours) see Histoire du Catholicisme en France.

Periodic, Large Doses of Vitamin A for the Prevention of Vitamin A Deficiency & Xerophthalmia: A Summary of Experiences. Keith P. West, Jr. & Alfred Sommer. (Illus.). 44p. (Orig.). 1984. pap. text ed. 3.50 (ISBN 0-935368-43-4). Nutrition Found.

Periodic Markets, Urbanization, & Regional Planning: A Case Study from Western Kenya. R. A. Obudho & P. P. Waller. LC 75-23867. (Contributions in Afro-American & African Studies: No. 22). (Illus.). 1976. lib. bdg. 36.95 (ISBN 0-8371-8375-8, OPM/). Greenwood.

Periodic Optimization: Proceedings of the CISM, Department of Automation & Information, 1972, 2 vols. CISM (International Center for Mechanical Sciences), Department of Automation & Information Staff. Ed. by A. Marzollo. (CISM Pubns. Ser.: No. 135). (Illus.). 532p. 1973. Set. pap. 50.70 (ISBN 0-387-81135-4). Springer-Verlag.

Periodic Orbits, Stability & Resonances: Proceedings. Symposium, University of Sao Paulo, 1969. Ed. by G. E. Giacaglia. LC 74-124848. 530p. 1970. lib. bdg. 50.00 (ISBN 90-277-0170-9, Pub. by Reidel Holland). Kluwer Academic.

Periodic Screening for Breast Cancer: The Health Insurance Plan Project & Its Sequelae, 1963-1986. Sam Shapiro et al. LC 88-9457. (Contemporary Medicine & Public Health Ser.). 224p. 1988. text ed. 35.00x (ISBN 0-8018-3689-1). Johns Hopkins.

Periodic Solutions of Perturbed Second-Order Autonomous Equations. Warren S. Loud. LC 52-42839. (Memoirs: No. 47). 133p. 1964. pap. 12.00 (ISBN 0-8218-1247-5, MEMO-47). Am Math.

Periodic Solutions of X Double Prime Plus C Times X Plus G of (X) Equals F of T. Warren S. Loud. LC 52-42839. (Memoirs: No. 31). 58p. 1966. pap. 11.00 (ISBN 0-8218-1231-9, MEMO-31). Am Math.

Periodic Table. Primo Levi. Tr. by Raymond Rosenthal from Ital. LC 84-5453. 160p. 1984. 16.95 (ISBN 0-8052-3929-4). Schocken.

Periodic Table. Primo Levi. Tr. by Raymond Rosenthal. 236p. 1986. pap. 7.95 (ISBN 0-8052-0811-9). Schocken.

Periodic Table of Elements. 2nd ed. R. J. Puddephatt & P. K. Monaghan. (Chemistry Ser.: No. 32). (Illus.). 100p. 1986. 27.50 (ISBN 0-19-855515-6); pap. 11.95 (ISBN 0-19-855516-4). Oxford U Pr.

Periodic Table with Nuclides & Reference Data. K. Yoshihara et al. (Illus.). 490p. 1985. pap. 80.00 (ISBN 0-387-15001-3). Springer-Verlag.

Periodical & Monographic Index to the Literature on the Gospels & Acts Based on the Files of Ecole Biblique in Jerusalem. LC 78-27276. (Bibliographia Tripotamopolitana: No.3). 1971. 12.00x (ISBN 0-931222-02-8). Pitts Theolog.

Periodical Classes. Harvard University Library Staff. LC 68-14152. (Widener Library Shelflist Ser: No. 15). 1968. 25.00x (ISBN 0-674-66300-4). Harvard U Pr.

Periodical Directories & Bibliographies. Ed. by Gary C. Tarbert. 1986. 60.00x (ISBN 0-8103-1474-6). Gale.

Periodical Essayist of the Eighteenth Century. George S. Marr. LC 76-93249. 264p. 1970. Repr. of 1923 ed. 30.00x (ISBN 0-87753-026-2). Phaeton.

Periodical Essayists of the Eighteenth Century. George S. Marr. LC 74-22089. 1974. Repr. of 1923 ed. lib. bdg. 39.00 (ISBN 0-8414-5978-9). Folcroft.

Periodical Essayists of the Eighteenth Century. George S. Marr. LC 77-99261. (English Book Trade). Repr. of 1923 ed. 27.50x (ISBN 0-678-00726-8). Kelley.

Periodical Essays of the Eighteenth Century. facsimile ed. Ed. by George Carver. LC 70-99621. (Essay Index Reprint Ser.). 1930. 25.50 (ISBN 0-8369-1555-0). Ayer Co Pubs.

Periodical Guide for Computerists, 1982: Annual Since 1975-76. Ellen Levine. 70p. (Orig.). 1982. pap. 15.95 (ISBN 0-686-40864-0). Applegate Comp Ent.

Periodical Indexes in the Social Sciences & Humanities: A Subject Guide. Lois A. Harzfeld. LC 78-5230. 188p. 1978. lib. bdg. 16.50 (ISBN 0-8108-1133-2). Scarecrow.

Periodical Letter on the Principles of the "Equity Movement". Josiah Warren. Bd. with Modern Times. Henry Edgar. LC 78-22601. (Free Love in America). Repr. of 1885 ed. 28.50 (ISBN 0-404-60975-9). AMS Pr.

Periodical Literature of Iceland Down to Year 1874, an Historical Sketch. Halldor Hermannsson. LC 19-7907. (Islandica Ser.: Vol. 11). 1918. 13.00 (ISBN 0-527-00341-7). Kraus Repr.

Periodical Literature on United States Cities: A Bibliography & Subject Guide. Barbara S. Shearer & Benjamin F. Shearer. LC 82-24211. xi, 574p. 1983. lib. bdg. 56.95 (ISBN 0-313-23511-2, SPL/). Greenwood.

Periodical Publishing in Wisconsin: Proceedings. Conference on Periodical Publishing in Wisconsin, May 11-12, 1978 et al. Ed. by Barbara J. Arnold & Jack A. Clarke. 233p. 1980. pap. 6.50 (ISBN 0-936442-08-5). U Wis Sch Lib.

Periodical Scholarship on Islamic Architecture Published 1973-1983: A Bibliography. Carole Cable. (Architecture Ser. Bibliography A-1307). 7p. 1985. pap. 2.00 (ISBN 0-89028-237-4). Vance Biblios.

Periodical Title Abbreviations: By Abbreviation, Vol. 1. 6th ed. Ed. by Leland G. Alkire. 872p. 1987. 165.00x (ISBN 0-8103-4367-3). Gale.

Periodical Title Abbreviations: By Title. 6th ed. Ed. by Leland G. Alkire. 872p. 1987. 165.00x (ISBN 0-8103-4368-1). Gale.

Periodicals & Their Guides, Vol. 4. Denis Grogan. (Grogan's Case Studies in Reference Work). 130p. 1988. 19.95x (ISBN 0-85157-414-9, B414-9, Pub. by C Bingley Ltd London). ALA.

Periodicals Current in Mainland China Held by the Science Reference Library. 2nd ed. R. Kyang. 91p. (Orig.). 1984. pap. 6.75 (ISBN 0-7123-0711-7, Pub. by British Lib). Longwood Pub Group.

Periodicals for School Media Programs. Selma K. Richardson. LC 77-25069. pap. 104.80 (ISBN 0-317-26568-7, 2023952). Bks Demand UMI.

Periodicals from Africa: A Bibliography & Union List of Periodicals Published in Africa, First Supplement. Ed. by David Blake & Carole Travis. 1984. lib. bdg. 66.00 (ISBN 0-8161-8525-5, Hall Reference). G K Hall.

Periodicals Holdings List of the American Hospital Association Resource Center. LC 86-17502. 115p. 1986. pap. text ed. 37.50 (ISBN 0-87258-445-3, 121053). Am Hospital.

Periodicals in College Libraries. Compiled by Jamie W. Hastreiter. (CLIP Note Ser.: No. 8). 116p. 1987. pap. text ed. 17.00x (ISBN 0-8389-7143-1). Ala.

Periodicals, Newsletters & Indexes in E. S. Bird Library & Clearinghouse of Resources for Educators of Adults. A. Charters & D. Holmwood. (MS Ser.: No. 8). 1978. 3.50 (ISBN 0-686-63883-2, MSS 8). Syracuse U Cont Ed.

Periodicals of American Transcendentalism. Clarence Gohdes. LC 77-136380. Repr. of 1931 ed. 26.00 (ISBN 0-404-02854-3). AMS Pr.

Periodicals of American Transcendentalism. Clarence L. Gohdes. LC 76-107803. (Select Bibliographies Reprint Ser). 1931. 19.00 (ISBN 0-8369-5206-5). Ayer Co Pubs.

Periodicals of Public Interest Organizations: A Citizen's Guide. Commission for the Advancement of Public Interest Organizations. LC 79-88697. (Illus.). 1982. pap. 5.00 (ISBN 0-9602744-1-3). Comm Adv Public Interest.

Periodicals of the Mid-West & West. Ed. by Carolyn Mueller. 1986. 35.00 (ISBN 0-87650-210-9). Pierian.

Periodicals on Agriculture Held by the Science Reference Library: Agricultural Research & Industry, Pt. 1. G. Jackson. 83p. (Orig.). 1981. pap. 7.50 (ISBN 0-902914-66-9, Pub. by British Lib). Longwood Pub Group.

Periodicals on Chemistry Held by the Science Reference Library. C. L. De Hamel. 73p. (Orig.). 1982. pap. 7.50 (ISBN 0-7123-0700-1, Pub. by British Lib). Longwood Pub Group.

Periodismo Literario De Jorge Manach. 1st ed. Jorge L. Marti. LC 76-27678. (Coleccion Mente y Palabra Ser.). 1976. 6.00 (ISBN 0-8477-0542-0); pap. 5.00 (ISBN 0-8477-0543-9). U of PR Pr.

Periodo: Libro Para Chicas Sobre la Menstruacion. JoAnn Gardner-Loulan et al. Tr. by Francisca M. Schneider. LC 82-10864. (Illus.). 96p. (Span.). (ps-5). 1986. pap. 7.00 (ISBN 0-912078-71-5). Volcano Pr.

Periodoniken. R. Knab. 83p. 1980. 12.50 (ISBN 0-89005-330-8). Ares.

Periodontal & Prosthetic Management for Advanced Cases. Marvin M. Rosenberg et al. (Illus.). 600p. 1988. text ed. write for info. (ISBN 0-86715-162-5, 1625). Quint Pub Co.

Periodontal Disease among Youths 12-17 Years, U. S. Marcus J. Sanchez. LC 74-4037. (Data from the Health Examination Survey Ser.11: No. 141). 60p. 1974. pap. text ed. 1.50 (ISBN 0-8406-0007-0). Natl Ctr Health Stats.

Periodontal Disease: Basic Phenomena, Clinical Management, & Occlusal & Restorative Interrelationships. 2nd ed. Saul Schluger et al. LC 87-3930. (Illus.). 750p. 1989. text ed. price not set (ISBN 0-8121-1084-6). Lea & Febiger.

Periodontal Disease: Immunological Factors, I. Irving Glickman et al. LC 72-10934. (Illus.). 220p. 1973. text ed. 29.50x (ISBN 0-8422-7061-2). Irvington.

Periodontal Disease: Immunological Factors, II. L. Ivanyi et al. LC 72-10934. (Illus.). 193p. 1973. text ed. 29.50x (ISBN 0-8422-7069-8). Irvington.

Periodontal Ligament in Health & Disease. Ed. by B. K. Berkovitz et al. (Illus.). 472p. 1982. pap. text ed. 65.00 (ISBN 0-08-024411-4). Pergamon.

Periodontal Prosthesis. Saul M. Hirshberg. (Illus.). 272p. 1977. photocopy ed. 37.00x (ISBN 0-398-03605-5). C C Thomas.

Periodontal Surgery: Biological Basis & Technique. photocopy ed. S. Sigmund Stahl. (Illus.). 480p. 1976. 61.25 (ISBN 0-398-03431-1). C C Thomas.

Periodontal Therapy. 6th ed. Henry M. Goldman & D. Walter Cohen. LC 79-13055. (Illus.). 1230p. 1979. cloth 54.95 (ISBN 0-8016-1875-4). Mosby.

Periodontic Syllabus. Ed. by Peter Fedi, Jr. LC 84-27787. (Illus.). 190p. 1985. pap. 23.50 (ISBN 0-8121-0982-1). Lea & Febiger.

Periodontics for the Dental Hygienist. 4th ed. Don L. Allen et al. LC 86-7305. (Illus.). 286p. 1987. 24.95 (ISBN 0-8121-1047-1). Lea & Febiger.

Periodontics in General Practice. William C. Hurt. (Illus.). 528p. 1976. photocopy ed. 66.00x (ISBN 0-398-03495-8). C C Thomas.

Periodontitis in Man & Other Animals. R. C. Page & H. E. Schroeder. (Illus.). x, 330p. 1982. 99.50 (ISBN 3-8055-2479-X). S Karger.

Periodontium. H. E. Schroeder. (Handbook of Microscopic Anatomy Ser.: Vol. 5; Pt. 5). (Illus.). 440p. 1986. 275.00 (ISBN 0-387-16604-1). Springer-Verlag.

Periodontology. 22.00 (ISBN 0-318-19105-9). Am Dental Hygienists.

Periodontology & Periodontics. Sigurd P. Ramfjord & Major M. Ash, Jr. LC 76-50150. pap. 160.00 (ISBN 0-317-26420-6, 2024972). Bks Demand UMI.

Periodontology & Periodontics: Modern Theory & Practice. rev. ed. Sigurd P. Ramfjord & M. Ash, Jr. 1989. 49.50 (ISBN 0-912791-40-3). Ishiyaku Euro.

Periodontology Today. Ed. by B. Guggenheim. (Illus.). viii, 312p. 1988. pap. 80.00 (ISBN 3-8055-4843-5). S Karger.

Periods in German Literature: A Symposium Vol. I: Problems of Periods & Movements from Baroque to Contemporary Literature. Ed. by J. M. Ritchie. 320p. (Orig.). 1966. pap. 16.95 (ISBN 0-85496-032-5, Pub. by Berg Pubs). St Martin.

Periods in German Literature: A Symposium Vol. 2: Texts & Contexts. Ed. by J. M. Richie. 264p. 1969. 29.95 (ISBN 0-85496-033-3, Pub. by Berg Pubs). St Martin.

Periods in Highland History. I. F. Grant & Hugh Cheape. LC 87-62815. (Illus.). 320p. 1988. 30.00 (ISBN 0-85683-057-7, Pub. by Shepheard-Walwyn UK). Dufour.

Periods of Hecke Characters. N. Schappacher. (Lecture Notes in Mathematics Ser.: Vol. 1301). xv, 160p. 1988. pap. 17.30 (ISBN 0-387-18915-7). Springer-Verlag.

Periods of Hilbert Modular Surfaces. Takayuki Oda. (Progress in Mathematics Ser.: Vol. 19). 1981. text ed. 16.95x (ISBN 0-8176-3084-8). Birkhauser.

Periods: Selected Writings, 1972-1987, No. 23. Phil Demise & Phil Smith. (Illus.). 472p. (Orig.). 1988. pap. 15.00 (ISBN 0-943783-00-3). Gegenschein.

Perioperative Assessment in Vascular Surgery. Flanigan. (Science & Practice of Surgery Ser.). 331p. 1986. 89.75 (ISBN 0-8247-7632-1). Dekker.

Perioperative Cardiac Dysfunction, Vol. 3. Ed. by Joe R. Utley. (Cardiothoracic Surgery Ser.). 250p. 1985. 57.95 (ISBN 0-683-08503-4). Williams & Wilkins.

Perioperative Chemotherapy. Ed. by U. Metzger et al. (Recent Results in Cancer Research Ser.: Vol. 98). (Illus.). 250p. 1985. 54.00 (ISBN 0-387-15124-9). Springer-Verlag.

Perioperative Management in Cardiothoracic Surgery. Benson B. Roe. 247p. 1980. text ed. 30.00 (ISBN 0-316-75376-9). Little.

Perioperative Patient Care: The Nursing Perspective. 2nd ed. Ed. by Julia A. Kneedler & Gwen H. Dodge. (Illus.). 570p. 1987. text ed. 44.95 (ISBN 0-86542-033-5). Blackwell Sci.

Peripatetic Astronomer: The Life of Charles Piazzi Smyth. Hermann Bruck & Mary Bruck. 264p. 1988. 80.00x (ISBN 0-85274-420-X, A Hilger UK). Taylor & Francis.

Peripatetic Diabetic: Good Health, Good Times, & Good Food for the Diabetic Who Wants to Have it All. June Biermann & Barbara Toohey. LC 83-24336. 264p. 1984. o. p. 14.95 (ISBN 0-87477-309-1); pap. 7.95 (ISBN 0-87477-308-3). J P Tarcher.

Peripatetic Saying: The Problem of the Thrice-Told Tale in the Canon of Talmudic Literature. Jacob Neusner. (Brown Judaic Studies: No. 89). 208p. 1985. 18.95 (ISBN 0-89130-830-X, 14 00 89); pap. 15.95 (ISBN 0-89130-831-8). Scholars Pr GA.

Peripatetics, Jonathan Greene. 48p. 1978. 15.00 (ISBN 0-916562-18-2); pap. 4.00 (ISBN 0-916562-14-X). Truck Pr.

Peripatos Uber das Greisenalter. Adolf Dyroff. 1939. pap. 12.00 (ISBN 0-384-13655-9). Johnson Repr.

Peripheral American: Destiny for the Coming Century. Matthew Carney. LC 80-68315. 278p. 1981. 14.95 (ISBN 0-937444-00-6); pap. 9.95 (ISBN 0-937444-01-4). Caislan Pr.

Peripheral Americans. Frank J. Cavaioli & Salvatore J. Lagumina. LC 82-14019. 268p. 1983. pap. 10.50 (ISBN 0-89874-542-X). Krieger.

Peripheral Array Processors. Ed. by Walter J. Karplus. (Simulation Ser.: Vol. 11, No. 1). 170p. 1982. 36.00 (ISBN 0-686-38787-2). Soc Computer Sim.

Peripheral Array Processors, Vol. 14, No. 2. Kaplus. (SCS Series). 1984. 36.00 (ISBN 0-317-17125-9). Soc Computer Sim.

Peripheral Arterial Chemoreceptors. Ed. by David J. Pallot. 1983. 45.00x (ISBN 0-19-520440-9). Oxford U Pr.

Peripheral Arterial Disease. 3rd ed. Max R. Gaspar & Wiley F. Barker. (Major Problems in Clinical Surgery Ser.: Vol. 4). (Illus.). 528p. 1981. text ed. write for info. (ISBN 0-7216-4054-0). Saunders.

Peripheral Arterial Diseases: Medical & Surgical Problems. Ed. by S. Stipa & A. Cavallaro. (Serono Symposia Ser.: No. 44). 1982. 93.00 (ISBN 0-12-671460-6). Acad Pr.

Peripheral Auditory Mechanisms. Ed. by J. B. Allen et al. (Lecture Notes in Biomathematics Ser.: Vol. 64). 400p. 1986. pap. 32.80 (ISBN 0-387-16095-7). Springer-Verlag.

Peripheral Campaigns & the Principles of War: The British Experience, 1914-1918. Charles T. Kamps. 147p. 1982. 20.00x (ISBN 0-89126-108-7). MA-AH Pub.

Peripheral Capitalism: The Transformation of Antigua in Postcolonial Caribbean Society. Paget Henry. (Latin America Today Ser.). (Illus.). 297p. 1984. 28.95 (ISBN 0-87855-490-4). Transaction Bks.

Peripheral Circulation. Ed. by S. Hunyor et al. (International Congress Ser.: No. 630). 300p. 1985. 99.50 (ISBN 0-444-80638-5, Excerpta Medica). Elsevier.

Peripheral Circulations. Ed. by Robert Zelis. LC 75-22237. (Clinical Cardiology Monographs). (Illus.). 440p. 1975. 84.50 (ISBN 0-8089-0890-1, 794962). Grune.

Peripheral Dopaminergic Receptors: Proceedings of Satellite Symposium, 7th International Congress of Pharmacology, Strasbourg, July 1978. Ed. by J. Imbs & J. Schwartz. LC 79-40355. (Advances in the Biosciences Ser.). (Illus.). 400p. 1979. 79.00 (ISBN 0-08-023189-6). Pergamon.

Peripheral Entrapment Neuropathies. rev. ed. Harvey P. Kopell & Walter A. Thompson. LC 76-5448. 198p. 1976. 19.50 (ISBN 0-88275-214-6). Krieger.

Peripheral Lymph: Formation & Immune Function. Waldemar L. Olszewski. 176p. 1985. 72.00 (ISBN 0-8493-6137-0). CRC Pr.

Peripheral Manipulation. 2nd ed. G. D. Maitland. (Illus.). 350p. 1977. pap. text ed. 29.95 (ISBN 0-407-35672-X). Butterworth.

Peripheral Metabolism of Thyroxine. U. Loos & L. Wartofsky. (Illus.). 140p. 1984. pap. 39.95 (ISBN 0-86577-174-X). Thieme Med Pubs.

Peripheral Nerve. Ed. by D. H. Landon. 1976. 86.00x (ISBN 0-412-11740-1, NO. 6173, Pub. by Chapman & Hall). Routledge Chapman & Hall.

Peripheral Nerve Block. F. L. Jenkner. LC 77-8317. (Illus.). 1977. 19.00 (ISBN 0-387-81426-4). Springer-Verlag.

Peripheral Nerve Disorders. Ed. by R. W. Gilliatt & A. K. Asbury. (Butterworth International Medical Reviews Neurology Ser.: Vol. 4). 320p. 1984. text ed. 55.00 (ISBN 0-407-02297-X). Butterworth.

Peripheral Nerve Injuries: Medical Subject Analysis with Reference Bibliography. Paul O. Parker. LC 85-48078. 1987. 34.50 (ISBN 0-88164-426-9); pap. 26.50 (ISBN 0-88164-427-7). ABBE Pubs Assn.

Peripheral Nerve Surgery. Julia K. Terzis. 1986. write for info. (ISBN 0-7216-1268-7). Saunders.

Peripheral Nervous System: Structure, Function, & Clinical Correlations. Lawrence J. Mathers, Jr. (Illus.). 227p. 1985. pap. text ed. 21.95 (ISBN 0-409-90074-5). Butterworth.

Peripheral Neuroendocrine Interaction. Ed. by R. E. Coupland & W. G. Forssmann. (Illus.). 1978. pap. 51.00 (ISBN 0-387-08779-6). Springer-Verlag.

Peripheral Neuropathy, 2 Vols. 2nd ed. Peter J. Dyck et al. (Illus.). 2491p. 1984. Two Vol. Set. 260.00 (ISBN 0-7216-3275-0); Vol. 1. 135.00 (ISBN 0-7216-3273-4); Vol. 2. 135.00 (ISBN 0-7216-3274-2). Saunders.

Peripheral Neuropathy: Proceedings of the International Symposium on Peripheral Neuropathy, Nagoya, 20-22 October 1983. Ed. by I. Sobue. (International Congress Ser.: No. 662). 442p. 1984. 169.00 (ISBN 0-444-80621-0, Excerpta Medica). Elsevier.

Peripheral Retina in Profile. Norman Byer. (Illus.). 159p. 1982. incl. 240 stereo slides (color) with stereo viewer & cassette (7 languages). 295.00 (ISBN 0-9609428-0-7). Criterion Pr.

Peripheral Vascular Diseases: Current Research & Clinical Applications. Ed. by Donald E. Strandness et al. 512p. 1987. 49.50 (ISBN 0-8089-1846-X, 794381). Grune.

Peripheral Visions. Gloria Pierce. LC 82-80581. (Illus.). 64p. (Orig.). 1982. pap. 4.95 (ISBN 0-943148-00-6). Nikki Pr.

Peripheral Worker. Dean Morse. LC 73-76251. pap. 57.80 (2030717). Bks Demand UMI.

Peripheralisation & Industrial Change Impacts on Nations, Regions, Firms, & People. Ed. by Godfrey Linge. 272p. 1988. lib. bdg. 57.50 (Pub. by Croom Helm UK). Routledge Chapman & Hall.

Peripherals Book: A Complete Guide to Microcomputer Accessories & Interfacing. Stan Veit. 1985. 16.95 (ISBN 0-452-25567-8, Plume). NAL.

Peripherals for the ISDN D-Channel. International Resource Development, Inc. Staff. 144p. 1986. 1650.00 (ISBN 0-88694-713-8). Intl Res Dev.

Peripheries & Center: Constitutional Development in the Extended Polities of the British Empire & the United States, 1607-1788. Jack P. Greene. LC 86-7802. (Richard B. Russell Lecture: No.2). 288p. 1986. 30.00x (ISBN 0-8203-0878-1). U of GA Pr.

Periphery. (Battletech Ser.). 80p. Date not set. pap. 15.00 (ISBN 0-317-55264-3). FASA Corp.

Periphery Is the Center: A Study of Community Development Practice in the West of Ireland 1983-84. Ian Scott. 93p. 1985. 27.00x (ISBN 0-317-54793-3, Pub. by Plunkett Foundation). State Mutual Bk.

Periphery of the Southeastern Classic Maya Realm. Ed. by Gary W. Pahl. LC 86-7502. (Latin American Ser.). 304p. (Orig.). 1986. pap. 48.50 (ISBN 0-87903-061-5). UCLA Lat Am Ctr.

Periphrastic Futures Formed by the Romance Reflexes of Valdo (ad) Plus Infinitive. James J. Champion. (Studies in the Romance Languages & Literatures: No. 202). 80p. 1978. pap. 7.50x (ISBN 0-8078-9202-5). U of NC Pr.

Periplum - Austin. (Orig.). 1987. pap. 10.00. Open theatre.

Periplus. Hanno the Carthaginian. Ed. by Al N. Oikonomides. (Ancient Greek & Roman Writers Ser.). 56p. 1982. pap. 15.00 (ISBN 0-89005-180-1). Ares.

Periplus: An Essay on the Early History of Charts & Sailing Directions. Nils A. Nordenskiold. Tr. by Francis A. Bather from Swedish. (Illus.). 1897. 189.00 (ISBN 0-8337-2572-6). B Franklin.

Periscope: Views of the Individualized Education Program. Ed. by Bluma B. Weiner. LC 78-57045. 1978. pap. text ed. 4.88 (ISBN 0-86586-061-0). Coun Exc Child.

Periscopio. Roberto Severino & Maria R. Falconi. (Illus.). 244p. (Orig., Ital.). 1986. 29.00 (ISBN 0-8191-5234-X). U Pr of Amer.

Perish the Thought: Intellectual Women in Romantic America 1830-1860. Susan P. Conrad. 1978. pap. 5.95 (ISBN 0-8065-0650-4, Pub. by Citadel Pr). Lyle Stuart.

Perish the Thought: Intellectual Women in Romantic America, 1830-1860. Susan P. Conrad. LC 75-25463. (Illus.). 1976. 22.50x (ISBN 0-19-501995-4). Oxford U Pr.

Perishing Republic. Jerome Bahr. LC 79-129182. 148p. 1971. 10.95 (ISBN 0-686-63593-0). Trempealeau.

Peritoneal Dialysis. Ed. by Karl D. Nolph. 1981. lib. bdg. 69.50 (ISBN 90-247-2477-5, Pub. by Martinus Nijhoff Netherlands). Kluwer Academic.

Peritoneal Dialysis. 2nd ed. Ed. by Karl D. Nolph. 1985. lib. bdg. 89.00 (ISBN 0-89838-685-3, Pub. by Martinus Nijhoff Netherlands). Kluwer Academic.

Peritoneum & Peritoneal Access. Stig Bengmark. (Illus.). 536p. 1988. price not set (ISBN 0-7236-0767-2). PSG Pub Co.

Peritonitis in CAPS. Ed. by R. Augustin. (Contributions to Nephrology Ser.: Vol. 57). (Illus.). viii, 256p. 1987. 98.00 (ISBN 3-8055-4519-3). S Karger.

Periwinkle. Roger Duvoisin. LC 76-8665. (ps-3). 1976. 5.95 (ISBN 0-394-83298-1). Knopf.

Periya Puranam. Sekkizhaar. Ed. by N. Mahalingam. Tr. by G. Vanmikanathan from Tamil. 612p. 1985. text ed. 11.50 (ISBN 0-87481-534-7, Pub. by RamaKrishna Math). Vedanta Pr.

Perjury: The Hiss-Chambers Case. Allen Weinstein. LC 77-75009. 1978. 20.00 (ISBN 0-394-49546-2). Knopf.

Perjury: The Hiss-Chambers Case. Allen Weinstein. LC 78-11048. (Illus.). 1979. (Vin). Random.

Perkey's Nebraska Place-Names, Vol. XXVIII. Elton Perkey. LC 82-80300. (Publications Ser.). 227p. 1982. 6.95. Nebraska Hist.

Perkin Warbeck. John Ford. Ed. by Donald K. Anderson, Jr. LC 65-15338. (Regents Renaissance Drama Ser). xx, 114p. 1965. 11.95x (ISBN 0-8032-0260-1); pap. 3.95x (ISBN 0-8032-5260-9, BB 213, Bison). U of Nebr Pr.

Perkins. Linda Yeatman. (Illus.). 64p. (gr. 2-5). 1988. pap. 2.95 (ISBN 0-8120-3993-9). Barron.

Perkins-Budd: Railway Statesmen of the Burlington. Richard C. Overton. LC 81-6961. (Contributions in Economic & Economic History Ser.: No. 45.). (Illus.). xxiv, 271p. 1982. lib. bdg. 35.00 (ISBN 0-313-23173-7, OPB/). Greenwood.

Perks & Parachutes: How to Get the Ideal Employment Package. John Tarrant. 320p. 1986. pap. 8.95 (ISBN 0-671-62807-0, Fireside). S&S.

Perks & Parachutes: Negotiating Your Executive Employment Contract. John Tarrant. 448p. 1985. 17.45 (ISBN 0-671-49851-7, Linden Pr). S&S.

Perle see Pearl.

Perle de la Canebiere. Eugene Labiche. 9.95 (ISBN 0-686-54245-2). French & Eur.

Perle Noire. Paul Claudel. 250p. 1947. 8.95 (ISBN 0-686-54416-1). French & Eur.

Perlevaus: Perceval - Le Haut Du Graal, 2 Vols. Ed. by A. Nitze & T. A. Jenkins. LC 71-159117. (Illus.). 926p. 1972. Repr. of 1932 ed. 125.00 (ISBN 0-87753-054-8). Phaeton.

Perley's Reminiscences of Sixty Years in the National Metropolis, 2 Vols. Benjamin P. Poore. LC 74-158970. Repr. of 1886 ed. Set. 74.50 (ISBN 0-404-05076-X). Vol. 1 (ISBN 0-404-05077-8). Vol. 2 (ISBN 0-404-05078-6). AMS Pr.

Perlycross: A Tale of the Western Hills, 3 vols. in 1. Richard D. Blackmore. LC 79-8239. Repr. of 1894 ed. 44.50 (ISBN 0-404-61790-5). AMS Pr.

Permafrost & Its Effect on Life in the North. Troy L. Pewe. LC 52-19235. (Illus.). 40p. 1970. pap. 3.95x (ISBN 0-87071-141-5). Oreg St U Pr.

Permafrost Environment. Stuart A. Harris. LC 85-22990. (Illus.). 288p. 1986. 31.50x (ISBN 0-389-20604-0). B&N Imports.

Permafrost Fourth International Conference: Final Proceedings. National Academy of Sciences Staff. 413p. 1985. text ed. 32.50x (ISBN 0-309-03533-3). Natl Acad Pr.

Permanence. (Bibliographic Ser.: No. 213). 115p. 1964. 13.00 (ISBN 0-317-34408-0); Supplement 1, 1970. 8.00 (ISBN 0-317-34409-9); Supplement 2, 1977. 12.00 (ISBN 0-317-34410-2). Inst Paper Chem.

Permanence & Care of Color Photographs: Prints, Negatives, Slides & Motion Pictures. Henry Wilhelm & Carol Brower. LC 84-6921. (Illus.). 600p. 1988. 65.00 (ISBN 0-911515-00-3); pap. price not set (ISBN 0-911515-01-1). Preserv Pub Co.

Permanence & Change: An Anatomy of Purpose. 3rd ed. Kenneth Burke. 1984. 38.00x (ISBN 0-520-04144-5); pap. 9.95x (ISBN 0-520-04146-1). U of Cal Pr.

Permanence in Child Care. June Thoburn et al. (Practice of Social Work Ser.). 224p. 1987. text ed. 45.00 (ISBN 0-631-15097-8). Basil Blackwell.

Permanence of Johann Gutenberg. Frederick R. Goff. LC 78-89558. (Bibliographical Monograph: No. 3). (Illus.). 1974. Repr. of 1970 ed. 5.95 (ISBN 0-87959-048-3). U of Tex H Ransom Ctr.

Permanence of Organic Coatings - STP 781. Ed. by G. G. Schurr. 132p. 1982. pap. 15.95 (ISBN 0-8031-0827-3, 04-781000-14). ASTM.

Permanency Planning for Children: Concepts & Methods. Anthony Maluccio et al. 350p. 1986. text ed. 29.95 (ISBN 0-422-78840-6, 4074, Pub. by Tavistock England); pap. text ed. 13.95 (ISBN 0-422-78850-3, 4075). Routledge Chapman & Hall.

Permanency Planning: Past, Present, & Future. Elizabeth Cole. write for info. (ISBN 0-87868-226-0, F-66, 2260). Child Welfare.

Perplexing Puzzles & Tantalizing Teasers. Martin Gardner. (Illus.). 256p. 1988. pap. 3.95 (ISBN 0-486-25637-5). Dover.

Perplexing Scriptures. Wade H. Phillips. 135p. (Orig.). 1984. pap. 4.50 (ISBN 0-934942-44-7, 2034). White Wing Pub.

Perplexing Trend of Major Contemporary Historical Forces & the Political Future of Mankind. Gustav Von Herschenfeld. (Illus.). 129p. 1982. 88.15x (ISBN 0-86722-009-0). Inst Econ Pol.

Perplexity in the Moral Life: Philosophical & Theological Considerations. Edmond N. Santurri. LC 87-16211. (Studies in Religion & Culture). 325p. 1987. 35.00 (ISBN 0-8139-1155-9). U Pr of Va.

Perquimans County: A Brief History. Alan D. Watson. (Illus.). xi, 122p. (Orig.). 1987. pap. 4.00 (ISBN 0-86526-220-9). NC Archives.

Perrault's Complete Fairy Tales. Charles Perrault. Tr. by A. E. Johnson from Fr. LC 82-19873. (Illus.). 184p. 1982. pap. 5.95 (ISBN 0-396-08108-8). Dodd.

Perrault's Fairy Tales. Charles Perrault. LC 72-79522. (Illus.). viii, 117p. (gr. 4-6). 1969. pap. 4.95 (ISBN 0-486-22311-6). Dover.

Perrault's Morals for Moderns. Jeanne Morgan. (American University Studies II (Romance Languages & Literature): Vol. 28). 187p. 1985. text ed. 23.45 (ISBN 0-8204-0230-3). P Lang Pubs.

Perrin & the Beginnings of French Opera, Pt. 1, Vol. XLI. L. Auld. (Wissenschaftliche Abhandlungen-Musicological Studies). 240p. lib. bdg. 60.00 (ISBN 0-931902-33-9). Inst Mediaeval Mus.

Perrin & the Beginnings of French Opera, Pt. 2, Vol. XLII. L. Auld. (Wissenschaftliche Abhandlungen-Musicological Studies). 208p. lib. bdg. 60.00 (ISBN 0-937902-35-7). Inst Mediaeval Mus.

Perrins Ledge Crematory. Jane E. Buikstra & Lynne Goldstein. (Reports of Investigations Ser.: No. 28). (Illus.). 40p. 1973. pap. 2.00x (ISBN 0-89792-052-X). Ill St Museum.

Perro Grande...Perro Pequeno. P. D. Eastman. Tr. by Ines Alvarez. LC 81-12070. (Bilingual Picturebacks Ser.). 32p. (Span.). (ps-3). 1982. lib. bdg. 4.99 (ISBN 0-394-95142-5). Random.

Perro Huevero Aunque le Quemen el Hocico. Juan F. Valerio. Ed. by Jose A. Escapanter & Jose A. Madrigal. LC 86-60602. 108p. (Span.). 1986. pap. 18.00 (ISBN 0-89295-045-5). Society Sp & Sp-Am.

Perry County, Arkansas Census 1850. Courtney York & Gerlene York. (Orig.). 1969. pap. 12.00x (ISBN 0-916660-03-6). Hse of York.

Perry Ellis: A Biography. Jonathan Moor. (Illus.). 256p. 1988. 17.95x (ISBN 0-312-01489-9, Pub. by Thomas Dunne Bks). St Martin.

Perry Mason TV Show Book. Brian Kelleher & Diana Merrill. (Illus.). 224p. Date not set. pap. 12.95 (ISBN 0-312-00669-1). St Martin.

Perry Preschool Program & Its Long-Term Effects: A Benefit-Cost Analysis. W. Steven Barnett. 115p. (Orig.). 1985. pap. 15.00 (ISBN 0-931114-34-9). High-Scope.

Perry, the Pet Pig. Eunice Pennington. (Illus.). (gr. 4-7). 1966. 3.00 (ISBN 0-685-19374-8, 911120-06-8); pap. 1.00 (ISBN 0-685-19375-6). Pennington.

Perry's Chemical Engineers' Handbook. 6th ed. Ed. by Robert H. Perry & Donald W. Green. (Illus.). 2336p. 1984. text ed. 102.00 (ISBN 0-07-049479-7). McGraw.

Perrywinkle & the Book of Magic Spells. Ross M. Madsen. LC 85-15932. (Easy-to-Read Bks.). (Illus.). 48p. (ps-3). 1986. 8.95 (ISBN 0-8037-0242-6, 0869-260); PLB 8.89 (ISBN 0-8037-0243-4). Dial Bks Young.

PerryWinkle & the Book of Magic Spells. Ross M. Madsen. LC 85-15932. (Easy-to-Read Ser.). (Illus.). 48p. (ps-3). 1988. pap. 4.95 (ISBN 0-8037-0501-8, 0481-140). Dial Bks Young.

Persatuan Islam: Islamic Reform in Twentieth Century Indonesia. Howard Federspiel. (Monograph Ser.). (Orig.). 1970. pap. 7.50 (ISBN 0-87763-013-5). Cornell Mod Indo.

Perse: A History of the Perse School 1615-1976. S. J. D. Mitchell. (Cambridge Town, Gown & County Ser.: Vol. 7). (Illus.). 1976. 25.00 (ISBN 0-902675-71-0). Oleander Pr.

Persecucion: Cinco Piezas de Teatro Experimental. Reinaldo Arenas. LC 86-80353. (Coleccion Teatro). 67p. (Orig., Span.). 1986. pap. 7.95 (ISBN 0-89729-391-6). Ediciones.

Persecuted & Prosecuted. Leon A. Mawson. 1986. 16.95 (ISBN 0-533-06851-7). Vantage.

Persecuted Church. Ann Ball. 1988. pap. write for info. (ISBN 0-940543-10-9). Magnificat Pr.

Persecution & Assassination of Jean-Paul Marat As Performed by the Inmates of the Asylum of Charenton Under the Direction of the Marquis De Sade. Peter Weiss. LC 65-15915. (Orig.). 1966. pap. text ed. 5.95x (ISBN 0-689-70568-9). Atheneum.

Persecution & Liberty: Essays in Honor of George Lincoln Burr. facs. ed. George L. Burr. LC 68-26467. (Essay Index Reprint Ser.). 1968. Repr. of 1931 ed. 17.50 (ISBN 0-8369-0783-3). Ayer Co Pubs.

Persecution & the Art of Writing. Leo Strauss. LC 73-1407. 204p. 1973. Repr. of 1952 ed. lib. bdg. 19.75 (ISBN 0-8371-6801-5, STPA). Greenwood.

Persecution & the Art of Writing. Leo Strauss. 214p. 1988. pap. 9.95 (ISBN 0-226-77711-1). U of Chicago Pr.

Persecution & Toleration. Ed. by W. J. Sheils. (Studies in Church History: Vol. 21). 500p. 1984. 45.00x (ISBN 0-631-13601-0). Basil Blackwell.

Persecutor. Sergei Kourdakov. (Illus.). 256p. 1974. pap. 3.50 (ISBN 0-8007-8177-5, Spire Bks). Revell.

Persee. Jean-Baptiste Lully. Ed. by Theodore De Lajarte. (Chefs-d'oeuvre classiques de l'opera francais Ser.: Vol. 22). (Illus.). 354p. (Fr.). 1972. pap. 27.50x (ISBN 0-8450-1122-7). Broude.

Persephone. Fred Ainsworth. (Illus.). 40p. (Director's Production Script). 1977. pap. 10.00 (ISBN 0-88680-150-8). I E Clark.

Persephone. Jenny Joseph. (Illus.). 304p. 1986. 30.00 (ISBN 0-906427-77-0, Pub. by Bloodaxe Bks); pap. 11.95 (ISBN 0-906427-78-9, Pub. by Bloodaxe Bks). Dufour.

Persephone see Theatre.

Persephone in a Front Yard. Jane Perrin. 59p. (Orig.). 1984. pap. 7.95 (ISBN 0-317-28515-7). St Andrews NC.

Persephone's Cave: Cultural Accumulations of the Early Greeks. Howard Baker. LC 77-11162. 352p. 1979. 25.00x (ISBN 0-8203-0438-7). U of Ga Pr.

Persephone's Flowers & Other Poems. Geoffrey Grigson. 64p. 1986. pap. 16.95 (ISBN 0-436-18807-4, Pub. by Secker & Warburg UK). David & Charles.

Persephone's Quest: Entheogens & the Origins of Religion. R. Gordon Wasson et al. LC 87-51547. (Illus.). 257p. 30.00t (ISBN 0-300-03877-1). Yale U Pr.

Persepolis - The Archaeology of Persa, Seat of the Persian Kings. rev. ed. Donald N. Wilber. LC 87-27438. (Illus.). 144p. 1988. 24.95 (ISBN 0-87850-062-6). Darwin Pr.

Persepolis & Ancient Iran. Oriental Institute Staff. LC 76-7942. 1976. 55.00 (ISBN 0-226-69493-3, Chicago Visual Lib); 1 color & 11 black-&-white fiches incl. U of Chicago Pr.

Persepolis Fortification Tablets. Richard T. Hallock. (Oriental Institute Pubns. Ser: No. 92). 1969. 50.00x (ISBN 0-226-62195-2, OIP92). U of Chicago Pr.

Persepolis, Third: The Royal Tombs & Other Monuments. Erich F. Schmidt. Bd. with Third Century Iran. Martin Sprengling. LC 53-4329. (Oriental Institute Pubns. Ser.: No. 70). 1970. 90.00x (ISBN 0-226-62170-7, OIP70). U of Chicago Pr.

Perseus, a Study in Greek Art & Legend. Jocelyn M. Woodward. LC 75-41299. Repr. of 1937 ed. 12.50 (ISBN 0-404-14633-3). AMS Pr.

Perseus & Medusa. Adapted by C. J. Naden. LC 80-50083. (Illus.). 32p. (gr. 4-8). 1980. PLB 10.79 (ISBN 0-89375-362-9); pap. 2.50 (ISBN 0-89375-366-1). Troll Assocs.

Perseus, or of Dragons. H. F. Stokes. 1973. Repr. of 1925 ed. 10.00 (ISBN 0-8274-0862-5). R West.

Perseverance. Robert E. Picirilli. 28p. 1973. pap. 0.95 (ISBN 0-89265-108-3). Randall Hse.

Perseverance for People under Pressure. Neva Coyle. 64p. (Orig.). 1986. pap. 2.95 saddle stitched (ISBN 0-87123-888-8). Bethany Hse.

Perseverance in Preservation. Ralph Staten. 36p. 1975. pap. 0.95 (ISBN 0-89265-109-1). Randall Hse.

Pershing: General of the Armies. Donald Smythe. LC 85-42529. (Illus.). 352p. 1986. 27.50x (ISBN 0-253-34381-X). Ind U Pr.

Pershing's Mission in Mexico. Haldeen Braddy. LC 66-26835. 1979. 14.00 (ISBN 0-87404-008-6). Tex Western.

Persia. Samuel G. Benjamin. LC 70-39191. (Select Bibliographies Reprint Ser.). 1887. 22.00 (ISBN 0-8369-6793-3). Ayer Co Pubs.

Persia. Arnold T. Wilson. 1976. lib. bdg. 69.95 (ISBN 0-8490-2421-8). Gordon Pr.

Persia & the Greeks: The Defense of the West, c. 546-478 B.C. rev. ed. A. R. Burn. LC 83-40516. (Illus.). 640p. 1984. Repr. of 1962 ed. 42.50x (ISBN 0-8047-1235-2). Stanford U Pr.

Persia & the Persian Question, 2 vols. new ed. George N. Curzon. 1966. 85.00x set (ISBN 0-7146-1969-8, F Cass Co). Biblio Dist.

Persia & the Persian Question, 2 vols. George N. Curzon. 1976. lib. bdg. 200.00 (ISBN 0-8490-2422-6). Gordon Pr.

Persia & the Victorians. Marzieh Gail. 1977. lib. bdg. 59.95 (ISBN 0-8490-2423-4). Gordon Pr.

Persia Past & Present. Abraham V. Jackson. LC 76-149392. (Illus.). Repr. of 1906 ed. 57.50 (ISBN 0-404-09014-1). AMS Pr.

Persian see Merchant.

Persian & the Turkish Tales, Pt. 2. Francois Petis De La Croix. LC 77-170535. (Novel in England, 1700-1775 Ser). lib. bdg. 61.00 (ISBN 0-8240-0536-8). Garland Pub.

Persian, Arabic, & Urdu Printing in Bengal, from 1778. Katharine S. Diehl. (Printers & Printing in the East Indies to 1850 Ser.: Vol. V). 1988. write for info. (ISBN 0-89241-394-8). Caratzas.

Persian Architecture. Arthur U. Pope. Ed. by Jay Gluck. (Illus.). 124p. 1976. 12.50 (ISBN 4-89360-027-3, Pub. by Personally Oriented Ltd.SoPA (Ashiya Japan)); pap. 7.50 (ISBN 4-89360-028-1). C E Tuttle.

Persian Art Before & after the Mongol Conquest. O. Grabar. (Illus.). 72p. 1959. pap. 0.50 (ISBN 0-912303-00-X). Michigan Mus.

Persian at the Court of King George, 1809-10: The Journal of Mirza Abul Hassan Khan. Ed. & tr. by Margaret Cloake. (Illus.). 320p. 1989. 34.95 (ISBN 0-7126-2105-9, Pub. by Century Hutchinson). David & Charles.

Persian Boy. Mary Renault. LC 72-3407. 1972. 15.45 (ISBN 0-394-48191-7). Pantheon.

Persian Boy. Mary Renault. LC 86-46179. 432p. 1988. pap. 6.95 (ISBN 0-394-75101-9, Vin). Random.

Persian Caravan. facsimile ed. Arthur C. Edwards. LC 70-110224. (Short Story Index Reprint Ser.). 1928. 17.00 (ISBN 0-8369-3311-7). Ayer Co Pubs.

Persian Carpet. A. Cecil Edwards. (Illus.). 384p. 1975. text ed. 110.00 (ISBN 0-7156-0256-X, Pub. by Duckworth London). Longwood Pub Group.

Persian Carpet Designs. Mehry M. Reid. (International Design Library). (Illus.). 48p. 1982. pap. 5.95 (ISBN 0-88045-005-3). Stemmer Hse.

Persian Carpets. Michael C. Hillmann. (Illus.). 112p. 1984. 24.95 (ISBN 0-292-76490-1). U of Tex Pr.

Persian Cats. Edward E. Esarde. Ed. by Ed Rugenstein. (Illus.). 96p. 1983. 9.95 (ISBN 0-87666-859-7, KW-061). TFH Pubns.

Persian Cats & Other Longhairs. Jeanne Ramsdale. (Illus.). 1964. 16.95 (ISBN 0-87666-179-7, H-918). TFH Pubns.

Persian Ceramic Designs. Mehry M. Reid. (International Design Library). (Illus.). 48p. (Orig.). 1983. pap. 5.95 (ISBN 0-88045-024-X). Stemmer Hse.

Persian Cooking: A Table of Exotic Delights. Nesta Ramazani. LC 73-90182. (Illus.). 206p. 1986. Repr. of 1974 ed. 13.95 (ISBN 0-8139-0962-7). U Pr of Va.

Persian Cuisine: Regional & Modern Foods, Bk. 2. M. R. Ghanoonparvar. LC 82-61268. (Illus., Orig.). 1984. pap. 12.95 (ISBN 0-939214-23-7). Mazda Pubs.

Persian Cuisine: Traditional Foods, Bk. 1. Mohammad R. Ghanoonparvar. LC 82-61281. (Illus.). 250p. (Orig.). 1982. write for info. (ISBN 0-939214-11-3); pap. 12.95 (ISBN 0-939214-10-5). Mazda Pubs.

Persian Designs & Motifs for Artists & Craftsmen. Ali Dowlatshahi. (Illus.). 1979. pap. 5.95 (ISBN 0-486-23815-6). Dover.

Persian Diary, 1939-1941. Walter N. Koelz & Henry T. Wright. (Anthropological Papers: No. 71). (Illus.). 227p. (Orig.). 1983. pap. 10.00x (ISBN 0-932206-93-X). U Mich Mus Anthro.

Persian Empire & the West see Cambridge Ancient History Series.

Persian Empire: Studies in Geography & Ethnography of the Ancient Near East. Ernst Herzfeld. Ed. by Gerold Walser. 415p. (Orig.). 1968. pap. 87.50x (ISBN 3-515-00091-7, Pub by Franz Steiner). Coronet Bks.

Persian-English Dictionary, Romanized. John A. Boyle. (Persian, Modern & Eng.). 32.50 (ISBN 0-87557-057-7, 057-7). Saphrograph.

Persian Etching Designs. Mehry M. Reid. (International Design Library). (Illus.). 48p. 1985. pap. 5.95 (ISBN 0-88045-061-4). Stemmer Hse.

Persian Expedition. rev. ed. Xuegin Cao. Tr. by Rex Warner. (Classics Ser.). 1950. pap. 6.95 (ISBN 0-14-044007-0). Penguin.

Persian for Beginners. Mohammad R. Ghanoonparvar & Fatemeh Givehchian. (Illus.). 112p. 1985. text ed. 12.95 (ISBN 0-939214-26-1). Mazda Pubs.

Persian Gardens & Garden Pavilions. 2nd ed. Donald N. Wilber & Elisabeth B. MacDougall. LC 78-13801. (Illus.). 1979. 15.00x (ISBN 0-88402-082-7). Dumbarton Oaks.

Persian Glass. Shinji Fukai. LC 77-23736. (Illus.). 200p. 1977. 50.00 (ISBN 0-8348-1515-X). Weatherhill.

Persian Grammar. Ann K. Lambton. 1953-1960. pap. 27.95x (ISBN 0-521-09124-1). Cambridge U Pr.

Persian Grammar: History & State of Its Study. Gernot L. Windfuhr. (Trends in Linguistics State of the Art Reports: No. 12). 303p. 1979. 51.20x (ISBN 90-279-7774-7). Mouton.

Persian Gulf. R. M. Burrell. (Washington Papers: Vol. I, No. 1). 86p. (Orig.). 1972. pap. text ed. 7.95 (ISBN 0-8191-5958-1, Pub. by CSIS). U Pr of Amer.

Persian Gulf: After Iran's Revolution. J. C. Hurewitz. LC 79-312. (Headline Ser.: No. 244). (Illus., Orig.). 1979. pap. 4.00 (ISBN 0-87124-054-8, 244). Foreign Policy.

Persian Gulf & American Policy. Emile A. Nakhleh. LC 82-13125. 172p. 1982. 35.00 (ISBN 0-275-90867-4, C0867). Praeger.

Persian Gulf & Indian Ocean in International Politics. Ed. by Abbas Amirie. LC 77-378100. pap. 111.60 (2030737). Bks Demand UMI.

Persian Gulf & South Asia: Prospects & Problems of Inter-Regional Cooperation. Bhabani G. Gupta. 244p. 1987. 21.00 (ISBN 81-7003-077-3, Pub. by South Asia Pubs). South Asia Bks.

Persian Gulf & the Strait of Hormuz. P. K. Ramazani. (International Straits of the World Ser.: No. 3). 200p. 1979. 35.00x (ISBN 90-286-0069-8, Pub. by Sijthoff & Noordhoff). Kluwer Academic.

Persian Gulf & the West: The Dilemmas of Security. Charles Kupchan. 272p. 1987. text ed. 39.95x (ISBN 0-04-497057-9); pap. text ed. 14.95x (ISBN 0-04-497058-7). Unwin Hyman.

Persian Gulf & United States Policy: A Guide to Issues & References. Bruce R. Kuniholm. LC 84-9853. (Guides to Contemporary Issues Ser.: No. 3). 228p. 1984. 21.95x (ISBN 0-941690-12-1); pap. 13.95x (ISBN 0-941690-11-3); pap. text ed. 8.75x. Regina Bks.

Persian Gulf: Iran's Role. Rouhollah K. Ramazani. LC 72-77262. (Illus.). pap. 43.80 (ISBN 0-317-08537-9, 2002291). Bks Demand UMI.

Persian Gulf States. Rupert Hay. LC 80-1926. Repr. of 1959 ed. 23.50 (ISBN 0-404-18966-0). AMS Pr.

Persian Gulf States: A General Survey. Ed. by Alvin J. Cottrell. LC 79-19452. 736p. 1980. text ed. 55.00x (ISBN 0-8018-2204-1). Johns Hopkins.

Persian Gulf States: Country Studies. 2nd ed. Ed. by Richard F. Nyrop. LC 85-6089. (DA Pam 550-185. Area Handbook Ser.). (Illus.). 564p. 1985. 17.00 (ISBN 0-318-18812-0, S/N 008-020-01051-1). USGPO.

Persian Illustrated Manuscripts. G. M. Meredith-Owens. (Illus.). 32p. (Orig.). 1973. 4.50 (ISBN 0-7141-0657-7, Pub. by British Lib); pap. 2.95 (ISBN 0-7141-0631-3). Longwood Pub Group.

Persian Kingship in Transition. E. A. Bayne. LC 68-30502. 1968. 7.50 (ISBN 0-910116-65-2). U Field Staff Intl.

Persian Letters. Charles Montesquieu. Tr. by C. J. Betts. (Classics Ser.). 1973. pap. 6.95 (ISBN 0-14-044281-2). Penguin.

Persian Letters. Charles D. Montesquieu. Tr. by George R. Healy from Fr. LC 62-21265. 1964. 29.50x (ISBN 0-672-51053-7). Irvington.

Persian Letters, Pt. 1. Charles D. Montesquieu. LC 73-170550. (Novel in England, 1700-1775 Ser). lib. bdg. 61.00 (ISBN 0-8240-0549-X). Garland Pub.

Persian Letters, Pt. 2. Charles D. Montesquieu. LC 73-170550. (Novel in England, 1700-1775 Ser). lib. bdg. 61.00 (ISBN 0-8240-0550-3). Garland Pub.

Persian Letters Before Montesquieu. G. L. Van Roosbroeck. 1932. 19.00 (ISBN 0-8337-4458-5). B Franklin.

Persian Letters: Montesquieu. George R. Healy. 1964. pap. text ed. write for info. (ISBN 0-02-352840-0). Macmillan.

Persian Life & Customs. 3rd ed. Samuel G. Wilson. LC 76-178305. Repr. of 1900 ed. 24.50 (ISBN 0-404-06996-7). AMS Pr.

Persian Lions, Persian Lambs: An American's Odyssey in Iran. Curtis Harnack. 280p. 1981. pap. 8.95 (ISBN 0-8138-1336-0). Iowa St U Pr.

Persian Literary Influence on English Literature. Hasan Javadi. (Illus.). 226p. 1983. 18.00x (ISBN 0-89410-629-5). Three Continents.

Persian Literature. Ed. by Ehsan Yarshater. (Persian Heritage Ser.). 540p. (Orig.). 1988. 59.50 (ISBN 0-88706-263-6); pap. 19.50x (ISBN 0-88706-264-4). State U NY Pr.

Persian Lustre Ware. Oliver Watson. LC 85-6833. (Illus.). 224p. 1985. 95.00 (ISBN 0-571-13235-9). Faber & Faber.

Persian Medical Manuscripts at the University of California, Los Angeles. Lutz Richter-Bernburg. LC 77-94986. (Humana Civilitas Ser.: Vol. 4). (Illus.). xxi, 297p. 1978. 45.00x (ISBN 0-89003-026-X). Undena Pubns.

Persian Metres. Laurence P. Elwell-Sutton. LC 75-39392. pap. 77.80 (2031646). Bks Demand UMI.

Persian Miniature Designs. Mojdeh B. Stephenson. (International Design Library Ser.). (Illus.). 48p. (Orig.). 1983. pap. 5.95 (ISBN 0-88045-033-9). Stemmer Hse.

Persian Miniature Painting & Its Influence on the Art of Turkey & India. Norah M. Titley. LC 83-81752. (Illus.). 272p. 1984. 35.00 (ISBN 0-292-76484-7). U of Tex Pr.

Persian Mythology. John R. Hinnells. LC 85-70554. (Library of the World's Myths & Legends). (Illus.). 144p. 1985. 18.95 (ISBN 0-87226-017-8). P Bedrick Bks.

Persian Nights. Diane Johnson. 1987. 17.95 (ISBN 0-394-55804-9). Knopf.

Persian Nights. Diane Johnson. 352p. 1988. pap. 4.50 (ISBN 0-449-21514-8, Crest). Fawcett.

Persian Notes. Robin Magowan. 1972. pap. 3.00 (ISBN 0-685-37095-X). Small Pr Dist.

Persian Oil: A Study in Power Politics. Laurence P. Elwell-Sutton. LC 75-6469. (History & Politics of Oil Ser). 343p. 1976. Repr. of 1955 ed. 21.45 (ISBN 0-88355-288-4). Hyperion Conn.

Persian Painting & the National Epic. B. W. Robinson. (Aspects of Art Lectures (Henriette Hertz Trust)). (Illus.). 24p. 1984. pap. 5.50 (ISBN 0-85672-455-6, Pub. by British Acad). Longwood Pub Group.

Persian Painting: Five Royal Safavid Manuscripts of the Sixteenth Century. Stuart C. Welch. LC 75-38508. (Illus.). 128p. 1976. 19.95 (ISBN 0-8076-0812-2); pap. 11.95 (ISBN 0-8076-0813-0). Braziller.

Persian Paintings. B. W. Robinson. (Orig.). pap. 3.95 (ISBN 0-317-02537-6, Pub. by Victoria & Albert Mus UK). Faber & Faber.

Persian Pearl & Other Essays. Clarence Darrow. LC 74-1199. (American Literature Ser., No. 49). 1974. lib. bdg. 49.95x (ISBN 0-8383-1770-7). Haskell.

Person to Person Evangelism. new ed. R. Edward Davenport. LC 77-23716. 1978. pap. 2.95 (ISBN 0-87148-691-1). Pathway Pr.

Person to Person: Helping Customers Make Financial Decisions. 320p. 1986. 19.95 (ISBN 0-912857-33-1). Inst Finan Educ.

Person to Person: How to Be Effective in Evangelism. Jim Berlucchi. 144p. (Orig.). 1984. pap. 3.95 (ISBN 0-89283-164-2). Servant.

Person to Person: The Problem of Being Human. Carl R. Rogers & Barry Stevens. LC 67-26674. 1967. pap. 6.50 (ISBN 0-911226-01-X). Real People.

Person to Person: The Problem of Being Human. Barry Stevens & Carl R. Rogers. pap. 2.95 (ISBN 0-671-42467-X). PB.

Person und Dasein. (Phaenomenologica Ser: No. 32). 1969. lib. bdg. 21.00 (ISBN 90-247-0271-2, Pub. by Martinus Nijhoff Netherlands); pap. 13.00 (ISBN 90-247-0270-4, Pub. by Martinus Nijhoff Netherlands). Kluwer Academic.

Person Who Chairs the Meeting. Paul O. Madsen. (Illus.). 96p. (Orig.). 1973. tanalin 2.50 (ISBN 0-8170-0582-X). Judson.

Person with AIDS: Nursing Perspectives. Jerry Durham & Felissa L. Cohen. 288p. 1987. 24.95 (ISBN 0-8261-5630-4). Springer Pub.

Person You Are. rev. ed. Linda Anderson et al. 1985. text ed. 16.60x (ISBN 0-913310-42-5). PAR Inc.

Person You Are. Richard H. Turner. (Follet Success Skills Ser.). 48p. pap. 3.75 (ISBN 0-8428-2268-2). Cambridge Bk.

Persona: A Style Study for Readers & Writers. Walker Gibson. 1969. pap. text ed. write for info (ISBN 0-394-30198-6, RanC). Random.

Persona & Shame: Two Screenplays. Ingmar Bergman. Tr. by Alan Blair from Swedish. (Cinema Ser.). (Illus.). 192p. 1984. pap. 6.95 (ISBN 0-7145-0757-1, Dist. by Scribner). M Boyars Pubs.

Persona: Social Role & Personality. Helen H. Perlman. LC 68-21892. 1968. 16.00x (ISBN 0-226-66030-3). U of Chicago Pr.

Persona: Social Role & Personality. Helen H. Perlman. LC 68-21892. x, 246p. 1986. pap. 15.00x (ISBN 0-226-66028-1). U of Chicago Pr.

Persona: The Transcendent Image. Marilyn J. Blackwell. LC 85-8664. 132p. 1986. 24.95 (ISBN 0-252-01320-4); pap. 9.95 (ISBN 0-252-01267-4). U of Ill Pr.

Persona: Vida y Mascara en el Teatro Puertorriqueno. Matias Montes-Huidobro. LC 84-19721. (Illus.). 560p. (Span.). 1984. pap. 15.00 (ISBN 0-913480-61-4). Inter Am U Pr.

Personae. Ezra Pound. LC 50-13308. 16.95 (ISBN 0-8112-0355-7). New Directions.

Personae & Poiesis: The Poet & the Poem in Medieval Love Lyric. Prospero Saiz. (De Proprietatibus Litterarum, Series Minor: No. 17). (Illus.). 1976. pap. text ed. 16.80x (ISBN 90-2793-494-0). Mouton.

Personae Comicae. G. M. Lyne. 48p. Repr. of 1956 ed. 5.00 (ISBN 0-86516-031-7). Bolchazy-Carducci.

Personae Non Gratae. Paul Mariah. 32p. 1977. pap. 1.95 (ISBN 0-686-19032-7). Man-Root.

Personajes Obra de Eduardo Barrios. Silvia Martinez-Dacosta. LC 87-61694. (Senda de Estudios y Ensayos Ser.). 176p. (Orig., Span.). 1987. pap. 17.95 (ISBN 0-918454-60-3). Senda Nueva.

Personal. Julie Sargel. 1985. pap. write for info. (ISBN 0-9614348-0-5). Baby Grande Prods.

Personal Accounts: New & Selected Poems, 1966-1986. Robert Phillips. LC 85-28350. (Ontario Review Press Poetry Ser.). 142p. 1986. 16.95 (ISBN 0-86538-050-3); pap. 9.95 (ISBN 0-86538-051-1). Ontario Rev NJ.

Personal Ad Portraits. Lonny Shavelson. (Illus.). 96p. 1983. pap. text ed. 13.95 (ISBN 0-912357-00-2). De Novo Pr.

Personal Adjustment & Growth: A Life-Span Approach. Harvey Barocas et al. LC 82-60476. 530p. 1983. text ed. write for info. (ISBN 0-312-60221-9); instr's. manual avail.; write for info. study guide (ISBN 0-312-60222-7). St Martin.

Personal Adjustment in Old Age. Ruth S. Cavan & Ernest W. Burgess. Ed. by Robert Kastenbaum. LC 78-22188. (Aging & Old Age Ser). (Illus.). 1979. Repr. of 1949 ed. lib. bdg. 17.00x (ISBN 0-405-11806-6). Ayer Co Pubs.

Personal Adjustment, Marriage & Family Living. 6th ed. Judson T. Landis et al. 1975. text ed. 26.48 (ISBN 0-13-657338-X). P-H.

Personal Adjustment: Selected Readings. Valerian Derlega & Louis H. Janda. 1979. pap. text ed. write for info. (ISBN 0-673-15288-X). Scott F.

Personal Adjustment: The Psychology of Everyday Life. 3rd ed. Valerian J. Derlega & Louis H. Janda. 1986. text ed. write for info. (ISBN 0-673-18197-9). Scott F.

Personal Adventures in Upper & Lower California, in 1848-9. William R. Ryan. LC 72-9466. (Far Western Frontier Ser.). (Illus.). 822p. 1973. Repr. of 1850 ed. 48.50 (ISBN 0-405-04994-3). Ayer Co Pubs.

Personal Airplanes. Don Berliner. LC 81-15658. (Superwheels & Thrill Sports Bks.). (Illus.). (gr. 4-9). 1982. PLB 8.95 (ISBN 0-8225-0447-2). Lerner Pubns.

Personal Alchemy: Course XXI, Lessons 216-25. (Illus.). 1976. pap. 12.50 (ISBN 0-87887-362-7). Church of Light.

Personal Alert Safety Systems (PASS) for Fire Fighters. National Fire Protection Association Staff. 1983. 10.50 (ISBN 0-317-63575-1, 1982-83). Natl Fire Prot.

Personal & Business Bartering. James Stout. (Illus.). 392p. (Orig.). 1985. pap. 14.95 (ISBN 0-8306-1676-4, 1676P). TAB Bks.

Personal & Business Tax & Financial Planning for Psychiatrists. Murray Bradford & Glenn B. Davis. LC 84-6189. (Private Practice Monograph). 192p. 1984. pap. text ed. 15.00x (ISBN 0-88048-102-1, 48-102-1). Am Psychiatric.

Personal & Career Exploration. George R. Schmidt. 240p. 1987. pap. text ed. 17.95 (ISBN 0-8403-4180-6). Kendall-Hunt.

Personal & Family Glimpses of Remarkable People: Lord Macaulay, George Borrow, the Lake Poets. Edward W. Whately. 312p. 1983. Repr. of 1889 ed. lib. bdg. 65.00 (ISBN 0-89987-887-3). Darby Bks.

Personal & Family Glimpses of Remarkable People: The Lake Poets, Lord Macaulay, George Borrow. Edward W. Whately. 1973. Repr. of 1889 ed. 30.00 (ISBN 0-8274-0686-X). R West.

Personal & Impersonal: Six Aesthetic Realists. Sheldon Kranz et al. LC 59-10629. (Orig.). 1959. 6.95 (ISBN 0-910492-06-9); pap. 4.95 (ISBN 0-910492-21-2). Definition.

Personal & Organizational Psychology. 2nd ed. Laurence Siegel & Irving M. Lane. 1987. 35.95x (ISBN 0-256-03369-2). Irwin.

Personal & Organizational Security Handbook: Annual. 424p. 1985. pap. 75.00. Gov Data Pubns.

Personal & Professional Recollections. George G. Scott. LC 77-1202. (Architecture & Decorative Arts Ser.). 1977. Repr. of 1879 ed. lib. bdg. 59.50 (ISBN 0-306-70873-6). Da Capo.

Personal & Public Speaking. Donald W. Klopf & Ronald E. Cambra. 256p. 1983. pap. text ed. 12.95x (ISBN 0-89582-085-4). Morton Pub.

Personal & Social Education in the Curriculum. Richard Pring. (Studies in Teaching & Learning). 184p. (Orig.). 1984. pap. text ed. 16.95 (ISBN 0-340-33422-3). Princeton Bk Co.

Personal & Vocational Relationships in Practical Nursing. 5th ed. Carmen F. Ross. (Illus.). 290p. 1981. pap. text ed. 14.95 (ISBN 0-397-54281-X, 64-02168, Lippincott Nursing). Lippincott.

Personal Anthology. Jorge L. Borges. Frwd. by Anthony Kerrigan. 224p. (Orig.). Date not set. pap. 8.95 (ISBN 0-8021-3077-1). Grove.

Personal Anthology. Jorge Luis Borges. Ed. & frwd. by Anthony Kerrigan. 1967. pap. 6.95 (ISBN 0-394-17270-1, E472, Ever). Grove.

Personal Appearance Identification. photocopy ed. Ed. by Albert Zavala & James J. Paley. (Illus.). 352p. 1972. spiral bdg. 39.25 (ISBN 0-398-02447-2). C C Thomas.

Personal Applications in Computer Education. 2nd ed. Ann Thompson. 192p. 1986. pap. text ed. 22.95 (ISBN 0-8403-4021-4). Kendall-Hunt.

Personal Art: Reading to Good Purposes (Victorian Novel & Victorian Theatre, Victorian Shakespeare, Shakespeare Novels) Robetson Davies. 268p. 1983. Repr. of 1961 ed. lib. bdg. 40.00. Darby Bks.

Personal Aspects of Jane Austen. Mary A. Austen-Leigh. 1978. Repr. of 1920 ed. lib. bdg. 29.50 (ISBN 0-8495-0057-5). Arden Lib.

Personal Aspects of Jane Austen. Mary A. Austen-Leigh. LC 74-5080. Repr. of 1920 ed. lib. bdg. 27.00 (ISBN 0-8414-2972-3). Folcroft.

Personal Autonomy: Beyond Negative & Postive Liberty. Robert Young. LC 85-18424. 176p. 1986. 22.50 (ISBN 0-312-60225-1). St Martin.

Personal Awareness: A Psychology of Adjustment. 3rd ed. Richard G. Warga. LC 82-81113. 528p. 1983. text ed. 35.16 (ISBN 0-395-32586-2); instr's. manual 2.00 (ISBN 0-395-32587-0). HM.

Personal Becoming: In Honor of Karl Rahner. Andrew Tallon. 188p. pap. 19.95 (ISBN 0-686-65691-1). Marquette.

Personal Being: A Theory for Individual Psychology. Rom Harre. (Illus.). 304p. 1984. text ed. 27.00x (ISBN 0-674-66313-6). Harvard U Pr.

Personal Being: A Theory for Individual Psychology. Rom Harre. 312p. 1986. pap. text ed. 9.95x (ISBN 0-674-66314-4). Harvard U Pr.

Personal Bible Study. William C. Lincoln. LC 75-2345. 160p. 1975. pap. 5.95 (ISBN 0-87123-458-0, 210458). Bethany Hse.

Personal Bible Study. Jim Townsend. (Complete Teacher Training Meeting Ser.). 48p. 1986. tchr's ed 9.95 (ISBN 0-89191-320-3). Cook.

Personal Bible Study Journal, 1989. 1988. pap. 6.95 spiral (ISBN 0-89066-105-7). World Wide Pubs.

Personal Business. Ellen W. Leroe. 144p. (YA) (gr. 6 up). 1987. pap. 2.95 (ISBN 0-553-26652-7, Starfire). Bantam.

Personal Business Management. Herbert M. Jelley & Robert O. Herrmann. 1985. text ed. 21.80 (ISBN 0-07-032336-4). McGraw.

Personal Career Consultant: A Step-by-Step Guide to Finding a Successful & Satisfying Career. Lehmann & Shapiro. (Education & Guidance Ser.). 256p. 1988. pap. 8.95 (ISBN 0-13-973041-9). Arco.

Personal Causation: The Internal Affective Determinants of Behavior. R. De Charms. 416p. 1983. pap. text ed. 24.95 (ISBN 0-89859-336-0). L Erlbaum Assocs.

Personal Change for Marriage, Sex & Social Happiness. E. Ulysses Watson. 160p. 1987. pap. 9.95 (ISBN 0-8059-3027-2). Dorrance.

Personal Change Through Self-Hypnosis. Pam Young. 261p. Date not set. pap. 8.95 (ISBN 0-89865-532-3). Donning Co.

Personal Characteristics of Assaulted & Non-Assaulted Officers. Charles D. Hale & Wesley R. Wilson. (Criminal Justice Policy & Administration Research Ser.: No. 4). 1974. pap. 4.50 (ISBN 0-686-18641-9). Univ OK Gov Res.

Personal Choice: A Celebration of Twentieth Century Photographs. Mark Haworth-Booth. (Illus.). 136p. (Orig.). 1984. pap. 18.95 (ISBN 0-905209-38-9, Pub. by Victoria & Albert Mus UK). Faber & Faber.

Personal Choice in Ethnic Identity Maintenance: Serbs, Croats & Slovenes in Washington, D. C. Linda A. Bennett. LC 77-93261. 230p. 1978. soft cover 10.00 (ISBN 0-918660-06-8). Ragusan Pr.

Personal Choices & Goals: Guidelines. Richard L. Crews. 66p. 1988. pap. text ed. write for info. (ISBN 0-945864-11-6); write for info. wkbk. (ISBN 0-945864-12-4). Columbia Pacific U Pr.

Personal Commitments: Making, Keeping, Breaking. Margaret A. Farley. 175p. 1985. 12.95 (ISBN 0-86683-476-1, HarpR). Har-Row.

Personal Communication Process. John R. Wenburg & William W. Wilmot. LC 79-26971. 252p. 1982. Repr. of 1973 ed. lib. bdg. 18.00 (ISBN 0-89874-111-4). Krieger.

Personal Computer: A New Tool for Ministers. Russell H. Dilday, Jr. LC 84-20360. 1985. pap. 8.95 (ISBN 0-8054-3111-X). Broadman.

Personal Computer: An Industry Sourcebook. 1985. looseleaf 295.00 (ISBN 0-317-19631-6). Chromatic Comm.

Personal Computer: An Industry Sourcebook. 1987. looseleaf 495.00. Chromatic Comm.

Personal Computer: An Introduction. ComputerKnowledge, Inc. Staff. 83p. 1986. pap. 150.00 (ISBN 0-471-84413-6). Wiley.

Personal Computer Applications. Bryan Pfaffenberger. 1987. pap. text ed. write for info. (ISBN 0-673-39242-2). Scott F.

Personal Computer Applications in the Gas Industry, 1st Symposium. Institute of Gas Technology Staff. 293p. 1985. 50.00 (ISBN 0-910091-55-2). Inst Gas Tech.

Personal Computer-Based CAD-CAM, CAE Markets & Opportunities. Autodesk, Inc. Staff et al. (Illus.). 225p. 1987. 3-ring loose-leaf 1395.00x (ISBN 0-938484-21-4). Daratech.

Personal Computer BASIC(s) Reference Manual. Donald A. Sordillo. (Illus.). 320p. 1983. pap. text ed. 27.50 (ISBN 0-13-658047-5). P-H.

Personal Computer BASIC(S) Reference Manual, Bk. II. Donald A. Sordillo. LC 83-9463. (Illus.). 300p. 1985. pap. text ed. 27.50 (ISBN 0-13-658428-4). P-H.

Personal Computer Book. Peter McWilliams. LC 84-10353. (Illus.). 416p. 1984. pap. 10.95 (ISBN 0-385-19683-0, Quantum Pr). Doubleday.

Personal Computer Buyer's Guide. Patrick Plemmons & David Myers. (Illus.). 180p. (Orig.). 1984. pap. 12.95 (ISBN 0-912213-04-3, 900600). Paladin.

Personal Computer Buyer's Guide. Patrick Plemmons & David Myers. 184p. pap. 12.95 (Visi Press). Random.

Personal Computer Dictionary. Paul Redlin. 256p. 1984. pap. 10.95 (ISBN 0-471-88714-5, Pub. by Wiley Pr). Wiley.

Personal Computer Glossary. George Ledin. 1982. 3.50 (ISBN 0-88284-233-1). Manusoft.

Personal Computer in Advertising: Using Technology to Increase Creativity. Robert W. Bly. 256p. 1984. pap. 14.95 (Banbury Bks). Putnam Pub Group.

Personal Computer Investment Handbook. Jon Zonderman. (Illus.). 160p. (Orig.). 1984. 17.95 (ISBN 0-8306-0807-9); pap. 11.95 (ISBN 0-8306-1807-4, 1807P). TAB Bks.

Personal Computer Logbook. E. L. S. Publishing Staff. (Applied Information Technology Ser.). 96p. (Orig.). text ed. 11.95 (ISBN 0-317-53764-4). Educ Lrn Syst.

Personal Computer Networks. John Barkley. LC 86-600564. (National Bureau of Standards Special Publication 500-140. Computer Science & Technology). (Illus.). 61p. (Orig.). 1986. pap. 3.25 (ISBN 0-318-21304-4, S.N 003-003-02746-4). USGPO.

Personal Computer Optical Disk Market. (Market Research Reports). 1986. write for info. (ISBN 0-86621-816-5, A1636). Frost & Sullivan.

Personal Computer Publicity Book. rev. ed. Ed. by Ron Gold. (Illus.). 340p. 1984. looseleaf 125.00; Incl. disks. looseleaf 200.00. R Gold.

Personal Computer Quality. Boris Beizer. 288p. 1986. 28.95x (ISBN 0-442-20992-4). Van Nos Reinhold.

Personal Computer Security Considerations. (NCSC Series WA-002-85). 17p. 1985. pap. 1.00 (ISBN 0-318-22597-2, S/N 008-000-00439-1). USGPO.

Personal Computer Systems for Automated Document Storage & Retrieval. Saffady. 1988. write for info. (ISBN 0-89258-119-0). Assn Inform & Image Mgmt.

Personal Computer to Mainframe Communications. Bouros. 1987. write for info. (ISBN 0-471-85602-9). Wiley.

Personal Computer Toolbox: Software Applications for the IBM PC. Patrick G. McKeown. 420p. 1987. pap. 22.00 spiral bd. (ISBN 0-15-569380-8); instr's. manual 7.25 (ISBN 0-15-569381-6). HarBraceJ.

Personal Computer Typesetting. Johann Guttenberg. (Illus.). 132p. 1985. pap. 14.95 (ISBN 0-934523-10-X). Middle Coast Pub.

Personal Computer Use in Credit & Finance. Credit Research Foundation. 18p. 1986. 40.00 (ISBN 0-939050-53-6). Credit Res NYS.

Personal Computers & Data Communications. Dimitris N. Chorafas. LC 84-19972. (Personal Computing Ser.). 341p. 1986. pap. text ed. 25.95 (ISBN 0-88175-052-2, Computer Sci Pr). W H Freeman.

Personal Computers & the Adult Learner. Ed. by Barry Heermann. LC 85-81882. (Continuing Education Ser.: No. 29). (Orig.). 1986. pap. text ed. 12.95x (ISBN 0-87589-711-8). Jossey-Bass.

Personal Computers & the Family. Ed. by Marvin B. Sussman. LC 85-8459. (Marriage & Family Review Ser.: Vol. 8, Nos. 1 & 2). 202p. 1985. text ed. 32.95 (ISBN 0-86656-361-X); pap. text ed. 22.95 (ISBN 0-86656-362-8). Haworth Pr.

Personal Computers for Education. Alfred Bork. 179p. 1985. pap. text ed. 14.95 scp (HarpC). Har-Row.

Personal Computers for Libraries. Howard Falk. 180p. 1985. 16.95 (ISBN 0-938734-10-5). Learned Info.

Personal Computers for Scientists. Glenn I. Ouchi. LC 86-24846. (Illus.). x, 250p. 1986. 34.95 (ISBN 0-8412-1000-4); pap. 22.95 (ISBN 0-8412-1001-2). Am Chemical.

Personal Computers Impact on the Test & Measurement Industry. Market Research Company Staff. 125p. 1985. pap. text ed. 895.00 (ISBN 0-317-19566-2). Market Res Co.

Personal Computers in Business. Donald P. Kenny. LC 84-45204. 224p. 1984. pap. 15.95 (ISBN 0-8144-7627-9). AMACOM.

Personal Computers in Chemistry. Peter Lykos. LC 80-25445. 262p. 1981. 35.95x (ISBN 0-471-08508-1, Pub. by Wiley-Interscience). Wiley.

Personal Computers in the Role of Testing. Network Staff. 1984. 110.00x (ISBN 0-907634-49-4, Pub. by Network Events Ltd). State Mutual Bk.

Personal Computing. B. Jackson. (Computer State of the Art Report, Series 12: No. 6). (Illus.). 350p. 1984. 350.00x (ISBN 0-08-028591-0). Pergamon.

Personal Computing & C. J.-A. Gainsborough. 1985. pap. text ed. 19.95 (ISBN 0-07-912645-6). McGraw.

Personal Computing & C. John A. Gainsborough. 200p. 1985. pap. 19.95 (ISBN 0-912677-45-7). Ashton-Tate Pub.

Personal Computing: BASIC Programming on the TRS-80. Robert R. Hare. LC 83-7502. (Computer Science Ser.). 500p. 1983. pap. text ed. 22.00 pub net (ISBN 0-534-02768-7). Brooks-Cole.

Personal Computing for Managers with Lotus 1-2-3. Philip H. Dybvig. 226p. 1986. pap. text ed. 25.00 (ISBN 0-89426-075-8). Scientific Pr.

Personal Computing for Professionals in Government & Business. P. Carr. 1989. pap. price not set. Meghan-Kiffer.

Personal Computing in Nuclear Medicine. D. P. Pretschner. (Lecture Notes in Medical Informatics: Vol. 18). 133p. 1982. pap. 13.50 (ISBN 0-387-11598-6). Springer-Verlag.

Personal Computing with the UCSD-P System. 2nd ed. Mark Overgaard & Stan Stringfellow. 320p. 1986. pap. text ed. 25.00 (ISBN 0-13-658030-0). P-H.

Personal Construct Counseling & Psychotherapy. Franz R. Epting. LC 83-6913. (Series on Methods in Psychotherapy). 216p. 1984. 42.95x (ISBN 0-471-90169-5, 1420, Pub. by Wiley-Interscience). Wiley.

Personal Construct Psychology. Ed. by Han Bonarius et al. 300p. 1981. 32.50x (ISBN 0-312-60228-6). St Martin.

Personal Construct Psychology & Education. Maureen Pope & Terence Keen. LC 81-66376. (Educational Psychology Ser.). 1981. 42.50 (ISBN 0-12-561520-5). Acad Pr.

Personal Construct Psychology: Clinical & Personality Assessment. Alvin W. Landfield & Franz R. Epting. LC 86-10477. 327p. 1987. text ed. 44.95 (ISBN 0-89885-315-X); pap. text ed. 19.95 (ISBN 0-89885-318-4). Human Sci Pr.

Personal Construct Theory & Mental Health: Theory, Research & Practice. Ed. by Eric Button. 394p. 1985. 39.95 (ISBN 0-914797-15-8, Co-Pub by Croom Helm Ltd). Brookline Bks.

Personal Construct Theory: Concepts & Applications. J. R. Adams-Webber. LC 78-8638. pap. 62.80 (ISBN 0-317-41952-8, 2025985). Bks Demand UMI.

Personal Construct Therapy Casebook. Ed. by Robert Neimeyer & Greg Neimeyer. LC 87-4601. 336p. 1987. text ed. 33.95 (ISBN 0-8261-5530-8); student 25.95. Springer Pub.

Personal Construction of Nature & the Natural Destruction of Culture. Michael Thompson. (Working Papers on Risk & Rationality). Date not set. 2.50 (RR9). IPPP.

Personal History. A. J. P. Taylor. LC 83-45086. 288p. 1983. 14.95 (ISBN 0-689-11412-5). Atheneum.

Personal History, Adventures, Experience, & Observation of David Copperfield, the Younger, of Blunderstone Rookery, 20 Nos. in 1 Vol. Charles Dickens. LC 72-1651. (Illus.). Repr. of 1850 ed. 45.00 (ISBN 0-404-09139-3). AMS Pr.

Personal History of David Copperfield see Oxford Illustrated Dickens.

Personal History of Douglas F. Roby. Joseph F. Clayton. 529p. 1986. write for info. After Thoughts Inc.

Personal History of Lord Bacon. William H. Dixon. 424p. 1984. Repr. of 1841 ed. lib. bdg. 82.50 (ISBN 0-8495-1146-1). Arden Lib.

Personal History of the Territorial Enterprise. Dave Basso. (Illus.). 40p. 1986. text ed. 169.00 (ISBN 0-936332-27-1). Falcon Hill Pr.

Personal History: The Afro-American Texans. Marian L. Martinello & Melvin M. Sance. (University of Texas Institute of Texan Culture Young Readers Ser.). (Illus.). 104p. (gr. 5-8). 8.95 (ISBN 0-86701-005-3). U of Tex Inst Tex Culture.

Personal Hygiene for College Students. Delbert Oberteuffer. LC 77-177126. (Columbia University. Teachers College. Contributions to Education: No. 407). Repr. of 1930 ed. 22.50 (ISBN 0-404-55407-5). AMS Pr.

Personal Identification from Human Remains. Spencer L. Rogers. (Illus.). 94p. 1987. 23.50x (ISBN 0-398-05307-3). C C Thomas.

Personal Identification of Living Individuals. Spencer L. Rogers. (Illus.). 104p. 1986. 21.50 (ISBN 0-398-05231-X). C C Thomas.

Personal Identity. Ed. by John Perry. (Topics in Philosophy: Vol. 2). 246p. 1975. pap. 10.95x (ISBN 0-520-02960-7). U of Cal Pr.

Personal Identity. Sydney Shoemaker & Richard Swinburne. 160p. 1984. pap. 14.95 (ISBN 0-631-13432-8). Basil Blackwell.

Personal Identity. Godfrey Vesey. LC 76-41208. (Problems of Philosophy, Cornell Paperback Ser.). 136p. 1977. pap. 6.95x (ISBN 0-8014-9162-2). Cornell U Pr.

Personal Impressions. Isaiah Berlin. Ed. by Henry Hardy. 1982. pap. 7.95 (ISBN 0-14-006313-7). Penguin.

Personal Impressions. Isaiah Berlin. Ed. by Henry Handy. 1988. 16.25 (ISBN 0-8446-6297-6). Peter Smith.

Personal Impressions of Edward Carpenter. Mrs. Havelock Ellis. 59.95 (ISBN 0-8490-0817-4). Gordon Pr.

Personal Income Distribution: A Multicapability Theory. Joop Hartog. 208p. 1980. lib. bdg. 22.00 (ISBN 0-89838-047-2, Pub. by Martinus Nijhoff Netherlands). Kluwer Academic.

Personal Income During Business Cycles. Daniel Creamer. LC 84-10763. xxx, 166p. 1984. Repr. of 1956 ed. lib. bdg. 38.50x (ISBN 0-313-24421-9, CRPI). Greenwood.

Personal Income Estimates for Virginia's Planning Districts, Counties & Cities, 1979-1984. (Statistical Ser.). 1986. write for info. U Va Ctr Pub Serv.

Personal Income Tax Practice Set. R. Armstrong. 1987. pap. text ed. 12.75 (ISBN 0-07-002529-0). McGraw.

Personal Income Tax Practice Set. Robert Armstrong. 1986. 5.50x (ISBN 0-916060-02-0). Math Alternatives.

Personal Income Tax Practice Set: 1988 Edition with 1987 Tax Return Forms. Robert E. Armstrong. 1988. 12.75 (ISBN 0-07-002530-4). McGraw.

Personal Income Tax Procedures. rev. ed. James B. Bower & Harold Q. Langenderfer. 1988. pap. text ed. write for info. (ISBN 0-538-80151-4, AG60HB1). SW Pub.

Personal Income Tax Reduction in a Business Contraction. Melvin I. White. LC 68-58638. (Columbia University. Studies Social Sciences: No. 564). Repr. of 1951 ed. 15.00 (ISBN 0-404-51564-9). AMS Pr.

Personal Income Tax Systems under Changing Economic Conditions. OECD. 382p. (Orig.). 1986. pap. 30.00x (ISBN 92-64-12789-5). OECD.

Personal Income Taxation: The Definition of Income As a Problem of Fiscal Policy. Henry C. Simons. LC 38-27193. pap. 62.50 (ISBN 0-317-20634-6, 2024125). Bks Demand UMI.

Personal Influence: The Part Played by People in the Flow of Mass Communications. Elihu Katz & Paul Lazarsfeld. LC 55-7334. 1964. pap. text ed. 11.95 (ISBN 0-02-917150-4). Free Pr.

Personal Information Book. Louis Marucci. 1975. pap. text ed. 1.00x (ISBN 0-8134-1759-7, 1759). Inter Print Pubs.

Personal Information: Privacy at the Workplace. Jack L. Osborn. LC 78-18223. (AMA Management Briefing Ser.). pap. 20.00 (ISBN 0-317-09614-1, 2050391). Bks Demand UMI.

Personal Injury: Actions, Defenses, Damages, 25 vols. Louis R. Frumer & R. L. Benoit. 1957. Set, updates avail. looseleaf 715.00 (530); Updates 1985. 583.50; Supplement 1986. 650.00. Bender.

Personal Injury & Product Liability Litigation. Howard R. Reis. LC 86-30250. 160p. 1986. write for info. (ISBN 0-13-657602-8). P-H.

Personal Injury Damages Deskbook. Martin. (Trial Practice Library). 1988. write for info. (ISBN 0-471-63604-5). Wiley.

Personal Injury Defense Techniques, 3 vols, No. 542. Mark A. Dombroff. 1987. 255.00 (ISBN 0-317-67048-4). Bender.

Personal Injury Deskbook. Ed. by Barry H. Nates et al. 1961. Updates avail. annually. 95.00 (545); Updates 1985 75.00,; 1986 90.00,; one year serv. with looseleaf binder 130.00. Bender.

Personal Injury Deskbook, 1961-1985. Bound set. 100.00x (ISBN 0-686-90014-6). Rothman.

Personal Injury Practice: Technique & Technology. Lawrence S. Charfoos & David W. Christensen. LC 85-82276. 1986. 72.50; Suppl. 1987. 28.00. Lawyers Co-Op.

Personal Injury Valuation Handbooks, 12 Vols. Jury Verdict Research Inc. Staff. 450.00 (ISBN 0-317-55323-2). Jury Verdict.

Personal Inspirations & Reflections. Gertrude T. Reisberg. LC 83-90251. 76p. 1984. 8.95 (ISBN 0-533-05757-4). Vantage.

Personal Instruments: Analog Input for PCs. 204p. 1985. 1285.00x (ISBN 0-88694-661-1). Intl Res Dev.

Personal Insurance. J. J. Launie et al. LC 87-80749. 339p. 1987. text ed. 25.00 (ISBN 0-89462-037-1). IIA.

Personal Insurance Guide. 1982. 15.00 (ISBN 0-942326-34-2, 30177). Rough Notes.

Personal Integrity. William Schuttle. Ed. by Erwin R. Steinberg. 7.00 (ISBN 0-8446-2889-1). Peter Smith.

Personal Investing. 5th ed. Widicus & Stitzel. 1988. 36.95 (ISBN 0-256-06797-X). Irwin.

Personal Investing. 4th ed. Wilbur W. Widicus & Thomas E. Stitzel. 1985. 31.95x (ISBN 0-256-03006-5). Irwin.

Personal Investing: A Complete Handbook. Benton G. Gup. Date not set. pap. 19.95 (ISBN 0-471-84971-5). Wiley.

Personal Investor's Complete Book of Bonds. Donald R. Nichols. 1988. 19.95 (ISBN 0-88462-627-X). Longman Finan.

Personal Justice Denied: Wartime Relocation & Internment Of Japanese-Americans During World War II. 1984. lib. bdg. 79.95 (ISBN 0-87700-619-9). Revisionist Pr.

Personal Kiwi-Yankee Dictionary. 1983 ed. Louis S. Leland, Jr. 115p. pap. 4.95 (ISBN 0-88289-414-5). Pelican.

Personal Knowledge: Towards a Post-Critical Philosophy. Michael Polanyi. LC 58-5162. xiv, 428p. 1974. pap. 12.00x (ISBN 0-226-67288-3, P583, Phoen). U of Chicago Pr.

Personal Landscape: An Anthology of Exile. Robin Fedden et al. 1977. Repr. of 1945 ed. 25.00. Century Bookbindery.

Personal Law. 2nd ed. Norbert J. Mietus & Bill W. West. LC 74-34192. (Illus.). 512p. 1981. text ed. write for info. (ISBN 0-574-19505-X, 13-2505); instr's. guide avail. (ISBN 0-574-19506-8, 13-2506). SRA.

Personal Law. Robert D. Rothenberg & Steven J. Blumenkrantz. LC 83-19773. 514p. 1984. pap. 32.95x (ISBN 0-471-09639-3); tchrs ed avail. (ISBN 0-471-88123-6). Wiley.

Personal Law: A Practical Legal Guide. Robert D. Rothenberg & Steven J. Blumenkrantz. LC 85-29577. 475p. 1986. pap. 16.95 (ISBN 0-471-84277-X). Wiley.

Personal Leadership in Marketing. Edwin J. Gross. 189p. 1968. pap. 4.50x (ISBN 0-912598-04-2). Florham.

Personal Legends of Formosa. Lou Tsu-K'uang. (Asian Folklore & Social Life Monographs: No. 66). 190p. (Chinese.). 1975. 14.00x (ISBN 0-89986-061-3). Oriental Bk Store.

Personal Letters for Business People. Isabel L. Bosticco. 290p. 1986. text ed. 39.95 (ISBN 0-566-02593-0). Gower Pub Co.

Personal Letters to Adventist Pastors & Others. Bert Brians. 40p. 1986. pap. 6.00 (ISBN 0-914009-85-0). VHI Library.

Personal Liability of Managers & Supervisors for Employment Discrimination. 2nd ed. Robert E. Williams. LC 86-62798. (Monograph Ser.). 1986. pap. 9.95 (ISBN 0-916559-05-X). NFSEP.

Personal Liability of Public Officials under Federal Law. 3rd ed. Paul T. Hardy & J. D. Weeks. LC 84-28088. 1985. pap. 3.95 (ISBN 0-89854-108-5). U of GA Inst Govt.

Personal Life Insurance Trusts. 3rd ed. Sherwin P. Simmons. (Tax Management Portfolio Ser.: No. 210). 1987. looseleaf 50.00. BNA.

Personal Life of David Livingstone. William G. Blaikie. LC 69-19353. (Illus.). 1880. 35.00x (ISBN 0-8371-0518-8, BLL&). Greenwood.

Personal Life of the Christian. Arthur W. Robinson. 1981. pap. 7.95X (ISBN 0-19-213427-2). Oxford U Pr.

Personal Life of the Psychotherapist. James D. Guy. LC 87-8254. (Personality Processes Ser.). 321p. 1987. 33.95 (ISBN 0-471-84854-9). Wiley.

Personal Lifeplan for Health & Fitness. David Singsank & Dennis Singsank. Ed. by Scott Knickelbine. LC 83-72757. (Illus.). 180p. (Orig.). 1984. pap. 5.95 (ISBN 0-914851-00-4). Amer Health Nutri.

Personal Lines Underwriting. 2nd ed. G. William Glendenning & Robert B. Holtom. LC 77-81989. 582p. 1982. text ed. 22.00 (ISBN 0-89462-003-7, UND62). IIA.

Personal Lunation Charts. Helen Paul-Wolf. LC 83-71152. 88p. 1984. 7.00 (2299-01). Am Fed Astrologers.

Personal Magnetism. T. Q. Dumont. 14.50x (ISBN 0-685-22069-9). Wehman.

Personal Management. (Illus.). 32p. (gr. 6-12). 1982. pap. 1.25x (ISBN 0-8395-3270-9, 3270). BSA.

Personal Management in Banking. D. B. Summers. 1981. text ed. 39.95 (ISBN 0-07-062558-1). McGraw.

Personal Manifesto. Jo Grimond. 200p. 1983. 34.95x (ISBN 0-85520-678-0). Basil Blackwell.

Personal, Marital, & Family Myths: Theoretical Formulations & Clinical Strategies. Dennis Bagarozzi & Stephen Anderson. (Illus.). 1988. 24.95 (ISBN 0-393-70065-8). Norton.

Personal Marketing Strategies: How to Sell Yourself, Your Ideas & Your Services. Mike McCaffrey & Jerry Derloshon. (Illus.). 219p. 1983. 21.95 (ISBN 0-13-657452-1); pap. 12.95 (ISBN 0-13-657114-X). P-H.

Personal Matter. Kenzaburo Oe. Tr. by John Nathan from Japanese. 1968. pap. 6.95 (ISBN 0-394-17141-1, B199, BC). Grove.

Personal Meanings of Death. Ed. by Franz R. Epting & Robert A. Neimeyer. LC 83-8529. (Death Education, Aging & Health Care Ser.). (Illus.). 246p. 1983. text ed. 37.25 (ISBN 0-89116-363-8). Hemisphere Pub.

Personal Memoirs, 2 Vols in 1. Ulysses S. Grant. Repr. of 1894 ed. 41.50 (ISBN 0-404-04599-5). AMS Pr.

Personal Memoirs & Recollections of Editorial Life. Joseph T. Buckingham. LC 76-125682. (American Journalists Ser). 1970. Repr. of 1852 ed. 24.00 (ISBN 0-405-01657-3). Ayer Co Pubs.

Personal Memoirs of a Residence of Thirty Years with the Indian Tribes on the American Frontiers: With Brief Notices of Passing Events, Facts & Opinions, A.D. 1812 to A.D. 1842. Henry R. Schoolcraft. LC 74-9021. Repr. of 1851 ed. 37.50 (ISBN 0-404-11899-2). AMS Pr.

Personal Memoirs of a Residence of Thirty Years with the Indian Tribes on the American Frontiers: 1812-1842. facsimile ed. Henry R. Schoolcraft. LC 75-119. (Mid-American Frontier Ser.). 1975. Repr. of 1851 ed. 54.00x (ISBN 0-405-06885-9). Ayer Co Pubs.

Personal Memoirs of Julia Dent Grant (Mrs. Ulysses S. Grant) Julia D. Grant. Ed. by John Y. Simon. (Illus.). 1988. Repr. of 1975 ed. 19.95 (ISBN 0-8093-1442-8); lib. bdg. 10.95 (ISBN 0-8093-1443-6). S Ill U Pr.

Personal Memoirs of U. S. Grant. U. S. Grant. (Quality Paperbacks Ser.). 608p. 1982. pap. 13.95 (ISBN 0-306-80172-8). Da Capo.

Personal Memories of P. H. Sheridan, General, 2 vols. Philip H. Sheridan. LC 72-78831. 1902. Repr. 95.00x (ISBN 0-403-02023-9). Somerset Pub.

Personal Memories, Social, Political & Literary. Edward D. Mansfield. LC 74-125707. (American Journalists). 1970. Repr. of 1879 ed. 32.00 (ISBN 0-405-01688-3). Ayer Co Pubs.

Personal Memories: Social, Political, & Literary. facsimile ed. Edward D. Mansfield. LC 72-133527. (Select Bibliographies Reprint Ser.). Repr. of 1879 ed. 21.00 (ISBN 0-8369-5559-5). Ayer Co Pubs.

Personal Ministry Handbook. Larry Richards. 224p. 1986. pap. 9.95 (ISBN 0-8010-7736-2). Baker Bk.

Personal Money Management. 5th, rev. ed. Thomas E. Bailard et al. 640p. (Orig.). 1986. text ed. write for info. (ISBN 0-574-19580-7, 13-2580); write for info. study guide (ISBN 0-574-19552-1, 13-2552); write for info. instr's guide (ISBN 0-574-19581-5, 13-2581). Sci Res Assoc Coll.

Personal Money Management. 2nd ed. Gale E. Hurley. (Illus.). 528p. 1981. text ed. write for info. (ISBN 0-13-657544-7). P-H.

Personal Money Management. James F. Tucker. (Illus.). 193p. 1985. 14.95 (ISBN 0-88258-145-7). Howard U Pr.

Personal Money Management for Physicians. 4th ed. Ed. by Lawrence Farber. 296p. 1986. 29.95 (ISBN 0-87489-416-6). Med Economics.

Personal Money Management with AppleWorks. Ruth K. Witkin. 418p. 1987. pap. 18.95 (ISBN 0-471-62575-2). Wiley.

Personal Monopoly: Lotos Compatible Tools for Building Your Personal Estate. Duncan Lindsey. 300p. (Orig.). 1987. pap. 19.95 (ISBN 0-317-56265-7); software 39.95 (ISBN 0-317-56266-5). Oregon Pr.

Personal Mythology: The Psychology of Your Evolving Self. David Feinstein & Stanley Krippner. 288p. 1988. 16.95 (ISBN 0-87477-483-7). J P Tarcher.

Personal Name Index to New Directions. Shelley Cox. LC 37-1751. 167p. 1979. 12.50x (ISBN 0-87875-180-7). Whitston Pub.

Personal Name Index to Orton's Records of California Men in the War of the Rebellion, 1861 to 1867. Compiled by J. Carlyle Parker. LC 78-15674. (Genealogy & Local History Ser.: Vol. 5). 168p. 1978. 68.00x (ISBN 0-8103-1402-9). Gale.

Personal Name Index to the Augusta Chronicle: Augusta, Georgia, 1800-1810, Vol. II. Compiled by Alice O. Walker. 542p. 1988. lib. bdg. 25.00 (ISBN 0-941877-02-7). Augusta-Richmond Cnty.

Personal Name Index to the Augusta Chronicle (Augusta, Georgia) 1786-1799, Vol. 1. Alice O. Walker. 488p. 1987. 25.00 (ISBN 0-941877-01-9). Augusta-Richmond Cnty.

Personal Name Index to the Eighteen Fifty-Six City Directories of California. Ed. by Nathan C. Parker. LC 79-24246. (Genealogy & Local History Ser.: Vol. 10). 280p. 68.00x (ISBN 0-8103-1414-2). Gale.

Personal Name Index to the Eighteen Fifty-Six City Directories of Iowa. LaVerne Sopp. (Genealogy & Local History Ser.: Vol. 13). 168p. 1980. 68.00x (ISBN 0-8103-1486-X). Gale.

Personal Name Index to the New York Times Index, 1851-1974, 22 vols. Byron A. Falk & Valerie R. Falk. Incl. Vol. 1. 351p. 1976. lib. bdg. 28.00 (ISBN 0-89902-101-8); Vol. 2. 602p. 1977. lib. bdg. 45.00 (ISBN 0-89902-102-6); Vol. 3. 569p. 1977. lib. bdg. 43.50 (ISBN 0-89902-103-4); Vol. 4. 494p. 1977. lib. bdg. 39.00 (ISBN 0-89902-104-2); Vol. 5. 436p. 1977. lib. bdg. 36.50 (ISBN 0-89902-105-0); Vol. 6. 639p. 1978. lib. bdg. 51.00 (ISBN 0-89902-106-9); Vol. 7. 769p. 1978. lib. bdg. 60.00 (ISBN 0-89902-107-7); Vol. 8. 674p. 1978. lib. bdg. 55.50 (ISBN 0-89902-108-5); Vol. 9. 455p. 1978. lib. bdg. 42.00 (ISBN 0-89902-109-3); Vol. 10. 492p. 1979. lib. bdg. 45.00 (ISBN 0-89902-110-7); Vol. 11. 838p. 1979. lib. bdg. 73.25 (ISBN 0-89902-111-5); Vol. 12. 648p. 1979. lib. bdg. 58.00 (ISBN 0-89902-112-3); Vol. 13. 600p. 1980. lib. bdg. 54.50 (ISBN 0-89902-113-1); Vol. 14. 600p. 1980. lib. bdg. 54.50 (ISBN 0-89902-114-X); Vol. 15. 417p. 1980. lib. bdg. 40.25 (ISBN 0-89902-115-8); Vol. 16. 624p. 1980. lib. bdg. 60.50; Vol. 17. 659p. 1981. lib. bdg. 64.00 (ISBN 0-89902-117-4); Vol. 18. 600p. 1981. lib. bdg. 64.00 (ISBN 0-89902-119-0); Vol. 20. 669p. 1982. lib. bdg. 65.00 (ISBN 0-89902-120-4); Vol. 21. 421p. 1982. lib. bdg. 61.00 (ISBN 0-89902-121-2); Vol. 22. 446p. 1983. lib. bdg. 62.00 (ISBN 0-89902-122-0). LC 76-12217. Vols. 1-22. lib. bdg. 899.00 (ISBN 0-89902-100-X). Roxbury Data.

Personal Name Index to the New York Times Index, 1975-1979 Supplement: Vol. 25, N-Z. Byron A. Falk & Valerie R. Falk. 434p. 1985. lib. bdg. 51.00 (ISBN 0-89902-125-5). Roxbury Data.

Personal Name Index to the New York Times Index, 1975-1984: A-D, Vol. 1. Byron A. Falk, Jr. & Valerie R. Falk. LC 76-12217. 538p. 1986. lib. bdg. 54.00 (ISBN 0-89902-126-3). Roxbury Data.

Personal Name Index to the New York Times Index, 1975-1984: E-K, Vol. 2. Byron A. Falk, Jr. & Valerie R. Falk. LC 76-12217. 523p. 1987. lib. bdg. 55.00 (ISBN 0-89902-127-1). Roxbury Data.

Personal Name Index to the New York Times Index, 1975-1984, Vol. 3, L-Q. Byron A. Falk & Valerie R. Falk. LC 76-12217. 462p. 1988. lib. bdg. 57.00 (ISBN 0-89902-128-X). Roxbury Data.

Personal Name Index to the New York Times Index 1975-1979 Supplement, Vol. 23, A-F. Byron A. Falk & Valerie R. Falk. 411p. 1984. lib. bdg. cancelled (ISBN 0-89902-123-9). Roxbury Data.

Personal Name Index to The New York Times Index, 1975-1979 Supplement, Vol. 24, G-M. Byron A. Falk & Valerie R. Falk. 412p. 1984. lib. bdg. cancelled. Roxbury Data.

Personal Names: A Bibliography. Elsdon C. Smith. LC 66-31855. 226p. 1965. Repr. of 1952 ed. 35.00x (ISBN 0-8103-3134-9). Gale.

Personal Names & Naming: An Annotated Bibliography. Compiled by Edwin D. Lawson. LC 86-31789. (Bibliographies & Indexes in Anthropology Ser.: No. 3). 198p. 1987. lib. bdg. 35.00 (ISBN 0-313-23817-0, LNN/). Greenwood.

Personal Names from Cuneiform Inscriptions of Cappadocia. Ferris J. Stephens. LC 78-63557. (Yale Oriental Ser. Researches: No. 13, Pt. 1). 1979. Repr. of 1928 ed. 24.00 (ISBN 0-404-60283-5). AMS Pr.

Personal Names from Cuneiform Inscriptions of Cappadocia. Ferris J. Stephens. (Yale Oriental Researches Ser.: No. XIII). 1928. pap. 19.50x (ISBN 0-685-69868-8). Elliots Bks.

Personal Names from Cuneiform Inscriptions of the Cassite Period. Albert T. Clay. LC 78-63543. (Yale Oriental Ser. Researches: No. I). Repr. of 1912 ed. 37.50 (ISBN 0-404-60271-1). AMS Pr.

Personal Narrative of a Pilgrimage to Al-Madinah & Meccah, 2 Vols. Richard F. Burton. (Illus.). 1893. Vol. 1. pap. 8.95 (ISBN 0-486-21217-3). Vol. 2. pap. 8.95 (ISBN 0-486-21218-1). Dover.

Personal Narrative of a Pilgrimage to Al-Madinah & Meccah, 2 Vols. Richard F. Burton. Ed. by Isabel Burton. Set. 33.50 (ISBN 0-8446-1781-4). Peter Smith.

Personal Narrative of Explorations & Incidents in Texas, New Mexico, California, Sonora & Chihuahua in Connection With the U. S. Mexican Boundary Survey, 1851-1853, 2 vols. John R. Bartlett. (Beautiful Rio Grande Classics Ser.). (Illus.). 1413p. 1983. Repr. of 1854 ed. 50.00 (ISBN 0-87380-018-4). Rio Grande.

Personal Narrative of James O. Pattie. James O. Pattie. Ed. by Timothy Flint. LC 83-27406. (Illus.). xvi, 269p. 1984. pap. 6.95 (ISBN 0-8032-8709-7, BB 853, Bison). U of Nebr Pr.

Personal Reminiscences by Moore & Jerdan. Richard H. Stoddard. Repr. of 1887 ed. 20.00 (ISBN 0-686-19858-1). Ridgeway Bks.

Personal Reminiscences, Eighteen Forty to Eighteen Ninety. facsimile ed. L. E. Chittenden. LC 72-37302. (Black Heritage Library Collection). Repr. of 1893 ed. 26.25 (ISBN 0-8369-8939-2). Ayer Co Pubs.

Personal Reminiscences of a Great Crusade. Josephine E. Butler. LC 74-33934. (Pioneers of the Woman's Movement: an International Perspective Ser.). 1976. Repr. 19.75 (ISBN 0-88355-257-4). Hyperion Conn.

Personal Reminiscences of Constable & Gillies. Richard H. Stoddard. 1978. Repr. of 1887 ed. lib. bdg. 25.00 (ISBN 0-8495-4875-6). Arden Lib.

Personal Reminiscences of Early Days in California. Stephen J. Field. LC 68-29601. (American Scene Ser). 1968. Repr. of 1893 ed. lib. bdg. 45.00 (ISBN 0-306-71157-5). Da Capo.

Personal Reminiscences of Henry Irving, 2 vols. Bram Stoker. 1970. Repr. of 1906 ed. Greenwood.

Personal Reminiscences of the Rebellion 1861-1866. facs. ed. Le Grand Cannon. LC 78-157363. (Black Heritage Library Collection Ser). 1895. 17.50 (ISBN 0-8369-8801-9). Ayer Co Pubs.

Personal Reminiscences of the War of 1861-5. facsimile ed. William H. Morgan. LC 74-146868. (Select Bibliographies Reprint Ser). Repr. of 1911 ed. 17.00 (ISBN 0-8369-5635-4). Ayer Co Pubs.

Personal Responsibility & Christian Morality. Josef Fuchs. Tr. by William Cleves et al from Ger. LC 83-1548. 238p. (Orig.). 1983. pap. 10.95 (ISBN 0-87840-405-8). Georgetown U Pr.

Personal Responsibilty & Therapy: A Intergrative Approach. Richard Nelson-Jones. 214p. 1987. 29.95 (ISBN 0-89116-777-3). Hemisphere Pub.

Personal Resume Preparation. Michael P. Jaquish. LC 68-20098. (Wiley Series on Human Communication). pap. 39.50 (2055730). Bks Demand UMI.

Personal Revolution & Picasso. Louis Danz. LC 74-3421. (Studies in Philosophy, No. 40). 1974. lib. bdg. 49.95x (ISBN 0-8383-2066-X). Haskell.

Personal Risk Management & Insurance, 2 Vols. 3rd ed. Glenn L. Wood et al. LC 84-72613. 846p. 1984. text ed. 22.00 ea. vol. (ISBN 0-89463-043-1). Vol.1. Vol.2. Am Inst Property.

Personal Risk Management & Insurance for CPCU Two. rev. ed. R. Robert Rackley. (CPCU Ser.). 1985. 155.00 (ISBN 0-88171-113-6). Insurance Achiev.

Personal Robot Book. Texe Marrs. (Illus.). 192p. 1985. pap. 12.95 (ISBN 0-8306-1896-1, 1896P). TAB Bks.

Personal Robot Book. Texe Marrs. (Illus.). 181p. (Orig.). 1985. pap. 14.95 (ISBN 0-317-39383-9). Robot Inst Am.

Personal Robot Market. International Resource Development Inc. 255p. 1984. 1650.00x (ISBN 0-88694-615-8). Intl Res Dev.

Personal Rule in Black Africa: Prince, Autocrat, Prophet, Tyrant. Robert H. Jackson & Carl G. Rosberg. LC 80-25439. 350p. 1982. 35.00x (ISBN 0-520-04185-2); pap. 12.95x (ISBN 0-520-04209-3). U of Cal Pr.

Personal Safety & Survival. John A. Banks. 204p. (Orig.). 1986. pap. 7.95 (ISBN 0-9616715-1-3). Highlight Bks.

Personal Security for Senior Citizens. Emerson Clarke. 1975. pap. 3.00x (ISBN 0-918384-00-1). Personal Security.

Personal Selection & Productivity. Mark Cook. LC 87-21070. (Psychology & Productivity at Work Ser.). 276p. 1988. 49.95 (ISBN 0-471-91148-8). Wiley.

Personal Selection of Graduate Engineers see Tentative Standardization of a Hard Opposites Test.

Personal Selling. 3rd ed. Marks. 624p. 1988. text ed. 37.00 (ISBN 0-205-11087-8). Allyn.

Personal Selling: A Professional Approach. Frank E. Brennan. 448p. 1983. text ed. write for info. (ISBN 0-574-20685-X, 13-3685); instr's. guide avail. (ISBN 0-574-20686-8, 13-3686). SRA.

Personal Selling: An Introduction. Robin Peterson. LC 84-937. 372p. 1984. Repr. of 1978 ed. lib. bdg. 28.95 (ISBN 0-89874-651-5). Krieger.

Personal Selling: Choice Against Chance. Edward Mazze. LC 75-35859. (Illus.). 331p. 1976. pap. text ed. 25.25 (ISBN 0-8299-0067-5). West Pub.

Personal Selling: Foundations, Process, & Management. Ben Enis. LC 78-12171. (Illus.). 1979. text ed. write for info. (ISBN 0-673-16132-3). Scott F.

Personal Selling: Function, Theory, & Practice. 2nd ed. James R. Young & Robert W. Mondy. LC 81-67246. 536p. 1981. text ed. 32.95x (ISBN 0-03-060291-2); instr's manual 20.00 (ISBN 0-03-060296-3). Dryden Pr.

Personal Selling: Theory, Research & Practice. Jacob Jacoby et al. LC 83-48825. (Advances in Retailing Ser.). 336p. 1984. 40.00x (ISBN 0-669-07606-6). Lexington Bks.

Personal Shorthand, 3 pts. Carl W. Salser & C. Theo Yerian. Incl. PS, Bk. 1. pap. text ed. 6.85 (ISBN 0-89420-106-9, 241050); Optional cassette recordings 314.05 (241000); PS, Bk 2. pap. text ed. 7.50 (ISBN 0-89420-107-7); Optional cassette recordings 311.45 (ISBN 0-89420-168-9); PS, Bk. 3. pap. text ed. 11.65 (ISBN 0-89420-108-5); Optional cassette recordings. 314.25 (ISBN 0-89420-169-7). (Personal Shorthand Cardinal Ser.). 1980. Set. text ed. write for info (ISBN 0-89420-105-0). 936.00 (ISBN 0-89420-170-0). Natl Book.

Personal Shorthand Combined Dictionary - Professional Edition. Carl W. Salser & C. Theo Yerian. 417p. 1984. pap. 16.95 (ISBN 0-89420-241-3, 213000). Natl Book.

Personal Shorthand for the Administrator, Executive, Manager & Supervisor. M. Herbert Freeman & Carl W. Salser. 136p. 1984. pap. text ed. 15.70 incl. key to exercises (ISBN 0-89420-237-5, 420125). Natl Book.

Personal Shorthand for the Executive Secretary: Syllabus. Piper et al. 211p. 1977. pap. text ed. 9.95 (ISBN 0-89420-030-5, 217150); cassette recordings 243.95 (ISBN 0-89420-171-9, 217100). Natl Book.

Personal Shorthand for the Journalist. Walter Blum & C. Theo Yerian. 176p. (Orig.). 1980. pap. text ed. 8.85 (ISBN 0-89420-214-6, 242032); optional cassettes recordings 237.20 (ISBN 0-89420-225-1, 242000). Natl Book.

Personal Shorthand: Individualized Syllabus. Carl W. Salser & C. Theo Yerian. (Personal Shorthand Cardinal Ser.: Bk. 1). 150p. (Orig.). 1983. pap. text ed. 7.95 (ISBN 0-89420-232-4, 241175); cassette 314.05 (241000). Natl Book.

Personal Shorthand: Ps-80, Bks. 1 & 2. Carl W. Salser & C. Theo. Yerian. (Personal Shorthand Cardinal Ser.). 369p. 1981. text ed. 12.85 (ISBN 0-89420-221-9, 241180); Optional cassette recordings 625.50 (241000). Natl Book.

Personal Shorthand Reverse Dictionary-Special Edition. Carl W. Salser & C. Theo Yerian. Ed. by Charlotte A. Butsch. 206p. 1984. pap. 10.80 (ISBN 0-89420-240-5, 213200). Natl Book.

Personal Shorthand Standard Dictionary. Carl W. Salser et al. Ed. by Charlotte Butsch. 207p. 1984. pap. 9.65 (ISBN 0-89420-239-1, 213100). Natl Book.

Personal Shorthand: Syllabus. Joanne Piper & Theo Yerian. 1975. pap. text ed. 12.95 (ISBN 0-89420-083-6, 217000); cassette recordings 248.60 (ISBN 0-89420-172-7, 178000). Natl Book.

Personal Shorthand: Teacher's Manual & Key to Syllabus. Joanne Piper & Theo Yerian. 1975. tchr's ed. 4.95 (ISBN 0-89420-094-1, 217007). Natl Book.

Personal Shorthand Theory Review Workbook. 2nd, rev. ed. Carl W. Salser & C. Theo Yerian. (Personal Shorthand Cardinal Ser.). 97p. 1983. pap. text ed. 5.25 (ISBN 0-89420-233-2, 216715). Natl Book.

Personal Side. Jessie A. Bloodworth & Elizabeth J. Greenwood. LC 71-137156. (Poverty U. S. A. Historical Record Ser). 1971. Repr. of 1939 ed. 26.50 (ISBN 0-405-03094-0). Ayer Co Pubs.

Personal Skills: For Home, School, Work, 1984. Valerie Chamberlain. (gr. 9-12). 1984. text ed. 22.40 (ISBN 0-02-665360-5). Bennett Il.

Personal Skills for the Manager. Leonard Nadler. LC 82-72869. 275p. 1982. ringed binder 29.95x (ISBN 0-87094-349-9). Dow Jones-Irwin.

Personal Skills in Public Speech. Stafford H. Thomas. (Illus.). 288p. 1985. pap. text ed. write for info. (ISBN 0-13-658576-0). P-H.

Personal, Social & Vocational Education. John MacBeath. (Professional Issues in Education Ser.: Vol. 3). 88p. 1987. pap. 7.95 (ISBN 0-7073-0531-4, Pub. by Scot Acad Pr). Longwood Pub Group.

Personal Social Services: Basic Information. 1977. 22.00x (ISBN 0-317-05798-7, Pub. by Natl Inst Social Work). State Mutual Bk.

Personal Social Services Bibliography. 2nd ed. Ed. by Gillian Stewart. 144p. 1980. pap. text ed. 29.50x (ISBN 0-85365-513-8, Pub. by Library Assn Pub London). ALA.

Personal Social Services Council: At Home in a Boarding House. Ed. by National Institue for Social Work Staff. 1981. 20.00x (ISBN 0-317-40623-X, Pub. by Natl Inst Social Work). State Mutual Bk.

Personal Social Services in an Unsuccessful Economy. Charles Carter. (Younghusband Lectrue Ser.: 1980). 1981. 25.00x (ISBN 0-317-40597-7, Pub. by Natl Soc Work). State Mutual Bk.

Personal Sociology. Ed. by Paul C. Higgins & John M. Johnson. LC 87-25894. 174p. 1988. lib. bdg. 37.95 (ISBN 0-275-92642-7, C2642). Praeger.

Personal Sphere Model. Raoul A. Schmiedeck. 240p. 1978. text ed. 39.50 (ISBN 0-8089-1093-0, 793915). Grune.

Personal Stories: A Book for Adults Who Are Beginning to Read. Kamla D. Koch et al. (Illus.). 78p. (Orig.). 1985. pap. 4.50 tchrs. ed. (ISBN 0-916591-03-4); 5.99 (ISBN 0-916591-02-6). Linmore Pub.

Personal Stories: A Book for Adults Who Are Beginning to Read, Bk. 2. Kamla D. Koch et al. (Illus.). 113p. (Orig.). 1986. pap. text ed. 6.50 (ISBN 0-916591-04-2); tchrs. ed. 4.50 (ISBN 0-916591-05-0). Linmore Pub.

Personal Stress Reduction Program. Jeffrey W. Forman & Dave Myers. (Illus.). 160p. 1987. pap. 9.95 (ISBN 0-13-659277-5). P-H.

Personal Style of Therapy. Irene Bloomfield. 1985. 10.00x (ISBN 0-317-62236-6, Guild of Pastoral Psych). State Mutual Bk.

Personal Styles & Effective Performance: Making Your Style Work for You. David W. Merill & Roger H. Reid. LC 80-70389. (Illus.). 256p. 1981. pap. 14.95 (ISBN 0-8019-6899-2). Chilton.

Personal Styles in Neurosis: Implications for Small Group Psychotherapy & Behavior Therapy. Tom Caine et al. (International Library of Group Psychotherapy & Group Process). 224p. 27.95x (ISBN 0-7100-0617-9). Routledge Chapman & Hall.

Personal Success: The Promise of God. Victor Matthews. 1989. price not set. Baker Bk.

Personal Tax Advisor: Understanding the New Tax Law. Cliff Roberson. LC 86-27850. 1987. pap. 12.95 (ISBN 0-8306-3134-8, Liberty Hse, 30134). TAB Bks.

Personal Tax Planning for Professionals & Owners of Small Businesses. 434p. 1983. 95.00 (ISBN 0-88124-115-6). Cal Cont Ed Bar.

Personal Tax Planning for Professionals & Owners of Small Businesses. 434p. 1987. 95.00 (36630); June '86 supp. 35.00; June '87 supp. 36.00. Cal Cont Ed Bar.

Personal Telecomputing. Donald Stoner. 232p. 1984. pap. 12.95 (ISBN 0-942386-47-7). Compute Pubns.

Personal Time Management. Marion E. Hayes. (CRISP Publications 50-Minute Ser.). Date not set. 6.95. Human Res Dev Pr.

Personal Time Management. Marion E. Haynes. Ed. by Michael G. Crisp. LC 86-72076. (Fifty-Minute Ser.). (Illus.). 88p. (Orig.). 1987. pap. 6.95 (ISBN 0-931961-22-X). Crisp Pubns.

Personal Time Management Manual. 11th ed ed. John S. Hoyt, Jr. 246p. 1981. 15.00 (ISBN 0-943000-08-4). Telstar Inc.

Personal Time Management Study Guide. 11th ed. John S. Hoyt, Jr. (Illus.). 50p. 1982. pap. text ed. 4.95 (ISBN 0-943000-02-5). Telstar Inc.

Personal Totem Pole: Animal Imagery, the Chakras, & Psychotherapy. Eligio S. Gallegos. LC 87-90620. 179p. (Orig.). 1987. pap. 12.00 (ISBN 0-944164-07-2). Moon Bear Pr.

Personal Traits & Success in Teaching. Elizabeth H. Morris. LC 76-177087. (Columbia University. Teachers College. Contributions to Education: No. 342). Repr. of 1929 ed. 22.50 (ISBN 0-404-55342-7). AMS Pr.

Personal Traits of British Authors. Edward F. Mason. 1891. Repr. lib. bdg. 37.50 (ISBN 0-8414-6486-3). Folcroft.

Personal Typing. 4th ed. Alan C. Lloyd & Russell J. Hosler. (Illus.). 1978. text ed. 19.32 (ISBN 0-07-038208-5). McGraw.

Personal Typing in Twenty-Four Hours: Learn to Type on Your Electric or Manual Typewriter or Personal Computer. 5th, rev. ed. Philip S. Pepe. 64p. 1984. pap. text ed. 6.95 (ISBN 0-07-049306-5). McGraw.

Personal Typing Thirty. 5th ed. Philip S. Pepe. 64p. 1974. text ed. 15.44 (ISBN 0-07-049299-9). McGraw.

Personal Values Analysis Handbook. Pref. by James J. Messina. (Professional Handbook Ser.). 26p. (Orig.). 1982. pap. text ed. 6.00 (ISBN 0-931975-16-6). Advanced Dev Sys.

Personal Values & Consumer Psychology. Robert E. Pitts, Jr. & Arch G. Woodside. LC 83-48123. 336p. 1984. 39.00x (ISBN 0-669-06937-X); pap. 18.00x (ISBN 0-669-09807-8). Lexington Bks.

Personal Values in Public Policy. John Haughey. LC 79-84401. (Woodstock Studies: No. 3). 288p. (Orig.). 1979. pap. 6.95 (ISBN 0-8091-2201-4). Paulist Pr.

Personal Valuing: An Introduction. Dale D. Simmons. LC 82-2191. 124p. 1982. text ed. 16.95x (ISBN 0-88229-565-9); pap. text ed. 9.95x (ISBN 0-88229-804-6). Nelson-Hall.

Personal View: Photography in the Collection of Paul F. Walter. John Pultz. 1985. pap. 9.95 (ISBN 0-87070-629-2). Museum Mod Art.

Personal View: Selections from the Joan Mannheimer Ceramic Collection. Elisabeth Kirsch. Ed. by Craig Subler. (Illus., Orig.). 1983. pap. 12.00 (ISBN 0-914489-00-3). Univ Miss KS Art.

Personal Vision Ingmar Bergman see Films of Ingmar Bergman.

Personal Vision of Ingmar Bergman. Jorn Donner. Tr. by Holger Lundbergh. (Biography Index Reprint Ser.). Repr. of 1964 ed. 20.25 (ISBN 0-8369-8119-7). Ayer Co Pubs.

Personal Vision of Ingmar Bergman. Jorn Donner. (Biography Index Reprint Ser.). (Illus.). 276p. Repr. of 1964 ed. lib. bdg. 19.25 (ISBN 0-8290-0832-2). Irvington.

Personal Vision of Ingmar Bergman. Jorn Donner. (Biography Index Reprint Ser.). (Illus.). 276p. 1964. pap. 4.95 (ISBN 0-8290-1760-7). Irvington.

Personal Voices: A Celebration of Dialogue. Ed. by Mary L. Bradford. 268p. 1987. pap. 8.95 (ISBN 0-941214-57-5). Signature Bks.

Personal Voices: Chinese Women in the 1980's. Emily Honig & Gail Hershatter. LC 87-18013. (Illus.). 450p. 1988. text ed. 42.50x (ISBN 0-8047-1416-9); pap. 14.95x (ISBN 0-8047-1431-2). Stanford U Pr.

Personal Vote: Constituency Service & Electoral Independence. Bruce Cain et al. LC 86-22839. (Illus.). 288p. 1987. text ed. 27.00x (ISBN 0-674-66317-9). Harvard U Pr.

Personal Watercraft Service Manual. Intertec Publishing Staff. (Illus.). 125p. (Orig.). 1988. pap. price not set (ISBN 0-87288-307-8, PWS-1). Intertec Pub.

Personal Weight Training for Fitness & Athletics: From Theory to Practice. 2nd ed. Frederick C. Hatfield & March L. Krotee. (Illus.). 208p. 1984. pap. text ed. 13.95 (ISBN 0-8403-3219-X). Kendall-Hunt.

Personal Witness. John Navone. LC 67-13761. 1967. 4.95 (ISBN 0-685-42652-1, Pub-by Sheed). Guild Bks.

Personal Work. Milo Kauffman. 1940. pap. 2.00 (ISBN 0-87813-951-6). Christian Light.

Personal Writings of Joseph Smith. Ed. by Dean C. Jessee. LC 83-18937. (Illus.). 737p. 1984. 19.95 (ISBN 0-87747-974-7). Deseret Bk.

Personalia. E. S. Haynes. 1973. Repr. of 1918 ed. 20.00 (ISBN 0-8274-0233-3). R West.

Personalia (Edward Thomas) E. S. Haynes. 128p. 1979. Repr. of 1918 ed. lib. bdg. 20.00 (ISBN 0-89987-352-9). Darby Bks.

Personalism. Borden P. Bowne. LC 75-949. Repr. of 1908 ed. 22.50 (ISBN 0-404-59073-X). AMS Pr.

Personalism. Emmanuel Mounier. Tr. by Philip Mairet. LC 75-122050. 1970. pap. 4.95 (ISBN 0-268-00434-X). U of Notre Dame Pr.

Personalism & Party Politics: Institutionalization of the Popular Democratic Party of Puerto Rico. Kenneth H. Farr. LC 73-75406. 143p. (Orig.). 1973. 4.95 (ISBN 0-913480-12-6); pap. 2.95 (ISBN 0-913480-13-4). Inter Am U Pr.

Personalism & the Problems of Philosophy: An Appreciation of the Works of Borden Parker Bowne. Ralph T. Flewelling. LC 75-3147. Repr. of 1915 ed. 21.00 (ISBN 0-404-59154-X). AMS Pr.

Personalism in Theology. Ed. by Edgar S. Brightman. LC 75-3088. (Philosophy in America Ser.). Repr. of 1943 ed. 24.50 (ISBN 0-404-59086-1). AMS Pr.

Personalismo y Politica De Partidos: La Institucionalizacion Del Partido Popular Democratico De Puerto Rico. Kenneth R. Farr. Tr. by Jesus Benitez from Eng. LC 73-75406. 268p. 1975. 4.95 (ISBN 0-913480-25-8); pap. 2.95 (ISBN 0-913480-26-6). Inter Am U Pr.

Personalist Challenge: Intersubjectivity & Ontology. Maurice Nedoncelle. Tr. by Francois C. Gerard et al. LC 83-26293. (Pittsburgh Theological Monographs: No. 27). 1984. pap. 15.00 (ISBN 0-915138-29-8). Pickwick.

Personalities. facs. ed. Arthur A. Baumann. LC 68-54323. (Essay Index Reprint Ser.). 1936. 18.00 (ISBN 0-8369-0177-0). Ayer Co Pubs.

Personalities & Cultures: Readings in Psychological Anthropology. Ed. by Robert Hunt. (Texas Press Sourcebooks: No. 3). (Illus.). 456p. 1976. pap. 10.95 (ISBN 0-292-76429-4). U of Tex Pr.

Personalities & Reminiscences of the War. Robert L. Bullard. 16.00 (ISBN 0-8369-6967-7, 7848). Ayer Co Pubs.

Personalities in American Art. William F. Paris. LC 72-107731. (Essay Index Reprint Ser.). 1930. 14.00 (ISBN 0-8369-1582-8). Ayer Co Pubs.

Personalities in Art. facs. ed. Royal Cortissoz. LC 68-55844. (Essay Index Reprint Ser). 1925. 24.50 (ISBN 0-8369-0339-0). Ayer Co Pubs.

Personalities of America. 3rd ed. Ed. by J. M. Evans. LC 79-51997. 500p. 1985. 69.50 (ISBN 0-934544-28-X). Am Biog Inst.

Personalities of America. 4th ed. Ed. by J. M. Evans. LC 79-51997. 500p. 1987. 49.50 (ISBN 0-934544-38-7). Am Biog Inst.

Personalities of Antiquity. Arthur Weigall. 235p. 1981. Repr. of 1928 ed. lib. bdg. 35.00. Century Bookbindery.

Personalities of Antiquity. facs. ed. Arthur E. Weigall. LC 77-90672. (Essay Index Reprint Ser.). 1928. 18.00 (ISBN 0-8369-1217-9). Ayer Co Pubs.

Personalities of the Eighteenth Century: (Samuel Foote, Christopher Smart, William Hazlitt) Grace A. Murray. 230p. 1980. Repr. of 1927 ed. lib. bdg. 25.00 (ISBN 0-8495-3772-X). Arden Lib.

Personalities of the Eighteenth Century. Grace A. Murray. LC 72-7299. Repr. of 1927 ed. lib. bdg. 35.00 (ISBN 0-8414-0316-3). Folcroft.

Personalities of the Socially & Mechanically Inclined see Effect of Manual Guidance upon Maze Learning.

Personalities of the South. 13th ed. Ed. by J. M. Evans. LC 73-4535. 500p. 1985. 55.00 (ISBN 0-934544-33-6). Am Biog Inst.

Personalities of the West & Midwest. 8th. ed. Ed. by J. M. Evans. LC 68-56857. 366p. 1985. 55.00x (ISBN 0-934544-26-3). Am Biog Inst.

Personality. 2nd ed. Seymour Feshbach & Bernard Weiner. LC 85-80721. 578p. 1986. text ed. 28.00 (ISBN 0-669-07550-7); instr's guide 2.00 (ISBN 0-669-07551-5). Heath.

Personality. Fay Fransella. (Psychology in Progress Ser.). 1981. 26.50x (ISBN 0-416-72770-0, NO. 2226); pap. 11.95x (ISBN 0-416-72780-8, NO. 2236). Routledge Chapman & Hall.

Personality. 3rd ed. Richard S. Lazarus & Alan Monat. (Foundations of Modern Psychology Ser.). (Illus.). 1979. write for info. (ISBN 0-13-657908-6). P-H.

Personality Orientation. Maria Neimark. LC 75-33931. 304p. 1976. 37.95 (ISBN 0-87778-088-9). Educ Tech Pubn.

Personality Patterns & Oral Reading: A Study of Overt Behavior in the Reading Situation As It Reveals Reactions of Dependence, Aggression, & Withdrawal in Children. Gladys Natchez. LC 60-6043. pap. 28.00 (ISBN 0-317-10337-7, 2050322). Bks Demand UMI.

Personality Plus. Florence Littauer. (Illus.). 192p. 1982. 7.95 (Power Ed.). Revell.

Personality Plus: Some Experiences of Emma McChesney & Her Son, Jock. facsimile ed. Edna Ferber. LC 77-150473. (Short Story Index Reprint Ser.). (Illus.). Repr. of 1914 ed. 15.00 (ISBN 0-8369-3813-5). Ayer Co Pubs.

Personality, Power & Authority: A View from the Behavioral Sciences. Leonard W. Doob. LC 83-1688. (Contributions in Psychology Ser.: No. 1). xiii, 218p. 1983. lib. bdg. 35.00 (ISBN 0-313-23920-7, DPA/). Greenwood.

Personality, Power, & Politics: The Historical Significance of Napoleon, Bismarck, Lenin, & Hitler. Anthony R. De Luca. 133p. 1983. 17.25 (ISBN 0-87073-616-7); pap. 11.95 (ISBN 0-87073-617-5). Schenkman Bks Inc.

Personality Power the Specific Action Way: A Complete Course in Management Styles. Owen Allen. LC 87-63535. (Illus.). 110p. 1988. text ed. 25.00 (ISBN 0-932569-01-3). Specific Action.

Personality Profile. Darrell Franken. 48p. 1986. pap. 3.95 (ISBN 0-934957-13-4). Wellness Pubns.

Personality Projection in the Drawing of the Human Figure: A Method of Personality Investigation. Karen Machover. (Illus.). 192p. 1980. 21.75 (ISBN 0-398-01184-2). C C Thomas.

Personality Psychology in Europe. Ed. by H. Bonarius et al. 398p. 1984. pap. text ed. 47.50 (ISBN 90-265-0559-0, Pub. by Swets Zeitlinger Netherlands). Hogrefe Intl.

Personality Psychology in Europe: Current Trends & Controversies. Ed. by A. Angleitner et al. 266p. (Orig.). 1986. pap. 33.50 (ISBN 9-02650-597-3). Hogrefe Intl.

Personality Research in Marketing: A Bibliography. Ed. by Dik W. Twedt et al. LC 76-45806. (American Marketing Association, Bibliography Ser.: No. 23). pap. 20.00 (ISBN 0-317-20079-8, 2023361). Bks Demand UMI.

Personality, Roles & Social Behavior. Ed. by W. Ickes & E. S. Knowles. (Springer Series in Social Psychology). (Illus.). 362p. 1982. 39.50 (ISBN 0-387-90637-1). Springer-Verlag.

Personality: Searching for the Sources of Human Behavior. William S. Samuel. (Illus.). 544p. 1981. text ed. 36.95 (ISBN 0-07-054520-0). McGraw.

Personality: Strategies & Issues. 5th ed. Robert M. Liebert & Michael D. Spiegler. 1987. 39.00x (ISBN 0-256-03397-8). Dorsey.

Personality Structure & Human Interaction: The Developing Synthesis of Psychodynamic Theory. Harry Guntrip. LC 61-12135. 456p. 1964. text ed. 47.50x (ISBN 0-8236-4120-1). Intl Univs Pr.

Personality Structure & Measurement. H. J. Eysenck & Sybil B. G. Eysenck. LC 68-15875. 1968. text ed. 12.95 (ISBN 0-912736-08-9). EDITS Pubs.

Personality Studies of Six-Year-Old Children in Classroom Situations. Alberta Munkres. LC 70-177096. (Columbia University. Teachers College. Contributions to Education: No. 681). Repr. of 1936 ed. 22.50 (ISBN 0-404-55681-7). AMS Pr.

Personality Styles & Brief Psychotherapy. Mardi Horowitz et al. 349p. 1984. 26.95x (ISBN 0-465-05575-3, 83-45378). Basic.

Personality Surgeon. Colin Wilson. LC 85-62423. 322p. (Orig.). 1986. 17.95 (ISBN 0-916515-04-4). Mercury Hse Inc.

Personality Survives Death. Lady Barrett. 59.95 (ISBN 0-8490-0819-0). Gordon Pr.

Personality Tests & Inventory: Medical Subject Analysis with Bibliography. American Health Research Institute Staff. LC 84-45659. 150p. 1985. 34.50 (ISBN 0-88164-212-6); pap. 26.50 (ISBN 0-88164-213-4). ABBE Pubs Assn.

Personality Tests & Reviews I. Ed. by Oscar K. Buros. xxxi, 1659p. 1970. 50.00x (ISBN 0-910674-10-8). U of Nebr Pr.

Personality Tests & Reviews II. Ed. by Oscar K. Buros. LC 74-13192. xxxi, 841p. 1975. 55.00x (ISBN 0-910674-19-1). U of Nebr Pr.

Personality: The Art of Being & Becoming. Hazrat I. Khan. LC 82-60284. (Collected Works of Hazrat Inayat Khan Ser.). (Illus.). 304p. (Orig.). 1982. pap. 10.95 (ISBN 0-930872-29-0, 1016P). Omega Pr NY.

Personality: The Human Potential. M. L. Weiner. 200p. 1973. 28.00 (ISBN 0-08-016946-5). Pergamon.

Personality: The Need for Liberty & Rights. Rubin Gotesky. 1967. 3.50 (ISBN 0-87212-012-0). Libra.

Personality Theories. 2nd, rev. ed. Larry A. Hjelle & Daniel J. Ziegler. (Illus.). 512p. 1981. text ed. 33.95 (ISBN 0-07-029063-6). McGraw.

Personality Theories. 5th ed. Maddi. 1988. text ed. 39.00 (ISBN 0-256-03245-9). Dorsey.

Personality Theories: A Comparative Analysis. 4th ed. Ed. by Salvatore R. Maddi. 1980. 37.00x (ISBN 0-256-02299-2). Dorsey.

Personality Theories Guides to Human Nature. 2nd ed. Nicholas S. DiCaprio. LC 82-15745. 564p. 1983. text ed. 32.95 (ISBN 0-03-059094-9). HR&W.

Personality Theories: Journeys into Self: An Experiential Workbook. Willard B. Frick. 1984. pap. text ed. 9.95x (ISBN 0-8077-6102-8). Tchrs Coll.

Personality Theories, Research & Assessment. Raymond J. Corsini & Anthony J. Marsella. LC 82-61261. 703p. 1983. text ed. 32.50 (ISBN 0-87581-288-0). Peacock Pubs.

Personality Theory & Clinical Practice. Peter Fonagy & Anna Higgitt. 194p. 1985. pap. 7.95 (ISBN 0-416-35630-3, NO. 9182). Routledge Chapman & Hall.

Personality Theory & Information Processing. Ed. by Peter Suedfeld et al. LC 77-123053. (Illus.). pap. 79.50 (ISBN 0-317-10383-0, 2012376). Bks Demand UMI.

Personality: Theory & Research. Jerry M. Burger. 510p. 1986. text ed. write for info. (ISBN 0-534-06126-5). Wadsworth Pub.

Personality Theory & Research. 5th ed. Pervin. 1989. price not set (ISBN 0-471-61219-7). Wiley.

Personality: Theory & Research. 4th ed. Lawrence A. Pervin. LC 83-21610. 569p. 1984. write for info. (ISBN 0-471-88577-0). Wiley.

Personality Theory & Social Work Practice. Herbert S. Strean. LC 75-1132. 190p. 1975. 16.50 (ISBN 0-8108-0797-1). Scarecrow.

Personality: Theory, Assessment, & Research. Robert J. Gatchel & Frederick G. Mears. LC 81-51856. 559p. 1982. text ed. write for info. (ISBN 0-312-60229-4); Instr's. manual avail. St Martin.

Personality Theory in Action: Handbook for the Objective-Analytic (O-A) Battery. Raymond B. Cattell & James M. Schuerger. LC 78-50146. 1978. 47.50 (ISBN 0-918296-11-0). Inst Personality & Ability.

Personality: Theory, Research & Applications. Charles R. Potkay & Bem P. Allen. LC 85-19477. (Psychology Ser.). 624p. 1986. text ed. 26.00 pub net (ISBN 0-534-05634-2). Brooks-Cole.

Personality Theory: The Personological Tradition. Robert Hagan. (Illus.). 256p. 1976. pap. text ed. write for info. (ISBN 0-13-658161-7). P-H.

Personality Types & Culture in Later Adulthood. J. Shanan. (Contributions to Human Development: Vol. 12). (Illus.). xiv, 146p. 1985. 42.75 (ISBN 3-8055-3998-3). S Karger.

Personality Types: Using the Enneagram for Self-Discovery. Don R. Riso. (Illus.). 400p. 1987. 19.95 (ISBN 0-395-40575-0); pap. 9.95 (ISBN 0-395-44484-5). HM.

Personality Types: Using the Enneagram for Self-Discovery. Don R. Riso. 1987. price not set. Ticknor & Fields.

Personality Unmasked. William A. Oribello. 1986. pap. 3.00 (ISBN 0-910433-05-4). Mystic Soc.

Personalized Care Model for the Elderly. Ed. by Clara Nicholson & Judith Nicholson. 540p. 1983. pap. text ed. 21.30. Elder.

Personalized Computational Skills Program. Combined & Condensed ed. Bryce R. Shaw. LC 79-90570. 544p. 1982. Set. pap. text ed. 33.16 (ISBN 0-395-30856-9); Mod. A. pap. text ed. 14.36 (ISBN 0-395-29033-3); Mod. B. pap. text ed. 14.36 (ISBN 0-395-29034-1); Mod. C. pap. text ed. 14.36 (ISBN 0-395-29035-X); Mod. D. pap. text ed. 14.36 (ISBN 0-395-29997-7); Mod. E. pap. text ed. 14.36 (ISBN 0-395-29998-5); Mod. F. pap. text ed. 14.36 (ISBN 0-395-29999-3); pap. text ed. 33.16 Vol. I (ISBN 0-395-29032-5); pap. text ed. 33.16 Vol. II (ISBN 0-395-29996-9). HM.

Personalized Guide to Establishing Associateships & Partnerships, Vol. 3. Thomas L. Snyder & Jeffrey C. Bauer. LC 82-14347. (Dental Practice Management Ser.). (Illus.). 152p. 1982. pap. text ed. 17.95 (ISBN 0-8016-4714-2). Mosby.

Personalized Guide to Financial Planning, Vol. 5. Ed. by Thomas L. Snyder et al. LC 82-14356. (Dental Practice Management Ser.). 122p. 1982. pap. text ed. 17.95 (ISBN 0-8016-4713-4). Mosby.

Personalized Guide to Legal Issues, Vol. 7. Thomas L. Snyder & Randall K. Berning. LC 84-8259. (Mosby's Dental Practice Management Ser.: Vol. 7). 140p. 1984. pap. text ed. 17.95 (ISBN 0-8016-4751-7). Mosby.

Personalized Guide to Marketing Strategy, Vol. 4. Ed. by Thomas L. Snyder & Charles J. Felmeister. LC 82-14158. (Dental Practice Management Ser.). (Illus.). 120p. 1983. pap. text ed. 17.95 (ISBN 0-8016-4725-8). Mosby.

Personalized Money Strategies: Fifteen No-Nonsense Investment Plans to Achieve Your Goals. Peter Passell. 192p. 1985. pap. 15.50 (ISBN 0-446-51335-0). Warner Bks.

Personalized Money Strategies: Fifteen No-nonsense Investment Plans to Achieve Your Goals. Peter Passell. 208p. 1986. pap. 3.95 (ISBN 0-446-30115-9). Warner Bks.

Personalized Reading Instruction: New Techniques That Increase Reading Skill and Comprehension. Walter Barbe & Jerry L. Abbott. 1975. 15.95 (ISBN 0-13-658104-8). P-H.

Personalized Stress Management: A Manual for Everyday Life & Work. Joseph L. Gill. LC 82-90115. (Illus.). 175p. 1983. 14.95 (ISBN 0-910819-00-9); pap. 9.95 (ISBN 0-910819-01-7). Counsel & Consult.

Personalized Student Instruction Units: Elements of Probability & Statistics, Vol. I. Ethel L. Lawrence. 336p. 1983. Shrink Wrapped 14.95 (ISBN 0-8403-3145-2). Kendall-Hunt.

Personalized System of Instruction. J. Gilmour Sherman & Robert S. Ruskin. Ed. by Danny G. Langdon. LC 77-25415. (Instructional Design Library). (Illus.). 128p. 1978. 23.95 (ISBN 0-87778-117-6). Educ Tech Pubns.

Personalizing Reading Efficiency. 2nd ed. Lyle L. Miller. 1981. pap. text ed. write for info. (ISBN 0-8087-3990-5). Burgess MN Intl.

Personals. Gisela Beker & Carol Rosenwald. 144p. 1985. pap. 2.95 (ISBN 0-8217-1512-7). Zebra.

Personals. Susan Lois. (Orig.). 1986. pap. 3.95 (ISBN 0-440-16945-3). Dell.

Personals. Lynn Nakkim. 240p. (Orig.). 1986. pap. 9.95 (ISBN 0-938787-00-4). Seahorse Pr.

Personas Escogidas de Dios. Margaret Ralph. (Serie Jirafa). Orig. Title: God's Special People. 28p. 1979. 3.95 (ISBN 0-311-38535-4, Edit Mundo). Casa Bautista.

Personenindex zu Kants Gesammelten Schriften see Kantindex Allgemeiner zu Kants Gesammelten Schriften.

Personhood. Leo Buscaglia. LC 78-66423. 160p. 1982. 9.95 (ISBN 0-03-063202-1, Pub by Slack Inc). H Holt & Co.

Personhood. Leo Buscaglia. 1988. pap. 6.95 (ISBN 0-449-90199-8, Columbine). Fawcett.

Personhood. Leo F. Buscaglia. LC 78-66423. 160p. 1978. 9.95 (ISBN 0-913590-63-0). Slack Inc.

Personhood. Mary A. Warren. Date not set. pap. (ISBN 0-918528-15-1). Edgepress.

Personhood, Creativity & Freedom. Eliot Deutsch. LC 82-4891. 167p. 1982. text ed. 20.00x (ISBN 0-8248-0800-2). UH Pr.

Personification & the Sublime: Milton to Coleridge. Steven Knapp. 192p. 1985. text ed. 18.50x (ISBN 0-674-66320-9). Harvard U Pr.

Personification in Eighteenth-Century English Poetry. Chester F. Chapin. 1967. lib. bdg. 18.50x (ISBN 0-374-91425-7, Octagon). Hippocrene Bks.

Personification in Piers Plowman. Lavinia Griffiths. (Piers Plowman Studies: No. III). 125p. 1985. 32.00 (ISBN 0-85991-184-5, Pub. by Boydell & Brewer). Longwood Pub Group.

Personnages. Francoise Mallet-Joris. 462p. 1973. 22.50 (ISBN 0-686-56310-7); pap. 3.95 (ISBN 0-686-56311-5). French & Eur.

Personnages Des Rougon-Macquart Pour Servir a la Lecture et a l'Etude De l'Oeuvre De Emile Zola. F. C. Ramond. LC 74-126396. (Bibliography & Reference Ser.: No. 351). (Fr., Literature & criticism, no. 73). 1970. lib. bdg. 32.00 (ISBN 0-8337-2901-2). B Franklin.

Personnel. 5th. ed. Dale S. Beach. 1985. text ed. write for info. (ISBN 0-02-307060-9); text ed. write for info. study guide (ISBN 0-02-307080-3). Macmillan.

Personnel. Marie-Elise Wheatwind. 16p. (Orig.). 1983. pap. 3.00 (ISBN 0-930012-45-3). J Mudfoot.

Personnel - Human Resource Management: An Environmental Approach. Vida G. Scarpello & James Ledvinka. 816p. 1988. text ed. 29.75 (ISBN 0-534-08346-3). PWS Kent Pub.

Personnel Administration. David Schrieber. 164p. 1984. 16.95 (ISBN 0-318-17597-5). Credit Union Natl Assn.

Personnel Administration: A Guide to the Effective Management of Human Resources. Betty Ream. 182p. 1984. 26.50 (ISBN 0-902197-14-2, Pub. by Woodhead-Faulkner). Longwood Pub Group.

Personnel Administration: A Point of View & a Method. 9th ed. Paul Pigors & Charles A. Myers. (Illus.). 560p. 1981. text ed. 39.95x (ISBN 0-07-049971-3). McGraw.

Personnel Administration: An Experiential Skill-Building Approach. Rev. ed. Richard W. Beatty & Craig E. Schneier. 576p. 1981. pap. text ed. write for info. (ISBN 0-201-00172-1); implemention manual o.p. 25.95 (ISBN 0-201-00176-4). Addison-Wesley.

Personnel Administration Handbook. Wilbert E. Scheer. 1985. 49.95 (ISBN 0-85013-028-X). Dartnell Corp.

Personnel Administration in Education: A Management Approach. 2nd ed. Ronald W. Rebore. (Illus.). 368p. 1987. text ed. write for info. (ISBN 0-13-657719-9). P-H.

Personnel Administration in Education: A Management Approach for Educational Organizations. Ronald W. Rebore. (Illus.). 336p. 1982. write for info. (ISBN 0-13-657742-3). P-H.

Personnel Administration in Education: Leadership for Instructional Improvement. 2nd ed. Ben M. Harris et al. 336p. 1985. 38.95x (ISBN 0-205-08200-9, 238200, Pub. by Longwood Div). Allyn.

Personnel Administration in Education: New Issues - New Needs. L. Dean Webb et al. 288p. 1987. text ed. 32.95 (ISBN 0-675-20439-9). Merrill.

Personnel Administration in Higher Education: Handbook of Faculty & Staff Personnel Practices. Ray T. Fortunato & D. Geneva Waddell. LC 81-47769. (Higher Education Ser.). 416p. 1981. text ed. 32.95x (ISBN 0-87589-506-9). Jossey-Bass.

Personnel Administration in the Christian School. J. Lester Brubaker. 168p. (Orig.). 1980. pap. 6.95 (ISBN 0-88469-130-6). BMH Bks.

Personnel Administration in the Health Services Industry: Theory & Practice. 2nd ed. Norman Metzger. LC 78-31330. (Illus.). 1979. 29.50 (ISBN 0-89335-074-5). PMA Pub Corp.

Personnel Administration in Three Non-Teaching Services of the Public Schools. Hazel Davis. LC 76-178802. (Columbia University. Teachers College. Contributions to Education: No. 784). Repr. of 1939 ed. 22.50 (ISBN 0-404-55784-8). AMS Pr.

Personnel Administration: Its Principles & Practice. Ordway Tead & Henry C. Metcalfe. Ed. by Alfred D. Chandler. LC 79-7556. (History of Management Thought & Practice Ser.). 1980. Repr. of 1926 ed. lib. bdg. 46.00x (ISBN 0-405-12342-6). Ayer Co Pubs.

Personnel Administration Today. Craig E. Schneier & Richard W. Beatty. 1978. pap. text ed. write for info. (ISBN 0-201-00503-4). Addison-Wesley.

Personnel Administrator. Jack Rudman. (Career Examination Ser.: C-647). (Cloth bdg. avail. on request). pap. 18.00 (ISBN 0-8373-0647-7). Natl Learning.

Personnel Administrator Index 1970-1981. 35p. 1985. pap. 12.00. Am Soc Personnel.

Personnel Analyst. Jack Rudman. (Career Examination Ser.: C-2344). (Cloth bdg. avail. on request). pap. 14.00 (ISBN 0-8373-2344-4). Natl Learning.

Personnel Analyst Trainee. Jack Rudman. (Career Examination Ser.: C-2395). (Cloth bdg. avail. on request). pap. 12.00 (ISBN 0-8373-2395-9). Natl Learning.

Personnel & Human Resource Management in Canada. Shimon D. Dolan & Randall S. Schuler. 620p. 1987. text ed. 38.25 (ISBN 0-314-32486-0); instr's manual avail. (ISBN 0-314-34766-6). West Pub.

Personnel & Human Resource Management. Jack Halloran. (Illus.). 576p. 1986. text ed. write for info. (ISBN 0-13-659020-9). P-H.

Personnel & Human Resource Management. 3rd ed. Randall S. Schuler. LC 86-15804. (Illus.). 735p. 1987. text ed. 41.00 (ISBN 0-314-25471-4); software manual avail. (ISBN 0-314-35244-9). West Pub.

Personnel & Human Resource Management (International Edition) 2nd ed. Randall S. Schuler. (Illus.). 700p. 1984. 17.00 (ISBN 0-314-77789-X). West Pub.

Personnel & Industrial Psychology. 2nd ed. Edwin E. Ghiselli & Clarence W. Brown. LC 54-10632. (McGraw-Hill Series in Psychology). pap. 126.00 (ISBN 0-317-08272-8, 2003754). Bks Demand UMI.

Personnel & Industrial Relations. 4th ed. John B. Miner & Mary G. Miner. 624p. 1985. text ed. write for info. (ISBN 0-02-381620-1). Macmillan.

Personnel & Labor Relations: Answers to the Questions on Subjects Matter, CEBS Course, No. 8. (Orig.). 1985. pap. text ed. 15.00 (ISBN 0-89154-280-9). Intl Found Employ.

Personnel & Labor Relations: Learning Guide, CEBS Course, No. 8. (Orig.). 1985. 18.00 (ISBN 0-89154-279-5). Intl Found Employ.

Personnel & Operating Efficiency in the Butler County (OH) Court: A Technical Assistance Report. National Center for State Courts Staff. 41p. 1986. manuscript 3.00 (NERO, T/A-532). Natl Ctr St Courts.

Personnel & Operations Manual for Travel Agencies. Douglas Thompson & Alexander Anolik. 200p. 1986. 65.00 (ISBN 0-936831-02-2). Dendrobium Bks.

Personnel Assistant. Jack Rudman. (Career Examination Ser.: C-577). (Cloth bdg. avail. on request). pap. 14.00 (ISBN 0-8373-0577-2). Natl Learning.

Personnel Associate. Jack Rudman. (Career Examination Ser.: C-648). (Cloth bdg. avail. on request). pap. 14.00 (ISBN 0-8373-0648-5). Natl Learning.

Personnel Classification Board: Its History, Activities & Organization. Paul V. Betters. LC 72-3081. (Brookings Institution. Institute for Government Research. Service Monographs of the U. S. Government: No. 64). Repr. of 1931 ed. 24.00 (ISBN 0-404-57164-6). AMS Pr.

Personnel Classification Schemes. (SPEC Kit & Flyer Ser.: No. 85). 98p. 1982. (10.00 for ARL members) 20.00 (ISBN 0-318-03469-7); members 10.00. OMS.

Personnel Clerk. Jack Rudman. (Career Examination Ser.: C-2461). (Cloth bdg. avail. on request). pap. 12.00 (ISBN 0-8373-2461-0). Natl Learning.

Personnel Development in Libraries. Ed. by R. Kay Maloney. (Issues in Library & Information Sciences: No. 3). 1977. pap. text ed. 15.00 (ISBN 0-8135-0843-6). Rutgers U SICLS.

Personnel Director's Legal Guide. Steven Kahn et al. 1984. 78.00 (ISBN 0-88712-127-6). Warren Gorham & Lamont.

Personnel Transactions Supervisor. Jack Rudman. (Career Examination Ser.: C-3150). (Cloth bdg. avail. on request). 1988. pap. 16.00 (ISBN 0-8373-3150-1). Natl Learning.

Personnel Utilization in Healthcare: A Systems Approach. Myrl Ricking. LC 74-8688. pap. 42.00 (ISBN 0-317-26570-9, 2023953). Bks Demand UMI.

Persons: A Comparative Account of the Six Possible Theories. F. F. Centore. LC 78-74653. (Contributions in Philosophy: No. 13). 1979. lib. bdg. 36.95 (ISBN 0-313-20817-4, CPE/). Greenwood.

Persons: A Study in Philosophical Psychology. Raziel Abelson. LC 76-19225. 1977. 22.50x (ISBN 0-312-60235-9). St Martin.

Persons & Minds: The Prospects of Nonreductive Materialism. Joseph Margolis. (Synthese Library: No. 121). 1977. lib. bdg. 34.00 (ISBN 90-277-0854-1, Pub. by Reidel Holland); pap. 16.00 (ISBN 90-277-0863-0, Pub. by Reidel Holland). Kluwer Academic.

Persons & Periods. George D. Cole. LC 73-75412. 1969. Repr. of 1938 ed. 35.00x (ISBN 0-678-00495-1). Kelley.

Persons & Periods: Studies. facs. ed. George D. Cole. LC 67-26726. (Essay Index Reprint Ser). 1938. 18.00 (ISBN 0-8369-0323-4). Ayer Co Pubs.

Persons & Personality: A Contemporary Enquiry. Arthur Peacocke & Grant Gillet. 208p. Date not set. text ed. 39.95 (ISBN 0-631-15102-8). Basil Blackwell.

Persons & Personality: An Introduction to Psychology. Sr. Annette Walters & Sr. Kevin O'Hara. LC 52-13695. (Century Psychology Ser). 1953. 36.00x (ISBN 0-89197-550-0). Irvington.

Persons & Places. George Santayana. Ed. by William G. Holzberger & Herman J. Saatkamp, Jr. 547p. (Orig.). 1988. 12.50 (ISBN 0-262-69114-0). MIT Pr.

Persons & Places in One Volume. George Sintayana. (Hudson River Edition Ser.). 1981. 35.00 (ISBN 0-684-16830-8). Scribner.

Persons & Places of the Bronte Novels. Herbert E. Wroot. (Research & Source Works Ser.: No. 403). 1970. Repr. of 1906 ed. lib. bdg. 24.50 (ISBN 0-8337-3897-6). B Franklin.

Persons & Places: The Autobiography of George Santayana. George Santayana. Ed. by Herman J. Saatkamp & William G. Holzberger. (Illus.). 650p. 1986. text ed. 35.00x (ISBN 0-262-19238-1, Pub. by Bradford). MIT Pr.

Persons & Their World: An Introduction to Philosophy. Jeffrey Olen. 608p. 1983. text ed. write for info (ISBN 0-394-32545-1, RanC). Random.

Persons & Values: Selected Papers, Vol. 2. John L. Mackie. Ed. by Joan Mackie & Penelope Mackie. 220p. 1985. text ed. 36.00x (ISBN 0-19-824678-1). Oxford U Pr.

Persons, Behavior, & the World: The Descriptive Psychology Approach. Mary M. Shideler. 362p. (Orig.). 1988. lib. bdg. 32.50 (ISBN 0-8191-6786-X); pap. text ed. 17.50 (ISBN 0-8191-6787-8). U Pr of Amer.

Persons-Exegese and Christologie bei Augustinus: Zur Herkunft der Formel una Persona. Hubertus R. Drobner. (Philosophia Patrum Ser.: Vol. 8). xiii, 353p. 1986. 47.25 (ISBN 90-04-07875-4, Pub. by E J Brill). Heinman.

Persons Hospitalized by Number of Episodes & Days Hospitalized in a Year: United States, 1972. Mary H. Wilder & Claudia S. Moy. Ed. by Taloria Stevenson. (Ser. 10, No. 116). 1977. pap. text ed. 1.50 (ISBN 0-8406-0104-2). Natl Ctr Health Stats.

Persons in Context: Developmental Processes. Ed. by Niall Bolger et al. (Human Development in Cultural & Historical Contexts Ser.). (Illus.). 267p. Date not set. price not set (ISBN 0-521-35577-X). Cambridge U Pr.

Persons in Groups: Social Behavior as Identity Formation in Medieval & Renaissance Europe. Ed. by Richard C. Trexler. LC 84-27211. (Medieval & Renaissance Texts & Studies: Vol. 36). (Illus.). 272p. 1985. 20.00 (ISBN 0-86698-069-5). Medieval & Renaissance NY.

Persons in Relation. John MacMurray. 1979. pap. text ed. 12.50x (ISBN 0-571-09404-X). Humanities.

Persons Injured & Disability Days by Detailed Type & Class of Accident, U. S. 1971 & 1972. Charles S. Wilder. Ed. by Audrey M. Shipp. LC 75-35509. (Ser. 10: No. 105). 53p. 1976. pap. text ed. 1.50 (ISBN 0-8406-0055-0). Natl Ctr Health Stats.

Persons, Passions & Politics. M. Yunus. 333p. 1980. 16.95. Asia Bk Corp.

Persons, Passions & Politics. Mohammad Yunus. (Illus.). 333p. 1980. text ed. 25.00x (ISBN 0-7069-1017-6, Pub. by Vikas India). Advent NY.

Persons, Rights & Corporations. Patricia H. Werhane. LC 84-23731. 208p. 1985. pap. text ed. 17.00 (ISBN 0-13-660341-6). P-H.

Persons, Rights & the Moral Community. Loren E. Lomasky. LC 86-18011. 297p. 1987. 29.95x (ISBN 0-19-504209-3). Oxford U Pr.

Persons with & Without a Regular Source of Medical Care: United States 1978. Barbara Bloom & Susan S. Jack. Ed. by Klaudia Cox. (Series Ten: No. 151). 80p. 1985. pap. text ed. 1.50 (ISBN 0-8406-0317-7). Natl Ctr Health Stats.

Persons with Impaired Hearing, U. S. 1971. Augustine Gentile. Ed. by Kathleen Knox. LC 75-619226. (Data from the Health Interview Survey Ser 10: No. 101). 65p. 1975. pap. text ed. 1.75 (ISBN 0-8406-0048-8). Natl Ctr Health Stats.

Perspecta: Papers of the Yale School of Architecture, No. 15. (Illus.). 175p. 1975. pap. 12.50x (ISBN 0-8150-0322-6). Wittenborn.

Perspecta: The Yale Architectural Journal, Vols 13, 14 (1971) 1972. pap. 25.00x (ISBN 0-8150-0170-3). Wittenborn.

Perspectiva Humoristica en la Trilogia de Gironelia. J. D. Suarez-Torres. 1975. 12.95 (ISBN 0-88303-021-7); pap. 10.95 (ISBN 0-685-73222-3). E Torres & Sons.

Perspectivas Criticas de la Psicologia Social. Maria M. Lopez & Ricardo Zuniga Burmester. LC 85-1053. viii, 450p. 1988. pap. 12.00 (ISBN 0-8477-2909-5). U of PR Pr.

Perspectivas Para la Planificacion Familiar En Areas Rurales de Guatemala see Communicating Family Planning to Rural Guatemala.

Perspectivas Politicas, Vol. II. Lynn D. Bender. LC 79-27350. 115p. 1979. pap. text ed. 4.55 (ISBN 0-913480-43-6). Inter Am U Pr.

Perspectivas Politicas. rev. ed. Lynn D. Bender. LC 83-82307. 167p. 1983. pap. text ed. 6.95 (ISBN 0-913480-59-2). Inter Am U Pr.

Perspectivas: Temas de Hoy y de Siempre. 3rd ed. Mary E. Kiddle & Brenda Wegmann. (Span.). 1983. pap. text ed. 16.95 (ISBN 0-03-061482-1). HR&W.

Perspectivas: Temas de Hoy y de Siempre. 4th ed. Mary E. Kiddle & Brenda Wegmann. (Illus.). 288p. 1988. pap. text ed. 14.50 (ISBN 0-03-004982-2). HR&W.

Perspective. J. M. Parramon. LC 80-83274. (Art Ser.). (Orig.). 1981. pap. 6.95 (ISBN 0-89586-082-1). Price Stern.

Perspective. Jan Vredeman De Vries. xv, 74p. 1968. pap. 4.95 (ISBN 0-486-20186-4). Dover.

Perspective Affrancie. Johann H. Lambert. (Perspective Ser.). (Illus.). 208p. (Fr.). 1987. Repr. of 1759 ed. 140.00 (ISBN 1-85297-028-6). Archival Facsimiles.

Perspective: Art, Literature, Participation. Ed. by Mark Neuman & Michael Payne. LC 85-24330. (Review Ser.: Vol. 30, No. 1). (Illus.). 160p. 1986. 16.50x (ISBN 0-8387-5104-0). Bucknell U Pr.

Perspective Design: Advanced Graphics & Mathematical Approaches. John Mauldin. LC 85-3231. (Illus.). 196p. 1985. pap. 27.95 (ISBN 0-442-26408-9). Van Nos Reinhold.

Perspective Drawing. Jane H. James. 1981. pap. 26.00 (ISBN 0-13-660357-2). P-H.

Perspective Drawing: A Point of View. 2nd ed. Jane H. James. (Illus.). 240p. 1988. pap. text ed. 22.00 (ISBN 0-13-660416-1). P-H.

Perspective Drawing: A Student Text-Workbook. Osamu A. Wakita. (Illus.). 288p. 1978. pap. 19.95 plastic comb. (ISBN 0-8403-1924-X). Kendall-Hunt.

Perspective Drawing & Applications. Charles A. O'Connor. (Illus.). 80p. 1985. pap. text ed. 22.00 (ISBN 0-13-660382-3). P-H.

Perspective Drawing Handbook. Joseph D'Amelio. (Illus.). 12.95. L Amiel Pub.

Perspective Drawing Handbook. Joseph D'Amelio. LC 83-12399. (Illus.). 96p. 1984. pap. 15.95 (ISBN 0-442-21828-1). Van Nos Reinhold.

Perspective for Artists. Pietro Accolti. (Printed Sources of Western Arts Ser.). (Illus.). 168p. (Ital.). 1981. pap. 35.00 slipcase (ISBN 0-915346-60-5). A Wofsy Fine Arts.

Perspective for Artists. Rex V. Cole. LC 77-15743. (Illus.). 288p. 1976. pap. 4.50 (ISBN 0-486-22487-2). Dover.

Perspective for Intellectual Development: Minnesota Symposium on Child Development, Vol. 19. Ed. by Marion Perlmutter. 280p. 1986. text ed. 29.95 (ISBN 0-89859-784-6). L Erlbaum Assocs.

Perspective for Interior Designers. John Pile. (Illus.). 160p. 1985. 24.95 (ISBN 0-8230-7420-X). Watson-Guptill.

Perspective for the Artist. Sal Amendola. (Illus.). 64p. (Orig.). 1983. pap. 4.95 (Pentalic). Taplinger.

Perspective in Alcohol & Drug Abuse: Similarities & Differences. Joel Solomon & Kim Keeley. 270p. 1982. pap. 28.00 (ISBN 0-88416-306-7). PSG Pub Co.

Perspective in American Education, & Doctors & Masters. Conrad Bergendoff & Mark Van Doren. (Augustana College Library Occasional Papers: No. 7). 20p. 1961. pap. 0.50 (ISBN 0-910182-28-0). Augustana Coll.

Perspective in Art. Michael Woods. (Illus.). 144p. 1988. pap. 11.95 (ISBN 0-89134-226-5). North Light Bks.

Perspective in Biomechanics, Vol. I. Ed. by D. N. Ghista et al. (Perspectives in Biomechanics Ser.). 891p. 1980. 212.00 (ISBN 3-7186-0013-7). Harwood Academic.

Perspective in Communications: Proceedings of the Workshop ICTP, Trieste, Italy, November 14-December 2, 1983, 2 vols. Ed. by U. R. Rao et al. 1504p. 1987. 176.00 (ISBN 9971-978-76-8). World Scientific Pub.

Perspective in Nonlinear Dynamics: Proceedings of the Conference Held at NSWC, Virginia May 28-30, 1985. M. G. Shlesinger et al. 368p. 1986. 61.00 (ISBN 9971-50-111-2); pap. 36.00 (ISBN 9971-50-114-7). World Scientific Pub.

Perspective in Personality, Vol. 3. Ed. by Robert Hogan & Warren Jones. 1988. price not set (ISBN 0-89232-890-8). Jai Pr.

Perspective in Whitehead's Metaphysics. Stephen D. Ross. LC 82-8332. (SUNY Series in Systematic Philosophy). 295p. 1983. 49.50x (ISBN 0-87395-657-5); pap. 19.50x (ISBN 0-87395-658-3). State U NY Pr.

Perspective in Zoosemiotics. Thomas A. Sebeok. LC 72-189708. (Janua Linguarum, Ser. Minor: No. 122). (Illus.). 188p. (Orig.). 1972. pap. text ed. 19.20x (ISBN 90-2792-121-0). Mouton.

Perspective Made Easie. Bernard Lamy. (Perspective Ser.). (Illus.). 256p. 1987. Repr. of 1710 ed. 140.00 (ISBN 1-85297-029-4). Archival Facsimiles.

Perspective of Environmental Pollution. M. W. Holdgate. LC 78-8394. (Illus.). 288p. 1981. pap. 15.95 (ISBN 0-521-29972-1). Cambridge U Pr.

Perspective of Environmental Pollution. M. W. Holdgate. LC 78-8394. (Illus.). 1979. o. p. 54.50 (ISBN 0-521-22197-8). Cambridge U Pr.

Perspective of Organized Labor on Improving America's Productivity. Kenneth R. Edwards. 18p. 1983. 2.50 (ISBN 0-318-22166-7, OC89). Natl Ctr Res Voc Ed.

Perspective of Physics, 2 vols. Rudolf Peierls. Incl. Vol. 1. Selections from 1976 Comments on Modern Physics. 280p. 1977. 67.00 (ISBN 0-677-13190-9); Vol. 2. Selections from 1977 Comments on Modern Physics. 294p. 1978. 67.00 (ISBN 0-677-12400-7). Gordon & Breach.

Perspective of Physics: Vol. 3, Selections from 1978 Comments on Modern Physics. H. Massey. (Perspective of Physics Ser.). 354p. 1979. 72.00 (ISBN 0-677-15970-6). Gordon & Breach.

Perspective of Physics: Volume 4, Selections from Nineteen Seventy-Nine Comments on Modern Physics. H. Massey. 384p. 1981. 82.00 (ISBN 0-677-16190-5). Gordon & Breach.

Perspective of the World: Civilisation & Capitalism, Vol. III. Fernand Braudel. LC 81-47653. (Illus.). 704p. 1986. Repr. of 1984 ed. 16.95 (ISBN 0-06-091296-0, PL 1296, PL). Har-Row.

Perspective of the World: Fifteenth to Eighteenth Century, Vol. III. Fernand Braudel. Tr. by Sian Reynolds. LC 81-47653. (Civilization & Capitalism Ser.). (Illus.). 704p. 1984. 34.50 (ISBN 0-06-015317-2, HarpT). Har-Row.

Perspective on Automation: Three Talks to Educators. R. Theobald et al. 1974. 2.50 (ISBN 0-8156-7023-0, NES 43). Syracuse U Cont Ed.

Perspective on Biology & Medicine in the 21st Century: Proceedings of Round-Table Discussion, Indianapolis, October 27-30, 1985, No. 121. Ed. by I. Johnson & Y. Rue. 1988. pap. 32.00 (ISBN 0-905958-53-5, Pub. by Royal Society of Medicine Services Ltd). Longwood Pub Group.

Perspective on Budgeting (Par Classics, Vol. II. Ed. by Allen Schick. LC 80-81208. 1980. 10.95 (ISBN 0-936678-01-1). Am Soc Pub Admin.

Perspective on Civil Procedure. Geoffrey C. Hazard, Jr. & Jan Vetter. LC 86-81528. 350p. (Orig.). 1987. pap. 12.95 (ISBN 0-316-35259-4). Little.

Perspective on Credit Risk. P. Henry Mueller. LC 88-436. (Illus.). 76p. 1988. pap. 37.00 (ISBN 0-936742-48-8, 34131). Robt Morris Assocs.

Perspective on Infantry. John A. English. LC 81-5230. 368p. 1981. 35.00 (ISBN 0-275-90609-4, C0609). Praeger.

Perspective On... Inflation. Richard DiPrima. LC 80-70424. 181p. (Orig.). 1980. pap. text ed. 5.95 (ISBN 0-86652-005-8). Know Unltd.

Perspective on Intelligent Systems: A Framework for Analysis & Design. Kohout. (Information Technology Ser.). (Illus.). 220p. 1985. 35.00 (ISBN 0-85626-423-7). Abacus Pr.

Perspective on Mycotoxins. (Food & Nutrition Papers: No. 13). 171p. (Eng. & Span.). 1979. pap. 12.00 (ISBN 92-5-100870-1, F1957, FAO). UNIPUB.

Perspective on New Techniques in Congenital & Acquired Heart Disease: Proceedings of the Cardiovascular Disease Conference, 4th, Snowmass at Aspen, Colorado, Jan. 1973. Cardiovascular Disease Conference Staff. Ed. by J. Vogel. (Advances in Cardiology: Vol. 11). 1974. 72.75 (ISBN 3-8055-1654-1). S Karger.

Perspective on Power, India & China: An Analysis of Attitudes Toward Political Power in the Two Countries Between the 7th & 2nd Centuries B.C. Padmanabh Pillai. LC 77-74488. 1977. 11.00x (ISBN 0-88386-889-X). South Asia Bks.

Perspective on Shakespeare. Alur J. Ram. 218p. 1988. text ed. 35.00x (ISBN 81-7044-062-9, Pub. by Printwell India). Advent NY.

Perspective on Social Communication. Stuart J. Sigman. LC 86-45036. 160p. 1987. 25.00x (ISBN 0-669-13012-5). Lexington Bks.

Perspective on the Nature of Geography. Richard Hartshorne. LC 59-7032. (Monograph: No. 1). 6.00 (ISBN 0-89291-080-1). Assn Am Geographers.

Perspective on the Nature of Geography. Richard Hartshorne. 201p. 1987. 75.00x (ISBN 0-317-62296-X, Pub. by Scientific). State Mutual Bk.

Perspective on U. S. Farm Problems & Agricultural Policy. Lance McKinzie et al. (Special Studies in Agriculture Science & Policy). 189p. 1986. pap. 22.50 (ISBN 0-8133-7376-X). Westview.

Perspective Rendering for Commercial Design: Exterior. Tokaski Mori. LC 84-13121. (Illus.). 156p. 1984. pap. 29.95 (ISBN 0-442-28301-6). Van Nos Reinhold.

Perspective Rendering for Commercial Design: Interior. Tokaski Mori. LC 84-13145. (Illus.). 156p. 1984. pap. 29.95 (ISBN 0-442-28302-4). Van Nos Reinhold.

Perspective Sketches. 4th, rev ed. Theodore D. Walker. LC 75-551. (Illus.). 250p. 1982. 29.00 (ISBN 0-914886-13-4); pap. 22.00 (ISBN 0-914886-14-2). PDA Pubs.

Perspective: Texte zu Kultur und Literaur. Manfred Bansleben. 272p. 1987. pap. text ed. write for info. (ISBN 0-03-063238-2). HR&W.

Perspectives. David Howard. LC 77-90787. (Illus.). 1978. lib. bdg. 13.95 (ISBN 0-930976-00-2). SF Center Vis Stud.

Perspectives. D. McCullin. 1986. 64.75X (ISBN 0-245-54368-6, Pub. by Harrap Ltd England). State Mutual Bk.

Perspectives. Edward Riccardo. (Illus.). 243p. 1985. pap. 12.95 (ISBN 0-911541-07-1). Gregory Pub.

Perspectives see Handbook of Cross-Cultural Psychology.

Perspectives: A Williams Anthology. Ed. by Frederick Rudolph. LC 83-51219. 340p. 1983. 17.50 (ISBN 0-915081-00-8). Williams Coll.

Perspectives: An Anthology of 1001 Architectural Quotations. Ed. by Charles Knevitt. (Illus.). 160p. 1986. pap. 17.50 (ISBN 0-85331-511-6, Pub. by Lund Humphries UK). Humanities.

Perspectives: An Intermediate Reader. Len Fox. 179p. 1980. pap. text ed. 10.00 net (ISBN 0-15-570486-9, HC). HarBraceJ.

Perspectives & Irony in American Slavery. 2nd ed. Ed. by Harry P. Owens. LC 76-18283. 1976. 10.50x (ISBN 0-87805-074-4). U Pr of Miss.

Perspectives & Patterns: Discourses on History. Warren B. Walsh. LC 62-16382. 1962. 19.95x (ISBN 0-8156-0027-5). Syracuse U Pr.

Perspectives & Points of View: The Early Works of Weiland & Their Background. Lieselotte E. Kurth-Voigt. LC 74-6829. pap. 52.00 (ISBN 0-317-41688-X, 2025855). Bks Demand UMI.

Perspectives: Angles on African Art. James Baldwin et al. Ed. by Michael J. Weber. (Illus.). 196p. (Orig.). 1987. text ed. 45.00 (ISBN 0-9614587-4-7, CAA); pap. text ed. 24.95 (ISBN 0-9614587-6-3). Center African Art.

Perspectives: Angles on African Art. James Baldwin et al. LC 86-26328. (Illus.). 196p. 1987. 45.00 (ISBN 0-8109-1491-3). Abrams.

Perspectives Cavaliere. Andre Breton. Ed. by Bonnet. 14.50 (ISBN 0-685-37235-9). French & Eur.

Perspectives: Collected Poems 1970-1986. George Bruce. 90p. 1987. pap. text ed. 12.50 (ISBN 0-08-035062-3, AUP). Pergamon.

Perspectives for Catholic Laity in the U. S. A. Stan M. Cusack. 59p. 1988. 7.95 (ISBN 0-533-07485-1). Vantage.

Perspectives for Development Through Industrialization in the 1980's: An Independent Viewpoint on Dependency. 20p. 1980. pap. 5.00 (ISBN 92-808-0151-1, TUNU102, UNU). UNIPUB.

Perspectives for Moral Decisions. John Howie. LC 80-6102. 192p. 1981. lib. bdg. 26.25 (ISBN 0-8191-1375-1); pap. text ed. 12.00 (ISBN 0-8191-1376-X). U Pr of Amer.

Perspectives for Peas & Lupins as Protein Crops. R. Thompson & R. Casey. 1983. 54.50 (ISBN 90-247-2792-8, Pub. by Martinus Nijhoff Netherlands). Kluwer Academic.

Perspectives for the Future: Social Work Practice in the 80s. Ed. by Kay Dea & Sixth NASW Professional Symposium, 1979. LC 80-83988. 192p. (Orig.). 1980. pap. text ed. 14.95x (ISBN 0-87101-089-5). Natl Assn Soc Wkrs.

Perspectives Francaises, No. 1. Sarah Vaillancourt. LC 80-12737. (Illus.). 1981. pap. text ed. 9.50 (ISBN 0-88436-755-X, 40250). EMC.

Perspectives Francaises, No. 2. Sarah Vaillancourt. LC 81-3311. (Illus.). 400p. (Fr.). 1982. pap. text ed. 9.95 (ISBN 0-88436-757-6, 40251). EMC.

Perspectives Francaises: 1984, No. 1. rev. ed. Sarah Vaillancourt. (Perspectives Francaises Ser.). (Illus.). 324p. (Fr.). 1983. text ed. 14.95 (ISBN 0-88436-971-4, 40452); pap. text ed. 11.95 (ISBN 0-88436-973-0, 40289); tchr's ed. 20.00 (ISBN 0-88436-977-3, 40813); wkbk. 3.95 (ISBN 0-88436-828-9, 40650); test booklet 4.25 (ISBN 0-88436-980-3, 40901). EMC.

Perspectives Francaises: 1984, No. 2. rev. ed. Sarah Vaillancourt. (Illus.). 404p. (Fr.). 1983. text ed. 15.95 (ISBN 0-88436-972-2, 40453); pap. text ed. 12.95 (ISBN 0-88436-974-9, 40290); tchr's ed. 20.00 (ISBN 0-88436-978-1, 40814); 3.95_wkbk. (ISBN 0-88436-829-7, 40651); test booklet 4.25 (ISBN 0-88436-979-X, 40902). EMC.

Perspectives from the Puerto Rican Faculty Training Project. Date not set. 3.30. Coun Soc Wk Ed.

Perspectives in Aesthetics: Plato to Camus. Ed. by Peyton E. Richter. LC 66-19066. (Orig.). 1967. pap. 12.04 scp (ISBN 0-672-63082-6). Odyssey Pr.

Perspectives in Psychopharmacology: A Collection of Papers in Honor of Earl Usdin. Ed. by Jack D. Barchas & William E. Bunney, Jr. LC 88-2762. (Neurology & Neurobiology Ser.: Vol. 40). 720p. 1988. 120.00 (ISBN 0-8451-2742-X, 2742). A R Liss.

Perspectives in Public Regulation: Essays on Political Economy. Ed. by Milton Russell. LC 73-9626. 159p. 1973. 6.95x (ISBN 0-8093-0645-X). S Ill U Pr.

Perspectives in Regional Geological Synthesis: Planning for the Geology of North America. Ed. by A. R. Palmer. LC 82-9331. (DNAG Special Pub. Ser.: No. 1). (Illus.). 1982. 5.00 (ISBN 0-8137-5201-9). Geol Soc.

Perspectives in Regional Problems & Regional Development in Nepal. D. B. Amatya. 106p. 1987. text ed. 17.95x (ISBN 81-207-0706-0, Pub. by Sterling Pubs India). Apt Bks.

Perspectives in Research on Headache. Ed. by Kenneth A. Holroyd & Barbara Schlote. 326p. 1983. text ed. 29.80 (ISBN 0-88937-006-0). Hogrefe Intl.

Perspectives in Ring Theory. Ed. by F. Van Oystaeyen & Lieven Le Bruyn. 1988. lib. bdg. 99.00 (ISBN 90-277-2736-8, Pub. by Reidel Holland). Kluwer Academic.

Perspectives In Running Water Ecology. Ed. by Maurice A. Lock & D. D. Williams. LC 81-17838. 440p. 1981. 69.50x (ISBN 0-306-40898-8, Plenum Pr). Plenum Pub.

Perspectives in Schizophrenia Research. Ed. by Claude Baxter & Theodore Melnechuk. 463p. 1980. text ed. 91.50 (ISBN 0-89004-517-8). Raven.

Perspectives in Shock Research. Ed. by Robert F. Bond. LC 88-530. (Progress in Clinical & Biological Research Ser.: Vol. 264). 452p. 1988. 90.00 (ISBN 0-8451-5114-2, 5114). A R Liss.

Perspectives in Social Science: Three Studies on the Agrarian Structure in Bengal, 1850-1947. Asok Sen et al. 1982. 16.95x (ISBN 0-19-561019-9). Oxford U Pr.

Perspectives in Social Sciences, 3: Economy, Polity, & Society: Essays in Honour of Professor Bhabatosh Datta. Ed. by Amiya Bagchi. (Illus.). 320p. 1988. 18.95 (ISBN 0-19-562059-3). Oxford U Pr.

Perspectives in Social Welfare in India. J. Bulsara. 226p. 1984. 22.95. Asia Bk Corp.

Perspectives in Sociology. 2nd ed. Ed. by E. C. Cuff & G. C. Payne. 1983. pap. text ed. 11.95x (ISBN 0-04-301157-8). Unwin Hyman.

Perspectives in Special Education: Personal Orientations. Burton Blatt & Richard J. Morris. (Scott, Foresman Special Education Ser.). 1984. text ed. write for info. (ISBN 0-673-16566-3). Scott F.

Perspectives in State School Support Programs. Ed. by K. Forbis Jordan. LC 81-8074. 408p. (American Education Finance Association). 1981. prof ref 35.00x (ISBN 0-88410-197-5). Ballinger Pub.

Perspectives in Statistical Physics. H. J. Raveche. (Studies in Statistical Mechanics: Vol. 9). 368p. 1981. 79.00 (ISBN 0-444-86026-6, North-Holland). Elsevier.

Perspectives in Steroid Receptor Research. Ed. by Francesco Bresciani. 334p. 1980. text ed. 55.00 (ISBN 0-89004-490-2). Raven.

Perspectives in String Theory: Proceedings of the Niels Bohr Institute-Nordita Meeting, Copenhagen, Denmark. Ed. by P. Di Vecchia & J. L. Petersen. 550p. (Orig.). 1988. 76.00 (ISBN 9971-50-526-6); pap. 48.00 (ISBN 9971-50-534-7). World Scientific Pub.

Perspectives in Surgery. Clare G. Peterson. LC 72-115025. pap. 67.50 (ISBN 0-317-07968-9, 2014577). Bks Demand UMI.

Perspectives in Temporomandibular Disorders. Clark & Solberg. (Illus.). 152p. 1987. text ed. 44.00 (ISBN 0-86715-176-5). Quint Pub Co.

Perspectives in the History of Religions. Jan De Vries. Tr. & intro. by Kees W. Bolle. LC 76-20154. 1977. pap. 7.95x (ISBN 0-520-03300-0). U of Cal Pr.

Perspectives in the History of Science & Technology. Ed. by Duane H. Roller. LC 77-144163. (Illus.). 1975. pap. text ed. 10.95x (ISBN 0-8061-1144-5). U of Okla Pr.

Perspectives in the Organic Chemistry of Sulfur: Invited Lectures of the Twelfth International Symposium, Nijmegen, The Netherlands, June 29-July 4, 1986. Ed. by B. Zwanenberg & A. J. H. Klunder. (Studies in Organic Chemistry: No. 28). 324p. 1987. 110.75 (ISBN 0-444-42739-2). Elsevier.

Perspectives in the Philosophy of Culture. Ed. by Sneh Pandit. 216p. 1978. text ed. 22.00x. Coronet Bks.

Perspectives in the Sociology of Science. Ed. by Stuart S. Blume. LC 76-30827. 245p. pap. 63.70 (2030484). Bks Demand UMI.

Perspectives in Theoretical Stereochemistry. I. Ugi et al. (Lecture Notes in Chemistry Ser.: Vol. 36). 265p. 1984. pap. 27.40 (ISBN 0-387-13391-7). Springer-Verlag.

Perspectives in Toxicology, Vol. 1. Robert L. Dixon. Date not set. price not set (ISBN 0-89004-436-8, 496). Raven.

Perspectives in Trypanosomiasis Research: Proceedings of the Twenty-First Trypanosomiasis Seminar: London 24 September 1981. John R. Baker. (Tropical Medicine Research Studies). 105p. 1982. 49.95 (ISBN 0-471-10478-7, Pub. by Res Stud Pr). Wiley.

Perspectives in Turbulence Studies. Ed. by H. U. Meier & P. Bradshaw. ix, 503p. 1987. 71.50 (ISBN 0-387-17448-6). Springer-Verlag.

Perspectives in Urban Entomology. Ed. by G. W. Frankie & C. S. Koehler. 1978. 65.00 (ISBN 0-12-265250-9). Acad Pr.

Perspectives in Urban Geography, Vol. 12: Perceptual & Cognitive Image of the City. C. S. Yadav. 1987. 57.00 (ISBN 0-8364-2253-8, Pub. by Concept India). South Asia Bks.

Perspectives in Urban Geography, Vol. 7: Slums, Urban Decline & Revitalization. C. S. Yadav. 1987. 41.00 (ISBN 0-8364-2260-0, Pub. by Concept India). South Asia Bks.

Perspectives in Urban Geography, Vol. 8: Contemporary Urban Issues. Ed. by C. S. Yadav. 1987. 54.00 (ISBN 0-8364-2241-4, Pub. by Concept India). South Asia Bks.

Perspectives in Vernacular Architecture, Vol. I. Camille Wells. 240p. 1987. pap. 15.00 (ISBN 0-8262-0631-X, 83-36372). U of Mo Pr.

Perspectives in Vernacular Architecture, Vol. 2. Ed. by Camille Wells. (Illus.). 256p. 1986. text ed. 35.00 (ISBN 0-8262-0628-X); pap. text ed. 14.00 (ISBN 0-8262-0613-1). U of Mo Pr.

Perspectives in Virology, Vol. 10. Ed. by Morris Pollard. LC 77-84126. (Gustav Stern Symposium Ser.). 276p. 1978. 58.00 (ISBN 0-89004-214-4). Raven.

Perspectives in Virology, Vol. 11: Proceedings of the Gustave Stern Symposium, 11th, New York, February, 1980. Stern Gustave Symposium on Perspectives in Virology Staff. Ed. by Morris Pollard. LC 59-8415. 324p. 1981. 49.00x (ISBN 0-8451-0800-X). A R Liss.

Perspectives in Western Civilization: Essays from Horizon, 2 Vols. Ed. by William L. Langer. (Illus.). 1972. scp ea. 19.50 (HarpC); Vol. 2. pap. text ed. (ISBN 0-06-043835-5). Har-Row.

Perspectives in Zoology. A. A. Boyden. LC 73-1279. 294p. 1973. 50.00 (ISBN 0-08-017122-2). Pergamon.

Perspectives: Legal Services & the Private Bar, 1982 & Beyond. 24p. 1982. pap. 1.00 (ISBN 0-317-31040-2). Amer Bar Assn.

Perspectives: Middle School Education, 1964-1984. Ed. by John H. Lounsbury. 184p. 1984. 9.95 (ISBN 0-318-17731-5). Natl Middle Schl.

Perspectives of a Regional Culture. Ed. by B. Beck. 212p. 1979. 19.95. Asia Bk Corp.

Perspectives of Antioxidant Treatment of Emphysema with N-Acetyloysteine. Ed. by V. Cichetti et al. (Vol. 50, Suppl. 1). vi, 74p. 1986. pap. 18.75 (ISBN 3-8055-4514-2). S Karger.

Perspectives of Biological Energy Transduction. Ed. by Yasuo Mukohata et al. 454p. 1988. 85.00 (ISBN 0-12-509855-3). Acad Pr.

Perspectives of Biophysical Ecology. Ed. by D. M. Gates & R. B. Schmere. LC 74-17493. (Illus.). 1975. 66.60 (ISBN 0-387-06743-4). Springer-Verlag.

Perspectives of Elementary Mathematics. G. P. Hochschild. 140p. 1983. pap. 27.00 (ISBN 0-387-90848-X). Springer-Verlag.

Perspectives of Fashion. George B. Sproles. 160p. (Orig.). 1981. pap. text ed. 10.95 (ISBN 0-8087-4510-7, Feffer & Simons). Burgess MN Intl.

Perspectives of Fundamental Physics. Ed. by C. Schaerf. (Studies in High Energy Physics: Vol. 1). 480p. 1979. lib. bdg. 68.00 flexicover (ISBN 3-7186-0007-2). Harwood Academic.

Perspectives of Intonation Analysis: Forum Linguisticum, Vol. 9. Dafydd Gibbon. 309p. 1976. pap. 33.95 (ISBN 3-261-01734-1). P Lang Pubs.

Perspectives of Irony in Medieval French Literature. Vladimir Rossman. (De Proprietatibus Litterarum, Ser Maior: No. 35). 198p. (Orig.). 1975. pap. text ed. 20.80x (ISBN 90-2793-291-3). Mouton.

Perspectives of New Music: An Index, 1962-1982. Ann P. Basart. (Reference Books in Music: No. 1). ix, 127p. (Orig.). 1984. pap. 13.95 (ISBN 0-914913-00-X, 83-82609). Fallen Leaf.

Perspectives of Nonlinear Dynamics, 2 vols, Vols. 1 & 2. E. Atlee Jackson. (Illus.). Date not set. Vol. 1, 400p. price not set (ISBN 0-521-34504-9); Vol. 2, 400p. price not set (ISBN 0-521-35458-7). Cambridge U Pr.

Perspectives of Psychiatry. Paul R. McHugh & Phillip R. Slavney. LC 83-6157. (Contemporary Medicine & Public Health Ser.). 176p. 1983. text ed. 20.00x (ISBN 0-8018-3039-7). Johns Hopkins.

Perspectives of Psychiatry. Paul R. McHugh & Phillip R. Slavney. LC 83-6157. 176p. 1986. pap. text ed. 8.95x (ISBN 0-8018-3302-7). Johns Hopkins.

Perspectives of the Scottish City, Eighteen Thirty-One to Nineteen Eighty-One. Ed. by George Gordon. (Illus.). 224p. 1985. 31.00 (ISBN 0-08-030371-4). Pergamon.

Perspectives of Tourism. Joseph Fridgen. (Illus.). 340p. 1989. text ed. 36.95 (ISBN 0-86612-049-1). Educ Inst Am Hotel.

Perspectives of Truth in Literature. John D. Martin & Lester E. Showalter. (Christian Day School Ser.). (gr. 9). 1982. 15.05 (ISBN 0-87813-921-4); tchr's. guide 10.95x (ISBN 0-87813-922-2). Christian Light.

Perspectives of Wages & Prices. Henry P. Brown & Sheila V. Hopkins. 256p. 1981. 30.00x (ISBN 0-416-31950-5, NO. 3478). Routledge Chapman & Hall.

Perspectives on a Decade of Small Business Research: Bolton Ten Years On. Ed. by John Stanworth & Ava Westrip. 199p. 1982. text ed. 36.50 (ISBN 0-566-00587-5). Gower Pub Co.

Perspectives on a Dynamic Earth. Thomas R. Paton. 176p. 1986. text ed. 34.95x (ISBN 0-04-550042-8); pap. text ed. 12.95x (ISBN 0-04-550043-6). Unwin Hyman.

Perspectives on a Grafted Tree. Patricia Irwin Johnston. LC 82-242541. (Illus.). 144p. 1983. 12.95 (ISBN 0-9609504-0-0). Perspect Indiana.

Perspectives on a U. S.-Canadian Free Trade Agreement. Ed. by Robert M. Stern et al. LC 87-17657. 266p. 1987. 32.95 (ISBN 0-8157-8132-6); pap. 12.95 (ISBN 0-8157-8131-8). Brookings.

Perspectives on Abortion. Ed. by Paul Sachdev. LC 84-10573. 293p. 1984. 22.50 (ISBN 0-8108-1708-X). Scarecrow.

Perspectives on Adult Career Development & Guidance. (gr. 5 up). 1980. 10.50 (ISBN 0-318-23262-6, RD 181). Natl Ctr Res Voc Ed.

Perspectives on Adult Learning. Ed. by E. Michael Brady. 92p. (Orig.). 1986. pap. text ed. 5.00 (ISBN 0-939561-00-X). Univ South ME.

Perspectives on African Literature. Ed. & intro. by Christopher Heywood. LC 71-169493. 172p. 1972. 29.50 (ISBN 0-8419-0093-0, Africana). Holmes & Meier.

Perspectives on Aging & Human Development Series, 3 vols. Ed. by Jon Hendricks. Incl. Vol. 1. Being & Becoming Old. 160p (ISBN 0-89503-014-4); Vol. 2. In the Country of the Old. 160p (ISBN 0-89503-015-2); Vol. 3. Institutionalization & Alternative Futures. 160p (ISBN 0-89503-016-0). 1979. Set. pap. 24.95 (ISBN 0-89503-024-1). Baywood Pub.

Perspectives on AIDS & Thanatology. Ed. by Leonard Liegner et al. (Current Thanatology Ser.). 150p. 1988. pap. 15.95 (ISBN 0-930194-43-8). Ctr Thanatology.

Perspectives on American & Texas Politics: A Collection of Essays. Tedin & Lutz. 384p. 1987. pap. text ed. 16.95 (ISBN 0-8403-4449-X). Kendall-Hunt.

Perspectives on American Business SEASA 81: Proceedings. Southeastern American Studies Association Wesleyean College, Macon, Ga., April 4-6, 1981. Ed. by Don Harkness. (Illus.). 75p. 1982. pap. 5.00 (ISBN 0-934996-15-6). American Studies Pr.

Perspectives on American English. Ed. by J. L. Dillard. (Contributions to the Sociology of Language Ser.: No. 29). 468p. 1980. 55.00 (ISBN 90-279-3367-7). Mouton.

Perspectives on American Folk Art. Ed. by Ian M. Quimby & Scott T. Swank. (Winterthur Bk.). (Illus.). 1980. 21.95 (ISBN 0-393-01273-5); pap. 9.95x (ISBN 0-393-95088-3). Norton.

Perspectives on American Foreign Policy. Ed. by Charles W. Kegley & Eugene R. Wittkopf. LC 82-60472. 510p. 1983. pap. text ed. write for info. (ISBN 0-312-60244-8). St Martin.

Perspectives on Anthropology 1976. A. F. Wallace. (Special Publication: No. 10). 1977. pap. 7.50 (ISBN 0-686-36566-6); pap. 5.00 members. Am Anthro Assn.

Perspectives on Anti-Trust Policy. A. Phillips. 1965. 49.50x (ISBN 0-691-04158-X). Princeton U Pr.

Perspectives on Applied Christianity: Essays in Honor of Thomas Buford Maston. Ed. by William M. Tillman, Jr. LC 85-26025. (National Association of Baptist Professors of Religion (NABPR) Festschrift Ser.). vi, 108p. 1986. 10.50 (ISBN 0-86554-196-5, MUP-H180). Mercer Univ Pr.

Perspectives on Applied Christianity: Essays in Honor of Thomas B. Matson. Ed. by William M. Tillman, Jr. (Festschriften Ser.: No. 2). vi, 108p. 10.50 (ISBN 0-317-61630-7). NABPR.

Perspectives on Applied Sociolinguistics. Robert St. Clair et al. 257p. 1979. pap. 10.00 (ISBN 0-87291-136-5). Coronado Pr.

Perspectives on Archaeological Resources Management in the Great Plains. Intro. by Alan J. Osborn & Robert C. Hassler. ix, 391p. 1987. pap. 16.00x (ISBN 0-9619168-0-X). I & O Pub NE.

Perspectives on Asian Music: Essays in Honor of Dr. Laurence E. R. Picken. Ed. by Fritz A. Kuttner & Fredric Lieberman. (Asian Music Ser.). (Illus.). viii, 230p. (Orig.). 1975. pap. 15.00 (ISBN 0-913360-08-2). Asian Music Pub.

Perspectives on Autoimmunity. Ed. by Irun r. Cohen. 272p. 1987. 145.00 (ISBN 0-8493-6431-0). CRC Pr.

Perspectives on Availability: A Symposium on Determining Protected Group Representation in Internal & External Labor Markets. Robert J. Flanagan et al. LC 78-63628. 243p. (Orig.). 1977. pap. 12.75 (ISBN 0-937856-02-9). Equal Employ.

Perspectives on Bacterial Pathogenesis & Host Defense. Ed. by Bernhard Urbaschek. 236p. 1988. 35.00x (ISBN 0-226-84275-4). U of Chicago Pr.

Perspectives on Behavior & Organizations. 2nd ed. R. Hackman et al. Ed. by Patricia S. Nave. (Illus.). 608p. 1983. text ed. 24.95 (ISBN 0-07-025414-1). McGraw.

Perspectives on Behavior in Organizations. Porter L. Hackman et al. 1977. pap. 20.95 (ISBN 0-07-025413-3, C). McGraw.

Perspectives on Behavior Therapy in the Eighties. Ed. by Michael Rosenbaum et al. (Springer Ser. in Behavior Therapy & Behavioral Medicine: Vol. 9). 480p. 1983. text ed. 39.50 (ISBN 0-8261-4070-X). Springer Pub.

Perspectives on Behavioral Medicine: Neuroendocrine Control & Behavior, Vol. 2. Ed. by Redford B. Williams. 1985. 59.00 (ISBN 0-12-532102-3); pap. 27.00 (ISBN 0-12-531954-1). Acad Pr.

Perspectives on Behavioral Medicine, Vol. 3: Prevention & Rehabilitation. Ed. by W. A. Gordon et al. 183p. 1988. 65.00 (ISBN 0-12-532103-1). Acad Pr.

Perspectives on Behavioral Medicine 1980, Vol. I. Ed. by Stephen M. Weiss et al. LC 80-2577. (Serial Publication). 1981. 59.00 (ISBN 0-12-532101-5). Acad Pr.

Perspectives on Bereavement. Irwin Gerber. 16.50 (ISBN 0-405-12481-3). Ayer Co Pubs.

Perspectives on Bereavement. Ed. by Irwin Gerber et al. (Thanatology Ser.). 1978. 14.95x (ISBN 0-8422-7304-2). Irvington.

Perspectives on Bias in Mental Testing. Ed. by Cecil R. Reynolds & Robert T. Brown. (Perspectives on Individual Differences Ser.). 594p. 1984. 55.00x (ISBN 0-306-41529-1, Plenum Pr). Plenum Pub.

Perspectives on Bilingualism & Bilingual Education. Ed. by James E. Alatis & John J. Staczek. 461p. (Orig.). 1985. pap. 12.95 (ISBN 0-87840-192-X). Georgetown U Pr.

Perspectives on Biomaterials. Ed. by O. C. Lin & E. Y. Chao. (Materials Science Monographs). 366p. 1986. 118.50 (ISBN 0-444-42672-8). Elsevier.

Perspectives on Black English. Ed. by J. L. Dillard. (Contributions to the Sociology of Language Ser: No. 4). 391p. 1975. text ed. 31.50x (ISBN 90-2797-811-5). Mouton.

Perspectives on Brazilian History. Ed. by E. Bradford Burns. LC 67-13779. (Institute of Latin American Studies). 235p. 1967. 27.50x (ISBN 0-231-02992-6). Columbia U Pr.

Perspectives on British Sign Language & Deafness. Ed. by B. Woll et al. (Illus.). 268p. 1981. 29.95 (ISBN 0-7099-2703-7, Pub. by Croom Helm Ltd). Routledge Chapman & Hall.

Perspectives on Canadian Health & Social Services Policy: History & Emerging Trends. Ed. by Carl A. Meilicke & Janet L. Storch. LC 80-12118. (Illus.). 534p. 1980. text ed. 39.00x (ISBN 0-914904-42-6, 0637). Health Admin Pr.

Perspectives on Charismatic Renewal. Ed. by Edward D. O'Connor. 228p. 1976. 7.95 (ISBN 0-268-01516-3). U of Notre Dame Pr.

Perspectives on Child Maltreatment in the Mid Eighties. 70p. 1984. pap. 2.75 (ISBN 0-318-11813-0, S/N 017-090-00076-3). USGPO.

Perspectives on Chinese Cinema. Ed. by Chris Berry. LC 86-133071. (East Asian Papers: No. 39). 159p. 1985. 8.00 (ISBN 0-939657-39-2). Cornell East Asia Pgm.

Perspectives on Clinical Decision Making. Suzanne B. Knoebel. (Illus.). 144p. 1987. 14.95 (ISBN 0-87993-287-2). Futura Pub.

Perspectives on Cognitive Dissonance. R. A. Wicklund & J. W. Brehm. 349p. 1976. 36.00x (ISBN 0-89859-419-7). L Erlbaum Assocs.

Perspectives on Cognitive Science. Ed. by Donald A. Norman. LC 80-21343. 320p. 1981. 24.95 (ISBN 0-89391-071-6). Ablex Pub.

Perspectives on Cognitive Science. Ed. by Donald A. Norman. LC 80-21343. (Illus.). 320p. 1981. 24.95x (ISBN 0-89859-106-6). L Erlbaum Assocs.

Perspectives on Communication. Louis Forsdale. (Illus.). 320p. 1981. pap. text ed. 14.50 (ISBN 0-394-34975-X, RanC). Random.

Perspectives on Communication Disorders. Barbaranne J. Benjamin. 298p. (Orig.). 1985. pap. text ed. 15.95x (ISBN 0-88133-181-3). Sheffield Wisc.

Perspectives on Community Health Education: A Series of Case Studies. Ed. by Raymond W. Carlaw. LC 80-54741. 224p. 1982. pap. text ed. 9.95x (ISBN 0-89914-007-6). Third Party Pub.

Perspectives on Computer Science. Ed. by Anita K. Jones. (Acm Ser.). 1977. 59.50 (ISBN 0-12-389450-6). Acad Pr.

Perspectives on Conflict of Laws: Choice of Law. James A. Martin. 1980. pap. text ed. 11.95 (ISBN 0-316-54853-7). Little.

Perspectives on Conservation: Essays on America's Natural Resources. John Kenneth Galbraith & Luther G. Griffith. Ed. by Henry Jarrett. pap. 68.00 (ISBN 0-317-26465-6, 2023801). Bks Demand UMI.

Perspectives on Contemporary Theatre. Oscar G. Brockett. LC 75-154268. viii, 158p. 1971. 20.00x (ISBN 0-8071-0939-8). La State U Pr.

Perspectives on Organization Theory. Anna Grandori. LC 87-11359. 240p. 1987. 32.00x (ISBN 0-88730-214-9). Ballinger Pub.

Perspectives on Organizational Communication. Tom Daniels & Barry Spiker. 304p. 1987. text ed. write for info. (ISBN 0-697-00444-9); pap. write for info. instr's manual (ISBN 0-697-00522-4). Wm C Brown.

Perspectives on Organizational Design & Behavior. Ed. by Andrew H. Van De Nen & William F. Joyce. LC 81-11550. (Wiley Ser. on Organizational Assessment & Change). 486p. 1981. 47.50x (ISBN 0-471-09358-0, Pub. by Wiley-Interscience). Wiley.

Perspectives on Our Age: Jacques Ellul Speaks on His Life & Work. Jacques Ellul. Ed. by William H. Vanderburg. Tr. by Joachim Neugroschel. 1981. 10.95 (ISBN 0-8164-0485-2, HarpR). Har-Row.

Perspectives on Particle Physics: From Mesons & Resonances to Quarks & Strings. Ed. by S. Matsuda et al. 450p. 1988. 68.00 (ISBN 9971-50-589-4). World Scientific Pub.

Perspectives on Patch. Ed. by Ian Sinclair & David N. Thomas. 1983. 25.00x (ISBN 0-317-40606-X, Pub. by Natl Soc Work). State Mutual Bk.

Perspectives on Paul. Ernst Kasemann. LC 79-157540. pap. 45.80 (ISBN 0-317-55776-9, 2029296). Bks Demand UMI.

Perspectives on Peirce: Critical Essays on Charles Sanders Peirce. Ed. by Richard J. Bernstein. LC 80-13703. ix, 148p. 1980. Repr. of 1965 ed. lib. bdg. 35.00x (ISBN 0-313-22414-5, BEPP). Greenwood.

Perspectives on Pentecost. Richard B Gaffin. 1979. pap. 5.95 (ISBN 0-87552-269-6). Presby & Reformed.

Perspectives on Pentecostalism: Case Studies from the Caribbean & Latin America. Ed. by Stephen D. Glazier. LC 80-7815. 207p. 1980. lib. bdg. 26.75 (ISBN 0-8191-1071-X); pap. text ed. 13.00 (ISBN 0-8191-1072-8). U Pr of Amer.

Perspectives on Person-Environment Interaction & Drug-Taking Behavior. Ed. & intro. by Bernard Segal. LC 87-26268. (Drugs & Society Ser.). 180p. 1988. text ed. 22.95 (ISBN 0-86656-716-X). Haworth Pr.

Perspectives on Personality. Michael Scheier & Charles Carver. 512p. 1987. text ed. 36.00 (ISBN 0-205-11120-3). Allyn.

Perspectives on Personnel: Human Resource Management. 3rd ed. Ed. by Herbert G. Heneman & Donald P. Schwab. 1986. pap. 19.95x (ISBN 0-256-03359-5). Irwin.

Perspectives on Philippine Historiography: A Symposium. Ed. by John A. Larkin. LC 78-59565. (Monograph Ser.: No. 21). iv, 74p. 1979. pap. 9.50x (ISBN 0-938692-09-7). Yale U SE Asia.

Perspectives on Photography. Ed. by Dave Oliphant & Thomas Zigal. (Illus.). 180p. 1982. pap. 14.95 (ISBN 0-87959-098-X). U of Tex H Ransom Ctr.

Perspectives on Photography: Essays in Honor of Beaumont Newhall. Ed. by Peter Walch & Thomas F. Barrow. LC 85-28824. (Illus.). 195p. 1986. 24.95x (ISBN 0-8263-0862-7); pap. 12.95 (ISBN 0-8263-0863-5). U of NM Pr.

Perspectives on Plant Population Ecology. Ed. by Rodolfo Dirzo & Jose Sarukhan. LC 83-20182. (Illus.). 450p. 1984. text ed. 55.00x (ISBN 0-87893-142-2); pap. text ed. 30.00x (ISBN 0-87893-143-0). Sinauer Assocs.

Perspectives on Political Economy. Ed. by R. J. Jones. LC 82-24027. 250p. 1983. 27.50x (ISBN 0-312-60258-8). St Martin.

Perspectives on Political Ethics: An Ecumenical Inquiry. Koson Srisang. 207p. 1983. pap. 8.95 (ISBN 0-87840-407-4). Georgetown U Pr.

Perspectives on Population: An Introduction to Concepts & Issues. Scott Menard & Elizabeth Moen. (Illus.). 512p. 1987. 39.95 (ISBN 0-19-504092-9); pap. text ed. 24.95 (ISBN 0-19-504190-9). Oxford U Pr.

Perspectives on Pornography: Sexuality in Film & Literature. Ed. by Gary Day & Clive Bloom. LC 88-4539. 192p. 1988. 35.00 (ISBN 0-312-01873-8). St Martin.

Perspectives on Postal Service Issues. Ed. by Roger Sherman. 1980. 23.00 (ISBN 0-8447-2173-5); pap. 7.25 (ISBN 0-8447-2174-3). Am Enterprise.

Perspectives on Postsecondary Education: An Annotated Bibliography. 56p. 3.50 (ISBN 0-318-18005-7, PS-81-141). Ed Comm States.

Perspectives on Poverty & Income Inequality in Brazil: An Analysis of the Changes During the 1970s. David Denslow, Jr. & William G. Tyler. (Working Paper: No. 601). 59p. 1983. 5.00 (ISBN 0-8213-0209-4, WP 0601). World Bank.

Perspectives on Presidential Selection. Ed. by Donald R. Matthews. LC 73-1078. (Brookings Insitution Studies in Presidential Selection). pap. 64.50 (ISBN 0-317-26737-X, 2025390). Bks Demand UMI.

Perspectives on Prevention & Treatment of Cancer in the Elderly. Ed. by Rosemary Yancik et al. (Aging Ser.: Vol. 24). 360p. 1983. text ed. 83.50 (ISBN 0-89004-878-9). Raven.

Perspectives on Project Management. Ed. by R. N. Burbridge. (IEE Management of Technology Ser.: No. 7). 180p. 1988. pap. 38.00 (ISBN 0-86341-105-3, MN007). Inst Elect Eng.

Perspectives on Prospective Payments. Marjorie Beyers. 260p. 1985. 51.95 (ISBN 0-87189-095-X). Aspen Pub.

Perspectives on Public Bureaucracy: A Reader on Organization. 3rd ed. Fred A. Kramer. 1981. pap. text ed. write for info. (ISBN 0-673-39457-3). Scott F.

Perspectives on Public Policy Making, Vol. 15. Ed. by William B. Gwyn & George C. Edwards, III. LC 75-321771. xi, 241p. 1975. lib. bdg. 15.00 (ISBN 0-930598-15-6); pap. text ed. 11.00 (ISBN 0-930598-14-8). Tulane Stud Pol.

Perspectives on Racial Minority & Women School Administrators. American Association of School Administrators Staff. 341p. (Orig.). 1983. pap. 6.50 (ISBN 0-87652-081-6, 021-00120). Am Assn Sch Admin.

Perspectives on Radio & Television: Telecommunication in the United States. 2nd ed. F. Leslie Smith. 588p. 1985. text ed. 37.95 scp (ISBN 0-06-046316-3, HarpC). Har-Row.

Perspectives on Receptor Classification. Ed. by J. W. Black et al. LC 86-15188. (Receptor Biochemistry & Methodology Ser.: Vol. 6). 306p. 1987. 69.50 (ISBN 0-8451-3705-0, 3705). A R Liss.

Perspectives on Research & Scholarship in Composition. Ed. by Ben W. McClelland & Timothy R. Donovan. LC 85-15401. 300p. 1985. 32.00x (ISBN 0-87352-144-7); pap. text ed. 16.50x (ISBN 0-87352-145-5). Modern Lang.

Perspectives on Resource Management. T. O'Riordan. (Illus.). 184p. 1971. 10.50x (ISBN 0-85086-024-5, NO. 2931, Pub by Pion England); pap. 10.50x (ISBN 0-85086-025-3, NO. 2920). Routledge Chapman & Hall.

Perspectives on Resource Policy Modeling: Energy & Minerals. Ed. by Raphael Amit & Mordecai Avriel. LC 81-12697. 456p. 1982. prof ref 42.00x (ISBN 0-88410-837-6). Ballinger Pub.

Perspectives on Revolution & Evolution. Ed. by Richard A. Preston. LC 78-74448. xii, 294p. 1979. 30.00 (ISBN 0-8223-0425-2). Duke.

Perspectives on Romanticism: A Transformational Analysis. David Morse. 324p. 1981. 29.50x (ISBN 0-389-20164-2). B&N Imports.

Perspectives on Safe & Sound Banking: Past, Present, & Future. George J. Benston et al. 352p. 1986. 21.95x (ISBN 0-262-02246-X). MIT Pr.

Perspectives on Schoenberg & Stravinsky. Ed. by Benjamin Boretz & Edward T. Cone. LC 83-12964. x, 284p. 1983. Repr. of 1972 ed. lib. bdg. 38.50x (ISBN 0-313-23204-0, B0PR). Greenwood.

Perspectives on School Learning: Selected Writings of John B. Carroll. Ed. by Lorin W. Anderson & John B. Carroll. 440p. 1985. text ed. 39.95 (ISBN 0-89859-343-3). L Erlbaum Assocs.

Perspectives on Schooling for Texas Educators. Charles W. Funkhouser & John N. Bruscemi. 216p. 1981. pap. text ed. 14.95 (ISBN 0-8403-2436-7). Kendall-Hunt.

Perspectives on Self Deception. Brian P. McLaughlin & Amelie O. Rorty. Date not set. 55.00 (ISBN 0-520-05208-0). U of Cal Pr.

Perspectives on Sexuality: A Literary Collection. Ed. by James L. Malfetti & Elizabeth Eidlitz. LC 78-144052. (Illus.). 611p. 1972. pap. text ed. 9.95x (ISBN 0-03-082826-0). Irvington.

Perspectives on Silence. Ed. by Deborah Tannen & Muriel Saville-Troike. LC 84-18465. 288p. 1985. text ed. 42.50 (ISBN 0-89391-255-7); pap. 19.95 (ISBN 0-89391-310-3). Ablex Pub.

Perspectives on Social Change, 3rd ed. Robert H. Lauer. 400p. text ed. 36.00 (ISBN 0-205-07561-4, 8175616). Allyn.

Perspectives on Social Group Work Practice: A Book of Readings. Ed. by Albert S. Alissi. LC 79-7633. 1980. pap. text ed. 16.95 (ISBN 0-02-900480-2). Free Pr.

Perspectives on Social Network Research. Ed. by Paul W. Holland & Sammuel Leinhardt. LC 78-4813. (Quantitative Studies in Social Relations Ser.). 1979. 33.00 (ISBN 0-12-352550-0). Acad Pr.

Perspectives on Social Psychology. Ed. by Clyde Hendrick. LC 77-22024. 362p. 1977. 19.95x (ISBN 0-470-99295-6). Halsted Pr.

Perspectives on Social Psychology. Ed. by Clyde Hendrick. 368p. 1977. 39.95 (ISBN 0-89859-469-3). L Erlbaum Assocs.

Perspectives on Social Welfare: An Introductory Anthology. 2nd ed. P. E. Weinberger. 1974. pap. write for info. (ISBN 0-02-425160-7). Macmillan.

Perspectives on Social Welfare in India. Jal F. Bulsara & E. R. Verma. 1984. text ed. 24.00x. Coronet Bks.

Perspectives on Sociolinguistics. Nessa Wolfson. 260p. 1988. pap. text ed. 18.95t (ISBN 0-06-632572-2). Har-Row.

Perspectives on Soviet Jewry. Anti-Defamation League Staff. 150p. pap. 2.50 (ISBN 0-686-95144-1). ADL.

Perspectives on Soviet Law of the Nineteen Eighties. Ed. by F. J. Feldbrugge & William B. Simons. 180p. 1981. lib. bdg. 32.50 (ISBN 90-247-2561-5, Pub. by Martinus Nijhoff Netherlands). Kluwer Academic.

Perspectives on Strategic Defense. Ed. by Steve W. Guerrier & Wayne C. Thompson. (WVSS in National Security & Defense Ser.). 192p. 1988. pap. 34.00 (ISBN 0-8133-7316-6). Westview.

Perspectives on Strategic Marketing Management. Roger Kerin & Robert M. Peterson. 480p. 1983. text ed. 27.00 (ISBN 0-205-07922-9, 087922). Allyn.

Perspectives on Stress & Stress Related Topics. Ed. by F. Lolas & H. Mayer. 230p. 1987. pap. 49.50 (ISBN 0-387-12371-7). Springer-Verlag.

Perspectives on Swedish Immigration. Ed. by Nils Hasselmo. 349p. 1978. 15.00 (ISBN 0-318-16619-4). Swedish-Am.

Perspectives on Teaching: Learning & Development. Andrew Garrod et al. 536p. 1984. pap. text ed. 25.95 (ISBN 0-8403-3482-6). Kendall Hunt.

Perspectives on Technological Development in the Arab World. Mujid Kazimi & John Makhoul. (Monograph: No. 8). 96p. (Orig.). pap. text ed. 4.95 (ISBN 0-937694-03-7). Assn Arab-Amer U Grads.

Perspectives on Technology. Nathan Rosenberg. LC 84-23495. 360p. 1984. pap. 14.95 (ISBN 0-87332-303-3). M E Sharpe.

Perspectives on Terrorism. Ed. by Lawrence Z. Freedman & Yonah Alexander. LC 83-3011. 258p. 1983. lib. bdg. 30.00 (ISBN 0-8420-2201-5). Scholarly Res Inc.

Perspectives on the Administrative Process. Robert L. Rabin. 1979. pap. 10.95 (ISBN 0-316-73001-7). Little.

Perspectives on the American Past, Vol. I. Michael Perman. 1988. pap. text ed. price not set (ISBN 0-673-18616-4). Scott F.

Perspectives on the American Past, Vol. II. Michael Perman. 1988. pap. text ed. price not set (ISBN 0-673-18617-2). Scott F.

Perspectives on the American Revolution: A Bicentennial Contribution. Ed. by George G. Suggs, Jr. LC 77-5737. 156p. 1977. 7.95x (ISBN 0-8093-0827-4). S Ill U Pr.

Perspectives on the American South. Merle Black & John S. Reed. (Perspectives on the American South Ser.: Vol. 2). 281p. 1984. 42.00 (ISBN 0-677-16450-5). Gordon & Breach.

Perspectives on the American South, Vol. 3. Ed. by James C. Cobb & Charles R. Wilson. 320p. 1985. text ed. 42.00 (ISBN 2-88124-108-5). Gordon & Breach.

Perspectives on the American South: An Annual Review, Vol. 1. Ed. by M. Black & J. Reed. 424p. 1981. 58.00 (ISBN 0-677-16260-X). Gordon & Breach.

Perspectives on the American South: An Annual Review of Society, Politics & Culture, Vol. IV. Ed. by James C. Cobb & Charles R. Wilson. 205p. 1986. 58.00 (ISBN 2-88124-157-3). Gordon & Breach.

Perspectives on the Battle of Kadesh. Ed. by Hans Goedicke. (Illus.). 216p. (Orig.). 1985. pap. 30.00. Halgo Inc.

Perspectives on the Christian Reformed Church. Ed. by Peter DeKlerk & Richard R. DeRidder. 1983. 14.95 (ISBN 0-8010-2934-1). Baker Bk.

Perspectives on the Code for Nurses. (No. G-132). 60p. 1978. pap. 10.25 (ISBN 0-686-09599-5). ANA.

Perspectives on the Costs & Benefits of Applied Social Research. Ed. by Clark C. Abt. 300p. 1984. Repr. of 1978 ed. lib. bdg. 29.00 (ISBN 0-8191-4103-8). U Pr of Amer.

Perspectives on the Costs & Benefits of Applied Social Research. Ed. by Clark C. Abt et al. LC 78-67240. 1979. text ed. 27.50 (ISBN 0-89011-520-6). Abt Bks.

Perspectives on the Cross. Jon L. Joyce. (Orig.). 1982. pap. 5.95 (ISBN 0-937172-33-2). JLJ Pubs.

Perspectives on the Development of a Comprehensive Labor Market Information System for Michigan. Rodgers Lawson. 74p. 1973. pap. 1.75 (ISBN 0-911558-42-X). W E Upjohn.

Perspectives on the Development of Memory & Cognition. Ed. by R. V. Kail, Jr. & J. W. Hagen. 512p. 1977. text ed. 39.95 (ISBN 0-89859-128-7). L Erlbaum Assocs.

Perspectives on the Education & Training System of the Future. Warren H. Groff. (Eric Information Analysis Ser.). 34p. 1986. 5.25 (ISBN 0-318-22358-9, IN 312). Natl Ctr Res Voc Ed.

Perspectives on the Educational Use of Animals. Mayer et al. (Illus.). 77p. 1980. pap. 3.00 (ISBN 0-913098-38-8). Myrin Institute.

Perspectives on the Emergence of Scientific Disciplines. Gerard Lemaine. 1977. text ed. 20.00x (ISBN 9-0279-7743-7). Mouton.

Perspectives on the Executive Personality. Virgil R. Lang & Samuel E. Krug. LC 78-27205. 1983. pap. text ed. 12.00 (ISBN 0-918296-12-9). Inst Personality Ability.

Perspectives on the Extraterritorial Application of U. S. Antitrust & Other Laws. LC 79-83502. 241p. 1979. pap. 20.00 (ISBN 0-686-48022-8). Amer Bar Assn.

Perspectives on the Holocaust. Randolph L. Braham. (Holocaust Studies). 1983. lib. bdg. 20.00 (ISBN 0-89838-124-X, Pub. by Kluwer-Nijhoff (Netherlands)). Kluwer Academic.

Perspectives on the Middle East, 1983: Proceedings of a Conference. Ed. by William G. Miller & Philip H. Stoddard. LC 83-62243. 150p. 1983. pap. 1.50 (ISBN 0-916808-23-8). Mid East Inst.

Perspectives on the Mitral Valve. John B. Barlow. LC 86-8834. (Illus.). 381p. 1986. text ed. 60.00 (ISBN 0-8036-0617-6). Davis Co.

Perspectives on the New Testament: Essays in Honor of Frank Stagg. Ed. by Charles H. Talbert. (Festschriften Ser.: No. 3). vi, 108p. 9.95 (ISBN 0-317-61633-1). NABPR.

Perspectives on the New Testament: Essays in Honor of Frank Stagg. Malcolm Tolbert et al. Ed. by Charles H. Talbert. vi, 108p. 1985. lib. bdg. 9.95x (ISBN 0-86554-152-3, MUP-H121). Mercer Univ Pr.

Perspectives on the Parables: An Approach to Multiple Interpretations. Mary Ann Tolbert. LC 78-54563. 144p. 1978. 4.95 (ISBN 0-8006-0527-6, 1-527). Fortress.

Perspectives on the Passion. William Grimbol. 1984. 5.95 (ISBN 0-89536-665-7, 1645). CSS of Ohio.

Perspectives on the Past: An Autobiography. Robert B. Downs. LC 84-5589. 240p. 1984. 18.50 (ISBN 0-8108-1703-9). Scarecrow.

Perspectives on the Philosophy of Wittgenstein. Ed. by Irving Block. (Studies in Contemporary German Social Thought). 224p. 1982. text ed. 32.50x (ISBN 0-262-02173-0); pap. 10.95x (ISBN 0-262-52087-7). MIT Pr.

Perspectives on the Preparation of Student Affairs Professionals. Gary Knock. (ACPA Monograph). 1977. pap. 7.00 (ISBN 0-911547-59-2, 72166W34); pap. 5.00 members. Am Assn Coun Dev.

Perspectives on the Reagan Years. Ed. by John L. Palmer. LC 86-13160. 235p. 1986. 24.95 (ISBN 0-87766-403-X); pap. 12.95 (ISBN 0-87766-402-1). Urban Inst.

Perspectives on the Regulation of Trucking in Texas. David L. Huff. (Research Monograph 1987: 3). (Orig.). 1987. pap. 9.50 (ISBN 0-87755-306-8). Bureau Busn UT.

Perspectives on the Second Republic in Nigeria. Ed. by C. S. Whitaker, Jr. 50p. (Orig.). 1981. pap. 10.00 (ISBN 0-918456-43-6, Crossroads). African Studies Assn.

Perspectives on the Sociology of Education. Philip Robinson. (Routledge Education Bks). 250p. 1981. (ISBN 0-7100-0786-8); pap. 13.95x (ISBN 0-7100-0787-6). Routledge Chapman & Hall.

Perspectives on the Study of Diplomacy. Smith Simpson. LC 86-82863. 32p. (Orig.). 1986. pap. 3.50 (ISBN 0-934742-32-4, Inst Study Diplomacy). Geo U Sch For Serv.

Perspectives on the Study of Speech. Ed. by Peter D. Eimas & Joanne L. Miller. LC 80-39499. 464p. 1981. text ed. 49.95x (ISBN 0-89859-052-3). L Erlbaum Assocs.

Perspectives on the T'ang. Ed. by Arther F. Wright. Denis Twitchett. LC 72-91310. 542p. 1981. pap. 13.95x (ISBN 0-300-02674-9). Yale U Pr.

Perspectives on the T'ang. Ed. by Arthur F. Wright et al. LC 72-91310. pap. 89.00 (ISBN 0-317-11178-7, 2010566). Bks Demand UMI.

Perspectives on the World Christian Movement: A Reader. Ed. by Ralph D. Winter & Steven C. Hawthorne. LC 81-69924. (Illus.). 864p. (Orig.). 1981. pap. 14.95x (ISBN 0-87808-189-5). William Carey Lib.

Perspectives on Topicalization: The Case of Japanese WA. Ed. by John Hinds. LC 87-29982. (Typological Studies in Language Ser.: Vol. 14). xi, 307p. 1987. 56.00x (ISBN 0-915027-97-6); pap. 29.95 (ISBN 0-915027-98-4). Benjamins North Am.

Perspectives on Tort Law. 2nd ed. Robert L. Rabin. 352p. 1983. pap. 12.00 (ISBN 0-316-73003-3). Little.

Perspectives on Treatment: The Minnesota Experience. Daniel J. Anderson. 60p. 1981. 4.95 (ISBN 0-89486-133-6). Hazelden.

Perspectives on Understanding & Working with Families. Kevin Swick. 129p. 1987. pap. text ed. 7.80x (ISBN 0-87563-306-4). Stipes.

Perspectives on U. S. Policy Toward Southern Africa: Policy Evaluations & Alternative Proposals. Michael A. Kamara & Salima S. Marriott. 158p. (Orig.). 1984. pap. 8.00 (ISBN 0-9610324-1-3). Morgan State.

Perspectives on U. S. Policy Toward the Law of the Sea: Prelude to the Final Session of the Third U. N. Conference of the Sea, OP35 Occasional Paper No. 35. Ed. by David D. Caron & Charles L. Buderi. 1985. 5.00 (ISBN 0-911189-12-2). Law Sea Inst.

Perspectives on Urban Affairs in North Carolina. Ed. by Warren J. Wicker. 290p. 1979. 3.00 (ISBN 0-686-39482-8). U of NC Inst Gov.

Perspectives on Urban America. Ed. by Melvin I. Urofsky. 8.75 (ISBN 0-8446-5091-9). Peter Smith.

Perspectives on Urban Infrastructure. National Research Council. 216p. 1984. pap. 17.50 (ISBN 0-309-03439-6). Natl Acad Pr.

Perspectives on Urbanization & Migration, India & U. S. S. R. Ed. by Manzoor Alam & Fatima Alikhan. xxiv, 538p. 1987. 26.50x (ISBN 0-8364-2155-8, Pub. by Allied India). South Asia Bks.

Perspectives on Violence. Ed. by Gene Usdin. 162p. 1976. pap. 3.95 (ISBN 0-8065-0518-4, Pub. by Citadel Pr). Lyle Stuart.

Perspectives on Vocational Education: Purposes & Performance. Ed. by Morgan V. Lewis & Frank C. Pratzner. 73p. 1984. 7.95 (ISBN 0-318-17788-9, RD247). Natl Ctr Res Voc Ed.

Peruvian Experiment Reconsidered. Ed. by Cynthia McClintock & Abraham F. Lowenthal. LC 82-61377. 484p. 1983. 55.50x (ISBN 0-691-07648-0); pap. 11.95x (ISBN 0-691-02214-3). Princeton U Pr.

Peruvian Industrial Labor Force. David Chaplin. 1967. 35.00x (ISBN 0-691-09324-5). Princeton U Pr.

Peruvian Literature: A Bibliography of Secondary Sources. David W. Foster. LC 81-6957. 352p. 1981. lib. bdg. 46.95 (ISBN 0-313-23097-8, FPL/). Greenwood.

Peruvian Mining Industry: Growth, Stagnation & Crisis. Elizabeth W. Dore. (WVSS on Latin America & the Caribbean Ser.). 195p. 1988. pap. 21.00x (ISBN 0-8133-7061-2). Westview.

Peruvian Nationalism: A Corporatist Revolution. Ed. by David Chaplin. LC 73-85099. (Third World Ser.). 600p. 1976. 39.95x (ISBN 0-87855-077-1); pap. 14.95 (ISBN 0-87855-573-0). Transaction Bks.

Peruvian Painting by Unknown Artists: 800 B. C. to 1700 A. D. Intro. by Junius B. Bird. (Illus.). 1973. pap. 3.00 (ISBN 0-913456-20-9, Pub. by Ctr Inter-Am Rel). Interbk Inc.

Peruvian Prehistory. Ed. by Richard W. Keatinge. (Illus.). 250p. 1988. 49.50 (ISBN 0-521-25560-0); pap. 15.95 (ISBN 0-521-27555-5). Cambridge U Pr.

Peruvian Revolution's Approach: Investment Policy & Investor Climate 1968-Present. Stanley F. Rose. LC 81-80767. xiii, 518p. 1981. lib. bdg. 40.00 (ISBN 0-89941-097-9). W S Hein.

Peruvian Textile Designs. Caren Caraway. (International Design Library). (Illus.). 48p. 1983. pap. 5.95 (ISBN 0-88045-026-6). Stemmer Hse.

Peruvians of Today. William B. Parker. (Illus.). 1919. 29.00 (ISBN 0-527-69824-5). Kraus Repr.

Pervasive Image: The Role of Analogy in the Poetry of Ausias March. Robert Archer. LC 85-13360. (Purdue University Monographs in Romance Languages: No. 17). xii, 220p. 1985. pap. 37.00x (ISBN 0-915027-56-9). Benjamins North Am.

Perversion: The Erotic Form of Hatred. Robert J. Stoller. LC 86-17296. 256p. 1986. pap. text ed. 14.95x (ISBN 0-88048-262-1, 48-262-1). Am Psychiatric.

Perversions of the Sex Instinct. Albert Moll. LC 72-11289. (Eng.). Repr. of 1931 ed. 38.50 (ISBN 0-404-57482-3). AMS Pr.

Perversity. Francis Carco. Tr. by Jean Rhys from Fr. 150p. 1986. pap. 7.95 (ISBN 0-88739-048-X, A Blacklizard Book). Creative Arts Bk.

Perversity. Francis Carco. Tr. by Jean Rhys from Fr. LC 85-73608. 160p. 1987. pap. 3.95. Creative Arts Bk.

Perversity of Politics. E. Beuhrig. 128p. 1985. 27.50 (ISBN 0-7099-3201-4, Pub. by Croom Helm Ltd). Routledge Chapman & Hall.

Pervert. Jose E. Contreras. 96p. 1986. 8.75 (ISBN 0-8062-3041-X). Carlton.

Perverted Love. Barbara H. Seguin. 62p. 1987. pap. 3.75 (ISBN 0-88144-109-0). Christian Pub.

Pervertidos Anonimos. new ed. Javier Lopez. (Pimienta Collection Ser). 160p. (Span.). 1975. pap. 1.00 (ISBN 0-88473-222-3). Fiesta Pub.

Perverts by Official Order: The Campaign Against Homosexuals by the United States Navy. Ed. by Lawrence R. Murphy. LC 87-33914. (Journal of Homosexuality Ser.). (Illus.). 280p. 1988. text ed. 29.95 (ISBN 0-86656-708-9). Haworth Pr.

Perverts by Official Order: The Campaign Against Homosexuality by the United States Navy. Ed. & intro. by Lawrence R. Murphy. LC 87-33452. (Journal of Homosexuality). (Illus.). 280p. 1988. pap. text ed. 19.95 (ISBN 0-918393-44-2). Harrington Pk.

Pervert's Diary. Carlos Amantea. 375p. 1991. pap. 16.95 (ISBN 0-917320-08-5). Mho & Mho.

Perverts in Paradise. J. S. Trevisan. Tr. by Martin Foreman from Port. (Illus.). 208p. 1986. pap. 9.95 (ISBN 0-907040-78-0, Pub. by GMP England). Alyson Pubns.

Pervigilium Veneris: A Late Latin Poem of Love & Springtime. Ed. by Vincent J. Cleary & Theodore W. Wells. 46p. (Lat.). (gr. 10-12). 1981. pap. text ed. 3.75x (ISBN 0-88334-151-4). Ind Sch Pr.

Pervoe Serbskoe Vosstanie 1804-1813. Ed. by Collet's Holdings, Ltd. Staff. 398p. (Rus.). 1983. 69.00x (ISBN 0-317-40832-1, Pub. by Collets (UK)). State Mutual Bk.

Pesach: A Holiday Funtext. Judy Bin-Nun & Nancy Cooper. (Illus.). 32p. (Orig.). (gr. 1-3). 1983. pap. text ed. 5.00 (ISBN 0-8074-0161-7, 101310). UAHC.

Pesah & the Young Child. 51p. 2.50 (ISBN 0-318-13631-7, 22-035). Board Jewish Educ.

Pesah Is Coming. Hyman Chanover & Alice Chanover. (Holiday Series of Picture Storybooks). (Illus.). (gr. k-2). 1956. 5.95 (ISBN 0-8381-0713-3, 10-713). United Syn Bk.

Pesah Is Here. Hyman Chanover & Alice Chanover. (Holiday Series of Picture Storybooks). (Illus.). (gr. k-2). 1956. 5.95 (ISBN 0-8381-0714-1). United Syn Bk.

Pesahim, 2 vols. (Hebrew & Eng.). 30.00 (ISBN 0-910218-55-2). Bennet Pub.

Pesharim: Qumran Interpretations of Biblical Books. Maurya P. Horgan. LC 78-12910. (Catholic Biblical Quarterly Monographs: No. 8). ix, 308p. 1979. pap. 6.00 (ISBN 0-915170-07-8). Catholic Biblical.

Peshchera Neozhidannostei ("The Fun House") Emil Draitser. LC 83-63368. 160p. (Rus.). 1984. pap. 7.95 (ISBN 0-911971-03-3, Pub. by Effect Pub Co). Effect Pub.

Peshitta: Its Early Text & History: Papers Read at the Peshitta Symposium Held at Leiden 30-31 August 1988. Ed. by P. B. Dirksen & M. J. Mulder. (Monographs of the Peshitta Institute Leiden: Vol. IV). (Illus.). x, 310p. 1988. 55.00 (ISBN 90-04-08769-9, Pub. by E J Brill). Heinman.

Peshitta of the Twelve Prophets. A. Gelston. 232p. 1987. 49.95 (ISBN 0-19-826179-9). Oxford U Pr.

Pesikta De-Rab Kahana. Tr. by William G. Braude. Israel J. Kapstein. LC 74-6563. 594p. 1975. 23.95 (ISBN 0-8276-0051-8, 365). JPS Phila.

Pesikta De Rav Kahana, 2 Vols. Bernard Mandelbaum. 1962. Set. 50.00x (ISBN 0-685-13742-2, Pub. by Jewish Theol Seminary). Ktav.

Pesikta Rabbati: Homiletical Discourses for Festal Days & Special Sabbaths, 2 Vols. Tr. by William G. Braude. LC 68-27748. (Judaica Ser.: No. 18). (Illus.). 1968. Set. 85.00t (ISBN 0-300-01071-0). Yale U Pr.

Pesimismo. Eduardo De Acha. LC 83-82918. 112p. (Orig., Span.). 1984. pap. 5.00 (ISBN 0-89729-340-1). Ediciones.

Pesiqta deRab Kahana: An Analytical Translation, 2 pts. Tr. by Jacob Neusner from Hebrew. LC 86-26042. (Brown Judaic Studies). 245p. 1987. 34.95 ea. Pt. 1, Pisqaot One Through Fourteen (ISBN 1-55540-072-8, 14-01-22). Pt. 2, Pisqaot Fifteen Through Twenty-Eight & an Introduction to Pesiqta de (ISBN 1-55540-073-6, 14-01-23). Scholars Pr GA.

Pesni I Stkhi: Songs & Poems. 3rd ed. Aleksandr Vertinskii. LC 83-82221. 100p. (Rus.). 1983. pap. 12.00 (ISBN 0-88669-000-5). Globus Pubs.

Pessimism. Joe Bailey. 200p. 1988. text ed. 39.95 (ISBN 0-415-00247-8, Pub. by Kegan Paul); pap. text ed. 12.95 (ISBN 0-415-00248-6, Pub. by Kegan Paul). Routledge Chapman & Hall.

Pessimism & Contemporary Bengali Literature. Diplab Chakraborti. 1985. 12.00x (ISBN 0-8364-1459-4, Pub. by KL Mukhopadhyay). South Asia Bks.

Pessimism of Thomas Hardy: A Social Study. G. W. Sherman. LC 74-4982. 518p. 1976. 37.50 (ISBN 0-8386-1582-1). Fairleigh Dickinson.

Pessimisme De Thomas Hardy. Louise De Ridder-Barzin. LC 76-16485. 1976. Repr. of 1932 ed. lib. bdg. 35.00 (ISBN 0-8414-3776-9). Folcroft.

Pessimistisches Theatre: Eine Studie Zur Entfremdung im Englischen Drama 1955-1975. Adolf Wimmer. Ed. by James Hogg. (Poetic Drama & Poetic Theory). 332p. (Orig.). 1979. pap. 15.00 (ISBN 3-7052-0867-5, Pub. by Salzburg Studies). Longwood Pub Group.

Pessimist's Handbook: A Collection of Popular Essays. Arthur Schopenhauer. Ed. by Hazel E. Barnes. LC 64-11583. pap. 160.00 (ISBN 0-317-08050-4, 2022476). Bks Demand UMI.

Pest & Pathogen Control: Strategic, Tactical & Policy Models. Ed. by Gordon R. Conway. LC 83-16962. (ILASA International Series on Applied Systems Analysis). 488p. 1984. 89.95x (ISBN 0-471-90349-3, 1-696). Wiley.

Pest Animals in Buildings: A World Review. N. Hickin. 398p. 1986. 127.00 (ISBN 0-470-20636-5, Co-Pub. with Longman). Wiley.

Pest Control Aide. Jack Rudman. (Career Examination Ser.: C-2030). (Cloth bdg. avail. on request). pap. 14.00 (ISBN 0-8373-2030-5). Natl Learning.

Pest Control: An Assesssment of Present & Alternative Technologies, Vols. 1-3 &5. National Research Council Staff. 1976. pap. 27.00 set (ISBN 0-309-02409-9). Natl Acad Pr.

Pest Control: Biological, Physical & Selected Chemical Methods. Wendell W. Kilgore & Richard L. Doutt. 1967. 91.00 (ISBN 0-12-406650-X). Acad Pr.

Pest Control: Operations & Systems Analysis in Fruit Fly Management. Ed. by M. Mangel et al. (NATO ASI Series, Series G: Ecological Sciences: No. 11). xii, 465p. 1986. 85.00 (ISBN 0-387-16088-4). Springer-Verlag.

Pest Control Strategies. Ed. by Edward H. Smith & David Pimentel. 1978. 46.50 (ISBN 0-12-650450-4). Acad Pr.

Pest Control Strategies for the Future. National Research Council, Agricultural Board. pap. 95.80 (ISBN 0-317-39635-8, 2055289). Bks Demand UMI.

Pest Control Supervisor. Jack Rudman. (Career Examination Ser.: C-3094). (Cloth bdg. avail. on request). 1988. pap. 16.00 (ISBN 0-8373-3094-7). Natl Learning.

Pest Control with Nature's Chemicals: Allelochemics & Pheromones in Gardening & Agriculture. Elroy L. Rice. LC 83-47838. (Illus.). 240p. 1985. 30.00x (ISBN 0-8061-1853-9). U of Okla Pr.

Pest Lepidopters of Europe. David J. Carter. (Entomologica Ser.). 1984. lib. bdg. 89.50 (ISBN 90-6193-504-0, Pub. by Junk Pubs Netherlands). Kluwer Academic.

Pest Management. G. A. Matthews. (Illus.). 288p. 1985. text ed. 36.95 (ISBN 0-582-47011-0). Wiley.

Pest Management. G. A. Matthews. 288p. 1986. 43.95 (ISBN 0-470-20541-5, Co-Pub. with Longman). Wiley.

Pest Management Guide for Insects & Nematodes of Cotton in California. N. C. Toscano et al. LC 78-73066. 1979. pap. 5.00 (ISBN 0-931876-30-3, 4089). ANR Pubns CA.

Pest Management: Proceedings of an International Conference, 25-29 October 1976, Laxenburg, Austria. Ed. by G. A. Norton & C. S. Hollings. LC 78-40825. 1979. text ed. 93.00 (ISBN 0-08-023427-5). Pergamon.

Pest Management Programs for Deciduous Tree Fruits & Nuts. Ed. by D. J. Boethal & R. D. Eikenbary. LC 79-12616. 268p. 1979. 52.50x (ISBN 0-306-40178-9, Plenum Pr). Plenum Pub.

Pest Management with Insect Sex Attractants. Ed. by Morton Beroza. LC 76-1873. (ACS Symposium Ser: No. 23). 1976. 24.95 (ISBN 0-8412-0308-3). Am Chemical.

Pest Resistance to Pesticides. Ed. by G. P. Georghiou & Tetsuo Saito. LC 82-22369. 822p. 1983. 115.00x (ISBN 0-306-41246-2, Plenum Pr). Plenum Pub.

Pest Resistance to Pesticides & Crop Loss Assessment: Report of the Third Session of the FAO Panel of Experts, Held in Kyoto, Japan, 6 August 1980. (Plant Production & Protection Papers: No. 6). 42p. (Eng., Fr. & Span.). 1981. pap. 7.50 (ISBN 92-5-101104-4, F2231, FAO). UNIPUB.

Pest Resistance to Pesticides & Crop Loss Assessment: Report of the 2nd Session of the FAO Panel of Experts Held in Rome, Aug.-Sept. 1978, Vol. 2. (Plant Production & Protection Papers: No. 6). 47p. (Eng., Fr. & Span.). 1979. pap. 7.50 (ISBN 92-5-100762-4, F1838, FAO). UNIPUB.

Pest Resistance to Pesticides in Agriculture. 38p. 1970. pap. 7.50 (ISBN 0-686-70624-2, F1984, FAO). UNIPUB.

Pest Slugs & Snails: Biology & Control. D. Goden. Tr. by S. Gruber from Ger. (Illus.). 470p. 1983. 98.00 (ISBN 0-387-11894-2). Springer-Verlag.

Pestalozzi. Compiled by Lewis F. Anderson. LC 75-130984. Repr. of 1931 ed. 19.00 (ISBN 0-404-00357-5). AMS Pr.

Pestalozzian Music Teacher. Lowell Mason. 1977. lib. bdg. 59.95 (ISBN 0-8490-2425-0). Gordon Pr.

Pestalozzi's Educational Writings. Ed. by J. A. Green. 59.95 (ISBN 0-8490-0822-0). Gordon Pr.

Pestalozzi's Educational Writings. Johann H. Pestalozzi. Tr. by John A. Green from Ger. Bd. with How Gertrude Teaches Her Children. (Contributions to the History of Psychology Ser., Vol. II, Pt. B: Psychometrics). 1978. Repr. of 1898 ed. 30.00 (ISBN 0-89093-163-1). U Pubns Amer.

Peste. Albert Camus. (Folio Ser.: No. 42). pap. 6.95 (ISBN 0-685-37269-3). Schoenhof.

Peste. Albert Camus. 1942. write for info. French & Eur.

Pesticidal Formulations Research: Physical & Colloidal Chemical Aspects. Ed. by J. W. Van Valkenburg. LC 74-81252. (Advances in Chemistry Ser: No. 86). 1969. 21.95 (ISBN 0-8412-0087-4). Am Chemical.

Pesticide Alert: A Guide to Pesticides in Fruits & Vegetables. Lawrie Mott & Karen Snyder. LC 87-42965. (Illus.). 128p. 1988. 15.95 (ISBN 0-87156-728-8); pap. 6.95 (ISBN 0-87156-726-1). Sierra.

Pesticide Analysis. Das. 1981. 69.75 (ISBN 0-8247-1087-8). Dekker.

Pesticide Analytical Methodology. Ed. by John Harvey, Jr. & Gunter Zweig. LC 80-19470. (ACS Symposium Ser.: No. 136). 1980. 44.95 (ISBN 0-8412-0581-7). Am Chemical.

Pesticide & Xenobiotic Metabolism in Aquatic Organisms. Ed. by M. A. Khan et al. LC 79-4598. (ACS Symposium Ser.: No. 99). 1979. 42.95 (ISBN 0-8412-0489-6). Am Chemical.

Pesticide Application & Safety Training. M. W. Stimmann. LC 80-52766. 1977. pap. text ed. 8.00x (ISBN 0-931876-17-6, 4070). ANR Pubns CA.

Pesticide Application Equipment & Techniques. Norman B. Akesson & Wesley E. Yates. (Agricultural Services Bulletins: No. 38). 261p. 1979. pap. 17.50 (ISBN 92-5-100835-3, F1894, FAO). UNIPUB.

Pesticide Application Methods. G. A. Matthews. LC 77-26033. (Illus.). 1979. 17.95x (ISBN 0-582-46351-3). Wiley.

Pesticide Application Methods. G. A. Matthews. 480p. 1979. pap. 22.95 (ISBN 0-470-20540-7, Co-Pub. with Longman). Wiley.

Pesticide Application: Principles & Practice. Ed. by P. T. Haskell. (Illus.). 1985. 85.00x (ISBN 0-19-854542-8). Oxford U Pr.

Pesticide Chemist & Modern Toxicology. Ed. by S. Kris Bandal et al. LC 81-10790. (ACS Symposium Ser.: No. 160). 1981. 49.95 (ISBN 0-8412-0636-8). Am Chemical.

Pesticide Chemistry - Human Welfare & the Environment: Mode of Action, Metabolism & Toxicology, Vol. 3. Ed. by J. Miyamoto & P. C. Kearney. (IUPAC Symposium Ser.). (Illus.). 1983. 120.00 (ISBN 0-08-029224-0). Pergamon.

Pesticide Chemistry - Human Welfare & the Environment: Pesticide Residues & Formulation Chemistry, Vol. 4. Ed. by J. Miyamoto & P. Kearney. (IUPAC Symposium Ser.). 1983. 120.00 (ISBN 0-08-029225-9). Pergamon.

Pesticide Chemistry - Human Welfare & the Environment: Synthesis & Structure Activity Relationships, Vol. 1. Ed. by J. Miyamoto & P. C. Kearney. (IUPAC Symposium Ser.). 1983. 120.00 (ISBN 0-08-029222-4). Pergamon.

Pesticide Chemistry: Human Welfare & the Environment, Vol. 2. Ed. by J. Miyamoto. (IUPAC Symposium Ser.). 1983. 120.00 (ISBN 0-08-029223-2). Pergamon.

Pesticide Chemistry: Human Welfare & the Environment: Proceedings of the 5th International Congress of Pesticide Chemistry, Kyoto, Japan, 29 August - 4 September 1982, 4 Vols. Ed. by J. Miyamoto & P. C. Kearney. (IUPAC Symposium Ser.). 1750p. 1983. Set. 475.00 (ISBN 0-08-029219-4). Pergamon.

Pesticide Chemistry in the Twentieth Century. Ed. by Jack R. Plimmer. LC 76-51748. (ACS Symposium Ser: No. 37). 1977. 19.95 (ISBN 0-8412-0532-9). Am Chemical.

Pesticide Chemistry: Proceedings of the International IUPAC Congress, 2nd Congress, 6 vols. International IUPAC Congress-2nd. Ed. by A. S. Tahori. Set. 600.00 (ISBN 0-677-12120-2); Vol. 1, 506p., 1972. 140.00 (ISBN 0-677-12130-X); Vol. 2, 310p., 1971. 90.00 (ISBN 0-677-12140-7); Vol. 3, 236p., 1971. 90.00 (ISBN 0-677-12150-4); Vol. 4, 618p., 1971. 165.00 (ISBN 0-677-12160-1); Vol. 5, 578p., 1972. 155.00 (ISBN 0-677-12170-9); Vol. 6, 584p., 1972. 155.00 (ISBN 0-677-12180-6). Gordon & Breach.

Pesticide Control Inspector. Jack Rudman. (Career Examination Ser.: C-2561). (Cloth bdg. avail. on request). pap. 16.00 (ISBN 0-8373-2561-7). Natl Learning.

Pesticide Decision Making. National Research Council. LC 77-94524. (Analytical Studies for the U. S. Environmental Protection Agency Ser.). (Illus.). 1978. pap. text ed. 7.50 (ISBN 0-309-02734-9). Natl Acad Pr.

Pesticide Effects on Soil Microflora. Ed. by L. Somerville & M. P. Greaves. 250p. 1987. 77.00x (ISBN 0-85066-365-2). Taylor & Francis.

Pesticide Fire & Spill Control. United States Fire Academy Environmental Protection Agency. Ed. by Ruth Harmon. LC 79-720315. (Illus.). 1979. pap. text ed. 250.00 (ISBN 0-87765-152-3, SL-45). Natl Fire Prot.

Pesticide Formulations. Ed. by W. Van Valkenburg. LC 72-86610. pap. 93.30 (ISBN 0-8357-9091-6, 2055053). Bks Demand UMI.

Pesticide Formulations & Application Systems, Vol. 7. Ed. by G. B. Beestman & D. I. Vander Hooven. LC 87-14461. (Special Technical Publications: No. 968). (Illus.). 275p. 1987. text ed. 39.00 (ISBN 0-8031-0970-9, 04-968000-48). ASTM.

Pesticide Formulations & Applications Systems, Vol. 6. Ed. by D. I. Vander Hooven et al. LC 87-11503. (Special Technical Publications: No. 943). (Illus.). 186p. 1987. text ed. 36.00 (ISBN 0-8031-0943-1, 04-943000-48). ASTM.

Pesticide Formulations & Application Systems: Fourth Symposium - STP 875. Ed. by Thomas M. Kaneko & Larry D. Spicer. LC 85-13390. (Illus.). 193p. 1985. text ed. 37.00 (ISBN 0-8031-0413-8, 04-875000-48). ASTM.

Pesticide Formulations & Application Systems: Fifth Symposium. Ed. by L. D. Spicer & T. M. Kaneko. LC 86-22358. (Special Technical Publications: No. 915). (Illus.). 154p. 1986. text ed. 32.00 (ISBN 0-8031-0481-2, 04-915000-48). ASTM.

Pesticide Formulations & Application Systems: Second Conference - STP 795. Ed. by K. G. Seymour. LC 82-72891. 111p. 1983. pap. text ed. 14.00 (ISBN 0-8031-0233-X, 04-795000-48). ASTM.

Pesticide Formulations & Application Systems: Third Symposium - STP 828. Ed. by T. M. Kaneko & N. B. Akesson. LC 83-71898. 152p. 1984. text ed. 19.00 (ISBN 0-8031-0221-6, 04-828000-48). ASTM.

Pesticide Formulations: Innovations & Developments. Ed. by Barrington Cross & Herbert B. Scher. LC 88-10419. (ACS Symposium Ser.: No. 371). (Illus.). xi, 288p. 1988. 64.95 (ISBN 0-8412-1483-2). Am Chemical.

Pesticide Handling: A Safety Manual. 144p. (Orig.). 1987. pap. text ed. 7.50 (ISBN 0-660-12311-8, SSC243, SSC). UNIPUB.

Pesticide Impact on Stream Fauna: With Special Reference to Macroinvertebrates. R. C. Muirhead-Thomson. LC 86-20696. (Illus.). 288p. 1987. 54.50 (ISBN 0-521-30967-0). Cambridge U Pr.

Pesticide Management & Insecticide Resistance. Ed. by David L. Watson & A. W. Brown. 1977. 66.00 (ISBN 0-12-738650-5). Acad Pr.

Pet for Kids. Sharon Boren. (Illus.). 200p. (gr. k up). pap. 12.95 (ISBN 0-517-56394-0); tchr's manual 14.95 (ISBN 0-517-56412-2); wkbk. 5.95 (ISBN 0-517-56413-0). Crown.

Pet for Mrs. Arbuckle. Gwenda Smyth. LC 84-1863. (Illus.). 32p. (ps-2). 1984. paper over boards with jacket 9.95 (ISBN 0-517-55434-8). Crown.

Pet for Pat. Pegeen Snow. LC 83-23159. (Rookie Readers). (Illus.). 32p. (ps-2). 1984. lib. bdg. 9.93 (ISBN 0-516-02049-8); pap. 2.50 (ISBN 0-516-42049-6). Childrens.

Pet for the Orphelines. Natalie S. Carlson. (gr. k-6). 1988. pap. 2.75 (ISBN 0-440-46838-8, YB). Dell.

Pet for the Orphelines. Natalie S. Carlson. (gr. 1-4). 1988. 2.75 (ISBN 0-440-40014-7, Pub. by Yearling Classics). Dell.

Pet Heroes: A Collection of True Stories for Animal Lovers. Elizabeth Seafoss. (Illus.). 80p. (Orig.). 1985. pap. 5.95 (ISBN 0-935253-00-9). Maynard-Thomas.

PET Index. Michael A. Ryan. 216p. 1982. pap. text ed. 17.95 (ISBN 0-566-03426-3). Gower Pub Co.

Pet Industry Outlook. Business Communications Staff. 140p. 1985. pap. 1500.00 (ISBN 0-89336-439-8, GA-034N). BCC.

Pet Loads, 2 Vol. set. 3rd ed. Ken Waters. Ed. by Dave Wolfe. (Illus.). 432p. 29.00 (ISBN 0-935632-33-6). Wolfe Pub Co.

Pet Loss: A Thoughtful Guide for Adults & Children. Herbert Nieburg & Arlene Fischer. LC 81-47670. 192p. 1982. 14.95i (ISBN 0-06-014947-7, HarpT). Har-Row.

Pet Loss & Human Bereavement. Ed. by William J Kay et al. 198p. 1984. text ed. 17.95x (ISBN 0-8138-1326-3). Iowa St U Pr.

Pet Loss & Human Bereavement. Ed. by William J. Kay et al. (Illus.). 210p. 1988. pap. 9.95t (ISBN 0-8138-1327-1). Iowa St U Pr.

Pet Mice. Jerome Wexler. Ed. by Kathleen Tucker. (Illus.). 48p. (gr. 2-8). 1988. PLB 12.95 (ISBN 0-8075-6524-5). A Whitman.

Pet Names. Rose Bianchina. Ed. by Paul Bianchina. (Illus.). 45p. (Orig.). 1984. pap. 3.95 (ISBN 0-918783-00-3). Golden Pubns.

Pet Names. Jean E. Taggart. LC 62-19730. 387p. 1962. 17.50 (ISBN 0-8108-0111-6). Scarecrow.

Pet of Frankenstein. Mel Gilden. 96p. (gr. 3-7). 1988. pap. 2.50 (ISBN 0-380-75185-2, Camelot). Avon.

Pet of the Met. Lydia Freeman & Don Freeman. (Illus.). 64p. (Orig.). (ps-3). Date not set. pap. 4.95 (ISBN 0-14-050892-9, Puffin Bks). Penguin.

Pet Owners' Guide to Dogs. Kay White. LC 86-27325. (Illus.). 160p. 1987. 10.95 (ISBN 0-87605-769-5). Howell Bk.

P.E.T. Parent Effectiveness Training. Thomas Gordon. 14.95 (ISBN 0-317-62733-3). McKay.

P.E.T, Parent Effectiveness Training: The Tested New Way to Raise Responsible Children. Thomas Gordon. 352p. 1975. pap. 7.95 (ISBN 0-452-25788-3, Z5252, Plume). NAL.

Pet Parts & Extra Things. Paul Woodbine. (Illus.). 24p. 1984. text ed. 98.00 (ISBN 0-916258-14-9). Mercury Print.

PET Personal Computer for Beginners. Seamus Dunn & Valerie Morgan. 1983. pap. 19.95 (ISBN 0-13-661827-8). P-H.

Pet Responsibility: Citizenship Lessons for Elementary Students. Thomas Fitzgerald & Barbara Miller. (Illus.). 132p. (Orig.). 1987. pap. 9.95 (ISBN 0-89994-319-5). Soc Sci Ed.

Pet Sematary. Stephen King. LC 82-45360. 384p. 1983. 19.95 (ISBN 0-385-18244-9). Doubleday.

Pet Sematary. Stephen King. 416p. 1984. pap. 4.95 (ISBN 0-451-15024-4, Sig). NAL.

Pet Sematary. Stephen King. 1984. 18.95 (ISBN 0-8161-3691-2, Large Print Bks); pap. 9.95 (ISBN 0-8161-3756-0). G K Hall.

Pet Shop. Harry Bornstein. (Signed English Ser.). 18p. 1976. pap. 3.50 (ISBN 0-913580-54-6, Clerc Bks). Gallaudet Univ Pr.

Pet Shop. Rod Campbell. (Play-Slots Ser.). (Illus.). 14p. (gr. 1-3). 1981. bds. 2.95 (ISBN 0-590-07940-9). Scholastic Inc.

Pet Shop. Frank Endersby. (Choices Ser.). (ps). 1984. 3.50 (ISBN 0-317-07210-2, Child's Play England). Playspaces.

Pet Show! Ezra J. Keats. LC 73-156843. 32p. (gr. k-3). 1972. 14.95 (ISBN 0-02-749620-1); pap. 3.95 (ISBN 0-02-044070-7, Collier). Macmillan.

Pet Show! Ezra J. Keats. LC 86-17225. (Illus.). 40p. (gr. k-4). 1987. pap. 4.50 (ISBN 0-689-71159-X, Aladdin Bks). Macmillan.

Pet Sitting for Profit. 1987 ed. Patti J. Moran. (Illus.). 72p. (Orig.). pap. 9.95 (ISBN 0-944165-00-1). New Beginnings.

Pet Sitting for Profit. rev., expanded ed. Patti J. Moran. (Illus.). 112p. (Orig.). 1988. pap. 9.95 (ISBN 0-944165-11-7). New Beginnings.

Pet-Sitting Peril. Willo D. Roberts. LC 82-13757. 192p. (gr. 3-7). 1983. 10.95 (ISBN 0-689-30963-5, Atheneum Childrens Bks). Macmillan.

Pet-Sitting Peril. Willo D. Roberts. 167p. (gr. 3-7). 1985. pap. 3.50 (ISBN 0-689-71042-9, Aladdin). Macmillan.

Pet Stories for Children. Sara Corrin & Stephen Corrin. (Illus.). 160p. (gr. 2-7). 1985. 11.95 (ISBN 0-571-13642-7). Faber & Faber.

Pet the Donkey. Illus. by Lucy C. Witherow & Michael Fleishman. (Touch & Do Ser.). 12p. (ps). 1987. bds. 5.95 (ISBN 0-8407-6705-6). Nelson.

Pet the Dove. Illus. by Lucy C. Witherow & Michael Fleishman. (Touch & Do Ser.). 12p. (ps). 1987. bds. 5.95 (ISBN 0-8407-6707-2). Nelson.

Pet the Duck. Illus. by Lucy C. Witherow & Michael Fleishman. (Touch & Do Ser.). 12p. (ps). 1987. bds. 5.95 (ISBN 0-8407-6706-4). Nelson.

Peta, Wild Rose of the Mountain. Marjorie Miller. (Illus.). 33p. (gr. 3-7). 1985. 4.95 (ISBN 0-533-06347-7). Vantage.

Petagwana to Pele: Point Edward to Point Pelee. 2nd ed. Al Plant. (Illus.). 113p. (Orig.). 1983. pap. 9.95 (ISBN 0-913611-00-X). W E C Plant Ent.

Petaled Sun. Mary A. Seguin. 48p. (Orig.). 1986. pap. 3.25 (ISBN 0-9616951-0-2). M A Seguin.

Petaloid Monocotyledons: Horticultural & Botanical Research. C. Brickell et al. (Linnean Society Symposium Ser.: No.8). 1980. 98.00 (ISBN 0-12-133950-5). Acad Pr.

Petals: Change Your Perspective Change Your Life. Annette Flad McMahon. (Illus.). 223p. (Orig.). 1987. 24.95 (ISBN 0-944005-21-7); lib. bdg. write for info. (ISBN 0-944005-23-3); pap. write for info. (ISBN 0-944005-22-5). Columbia NY.

Petals Fall Softly. Priscilla Klepser. LC 84-91293. 129p. 1985. 10.95 (ISBN 0-533-06385-X). Vantage.

Petals from the Moon. Guanetta Gordon. LC 72-15540. (Illus.). 96p. 1971. 4.50 (ISBN 0-8233-0162-1). Golden Quill.

Petals from the Womanflower. Margaret K. Biggs. 20p. (Orig.). 1983. pap. 2.50 (ISBN 0-938566-14-8). Adastra Pr.

Petals of Blood. Ngugi Wa Thiong'O. 1978. pap. 10.95 (ISBN 0-525-48235-0). Dutton.

Petals of the Rose: Poems & Epigrams. facsimile ed. Louis V. Burrell. LC 70-168513. (Black Heritage Library Collection). Repr. of 1917 ed. 11.50 (ISBN 0-8369-8876-0). Ayer Co Pubs.

Petals on the Wind. V. C. Andrews. 1982. pap. 4.95 (ISBN 0-671-60638-7). PB.

Petals on the Wind. V. C. Andrews. 448p. 1987. pap. 4.95 (ISBN 0-671-64813-6). PB.

Petals on the Wind see Flowers in the Attic.

Petals Plucked from Sunny Climes. Silvia Sunshine, pseud. Intro. by Richard A. Martin. LC 76-10700. (Floridiana Facsimile & Reprint Ser.). 1976. Repr. of 1880 ed. 13.50 (ISBN 0-8130-0414-4). U Presses Fla.

Petcetera: The Pet Riddle Book. Meyer Seltzer. Ed. by Ann Fay. (Illus.). 32p. (gr. 1-5). 1988. PLB 7.95 (ISBN 0-8075-6515-6). A Whitman.

Pete & Johnny to the Rescue. Jorgen Clevin. LC 74-4926. (Illus.). 64p. (ps-k). 1974. Random.

Pete & Lily. Amy Hest. LC 85-13992. 120p. (gr. 4-7). 1986. 11.95 (ISBN 0-89919-354-4, Pub. by Clarion). Ticknor & Fields.

Pete & Lily. Amy Hest. (gr. k-6). 1989. pap. price not set (ISBN 0-440-40145-3, YB). Dell.

Pete & Roland. Bob Graham. (Illus.). 28p. (gr. 1). 1983. lib. bdg. 9.95 (ISBN 0-00-184344-3, Pub. by W Collins Australia). Intl Spec Bk.

Pete & Roland. Bob Graham. LC 83-23402. (Illus.). 32p. (ps-2). 1984. 5.95 (ISBN 0-670-54912-6, Viking Kestrel). Viking.

Pete & Roland. Bob Graham. (ps-3). 1988. pap. 3.95 (ISBN 0-14-050798-1, Puffin Bks). Penguin.

Pete Culler's Boats: The Complete Design Catalog. John Burke. LC 82-48429. (Illus.). 322p. 1984. 24.95 (ISBN 0-87742-142-0, P566). Intl Marine.

Pete Maravich: Basketball Whiz. Musemeche & Ellis. 1969. 2.95 (ISBN 0-685-00420-1). Claitors.

Pete Rose. Nathan Aaseng. LC 79-27377. (Lerner Achievers Ser.). (Illus.). (gr. 4-9). 1981. PLB 7.95 (ISBN 0-8225-0480-4). Lerner Pubns.

Pete Rose: "Charlie Hustle". Ray Buck. LC 82-23482. (Sports Stars Ser.). (Illus.). 48p. (gr. 2-8). 1983. PLB 11.27 (ISBN 0-516-04329-3); pap. 2.95 (ISBN 0-516-44329-1). Childrens.

Pete Rose on Hitting. Pete Rose & Peter Golenbock. (Illus.). 96p. 1985. pap. 7.95 (ISBN 0-399-51164-4, Perigee). Putnam Pub Group.

Pete Rose's Winning Baseball. Pete Rose & Bob Hertzel. (Illus.). 192p. 1986. pap. 6.95 (ISBN 0-8092-8102-3). Contemp Bks.

Pete the Parakeet. Sharon Gordon. (Illus.). 32p. (gr. k-2). 1980. PLB 5.41 (ISBN 0-89375-384-X); pap. 1.50 (ISBN 0-89375-284-3). Troll Assocs.

Pete the Penguin. Jane Hammond. (God's Animals Story Bks.). (ps-k). 1984. pap. 1.50 (ISBN 0-87162-394-3, D5607). Warner Pr.

Pete: The Story of Peter V. Cacchione, New York's First Communist Councilman. Simon W. Gerson. LC 76-29039. 215p. 1976. pap. 3.50 (ISBN 0-7178-0473-9). Intl Pubs Co.

Pete Turner. Gruppo Editoriale Fabbri Staff. (Great Photographer's Ser.). Date not set. price not set. P-H.

Pete Turner Photographs. Owen Edwards. (Illus.). 144p. 1987. 29.95 (ISBN 0-8109-1691-6). Abrams.

Peter. Ethel Barrett. LC 81-52942. (Bible Biography Ser.). 128p. (Orig.). (gr. 3 up). 1982. pap. text ed. 2.95 (ISBN 0-8307-0768-9, 5810809). Regal.

Peter. William Coleman. LC 81-85894. 160p. (Orig.). 1982. pap. 4.95 (ISBN 0-89081-305-1). Harvest Hse.

Peter. F. B. Meyer. 1968. pap. 4.50 (ISBN 0-87508-349-8). Chr Lit.

Peter - Revelation: Commentary. Paul Gardner. 1988. pap. 4.95 (ISBN 0-87508-175-4). ChR Lit.

Peter: A Journey in Faith. R. Scott Sullender. 47p. (Orig.). 1986. pap. 6.95 (ISBN 0-940754-37-1). Ed Ministries.

Peter Abelard. facsimile ed. Joseph McCabe. LC 74-148889. (Select Bibliographies Reprint Ser). Repr. of 1901 ed. 22.00 (ISBN 0-8369-5655-9). Ayer Co Pubs.

Peter Abelard. Helen Waddell. (Thomas More Books to Live Ser.). 277p. 1987. Repr. of 1933 ed. 14.95 (ISBN 0-88347-217-1). Thomas More.

Peter Abelard & the Rise of the Modern Universities, 2 vols. Gabriel Compayre' (Illus.). 327p. 1987. Set. 187.75 (ISBN 0-89901-297-3). Found Class Reprints.

Peter Abelard, Letters IX-XIV. Edme R. Smits. xii, 315p. (Orig.). 1983. pap. 24.00x (ISBN 90-6088-085-4, Pub. by Boumas Boekhuis Netherlands). Benjamins North AM.

Peter Abelard (1079-1142) Joseph McCabe. LC 72-85102. ix, 402p. 1972. Repr. of 1901 ed. lib. bdg. 23.50 (ISBN 0-8337-4244-2). B Franklin.

Peter Alliss' Most Memorable Golf. Peter Alliss. (Illus.). 146p. 1987. 17.95 (ISBN 0-09-166050-5, Pub. by Century Hutchinson). David & Charles.

Peter & Anthony Shaffer: A Reference Guide. Dennis A. Klein. 1982. lib. bdg. 23.00 (ISBN 0-8161-8574-3, Hall Reference). G K Hall.

Peter & George & Uncle Henry. Elizabeth Delavan. (Illus.). 48p. (gr. 3-4). pap. cancelled (ISBN 1-55787-020-9). Heart of the Lakes.

Peter & His Oak. Claude Levert. Tr. by Leland Northam from Span. LC 85-40499. (Illus.). 26p. (ps-4). 1985. 6.45 (ISBN 0-382-09141-8). Silver.

Peter & Polly. David Lloyd. 32p. (ps-3). 1988. pap. 3.95 (ISBN 0-590-33652-5). Scholastic Inc.

Peter & Susie Find a Family. Edith Hess & Jacqueline Blass. (Illus.). 28p. (gr. 2-4). 1985. Repr. of 1981 ed. 10.95 (ISBN 0-687-30848-8). Abingdon.

Peter & the First Christians. Laurent Lalo. LC 84-42946. (Illus.). 24p. (gr. 1-4). 1985. 4.95 (ISBN 0-88070-084-X). Multnomah.

Peter & the North Wind. Retold by Freya Littledale. LC 87-4817. 32p. 1988. 12.95 (ISBN 0-590-40756-2). Scholastic Inc.

Peter & the Wolf. Ed. by Warren Chappell. LC 81-40404. (Illus.). 36p. 1981. pap. 5.95 (ISBN 0-8052-0684-1). Schocken.

Peter & the Wolf. David Eastman. LC 87-11275. (Illus.). 32p. (gr. k-3). 1987. PLB 9.79 (ISBN 0-8167-1057-0); pap. text ed. 1.95 (ISBN 0-8167-1058-9). Troll Assocs.

Peter & The Wolf. S. Hasting. LC 86-27004. (Illus.). 32p. (gr. k-2). 1987. 12.95 (ISBN 0-8050-0408-4). H Holt & Co.

Peter & the Wolf. Adapted by Margaret A. Hughes & Ken Forsse. (Talking Mother Goose Ser.). (Illus.). 26p. (ps). 1986. packaged with preprogrammed audio cassette tapes 9.95 (ISBN 0-934323-33-X). Alchemy Comms.

Peter & the Wolf. Serge Prokofieff. (Tell Me a Story Ser.). (Illus.). 26p. (ps). 1988. incl. cassette 9.95. Worlds Wonder.

Peter & the Wolf. Sergei Prokofiev. (Illus.). 32p. (gr. 1-2). 1979. 4.95 (ISBN 0-571-18004-3). Faber & Faber.

Peter & the Wolf. Sergei Prokofiev. LC 86-7462. (Knopf Book & Cassette Classics). (Illus.). 24p. (ps-6). 1986. Set. 14.95 (ISBN 0-394-88417-5); bk. & cassette 19.95 (ISBN 0-394-88418-3). Knopf.

Peter & the Wolf. Sergei Prokofiev. Tr. by Maria Carlson. (Picture Puffins Ser.). (Illus.). 32p. (ps-3). 1986. pap. 3.95 (ISBN 0-14-050633-0, Puffin). Penguin.

Peter & the Wolf. Sergei Prokofiev. Tr. by Maria Carlson. (Illus.). (gr. 2-5). 1987. incl. cassette 19.95 (ISBN 0-87499-074-2); pap. 12.95 incl. cassette (ISBN 0-87499-073-4); 4 paperbacks, cassette & guide 27.95 (ISBN 0-87499-075-0). Live Oak Media.

Peter & the Wolf. Sergei Prokofiev. Tr. by Patricia Crampton. LC 87-13915. (Illus.). (ps up). 1987. 12.95 (ISBN 0-88708-049-9). Picture Bk Studio.

Peter & the Wolf. Sergei Prokofiev. LC 79-92902. (Illus.). 32p. 1987. 12.95 (ISBN 0-317-62883-6). Godine.

Peter & the Wolf. Sergei Prokofiev & Warren Chappell. (Illus.). (gr. 4 up). 1973. pap. 1.95 (ISBN 0-394-82613-2). Knopf.

Peter & the Wolf. Retold by James Riordan. (Illus.). 24p. (ps-6). 1987. 12.95 (ISBN 0-19-279824-3). Oxford U Pr.

Peter & the Wolf Pop-up-Book. Sergei Prokofiev. (Illus.). (gr. k-12). 1986. 13.95 (ISBN 0-670-80849-0, Viking Kestrel). Viking.

Peter & Veronica. Marilyn Sachs. (Illus.). 176p. (gr. 4-6). 1987. pap. 2.50 (ISBN 0-590-40404-0, Apple Paperbacks). Scholastic Inc.

Peter: Apostle of Contrast. James T. Dyet. LC 81-70776. (Chosen Messengers Ser.). 128p. (Orig.). 1982. pap. text ed. 3.50 (ISBN 0-89636-077-6). Accent Bks.

Peter Arbiter: The Adventures of a Young Man in Texas. Edwin Shrake. (Illus.). 152p. 1973. 12.50 (ISBN 0-88426-030-5). Encino Pr.

Peter Arno. Intro. by Charles Saxon. (Peter Weed Bks.). (Illus.). 256p. 1986. pap. 14.95 (ISBN 0-8253-0401-6). Beaufort Bks NY.

Peter Ashley. Du Bose Heyward. 316p. Repr. of 1932 ed. lib. bdg. 25.00 (ISBN 0-89984-715-3). Century Bookbindery.

Peter Aureoli: Scriptum Super Primum Sententiarum, 2 vols. Ed. by Eligius M. Buytaert. (Text Ser). 1956. Vol. 1, Prologue-dist. 1. 20.00 (ISBN 0-686-11547-3); Vol. 2, Dist. 2-8. 23.00 (ISBN 0-686-11548-1). Franciscan Inst.

Peter Beagle. Kenneth J. Zahorski. (Starmont Reader's Guide Ser.: No. 44). 124p. 1988. lib. bdg. 17.95x (ISBN 0-89370-971-9). Borgo Pr.

Peter Beagle. Kenneth J. Zahorski. LC 87-9924. (Reader's Guide to Contemporary Science Fiction & Fantasy Authors Ser.: Vol. 44). (Orig.). 1988. 17.95x (ISBN 1-55742-009-2); pap. 9.95x (ISBN 1-55742-008-4). Starmont Hse.

Peter Bell. William Wordsworth. Ed. by John E. Jordan. LC 83-21042. (Wordsworth Ser.). (Illus.). 648p. 1985. 65.00x (ISBN 0-8014-1620-5). Cornell U Pr.

Peter Bently: The Super Sleuth Cat. Al Montesi. 60p. 1987. pap. 5.00 (ISBN 0-918476-15-1). Cornerstone Pr.

Peter Blake. Marina Vaizey. (Royal Academy Painters & Sculptors Ser.). (Illus.). 92p. 1986. 16.95 (ISBN 0-89733-182-6). Academy Chi Pubs.

Peter Blume. Frank A. Trapp. LC 87-45385. (Illus.). 144p. 1987. 40.00 (ISBN 0-8478-0854-8). Rizzoli Intl.

Peter Blume: The Italian Drawings. Frank A. Trapp. (Illus.). 42p. (Orig.). 1985. pap. 5.00 (ISBN 0-914337-06-8). Mead Art Mus.

Peter Brereton's Touring Guide to English Villages. Peter Brereton. (One-of-a-Kind Travel Guides Ser.). (Illus.). 9.95 (ISBN 0-13-661802-2). P-H.

Peter Brooks: A Theatrical Casebook. David Williams. 256p. 1988. pap. 13.95 (ISBN 0-413-15700-8). Heinemann Ed.

Peter Buchan, & Other Papers on Scottish & English Ballads & Songs. William Walker. 1980. Repr. of 1915 ed. lib. bdg. 30.50 (ISBN 0-8414-2838-7). Folcroft.

Peter Burwash's Aerobic Workout Book for Men. Peter Burwash & John Tullius. (Illus.). 1984. pap. 11.95 (ISBN 0-396-08380-3). Dodd.

Peter C. Tamony: Word Man of San Francisco's Mission. Marjorie W. McLain. LC 87-50071. 135p. (Orig.). 1986. pap. 10.50 (ISBN 0-931703-01-8). Wellman Pub.

Peter Calvay -- Hermit: A Personal Rediscovery of Prayer. Rayner Torkington. LC 80-13188. 107p. (Orig.). 1980. pap. 3.95 (ISBN 0-8189-0404-6). Alba.

Peter Camenzind. Hermann Hesse. Tr. by Michael Roloff from Ger. 208p. 1969. pap. 7.95 (ISBN 0-374-50784-8). FS&G.

Peter Campus - Photographs, David Deutsch - Paintings & Drawings. Kathy Halbreich & Katy Kline. (Illus.). 28p. (Orig.). 1983. pap. 4.00 (ISBN 0-938437-07-0). MIT List Visual Arts.

Peter Campus: Selected Works, 1973-1987. Judith E. Tannenbaum & David S. Rubin. LC 87-80140. (Illus.). 36p. (Orig.). 1987. pap. text ed. 8.00 (ISBN 0-941972-04-6). Freedman.

Peter Capstick's Africa: Return to the Long Grass. Peter H. Capstick. 320p. 1987. 29.95 (ISBN 0-312-00670-5). St Martin.

Peter Chan's Magical Landscape: Transforming Any Small Space into a Place of Beauty. Peter Chan. Ed. by Gwen Steege. LC 86-45975. (Illus.). 128p. 1988. 21.95 (ISBN 0-88266-454-9); pap. 10.95 (ISBN 0-88266-455-7). Storey Comm Inc.

Peter Charlie: The Cruise of the PC 477. Arthur S. Bell, Jr. LC 82-71794. (Illus.). 384p. 1982. 14.95 (ISBN 0-910355-00-2). Courtroom Comp.

Peter Christian's Recipes. Shirley Edes & Julia Philipson. LC 83-374. (Illus.). vii, 173p. (Orig.). 1983. pap. 10.50 comb bdg. (ISBN 0-936988-09-6, Dist. by Shoe String Press). Tompson Rutter Inc.

Peter Collingwood: His Weaves & Weaving. Peter Collingwood. Ed. by Harriet Tidball. LC 63-2332. (Shuttle Craft Guild Monograph: No. 8). (Illus.). 46p. 1963. pap. 8.95 (ISBN 0-916658-08-2). Shuttle Craft.

Peter Cooper. Rossiter W. Raymond. LC 72-1252. (Select Bibliographies Reprints Ser.). 1972. Repr. of 1901 ed. 12.00 (ISBN 0-8369-6835-2). Ayer Co Pubs.

Peter Cottontail. Illus. by Patrick McRae. (Illus.). 24p. (Orig.). (gr. k-6). 1986. pap. 2.95 (ISBN 0-8249-8106-5). Ideals.

Peter Cottontail's Surprise. Bonnie Worth. LC 84-28031. (Illus.). 48p. (ps up). 1985. 11.95 (ISBN 0-88101-015-4). Unicorn Pub.

Peter De Vries: A Bibliography Nineteen Thirty-Four to Nineteen Seventy-Seven. Compiled by Edwin T. Bowden. LC 76-620049. (Tower Bibliographical Ser.: No. 14). 1978. 12.95 (ISBN 0-87959-079-3). U of Tex H Ransom Ctr.

Peter Dominic's Practical Cocktails. John Doxat. 160p. 1986. pap. 7.95 (ISBN 0-907621-40-6, Pub. by Quiller Pr England). Intl Spec Bk.

Peter Duck. Arthur Ransome. LC 86-46247. (Illus.). 414p. 1987. pap. 9.95 (ISBN 0-87923-660-4) (ISBN 0-87923-633-7). Godine.

Peter Eisenman: A Bibliography of Periodical Literature, 1967-1985. Patricia Weisenburger & Douglas Levey. (Architecture Ser.: A 1705). 7p. 1986. 3.00 (ISBN 1-55590-075-5). Vance Biblios.

Peter Ellenshaw: Selected Works, 1929-1983. Illus. by Peter Ellenshaw. LC 83-13358. (Contemporary Realists Ser.). (Illus.). 72p. 1983. pap. 11.50x (ISBN 0-913060-21-6). Norton Art.

Peter Rabbit's ABC. Beatrix Potter. (Illus.). 48p. (ps-2). 1987. 6.95 (ISBN 0-7232-3423-X). Warne.

Peter Rabbit's Big Adventure. Illus. by Tony Tallarico. (Tote Bks). (Illus.). 12p. (ps). 1988. price not set (ISBN 0-89828-324-8). Tuffy Bks.

Peter Rabbit's Colors. Beatrix Potter. (ps-k). 1988. 6.95 (ISBN 0-7232-3612-7); frieze 5.00. Warne.

Peter Rabbit's Cookery Book. Anne Emerson. (Non-Fiction Ser.). (Illus.). 48p. (gr. k-3). 1986. 6.95 (ISBN 0-7232-3328-4). Warne.

Peter Rabbit's Family. Illus. by Tony Tallarico. (Tote Bks). (Illus.). 12p. (ps). 1988. price not set (ISBN 0-89828-312-4). Tuffy Bks.

Peter Rabbit's First Library. Illus. by Donna Lampell. Incl. Surprise for Mrs. Rabbit. 10p (ISBN 1-55580-006-8); Tom Kitten's New Sweater. 10p (ISBN 1-55580-007-6); Birthday Party for Mrs. Tiggy-Winkle. 10p (ISBN 1-55580-008-4); Mr. Jeremy Fisher Dives for Treasure. 10p (ISBN 1-55580-009-2). (Illus.). (ps-k). 1986. Set of 4 bks. write for info. (ISBN 1-55580-010-6). Octopus Bks.

Peter Rabbit's Gardening Book. Sarah Galland. (Illus.). 48p. (gr. 5-9). 1983. 6.95 (ISBN 0-7232-2994-5). Warne.

Peter Rabbit's Natural Foods Cookbook. Arnold Dobrin. LC 76-45309. (Illus.). 1977. 10.95 (ISBN 0-7232-6142-3). Warne.

Peter Rabbit's One Two Three. Beatrix Potter. (ps-k). 1988. 6.95 (ISBN 0-7232-3424-8). Warne.

Peter Rabbit's Pockets. Carolyn Bracken. (Illus.). 8p. (ps). 1982. 3.95 (ISBN 0-671-44528-6, Little Simon). S&S.

Peter Rabbit's Puzzle Book. 1987. pap. 3.95 (ISBN 0-7232-3441-8). Warne.

Peter Rabbit's Sniffy Adventure. Jane E. Gerver. LC 83-62606. (Sniffy Bks.). (Illus.). 24p. (gr. k-2). 1984. 3.95 (ISBN 0-394-86352-6, BYR). Random.

Peter Rugg, the Missing Man. William Austin. LC 72-104409. Repr. of 1824 ed. lib. bdg. 19.00 (ISBN 0-8398-0071-1). Irvington.

Peter Rugg: The Missing Man. William Austin. 1988. pap. text ed. 6.95 (ISBN 0-317-66458-1). Irvington.

Peter Shaffer: Roles, Rites, & Rituals in the Theater. Gene A. Plunka. LC 87-46010. 256p. 1988. 34.50x (ISBN 0-8386-3329-3). Fairleigh Dickinson.

Peter Simple. Frederick Marryat. 1970. Repr. of 1907 ed. 14.95x (ISBN 0-460-00232-5, Evman). Biblio Dist.

Peter Sinks in the Water. Joyce Morse. (Books I Can Read). 32p. (Orig.). (gr. 2). 1980. pap. 1.95 (ISBN 0-8127-0281-6). Review & Herald.

Peter Skene Ogden & the Hudson's Bay Company. Gloria G. Cline. LC 72-9266. (American Exploration & Travel Ser.). pap. 77.80 (ISBN 0-317-55779-3, 2029302). Bks Demand UMI.

Peter Skene Ogden, Fur Trader. Archie Binns. LC 67-23627. (Illus.). 1967. 10.95 (ISBN 0-8323-0054-3). Binford-Metropolitan.

Peter Skene Ogden's Snake Country Journals, Eighteen Twenty-Four to Eighteen Twenty-Five & Eighteen Twenty-Five to Eighteen Twenty-Six. Ed. by E. E. Rich & A. M. Johnson. (Hudson's Bay Record Society Publication Ser.: Vol. 13). pap. 52.00 (ISBN 0-8115-3187-2). Kraus Repr.

Peter Skene Ogden's Snake Country Journal 1826-1827. Ed. by Davies & A. M. Johnson. (Hudson's Bay Record Society Publications Ser.: Vol. 23). pap. 52.00 (ISBN 0-8115-3191-0). Kraus Repr.

Peter, Speak for God. Charlotte Graeber. (Speak for Me Ser.). (Illus.). 24p. (gr. 1-4). 1986. 3.95 (ISBN 0-8407-6701-3). Nelson.

Peter Spier's Cars & Trucks, 4 bks. Peter Spier. 1988. Boxed Set. 8.95. Random.

Peter Spier's Christmas! Peter Spier. LC 80-2875. (Illus.). 40p. (ps up). 1983. 12.95 (ISBN 0-385-13184-4); pap. 12.95 (ISBN 0-385-13183-6). Doubleday.

Peter Spier's Christmas. Peter Spier. (Illus.). 40p. (ps-3). 1988. pap. 6.95 (ISBN 0-385-24580-7). Doubleday.

Peter Spier's Little Animal Books, 4 bks. Peter Spier. (Illus.). (ps). 1987. Boxed Set. bds. 10.00 laminated (ISBN 0-385-19715-2). Doubleday.

Peter Spier's Little Cats. Peter Spier. LC 82-45494. (Peter Spier's Little Animals Ser.). (Illus.). 14p. (ps-1). 1984. 2.50 (ISBN 0-385-18197-3). Doubleday.

Peter Spier's Rain. Peter Spier. LC 81-43056. (Illus.). 40p. (gr. k-3). 1982. 12.95 (ISBN 0-385-15485-2); pap. 12.95 (ISBN 0-385-15484-4). Doubleday.

Peter Spier's Rain. Peter Spier. LC 81-43506. (Illus.). (gr. k-3). 1987. pap. 6.95 (ISBN 0-385-24105-4, Pub. by Zephyr-BFYR). Doubleday.

Peter Stein: Germany's Leading Theatre Director. Michael Patterson. LC 81-6084. (Directors in Perspective Ser.). (Illus.). 220p. 1982. 37.50 (ISBN 0-521-22442-X); pap. 14.95 (ISBN 0-521-29502-5). Cambridge U Pr.

Peter, Stephen, James & John: Studies in Non-Pauline Christianity. F. F. Bruce. (Orig.). 1980. 9.95 (ISBN 0-8028-3532-5). Eerdmans.

Peter Stuyvesant of Old New York. Anna Crouse & Russel Crouse. (Landmark Ser.: No. 3). (gr. 4-6). 1963. pap. 2.95 (ISBN 0-394-80343-4). Random.

Peter Taylor: A Descriptive Bibliography, 1934-87. Stuart Wright. LC 87-32044. (Illus.). 340p. 1988. 40.00x (ISBN 0-8139-1168-0). U Pr of Va.

Peter Taylor: A Study of the Short Fiction. James C. Robinson. 192p. 1988. lib. bdg. 18.95x (ISBN 0-8057-8303-2, Twayne). G K Hall.

Peter Testman's Account of His Experiences in North America. Ed. by Theodore C. Blegen. 60p. 1927. 3.00 (ISBN 0-87732-004-7). Norwegian-Am Hist Assn.

Peter the Caterpillar. Joanne Keegan. 32p. (ps-3). 1986. 5.95 (ISBN 0-8062-2866-0). Carlton.

Peter the Cruel: Don Pedro of Castille. E. Storer. 1976. lib. bdg. 69.75 (ISBN 0-8490-2426-9). Gordon Pr.

Peter the Great. Nina B. Baker. (Illus.). 310p. (gr. 7 up). 1943. 12.95 (ISBN 0-8149-0263-4). Vanguard.

Peter the Great. Vasili Klyuchevsky. Tr. by Liliana Archibald. LC 84-45072. 294p. 1984. pap. 12.95x (ISBN 0-8070-5647-2, BP678). Beacon Pr.

Peter the Great. Robert Massie. 924p. 1981. pap. 9.95 (ISBN 0-345-29806-3). Ballantine.

Peter the Great. Robert K. Massie. pap. 5.95 (ISBN 0-345-33619-4). Ballantine.

Peter the Great. Diane Stanley. LC 85-13060. (Illus.). 32p. (gr. 1-4). 1986. 12.95 (ISBN 0-02-786790-0, Four Winds). Macmillan.

Peter the Great. Diane Stanley. Date not set. price not set. Morrow.

Peter the Great. K. Waliszewski. LC 68-25279. (World History Ser., No. 48). 1968. Repr. of 1897 ed. lib. bdg. 79.95x (ISBN 0-8383-0265-3). Haskell.

Peter the Great: A Biography. Henri Troyat. LC 86-19694. (Illus.). 432p. 1987. 22.95 (ISBN 0-525-24547-2). Dutton.

Peter the Great & Marlborough: Politics & Diplomacy in Converging Wars. Andrew Rothstein. LC 85-22125. 224p. 1986. 27.50 (ISBN 0-312-60363-0). St Martin.

Peter the Great & the Emergence of Russia. Benedict H. Sumner. 1962. pap. 4.95 (ISBN 0-02-037760-6, Collier). Macmillan.

Peter the Great Changes Russia. 2nd ed. Ed. by Marc Raeff. (Problems in European Civilization Ser.). 1972. pap. text ed. 8.00 (ISBN 0-669-82701-0). Heath.

Peter the Great: His Life & His World. Robert K. Massie. LC 80-7635. (Illus.). 864p. 1980. 29.95 (ISBN 0-394-50032-6). Knopf.

Peter the Great: Russian Emperor. Ed. by Arthur M. Schlesinger, Jr. (World Leaders - Past & Present Ser.). (Illus.). (gr. 5-12). 1989. 16.95 (ISBN 1-55546-821-7). Chelsea Hse.

Peter: The Little Fish Book Ser. see Pedro.

Peter: The Prince of Apostles. Muriel Blackwell. (BibLearn Ser.). (Illus.). (gr. 1-6). 5.95 (ISBN 0-8054-4227-8, 4242-27). Broadman.

Peter the Rock: Extraordinary Lessons from an Ordinary Man. David Gill. LC 86-7383. 192p. (Orig.). 1986. pap. 7.95 (ISBN 0-87784-609-X). Inter-Varsity.

Peter Third, Emperor of Russia. Robert N. Bain. 1902. 12.00 (ISBN 0-403-00465-9). Scholarly.

Peter Third, Emperor of Russia: The Story of a Crisis & a Crime. Robert N. Bain. LC 72-156962. (BCL Ser.: No. II). Repr. of 1902 ed. 14.50 (ISBN 0-404-00448-2). AMS Pr.

Peter Three Eight: The Pilot's Story. John Stanaway. LC 86-60128. (Illus.). 140p. 1986. pap. 9.95 (ISBN 0-317-57659-3). Pictorial Hist.

Peter Townsend Story. Norman Barrymaine. (Illus.). 1957. 14.95 (ISBN 0-685-84238-X). Beachcomber Bks.

Peter Tudebode: Historia De Hierosolymitano Itinere. John H. Hill & Laurita L. Hill. LC 74-78091. (Memoirs Ser.: Vol. 101). 1974. 12.00 (ISBN 0-87169-101-9). Am Philos.

Peter Ujvari's by Candlelight. Tr. by Andrew Handler. 252p. 1977. 24.50 (ISBN 0-8386-1895-2). Fairleigh Dickinson.

Peter Ustinov & His World. V. Lorne Stewart. Ed. by Helen Graves. LC 88-50116. 195p. 1988. 12.95 (ISBN 1-55523-144-6). Winston-Derek.

Peter Ustinov in Russia. Peter Ustinov. (Illus.). 160p. 1988. 22.95 (ISBN 0-671-65954-5). Summit Bks.

Peter Viereck. Marie Henault. (Twayne's United States Author's Ser.). 1969. pap. 8.95x (ISBN 0-8084-0008-8, T133, Twayne). New Coll U Pr.

Peter Waring. Forrest Reid. LC 83-45463. Repr. of 1937 ed. 37.50 (ISBN 0-404-20212-8). AMS Pr.

Peter Watkins: A Guide to References & Resources. James M. Welsh. (Film Directors Ser.). 293p. 1986. lib. bdg. 45.00x (ISBN 0-8161-8179-9, Hall Reference). G K Hall.

Peter Weiss. Otto F. Best. Tr. by Ursule Molinaro from Ger. LC 75-10104. (Literature and Life Ser.). 170p. 1976. 16.95x (ISBN 0-8044-2038-6). Ungar.

Peter Weiss in Exile: A Critical Study of His Works. Roger Ellis. Ed. by Oscar Brockett. LC 86-19241. (Theater & Dramatic Studies: No. 37). 198p. 1986. 39.95 (ISBN 0-8357-1764-X); pap. write for info. (ISBN 0-8357-1921-9). UMI Res Pr.

Peter Whiffle. Carl Van Vechten. LC 77-78306. Repr. of 1927 ed. 29.50 (ISBN 0-404-15126-4). AMS Pr.

Peter Wilson: Paintings 1982-1985. 28p. 1985. 30.00x (Pub. by Third Eye Control). State Mutual Bk.

Peterborough: A History. Herbert F. Tebbs. (Cambridge Town, Gown & County Ser.: Vol. 24). (Illus.). 1979. 25.00 (ISBN 0-900891-30-0). Oleander Pr.

Peterborough Chronicle see Early English Manuscripts in Facsimile.

Peterborough Postgraduate Symposia: Cardiology. Pitman Publishing Ltd. Editors. (Pitman Medical Conference Reports Ser.). (Illus.). 128p. 1975. pap. text ed. 19.95 (ISBN 0-8464-0713-2). Beekman Pubs.

Peterborough Psalter in Brussells & Other Fenland Manuscripts. Lucy F. Sandler. (Illus.). 1974. 49.00x (ISBN 0-19-921005-5). Oxford U Pr.

Peterborough Symposium on Cardiology. F. J. Fawcet. 1975. pap. text ed. 30.00x. State Mutual Bk.

Peterborough: The Electric City. Elwood Jones & Bruce Dyer. Ed. by Lane Powell. (Illus.). 176p. 1987. 28.95 (ISBN 0-89781-224-7). Windsor Pubns Inc.

Peterburg V. Russkom Ocherke XiX Veka. Ed. by Collet's Holdings, Ltd. Staff. 376p. 1984. 49.00x (ISBN 0-317-40739-2, Pub. by Collets UK). State Mutual Bk.

Peterkin Meets a Star. Emilie Boon. LC 83-9691. (Illus.). 32p. (gr. k-2). 1984. 4.95 (ISBN 0-394-86284-8, BYR); lib. bdg. 6.99 (ISBN 0-394-96284-2). Random.

Peterkin Meets a Star: Random House Picturebacks Ser. Emilie Boon. LC 84-29810. (Illus.). 32p. (ps-1). 1985. pap. 1.95 (ISBN 0-394-87505-2). Random.

Peterkin Papers. Lucretia P. Hale. (Bambi Classics Ser.). (Illus.). 256p. (Orig.). (YA) (gr. 9-12). 1981. pap. 3.95 (ISBN 0-89531-065-1, 0221-48). Sharon Pubns.

Peterkin's Very Own Garden. Emilie Boon. LC 86-62244. (Great Big Board Bks.). (Illus.). 14p. (ps). 1987. 3.95 (ISBN 0-394-88666-6, BYR). Random.

Peterkin's Wet Walk. Emilie Boon. LC 83-8937. (Illus.). 32p. (gr. k-2). 1984. 4.95 (ISBN 0-394-86285-6); lib. bdg. 6.99 (ISBN 0-394-96285-0). Random.

Peterloo. Donald Read. LC 72-7212. 1973. Repr. of 1958 ed. 29.50x (ISBN 0-678-06791-0). Kelley.

Peterloo: The Case Reopened. Robert Walmsley. LC 73-81146. (Illus.). 1969. 45.00x (ISBN 0-678-06777-5). Kelley.

Peter's Chair. Ezra J. Keats. LC 67-4816. (Illus.). (gr. k-3). 1967. 12.95i (ISBN 0-06-023111-4); PLB 12.89 (ISBN 0-06-023112-2). HarpJ.

Peter's Chair. Ezra J. Keats. LC 67-4816. (Trophy Picture Bks.). (Illus.). 32p. (ps-3). 1983. pap. 4.95 (ISBN 0-06-443040-5, Trophy). HarpJ.

Peter's Pentecost Discourse: Tradition & Lukan Reinterpretation in Peter's Speeches of Acts 2 & 3. Richard F. Zehnle. 144p. 1972. 8.95 (ISBN 0-89130-322-7, 06-00-15); members 5.95 (ISBN 0-317-35713-1). Scholars Pr GA.

Peter's People. Laurence J. Peter. 1981. pap. 2.25 (ISBN 0-505-51751-5, T51751, Pub. by Tower Bks). Leisure NY.

Peter's Pockets. L. Morgan. LC 65-27622. (Illus.). 32p. (gr. k-2). 1968. PLB 9.95 (ISBN 0-87783-029-0). Oddo.

Peter's Pockets. Leonore Morgan. (Illus.). (gr. k-2). 1978. pap. 1.25 (ISBN 0-89508-063-X). Rainbow Bks.

Peter's Portrait of Jesus. J. B. Phillips. (Festival Ser.). 192p. 1981. pap. 1.95 (ISBN 0-687-30850-X). Abingdon.

Peter's Quotations: Ideas for Our Time. Laurence J. Peter. 1979. pap. 5.50 (ISBN 0-553-23910-4). Bantam.

Peters Third Black & Blue Guide to Literary Journals. 3rd ed. Robert Peters. 164p. pap. 5.95 (ISBN 0-916685-03-9). Dustbooks.

Petersburg. Andrei Bely. Tr. by Robert A. Maguire & John E. Malmstad. LC 77-74442. (Midland Bks.: No. 219). 384p. 1978. 27.50x (ISBN 0-253-34410-7); pap. 10.95X (ISBN 0-253-20219-1). Ind U Pr.

Petersburg. Emily Hanlon. 544p. 1988. 19.95 (ISBN 0-399-13374-7). Putnam Pub Group.

Petersburg & Paris Period, 2 vols. Mihail Chemiakin. Incl. Vol. II. Transformation: New York Period. 286p. (Illus.). 504p. 1986. pap. 250.00 sold as boxed set only (ISBN 0-317-56275-4, Pub. by Mosaic Pr Canada). Riverrun NY.

Petersburg Nebraska. Petersburg Centennial Committee. (Illus.). 447p. 1987. 47.50 (ISBN 0-88107-092-0). Curtis Media.

Petersen's Basic How to Tune Your Car. 7th, rev. ed. Petersen Pub. Co. LC 80-644753. (Illus.). 256p. 1985. pap. 9.95 (ISBN 0-89803-126-5, Dist. by Kampmann). Green Hill.

Petersen's Basic Ignition & Electrical Systems. 6th ed. LC 75-15282. 256p. 1985. pap. 9.95 (ISBN 0-89803-141-9, Dist. by Kampmann). Green Hill.

Petersen's Big Book of Auto Repair. 10th ed. 896p. 1985. pap. 14.95 (ISBN 0-89803-157-5, Dist. by Kampmann). Green Hill.

Petersen's Big Book of Photography. Ed. by Kalton Lahue. LC 77-86527. (Petersen "How-to" Photographic Library). (Illus.). (gr. 9-12). 1977. pap. 12.95 (ISBN 0-8227-4029-X). Petersen Pub.

Peterson First Guide to Astronomy. Jay M. Pasachoff. (Illus.). 128p. 1988. pap. 3.95 (ISBN 0-395-46790-X). HM.

Peterson First Guide To Insects. Christopher Leahy. (Illus.). 128p. (Orig.). 1987. pap. 3.95 (ISBN 0-395-35640-7). HM.

Peterson First Guide to Mammals. Peter Alden. (Illus.). 128p. (Orig.). 1987. pap. 3.95 (ISBN 0-395-42767-3). HM.

Peterson's Business & Management Jobs, 1989. 5th ed. Ed. by Christopher Billy & Donna L. Snyder. 350p. 1988. 32.95 (ISBN 0-87866-827-6); pap. 17.95 (ISBN 0-87866-691-5). Petersons Guides.

Peterson's College Money Handbook, 1989: The Only Complete Guide to Scholarships, College Costs, & Financial Aid. 6th ed. Ed. by Andrea E. Lehman & Eric A. Suber. 600p. 1988. 32.95 (ISBN 0-87866-760-1); pap. 17.95 (ISBN 0-87866-702-4). Petersons Guides.

Peterson's Competitive Colleges 1988-89. 7th ed. 356p. (Orig.). 1988. pap. 9.95 (ISBN 0-87866-682-6). Petersons Guides.

Peterson's Engineering, Science, & Computer Jobs 1989. 10th ed. 613p. (Orig.). 1988. lib. bdg. 34.95 (ISBN 0-87866-828-4); pap. 19.95 (ISBN 0-87866-692-3). Petersons Guides.

Peterson's First Guide to Birds. Roger T. Peterson. 1986. pap. 3.95 (ISBN 0-395-40684-6). HM.

Peterson's First Guide to Birds. Roger T. Peterson. 1985. pap. write for info. HM.

Peterson's First Guide to Wildflowers. Roger T. Peterson. 1986. pap. 3.95 (ISBN 0-395-40777-X). HM.

Peterson's First Guide to Wildflowers. Roger T. Peterson. 1985. pap. write for info. HM.

Peterson's Graduate Education Directory. LC 86-1306. 641p. (Orig.). 1986. pap. 29.95 (ISBN 0-87866-445-9). Petersons Guides.

Peterson's Guide to Certificate Programs at American Colleges & Universities. 650p. 1988. pap. 35.95 (ISBN 0-87866-741-5). Petersons Guides.

Peterson's Guide to College Admissions: Getting into the College of Your Choice. 3rd. ed. R. Fred Zuker & Karen C. Hegener. LC 83-4219. 366p. (Orig.). 1983. pap. 9.95 (ISBN 0-87866-224-3). Peterson's Guides.

Peterson's Guide to College Admissions: How to Plan Your Admissions Strategy & Get into the College of Your Choice. 4th ed. R. Fred Zuker & Karen C. Hegener. LC 87-7763. 412p. (Orig.). 1987. pap. 11.95 (ISBN 0-87866-463-7). Petersons Guides.

Peterson's Guide to Colleges in New England 1988. 4th ed. (Peterson's Regional Guides to Colleges Ser.). 136p. (Orig.). 1987. pap. 7.95 (ISBN 0-87866-564-1). Petersons Guides.

Peterson's Guide to Colleges in New England 1989. 5th ed. 140p. (Orig.). 1988. pap. 9.95 (ISBN 0-87866-721-0). Petersons Guides.

Peterson's Guide to Colleges in New York 1988. 4th ed. (Peterson's Regional Guides to Colleges Ser.). 131p. (Orig.). 1987. pap. 7.95 (ISBN 0-87866-565-X). Petersons Guides.

Peterson's Guide to Colleges in New York 1989. 5th ed. 140p. (Orig.). 1988. pap. 9.95 (ISBN 0-87866-722-9). Petersons Guides.

Peterson's Guide to Colleges in the Middle Atlantic States 1988. 4th ed. (Peterson's Regional Guides to Colleges Ser.). 216p. (Orig.). 1987. pap. 7.95 (ISBN 0-87866-566-8). Petersons Guides.

Peterson's Guide to Colleges in the Middle Atlantic States 1989. 5th ed. 220p. (Orig.). 1988. pap. 9.95 (ISBN 0-87866-723-7). Petersons Guides.

Peterson's Guide to Colleges in the Midwest 1988. 4th ed. (Peterson's Regional Guides to Colleges Ser.). 318p. (Orig.). 1987. pap. 8.95 (ISBN 0-87866-568-4). Petersons Guides.

Peterson's Guide to Colleges in the Midwest 1989. 5th ed. 320p. (Orig.). 1988. pap. 9.95 (ISBN 0-87866-725-3). Petersons Guides.

Peterson's Guide to Colleges in the Southwest 1988. 3rd ed. (Peterson's Regional Guides to Colleges Ser.). 116p. (Orig.). 1987. pap. 7.95 (ISBN 0-87866-570-6). Petersons Guides.

Peterson's Guide to Colleges in the Southeast 1988. 3rd ed. (Peterson's Regional Guides to Colleges Ser.). 224p. (Orig.). 1987. pap. 7.95 (ISBN 0-87866-567-6). Petersons Guides.

Peterson's Guide to Colleges in the Southeast 1989. 4th ed. 230p. (Orig.). 1988. pap. 9.95 (ISBN 0-87866-724-5). Petersons Guides.

Peterson's Guide to Colleges in the Southwest 1989. 4th ed. 120p. (Orig.). 1988. pap. 9.95 (ISBN 0-87866-726-1). Petersons Guides.

Peterson's Guide to Colleges in the West 1988. 2nd ed. (Peterson's Regional Guides to Colleges Ser.). 185p. (Orig.). 1987. pap. 7.95 (ISBN 0-87866-569-2). Petersons Guides.

Peterson's Guide to Colleges in the West 1989. 3rd ed. 190p. (Orig.). 1988. pap. 9.95 (ISBN 0-87866-727-X). Petersons Guides.

Peterson's Guide to Colleges with Programs for Learning-Disabled Students. 2nd ed. Ed. by Charles T. Mangrum, II & Stephen S. Strichart. 350p. (Orig.). 1988. pap. 19.95 (ISBN 0-87866-689-3). Petersons Guides.

Peterson's Guide to Colleges with Programs for Learning-Disabled Students. LC 85-3497. 322p. (Orig.). 1985. pap. 13.95 (ISBN 0-87866-327-4). Petersons Guides.

Peterson's Guide to Four-Year Colleges 1989. 19th ed. 2363p. (Orig.). 1988. lib. bdg. 30.95 (ISBN 0-87866-758-X); pap. 15.95 (ISBN 0-87866-718-0). Petersons Guides.

Peterson's Guide to Graduate & Professional Programs: An Overview, 1989. 23rd ed. (Annual Guides to Graduate Study Ser.: Bk. 1). 1150p. (Orig.). 1988. lib. bdg. 34.95 (ISBN 0-87866-744-X); pap. 19.95 (ISBN 0-87866-743-1). Petersons Guides.

Petrified Forest Through the Ages: Seventy-Fifth Anniversary Symposium. Ed. by Edwin H. Colbert & R. Roy Johnson. LC 84-62519. (Bulletin Ser.: No. 54). (Illus.). 104p. (Orig.). pap. 12.50 (ISBN 0-89734-056-6). Mus Northern Ariz.

Petrikivka Painting: A Ukrainian Heritage. Rose Tanasichuk. (Illus.). 48p. 1986. pap. 8.95 (ISBN 0-941284-31-X). Deco Design Studio.

Petrine Controversies in Early Christianity: Attitudes Towards Peter in Christian Writings for the First Two Centuries. Terrence V. Smith. 259p. (Orig.). 1985. pap. 57.50x (ISBN 3-16-144876-6, Pub. by J C B Mohr BRD). Coronet Bks.

Petrine Revolution in Russian Architecture. James Cracraft. (Illus.). 400p. 1988. 35.00x (ISBN 0-226-11664-6). U of Chicago Pr.

Petroanalysis 81: Advances in Analytical Chemistry in the Petroleum Industry. Proceedings of the Institute of Petroleum (IP) Ed. by G. B. Crump. 456p. 1983. 116.00 (ISBN 0-471-26217-X, Pub. by Wiley Interscience). Wiley.

PETROCALC (R) 1: Reservoir Engineering & Formation Evaluation. R. L. McCoy. LC 82-24233. (PETROCALC (R) Software for Petroleum Engineers Ser.). 144p. 1983. 35.00x (ISBN 0-87201-553-X); disk 250.00x (ISBN 0-87201-554-8). Gulf Pub.

PETROCALC (R) 2: Drilling Engineering. Martin Chenevert & Walter A. Braunlin. LC 83-18562. (PETROCALC (R) Software for Petroleum Engineers Ser.). 1984. incl. disk 275.00x (ISBN 0-87201-728-1). Gulf Pub.

PETROCALC (R) 3: Reservoir Economics & Evaluation. R. L. McCoy. LC 84-558. (PETROCALC (R) TM Software for Petroleum Engineers Ser.). 1984. incl. disk 450.00x (ISBN 0-87201-729-X). Gulf Pub.

PETROCALC (R) 4: Well History Record Keeping System. Sigma Energy Consultants. LC 85-937. (PETROCALC (R) Software for Petroleum Engineers Ser.). 1985. 3-ring binder incl. disk 550.00x (ISBN 0-87201-730-3). Gulf Pub.

PETROCALC (R) 5: Production History & Future Projection. Sigma Energy Consultants. LC 85-938. (PETROCALC (R) Software for Petroleum Engineers Ser.). 1985. 3-ring binder incl. disk 550.00x (ISBN 0-87201-731-1). Gulf Pub.

PETROCALC (R) 6: Wellbore Stimulation. Richard Sinclair & Martin Chenevert. LC 85-9806. (PETROCALC (R) Software for Petroleum Engineers Ser.). (Illus.). 64p. 1985. incl. floppy disk 450.00x (ISBN 0-87201-732-X). Gulf Pub.

PETROCALC (R) 7: Applied Well Log Analysis. R. L. McCoy. LC 85-12564. (PETROCALC (R) Software for Petroleum Engineers Ser.). 80p. 1985. incl. floppy disk 550.00x (ISBN 0-87201-734-6). Gulf Pub.

Petrochemical Calculations. Conrad Burri. 312p. 1964. text ed. 63.00x (ISBN 0-7065-0622-7, Pub. by Keter Pub Jerusalem). Coronet Bks.

Petrochemical Industry. (Guides to Information Sources: No. 29). pap. 4.00 (ISBN 92-1-106164-4, ID/199). UN.

Petrochemical Industry & Possibilities of Its Establishment in Developing Countries. C. Mercier. 202p. 1971. 108.00 (ISBN 0-677-61370-9). Gordon & Breach.

Petrochemical Industry: Energy Aspects of Structural Change. OECD. 161p. (Orig.). 1985. pap. 19.00x (ISBN 92-64-12683-X). OECD.

Petrochemical Industry: Trends in Production & Investment to 1985. 1979. 8.00 (ISBN 92-64-11890-X). OECD.

Petrochemical Manufacturing & Marketing Guide. Robert B. Stobaugh. LC 67-24629. Vol. 1: Aromatics & Derivatives. pap. 65.80 (ISBN 0-317-58212-7, 2052218). Bks Demand UMI.

Petrochemical Manufacturing & Marketing Guide, 2 vols. Robert B. Stobaugh, Jr. Incl. Vol. 1. Aromatics & Derivatives. 1967. (ISBN 0-87201-665-X); Vol. 2. Olefins, Diolefins & Acetylene. 1968. (ISBN 0-87201-666-8). 12.95x ea. Gulf Pub.

Petrochemical Manufacturing & Marketing Guide, Vol. 2: Olefins, Diolefins, & Acetylene. Robert B. Stobaugh. LC 67-24629. (Illus.). 236p. pap. 61.40 (2029925). Bks Demand UMI.

Petrochemical Technology: An Overview for Decision Makers in the International Petrochemical Industry. Harvey L. List. (Illus.). 256p. 1986. text ed. 80.00 (ISBN 0-13-661992-4). P-H.

Petrochemical Technology Assessment. D. F. Rudd. 382p. 1981. 53.50 (ISBN 0-471-08912-5, JW). Krieger.

Petrochemicals. P. Wiseman. LC 85-24843. (Umist Series in Science & Technology). 1986. 41.95 (ISBN 0-470-20279-3); pap. 19.95 (ISBN 0-470-20284-X). Halsted Pr.

Petrochemicals for the Nontechnical Person. Donald L. Burdick & William L. Leffler. 238p. 1983. 46.95 (ISBN 0-87814-207-X, P-4296). PennWell Bks.

Petrochemicals: The Rise of an Industry. Peter H. Spitz. LC 87-23019. 588p. 1988. 29.95 (ISBN 0-471-85985-0). Wiley.

Petrodvorets: Palaces, Gardens, Fountains, Sculpture. Abram Raskin. 346p. 1979. 155.00x (ISBN 0-317-57407-8, Pub. by Collets UK). State Mutual Bk.

Petrogenesis of Metamorphic Rocks: Springer Study Edition. 5th ed. H. G. Winkler. LC 79-14704. (Illus.). 1979. pap. 21.00 (ISBN 0-387-90413-1). Springer-Verlag.

Petroglyphes de l'Ile de Paques: Ouvrage publie avec le concours de la Fondation Universitaire de Belgique. Henri A. Lavachery. LC 75-35198. Repr. of 1939 ed. 16.50 (ISBN 0-404-14226-5). AMS Pr.

Petroglyphs. Barney Bush. LC 82-82422. (Illus.). 84p. (Orig.). 1982. pap. 6.00 (ISBN 0-912678-54-2). Greenfld Rev Pr.

Petroglyphs. Sam Hamill. LC 75-24583. (Three Rivers Poetry Ser.). (Orig.). 1976. pap. 2.95x (ISBN 0-915606-01-1). Three Rivers Pr.

Petroglyphs & Pictographs of Utah, Vol. 2. Kenneth B. Castleton. (Illus.). 1980. 15.00 (ISBN 0-686-26976-4). Utah Mus Natural Hist.

Petroglyphs in the Guianas & Adjacent Areas of Brazil & Venezuela: An Inventory with a Comprehensive Bibliography of South American & Antillean Petroglyphs. C. N. Dubelaar. LC 85-11914. (Monumenta Archaeologica: 12). (Illus.). 327p. 1986. text ed. 35.00x (ISBN 0-917956-50-8). UCLA Arch.

Petroglyphs of Hawaii. L. R. McBride. (Illus.). 1969. pap. 3.95 (ISBN 0-912180-12-9). Petroglyph.

Petroglyphs of Ohio. James L. Swauger. (Illus.). xxii, 341p. 1984. Cloth 49.95x (ISBN 0-8214-0678-7, 83-19440). Ohio U Pr.

Petrograd Codex of the Hebrew Bible: The Latter Prophets, Prophetarum Posteriorum. rev. ed. Hermann L. Strack. (Library of Biblical Studies Ser). 1970. 50.00x (ISBN 0-87068-111-7). Ktav.

Petrograd Workers & the Fall of the Old Regime: From the February Revolution to the July Days, 1917. David Mandel. LC 81-21237. 224p. 1984. 27.50 (ISBN 0-312-60393-2). St Martin.

Petrograd Workers & the Soviet Seizure of Power: From the July Days, 1917 to July 1918. David Mandel. LC 83-13960. 1984. 27.50 (ISBN 0-312-60395-9). St Martin.

Petrographs of the Glen Canyon Region. Christy Turner, II. (MNA Bulletin Ser.: No. 38). 74p. 1964. pap. 5.00 (ISBN 0-685-76475-3). Mus Northern Ariz.

Petrography: An Introduction to the Study of Rocks in Thin Sections. 2nd ed. Howel Williams et al. LC 82-5072. (Illus.). 626p. 1983. text ed. 38.95 (ISBN 0-7167-1376-4). W H Freeman.

Petrography of Kentucky Coals in the Princess Reserve District. James Hower & Garry Wild. (Resource Characterization Ser.). 27p. (Orig.). 1981. pap. 4.00 (ISBN 0-86607-004-4). KY Energy Cabnt Lab.

Petroleo Moderno. Bill Berger & Ken Anderson. Tr. by Gus Pena from Eng. 284p. (Span.). 1980. 15.95 (ISBN 0-87814-136-7, P-4233). PennWell Bks.

Petroleum. Wilbur Cross. (Science & Technology Ser.). (Illus.). 100p. (gr. 5 up). 1983. PLB 17.27 (ISBN 0-516-00509-X). Childrens.

Petroleum. 584p. 1975. text ed. 59.00x (ISBN 0-909520-25-9, Pub. by Australasian Inst M&M). Brookfield Pub Co.

Petroleum: A Resource Interpretation. Chester G. Gilbert & Joseph E. Pogue. 1980. lib. bdg. 49.95 (ISBN 0-8490-3109-5). Gordon Pr.

Petroleum Accounting: Principles, Procedures & Issues. Horace R. Brock et al. LC 85-60604. 600p. 1985. 49.95x (ISBN 0-940966-08-5). UNTX Pro Dev Inst.

Petroleum & Economic Development: The Cases of Mexico & Norway. Ragaei El Mallakh & Oystein Noreng. LC 83-48148. 224p. 1983. 30.00x (ISBN 0-669-07002-5). Lexington Bks.

Petroleum & Medicine: Scientific Subject Index with Research Bibliography. American Health Research Institute Staff. LC 88-47604. 150p. 1988. 34.50 (ISBN 0-88164-742-X); pap. 26.50 (ISBN 0-88164-743-8). ABBE Pubs Assn.

Petroleum & Mexico's Future. Ed. by Pamela S. Falk. (Special Studies on Latin America & the Caribbean). 124p. 1987. 23.50 (ISBN 0-8133-0339-7). Westview.

Petroleum & Mining Taxation: Handbook on a Method for Equitable Sharing of Profits & Risk. Christopher Goss. 86p. 1986. text ed. 39.00 (ISBN 0-566-05269-5, Pub. by Gower Pub England). Gower Pub Co.

Petroleum & National Development in the Middle East: The Case of Saudi Arabia. 1979. 10.00 (ISBN 0-317-56399-8). UM Ctr NENAS.

Petroleum & Organic Chemicals see Chemical Technology: An Encyclopedic Treatment.

Petroleum & Structural Change in a Developing Country: The Case of Nigeria. Peter O. Olayiwola. LC 86-21216. 225p. 1986. lib. bdg. 40.95 (ISBN 0-275-92115-8, C2115). Praeger.

Petroleum & the Continental Shelf of Northwest Europe, Vol. 2. Ed. by H. A. Cole. (Illus.). 126p. 1975. 32.50 (ISBN 0-85334-656-9, Pub. by Elsevier Applied Sci England). Elsevier.

Petroleum & the Continental Shelf of Northwest Europe: Geology, Vol. 1. Ed. by A. W. Woodland. (Illus.). 501p. 1975. 122.50 (ISBN 0-85334-648-8, Pub. by Elsevier Applied Sci England). Elsevier.

Petroleum & the Economy of the United Arab Emirates. Mana Saeed Al-Otaiba. 304p. 1977. 90.00 (ISBN 0-85664-519-2, Pub. by Croom Helm Ltd). Routledge Chapman & Hall.

Petroleum & the Nigerian Economy. Scott R. Pearson. LC 76-130830. 1970. 25.00x (ISBN 0-8047-0749-9). Stanford U Pr.

Petroleum Basins of China, the U. S. S. R. & Mongolia. A. A. Meyerhoff. 1986. 79.00 (ISBN 0-86010-569-5). Graham & Trotman.

Petroleum: Canadian Markets & United States Foreign Trade Policy. Alan R. Plotnick. LC 64-25731. 175p. 1965. 16.50x (ISBN 0-295-73876-6). U of Wash Pr.

Petroleum Company Operations & Agreements in the Developing Countries. Raymond F. Mikesell. LC 83-43265. 160p. 1984. pap. text ed. 20.00 (ISBN 0-915707-07-1). Resources Future.

Petroleum Concession Agreements of the United Arab Emirates: Adu Dhabi 1939-1981, 2 vols. Mana S. Al-Otaiba. 578p. 1982. Set. 165.00 (ISBN 0-7099-1915-8, Pub. by Croom Helm Ltd). Routledge Chapman & Hall.

Petroleum Conservation in Eastern Europe. Victor Merkin. Ed. by Andreas Tamberg. 197p. (Orig.). Date not set. pap. text ed. 42.50 (ISBN 1-55831-080-0). Delphic Associates.

Petroleum Conservation in the United States: An Economic Analysis. Stephen L. McDonald. LC 71-149242. (Resources for the Future Ser.). (Illus.). 288p. 1971. 22.50x. Johns Hopkins.

Petroleum Conservation in the United States: An Economic Analysis. Stephen L. McDonald. 279p. 1971. 22.50 (ISBN 0-8018-1261-5). Resources Future.

Petroleum Contaminated Soils: Remediation Techniques, Environmental Fate & Risk Assessment. Ed. by Paul T. Kostecki & Edward J. Calabrese. (Illus.). 260p. Date not set. 55.00 (ISBN 0-87371-135-1). Lewis Pubs Inc.

Petroleum Cooperation Among Developing Countries. pap. 11.00 (ISBN 92-1-104109-0, E.77.11.A.3). UN.

Petroleum Deposits: Origin, Evolution, & Present Characteristics. J. H. Tatsch. LC 73-93625. (Illus.). 378p. 1974. 50.00 (ISBN 0-912890-06-1). Tatsch.

Petroleum Derivatives, 2 vols. Incl. Vol. 1. William R. Jones et al (ISBN 0-8422-7291-7); Vol. 2. John G. Ditman et al (ISBN 0-8422-7292-5). (Energy Ser.). 1976. text ed. 34.50x ea. Irvington.

Petroleum-Derived Carbons. Ed. by John D. Bacha et al. LC 86-7894. (ACS Symposium Ser.: No. 303). (Illus.). x, 406p. 1986. 74.95 (ISBN 0-8412-0964-2, PA 410). Am Chemical.

Petroleum Development Geology. 3rd ed. Parke A. Dickey. LC 81-11943. 560p. 1986. 59.95 (ISBN 0-87814-307-6). PennWell Bks.

Petroleum Divestiture & the Use & Misuse of Business Segment Financial Statistics. Bernell K. Stone. (LEC Occasional Paper). 1978. pap. 2.50 (ISBN 0-916770-07-9). Law & Econ U Miami.

Petroleum Drilling Equipment Terms & Phrases: English-Spanish, Spanish-English. Arthur E. Thomann. LC 80-82143. 423p. 1980. lib. bdg. 50.00x (ISBN 0-930624-02-5). Marlin.

Petroleum Economics & Engineering. Abdel-Aal & Smelzlee. (Chemical Processing & Engineering Ser.: Vol. 6). 1976. 59.75 (ISBN 0-8247-6293-2). Dekker.

Petroleum Effects in the Arctic Environment. Ed. by F. R. Engelhardt. 272p. 1985. 86.50 (ISBN 0-85334-356-X, Pub. by Elsevier Applied Sci England). Elsevier.

Petroleum Engineering: Drilling & Well Completion. reference ed. Carl Gatlin. 1960. 56.00 (ISBN 0-13-662155-4). P-H.

Petroleum Engineering Practice Problem Manual. David S. Goldstein & Rhonda A. Jones. (Engineering Review Manual Ser.). 138p. 1987. pap. text ed. 19.50 (ISBN 0-932276-65-2). Prof Pubns CA.

Petroleum Engineering: Principles & Practice. John S. Archer & Colin G. Wall. (Illus.). 350p. 1986. 83.00 (ISBN 0-86010-665-9); pap. 37.00 (ISBN 0-86010-715-9). Graham & Trotman.

Petroleum Evaluations & Economic Decision. A. W. McCray. (Illus.). 544p. 1975. 56.00 (ISBN 0-13-662213-5). P-H.

Petroleum Exploitation Strategy. Derek A. Fee. 200p. 1988. 35.00 (ISBN 0-317-68230-X, Pub. by Pinter Pubs UK). Columbia U Pr.

Petroleum Exploration: A Quantitative Introduction. L. Ray Sengbush. LC 85-8207. (Illus.). 238p. 1986. text ed. 56.00 (ISBN 0-88746-047-X). Intl Human Res.

Petroleum Exploration Strategies in Developing Countries. 300p. 1982. 46.00 (ISBN 0-86010-346-3). Graham & Trotman.

Petroleum Exploration Worldwide. John C. McCaslin. LC 82-22499. 192p. 1983. 59.95 (ISBN 0-87814-220-7, P-4307). Pennwell Bks.

Petroleum Explorationist's Guide to Contracts Used in Oil & Gas Operations. Ed. by Lewis G. Mosburg, Jr. (Illus.). 458p. (Orig.). 1985. pap. 48.00 (ISBN 0-910649-18-9). Energy Textbks.

Petroleum Explorationist's Guide to Contracts Used in Oil & Gas Operations. Ed. by Lewis G. Mosburg, Jr. 600p. Date not set. 48.00 (P7109). PennWell Bks.

Petroleum Explorationist's Guide to Titles, Leases & Contracts. Ed. by Lewis G. Mosburg, Jr. (Illus.). 567p. (Orig.). 1984. pap. 42.50x (ISBN 0-910649-15-4). Energy Textbks.

Petroleum Formation & Occurence. rev. & enl. ed. B. P. Tissot & D. H. Welte. (Illus.). 610p. 1984. 49.50 (ISBN 0-387-13281-3). Springer-Verlag.

Petroleum Geochemistry & Exploration in the Afro-Asian Region: Proceedings of the International Conference, Dehra Dun, India, 1st, 25-27 November 1985. Ed. by Ruby K. Kumar et al. 558p. 1987. text ed. 89.00 (ISBN 90-6191-791-3, Pub. by A A Balkema). Brookfield Pub Co.

Petroleum Geochemistry & Exploration of Europe. Ed. by J. Brooks. (Illus.). 396p. 1983. text ed. 66.00x (ISBN 0-632-01076-2). Blackwell Pubns.

Petroleum Geochemistry & Geology. John M. Hunt. LC 79-1281. (Illus.). 617p. 1979. text ed. 46.95 (ISBN 0-7167-1005-6). W H Freeman.

Petroleum Geochemistry, Genesis & Migration. Ed. by Hollis D. Hedberg et al. (AGI Reprint Ser.). (Illus.). 287p. 1983. pap. 17.95 (ISBN 0-913312-77-0). Am Geol.

Petroleum Geochemistry in Exploration of the Norwegian Shelf: Proceedings of a Norwegian Petroleum Society Conference held in Stavanger, 22-24 October 1984. Ed. by Bruce M. Thomas. (Illus.). 500p. 1985. 97.50 (ISBN 0-86010-706-X). Graham & Trotman.

Petroleum Geology. R. E. Chapman. (Developments in Petroleum Science Ser.: Vol. 16). 416p. 1983. 44.25 (ISBN 0-444-42165-3, I-424-83). Elsevier.

Petroleum Geology. 2nd ed. Kenneth K. Landes. LC 74-26700. 458p. 1975. Repr. of 1959 ed. 34.50 (ISBN 0-88275-226-X). Krieger.

Petroleum Geology. F. K. North. (Illus.). 750p. 1985. text ed. 70.00x (ISBN 0-04-553003-3); pap. text ed. 44.95x (ISBN 0-04-553004-1). Unwin Hyman.

Petroleum Geology & Reservoirs. (Well Servicing & Workover Ser.: Lesson 2). (Illus.). 65p. (Orig.). 1971. pap. text ed. 5.95 (ISBN 0-88698-058-5, 3.70210). PETEX.

Petroleum Geology for Geophysicists & Engineers. Richard C. Selley. LC 82-81124. (Short Course Handbooks). (Illus.). 88p. 1983. text ed. 23.00 (ISBN 0-934634-49-1); pap. 15.00 (ISBN 0-934634-42-4). Intl Human Res.

Petroleum Geology in China. Ed. by John F. Mason. 263p. 1981. 44.95 (ISBN 0-87814-163-4, P-4272). PennWell Bks.

Petroleum Geology of Northwestern Europe. Ed. by J. Brooks & K. Glennie. 1987. lib. bdg. 245.00 (ISBN 0-86010-703-5, Pub. by Graham & Trotman UK). Kluwer Academic.

Petroleum Geology of the Continental Shelf of North West Europe. Ed. by L. V. Illing & G. D. Hobson. 1981. 220.00x (ISBN 0-471-25779-6). Wiley.

Petroleum Geology of the North European. Norwegian Petroleum Society Staff. 444p. 1984. 105.00 (ISBN 0-86010-486-9). Graham & Trotman.

Petroleum Geology of the United States. Kenneth K. Landes. LC 77-101975. 571p. 1970. 87.95x (ISBN 0-471-51335-0, Pub. by Wiley-Interscience). Wiley.

Petroleum Handbook. 6th, rev. ed. Royal Dutch-Shell Group of Companies. 710p. 1983. 166.00 (ISBN 0-444-42118-1). Elsevier.

Petroleum: How It Is Found & Used. William R. Pampe. LC 84-1531. (Illus.). 64p. (gr. 5-9). 1984. PLB 12.95 (ISBN 0-89490-100-1). Enslow Pubs.

Petroleum Hydrocarbons. A. A. Petrov. (Illus.). 325p. 1987. 95.00 (ISBN 0-387-17329-3). Springer-Verlag.

Petroleum in Mexico. J. Ranolph. 1976. lib. bdg. 34.95 (ISBN 0-8490-2427-7). Gordon Pr.

Petroleum in the Marine Environment. Ed. by Leon Petrakis & F. T. Weiss. LC 79-25524. (ACS Advances in Chemistry Ser.: No. 185). 1980. 54.95 (ISBN 0-8412-0475-6). Am Chemical.

Petroleum in Venezuela: A Partially Annotated Bibliography to 1980. William Sullivan & Brian S. McBeth. (Latin American Studies). 550p. 1985. lib. bdg. 83.00 (ISBN 0-8161-8522-0). G K Hall.

Petroleum Industry & the Future Petroleum Province in Pennsylvania. 3rd ed. Dana R. Kelley et al. (Mineral Resource Report Ser.: No. 65). (Illus.). 39p. 1983. pap. 2.05 (ISBN 0-8182-0037-5). Commonweal PA.

Petroleum Industry: General Problems see Proceedings.

Petroleum Industry in Oil-Importing Developing Countries. Fariborz Ghadar & Robert Stobaugh. LC 81-48556. 240p. 1983. 30.00x (ISBN 0-669-05419-4). Lexington Bks.

Petroleum Industry in the United Kingdom: Proceedings of the Joint Meeting of the Institute of Petroleum & the Deutsche Gesellschaft fur Mineralolwissenschaft und the Kohlechemie e V., London, 11-12 November, 1965. Ed. by Peter Hepple. LC 66-6024. pap. 49.50 (ISBN 0-317-28997-7, 2023697). Bks Demand UMI.

Petroleum Industry in Western Europe: A Guide to Information Sources. Lawrence G. Franco et al. LC 75-20065. (Reference Library of Social Science: Vol. 13). 178p. 1975. lib. bdg. 34.00 (ISBN 0-8240-9990-7). Garland Pub.

Petroleum Industry of the People's Republic of China. Hsien C. Ling. LC 74-22168. (Publications Ser.: No. 142). 264p. 1975. 11.95x (ISBN 0-8179-6421-5). Hoover Inst Pr.

Petroleum Industry Risk & Insurance Managment Manual. Keith Kakacek & Roy Adams. 250p. 3-ring loose-leaf binder 125.00 (ISBN 0-940966-11-5). UNTX Pro Dev Inst.

Petroleum Lands & Leasing. Joan Burk. 184p. 1983. 43.95 (ISBN 0-87814-239-8, P-4315). PennWell Bks.

Pettis Integrals & Measure Theory, Vol. 51. Michel Talagrand. LC 84-14614. (Memoirs of the American Mathematical Society: No. 307). 226p. 1984. pap. 21.00 (ISBN 0-8218-2307-8). Am Math.

Pettranella. Betty Waterton. LC 80-52829. (Illus.). 32p. (gr. 1-4). 1981. 12.95 (ISBN 0-8149-0844-6). Vanguard.

Petty-Bourgeois & Proletarian Socialism. V. I. Lenin. 15p. 1977. pap. 0.75 (ISBN 0-8285-2264-2, Pub. by Progress Pubs USSR). Imported Pubns.

Petty Capitalism in Spanish America: The Pulperos of Puebla, Mexico City, Caracas, & Buenos Aires. Jay Kinsbruner. (Dellplain Latin American Studies). 150p. 1986. pap. 19.95X (ISBN 0-8133-7272-0). Westview.

Petty Demon. Fyodor Sologub. Tr. by Sam Cioran from Rus. 400p. 1983. pap. 7.95 (ISBN 0-88233-808-0). Ardis Pubs.

Petty Papers, 2 Vols. in 1. William Petty. Ed. by Marquis Landsdowne. LC 66-22634. 1967. Repr. of 1927 ed. 49.50x (ISBN 0-678-00237-1). Kelley.

Petty-Southwell Correspondence, 1676-1687. William Petty. Ed. by Marquis Of Landsdowne. LC 67-27557. 1967. Repr. of 1928 ed. 39.50x (ISBN 0-678-00314-9). Kelley.

Petty: The Origins of Political Economy. Alessandro Roncaglia. Tr. by Isabella Cherubini from Ital. LC 84-2359. 140p. 1985. 32.50 (ISBN 0-87332-315-7). M E Sharpe.

Pettyfoggers & Vipers of the Commonwealth: The "Lower Branch" of the Legal Profession in Early Modern England. C. W. Brooks. LC 85-26896. (Cambridge Studies in English Legal History). 410p. 1986. 54.50 (ISBN 0-521-30574-8). Cambridge U Pr.

Petulant Children. Baxter Hathaway. LC 78-14869. 36p. 1978. 3.50 (ISBN 0-87886-099-1). Greenfld Rev Pr.

Petunia. Roger Duvoisin. (Illus.). (gr. k-3). 1962. lib. bdg. 8.99 (ISBN 0-394-90865-1). Knopf.

Petunia. Ed. by K. C. Sink. (Monographs on Theoretical & Applied Genetics: Vol. 9). (Illus.). 290p. 1984. 52.00 (ISBN 0-387-13472-7). Springer Verlag.

Petunia, Beware! Roger Duvoisin. (Illus.). (gr. 1-3). 1964. lib. bdg. 10.99 (ISBN 0-394-90867-8). Knopf.

Petunia, I Love You. Roger Duvoisin. (Illus.). (gr. k-3). 1965. lib. bdg. 9.99 (ISBN 0-394-90870-8). Knopf.

Petunia the Silly Goose Stories: Five Read-Aloud Classics. Roger Duvoisin. LC 86-2783. (Illus.). 160p. (ps-3). 1987. 15.95 (ISBN 0-394-88292-X); lib. bdg. 15.99 (ISBN 0-394-98292-4). Knopf.

Petunia's Christmas. Roger Duvoisin. (Illus.). (gr. k-3). 1963. lib. bdg. 10.99 (ISBN 0-394-90868-6). Knopf.

Peu de Soleil dans l'Eau Froide. Francoise Sagan. 14.95 (ISBN 0-685-37083-6). French & Eur.

Peugeot 205: The Story of a Challenge. Jean Todt & Jean-Louis Moncet. (Foulis Motoring Bk.). (Illus.). 128p. 1986. 22.95 (ISBN 0-85429-554-2, Pub. by G T Foulis Ltd). Haynes Pubns.

Peugeot 205GTI Enthusiast's Companion. Ray Hutton. (Illus.). 112p. 1987. pap. 27.95 (ISBN 0-947981-18-7, Pub. by Motor Racing England). Motorbooks Intl.

Peuplades de la Senegambie: Histoire, Ethnographie, Moeurs et Coutumes, Legendes, etc. Laurent J. Berenger-Feraud. (Fr.). 1879. 41.00 (ISBN 0-8115-3081-7). Kraus Repr.

Peuple Esquimau Aujourd'hui et Demain-The Eskimo People Today & Tomorrow: Quatrieme Congres International De la Fondation Francaise D'etudes Nordiques. Ed. by Jean Malaurie. (Bibliotheque Arctique et Antarctique: No. 4). 1973. pap. 40.40x (ISBN 90-2797-242-7). Mouton.

Peuples de l'Oubangui-Chari. Adolphe F. Eboue. LC 74-15034. (Illus., Fr.). Repr. of 1933 ed. 20.00 (ISBN 0-404-12039-3). AMS Pr.

Peuples et les civilisations de l'Afrique. Hermann Baumann. LC 74-15010. Repr. of 1948 ed. AMS Pr.

Peuples et les Civilisations du Proche-Orient: Essai d'une Histoire Comparee, des Origines a nos Jours, Tomes II-V. Jawad Boulos. Incl. Tome II. De 1600 a 64 Avant J.-C. 430p. 1962. pap. text ed. 21.60x (ISBN 0-686-27788-0); Tome III. De la Conquete Romaine a l'Expansion Arabo-Islamique (64 av. J.-C. to 640 ap. J.-C.) 400p. 1964. pap. text ed. 21.60x (ISBN 0-686-27789-9); Tome IV. De l'Expansion Arabo-Islamique a la Conquete Turco-Ottomane (640-1517) 550p. 1964. pap. text ed. 27.20 (ISBN 0-686-27790-2); Le Proche-Orient Ottoman (1517-1918) et Postottoman (1918-1930) 300p. 1968. pap. text ed. 16.80 (ISBN 0-686-27791-0). pap. Mouton.

Peuples Noirs Peuples Africains, Nos. 1-26. Ed. by Mongo Beti. 150p. (Fr.). 1983. pap. 8.00 per issue (ISBN 0-686-88947-9, Pub. by Edit Peuples Noirs France); pap. 185.00 for set. Three Continents.

Peur en Dauphine: Juillet-Aout 1789. Pierre Conrad. 283p. (Fr.). Repr. of 1904 ed. lib. bdg. 52.50x. Coronet Bks.

Peux-tu Attraper Josephine? Stephane Poulin. (Illus.). 24p. (Orig., Fr.). (gr. k-4). 1987. 12.95 (ISBN 0-88776-199-2); pap. 5.95 (ISBN 0-88776-225-5). Tundra Bks.

Peverel Papers: A Yearbook of the Countryside. Flora Thompson. (Illus.). 224p. 1987. 24.95 (ISBN 0-7126-1296-3, Pub. by Century Hutchinson). David & Charles.

Pevsner, Nikolaus Berhard Leon, 1902-1983. Peter Murray. (Memoirs of the Fellows of the Academy Ser.). (Illus.). 1986. pap. 2.25 (ISBN 0-85672-526-9, Pub. by British Acad). Longwood Pub Group.

Pew Group. Anthony Oliver. 224p. 1985. pap. 2.95 (ISBN 0-449-20594-0, Crest). Fawcett.

Pew Peeves. Compiled by Thom Schultz. LC 82-50731. (Illus.). 80p. (Orig.). 1982. pap. 3.95 (ISBN 0-936664-07-X). Group Bks.

Pewter. Ed. by Tony Curtis. (Illus.). 1978. 2.00 (ISBN 0-902921-54-1). Apollo.

Pewter & the Revival of Its Use. facs. ed. Arthur L. Liberty. (Shorey Lost Arts Ser.). 28p. pap. 3.95 (ISBN 0-8466-6007-5, U7). Shorey.

Pewter of the Western World, Sixteen Hundred to Eighteen Fifty. Peter R. Hornsby. LC 83-61251. (Illus.). 381p. 1983. 60.00 (ISBN 0-916838-83-8). Schiffer.

Pewter Wares from Sheffield. Jack L. Scott. LC 80-68670. (Illus.). 260p. 1980. 28.00 (ISBN 0-937864-00-5). Antiquary Pr.

Pewter Wares from Sheffield. Jack L. Scott. 262p. 28.00 (ISBN 0-916838-00-5). Schiffer.

Pewter Wheel. Susan Bright. 1982. 3.00 (ISBN 0-911051-04-X); chapbook & VHS video. Plain View.

Pewter-Working: Instructions & Projects. Burl N. Osburn & Gordon O. Wilber. LC 78-74121. (Illus.). 1979. pap. 4.50 (ISBN 0-486-23786-9). Dover.

Peyote Hunt: The Sacred Journey of the Huichol Indians. Barbara G. Myerhoff. LC 73-16923. (Symbol, Myth & Ritual Ser.). (Illus.). 288p. 1976. pap. 9.95x (ISBN 0-8014-9137-1). Cornell U Pr.

Peyote Music. David P. McAllester. pap. 19.00 (ISBN 0-384-36490-X). Johnson Repr.

Peyote Religion. Omer C. Stewart. LC 87-5941. (Civilization of the American Indian Ser.: Vol. 181). (Illus.). 464p. 1987. 29.95 (ISBN 0-8061-2068-1). U of Okla Pr.

Peyote Religion among the Navaho. 2nd ed. David F. Aberle. LC 82-2562. (Illus.). 454p. 1982. lib. bdg. 35.00x (ISBN 0-226-00082-6); pap. text ed. 15.00x (ISBN 0-226-00083-4). U of Chicago Pr.

Peyote: The Divine Cactus. Edward F. Anderson. LC 79-20173. 248p. 1980. pap. 10.95 (ISBN 0-8165-0613-2). U of Ariz Pr.

Peyote Toad. Charles Foster. LC 75-44699. 1976. perfect bdg. 2.00 (ISBN 0-915214-09-1). Litmus.

Peyotism in the West: A Historical & Cultural Perspective. Ed. by Omer C. Stewart. (Anthropological Papers: No. 108). (Illus.). 168p. (Orig.). 1984. pap. 17.50x (ISBN 0-87480-235-0). U of Utah Pr.

Peyronie's Disease: Induratio Penis Plastica. Ed. by A. Kelami & J. P. Pryor. (Progress in Reproductive Biology & Medicine: Vol. 9). (Illus.). viii, 116p. 1983. 75.50 (ISBN 3-8055-3513-9). S Karger.

Peyton Randolph, 1721-1775: One Who Presided. John J. Reardon. LC 81-70431. (Illus.). 112p. 1982. lib. bdg. 12.95 (ISBN 0-89089-201-6). Carolina Acad Pr.

Pezzettino. Leo Lionni. LC 75-9669. (Illus.). 40p. (gr. k-3). 1975. 9.95 (ISBN 0-394-83156-X). Pantheon.

Pfaff's Problem & Its Generalizations. Jan A. Schouten & W. Van Der Kulk. LC 75-77140. 1969. Repr. of 1949 ed. 19.50 (ISBN 0-8284-0221-3). Chelsea Pub.

Pfander-Studien. H. Spiegelberg & E. Ave-Lallemant. 1982. 69.50 (ISBN 90-247-2490-2, Pub. By Martinus Nijhoff Netherlands). Kluwer Academic.

Pfeiffers' Official Frequent Flyers Guide: The Comprehensive Source for Discovering the Full Benefits Available to Frequent Travelers. J. William Pfeiffer & Judith A. Pfeiffer. (North American Edition, 1989 Ser.). (Illus.). 304p. (Orig.). 1988. pap. 24.95 (ISBN 0-9620496-0-3). Pegasus Pr CA.

Pfizer Guide: Medical Career Opportunities. 204p. 1983. pap. write for info. (ISBN 0-943378-02-8). M Powley.

Pflanzenfasern: Neue Wege in der Stoffwechseltherapie. Ed. by K. Huth & Christiane Braeuning. (Beitraege zu Infusionstherapie und Klinische Ernaehrung: Vol. 12). (Illus.). viii, 224p. 1983. 36.00 (ISBN 3-8055-3723-9). S Karger.

Pflanzengesellschaften Westdeutschlands. R. Tuexen. 1970. Repr. of 1937 ed. 15.00x (ISBN 3-7682-0702-1). Lubrecht & Cramer.

Pflanzenlexikon. W. Baumeister. 1280p. (Ger.). 1969. pap. 99.95 (ISBN 3-499-16100-1, M-7580). French & Eur.

Pflanzenoekologische Untersuchungen in den Subalpinen Dornpolsterfluren Kretas. J. Hager. (Dissertationes Botanicae Ser.: Vol. 89). (Illus.). 196p. 1985. pap. 36.00x (ISBN 3-7682-1449-4). Lubrecht & Cramer.

Pflanzensociologische Studien in Chile. E. Oberdorfer. (Illus.). 1960. 36.00x (ISBN 3-7682-0011-6). Lubrecht & Cramer.

PFS: FILE Instruction Manual: For IBM PC & Apple Computers. Ellen Matrose. 55p. 1985. 6.00 (ISBN 0-9619731-2-9). Ram Pub IA.

PFS: First Choice-Applications Made Easy. Paul Dlug. (Illus.). 220p. 1988. pap. 14.95. TAB BKS.

PFS on the IBM PC, Using. Linda L. Rice. (Illus.). 147p. (Orig.). 1984. pap. text ed. 12.95 (ISBN 0-942728-20-3). Custom Pub Co.

PFS: REPORT Instruction Manual: For IBM PC & Apple Computers. Ellen Matrose. 34p. 1985. 4.00 (ISBN 0-9619731-3-7). Ram Pub IA.

PFS: Software Made Easy: Write, File, Report, Access, Graph. Carl Townsend. 250p. (Orig.). 1984. pap. text ed. 17.95 (ISBN 0-07-881147-3). Osborne-McGraw.

PFS: WRITE-IBM Writing Assistant Instruction Manual: For IBM PC & Apple Computers. 2nd ed. Ellen Matrose. 81p. 1987. 5.00 (ISBN 0-9619731-5-3). Ram Pub IA.

PFS: WRITE Instruction Manual: For IBM PC & Apple Computers. Ellen Matrose. 55p. 1985. 6.00 (ISBN 0-9619731-4-5). Ram Pub IA.

PF474 Product Data Book. 148p. (Orig.). 1984. pap. write for info. (ISBN 0-926390-00-7). Proximity Tech.

PG: A Parental Guide to Rock. David Scheer. 275p. 1986. pap. 7.95 (ISBN 0-87509-378-7). Chr Pubns.

PGL-2, Over the P-Adics: Its Representations, Spherical Functions, & Fourier Analysis. A. J. Silberger. LC 70-139951. (Lecture Notes in Mathematics: Vol. 166). 1970. pap. 14.00 (ISBN 0-387-05193-7). Springer-Verlag.

PH & pION Control in Process & Waste Streams. F. G. Shinskey. LC 73-7853. (Environmental Science & Technology Ser.). 259p. 1973. 50.00 (ISBN 0-471-78640-3, Pub. by Wiley-Interscience). Wiley.

PH Control: An Independent Learning Module of the Instrument Society of America. Gregory K. McMillan. 272p. 1985. pap. text ed. 39.95x (ISBN 0-87664-725-5). Instru Soc.

PH. D.'s & the Academic Labor Market. Allan Cartter. LC 75-38700. pap. 70.00 (ISBN 0-317-29023-1, 2020884). Bks Demand UMI.

PH Homeostatis: Mechanisms & Control. Ed. by D. Haussinger. 479p. 1988. 96.00 (ISBN 0-12-333065-3). Acad Pr.

PH Measurement. C. Clarke Westcott. 1978. 35.00 (ISBN 0-12-745150-1). Acad Pr.

Phacomatoses see Handbook of Clinical Neurology.

Phaedo. Plato. Tr. by F. J. Church. LC 51-10496. 1951. pap. 4.24 scp (ISBN 0-672-60192-3, LLA30). Bobbs.

Phaedo. Plato. Ed. by R. Hackforth. 200p. 1972. pap. 10.95x (ISBN 0-521-09702-9). Cambridge U Pr.

Phaedo. Plato. Tr. by G. M. Grube. LC 76-49565. (HPC Philosophical Classics Ser.). 72p. 1977. pap. 2.95 (ISBN 0-915144-18-2). Hackett Pub.

Phaedo. Plato. Ed. by John Burnet. 1979. pap. 13.95x (ISBN 0-19-814014-2). Oxford U Pr.

Phaedo. Plato. Tr. & notes by David Gallop. (Clarendon Plato Ser). 1975. pap. 12.95x (ISBN 0-19-872049-1). Oxford U Pr.

Phaedo see Republic & Other Works.

Phaedo: A Platonic Labyrinth. Ronna Burger. LC 84-40191. 288p. 1984. text ed. 29.50t (ISBN 0-300-03163-7). Yale U Pr.

Phaedo Church Plato. F. J. Church. 1951. pap. text ed. write for info. (ISBN 0-02-322400-2). Macmillan.

Phaedo of Plato. Plato. LC 72-9280. (Philosophy of Plato & Aristotle Ser.). Repr. of 1894 ed. 14.00 (ISBN 0-405-04831-9). Ayer Co Pubs.

Phaedon; or, the Death of Socrates. Moses Mendelssohn. LC 73-2219. (Jewish People; History, Religion, Literature Ser.). Repr. of 1789 ed. 22.00 (ISBN 0-405-05282-0). Ayer Co Pubs.

Phaedra. (Illus.). 35p. (Director's Production Script). 1966. pap. 5.00 (ISBN 0-88680-152-4). I E Clark.

Phaedra. Jean Racine. Tr. by Bernard Grebanier from Fr. (gr. 9 up). 1958. pap. text ed. 4.95 (ISBN 0-8120-0143-5). Barron.

Phaedra. Jean Racine. Ed. & tr. by Oreste F. Pucciani. LC 59-13086. (Crofts Classics Ser.). 1950. pap. text ed. 3.75x (ISBN 0-88295-069-X). Harlan Davidson.

Phaedra. Jean Racine. Tr. by Robert Lowell. 1972. lib. bdg. 12.00x (ISBN 0-374-95132-2, Octagon). Hippocrene Bks.

Phaedra. Jean Racine. Tr. by Richard Wilbur. (Illus.). 128p. 1986. 15.95 (ISBN 0-15-171731-1). HarBraceJ.

Phaedra. Jean Racine. Tr. by Richard Wilbur. (Illus.). 1987. pap. 5.95 (ISBN 0-15-675780-X, Harv). HarBraceJ.

Phaedra. Lucius Annaeus Seneca. Tr. & intro. by Frederick Ahl. LC 86-47634. (Masters of Latin Literature Ser.). 128p. 1986. pap. 5.95x (ISBN 0-8014-9433-8). Cornell U Pr.

Phaedra: A Novel of Ancient Athens. June R. Brindel. 256p. 1985. 14.95 (ISBN 0-312-60399-1). St Martin.

Phaedra: A Novel of Ancient Athens. June R. Brindel. 240p. 1987. pap. 7.95 (ISBN 0-312-00174-6). St Martin.

Phaedra & Iphigenia. Tr. by William L. Crain from Fr. LC 82-81873. (Illus.). 150p. (Orig.). 1982. pap. 14.50 (ISBN 0-88127-002-4). Oracle Pr LA.

Phaedra & Other Plays. Jean Racine. Tr. by John Cairncross. Incl. Iphigenia; Athaliah. (Classics Ser.). 1964. pap. 3.95 (ISBN 0-14-044122-0). Penguin.

Phaedra of Seneca. Gilbert Lawall & Gerda Kundel. 238p. pap. text ed. 13.00 (ISBN 0-86516-016-3). Bolchazy-Carducci.

Phaedrus. Plato. Tr. by W. C. Helmbold & W. G. Rabinowitz. 1956. pap. 3.56 scp (ISBN 0-672-60207-5, LLA40). Bobbs.

Phaedrus. Plato. Ed. by R. Hackforth. 200p. 1972. pap. 12.95x (ISBN 0-521-09703-7). Cambridge U Pr.

Phaedrus & Letters VII & VIII. Plato. Tr. by Walter Hamilton. (Classics Ser.). (Orig.). 1973. pap. 4.95 (ISBN 0-14-044275-8). Penguin.

Phaedrus of Plato. Plato. LC 72-9307. (Philosophy of Plato & Aristotle Ser.). (Gr. & Eng.). Repr. of 1868 ed. 15.00 (ISBN 0-405-04866-1). Ayer Co Pubs.

Phaedrus Plato. W. C. Helmbold & W. G. Rabinowitz. 1956. pap. text ed. write for info. (ISBN 0-02-352960-1). Macmillan.

Phaenomen: Tourismus. Stefan J. Wirtz. (European University Studies: No. 10, Vol. 5). 460p. (Ger.). 1982. 42.10 (ISBN 3-8204-5794-1). P Lang Pubs.

Phaeton. Jean-Baptiste Lully. Ed. by Theodore De Lajarte. (Chefs-d'oeuvre classiques de l'opera francais Ser.: Vol. 23). (Illus.). 346p. (Fr.). 1972. pap. 27.50x (ISBN 0-8450-1123-5). Broude.

Phage Mu. Ed. by Neville Symonds et al. LC 87-15102. (Illus.). 354p. 1987. text ed. 75.00 (ISBN 0-87969-306-1). Cold Spring Harbor.

Phagocytes & Cellular Immunity. Hans H. Gadebusch. 176p. 1979. 85.00 (ISBN 0-8493-5349-1). CRC Pr.

Phagocytosis: Past & Future. Ed. by Manfred L. Karnovsky & Lian Bolis. LC 82-11461. 586p. 1982. 65.50 (ISBN 0-12-400050-9). Acad Pr.

Phaid the Gambler. Mick Farren. 1986. pap. 3.50 (ISBN 0-441-66232-3). Ace Bks.

Phaidon Guide to Antique Weapons & Armour. Robert Wilkinson-Latham. write for info. P-H.

Phaidon Guide to Furniture. Andrew Brunt. (Phaidon Guide Ser.). (Illus.). 256p. 1984. pap. 6.95 (ISBN 0-13-661959-2). P-H.

Phaidon Guide to Glass. Felice Mehlman. (Illus.). 256p. 1983. pap. 6.95 (ISBN 0-13-662015-9). P-H.

Phaidon Guide to Silver. Margaret Holland. (Phaidon Guide Ser.). (Illus.). 256p. 1983. pap. 6.95 (ISBN 0-13-662122-8). P-H.

Phalaenopsis Culture: A Worldwide Survey. Ed. by Bob Gordon. (Illus.). 312p. 1988. spiral bound 27.95 (ISBN 0-9615714-4-6). Laid Back Pubns.

Phalanx, Vol 1, Nos. 1-23. Repr. of 1845 ed. lib. bdg. 72.50 (ISBN 0-404-19539-3). AMS Pr.

Phalanx, or Journal of Social Science, Vol. 1, Nos. 1 To 23. Charles Fourier. LC 68-56770. Repr. of 1845 ed. 35.50 (ISBN 0-8337-2734-6). B Franklin.

Phallic Critiques: Masculinity & Twentieth Century Literature. Peter Schwenger. 256p. 1984. 24.95x (ISBN 0-7102-0164-8). Routledge Chapman & Hall.

Phallism in Ancient Worships: Ancient Symbol Worship. 2nd ed. Hodder M. Westropp & Wake C. Staniland. (Illus.). 111p. pap. 8.95 (ISBN 0-88697-017-2). Life Science.

Phallos: A Symbol & Its History in the Male World. Thorkil Vanggaard. LC 72-80553. (Illus.). 266p. 1972. text ed. 22.50x (ISBN 0-8236-4135-X); pap. text ed. 17.95 (ISBN 0-8236-8192-0, 24135). Intl Univs Pr.

Phanerozoic Diversity Patterns: Profiles in Macroevolution. Ed. by James W. Valentine. LC 84-42905. (Series in Geology & Paleontology). (Illus.). 430p. 1985. text ed. 55.50x (ISBN 0-691-08374-6); pap. text ed. 17.50x (ISBN 0-691-08375-4). Princeton U Pr.

Phanerozoic Earth History of Australia. J. J. Veevers. (Oxford Geological Sciences Ser.). (Illus.). 1984. 80.00x (ISBN 0-19-854459-6). Oxford U Pr.

Phanerozoic Earth History of Australia. Ed. by J. J. Veevers. (Oxford Monographs on Geology & Geophysics: No. 2). (Illus.). 442p. 1987. pap. 49.95 (ISBN 0-19-854488-X). Oxford U Pr.

Phanerozoic Geology of the World: The Mesozoic, Vol. 2A. Ed. by M. Moullade & A. E. Nairn. 530p. 1978. 152.75 (ISBN 0-444-41671-4). Elsevier.

Phanerozoic Geology of the World: The Mesozoic, Vol. 2B. Ed. by M. Moullade & A. E. Nairn. 450p. 1983. 147.50 (ISBN 0-444-41672-2, I-343-83). Elsevier.

Phanerozoic Paleocontinental World Maps. A. G. Smith et al. LC 79-42669. (Cambridge Earth Science Ser.). 96p. 1981. pap. 17.95 (ISBN 0-521-23258-9). Cambridge U Pr.

Phanerozoic Stromatolites: Case Histories. Ed. by C. Monty. (Illus.). 249p. 1981. 55.00 (ISBN 0-387-10474-7). Springer-Verlag.

Phanomelogie Heute. Biemel. (Phaenomenologica Ser: No. 51). 1972. lib. bdg. 22.50 (ISBN 90-247-1336-6, Pub. by Martinus Nijhoff Netherlands). Kluwer Academic.

Phanomenologie der Assoziation. Holenstein. (Phaenomenologica Ser: No. 44). 1972. lib. bdg. 42.00 (ISBN 90-247-1175-4, Pub. by Martinus Nijhoff Netherlands). Kluwer Academic.

Phanomenologie und Egologie. Broekman. (Phaenomenologica Ser: No. 12). 1963. lib. bdg. 26.00 (ISBN 90-247-0245-3, Pub. by Martinus Nijhoff Netherlands). Kluwer Academic.

Phanomenologische Idealismus Husserls. Theodor Celms. Ed. by Natanson. LC 78-66733. (Phenomenology: Vol. 3). 192p. 1979. lib. bdg. 26.00 (ISBN 0-8240-9567-7). Garland Pub.

Pharmaceutical Microbiology. 4th ed. A. D. Russell. Ed. by W. B. Hugo. (Illus.). 520p. 1987. text ed. 90.00 (ISBN 0-632-01909-3); pap. text ed. 39.50 (ISBN 0-632-01896-8). Blackwell Pubns.
Pharmaceutical Packaging Technologies & Materials Seminar: TAPPI Notes, Adam's Mark, Philadelphia, PA, June 10-11, 1986. Technical Association of the Pulp & Paper Industry. pap. 20.00 (ISBN 0-317-55373-9, 2029174). Bks Demand UMI.
Pharmaceutical Products Market. Frost & Sullivan, Inc. Staff. 253p. 1986. 2375.00 (ISBN 0-86621-749-5, E819). Frost & Sullivan.
Pharmaceutical Quality Control. William F. Head, Jr. (Illus.). 99p. 1983. 20.00 (ISBN 0-682-49983-8). Exposition-Phoenix.
Pharmaceutical Reformulation. James I. Wells. (Pharmaceutical Technology Ser.). 240p. 1988. 59.95 (ISBN 0-470-21114-8). Wiley.
Pharmaceutical Statistics: Practical & Clinical Applications. Sanford Bolton. (Drugs & the Pharmaceutical Sciences Ser.: Vol. 25). (Illus.). 544p. 1984. 85.00 (ISBN 0-8247-7218-0); text ed. 39.75. Dekker.
Pharmaceutical Technology Conference Proceedings, 1984. (Orig.). 1984. pap. 60.00x (ISBN 0-943330-09-2). Aster Pub Corp.
Pharmaceutical Technology: Controlled Drug Release. M. H. Rubinstein. LC 87-2847. (Pharmaceutical Technology Ser.). 126p. 1987. 57.95 (ISBN 0-470-20881-3). Halsted Pr.
Pharmaceutical Technology: Tableting Technology, Vol. 1. Michael Rubinstein. 200p. 1988. 59.95 (ISBN 0-470-21001-X). Halsted Pr.
Pharmaceutical Word Book. DeLorenzo & Fedun. LC 87-43343. 1988. pap. text ed. 16.95 (ISBN 1-55642-042-0). Slack Inc.
Pharmaceuticals among the Sunrise Industries: Proceedings of an Office of Health Economics International Symposium Held at the Royal College of Physicians, London, Oct 22-23,1984. Ed. by Nicholas Wells. LC 85-11879. 240p. 1985. 29.95 (ISBN 0-312-60401-7). St Martin.
Pharmaceuticals & Cosmetics Manufacturing Expo: Proceedings of Technical Program May 13-15, 1980, Rosemont, Illinois. Pharmaceuticals & Cosmetics Manufacturing Expo(1980: Rosemont IL) pap. 79.50 (ISBN 0-317-39629-3, 2020833). Bks Demand UMI.
Pharmaceuticals & Health Policy: International Perspectives on Provision & Control of Medicines. Ed. by Blum et al. LC 80-26498. 387p. 1981. 44.50 (ISBN 0-8419-0682-3). Holmes & Meier.
Pharmaceuticals & the Sea. Charles W. Jefford et al. LC 87-51603. 168p. 1988. 65.00 (ISBN 0-87762-581-6). Technomic.
Pharmaceuticals in the EEC. K. Collins & S. A. Mclean. (Medico-Legal Issues Ser.: Vol. 7). 1989. text ed. 50.00 (ISBN 0-566-05394-2, Pub. by Gower Pub England). Gower Pub Co.
Pharmaceutics of Solids & Solid Dosage Forms. Jens T. Carstensen. LC 76-22754. 256p. 1977. 46.95 (ISBN 0-471-13726-X, Pub. by Wiley-Interscience). Wiley.
Pharmacist. Jack Rudman. (Career Examination Ser.: C-580). (Cloth bdg. avail. on request). pap. 18.00 (ISBN 0-8373-0580-2). Natl Learning.
Pharmacist, No. I. Jack Rudman. (Career Examination Ser.: C-1836). (Cloth bdg. avail. on request). pap. 18.00 (ISBN 0-8373-1836-X). Natl Learning.
Pharmacist, No. II. Jack Rudman. (Career Examination Ser.: C-1837). (Cloth bdg. avail. on request). pap. 18.00 (ISBN 0-8373-1837-8). Natl Learning.
Pharmacist, No. III. Jack Rudman. (Career Examination Ser.: C-1838). (Cloth bdg. avail. on request). pap. 20.00 (ISBN 0-8373-1838-6). Natl Learning.
Pharmacist & Family Planning. Carl F. Grindstaff. 192p. 1980. pap. 8.95 (ISBN 0-8158-0396-6). Chris Mass.
Pharmacist Trainee. Jack Rudman. (Career Examination Ser.: C-649). (Cloth bdg. avail. on request). pap. 14.00 (ISBN 0-8373-0649-3). Natl Learning.
Pharmacist's Answer Book. John M. Fischer et al. LC 85-51487. 267p. 1986. 35.00 (ISBN 0-87762-441-0). Technomic.
Pharmacist's Guide to the Misused & Abused Drugs in America: Prescription Drugs-Over-the-Counter Drugs-Designer Drugs. Ken Liska. 1988. (Collier); pap. 9.95 (ISBN 0-02-059340-6, Collier). Macmillan.
Pharmacists Prescription: Your Complete Guide to Over-The-Counter Remedies. F. James Grogan. LC 85-82609. 1987. 19.95 (ISBN 0-89256-311-7). Rawson Assocs.
Pharmacist's Prescription: Your Complete Guide to the Over-the-Counter Remedies that Work Best. F. James Grogan. 384p. 1988. pap. 4.95 (ISBN 0-380-70550-8). Avon.
Pharmacoangiography in the Diagnosis of Tumours. G. Vargha. 254p. 1981. 150.00x (ISBN 0-569-08708-2, Pub. by Collets (UK)). State Mutual Bk.
Pharmacoangiography in the Diagnosis of Tumors. Gy Vargha. 1982. cancelled 37.00 (ISBN 963-05-2912-2, Pub. by Akademiai Kaido Hungary). IPS.
Pharmacochemistry of One, Three-Indandiones. Ed. by W. T. Nauta & R. F. Rekker. (Pharmacochemistry Library: Vol. 3). 346p. 1981. 94.75 (ISBN 0-444-41976-4). Elsevier.
Pharmacodynamic Models of Selected Toxic Chemicals in Man. A. D. Smith & M. C. Thorne. 1986. lib. bdg. 109.00 (ISBN 0-85200-953-4, Pub. by MTP Pr England). Kluwer Academic.
Pharmacogenetics. David J. Gerrick. (Illus.). 1978. 20.00 (ISBN 0-916750-43-4). Dayton Labs.
Pharmacogenetics Principles & Pediatric Aspects. I. Szoraby. 240p. 1973. 56.00x (ISBN 0-569-08007-X, Pub. by Collets (UK)). State Mutual Bk.
Pharmacogenetics: Report. WHO Scientific Group. Geneva, 1972. (Technical Report Ser.: No. 524). (Also avail. in French & Spanish). 1973. pap. 1.60 (ISBN 92-4-120524-5). World Health.
Pharmacognosy. 12th ed. G. E. Trease & W. C. Evans. (Illus.). 1983. text ed. 67.95 (Pub. by Bailliere-Tindall). Saunders.
Pharmacognosy. 9th ed. Varro E. Tyler et al. LC 86-27400. (Illus.). 519p. 1988. text ed. 39.50 (ISBN 0-8121-1071-4). Lea & Febiger.
Pharmacographia Indica: A History of Principal Drugs of Vegetable Origin Met with in British India, 3 vols. William Dymock et al. 1978. Repr. of 1890 ed. Set. 225.00x (ISBN 0-89955-296-X, Pub. by Intl Bk Dist). Intl Spec Bk.
Pharmacokinetic Basis for Drug Treatment. Ed. by Leslie Z. Benet et al. 480p. 1984. text ed. 60.50 (ISBN 0-89004-874-6). Raven.
Pharmacokinetic Basis of Therapeutics. David J. Greenblatt & Richard I. Shader. (Illus.). 144p. 1985. pap. 25.95 (ISBN 0-7216-1148-6). Saunders.
Pharmacokinetics. Gibaldi & Perrier. (Drugs & the Pharmaceutical Sciences Ser.). 432p. 1982. 39.75 (ISBN 0-8247-1042-8). Dekker.
Pharmacokinetics. E. Gladtke et al. Tr. by P. J. Wilkinson from Ger. (Illus.). 1979. pap. 19.50 (ISBN 0-387-09183-1). Springer-Verlag.
Pharmacokinetics. Ed. by H. Schoenfeld et al. (Antibiotics and Chemotherapy: Vol. 25). (Illus.). 1977. 106.00 (ISBN 3-8055-2752-7). S Karger.
Pharmacokinetics: A Modern View. Ed. by Leslie Z. Benet et al. LC 84-15011. 548p. 1984. 75.00x (ISBN 0-306-41810-X, Plenum Pr). Plenum Pub.
Pharmacokinetics & Clinical Pharmacology of Beta-Blockers in Hypertension. Ed. by P. M. Galletti. (Cardiology: Vol. 64, Suppl. 1). (Illus.). 1979. pap. 22.00 (ISBN 3-8055-3061-7). S Karger.
Pharmacokinetics & Clinical Pharmacology of Cardiac Clyscosides. Ed. by K. Greeff. (Handobook of Experimental Pharmacology Ser.: Vol. 56). (Illus.). 394p. 1982. 135.00 (ISBN 0-387-10918-8). Springer-Verlag.
Pharmacokinetics & Pharmacodynamics of Psychoactive Drugs. Ed. by Gene Barnett & C. Nora Chang. LC 85-70734. (Illus.). 500p. 1985. text ed. 48.00 (ISBN 0-931890-20-9, Biomed Pubns). PSG Pub Co.
Pharmacokinetics & Pharmacodynamics, Vols. 1 & 2. pap. 33.00 (ISBN 0-9606488-8-7). H W Bks.
Pharmacokinetics & Pharmacodynamics, Vol. 1: Research Design & Analysis. Ed. by Randall B. Smith et al. LC 86-50775. (Illus.). viii, 104p. (Orig.). 1986. pap. 8.00 (ISBN 0-9606488-4-4). H W Bks.
Pharmacokinetics & Pharmacodynamics, Vol. 2: Current Problems, Potential Solutions. Ed. by Patricia D. Kroboth et al. LC 88-50443. (Illus.). x, 278p. 1988. pap. 28.00 (ISBN 0-9606488-7-9). H W Bks.
Pharmacokinetics: Classic & Modern. Ed. by J. H. Van Rossum & A. A. Maes. (Illus.). 63p. 1986. pap. 13.00 (ISBN 0-89573-542-3). VCH Pubs.
Pharmacokinetics for the Non-Mathematical. D. W. Bourne et al. 1986. lib. bdg. 43.00 (ISBN 0-85200-712-4, Pub. by MTP Pr England). Kluwer-Academic.
Pharmacokinetics II. Ed. by H. Schoenfeld. (Antibiotics & Chemotherapy: Vol. 31). (Illus.). xiv, 226p. 1981. 98.75 (ISBN 3-8055-2448-X). S Karger.
Pharmacokinetics: Mathematical & Statistical Approaches. Ed. by A. Pecile & A. Rescigno. LC 87-36043. (NATO ASI Series A, Life Sciences: Vol. 145). (Illus.). 358p. 1988. 65.00x (ISBN 0-306-42806-7, Plenum Pr). Plenum Pub.
Pharmacokinetics of Anticancer Agents in Humans. Ed. by M. A. Ames et al. 300p. 1984. 178.50 (ISBN 0-444-80518-4, I-021-84, Biomedical Pr). Elsevier.
Pharmacokinetics of Cardiovascular, Central Nervous System & Antimicrobial Drugs. Ed. by P. G. Welling & F. L. Tse. 472p. 1985. text ed. 71.00x (ISBN 0-85186-937-8, Pub. by Royal Soc Chem). Scholium Intl.
Pharmacokinetics of Psychoactive Drugs: Further Studies. Ed. by Louis Gottschalk. LC 79-9430. 140p. 1979. text ed. 35.00 (ISBN 0-88331-176-3). Luce.
Pharmacokinetics of Sulfonamides Revisited. T. B. Vree et al. (Antibiotics & Chemotherapy: Vol. 34). (Illus.). x, 220p. 1985. 113.50 (ISBN 3-8055-3949-5). S Karger.
Pharmacokinetics: Processes & Mathematics. Peter G. Welling. LC 86-20644. (ACS Monograph Ser.: No. 185). (Illus.). xiv, 268p. 1986. 59.95 (ISBN 0-8412-0967-7). Am CHemical.
Pharmacokinetics: Regulatory-Industrial-Academic Perspectives. Welling & Tse. (Drugs & the Pharmaceutical Sciences Ser.). 560p. 1988. 125.00 (ISBN 0-8247-7945-2). Dekker.
Pharmacokinetics: Theory & Methodology. Ed. by M. Rowland & G. T. Tucker. (International Encyclopedia of Pharmacology & Therapeutics Ser.: Section 122). 1986. 200.00 (ISBN 0-08-032020-1, PBL). Pergamon.
Pharmacologic Analysis of Drug-Receptor Interaction. Terrence P. Kenakin. (Illus.). 350p. 1987. text ed. 82.00 (ISBN 0-88167-277-7). Raven.
Pharmacologic Approach to the Critically Ill Patient. 2nd ed. Bart Chernow. 1988. 116.50 (ISBN 0-683-01521-4). Williams & Wilkins.
Pharmacologic Aspects of Aging. Ed. by Louis A. Pagliaro & Ann M. Pagliaro. LC 81-14096. (Illus.). 381p. 1983. 32.95 (ISBN 0-8016-3748-1). Mosby.
Pharmacologic Aspects of Nursing. Pagliaro. (Illus.). 1986. 52.50 (ISBN 0-8016-3747-3). Mosby.
Pharmacologic Basis of Patient Care. 5th ed. Mary K. Asperheim. (Illus.). 620p. 1985. 39.95 (ISBN 0-7216-2004-3); instr's. manual avail. (ISBN 0-7216-1229-6). Saunders.
Pharmacologic Principles of Cancer Treatment. Bruce A. Chabner. (Illus.). 480p. 1982. write for info. (ISBN 0-7216-2477-4). Saunders.
Pharmacological Adjuncts in Smoking Cessation. Ed. by John Grabowski & Sharon M. Hall. (National Institute on Drug Abuse Research Ser.: No. 53). (Illus.). 156p. 1985. pap. 3.50 (ISBN 0-318-18815-5, S/N 017-024-01266-1). USGPO.
Pharmacological & Behavioral Treatment: An Integrated Approach. Ed. by Michel Hersen. LC 84-11823. (Personality Processes Ser.). 400p. 1986. 40.00 (ISBN 0-471-87471-X, 1-341, Pub. by Wiley-Interscience). Wiley.
Pharmacological & Biochemical Properties of Drug Substances, Vol. 1. Ed. by Morton E. Goldberg. LC 77-88184. 413p. 1977. 15.00 (ISBN 0-917330-17-X). Am Pharm Assn.
Pharmacological & Biochemical Properties of Drug Substances, Vol. 2. Ed. by Morton E. Goldberg. 576p. 1977. 18.00 (ISBN 0-917330-25-0). Am Pharm Assn.
Pharmacological & Biochemical Properties of Drug Substances, Vol. 3. Ed. by Morton E. Goldberg. 495p. 1981. 19.50 (ISBN 0-917330-37-4). Am Pharm Assn.
Pharmacological & Chemical Synonyms: A Collection of Names of Drugs, Pesticides & Other Compounds Drawn from the Medical Literature of the World. 7th ed. Compiled by E. E. Marler. 514p. 1983. 81.00 (ISBN 0-444-90227-9, Excerpta Medica). Elsevier.
Pharmacological & Chemical Synonyms. 8th, rev. ed. E. E. Marler. 1984. 94.25. Elsevier.
Pharmacological & Therapeutic Aspects of Hypertension. Austin E. Doyle. LC 78-27898. 232p. 1980. Vol. 1, 224p. 72.00 (ISBN 0-8493-5385-8); Vol. 2, 256p. 69.00 (ISBN 0-8493-5386-6). CRC Pr.
Pharmacological Approach to the Treatment of Limb Ischemia. Ed. by John A. Spitell, Jr. (Symposia on Frontiers of Pharmacology Ser.). (Illus.). 203p. 1983. text ed. 45.00 (ISBN 0-943060-02-8). C P P.
Pharmacological Approaches to the Treatment of Brain & Spinal Cord Injury. Ed. by D. G. Stein & B. A. Sabel. LC 88-5942. (Illus.). 408p. 1988. 75.00x (ISBN 0-306-42732-X, Plenum Pr). Plenum Pub.
Pharmacological Aspects & Neurological Potentials of Calcium Entry Blockers: Journal: European Neurology. Ed. by A. Hartmann & P. A. Van Zwieten. (Vol. 25, Suppl. 1, 1986). 128p. 1986. pap. 30.75 (ISBN 3-8055-4365-4). S Karger.
Pharmacological Aspects of Heart Disease. Ed. by N. Dhalla et al. (Developments in Cardiovascular Medicine Ser.). 1987. lib. bdg. 75.95 (ISBN 0-89838-867-8, Pub. by Martinus Nijhoff Netherlands). Kluwer Academic.
Pharmacological Aspects of Nursing Care. Barry S. Reiss & Mary E. Melick. LC 83-71045. 1984. text ed. 30.95 (ISBN 0-8273-1746-8). Delmar.
Pharmacological Aspects of Nursing Care. 2nd ed. Barry S. Reiss & Mary E. Melick. 640p. 1987. pap. text ed. 30.95 (ISBN 0-8273-2690-4); instr's. guide 9.00 (ISBN 0-8273-2691-2). Delmar.
Pharmacological Basis of Anesthesiology: Clinical Pharmacology of New Analgesics & Anesthetics. Ed. by Mario Tiengo & Michael J. Cousins. (Progress in Anesthesiology Ser.: Vol. 3). 352p. 1983. text ed. 60.50 (ISBN 0-89004-973-4). Raven.
Pharmacological Basis of Nursing Practice. 2nd ed. Clark et al. 1986. 40.95 (ISBN 0-8016-0984-4). Mosby.
Pharmacological Calculations for Nurses: A Worktext. Peggy H. Batastini & Judy K. Davidson. 202p. 1985. pap. 16.50 (ISBN 0-471-81961-1). Wiley.
Pharmacological Control of Heart & Circulation: Proceedings of the Third Congress of the Hungarian Pharmacological Society, Budapest, 1979. Ed. by. Tardos et al. LC 80-41281. (Advances in Pharmacological Research & Practice Ser.: Vol. I). 445p. 1981. 110.00 (ISBN 0-08-026386-0). Pergamon.
Pharmacological Denervation & Glaucoma. Philip F. Hoyng. 1981. lib. bdg. 34.50 (ISBN 90-6193-802-3, Pub. by Junk Pubs Netherlands). Kluwer Academic.
Pharmacological Dictionary. Latin-Russian, Russian-Latin. 463p. (Lat. & Rus.). 1977. 39.95 (ISBN 0-686-92090-2, M-9078). French & Eur.
Pharmacological Effect of Lipids. Jon J. Kabara & American Oil Chemists Society. 216p. 1985. 24.00 (ISBN 0-318-12898-5); members 17.00 (ISBN 0-318-12899-3). Am Oil Chemists.
Pharmacological Effects of Lipids II. Ed. by Jon J. Kabara. 354p. 1985. 45.00 (ISBN 0-317-59766-3). Am Oil Chemists.
Pharmacological Facts & Figures. F. Lembeck et al. Tr. by H. Heller & D. R. Ferguson. LC 75-82689. (Heidelberg Science Library: Vol. 9). 1969. pap. 12.00 (ISBN 0-387-90010-1). Springer-Verlag.
Pharmacological Issues in Alcohol & Substance Abuse. Ed. by Barry Stimmel. LC 87-36672. (Advances in Alcohol & Substance Abuse Ser.). (Illus.). 80p. 1988. text ed. 14.95 (ISBN 0-86656-717-8). Haworth Pr.
Pharmacological Methods in Toxicology. Ed. by G. Zbinden & F. Gross. 1979. Pergamon.
Pharmacological Methods, Receptors & Chemotherapy. Ed. by M. J. Parnham & J. Bruinvels. (Monographs in Primatology: Vol. 5). 404p. 1986. 193.75 (ISBN 0-444-80752-7). Elsevier.
Pharmacological Protection of the Myocardium & Pharmacology of the Vascular System: Proceedings of the 4th Congress of the Hungarian Pharmacological Society, Budapest, 1985, Vol. 1. Ed. by L. Szekeres et al. LC 86-9349. 429p. 1987. 99.00 (ISBN 0-08-034190-X, PBL). Pergamon.
Pharmacological Treatment of Cardiovascular Diseases. Ed. by J. B. Kostis & E. A. DeFelice. (Other Medical Bks.: Vol. 21). 408p. 1986. 39.50 (ISBN 0-444-01033-5). Elsevier.
Pharmacological Treatments for Alcoholism. Ed. by Griffith Edwards & John Littleton. LC 83-26488. 400p. 1984. 49.95x (ISBN 0-416-00921-2, 5075). Routledge Chapman & Hall.
Pharmacologist. Jack Rudman. (Career Examination Ser.: C-581). (Cloth bdg. avail. on request). pap. 20.00 (ISBN 0-8373-0581-0). Natl Learning.
Pharmacology. 9th ed. John Gaddum. Ed. by J. F. Mitchell & A. S. Burgen. (Illus.). 1985. 17.95x (ISBN 0-19-261423-1). Oxford U Pr.
Pharmacology. Ed. by J. I. Moore. (Oklahoma Notes Ser.). xi, 247p. 1987. pap. 13.95 (ISBN 0-387-96332-4). Springer-Verlag.
Pharmacology. 2nd ed. (National Medical Series for Independent Study). 284p. 1987. pap. 20.00 (ISBN 0-471-85806-4). Wiley.
Pharmacology. 1988. pap. price not set (ISBN 0-471-85259-7). Wiley.
Pharmacology. M. J. Rand & C. Raper. (International Congress Ser.: Vol. 750). 210.75 (ISBN 0-444-80949-X). Elsevier.
Pharmacology. H. P. Rang & M. M. Dale. LC 86-12914. (Illus.). 736p. (Orig.). 1987. pap. text ed. 36.95 (ISBN 0-443-03407-9). Churchill.
Pharmacology. Robert S. Sloviter. Ed. by The Council on Resident Education in Obstetrics & Gynecology. (CREOG Basic Science Monograph in Obstrtrics & Gynecology Ser.). 160p. 1984. pap. 5.00 (ISBN 0-915473-00-3). Am Coll Obstetric.
Pharmacology: A Review. 2nd ed. B. G. Katzung & A. J. Trevor. (Illus.). 502p. 1987. 16.50 (ISBN 0-317-66375-5). Appleton & Lange.
Pharmacology: A Self-Instructional Approach. Alberta Tedford & Helen Van Hoozer. (Illus.). 1979. text ed. 34.95 (ISBN 0-07-063385-1). McGraw.
Pharmacology: An Introduction to Drugs. Michael C. Gerald. (Illus.). 720p. 1981. 29.95 (ISBN 0-13-662098-1). Appleton & Lange.
Pharmacology: An Introductory Text. 6th ed. Mary K. Asperheim. (Illus.). 288p. 1987. pap. 20.95 (ISBN 0-7216-2152-X); instr's. manual avail. (ISBN 0-03-013298-3). Saunders.
Pharmacology & Applications of Chinese Materia Medica, Vol. II. Ed. by H. M. Chang & P. P. But. Tr. by S. C. Yao et al from Chinese. 556p. 1987. 68.00 (ISBN 9971-50-167-8). World Scientific Pub.
Pharmacology & Applications of Chinese Materia Medica, Vol. 1. Ed. by H. M. Chang & P. P. But. LC 86-9278. 792p. 1986. 78.00 (ISBN 9971-50-121-X). World Scientific Pub.
Pharmacology & Biochemistry of Psychiatric Disorders. A. Richard Green & David W. Costain. 217p. 1981. 39.95x (ISBN 0-471-09998-8); pap. 21.95 (ISBN 0-471-10000-5). Wiley.
Pharmacology & Clinical Uses of Inhibitors of Hormone Secretion & Action. B. J. Furr & A. E. Wakeling. (Illus.). 510p. 1986. 68.00 (ISBN 0-7020-1136-3, Bailliere-Tindall). Saunders.
Pharmacology & Drug Therapy in Nursing. 3rd ed. Morton J. Rodman & Amy M. Karch. LC 64-2978. (Illus.). 1264p. 1985. text ed. 39.95 (ISBN 0-397-54356-5, Nursing). Lippincott.
Pharmacology & Endocrinology of Sexual Function. Ed. by J. M. Sitsen. (Handbook of Sexology Ser.: Vol. 6). 570p. 1987. 180.50 (ISBN 0-444-90460-3). Elsevier.
Pharmacology & Medications. 4th ed. Eloise Worley. LC 82-1502. (Illus.). 282p. 1982. pap. text ed. 11.95x (ISBN 0-8036-9593-4). Davis Co.

Pharmacology & Pharmaco-Therapeutics. rev. ed. V. Iswaran & M. N. Guruswami. 1979. text ed. 45.00x (ISBN 0-7069-0803-1, Pub. by Vikas India). Advent NY.

Pharmacology & Physiology in Anesthetic Practice. Stoelting. LC 65-9350. 1987. text ed. 69.50 (ISBN 0-397-50771-2, Lippincott Medical). Lippincott.

Pharmacology & the Future of Man: Proceedings, 5 vols. International Congress on Pharmacology, 5th, San Francisco, 1972. Incl. Vol. 1. Drug Abuse & Contraception. Ed. by J. Cochin. 252p. 48.00 (ISBN 3-8055-1470-0); Vol. 2. Toxicological Problems. Ed. by T. A. Loomis. 204p. 39.50 (ISBN 3-8055-1471-9); Vol. 3. Problems of Therapy. Ed. by G. T. Okita & G. H. Acheson. 400p. 77.50 (ISBN 3-8055-1472-7); Vol. 4. Brain, Nerves, & Synapses. Ed. by F. E. Bloom & G. H. Acheson. 430p. 72.75 (ISBN 3-8055-1473-5); Vol. 5. Cellular Mechanisms. Ed. by R. A. Maxwell & G. H. Acheson. 380p. 69.50 (ISBN 3-8055-1474-3). 1973. Set. 238.00 (ISBN 3-8055-1387-9). S Karger.

Pharmacology & the Nursing Process. 2nd ed. Gordon Johnson & Kathryn J. Hannah. 744p. 1986. pap. 31.95 (ISBN 0-920513-01-8); instr's. manual avail. Saunders.

Pharmacology & Therapeutics for Dentistry. 3rd ed. Neidle & Yagiela. (Illus.). 850p. 1989. text ed. 44.95 (ISBN 0-8016-3262-5). Mosby.

Pharmacology & Therapeutics for Dentistry. 2nd ed. Enid A. Neidle et al. LC 80-10522. (Illus.). 770p. 1984. 49.95 (ISBN 0-8016-3743-0). Mosby.

Pharmacology & Therapeutics in Emergency Care. Stephen Margolis & Jonathan Wasserberger. LC 82-122. (Illus.). 410p. (Orig.). 1982. pap. 16.95x (ISBN 0-940122-03-0). Mosby Multi-Media.

Pharmacology & Toxicology of Naturally Occurring Toxins, 2 vols. Ed. by H. Raskova. LC 77-130797. 1971. Vol. 2. 93.00 (ISBN 0-08-016798-5). Pergamon.

Pharmacology & Toxicology of Proteins. Ed. by John C. Holcenberg & Jeffery L. Winkelhake. LC 87-22654. (UCLA Symposia on Molecular & Cellular Biology Ser.: Vol. 65). 404p. 1987. 70.00 (ISBN 0-8451-2664-4, 2664). A R Liss.

Pharmacology: Drug Actions & Reactions. 3rd ed. Ruth R. Levine. (Illus.). 1983. pap. 21.00 (ISBN 0-316-52222-8). Little.

Pharmacology: Drug Actions & Reactions. 3rd ed. Ruth R. Levine. 526p. 1983. pap. text ed. 21.00. Little.

Pharmacology: Drug Therapy & Nursing Considerations. 2nd ed. Roger T. Malseed. LC 64-4016. 1985. 25.95 (ISBN 0-397-54460-X, Lippincott Nursing). Lippincott.

Pharmacology for Medical Assistants. E. A. Watts. 100p. 1986. pap. text ed. 12.95x (ISBN 0-935920-28-5). Natl Pub Black Hills.

Pharmacology for Nurses. 5th ed. James Connechen et al. 384p. 1983. pap. 11.95 (ISBN 0-7216-0803-5). Saunders.

Pharmacology for the Dental Hygienist. 2nd ed. Ed. by Austin H. Kutscher et al. LC 81-19395. (Illus.). 389p. 1982. text ed. 19.50 (ISBN 0-8121-0802-7). Lea & Febiger.

Pharmacology for the Elderly: A Nurse's Guide to Quality Care. Majorie Crow. (Nursing Education Ser.). 1984. pap. text ed. 16.95x (ISBN 0-8077-2752-0). Tchrs Coll.

Pharmacology for the Health Professional. Daniel E. Becker. 1985. text ed. 27.95 (ISBN 0-8359-5531-1); instr's. manual avail. (ISBN 0-8359-5532-X). Appleton & Lange.

Pharmacology IBM. Pogue. 1987. 546.00 (ISBN 0-8016-3973-5). Mosby.

Pharmacology in Medicine: Principles & Practice. Ed. by Sachin N. Pradhan et al. 1100p. 1986. text ed. 55.00 (ISBN 0-9617129-0-2). SP Press Intl.

Pharmacology in Nursing. 16th ed. Anne B. Hahn et al. (Illus.). 1985. 42.95 (ISBN 0-8016-2034-1). Mosby.

Pharmacology of Adrenal Cortical Hormones. Ed. by Gordon N. Gill. LC 78-40135. 1979. 79.00 (ISBN 0-08-019619-5). Pergamon.

Pharmacology of Adrenoceptors: Satellite Symposium of the 9th IUPHAR Congress. E. Szabadi et al. LC 85-11260. (Illus.). 352p. 1985. lib. bdg. 59.00 (ISBN 0-89573-445-1). VCH Pubs.

Pharmacology of Alcohol. Dora B. Goldstein. (Illus.). 1983. text ed. 19.95x (ISBN 0-19-503111-3); pap. text ed. 18.95x (ISBN 0-19-503112-1). Oxford U Pr.

Pharmacology of Anesthetic Drugs: A Syllabus for Students & Clinicians. 5th ed. John Adriani. (Illus.). 320p. 1977. 33.00 (ISBN 0-398-00013-1). C C Thomas.

Pharmacology of Antiarrhythmic Agents. Ed. by L. Szekeres. (Intermnational Encyclopedia of Pharmacology & Therapeutics Ser.: Section 105). (Illus.). 328p. 1981. 115.00 (ISBN 0-08-025897-2). Pergamon.

Pharmacology of Antihypertensive Drugs. P. A. Van Zwieten. (Handbook of Hypertension Ser.: Vol. 3). 1984. 133.75 (ISBN 0-444-90313-5, I-527-83). Elsevier.

Pharmacology of Asthma. Ed. by John Morley & Kim Rainsford. (Agents & Actions Supplements: Vol. 13). 228p. 1983. 43.00 (ISBN 0-8176-1503-2). Birkhauser.

Pharmacology of Bacterial Toxins. Ed. by F. Dorner & J. Drews. (International Encyclopedia of Pharmacology & Therapeutics: Section 119). (Illus.). 790p. 1986. 235.00 (ISBN 0-08-031988-2, PBL). Pergamon.

Pharmacology of Benzodiazepines. Ed. by Earl Usdin et al. 670p. 1983. lib. bdg. 98.00 (ISBN 0-89573-179-7). VCH Pubs.

Pharmacology of Benzopyrone Derivatives & Related Compounds. Miklos Gabor. (Illus.). xviii, 254p. 1986. 39.00 (ISBN 963-05-4124-6, Pub. by Akademiai Kiado Budapest). Stillman Pubs.

Pharmacology of Central Synapses. V. V. Zakusov. (Illus.). 1980. 85.00 (ISBN 0-08-020549-6). Pergamon.

Pharmacology of Cerebral Ischemia: Proceedings of the International Symposium, Marburg, FRG, July 16-17, 1986. Ed. by J. Krieglstein. 450p. 1986. 138.50 (ISBN 0-444-80845-0). Elsevier.

Pharmacology of Eating Disorders: Theoretical & Clinical Developments. Ed. by Michele O. Carruba & John E. Blundell. 192p. 1986. text ed. 40.00 (ISBN 0-88167-201-7). Raven.

Pharmacology of Estrogens. Ed. by R. R. Chaudhury. (International Encyclopedia of Pharmacology & Therapeutics: Section. 106). (Illus.). 180p. 1981. 67.00 (ISBN 0-08-026869-2). Pergamon.

Pharmacology of Extrapyramidal Movement Disorders. Ed. by H. L. Klawans, Jr. (Monographs in Neural Sciences: Vol. 2). 1973. 32.75 (ISBN 3-8055-1421-2). S Karger.

Pharmacology of Fluorides. Ed. by F. A. Smith. (Handbook of Experimental Pharmacology: Vol. 20). (Illus.). 1966-70. Pt. 1. 103.30 (ISBN 0-387-03537-0); Pt. 2. 97.40 (ISBN 0-387-04846-4). Springer-Verlag.

Pharmacology of Ganglionic Transmission. Ed. by D. A. Kharkevich. LC 79-9406. (Handbook of Experimental Pharmacology: Vol. 53). (Illus.). 1979. 144.00 (ISBN 0-387-09592-6). Springer-Verlag.

Pharmacology of Histamine Receptors. C. Ganellin. (Illus.). 544p. 1982. 102.50 (ISBN 0-7236-0589-0). PSG Pub Co.

Pharmacology of Hydroxyehty Starch: Use in Therapy & Blood Banking. John M. Mishler, IV. (Illus.). 1982. text ed. 45.00x (ISBN 0-19-261239-5). Oxford U Pr.

Pharmacology of Immunoregulation: Present Concepts As a Basis for the Development of Immunopharmacological Agents. Ed. by G. H. Werner & F. Floc'h. 1979. 89.00 (ISBN 0-12-745650-3). Acad Pr.

Pharmacology of Inflammation. Ed. by I. L. Bonta & M. A. Bray. (Handbook of Inflammation Ser.: No. 5). 1985. 138.50 (ISBN 0-444-90312-7, Excerpta Medica). Elsevier.

Pharmacology of Intestinal Permeation I. Ed. by T. Z. Csaky. (Handbook of Experimental Pharmacology Ser.: Vol. 70, Pt. 1). (Illus.). 800p. 1984. 241.70 (ISBN 0-387-13100-0). Springer-Verlag.

Pharmacology of Intestinal Permeation 2. Ed. by T. Z. Csaky. (Handbook of Experimental Pharmacology Ser.: Vol. 70, Pt. 2). (Illus.). 640p. 1984. 240.00 (ISBN 0-387-13101-9). Springer Verlag.

Pharmacology of Lymphocytes. Ed. by M. A. Bray & J. Morley. (Handbook of Experimental Pharmacology Ser.: Vol. 85). (Illus.). 700p. 1988. 412.00 (ISBN 0-387-18609-3). Springer-Verlag.

Pharmacology of Marihuana, 2 vols. Ed. by Monique C. Braude & Stephen Szara. LC 75-14562. (National Institute on Drug Abuse Monograph). 901p. 1976. Set. 112.00 (ISBN 0-89004-067-2). Raven.

Pharmacology of Nerve & Muscle in Tissue Culture. Alan L. Harvey. LC 83-23878. 260p. 1984. 53.00 (ISBN 0-8451-3011-0). A R Liss.

Pharmacology of Psychotherapeutic Drugs. Franz Von Bruecke et al. Tr. by E. B. Sigg. (Heidelberg Science Library: Vol. 8). 1969. pap. 12.00 (ISBN 0-387-90009-8). Springer-Verlag.

Pharmacology of Reproduction, Vol. 2. Ed. by E. Diczfalusy. LC 67-19416. 1968. 50.00 (ISBN 0-08-012368-6). Pergamon.

Pharmacology of Respiratory Care. Bruce E. Lehnert & E. Neil Schachter. LC 79-28446. (Illus.). 344p. 1980. pap. text ed. 24.95 (ISBN 0-8016-2921-7). Mosby.

Pharmacology of Steroid Contraceptive Drugs. Ed. by S. Garattini & H. W. Berendes. LC 77-6100. (Monographs of the Mario Negri Institute for Pharmacological Research). 391p. 1977. 65.00 (ISBN 0-89004-187-3). Raven.

Pharmacology of the Eye. Ed. by M. L. Sears. (Handbook of Experimental Pharmacology Ser.: Vol. 69). 784p. 1984. 245.00 (ISBN 0-387-12578-7). Springer-Verlag.

Pharmacology of the States of Alertness: Proceedings. International Congress of Pharmacology, 7th, Paris, 1978. Satellite Symposium. Ed. by P. Passcuant & I. Oswald. (Illus.). 1979. 63.00 (ISBN 0-08-023753-3). Pergamon.

Pharmacology of the Urinary Tract: Clinical Practice in Urology. Ed. by M. Caine. (Illus.). 180p. 1984. 52.50 (ISBN 0-387-13238-4). Springer-Verlag.

Pharmacology of Thermoregulation: Proceedings of a Satellite Symposium. International Congress on Pharmacology, 5th, San Francisco, 1972. Ed. by E. Schoenbaum & P. Lomax. 300p. 1973. 125.50 (ISBN 3-8055-1391-7). S Karger.

Pharmacology: PreTest Self-Assessment & Review. 4th ed. Ed. by Joseph DiPalma et al. 192p. 1985. pap. 14.95 (ISBN 0-07-051945-5). McGraw-Pretest.

Pharmacology Review. Sydney Ellis. LC 79-13485. (Medical Review Ser.). 1980. pap. 17.95 (ISBN 0-668-04108-0). Appleton & Lange.

Pharmacology: Self Assessment Questions for Students. Rosemarie Einstein. 168p. 1985. pap. text ed. 13.95 (ISBN 0-409-49054-7). Butterworth.

Pharmacology Textbook for Nurses. Spratto. 1987. write for info. (ISBN 0-471-08733-5). Wiley.

Pharmacotherapeutics: A Nursing Process Approach. Merrily K. Mathewson. LC 85-10208. (Illus.). 1409p. 1986. text ed. 44.95 (ISBN 0-8036-5921-0). Davis Co.

Pharmacotherapeutics in Primary Care. M. F. Ivey. 1984. 40.00 (ISBN 0-444-00739-3). Elsevier.

Pharmacotherapy & Mental Retardation. Ed. by Kenneth D. Gadow & Alan D. Poling. 400p. (Orig.). 1988. pap. text ed. 24.50 (ISBN 0-316-30149-3, 301493). College-Hill.

Pharmacotherapy of Affective Disorders: Theory & Practice. Ed. by W. G. Dewhurst & G. B. Baker. 500p. 1985. 55.00x (ISBN 0-8147-1777-2). NYU Pr.

Pharmacotherapy of Renal Disease & Hypertension: Vol. 17, CIN. Bennett & McCarron. 1987. 75.00 (ISBN 0-443-08541-2). Churchill.

Pharmacy Aide. Jack Rudman. (Career Examination Ser.: C-2576). (Cloth bdg. avail. on request). pap. 16.00 (ISBN 0-8373-2576-5). Natl Learning.

Pharmacy & the Law. 2nd ed. Carl DeMarco. LC 84-2991. 464p. 1984. 57.50 (ISBN 0-89443-591-4). Aspen Pub.

Pharmacy Assistant. Jack Rudman. (Career Examination Ser.: C-1388). (Cloth bdg. avail. on request). pap. 16.00 (ISBN 0-8373-1388-0). Natl Learning.

Pharmacy Assistant II. Jack Rudman. (Career Examination Ser.: C-2943). (Cloth bdg. avail. on request). pap. 16.00 (ISBN 0-8373-2943-4). Natl Learning.

Pharmacy College Admission Test (PCAT) D. R. Gourley. 208p. (Orig.). 1983. pap. 12.95 (ISBN 0-668-05682-7). Arco.

Pharmacy College Admission Test (PCAT) Jack Rudman. (Admission Test Ser.: ATS-52). (Cloth bdg. avail. on request). pap. 15.00 (ISBN 0-8373-5052-2). Natl Learning.

Pharmacy College Admission Test Student Guide. David M. Tarlow. (Illus.). 1987. pap. 14.95 (ISBN 0-931572-05-3). Datar Pub.

Pharmacy, Drugs & Medical Care. 4th ed. Smith & Knapp. (Illus.). 284p. 1986. pap. text ed. 24.95 (ISBN 0-683-07762-7). Williams & Wilkins.

Pharmacy Education & Careers: The APhA Resource Book. Ed. by Vicki L. Meade. 88p. 1988. pap. 15.00 (ISBN 0-917330-59-5). Am Pharm Assn.

Pharmacy Examination Review, Vol. 31. 9th ed. R. J. Gerraughty. 287p. 1986. pap. 19.50 (ISBN 0-444-01025-4). Elsevier.

Pharmacy Inspector. Jack Rudman. (Career Examination Ser.: C-2536). (Cloth bdg. avail. on request). pap. 20.00 (ISBN 0-8373-2536-6). Natl Learning.

Pharmacy, Law & Ethics. 3rd ed. Dale. 604p. 1983. 26.00 (ISBN 0-85369-168-1, Pub. by Pharmaceutical Pr England). Rittenhouse.

Pharmacy Law Cases & Materials. Helen Wetherbee & Bruce D. White. LC 80-14608. 592p. 1980. text ed. 36.50 (ISBN 0-8299-2091-9). West Pub.

Pharmacy Manual: Policies, Procedures & Quality Assurance Provisions for Long-Term Care Facilities. Date not set. price not set (ISBN 0-938485-03-2). Beverly Found.

Pharmacy Museums & Collections in the United States & Canada. rev. ed. George Griffenhagen & Ernst Stieb. 130p. 1988. pap. price not set. Am Inst Hist Pharm.

Pharmacy Review. 3rd. ed. Walter Singer. 213p. (Orig.). 1984. pap. 15.95 (ISBN 0-8385-7840-3). Appleton & Lange.

Pharmacy Services in Correctional Institutions. 168p. Date not set. 7.00. NCCHC.

Pharmacy-Thermomechanics-Elastomers-Telechelics. K. Dusek. (Advances in Polymer Science Ser.: Vol. 76). (Illus.). 200p. 1986. 54.00 (ISBN 0-387-15830-8). Springer-Verlag.

Pharmakotherapie der Depression: Bedeutung von Serotonin und Melatonin. Ed. by P. Kielholz & B. Muller-Oerlinghausen. (Advances in Pharmacotherapy Ser.: Band 3). (Illus.). x, 150p. 1987. 92.75 (ISBN 3-8055-4539-8). S Karger.

Pharmer's Almanac. Anthony B. Radcliffe et al. (Illus., Orig.). 1985. pap. 8.95 (ISBN 0-910223-05-X). MAC Pub.

Pharo Village. John P. Marwitt. (Utah Anthropological Papers: No. 91). Repr. of 1968 ed. 20.00 (ISBN 0-404-60691-1). AMS Pr.

Pharoahs & Mortals: Egyptian Art in the Middle Kingdom. FitzWilliam Museum Staff. Compiled by Janine Bourriau. (Illus.). 148p. 1988. 49.50 (ISBN 0-521-35319-X); pap. 17.95 (ISBN 0-521-35846-9). Cambridge U Pr.

Pharos & Pharillon. E. M. Forster. LC 62-1459. 101p. 1980. pap. 4.95 (ISBN 0-916870-28-6). Creative Arts Bk.

Pharos, the Egyptian. Guy Boothby. Ed. by R. Reginald & Douglas Menville. LC 75-46256. (Supernatural & Occult & Fiction Ser.). (Illus.). 1976. Repr. of 1899 ed. lib. bdg. 30.00x (ISBN 0-405-08115-4). Ayer Co Pubs.

Pharyngitis: Management in an Era of Declining Rheumatic Fever. Ed. by Stanford T. Shulman. 320p. 1984. 36.95 (ISBN 0-275-91452-6, C1452). Praeger.

Phase & Caste Determination in Insects - Endocrine Aspects: Proceedings of the International Congress of Entomology, 15th, Washington, D.C., 1976. Ed. by Martin Luscher. 1976. 37.00 (ISBN 0-08-021256-5). Pergamon.

Phase & Flow Behavior in Petroleum Production. E. J. Hoffman. LC 81-68122. (Illus.). 915p. 1981. 225.00x (ISBN 0-9601552-3-6). Energon Co.

Phase Behavior. (SPE Reprint Ser.). 304p. 1981. 24.00x (ISBN 0-317-36509-6, 30515). Soc Petrol Engineers.

Phase Conjugation, Beam Combining, & Diagnostics. Ed. by Fisher & Abramowitz. 224p. 1987. 50.00 (ISBN 0-89252-774-9, 739). SPIE.

Phase Conjugation of Laser Emission. Ed. by N. G. Basov. (Proceedings of the Lebedev Physics Institute of the Academy of Sciences of the U. S. S. R. Ser.: Vol. 172). 240p. 1987. text ed. 76.00 (ISBN 0-941743-07-1). Nova Sci Pubs.

Phase Contrast & Interference Microscopy. K. F. Ross. 1969. 26.00 (ISBN 0-312-60410-6). St Martin.

Phase Diagram for Ceramists, Vol. II. Ed. by Ernest M. Levin & Howard F. McMurdie. 625p. 1969. 80.00 (ISBN 0-916094-05-7). Am Ceramic.

Phase Diagram for Ceramists 1964 Basic Volume, Vol. 1. Ernest M. Levin et al. (Illus.). 80.00 (ISBN 0-916094-04-9). Am Ceramic.

Phase Diagrams: A Literature Source Book, 2 vols. J. Wisniak. (Physical Sciences Data Ser.: Vol. 10). 2102p. 1981. Set. 387.00 (ISBN 0-444-41981-0). Elsevier.

Phase Diagrams: A Literature Source Book, Supplement 1. J. Wisniak. (Physical Sciences Data Ser.: No. 27). 1036p. 1986. 292.00 (ISBN 0-444-42613-2). Elsevier.

Phase Diagrams, Alloy Phase Stability & Thermodynamic Aspects of Noble Metal Alloys. Ed. by T. B. Massalski & L. H. Bennett. cancelled. Metal Soc.

Phase Diagrams & Thermodynamic Properties of Ternary Copper-Metal Systems. University of Wisconsin-Milwaukee Staff. (INCRA Monograph). 701p. 1979. 30.00 (ISBN 0-317-42806-3). Intl Copper.

Phase Diagrams & Thermodynamic Properties of Ternary Copper-Sulfur-Metal Systems. University of Wisconsin-Milwaukee. (INCRA Mononograph). 191p. 1979. 30.00 (ISBN 0-317-42814-4). Intl Copper.

Phase Diagrams for Ceramists, Vol. III. Ed. by Ernest M. Levin & Howard F. McMurdie. 513p. 1975. 80.00 (ISBN 0-916094-06-5). Am Ceramic.

Phase Diagrams for Ceramists. Ed. by C. G. Messa et al. (Bibliographic Update for Oxides & Salts Through January 1st, 1984). 182p. 1986. 24.00 (ISBN 0-916094-80-4). Am Ceramic.

Phase Diagrams for Ceramists, Vol. V. Ed. by R. S. Roth. 1983. 80.00 (ISBN 0-916094-47-2). Am Ceramic.

Phase Diagrams for Ceramists, Vol. VI. Robert S. Roth. 528p. 1987. 125.00 (ISBN 0-916094-90-1). Am Ceramic.

Phase Diagrams for Ceramists, Vol IV, 1981. Ed. by R. S. Roth. (Illus.). 80.00 (ISBN 0-916094-40-5). Am Ceramic.

Phase Diagrams for Ceramists: Cumulative Index. Ed. by Geraldine Smith. 1984. 15.00 (ISBN 0-916094-60-X). Am Ceramic.

Phase Diagrams: Materials Science & Technology. Ed. by Allen Alper. Incl. Part 1. Theory, Principles & Techniques of Phase Diagrams. 1970. 77.00 (ISBN 0-12-053201-8); Part 2. Use of Phase Diagrams in Metals, Refractories, Ceramics, Glass & Electronic Materials. 1970. 77.00 (ISBN 0-12-053202-6); Part 3. Use of Phase Diagrams in Electronic Materials & Glass Technology. 1970. 77.00 (ISBN 0-12-053203-4); Pt. 4. Use of Phase Diagrams in Technical Materials. 1976. 72.00 (ISBN 0-12-053204-2). (Refractory Materials Ser: Vol. 6). Acad Pr.

Phase Diagrams: Materials Science & Technology Vol. 5: Crystal Chemistry, Stoichiometry, Spinodal Decomposition, Properties of Inorganic Phases. Ed. by Allan M. Alper. (Refractory Materials Ser.: Vol. 6-V). 1978. 91.50 (ISBN 0-12-053205-0). Acad Pr.

Phase Diagrams of Titanium Alloys. E. K. Molchanova. 320p. 1965. text ed. 65.00x (ISBN 0-7065-0575-1, Pub. by Keter Pub Jerusalem). Coronet Bks.

Phase Equilibria. Arnold Reisman. (Physical Chemistry Ser: Vol. 19). 1970. 98.50 (ISBN 0-12-586350-0). Acad Pr.

Phase Equilibria - Collected Research Papers. 113p. 1953. pap. 24.00 (ISBN 0-8169-0297-6, S-6). Am Inst Chem Eng.

Phase Equilibria - Pittsburgh & Houston. 138p. 1952. pap. 22.00 (ISBN 0-8169-0298-4, S-2). Am Inst Chem Eng.

Phase Equilibria & Fluid Properties in the Chemical Industry: Estimation & Correlation. Ed. by Truman S. Storvick & Stanley I. Sandler. LC 77-13804. (ACS Symposium Ser.: No. 60). 1977. 49.95 (ISBN 0-8412-0393-8). Am Chemical.

Phase Equilibria & Fluid Properties in the Chemical Industry: Proceedings of the International Conference, 2nd, Berlin, 1980, Pts. 1 & 2. European Federation of Chemical Engineering Staff. (EFCE Publication Ser.: No. 11). 1012p. 1980. text ed. 125.00x (ISBN 3-921567-35-1, Pub. by Dechema Germany). Scholium Intl.

Phase Equilibria in Binary Halides. Ed. by V. I. Posypaiko & E. A. Alekseeva. Tr. by B. Indyk from Rus. LC 87-29267. (Illus.). 496p. 1988. 115.00x (ISBN 0-306-65211-0, IFI-Plenum). Plenum Pub.

Phase Equilibria in Chemical Engineering. Stanley M. Walas. (Illus.). 736p. 1984. text ed. 54.95 (ISBN 0-409-95162-5). Butterworth.

Phase Equilibrium in Process Design. Harold R. Null. LC 78-23527. 288p. 1980. Repr. of 1970 ed. lib. bdg. 21.50 (ISBN 0-88275-808-X). Krieger.

Phase II in Review: The Price Commission Experience. Robert F. Lanzillotti & Mary T. Hamilton. LC 75-5164. (Brookings Institution Studies in Wage-Price Policty). pap. 55.80 (ISBN 0-317-26731-0, 2025387). Bks Demand UMI.

Phase-Locked Loops. rev. ed. Heath Company Staff. (Electronic Technology Ser.). (Illus.). 268p. 1979. looseleaf with experimental pts. 49.95 (ISBN 0-87119-025-7); pap. text ed. 18.95 (ISBN 0-87119-023-0); tchr's. ed 9.95 (ISBN 0-87119-024-9). Heathkit-Zenith Ed.

Phase-Locked Loops. Ed. by W. C. Lindsey & C. M. Chie. 352p. 1985. 46.20 (ISBN 0-87942-200-9, PC01917). Inst Electrical.

Phase-Locked Loops & Their Application. Ed. by William C. Lindsey & Mark K. Simon. LC 85-19725. 1978. 47.45 (ISBN 0-87942-101-0, PC00984). Inst Electrical.

Phase-Locked Loops: Application to Coherent Receiver Design. Alain A. Blanchard. LC 75-30941. 389p. 1976. 54.95x (ISBN 0-471-07941-3, Pub. by Wiley-Interscience). Wiley.

Phase Noise in Signal Sources (Theory & Application) rev. ed. W. P. Robins. Ed. by J. E. Flood & C. J. Hughes. 336p. 1984. pap. 50.00 (ISBN 0-86341-026-X, TER09). Inst Elect Eng.

Phase One Evaluation of Pretrial Delay Release Programs, 7 vols. National Center for State Courts Staff. 1976. Vol. I, 84 pgs. manuscript 5.04 (MAB-080); Vol. II, 33 pgs. manuscript 19.98 (MAB-081); Vol. III, 51 pgs. manuscript 3.06 (MAB-082); Vol. IV, 48 pgs. manuscript 2.88 (MAB-083); Vol. V, 35 pgs. manuscript 2.10 (MAB-084); Vol. VI, 33 pgs. manuscript 1.98 (MAB-085); Vol. VII, 54 pgs. manuscript 3.24 (MAB-086). Natl Ctr St Courts.

Phase Separation in Glass. Ed. by O. V. Mazurin & E. A. Poraikoshits. 1985. 116.00 (ISBN 0-444-86810-0). Elsevier.

Phase Space Approach to Nuclear Dynamics: Proceedings to the Topical Meeting on Phase Space Approach to Nuclear Dynamics, Sept. 3-Oct. 4, 1985, Trieste, Italy. Ed. by M. Di Toro et al. 812p. 1986. 105.00 (ISBN 9971-50-015-9). World Scientific Pub.

Phase Stability & Phase Transformations. Ed. by R. Krishnan. (Materials Science Forum Ser.: Vol. 3). 474p. 1985. pap. text ed. 80.00x (ISBN 0-87849-535-5). Trans Tech.

Phase Stability in High Temperature Alloys. Ed. by V. Guttman. (Illus.). vii, 155p. 1981. 57.75 (ISBN 0-85334-946-0, Pub. by Elsevier Applied Sci England). Elsevier.

Phase Theory: The Thermodynamics of Heterogeneous Equilibria. H. A. Oonk. (Studies in Modern Thermodynamics: Vol. 3). 270p. 1981. 100.00 (ISBN 0-444-42019-3). Elsevier.

Phase Transfer Catalysis. 2nd ed. Ekkehard Dehmlow & Sigrid Dehmlow. Ed. by Hans F. Ebel. (Monographs in Modern Chemistry: Vol. 11). (Illus.). xi, 386p. 1983. 75.00 (ISBN 0-89573-035-9). VCH Pubs.

Phase-Transfer Catalysis: New Chemistry, Catalysts, & Applications. Ed. by Charles M. Starks. LC 86-25957. (ACS Symposium Ser.: No. 326). (Illus.). ix, 184p. 1986. 36.95 (ISBN 0-8412-1007-1). Am Chemical.

Phase Transformation in Ferrous Alloys. Ed. by A. R. Marder & J. I. Goldstein. LC 84-61582. (Illus.). 411p. 1984. 38.00 (ISBN 0-89520-481-9). Metal Soc.

Phase Transformations. Ed. by E. C. Aifantis & J. Gittus. 272p. 1986. 84.75 (ISBN 0-85334-425-6). Elsevier.

Phase Transformations, 2 Vols. 342p. 1979. pap. text ed. 56.00x (ISBN 0-901462-04-7, Pub. by Inst Metals). Brookfield Pub Co.

Phase Transformations & Material Instabilities in Solids. Ed. by Morton E. Gurtin. (Mathematics Research Center Symposium Ser.). 1985. 29.95 (ISBN 0-12-309770-3). Acad Pr.

Phase Transformations & Related Phenomena in Steels: Papers Presented at the E. C. Bain Seminar of the American Society for Metals. American Society for Metals Staff. LC 72-95849. pap. 24.50 (ISBN 0-317-27682-4, 2019496). Bks Demand UMI.

Phase Transformations During Irradiation. Ed. by Frank V. Nolfi, Jr. (Illus.). 363p. 1983. 83.00 (ISBN 0-85334-179-6, Pub. by Elsevier Applied Sci England). Elsevier.

Phase Transformations in Crystalline & Amorphous Alloys. Ed. by Barry L. Mordike. (Illus.). 260p. 1983. lib. bdg. 45.00x (ISBN 3-88355-060-4, Pub. by DGM Metallurgy Information). IR Pubns.

Phase Transformations in Crystalline & Amorphous Alloys: Proceedings. Ed. by B. L. Morkike. 266p. 1983. cancelled 70.00 (ISBN 3-88355-060-4, Pub. by Aluminium W Germany). IPS.

Phase Transformations in Metals Alloys. Porter. pap. 27.95 (ISBN 0-317-64236-7). Van Nos Reinhold.

Phase Transformations in Metals & Alloys. D. Porter & K. Easterling. 1981. pap. 29.95 (ISBN 0-442-30440-4). Van Nos Reinhold.

Phase Transformations in Solids. T. Tsakalakos. (Materials Research Society Ser.: Vol. 21). 1984. 132.75 (ISBN 0-444-00901-9). Elsevier.

Phase Transition & Critical Phenomena, Vol. 12. Ed. by C. Domb & J. L. Lebowitz. 498p. 1988. 100.00 (ISBN 0-12-220312-7). Acad Pr.

Phase Transitions - Lectures On. A. Shumovsky & X. Yukalov. 450p. 1988. 78.00 (ISBN 9971-50-492-8); pap. 44.00 (ISBN 9971-50-474-X). World Scientific Pub.

Phase Transitions & Critical Phenomena, Vol. 7. Ed. by C. M. Domb & Joel L. Lebowitz. 1983. 82.00 (ISBN 0-12-220307-0). Acad Pr.

Phase Transitions & Critical Phenomena, Vol. 9. C. Domb & J. L. Lebowitz. LC 77-170760. 1984. 82.00 (ISBN 0-12-220309-7). Acad Pr.

Phase Transitions & Critical Phenomena, Vol. 10. Ed. by Cyril Domb & Joel Lebowitz. 363p. 1987. 88.00 (ISBN 0-12-220310-0). Acad Pr.

Phase Transitions & Critical Phenomena, Vol. 11. Ed. by Cyril Domb & Joel Lebowitz. 240p. 1987. 76.00 (ISBN 0-12-220311-9). Acad Pr.

Phase Transitions & Critical Phenomena: Series Expansion for Lattice Models, Vol. 3. Ed. by C. Domb & M. Green. 1974. 141.00 (ISBN 0-12-220303-8). Acad Pr.

Phase Transitions & Their Applications in Materials Science. Ed. by H. K. Henisch et al. LC 73-14411. 300p. 1974. 59.00 (ISBN 0-08-017955-X). Pergamon.

Phase Transitions: Cargese 1980. Ed. by Maurice Levy et al. LC 81-15838. (NATO ASI Series B, Physics: Vol. 72). 462p. 1982. 79.50x (ISBN 0-306-40825-2, Plenum Pr). Plenum Pub.

Phase Transitions in Condensed Systems: Experiments & Theory (In Honor of David Turnbull, Vol. 57. Ed. by G. S. Cargill, III et al. (Materials Research Society Symposia Proceedings Ser.). 1987. text ed. 46.00 (ISBN 0-931837-22-7). Materials Res.

Phase Transitions in Surface Films. Ed. by J. G. Dash & J. Ruvalds. LC 79-28484. (NATO ASI Series B, Physical Sciences: Vol. 51). 380p. 1980. 69.50x (ISBN 0-306-40348-X, Plenum Pr). Plenum Pub.

Phase Transitions of the Second Order: Collective Variables Method. I. R. Yukhnovskii. 350p. 1987. 55.00 (ISBN 9971-50-087-6). World Scientific Pub.

Phased Array Antennas: Proceedings of the 1970 Phased Array Antenna Symposium. Phased Array Antenna Symposium (1970: Polytechnic Institute of Brooklyn. Ed. by Arthur A. Oliner. (Modern Frontiers in Applied Science Ser.). pap. 98.30 (2027162). Bks Demand UMI.

Phased Retirement: The European Experience. 228p. 1982. 8.50 (ISBN 0-911583-04-1). New Ways Work.

Phaselock Loops for DC Motor Speed Control. Dana F. Geiger. LC 80-29578. 206p. 1981. 32.50 (ISBN 0-471-08548-0, Pub. by Wiley-Interscience). Wiley.

Phaselock Techniques. 2nd ed. Floyd M. Gardner. LC 78-20777. 285p. 1979. 36.95x (ISBN 0-471-04294-3, Pub by Wiley-Interscience). Wiley.

Phases. Caroline B. Robison. 1987. 4.95 (ISBN 0-533-07278-6). Vantage.

Phases of American Culture. facs. ed. Jesuit Philosophical Association Of The Eastern States. LC 69-17579. (Essay Index Reprint Ser). 1942. 14.00 (ISBN 0-8369-0021-9). Ayer Co Pubs.

Phases of Burnout: Developments in Concepts & Applications. Robert T. Golembiewski & Robert F. Munzenrider. 1988. 49.85 (ISBN 0-275-92980-9, C2980). Praeger.

Phases of Capitalism & Economic Theory & Other Essays. A. K. Dasgupta. 1983. 18.95x (ISBN 0-19-561565-4). Oxford U Pr.

Phases of Capitalist Development. Angus Maddison. (Illus.). 1982. pap. 11.95x (ISBN 0-19-828451-9). Oxford U Pr.

Phases of Dickens: The Man, His Message & His Mission. John C. Walters. LC 73-176491. (Studies in Dickens, No. 52). 1971. Repr. of 1911 ed. lib. bdg. 52.95x (ISBN 0-8383-1358-2). Haskell.

Phases of Economic Growth 1850-1973: Kondratieff Waves & Kuznets Swings. Solomos Solomou. (Illus.). 224p. 1988. 44.50 (ISBN 0-521-33457-8). Cambridge U Pr.

Phases of English Poetry. Herbert Read. LC 72-187213. 1928. lib. bdg. 29.50 (ISBN 0-8414-7414-1). Folcroft.

Phases of Harry Moon. Thomas Sullivan. 320p. 1988. 18.95 (ISBN 0-525-24656-8). Dutton.

Phases of Modern Music. facs. ed. Lawrence Gilman. LC 68-22915. (Essay Index Reprint Ser). 1904. 15.00 (ISBN 0-8369-0476-1). Ayer Co Pubs.

Phases of Pre-Pagan Burma: Languages & History, 2 vols. G. H. Luce. (Illus.). 1985. Set. 155.00x (ISBN 0-19-713595-1). Oxford U Pr.

Phases of Rilke. Norbert Fuerst. LC 72-6786. (Studies in German Literature, No. 13). 1972. Repr. of 1958 ed. lib. bdg. 49.95x (ISBN 0-8383-1663-8). Haskell.

Phases of Silica. Robert B. Sosman. LC 65-19405. pap. 100.00 (ISBN 0-317-10761-5, 2050311). Bks Demand UMI.

Phases of the Heart. Thomas J. Shaw. 32p. 1987. cancelled (ISBN 0-8062-3110-6). Carlton.

Phases of the Moon. Busteed & Wergin. LC 82-73123. 224p. 12.50 (2644-01). Am Fed Astrologers.

Phases of the Moon. James Magorian. LC 77-82560. (Illus.). 40p. 1978. 6.00 (ISBN 0-930674-01-4). Black Oak.

Phases of Thought & Criticism: Emerson, Dante, Newman. Azarias. 273p. 1983. Repr. of 1892 ed. lib. bdg. 40.00. Darby Bks.

Phasor Diagrams. Marcus G. Scroggie. 12.50x (ISBN 0-685-20612-2). Transatl Arts.

Phasors. Attilya J. Roos. (Operations in Electrical Engineering Ser.: Vol. VII). 83p. 1984. pap. text ed. cancelled. IPS.

Phatik Chand. Satyajit Ray. Tr. by Lila Ray from Bengali. 108p. (gr. 6-8). 1984. pap. 8.00 (ISBN 0-86578-230-X). Ind-US Inc.

PhD Experience: A Woman's Point of View. Ed. by Sue Vartuli. LC 81-17797. 160p. 1982. 35.00 (ISBN 0-275-90919-0, C0919). Praeger.

Pheasant. Kimio Endo. Ed. by Kathy Pohl. LC 85-28207. (Nature Close-Ups Ser.). (Illus.). 32p. (gr. 4). 1986. PLB 15.33 (ISBN 0-8172-2549-8); pap. text ed. 9.27 (ISBN 0-8172-2574-9). Raintree Pubs.

Pheasant. Virginia Holmgren. Ed. by Howard Schroeder. LC 82-23672. (Wildlife (Habits & Habitat) Ser.). (Illus.). 48p. (gr. 4 up). 1983. lib. bdg. 10.95 (ISBN 0-89686-222-4). Crestwood Hse.

Pheasant Book. Keith Proud & John Foyster. (Illus.). 208p. 1988. 34.95 (ISBN 0-7153-8981-5). David & Charles.

Pheasant Breeding & Care. Jean Delacour. (Illus.). 1978. 19.95 (ISBN 0-87666-434-6, AP-6450). TFH Pubns.

Pheasant Flower. Sandra McPherson. (Poetry Chapbook Ser.). 32p. (Orig.). 1985. pap. 4.00 (ISBN 0-937669-18-0). Owl Creek Pr.

Pheasant Hunter. William Saroyan. (Perfect Presents Story-Gifts Ser.). (Illus.). 44p. 1986. pap. 5.95 (ISBN 1-55628-010-6). Redpath Pr.

Pheasant Run Pubns. Walter J. Schenck, Sr. LC 77-4567. (Illus.). 1977. 15.95 (ISBN 0-669-01372-2). Pheasant Run.

Pheasants of the World. Paul A. Johnsgard. LC 85-7218. (Illus.). 350p. 1986. 75.00x (ISBN 0-19-857185-2). Oxford U Pr.

Phebus Lane. Alec Bond. 89p. 1987. pap. 5.95 (ISBN 0-317-69927-X). Spoon Riv Poetry.

Phedra. Jean Racine & Robert D. McDonald. Tr. by Robert D. McDonald from Fr. 72p. (Orig.). 1988. pap. 7.95 (ISBN 0-317-65858-1). Applause Theatre Bk Pubs.

Phedre. Jean Racine. Tr. by Margaret Rawlings. (Bilingual). 1962. pap. 6.95 (ISBN 0-525-47099-9, 0674-210); pap. 7.50 (ISBN 0-525-48270-9). Dutton.

Phedre. Jean Racine. (Illus.). 1964. pap. 5.95 (ISBN 0-685-11490-2). French & Eur.

Phellinus Pachyphloeus & Its Allies see Memoirs of the New York Botanical Garden.

Phelon's Discount - Sheldon's Jobbing Trade, 1985-1986. 385p. 1986. 85.00 (ISBN 0-317-55709-2). B Klein Pubns.

Phelon's Discount & Jobbing Trade, 1988-1989. 11th ed. Ed. by Kenneth W. Phelon, Jr. 386p. Date not set. pap. 95.00 (ISBN 0-942239-01-6). P S & M Inc.

Phelon's Discount & Jobbing Trade, 1988-1989. 11th ed. Phelon, Sheldon & Marsar, Inc. Staff. 1987. 95.00 (ISBN 0-317-57737-9). P S & M Inc.

Phelon's Womens Apparel Shops, 1986-1987. 9th ed. Ed. by Kenneth W. Phelon, Jr. 436p. Date not set. pap. 90.00 (ISBN 0-942239-00-8). P S & M Inc.

Phelon's Women's Apparel Shops: 1986-1987. 9th, rev. ed. 429p. 1986. pap. 90.00 (ISBN 0-939300-28-1). P S & M Inc.

Phelon's Women's Apparel Shops, 1986-1987. 400p. 1987. 95.00 (ISBN 0-317-55711-4). B Klein Pubns.

Phemomena of Astral Projection. Sylvan Muldoon & Hereward Carrington. 222p. 1970. pap. 10.95 (ISBN 0-87728-068-1). Weiser.

Phencyclidine: An Update. Ed. by Doris H. Clouet. (National Institute on Drug Abuse Research Monograph Ser.: No. 64). 288p. 1986. pap. 6.50 (S/N 017-024-01281-5). USGPO.

Phencyclidine & Related Arylcyclohexylamines: Present & Future Applications. Ed. by J. M. Kamenka et al. LC 83-61728. (Illus.). 690p. 1983. 50.00x (ISBN 0-916182-04-5). NPP Bks.

Phenetic Variation in the Avian Subfamily Cardinalinae. Jenna J. Hellack. (Occasional Papers: No. 57). 22p. 1976. pap. 1.25 (ISBN 0-317-04589-X). U of KS Mus Nat Hist.

Phenetics & Ecology of Hybridization in Buckeye Butterflies (Lepidoptera, Nymphalidae) John E. Hafernik, Jr. (University of California Publications in Entomology: Vol. 96). 221p. 1982. pap. 25.00x (ISBN 0-520-09649-5). U of Cal Pr.

Phenetics: Evolution, Population, Trait. A. V. Yablokov. Tr. by Marie J. Hall from Rus. LC 85-31420. 192p. 1986. 25.00 (ISBN 0-231-05990-6). Columbia U Pr.

Phenix, or a Revival of Scarce & Valuable Tracts, 2 vols. Ed. by Gerald M. Straka. LC 72-83168. (English Studies Ser.). 1972. Repr. of 1707 ed. Set. lib. bdg. 81.00 (ISBN 0-8420-1425-X). Scholarly Res Inc.

Phenol Oxidase (EC 1.14.18.1)-A Marker Enzyme for Defense Cells. Hans Schmidt. (Progress in Histochemistry & Cytochemistry Ser.: Vol. 17/3). 165p. (Orig.). 1988. pap. text ed. 74.50 (ISBN 0-89574-256-X, Pub. by Gustav Fischer Verlag). VCH Pubs.

Phenolic Resins. A. Knop & L. A. Pilato. (Illus.). 350p. 1985. 69.50 (ISBN 0-387-15039-0). Springer-Verlag.

Phenolic Substances in Grapes & Wine & Their Significance see Advances in Food Research: Supplements.

Phenolic, Sulfur, & Nitrogen Compounds in Food Flavors. Ed. by George Charalambous & Ira Katz. LC 76-16544. (ACS Symposium Ser: No. 26). 1976. 23.95 (ISBN 0-8412-0330-X). Am Chemical.

Phenologies. Richard Dauenhauer. (Orig.). 1988. pap. 6.00 (ISBN 0-914476-90-4). Thorp Springs.

Phenology & Seasonality Modeling. Ed. by H. Lieth. LC 73-23022. (Ecological Studies - Analysis & Synthesis Ser.: Analysis & Synthesis, Vol. 8). (Illus.). 480p. 1974. 90.80 (ISBN 0-387-06524-5). Springer-Verlag.

Phenology of Cultivated Rhododendrons in Lower Mainland of British Columbia. L. Keith Wade. (Illus.). 225p. (Orig.). 1979. pap. 8.25 (ISBN 0-89955-412-1, Pub. by U BC Pr Canada). Intl Spec Bk.

Phenols & Medicine: Subject, Reference & Research Guidebook. Mary S. Fayette. LC 87-47653. 160p. 1987. 34.50 (ISBN 0-88164-606-7); pap. 26.50 (ISBN 0-88164-607-5). ABBE Pubs Assn.

Phenomena. Henry Billings & Melissa Billings. (Illus.). 160p. (gr. 6-8). 1984. pap. text ed. 7.20x (ISBN 0-89061-363-X, 762). Jamestown Pubs.

Phenomena & Culture of Mediumship for Sensitive Personalities. M. H. Wallis. (Illus.). 137p. 1988. 117.75 (ISBN 0-89920-184-9). Am Inst Psych.

Phenomena in Ionized Gases: Eigtheenth International Conference, Swansea, July 1987, 2 vols. W. T. Williams. 1987. Set. 216.00x (ISBN 0-9511848-2-2, Pub by A Hilger UK); Vol. 1, 1000 pgs. 135.00x (ISBN 0-9511848-0-6); Vol 2,400 pgs. 135.00x (ISBN 0-9511848-1-4). Taylor & Francis.

Phenomena in Mixed Surfactant Systems. Ed. by John F. Scamehorn. LC 86-8062. (ACS Symposium Ser.: No. 311). (Illus.). ix, 349p. 1986. 66.95 (ISBN 0-8412-0975-8). Am Chemical.

Phenomena Induced by Intermolecular Interactions. Ed. by G. Birnbaum. (NATO ASI Series B, Physics: Vol. 127). 782p. 1985. 125.00x (ISBN 0-306-42071-6, Plenum Pr.). Plenum Pub.

Phenomena of Astral Projection. Sylvia Muldoon & Hereward Carrington. 222p. 1981. pap. 13.00 (ISBN 0-89540-112-6, SB-112). Sun Pub.

Phenomena of Fluid Motions. rev. ed. Robert S. Brodkey. (Illus.). 737p. 1986. Repr. 15.00 (ISBN 0-9616374-0-4). R S Brodkey.

Phenomena of Life. Ed. by Mystic Jhamom Staff. (Conversations with a Mystic Ser.: No. 4). (Illus.). 1986. pap. write for info. (ISBN 0-933961-09-X). Mystic Jhamom.

Phenomena of Life: A Radio-Electric Interpretation. George Crile. Ed. by Amy Rowland. 377p. Repr. of 1936 ed. lib. bdg. 60.00 (ISBN 0-89984-026-4). Century Bookbindery.

Phenomena of Life: A Radio-Electric Interpretation. George Crile. Ed. by Amy Rowland. (Illus.). 379p. 1985. Repr. of 1936 ed. lib. bdg. 50.00 (ISBN 0-89987-193-3). Darby Bks.

Phenomena of Life Illustrations Booklet: Supplement. Ed. by Mystic Jhamom Staff. (Conversations with a Mystic Ser.: No. 4). (Illus.). 24p. 1986. pap. write for info. (ISBN 0-933961-10-3). Mystic Jhamom.

Phenomena of Materialisation: A Contribution to the Investigation of Mediumistic Teleplastics. A. Von Schrenck Notzing. LC 75-7408. (Perspectives in Psychical Research Ser.). (Illus.). 1975. Repr. of 1920 ed. 47.50x (ISBN 0-405-06995-2). Ayer Co Pubs.

Phenomena of Physics: A Conceptual Laboratory Program. Karen Johnston & Cecil G. Shugart. 120p. 1982. pap. text ed. 14.95 (ISBN 0-8403-2771-4). Kendall-Hunt.

Phenomena: Poems. Cathryn Hankla. LC 82-11013. (Breakthrough Bks.: No. 40). 80p. (Orig.). 1983. pap. 5.95 (ISBN 0-8262-0386-8). U of Mo Pr.

Phenomenal Architecture: Cesar Pelli. Ed. by Ching-Yu Chang. (Stylos: Architecture International Ser.: No. 1). (Illus.). 1979. pap. 18.50 (ISBN 0-89860-029-4). Eastview.

Phil Flasche: Male Photographer. Phil Flasche. (Illus.). 96p. (Orig.). 1987. pap. 20.00 (ISBN 0-85449-060-4, Pub. by GMP England). Alyson Pubns.
Phil May: The Artist & His Wit. David Cuppleditch. (Illus.). 127p. 1982. 27.50 (ISBN 0-8390-0292-0). Abner Schram Ltd.
Phil Sheridan & His Army. Paul A. Hutton. LC 84-7216. (Illus.). xviii, 479p. 1985. 35.00x (ISBN 0-8032-2329-3); pap. 14.95 (ISBN 0-8032-7227-8, BB 922, Bison). U of Nebr Pr.
Phil the Fiddler: Or, the Story of a Young Street Musician. Horatio Alger. 1976. Repr. of 1872 ed. lib. bdg. 17.95x (ISBN 0-88411-815-0, Pub. by Aeonian Pr). Amereon Ltd.
Phil Weyerhaeuser: Lumberman. Charles E. Twining. LC 84-40663. (Illus.). 420p. 1985. 25.00 (ISBN 0-295-96218-6). U of Wash Pr.
Philadelphia. Bernadette Balcer & Fran Pelham. (Downtown America Bks.). (Illus.). 60p. (gr. 3 up). 1988. PLB 12.95 (ISBN 0-87518-388-3). Dillon.
Philadelphia. Horace M. Lippincott & Thornton Oakley. LC 78-124995. (Keystone State Historical Publications Ser). 1970. Repr. of 1926 ed. 20.50x (ISBN 0-87198-511-X, Ira J Friedman). Assoc Faculty Pr.
Philadelphia. Robert Llewellyn. Ed. by James B. Patrick. (Scenic Discovery Ser.). (Illus.). 128p. 1986. 30.00 (ISBN 0-89909-097-4). Yankee Bks.
Philadelphia. rev. ed. (Frommer's City Guides Ser.). (Illus.). 224p. 1988. pap. 5.95 (ISBN 0-13-047630-7). Prentice Hall Pr.
Philadelphia: A Chronological & Documentary History. Adrienne Siegel. LC 74-23205. (American Cities Chronology Ser.). 154p. 1975. 8.50 (ISBN 0-379-00621-9). Oceana.
Philadelphia: A Guide to the Nation's Birthplace. Federal Writers' Project Staff. LC 39-4271. (American Guidebook). 1982. Repr. of 1939 ed. 79.00x (ISBN 0-403-02204-5). Somerset Pub.
Philadelphia: A Three Hundred Year History. Ed. by Russell F. Weigley et al. (Barra Foundation Bk). (Illus.). 1982. 17.95 (ISBN 0-393-01610-2). Norton.
Philadelphia & Erie Railroad: Its Place in American Economic History. Homer T. Rosenberger. LC 74-75110. (Illus.). 748p. 1975. 22.50 (ISBN 0-914932-02-0). Fox Hills Pr.
Philadelphia & Erie Railroad: Its Place in American Economic History. Homer T. Rosenberger. LC 74-75110. (Illus.). 748p. 1975. lib. bdg. 22.50. Rose Hill.
Philadelphia & the China Trade, Sixteen Eighty-Two to Eighteen Forty-Six: Commercial, Cultural, & Attitudinal Effects. Jonathan Goldstein. LC 77-1638. (Illus.). 1978. 20.00x (ISBN 0-271-00512-2). Pa St U Pr.
Philadelphia Architecture: A Guide to the City. Group for Environmental Education, Inc. Staff. Ed. by John Andrew Gallery. (Illus.). 176p. (Orig.). 1984. pap. 14.95 (ISBN 0-262-56030-5). MIT Pr.
Philadelphia Architecture in the Nineteenth Century. rev. ed. Ed. by Theo B. White. (Illus.). 121p. 1974. 20.00 (ISBN 0-87982-005-5). Art Alliance.
Philadelphia-Baltimore Trade Rivalry 1780-1860. James W. Livingood. LC 70-112557. (Rise of Urban America). (Illus.). 1970. Repr. of 1947 ed. 19.00 (ISBN 0-405-02463-0). Ayer Co Pubs.
Philadelphia-Baltimore Trade Rivalry, 1780-1860. James W. Livingood. LC 47-29. 195p. 1947. 5.50 (ISBN 0-911124-35-7). Pa Hist & Mus.
Philadelphia Church. 27p. (Orig.). pap. 0.95 (ISBN 0-937408-19-0). GMI Pubns Inc.
Philadelphia Collects: Art Since Nineteen Forty. Mark Rosenthal. (Philadelphia Museum of Arts Ser.). (Illus.). 112p. 1986. 39.95 (ISBN 0-8122-7955-7). U of Pa Pr.
Philadelphia Collects: Art since 1940. Philadelphia Museum of Art Staff. LC 86-22490. (Illus.). 128p. (Orig.). 1986. pap. 12.95 (ISBN 0-87633-066-9). Phila Mus Art.
Philadelphia Communists, 1936-1956. Paul Lyons. 244p. 1982. 25.95 (ISBN 0-87722-259-2). Temple U Pr.
Philadelphia Eagles. James R. Rothaus. (NFL Today Ser.). 48p. (gr. 4 up). 1986. PLB 10.45 (ISBN 0-88682-044-8). Creative Ed.
Philadelphia Epicure. Turquoise Erving. (Epicure Ser.). 180p. (Orig.). 1986. pap. 7.95 (ISBN 0-89716-146-7). Peanut Butter.
Philadelphia Family: The Houstons & Woodwards of Chestnut Hill. David R. Contosta. (Illus.). 256p. 1988. 19.95 (ISBN 0-8122-8136-5). U of Pa Pr.
Philadelphia Folks. Cornelius Weygandt. LC 75-124997. (Keystone State Historical Publications Ser). 1970. Repr. of 1938 ed. 21.50 (ISBN 0-8046-8513-4, Ira J Friedman). Assoc Faculty Pr.
Philadelphia Folly. Nancy Richards-Akers. 1988. pap. 2.95 (ISBN 0-446-34894-5). Warner Bks.
Philadelphia Homestyle Cookbook. Norwood-Fontbonne Home & School Association Staff. Ed. by Wimmer Brothers Books Staff. (Illus.). 288p. (Orig.). 1985. 12.95. Norwood-Fontbonne.
Philadelphia Houston Exchange. Suzanne Delehanty & James Harithas. (Illus.). 1976. pap. 7.00 (ISBN 0-88454-020-0). U of Pa Contemp Art.
Philadelphia in Color. John P. Hayes. (Illus., Orig.). 1983. 10.95 (ISBN 0-8038-5898-1). Hastings.
Philadelphia Inquirer in a Hurry Cookbook. Elaine Tait. (Illus.). 224p. (Orig.). 1988. pap. 9.95 (ISBN 0-912608-60-9). Mid Atlantic.
Philadelphia Lawyer in the London Courts. Thomas Leaming. (Illus.). xiii, 199p. 1987. Repr. of 1911 ed. lib. bdg. 30.00x (ISBN 0-8377-2408-2). Rothman.
Philadelphia Magazines & Their Contributors, 1741-1850. facs. ed. Albert H. Smyth. LC 70-119944. (Select Bibliographies Reprint Ser). 1892. 19.00 (ISBN 0-8369-5387-8). Ayer Co Pubs.
Philadelphia Maritime Museum 1961-1986. John W. Jackson. (Illus.). 79p. (Orig.). 1987. pap. 10.00 (ISBN 0-913346-13-6). Phila Maritime Mus.
Philadelphia Marriages & Obituaries, 1857-1860 Philadelphia Saturday Bulletin. Ed. & compiled by Maryly B. Penrose. LC 74-84453. 294p. 1974. 35.00 (ISBN 0-918940-03-6); softcover 30.00 (ISBN 0-918940-04-4). Libty Bell Assoc.
Philadelphia Meno Directory. 2nd ed. Ed. by James D. Senker. 160p. pap. 4.95 (ISBN 0-686-46012-X). Senkers Whim Ent.
Philadelphia Merchant: The Diary of Thomas P. Cope, 1800-1851. Thomas P. Cope. Intro. by Eliza Cope Harrison. LC 78-60231. (Illus.). 1978. 19.95 (ISBN 0-89526-689-X). Regnery Gateway.
Philadelphia Naturalization Records, 1789-1880: Index to Records of Aliens' Declarations of Intention and - or Oaths of Allegiance. Ed. by P. William Filby. 736p. 1982. 295.00x (ISBN 0-8103-1116-X). Gale.
Philadelphia Negro: A Social Study. Together with a Special Report on Domestic Service by Isabel Eaton. W. E. B. Dubois. 520p. 1973. Repr. of 1899 ed. 31.00 (ISBN 0-527-25320-0). Kraus Intl.
Philadelphia on the River. Smith. 33.95. U of PA Pr.
Philadelphia One-Day Trip Book. Jane O. Smith. 1985. pap. 8.95 (ISBN 0-914440-82-9). EPM Pubns.
Philadelphia Orchestra Cookbook. Compiled by Philadephia Orchestra, West Philadelphia Volunteer Committee & Anne M. Krout. (Illus.). 400p. 1980. pap. 11.95 (ISBN 0-9607586-0-7). W Phila Comm.
Philadelphia: Patricians & Philistines 1900-1950. John Lukacs. (Illus.). 368p. 1981. 17.50 (ISBN 0-374-23161-3). FS&G.
Philadelphia: Patricians & Philistines, 1900 to 1950. John Lukacs. LC 81-15754. (Illus.). 360p. 1982. pap. 9.50 (ISBN 0-89727-044-4). ISHI PA.
Philadelphia Phillies. Martin. LC 82-13972. (Baseball Today Ser.). 48p. (gr. 4 up). 1982. PLB 11.45 (ISBN 0-87191-870-6). Creative Ed.
Philadelphia Phillies. James R. Rothaus. (Baseball: The Great American Game Ser.). 48p. (gr. 4-10). 1987. PLB 14.89 (ISBN 0-88682-146-0). Creative Ed.
Philadelphia Plus One: A Traveler's Guide. Nancy Sokoloff. (Illus.). 309p. (Orig.). 1987. pap. 10.95 (ISBN 0-943495-00-8). WhyNot Pr.
Philadelphia Police, Past & Present. Howard O. Sprogle. LC 77-156032. Repr. of 1887 ed. 35.00 (ISBN 0-404-09134-2). AMS Pr.
Philadelphia Police, Past & Present. Howard O. Sprogle. LC 72-154590. (Police in America Ser). (Illus.). 1971. Repr. of 1887 ed. 36.00 (ISBN 0-405-03387-7). Ayer Co Pubs.
Philadelphia Police: Past & Present. Howard O. Sprogle. LC 70-172570. (Criminology, Law Enforcement, & Social Problems Ser.: No. 151). (Illus.). Date not set. Repr. of 1887 ed. lib. bdg. price not set (ISBN 0-87585-151-7). Patterson Smith.
Philadelphia: Port of History 1609-1837. Charles L. Chandler et al. (Illus.). 82p. 1976. pap. 2.00 (ISBN 0-913346-02-0). Phila Maritime Mus.
Philadelphia Preserved: Catalog of the Historic American Building Survey. Richard J. Webster. 445p. 1981. pap. 12.95 (ISBN 0-87722-215-0). Temple U Pr.
Philadelphia Preserved: Catalog of the Historic American Building Survey. Richard J. Webster. LC 76-18669. (Illus.). 512p. 1976. 29.95 (ISBN 0-87722-089-1). Temple U Pr.
Philadelphia Rebel: The Education of a Bourgeoise. Clara Jaeger. LC 87-182089. 240p. 1988. pap. 7.95 (ISBN 1-85239-502-8). Grosvenor USA.
Philadelphia Revisions: The Print Department Collects. Kenneth Finkel. (Illus.). 50p. 1983. pap. 5.00 (ISBN 0-914076-71-X). Lib Co Phila.
Philadelphia Riots of Eighteen Forty-Four: A Study of Ethnic Conflict. Michael Feldberg. LC 75-65. (Contributions in American History: No. 43). (Illus.). 209p. 1975. lib. bdg. 35.00 (ISBN 0-8371-7876-2, FGC/). Greenwood.
Philadelphia Sampler. Vincent P. Dowdle & Anthony Dowdle. 80p. (Orig.). 1982. pap. 4.95 (ISBN 0-9611304-0-7). Earpacker Pr.
Philadelphia: Seventeen Seventy-Six to Two Thousand Seventy-Six, a Three Hundred Year View. Ed. by Dennis J. Clark. (Interdisciplinary Urban Ser.). 130p. 1975. 18.00x (ISBN 0-8046-9141-X, Pub. by Kennikat). Assoc Faculty Pr.
Philadelphia Seventy-Sixers. Pam Banks. (NBA Today Ser.). (Illus.). 48p. (gr. 4 up). 1984. PLB 10.45 (ISBN 0-87191-985-0). Creative Ed.
Philadelphia Shakespeare Story: Horace Howard Furness & the Variorum Shakespeare. LC 87-45801. (Studies in the Renaissance: No. 23). 1987. 42.50 (ISBN 0-404-62293-3). AMS Pr.
Philadelphia, Sixteen Eighty-One to Eighteen Eighty-Seven: A History of Municipal Development. Edward P. Allinson. LC 78-64246. (Johns Hopkins University. Studies in the Social Sciences. Extra Volumes: 2). Repr. of 1887 ed. 30.50 (ISBN 0-404-61351-9). AMS Pr.
Philadelphia Standards & Goals Exemplary Court Project: Final Evaluation. National Center for State Courts Staff. 137p. 1978. manuscript 8.22 (NERO-027). Natl Ctr St Courts.
Philadelphia Stories: A Photographic History, 1920-1960. Fredric M. Miller et al. (Illus.). 336p. 1988. 29.95 (ISBN 0-87722-551-6). Temple U Pr.
Philadelphia Story: A City of Winners. Frank Dolson. (Illus.). 336p. 1981. 12.95 (ISBN 0-89651-600-8). B L Pub.
Philadelphia Story: A Comedy in Three Acts. Philip Barry. LC 83-45700. Repr. of 1939 ed. 24.50 (ISBN 0-404-20018-4). AMS Pr.
Philadelphia Taxes on Business & Related Activities. Pennsylvania Bar Institute Staff. 92p. 1984. 25.00 (ISBN 0-318-02182-X, 248). PA Bar Inst.
Philadelphia: The City & the Bell. Barbara Ratner-Gantshar. LC 76-43573. (Grasshopper Ser.). (Illus.). (gr. 4-8). 1976. 3.98 (ISBN 0-686-16319-2); tchr & research guide 3.48 (ISBN 0-686-16320-6). Artistic Endeavors.
Philadelphia the Federalist City: A Study of Urban Politics, 1789-1801. Richard G. Miller. (National University Publications Ser. in American Studies). 1976. 21.50x (ISBN 0-8046-9135-5, Pub. by Kennikat). Assoc Faculty Pr.
Philadelphia Theatre in the Eighteenth Century, Together with the Day Book of the Same Period. Wilson. LC 69-10147. (Illus.). 1968. Repr. of 1933 ed. lib. bdg. 31.50 (ISBN 0-8371-0272-3, WIPT). Greenwood.
Philadelphia Theatres A-Z: A Comprehensive, Descriptive Record of 813 Theatres Constructed Since 1724. Irvin R. Glazer. LC 85-27131. (Illus.). lxxxv, 225p. 1986. lib. bdg. 46.95 (ISBN 0-313-24054-X, GPT/). Greenwood.
Philadelphia Trivia Quiz. Bernard Stiefel. (American Metropolitan Area Trivia Quizzes Ser.). (Illus.). 1984. pap. 4.95 (ISBN 0-916399-01-X). Normandy Pubns.
Philadelphia: Work, Space, Family & Group Experience in the Nineteenth Century. Essays Toward an Interdisciplinary History of the City. Ed. by Theodore Hershberg. (Illus.). 1981. 39.95x (ISBN 0-19-502752-3). Oxford U Pr.
Philadelphia: Work, Space, Family & Group Experience in the Nineteenth Century. Essays Toward an Interdisciplinary History of the City. Ed. by Theodore Hershberg. (Illus.). 1981. pap. 13.95 (ISBN 0-19-502753-1). Oxford U Pr.
Philadelphia 1987-1988. (Frommer's City Guides). 224p. 5.95 (ISBN 0-671-62361-3). Prentice Hall Pr.
Philadelphians & the China Trade, Seventeen Eighty-Four to Eighteen Forty-Four. Jean G. Lee. (Illus.). 232p. (Orig.). 1984. pap. 22.50 (ISBN 0-87633-060-X). Phila Mus Art.
Philadelphians & the China Trade: 1784 to 1840. Jean G. Lee. (Illus.). 304p. 1984. 52.95 (ISBN 0-8122-1172-3, Pub. by PA Mus Art); 45.00. U of Pa Pr.
Philadelphia's Black Elite. Julie Winch. LC 87-10135. (Activism, Accommodation, & the Struggle for Autonomy, 1787-1848). 248p. 1988. 34.95 (ISBN 0-87722-515-X). Temple U Pr.
Philadelphia's First Fuel Crisis: Jacob Cist & the Developing Market for Pennsylvania Anthracite. H. Benjamin Powell. LC 77-88471. (Illus.). 1978. 22.00x (ISBN 0-271-00533-5). Pa St U Pr.
Philadelphia's Outdoor Art: A Walking Tour. Roslyn F. Brenner. LC 86-19989. (Illus.). 128p. (Orig.). 1987. pap. 8.95 (ISBN 0-940159-00-7). Camino Bks.
Philadelphia's Philosopher Mechanics: A History of the Franklin Institute, 1824-1865. Bruce A. Sinclair. LC 74-6843. (History of Technology Ser). (Illus.). 352p. 1974. 37.50x (ISBN 0-8018-1636-X). Johns Hopkins.
Philadelpia on the River. Philip C. Smith. LC 85-60100. (Illus.). 176p. 1986. 29.00 (ISBN 0-913346-10-1). Phila Maritime Mus.
Philanderer. George Bernard Shaw. Ed. by Julius Novick. LC 79-56700. (Bernard Shaw Early Texts: Play Manuscripts in Facsimile). 1981. lib. bdg. 113.00 (ISBN 0-8240-4576-9). Garland Pub.
Philanthropic Foundations ABD Resources for Health. Ed. by Rosenkrantz & Barbara Gutmann. (Medical Care in the United States Ser.). 200p. 1988. lib. bdg. 40.00 (ISBN 0-8240-8343-1). Garland Pub.
Philanthropic Foundations in Latin America. Ed. by Ann Stromberg. LC 68-54409. 223p. 1968. 17.50x (ISBN 0-87154-837-2). Russell Sage.
Philanthropic Giving. F. Emerson Andrews. 318p. 1950. 27.50x (ISBN 0-87154-022-3). Russell Sage.
Philanthropic Work of Josephine Shaw Lowell, Containing a Biographical Sketch of Her Life Together with a Selection of Her Public Papers & Private Letters. William R. Stewart. LC 71-172576. (Criminology, Law Enforcement, & Social Problems Ser.: No. 163). (Illus.). 1974. Repr. of 1911 ed. 20.00x (ISBN 0-87585-163-0). Patterson Smith.
Philanthropist, Vols. 1-7. 1971. Repr. of 1811 ed. Set. lib. bdg. 185.00x o. p. (ISBN 0-8371-9383-4, PT00); Vol. 1. lib. bdg. 31.00 (ISBN 0-313-21929-X, PT01); Vol. 2. lib. bdg. 31.00 (ISBN 0-313-21930-3, PT02); Vol. 3. lib. bdg. 31.00 (ISBN 0-313-21931-1, PT03); Vol. 4. lib. bdg. 31.00 (ISBN 0-313-21932-X, PT04); Vol. 5. lib. bdg. 31.00 (ISBN 0-313-21933-8, PT05); Vol. 6. lib. bdg. 31.00 (ISBN 0-313-21934-6, PT06); Vol. 7. lib. bdg. 31.00 (ISBN 0-313-21935-4, PT07). Greenwood.
Philanthropist: A Bourgeois Comedy. 2nd ed. Christopher Hampton. 72p. 1985. pap. 8.95 (ISBN 0-571-13488-2). Faber & Faber.
Philanthropists, Therapists & Activists. Gerald C. Rothman. LC 84-23514. 256p. 1985. 18.95 (ISBN 0-87073-521-7); pap. 11.95 (ISBN 0-87073-524-1). Schenkman Bks Inc.
Philanthropy & Cultural Imperialism: The Foundations at Home & Abroad. Ed. by Robert F. Arnove. LC 82-48055. (Midland Bks.: No. 303). 488p. 1982. pap. 10.95x (ISBN 0-253-20303-1). Ind U Pr.
Philanthropy & Culture: The International Foundation Perspective. Kathleen D. McCarthy. LC 84-2356. 190p. 1984. pap. 15.95 (ISBN 0-8122-1173-1). U of Pa Pr.
Philanthropy & Jim Crow in American Social Science. John H. Stanfield. LC 84-8995. (Contributions in Afro-American & African Studies: No. 82). (Illus.). xii, 216p. 1985. lib. bdg. 35.00 (ISBN 0-313-23894-4, SNE/). Greenwood.
Philanthropy & Learning with Other Papers. Frederick P. Keppel. LC 36-14158. Repr. of 1936 ed. 16.50 (ISBN 0-404-03660-0). AMS Pr.
Philanthropy & Marketing: New Strategies for Fund Raising. James G. Lord. LC 81-50197. 203p. 1981. lib. bdg. 47.50 (ISBN 0-939120-00-3); 3-ring notebook 47.50 (ISBN 0-939120-01-1). Third Sector.
Philanthropy & Peace. Francis Neilson. 1979. lib. bdg. 39.95 (ISBN 0-685-96634-8). Revisionist Pr.
Philanthropy & Social Progress: Seven Essays by Jane Addams, Robert A. Woods, Father J. O. S. Huntington, Prof. Franklin H. Giddings, & Bernard Bosanquet, Delivered Before the School of Applied Ethics at Plymouth, Mass. During the Session of 1892. facsimile ed. Jane Addams et al. LC 79-95059. (Select Bibliographies Reprint Ser). 1893. 19.00 (ISBN 0-8369-5061-5). Ayer Co Pubs.
Philanthropy & Social Progress: Seven Essays. Jane Addams et al. LC 75-108221. (Criminology, Law Enforcement, & Social Problems Ser.: No. 104). (Index added). 1970. Repr. of 1893 ed. 10.00x (ISBN 0-87585-104-5). Patterson Smith.
Philanthropy & the Business Corporation. Marion R. Fremont-Smith. LC 72-83835. 110p. 1972. pap. 7.95x (ISBN 0-87154-279-X). Russell Sage.
Philanthropy & Voluntarism: An Annotated Bibliography. Daphne N. Layton. LC 87-12032. 308p. 1987. 18.50 (ISBN 0-87954-198-9). Foundation Ctr.
Philanthropy: Four Views. Robert Payton et al. 100p. (Orig.). 1988. 19.95 (ISBN 0-912051-20-5); pap. 12.95 (ISBN 0-912051-21-3). Transaction Bks.
Philanthropy in Action. Brian O'Connell. LC 87-17729. 337p. 1987. 24.95 (ISBN 0-87954-230-6); pap. 19.95 (ISBN 0-87954-231-4). Foundation Ctr.
Philanthropy in Action. Brian O'Connell. 337p. Date not set. 24.95; pap. 19.95. Ind Sector.
Philanthropy in an Age of Transition: The Essays of Alan Pifer. Alan Pifer. LC 84-80697. 207p. (Orig.). 1984. pap. text ed. 12.50 (ISBN 0-87954-104-0). Foundation Ctr.
Philanthropy in England, Fourteen Eighty to Sixteen Sixty: A Study of the Changing Pattern of English Social Aspirations. Wilbur K. Jordon. LC 78-5651. (Illus.). 1978. Repr. of 1959 ed. lib. bdg. 30.00x (ISBN 0-313-20467-5, JOPH). Greenwood.
Philanthropy in the Shaping of American Higher Education. Gurti & Nash. LC 65-19399. 8.50 (ISBN 0-910294-27-5). Brown Bk.
Philanthropy: Private Means, Public Ends. Ed. by Kenneth W. Thompson. (Exxon Education Foundation Series on Rhetoric & Political Discourse: Vol. 4). 176p. (Orig.). 1987. lib. bdg. 23.50 (ISBN 0-8191-5816-X, Pub. by White Miller Center); pap. text ed. 11.25 (ISBN 0-8191-5817-8, Pub. by White Muller Center). U Pr of Amer.
Philanthropy Volunteering Action & the Public Good, 1986. (Working Papers for Spring Research Forum). 633p. Date not set. 75.00 ea. Ind Sector.
Philaster. Francis Beaumont & John Fletcher. Ed. by Dora J. Ashe. LC 75-127980. (Regents Renaissance Drama Ser). xxxii, 152p. 1974. 15.95x (ISBN 0-8032-0291-1). U of Nebr Pr.
Philaster. Francis Beaumont & John Fletcher. Ed. by Andrew Gurr. (Revels Plays Ser.). 142p. 1973. pap. 11.00 (ISBN 0-7190-1603-7, Pub. by Manchester Univ Pr). St Martin.
Philatelic Agencies, 1982. Leonard I. Kindler. ii, 20p. (Orig.). 1982. pap. 3.95 (ISBN 0-943502-02-0). Kindler.
Philatelic Gems. Donna O'Keefe. (Illus.). 168p. 1987. pap. 7.95 (ISBN 0-940403-04-8). Linns Stamp News.
Philatelic Gems, Three. Donna O'Keefe. (Illus.). 168p. (Orig.). 1987. pap. 7.95 (ISBN 0-940403-02-1). Linns Stamp News.

Philippians--Thessalonians. Gary Weedman. (Standard Bible Studies). 1988. pap. price not set (ISBN 0-87403-170-2, 11-40110). Standard Pub.

Philippians: A Bible Study Commentary. Howard F. Vos. (Study Guide Commentary Ser.). 96p. (Orig.). 1980. pap. 5.95 (ISBN 0-310-33863-8, 10967P). Zondervan.

Philippians: A Study Guide. Roger Van Harn. (Revelation Series for Adults). 1983. pap. text ed. 2.75 (ISBN 0-933140-84-3). CRC Pubns.

Philippians: A Translation with Notes. R. Paul Caudill. LC 80-70403. (Orig.). 1981. pap. 2.25 (ISBN 0-938980-00-9). Blue Ridge.

Philippians: An Expositional Commentary. James M. Boice. 320p. 1982. pap. 11.95 (ISBN 0-310-21501-3, 10310P). Zondervan.

Philippians & Colossians. Marilyn Kunz & Catherine Schell. (Neighborhood Bible Studies). 1974. pap. 2.95 (ISBN 0-8423-4825-5). Tyndale.

Philippians & Philemon. Mary-Ann Getty. LC 80-65637. (New Testament Message Ser.: Vol. 14). 10.95 (ISBN 0-89453-202-2); pap. 5.95 (ISBN 0-89453-137-9). M Glazier.

Philippians & Philemon: Critical & Exegetical Commentary. Marvin R. Vincent. Ed. by Samuel R. Driver & Charles A. Briggs. (International Critical Commentary Ser.). 248p. 1897. 29.95 (ISBN 0-567-05031-9, Pub. by T & T Clark Ltd UK). Fortress.

Philippians & Thessalonians. Kenneth Grayston. (Cambridge Bible Commentary on the New English Bible, New Testament Ser.). 1967. 16.95 (ISBN 0-521-04224-0); pap. 8.95 (ISBN 0-521-09409-7, 409). Cambridge U Pr.

Philippians: Be Glad. Ron Klug. (Young Fisherman Bible Studyguide Ser.). (Illus.). 64p. (gr. 7-12). 1983. tchr's ed. 4.95 (ISBN 0-87788-682-2); saddle-stitched student's ed. 2.95 (ISBN 0-87788-681-4). Shaw Pubs.

Philippians, Colossians, & First & Second Thessalonians. Edward P. Blair. Ed. by Lynne M. Deming & Margaret Rogers. (Cokesbury Basic Bible Commentary Ser.). (Illus.). 157p. (Orig.). 1988. pap. text ed. 4.95 (ISBN 0-939697-33-5). Graded Pr.

Philippians, Colossians, & Philemon. William Hendriksen. (New Testament Commentary). 243p. 1979. 19.95 (ISBN 0-8010-4212-7). Baker Bk.

Philippians, Colossians, Philemon, Vol. IX. Beacon Bible Expositions Staff. 300p. 1985. text ed. 6.95 (ISBN 0-8010-0788-7). Baker Bk.

Philippians, Colossians, Philemon. Wilbur Fields. LC 78-8763. (Bible Study Textbook Ser.). (Illus.). 1969. 12.95 (ISBN 0-89900-041-X). College Pr Pub.

Philippians, Colossians, Thessalonians. H. A. Ironside. 433p. 11.95 (ISBN 0-87213-398-2). Loizeaux.

Philippians: God's Guide to Joy. Ronald Klug. (Fisherman Bible Studyguide). 40p. 1981. saddle stitch 2.95 (ISBN 0-87788-680-6). Shaw Pubs.

Philippians: Interpretation: A Bible Commentary for Teaching & Preaching. Fred Craddock. Ed. by James L. Mays & Patrick D. Miller. LC 84-47797. 96p. 1984. 12.95 (ISBN 0-8042-3140-0, John Knox). Westminster John Knox.

Philippians: Joy & Peace. John F. Walvoord. (Everyman's Bible Commentary). 1971. pap. 5.95 (ISBN 0-8024-2050-8). Moody.

Philippians: Joy in the Lord. Ed. by Gary Wilde. (Basic Bible Ser.). 96p. 1986. pap. 4.95 (ISBN 0-89191-482-X). Cook.

Philippians: Our High Calling. Richard A. Hufton. LC 85-70134. 116p. (Orig.). 1985. pap. 4.00 (ISBN 0-933643-01-2). Grace World Outreach.

Philippians: Studies. Lehman Strauss. 1959. 7.50 (ISBN 0-87213-823-2). Loizeaux.

Philippians, The Epistle of Christian Joy. Keith L. Brooks. (Teach Yourself the Bible Ser.). 1964. pap. 2.95 (ISBN 0-8024-6506-4). Moody.

Philippians: The Joyful Life. William W. Menzies. LC 81-80302. (Radiant Life Ser.). 128p. (Orig.). 1981. pap. 2.50 (ISBN 0-88243-880-8, 02-0880); tchr's. guide 3.95 (ISBN 0-88243-191-9, 32-0191). Gospel Pub.

Philippians: Triumph in Christ (Everyman's Bible Commentary) see Filipenses: Triunfo en Cristo (Comentario Biblico Portavoz).

Philippians: Twenty-Six Daily Bible Studies. David Jeremiah. (Steps to Higher Ground Ser.). 1983. pap. 1.95 (ISBN 0-86508-208-1). BCM Pubn.

Philippians: Where Life Advances. Roy L. Laurin. LC 86-7177. 208p. 1987. pap. 8.95 (ISBN 0-8254-3134-4). Kregel.

Philippics. Cicero. (Loeb Classical Library: No. 189). 1926. 13.95x (ISBN 0-674-99208-3). Harvard U Pr.

Philippine-American Relations: A Guide to Manuscript Sources in the United States. Ed. by Shiro Saito. LC 82-12140. xx, 256p. 1982. lib. bdg. 85.00 (ISBN 0-313-23632-1, SPH/). Greenwood.

Philippine Answer to Communism. Alvin H. Scaff. (Illus.). 1955. 17.50x (ISBN 0-8047-0470-8). Stanford U Pr.

Philippine Bases: Negotiating for the Future. Ed. by Fred Greene. 160p. 1988. pap. 9.95 (ISBN 0-87609-043-9). Coun Foreign.

Philippine Bases: U. S. Security at Risk. A. James Gregor & Virgilio Aganon. LC 87-8910. 146p. (Orig.). 1987. Deccember 1987. lib. bdg. 17.50 (ISBN 0-89633-110-5); pap. text ed. 7.95 (ISBN 0-89633-111-3). Ethics & Public Policy.

Philippine Colonial Democracy. Intro. by Ruby R. Paredes. LC 87-51575. (Monograph Ser.: No. 32). (Illus.). 200p. (Orig.). Date not set. pap. price not set (ISBN 0-938692-34-8). Yale U SE Asia.

Philippine Cookbook. Reynaldo Alejandro. (Illus.). 288p. 1983. 17.95 (ISBN 0-698-11174-5, Coward). Putnam Pub Group.

Philippine Cookbook. Reynaldo Alejandro. (Illus.). 256p. 1985. pap. 10.95 (ISBN 0-399-51144-X, Perigee). Putnam Pub Group.

Philippine Cookery & Household Hin ts. H. Villacorta-Alvarez. (Illus.). 256p. 1977. 8.95. Asia Bk Corp.

Philippine Cooking in America. M. R. Doanto. 134p. 1980. 12.95. Asia Bk Corp.

Philippine Coral Reefs: A Natural History Guide. Alan White. (Illus.). xv, 223p. (Orig.). 1987. pap. 25.50 (ISBN 971-10-0338-4, Pub. by New Day Pub Philippines). Cellar.

Philippine Economy & the United States: Studies in Past & Present Interactions. Ed. by Norman G. Owen. LC 82-74314. (Michigan Papers on South & Southeast Asia: No. 22). xvi, 208p. (Orig.). 1984. pap. 13.95 (ISBN 0-89148-025-0). Ctr S&SE Asian.

Philippine Ethnography: A Critically Annotated & Selected Bibliography. Shiro Saito. LC 72-92068. (East-West Bibliographic Ser.: No. 2). 543p. (Orig.). 1973. pap. text ed. 20.00x (ISBN 0-8248-0258-6). UH Pr.

Philippine Folk Fiction & Tales. Teresita V. Pil. 1977. wrps. 4.25 (ISBN 0-686-09443-3, Pub. by New Day Pub.). Cellar.

Philippine Folk Tales. Mabel Cole. LC 78-67699. (Folktale). (Illus.). Repr. of 1916 ed. 30.00 (ISBN 0-404-16073-5). AMS Pr.

Philippine Foreign Policy Toward the U. S., 1972-1980: Reorientation? Virginia S. Capulong-Hallenberg. (Stockholm Studies in Politics: No. 33). 292p. (Orig.). 1987. pap. 67.50x (ISBN 91-7146-478-6, Pub. by Stockholms Universitet (Stockholm Sweden)). Coronet Bks.

Philippine Hospitality: A Gracious Tradition of the East. Lily G. O'Boyle & Reynaldo Alejandro. Ed. by Sonia Ner & Lyn Almario. 224p. 1988. 50.00 (ISBN 0-944863-00-0). Acacia Corp.

Philippine Independence: Motives, Problems & Prospects. Grayson L. Kirk. LC 72-2377. (FDR & the Era of the New Deal Ser.). 278p. 1974. Repr. of 1936 ed. lib. bdg. 37.50 (ISBN 0-306-70486-2). Da Capo.

Philippine Industrialization: Foreign & Domestic Capital. Kunio Yoshihara. 1985. pap. 17.95x (ISBN 0-19-582620-5). Oxford U Pr.

Philippine Insects: An Introduction. Clare R. Baltazar & Nelia P. Salazar. (Illus.). 1980. text ed. 17.00x (ISBN 0-8248-0675-1, Pub. by U of Philippines Pr); pap. text ed. 12.00x (ISBN 0-8248-0676-X). UH Pr.

Philippine Invasion Nineteen Forty-One to Nineteen Forty-Two: A Matter of Time. rev. ed. Robert H. Firth. LC 80-68365. 143p. 1981. pap. 6.50 (ISBN 0-9605060-0-4). Firth.

Philippine Island World: A Physical, Cultural & Regional Geography. Frederick L. Wernstedt & Joseph E. Spencer. 1978. Repr. of 1967 ed. 53.00x (ISBN 0-520-03513-5). U of Cal Pr.

Philippine Islands: Moluccas, Siam, Cambodia, Japan & China at the Close of the Sixteenth Century. Antonio De Morga. Tr. by Henry J. Stanley. 1964. 32.00 (ISBN 0-8337-2460-6). B Franklin.

Philippine Land Vertebrates: Field Biology. Angel C. Alcala. 1976. newsprint 5.25x (ISBN 0-686-09425-5). Cellar.

Philippine Languages: Discourse, Paragraph & Sentence Structure. Robert E. Longacre. (Publications in Linguistics & Related Fields Ser.: No. 21). 456p. 1968. microfiche (6) 10.80 (ISBN 0-88312-423-8). Summer Inst Ling.

Philippine Law Journal: 1914-1931, Vols. 1-10. Bound set. 250.00x (ISBN 0-686-90016-2). Rothman.

Philippine Literature in English. L. Y. Yabes. lib. bdg. 79.95 (ISBN 0-87968-568-9). Krishna Pr.

Philippine Migration: The Settlement of the Digos-Padada Valley, Davao Province. Paul D. Simkins & Frederick L. Wernstedt. LC 73-154010. (Monograph Ser.: No. 16). (Illus.). 147p. 1970. 8.50x (ISBN 0-938692-13-5). Yale U SE Asia.

Philippine Municipal Fisheries: A Review of Resources Technology & Socioeconomics. Ian R. Smith et al. (Illus.). 87p. 1983. pap. text ed. 12.00x (ISBN 0-89955-388-5, Pub. by ICLARM Philippines). Intl Spec Bk.

Philippine Pagans: The Autobiographies of Three Ifugaos. Roy F. Barton. LC 76-44686. Repr. of 1938 ed. 30.00 (ISBN 0-404-15903-6). AMS Pr.

Philippine Permanent & General Statutes, 5 vols. University Of The Philippines Law Center Editors. (Illus.). 1971-73. Set. lib. bdg. 250.00 (ISBN 0-379-20125-9); lib. bdg. 50.00 ea. Oceana.

Philippine Policy Toward Sabah: A Claim to Independence. Lela G. Noble. LC 77-77849. (Association for Asian Studies Monograph: No. 33). 267p. 1977. 10.50x (ISBN 0-8165-0597-7). U of Ariz Pr.

Philippine Postage Stamp Handbook, 1854-1982. Peter W. Harradine. LC 84-43212. (Illus.). 475p. 1987. lib. bdg. 29.95 (ISBN 0-89950-178-8). McFarland & Co.

Philippine Republic. Leandro H. Fernandez. LC 68-57571. (Columbia University. Studies in the Social Sciences: No. 268). Repr. of 1926 ed. 18.50 (ISBN 0-404-51268-2). AMS Pr.

Philippine Revolution Nineteen Eighty-Six: Model of Nonviolent Change. Douglas J. Elwood. (Illus.). vi, 60p. (Orig.). 1986. pap. 5.00 (ISBN 971-10-0303-1, Pub. by New Day Philippines). Cellar.

Philippine Rural School: Its Cultural Dimension. Priscilla S. Manalang. 265p. 1976. 13.50x (ISBN 0-8248-0473-2). UH Pr.

Philippine Short Stories, 1941-1955. Ed. by Leopoldo Y. Yabes. 1400p. 1981. Set, 2 vols. text ed. 48.00x (ISBN 0-8248-0650-6). UH Pr.

Philippine Social History: Global Trade & Local Transformations. Ed. by Alfred W. McCoy & Ed. C. De Jesus. 488p. 1982. pap. text ed. 12.95x (ISBN 0-8248-0803-7). UH Pr.

Philippine Society & the Individual: Selected Essays of Frank Lynch, 1949-1976. Ed. by Aram A. Yengoyan & Perla Q. Makil. LC 82-72447. (Michigan Papers on South & Southeast Asia: No. 24). xvii, 469p. 1984. 26.95 (ISBN 0-89148-028-5); pap. 14.95 (ISBN 0-89148-029-3). Ctr S&SE Asian.

Philippine State & the Marcos Regime: The Politics of Export. Gary Hawes. LC 86-29218. (Cornell Studies in Political Economy). 216p. 1987. 25.00x (ISBN 0-8014-2012-1). Cornell U Pr.

Philippine Studies: Political Science, Economics, & Linguistics, No. 8. Ed. by Donn V. Hart. (NIU Center for SEAsian Studies, Occasional Papers). 294p. 1981. pap. 14.00x (ISBN 0-686-35858-9). North Ill U Ctr SE Asian.

Philippine Supreme Court Reports Annotated, 1961-1980, 113 vols. 40.00 ea. (ISBN 0-379-12500-5); Set 3 vols. quick index digest. 75.00. Oceana.

Philippine Treaty Series, 4 Vols. University of the Philippines Law Center Editors. 1968-81. Set. 175.00 (ISBN 0-379-16050-1). Oceana.

Philippine World-View. Virgilio G. Enriquez. 148p. 1986. pap. text ed. 21.50x (ISBN 9971-988-19-4, Pub. by Inst Southeast Asian Stud). Gower Pub Co.

Philippine Writing: An Anthology. Ed. by T. D. Agcaoili. LC 76-98742. 1971. Repr. of 1953 ed. lib. bdg. 35.00x (ISBN 0-8371-3063-8, AGPW). Greenwood.

Philippine Yearbook, 1982-83. cancelled. Intl Pubns Serv.

Philippines. Richard Z. Chesnoff. LC 77-99197. (Illus.). 288p. 1978. 125.00 (ISBN 0-8109-1458-1). Abrams.

Philippines. Ed. by Harrap Limited Staff. 1986. pap. 49.75X (ISBN 0-245-54017-2, Pub. by Harrap Ltd England). State Mutual Bk.

Philippines. Insight Guides Staff. (Illus.). 338p. 1983. pap. 16.95 (ISBN 0-13-662197-X). P-H.

Philippines. Emilie U. Lepthien. LC 83-23152. (Enchantment of the World Ser.). (Illus.). 128p. (gr. 5-9). 1984. lib. bdg. 22.60 (ISBN 0-516-02782-4). Childrens.

Philippines. (Let's Visit Places & Peoples - - Nations, Dependencies, & Sovereignties of the World Ser.). (Illus.). (gr. 5 up). 1988. 12.95 (ISBN 0-7910-0105-9). Chelsea Hse.

Philippines: A Country in Crisis. 1983. write for info. (ISBN 0-934143-10-2). Lawyers Comm Intl.

Philippines: A Country Study. 3rd ed. Ed. by Frederica M. Bunge. LC 84-6382. (Area Handbook Ser.: DA Pam 550-72). (Illus.). 404p. 1984. 15.00 (ISBN 0-318-21886-0, S/N 008-020-01004-9). USGPO.

Philippines: A Framework for Economic Recovery. World Bank Staff. 1987. 10.00 (ISBN 0-8213-0942-0, BK0942). World Bank.

Philippines: A Nation in the Making. Felix M. Keesing. LC 71-179211. Repr. of 1937 ed. 23.50 (ISBN 0-404-54839-3). AMS Pr.

Philippines: A Singular & a Plural Place. David J. Steinberg. LC 82-8407. (Illus.). 160p. 1982. lib. bdg. 28.50x (ISBN 0-89158-990-2); pap. 14.95x (ISBN 0-86531-751-8). Westview.

Philippines: A Study in National Development. Joseph R. Hayden. LC 72-4276. (World Affairs Ser.: National & International Viewpoints). (Illus.). 1050p. 1972. Repr. of 1942 ed. 57.00 (ISBN 0-405-04570-0). Ayer Co Pubs.

Philippines: A Travel Survival Kit. 3rd ed. Jens Peters. (Illus.). 360p. (Orig.). 1987. pap. 8.95 (ISBN 0-908086-92-X). Lonely Planet.

Philippines: A Treasure & a Problem. Nicholas Roosevelt. LC 71-100510. Repr. of 1926 ed. 24.00 (ISBN 0-404-00618-3). AMS Pr.

Philippines after Marcos. Ed. by R. J. May & Francisco Nemenzo. LC 85-1851. 288p. 1985. 29.95 (ISBN 0-312-60419-X). St Martin.

Philippines: An Annotated Bibliography on Regional Development. (Country Bibliography Ser.: No. 3). 83p. 1979. pap. 7.50 (ISBN 0-686-75156-6, CRD005, UNCRD). UNIPUB.

Philippines: Democracy in Asia. Salvador R. Gonzales. LC 87-63563. 186p. 1987. pap. 8.50 (ISBN 0-945197-00-4). Burgos & Burgos Ltd.

Philippines Facing the Future: An Assessment of the Prospects for the Philippines & the Philippine-American Relations. The Asia Society. (Asian Agenda Report: No. 4). (Illus.). 48p. 1986. pap. text ed. 4.25 (ISBN 0-8191-5550-0, Pub. by the Asia Soc). U Pr of Amer.

Philippines Handbook. Peter Harper. 600p. Date not set. price not set (ISBN 0-918373-01-8). Moon Pubns CA.

Philippines: Housing Finance. Madhusudan Joshi et al. 137p. 1983. 5.00 (ISBN 0-8213-0108-X, BK 0108). World Bank.

Philippines in Focus. Simon Barnes. ("In Focus" Ser.). (Illus.). 64p. (Orig.). 1981. pap. 5.95 (ISBN 962-7031-13-5, Pub. by CFW Pubns Hong Kong). C E Tuttle.

Philippines Is in the Heart: A Collection of Short Stories. Carlos Bulosan, Jr. (Illus.). 1979. pap. 4.50x newsprint (ISBN 0-686-25219-5, Pub. by New Day Pub). Cellar.

Philippines: People, Poverty & Politics. Leonard Davis. 320p. 1987. 29.95 (ISBN 0-312-00412-5). St Martin.

Philippines: Priorities & Prospects for Development. World Bank. LC 76-17243. (World Bank Country Economic Report Ser.). (Illus.). 596p. 1976. pap. 10.00x (ISBN 0-8018-1893-1). Johns Hopkins.

Philippines Reader: A History of Colonialism, Neocolonialism Dictatorship, & Resistance. Ed. by Daniel B. Schirmer & Stephen R. Shalom. 400p. (Orig.). 1987. 30.00 (ISBN 0-89608-276-8); pap. 11.00 (ISBN 0-89608-275-X). South End Pr.

Philippines Report. (Working Papers Ser.: No. 79-20). 51p. 1978. pap. 6.00 (ISBN 0-686-78215-1, CRD049, UNCRD). UNIPUB.

Philippines Report, Pt. III: Barangay Profile. (Working Papers Ser.: No. 79-22). 137p. 1979. pap. 7.50 (ISBN 0-686-78246-1, CRD030, UNCRD). UNIPUB.

Philippines: Survey of Trends on Urbanization & Regionalization. (Working Papers Ser.: No. 74-2). 86p. 1979. pap. 6.00 (ISBN 0-686-78247-X, CRD029, UNCRD). UNIPUB.

Philippines to the End of the Commission Government: A Study in Tropical Democracy. Charles B. Elliott. LC 69-10088. 1969. Repr. of 1917 ed. lib. bdg. 35.00x (ISBN 0-8371-0406-8, ELPH). Greenwood.

Philippines under Aquino: Crisis & Response. Larry Niksch. (CSIS Washington Papers). 1988. write for info. CSI Studies.

Philippines: Unlawful Killings by Military & Paramilitary. Amnesty Interantional Staff. 66p. (Orig., Span.). 1988. pap. 6.00 (ISBN 0-939994-36-4, Pub. by Amnesty Intl Pubns UK). Amnesty Intl USA.

Philippus see De Pace.

Philip's Chair: Life with a Younger Man. Dale Eunson. 1988. 18.95 (ISBN 0-916515-48-6). Mercury Hse Inc.

Philip's Cousin Jesus: The Untold Story. Fenwicke Holmes & Margaret McEathron. LC 81-65247. 425p. 1982. pap. 9.95. Reading Hse.

Philip's Cousin Jesus: The Untold Story. Fenwicke Holmes & Margaret McEathron. LC 82-65247. 425p. 1982. pap. 9.95 (ISBN 0-87516-494-3). DeVorss.

Philips Family Record 1978. George O. Philips. (Illus.). 520p. (Orig.). 1979. pap. 17.50 (ISBN 0-940846-00-4). Hastings Bks.

Philistine, 10 vols. Elbert Hubbard. 1000.00 (ISBN 0-8490-0824-7). Gordon Pr.

Philistines. Arlo Bates. LC 74-104412. 442p. Repr. of 1889 ed. lib. bdg. 29.00 (ISBN 0-8398-0154-8). Irvington.

Philistines. Arlo Bates. 442p. 1986. pap. text ed. 8.95x (ISBN 0-8290-1880-8). Irvington.

Philistines & the Old Testament. Edward E. Hindson. (Baker Studies in Biblical Archaeology). pap. 6.95 (ISBN 0-8010-4034-5). Baker Bk.

Philistines & Their Material Culture. Trude Dothan. LC 80-22060. 352p. 1982. 55.00t (ISBN 0-300-02258-1). Yale U Pr.

Philistines: Their History & Civilization. R. A. Macalister. (British Academy, London, Schweich Lectures on Biblical Archaeology Series 1911). pap. 19.00 (ISBN 0-8115-1253-3). Kraus Repr.

Philistinism in England & America see Complete Prose Works of Matthew Arnold.

Phillimore Atlas & Index of Parish Registers. Cecil R. Humphery-Smith. LC 84-81205. (Illus.). 304p. 1984. 50.00 (ISBN 0-8063-1088-X). Genealog Pub.

Phillip Blanc in San Francisco. Steve Brooks. (Illus.). 20p. 1972. pap. 3.00 (ISBN 0-915572-12-5). Panjandrum.

Phillip Brooks: The Man, the Preacher, & the Author. Newell Dunbar. 1978. Repr. of 1893 ed. lib. bdg. 35.00 (ISBN 0-8492-0668-5). R West.

Phillip Mazzei: Selected Writings & Correspondence, 3 vols. Ed. by Margherita Marchione & B. J. Idzerda. (Illus.). Set. 200.00x. Mazzei.

Phillipines. rev. ed. (Hildebrand Travel Guides). (Illus.). 320p. (Orig.). 1988. pap. 10.95 (ISBN 3-88989-089-X). Hunter Pub NY.

Phillipians: Commentary see Filipenses: Un Comentario Exegetico y Practico.

Phillipps Manuscripts: Catalogus Liberorum Maniscriptorum in Bibliotheca, 1837-71. D. Thomas Phillipps. 300.00 (ISBN 0-87556-663-4). Saifer.

Philosophers of China. Clarence B. Day. 1978. pap. 5.95 (ISBN 0-8065-0622-9, Pub. by Citadel Pr). Lyle Stuart.

Philosophers of Consciousness: Polanyi, Lonergan, Voegelin, Ricoeur, Girard, Kierkegaard. Eugene Webb. 336p. 1988. 30.00 (ISBN 0-295-96621-1). U of Wash Pr.

Philosophers of East & West: The Quest for the Meaning of Existence in Eastern & Western Thought. E. W. Tomlin. 528p. 1988. 48.00x (ISBN 81-202-0197-3, Pub. by Ajanta). South Asia Bks.

Philosophers of Greece. Robert S. Brumbaugh. LC 81-9120. (Illus.). 274p. 1981. 34.50x (ISBN 0-87395-550-1); pap. 8.95x (ISBN 0-87395-551-X). State U NY Pr.

Philosophers of Peace & War. W. B. Gallie. LC 77-23553. 1979. pap. 11.95 (ISBN 0-521-29651-X). Cambridge U Pr.

Philosophers of the Scottish Enlightenment. Ed. by Vincent Hope. 261p. 1984. 24.00x (ISBN 0-85224-477-0, Pub. by Edinburgh U Pr Scotland). Columbia U Pr.

Philosophers on Education. Ed. by Roger Straughan & John Wilson. LC 86-3297. 220p. 1986. 28.50x (ISBN 0-389-20621-0). B&N Imports.

Philosophers on Education: Six Essays on the Foundations of Western Thought. Robert S. Brumbaugh & Nathaniel M. Lawrence. 222p. 1986. pap. text ed. 9.75 (ISBN 0-8191-5131-9). U Pr of Amer.

Philosophers on their Own Work, 11 vols. Ed. by Maja Svilar & Andre Mercier. 309p. 1983. Vol. 10. 34.20 (ISBN 3-261-05090-X). P Lang Pubs.

Philosopher's Pupil. Iris Murdoch. 1983. 17.75 (ISBN 0-670-55186-4). Viking.

Philosopher's Pupil. Iris Murdoch. (Penguin Fiction Ser.). 592p. 1984. pap. 7.95 (ISBN 0-14-007614-X). Penguin.

Philosopher's Search for the Infinite. Jules M. Brady. 96p. 1983. 10.00 (ISBN 0-8022-2410-5). Philos Lib.

Philosophers Speak for Themselves: Berkeley, Hume & Kant. 2nd ed. Ed. by Thomas V. Smith & Marjorie Grene. LC 57-7905. 1957. pap. 9.00X (ISBN 0-226-76482-6, P18, Phoen). U of Chicago Pr.

Philosophers Speak for Themselves: From Descartes to Locke. 2nd ed. Ed. by Thomas V. Smith & Marjorie Grene. LC 57-7905. 1957. pap. 11.00x (ISBN 0-226-76481-8, P17, Phoen). U of Chicago Pr.

Philosophers Speak of God. Charles Hartshorne & William L. Reese. LC 53-10041. (Midway Reprint Ser.). 1976. pap. 24.00x (ISBN 0-226-31862-1). U of Chicago Pr.

Philosopher's Stone. Colin Wilson. 320p. 1974. pap. 2.95 (ISBN 0-446-33030-2). Warner Bks.

Philosopher's World Model. Archie J. Bahm. LC 78-67569. (Contributions in Philosophy: No. 12). (Illus.). 1979. lib. bdg. 35.00 (ISBN 0-313-21198-1, BPW/). Greenwood.

Philosophers's Index, 1985: Cumulative Edition, Vol. XIX. Ed. by Richard H. Lineback. 488p. 1986. lib. bdg. 89.00 (ISBN 0-912632-19-4). Philos Document.

Philosophes & the People. Harry C. Payne. LC 75-18181. (Historical Publications, Miscellany Ser: No. 109). 240p. 1976. 26.00x (ISBN 0-300-01907-6). Yale U Pr.

Philosophes-Geometres de la Grece: Platon & Ses & Predecesseurs. facsimile ed. Gaston Milhaud. LC 75-13280. (History of Ideas in Ancient Greece Ser.). (Fr.). 1976. Repr. of 1900 ed. 24.50x (ISBN 0-405-07323-2). Ayer Co Pubs.

Philosophia Botanica. C. Linnaeus. (Illus.). 1966. Repr. of 1751 ed. 90.00x (ISBN 3-7682-0350-6). Lubrecht & Cramer.

Philosophia Perennis, Vol. 1. Bhagwan Shree Rajneesh. Ed. by Ma Yoga Anurag. (Western Mystics Ser.). (Illus.). 392p. (Orig.). 1981. 8.95 (ISBN 0-88050-115-4); pap. 15.95 428p (ISBN 0-88050-615-6). Chidvilas Inc.

Philosophia Perennis, Vol. 2. Bhagwan Shree Rajneesh. Ed. by Ma Yoga Anurag. (Western Mystics Ser.). (Illus.). 436p. (Orig.). 1981. pap. 8.95 (ISBN 0-88050-616-4). Chidvilas Inc.

Philosophia Ultima. Bhagwan Shree Rajneesh. Ed. by Ma Yoga Anurag. LC 83-43216. (Upanishads Ser.). 384p. (Orig.). 1983. pap. 4.95 (ISBN 0-88050-617-2). Chidvilas Inc.

Philosophic Classics, 2 vols. 2nd ed. Walter Kaufmann. Incl. Vol. 1. Thales to Ockham. text ed. write for info. (ISBN 0-13-662403-0); Vol. 2. Bacon to Kant. text ed. write for info. (ISBN 0-13-662411-1). LC 68-15350. 1968. text ed. write for info. (ISBN 0-685-73716-0). P-H.

Philosophic Foundations of American Education. Don-chean Chu. LC 70-150045. 392p. 1971. pap. 7.00 (ISBN 0-913973-08-4). Inst Sino-Amer.

Philosophic Foundations of Quantum Mechanics. Hans Reichenbach. 192p. 1982. Repr. of 1950 ed. 25.00x (ISBN 0-520-04765-6). U of Cal Pr.

Philosophic Initiation: Soul Conciousness. R. Swinburne Clymer. 268p. 1955. 8.95 (ISBN 0-932785-37-9). Philos Pub.

Philosophic Inquiry in Sport. Ed. by William J. Morgan & Klaus V. Meier. LC 87-2767. 560p. 1987. text ed. 32.00x (ISBN 0-87322-119-2, BMOR0119). Human Kinetics.

Philosophic Nights in Paris. facsimile ed. Remy De Gourmont. Tr. by I. Goldberg. LC 68-8465. (Essay Index Reprint Ser). 1920. 17.00 (ISBN 0-8369-1293-4). Ayer Co Pubs.

Philosophic Problems of Nuclear Science see Philosophical Problems of Quantum Physics.

Philosophic Process in Physical Education. 3rd ed. William A. Harper. LC 76-10373. pap. 87.50 (2056188). Bks Demand UMI.

Philosophic Roots of Modern Ideology: Liberalism, Communism, Fascism. David E. Ingersoll & Richard K. Matthews. 304p. 1986. pap. text ed. write for info. (ISBN 0-13-662503-7). P-H.

Philosophic Thought in France & the United States: Essays Representing Major Trends in Contemporary French & American Philosophy. Ed. by Marvin Farber. pap. 160.00 (ISBN 0-317-09067-4, 2010107). Bks Demand UMI.

Philosophic Thought of Ayn Rand. Intro. by Douglas J Den Uyl & Douglas B. Rasmussen. LC 83-5844. 248p. 1984. 21.95 (ISBN 0-252-01033-7); pap. 12.95 (ISBN 0-252-01407-3). U of Ill Pr.

Philosophic Way of Life. T. V. Smith. 1978. Repr. of 1929 ed. 25.00 (ISBN 0-8492-8236-5). R West.

Philosophic Way of Life in America. 2nd ed. Thomas V. Smith. LC 68-15836. 1968. Repr. of 1943 ed. 23.00x (ISBN 0-8046-0431-2, Pub. by Kennikat). Assoc Faculty Pr.

Philosophic Words, a Study of Style & Meaning in the Rambler & Dictionary of Samuel Johnson. William K. Wimsatt, Jr. LC 68-16343. xvi, 167p. 1968. Repr. of 1948 ed. 21.00 (ISBN 0-208-00086-0, Archon). Shoe String.

Philosophical Adventures with Children. Michael S. Pritchard. LC 85-15795. 166p. (Orig.). 1985. lib. bdg. 26.25 (ISBN 0-8191-4896-2); pap. text ed. 11.50 (ISBN 0-8191-4897-0). U Pr of Amer.

Philosophical Analysis: A Collection of Essays. facsimile ed. Ed. by Max Black. LC 78-152158. (Essay Index Reprint Ser). Repr. of 1950 ed. 27.50 (ISBN 0-8369-2214-X). Ayer Co Pubs.

Philosophical Analysis: A Collection of Essays. Ed. by Max Black. LC 78-152158. (Essay Index Reprint Ser.). 405p. Repr. of 1950 ed. lib. bdg. 49.00 (ISBN 0-8290-0796-2). Irvington.

Philosophical Analysis: A Defense by Example. Ed. by David F. Austin. 1988. lib. bdg. 79.00 (ISBN 90-277-2674-4, Pub. by Reidel Holland). Kluwer Academic.

Philosophical Analysis: An Introduction to Its Language & Techniques. 3rd ed. Samuel Gorovitz et al. LC 78-5661. 1979. pap. text ed. write for info (ISBN 0-394-32284-3, RanC). Random.

Philosophical Analysis & Human Welfare. Dickinson S. Miller. Ed. by Loyd D. Easton. LC 75-4832. (Philosophical Studies: No. 3). x, 335p. 1975. lib. bdg. 55.00 (ISBN 90-277-0566-6, Pub. by Reidel Holland). Kluwer Academic.

Philosophical Analysis & Illustration of Some of Shakespeare's Remarkable Characters. new corr. ed. William Richardson. LC 17-30453. Repr. of 1780 ed. 17.50 (ISBN 0-404-05309-2). AMS Pr.

Philosophical Analysis in Latin America. Ed. by Jorge J. Garcia et al. 1984. lib. bdg. 55.00 (ISBN 90-277-1749-4, Pub. by Reidel Holland). Kluwer Academic.

Philosophical Analysis: Its Development Between the Two World Wars. J. O. Urmson. 1956. 19.95x (ISBN 0-19-824172-0). Oxford U Pr.

Philosophical Analysis of Buddhist Notions. A. D. Kalasuriya. 255p. 1987. 28.00 (ISBN 0-317-60652-2, Pub. by SRI SATGURU Pubns India). Orient Bk Dist.

Philosophical Anarchism of William Godwin. John P. Clark. LC 76-24291. 1977. 45.50x (ISBN 0-691-07217-5). Princeton U Pr.

Philosophical & Historical Roots of Occupational Therapy. Ed. by Karen Diasio Serrett. LC 85-8838. (Occupational Therapy & Mental Health Ser.: Vol. 5, No. 3). 113p. 1985. text ed. 22.95 (ISBN 0-86656-456-X, B456); pap. text ed. 17.95 (ISBN 0-86656-527-2, B527). Haworth Pr.

Philosophical & Ideological Perspectives on Education. Gerald L. Gutek. (Illus.). 336p. 1988. text ed. price not set (ISBN 0-13-662594-0). P-H.

Philosophical & Literary Commentary on Martianus Capella's De Nuptiis Philologiae Et Mercurii. Danuta Shanzer. (UC Publications in Classical Studies: Vol. 32). 1987. pap. 30.00x (ISBN 0-520-09716-5). U of Cal Pr.

Philosophical & Literary Pieces. facsimile ed. Samuel Alexander. LC 70-93313. (Essay Index Reprint Ser). 1940. 24.50 (ISBN 0-8369-1269-1). Ayer Co Pubs.

Philosophical & Mathematical Correspondence. Gottlob Frege. Ed. by Brian McGuinness. Tr. by Hans Kaal. LC 79-23199. 1980. lib. bdg. 31.00x (ISBN 0-226-26197-2). U of Chicago Pr.

Philosophical & Radical Thought in Marketing. Ed. by A. Fuat Firat & Nikhilesh Dholakia. LC 86-45791. 384p. 1987. 45.00x (ISBN 0-669-14301-4). Lexington Bks.

Philosophical Anthropology of George Herbert Mead. George Cronk. (American University Studies Series V Philosophy: Vol. 27). 200p. 1987. text ed. 26.00 (ISBN 0-8204-0404-7). P Lang Pubs.

Philosophical Apprenticeships. Hans-Georg Gadamer. Tr. by Robert R. Sullivan from Ger. (Studies in Contemporary German Social Thought). 205p. 1985. 19.50 (ISBN 0-262-07092-8). MIT Pr.

Philosophical Apprenticeships. Hans-Georg Gadamer. 232p. 1987. pap. 9.95 (ISBN 0-262-57066-1). MIT Pr.

Philosophical Approach to the Management of Occupational Health Hazards. June Fessenden-Raden & Bernard Gert. 43p. 1984. pap. text ed. 2.00x (ISBN 0-88738-641-5). Transaction Bks.

Philosophical Approaches to Literature: New Essays on Nineteenth & Twentieth Century Texts. Ed. by William E. Cain. LC 82-48652. 256p. 1984. 29.50 (ISBN 0-8387-5055-9). Bucknell U Pr.

Philosophical Artwork & Other Writings. Richard Schain. LC 83-81441. 170p. (Orig.). 1983. pap. 6.00 (ISBN 0-9609922-1-9). Garric Pr.

Philosophical Aspects of Modern Science. Cyril E. Joad. (Select Bibliographies Reprint Ser.). 1972. Repr. of 1932 ed. 21.00 (ISBN 0-8369-6886-7). Ayer Co Pubs.

Philosophical Aspects of Thanatology, Vol. 1. Florence M. Hetzler & Austin H. Kutscher. 17.50 (ISBN 0-405-12515-1). Ayer Co Pubs.

Philosophical Aspects of Thanatology, Vol. 2. Florence M. Hetzler & Austin H. Kutscher. 17.50 (ISBN 0-405-12516-X). Ayer Co Pubs.

Philosophical Aspects of the Mind-Body Problem. Ed. by Chung-ying Cheng. 226p. 1975. text ed. 16.00x (ISBN 0-8248-0342-6). UH Pr.

Philosophical Assessment of Theology: Essays in Honour of Frederick C. Copleston. Ed. by Gerard J. Hughes. LC 87-94. (Orig.). 1987. pap. 29.95 (ISBN 0-87840-449-X). Georgetown U Pr.

Philosophical Background to Friedrich Schiller's Aesthetics of Living Form, Vol. 578. Leonard P. Wessell, Jr. (European University Ser. 1: German Language & Literature Ser.). 174p. 1982. pap. 23.15 (ISBN 3-8204-7195-2). P Lang Pubs.

Philosophical Bases of Theism. George D. Hicks. LC 77-27142. (Hibbert Lectures: 1931). Repr. of 1937 ed. 31.00 (ISBN 0-404-60427-7). AMS Pr.

Philosophical Basis of Biology. J. B. Haldane. 1931. 25.00 (ISBN 0-8274-4213-0). R West.

Philosophical Basis of Medical Practice: Toward a Philosophy & Ethic of the Healing Professions. Edmund D. Pellegrino & David C. Thomasma. (Illus.). 1981. 29.95x (ISBN 0-19-502790-6); text ed. 12.95x (ISBN 0-19-502789-2). Oxford U Pr.

Philosophical Biographer: Doubt & Dialectic in Johnson's Lives of the Poets. Martin Maner. LC 87-34296. 168p. 1989. 26.00x (ISBN 0-8203-1038-7). U of Ga Pr.

Philosophical Chemistry. A. Donovan. 343p. 1983. 24.00x (ISBN 0-85224-281-6, Pub. by Edinburgh U Pr Scotland). Columbia U Pr.

Philosophical Commentaries, Transcribed from the Manuscript & Edited, with an Introduction & Index by George H. Thomas: Explanatory Notes by A. A. Luce. Ed. by George Pitcher. (Philosophy of George Berkeley Ser.). 387p. 1988. lib. bdg. 60.00 (ISBN 0-8240-2440-0). Garland Pub.

Philosophical Concepts & Values in Adult Education. K. H. Lawson. 128p. 1979. pap. 24.00x (ISBN 0-335-00254-4, Pub. by Open Univ Pr). Taylor & Francis.

Philosophical Correspondence, 1759-99. Immanuel Kant. Ed. by Arnulf Zweig. LC 66-23705. 1986. Repr. of 1967 ed. 67.50 (ISBN 0-317-08046-6, 2022503). Bks Demand UMI.

Philosophical Correspondence: 1759-99. Immanuel Kant. Ed. by Arnulf Zweig. x, 260p. 1986. pap. 15.00x (ISBN 0-226-42361-1, Midway Reprint). U of Chicago Pr.

Philosophical Critiques of Policy Analysis: Lindblom, Habermas, & the Great Society. Lance De Haven-Smith. Date not set. text ed. price not set (ISBN 0-8130-0907-3). U Presses Fla.

Philosophical Dictionary. Voltaire. Tr. by Theodore Besterman. (Penguin Classics Ser.). 400p. 1984. pap. 6.95 (ISBN 0-14-044257-X). Penguin.

Philosophical Dilemma & the Conception of Truth, 2 vols. William James. 315p. (Orig.). 1985. Repr. Set. 167.85 (ISBN 0-89901-216-7). Found Class Reprints.

Philosophical Dimensions of Privacy: An Anthology. Ed. by Ferdinand D. Schoeman. 350p. 1984. 47.50 (ISBN 0-521-25555-4); pap. 15.95 (ISBN 0-521-27554-7). Cambridge U Pr.

Philosophical Dimensions of the Constitution. Ed. by Kenneth Kipnis & Diana T. Meyers. 256p. 1988. 45.95 (ISBN 0-8133-0675-2). Westview.

Philosophical Dimensions of the Neuro-Medical Sciences. Stuart F. Spicker & H. Tristram Engelhardt, Jr. LC 76-1204. (Philosophy & Medicine Ser.: Vol. 2). 1976. lib. bdg. 34.00 (ISBN 90-277-0672-7, Pub. by Reidel Holland). Kluwer Academic.

Philosophical Discourse Concerning Speech. Geraud De Cordemoy. Bd. with Discourse Written by a Learned Frier. Repr. of 1670 ed. LC 78-147961. Repr. of 1668 ed. 15.00 (ISBN 0-404-08211-4). AMS Pr.

Philosophical Discourse Concerning Speech (1668) & a Discourse Written to a Learned Frier (1670) Geraud de Cordemoy. LC 72-6400. (History of Psychology Ser.). 232p. 1972. Repr. 35.00x (ISBN 0-8201-1106-6). Schol Facsimiles.

Philosophical Discourse of Modernity: Twelve Lectures. Jurgen Habermas. Tr. by Frederick G. Lawrence from Ger. (Studies in Contemporary German Social Thought). 600p. 1987. text ed. 27.50x (ISBN 0-262-08163-6). MIT Pr.

Philosophical Discussions. Chauncey Wright. 1971. Repr. of 1877 ed. lib. bdg. 29.00 (ISBN 0-8337-3895-X). B Franklin.

Philosophical Disenfranchisement of Art. Arthur C. Danto. LC 86-2260. 1986. 25.00x (ISBN 0-231-06364-4). Columbia U Pr.

Philosophical Disenfranchisement of Art. Arthur C. Danto. 216p. 1988. pap. 13.00x (ISBN 0-231-06365-2). Columbia U Pr.

Philosophical Enquiries. Margaret Chatterjee. 294p. 1988. Repr. of 1968 ed. 16.50x (ISBN 0-317-67680-6, Pub. by Motilal Banarsidass). South Asia Bks.

Philosophical Essay: Declaring the Probable Causes Whence Stones Are Produced in the Greater World. Thomas Sherley. Ed. by Claude C. Albritton, Jr. LC 77-6541. (History of Geology Ser.). 1978. Repr. of 1672 ed. lib. bdg. 17.00x (ISBN 0-405-10460-X). Ayer Co Pubs.

Philosophical Essays. Alfred J. Ayer. LC 79-24852. 289p. 1980. Repr. of 1954 ed. lib. bdg. 35.00x (ISBN 0-313-20902-2, AYPE). Greenwood.

Philosophical Essays. O. K. Bouwsma. LC 82-70014. (Landmark Edition). x, 209p. 1982. Repr. of 1965 ed. 18.95x (ISBN 0-8032-1179-1). U of Nebr Pr.

Philosophical Essays. Richard Cartwright. 312p. 1987. text ed. 25.00x (ISBN 0-262-03130-2). MIT Pr.

Philosophical Essays. Bertrand Russell. 1984. pap. 5.95 (ISBN 0-671-50583-1, Touchstone). S&S.

Philosophical Essays. Descartes. Laurence J. Lafleur. (LLA Ser.: No. 99). 1964. pap. text ed. write for info. (ISBN 0-02-367240-4). Macmillan.

Philosophical Essays: Discourse on Method; Meditations; Rules for the Direction of the Mind. Rene Descartes. Tr. by Laurence J. Lafleur. LC 63-16951. (Orig.). 1964. pap. 7.87 scp (ISBN 0-672-60292-X, LLA99). Bobbs.

Philosophical Essays for Alfred North Whitehead. Alfred N. Whitehead. Ed. by Otis H. Lee. LC 66-24769. 1967. Repr. of 1936 ed. 8.50x (ISBN 0-8462-0970-5). Russell.

Philosophical Essays: From Ancient Creed to Technological Man. Hans Jonas. pap. 18.00x (ISBN 0-226-40591-5, Midway Reprint). U of Chicago Pr.

Philosophical Essays in Honor of James Edwin Creighton. facs. ed. Ed. by George H. Sabine. LC 67-23258. (Essay Index Reprint Ser). 1917. 21.50 (ISBN 0-8369-0789-2). Ayer Co Pubs.

Philosophical Essays in the Honor of Edgar Arthur Singer Jr. F. P. Clarke & M. C. Nahm. LC 78-80394. (Essay Index Reprint Ser). 1942. 23.75 (ISBN 0-8369-1062-1). Ayer Co Pubs.

Philosophical Essays on Dance: With Responses from Choreographers, Critics & Dancers. Ed. by Gordon Fancher & Gerald Myers. LC 81-67061. 178p. (Orig.). 1981. pap. 14.95 (ISBN 0-87127-126-5, Pub. by Dance Horiz). Princeton Bk Co.

Philosophical Essays on Dreaming. Ed. by Charles E. Dunlop. LC 77-4582. 372p. 1977. 32.50x (ISBN 0-8014-1015-0). Cornell U Pr.

Philosophical Essays on Freud. R. Wollheim & J. Hopkins. LC 82-1123. 250p. 1983. 47.50 (ISBN 0-521-24076-X); pap. 16.95 (ISBN 0-521-28425-2). Cambridge U Pr.

Philosophical Essays on the Ideas of a Good Society, No. 1. Ed. by Yeager Hudson & Creighton Peden. LC 87-31358. (Studies in Social & Political Theory: Vol. 2). 354p. 1988. lib. bdg. 49.95x (ISBN 0-88946-102-3). E Mellen.

Philosophical Essays Presented to John Watson. facsimile ed. Queen's University, Faculty of the Arts. LC 70-156704. (Essay Index Reprint Ser). Repr. of 1922 ed. 21.00 (ISBN 0-8369-2291-3). Ayer Co Pubs.

Philosophical Essence of Islam. Mohamed. (Essential Library of the Great Philosophies). (Illus.). 143p. 1985. 117.50 (ISBN 0-317-19583-2). Am Inst Psych.

Philosophical Essence of the Oriental World. Georg Hegel & Georg W. Friedrich. (Illus.). 133p. 1984. 127.75 (ISBN 0-89266-437-1). Am Classical Coll Pr.

Philosophical Ethics: An Introduction to Moral Philosophy. Tom L. Beauchamp. Ed. by Kaye Pace. 416p. 1982. text ed. 32.95x (ISBN 0-07-004203-9). McGraw.

Philosophical Experiments & Observations. Robert Hooke. Ed. by W. Derham. (Illus.). 398p. 1967. 55.00x (ISBN 0-7146-1115-8, F Cass Co). Biblio Dist.

Philosophical Explanations. Robert Nozick. LC 81-1369. 768p. 1981. 32.00x (ISBN 0-674-66448-5, Belknap Pr). Harvard U Pr.

Philosophical Explanations. Robert Nozick. 792p. 1983. pap. 10.95 (ISBN 0-674-66479-5, Belknap Pr). Harvard U Pr.

Philosophical Explorations: Freedom, God, & Goodness. Steven Cahn. 230p. 1988. pap. text ed. 14.95 (ISBN 0-87975-487-7). Prometheus Bks.

Philosophical Fact & Paradox. Francis Schwanauer. (American University Studies V: Philosophy). 244p. 1987. text ed. 37.50 (ISBN 0-8204-0429-2). P Lang Pubs.

Philosophical Fisherman. Harold Blaisdell. 384p. 1986. pap. 12.95 (ISBN 0-941130-13-4). N Lyons Bks.

Philosophical Foundations of Adult Education. Ed. by John L. Elias & Sharan Merriam. LC 79-21655. 218p. 1980. 15.50 (ISBN 0-88275-971-X). Krieger.

Philosophical Sketches of the Principles of Society & Government. William Drummond. LC 86-17791. 1986. Repr. of 1795 ed. 50.00x (ISBN 0-8201-1418-9). Schol Facsimiles.

Philosophical Sovietology. Thomas Blakeley. 1988. lib. bdg. 69.00 (ISBN 90-277-2637-X, Pub. by Reidel Holland). Kluwer Academic.

Philosophical Statements. Lonnie Gardner. 1986. 5.95 (ISBN 0-533-06605-0). Vantage.

Philosophical Studies. facs. ed. John M. McTaggart. Ed. by S. V. Keeling. LC 67-22104. (Essay Index Reprint Ser). 1934. 17.75 (ISBN 0-8369-0660-8). Ayer Co Pubs.

Philosophical Studies. facsimile ed. A. E. Taylor. LC 75-13298. (History of Ideas in Ancient Greece Ser.). 1976. Repr. of 1934 ed. 26.50x (ISBN 0-405-07342-9). Ayer Co Pubs.

Philosophical Studies. facs. ed. Alfred E. Taylor. LC 68-26480. (Essay Index Reprint Ser). 1968. Repr. of 1934 ed. 20.00 (ISBN 0-8369-0926-7). Ayer Co Pubs.

Philosophical Study of the Mysticism of Sankara. G. Sundara Ramaiah. 1983. 12.00x (ISBN 0-686-88924-X, Pub. by KP Bagchi India). South Asia Bks.

Philosophical Style: An Anthology about the Reading & Writing of Philosophy. Berel Lang. LC 85-20424. 560p. 1980. 12.50; lib. bdg. 12.50 (ISBN 0-317-39883-0). Hackett Pub.

Philosophical Style: An Anthology About the Writings, & Readings of Philosophy. Berel Lang. LC 79-20424. 544p. 1980. 29.95x (ISBN 0-88229-230-7). Nelson-Hall.

Philosophical Subjects: Essays Presented to P. F. Strawson. Ed. by Zak Van Straaten. 1980. 45.00x (ISBN 0-19-824603-X). Oxford U Pr.

Philosophical Systems: A Categorical Analysis. Everett W. Hall. LC 60-11824. 1960. 12.50x (ISBN 0-226-31321-2). U of Chicago Pr.

Philosophical Tales. Jonathan Ree. 192p. 1988. pap. text ed. 11.95 (ISBN 0-416-42620-4). Routledge Chapman & Hall.

Philosophical Teachings in the Upanisats. Mohan L. Sandal. LC 73-3831. (Sacred Books of the Hindus: Extra Vol. 5). Repr. of 1926 ed. 17.00 (ISBN 0-404-57849-7). AMS Pr.

Philosophical Terms in the Moreh Nebukim. Israel I. Efros. LC 73-164764. (Columbia University. Oriental Studies: No. 22). Repr. of 1924 ed. 17.00 (ISBN 0-404-50512-0). AMS Pr.

Philosophical Themes in Modern Education. Robert S. Brumbaugh & Nathaniel M. Lawrence. (Illus.). 304p. 1985. pap. text ed. 13.50 (ISBN 0-8191-4718-4). U Pr of Amer.

Philosophical Theology. James F. Ross. 366p. 1982. 49.50x (ISBN 0-8290-0335-5). Irvington.

Philosophical Theology of Jonathan Edwards. Sang Hyun Lee. 272p. 1988. text ed. 35.00 (ISBN 0-691-07325-2). Princeton U Pr.

Philosophical Theories. M. Lazerowitz & A. Ambrose. 1976. text ed. 22.00x (ISBN 90-2797-501-9). Mouton.

Philosophical Theory & Psychological Fact: An Attempt at Synthesis. Charles F. Wallraff. LC 61-15392. 218p. 1961. 6.00x (ISBN 0-8165-0071-1). U of Ariz Pr.

Philosophical Theory & Social Reality. Ed. by Ravinder Kumar. 200p. 1984. 22.95 (ISBN 0-8364-1171-4, Pub. by Allied India). South Asia Bks.

Philosophical Theory & Social Reality. Ed. by Ravinder Kumar. 201p. 1984. 24.95. Asia Bk Corp.

Philosophical Theory of the State. 2nd ed. Bernard Bosanquet. 1986. lib. bdg. 25.00X (ISBN 0-935005-19-6); pap. text ed. 14.00X (ISBN 0-935005-20-X). Ibis Pub VA.

Philosophical Thought in America, 3 vols. Incl. Vol. 1. Panorama of Ideas in Latin America. 24p. 1971. pap. 1.00 (ISBN 0-8270-5860-8); Vol. 2. Thinkers of Latin America - Andres Bello, Domingo Faustino Sarmiento, Silvio Romero. 16p. 1972. pap. 1.00 (ISBN 0-8270-5865-9); Vol. 3. Inter-American Idea in the United States. 1976. pap. 3.00 (ISBN 0-8270-5885-3). OAS.

Philosophical Trends in the Contemporary World. Michele F. Sciacca. Tr. by Attilio M. Salerno. LC 64-20845. 1964. 49.50x (ISBN 0-268-00210-X). Irvington.

Philosophical Understanding & Religious Truth. Erich Frank. LC 82-8476. 220p. 1982. pap. text ed. 12.50 (ISBN 0-8191-2510-5). U Pr of Amer.

Philosophical Works, 5 vols. Henry Viscount Bolingbroke. Ed. by Rene Wellek. LC 75-11198. (British Philosophers & Theologians of the 17th & 18th Centuries: Vol. 5). 1976. Repr. of 1777 ed. Set. lib. bdg. 231.00 (ISBN 0-8240-1754-4); lib. bdg. 254.00. Garland Pub.

Philosophical Works, 2 Vols. Rene Descartes. Ed. by E. S. Haldane & G. R. Ross. 1967. Vol. 2. 59.50 (ISBN 0-521-06944-0); Vol. 1. pap. 16.95 (ISBN 0-521-09416-X); Vol. 2. pap. 14.95 (ISBN 0-521-09417-8). Cambridge U Pr.

Philosophical Works, 4 Vols. David Hume. Ed. by Hill Green & H. Hodge Grose. Repr. of 1882 ed. Set. half lea. 382.25x (ISBN 3-511-01210-4). Adlers Foreign Bks.

Philosophical Works. Philo. Incl. Vol. 1 (ISBN 0-674-99249-0); Vol. 2 (ISBN 0-674-99250-4); Vol. 3 (ISBN 0-674-99272-5); Vol. 4 (ISBN 0-674-99287-3); Vol. 5 (ISBN 0-674-99303-9); Vol. 6 (ISBN 0-674-99319-5); Vol. 7 (ISBN 0-674-99353-5); Vol. 8 (ISBN 0-674-99376-4); Vol. 9 (ISBN 0-674-99400-0); Vol. 10 (ISBN 0-674-99417-5); Suppl. 1 (ISBN 0-674-99418-3); Suppl. 2 (ISBN 0-674-99442-6). (Loeb Classical Library: No. 226-227, 247, 261, 289, 320, 341, 363, 379, 380, 401). 13.95x ea. Harvard U Pr.

Philosophical Works, 4 vols. Sextus Empiricus. (Loeb Classical Library: No. 273, 291, 311, 382). 13.95x ea. Vol. 1 (ISBN 0-674-99301-2). Vol. 2 (ISBN 0-674-99321-7). Vol. 3 (ISBN 0-674-99344-6). Vol. 4 (ISBN 0-674-99420-5). Harvard U Pr.

Philosophical Works Including the Works of Vision. George Berkeley. 358p. 1975. 22.50x (ISBN 0-460-10483-7, DEL-05137, Evman); pap. 8.95x. Biblio Dist.

Philosophical Works of Descartes, Vol. 1. Rene Descartes & G. R. Ross. Ed. by Elizabeth S. Haldane. pap. 115.00 (ISBN 0-317-20587-0, 2024470). Bks Demand UMI.

Philosophical Works of Etienne Bonnot de Condillac. Etienne Bonnot De Condillac. Tr. by Franklin Philip & Harlan Lane. 448p. 1982. text ed. 49.95x (ISBN 0-89859-181-3). L Erlbaum Assocs.

Philosophical Works of Francis Bacon. facs. ed. Francis Bacon. LC 70-119952. (Select Bibliographies Reprint Ser). 1905. 38.00 (ISBN 0-8369-5395-9). Ayer Co Pubs.

Philosophical Works: Phenomenology-Background, Foreground & Influences, 3 vols. James F. Ferrier. Ed. by Maurice Natanson. LC 78-66732. 1980. lib. bdg. 200.00 set (ISBN 0-8240-9566-9). Garland Pub.

Philosophical Writing: Locke, Berkeley, Hume. John J. Richetti. 304p. 1983. 27.00x (ISBN 0-674-66482-5). Harvard U Pr.

Philosophical Writings. Rene Descartes. Ed. by Elizabeth Anscombe & Peter T. Geach. Tr. by Elizabeth Anscombe & Peter T. Geach. LC 79-171798. 1971. pap. 7.20 scp (ISBN 0-672-61274-7, LLA198). Bobbs.

Philosophical Writings. Rene Descartes et al. Tr. by John Cottingham & Dugald Murdoch. 456p. 1985. Vol. 1. 49.50 (ISBN 0-521-24594-X); Vol. 1. pap. 12.95 (ISBN 0-521-28807-X); Vol. 2. 49.50 (ISBN 0-521-24595-8); Vol. 2. pap. 12.95 (ISBN 0-521-28808-8). Cambridge U Pr.

Philosophical Writings, Vol 13. Immanuel Kant. Ed. by Volkmar Sander. (German Library). 320p. 1986. 27.50x (ISBN 0-8264-0298-4); pap. 10.95 (ISBN 0-8264-0299-2). Continuum.

Philosophical Writings: A Selection. Duns Scotus. Tr. by Allan Wolter. (HPC Philosophical Classics Ser.). 400p. 1987. lib. bdg. 28.50 (ISBN 0-87220-019-1); pap. text ed. 7.95 (ISBN 0-87220-018-3). Hackett Pub.

Philosophical Writings: Descartes. Elizabeth Anscombe et al. 1971. pap. text ed. write for info. (ISBN 0-02-303600-1). Macmillan.

Philosophical Writings of Etienne Bonnot, Abbe' de Condillac, Vol. 2. Tr. by Franklin Philip & Harlan Lane. 192p. 1986. text ed. 29.95 (ISBN 0-89859-616-5). L Erlbaum Assocs.

Philosophical Writings of Henry More. Henry More. Ed. by Flora I. MacKinnon. LC 78-95151. Repr. of 1925 ed. 26.00 (ISBN 0-404-04409-3). AMS Pr.

Philosophical Writings of Peirce. Charles S. Peirce. Ed. by Justus Buchler. 1940. pap. 6.95 (ISBN 0-486-20217-8). Dover.

Philosophical Writings of Percy William Bridgman: An Original Anthology, 2 vols. in 1. Percy W. Bridgman. Ed. by I. Bernard Cohen. LC 79-7952. (Three Centuries of Science in America Ser.). 1980. lib. bdg. 19.00x (ISBN 0-405-12532-1). Ayer Co Pubs.

Philosophiches Woerterbuch. 6th ed. Max Apel & Peter Luds. (Sammlung Goeschen: 2202). (Ger.). 1980. pap. 5.10x (ISBN 3-11-006729-3). De Gruyter.

Philosophie Bergsonienne. Jacques Maritain. 384p. 1947. 14.95 (ISBN 0-686-56361-1). French & Eur.

Philosophie Contemporaine, 1850 a Nos Jours see Histoire de la Philosophie.

Philosophie dans le Boudoir: Les Instituteurs Amoureaux. Donatien Alphonse Francois de Sade. (Folio 800). 1976. 4.50 (ISBN 0-686-55371-3). French & Eur.

Philosophie De Gassendi. P. Felix Thomas. 1889. lib. bdg. 23.50 (ISBN 0-8337-3514-4). B Franklin.

Philosophie De Jacob Boehme. Alexandre Koyre. 1929. 32.00 (ISBN 0-8337-1953-X). B Franklin.

Philosophie de la Nature. Jacques Maritain. 1935. 9.95 (ISBN 0-686-56362-X). French & Eur.

Philosophie De la Science Economique. James Forbes. LC 72-150157. 32p. 1973. Repr. of 1897 ed. lib. bdg. 13.50 (ISBN 0-8337-1172-5). B Franklin.

Philosophie De L'amour Chez Raymond Lulle. Louis Sala-Molins. (Illus.). 1974. pap. 20.80x (ISBN 90-2797-301-6). Mouton.

Philosophie De Leibniz. B. Russell. (Reimpressions G & B Ser.). 250p. 1971. pap. 40.00x. Gordon & Breach.

Philosophie De Saint Thomas D'Aquin, 2 vols. Charles Jourdain. (Reprints in Philosophy Ser.). (Fr.). Repr. of 1858 ed. Set. lib. bdg. 98.00 (ISBN 0-89197-885-2); lib. bdg. 49.00 ea. Vol. 1 (ISBN 0-697-00009-5). Vol. 2 (ISBN 0-697-00010-9). Irvington.

Philosophie der Arithmetik. Husserl. (Husserliana Ser: No. 12). 1970. lib. bdg. 50.00 (ISBN 90-247-0230-5, Pub. by Martinus Nijhoff Netherlands). Kluwer Academic.

Philosophie des Deutschen Idealismus. 3rd ed. Nicolai Hartmann. vi, 575p. (Ger.). 1972. 46.40x (ISBN 3-11-004878-7). De Gruyter.

Philosophie des Thomas von Aquino see Redemption of Thinking: A Study in the Philosophy of Thomas Aquinas.

Philosophie du Bon-Sens, ou Reflexions Philosophiques sur l'Incertitude des Connaissances Humaines. Jean B. De Boyer Argens. 1056p. (Fr.). Repr. of 1768 ed. text ed. 124.20x (ISBN 0-576-12360-9, Pub. by Gregg Intl Pubs England). Gregg Intl.

Philosophie et les Experiences Naturelles. De Waelhens. (Phaenomenologica Ser: No. 9). 1961. lib. bdg. 24.00 (ISBN 90-247-0243-7, Pub. by Martinus Nijhoff Netherlands). Kluwer Academic.

Philosophie et les Philosophes: Ouvrages Generaux. Jean Hoffmans. LC 68-56798. (Bibliography & Reference Ser: No. 204). (Fr). 1968. Repr. of 1920 ed. 26.00 (ISBN 0-8337-1720-0). B Franklin.

Philosophie Europeene Antique et Medievale see Histoire de la Philosophie.

Philosophie Fieldings. Maria Joesten. 1932. pap. 10.00 (ISBN 0-384-27580-X). Johnson Repr.

Philosophie Geschichtliches Lexikon. 2nd ed. Ludwig Noack. (Ger.). 1968. 195.00 (ISBN 3-7728-0232-X, M-7585, Pub. by Frommann-Holzboog). French & Eur.

Philosophie im 14. und 15. Jahrhundert: In Memoriam Konstanty Michalski (1879-1947) Ed. by Olaf Pluta. (Bochumer Studien zur Philosophie: Vol. 10). lx, 613p. (Ger.). 1988. 55.00x (ISBN 90-6032-297-5, Pub. by B R Gruener Netherlands). Benjamins North Am.

Philosophie Moderne, de la Renaissance a 1850 see Histoire de la Philosophie.

Philosophie Morale: Examen Historique et Critique des Grandes Systemes. Jacques Maritain. 592p. 1960. 17.95 (ISBN 0-686-56363-8). French & Eur.

Philosophie Politique et L'etat D'israel. R. Misrahi. (Archives Positivistes: No. 7). 391p. 1976. pap. text ed. 23.20x (ISBN 90-2797-942-1). Mouton.

Philosophie und Mythos. Hans Poser. 1979. text ed. 35.20x (ISBN 3-11-007601-2). De Gruyter.

Philosophie und Wissenschaften, Kuenste see Aufstieg und Niedergang der romischen Welt: Section 1, von den Anfangen Roms bis zum Ausgang der Republik.

Philosophie Zoologique, 2 vols. in 1. J. B. Lamarck. 1960. Repr. of 1809 ed. 74.00x (ISBN 3-7682-0028-0). Lubrecht & Cramer.

Philosophies & Cultures. Frederick Copleston. 1980. 24.95x (ISBN 0-19-213960-6). Oxford U Pr.

Philosophies & Post-Revolutionary France. John Lough. 1982. 52.00x (ISBN 0-19-821921-0). Oxford U Pr.

Philosophies & Religions of India. Y. Ramacharaka. 212p. 1963. 11.95. Asia Bk Corp.

Philosophies & Religions of India. Yogi Ramacharaka. 8.00 (ISBN 0-911662-05-7). Yoga.

Philosophies in Modern Fiction. facs. ed. Patrick Braybrooke. LC 67-22077. (Essay Index Reprint Ser.). 1929. 14.00 (ISBN 0-8369-1322-1). Ayer Co Pubs.

Philosophies of Administration Current in the Deanship of the Liberal Arts College. Merle S. Ward. LC 79-177661. (Columbia University. Teachers College. Contributions to Education: No. 632). Repr. of 1934 ed. 22.50 (ISBN 0-404-55632-9). AMS Pr.

Philosophies of American Education. Max G. Wingo. 1974. text ed. 19.50 (ISBN 0-669-06143-3). Heath.

Philosophies of Art & Beauty: Selected Readings in Aesthetics from Plato to Heidegger. Ed. by Albert Hofstadter & Richard Kuhns. 1976. pap. 15.95 (ISBN 0-226-34812-1, P685, Phoen). U of Chicago Pr.

Philosophies of Beauty, from Socrates to Robert Bridges. Ed. by Edgar F. Carritt. LC 76-5885. 334p. 1976. Repr. of 1931 ed. lib. bdg. 60.00x (ISBN 0-8371-8812-1, CAPB). Greenwood.

Philosophies of Education. 2nd ed. William H. Howick. xiv, 150p. 1980. pap. 8.95x (ISBN 0-8134-2146-2). Inter Print Pubs.

Philosophies of Education Current in the Preparation of Teachers in the United States. Francis E. Peterson. LC 74-177152. (Columbia University. Teachers College. Contributions to Education: No. 528). Repr. of 1933 ed. 22.50 (ISBN 0-404-55528-4). AMS Pr.

Philosophies of Education from the Standpoint of the Philosophy of Experimentalism. John P. Wynne. Repr. of 1947 ed. lib. bdg. 35.00 (ISBN 0-8371-2793-9, WYPE). Greenwood.

Philosophies of Existence: Ancient & Medieval. Ed. by Parviz Morewedge. LC 81-66643. 344p. 1982. 45.00 (ISBN 0-8232-1059-6); pap. 25.00 (ISBN 0-8232-1060-X). Fordham.

Philosophies of History. Grace E. Cains. LC 62-12617. 519p. 1962. 6.00 (ISBN 0-8022-0208-X). Philos Lib.

Philosophies of History. Rolf Gruner. 190p. 1985. text ed. 34.95 (ISBN 0-566-05021-8). Gower Pub Co.

Philosophies of History: Meeting of East & West in Cycle-Pattern Theories of History. Grace E. Cairns. LC 71-139126. xxiii, 496p. 1971. Repr. of 1962 ed. lib. bdg. 27.50x (ISBN 0-8371-5742-0, CAPH). Greenwood.

Philosophies of India. Heinrich Zimmer. Ed. by Joseph Campbell. (Bollingen Ser.: Vol. 26). (Illus.). 1969. 57.00x (ISBN 0-691-09811-5); pap. 12.50 (ISBN 0-691-01758-1, 182). Princeton U Pr.

Philosophies of Judaism: The History of Jewish Philosophy from Biblical Times to Franz Rosenzweig. Julius Guttmann. LC 63-11875. 560p. 1973. pap. 13.50 (ISBN 0-8052-0402-4). Schocken.

Philosophies of Language in 18th Century France. Pierre Juliard. LC 77-111622. (Janua Linguarum Ser: No. 18). (Orig.). 1970. pap. text ed. 10.40x (ISBN 0-686-22419-1). Mouton.

Philosophies of Life. William S. Sahakian. LC 63-11487. 470p. 1963. 12.95 (ISBN 0-8022-1466-5). Philos Lib.

Philosophies of Life of the Ancient Greeks & Israelites. Ben F. Kimpel. LC 80-81697. 349p. 1981. 17.50 (ISBN 0-8022-2371-0). Philos Lib.

Philosophies of Love. Ed. by David L. Norton & Mary F. Kille. (Helix Bk.: No. 376). 296p. 1983. pap. 10.95 (ISBN 0-8226-0376-4, Helix). Rowman.

Philosophies of Music History: A Study of General Histories of Music, 1600-1960. Warren D. Allen. (Illus.). 1962. pap. 7.50 (ISBN 0-486-20282-8). Dover.

Philosophies of Science: An Introductory Survey. 2nd ed. Rom Harre. 212p. 1986. pap. 8.95x (ISBN 0-19-289201-0). Oxford U Pr.

Philosophische Anthropologie: Menschliche Selbstdeutung in Geschichte und Gegenwart. 5th ed. Michael Landmann. (Sammlung Goeschen: Vol. 2201). 228p. 1976. pap. 7.90x (ISBN 3-11-002739-9). De Gruyter.

Philosophische Grundlegung Zu Einer Enzyklopaedie des Glaubens. Guenther Keil. (Ger.). 1975. 115.00 (ISBN 3-445-01173-7, M-7093). French & Eur.

Philosophische Probleme der Physik see Philosophical Problems in Physical Science.

Philosophische Psychologie des Peter von Ailly. Olaf Pluta. (Beitrag zur Geschichte der Philosophie des Spaten Mittelalters Bochumer Studien zur Philosophie: Vol. 6). 1987. 45.00 (ISBN 90-6032-275-4, Pub. by B R Gruner Netherlands). Benjamins North Am.

Philosophische Schriften: Band I Werttheorie, 4 Vols. Christian Von Ehrenfels. Ed. by Reinhard Fabian. (Philosophia Resources Library Ser.). 615p. 1983. vol 175.00 ea. (ISBN 3-88405-033-8); subscription 149.50. Philosophia Pr.

Philosophische Schriften: Band II Asthetik, 4 Vols. Christian Von Ehrenfels. Ed. by Reinhard Fabian. (Philosophia Resources Library). viii, 502p. 1986. 116.50ea. (ISBN 3-88405-032-X); subscription 99.00. Philosophia Pr.

Philosophische Schriften: Band III Psychologie, Ethik, Erkenntnistheorie. Christian Von Ehrenfels. Ed. by Reinhard Fabian. (Philosophia Resources Library). 540p. 1988. 134.00 (ISBN 3-88405-034-6). Philosophia Pr.

Philosophische Theologie im Schatten des Nihilismus. Wilhelm Weischedel et al. Ed. by Joerg Salaquarda. (Ger). 1971. pap. 9.60x (ISBN 3-11-001604-4). De Gruyter.

Philosophischen Analysen Zur Kunst der Gegenwart. Biemel. (Phaenomenologica Ser: No. 28). 1968. lib. bdg. 34.00 (ISBN 90-247-0263-1, Pub. by Martinus Nijhoff Netherlands); pap. 18.50 (ISBN 90-247-0262-3, Pub. by Martinus Nijhoff Netherlands). Kluwer Academic.

Philosophischer Phoenix, Rettung des Phoenix, Teutsche Hauptsprache, Adelicher Hausvatter see Saemtliche Werke.

Philosophisches Woerterbuch. 14th ed. W. Brugger. 592p. 1976. pap. 110.00 (ISBN 0-686-56637-8, M-7587, Pub. by Herder). French & Eur.

Philosophisches Woerterbuch. 19th ed. Heinrich Schmidt. 1974. 17.50 (ISBN 3-520-01319-3, M-7586, Pub. by Kroener). French & Eur.

Philosophizing with Socrates: An Introduction to the Study of Philosophy. Gary Bedell. LC 80-5626. 262p. 1980. pap. text ed. 9.75 (ISBN 0-8191-1203-8). U Pr of Amer.

Philosophy, 3 Vols. Karl Jaspers. Tr. by E. B. Ashton. LC 69-19922. Vol. 1. 1969 ed. 19.00x (ISBN 0-226-39489-1); Vol. 2. 1970 ed. 21.00x (ISBN 0-226-39491-3); Vol. 3. 1971 ed. 14.00x (ISBN 0-226-39494-8). U of Chicago Pr.

Philosophy. Jack Rudman. (Graduate Record Examination Ser.: GRE-14). (Cloth bdg. avail. on request). pap. 13.95 (ISBN 0-8373-5214-2). Natl Learning.

Philosophy. Jack Rudman. (Undergraduate Program Field Test Ser.: UPFT-17). (Cloth bdg. avail. on request). pap. 13.95 (ISBN 0-8373-6017-X). Natl Learning.

Philosophy: A Contemporary, Tough-Minded Approach. Keith Halbasch. LC 86-25200. 123p. 1986. lib. bdg. 16.95 (ISBN 0-87975-352-8). Prometheus Bks.

TITLE INDEX PHILOSOPHY & THE EXPERIMENTAL

Philosophy: A Guide to Reference Literature. Hans E. Bynagle. LC 86-2942. (Reference Sources in the Humanities Ser.). x, 170p. 1986. lib. bdg. 35.00 (ISBN 0-87287-464-8). Libs Unl.
Philosophy: A Literary & Conceptual Approach. 2nd ed. Burton F. Porter. 496p. 1980. pap. text ed. 14.00 net (ISBN 0-15-570553-9, HC). HarBraceJ.
Philosophy: A Modern Encounter. Robert Wolff. LC 76-25427. 1976. pap. text ed. write for info. (ISBN 0-13-663377-3). P-H.
Philosophy: A Select, Classified Bibliography of Ethics, Economics, Law, Politics, Sociology. Sebastian A. Matczak. LC 72-80678. (Philosophical Questions Ser.: No. 3). 1970. 45.00x (ISBN 0-912116-02-1). Learned Pubns.
Philosophy: A Text with Readings. 3rd ed. Manuel Velasquez & Vincent Barry. 454p. 1988. text ed. write for info. (ISBN 0-534-08526-1). Wadsworth Pub.
Philosophy After Darwin: Chapters for the Career of Philosophy & Other Essays, Vol. 3. John H. Randall, Jr. Ed. by Beth J. Singer. LC 62-10454. 1977. 35.00x (ISBN 0-231-04114-4). Columbia U Pr.
Philosophy: An Introduction. J. M. Bochenski. Tr. by William M. Newell from Ger. 112p. 1963. lib. bdg. 16.00 (ISBN 90-277-0005-2, Pub. by Reidel Holland). Kluwer Academic.
Philosophy: An Introduction. Antony Flew. LC 79-93076. 194p. 1980. pap. text ed. 11.95 (ISBN 0-87975-127-4). Prometheus Bks.
Philosophy: An Introduction. rev. ed. John H. Randall, Jr. & Justus Buchler. 1971. pap. 7.95 (ISBN 0-06-460041-6, CO 41, B&N Bks). Harper Row.
Philosophy: An Introduction Through Original Fiction & Discussion. Thomas D. Davis. LC 78-12329. 1978. pap. text ed. 9.00x (ISBN 0-394-32048-4). Random.
Philosophy: An Introduction Through Original Fiction, Discussion & Readings. 2nd ed. Thomas D. Davis. 320p. 1986. pap. text ed. write for info. (ISBN 0-394-36289-6, RanC). Random.
Philosophy: An Introduction to the Central Issues. Charles Landesman. 335p. 1985. text ed. 23.95 (ISBN 0-03-063801-1, HoltC). HR&W.
Philosophy: An Orthodox Christian Understanding. Apostolos Makrakis. Ed. by Orthodox Christian Educational Society. Tr. by Denver Cummings from Hellenic. (Logos & Holy Spirit in the Unity of Christian Thought Ser.: Vol. 5). 279p. 1977. pap. 5.50x (ISBN 0-938366-02-5). Orthodox Chr.
Philosophy: An Outline for the Intending Student. Ed. by R. J. Hirst. (Outlines Ser). 1968. cased o.p. 16.95x (ISBN 0-7100-2038-4); pap. 6.95 (ISBN 0-7100-6099-8). Routledge Chapman & Hall.
Philosophy & an African Culture. K. Wiredu. LC 79-51230. 1980. 39.50 (ISBN 0-521-22794-1); pap. 12.95 (ISBN 0-521-29647-1). Cambridge U Pr.
Philosophy & Archaeology. Merrilee H. Salmon. (Studies in Archaeology Ser.). 1982. 19.50 (ISBN 0-12-615650-6). Acad Pr.
Philosophy & Argument in Late Vedanta. Phyllis Granoff. (Studies of Classical India: No. 1). 1978. lib. bdg. 53.00 (ISBN 90-277-0878-9, Pub. by Reidel Holland). Kluwer Academic.
Philosophy & Argumentation in Third-Century China: The Essays of Hsi K'ang. Tr. by Robert C. Henricks. K'ang Hsi. LC 82-61367. (Princeton Library of Asian Translations). 224p. 1983. 35.50x (ISBN 0-691-05378-2). Princeton U Pr.
Philosophy & Atheism. Kai Nielsen. LC 84-63084. (Skeptic's Bookshelf Ser.). 231p. 1985. 21.95 (ISBN 0-87975-289-0). Prometheus Bks.
Philosophy & Background of Team Teaching see Team Teaching Modules.
Philosophy & Christian Theology. Ed. by George F. McLean & Jude P. Dougherty. (Proceedings of the American Catholic Philosophical Association: Vol. 44). 1970. pap. 15.00 (ISBN 0-918090-04-0). Am Cath Philo.
Philosophy & Civil Law. Ed. by George F. McLean. LC 76-150281. (Proceedings of the American Catholic Philosophical Association: Vol. 49). 1975. pap. 15.00 (ISBN 0-918090-09-1). Am Cath Philo.
Philosophy & Civilization in the Middle Ages. Maurice M. De Wulf. Repr. of 1922 ed. lib. bdg. 25.00x (ISBN 0-8371-2521-9, WUMA). Greenwood.
Philosophy & Class Struggle. Dialego. 1978. pap. 1.50 (ISBN 0-8285-1045-8, Pub. by Inkululeko). Imported Pubns.
Philosophy & Common Sense: A Study in the Philosphy of C. S. Peirce. Indira Prasad. 1983. text ed. 24.00x. Coronet Bks.
Philosophy & Contempoary Problems: A Reader. Richard H. Popkin & Avrum Stroll. 1984. pap. text ed. 22.95 (ISBN 0-03-061701-4). HR&W.
Philosophy & Contemporary Issues. 5th ed. John R. Burr & Milton Goldinger. 568p. 1988. text ed. write for info. (ISBN 0-02-317260-6). Macmillan.
Philosophy & Culture, East & West: East-West Philosophy in Practical Perspective. Ed. by Charles A. Moore. 627p. 1962. 25.00x (ISBN 0-87022-541-3). UH Pr.
Philosophy & Culture: Studies from Hungary Published on the Occasion of the 17th World Congress of Philosophy. Jozset Lukacs & Ference Tokei. 368p. 1983. 67.50x (ISBN 0-317-53780-6, Pub. by Collets (UK)). State Mutual Bk.
Philosophy & Culture-Studies from Hungary. Ed. by J. Lukacs. 368p. 1983. text ed. 28.50x (ISBN 963-05-3449-5, Pub. by Akademiai Kiado UK). Humanities.
Philosophy & Development of Religion, 2 vols. Otto Pfleiderer. LC 77-27229. (Gifford Lectures: 1894). Repr. of 1894 ed. Set. 65.00 (ISBN 0-404-60470-6). AMS Pr.
Philosophy & Economic Prophecy. Shirley Telford. LC 74-11231. (Orig.). 1974. pap. 2.00 (ISBN 0-9600202-8-4). William & Rich.
Philosophy & Economic Theory. Ed. by Frank Hahn & Martin Hollis. (Oxford Readings in Philosophy Ser.). 1979. pap. text ed. 8.95x (ISBN 0-19-875042-0). Oxford U Pr.
Philosophy & Economics: The Origins & Development of Economic Theory. Piero V. Mini. LC 74-7122. 1974. 15.00x (ISBN 0-8130-0381-4). U Presses Fla.
Philosophy & Education. Ed. by Jonas Soltis. LC 80-83743. (National Society for the Study of Education 80th Yearbooks: Pt. I). 288p. 1981. lib. bdg. 17.50x (ISBN 0-226-60130-7). U of Chicago Pr.
Philosophy & Education: Alternatives in Theory & Practice. 2nd ed. Russell L. Hamm. xviii, 330p. 1981. pap. text ed. 9.95x (ISBN 0-8134-2203-5, 2203). Inter Print Pubs.
Philosophy & Education: An Introduction in Christian Perspective. George R. Knight. LC 81-117900. (Illus.). xii, 244p. 1980. pap. text ed. 10.95 (ISBN 0-943872-79-0). Andrews Univ Pr.
Philosophy & Environmental Crisis. Ed. by William T. Blackstone. LC 73-90842. 148p. 1974. pap. 6.00x (ISBN 0-8203-0343-7). U of Ga Pr.
Philosophy & Feminist Thinking. Jean Grimshaw. LC 86-6993. 288p. (Orig.). 1986. 35.00x (ISBN 0-8166-1545-4); pap. 14.95 (ISBN 0-8166-1546-2). U of Minn Pr.
Philosophy & Freedom. Heydar Reghaby. LC 71-104386. 1970. 5.95 (ISBN 0-8022-2324-9). Philos Lib.
Philosophy & Future of Graduate Education. Ed. by William K. Frankena. LC 80-14804. (Michigan Faculty Ser.). 272p. 1980. text ed. 15.00x (ISBN 0-472-09321-5); pap. 8.50x (ISBN 0-472-06321-9). U of Mich Pr.
Philosophy & Grammar. Ed. by Stig Kanger & Sven Ohman. (Synthese Library: No. 143). 168p. 1980. lib. bdg. 28.50 (ISBN 90-277-1091-0, Pub. by Reidel Holland). Kluwer Academic.
Philosophy & History. Ed. by R. Klibansky & H. J. Paton. 12.00 (ISBN 0-8446-2387-3). Peter Smith.
Philosophy & History: A Symposium see New York University Institute of Philosophy Symposia.
Philosophy & Homosexuality. Ed. by Noretta Koertge. LC 84-22470. 98p. 1985. pap. text ed. 7.95 (ISBN 0-918393-12-4). Harrington Pk.
Philosophy & Human Development. Ed. by Anand Amaladass. 333p. 1986. 19.95. Asia Bk Corp.
Philosophy & Human Movement. David Best. (Unwin Education Bks.). 1979. text ed. 21.95x (ISBN 0-04-370088-8). Unwin Hyman.
Philosophy & Humanism: Renaissance Essays in Honor of Paul Oskar Kristeller. Ed. by Edward P. Mahoney. LC 75-42285. 624p. 1976. 65.00 (ISBN 0-231-03904-2). Columbia U Pr.
Philosophy & Ideology: An Adventure. 2nd ed. Larry Azar. 200p. 1985. pap. 14.95 (ISBN 0-8403-4120-2). Kendall-Hunt.
Philosophy & Ideology in Hume's Political Thought. David Miller. 1981. pap. 13.95x (ISBN 0-19-824742-7). Oxford U Pr.
Philosophy & Ideology: The Development of Philosophy & Marxism-Leninism in Poland Since the Second World War. Z. A. Jordan. (Sovietica Ser.: No. 12). 600p. 1963. lib. bdg. 45.00 (ISBN 90-277-0054-0, Pub. by Reidel Holland). Kluwer Academic.
Philosophy & Its Place in Our Culture. new ed. J. O. Wisdom. (Current Topics of Contemporary Thought Ser.). 282p. 1975. 50.00 (ISBN 0-677-05150-6). Gordon & Breach.
Philosophy & Its Shadow. Eugenio Trias. Tr. by Kenneth Krabbenhoft. LC 82-12803. (European Perspectives Ser.). 160p. 1983. 27.50x (ISBN 0-231-05288-X). Columbia U Pr.
Philosophy & Journalism. John C. Merrill & Jack S. Odell. LC 82-7770. (Public Communication Ser.). 256p. 1982. pap. text ed. 16.95 (ISBN 0-582-28383-3). Longman.
Philosophy & Law. Ed. by Jules Coleman & Ellen F. Paul. 240p. 1987. pap. text ed. 14.95 (ISBN 0-631-15257-1). Basil Blackwell.
Philosophy & Law: Essays Toward the Understanding of Maimonides His Predecessors. Leo Strauss. Tr. by Fred Baumann from Ger. 120p. 1987. 18.95 (ISBN 0-8276-0273-1). JPS Phila.
Philosophy & Life. Ed. by Ilham Dilman. LC 84-14685. 1984. lib. bdg. 56.00 (ISBN 90-247-2996-3, Pub. by Martinus Nijhoff Netherlands). Kluwer Academic.
Philosophy & Literature. Bolling. 210p. 1986. 65.00 (ISBN 0-930586-22-0). Haven Pubns.
Philosophy & Literature. A. Phillips Griffiths. LC 84-5894. 1984. 12.95 (ISBN 0-521-27411-7). Cambridge U Pr.
Philosophy & Logical Syntax. Rudolf Carnap. LC 75-41050. (BCL Ser. II). Repr. of 1935 ed. 11.50 (ISBN 0-404-14518-3). AMS Pr.
Philosophy & Mathematics: From Plato to the Present. Ed. by Robert J. Baum. LC 73-84704. 320p. 1973. pap. 12.00x (ISBN 0-87735-514-2). Freeman Cooper.
Philosophy & Medicine. E. K. Ledermann. (Avebury Series in the Philosophy of Science). 196p. 1986. text ed. 41.50 (ISBN 0-566-05062-5, Pub. by Gower Pub England). Gower Pub Co.
Philosophy & Medicine in Ancient Greece. W. H. Jones. 100p. 1980. 15.00 (ISBN 0-89005-286-7). Ares.
Philosophy & Medicine in Ancient Greece: With an Edition of Peri Archaiees Ieetrikees. William H. Jones. 1979. 12.00 (ISBN 0-405-10606-8). Ayer Co Pubs.
Philosophy & Miracle: The Contemporary Debate. David Basinger & Randall Basinger. LC 86-12766. (Problems in Contemporary Philosophy: Vol. 2). 130p. 1986. lib. bdg. 39.95x (ISBN 0-88946-327-1). E Mellen.
Philosophy & Mysticism. Ed. by Herbert Guerry. Dell.
Philosophy & Myth in Karl Marx. 2nd ed. Robert C. Tucker. LC 70-180022. 250p. 1972. 47.50 (ISBN 0-521-08455-5); pap. 15.95 (ISBN 0-521-09701-0). Cambridge U Pr.
Philosophy & Non-Philosophy since Merleau-Ponty. Ed. by Hugh J. Silverman. 320p. 1988. text ed. 40.00 (ISBN 0-415-00178-1, Pub. by Kegan Paul); pap. text ed. 13.95 (ISBN 0-415-00179-X, Pub. by Kegan Paul). Routledge Chapman & Hall.
Philosophy & Opinions of Marcus Garvey, or Africa for the Africans. Marcus Garvey. Ed. by Amy J. Garvey. (New Marcus Garvey Library: No. 9). (Illus.). xxvii, 518p. (Orig.). 1986. pap. text ed. 10.95 (ISBN 0-912469-24-2). Majority Pr.
Philosophy & Opinions of Marcus Garvey, Or, Africa for the Africans, 2 vols. in 1. 2nd, rev. ed. Ed. by Amy Jacques-Garvey. (Illus.). 412p. 1977. 32.50x (ISBN 0-7146-1143-3, F Cass Co); pap. 13.50x (ISBN 0-7146-2120-X). Biblio Dist.
Philosophy & Opinions of Marcus Garvey. Marcus Garvey. Ed. by Amy Jacques-Garvey. LC 69-15523. (Studies in American Negro Life Ser). 1969. pap. text ed. 9.95x (ISBN 0-689-70079-2, NL14). Atheneum.
Philosophy & Opinions of Marcus Garvey, Vol. 2. Ed. by Amy Jacques-Garvey. LC 69-19115. (American Negro: His History & Literature Ser., No. 2). 1969. Repr. of 1925 ed. 14.00 (ISBN 0-405-01873-8). Ayer Co Pubs.
Philosophy & Ordinary Language. Charles E. Caton. LC 63-7250. pap. 65.00 (ISBN 0-317-09788-1, 2020860). Bks Demand UMI.
Philosophy & Parapsychology. Ed. by Jan K. Ludwig. LC 77-91852. 454p. 1978. 21.95 (ISBN 0-87975-075-8); pap. 12.95 (ISBN 0-87975-076-6). Prometheus Bks.
Philosophy & Philosophers. Lois Roets. 48p. (gr. 5-12). 1987. pap. 8.00 tchr's. manual & text in one volume (ISBN 0-911943-12-9). Leadership Pub.
Philosophy & Philosophical Authors of the Jews: A Historical Sketch with Explanatory Notes. S. Munk. Tr. by Isidor Kalisch. (Reprints in Philosophy Ser.). Repr. of 1881 ed. lib. bdg. 26.50 (ISBN 0-697-00012-5). Irvington.
Philosophy & Policies of Woodrow Wilson. Ed. by Earl Latham. (Midway Reprint Ser). xvi, 268p. 1975. pap. text ed. 11.50x (ISBN 0-226-46924-7). U of Chicago Pr.
Philosophy & Politics. Adriaan T. Peperzak. 1987. lib. bdg. 40.95 (ISBN 90-247-3337-5, Pub. by Martinus Nijhoff Netherlands); pap. text ed. 15.00 (ISBN 90-247-3338-3, Pub. by Martinus Nijhoff Netherlands). Kluwer Academic.
Philosophy & Politics of Freedom. Richard E. Flathman. LC 86-16128. (Illus.). x, 360p. 1987. text ed. 42.50x (ISBN 0-226-25316-3); pap. text ed. 16.95x (ISBN 0-226-25317-1). U of Chicago Pr.
Philosophy & Practice. Ed. by Phillips A. Griffiths. (Royal Institute of Philosophy Lecture: No. 18). 250p. 1985. pap. 13.95 (ISBN 0-521-31231-0). Cambridge U Pr.
Philosophy & Practice of Wildlife Management. Frederick F. Gilbert & Donald G. Dodds. LC 85-23956. 292p. 1987. text ed. 24.50 (ISBN 0-89874-911-5). Krieger.
Philosophy & Practice of Yoga. Roy E. Davis. 192p. 1983. pap. 4.95 (ISBN 0-317-20862-4). CSA Pr.
Philosophy & Psycholinguistics. Edmund L. Erde. LC 72-94464. (Janua Linguarum: Series Minor Ser: No. 160). 1973. pap. 21.20x (ISBN 90-2792-444-9). Mouton.
Philosophy & Psychology of Pietro Pomponazzi. Andrew H. Douglas. Ed. by C. Douglas & R. P. Hardie. 328p. Repr. of 1910 ed. lib. bdg. 57.50x (Pub. by G. Olms BRD). Coronet Bks.
Philosophy & Public Policy. Sidney Hook. LC 79-16825. 296p. 1980. 19.50x (ISBN 0-8093-0937-8); pap. 11.95x (ISBN 0-8093-1041-4). S Ill U Pr.
Philosophy & Religion see Comprehensive Dissertation Index 1861-1972: Supplement, 1973.
Philosophy & Religion in Colonial America. Claude M. Newlin. LC 68-23317. 1968. Repr. of 1962 ed. lib. bdg. 35.00 (ISBN 0-8371-0184-0, NEPR). Greenwood.
Philosophy & Religion: Some Contemporary Perspectives. Jerry H. Gill. LC 68-54894. pap. 95.50 (ISBN 0-317-08950-1, 2003459). Bks Demand UMI.
Philosophy & Revolutionary Theory, Vol. I. Ed. by Dale Riepe et al. (Philosopical Currents Ser.: Vol. 32). 260p. 1987. pap. text ed. 45.00 (ISBN 90-6032-278-9, Pub. by Gruner). Humanities.
Philosophy & Romantic Nationalism: The Case of Poland. Andrzej Walicki. (Illus.). 1982. 45.00x (ISBN 0-19-827250-2). Oxford U Pr.
Philosophy & Science As Modes of Knowing: Selected Essays. Ed. by Alden L. Fisher & George B. Murray. LC 69-18680. (Orig.). 1969. pap. text ed. 19.95x (ISBN 0-89197-340-0). Irvington.
Philosophy & Science Fiction. Ed. by Michael Philips. LC 83-62874. 392p. 1984. pap. 16.95 (ISBN 0-87975-248-3). Prometheus Bks.
Philosophy & Science in Phenomenological Perspective. Ed. by Kah Kyung Cho. 1984. lib. bdg. 45.50 (ISBN 90-247-2922-X, Pub. by Martinus Nijhoff Netherlands). Kluwer Academic.
Philosophy & Science in the Islamic World: From Origins to the Present Day. C. A. Quadir. 224p. 1988. lib. bdg. 65.00 (ISBN 0-7099-2108-X, Pub. by Croom Helm UK). Routledge Chapman & Hall.
Philosophy & Science: The Wide Range of Interaction. F. Mosedale. 1979. pap. write for info. (ISBN 0-13-662577-0). P-H.
Philosophy & Sex. rev. ed. Robert Baker & Frederick Elliston. LC 84-63548. 525p. 1984. pap. text ed. 17.95 (ISBN 0-87975-246-7). Prometheus Bks.
Philosophy & Social Issues: Five Studies. Richard Wasserstrom. LC 79-9486. 224p. 1980. text ed. 8.95x (ISBN 0-268-01535-X). U of Notre Dame Pr.
Philosophy & Social Theory: An Introduction to Historical Materialism. Valery Deyev. 196p. 1987. 8.95 (ISBN 0-8285-3721-6, Pub. by Progress Pubs USSR). Imported Pubns.
Philosophy & Sociology of Science: An Introduction. 2nd ed. Stewart Richards. 240p. 1987. pap. text ed. 15.95 (ISBN 0-631-13414-X). Basil Blackwell.
Philosophy & Spacetime Physics. Lawrence Sklar. LC 84-24128. 1985. 35.00x (ISBN 0-520-05374-5). U of Cal Pr.
Philosophy & Spacetime Physics. Lawrence Sklar. 345p. 1987. pap. 10.95 (ISBN 0-520-06180-2). U of Cal Pr.
Philosophy & Structure of the Middos Program. Mordechai Gifter. (Annual Fryer Memorial Lecture Ser.). 0.75 (ISBN 0-914131-48-6, 131). Torah Umesorah.
Philosophy & Teaching of Reading. B. Robert Ross. 75p. 1988. 30.00 (ISBN 0-87916-007-1); pap. 15.00 (ISBN 0-87916-008-X). Upstat.
Philosophy & Technology. Ed. by Paul T. Durbin & Friedrich Rapp. 1983. lib. bdg. 59.00 (ISBN 90-277-1576-9, Pub. by Reidel Holland). Kluwer Academic.
Philosophy & Technology. Alexander S. Kohanski. LC 77-75257. 215p. 1977. 9.95 (ISBN 0-8022-2202-1). Philos Lib.
Philosophy & Technology II. Ed. by Carl Mitcham & Alois Huning. 1986. lib. bdg. 59.00 (ISBN 90-277-1975-6, Pub. by Reidel Holland). Kluwer-Academic.
Philosophy & Technology: Readings in the Philosophical Problems of Technology. Ed. by Carl Mitcham & Robert Mackey. LC 82-19818. 416p. 1983. pap. text ed. 14.95 (ISBN 0-02-921430-0). Free Pr.
Philosophy & the Absolute: The Modes of Hegel's Speculation. Robert Grant McRae. 1985. lib. bdg. 31.00 (ISBN 90-247-3151-8, Pub. by Martinus Nijhoff Netherlands). Kluwer Academic.
Philosophy & the American School. 2nd ed. Van C. Morris & Young Pai. LC 75-26083. (Illus.). 544p. 1976. text ed. 39.96 (ISBN 0-395-18620-X). HM.
Philosophy & the Art of Writing: Studies in Philosophical & Literary Style. Berel Lang. LC 81-65865. 248p. 1982. 28.50 (ISBN 0-8387-5030-3). Bucknell U Pr.
Philosophy & the Brain. J. Z. Young. 224p. 1987. 23.50 (ISBN 0-19-219215-9). Oxford U Pr.
Philosophy & the Brain. J. Z. Young. 256p. 1988. pap. 8.95 (ISBN 0-19-282167-9). Oxford U Pr.
Philosophy & the Christian Faith. Colin Brown. LC 68-58083. (Orig.). 1969. pap. 11.95 (ISBN 0-87784-712-6). Inter-Varsity.
Philosophy & the Christian Faith. Ed. by Thomas V. Morris. LC 87-40618. (Studies in Philosophy of Religion: No. 5). 336p. 1988. text ed. 31.95x (ISBN 0-268-01570-8). U of Notre Dame Pr.
Philosophy & the Community of Speech. Donald Stoll. LC 87-25252. (Social Philosophy Research Institute Ser.: No. 6). 84p. (Orig.). 1988. lib. bdg. 17.50 (ISBN 0-8191-6683-9); pap. text ed. 7.50 (ISBN 0-8191-6684-7). U Pr of Amer.
Philosophy & the Criminal Law. Association for Legal & Social Philosophy. Ed. by Anthony Duff & Nigel Simmond. 120p. (Orig.). 1984. pap. 33.00x (ISBN 3-515-04169-9, Pub by Franz Steiner). Coronet Bks.
Philosophy & the Experimental Sciences: Proceedings, Vol. 26. American Catholic Philosophical Association Staff. 1952. 18.00 (ISBN 0-384-46400-9). Johnson Repr.

Philosophy & the Future of Man. Ed. by George F. McLean. (Proceedings of the American Catholic Philosophical Association: Vol. 42). 1968. pap. 15.00 (ISBN 0-918090-02-4). Am Cath Philo.

Philosophy & the Human Condition. Tom L. Beauchamp et al. (Illus.). 640p. 1980. text ed. write for info. (ISBN 0-13-662528-2). P-H.

Philosophy & the Human Sciences. R. J. Anderson et al. LC 86-3415. 274p. 1986. 28.95x (ISBN 0-389-20619-9). B&N Imports.

Philosophy & the Mind. Jenny Teichman. 224p. Date not set. text ed. 55.00 (ISBN 0-631-15752-2); pap. text ed. 16.95 (ISBN 0-631-15753-0). Basil Blackwell.

Philosophy & the Mirror of Nature. Richard Rorty. LC 79-84013. 401p. 1979. 41.00x (ISBN 0-691-07236-1); pap. 9.95x (ISBN 0-691-02016-7). Princeton U Pr.

Philosophy & the Modern Mind: A Philosophical Critique of Modern Western Civilization. E. M. Adams. 244p. 1985. pap. text ed. 13.00 (ISBN 0-8191-4754-0). U Pr of Amer.

Philosophy & the Nature of Language. David E. Cooper. LC 86-29423. (Longman Linguistics Library). 230p. 1987. Repr. of 1973 ed. lib. bdg. 39.75x (ISBN 0-313-25641-1, COPN). Greenwood.

Philosophy & the New Physics. Jonathan Powers. (Methuens Ideas Ser.). (Illus.). 150p. 1982. pap. 9.50x (ISBN 0-416-73480-4, NO. 3795). Routledge Chapman & Hall.

Philosophy & the Oriental Mind. Georg W. Hegel. (Illus.). 1980. 117.75 (ISBN 0-89266-212-3). Am Classical Coll Pr.

Philosophy & the Real World: An Introduction to Karl Popper. Bryan Magee. 120p. 1985. pap. 7.95 (ISBN 0-87548-436-0). Open Court.

Philosophy & the Science of Behavior, Including Psychology & the Philosophy of Science. Merle B. Turner. LC 66-25267. (Century Psychology Ser.). (Illus.). 1967. 49.50x (ISBN 0-89197-341-9); pap. text ed. 12.95x (ISBN 0-89197-342-7). Irvington.

Philosophy & the Self: East & West. Troy W. Organ. LC 86-62506. 240p. 1987. 33.50x (ISBN 0-941664-80-5). Susquehanna U Pr.

Philosophy & the State in France: The Renaissance to the Enlightenment. Nannerl O. Keohane. LC 79-3219. 1980. 51.50x (ISBN 0-691-07611-1); pap. 21.50x ltd. ed. (ISBN 0-691-10078-0). Princeton U Pr.

Philosophy & the Teacher. Ed. by D. I. Lloyd. (Students' Library of Education). 180p. 1975. pap. 8.95x (ISBN 0-7100-8288-6). Routledge Chapman & Hall.

Philosophy & the Visual Arts. Ed. by Andrew Harrison. 1987. lib. bdg. 69.00 (ISBN 90-277-2468-7, Pub. by Reidel Holland). Kluwer Academic.

Philosophy & the Young Child. Gareth B. Matthews. LC 80-14494. 123p. 1980. text ed. 11.00x (ISBN 0-674-66605-4). Harvard U Pr.

Philosophy & the Young Child. Gareth B. Matthews. 128p. 1982. pap. 3.95 (ISBN 0-674-66606-2). Harvard U Pr.

Philosophy & Theology. James H. Stirling. LC 77-27233. (Gifford Lectures: 1890). 1978. Repr. of 1890 ed. 39.00 (ISBN 0-404-60451-X). AMS Pr.

Philosophy & Theology of Anders Nygren. Kegley. 12.95 (ISBN 0-8298-0486-2). Pilgrim NY.

Philosophy & Unified Science. George Talbott. 1435p. 1982. Repr. of 1978 ed. 36.50 (ISBN 0-941524-18-3). Lotus Light.

Philosophy & Women. Ed. by Sharon Bishop & Marjorie Weinzweig. 270p. 1979. pap. text ed. write for info. (ISBN 0-534-00609-4). Wadsworth Pub.

Philosophy Applied to Controversial Issues in a Democratic Society. Bradley G. Moore. LC 79-84650. 1979. pap. text ed. 10.00 (ISBN 0-8191-0741-7). U Pr of Amer.

Philosophy As a Science. Paul Carus. LC 75-3106. Repr. of 1909 ed. AMS Pr.

Philosophy As Dramatic Theory. Julian Marias. Tr. by James Parsons. LC 72-84669. 1970. 24.50x (ISBN 0-271-00100-3). Pa St U Pr.

Philosophy As Metanoetics. Hajime Tanabe. (Nanzan Studies in Religion & Culture: No. 2). 224p. 1987. text ed. 42.00x (ISBN 0-520-05490-3). U of Cal Pr.

Philosophy As Scientia Scientiarum: A History of Classifications of the Sciences. Robert Flint. LC 74-26261. (History, Philosophy & Sociology of Science Ser). 1975. Repr. 25.00x (ISBN 0-405-06589-2). Ayer Co Pubs.

Philosophy As Social Expression. Albert W. Levi. LC 73-84191. xii, 328p. 1976. pap. 4.25x (ISBN 0-226-47390-2, P668, Phoen). U of Chicago Pr.

Philosophy, B-BJ. Ed. by James Larrabee. (LC Cumulative Classification Ser.). 300p. 1985. looseleaf 38.00 (ISBN 0-933949-14-6); microfiche 13.00 (ISBN 0-933949-18-9). Livia Pr.

Philosophy: Basic Judaism. (Home Study Program Ser.: No. 601). 5.00 (ISBN 0-686-96129-3). United Syn Bk.

Philosophy, Being & the Good: An Historical Anthology. Ed. by Joel W. Lidz. 490p. (Orig.). 1983. lib. bdg. 39.25 (ISBN 0-8191-3398-1); pap. text ed. 17.75 (ISBN 0-8191-3399-X). U Pr of Amer.

Philosophy Beside Itself: On Deconstruction & Modernism. Stephen W. Melville. LC 85-14025. (Theory & History of Literature Ser.: Vol. 27). 208p. (Orig.). 1986. 25.00x (ISBN 0-8166-1437-7); pap. 10.95 (ISBN 0-8166-1438-5). U of Minn Pr.

Philosophy Beyond the Classroom. Vergilius Ferm. 411p. 1974. 12.95 (ISBN 0-8158-0314-1). Chris Mass.

Philosophy Born of Struggle: Anthology of Afro-American Philosophy from 1917. Leonard Harris. 344p. 1985. pap. 22.95 (ISBN 0-8403-3328-5). Kendall-Hunt.

Philosophy by Way of the Sciences: An Introductory Textbook. Ray H. Dotterer. (Select Bibliographies Reprint Ser). Repr. of 1929 ed. 26.50 (ISBN 0-8369-6642-2). Ayer Co Pubs.

Philosophy by Way of the Sciences: An Introductory Textbook. Ray H. Dotterer. 484p. Repr. of 1929 ed. lib. bdg. 23.50 (ISBN 0-8290-0823-3). Irvington.

Philosophy Can Be Verse: The Re-Sounds & Re-Motions of Man's Loco-Notions. Sid Greenberg. (Illus.). 1979. pap. 6.95 (ISBN 0-915358-26-3). Bridgeberg.

Philosophy (Concepts) of Scientific & Technological Development. 17p. 1980. pap. 5.00 (ISBN 92-808-0176-7, TUNU109, UNU). UNIPUB.

Philosophy, Cosmology & Religion: Ten Lectures. Rudolf Steiner. Ed. by Stewart C. Easton et al. 180p. (Orig.). 1984. 16.00 (ISBN 0-88010-109-1); pap. 9.95 (ISBN 0-88010-110-5). Anthroposophic.

Philosophy: East & West. Ed. by Charles A. Moore. LC 72-119008. (Essay Index Reprint Ser). 1944. 24.50 (ISBN 0-8369-1677-8). Ayer Co Pubs.

Philosophy, Evolution & Human Nature. Florian Von Schilcher & Neil Tennant. 269p. 1984. 29.95X (ISBN 0-7100-9767-0). Routledge Chapman & Hall.

Philosophy for a Changing Society. Ed. by Creighton Peden. (Orig.). 1985. pap. text ed. 13.95x (ISBN 0-89894-003-6). Advocate Pub Group.

Philosophy for a Modern Man. H. Levy. 1978. Repr. of 1938 ed. lib. bdg. 25.00 (ISBN 0-8492-1589-7). R West.

Philosophy for a New Generation. 4th ed. Arthur K. Bierman & James A. Gould. 1980. pap. write for info. (ISBN 0-02-309640-3). Macmillan.

Philosophy for Adults. Thomas O. Buford. LC 80-5524. 639p. 1980. pap. text ed. 20.75 (ISBN 0-8191-1118-X). U Pr of Amer.

Philosophy for Children: An Approach to Critical Thinking. Tony W. Johnson. LC 83-83088. (Fastback Ser.: No. 206). 50p. 1984. pap. 0.90 (ISBN 0-87367-206-2). Phi Delta Kappa.

Philosophy for Education. Ed. by Seymour Fox. 120p. 1983. text ed. 12.50x (Pub. by Van Leer Jerusalem). Humanities.

Philosophy for Education. John Harris. 196p. 1986. 34.95x (ISBN 0-631-13702-5); pap. 9.95x (ISBN 0-631-14292-4). Basil Blackwell.

Philosophy for Everyman: From Socrates to Sartre. Dagobert D. Runes. (Quality Paperback: No. 276). 148p. 1974. pap. 4.95 (ISBN 0-8226-0276-8). Littlefield.

Philosophy for Living: A Sketch of Aquinate Philosophy. Johnemery Konecsni. 184p. 1977. pap. text ed. 12.00 (ISBN 0-8191-0138-9). U Pr of Amer.

Philosophy for Managers: Selected Papers of Chester I. Barnard. Ed. by William B. Wolf & Haruki Iino. 200p. 1988. 18.00 (ISBN 0-87546-141-7). ILR Pr.

Philosophy for the New Age. Alan F. Markun. LC 79-169243. 85p. 1972. 8.95 (ISBN 0-8022-2066-5). Philos Lib.

Philosophy for the Sick. Manly P. Hall. pap. 2.50 (ISBN 0-89314-340-5). Philos Res.

Philosophy for Understanding Theology. Diogenes Allen. LC 84-48510. 252p. 1985. pap. 14.95 (ISBN 0-8042-0688-0, John Knox). Westminster John Knox.

Philosophy for Young Thinkers. Joseph P. Hester & Philip F. Vincent. 15.00 (ISBN 0-89824-075-1). Trillium Pr.

Philosophy Goes to School. Matthew Lipman. LC 87-18071. 250p. 1988. 34.95 (ISBN 0-87722-537-0); pap. 14.95 (ISBN 0-87722-555-9). Temple U Pr.

Philosophy Gone Wild: Essays in Environmental Ethics. Holmes Rolston, III. LC 86-60106. 269p. 1986. 19.95 (ISBN 0-87975-329-3). Prometheus Bks.

Philosophy, History & Politics. Rotenstreich. (Melbourne International Philosophy Ser: No. 1). 1976. pap. 24.00 (ISBN 90-247-1743-4, Pub. by Martinus Nijhoff Netherlands). Kluwer Academic.

Philosophy: History & Problems. 3rd ed. Samuel Stumpf. (Illus.). 912p. 1983. text ed. 33.95 (ISBN 0-07-062181-0). Mcgraw.

Philosophy: History & Problems. Samuel E. Stumpf. 1971. text ed. 16.95 (ISBN 0-07-062198-5, C). McGraw.

Philosophy: History & Problems. 4th ed. Samuel E. Stumpf. 960p. 1988. text ed. price not set (ISBN 0-07-062187-X). McGraw.

Philosophy, History, & the Image of Man. N. A. Nikam. 160p. 1973. 11.25x (ISBN 0-89684-441-2). Orient Bk Dist.

Philosophy, History, & the Sciences: Selected Critical Essays. Maurice Mandelbaum. LC 83-18721. 336p. 1984. text ed. 35.00x (ISBN 0-8018-3112-1). Johns Hopkins.

Philosophy, Ideology & Social Science: Essays in Negation & Affirmation. Istvan Meszaros. LC 86-21996. 304p. 1986. 29.95 (ISBN 0-312-00230-0); pap. 12.95 (ISBN 0-312-00231-9). St Martin.

Philosophy in a New Key: A Study in the Symbolism of Reason, Rite & Art. 3rd ed. Susanne K. Langer. LC 57-1386. 1957. 21.00x (ISBN 0-674-66500-7); pap. 7.95 (ISBN 0-674-66503-1). Harvard U Pr.

Philosophy in America, 217 vols. (AMS Reprint Ser.). Repr. of 1953 ed. Set. write for info. (ISBN 0-404-59000-4). AMS Pr.

Philosophy in America from Puritans to James. Paul R. Anderson & Max H. Fisch. 1969. lib. bdg. 31.50x (ISBN 0-374-90248-8, Octagon). Hippocrene Bks.

Philosophy in American Education, Its Tasks & Opportunities. Curt J. Ducasse et al. LC 75-3317. Repr. of 1945 ed. 21.50 (ISBN 0-404-59297-X). AMS Pr.

Philosophy in & out of Europe. Ed. by Marjorie Grene. (Current Continental Research: No. 804). 182p. (Orig.). 1987. pap. text ed. 9.75 (ISBN 0-8191-6324-4, Pub. by Ctr Adv Res). U Pr of Amer.

Philosophy in Britain Today. Ed. by S. G. Shanker. 315p. 1986. 49.50 (ISBN 0-88706-489-2); pap. 18.95x (ISBN 0-88706-490-6). State U NY Pr.

Philosophy in Economics. Ed. by Joseph C. Pitt. 210p. 1981. 34.00 (ISBN 90-277-1210-7, Pub. by Reidel Holland). Kluwer Academic.

Philosophy in France Today. Ed. by Alan Montefiore. LC 82-9730. 200p. 1983. 42.50 (ISBN 0-521-22838-7); pap. 12.95 (ISBN 0-521-29673-0). Cambridge U Pr.

Philosophy in Geography. Ed. by Stephen Gale & Gunnar Olsson. (Theory & Decision Library: No. 20). 1979. lib. bdg. 40.00 (ISBN 9-0277-0948-3, Pub. by Reidel Holland). Kluwer Academic.

Philosophy in History: Essays in the Historiography of Philosophy. Ed. by Richard Rorty et al. (Ideas in Context Ser.). 380p. 1984. pap. 11.95 (ISBN 0-521-27330-7). Cambridge U Pr.

Philosophy in India: Traditions, Teaching & Research. K. Satchidanada Mutry. 237p. 1985. 16.95 (ISBN 81-208-0002-8, Pub. by Motilal Banarsidass India). Orient Bk Dist.

Philosophy in Medicine: Conceptual & Ethical Issues in Medicine & Psychiatry. Charles M. Culver & Bernard Gert. 1982. lib. bdg. 29.95x (ISBN 0-19-502979-8); pap. text ed. 12.95x (ISBN 0-19-502980-1). Oxford U Pr.

Philosophy in Medicine, Science & Health: Subject Analysis Index with Reference Bibliography. Rocco Z. De Forto. LC 84-47864. 150p. 1987. 34.50 (ISBN 0-88164-402-1); pap. 26.50 (ISBN 0-88164-403-X). ABBE Pubs Assn.

Philosophy in Poetry. facs. ed. Elias H. Sneath. LC 79-119965. (Select Bibliographies Reprint Ser). 1903. 19.00 (ISBN 0-8369-5408-4). Ayer Co Pubs.

Philosophy in Poetry: A Study of Sir John Davies' Poem "Nosce Teipsum". Elias H. Sneath. 1970. Repr. of 1903 ed. lib. bdg. 35.00x (ISBN 0-8371-1934-0, SNPP). Greenwood.

Philosophy in Process, Vols. 1-7. Paul Weiss. Incl. Vol. 1. June 24, 1955 - December 25, 1960. 800p. 1966 (ISBN 0-8093-0190-3); Vol. 2. December 26, 1960-March 6, 1964. 736p. 1966; Vol. 3. March-November 1964. 700p. 1968. 25.00 (ISBN 0-8093-0329-9); Vol. 4. November 26, 1964-September 2, 1965. 634p. 1969 (ISBN 0-8093-0401-5); Vol. 5. September 3, 1965-August 27, 1968. 832p. 1971. 25.00 (ISBN 0-8093-0465-1); Vol. 6. August 28, 1968-May 22, 1971. 761p. 1975 (ISBN 0-8093-0678-6); Vol. 7. April 13, 1975 - June 21, 1976. 643p. 1978 (ISBN 0-8093-0821-5). LC 63-14293. 25.00x ea. S Ill U Pr.

Philosophy in Process, Vol. 8. Paul Weiss. LC 63-14293. (Philosophy Ser.). 475p. 1985. 76.95x (ISBN 0-87395-824-1); pap. 24.50x (ISBN 0-87395-825-X). State U NY Pr.

Philosophy in Process, Vol. 10: April 15, 1984-January 18, 1986. Paul Weiss. (Philosophy Ser.). 480p. 1987. 76.95x (ISBN 0-88706-497-3); pap. 24.50x (ISBN 0-88706-499-X). State U NY Pr.

Philosophy in Process, Vol. 11: 19 January 1986 - 27 May 1987. Paul Weiss. (Philosophy Ser.). 567p. 1988. 76.95x (ISBN 0-88706-762-X); pap. 24.50x (ISBN 0-88706-767-0). State U NY Pr.

Philosophy in Process, Vol. 9: August 16, 1980-March 15, 1984. Paul Weiss. LC 63-14293. (Philosophy Ser.). 474p. (Orig.). 1986. 76.95x (ISBN 0-88706-293-8); pap. 24.50x (ISBN 0-88706-294-6). State U NY Pr.

Philosophy in Process: 17 September 1977-26 February 1978 & an Appendix, Vol. 7, Pt. 2. Paul Weiss. LC 63-14293. (Series in Philosophy). 291p. 1985. 76.95x (ISBN 0-88706-080-3); pap. 24.50 (ISBN 0-88706-082-X). State U NY Pr.

Philosophy in Question: Essays on a Pyrrhonian Theme. David R. Hiley. 224p. 1988. 24.95x (ISBN 0-226-33433-3). U of Chicago Pr.

Philosophy in Russia: From Herzen to Lenin & Berdyaev. Frederick C. Copleston. LC 85-40601. 445p. 1988. pap. text ed. 15.95x (ISBN 0-268-01569-4). U of Notre Dame Pr.

Philosophy in Russia: Herzen to Lenin to Berdyaev. Fredrick C. Copleston. LC 85-40601. 320p. 1986. text ed. 29.95x (ISBN 0-268-01558-9). U of Notre Dame Pr.

Philosophy in Science, Vol. 1. Ed. by M. Heller et al. 191p. 1983. 28.00 (ISBN 0-88126-631-0). Pachart Pub Hse.

Philosophy in the Bedroom see **Justine.**

Philosophy in the Classroom. 2nd ed. Matthew Lipman & Ann M. Sharp. 248p. 1980. 34.95 (ISBN 0-87722-177-4); pap. 12.95 (ISBN 0-87722-183-9). Temple U Pr.

Philosophy in the Classroom. 177p. 11.95 (ISBN 0-686-74922-7). ADL.

Philosophy in the Development of Law. Pierre De Tourtoulon. Ed. by Morris R. Cohen. Tr. by M. M. Read. 1977. lib. bdg. 59.95 (ISBN 0-8490-2428-5). Gordon Pr.

Philosophy in the Development of Law. Pierre De Tourtoulon. (Modern Legal Philosophy Ser.: Vol. 13). lxii, 654p. 1969. Repr. of 1922 ed. 37.50x (ISBN 0-8377-2626-3). Rothman.

Philosophy in the Middle Ages: The Christian, Islamic & Jewish Traditions. 2nd ed. Ed. by Arthur Hyman & James J. Walsh. LC 82-23337. 816p. (Orig.). 1983. lib. bdg. 37.50 (ISBN 0-915145-81-2); pap. text ed. 17.50 (ISBN 0-915145-80-4). Hackett Pub.

Philosophy in the Open. Godfrey Vesey. 144p. 1974. pap. 19.00x (ISBN 0-335-00909-3, Pub. by Open Univ Pr). Taylor & Francis.

Philosophy in the Poetry of Edwin Arlington Robinson. Estelle Kaplan. LC 70-173125. Repr. of 1940 ed. 17.45 (ISBN 0-404-03635-X). AMS Pr.

Philosophy in the Renaissance of Islam: Abu Sulayman Al-Sijistani & His Circle. Joel L. Kraemer. xvi, 354p. 1986. 63.75 (ISBN 90-04-07258-6, Pub. by E J Brill). Heinman.

Philosophy in the Soviet Union: A Survey of the Mid-Sixties. Ed. by E. Laszlo. (Sovietica Ser: No.25). 208p. 1967. lib. bdg. 21.00 (ISBN 90-277-0057-5, Pub. by Reidel Holland). Kluwer Academic.

Philosophy in the Tragic Age of the Greeks. Friedrich Nietzsche. Tr. by Marianne Cowan. 117p. 1962. pap. 7.95 (ISBN 0-89526-944-9). Regnery Gateway.

Philosophy in the Twentieth Century. A. J. Ayers. LC 82-40131. 283p. 1982. 22.00 (ISBN 0-394-50454-2). Random.

Philosophy in the Twentieth Century. A. J. Ayers. LC 83-47822. 304p. 1983. pap. 8.95 (ISBN 0-394-71655-8, Vin). Random.

Philosophy, Its History & Historiography. Ed. by A. J. Holland. 1985. lib. bdg. 49.00 (ISBN 90-277-1945-4, Reidel Holland). Kluwer Academic.

Philosophy: Its Nature, Methods & Basic Sources. Sebastian A. Matczak. LC 70-183043. (Philosophical Questions Ser: No. 4). 300p. 1976. 45.00x (ISBN 0-912116-09-9). Learned Pubns.

Philosophy, Its Scope & Relations: An Introductory Course of Lectures. Henry Sidgwick. Ed. by James Ward. LC 2-21241. 1968. Repr. of 1902 ed. 20.00 (ISBN 0-527-82830-0). Kraus Repr.

Philosophy Journals & Serials: An Analytical Guide. Compiled by Douglas H. Ruben. LC 84-29021. (Annotated Bibliographies of Serials: A Subject Approach Ser.: No. 2). xx, 147p. 1985. lib. bdg. 36.95 (ISBN 0-313-23958-4, RPJ/). Greenwood.

Philosophy, Language, & Artificial Intelligence. Ed. by Jack Kulas et al. 1988. lib. bdg. 99.00 (ISBN 1-55608-073-5, Pub. by Reidel Holland). Kluwer Academic.

Philosophy, Language & Skepticism. D. J. O'Connor. 75p. 1985. Repr. of 1949 ed. lib. bdg. 5.00 (ISBN 0-8495-4236-7). Arden Lib.

Philosophy, Letters & the Fine Arts in Klopstock's Thought. Kevin Hilliard. (Bithell of Dissertations Ser.: Vol. 12). 220p. 1987. pap. text ed. 35.00 (ISBN 0-85457-133-7, Pub. by Inst Germanic UK). Humanities.

Philosophy Looks at the Arts: Contemporary Readings in Aesthetics. 3rd ed. Joseph Margolis. 592p. 1987. 37.95 (ISBN 0-87722-439-0); pap. 16.95 (ISBN 0-87722-440-4). Temple U Pr.

Philosophy Looks at the Arts: Contemporary Readings in Aesthetics. rev. ed. Ed. by Joseph Margolis. LC 77-95028. 492p. 1978. 34.95 (ISBN 0-87722-123-5); pap. 14.95 (ISBN 0-87722-134-0). Temple U Pr.

Philosophy Looks to the Future: Confrontation, Commitment & Utopia. 2nd ed. Peyton E. Richter & Walter L. Fogg. 576p. 1985. pap. text ed. 21.95x (ISBN 0-88133-185-6). Waveland Pr.

Philosophy Now. 3rd ed. Karsten J. Struhl & Paula R. Struhl. 608p. 1980. pap. text ed. write for info (ISBN 0-394-32354-8, RanC). Random.

Philosophy Now: An Introductory Reader. 3rd ed. Ed. by Paula R. Struhl & Karsten J. Struhl. 1980. pap. text ed. write for info (ISBN 0-394-31852-8, RanC). Random.

Philosophy of a Biologist. J. B. Haldane. 1955. 47.00 (ISBN 0-8274-4211-4). R West.

Philosophy of Abraham Shalom: A Fifteenth-Century Exposition & Defense of Maimonides. Herbert A. Davidson. LC 65-63470. (University of California Publications. Near Eastern Studies: Vol. 5). pap. 29.80 (ISBN 0-317-08847-5, 2014820). Bks Demand UMI.

Philosophy of Accounts. Charles E. Sprague. LC 72-81869. 1972. Repr. of 1919 ed. text ed. 13.00 (ISBN 0-914348-09-4). Scholars Bk.

Philosophy of Goethe's Faust. Thomas Davidson. LC 68-24963. (Studies in German Literature, No. 13). 1969. Repr. of 1906 ed. lib. bdg. 49.95x (ISBN 0-8383-0933-X). Haskell.

Philosophy of Good Life. Charles Gore. 1963. Repr. of 1935 ed. 14.95x (ISBN 0-460-00924-9, Evman). Biblio Dist.

Philosophy of "Hamlet". Thomas Tyler. LC 74-2056. 1974. Repr. of 1874 ed. lib. bdg. 16.50 (ISBN 0-8414-8568-2). Folcroft.

Philosophy of Hatha Yoga. 2nd ed. Pandit U. Arya. 95p. pap. 5.95 (ISBN 0-89389-088-X). Himalayan Pubs.

Philosophy of Hegel. Georg W. Hegel. Ed. by Carl J. Friedrich. LC 54-13055. (Modern Library College Editions Ser.). 1965. pap. text ed. write for info (ISBN 0-394-30976-6, T76, RanC). Random.

Philosophy of Hegel: A Systematic Exposition. Walter T. Stace. 1923. pap. text ed. 8.95 (ISBN 0-486-20254-2). Dover.

Philosophy of Helvetius with Special Emphasis on the Educational Implications of Sensationalism. Mordecai Grossman. LC 79-176822. (Columbia University. Teachers College. Contributions to Education: No. 210). Repr. of 1926 ed. 22.50 (ISBN 0-404-55210-2). AMS Pr.

Philosophy of Henry George. George R. Geiger. LC 75-317. (Radical Tradition in America Ser.). 603p. 1975. Repr. of 1933 ed. 35.75 (ISBN 0-88355-220-5). Hyperion Conn.

Philosophy of Henry James Sr. Frederic H. Young. (Orig.). 1951. pap. 11.95x (ISBN 0-8084-0245-5). New Coll U Pr.

Philosophy of Herbert Spencer. Borden O. Bowne. 59.95 (ISBN 0-8490-0827-1). Gordon Pr.

Philosophy of Herbert Spencer. W. H. Hudson. LC 74-30102. (Studies in Philosophy, No. 40). 1974. lib. bdg. 75.00x (ISBN 0-8383-1794-4). Haskell.

Philosophy of Higher Education. Louis Wildman. LC 76-360049. 1974. 10.00 (ISBN 0-939630-00-1). Inst Qual Hum Life.

Philosophy of History. Benedetto Croce. (Illus.). 123p. 1983. 127.75 (ISBN 0-89901-128-4). Found Class Reprints.

Philosophy of History. reference ed. William H. Dray. (Orig.). 1964. pap. write for info. (ISBN 0-13-663849-X). P-H.

Philosophy of History. Ed. by Patrick Gardiner. (Oxford Readings in Philosophy). 1974. pap. text ed. 9.95x (ISBN 0-19-875031-5). Oxford U Pr.

Philosophy of History. Georg W. Hegel. 15.50 (ISBN 0-8446-2232-X). Peter Smith.

Philosophy of History. Georg W. Hegel et al. Tr. by J. Sibree. 457p. Repr. of 1900 ed. 45.00 (ISBN 0-8495-2407-5). Arden Lib.

Philosophy of History. Voltaire. 1965. pap. 3.45 (ISBN 0-8065-0078-6, 175, Pub. by Citadel Pr). Lyle Stuart.

Philosophy of History. Fredreick Von Schlegel. Tr. by James B. Robertson from Ger. 498p. 1985. Repr. of 1846 ed. lib. bdg. 200.00 (ISBN 0-89987-926-8). Darby Bks.

Philosophy of History. Friedrich Von Schlegel. LC 72-144683. Repr. of 1873 ed. 18.00 (ISBN 0-404-05606-7). AMS Pr.

Philosophy of History & Action. Ed. by Irmiahu Yovel. (Philosophical Studies in Philosophy: No. 11). 1978. lib. bdg. 36.50 (ISBN 90-277-0890-8, Pub. by Reidel Holland). Kluwer Academic.

Philosophy of History: In a Course of Lectures, Delivered in Vienna. Frederick Von Schlegel. Tr. by James B. Robertson from Ger. LC 77-145282. 1971. Repr. of 1883 ed. 16.00x (ISBN 0-403-01196-5). Scholarly.

Philosophy of History in Our Time. Ed. by Hans Meyerhoff & Robin W. Wicks. LC 83-49157. (History & Historiography Ser.). 350p. 1985. lib. bdg. 45.00 (ISBN 0-8240-6371-6). Garland Pub.

Philosophy of History with Reflections & Aphorisms. John W. Miller. LC 80-29179. 192p. 1981. 20.00x (ISBN 0-393-01464-9). Norton.

Philosophy of History: With Reflections & Aphorisms. John W. Miller. 192p. 1983. pap. 6.50x (ISBN 0-393-30060-9). Norton.

Philosophy of Hope. C. C. Brown. 1972. 2.95; pap. 2.00 (ISBN 0-9600378-3-7). C C Brown Pub.

Philosophy of Human Hope. Joseph J. Godfrey. 1987. lib. bdg. 50.50 (ISBN 90-247-3353-7, Pub. by Martinus Nijhoff Netherlands); pap. 19.50 (ISBN 90-247-3354-5, Pub. by Martinus Nijhoff Netherlands). Kluwer Academic.

Philosophy of Human Nature. Joseph Buchanan. Ed. by James F. Adams. 368p. 1971. 20.00x (ISBN 0-87730-005-4). M&S Pr.

Philosophy of Human Nature. Joseph Buchanan. LC 71-90941. (History of Psychology Ser.). (Illus.). 1969. Repr. of 1812 ed. 50.00x (ISBN 0-8201-1064-7). Schol Facsimiles.

Philosophy of Human Nature. Chu Hsi. Tr. by J. Percy Bruce. LC 73-38057. (BCL Ser.: No. II). Repr. of 1922 ed. 42.50 (ISBN 0-404-56913-7). AMS Pr.

Philosophy of Human Nature. Chu Hsi. 1976. lib. bdg. 59.95 (ISBN 0-8490-2432-3). Gordon Pr.

Philosophy of Human Rights. Ed. by Morton E. Winston. Date not set. pap. text ed. write for info. (ISBN 0-534-10020-1). Wadsworth Pub.

Philosophy of Human Rights: International Perspectives. Ed. by Alan S. Rosenbaum. LC 79-6191. (Contributions in Philosophy: No. 15). xv, 272p. 1980. lib. bdg. 38.95 (ISBN 0-313-20985-5, RHR/). Greenwood.

Philosophy of Humanism. 6th ed. Corliss Lamont. LC 81-70127. 340p. 1982. 15.95 (ISBN 0-8044-5997-5); pap. 9.95 (ISBN 0-8044-6379-4). Ungar.

Philosophy of Humanism. 5th ed. Corliss Lamont. LC 65-16612. 10.50 (ISBN 0-8044-5595-3); pap. 10.95 (ISBN 0-8044-6378-6). Ungar.

Philosophy of Idealism in Its Structure & Objectives. Bernard Bosanquet. 121p. 1985. 84.65 (ISBN 0-89266-513-0). Am Classical Coll Pr.

Philosophy of Ideological Conflict. Charles E. Seely. LC 85-28657. 1953. 5.95 (ISBN 0-8022-1528-9). Philos Lib.

Philosophy of Immanuel Kant. Ed. by Richard Kennington. LC 84-23887. (Studies in Philosophy & the History of Philosophy: Vol. 12). 300p. 1985. 31.95 (ISBN 0-8132-0607-3). Cath U Pr.

Philosophy of Immanuel Kant Series, 14 vols. 1977. lib. bdg. 350.00 set (ISBN 0-685-83865-X). Garland Pub.

Philosophy of Immortality. R. Swinburne Clymer. 208p. 1960. 6.95 (ISBN 0-932785-39-5). Philos Pub.

Philosophy of India & Its Impact on American Thought. Dale Riepe. (Illus.). 354p. 1970. 32.50x (ISBN 0-398-01590-2). C C Thomas.

Philosophy of Individual Freedom: The Political Thought of F. A. Hayek. Calvin M. Hoy. LC 84-8973. (Contributions in Political Science Ser.: No. 119). (Illus.). ix, 144p. 1984. lib. bdg. 35.00 (ISBN 0-313-24361-1, HPI/). Greenwood.

Philosophy of Integralism see Being, Evolution & Immortality.

Philosophy of Islam. Ayatullah Behishti. Tr. by M. A. Ansari from Farsi. 580p. 25.00 (ISBN 0-941724-22-0). Islamic Seminary.

Philosophy of J. Krishnamurti: A Systematic Study. R. K. Shringy. LC 78-670076. 1977. 24.00x (ISBN 0-89684-442-0). Orient Bk Dist.

Philosophy of J. S. Mill. R. P. Anschutz. LC 85-27075. (Illus.). 206p. 1986. Repr. of 1953 ed. lib. bdg. 38.50x (ISBN 0-313-25040-5, ANPM). Greenwood.

Philosophy of Jacques Maritain. Charles A. Fecher. LC 70-90705. Repr. of 1953 ed. lib. bdg. 35.00x (ISBN 0-8371-2287-2, FEJM). Greenwood.

Philosophy of Jean-Paul Sartre. Robert D. Cumming. 1972. pap. 5.95 (ISBN 0-394-71808-9, V808, Vin). Random.

Philosophy of Jean-Paul Sartre. Intro. by Paul A. Schilpp. (Library of Living Philosophers: Vol. XVI). 754p. 1981. 29.95 (ISBN 0-87548-354-2). Open Court.

Philosophy of Jesus. Ernest Holmes. Ed. by Willis Kinnear. 94p. 1973. pap. 4.50 (ISBN 0-911336-51-6). Sci of Mind.

Philosophy of Jesus: Real Love. Jules A. Delanghe. LC 72-96805. 1973. 4.95 (ISBN 0-8059-1821-3). Dorrance.

Philosophy of John Dewey, 2 vols. John Dewey. Ed. by John J. McDermott. LC 80-39766. xiii, 724p. (Vol. 1, The Structure of Experience; Vol. 2, The Lived Experience). 1981. pap. 14.00x (ISBN 0-226-14401-1). U of Chicago Pr.

Philosophy of John Scottus Eriugena. Dermot Moran. (Illus.). 450p. Date not set. price not set (ISBN 0-521-34549-9). Cambridge U Pr.

Philosophy of Josiah Royce. Josiah Royce. Ed. & intro. by John K. Roth. LC 82-2932. (HPC Philosophical Classics Ser.). 430p. 1982. lib. bdg. 25.00 (ISBN 0-915145-42-1); pap. text ed. 9.95 (ISBN 0-915145-41-3). Hackett Pub.

Philosophy of Judaism. Joshua Adler. 5.95 (ISBN 0-8022-0008-7). Philos Lib.

Philosophy of Judaism: The History of Jewish Philosophy from Biblical Times to Franz Rosenzweig. Julius Guttmann. LC 88-26214. 480p. 1988. 30.00 (ISBN 0-87668-872-5). Aronson.

Philosophy of Justice Between God & Man. Benjamin P. Blood. LC 75-3056. Repr. of 1851 ed. 20.50 (ISBN 0-404-59054-3). AMS Pr.

Philosophy of Kant. Immanuel Kant. Ed. & tr. by John Watson. 1934. Repr. lib. bdg. 59.50 (ISBN 0-8414-5551-1). Folcroft.

Philosophy of Kant. Immanuel Kant. Ed. by Carl J. Friedrich. LC 50-267. 1949. 8.95 (ISBN 0-394-60465-2). Modern Lib.

Philosophy of Kant & Our Modern World. Charles W. Hendel. LC 81-4693. vii, 132p. 1981. Repr. of 1957 ed. lib. bdg. 35.00x (ISBN 0-313-23051-X, HEPK). Greenwood.

Philosophy of Kant Explained. John Watson. 515p. 1981. Repr. of 1908 ed. lib. bdg. 50.00 (ISBN 0-8495-5659-7). Arden Lib.

Philosophy of Kant Explained. John Watson. LC 78-14918. 1978. Repr. of 1908 ed. lib. bdg. 62.00 (ISBN 0-8414-9708-7). Folcroft.

Philosophy of Kant Explained. John Watson. Ed. by Lewis W. Beck. LC 75-32047. (Philosophy of Immanual Kant Ser.: Vol. 11). 1977. Repr. of 1908 ed. lib. bdg. 48.00 (ISBN 0-8240-2335-8). Garland Pub.

Philosophy of Karl Jaspers. augmented ed. Ed. by Paul A. Schilpp. LC 57-14578. (Library of Living Philosophers: Vol. IX). 992p. 1981. 39.95 (ISBN 0-87548-361-5). Open Court.

Philosophy of Karl Popper, 2 vols. Ed. by Paul A. Schilpp. LC 78-186983. (Library of Living Philosophers: Vol. XIV). 1357p. 1974. Set. 39.95 (ISBN 0-87548-353-4). Open Court.

Philosophy of Knowledge. 2nd ed. Kenneth T. Gallagher. LC 64-19903. xii, 307p. 1984. pap. 10.00 (ISBN 0-8232-1095-2). Fordham.

Philosophy of Knowledge. rev. ed. Vincent G. Potter. LC 85-81101. xii, 249p. 1986. pap. 6.25x (ISBN 0-8232-1170-3). Fordham.

Philosophy of Knowledge: An Inquiry into the Nature, Limits & Validity of Human Cognitive Faculty. George T. Ladd. LC 75-3223. Repr. of 1897 ed. 57.50 (ISBN 0-404-59219-8). AMS Pr.

Philosophy of Language. reference ed. William P. Alston. (Orig.). 1964. pap. write for info. (ISBN 0-13-663799-X). P-H.

Philosophy of Language. Ed. by G. Floistad. 1986. pap. 21.50 (ISBN 90-247-3297-2, Pub. by Martinus Nijhoff Netherlands). Kluwer Academic.

Philosophy of Language. Ed. by A. P. Martinich. 1985. 26.00x (ISBN 0-19-503553-4). Oxford U Pr.

Philosophy of Language. Ed. by J. R. Searle. (Oxford Readings in Philosophy Ser). (Orig.). 1971. pap. text ed. 8.95x (ISBN 0-19-875015-3). Oxford U Pr.

Philosophy of Language & the Theory of Aesthetics, 2 vols. Benedetto Croce. (Illus.). 237p. 1987. Set. 167.45 (ISBN 0-89901-310-4). Found Class Reprints.

Philosophy of Language in Britain: Major Theories from Hobbes to Thomas Reid. Stephen K. Land. LC 83-45287. (Studies in the Seventeenth Century: No. 2). 1986. 39.50 (ISBN 0-404-61722-0). AMS Pr.

Philosophy of Language, Linguistic Pragmatics & Formative Pragmatics, Vol. IV. (Pragmatics: Handbook of Pragmatic Thought Ser.). Date not set. price not set. Transaction Bks.

Philosophy of Language: Philosophical Logic. Ed. by Guttorm Floistad & G. H. Von Wright. (Contemporary Philosophy: a New Survey Ser.: No. 1). 320p. 1981. 43.20 (ISBN 0-686-31875-7, Pub. by Martinus Nijhoff Netherlands). Kluwer Academic.

Philosophy of Language Primer. Thomas S. Vernon. LC 80-489. 136p. 1980. text ed. 24.25 (ISBN 0-8191-1023-X); pap. text ed. 9.25 (ISBN 0-8191-1024-8). U Pr of Amer.

Philosophy of Laughter & Humor. Ed. by John Morreall. LC 86-14498. (Philosophy Ser.). 270p. (Orig.). 1986. 52.50 (ISBN 0-88706-326-8); pap. 17.95 (ISBN 0-88706-327-6). State U NY Pr.

Philosophy of Laughter & Smiling. George Vasey. 166p. 1982. Repr. of 1875 ed. lib. bdg. 65.00 (ISBN 0-89984-479-0). Century Bookbindery.

Philosophy of Laughter & Smiling. George Vassey. Repr. of 1875 ed. 30.00 (ISBN 0-8274-4178-9). R West.

Philosophy of Law. Ed. by Ronald M. Dworkin. (Oxford Readings in Philosophy). 1977. pap. 9.95x (ISBN 0-19-875022-6). Oxford U Pr.

Philosophy of Law. 3rd ed. Ed. by Joel Feinberg & Hyman Gross. 708p. 1986. text ed. write for info. (ISBN 0-534-06198-2). Wadsworth Pub.

Philosophy of Law. Martin P. Golding. (Foundation of Philosophy Ser.). 176p. 1975. pap. text ed. write for info. (ISBN 0-13-664128-8). P-H.

Philosophy of Law. Immanuel Kant. Tr. by W. Hastie. LC 77-146882. 265p. 1974. Repr. of 1887 ed. lib. bdg. 35.00x (ISBN 0-678-01152-4). Kelley.

Philosophy of Law. Josef Kohler. (Modern Legal Philosophy Ser: Vol. 12). xliv, 390p. 1969. Repr. of 1914 ed. 37.50x (ISBN 0-8377-2326-4). Rothman.

Philosophy of Law. Paul Sayre. vi, 148p. 1981. Repr. of 1954 ed. lib. bdg. 22.50x (ISBN 0-8377-1121-5). Rothman.

Philosophy of Law: An Introduction to Jurisprudence. Jeffrie G. Murphy & Jules L. Coleman. LC 84-6870. (Texts in Philosophy Ser.). 312p. 1984. 32.50x (ISBN 0-8476-6277-2, Rowman & Allanheld); pap. 15.95x (ISBN 0-8476-6278-0). Rowman.

Philosophy of Law: Being Notes of Lectures Delivered During Twenty-Three Years (1852 to 1875) in the Inner Temple Hall Adapted for Students & the Public. Herbert Broom. xi, 338p. 1980. Repr. of 1878 ed. lib. bdg. 27.50x (ISBN 0-8377-0310-7). Rothman.

Philosophy of Law in Historical Perspective. 2nd ed. Carl J. Friedrich. LC 57-9546. 1963. pap. 10.00x (ISBN 0-226-26466-1, P135, Phoen). U of Chicago Pr.

Philosophy of Leadership. Christopher Hodgkinson. LC 83-10943. 260p. 1983. 27.50 (ISBN 0-312-60672-9). St Martin.

Philosophy of Leibniz & the Modern World. Ed. by Ivor Leclerc. LC 72-1346. 306p. 1973. 17.95x (ISBN 0-8265-1181-3). Vanderbilt U Pr.

Philosophy of Leibniz: Metaphysical Underpinnings. Benson Mates. 336p. 1986. 29.95x (ISBN 0-19-503696-4). Oxford U Pr.

Philosophy of Liberation. Enrique Dussel. Tr. by Aquilina Martinez & Christine Morkovsky. LC 85-5103. 240p. (Orig.). 1985. pap. 10.95 (ISBN 0-88344-405-4). Orbis Bks.

Philosophy of Life & Philosophy of Language. Frederick Von Schlegel. Tr. by Reverend A. J. Morrison from Ger. 567p. 1985. Repr. of 1847 ed. lib. bdg. 250.00 (ISBN 0-89987-925-X). Darby Bks.

Philosophy of Life & Philosophy of Language. Friedrich Von Schlegel. Tr. by A. J. Morrison. LC 70-147991. Repr. of 1847 ed. 27.50 (ISBN 0-404-08249-1). AMS Pr.

Philosophy of Life & Philosophy of Language, in a Course of Lectures. F. Von Schlegel. Tr. by A. J. Morrison. 1847. Repr. 35.00 (ISBN 0-8274-3132-5). R West.

Philosophy of Life & the Philosophy of Death: Considerations & Anticipations of the Future Universe & of Man's Existence in It. 2nd ed. (Illus.). 1977. 88.85 (ISBN 0-89266-058-9). Am Classical Coll Pr.

Philosophy of Life & the Philosophy of Death. C. M. Flumiani. 89p. 1987. pap. 37.50 (ISBN 0-86650-223-8). Gloucester Art.

Philosophy of Life & the Philosophy of Death. Lucretius. (Illus.). 117p. 1984. Repr. of 1911 ed. 117.75 (ISBN 0-89901-167-5). Found Class Reprints.

Philosophy of Lifelong Education. Kenneth Wain. (International Perspectives on Adult & Continuing Education Ser.). 220p. 1986. 33.95 (ISBN 0-7099-3675-3, Pub. by Croom Helm UK). Routledge Chapman & Hall.

Philosophy of Light: An Introductory Treatise. Floyd I. Lorbeer. 259p. 1981. pap. 15.00 (ISBN 0-89540-102-9, SB-102). Sun Pub.

Philosophy of Linguistics. Ed. by Jerrold J. Katz. (Oxford Readings in Philosophy Ser.). 270p. 1985. 22.00x (ISBN 0-19-875070-6); pap. 9.95x (ISBN 0-19-875065-X). Oxford U Pr.

Philosophy of Literary Form. Kenneth Burke. 1974. pap. 11.95x (ISBN 0-520-02483-4). U of Cal Pr.

Philosophy of Literature. Gustar E. Mueller. LC 72-14195. (Essay Index Reprint Ser.). Repr. of 1948 ed. 18.75 (ISBN 0-518-10021-9). Ayer Co Pubs.

Philosophy of Literature. Raymond Tschumi. LC 62-12798. 1968. 22.50 (ISBN 0-900001-03-8, Pub. by Centaur Bks). State Mutual Bk.

Philosophy of Literature. Raymond Tschumi. 20.00 (ISBN 0-87556-338-4). Saifer.

Philosophy of Literature. Raymond Tschumi. 1983. 40.00x (Pub. by Centaur Bks). State Mutual Bk.

Philosophy of Living or, the Way to Enjoy Life & Its Comforts. Caleb Ticknor. LC 72-180595. (Medicine & Society in America Ser). 342p. 1972. Repr. of 1836 ed. 23.50 (ISBN 0-405-03977-8). Ayer Co Pubs.

Philosophy of Logic. Ed. by Stephen Korner. LC 76-6020. (Studies in the Logic of Science). 1976. 40.00x (ISBN 0-520-03235-7). U of Cal Pr.

Philosophy of Logic. 2nd ed. W. V. Quine. 128p. 1986. pap. text ed. 6.95x (ISBN 0-674-66563-5). Harvard U Pr.

Philosophy of Logical Atomism. Bertrand Russell. LC 85-18750. 192p. 1985. pap. 6.95 (ISBN 0-87548-443-3). Open Court.

Philosophy of Logical Atomism & Other Essays, 1914-1919. Bertrand Russell. Ed. by John G. Slater. (Collected Papers of Bertrand Russell: Vol. 8). 418p. 1986. lib. bdg. 60.00 (ISBN 0-04-920074-7). Unwin Hyman.

Philosophy of Logics. Susan Haack. LC 77-17071. (Illus.). 1978. o. p. 44.50 (ISBN 0-521-21988-4); pap. 15.95x (ISBN 0-521-29329-4). Cambridge U Pr.

Philosophy of Love. Judah Abarbanel. Tr. by F. Friedeberg-Seeley & J. H. Barnes. 1977. lib. bdg. 59.95 (ISBN 0-8490-2433-1). Gordon Pr.

Philosophy of Love in Spanish Literature. A. A. Parker. 245p. 1985. 15.00x (ISBN 0-85224-491-6, Pub. by Edinburgh Scotland). Columbia U Pr.

Philosophy of Love, the Narada Sutras. Hari P. Shastrim. 59.95 (ISBN 0-8490-0828-X). Gordon Pr.

Philosophy of Loyalty. Josiah Royce. xiv, 409p. 1971. Repr. of 1908 ed. 20.95x (ISBN 0-02-851160-3). Hafner.

Philosophy of Loyalty. Josiah Royce. 409p. 1985. lib. bdg. 30.00 (ISBN 0-8492-7733-7). R West.

Philosophy of Machiavelli on the Art of Entrepreneurship. Niccolo Machiavelli. (Illus.). 119p. 1983. 147.75 (ISBN 0-86654-092-X). Inst Econ Finan.

Philosophy of Magic. large type ed. Eusebe Salverte. pap. 6.95 (ISBN 0-910122-41-5). Amherst Pr.

Philosophy of Magic. Arthur Versluis. (Illus.). 166p. 1985. pap. 7.95 (ISBN 0-317-40548-9). Routledge Chapman & Hall.

Philosophy of Mahatma Gandhi. Dhirendra M. Datta. 168p. 1953. pap. 10.95x (ISBN 0-299-01014-7). U of Wis Pr.

Philosophy of Man: A New Introduction to Some Perennial Issues. Howard P. Kainz. LC 79-14716. (Illus.). 224p. 1981. pap. text ed. 9.50 (ISBN 0-8173-0066-X). U of Ala Pr.

Philosophy of Man & Society. Forrest H. Peterson. LC 76-136014. 238p. 1970. 10.00 (ISBN 0-8022-2043-6); pap. 9.95 (ISBN 0-8022-2548-9). Philos Lib.

Philosophy of Man & the Universe. Fred Loeschmann. LC 75-393404. 1976. 7.95 (ISBN 0-87212-052-X). Libra.

Philosophy of Science & Belief in God. 2nd rev. ed. Gordon H. Clark. (Trinity Papers: No. 18). 150p. pap. 5.95 (ISBN 0-940931-18-4). Trinity Found.

Philosophy of Science & Historical Enquiry. John Losee. LC 86-23550. 152p. 1987. 32.00 (ISBN 0-19-824946-2). Oxford U Pr.

Philosophy of Science & Its Discontents. Steve W. Fuller. 192p. 1989. 28.50 (ISBN 0-8133-0611-6). Westview.

Philosophy of Science & Sociology: From the Methodological Doctrine to Research Practice. E. Mokrzycki. (International Library of Sociology). 180p. 1983. 21.95x (ISBN 0-7100-9444-2). Routledge Chapman & Hall.

Philosophy of Science & the Occult. Patrick Grim. LC 81-13552. 336p. 1983. 44.50x (ISBN 0-87395-572-2); pap. 10.95x (ISBN 0-87395-573-0). State U NY Pr.

Philosophy of Science for Personality Theory. 2nd ed. Joseph F. Rychlak. LC 80-15614. 584p. 1981. 31.50 (ISBN 0-88275-889-6). Krieger.

Philosophy of Science of Ruder Boskovic. Ed. by Valentin Posaic. 1988. text ed. 25.00x (ISBN 0-268-01572-4). U of Notre Dame Pr.

Philosophy of Sex: Contemporary Readings. Ed. by Alan Soble. (Quality Paperback Ser.: No. 351). 412p. (Orig.). 1980. pap. 9.95 (ISBN 0-8226-0351-9). Littlefield.

Philosophy of Sex: Contemporary Readings. Ed. by Alan Soble. 412p. 1980. 18.50x (ISBN 0-8476-6292-6). Rowman.

Philosophy of Sikh Religion. Wazir Singh. 127p. 1981. 14.95x (ISBN 0-940500-09-4, Pub. by Ess Ess Pubns India). Asia Bk Corp.

Philosophy of Sin. Oswald Chambers. 1961. pap. 3.95 (ISBN 0-87508-122-3). Chr Lit.

Philosophy of Sleep see Mesmerism in India.

Philosophy of Small Scale Industrial Management. K. S. Iyengar. 215p. 1970. 5.00 (ISBN 0-88065-134-2, Pub. by Messers Today & Tomorrows Printers & Publishers India). Scholarly Pubns.

Philosophy of Social Explanation. Ed. by Alan Ryan. (Oxford Readings in Philosophy). 1973. pap. text ed. 8.95x (ISBN 0-19-875025-0). Oxford U Pr.

Philosophy of Social Science. David Braybrooke. (Illus.). 144p. 1987. pap. text ed. write for info. (ISBN 0-13-663394-3). P-H.

Philosophy of Social Science. Alexander Rosenberg. (Dimensions of Philosophy Ser.). 224p. 1988. 34.50 (ISBN 0-8133-0616-7); pap. 14.95 (ISBN 0-8133-0617-5). Westview.

Philosophy of Society. Ed. by Roger Beehler & Alan R. Drengson. 1978. pap. 15.50x (ISBN 0-416-83490-6, NO. 2083). Routledge Chapman & Hall.

Philosophy of Socrates: A Collection of Critical Essays. Ed. by Gregory Vlastos. LC 80-308. (Modern Studies in Philosophy). 360p. 1980. pap. text ed. 10.95 (ISBN 0-268-01540-6). U of Notre Dame Pr.

Philosophy of Space & Time. Hans Reichenbach. Tr. by Maria Reichenbach. 1957. pap. text ed. 5.95 (ISBN 0-486-60443-8). Dover.

Philosophy of Spinoza: The Unity of His Thought. Richard McKeon. LC 86-28563. 345p. 1987. 30.00 (ISBN 0-918024-47-1); pap. 16.00 (ISBN 0-918024-48-X). Ox Bow.

Philosophy of Spinoza: Unfolding the Latent Processes of His Reasoning. Harry A. Wolfson. 872p. 1983. pap. text ed. 17.50x (ISBN 0-674-66595-3). Harvard U Pr.

Philosophy of Spirit Intercourse. Richard W. Cromwell. 225p. 1988. 117.75 (ISBN 0-89901-362-7). Found Class Reprints.

Philosophy of Spiritual Activity. Rudolf Steiner. Tr. by William Lindeman from Ger. 200p. 1987. 18.00 (ISBN 0-88010-157-1); pap. 8.95 (ISBN 0-88010-156-3). Anthroposophic.

Philosophy of Spiritual Activity, Vol. 2. 2nd ed. Rudolf Steiner. LC 80-65627. (Spiritual Science Library). 304p. 1980. lib. bdg. 20.00 (ISBN 0-89345-030-8, Spiritual Sci Lib); pap. 11.50 (ISBN 0-89345-208-4). Garber Comm.

Philosophy of Sri Madhavacarya. B. N. Sharma. 483p. 1986. Repr. of 1962 ed. 38.50x (ISBN 81-208-0068-0, Pub. by Motilal Banarsidass India). Orient Bk Dist.

Philosophy of Strategy for Breeding Tropical Forest Trees. G. Namkoong et al. 1980. 30.00x (ISBN 0-85074-034-7, Pub. by For Lib Comm England). State Mutual Bk.

Philosophy of Symbolic Forms, Vol. 1, Language. Ernst Cassirer. Tr. by Ralph Manheim. 1965. pap. 13.95x (ISBN 0-300-00037-5, Y146). Yale U Pr.

Philosophy of Symbolic Forms, Vol. 2, Mythical Thought. Ernst Cassirer. Tr. by Ralph Manheim. 1955. pap. 13.95x (ISBN 0-300-00038-3, Y147). Yale U Pr.

Philosophy of Symbolic Forms, Vol. 3, The Phenomenology Of Knowledge. Ernst Cassirer. Tr. by Ralph Manheim. 1965. pap. 13.95x (ISBN 0-300-00039-1, Y148). Yale U Pr.

Philosophy of T. S. Eliot: From Skepticism to a Surrealist Poetic, 1909-1927. William Skaff. LC 85-31477. (Illus.). 256p. 1986. 28.95 (ISBN 0-8122-8017-2). U of PA Pr.

Philosophy of Teaching. E. J. Ortman. LC 61-18688. 1962. 5.95 (ISBN 0-8022-1244-1). Philos Lib.

Philosophy of Teaching. John Passmore. 259p. 1980. pap. 12.75 (ISBN 0-7156-1465-7, Pub. by Duckworth London). Longwood Pub Group.

Philosophy of Technology. Frederick Ferre. 144p. 1988. pap. text ed. price not set (ISBN 0-13-662586-X). P-H.

Philosophy of the Act. George H. Mead. Ed. by Charles W. Morris. LC 38-15971. 696p. 1972. pap. 3.95x (ISBN 0-226-51669-5, P476, Phoen). U of Chicago Pr.

Philosophy of the American Constitution: A Reinterpretation of the Intentions of the Founding Fathers. Paul Eidelberg. LC 86-5532. 356p. 1986. pap. text ed. 15.50 (ISBN 0-8191-5341-9). U Pr of Amer.

Philosophy of the American Revolution. Morton White. LC 77-18081. (American Social Thought Ser.). 1978. 22.50x (ISBN 0-19-502381-1); pap. 8.95 (ISBN 0-19-502891-0). Oxford U Pr.

Philosophy of the Christian Religion. Edward J. Carnell. (Twin Brooks Ser.). 525p. 1981. pap. 10.95 (ISBN 0-8010-2464-1). Baker Bk.

Philosophy of the Church Fathers: Faith, Trinity, Incarnation. 3rd rev. ed. Harry A. Wolfson. LC 70-119077. 1970. 32.50x (ISBN 0-674-66551-1). Harvard U Pr.

Philosophy of the Curriculum. Ed. by Sidney Hook et al. LC 75-3921. 280p. 1975. 18.95 (ISBN 0-87975-051-0). Prometheus Bks.

Philosophy of the Enlightenment. Ernst Cassirer. Tr. by F. Koelin & J. Pettegrove. 1951. pap. 10.50 (ISBN 0-691-01963-0). Princeton U Pr.

Philosophy of the Enlightenment: The Burgess & the Enlightenment. Lucien Goldmann. Tr. by Henry Maas from Fr. 1973. 17.50x (ISBN 0-262-07060-X). MIT Pr.

Philosophy of the Film. Ed. by Ian Jarvie. LC 86-26226. 312p. 1987. pap. 35.00 (ISBN 0-7102-1016-7, 10167, Pub. by Routledge UK). Routledge Chapman & Hall.

Philosophy of the Good Life. Charles Gore. LC 77-27197. (Gifford Lectures: 1929-30). Repr. of 1930 ed. 24.00 (ISBN 0-404-60484-6). AMS Pr.

Philosophy of the Human Voice. James Rush. 634p. (Orig.). 1900. 15.00 (ISBN 0-914076-60-4). Lib Co Phila.

Philosophy of the Humanistic Society. Ed. by Alfred E. Koenig et al. LC 80-1425. 290p. (Orig.). 1981. pap. text ed. 14.50 (ISBN 0-8191-1415-4). U Pr of Amer.

Philosophy of the I Ching. Carol K. Anthony. LC 81-69537. 160p. 1981. pap. 7.50 (ISBN 0-9603832-1-2). Anthony Pub Co.

Philosophy of the Inductive Sciences, 2 vols. William Whewell. 1967. Repr. of 1847 ed. 95.00x (ISBN 0-7146-1156-5, BHA-01156, F Cass Co). Biblio Dist.

Philosophy of the Inductive Sciences, 2 Vols. 2nd facsimile ed. William Whewell. Repr. of 1847 ed. Set. 62.00 (ISBN 0-384-67940-4). Johnson Repr.

Philosophy of the Inner Light. Michael Marsh. LC 76-50674. (Orig.). 1976. pap. 2.50x (ISBN 0-87574-209-2). Pendle-Hill.

Philosophy of the Kalam. Harry A. Wolfson. LC 74-78718. 864p. 1976. 42.00x (ISBN 0-674-66580-5). Harvard U Pr.

Philosophy of the Language Laboratory see Language Classroom.

Philosophy of the Literary Symbolic. Hazard Adams. LC 82-24785. (Illus.). xiv, 466p. 1983. pap. 29.00x (ISBN 0-8130-0771-2). U Presses Fla.

Philosophy of the Mind. J. Richardson. 1985. 60.00 (ISBN 0-317-68632-1, Pub. by J Richardson); pap. 40.00 (ISBN 0-317-68633-X). State Mutual Bk.

Philosophy of the Mind - Philosophy of Psychology. Ed. by Chisholm et al. 1985. pap. text ed. 73.00 (ISBN 90-277-9148-1, Pub by Reidel Holland). Kluwer Academic.

Philosophy of the Novel: Lukacs, Marxism & the Dialectics of Form. J. M. Bernstein. 320p. 1984. 35.00x (ISBN 0-8166-1304-4); pap. 14.95 (ISBN 0-8166-1307-9). U of Minn Pr.

Philosophy of the Plays of Shakspere Unfolded. Delia S. Bacon. LC 73-113547. Repr. of 1857 ed. 34.50 (ISBN 0-404-00443-1). AMS Pr.

Philosophy of the Practical. Benedetto Croce. Tr. by Douglas Ainslie. LC 66-30790. 1913. 18.00 (ISBN 0-8196-0192-6). Biblo.

Philosophy of the Practice of Dentistry. Lindsey D. Pankey & William J. Davis. Ed. by Veronica Sanitate. (Illus.). 323p. 1987. text ed. 69.50 (ISBN 0-944742-01-7); tapes 127.50 (ISBN 0-944742-02-5). Med Coll of OH Pr.

Philosophy of the Present. George H. Mead. Ed. by Arthur E. Murphy. LC 80-16334. 240p. 1980. pap. 5.95x (ISBN 0-226-51670-9, P909, Phoen). U of Chicago Pr.

Philosophy of the Quran. H. G. Sarwar. 4.50 (ISBN 0-686-18604-4). Kazi Pubns.

Philosophy of the Qur'an. H. G. Sarwar. 1969. 7.25x (ISBN 0-87902-187-X). Orientalia.

Philosophy of the Real & the Possible. Harry T. Costello. LC 72-972. Repr. of 1954 ed. 15.00 (ISBN 0-404-01737-1). AMS Pr.

Philosophy of the Recent Past: An Outline of European & American Philosophy Since 1860. Ralph B. Perry. LC 75-3314. Repr. of 1926 ed. 29.00 (ISBN 0-404-59295-3). AMS Pr.

Philosophy of the Religions of Ancient Greeks & Israelites. Ben Kimpel. LC 83-6512. 362p. (Orig.). 1983. lib. bdg. 31.50 (ISBN 0-8191-3225-X); pap. text ed. 16.50 (ISBN 0-8191-3226-8). U Pr of Amer.

Philosophy of the Sciences; or, the Relations Between the Departments of Knowledge. F. R. Tennant. LC 73-1828. ix, 191p. 1973. Repr. of 1932 ed. 25.00 (ISBN 0-208-01317-2, Archon). Shoe String.

Philosophy of the Sciences or the Relations Between the Departments of Knowledge. Frederick R. Tennant. 1970. Repr. of 1932 ed. lib. bdg. 35.00x (ISBN 0-8371-4353-5, TEPS). Greenwood.

Philosophy of the Second Advent. Howard Redmond. Ed. by Leonard G. Goss. 160p. 1985. write for info. (ISBN 0-88062-070-6); pap. write for info. (ISBN 0-88062-067-6). Mott Media.

Philosophy of the Second Advent. Howard A. Redmond. 1986. text ed. 12.95 (ISBN 0-8010-7740-0). Baker Bk.

Philosophy of the Self. Ghanshamdas R. Malkani. 15.00 (ISBN 0-384-35112-3); pap. 10.00 (ISBN 0-685-13549-7). Johnson Repr.

Philosophy of the Short Story. Brander Matthews. LC 72-187105. 1912. lib. bdg. 20.00 (ISBN 0-8414-0533-6). Folcroft.

Philosophy of the Sixteenth & Seventeenth Centuries. Richard H. Popkin. LC 66-10365. (Orig.). 1966. pap. text ed. 14.95 (ISBN 0-02-925490-6). Free Pr.

Philosophy of the Social Sciences. Vernon Pratt. 1978. pap. 12.95x (ISBN 0-416-76380-4, NO. 2392). Routledge Chapman & Hall.

Philosophy of the Social Sciences: Scheimater, Vol. 2. J. Wisdom. (Avebury Series in the History & Philosophy of Science). 180p. 1986. text ed. 33.00x (ISBN 0-566-05158-3, Pub. by Gower England). Gower Pub Co.

Philosophy of the Upanishads. Paul Deussen. Tr. by A. S. Geden. (Orig.). 1966. pap. 8.50 (ISBN 0-486-21616-0). Dover.

Philosophy of the Upanishads. Edward Gough. 268p. 1979. Repr. of 1882 ed. 19.95 (ISBN 0-89684-158-8). Orient Bk Dist.

Philosophy of the Waverly Novels. Albert S. Canning. 1973. Repr. of 1879 ed. 25.00 (ISBN 0-8274-1784-5). R West.

Philosophy of Theism. Alexander C. Fraser. LC 77-27228. (Gifford Lectures: 1894-95). Repr. of 1895 ed. 30.00 (ISBN 0-404-60453-6). AMS Pr.

Philosophy of Theism: Second Series. Alexander C. Fraser. LC 77-27227. (Gifford Lectures: 1895-96). Repr. of 1896 ed. 22.50 (ISBN 0-404-60454-4). AMS Pr.

Philosophy of Thomas Aquinas: Introductory Readings. Thomas Aquinas. Tr. by Christopher Martin. (Croom Helm Philosophy Ser.). 256p. 1988. text ed. 45.00 (ISBN 0-415-00295-8); pap. text ed. 17.95 (ISBN 0-415-00296-6). Routledge Chapman & Hall.

Philosophy of Universality. rev. ed. Omraam M. Aivanhov. (Izvor Collection: Vol. 206). 178p. (Orig.). 1988. pap. 6.95 (ISBN 2-85566-420-9, Pub. by Prosveta France). Prosveta USA.

Philosophy of Upanishads. B. Singh. 160p. 1983. text ed. 10.50x (ISBN 0-391-02935-5). Humanities.

Philosophy of Utilitarianism. John S. Mill. (Illus.). 129p. (Orig.). 1988. 117.50 (ISBN 0-89266-620-X). Am Classical Coll Pr.

Philosophy of Vaisnava Religion. G. N. Mallik. 59.95 (ISBN 0-8490-0829-8). Gordon Pr.

Philosophy of Vegetarianism. Daniel A. Dombrowski. LC 83-18125. 192p. 1984. lib. bdg. 20.00x (ISBN 0-87023-430-7); pap. 9.95x (ISBN 0-87023-431-5). U of Mass Pr.

Philosophy of Visistadvaita. P. N. Srinivasachari. 648p. 1978. 15.00 (ISBN 0-8356-7495-9). Orient Bk Dist.

Philosophy of W. V. Quine. Ed. by Lewis Hahn & Paul A. Schilpp. LC 86-17980. (Library of Living Philosophers: Vol. XVIII). 728p. 1986. 49.95 (ISBN 0-8126-9010-9); pap. 24.95 (ISBN 0-8126-9012-5). Open Court.

Philosophy of W. V. Quine: An Expository Essay. Roger F. Gibson. LC 81-16338. 1982. 26.00x (ISBN 0-8130-0707-0); pap. 18.00x. U Presses Fla.

Philosophy of Wang Yang Ming. Frederick G. Henke. 1976. lib. bdg. 59.95 (ISBN 0-8490-2436-6). Gordon Pr.

Philosophy of Wealth. 2nd ed. John B. Clark. LC 67-25955. 1967. Repr. of 1887 ed. 27.50x (ISBN 0-678-00275-4). Kelley.

Philosophy of Welfare: Selected Writing of Richard M. Titmuss. Ed. by Brian Abel-Smith & Kay Titmuss. 240p. 1987. text ed. 39.95x (ISBN 0-04-361063-3); pap. text ed. 14.95X (ISBN 0-04-361064-1). Unwin Hyman.

Philosophy of Wilfrid Sellars: Queries & Extensions. Ed. by J. C. Pitt. (Philosophical Studies in Philosophy: No. 12). 1978. lib. bdg. 34.00 (ISBN 90-277-0903-3, Pub. by Reidel Holland). Kluwer Academic.

Philosophy of Wilhelm Dilthey. Herbert A. Hodges. LC 73-13024. (International Library of Sociology & Social Reconstruction). 368p. 1974. Repr. of 1952 ed. lib. bdg. 35.00x (ISBN 0-8371-7112-1, HOWD). Greenwood.

Philosophy of William Ellery Channing. Robert L. Patterson. LC 76-153342. Repr. of 1952 ed. 23.50 (ISBN 0-404-04916-8). AMS Pr.

Philosophy of William James. Ed. by W. Corti. 1977. pap. 32.25x (ISBN 3-7873-0352-9). Adlers Foreign Bks.

Philosophy of William James. T. Flournoy. LC 78-99658. (Select Bibliographies Reprint Ser). 1917. 22.00 (ISBN 0-8369-5087-9). Ayer Co Pubs.

Philosophy of Wittgenstein: Aesthetics, Ethics & Religion. Ed. by John V. Canfield. (Philosophy of Wittgenstein Ser.). 342p. 1987. lib. bdg. 42.00 (ISBN 0-8240-6497-6). Garland Pub.

Philosophy of Wittgenstein: Criteria. Ed. by John V. Canfield. (Philosophy of Wittgenstein Ser.). 434p. 1987. lib. bdg. 52.00 (ISBN 0-8240-6490-9). Garland Pub.

Philosophy of Wittgenstein: Elective Affinities. John V. Canfield. (Philosophy of Wittgenstein Ser.). 355p. 1987. lib. bdg. 42.00 (ISBN 0-8240-6498-4). Garland Pub.

Philosophy of Wittgenstein: Knowing, Naming, Certainty & Idealism. Ed. by John V. Canfield. (Philosophy of Wittgenstein). 324p. 1987. lib. bdg. 40.00 (ISBN 0-8240-6491-7). Garland Pub.

Philosophy of Wittgenstein: Logic & Ontology. Ed. by John V. Canfield. (Philosophy of Wittgenstein Ser.). 342p. 1987. lib. bdg. 42.00 (ISBN 0-8240-6485-2). Garland Pub.

Philosophy of Wittgenstein: Logical Necessitiy & Rules. Ed. by John V. Canfield. (Philosophy Wittgenstein Ser.). 384p. 1987. lib. bdg. 47.00 (ISBN 0-8240-6493-3). Garland Pub.

Philosophy of Wittgenstein: Meaning. Ed. by John V. Canfield. (The Philosophy Wittgenstein Ser.). 335p. 1987. lib. bdg. 40.00 (ISBN 0-8240-6489-5). Garland Pub.

Philosophy of Wittgenstein: Method & Essence. Ed. by John V. Canfield. (Philosophy of Wittgenstein Ser.). 379p. 1987. lib. bdg. 45.00 (ISBN 0-8240-6488-7). Garland Pub.

Philosophy of Wittgenstein: My World & Its Value. Ed. by John V. Canfield. (Philosophy of Wittgenstein Ser.). 325p. 1987. lib. bdg. 40.00 (ISBN 0-8240-6486-0). Garland Pub.

Philosophy of Wittgenstein: Persons. Ed. by John V. Canfield. (Philosophy of Wittgenstein Ser.). 306p. 1987. lib. bdg. 37.00 (ISBN 0-8240-6495-X). Garland Pub.

Philosophy of Wittgenstein: Philosophy of Mathematics. Ed. by John V. Canfield. (Philosophy of Wittgenstein Ser.). 408p. 1987. lib. bdg. 47.00 (ISBN 0-8240-6494-1). Garland Pub.

Philosophy of Wittgenstein: Psychology & Conceptual Relativity. Ed. by John V. Canfield. (Philosophy of Wittgenstein Ser.). 349p. 1987. lib. bdg. 42.00 (ISBN 0-8240-6496-8). Garland Pub.

Philosophy of Wittgenstein: The Early Philosophy--Language As Picture. Ed. by John V. Canfield. (Philosophy of Wittgenstein Ser.). 393p. 1987. lib. bdg. 47.00 (ISBN 0-8240-6484-4). Garland Pub.

Philosophy of Wittgenstein: The Later Philosophy--Views & Reviews. Ed. by John V. Canfield. (Philosophy of Wittgenstein Ser.). 335p. 1987. lib. bdg. 42.00 (ISBN 0-8240-6487-9). Garland Pub.

Philosophy of Wittgenstein: The Private Language Argument. Ed. by John V. Canfield. (Philosophy of Wittgenstein Ser.). 364p. 1987. lib. bdg. 42.00 (ISBN 0-8240-6492-5). Garland Pub.

Philosophy of Woman: An Anthology of Classic & Current Concepts. 2nd ed. Ed. by Mary B. Mahowald. LC 83-8433. 480p. 1983. lib. bdg. 24.50 (ISBN 0-915144-49-2); pap. text ed. 12.50 (ISBN 0-915144-48-4). Hackett Pub.

Philosophy of Worship in Islam. F. R. Ansari. pap. 1.00 (ISBN 0-686-18603-6). Kazi Pubns.

Philosophy: Paradox & Discovery. 2nd ed. Arthur J. Minton & Thomas A. Shipka. 496p. 1982. pap. 26.95x (ISBN 0-07-042413-6). McGraw.

Philosophy, Policies & Programs for Early Adolescent Education: An Annotated Bibliography. Compiled by Dale A. Blyth & Elizabeth L. Karnes. LC 81-4237. 704p. 1981. lib. bdg. 56.95 (ISBN 0-313-22687-3, BEA/). Greenwood.

Philosophy, Politics & Citizenship: The Life & Thought of the British Idealists. Andrew Vincent & Raymond Plant. 232p. 1985. 39.95 (ISBN 0-85520-693-4). Basil Blackwell.

Philosophy, Politics & Society, Vol. 5. Ed. by Peter Laslett & James Fishkin. LC 78-64392. 1979. 34.00x (ISBN 0-300-02337-5). Yale U Pr.

Philosophy, Psychology & Mysticism. Inayat Khan. (Sufi Message of Hazrat Inayat Khan Ser.: Vol. 11). 256p. 1979. (Pub. by Servire BV Netherlands). Hunter Hse.

Philosophy, Psychology & Spirituality. Ed. by James W. Kidd. LC 83-80836. 87p. (Orig.). 1984. pap. text ed. 12.00 (ISBN 0-910727-05-8). Golden Phoenix.

Philosophy: Ritual-Shabbat & Kashrut. (Home Study Program Ser.: No. 602). 6.00 (ISBN 0-686-96133-1). United Syn Bk.

Philosophy, Science, & Sense Perception: Historical and Critical Studies. Maurice Mandelbaum. 288p. 1964. 32.50x (ISBN 0-8018-0450-7); pap. 10.95x (ISBN 0-8018-0451-5). Johns Hopkins.

Philosophy, Science & Social Inquiry: Contemporary Methodological Controversies in Social Science & Related Applied Fields of Research. D. C. Phillips. 245p. 1987. text ed. 35.00 (ISBN 0-08-033410-5, PBL); pap. text ed. 15.95 (ISBN 0-08-033411-3, PBL). Pergamon.

Philosophy, Science & the Sociology of Knowledge. Irving L. Horowitz. LC 76-27756. 1976. Repr. of 1961 ed. lib. bdg. 35.00x (ISBN 0-8371-9051-7, HOPS). Greenwood.

Phonemics: A Technique for Reducing Language to Writing. Kenneth L. Pike. 1947. pap. 13.95x (ISBN 0-472-08732-0). U of Mich Pr.

Phones on Your Own. Louis Ance & Robert Hazenfield. 1984. pap. 10.05 (Reston). P-H.

Phonetic Alphabet. 3rd ed. Francis A. Cartier & Martin T. Todaro. 112p. 1982. pap. text ed. write for info. (ISBN 0-697-04218-9); avail. instr's. guide & answer key (ISBN 0-697-04231-6). Wm C Brown.

Phonetic Approaches to Speech Production in Aphasia & Related Disorders. Ed. by John H. Ryalls. 352p. (Orig.). 1987. pap. text ed. 35.00 (ISBN 0-316-76371-3, 763713). College-Hill.

Phonetic Bases of Speaker Recognition. Francis Nolan. LC 83-1828. (Cambridge Studies in Speech Science & Communication). (Illus.). 225p. 1983. 44.50 (ISBN 0-521-24486-2). Cambridge U Pr.

Phonetic Basis of Perceptual Ratings of Running Speech. L. Boves. (Netherlands Phonetic Archives Ser.). xii, 188p. 1984. write for info. (ISBN 90-6765-034-X); pap. write for info. (ISBN 90-6765-035-8). Foris Pubns.

Phonetic Context. Cynthia F. Farell. 146p. 1987. pap. text ed. 16.95 (ISBN 0-88450-974-5, 7325). Communication SKill.

Phonetic Context Drill Book. Jerry Griffith & Lynn E. Miner. 1979. pap. 16.95. P-H.

Phonetic Description of the Ukrainian Language. Ivan Zilyns'Kyj. Tr. by Wolodymyry T. Zyla & Wendell M. Aycock. LC 77-73711. (Harvard Ukrainian Research Institute Monograph). (Illus.). 1979. 15.00x (ISBN 0-674-66612-7). Harvard U Pr.

Phonetic Description of Voice Quality. J. Laver. LC 77-82501. (Cambridge Studies in Linguistics: No. 31). (Illus.). 225p. 1980. 44.50 (ISBN 0-521-23176-0). Cambridge U Pr.

Phonetic Dictionary of Medical Terminology: A Spelling Guide. Elaine Rice. LC 85-62428. 200p. 1985. text ed. 19.00 (ISBN 0-932500-37-4). Natl Hlth Pub.

Phonetic French Dictionary: Contrasting French-English Sounds. Jeanne V. Pleasants. 1959p. (Fr. & Eng.). pap. text ed. 5.95 (ISBN 0-940630-01-X, T-7010). Playette Corp.

Phonetic Linguistics: Essays in Honor of Peter Ladefoged. Ed. by Victoria A. Fromkin. 1985. 27.50 (ISBN 0-12-268990-9). Acad Pr.

Phonetic Music with Electronic Music. Ernest Robson & Larry Wendt. LC 81-90189. 1981. bk. only 19.45 (ISBN 0-934982-02-3); with book & cassette 23.45 (ISBN 0-686-31759-9); cass. only 12.00 (ISBN 0-686-34446-4). Primary Pr.

Phonetic Puzzles: Grade 3. Fred Justus. (Puzzles Ser.). 24p. 1980. wkbk. 5.00 (ISBN 0-8209-0289-6, PU-3). ESP.

Phonetic Puzzles: Grade 4. Fred Justus. (Puzzles Ser.). 24p. 1980. 5.00 (ISBN 0-8209-0290-X, PU-4). ESP.

Phonetic Puzzles: Grade 5. Fred Justus. (Puzzles Ser.). 24p. 1980. wkbk. 5.00 (ISBN 0-8209-0291-8, PU-5). ESP.

Phonetic Puzzles: Grade 6. Fred Justus. (Puzzles Ser.). 24p. 1980. 5.00 (ISBN 0-8209-0292-6, PU-6). ESP.

Phonetic Puzzles: Grade 7. Fred Justus. (Puzzles Ser.). 24p. 1980. wkbk. 5.00 (ISBN 0-8209-0293-4, PU-7). ESP.

Phonetic Puzzles: Grade 8. Fred Justus. (Puzzles Ser.). 24p. 1980. wkbk. 5.00 (ISBN 0-8209-0294-2, PU-8). ESP.

Phonetic Readers for the Short Vowels: Jan & Pam, The Van, Rex & Tex, The Bed, Siz & Liz, The Pit, Dod & Bob, The Box, Hun & Sum, The Hut, & Pals, 11 bks. Trish Mylet & Antoinette Sheffield. Ed. by Barry W. Burton. (Illus.). 180p. (ps-2). 1988. Set. pap. text ed. 16.00 (ISBN 0-945590-00-8). Sizzy Bks.

Phonetic Readings of Brahms Lieder. Candace A. Magner. LC 87-17620. (Illus.). 424p. 1987. 25.00 (ISBN 0-8108-2059-5). Scarecrow.

Phonetic Readings of Songs & Arias: With Revised German Transcriptions. 2nd ed. Berton Coffin & Ralph Errolle. LC 82-874. 400p. 1982. pap. text ed. 21.50 (ISBN 0-8108-1533-8). Scarecrow.

Phonetic Science: A Program of Instruction. Samuel R. Faircloth & Marjorie A. Faircloth. (Illus.). 144p. 1973. pap. text ed. 16.95. P-H.

Phonetic Sounds. Bearl Brooks. (Phonics Ser.). 24p. (gr. 2). 1979. wkbk. 5.00 (ISBN 0-8209-0331-0, P-3). ESP.

Phonetic Sounds & Symbols: Part 1. Bearl Brooks. (Phonics Ser.). 24p. (gr. 1). 1978. wkbk. 5.00 (ISBN 0-8209-0335-3, P-7). ESP.

Phonetic Sounds & Symbols: Part 2. Bearl Brooks. (Phonics Ser.). 24p. (gr. 1). 1978. wkbk. 5.00 (ISBN 0-8209-0336-1, P-8). ESP.

Phonetic Spelling for College Students. Ralph M. Williams. LC 80-24084. 180p. 1980. Repr. of 1960 ed. lib. bdg. 41.50 (ISBN 0-313-22650-4, WIPS). Greenwood.

Phonetic Storybook Readers, 17 vols. rev. ed. Sue Dickson. (Illus.). 960p. (gr. k-3). 1984. pap. 48.00 (ISBN 1-55574-003-0, SR-310). CBN Publishing.

Phonetic Structure of Somali. Lillias E. Armstrong. 48p. Repr. text ed. 20.70x (ISBN 0-576-11443-X, Pub. by Gregg Intl Pubs England). Gregg Intl.

Phonetic Symbol Guide. Geoffrey K. Pullum & William A. Ladusaw. LC 86-7036. xxx, 266p. 1986. text ed. 35.00x (ISBN 0-226-68531-4); pap. text ed. 9.95x (ISBN 0-226-68532-2). U of Chicago Pr.

Phonetic Value of Certain Characters in Maya Writing. B. L. Whorf. (Harvard University Peabody Museum of Archaeology & Ethnology Papers Ser). pap. 14.00 (ISBN 0-527-01229-7). Kraus Repr.

Phonetic Variation & Acoustic Distinctive Features. Clara N. Bush. (Janua Linguarum, Ser. Practica: No. 12). (Orig.). 1964. pap. text ed. 23.20x (ISBN 90-2790-631-9). Mouton.

Phonetical Study of the Eskimo Language, Based on Observations Made on a Journey in North Greenland 1900-1901. William C. Thalbitzer. LC 74-5883. (Illus.). Repr. of 1904 ed. 30.00 (ISBN 0-404-11662-7). AMS Pr.

Phoneticism in Mayan Hieroglyphic Writing. John S. Justeson & Lyle Campbell. LC 84-62430. (Monographs: No. 9). (Illus.). 389p. (Orig.). 1984. pap. text ed. 27.00 (ISBN 0-942041-08-9). SUNYA Inst Mesoam.

Phonetics. 3rd ed. Bertil Malmberg. (Illus.). 1954. pap. 2.95 (ISBN 0-486-21024-3). Dover.

Phonetics: A Critical Analysis of Phonetic Theory & a Technic for the Practical Description of Sounds. Kenneth L. Pike. 1943. pap. 10.95x (ISBN 0-472-08733-9). U of Mich Pr.

Phonetics & Diction in Singing: Italian, French, Spanish, German. Kurt Adler. LC 67-25073. (Illus., Orig.). 1967. pap. 7.95x (ISBN 0-8166-0446-0). U of Minn Pr.

Phonetics & Phonology of Modern German: An Introduction. Wilbur A. Benware. 256p. (Orig.). 1986. pap. 12.95x (ISBN 0-87840-193-8). Georgetown U Pr.

Phonetics: Instructional Aid in Language Arts. Barbara B. Dreher & Charles J. Gervase. 1976. perfect bdg. 7.95 (ISBN 0-8403-1310-1). Kendall-Hunt.

Phonetics of English. Ida C. Ward. 1979. Repr. of 1931 ed. lib. bdg. 22.50 (ISBN 0-8495-5707-0). Arden Lib.

Phonetics of Russian. D. Jones & Dennis Ward. 1969. text ed. 70.00 (ISBN 0-521-06736-7). Cambridge U Pr.

Phonetics: Principles & Practices. 2nd ed. Sadanand Singh & Kala S. Singh. LC 81-13031. (Illus.). 288p. 1982. pap. 19.00x (ISBN 0-8391-1701-9, 1326). Pro Ed.

Phonetics: The Science of Speech Production. Ian R. MaKay. 336p. 1986. 24.00 (ISBN 0-316-54238-5). College-Hill.

Phonetics: Theory & Application. 2nd ed. William R. Tiffany & James Carrell. (Speech Ser.). (Illus.). 1977. text ed. 39.95 (ISBN 0-07-064575-2). McGraw.

Phonetikkurs Deutsch: Aussprache, Artikulation und Intonation. Theodor Kriesch. (Illus.). 1964. pap. text ed. 4.95 (ISBN 0-940630-10-9, T-7097). Playette Corp.

Phonetique et Phonologie du Judeo - Espagnol de Bucarest. Marius Sala. (Janua Linguarum, Practica Ser.: No. 142). 1971. pap. text ed. 30.80x (ISBN 90-2791-708-6). Mouton.

Phonetique Generale et Romane: Etudes En Allemand, Anylais, Es Paynol et Francais. Bertil Malmberg. LC 75-141182. (Janua Linguarum, Ser. Major: No. 42). 478p. 1971. text ed. 59.20x (ISBN 90-2791-790-6). Mouton.

Phonetisch-Phonologische Untersuchungen zur Vokalentwicklung in den deutschen Dialekten. Peter Wiesinger. Incl. Vol. 1. Langvokale im Hochdeutschen. (Illus.). xxx, 423p (ISBN 3-11-001895-0); Vol. 2. Diphtonge im Hochdeutschen. (Illus.). viii, 361p (ISBN 3-11-001896-9). (Studia Linguistica Germanica: Zweiter Deutscher Sprachatlas, Gesamtdarstellungen Volkalismus, Vols. 1 & 2). (Ger.). 1970. Set. 82.00x (ISBN 0-685-24226-9). De Gruyter.

Phonewriting: A Consumer's Guide to the New World of Electronic Information Services. Samuel A. Simon & Michael J. Whalen. (Orig.). 1986. pap. text ed. 7.00 (ISBN 0-943444-03-9). T R A C.

Phonic Analysis Activity Sheets for Grades 2-4. Wilma H. Miller. (Corrective Reading Skills Activity File Ser.). (Orig.). 1977. pap. 7.30x (ISBN 0-87628-221-4, C-2214-9). Ctr Appl Res.

Phonic Analysis Activity Sheets for Grades 4-6. Wilma H. Miller. (Corrective Reading Skills Activity File Ser.). (Orig.). 1977. pap. 7.30x (ISBN 0-87628-222-2, C-2222-2). Ctr Appl Res.

Phonic Dictionary. Linda Hayward. (Illus.). 96p. (gr. k-4). 1981. PLB 3.99 (ISBN 0-448-13923-5, G&D); pap. 4.95 (ISBN 0-448-47336-4). Putnam Pub Group.

Phonic Grab Bag. Mary F. Pecci. (Super Seatwork Ser.). (Illus.). 138p. 1984. 9.95 (ISBN 0-943220-09-2). Pecci Educ Pubs.

Phonic Word Builder. Hy Ruchlis. (Hip Reader Program Ser.). 32p. (gr. 1-5). 1972. 2.75 (ISBN 0-87594-191-5, 2046); tchr's manual 2.75 (ISBN 0-685-56184-4). Book-Lab.

Phonics. Annette Taulbee. (Be Smart Bks.). (Illus.). 24p. (ps-k). 1986. 2.50 (ISBN 0-86734-066-5, FS-3058). Schaffer Pubns.

Phonics: A Handbook of Classroom Ideas to Motivate the Teaching of Elementary Phonics. 1980. 8.95 (ISBN 0-89273-130-3). Educ Serv.

Phonics & Spelling. Beverly Cory. (gr. 4-6). pap. 1.95 (ISBN 0-8224-4176-4). D S Lake Pubs.

Phonics Art Projects. Marilyn Bruch. (gr. 1-3). 1985. pap. 6.95 (ISBN 0-8224-5541-2). D S Lake Pubs.

Phonics: Blends & Digraphs. Schaffer, Frank, Publications Staff. (Schaffer Basic Learning Ser.). (Illus.). 48p. (gr. 1-3). 1983. wkbk. 3.98 (ISBN 0-86734-027-4, FS-2656). Schaffer Pubns.

Phonics Bulletin Boards. Marilyn Burch. (gr. 1-3). 1985. pap. 6.95 (ISBN 0-8224-5542-0). D S Lake Pubs.

Phonics Combinations. Compiled by Constance McAllister. (Illus., Orig.). (gr. 1-4). 1978. pap. 2.50 (ISBN 0-87534-173-X). Highlights.

Phonics Competencies for Reading Teachers. John W. Logan. 80p. 1985. pap. 8.95 (ISBN 0-8403-3654-3). Kendall Hunt.

Phonics: Consonants. Schaffer, Frank, Publications Staff. (Help Your Child Learn Ser.). (Illus.). 24p. (ps-2). 1978. wkbk. 2.50 (ISBN 0-86734-003-7, FS 3004). Schaffer Pubns.

Phonics-Consonants. Schaffer, Frank, Publications Staff. (Schaffer Basic Learning Ser.). (Illus.). 48p. (gr. 1-3). 1983. wkbk. 3.98 (ISBN 0-86734-026-6, FS-2655). Schaffer Pubns.

Phonics Duplicating Masters: Elementary Phonics. (Vols. 2). 1980. 8.95 ea. Vol. 1 (ISBN 0-89273-564-3). Vol. II (ISBN 0-89273-565-1). Educ Serv.

Phonics for Reading & Spelling: Grade 2. Bearl Brooks. (Phonics Ser.). 24p. 1978. wkbk. 5.00 (ISBN 0-8209-0337-X, P-9). ESP.

Phonics for Reading & Spelling: Grade 3. Bearl Brooks. (Phonics Ser.). 24p. 1978. wkbk. 5.00 (ISBN 0-8209-0338-8, P-10). ESP.

Phonics for Reading & Spelling: Grade 4. Bearl Brooks. (Phonics Ser.). 24p. 1978. wkbk. 5.00 (ISBN 0-8209-0339-6, P-11). ESP.

Phonics for Teachers for Teachers of Reading. 5th ed. Marion Hull. 160p. 1988. pap. 14.95 (ISBN 0-675-21071-2). Merrill.

Phonics for the Teacher of Reading. 4th ed. Marion A. Hull. 160p. 1985. pap. 14.95 (ISBN 0-675-20406-2). Merrill.

Phonics Fun for Beginners. Compiled by Constance McAllister. (Illus., Orig.). (gr. 1-3). 1977. pap. 2.50 (ISBN 0-87534-167-5). Highlights.

Phonics Guidelines: An Introduction. Paul C. Holmes. 320p. 1980. pap. text ed. 20.50 (ISBN 0-8403-2225-9). Kendall-Hunt.

Phonics Handbook for the Primary Grades. Alta Mellin. 1962. pap. 4.95 (ISBN 0-8224-5400-9). D S Lake Pubs.

Phonics in Proper Perspective. 5th ed. Arthur W. Heilman. 128p. 1985. pap. 14.95 (ISBN 0-675-20376-7). Merrill.

Phonics in Proper Perspective. 6th ed. Arthur W. Heilman. 128p. 1988. pap. 14.95 (ISBN 0-675-21068-2). Merrill.

Phonics Is Fun. Louis Krane. Incl. Bk. 1. (gr. 1). 1978. pap. text ed. 5.84 (ISBN 0-8136-0201-7); tchrs.' ed. 2.70 (ISBN 0-8136-0214-9); Bk. 2. (gr. 2). 1978. pap. text ed. 5.76 (ISBN 0-8136-0202-5); tchrs.' ed. 2.70 (ISBN 0-8136-0215-7); answer key o.p. 1.00; Bk. 3. (gr. 3). 1978. pap. text ed. 5.72 (ISBN 0-8136-0203-3); tchrs.' ed. 2.70 (ISBN 0-8136-0216-5). (Phonics Is Fun Ser.). pap. Modern Curr.

Phonics Is Fun, Pre-Primer 2: In the Tent. pap. text ed. 1.35. Modern Curr.

Phonics, Linguistics, & Reading. Dolores Durkin. LC 72-87115. 1972. pap. 6.95x (ISBN 0-8077-1258-2). Tchrs Coll.

Phonics Manual & Lesson Plans, Level D. Jane Ervin. (gr. 4). 1977. 2.00. Modern Curr.

Phonics One-Three, 3 bks. (gr. k-3). 1970. Bk. 2. pap. 0.99 (ISBN 0-440-03393-4); Bk. 3. pap. 0.99 (ISBN 0-440-03396-9); Bk. 1. pap. text ed. 1.29 (ISBN 0-440-07085-6). Dell.

Phonics Practice Readers. 1978. Set 4 Digraphs 10 Bks. pap. text ed. 11.48 (ISBN 0-8136-0608-X). Modern Curr.

Phonics Practice Readers. Janis Raabe. 1978. Set 3 Blends 10 Bks. pap. text ed. 11.48 (ISBN 0-8136-0607-1). Modern Curr.

Phonics Practice Readers, Set 1: Short Vowels. Janis A. Raabe. (Illus.). (gr. k-1). 1974. pap. text ed. 11.48 incl. tchrs' guide (ISBN 0-8136-0605-5). Modern Curr.

Phonics Practice Readers, Set 2: Long Vowels. Janis A. Raabe. (Illus.). (gr. k-1). 1975. pap. text ed. 11.48 (ISBN 0-8136-0606-3); tchr's. guide avail. Modern Curr.

Phonics Primer for Teens & Adults (for the Reading Helper) rev ed. Margaret McEathron. Incl. Bk. 1. Helper's Instruction Book. 160p. pap. 9.95 (ISBN 0-9604388-1-5); Bk. 2. Student's Account Book. 120p. wkbk. 4.95 (ISBN 0-9604388-2-3). (Illus., Orig.). (gr. 4 up). 1980. Set. pap. 14.90 (ISBN 0-9604388-0-7). Reading Hse.

Phonics Review. Arlene Henkel. Ed. by Joan Hoffman. (I Know It! Bks.). (Illus.). 32p. (gr. 2-3). 1980. wkbk. 1.95 (ISBN 0-938256-08-4). Sch Zone Pub Co.

Phonics Seatwork. Marilyn Burch. (gr. 1-3). 1985. pap. 6.95 (ISBN 0-8224-5543-9). D S Lake Pubs.

Phonics: Vowels. Schaffer, Frank, Publications Staff. (Help Your Child Learn Ser.). (Illus.). 24p. (gr. 1-3). 1978. wkbk. 2.50 (ISBN 0-86734-004-5, FS 3005). Schaffer Pubns.

Phonics: Vowels. Schaffer, Frank, Publications Staff. (Schaffer Basic Learning Ser.). (Illus.). 48p. (gr. 1-3). 1983. wkbk. 3.98 (ISBN 0-86734-028-2, FS-2657). Schaffer Pubns.

Phonics Workbook, Level D. Jane Ervin. (MCP Basic Phonics Program Ser.). (gr. 4). 1988. 6.21 (ISBN 0-8136-0116-9). Modern Curr.

Phonix: Fruhlings-Zeitung Fur Deutschland, 2 vols. Ed. by Edward Duller & Karl Gutzkow. 1973. Repr. of 1835 ed. vol. 1 nos. 1-309 77.00 (ISBN 0-384-46413-0). Johnson Repr.

Phonogram in Cultural Communications. Ed. by K. Blaukopf. (Illus.). 180p. 1982. pap. 26.70 (ISBN 0-387-81725-5). Springer-Verlag.

Phonograph & Our Musical Life: Proceedings of a Centennial Conference. Ed. by H. Wiley Hitchcock. LC 80-82409. (I. S. A. M. Monographs: No. 14). 91p. 1980. pap. 7.50 (ISBN 0-914678-14-0). Inst Am Music.

Phonograph & Radio-Phonograph Diagrams & Servicing Information, 1927-1946. Hartford Beitman. Ed. by K. H. Beitman. (Supreme Specialty Servicing Manuals Ser.). (Illus.). 240p. (Orig.). 1988. pap. text ed. 26.00 (ISBN 0-938630-78-4, SM-19). ARS Enterprises.

Phonologic-Articulatory Disorders: Current Therapy of Communication Disorders, Vol. 5. Ed. by William H. Perkins. 114p. 1983. 17.50 (ISBN 0-86577-099-9). Thieme Med Pubs.

Phonologica Nineteen Eighty-Four: Proceedings of the Fifth International Phonology Meeting, Eisenstadt, 25-28 June 1984. Ed. by Wolfgang Dressler et al. (Illus.). 400p. 1987. 49.50 (ISBN 0-521-30291-9). Cambridge U Pr.

Phonological Acquisitions & Change (Symposium) Ed. by John L. Locke. 1983. 33.00 (ISBN 0-12-454180-1). Acad Pr.

Phonological Analysis. Joseph E. Grimes. 187p. 1969. microfiche (2) 4.00 (ISBN 0-88312-360-6). Summer Inst Ling.

Phonological Analysis: Focus on American English. Walt Wolfram & Robert Johnson. 250p. 1982. 16.00x (ISBN 0-13-665043-0, Dist. by P-H); pap. 14.67x (ISBN 0-13-664988-2). Ctr Appl Ling.

Phonological & Lexical Aspects of Colloquial Finnish. Melvin J. Luthy. (Uralic & Altaic Ser.: No. 119). 93p. 1973. pap. text ed. 13.60x (ISBN 0-686-27754-6). Mouton.

Phonological & Lexical Aspects of Colloquial Finnish, Vol. 119. Melvin J. Luthy. (Uralic & Altaic Ser.). x, 94p. 1973. pap. text ed. 19.95x (ISBN 0-87750-173-4). Res Ctr Lang Semiotic.

Phonological & Lexical Study of the Speech of Tuscaloosa County. Lawrence M. Foley. (Publications of the American Dialect Society: No. 58). 68p. 1972. pap. 7.45 (ISBN 0-8173-0658-7). U of Ala Pr.

Phonological & Morphological Study of the Speech of the Negro of Memphis, Tennessee. Juanita Williamson. (Publications of the American Dialect Society: No. 50). 60p. 1968. pap. 6.85 (ISBN 0-8173-0650-1). U of Ala Pr.

Phonological Assessment of Child Speech: PACS. Pamela Grunwell. LC 85-3734. 172p. 1985. incl. forms 42.00 (ISBN 0-316-33050-7, 330507). College-Hill.

Phonological Development in Children 18 to 72 Months. Ed. by John V. Irwin & Seok P. Wong. LC 82-5893. 256p. 1983. 24.95x (ISBN 0-8093-1057-0). S Ill U Pr.

Phonological Disorders. John V. Irwin. Ed. by Harvey Halpern. LC 86-2616. (Pro-Ed Studies in Communicative Disorders). (Illus.). 48p. (Orig.). 1986. pap. text ed. 7.00x (ISBN 0-89079-090-6, 1380). Pro Ed.

Phonological Interpretation of Ancient Greek: A Pandialectal Analysis. Vit Bubenik. (Phoenix Supplementary Ser.: Vol. 19). 352p. 1983. 37.50x (ISBN 0-8020-5476-5). U of Toronto Pr.

Phonological Intervention: Concepts & Procedures. Ed. by Michael A. Crary. LC 81-21706. (Illus.). 128p. 1982. pap. 18.00 (ISBN 0-316-16049-0). College-Hill.

Phonological Investigation of Aphasic Speech. Sheila E. Blumstein. (Janua Linguarum Ser. Minor: No. 153). 1973. pap. text ed. 14.00x (ISBN 90-2792-448-1). Mouton.

Phonological Issues in North Alaskan Inupiaq. Lawrence D. Kaplan. (Alaska Native Language Center Research Papers Ser.: No. 6). 282p. 1981. pap. 15.00 (ISBN 0-933769-36-9). Alaska Native.

Phonological Markedness & Distinctive Features. Arthur Brakel. LC 82-49348. (Illus.). 144p. 1983. 22.50x (ISBN 0-253-34450-6). Ind U Pr.

Phonological Parsing in Speech Recognition. Kenneth W. Church. 1987. lib. bdg. 49.95 (ISBN 0-89838-250-5). Kluwer Academic.

Phonological Process Analysis. Weiner. (Illus.). 224p. 1979. 26.00x (ISBN 0-8391-1300-5, 1331). Pro Ed.

Phonological Reconstruction of Proto-North-Bahnaric. Ken D. Smith. (Language Data, Asia-Pacific Ser.: No. 2). 109p. 1972. microfiche (2) 4.00 (ISBN 0-88312-302-9). Summer Inst Ling.

Photo-Electronics Image Devices: Proceedings see Advances in Electronics & Electron Physics.

Photo Equipment. Ed. by Michael L. Green. 1978. pap. 1.95 (ISBN 0-89552-017-6). DMR Pubns.

Photo Equipment. rev. ed. (Illus.). pap. 1.95 (ISBN 0-89552-004-4). DMR Pubns.

Photo Equipment You Can Make, Vol. 2. Parry Yob. LC 73-82539. (Photography How-to Ser.). 1977. 3.95 (ISBN 0-8227-4013-3). Petersen Pub.

Photo-Fashion. Ed. by Wolfgang Hageney. (Illus.). 208p. (Eng., Ital., Ger., Span. & Fr.). 1982. pap. 44.95 (ISBN 88-7070-013-5). R Silver.

Photo-Fiends. Patrick Smith. (Moon Books: No. 37). (Illus.). 36p. (Orig.). 1977. pap. text ed. 5.00 (ISBN 0-942908-00-7). Pancake Pr.

Photo Filters & Lens Attachments. Kalton C. Lahue. (Petersen's Photographic Library: Vol. 5). (Illus.). 160p. 1981. pap. 8.95 (ISBN 0-8227-4044-3). Petersen Pub.

Photo Finish. Ngaio Marsh. (Ngaio Marsh Mystery Ser.). 224p. 1987. pap. 3.50 (ISBN 0-515-07505-1). Jove Pubns.

Photo Identification for Photogrammetric Mapping. Herbert W. Stoughton. 1981. 10.00 (ISBN 0-317-60443-0, G425). Am Congrs Survey.

Photo-Lab Index. 39th ed. LC 40-847. 1400p. 1985. looseleaf 65.00 (ISBN 0-87100-051-2, 2051). Morgan.

Photo Laboratory Technician. Jack Rudman. (Career Examination Ser.: C-1389). (Cloth bdg. avail. on request). pap. 10.00 (ISBN 0-8373-1389-9). Natl Learning.

Photo Language Stimulation for Aphasic Patients. Robert Canetta. LC 74-76839. 1974. pap. text ed. 16.95x (ISBN 0-8134-1641-8, 1641). Inter Print Pubs.

Photo Machine Operator. Jack Rudman. (Career Examination Ser.: C-1390). (Cloth bdg. avail. on request). pap. 10.00 (ISBN 0-8373-1390-2). Natl Learning.

Photo Manual & Dissection Guide of the Shark. Fred Bohensky. (Avery's Anatomy Ser.). (Illus.). 144p. (Orig.). 1981. pap. text ed. 8.95 (ISBN 0-89529-140-1). Avery Pub.

Photo Manual & Dissection Guide of the Rat. Fred Bohensky. (Avery's Anatomy Ser.). (Illus.). 160p. (Orig.). 1986. lab manual 7.95 (ISBN 0-89529-213-0). Avery Pub.

Photo Manual & Dissection Guide of the Frog. Fred Bohensky. (Avery's Anatomy Ser.). (Illus.). 88p. (Orig.). 1982. lab manual 6.95 (ISBN 0-89529-162-2). Avery Pub.

Photo Manual & Dissection Guide of the Fetal Pig: With Sheep Heart, Brain, Eye. Fred Bohensky. (Illus.). 1978. 7.95 (ISBN 0-89529-058-8). Avery Pub.

Photo Manual of the Cat: With Sheep Heart, Brain, Eye. Fred Bohensky. (Illus.). 1977. lab manual 7.95 (ISBN 0-89529-019-7). Avery Pub.

Photo-Micrography 1899. Edmund Spitta. (Illus.). 163p. pap. 35.00 (ISBN 0-87556-580-8). Saifer.

Photo Notes & Film Front. Ed. by Ann Tucker. 440p. 1977. lib. bdg. 75.00. Visual Studies.

Photo Notes... FilmFront. Ed. by Anne Tucker & Nathan Lyons. (Visual Studies Reprint Ser.). 440p. 1977. Repr. of 1934 ed. lib. bdg. 75.00x (ISBN 0-89822-003-3). Visual Studies.

Photo-Offset. Irvin T. Lathrop & Robert J. Kunst. LC 78-69688. (Graphic Arts Ser.). pap. 56.00 (ISBN 0-317-19780-0, 2023204). Bks Demand UMI.

Photo-Offset Fundamentals. 4th ed. John E. Cogoli. (Illus.). (gr. 10-12). 1980. text ed. 23.95 (ISBN 0-02-672180-5); study guide 7.96 (ISBN 0-02-672190-2); filmstrips & ans. avail. 546.64 (ISBN 0-02-672070-1); ans. key 2.20 (ISBN 0-02-672200-3); 8.40 (ISBN 0-02-672170-8). Glencoe Bennett & McKnight.

Photo-Offset Lithography. Z. A. Prust. LC 77-21607. (Illus.). (YA) (gr. 9 up). text ed. 10.80 (ISBN 0-87006-240-9). Goodheart.

Photo Oil Painting. 1988. write for info. (ISBN 0-935333-01-0). VC Pub.

Photo One. 2nd ed. Kenneth Muse. (Illus.). 240p. 1987. pap. 21.00 (ISBN 0-13-665340-5). P-H.

Photo One: Basic Photo Text. Kenneth Muse. (Illus.). 240p. 1973. pap. text ed. 23.33 (ISBN 0-13-665331-6). P-H.

Photo-Optical Instrumentation Applications & Theory: 14th Annual Technical Symposium. Society of Photo-Optical Instrumentation Engineers. LC 73-19674. (SPIE Ser.: Vol. 2). (Illus.). pap. 137.50 (ISBN 0-317-41789-4, 2025647). Bks Demand UMI.

Photo Oxidation of Organo-Sulfur Compounds. W. Ando. (Sulfur Reports Ser.). 80p. 1981. flexicover 22.00 (ISBN 3-7186-0073-0). Harwood Academic.

Photo Poems. Edward Scott. 36p. (Orig.). 1985. pap. 5.95 (ISBN 0-937067-06-7). Inst Study Hum Aware.

Photo-Realist Statement: Recent Paintings by Robert Cottingham. Howard DaLee Spencer. LC 83-51541. (Illus.). 5p. 1983. pap. 3.00 (ISBN 0-939324-12-1). Wichita Art Mus.

Photo Retouching & Restoration. Kalton C. Lahue. LC 78-78395. (Photography How-to Ser.). (Illus.). 1979. pap. 4.50 (ISBN 0-8227-4034-6). Petersen Pub.

Photo School: A Step by Step Course in Photography. Michael Freeman. (Illus.). 224p. 1982. 27.50 (ISBN 0-8174-5402-0, Amphoto). Watson-Guptill.

Photo-Secession: Stieglitz & the Fine Art Movement in Photography. Robert Doty. LC 77-20467. (Illus.). 1978. pap. 8.95 (ISBN 0-486-23588-2). Dover.

Photo Source: A Working Photographer's Guide. Ed. by Will Rhyins & Dorothy McNeill. 300p. (Orig.). Date not set. pap. 12.95 (ISBN 0-945615-00-0). Prof Photo Source.

Photo Specialist. Jack Rudman. (Career Examination Ser.: C-1391). (Cloth bdg. avail. on request). pap. 10.00 (ISBN 0-8373-1391-0). Natl Learning.

Photo Technology. 3rd ed. Marshall LaCour & Irvin T. Lathrop. LC 77-73215. pap. 86.00 (ISBN 0-317-55666-5, 2029412). Bks Demand UMI.

Photo Technology Laboratory Manual. Irvin I. Lathrop & Marshall LeCour. pap. 28.00 (ISBN 0-317-10693-7, 2011577). Bks Demand UMI.

Photo Typesetter Comparison Charts: 1988 Edition. Harold Durbin. 1988. pap. 25.00. Durbin Assoc.

Photo Voltaics. Robert Seippel. 1983. text ed. 41.00 (ISBN 0-8359-5538-9, Reston). P-H.

Photoabsorption, Photoionization & Photoelectron Spectroscopy. Joseph Berkowitz. (Pure & Applied Physics Ser.). 1979. 70.50 (ISBN 0-12-091650-9). Acad Pr.

Photoacoustic & Photothermal Phenomena. Ed. by P. Hess & J. Pelzl. (Optical Science Ser.: Vol. 58). (Illus.). 560p. 1988. 65.00 (ISBN 0-387-18782-0). Springer-Verlag.

Photoacoustic & Thermal Wave Phenomena in Semiconductors. Ed. by A. Mandelis. 480p. 1987. 79.50 (ISBN 0-444-01226-5, North Holland). Elsevier.

Photoacoustic Effect: Principles & Applications. E. Luescher et al. LC 83-10233. 183p. 1984. 55.00 (ISBN 3-528-08573-8). IPS.

Photoacoustics & Photoacoustic Spectroscopy, Vol. 57. Allan Rosencraig. LC 80-17286. (Chemical Analysis: A Series of Monographs on Analytical Chemistry & Its Applications). 309p. 1980. 79.00 (ISBN 0-471-04495-4). Krieger.

Photoatlas of Inclusions in Gemstones. E. J. Gubelin & J. I. Koivula. 1986. 195.00 (ISBN 3-85504-095-8). Gemological.

Photobiology, Ionizing Radiation see Comprehensive Biochemistry, Section 5: Chemical Biology.

Photobiology 1984. Ed. by J. W. Longworth et al. LC 85-604. 1985. 40.95 (ISBN 0-275-90189-0, C0189). Praeger.

Photobooks: Ontario. Harrap Columbus Sales Staff. (Illus.). 1988. 65.00x (ISBN 0-7471-0135-3, Pub. by Harrap Ltd England). State Mutual Bk.

Photobooks: Rajasthan. Harrap Columbus Sales Staff. (Illus.). 1988. 65.00x (ISBN 0-7471-0136-1, Pub. by Harrap Ltd England). State Mutual Bk.

Photocabulary. Johnson. (Illus.). (gr. 3-9). pap. 2.79x (ISBN 0-87783-075-4). Oddo.

Photocatalysis. Serpone. 1988. price not set (ISBN 0-471-62603-1). Wiley.

Photocatalytic Production of Energy-Rich Compounds: Proceedings of Second EC Workshop, Seville, Spain, 22-25, Sept., 1987. Ed. by G. Grassi & D. O. Hall. 254p. 1988. 52.25 (ISBN 1-85166-216-2). Elsevier.

Photochemical & Photobiological Reviews, Vol. 4. Ed. by Kendric C. Smith. LC 75-43689. 344p. 1979. 75.00x (ISBN 0-306-40225-4, Plenum Pr). Plenum Pub.

Photochemical & Photobiological Reviews, Vol. 5. Ed. by Kendric C. Smith. LC 75-43689. (Illus.). 326p. 1980. 75.00x (ISBN 0-306-40360-9, Plenum Pr). Plenum Pub.

Photochemical & Photobiological Reviews, Vol. 6. Ed. by Kendric C. Smith. LC 75-43689. 214p. 1981. 55.00x (ISBN 0-306-40662-4, Plenum Pr). Plenum Pub.

Photochemical & Photobiological Reviews, Vol. 7. Ed. by Kendric C. Smith. LC 75-43689. 384p. 1983. 75.00x (ISBN 0-306-41289-6, Plenum Pr). Plenum Pub.

Photochemical Conversion & Stabilization of Polymers. V. Shlyapintokh. LC 83-62287. (Hanser Publications). (Illus.). 484p. 1985. 90.00 (ISBN 0-19-520738-6). Oxford U Pr.

Photochemical Conversion & Storage of Solar Energy. John S. Connolly. LC 81-12853. 1981. 72.50 (ISBN 0-12-185880-4). Acad Pr.

Photochemical Oxidants & Their Precursors in the Atmosphere: Effects, Formation, Transport & Abatement. (Document Ser.). 120p. 1979. 7.50x (ISBN 92-64-11838-1). OECD.

Photochemical, Photoelectrochemical & Photobiological Processes. Ed. by D. O. Hall & W. Palz. 1982. 32.50 (ISBN 90-277-1371-5, Pub. by Reidell Holland). Kluwer Academic.

Photochemical, Photoelectrochemical & Photobiological Processes. Ed. by D. O. Hall et al. 1983. lib. bdg. 46.00 (ISBN 90-277-1614-5, Pub. by Reidel Holland). Kluwer Academic.

Photochemical Smog: Contribution of Volatile Organic Compounds. 98p. 1982. pap. 9.50 (ISBN 92-64-12297-4). OECD.

Photochemical Synthesis. I. Ninomiya & T. Naito. (Best Synthetic Methods Ser.). 350p. 1988. price not set (ISBN 0-12-519490-0). Acad Pr.

Photochemistry, Vols. 1-10. D. Bryce-Smith. Incl. Vol. 1. 1968-69 Literature. 1970. 30.00 (ISBN 0-85186-005-2); Vol. 2. 1969-70 Literature. 1971. 47.00 (ISBN 0-85186-015-X); Vol. 3. 1970-71 Literature. 1972. 47.00 (ISBN 0-85186-025-7); Vol. 4. 1971-72 Literature. 1973. 50.00 (ISBN 0-85186-035-4); Vol. 5. 1972-73 Literature. 1974. 56.00 (ISBN 0-85186-045-1); Vol. 6. 1973-74 Literature. 1975. 70.00 (ISBN 0-85186-055-9); Vol. 7. 1974-75 Literature. 1976. 82.00 (ISBN 0-85186-065-6); Vol. 8. 1975-76 Literature. 1977. 95.00 (ISBN 0-85186-075-3); Vol. 9. 1976-77 Literature. 1978. 97.00 (ISBN 0-85186-085-0); Vol. 10. 1979. 102.00 (ISBN 0-85186-590-9). LC 73-17909. Am Chemical.

Photochemistry, Vol. 18. Ed. by D. Bryce-Smith. 592p. 1987. text ed. 190.00x (ISBN 0-85186-165-2, Pub. by Royal Soc Chem). Scholium Intl.

Photochemistry: A Review of the Literature Published Between July 1984 & June 1985, Vol. 17. Ed. & intro. by D. Bryce-Smith. (Specialist Periodical Reports). (Illus.). 688p. 1986. text ed. 173.00x (ISBN 0-85186-155-5). Scholium Intl.

Photochemistry: An Introduction. D. R. Arnold et al. 1974. 53.50 (ISBN 0-12-063350-7). Acad Pr.

Photochemistry & Luminescence of Proteins. yu. A. Vladimirov. 210p. 1969. text ed. 41.50x (ISBN 0-7065-0711-8). Coronet Bks.

Photochemistry & Organic Synthesis. (Topics in Current Chemistry Ser.: Vol. 129). (Illus.). 280p. 1985. 59.00 (ISBN 0-387-15141-9). Springer-Verlag.

Photochemistry & Photobiology, 2 vols. Ed. by Ahmed Zewail. LC 83-12618. 1504p. 1984. Set. text ed. 175.00 (ISBN 3-7186-0205-9). Harwood Academic.

Photochemistry & Photobiology, Vol. 1. Ed. by Ahmed Zewail. 784p. 1984. text ed. 115.00 (ISBN 3-7186-0173-7). Harwood Academic.

Photochemistry & Photobiology, Vol. 2. Ed. by Ahmed Zewail. 720p. 1984. text ed. 115.00 (ISBN 3-7186-0179-6). Harwood Academic.

Photochemistry & Photophysics of Coordination Compounds. H. Yerson & A. Vogler. (Illus.). xii, 344p. 1987. pap. 59.20 (ISBN 0-387-17808-2). Springer Verlag.

Photochemistry & Photophysics of Polymers. Ed. by N. S. Allen & W. Schnabel. 440p. 1984. 174.75 (ISBN 0-85334-269-5, I-256-84, Pub. by Elsevier Applied Sci England). Elsevier.

Photochemistry & Reaction Kinetics. Ed. by Philip G. Ashmore et al. LC 67-105417. pap. 98.50 (ISBN 0-317-26113-4, 2024403). Bks Demand UMI.

Photochemistry in Microheterongeous Systems. K. Kalyanasundaram. 1987. 49.95 (ISBN 0-12-394995-5). Acad Pr.

Photochemistry in Organic Synthesis. Ed. & intro. by J. D. Coyle. (Royal Society of Chemistry Special Publication: No. 57). (Illus.). 342p. 1986. pap. 71.00x flex-text (ISBN 0-85186-656-5, Pub. by Royal Soc Chem). Scholium Intl.

Photochemistry of Atmospheres: Earth, the Other Planets, & Comets. Ed. by Joel S. Levine. 1985. 87.50 (ISBN 0-12-444920-4). Acad Pr.

Photochemistry of Dyed & Pigmented Polymers. Ed. by N. S. Allen & J. F. McKellar. 296p. 1980. 77.50 (ISBN 0-85334-898-7, Pub. by Elsevier Applied Sci England). Elsevier.

Photochemistry of Environmental Aquatic Systems. Ed. by Rod G. Zika & William J. Cooper. LC 86-26489. (ACS Symposium Ser.: No. 327). (Illus.). vii, 280p. 1986. 54.95 (ISBN 0-8412-1008-X). Am Chemical.

Photochemistry of Man Made Polymers. J. F. McKellar & N. S. Allen. (Illus.). 306p. 1975. 72.00 (ISBN 0-85334-799-9, Pub. by Elsevier Applied Sci England). Elsevier.

Photochemistry of Molecular Reactions. M. Mousseron-Canet & J. C. Mani. 278p. 1972. text ed. 55.00x (ISBN 0-7065-1120-4, Pub. by Keter Pub Jerusalem). Coronet Bks.

Photochemistry of Small Molecules. Hideo Okabe. LC 78-6704. (Illus.). 445p. pap. 115.70 (2056455). Bks Demand UMI.

Photochemistry of the Atmosphere of Mars & Venus. V. A. Krasnopolsky. (Physics & Chemistry in Space Ser.: Vol. 13). (Illus.). 380p. 1986. 90.00 (ISBN 0-387-15336-5). Springer-Verlag.

Photochemistry of Vision see Handbook of Sensory Physiology.

Photochemistry Seven: IUPAC Symposium on Photochemistry, Leuven, Belgium, 24-28 July, 1978, Seventh IUPAC Symposium. Ed. by A. Reiser. (IUPAC Symposia Ser.). 1979. 55.00 (ISBN 0-08-022358-3). Pergamon.

Photocommunication: A Guide to Creative Photography. rev. ed. David H. Curl. LC 76-19049. (Illus.). 320p. (Orig.). 1984. pap. 16.95 (ISBN 0-88196-000-4). Oak Woods Media.

Photoconductivity & Related Phenomena. Ed. by J. Mort & C. M. Pai. LC 76-16160. 502p. 1976. 116.00 (ISBN 0-444-41463-0). Elsevier.

Photoconductivity in Polymers. A. V. Patsis & D. A. Seanor. LC 74-80461. (Illus.). 349p. (Orig.). 1976. 19.95 (ISBN 0-87762-136-5). Technomic.

Photocopy Machine Operator. Jack Rudman. (Career Examination Ser.: C-2971). 1988. pap. 10.00 (ISBN 0-8373-2971-X). Natl Learning.

Photocrafts Book of Guides, Vol. 1. Mark Baczynsky. (Illus.). 100p. 1978. pap. 19.95 (ISBN 0-89816-001-4). Embee Pr.

Photocrafts Book of Guides, Vol. 2. Mark Baczynsky. LC 78-70581. (Illus.). 104p. 1980. pap. 19.95 (ISBN 0-89816-002-2). Embee Pr.

Photodegradation & Photostabilization of Coatings. Ed. by S. Peter Pappas & F. H. Winslow. LC 81-467. (ACS Symposium Ser: No. 151). 1981. 39.95 (ISBN 0-8412-0611-2). Am Chemical.

Photodegradation, Photo-Oxidation, & Photostabilization of Polymers: Principles & Applications. Bengt G. Ranby & J. F. Rabek. LC 74-2498. pap. 111.20 (ISBN 0-317-09017-8, 2016183). Bks Demand UMI.

Photodetectors. P. N. Dennis. (Updates in Applied Physics & Electrical Technology Ser.). 192p. 1986. 35.00x (ISBN 0-306-42217-4, Plenum Pr). Plenum Pub.

Photodocumentation for Conservation: Procedural Guidelines & Photographic Concepts & Techniques. Dan. Kushel. 1980. 9.00 (ISBN 0-318-18697-7). Am Inst Conser Hist.

Photodrama. Henry A. Phillips. LC 70-124032. (Literature of Cinema, Ser. 1). Repr. of 1914 ed. 11.00 (ISBN 0-405-01632-8). Ayer Co Pubs.

Photodrama: Its Place Among the Fine Arts. W. H. Hannon. 59.95 (ISBN 0-8490-0830-1). Gordon Pr.

Photodynamic Therapy, No. 271. C. J. Gomer. (Photochemistry & Photobiology Ser.: Vol. 46). 391p. 1989. price not set (ISBN 0-08-036081-5). Pergamon.

Photoeffects at Semiconductor-Electrolyte Interfaces. Ed. by Arthur J. Nozik. LC 80-27773. (Symposium Ser.: No. 146). 1981. 44.95 (ISBN 0-8412-0604-X). Am Chemical.

Photoelastic & Electro-Optic Properties of Crystals. T. S. Narasimhamurty. LC 79-409. (Illus.). 544p. 1981. 69.50x (ISBN 0-306-31101-1, Plenum Pr). Plenum Pub.

Photoelastic Coatings. Felix Zandman et al. LC 76-46984. (Society for Experimental Stress Analysis. Monograph: No. 3). pap. 47.30 (2026697). Bks Demand UMI.

Photoelastic Effect & Its Applications: Proceedings. Symposium of International Union of Theoretical & Applied Mechanics, Brussels, Belgium, 1973. Ed. by J. Kestens. (Illus.). 650p. 1975. 66.10 (ISBN 0-387-07278-0). Springer-Verlag.

Photoelasticity, Vol. 2. Max M. Frocht. LC 41-15564. (Illus.). pap. 130.80 (ISBN 0-317-08372-4, 2017833). Bks Demand UMI.

Photoelasticity in Engineering Practice. Ed. by S. A. Paipetis & G. S. Holister. LC 85-6914. 244p. 1985. 59.50 (ISBN 0-85334-363-2, Pub. by Elsevier Applied Sci England). Elsevier.

Photoelasticity in Theory & Practice: Proceedings of CISM, Department for Mechanics of Defable Bodies, 1970. CISM (International Center for Mechanical Sciences), Department for Mechanics of Deformable Bodies Staff. Ed. by V. Brcic. (CISM International Center for Mechanical Sciences Ser.: No. 59). (Illus.). 242p. 1975. pap. 23.30 (ISBN 0-387-81081-1). Springer-Verlag.

Photoelasticity '86. Ed. by M. Nisida. 250p. 1986. 51.60 (ISBN 0-387-70012-9). Springer-Verlag.

Photoelectric Photometry Handbook. Ed. by Karen A. Genet et al. 250p. (Orig.). 1987. pap. 23.95 (ISBN 0-911351-09-4). Fairborn AZ.

Photoelectric Sensors & Controls Selection & Applications. Juds. (Mechanical Engineering Ser.). 1988. 99.75 (ISBN 0-8247-7886-3). Dekker.

Photoelectrochemical Solar Cells. Suresh Chandra. (Electrocomponent Science Monographs: Vol. 5). 245p. 1985. text ed. 59.00 (ISBN 2-88124-014-3). Gordon & Breach.

PhotoElectrochemical Solar Cells. K. S. Santhanam. (Studies in Physical & Theoretical Chemistry: Vol. 50). 1987. 144.75 (ISBN 0-444-42910-7). Elsevier.

Photoelectrochemistry, Photocatalysis & Photoreactors Fundamentals & Developments. Mario Schiavello. 1985. lib. bdg. 84.00 (ISBN 90-277-1946-2, Pub. by Reidel Holland). Kluwer Academic.

Photoelectron & Auger Spectroscopy. Thomas A. Carlson. LC 72-28025. (Modern Analytical Chemistry Ser.). (Illus.). 418p. 1975. 69.50x (ISBN 0-306-33901-3, Plenum Pr). Plenum Pub.

Photoelectron Spectra. G. Wendin. (Structure & Bonding Ser.: Vol. 45). (Illus.). 150p. 1981. 40.00 (ISBN 0-387-10584-0). Springer-Verlag.

Photoelectron Spectra of Nonmetallic Solids & Consequences for Quantum Chemistry see Photoelectron Spectrometry.

Photoelectron Spectrometry. Incl. Photoelectron Spectra of Nonmetallic Solids & Consequences for Quantum Chemistry. C. K. Jrgensen; Fractional Prentage Methods for Ionisation of Open Shells of D & F Electrons. P. A. Cox; X-Ray Photoelectron Spectroscopy: Application to Metals & Alloys. R. E. Watson & M. L. Perlman; Ultraviolet Photoelectron Spectroscopy of Gases Absorbed on Metal Surfaces. A. M. Bradshaw et al. (Structure & Bonding: Vol. 24). (Illus.). iv, 170p. 1975. 40.00 (ISBN 0-387-07364-7). Springer-Verlag.

Photoelectron Spectroscopy. 2nd ed. J. H. Eland. (Illus.). 272p. 1983. text ed. 49.95 (ISBN 0-408-71057-8). Butterworth.

Photographic Techniques for Accident Investigation. 1984. 10.00 (ISBN 0-939874-60-1). ASSE.
Photographic Techniques in Scientific Research, Vol. 2. Ed. by A. A. Newman. 1976. 99.00 (ISBN 0-12-517960-X). Acad Pr.
Photographic Techniques in Scientific Research, Vol. 3. Ed. by A. A. Newman. 1979. 115.00 (ISBN 0-12-517963-4). Acad Pr.
Photographic Theory for the Motion Picture Cameraman. Compiled by Russell Campbell. LC 70-130298. (Illus.). 160p. 1981. pap. 7.95 (ISBN 0-498-07776-4). A S Barnes.
Photographic Tone Control. Norman Sanders. LC 77-83265. 1977. pap. 12.95 (ISBN 0-87100-117-9). Morgan.
Photographic Viewpoints: Selections from the Collection of the Museum of Fine Arts, Boston. Clifford S. Ackley. (MFA Bulletin Ser.: Vol. 80). (Illus.). 72p. (Orig.). 1984. pap. 6.95 (ISBN 0-87846-245-7). Mus Fine Arts Boston.
Photographic Views of Sherman's Campaign. George N. Barnard. LC 76-45964. (Illus.). 1977. pap. 6.00 (ISBN 0-486-23445-2). Dover.
Photographic Views of Sherman's Campaign. George N. Barnard. 15.25 (ISBN 0-8446-5553-8). Peter Smith.
Photographic Whitewash: Suppressed Kennedy Assassination Pictures. Harold Weisberg. 1967. 8.00 (ISBN 0-911606-03-3). Weisberg.
Photographie, 2 vols. in 1. A. Davanne. Ed. by Peter C. Bunnell & Robert A. Sobieszek. LC 76-23052. (Sources of Modern Photography Ser.). (Illus., Fr.). 1979. lib. bdg. 37.00x (ISBN 0-405-09615-1). Ayer Co Pubs.
Photographie. L. D. Evrard-Blanquart. Ed. by Peter C. Bunnell & Robert A. Sobieszk. LC 76-23042. (Sources of Modern Photography Ser.). 1979. Repr. of 1870 ed. lib. bdg. 14.00x (ISBN 0-405-09604-6). Ayer Co Pubs.
Photographie als Medium der Architekturinterpretation. Rolf Sachsse. 469p. (Ger.). 1984. lib. bdg. 62.00 (ISBN 3-598-10564-9). K G Saur.
Photographie au Salon de 1859 et "La Photographie" et Le Stereoscope", 2 vols. in 1. Louis Figuier. Ed. by Peter C. Bunnell & Robert A. Sobieszek. LC 76-24661. (Sources of Modern Photography Ser.). (Illus., Fr.). 1979. Repr. of 1868 ed. lib. bdg. 28.50x (ISBN 0-405-09639-9). Ayer Co Pubs.
Photographie Consideree Comme Art et Comme Industrie. Pierson & Mayer. Ed. by Peter C. Bunnell & Robert A. Sobieszk. LC 76-24666. (Sources of Modern Photography Ser.). (Fr.). 1979. Repr. of 1862 ed. lib. bdg. 21.00x (ISBN 0-405-09643-7). Ayer Co Pubs.
Photographie Farbiger Gegenstande in Den Richtigen Tonverhaltnissen. Hermann Vogel. Ed. by Peter C. Bunnell & Robert A. Sobieszek. LC 78-19590. (Sources of Modern Photography Ser.). (Illus., Ger.). 1979. Repr. lib. bdg. 17.00x (ISBN 0-405-09663-1). Ayer Co Pubs.
Photographie Instantanee. Josef M. Eder. Ed. by Peter C. Bunnell & Robert A. Sobieszek. LC 76-23056. (Sources of Modern Photography Ser.). (Illus., Fr.). 1979. Repr. of 1888 ed. lib. bdg. 19.00x (ISBN 0-405-09619-4). Ayer Co Pubs.
Photographierte Augenhintergrund. H. Huismans. (Illus.). x, 216p. 1986. 217.50 (ISBN 3-8055-3985-1). S Karger.
Photographing Assignments on Location. Adrian Taylor. (Illus.). 144p. 1987. 27.50 (ISBN 0-8174-5425-X, Amphoto); pap. 18.95 (ISBN 0-8174-5426-8, Amphoto). Watson-Guptill.
Photographing Buildings & Cityscapes. LC 82-62982. (Kodak Library of Creative Photography). 1984. lib. bdg. 17.27 (ISBN 0-86706-228-2, Pub. by Time-Life). Silver.
Photographing Buildings Inside & Out. Norman McGrath. (Illus.). 176p. 1987. 32.50 (ISBN 0-8230-7413-7, Whitney Lib); pap. 22.50 (ISBN 0-8230-7410-2, Whitney Lib). Watson-Guptill.
Photographing for Publication: A Guide for Photographers, Editors, & Graphic Arts Professionals. Norman Sanders. 112p. 1983. pap. 44.95 (ISBN 0-8352-1734-5). Bowker.
Photographing Friends & Family. LC 82-62975. (Kodak Library of Creative Photography). (gr. 7 up). 1984. lib. bdg. 17.27 (ISBN 0-86706-207-X). Silver.
Photographing Horses & Other Livestock: The Complete Guide. Darol Dickinson. LC 79-88468. (Illus.). 104p. 1980. pap. 9.95 (ISBN 0-87358-200-4). Northland.
Photographing Indoors with Your Automatic Camera. Barbara London & Richard Boyer. (Your Automatic Camera Ser.). (Illus.). 144p. (Orig.). 1981. pap. 6.95 (ISBN 0-930764-18-8). Curtin & London.
Photographing Infants & Children. Eric Erickson. (Illus.). 96p. (Orig.). 1985. pap. text ed. 24.95 (ISBN 0-937649-02-3). Am Passage Mktg.
Photographing Infants & Children. Eric Ericson. (Seattle FilmWorks Photo Home Study Continuity Ser.). (Illus.). 96p. (Orig.). 1986. pap. 13.90 (ISBN 0-937649-09-0). Am Passage Mktg.
Photographing Medicine: Images & Power in Britain & America Since Eighteen Forty. Daniel M. Fox & Christopher J. Lawrence. LC 87-25088. (Contributions in Medical Studies: No. 21). (Illus.). 360p. 1988. lib. bdg. 49.95 (ISBN 0-313-23719-0, FMC/). Greenwood.
Photographing Nature. G. J. Moon. LC 70-118605. (Illus.). (YA) (gr. 9 up). 1970. 10.00 (ISBN 0-8048-0921-6). C E Tuttle.
Photographing Nature. Arlyn Powell. (Illus.). 144p. (Orig.). pap. cancelled (ISBN 0-240-51720-2). Focal Pr.
Photographing Nature. Art Wolfe. (Seattle FilmWorks Photo Home Study Continuity Ser.). (Illus.). 96p. (Orig.). 1986. pap. 13.90 (ISBN 0-937649-12-0); pap. text ed. 24.95 (ISBN 0-937649-05-8). Am Passage Mktg.
Photographing Nature. Art Wolfe. (Home Study School Continuity Ser.). (Illus.). 96p. (Orig.). 1987. pap. 13.90 (ISBN 0-937649-19-8). Am Passage Mktg.
Photographing Oregon with Professional Results. LC 84-80434. (Illus.). 96p. (Orig., Photos & Text by Bryan F. Peterson). 1984. pap. 9.95 (ISBN 0-912856-90-4). Gr Arts Ctr Pub.
Photographing Outdoors with Your Automatic Camera. Barbara London & Richard Boyer. (Your Automatic Camera Ser.). (Illus.). 144p. (Orig.). 1981. pap. 6.95 (ISBN 0-930764-19-6). Curtin & London.
Photographing People. Cliff Hollenbeck. (Illus.). 96p. (Orig.). 1985. pap. text ed. 24.95 (ISBN 0-937649-03-1). Am Passage Mktg.
Photographing People. Cliff Hollenbeck. (Seattle FilmWorks Photo Home Study Continuity Ser.). (Illus.). 96p. (Orig.). 1986. pap. 13.90 (ISBN 0-937649-10-4). Am Passage Mktg.
Photographing People. Cliff Hollenbeck. (Home Study Photography School Continuity Ser.). (Illus.). 96p. (Orig.). 1987. pap. 13.90 (ISBN 0-937649-17-1). Am Passage Mktg.
Photographing People for Advertising. Nancy Brown. (Illus.). 144p. 1986. 27.50 (ISBN 0-8174-5438-1, Amphoto); pap. 18.95 (ISBN 0-8174-5439-X, Amphoto). Watson-Guptill.
Photographing the Drama of Daily Life. LC 82-62981. (Kodak Library of Creative Photography). 1984. lib. bdg. 17.27 (ISBN 0-86706-225-8, Pub. by Time-Life). Silver.
Photographing the Invisible. James Coates. LC 72-9189. (Literature of Photography Ser.). Repr. of 1911 ed. 31.00 (ISBN 0-405-04899-8). Ayer Co Pubs.
Photographing the North American West: How & Where to Capture Nature on Film. Erwin & Peggy Bauer. LC 87-6931. (Illus.). 146p. 1987. casebound 24.95 (ISBN 0-931397-16-2); pap. 14.95 (ISBN 0-931397-15-4). Globe Pequot.
Photographing Urban Landscapes. David Chamberlain. (Illus.). 160p. 1988. 29.95 (ISBN 0-7137-1849-8, Pub. by Blandford Pr England). Sterling.
Photographing Wild Texas. Erwin Bauer & Peggy Bauer. (Illus.). 112p. 1985. 24.95 (ISBN 0-292-76495-2); pap. 14.95 (ISBN 0-292-76497-9). U of Tex Pr.
Photographing Wildflowers. Craig Blacklock & Nadine Blacklock. (Illus.). 64p. 1987. pap. 9.95 (ISBN 0-89658-069-5). Voyageur Pr Inc.
Photographing Wildlife. Patricia Caulfield. (Illus.). 144p. 1988. 27.50 (ISBN 0-8174-5442-X, Amphoto); pap. 18.95 (ISBN 0-8174-5443-8, Amphoto). Watson-Guptill.
Photographing with Automatic Cameras. Hubert C. Birnbaum. LC 81-67431. (Kodak Workshop Ser.). (Illus.). 96p. 1987. pap. 9.95 (KW-11). Eastman Kodak.
Photographing Your Artwork. Russell Hart. (Illus.). 128p. (Orig.). 1987. pap. 15.95 (ISBN 0-89134-187-0). North Light Bks.
Photographing Your Baby: Tips for Taking Better Pictures. Eastman Kodak Editors. LC 84-16788. 1984. write for info. (ISBN 0-201-11698-7). Addison-Wesley.
Photographing Your Church's History. John Hack. Ed. by Charles W. Deweese. (Resource Kit for Your Church's History ser.). 7p. 1984. pap. 0.50 (ISBN 0-939804-18-2). Hist Comm S Baptist.
Photographing Your Craftwork: A Hands-On Guide for Craftspeople. Steve Meltzer. LC 86-2970. (Crafts Business Bks.). (Illus.). 144p. (Orig.). 1986. pap. 9.95 (ISBN 0-88089-012-6). Madrona Pubs.
Photographing Your Heritage. Wilma S. Shull. LC 88-70335. (Illus.). 120p. (Orig.). 1988. pap. 7.95 (ISBN 0-916489-31-0, 231). Ancestry.
Photographs Eighty-Six: The International Annual of Advertising & Editorial Photography. Ed. by Walter Herdeg. (Illus.). 228p. 1986. 59.50 (ISBN 0-8230-4004-6). Watson-Guptill.
Photographische Industrie Deutschland. Willy Kuhn. Ed. by Peter C. Bunnell & Robert A. Sobieszek. LC 78-67657. (Sources of Modern Photography Ser.). (Ger.). 1979. Repr. of 1929 ed. lib. bdg. 17.00x (ISBN 0-405-09899-5). Ayer Co Pubs.
Photographs. Annie Leibovitz. LC 83-2385. (Illus.). 144p. 1983. 34.50 (ISBN 0-394-53208-2); pap. 15.95 (ISBN 0-394-72597-2). Pantheon.
Photographs. Linda McCartney. 1982. 29.95 (ISBN 0-671-45985-6); pap. 12.95 (ISBN 0-671-45986-4). S&S.
Photographs. Elliott McDowell. LC 81-86604. (Illus.). 88p. 1981. 40.00 (ISBN 0-87923-422-9). Godine.
Photographs. Prince Andrew. (Illus.). 160p. 1986. 29.95 (ISBN 0-241-11644-9, Pub. by Hamish Hamilton England). David & Charles.
Photographs. Joyce Tenneson. LC 83-81725. 80p. 1984. pap. 20.00 (ISBN 0-87923-502-0). Godine.
Photographs & Other Stories. Geraldine C. Maayo. 99p. 1981. pap. 3.50x (ISBN 0-686-32577-X, Pub. by New Day Phillipines). Cellar.
Photographs & Words. Wright Morris. Ed. by James Alinder. LC 82-82471. (Illus.). 120p. 1982. 32.50 (ISBN 0-933286-28-7). Friends Photography.
Photographs By Bill Brandt. Intro. by Mark Haworth Booth. (Illus.). 16p. 1980. pap. 4.25 (ISBN 0-88397-035-X). Intl Exhibitions.
Photographs by David Hockney. Ed. by B. J. Bradley. (Illus.). 48p. (Orig.). 1986. pap. 11.00 (ISBN 0-88397-087-2). Intl Exhibitions.
Photographs by Man Ray: Nineteen Twenty to Nineteen Thirty-Four. Man Ray. LC 79-50461. (Illus.). 1980. pap. 8.95 (ISBN 0-486-23842-3). Dover.
Photographs by the Wright Brothers: Prints from the Glass Negatives in the Library of Congress. LC 78-606137. (Illus.). vi, 21p. 1978. pap. 5.00 (ISBN 0-317-60010-9). Lib Congress.
Photographs from Detroit Collections. Commentary by Ellen Sharp. (Illus.). 38p. 1983. pap. 5.00 (ISBN 0-89558-099-3). Detroit Inst Arts.
Photographs from One Year. Nicholas Nixon. Ed. by James Alinder. LC 82-84610. (Untitled Ser.: No. 31). (Illus.). 52p. (Orig.). 1983. pap. 16.00 (ISBN 0-933286-33-3). Friends Photography.
Photographs: Negatives; History As Apple Tree. Michael S. Harper. 32p. 1972. 10.00x (ISBN 0-912962-00-3). Scarab Pr.
Photographs, Nineteen Seventy-Three to Nineteen Eighty. Christopher Rauschenberg. LC 82-81916. (Illus.). 139p. (Orig.). 1982. pap. 10.00 (ISBN 0-943446-00-7). Pair O Dice.
Photographs Nineteen Seventy-Three to Nineteen Eighty-Three. John Mckee & Philip M. Isaacson. (Illus.). 1984. pap. 7.50 (ISBN 0-916606-06-6). Bowdoin Coll.
Photographs of Alvan S. Harper: Tallahassee, 1885-1910. Ed. by Joan P. Morris & Lee H. Warner. LC 82-24765. 152p. 1983. 30.00 (ISBN 0-8130-0737-2). U Presses Fla.
Photographs of American Civil War Cavalry. Harris Andrews et al. (Illus.). 100p. (Orig.). 1988. pap. 9.95. Guidon Pr.
Photographs of Chachaji: The Making of a Documentary Film. Ved Mehta. (Illus.). 1980. 22.50x (ISBN 0-19-502792-2). Oxford U Pr.
Photographs of Harriet V. S. Thorne. Rosalie McKenna & James Burke. (Illus.). 1979. pap. 3.50x (ISBN 0-89467-008-5). Yale Art Gallery.
Photographs of Lyle Bonge. Lyle Bonge. 32.50 (ISBN 0-912330-53-8). Jargon Soc.
Photographs of Moholy-Nagy from the William Larson Collection. 2nd ed. Ed. by Leland D. Rice & David W. Steadman. LC 75-4035. (Illus.). 64p. 1977. 8.50 (ISBN 0-915478-08-0). Galleries Coll.
Photographs of Mother St. Croix. Tina Freeman. LC 82-61400. (Illus.). 39p. 1982. pap. 8.95 (ISBN 0-89494-015-5). New Orleans Mus Art.
Photographs of Old Bolton. Hendon Publishing Co., Ltd. Staff. 1986. 16.10x (ISBN 0-317-54156-0, Pub. by Hendon Pub UK). State Mutual Bk.
Photographs of Palace Buildings of Peking. Compiled by Imperial Museum Staff. (Illus.). 1906. 17150.00 (Pub. by Han-Shan Tang Ltd). State Mutual Bk.
Photographs of the Old Closes & Streets of Glasgow, 1868-1877. Thomas Annan. (Eighteen Sixty-Eight to Eighteen Seventy-Seven). (Illus.). 96p. 1977. pap. 6.50 (ISBN 0-486-23442-8). Dover.
Photographs of the Southwest. Ansel Adams. LC 76-10034. (Illus.). 1984. 45.00 (ISBN 0-8212-0699-0, 706914); pap. 25.00i (ISBN 0-8212-1574-4, 702617). NYGS.
Photographs: Robert Capa. Ed. by Cornell Capa & Richard Whelan. LC 85-40213. (Illus.). 252p. 1985. 35.00 (ISBN 0-394-54421-8). Knopf.
Photographs Underwater. Bob Kendall. LC 76-15705. (Illus.). 104p. 1976. 24.50 (ISBN 0-914704-02-8). ICER Pr.
Photographs 87. Ed. by B. Martin Pederson. (Illus.). 228p. 1987. 59.50 (ISBN 0-317-56325-4). Watson-Guptill.
Photography. Sr. Robert V. Bullough. Ed. by James E. Duane. LC 80-21333. (Instructional Media Library: Vol. 11). (Illus.). 104p. 1981. 23.95 (ISBN 0-87778-171-0). Educ Tech Pubns.
Photography. 5th ed. Philip Davis. 400p. 1986. pap. text ed. write for info. plastic comb. (ISBN 0-697-00300-0); instr's. manual avail. (ISBN 0-697-00301-9). Wm C Brown.
Photography. Duncan Fraser. LC 86-70972. (Topics Ser.). (Illus.). 32p. (gr. k-6). 1987. lib. bdg. 11.90 (ISBN 0-531-18114-6, Pub. by Bookwright Pr). Watts.
Photography. Tony Freeman. LC 83-7359. (New True Bks.). (Illus.). 48p. (gr. k-4). 1983. PLB 12.60 (ISBN 0-516-01704-7). Childrens.
Photography. (Illus.). 64p. (gr. 6-12). 1983. pap. 1.25x (ISBN 0-8395-3334-9, 3334). BSA.
Photography. 3rd ed. Barbara L. Upton & John Upton. 1985. pap. text ed. write for info. (ISBN 0-673-39618-5). Scott F.
Photography. 4th ed. Barbara L. Upton & John Upton. 1988. pap. text ed. price not set (ISBN 0-673-39842-0). Scott F.
Photography - A Facet of Modernism: Photographs from the San Francisco Museum of Modern Art. Van Deren Coke & Diana C. Du Pont. LC 86-15261. (Illus.). 196p. 1987. 45.00 (ISBN 0-933920-73-3, Dist. by Rizzoli); pap. 25.00 (ISBN 0-933920-74-1, Dist. by Rizzoli). Hudson Hills.
Photography: A Concise History. Ian Jeffrey. (World of Art Ser.). (Illus.). 248p. 1985. 19.95f (ISBN 0-500-18187-X); pap. 11.95 (ISBN 0-500-20187-0). Thames Hudson.
Photography: A Manual for Shutterbugs. Eugene Kohn. (Illus.). (gr. 3-7). 1965. pap. 1.25. P-H.
Photography A-V Program Directory. A. D. Coleman et al. LC 80-83469. (Illus.). 224p. 1980. 28.00x (ISBN 0-936524-00-6). PMI Inc.
Photography Album, No. 1. Ed. by Pierre De Fenoyl. LC 79-20063. (Illus.). 232p. (Fr. & Eng.). 50.00 (ISBN 0-9601068-3-9). Agrinde Pubns.
Photography & Architecture: Eighteen Thirty-Nine to Nineteen Thirty-Nine. Richard Pare. (Illus.). 282p. 1985. Repr. of 1982 ed. 60.00 (ISBN 0-262-16101-X). MIT Pr.
Photography & Art: Interactions since 1946. Andy Grundberg & Kathleen Gauss. LC 86-32104. (Illus.). 272p. 1987. 45.00 (ISBN 0-89659-683-4). Abbeville Pr.
Photography & Language. Ed. & intro. by Lew Thomas. LC 76-43622. (Illus.). pap. 15.95 (ISBN 0-917986-01-6). NFS Pr.
Photography & Layout for Reproduction. (Illus.). 1978. pap. 5.50 (ISBN 0-87985-218-6, Q-74). Eastman Kodak.
Photography & Philosophy of Wynn Bullock. Clyde H. Dilley. LC 81-65881. (Illus.). 129p. 1984. 30.00 (ISBN 0-87982-042-X). Art Alliance.
Photography & Photographers to Nineteen Hundred: An Annotated Bibliography. Robert S. Sennett. 200p. lib. bdg. 30.00 (ISBN 0-8240-8728-3). Garland Pub.
Photography & Society. Gisele Freund. 256p. 1981. 35.00x (ISBN 0-86092-049-6, Pub. by Fraser Bks). State Mutual Bk.
Photography & the Art of Seeing. Freeman Patterson. (Illus.). 156p. 1987. pap. 16.95 (ISBN 0-919493-81-5, Pub. by Key Porter Canada). U of Toronto Pr.
Photography & the Book. Beaumont Newhall. 1983. pap. 10.00 (ISBN 0-89073-066-0). Boston Public Lib.
Photography & the Law. Christopher DuVernet. 160p. 1986. pap. 7.95 (ISBN 0-88908-615-X, 9539, Pub. by Intl Self-Counsel Pr). TAB Bks.
Photography & the Old West. Karen Current. (Illus.). 272p. 1986. 16.98 (ISBN 0-8109-8074-6). Abrams.
Photography: Art & Technique. Alfred A. Blaker. LC 79-23536. (Illus.). 460p. 1980. text ed. 34.95 (ISBN 0-7167-1115-X); reference manual incl. W H Freeman.
Photography: Art & Technique. Alfred A. Blaker. (Illus.). 460p. (Orig.). 1980. 32.95x (ISBN 0-240-51748-2); pap. 22.95x (ISBN 0-240-51741-5). Focal Pr.
Photography: Art & Technique. 2nd ed. Alfred A. Blaker. (Illus.). 480p. 1988. pap. 26.00X (ISBN 0-317-54394-6). Focal Pr.
Photography As a Fine Art. facsimile ed. Charles H. Caffin. LC 73-167715. 192p. 1981. pap. 15.95 (ISBN 0-87100-019-9, 2019). Morgan.
Photography As Fine Art. Intro. by Douglas Davies. (Library of World Photography). (Illus.). 224p. 1987. pap. 16.95 (ISBN 0-940595-01-X). Hill & Co Pubs.
Photography Basics: An Introduction for Young People. Vic Owens-Knudsen. LC 83-9775. (Illus.). 48p. (gr. 5-9). 1983. PLB 9.95 (ISBN 0-13-664995-5). P-H.
Photography Best Sellers. James Ong. (Illus.). 128p. 1987. 29.95 (Pub. by Moore & Moore). R Silver.
Photography Best Sellers: One Hundred Top Moneymaking Stock Photos. James Ong. LC 87-16193. (Illus.). 128p. 1987. 29.95 (ISBN 0-942485-01-7). Moore & Moore Pub.
Photography Between Covers. Thomas Dugan. Date not set. 7.50. Visual Studies.
Photography: Beyond Simple Truth: An Advanced Workbook for Teachers & Students. Philip Krejcarek. 1984. pap. 25.00 (slide edition) (ISBN 0-318-03706-8); pap. 6.00. P Krejcarek.
Photography Books Index: A Subject Guide to Photo Anthologies. Martha Moss. LC 79-26938. 298p. 1980. lib. bdg. 21.00 (ISBN 0-8108-1283-5). Scarecrow.
Photography Books Index: A Subject Guide to Photo Anthologies, Vol. II. Martha Moss. LC 84-23652. 276p. 1985. 19.50 (ISBN 0-8108-1773-X). Scarecrow.
Photography: Essays & Images; Illustrated Readings in the History of Photography. Ed. by Beaumont Newhall. (Illus.). 328p. 1980. 32.50 (ISBN 0-87070-387-0, 706949, Pub. by Museum Mod Art); pap. 16.95 (ISBN 0-87070-385-4, 706957, Pub. by Museum Mod Art). NYGS.
Photography: Experiments & Projects. Dwight R. Dixon & Paul B. Dixon. (Illus.). 1976. pap. text ed. write for info. (ISBN 0-02-329840-5). Macmillan.

Photophonics I. Piersel. (Illus.). (gr. 1-5). 1968. pap. 1.99x (ISBN 0-87783-073-8); tchr's guide 0.29x. Oddo.

Photophonics II. Piersel. (Illus.). (gr. 1-5). 1968. pap. 2.39x (ISBN 0-87783-074-6); tchr's guide 0.29x. Oddo.

Photophysical & Photochemical Tools in Polymer Science. Ed. by Mitchell A. Winnik. 1986. lib. bdg. 124.00 (ISBN 90-277-2307-9, Pub. by Reidel Holland). Kluwer Academic.

PhotoPhysical Processes Membrane Energization, Vol. 1. Ed. by George Akoyunoglou. 792p. cancelled 75.00 (Pub. by Balaban Intl Sci Serv). IPS.

Photophysics & Photochemistry above 6 EV: Proceedings of the International Meeting of the Societe de Chimie Physique, 38th, Bombannes, 21-27 September, 1984. Ed. by F. Lahmani. (Studies in Physical & Theoretical Chemistry: Vol. 35). 672p. 1985. 197.50 (ISBN 0-444-42463-6). Elsevier.

Photophysics of Polymers. Ed. by Charles E. Hoyle & John M. Torkelson. LC 87-27303. (Symposium Ser.: No. 358). (Illus.). xi, 531p. 1987. 99.95 (ISBN 0-8412-1439-5). Am Chemical.

Photopion Nuclear Physics. Ed. by P. Stoler. LC 78-31569. 448p. 1979. 75.00x (ISBN 0-306-40148-7, Plenum Pr). Plenum Pub.

Photoplay: A Psychological Study. Hugo Munsterberg. LC 79-124021. (Literature of Cinema, Ser. 1). Repr. of 1916 ed. 11.50 (ISBN 0-405-01628-X). Ayer Co Pubs.

Photoplay Plot Encyclopedia. F. Palmer. 1976. lib. bdg. 59.95 (ISBN 0-8490-2437-4). Gordon Pr.

Photopolymerization of Surface Coatings. C. G. Roffey. LC 81-12916. 353p. 1982. 79.95 (ISBN 0-471-10063-3, Pub. by Wiley-Interscience). Wiley.

Photopolymers, Principles, Processes & Materials: Technical Papers: Regional Technical Conference, November 8-10 1982. Society of Plastics Engineers. (Illus.). pap. 107.30 (ISBN 0-317-09315-0, 2021695). Bks Demand UMI.

Photopolymers: Principles, Processes & Materials: Technical Papers, Regional Technical Conference, Nevele Country Club, Ellenville, New York, October 28-30, 1985. Society of Plastics Engineers. pap. 97.30 (2027693). Bks Demand UMI.

Photoproduction & Scattering of Pi-Mesons. N. F. Nelipa. (Russian Tracts on the Physical Sciences Ser). (Illus.). 108p. 1961. 48.00 (ISBN 0-677-20430-2). Gordon & Breach.

Photoproduction of Elementary Particles see Landolt-Boernstein Numerical Data & Functional Relationships in Science & Technology, New Series, Group 1: Nuclear Particle & Physics.

Photopublication Manual. Steven T. Puglia. 1988. pap. price not set (ISBN 0-910050-95-3). AASLH Pr.

Photorealism. Louis K. Meisel. (Illus.). 528p. 1980. 125.00 (ISBN 0-8109-1464-6). Abrams.

Photoreception & Vision in Invertebrates. Ed. by M. A. Ali. (NATO ASI Series A, Life Sciences: Vol. 74). 868p. 1984. 115.00x (ISBN 0-306-41626-3, Plenum Pr). Plenum Pub.

Photoreceptors. Ed. by A. Borsellino & L. Cervetto. (NATO ASI Series A, Life Sciences: Vol. 75). 368p. 1984. 65.00x (ISBN 0-306-41629-8, Plenum Pr). Plenum Pub.

Photoreceptors: Their Role in Vision. Alan Fein & Ete Z. Szuts. LC 81-24209. (International Union of Pure & Applied Physics Biophysics Ser.: No. 5). (Illus.). 1982. 39.50 (ISBN 0-521-24433-1); pap. 17.95 (ISBN 0-521-28684-0). Cambridge U Pr.

Photorefractive Materials. LC 87-60688. (Technical Digest Series 1987: Vol. 17). 241p. (Orig.). 1987. lib. bdg. 62.00 postconference ed. (ISBN 0-936659-73-4); pap. 35.00 conference ed. (ISBN 0-936659-53-X). Optical Soc.

Photorefractive Materials & Their Applications, Vol. I. Ed. by P. Gunter Eth & J. P. Huignard. (Topics in Applied Physics Ser.: Vol. 61). (Illus.). 310p. 1988. 69.50 (ISBN 0-387-18332-9). Springer-Verlag.

Photoresist: Materials & Processes. W. S. DeForest. 1975. text ed. 54.95 (ISBN 0-07-016230-1). McGraw.

Photorespiration in Marine Plants. Ed. by N. E. Tolbert & C. B. Osmond. (Illus.). 139p. 1976. 7.50x (ISBN 0-643-00201-4). Sabbot-Natural Hist Bks.

Photos at the Archives. Charles E. Magoon. LC 81-4473. 274p. (Orig.). 1981. pap. 8.50. Macmillan.

Photos at the Archives. Ed. by Charles E. Magoon. 262p. pap. cancelled. McNally & Loftin.

Photos from Wisconsin's Past. Malcolm Rosholt. (Illus.). 176p. 1986. 24.95 (ISBN 0-910417-08-3). Rosholt Hse.

Photoscope: Stimulating Communication from Personal Experience: A Pragmatic Approach to Restoring Memory & Communication. Mary Jo Santo Pietro. (Illus.). 60p. 1987. pap. 10.00 (ISBN 0-937857-04-1, 1332). Speech Bin.

Photosensitisation. Ed. by G. Moreno et al. (NATO ASI Ser.: No. H15). 521p. 1988. 132.10 (ISBN 0-387-18554-2). Springer-Verlag.

Photosensitive Epilepsy. P. Jeavons & G. F. Harding. (Clinics in Developmental Medicine Ser.: Vol. 56). 130p. 1975. text ed. 23.00 (ISBN 0-433-17201-0, Pub. by Spastics Intl England). Lippincott.

Photosensitivity & Epilepsy. M. Newmark & J. K. Penry. 232p. 1979. 36.50 (ISBN 0-89004-393-0). Raven.

Photostat Operator. Jack Rudman. (Career Examination Ser.: C-1878). (Cloth bdg. avail. on request). pap. 10.00 (ISBN 0-8373-1878-5). Natl Learning.

Photosynthesis, 6 vols. Ed. by George Akoyunoglou. (Illus.). 5570p. 1981. Set. text ed. 499.00 cancelled (Pub. by Balaban Intl Sci Serv); Vol. 1. text ed. 75.00 cancelled (ISBN 0-86689-012-2); Vol. 2. text ed. 108.00 cancelled; Vol. 3. text ed. 109.00 cancelled; Vol. 4. text ed. 79.00 cancelled (ISBN 0-86689-009-2); Vol. 5. text ed. 102.00 cancelled; Vol. 6. text ed. 75.00 cancelled (ISBN 0-86689-011-4). IPS.

Photosynthesis. J. Amesz. (Van Comprehensive Biochemistry Ser.: Vol. 15). 355p. 1987. 90.75 (ISBN 0-444-80864-7). Elsevier.

Photosynthesis. Christine H. Foyer. LC 83-21764. (Cell Biology Ser.). 219p. 1984. 34.95x (ISBN 0-471-86473-0, 1-570). Wiley.

Photosynthesis. Herbert Y. Nakatani. Ed. by J. J. Head. LC 84-45838. (Carolina Biology Readers Ser.: No. 193). (Illus.). 16p. (Orig.). (YA) (gr. 10 up). 1987. pap. text ed. 1.75 (ISBN 0-89278-109-2, 45-9793). Carolina Biological.

Photosynthesis. rev. ed. C. P. Whittingham. Ed. by J. J. Head. LC 76-50840. (Carolina Biology Readers Ser.). (Illus.). 16p. (gr. 10 up). 1977. pap. 1.65 (ISBN 0-89278-209-9, 45-9609). Carolina Biological.

Photosynthesis & Chemosynthesis see Plant Physiology: A Treatise.

Photosynthesis & Plant Development. Ed. by R. Marcelle et al. 1979. lib. bdg. 67.00 (ISBN 90-6193-595-4, Pub. by Junk Pubs Netherlands). Kluwer Academic.

Photosynthesis & Respiration in White Spruce & Balsam Fir, No. 85. 1961. 0.65 (ISBN 0-686-20697-5). SUNY Environ.

Photosynthesis Bibliography, Vol. III. Ed. by Z. Sestak & J. Catsky. 1977. pap. 55.00 (ISBN 90-6193-042-1, Pub. by Junk Pubs Netherlands). Kluwer Academic.

Photosynthesis Bibliography: Publications 1974, References No. 18421-21504 ABD-ZYL & Cumulative Indexes to Volumes 2-5, Vol. 5. Ed. by Z. Sestak & J. Catsky. 1980. pap. 74.00 (ISBN 90-6193-044-8, Pub. by Junk Pubs Netherlands). Kluwer Academic.

Photosynthesis: Energy Tranduction: A Practical Approach. Ed. by M. F. Hipkins & N. R. Baker. 208p. 1986. 45.00 (ISBN 0-947946-63-2); pap. 28.00 (ISBN 0-947946-51-9). IRL Pr US.

Photosynthesis III. Ed. by L. A. Staehelin & C. J. Arntzen. (Encyclopedia of Plant Physiology Ser.: Vol. 19). (Illus.). 810p. 1986. 239.00 (ISBN 0-387-16140-6). Springer-Verlag.

Photosynthesis in Contrasting Environments. N. R. Baker & S. P. Long. (Topics in Photosynthesis Ser.: Vol. 7). 426p. 1986. 171.75 (ISBN 0-444-80772-1). Elsevier.

Photosynthesis in Relation to Model Systems. Ed. by J. Barber. (Topics in Photosynthesis Ser.: Vol. 3). 534p. 1979. 186.50 (ISBN 0-444-80066-2, North Holland). Elsevier.

Photosynthesis: Metabolism, Control, Physiology. D. W. Lawlor. LC 85-15888. 262p. 1986. pap. 39.95 (ISBN 0-470-20681-0). Halsted Pr.

Photosynthesis of Protective Systems. Ed. by A. A. Nichiporovich. 192p. 1967. text ed. 41.00x (ISBN 0-7065-0589-1, Pub. by Keter Pub Jerusalem). Coronet Bks.

Photosynthesis One: Photosynthetic Electron Transport & Photophosphorylation. Ed. by A. Trebst & M. Avron. (Encyclopedia of Plant Physiology Ser.: Vol. 5). 1977. 127.00 (ISBN 0-387-07962-9). Springer-Verlag.

Photosynthesis, Photorespiration & Plant Productivity. Israel Zelitch. 1971. 66.50 (ISBN 0-12-779250-3). Acad Pr.

Photosynthesis: Physical Mechanisms & Chemical Patterns. R. K. Clayton. LC 79-27543. (IUPAB Biophysics Ser.: No. 4). 295p. 1981. 52.50 (ISBN 0-521-22300-8); pap. 18.95 (ISBN 0-521-29443-6). Cambridge U Pr.

Photosynthesis, Productivity & Growth: The Physiological Ecology of Phytoplankton. G. P. Harris. (Ergebnisse der Limnologie Ser.: No. 10). (Illus.). 171p. 1978. pap. text ed. 37.70x. Lubrecht & Cramer.

Photosynthesis, Productivity, & Growth: The Physiological Ecology of Phytoplankton. Ed. by Graham P. Harris. (Limnology Report: No. 10). (Illus.). 175p. (Orig.). 1978. pap. text ed. 47.50x (ISBN 3-510-47008-7, Pub. by E Schweizerbartsche). Coronet Bks.

Photosynthesis Two: Photosynthetic Carbon Metabolism & Related Processes. Ed. by M. Gibbs & E. Latzko. (Encyclopedia of Plant Physiology, New Ser.: Vol. 6). (Illus.). 1979. 118.00 (ISBN 0-387-09288-9). Springer-Verlag.

Photosynthesis: Vol. 1: Energy Conversion by Plants & Bacteria. Ed. by Govindjee. (Cell Biology: A Series of Monographs). 690p. 1982. 103.50 (ISBN 0-12-294301-5). Acad Pr.

Photosynthesis: Vol. 2, Carbon Metabolism and Plant Productivity. Ed. by Govindjee. (Cell Biology: Monographs). 1983. 85.00 (ISBN 0-12-294302-3). Acad Pr.

Photosynthetic Bacteria. Ed. by R. K. Clayton & W. R. Sistrom. LC 78-2835. (Illus.). 968p. 1978. 135.00x (ISBN 0-306-31133-X, Plenum Pr). Plenum Pub.

Photosynthetic Bacteria. E. N. Kondrat'eva. 252p. 1965. 54.00x (ISBN 0-7065-0337-6, Pub. by Keter Pub Jerusalem). Coronet Bks.

Photosynthetic Bacterial Reaction Center: Structure & Dynamics. Ed. by J. Breton & A. Vermeglio. (NATO ASI Series A, Life Sciences: Vol. 149). (Illus.). 440p. 1988. 85.00x (ISBN 0-306-42917-9, Plenum Pr). Plenum Pub.

Photosynthetic Light-Harvesting Systems Organization & Function: Proceedings of an International Workshop, October 12-16 1987, Freising, Federal Republic of Germany. Ed. by Hugo Scheer & Siegfried Schneider. 636p. 1988. lib. bdg. 188.00x (ISBN 0-89925-427-6). De Gruyter.

Photosynthetic Picoplankton. Ed. by Trevor Platt & William Li. (Canadian Bulletin of Fisheries & Aquatic Sciences Ser.: No. 214). 583p. (Orig.). 1987. pap. text ed. 24.00 (ISBN 0-317-66573-1, SSC226, SSC). UNIPUB.

Photosynthetic Prokaryotes: Cell Differentiation & Function. Papageorgiou. 408p. 1983. 99.00 (ISBN 0-444-00732-6, Biomedical Pr). Elsevier.

Photosynthetic Systems: Structure, Function & Assembly. Susan M. Danks et al. LC 85-5831. 162p. 1985. 47.00 (ISBN 0-471-10250-4); pap. 21.95 (ISBN 0-471-90178-4). Wiley.

Phototherapy & Photochemotherapy of Skin Disease. Warwick L. Morison. LC 82-16692. 160p. 1983. 36.95 (ISBN 0-275-91375-9, C1375). Praeger.

Phototherapy in Mental Health. David A. Krauss & Jerry L. Fryrear. (Illus.). 260p. 1983. 32.75x (ISBN 0-398-04785-5). C C Thomas.

Photothermal Investigations of Solids & Fluids. Ed. by Jeffrey A. Sell. 350p. 1988. price not set (ISBN 0-12-636345-5). Acad Pr.

Phototrophic Bacteria. Ed. by J. G. Ormerod. LC 83-47855. (Studies in Microbiology: Vol. 3). (Illus.). 320p. 1983. text ed. 48.00x (ISBN 0-520-05092-4). U of Cal Pr.

Phototropic Woman: The 1981 Iowa Short Fiction Award. Annabel Thomas. LC 81-10469. 168p. (Orig.). 1981. 14.95 (ISBN 0-87745-113-3); pap. 8.95 (ISBN 0-87745-114-1). U of Iowa Pr.

Phototypesetting: A Design Manual. James Craig. Ed. by Margit Malmstrom. (Illus.). 224p. 1978. 27.95 (ISBN 0-8230-4011-9). Watson-Guptill.

Phototypesetting with Kodak Products, 1980. Eastman Kodak Company. LC 75-36853. (Illus.). 48p. 1982. 8.00 (ISBN 0-87985-166-8, Q-5). Eastman Kodak.

Phototypography & Graphic Arts Dimension Control Photography. Jozef Bruyninckx. LC 74-115394. (Illus.). 150p. 1976. 18.25 (ISBN 0-911126-03-1). Perfect Graphic.

Photovisions. Sarah R. Lafferty. (Illus.). 1987. 9.95 (ISBN 0-917562-48-8). Contemp Arts.

Photovoltaic & Photoelectrochemical Solar Energy Conversion. Ed. by F. Cardon et al. LC 81-10666. (NATO ASI Series B, Physics: Vol. 69). 436p. 1981. 75.00x (ISBN 0-306-40800-7, Plenum Pr). Plenum Pub.

Photovoltaic Demonstration Projects: Proceedings of a Second Contractors' Meeting Organized by the Commission of the European Communities, Directorate-General for Energy, Brussels, Belgium, 28-29 April 1987. Ed. by W. B. Gillet et al. 235p. 1988. 45.00 (ISBN 1-85166-190-5). Elsevier.

Photovoltaic Energy Systems: Design & Installation. M. Buresch. 352p. 1983. text ed. 39.00 (ISBN 0-07-008952-3). McGraw.

Photovoltaic Markets. 316p. 1985. 1775.00 (ISBN 0-86621-255-8, A1327). Frost & Sullivan.

Photovoltaic Materials & Devices. Ed. by B. K. Das & S. N. Singh. LC 85-8631. 448p. 1985. 39.95 (ISBN 0-470-20224-6). Halsted Pr.

Photovoltaic Power for Europe. Michael R. Starr & W. Palz. 1983. PLB 32.50 (ISBN 90-277-1556-4, Pub. by Reidel Holland). Kluwer Academic.

Photovoltaic Power Generation. W. Palz. 1982. 49.50 (ISBN 90-277-1386-3, Pub. by Reidel Holland). Kluwer Academic.

Photovoltaic Power Generation. Ed. by W. Palz. 1984. lib. bdg. 42.00 (ISBN 90-277-1725-7, Pub. by Reidel Holland). Kluwer Academic.

Photovoltaic Power Generation. David L. Pulfrey. LC 77-18220. 234p. 1978. 24.95 (ISBN 0-442-26640-5). Krieger.

Photovoltaic Power Generation. R. Van Overstraeten & G. Caratti. 1988. lib. bdg. 89.00 (ISBN 90-277-2691-4, Pub. by Reidel Holland). Kluwer Academic.

Photovoltaic Power Generation. Ed. by R. Van Overstraeten. 1983. lib. bdg. 46.00 (ISBN 90-277-1585-8, Pub. by Reidel Holland). Kluwer Academic.

Photovoltaic Power Generation. Ed. by G. Willeke & G. Grassi. 1987. lib. bdg. 58.00 (ISBN 90-277-2448-2, Pub. by Reidel Holland). Kluwer Academic.

Photovoltaic Product Directory & Buyers Guide. 2nd ed. R. L. Watts et al. 144p. 1984. pap. 14.95 (ISBN 0-442-29274-0). Van Nos Reinhold.

Photovoltaic Solar Energy Conference. Ed. by Albert Strub. 1977. lib. bdg. 76.00 (ISBN 90-277-0889-4, Pub. by Reidel Holland). Kluwer Academic.

Photovoltaic Solar Energy Conference, Fifth E. C. Ed. by W. Palz & F. Fittipaldi. 1984. lib. bdg. 125.00 (ISBN 90-277-1724-9, Pub. by Reidel Holland). Kluwer Academic.

Photovoltaic Solar Energy Conference, Second E.C. Proceedings. International Conference, West Berlin, April 23-26, 1979. Ed. by R. Van Overstraeten & W. Palz. 1979. lib. bdg. 71.00 (ISBN 90-277-1021-X, Pub. by Reidel Holland). Kluwer Academic.

Photovoltaic System Design. (Illus.). 1982. 59.95 (ISBN 0-918984-04-1). Solarvision.

Photovoltaics: Critical Reviews. Ed. by S. K. Deb. 145p. 1985. 43.00 (ISBN 0-89252-578-9, 543). SPIE.

Photovoltaics for Commercial Solar Power Applications. Ed. by Adler. 115p. 1986. 36.00 (ISBN 0-89252-741-2, 706). SPIE.

Photovoltaics: Sunlight to Electricity in One Step. Paul D. Maycock & Edward N. Stirewalt. LC 81-6157. 244p. 1981. pap. 12.95 (ISBN 0-931790-17-4). Brick Hse Pub.

Photoxidation of Organosulfur Compounds. W. Ando. (Sulfur Reports Ser.). 80p. 1981. pap. 17.00 (ISBN 3-7186-0073-0). Harwood Academic.

Phra the Phoenician. Edwin L. Arnold. (Forgotten Fantasy Library: Vol. 11). (Illus.). 1977. pap. 5.95 (ISBN 0-87877-110-7, F-110). Newcastle Pub.

Phra the Phoenician. Edwin P. Arnold. 1976. lib. bdg. 12.95x (ISBN 0-89968-174-3). Lightyear.

Phrase & Word Origins: A Study of Familiar Expressions. 2nd ed. Alfred H. Holt. Orig. Title: Phrase Origins. 1961. pap. 5.95 (ISBN 0-486-20758-7). Dover.

Phrase Book from the Poetic & Dramatic Works of Robert Browning. Marie A. Molineux. 59.95 (ISBN 0-8490-0831-X). Gordon Pr.

Phrase Books for Travellers. (Illus.). 192p. 1984. 4.95 (ISBN 0-317-07017-7, Berlitz). Macmillan.

Phrase by Phrase: Pronunciation & Listening in American English. Marsha Chan. (Illus.). 176p. 1987. pap. text ed. write for info. (ISBN 0-13-665852-0). P-H.

Phrase Concordance of the Bible. LC 86-16314. 736p. 1986. 17.95 (ISBN 0-8407-4948-1). Nelson.

Phrase-Locked Loops: Theory, Design & Applications. R. G. Best. 1984. text ed. 43.95 (ISBN 0-07-005050-3). McGraw.

Phrase Origins see Phrase & Word Origins: A Study of Familiar Expressions.

Phrase Structure Theory in Generative Grammar. Frits Stuurman. (Language Science Ser.: No. 20). 265p. 1985. pap. 24.90 (ISBN 9-067-65129-X). Foris Pubns.

Phraseologie Im Schulalter. Thomas Scherer. (European University Studies: No. 1, Vol. 515). 174p. (Ger.). 1982. 18.40 (ISBN 3-261-05015-2). P Lang Pubs.

Phrases & Fragments. E. K. Wilson. 136p. 1980. 6.50 (ISBN 0-86690-176-0, 1531-01). Am Fed Astrologers.

Phrases of Modern Music. Lawrence Gilman. 59.95 (ISBN 0-8490-0832-8). Gordon Pr.

Phrasing & Articulation: A Contribution to a Rhetoric of Music. Hermann Keller. Tr. by Leigh Gerdine. (Illus.). 128p. 1973. pap. 6.95x (ISBN 0-393-00681-6, N681, Norton Lib). Norton.

Phrenological Dictionary of Nineteenth-Century Americans. Compiled by Madeleine B. Stern. LC 82-991. (Documentary Reference Collection Ser.). (Illus.). xx, 430p. 1982. lib. bdg. 55.00 (ISBN 0-313-23286-5, STN/). Greenwood.

Phrenology & Palmistry. St. Germain. (Illus.). 137p. 1980. Repr. deluxe ed. 145.75 (ISBN 0-89901-018-0). Found Class Reprints.

Phrenology Examined see Physiological Researches on Life & Death.

Phrenology: Fad & Science: A Nineteenth Century American Crusade. John D. Davies. LC 70-122405. (Illus.). xiii, 203p. 1971. Repr. of 1955 ed. 22.50 (ISBN 0-208-00952-3, Archon). Shoe String.

Phrygian. I. M. Diakonov & V. P. Neroznak. LC 85-453. 1986. 50.00x (ISBN 0-88206-042-2). Caravan Bks.

Phsysics of Intermediate & High Energy Heavy-Ion Reactions: Proceedings of the Workshop. Ed. by M. Kutschers & M. Plossajcsak. 264p. 1988. 48.00 (ISBN 9971-50-498-7). World Scientific Pub.

Phthalate Esters: Toxicity & Metabolism. Kevin N. Woodward. 1988. 99.50 ea. Vol. I, 192 pgs (ISBN 0-8493-6692-5, 6692). Vol. II, 192 pgs (ISBN 0-8493-6693-3, 6693). CRC Pr.

Phthalocyanines. Frank H. Moser & Arthur L. Thomas. 1983. Vol. I: Properties, 248p. 85.00 (ISBN 0-8493-5677-6); Vol. II: Manufacture & Applications, 184p. 75.00 (ISBN 0-8493-5678-4). CRC Pr.

Phthor. Piers Anthony. 240p. pap. 2.95 (ISBN 0-441-66238-2, Pub. by Ace Science Fiction). Ace Bks.

Phu Nham. Barry Sadler. 320p. (Orig.). 1985. pap. 3.50 (ISBN 0-8125-8825-8, Dist. by Warner Pub Services & St. Martin's Press). Tor Bks.

Physical Anthropology of Afghanistan. G. F. Debets. LC 72-116739. (Russian Translation Ser.: Vol. 5, No. 1). 1970. pap. 15.00x (ISBN 0-87365-763-2). Peabody Harvard.

Physical Anthropology of European Populations. Ed. by Ilse Schwidetzky et al. (World Anthropology Ser.). xii, 440p. 1980. text ed. 59.50 (ISBN 90-279-7900-6). Mouton.

Physical Anthropology of Ireland, 2 vols. E. A. Hooton & C. Wesley Dupertius. (Harvard University Peabody Museum of Archaeology & Ethnology Papers Ser). 1955. Set. 103.00 (ISBN 0-527-01275-0). Kraus Repr.

Physical Anthropology of the Eastern Highlands of New Guinea. Robert A. Littlewood. LC 70-117730. (Anthropological Studies in the Eastern Highlands of New Guinea: No. 2). (Illus.). 264p. 1972. 35.00x (ISBN 0-295-95133-8). U of Wash Pr.

Physical Applications of Stationary Time-Series. Enders A. Robinson. (Charles Griffin Bk.). (Illus.). 313p. 1987. 45.00 (ISBN 0-19-520583-9). Oxford U Pr.

Physical Aspects of Brachytherapy. T. J. Godden. (Medical Physics Handbooks: No. 19). 344p. 1988. 102.00x (ISBN 0-85274-511-7, A Hilger UK). Taylor & Francis.

Physical Aspects of Diagnostic Radiology. Michel M. Ter-Pogossian. LC 66-19240. pap. 112.00 (ISBN 0-317-30001-6, 2051853). Bks Demand UMI.

Physical Aspects of Irradiation. 1964. 7.00. Intl Comm Rad Meas.

Physical Aspects of Medical Imaging: Proceedings of a Meeting Held at the University of Manchester, June 25-27, 1980. Ed. by B. M. Moores et al. 342p. 1981. 64.95x (ISBN 0-471-10039-0). Wiley.

Physical Aspects of Natural Catastrophes. A. E. Scheidegger. 300p. 1975. 94.75 (ISBN 0-444-41216-6). Elsevier.

Physical Aspects of Piano Playing. Claire Le Guerrier. 1987. 12.95 (ISBN 0-533-06935-1). Vantage.

Physical Aspects of Radioisotope Brachytherapy. (Technical Reports Ser.: No. 75). (Illus.). 63p. 1967. pap. 9.50 (ISBN 92-0-115167-5, IDC75, IAEA). UNIPUB.

Physical Assessment of the Gerontologic Client. Rosine Carotenuto & John Bullock. LC 80-15247. 157p. 1981. pap. text ed. 10.95x (ISBN 0-8036-1680-5). Davis Co.

Physical Attractiveness. Gerald Adams & Sharyn Crossman. LC 78-56850. 1979. 7.95 (ISBN 0-87212-122-4). Libra.

Physical Attractiveness Phenomena. Gordon L. Patzer. LC 85-6593. (Perspectives in Social Psychology Ser.). 320p. 1985. 42.50x (ISBN 0-306-41783-9, Plenum Pr). Plenum Pub.

Physical Basis of Cell-Cell Adhesion. Ed. by Pierre Bongrand. 280p. 1988. 145.00 (ISBN 0-8493-6554-6, 6554). CRC Pr.

Physical Basis of Computerized Tomography. Christopher Marshall. 171p. 1982. 37.50 (ISBN 0-87527-314-9). Green.

Physical Basis of Mind see Problems of Life & Mind.

Physical Basis of Musical Sound. Joseph Morgan. LC 78-5508. (Illus.). 168p. (Orig.). 1980. lib. bdg. 12.50 (ISBN 0-88275-656-7). Krieger.

Physical Basis of Organic Chemistry. Howard Maskill. (Illus.). 1985. 55.00x (ISBN 0-19-855192-4); pap. 24.95x (ISBN 0-19-855199-1). Oxford U Pr.

Physical Basis of Rime: An Essay on the Aesthetics of Sound. Henry Lanz. LC 69-10115. (Illus.). 1969. Repr. of 1931 ed. lib. bdg. 35.00x (ISBN 0-8371-0136-0, LABR). Greenwood.

Physical Behavior of PCBs in the Great Lakes. Ed. by S. Eisenreich. LC 82-72347. (Illus.). 442p. 1983. 52.95 (ISBN 0-250-40584-9). Butterworth.

Physical Behaviour of Macromolecules with Biological Functions. S. P. Spragg. LC 80-40280. (Monographs in Molecular Biophysics & Biochemistry). 218p. pap. 56.70 (2030452). Bks Demand UMI.

Physical Behaviour of Radioactive Contaminants in the Atmosphere. (Illus.). 532p. (Orig., Eng. & Fr.). 1974. pap. 41.00 (ISBN 92-0-020274-8, ISP354, IAEA). UNIPUB.

Physical Biochemistry. 2nd ed. David M. Freifelder. LC 81-19521. (Illus.). 761p. 1982. pap. text ed. 32.95 (ISBN 0-7167-1444-2). W H Freeman.

Physical Biochemistry. 2nd ed. K. E. Van Holde. (Illus.). 320p. 1985. pap. text ed. 22.95 (ISBN 0-13-666272-2). P-H.

Physical Capacity Tests in the Administration of Physical Education. Frederick R. Rogers. LC 70-177203. (Columbia University. Teachers College. Contributions to Education: No. 173). Repr. of 1926 ed. 22.50 (ISBN 0-404-55173-4). AMS Pr.

Physical Ceramics for Engineers. Lawrence H. Van Vlack. (Illus.). 1964. write for info. (ISBN 0-201-08068-0). Addison-Wesley.

Physical Change & Aging: A Guide for the Helping Professions. 2nd ed. Sue V. Saxon & Mary J. Etten. LC 87-50554. (Illus.). 288p. 1987. pap. text ed. 11.95. Tiresias Pr.

Physical Characteristics of Comets. S. K. Vsekhsvyatskii. 600p. 1964. text ed. 120.00x (ISBN 0-7065-0226-4, Pub. by Keter Pub Jerusalem). Coronet Bks.

Physical Characters of the Cook Islanders. H. L. Shapiro & P. H. Buck. (BMM). pap. 10.00 (ISBN 0-527-01669-1). Kraus Repr.

Physical Characters of the Indians of Southern Mexico. Frederick Starr. LC 74-9008. (Illus.). Repr. of 1902 ed. 19.00 (ISBN 0-404-11906-9). AMS Pr.

Physical, Chemical & Biological Changes in Food Caused by Thermal Processing. Ed. by T. Hoyem & O. Kvale. (Illus.). 398p. 1977. 133.25 (ISBN 0-85334-729-8, Pub. by Elsevier Applied Sci England). Elsevier.

Physical, Chemical, & Biological Properties of Radiocerium Relevant to Radiation Protection Guidelines. LC 79-84485. (NCRP Reports Ser.: No. 60). 1978. 14.00 (ISBN 0-913392-44-8). NCRP Pubns.

Physical Chemical Aspects of Cell Surface Events in Cellular Regulation. Ed. by C. DeLisi & R. Blumenthal. (Developments in Cell Biology Ser.: Vol. 4). 394p. 1979. 79.25 (ISBN 0-444-00311-8, Biomedical Pr). Elsevier.

Physical, Chemical Properties of Drugs. Ed. by Samuel H. Yalkowsky et al. LC 80-22598. (Medicinal Research Ser.: No. 10). pap. 94.80 (ISBN 0-317-42096-8, 2025951). Bks Demand UMI.

Physical-Chemical Properties of Ethane-Nitrogen Mixtures. B. E. Eakin et al. (Research Bulletin Ser.: No. 26). iv, 40p. 1955. 5.00 (ISBN 0-317-56877-9). Inst Gas Tech.

Physical-Chemical Properties of Methane-Ethane Mixtures. O. T. Bloomer et al. (Research Bulletin Ser.: 22). iv, 39p. 1953. 3.50 (ISBN 0-317-56869-8). Inst Gas Tech.

Physical-Chemical Properties of Methane-Nitrogen Mixtures. O. T. Bloomer & J. D. Parent. (Research Bulletin Ser.: No. 17). iv, 35p. 1952. 3.50 (ISBN 0-317-56842-6). Inst Gas Tech.

Physical Chemistry. 7th ed. Alberty. LC 86-15681. 934p. 1987. write for info. (ISBN 0-471-82577-8). Wiley.

Physical Chemistry. 3rd ed. Peter W. Atkins. LC 85-7048. (Illus.). 528p. 1985. text ed. 44.95 (ISBN 0-7167-1749-2). W H Freeman.

Physical Chemistry. 4th ed. Gordon M. Barrow. (Illus.). 1979. text ed. 44.95 (ISBN 0-07-003825-2). McGraw.

Physical Chemistry. 5th ed. Gordon M. Barrow. 800p. 1987. text ed. 47.95 (ISBN 0-07-003905-4). McGraw.

Physical Chemistry. R. Stephen Berry et al. LC 79-790. 1281p. 1980. Combined Ed. text ed. write for info. (ISBN 0-471-04829-1); pap. 18.45 solutions manual (ISBN 0-471-04844-5). Wiley.

Physical Chemistry. 2nd ed. J. Philip Bromberg. 1983. text ed. 49.25 (ISBN 0-205-08019-7, 688020). Allyn.

Physical Chemistry. 3rd ed. Gilbert W. Castellan. LC 82-22754. (Chemistry Ser.). (Illus.). 960p. 1983. text ed. write for info. (ISBN 0-201-10386-9); write for info. solutions manual (ISBN 0-201-10387-7). Addison-Wesley.

Physical Chemistry. 6th ed. Farrington Daniels. 700p. (Arabic.). 1987. S. I. Version. pap. 19.00 (ISBN 0-471-09653-9). Wiley.

Physical Chemistry. V. Kireev. Tr. by MIR Publishers. (Illus.). 640p. 1975. 24.00 (ISBN 0-8464-0716-7). Beekman Pubs.

Physical Chemistry. Laidler & Meiser. 1982. 43.95 (ISBN 0-8053-5682-7); solns. manual 13.95 (ISBN 0-8053-5683-5). Benjamin-Cummings.

Physical Chemistry. 2nd ed. Ira N. Levine. (Illus.). 912p. 1983. text ed. 49.95 (ISBN 0-07-037421-X). McGraw.

Physical Chemistry. 3rd, rev. ed. Ira N. Levine. 920p. 1988. text ed. 49.95 (ISBN 0-07-037474-0). McGraw.

Physical Chemistry. Y. S. Lipatov et al. LC 61-642. (Advances in Polymes Science Ser.: Vol. 22). (Illus.). 1977. 41.00 (ISBN 0-387-07942-4). Springer-Verlag.

Physical Chemistry. Clyde Metz. (Schaum's Outline Ser). 256p. (Orig.). 1975. pap. text ed. 10.95 (ISBN 0-07-041709-1). McGraw.

Physical Chemistry. 2nd rev. ed. E. A. Moelwyn-Hughes. 1964. text ed. 93.00 (ISBN 0-08-010846-6). Pergamon.

Physical Chemistry. Joseph H. Noggle. 1984. text ed. write for info. (ISBN 0-673-39550-2). Scott F.

Physical Chemistry. 2nd ed. Joseph H. Noggle. 1988. text ed. price not set (ISBN 0-673-39817-X). Scott F.

Physical Chemistry. (Advances in Polymer Science: Vol. 30). (Illus.). 1979. 56.00 (ISBN 0-387-09199-8). Springer-Verlag.

Physical Chemistry. Jed White. 486p. 1988. pap. 11.95 (ISBN 0-15-601657-5, BFP). HarBraceJ.

Physical Chemistry, Vol. 2. Nagakura. (Organic Synthesis--Today & Tomorrow Ser.). 1979. 48.00 (ISBN 0-08-022036-3). Pergamon.

Physical Chemistry: A Step by Step Approach. Kemp. (Undergraduate Chemistry - A Series of Textbooks: Vol. 6). 1979. 39.75 (ISBN 0-8247-6640-7). Dekker.

Physical Chemistry: An Advanced Treatise in Eleven Volumes. Ed. by H. Eyring et al. Incl. Vol. 1. Thermodynamics. Ed. by W. Jost. 1971. 95.00 (ISBN 0-12-245601-7); Vol. 2, Statistical Mechanics. Ed. by H. Eyring. 1967. 87.00, by subscription 70.50 (ISBN 0-12-245602-5); Vol. 3. Electronic Structure of Atoms & Molecules. Ed. by D. Henderson. 1969. 95.00 (ISBN 0-12-245603-3); Vol. 4. Molecular Properties. Ed. by D. Henderson. 1970. 99.50 (ISBN 0-12-245604-1); Vol. 5. Valency. Ed. by H. Eyring. 1970. 99.50 (ISBN 0-12-245605-X); Vol. 6A. General Introduction & Gas Reactions. Ed. by W. Jost. 1974. Pt. A. 95.00 (ISBN 0-12-245606-8); Pt. B, 1975. 95.00 (ISBN 0-12-245656-4); Vol. 7. Reactions in Condensed Phases. Ed. by H. Eyring. 1975. 95.00 (ISBN 0-12-245607-6); Vol. 8. Liquid State. Ed. by D. Henderson. Pt. A, 1971. 70.00 (ISBN 0-12-245608-4); Pt. B. 87.00 (ISBN 0-12-245658-0); Vol. 9. Electrochemistry. Ed. by H. Eyring. 1970. Pt. A. 87.00 (ISBN 0-12-245609-2); Pt. B. 87.00 (ISBN 0-12-245659-9). Pt. B; Vol. 10. Solid State Chemistry. Ed. by W. Jost. 1970. 95.00 (ISBN 0-12-245610-6); Vol. 11 Pt. A. Mathematical Applications. Ed. by D. Henderson. 1975. 95.00 (ISBN 0-12-245611-4); Pt. B. 101.50 (ISBN 0-12-245661-0). Acad Pr.

Physical Chemistry & Mineralogy of Soils: Soils in Place, Vol. II. C. Edmund Marshall. LC 64-20074. 330p. 1977. 45.50 (ISBN 0-471-02957-2, Pub. by Wiley-Interscience). Krieger.

Physical Chemistry & Mineralogy of Soils: Volume 1: Soil Materials. C. Edmund Marshall. LC 75-22180. 398p. 1975. Repr. of 1964 ed. 26.50 (ISBN 0-88275-351-7). Krieger.

Physical Chemistry: Enriching Topics from Colloid & Surface Science. H. Van Olphen & Karol J. Mysels. LC 75-23217. (Illus.). xvi, 404p. 1975. pap. text ed. 7.50x (ISBN 0-916004-01-5). Theorex.

Physical Chemistry for the Life Sciences. 2nd ed. Gordon M. Barrow. (Illus.). 448p. 1981. text ed. 39.95 (ISBN 0-07-003858-9). McGraw.

Physical Chemistry of Alloys & Refractory Compounds of Thorium & Uranium. Ed. by D. S. Ivanov. 264p. 1972. text ed. 50.00x (ISBN 0-7065-1224-3, Pub. by Keter Pub Jerusalem). Coronet Bks.

Physical Chemistry of Extractive Metallurgy. Ed. by V. Kudryk & Y. K. Rao. LC 84-29561. (Illus.). 497p. 1985. 70.00 (ISBN 0-89520-486-X). Metal Soc.

Physical Chemistry of Fast Reactions, Vol. 1: Gas Phase Reactions of Small Molecules. Ed. by B. P. Levitt. LC 74-161304. 332p. 1974. 55.00x (ISBN 0-306-35091-2, Plenum Pr). Plenum Pub.

Physical Chemistry of Fast Reactions, Vol. 2: Reaction Dynamics. Ed. by I. W. Smith. LC 79-12248. (Illus.). 290p. 1980. 55.00x (ISBN 0-306-40227-0, Plenum Pr). Plenum Pub.

Physical Chemistry of High Temperature Technology. E. T. Turkdogan. LC 79-26880. 1980. 57.00 (ISBN 0-12-704650-X). Acad Pr.

Physical Chemistry of Inorganic Crystalline Solids. H. F. Franzen. (Illus.). 160p. 1986. 49.00 (ISBN 0-387-16580-0). Springer-Verlag.

Physical Chemistry of Leather Making. Krzysztof J. Bienkiewicz. LC 80-27191. 556p. 1983. 52.50 (ISBN 0-89874-304-4). Krieger.

Physical Chemistry of Lipids-From Alkanes to Phospholipids. Donald M. Small. LC 85-19420. (Handbook of Lipid Research Ser.: Vol. 4). 692p. 1986. 89.50x (ISBN 0-306-41763-4, Plenum Pr.). Plenum Pub.

Physical Chemistry of Macromolecules. Charles Tanford. LC 61-11511. 710p. 1961. 54.50x (ISBN 0-471-84447-0, Wiley-Interscience). Wiley.

Physical Chemistry of Membranes: An Introduction to the Structure & Dynamics of Biological Membranes. Brian L. Silver. (Illus.). 432p. 1985. text ed. 65.00x (ISBN 0-04-574028-3). Unwin Hyman.

Physical Chemistry of Membranes (Monograph) Michael E. Starzak. LC 83-4628. 1984. 55.50 (ISBN 0-12-664580-9). Acad Pr.

Physical Chemistry of Organic Solvent Systems. Ed. by A. K. Covington & T. Dickinson. LC 72-77042. 824p. 1973. 125.00x (ISBN 0-306-30569-0, Plenum Pr). Plenum Pub.

Physical Chemistry of Paddy Soils. Ed. by T. Yu. (Illus.). 1985. 75.00 (ISBN 0-387-13001-2). Springer-Verlag.

Physical Chemistry of Process Metallurgy: The Richardson Conference. Ed. by J. H. Jeffes & R. J. Tait. 266p. 1974. text ed. 72.00x (ISBN 0-900488-22-0). IMM North Am.

Physical Chemistry of Process Metallurgy, Pt. 1. Ed. by George R. St. Pierre. LC 60-10587. (Metallurgical Society Conferences Ser.: Vol. 7). pap. 160.00 (ISBN 0-317-10237-0, 2000670). Bks Demand UMI.

Physical Chemistry of Process Metallurgy, Pt. 2. Ed. by George R. St. Pierre. LC 60-10587. (Metallurgical Society Conferences Ser.: Vol. 8). pap. 160.00 (ISBN 0-317-10836-0, 2000671). Bks Demand UMI.

Physical Chemistry of Surfaces. 5th ed. Adamson. 1990. price not set (ISBN 0-471-61019-4). Wiley.

Physical Chemistry of Surfaces. 4th ed. Arthur W. Adamson. LC 82-2711. 664p. 1982. 49.50 (ISBN 0-471-07877-8). Wiley.

Physical Chemistry of the Solid State: Applications to Metals & Their Compounds. Lacombe. 1984. 189.50 (ISBN 0-444-42370-2). Elsevier.

Physical Chemistry of Transmembrane Ion Motions: Proceedings of the International Meeting of the Societe de Chimie Physique, 36th, Paris, Sept. 27-Oct. 1, 1982. Ed. by G. Spach et al. (Studies in Physical & Theoretical Chemistry: Vol. 24). 856p. 1983. 179.00 (ISBN 0-444-42176-9). Elsevier.

Physical Chemistry of 1, 2-Dithiole Compounds: The Question of Aromaticity. Carl Pedersen. (Sulfur Reports). 96p. 1980. flexicover 40.00 (ISBN 3-7186-0031-5). Harwood Academic.

Physical Chemistry on a Microcomputer. Joseph H. Noggle. 1985. pap. text ed. write for info. (ISBN 0-673-39549-9). Scott F.

Physical Chemistry: Principles & Applications in Biological Sciences. Ignacio Tinoco, Jr. et al. LC 77-25417. 1978. solutions 9.95. P-H.

Physical Chemistry: Principles & Applications in Biological Sciences. 2nd ed. Ignacio Tinoco, Jr. et al. (Illus.). 656p. 1985. text ed. write for info. (ISBN 0-13-666280-3). P-H.

Physical Chemistry Problem Solver. rev. ed. Research & Education Assn. LC 81-522778. (Illus.). 800p. (Orig.). 1986. pap. text ed. 23.85 (ISBN 0-87891-532-X). Res & Educ.

Physical Chemistry Source Book. (Science Reference Ser.). (Illus.). 500p. Date not set. 45.00 (ISBN 0-07-045504-X). McGraw.

Physical Chemistry with Applications to Biological Systems. 2nd ed. Raymond Chang. (Illus.). 1981. text ed. write for info. (ISBN 0-02-321040-0). Macmillan.

Physical Chemistry with Applications to the Life Sciences. David Eisenberg & Donald M. Crothers. 1979. 45.95 (ISBN 0-8053-2402-X); instrs'. guide 9.95 (ISBN 0-8053-2403-8). Benjamin-Cummings.

Physical Chemistry with Tront Eureka. 7th ed. Robert A. Alberty. 1988. write for info. bk. & disk pak (ISBN 0-471-61063-1). Wiley.

Physical Child Abuse: An Expanded Analysis. James R. Seaberg. LC 79-93293. 145p. 1980. 12.00 (ISBN 0-86548-021-4). R & E Pubs.

Physical Cleaning of Coal. Liu. (Energy, Power & Environment Ser.). 664p. 1982. 95.00 (ISBN 0-8247-1862-3). Dekker.

Physical Climatology. William D. Sellers. LC 65-24983. 1965. 22.00x (ISBN 0-226-74699-2). U of Chicago Pr.

Physical Climatology for Solar & Wind Energy: Course on Physical Climatology for Solar & Wind Energy. Ed. by R. Guzzi & C. G. Justus. 1096p. 1988. 85.00 (ISBN 9971-50-551-7). World Scientific Pub.

Physical Conditioning for Winning Football. William A. Kroll. 299p. 1983. text ed. write for info. (ISBN 0-205-07940-7, Pub. by Longwood Div). Wm C Brown.

Physical Conditions & Public Service. (Metropolitan America Ser.: Vol. 10). 216p. 1974. 13.00x (ISBN 0-405-05423-8). Ayer Co Pubs.

Physical Conditions Guide for Inspections. LC 78-57046. 1984. pap. 2.00 (ISBN 0-318-19241-1). Institute Pr.

Physical Conditions of the Elizabethan Public Playhouse. William J. Lawrence. LC 68-31297. 1968. Repr. of 1927 ed. 13.75x (ISBN 0-8154-0135-3). Cooper Sq.

Physical Constants of Hydrocarbons C Subscript 1 to C Subscript 10 - DS-04A. 76p. 1971. 12.00 (ISBN 0-8031-0818-4, 05-004010-12). ASTM.

Physical Control of the Mind: Toward a Psychocivilized Society. Jose M. Delgado. Ed. by Ruth N. Anshen. (Illus.). 280p. 1971. 29.50x (ISBN 0-8290-0574-9). Irvington.

Physical Control of the Mind: Toward a Psychocivilized Society. Jose M. Delgado. Ed. by Ruth N. Anshen. (Illus.). 280p. pap. text ed. 12.95x (ISBN 0-8290-1765-8). Irvington.

Physical Cosmology. R. Balian & J. Adouse. (Houches Summer School Ser.: Vol. 32). 668p. 1980. 173.75 (ISBN 0-444-85433-9). Elsevier.

Physical Culture. Richard Friedman. LC 79-14604. 1979. pap. 3.00 (ISBN 0-916328-14-7). Yellow Pr.

Physical Data Base Record Design. Jon Clark & Jeffrey A. Hoffer. (Data Base Monograph Ser.: No. 7). (Illus.). 1979. pap. 15.00x (ISBN 0-89435-008-0). QED Info Sci.

Physical Data Base Record Design. Jon Clark & Jeffrey A. Hoffer. LC 79-113431. (QED Monograph Series. Data Base Management: No. 7). pap. 30.70 (2031751). Bks Demand UMI.

Physical Demands Job Analysis: A New Approach. Robert B. Lytel & Karl F. Botterbusch. (Illus.). 166p. (Orig.). 1981. pap. 18.50x (ISBN 0-916671-34-8). Material Dev.

Physical Design Automation of VLSI Systems. Ed. by Bryan Preas & Michael Lorenzetti. (Illus.). 510p. Date not set. text ed. 38.95 (ISBN 0-8053-0412-9). Benjamin-Cummings.

Physical Diagnosis: A Concise Textbook. Ed. by Siegfried J. Kra. (Concise Textbook Ser.: Vol. 19). 384p. 1987. pap. 29.25 (ISBN 0-444-01044-0). Elsevier.

Physical Geography of Canada - Climate, Ice & Water Studies: A Selected Bibliography. Thomas A. Rumney. (Public Administration Ser.: P 2275). 50p. 1987. 12.50 (ISBN 1-55590-535-8). Vance Biblios.

Physical Geography of Canada - Geomorphology: A Selected Bibliography. Thomas A. Rumney. (Public Administration Ser.: P 2241). 98p. 1987. 22.50 (ISBN 1-55590-481-5). Vance Biblios.

Physical Geography of China. Ed. by Sonegiao Zhao. LC 85-15574. 200p. 1986. text ed. 44.05 (ISBN 0-471-09597-4). Wiley.

Physical Geography of the Sea, 3 vols. M. F. Maury. (Illus.). 460p. 1985. Set. 327.75x (ISBN 0-86722-087-2). Inst Econ Pol.

Physical Geography of the Sea, & Its Meteorology. Matthew F. Maury. Ed. by John Leighly. LC 63-10870. (John Harvard Library). (Illus.). 1963. pap. 10.95x (ISBN 0-674-66652-6). Harvard U Pr.

Physical Geography of Wisconsin. 3rd ed. Lawrence Martin. (Illus.). 636p. 1965. text ed. 30.00 (ISBN 0-299-03472-0); pap. 11.75t (ISBN 0-299-03475-5). U of Wis Pr.

Physical Geography Today. 3rd ed. Robert A. Muller & Theodore M. Oberlander. 608p. 1984. text ed. write for info (ISBN 0-394-33264-4, RanC). Random.

Physical Geography Workbook. rev. ed. John A. Carthew. (Illus.). 68p. 1981. pap. text ed. 7.00x (ISBN 0-89179-218-X). Tam's Bks.

Physical Geology. 2nd ed. Robert F. Flint & Brian J. Skinner. LC 76-23206. 671p. 1977. text ed. write for info. (ISBN 0-471-26442-3); study guide o.p. 12.45 (ISBN 0-471-02593-3); tchr's. manual avail. (ISBN 0-471-03075-9). Wiley.

Physical Geology. 4th ed. Robert J. Foster. 460p. 1983. text ed. 37.95 (ISBN 0-675-20021-0). Additional supplments may be obtained from publisher. Merrill.

Physical Geology. G. Gorshkov & A. Yakushova. Tr. by A. Gurevich. (Russian Monographs Ser.). 596p. 1969. 168.00 (ISBN 0-677-20790-5). Gordon & Breach.

Physical Geology. George Gorshkov & Alexandra Yakushova. (Illus.). 596p. 1975. text ed. 22.00 (ISBN 0-8464-0718-3). Beekman Pubs.

Physical Geology. 7th ed. Sheldon Judson et al. (Illus.). 528p. 1987. text ed. write for info. (ISBN 0-13-669698-8); write for info. study guide (ISBN 0-13-669722-4). P-H.

Physical Geology. Allan Ludman et al. (Illus.). 576p. 1982. text ed. 38.95 (ISBN 0-07-011510-9). McGraw.

Physical Geology. Carla W. Montgomery. 560p. 1987. text ed. write for info. (ISBN 0-697-00851-7); write for info. instr's manual (ISBN 0-697-00852-5); write for info. student study guide (ISBN 0-697-01066-X); write for info. transparencies (ISBN 0-697-00853-3); write for info. slides (ISBN 0-697-00870-3). Wm C Brown.

Physical Geology. 3rd ed. Charles C. Plummer & David McGeary. 528p. 1985. text ed. write for info. (ISBN 0-697-00794-4); pap. write for info. (ISBN 0-697-05046-7); instr's. manual avail. (ISBN 0-697-00566-6); student study guide avail. (ISBN 0-697-00564-X); lab manual avail. (ISBN 0-697-00351-5); transparencies avail. (ISBN 0-697-00565-8); slides avail. (ISBN 0-697-00596-8); instr's. lab manual avail. (ISBN 0-697-00595-X). Wm C Brown.

Physical Geology. 4th ed. Charles C. Plummer & David McGeary. 560p. 1988. text ed. write for info. (ISBN 0-697-05093-9); pap. text ed. write for info. (ISBN 0-697-05092-0). Instr's Manual (ISBN 0-697-05094-7). Student study guide (ISBN 0-697-05090-4). Lab Manual (ISBN 0-697-05095-5). Transparencies (ISBN 0-697-05091-2). Slides (ISBN 0-697-05087-4). Wm C Brown.

Physical Geology. Jack Rudman. (ACT Proficiency Examination Program Ser.: PEP-56). 1988. 25.95 (ISBN 0-8373-5956-2); pap. 13.95 (ISBN 0-8373-5906-6). Natl Learning.

Physical Geology. Brian Skinner & Stephen Porter. LC 86-32533. 750p. 1987. write for info. (ISBN 0-471-05668-5); study guide avail. (ISBN 0-471-84796-8); apple software avail. (ISBN 0-471-63550-2); IBM software avail. (ISBN 0-471-63548-0); slides avail. (ISBN 0-471-63489-1); study guide avail. (ISBN 0-471-62946-4). Wiley.

Physical Geology. Edgar W. Spencer. (Biology Ser.). (Illus.). 656p. 1983. text ed. write for info. (ISBN 0-201-06423-5); lab. manual avail.; write for info. instr's. manual (ISBN 0-201-06424-3); Study Guide avail. Addison-Wesley.

Physical Geology Laboratory Course. 2nd ed. C. M. Gilbert & M. N. Christensen. 1967. text ed. 24.95 (ISBN 0-07-023206-7). McGraw.

Physical Geology Laboratory Manual. American Geological Institute Staff & National Association of Geology Teachers Staff. Ed. by Bob Bates. (Illus.). 224p. 1986. text ed. 21.95 (ISBN 0-675-20478-X). Merrill.

Physical Geology Laboratory Manual. 3rd ed. Charles J. Cazeau & Francis T. Siemankowski. 184p. 1982. wire coil bdg. 14.95 (ISBN 0-8403-3690-X, 40279101). Kendall-Hunt.

Physical Geology Laboratory Manual. Frederic Goldstein. 1976. spiral bdg. 7.50 (ISBN 0-88252-049-0). Paladin Hse.

Physical Geology Laboratory Text & Manual: A Guide for the Study of Earth. 2nd ed. R. David Dallmeyer. 1980. wire coil bdg. 15.95 (ISBN 0-8403-1231-8). Kendall-Hunt.

Physical Geology: Principles & Perspectives. 2nd ed. Edward A. Hay & A. Lee McAlester. (Illus.). 432p. 1984. write for info. (ISBN 0-13-669549-3). P-H.

Physical Geology: Principles & Perspectives. A. Lee McAlester & Edward A. Hay. (Illus.). 448p. 1975. 26.95. P-H.

Physical Geology: Student Handbook & Study Guide. 6th ed. Richard Gerfin & Robert Koch. 320p. 1982. pap. text ed. write for info. (ISBN 0-13-669788-7). P-H.

Physical Geology Study Guide. Steven G. Spear. 1977. wire coil bdg. 5.00 (ISBN 0-88252-068-7). Paladin Hse.

Physical Geology: The Structure & Processes of the Earth. B. Clark Burchfiel et al. 496p. 1982. text ed. 37.95 (ISBN 0-675-09913-7). Merrill.

Physical Growth & Development: From Conception to Maturity. Isabelle Valadian & Douglas Porter. LC 75-41572. 1977. text ed. 18.50 (ISBN 0-316-89525-3). Little.

Physical Growth of Children: An Appraisal of Studies. W. M. Krogman. (SRCD M Ser.). 1955. pap. 15.00 (ISBN 0-527-01563-6). Kraus Repr.

Physical Growth of Mentally Deficient Boys. Charles D. Flory. (SRCD M). 1936. 12.00 (ISBN 0-527-01491-5). Kraus Repr.

Physical Growth of White Children. H. V. Meredith. (SRCD M Ser.). 1936. pap. 15.00 (ISBN 0-527-01487-7). Kraus Repr.

Physical Handicaps. Ed. by Dale C. Garell & Solomon H. Snyder. (Encyclopedia of Health Ser.). (Illus.). (YA) (gr. 7-12). 1989. 17.95 (ISBN 0-7910-0073-7). Chelsea Hse.

Physical Health see Individualized Health Incentive Program Modules For Physically Disabled Students.

Physical Hydrogeology. Ed. by R. A. Freeze & W. Back. LC 82-2976. (Benchmark Papers in Geology: Vol. 72). 431p. 1983. 57.95 (ISBN 0-87933-431-2). Van Nos Reinhold.

Physical Illness & Handicap in Childhood: An Anthology of the Psychoanalytic Study of the Child. Ed. by Ruth S. Eissler et al. Marianne Kris & Albert J. Solnit. LC 75-34811. 375p. 1977. 15.95x (ISBN 0-300-02005-8); pap. 15.95x (ISBN 0-300-02006-6). Yale U Pr.

Physical Illness in the Psychiatric Patient. Erwin K. Koranyi. (Illus.). 236p. 1982. 26.00x (ISBN 0-398-04558-5). C C Thomas.

Physical Immortality & Transfiguration. Leonard Orr. pap. write for info. L Orr.

Physical Immortality & Transfiguration. Leonard D. Orr. (YA) (gr. 7 up). 1988. pap. 15.00 (ISBN 0-945793-01-4). Inspir Univ.

Physical Immortality for Christians. Leonard D. Orr. (YA) (gr. 7 up). 1988. pap. 10.00 (ISBN 0-945793-03-0). Inspir Univ.

Physical Interpretation of the Universe: The Doctrines of Zeno the Stoic. H. A. Hunt. 1976. pap. 2.50 (ISBN 0-522-84100-7, Pub. by Melbourne U Pr). Intl Spec Bk.

Physical Interrogation Techniques. Richard Krousher. LC 84-52485. 88p. (Orig.). 1985. pap. 12.00 (ISBN 0-915179-23-7). Loompanics.

Physical Kinetics. E. M. Lifshitz & L. P. Pitaevskii. Tr. by J. B. Sykes & R. N. Franklin. (Course of Theorectical Physics Ser.: Vol. 10). (Illus.). 625p. 1981. text ed. 83.00 (ISBN 0-08-020641-7); pap. text ed. 32.50 (ISBN 0-08-026480-8). Pergamon.

Physical Knowledge in Preschool Education: Implications of Piaget's Theory. reference ed. Constance Kamii & Rheta DeVries. (Illus.). 1978. write for info. (ISBN 0-13-669804-2). P-H.

Physical Level Interfaces & Protocols: Monograph. Uyless Black. 250p. 1988. write for info. (FE824). IEEE Comp Soc.

Physical Logistics Management. Grant M. Davis & John E. Dillard, Jr. LC 83-10300. (Illus.). 566p. 1983. lib. bdg. 41.75 (ISBN 0-8191-3342-6); pap. text ed. 23.50 (ISBN 0-8191-3343-4). U Pr of Amer.

Physical Management for the Quadriplegic Patient. 2nd ed. Jack R. Ford & Bridget Duckworth. LC 87-479. (Illus.). 661p. 1987. 59.00 (ISBN 0-8036-3676-8). Davis Co.

Physical Management of Multiple Handicaps: A Professional's Guide. Beverly A. Fraser et al. LC 86-13714. 288p. 1986. text ed. 27.00 (ISBN 0-933716-67-2, 672). P H Brookes.

Physical Manifestations & Philosophy of Christ. Thomson J. Hudson. 1978. pap. 4.50 deluxe (ISBN 0-87852-003-1). Inst Human Growth.

Physical Mathematics & Nonlinear Partial Differential Equations. Rankin & Lightbourne. (Lecture Notes in Pure & Applied Mathematics Ser.). 296p. 1985. 59.75 (ISBN 0-8247-7343-8). Dekker.

Physical Measurements. Ed. by J. F. Liebman & A. Greenberg. (Molecular Structure & Energetics Ser.). 388p. 1987. lib. bdg. 84.00 (ISBN 0-89573-140-1). VCH Pubs.

Physical Measurements in Flooded Rice Soils: The Japanese Methodologies. (Illus.). 65p. (Orig.). 1987. pap. 5.00x (ISBN 971-104-163-4, Pub. by Intl Rice Res Philippines). Agribookstore.

Physical Measurements in Gas Dynamics & Combustion. Ed. by R. W. Ladenburg et al. LC 54-13127. pap. 151.50 (ISBN 0-317-09134-4, 2000097). Bks Demand UMI.

Physical Mechanisms in Radiation Biology: Proceedings. AEC Technical Information Center Staff. Ed. by Robert W. Wood & Raymond D. Cooper. LC 74-600124. 332p. 1974. pap. 16.25 (CONF-721001); microfiche 6.50 (ISBN 0-87079-303-9, CONF-721001). DOE.

Physical Medicine & Rehabilitation. Gary A. Okamoto & Theodore J. Phillips. (Saunders Blue Book Ser.). (Illus.). 320p. 1984. pap. 24.95 (ISBN 0-7216-6957-3). Saunders.

Physical Medicine & Rehabilitation. 2nd ed. Kenneth B. Washburn. (Essentials of Primary Care Ser.: Vol. 9). 1981. 22.75 (ISBN 0-87488-713-5). Med Exam.

Physical Medicine & Rehabilitation Approaches in Spinal Cord Injury: 1929, C. Ed. by John G. Cull & Richard E. Hardy. (M). (Illus.). 336p. 1977. 44.75x (ISBN 0-398-03609-8, CHMN DEPT MARINE SCI, 68-74, PROF MARINE SCI & DIR SEA GRANT DEVELOP, LA STATE UNIV, BATON ROUGE, 68-, DEAN, CTR WETLAND RESOURCES, 70-). C C Thomas.

Physical Metallurgy. Bruce Chalmers. LC 59-14983. (Wiley Series on the Science & Technology of Materials). pap. 117.00 (ISBN 0-317-10463-2, 2055140). Bks Demand UMI.

Physical Metallurgy. 2nd ed. Peter Haasen. (Illus.). 416p. 1986. 75.00 (ISBN 0-521-32489-0); pap. 24.95 (ISBN 0-521-31027-X). Cambridge U Pr.

Physical Metallurgy & Heat Treatment. Ed. by N. V. Ageev. 200p. 1970. text ed. 43.00x (ISBN 0-7065-0689-8, Pub. by Keter Pub Jerusalem). Coronet Bks.

Physical Metallurgy & the Design of Steels. F. B. Pickering. (Illus.). 275p. 1978. text ed. 65.00 (ISBN 0-85334-752-2, Pub. by Elsevier Applied Sci England). Elsevier.

Physical Metallurgy of Cast Iron. I. Minkoff. LC 82-21984. 305p. 1983. 76.95x (ISBN 0-471-90006-0, Pub. by Wiley-Interscience). Wiley.

Physical Metallurgy of Cast Iron: Materials Research Society Symposia Proceedings, Vol. 34. Ed. by H. Fredriksson & M. Hillert. xxi, 500p. 1985. 114.25 (ISBN 0-444-00938-8, North-Holland). Elsevier.

Physical Metallurgy of Metal Joining: Proceedings of a Symposium. The Metallurgical Society of AIME. Ed. by Ram Kossowsky & M. E. Glicksman. LC 80-82303. pap. 69.50 (ISBN 0-317-26075-8, 2023772). Bks Demand UMI.

Physical Metallurgy of Platinum Metals. E. Savitsky et al. 1979. 85.00 (ISBN 0-08-023259-0). Pergamon.

Physical Metallurgy of Steels. Leslie. 396p. 1981. 51.00 (ISBN 0-89116-497-9). Hemisphere Pub.

Physical Metallurgy of Stress Corrosion Fracture. Ed. by Thor N. Rhodin. LC 59-14890. (Metallurgical Society Conferences Ser.: Vol. 4). pap. 102.30 (ISBN 0-317-10921-9, 2000667). Bks Demand UMI.

Physical Metallurgy: Part 1: Chapters 1-13; Part 2: Chapters 14-30, 2 pts. 3rd, rev. ed. Ed. by R. W. Cahn. 2050p. 1984. Set. 200.00 (ISBN 0-444-86628-0, I-005-83, North-Holland); Pt. 1. write for info. (ISBN 0-444-86786-4); Pt. 2. write for info. (ISBN 0-444-86787-2). Elsevier.

Physical Meteorology. Herny G. Houghton. (Illus.). 450p. 1985. text ed. 37.50x (ISBN 0-262-08146-6). MIT Pr.

Physical Methods for Fossil Fuels Characterization, Coal Gasification, Pyrolysis & Biomass: Presented at Miami Beach, FL, April 28-May 3, 1985, Vol. 7. American Chemical Society, Division of Fuel Chemistry Staff. (American Chemical Society Division of Fuel Chemistry Preprints of Papers Ser.: Vol. 30, No. 1). pap. 108.80 (ISBN 0-317-28033-3, 2025564). Bks Demand UMI.

Physical Methods for Inorganic Biochemistry, Vol. 5. John R. Wright et al. (Biochemistry of the Elements Ser.). 400p. 1986. 59.50x (ISBN 0-306-42049-X, Plenum Pr). Plenum Pub.

Physical Methods in Chemistry. 2nd ed. Russell S. Drago. 1977. text ed. 53.25 (ISBN 0-7216-3184-3, CBS C). SCP.

Physical Methods in Determinative Mineralogy. 2nd ed. Ed. by J. Zussman. 1978. 90.00 (ISBN 0-12-782960-1). Acad Pr.

Physical Methods in Heterocyclic Chemistry. R. R. Gupta. LC 83-14609. (General Heterocyclic Chemistry Ser.). 682p. 1984. 178.00x (ISBN 0-471-09855-8). Wiley.

Physical Methods in Heterocyclic Chemistry, Vol 6. Katritsky. 1974. 81.50 (ISBN 0-12-401106-3). Acad Pr.

Physical Methods in Macromolecular Chemistry. Ed. by Benjamin Carroll. LC 69-12679. Vol. 1. pap. 99.30 (2027104); Vol. 2. pap. 95.30. Bks Demand UMI.

Physical Methods in Modern Chemical Analysis, Vol. 1. Ed. by Ted Kuwana & Tetsuo Osa. 1978. 49.50 (ISBN 0-12-430801-5). Acad Pr.

Physical Methods in Modern Chemical Analysis, Vol. 2. Ed. by Theodore Kuwana. LC 77-92242. 1980. 49.50 (ISBN 0-12-430802-3). Acad Pr.

Physical Methods in Modern Chemical Analysis, Vol. 3. Ed. by Theodore Kuwana. 320p. 1983. 55.00 (ISBN 0-12-430803-1). Acad Pr.

Physical Methods of Chemistry. 2nd ed. Bryant W. Rossiter & John F. Hamilton. LC 85-6386. (Techniques of Chemistry Ser.). 1986. Vol. 1, Components of Scientific Instruments & Applications of Computers to Chemical Research. 150.00 (ISBN 0-471-08034-9); Vol. 2, Electronic Methods. 150.00 (ISBN 0-471-08027-6). Wiley.

Physical Methods of Chemistry: Determination of Chemical Composition & Molecular, Vol. 3. 2nd ed. Rossiter. (Physical Methods of Chemistry Ser.). 1987. write for info. (ISBN 0-471-85051-9). Wiley.

Physical Methods of Chemistry, Electrochemical Methods, Vol. 1, Pt. 2a. Ed. by Arnold Weissberger & Bryant W. Rossiter. (Techniques of Chemistry Ser.). 723p. 1971. 112.95 (ISBN 0-471-92727-9). Wiley.

Physical Methods of Investigating Textiles. Ed. by R. Meredith & J. W. Hearle. LC 59-13795. (Illus.). pap. 110.30 (ISBN 0-317-10818-2, 2011955). Bks Demand UMI.

Physical Methods on Biological Membranes & Their Model Systems. Ed. by F. Conti et al. LC 83-22909. (NATO ASI Series A, Life Sciences: Vol. 71). 470p. 1985. 85.00x (ISBN 0-306-41480-5, Plenum Pr). Plenum Pub.

Physical Modalities in Dermatologic Therapy: Radiotherapy, Electrosurgery, Phototherapy, Cryosurgery. Ed. by H. Goldschmidt. 1978. 69.00 (ISBN 0-387-90267-8). Springer-Verlag.

Physical Modeling of Metalworking Processes. Ed. by E. Erman & S. L. Semiatin. LC 87-73245. (Illus.). 400p. 1988. 110.00 (ISBN 0-87339-029-6). Metal Soc.

Physical Modelling in Costal Engineering: Proceedings of an International Conference, Newark, Delaware, August 1981. Ed. by R. A. Dalrymple. 320p. 1984. text ed. 68.50 (ISBN 90-6191-516-3, Pub. by A A Balkema). Brookfield Pub Co.

Physical Models & Equilibrium Methods in Programming & Economics. B. S. Razumikhin. (Mathematics & Its Applications Soviet Ser.). 372p. 1984. lib. bdg. 64.00 (ISBN 90-277-1644-7, Pub. by Reidel Holland). Kluwer Academic.

Physical Nature & Structure of Oceanic Fronts. K. N. Fedorov. (Lecture Notes on Coastal & Estuarine Studies: Vol. 19). viii, 333p. 1986. pap. 53.30 (ISBN 0-387-96445-2). Springer-Verlag.

Physical Nature of the Skin. Ed. by R. M. Marks & S. P. Barton. 1988. lib. bdg. 64.00 (ISBN 0-85200-977-1, Pub. by MTP Pr England). Kluwer Academic.

Physical Non-Linearities in Structural Analysis Symposium. Ed. by J. Hult & J. Lemaitre. (IUTAM Ser.). (Illus.). 287p. 1981. 37.00 (ISBN 0-387-10544-1). Springer-Verlag.

Physical Oceanography of Coastal & Shelf Seas. Ed. by B. Johns. 470p. 1983. 123.75 (ISBN 0-444-42153-X, I-419-83). Elsevier.

Physical Oceanography of Coastal Waters. K. F. Bowden. 302p. 1984. 74.95x (ISBN 0-470-27505-7). Halsted Pr.

Physical Optics of Dynamic Phenomena & Processes in Macromolecular Systems: Proceedings of the 27th Microsymposium on Macromolecules, Prague, Czechoslovakia, July 16-19, 1984. Ed. by B. Sedlacek. (Illus.). xv, 555p. 1985. 137.00 (ISBN 3-11-010234-X). De Gruyter.

Physical Order & Moral Liberty: Previously Unpublished Essays of George Santayana. George Santayana. Ed. by John Lachs & Shirley Lachs. LC 70-87255. 1969. 15.95x (ISBN 0-8265-1131-7). Vanderbilt U Pr.

Physical Organic Chemistry. Ed. by M. J. Dewar et al. (Topics in Current Chemistry Ser.: Vol. 146). (Illus.). 270p. 1988. 89.70 (ISBN 0-387-18541-0). Springer-Verlag.

Physical Organic Chemistry. Neil S. Issacs. LC 87-3848. 828p. 1987. 49.95 (ISBN 0-470-20787-6). Halsted Pr.

Physical Organic Chemistry. C. D. Ritchie. (Organic Chemical Ser.: Vol. 4). 39.75 (ISBN 0-8247-6323-8). Dekker.

Physical Organic Chemistry. 2nd ed. Wiberg. 1988. write for info. (ISBN 0-471-85363-1). Wiley.

Physical Organic Chemistry, Nineteen Eighty-Six. Ed. by M. Kobayashi. (Studies in Organic Chemistry: No. 31). 654p. 1987. 192.75 (ISBN 0-444-42806-2). Elsevier.

Physical Organic Chemistry Through Solved Problems. Joseph B. Lambert. 1978. pap. text ed. 22.95x (ISBN 0-8162-4921-0). Holden-Day.

Physical Organic Chemistry-2: Proceedings, Leyden, 1974. International Union of Pure & Applied Chemistry. 1976. 43.00 (ISBN 0-08-020814-2). Pergamon.

Physical Paradoxes & Sophisms. V. N. Lange. 232p. 1987. pap. 0.95 (ISBN 0-8285-3581-7, Pub. by Mir Pubs USSR). Imported Pubns.

Physical Pharmacy: Physical Chemical Principles in the Pharmaceutical Sciences. 3rd ed. Alfred Martin et al. LC 82-22872. (Illus.). 664p. 1983. text ed. 42.50 (ISBN 0-8121-0877-9). Lea & Febiger.

Physical Planning Report: Murdoch University 1973. R. J. Ferguson & Gordon Stephenson. LC 73-93913. (Illus.). 72p. 1974. pap. 11.50x (ISBN 0-85564-080-4, Pub. by U of W Austral Pr). Intl Spec Bk.

Physical Testing & Quality Control. H. Weston. 150p. 1974. 70.00x (ISBN 0-686-63780-1). State Mutual Bk.

Physical Testing of Plastics - STP 736. Ed. by R. Evans. 125p. 1981. 15.00 (ISBN 0-8031-0768-4, 04-736000-19). ASTM.

Physical Testing of Pulp: Fibers & Slurries, Vol. 1. Jack Weiner & Vera Pollock. LC 65-20872. (Bibliographic Ser.: No. 218, Suppl. 1). 1973. pap. 13.00 (ISBN 0-87010-017-3). Inst Paper Chem.

Physical Testing of Pulp: Fibers & Slurries, Vol. 1. Jack Weiner & Vera Pollock. (Bibliographic Ser.: No. 218). 161p. 1965. 12.00 (ISBN 0-317-34415-3). Inst Paper Chem.

Physical Testing of Pulp: Handsheets, Vol. 2. (Bibliographic Ser.: No. 219). 82p. 1965. 8.00 (ISBN 0-317-34416-1). Inst Paper Chem.

Physical Testing of Rubber. 2nd ed. R. P. Brown. 348p. 1986. 79.25 (ISBN 1-85166-047-X, Pub. by Elsevier Applied Sci England). Elsevier.

Physical Testing of Rubbers. R. P. Brown. (Illus.). 327p. 1979. 61.00 (ISBN 0-85334-788-3, Pub. by Elsevier Applied Sci England). Elsevier.

Physical, the Mental, the Spiritual. Joel Jessen. 185p. 1978. pap. 10.00 (ISBN 0-942958-05-5). Kappeler Inst Pub.

Physical Theory As Logico-Operational Structure. Ed. by Clifford A. Hooker. (Western Ontario Ser.: No. 7). 1978. lib. bdg. 50.00 (ISBN 90-277-0711-1, Pub. by Reidel Holland). Kluwer Academic.

Physical Theory of Neutron Chain Reactors. Alvin M. Weinberg & Eugene P. Wigner. LC 58-8507. (Illus.). 1958. 45.00x (ISBN 0-226-88517-8). U of Chicago Pr.

Physical Therapist. Jack Rudman. (Career Examination Ser.: C-585). (Cloth bdg. avail. on request). pap. 14.00 (ISBN 0-8373-0585-3). Natl Learning.

Physical Therapy. John S. Coulter. LC 75-23658. (Clio Medica: 8). (Illus.). Repr. of 1932 ed. 20.00 (ISBN 0-404-58908-1). AMS Pr.

Physical Therapy & Health Sciences: Medical Analysis Index with Research Bibliography. Richard G. Lydecki. LC 88-47603. 150p. 1988. 34.50 (ISBN 0-88164-358-0); pap. 26.50 (ISBN 0-88164-359-9). ABBE Pubs Assn.

Physical Therapy & the Arthritis Patient: Clinical Aspects & Approaches to Management. Ed. by Mary Singleton & Eleanor F. Branch. LC 88-563. (Physical Therapy in Health Care Ser.: Vol. 2, Nos. 1-2). (Illus.). 90p. 1988. text ed. 22.95 (ISBN 0-86656-728-3). Haworth Pr.

Physical Therapy & the Pulmonary Patient: Aspects of Evaluation & Treatment. Ed. by Mary C. Singleton & Eleanor F. Branch. LC 87-21224. (Physical Therapy in Health Care Ser.). 105p. 1987. text ed. 18.95 (ISBN 0-86656-705-4). Haworth Pr.

Physical Therapy & the Stroke Patient: Pathologic Aspects & Clinical Management. Ed. by Mary C. Singleton & Eleanor F. Branch. LC 87-26668. (Physical Therapy in Health Care). 80p. 1987. text ed. 22.95 (ISBN 0-86656-740-2). Haworth Pr.

Physical Therapy Examination Review: Allied Health Bk. 4th ed. Ronald A. Hershey & Helen K. Seibert. (Vol. 18, No. 1). 1984. pap. text ed. 27.50 (ISBN 0-87488-142-0). Med Exam.

Physical Therapy Examination Review: Clinical Applications, Vol. 2. 3rd. ed. Eugene C. Rembe. (Allied Health Bks.: Vol. 18, No. 3). 1985. pap. 31.25 (ISBN 0-87488-164-1). Med Exam.

Physical Therapy for Sports. Ed. by Werner Kuprian. (Illus.). 400p. 1982. 55.00 (ISBN 0-7216-5553-X). Saunders.

Physical Therapy in the Home: Management, Evaluation & Treatment of Patients. Gretchen Veigh. (Illus.). 150p. cancelled (ISBN 0-932426-27-1). Trado-Medic.

Physical Therapy Licensure Examination Review. Jane E. Hogencamp & Patricia R. Evans. Date not set. price not set. Appleton & Lange.

Physical Therapy Management of Lower Extremity Amputations. Gertrude Mensch & Patricia Ellis. 384p. 1986. 44.50 (ISBN 0-87189-372-X). Aspen Pub.

Physical Therapy Manual. Homer Greene. LC 76-715. 1976. pap. 8.00 (ISBN 0-87125-032-2). Cath Health.

Physical Therapy of the Foot & Ankle: Vol. 15, CPT. Hunt. 1987. 35.00 (ISBN 0-443-08467-X). Churchill.

Physical Therapy of the Shoulder. Ed. by Robert Donatelli. (Clinics in Physical Therapy Ser.: Vol. 11). (Illus.). 317p. 1986. text ed. 36.00 (ISBN 0-443-08458-0). Churchill.

Physical Therapy Patient Care Audit Manual. 1980. looseleaf vinyl 17.50 (ISBN 0-912452-15-3). Am Phys Therapy Assn.

Physical Therapy Practice in Educational Environments: Policies, Guidelines, & Background Information-an Anthology. 1981. pap. 8.00 (ISBN 0-912452-31-5). Am Phys Therapy Assn.

Physical Therapy Procedures: Selected Techniques. 3rd ed. Ann H. Downer. (Illus.). 320p. 1981. 21.75x (ISBN 0-398-03840-6). C C Thomas.

Physical Therapy Procedures: Selected Techniques. 4th ed. Ann H. Downer. (Illus.). 336p. 1988. text ed. 24.75x (ISBN 0-398-05457-6). C C Thomas.

Physical Therapy Services in the Developmental Disabilities. Ed. by Paul H. Pearson & Carol E. Williams. (Illus.). 486p. 1980. 30.25 (ISBN 0-398-02377-8). C C Thomas.

Physical Training of the Soviet Soldier. Defense Intelligence Agency. (Illus.). 48p. 1987. pap. text ed. 8.00 (ISBN 0-87364-433-6). Paladin Pr.

Physical Treatises of Pascal. Blaise Pascal. Ed. by Frederick Barry. 1969. lib. bdg. 20.50x (ISBN 0-374-90418-9, Octagon). Hippocrene Bks.

Physical Ultrasonics. R. T. Beyer & S. V. Letcher. (Pure & Applied Physics Ser.: Vol. 32). 1969. 90.50 (ISBN 0-12-095050-2). Acad Pr.

Physical Universe. 4th ed. Konrad B. Krauskopf & Arthur Beiser. (Illus.). 1979. text ed. 38.95 (ISBN 0-07-035460-X). McGraw.

Physical Universe. 5th ed. Konrad B. Krauskopf & Arthur Beiser. 800p. 1986. text ed. 38.95 (ISBN 0-07-035484-7). McGraw.

Physical Universe. Frank H. Shu. LC 81-51271. (Astronomy Ser.). (Illus.). 584p. 1982. text ed. 44.00 (ISBN 0-935702-05-9). Univ Sci Bks.

Physical Volcanology. L. Civetta et al. (Developments in Solid Earth Geophysics Ser.: Vol. 6). 333p. 1974. 121.00 (ISBN 0-444-41141-0). Elsevier.

Physical Work Effort. Ed. by Gunnar Borg. LC 76-45405. 1977. 77.00 (ISBN 0-08-021373-1). Pergamon.

Physical World. Tony Seddon & Jill Bailey. LC 87-6855. (Illus.). 160p. (gr. 3 up). 1987. 12.95 (ISBN 0-385-24179-8). Doubleday.

Physical World. Ed. by Martin Sherwood & Christine Sutton. (Illus.). 256p. 1988. 35.00 (ISBN 0-19-520632-0). Oxford U Pr.

Physical World of Late Antiquity. S. Sambursky. 202p. 1987. text ed. 21.00 (ISBN 0-691-08476-9); pap. 8.95 (ISBN 0-691-02410-3). Princeton U Pr.

Physical World of the Greeks. S. Sambursky. 272p. 1987. text ed. 21.00 (ISBN 0-691-08477-7); pap. text ed. 8.95 (ISBN 0-691-02411-1). Princeton U Pr.

Physicality. Richard Benyo. 1987. write for info. (ISBN 0-8289-0612-2). Greene.

Physicality. Richard Benyo. 1987. pap. write for info. (ISBN 0-8289-0613-0). Greene.

Physically & Sexually Abused Child: Evaluation & Treatment. C. Eugene Walker et al. 208p. 1988. 23.50 (ISBN 0-08-032769-9, PBI); pap. 13.95 (ISBN 0-08-032768-0, PBI). Pergamon.

Physically Disabled Women & New Directions in Public Policy, 1977-1987. Mary J. Deegan. (Public Administration Ser.: P 2307). 17p. 1987. 5.00 (ISBN 1-55590-607-9). Vance Biblios.

Physically Handicapped Child: An Interdisciplinary Approach to Management. Gillian T. McCarthy. (Illus.). 384p. 1984. 29.95 (ISBN 0-571-13263-4); pap. 15.95 (ISBN 0-571-13204-9). Faber & Faber.

Physically Handicapped Children: A Medical Atlas for Teachers. 2nd ed. Ed. by Eugene E. Bleck & Donald Nagel. 560p. 1981. 39.50 (ISBN 0-8089-1391-3, 790623). Grune.

Physically Handicapped in India. Rama Mani. 1987. 32.00x (ISBN 0-317-67675-X, Pub. by Ashish India). South Asia Bks.

Physically Handicapped in India: Policy & Programme. Mani Rama. 223p. 1988. 26.50x (ISBN 81-7024-164-2, Pub. by Ashish India). South Asia Bks.

Physically Handicapped in Society Series, 39 bks. Ed. by William R. Phillips & Janet Rosenberg. 1980. Set. lib. bdg. 965.00x (ISBN 0-405-13100-3). Ayer Co Pubs.

Physician. Noah Gordon. 624p. 1986. 18.95 (ISBN 0-671-47748-X). S&S.

Physician. Noah Gordon. 640p. 1987. pap. 4.95 (ISBN 0-449-21426-5, Crest). Fawcett.

Physician. Jack Rudman. (Career Examination Ser.: C-1392). (Cloth bdg. avail. on request). pap. 27.95 (ISBN 0-8373-1392-9). Natl Learning.

Physician & Child-Rearing: Two Guides 1809-1894. William Buchan & Luther E. Holt. 1974. 16.00 (ISBN 0-405-03965-4, 15717). Ayer Co Pubs.

Physician & Cost Control. Edward Carels et al. LC 79-21736. 196p. 1979. text ed. 35.00 (ISBN 0-89946-005-4). Oelgeschlager.

Physician & Patient or a Practical View of the Mutual Duties, Relations & Interests of the Medical Profession & the Community. Worthington Hooker. LC 75-180577. (Medicine & Society in America Ser.). 456p. 1972. Repr. of 1849 ed. 25.00 (ISBN 0-405-03954-9). Ayer Co Pubs.

Physician & Sexuality in Victorian America. John S. Haller & Robin M. Haller. (Illus.). 1977. pap. 7.95x (ISBN 0-393-00845-2, Norton Lib). Norton.

Physician & Sexuality in Victorian America. John S. Haller, Jr. & Robin M. Haller. LC 73-2456. (Illus.). 346p. 1974. 29.95 (ISBN 0-252-00207-5). U of Ill Pr.

Physician & Sports Medicine Guide to Running. Allan J. Ryan. (Physician & Sports Medicine Guides). (Illus.). 1980. text ed. 7.95 (ISBN 0-07-054358-5). McGraw.

Physician & the Hopelessly Ill Patient: Legal, Medical & Ethical Guidelines. 96p. (Orig.). 1985. pap. 5.00x (ISBN 0-9613825-1-1). Soc Right to Die.

Physician As Captain of the Ship: A Critical Appraisal. Ed. by Nancy M. P. King et al. 270p. 1988. 59.00 (ISBN 1-55608-044-1, Pub. by Reidel Holland). Kluwer Academic.

Physician As Manager. 2nd ed. J. J. Aluise. (Illus.). xvi, 260p. 1986. 35.00 (ISBN 0-387-96381-2). Springer-Verlag.

Physician as Manager. John J. Aluise. 357p. 1980. 10.00 (ISBN 0-89303-006-6). Soc Tchrs Fam Med.

Physician As Teacher. Schwenk & Whitman. 203p. 1987. pap. 22.95 (ISBN 0-683-07613-2). Williams & Wilkins.

Physician Assistant in a Changing Health Care Environment. Gretchen E. Schafft & James F. Cawley. 1987. 32.00 (ISBN 0-87189-870-5). Aspen Pub.

Physician Assistants: Their Contribution to Health Care. Henry B. Perry & Bina Breitner. LC 81-6260. 331p. 1982. 39.95 (ISBN 0-89885-066-5). Human Sci Pr.

Physician Characteristics & Distribution in the U. S. American Medical Association Staff. (Orig.). 1987. pap. 45.00 (ISBN 0-89970-302-X, OP-180/7). AMA.

Physician Contacts by Sociodemographic & Health Characteristics, United States, 1982-1983 (PHS) 87-1589. Peter Ries. Ed. by Mary Olmsted. (Series 10: No. 161). 110p. Date not set. pap. text ed. 4.75 (ISBN 0-8406-0360-6). Natl Ctr Health Stats.

Physician Executive Compensation Report: A 1986 Survey of Salary & Benefits. David Kirschman & Jennifer Grebenschikoff. Ed. by Wesley Curry. 83p. (Orig.). 1987. pap. 95.00 (ISBN 0-9605218-2-8). Am Acad Med Dir.

Physician Extraordinary: Dr. Richard Bright (1789-1858) R. M. Kark. LC 86-62925. (Illus., Orig.). 1986. pap. text ed. 5.00 (ISBN 0-9614070-1-8). Horn Moon Ent.

Physician Faces Cancer in Himself. Samuel Sanes. LC 79-13124. 201p. 1979. 14.95x (ISBN 0-87395-395-9); pap. 8.95x (ISBN 0-87395-449-1). State U NY Pr.

Physician-Generals in the Civil War: A Study in Nineteenth Mid-Century American Medicine. photocopy ed. Paul E. Steiner. (Illus.). 216p. 1966. 24.75 (ISBN 0-398-01853-7). C C Thomas.

Physician, Heal Thyself. John Allegro. LC 85-43081. 93p. 1985. 15.95 (ISBN 0-87975-305-6). Prometheus Bks.

Physician, Heal Thyself! Thirty-Five Years of Adventures in Sobriety by an AA "Old-Timer". Earlem. 250p. (Orig.). 1988. pap. 9.95 (ISBN 0-89638-152-8). CompCare.

Physician Health & Effectiveness: New Directions. 170p. 1985. pap. 15.00 (ISBN 0-89970-259-7, OP-215). AMA.

Physician Himself & What He Should Add to His Scientific Acquirements. 2nd ed. D. W. Cathell. LC 70-180562. (Medicine & Society in America Ser). 216p. 1972. Repr. of 1882 ed. 16.00 (ISBN 0-405-03941-7). Ayer Co Pubs.

Physician-Hospital Joint Ventures. 59p. 1986. pap. 12.50 (ISBN 0-89970-222-8, OP-124). AMA.

Physician in Industry. William P. Shepard. Ed. by Leon Stein. LC 77-70532. (Work Ser.). 1977. Repr. of 1961 ed. lib. bdg. 30.00x (ISBN 0-405-10200-3). Ayer Co Pubs.

Physician in Literature. Norman Cousins. 500p. 1982. text ed. 17.95 (ISBN 0-7216-2739-0). Saunders.

Physician Location & Specialty Choice. Richard L. Ernst & Donald E. Yett. LC 85-5469. 338p. 1985. text ed. 20.00x (ISBN 0-910701-03-2, 0655). Health Admin Pr.

Physician Managers & the Law: Employment & Personal Service Contracts. Wesley Curry. 113p. 1988. pap. 48.00 (ISBN 0-9605218-4-4). Am Acad Med Dir.

Physician Marketplace Statistics. American Medical Association Staff. Ed. by Martin L. Gonzalez. (Orig.). 1988. pap. 295.00 (ISBN 0-89970-317-8, OP-229). AMA.

Physician of the Dance of Death: A Historical Study of the Evolution of the Dance of Death Mythus in Art. Alfred S. Warthin. Ed. by Robert Kastenbaum. LC 76-19592. (Death & Dying Ser.). (Illus.). 1977. Repr. of 1931 ed. lib. bdg. 17.00x (ISBN 0-405-09587-2). Ayer Co Pubs.

Physician-Oriented Review: Criteria Development & Analysis of Patient Care: QRB Special Edition. 64p. 1981. pap. 20.00 (ISBN 0-86688-049-6). Joint Comm Hlthcare.

Physician-Patient Decision-Making: A Study in Medical Ethics. Douglas N. Walton. LC 85-5412. (Contributions in Philosophy Ser.: No. 27). (Illus.). xv, 265p. 1985. lib. bdg. 36.95 (ISBN 0-313-24888-5, WPH/). Greenwood.

Physician-Patient Relations: Subject, Reference & Research Guidebook. Wayne C. Heier. LC 87-47637. 160p. 1987. 34.50 (ISBN 0-88164-576-1); pap. 26.50 (ISBN 0-88164-577-X). ABBE Pubs Assn.

Physician Practice Monitors. Eric D. Joseph et al. (Monitoring Sourcebook Ser.: Vol. 3). 1986. 98.00 (ISBN 0-916499-35-9). Care Comm Inc.

Physician Recruitment: Strategies That Work. Suzanne M. Lewitt. LC 82-4088. 222p. 1982. 35.95 (ISBN 0-89443-693-7). Aspen Pub.

Physician Services in the Long Term Care Facility. Carl E. Adman. 100p. 9.00 (ISBN 0-318-12750-4, 110023). Am Health Care Assn.

Physician Services: Productivity (PSP) Administrator's Handbook. Steven S. Layarus. Ed. by Center for Research in Ambulatory Health Care Administration Staff. 1987. pap. 48.00 (ISBN 0-933948-95-6). Ctr Res Ambulatory.

Physician Services: Productivity (PSP) User's Manual. Ed. by Center for Research in Ambulatory Health Care Administration Staff. 1987. pap. 48.00 (ISBN 0-933948-96-4). Ctr Res Ambulatory.

Physician Signers of the Declaration of Independence. Ed. by George E. Gifford, Jr. (Illus.). 1976. 14.95 (ISBN 0-88202-159-1). Watson Pub Intl.

Physician Supply & Utilization by Specialty. American Medical Association Staff & William D. Marder. LC 88-6272. (Orig.). 1988. pap. 30.00 (ISBN 0-89970-315-1). AMA.

Physician Visits: Volume & Interval Since Last Visit, United States, 1980. John G. Collins. Ed. by Audrey Shipp. 55p. 1983. pap. text ed. 4.50 (ISBN 0-8406-0276-6). Natl Ctr Health Stats.

Physician Visits: Volume & Interval Since Last Visit, U.S. 1971. Kathleen M. Danchik. LC 72-20716. (Data from the Health Interview Survey Ser. 10: No. 97). 55p. 1975. pap. text ed. 1.50 (ISBN 0-8406-0032-1). Natl Ctr Health Stats.

Physician Visits: Volume & Interval Since the Last Visit, United States-1975. Augustine Gentile. Ed. by Taloria Stevenson. (Ser. 10: No. 128). 1978. pap. text ed. 1.75 (ISBN 0-8406-0150-6). Natl Ctr Health Stats.

Physician Within. Cathy Feste. Ed. by Mike Moore. (Wellness Ser.). 176p. (Orig.). 1987. pap. 8.95 (ISBN 0-937721-19-0). Diabetes Ctr MN.

Physicians & Hospitals: Easing Adversary Relationships. Richard E. Thompson. LC 84-60124. 176p. 1984. text ed. 22.95 (ISBN 0-931028-49-3). Pluribus Pr.

Physicians & Hospitals: The Great Partnership at the Crossroads Based on the Ninth Private Sector Conference Held at Duke University in March 1984. Ed. by Duncan Yaggy & Patricia Hodgson. LC 84-25928. (Policy Studies). xxiii, 202p. 1985. 27.50 (ISBN 0-8223-0639-5). Duke.

Physicians & Social Change. John Colombotos & Corinne Kirchner. (Illus.). 282p. 1986. 35.00x (ISBN 0-19-503685-9). Oxford U Pr.

Physicians & Sportsmedicine Guide to Raquetball & Squash. Robert S. Scott. (Physician & Sportsmedicine Guides). (Illus.). 1980. text ed. 7.95 (ISBN 0-07-055586-9). McGraw.

Physicians & the Military: A Study of Contact, Awareness, & Interest. Richard J. Willke & Phillip R. Kletke. LC 87-30835. 80p. (Orig.). 1987. pap. write for info. (ISBN 0-89970-287-2). AMA.

Physician's Anthology of English & American Poetry. Casey A. Wood & Fielding H. Garrison. 1979. Repr. of 1920 ed. lib. bdg. 25.00 (ISBN 0-8495-5734-8). Arden Lib.

Physician's Assistant. Jack Rudman. (Career Examination Ser.: C-2557). (Cloth bdg. avail. on request). pap. 19.95 (ISBN 0-8373-2557-9). Natl Learning.

Physician's Assistant, No. 1210-1211. Diane V. Lloyd & Marta B. Stavrou. 1977. 10.00 (ISBN 0-686-19685-6). CPL Biblios.

Physician's Assistant Examination Review & Patient Management Problems. Ed. by R. R. Rahr & B. R. Niebuhr. (Allied Health Ser.: Vol. 29). 284p. 1986. pap. 32.50 (ISBN 0-444-01071-8, Med Exam). Elsevier.

Physicians Assistant Examination Review. Thomas D. Aschenbrener & Paul Mosan. LC 78-26893. 144p. 1980. pap. 16.95 (ISBN 0-668-04026-2). Appleton & Lange.

Physician's Book Compendium, 1969-1970: The Medical Book Reference for Physicians. Ed. by Max Celnik. Inaugural Edition. pap. 160.00 (2027106). Bks Demand UMI.

Physician's Book of Lists. David Margulies & Malcolm Thaler. (Illus.). 288p. 1983. pap. 22.00 (ISBN 0-443-08178-6). Churchill.

Physician's Covenant: Images of the Healer in Medical Ethics. William F. May. LC 83-16992. 204p. 1983. pap. 10.95 (ISBN 0-664-24497-1). Westminster John Knox.

Physicians' Desk Reference, 1988. 42nd ed. Ed. by Ed Barnhart. 1988. 38.95 (ISBN 0-87489-844-7). Med Economics.

Physicians Drug Handbook. 21.95 (ISBN 0-317-66164-7). Springhouse Pub.

Physicians' Guide to Aging: The Immune System & Free Radical Damage. Lee-Benner. 1986. lib. bdg. 125.00 (ISBN 0-944213-00-6). World Hlth Found.

Physician's Guide to Better Communication. Barbara F. Sharf. (PROCOM Ser.). 1984. pap. 9.95 (ISBN 0-673-15559-5). Scott F.

Physicians Guide to Cancer Care Complications. Laszlo. (Fundamentals of Cancer Management Ser.). 480p. 1986. 69.75 (ISBN 0-8247-7547-3). Dekker.

Physician's Guide to Diving Medicine. Ed. by Charles W. Shilling et al. LC 84-14817. 768p. 1984. 125.00x (ISBN 0-306-41428-7, Plenum Pr). Plenum Pub.

Physician's Guide to Drugs. Ed. by Robert J. Shakno. LC 83-62695. 248p. 1984. pap. text ed. 24.95 (ISBN 0-931028-41-8). Pluribus Pr.

Physics, Pt. 2. 3rd ed. Robert Resnick. 1089p. (Bahasa-Malaysia.). 1986. pap. write for info. (ISBN 0-471-08322-4). Wiley.

Physics: A Basic Course, High School Sophomore Level (Grade 10) Dale Crane. LC 86-22225. (ABC (A Basic Course) Ser.). (Illus., Orig.). 1986. pap. text ed. 8.95 (ISBN 0-914565-23-0). Capstan Pubns.

Physics: A General Course, Vol. 1. I. Savelyev. 1980. 9.45 (ISBN 0-8285-1829-7, Pub. by Mir Pubs USSR). Imported Pubns.

Physics: A General Course, Vol. 2. I. Savelyev. 1980. 9.45 (ISBN 0-8285-1832-7, Pub. by Mir Pubs USSR). Imported Pubns.

Physics: A General Course, Vol. 3. I. Savelyev. 1981. 12.00 (ISBN 0-8285-1935-8, Pub. by Mir Pubs USSR). Imported Pubns.

Physics: A General Introduction. 2nd ed. Alan Van Heuvelen. 1986. text ed. write for info. (ISBN 0-673-39556-1). write for info. study guide (ISBN 0-673-39557-X). Scott F.

Physics: A Laboratory Textbook. 2nd ed. Howard Carr & Marllin Simon. (Illus.). 1981. pap. text ed. 17.95x lab. manual (ISBN 0-89892-039-6). Contemp Pub Co of Raleigh.

Physics: An Introduction. Jay S. Bolemon. (Illus.). 692p. 1985. text ed. write for info. (ISBN 0-13-672221-0). P-H.

Physics & Applications of Amorphous Semiconductors. Arun Madan & Melvin P. Shaw. 450p. 1988. 69.50 (ISBN 0-12-464960-2). Acad Pr.

Physics & Applications of Amorphous Semiconductors: Proceedings of the Workshop, Torino, Villa Gualino, Italy. Ed. by F. Demichells. 408p. 1988. 62.00 (ISBN 9971-50-550-9). World Scientific Pub.

Physics & Applications of Quantum Wells & Superlattices. Ed. by E. E. Mendez & K. Von Klitzing. (NATO ASI Series B, Physics: Vol. 170). (Illus.). 442p. 1988. 89.50x (ISBN 0-306-42823-7, Plenum Pr). Plenum Pub.

Physics & Applications of the Josephson Effect. Antonio Barone & Gianfranco Paterno. LC 81-7554. 529p. 1982. 74.95x (ISBN 0-471-01469-9). Wiley.

Physics & Astrophysics: A Selection of Key Problems. V. L. Ginzburg. Tr. by O. Glebov & G. Ter Haar. 144p. 1985. pap. text ed. 17.50 (ISBN 0-08-026499-9). Pergamon.

Physics & Astrophysics of Neutron Stars & Black Holes: Proceedings. Giacconi & R. Ruffini. (Enrico Fermi Summer School Ser.: Vol. 65). 876p. 1980. pap. 81.75 (ISBN 0-444-85446-0, North-Holland). Elsevier.

Physics & Beyond. Werner Heisenberg. (World Perspectives Ser.). pap. 8.95x (ISBN 0-06-131622-9, TB1622, Torch). Har-Row.

Physics & Biology. M. V. Volkenstein. 1982. 31.00 (ISBN 0-12-723140-4). Acad Pr.

Physics & Chemistry at Upper Atmospheres: Proceedings. Summer Advanced Study Institute Symposium, University of Orleans, France, July 31-Aug. 11, 1972. Ed. by B. M. McCormac. LC 72-92533. (Astrophysics & Space Science Library: No. 35). 385p. 1973. lib. bdg. 60.50 (ISBN 90-277-0283-7, Pub. by Reidel Holland). Kluwer Academic.

Physics & Chemistry of Aqueous Ionic Solutions. M. C. Bellisent-Funel & G. W. Neilson. 1987. lib. bdg. 99.00 (ISBN 90-277-2534-9, Pub. by Reidel Holland). Kluwer Academic.

Physics & Chemistry of Baking. 3rd ed. Ed. by K. J. Dean et al. (Illus.). vii, 230p. 1980. 36.00 (ISBN 0-85334-867-7, Pub. by Elsevier Applied Sci England). Elsevier.

Physics & Chemistry of Ceramics. Ed. by Cyrus Klingsberg. 372p. (Orig.). 1963. 125.00 (ISBN 0-677-10210-0). Gordon & Breach.

Physics & Chemistry of Color: The Fifteen Causes of Color. Kurt Nassau. LC 83-10580. (Pure & Applied Optics Ser.). 454p. 1983. 54.95x (ISBN 0-471-86776-4, 1-349). Wiley.

Physics & Chemistry of Electrons & Ionsin Condensed Matter. Ed. by J. V. Acrivos. 768p. 1984. 99.00 (ISBN 90-277-1799-0, Pub. by Reidel Holland). Kluwer Academic.

Physics & Chemistry of Fission: 1969. (Proceedings Ser.). (Illus.). 983p. (Orig.). 1969. pap. 68.00 (ISBN 92-0-030269-6, ISP234, IAEA). UNIPUB.

Physics & Chemistry of Fission: 1973, 2 vols. (Proceedings Ser.). (Illus.). 579p. (Orig.). 1974. Vol. 1. pap. 49.25 (ISBN 92-0-030074-X, ISP347-1, IAEA); Vol. 2. pap. 45.75 (ISBN 92-0-030174-6, ISP347-2). UNIPUB.

Physics & Chemistry of Fission: 1979, 2 vols. (Proceedings Ser.). 1980. pap. 87.75 (ISBN 92-0-030080-4, ISP526 1, IAEA); pap. 70.75 (ISBN 92-0-030180-0, ISP526 2). UNIPUB.

Physics & Chemistry of III-V Compound Semiconductor Interfaces. Ed. by Carl W. Wilmsen. LC 85-6598. 480p. 1985. 69.50x (ISBN 0-306-41769-3, Plenum Pr). Plenum Pub.

Physics & Chemistry of Liquid Crystal Devices. Ed. by Gerald J. Sprokel. LC 80-12097. (IBM Research Symposia Ser.). 362p. 1980. 65.00x (ISBN 0-306-40440-0, Plenum Pr). Plenum Pub.

Physics & Chemistry of Low Dimensional Solids. Ed. by Luis Alcacer. (NATO Advanced Study Institute Ser. C: Mathematical & Physical Sciences: No. 56). 436p. 1980. lib. bdg. 50.00 (ISBN 90-277-1144-5, Pub. by Reidel Holland). Kluwer Academic.

Physics & Chemistry of Minerals & Rocks. NATO Advanced Study Institute (1974: Newcastle upon Tyne) Staff. Ed. by R. G. Strens. LC 75-6930. (Illus.). 715p. pap. 160.00 (2030471). Bks Demand UMI.

Physics & Chemistry of Porous Media II. Ed. by Jayanth R. Banavar et al. LC 83-73640. (AIP Conference Proceedings: No. 154). 336p. 1987. lib. bdg. 55.50 (ISBN 0-88318-354-4). Am Inst Physics.

Physics & Chemistry of Porous Media: Schlumberger-Doll Research, 1983. Ed. by D. L. Johnson & P. N. Sen. LC 83-73640. (AIP Conference Proceedings: No. 107). 223p. 1984. lib. bdg. 37.50 (ISBN 0-88318-306-4). Am Inst Physics.

Physics & Chemistry of Protective Coatings. Ed. by W. D. Sproul et al. LC 86-72019. (AIP Conference Proceedings Ser.: No. 149). 192p. 1986. lib. bdg. 48.00 (ISBN 0-88318-348-X). Am Inst Physics.

Physics & Chemistry of Small Clusters. Ed. by P. Jena et al. LC 87-14199. (NATO ASI Series B, Physics: Vol. 158). (Illus.). 972p. 1987. 145.00x (ISBN 0-306-42606-4, Plenum Pr). Plenum Pub.

Physics & Chemistry of Sugar-Beet in Sugar Manufacture. Konstantin Vukov. LC 76-7400. 596p. 1977. 147.50 (ISBN 0-444-99836-5). Elsevier.

Physics & Chemistry of the Inorganic Azides see Energetic Materials.

Physics & Chemistry of the Upper Atmosphere. M. H. Rees. (Illus.). 350p. Date not set. price not set (ISBN 0-521-32305-3); pap. price not set (ISBN 0-521-36848-0). Cambridge U Pr.

Physics & Contemporary Needs, Vol. 5. Ed. by Riazuddin & Asghar Qadir. 638p. 1982. 95.00x (ISBN 0-306-40905-4, Plenum Pr). Plenum Pub.

Physics & Contemporary Needs, Vol. 6. Ed. by A. M. Khan et al. 476p. 1984. 85.00x (ISBN 0-306-41631-X, Plenum Pr). Plenum Pub.

Physics & Contemporary Needs: Proceedings of the International Nathiagali Summer College, Islamabad, August 1982, Vol. 7. Ed. by M. N. Qazi. 400p. 1985. 51.00 (ISBN 9971-966-83-2). World Scientific Pub.

Physics & Dynamics of Meteors: Proceedings of the I.A.U. Symposium, No. 33, Tatransks, Lomnica, Czechoslovakia, 1967. International Astronomical Union Staff. Ed. by L. Kresak & P. M. Millman. LC 68-26965. (IAU Symposia). 525p. 1968. lib. bdg. 53.00 (ISBN 90-277-0127-X, Pub. by Reidel Holland). Kluwer Academic.

Physics & Engineering of Computerized Multidimensional Imaging & Processing. Ed. by Nalcioglu. 337p. 1986. 57.00 (ISBN 0-89252-706-4, 671). SPIE.

Physics & Engineering of Medical Imaging. Ed. by Riccardo Guzzardi. 1987. lib. bdg. 210.00 (ISBN 90-247-3454-1, Pub. by Martinus Nijhoff Netherlands). Kluwer Academic.

Physics & Fabrication of Microstructures & Microdevices. Ed. by M. J. Kelly & C. Weisbuch. (Springer Proceedings in Physics Ser.: Vol. 13). (Illus.). 480p. 1986. 54.50 (ISBN 0-387-16898-2). Springer-Verlag.

Physics & General Science. (National Teachers Examination Ser.: NT-7B). Date not set. pap. 13.95 (ISBN 0-8373-8410-9). Natl Learning.

Physics & General Science - Sr. H.S. Jack Rudman. (Teachers License Examination Ser.: T-46). (Cloth bdg. avail. on request). pap. 13.95 (ISBN 0-8373-8046-4). Natl Learning.

Physics & Geometry of Disorder: Percolation Theory. A. L. Efros. 259p. 1986. 5.95 (ISBN 0-8285-3291-5, Pub. by Mir Pubs USSR). Imported Pubns.

Physics & Heat Technology of Reactors. Consultants Bureau Staff. LC 59-958. (Soviet Journal of Atomic Energy. Supplement 1958: No. 1). pap. 45.00 (ISBN 0-317-08314-7, 2020654). Bks Demand UMI.

Physics & Human Affairs. Art Hobson. LC 81-11407. 418p. 1982. text ed. 33.50 (ISBN 0-471-04746-5); tchrs.' ed. avail. (ISBN 0-471-09706-3). Wiley.

Physics & Its Fifth Dimension: Society. Dietrich Schroeer. LC 75-184158. 1972. pap. text ed. write for info. (ISBN 0-201-06767-6). Addison-Wesley.

Physics & Material Problems of Reactor Control Rods. (Proceedings Ser.). (Illus.). 792p. 1964. 43.00 (ISBN 92-0-050364-0, ISP81, IAEA). UNIPUB.

Physics & Mechanics of Ice: Proceedings. Symposium Copenhagen, Technical University of Denmark, August 6-10, 1979. Ed. by P. Tryde. (IUTAM Ser.). (Illus.). 378p. 1980. 43.70 (ISBN 3-540-09906-9). Springer-Verlag.

Physics & Nondestructive Testing, Vol. 1. Ed. by Warren J. McGonnagle. 578p. 1967. 138.00 (ISBN 0-677-10580-0). Gordon & Breach.

Physics & Nondestructive Testing, Vol. 2. Ed. by Warren J. McGonnagle. LC 65-27852. (Illus.). 302p. 1972. 92.00x (ISBN 0-677-15250-7). Gordon & Breach.

Physics & Nondestructive Testing, Vol. 3. Ed. by Warren J. McGonnagle. LC 65-27852. (Illus.). 338p. 1972. 92.00 (ISBN 0-677-15260-4). Gordon & Breach.

Physics & Our World: A Symposium in Honor of Victor F. Weisskopf MIT 1974. Ed. by Kerson Huang. LC 76-7207. (AIP Conference Proceeding: No. 28). 164p. 1976. 15.00 (ISBN 0-88318-127-4). Am Inst Physics.

Physics & Philosophy. James Jeans. 232p. 1981. pap. 4.95 (ISBN 0-486-24117-3). Dover.

Physics & Philosophy: Selected Essays. Henry Margenau. (Episteme: No. 6). 1978. lib. bdg. 39.50 (ISBN 90-277-0901-7, Pub. by Reidel Holland). Kluwer Academic.

Physics & Philosophy: The Revolution in Modern Science. Werner Heisenberg. (World Perspectives Ser.). pap. 8.95x (ISBN 0-06-130549-9, TB549, Torch). Har-Row.

Physics & Physical Chemistry of Water see Water: A Comprehensive Treatise.

Physics & Politics. Walter Bagehot. 1881. 39.00 (ISBN 0-932062-08-3). Sharon Hill.

Physics & Politics or Thoughts on the Application of the Principles of "Natural Selection" & "Inheritance" to Political Society. Walter Bagehot. (Illus.). 138p. 1986. Repr. of 1900 ed. lib. bdg. 50.00 (ISBN 0-8495-0644-1). Arden Lib.

Physics & Psyche. C. D. Curling. 1985. 10.00x (ISBN 0-317-62095-9, Guild of Pastoral Psych). State Mutual Bk.

Physics & Technology of Amorphous SiO2. Ed. by R. A. Devine. (Illus.). 578p. 1988. 97.50x (ISBN 0-306-42929-2, Plenum Pr). Plenum Pub.

Physics & Technology of Hyperthermia. Ed. by Stanley B. Field & Cafiero Franconi. 1987. lib. bdg. 134.00 (ISBN 90-247-3509-2, Pub. by Martinus Nijhoff Netherlands). Kluwer Academic.

Physics & Technology of Ion Motors. AGARD-NATO Staff. (Agardographs Ser.: No. 88). (Illus.). 438p. 1966. 152.00 (ISBN 0-677-10570-3). Gordon & Breach.

Physics & Technology of Low-Temperature Plasmas. A. V. Donski et al. Ed. by S. V. Dresvin & H. U. Eckert. Tr. by T. Cheron from Rus. (Illus.). 1977. text ed. 29.95x (ISBN 0-8138-1950-4). Iowa St U Pr.

Physics & Technology of Nuclear Materials. I. Ursu. (Illus.). 534p. 1985. text ed. 83.00 (ISBN 0-08-032601-3, Pub. by PPL). Pergamon.

Physics & Technology of Semiconductor Devices. A. S. Grove. 366p. 1967. 46.25 (ISBN 0-471-32998-3). Wiley.

Physics & Technology of Xerographic Processes. Edgar M. Wlliams. LC 83-26077. 288p. 1984. text ed. 46.95x (ISBN 0-471-88080-9, Pub. by Wiley Interscience). Wiley.

Physics & the Architecture of Cell Membranes. R. C. Warren. 240p. 1987. pap. 41.00x (ISBN 0-85274-446-3, Pub. by A Hilger UK). Taylor & Francis.

Physics & the Circulation. J. O. Rowan. Ed. by J. A. Leniham. (Medical Physics Handbooks Ser.: No. 9). (Illus.). 148p. 1981. 36.00x (ISBN 0-85274-508-7, Pub. by A Hilger UK). Taylor & Francis.

Physics & the Earth's Interior. Ed. by A. Dziewonski & E. Boschi. (Enrico Fermi Summer School Ser.: No. 78). 720p. 1980. 210.75 (ISBN 0-444-85461-4, North-Holland). Elsevier.

Physics & the Physical Universe. 3rd ed. Jerry B. Marion. LC 79-9387. 446p. 1980. text ed. 38.95 (ISBN 0-471-03430-4); pap. 13.45 study guide (ISBN 0-471-05815-7); answers avail. (ISBN 0-471-05818-1). Wiley.

Physics & the Sound of Music. 2nd ed. John S. Rigden. LC 84-10401. 353p. 1985. 29.95x (ISBN 0-471-87412-4). Wiley.

Physics & the Ultimate Significance of Time: Bohm, Prigogine, & Process Philosophy. Ed. by David R. Griffin. LC 85-2782. 322p. 1985. 49.50 (ISBN 0-88706-113-3); pap. 16.95x (ISBN 0-88706-115-X). State U NY Pr.

Physics: Answers to Problems. Hans C. Ohanian. (Orig.). 1986. pap. text ed. 2.95x (ISBN 0-393-95587-7). Norton.

Physics Applied to Anaesthesia. 4th ed. D. W. Hill. LC 80-40011. (Illus.). 420p. 1980. text ed. 75.00 (ISBN 0-407-00188-3). Butterworth.

Physics Around You. 2nd ed. Dale D. Long. 587p. 1988. text ed. write for info. (ISBN 0-534-08670-5). Wadsworth Pub.

Physics As Metaphor. Roger S. Jones. LC 81-16496. (Illus.). 256p. 1982. 15.95 (ISBN 0-8166-1076-2). U of Minn Pr.

Physics As Metaphor. Roger S. Jones. 1983. pap. 7.95 (ISBN 0-452-00721-6, Mer). NAL.

Physics As Natural Philosophy: Essays in Honor of Laszlo Tisza. Ed. by Abner Shimony & Herman Feshbach. 448p. 1983. text ed. 60.00x (ISBN 0-262-19208-X). MIT Pr.

Physics at DePauw University. Ed. by Clifton J. Phillips. (Sesquicentennial Ser.: No. 6). (Illus.). 44p. (Orig.). 1987. pap. write for info. (ISBN 0-936631-05-8). DePauw Univ.

Physics at LEAR with Low-Energy Cooled Antiprotons. Ed. by Ugo Gastaldi & Robert Klapisch. (Ettore Majorana International Science Series, Physical Sciences: Vol. 17). 902p. 1984. 135.00x (ISBN 0-306-41384-1, Plenum Pr). Plenum Pub.

Physics at Surfaces. A. Zangwill. (Illus.). 350p. 1988. 69.50 (ISBN 0-521-32147-6); 27.95 (ISBN 0-521-34752-1). Cambridge U Pr.

Physics-Based Modeling of Lakes, Reservoirs & Impoundments. Ed. by William G Gray. 308p. 1986. 38.00x (ISBN 0-87262-531-1). Am Soc Civil Eng.

Physics: Building a World View. reference ed. Gerald Wheeler & Larry Kirkpatrick. (Illus.). 576p. 1983. write for info. (ISBN 0-13-672204-0). P-H.

Physics Careers, Employment & Education. Conference on Changing Career Opportunities, Pennsylvania State Univ., Aug. 1977. Ed. by Martin L. Perl. LC 77-9403. (AIP Conference Proceedings: No. 39). (Illus.). 1978. lib. bdg. 18.50 (ISBN 0-88318-138-X). Am Inst Physics.

Physics: Concepts & Consequences. R. L. Murray & G. C. Cobb. (American Nuclear Society Textbook Ser.). 710p. text ed. 13.95 (ISBN 0-13-672501-5, 350004). Am Nuclear Soc.

Physics: Demonstration Experiments, 2 vols. Ed. by Harry F. Meiners. LC 84-23409. 1518p. 1985. Repr. of 1970 ed. lib. bdg. 106.50 (ISBN 0-89874-821-6). Krieger.

Physics Dictionary, 3 vols. R. Sube & G. Eisenreich. 2895p. 1980. 185.00x (ISBN 0-569-07879-2, Pub. by Collets (UK)). State Mutual Bk.

Physics Dictionary, 3 vols. Ed. by R. Sube & G. Eisenreich. (Eng., Ger., Fr. & Rus.). 1974. 390.00x (ISBN 3-87144-143-0). Adlers Foreign Bks.

Physics: Elementary. 3rd, rev. ed. Weidner & Sells. 1988. Physics Part II. pap. text ed. 60.00 (ISBN 0-205-10455-X). Allyn.

Physics Experiments for Children. Muriel Mandell. LC 68-9308. Orig. Title: Science for Children. (Illus.). (gr. 3-10). 1968. pap. 2.75 (ISBN 0-486-22033-8). Dover.

Physics Experiments for Laboratory & Life. Philip R. Hetland. 144p. 1978. pap. text ed. 12.95 (ISBN 0-8403-1907-X). Kendall-Hunt.

Physics: Extended Version. Richard Wolfson & Jay M. Pasachoff. 1989. text ed. price not set (ISBN 0-673-39836-6). Scott F.

Physics, Fabrication, & Applications of Multilayered Structures. Ed. by P. Dhez & C. Weisbuch. (NATO ASI Series B, Physics: Vol. 182). (Illus.). 404p. 1988. 89.50x (ISBN 0-306-42995-0, Plenum Pr). Plenum Pub.

Physics for a New Century: Papers Presented at the 1904 St. Louis Congress. Intro. by Katherine R. Sopka. LC 85-28623. (History of Modern Physics, 1800-1950 Ser.). (Illus.). 320p. 1986. Repr. text ed. 30.00 (ISBN 0-88318-487-7). Am Inst Physics.

Physics for Anaesthetists. James Duffin. (Illus.). 296p. 1976. 34.00x (ISBN 0-398-03451-6). C C Thomas.

Physics for Biology & Medicine. I. W. Richardson & Ejler B. Neergaard. LC 76-180711. (Illus.). 257p. pap. 66.90 (2030538). Bks Demand UMI.

Physics for Career Education. 2nd ed. Dale Ewen & Neill Schurter. (Illus.). 448p. 1982. write for info. (ISBN 0-13-672329-2). P-H.

Physics for Career Education. 3rd ed. Dale Ewen et al. (Illus.). 448p. 1988. text ed. price not set (ISBN 0-13-672429-9). P-H.

Physics for Computer Science Students: With Emphasis on Atomic & Semiconductor Physics. Narciso Garcia & Arthur C. Damask. LC 85-31527. 528p. 1986. 34.95 (ISBN 0-471-82131-4). Wiley.

Physics for Divers. Fred Calhoun. (Illus.). 1978. pap. 4.50 (ISBN 0-916974-28-6). NAUI.

Physics for Engineering Technology. 2nd ed. Alexander Joseph et al. LC 76-55696. 629p. 1978. write for info. (ISBN 0-471-45075-8). Wiley.

Physics for Everyone. L. D. Landau & A. J. Kitaigorsky. 250p. 1980. Set. 63.00x (ISBN 0-317-46679-8, Pub. by Collets (UK)). State Mutual Bk.

Physics for Everyone: Electrons. A. I. Kitaigorodsky. 1981. 6.60 (ISBN 0-8285-1904-8, Pub. by Mir Pubs USSR). Imported Pubns.

Physics for Everyone: Molecules. L. Landau & A. I. Kitaigorodsky. 224p. 1980. 6.60 (ISBN 0-8285-1725-8, Pub. by Mir Pubs USSR). Imported Pubns.

Physics for Everyone: Photons & Nuclei. A. I. Kitaigorodsky. 235p. 1981. 6.60 (ISBN 0-8285-1996-X, Pub. by Mir Pubs USSR). Imported Pubns.

Physics for Everyone: Physical Bodies. L. Landau & A. I. Kitaigorodsky. 248p. 1980. 6.60 (ISBN 0-8285-1716-9, Pub. by Mir Pubs USSR). Imported Pubns.

Physics for Modern Architecture. David Hafemeister & A. Buffa. 1983. perfect bdg. 10.75 (ISBN 0-317-11346-1). Paladin Hse.

Physics for Modern World. A. J. Hirsch. 642p. 1986. 37.45 (ISBN 0-471-79747-2). Wiley.

Physics for Poets. 2nd ed. Robert H. March. (Illus.). 1977. text ed. 38.95 (ISBN 0-07-040243-4). McGraw.

Physics for Poets. Robert H. March. (Illus.). 304p. 1983. pap. 11.95 (ISBN 0-8092-5532-4). Contemp Bks.

Physics for Radiologists. Dendy & Heaton. 1986. 35.50 (ISBN 0-8016-1411-2). Mosby.

Physics for Rural Development: A Sourcebook for Teachers & Extension Workers in Developing Countries. Digby G. Swift. LC 82-2748. 257p. 1983. 48.95x (ISBN 0-471-10364-0, Pub. by Wiley-Interscience). Wiley.

Physics for Scientists & Engineers. 2nd ed. Douglas C. Giancoli. (Illus.). 992p. 1988. text ed. price not set (ISBN 0-13-669201-X). P-H.

Physics of Geomagnetic Phenomena, 2 Vols. Ed. by S. Matsushita & W. H. Campbell. (International Geophysics Ser.: Vol. 11). 1967. Vol. 1. 98.00 (ISBN 0-12-480301-6); Vol. 2, 1968. 98.50 (ISBN 0-12-480302-4). Acad Pr.

Physics of Glaciers 2nd ed. W. S. Paterson. (Illus.). vii, 380p. 1981. text ed. 65.00 (ISBN 0-08-024005-4); pap. text ed. 21.95 (ISBN 0-08-024004-6). Pergamon.

Physics of Glassy Polymers. Ed. by R. N. Haward. (Illus.). 620p. 1973. 133.25 (ISBN 0-85334-565-1, Pub. by Elsevier Applied Sci England). Elsevier.

Physics of Graphite. B. T. Kelly. (Illus.). 477p. 1981. 126.00 (ISBN 0-85334-960-6, Pub. by Elsevier Applied Sci England). Elsevier.

Physics of Gravitating Systems: Vol. 1 - Equilibrium & Stability of Gravitating Systems. A. M. Fridman & V. I. Polyachenko. Tr. by A. B. Aries & I. N. Poliakoff. (Illus.). 480p. 1984. 110.00 (ISBN 0-387-11045-3). Springer Verlag.

Physics of Gravitating Systems: Vol. 2 - The Nonlinear Theory of Collective Processes in a Gravitating Medium: Astrophysical Application. A. M. Fridman & V. L. Polyachenko. Tr. by A. B. Aries & I. N. Poliakoff. (Illus.). 385p. 1984. 100.00 (ISBN 0-387-13103-5). Springer Verlag.

Physics of High Energy Density. Ed. by P. Caldirola & H. Knoepfel. (Italian Physical Society: Course 48). 1971. 95.00 (ISBN 0-12-368848-5). Acad Pr.

Physics of High Energy Particle Accelerators: BNL-SUNY Summer School. Ed. by Melvin Month et al. LC 85-70057. (AIP Conference Proceedings: No. 127). 970p. 1985. lib. bdg. 65.00 (ISBN 0-88318-326-9). Am Inst Physics.

Physics of High Energy Particle Accelerators: Proceedings of the AIP Conference, No. 87, Fermilab School. American Institute of Physics. Ed. by R. A. Carrigan et al. LC 82-72421. 960p. 1982. lib. bdg. 48.00 (ISBN 0-88318-186-X). Am Inst Physics.

Physics of High Energy Particle Accelerators: SLAC Summer School, 1982, No. 105. Melvin Month. LC 83-72986. (AIP Conference Proceedings: No. 105). 1102p. 1983. lib. bdg. 55.50 (ISBN 0-88318-304-8). Am Inst Physics.

Physics of High Temperature Plasmas. 2nd ed. George Schmidt. 1979. 47.00 (ISBN 0-12-626660-3). Acad Pr.

Physics of High Temperature Reactors. L. Massimo. 1975. 57.00 (ISBN 0-08-019616-0). Pergamon.

Physics of Highly Charged Ions. R. K. Janev et al. (Springer Series in Electrophysics: Vol. 13). (Illus.). 350p. 1985. 62.00 (ISBN 0-387-12559-0). Springer-Verlag.

Physics of Highly Excited States in Solids: Proceedings. Oji Seminar, Tomakomai, Japan, Sept. 9-13, 1975. Ed. by M. Ueta & Y. Nishina. (Lecture Notes in Physics: Vol. 57). 1976. soft cover 21.00 (ISBN 0-387-07991-2). Springer-Verlag.

Physics of Hydrogenated Amorphous Silicon II. Ed. by J. D. Joannopoulos & G. Lucovsky. (Topics in Applied Physics Ser.: No. 56). (Illus.). 385p. 1984. 59.00 (ISBN 0-387-12808-5). Springer-Verlag.

Physics of Hydrogenated Amorphous Silicon I. Ed. by J. D. Joannopoulos & G. Lucovsky. (Topics in Applied Physics: Vol. 55). (Illus.). 320p. 1984. 59.00 (ISBN 0-387-12807-7). Springer Verlag.

Physics of Intercalation Compounds: Proceedings. Ed. by L. Pictronero & E. Tosatti. (Springer Series in Solid-State Sciences: Vol. 38). (Illus.). 323p. 1981. 31.00 (ISBN 0-387-11283-9). Springer-Verlag.

Physics of Ion-Ion & Electron-Ion Collisions. Ed. by F. Brouillard. (NATO ASI Series B, Physics: Vol. 83). 550p. 1983. 89.50x (ISBN 0-306-41105-9, Plenum Pr). Plenum Pub.

Physics of Ionized Gases: Proceeding of the XII International Symposium on the Physics of Ionized Gases (SPIG) 84 Yugoslavia, Sept. 1984. Ed. by M. Popovic. 1024p. 1985. 109.00 (ISBN 9971-50-001-9). World Scientific Pub.

Physics of Ionized Glass: Proceedings of the XIII Symposium on Sibenik, Yugoslavia, September 1-5, 1986. Ed. by M. Popovic. 528p. 1987. 90.00 (ISBN 9971-50-292-5). World Scientific Pub.

Physics of Laser Fusion. H. Motz. 1979. 78.50 (ISBN 0-12-509350-0). Acad Pr.

Physics of Laser Plasma Interactions. William L. Kruer. 182p. 1988. 40.95 (ISBN 0-201-15672-5). Addison-Wesley.

Physics of Latent Image Formation in Silver Halides: Proceedings of the 3rd Symposium, Trieste Italy, 1983. Ed. by W. Czaja & A. Baldereschi. 240p. 1984. 31.00 (ISBN 9971-966-34-4). World Scientific Pub.

Physics of Magmatic Processes. Ed. by R. B. Hargraves. LC 80-7525. (Illus.). 800p. 1980. 73.00x (ISBN 0-691-08259-6); pap. 26.95x (ISBN 0-691-08261-8). Princeton U Pr.

Physics of Magnetic Garnets. Ed. by A. Paoletti. (Enrico Fermi International Summer School of Physics Ser.: Course 70, 1977). 546p. 1979. 147.50 (ISBN 0-444-85200-X, North Holland). Elsevier.

Physics of Magnetic Materials. Ed. by J. Rauluszkiewicz et al. LC 85-2300. 592p. 1985. 69.00 (ISBN 9971-978-34-2). World Scientific Pub.

Physics of Magnetic Materials: Proceedings of the International Symposium on Physics of Magnetic Materials. Ed. by S. Mackawa. 620p. 1987. 83.00 (ISBN 9971-50-358-1). World Scientific Pub.

Physics of Magnetic Materials: Proceedings of the Third International Conference on Physics of Magnetic Materials, Szczyrk-Bila, Poland 9-14 September 1986. Ed. by W. Gorzkowski et al. 600p. 1987. 85.00 (ISBN 9971-50-188-0, Z0329P-P). World Scientific Pub.

Physics of Magnetic Materials: Proceedings of the 4th International Conference. Ed. by W. Gorzkowski et al. 600p. 1989. 78.00 (ISBN 9971-50-696-3). World Scientific Pub.

Physics of Magnetic Recording. C. D. Mee. (North-Holland Personal Library). 286p. 1987. pap. 29.50 (ISBN 0-444-87043-1, North Holland). Elsevier.

Physics of Magnetic Semiconductors. Ed. by E. Nagev. 388p. 1983. 11.95 (ISBN 0-8285-5123-5, Pub. by Mir Pubs USSR). Imported Pubns.

Physics of Magnetism. Sushin Chikazumi & Stanley H. Charap. LC 78-2315. 566p. 1978. Repr. of 1964 ed. lib. bdg. 40.50 (ISBN 0-88275-662-1). Krieger.

Physics of Magnetospheric Substorms. new ed. Syun-Ichi Akasofu. (Astrophysics & Space Science Library: No. 47). 1976. lib. bdg. 95.00 (ISBN 90-277-0748-0, Pub. by Reidel Holland). Kluwer Academic.

Physics of Many-Particle Systems. Ed. by E. Meeron. (Many-Body Problem: Current Research & Reviews Ser.). 698p. 1966. 177.00 (ISBN 0-677-10330-1). Gordon & Breach.

Physics of Massive Neutrinos. F. Boehm & P. Vogel. 180p. 1988. 34.50 (ISBN 0-521-30567-5). Cambridge U Pr.

Physics of Massive Neutrinos. B. Kayser & F. Gibrat-Debu. 180p. 1988. 42.00 (ISBN 9971-50-661-0, ZB0655PB); pap. 22.00 (ISBN 9971-50-662-9). World Scientific Pub.

Physics of Materials: Proceedings of the Fourth & Fifth International Courses. Ed. by S. Radhakrishna & K. Srinivasan. 476p. 1988. 64.00 (ISBN 9971-50-398-0). World Scientific Pub.

Physics of Medical Imaging. Ed. by Steve Webb. (Medical Science Ser.). 600p. 1988. 203.00 (ISBN 0-85274-361-0, Pub. by A Hilger UK). Taylor & Francis.

Physics of Membrane Transport. A. Iberall & A. Schindler. LC 73-87972. (Illus.). 266p. (Orig.). 1973. pap. 6.00 (ISBN 0-914780-02-6). Gen Tech Serv.

Physics of Mesospheric (Noctilucent) Clouds. Ed. by Y. Ikaunieks. 164p. 1974. text ed. 38.00x (ISBN 0-7065-1373-8, Pub. by Keter Pub Jerusalem). Coronet Bks.

Physics of Metals, Vol. 2: Defects. P. B. Hirsch. LC 74-14439. (Illus.). 304p. 1976. 82.50 (ISBN 0-521-20077-6). Cambridge U Pr.

Physics of Microfabrication. Ivor Brodie & Julius J. Muray. LC 82-3835. 522p. 1982. 65.00x (ISBN 0-306-40863-5, Plenum Pr). Plenum Pub.

Physics of Minerals & Inorganic Materials: An Introduction. A. S. Marfunin. Tr. by G. Egorova & A. G. Mishchenko. (Illus.). 1979. 58.00 (ISBN 0-387-08982-9). Springer-Verlag.

Physics of Modern Materials, 2 vols. (Proceedings Ser.). 1980. pap. 73.50 (ISBN 92-0-130080-8, ISP538 1, IAEA); pap. 95.00 (ISBN 92-0-130180-4, ISP538 2). UNIPUB.

Physics of MOS Insulators. Lucovsky et al. 400p. 1980. 83.00 (ISBN 0-08-025969-3). Pergamon.

Physics of Music. 7th ed. Ed. by Alexander Wood. 1975. pap. 15.95x (ISBN 0-412-21140-8, NO. 6326, Pub. by Chapman & Hall). Routledge Chapman & Hall.

Physics of Narrow Gap Semiconductors. J. Rauluskiewicz et al. (Proceedings). 1978. 105.25 (ISBN 0-444-99801-2). Elsevier.

Physics of Narrow Gap Semiconductors: Proceedings. Ed. by E. Gornik et al. (Lecture Notes in Physics Ser.: Vol. 152). 485p. 1982. 30.00 (ISBN 0-387-11191-3). Springer-Verlag.

Physics of New Laser Sources. Ed. by Neal B. Abraham et al. (NATO ASI Series B, Physics: Vol. 132). 460p. 1985. 75.00x (ISBN 0-306-42105-4, Plenum Pr). Plenum Pub.

Physics of Non-Conventional Energy Sources & Material Science for Energy: Proceedings of the International Workshop. Ed. by G. Furlan et al. 608p. 1987. 78.00 (ISBN 9971-50-252-6); pap. 41.00 (ISBN 9971-50-346-8). World Scientific Pub.

Physics of Non-Thermal Radio Sources: Proceedings of the NATO Advanced Study Institute, Urbino, 1975. NATO Advanced Study Institute Staff. Ed. by Giancarlo Setti. (Mathematical & Physical Sciences Ser.: No. 28). 1976. lib. bdg. 34.00 (ISBN 90-277-0753-7, Pub. by Reidel Holland). Kluwer Academic.

Physics of Nonlinear Transport in Semiconductors. Ed. by D. K. Ferry et al. LC 79-28383. (NATO ASI Series B, Physics: Vol. 52). 634p. 1980. 95.00x (ISBN 0-306-40356-0, Plenum Pr). Plenum Pub.

Physics of Nuclear Fission. N. A. Perfilov & V. P. Eismont. 216p. 1964. text ed. 46.50 (ISBN 0-7065-0336-8, Pub. by Keter Pub Jerusalem). Coronet Bks.

Physics of Nuclear Reactions. W. Martin Gibson. LC 79-40063. (Illus.). 288p. 1980. text ed. 69.00 (ISBN 0-08-023078-4); pap. text ed. 21.00 (ISBN 0-08-023077-6). Pergamon.

Physics of Particle Accelerators, 2 vols. Melvin Month & Margaret Dienes. LC 87-70103. (AIP Conference Proceedings Ser.: No. 153). 1748p. 1987. Set. lib. bdg. 153.75 (ISBN 0-88318-353-6). Am Inst Physics.

Physics of Phase Space. Ed. by Y. S. Kim & W. ZAchary. (Lecture Notes in Physics Ser.: Vol. 278). ix, 449p. 1987. 45.70 (ISBN 0-387-17894-5). Springer-Verlag.

Physics of Phonons. Ed. by T. Paszkiewicz. (Lecture Notes in Physics,: Vol. 285). x, 486p. 1987. 45.70 (ISBN 0-387-18244-6). Springer Verlag.

Physics of Planetary Atmospheres. Abbas. 1987. write for info. (ISBN 0-471-88722-6). Wiley.

Physics of Planetary Interiors. G. H. Cole. 224p. 1984. 67.00x (ISBN 0-85274-444-7, Pub. by A Hilger Techo Hse UK); pap. 27.00x (ISBN 0-85274-445-5, Pub. by A Hilger Techo Hse UK). Taylor & Francis.

Physics of Planetary Interiors. V. N. Zharkov & V. P. Triubitsyn. (Astronomy & Astrophysics Ser.: Vol. .6). 38.00 (ISBN 0-686-87510-9). Pachart Pub Hse.

Physics of Planetary Ionospheres. S. J. Bauer. LC 72-15455. (Physics & Chemistry in Space Ser.: Vol. 6). (Illus.). 230p. 1973. 55.00 (ISBN 0-387-06173-8). Springer-Verlag.

Physics of Plasma Close to Thermonuclear Conditions, 2 vols. Ed. by B. Coppi et al. (Commission of the European Communities). 750p. 1981. pap. 115.00 (ISBN 0-08-024475-0). Pergamon.

Physics of Plasma-Wall Interactions in Controlled Fusion. Ed. by D. E. Post & R. Behrisch. (NATO ASI Series B, Physics: Vol. 131). 1196p. 1986. 145.00x (ISBN 0-306-42097-X, Plenum Pr). Plenum Pub.

Physics of Pulsars. Allen M. Lenchek. (Topics in Astrophysics & Space Physics Ser.). 184p. 1972. 52.00x (ISBN 0-677-14295-1). Gordon & Breach.

Physics of Quasicrystals: Lectures & Reprints. Ed. by P. Steinhardt & S. Ostlund. 600p. 1987. 79.00 (ISBN 9971-50-296-8); pap. 56.00 (ISBN 9971-50-297-6). World Scientific Pub.

Physics of Radiation Effects in Crystals. Ed. by R. A. Johnson & A. N. Orlov. (Modern Problems in Condensed Matter Sciences Ser.: Vol. 13). 686p. 1986. 208.00 (ISBN 0-444-86946-8, North-Holland). Elsevier.

Physics of Radiology. 4th ed. Harold E. Johns & John R. Cunningham. (Illus.). 816p. 1983. 54.50 (ISBN 0-398-04669-7). C C Thomas.

Physics of Rainclouds. Neville H. Fletcher. pap. 101.00 (ISBN 0-317-08923-4, 2051499). Bks Demand UMI.

Physics of Reactor Shielding. Y. A. Kazanskii et al. 360p. 1968. text ed. 73.50 (ISBN 0-7065-0653-7, Pub. by Keter Pub Jerusalem). Coronet Bks.

Physics of Selenium & Tellurium. Ed. by E. Gerlach. (Springer Series in Solid State Sciences: Vol.13). (Illus.). 1979. 37.00 (ISBN 0-387-09692-2). Springer-Verlag.

Physics of Semiconductor Devices. 4th ed. D. A. Fraser. (Oxford Physics Ser.). 1986. 39.95x (ISBN 0-19-851867-6); pap. text ed. 16.95x (ISBN 0-19-851866-8). Oxford U Pr.

Physics of Semiconductor Devices. 2nd ed. S. M. Sze. LC 81-213. 868p. 1981. 59.95 (ISBN 0-471-05661-8). Wiley.

Physics of Semiconductor Devices: Proceedings of the IV Int'l Workshop, Madras, India. Ed. by S. C. Jain & S. Radhakrishra. 544p. (Orig.). 1987. 86.00 (ISBN 9971-50-531-2); pap. 48.00 (ISBN 9971-50-532-0). World Scientific Pub.

Physics of Semiconductor Devices: Proceedings of the International Workshop. Ed. by S. C. Jain & S. Radhakrishna. 803p. 1982. 62.95 (ISBN 0-470-27512-X). Halsted Pr.

Physics of Semiconductor Devices: Proceedings of the Third International Workshop on Physics of Semiconductor Devices, Madras, India, Nov 27 - Dec 2, 1985. Ed. by S. Radhakrishna. 500p. 1986. 54.00 (ISBN 9971-50-082-5). World Scientific Pub.

Physics of Semiconductor Laser Devices. G. H. B. Thompson. LC 79-41217. 549p. 1980. 114.00 (ISBN 0-471-27685-5). Wiley.

Physics of Semiconductors: Edinburgh 1978. (Institute of Physics Conference Ser.: No. 43). 1979. cancelled 78.00 (ISBN 0-85498-134-9, Pub. by Inst Physics England). IPS.

Physics of Semiconductors: Proceedings of the International Conference, 18th, Stockholm, Sweden, August 11-15, 1986, 2 vols. Ed. by O. Engstrom. 1964p. 1987. 221.00 (ISBN 9971-50-197-X); pap. 88.00 (ISBN 9971-50-198-8). World Scientific Pub.

Physics of Semiconductors: Proceedings of the 13th International Conference, Rome, 1976. F. G. Fumi. 1977. 171.00 (ISBN 0-7204-0571-8, North-Holland). Elsevier.

Physics of Semiconductors: Proceedings. International Conference on Physics of Semiconductors. Ed. by Michel Hulin. (Vol. 1). 1965. 114.00 (ISBN 0-12-532301-8). Acad Pr.

Physics of Shallow Estuaries & Bays. Ed. by J. Van de Kreeke. (Lecture Notes on Coastal & Estuarine Studies: Vol. 16). ix, 280p. 1986. pap. 24.50 (ISBN 0-387-96328-6). Springer-Verlag.

Physics of Shock Waves & High Temperature Hydrodynamic Phenomena, 2 Vols. Ya B. Zel'Dovich et al. Vol. 1 1966. 91.00 (ISBN 0-12-778701-1); Vol. 2 1967. 91.00 (ISBN 0-12-778702-X). Acad Pr.

Physics of Shock Waves in Gases & Plasmas. M. A. Liberman & A. L. Velikovich. (Springer Series in Electrophysics: Vol. 19). (Illus.). 400p. 1986. 49.00 (ISBN 0-387-15605-4). Springer-Verlag.

Physics of Silicon Dioxide & Its Interfaces: An International Topical Conference. Ed. by Sokrates T. Pantelides. 1978. pap. 53.00 (ISBN 0-08-023049-0). Pergamon.

Physics of Solar Continuum Radio Bursts. A. Krueger. 200p. 1973. cancelled 26.50x (ISBN 0-685-39164-7). Adlers Foreign Bks.

Physics of Solar Flares. Einar Tandberg-Hanssen & A. Gordon Emslie. (Cambridge Astrophysics Ser.: No. 14). (Illus.). 400p. Date not set. price not set (ISBN 0-521-30804-6). Cambridge U Pr.

Physics of Solar Planetary Environments: Proceedings, 2 vols. International Symposium on Solar Terrestrial Physics. Ed. by Donald J. Williams. LC 76-29443. (Illus.). 1038p. 1976. pap. 10.00. Am Geophysical.

Physics of Solid and Liquid Helium, Pt. 2. Ed. by K. H. Benneman & J. B. Ketterson. LC 75-20235. 760p. 1978. text ed. 80.95 (ISBN 0-471-06601-X, JW). Krieger.

Physics of Solid Dielectrics. I. Bunget & M. Popescu. (Materials Science Monographs: No. 19). 446p. 1984. 134.25 (ISBN 0-444-99632-X, I-039-84). Elsevier.

Physics of Solid Surfaces. M. Laznicka. (Studies in Surface Science & Catalysts: Vol. 9). 282p. 1982. 87.00 (ISBN 0-444-99716-4). Elsevier.

Physics of Solid Surfaces Surfaces 1987: Proceedings of the 4th Symposium, Bechyne Caslte, Czechoslovakia, 7-11 Sept., 1987. Ed. by J. Koukal. (Studies in Surface Science & Catalysis: No. 40). 366p. 1988. 142.00 (ISBN 0-444-42972-7). Elsevier.

Physics of Solid Surfaces 1984: Proceedings of the Third Symposium on Surface Physics, Smolenice Castle, Czechoslovakia, 3-7 September, 1984. Ed. by J. Koukal. (No. 23). 240p. 1985. 102.75 (ISBN 0-444-42529-2). Elsevier.

Physics of Solids. 2nd ed. Charles A. Wert & Robb W. Thomson. LC 77-98055. (Materials Science & Engineering Ser.). 1970. text ed. 59.95 (ISBN 0-07-069435-4). McGraw.

Physics of Solids under High Pressure. Ed. by J. S. Schilling & R. N. Shelton. 420p. 1982. 108.00 (ISBN 0-444-86326-5, North-Holland). Elsevier.

Physics of Sound. Richard E. Berg & David G. Stork. (Illus.). 416p. 1982. write for info. (ISBN 0-13-674283-1). P-H.

Physics of Sound in the Sea, 4 pts. P. G. Bergmann et al. Incl. Pt. 1. Transmission. P. G. Bergmann & A. Yaspan. 266p. 1968. 75.00 (ISBN 0-677-01890-8); Pts. 2 & 3. Reverbreration: Refelection of Sound from Submarines & Surface Vessels. Ed. by E. Gerjuoy et al. 218p. 1968. 49.00 (ISBN 0-677-01900-9); Pt. 4. Acoustic Properties of Wakes. Ed. by R. Wildt. 128p. 30.00 (ISBN 0-677-01910-6). (Documents on Modern Physics Ser.). 612p. 1968. Set. 110.00 (ISBN 0-677-01920-3). Gordon & Breach.

Physics of Speech. Dennis B. Fry. LC 78-56752. (Textbooks in Linguistics Ser.). (Illus.). 1979. 32.50 (ISBN 0-521-22173-0); pap. 12.95 (ISBN 0-521-29379-0). Cambridge U Pr.

Physics of Stars. S. A. Kaplan. LC 82-2651. 158p. 1983. 51.95x (ISBN 0-471-10327-6). Wiley.

Physics of Stars & Stellar Systems, 2 Vols. Ed. by A. A. Mikhailov. 856p. 1969. Set. text ed. 175.00x (ISBN 0-7065-0654-5, Pub. by Keter Pub Jerusalem). Coronet Bks.

Physics of Stellar Evolution & Cosmology. Howard S. Goldberg & Michael D. Scadron. 405p. 1982. 69.00 (ISBN 0-677-05540-4). Gordon & Breach.

Physics of Stereo Quad Sound. Joseph G. Traylor. (Illus.). 1977. pap. 10.95x (ISBN 0-8138-0025-0). Iowa St U Pr.

Physics of Strong Fields. Ed. by W. Greiner. (NATO ASI Series B, Physics: Vol. 153). (Illus.). 1003p. 1987. 135.00x (ISBN 0-306-42577-7, Plenum Pr). Plenum Pub.

Physics of Structurally Disordered Matter: An Introduction. N. E. Cusack. (Graduate Student Series in Physics). 432p. 1987. 162.00x (ISBN 0-85274-591-5, Pub. by A Hilger UK). Taylor & Francis.

Physics of Structure Formation: Theory & Simulation. Ed. by W. Guttinger & G. Dangelmayr. (Syergentics Ser.: Vol. 37). (Illus.). 450p. 1987. 55.00 (ISBN 0-387-18383-3). Springer-Verlag.

Physics of Submicron Semiconductor Devices. Ed. by H. L. Grubin et al. (NATO ASI Series B, Physics: Vol. 180). (Illus.). 730p. Date not set. 125.00x (ISBN 0-306-42986-1, Plenum Pr). Plenum Pub.

Physics of Submicron Structures. Ed. by H. L. Grubin et al. 370p. 1984. 67.50x (ISBN 0-306-41715-4, Plenum Pr). Plenum Pub.

Physics of Superionic Conductors. Ed. by M. B. Salamon. (Topics in Current Physics Ser.: Vol. 15). (Illus.). 1979. 37.00 (ISBN 0-387-09333-8). Springer-Verlag.

Physiologic Foundations of Perinatal Care. Ed. by Leo Stern et al. LC 84-24813. 398p. 1985. 50.95 (ISBN 0-275-91454-2, C14541). Praeger.

Physiologic Foundations of Perinatal Care, Vol. 2. Ed. by L. Stern & W. Oh. 400p. 1987. 63.00 (ISBN 0-317-62774-0). Elsevier.

Physiologic, Metabolic, & Immunolog Actions of Interleukin-1. Matthew J. Kluger et al. LC 85-19688. (PLB Ser.: Vol. 2). 576p. 1985. 84.00 (ISBN 0-8451-4101-5). A R Liss.

Physiologic Principles of Functional Appliances. Graber. 1985. pap. 12.95 (ISBN 0-8016-1950-5). Mosby.

Physiological Acoustics. Glen Wever & M. Lawrence. 1954. 52.50x (ISBN 0-691-08018-6). Princeton U Pr.

Physiological Activity of the Speech Organs: An Analysis of the Speech-Organs During the Phonation of Sung, Spoken, & Whispered Czech Vowels on the Basis of X-Ray Methods. Jana Ondrackova. Tr. by D. Short from Dutch. LC 72-94494. (Illus.). 105p. 1973. text ed. 24.00x (ISBN 90-2792-374-4). Mouton.

Physiological Adaptability & Nutritional Status of the Japanese (A, Vol. 3. Ed. by H. Yoshimura & S. Kobayashi. (Japan International Biological Program Synthesis Ser.). 276p. 1975. 39.50 (ISBN 0-86008-213-X, Pub. by U of Tokyo Japan). Columbia U Pr.

Physiological Adaptability & Nutritional Status of the Japanese (B, Vol. 4. Ed. by K. Asahina & R. Shigiya. (Japan International Biological Program Synthesis Ser.). 250p. 1975. 39.50 (ISBN 0-86008-214-8, Pub. by U of Tokyo Japan). Columbia U Pr.

Physiological Adaptations of Marine Animals. Ed. by M. S. Laverack. (Society for Experimental Biology Symposium: No. 39). 540p. 1985. text ed. 60.00x (ISBN 0-948601-00-0, Biochemical Society). Rsrch Bks CT.

Physiological Aesthetics. Grant Allen. 283p. 1980. Repr. of 1877 ed. lib. bdg. 35.00 (ISBN 0-8495-0064-8). Arden Lib.

Physiological & Behavioral Effects of Food Constituents. Ed. by Richard J. Wurtman & Judith J. Wurtman. (Nutrition & the Brain Ser.: Vol. 6). 292p. 1983. text ed. 67.50 (ISBN 0-89004-733-2). Raven.

Physiological & Biochemical Basis for Perinatal Medicine. Ed. by A. Minkowski & M. Monset-Couchard. (Illus.). xiv, 370p. 1981. 104.00 (ISBN 3-8055-1283-X). S Karger.

Physiological & Biochemical Foundations of Therapeutics. Shirley D. Kraus. LC 80-67378. (Illus.). 259p. (Orig.). 1982. pap. text ed. 19.00x (ISBN 0-932126-33-2). Graceway.

Physiological & Clinical Anatomy of the Domestic Mammals, Vol. 1, Central Nervous System. A. S. King. (Illus.). 212p. 1987. pap. 19.95 (ISBN 0-19-854187-2). Oxford U Pr.

Physiological & Genetical Aspects of Egg Production in White Plymouth Rock Pullets. J. H. Van Middelkoop. (Illus.). 76p. 1978. pap. 13.75 (ISBN 90-220-0495-3, PDC65, Pudoc). UNIPUB.

Physiological & Morphological Adaption & Evolution. Ed. by William A. Stini. (World Anthropology Ser.). xiv, 526p. 1979. text ed. 60.75 (ISBN 90-279-7710-0). Mouton.

Physiological & Pathological Aspects of Eye Movements. A. Roucoux & M. Crommelinck. 1983. 76.00 (ISBN 90-619-3730-2, Pub. by Junk Pubs Netherlands). Kluwer Academic.

Physiological & Performance Determinants in Manned Space Systems. Ed. by Paul Horowitz. (Science & Technology Ser.: Vol. 5). 1965. 20.00x (ISBN 0-87703-033-2, Pub. by Am Astronaut). Univelt Inc.

Physiological & Pharmacological Aspects of the Reticulo-rumen. Ed. by L. A. Ooms & A. D. Degryse. (Current Topics in Veterinary Medicine & Animal Science Ser.). 1987. lib. bdg. 95.00 (ISBN 0-89838-878-3, Pub. by Martinus Nijhoff Netherlands). Kluwer Academic.

Physiological & Psychological Considerations in the Management of Stroke. Arnold Brown. LC 72-7682. 160p. 1976. 12.50 (ISBN 0-87527-094-8). Green.

Physiological & Technical Basis of Electromyography. William F. Brown. (Illus.). 448p. 1984. text ed. 70.00 (ISBN 0-409-95042-4). Butterworth.

Physiological Applications. Harold J. Benson & Arthur Talaro. 318p. 1982. wire coil (ISBN 0-697-04717-2); instr's. handbook (ISBN 0-697-04723-7). Wm C Brown.

Physiological Approach to Clinical Neurology. 3rd ed. James W. Lance & James G. McLeod. (Illus.). 368p. 1981. text ed. 59.95 (ISBN 0-407-00196-4). Butterworth.

Physiological Aspects of Clinical Neuro-Ophthalmology. Kennard. 1988. 95.00 (ISBN 0-8151-7384-9). Year Bk Med.

Physiological Aspects of Copper: Copper in Organs & Systems. Charles A. Owen, Jr. LC 82-3421. (Copper in Biology & Medicine Ser.). 286p. 1982. 28.00 (ISBN 0-8155-0904-9). Noyes.

Physiological Aspects of Crop Yield. Ed. by J. D. Eastin. (Illus.). 1969. 10.00 (ISBN 0-89118-004-4). Am Soc Agron.

Physiological Aspects of Deep Sea Biology. Alister G. Macdonald. LC 73-90652. (Physiological Society. Monographs: No. 31). pap. 120.70 (2031685). Bks Demand UMI.

Physiological Aspects of Photosynthesis. O. V. Heath. 1969. 32.50x (ISBN 0-8047-0745-6). Stanford U Pr.

Physiological Aspects of the Liquor Problem, 2 Vols. John S. Billings & Wilbur O. Atwater. 37.00 (ISBN 0-8369-6965-0, 7846). Ayer Co Pubs.

Physiological Basis for Crop Growth & Develpment. Ed. by M. B. Tesar. 341p. 1984. 20.00 (ISBN 0-89118-037-0). Am Soc Agron.

Physiological Basis of Anxiety. (Journal: Psychopathology: Vol. 17, Suppl. 1). (Illus.). 120p. 1984. pap. 24.00 (ISBN 3-8055-3812-X). S Karger.

Physiological Basis of Diuretic Therapy in Clinical Medicine. Ed. by Garabed Eknoyan & Manueal Martinez-Maldonado. LC 79-1152. 432p. 1986. 74.50 (ISBN 0-8089-1744-7, 791152). Grune.

Physiological Basis of Geriatrics. Paola S. Timiras. 448p. 1988. 49.95 (ISBN 0-02-420810-8). Macmillan.

Physiological Basis of Health Standards for Dwellings. M. S. Goromosov. (Public Health Papers Ser: No. 33). 99p. 1968. pap. 2.80 (ISBN 92-4-130033-7, 761). World Health.

Physiological Basis of Hearing. Wolfgang D. Keidel. (Illus.). 262p. 1983. 32.50 (ISBN 0-86577-072-7). Thieme Med Pubs.

Physiological Basis of Memory. Ed. by J. A. Deutsch. 1973. 55.00 (ISBN 0-12-213450-8). Acad Pr.

Physiological Basis of Memory. 2nd ed. Ed. by J. Anthony Deutsch. 448p. 1983. 49.95 (ISBN 0-12-213460-5). Acad Pr.

Physiological Basis of Physical Education & Athletics. 4th ed. Edward L. Fox et al. 734p. 1988. text ed. write for info. (ISBN 0-697-05995-2). Wm C Brown.

Physiological Basis of Salt Tolerance in Plants. B. P. Strogonov. 286p. 1964. text ed. 66.75x (ISBN 0-7065-0524-7, Pub. by Keter Pub Jerusalem). Coronet Bks.

Physiological Basis of Starling's Law of the Heart. Ciba Foundation Staff. LC 74-77177. (Ciba Foundation Symposium: New Ser.: No. 24). pap. 77.00 (ISBN 0-317-29186-6, 2022153). Bks Demand UMI.

Physiological Causes of Yield Variation in Cassava (Manihot Esculenta Crantz) H. J. Veltkamp. (Agricultural University Wageningen Papers: No. 85-6, 1985). (Illus.). 103p. (Orig.). 1987. pap. text ed. 16.00 (ISBN 90-6754-070-6, PDC326, Pub. by PUDOC). UNIPUB.

Physiological Chemistry of Carbohydrates in Mammals. Walton W. Shreeve. LC 73-88265. (Illus.). Repr. of 1974 ed. 65.40 (ISBN 0-8357-9553-5, 2016687). Bks Demand UMI.

Physiological Chemistry of Exercise & Training. Ed. by P. E. Di Prampero & J. Poortsmans. (Medicine & Sport Ser.: Vol. 13). (Illus.). viii, 216p. 1981. 65.50 (ISBN 3-8055-2028-X). S Karger.

Physiological Chemistry of Training & Detraining. Ed. by P. Marconnet & J. Poortmans. (Medicine & Sport Science: Vol. 17). (Illus.). xii, 264p. 1984. 132.00 (ISBN 3-8055-3764-6). S Karger.

Physiological Concept of Love in the Elizabethan & Early Stuart Drama. L. Babb. 59.95 (ISBN 0-8490-0833-6). Gordon Pr.

Physiological Concepts & the Critically Ill Patient. Sharon L. Roberts. (Illus.). 512p. 1985. text ed. 32.50 (ISBN 0-13-674813-9). Appleton & Lange.

Physiological Control of Mammalian Vocalization. Ed. by J. D. Newman. (Illus.). 438p. 1988. 85.00x (ISBN 0-306-43003-7, Plenum Pr). Plenum Pub.

Physiological Correlates of Human Behaviour, Vol. 1. Ed. by Anthony Gale. John A. Edwards. 1983. Vol. 1. 49.50 (ISBN 0-12-273901-9); Vol. 2. 49.50 (ISBN 0-12-273902-7); Vol. 3, 1984. 49.50 (ISBN 0-12-273903-5). Acad Pr.

Physiological Correlates of Human Behaviour, Vol. 2. Ed. by Anthony Gale & John A. Edwards. 272p. 1986. pap. 24.00 (ISBN 0-12-273905-1). Acad Pr.

Physiological Correlates of Human Behaviour, Vol. 3. Ed. by Anthony Gale & John A. Edwards. 308p. 1986. pap. 24.00 (ISBN 0-12-273906-X). Acad Pr.

Physiological Correlates of Human Behavior, Vol. 1: Basic Issues. Ed. by Anthony Cale & John Edwards. 350p. 1986. pap. 24.00 (ISBN 0-12-273904-3). Acad Pr.

Physiological Correlates of Psychological Disorder: Proceedings of an Interdisciplinary Research Conference Sponsored by the Wisconsin Psychiatric Institute & the Dept. of Psychiatry of the University of Wisconsin Medical Center, August 29-31, 1961. Ed. by Robert Roessler & Norman S. Greenfield. LC 62-15990. pap. 73.50 (ISBN 0-317-30077-6, 2021145). Bks Demand UMI.

Physiological Correspondences. John Worcester. (Illus.). 432p. 1987. Repr. of 1931 ed. 8.85 (ISBN 0-915221-64-0). Swedenborg Sci Assn.

Physiological Determinants of Crop Growth. Ed. by D. Charles-Edwards. 1983. 44.00 (ISBN 0-12-169360-0). Acad Pr.

Physiological Development of the Fetus & Newborn. C. T. Jones & P. W. Nathanielsz. 1985. 84.00 (ISBN 0-12-389080-2). Acad Pr.

Physiological Ecology: An Evolutionary Approach to Resource Use. Ed. by Colin R. Townsend & Peter Calow. LC 81-13559. (Illus.). 480p. 1981. pap. text ed. 29.95x (ISBN 0-87893-828-1). Sinauer Assocs.

Physiological Ecology of Estuarine Organisms. Ed. by F. John Vernberg. LC 74-14572. (Belle W. Baruch Library in Marine Science Ser.: No. 3). (Illus.). xiv, 400p. 1975. lib. bdg. 42.95x (ISBN 0-87249-320-2). U of SC Pr.

Physiological Ecology of Forest Production. J. J. Landsberg. (Applied Botany & Crop Science Ser.). 1986. 45.00 (ISBN 0-12-435965-5). Acad Pr.

Physiological Ecology of Lichens. Kenneth A. Kershaw. (Cambridge Studies in Ecology). (Illus.). 256p. 1985. 59.50 (ISBN 0-521-23925-7). Cambridge U Pr.

Physiological Ecology of North American Plant Communities. Ed. by Brain F. Chabot & Hal. A Mooney. 400p. 1985. 39.95 (ISBN 0-412-23240-5, NO. 6536, Pub. by Chapman & Hall England). Routledge Chapman & Hall.

Physiological Ecology of Phytoplankton. Ed. by I. Morris. (Studies in Ecology: Vol. 7). 1981. 85.00x (ISBN 0-520-04308-1). U of Cal Pr.

Physiological Ecology of Phytoplankton. Rhee. 1987. write for info. (ISBN 0-471-80316-2). Wiley.

Physiological Ecology of Plants of the Wet Tropics. Ed. by E. Medina et al. (Tasks for Vegetation Science). 1984. lib. bdg. 60.00 (ISBN 90-6193-952-6, Pub. by Junk Pubs Netherlands). Kluwer Academic.

Physiological Ecology of Seaweeds. Christopher S. Lobban et al. (Illus.). 300p. 1985. 47.50 (ISBN 0-521-26508-8). Cambridge U Pr.

Physiological Ecology of the Alpine Timberline. W. Tranquillini. (Ecological Studies: Vol. 31). (Illus.). 1979. 37.00 (ISBN 0-387-09065-7). Springer-Verlag.

Physiological Ecology of the Tunas. Ed. by Gary D. Sharp & Andrew E. Dizon. LC 78-26514. 1979. 66.50 (ISBN 0-12-639180-7). Acad Pr.

Physiological Effects of Exercise Programs on Adults. Thomas K. Cureton. (Illus.). 228p. 1971. photocopy ed. 25.50x (ISBN 0-398-00377-7). C C Thomas.

Physiological Effects of Wheat Germ Oil on Humans in Exercise: Forty-Two Physical Training Programs Utilizing 894 Humans. Thomas K. Cureton. (Illus.). 552p. 1972. 52.25x (ISBN 0-398-02270-4). C C Thomas.

Physiological Fluid Mechanics. CISM (International Center for Mechanical Sciences) Staff. Ed. by J. Lighthill. (CISM Pubns. Ser: No. 111). 59p. 1973. pap. 9.80 (ISBN 0-387-81133-8). Springer Verlag.

Physiological Function see Isozymes.

Physiological Genetics. Ed. by John G. Scandalios. (Physiological Ecology Ser.). 1979. 43.00 (ISBN 0-12-620980-4). Acad Pr.

Physiological Genetics of Agricultural Crops. Andor Balint. 167p. 15.00_cancelled (ISBN 9-63053-288-3). IPS.

Physiological Genetics of Agricultural Crops. Andor Balint. 168p. 1984. 81.00x (Pub. by Collets (UK)). State Mutual Bk.

Physiological Limitations & the Genetic Improvement of Symbiotic Nitrogen Fixation. Ed. by F. O. Gara et al. (Advances in Agricultural Biotechnology Ser.). 1988. lib. bdg. 54.00 (ISBN 90-247-3692-7, Pub. by Kluwer Tech Netherlands). Kluwer Academic.

Physiological Management of Diabetes in Children. Robert L. Jackson & Richard A. Guthrie. (Other Medical Bks.: Vol. 6). 1985. pap. text ed. 30.00 (ISBN 0-87488-308-3). Med Exam.

Physiological Measures of the Audiovestibular System. Ed. by Larry J. Bradford. 1975. 49.95 (ISBN 0-12-123650-1). Acad Pr.

Physiological Mechanics of Piano Technique. Otto Ortmann. LC 80-26521. (Music Ser.). (Illus.). xvi, 396p. 1981. Repr. of 1929 ed. lib. bdg. 52.50 (ISBN 0-306-76058-4). Da Capo.

Physiological Mechanisms of Marine Pollutant Toxicity. Ed. by Winona B. Vernberg et al. 1982. 53.50 (ISBN 0-12-718460-0). Acad Pr.

Physiological Mechanisms of Motivation. D. E. Pfaff. (Illus.). 512p. 1982. 46.50 (ISBN 0-387-90650-9). Springer-Verlag.

Physiological Models in Microbiology, 2 vols. Ed. by Michael J. Bazin & James I. Prosser. 1988. Vol. I, Regulation & Control of Metabolic Pathways, 160 pgs. 92.50 (ISBN 0-8493-5954-6, 5954); Vol. II, Microbial Death, 160 pgs. 92.50 (ISBN 0-8493-5955-4, 5955). CRC Pr.

Physiological NMR Spectroscopy: From Isolated Cells to Man. Intro. by Sheila M. Cohen. (Annals of the New York Academy of Sciences: Vol. 508). (Illus.). 537p. 1987. 134.00 (ISBN 0-89766-411-6). NY Acad Sci.

Physiological Optics. Y. LeGrand & S. G. El Hage. (Springer Ser. in Optical Sciences: Vol. 13). (Illus.). 350p. 1980. pap. 52.00 (ISBN 0-387-09919-0). Springer-Verlag.

Physiological Optics of the Human Eye. Gurland. (Pure & Applied Optics Ser.). 1988. write for info. (ISBN 0-471-01565-2). Wiley.

Physiological-Pathological Interactions Affecting Seed Deterioration. write for info. Crop Sci Soc Am.

Physiological Peptides & New Trends in Radioimmunology. Ed. by C. A. Bizollon. 370p. 1981. 84.75 (ISBN 0-444-80358-0, Biomedical Pr). Elsevier.

Physiological Pharmacology: A Comprehensive Treatise, 4 vols. Ed. by W. S. Root & F. G. Hoffman. Incl. Vol. 1. The Nervous System, Part A. 1963; Vol. 2. The Nervous System, Part B. 1965; Vol. 3. The Nervous System, Part C. 1967; Vol. 4. The Nervous System, Part D. 1967; Vol. 5. The Nervous System, Part E. 1974. Acad Pr.

Physiological Plant Anatomy. 4th ed. G. Haberlandt. Tr. by M. Drummond from Ger. 398p. 1979. Repr. of 1928 ed. lib. bdg. 15.00x (ISBN 0-934454-89-2). Lubrecht & Cramer.

Physiological Plant Anatomy. G. Haberlandt. 777p. 1979. Repr. of 1965 ed. 20.00 (ISBN 0-88065-098-2, Pub. by Messers Today & Tomorrow Printers & PublishersIndia). Scholarly Pubns.

Physiological Plant Biology IV: Ecosystems Processes - Mineral Cycling, Productivity, & Man's Influence. Ed. by O. L. Lange et al. (Encylopedia of Plant Physiology Ser.: Vol. 12 D). (Illus.). 690p. 1983. 151.00 (ISBN 0-387-10908-0). Springer-Verlag.

Physiological Plant Ecology. Kapustka. 1988. write for info. (ISBN 0-471-89611-X). Wiley.

Physiological Plant Ecology. rev. ed. W. Larcher. Tr. by M. A. Biederman-Thorson. LC 79-26396. (Illus.). 304p. 1980. 34.00 (ISBN 3-540-09795-3). Springer-Verlag.

Physiological Plant Ecology I: Responses to the Physical Environment. Ed. by O. L. Lange et al. (Encylopedia of Plant Physiology Ser.: Vol. 12 A). (Illus.). 625p. 1981. 130.00 (ISBN 0-387-10763-0). Springer-Verlag.

Physiological Plant Ecology II: Water Relations & Carbon Assimilation. O. L. Lange et al. (Encyclopedia of Plant Physioilogy Ser.: Vol. 12 B). (Illus.). 153p. 1982. 151.00 (ISBN 0-387-10906-4). Springer-Verlag.

Physiological Plant Ecology III: Responses to the Chemical & Biological Environment. Ed. by O. L. Lange et al. (Encyclopedia of Plant Physiology Ser.: Vol. 12C). (Illus.). 850p. 1983. 151.00 (ISBN 0-387-10907-2). Springer-Verlag.

Physiological Plant Pathology. Ed. by R. Heitefuss & P. H. Willaims. (Encyclopedia of Plant Physiology: Vol. 4). 1976. 120.00 (ISBN 0-387-07557-7). Springer-Verlag.

Physiological Processes in Plant Ecology: Towards a Synthesis with Atriplex. C. B. Osmond et al. (Ecololgical Studies: Vol. 36). (Illus.). 500p. 1980. 64.00 (ISBN 0-387-10060-1). Springer-Verlag.

Physiological Processes Limiting Plant Productivity. Christopher B. Johnson. 1981. text ed. 99.95 (ISBN 0-408-10649-2). Butterworth.

Physiological Programmatics of the Nineteenth Century. Ed. by William Coleman & I. Bernard Cohen. LC 80-2107. (Development of Science Ser.). (Illus.). 1981. lib. bdg. 50.00x (ISBN 0-405-13872-5). Ayer Co Pubs.

Physiological Properties of Plant Protoplasts. Ed. by P. E. Pilet. (Proceedings in Life Sciences Ser.). (Illus.). 300p. 1985. 57.50 (ISBN 0-387-15017-X). Springer-Verlag.

Physiological Psychology. John Blundell. (Essential Psychology Ser.). 1975. pap. 4.95x (ISBN 0-416-81950-8, NO. 2610). Routledge Chapman & Hall.

Physiological Psychology. Abridged ed. Mark R. Rosenzweig & Arnold L. Leiman. 640p. 1988. text ed. 34.00 (ISBN 0-394-37237-9, RanC); wkbk. 10.50 (ISBN 0-394-37617-X). Random.

Physiological Psychology. 3rd ed. Allen M. Schneider & Barry Tarshis. 500p. 1985. text ed. write for info (ISBN 0-394-33542-2, RanC); pap. text ed. write for info. Random.

Physiological Psychology. 2nd ed. Marvin Schwartz. LC 77-17438. (Century Psychology Ser.). (Illus.). 1978. ref. ed. 27.95. P-H.

Physiological Psychology: An Introduction. William C. Watson. LC 80-82838. (Illus.). 592p. 1981. text ed. 34.50 (ISBN 0-395-30221-8); instr's. manual 1.00 (ISBN 0-395-30222-6); study guide 8.95 (ISBN 0-395-30223-4). HM.

Physiological Regulation of Membrane Fluidity. Ed. by Roland C. Aloia et al. LC 88-780. (Advances in Membrane Fluidity: Vol. 3). 379p. 1988. 120.00 (ISBN 0-8451-4602-5, 4602). A R Liss.

Physiological Researches on Life & Death. Marie F. Bichat. Ed. by Robert Kastenbaum. Tr. by F. Gold & F. Magendie. LC 76-19561. (Death & Dying Ser.). 1977. Repr. lib. bdg. 30.00x (ISBN 0-405-09557-0). Ayer Co Pubs.

Physiological Researches on Life & Death. Xavier Bichat. Tr. by F. Gold from Fr. Bd. with Outlines of Phrenology; Phrenology Examined. LC 77-72191. (Contributions to the History of Psychology, Vol. II, Pt. E: Physiological Psychology). 516p. 1978. Repr. of 1827 ed. 30.00 (ISBN 0-89093-175-5). U Pubns Amer.

Physiological Response of the Surgical Patient. (Modular Independent Learning Systems Ser.). 1985. 15.00 (ISBN 0-939583-14-3). Assn Oper Rm Nurses.

Physiological Responses to Burning Injury. J. W. Davies. 1982. 108.00 (ISBN 0-12-206080-6). Acad Pr.

Physiology of Excitable Membranes: Proceedings of the 28th International Congress of Physiological Sciences, Budapest, 1980. Ed. by J. Salanki et al. LC 80-41853. (Advances in Physiological Sciences: Vol. 4). (Illus.). 350p. 1981. 57.00 (ISBN 0-08-026816-1). Pergamon.

Physiology of Exercise. Ernst Jokl. (Illus.). 156p. 1971. photocopy ed. 17.50x (ISBN 0-398-02152-X). C C Thomas.

Physiology of Exercise & Sport. Noble. 1986. 34.95 (ISBN 0-8016-3711-2). Mosby.

Physiology of Exercise for Physical Education & Athletics. 4th ed. Herbert A. DeVries. 608p. 1986. text ed. write for info. (ISBN 0-697-00988-2). Wm C Brown.

Physiology of Exercises: Responses & Adaptations. 2nd ed. David R. Lamb. 464p. 1984. text ed. write for info. (ISBN 0-02-367210-2); write for info. lab manual (ISBN 0-02-367220-X). Macmillan.

Physiology of Fitness. 2nd ed. Brian J. Sharky. LC 84-3850. 384p. 1984. pap. text ed. 15.00x (ISBN 0-931250-66-8, BSHA0066). Human Kinetics.

Physiology of Flowering, 2 vols. Ed. by Georges Bernier. 1981. Vol. I, 168p. 85.00 (ISBN 0-8493-5709-8); Vol. II 248p. 110.00 (ISBN 0-8493-5710-1). CRC Pr.

Physiology of Flowering Plants. Rev. ed. H. Street & H. Opik. 1976. 18.50 (ISBN 0-444-19505-X). Elsevier.

Physiology of Flowering: The Development of Flowers, Vol. III. Jean M. Kinet et al. 288p. 1985. 125.00 (ISBN 0-8493-5711-X). CRC Pr.

Physiology of French Consonant Changes. Ernest F. Haden. (LD). 1938. 13.00 (ISBN 0-527-00772-2). Kraus Repr.

Physiology of Fungi. K. S. Bilgrami & R. N. Verma. 307p. 1986. pap. text ed. 15.95x (ISBN 0-7069-1325-6, Pub. by Vikas India). Advent NY.

Physiology of Fungi. Lilian E. Hawker. (Illus.). 1968. Repr. of 1950 ed. 48.00x (ISBN 3-7682-0530-4). Lubrecht & Cramer.

Physiology of Giant Algal Cells. A. B. Hope & N. A. Walker. LC 74-77832. (Illus.). 224p. 1975. 42.50 (ISBN 0-521-20513-1). Cambridge U Pr.

Physiology of Growth. Richard J. Goss. 1978. 72.50 (ISBN 0-12-293055-X). Acad Pr.

Physiology of Growth & Nutrition. Ed. by M. Rechcigl, Jr. (Comparative Animal Nutrition: Vol. 4). (Illus.). xii, 344p. 1981. pap. 166.00 (ISBN 3-8055-1199-X). S Karger.

Physiology of Hemostasis. Derek Ogston. (Illus.). 384p. 1983. text ed. 32.00x (ISBN 0-674-66660-7). Harvard U Pr.

Physiology of Human Growth. Ed. by J. M. Tanner & M. A. Preece. (Society for the Study of Human Biology Symposium Ser.: No. 29). (Illus.). 275p. Date not set. price not set (ISBN 0-521-34410-7). Cambridge U Pr.

Physiology of Immunoglobulins: Diagnostic & Clinical Aspects. Ed. by Stephen E. Ritzmann. LC 82-13101. (Protein Abornormalities Ser.: Vol. 1). 376p. 1982. 42.00 (ISBN 0-8451-2800-0). A R Liss.

Physiology of Industrial Organization & the Re-Employment of the Disabled. Jules Amar. Ed. by A. F. Kent. Tr. by Bernard Miall. LC 73-10379. (Management History Ser.: No. 34). (Illus.). 400p. 1973. Repr. of 1918 ed. 25.00 (ISBN 0-87960-036-5). Hive Pub.

Physiology of Lactation. T. B. Mepham. LC 86-8504. 100p. 1987. 104.00x (ISBN 0-335-15152-3, Open Univ Pr); pap. 46.00x (ISBN 0-335-15151-5, Open Univ Pr). Taylor & Francis.

Physiology of Large Reptiles: With Special Reference to the Heat Production of Snakes, Tortoises, Lizards & Alligators. F. C. Benedict. (Illus.). 1973. Repr. of 1932 ed. 82.50x (ISBN 90-6123-263-5). Lubrecht & Cramer.

Physiology of Mammals & Other Vertebrates. 2nd ed. Patricia T. Marshall & George M. Hughes. LC 78-73810. (Illus.). 1981. 49.50 (ISBN 0-521-22633-3); pap. 23.95 (ISBN 0-521-29586-6). Cambridge U Pr.

Physiology of Marriage. William A. Alcott. LC 79-180551. (Medicine & Society in America Ser). 266p. 1972. Repr. of 1866 ed. 18.00 (ISBN 0-405-03931-X). Ayer Co Pubs.

Physiology of Marriage. Honore De Balzac. (Black & Gold Lib). 1943. 6.95 (ISBN 0-87140-983-6, Co-Pub with Tudor). Liveright.

Physiology of Mastication. Ed. by Y. Kawamura. (Frontiers of Oral Physiology: Vol. 1). 1974. 116.00 (ISBN 3-8055-1281-3). S Karger.

Physiology of Membrane Disorders. 2nd ed. Ed. by Thomas E. Andreoli et al. LC 85-19367. 1094p. 1986. 135.00x (ISBN 0-306-41774-X, Plenum Med). Plenum Pub.

Physiology of Membrane Fluidity, 2 vols. Meir Shinitzky. 1984. Vol. I, 208p. 85.00 (ISBN 0-8493-6141-9); Vol. II, 144p. 66.00 (ISBN 0-8493-6142-7). CRC Pr.

Physiology of Mollusca, 2 vols. Ed. by Karl M. Wilbur & C. M. Yonge. Vol. 1, 1966. 96.50 (ISBN 0-12-751302-7); Vol. 2, 1964. 78.00 (ISBN 0-12-751301-9). Acad Pr.

Physiology of Movements. Ed. by W. Haupt & M. E. Feinleib. (Encyclopedia of Plant Physiology: Vol. 7). (Illus.). 1979. 118.00 (ISBN 0-387-08776-1). Springer-Verlag.

Physiology of Nematodes. 2d ed. Donald Lewis Lee & H. J. Atkinson. LC 77-1232. (Illus.). 215p. 1977. 36.00x (ISBN 0-231-04358-9). Columbia U Pr.

Physiology of Nerve Cells. John C. Eccles. LC 68-9181. 288p. 1957. pap. 9.95x (ISBN 0-8018-0182-6). Johns Hopkins.

Physiology of Non-Excitable Cells: Proceedings of the 28th International Congress of Physiological Sciences, Budapest, 1980. Ed. by J. Salanki et al. LC 80-41874. (Advances in Physiological Sciences: Vol. 3). (Illus.). 350p. 1981. 57.00 (ISBN 0-08-026815-3). Pergamon.

Physiology of Oral Reconstruction. Dubrul & Menekratis. 1981. 52.00 (ISBN 0-931386-47-0). Quint Pub Co.

Physiology of Oral Tissues. Ed. by Y. Kawamura. (Frontiers of Oral Physiology: Vol. 2). (Illus.). 350p. 1976. 77.50 (ISBN 3-8055-1360-7). S Karger.

Physiology of Oxygen Radicals. Ed. by Aubrey E. Taylor et al. (American Physiological Society Book). (Illus.). 313p. 1986. 49.50 (ISBN 0-19-520686-X). Oxford U Pr.

Physiology of Parasitism: Proceedings of the All India Symposium, Jabalpur, Feb. 24-27, 1978. All India Symposium Staff. Ed. by G. P. Agarwal & K. S. Bilgrami. (Current Trends in Life Sciences: Vol. 7). vi, 478p. 1979. 50.00 (ISBN 0-88065-004-4, Pub. by Messers Today & Tomorrows Printers & Publishers India). Scholarly Pubns.

Physiology of Peripheral Nerve Disease. Austin J. Sumner. (Illus.). 544p. 1980. text ed. write for info. (ISBN 0-7216-8639-7). Saunders.

Physiology of Photoreceptor Organs see Handbook of Sensory Physiology.

Physiology of Physical Stress: A Selective Bibliography, 1500-1964. Carl B. Chapman & Elinor C. Reinmiller. LC 74-15565. 400p. 1974. text ed. 27.00x (ISBN 0-674-66670-4). Harvard U Pr.

Physiology of Plants under Stress. Maynard G. Hale & David M. Orcutt. LC 87-17609. 206p. 1987. 39.95 (ISBN 0-471-88997-0); pap. 22.50 (ISBN 0-471-63247-3). Wiley.

Physiology of Reproduction, 2 vols. Ed. by Ernst Knobil et al. 2640p. 1988. Set. text ed. 290.00 (ISBN 0-88167-281-5). Raven.

Physiology of Reproduction: Proceedings of the Biology Colloquium, 22nd, Oregon State University, 1961. Biology Colloquium Staff. Ed. by Frederick L. Hisaw, Jr. LC 52-19235. (Illus.). 152p. 1963. 10.95x (ISBN 0-87071-161-X). Oreg St U Pr.

Physiology of Respiration. 2nd ed. Julius H. Comroe, Jr. (Illus.). 316p. 1974. 25.00 (ISBN 0-8151-1826-0); pap. 22.00 (ISBN 0-8151-1827-9). Year Bk Med.

Physiology of Rubber Tree Latex, 2 vols. Ed. by J. D'Auzac et al. 1988. 197.00; Vol. I, 224 pgs. cancelled (ISBN 0-8493-4893-5, 4893). Vol. II, 256 pgs (ISBN 0-8493-4894-3, 4894). CRC Pr.

Physiology of Seed Detenovation. Ed. by M. B. McDonald, Jr. & C. J. Nelson. 123p. 1986. 18.00 (ISBN 0-89118-522-4). Crop Sci Soc Am.

Physiology of Smooth Muscle. Ed. by E. Bulbring & M. F. Shuba. LC 75-14566. 448p. 1976. 68.00 (ISBN 0-89004-051-6). Raven.

Physiology of Speech & Hearing: An Introduction. Raymond G. Daniloff & Gordon H. Schuckers. 1980. text ed. write for info. (ISBN 0-13-674747-7). P-H.

Physiology of Speech Production: An Introduction for Speech Scientists. W. J. Hardcastle. 1977. 29.00 (ISBN 0-12-324950-3). Acad Pr.

Physiology of Standing: Postural Reactions & Equilibrium with Special Reference to the Behavior of Decerebellate Animals. G. G. Rademaker. 680p. 1981. 35.00x (ISBN 0-8166-0857-1). U of Minn Pr.

Physiology of Strength. Theodor Hettinger. (Illus.). 96p. 1961. 13.75x (ISBN 0-398-04281-0). C C Thomas.

Physiology of Stress. Mary F. Asterita & Donald D. Macchia. Ed. by Mary Didelot. (Illus.). 1985. incl. tapes & slides 140.00 (ISBN 0-933019-00-9). Aster Pub Co.

Physiology of Stress: With Special Reference to the Neuroendocrine System. Mary F. Asterita. 240p. 1984. text ed. 34.95 (ISBN 0-89885-176-9); pap. 16.95 (ISBN 0-89885-187-4). Human Sci Pr.

Physiology of Synapses. John C. Eccles. (Illus.). 1964. Repr. 38.00 (ISBN 0-387-03112-X). Springer-Verlag.

Physiology of Taste. Brillat-Savarin. Tr. by M. F. Fisher. LC 78-7199. 1978. pap. 9.95 (ISBN 0-15-671770-0, Harv). HarBraceJ.

Physiology of Taste. Anselme Brillat-Savarin. Orig. Title: Physiologie du Gout. (Illus.). 350p. 1982. pap. 9.95 (ISBN 0-918172-11-X). Leetes Isl.

Physiology of Taste: Or, Meditations on Transcendental Gastronomy. Jean A. Brillat-Savarin. Tr. & annotations by M. F. Fisher. LC 86-61002. 464p. 1986. pap. 13.95 (ISBN 0-86547-249-1). N Point Pr.

Physiology of Temperate Zone Fruit Trees. Faust. 1987. write for info. (ISBN 0-471-81781-3). Wiley.

Physiology of the Amino Acids. Frank P. Underhill. 1915. 49.50x. Elliots Bks.

Physiology of the Amphibia. Ed. by Brian Lofts. 1974. Vol. 2. 106.50 (ISBN 0-12-455402-4); Vol. 3, 1976. 113.00 (ISBN 0-12-455403-2). Acad Pr.

Physiology of the Body Fluids. Ed. by David Ramsay. (Series in Physiology). Date not set. price not set (ISBN 0-89004-328-0). Raven.

Physiology of the Cornea & Contact Lens Applications. Hikaru Hamano & Herbert E. Kaufman. (Illus.). 100p. 1986. text ed. 40.00 (ISBN 0-443-08519-6). Churchill.

Physiology of the Digestive Tract. 5th ed. Horace W. Davenport. (Illus.). 1982. 37.50 (ISBN 0-8151-2330-2); pap. 29.00 (ISBN 0-8151-2329-9). Year Bk Med.

Physiology of the Ear. Ed. by Anthony F. Jahn & Joseph Santos-Sacchi. (Illus.). 544p. 1988. text ed. 99.00 (ISBN 0-88167-437-0). Raven.

Physiology of the Eye. 4th ed. H. Davson. 1980. 85.00 (ISBN 0-12-206745-2). Acad Pr.

Physiology of the Eye & of Vision see System of Ophthalmology Series.

Physiology of the Fetal & Neonatal Lung. Ed. by D. V. Walters et al. 1987. lib. bdg. 79.00 (ISBN 0-85200-948-8, Pub. by MTP Pr England). Kluwer Academic.

Physiology of the Garden Pea. Ed. by J. F. Sutcliffe & J. S. Pate. 1978. 99.00 (ISBN 0-12-677550-8). Acad Pr.

Physiology of the Gastro-Intestinal Lymphatic System. J. A. Barrowman. LC 77-22823. (Physiological Society Monographs: No. 33). (Illus.). 1978. 67.50 (ISBN 0-521-21710-5). Cambridge U Pr.

Physiology of the Gastro-Intestinal Lymphatic System. J. A. Barrowman. LC 77-22823. (Monographs of the Physiological Society: No. 33). pap. 85.00 (2027280). Bks Demand UMI.

Physiology of the Gastrointestinal Tract, 2 Vols. 2nd ed. Ed. by Leonard R. Johnson et al. (Illus.). 1880p. 1987. Set. text ed. 262.50 (ISBN 0-88167-165-7). Raven.

Physiology of the Heart. Arnold M. Katz. LC 75-14580. 464p. 1977. pap. 29.00 (ISBN 0-686-67627-0). Raven.

Physiology of the Heart & Circulation. 4th ed. Robert C. Little. 1988. 22.95 (ISBN 0-8151-5478-X). Year Bk Med.

Physiology of the Human Body. 6th ed. Arthur C. Guyton. 1984. text ed. 46.00 (ISBN 0-03-058339-X, CBS C). SCP.

Physiology of the Human Body. 3rd ed. J. Robert Mcclintic. LC 84-23448. 615p. 1985. 36.95 (ISBN 0-471-87483-3); pap. 19.95 study guide (ISBN 0-471-83099-2). Wiley.

Physiology of the Hypothalmus: Handbook of the Hypothalamus, Vol. 2. Morgane & Panskepp. 688p. 1980. 155.00 (ISBN 0-8247-6881-7). Dekker.

Physiology of the Insecta. 2nd ed. Rockstein. 1974. Vol. 1, 1973. 99.00 (ISBN 0-12-591601-9); Vol. 2, 1974. 99.00 (ISBN 0-12-591602-7); Vol. 3, 1974. 99.00 (ISBN 0-12-591603-5); Vol. 4, 1974. 92.00 (ISBN 0-12-591604-3); Vol. 5, 1974. 106.00 (ISBN 0-12-591605-1); Vol. 6, 1974. 103.50 (ISBN 0-12-591606-X). Acad Pr.

Physiology of the Intestinal Circulation. Ed. by A. P. Shepherd & D. N. Granger. LC 84-9858. (Illus.). 440p. 1984. text ed. 104.00 (ISBN 0-88167-025-1). Raven.

Physiology of the Joints, 3 vols. I. A. Kapandji. Incl. Vol. 1, 5E. Upper Limb. 2nd ed. 1982. 22.00 (ISBN 0-443-02504-5); Vol. 2. Lower Limb. 5th ed. (Illus.). 1987. 22.00 (ISBN 0-443-03618-7); Vol. 3. Truck & Vertebral Column. 2nd ed. 1974. 22.00 (ISBN 0-443-01209-1). (Illus.). Churchill.

Physiology of the Kidney. 2nd ed. Lawrence P. Sullivan & Jared J. Grantham. LC 81-18569. (Illus.). 236p. 1982. pap. 14.50 (ISBN 0-8121-0839-6). Lea & Febiger.

Physiology of the Kidney & Body Fluids. 3rd ed. Robert F. Pitts. (Illus.). 307p. 1974. pap. 20.00 (ISBN 0-8151-6703-2). Year Bk Med.

Physiology of the Kidney & of Water Balance. P. Deetjen et al. LC 72-85949. (Illus.). 145p. 1975. pap. 24.00 (ISBN 0-387-90048-9). Springer-Verlag.

Physiology of the Lower Urinary Tract. Ed. by M. J. Torrens & J. F. Morrison. (Illus.). 255p. 1987. 135.00 (ISBN 0-387-17486-9). Springer Verlag.

Physiology of the Lung. Thomas P. Lim. (Illus.). 196p. 1983. spiral bdg. 18.50x (ISBN 0-398-04727-8). C C Thomas.

Physiology of the Nervous System. C. Eyzaguirre. 17.50 (ISBN 0-8151-3185-2). Year Bk Med.

Physiology of the Nervous System. David Ottoson. (Illus.). 1983. 45.00x (ISBN 0-19-520409-3); pap. 28.95x (ISBN 0-19-520410-7). Oxford U Pr.

Physiology of the Newborn Infant. 4th ed. Ed. by Clement A. Smith & Nicholas M. Nelson. (Illus.). 784p. 1976. 86.50 (ISBN 0-398-03232-7). C C Thomas.

Physiology of the Opera by Scrici (Philadelphia: Willis P. Hazard, 1852) Intro. by D. W. Krummel. LC 81-81546. (I.S.A.M. Special Publications: No. 2). 125p. 1981. pap. 6.00 (ISBN 0-914678-16-7). Inst Am Music.

Physiology of the Peripheral Arterial Chemoreceptors. Ed. by H. Acker & R. G. O'Regan. xii, 494p. 1984. 211.00 (ISBN 0-444-80494-3, I-179-84, Biomedical Pr). Elsevier.

Physiology of Thirst & Sodium Appetite. Ed. by G. De Caro et al. LC 86-4982. (NATO ASI Series A, Life Sciences: Vol. 105). 586p. 1986. 89.50x (ISBN 0-306-42265-4, Plenum Pr). Plenum Pub.

Physiology of Thirst & Sodium Appetite. J. T. Fitzsimons. LC 78-16212. (Physiological Society Monographs: No. 35). 1979. 95.00 (ISBN 0-521-22292-3). Cambridge U Pr.

Physiology of Ticks. Ed. by F. D. Obenchain & R. Galun. (Current Themes in Tropical Science Ser.: Vol. 1). (Illus.). 450p. 1982. 180.00 (ISBN 0-08-024937-X). Pergamon.

Physiology of Trematodes. 2nd ed. James D. Smyth & D. W. Halton. LC 82-12961. (Illus.). 460p. pap. 119.60 (2030621). Bks Demand UMI.

Physiology of Tropical Field Crops. Ed. by Peter R. Goldsworthy & N. M. Fisher. LC 83-21624. 664p. 1984. 116.00 (ISBN 0-471-10267-9). Wiley.

Physiology of Violin Bowing. Otto Szende & Mihaly Nemessuri. 15.95 (ISBN 0-318-18113-4). Am String Tchrs.

Physiology of Woody Plants. Paul J. Kramer & Theodore T. Kozlowski. LC 78-27356. 1979. 39.95 (ISBN 0-12-425050-5). Acad Pr.

Physiology of Work Capacity & Fatigue. photocopy ed. Ernst Simonson. (Illus.). 592p. 1971. 65.75 (ISBN 0-398-01750-6). C C Thomas.

Physiology; or, an Attempt to Explain the Functions & Laws of the Nervous System see First Lines for the Practice of Physic.

Physiology: Past, Present, & Future: A Symposium in Honour of Yngve Zotterman, University of Bristol, July 11 & 12, 1979. Ed. by D. J. Anderson. LC 80-40957. (Illus.). 168p. 1980. 42.00 (ISBN 0-08-025480-2). Pergamon.

Physiology: PreTest Self-Assessment & Review. 4th ed. Ed. by Craig A. Dise. 196p. 1986. write for info. McGraw-Pretest.

Physiology Workbook. Oosthuizen. 1984. text ed. 14.95 (ISBN 0-409-08631-2). Butterworth.

Physionomie du Theatre de l'Odeon. Ed. by John R. Williams. 30p. 1982. pap. 3.95 (ISBN 0-917786-27-0). Summa Pubns.

Physiopathogenesis of the Epilepsies. Henri Gastaut et al. (Illus.). 340p. 1969. photocopy ed. 40.25x (ISBN 0-398-00656-3). C C Thomas.

Physiopathology & Treatment of Functional Disorders. George B. Whatmore & Daniel R Kohli. LC 74-17154. (Illus.). 256p. 1974. 56.50 (ISBN 0-8089-0851-0, 794810). Grune.

Physiopathology of Endocrine Diseases & Mechanisms of Hormone Action. Robert J. Soto et al. LC 81-17158. (Progress in Clinical & Biological Research Ser.: Vol. 74). 526p. 1981. 86.00 (ISBN 0-8451-0074-2). A R Liss.

Physiopathology of Hypophysial Disturbances & Diseases of Reproduction. Alejandro F. DeNicola & Jorge A. Blaquier. LC 82-15219. (Progress in Clinical & Biological Research Ser.: Vol. 87). 352p. 1982. 40.00 (ISBN 0-8451-0087-4). A R Liss.

Physiopathology of the Cardiovascular System. Joseph S. Alpert. (Physiopathology Ser.). 348p. 1984. pap. text ed. 22.50 (ISBN 0-316-03504-1). Little.

Physiotheraphy in Pediatrics. 2nd ed. Roberta B. Shepherd. 524p. 1980. 38.00 (ISBN 0-89443-813-1). Aspen Pub.

Physiotherapy & the Asthmatic Child. Myra Kendall. 176p. 1988. text ed. 21.95 (ISBN 0-8385-7866-7). Appleton & Lange.

Physiotherapy Assessment. 2nd ed. Anne Parry. LC 85-4615. 168p. (Orig.). 1985. pap. 11.95 (ISBN 0-7099-4009-2, Pub. by Croom Helm Ltd). Routledge Chapman & Hall.

Physiotherapy Equipment Markets. 278p. 1984. 1750.00 (ISBN 0-86621-609-X, E681). Frost & Sullivan.

Physiotherapy in Cerebral Palsy: A Handbook. Sophie Levitt. (Illus.). 148p. 1962. photocopy ed. 16.25x (ISBN 0-398-04337-X). C C Thomas.

Physiotherapy in Disorders of the Brain. Janet H. Carr & Roberta B. Shepherd. 408p. 1980. 37.00 (ISBN 0-89443-656-2). Aspen Pub.

Physiotherapy in the Community. Ann Gibson. 1988. text ed. 45.00 (ISBN 0-85941-446-9, Pub. by Woodhead-Faulkner); pap. text ed. 26.95 (ISBN 0-85941-412-4, Pub. by Woodhead-Faulkner). Longwood Pub Group.

Physique: A Pictorial History of the Athletic Model Guild. Photos by Bob Mizer. Ed. by Winston Leyland. (Illus.). 96p. (Orig.). 1982. pap. 18.95 (ISBN 0-917342-94-1). Gay Sunshine.

Physique & Character: An Investigation of the Nature of Constitution & of the Theory of Temperament. Ernst Kretschmer. LC 73-119165. Repr. of 1936 ed. 25.00x (ISBN 0-8154-0332-1). Cooper Sq.

Physique & Delinquency. Sheldon S. Glueck & Eleanor T. Glueck. 1956. 45.00 (ISBN 0-527-34104-5). Kraus Repr.

Physique & Delinquent Behavior: A Thirty Year Followup of W. H. Sheldon's Varieties of Delinquent Youth. Emil Hartl et al. (Personality & Psychopathology Ser.). 582p. 1982. 65.00 (ISBN 0-12-328480-5). Acad Pr.

Physique & Intellect. Donald G. Paterson. Repr. of 1930 ed. lib. bdg. 35.00x (ISBN 0-8371-2886-2, PAPI). Greenwood.

Piano for Fun: A Creative Chord Approach for Kids, Bk. 1. 2nd ed. Anita Barr. (Illus.). 64p. (Orig.). (gr. k-8). 1984. pap. 9.95 incl. cass. (ISBN 0-9611130-4-9). Funn Music.

Piano for Julie. Eleanor Schick. LC 83-14154. (Illus.). 32p. (gr. k-3). 1984. 10.25 (ISBN 0-688-01818-1); PLB 10.88 (ISBN 0-688-01819-X). Greenwillow.

Piano for Pleasure: A Basic Course for Adults. Martha Hilley & Lynn F. Olson. LC 85-20208. (Illus.). 346p. (Orig.). 1986. pap. text ed. 26.75 (ISBN 0-314-93533-9). West Pub.

Piano for the Developing Musician, Vol. 1. Martha Hilley & Lynn F. Olson. (Illus.). 256p. 1985. pap. text ed. 26.75 (ISBN 0-314-85247-6). West Pub.

Piano for the Developing Musician, Vol. 2. Martha Hilley & Lynn F. Olson. 292p. 1985. pap. text ed. 26.75 (ISBN 0-314-87394-5). West Pub.

Piano-Forte. Rosamond E. Harding. LC 69-15634. (Music Ser.). 1973. Repr. of 1933 ed. lib. bdg. 49.50 (ISBN 0-306-71084-6). Da Capo.

Piano-Forte. Rosamond E. Harding. 1988. Repr. lib. bdg. 75.00x. Am Biog Serv.

Piano-Forte: Its History Traced to the Great Exhibition of 1851. Rosamond E. Harding. LC 71-181171. 1933. Repr. 69.00x (ISBN 0-403-01574-X). Scholarly.

Piano: Guided Sight-Reading: A New Approach to Piano Study. Leonhard Deutsch. (Illus.). 1978. 18.95x (ISBN 0-88229-555-1); pap. 9.95 (ISBN 0-88229-556-X). Nelson-Hall.

Piano Hammer. Walter Pfeifer. Tr. by J. Englehardt from Ger. (Illus.). 120p. (Orig.). 1979. pap. 49.43 (ISBN 3-920-11261-X). Bold Strummer Ltd.

Piano Improvisation on Rhythm & Dissonant Chords: For Individual & Class Instruction. Carmen P. Rummo. LC 79-91854. 70p. (Orig.). 1979. pap. text ed. 6.95 (ISBN 0-913650-12-9). Columbia Pictures.

Piano in Chamber Ensemble: An Annotated Guide. Maurice Hinson. LC 77-9862. 608p. 1978. 32.50 (ISBN 0-253-34493-X). Ind U Pr.

Piano: Its Story, from Zither to Grand. David S. Grover. (Illus.). 1978. 4.95 (ISBN 0-684-15781-0, ScribT). Scribner.

Piano Literature of the 17th, 18th, & 19th Centuries. Ed. by Frances Clark & Louise Goss. Incl. Bk. 1. 32p. 1964. pap. text ed. 5.95 (ISBN 0-87487-125-5); Bk. 2. (Illus.). 64p. 1954. pap. text ed. 5.95 (ISBN 0-87487-126-3); Bks. 3, 4a & 4b. (Illus.). 64p. 1957. pap. text ed. 9.95 (ISBN 0-87487-127-1); Bks. 5a & 6a. (Illus.). 48p. 1974. pap. text ed. 7.95 (ISBN 0-87487-128-X); Bk. 5b. (Illus.). 48p. 1957. pap. text ed. 7.95 (ISBN 0-87487-129-8); Bk. 6b. (Illus.). 64p. 1956. pap. text ed. 9.95 (ISBN 0-87487-130-1). (Frances Clark Library for Piano Students). pap. text ed. Birch Tree Gr.

Piano Man's Christmas & Other Stories for Christmas. Ira Williams, Jr. 80p. (Orig.). 1986. pap. 4.95 (ISBN 0-687-30920-4). Abingdon.

Piano Masterpieces of Maurice Ravel. Maurice Ravel. 128p. 1986. pap. 5.95 (ISBN 0-486-25137-3). Dover.

Piano Music. Agathe Backer-Grondahl. LC 81-19523. (Women Composers Ser.: No. 9). 145p. 1983. lib. bdg. 29.50 (ISBN 0-306-76133-5). Da Capo.

Piano Music. Amy Beach. LC 81-12551. (Women Composers Ser.: No. 10). 1982. Repr. lib. bdg. 29.50 (ISBN 0-306-76088-6). Da Capo.

Piano Music Eighteen Eighty-Eight to Nineteen Hundred Five. Claude Debussy. 175p. 1972. pap. 6.95 (ISBN 0-486-22771-5). Dover.

Piano Music from New Orleans Eighteen Fifty-One to Eighteen Ninety-Eight. Compiled by John Baron. LC 80-12645. (Music Reprint Ser.). (Illus.). 194p. 1980. Repr. lib. bdg. 32.50 (ISBN 0-306-76034-7). Da Capo.

Piano Music in Collections: An Index. Rita M. Fuszek. LC 78-70023. 1982. 50.00 (ISBN 0-89990-012-7). Harmonie Pk Pr.

Piano Music of Bela Bartok. Bela Bartok. Ed. by Benjamin Suchoff. (Series I-Archive Edition). 18.00 (ISBN 0-8446-5875-8). Peter Smith.

Piano Music of Bela Bartok. Bela Bartok. Ed. by Benjamin Suchoff. (Series II-Archive Edition). 18.00 (ISBN 0-8446-5876-6). Peter Smith.

Piano Music of Bela Bartok, Series I. Bela Bartok. 1982. pap. 6.95 (ISBN 0-486-24108-4). Dover.

Piano Music of Bela Bartok, Series II. Bela Bartok. 1982. pap. 6.95 (ISBN 0-486-24109-2). Dover.

Piano Music of Louis Moreau Gottschalk: 26 Complete Pieces from Original Editions. Louis M. Gottschalk. Ed. by Richard Jackson. LC 73-75872. 320p. (Orig.). 1973. pap. 10.95 (ISBN 0-486-21683-7). Dover.

Piano Music of Louis Moreau Gottschalk: 26 Complete Pieces from Original Editions. Louis M. Gottschalk. Ed. & intro. by Richard Jackson. 13.25 (ISBN 0-8446-4746-2). Peter Smith.

Piano Music of Robert Schumann. Robert Schumann. Incl. Series I. 274p. pap. 9.95 (ISBN 0-486-21459-1); Series 2. 272p. pap. 9.95 (ISBN 0-486-21461-3). 1972. pap. Dover.

Piano Music of Robert Schumann: Series III. Robert Schumann. Ed. by Clara Schumann. 1980. Repr. of 1887 ed. 7.95 (ISBN 0-486-23906-3). Dover.

Piano Music of Six Great Composers. facs. ed. Donald N. Ferguson. LC 73-111830. (Essay Index Reprint Ser). 1947. 24.50 (ISBN 0-8369-1652-2). Ayer Co Pubs.

Piano Nomenclatur: Deutch, English, Francais, Italiano, Norsk, Espanol. N. Schimmel. Ed. by H. K. Herzog. 130p. 1983. pap. text ed. 60.16 (ISBN 3-920-11219-9). Bold Strummer Ltd.

Piano-Owner's Guide. Carl D. Schmeckel. LC 74-7362. (Illus.). 120p. 1974. 7.95 (ISBN 0-684-13869-7, ScribT); pap. 6.95 (ISBN 0-684-13872-7, ScribT). Scribner.

Piano Pieces, (Opus 51, 55, 61, 62) Edward MacDowell. LC 70-170391. (Earlier American Music Ser.: No. 8). 144p. 1972. Repr. lib. bdg. 32.50 (ISBN 0-306-77308-2). Da Capo.

Piano Player's Jazz Handbook. Ray Spencer. LC 84-20289. (Illus.). 1985. pap. 14.00 (ISBN 0-8108-1778-0). Scarecrow.

Piano Playing: A Positive Approach. Richard Collins. 76p. 1986. lib. bdg. 19.50 (ISBN 0-8191-5367-2); pap. text ed. 8.00 (ISBN 0-8191-5368-0). U Pr of Amer.

Piano Playing with Piano Questions Answered. Josef Hofmann. (Illus.). 1976. pap. 4.95 (ISBN 0-486-23362-6). Dover.

Piano Progress, Bk. I. June Davison & Ardella Schaub. Ed. by Leo Podolsky. 1967. 4.50 (ISBN 0-913650-43-9). Columbia Pictures.

Piano Progress, Bk. II. June Davison & Ardella Schaub. Ed. by Leo Podolsky. 1967. 5.00 (ISBN 0-913650-44-7). Columbia Pictures.

Piano Progress for the Partially Sighted, Bk. IA. June Davison & Ardella Schaub. Ed. by Leo Podolsky. 1972. 5.00 (ISBN 0-913650-13-7). Columbia Pictures.

Piano Progress for the Partially Sighted, Bk. IB. June Davison & Ardella Schaub. Ed. by Leo Podolsky. 1972. 5.00 (ISBN 0-913650-14-5). Columbia Pictures.

Piano Progress for the Partially Sighted, Bk. 2A. June Davison & Ardella Schaub. Ed. by Leo Podolsky. 1967. 5.00 (ISBN 0-913650-15-3). Columbia Pictures.

Piano Progress for the Partially Sighted, Bk. 3B. June Davison & Ardella Schaub. Ed. by Leo Podolsky. 1974. 6.95 (ISBN 0-913650-18-8). Columbia Pictures.

Piano Progress-Primary Book. June Davison & Ardella Schaub. Ed. by Leo Podolsky. 1968. 5.00 (ISBN 0-913650-42-0). Columbia Pictures.

Piano Repertoire: A Guide to Interpretation & Performance. Bela Siki. LC 81-50526. (Illus.). 352p. 1981. 22.95 (ISBN 0-02-872390-2). Schirmer Bks.

Piano Servicing, Tuning & Rebuilding. Arthur A. Reblitz. LC 76-21796. (Illus.). 179p. 1986. pap. 15.95 (ISBN 0-911572-58-9, B-55). Vestal.

Piano Sonata, No. 1. Harold Zabrack. 1978. 5.00 (ISBN 0-934286-06-X). Kenyon.

Piano Sonata, No. 2. Harold Zabrack. 1981. pap. 7.50 (ISBN 0-934286-61-2). Kenyon.

Piano Sonata No. I. Albert DeVito. (Orig.). 1979. pap. 5.00 (ISBN 0-934286-12-4). Kenyon.

Piano Sonatina. Albert DeVito. (Illus.). 16p. (Orig.). 1985. 5.00 (ISBN 0-934286-65-5). Kenyon.

Piano Stool: Footnotes. Simon Cutts. pap. 10.00 (ISBN 0-912330-55-4). Jargon Soc.

Piano Stylings. Edward Shanaphy. 1985. book of special music arrangements 9.95 (ISBN 0-943748-09-7). Ekay Music.

Piano Teacher. Elfriede Jelinek. Ed. by Mark Polizzotti. 1988. price not set (ISBN 1-55584-052-3). Weidenfeld.

Piano Teacher. Robert K. Tanenbaum & Peter S. Greenberg. 304p. (Orig.). 1988. pap. 4.50 (ISBN 0-451-15468-1, Sig). NAL.

Piano Teacher: The True Story of a Psychotic Killer. Robert K. Tanenbaum & Peter S. Greenberg. 1987. 18.95 (ISBN 0-453-00547-0). NAL.

Piano Teacher's Art (Guideline for Successful Piano Teaching) Isabelle Y. Byman. Ed. by Albert K. De Vito. 1979. 13.50 (ISBN 0-934286-13-2). Kenyon.

Piano Technic, 6 bks. Ed. by Frances Clark & Louise Goss. Incl. Bk. 1. 48p. 1954. pap. text ed. 7.95 (ISBN 0-87487-131-X); Bk. 2. 40p. 1955. pap. text ed. 7.95 (ISBN 0-87487-132-8); Bk. 3. 40p. 1955. pap. text ed. 7.95 (ISBN 0-87487-133-6); Bk. 4. 40p. 1960. pap. text ed. 7.95 (ISBN 0-87487-134-4); Bk. 5. 40p. 1960. pap. text ed. 7.95 (ISBN 0-87487-135-2); Bk. 6. 40p. 1960. pap. text ed. 7.95 (ISBN 0-87487-136-0). (Frances Clark Library for Piano Students). pap. text ed. Birch Tree Gr.

Piano Technique. Walter Gieseking & Karl Leimer. (Illus.). 140p. pap. 3.50 (ISBN 0-486-22867-3). Dover.

Piano Technique: Tone, Touch, Phrasing & Dynamics. Lillie H. Philipp. (Illus.). 90p. (gr. 7 up). 1982. pap. 4.95 (ISBN 0-486-24272-2). Dover.

Piano Tone Building see Secrets of Piano Construction.

Piano Transcriptions from French & Italian Operas. Franz Liszt. (Illus.). 256p. 1982. pap. 8.95 (ISBN 0-486-24273-0). Dover.

Piano Tuner. Peter Meinke. LC 85-28864. (Flannery O'Connor Award for Short Fiction Ser.). 176p. 1986. 13.95 (ISBN 0-8203-0844-7). U of GA Pr.

Piano Tuning: A Simple & Accurate Method for Amateurs. J. Cree Fischer. LC 75-14759. 224p. 1976. pap. 3.50 (ISBN 0-486-23267-0). Dover.

Piano Variations. Harold Zabrack. 1981. pap. 5.00 (ISBN 0-934286-60-4). KENYON.

Piano Way to Music Piano Speller. June Davison & Ardella Schaub. Ed. by Leo Podolsky. 1957. 5.00 (ISBN 0-913650-46-3). Columbia Pictures.

Piano Way to Music Reader, Bk. II. June Davison & Ardella Schaub. Ed. by Leo Podolsky. 1957. 3.50 (ISBN 0-913650-48-X). Columbia Pictures.

Piano Way to Music Reader, Bk. III. June Davison & Ardella Schaub. Ed. by Leo Podolsky. 1957. 3.50 (ISBN 0-913650-49-8). Columbia Pictures.

Piano Works of Claude Debussy. E. Robert Schmitz. LC 82-23642. (Music Reprint Ser.). 238p. 1983. Repr. of 1950 ed. lib. bdg. 29.50 (ISBN 0-306-76199-8). Da Capo.

Piano Works of Claude Debussy. Elie R. Schmitz. (Illus.). 1966. pap. 5.50 (ISBN 0-486-21567-9). Dover.

Pianoforte: A Social History of the Piano. Dieter Hildebrandt. Tr. by Harriet Goodman from Ger. 224p. 1988. 19.95 (ISBN 0-8076-1182-4). Braziller.

Pianoforte & Its Music. Henry E. Krehbiel. LC 76-22338. 1976. Repr. of 1911 ed. lib. bdg. 35.00 (ISBN 0-89341-016-0). Longwood Pub Group.

Pianoforte & Its Music. Henry E. Krehbiel. 324p. 1984. pap. 6.75 cancelled (ISBN 0-317-01741-1). Longwood Pub Group.

Pianoforte Music: Its History. John C. Fillmore. LC 77-92444. 1978. Repr. of 1884 ed. lib. bdg. 25.00 (ISBN 0-89341-428-X). Longwood Pub Group.

Pianoforte Sonata: Its Origin & Development. 2nd ed. J. S. Shedlock. LC 64-18993. (Music Ser). 1964. Repr. of 1895 ed. lib. bdg. 29.50 (ISBN 0-306-70900-7). Da Capo.

Pianola: The History of the Self-Playing Piano. Arthur W. Ord-Hume. (Illus.). 360p. 1984. 65.00x (ISBN 0-04-789009-6). Unwin Hyman.

PianoLab: An Introduction to Class Piano. Carolynn A. Lindeman. 292p. 1983. Spiralbound. text ed. write for info. (ISBN 0-534-01305-8). Wadsworth Pub.

Pianoplayers. Anthony Burgess. 256p. 1986. 16.95 (ISBN 0-87795-832-7). Morrow.

Pianoplayers. Anthony Burgess. 1987. pap. 4.95. WSP.

Pianos & Player Pianos: An Informative Guide for Owners & Prospective Buyers. Adrian Bezdechi. LC 79-318082. (Illus.). 63p. (Orig.). 1979. pap. 7.75 (ISBN 0-9604092-0-3). Interstate Piano.

Pianos & Their Makers. Alfred Dolge. (Illus.). 581p. 1972. pap. 9.95 (ISBN 0-486-22856-8). Dover.

Pianos & Their Makers: A Comprehensive History of the Development of the Piano from the Monochord to the Concert Grand Player Piano. Alfred Dolge. (Illus.). 14.75 (ISBN 0-8446-4540-0). Peter Smith.

Pianos in Practice: An Owner's Manual. 120p. 1978. text ed. 8.95x (ISBN 0-317-62614-0, Pub. by Scolar Pr). Gower Pub Co.

Pianos in Practice: An Owner's Manual. Eric Smith. 1978. 15.95 (ISBN 0-85967-393-6); pap. 7.95 (ISBN 0-317-12599-0). Scolar.

Piast Poland. Pawel Jasienica. Tr. by Alexander T. Jordan from Pol. (Illus.). 238p. 1985. 19.50 (ISBN 0-87052-134-9). Hippocrene Bks.

Piazza see Piazza Tales.

Piazza Armerina. R. J. Wilson. (Illus.). 124p. 1983. 12.50 (ISBN 0-292-76472-3). U of Tex Pr.

Piazza Tales. Herman Melville. Ed. by Egbert S. Oliver. Incl. Piazza; Bartleby; Benito Cereno; Lightning-Rod Man; Encantadas; Bell-Tower. (Complete Works of Herman Melville Ser.). 268p. 1962. 13.00 (ISBN 0-87532-005-8). Hendricks House.

Piazza Tales. Herman Meville. 14.95 (ISBN 0-89190-877-3, Pub. by Am Repr). Amereon Ltd.

Piazza Tales see Pierre, Israel Potter, the Confidence-Man, Tales & Billy Budd.

Piazza Tales & Other Prose Pieces, 1839-60. Herman Melville. Ed. by Hershel Parker & G. Thomas Tanselle. (Writings of Herman Melville Ser.: Vol. 9). (Illus.). 848p. 1987. 82.95x (ISBN 0-8101-0550-0); pap. 21.95 (ISBN 0-8101-0551-9). Northwestern U Pr.

Piazzetta: A Tercentenary Exhibition of Drawings, Prints, & Books. George Knox. LC 83-17484. (Illus.). pap. 9.95 (ISBN 0-89468-071-4). Natl Gallery Art.

Piazzetta: A Tercentenary Exhibition of Drawings, Prints, & Books. Ed. by George Knox. LC 83-17484. 258p. 1984. 57.50 (ISBN 0-521-26431-6). Cambridge U Pr.

Pic. Jack Kerouac. LC 71-166459. 1971. pap. 4.95 (ISBN 0-394-62440-8, E839, Ever). Grove.

Pica. David J. Gerrick. (Illus.). 1978. 20.00 (ISBN 0-916750-45-0). Dayton Labs.

Picacho: Life & Death of a Great Gold Mining Camp. Peter Odens. (Illus.). 44p. 1982. Repr. of 1973 ed. lib. bdg. 3.50 (ISBN 0-9609484-4-9). P R Odens.

Picara y la Dama: La Imagen de las Nujeres en las Novelas Picaresco Cortesanas de Maria de Zayas y Sotomayor. Mireya Perez-Erdelyi. LC 78-74597. (Coleccion Polymita Ser.). (Illus.). 128p. (Span.). 1979. pap. 10.00 (ISBN 0-89729-216-2). Ediciones.

Picaresque. Harry Sieber. (Critical Idiom Ser.). 1977. 9.95x (ISBN 0-416-82710-1, NO. 2509). Routledge Chapman & Hall.

Picaresque Hero in European Fiction. Richard Bjornson. LC 76-11312. (Illus.). 320p. 1977. 27.50x (ISBN 0-299-07100-6); pap. 13.95x (ISBN 0-299-07104-9). U of Wis Pr.

Picaresque Narrative, Picaresque Fictions: A Theory & Research Guide. Ulrich Wicks. 1989. 55.85 (ISBN 0-313-24934-2, WPI/). Greenwood.

Picaro or Me. Arindam Basu. (Writers Workshop Greenbird Ser.). 90p. 1975. 12.00 (ISBN 0-88253-608-7); pap. text ed. 4.80 (ISBN 0-88253-607-9). Ind-US Inc.

Picaroons. facsimile ed. Richard Hill. LC 77-37306. (Black Heritage Library Collection). Repr. of 1869 ed. 12.00 (ISBN 0-8369-8943-0). Ayer Co Pubs.

Picaros, Madmen, Naifs, & Clowns: The Unreliable First-Person Narrator. William Riggan. LC 81-2791. 216p. 1981. 17.95x (ISBN 0-8061-1714-1). U of Okla Pr.

Picasso. George Bloch. (Catalogue of the Printed Graphic Work: Vols. 1 & 2). (Illus.). 1971. 82.50x ea. Vol. 1, 1904-1967 (ISBN 0-8150-0467-2). Vol. 2, 1967-1969 (ISBN 0-8150-0468-0). Wittenborn.

Picasso. Gaston Diehl. (Q L P Art Ser.). (Illus.). 1960. 12.95 (ISBN 0-517-00501-8). Crown.

Picasso. Josep P. Fabre. LC 85-42962. (Illus.). 128p. 1985. 19.95 (ISBN 0-8478-0652-9). Rizzoli Intl.

Picasso. Timothy Hilton. (World of Art Ser.). (Illus.). 288p. 1985. pap. 11.95 (ISBN 0-500-20144-7). Thames Hudson.

Picasso. Hans L. Jaffe. (Library of Great Painters). 1964. 45.00 (ISBN 0-8109-0368-7). Abrams.

Picasso. Hans L. Jaffe. (Masters of Art Ser.). 1984. 19.95 (ISBN 0-8109-1480-8). Abrams.

Picasso. (Grosset Art Library: No. 4). (Illus.). 120p. pap. write for info. (ISBN 0-448-00455-0, G&D). Putnam Pub Group.

Picasso. Gertrude Stein. 128p. 1984. pap. 3.95 (ISBN 0-486-24715-5). Dover.

Picasso: A Postcard Book. (Illus.). 64p. (Orig.). 1988. pap. 6.95 (ISBN 0-89471-645-X). Running Pr.

Picasso: An Annotated Bibliography. Ray A. Kibbey. LC 76-24732. (Reference Library of the Humanities Ser.: Vol. 45). 1976. lib. bdg. 39.00 (ISBN 0-8240-9944-3). Garland Pub.

Picasso: An Intimate Portrait. Jaime Sabartes. Tr. by Angel Flores. LC 83-45789. Repr. of 1948 ed. 32.50 (ISBN 0-404-20223-3, ND553). AMS Pr.

Picasso Anthology: Documents, Criticism, Reminiscences. Ed. by Marilyn McCully. LC 82-47632. (Illus.). 288p. 1982. 33.50x (ISBN 0-691-04001-X); pap. 12.95x (ISBN 0-691-00348-3). Princeton U Pr.

Picasso: Art As Autobiography. Mary M. Gedo. LC 80-11126. (Illus.). 288p. 1980. pap. 12.50 (ISBN 0-226-28483-2). U of Chicago Pr.

Picasso: Blue & Rose Periods. Denys Chevalier. (Q L P Art Ser.). (Illus.). 1969. 12.95 (ISBN 0-517-00904-8). Crown.

Picasso Catalogue of the Printed Graphic Work, Vol. 4. Georges Bloch. (Illus.). 253p. (Eng., Fr. & Ger.). 1979. 82.50x (ISBN 3-8577-3009-9). Wittenborn.

Picasso Ceramics. Georges Bloch. (Catalogue of the Printed Graphic Work Ser: Vol. 3, Ceramiques 1949-1971). (Illus., Tri-"lingual). 1972. 145.00x (ISBN 0-8150-0646-2). Wittenborn.

Picasso Ceramics. Roland Doschka. LC 86-40211. (Illus.). 252p. (Orig.). 1986. pap. 35.00 (ISBN 0-87663-897-3). Universe.

Picasso: Creator & Destroyer. Arianna Stassinopoulos. 1988. 22.95 (ISBN 0-671-45446-3). S&S.

Picasso, Dessins. Rene Char & Charles Feld. 256p. 1969. 65.00 (ISBN 0-686-54165-0). French & Eur.

Picasso Drawings & Watercolors, 1899-1907 in the Collection of the Baltimore Museum of Art. Victor I. Carlson. LC 76-41022. 1977. pap. 25.00 (ISBN 0-912298-43-X); pap. 17.50 (ISBN 0-912298-42-1). Baltimore Mus.

Picasso Fifty Years of His Art. Alfred H. Barr, Jr. LC 66-26126. (Museum of Modern Art Publications in Repr. Ser). Repr. of 1955 ed. 14.95 (ISBN 0-405-01519-4). Ayer Co Pubs.

Picasso: Genius of the Century. Ingo F. Walther. (Illus.). 96p. (Orig.). 1987. pap. 7.95 (ISBN 3-8228-0038-4). Parkwest Pubns.

Picasso Had the Bream: Reminiscences & Some Rather Special Recipes. Michael Edmonds. (Illus.). 117p. 1988. pap. 5.95 (ISBN 0-533-07477-0). Vantage.

Picasso: His Life & Work. 3rd ed. Roland Penrose. (Illus.). 550p. 1981. 35.00x (ISBN 0-520-04182-8); pap. 12.95 (ISBN 0-520-04207-7). U of Cal Pr.

Picasso in Retrospect. Roland Penrose & John Golding. LC 79-3042. (Icon Edns.). 1980. pap. 6.95 (ISBN 0-06-430101-X, IN-101, HarpT). Har-Row.

Picasso Line Drawings & Prints. Pablo Picasso. (Dover Art Library). (Illus.). 48p. (Orig.). 1982. pap. 3.50 (ISBN 0-486-24196-3). Dover.

Picasso Linoleum Cuts: Bacchanals, Women, Bulls, & Bullfighters. 1988. 75.00 (ISBN 0-8109-0386-5); until 1/89 67.50. Abrams.

Picasso Linoleum Cuts: The Mr. & Mrs. Charles Kramer Collection in the Metropolitan Museum of Art. Ed. by L. Donald McVinney. 1985. 59.50 (ISBN 0-394-54692-X). Random.

Picasso Linoleum Cuts: The Mr. & Mrs. Charles Kramer Collection. Ed. by William S. Lieberman. (Illus.). 168p. 1985. 19.95 (ISBN 0-87099-404-2, Co-pub. by Random House, Inc.). Metro Mus Art.

Picasso Lithographs: Sixty-One Works. Pablo Picasso. (Dover Art Library). (Illus.). 64p. (Orig.). 1980. pap. 3.50 (ISBN 0-486-23949-7). Dover.

Picnic Gourmet. Joan Hemingway & Connie Maricich. (Illus.). 1978. pap. 10.95 (ISBN 0-394-72164-0, Vin). Random.

Picnic: How Do You Say It? Meredith Dunham. LC 86-27490. (Illus.). 24p. (ps-3). 1987. 9.25 (ISBN 0-688-07096-5); PLB 9.88 (ISBN 0-688-07097-3). Lothrop.

Picnic in the Cemetery. Constance Urdang. LC 75-7653. 80p. 1975. pap. 3.95 (ISBN 0-8076-0796-7). Braziller.

Picnic on the Battlefield see Guernica & Other Plays.

Picnic: Teddy Horsley Goes to Communion. Leslie J. Francis & Nicola M. Slee. (Teddy Horsley Books for Young Christians). (Illus.). 24p. (ps-2). 1986. pap. 1.25 (ISBN 0-00-599771-2, Collins Liturgical). HarpR.

Picnic with Piggins. Jane Yolen. (Illus.). 32p. (gr. 4-8). 1988. 14.95 (ISBN 0-15-261534-2). HarBraceJ.

Picnics. David Breeden. Ed. by Bradley R. Strahan. (Black Buzzard Illustrated Poetry Chapbooks Ser.). (Illus.). 24p. (Orig.). 1985. pap. 3.50 (ISBN 0-938872-08-7). Black Buzzard.

Picnics. Joan Chatfield-Taylor. LC 79-64872. (Illus.). 1980. pap. 5.95 (Dist. by Random). Taylor & NG.

Picnics. Marilyn Myers. LC 87-42998. (Illus.). 128p. 1988. 19.95 (ISBN 0-89471-583-6). Running Pr.

Picnics. Joan C. Taylor. LC 79-64872. (Illus.). 88p. 1979. 4.95. Random.

Picnics & Barbecues. Bon Appetit Magazine Editors. LC 85-23986. (Cooking with Bon Appetit Ser.). (Illus.). 144p. 1986. 12.95 (ISBN 0-89535-174-9). Knapp Pr.

Picnics & Barbecues. Bon Appetit Magazine Editors. LC 85-23986. (Cooking with Bon Appetit Ser.). (Illus.). 144p. 12.95. Knapp Pr.

Picnics, Coffins, Shooflies. John Thomas. (Illus.). 136p. (Orig.). 1977. pap. 8.95 (ISBN 0-89288-009-0). Maverick.

Picnics for Lovers see Romantic Meals for Lovers: Recipes for 50 Intimate Occasions.

Pico Della Mirandola: Of Being & Unity. Giovanni Pico Della Mirandola Tr. by Victor M. Hamm. (Medieval Philosophical Texts in Translation: No. 3). 1943. pap. 5.95 (ISBN 0-87462-203-4). Marquette.

Pico della Mirandola's Encounter with Jewish Mysticism. Chaim Wirszubski. (Illus.). 304p. 1988. text ed. 35.00 (ISBN 0-674-66730-1). Harvard U Pr.

Picolinis. Anne G. Eastern. 160p. (Orig.). (gr. 2-5). 1988. pap. 2.75 (ISBN 0-553-15566-0, Skylark). Bantam.

Picosecond Electronics & Optoelectronics II. Ed. by F. J. Leonberger et al. (Electronics & Photonics Ser.: Vol. 24). (Illus.). 280p. 1987. 44.00 (ISBN 0-387-18329-9). Springer-Verlag.

Picosecond Electronics & Optoelectronics. LC 86-63501. (Technical Digest Series 1987: Vol. 1). 200p. (Orig.). 1987. lib. bdg. 65.00 postconference ed. (ISBN 0-936659-36-X); pap. 37.00 conference ed. (ISBN 0-936659-16-5). Optical Soc.

Picosecond Optoelectronic Devices. Ed. by Chi H. Lee. LC 84-3016. 1984. 68.00 (ISBN 0-12-440880-X). Acad Pr.

Picosecond Phenomena II: Proceedings. Ed. by R. M. Hochstrasser et al. (Springer Series in Chemical Physics: Vol. 14). (Illus.). 382p. 1980. 46.00 (ISBN 0-387-10403-8). Springer-Verlag.

Picosecond Phenomena III, Garmisch Partenkirchen, FRG, 1982: Proceedings. Ed. by K. B. Eisenthal et al. (Springer Series in Chemical Physics: Vol. 23). (Illus.). 401p. 1982. 33.00 (ISBN 0-387-11912-4). Springer-Verlag.

Picosescond Electronics & Optoelectronics. Ed. by G. A. Mourou & D. M. Bloom. (Electrophysics Ser.: Vol. 21). (Illus.). x, 258p. 1985. 34.00 (ISBN 0-387-15884-7). Springer-Verlag.

PICSYMS Categorical Dictionary. Faith Carlson. LC 84-72946. (Illus.). 192p. 1985. pap. 25.00 (ISBN 0-932591-01-9); small symbol packet 10.00 (ISBN 0-932591-02-7); reg. symbol packet 15.00 (ISBN 0-932591-03-5); large symbol packet 20.00 (ISBN 0-932591-04-3). Baggeboda Pr.

Pictish Nation, Its People & Church. Archibald B. Scott. 1977. lib. bdg. 69.95 (ISBN 0-8490-2439-0). Gordon Pr.

Picto-Cabulary Series, 7 sets. Richard A. Boning. Incl. Basic Word Set-A. (gr. 1-2); Words to Eat. (gr. 4-6); Words to Wear. (gr. 4-6); Words to Meet. (gr. 4-6); Descriptive Words. (gr. 5-9). 84.20 (ISBN 0-87965-421-X); Words Around the House. (gr. 4-6); Words Around the Neighborhood. (gr. 4-6). 1980. B Loft.

Pictographic History of the Oglala Sioux. Amos Bad Heart Bull & Helen H. Blish. LC 66-13404. (Illus.). xxii, 530p. 1968. 35.00 (ISBN 0-8032-0002-1). U of Nebr Pr.

Pictographs & Petrographs of the Oregon Country: Southern Oregon, Pt. 2. J. Malcolm Loring & Louise Loring. (Monographs: No. XXIII). (Illus.). 355p. 1983. pap. 22.50x (ISBN 0-917956-43-5). UCLA Arch.

Pictor Succensor: A Study of Salvator Rosa As Satirist, Cynic, & Painter. Wendy W. Roworth. LC 77-94726. (Outstanding Dissertations in the Fine Arts Ser.). 1978. lib. bdg. 56.00 (ISBN 0-8240-3248-9). Garland Pub.

Pictoral Library of the Landscape Plants, Vol. I. 4th ed. M. Jane Helmer. LC 81-82113. (Northern Hardiness Zones 1-5). (Illus.). 352p. 1985. text ed. 85.00 (ISBN 0-89484-027-4). Merchants Pub Co.

Pictorial Americana: The National Road. Harry G. Black. LC 83-90398. (Illus.). 88p. (Orig.). 1984. pap. 5.50 (ISBN 0-937086-02-9). HMB Pubns.

Pictorial Analysis, Communication & Storage (PACS) Systems in the Medical Imaging Area. Frost & Sullivan Inc., Staff. 240p. 1986. 1900.00 (ISBN 0-86621-769-X, A1586). Frost & Sullivan.

Pictorial Anatomy of the Cat. rev. ed. Stephen G. Gilbert. LC 67-21200. (Illus.). 128p. 1975. pap. 9.95x (ISBN 0-295-95454-X). U of Wash Pr.

Pictorial Anatomy of the Dogfish. Stephen G. Gilbert. LC 74-152331. (Illus.). 66p. (Orig.). 1973. pap. text ed. 7.95x (ISBN 0-295-95148-6). U of Wash Pr.

Pictorial Anatomy of the Fetal Pig. 2nd, rev. ed. Stephen G. Gilbert. LC 63-10797. (Illus.). 96p. 1966. pap. 7.95x (ISBN 0-295-73877-4). U of Wash Pr.

Pictorial Anatomy of the Frog. Stephen G. Gilbert. LC 65-14843. (Illus.). 71p. 1965. pap. 7.95x (ISBN 0-295-73878-2). U of Wash Pr.

Pictorial Anatomy of the Human Embryo. Stephen G. Gilbert. (Illus.). 176p. 1988. 15.00 (ISBN 0-295-96632-7). U of Wash Pr.

Pictorial Anatomy of the Necturus. Stephen G. Gilbert. LC 78-152332. (Illus.). 54p. (Orig.). 1973. pap. text ed. 7.95x (ISBN 0-295-95149-4). U of Wash Pr.

Pictorial Approach to Molecular Bonding. J. G. Verkade. (Illus.). 280p. 1986. 44.50 (ISBN 0-387-96271-9). Springer-Verlag.

Pictorial Archive of Decorative & Illustrative Mortised Cuts: 551 Eye-Catching Designs for Advertising & Other Uses. Ed. by Carol B. Grafton. (Pictorial Archive Ser.). 112p. (Orig.). 1984. pap. 4.95 (ISBN 0-486-24540-3). Dover.

Pictorial Archive of Decorative Frames & Labels: 550 Copyright-Free Designs. Ed. by Carol B. Grafton. (Illus.). 128p. 1982. pap. 4.95 (ISBN 0-486-24277-3). Dover.

Pictorial Archive of Printer's Ornaments from the Renaissance to the 20th Century. Ed. by Carol B. Grafton. (Pictorial Archive Ser.). (Illus., Orig.). 1980. pap. 5.95 (ISBN 0-486-23944-6). Dover.

Pictorial Art of Japan as Expressed in Its Most Famous Color-Prints Fully Illustrated. Ludovic Bartlett. (Illus.). 111p. 1988. 147.55 (ISBN 0-86650-247-5). Gloucester Art.

Pictorial Arts of Japan. William Anderson. LC 77-94540. 1979. Repr. of 1886 ed. lib. bdg. 35.00 (ISBN 0-89341-222-8). Longwood Pub Group.

Pictorial Arts of Japan. William Anderson. (Illus.). 276p. 1750.00x (ISBN 0-317-69139-2, Pub. by Han-Shan Tang Ltd). State Mutual Bk.

Pictorial Atlas of Australian Wine. Thomas Hardy & Mil Roden. (Illus.). 208p. Date not set. pap. 21.95 (ISBN 0-932664-57-1). Wine Appreciation.

Pictorial Beauty on the Screen. Victor O. Freeburg. LC 76-124007. (Literature of Cinema, Ser. 1). Repr. of 1923 ed. 12.50 (ISBN 0-405-01613-1). Ayer Co Pubs.

Pictorial Beauty on the Screen. Victor O. Freeburg. 1972. 12.50 (ISBN 0-405-08533-8, 1482). Ayer Co Pubs.

Pictorial Bible Atlas. J. Catling Allen. (gr. 7-12). 14.95 (ISBN 0-7175-0991-5); pap. 9.95 (ISBN 0-7175-0857-9). Dufour.

Pictorial Biography of C. H. Spurgeon. Bob L. Ross. 1981. 5.95 (ISBN 0-686-16830-5); pap. 3.95 (ISBN 0-686-16831-3). Pilgrim Pubns.

Pictorial Biography of the Venerable Master Hsu Yun, Vol. 1. Tr. by Buddhist Text Translation Society Staff. (Illus.). 120p. (Orig.). 1983. pap. 8.00 (ISBN 0-88139-008-9). Buddhist Text.

Pictorial Biography of the Venerable Master Hsu Yun, Vol. 2. Tr. by Buddhist Text Translation Society Staff. (Illus.). 120p. (Orig.). 1985. pap. 8.00 (ISBN 0-88139-116-6). Buddhist Text.

Pictorial Biography of Toyotomi Hideyoshi. Kuniyoshi. 1986. Repr. of 1975 ed. 85.00 (ISBN 0-910704-68-6). Hawley.

Pictorial Calligraphy & Ornamentation. Edmund V. Gillon, Jr. (Illus.). 96p. (Orig.). 1972. pap. 4.00 (ISBN 0-486-22788-X). Dover.

Pictorial Catalogue: Mural Decoration In Libraries. Andre Masson. Tr. by David Gerard. (Illus.). 1981. text ed. 29.95x (ISBN 0-19-818159-0). Oxford U Pr.

Pictorial Chronology of Events in the Life of Thomas Alva Edison 1847-1931. Lawrence Frost. 1985. 27.95 (ISBN 0-89190-406-9, Pub. by J M C & Co). Amereon Ltd.

Pictorial Compositions & the Critical Judgment of Pictures. Henry R. Poore. Ed. by Robert A. Sobieszek & Peter C. Bunnell. LC 76-24676. (Sources of Modern Photography Ser.). (Illus.). 1979. Repr. of 1903 ed. lib. bdg. 25.50x (ISBN 0-405-09652-6). Ayer Co Pubs.

Pictorial Connecticut. Lawrence F. Willard & Alvin V. Sizer. 1962. 16.95x (ISBN 0-8084-0246-3). New Coll U Pr.

Pictorial Data Analysis. Ed. by R. M. Haralick. (NATO ASI Series F: Computer & Systems Sciences, No. 4). 480p. 1983. 60.00 (ISBN 0-387-12288-5). Springer-Verlag.

Pictorial Dictionary of Ancient Athens. John Travlos. LC 79-91823. (Illus.). 590p. 1980. Repr. of 1971 ed. lib. bdg. 100.00 (ISBN 0-87817-267-X). Hacker.

Pictorial Dictionary of Ancient Rome, 2 vols. Ernest Nash. LC 79-91827. (Illus.). 1076p. 1980. Repr. of 1968 ed. Set. lib. bdg. 150.00 (ISBN 0-87817-265-3). Hacker.

Pictorial Dictionary of British Nineteenth Century Furniture Designs. Edward Joy. (Illus.). 578p. 1980. 69.50 (ISBN 0-686-65051-4). Hacker.

Pictorial Dictionary of British Nineteenth Century Furniture Design. (Illus.). 683p. 1977. 89.50. Antique Collect.

Pictorial Dictionary of Nineteeth Century Furniture Design. E. Jay. (Illus.). 1980. 89.50 (ISBN 0-902028-47-2). Apollo.

Pictorial Encyclopedia of Civil War Medical Instruments & Equipment, Vol. II. Gordon Dammann. LC 88-60472. (Illus.). 96p. 1988. pap. 8.95 (ISBN 0-933126-94-8). Pictorial Hist.

Pictorial Encyclopedia of Historic Architectural Plans, Details & Elements. John T. Haneman. (Architecture, Interior Design, Period Style Ser.). 140p. 1984. pap. 6.95 (ISBN 0-486-24605-1). Dover.

Pictorial Encyclopedia of Modern Japan. Gakken Staff. (Illus.). 200p. 1986. 24.95 (ISBN 0-87040-712-0). Japan Pubns USA.

Pictorial Family Tree of Brass Instruments in Europe Since the Early Middle Ages. Emilie Mende. (Illus., Eng., Fr. & Ger.). 1978. 20.00x (ISBN 2-88039-003-6). Brass Pr.

Pictorial Field-Book of the Revolution or Illustrations, by Pen & Pencil, of the History, Biography, Scenery, Relics & Traditions of the War for Independence, 2 Vols. facsimile ed. Benson J. Lossing. LC 72-85457. (Select Bibliogrpahies Reprint Ser). 82.50 (ISBN 0-8369-5029-1). Ayer Co Pubs.

Pictorial Field-Book of the Revolution or, Illustrations, by Pen & Pencil, of the History, Biography, Scenery, Relics, & Traditions of the War for Independence, 2 vols. Benson J. Lossing. LC 76-89658. 1969. Repr. of 1860 ed. 17.50 ea. Vol. 1 (ISBN 0-87152-055-9). Vol. 2 (ISBN 0-87152-056-7). Set. 35.00 (ISBN 0-87152-311-6). Reprint.

Pictorial Field Book of the Revolution. Benson Lossing. 69.95 (ISBN 0-8490-0834-4). Gordon Pr.

Pictorial Field-Book of the War of 1812. Benson J. Lossing. LC 73-76395. (Illus.). 1096p. 1976. Repr. of 1868 ed. 55.00 (ISBN 0-912274-31-X). NH Pub Co.

Pictorial Folk History of Jefferson City, Missouri 1890-1900. rev. ed. Joseph S. Summers, Jr. 100p. (Orig.). 1984. pap. 9.95 (ISBN 0-916109-00-3). Summers Pub.

Pictorial Guide to American Spinning Wheels. David A. Pennington & Michael B. Taylor. LC 75-15298. (Illus.). 100p. (Orig.). 1975. pap. 5.95 (ISBN 0-915836-01-7). United Soc Shakers.

Pictorial Guide to Fossils. Gerard R. Case. LC 81-10504. (Illus.). 514p. 1982. 34.95 (ISBN 0-442-22651-9). Van Nos Reinhold.

Pictorial Guide to Hardy Perennials. John K. Drew. (Illus.). 96p. 1984. text ed. 14.95 (ISBN 0-89484-091-6). Merchants Pub Co.

Pictorial Guide to Hardy Perennials. 2nd ed. John K. Drew. (Illus.). 96p. (Orig.). pap. text ed. 8.95 (ISBN 0-89484-093-2). Merchants Pub Co.

Pictorial Guide to the Hungarian Cinema (1901-1984) Istvan Nemeskurty & Tibor Szanto. 210p. 1985. 60.00x (ISBN 0-317-61348-0, Pub. by Collets (UK)). State Mutual Bk.

Pictorial Guide to the Identification of Fusarium Species. 2nd ed. T. A. Tousson & Paul E. Nelson. LC 76-2027. (Illus.). 1976. pap. 9.75x (ISBN 0-271-01225-0). Pa St U Pr.

Pictorial Guide to the Planets. 3rd ed. Joseph H. Jackson & John H. Baumert. LC 80-7897. (Illus.). 256p. 1981. 22.50i (ISBN 0-06-014869-1, HarpT). Har-Row.

Pictorial Guide to Victorian New Jersey. Ed. by Robert B. Burnett. LC 85-63720. (Illus.). 192p. 1986. 29.95 (ISBN 0-911020-16-0); pap. 14.95x (ISBN 0-911020-15-2). NJ Hist Soc.

Pictorial Guide to Woodworking Tools & Joints. rev. ed. H. F. Marfleet. (Illus.). 1979. pap. 3.95 (ISBN 0-7100-0177-0). Routledge Chapman & Hall.

Pictorial Guide to Yosemite. Maryann Olsen & Henry Berrey. (Illus.). 22p. (Orig.). 1981. pap. 2.95 (ISBN 0-939666-37-5). Yosemite Assn.

Pictorial Guide to Yosemite see Guide Illustre de Yosemite.

Pictorial Guide to Yosemite: Japanese. (Illus.). 22p. (Japanese.). pap. 2.95 (ISBN 0-939666-09-X). Yosemite Assn.

Pictorial Handbook of Creative Graphic Design. Ed. by Wolfgang Hageney. (Illus.). 264p. 1986. 49.95 (ISBN 88-7070-071-2). R Silver.

Pictorial Handbook of Medically Important Fungi & Aerobic Actinomycetes. Michael R. McGinnis & Richard F. D'Amoto. LC 81-5306. (Illus.). 172p. 1981. pap. 24.95 (ISBN 0-275-91514-X, B1514). Praeger.

Pictorial Handbook of Technical Devices. Paul Grafstein & Otto M. Schwarz. (Illus.). 1971. 14.00 (ISBN 0-8206-0234-5). Chem Pub.

Pictorial History of Ancient Japanese Weapons, Armour, & Artifacts. M. Suenaga. (Illus.). 100p. 1983. pap. 17.50 (ISBN 0-87556-582-4). Saifer.

Pictorial History of Arkansas from Earliest Times to 1890. Fay Hempstead. 1256p. 1978. Repr. of 1890 ed. 40.00 (ISBN 0-89308-074-8). Southern Hist Pr.

Pictorial History of Black Servicemen: Air Force, Army, Navy, Marines. Jesse J. Johnson. LC 70-130752. (Illus.). 10.00 (ISBN 0-915044-09-9). Carver Pub.

Pictorial History of Boxing from the Bare Knuckle Days to the Present. rev.& updated ed. Nat Fleisher et al. (Illus.). 400p. 1987. Repr. of 1974 ed. 19.95 (ISBN 0-8065-1048-X, Pub. by Citadel Pr). Lyle Stuart.

Pictorial History of Chinese Architecture: A Study of the Development of Its Structural System & the Evolution of Its Types. Liang Ssu-ch'eng. Compiled by Wilma Fairbank. (Illus.). 200p. 1984. 42.50 (ISBN 0-262-12103-4). MIT Pr.

Pictorial History of Civil War, 3 vols. Benson Lossing. 300.00 (ISBN 0-8490-0835-2). Gordon Pr.

Pictorial History of Civil War Era Musical Instruments & Military Bands. Robert Garofalo & Mark Elrod. LC 85-60321. (Illus.). 1985. pap. 9.95 (ISBN 0-933126-60-3). Pictorial Hist.

Pictorial History of Delta State University. Jack W. Gunn & Gladys C. Castle. LC 80-19085. 216p. 1980. 25.00x (ISBN 0-87805-112-0). U Pr of Miss.

Pictorial History of Downhill Skiing. Stan B. Cohen. Ed. by Peter Stark. LC 84-62203. (Illus.). 256p. 1985. pap. 14.95 (ISBN 0-933126-55-7). Pictorial Hist.

Pictorial History of European Medicine & Pharmaceutics. J. Antall. 1981. 51.00x (ISBN 0-317-57334-9, Pub. by Collets UK). State Mutual Bk.

Pictorial History of Florida. 3rd ed. Richard J. Bowe. 1970. 10.00 (ISBN 0-913122-14-9). Mickler Hse.

Pictorial History of Glenwood. E. H. Goodwin & Nellie Duffy. 56p. 1983. pap. 5.00 (ISBN 0-937080-10-1). Century One.

Pictorial History of Indiana. Dwight W. Hoover. LC 80-7806. (Illus.). 304p. 1981. 25.00 (ISBN 0-253-14693-3). Ind U Pr.

Pictorial History of Medicine. Otto L. Bettmann. (Illus.). 336p. 1979. 25.25x (ISBN 0-398-00149-9). C C Thomas.

Pictorial History of Music. Paul H. Lang & Otto L. Bettmann. (Illus.). (gr. 9 up). 1960. 19.95 (ISBN 0-393-02107-6). Norton.

Pictorial History of Our English Bible. David Beale. (Illus.). 79p. (Orig.). 1982. pap. 3.15 (ISBN 0-89084-149-7). Bob Jones Univ Pr.

Pictorial History of Pikesville, Maryland. Beryl Frank. (Baltimore County Heritage Publication). (Illus.). 140p. 1982. 9.95 (ISBN 0-937076-02-3). Baltimore Co Pub Lib.

Pictorial History of St. Francias Desales & St. Emma Military Academy. Carl Baker. Ed. by Pictorial History Committee Staff. 1989. 46.00x (ISBN 0-9618214-2-6); lib. bdg. 100.00x; History clases 32.00. UNIAC Pub.

Pictorial History of Science-Fiction Films. Jeff Rovin. (Illus.). 1975. 12.00 (ISBN 0-8065-0475-7, Pub. by Citadel Pr). Lyle Stuart.

Pictorial History of Science Fiction Films. Jeff Rovin. (Illus.). 1976. pap. 9.95 (ISBN 0-8065-0537-0, Pub. by Citadel Pr). Lyle Stuart.

Pictorial History of Science Fiction Films. David Shipman. (Illus.). 172p. 1986. 17.95 (ISBN 0-600-38520-5). Salem Hse Pubs.

Pictorial History of Self-Realization Fellowship. (Illus.). 80p. 1982. pap. 5.50 (ISBN 0-87612-196-2). Self Realization.

Pictorial History of Sex in Films. Parker Tyler. (Illus.). 256p. 1974. 14.95 (ISBN 0-8065-0443-9, Pub. by Citadel Pr). Lyle Stuart.

Pictorial History of Sex in Films. Parker Tyler. (Illus.). 1976. pap. 9.95 (ISBN 0-8065-0540-0, Pub. by Citadel Pr). Lyle Stuart.

Pictorial History of Shakespearean Production in England, 1576-1946. facsimile ed. Arts Council Of Great Britain. Ed. by M. St. Clare Byrne. LC 70-109640. (Select Bibliographies Reprint Ser). 1948. 11.00 (ISBN 0-8369-5249-9). Ayer Co Pubs.

Pictorial History of Smoke Jumping. Stan B. Cohen. LC 83-62751. (Illus.). 180p. 1983. pap. 10.95 (ISBN 0-933126-40-9). Pictorial Hist.

Pictorial History of Swansea. W. C. Rogers. 146p. 1985. 30.00x (ISBN 0-85088-516-7, Pub. by Gomer Pr). State Mutual Bk.

Pictorial History of Texas A&M University: 1876-1976. Henry C. Dethloff. LC 75-19559. (Centennial Ser. of the Association of Former Students: No. 2). (Illus.). 232p. 1975. 15.00 (ISBN 0-89096-006-2). Tex A&M Univ Pr.

Pictorial History of the American Theatre 1860-1985. Daniel Blum. Ed. by John Willis. LC 81-3269. (Illus.). 496p. 1986. 29.95 (ISBN 0-517-56258-8). Crown.

Pictorial History of the Black Soldier in the United States (1619-1969) in Peace & War. Jesse J. Johnson. LC 72-130446. 1976. Pages 130. 10.00 (ISBN 0-915044-08-0). Carver Pub.

Pictorial History of the Carousel. Frederick Fried. (Illus.). 240p. 1983. 29.95 (ISBN 0-911572-29-5, A-15). Vestal.

Picture History of the Brooklyn Bridge. Mary J. Shapiro. 1984. 17.25 (ISBN 0-8446-6108-2). Peter Smith.

Picture History of the "Normandie". Frank O. Braynard. (Illus.). 144p. 1987. pap. 9.95 (ISBN 0-486-25257-4). Dover.

Picture History of the World. W. D. Townson et al. (Illus.). 224p. (gr. 5 up). 1986. pap. 19.95 (ISBN 0-448-18988-7, G&D). Putnam Pub Group.

Picture Indexing for Local History Materials. new ed. Karen D. Gilbert. LC 73-91411. (Illus.). 36p. 1974. pap. text ed. 3.45 (ISBN 0-912526-12-2). Lib Res.

Picture It. Ed. by John Dumicich. (Illus.). 194p. (gr. 10-12). 1981. pap. text ed. 7.00 (ISBN 0-13-676149-6, 18677). Prentice ESL.

Picture It in Cross-Stitch. Jo Verso. (Illus.). 1988. 19.95 (ISBN 0-7153-9098-8, Pub. by David & Charles Pub England). Sterling.

Picture Languages: Formal Models for Picture Recognition. Azriel Rosenfeld. (Computer Science & Applied Mathematics Ser.). 1979. 54.50 (ISBN 0-12-597340-3). Acad Pr.

Picture Librarianship. Hilary Evans. (Outlines of Modern Librarianship Ser.). 136p. 1980. text ed. 12.00 (ISBN 0-85157-294-4, Pub. by Bingley England). ALA.

Picture Librarianship. Helen P. Harrison. 554p. 1981. lib. bdg. 39.50x (ISBN 0-89774-011-4). Oryx Pr.

Picture Life of Bill Cosby. Barbara Johnston Adams. LC 85-29487. (Picture Life Books Ser.). 48p. (gr. k-6). 1986. lib. bdg. 10.90 (ISBN 0-531-10168-1). Watts.

Picture Life of Bruce Springsteen. Geri Bain & Michael Leather. (Picture Life Ser.). 48p. (gr. 1-6). 1986. PLB 10.90 (ISBN 0-531-10204-1). Watts.

Picture Life of Charles & Diana. Henry Rasof. Ed. by Maury Solomon. (Picture Life Ser.). (Illus.). 64p. (gr. 4 up). 1988. 9.90 (ISBN 0-531-10496-6). Watts.

Picture Life of Corazon Aquino. Margaret M. Scariano. (Picture Life Ser.). (Illus.). 64p. (gr. 1-3). 1987. PLB 10.90 (ISBN 0-531-10296-3). Watts.

Picture Life of Cyndi Lauper. Carol Nicklaus. LC 85-13802. (Picture Life Books Ser.). (Illus.). 47p. (gr. 4-6). 1985. PLB 10.90 (ISBN 0-531-10079-0). Watts.

Picture Life of Dwight Gooden. Maury Solomon. (Picture Life Books Ser.). 48p. (gr. k-6). 1986. lib. bdg. 10.90 (ISBN 0-531-10193-2). Watts.

Picture Life of Michael Jackson. Warren J. Halliburton. (Picture Life Bks.). (Illus.). 48p. (gr. k-6). 1984. lib. bdg. 10.90 (ISBN 0-531-04879-9). Watts.

Picture Life of Mikhail Gorbachev. Janet Caulkins. LC 85-15023. (Picture Life Books Ser.). (Illus.). 47p. (gr. 2-4). 1985. PLB 10.90 (ISBN 0-531-10085-5). Watts.

Picture Life of Muhammad Ali. A. Edwards & G. Wohl. (YA) (gr. 3-7). 1984. pap. 1.75 (ISBN 0-380-01904-3, 51623, Camelot). Avon.

Picture Life of O. J. Simpson. J. Jameson. (gr. 3-7). 1984. pap. 1.95 (ISBN 0-380-01906-X, 60962-2, Camelot). Avon.

Picture Life of Pope John Paul II. Bonic. Date not set. lib. bdg. 10.90 (ISBN 0-531-04806-3). Watts.

Picture Life of Reggie Jackson. Bill Gutman. (gr. 1 up). 1984. pap. 1.95 (ISBN 0-380-40345-5, 58743-2, Camelot). Avon.

Picture Life of Ronald Reagan. rev. ed. Don Lawson. LC 84-673. (Picture Life Ser.). (Illus.). 48p. (gr. k-3). 1985. lib. bdg. 10.90 (ISBN 0-531-04953-1). Watts.

Picture Life of Steven Spielberg. Michael Leather. (Picture Life Ser.). (Illus.). 64p. (gr. 3 up). 1988. 10.90 (ISBN 0-531-10497-4). Watts.

Picture Life of Stevie Wonder. A. Edwards & G. Wohl. 48p. (ps-5). 1984. pap. 1.75 (ISBN 0-380-01907-8, 51656-X, Camelot). Avon.

Picture Life of Tina Turner. Gene Busner. (Picture Life Ser.). (Illus.). 64p. 1987. lib. bdg. 10.90 (ISBN 0-531-10297-1). Watts.

Picture Life of Whitney Houston. Gene Busnar. Ed. by Jennie Rakos. (Picture Life Ser.). (Illus.). 64p. (gr. k-6). 1988. 10.90 (ISBN 0-531-10498-2). Watts.

Picture-Making by Photography. 5th ed. Henry P. Robinson. LC 72-9230. (Literature of Photography Ser.). Repr. of 1897 ed. 16.00 (ISBN 0-405-04936-6). Ayer Co Pubs.

Picture Me Perfect. Dennis Marthaler. 176p. (Orig.). 1985. pap. 7.95 (ISBN 0-87877-078-X). Newcastle Pub.

Picture Me Perfect: Self-Hypnosis & Imaging for Improving Your Life. Dennis Marthaler. LC 85-11646. 141p. 1985. Repr. lib. bdg. 19.95x (ISBN 0-89370-678-7). Borgo Pr.

Picture of a Papist: Whereunto Is Annexed a Certain Treatise, Intituled Pagano-Papismus. Oliver Ormerod. LC 74-28878. (English Experience Ser.: No. 756). 1975. Repr. of 1606 ed. 35.00 (ISBN 90-221-0756-6). Walter J Johnson.

Picture of a Puritane: Or, a Relation of the Opinions - of the Anabaptists in Germanie, & of the Puritanes in England. Oliver Ormerod. LC 74-28879. (English Experience Ser.: No. 757). 1975. Repr. of 1605 ed. 35.00 (ISBN 90-221-0757-4). Walter J Johnson.

Picture of Dorian Gray. Oscar Wilde. (Airmont Classics Ser.). (gr. 9 up). 1964. pap. 1.75 (ISBN 0-8049-0039-6, CL-39). Airmont.

Picture of Dorian Gray. Oscar Wilde. (Literature Ser). (gr. 10-12). 1970. pap. text ed. 7.00 (ISBN 0-87720-734-8). AMSCO Sch.

Picture of Dorian Gray. Oscar Wilde. 1976. pap. 3.95x (ISBN 0-460-01198-7, DEL-04288, Evman). Biblio Dist.

Picture of Dorian Gray. Oscar Wilde. Ed. by Isobel Murray. (World's Classics Paperback Ser.). 1981. pap. 2.95 (ISBN 0-19-281553-9). Oxford U Pr.

Picture of Dorian Gray. Oscar Wilde. LC 84-25541. 1985. pap. 6.95 (ISBN 0-394-60514-4). Modern Lib.

Picture of Dorian Gray. Oscar Wilde. 1962. pap. 2.95 (ISBN 0-451-51967-1, Sig Classics). NAL.

Picture of Dorian Gray. Oscar Wilde. Ed. by Peter Ackroyd. (Classics Ser.). 272p. 1986. pap. 2.95 (ISBN 0-14-043187-X). Penguin.

Picture of Dorian Gray. Oscar Wilde. Ed. by Donald Lawler. (Critical Editions Ser.). 672p. (Orig.). 1988. pap. text ed. 7.95x (ISBN 0-393-95568-0). Norton.

Picture of Dorian Gray & Other Stories. Oscar Wilde. Repr. lib. bdg. 17.95x (ISBN 0-88411-893-2, Pub. by Aeonian Pr). Amereon Ltd.

Picture of Dorian Gray & Other Stories. Oscar Wilde. 318p. 1988. 21.95x (ISBN 0-86225-014-5). Queens Hse-Focus Serv.

Picture of Dorian Gray & Other Writings. Oscar Wilde. Ed. by Richard Ellmann. (Bantam Classics Ser.). 512p. (gr. 9-12). 1983. pap. 3.50 (ISBN 0-553-21254-0). Bantam.

Picture of Dorian Gray & Selected Stories. Oscar Wilde. 1962. pap. 1.95 (Ment). NAL.

Picture of Dorian Gray: Original Text-1890. Oscar Wilde. 172p. 1964. pap. 33.50x (ISBN 3-418-00018-5). Adlers Foreign Bks.

Picture of Evil. Graham Masterton. 384p. (Orig.). 1985. pap. 3.95 (ISBN 0-8125-2199-4, Dist. by Warner Pub Services & St. Martin's Press). Tor Bks.

Picture of Guilt: A Sir John Appleby Mystery. Michael Innes. LC 87-45628. 224p. 1988. pap. 3.95 (ISBN 0-06-080878-0, P-878, PL). Har-Row.

Picture of Health: Environmental Sources of Disease. Erik P. Eckholm. 1977. pap. 5.95 (ISBN 0-393-06440-9). Norton.

Picture of Persia. Mohammed Ali Issari & Doris A. Paul. LC 76-678. 1977. 15.00 (ISBN 0-682-48410-5, University). Exposition-Phoenix.

Picture of Philadelphia. James Mease. LC 75-112561. (Rise of Urban America Ser.). (Illus.). 1970. Repr. of 1811 ed. 21.00 (ISBN 0-405-02466-5). Ayer Co Pubs.

Picture of Slavery in the United States. George Bourne. LC 74-92420. (Illus.). 228p. 1972. Repr. of 1834 ed. 29.00 (ISBN 0-403-00179-X). Scholarly.

Picture Painting Self Taught. D. M. Campana. 9.50 (ISBN 0-939608-28-6). Campana Art.

Picture Palace. Paul Theroux. 1978. 9.95 (ISBN 0-395-26475-8). HM.

Picture Palace. Paul Theroux. 1987. pap. 4.95 (ISBN 0-317-56920-1). PB.

Picture Palaces: Views from America's Past. Intro. by David Naylor. (Past-Age Postcard Ser.). (Illus.). 32p. (Orig.). 1988. pap. 6.95 (ISBN 0-89133-143-3). Preservation Pr.

Picture Parade of Jewish History. Morris Epstein. 1977. pap. 4.95 (ISBN 0-8197-0024-X). Bloch.

Picture Past: A Centennial Celebration of Utah State University. A. J. Simmonds. (Illus.). 126p. 1988. 27.50 (ISBN 0-87421-134-4). Utah St U Pr.

Picture Perfect. M. E. Cooper. (Couples Ser.: No. 14). 192p. (Orig.). (gr. 7 up). 1986. pap. 2.50 (ISBN 0-590-40237-4). Scholastic Inc.

Picture-Perfect Murders. Bill Adler & Thomas Chastain. LC 85-15480. 1987. 12.95 (ISBN 0-688-04797-1). Morrow.

Picture Perfect One. Monica Gustafson. 256p. 1987. pap. text ed. 24.95 (ISBN 0-88450-212-0, 7368). Communication Skill.

Picture Perfect Two. Monica Gustafson. 256p. 1987. pap. text ed. 24.95 (ISBN 0-88450-213-9, 7369). Communication Skill.

Picture Play: Kintaro's Adventures. Genichi Kume. LC 64-20366. (Illus.). 5.50 (ISBN 0-8048-0342-0). C E Tuttle.

Picture-Play Magazine Anthology, 6 vols. Ed. by R. Gordon. 1976. lib. bdg. 995.00 (ISBN 0-8490-2440-4). Gordon Pr.

Picture Pointers for Piano Technic. Ed. by Maxwell Eckstein. 1947. pap. 4.95 (ISBN 0-8258-0175-3, 03451). Fischer Inc NY.

Picture Post Nineteen Thirty-Eight to Nineteen Fifty. Tom Hopkinson. (Illus.). 288p. 1985. pap. 12.95 (ISBN 0-7011-2858-5, Pub. by Chatto & Windus-Hogarth Pr). Salem Hse Pubs.

Picture-Postcard History of New York's Broome Country Area. Kiwanis Club of Binghamton, N. Y. LC 85-20880. (Illus.). 82p. (Orig.). 1985. pap. 7.95 (ISBN 0-911572-48-1, A-297). Vestal.

Picture Postcard History of New York's Elmira, Corning, & Vicinity. Alfred N. Weiner. (Illus., Orig.). 1988. pap. 9.95 (ISBN 0-930256-17-4). Almar.

Picture Postcard History of Princeton & Princeton University. William K. Evans. (Illus.). 101p. (Orig.). Date not set. pap. price not set (ISBN 0-930256-18-2). Almar.

Picture Postcards in the United States. George Miller & Dorothy Miller. (Illus.). 1976. 12.98 (ISBN 0-517-52400-7, C N Potter Bks). Crown.

Picture Postcards of Old Brooklyn: Twenty-Four Ready-to-Mail Views. (Illus.). 18p. (Orig.). 1983. pap. 3.50 (ISBN 0-486-24489-X). Dover.

Picture Posters. Charles Hiatt. (Illus.). 1977. Repr. of 1895 ed. 29.00x (ISBN 0-7158-1150-9). Charles River Bks.

Picture Processing & Digital Filtering. T. S. Huang. LC 75-5770. (Illus.). 270p. 1979. 27.00 (ISBN 0-387-09339-7). Springer-Verlag.

Picture Processing & Psychopictorics. Ed. by Bernice S. Lipkin & Azriel Rosenfeld. 1970. 39.95 (ISBN 0-12-451550-9). Acad Pr.

Picture Profits: Let Your Camera Make Money for You. 4th ed. Andrew S. Linick. 1981. pap. 7.95 (ISBN 0-917098-02-1). LKA Inc.

Picture Puzzle Riddle Book. Joyce Behr. LC 83-9160. (Illus.). 128p. (gr. 3 up). 1983. 10.95 (ISBN 0-8069-4676-8); PLB 13.29 (ISBN 0-8069-4677-6). Sterling.

Picture Puzzles. The Diagram Group. 96p. (Orig.). 1983. pap. 1.75 (ISBN 0-345-30476-4). Ballantine.

Picture Puzzles. Tyler. (Brain Benders Ser.). (gr. 2-5). 1980. (Usborne-Hayes); PLB 11.96 (ISBN 0-88110-049-8); pap. 2.95 (ISBN 0-86020-433-2). EDC.

Picture Puzzles for the Super-Smart. Illus. by Studio D Staff & Irit Adler. LC 85-2596. (Illus.). 136p. (gr. 8 up). 1985. pap. 4.95 (ISBN 0-8069-7952-6). Sterling.

Picture Quilts. Joan Masters. LC 86-19966. (Illus.). 128p. 1986. 22.50 (ISBN 1-55562-013-2); pap. 14.95 (ISBN 1-55562-012-4). Main Street.

Picture Researcher's Handbook. 3rd ed. Evans. 1986. 57.95 (ISBN 0-442-31737-9). Van Nos Reinhold.

Picture Rhymes. Jan Gleiter. (Teddies Ser.). (Illus.). 32p. (gr. k-3). 1986. PLB 13.31 (ISBN 0-8172-2443-2); pap. 9.27 (ISBN 0-8172-2448-3). Raintree Pubs.

Picture Searching: Techniques & Tools. Renate V. Shaw. LC 72-13234. (SLA Bibliographies Ser.: No. 6). pap. 20.00 (ISBN 0-317-09419-X, 2017282). Bks Demand UMI.

Picture Sourcebook for Collage & Decoupage. Edmund V. Gillon, Jr. LC 74-82206. (Illus.). 144p. (Orig.). 1974. pap. 6.95 (ISBN 0-486-23095-3). Dover.

Picture Sources Four. Ed. by Ernest H. Robl. LC 83-625. (Illus.). 200p. 1983. pap. text ed. 35.00 (ISBN 0-87111-274-4). SLA.

Picture Sources Three: Collections of Prints & Photographs in the U. S. & Canada. Special Libraries Association, Picture Division. Ed. by Ann Novotny & Rosemary Eakins. LC 75-6582. pap. 101.80 (ISBN 0-317-10135-8, 2012011). Bks Demand UMI.

Picture South Florida: Sunrise to Sunrise. 1988. 29.95 (ISBN 0-937047-13-9). United Comns.

Picture Squares. (Let's Draw Ser.). (Illus.). 24p. (gr. k up). 1988. pap. 2.95 (ISBN 0-8249-8200-2). Ideals.

Picture Stories for Beginning Composition. Sandra Heyer. 144p. 1983. pap. text ed. 6.25 (ISBN 0-13-675810-X, 21321). Prentice ESL.

Picture Stories for Children. Irmengarde Eberle. (gr. k-6). 1988. pap. 2.95 (ISBN 0-440-40031-7, YB). Dell.

Picture Stories for Speech Correction, Set 1. Bethanie Valentine. 1972. text ed. 11.95x (ISBN 0-8134-1443-1). Inter Print Pubs.

Picture Stories for Speech Correction, Set 2. Bethanie Valentine-Millstein. 1978. text ed. 11.95x (ISBN 0-8134-2010-5). Inter Print Pubs.

Picture Stories from the Bible. M. C. Gaines. Old Testament. pap. 2.95 (ISBN 0-345-34031-0); Nwe Testament. pap. 2.95 (ISBN 0-345-34030-2). Ballantine.

Picture Stories from the Bible. (gr. 4). pap. 5.00 (ISBN 0-87068-598-8). Ktav.

Picture Stories from the Bible: The New Testament in Full-Color Comic-Strip Form. Ed. by M. C. Gaines. LC 80-51593. (Comic-Book Bible Ser.: Vol. 2). (Illus.). 144p. (gr. 3-10). 1980. Repr. of 1946 ed. 9.95 (ISBN 0-934386-02-1). Scarf Pr.

Picture Stories from the Bible: The Old Testament in Full-Color Comic-Strip Form. Ed. by M. C. Gaines. LC 79-66064. (Illus.). 224p. (gr. 3-10). 1979. Repr. of 1943 ed. 9.95 (ISBN 0-934386-01-3). Scarf Pr.

Picture Story Bible ABC Book. rev. ed. Elsie E. Egermeier. (Illus.). (ps-1). 1963. 5.95 (ISBN 0-87162-262-9, D1703). Warner Pr.

Picture Story Language Test. Ed. by Helmer R. Myklebust. 4p. 1985. 22.50 (ISBN 0-8089-1745-5, 793019). Grune.

Picture Story of George Brett. George Sullivan. LC 82-3505. (Illus.). 64p. (gr. 4-6). 1982. PLB 9.29 (ISBN 0-671-44272-4). Messner.

Picture Story of Wayne Gretzky. Jim Benagh. LC 82-60640. (Illus.). 64p. (gr. 4 up). 1982. PLB 9.29g (ISBN 0-671-45949-X). Messner.

Picture Taking in Glacier Park. Winton Weydemeyer. 160p. (Orig.). 1986. pap. 7.95 (ISBN 0-934318-71-9). Falcon Pr MT.

Picture the Dawning (Songbook) Paul F. Page. 1976. pap. 4.96 (ISBN 0-89390-002-8). Resource Pubns.

Picture the People of the Caribbean. Joyce Bailey & Michael Dash. (Illus., Orig.). 1977. pap. 2.95 (ISBN 0-377-00065-5). Friendship Pr.

Picture Them Dead. Margaret Maron. 224p. (Orig.). 1988. pap. 3.50 (ISBN 0-553-27410-4). Bantam.

Picture Theory of Meaning: An Interpretation of Wittgenstein's Tractatus Logico-Philosophicus. Scott R. Stripling. LC 78-62176. 1978. pap. text ed. 10.00 (ISBN 0-8191-0109-5). U Pr of Amer.

Picture This. Joseph Heller. 336p. 1988. 19.95 (ISBN 0-399-13355-0, Putnam). Putnam Pub Group.

Picture This: An Illustrated Guide to Complete Dinners. Susan Bachner. (Illus.). 72p. 1984. 27.50 (ISBN 0-9613439-0-7). Spec Addns.

Picture This Book, Bk. 1. Carl E. Klitgaard. pap. 7.95 (ISBN 0-686-97148-0). Cardot Entpr Inc.

Picture This: Films Chosen by Artists. Barbara Kruger et al. Ed. by Steve Gallagher. (Illus.). 108p. (Orig.). Date not set. pap. 5.00 (ISBN 0-936739-05-3). Hallwalls Inc.

Picture Tour of the Smithsonian. 1986. 5.98 (ISBN 0-517-62609-8). Outlet Bk Co.

Picture: Welsh Poets. Stuart Smith. LC 87-62942. (Illus.). 60p. (Orig.). 1988. pap. 15.95 (ISBN 0-907476-83-X, Pub. by Poetry Wales Pr UK). Dufour.

Picture Windows. John Pfahl. LC 87-3273. (Illus.). 112p. 1987. 40.00 (ISBN 0-8212-1665-1). NYGS.

Picture Windows on the Christ. Charles C. Wise, Jr. LC 78-69928. (Illus.). 354p. 1979. 11.95 (ISBN 0-917023-03-X); pap. 5.95 (ISBN 0-917023-04-8). Magian Pr.

Picture-Writing of the American Indians, 2 vols. Garrick Mallery. (Illus.). 822p. 1972. pap. 9.95; Vol. 1. pap. (ISBN 0-486-22842-8); Vol. 2. pap. 9.95 (ISBN 0-486-22843-6). Dover.

Picture-Writing of the American Indians. Garrick Mallery. 39.95 (ISBN 0-8490-0836-0). Gordon Pr.

Picture-Writing of the American Indians, 2 vols. Garrick Mallery. (Illus.). Set. 34.00 (ISBN 0-8446-4582-6). Peter Smith.

Picture-Writings & Other Documents by Nele, Paramount Chief of the Cuna Indians, & Ruben Perez Kantule, His Secretary, 2 pts. in 1 vol. Erland Nordenskiold. LC 75-46061. (Comparative Ethnographical Studies Ser.: Vol. 7). Repr. of 1930 ed. 39.50 (ISBN 0-404-15147-7). AMS Pr.

Picture Yourself a Winner. R. Eugene Nichols. LC 85-90039. 267p. 1985. 12.95 (ISBN 0-533-06570-4). Vantage.

Picturebook Ramayana: An Illustrated Version of Valmiki's Story. Ed. by H. Daniel Smith. M. Narasimhachary. LC 81-13602. (Foreign & Comparative Studies Program: South Asian Special Publications, No. 3). (Illus., Orig.). 1981. pap. text ed. 12.00x (ISBN 0-915984-83-0). Syracuse U Foreign Comp.

Pictured Rocks Cruises. John S. Penrod. 1988. pap. 2.95 (ISBN 0-942618-14-9). Penrod Hiawatha.

Picturegoers Who's Who & Encyclopedia of the Screen. G. Arliss. 608p. 1976. lib. bdg. 95.00 (ISBN 0-8490-0837-9). Gordon Pr.

Pictures. Kate Petty. LC 85-81979. (Micro Fun Ser.). 32p. (gr. k-6). 1986. lib. bdg. 10.40 (ISBN 0-531-17018-7, Gloucester Pr). Watts.

Pictures & Biographies of Brigham Young & His Wives. J. H. Crockwell. 1980. lib. bdg. 59.95 (ISBN 0-8490-3158-3). Gordon Pr.

Pictures & Other Passages from Henry James. Henry James. LC 76-22796. 1976. Repr. of 1916 ed. lib. bdg. 37.00 (ISBN 0-8414-4831-0). Folcroft.

Pictures & Plans. rev. ed. Philip Sauvain. (Practical Geography Ser.: Bk. 1). (Illus.). 100p. 1976. 12.95 (ISBN 0-7175-0485-9). Dufour.

Pictures & Poems in Rhythm. Joseph Karbownicsk. (Illus.). 32p. 1988. 6.95 (ISBN 0-89962-692-0). Todd & Honeywell.

Pictures & Punishment: Art & Criminal Prosecution During the Florentine Renaissance. Samuel Y. Edgerton, Jr. LC 84-45144. (Illus.). 244p. 1984. 39.95x (ISBN 0-8014-1705-8). Cornell U Pr.

Pictures & Stories from Forgotten Children's Books. Arnold Arnold. (Illus., Orig.). (gr. k-6). 1970. pap. 5.95 (ISBN 0-486-22041-9). Dover.

Pictures & Texts: Henry James, A. L. Coburn, & New Ways of Seeing in Literary Culture. Ralph F. Bogardus. Ed. by Diane Kirkpatrik. LC 84-8844. (Studies in Photography: No. 2). 266p. 1984. 42.95 (ISBN 0-8357-1471-3). UMI Res Pr.

Pictures & Their Use in Communication. Novitz. 1977. pap. 26.00 (ISBN 90-247-1942-9, Pub. by Martinus Nijhoff Netherlands). Kluwer Academic.

Pictures Are Fun to Look at. (Shorewood Art Programs for Education Ser.). 8p. 1974. tchr's. ed. 86.00 (ISBN 0-88185-002-0); mounted prints 119.00. Shorewood Fine Art.

Pictures at an Exhibition: A Science Fiction Anthology. Ed. by Ian Watson. LC 87-33754. 168p. 1987. lib. bdg. 19.95x (ISBN 0-8095-6107-7). Borgo Pr.

Pictures at Play or Dialogues of the Galleries. Andrew Lang & W. E. Henley. LC 70-112940. (Illus.). Repr. of 1888 ed. 10.00 (ISBN 0-404-03829-8). AMS Pr.

Pictures at the Abbey: The Collection of the Irish National Theatre. Lennox Robinson & M. O'Haoda. 1983. pap. 11.95 (Pub. by Colin Smythe Ltd Britain). Dufour.

Pieces Baroques. Jean Anouilh. Incl. Cher Antoine; Ne Reveillez Pas, Madam; Directeur de l'Opera. 1974. 39.95 (ISBN 0-686-50202-7). French & Eur.

Pieces Brillantes. Jean Anouilh. Incl. Invitation au Chateau; Colombe; Repetition ou L'amour Puni; Cecile ou L'ecole des Peres. 39.95 (ISBN 0-685-37149-2). French & Eur.

Pieces Costumees: L'alouette, Becket, la Foire D'empoigne. Jean Anouilh. 39.95 (ISBN 0-685-37150-6). French & Eur.

Pieces de Clavecin see Monuments of Music & Music Literature in Facsimile: Series One.

Pieces de clavecin see Oeuvres Completes De Jean-Philippe Rameau.

Pieces de clavecin (Livre Premier) see Monuments of Music & Music Literature in Facsimile: Series One.

Pieces de Clavecin: Premier, Second, Troisieme et Quatrieme Livres see Monuments of Music & Music Literature in Facsimile: Series One.

Pieces De Clavessin see Monuments of Music & Music Literature in Facsimile: Series One.

Pieces Diverses see Poesies Album De Vers Anciens Avec.

Pieces en un Acte: Avec: La Scintillante, Amedes et les Messieurs en rang. Jules Romains. 176p. 1930. 3.95 (ISBN 0-686-55283-0). French & Eur.

Pieces for Prize Speaking. Ed. by A. H. Craig & Binney Gunnison. LC 75-5592. (Granger Index Reprint Ser.). 1972. Repr. of 1899 ed. 23.00 (ISBN 0-8369-6371-7). Ayer Co Pubs.

Pieces Grincantes. Jean Anouilh. Incl. Ardele ou la Marguerite; Valse des Toreadors; Ornifle Ou le Courant D'air; Pauvre Bitos Ou le Diner De Tetes. 39.95 (ISBN 0-685-37151-4). French & Eur.

Pieces in Context: An Approach to the Study of Chinese Furniture Through an Analysis of Ming Dynasty Domestic Hardwood Examples in Kansas City. Sarah A. Handler. 296p. 1985. 420.00x (ISBN 0-317-68974-6, Pub. by Han-Shan Tang Ltd). State Mutual Bk.

Pieces Noires. Jean Anouilh. Incl. Hermine; Sauvage; Voyageur sans Bagage; Eurydice. 39.95 (ISBN 0-685-37152-2). French & Eur.

Pieces of a Dream: The Ethnic Worker's Crisis with America. Ed. by Michael G. Wenk et al. LC 72-93362. (Illus.). 212p. 1977. pap. 9.95 (ISBN 0-913256-08-0). Ctr Migration.

Pieces of a Woman. Barbara Holley. (Illus.). 12p. 1982. pap. 2.50 (ISBN 0-943696-01-1). Red Key Pr.

Pieces of Bread. Jimmie Canfeld. 1987. 10.00. White Pine.

Pieces of Cream. Richard Rodino & Hilary Connor. 224p. (Orig.). 1987. pap. 3.50 (ISBN 0-553-26666-7). Bantam.

Pieces of Dreams. Charlotte V. Allen. 1985. pap. 3.95 (ISBN 0-425-07582-6). Berkley Pub.

Pieces of Dreams. Charlotte V. Allen. (Large Print Books (General Ser.)). 514p. 1985. lib. bdg. 18.95 (ISBN 0-8161-3958-X). G K Hall.

Pieces of Eight. Becky Blackley. (Illus.). 52p. (Orig.). Date not set. pap. 7.95 (ISBN 0-912827-04-1). I A D Pubns.

Pieces of Eight. Sydney J. Harris. 300p. 1982. 12.95 (ISBN 0-395-32512-9). HM.

Pieces of Eight. Sydney J. Harris. 1985. pap. 7.95. HM.

Pieces of Eight. Robert Nisbet. 145p. 1982. 23.00x (ISBN 0-85088-555-8, Pub. by Gomer Pr). State Mutual Bk.

Pieces of Eight: Monetary Powers & Disabilities of the United States Constitution: A Study in Constitutional Law. Edwin Vieira, Jr. LC 83-18898. 1983. 24.95 (ISBN 0-8159-6226-6). Devin.

Pieces of Hate. Richard Franks. 1982. 15.00x (ISBN 0-906660-51-3, Pub. by New Playwrights Network). State Mutual Bk.

Pieces of Life. Larry Fotine. LC 86-90707. Date not set. pap. 10.00 (ISBN 0-933830-07-6). Poly Tone.

Pieces of Life. Larry Fotine. LC 86-90707. 1987. 15.95 (ISBN 0-933830-06-8). Poly Tone.

Pieces of Map, Pieces of Music. Robert Bringhurst. LC 86-73199. 128p. (Orig.). 1987. pap. 9.00 (ISBN 1-55659-003-2). Copper Canyon.

Pieces of Modesty. Peter O'Donnell. 192p. 1986. Repr. 15.95 (ISBN 0-89296-172-4); ltd. ed. 45.00 (ISBN 0-89296-267-4). Mysterious Pr.

Pieces of My Mind. Andrew A. Rooney. (General Ser.). 1985. lib. bdg. 14.95 (ISBN 0-8161-3802-8, Large Print Bks). G K Hall.

Pieces of My Mind. Andrew A. Rooney. 1985. pap. 4.95 (ISBN 0-380-69885-4). Avon.

Pieces of Peace. W. Calvin McCain. LC 74-25235. 80p. 1983. pap. text ed. 5.95 (ISBN 0-931680-01-8). Dunbar Pub.

Pieces of Resistance: Selected Essays. Eugene Goodheart. 200p. 1987. 29.95 (ISBN 0-521-34036-5). Cambridge U Pr.

Pieces of Silver & Gold. Aglow Staff. (Prayer Diary Ser.: No.3). 40p. 1984. pap. 2.95 (ISBN 0-930756-86-X, 533009). Aglow Pubns.

Pieces of Sky. Marianne Willman. 400p. Date not set. pap. 4.50 (ISBN 0-373-97022-6). Harlequin Bks.

Pieces of String & Other Stories. Tita Lacambra-Ayala. 138p. (Orig.). 1984. pap. 9.25x (ISBN 971-10-0186-1, Pub. by New Day Philippines). Cellar.

Pieces of the Bone-Text Still There. Ivan Arguelles. (Illus.). 28p. 1987. pap. 3.00 (ISBN 0-318-23467-X). Skydog OR.

Pieces of the Frame. John McPhee. 320p. 1975. 14.95 (ISBN 0-374-23281-4); pap. 9.95. FS&G.

Pieces of the Game: The Human Drama of Americans Held Hostage in Iran. Charles W. Scott. (Illus.). 350p. 1984. 14.95 (ISBN 0-931948-51-7). Peachtree Pubs.

Pieces of the Global Puzzle: International Approaches to Environmental Concerns. Ed. by Anne M. Blackburn. 210p. 1986. 13.95 (ISBN 1-55591-002-5). Fulcrum Inc.

Pieces of the Past. Nancy J. Martin. LC 86-50463. (Illus.). 152p. 1986. pap. 18.95 (ISBN 0-943574-38-2). That Patchwork.

Pieces of the Past, Pioneer Life in Burnett County. Eunice Kanne. (Illus.). 100p. (Orig.). 1986. pap. 7.95x (ISBN 0-938627-00-7). New Past Pr.

Pieces of White Shell. Terry T. Williams. LC 86-24915. (Illus.). 176p. 1987. pap. 9.95 (ISBN 0-8263-0969-0). U of NM Pr.

Pieces of White Shell: A Journey to Navajoland. Terry T. Williams. (Illus.). 160p. 1984. 14.95 (ISBN 0-684-18232-7, ScribT). Scribner.

Pieces Roses. Jean Anouilh. Incl. Humulus le Monet; Bal des Voleurs; Rendez-vous de Senlis; Leocadia. 39.95 (ISBN 0-685-37153-0). French & Eur.

Pieces Secretes. Jean Anouilh. Incl. Tu estais Si Gentil Quand Tu Etais Petit; Arrestation; Scenario. 1977. 39.95 (ISBN 0-686-52219-2). French & Eur.

Pieces sur L'art. Paul Valery. pap. 4.95 (ISBN 0-685-36622-7). French & Eur.

Pieces sur l'Art see Oeuvres.

Pieces That Have Won Prizes: Also Many Encore Pieces; Enlarged Edition. Compiled by Frank McHale. LC 79-39381. (Granger Index Reprint Ser.). Repr. of 1930 ed. 19.00 (ISBN 0-8369-6346-6). Ayer Co Pubs.

Piecewise Constant Orthogonal Functions & Their Application to Systems & Control. G. P. Rao. (Lecture Notes in Control & Information Sciences: Vol. 55). 254p. 1983. pap. 20.50 (ISBN 0-387-12556-6). Springer-Verlag.

Piecewise Linear Concordances & Isotopies. Kenneth C. Millet. LC 74-18328. (Memoirs Ser.: No. 153). 74p. 1974. pap. 12.00 (ISBN 0-8218-1853-8, MEMO-153). Am Math.

Piecewise Methods & Applications to Power Systems. Ed. by H. H. Happ & A. H. Gibson. LC 79-901. 428p. 1980. 56.95 (ISBN 0-471-35131-8, Pub. by Wiley). Krieger.

Piecework Abandoned: The Effect of Wage Incentive Systems on Managerial Authority. Wilfred Brown. (Glacier Project Ser.). 127p. 1962. 5.95x (ISBN 0-8093-0371-X). S Ill U Pr.

Piecework: Nineteen Fresno Poets. Ed. by Jon Veinberg & Ernesto Trejo. (Illus.). 221p. (Orig.). 1987. pap. 9.95 (ISBN 0-936105-00-3). Silver Skates.

Piecing It Together: Feminism & Nonviolence. British Feminism & Nonviolence Study Group Staff. (Illus.). 60p. 1983. 3.00 (ISBN 0-9508602-0-4). J Tiffany.

Pied dans le Crime. Eugene Labiche. 9.95 (ISBN 0-686-54249-5). French & Eur.

Pied Piper. William Glennon. (Children's Theatre Playscript Ser.). (gr. k-12). 1968. pap. 2.25x (ISBN 0-88020-017-0). Coach Hse.

Pied Piper. Robert Paier. 1979. text ed. 9.95 (ISBN 0-07-048091-5). McGraw.

Pied Piper. (Once Upon A Story Time Ser.). (Illus.). (ps-1). 1985. 1.98 (ISBN 0-517-47105-1). Outlet Bk Co.

Pied Piper. Nevil Shute. 19.95 (ISBN 0-88411-323-X, Pub. by Aeonian Pr). Amereon Ltd.

Pied Piper: Allard K. Lowenstein & the Liberal Dream. Richard Cummings. LC 83-49377. 565p. 1985. 17.95 (ISBN 0-394-53848-X, GP 895). Grove.

Pied Piper of Hamelin. Barbara Bartos-Hoppner. LC 87-45150. (Illus.). 32p. (gr. k-3). 1987. 9.95i (ISBN 0-397-32239-9, Lipp Jr Bks); PLB 11.89 (ISBN 0-397-32240-2). HarpJ.

Pied Piper of Hamelin. Melvin Bernhardt. (Children's Theatre Playscript Ser.). (gr. k-12). 1963. pap. 2.50x (ISBN 0-88020-043-X). Coach Hse.

Pied Piper of Hamelin. Val Biro. LC 84-52469. (Illus.). 30p. (ps-3). 1985. 9.45 (ISBN 0-382-09014-4). Silver.

Pied Piper of Hamelin. Robert Browning. LC 85-24168. (Illus.). 40p. (ps-4). 1986. 13.00 (ISBN 0-688-03809-3); lib. bdg. 12.88 (ISBN 0-688-03810-7). Lothrop.

Pied Piper of Hamelin. rev. ed. Robert Browning. (Illus.). 64p. (gr. 1 up). 1988. 10.95 (ISBN 0-15-200566-8, Gulliver Bks). HarBraceJ.

Pied Piper of Hamelin. Mercer Mayer. LC 87-1607. (Illus.). 48p. (gr. k-3). 1987. PLB 16.95 (ISBN 0-02-765361-7). Macmillan.

Pied Piper of Hamelin. (Derrydale Fairytale Library). (Illus.). (ps-3). 1985. 2.98 (ISBN 0-517-28805-2). Outlet Bk Co.

Pied Piper of Hamelin. Illus. by Maria Rius. LC 84-52785. (Tell Me a Story Ser.). (Illus.). 18p. (ps-1). 1985. 3.75 (ISBN 0-382-09070-5). Silver.

Pied Piper of Hamelin. Retold by Catherine Storr. LC 84-26971. (Stories Clippers Ser.). (Illus.). 32p. (gr. k-4). 1984. PLB 15.33 (ISBN 0-8172-2107-7); PLB 27.99 incl. cassette (ISBN 0-8172-2238-3); pap. 9.27 (ISBN 0-8172-2251-0); pap. 23.95g incl. cassette (ISBN 0-8172-2266-9); cassette 14.00. Raintree Pubs.

Pied Piper of Hamelin. Geoffrey Thornber. 1982. 15.00x (ISBN 0-906660-55-6, Pub. by New Playwrights Network). State Mutual Bk.

Pied Piper of Hamlin: Fairy Tales. Ed. by Tony Tallarico. (Tuffy Story Bks). (Illus.). 32p. (ps-3). 1987. pap. text ed. 2.95 (ISBN 0-89828-332-9, 83329). Tuffy Bks.

Pied Tendre. Rene de Goscinny. (Lucky Luke Series). (Fr.). 1976. 7.95x (ISBN 2-205-00305-4). Intl Learn Syst.

Piedmont Garden: How to Grow by the Calendar. Juanita B. Garrison. LC 80-23218. 1981. pap. text ed. 10.95 mechanical (ISBN 0-87249-403-9). U of SC Pr.

Piedmont Plantation: The Bennehan-Cameron Family & Lands in North Carolina. Jean B. Anderson. LC 85-81002. (Illus.). xix, 227p. 1985. 24.95x (ISBN 0-9615577-1-0). HPS Durham.

Piedras Negras Archaeology: Artifacts, Caches & Burials. William R. Coe. (University Museum Monographs: No. 18). (Illus.). x, 245p. 1959. pap. 25.00 (ISBN 0-934718-11-3). Univ Mus of U PA.

Piedras Negras Pottery. Mary Butler. LC 36-19557. (Piedras Negras Preliminary Papers: No. 4). pap. 25.00 (ISBN 0-317-26206-8, 2052124). Bks Demand UMI.

Pieface & Daphne. Lila Perl. 184p. (gr. 3-6). 1980. 7.95 (ISBN 0-395-29105-4, Clarion). HM.

Pieface & Daphne. Lila Perl. (gr. 4-6). 1982. pap. 2.25 (ISBN 0-671-52693-6). Archway.

Pien Chih-Lin: A Study in Modern Chinese Poetry. Lloyd Halt. (Publications in Modern Chin. Lang. & Literature). xii, 210p. 1983. pap. write for info. (ISBN 90-70176-92-0). Foris Pubns.

Piensa Estas Cosas. Orig. Title: Think on These Things. 12p. 1969. pap. 0.15x (ISBN 0-8361-1133-8). Herald Pr.

Pienza: The Creation of a Renaissance City. Charles R. Mack. LC 86-24269. (Illus.). 256p. 1987. 39.95x (ISBN 0-8014-1699-X). Cornell U Pr.

Pier. Rayner Heppenstall. 192p. 1987. 15.95 (ISBN 0-85031-450-X, Pub. by Allison & Busby England); pap. 7.95 (ISBN 0-85031-451-8, Pub. by Allison & Busby England). Schocken.

Pier-Glass. Robert Graves. LC 73-11339. Repr. of 1921 ed. lib. bdg. 35.00 (ISBN 0-8414-2047-5). Folcroft.

Pier Paolo Pasolini. Pia Friedrich. (World Authors Ser.). 1982. lib. bdg. 20.95 (ISBN 0-8057-6500-X, Twayne). G K Hall.

Pier Paolo Pasolini: The Poetics of Heresy. Beverly Allen. (Illus.). 144p. (Orig.). 1982. pap. 29.50 (ISBN 0-915838-11-7). Anma Libri.

Pieracci & Shelley: An Italian Ur-Cenci. George Yost. 27.50 (ISBN 0-916379-33-7). Scripta.

Pierce Arrow. Mark A. Ralston. LC 80-15214. (Illus.). 366p. 1980. 25.00 (ISBN 0-498-02451-2). A S Barnes.

Pierce Chronicle. Ed. by J. Gary Williams & Ronald W Stark. 127p. 1975. 10.95 (ISBN 0-89301-028-6). U of Idaho Pr.

Pierce County Street Guide & Directory, 1989. Thomas Bros. Maps Staff. (Illus.). 84p. 1988. pap. 12.95. Thomas Bros Maps.

Pierce, Pace, Hall, Minton, & Huie Families. Virginia C. Jantz. LC 86-80864. (Illus.). 442p. 1986. 30.00 (ISBN 0-9607170-1-3). V C Jantz.

Pierce Penilesse. Thomas Nash. 1975. Repr. of 1924 ed. 15.00 (ISBN 0-8274-4011-1). R West.

Pierce's Register: Register of the Certificates Issued by John Pierce, Esquire, Paymaster General & Commissioner of Army Accounts for the United States, to Officers & Soldiers of the Continental Army under Act of July 4, 1783. 566p. 1987. Repr. of 1915 ed. 25.00 (5935). Genealog Pub.

Pierce's Register: Register of the Certificates Issued by John Pierce, Esquire, Paymaster General & Commissioner of Army Accounts... to Officers & Soldiers of the Continental Army. United States Pay Department. LC 72-10551. 566p. 1984. Repr. of 1915 ed. 25.00 (ISBN 0-8063-0527-4). Genealog Pub.

Piercing. John Coyne. 272p. 1986. pap. 3.50 (ISBN 0-441-66310-9, Pub. by Charter Bks). Ace Bks.

Piercing the Reich. Joseph Persico. 1979. pap. 2.50 (ISBN 0-345-28280-9). Ballantine.

Piercing the Surface: X Rays of Nature. Carlo Greco & Stefano Greco. (Illus.). 144p. 1987. 29.95 (ISBN 0-8109-1495-6). Abrams.

Piero della Francesca. Alessandro Angelini. LC 85-50364. (Illus.). 80p. 1985. pap. 13.95 (ISBN 0-935748-65-2). Scala Books.

Piero Della Francesca. V. Tatrai. 70p. (Ger.). 1981. 33.00x (ISBN 0-317-57409-4, Pub. by Collets UK). State Mutual Bk.

Piero della Francesca's Baptism of Christ. Marilyn A. Lavin. LC 81-3371. (Publications in the History of Art Ser.: No. 29). (Illus.). 204p. 1981. 33.00x (ISBN 0-300-02619-6). Yale U Pr.

Piero di Cosimo's Forest Fire. Ed. by Christopher Lloyd. (Illus.). 28p. (Orig.). 1984. pap. 7.50 (ISBN 0-317-58644-0, Pub. by Ashmolean Mus). Longwood Pub Group.

Piero Di Cosmos's Forest Fire. Ed. by Christopher Lloyd. 28p. 1984. 4.50x (ISBN 0-907849-07-5, Pub. by Ashmolean Museum). State Mutual Bk.

Piero Ventura's Book of Cities. Piero Ventura. (Illus.). (ps up). 1975. Random.

Pierpont Morgan As Collector & Patron, 1837-1913. rev. ed. Francis H. Taylor. (Illus.). 39p. 1957. pap. 4.00 (ISBN 0-87598-033-3). Pierpont Morgan.

Pierpont Morgan Library: A Review of Acquisitions, 1949-1968. Compiled by Morgan Library Curators. (Illus.). 1969. 15.00 (ISBN 0-87598-005-8). Pierpont Morgan.

Pierpont Morgan Library: Eighteenth Report to the Fellows, 1975-1977. Herbert Cahoon. Ed. by Charles Ryskamp. (Illus.). 421p. 1978. 50.00 (ISBN 0-87598-066-X). Pierpont Morgan.

Pierpont Morgan Library: Gifts in Honor of the Fiftieth Anniversary. Pref. by Charles Ryskamp. 1974. pap. 5.00 (ISBN 0-87598-048-1). Pierpont Morgan.

Pierpont Morgan Library: Twentieth Report to the Fellows, 1981-1983. Ed. by Charles Ryskamp. (Illus.). xxxiii, 432p. 1984. 27.95 (ISBN 0-87598-081-3). Pierpont Morgan.

Pierre. Herman Melville. (Writings of Herman Melville Ser.). 435p. 1972. 36.95x (ISBN 0-8101-0266-8); pap. 13.95 (ISBN 0-8101-0267-6). Northwestern U Pr.

Pierre. Maurice Sendak. (Illus.). 48p. (ps-3). 1962. PLB 11.89 (ISBN 0-06-025965-5). HarpJ.

Pierre see Nutshell Library.

Pierre Alechinsky; les Estampes, 1946-1972. Pierre Alechinsky. 1973. 60.00 (ISBN 0-915346-17-6). A Wofsy Fine Arts.

Pierre Alechinsky: Margin & Center. Michael Gibson & Pierre Alechinsky. (Illus.). 144p. 1987. 18.00 (ISBN 0-89207-061-7). S R Guggenheim.

Pierre & His People. facsimile ed. Gilbert Parker. LC 74-101287. (Short Story Index Reprint Ser.). 1894. 19.00 (ISBN 0-8369-3224-2). Ayer Co Pubs.

Pierre & Jean. Guy De Maupassant. LC 76-48441. (Library of World Literature Ser.). 1988. Repr. of 1923 ed. lib. bdg. 27.00 (ISBN 0-88355-578-6). Hyperion Conn.

Pierre & Jean. Guy De Maupassant. Tr. by Leonard W. Tancock. (Penguin Classics Ser.). 1979. pap. 4.95 (ISBN 0-14-044358-4). Penguin.

Pierre Attaingnant, Royal Printer of Music: A Historical Study & Bibliographical Catalogue. Daniel Heartz. LC 68-13959. 1970. 75.00x (ISBN 0-520-01563-0). U of Cal Pr.

Pierre-Auguste Renoir. Ernest Raboff. LC 87-45154. (Art for Children Ser.). (Illus.). 32p. (gr. 1 up). 1987. 11.70i (ISBN 0-397-32217-8, Lipp Jr Bks). HarpJ.

Pierre-Auguste Renoir. Ernest Raboff. LC 87-45145. (Trophy Nonfiction Art for Children Bks.). (Illus.). 32p. (gr. 1 up). 1987. pap. 5.95 (Trophy). HarpJ.

Pierre Bayle's Philosophical Commentary: A Modern Commentary Translation & Critical Interpretation. Amie G. Tannenbaum. (American University Studies Series V Philosophy). 311p. 1987. text ed. 43.00 (ISBN 0-8204-0347-4). P Lang Pubs.

Pierre Boaistuau's "Histoires Tragiques" A Study of Narrative Form & Tragic Vision. Richard A. Carr. (Studies in the Romance Languages & Literatures: No. 210). 258p. 1979. 15.00x (ISBN 0-8078-9210-6). U of NC Pr.

Pierre Bonnard. Alexander Babin. 1986. 30.00x (ISBN 0-317-61349-9, Pub. by Collets (UK)). State Mutual Bk.

Pierre Bonnard: Photographer & Painter. Philippe Neagu & Francoise Heilbrun. (Illus.). 144p. 1988. 50.00 (ISBN 0-89381-322-2). Aperture.

Pierre Bouguer's Optical Treatise on the Gradation of Light. Pierre Bouguer. Tr. by W. E. Middleton. LC 61-19105. pap. 66.00 (ISBN 0-317-08928-5, 2014140). Bks Demand UMI.

Pierre Chareau. Marc Vellay & Kenneth Frampton. LC 85-42815. (Illus.). 232p. 1986. 75.00 (ISBN 0-8478-0614-6). Rizzoli Intl.

Pierre Corneille. Claude Abraham. LC 76-186715. (Twayne's World Authors Ser.). 169p. 1972. lib. bdg. 17.95 (ISBN 0-8290-1745-3). Irvington.

Pierre Courtin. L'Oeuvre Grave 1944-1972. Yves Riviere. 240p. 1973. 50.00 (ISBN 0-915346-18-4). A Wofsy Fine Arts.

Pierre d'Ailly & the Council of Constance. John P. McGowan. 110p. 1984. Repr. of 1936 ed. 22.00x (ISBN 0-939738-34-1). Zubal Inc.

Pierre de Boisguilbert, precurseur des economistes, 1646-1714: sa vie, ses travaux, son influence. Felix Cadet. LC 68-56731. Repr. of 1870 ed. 25.50 (ISBN 0-8337-0449-4). B Franklin.

Pierre De la Folie: Poemes. Fernando Arrabal. 1970. pap. 9.95 (ISBN 0-686-54461-7). French & Eur.

Pierre de Ronsard. K. R. Jones. LC 75-120502. (Twayne's World Authors Ser.). 1970. lib. bdg. 17.95 (ISBN 0-8057-2778-7). Irvington.

Pierre Des Voeux. Sara Craven. (Harlequin Collection Ser.). 192p. 1983. pap. 1.95 (ISBN 0-373-49337-1). Harlequin Bks.

Pierre Deux's French Country. Pierre Moulin et al. (Illus.). 1984. 35.00 (ISBN 0-517-54787-2, C N Potter Bks). Crown.

Pierre Deux's Normandy: A French Country Style & Source Book. Linda Dannenberg et al. (Illus.). 1988. 35.00 (ISBN 0-517-56079-8, C N Potter Bks). Crown.

Pierre d'Horeb. Georges Duhamel. (Folio Ser.: No. 594). 286p. 1947. 6.95 (ISBN 0-686-55189-3). Schoenhof.

Pig Iron, Number 8: The New Beats. Ed. by Jim Villani & Rose Sayre. (Literary & Art Anthology Ser.). 96p. 1980. pap. 4.95 (ISBN 0-917530-16-0). Pig Iron Pr.

Pig Jokes & Puzzles. Lisa Eisenberg & Katy Hall. 96p. (gr. 4-7). pap. 1.95 (ISBN 0-590-32566-3). Scholastic Inc.

Pig Management & Production: A Practical Guide for Farmers & Students. Derek H. Goodwin. 203p. (Orig.). 1982. pap. text ed. 12.25 (ISBN 0-09-110891-8, Hutchinson & Co). Brookfield Pub co.

Pig or Pork Dead or Alive. Dennis Williams. 104p. 1987. 8.95 (ISBN 0-8062-3095-9). Carlton.

Pig Out. Christina Hanley. 1983. pap. 5.95 (ISBN 0-8065-0843-4, Pub. by Citadel Pr). Lyle Stuart.

Pig-Out Blues. Jan Greenberg. LC 82-2552. 121p. (gr. 7 up). 1982. 9.95 (ISBN 0-374-35937-7). FS&G.

Pig-Out Inn. Lois Ruby. LC 86-21433. 180p. (gr. 5 up). 1987. 12.95 (ISBN 0-395-42714-2). HM.

Pig Parade. (Illus.). 64p. 1987. 13.95 (ISBN 0-241-11692-9, Pub. by Hamish Hamilton England). David & Charles.

Pig Pickin' Country Carving. Tom Wolfe. (Illus.). 136p. 1988. pap. 15.95 (ISBN 0-88740-130-9). Schiffer.

Pig Pig & the Magic Photo Album. David McPhail. LC 85-20459. (Illus.). 24p. (ps-3). 1986. 10.95 (ISBN 0-525-44238-3). Dutton.

Pig Pig Goes to Camp. David McPhail. LC 83-1412. (Illus.). 24p. (ps-3). 1983. 9.95 (ISBN 0-525-44064-X, 0966-290). Dutton.

Pig Pig Goes to Camp. David McPhail. (Unicorn Paperback Ser.). (Illus.). 24p. (ps-3). 1987. pap. 3.95 (ISBN 0-525-44302-9). Dutton.

Pig Pig Grows up. David McPhail. LC 80-377. (Unicorn Paperbacks Ser.). (Illus.). 32p. (ps-2). 1980. 11.95 (ISBN 0-525-37027-7); pap. 3.95 (ISBN 0-525-44195-6). Dutton.

Pig Pig Grows up. David McPhail. (ps-2). 1985. pap. 12.95 incl. cassette (ISBN 0-941078-94-9); incl. cassette 19.95 (ISBN 0-941078-96-5); incl. cassette 4 paperbacks guide 27.95 (ISBN 0-941078-95-7). Live Oak Media.

Pig Pig Grows Up. David McPhail. 24p. (gr. k-3). pap. 2.50 (ISBN 0-590-40416-4). Scholastic Inc.

Pig Pig Rides. David McPhail. (Illus.). 32p. (ps-3). 1982. 11.95 (ISBN 0-525-44024-0, Unicorn Bk). Dutton.

Pig Pig Rides. David McPhail. LC 82-9777. (Unicorn Paperback Ser.). (Illus.). 24p. (ps-3). 1985. pap. 3.95 (ISBN 0-525-44222-7). Dutton.

Pig Plantagenet. Allen Andrews. 288p. 1984. pap. 2.95 (ISBN 0-8125-3094-2, Dist. by Warner Pub Services & St. Martin's Press). Tor Bks.

Pig Production. Ed. by D. J. Cole. LC 70-38754. (Illus.). 434p. 1972. 32.50x (ISBN 0-271-01114-9). Pa St U Pr.

Pig-Tail Days in Old Seattle. Sophie F. Bass. LC 72-77591. (Illus.). 190p. (gr. 4-6). 1973. 12.50 (ISBN 0-8323-0206-6). Binford-Metropolitan.

Pig, the Prince & the Unicorn. Karen Brush. 224p. 1987. pap. 2.95 (ISBN 0-380-75062-7). Avon.

Pig War. Betty Baker. LC 69-10212. (I Can Read History Bks.). (Illus.). 64p. (gr. k-3). 1969. PLB 10.89 (ISBN 0-06-020333-1). HarpJ.

Pig War. Keith A. Murray. LC 68-7256. (Illus.). 84p. 1968. pap. 2.00 (ISBN 0-917048-23-7). Wash St Hist Soc.

Pig Who Saved the Day. Thomas Crawford. (Illus.). (gr. 3-4). 1972. pap. 1.50 (ISBN 0-89375-049-2). Troll Assocs.

Pig Who Saw Everything. Dick Gackenbach. LC 77-12741. (Illus.). 40p. 1978. 6.95 (ISBN 0-395-28798-7, Clarion). HM.

Pig Will & Pig Won't. Richard Scarry. (Book & Doll Packages Ser.). (Illus.). (ps-1). 1985. doll incl. 9.95 (ISBN 0-394-87530-3). Random.

Pig Will & Pig Won't: A Book of Manners. Richard Scarry. LC 83-19177. (Knee-High Bks.). (Illus.). 24p. (ps-1). 1984. 3.95 (ISBN 0-394-86585-5, BYR); lib. bdg. 4.99 (ISBN 0-394-96585-X). Random.

Pig William. Arlene Dubanevich. LC 85-5776. (Illus.). 32p. (ps-2). 1985. 12.95 (ISBN 0-02-733200-4). Bradbury Pr.

Pigalee Pink & Other Stories. Evelyn Dorio. LC 79-56540. (Illus.). 95p. (gr. 3-6). 1979. 4.50x (ISBN 0-9603118-5-8); pap. text ed. 1.25 (ISBN 0-9603118-4-X). Davenport.

Pigalev. Nanette Newman. (Illus.). 28p. (ps-1). 1987. 6.95 (ISBN 0-340-33855-5, Pub. by Hodder & Stoughton UK). David & Charles.

Pigboat Thirty-Nine: An American Sub Goes to War. Bobette Gugliotta. LC 84-15295. (Illus.). 264p. 1984. 20.00 (ISBN 0-8131-1524-8). U Pr of KY.

Pigeon. Jay Bennett. 144p. (YA) (gr. 7 up). 1981. pap. 2.50 (ISBN 0-380-55848-3, 60163-X, Flare). Avon.

Pigeon. Jay Bennett. LC 79-26270. 1980. 8.95 (ISBN 0-416-30631-4, NO. 0151). Routledge Chapman & Hall.

Pigeon. Wendell M. Levi. 1986. Repr. 52.00 (ISBN 0-910876-01-0). Levi Pub.

Pigeon. Patrick Suskind. Tr. by John E. Woods. LC 87-46106. 1988. 14.45 (ISBN 0-394-56315-8). Knopf.

Pigeon & Will. Mryl Ijams. 1988. 13.95 (ISBN 0-533-07667-6). Vantage.

Pigeon Blood. Gary Alexander. 16.95 (ISBN 0-8027-5700-6). Walker Educ.

Pigeon Factory. John Richards. (Illus., Orig.). 1987. pap. 6.95 (ISBN 0-932274-40-4). Cadmus Eds.

Pigeon Fancying: Racing & Exhibiting. Ron Bissett. (Illus.). 173p. 1985. 19.95 (ISBN 0-7153-8427-9). David & Charles.

Pigeon Feathers. John Updike. 1986. pap. 3.50 (ISBN 0-449-21132-0, Crest). Fawcett.

Pigeon Feathers & Other Stories. John Updike. 1962. 12.95 (ISBN 0-394-44056-0). Knopf.

Pigeon Holes of Memory: The Life & Times of Dr. John Mackenzie (1803-1886) Intro. by Christina B. Shaw. (Illus.). 436p. 1988. text ed. 36.00x (ISBN 0-930664-07-8, Pub. by Constable UK). SPOSS.

Pigeon Pair. Elizabeth Ogilvie. Repr. lib. bdg. 14.95x (ISBN 0-88411-336-1, Pub. by Aeonian Pr). Amereon Ltd.

Pigeon Pie. Nancy Mitford. 186p. 1987. pap. 3.95 (ISBN 0-88184-332-6). Carroll & Graf.

Pigeon Racing. Wilson Stephens. (Illus.). 94p. 1988. 17.95 (ISBN 0-7063-6197-0, Pub. by Ward Lock). David & Charles.

Pigeon Shooting. Albert W. Money. Ed. & intro. by A. C. Gould. (Illus.). 109p. 1987. Repr. of 1896 ed. 19.95 (ISBN 0-936075-12-0). Gunnerman Pr.

Pigeon with Nine Heads. Glen Wright. Ed. by Carol Murphy. (Illus.). (gr. 3-6). 1981. PLB 6.95 (ISBN 0-89868-115-4, Read Res); pap. text ed. 4.95 (ISBN 0-89868-122-7, Read Res). ARO Pub.

Pigeons. Carl Naether. (Illus.). 96p. 1984. 9.95 (ISBN 0-87666-837-6, KW-148). TFH Pubns.

Pigeons see Brazilian Tales.

Pigeons & Doves of the World. 3rd ed. Derek Goodwin. LC 76-55484. (A Comstock Bk Ser). (Illus.). 496p. 1983. 48.50x (ISBN 0-8014-1434-2). Cornell U Pr.

Pigeons for Pleasure & Profit. Charles Foy. (Illus.). 1972. pap. 4.00 (ISBN 0-911466-19-3). Swanson.

Pigeons, Marks, Hustlers & Other Golf Bettors You Can Beat. Sam Snead & Jerry Tarde. LC 86-19516. (Illus.). 112p. 1986. 15.95 (ISBN 0-394-56194-5, Dist. by Random House). Golf Digest.

Pigeons on the Grass. Wolfgang Koeppen. Tr. by David Ward. (Modern German Voices Ser.). 210p. 1988. 24.95 (ISBN 0-8419-1163-0). Holmes & Meier.

Pigeons, Racing Homer Facts & Secrets. Leslie C. Swanson. 1958. pap. 3.00 (ISBN 0-911466-17-7). Swanson.

Pigeons, Racing Homer Topics. Leslie C. Swanson. 1955. pap. 3.00 (ISBN 0-911466-18-5). Swanson.

Pigeons That Went to War. Gordon Hayes. LC 81-90046. (Illus.). 160p. 1981. 9.95 (ISBN 0-9605880-1-9). G H Hayes.

Pigfoot Rebellion. Charles O. Hartman. LC 80-83946. (Poetry Chapbook, Fourth Ser.). 42p. 1981. 8.95 (ISBN 0-87923-364-8). Godine.

Piggety Pig Books, 6 of ea. title. Harriet Ziefert. 96p. (ps-k). 1988. 2.95 (ISBN 0-316-98758-1). Little.

Piggety Pig from Morning 'til Night. Harriet Ziefert. (Piggety Pig Bks.). (Illus.). (ps-k). 2.95 (ISBN 0-316-98764-6). Little.

Piggins. Jane Yolen. LC 86-22915. (Illus.). 32p. (ps-3). 1987. 13.95 (ISBN 0-15-261685-3). HarBraceJ.

Piggle. Crosby N. Bonsall. LC 73-5478. (Harper I Can Read Bks.). (Illus.). 64p. (gr. k-3). 1973. PLB 10.89 (ISBN 0-06-020580-6). HarpJ.

Piggle. D. W. Winnicott. LC 76-46815. 201p. 1977. text ed. 26.00x (ISBN 0-8236-4137-6). Intl Univs Pr.

Piggy at the Wheel. Derek Radford. (Illus.). 16p. (ps-2). 1988. 6.95 (ISBN 0-671-65265-6, Little Simon). S&S.

Piggy Back Concept: Reference Pages. Ed. by Barter Publishing Staff. LC 83-90676. 10p. 1983. pap. text ed. 3.00 (ISBN 0-911617-03-5, Pub. by Barter Pub). Prosperity & Profits.

Piggy in the Puddle. Charlotte Pomerantz. LC 73-6047. (Illus.). 32p. (ps-2). 1974. 13.95 (ISBN 0-02-774900-2). Macmillan.

Piggyback & Peek-a-Boo. Illus. by San Diego Zoological Society. (San Diego Zoo Series of Picture Bks.). (Illus.). 12p. (ps-2). 1983. board 3.50 (ISBN 0-89346-217-9). Heian Intl.

Piggyback Songs in Praise of God. Compiled by Jean Warren & Elizabeth S. McKinnon. (Piggyback songs Ser.). (Illus.). 80p. (Orig.). 1986. pap. 6.95 (ISBN 0-911019-10-3). Warren Pub Hse.

Piggyback Songs in Praise of Jesus: New Songs Sung to the Tunes of Childhood Favorites. Compiled by Jean Warren & Elizabeth S. McKinnon. (Piggyback Songs Series). (Illus.). 96p. (Orig.). 1986. pap. 7.95 (ISBN 0-911019-11-1). Warren Pub Hse.

Piggyback Songs: New Song Sung to the Tunes of Childhood Favorites. Compiled by Jean Warren. LC 83-90111. (Piggyback Songs Ser.). (Illus.). 64p. 1983. pap. 4.95 (ISBN 0-911019-01-4). Warren Pub Hse.

Piggyback Songs: New Song Sung to the Tunes of Childhood Favorites. Compiled by Jean Warren & Elizabeth S. McKinnon. LC 85-50433. (Piggyback Songs Ser.). (Illus.). 80p. (Orig.). 1985. pap. 6.95 (ISBN 0-911019-07-3). Warren Pub Hse.

Piggybook. Anthony Browne. LC 86-3008. (Illus.). 32p. (ps-3). 1986. 9.95 (ISBN 0-394-88416-7); lib. bdg. 10.99 (ISBN 0-394-98416-1). Knopf.

Piggy's Good Food: A Mealtime Word Book. Maida Silverman. (Little Poke & Look Bks.). (Illus.). (ps-1). 1987. 3.95 (ISBN 0-448-10557-8, G&D). Putnam Pub Group.

Pigkeeper's Guide. Peter Michelmore. LC 80-68686. (Illus.). 136p. 1981. 18.95 (ISBN 0-7153-7995-X). David & Charles.

Piglet Goes to the Rescue. Rod Hunt. (Little Stories Ser.). (Illus.). 32p. (ps). 1987. 5.95 (ISBN 0-09-167240-6, Pub. by Century Hutchinson). David & Charles.

Pigman. Paul Zindel. 176p. 1983. pap. 2.95 (ISBN 0-553-26321-8). Bantam.

Pigman. Paul Zindel. LC 68-10784. 192p. (YA) (gr. 7 up). 1968. 13.70i (ISBN 0-06-026827-1); PLB 12.89 (ISBN 0-06-026828-X). HarpJ.

Pigmania. Emil Van Beest. (Illus.). 96p. pap. 6.95 (ISBN 0-85236-167-X, Farming Press UK). Diamond Farm Bk.

Pigman's Handbook. Gerry Brent. (Illus.). 240p. pap. 22.95 (ISBN 0-85236-126-2, Pub. by Farming Pr UK). Diamond Farm Bk.

Pigman's Legacy. Paul Zindel. 128p. (gr. 12 up). 1984. pap. 2.95 (ISBN 0-553-26599-7). Bantam.

Pigman's Legacy. Paul Zindel. LC 79-2684. 192p. (YA) (gr. 7 up). 1980. 11.70i (ISBN 0-06-026853-0); PLB 11.89 (ISBN 0-06-026854-9). HarpJ.

Pigment Cell 1985. Ed. by Joe Bagnara et al. 1986. 175.00 (ISBN 0-86008-373-X, Pub. by U of Tokyo Japan). Columbia U Pr.

Pigment Handbook. Ed. by Robert Feller. (Illus.). 320p. 1987. 49.50 (ISBN 0-521-30374-5). Cambridge U Pr.

Pigment Handbook. 2nd ed. Ed. by Peter A. Lewis. 1988. 460.00 (ISBN 0-471-60021-0). Wiley.

Pigment Handbook: Application & Markets, Vol. 2. 2nd ed. Ed. by Peter A. Lewis. 1973. 160.00 (ISBN 0-471-67124-X). Wiley.

Pigment Handbook: Characterization & Physical Relationships, Vol. 3. 2nd ed. Ed. by Peter A. Lewis. 1973. 135.00 (ISBN 0-471-67126-6). Wiley.

Pigment Handbook: Properties & Economics, Vol. 1. 2nd ed. Ed. by Peter A. Lewis. LC 87-13358. 945p. 1988. 195.00 (ISBN 0-471-82833-5). Wiley.

Pigmentation: Its Genesis & Biologic Control. International Pigment Cell Conference (7th: 1969: Seattle) Ed. by Vernon Riley. LC 77-150501. pap. 160.00 (ISBN 0-317-26289-0, 2055693). Bks Demand UMI.

Pigmented Lesions of the Skin: Clinicopathologic Correlations. John C. Maize & A. Bernard Ackerman. LC 85-19886. (Illus.). 328p. 1987. text ed. 89.50 (ISBN 0-8121-0969-4). Lea & Febiger.

Pigments, Pt.1. R. Myers & J. S. Long. (Treatise on Coatings Ser.: Vol. 3). (Illus.). 592p. 1975. 175.00 (ISBN 0-8247-1475-X). Dekker.

Pigments: An Introduction to Their Physical Chemistry. Ed. by David Patterson. (Illus.). 210p. 1967. 27.75 (ISBN 0-444-20009-6, Pub. by Elsevier Applied Sci England). Elsevier.

Pigments, & Pigmented Coatings for Architectural & Industrial Applications see Organic Coating Technology.

Pigments for Paper: A Project of the Coating Pigments & the Papermaking Additives Committee. Technical Association of the Pulp & Paper Industry. Ed. by Robert W. Hagemeyer. LC 84-50800. pap. 77.50 (ISBN 0-317-30448-8, 2024921). Bks Demand UMI.

Pigments for Printing Ink. Ed. by D. Sanders. (Illus.). 200p. 1988. 100.00x (ISBN 0-947798-07-2, Selective Industrial Training Associates Ltd London). Rsrch Bks CT.

Pigments in Fruits. Jeana Gross. (Food Science & Technology Ser.). 303p. 1987. 78.00 (ISBN 0-12-304200-3). Acad Pr.

Pigments of Your Imagination, Vol. 1 - 2. Jackie Shaw. (Illus., Orig.). 1978. Vol. 1. pap. 5.95 (ISBN 0-941284-06-9); Vol. 2. pap. 5.95 (ISBN 0-941284-07-7). Deco Design Studio.

Pigors Incident Process of Case Study. Paul Pigors & Faith Pigors. LC 79-23530. (Instructional Design Library). 128p. 1980. 23.95 (ISBN 0-87778-149-4). Educ Tech Pubns.

Pig's Alphabet. Leah P. Preiss. 1988. price not set. Godine.

Pigs & Other Animals. Roger Martin. LC 79-92628. 300p. 1980. 10.95 (ISBN 0-936634-00-6). Myco Pub Hse.

Pigs Are Flying! Emily Rodda. LC 88-2449. Orig. Title: Pigs Might Fly. (Illus.). 160p. (gr. 4-6). 1988. Repr. of 1986 ed. 10.95 (ISBN 0-688-08130-4). Greenwillow.

Pigs at Christmas. Arlene Dubanevich. LC 86-6891. (Illus.). 32p. (ps-2). 1986. 13.95 (ISBN 0-02-733160-1). Bradbury Pr.

Pigs at Home: A Picture Word Book. Ron Van Der Meer & Atie Van Der Meer. LC 88-831. (Illus.). 20p. (ps-1). 1988. bds. 9.95 (ISBN 0-689-71232-4, Aladdin Bks). Macmillan.

Pigs' Book of World Records. Bob Stine. LC 79-5239. (Illus.). 96p. (gr. 3 up). 1980. pap. 4.99 (ISBN 0-394-94402-X, BYR). Random.

Pigs for the Ancestors: Ritual in the Ecology of a New Guinea People. 2nd ed. Roy A. Rappaport. LC 83-51294. (Illus.). 496p. 1984. text ed. 35.00t (ISBN 0-300-03204-8); pap. 13.95x (ISBN 0-300-03205-6). Yale U Pr.

Pigs from A to Z. Arthur Geisert. LC 86-18542. (Illus.). 64p. (gr. 2 up). 1986. 15.95 (ISBN 0-395-38509-1). HM.

Pigs Get Fat. Warren Murphy. (Trace Ser.: No. 5). 1985. pap. 2.95 (ISBN 0-451-13851-1, Sig). NAL.

Pigs in Hiding. Arlene Dubanevich. (Illus.). 32p. (ps-1). 1983. 10.95 (ISBN 0-02-732140-1, Four Winds). Macmillan.

Pigs in the House. Steven Kroll. LC 83-13310. (Illus.). 48p. (ps-3). 1983. 5.95 (ISBN 0-8193-1111-1). Parents.

Pigs in the House. Steven Kroll. (Illus.). (ps-2). 1987. pap. 2.95 (ISBN 0-517-56744-X). Crown.

Pigs in the Parlor. Frank Hammond & Ida M. Hammond. 153p. (Orig.). 1973. pap. 5.95 (ISBN 0-89228-027-1). Impact Bks MO.

Pigs in the Playground. John Terry. (Illus.). 208p. 1986. pap. 7.95 (ISBN 0-85236-158-0, Pub by Farming Pr UK); pap. text ed. 6.95 (ISBN 0-317-47058-2, Pub. by Farming Pr UK). Diamond Farm Bk.

Pigs Is Pigs. Ellis P. Butler. 1907. 30.00 (ISBN 0-932062-20-2). Sharon Hill.

Pigs Is Pigs & Other Favorites. Ellis P. Butler. (Illus.). 109p. pap. 3.50 (ISBN 0-486-21532-6). Dover.

Pigs' Meat: Selected Writings of Thomas Spence. Thomas Spence. 1982. pap. 12.95 (ISBN 0-85124-424-6). Dufour.

Pigs' Meat: The Selected Writings of Thomas Spence, Radical & Pioneer Land Reformer. Intro. by G. I. Gallop. 194p. 90.00x (ISBN 0-85124-315-0, Pub. by Bertrand Russell Hse); pap. 30.00x. State Mutual Bk.

Pigs Might Fly. Dick King-Smith. LC 81-11525. (Illus.). 156p. (gr. 3-7). 1982. 12.95 (ISBN 0-670-55506-1). Viking.

Pigs Might Fly. Dick King-Smith. (Illus.). 168p. (gr. 4-6). 1984. pap. 2.50 (ISBN 0-590-40839-9, Apple Paperbacks). Scholastic Inc.

Pigs Might Fly see Pigs Are Flying!.

Pig's New Hat. Ethel Kessler & Leonard Kessler. LC 80-17373. (Begin to Read with Duck & Pig Ser.). (Illus.). 32p. (gr. 1-2). 1981. PLB 6.69 (ISBN 0-8116-7551-3). Garrard.

Pigs on the Farm. Cliff Moon. LC 83-71630. (Down on the Farm Bks.). (Illus.). 33p. (ps-2). 1983. PLB 9.40 (ISBN 0-531-04696-6). Watts.

Pig's Orange House. Ethel Kessler & Leonard Kessler. LC 80-24222. (Begin to Read with Duck & Pig Ser.). (Illus.). 32p. (gr. 1-2). 1981. PLB 6.69 (ISBN 0-8116-7553-X). Garrard.

Pigs' Picnic. Keiko Kasza. (Illus.). 32p. (ps-1). 1988. PLB 13.95 (ISBN 0-399-21543-3, Putnam). Putnam Pub Group.

Pig's Ploughman. Bernard Evslin. (Monsters of Mythology Ser.). (Illus.). 104p. Date not set. lib. bdg. 19.95x (ISBN 1-55546-256-1). Chelsea Hse.

Pigs Say Oink. Martha Alexander. (Illus.). 32p. (ps-3). 1981. pap. 1.95 (ISBN 0-394-83838-6). Random.

Pig's Tale. Geoffrey Patterson. LC 82-72113. (Illus.). 32p. (gr. k-3). 1984. 9.95 (ISBN 0-233-97477-6). Andre Deutsch.

Pigs with Wings: Poems. Tim Longville. 1971. sewn in wrappers 2.25 (ISBN 0-685-78937-3, Pub. by Grosseteste). Small Pr Dist.

Pigs's Wedding. Helme Heine. LC 86-60471. (Illus.). 32p. (ps-4). 1986. 12.95 (ISBN 0-689-50409-8, M K McElderry). Macmillan.

Pigtail War: American Involvement in the Sino-Japanese War of 1894-1895. Jeffery M. Dorwart. LC 75-8446. (Illus.). 168p. 1975. 12.50x (ISBN 0-87023-183-9). U of Mass Pr.

Pigtails & Gold Dust. Alexander McLeod. 326p. 1948. 315.00x (Pub. by Han-Shan Tang Ltd). State Mutual Bk.

Pigtails, Petticoats & the Old School Tie. Sheila Miller. 1981. pap. 3.95 (ISBN 0-85363-140-9). OMF Bks.

Pike: A Fortress in the Wetlands. Bertram H. Groene. (Illus.). 60p. (Orig.). 1988. pap. 10.95x (ISBN 0-318-24021-1). SE LA Univ Pr.

Pike: An In-Fisherman Handbook of Strategies. Al Lindner et al. (Illus.). 234p. (Orig.). 1983. pap. 11.95. In-Fisherman.

Pike County Arkansas Census 1850. Courtney York & Gerlene York. 52p. 1969. pap. 12.00x (ISBN 0-916660-04-4). Hse of York.

Pike County (PA) Data Processing: A Technical Assistance Report. National Center for State Courts Staff. 9p. 1984. manuscript 0.54 (NERO, T/A-521). Natl Ctr St Courts.

Pike Family. G. T. Ridlon. LC 77-133878. (Saco Valley Settlements Ser). 1970. pap. 1.50 (ISBN 0-8048-0824-4). C E Tuttle.

Pike Fishing in the 80's. Neville Fickling. 1985. 40.00x (ISBN 0-317-39183-6, Pub. by BeeKay Pubs Ltd); pap. 32.00x (ISBN 0-317-39184-4, Pub. by BeeKay Pubs Ltd). State Mutual Bk.

Pike in Colorado. Carrol J. Carter. LC 78-60399. (Illus.). 1978. 12.95 (ISBN 0-88342-058-9); pap. 5.95 (ISBN 0-88342-241-7). Old Army.

Pike Place Market: People, Politics, & Produce. Alice Shorett & Murray Morgan. LC 82-8163. (Illus.). 160p. (Orig.). 1982. pap. 14.95 (ISBN 0-914718-70-3). Pacific Search.

Pike River Phantom. Betty R. Wright. LC 88-45276. 192p. (gr. 4-7). 1988. 12.95 (ISBN 0-8234-0721-7). Holiday.

Pikes Peak: A Family Saga. Frank Waters. LC 77-150753. 743p. 1971. 17.95 (ISBN 0-8040-0503-6, Swallow); pap. 36.95. Ohio U Pr.

Pike's Peak: A Mining Saga. Frank Waters. 743p. 1987. pap. 17.95 (ISBN 0-8040-0900-7, Pub. by Swallow Pr). Ohio U Pr.

Pike's Peak Country. Jim Scott. (Colorado Georgraphic Ser.). (Illus.). 120p. (Orig.). 1987. 24.95 (ISBN 0-937959-11-1); pap. 14.95 (ISBN 0-937959-09-X). Falcon Pr MT.

Pikes Peak Country: The Complete Guide to Natural Wonders, Historic Sites, Attractions & Outdoor Recreation. Stewart M. Green. LC 85-60701. (Illus.). 104p. (Orig.). 1985. pap. 6.95 (ISBN 0-933393-07-5). Ponderosa Pr.

Pikes Peak Pioneers. Ivan Brunk. Ed. by Leland Feitz. (Illus.). 64p. 1987. pap. 3.95 (ISBN 0-936564-35-0). Little London.

Pikes Peak Trolleys. Morris Cafky & John A. Haney. LC 83-73227. (Illus.). 112p. 1984. 22.95 (ISBN 0-937080-13-6); pap. 16.95 (ISBN 0-937080-14-4). Century One.

Pilates Method of Physical & Mental Conditioning. Philip Friedman & Gail Eisen. (Illus.). 1981. pap. 6.95 (ISBN 0-446-97859-0). Warner Bks.

Pilbara see Vegetation Surveys of Western Australia: Map & Memoir.

Pilchuck, the Life of a Mountain. Harry W. Higman & Earl J. Larrison. (Shorey Historical Ser.). 288p. 12.95 (ISBN 0-8466-2307-2, S307); pap. 8.95 (ISBN 0-8466-0307-1). Shorey.

Pile Design & Construction Practice. 3rd ed. M. J. Tomlinson. (Illus.). 400p. 1987. text ed. 59.50x (ISBN 0-86310-024-4, Pub. by Palladian). Scholium Intl.

Pile Driving: Construction Guide. W. A. Dawson. 30p. 1981. 8.00 (ISBN 0-7277-0093-6, Pub. by T Telford UK). Am Soc Civil Eng.

Pile Driving Engineer. Jack Rudman. (Career Examination Ser.: C-2558). (Cloth bdg. avail. on request). pap. 16.00 (ISBN 0-8373-2558-7). Natl Learning.

Pile Neutron Research in Physics. (Proceedings Ser.). (Illus.). 656p. 1962. 30.75 (ISBN 92-0-030062-6, ISP36, IAEA). UNIPUB.

Pile Weaves: Twenty Six Techniques & How to Do Them. rev. ed. Jean Wilson. (Illus., Orig.). 1979. pap. 3.95 Encore ed. (ISBN 0-684-17740-4, ScribT). Scribner.

Pileated Woodpecker. Seliesa Pembleton. (Remarkable Animals Ser.). (Illus.). 60p. (gr. 3 up). 1988. PLB 12.95 (ISBN 0-87518-392-1). Dillon.

Piles & Foundations. Ed. by F. E. Young. 341p. 1981. 36.00 (ISBN 0-7277-0118-5, Pub. by T Telford UK). Am Soc Civil Eng.

Pileup on Death Row. Burton H. Wolfe. LC 82-45676. (Capital Punishment Ser.). (Illus.). Date not set. Repr. of 1973 ed. 46.50 (ISBN 0-404-62436-7). AMS Pr.

Pilgermann. Russell Hoban. 1983. 13.95 (ISBN 0-671-45968-6). Summit Bks.

Pilgermann. Russell Hoban. pap. 2.95 (ISBN 0-671-61893-8). PB.

Pilgerreise der Aetheria. August Bludau. pap. 22.00 (ISBN 0-384-04760-2). Johnson Repr.

Pilgrim. Ray Hogan. 1981. pap. 1.75 (ISBN 0-451-09576-6, E9576, Sig). NAL.

Pilgrim: A Biography of William Brewster. Mary B. Sherwood. LC 82-80574. 272p. 1982. 25.00 (ISBN 0-9608234-0-9). Great Oak Pr Va.

Pilgrim Aflame. Myron S. Augsburger. LC 67-15993. (Illus.). 288p. 1967. pap. 2.25 (ISBN 0-8361-1840-5). Herald Pr.

Pilgrim & Dreamer: John Bunyan: His Life & Work. Ernest W. Bacon. 176p. pap. text ed. 8.95 cancelled (ISBN 0-85364-309-1). Attic Pr.

Pilgrim & the Book: A Study of Dante, Langland & Chaucer. Julia B. Holloway. (American University Studies IV- English Language & Literature: Vol. 42). 321p. 1987. text ed. 49.95 (ISBN 0-8204-0345-8). P Lang Pubs.

Pilgrim Artifacts & Genre Paintings. L. D. Geller. 1970. 0.25 (ISBN 0-940628-26-0). Pilgrim Soc.

Pilgrim at Sea. Par Lagerkvist. Tr. by Naomi Walford from Swedish. LC 81-69683. (Illus.). 128p. 1982. pap. 2.95 (ISBN 0-394-70821-0, Vin). Random.

Pilgrim Centenary: A Remembrance. Santha Rungachary. LC 73-904628. (Illus.). 317p. 1973. 11.25x (ISBN 0-89684-443-9). Orient Bk Dist.

Pilgrim Century Furniture: An Historical Survey. Ed. by Robert Trent. LC 76-5095. (Antiques Magazine Library). (Illus.). 168p. 1976. 15.00x (ISBN 0-87663-239-8). Universe.

Pilgrim Children Come to Plymouth. Ida DeLage. LC 80-29180. (Ida DeLage Bks.). (Illus.). 48p. (gr. 1-5). 1981. PLB 6.69 (ISBN 0-8116-6084-2). Garrard.

Pilgrim Children on the Mayflower. Ida DeLage. LC 79-21812. (Ida DeLage Bks.). (Illus.). 48p. (gr. 1-5). 1980. PLB 6.69 (ISBN 0-8116-4315-8). Garrard.

Pilgrim Church. William J. Bausch. LC 73-6608. 560p. 1980. pap. 9.95 (ISBN 0-89622-140-7). Twenty-Third.

Pilgrim Church. E. H. Broadbent. 422p. 1987. pap. 12.95 (ISBN 0-310-55171-4, 19017P). Zondervan.

Pilgrim Church & the Easter People. Norman Pittenger. (Theology & Life Ser.: Vol. 20). 112p. (Orig.). 1987. pap. 8.95 (ISBN 0-89453-598-6). M Glazier.

Pilgrim Experiences the World's Religions. Aaron Milavec. LC 84-9024. (Mellen Lives Ser.: Vol. 1). 96p. 1984. pap. 9.95x (ISBN 0-88946-010-8). E Mellen.

Pilgrim Fathers. Peach. (Ladybird Ser.). (gr. 2-7). 1972. 2.50 (ISBN 0-87508-855-4). Chr Lit.

Pilgrim Fathers from a Dutch Point of View. D. Plooij. LC 71-100509. Repr. of 1932 ed. 8.50 (ISBN 0-404-05065-4). AMS Pr.

Pilgrim Fathers from a Dutch Point of View. Daniel Plooij. LC 79-131801. 1970. Repr. of 1932 ed. 7.00x (ISBN 0-403-00688-0). Scholarly.

Pilgrim Fathers of New England. John Brown. 352p. 1970. 6.95 (ISBN 0-686-09112-4). Pilgrim Pubns.

Pilgrim Fathers of New England & Their Puritan Successors. 4th ed. J. Brown. (Illus.). Repr. of 1920 ed. 39.00 (ISBN 0-527-12050-2). Kraus Repr.

Pilgrim Fort of Sixteen Twenty-Three. Allen D. Russell. (Pilgrim Society Notes Ser.: No. 24). 2.00 (ISBN 0-940628-27-9). Pilgrim Soc.

Pilgrim from a Red Land. Quentin K. Y. Huang. 1981. 8.00 (ISBN 0-682-49669-3). Exposition-Phoenix.

Pilgrim God: A Biblical Journey. Brother John of Taize. (Orig.). 1985. pap. 12.95 (ISBN 0-912405-18-X). Pastoral Pr.

Pilgrim Goes Forth. John Robson. 276p. (Orig.). 1986. pap. 8.75. Lake Crest Hse.

Pilgrim Hawks see Six Great Modern Short Novels.

Pilgrim Hymnal. Blue. 1958. 9.95x (ISBN 0-8298-0460-9). Pilgrim NY.

Pilgrim Hymnal. Red. 1958. 9.95x (ISBN 0-8298-0107-3). Pilgrim NY.

Pilgrim Hymnal: Organist's Edition. UCC. 1981. 15.00 (ISBN 0-8298-0454-4). Pilgrim NY.

Pilgrim in China. Thomas. 1988. pap. 4.95 (ISBN 0-946616-39-6). OMF Bks.

Pilgrim in Love: An Introduction to Dante & His Spirituality. James Collins. 312p. 1984. 12.95 (ISBN 0-8294-0453-8). Loyola.

Pilgrim in the Microworld. David Sudnow. LC 82-61877. 240p. (Orig.). 1984. 15.50 (ISBN 0-446-51261-3); pap. 7.95 (ISBN 0-446-37521-7). Warner Bks.

Pilgrim in the Parish: Spirituality for Lay Ministers. Virginia S. Finn. 208p. (Orig.). 1986. pap. 8.95 (ISBN 0-8091-2742-3). Paulist Pr.

Pilgrim in the Sky. Helmer Bjerkebek. 1985. 6.95 (ISBN 0-934860-40-8). Adventure Pubns.

Pilgrim in the Sun: A Southwestern Omnibus. C. L. Sonnichsen. 320p. 1988. pap. 15.00 (ISBN 0-87404-205-4); 25.00 (ISBN 0-87404-204-6). Tex Western.

Pilgrim John Alden's Progress: Archaeological Excavations in Duxbury. Roland W. Robbins. 1969. 2.00 (ISBN 0-940628-28-7). Pilgrim Soc.

Pilgrim Journey. Frank Dearing. 214p. (Orig.). 1987. pap. 4.95 (ISBN 0-914903-22-5). Destiny Image.

Pilgrim of Faith: Words of Inspiration from Pope John Paul II. Ed. by K. S. Giniger. 48p. 1987. 7.95 (ISBN 0-8378-1829-X). Gibson.

Pilgrim of the Absolute. Leon Bloy. 1977. Repr. of 1947 ed. lib. bdg. 35.00 (ISBN 0-8495-0318-3). Arden Lib.

Pilgrim of the Clouds: Poems & Essays from Ming China by Yuan Hung-Tao & His Brothers. Yuan Hung-Tao. Tr. & intro. by Jonathan Chaves. LC 78-17455. (Illus.). 144p. 1978. pap. 6.95 (ISBN 0-8348-0134-5). Weatherhill.

Pilgrim of the Himalayas. Edmond B. Szekely. (Illus.). 32p. 1974. pap. 2.95 (ISBN 0-89564-061-9). IBS Intl.

Pilgrim on a Bicycle. Barbara M. Johnson. LC 81-68637. 144p. 1982. write for info. (ISBN 0-86693-001-9). B M Johnson.

Pilgrim; or, a Picture of Life, 1775, 2 vols. in 1. Charles Johnstone. LC 74-16216. (Novel in England, 1700-1775 Ser). 1974. lib. bdg. 61.00 (ISBN 0-8240-1208-9). Garland Pub.

Pilgrim People: Learning Through the Church Year. John H. Westerhoff, III. 128p. (Orig.). 1984. pap. 7.95 (ISBN 0-86683-884-8, 7462, HarpR). Har-Row.

Pilgrim Possessions, Sixteen Twenty to Sixteen Forty. Richard B. Bailey. (Pilgrim Society Notes Ser.: No. 7). 1957. 2.00 (ISBN 0-940628-29-5). Pilgrim Soc.

Pilgrim Primer. Jan P. Pierce. 32p. 1985. pap. text ed. 1.50 (ISBN 0-932050-28-X). New Puritan.

Pilgrim Recipes. 3rd ed. Anthony Gauquier & Beverly Gauguier. 27p. 1983. pap. 3.00 (ISBN 0-9609574-0-5). A Gauquier.

Pilgrim Route to Santiago. Brian Tate & Marcus Tate. (Illus.). 160p. 1987. 50.00 (ISBN 0-7148-2425-9, Pub. by Salem House-Phaidon). Salem Hse Pubs.

Pilgrim Society. Ed. by Peter Gomes. 1971. 0.75 (ISBN 0-940628-30-9). Pilgrim Soc.

Pilgrim Study Bible. 1984. write for info. Oxford U Pr.

Pilgrim to Poland. Pope John Paul II. 1979. 5.00 (ISBN 0-686-63640-6); pap. 3.50 (ISBN 0-8198-0627-7). Dghtrs St Paul.

Pilgrim to the Russian Church. Jim Forest. (Illus.). 192p. 1988. 15.95 (ISBN 0-8245-0898-X). Crossroad NY.

Pilgrim Way. Robert M. Bartlett. LC 70-172790. 384p. 1971. 15.00 (ISBN 0-8298-0222-3). Pilgrim NY.

Pilgrim Wind. Mollie M. O'Brien. LC 85-60237. 64p. (Orig.). 1985. pap. 5.95 (ISBN 0-89390-062-1). Resource Pubns.

Pilgrimage. Kathryn Anger. LC 84-73307. (Feminist Novels Ser.). 98p. (Orig.). 1982. 4.95 (ISBN 0-935772-04-9). Diotima Bks.

Pilgrimage. Johan Bojar. Tr. by Jessie Muir. 246p. 1981. Repr. of 1924 ed. lib. bdg. 35.00. Darby Bks.

Pilgrimage. Zenna Henderson. 1970. pap. 3.50 (ISBN 0-380-01507-2). Avon.

Pilgrimage. J. Ellsworth Kalas. Ed. by Michael L. Sherer. LC 86-28349. (Orig.). 1987. pap. 3.95 (ISBN 0-89536-845-5, 7804). CSS of Ohio.

Pilgrimage. Kinnara Inc. (Illus., Orig.). 1977. pap. 4.95 (ISBN 0-89346-011-7). Heian Intl.

Pilgrimage. Jon Mayled. (Religious Topics Ser.). (Illus.). 32p. (gr. 4-6). 1987. PLB 11.95 (ISBN 0-382-09450-6). Silver.

Pilgrimage: A Journey Through Colorado's History & Culture. Stephen May. LC 82-76537. (Illus.). 200p. 1986. text ed. 18.95x (ISBN 0-8040-0882-5, Pub. by Swallow); pap. 8.95 (ISBN 0-8040-0883-3, Pub. by Swallow). Ohio U Pr.

Pilgrimage: A Tale of Old Natchez. Louise W. Collier. 424p. (Orig.). 1983. pap. 9.95 (ISBN 0-918518-26-1, St Luke TN). Peachtree Pubs.

Pilgrimage: A Tale of Old Natchez. Louise W. Collier. LC 82-16977. 432p. 1984. 14.95 (ISBN 0-918518-32-6, St Luke TN). Peachtree Pubs.

Pilgrimage: A Workbook on Christian Growth. Richard Peace. 1985. pap. 6.95 (ISBN 0-8010-7087-2). Baker Bk.

Pilgrimage & Service. Joseph Krimsky. Ed. by Moshe Davis. LC 77-70712. (America & the Holy Land Ser.). 1977. Repr. of 1919 ed. lib. bdg. 17.00x (ISBN 0-405-10261-5). Ayer Co Pubs.

Pilgrimage & Storytelling in the Canterbury Tales: The Dialectic of "Ernest" & "Game". Charles A. Owen, Jr. LC 76-53814. 1977. 18.95x (ISBN 0-8061-1323-5). U of Okla Pr.

Pilgrimage: Being the Narrative of Emma Louise Heath with Excerpts from the Private Journal of Jessie Elizabeth Heath. Ann Ross. 256p. 1987. 18.95 (ISBN 0-02-605140-0). Macmillan.

Pilgrimage from Rome. rev. ed. Bartholomew F. Brewer & Alfred W. Furrell. (Illus.). 1986. pap. 7.95 (ISBN 0-89084-327-9). Bob Jones Univ Pr.

Pilgrimage Home. Gerald May. LC 78-61720. 196p. 1979. pap. 6.95 (ISBN 0-8091-2143-3). Paulist Pr.

Pilgrimage in Faith: An Introduction to the Episcopal Church. rev. ed. Franklin C. Ferguson. LC 75-5220. 180p. (Orig.). 1979. pap. 6.95 (ISBN 0-8192-1277-6). Morehouse.

Pilgrimage in Mission. Donald R. Jacobs. LC 83-306. 168p. 1983. pap. 6.50 (ISBN 0-8361-3324-2). Herald Pr.

Pilgrimage in Mission: Leader's Guide. Richard A. Kauffman. 60p. 1983. pap. 4.95x (ISBN 0-8361-1260-1). Herald Pr.

Pilgrimage in the Hindu Tradition: A Case Study of West Bengal. Ed. by E. Alan Morinis. (Illus.). 1984. 34.95x (ISBN 0-19-561412-7). Oxford U Pr.

Pilgrimage: Limited Commerative Edition of the Third Annual JHG Festival of the Arts. John H. Griffin. 1985. pap. 4.00. Latitudes Pr.

Pilgrimage of Arnold Von Harff, Knight, 1496 to 1499. Ed. by Malcolm Letts. (Hakluyt Society Works Ser.: No. 2,Vol. 94). Repr. of 1946 ed. 52.00 (ISBN 0-8115-0390-9). Kraus Repr.

Pilgrimage of Buddhism & a Buddhist Pilgrimage. James B. Pratt. LC 75-3325. (Philosophy of America Ser.). Repr. of 1928 ed. 57.50 (ISBN 0-404-59320-8). AMS Pr.

Pilgrimage of Buddhism & a Buddhist Pilgrimage. James B. Pratt. 758p. 1982. Repr. of 1928 ed. lib. bdg. 75.00 (ISBN 0-89984-828-1). Century Bookbindery.

Pilgrimage of Charle Magne & Aucassin & Nicolette. Anne E. Glyn Bargess. (GLML Ser.). 1987. lib. bdg. write for info. (ISBN 0-8240-8637-6). Garland Pub.

Pilgrimage of Faith of Tanzania Mennonite Church, 1934-83. Mahlon M. Hess. (Illus.). 176p. 1985. 5.00 (ISBN 0-9613368-2-X). E Mennonite Bd.

Pilgrimage of Faith: The Legacy of the Otterbeins. J. Steven O'Malley. LC 73-5684. (ATLA Monograph: No. 4). 226p. 1973. 18.00 (ISBN 0-8108-0626-6). Scarecrow.

Pilgrimage of Henry James. Van Wyck Brooks. LC 75-159169. vii, 170p. 1972. Repr. of 1925 ed. lib. bdg. 18.50x (ISBN 0-374-91004-9, Octagon). Hippocrene Bks.

Pilgrimage of Love, Book I. Shri Kripalvanandji. LC 81-82015. 86p. (Orig.). 1981. pap. 4.50 (ISBN 0-940258-02-1). Kripalu Pubns.

Pilgrimage of Love, Book II. Shri Kripalvanandji. LC 81-82015. 416p. (Orig.). 1982. pap. 7.50 (ISBN 0-940258-05-6). Kripalu Pubns.

Pilgrimage of Love: Premyatra, Bk. III. Shri Kripalvanandji. LC 81-82015. (Illus.). 136p. (Orig.). 1984. pap. 5.50 (ISBN 0-940258-12-9). Kripalu Pubns.

Pilgrimage of Peace: John Paul II in Ireland & the United States. Pope John Paul II. (Illus.). 175p. 1980. 17.50 (ISBN 0-374-23307-1); pap. 9.95 (ISBN 0-374-51578-6). FS&G.

Pilgrimage of Sudhana. J. Fontein. 1967. text ed. 35.60x (ISBN 90-2796-387-8). Mouton.

Pilgrimage of the Abbot Daniel in the Holy Land 1106-1107 AD. Abbot Daniel. pap. 12.95 (ISBN 0-317-60811-8). Eastern Orthodox.

Pilgrimage of the Heart. Thomas McGuiness. LC 83-63477. 74p. (Orig.). 1984. pap. text ed. 2.95 (ISBN 0-911905-19-7). Past & Mat Rene Ctr.

Pilgrimage of the Heart: A Treasury of Eastern Christian Spirituality. Ed. by George A. Maloney. LC 82-48933. 256p. (Orig.). 1983. pap. 8.95 (ISBN 0-06-065413-9, RD/444, HarpR). Har-Row.

Pilgrimage of the Life of Man, Pts. 1-3. Guillaume De Deguilleville. Ed. by F. J. Furnivall & K. B. Locock. (EETS, ES Ser.: Nos. 77, 83, & 92). Repr. of 1904 ed. 90.00 (ISBN 0-527-00279-8). Kraus Repr.

Pilgrimage of the Life of Man, Vol. 1. Ed. by Avril Henry. (Early English Text Society Original Ser.: No. 288). (Illus.). 1985. 59.00x (ISBN 0-19-722290-0). Oxford U Pr.

Pilgrimage of the Lyf of the Manhode. Guillaume de Deguilleville. Ed. by W. A. Wright. LC 78-178536. (Eng.). Repr. of 1869 ed. 28.50 (ISBN 0-404-56613-8). AMS Pr.

Pilgrimage of the Lyfe of the Manhode, Vol. 2. Ed. by Avril Henry. (Early English Text Society - Original Ser.: No. 292). 250p. 1989. 29.95 (ISBN 0-19-722294-3). Oxford U Pr.

Pilgrimage of Western Man. Stringfellow Barr. LC 73-21283. 369p. 1974. Repr. of 1962 ed. lib. bdg. 25.00x (ISBN 0-8371-6152-5, BAPI). Greenwood.

Pilgrimage Project: Leader's Guide. John & Adrienne Carr. 64p. (Orig.). 1987. pap. 4.95 (ISBN 0-8358-0550-6). Upper Room.

Pilgrimage Project: Participant's Notebook. John Carr & Adrienne Carr. 48p. (Orig.). 1987. pap. 2.95 (ISBN 0-8358-0549-2). Upper Room.

Pilgrimage to Al-Madinah & Meccah, Vols. 1 & 2. R. F. Burton. 1986. 350.00x ea. (Pub. by Darf). Vol. 1, 488p (ISBN 1-85077-125-1). Vol. 2, 512p (ISBN 1-85077-126-X). State Mutual Bk.

Pilgrimage to Canterbury. Howard Loxton. (Illus.). 208p. 1978. 18.50x (ISBN 0-8476-6072-9). Rowman.

Pilgrimage to Humanity. Albert Schweitzer. (Philosophical Paperbook). 107p. 1983. pap. 4.95 (ISBN 0-8022-2437-7). Philos Lib.

Pilgrimage to Luther's Germany. Herbert F. Brokering & Roland Bainton. 80p. 1983. 14.95 (ISBN 0-86683-629-2, HarpR). Har-Row.

Pilgrimage to Nejd, 2 vols. Anne Blunt. (Illus.). 1968. Repr. of 1881 ed. 85.00x (ISBN 0-7146-1979-5, F Cass Co). Biblio Dist.

Pilgrimage to Nejd, 2 vols. Anne Blunt. 600p. Repr. of 1881 ed. Set. text ed. 124.20x (ISBN 0-576-03993-4, Pub. by Gregg Intl Pubs England). Gregg Intl.

Pilgrimage to Nejd. Anne Blunt. 632p. 1986. 60.00x (ISBN 0-317-39198-4, Pub. by Luzac & Co Ltd). State Mutual Bk.

Pilgrimage to Nejd. Anne Blunt. (Century Classic Ser). 557p. 1988. pap. 15.95 (ISBN 0-7126-0989-X, Pub. by Century Hutchinson). David & Charles.

Pilgrimage to Nejd. Anne Blunt. 632p. 1984. 350.00x (ISBN 1-85077-016-6, Pub. by Darf Pubs Ltd). State Mutual Bk.

Pilgrimage to Palestine. Harry E. Fosdick. Ed. by Moshe Davis. LC 77-70688. (America & the Holy Land Ser.). 1977. Repr. of 1927 ed. lib. bdg. 30.00x (ISBN 0-405-10247-X). Ayer Co Pubs.

Pilgrimage to Parnassus. Incl. Return from Parnassus, Part 1. LC 77-133721. (Tudor Facsimile Tets. Old English Plays: No. 80). (Printed in leaf form). Repr. of 1912 ed. 49.50 (ISBN 0-404-53380-9). AMS Pr.

Pilgrimage to Personhood. Fount Shults. (Illus.). 149p. (Orig.). 1987. pap. 4.95 (ISBN 0-914903-20-9). Destiny Image.

Pilgrimage to Priesthood. Elizabeth Canham. 128p. (Orig.). 1985. pap. 9.95 (ISBN 0-8164-2492-6, 8603, HarpR). Har-Row.

Pilgrimage to Rebirth. Erlo Van Waveren. 125p. 1978. 7.95 (ISBN 0-87728-420-2); pap. 3.95. Weiser.

Pilgrimage to Renewal. Herbert F. Brokering. 96p. (Orig.). 1979. pap. 1.95 (ISBN 0-03-053791-6, HarpR). Har-Row.

Pilgrimage to Russia: The Soviet Union & the Treatment of Foreigners, 1924-1937. Sylvia R. Margulies. 302p. 1968. 30.00x (ISBN 0-299-04720-2). U of Wis Pr.

Pilgrimage to the Holy Land. Alphonse de Lamartine. LC 78-14368. 1978. Repr. of 1838 ed. 75.00x (ISBN 0-8201-1323-9). Schol Facsimiles.

Pilgrimage to the Tree of Life. 2nd ed. Albert Steffen. 66p. 1978. 5.00 (ISBN 0-932776-01-9). Adonis Pr.

Pilgrimage to the West. Mario M. Rossi. Tr. by J. M. Hone. 68p. 1971. Repr. of 1933 ed. 15.00x (ISBN 0-7165-1376-5, BBA 02079, Pub. by Cuala Press Ireland). Biblio Dist.

Pilgrimage: Visiting Richard Brautigan, August, 1982. David F. Curran. Ed. by Patricia A. Curran. (Illus.). 50p. (Orig.). 1985. pap. 6.00 (ISBN 0-318-04402-1). D F Curran Prods.

Pilgrimages: Aspects of Japanese Literature & Culture. J. Thomas Rimer. LC 88-21621. (Illus.). 168p. 1988. text ed. 17.00x (ISBN 0-8248-1148-8). UH Pr.

Pilgrimages to Home & Beyond: A Guide to the Holy Places of Southern Europe for Today's Traveler. Paul L. Higgins. Date not set. write for info. S&S.

Pilgrimages to Rome & Beyond: A Guide to the Holy Places of Southern Europe for Today's Traveler. Paul L. Higgins. (Illus.). 156p. 1985. 17.95 (ISBN 0-13-676073-2). P-H.

Pilgrimages to Rome & Beyond: A Guide to the Holy Places of Southern Europe for Today's Traveler. 1985. pap. 7.95. S&S.

Pilgrims. Peter Makuck. 1987. pap. 3.50 (ISBN 0-935331-03-4). Ampersand RI.

Pilgrims & Pioneers: New England Women in the Arts. Ed. by Alicia Faxon & Sylvia Moore. LC 87-60021. (Illus.). 176p. (Orig.). 1987. pap. 12.00 (ISBN 0-9602476-6-1). Midmarch Arts-WAN.

Pilgrims & Strangers: Essays in Mennonite Brethren History. Paul Toews. (Perspective on Mennonite Life & Thought Ser.: Vol. 1). 183p. (Orig.). 1977. pap. 5.95 (ISBN 0-919797-36-9). Kindred Pr.

Pilgrims & Thanksgiving. Rae Bains. LC 84-2686. (Illus.). 32p. (gr. 3-6). 1985. PLB 8.45 (ISBN 0-8167-0222-5); pap. text ed. 1.95 (ISBN 0-8167-0223-3). Troll Assocs.

Pilgrims & the Wampanoags: A Survey of Attitudes & Behavior in the Early Years. George R. Horner. (Pilgrim Society Notes Ser.: No. 29). 1981. 2.00 (ISBN 0-940628-46-5). Pilgrim Soc.

Pilgrims & Their History. Roland G. Usher. (Illus.). 310p. 1977. Repr. of 1918 ed. 21.00 (ISBN 0-87928-082-4). Corner Hse.

Pilgrims & Their Times. rev. ed. Ed. by Elizabeth M. Brown et al. (Illus.). 32p. (gr. 2-6). 1973. pap. 2.50 (ISBN 0-87534-121-7). Highlights.

Pilgrims: Explorations in Life Science. C. Margaret Hall. LC 77-91663. 1978. 6.00 (ISBN 0-87212-083-X). Libra.

Pilgrims' First Thanksgiving. Ann McGovern. 48p. (gr. 2-5). pap. 2.50 (ISBN 0-590-04835-X). Scholastic Inc.

Pilgrim's First Thanksgiving. Ann Mcgovern. 48p. (gr. k-3). 1988. pap. 2.50 (ISBN 0-590-40617-5). Scholastic Inc.

Pilgrim's Guide to Forty-Six Temples. Shiro Usui. (Illus.). 336p. (Orig.). 1986. pap. 12.50 (ISBN 0-8348-0211-2). Weatherhill.

Pilgrim's Guide to Planet Earth: Traveler's Handbook & Spiritual Directory. LC 85-11046. 320p. 1985. Repr. of 1981 ed. lib. bdg. 19.95x (ISBN 0-89370-888-7). Borgo Pr.

Pilgrim's Guide to Prayer. Edward C. Briggs. (Orig.). 1987. pap. 3.95 (ISBN 0-8054-8156-7). Broadman.

Pilgrim's Guide to the New Age. Alice Lawhead & Steve Lawhead. 128p. 1986. pap. 9.95 (ISBN 0-85648-955-7). Lion USA.

Pilgrims in a New Land. Lee M. Friedman. LC 78-26208. (Illus.). 1979. Repr. of 1948 ed. lib. bdg. 35.00x (ISBN 0-313-20877-8, FRPI). Greenwood.

Pilgrims in a Strange Land: Hausa Communities in Chad. John A. Works, Jr. LC 76-23138. 1976. 35.00x (ISBN 0-231-03976-X). Columbia U Pr.

Pilgrims in the Region of Faith (Amiel, Tolstoy, Pater, Newman) John A. Hutton. 1973. lib. bdg. 30.00 (ISBN 0-8414-5241-5). Folcroft.

Pilgrims in Their Own Land. Martin E. Marty. 512p. 1985. pap. 7.95 (ISBN 0-14-008268-9). Penguin.

Pilgrims in Their Own Land: Five Hundred Years of Religion in America. Martin E. Marty. (Illus.). 416p. 1984. 25.00 (ISBN 0-316-54867-7). Little.

Pilgrim's Journey: The Autobiography of Ignatius of Loyola. Tr. & intro. by Joseph N. Tylenda. LC 85-47757. 1985. pap. 8.95 (ISBN 0-89453-468-8). M Glazier.

Pilgrim's Letter Home. Dorothy B. Eaton. LC 87-71480. 64p. 1987. 7.50x (ISBN 0-8233-0432-9). Golden Quill.

Pilgrim's New Guide to the Holy Land. Stephen Doyle. LC 84-81244. 1985. pap. 7.95 (ISBN 0-89453-440-8). M Glazier.

Pilgrims of a Common Life. Trevor J. Saxby. LC 86-27043. 208p. (Orig.). 1987. pap. 17.95 (ISBN 0-8361-3426-5). Herald Pr.

Pilgrims of Blind Island, 3 Bks. James L. Davis. (Illus.). 56p. (gr. k-6). 1986. 6.95 ea. Bk. I (ISBN 0-937653-01-2). Bk. II (ISBN 0-937653-02-0). BK. III. Bollenbaugh Hill.

Pilgrims of Forty-Eight. facsimile ed. Josephine Goldmark. LC 74-27989. (Modern Jewish Experience Ser.). (Illus.). 1975. Repr. of 1930 ed. 29.00x (ISBN 0-405-06716-X). Ayer Co Pubs.

Pilgrims of Plimoth. Marcia Sewall. LC 86-3362. (Illus.). 48p. (gr. 2 up). 1986. 14.95 (ISBN 0-689-31250-4, Atheneum Childrens Bks). Macmillan.

Pilgrims of Russian-Town: The Community of Spiritual Christian Jumpers in America. Pauline V. Young. LC 66-27375. (Illus.). 1967. Repr. of 1932 ed. 9.00x (ISBN 0-8462-1001-0). Russell.

Pilgrims of the Andes: Regional Cults in Cusco. Micheal Sallnow. LC 87-43043. (Ethnographic Inquiry Ser.). (Illus.). 330p. 1987. 29.95x (ISBN 0-87474-826-7). Smithsonian.

Pilgrims of the Lonely Road. facs. ed. Gaius G. Atkins. LC 67-28741. (Essay Index Reprint Ser). 1913. 18.00 (ISBN 0-8369-0162-2). Ayer Co Pubs.

Pilgrims of the Prairie. Andrew Dubovy. Tr. by Marie H. Bloch from Ukrainian. Date not set. price not set. Ukrainian Cult Inst.

Pilgrims of the Prairie: Pioneer Ukrainian Baptists in North Dakota. Andrew Dubovy. Ed. by Marie H. Bloch. (Illus.). 72p. (Orig.). 1983. lib. bdg. 8.50; pap. 4.50. Ukrainian Cult Inst.

Pilgrims of the Stars. 2nd ed. Indira Devi & Dilip K. Roy. (Illus.). 406p. 1985. pap. 14.95 (ISBN 0-931454-10-7). Timeless Bks.

Pilgrims of the Thames in Search of the National! Pierce Egan. LC 79-8261. Repr. of 1838 ed. 44.50 (ISBN 0-404-61842-1). AMS Pr.

Pilgrim's Progress. John Bunyan. (Airmont Classics Ser.). (gr. 9 up). 1968. pap. 1.50 (ISBN 0-8049-0183-X, CL-183). Airmont.

Pilgrim's Progress. John Bunyan. (Giant Summit Bks). pap. 8.95 (ISBN 0-8010-0732-1). Baker Bk.

Pilgrim's Progress. John Bunyan. 1979. Repr. 23.95 (ISBN 0-85151-259-3). Banner of Truth.

Pilgrim's Progress. John Bunyan. 1978. 14.95x (ISBN 0-460-00204-X, Evman); pap. 2.95x (ISBN 0-460-01204-5, Evman). Biblio Dist.

Pilgrim's Progress. John Bunyan. (Illus.). 232p. (gr. 9 up). 1981. pap. text ed. 2.95 (ISBN 0-89323-016-2, 119). Bible Memory.

Pilgrim's Progress. John Bunyan. (Great Illustrated Classics Ser.). (Illus.). (YA) (gr. 9 up). 1979. 10.95 (ISBN 0-396-07754-4). Dodd.

Pilgrim's Progress. John Bunyan. 1976. lib. bdg. 18.95. (ISBN 0-89968-156-5). Lightyear.

Pilgrim's Progress. John Bunyan. (Moody Classics Ser.). 1984. pap. 3.95 (ISBN 0-8024-0012-4). Moody.

Pilgrim's Progress. John Bunyan. (YA) (RL 10). pap. 2.95 (ISBN 0-451-51930-2, CE1813, Sig Classics). NAL.

Pilgrim's Progress. John Bunyan. Ed. by Roger Shattock. (English Library Ser.). 1965. pap. 2.95 (ISBN 0-14-043004-0). Penguin.

Pilgrim's Progress. John Bunyan. 1975. 18.95 (ISBN 0-685-52821-9). Reiner.

Pilgrim's Progress. John Bunyan. 288p. 1965. pap. 3.95 (ISBN 0-8007-8032-9, Spire Bks). Revell.

Pilgrim's Progress. John Bunyan. 416p. 1981. pap. 3.95 (ISBN 0-88368-096-3). Whitaker Hse.

Pilgrim's Progress. John Bunyan. 320p. pap. 2.50 (ISBN 0-671-42460-2). WSP.

Pilgrim's Progress. John Bunyan. Ed. by Hal M. Helms. LC 81-85770. (Living Library Ser.). (Illus.). 268p. 1982. 7.95. Paraclete Pr.

Pilgrim's Progress. John Bunyan. (World's Classics-Paperback Ser.). 1984. pap. 2.95 (ISBN 0-19-281607-1). Oxford U Pr.

Pilgrim's Progress. John Bunyan. Ed. by Hal M. Helms. (Illus.). 268p. pap. 6.95 (ISBN 0-941478-02-5, Pub. by Paraclete Pr). Upper Room.

Pilgrim's Progress. John Bunyan. 1985. pap. 4.95 (ISBN 0-317-18945-X). Barbour & Co.

Pilgrims' Progress. Franklin Jones, Sr. (Hindsight Saga Ser.). (Illus.). 160p. 1988. 16.95 (ISBN 0-915433-15-X). Packrat WA.

Pilgrim's Progress. 2.95 (ISBN 0-318-18180-0). WCTU.

Pilgrim's Progress. (Christian Library). 379p. 1984. Repr. 6.95 (ISBN 0-916441-00-8). Barbour & Co.

Pilgrim's Progress. Retold by James Reeves. LC 86-25902. (Children's Classics from World Literature Ser.). (Illus.). 160p. (gr. 4 up). 1987. 12.95 (ISBN 0-87226-147-6); pap. 6.95 (ISBN 0-87226-148-4). P Bedrick Bks.

Pilgrim's Progress. Ralph Vaughan Williams. (Libretto only). 1951. 2.25 (ISBN 0-19-339227-5). Oxford U Pr.

Pilgrim's Progress: Critical & Historical Views. Ed. by Vincent Newey. (English Texts & Studies). 302p. 1980. 30.00x (ISBN 0-389-20016-6). B&N Imports.

Pilgrim's Progress Guides. Ed. by Diane Zimmerman. (LifeView: a Christian Approachto Literature Studies). (gr. 10-12). 1977. pap. 0.85 student guide (ISBN 0-915134-32-2); tchrs. ed. 1.50 (ISBN 0-915134-36-5). Mott Media.

Pilgrims Progress Illustrated see Progreso del Peregrino Ilustrado.

Pilgrim's Progress in Today's English. John Bunyan. LC 64-25255. 1964. pap. 6.95 (ISBN 0-8024-6520-X). Moody.

Pilgrims Progress: Notes. George F. Willison. (Orig.). 1968. pap. 3.75 (ISBN 0-8220-1030-5). Cliffs.

Pilgrim's Progress (Retold for Children) Laurence Morris. (gr. 1-5). 1962. pap. 1.95 (ISBN 0-87508-747-7). Chr Lit.

Pilgrims Progress, Sixteen Seventy-Eight. John Bunyan. 288p. 1984. 30.00x (ISBN 0-905418-29-8, Pub. by Gresham England). State Mutual Bk.

Pilgrim's Progress: Three Generations of Migration Among Mayflower Settlers & Their Descendants. Ralph J. Crandall & Lawrence Kilbourne. (Pilgrim Society Notes Ser.: No. 32). 1984. 2.00. Pilgrim Soc.

Pilgrims, Puritans & Patriots: Our Christian Heritage. Don Boys. 1983. pap. 9.00x (ISBN 0-686-40717-2). Freedom Univ-FSP.

Pilgrim's Quest. Dukki Brown. 90p. (Orig.). 1986. pap. 7.45 (ISBN 0-934501-02-5). Kairos Inc.

Pilgrim's Regress. C. S. Lewis. 224p. 1981. pap. 3.50 (ISBN 0-553-26063-4). Bantam.

Pilgrim's Regress. C. S. Lewis. 1958. pap. 6.95 (ISBN 0-8028-6018-4). Eerdmans.

Pilgrim's Regress: An Allegorical Apology for Christianity, Reason, & Romanticism. C. S. Lewis. LC 82-101595. pap. 55.30 (ISBN 0-317-30149-7, 2025332). Bks Demand UMI.

Pilgrim's Rest. Patricia Wentworth. 240p. 1988. pap. 3.50 (ISBN 0-446-31463-3). Warner Bks.

Pilgrim's Rest. Patricia Wentworth. 17.95 (ISBN 0-88411-721-9, Pub. by Aeonian Pr). Amereon Ltd.

Pilgrims' Road (Songbook) Mike Wood. 1976. pap. 3.95 (ISBN 0-89390-015-X). Resource Pubns.

Pilgrim's Scrip: Wit & Wisdom of George Meredith. George Meredith. LC 78-31730. 1978. lib. bdg. 38.50 (ISBN 0-8414-6334-4). Folcroft.

Pilgrim's Staff. Rose Porter. 1897. 20.00 (ISBN 0-686-17690-1). Quaker City.

Pilgrim's Staff or Daily Steps Heavenward by the Pathway of Faith. 1979. Repr. of 1897 ed. lib. bdg. 20.00 (ISBN 0-8495-4332-0). Arden Lib.

Pilgrims Through Space & Time: Trends & Patterns in Scientific & Utopian Fiction. James O. Bailey. LC 76-38126. 341p. 1972. lib. bdg. 35.00x (ISBN 0-8371-6323-4, BAPS). Greenwood.

Pilgrim's Way. John Buchan. 352p. 1984. pap. 10.95 (ISBN 0-88184-107-2). Carroll & Graf.

Pilgrim's Way: An Essay in Recollection. John Buchan. LC 76-6591. (BCL Ser. II). Repr. of 1940 ed. 32.50 (ISBN 0-404-15278-3). AMS Pr.

Pilgrims' Way Between Psychotherapy & Religion. Erastus Evans. 1985. 10.00x (ISBN 0-317-62244-7, Guild of Pastoral Psych). State Mutual Bk.

Pilgrim's Way from Winchester to Canterbury. Julia M. Ady. LC 71-158231. Repr. of 1893 ed. 17.50 (ISBN 0-404-01399-6). AMS Pr.

Pilgrim's Way: Shrines & Saints in Britain & Ireland. John Adair. (Illus.). 1978. 12.98 (ISBN 0-500-25061-8). Thames Hudson.

Piling & Ground Treatment: Proceedings of a Conference Organized by the Institution of Civil Engineers. 297p. 1984. 49.50 (ISBN 0-7277-0185-1, Pub. by T Telford UK). Am Soc Civil Eng.

Piling Engineering. W. G. Fleming et al. 1985. 69.95 (ISBN 0-470-20144-4). Halsted Pr.

Piling in Rock. Joram M. Amir. 112p. 1985. text ed. 50.00 (ISBN 0-317-64963-9, Pub. by A A Balkema). Brookfield Pub Co.

Piling: Model Procedures & Specifications. 171p. 1978. 20.00 (ISBN 0-7277-0036-7, Pub. by T Telford UK). Am Soc Civil Eng.

Piling Practice. A. S. West. (Illus.). 122p. 1975. 17.50 (ISBN 0-408-70288-5). Transatl Arts.

Pilipino Phrasebook. John U. Wolff. 80p. (Orig.). 1988. pap. 2.95 (ISBN 0-86442-064-1). Lonely Planet.

Pilipinos in America: Macro-Micro Dimensions of Immigration & Integration. Antonio J. Pido. (CMS Migration & Ethnicity Ser.). 300p. 1986. pap. 12.95 (ISBN 0-913256-83-8). Ctr Migration.

Pilippino-English: English-Pilippino Concise Dictionary. Sam Bickford. (Hippocrene Concise Dictionaries Ser.). 550p. 1985. pap. 6.95 (ISBN 0-87052-028-8). Hippocrene Bks.

Pili's Wall. Philip Levine. LC 72-134741. 1971. 12.50 (ISBN 0-87775-007-6); pap. 5.00 (ISBN 0-685-04900-0). Unicorn Pr.

Pili's Wall. rev. ed. Philip Levine. (Illus.). 1980. 10.00; pap. 5.00 (ISBN 0-87775-125-0). Unicorn Pr.

Pilkington's Royal Lancastrian Pottery & Tiles. A. J. Cross. (Illus.). 96p. 55.00 (ISBN 0-317-55035-7). Apollo.

Pill. John Guillebaud. (Illus.). 1980. pap. 9.95x (ISBN 0-19-286002-X). Oxford U Pr.

Pill Book. 3rd, rev. ed. Harold Silverman & Gilbert I. Simon. (Orig.). 1986. pap. 4.95 (ISBN 0-553-24955-X). Bantam.

Pill Book. 3rd, rev. ed. Gilbert I. Simon & Harold Silverman. (Illus.). 1986. pap. 12.95 (ISBN 0-553-34242-8). Bantam.

Pill Popping: How You Can Get Clear. Valerie Curran & Susan Golombok. 176p. (Orig.). 1985. pap. 7.95 (ISBN 0-571-13508-0). Faber & Faber.

Pill Versus the Springhill Mine Disaster see Trout Fishing in America.

Pillage of the Third World. Pierre Jalee. LC 68-13069. 128p. 1968. pap. 4.95 (ISBN 0-85345-118-4). Monthly Rev.

Pillar & Tinderbox: The Greek Press & the Dictatorship. Robert McDonald. LC 82-14748. (Open Forum Ser.). 240p. 1983. 25.00 (ISBN 0-7145-2781-5, Dist. by Scribner). M Boyars Pubs.

Pillar & Tinderbox: The Greek Press & the Dictatorship. Robert McDonald. 242p. 1985. pap. 12.00 (ISBN 0-7145-2833-1, Dist. by Kampmann & Co). M Boyars Pubs.

Pillar House Cookbook. David P. Larousse & Alan R. Gibson. (Illus.). 248p. (Orig.). 1988. pap. 14.95 (ISBN 1-55832-005-9). Harvard Common Pr.

Pillar in the Twilight. Daughters of St. Paul. (Encounter Ser.). 3.00 (ISBN 0-8198-0591-2); pap. 2.00 (ISBN 0-8198-0592-0). Dghtrs St Paul.

Pillar Mountain. Max Brand. 1978. pap. 1.50 (ISBN 0-671-81758-2). PB.

Pillar Mountian. Max Brand. pap. 2.75 (ISBN 0-671-63306-6). PB.

Pillar of Fire to Follow: American Indian Dramas, 1808-1859. Priscilla F. Sears. LC 81-85523. 149p. 1982. 11.95 (ISBN 0-87972-193-6); pap. 5.95 (ISBN 0-87972-194-4). Bowling Green Univ.

Pillar of Flame: The Mythological Foundations of D. H. Lawrence's Sexual Philosophy. Barbara A. Miliaras. (American University Studies IV-English Language & Literature: Vol. 33). 308p. 1987. text ed. 42.00 (ISBN 0-8204-0271-0). P Lang Pubs.

Pillar of Night. Robert E. Vardeman. (Cenotaph Road Ser.: No. 6). 1984. pap. 2.75 (ISBN 0-441-66397-4, Pub. by Ace Science Fiction). Ace Bks.

Pillar of the Sky. Cecelia Holland. LC 84-48659. (Illus.). 544p. 1985. 17.45 (ISBN 0-394-53538-3). Knopf.

Pillar Stability in Large Underground Openings: Applications from a Case Study in Competent, Jointed Rock. J. F. Agapito. Ed. by Jon W. Raese. (Colorado School of Mines Quarterly Ser.: Vol. 81 No. 3 1986). (Illus.). 90p. 1986. pap. text ed. 17.00 (ISBN 0-918062-70-5). Colo Sch Mines.

Pillar to Post: Looking at Street Furniture. Henry Aaron. (Illus.). 192p. 1982. 60.00x (ISBN 0-7232-2762-4, Pub. by F Warne England). State Mutual Bk.

Pillars in Ethiopian History: The William Leo Hansberry African History Notebook, Vol. I. Ed. by Joseph E. Harris. LC 73-88970. 1981. pap. 6.95 (ISBN 0-88258-090-6). Howard U Pr.

Pillars in Ethiopian History: The William Leo Hansberry African History Notebook, Vol. 1. Ed. by Joseph E. Harris. LC 73-88970. 154p. 1974. 10.95 (ISBN 0-88258-009-4). Howard U Pr.

Pillars of Atonia: A Journey Through Time & Space. Fouad E. Shaker. (Illus.). 184p. 1983. 10.50 (ISBN 0-682-49995-1). Exposition-Phoenix.

Pillars of Faith. Herman O. Wilson & Morris M. Womack. 6.95 (ISBN 0-8010-9540-9); pap. 4.95 (ISBN 0-8010-9538-7). Baker Bk.

Pillars of Flame: Power, Priesthood, & Spiritual Maturity. Maggie Ross. LC 87-46227. 160p. 1988. 15.95 (ISBN 0-06-254840-9, HarpR). Har-Row.

Pillars of Hercules. Jeffrey Saltzman. LC 77-93668. (Illus.). 1978. pap. 12.50 (ISBN 0-915346-32-X). A Wofsy Fine Arts.

Pillars of Marriage. H. Norman Wright. LC 78-68849. 176p. 1979. pap. 6.95 (ISBN 0-8307-0698-4, 5412501); leader's guide 12.95 (ISBN 0-8307-0699-2, 5202418). Regal.

Pillars of Pentecost. Charles W. Conn. 148p. 1979. 6.95 (ISBN 0-87148-681-4). Pathway Pr.

Pillars of Society see Ibsen Plays.

Pillars of the Church. Theodore Maynard. LC 76-136763. (Essay Index Reprint Ser). 1945. 19.00 (ISBN 0-8369-1940-8). Ayer Co Pubs.

Pillars of the House: An Anthology of Irish Women's Poetry. Intro. by A. A. Kelly. 192p. (Orig.). 1988. pap. 15.95 (ISBN 0-86327-143-X, Pub. by Wolfhound Pr Ireland). Irish Bks Media.

Pillars of the Pentagon. Nita Scoggan. (Illus.). 192p. 1982. pap. 4.95 (ISBN 0-934588-05-8). Ranger Assocs.

Pillars of the Pentagon. Nita Scoggan. LC 82-50507. (Illus.). 178p. (Orig.). 1982. pap. 4.95 (ISBN 0-910487-00-6). Royalty Pub.

Pillars of the Post: The Making of a News Empire. Howard Bray. 1980. 7.95 (ISBN 0-393-01313-8); pap. write for info. (ISBN 0-393-30020-X). Norton.

Pillars of the Republic: Common Schools & American Society, 1780-1860. Carl Kaestle. Ed. by Eric Foner. (American Century Ser.). 280p. 1983. 17.95 (ISBN 0-8090-7620-9); pap. 7.95 (ISBN 0-8090-0154-3). Hill & Wang.

Pillars of Zen. Roshi P. Kapleau. 1989. pap. 10.95 (ISBN 0-385-26093-8, Anchor Pr). Doubleday.

Pillboxes: A Study of U. K. Defences 1940. Henry Wills. (Illus.). 128p. 1985. 30.95 (ISBN 0-436-57360-1, Pub. by Secker & Warburg UK). David & Charles.

Pillory Poetics. 3rd rev. ed. Ed. by Merritt Clifton. 24p. 1979. pap. 1.00 (ISBN 0-686-27505-5). Samisdat.

Pillow & Placemats. 1983. pap. 4.98 (ISBN 0-317-03202-X). Gick.

Pillow Book. Charles Blackburn. LC 77-93302. (Illus.). 156p. 1979. pap. 14.95 (ISBN 0-8149-0801-2). Vanguard.

Pillow Book of Carol Tinker. Carol Tinker. LC 79-57557. 100p. 1980. sign ed ltd. ed. 20.00 (ISBN 0-932274-09-9); pap. 5.00 (ISBN 0-932274-08-0). Cadmus Eds.

Pillow Book of Sei Shonagon. Sei Shonagon. Tr. by Ivan Morris. (Classics Ser). 1971. pap. 6.95 (ISBN 0-14-044236-7). Penguin.

Pillow Ideas. Ed. by Janet DuBane & Alexandra Kuman. (Illus.). 64p. (Orig.). 1980. pap. 2.50 (ISBN 0-918178-19-3). Simplicity.

Pillow Lace: A Practical Handbook. Elizabeth Mincoff & Margaret S. Marriage. 22.95 (ISBN 0-903585-10-3). Robin & Russ.

Pillow of Fire. Betty Leemisa. 80p. 1988. 7.75 (ISBN 0-8062-3275-7). Carlton.

Pillow of Gold. George A. Montgomery. 256p. 1985. pap. 3.95 (ISBN 0-939332-13-2). J Pohl Assocs.

Pillow of the Community. Richard Hilary. 208p. (Orig.). 1988. pap. 3.50 (ISBN 0-553-27172-5). Bantam.

Pillow or Bobbin Lace - Techniques, Patterns, History. Elizabeth Mincoff & Margaret S. Marriage. 1988. 16.00 (ISBN 0-8446-6327-1). Peter Smith.

Pillow or Bobbin Lace: Technique, Patterns, History. Elizabeth Mincoff & Margaret S. Marriage. (Illus.). 288p. 1987. pap. 6.95 (ISBN 0-486-25505-0). Dover.

Pillow Problems & A Tangled Tale. Lewis Carroll. pap. 4.95 (ISBN 0-486-20493-6). Dover.

Pillow Talk. Susan Kalish & Nancy Kallish. 144p. 1985. pap. 9.95 (ISBN 0-671-54565-5). S&S.

Pillows. Benny Andersen. LC 83-7166. 182p. 1983. 7.50 (ISBN 0-915306-37-9). Curbstone.

Pillows & Placemats. 4.98 (ISBN 0-317-38600-X). Gick.

Pillows: How to Make. Sunset Editors. LC 80-80859. (Illus.). 80p. 1980. pap. 5.95 (ISBN 0-376-01432-6, Sunset Bks). Sunset-Lane.

Pills Against Poverty: A Study of the Introduction of Western Medicine in a Tamil Village. Linberg S. Djurfeldt. 1981. 11.00x (ISBN 0-8364-0681-8, Pub. by Macmillan India). Asia Bks.

Pills & the Public Purse: The Routes to National Drug Insurance. Milton Silverman et al. LC 80-6058. 300p. 1981. 27.50x (ISBN 0-520-04381-2). U of Cal Pr.

Pilot's Weight & Balance Handbook. rev. ed. Federal Aviation Administration Staff. 68p. 1977. pap. text ed. 5.00. Flightshops.
Pilot's Weight & Balance Handbook. (Advisory Circular 91-23A). (Illus.). 76p. 1977. pap. 5.00 (ISBN 0-318-20390-1, S/N 050-007-00405-2). USGPO.
Pilots Weight & Balance Handbook: FAA AC 91-23A. Federal Aviation Administration Staff. (Illus.). 1977. pap. 5.00 (ISBN 0-939158-22-1, Pub. by Cooper). Aviation.
Pilsen & the West Side. William Adelman. (Illus.). 112p. 1982. 24.95 (Pub. by Illinois Labor History Society); pap. 10.95. C H Kerr.
Pilsen & the West Side. William Adelman. (Illus.). 100p. 1983. pap. 6.95. Ill Labor Hist Soc.
Pilsudski: A Biography by His Wife. Alexandra Pilsudska. LC 76-135829. (Eastern Europe Collection Ser). 1970. Repr. of 1941 ed. 22.00 (ISBN 0-405-02771-0). Ayer Co Pubs.
Piltdown Forgery. J. S. Weiner. (Illus.). 240p. 1981. pap. 4.95 (ISBN 0-486-24075-4). Dover.
Piltdown Inquest. Charles Blinderman. LC 86-20485. (Illus.). 261p. 1986. 22.95 (ISBN 0-87975-359-5). Prometheus Bks.
Pilz-Taschenatlas. A. Pilat. (Illus.). 118p. (Ger.). 1976. lib. bdg. 10.00x (ISBN 3-7684-2480-4). Lubrecht & Cramer.
Pilze. Aurel Dermek. (Illus.). 228p. (Ger.). 1981. lib. bdg. 10.00x (ISBN 3-7684-2114-7). Lubrecht & Cramer.
Pilze: Alle wichtigen Pilze nach Farbfotos bestimmen. A. Neuner. (Illus.). 143p. 1983. pap. text ed. 10.00x (ISBN 3-405-12048-9). Lubrecht & Cramer.
Pilze auf Holz. Speisepilze, Holzzersetzer, Baumschaedlinge. M. Enderle & H. E. Laux. (Illus., Ger.). 1980. pap. text ed. 10.00x (ISBN 3-440-04823-3). Lubrecht & Cramer.
Pilze Erkennen-Leicht Gemancht. R. Rayner. (Illus., Ger.). 1979. pap. text ed. 7.95x (ISBN 3-440-04748-2). Lubrecht & Cramer.
Pilze im Garten. 2nd ed. H. Steineck. (Illus.). 148p. 1981. lib. bdg. 15.00x (ISBN 3-8001-6122-2). Lubrecht & Cramer.
Pilze in Wald und Flur. 5th ed. H. Haas & H. Schrempp. (Illus., Ger.). 1984. pap. text ed. 7.95x (ISBN 3-440-05328-8). Lubrecht & Cramer.
Pilze Mitteleuropas: Vol. 28, Die Milchlinge (Lactarii) Walther Neuhoff. (Illus.). 1956. 120.00x (ISBN 3-7682-0520-7). Lubrecht & Cramer.
Pilze Mitteleuropas: Vol. 4, Die Gattung Phlegmacium (Schleimkoepfe) Meinhard Moser. (Illus.). 1960. 125.00x (ISBN 3-7682-0523-1). Lubrecht & Cramer.
Pilze Mitteleuropas: Vol. 5, Die Roehrlinge- Pt. 1, Die Boletaceae (Ohne Boletoideae) Rolf Singer. (Illus.). 1965. 74.00x (ISBN 3-7682-0526-6). Lubrecht & Cramer.
Pilze Mitteleuropas: Vol. 5, Die Roehrlinge- Pt. 2, Die Boletoiceae una Strobilomycetaceae. Rolf Singer. (Illus.). 1967. 108.00x (ISBN 3-7682-0529-0). Lubrecht & Cramer.
Pilze Mitteluropas. Herve Chaumeton. Tr. by Ute Juelich from Fr. (Illus.). 484p. (Ger.). 1987. lib. bdg. 37.75x. Lubrecht & Cramer.
Pilze Schlesiens, 2 vols. J. Schroeter. (Illus.). 1973. Repr. of 1908 ed. Set. 150.00x (ISBN 3-7682-0761-7). Lubrecht & Cramer.
Pilze, Vol. 1: Lamellenpilze, Taeublinge, Milchlinge und andere Gruppen mit Lamellen. E. Gerhardt. (Illus.). 318p. (Ger.). 1984. pap. 25.00x (ISBN 3-405-12927-3). Lubrecht & Cramer.
Pilze, Vol. 2: Roehrlinge, Porlinge, Bauchpilze, und Schlauchpilze und Andere. E. Gerhardt. (Illus.). 320p. (Ger.). 1985. pap. 25.00x (ISBN 3-405-12965-6). Lubrecht & Cramer.
Pilzflora der Deutschen Demokratischen Republik Basidiomycetes (Gallert-Hut-und Bauchpilze) Ed. by Hans Kreisel. 261p. (Ger.). 1987. lib. bdg. 37.50x (ISBN 3-334-00025-7). Lubrecht & Cramer.
Pilzfuehrer: 245 wichtige Speise- und Giftpilze in 267 Farbfotos abgebildet un beschrieben. 2nd ed. E. Gerhardt. (Illus.). 326p. 1981. pap. text ed. 15.00x (ISBN 3-405-12484-0). Lubrecht & Cramer.
Pilzkunde: Ein Kurzer Abriss der Mykologie Unter Besonderer Beruecksichtigung der Pilze in Reinkultur. 3rd ed. J. A. von Arx. (Illus.). 1976. 18.00x (ISBN 3-7682-1067-7). Lubrecht & Cramer.
Pilzmikroskopie: Praeparation und Untersuchung von Pilzen. Bruno Erb & W. Matheis. (Illus.). 166p. lib. bdg. 40.00x (ISBN 3-440-05127-7). Lubrecht & Cramer.
Pima & Papago Indian Agriculture. Edward F. Castetter et al. LC 76-43674. Repr. of 1942 ed. 21.00 (ISBN 0-404-15510-3). AMS Pr.
Pima Bajo Nevome of Central Sonora, Mexico: Vol. 1, The Material Culture. Campbell W. Pennington. (Illus.). 372p. 1980. 30.00x (ISBN 0-87480-126-5). U of Utah Pr.
Pima Bajo (Nevome) of Central Sonora, Mexico, Vol. 2: Vocabulario en la Lengua Nevome. Campbell W. Pennington. 1979. 16.00x (ISBN 0-87480-125-7). U of Utah Pr.
Pima-Marciopa: Southwest. Ed. by Frank W. Porter, III. (Indians of North America Ser.). (Illus.). (gr. 5 up). 1989. 16.95 (ISBN 1-55546-724-5). Chelsea Hse.
Pima Remembers. rev. ed. George Webb. LC 59-4914. 126p. 1982. pap. 7.50 (ISBN 0-8165-0786-4). U of Ariz Pr.
Piman & Papago Ritual Oratory. Don Bahr. 1975. pap. 7.00 (ISBN 0-685-64956-3). Indian Hist Pr.
Piman Shamanism & Staying Sickness: Ka: cim Mumkidag. Donald M. Bahr et al. LC 72-92103. 332p. 1974. pap. 9.95 (ISBN 0-8165-0303-6). U of Ariz Pr.
Pimlico Plot. Mary McMullen. 1988. pap. 3.50 (ISBN 0-515-09544-3). Jove Pubns.
Pimp. Iceberg Slim. 1985. pap. 3.25 (ISBN 0-87067-850-7, BH850). Holloway.
Pimp: The Story of My Life. Robert Beck. (Orig.). 1969. pap. 2.95 (ISBN 0-87067-806-X, BH806). Holloway.
Pimpernel & Rosemary. E. Orczy. 341p. 1983. Repr. lib. bdg. 18.95x (ISBN 0-686-47487-2). Buccaneer Bks.
Pimpernel Plot. Simon Hawke. (Time War Ser.: No. 3). 224p. 1986. pap. 2.95 (ISBN 0-441-66411-3). Ace Bks.
Pimps & Pimping: A Comprehensive Bibliography. John Deer. 53p. (Orig.). 1988. pap. 9.95 (ISBN 0-940519-09-7). Res Discover Pubns.
PIMS Principles: Linking Strategy to Performance. Robert D. Buzzell & Bradley T. Gale. 352p. 1987. 24.95 (ISBN 0-02-904430-8). Free Pr.
Pimsleur's Checklists of Basic American Legal Publications, 5 pts. Ed. by Marcia S. Zubrow. Incl. Pt. 1. Statutes; Pt. 2. Session Laws; Pt. 3. Attorneys General Opinions & Reports; Pt. 4. Judicial Councils; Pt. 5. Restatements. (AALL Publications Ser: No. 4). (5 sections with 1983 supplement). looseleaf bdg., 1983 supplement incl. 150.00x (ISBN 0-8377-0104-X). Rothman.
Pin Prick Press Annual Index of Serial & Chapbook Publications, 1980. Roberta Mendel. 27p. (Orig.). 1981. pap. 2.00 (ISBN 0-936424-07-9). Pin Prick.
Pin-Up. Hajime Sorayama. 88p. 1986. 24.95 (ISBN 0-88715-015-2). Putnam Pub Group.
Pin-up: A Modest History. Mark Gabor. LC 73-189116. (Illus.). 272p. 1973. pap. 6.95 (ISBN 0-87663-910-4). Universe.
Pin-Up: The Tragedy of Betty Grable. Spero Pastos. (Illus.). 176p. Date not set. 16.95 (ISBN 0-399-13189-2, Putnam). Putnam Pub Group.
Pin-Up: The Tragedy of Betty Grable. Spero Pastos. 1987. pap. 3.95 (ISBN 0-425-10422-2). Berkley Pub.
Pina: Etude D'un Terroir De Front Pionnier En Pays Dagari (Haute-Volta) Georges Savonnet. (Atlas Des Structures Agraires Au Sud Du Sahara: No. 4). (Illus.). 1971. pap. 19.60x (ISBN 90-2796-885-3). Mouton.
Pinafore Palace: A Book of Rhymes for the Nursery. Ed. by Kate D. Wiggin et al. LC 72-8290. (Granger Index Reprint Ser.). (YA) (ps-1). Repr. of 1907 ed. 21.00 (ISBN 0-8369-6399-7). Ayer Co Pubs.
Pinal Dome Oil Company: An Adventure in Business, 1901-1917. Richard C. Schwatzman. LC 75-41782. (Companies & Men: Business Enterprises in America). 1976. 29.00x (ISBN 0-405-08097-2). Ayer Co Pubs.
Pinatas & Paper Flowers-Pinatas y Flores de Papel: Holidays of the Americas in English & Spanish. Lila Perl & Alma F. Ada. LC 82-12211. (Illus.). 96p. (gr. 3-6). 1983. 11.50 (ISBN 0-89919-112-6, Pub. by Clarion); pap. 4.50 (ISBN 0-89919-155-X). Ticknor & Fields.
Pinball Player. Pat M. Kuras. 1982. pap. 3.50 (ISBN 0-914852-11-6). Good Gay.
Pinball Reference Guide. Donald Mueting & Robert Hawkins. (Orig.). 1979. pap. 7.95 (ISBN 0-934422-19-2). Mead Pub Corp.
Pinballs. Betsy Byars. LC 76-41518. 144p. (gr. 5 up). 1977. 12.70i (ISBN 0-06-020917-8); PLB 12.89 (ISBN 0-06-020918-6). HarpJ.
Pinballs. Betsy Byars. (gr. 4-6). 1979. pap. 2.50 (ISBN 0-590-33785-8, Apple Paperbacks). Scholastic Inc.
Pinballs. Betsy Byars. LC 76-41518. (Trophy Bks.). 144p. (gr. 5 up). 1987. pap. 2.95 (ISBN 0-06-440198-7, Trophy). HarpJ.
Pinballs see Betsy Byars Boxed Set.
Pinceladas Criollas. Jorge R. Plasencia. LC 87-83348. (Coleccion Caniqui). 88p. (Orig., Span.). 1988. pap. 9.95 (ISBN 0-89729-472-6). Ediciones.
Pincers. Philip Ward. (Oleander Dramascripts Ser.: Vol. 5). 1973. 4.50 (ISBN 0-902675-30-3). Oleander Pr.
Pinch. Larry Callen. (Illus.). (gr. 5 up). 1976. 13.95 (ISBN 0-316-12495-8, Joy St Bks). Little.
Pinch & Ouch: English Through Drama. Yoko Nomura. (Illus.). 136p. 1982. pap. text ed. 7.95 (ISBN 0-940264-13-7); cassette tape 13.50 (ISBN 0-940264-15-3). Lingual Hse Pub.
Pinch & Ouch: English Through Drama with Acting Games. Yoko Nomura. 182p. 1982. pap. text ed. 9.50 (ISBN 0-940264-30-7). Lingual Hse Pub.
Pinch of Poison. Frances Lockridge & Richard Lockridge. 13.95 (ISBN 0-89190-917-6, Pub. by Am Repr). Amereon Ltd.
Pinch of Salt Lake. The Junior League of Salt Lake City, Inc. Staff. Ed. by Kristine E. Widner & Shonnie S. Hays. LC 86-81537. 272p. 1986. 16.95 (ISBN 0-9616972-0-2). Jr League Salt Lake City.
Pinch of Sunshine. Junior Service League of Brooksville Florida. Ed. by Beth Bartos. (Illus.). 336p. 1982. pap. 9.95 (ISBN 0-939114-63-1). Wimmer Bks.
Pinch of This. Marie P. Kilpatrick. (Illus.). 104p. 1987. 9.95 (ISBN 0-8487-0824-5). Oxmoor Hse.
Pinch of This & a Dash of That. Kaye Johns. (Illus.). 1988. 24.95 (ISBN 0-9615390-5-4). Aspen West Pub.
Pinch of This & a Handful of That. Daughters of the Republic of Texas District VIII Staff. 160p. 1988. 12.95 (ISBN 0-89015-649-2). Eakin Pr.
Pincher Martin. William Golding. LC 57-10059. Orig. Title: Two Deaths of Christopher Martin. 216p. 1968. pap. 4.95 (ISBN 0-15-671833-2, Harv). HarBraceJ.
Pinchpenny John. Lee Lorenz. (Illus.). 32p. 1984. pap. 5.95 (ISBN 0-13-676172-0). P-H.
Pinckert's Practical Grammar: A Lively, Unintimidating Guide to Usage, Punctuation & Style. Robert C. Pinckert. LC 85-29618. 179p. 1986. 14.95 (ISBN 0-89879-211-8). Writers Digest.
Pinckney's Treaty: America's Advantage from Europe's Distress, 1783-1800. Samuel F. Bemis. LC 73-8148. (Illus.). xvi, 372p. 1973. Repr. of 1960 ed. lib. bdg. 65.00x (ISBN 0-8371-6954-2, BEPT). Greenwood.
Pinco mil Palabras Inglesas de Uso Comun Que Usted Ya Sabe: Five Thousand Everyday Spanish Words You Already Know. Carlos B. Vega. 200p. (Span. & Eng.). pap. write for info. C B Vega.
Pincushions. Averil Colby. (Illus.). 124p. 1988. pap. 15.95 (ISBN 0-7134-5880-1, Pub. by Batsford England). David & Charles.
Pincushion's Strawberry. Jared Carter. (Illus.). 31p. (Orig.). 1984. pap. 3.50 (ISBN 0-914946-43-9). Cleveland St Univ Poetry Ctr.
Pindar. C. Maurice Bowra. 1964. 32.50x (ISBN 0-19-814338-9). Oxford U Pr.
Pindar. D. S. Carne-Ross. LC 84-40668. (Hermes Bk.). 224p. 1985. text ed. 27.50t (ISBN 0-300-03383-4); 9.95x (ISBN 0-300-03393-1, Y-531). Yale U Pr.
Pindar. Hugh Lloyd-Jones. (Master-Mind Lectures (Henriette Hertz Trust)). 26p. 1984. pap. 5.50 (ISBN 0-85672-450-5, Pub. by British Acad). Longwood Pub Group.
Pindar. Gilbert Norwood. (Sather Classical Lectures: No. 19). 1974. 32.00x (ISBN 0-520-01952-0). U of Cal Pr.
Pindar. William H. Race. (Twayne's World Authors Ser.: 773). 176p. 1986. lib. bdg. 18.95x (ISBN 0-8057-6624-3, Twayne). G K Hall.
Pindar & Aeschylus. John H. Finley, Jr. LC 54-11110. (Martin Classical Lectures Ser.: No. 14). 1955. 22.50x (ISBN 0-674-66800-6). Harvard U Pr.
Pindar, the Olympian & Pythian Odes. Pindarus. Ed. by Basil L. Gildersleeve. 1885. 59.00x (ISBN 0-403-00331-8). Scholarly.
Pindar TV Viewer's Guide to the 1984 Olympic Games. (Illus.). 112p. 1984. pap. 6.95 (ISBN 0-918223-33-4). Pindar Pr.
Pindar's Mythmaking: The Fourth Pythian Ode. Charles Segal. LC 85-43312. 196p. 1986. text ed. 24.00 (ISBN 0-691-05473-8). Princeton U Pr.
Pindar's Odes. Pindar. Tr. by Roy A. Swanson from Gr. 416p. pap. 12.95 (ISBN 0-8290-0332-0). Irvington.
Pindar's Olympian I: A Commentary. Douglas E. Gerber. (Phoenix Supplementary Volumes Ser.). 264p. 1981. 50.00x (ISBN 0-8020-5507-9). U of Toronto Pr.
Pindar's Victory Songs. Frank J. Nisetich. LC 79-3739. 384p. 1980. text ed. 42.50x (ISBN 0-8018-2350-1); pap. text ed. 14.95x (ISBN 0-8018-2356-0). Johns Hopkins.
Pindharee. Joel Richards. 224p. (Orig.). 1986. pap. 2.95 (ISBN 0-8125-5141-9, Dist. by Warner Pub Services & St. Martin's Press). Tor Bks.
Pine Barrens. spec. ed. John McPhee. (Illus.). 212p. 1981. 25.00 (ISBN 0-374-23362-4). FS&G.
Pine Barrens. John McPhee. LC 67-22439. (Illus.). 157p. 1968. 11.95 (ISBN 0-374-23360-8); pap. 5.95 (ISBN 0-374-51442-9). FS&G.
Pine Barrens: Ecosystem & Landscape. Ed. by Richard R. Forman. LC 79-9849. (Natural Resource Management Ser.). 1979. 72.50 (ISBN 0-12-263450-0). Acad Pr.
Pine Barrens Legends, Lore & Lies. William McMahon. (Illus.). 149p. (gr. 6 up). Date not set. pap. 6.95 (ISBN 0-912608-19-6). Mid Atlantic.
Pine Barrens of Ronkonkoma: A Guide for the Hiker to the Long Island Pine Barrens. 2nd ed. Lawrence G Paul. 1986. pap. 3.95 (ISBN 0-9603966-5-9). NY-NJ Trail Confer.
Pine Cone Book. Nancy L. Boyd. LC 83-62035. (Illus.). 80p. 1983. 12.95 (ISBN 0-941526-01-1); pap. 7.95 (ISBN 0-941526-02-X). Prospect Hill.
Pine Figures. Stephen Knauth. (Illus.). 80p. 1986. 14.95 (ISBN 0-937160-15-6); pap. 8.00 (ISBN 0-937160-14-8). Dooryard.
Pine Furniture of Early New England. Russell H. Kettell. 1929. 14.95 (ISBN 0-486-20145-7). Dover.
Pine Gate. Thich N. Hanh. Tr. by Vo Dinh & Jim Forest. 1988. 7.00 (ISBN 0-934834-27-X). White Pine.
Pine Hut Poems. Dennis Maloney. 1983. pap. 4.00 (ISBN 0-934834-41-5). White Pine.
Pine Needle Basketry: How to Do Hand Crafts. rev. ed. M. Loffborough & E. Cain. LC 76-25409. (Illus.). 1978. pap. 12.95 (ISBN 0-87282-110-2). Am Life Foun.
Pine Needle Basketry in Schools. facs. ed. William Hammell. (Shorey Lost Arts Ser.). (Illus.). 20p. pap. 2.95 (ISBN 0-8466-6008-3, U8). Shorey.
Pine Needle Baskets. Linna L. Milliken. (Shorey Lost Arts Ser.). (Illus.). 86p. pap. 4.95 (ISBN 0-8466-4076-7, I76). Shorey.
Pine Needle Raffia Basketry. rev. ed. Jeannie McFarland. (Illus.). 48p. 1987. pap. 6.50 (ISBN 0-9618828-0-8). Baskets & Bullets.
Pine Ridge Plantation. facsimile ed. William Drysdale. LC 75-38647. (Black Heritage Library Collection Series). Repr. of 1901 ed. 20.75 (ISBN 0-8369-9005-6). Ayer Co Pubs.
Pine-Tarred & Feathered: A Year on the Baseball Beat. Jim Kaplan. (Illus.). 280p. 1985. 15.95 (ISBN 0-912697-15-6). Algonquin Bks.
Pine Tree Resorts: An Office Communications Simulation. Ella E. Butler et al. 1988. 12.95 (ISBN 0-88462-749-7); tchr's. manual 5.95 (ISBN 0-88462-051-4). Longman Finan.
Pine Trees & Politics. Joseph J. Malone. Ed. by Stuart Bruchey. LC 78-53552. (Development of Public Land Law in the U. S. Ser.). 1979. Repr. of 1964 ed. lib. bdg. 17.00x (ISBN 0-405-11380-3). Ayer Co Pubs.
Pine Vole in North Carolina. John R. Paul. (Reports of Investigations Ser: No. 20). (Illus.). 28p. 1970. pap. 1.00x (ISBN 0-89792-044-9). Ill St Museum.
Pineal & Its Hormones. Russel J. Reiter. LC 82-7154. (Progress in Clinical & Biological Research Ser.: Vol. 92). 310p. 1982. 33.00 (ISBN 0-8451-0092-0). A R Liss.
Pineal & Midbrain Lesions. G. Pendl. (Illus.). 280p. 1985. 59.00 (ISBN 0-387-81858-8). Springer-Verlag.
Pineal & Reproduction. Ed. by R. J. Reiter. (Progress in Reproductive Biology: Vol. 4). (Illus.). 1978. 79.50 (ISBN 3-8055-2815-9). S Karger.
Pineal & Retinal Relationships. Ed. by Paul O'Brein & David Klein. 475p. 1986. 59.00 (ISBN 0-12-523970-X). Acad Pr.
Pineal Function. Ed. by C. D. Matthews & R. F. Seamark. 272p. 1981. 105.25 (ISBN 0-444-80313-0, Biomedical Pr). Elsevier.
Pineal Gland. Ed. by Russel J. Reiter. (Comprehensive Endocrinology Ser.). (Illus.). 394p. 1984. text ed. 80.50 (ISBN 0-89004-314-0). Raven.
Pineal Gland & Its Endocrine Role. Ed. by J. Axelrod et al. LC 83-9134. (NATO ASI Series A, Life Sciences: Vol. 65). 614p. 1983. 95.00x (ISBN 0-306-41359-0, Plenum). Plenum Pub.
Pineal Gland & Its Endocrine Role: Proceedings of a Symposium on the Pineal Gland Held in Canada, April 1984. Ed. by M. Brown & S. D. Wainwright. (Illus.). 368p. 1985. 83.00 (ISBN 0-08-031992-0, Pub. by PPL); pap. 55.00 (ISBN 0-08-031991-2, Pub. by PPL). Pergamon.
Pineal Gland: Current Endocrinology-Basic & Clinical Aspects. R. Relkin. 320p. 1982. 69.25 (ISBN 0-444-00714-8, Biomedical Pr). Elsevier.
Pineal Gland: Current State of Pineal Research. Ed. by R. Mess et al. (Developments in Endocrinology Ser.: Vol. 16). 372p. 1985. 125.25 (ISBN 0-444-80629-6). Elsevier.
Pineal Gland During Development: From Fetus to Adult. Ed. by Derek Gupta & Russel J. Reiter. (Illus.). 288p. 1986. text ed. 90.00x (ISBN 0-7099-3837-3, Pub. by Croom Helm UK). Sheridan Med Bks.
Pineal Gland: Extra-Reproductive Effects, Vol. III. Ed. by Russel J. Rieter. 248p. 1982. 89.00 (ISBN 0-8493-5717-9). CRC Pr.
Pineal Gland of Vertebrates Including Man. Ed. by J. Ariens-Kappers & P. Pevet. (Progress in Brain Research Ser.: Vol. 52). 534p. 1980. 143.75 (ISBN 0-444-80114-6). Elsevier.
Pineal Gland: Reproductive Effects, Vol. II. Ed. by Russel J. Reiter. 240p. 1981. 89.00 (ISBN 0-8493-5716-0). CRC Pr.
Pineal Organ. L. E. Vollrath. (Hanbuch der Mikroskopischen Anatomie: Vol. VI-7). (Illus.). 670p. 1981. 220.00 (ISBN 0-387-10313-9). Springer-Verlag.
Pineal Organ: Photobiology, Biochronometry & Endocrinology. Oksche & Pevet. (Developments in Endocrinology Ser.: Vol. 14). 366p. 1982. 97.00 (ISBN 0-444-80387-4, Biomedical Pr). Elsevier.
Pineal Research Reviews, Vol. 1. Russel J. Reiter. 274p. 1983. 62.00 (ISBN 0-8451-3600-3). A R Liss.
Pineal Research Reviews, Vol. 2. Russel J. Reiter. 224p. 1984. 62.00 (ISBN 0-8451-3601-1). A R Liss.
Pineal Research Reviews, Vol. 3. Russel J. Reiter. 278p. 1985. 76.00 (ISBN 0-8451-3602-X). A R Liss.
Pineal Research Reviews, Vol. 4. Russel J. Reiter. 266p. 1986. 86.00 (ISBN 0-8451-3603-8). A R Liss.
Pineal Research Reviews, Vol. 5. Russel J. Reiter. 290p. 1987. 89.00 (ISBN 0-8451-3604-6). A R Liss.
Pineal Research Reviews, Vol. 6. Reiter. 1988. write for info. (ISBN 0-471-61264-2). Wiley.
Pineal Research Reviews, Vol. 6. Ed. by Russel J. Reiter. 328p. 1988. 120.00 (ISBN 0-8451-3605-4, 3605). A R Liss.
Pineapple Crochet Designs. Ed. by Rita Weiss. (Illus.). 48p. (Orig.). 1980. pap. 2.75 (ISBN 0-486-23939-X). Dover.

Pioneer see Two by Terry Plus One: An Anthology of Plays by Women.

Pioneer Aboriginal Mission. William McNair & Hilary Rumley. (Illus.). 162p. (Orig.). pap. 27.95 (ISBN 0-85564-178-9, Pub. by U of W Austral Pr). Intl Spec Bk.

Pioneer Agricultural Journalists: Brief Biographical Sketches of Some of the Early Editors in the Field of Agricultural Journalism. William E. Ogilvie. LC 72-89071. (Rural America Ser.). 1973. Repr. of 1927 ed. 16.00 (ISBN 0-8420-1492-6). Scholarly Res Inc.

Pioneer Agriculture Journalists. William E. Ogilvie. (American Newspapermen 1790-1933 Ser.). (Illus.). vii, 128p. 1973. Repr. of 1927 ed. 10.50x (ISBN 0-8464-0010-3). Beekman Pubs.

Pioneer Airplane Mails of the United States. Thomas J. O'Sullivan. 346p. 25.00 (ISBN 0-318-19121-0). Am Air Mail.

Pioneer American Merchants in Japan. 2nd ed. Howard F. Van Zandt. (Illus.). 404p. 1981. pap. 8.95 (Pub. by Lotus Pr Japan). C E Tuttle.

Pioneer Artists of Taos. rev. ed. Laura Bickerstaff. 1984. 25.00 (ISBN 0-912094-21-4). Old West.

Pioneer Arts & Artists. C. Drepperd. LC 70-121195. 1970. 12.00 (ISBN 0-87282-026-2). Am Life Foun.

Pioneer Banking. Carl A. Zapffe. LC 82-91046. (Illus.). 60p. pap. cancelled (ISBN 0-910623-01-5). Hist Heart Assoc Inc.

Pioneer Book of Nature Crafts. Harlan G. Metcalf. Orig. Title: Whittlin, Whistlin & Thingama Jigs. 1977. pap. 4.95 (ISBN 0-8065-0568-0, Pub. by Citadel Pr). Lyle Stuart.

Pioneer Cat. William J. Hooks. LC 88-4708. (Stepping Stone Bks.). (Illus.). 64p. (Orig.). (gr. 2-4). 1988. PLB 5.99 (ISBN 0-394-92038-4, BYR); pap. 1.95 (ISBN 0-394-82038-X, BYR). Random.

Pioneer Children of Appalachia. Joan Anderson. LC 86-2624. (Illus.). 48p. (gr. 2-5). 1986. 13.95 (ISBN 0-89919-440-0, Pub. by Clarion). Ticknor & Fields.

Pioneer Churchman: The Narrative & Journal of J. W. C. Dietrichson, 1844-1850. Tr. by Harris Kaasa & Malcolm Rosholt. Ed. by Clifford Nelson. 265p. 1973. 10.00 (ISBN 0-87732-053-5). Norwegian-Am Hist Assn.

Pioneer Colored Christians. facsimile ed. Harriet P. Miller. LC 73-37313. (Black Heritage Library Collection). Repr. of 1911 ed. 13.50 (ISBN 0-8369-8950-3). Ayer Co Pubs.

Pioneer Conservationists of Early America. Peter Wild. (Pioneer Conservation Ser.). (Illus.). 256p. 1988. 15.95 (ISBN 0-87842-187-4); pap. cancelled (ISBN 0-87842-188-2). Mountain Pr.

Pioneer Conservationists of Eastern America. Peter Wild. LC 87-10354. (Illus.). 304p. 1987. 14.95 (ISBN 0-87842-126-2). Mountain Pr.

Pioneer Conservationists of Western America. Peter Wild. LC 78-15042. (Illus.). 271p. 1979. 12.95 (ISBN 0-87842-107-6). Mountain Pr.

Pioneer Cooking. Kathryn S. Maxwell. (Illus.). 184p. (Orig.). 1987. pap. 4.95 (ISBN 0-940649-02-0). Parnell Pub.

Pioneer Cooking in Ontario: Tested Recipes from Ontario's Pioneer Villages & Historic Sites. 2nd ed. Illus. by C. W. Jeffreys. (Illus.). 64p. (Orig.). 1988. pap. 4.95 (ISBN 1-55021-015-7, Pub. by NC Press Ltd). U of Toronto Pr.

Pioneer Daughter. 209p. 1985. pap. 8.95 (ISBN 0-317-68253-9). Big Horn Bks.

Pioneer Days. Mary Hayden. 68p. 1980. 14.95 (ISBN 0-87770-203-9). Ye Galleon.

Pioneer Days see Syracuse University History.

Pioneer Days at Tekoa. Bertha E. Williams. (Illus.). 28p. 1986. 3.00 (ISBN 0-87770-383-3). Ye Galleon.

Pioneer Days in San Francisco. John W. Palmer. Ed. by William R. Jones. (Illus.). 24p. 1977. pap. 2.95 (ISBN 0-89646-015-0). Outbooks.

Pioneer Days in Upper Canada. Edwin C. Guillet. LC 66-37656. (Canadian University Paperbooks: 30). pap. 54.00 (ISBN 0-317-41792-4, 2055823). Bks Demand UMI.

Pioneer Days on Puget Sound. rev. ed. Arthur A. Denny. 101p. 1980. 16.95 (ISBN 0-87770-226-8). Ye Galleon.

Pioneer Decoy Carvers: A Biography of Lemuel & Stephen Ward. Barry R. Berkey et al. LC 77-13075. (Illus.). 172p. 1977. 17.50 (ISBN 0-87033-243-0). Tidewater.

Pioneer Efforts in Rural Social Welfare: Firsthand Views Since 1908. Ed. by Emilia E. Martinez-Brawley. LC 79-5142. 1980. lib. bdg. 29.50x (ISBN 0-271-00233-6); pap. text ed. 14.50x (ISBN 0-271-00245-X). Pa St U Pr.

Pioneer Evangelists of the Church of God in the Pacific Northwest. John L. Green. 164p. pap. 2.00 (ISBN 0-686-29135-2). Faith Pub Hse.

Pioneer Experience. Trudy Rodine Pederson. (Illus.). 116p. (Orig.). 1982. 10.00 (ISBN 0-686-95352-5). Directed Media.

Pioneer Experiences. Ed. by Phoebe Palmer & Donald W. Dayton. (Higher Christian Life Ser.). 368p. 1985. 45.00 (ISBN 0-8240-6433-X). Garland Pub.

Pioneer Families of Eastern & Southeastern Kentucky. William C. Kozee. LC 73-9090. 272p. 1980. Repr. of 1957 ed. 15.00 (ISBN 0-8063-0576-2). Genealog Pub.

Pioneer Flights of Garden City Estates, New York: The First U. S. Airmail Service. Robert Schoendorf. Ed. by Peter S. Lemmo. (Illus.). 75p. (Orig.). 1982. pap. 19.95 (ISBN 0-686-39388-0). A Zimmerman.

Pioneer Fringe. facsimile ed. Isaiah Bowman. LC 71-160960. (Select Bibliographies Reprint Ser.). Repr. of 1931 ed. 38.50 (ISBN 0-8369-5828-4). Ayer Co Pubs.

Pioneer Ghosts of Kentucky: Rest in Peace John Jay Dickey. rev. ed. Wilma Winton. LC 87-70773. (History & Genealogy of Kentucky Families Ser.: Vol. I). 250p. 1987. pap. price not set (ISBN 0-9618206-2-4). Pearl Bullock.

Pioneer Ghosts of Kentucky: Rest in Peace John Jay Dickey. Wilma Winton. (History & Genealogy of Kentucky Families Ser.: Vol. II). 250p. 1987. pap. price not set (ISBN 0-9618206-3-2). Pearl Bullock.

Pioneer Ghosts of Kentucky: Rest in Peace John Jay Dickey. Wilma Winton. (History & Genealogy of Kentucku Families Ser.: Vol. III). 250p. 1987. pap. price not set (ISBN 0-9618206-4-0). Pearl Bullock.

Pioneer Ghosts of Kentucky: Rest in Peace John Jay Dickey. Wilma Winton. (History & Genealogy of Kentucky Families Ser.: Vol. IV). 250p. 1987. pap. price not set (ISBN 0-9618206-5-9). Pearl Bullock.

Pioneer Ghosts of Kentucky: Rest in Peace John Jay Dickey, 5 vols. Wilma Winton. (History & Genealogy of Kentucky Families Ser.). 1987. Set, 250 pp. per volume. pap. price not set (ISBN 0-9618206-0-8). Pearl Bullock.

Pioneer, Go Home! Richard Powell. 246p. 1985. pap. 2.75 (ISBN 0-89176-008-3, 6008). Mockingbird Bks.

Pioneer Healers: History of Women Religious in U. S. Health Care. M. U. Stepsis & Delores Liptak. 376p. 1988. 24.50 (ISBN 0-8245-0894-7). Crossroad NY.

Pioneer Heritage: The First Century of the Arizona Historical Society. C. L. Sonnichsen. LC 83-17264. (Illus.). 240p. 1984. 15.00 (ISBN 0-910037-21-3). AZ Hist Soc.

Pioneer Heritage Wild Game Cookbook. Jack French. LC 86-62881. (Illus.). 416p. (Orig.). 1987. pap. 14.95. Realco Pub.

Pioneer History: Being an Account of the First Examinations of the Ohio Valley, & the Early Settlement of the Northwest Territory. S. P. Hildreth. LC 79-146400. (First American Frontier Ser). (Illus.). 1971. Repr. of 1848 ed. 29.00 (ISBN 0-405-02854-7). Ayer Co Pubs.

Pioneer History of Custer County. Solomon D. Butcher. 15.50 (ISBN 0-931068-05-3); pap. 10.00. Purcells.

Pioneer History of Greene County, Pennsylvania. L. K. Evans. 1969. Repr. of 1941 ed. 10.00 (ISBN 0-87012-043-3). McClain.

Pioneer History of the Township of Grand Blanc. Alvah Brainerd. LC 64-1263. (Local History Reprints Ser.). 73p. 1964. pap. 3.25 (ISBN 0-916699-00-5). CMU Clarke Hist Lib.

Pioneer Homesteaders in Union County New Mexico. Olive D. Slocum. 40p. 1986. 5.75 (ISBN 0-8062-2773-7). Carlton.

Pioneer Homesteaders of the Fort Rock Valley. Raymond R. Hatton. LC 82-71119. (Illus.). 1982. 9.50 (ISBN 0-8323-0407-7); pap. 6.50 (ISBN 0-8323-0404-2). Binford-Metropolitan.

Pioneer Humanists. John M. Robertson. LC 77-2881. 1977. Repr. of 1907 ed. lib. bdg. 49.00 (ISBN 0-8414-7202-5). Folcroft.

Pioneer in Madagascar, Joseph Pearse of the L. M. S. Charles F. Moss. LC 70-98738. Repr. of 1913 ed. cancelled (ISBN 0-8371-2781-5, MOP&, Pub. by Negro U Pr). Greenwood.

Pioneer in Marketing: L. D. H. Weld. an orginal anthology ed. Ed. by Henry Assael. LC 78-283. (Century of Marketing Ser.). 1978. lib. bdg. 40.00x (ISBN 0-405-11157-6). Ayer Co Pubs.

Pioneer in Modern Medicine: David Linn Edsall of Harvard. Joseph C. Aub & Ruth K. Hapgood. LC 78-145896. (Illus.). 1970. 22.50x (ISBN 0-674-66875-8). Harvard U Pr.

Pioneer in Northwest America 1841-1858, 2 vols. Ed. by Nils W. Olsson. LC 60-11209. 1960. 16.00 (ISBN 0-318-03680-0). Swedish Am.

Pioneer in the American Novel, Nineteen Hundred to Nineteen Fifty. Nicholas J. Karolides. 1967. 17.50x (ISBN 0-8061-0745-6). U of Okla Pr.

Pioneer in the U. S. Air Corps. George H. Beverley. (Illus.). 70p. (Orig.). 1982. pap. text ed. 9.95x (ISBN 0-89745-029-9). Sunflower U Pr.

Pioneer Irish in New England. Michael J. O'Brien. 325p. 1988. pap. 18.00 (ISBN 1-55613-106-2). Heritage Bk.

Pioneer Jesuits in Northern Mexico. Peter M. Dunner. LC 78-10566. (Illus.). 1979. Repr. of 1944 ed. lib. bdg. 35.00x (ISBN 0-313-20653-8, DUPJ). Greenwood.

Pioneer Jewish Texans: Their Contributions to Texas & American History for 400 Years, 1590-1990. Natalie Ornish. (Illus.). 320p. 1988. 29.95 (ISBN 0-9620755-0-7). TX Heritage Pr.

Pioneer Jews: A New Life in the Far West. Harriet Rechlin & Fred Rechlin. (Illus.). 256p. pap. 12.95 (ISBN 0-395-42639-1). HM.

Pioneer Jews: A New Life in the Far West. Harriet Rochlin. LC 83-12647. (Illus.). 1984. 17.95 (ISBN 0-395-31832-7). HM.

Pioneer Jews of the California Mother Lode: 1849 to 1880. Compiled by Sara G. Cogan. (Western Jewish Americana Ser.: No. 1). 1968. 7.50 (ISBN 0-943376-01-7). Magnes Mus.

Pioneer Lady's Country Kitchen: A Seasonal Treasury of Time-Honored American Recipes. Jane W. Hopping. 1988. 18.95 (ISBN 0-394-57197-5, Villard Bks). Random.

Pioneer Leaders & Early Institutions in Louisiana Education. Rodney Cline. 1969. 12.50 (ISBN 0-87511-018-5). Claitors.

Pioneer Letters: The Letter As Literature. Ed. by John Witte. LC 81-1903. (Illus.). 1981. pap. 6.95 (ISBN 0-918402-05-0). NW Review Bks.

Pioneer Life in Southeast Florida. Charles W. Pierce. Ed. by Donald W. Curl. LC 70-122290. 1981. 12.95 (ISBN 0-87024-304-7). U of Miami Pr.

Pioneer Life in Western Pennsylvania. J. E. Wright & Doris S. Corbett. LC 40-10730. (Illus.). 1968. pap. 8.95 (ISBN 0-8229-6044-3). U of Pittsburgh Pr.

Pioneer Life or Thirty Years a Hunter: Being Scenes & Adventures in the Life of Philip Tome. Philip Tome. LC 78-146424. (First American Frontier Ser). (Illus.). 1971. Repr. of 1854 ed. 20.00 (ISBN 0-405-02893-8). Ayer Co Pubs.

Pioneer Lutheran Ministry - L.P. Esbjorn & His Family in Andover Illinois. Lilly Setterdahl. LC 86-80107. (Augustana College Library Occasional Paper: No. 15). 1986. pap. 4.00x (ISBN 0-910182-42-6). Augustana Coll.

Pioneer Merchant in Mid-America. Lewis E. Atherton. LC 75-77700. (American Scene Ser). 1969. Repr. of 1939 ed. 24.50 (ISBN 0-306-71338-1). Da Capo.

Pioneer Merchant of St. Louis, 1810-1820. Sr. Marietta Jennings. LC 68-58594. (Columbia University. Studies in the Social Sciences: No. 462). Repr. of 1939 ed. 18.50 (ISBN 0-404-51462-6). AMS Pr.

Pioneer Merchants: The Letters of James Graham, 1839-54. Sally Graham. 240p. 1986. 25.00 (ISBN 0-908090-85-4, Pub. by Hyland Australia). Intl Spec Bk.

Pioneer Michigan City & Pictorial History. Edna P. Kitchell & Gwalter Calvert. (Illus.). 16p. 1969. 1.50 (ISBN 0-935549-00-5). MI City Hist.

Pioneer Miner & the Pack Mule Express. Ernest A. Wiltsee. LC 76-4134. (Illus.). 160p. 1976. Repr. 40.00x (ISBN 0-88000-084-8). Quarterman.

Pioneer Missionary to the Bering Strait Eskimos: Bellarmine Lafortune, S. J. Louis L. Renner. LC 79-53362. (Illus.). 1979. 12.50 (ISBN 0-8323-0343-7). Binford-Metropolitan.

Pioneer Mother. Hamlin Garland. (Collected Works of Hamlin Garland). 1988. Repr. of 1922 ed. lib. bdg. 59.00x. Am Biog Serv.

Pioneer Mother see Collected Works.

Pioneer Mothers of the West; or, Daring & Heroic Deeds of American Women, Comprising Thrilling Examples of Courage, Fortitude, Devotedness & Self-Sacrifice. John Frost. LC 74-3950. (Women in America Ser). (Illus.). 360p. 1974. Repr. of 1869 ed. 26.00x (ISBN 0-405-06097-1). Ayer Co Pubs.

Pioneer Museum Book. 5.00 (ISBN 0-318-01715-6). Daughters Utah.

Pioneer of Sociology: The Life & Letters of Patrick Geddes. Philippe Mairet. LC 78-20482. 1980. Repr. of 1957 ed. 23.00 (ISBN 0-88355-859-9). Hyperion Conn.

Pioneer Ohio Newspapers: Genealogical & Historical Abstracts, 1802-1818, 2 vols, Vol. 2. Karen M. Green. 362p. 1988. lib. bdg. 27.00 (ISBN 0-932231-04-7). Frontier Pr.

Pioneer Ohio Newspapers, 1793-1810: Genealogical & Historical Abstracts, 2 vols. Karen M. Green. 1986. Set. lib. bdg. 50.00 (ISBN 0-932231-05-5); Vol. 1, 384 pgs. lib. bdg. 27.00 (ISBN 0-932231-03-9). Frontier Pr.

Pioneer: Or, Leaves from an Editor's Portfolio. Henry Clapp. 1969. Repr. of 1846 ed. 19.00 (ISBN 0-384-09195-4). Johnson Repr.

Pioneer Painters of Indiana. Wilbur D. Peat. (Illus.). 253p. 1954. 40.00 (ISBN 0-317-29200-5). Ind Mus Art.

Pioneer Parade: A Collection of Newspapers & Magazine Articles on Eastern Laramie County Wyoming History, Vol. II. Martha Thompson. 200p. (Orig.). 1986. pap. text ed. 25.00 (ISBN 0-9616768-0-9). Deercreek Pubs.

Pioneer Pentecostal Women. Mary H. Wallace. (Pioneer Pentecostal Women Ser.: Vol. 1). (Illus.). 272p. (Orig.). 1983. pap. 5.95 (ISBN 0-912315-18-0). Word Aflame.

Pioneer Pentecostal Women. Mary H. Wallace. LC 85-20981. (Pioneer Pentecostal Women: Vol. II). (Illus.). 288p. (Orig.). 1981. pap. 5.95 (ISBN 0-912315-19-9). Word Aflame.

Pioneer Photographers of Brazil. Gilberto Ferrez & Weston J. Naef. (Illus.). 144p. 1976. 12.50 (ISBN 0-89192-160-5, Pub. by Ctr Inter-Am Rel). Interbk Inc.

Pioneer Photographs of Brazil, Eighteen Forty to Nineteen Twenty. Gilberto Ferrez & Weston J. Naef. LC 76-25710. (Center for Inter-American Relations &The American Federation of Arts). (Illus.). 144p. 1980. 16.95 (ISBN 0-295-95737-9). U of Wash Pr.

Pioneer Plastic: The Making & Selling of Celluloid. Robert Friedel. LC 81-69818. (Illus.). 192p. 1983. 22.50x (ISBN 0-299-09170-8). U of Wis Pr.

Pioneer Policewomen. Mary S. Allen. Ed. by Julie H. Heyneman. LC 71-156001. Repr. of 1925 ed. 23.50 (ISBN 0-404-09100-8). AMS Pr.

Pioneer Preacher in Idaho. James A. Hedges. 87p. 1981. 9.95 (ISBN 0-87770-249-7). Ye Galleon.

Pioneer Primer. Jan P. Pierce. 80p. Date not set. pap. text ed. 2.50 (ISBN 0-932050-31-X). New Puritan.

Pioneer Publisher: The Life & Times of J. F. Harms. Orlando Harms. LC 84-82050. 116p. (Orig.). 1984. pap. 5.95 (ISBN 0-919797-33-4). Kindred Pr.

Pioneer Reminiscences of Jefferson County. Thomas J. Russell. Ed. by Bertie H. Boodry. LC 86-62792. 160p. 1987. 28.00x (ISBN 0-318-22096-2); pap. 20.00 (ISBN 0-318-22097-0). SE Tex G&H.

Pioneer Reminiscenses of Puget Sound. Ezra Meeker. (Northwest Historical Classics Ser.). (Illus.). 199p. 1980. pap. 9.95 (ISBN 0-939806-01-0). Hist Soc Seattle.

Pioneer Roads: Pt. 1 see Historic Highways of America.

Pioneer Roads: Pt. 2 see Historic Highways of America.

Pioneer Saddle Mystery. Dorothy K. French. LC 75-12428. 192p. (gr. 5-10). 1975. PLB 6.19 (ISBN 0-8313-0113-9). Lantern.

Pioneer Settlement. facsimile ed. American Geographical Society of New York Staff. LC 74-90599. (Essay Index Reprint Ser). 1932. 31.00 (ISBN 0-8369-1241-1). Ayer Co Pubs.

Pioneer Settlement in Northeast Argentina. Robert C. Eidt. LC 71-138058. (Illus.). 294p. 1971. 30.00x (ISBN 0-299-05920-0). U of Wis Pr.

Pioneer Settlement in the Asiatic Tropics: Studies in Land Utilization & Agricultural Colonization in Southeastern Asia. Karl J. Pelzer. LC 83-1484. (American Geographical Society Ser.-Special publication). (Illus.). xviii, 288p. 1983. Repr. of 1945 ed. lib. bdg. 41.50x (ISBN 0-313-23853-7, PEPI). Greenwood.

Pioneer Settlement in the Twenties: An Original Anthology. Ed. by Moshe Davis. LC 77-70699. (America & the Holy Land Ser.). 1977. lib. bdg. 20.00x (ISBN 0-405-10250-X). Ayer Co Pubs.

Pioneer Settlers of Grayson County, Virginia. Benjamin F. Nuckolls. LC 74-18309. 219p. 1982. Repr. of 1914 ed. 17.50 (ISBN 0-8063-0640-8). Genealog Pub.

Pioneer Spirit. Lyle A. White. LC 86-82704. (Illus.). 208p. 1987. 29.95 (ISBN 0-932845-22-3). Lowell Pr.

Pioneer Spirit: A Prairie Portrait. Lyle A. White. LC 86-82704. (Illus.). 208p. 1987. 29.95 (ISBN 0-9617622-0-9). Walter Pubns.

Pioneer Stage of Railroad Electrification. Carl W. Condit. LC 77-76428. (Transactions Ser.: Vol. 67, Pt. 7). 1977. pap. 10.00 (ISBN 0-87169-677-0). Am Philos.

Pioneer Stories of Linn County, Oregon, Vol. 1. 115p. write for info. (ISBN 0-939509-34-2); pap. 12.00 (ISBN 0-317-58904-0). L Benton Geneal.

Pioneer Stories of Linn County, Oregon, Vol. 2. 115p. write for info. (ISBN 0-939509-35-0); pap. 12.00 (ISBN 0-317-58906-7). L Benton Geneal.

Pioneer Stories of Linn County, Oregon, Vol. 3. 115p. write for info. (ISBN 0-939509-36-9); pap. 12.00 (ISBN 0-317-58912-1). L Benton Geneal.

Pioneer Stories of Linn County, Oregon Series. Set. write for info. (ISBN 0-939509-33-4); pap. write for info. L Benton Geneal.

Pioneer Ststurn. (Illus.). 308p. 1980. Repr. 12.00 (ISBN 0-317-66488-3). Am Geophysical.

Pioneer Swedish Settlements & Swedish Lutheran Churches in America 1845-1860. Eric Norelius. Tr. by Conrad Bergendoff from Swedish. LC 84-71391. (Publication Ser.: No. 31). Orig. Title: De Svenska Luterska Forsamlingarnas och Svenska Historia i Amerika. 419p. 1984. 15.00 (ISBN 0-910184-31-3). Augustana.

Pioneer Telegraphy in Chile, 1852-1876. John J. Johnson. LC 68-54275. (Stanford University. Stanford Studies in History, Economics & Political Science: Vol. 6 No. 1). Repr. of 1948 ed. 19.50 (ISBN 0-404-50971-1). AMS Pr.

Pioneer to the Past: The Story of James Henry Breasted, Archaeologist. Charles Breasted. 1977. pap. 5.95x (ISBN 0-226-07186-3, P710, Phoen). U of Chicago Pr.

Pioneer Trails of the Oregon Coast. 2nd ed. Samuel N. Dicken. LC 70-176249. (Illus.). 78p. 1978. pap. 4.95 (ISBN 0-87595-030-2). Oregon Hist.

Pioneer Trails West: Great Stories of the Westering Americans & the Trails They Followed. Western Writers of America Staff. Ed. by Donald Worcester. LC 84-15592. (Illus.). 283p. 1985. 24.95 (ISBN 0-87004-304-8). Caxton.

Pioneer Travel. Edwin C. Guillet. LC 66-4464. (Illus.). 1966. pap. 8.95 (ISBN 0-8020-6052-8). U of Toronto Pr.

Pioneer Twins. Lucy F. Perkins. 16.95 (ISBN 0-89190-472-7, Pub. by Am Repr). Amereon Ltd.

Pioneer Woman. Pat Enders. 1979. 6.25 (ISBN 0-941490-13-0). Solo Pr.

Pioneer Women. Joanna Stratton. 1982. pap. 10.95 (ISBN 0-671-44748-3, Touchstone Bks). S&S.

Pioneer Women of the West. Elizabeth F. Ellet. LC 72-13219. (Essay Index Reprint Ser.). Repr. of 1852 ed. 22.50 (ISBN 0-8369-8157-X). Ayer Co Pubs.

Pioneer Women of the West. Elizabeth F. Ellet. 1979. Repr. of 1879 ed. lib. bdg. 45.00 (ISBN 0-89341-325-9). Longwood Pub Group.

Pioneer Youth in Palestine. Shlomo Bardin. LC 75-6420. (Rise of Jewish Nationalism & the Middle East Ser.). 182p. 1976. Repr. of 1932 ed. 18.70 (ISBN 0-88355-308-2). Hyperion Conn.

Pioneering a Modern Small Business: Wakefield Seafoods & the Alaskan Frontier. Mansel G. Blackford. Ed. by Glenn Porter. LC 77-7794. (Industrial Development & the Social Fabric Ser.: Vol. 6). 222p. 1979. 52.50 (ISBN 0-89232-088-5). Jai Pr.

Pioneering Adventures of Johan Edvard Lilljeholm in America, 1846-1850. Tr. by Arthur Wald. (Augustana Historical Society Ser.: Vol. 19). xii, 53p. 1962. pap. 3.00 (ISBN 0-910184-19-4). Augustana.

Pioneering Economic Theory, 1630-1980: A Mathematical Restatement. Hans Brems. LC 85-19819. 432p. 1986. text ed. 47.50x (ISBN 0-8018-2667-5). Johns Hopkins.

Pioneering for Peace: A Study of American Peace Efforts to 1846. W. Freeman Galpin. LC 73-143429. (Peace Movement in America Ser). x, 237p. 1972. Repr. of 1933 ed. lib. bdg. 18.95x (ISBN 0-89198-069-5). Ozer.

Pioneering in Delinquency Prevention: The California Experience. Barry Krisberg et al. 1978. 7.50 (ISBN 0-318-02057-2). Natl Coun Crime.

Pioneering in Education Requires Pioneering in Community. Community Service Editors. 1973. pap. 1.50 (ISBN 0-910420-15-7). Comm Serv OH.

Pioneering in Montana: The Making of a State 1864-1887. Granville Stuart. Ed. by Paul C. Phillips. LC 77-7651. Orig. Title: Forty Years on the Frontier. (Illus.). 265p. 1977. 21.50x (ISBN 0-8032-0933-9); pap. 7.95 (ISBN 0-8032-5870-4, BB 648, Bison). U of Nebr Pr.

Pioneering in Oregon's Coast Range: Surviving the Depression Years. Ione Reed. (Illus.). 140p. (Orig.). 1983. pap. 7.95 (ISBN 0-934784-31-0). Calapooia Pubns.

Pioneering in South Brazil: Three Years of Forest & Prairie Life in the Province of Parana, 2 vols. Thomas P. Bigg-Wither. LC 68-55177. (Illus.). 1971. Repr. of 1878 ed. Vol. 1. lib. bdg. 15.75 (ISBN 0-8371-0313-4, BISC); Vol. 2. lib. bdg. 15.75 (ISBN 0-8371-0783-0, BISD). Greenwood.

Pioneering in Steel Research. E C. Bain. 1975. 8.00 (ISBN 0-686-95117-4). ASM.

Pioneering MBP. (Illus.). 48p. (gr. 6-12). 1967. pap. 1.25x (ISBN 0-8395-3382-9, 3382). BSA.

Pioneering New Products. Edwin E. Bobrow & Dennis W. Shafer. 225p. 1986. 29.95 (ISBN 0-87094-621-8). Dow Jones-Irwin.

Pioneering on Social Frontiers. Graham Taylor. LC 75-17246. (Social Problems & Social Policy Ser.). 1976. Repr. of 1930 ed. 35.50x (ISBN 0-405-07517-0). Ayer Co Pubs.

Pioneering on the Congo, 2 Vols. W. Holman Bently. (Landmarks in Anthropology Ser). 1970. Repr. of 1900 ed. Set. lib. bdg. 85.00 (ISBN 0-384-03943-X). Johnson Repr.

Pioneering on the Plains. Edith McCall. LC 62-15638. (Frontiers of America Ser.). (Illus.). 128p. (gr. 3-10). 1980. PLB 11.93 (ISBN 0-516-03358-1). Childrens.

Pioneering Research in Surgical Shock & Cardiovascular Surgery: Vivien Thomas & His Work with Alfred Blalock. Vivien T. Thomas. (Illus.). 304p. 1985. 34.95 (ISBN 0-8122-7989-1). U of Pa Pr.

Pioneering Salvationists. John D. Waldron. 170p. (Orig.). 1987. pap. 5.50 (ISBN 0-89216-074-8). Salvation Army.

Pioneering Space: Living on the Next Frontier. James E. Oberg & Alcestis R. Oberg. 352p. 1987. pap. text ed. 4.95 (ISBN 0-07-048039-7). McGraw.

Pioneering Space: Living on the Next Threshold. James E. Oberg & Alcestis R. Oberg. (Illus.). 352p. 1986. text ed. 16.95 (ISBN 0-07-048034-6). McGraw.

Pioneering the Space Frontier: The Report of the National Commission on Space. 1986. pap. 14.95 (ISBN 0-553-34314-9). Bantam.

Pioneering with Taconite. Edward W. Davis. LC 64-64494. (Illus.). 246p. 1964. 8.50 (ISBN 0-87351-023-2). Minn Hist.

Pioneers. John Artman. (Illus.). 64p. (gr. 4-8). 1987. pap. 6.95 (ISBN 0-86653-401-6). Good Apple.

Pioneers. James Fenimore Cooper. (Airmont Classics Ser.). (gr. 8 up). 1964. pap. 1.95 (ISBN 0-8049-0049-3, CL-49). Airmont.

Pioneers. James Fenimore Cooper. 1976. lib. bdg. 18.95x (ISBN 0-89968-157-3). Lightyear.

Pioneers. James Fenimore Cooper. 448p. (YA) (RL 10). pap. 3.95 (ISBN 0-451-52145-5, Sig Classics). NAL.

Pioneers. James Fenimore Cooper. Ed. by James F. Beard. LC 77-21795. (Writings of James Fenimore Cooper Ser.). 565p. 1980. 49.50 (ISBN 0-87395-359-2); pap. 18.95 (ISBN 0-87395-423-8). State U NY Pr.

Pioneers. James Fenimore Cooper. 493p. 1984. Repr. lib. bdg. 19.95 (ISBN 0-89966-492-X). Buccaneer Bks.

Pioneers. James Fenimore Cooper. 448p. 1988. pap. 4.95 (ISBN 0-14-039007-3). Penguin.

Pioneers. Dennis Fradin. LC 84-9418. (New True Bks.). (Illus.). 48p. (gr. k-4). 1984. lib. bdg. 12.60 (ISBN 0-516-01927-9); pap. 3.95 (ISBN 0-516-41927-7). Childrens.

Pioneers. Marie Gorsline & Douglas Gorsline. LC 78-54960. (Picturebacks Ser.). (Illus.). 32p. (ps-3). 1982. lib. bdg. 5.99 (ISBN 0-394-93905-0); pap. 1.95 saddle stitched (ISBN 0-394-83905-6). Random.

Pioneers. Huston Horn. LC 73-94242. (Old West Ser.). (Illus.). (gr. 7 up). 1974. 19.94 (ISBN 0-8094-1477-5, Pub. by Time-Life). Silver.

Pioneers. Huston Horn. (Old West Ser.). (Illus.). 1974. 14.95 (ISBN 0-8094-1475-9). Time-Life.

Pioneers. L. Matthews. (Wild West in American History Ser.). (Illus.). 32p. (gr. 3-8). Date not set. PLB 15.93 (ISBN 0-86625-362-9). Rourke Corp.

Pioneers. Francene Sabin. LC 84-2580. (Illus.). 32p. (gr. 3-6). 1985. PLB 8.45 (ISBN 0-8167-0120-2); pap. text ed. 1.95 (ISBN 0-8167-0121-0). Troll Assocs.

Pioneers see Leatherstocking Tales.

Pioneers Along the Manatawny. W. Edmunds Claussen. (Illus.). 52p. (Orig.). 1968. pap. text ed. 2.50 (ISBN 0-9616068-4-3). Boyertown Hist.

Pioneers & Caretakers: A Study of Nine American Women Novelists. Louis Auchincloss. LC 65-17016. pap. 52.00 (2056197). Bks Demand UMI.

Pioneers & Explorers in North America: Summaries of Biographical Articles in History Journals. Pamela R. Byrne & Susan K. Kinnell. (People in History Ser.). 132p. (YA) (gr. 9-12). 1988. pap. text ed. 18.00 (ISBN 0-87436-540-6). ABC Clio.

Pioneers & Peers (ESC 1988, Orlando) Date not set. 28.00 (ISBN 0-911801-37-5). Soc Computer Sim.

Pioneers & Preachers: Stories of the Old Frontier. Robert W. Mondy. LC 79-16906. (Illus.). 272p. 1980. 29.95x (ISBN 0-88229-619-1). Nelson-Hall.

Pioneers East: The Early American Experience in the Middle East. David H. Finnie. LC 67-20875. (Middle Eastern Studies: No. 13). (Illus.). 1967. 24.50x (ISBN 0-674-66900-2). Harvard U Pr.

Pioneers, Eighteen Twenty-Five to Nineteen Hundred: The Early British Tea & Coffee Planters & Their Way of Life. John Weatherstone. (Illus.). 224p. 1987. 40.00 (ISBN 0-907621-68-6). Salem Hse Pubs.

Pioneers for Peace. Gertrude Bussey & Margaret Tims. 255p. 2.00 (ISBN 0-686-30387-3, Co-Pub. by Addams Peace). WILPF.

Pioneers for Profit: Foreign Entrepreneurship & Russian Industrialization, 1885-1913. John P. McKay. LC 79-103932. 1970. 30.00x (ISBN 0-226-55990-4). U of Chicago Pr.

Pioneers Go West. George R. Stewart. LC 87-4568. (Landmark Bks.). 160p. (gr. 5-9). 1964. lib. bdg. 8.99 (ISBN 0-394-90342-0, BYR); pap. 2.95 (ISBN 0-394-89180-5, BYR). Random.

Pioneers in a Frontier Land: The Strabane Knoxes & Other Families. Daryl K. Knox. LC 78-108863. 165p. 1978. 11.00 (ISBN 0-9605790-0-1). D Knox.

Pioneers in Adult Education. Willis D. Moreland & Erwin H. Goldenstein. (Illus.). 280p. 1985. 23.95x (ISBN 0-8304-1082-1). Nelson-Hall.

Pioneers in American Anthropology: The Bandelier-Morgan Letters, 1873-1883, 2 vols. Adolf F. Bandelier. Ed. by Leslie A. White. LC 74-7921. Repr. of 1940 ed. Set. 49.50 (ISBN 0-404-11806-2). AMS Pr.

Pioneers in Angiography. 2nd ed. Ed. by J. A. Veiga-Pires & Ronald G. Grainger. 1987. lib. bdg. 38.75 (ISBN 0-85200-828-7, Pub. by MTP Pr England). Kluwer Academic.

Pioneers in Angiography: The Portugese School of Angiography. Ed. by J. A. Veiga-Pires & Ronald G. Grainger. (Illus.). 131p. 1981. text ed. 24.95 (ISBN 0-85200-448-6, Pub. by MTP Pr England). Kluwer Academic.

Pioneers in Development. Ed. by Gerald M. Meier & Dudley Seers. 372p. 1985. pap. 12.95x (ISBN 0-19-520479-4). Oxford U Pr.

Pioneers in Development: Second Series. Ed. by Gerald M. Meier. LC 86-23511. (World Bank Paper). 256p. 1987. 29.95x (ISBN 0-19-520542-1). Oxford U Pr.

Pioneers in Marketing. John S. Wright & Parks B. Dimsdale. LC 73-620235. 1974. pap. 12.95 (ISBN 0-88406-016-0). Ga St U Busn Pub.

Pioneers in Modern Factory Management: An Original Anthology. Ed. by Alfred Chandler. LC 79-7526. (History of Management Thought & Practice Ser.). 1980. lib. bdg. 19.00x (ISBN 0-405-12310-8). Ayer Co Pubs.

Pioneers in Music. David Ewen. LC 72-6816. (Essay Index Reprint Ser.). 1972. Repr. of 1940 ed. 27.50 (ISBN 0-8369-7262-7). Ayer Co Pubs.

Pioneers in Nation-Building in a Caribbean Mini-State. Rupert John. (Regional Studies Ser.: No. 8). pap. 12.00 (UN7915RS8, UN). UNIPUB.

Pioneers in Nation-Building in the Caribbean Mini-State. Date not set. 12.00 (ISBN 92-1-157064-6, E.79.XV.RS/8). UN.

Pioneers in Palestine. Hannah Trager. LC 75-6440. (Rise of Jewish Nationalism in the Middle East Ser.). xx, 208p. 1975. Repr. of 1923 ed. 21.50 (ISBN 0-88355-345-7). Hyperion Conn.

Pioneers in Policing. Ed. by Philip J. Stead. LC 75-14556. (Ser. in Criminology, Law Enforcement & Social Problems: No. 213). (Illus.). 1978. 22.00x (ISBN 0-87585-213-0). Patterson Smith.

Pioneers in Protest. Lerone Bennett, Jr. 1968. 5.95 (ISBN 0-87485-026-6). Johnson Chi.

Pioneers In Psychology. Raymond E. Fancher. (Illus.). 1979. pap. text ed. 9.95x (ISBN 0-393-09082-5). Norton.

Pioneers in Radiology. Ed. by J. A. Veiga-Pires & Ronald G. Grainger. 1982. text ed. 19.50 (ISBN 0-686-37440-1, Pub. by MTP Pr England). Kluwer Academic.

Pioneers in the Arab World. Dorothy Van Ess. 1974. pap. 4.95 (ISBN 0-8028-1585-5). Eerdmans.

Pioneers in the Tropics. Philip Staniford. (London School of Economics Monographs on Social Anthropology Ser: No. 45). (Illus.). 210p. 1973. text ed. 36.50x (Athlone Pr). Humanities.

Pioneers in the Tropics: The Political Organization of Japanese in an Immigrant Community in Brazil. Philip Staniford. (London School of Economics Monographs on Social Anthropology: No. 45). (Illus.). 201p. 1973. 36.50 (ISBN 0-485-19545-3, Pub. by Athlone Pr UK). Humanities.

Pioneers in World Order. facs. ed. Ed. by Harriet E. Davis. LC 70-128232. (Essay Index Reprint Ser). 1944. 19.00 (ISBN 0-8369-1913-0). Ayer Co Pubs.

Pioneers: Notes from the Diaries of Judge Benjamin Hayes, 1849-1875. Benjamin Hayes. Ed. by Carlos E. Cortes. LC 76-1274. (Chicano Heritage Ser.). (Illus.). Repr. of 1929 ed. lib. bdg. 25.50x (ISBN 0-405-09506-6). Ayer Co Pubs.

Pioneers: Novels of the American Frontier. Ed. by Reader's Digest Editors. LC 85-23236. (Illus.). 640p. 1988. 19.95 (ISBN 0-89577-229-9). RD Assn.

Pioneers of a Peaceable Kingdom: The Quaker Peace Testimony from the Colonial Era to the First World War. Peter Brock. 1970. pap. 13.95x (ISBN 0-691-00573-7). Princeton U Pr.

Pioneers of American Anthropology: The Uses of Biography. Ed. by June Helm. LC 84-45536. (American Ethnological Society Monographs: No. 43). 1988. Repr. of 1966 ed. 32.50 (ISBN 0-404-62941-5). AMS Pr.

Pioneers of American Freedom. Rudolf Rocker. 69.95 (ISBN 0-87700-077-8). Revisionist Pr.

Pioneers of Anglo-Irish Fiction 1800-1850. Barry Sloan. LC 86-17438. 378p. 1986. 26.50x (ISBN 0-389-20662-8). B&N Imports.

Pioneers of CAD in Architecture. Alfred M. Kemper. (Illus.). 654p. 1985. 78.00 (ISBN 0-9614667-0-7); pap. 49.95 (ISBN 0-9614667-1-5). Hurland-Swenson.

Pioneers of Catholic Europe. Frederick J. Cowie. LC 84-62160. 190p. 1985. pap. 3.45 (ISBN 0-87973-713-1, 713). Our Sunday Visitor.

Pioneers of Christian Thought. facs. ed. Frederick D. Kershner. LC 68-57327. (Essay Index Reprint Ser). 1930. 20.00 (ISBN 0-8369-0594-6). Ayer Co Pubs.

Pioneers of Crawford County, Pennsylvania, 1788-1800. Ed. by Robert D. Ilisevich. vi, 47p. (Orig.). 1985. pap. 8.00 (ISBN 0-917890-67-1). Heritage Bk.

Pioneers of Criminology. 2nd, enl. ed. Hermann Mannheim. LC 78-108238. (Criminology, Law Enforcement, & Social Problems Ser.: No. 121). 1972. 24.00x (ISBN 0-87585-121-5); pap. 12.00x (ISBN 0-87585-902-X). Patterson Smith.

Pioneers of Davidson County, Tennessee. Edythe R. Whitley. LC 79-50041. 84p. 1981. pap. 6.00 (ISBN 0-8063-0840-0). Genealog Pub.

Pioneers of Education in Western Australia. Ed. by Laadan Fletcher. (Illus.). 360p. 1983. 52.50x (ISBN 0-85564-220-3, Pub. by U of W Austral Pr); pap. 24.95 (ISBN 0-85564-222-X). Intl Spec Bk.

Pioneers of Electrical Communication. facs. ed. Rollo Appleyard. LC 68-54322. (Essay Index Reprint Ser). 1930. 24.50 (ISBN 0-8369-0156-8). Ayer Co Pubs.

Pioneers of English Learning. Thomas Allison. 1978. lib. bdg. 27.50 (ISBN 0-8495-0104-0). Arden Lib.

Pioneers of English Learning. Thomas Allison. LC 74-22133. 1974. Repr. of 1932 ed. lib. bdg. 20.00 (ISBN 0-8414-3004-7). Folcroft.

Pioneers of Evolution: From Thales to Huxley; with an Intermediate Chapter on the Causes of Arrest of the Movement. facsimile ed. Edward Clodd. LC 74-37470. (Essay Index Reprint Ser). Repr. of 1897 ed. 19.00 (ISBN 0-8369-2540-8). Ayer Co Pubs.

Pioneers of Excellence: The History of the Chilton Corporation. William Simon. 1986. write for info. (ISBN 0-9616037-0-4). Chilton Corp.

Pioneers of Forest & City. Harry Stapler. LC 85-62817. (Illus.). 227p. (gr. 4-8). 1985. 12.00 (ISBN 0-935719-00-8). MI Dept Hist.

Pioneers of France in the New World. Francis Parkman. 493p. 1970. Repr. of 1865 ed. 22.50 (ISBN 0-87928-017-4). Corner Hse.

Pioneers of France in the New World; Jesuits in North America in the Seventeenth Century; La Salle & the Discovery of the Great West; Old Regime in Canada see France & England in North America.

Pioneers of Freedom. facs. ed. McAlister Coleman. LC 68-20292. (Essay Index Reprint Ser). 1968. Repr. of 1929 ed. 17.00 (ISBN 0-8369-0326-9). Ayer Co Pubs.

Pioneers of Freedom & Social Change in India. Brijendra Sankhder. 1986. 18.00 (ISBN 0-8364-1905-7, Pub. by Deep). South Asia Bks.

Pioneers of Land Reform. Thomas Spence et al. 34.95 (ISBN 0-8490-0838-7). Gordon Pr.

Pioneers of Maine & New Hampshire. Charles H. Pope. 252p. 1985. pap. text ed. 5.50 (ISBN 0-935207-19-8). DanBury Hse Bks.

Pioneers of Massachusetts. Charles H. Pope. 551p. 1985. pap. 15.00 (ISBN 0-935207-36-8). DanBury Hse Bks.

Pioneers of Modern Design. Nikolaus Pevsner. 1986. pap. 7.95 (ISBN 0-14-055211-1). Penguin.

Pioneers of Modern Economics in Britain. Ed. by D. P. O'Brien & John R. Presley. LC 79-55496. (Illus.). 292p. 1981. text ed. 28.50x (ISBN 0-389-20181-2). B&N Imports.

Pioneers of Modern Typography. Herbert Spencer. (Illus.). 160p. 1983. pap. 16.50 (ISBN 0-262-69081-0). MIT Pr.

Pioneers of New France in New England. James P. Baxter. 450p. 1980. Repr. of 1894 ed. 25.00 (ISBN 0-917890-20-5). Heritage Bk.

Pioneers of Old Monocacy: The Early Settlement of Frederick County, Maryland, 1721-1743. Grace L. Tracey & John P. Dern. LC 86-83226. (Illus.). 1987. 37.50 (ISBN 0-8063-1183-5). Monocacy.

Pioneers of Peace Research. William Eckhardt. 1983. 25.00 (ISBN 0-933061-08-0). Lentz Peace Res.

Pioneers of Plant Study. facs. ed. Ellison Hawks & George S. Boulger. LC 75-86759. (Essay Index Reprint Ser). 1928. 19.00 (ISBN 0-8369-1139-3). Ayer Co Pubs.

Pioneers of Popular Education: 1760-1850. Hugh M. Pollard. LC 73-20922. 297p. 1974. Repr. of 1956 ed. lib. bdg. 35.00x (ISBN 0-8371-5871-0, POPP). Greenwood.

Pioneers of Prefabrication: The British Contribution in the Nineteenth Century. Gilbert Herbert. LC 76-47372. (Studies in Nineteenth-Century Architecture). (Illus.). 1978. text ed. 27.50x (ISBN 0-8018-1852-4). Johns Hopkins.

Pioneers of Prehistory: Leaders & Landmarks in English Archaeology, 1500-1900. 1985. 32.00x (ISBN 0-317-54390-3, Pub. by Hesketh UK). State Mutual Bk.

Pioneers of Psychology. 2nd ed. Raymond E. Fancher. (Illus.). 1989. pap. price not set (ISBN 0-393-95648-2). Norton.

Pioneers of Public Health: The Story of Some Benefactors of the Human Race. facs. ed. M. E. Walker. LC 68-26483. (Essay Index Reprint Ser). 1930. 20.00 (ISBN 0-8369-0965-8). Ayer Co Pubs.

Pioneers of Quarry Hill. Maurice L. Patterson. (Illus.). 280p. 1984. 19.75 (ISBN 0-932334-40-7); pap. 16.00 (ISBN 0-932334-42-3). Heart of the Lakes.

Pioneers of Reform: Corbett, Owen, Place, Shaftesbury, Cobden, Bright. Dorothy C. Johnson. LC 68-56796. (Research & Source Works Ser.: No. 289). (Illus.). 1968. Repr. of 1929 ed. 14.50 (ISBN 0-8337-1853-3). B Franklin.

Pioneers of Religious Education. facs. ed. Tom F. Kinlock. LC 69-18929. (Essay Index Reprint Ser). 1939. 14.00 (ISBN 0-8369-0045-6). Ayer Co Pubs.

Pioneers of Rocketry. Michael Stoiko. 13.95 (ISBN 0-89190-722-X, Pub. by Am Repr). Amereon Ltd.

Pioneers of Science. facs. ed. Amelia D. Defries. LC 74-117782. (Essay Index Reprint Ser). 1928. 17.00 (ISBN 0-8369-1646-8). Ayer Co Pubs.

Pioneers of Science in America: Sketches of Their Lives & Scientific Work. rev. ed. Ed. by William J. Youmans & Keir B. Sterling. LC 77-83845. (Biologists & Their World Ser.). (Illus.). 1978. Repr. of 1896 ed. lib. bdg. 46.50x (ISBN 0-405-10743-9). Ayer Co Pubs.

Pioneers of Science: Nobel Prize Winners in Physics. Robert L. Weber. Ed. by J. M. Lenihan. 285p. 1980. 33.00x (ISBN 0-85498-036-9, Pub. by A Hilger UK). Taylor & Francis.

Pioneers of Soviet Architecture. S. O. Khan-Magomedov. LC 87-26150. (Illus.). 618p. 1987. 75.00 (ISBN 0-8478-0744-4). Rizzoli Intl.

Pioneers of the British Film. John Barnes. 1988. 90.00x (ISBN 1-85219-012-4, Pub. by Bishopgate Pr Ltd). State Mutual Bk.

Pioneers of the Columbia. Greenwood Park Grange Staff et al. (Illus.). 114p. 1987. pap. 9.95 (ISBN 0-940151-02-2). Statesman Exam.

Pioneers of the French Revolution. Marius Roustan. LC 68-9659. 1970. Repr. of 1926 ed. 35.00x (ISBN 0-86527-150-X). Fertig.

Pioneers of the Old South. Mary Johnston. 1918. 8.50x (ISBN 0-686-83699-5). Elliots Bks.

Pioneers of the Old South see Chronicles of America.

Pioneers of the Old Southwest see Chronicles of America.

Pioneers of Wireless. Ellison Hawks. LC 74-4685. (Telecommunications Ser). (Illus.). 400p. 1974. Repr. of 1927 ed. 27.00x (ISBN 0-405-06049-1). Ayer Co Pubs.

Pioneers of Women's Education in the United States. Ed. by Willystine Goodsell. (Illus.). Repr. of 1931 ed. 32.50 (ISBN 0-404-02864-0). AMS Pr.

Pioneers on Early Waterways. Edith McCall. LC 61-10104. (Frontiers of America Ser.). (Illus.). 128p. (gr. 3-10). 1980. PLB 11.93 (ISBN 0-516-03357-3). Childrens.

Pioneers, Peddlers, & Tsadikim: The Story of the Jews in Colorado. 2nd ed. Ida L. Uchill. LC 57-57817. 327p. 1979. pap. 9.95 (ISBN 0-9604468-0-X). Uchill.

Pioneer's Search for an Ideal Home. Phoebe G. Judson. LC 84-7478. iv, 314p. 1984. 25.00x (ISBN 0-8032-2563-6); pap. 7.50 (ISBN 0-8032-7559-5, BB 872, Bison). U of Nebr Pr.

Pioneros del Desarrollo. Ed. by Gerald M. Meier & Dudley Seers. 368p. 1986. Spanish. pap. write for info. (IBO876); English. pap. write for info. (OX520479). World Bank.

Pionniers du Developpement. Ed. by Gerald M. Meier & Dudley Seers. 408p. (Fr.). 1988. 14.95 (IB0957). World Bank.

Pionniers du Developpement. Ed. by Gerald M. Meier & Dudley Seers. 408p. (Span.). 1988. 14.95 (IB0876). World Bank.

Pionniers du Developpement. Ed. by Gerald M. Meier & Dudley Seers. 408p. 1988. pap. 14.95 (ISBN 2-7178-1252-0, IB095752). World Bank.

Piotruszek: How Little Peter Got into Heaven. (Illus.). (gr. 2-6). 1957. 1.50 (ISBN 0-685-19451-5). Polanie.

Pious & Secular America. Reinhold Niebuhr. LC 79-128063. 1977. Repr. of 1958 ed. 19.50x (ISBN 0-678-02756-0). Kelley.

Pious Brief Narrative in Medieval Castilian & Galician Verse: From Berceo to Alfonso X. John E. Keller. LC 77-84064. (Studies in Romance Languages: No. 21). 152p. 1978. 16.00x (ISBN 0-8131-1381-4). U Pr of Ky.

Pious Dance: The Adventure Story of a Young Man. Klaus Mann. Tr. by Laurence Senelick. 180p. 1987. 15.95 (ISBN 1-55554-017-1). PAJ Pubns.

Pious Prentice, or, the Prentices Piety. Abraham Jackson. LC 74-28866. (English Experience Ser.: No. 746). 1975. Repr. of 1640 ed. 7.00 (ISBN 90-221-0746-9). Walter J Johnson.

Pious Traitors of Belgium & France. Joseph McCabe. 32p. pap. cancelled (ISBN 0-911826-86-6). Am Atheist.

Piozzi Marginalia: Comprising Some Extracts from Hanuscripts of Hester Lynch Piozzi & Annotations from Her Books. Percival Meritt. 1891. Repr. 20.00 (ISBN 0-8274-3905-9). R West.

Pip & Emma. Katharine J. Bacon. LC 85-20059. 164p. (gr. 4-7). 1986. 11.95 (ISBN 0-689-50385-7, M K McElderry). Macmillan.

PIP College "HELPS" - Handicapped & Exceptional Learners Programs & Services. P. Fielding. (College Handicapped & Exceptional Programs & Services Ser.: Vol. 3). 1978. pap. 8.95 (ISBN 0-937660-04-3). PIP.

PIP College "HELPS" - Handicapped & Exceptional Learners Programs & Services, Vol. 2. P. P. Fielding. 1977. pap. 7.95 (ISBN 0-937660-03-5). PIP.

Pipe. Georges Herment. 1962. pap. 2.95 (ISBN 0-671-57751-4, Fireside). S&S.

Pipe All Hands! Aylward E. Dingle. LC 74-101279. (Short Story Index Reprint Ser.). 1935. 20.00 (ISBN 0-8369-3216-1). Ayer Co Pubs.

Pipe & Excavation Contracting. Dave Roberts. 400p. (Orig.). 1987. pap. 23.50 (ISBN 0-934041-22-9). Craftsman.

Pipe & Pouch. Ed. by Joseph Knight. LC 74-108584. (Granger Index Reprint Ser.). 1894. 17.00 (ISBN 0-8369-6112-9). Ayer Co Pubs.

Pipe & Tube Bending Manual. John Gillanders. LC 84-631. 220p. 1984. 29.00x (ISBN 0-87201-493-2). Gulf Pub.

Pipe & Tube Fabrication. 2nd ed. Ed. by D. Anderson et al. (Engineering Craftsmen: No. D3). (Illus.). 1978. spiral bdg. 39.95x (ISBN 0-85083-415-5). Trans-Atl Phila.

Pipe & Tube Fabrication. 50.00x (ISBN 0-85083-017-6, Pub. by Engineering Ind). State Mutual Bk.

Pipe & Tube Welding. 49.00x (Pub. by Engineering Ind). State Mutual Bk.

Pipe Caulker. Jack Rudman. (Career Examination Ser.: C-641). (Cloth bdg. avail. on request). pap. 12.00. Natl Learning.

Pipe De Maigret et Maigret se fache. Georges Simenon. pap. 3.95 (ISBN 0-685-11496-1). French & Eur.

Pipe Drafting. W. Hartman & F. Williams. 1981. text ed. 29.95 (ISBN 0-07-026945-9). McGraw.

Pipe Dream of Peace: The Story of the Collapse of Disarmament. John W. Wheeler-Bennett. LC 76-80601. 1971. Repr. 28.50x (ISBN 0-86527-151-8). Fertig.

Pipe Dreams. Don Raye. Ed. by Una King & Delia Moon. LC 81-2507. 110p. 1980. pap. 12.00 (ISBN 0-686-75463-8). Family Pub CA.

Pipe Fitter's & Pipe Welder's Handbook. Thomas N. Frankland. 175p. 1981. 25.00x (ISBN 0-561-00012-3, Pub. by Bailey Bros & Swinfen Ltd). State Mutual Bk.

Pipe Fitter's & Welder's Handbook. Thomas W. Frankland. (Illus., Orig.). 1984. pap. 8.76 (ISBN 0-02-802500-8). Glencoe.

Pipe Frames for Awnings. 1979. 10.00 (ISBN 0-318-01555-2, 21045). Indus Fabrics.

Pipe Jointing Methods. EEMUA Staff. 1968. 75.00x (ISBN 0-85931-052-3, Pub. by EEMUA). State Mutual Bk.

Pipe Line Corrosion & Cathodic Protection. 3rd ed. Marshall E. Parker & Edward G. Peattie. LC 83-22630. 170p. 1984. 29.00x (ISBN 0-87201-149-6). Gulf Pub.

Pipe Line Rules of Thumb Handbook. LC 76-52237. 198p. (Orig.). 1978. pap. 25.00x (ISBN 0-87201-698-6). Gulf Pub.

Pipe Loops & Bends: Design for Flexibility Tables. K. Bendisz. Ed. by Anna Bendisz-Siekierski. LC 84-90195. (Illus.). 288p. (Orig.). 1984. 27.00 (ISBN 0-9613395-0-0). Siren.

Pipe Organs of Slovenia. M. Bizjak & E. Skulj. (Illus.). 232p. 1985. 50.00x. Heinman.

Pipe Protection: A Review of Current Practice in the U. K. V. Hassan et al. (Illus.). 183p. 1979. pap. 91.00x lib. ed. (ISBN 0-900983-92-2, Dist. by Air Sciencec Co.). BHRA Fluid.

Pipe Protection Bibliography. Ed. by N. G. Guy. 285p. 1987. 74.25 (ISBN 1-85166-077-1, Pub. by Elsevier Applied Sci England). Elsevier.

Pipe Spring & the Arizona Strip. David S. Lavender. 64p. 1984. pap. 2.95 (ISBN 0-915630-20-6). Zion.

Pipe Template Layout. Thomas W. Frankland. (Illus., Orig.). 1967. pap. 8.76 (ISBN 0-02-802400-1). Glencoe.

Pipe Trades Pocket Manual. Thomas W. Frankland. (Illus., Orig.). 1969. pap. 9.24 (ISBN 0-02-802410-9). Glencoe.

Pipe Welding. Richard Hunter & Robert O'Con. (Series 911). (Orig.). 1985. pap. 8.00 wkbk. (ISBN 0-8064-0389-6); audio visual pkg. 399.00 (ISBN 0-8064-0390-X). Bergwall.

Pipe Welding Procedures. Hoobasar Rampaul. LC 73-7849. (Illus.). 238p. 1973. 24.95x (ISBN 0-8311-1100-3). Indus Pr.

Pipe Welding Techniques. 4th ed. I. H. Griffin et al. LC 85-1513. 128p. 1985. pap. text ed. 17.95 (ISBN 0-8273-2248-8); instr's. guide 5.00 (ISBN 0-8273-2249-6). Delmar.

PIPECALC (TM) 1: Version 20--Practical Pipeline Hydraulics. Martin Chenevert & J. Roye. LC 84-9007. (Microcomputer Software for Pipeline Engineers Ser.). 1984. incl. disk 495.00x (ISBN 0-87201-741-9); disk incl. Gulf Pub.

Pipedreams: Poems. Debra Williams-Garner. LC 88-90092. (Orig.). 1988. pap. 3.50 (ISBN 0-9620332-0-0). D Williams-Garner.

Pipefitter. Jack Rudman. (Career Examination Ser.: C-587). (Cloth bdg. avail. on request). pap. 12.00 (ISBN 0-8373-0587-X). Natl Learning.

Pipefitters Handbook. 3rd ed. Forrest R. Lindsey. LC 59-14725. (Illus.). 464p. 1967. 19.95x (ISBN 0-8311-3019-9). Indus Pr.

Pipeflow Analysis. D. Stephenson. (Developments in Water Science Ser.: Vol. 19). 1984. 66.00 (ISBN 0-444-42283-8, I-046-84). Elsevier.

Pipeline & Energy Plant Piping--Design & Construction: Proceedings of the International Conference on Pipeline & Energy Plant Piping, Calgary, Alberta, Nov. 10-13, 1980. Ed. by Welding Institute of Canada, Toronto, Ontario. (Illus.). 360p. 1981. 77.00 (ISBN 0-08-025368-7). Pergamon.

Pipeline Construction. 3rd ed. Max Hosmanek. Ed. by Cinda Cyrus. (Illus.). 122p. 1984. pap. text ed. 10.50 (ISBN 0-88698-096-8, 4.00030). PETEX.

Pipeline Design for Hydrocarbon Gases & Liquids. 87p. 1975. pap. 9.00x (ISBN 0-87262-118-9). Am Soc Civil Eng.

Pipeline Design for Water & Wastewater. 136p. 1975. pap. 8.00x (ISBN 0-87262-106-5). Am Soc Civil Eng.

Pipeline Design for Water Engineers. 2nd ed. D. Stephenson. (Developments in Water Science Ser.: Vol. 15). 234p. 1981. 73.75 (ISBN 0-444-41991-8). Elsevier.

Pipeline Dictionary. H. Bucksch & A. P. Altmeyer. 288p. (Eng., Ger. & Fr.). 1969. 150.00 (ISBN 3-7625-1166-7, M-7588, Pub. by Bauverlag). French & Eur.

Pipeline Engineering Symposium. Ed. by K. Chickering. 96p. 1983. pap. text ed. 24.00 (ISBN 0-317-02640-2, I00157). ASME.

Pipeline from Hell. David Bannerman. (Magic Man Ser.: No. 3). 1984. pap. 2.50 (ISBN 0-8217-1327-2). Zebra.

Pipeline Gas from Coal by Methanation of Synthesis Gas. H A. Dirksen & H R. Linden. (Research Bulletin Ser.: No. 31). vi, 137p. (B). 1963. 10.00. Inst Gas Tech.

Pipeline Infrastructure. Ed. by Bruce A. Bennett. (Conference Proceedings Ser.). 536p. 1988. 44.00 (ISBN 0-87262-662-8). Am Soc Civil Eng.

Pipeline Materials & Design: Proceedings of a Session Sponsored by the Pipeline Division. Ed. by Jay B. Schrock. 70p. 1984. 15.00x (ISBN 0-87262-418-8). Am Soc Civil Eng.

Pipeline Politics: The Complex Political Economy of East-West Energy Trade. Bruce W. Jentleson. LC 86-47643. (Cornell Studies in Political Economy). 272p. 1986. 29.95x (ISBN 0-8014-1923-9). Cornell U Pr.

Pipeline Welding & Inspection, PWI: Proceedings of the AWS Pipeline Conference, 1980. AWS Pipeline Conference Staff. 108p. 1980. 25.00 (ISBN 0-87171-199-0). Am Welding.

Pipeliners. Frank Mangan. LC 77-73481. (Illus.). 1977. 20.00 (ISBN 0-930208-06-4, Pub. by Guynes Press). Mangan Bks.

Pipelines: A Study in Private Enterprise & Public Policy, 1862-1906. Arthur M. Johnson. LC 81-23728. (Illus.). xiii, 307p. 1982. Repr. of 1956 ed. lib. bdg. 41.50x (ISBN 0-313-23409-4, JODEV). Greenwood.

Pipelines & Permafrost: Science in a Cold Climate. 2nd, rev. & enl. ed. Peter J. Williams. (Illus.). 140p. 1988. pap. 14.95 (ISBN 0-88629-056-2). Oxford U Pr.

Pipelines: Design, Construction & Operation. Pipline Industries Guild. 192p. 1984. pap. 41.95 (ISBN 0-470-20563-6, Co-Pub. with Longman). Wiley.

Pipelines in Adverse Environments, 2 vols. 562p. 1979. pap. 40.00x (ISBN 0-87262-176-6). Am Soc Civil Eng.

Pipelines in Adverse Environments II. Ed. by Mark B. Pickell. 748p. 1983. 54.00x (ISBN 0-87262-385-8). Am Soc Civil Eng.

Pipelines in the Ocean. 114p. 1974. pap. 6.00x (ISBN 0-87262-062-X). Am Soc Civil Eng.

Pipemaker's Book. E. Nachwalter. 1986. cancelled (ISBN 0-442-26909-9). Van Nos Reinhold.

Pipemaker's Book: A Step-by-Step Guide to Making & Appreciating Fine Pipes. Elliott Nachwalter & Fred Poole. Date not set. write for info. S&S.

Piper. Campbell Black. 1986. pap. 3.50 (ISBN 0-671-55508-1). PB.

Piper. Brett Rutherford & John Robertson. 480p. 1987. pap. 3.95 (ISBN 0-8217-1967-X). Zebra.

Piper Classics. Joe Christy. (Illus.). 160p. 1987. 19.95 (ISBN 0-8306-9457-9, 2457); pap. 13.95 (ISBN 0-8306-2457-0). TAB Bks.

Piper in Peace & War. C. A. Malcolm. 282p. 1985. pap. 7.50 (ISBN 0-912951-35-4). ScotPr.

Piper Indians. Bill Clarke. (Illus.). 288p. 1987. 24.95 (ISBN 0-8306-0232-1, 2432); pap. 16.95 (ISBN 0-8306-2432-5). TAB Bks.

Piper Pays. Eugene O. Cody. 1984. cancelled (ISBN 0-8062-2245-X). Carlton.

Piper: Selection of Estonian Fairy Tales. Ed. by J. Talvet. 199p. 1987. 7.95 (ISBN 0-8285-3785-2, Pub. by Periodika Tallinn). Imported Pubns.

Piper Tuning Manual. Bob Gayler. (Illus.). 44p. pap. 6.95 (ISBN 0-85429-292-6, F292, Pub. by G T Foulis Ltd). Haynes Pubns.

Pipers at the Gates of Dawn: The Wisdom of Children's Literature. J. Cott. (Paperbacks Ser.). 352p. 1984. pap. text ed. 8.95 (ISBN 0-07-013220-8). McGraw.

Pipers at the Gates of Dawn: The Wisdom of Children's Literature. Jonathan Cott. 1983. 19.45 (ISBN 0-394-50464-X). Random.

Piper's Pocket Handbook. Rip Weaver. LC 79-50250. 120p. (Orig.). 1979. pap. 15.00x (ISBN 0-87201-701-X). Gulf Pub.

Piper's Song. Sesyle Joslin. 320p. 1986. 16.95 (ISBN 0-15-171977-2). HarBraceJ.

Piper's Tune. Dallas Miller. LC 87-11283. 416p. 1987. 18.95 (ISBN 0-688-06476-0). Morrow.

Pipes That Won't Smoke; Coal That Won't Burn: Haida Sculpture in Argillite. Carol Sheehan. (Illus.). 214p. 1983. pap. 19.95 (ISBN 0-919224-20-2, 28739-4, Glenbow Museum). U of Chicago Pr.

PIPESTAR (TM) 1: Pipe Stress Analysis for HP-41C-CV Calculators. Jack Stone. 1986. manual & magnetic cards 150.00x (ISBN 0-87201-465-7). Gulf Pub.

Pipil Language of El Salvador. Lyle Campbell. (Grammar Library: No. 1). xiv, 957p. 1985. 89.50x (ISBN 0-89925-040-8). Mouton.

Piping & Pipe Support Systems: Design & Engineering. 4th ed. R. P. Smith & T. Van Laan. 384p. 1987. text ed. 46.50 (ISBN 0-07-058931-3). McGraw.

Piping & Pressure Vessels see Mechanical Design of Process Systems.

Piping Components. (Principles of Steam Generation Ser.: Module 9). (Illus.). 100p. 1982. pap. text ed. 21.50x spiral bdg. (ISBN 0-87683-259-1). GP Pub.

Piping Design for Process Plants. Howard F. Rase & M. H. Barrow. LC 63-17483. 1963. 59.50 (ISBN 0-471-70920-4, Pub. by Wiley-Interscience). Wiley.

Piping Down the Valleys Wild. Ed. by Nancy Larrick. 247p. (gr. 10 up). 1982. pap. 3.50 (ISBN 0-440-46952-X, YB). Dell.

Piping Down the Valleys Wild. Intro. by Nancy Larrick. LC 68-27742. (Illus.). 256p. (ps-3). 1985. 14.95 (ISBN 0-385-29429-8). Delacorte.

Piping, Flexibility & Stresses. Spiros D. Vinieratos & D. R. Zeno. LC 41-19398. pap. 22.80 (ISBN 0-317-08190-X, 2015258). Bks Demand UMI.

Piping Guide: A Compact Reference for the Design & Drafting of Piping Systems. 2nd, rev. ed. David R. Sherwood. (Illus.). 232p. 1988. price not set (ISBN 0-914082-19-1). Syentek Bks.

Piping Guide: A Compact Reference for the Design & Drafting of Industrial Piping Systems. David R. Sherwood & Dennis J. Whistance. 209p. 1986. 29.95 (ISBN 0-419-11510-2, 9869, Pub. by Chapman & Hall England). Routledge Chapman & Hall.

Piping Handbook. 5th ed. Sabin Crocker. Ed. by R. C. King. 1967. text ed. 94.50 (ISBN 0-07-013841-9). McGraw.

Piping Problems. S. D. Bowman. 1970. 4.00 (ISBN 0-87511-009-6). Claitors.

Piping Stress Handbook. 2nd ed. Victor Helguero. LC 85-17716. (Illus.). 400p. 1985. 69.00x (ISBN 0-87201-703-6). Gulf Pub.

Pipline Supervisory & Control Systems Workshop. Ed. by E. J. Seiders. 90p. 1982. 25.00 (I00149). ASME.

Pippa. Norma L. Clark. 224p. 1987. pap. 2.50 (ISBN 0-451-15045-7, Sig). NAL.

Pippa Pops Out! Betty Boegehold. LC 78-12491. (Illus.). (ps-3). 1979. Knopf.

Pippa Pops Out! Betty Boegehold. (Illus.). 64p. (ps-3). 1980. pap. 0.95 (ISBN 0-440-46865-5, YB). Dell.

Pippi Goes on Board. Astrid Lindgren. 192p. 1981. Repr. PLB 16.95x (ISBN 0-89966-339-7). Buccaneer Bks.

Pippi Goes on Board. Astrid Lindgren. 172p. 1980. PLB 12.95x (ISBN 0-89967-014-8). Harmony Raine.

Pippi Goes on Board. Astrid Lindgren. (Illus.). (gr. 3-6). 1977. pap. 3.95 (ISBN 0-14-030959-4, Puffin). Penguin.

Pippi Goes on Board. Astrid Lindgren. (Illus.). (gr. 4-6). 1957. lib. bdg. 10.95 (ISBN 0-670-55677-7). Viking.

Pippi Goes on Board. Astrid Lindgren. 128p. (gr. 4-6). 1987. pap. 2.25 (ISBN 0-590-41177-2). Scholastic Inc.

Pippi Goes on Board. Astrid Lindgren. (Orig.). 1988. pap. 3.95 (ISBN 0-14-032774-6, Puffin Bks). Penguin.

Pippi in the South Seas. Astrid Lindgren. Tr. by Gerry Bothmer. (Illus.). (gr. 3-7). 1977. pap. 3.95 (ISBN 0-14-030958-6, Puffin). Penguin.

Pippi in the South Seas. Astrid Lindgren. Tr. by Gerry Bothmer. (Illus.). (gr. 4-6). 1959. lib. bdg. 10.95 (ISBN 0-670-55711-0). Viking.

Pippi in the South Seas. Astrid Lindgren. 116p. (gr. 4-6). 1987. pap. 2.25 (ISBN 0-590-01583-4). Scholastic Inc.

Pippi in the South Seas. Astrid Lindgren. (Orig.). 1988. pap. 3.95 (ISBN 0-14-032773-8, Puffin Bks). Penguin.

Pippi Longstocking. Astrid Lindgren. 192p. 1981. Repr. PLB 16.95x (ISBN 0-89966-338-9). Buccaneer Bks.

Pippi Longstocking. Astrid Lindgren. 175p. 1980. Repr. PLB 12.95x (ISBN 0-89967-013-X). Harmony Raine.

Pippi Longstocking. Astrid Lindgren. Tr. by Florence Lamborn. (Illus.). (gr. 4-6). 1977. pap. 3.95 (ISBN 0-14-030957-8, Puffin). Penguin.

Pippi Longstocking. Astrid Lindgren. Tr. by Florence Lamborn. (Illus.). (gr. 4-6). 1950. lib. bdg. 10.95 (ISBN 0-670-55745-5). Viking.

Pippi Longstocking. Astrid Lindgren. (Orig.). 1988. pap. 3.95 (ISBN 0-14-032772-X, Puffin Bks). Penguin.

Pippi on the Run. Astrid Lindgren. (Illus.). 48p. (gr. 4-6). 1976. 10.95 (ISBN 0-670-55751-X). Viking.

Pippin at the Gym. Phylliss Adams et al. (BTR Ser.). (Illus.). 32p. (gr. k-3). 1983. PLB 4.95 (ISBN 0-8136-5156-5, Dist. by Caroline Hse); pap. 2.25 (ISBN 0-8136-5656-7). Modern Curr.

Pippin Cleans Up. Phylliss Adams et al. (BTR Ser.). (Illus.). 32p. (gr. k-3). 1983. PLB 4.95 (ISBN 0-8136-5152-2, Dist. by Caroline Hse); pap. 2.25 (ISBN 0-8136-5652-4). Modern Curr.

Pippin Eats Out. Phylliss Adams et al. (BTR Ser.). (Illus.). 32p. (gr. k-3). 1983. PLB 4.95 (ISBN 0-8136-5155-7, Dist. by Caroline Hse); pap. 2.25 (ISBN 0-8136-5655-9). Modern Curr.

Pippin Goes to Work. Phylliss Adams et al. (BTR Ser.). (Illus.). 32p. (gr. k-3). 1983. PLB 4.95 (ISBN 0-8136-5153-0, Dist. by Caroline Hse); pap. 2.25 (ISBN 0-8136-5653-2). Modern Curr.

Pippin Learns a Lot. Phylliss Adams et al. (BTR Ser.). (Illus.). 32p. (gr. k-3). 1983. PLB 4.95 (ISBN 0-8136-5151-4, Dist. by Caroline Hse); pap. 2.25 (ISBN 0-8136-5651-6). Modern Curr.

Pippin's Lucky Penny. Phylliss Adams et al. (BTR Ser.). (Illus.). 32p. (gr. k-3). 1983. PLB 4.95 (ISBN 0-8136-5154-9, Dist. by Caroline Hse); pap. 2.25 (ISBN 0-8136-5654-0). Modern Curr.

PIP's Freebie Guide: A Guide to Free & Inexpensive Publications, Products & Aids to Successful Completion of College or Career Training for Learning Disabled Youth. P. M. Fielding & M. E. Alexander. 1978. pap. 5.95 (ISBN 0-937660-06-X). PIP.

Pique: Plain & Patterned. Donna L. Sullivan. (Illus.). 1988. 12.95 (ISBN 0-9620118-0-0). Sullivan Pubns.

Piracy in the Ancient World. H. A. Ormerod. (Dorset Press Reprints Ser.). 291p. 1988. 18.95 (ISBN 0-88029-163-X). Hippocrene Bks.

Piracy in the Ancient World - An Essay on Mediterranean History. H. A. Ormerod. 286p. 1924. pap. text ed. 12.50x (ISBN 0-85323-044-7, Pub. by Liverpool U Pr). Humanities.

Piracy in the Ancient World: An Annotated History of the Mediterranean Covering All of the Countries to 250 A. D. Henry Omerod. 1977. lib. bdg. 69.95 (ISBN 0-8490-2445-5). Gordon Pr.

Piracy in the Levant, 1827-1828. Ed. by C. G. Jones. 69.00x (ISBN 0-317-44207-4, Pub. by Navy Rec Soc). State Mutual Bk.

Piracy of Phonograms. 2nd ed. Gillian Davies. 1987. pap. 90.00x (ISBN 0-906214-42-4, Pub. by ESC Ltd UK). State Mutual Bk.

Piraeus: From the Fifth to the First Century B. C. Robert Garland. LC 87-47596. 272p. 1987. text ed. 39.50x (ISBN 0-8014-2041-5). Cornell U Pr.

Pirandellian Mode in Spanish Literature: From Cervantes to Sastre. Wilma Newberry. LC 77-171181. 227p. 1973. 49.50x (ISBN 0-87395-089-5). State U NY Pr.

Pistachio Prescription. Paula Danziger. LC 77-86330. 168p. (gr. 7 up). 1978. pap. 12.95 (ISBN 0-385-28784-4). Delacorte.

Pistachio Prescription. Paula Danziger. 160p. (YA) (gr. 5 up). 1978. pap. 2.95 (ISBN 0-440-96895-X, LFL). Dell.

Pistachio Prescription. Paula Danziger. (gr. k-12). 1988. pap. 2.95 (ISBN 0-317-67249-5). Dell.

Pistis Sophia: A Gnostic Gospel, Vol. 21. 3rd ed. G. R. Mead. LC 83-83170. (Spiritual Science Library). 408p. 1984. Repr. of 1921 ed. lib. bdg. 25.00 (ISBN 0-89345-041-3, Spiritual Sci Lib). Garber Comm.

Pistol & Revolver Shooting. A. Himmelwright. (Library Classics Ser.). (Illus.). 496p. Date not set. Repr. of 1928 ed. deluxe ed. price not set (ISBN 0-935632-59-X). Wolfe Pub Co.

Pistol: Browning, F. N. 9mm. No. 2, Mark 1. Command of the Army Council Staff. 1982. pap. text ed. 0.95 (ISBN 0-86663-991-8). Ide Hse.

Pistol Grip. Kit Dalton. (Buckskin Ser.: No. 20). 224p. (Orig.). 1987. pap. 2.95 (ISBN 0-8439-2551-5). Leisure NY.

Pistol Guide. George C. Nonte, Jr. (Illus.). 280p. pap. 11.95 (ISBN 0-88317-095-7). Stoeger Pub Co.

Pistol Instruction Handbook. write for info. Looseleaf Law.

Pistol Pete. Peter Finney. 1969. pap. 1.95 (ISBN 0-88289-102-2). Pelican.

Pistol Pete - Veteran of the Old West. Frank Eaton. LC 79-109054. (Illus.). 1979. Repr. of 1952 ed. text ed. 14.95 (ISBN 0-934188-01-7). Evans Pubns.

Pistolero. Walt Denver. 1984. pap. 2.25 (ISBN 0-8217-1331-0). Zebra.

Pistolero Fantasma. new ed. John Benteen. Tr. by Alvaro De Villa from Eng. (Compadre Collection, Fargo Ser.: No. 3). Orig. Title: Phantom Gunman. 160p. 1974. pap. 0.85 (ISBN 0-88473-513-3). Fiesta Pub.

Pistoleros. John Benteen. (Sundance: No. 5). 1979. pap. 0.95 (ISBN 0-8439-0706-1, Leisure Bks). Leisure NY.

Pistols & Pointed Pens: The Dueling Editors of Old Virginia. Virginius Dabney. 248p. 1987. 15.95 (ISBN 0-912697-70-9). Algonquin Bks.

Pistols for Two. Owen Hatteras, pseud. LC 77-4002. 1973. lib. bdg. 30.50 (ISBN 0-8414-4910-4). Folcroft.

Pistols for Two. Georgette Heyer. 341p. 1983. Repr. lib. bdg. 16.95x (ISBN 0-89966-449-0). Buccaneer Bks.

Pistols for Two. Georgette Heyer. 1984. pap. 2.50 (ISBN 0-451-13248-3, Sig). NAL.

Pistols for Two. Georgette Heyer. 15.95 (ISBN 0-89190-638-X, Pub. by Am Repr). Amereon Ltd.

Pistolsmithing. George C. Nonte, Jr. LC 74-10783. (Illus.). 560p. 1974. 27.95 (ISBN 0-8117-1265-6). Stackpole.

Pistoltown. Roy LeBeau. (Buckskin Ser.: No. 3). 240p. (Orig.). 1984. pap. 2.75 (ISBN 0-8439-2126-9, Leisure Bks). Leisure NY.

Pit. Trish Mylet & Antoinette Sheffield. Ed. by Barry W. Burton. (Phonetic Readers for the Short Vowels Ser.: Bk. 6). (Illus.). 16p. (ps-2). 1988. pap. text ed. 5.00 (ISBN 0-945590-06-7). Sizzy Bks.

Pit. Frank Norris. (Literature Ser.). (gr. 10-12). 1970. pap. text ed. 7.17 (ISBN 0-87720-735-6). AMSCO Sch.

Pit. Frank Norris. 1976. lib. bdg. 19.95x (ISBN 0-89968-069-0). Lightyear.

Pit: A Story of Chicago. Frank Norris. LC 70-184738. 432p. 1971. Repr. of 1903 ed. lib. bdg. 14.00x (ISBN 0-8376-0407-9). Bentley.

Pit: A Story of Chicago. Frank Norris. 1978. Repr. of 1902 ed. lib. bdg. 25.00 (ISBN 0-8492-1960-4). R West.

Pit & Fissure Sealants. Norman O. Harris & Linda S. Scheirton. 1985. 39.00 (ISBN 0-318-19100-8). Am Dental Hygienists.

Pit & the Pendulum. Edgar Allan Poe. (Creative's Classics Ser.). (Illus.). 48p. (YA) (gr. 9 up). 1980. PLB 8.95 (ISBN 0-87191-771-8). Creative Ed.

Pit & the Pendulum. Edgar Allan Poe. LC 81-16432. (Illus.). 32p. (gr. 5-10). 1982. PLB 9.79 (ISBN 0-89375-626-1); pap. text ed. 2.50 (ISBN 0-89375-627-X); cassettes avail. Troll Assocs.

Pit & the Pendulum. Edgar Allan Poe. Ed. by Raymond Harris. (Classics Ser.). (Illus.). 48p. (Orig.). (gr. 6-12). 1982. pap. text ed. 3.00x (ISBN 0-89061-265-X, 471); tchr's ed. 4.00x (ISBN 0-89061-266-8, 473); cassette 12.00 (472). Jamestown Pubs.

Pit & the Trap: Leyb Rochman. Ed. by Sheila Friedling. Tr. by Moshe Kohn. (Illus.). 288p. (Orig., Yiddish.). 1983. 16.95 (ISBN 0-8052-5044-1); pap. 10.95 (ISBN 0-8052-5045-X). Holocaust Pubns.

Pit Bull. Scott Ely. Ed. by John Herman. LC 87-37161. 192p. 1988. 15.95 (ISBN 1-55584-046-9). Weidenfeld.

Pit Bull: Fact & Fable. K. S. Matz. LC 84-73192. (Illus.). 236p. (Orig.). 1985. pap. 19.95 (ISBN 0-932501-00-1). De Mortmain.

Pit Bull Sting: The Other Side of the Story. Boen Hallum. 190p. 1987. pap. 12.00. B Hallum.

Pit-Men, Preachers & Politics. R. Moore. LC 73-88307. 42.50x (ISBN 0-521-20356-2). Cambridge U Pr.

Pit of Babel. Joseph Zsuffa. LC 75-8097. 190p. 1975. 12.95 (ISBN 0-915648-00-8). Orpheus Pr.

Pit Ponies. John Bright. (Illus.). 144p. 1986. 25.95 (ISBN 0-7134-5226-9, Pub. by Batsford England). David & Charles.

Pit-Prop Syndicate. Freeman W. Crofts. (Crime Ser.). 1978. pap. 3.95 (ISBN 0-14-000512-9). Penguin.

Pit Stop. Illus. by Mones. (Fast Rolling Race Cars Ser.). (Illus.). (ps-2). 1987. 3.95 (ISBN 0-448-09888-1, G&D). Putnam Pub Group.

Pit Village & the Store: The Portrait of a Mining Past. Linda M. Thew. 226p. 1985. pap. 9.50 (ISBN 0-7453-0069-3, Pub. by Pluto Pr). Longwood Pub Group.

Pita Breads & Pocket Fillings. Darcy Williamson & John Allgair. 140p. (Orig.). 1981. pap. 5.95 (ISBN 0-89288-067-8). Maverick.

Pita the Great. Virginia Habeeb. LC 85-40902. (Illus.). 224p. 1986. pap. 6.95 (ISBN 0-89480-039-6). Workman Pub.

Pitcairn Island Register Book. Ed. by Charles Lucas. LC 75-3444. (Illus.). Repr. of 1929 ed. 22.50 (ISBN 0-404-14447-0). AMS Pr.

Pitcairnioideae (Bromeliaceae) Lyman B. Smith & Robert J. Downs. (Flora Neotropica Monograph: No. 14(1)). 660p. (Orig.). 1986. pap. 45.00x (ISBN 0-89327-296-5). NY Botanical.

Pitcairn's Island. Thomas Murray. LC 72-281. (World History Ser., No. 48). 1972. Repr. of 1860 ed. lib. bdg. 52.95x (ISBN 0-8383-1410-4). Haskell.

Pitcairn's Island, & the Islanders, in 1850. 3rd ed. Walter Brodie. LC 75-3441. Repr. of 1851 ed. 28.50 (ISBN 0-404-14445-4). AMS Pr.

Pitch. Hugh Rank. 207p. 1982. 17.00 (ISBN 0-8141-3557-9). NCTE.

Pitch Analysis: Journal: Phonetica, Vol. 39, No. 4-5, 1982. Ed. by K. Kohler. (Illus.). viii, 156p. 1982. pap. 62.75 (ISBN 3-8055-3670-4). S Karger.

Pitch & Hasty Check It Out. Eric Deleon. LC 88-1483. (Illus.). 96p. (gr. 3-5). 1988. 11.95 (ISBN 0-531-05768-2); PLB 11.99 (ISBN 0-531-08368-3). Orchard Bks Watts.

Pitch Dark. Renata Adler. LC 83-48133. 192p. 1983. 12.45 (ISBN 0-394-50374-0). Knopf.

Pitch Dark. Renata Adler. LC 87-45590. 160p. 1988. pap. 6.95 (ISBN 0-06-097144-4, PL-7144, PL). Har-Row.

Pitch Determination of Speech Signals: Algorithms & Devices. W. Hess. (Springer Series in Information Sciences: Vol. 3). (Illus.). 698p. 1983. 46.50 (ISBN 0-387-11933-7). Springer-Verlag.

Pitch: How To Analyze Advertising. Hugh Rank. LC 82-8107. (Illus.). 208p. (Orig.). 1982. pap. 11.95 (ISBN 0-943468-00-0). Counter-Prop Pr.

Pitch in & Play Fair. Lynn Hartsell. (Huddles Ser.). (Illus.). 40p. (ps-3). write for info (ISBN 0-910313-75-X). Parker Bros.

Pitch in & Play Fair. Lynn Hartsell. (Huddles Ser.). (Illus.). 40p. (ps-3). write for info. Parker Bros.

Pitch Pine & Brass Handles. Ted Sharpe. 1982. 15.00x (ISBN 0-906660-23-8, Pub. by New Playwrights Network). State Mutual Bk.

Pitch, Power, & Luck: A Helicopter Log. Gary Traylor. Ed. by By Fish. (Illus.). 111p. (Orig.). 1987. pap. 8.95 (ISBN 0-939177-02-1). Heli World Pr.

Pitch: Problems & Control. Vera Pollock & Jack Weiner. LC 76-3081. (Bibliographic Ser.: No. 268). 1976. pap. 17.00 (ISBN 0-87010-041-6). Inst Paper Chem.

Pitcher. George Sullivan. LC 85-47939. (Illus.). 64p. (gr. 4-7). 1986. 10.70i (ISBN 0-690-04538-7, Crowell Jr Bks); PLB 10.89 (ISBN 0-690-04539-5). HarpJ.

Pitcher. John Thorn & John Holway. (Illus.). 320p. 1987. 19.95 (ISBN 0-13-157652-6). P-H.

Pitcher. John Thorn & John Holway. (Illus.). 320p. 1988. pap. 12.95 (ISBN 0-13-676990-X). Prentice Hall Pr.

Pitcher Mountain Inn Cookbook. Bill Matthews & Dawn Matthews. LC 84-51153. (Illus.). 160p. (Orig.). 1985. pap. 8.95 (ISBN 0-89909-047-8). Yankee Bks.

Pitcher Plants: The Elegant Insect Traps. Carol Lerner. LC 82-12514. (Illus.). 64p. (gr. k up). 1983. 11.75 (ISBN 0-688-01717-7); PLB 11.88 (ISBN 0-688-01718-5). Morrow.

Pitchers Do Get Lonely: And Other Sports Stories. Ira Berkow. LC 88-3387. 256p. 1988. 17.95 (ISBN 0-689-11964-X). Atheneum.

Pitchfork Ben Tillman: South Carolinian. Francis B. Simkins. LC 44-9640. (Southern Biography Ser.). xii, 578p. 1967. pap. text ed. 12.95 (ISBN 0-8071-0119-2). La State U Pr.

Pitchfork Ben Tillman: South Carolinian. Francis B. Simkins. 1964. 13.25 (ISBN 0-8446-1409-2). Peter Smith.

Pitching. Bob Shaw. (Illus.). 1981. pap. 10.95 (ISBN 0-8092-5913-3). Contemp Bks.

Pitchman's Melody: Shaw About Shakespeare. Jerry Lutz. LC 72-3529. 175p. 1974. 18.00 (ISBN 0-8387-1247-9). Bucknell U Pr.

Pitfall (Alien Speedway, No. 2. Thomas Wylde. (Spectra Ser). 160p. (Orig.). 1988. pap. 3.50 (ISBN 0-553-26946-1, Spectra). Bantam.

Pitfalls in Development. H. McKinley Conway. LC 78-62198. 350p. 1981. pap. 11.95 (ISBN 0-910436-06-1). Conway Data.

Pitfalls in Genealogical Research. Milton Rubincam. LC 87-70105. (Illus.). 74p. (Orig.). 1987. pap. 5.95 (ISBN 0-916489-28-0, 143). Ancestry.

Pitfalls in Seismic Interpretation. Paul M. Tucker & Howard J. Yorston. LC 73-84680. (SEG Monographs: No. 2). 56p. 1973. pap. 5.00 (ISBN 0-931830-11-7). Soc Expl Geophys.

Pitfalls of Analysis. Giandomenico Majone & Edward S. Quade. LC 79-41700. (Wiley IIASA International Series on Applied Systems Analysis). 213p. 1980. 65.95x (ISBN 0-471-27746-0, Pub. by Wiley-Interscience). Wiley.

Pitfalls of Christian Liberty: First Corinthians 10, 1-22. John MacArthur, Jr. (John MacArthur Bible Studies). 1988. pap. 3.95 (ISBN 0-8024-5360-0). Moody.

Pithole: The Vanished City. William C. Darrah. LC 72-78194. (Illus.). 260p. 1972. 8.50 (ISBN 0-913116-03-3). W C Darrah.

Pithy Sayings from FORMAT Interviews, Vol. II. Ed. by C. L. Morrison. 1980. pap. 3.49 (ISBN 0-932508-07-3). Seven Oaks.

Pithy Sayings from FORMAT Interviews, Vol. I. 1979. pap. 3.49 (ISBN 0-932508-06-5). Seven Oaks.

Pitia: An Archaeological Series in Northwestern Venezuela. Patrick Gallagher. LC 75-21042. (Publications in Anthropology: No.76). 1976. pap. 12.00 (ISBN 0-913516-09-0). Yale U Anthro.

Pitie pour les Femmes. Henry de Montherlant. (Folio Ser.: No. 156). 224p. 1972. 6.95 (ISBN 0-686-55528-7). Schoenhof.

Pitie pour les Femmes see Jeunes Filles.

Pitman New Era Shorthand: A Student's Review. Ed. by Pitman Publishing Ltd Staff. 160p. (Orig.). 1970. pap. text ed. 42.95x (ISBN 0-273-43111-0, Pub. by Pitman Pub). Trans-Atl Phila.

Pitman New Era Shorthand: Anniversary Edition. Ed. by Pitman Publishing Staff. 192p. (Orig.). 1988. Set. pap. 22.00 wkbk. (ISBN 0-273-02902-9, Pub. by Pitman Pub Ltd London). Two Vols., 200 Pages. Trans-Atl Phila.

Pitman New Era Shorthand. Facility Drills: Anniversary Edition. Julie Watson. 64p. (Orig.). 1988. pap. 9.95x (ISBN 0-273-02904-5, Pub. by Pitman Pub Ltd London). Trans-Atl Phila.

Pitman New Era Shorthand Pocket Dictionary. Ed. by Pitman Publishing Ltd Staff. 221p. (Orig.). 1985. pap. text ed. 9.95x (ISBN 0-273-40954-9, Pub. by Pitman Pub). Trans-Atl Phila.

Pitman Puzzles. M. M. Treacy. 82p. 1987. 7.95 (ISBN 0-533-07008-2). Vantage.

Pitman Shorthand Speedbuilder. Bryan Coombs. (Illus.). 128p. (Orig.). 1975. pap. 7.95x (ISBN 0-8464-0721-3). Beekman Pubs.

Pitman Two Thousand Shorthand: Realistic Business Dictation. Doreen Sharp & Doreen Trimnell. 116p. (Orig.). 1985. pap. text ed. 17.50x (ISBN 0-318-22515-8, Pub. by Pitman Pub Ltd London). Trans-Atl Phila.

Pitman Two Thousand Shorthand: Reporting Style. Janet Job & Bert Canning. 134p. (Orig.). 1986. pap. text ed. 21.00x (ISBN 0-318-22514-X, Pub. by Pitman Pub Ltd London). Trans-Atl Phila.

Pitman 2000 Shorthand: Realistic Business Dictation. Doreen Sharp & Doreen Trimnell. 116p. (Orig.). 1985. pap. text ed. 17.50x (ISBN 0-273-02173-7, Pub. by Pitman Pub). Trans-Atl Phila.

Pitman 2000 Shorthand: Reporting Style. Janet Job & Bert Canning. 134p. (Orig.). 1986. pap. text ed. 21.00x (ISBN 0-273-02508-2, Pub. by Pitman Pub). Trans-Atl Phila.

Pitman's Dictionary of Industrial Administration: A Comprehensive Encyclopedia of the Organization, Administration, & Management of Modern Industry, 2 vols. Ed. by John Lee & Alfred D. Chandler. LC 79-7552. (History of Management Thought & Practice Ser.). 1980. Repr. of 1928 ed. Set. lib. bdg. 144.00x (ISBN 0-405-12336-1); lib. bdg. 72.00x ea. Vol. 1 (ISBN 0-405-12337-X). Vol. 2 (ISBN 0-405-12338-8). Ayer Co Pubs.

Pitmen of the Northern Coalfield: Work, Culture & Protest from the Late 18th to the Mid-19th Centuries. Robert Colls. 288p. 1987. 60.00 (ISBN 0-7190-2202-9, Pub. by Manchester Univ Pr). St Martin.

Pitseolak: Pictures Out of My Life. Pitseolak. Ed. by Dorothy Eber. LC 72-4111. (Illus.). 96p. 1979. pap. 8.95 (ISBN 0-295-95632-1). U of Wash Pr.

Pitt. Archibald Rosebery. LC 68-25264. (English Biography Ser., No. 31). 1969. Repr. lib. bdg. 49.95x (ISBN 0-8383-0236-X). Haskell.

Pitt. Archibald P. Rosebery. LC 78-106521. Repr. of 1892 ed. 34.00 (ISBN 0-404-05405-6). AMS Pr.

Pitt & Fox. Preston W. Slosson. 1979. 3.75 (ISBN 0-686-78142-2). Wahr.

Pitt & Popularity: The Patriot Minister & London Opinion During the Seven Years War. Marie Peters. (Illus.). 1980. 55.00x (ISBN 0-19-822498-2). Oxford U Pr.

Pitt: The Story of the University of Pittsburgh, 1787-1987. Robert C. Alberts. LC 86-5461. (Illus.). 596p. 1986. 29.95 (ISBN 0-8229-1150-7). U of Pittsburgh Pr.

Pitt Versus Fox: Father & Son, 1735-1806. Erich Eyck. LC 72-13742. viii, 396p. 1972. Repr. lib. bdg. 27.50x (ISBN 0-374-92673-5, Octagon). Hippocrene Bks.

Pittman-Robertson Program: Fifty Years of Dollarsand Sense for Wildlife. 20p. 1986. 1.00 (ISBN 0-318-23134-4). Wildlife Mgmt.

Pittock Mansion Through the Ages. Bennet Norbo. (Illus.). 48p. (Orig.). 1986. pap. 2.00 (ISBN 0-911518-23-1). Touchstone Oregon.

Pittock Mansion Through the Ages. Bennett Norrbo. 1973. pap. 2.00 (ISBN 0-911518-24-X). Touchstone Pr Ore.

Pittori Viterbesi Di Cinque Secoli. Italo Faldi. LC 77-106770. (Illus., Ital.). 1970. 87.50x (ISBN 0-271-00119-4). Pa St U Pr.

Pittsburgh. Lynn Johnson. Ed. by Ross A. Howell, Jr. & Kathleen D. Valenzi. LC 86-82618. 104p. 1987. 32.00 (ISBN 0-9616878-3-5). Howell Pr VA.

Pittsburgh. Ed. by Lubove. LC 76-3119. (Documentary History of American Cities Ser.). 1976. pap. 6.95 (ISBN 0-531-05590-6). Wiener Pub Inc.

Pittsburgh: A Chronological & Documentary History 1682-1976. Robert I. Vexler. LC 77-8948. (American Cities Chronology Ser.). 154p. 1977. 8.50 (ISBN 0-379-00606-5). Oceana.

Pittsburgh: An Urban Portrait. Franklin Toker. LC 85-71786. (Illus.). 359p. 1986. 29.95x (ISBN 0-271-00415-0); pap. 16.95x (ISBN 0-271-00438-X). Pa St U Pr.

Pittsburgh & Lake Erie. Harold McLean. LC 80-26230. (Illus.). 224p. 32.95 (ISBN 0-87095-080-0). Gldn West Bks.

Pittsburgh District Civic Frontage, Vol. 5. Ed. by Paul U. Kellogg. LC 73-11904. (Metropolitan America Ser.). 678p. 1974. Repr. 45.50x (ISBN 0-405-05397-5). Ayer Co Pubs.

Pittsburgh: Fulfilling Its Destiny. Vince Gagetta. Ed. by Karl Stull. LC 86-22382. (Illus.). 624p. 1986. 34.95 (ISBN 0-89781-189-5). Windsor Pubns Inc.

Pittsburgh Gazette Abstracts, 1797-1803. Clara E. Duer. 430p. 1986. 24.95 (ISBN 0-933227-51-5). Closson Pr.

Pittsburgh Graded Tax Plan. Percy R. Williams. 71p. 1964. pap. 1.00 (ISBN 0-911312-38-2). Schalkenbach.

Pittsburgh in the Year Eighteen Twenty-Six. Samuel Jones. LC 70-125749. (American Environmental Studies). 1970. Repr. of 1826 ed. 16.00 (ISBN 0-405-02673-0). Ayer Co Pubs.

Pittsburgh Internationals: A Selection of 5 of the Annual Exhibition of Paintings Catalogues from the 1920s-1930s, 5 vols. Carnegie Institute Staff. 150p. Set. 95.00 (ISBN 0-686-87742-X). A Wofsy Fine Arts.

Pittsburgh Moments. Lynn Johnson et al. LC 84-40227. (Illus.). 124p. 1984. 19.95 (ISBN 0-8229-3501-5). U of Pittsburgh Pr.

Pittsburgh, Pa. Gazette Genealogical Gleanings, 1786-1820, Vol. I. Mark Welchley. 81p. (Orig.). perfect bdg. 11.00 (ISBN 0-933227-66-3). Closson Pr.

Pittsburgh Photography: A New Generation. John Caldwell & Annegreth Nill. (Illus., Orig.). 1987. pap. 6.00 (ISBN 0-88039-015-8). Mus Art Carnegie.

Pittsburgh Pirates. rev. ed. Martin. LC 82-13027. (Baseball Today Ser.). 48p. (gr. 4 up). 1982. PLB 11.45 (ISBN 0-87191-871-4). Creative Ed.

Pittsburgh Pirates. James R. Rothaus. (Baseball: The Great American Game Ser.). 48p. (gr. 4-10). 1987. PLB 14.89 (ISBN 0-88682-147-9). Creative Ed.

Pittsburgh Portraits. Elizabeth Moorhead. (Orig.). 1955. pap. 1.95 (ISBN 0-910286-25-6). Boxwood.

Pittsburgh Steelers. James R. Rothaus. (NFL Today Ser.). (gr. 4 up). 1986. PLB 10.45 (ISBN 0-88682-045-6). Creative Ed.

Pittsburgh Steelers: A Pictorial History. Pat Livinston. LC 79-91292. (Illus.). 198p. 1980. 14.95 (ISBN 0-918908-11-6). JCP Corp VA.

Pittsburgh: The Story of a City, 1750-1865. rev. ed. Leland D. Baldwin. LC 73-104172. (Illus.). 1970. pap. 8.95 (ISBN 0-8229-5216-5). U of Pittsburgh Pr.

Pittsburgh: The Story of an American City. Stefan Lorant. LC 75-24970. (Illus.). 1986. Repr. of 1980 ed. 24.95 (ISBN 0-317-56929-5). Authors Edn MA.

Pittsburgh: The Story of the City of Champions. Marty Wolfson & Jim O'Brien. LC 80-52074. (Illus.). 1980. 14.95 (ISBN 0-916114-07-4). Wolfson.

Pittsburgh Walking Map & Guide (The One & Only) Rosemary Parlak & Dorothy Miller. pap. 2.50 (ISBN 0-944101-01-1). New Pittsburgh.

Pittsburgh's Commercial Development, 1800-1850. Catherine L. Reiser. LC 51-9480. 247p. 1951. 6.00 (ISBN 0-911124-36-5). Pa Hist & Mus.

Pittsburgh's Post-Gazette: The First Newspaper West of the Alleghenies. J. Cutler Andrews. (American Studies Ser.). 1969. Repr. of 1936 ed. 24.00 (ISBN 0-384-01455-0). Johnson Repr.

Pittsylvania County Inventory: Circuit Court Clerk. Compiled by B. Kirke White. 50p. (Orig.). 1977. pap. 2.00 (ISBN 0-686-98188-X). VA State Lib.

Pittsylvania County Marriages, 1767-1805. Catherine L. Knorr. 136p. 1982. Repr. of 1956 ed. 17.50 (ISBN 0-89308-260-0, VA 53). Southern Hist Pr.

Pittura e Misericordia: The Oratory of S. Giovanni Decollato in Rome. Jean S. Weisz. Ed. by Linda Seidel. LC 84-151. (Studies in the Fine Arts: Art Patronage: No. 2). 198p. 1984. 42.95 (ISBN 0-8357-1461-6). UMI Res Pr.

Place Names of Sumter County, Alabama. Virginia O. Foscue. Ed. by James W. Hartman. (Publication of the American Dialect Society Ser.: No. 65). (Illus.). 75p. 1978. pap. 5.90 (ISBN 0-8173-0663-3). U of Ala Pr.

Place Names of the Avalon Peninsula of the Island of Newfoundland. E. R. Seary. LC 73-151390. (Memorial University Ser.: No. 2). pap. 101.00 (2026372). Bks Demand UMI.

Place Names of the Death Valley Region in California & Nevada. T. S. Palmer. LC 80-51783. (Illus.). 1980. wrappers 7.50 (ISBN 0-930704-04-5). Sagebrush Pr.

Place-Names of the Northern Neck of Virginia. Mary R. Miller. xiv, 189p. 1983. pap. 10.00 (ISBN 0-88490-099-1). VA State Lib.

Place Names of the Sierra Nevada. Peter Browning. LC 84-52655. 264p. (Orig.). 1986. pap. 12.95 (ISBN 0-89997-047-8); 19.95 (ISBN 0-89997-072-9). Wilderness Pr.

Place Names of the White Mountains. Hixson. 446p. 1980. pap. 8.95 (ISBN 0-89272-069-7). Down East.

Place-Names of the World. Adrian Room. 1988. pap. 12.95 (ISBN 0-207-15539-9, Pub. by Angus & Robertson). Salem Hse Pubs.

Place Names of Upper Deeside. Adam Watson & Elizabeth Allan. 256p. 1984. text ed. 32.00 (ISBN 0-08-030403-6). Pergamon.

Place Names of Washington State. Robert Hitchman. LC 85-24683. 1986. 24.95 (ISBN 0-917048-57-1). Wash St Hist Soc.

Place Names of West Penwith. P. A. Pool. 1985. 15.00x (ISBN 0-317-58007-8, Pub. by Dyllansow & Truran). State Mutual Bk.

Place Names of Westchester County, New York. Richard M. Lederer, Jr. LC 78-13727. (Illus.). 1978. 9.75 (ISBN 0-916346-30-7). Harbor Hill Bks.

Place No One Knew: Glen Canyon on the Colorado River. Eliot Porter. 1988. 45.00 (ISBN 0-87905-249-X). Gibbs Smith Pub.

Place of Animal Behavioural Studies in Agricultural Training. R. Ewbank. 1976. 16.00x (ISBN 0-317-43889-1, Pub. by Univ Federation Animal). State Mutual Bk.

Place of Art in the World of Architecture. Donald W. Thalacker. LC 79-3322. (Illus.). 1980. 35.00 (ISBN 0-87754-098-5). Chelsea Hse.

Place of Astronomy in the Ancient World: A Joint Symposium of the Royal Society & the British Academy. Ed. by F. R. Hodson. (Illus.). 1974. 69.00x (ISBN 0-19-725944-8). Oxford U Pr.

Place of Birth. Ed. by Sheila Kitzinger & John A. Davis. (Illus.). 1978. text ed. 34.50x (ISBN 0-19-261125-9); pap. text ed. 19.95x (ISBN 0-19-261238-7). Oxford U Pr.

Place of Blessed Augustine in the Orthodox Church. Seraphim Rose. (Illus.). 50p. Date not set. pap. 3.00. St Herman AK.

Place of Bonhoeffer: Problems & Possibilities in His Thought. Ed. by Martin E. Marty. LC 79-8718. 224p. 1981. Repr. of 1962 ed. lib. bdg. 35.00x (ISBN 0-313-20812-3, MAPL). Greenwood.

Place of Book Illumination in Byzantine Art. Kurt Weitzmann et al. (Princeton Univ., Publications of the Art Museum Ser.). 240p. 1975. 58.50x (ISBN 0-691-03910-0). Princeton U Pr.

Place of Culture & Civilization in Foreign Language Teaching see Culture, Literature, & Articulation.

Place of Dead Roads. William Burroughs. (Owl Bk.). 1985. pap. 7.95 (ISBN 0-03-003684-4). H Holt & Co.

Place of Dreams: Houston, an American City. Geoff Winningham & Al Reinert. LC 86-61304. (Illus.). 192p. 1986. 39.95 (ISBN 0-89263-263-1). Rice Univ.

Place of Endocrine Therapy in Breast Disease: Proceedings from a Conference, No. 111. 1988. pap. 12.50 (ISBN 0-905958-46-2, Pub. by Royal Society of Medicine Services Ltd). Longwood Pub Group.

Place of Exile: The European Settlement of New South Wales. David McKay. 184p. 1985. 29.95x (ISBN 0-19-554632-6). Oxford U Pr.

Place of Faith & Grace in Judaism. David R. Blumenthal. 29p. (Orig.). 1985. pap. 3.95 (ISBN 0-918873-03-7). Ctr Judaic-Christ Studies.

Place of Grammar & the Use of English in the Teaching of Foreign Languages see Language Classroom.

Place of Help. Oswald Chambers. 1973. pap. 3.95 (ISBN 0-87508-139-8). Chr Lit.

Place of Her Own: The Story of Elizabeth Garrett. rev. ed. Ruth K. Hall. LC 83-5104. (Illus.). 171p. 1983. pap. 8.95 (ISBN 0-913270-68-7). Sunstone Pr.

Place of Hope. Carol Gino. 368p. Date not set. 15.95 (ISBN 0-671-49499-6, Linden). S&S.

Place of Houses. rev. ed. Charles W. Moore et al. LC 70-182776. (Illus.). 288p. 1979. pap. 9.95 (ISBN 0-03-052361-3, Owl Bks.). H Holt & Co.

Place of Iceland in the History of European Institutions, Being the Lothian Prize Essay, 1877. Charles A. Conybeare. Repr. of 1877 ed. 15.00 (ISBN 0-404-01696-0). AMS Pr.

Place of Ideology in Political Life. D. J. Manning & T. J. Robinson. LC 84-45822. 128p. 1985. 31.00 (ISBN 0-7099-1796-1, Pub. by Croom Helm Ltd). Routledge Chapman & Hall.

Place of Information in Educational Development. Leo Fernig. (IBE Studies & Surveys in Comparative Education). (Illus.). 135p. 1980. pap. 5.00 (ISBN 92-3-101822-1, U1059, UNESCO). UNIPUB.

Place of James Thomson. D. W. Jefferson. (Warton Lectures on English Poetry). 1978. pap. 5.50 (ISBN 0-85672-181-6, Pub. by British Acad). Longwood Pub Group.

Place of Law in Lukacs' World Concept. Csaba Varga. Tr. by Judit Petranyi & Sandor Eszenyi. Rev. by Jeremy Payne. 196p. 1985. text ed. 17.50 (ISBN 963-05-3877-6, Pub. by Akademiai Kiado Hungary). Humanities.

Place of Literature in the Teaching of English As a Second or Foreign Language. Albert H. Marckwardt. LC 77-25360. 86p. 1978. pap. text ed. 4.50x (ISBN 0-8248-0606-9, Eastwest Ctr). UH Pr.

Place of Magic in the Intellectual History of Europe. Lynn Thorndike. LC 70-177455. (Columbia University Studies in the Social Sciences: No. 62). Repr. of 1905 ed. 14.50 (ISBN 0-404-51062-0). AMS Pr.

Place of "Measure for Measure" in Shakespeare's Universe of Comedy. William J. Martz. 150p. 1982. 10.00x (ISBN 0-686-88126-5). Coronado Pr.

Place of Minds in the World. William Mitchell. LC 77-27201. (Gifford Lectures: 1924-26). 400p. Repr. of 1933 ed. 35.00 (ISBN 0-404-60477-3). AMS Pr.

Place of Musicology in American Institutions of Higher Learning, 2 vols. in one. Ed. by Manfred Bukofzer et al. Incl. Some Aspects of Musicology. LC 77-4226. (Music Reprint Ser.). 1977. Repr. of 1957 ed. lib. bdg. 27.50 (ISBN 0-306-77407-0). Da Capo.

Place of Oral Reading in the School Program: Its History & Development from 1880-1941. Ada Hyatt. LC 76-176891. (Columbia University. Teachers College. Contributions to Education Ser.: No. 872). Repr. of 1943 ed. 22.50 (ISBN 0-404-55872-0). AMS Pr.

Place of Poetry: Two Centuries of an Art in Crisis. Christopher Clausen. LC 80-5172. 160p. 1981. 15.00x (ISBN 0-8131-1429-2). U Pr of Ky.

Place of Power. Marilyn Cunningham. Ed. by Betty L. Kratoville. (Meridian Bks.). (Illus.). 64p. (gr. 3-9). 1989. lib. bdg. 4.95 (ISBN 0-87879-651-7, High Noon Books). Acad Therapy.

Place of Power: The American Episode in Human Evolution. Walter Anderson. LC 76-12809. 1976. pap. text ed. write for info. (ISBN 0-673-16268-0). Scott F.

Place of Prejudice in Modern Civilization. Arthur Keith. 1982. lib. bdg. 59.95 (ISBN 0-87700-336-X). Revisionist Pr.

Place of Pride: The Role of the Bishops in the Development of Catechesis in the United States. Mary C. Bryce. LC 84-17065. 227p. 1985. 25.95x (ISBN 0-8132-0595-6). Cath U Pr.

Place of Reason in Education. Bertram Bandman. LC 66-25169. (Studies in Educational Theory of the John Dewey Society: No. 4). 218p. 1967. 5.00 (ISBN 0-8142-0020-6). Ohio St U Pr.

Place of Reason in Ethics. Stephen Toulmin. 256p. 1986. text ed. 25.00x (ISBN 0-226-80843-2); pap. 10.95 (ISBN 0-226-80844-0). U of Chicago Pr.

Place of Residence. Christopher Bursk. (Sparrow Poverty Pamphlets Ser.: No. 44). 32p. (Orig.). 1983. pap. 2.00x (ISBN 0-935552-16-2). Sparrow Pr.

Place of St. Patrick in History & His Life. J. B. Burg. 59.95 (ISBN 0-8490-0839-5). Gordon Pr.

Place of Saint Thomas More in English Literature & History. Raymond W. Chambers. LC 65-15870. (English Biography Ser., No. 31). 1969. Repr. of 1937 ed. lib. bdg. 75.00x (ISBN 0-8383-0523-7). Haskell.

Place of Sense: Essays in Search of the Midwest. Ed. by Michael Martone. LC 88-15058. (Bur Oak Original Ser.). (Illus.). 170p. (Orig.). 1988. 17.50 (ISBN 0-87745-211-3); pap. 8.50 (ISBN 0-87745-217-2). U of Iowa Pr.

Place of Shelley. Robert P. Scott. LC 72-191829. 1878. lib. bdg. 17.50 (ISBN 0-8414-8152-0). Folcroft.

Place of Shelley Among English Poets. R. P. Scott. LC 76-116800. (Studies in Shelley, No. 25). 1970. Repr. of 1878 ed. lib. bdg. 43.95x (ISBN 0-8383-1042-7). Haskell.

Place of Silver Silence. Ardath Mayhar. (Millenium Science Fiction Ser.). (Illus.). (YA) (gr. 7 up). Date not set. 15.95. Walker & Co.

Place of Social Security in Welfare Policy: An Assessment of Federal Policy Changes & Their Impact on Texas, No. 5. (Policy Research Project Reports). 66p. 1974. 3.00 (ISBN 0-318-00183-7). LBJ Sch Pub Aff.

Place of Sodium Valproate in the Treatment of Epilepsy. Ed. by M. J. Parsonage & A. D. Caldwell. (International Congress & Symposium Ser.: No. 30). 208p. 1980. pap. 24.00 (ISBN 1-85315-046-0, Pub. by Royal Society of Medicine Services Ltd). Longwood Pub Group.

Place of Space & Other Themes. Jan T. Srzednicky. 1983. lib. bdg. 32.50 (ISBN 90-247-2844-4, Pub. by Martinus Nijhoff Netherlands). Kluwer Academic.

Place of Sport in Education: A Comparative Study. (Education Studies & Documents: No. 21). pap. 15.00 (ISBN 0-8115-1345-9). Kraus Repr.

Place of Springs. Viola G. Liddell. LC 78-31572. vii, 177p. 1982. pap. 7.50 (ISBN 0-8173-0121-6). U of Ala Pr.

Place of Suffering. John Ferguson. 137p. 1972. 7.95 (ISBN 0-227-67803-6). Attic Pr.

Place of the Dream in Clinical Psychoanalysis see Indications for Psychoanalysis.

Place of the Elementary Calculus in the Senior High School Mathematics. Noah B. Rosenberger. LC 71-177209. (Columbia University. Teachers College. Contributions to Education: No. 117). Repr. of 1921 ed. 22.50 (ISBN 0-404-55117-3). AMS Pr.

Place of the Humanities in Medicine. Eric J. Cassell. 1984. 7.00 (ISBN 0-317-07448-2). Hastings Ctr.

Place of the Lion see Novels.

Place of the Merchant of Venice in Shakespeare's Universe of Comedy. William J. Martz. lib. bdg. 69.95 (ISBN 0-87700-233-9). Revisionist Pr.

Place of the Pots in Akan Funerary Custom. James Bellis. LC 82-74220. 59p. (Orig.). 1982. pap. 5.00 (ISBN 0-686-46683-7). Indiana Africa.

Place of the Stage: License, Play, & Power in Rennaissance England. Steven Mullaney. (Illus.). 192p. 1988. 24.95x (ISBN 0-226-54760-4). U of Chicago Pr.

Place of the Swan. Lola Irish. 448p. 1986. 16.95 (ISBN 0-531-15029-1). Watts.

Place of the Tempest in Shakespeare's Universe of Comedy. William Martz. 8.00x (ISBN 0-87291-098-9). Coronado Pr.

Place of Value in a World of Facts. Wolfgang Kohler. 320p. 1976. pap. 3.95 (ISBN 0-87140-107-X). Liveright.

Place of Wesley in the Christian Tradition: Essays Delevered at Drew University in Celebration of the Commencement of the Publication of the Oxford Edition of the Works of John Wesley. Ed. by Kenneth E. Rowe. LC 76-27659. 168p. 1976. 16.50 (ISBN 0-8108-0981-8). Scarecrow.

Place of Your Own. Elizabeth James & Carol Barkin. (Skinny Bks.). (Illus.). 96p. (gr. 9 up). 1981. 9.75 (ISBN 0-525-37100-1, 0947-280). Dutton.

Place of Your Own. Virginia S. Strain. (Independent Living Ser.). (Illus.). 1978. pap. 12.00 (ISBN 0-07-061972-7). McGraw.

Place of Your Own Making: How to Build a One-Room Cabin, Studio, Shack, or Shed. Stephen Taylor. (Illus.). 96p. 1988. 14.95 (ISBN 0-8050-0364-9). H Holt & Co.

Place on Earth. Rev. ed. Wendell Berry. LC 82-81478. 352p. 1983. pap. 15.00 (ISBN 0-86547-083-9). N Point Pr.

Place on the Corner: Identity & Rank Among Black Streetcorner Men. Elijah Anderson. LC 78-1879. (Studies of Urban Society). 1978. 20.00x (ISBN 0-226-01953-5); pap. 9.00x (ISBN 0-226-01954-3). U of Chicago Pr.

Place Over Time: The Continuity of Southern Distinctiveness. Carl N. Degler. LC 77-586. (Walter Lynwood Fleming Lectures in Southern History Ser.). xiv, 138p. 1977. 12.95x (ISBN 0-8071-0299-7); pap. 6.95x. La State U Pr.

Place, Practice & Structure: Social & Spatial Transformation in Southern Sweden, 1750-1850. Allan Pred. LC 85-30652. 300p. 1986. 33.50x (ISBN 0-389-20615-6). B&N Imports.

Place Sous le Ciel Mauve. Anne Hampson. (Collection Harlequin Ser.). 192p. 1983. pap. 1.95 (ISBN 0-373-49364-9). Harlequin Bks.

Place to Begin: The New England Experience. LC 76-21312. 1976. 20.00 (ISBN 0-87156-182-4, Pub. by Sierra). Black Ice.

Place to Belong. Marilyn Donahue. LC 88-14808. (Quick Fox Line Ser.). Orig. Title: Violets Grow in Secret Places. (gr. 3-7). 1988. pap. 3.95 (ISBN 1-55513-757-1, Chariot Bks). Cook.

Place to Belong. Wendell Willis. LC 82-80356. (Journey Adult Ser.). 144p. 1982. pap. text ed. 4.95 (ISBN 0-8344-0119-3, Sweet). Worthy TX.

Place to Celebrate! Wedding & Party Locations for Southern California. Dawn Carter. 116p. (Orig.). 1986. pap. write for info. (ISBN 0-9616630-2-2). Love in Bloom Pub.

Place to Come Back To. Nancy Bond. LC 83-48745. 204p. (gr. 7 up). 1984. 13.95 (ISBN 0-689-50302-4, M K McElderry). Macmillan.

Place to Come to. Robert Penn Warren. 1977. 12.95 (ISBN 0-394-41064-5). Random.

Place to Dig In. William H. Hinson. 1987. 10.95t (ISBN 0-687-31549-2). Abingdon.

Place to Go Back To: Ronald Reagan in Dixon, Illinois. Norman E. Wymbs. 1987. 12.50 (ISBN 0-533-07196-8). Vantage.

Place to Grow Old: The Meaning of Environment in Old Age. Stephen M. Golant. LC 84-5042. (Columbia Studies of Social Gerontology & Aging). 420p. 1984. 42.50x (ISBN 0-231-04840-8); pap. 17.50 (ISBN 0-231-04841-6). Columbia U Pr.

Place to Hide. Evelyn Anthony. 256p. 1987. 17.95 (ISBN 0-399-13207-4, Putnam). Putnam Pub Group.

Place to Hide. Bill Gillham. (Illus.). 112p. (gr. 2-6). 1983. 9.95 (ISBN 0-233-97496-2). Andre Deutsch.

Place to Live: A Study of Housing for Women. YMCA of India Staff. 136p. Date not set. 4.50. Asia Bk Corp.

Place to Live: More Effective Low-Cost Housing in Asia. 216p. 1983. pap. text ed. 15.00 (ISBN 0-88936-371-4, IDRC209, IDRC). UNIPUB.

Place to Meet: A History of the Shire of Katanning Western Australia. Merle Bignell. 350p. 1983. 25.95 (ISBN 0-85564-202-5, Pub. by U of W Austral Pr). Intl Spec Bk.

Place to Place Indexes of the Price of Housing: Some New Estimates & a Comparative Analysis. James Follain et al. 98p. 1979. pap. text ed. 6.00x (ISBN 0-87766-265-7). Urban Inst.

Place to Raise Hell-Cheyenne Saloons. Scott Dial. 62p. 1977. pap. 2.95 (ISBN 0-933472-52-8). Johnson Bks.

Place to Stand. Philip Holmes. 1977. sewn in wrappers 4.95 (ISBN 0-685-04186-7, Pub. by Anvil Pr). Small Pr Dist.

Place to Stand. Philip Holmes. 96p. (Orig.). 1977. pap. 5.95 (ISBN 0-85646-034-6, Pub. by Anvil Pr Poetry). Longwood Pub Group.

Place to Stand: A Reformed Study of Creeds & Confessions. Cornelius Plantinga, Jr. LC 79-371. (Illus.). 1979. pap. text ed. 9.50 (ISBN 0-933140-01-0). CRC Pubns.

Place to Stand: When Life Throws You Off Balance. Mark Littleton. LC 86-3041. (Christian Living Ser.). 1986. pap. 6.95 (ISBN 0-88070-141-2). Multnomah.

Place to Start. Marilyn Levinson. LC 87-11414. 192p. (YA) (gr. 7 up). 1987. 12.95 (ISBN 0-689-31325-X, Atheneum Childrens Bks). Macmillan.

Place to Start: An Anthology for Living. Pauline L. Dixon. 80p. 1987. 6.95 (ISBN 0-8059-3095-7). Dorrance.

Place to Start: The Bible As a Guide for Today. R. T. Brooks. 120p. 1983. pap. 4.95 (ISBN 0-86683-708-6, HarpR). Har-Row.

Place Value & Regrouping Games. Lee Jenkins & Marion Nordberg. (Illus., Orig.). (gr. 1-4). 1976. pap. 6.95 (ISBN 0-918932-39-4). Activity Resources.

Place Where I Am Standing. Theodore Enslin. 1964. pap. 3.00 (ISBN 0-685-00997-1). Elizabeth Pr.

Place Where the Eelgrass Flows. Norman S. Reed. Ed. by Vineyard Gazette Editors. (Illus.). 81p. pap. 7.95. Quill Pubns GA.

Place with Promise. Edward Swift. LC 87-6677. 264p. 1987. 16.95 (ISBN 0-385-24287-5). Doubleday.

Place Your Body Is. Marjorie Edel. 98p. 1984. pap. 6.00 (ISBN 0-932136-07-9). Petronium Pr.

Placebo Play. E. A. Davis. 1980. 5.50 (ISBN 0-682-49646-4). Exposition-Phoenix.

Placebo: Theory, Research, & Mechanisms. Ed. by Leonard White et al. LC 84-19829. 474p. 1985. text ed. 50.00 (ISBN 0-89862-649-8). Guilford Pr.

Placebos & the Philosophy of Medicine: Clinical, Conceptual, & Ethical Issues. Howard Brody. LC 79-18481. 1980. lib. bdg. 15.00x (ISBN 0-226-07531-1). U of Chicago Pr.

Placemat Pets 'n Playmates. Pam Aulson. (Illus.). 24p. (gr. 6 up). 1980. pap. 3.00 (ISBN 0-9601896-2-9). Patch As Patch.

Placement & Compaction of Asphalt Mixtures- STP 829. Ed. by F. T. Wagner. LC 83-71927. 149p. 1984. text ed. 21.00 (ISBN 0-8031-0223-2, 04-829000-08). ASTM.

Placement & Improvement of Soil to Support Structures: Specialty Conference held at Cambridge, MA, August 26-28, 1968. American Society of Civil Engineers Staff. LC 72-185397. (Illus.). pap. 111.50 (ISBN 0-317-08328-7, 2019535). Bks Demand UMI.

Placement Handbook for Counseling Disabled Persons. Chrisann S. Geist & William Calzaretta. (Illus.). 346p. 1982. 41.25x (ISBN 0-398-04592-5). C C Thomas.

Placement in Rehabilitation. David Vandergoot & John Worrall. LC 79-10700. 252p. 1979. pap. text ed. 19.00x (ISBN 0-936104-58-9, 1147). Pro Ed.

Placement Plus & Plenty More. Pam Aulson. (Illus.). 64p. 1982. pap. 3.50 (ISBN 0-9601896-5-3). Patch As Patch.

Placement Representative I. Jack Rudman. (Career Examination Ser.: C-868). (Cloth bdg. avail. on request). pap. 14.00 (ISBN 0-8373-0868-2). Natl Learning.

Placement Representative II. Jack Rudman. (Career Examination Ser.: C-869). (Cloth bdg. avail. on request). pap. 14.00 (ISBN 0-8373-0869-0). Natl Learning.

Placement Services & Techniques. James T. Bowman & W. H. Graves. 1976. pap. 9.20x (ISBN 0-87563-124-X). Stipes.

Placenames in Maryland. Hamill Kenny. LC 84-60803. 368p. (Orig.). 1984. pap. 17.50 (ISBN 0-938420-28-3). Md Hist.

Placenames of the West Riding of Yorkshire. Frederic W. Moorman. pap. 34.00 (ISBN 0-384-40020-5). Johnson Repr.

Placenta - a Neglected Experimental Animal. P. Beaconsfield. 1979. 105.00 (ISBN 0-08-024430-0); pap. 40.00 (ISBN 0-08-024435-1). Pergamon.

Placenta: Human & Animal. Elizabeth M. Ramsey. LC 81-23372. 204p. 1982. 44.95 (ISBN 0-275-91378-3, C1378). Praeger.

Placenta: Receptors, Pathology & Toxicology. R. K. Miller. Ed. by H. Thiede. 390p. 1982. 76.50 (ISBN 0-275-91350-3, C1350). Praeger.

Plain English Repair & Maintenance Guide for Home Computers. Henry F. Beechhold. (Illus.). 224p. 1984. pap. 14.95 (ISBN 0-671-49293-4, Pub. by Computer Bks). S&S.

Plain Facts for Old & Young: Natural History & Hygiene of Organic Life. J. H. Kellogg. LC 73-20633. (Sex, Marriage & Society Ser.). 648p. 1974. Repr. 43.00x (ISBN 0-405-05808-X). Ayer Co Pubs.

Plain Film Approach to Abdominal Calcifications. Stephen R. Baker & Milton Elkin. (Saunders Monographs in Clinical Radiology: Vol. 21 c). (Illus.). 240p. 1983. 51.00 (ISBN 0-7216-1498-1). Saunders.

Plain Folk & Gentry in a Slave Society: White Liberty & Black Slavery in Augusta's Hinterlands. J. William Harris. (Illus.). viii, 224p. 1985. 28.50 (ISBN 0-8195-5125-2); pap. 12.95. Wesleyan U Pr.

Plain Folk in the New South: Social Change & Cultural Persistence, 1880-1915. I. A. Newby. 608p. 1988. text ed. 35.00 (ISBN 0-8071-1456-1). La State U Pr.

Plain Folk of the Old South. Frank L. Owsley. LC 82-9903. (Walter Lynwood Fleming Lectures in Southern History Ser.). 234p. 1982. text ed. 25.00 (ISBN 0-8071-1062-0); pap. 7.95 (ISBN 0-8071-1063-9). La State U Pr.

Plain Folk: The Life Stories of Undistinguished Americans. Ed. by David M. Katzman & William H. Tuttle, Jr. LC 81-3026. 224p. 1982. 22.95 (ISBN 0-252-00884-7); pap. 8.95 (ISBN 0-252-00906-1). U of Ill Pr.

Plain Girl. Virginia Sorensen. 156p. (gr. 3-7). 1988. 5.95 (HJ). HarBraceJ.

Plain Good Cookin' Ginnie Bedell. (Illus.). 7.50 (ISBN 0-918544-79-3). Wimmer Bks.

Plain Jane. Marion Chesney. (Nightingale Paperbacks Ser.). 280p. 1987. pap. 11.95 (ISBN 0-8161-4319-6, Large Print Bks). G K Hall.

Plain Jane. Marion Chesney. 1988. pap. 2.95 (ISBN 0-312-90323-5). St Martin.

Plain Jane: Being the Second Volume of a House for the Season. Marion Chesney. 192p. 1986. 12.95 (ISBN 0-312-61381-4). St Martin.

Plain Jane Vanilla. Missy McConnell. (Illus.). 48p. 20.00 (ISBN 0-88014-018-6). Mosaic Pr OH.

Plain Language from Truthful James. Bret Harte. 15.95 (ISBN 0-88411-593-3, Pub. by Aeonian Pr). Amereon Ltd.

Plain-Language Law Dictionary. Robert Rothenberg. (Reference Ser.). 1981. pap. 8.95 (ISBN 0-14-051109-1). Penguin.

Plain Language Movement Away from Legalese & Federalese: A Bibliography. Martha J. Birchfield & Wallis D. Hoffsis. (Public Administration Ser.: P 1898). 7p. 1986. 3.00 (ISBN 0-89028-818-6). Vance Biblios.

Plain Man & the Novel. Arthur A. Eaglestone, pseud. LC 78-105776. 1970. Repr. of 1940 ed. 21.50x (ISBN 0-8046-0946-2, Pub. by Kennikat). Assoc Faculty Pr.

Plain Man's Talk on the Labor Question. Simon Newcomb. LC 77-89756. (American Labor, from Conspiracy to Collective Bargaining, Ser. 1). 195p. 1969. Repr. of 1886 ed. 14.00 (ISBN 0-405-02143-7). Ayer Co Pubs.

Plain Murder. C. S. Forester. 15.95 (ISBN 0-8488-0097-4, Pub. by Amereon Hse). Amereon Ltd.

Plain of Smokes. Harvey Mudd. LC 82-14792. (Illus.). 98p. 1982. 14.00 (ISBN 0-87685-567-2); signed ed. 20.00 (ISBN 0-87685-568-0); pap. 6.50 (ISBN 0-87685-566-4). Black Sparrow.

Plain Ol' Charlie Deam: Pioneer Hoosier Botanist. Robert C. Kriebel. (Illus.). 208p. (Orig.). 1987. pap. 12.95 (ISBN 0-911198-85-7). Purdue U Pr.

Plain Old Man. Charlotte MacLeod. 224p. 1986. pap. 2.95 (ISBN 0-380-70148-0). Avon.

Plain Painters: Making Sense of American Folk Art. John M. Vlach. LC 88-600013. (New Directions in American Art Ser.). (Illus.). 256p. 1988. 45.00x (ISBN 0-87474-926-3); pap. 21.95. Smithsonian.

Plain Pathway to Plantations (1624) Richard Eburne. Ed. by Louis B. Wright. (Documents Ser.). 1978. 12.00x (ISBN 0-918016-37-1). Folger Bks.

Plain People see Collected Works.

Plain People: An Ethnography of the Holdeman Mennonites. Linda L. Boynton. (Illus.). 222p. (Orig.). 1986. pap. text ed. 9.95x (ISBN 0-88133-198-8). Sheffield Wisc.

Plain People of the Confederacy. B. I. Wiley. 11.25 (ISBN 0-8446-0294-9). Peter Smith.

Plain Pictures of Plain Doctoring: Vernacular Expression in New Deal Medicine & Photography. John D. Stoeckle & George Abbott White. 239p. 1985. 25.00 (ISBN 0-262-19236-5). MIT Pr.

Plain Pine Box: A Return to Simple Jewish Funerals & Eternal Traditions. Arnold M. Goodman. 8.95x (ISBN 0-87068-895-2). Ktav.

Plain Prayers for a Complicated World. Avery Brooke. 124p. 1983. 5.95 (ISBN 0-8164-0501-8, HarpR); pap. 2.95 (ISBN 0-8164-2428-4). Har-Row.

Plain Public Speaking. Charles R. Gruner. 192p. 1983. pap. text ed. write for info. (ISBN 0-02-348340-7). Macmillan.

Plain Sailing. Douglas Clark. 208p. cancelled (ISBN 0-575-04055-6, Pub. by Gollancz England). David & Charles.

Plain Sailing: A Masters & Green Mystery. Douglas Clark. LC 87-46127. 272p. 1988. pap. 3.95 (ISBN 0-06-080917-5, P-917, PL). Har-Row.

Plain Song. Brian Meehan. 24p. 1982. pap. 25.00 (ISBN 0-936576-07-3). Symposium Pr.

Plain Song: Collected Poems. Cliff Ashby. 154p. 1985. text ed. 15.95 (ISBN 0-85635-562-3). Carcanet.

Plain Southern Eating: Reminiscences of A.L. "Tommie" Bass, Herbalist. Ed. by John K. Crellin. LC 87-31765. (Illus.). 136p. 1988. 12.95 (ISBN 0-8223-0828-2). Duke.

Plain Speaking: An Oral Biography of Harry S. Truman. Merle Miller. 480p. 1986. pap. 4.95 (ISBN 0-425-09499-5). Berkley Pub.

Plain Tales from the Hills. Rudyard Kipling. Ed. by H. R. Woudhuysen. 288p. 1987. pap. 5.95 (ISBN 0-14-043287-6). Penguin.

Plain Tales from the Hills. Rudyard Kipling. Intro. by Andrew Rutherford. (World's Classics Ser.). 368p. 1987. pap. 5.95 (ISBN 0-19-281652-7). Oxford U Pr.

Plain Talk about Acupuncture. Ellinor R. Mitchell. (Illus.). 123p. (Orig.). 1987. pap. 8.95 (ISBN 0-9617918-0-2). Whalehall Inc.

Plain Talk About Word Business. 1970. 12.00 (ISBN 0-8183-0191-0). Pub Aff Pr.

Plain Talk: Clear Communication for International Development. David Jarmul. 76p. 1980. write for info (ISBN 0-86619-131-3). Vols Tech Asst.

Plain Talk, Guidelines for Speaking Out to Your Community About Health Care Costs. 58p. 1984. 15.00 (ISBN 0-317-36952-0, C-166556). Am Hospital.

Plain Talks on Parenting. William S. Deal. 1984. pap. 3.95 (ISBN 0-318-18715-9). Crusade Pubs.

Plain Truth about Armstrongism. 2nd ed. Roger R. Chambers. 176p. 1988. pap. 7.95 (ISBN 0-8010-2525-7). Baker Bk.

Plain Truth about Seventh Day Adventists. Hoehn. 36p. 1988. pap. 6.00 (ISBN 0-914009-87-7). VHI Library.

Plain Truth About the Plain Truth. Salem Kirban. (Illus.). 1972. pap. 4.95 (ISBN 0-912582-12-X). Kirban.

Plain Truth & Redirection of the Cold War. rev. ed. Edward F. Haskell & Harold G. Cassidy. 170p. 1984. write for info. CURE.

Plain Words About AIDS: With a Glossary of Related Terms. W. Hovey Smith. (Illus.). 134p. (Orig.). 1986. pap. 9.95 (ISBN 0-916565-08-4). Whitehall Pr.

Plain Words about AIDS: With a Glossary of Related Terms. 3rd ed. W. Hovey Smith. (Illus.). 200p. (Orig.). 1988. pap. 19.50 (ISBN 0-916565-11-4). Whitehall Pr.

Plain Words about AIDS: With Glossary of Related Terms. 2nd ed. Ed. by Hovey Smith. (Illus.). 200p. (Orig.). 1987. pap. 17.50 (ISBN 0-916565-09-2). Whitehall Pr.

Plain X-Ray Diagnosis of the Acute Abdomen: A Surgical Handbook with Notes on Clinical Presentation & Differential Diagnosis. 2nd ed. Gough et al. (Illus.). 224p. 1986. cancelled (ISBN 0-632-01432-6, B-1934-3). Mosby.

Plainchant Tradition of Southwester Rus. Joan L. Roccasalvo. 200p. 1986. 20.00 (ISBN 0-88033-096-1). East Eur Quarterly.

Plaine Declaration That Our Brownists Be Full Donatists. George Gifford. LC 74-80180. (English Experience Ser.: No. 661). 1974. Repr. of 1590 ed. 14.00 (ISBN 90-221-0661-6). Walter J Johnson.

Plaine Description of the Barmudas Now Called Sommer Islands: With an Addition Etc. Silvester Jourdan. LC 75-171770. (English Experience Ser.: No. 394). 52p. 1971. Repr. of 1613 ed. 8.00 (ISBN 90-221-0394-3). Walter J Johnson.

Plaine Mans Path-Way to Heaven. Arthur Dent. LC 74-80173. (English Experience Ser.: No. 652). 430p. 1974. Repr. of 1601 ed. 45.00 (ISBN 90-221-0652-7). Walter J Johnson.

Plainer Translation: Joseph Smith's Translation of the Bible, a History & Commentary. Robert J. Matthews. LC 75-5937. 1975. 15.95 (ISBN 0-8425-1411-2). Brigham.

Plains Across: The Overland Emigrants & the Trans-Mississippi West, 1840-60. John D. Unruh, Jr. LC 78-9781. (Illus.). 384p. 1982. 32.50 (ISBN 0-252-00698-4); pap. 8.95 (ISBN 0-252-00968-1). U of Ill Pr.

Plains & Southwest see Ethnographic Bibliography of North America.

Plains & the Rockies. 4th ed. Henry R. Wagner. Ed. by Robert H. Becker. LC 81-86051. (Illus.). 765p. 1982. 150.00 (Pub. by J Howell). Brick Row.

Plains Archaeology Sourcebook: Selected Papers of the Nebraska State Historical Society. Nebraska State Historical Society Staff. Ed. by Waldo R. Wedel. LC 83-47639. (North American Indian Ser.). 314p. 1985. lib. bdg. 40.00 (ISBN 0-8240-5887-9). Garland Pub.

Plains Country Towns. John C. Hudson. LC 84-13049. 200p. 1985. 25.00xx (ISBN 0-8166-1347-8); pap. 13.95 (ISBN 0-8166-1348-6). U of Minn Pr.

Plains Cree. David G. Mandelbaum. LC 76-43772. (Vol. 37.Pt 2). Repr. of 1940 ed. 21.00 (ISBN 0-404-15626-6). AMS Pr.

Plains Cree Texts. Leonard Bloomfield. LC 73-3552. (American Ethnological Society. Publications Ser.: No. 16). Repr. of 1934 ed. 36.00 (ISBN 0-404-58166-8). AMS Pr.

Plains Families: Exploring Sociology Through Social History. Scott G. McNall & Sally A. McNall. LC 82-60479. 384p. 1983. pap. text ed. write for info. (ISBN 0-312-61393-8); write for info. instr's. manual. St Martin.

Plains Folk: A Commonplace of the Great Plains. Jim Hoy & Tom Isern. LC 87-5082. (Illus.). 214p. 1987. 17.95 (ISBN 0-8061-2064-9). U of Okla Pr.

Plains Indian Autobiographies. Lynne W. O'Brien. LC 73-8339. (Western Writers Ser: No. 10). 1973. pap. 2.95x (ISBN 0-88430-009-9). Boise St Univ.

Plains Indian Book. (gr. 1-6). 1974. pap. 3.95 (ISBN 0-918858-02-X). Fun Pub AZ.

Plains Indian Designs. Caren Caraway. (International Design Library). (Illus.). 48p. (Orig.). 1984. pap. 5.95 (ISBN 0-88045-050-9). Stemmer Hse.

Plains Indian Mythology. Carol K. Rachlin & Alice Marriott. 224p. 1977. pap. 3.95 (ISBN 0-452-00766-6, Mer). NAL.

Plains Indian Painting: A Description of Aboriginal American Art. John C. Ewers. LC 76-43701. Repr. of 1939 ed. 24.50 (ISBN 0-404-15533-2). AMS Pr.

Plains Indian Raiders: The Final Phases of Warfare from the Arkansas to the Red River. Wilbur S. Nye. LC 67-24624. (Illus.). 438p. 1984. pap. 14.95 (ISBN 0-8061-1175-5). U of Okla Pr.

Plains Indian Sculpture: A Traditional Art from America's Heartland. John C. Ewers. LC 85-600247. (Illus.). 240p. 1986. 39.95 (ISBN 0-87474-422-9, EWPI); pap. 24.95 (ISBN 0-87474-423-7, EWPIP). Smithsonian.

Plains Indian Warrior. R. May. (How They Lived Ser.). (Illus.). 32p. (gr. 3-8). Date not set. PLB 12.67 (ISBN 0-86592-147-4). Rourke Corp.

Plains Indians. rev. ed. Kate Petty. (Small World Ser.). (Illus.). 32p. (gr. 3 up). 1988. 9.90 (ISBN 0-531-17096-9). Watts.

Plains Indians see West on Wood: Antique Wood Engravings of the Old West.

Plains Indians: An Educational Coloring Book. Spizzirri Publishing Co. Staff. Ed. by Linda Spizzirri. (Illus.). 32p. (gr. 1-8). 1981. pap. 1.49 (ISBN 0-86545-025-0). Spizzirri.

Plains Indians of North America. Robin May. (Original People Ser.). (Illus.). 48p. (gr. 4-8). 1987. PLB 75.96 6 bk. set (ISBN 0-317-60597-6); PLB 12.66 (ISBN 0-86625-258-4). Rourke Corp.

Plains Indians of the Twentieth Century. Ed. & intro. by Peter Iverson. LC 85-40475. (Illus.). 267p. (Orig.). 1985. 21.95 (ISBN 0-8061-1866-0); pap. 9.95 (ISBN 0-8061-1959-4). U of Okla Pr.

Plains Miwok Dictionary. Catherine A. Callaghan. LC 83-18034. (UC Publications in Linguistics Ser.: Vol. 105). 318p. 1984. pap. 25.00x (ISBN 0-520-09952-4). U of Cal Pr.

Plains Rifle. Hanson. 19.95 (ISBN 0-88227-015-X). Gun Room.

Plains Song. Wright Morris. LC 79-2655. (Illus.). 1980. 12.45i (ISBN 0-06-013047-4, HarpT). Har-Row.

Plains Song. Wright Morris. (Contemporary American Fiction Ser.). 241p. 1981. pap. 6.95 (ISBN 0-14-005778-1). Penguin.

Plains Woman: The Diary of Martha Farnsworth, 1882-1922. Ed. by Marlene Springer & Haskell Springer. LC 84-43169. (Illus.). 352p. 1986. 27.50x (ISBN 0-253-34510-3). Ind U Pr.

Plains Woman: The Diary of Martha Farnsworth, 1882-1922. Ed. by Marlene Springer & Haskell Springer. LC 84-43169. 352p. 1988. pap. 9.95 (ISBN 0-253-20480-1). Ind U Pr.

Plainsmen of the Yellowstone: A History of the Yellowstone Basin. Mark H. Brown. LC 60-5262. (Illus.). 480p. 1969. pap. 10.95 (ISBN 0-8032-5026-6, BB 397, Bison). U of Nebr Pr.

Plainsongs. John B. Gerald. (Illus.). 53p. (Orig.). 1985. pap. 7.00 (ISBN 0-941917-09-6). Gerald & Maas.

Plainswoman. Anne Jordan. (Orig.). 1980. pap. 1.75 (ISBN 0-505-51545-8, Pub. by Tower Bks). Leisure NY.

Plaintext. Nancy Mairs. LC 85-27043. 154p. 1986. 15.95 (ISBN 0-8165-0892-5). U of Ariz Pr.

Plaintext: Deciphering a Woman's Life. Nancy Mairs. LC 86-46085. 160p. 1987. pap. 6.95 (ISBN 0-06-097094-5, PL 7094, PL). Har-Row.

Plaintiff's Master Exhibit on Conditions in Haiti. Haitian Refugee Center Staff. 85.00. Natl Lawyers Guild.

Plaintiff's Proof of a Prima Facie Case: 1982, 1 Vol. Ed. by D. Kirk Drussel & Judith A. Wade. LC 82-4177. 521p. 90.00 (ISBN 0-317-12039-5); Suppl., 1983. 20.00. Callaghan.

Plainville, U. S. A. James West. LC 45-1863. 1945. pap. 14.50x (ISBN 0-231-08514-1). Columbia U Pr.

Plaisir D'Amour: An Erotic Memoir of Paris in the 1920s. Anne-Marie Villefranche. 252p. 1984. pap. 3.95 (ISBN 0-88184-096-3); cloth 12.95 (ISBN 0-88184-022-X). Carroll & Graf.

Plaisir du Texte. Roland Barthes. 1973. 9.95 (ISBN 0-686-53940-0). French & Eur.

Plaisirs Et Les Jours. Marcel Proust. (Imaginaire Ser.). 1924. 6.50 (ISBN 0-685-11499-6). Schoenhof.

Plaisted Family. G. T. Ridlon. LC 75-133880. (Saco Valley Settlements Ser.). 1970. pap. 2.00 (ISBN 0-8048-0826-0). C E Tuttle.

Plaited Basketry: The Woven Form. Shereen LaPlantz. LC 82-90066. 1982. pap. 17.95 (ISBN 0-942002-00-8). Press LaPlantz.

Plakate-Fotomontagen. John Heartfield. 33.00x (ISBN 0-317-57335-7, Pub. by Collets UK). State Mutual Bk.

Plan Administrator's Compliance Manual, 2 vols. (Information Services Ser.). 1987. looseleaf 444.00; looseleaf 396.00; write for info. P-H.

Plan & Market: Economic Reform in Eastern Europe. Intro. by Morris Bornstein. LC 72-91289. (Yale Russian & East European Studies Ser.: No. 12). (Illus.). pap. 106.00 (ISBN 0-317-09696-6, 2021982). Bks Demand UMI.

Plan & Market in Yugoslav Economic Thought. Deborah D. Milenkovitch. LC 78-140534. (Russian & East European Studies: No. 9). Repr. of 1971 ed. 83.30 (ISBN 0-8357-9440-7, 2011104). Bks Demand UMI.

Plan & Market under Socialism. Ota Sik. LC 66-23896. pap. 95.50 (ISBN 0-317-41938-2, 2026138). Bks Demand UMI.

Plan & Operation of the Epidemiologic Follow-up Study to the First National Health & Nutrition Examination Survey. Bruce B. Cohen & Helen E. Barbano. Ed. by Mary Olmsted. LC 87-1324. (Series One: No. 22). 106p. pap. text ed. 4.00 (ISBN 0-8406-0366-5). Natl Ctr Health Stats.

Plan & Operation of the Hanes I Augmentation Survey of Adults 25-74 Years: United States 1974-1975. Arnold Engel et al. Ed. by Taloria Stevenson. (Series 1: No. 14). 1978. pap. text ed. 1.75 (ISBN 0-8406-0124-7). Natl Ctr Health Stats.

Plan & Operation of the Hispanic Health & Nutrition Examination Survey: 1982-84 (PHS) 85-1321. Kurt R. Maurer. Ed. by Mary Olmsted. (Series 1: No. 19). 448p. 1985. pap. text ed. 10.25 (ISBN 0-8406-0315-0). Natl Ctr Health Stats.

Plan & Operation of the Second National Health & Nutrition Examination Survey, 1976-80. (Series 1: No. 15). 144p. 6.50. Natl Ctr Health Stats.

Plan & Section Drawing. Thomas C. Wang. (Illus.). 100p. 1979. pap. 14.95 (ISBN 0-442-29178-7). Van Nos Reinhold.

PlAN & the Austrian Rebirth: A Journal of Literature, Art, & Culture. Ruth V. Gross. LC 81-66918. (Studies in German Literature, Linguistics, & Culture: Vol. 6). (Illus.). 170p. 1982. 24.00x (ISBN 0-938100-03-3). Camden Hse.

Plan "B" Protecting Your Career from the Winds of Change. Elwood N. Chapman. Ed. by Michael G. Crisp. LC 87-73560. (Illus.). 72p. 1988. pap. 7.95 (ISBN 0-931961-48-3). Crisp Pubns.

Plan Changes & Terminations. (Basic Concepts of Qualified Plans Ser.). write for info. Am Law Inst.

Plan de la Senorita Monstruo see Monstruo.

Plan Examiner. Jack Rudman. (Career Examination Ser.: C-651). (Cloth bdg. avail. on request). pap. 16.00 (ISBN 0-8373-0651-5). Natl Learning.

Plan for Automating the York County (PA) Court of Common Pleas: Final Report. National Center for State Courts Staff. 103p. 1985. manuscript 6.00 (NERO-170). Natl Ctr St Courts.

Plan for Escape. Adolfo Bioy-Casares. Tr. by Suzanne J. Levine from Span. 128p. 1988. pap. 7.50 (ISBN 1-55597-107-5). Graywolf.

Plan for Improving Female Education. Emma Willard. 44p. 1987. pap. 4.95 (ISBN 0-89783-044-X). Larlin Corp.

Plan for Lawyer Development: A Comprehensive Manual on Establishing & Administering CLE Programs in the Office. 250p. 1986. looseleaf 50.00 (ISBN 0-317-63631-6, 241-0012-01). Amer Bar Assn.

Plan for New York City. New York City Planning Commission. Ed. by Peter Richards. Incl. Vol. 1. Critical Issues. 1970. pap. 22.00 (ISBN 0-262-64004-X); Vol. 2. Bronx. 1970. pap. 22.00x (ISBN 0-262-64005-8); Vol. 3. Brooklyn. 1970; Vol. 4. Manhattan. 1970. o.p. (ISBN 0-262-64007-4); Vol. 5. Queens; Vol. 6. Staten Island. 24.00x (ISBN 0-262-64009-0). pap. MIT Pr.

Plan for Planning: The Need for a Better Method of Assisting Underdeveloped Countries on Their Economic Policies. Gustav F. Papanek. LC 78-38759. (Harvard University. Center for International Affairs. Occasional Papers: No. 1). Repr. of 1961 ed. 11.50 (ISBN 0-404-54601-3). AMS Pr.

Plan for Promotion: Advancement & the Manager. Tom Watling. 237p. 1977. text ed. 24.50x (ISBN 0-220-66327-0, Pub. by Busn Bks England). Brookfield Pub Co.

Plan for Success. James R. Sherman. (Do It! Success Ser.). 72p. 1988. pap. 2.95 (ISBN 0-935538-12-7). Pathway Bks.

Plan for Success: Time Management for the Pre-Med Student. Charles E. Kozoll. (Illus.). 65p. (Orig.). 1984. pap. 5.00 (ISBN 0-911899-01-4). NAAHP Inc.

Plan for the Dictionary of Old English. Ed. by Roberta Frank & Angus Cameron. LC 72-97152. (Toronto Old English Ser.). 1973. 35.00x (ISBN 0-8020-3303-2). U of Toronto Pr.

Plan for Writing. 3rd ed. John Brereton. 256p. 1987. pap. text ed. write for info. (ISBN 0-03-001432-8). HR&W.

Plan Graphics. 3rd ed. Theodore D. Walker. LC 75-12051. (Illus.). 235p. 1985. 28.00 (ISBN 0-914886-26-6); pap. 19.95 (ISBN 0-914886-27-4). PDA Pubs.

Plan Like a Grandmaster. Alexei Suetin. (Illus.). 272p. 1988. pap. 17.95 (ISBN 0-7134-5830-5, Pub. by Batsford England). David & Charles.

Plan Marshall: Mouvements de Capitaux et Liquidites Internationales. J. Mouly. (Economies et Societes Serie A: No. 10). 1955. pap. 19.00 (ISBN 0-8115-0611-8). Kraus Repr.

Plan of a Novel. Jane Austen. 1979. 42.50 (ISBN 0-685-94338-0). Bern Porter.

Plan of a Novel According to Hints from Various Quarters. Jane Austen. LC 72-188492. 1973. lib. bdg. 20.00 (ISBN 0-8414-1677-X). Folcroft.

Plan of Action for Personnel Generalists & Corporate Managers with Supervisory Responsibilities. Jean M. DuBois & Patricia J. Bestler. 138p. 1986. 3-ring binder 99.95 (ISBN 0-9615775-0-9). Raleigh Pub.

Plan of Chicago Prepared Under the Direction of the Commercial Club During the Years 1906, 1907, 1908. Daniel H. Burnham & Edward H. Bennett. Ed. by Charles Moore. LC 71-75303. (Architecture & Decorative Art Ser.: Vol. 29). (Illus.). 1970. Repr. of 1909 ed. lib. bdg. 125.00 (ISBN 0-306-71261-X). Da Capo.

Plan of Chicago: 1909-1979. Robert Bruegmann et al. LC 79-55997. (Illus.). 52p. (Orig.). 1979. pap. 4.95 (ISBN 0-86559-039-7). Art Inst Chi.

Plan of Mr. Pope's Garden with Gardens at Richmond, Kew & Environs. John Seris. Ed. by John D. Hunt. LC 79-56992. (English Landscape Graden Ser.). 115p. 1982. lib. bdg. 24.00 (ISBN 0-8240-0163-X). Garland Pub.

Plan of Parliamentary Reform, in the Form of a Catechism, with Reasons for Each Article. Jeremy Bentham. LC 75-41027. (BCL Ser. II). Repr. of 1818 ed. 16.50 (ISBN 0-404-14777-1). AMS Pr.

Plan of St. Gall in Brief: An Overview Based on the Three-Volume Work by Walter Horn & Ernest Born. Lorna Price. LC 82-70215. (Illus.). 120p. 1982. 65.00 (ISBN 0-520-04736-2); pap. 35.00 (ISBN 0-520-04334-0). U of Cal Pr.

Plan of Salvation. Ostis B. Wilson. 64p. pap. 0.50 (ISBN 0-686-29160-3). Faith Pub Hse.

Plan of Salvation & the Future in Prophecy. Duane S. Crowther. LC 72-173391. (Scripture Guide Ser.). 228p. 1971. pap. 6.95 (ISBN 0-88290-005-6). Horizon Utah.

Plan of the English Commerce, 3 Pts. 2nd ed. Daniel Defoe. LC 67-20365. 1967. Repr. of 1730 ed. 49.50x (ISBN 0-678-00316-5). Kelley.

Plan of the Snake: A Look at Our Government Today. James A. Fisher, Jr. LC 79-51483. 94p. (Orig.). 1979. pap. 4.95 (ISBN 0-933886-00-4). Black-A-Moors.

Plan Para Memorizar las Escrituras. J. W. Alexander. Orig. Title: Fire in My Bones. 48p. 1981. Repr. of 1979 ed. 1.75 (ISBN 0-311-03660-0). Casa Bautista.

Plan Paris, No. 12. 5th ed. 1986. pap. 5.95 (ISBN 2-060-00124-2). Michelin.

Plan Provisions Determining Benefits Payable. (Basic Concepts of Qualified Plans Ser.). 69p. 1979. pap. 9.00 (ISBN 0-317-32247-8, B341). Am Law Inst.

Plan Provisions Determining Benefits Payable. David C. Rothman. (Basic Concepts of Qualified Plans). 69p. 1979. pap. 3.00 (ISBN 0-317-31092-5, B341). Am Law Inst.

Plan Provisions Determining Eligibility to Participate. David C. Rothman. (Basic Concepts of Qualified Plans). 11p. 1978. pap. 1.50 (ISBN 0-317-31091-7, B340). Am Law Inst.

Plan Reading & Nonstructural Plan Review. instr's. guide 75.00 (ISBN 0-318-00070-9, BIT-101). Intl Conf Bldg Off.

Plan Reading & Nonstructural Plan Review. 1988. 14.00. Intl Conf Bldg Off.

Plan Reading for Home Builders. 2nd ed. Ralph J. Dalzell & Frederick Merritt. LC 82-14057. 186p. 1983. Repr. of 1972 ed. 14.50 (ISBN 0-89874-393-1). Krieger.

Plan Review Manual, 1986. 17.50 (ISBN 0-318-00052-0). Intl Conf Bldg Off.

Plan Review Manual, 1987. 1987. 16.00. Intl Conf Bldg Off.

Plan Septennal Sovietique: Etudes et Documents. (Economies et Societes Series G: No. 10). 1960. pap. 34.00 (ISBN 0-8115-0701-7). Kraus Repr.

Plan Termination Insurance. Henry Rose. (Qualified Plan Changes & Terminations Ser.). 35p. 1978. pap. 2.00 (ISBN 0-317-31235-9, B372). Am Law Inst.

Plan Terminations. Goodman. 24p. (Orig.). 1987. pap. 2.00 (5269). Commerce.

Plan Terminations Under the Internal Revenue Code Ser. James T. Tilton. (Qualified Plan Changes & Terminations). 134p. 1981. pap. 7.50 (ISBN 0-317-31225-1, B371). Am Law Inst.

Plan to Be Spiritual: The Wonderful Blessing of God's Direction & God's Power. David A. Norris. (Illus.). 31p. 1987. pap. 1.95x (ISBN 0-943177-05-7). Heartland Pr.

Plan to Promote Proper Traffic Operation on Crossroads Near Interchanges. 1963. 2.00 (ISBN 0-686-32366-1, TNI-1). AASHTO.

Plan: To Restore the Constitution & Help Us All Get Out of Debt. Paul Fisher. (Illus.). 300p. (Orig.). 1988. pap. 10.00 (ISBN 0-9619843-0-9). P Fisher.

Plan to Succeed: A Guide to Strategic Planning. Steven C. Stryker. (Illus.). 330p. 1986. text ed. 32.95 (ISBN 0-89433-251-1). Petrocelli.

Plan to Win. Bill Glass & James E. McEachern. 160p. 1984. 8.95 (ISBN 0-8499-0431-5, 0431-5). Word Bks.

Plan Two Thousand. Sean F. Mooney & Ruth Gastel. 184p. 1983. 150.00 (ISBN 0-932387-08-X). Insur Info.

Plan Your Estate: Wills, Probate Avoidance, Trusts & Taxes. National ed. Denis Clifford. 220p. (Orig.). 1988. pap. 17.95 (ISBN 0-87337-050-3). Nolo Pr.

Plan Your Estate, Wills, Probate, Avoidance, Trusts & Taxes: California Edition. 6th, rev. ed. Denis Clifford. 230p. 1987. pap. 15.95 (ISBN 0-87337-057-0). Nolo Pr.

Plan Your Route: New Approach to Map Reading. Victor Selwyn. (Illus.). 196p. 1988. 17.95 (ISBN 0-7153-8892-4, Pub. by David & Charles England). Hippocrene Bks.

Planar Circuits. T. Okoshi. (Springer Series in Electrophysics: Vol. 18). (Illus.). 220p. 1985. 49.50 (ISBN 0-387-13853-6). Springer-Verlag.

Planar Dimension: Europe, 1912-1932. Margit Rowell. LC 78-74711. 1981. pap. 12.95 (ISBN 0-89207-017-X). S R Guggenheim.

Planar Dimension: Europe, 1912-1932. Margit Rowell. LC 78-74711. (Illus.). 160p. 1979. pap. 14.95 (ISBN 0-295-96290-9). U of Wash Pr.

Planar Graphs: Theory & Algorithms. T. Nishizeki & N. Chiba. (Mathematics Studies, Vol.140:-Annals of Discrete Mathematics, Vol. 32). 410p. 1988. 100.00 (ISBN 0-444-70212-1, North Holland). Elsevier.

Planar Optical Waveguides & Fibres. H. G. Unger. (Oxford Engineering Science Ser.). (Illus.). 1977. 76.00x (ISBN 0-19-856133-4). Oxford U Pr.

Planar Transmission Line Structures. Tatsuo Itoh. LC 87-17277. 424p. 1988. 59.95 (ISBN 0-87942-232-7, PCO2196). Inst Electrical.

Planctus Mariae in the Dramatic Tradition of the Middle Ages. Sandro Sticca. Tr. by Joseph R. Berrigan. LC 87-12537. 288p. 1988. 35.00x (ISBN 0-8203-0983-4). U of GA Pr.

Plane Algebraic Curves. E. Brieskorn & Horst Knorrer. 864p. 1986. 58.95 (ISBN 0-8176-1769-8). Birkhauser.

Plane Algebraic Curves. Orzech. (Pure & Applied Mathematics Ser.: Vol. 67). 240p. 1981. 55.00 (ISBN 0-8247-1159-9). Dekker.

Plane Analytic Geometry. Walter W. Graham & William H. Rowan. (Quality Paperback Ser.: No. 47). 169p. (Orig.). 1968. pap. 3.50 (ISBN 0-8226-0047-1). Littlefield.

Plane & Coordinate Geometry Study Aid. Joseph A. Vellozi. 1974. pap. 2.50 (ISBN 0-87738-040-6). Youth Ed.

Plane Answers to Complex Questions: The/Theory of Linear Models. R. Christensen. LC 87-4978. (Texts in Statistics Ser.). (Illus.). 390p. 1987. 42.00 (ISBN 0-387-96487-8). Springer-Verlag.

Plane Crazy: A Celebration of Flying. Burton Bernstein. LC 85-8155. (Illus.). 165p. 1985. 16.95 (ISBN 0-89919-390-0). Ticknor & Fields.

Plane Crazy: A Celebration of Flying. Burton Bernstein. (Illus.). 192p. 1985. 16.95. HM.

Plane Ellipticity & Related Problems. Ed. by Robert P. Gilbert. LC 82-11562. (Contemporary Mathematics Ser.: Vol. 11). 256p. 1982. 25.00 (ISBN 0-8218-5012-1, CONM/11). Am Math.

Plane Figures & Sections: How to Construct Them Given Specific Conditions. P. V. Pritulenko. 1980. 8.45 (ISBN 0-8285-1778-9, Pub. by Mir Pubs USSR). Imported Pubns.

Plane Geometry. Barnett Rich. (Shaum Outline Ser.). (Orig.). 1963. pap. text ed. 7.95 (ISBN 0-07-052245-6). McGraw.

Plane Geometry & Other Affairs of the Heart: Stories. R. M. Berry. LC 84-8172. 189p. 1985. 13.95 (ISBN 0-914590-88-X); pap. 7.95 (ISBN 0-914590-89-8). Fiction Coll.

Plane Ride. Florance W. Taylor. LC 71-165321. (Felipe Adventure Stories Ser.). (Illus.). (gr. 2-4). 1971. PLB 3.95g (ISBN 0-8225-0147-3). Lerner Pubns.

Plane Safety & Survival. Eric G. Anderson. LC 78-8247. 1978. pap. 9.95h (ISBN 0-8168-7508-1, 27508, TAB-Aero); pap. 6.95 (ISBN 0-8168-7510-3). TAB Bks.

Plane Strain Crack Toughness: Testing of High Strength Metallic Materials. American Society for Testing & Materials Staff. LC 66-29517. (American Society for Testing & Materials, Special Technical Publication Ser.: No. 410). pap. 34.00 (ISBN 0-317-08331-7, 2051707). Bks Demand UMI.

Plane Strain Slip Line Fields for Metal Deformation Processes: A Source Book & Bibliography. W. Johnson et al. (Illus.). 270p. 1982. 65.00 (ISBN 0-08-025452-7). Pergamon.

Plane Table Manual for Geologists. Kenneth K. Landes. 1951. 3.00x (ISBN 0-685-21796-5). Wahr.

Plane Talk: Aviators' & Astronauts' Own Stories. Carl Oliver. (gr. 7 up). 1980. 7.95 (ISBN 0-395-29743-5). HM.

Plane Trigonometry. Walter Fleming & Dale E. Varberg. 1980. text ed. write for info. (ISBN 0-13-679043-7). P-H.

Plane Trigonometry. 2nd ed. Walter Fleming & Dale E. Varberg. (Illus.). 320p. 1988. text ed. write for info. (ISBN 0-13-679051-8). P-H.

Plane Trigonometry. 2nd ed. David R. Gustafson. LC 84-9446. 1984. text ed. 24.50 pub net (ISBN 0-534-03606-6). Brooks-Cole.

Plane Trigonometry. 5th ed. E. Richard Heineman. (Illus.). 1980. text ed. 38.95 (ISBN 0-07-027932-2). McGraw.

Plane Trigonometry. 6th ed. E. Richard Heineman. 352p. 1988. text ed. 33.95 (ISBN 0-07-027935-7). McGraw.

Plane Trigonometry. 4th ed. Rice & Strange. 1986. text ed. 27.50 (ISBN 0-87150-913-X, 33L4040, Prindle). PWS Kent Pub.

Plane Trigonometry. 3rd ed. Bernard J. Rice & Jerry D. Strange. LC 80-26108. 322p. 1981. text ed. 24.00 (ISBN 0-87150-297-6, 2381, Prindle). PWS Kent Pub.

Plane Trigonometry. Jack Rudman. (DANTES Ser.: No. 29). 1988. 25.95 (ISBN 0-8373-6679-8); pap. 13.95 (ISBN 0-8373-6629-1). Natl Learning.

Plane Trigonometry. 8th ed. Fred W. Sparks et al. (Illus.). 352p. 1984. text ed. write for info. (ISBN 0-13-679225-1). P-H.

Plane Trigonometry. Allyn J. Washington & Carolyn E. Edmond. LC 76-7883. 1977. 27.95 (ISBN 0-8465-8622-3); instr's. guide 10.95 (ISBN 0-8465-8623-1). Benjamin-Cummings.

Plane Trigonometry: A New Approach. 2nd ed. Carol Johnston. LC 77-16841. 1978. text ed. write for info. (ISBN 0-13-677666-3). P-H.

Plane Trigonometry & Four-Place Tables. William A. Granville. LC 52-3178. pap. 69.00 (ISBN 0-317-08698-7, 2000160). Bks Demand UMI.

Plane Trigonometry with Practical Applications. Leonard E. Dickson. LC 70-114597. (Illus.). (gr. 10-12). 1970. Repr. of 1922 ed. text ed. 14.95 (ISBN 0-8284-0230-2). Chelsea Pub.

Plane Trigonometry with Tables. 5th ed. Gordon Fuller. LC 77-22329. (Illus.). 1977. text ed. 36.95 (ISBN 0-07-022612-1). McGraw.

Plane Trigonometry with Tables. 7th ed. Charles S. Rees et al. (Illus.). 1977. text ed. 23.95. P-H.

Plane: Watch It Work! Ray Marshall & John Bradley. LC 85-3263. (Illus.). 10p. 1985. 13.95 (ISBN 0-670-80695-1). Viking.

Plane Waves & Spherical Means Applied to Partial Differential Equations. F. John. (Illus.). 172p. 1981. pap. 28.00 (ISBN 0-387-90565-0). Springer-Verlag.

Planeamiento Nacional De Servicios Bibliotecarios, Vol. 2. (Span.). 1972. pap. 1.00 (ISBN 0-8270-3055-X). OAS.

Planecraft. C. W. Hampton & E. Clifford. LC 79-57129. (Illus.). 1982. pap. 6.00 (ISBN 0-918036-00-3). Woodcraft Supply.

Planecraft: A Woodworker's Handbook. John Sainsbury. LC 83-24217. (Illus.). 192p. 1984. pap. 11.95 (ISBN 0-8069-7848-1). Sterling.

Planemakers: Boeing. Ed. by Michael J. Taylor. (Planemakers Ser.). (Illus.). 160p. 1982. 17.95 (ISBN 0-86720-554-7). Janes Info Group.

Planen und Auswerten von Versuchen. 3rd ed. A. Linder. (Reihe der Experimentellen Biologie Ser.: No. 13). (Illus.). 344p. (Ger.). 1969. 52.95x (ISBN 0-8176-0248-8). Birkhauser.

Planes. Anne Rockwell. LC 84-13732. (Illus.). 24p. (ps-1). 1985. 9.95 (ISBN 0-525-44159-X). Dutton.

Planes & Airports. Chris McAllister. (Illus.). 64p. 1981. pap. 7.95 (ISBN 0-7134-3911-4, Pub. by Batsford England). David & Charles.

Planes, Planebuilders & Pilots. Hoff. 1987. write for info. (ISBN 0-471-08204-X). Wiley.

Planet Beyond. Littman. (Science Editions Ser.). 1988. 22.95 (ISBN 0-471-61128-X). Wiley.

Planet Called Utopia. J. T. McIntosh. (Orig.). 1979. pap. 1.95 (ISBN 0-89083-503-9). Zebra.

Planet Earth. Martyn Bramwell. (Earth Science Library). (Illus.). 32p. (gr. 4-9). 1987. PLB 9.90 (ISBN 0-531-10346-3). Watts.

Planet Earth. David Lambert. (Gateway Fact Bks.). (Illus.). 96p. (gr. 4-6). 1983. PLB 9.90 (ISBN 0-531-09215-1). Watts.

Planet Earth. Mark Pettigrew. (Science Today Ser.). (Illus.). 32p. (gr. k-6). 1987. lib. bdg. 11.90 (ISBN 0-531-17043-8, Gloucester Pr). Watts.

Planet Earth. Karl Stumpff. Tr. by Philip Wayne. LC 59-5266. (Ann Arbor Science Library Ser.). pap. 47.80 (ISBN 0-317-09526-9, 2055653). Bks Demand UMI.

Planet Earth. Jonathan Weiner. LC 85-47795. 384p. 1986. pap. 14.95 (ISBN 0-553-34358-0). Bantam.

Planet Earth. Jonathan Wiener. LC 85-47795. (Illus.). 356p. 1986. 24.95 (ISBN 0-553-05096-6). Bantam.

Planet Earth & the New Geoscience. Victor A. Schmidt. 576p. 1986. pap. 25.95 (ISBN 0-8403-3809-0). Kendall-Hunt.

Planet Earth in Jeopardy: Environmental Consequences of Nuclear War. Lydia Dotto. LC 85-22747. 134p. 1986. 14.95 (ISBN 0-471-99836-2). Wiley.

Planet Earth in Jeopardy: Environmental Consequences of Nuclear War (SCOPE 28) Lydia Dotto. LC 85-22747. 1986. pap. write for info. (ISBN 0-471-90908-4). Wiley.

Planet Earth 2000. David Lambert. (Your World 2000 Ser.). (Illus.). 64p. (YA) (gr. 7 up). 1986. 12.95 (ISBN 0-8160-1153-2). Facts on File.

Planet Hunters. Seth McEvoy. (Be An Interplanetary Spy Ser.: No. 10). 128p. (Orig.). (gr. 3 up). 1985. pap. 1.95 (ISBN 0-553-24532-5). Bantam.

Planet in Arms. Donald Barr. 288p. 1981. pap. 2.25 (ISBN 0-449-24407-5, Crest). Fawcett.

Planet in Peril. Kim Mohan & Pamela O'Neil. 1987. pap. 3.50 (ISBN 0-441-66883-6, Pub. by Ace Science Fiction). Ace Bks.

Planet Medicine: From Stone-Age Shamanism to Post-Industrial Healing. 3rd, rev. ed. Richard Grossinger. LC 82-50278. 486p. 1987. 25.00; pap. 14.95 (ISBN 1-55643-019-1). North Atlantic.

Planet News: Poems, 1961-1964. Allen Ginsberg. LC 68-25477. (Pocket Poet Ser.: No. 23). (Orig.). 1968. pap. 3.50 (ISBN 0-87286-020-5). City Lights.

Planet Noise. Liam O'Gallagher. (Nova Broadcast Ser.: No. 4). (Illus.). 43p. (Orig.). 1969. pap. 3.50 (ISBN 0-89366-022-1). Ultramarine Pub.

Planet of Exile. Ursula K. Le Guin. (Orig.). 1983. pap. 1.95 (ISBN 0-441-66957-3, Pub. by Ace Science Fiction). Ace Bks.

Planet of Gold. Russell A. Byrd. (Illus.). 88p. 1983. pap. 5.95 (ISBN 0-911096-02-7). Pacific-West.

Planet of Ice. Harriette S. Abels. Ed. by Howard Schroeder. LC 79-9920. (Galaxy I Ser.). (Illus.). 48p. (gr. 3-5). 1979. PLB 7.95 (ISBN 0-89686-026-4). Crestwood Hse.

Planet of Junior Brown. Virginia Hamilton. LC 71-155264. (Illus.). 240p. (gr. 7 up). 1971. 14.95 (ISBN 0-02-742510-X). Macmillan.

Planet of Junior Brown. Virginia Hamilton. LC 85-16651. (Illus.). 224p. (gr. 5-9). 1986. pap. 3.95 (ISBN 0-02-043540-1, Collier). Macmillan.

Planet of Lost Things. Mark Strand. LC 81-19138. (Illus.). 32p. (ps-3). 1983. 9.95 (ISBN 0-517-54184-X, C N Potter). Crown.

Planet of No Return. Harrison. 2.75 (ISBN 0-523-48557-3, Dist. by Warner Pub Services & St Martin's Press). Tor Bks.

Planet of No Return. Harry Harrison. 256p. 1981. pap. 6.95 (ISBN 0-671-43138-2, Wallaby). S&S.

Planet of Reason: A Sociological Study of Man-Nature Relationship. I. Laptev. Tr. by Jane Sayer. 220p. 1977. 7.50x (ISBN 0-317-53779-2, Pub. by Collets (UK)). State Mutual Bk.

Planet of Reason: A Sociological Study of the Interrelation of Society & Nature. I. Laptev. (Current Problems Ser.). 1977. 4.95 (ISBN 0-8285-3327-X, Pub. by Progress Pubs USSR). Imported Pubns.

Planet of Sorrows. R. A. Montgomery. (Choose Your Own Adventure Ser.: No. 87). 176p. (Orig.). 1989. pap. 2.50 (ISBN 0-553-27651-4). Bantam.

Planet of Tears. Trish Reinius. (Illus.). 157p. 1985. pap. 8.00 (ISBN 0-932987-00-1). Iris IO.

Planet of Terror. Walker Books Staff. (Illus.). 48p. (gr. 1-5). 1986. bds. 4.95 (ISBN 0-671-60717-0, Little Simon). S&S.

Planet of the Apes. Pierre Boulle. 128p. (RL 7). 1968. pap. 2.50 (ISBN 0-451-14324-8, AJ2318, Sig). NAL.

Planet of the Apes. Pierre Boulle. LC 63-21843. 224p. 1963. 14.95 (ISBN 0-8149-0064-X). Vanguard.

Planet of the Condemned see Ten Top Stories.

Planet of the Damned. Harrison. pap. 2.95 (ISBN 0-523-48565-4, Dist. by Warner Pub Services & St. Martin's Press). Tor Bks.

Planet of the Dead. Donald Wismer. (Orig.). 1988. pap. 2.95 (ISBN 0-671-65400-4). Baen Bks.

Planet of the Dinosaurs. Stephanos Attalides. (Adventure Box Ser.: No. III). (Illus.). 12p. (ps up). 1988. 4.95 (ISBN 0-694-00265-8). HarpJ.

Planet of the Double Sun. Neil R. Jones. Ed. by Lester Del Ray. LC 75-413. (Library of Science Fiction). 1975. lib. bdg. 21.00 (ISBN 0-8240-1418-9). Garland Pub.

Planet of the Dragons. Richard Brightfield. (Choose Your Own Adventure Ser.: No. 75). (gr. 5 up). 1988. pap. 2.50 (ISBN 0-553-26887-2). Bantam.

Planet of the Financial Planners (and other aberrations) Michael Silverstein. (Illus.). 88p. (Orig.). 1987. pap. 5.95 (ISBN 0-943209-00-5). Silverwood Pubns.

Planet of the Gawfs. Steve Vance. (Inflation Fighter Ser.). 176p. pap. 1.50 (ISBN 0-8439-1113-1, Leisure Bks). Leisure NY.

Planet of the Warlord. Douglas Hill. (YA) (gr. 7 up). 1987. pap. 2.50 (ISBN 0-440-97126-8). Dell.

Planet of Trash. George Poppel. (Illus.). 32p. (ps-3). 1987. 9.95 (ISBN 0-915765-42-X, Pub. by Panda Monium Bks.). Natl Pr Inc.

Planet of Waters. Douglas Anderson. 135p. (Orig.). 1983. pap. 6.95 (ISBN 0-912549-00-9). Bread and Butter.

Planet of Whispers. James P. Kelly. (Messengers Chronicles Ser.: Vol. 1). 240p. 1984. 14.95 (ISBN 0-312-94369-5). Bluejay Bks.

Planet of Whispers. James P. Kelly. 240p. 1985. 2.95 (ISBN 0-8125-4291-6, Dist. by Warner Pub. Services & St. Martin's Press). Tor Bks.

Planet of Youth. Coblentz. 1952. 3.50 (ISBN 0-686-21530-3); pap. 1.00 (ISBN 0-686-21531-1). Fantasy Pub Co.

Planet on the Table. Kim S. Robinson. 256p. 1986. 14.95 (ISBN 0-312-93595-1, Dist. by St. Martin's Press). Tor Bks.

Planet on the Table. Kim S. Robinson. 256p. 1987. pap. 3.50 (ISBN 0-8125-5237-7, Dist. by St Martin's Pr & Warner Pub Servs). Tor Bks.

Planet out of the Past. James L. Collier. LC 83-9365. 168p. (gr. 5-9). 1983. 10.95 (ISBN 0-02-722860-6). Macmillan.

Planet Pluto. Anthony J. Whyte & Herbert A. Wise. LC 79-23998. 1980. 32.00 (ISBN 0-08-024648-6). Pergamon.

Planet Run. Laumer & Dickson. 2.75 (ISBN 0-523-48525-5, Dist. by Warner Pub. Services & St. Martin's Press). Tor Bks.

Planet Savers: The Sword of Aldones. Marion Zimmer Bradley. 1984. pap. 2.75 (ISBN 0-441-67025-3). Ace Bks.

Planet That Wasn't. Isaac Asimov. LC 75-40710. 216p. 1976. pap. 7.95 (ISBN 0-385-11687-X). Doubleday.

Planet That Wasn't There. Isaac Asimov. 1983. pap. 1.75 (ISBN 0-380-01813-6, 35709-7, Discus). Avon.

Planet Venus. Garry Hunt & Patrick Moore. LC 82-5045. (Illus.). 240p. 1983. 22.00 (ISBN 0-571-09050-8). Faber & Faber.

Planet Vulcan: History, Nature, Tables. L. Weston. 35p. 1941. 3.50 (ISBN 0-317-66052-7, 1515-01). Am Fed Astrologers.

Planeta Fantasma. new ed. Harris Moore. Tr. by Javier Lopez from Eng. (Compadre Collection). Orig. Title: Slater's Planet. 160p. (Span.). 1974. pap. 0.75 (ISBN 0-88473-603-2). Fiesta Pub.

Planetanimals: Mission Zapton. Nancy Fornatora. Ed. by Jean Lewis. LC 84-61163. (Illus.). 48p. (ps-3). 1984. 5.95 (ISBN 0-448-18965-8). Putnam Pub Group.

Planetarium. Nathalie Sarraute. (Folio Ser.: No. 92). 1972. 6.95 (ISBN 0-686-54967-8). Schoenhof.

Planetarium. Nathalie Sarraute. Tr. by Maria Jolas from Fr. (Orig.). 1980. pap. 4.95 (ISBN 0-7145-0444-0). Riverrun NY.

Planetariums: A Bibliography on Their Architecture, Construction & Development. Glenna Dunning. (Architecture Ser.: A 1489). 23p. 1985. 3.75 (ISBN 0-89028-619-1). Vance Biblios.

Planetarization of Consciousness. (Dane Rudhyar Ser.). 320p. pap. 9.95 (ISBN 0-943358-16-7). Aurora Press.

Planetarnoe Soznanie. Mihailo Mihailov. 230p. (Rus.). 1982. 20.00 (ISBN 0-88233-752-1). Ardis Pubs.

Planetary & Lunar Exploration. National Research Council. (Space Science in the Twenty-First Century Series: Imperatives for the Decades 1995 to 2015). 128p. 1988. pap. text ed. 12.00x (ISBN 0-309-03885-5). Natl Acad Pr.

Planetary & Proto-Planetary Nebulae: From IRAS to ISO. Ed. by Andrea P. Martinez. 1987. lib. bdg. 74.00 (ISBN 90-277-2517-9, Pub. by Reidel Holland). Kluwer Academic.

Planetary & Stellar Worlds: A Popular Exposition of the Great Discoveries & Theories of Modern Astronomy. Ormsby M. Mitchel. Ed. by I. Bernard Cohen. LC 79-7976. (Three Centuries of Science in America Ser.). (Illus.). 1980. Repr. of 1848 ed. lib. bdg. 23.00x (ISBN 0-405-12559-3). Ayer Co Pubs.

Planetary Aspects: From Conflict to Cooperation. Rev. ed. Tracy Marks. LC 86-26445. 220p. (Orig.). 1987. pap. 8.95 (ISBN 0-916360-32-6). CRCS Pubns CA.

Planetary Atmospheres: Proceedings of the I.A.U. Symposium, No. 40,Marfa, Texas, 1969. International Astronomical Union Staff. Ed. by C. Sagan et al. LC 77-140566. (I.A.U. Symposia: No. 40). 408p. 1971. lib. bdg. 42.00 (ISBN 90-277-0165-2, Pub. by Reidel Holland). Kluwer Academic.

Planetary Commission. John R. Price. LC 84-61264. 176p. (Orig.). 1984. pap. 7.95 (ISBN 0-942082-05-2). Quartus Bks.

Planetary Containment. Alexander Volguine. Tr. by John Broglio from Fr. (French Astrology Ser.). (Illus.). 1987. write for info. (ISBN 0-88231-006-2). ASI Pubs Inc.

Planetary Containments: A Study of 990 Combinations. John Sandbach & Ronn Ballard. 336p. 1980. pap. 10.95 perfect bdg. (ISBN 0-930706-05-6). Seek-It Pubns.

Planetary Cycles: Astrological Indicators of Crises & Change. Betty Lundsted. LC 84-51107. (Illus.). 192p. (Orig.). 1984. pap. 8.95 (ISBN 0-87728-630-2). Weiser.

Planetary Ecology. Ed. by Douglas E. Caldwell et al. (Illus.). 544p. 1985. 62.95 (ISBN 0-442-24007-4). Van Nos Reinhold.

Planetary Effects on Stock Market & Commodity Prices: The Influence of Certain Planetary Positions & Commodity Futures Prices, 2 vols. in 1. James M. Langham. (Illus.). 1979. Repr. deluxe ed. 287.50x (ISBN 0-86654-269-8). Inst Econ Finan.

Planetary Electrodynamics, 2 Vols. Ed. by Samuel C. Coroniti & J. Hughes. (Illus.). 1132p. 1969. Set. 275.00 (ISBN 0-677-13600-5). Gordon & Breach.

Planetary Emotions. Charles Reid. 1980. 18.00x (ISBN 0-85032-172-7, Pub. by Daniel Co England). State Mutual Bk.

Planetary Equatorium of Jamshid Ghiath al-Din al-Kashi. Tr. by Edward S. Kennedy. (Princeton Studies on the Near East). 1960. 43.00x (ISBN 0-691-08019-4). Princeton U Pr.

Planetary Exploration. Arthur Smith. (Illus.). 192p. (Orig.). 1988. pap. 12.95 (ISBN 0-85059-915-6, Pub. by PSL P Stephens England). Sterling.

Planetary Exploration: Proceedings. Ed. by Harry Massey & S. K. Runcorn. (Royal Society of London Ser.). (Illus.). 167p. 1982. text ed. 55.00x (ISBN 0-85403-185-5, Pub. by Royal Soc London). Scholium Intl.

Planetary Exploration: Thirty Years of Unmanned Space Probes. Arthur Smith. (Illus.). 192p. 1988. Repr. lib. bdg. 28.95x (ISBN 0-8095-7067-X). Borgo Pr.

Planetary Exploration Through Year 2000: An Augmented Program, Pt. 2. (Illus.). 239p. (Orig.). 1986. pap. 12.00 (ISBN 0-318-21305-2, S/N 033-000-00987-9). USGPO.

Planetary Exploration Through Year 2000, A Core Program: Mission Operations, A Report by the Solar Exploration Committee of the NASA Advisory Council. (Illus.). 55p. 1986. pap. 4.00 (ISBN 0-318-22422-4, S/N 033-000-00993-3). USGPO.

Planetary Forces Ruling the Course of History & the Actions of Men. Heraclitus. (Illus.). 147p. 1985. Repr. of 1901 ed. 127.75 (ISBN 0-89901-203-5). Found Class Reprints.

Planetary Gods & Planetary Orders in the Mysteries of Mithras. Roger Beck. LC 87-30906. (Etudes Preliminaires Aux Religions Orientales Dans L'Empire Romain Ser.: Vol. 109). (Illus.). xiii, 120p. (Orig.). 1988. pap. 24.00 (ISBN 90-04-08450-9, Pub. by E J Brill). Heinman.

Planetary Herbology. Michael Tierra. Ed. by David Frawley. LC 87-80889. (Illus.). 490p. (Orig.). 1988. pap. 16.95 (ISBN 0-941524-27-2). Lotus Light.

Planetary Heredity. rev ed. Michel Gauquelin. (Illus., Orig.). 1988. pap. 8.95 (ISBN 0-935127-01-1). A C S Pubns Inc.

Planetary Influence & Human Soul. Manly P. Hall. pap. 2.50 (ISBN 0-89314-341-3). Philos Res.

Planetary Influences & Therapeutic Uses of Precious Stones. George F. Kunz. 63p. pap. 4.50 (ISBN 0-89540-153-3). Sun Pub.

Planetary Influences Upon Plants: Cosmological Botany. Ernst M. Kranich. 184p. (Orig.). pap. 12.50 (ISBN 0-938250-20-5). Anthroposophic.

Planetary Interiors. William B. Hubbard. 1984. 49.95 (ISBN 0-442-23704-9). Van Nos Reinhold.

Planetary Interiors. V. N. Zharkov & V. P. Trubitsyn. Ed. by W. B. Hubbard. (Astronomy & Astrophysics Ser.: Vol. 6). 399p. 1978. pap. text ed. 24.00 (ISBN 0-912918-15-2, 0015). Pachart Pub Hse.

Planetary Landscapes. Ronald Greeley. (Illus.). 256p. 1985. 60.00x (ISBN 0-04-551080-6). Unwin Hyman.

Planetary Landscapes. rev ed. Ronald Greeley. (Illus.). 288p. 1987. pap. text ed. 29.95x (ISBN 0-04-551081-4). Unwin Hyman.

Planetary, Lunar & Solar Positions A. D. 2 to A. D. 1649 at Five Day & Ten Day Intervals. Bryant Tuckerman. LC 64-14093. (Memoirs Ser.: Vol. 59). 842p. 1964. 25.00 (ISBN 0-317-65165-X). Am Philos.

Planetary, Lunar & Solar Positions Six Hundred-One B. C to A. D One at Five-Day & Ten-Day Intervals. Bryant Tuckerman. (Memoirs Ser.: Vol. 56). 333p. 1979. Repr. of 1962 ed. 20.00 (ISBN 0-87169-056-X). Am Philos.

Planetary, Lunar & Solar Positions, 1650-1805. Owen Gingerich & Barbara L. Welther. LC 83-1805. (Memoirs: Vol. 59S). 1983. 20.00 (ISBN 0-87169-590-1). Am Philos.

Planetary Man. Wilfrid Desan. 380p. 1987. pap. 12.95 (ISBN 0-87840-437-6). Georgetown U Pr.

Planetary Mysteries. Ed. by Richard Grossinger. (Io Ser.). (Illus.). 192p. 1986. 20.00 (ISBN 0-938190-71-7). North Atlantic.

Planetary Mysteries. 2nd ed. Ed. by Richard Grossinger. (Illus.). pap. 12.95 (ISBN 0-938190-90-3). North Atlantic.

Planetary Nebulae. Ed. by David Flower. 1983. 65.00 (ISBN 90-277-1557-2, Pub. by Reidel Holland). Kluwer Academic.

Planetary Nebulae. G. A. Gurzadyan. 328p. 1969. 108.00 (ISBN 0-677-20220-2). Gordon & Breach.

Planetary Nebulae. G. A. Gurzadyan. Ed. & tr. by D. G. Hummer. LC 69-11664. 314p. 1971. lib. bdg. 45.00 (ISBN 90-277-0117-2, Pub. by Reidel Holland). Kluwer Academic.

Planetary Nebulae. Stuart R. Pottasch. 1984. lib. bdg. 43.00 (ISBN 90-277-1672-2, Pub. by Reidel Holland). Kluwer Academic.

Planetary Nebulae: Proceedings of the I.A.U. Symposium, No. 34, Tatranska, Lomnica, Czechoslovakia, 1967. International Astronomical Union Staff. Ed. by D. E. Osterbrock & C. R. O'Dell. (IAU Symposia: No. 34). 469p. 1968. lib. bdg. 45.00 (ISBN 90-277-0134-2, Pub. by Reidel Holland). Kluwer Academic.

Planetary Nebulae: Proceedings of the I.A.U. Symposium, No. 78. International Astronomical Union Staff. Ed. by Yervant Terzian. 1978. lib. bdg. 47.50 (ISBN 90-277-0872-X, Pub. by Reidel Holland); pap. 31.50 (ISBN 90-277-0873-8, Pub. by Reidel Holland). Kluwer Academic.

Planetary Planting. 2nd ed. Louise Riotte. (American Gardening Ser.: No. 13). 352p. 1982. pap. 9.95 (ISBN 0-917086-38-4). A C S Pubns Inc.

Planetary Product in Nineteen Eighty-Two: World Economic Output, 1970-1982. Herbert Block & Ray S. Cline. LC 83-21067. (Significant Issues Ser.: Vol V, No. 8). 31p. 1983. 5.95 (ISBN 0-89206-051-4). CSI Studies.

Planetary Product in 1982: World Economic Output, 1970-1982. Herbert Block & Ray S. Cline. (Significant Issues Ser.: Vol. V, No. 8). 38p. 1983. pap. text ed. 6.95 (ISBN 0-8191-5923-9, Pub. by CSIS). U Pr of Amer.

Planetary Programs & Tables. Pierre Bretagnon & Jean L. Simon. LC 86-9099. 160p. 1986. pap. text ed. 19.95x (ISBN 0-943396-08-5). Willmann-Bell.

Planetary Quarantine: Principles, Methods & Problems. Ed. by Lawrence B. Hall & Charles W. Shilling. LC 71-158834. (Illus.). 184p. 1971. 79.00 (ISBN 0-677-15100-4). Gordon & Breach.

Planetary Rings. Ed. by Richard Greenberg & Andre Brahic. LC 84-125. 785p. 1983. 50.00x (ISBN 0-8165-0828-3). U of Ariz Pr.

Planetary Satellites. Ed. by Joseph A. Burns. LC 76-7475. 598p. 1977. text ed. 29.50x (ISBN 0-8165-0552-7). U of Ariz Pr.

Planetary Science: A Lunar Perspective. Stuart R. Taylor. LC 82-193. (Illus.). 512p. 1982. 30.00X (ISBN 0-942862-00-7). Lunar & Planet Inst.

Planetary Service. Eugen Rosenstock-Huessy. Tr. by Mark Huessy & Freya Von Moltke. 1978. pap. 6.00 (ISBN 0-912148-09-8). Argo Bks.

Planetary Spheres & Their Influence on Man's Life on Earth & in Spiritual Worlds. Rudolf Steiner. Tr. by George Adams et al from Ger. 120p. 1982. pap. 10.95 (ISBN 0-85440-392-2, Pub by Steinerbooks). Anthroposophic.

Planetary Symbolism in the Horoscope, Vol. 2. Karen Hamaker-Zondag. LC 84-52312. (Jungian Symbolism & Astrology Ser.: Vol. 2). (Illus.). 224p. (Orig.). 1985. pap. 8.95 (ISBN 0-87728-623-X). Weiser.

Planetary System. Tobias Owen & David Morrison. (AW Physics Ser.). 600p. 1987. text ed. price not set (ISBN 0-201-10487-3). Addison-Wesley.

Planetary Theology. Tissa Balasuriya. LC 83-19339. 288p. (Orig.). 1984. pap. 10.95 (ISBN 0-88344-400-3). Orbis Bks.

Planete des Fleurs see King's Garden.

Planete des Singes. Pierre Boulle. 9.95 (ISBN 0-686-54110-3). French & Eur.

Planetfall. Douglas Hill. (Illus.). 96p. (gr. 3-7). 1987. 13.95 (ISBN 0-19-278113-8). Oxford U Pr.

Planetfall: In Search of Floyd, Pt. 1. Arthur B. Cover. 304p. 1988. pap. 3.95 (ISBN 0-380-75384-7). Avon.

PlanetHood. Benjamin B. Ferencz. 192p. (Orig.). 1988. pap. 2.50 (ISBN 0-915972-14-X, Vsn Bks). Love Line Bks.

Planets. Norman Barrett. LC 85-50159. (Picture Library Ser.). (Illus.). 32p. (gr. 3-5). 1985. PLB 10.90 (ISBN 0-531-10005-7). Watts.

Planets. Kim Jackson. LC 84-16451. (Illus.). 32p. (gr. k-2). 1985. lib. bdg. 9.89 (ISBN 0-8167-0450-3); pap. text ed. 2.95 (ISBN 0-8167-0451-1). Troll Assocs.

Planets. Michael Jay. (Easy-Read Fact Book Ser.). (Illus.). 32p. (gr. k-3). 1987. PLB 9.90 (ISBN 0-531-10278-5). Watts.

Planets. Kate Petty. (First Library Ser.). (Illus.). 32p. (gr. k-3). 1984. lib. bdg. 10.90 (ISBN 0-531-04734-2). Watts.

Planets. Byron Preiss. LC 85-47649. (Spectra Ser.). 304p. (Orig.). 1985. pap. 24.95 (ISBN 0-553-05109-1, Spectra). Bantam.

Planets. Ruth Radlauer & Charles Stembridge. LC 83-21043. (GEO Bks.). (Illus.). 48p. (gr. 3 up). 1984. lib. bdg. 13.27 (ISBN 0-516-07838-0); pap. 3.95 (ISBN 0-516-47838-9). Childrens.

Planets. Jonathan Rutland. LC 86-26219. (All About Bks.). (Illus.). 24p. (gr. 2-5). 1987. lib. bdg. 6.99 (ISBN 0-394-98972-4, BYR); pap. 2.95 (ISBN 0-394-88972-X). Random.

Planets: An Educational Coloring Book. Spizzirri Publishing Co. Staff. Ed. by Linda Spizzirri. (Illus.). 32p. (gr. 1-8). 1982. pap. 1.49 (ISBN 0-86545-043-9). Spizzirri.

Planets & Galaxies. Dan Mackie. (Technology Ser.). (Illus.). 32p. (gr. 5-9). 1986. PLB 10.99 (ISBN 0-87617-006-8, Pub. by C Hayes Pr). Penworthy Pub.

Planets & Galaxies. Dan Mackie. (Hayes Technology Ser.). (Illus.). 32p. (gr. 5-9). 1985. pap. 5.95 (ISBN 0-88625-102-8). C Hayes Pr.

Planets & Human Behavior. Jeff Mayo. LC 85-22367. 182p. 1986. pap. 7.95 (ISBN 0-916360-27-X). CRCS Pubns CA.

Planets & Moons. William J. Kaufmann, III. LC 78-21156. (Illus.). 219p. 1979. pap. text ed. 12.95 (ISBN 0-7167-1040-4). W H Freeman.

Planets & Perception: Telescopic Views & Interpretations, 1609-1909. William Sheehan. LC 88-20501. 330p. 1988. 35.00x (ISBN 0-8165-1059-8). U of Ariz Pr.

Planets & Pulleys: Studies of Class Visits to Science Museums. Minda Borun et al. (Illus.). 128p. (Orig.). 1983. pap. 12.50 (ISBN 0-944040-04-7). AST Ctrs.

Planets & Satellites. Ed. by Gerard P. Kuiper & Barbara M. Middlehurst. LC 54-7183. (Solar System Ser.: Vol. 3). 1961. 50.00x (ISBN 0-226-45927-6). U of Chicago Pr.

Planets & the Solar System. Keith Brandt. LC 84-2714. (Illus.). 32p. (gr. 3-6). 1985. PLB 8.45 (ISBN 0-8167-0300-0); pap. text ed. 1.95 (ISBN 0-8167-0301-9). Troll Assocs.

Planets & Their Atmospheres: Origin & Evolution (Monograph) John S. Lewis & Ronald G. Primm. LC 83-10001. (International Geophysics Ser.). 1983. 65.00 (ISBN 0-12-446580-3); pap. 35.00 (ISBN 0-12-446582-X). Acad Pr.

Planets: Exploring the Solar System. Roy A. Gallant. LC 84-29725. (Illus.). 192p. (gr. 7 up). 1985. Repr. of 1982 ed. 15.95 (ISBN 0-02-736930-7, Four Winds). Macmillan.

Planets in Aspect: Understanding Your Inner Dynamics. Robert Pelletier. LC 74-82711. (Planets Ser.). 1974. pap. 19.95 (ISBN 0-914918-20-6). Para Res.

Planets in Combination. Lynne Burmyn. (Orig.). 1987. pap. 12.95 (ISBN 0-917086-78-3). A C S Pubns Inc.

Planets in Composite: Analyzing Human Relationships. Robert Hand. LC 75-17260. (Planets Ser.). 1975. 19.95 (ISBN 0-914918-22-2). Para Res.

Planets in Houses: Experiencing Your Environment Planets. Robert Pelletier. Ed. by Margaret Anderson. (Planets Ser.). (Illus.). 1978. pap. 19.95 (ISBN 0-914918-27-3). Para Res.

Planets in Locality. Steve Cozzi. Ed. by Tom Streissguth. LC 88-45190. (Modern Astrology Ser.). 250p. (Orig.). 1988. pap. 12.95 (ISBN 0-87542-098-2). Llewellyn Pubns.

Planets in Love: Exploring Your Emotional & Sexual Needs. John Townley. (Planets Ser.). 1978. pap. 18.95 (ISBN 0-914918-21-4). Para Res.

Planets in Our Solar System. Franklyn M. Branley. LC 79-7894. (Let's Read & Find out Science Bks.). (Illus.). 40p. (gr. k-3). 1981. (Crowell Jr Bks); PLB 12.89 (ISBN 0-690-04026-1). HarpJ.

Planets in Our Solar System. rev. ed. Franklyn M. Branley. LC 86-47530. (Let's-Read-&-Find-Out Science Bks.). (Illus.). 32p. (ps-3). 1987. 12.95i (ISBN 0-690-04579-4, Crowell Jr Bks); PLB 12.89 (ISBN 0-690-04581-6). HarpJ.

Planets in Our Solar System. Franklyn M. Branley. LC 86-45171. (Trophy Let's-Read-&-Find-out Bks.). (Illus.). 32p. (ps-3). 1987. pap. 3.95 (ISBN 0-06-445064-3, Trophy). HarpJ.

Planets in Signs. Skye Alexander. Ed. by Marah Ren & Julie Lockhart. 300p. (Orig.). 1988. pap. 18.95 (ISBN 0-914918-79-6, Pub. by Whitford Pr). Schiffer.

Planets in Transit: Life Cycles for Living. Robert Hand. LC 76-12759. (Planets Ser.). 1980. pap. 22.95 (ISBN 0-914918-24-9). Para Res.

Planets in Work. Jamie Binder. 1988. pap. 17.95 (ISBN 0-917086-89-9). A C S Pubns Inc.

Planets in Youth: Patterns of Early Development. Robert Hand. (Planets Ser.). 1981. pap. 18.95 (ISBN 0-914918-26-5). Para Res.

Planets, Stars & Galaxies. Melvin Berger. LC 78-16688. (Illus.). (gr. 6-8). 1978. PLB 7.99 (ISBN 0-399-61104-5, Putnam). Putnam Pub Group.

Planets, Stars & Galaxies. Anthony E. Fanning. (Illus.). 1966. pap. 4.95 (ISBN 0-486-21680-2). Dover.

Planets, Stars & Galaxies: Descriptive Astronomy for Beginners. Anthony E. Fanning. (Illus.). 13.00 (ISBN 0-8446-2042-4). Peter Smith.

Planets, Stars & Nebulae Studied With Photopolarimetry. Ed. by T. Gehrels. LC 73-86446. 1133p. 1974. 27.50x (ISBN 0-8165-0428-8). U of Ariz Pr.

Planets: The Next Frontier. David J. Darling. LC 84-12668. (Discovering Our Universe Ser.). (Illus.). 64p. (gr. 4 up). 1984. PLB 10.95 (ISBN 0-87518-263-1). Dillon.

Planets Through the Signs: Astrology for Living. Abbe Bassett. 160p. 1987. pap. 10.00 (ISBN 0-89540-170-3, SB-170). Sun Pub.

Planets Through the Signs: Astrology for Living. Abbe Bassett. 152p. 1987. pap. 10.00 (ISBN 0-317-66692-4, SB-170). Sun Pub.

Planets Within: Ficino's Astrological Psychology. Thomas Moore. LC 81-65457. (Illus.). 224p. 1982. 26.50 (ISBN 0-8387-5022-2). Bucknell U Pr.

Planets "X" & Pluto. William G. Hoyt. LC 79-15665. 302p. 1980. pap. 10.95 (ISBN 0-8165-0664-7). U of Ariz Pr.

Planforms: Model Documents for Legal Services Plans. 2nd ed. Ed. by William A. Bolger. Date not set. price not set. NRCCLS.

Planificacion Para Computadoras: Evaluacion de las Necesidades de Procesamiento de Datos para Bufetes de Abogados Medianos y Grandes. ABA, Economics of Law Practice Section. 133p. (Span.). 1986. pap. 30.00. Amer Bar Assn.

Planification, Banque et Gestion Economique en U. R. S. S. (Economies et Societes Series G: No. 18). 1963. pap. 19.00 (ISBN 0-8115-0709-2). Kraus Repr.

Planification Dans les Pays D'economie Capitaliste. Jean-Pierre Delilez. (Confluence Ser.: No. 14). 1968. pap. 14.00x (ISBN 90-2796-011-9). Mouton.

Planification de l'Agriculture en Pologne see Cahiers de l'Institut de Science Economique Appliquee.

Planification et Analyse Economiques. (Economies et Societes Series G: No. 20). 1964. pap. 34.00 (ISBN 0-8115-0711-4). Kraus Repr.

Planning & Design of Townhouses & Condominiums. Robert E. Engstrom & Marc Putman. LC 79-64813. (Illus.). 246p. 1979. pap. 38.00 (ISBN 0-87420-587-5, P20). Urban Land.
Planning & Designing Correctional Facilities. Jay Farbstein. (Illus.). 384p. 1986. 68.95x (ISBN 0-442-22619-5). Van Nos Reinhold.
Planning & Designing Lighting. Edward Effron. (Illus.). 144p. 1987. 22.95 (ISBN 0-316-21235-0). Little.
Planning & Designing Plumbing Systems. John E. Traister. LC 85-17189. (Illus.). 224p. 1983. pap. 13.00 (ISBN 0-910460-39-6). Craftsman.
Planning & Designing the Data Base Environment. Thomas A. Turk. (Illus.). 240p. 1985. 37.95 (ISBN 0-442-28528-0). Van Nos Reinhold.
Planning & Developing a Library Orientation Program: Proceedings. Ed. by Mary Bolner. LC 75-676. (Library Orientation Ser.: No. 3). 1975. 19.50 (ISBN 0-87650-061-0). Pierian.
Planning & Development in Iran. George B. Baldwin. LC 67-18377. pap. 57.80 (ISBN 0-317-19825-4, 2023082). Bks Demand UMI.
Planning & Development in Modern Libya. Mukhtar Buru et al. 234p. 1985. lib. bdg. 27.50x (ISBN 0-906559-19-7). Lynne Rienner.
Planning & Development of Educational Programmes for Personnel in Oral Health. H. Allred & M. H. Hobdell. (WHO Offset Publication Ser.: No. 93). 101p. 1986. pap. 9.60 (ISBN 92-4-170093-9). World Health.
Planning & Development of Nuclear Power Programmes. (Nuclear Power Experience Ser.: Vol. 1). 459p. 1983. pap. text ed. 72.00 (ISBN 92-0-050083-8, ISP627 1, IAEA). UNIPUB.
Planning & Development of Towns. R. G. Gupta. 1984. 22.50x (ISBN 0-8364-1233-8, Pub. by Oxford IBH). South Asia Bks.
Planning & Drafting Marital Termination Agreements. 600p. 1988. 95.00 (FA-30890). Cal Cont Ed Bar.
Planning & Drafting of Wills & Trusts: 2nd ed. 1982 Supplement. Thomas L. Shaffer. (University Textbook). 68p. 1982. pap. text ed. 3.75 (ISBN 0-88277-083-7). Foundation Pr.
Planning & Ecology. Ed. by R. D. Roberts & T. M. Roberts. (Illus.). 400p. 1984. 55.00x (ISBN 0-412-23560-9, NO. 6896). Routledge Chapman & Hall.
Planning & Ecology. Ed. by R. D. Roberts & T. M. Roberts. 480p. 1986. pap. text ed. 39.95 (ISBN 0-412-28470-7, 9975, Pub. by Chapman & Hall England). Routledge Chapman & Hall.
Planning & Economic Policy in India: Enlarged & Revised Edition. D. R. Gadgil. 1972. 19.50x (ISBN 0-8046-8809-5, Pub. by Kennikat). Assoc Faculty Pr.
Planning & Economic Policy: Socialist Mali & Her Neighbors. William I. Jones. LC 76-8048. (Illus.). 1976. cased 18.00 (ISBN 0-914478-70-2); pap. 10.00 (ISBN 0-914478-71-0). Three Continents.
Planning & Engineering Interface with a Modernized Land Data System. Ed. by G. Warren Marks. LC 80-66123. 269p. 1980. pap. 26.00x (ISBN 0-87262-243-6). Am Soc Civil Eng.
Planning & Engineering of Radio Relay Links. H. Brodhage & W. Hormuth. 1977. 160.00 (ISBN 0-471-25615-3, Wiley Heyden). Wiley.
Planning & Engineering of Shortwave Links. 2nd ed. Gerhard Braun. LC 86-4108. 338p. 1986. 41.95 (ISBN 0-471-90868-1). Wiley.
Planning & Equipping Educational Music Facilities. Harold P. Geerdes. LC 75-15271. (Illus.). 96p. (Orig.). 1975. pap. 8.75 (ISBN 0-940796-13-9, 1036). Music Ed Natl.
Planning & Estimating Heavy Construction. A. D. Parker & D. S. Barrie. 1984. text ed. 49.50 (ISBN 0-07-048489-9). McGraw.
Planning & Evaluating Computer Education Programs. Ed. by Randy E. Bennett. 256p. 1987. pap. text ed. 20.95 (ISBN 0-675-20499-2). Merrill.
Planning & Evaluating Nursing Care. 2nd ed. Jona. 64p. 1976. pap. 25.25 (ISBN 0-913654-29-9). Aspen Pub.
Planning & Evaluating Rural Reconstruction Projects: A Practical Manual for Project Managers. International Institute of Rural Reconstruction, Research Division Staff. 77p. 1984. pap. text ed. 3.00 (ISBN 0-942717-12-0). Intl Inst Rural.
Planning & Evaluating Special Education Services. Charles A. Maher & Randy E. Bennett. (Illus.). 288p. 1984. text ed. 21.75 (ISBN 0-13-679481-5). P-H.
Planning & Evaluating Student Activity Programs. Douglas D. Christensen. 1978. pap. 5.00 (ISBN 0-88210-085-8). Natl Assn Principals.
Planning & Evaluation Assistant. Jack Rudman. (Career Examination Ser.: C-549). (Cloth bdg. avail. on request). pap. 16.00 (ISBN 0-8373-0549-7). Natl Learning.
Planning & Evaluation in Aid Organizations. Kim Forss. 406p. 1985. pap. 55.00x (ISBN 91-7258-196-4, Pub. by Almqvist & Wiksell). Coronet Bks.
Planning & Evaluation of Applied Nutrition Programmes. M. C. Latham. (Food & Nutrition Papers: No. 16). 125p. (Orig., 3rd Printing 1977). 1972. pap. 11.25 (ISBN 92-5-100439-0, F319, FAO). UNIPUB.
Planning & Evaluation of Applied Nutrition Programs: Planification Y Evaluacion de Los Programas de Nutricion Aplicada. (Span.). pap. 10.25 (F1302, FAO). UNIPUB.
Planning & Evaluation of Forestry Projects. G. Watt. 1973. 30.00x (ISBN 0-85074-014-2, Pub. by For Lib Comm). State Mutual Bk.
Planning & Evaluation of Health Education Services: Report. WHO Expert Committee. Geneva, 1967. (Technical Report Ser.: No. 409). (Also avail. in French, Russian & Spanish). 1969. pap. 2.40 (ISBN 92-4-120409-5). World Health.
Planning & Evaluation of Public Dental Health Services: Report. WHO Expert Committee, Geneva, 1975. (Technical Report Ser.: No. 589). (Also avail. in French & Spanish). 1976. pap. 2.40 (ISBN 92-4-120589-X). World Health.
Planning & Executing Computer Applications Development. 1984. write for info. loose-leaf (ISBN 0-935506-23-3). Carnegie Pr.
Planning & Federalism: Australian & Canadian Experience. Kenneth Wiltshire. LC 85-16521. (Scholars' Library). (Illus.). 335p. 1987. text ed. 42.50 (ISBN 0-7022-1958-4). U of Queensland Pr.
Planning & Finance in China's Economic Reforms. Thomas P. Lyons & Wang Yan. (Cornell University East Asia Papers: No. 46). 57p. (Orig.). 1988. pap. 5.00 (ISBN 0-939657-46-5). Cornell East Asia Pgm.
Planning & Financial Management for the School Principal. Howard M. Johnson. 1982. text ed. 24.95x (ISBN 0-8077-2719-9). Tchrs Coll.
Planning & Implementation of Drought-Prone Areas Programme. U. K. Srivastava. 1978. 12.50x (ISBN 0-8364-0299-5). South Asia Bks.
Planning & Implementing Health Education in Schools. Marion Pollock et al. 400p. 1987. text ed. 26.95 (ISBN 0-87484-563-7). Mayfield Pub.
Planning & Implementing Information Resource Centers for End-User Computing. Robert V. Head. LC 84-61536. 186p. (Orig.). 1985. pap. 34.95 (ISBN 0-89435-123-0, IC 1230). QED Info Sci.
Planning & Implementing Vocational Education in Nepal. Lekh N. Belbase. 326p. 1981. 30.00 (ISBN 0-318-12884-5, 41). Am-Nepal Ed.
Planning & Implementing Vocational Readiness in Occupational Therapy (PIVOT) Ed. by Martha Kirkland & Susan C. Robertson. (Illus.). 375p. 1985. 3-ring looseleaf binder 39.00 (ISBN 0-910317-12-7). Am Occup Therapy.
Planning & Implementing Your Neighborhood Projects Through the City Budget: A Primer of Community Planning Boards. 1979. pap. 3.00 (ISBN 0-88156-043-X). Comm Serv Soc NY.
Planning & Internal Control Under Prospective Payment. Robert W. Broyles & Michael D. Rosko. 1986. 51.95 (ISBN 0-87189-266-9). Aspen Pub.
Planning & Management for Health. (EURO Reports & Studies: No. 102). 65p. 1986. pap. 4.80 (ISBN 92-890-1268-4). World Health.
Planning & Management of Agricultural Research. Ed. by Dieter Elz. (Symposium Ser.). 160p. 1985. 12.50 (ISBN 0-8213-0430-5, BK 0430). World Bank.
Planning & Management of Distance Education. Greville Rumble. LC 86-13847. 259p. 32.50 (ISBN 0-312-61403-9). St Martin.
Planning & Management of Environmentally Sensitive Areas. Paul F. Eagles. pap. text ed. 15.95 (ISBN 0-582-30074-6). Wiley.
Planning & Management of Environmentally Sensitive Areas. Paul F. Eagles. 224p. 1984. pap. 18.95 (ISBN 0-470-20471-0, Co-Pub. with Longman). Wiley.
Planning & Management of Special Education in Nepal. Harsha N. Dhaubhadel. 60p. 1983. pap. 10.00 (ISBN 0-318-03447-6). Am-Nepal Ed.
Planning & Management of Zoological Parks: A Selected Annotated Bibliography. Jerry E. Green. (Architecture Ser.: A 1430). 18p. 1985. 3.00 (ISBN 0-89028-480-6). Vance Biblios.
Planning & Managing Adult Day Care. Linda C. Webb. 300p. 1988. 28.00 (ISBN 0-932500-95-1). Natl Hlth Pub.
Planning & Managing Housing for the Elderly. Mortimer P. Lawton. LC 74-28099. (Illus.). pap. 87.50 (ISBN 0-317-09607-9, 2022488). Bks Demand UMI.
Planning & Managing Interior Projects. Carol E. Farren. Ed. by William D. Mahoney. (Illus.). 225p. 1988. text ed. 44.95 (ISBN 0-87629-097-7, 67245). R S Means.
Planning & Managing Major Construction Projects: A Guide for Hospitals. Deborah J. Rohde et al. LC 84-28997. 112p. 1985. pap. text ed. 18.00 (ISBN 0-910701-01-6, 0651, Pub. by Health Administration Press Perspectives). Health Admin Pr.
Planning & Managing the Economy of the City: Policy Guidelines for the Metropolitan Mayor. Joseph Oberman & Robert Bingham. LC 72-79544. (Special Studies in U. S. Economic, Social & Political Issues). 1972. 29.50x (ISBN 0-275-06160-4). Irvington.
Planning & Market Relations: Proceedings of a Conference Held by the International Economic Association at Liblice, Czechoslovakia. Ed. by Michael Kaser & Richard Portes. LC 75-163474. (Illus.). 261p. 1971. text ed. 29.50x (ISBN 0-333-12825-7). Irvington.
Planning & Operating a Successful Food Service Operation. William L. Kahrl. LC 72-92136. (Chain Store Age Bks.). (Illus.). 1973. 15.95 (ISBN 0-86730-219-4). Lebhar Friedman.
Planning & Operation of Electric Energy Systems: Proceedings of the IFAC Symposium, Rio de Janeiro, Brazil, 22-25 July 1985. Ed. by S. H. Da Cunha. (IFAC Proceedings Ser.). 494p. 1986. 130.00 (ISBN 0-08-032543-2, Pub. by PPL). Pergamon.
Planning & Organising Business Functions. Stuart Turner. 176p. 1983. text ed. 33.95x (ISBN 0-566-02394-6). Gower Pub Co.
Planning & Organization of Fertilizer Use Development in Africa: Papers Presented at the FAO-DANIDA Regional Seminar on Planning & Organization of Fertilizer Use in Africa, Nairobi, Kenya, Dec. 1-16, 1972. (Soils Bulletins: No. 26). (Illus.). 184p. 1975. pap. 12.00 (ISBN 0-685-57607-8, F1168, FAO). UNIPUB.
Planning & Organization of Geriatric Services: Report. WHO Expert Committee. Geneva, 1973. (Technical Report Ser.: No. 548). (Also avail. in French & Spanish). 1974. pap. 2.00 (ISBN 92-4-120548-2). World Health.
Planning & Organization of Health Laboratory Services: Report. WHO Expert Committee on Health Laboratory Services. Geneva, 1971, 5th. (Technical Report Ser.: No. 491). (Also avail. in French, Russian & Spanish). 1972. pap. 1.60 (ISBN 92-4-120491-5). World Health.
Planning & Organizing Career Curricula. Larry J. Kenneke & Dennis C. Nystrom. LC 72-92619. 1975. scp 19.96 (ISBN 0-672-97533-5). Bobbs.
Planning & Organizing for Multicultural Instruction. Gwendolyn C. Baker. LC 82-8910. (Illus.). 288p. 1983. pap. text ed. write for info. (ISBN 0-201-10188-2). Addison-wesley.
Planning & Organizing for Social Change: Action Principles from Social Service Research. Jack Rothman. LC 74-4434. 1974. pap. 32.50 (ISBN 0-231-08335-1). Columbia U Pr.
Planning & Organizing Leisure Resources. D. L. Groves & S. L. Groves. 15p. 1978. pap. text ed. 3.00 (ISBN 0-940414-02-3). Appalach Assoc.
Planning & Politics in Western Europe. David McKay. LC 81-21233. 256p. 1983. 27.50x (ISBN 0-312-61399-7). St Martin.
Planning & Politics: The Metro Toronto Transportation Plan Review. Juri Pill. (MIT Center for Transportation Studies: No. 5). (Illus.). 1979. 32.50x (ISBN 0-262-16073-0). MIT Pr.
Planning & Pollution: An Examination of the Role of Land Planning in the Protection of Environmental Quality. Christopher Miller & Christopher Wood. (Illus.). 1983. text ed. 36.00x (ISBN 0-19-823245-4). Oxford U Pr.
Planning & Productivity in Sweden. Harold G. Jones. 212p. 1976. 19.50x (ISBN 0-87471-758-2). Rowman.
Planning & Profit in Socialist Economies. Jean-Charles Asselain. (International Library of Economics). 256p. 1984. 35.00x (ISBN 0-7102-0257-1). Routledge Chapman & Hall.
Planning & Profit in the Urban Economy. T. A. Broadbent. 1977. 13.95x (ISBN 0-416-56320-1, NO. 2768). Routledge Chapman & Hall.
Planning & Programming for Nursing Services. (Public Health Paper: No. 44). (Also avail. in French & Spanish). 1971. pap. 3.60 (ISBN 92-4-130044-2). World Health.
Planning & Programming for Transportation: Five Reports. (Transportation Research Record Ser.). 58p. 1976. 2.60 (ISBN 0-309-02488-9). Transport Res Bd.
Planning & Programming of Agricultural Research. I. Arnon. 122p. (2nd Printing 1978). 1975. pap. 7.50 (ISBN 92-5-100850-7, F320, FAO). UNIPUB.
Planning & Reasoning about Time. Thomas Dean & Yoav Shoham. (Illus.). 75p. 1988. pap. text ed. 5.00x (ISBN 0-929280-13-X). Amer Artificial.
Planning & Reviewing Employee Performance. rev. ed. Glenn H. Varney. 46p. 1974. pap. 7.00 (ISBN 0-686-05625-6). Mgmt Advisory Assoc Inc.
Planning & Role Setting for Public Libraries: A Manual of Options & Procedures. Charles R. McClure et al. LC 87-11445. 140p. 1987. pap. text ed. 14.00x (ISBN 0-8389-3341-6). ALA.
Planning & Supplying a Hotel Bar-Lounge. Ad Wittemann. 16p. (Orig.). 1985. pap. 35.00 (ISBN 0-938481-33-9). Camelot Consult.
Planning & the Civil Engineer: Proceedings of a Conference Sponsored by the American Society of Civil Engineers, the Canadian Society of Civil Engineering, & the Institution of Civil Engineers. 154p. 1982. 36.00 (ISBN 0-7277-0152-5, Pub. by T Telford UK). Am Soc Civil Eng.
Planning & the Corporate Planning Director. James K. Brown & Rochelle O'Connor. (Report Ser.: No. 627). 94p. 1974. pap. 22.50 (ISBN 0-8237-0045-3). Conference Bd.
Planning & the Educational Administrator. C. Beeby. (Fundamentals of Educational Planning: No. 4). 36p. (2nd Printing 1980). 1967. pap. 5.00 (ISBN 92-803-1009-7, U1065, UNESCO). UNIPUB.
Planning & the Growth of the Firm. John Bridge & J. C. Dodds. 211p. 1978. 28.00 (ISBN 0-85664-362-9, Pub. by Croom Helm Ltd). Routledge Chapman & Hall.
Planning & the Innovative Process see **Progress in Planning.**
Planning & the Politicians. Albert H. Hanson. LC 75-95618. 1969. lib. bdg. 37.50x (ISBN 0-678-06524-1). Kelley.
Planning & the Rural Environment, Vol. 18. Gerald Wibberley & Joan Davidson. 1977. pap. text ed. 17.50 (ISBN 0-08-020526-7). Pergamon.
Planning & Urban Affairs Library Manual. 3rd ed. Mary L. Knobbe. 1975. 15.00 (ISBN 0-87326-015-5). Intl City Mgt.
Planning & Urban Growth: An Anglo-American Comparison. Marion Clawson & Peter Hall. LC 72-12364. (Resources for the Future Ser.). (Illus.). 312p. 1973. 26.95x (ISBN 0-8018-1496-0). Johns Hopkins.
Planning & Urban Growth in Southern Europe. Martin Wynn. LC 84-7859. 210p. 1984. 38.00x (ISBN 0-7201-1608-2). Mansell.
Planning & Using a Total Personnel System. Richard A. Kaumeyer. 256p. 1981. 25.95 (ISBN 0-442-21370-0). Van Nos Reinhold.
Planning & Using Skills Inventory Systems. Richard A. Kaumeyer. LC 78-25959. 1979. 26.95 (ISBN 0-442-24240-9). Van Nos Reinhold.
Planning & Using the Blackboard. Patricia Mugglestone. (Practical Language Teaching Ser.). (Orig.). 1981. pap. text ed. 9.00x (ISBN 0-435-28965-9). Heinemann Ed.
Planning & Vocational Education. G. Copa & J. Moss. 208p. 1983. text ed. 24.95 (ISBN 0-07-013049-3). McGraw.
Planning & Zoning in the United States. Beverly J. Pooley. LC 61-63301. (Michigan Legal Publications Ser.). 123p. 1982. Repr. of 1961 ed. lib. bdg. 35.00 (ISBN 0-89941-243-2). W S Hein.
Planning Around the Key Experiences. Michelle Graves. 1988. pap. text ed. 15.00 (ISBN 0-931114-80-2). High-Scope.
Planning at the Grassroots. Kamta Prasad. xii, 200p. 1988. text ed. 27.50x (ISBN 81-207-0782-6, Pub. by Sterling Pubs India). Apt Bks.
Planning Basics for Managers. D. Ellis & P. Pekar. 1983. pap. 6.95 (ISBN 0-317-31398-3). AMACOM.
Planning Better Programs. Patrick G. Boyle. Ed. by Alan Pardoen & Don Seaman. (Adult Education Association Professional Development Ser.). (Illus.). 272p. 1981. text ed. 24.95 (ISBN 0-07-000552-4). McGraw.
Planning Big with MacProject. James Halcomb. (Illus.). 250p. (Orig.). 1986. pap. text ed. 16.95 (ISBN 0-07-881219-4). Osborne-McGraw.
Planning, Budgeting & Control for Data Processing: Making Zero Base Budgeting Work for You. Thomas J. Francl et al. 248p. 1984. 28.95 (ISBN 0-442-22550-4). Van Nos Reinhold.
Planning Bulletin Boards for Church & Synagogue Libraries. Janelle A. Paris. LC 83-7331. (CSLA Guide Two Ser. No. 11). 48p. (Orig.). 1983. pap. 6.95 (ISBN 0-915324-20-2); pap. 5.50 members. CSLA.
Planning Business Combinations: Guide for Buyers & Sellers. Wintrub et al. 1985. write for info. (ISBN 0-471-05622-7). Wiley.
Planning by Mathematics. S. Vajda. LC 73-330815. (Topics in Operational Research Ser.). (Illus.). pap. 37.50 (ISBN 0-317-10739-9, 2051913). Bks Demand UMI.
Planning by Network. H. S. Woodgate. 330p. 1977. text ed. 36.75x (ISBN 0-220-66312-2, Pub. by Busn Bks England). Brookfield Pub Co.
Planning Cash Flow: A Problem Solving Approach. Joseph E. Finnerty. 237p. 1986. pap. text ed. 55.00 comb bound (ISBN 0-8144-7652-X). AMACOM.
Planning Challenges of the Seventies in Space. Ed. by George W. Morgenthaler & Robert Morra. LC 57-43769. (Advances in the Astronautical Sciences Ser.: Vol. 26). (Illus.). 1970. lib. bdg. 35.00x (ISBN 0-87703-053-7, Pub. by Am Astronaut); microfiche suppl. 15.00x. Univelt Inc.
Planning Challenges of the 70's in the Public Domain. Ed. by W. Bursnall. (Science & Technology Ser.: Vol. 22). (Illus.). 1969. lib. bdg. 40.00x (ISBN 0-87703-050-2, Pub. by Am Astronaut); microfiche suppl. 20.00x. Univelt Inc.
Planning Christian Education in Your Church. Kenneth D. Blazier & Evelyn M. Huber. LC 73-19585. 32p. (Orig.). 1974. pap. 1.00 (ISBN 0-8170-0633-8); pap. 2.95 spanish ed (ISBN 0-8170-0685-0). Judson.
Planning Cities: Selected Writings on Principles & Practice. Ed. by Frederick H. Bair & Virginia Curtis. 499p. 1970. pap. 10.95 (ISBN 0-318-13048-3); pap. 8.95 members (ISBN 0-318-13049-1). Am Plan Assn.
Planning Cogeneration Systems. Dilip R. Limaye. LC 84-48107. 250p. 1985. text ed. 39.00 (ISBN 0-915586-95-9). Fairmont Pr.
Planning College Geography Facilities. R. H. Stoddard. LC 73-83739. (General Ser.: No. 12). 1973. pap. 1.50 (ISBN 0-89291-043-7). Assn Am Geographers.
Planning Colleges for the Community. Dorothy M. Knoell & Charles McIntyre. LC 73-10943. (Jossey-Bass Series in Higher Education). pap. 42.80 (ISBN 0-317-41814-9, 2025659). Bks Demand UMI.

Planning for Play. Lady Allen of Hurtwood. LC 69-16908. 144p. 1969. pap. 9.95x (ISBN 0-262-51013-8). MIT Pr.

Planning for Population Change. Ed. by W. T. Gould & R. Lawton. LC 85-26828. 228p. 1986. 27.50x (ISBN 0-389-20606-7). B&N Imports.

Planning for Population, Labour Force & Service Demand: A Microcomputer-based Training Module. Geoffrey Greene. (Training Population, Human Resources & Development Planning Ser.: No. 3). v, 100p. (Orig.). 1986. pap. 10.50 (ISBN 92-2-105622-8). Intl Labour Office.

Planning for Presidential Succession. Robert Fulmer. (Presidents Association Special Study Ser.: No. 71). 1979. pap. 20.00 (ISBN 0-8144-4072-X). AMACOM.

Planning for Profits: The Retailers Guide to Success. Anita Goldwasser. 1981. 20.95 (ISBN 0-86730-531-2). Lebhar Friedman.

Planning for Rare Events: Nuclear Accident Preparedness & Management-Proceedings. International Workshop, IIASA, Laxenburg, Austria, 28-31 January 1980 & J. W. Lathrop. (IIASA Proceedings Ser.: Vol. 14). (Illus.). 280p. 1981. 44.00 (ISBN 0-08-028703-4). Pergamon.

Planning for Research: A Guide for the Helping Professions. Raymond M. Berger & Michael A. Patchner. (Human Service Guides: Vol. 50). 160p. 1988. pap. text ed. 12.95 (ISBN 0-8039-3033-X). Sage.

Planning for Rural Development. R. B. Singh. 1987. 11.50x (ISBN 0-8364-2171-X, Pub. by Discovery Pub Hse India). South Asia Bks.

Planning for Rural Development: The Case of Bangladesh. (Working Papers Ser.: No. 78-22). 42p. 1978. pap. 6.00 (ISBN 0-686-78492-8, CRD108, UNCRD). UNIPUB.

Planning for Satellite Broadcasting: The Indian Instructional Television Experiment. Romesh Chander & Kiran Karnik. (Reports & Papers on Mass Communication: No. 78). 71p. 1976. pap. 5.00 (ISBN 92-3-101392-0, U453, UNESCO). UNIPUB.

Planning for Single Young Adult Ministry: Directions for Ministerial Outreach. 65p. 1981. pap. 4.95 (ISBN 1-55586-738-3). US Catholic.

Planning for Small Enterprises in Third World Cities. Ed. by R. Bromley. (Urban & Regional Planning Ser.: Vol. 34). 360p. 1984. text ed. 63.00 (ISBN 0-08-025236-2); pap. text ed. 40.00 (ISBN 0-08-031333-7). Pergamon.

Planning for Software Validation, Verification & Testing. 1986. lib. bdg. 79.95 (ISBN 0-8490-3760-3). Gordon Pr.

Planning for Solid Waste Management. Mary McLean. (PAS Reports: No. 275). 52p. 1971. 6.00 (ISBN 0-318-13050-5). Am Plan Assn.

Planning for Stewardship: Developing a Giving Program for Congregations. Thomas Heyd. (Administration for Churches Ser.). 40p. (Orig.). 1980. pap. 4.95 (ISBN 0-8066-1782-9, 10-4992). Augsburg.

Planning for Strikes: Obtaining Maximum Performance with Minimum Personnel. Stephen R. Levine. 54p. 1975. pap. 25.00 (ISBN 0-941496-00-7). Model Cities.

Planning for Study Abroad. Alice K. Swinger. LC 85-61793. (Fastback Ser.: No. 228). 50p. 1985. pap. 0.90 (ISBN 0-87367-228-3). Phi Delta Kappa.

Planning for Sunday School Progress. Ray H. Hughes & Bernice Stout Woodard. 5.25 (ISBN 0-87148-682-2). Pathway Pr.

Planning for Survival: A Handbook for Hospital Trustees. 2nd ed. Norman H. McMillan. LC 84-245781. 132p. 1985. pap. 20.00 (ISBN 0-939450-53-4, 127174). AHPI.

Planning for Teaching: An Introduction to Education. 6th ed. Robert W. Richey. (Illus.). 1979. text ed. 35.95 (ISBN 0-07-052360-6). McGraw.

Planning for Teaching Church School. Donald L. Griggs. LC 85-12588. 64p. 1985. pap. 5.95 (ISBN 0-8170-1079-3). Judson.

Planning for Teaching Preprimary Motor & Play Skills. Ellen Curtis-Pierce & Janet Wessel. (ps). 1988. pap. 7.95 (ISBN 0-8224-5355-X). D S Lake Pubs.

Planning for Telecommunications. Ed. by Alan Simpson. (Office of the Future Ser.: Vol. 4). 164p. (Orig.). 1982. pap. text ed. 23.50x (ISBN 0-566-03415-8). Gower Pub Co.

Planning for the Aging in Local Communities: An International Perspective. Arthur Dunham & Charlotte Nusberg. 49p. 4.00 (ISBN 0-318-14567-7). Intl Fed Ageing.

Planning for the Archival Profession. SAA Task Force on Goals & Priorities Staff. 42p. (Orig.). 1986. pap. text ed. 8.00 (ISBN 0-931828-34-1). Soc Am Archivists.

Planning for the Elderly: Alternative Community Analysis Techniques. Victor Regnier. LC 79-90975. 152p. 1980. pap. 8.00x (ISBN 0-88474-093-5, 05748-7). Lexington Bks.

Planning for the Elderly in New York City - An Assessment of Depression, Dementia & Isolation: Report of Proceedings of a Second Research Utilization Workshop on the US-UK Cross-National Geriatric Community Study. 68p. 1980. 4.00 (ISBN 0-318-13710-0). Comm Coun Great NY.

Planning for the Elderly in New York City: Report of a Research Utilization Workshop. 1980. 4.00 (ISBN 0-86671-065-5). Comm Coun Great NY.

Planning for the Electronic Mail. Ed. by Alan Simpson. (Office of the Future Ser.: Vol. 2). 144p. 1981. pap. text ed. 23.50x (ISBN 0-566-03406-9). Gower Pub Co.

Planning for the Factory of the Future. 1984. write for info. C I M Systems.

Planning for the Internal Audit Function. J. Efrim Boritz. Ed. by Richard Holman. (Illus.). 339p. 1983. text ed. 37.50 (ISBN 0-89413-107-9, 522). Inst Inter Aud.

Planning for the Lower East Side. Harry Schwartz & Peter Abeles. LC 72-88988. (Special Studies in U. S. Economic, Social & Political Issues). 1973. 29.00x (ISBN 0-275-28805-6). Irvington.

Planning for the Mobilization of the Nation's Medical Resources. John R. Beatty. (Illus.). 208p. 1985. pap. 7.50 (ISBN 0-318-22424-0, S/N 008-020-01058-8). USGPO.

Planning for the Nation's Health: A Study of Twentieth-Century Developments in the United States. Grace Budrys. LC 86-12142. (Contributions in Medical Studies: No. 19). 168p. 1987. 29.95 (ISBN 0-313-25348-X, BYP/). Greenwood.

Planning for the Office of the Future. Ed. by Alan Simpson. (Office of the Future Ser.: Vol. 1). 152p. 1981. pap. text ed. 23.50x (ISBN 0-566-03404-2). Gower Pub Co.

Planning for the Poor: A Case Study of Mahaweli, Sri Lanka. Shoaib Sultan Khan. (Working Papers Ser.: No. 82-2). 30p. 1982. pap. 6.00 (ISBN 0-686-95380-0, CRD136, UNCRD). UNIPUB.

Planning for the Theatre. Ned A. Bowman et al. 1965. spiral bdg. 4.95x (ISBN 0-913868-08-6). Scenographic.

Planning for the Word Processing. Ed. by Alan Simpson. (Office of the Future Ser.: Vol. 3). 160p. 1982. pap. text ed. 23.50x (ISBN 0-566-03414-X). Gower Pub Co.

Planning for Tomorrow. Michael J. Klein. LC 79-11308. 1979. text ed. 35.00 3-ring binder (ISBN 0-07-035031-0). McGraw.

Planning For Tomorrow's Schools: Problems & Solutions. 12.95 (ISBN 0-318-01770-9, 021-00832). Am Assn Sch Admin.

Planning for Vegetation in Urbanizing Areas. Lisa Rosenberger & Robert E. Coughlin. (Discussion Paper Ser.: No. 115). 1979. pap. 5.50 (ISBN 0-686-32280-0). Regional Sci Res Inst.

Planning for Water Reuse. Ed. by Duane D. Baumann & Daniel M. Dworkin. 1980. 25.00x (ISBN 0-416-60121-9, NO. 2864). Routledge Chapman & Hall.

Planning for Wellness: A Guidebook for Achieving Optimal Health. 2nd ed. Donald Ardell & Mark J. Tager. 208p. 1982. pap. text ed. 13.50 (ISBN 0-8403-2717-X). Kendall-Hunt.

Planning for Your Church. Douglas A. Walrath. LC 84-5211. (Pastor's Handbooks: Vol. 4). 112p. 1984. pap. 7.95 (ISBN 0-664-24554-4). Westminster John Knox.

Planning for Your Retirement: IRAs & Keoghs. LC 84-151079. 96p. 1983. pap. 2.50 (4761). Commerce.

Planning for Your Retirement: IRAs & KEOGHs. 118p. (Orig.). 1987. pap. 3.00 (5330). Commerce.

Planning Forest Roads & Harvesting Systems. (Forestry Papers: No. 2). (Illus.). 158p. (Eng., Fr. & Span., 2nd Printing 1979). 1977. pap. 11.25 (ISBN 92-5-100407-2, F1343, FAO). UNIPUB.

Planning Fundamentals of Thermal Power Plants. F. S. Ashner. 750p. 1978. 144.00x (ISBN 0-7065-1579-X, Pub. by Keter Pub Jerusalem). Coronet Bks.

Planning Future Land Uses. Ed. by Gary W. Petersen & Marvin T. Beatty. (ASA Special Publications Ser.). 71p. 1981. pap. 5.50 (ISBN 0-89118-067-2). Am Soc Agron.

Planning Games: Case Study Simulations in Land Management & Development. Martin Wynn. (Illus.). 200p. 1985. 35.00 (ISBN 0-419-12810-7, NO. 9153). Routledge Chapman & Hall.

Planning, Geometry, & Complexity of Robot Motion. Jacob T. Schwartz et al. Ed. by Jerry R. Hobbs. (Ablex Series in Artificial Intelligence: Vol. 4). 352p. 1987. text ed. 49.50 inst. ed. (ISBN 0-89391-361-8); pers. ed. 35.00. Ablex Pub.

Planning Growth in Your Church. Duncan McIntosh & Richard E. Rusbuldt. 224p. 1983. pap. 16.95 (ISBN 0-8170-1007-6). Judson.

Planning Guide for Information System Evaluation Studies. William A. Smith, Jr. & Ben L. Wechsler. 1983. 13.00 (ISBN 0-89806-016-8, 108). Inst Indus Eng.

Planning Guide for Physicians' Medical Facilities. 1986. pap. 9.50 (ISBN 0-89970-261-9, OP-439-6). AMA.

Planning Guide for the Beginning Retailer. Albert Smart. LC 79-25510. 1979. 6.95 (ISBN 0-86730-540-1). Lebhar Friedman.

Planning Guide for Voluntary Human Service Delivery Agencies. 2nd ed. Stephen M. Drezner & William B. McCurdy. LC 78-26125. 1979. pap. 15.95 (ISBN 0-87304-167-4). Family Serv.

Planning Guide to Office Automation. Ed. by Gower Publishing Co., Ltd. Staff. 123p. 1984. text ed. 41.95x (ISBN 0-566-02503-5). Gower Pub Co.

Planning Guide to Successful Computer Instruction. G. David Peters & John M. Eddins. 1981. 19.95 (ISBN 0-942132-00-9). Electron Course.

Planning Health Promotion at the Worksite. David H. Chenoweth. LC 86-73126. (Illus.). 211p. 1987. pap. text ed. 17.95 (ISBN 0-936157-16-X). Benchmark Pr.

Planning Healthy Meals. Bostick & Echaorce. (Food & Nutrition Ser.). (Illus.). 80p. 1986. pap. text ed. 14.95 (ISBN 0-88102-034-6). Janus Bks.

Planning Home Care with the Elderly: Patient, Family & Professional Views of An Alternative to Institutionalization. Alan Sager. LC 66-7006. 320p. 1983. prof ref 35.00x (ISBN 0-88410-725-6). Ballinger Pub.

Planning Hospital Health Promotion Services for Business & Industry. LC 82-18489. 140p. 1982. pap. 33.75 (ISBN 0-939450-36-4, 070175). AHPI.

Planning Human Activities on Protected Natural Ecosystems. W. Lusigi. (Dissertationes Botanica Ser.: No. 48). (Illus.). 1979. pap. 24.00x (ISBN 3-7682-1214-9). Lubrecht & Cramer.

Planning Implementation & Control in Product Test Assurance. Richard H. Spencer. (Illus.). 240p. 1983. text ed. 46.00 (ISBN 0-13-679506-4). P-H.

Planning, Implementing, & Evaluating Targeted Communication Programs: A Manual for Business Communicators. Gary W. Selnow & William D. Crano. LC 86-30418. 300p. 1987. lib. bdg. 45.00 (ISBN 0-89930-208-4, SPQ/, Quorum Bks). Greenwood.

Planning in a Nutshell see High Performance Planning: A Guide to Planning Anything.

Planning in America: Learning from Turbulence. Ed. by David R. Godschalk. 240p. 1974. pap. 10.00 (ISBN 0-318-13052-1); pap. 8.00 members (ISBN 0-318-13053-X). Am Plan Assn.

Planning in Brazil: Monographs Published since 1950. Mary Vance. (Architecture Ser.: A 1419). 25p. 1985. 3.75 (ISBN 0-89028-469-5). Vance Biblios.

Planning in Chess. Janos Flesch. (Illus.). 96p. 1983. pap. 18.95 (ISBN 0-7134-1597-5, Pub. by Batsford England). David & Charles.

Planning in Chinese Agriculture: Socialisation & the Private Sector 1956-1962. Kenneth R. Walker. 109p. 1965. 26.00x (ISBN 0-7146-1256-1, F Cass Co). Biblio Dist.

Planning in Criminal Justice Organizations & Systems. John Hudzik & Gary W. Cordner. 352p. 1983. text ed. write for info. (ISBN 0-02-475170-7). Macmillan.

Planning in Decentralized Firms. B. R. Meijboom. (Lecture Notes in Economics & Mathematical Systems Ser.: Vol. 289). x, 168p. 1987. pap. 21.70 (ISBN 0-387-17795-7). Springer-Verlag.

Planning in Developing Countries: Lessons of Experience. Ramgopal Agarwala. (Working Paper: No. 576). 71p. 1983. 5.00 (ISBN 0-8213-0303-1, WP 0576). World Bank.

Planning in Developing Countries: Theory & Methodology. (United Nations Studies). 18.50 (ISBN 92-1-157052-2, E.80.XV.ST/17). UN.

Planning in Eastern Europe. Ed. by Andrew Dawson. LC 86-17654. 320p. 1986. 35.00 (ISBN 0-312-61412-8). St Martin.

Planning in Europe. Jack Hayward & Olga A. Narkiewicz. LC 77-25975. 1978. 25.00x (ISBN 0-312-61406-3). St Martin.

Planning in Europe. R. H. Williams. (Urban & Regional Studies: No. 11). 208p. 1984. text ed. 39.95x (ISBN 0-04-711012-0). Unwin Hyman.

Planning in France: Monographs Published since 1950. Mary Vance. (Architecture Ser.: A 1420). 32p. 1985. 4.50 (ISBN 0-89028-470-9). Vance Biblios.

Planning in Germany: Monographs Published since 1950. Mary Vance. (Architecture Ser.: A 1421). 45p. 1985. 6.75 (ISBN 0-89028-471-7). Vance Biblios.

Planning in Goverment: Shaping Programs that Succeed. Melvin R. Levin. (Illus.). 257p. (Orig.). 1987. lib. bdg. 39.95; pap. 19.95 (ISBN 0-918286-44-1). Planners Pr.

Planning In-House Training: A Personal System with an Organizational Perspective. Stephen F. Sauer & Ronald E. Holland. LC 81-11818. 173p. 1981. 8.95 (ISBN 0-89384-049-1). Univ Assocs.

Planning in India. P. B. Desai. 1980. text ed. 17.95x (ISBN 0-7069-0832-5, Pub. by Vikas India). Advent NY.

Planning in India. H. V. Iengar & V. T. Krishnamachari. LC 75-903517. 1974. 5.00x (ISBN 0-89684-507-9). Orient Bk Dist.

Planning in India. S Venu et al. cancelled (ISBN 0-8364-0066-6, Orient Longman). South Asia Bks.

Planning in India: A Critique. R. K. Sinha. ix, 247p. 1987. 18.00x (ISBN 81-7003-079-X). South Asia Bks.

Planning in India: Monographs Published since 1950. Mary Vance. (Architecture Ser.: A 1422). 20p. 1985. 3.00 (ISBN 0-89028-472-5). Vance Biblios.

Planning in Italy: Monographs Published since 1950. Mary Vance. (Architecture Series Bibliography: A 1423). 51p. 1985. pap. 7.50 (ISBN 0-89028-473-3). Vance Biblios.

Planning in Morocco: Organization & Implementation. Albert Waterston. (World Bank Ser). 73p. 1962. pap. 3.50x (ISBN 0-8018-0664-X). Johns Hopkins.

Planning in OCLC Member Libraries. (Library, Information, & Computer Science). 130p. (Orig.). 1988. pap. 16.00 (ISBN 1-55653-051-X). OCLC Online Comp.

Planning in Pakistan: Organization & Implementation. Albert Waterston. (World Bank Ser). 160p. 1963. pap. 4.50x (ISBN 0-8018-0665-8). Johns Hopkins.

Planning in Rural Environments. William R. Lassey. (McGraw-Hill Publications in the Agricultural Sciences Ser.). 1977. text ed. 42.95 (ISBN 0-07-036580-6). McGraw.

Planning in State Courts: A Survey of the State of the Art. 76p. 1976. pap. 2.75 (ISBN 0-89656-011-2, R-029). Natl Ctr St Courts.

Planning in State Courts: Trends & Developments 1976-78. 64p. 1978. pap. 2.75 (ISBN 0-89656-028-7, R-040). Natl Ctr St Courts.

Planning in the Netherlands: Monographs. Mary Vance. (Architecture Ser.: Bibliography A-1302). 42p. 1985. pap. 6.00 (ISBN 0-89028-232-3). Vance Biblios.

Planning in the Public Domain. John Friedmann. LC 87-3194. (Illus.). 480p. 1987. text ed. 55.00 (ISBN 0-691-07743-6); pap. text ed. 16.95 (ISBN 0-691-02268-2). Princeton U Pr.

Planning in the Soviet Union. Judith Pallot & Denis Shaw. LC 80-24723. 320p. 1981. 30.00x (ISBN 0-8203-0550-2). U of Ga Pr.

Planning in Urban India. John Van Willigen & Jacqueline Van Willigen. 1975. 5.50 (ISBN 0-686-20339-9, 743). CPL Biblios.

Planning Individualized Education Programs in Special Education: With Examples from I CAN Physical Education. Janet A. Wessel. (Illus.). 1977. pap. 5.95 (ISBN 0-8331-1217-1). Hubbard Sci.

Planning Instruction & Monitoring Classroom Processes with Computer Assistance. Margaret C. Wang & Robert J. Fitzhugh. 56p. 1977. 1.50 (ISBN 0-318-14726-2). Learn Res Dev.

Planning Integrated Development: Methods Used in Asia. (Socio-Economic Studies: No. 11). (Illus.). 271p. (Orig.). 1987. pap. text ed. 18.00 (ISBN 92-3-102390-X, U1568, UNESCO). UNIPUB.

Planning Is the Key. Billie I. Reynolds. 1983. 10.00 (ISBN 0-915807-00-9). Hidden Valley Bks.

Planning Law in Western Europe. J. F. Garner. LC 74-30920. 353p. 1975. 47.50 (ISBN 0-444-10833-5, North-Holland). Elsevier.

Planning Law in Western Europe. 2nd, rev. ed. Ed. by J. F. Garner & N. P. Gravells. LC 86-4423. 430p. 1986. 100.00 (ISBN 0-444-87996-X, North-Holland). Elsevier.

Planning, Layout, & Construction of the Printing Plant. 89p. 85.00 (ISBN 0-318-14968-0). NAPL.

Planning LDS Weddings & Receptions. Lois F. Worlton & Opal D. Jasinski. LC 72-88908. (Illus.). 73p. 1972. pap. 6.95 (ISBN 0-88290-014-5). Horizon Utah.

Planning Learning Resource Centres in Schools & Colleges. Rosemary Raddon. 256p. 1984. text ed. 33.95x (ISBN 0-566-03435-2). Gower Pub Co.

Planning Library Buildings: From Decision to Design. Ed. by Lester K. Smith. 194p. 1986. 25.00 (ISBN 0-8389-7031-1). Library Admin.

Planning Library Services see Planning of Library & Documentation Services.

Planning Local Economic Development: A Guide for Policymakers, Professionals & Students. Edward J. Blakely. (Library of Social Research: Vol. 168). 320p. 1988. text ed. 35.00 (ISBN 0-8039-3275-8); pap. text ed. 16.95 (ISBN 0-8039-3276-6). Sage.

Planning Manual for Colleges. rev. ed. National Association of College & University Business Officers et al. Ed. by Jeanne Nevin. LC 80-12096. 73p. 1980. pap. text ed. 20.00 (ISBN 0-915164-09-4); pap. text ed. 17.50 ea. 2-4 copies; pap. text ed. 12.50 ea. 5 or more copies. NACUBO.

Planning Medical Center Facilities for Education, Research, & Public Service. George T. Harrell. LC 73-12293. 232p. 1974. 24.95x (ISBN 0-271-01163-7, Penn State). Pa St U Pr.

Planning Meeting of the Human & Social Development Programme. (Human & Social Development Programme - Programme Documents). 37p. 1979. pap. 5.00 (ISBN 92-808-0003-5, TUNU038, UNU). UNIPUB.

Planning Methods & the Human Environment. Giberte Gallopin. (Socio-Economic Studies: No. 4). 68p. 1981. pap. 5.00 (ISBN 92-3-101894-9, U1106, UNESCO). UNIPUB.

Planning Methods: For Health & Related Organizations. Paul C. Nutt. LC 83-17105. 587p. 1984. 38.50x (ISBN 0-471-08648-7, Pub. by Wiley Med). Wiley.

Planning Models for Colleges & Universities. David S. Hopkins & William F. Massy. LC 78-66176. 572p. 1981. 45.00x (ISBN 0-8047-1023-6). Stanford U Pr.

Planning Multicultural Education. (Ethnic Studies Bulletins: No. 1). 8p. 1982. 1.00. I N Thut World Educ Ctr.

Planning My Career, Occupational Guidance. Vincent Capozziello, Jr. LC 75-20074. (gr. 7 up). 1985. 3.75 (ISBN 0-912486-43-0). Finney Co.

Planning National Infrastructures for Documentation, Libraries, & Archives. J. D'Olier & B Delmas. (Documentation, Libraries & Archives: Studies & Research: No. 4). 328p. 1975. pap. 8.00 (ISBN 92-3-101144-8, U454, UNESCO). UNIPUB.

Planning under Pressure: The Strategic Choice Approach. J. K. Friend & A. Hickling. (URPS Ser.: No. 37). (Illus.). 350p. 1987. text ed. 78.00 (ISBN 0-08-018766-8, PBL); pap. text ed. 29.75 (ISBN 0-08-018765-X, PBL). Pergamon.

Planning under Uncertainty: Multiple Scenarios & Contingency Planning. Rochelle O'Connor. (Report Ser: No. 741). (Illus.). 26p. 1978. pap. 22.50 (ISBN 0-8237-0175-1). Conference Bd.

Planning U. S. Security: Defense Policy in the Eighties. Ed. by Philip S. Kronenberg. LC 81-13791. (Pergamon Policy Studies on Security Affairs). 232p. 1982. text ed. 35.00 (ISBN 0-08-028082-X); pap. text ed. 10.75 (ISBN 0-08-028081-1). Pergamon.

Planning Urban Education: New Techniques to Transform Learning in the City. Ed. by Dennis L. Roberts, 2nd. LC 73-160895. 384p. 1972. 34.95 (ISBN 0-87778-024-2). Educ Tech Pubns.

Planning Useful Evaluations: Evaluability Assessment. Leonard Rutman. LC 79-24116. (Sage Library of Social Research: Vol. 96). (Illus.). 1980. 29.95 (ISBN 0-8039-1252-8); pap. 14.95 (ISBN 0-8039-1253-6). Sage.

Planning with Neighborhoods. William M. Rohe & Lauren B. Gates. LC 84-17221. (Urban & Regional Policy & Development Studies). 260p. 1985. 13.95x (ISBN 0-8078-1638-8); pap. 12.95x (ISBN 0-8078-4133-1). U of NC Pr.

Planning with the Semi Input-Output Method. Arie Kuyvenhoven. (Studies in Development & Planning: Vol. 10). 266p. 1978. lib. bdg. 26.00 (ISBN 90-207-0798-1, Pub. by Martinus Nijhoff Netherlands). Kluwer Academic.

Planning with the Small Computer: An Applications Reader. Ed. by Mathew E. MacIver & Jan Schreiber. LC 86-8462. (Lincoln Institute of Land Policy-OG&H Ser.). (Illus.). 168p. text ed. 30.00x (ISBN 0-89946-215-4, 215-4). Oelgeschlager.

Planning Workbook for Law Firm Management. 2nd ed. ABA, Economics of Law Practice Section Staff. LC 84-72362. 157p. 1985. looseleaf 89.95 (ISBN 0-89707-156-5). Amer Bar Assn.

Planning Your Career. Robert Calvert, Jr. & John E. Steel. 1963. pap. text ed. 3.95 (ISBN 0-07-009658-9). McGraw.

Planning Your Career: A Workshop Series for Women. Carole M. Davis & Dorothy Graham. 138p. (Orig.). 1981. pap. 9.50 participant's manual (ISBN 1-55719-102-6); pap. 12.00 leader's manual (ISBN 1-55719-106-9). U NE Ctr Applied Urban Rsch.

Planning Your Career Change. Kent Banning & Ardelle Friday. 1986. pap. 6.95 (ISBN 0-8442-6688-4, Passport Bks). Natl Textbk.

Planning Your Career of Tomorrow. A. Paradis. 1986. 6.95 (ISBN 0-8442-6678-7, Passport Bks). Natl Textbk.

Planning Your Career Pathways: Employee's Career Development Workbook. rev. ed. Ed. by Carol Nalbandian & Colleen Ryan. 50p. 1981. wkbk. 8.00 (ISBN 0-936352-11-6). U of KS Cont Ed.

Planning Your Career Pathways: Supervisor's Manual. rev. ed. Ed. by Colleen Ryan & Carol Nalbandian. 85p. (Orig.). 1981. pap. 14.00 spiral bdg. (ISBN 0-936352-12-4). U of KS Cont Ed.

Planning Your Career Success: Nine Self-Guided Steps. Terry D. Schmidt. (Career Development Ser.). (Illus.). 162p. 1984. 10.95 (ISBN 0-534-97947-5, Lifetime Learn). Van Nos Reinhold.

Planning Your College Education. William A. Rubinfield. LC 76-5713. (Illus.). 160p. (gr. 8-12). 1981. pap. 6.95 (ISBN 0-8442-6673-6). Natl Textbk.

Planning your Family: How To Decide What's Best for You. Peter DeJong & William Smit. 208p. 1987. pap. 6.95 (ISBN 0-310-37961-X, 12500P). Zondervan.

Planning Your Family Reunions, Weddings & Anniversaries. Margaret Ward. 33p. (Orig.). 1985. 2.50 (ISBN 0-932641-00-8). Kitwardo Pubs.

Planning Your Financial Future. H. Stanley Jones. LC 88-232. 236p. 1988. 29.95 (ISBN 0-471-85650-9); pap. 14.95 (ISBN 0-471-63392-5). Wiley.

Planning Your First Vacation to Australia. Brian Lewis. (Illus.). 50p. 1987. pap. 2.95 (ISBN 0-940749-01-7). A A Pub.

Planning Your Future. Credit Research Foundation. 64p. 1963. 40.00 (ISBN 0-939050-36-6). Credit Res NYS.

Planning Your Future: A Workbook for Personal Goal Setting. George A. Ford & Gordon L. Lippitt. LC 76-11357. Orig. Title: Life Planning Workbook for Guidance in Planning & Personal Goal Setting. 49p. 1976. pap. 8.50 (ISBN 0-88390-120-X). Univ Assocs.

Planning Your Garden. Anne De Verteuil & Val Burton. (Illus.). 192p. 1988. 24.95 (ISBN 0-525-24623-1). Dutton.

Planning Your High-Tech Career. Sandra Grundfest. 12p. (Orig.). 1984. pap. 1.25 (ISBN 0-87866-276-6). Petersons Guides.

Planning Your Medical Career: Traditional & Alternative Opportunities. T. Donald Rucker & Martin D. Keller. LC 86-80772. 346p. (Orig.). 1986. pap. 15.95 (ISBN 0-912048-40-9). Garrett Pk.

Planning Your Military Career. Robert McKay. 160p. pap. 6.95 (ISBN 0-8442-6672-8, NTC Busn Bks). Natl Textbk.

Planning Your Ornamental Fish Pond. Robert G. Sims. 1987. 9.95 (ISBN 0-533-06729-4). Vantage.

Planning Your Own Home Business. Coralee Smith Kern & Tammara Hoffman Wolfgram. (Illus.). 160p. pap. 6.95 (ISBN 0-8442-6677-9, NTC Busn Bks). Natl Textbk.

Planning Your Paintings Step-by-Step. Carole Katchen. (Illus.). 144p. 1988. 27.50 (ISBN 0-8230-4022-4). Watson-Guptill.

Planning Your Preaching. J. Winston Pearce. LC 78-73135. 1979. pap. 6.95 (ISBN 0-8054-2108-4). Broadman.

Planning Your Professional Development: A Self-Administered Workbook. American Physical Therapy Association Staff. 1985. pap. 6.00 (ISBN 0-912452-53-6). Am Phys Therapy Assn.

Planning Your Retirement Housing. Michael Sumichrast et al. LC 83-24702. 270p. 1984. pap. 8.95 (ISBN 0-673-24810-0). Am Assn Retire.

Planning Your School PR Investment. (Public Relations Professional Development Ser.). 1987. 24.95 (ISBN 0-317-59089-8, 411-13372). Natl Sch PR.

Planning Your Store for Maximum Sales & Profits. rev. ed. Charles S. Telchin & Seymour Helfant. 165p. 1975. cancelled (ISBN 0-685-44077-X, SM71969). Natl Ret Merch.

Planning Your Vacation in Florida: Miami & Dade County, Including Miami Beach & Coral Gables. Writers Program, Florida. LC 73-3603. Repr. of 1941 ed. 13.50 (ISBN 0-404-57907-8). AMS Pr.

Planning Your Veterinary Career. Ed. by John McCarthy. 115p. 1987. 15.00 (ISBN 0-941451-00-3). Am Animal Hosp Assoc.

Planning Your Young Child's Education. R. Parkinson. 1986. 6.95 (ISBN 0-8442-6683-3, Passport Bks). Natl Textbk.

Plannning India's Future. K. Ghosh. 1978. 15.00x (ISBN 0-88386-906-3). South Asia Bks.

Plano de Deus para a Familia. Elvin Irwin. Orig. Title: Living on God's Family Plan. (Port.). 1986. write for info. (ISBN 0-8297-0708-5). Life Pubs Intl.

Plano Diet. Max Morales, Jr. (Illus.). 87p. (Orig.). 1984. pap. 6.95 (ISBN 0-934157-00-6). Morales Pubns.

Planpak Number 83131: Model Rocket Launch Panel. Howard A. Goodman. (Illus.). 24p. (Orig.). 1984. pap. text ed. 3.95 (ISBN 0-914465-00-7, 83131). S S J Pubns.

Plans & Disequilibria in Centrally Planned Economies: Empirical Investigations for Poland. W. Charemza & M. Gronicki. (Contributions to Economic Analysis Ser.: No. 159). 159p. 1988. 94.75 (ISBN 0-444-70100-1, North Holland). Elsevier.

Plans & Early Operations: January 1939 to August 1942, Vol. 1. 2nd ed. Ed. by Wesley F. Craven & James L. Cate. (Army Air Forces in World War II Ser.). (Illus.). 788p. 1983. Repr. of 1948 ed. write for info. Off Air Force.

Plans & Projects for Nagoya Port. Akio Yamada. (Working Papers Ser.: No. 73-2). 58p. 1973. pap. 6.00 (ISBN 0-686-78493-6, CRD075, UNCRD). UNIPUB.

Plans & Provisions for the Mentally Handicapped. M. Bone et al. 1972. 30.00x (ISBN 0-317-05812-6, Pub. by Natl Inst Social Work). State Mutual Bk.

Plans & Situated Actions: The Problem of Human-Machine Communication. Lucy A. Suchman. (Illus.). 200p. 1987. 34.50 (ISBN 0-521-33137-4); pap. 11.95 (ISBN 0-521-33739-9). Cambridge U Pr.

Plans & the Structure of Behavior. George A. Miller et al. (Illus.). 226p. 1986. Repr. of 1960 ed. text ed. 19.95x (ISBN 0-937431-00-1). Adams Bannister Cox.

Plans Covering Self-Employed Persons or Shareholder-Employees of Subchapters Corporations. (Kinds of Qualified Plans Ser.: A). write for info. Am Law Inst.

Plans for City Police Jails & Village Lockups. Hastings H. Hart. (Russell Sage Foundation Reprint Ser). (Illus.). Repr. of 1932 ed. lib. bdg. 34.50 (ISBN 0-697-00203-9). Irvington.

Plans for Departure. Nayantara Sahgal. LC 85-3037. 1985. 14.95 (ISBN 0-393-02221-8). Norton.

Plans for the Night. M. Kasper. Ed. by Allan Bealy. (Illus.). 64p. (Orig.). 1987. pap. 7.50 (ISBN 0-939194-04-X). Benzene Edns.

Plans of Men. Leonard W. Doob. LC 68-11253. xix, 411p. 1968. Repr. of 1940 ed. 37.50 (ISBN 0-208-00126-3, Archon). Shoe String.

Plans, Programs, & the Defense Budget. Robert P. Meehan. LC 85-600612. (National Security Essay Ser.). 65p. 1988. pap. 1.00 (S/N 008-020-01043-0). USGPO.

Plans, Specs & Contracts for Building Professionals. Waller S. Poage. Ed. by William D. Mahoney. (Illus.). 336p. 1987. text ed. 42.95 (ISBN 0-87629-068-3, 67243). R S Means.

Plant - Microbe Interactions: Molecular & Genetic Perspectives, Vol. 1. Ed. by Eugene Nester & Tsaune Kosuge. LC 84-12260. 400p. 1984. text ed. 40.00x (ISBN 0-02-949470-2). Macmillan.

Plant - the Living Plant - the Root. (Economic & Social Development Papers: No. 1). (Illus.). 1977. pap. 7.50 (ISBN 92-5-100140-5, F59, FAO). UNIPUB.

Plant Accounting Regulations of the Federal Power Commission: A Critical Analysis. Sydney Davidson. Ed. by Richard P. Brief. LC 77-87296. (Development of Contemporary Accounting Thought Ser). 1978. Repr. of 1952 ed. lib. bdg. 20.00x (ISBN 0-405-10936-9). Ayer Co Pubs.

Plant Agriculture: Federal Biotechnology Activities. Carolyn Bloch. LC 85-24665. 210p. 1986. 39.00 (ISBN 0-8155-1058-6). Noyes.

Plant Analysis: An Interpretation Manual. Ed. by D. J. Reuter & J. B. Robinson. (Illus.). 224p. 1987. pap. 50.00x (ISBN 0-909605-41-6, Pub. by Inkata Pr Australia). Intl Spec Bk.

Plant Anatomy. 3rd ed. Esau. 1988. write for info. (ISBN 0-471-04765-1). Wiley.

Plant Anatomy. 3rd ed. A. Fahn. LC 81-13813. (Illus.). 528p. 1982. text ed. 87.00 (ISBN 0-08-028030-7); pap. text ed. 35.00 (ISBN 0-08-028029-3). Pergamon.

Plant Anatomy. James Mauseth. 600p. 1988. text ed. 49.95 (ISBN 0-8053-4570-1). Benjamin-Cummings.

Plant Anatomy, Pt. I: Experiment & Interpretation. 2nd ed. Elizabeth G. Cutter. (Illus.). 1978. text ed. write for info. (ISBN 0-201-01236-7). Addison-Wesley.

Plant & Animal Products in the U. S. Food System. National Research Council. 254p. 1978. pap. 12.25x (ISBN 0-309-02769-1). Natl Acad Pr.

Plant & Animal Ways see Child Horizons.

Plant & Floral Woodcuts for Designers & Craftsmen. Carolus Clusius. Ed. by Theodore Menten. LC 74-77539. (Illus.). 192p. 1974. pap. 6.95 (ISBN 0-486-20722-6). Dover.

Plant & Floral Woodcuts for Designers & Craftsmen: 419 Illustrations from the Renaissance Herbal of Clusius. Carolus Clusius. 11.25 (ISBN 0-8446-5170-2). Peter Smith.

Plant & Insect Mycoplasma Techniques. Ed. by M. J. Daniels & P. G. Markham. 368p. 1982. 37.00 (ISBN 0-7099-0272-7, Pub. by Croom Helm Ltd). Routledge Chapman & Hall.

Plant & Insect Nematodes. Nickle. 736p. 1984. 145.00 (ISBN 0-8247-7079-X). Dekker.

Plant & Planet. Anthony Huxley. 440p. 1987. pap. 6.95 (ISBN 0-14-007946-7). Penguin.

Plant & Power Engineering, Vol. 8. Date not set. 2.00 (ISBN 92-1-106039-7, E.70.II.B.6). UN.

Plant & Process Ventilation. 2nd ed. Wesley C. Hemeon. LC 63-3486. pap. 123.30 (ISBN 0-317-42402-5, 2056075). Bks Demand UMI.

Plant & Soil: Interfaces & Interactions: Proceedings of the International Symposium Plant & Soil, Wageningen, the Netherlands, August 6-8, 1986. (Developments in Plant & Soil Sciences Ser.). 1987. lib. bdg. 110.00 (ISBN 90-247-3535-1, Pub. by Martin Nijhoff Netherlands). Kluwer Academic.

Plant Animal Biotechnology Conference: Proceedings. 1985. pap. 150.00 (ISBN 0-89336-446-0). BCC.

Plant-Animal Interactions. Ed. by Warren G. Abrahamson. 400p. 1988. 48.00x (ISBN 0-02-948050-7). Macmillan.

Plant-Atmosphere Relationships. J. Grace. LC 82-19177. (Outline Studies in Ecology). 80p. 1983. pap. 8.50 (ISBN 0-412-23180-8, NO. 6783, Pub. by Chapman & Hall). Routledge Chapman & Hall.

Plant Between Sun & Earth & the Science Physical & Ethereal Spaces. 2nd ed. George Adams & Olive Whicher. (Illus.). 1980. pap. 40.00 (ISBN 0-85440-360-4, Pub. by Steinerbooks). Anthroposophic.

Plant Biochemistry. 3rd ed. Ed. by James Bonner & Joseph Varner. 1976. text ed. 47.00 (ISBN 0-12-114860-2). Acad Pr.

Plant Biology Lab Manual for a One Semester Course: Form & Function. Jean Gerrath et al. 152p. 1982. pap. text ed. 7.95 (ISBN 0-8403-2814-1). Kendall-Hunt.

Plant Biology Lab Manual: Form & Function. 3d ed. Ann T. Middleton et al. 160p. 1986. shrink wrap 9.95 (ISBN 0-8403-4111-3). Kendall Hunt.

Plant Biology Laboratory. Thomas McInnis, Jr. 1975. wire coil bdg. 7.00 (ISBN 0-88252-024-5). Paladin Hse.

Plant Biology Laboratory Manual. 3rd ed. Curt M. Peterson. 224p. 1987. pap. text ed. 15.95 (ISBN 0-8403-4237-3). Kendall-Hunt.

Plant Biosystematics: Symposium. William F. Grant. 1984. 65.00 (ISBN 0-12-295680-X). Acad Pr.

Plant Biotechnology: Society for Experimental Biology Seminar 18. Ed. by S. H. Mantell & H. Smith. (Illus.). 334p. 1985. pap. 20.95 (ISBN 0-521-28782-0). Cambridge U Pr.

Plant Book: A Portable Dictionary of the Higher Plants. D. J. Mabberley. 700p. 1987. 34.50 (ISBN 0-521-34060-8). Cambridge U Pr.

Plant Breeding: A Symposium. Plant Breeding Symposium (1965: Iowa State University) Ed. by Kenneth J. Frey. LC 66-21642. pap. 109.50 (ISBN 0-317-30428-3, 2024932). Bks Demand UMI.

Plant Breeding for Stress Environments. Abraham Blum. 208p. 1988. 120.00 (ISBN 0-8493-6388-8, 6388). CRC Pr.

Plant Breeding II. Ed. by Kenneth J. Frey. 498p. 1981. 25.95x (ISBN 0-8138-1550-9). Iowa St U Pr.

Plant Breeding in New Zealand. Ed. by H. C. Smith & G. S. Wratt. (Illus.). 300p. (Orig.). 1984. 34.95 (ISBN 0-409-70137-8). Butterworth.

Plant Breeding Methodology. Neal F. Jensen. 1988. price not set (ISBN 0-471-60190-X). Wiley.

Plant Breeding Perspectives. Ed. by A. J. T. Hendriksen & J. Sneep. 460p. (13 colour plates, over 700 refs.). 1979. 63.50 (ISBN 90-220-0697-2, PDC122, PUDOC). UNIPUB.

Plant Breeding Reviews, Vol. 4. Janick. 59.95 (ISBN 0-317-64240-5). Van Nos Reinhold.

Plant Breeding Reviews, Vol. 5. Ed. by Jules Janick. (Illus.). 650p. 1987. 62.95 (ISBN 0-442-24376-6). Van Nos Reinhold.

Plant Breeding Reviews, Vol. 6. Ed. by Jules Janick. (Illus.). 400p. 1989. text ed. 57.95x (ISBN 0-88192-116-5). Timber.

Plant Breeding Systems in Seed Plants. A. J. Richards. (Illus.). 320p. 1986. text ed. 85.00x (ISBN 0-04-581020-6); pap. text ed. 34.95x (ISBN 0-04-581021-4). Unwin Hyman.

Plant Buyer's Directory. Allan Sawyer. (Illus.). 1985. 10.95 (ISBN 0-88162-107-2). Salem Hse Pubs.

Plant Canopies: Their Growth, Form & Function. Ed. by G. Russell et al. (Society for Experimental Biology Seminar Ser.: No. 31). 300p. Date not set. price not set (ISBN 0-521-32838-1). Cambridge U Pr.

Plant Carbohydrates I: Intracellular Carbohydrates. Ed. by F. A. Loewus & W. Tanner. (Encyclopedia of Plant Physiology Ser.: Vol. 13 a). (Illus.). 880p. 1982. 155.00 (ISBN 0-387-11060-7). Springer-Verlag.

Plant Carbohydrates II: Extracellular Carbohydrates. Ed. by W. Tanner & F. A. Loewus. (Encyclopedia of Plant Physiology: Vol. 13 B). (Illus.). 800p. 1981. 145.00 (ISBN 0-387-11007-0). Springer-Verlag.

Plant Cast Precast & Prestressed Concrete a Design Guide. 560p. softcover 24.00x (ISBN 0-937040-17-7, MNL-125-80). Prestressed Concrete.

Plant Cast Precast & Prestressed Concrete: A Design Guide. David A. Sheppard & William R. Phillips. 576p. 1989. 59.50 (ISBN 0-07-056760-3). McGraw.

Plant Cell & Tissue Culture: A Laboratory Manual. J. Reinert & M. M. Yeoman. (Illus.). 90p. 1982. 27.00 (ISBN 0-387-11316-9). Springer-Verlag.

Plant Cell-Cell Interactions. Ed. by I. Sussex et al. (Current Communications in Molecular Biology Ser.). 151p. (Orig.). 1985. pap. 27.00 (ISBN 0-87969-189-1). Cold Spring Harbor.

Plant Cell Culture. R. G. Butenko. 207p. 1985. 6.96 (ISBN 0-8285-3408-X, Pub. by Mir Pubs USSR). Imported Pubns.

Plant Cell Culture. (Advances in Biochemical Engineering - Biotechnology Ser.: Vol. 31). (Illus.). 140p. 1985. 39.00 (ISBN 0-387-15489-2). Springer-Verlag.

Plant Cell Culture in Crop Improvement. Ed. by Kenneth L. Giles & S. K. Sen. (Basic Life Sciences Ser.: Vol. 22). 514p. 1982. 75.00x (ISBN 0-306-41160-1, Plenum Pr). Plenum Pub.

Plant Cell Structure & Metabolism. 2nd ed. J. L. Hall & T. J. Flowers. (Illus.). 480p. (Orig.). 1982. pap. 22.00x (ISBN 0-582-44408-X). Wiley.

Plant Cell Structure & Metabolism. 2nd ed. J. L. Hall et al. 480p. 1986. pap. 28.95 (ISBN 0-470-20487-7, Co-Pub. with Longman). Wiley.

Plant Cell Wall. 3rd, rev. ed. A. Frey-Wyssling. 1976. 125.00x (ISBN 3-443-14009-2). Lubrecht & Cramer.

Plant Chemosystematics. Jeffrey B. Harborne & Billie L. Turner. 1984. 109.50 (ISBN 0-12-324640-7). Acad Pr.

Plant Chromosomes. A. Love & D. Love. 1975. 22.50x (ISBN 3-7682-0966-0). Lubrecht & Cramer.

Plant Closing & Worker Displacement: The Regional Issues. Marie Howland. LC 88-17032. 170p. 1988. text ed. write for info. (ISBN 0-88099-063-5); pap. text ed. write for info. (ISBN 0-88099-062-7). W E Upjohn.

Plant Closing Legislation. Ed. by Antone Aboud. LC 84-6891. (Key Issues Ser.: No. 27). 68p. 1984. pap. 6.00 (ISBN 0-87546-108-5). ILR Pr.

Plant Closing Legislation in the United States: A Bibliogrphy. Edward Duensing. LC 85-184586. (Public Administration Ser.: P 1691). 1985. 2.00 (ISBN 0-89028-421-0). Vance Biblios.

Plant Closings: A Selected Bibliography of Materials Published Through 1985. LC 87-31762. 194p. 1988. pap. 15.00. ILR Pr.

Plant Closings & Economic Dislocation. Jeanne P. Gordus et al. LC 81-16188. 173p. 1981. text ed. 18.95 (ISBN 0-911558-89-6); pap. text ed. 11.95 (ISBN 0-911558-90-X). W E Upjohn.

Plant Closings in the New Industrial Revolution. Robert W. Burchell & George Sternleib. 412p. 1988. 32.50 (ISBN 0-317-64577-3). Ctr Urban Pol Res.

Plant Closings in the New Industrial Revolution. Robert W. Burchell & George Sternlieb. 412p. 1988. 32.50 (ISBN 0-88285-124-1); pap. 12.95. Transaction Bks.

Plant Closings: International Context & Social Costs. Robert Perrucci et al. (Social Institutions & Social Change Ser.). 256p. (Orig.). 1988. lib. bdg. 38.95 (ISBN 0-202-30338-1); pap. text ed. 15.95 (ISBN 0-202-30339-X). Aldine de Gruyter.

Plant Closings: Myths, Power, Politics. Lawrence E. Rothstein. 250p. 1986. 27.95 (ISBN 0-86569-121-5). Auburn Hse.

Plant Closings: Public or Private Choices? Ed. by Richard McKenzie. LC 84-14957. 326p. 1984. pap. 9.50 (ISBN 0-932790-42-9). Cato Inst.

Plant Manager's Handbook. Water Pollution Control Federation Staff. (Manual & Practice: Systems Management). (Illus.). 168p. 1986. pap. 32.00 (ISBN 0-943244-66-8). Water Pollution.

Plant Manager's Manual & Guide. Charles H. Becker. 464p. 1987. 49.95 (ISBN 0-13-680703-8). P-H.

Plant Materials in Urban Design: A Selected Bibliography. J. Wayne Pratt. (Architecture Ser.: A 1575). 9p. 1986. 3.00 (ISBN 0-89028-785-6). Vance Biblios.

Plant Membranes: Endo- & Plasma Membranes. David G. Robinson. LC 84-7539. (Cell Biology: A Series of Monographs: Vol. 3). 1075p. 1985. 78.00x (ISBN 0-471-86210-X). Wiley.

Plant Membranes: Structure, Assembly & Functions. Ed. by J. L. Harwood. 252p. 1988. lib. bdg. 50.00 (ISBN 0-904498-23-9, Biochemical Society, London). Rsrch Bks Ct.

Plant Microbe Interactions, Vol. 3. Ed. by T. Kosuge & E. Nester. 400p. 1988. 45.00 (ISBN 0-02-947992-4). Macmillan.

Plant Microbe Interactions: Molecular & Genetic Perspectives, Vol. 2. Tsune Kosuge & Eugene Nester. (Illus.). 448p. 1986. text ed. 40.00 (ISBN 0-02-947990-8). Macmillan.

Plant Migration: The Dynamics of Geographic Patterning in Seed Plant Species. Jonathan D. Sauer. 1988. 45.00x (ISBN 0-520-06003-2). U of Cal Pr.

Plant, Mineral, Nutrition. Anthony D. Glass. 1988. pap. text ed. 31.25 (ISBN 0-86720-080-4). Jones & Bartlett.

Plant Mitochondria: Structural, Functional, & Physiological Aspects. Ed. by A. L. Moore & R. B. Beechey. LC 87-15303. (Illus.). 424p. 1987. 79.50x (ISBN 0-306-42572-6, Plenum Pr). Plenum Pub.

Plant Modernization & Community Economic Stability: Proceedings. University of Oregon Conference, 1982. 7.00 (ISBN 0-318-01115-8). U OR BGR.

Plant Modification for More Efficient Water Use, Vol. 14. John F. Stone. (Developments in Agricultural & Managed Forest Ecology Ser.: Vol. 1). 330p. 1975. Repr. 92.00 (ISBN 0-444-41273-5). Elsevier.

Plant Molecular Biology. Robert B. Goldberg. LC 83-19530. (UCLA Symposia on Molecular & Cellular Biology Ser.: Vol. 12). 520p. 1983. 78.00 (ISBN 0-8451-2611-3). A R Liss.

Plant Molecular Biology. D. Grierson & S. Covey. (Tertiary Level Biology Ser.). 200p. 1988. text ed. 57.50 (ISBN 0-412-01681-8, Pub. by Chapman & Hall England); pap. text ed. 27.50 (ISBN 0-412-01691-5, Pub. by Chapman & Hall England). Routledge Chapman & Hall.

Plant Molecular Biology. Ed. by D. Von Wettstein & N. H. Chua. LC 87-24389. (NATO ASI Series A, Life Sciences: Vol. 140). 710p. 1987. 125.00x (ISBN 0-306-42696-X, Plenum Pr). Plenum Pub.

Plant Monster. Jim Razzi. (Double Dinomite Ser.: No. 4). (gr. 1-3). 1987. pap. 2.50 (ISBN 0-671-62094-0, Minstrel Bks). S&S.

Plant Morphogenesis. Edmund W. Sinnott. LC 79-4660. 560p. 1979. Repr. of 1960 ed. lib. bdg. 19.50 (ISBN 0-88275-922-1). Krieger.

Plant Names. Thomas Lindsay. LC 75-16423. viii, 100p. 1976. Repr. of 1923 ed. 40.00x (ISBN 0-8103-4160-3). Gale.

Plant Nonprotein Amino & Imino Acids: Biological, Biochemical & Toxicological Properties. Gerald Rosenthal. LC 82-1651. (American Society of Plant Physiologists Monograph). 1982. 51.00 (ISBN 0-12-597780-8). Acad Pr.

Plant Nurseries: Training Element & Technical Guide for SPWP Workers. (Special Labour-Intensive Public Works Programme Ser.: No. 6). (Illus.). 61p. (Orig.). 1985. pap. 7.00 (ISBN 92-2-105236-2). Intl Labour Office.

Plant Nutrient Supply & Movement. (Technical Reports Ser.: No. 48). 160p. 1965. pap. 15.00 (ISBN 92-0-115265-5, IDC48, IAEA). UNIPUB.

Plant Operations Training, Vol. 1. Bill D. Berger & Ken E. Anderson. 157p. 1979. 39.95 (ISBN 0-87814-109-X). Pennwell Bks.

Plant Operations Training, Vol. 2. Bill D. Berger & Ken E. Anderson. 165p. 1979. 39.95 (ISBN 0-87814-110-3, P-4225). Pennwell Bks.

Plant Operations Training, Vol. 3. Bill D. Berger & Ken E. Anderson. 162p. 1980. 39.95 (ISBN 0-87814-111-1, P-4226). Pennwell Bks.

Plant Organelles. Ed. by E. Reid. LC 79-40730. (Methodological Surveys in Biochemistry Ser.: Vol. 9). 232p. 1979. 79.95x (ISBN 0-470-26810-7). Halsted Pr.

Plant-Parasitic Nematodes, 2 vols. A. A. Paramonov. 408p. 1972. Set, vol. 1, vol. 3. text ed. 97.00x (ISBN 0-7065-1250-2, Pub. by Keter Pub Jerusalem). Coronet Bks.

Plant Parasitic Nematodes, Vol. 3. Ed. by Bert M. Zuckerman & Richard A. Rohde. 508p. 1981. 91.00 (ISBN 0-12-782203-8). Acad Pr.

Plant Parasitic Nematodes - A Check List 1981-1985. R. L. Rajak et al. (International Bioscience Monographs: Vol. XVIII). (Illus.). 135p. 1987. 17.00 (ISBN 1-55528-143-5, Pub. by Messers Today & Tomorrow Printers & Publishers). Scholarly Pubns.

Plant Parasitic Nematodes: Morphology, Anatomy, Taxonomy, & Ecology, Vols. 1 & 2. Ed. by B. M. Zuckerman et al. 1971. Vol. 1. 77.00 (ISBN 0-12-782201-1); Vol. 2. 77.00 (ISBN 0-12-782202-X). Acad Pr.

Plant Parasitic Nematodes of India. K. Sitaramaiah. (International Bioscience Monograph: No. XV). xxii, 292p. 1984. 25.00 (ISBN 1-55528-042-0, Pub. by Messers Today & Tomorrow Printers & Publishers). Scholarly Pubns.

Plant Pathogenesis. H. Wheeler. LC 75-19318. (Advanced Series in Agricultural Sciences: Vol. 2). (Illus.). 140p. 1975. 29.00 (ISBN 0-387-07358-2). Springer-Verlag.

Plant Pathogenic Bacteria. Ed. by E. L. Civerolo et al. (Current Plant Science & Biotechnology in Agriculture). 1987. lib. bdg. 175.00 (ISBN 90-247-3476-2, Pub. by Martinus Nijhoff Netherlands). Kluwer Academic.

Plant Pathogenic Fungi. J. A. Von Arx. (Nova Hedwigia Beiheft Eighty-Seven Ser.). (Illus.). 288p. 1987. pap. text ed. 84.00x (ISBN 3-443-51009-4). Lubrecht & Cramer.

Plant Pathogens. Ed. by D. W. Lovelock. (Society of Applied Bacteriology Technical Ser.). 1979. 38.50 (ISBN 0-12-457050-X). Acad Pr.

Plant Pathogens & Their Control in Horticulture. G. R. Dixon. (Sciences in Horticulture Ser.). (Illus.). 265p. (Orig.). 1984. pap. text ed. 18.50x (ISBN 0-333-35912-7, Pub. by Macmillan England). Scholium Intl.

Plant Pathologist's Pocketbook. Ed. by A. Johnston & C. Booth. 439p. 1983. lib. bdg. 25.20 (ISBN 0-85198-460-6); pap. text ed. 12.60 (ISBN 0-85198-517-3). Lubrecht & Cramer.

Plant Pathology. 2nd ed. George N. Agrios. 1978. 47.95 (ISBN 0-12-044560-3). Acad Pr.

Plant Pathology. 3rd ed. George N. Agrios. 803p. 1988. 45.00 (ISBN 0-12-044563-8). Acad Pr.

Plant Pathology & Plant Pathogens. 2nd ed. J. A. Lucas & C. H. Dickinson. (Illus.). 238p. 1982. pap. text ed. 24.95x (ISBN 0-632-00918-7). Blackwell Pubns.

Plant Pathology: Principles & Practice. D. Gareth Jones. (Illus.). 208p. 1987. pap. text ed. 21.00 (ISBN 0-13-680760-7). P-H.

Plant Pathosystems. R. A. Robinson. (Advanced Series in Agricultural Sciences: Vol. 3). (Illus.). 1976. 33.00 (ISBN 0-387-07712-X). Springer-Verlag.

Plant People. Dale Carlson. 96p. (YA) (gr. 5 up). 1979. pap. 1.25 (ISBN 0-440-96959-X, LFL). Dell.

Plant Peroxisomes. Anthony H. Huang et al. LC 82-22777. (American Society of Plant Physiologists Monograph Ser.). 1983. 45.00 (ISBN 0-12-358260-1). Acad Pr.

Plant Pests & Their Control. Peter G. Fenemore. (Illus.). 292p. 1983. pap. text ed. 29.95 (ISBN 0-409-60087-3). Butterworth.

Plant Photoplasts: A Biotechnological Tool for Plant Improvement. Tessa Bengochea & John H. Dodds. 128p. 1986. 37.00 (ISBN 0-412-26890-6, Pub. by Chapman & Hall England); pap. 17.95 (ISBN 0-412-26640-7). Routledge Chapman & Hall.

Plant Physiognomies. Elisee Reclus. 69.95 (ISBN 0-8490-0840-9). Gordon Pr.

Plant Physiology. 4th ed. Robert M. Devlin & Francis H. Witham. 577p. 1983. text ed. write for info. (ISBN 0-87150-765-X). Wadsworth Pub.

Plant Physiology. rev. ed. S. N. Pandey & B. K. Sinha. 594p. 1986. text ed. 45.00x (ISBN 0-7069-2967-5, Pub. by Vikas India). Advent NY.

Plant Physiology. 1987. 5.00 (ISBN 0-471-63908-7). Wiley.

Plant Physiology. 3rd ed. Frank B. Salisbury & Cleon W. Ross. 540p. 1985. text ed. write for info. (ISBN 0-534-04482-4). Wadsworth Pub.

Plant Physiology. Irwin P. Ting. LC 80-16448. (Illus.). 635p. 1982. text ed. write for info. (ISBN 0-201-07406-0). Addison-Wesley.

Plant Physiology. William Woodbury. 1984. text ed. 27.67 (ISBN 0-8359-5556-7, Reston). P-H.

Plant Physiology: A Treatise, 6 vols. Ed. by F. C. Steward. Incl. Vol. 1A. Cellular Organization & Respiration. 1960. 52.00 (ISBN 0-12-668601-7); Vol. 1B. Photosynthesis & Chemosynthesis. 1960. 54.00 (ISBN 0-12-668641-6); Vol. 2. Plants in Relation to Water & Solutes. 1959. 90.00 (ISBN 0-12-668602-5); Vol. 3. Inorganic Nutrition of Plants. 1963. 91.50 (ISBN 0-12-668603-3); Vol. 4A. Metabolism: Organic Nutrition & Nitrogen Metabolism. 1965. 86.50 (ISBN 0-12-668604-1); Vol. 4B. Metabolism: Intermediary Metabolism & Pathology. 1966. 81.00 (ISBN 0-12-668644-0); Vol. 5A. Analysis of Growth: Behavior of Plants & Their Organs. 1969. 67.50 (ISBN 0-12-668605-X); Vol. 5B. Analysis of Growth: The Responses of Cells & Tissues in Culture. 1969. 65.00 (ISBN 0-12-668645-9); Vol. 6A. Physiology of Development: Plants & Their Reproduction. 1972. 81.00 (ISBN 0-12-668606-8); Vol. 6B. Physiology of Development: the Hormones. 1972. 60.00 (ISBN 0-12-668646-7); Vol. 6C. From Seeds to Sexuality. 1972. 65.00 (ISBN 0-12-668656-4). Acad Pr.

Plant Physiology: A Treatise: Energy & Carbon Metabolism, Vol. 7. Ed. by F. C. Steward & R. G. Bidwell. 1983. 80.50 (ISBN 0-12-668607-6). Acad Pr.

Plant Physiology: A Treatise Vol. 8: Nitrogen Metabolism. Ed. by F. C. Steward & R. G. Bidwell. 1983. 83.00 (ISBN 0-12-668608-4). Acad Pr.

Plant Physiology: A Treatise: Water & Solutes in Plants, Vol. 9. F. C. Steward et al. 1986. 95.00 (ISBN 0-12-668609-2). Acad Pr.

Plant Physiology Laboratory Manual. Cleon W. Ross. 200p. 1974. pap. text ed. write for info. (ISBN 0-534-00351-6). Wadsworth Pub.

Plant Pigments. T. W. Goodwin. 325p. 1988. price not set (ISBN 0-12-289847-8). Acad Pr.

Plant Pigments, Flavors & Textures: The Chemistry & Biochemistry of Selected Compounds. N. Michael Eskin. LC 78-22523. (Food Science & Technology Ser.). 1979. 46.00 (ISBN 0-12-242250-3). Acad Pr.

Plant Poisoning in Animals: A Bibliography of World Literature, No. 2: 1980-1982. Michael R. Hails. (Annotated Bibliography Ser.: Vol. 39). 92p. 1986. pap. text ed. 28.50x (ISBN 0-85198-578-5). Lubrecht & Cramer.

Plant Portraits. Beth Chatto. LC 85-80531. 112p. 1986. 25.00 (ISBN 0-87923-595-0). Godine.

Plant Portraits from the Flora Danica, 1761-1769. William T. Stearn. 75.00x (ISBN 0-900751-20-7, Pub. by Trade & Travel UK). State Mutual Bk.

Plant Printing. Ida Geary. (Illus.). 1978. pap. 3.50 (ISBN 0-912908-03-3). Tamal Land.

Plant Processing of Natural Gas. Curtis Kruse & Hank Haas. (Illus.). 114p. (Orig.). 1975. pap. text ed. 8.00 (ISBN 0-88698-115-8, 3.11010). PETEX.

Plant Production & Management under Drought Conditions: Papers Presented at the Symposium, 4-6 Oct., 1982, Held at Tulsa, OK. Ed. by J. F. Stone & W. O. Willis. (Developments in Agricultural & Managed-Forest Ecology Ser.: Vol. 12). 398p. 1986. Repr. 65.00 (ISBN 0-444-42214-5). Elsevier.

Plant Production in Containers. Carl. E. Whitcomb. (Illus.). 640p. 1984. 28.00 (ISBN 0-9613109-1-X). Lacebark Pubns.

Plant Propagation. 1987. 7.00 (ISBN 0-471-63911-7). Wiley.

Plant Propogation. Phillip M. Browse. 1988. pap. 9.95 (ISBN 0-671-65840-9, Fireside). S&S.

Plant Protection: An Integrated Interdisciplinary Approach. Webster H. Sill, Jr. (Illus.). 298p. 1982. 28.95x (ISBN 0-8138-1665-3). Iowa St U Pr.

Plant Protection Legislation. Luis M. Bombin. (Legislative Study Ser.: No. 28). 165p. 1985. pap. 12.00 (ISBN 92-5-101460-4, F2732, FAO). UNIPUB.

Plant Proteins: Applications, Biological Effects, & Chemistry. Ed. by Robert L. Ory. LC 86-10848. (ACS Symposium Ser.: No. 312). (Illus.). 285p. 1986. 59.95 (ISBN 0-8412-0976-6). Am Chemical.

Plant Proteolytic Enzymes. Ed. by Michael J. Dalling. 1986. Vol. I, 192p. 2 vol. set 164.00 (ISBN 0-8493-5684-9). Vol. II, 192p. CRC Pr.

Plant Protoplasts. Ed. by Larry C. Fowke & Fred Constabel. 256p. 1985. 99.00 (ISBN 0-8493-6473-6). CRC Pr.

Plant Quarantine & Control Administration: Its History, Activities & Organization. Gustavus A. Weber. LC 72-3076. (Brookings Institution. Institute for Government Research. Service Monographs of the U. S. Government: No. 59). Repr. of 1930 ed. 29.00 (ISBN 0-404-57159-X). AMS Pr.

Plant Regulation & World Agriculture. Ed. by Tom Scott. LC 79-14597. (NATO ASI Series A, Life Sciences: Vol. 22). 586p. 1979. 95.00x (ISBN 0-306-40180-0, Plenum Pr). Plenum Pub.

Plant Relocation: Industrial Relations Implications: a Review Based on the Glidden Decision. 1962. pap. 1.75 (ISBN 0-87330-008-4). Indus Rel.

Plant Reproductive Ecology. Mary F. Willson. LC 82-24826. 282p. 1983. 45.00 (ISBN 0-471-08362-3). Wiley.

Plant Reproductive Ecology: Patterns & Strategies. Ed. by Jon L. Doust. Lesley L. Doust. (Illus.). 352p. 1988. 49.95 (ISBN 0-19-505175-0). Oxford U Pr.

Plant Resistance to Insects. Ed. by Paul A. Hedin. LC 82-22622. (ACS Symposium Ser.: No. 208). 375p. 1983. lib. bdg. 49.95 (ISBN 0-8412-0756-9). Am Chemical.

Plant Resistance to Insects: A Fundamental Approach. Smith. 1988. price not set (ISBN 0-471-84938-3). Wiley.

Plant Resistance to Viruses: Symposium No. 133. Ciba Foundation Symposium Staff. LC 87-25447. (CIBA Foundation Symposia Ser.). 215p. 1988. 49.95 (ISBN 0-471-91263-8). Wiley.

Plant Resources of Arid & Semiarid Lands: A Global Perspective. Edited Treatise ed. Ed. by J. R. Goodin & David K. Northington. 1985. 65.50 (ISBN 0-12-289745-5). Acad Pr.

Plant Response to Stress. Ed. by J. D. Tenhunen & E. M. Catarino. (NATO ASI Ser.: Vol G 15). 680p. 1987. 168.50 (ISBN 0-387-16082-5). Springer Verlag.

Plant Response to Wind. J. Grace. (Experimental Botany Ser.). 1978. 73.00 (ISBN 0-12-294450-X). Acad Pr.

Plant Root & Its Environment. Ed. by E. W. Carson, Jr. LC 72-92877. (Illus.). xxiii, 425p. 1974. 30.00x (ISBN 0-8139-0411-0). U Pr of Va.

Plant Root Systems: Their Function & Interaction with the Soil. R. Scott Russell. LC 77-6394. 1977. text ed. 46.95 (ISBN 0-07-084068-7). McGraw.

Plant Science. J. Barden & R. Gordon Halfacre. 592p. 1986. text ed. 39.95 (ISBN 0-07-003669-1). McGraw.

Plant Science. (Illus.). 48p. (gr. 6-12). 1975. pap. 1.25x (ISBN 0-8395-3396-9, 3396). BSA.

Plant Science: An Introduction to World Crops. 3rd ed. Jules Janick et al. LC 81-4897. (Illus.). 868p. 1981. text ed. 36.95 (ISBN 0-7167-1261-X). W H Freeman.

Plant Science: Growth, Development & Utilization of Cultivated Plants. William J. Flocker & Hudson T. Hartmann. (Illus.). 688p. 1981. text ed. write for info. (ISBN 0-13-681056-X). P-H.

Plant Science: Growth, Development & Utilization of Cultivated Plants. 2nd ed. Hudson T. Hartmann et al. (Illus.). 720p. 1988. text ed. 40.00 (ISBN 0-13-680307-5). P-H.

Plant Seed: Development, Preservation & Germination. Ed. by Irwin Rubenstein et al. 1979. 29.95 (ISBN 0-12-602050-7). Acad Pr.

Plant Senescence: Its Biochemistry & Physiology. Ed. by W. W. Thomson & E. A. Nothnagel. LC 87-70735. 269p. pap. 20.00 (ISBN 0-943088-10-0). Am Soc of Plan.

Plant Sociology of Alpine Tundra, Trail Ridge, Rocky Mountain National Park, Colorado. Beatrice L. Willard. Ed. by Jon W. Raese. LC 79-26590. (CSM Quarterly Ser.: Vol. 74, No. 4). (Illus.). 119p. 1980. pap. 6.00 (ISBN 0-686-63162-5). Colo Sch Mines.

Plant Sociology: The Study of Plant Communities. J. Braun-Blanquet. Tr. by George D. Fuller & Henry S. Conard. (Illus.). 439p. 1983. Repr. of 1932 ed. lib. bdg. 60.00x (ISBN 3-87429-208-8). Lubrecht & Cramer.

Plant Speciation. 2nd ed. Verne Grant. LC 81-6159. (Illus.). 544p. 1981. 60.00x (ISBN 0-231-05112-3); pap. 20.00x (ISBN 0-231-05113-1). Columbia U Pr.

Plant Species & Plant Communities. Ed. by Eddy Van Der Maarel & Marinus J. Werger. 1978. lib. bdg. 37.00 (ISBN 90-6193-591-1, Pub. by Junk Pubs Netherlands). Kluwer Academic.

Plant Species Reportedly Possessing Pest-Control Properties: A Database. Michael Grainge et al. (East-West Resource Systems Institute RM Ser.: NO. 84-1). vi, 240p. 1984. 25.00 (ISBN 0-86638-057-4). EW Ctr HI.

Plant Strategies & the Dynamics & Structure of Plant Communities. David Tilman. Ed. by Robert M. May. (Monographs in Population Biology: No. 26). (Illus.). 92p. Date not set. text ed. 45.00 (ISBN 0-691-08488-2); pap. text ed. 15.95 (ISBN 0-691-08489-0). Princeton U Pr.

Plant Strategies & Vegetation Processes. J. P. Grime. LC 78-18523. 222p. 1979. 67.95x (ISBN 0-471-99695-5); pap. 32.95x (ISBN 0-471-99692-0). Wiley.

Plant Stress: Insect Interactions. Ed. by E. A. Heinrichs. LC 88-255. (Environmental Science & Technology: A Wiley-Interscience Series of Texts & Monographs). (Illus.). 1988. 60.00 (ISBN 0-471-82648-0). Wiley.

Plant Succession & Indicators: A Definitive Edition of Plant Succession & Plant Indicators. Frederic E. Clements. (Illus.). 1973. Repr. 23.95x (ISBN 0-02-843020-4). Hafner.

Plant Superintendent. Jack Rudman. (Career Examination Ser.: C-1935). (Cloth bdg. avail on request), 1988. pap. 16.00 (ISBN 0-8373-1935-8). Natl Learning.

Plant Superintendent - A. Jack Rudman. (Career Examination Ser.: C-2046). (Cloth bdg. avail. on request). pap. 14.00 (ISBN 0-8373-2046-1). Natl Learning.

Plant Superintendent - B. Jack Rudman. (Career Examination Ser.: C-2047). (Cloth bdg. avail. on request). pap. 14.00 (ISBN 0-8373-2047-X). Natl Learning.

Plant Superintendent - C. Jack Rudman. (Career Examination Ser.: C-2048). (Cloth bdg. avail. on request). pap. 14.00 (ISBN 0-8373-2048-8). Natl Learning.

Plant Systematics. 2nd ed. Samuel B. Jones & Arlene E. Luchsinger. 512p. 1986. text ed. 37.95 (ISBN 0-07-032796-3). McGraw.

Plant Taxonomic Literature in Australian Libraries. Nancy T. Burbidge. 1979. 30.00 (ISBN 0-643-00286-3, Pub. by CSIRO). Intl Spec Bk.

Plant, Technology, & Safety Management Handbook. 144p. 1985. pap. 50.00 (ISBN 0-86688-081-X). Joint Comm Hlthcare.

Plant That Ate Dirty Socks. Nancy McArthur. 128p. (Orig.). 1988. pap. 2.50 (ISBN 0-380-75493-2, Camelot). Avon.

Plant: The Flower. (Better Farming Ser.: No. 3). 29p. 1976. pap. 9.50 (ISBN 92-5-100142-1, F61, FAO). UNIPUB.

Plant: The Stem, the Buds, & the Leaves. Rev. ed. (Better Farming Ser.: No. 2). (Illus.). 30p. 1977. pap. 7.50 (ISBN 92-5-100141-3, F60, FAO). UNIPUB.

Plant Tissue & Cell Culture. Ed. by C. E. Green et al. LC 86-27527. (Plant Biology Ser.: Vol. 3). 520p. 1987. 47.00 (ISBN 0-8451-1802-1, 1802). A R Liss.

Plants. Lillian Savage-Harrington & Anne Maassen-Nickel. (Just What We Need Ser.). 56p. 1988. pap. 5.00 (ISBN 0-930599-20-9). Thinking Pubns.

Plants see Illustrated Biology.

Plants see Rare & Endangered Biota of Florida.

Plants, Agriculture, & Human Society. Norman Richardson & Thomas Stubbs. LC 77-72644. 1978. pap. text ed. 21.95 (ISBN 0-8053-8215-1). Benjamin-Cummings.

Plants: An Evolutionary Survey. R. F. Scagel et al. 757p. 1984. text ed. write for info. (ISBN 0-534-02802-0). Wadsworth Pub.

Plants: An Integrated Unit for Grade One. Linda Enas. (Illus.). 45p. 1987. 5.00 (ISBN 0-941221-04-0). Reformed Educ Pub.

Plants & Ancient Man - Studies in Palaeoethnobotany: Proceedings of the 6th Symposium of the International Work Group for Palaeoethnobotany, Groningen, 30 May - 3 June 1983. Ed. by W. Van Zeist & W. A. Casarie. 374p. 1984. text ed. 48.50 (ISBN 90-6191-528-7, Pub. by A A Balkema). Brookfield Pub Co.

Plants & Animals in Nature. Lorraine Conway. (Superific Science Ser.). 64p. (gr. 5-8). 1986. wkbk. 6.95 (ISBN 0-86653-356-7). Good Apple.

Plants & Animals of the Pacific Northwest: An Illustrated Guide to the Natural History of Western Oregon, Washington, & British Columbia. Eugene N. Kozloff. LC 75-40875. (Illus.). 280p. 1976. 30.00x (ISBN 0-295-95449-3); pap. 19.95 (ISBN 0-295-95597-X). U of Wash Pr.

Plants & Animals Rare in South Dakota: A Field Guide. Michael M. Melius. LC 87-50402. (Illus.). 120p. (Orig.). 1987. pap. 3.00 (ISBN 0-937603-05-8). Melius Peterson Pub.

Plants & Environment: A Textbook of Plant Autecology. 3rd ed. Rexford Daubenmire. LC 73-13826. 422p. 1974. 39.95 (ISBN 0-471-19636-3). Wiley.

Plants & Flowers. Brian Holley. (Discover Nature Ser.). (Illus.). 32p. (gr. 3-7). 1986. PLB 14.25 (ISBN 0-87617-018-1, Pub. by C Hayes Pr). Penworthy Pub.

Plants & Flowers of Hawai'i. S. H. Sohmer. LC 86-19231. (Illus.). 144p. 1987. 14.95 (ISBN 0-8248-1096-1). UH Pr.

Plants & Gardens in Persian, Mughal & Turkish Art. Norah M. Titley. (Illus.). 32p. (Orig.). 1979. pap. 2.95 (ISBN 0-904654-27-3, Pub. by British Lib). Longwood Pub Group.

Plants & Islands. D. Bramwell. LC 79-50299. 1980. 91.50 (ISBN 0-12-125460-7). Acad Pr.

Plants & Microclimate: A Quantitative Approach to Environmental Plant Physiology. Hamlyn G. Jones. LC 82-22043. 350p. 1983. 65.00 (ISBN 0-521-24849-3); pap. 24.95 (ISBN 0-521-27016-2). Cambridge U Pr.

Plants & People. (Wonders of Learning Kits Ser.). (gr. 3-6). 1981. incl. cass. & tchr's. guide 28.95 (ISBN 0-686-73889-6, 04915). Natl Geog.

Plants & People of the Sonoran Desert. 1988. 0.50 (ISBN 0-9605656-5-5). Desert Botanical.

Plants & People: Vegetation Change in North America. Thomas R. Vale. Ed. by C. Gregory Knight. LC 82-8865. (Resource Publications in Geography Ser.). (Illus., Orig.). 1982. pap. 6.00 (ISBN 0-89291-151-4). Assn Am Geographers.

Plants & the Daylight Spectrum. Ed. by H. Smith. LC 81-66697. 1982. 70.00 (ISBN 0-12-650980-8). Acad Pr.

Plants & the Home Gardener. 3.95 (ISBN 0-318-04566-4). Bklyn Botanic.

Plants Are for People, Pt. 1. Don Watson. LC 72-95083. 1973. soft bdg. 3.50 (ISBN 0-930492-09-9). Hawaiian Serv.

Plants Are for People, Pt. 2. Don Watson. LC 75-33750. 1976. soft bdg. 3.50 (ISBN 0-930492-10-2). Hawaiian Serv.

Plants Are Waters' Factories: A Book About Drouth. Michael A. Weinberg. LC 75-4850. (Illus.). 110p. 1976. pap. 1.95 (ISBN 0-9601014-1-1). Weinberg.

Plants As Solar Collectors: Optimizing Productivity for Energy. J. Coombs et al. 1983. lib. bdg. 32.50 (ISBN 90-277-1625-0, Pub. by Reidel Holland). Kluwer Academic.

Plants, Chemicals & Growth. F. C. Steward & A. D. Krikorian. 1971. 39.50 (ISBN 0-12-668662-9); pap. 8.95. Acad Pr.

Plants Collected by the Vernay Nyasaland Expedition of 1946: Conclusion: Angiospermae & General Index. J. P. M. Brenan et al. (Memoirs of the New York Botanical Garden Series: Vol. 9 (1)). 132p. 1954. 10.00x (ISBN 0-89327-028-8). NY Botanical.

Plants Collected by the Vernay Nyasaland Expedition of 1946: Continuation: Angiospermae. J. P. M. Brenan et al. (Memoirs of the New York Botanical Garden Series: Vol. 8 (5)). 102p. 1954. 10.00x (ISBN 0-89327-033-4). NY Botanical.

Plants Collected by the Vernay Nyasaland Expedition of 1946: Introduction: Musi, Pteridophyta, Gymnospermae, Angiospermae. L. J. Brass et al. (Memoirs of the New York Botanical Garden Series: Vol. 8 (3)). 96p. 1953. 10.00x (ISBN 0-89327-031-8). NY Botanical.

Plants Collected in Ecuador by W. H. Camp: Bromeliaceae, Cannaceae, Zingiberaceae, Musaceae, Marantaceae, Xyridaceae, Begoniaceae, Vacciniaceae. W. H. Camp et al. (Memoirs of the New York Botanical Garden Series: Vol. 8 (1)). 85p. 1952. 10.00x (ISBN 0-89327-027-X). NY Botanical.

Plants Collected in Ecuador by W. H. Camp: Gramineae, Piperaceae, Umbelliferae, Eriocaulaceae, Verbenaceae see Memoirs of the New York Botanical Garden.

Plants Collected in Ecuador by W. H. Camp: Melastomataceae see Memoirs of the New York Botanical Garden.

Plants Consumed by Man. B. Brouk. 1975. 112.00 (ISBN 0-12-136450-X). Acad Pr.

Plants Do Amazing Things. Hedda Nussbaum. LC 75-36471. (Step-up Bk.: No. 24). (Illus.). 72p. (gr. 2-3). 1977. 6.95 (ISBN 0-394-83232-9, BYR); lib. bdg. 8.99 (ISBN 0-394-93232-3). Random.

Plants: Evolution & Diversity. Raymond E. Stotler & Barbara Crandall-Stotler. 224p. 1986. pap. text ed. 16.95 (ISBN 0-8403-4055-9). Kendall-Hunt.

Plants Facts & Fancies. Sylvia Woods. (Illus.). 96p. (YA) (gr. 8-11). 10.95 (ISBN 0-571-13436-X). Faber & Faber.

Plants for Dry Climates: How to Select, Grow & Enjoy. Mary R. Duffield & Warren D. Jones. LC 80-82535. (Illus.). 176p. 1981. pap. 12.95 (ISBN 0-89586-042-2). Price Stern.

Plants for Ground-Cover. rev. ed. Graham S. Thomas. (Illus.). 308p. 1977. 22.50x (ISBN 0-460-03994-6, Pub. by J M Dent England). Biblio Dist.

Plants for Human Consumption: Annotated Checklist of Edible Phanerogams & Ferns. G. Kunkel. 393p. 1984. lib. bdg. 70.00x (ISBN 3-87429-216-9). Lubrecht & Cramer.

Plants for Problem Places. Graham Rice. LC 87-27465. (Illus.). 1988. 29.95 (ISBN 0-88192-090-8). Timber.

Plants for the Home, Vol. 1. John J. Bagnasco. 1975. 15.00 (ISBN 0-918134-01-3). Nature Life.

Plants from Test Tubes: An Introduction to Micropropagation. Lydiane Kyte. LC 87-24607. (Illus.). 132p. 1988. text ed. 24.95x (ISBN 0-88192-040-1). Timber.

Plants Humanity & the Environment: Discussion Guide. 2nd ed. Lawrence Kapustka. 148p. 1984. pap. text ed. 10.95 (ISBN 0-89917-407-8, Pub. by College Town Pr). Tichenor Pub.

Plants in Danger. Edward R. Ricciuti. LC 77-25669. (Illus.). (YA) (gr. 7-9). 1979. PLB 11.89 (ISBN 0-06-024979-X). HarpJ.

Plants in Indigenous Medicine & Diet: Biobehavioral Approaches. Nina L. Etkin et al. (Illus.). xii, 336p. (Orig.). 1986. 24.95 (ISBN 0-913178-02-0). Redgrave Pub Co.

Plants in Relation to Water & Solutes see Plant Physiology: A Treatise.

Plants in the Development of Modern Medicine. Tony Swain. LC 79-169862. (Illus.). 548p. 1972. 27.00x (ISBN 0-674-67330-1). Harvard U Pr.

Plants in the Landscape. Philip L. Carpenter et al. LC 74-32292. (Illus.). 481p. 1975. text ed. 33.95 (ISBN 0-7167-0778-0). W H Freeman.

Plants in Winter. Joanna Cole. LC 73-1771. (Let's Read & Find Out Science Bks.). (Illus.). (ps-3). 1973. (Crowell Jr Bks); PLB 12.89 (ISBN 0-690-62886-2, Crowell Jr Bks). HarpJ.

Plants, Man & Life. rev. ed. Edgar Anderson. LC 52-5870. (YA) (gr. 9 up). 1967. pap. 6.95x (ISBN 0-520-00021-8). U of Cal Pr.

Plants of Christmas. Hal Borland. LC 87-552. (Illus.). 32p. (gr. 3 up). 1987. Repr. of 1969 ed. 12.70i (ISBN 0-690-04649-X, Crowell Jr Bks); PLB 12.89 (ISBN 0-690-04650-2). HarpJ.

Plants of Colonial Williamsburg. Joan P. Dutton. LC 76-50633. (Illus.). 193p. 1979. pap. 12.95 (ISBN 0-87935-042-3). Williamsburg.

Plants of Deep Canyon. Jan Zabriskie. (Illus.). 175p. (Orig.). 1985. pap. 8.95 (ISBN 0-937794-05-8). Nature Trails.

Plants of Deep Canyon: The Central Coachella Valley of California. LC 79-63644. 1979. 14.95 (ISBN 0-942290-03-8). Boyd Deep Canyon.

Plants of Hawaii. Fortunato Teho. (Illus.). pap. 3.95 (ISBN 0-912180-13-7). Petroglyph.

Plants of Hope. Robert Muller. (Chrysalis Bk). (Illus.). 128p. 1986. pap. 7.95 (ISBN 0-916349-04-7). Amity Hse Inc.

Plants of India. Cecil J. Saldhana & J. Dhawan. 1987. 28.50x (ISBN 0-8364-2116-7, Pub. by Oxford IBH). South Asia Bks.

Plants of Nineteen Seventeen. Ed. by Wolfgang Hageney. (Illus.). 192p. (Eng., Ital., Ger., Span. & Fr.). 1986. 54.95 (ISBN 88-7070-017-8). R Silver.

Plants of Nineteen Seventeen, Vol. 1-Spring 1. Ed. by Wolfgang Hageney. (Illus.). 55p. 1986. pap. 16.95 (ISBN 88-7070-087-9). R Silver.

Plants of Nineteen Seventeen, Vol. 2-Spring 2. Ed. by Wolfgang Hageney. (Illus.). 55p. 1986. pap. 16.95 (ISBN 88-7070-088-7). R Silver.

Plants of Nineteen Seventeen, Vol. 3-Summer 1. Ed. by Wolfgang Hageney. (Illus.). 55p. 1986. pap. 16.95 (ISBN 88-7070-089-5). R Silver.

Plants of Nineteen Seventeen, Vol. 4-Summer 2. Ed. by Wolfgang Hageney. (Illus.). 55p. 1986. pap. 16.95 (ISBN 88-7070-090-9). R Silver.

Plants of Nineteen Seventeen, Vol. 5-Autumn-Winter. Ed. by Wolfgang Hageney. (Illus.). 55p. 1986. pap. 16.95 (ISBN 88-7070-091-7). R Silver.

Plants of Old Hawaii. Lois Lucas. LC 82-72199. (Illus.). 112p. (Orig.). 1982. pap. 5.95 (ISBN 0-935848-11-8). Bess Pr.

Plants of Prey. Rica Erickson. 1977. 34.90 (ISBN 0-85564-099-5, Pub. by U of W Austral Pr). Intl Spec Bk.

Plants of Quetico & the Ontario Shield. Shan Walshe. (Illus.). 216p. 1980. 25.00x (ISBN 0-8020-3370-9); pap. 12.95 (ISBN 0-8020-3371-7). U of Toronto Pr.

Plants of the Bible. G. Henslow. 294p. 1981. Repr. of 1900 ed. lib. bdg. 75.00 (ISBN 0-8495-2375-3). Arden Lib.

Plants of the Bible. Harold N. Moldenke & Alma L. Moldenke. 384p. 1986. pap. 8.95 (ISBN 0-486-25069-5). Dover.

Plants of the Bible. Nancy Peelman. LC 75-14607. (Illus.). 40p. (Orig.). (gr. 1-8). 1975. pap. 4.50 (ISBN 0-8192-1196-6). Morehouse.

Plants of the Bible: A Complete Handbook to all the Plants with 200 Full-Color Plates taken in the Natural Habitat. Michael Zohary. LC 82-4535. (Illus.). 224p. 1982. 19.95 (ISBN 0-521-24926-0). Cambridge U Pr.

Plants of the Coast of Coromandel: Selected from Drawings & Descriptions Presented to the Hon. Court of Directors of the East India Company, under the Order of Sir Joseph Banks, 3 vols. William Roxburgh. (Illus.). 20p. 1982. Repr. of 1795 ed. Set. lib. bdg. 1200.00x. Lubrecht & Cramer.

Plants of the Gods: Origins of Hallucinogenic Use. Richard E. Schultes & Albert Hofmann. LC 86-40445. (Illus.). 192p. 1987. pap. 16.95 (ISBN 0-912383-37-2). Van der Marck.

Plants of the Kimberly Region of Western Australia. R. J. Petheram & B. Kok. (Illus.). 556p. (Orig.). 1983. pap. text ed. 35.00x (ISBN 0-85564-215-7, Pub. by U of W Austral Pr). Intl Spec Bk.

Plants of the Manua Islands. T. G. Yuncker. (BMB). Repr. 12.00 (ISBN 0-527-02292-6). Kraus Repr.

Plants of the Oregon Coastal Dunes. Alfred M. Weidemann. 1969. pap. text ed. 6.20X (ISBN 0-88246-117-6). Oreg St U Bkstrs.

Plants of the Past, a Popular Account of Fossil Plants. Frank H. Knowlton. LC 76-94246. (Illus.). Repr. of 1927 ed. 19.50 (ISBN 0-404-03735-6). AMS Pr.

Plants of the Punjab: A Descriptive Key to the Flora of the Punjab, Northwest Frontier Province & Kashmir. C. J. Bamber. 1978. Repr. of 1916 ed. 56.25x (ISBN 0-89955-298-6, Pub. by Intl Bk Dist). Intl Spec Bk.

Plants of the Tampa Bay Area. rev. & supplemented ed. Olga Lakela et al. 1976. pap. 7.95 (ISBN 0-916224-10-4). Banyan Bks.

Plants of the Texas Shore: A Beachcomber's Guide. Mary M. Cannatella & Rita E. Arnold. LC 84-40553. (Illus.). 78p. 1985. pap. 5.95 (ISBN 0-89096-214-6). Tex A&M Univ Pr.

Plants of Tonga. T. G. Yuncker. (BMB). Repr. of 1959 ed. 37.00 (ISBN 0-527-02328-0). Kraus Repr.

Plants of Waterton-Glacier National Parks & the Northern Rockies. Richard J. Shaw & Danny On. LC 79-9912. (Illus.). 160p. 1987. pap. 8.95 (ISBN 0-87842-114-9). Mountain Pr.

Plants of Yellowstone & Grand Teton National Parks. (Nature & Scenic Bks.). pap. 5.95 (ISBN 0-937512-02-8). Wheelwright UT.

Plants of Zion National Park: Wildflowers, Trees, Shrubs & Ferns. Ruth A. Nelson. LC 74-28958. (Illus.). 344p. 1976. pap. text ed. 9.95 (ISBN 0-915630-01-X). Zion.

Plants on Stamps. 164p. 10.00 (ISBN 0-318-13307-5). Am Topical Assn.

Plants, People, & Environmental Quality: Syllabus. 1977. pap. text ed. 5.65 (ISBN 0-89420-021-6, 140014); cassette recordings 70.90 (ISBN 0-89420-173-5, 140000). Natl Book.

Plants, People & Paleoecology. Frances B. King. (Scientific Papers Ser.: Vol. XX). (Illus.). 224p. (Orig.). 1985. pap. 10.00x (ISBN 0-89792-100-3). Ill St Museum.

Plants Plus: A Comprehensive Guide to Successful Plant Propagation. George Seddon & Andrew Bicknell. (Illus.). 160p. 1987. pap. 14.95 (ISBN 0-87857-717-3). Rodale Pr Inc.

Plants Poisonous to People in Florida & Other Warm Areas. 2nd Rev. ed. Julia F. Morton. LC 81-71614. (Illus.). 170p. 1982. pap. 19.75 (ISBN 0-9610184-0-2). J F Morton.

Plants, Seeds & Flowers. Louis Sabin. LC 84-2720. (Illus.). 32p. (gr. 3-6). 1985. PLB 8.45 (ISBN 0-8167-0226-8); pap. text ed. 1.95 (ISBN 0-8167-0227-6). Troll Assocs.

Plants That Merit Attention: Trees, Vol. 1. The Horticultural Committee of the Garden Club of America. (Illus.). 360p. 1984. 44.95 (ISBN 0-917304-75-6). Timber.

Plants That Never Ever Bloom. Ruth Heller. (Illus.). 48p. (ps-2). 1984. 8.95 (ISBN 0-448-18964-X, G&D). Putnam Pub Group.

Plants That Poison: An Illustrated Guide. Ervin M. Schmutz. LC 78-74037. (Illus.). 250p. 1986. pap. 11.95 (ISBN 0-87358-193-8). Northland.

Plants: The Potentials for Extracting Protein, Medicines & Other Useful Chemicals. 1984. lib. bdg. 79.95 (ISBN 0-87700-537-0). Revisionist Pr.

Plants Up Close. Joan E. Rahn. (Illus.). (gr. 2-5). 1981. 8.95 (ISBN 0-395-31677-4). HM.

Plants Used Against Cancer. Jonathan L. Hartwell. LC 81-85230. (Bio-Active Plants Ser.: Vol. 2). 754p. 1984. Repr. lib. bdg. 75.00x (ISBN 0-88000-130-5). Quarterman.

Plants Used As Curatives by Certain Southeastern Tribes. Lyda A. Taylor. LC 76-43866. (Botanical Museum of Harvard Univ.). Repr. of 1940 ed. 14.50 (ISBN 0-404-15725-4). AMS Pr.

Plants Used in Basketry by the California Indians. Ruth E. Merrill. (Illus.). 1980. Repr. 2.95 (ISBN 0-686-77544-9). Acoma Bks.

Plants We Eat & Wear. H. E. Jaques. (Illus.). 7.75 (ISBN 0-8446-5207-5). Peter Smith.

Plants We Know. O. Irene Miner. LC 81-9929. (New True Bks.). 48p. (gr. k-4). 1981. PLB 12.60 (ISBN 0-516-01642-3); pap. 3.95 (ISBN 0-516-41642-1). Childrens.

Plants Without Seeds. Helen Challand. LC 85-30935. (New True Bks.). (Illus.). 48p. (gr. k-4). 1986. PLB 12.60 (ISBN 0-516-01286-X); pap. 3.95 (ISBN 0-516-41286-8). Childrens.

Plants Your Mother Never Told You About: Interesting Edible & Poisonous Plants of the Bay Area. James Wiltens. (Illus.). 160p. (Orig.). 1986. pap. 8.50 (ISBN 0-938525-00-X). Deer Xing Camp.

Plants 1945-1966. pap. 12.25 (F938, FAO). UNIPUB.

Plantsman in China. Roy Lancaster. (Illus.). 500p. 1988. 59.50 (ISBN 1-85149-019-1). Antique Collect.

Plantworks: Indoor Gardening Made Easy. Jan Aaron. LC 74-21357. 208p. Date not set. 14.95 (ISBN 0-8303-0146-1). Fleet.

Planty's Encyclopedia of Cacheted F. D. C.'s, 10 vols. Earl Planty & Michael Mellone. (Illus.). 1979. Set. pap. 99.98 (ISBN 0-89794-008-3). FDC Pub.

Planty's Encyclopedia of Cacheted F. D. C.'s: 1923-28, Vol. 1. Earl Planty & Michael Mellone. (Illus.). 1977. pap. 9.95 (ISBN 0-89794-009-1). FDC Pub.

Planty's Encyclopedia of Cacheted F. D. C.'s: 1928-1929, Vol. 2. Earl Planty & Michael Mellone. (Illus.). 1977. pap. 9.95 (ISBN 0-89794-010-5). FDC Pub.

Planty's Encyclopedia of Cacheted F. D. C.'s, Vol. 3. Earl Planty & Michael Mellone. (Illus.). 1978. pap. 8.95 (ISBN 0-89794-011-3). FDC Pub.

Planty's Encyclopedia of Cacheted F. D. C.'s, Vol. 4. Earl Planty & Michael Mellone. (Illus.). 1978. pap. 9.95 (ISBN 0-89794-012-1). FDC Pub.

Planty's Encyclopedia of Cacheted F. D. C.'s, Vol. 5. Earl Planty & Michael Mellone. (Illus.). 1978. pap. 9.95 (ISBN 0-89794-013-X). FDC Pub.

Planty's Encyclopedia of Cacheted F. D. C.'s, Vol. 6. Earl Planty & Michael Mellone. (Illus.). 1978. pap. 9.95 (ISBN 0-89794-014-8). FDC Pub.

Planty's Encyclopedia of Cacheted F. D. C.'s, Vol. 7. Earl Planty & Michael Mellone. (Illus.). 1979. pap. 9.95 (ISBN 0-89794-015-6). FDC Pub.

Planty's Encyclopedia of Cacheted F. D. C.'s, Vol. 8. Earl Planty & Michael Mellone. (Illus.). 1979. pap. 9.95 (ISBN 0-89794-016-4). FDC Pub.

Planty's Encylopedia of Cacheted F. D. C.'s, Vol. 9. Earl Planty & Michael Mellone. (Illus.). 1978. pap. 9.95 (ISBN 0-317-16573-9). FDC Pub.

Planty's Encylopedia of Cacheted F. D. C.'s, Vol. 10. Earl Planty & Michael Mellone. (Illus.). 1978. pap. 9.95 (ISBN 0-317-16574-7). FDC Pub.

Planung & Verwirklichung Von Freizeitangeboten. Moeglichkeiten & Formen der Partizipation. S. Agricola & B. Von Schmettow. Ed. by R. Schmitz-Scherzer. (Psychologische Praxis: Band 50). 1976. 16.75 (ISBN 3-8055-2361-0). S Karger.

Plaques & People. William H. McNeill. LC 76-2798. (Illus.). 1977. pap. 6.95 (ISBN 0-385-12122-9, Anch). Doubleday.

Plasir de Rompre see Oeuvres.

Plasm. Charles Platt. 288p. 1987. pap. 3.50 (ISBN 0-451-15015-5, Sig). NAL.

Plasma Acceleration. Ed. by Sidney W. Kash. LC 60-13869. pap. 31.30 (ISBN 0-317-09232-4, 2000312). Bks Demand UMI.

Plasma & Current Instabilities in Semiconductors. J. Pozhela. Tr. by O. A. Germogenova. (International Series in the Science of the Solid State: Vol. 18). (Illus.). 314p. 1981. 89.00 (ISBN 0-08-025048-3). Pergamon.

Plasma & the Universe: Dedicated to Hannes Alfven. Ed. by Carl-Gunne Falthammar et al. 1988. lib. bdg. 139.00 (ISBN 90-277-2764-3). Kluwer Academic.

Plasma Arc Metalworking Processes, PMP. R. L. O'Brien. 160p. 1967. 10.00 (ISBN 0-685-65957-7). Am Welding.

Plasma Astrophysics. S. A. Kaplan & V. N. Tsytovich. LC 73-5785. 316p. 1973. 110.00 (ISBN 0-08-017190-7). Pergamon.

Plasma Astrophysics: Nonthermal Processes in Diffuse Magnetized Plasmas, Vol.1: The Emission, Absorption & Transfer of Waves in Plasmas. D. B. Melrose. 280p. 1979. 91.00 (ISBN 0-677-02340-5). Gordon & Breach.

Plastering: A Craftsman's Encyclopedia. William D. Stagg & Brian F. Pegg. 1985. 8.95 (ISBN 0-517-55652-9). Crown.

Plastering Skill & Practice. Felicien Van Den Branden & Thomas L. Hartsell. LC 72-165182. (Illus.). pap. 137.50 (ISBN 0-317-10858-1, 2010124). Bks Demand UMI.

Plastering Skills. F. Van Den Branden & T. L. Hartsell. (Illus.). 544p. (Orig.). 1984. pap. 24.96 (ISBN 0-8269-0657-5). Am Technical.

Plastic Additive Market. 304p. 1985. 1850.00 (ISBN 0-86621-385-6, A1460). Frost & Sullivan.

Plastic Age: A Novel. Percy Marks. LC 80-17959. (Lost American Fiction Ser.). 352p. 1980. Repr. of 1924 ed. 12.95 (ISBN 0-8093-0984-X). S Ill U Pr.

Plastic Alternatives to the Metal Can. Business Communications Staff. 136p. 1984. 1950.00 (ISBN 0-89336-386-3, P-077). BCC.

Plastic Analysis & Design of Plates, Shells & Disks, Vol. 15. M. A. Save & C. C. Massonnet. 478p. 1972. 126.50 (ISBN 0-444-10113-6, North-Holland). Elsevier.

Plastic Analysis of Concrete Frames. M. Tichy & J. Rakosnik. 320p. 1977. 77.00x (Pub. by Collets (UK)). State Mutual Bk.

Plastic Analysis of Concrete Frames: With Particular Reference to Limit States Des. M. Tichy & J. Rakosnik. Tr. by Dagmar et al from Czech. (Illus.). 320p. 1977. text ed. 40.00x (ISBN 0-569-08199-8, Pub. by Collets England). Scholium Intl.

Plastic Analysis of Reinforced Concrete Beams. Bruno Thverlimann. (IBA Ser.: No. 86). 20p. 1979. pap. text ed. 9.95x (ISBN 0-8176-1064-2). Birkhauser.

Plastic Analysis of Reinforced Concrete Shear Walls. Peter Marti. (IBA Ser.: No. 87). 19p. 1979. pap. text ed. 8.95x (ISBN 0-8176-1065-0). Birkhauser.

Plastic Analysis of Structures. rev. ed. Philip G. Hodge. LC 80-26340. 444p. 1981. 34.50 (ISBN 0-89874-161-0). Krieger.

Plastic & Competitive Pipe. John J. Breckling. (Illus.). 290p. (Orig.). 1987. Market Research Study. 1500.00 (ISBN 0-945235-00-3). Lead Edge Reports.

Plastic & Competitive Pipe: A Product-by-Product Marketing Analysis & Competitior Profile. (Illus.). 275p. 1987. 3-ring binder 1500.00 (ISBN 0-317-65751-8). Busn Trend.

Plastic & Electronic Money: New Payment Systems & Their Implications. Patrick Frazer. LC 85-22552. 304p. 1985. 37.50 (ISBN 0-85941-290-3, Pub. by Woodhead-Faulkner). Longwood Pub Group.

Plastic & Other Limit State Methods for Design Evaluation: Proceedings of a Session Sponsored by the Committee on Analysis & Design of Structurs the Structural Division. Ed. by V. B. Watwood, Jr. 94p. 1984. 17.00x (ISBN 0-87262-423-4). Am Soc Civil Eng.

Plastic & Reconstructive Surgery. I. F. Muir. (Illus.). 190p. 1986. 58.00 (ISBN 0-7216-9995-2, Bailliere-Tindall). Saunders.

Plastic & Reconstructive Surgery of the Eyelids. Charles Beyer-Machule. (Illus.). 135p. 1983. 37.00 (ISBN 0-86577-080-8). Thieme Med Pubs.

Plastic & Reconstructive Surgery of the Breast. Robert M. Goldwyn. LC 75-25159. 1976. text ed. 82.00 (ISBN 0-316-31971-6). Little.

Plastic & Reconstructive Surgery of the Face & Neck. American Academy of Facial Plastic & Reconstructive Surgery Staff. 1984. 175.00 (ISBN 0-8016-0067-7). Mosby.

Plastic & Reconstructive Surgery of the Face & Neck, 2 vols. Ed. by John Conley & John T. Dickinson. Incl. Vol. 1. Aesthetic Surgery. 264p; Vol. 2. Rehabilitative Surgery. 392p. (Illus.). 1972. Grune.

Plastic & Reconstructive Surgery of the Genital Area. Ed. by Charles E. Horton. (Illus.). 1973. 82.00 (ISBN 0-316-37381-8). Little.

Plastic & Reconstructive Surgery of the Head & Neck: Rehabilitative Surgery, Vol. 2. Ed. by Leslie Bernstein. 576p. 1981. 94.50 (ISBN 0-8089-1373-5, 790577). Grune.

Plastic Card Float. 111p. 1986. 69.00 (ISBN 1-55520-008-7, 245). Bank Admin Inst.

Plastic Coating for Electronics. James J. Licari. LC 79-26923. 398p. 1980. Repr. of 1970 ed. lib. bdg. 32.50 (ISBN 0-89874-107-6). Krieger.

Plastic Containers for Pharmaceuticals: Testing & Control. J. Cooper. (Offset Pub.: No. 4). (Also avail. in French). 1974. pap. 12.80 (ISBN 92-4-170004-1). World Health.

Plastic Deformation of Materials see Treatise on Materials Science.

Plastic Deformation of Simple Ionic Crystals. M. T. Sprackling. 1977. 66.00 (ISBN 0-12-657850-8). Acad Pr.

Plastic Design: An Imposed Hinge Rotation Approach. P. Zeman & H. M. Irvine. 128p. 1986. text ed. 29.95x (ISBN 0-04-624009-8). Unwin Hyman.

Plastic Design in Steel: A Guide & Commentary. 2nd ed. (Manual & Report of Engineering Practice Ser.: No. 41). 348p. 1971. pap. 19.00x (ISBN 0-87262-217-7). Am Soc Civil Eng.

Plastic Design of Braced Multistory Steel Frames. 124p. 1968. 10.00 (ISBN 0-318-12809-8, M004). Am Inst Steel Construct.

Plastic Design of Frames, 2 vols. John Baker & J. Heyman. Incl. Vol. 1. Fundamentals; Vol. 2. Applications. 49.50 (ISBN 0-521-07984-5). LC 69-19370. (Illus.). 1969-1971. Cambridge U Pr.

Plastic Design of Low Rise Frames. M. R. Horne & L. J. Morris. 238p. 1981. text ed. 61.25x (ISBN 0-246-11199-2, Pub. by Granada England). Brookfield Pub Co.

Plastic Design of Low-Rise Frames. M. R. Horne & L. J. Morris. (Structural Mechanics Ser.). (Illus.). 256p. 1982. 60.00x (ISBN 0-262-08123-7). MIT Pr.

Plastic Design of Steel. Mrazik et al. LC 85-5623. 420p. 1986. 110.00 (ISBN 0-470-20132-0). Wiley.

Plastic Design of Steel Frames. Lynn S. Beedle. LC 58-13454. 406p. 1958. 56.95x (ISBN 0-471-06171-9, Pub. by Wiley-Interscience). Wiley.

Plastic Father. C. W. Truesdale. (Illus.). 1971. saddlestitched in wrappers 2.00 (ISBN 0-912284-19-6). New Rivers Pr.

Plastic Films & Packaging. C. R. Oswin. (Illus.). xi, 214p. 1975. 37.00 (ISBN 0-85334-641-0, Pub. by Elsevier Applied Sci England). Elsevier.

Plastic Films for Packaging: Technology Applications & Process Economics. Calvin J. Benning. 192p. 1983. 35.00 (ISBN 0-87762-320-1). Technomic.

Plastic Flowers in the Holy Water. George M. Bass. 1981. 4.35 (ISBN 0-89536-480-8, 1605). CSS of Ohio.

Plastic Foams, Pt.1. Ed. by Kurt C. Frisch & J. H. Saunders. LC 71-157837. (Monographs on Plastics). Repr. of 1972 ed. 116.00 (ISBN 0-8357-9092-4, 2055059). Bks Demand UMI.

Plastic Foams, Pt.2. Ed. by Kurt C. Frisch & J. H. Saunders. (Monographs on Plastics: Vol. 1). 592p. 1973. 115.00 (ISBN 0-8247-1219-6). Dekker.

Plastic Foams: Proceedings of a Special Conference, Los Angeles. (Illus.). 188p. 1980. 37.00 (ISBN 0-938648-03-9). T-C Pubns CA.

Plastic Gearing: Selection & Application. Adams. (Mechanical Engineering Ser.). 416p. 1986. 69.75 (ISBN 0-8247-7498-1). Dekker.

Plastic Greenhouses for Warm Climates. Kjell Virhammar. (Agricultural Services Bulletins: No. 48). 52p. 1982. pap. 9.00 (ISBN 92-5-101168-0, F2302, FAO). UNIPUB.

Plastic Jewelry. Lyngerda Kelley & Nancy Schiffer. (Illus.). 128p. 1987. pap. 12.95 (ISBN 0-88740-109-0). Schiffer.

Plastic Machinery Market. 277p. 1984. 1600.00 (ISBN 0-86621-614-6, E686). Frost & Sullivan.

Plastic Methods for Steel & Concrete Structures. S. S. Moy. LC 81-552. 221p. 1981. pap. 31.95x (ISBN 0-470-27079-9). Halsted Pr.

Plastic Methods of Structural Analysis: SI Version. 3rd ed. B. G. Neal. 1977. 18.95x (ISBN 0-412-21450-4, NO. 6208, Pub. by Chapman & Hall). Routledge Chapman & Hall.

Plastic Mortars, Sealants, & Caulking Compounds. Ed. by Raymond B. Seymour. LC 79-19752. (ACS Symposium Ser.: No. 113). 1979. 29.95 (ISBN 0-8412-0523-X). Am Chemical.

Plastic Package Integrity: Proceedings. Food Processors Institute Staff. 56p. (Orig.). 1988. pap. text ed. 50.00 (ISBN 0-937774-18-9). Food Processors.

Plastic Pipe for Subsurface Drainage of Transportation Facilities. (National Cooperative Highway Research Program Report). 153p. 1980. 9.60 (ISBN 0-309-03030-7). Transport Res Bd.

Plastic Piping Systems. David A. Chasis. LC 75-45420. 216p. 1976. 25.00 (ISBN 0-8311-1111-9). Krieger.

Plastic Piping Systems. 2nd ed. David A. Chasis. 200p. 1988. 26.95 (ISBN 0-8311-1181-X). Indus Pr.

Plastic Piping Systems Development for Natural Gas Applications. H. W. Kuhlman et al. 50p. 1970. pap. 4.00 (ISBN 0-318-12668-0, X10180). Am Gas Assn.

Plastic Product Design. 2nd ed. Ronald D. Beck. 424p. 1980. 37.95 (ISBN 0-442-20632-1). Van Nos Reinhold.

Plastic Products Design Handbook, Pt. B. Miller. (Mechanical Engineering Ser.). 400p. 1983. 65.00 (ISBN 0-8247-1886-0). Dekker.

Plastic Reconstruction in the Head & Neck. Tony Bull & Eugene N. Myers. (Butterworths International Medical Reviews; Otolaryngology Ser.: Vol. 2). (Illus.). 320p. 1986. text ed. 55.00 (ISBN 0-407-02328-3). Butterworth.

Plastic Redirections in Twentieth Century Painting: The Meaning of Unintelligibility in Modern Art. James J. Sweeney & Edward F. Rothschild. 15.00 (11380). Ayer Co Pubs.

Plastic Rulers. Steven P. LaVoie. (Famous Last Words Ser.: No. VI). 40p. (Orig.). 1985. pap. 3.00 (ISBN 0-916331-01-6). Famous Last Wds.

Plastic Surgery. 4th ed. Barclay & Kernahan. (Rob & Smith's Operative Surgery Ser.). 1986. 112.00 (ISBN 0-8016-4416-X, C-4416-X). Mosby.

Plastic Surgery. 3rd ed. Ed. by William X. Grabb & James W. Smith. 1980. text ed. 56.00 (ISBN 0-316-32269-5). Little.

Plastic Surgery Atlas, 3 Vols. F. Burian. 1968. write for info. Vol. 1 (ISBN 0-02-317050-6). Vol. 2 (ISBN 0-02-317060-3). Set. write for info. (ISBN 0-02-317080-8). Macmillan.

Plastic Surgery in Infancy & Childhood. 2nd ed. Ed. by John C. Mustarde. (Illus.). 1979. text ed. 120.00 (ISBN 0-443-01629-1). Churchill.

Plastic Surgery of the Facial Skeleton. S. Anthony Wolfe. 500p. 1988. text ed. 225.00 (ISBN 0-316-95105-6). Little.

Plastic Surgery of the Head & Neck, 2 vols. Ed. by Richard B. Stark. (Illus.). 1580p. 1986. Set. text ed. 275.00 (ISBN 0-443-08249-9). Churchill.

Plastic Surgery: Past & Present. J. Gabka & E. Vaubel. (Illus.). viii, 180p. 1983. 196.75 (ISBN 3-8055-3651-8). S Karger.

Plastic Surgery: Principles & Practice. Jurkiewicz et al. (Illus.). 1630p. 1990. text ed. 125.00 (ISBN 0-8016-2602-1). Mosby.

Plastic Surgical & Burns Nursing. Harvey Kemble & Brenda Lamb. 1985. write for info. (ISBN 0-7216-0953-8, Bailliere-Tindall). Saunders.

Plastic Technology, Basic Materials & Processes. Robert S. Swanson. (gr. 11-12). 1965. text ed. 24.40 (ISBN 0-02-672300-X). Glencoe Bennett & McKnight.

Plastic Technology Dictionary. H. Y. El-Desouti. 331p. (Eng., Fr., Ger. & Arabic.). 1980. 75.00 (ISBN 0-686-92400-2, M-9754). French & Eur.

Plastic Technology Handbook. Chanda. Ed. by Roy. (Plastics Engineering Ser.). 568p. 1987. 99.75 (ISBN 0-8247-7564-3). Dekker.

Plastic Templates for Traditional Patchwork Quilt Patterns: Instructions for 27 Easy-to-Make Designs. Rita Weiss. 32p. (Orig.). 1985. pap. 3.95 (ISBN 0-486-24984-0). Dover.

Plastically Crystalline State: (Orientationally-Disordered Crystals) Ed. by John N. Sherwood. LC 78-16086. 409p. pap. 106.40 (2030386). Bks Demand UMI.

Plasticity & Recovery of Function in the Central Nervous System. Ed. by Donald G. Stein et al. 1974. 29.95 (ISBN 0-12-664350-4). Acad Pr.

Plasticity for Engineers. C. R. Calladine. LC 85-14057. 318p. 1985. pap. 23.95 (ISBN 0-470-20235-1). Halsted Pr.

Plasticity for Structural Engineers. W. F. Chen & D. J. Han. (Illus.). 415p. 1988. 59.00 (ISBN 0-387-96711-7). Springer-Verlag.

Plasticity in Plants. D. H. Jennings. (Society for Experimental Biology Symposia Ser.: No. 40). (Illus.). 372p. 1986. 60.00 (ISBN 0-948601-03-5). Rsrch Bks Ct.

Plasticity in Reinforced Concrete. Wayne F. Chen. (Illus.). 576p. 1982. text ed. 55.95 (ISBN 0-07-010687-8). McGraw.

Plasticity in Structural Engineering, Fundamentals & Applications. C. Massonnet et al. (CISM,, International Center for Mechanical Sciences: Vol. 241). (Illus.). 302p. 1979. pap. 35.00 (ISBN 0-387-81350-0). Springer-Verlag.

Plasticity into Power: Variations on Themes of Politics, a Work in Constructive Social Theory. Roberto M. Unger. 231p. 1987. 37.50 (ISBN 0-521-32976-0); pap. 10.95 (ISBN 0-521-33864-6). Cambridge U Pr.

Plasticity of Muscle. Ed. by D. Pette. 1979. 104.00 (ISBN 3-1100-7961-5). De Gruyter.

Plasticity of the Central Nervous System. Ed. by K. Sano & S. Ishii. (Acta Neurochirurgica Ser.: Supplementum 41). (Illus.). 140p. 1988. 100.00 (ISBN 0-387-82027-2). Springer-Verlag.

Plasticity: Theory & Application. Alexander Mendelson. LC 82-21231. 368p. 1983. Repr. of 1968 ed. lib. bdg. 29.50 (ISBN 0-89874-582-9). Krieger.

Plasticity: Theory & Application. Alexander Mendelson. LC 68-12718. (Macmillan Series in Applied Mechanics). pap. 91.80 (ISBN 0-317-10993-6, 2003540). Bks Demand UMI.

Plasticity Today-Modelling, Methods & Applications: Proceedings of an International Symposium on Current Trends & Results in Plasticity, Held at the International Centre for Mechanical Sciences, Udine, Italy, 27-30 June 1983. Ed. by A. Sawczuk & G. Bianchi. (Illus.). 864p. 1985. 194.50 (ISBN 0-85334-302-0, Pub. by Elsevier Applied Sci England). Elsevier.

Plastics. Dwight W. Cope & Lee E. Schaude. LC 77-21618. (Illus.). 112p. 1982. text ed. 7.20 (ISBN 0-87006-426-6). Goodheart.

Plastics. M. Lambert. (Spotlight on Resources Ser.). (Illus.). 48p. (gr. 5 up). Date not set. PLB 14.60 (ISBN 0-86592-269-1). Rourke Corp.

Plastics. McKnight Staff Members & Wilbur R. Miller. LC 78-53391. (Basic Industrial Arts Ser.). (Illus.). 1978. softbound 6.60 (ISBN 0-02-672850-8). Glencoe Bennett & McKnight.

Plastics. Kathryn Whyman. Ed. by Franklin Watts Ltd. (Resources Today Ser.). (Illus.). 32p. (gr. k-9). 1988. 10.90 (ISBN 0-531-17084-5, Gloucester Pr). Watts.

Plastics--Value Through Technology: ANTEC 86. Conference Proceedings Sponsored by SPE. 1500p. 1986. pap. 100.00 (ISBN 0-87762-472-0). Technomic.

Plastics: A Bibliographical Overview of Plastic in Building Materials, Plastic Strength, Aging, Failure & Fire Resistance. Coppa & Avery Consultants Staff. (Architecture Ser.: A 1530). 11p. 1986. 3.75 (ISBN 0-89028-700-7). Vance Biblios.

Plastics ABC's: Polymer Alloys, Blends & Composites; National Technical Conference, Sheraton Bal Harbour, Bal Harbour, Florida, October 25-27, 1982. Society of Plastics Engineers. pap. 83.00 (ISBN 0-317-29830-5, 2019654). Bks Demand UMI.

Plastics Additives: An Industrial Guide. Ernest W. Flick. LC 86-17988. 745p. 1987. 86.00 (ISBN 0-8155-1093-4). Noyes.

Plastics Additives Handbook. R. Gaechter & H. Mueller. LC 83-62289. 320p. 1984. text ed. 68.00x (ISBN 0-02-949430-3, Pub. by Hanser International). Macmillan.

Plastics Additives Handbook: Stabilizers, Processing Aids, Plasticizers, Fillers, Reinforcements, Colorants for Thermoplastics. 2nd ed. Ed. by R. Gachter & H. Muller. (Hanser Publications). (Illus.). 788p. 1987. 80.00 (ISBN 0-19-520764-5). Oxford U Pr.

Plastics Alternatives to the Metal Can - Update. Business Communications Staff. 1988. 2450.00 (ISBN 0-89336-676-5, P-077R). BCC.

Plastics Analysis Guide: Chemical & Instrumental Methods. A. Krause et al. Tr. by Kathleen Ruby. LC 83-62183. (Hanser Publications). (Illus.). 358p. 1983. 65.00 (ISBN 0-19-520727-0). Oxford U Pr.

Plastics & Passenger Cars. 1984. 44.00 (ISBN 0-89883-337-X, SP566). Soc Auto Engineers.

Plastics & Plastic Products. LC 75-39854. (Illus.). 126p. 1975. pap. 5.50 (ISBN 0-87765-064-0, SPP-35). Natl Fire Prot.

Plastics & Polymer Processing Automation. Ed. by The Plastics & Rubber Institute Staff. LC 87-12401. (Illus.). 251p. 1988. 39.00 (ISBN 0-8155-1140-X). Noyes.

Plastics & Rubbers: World Sources of Information. E. R. Yescombe. 512p. 1976. 73.00 (ISBN 0-85334-675-5, Pub. by Elsevier Applied Sci England). Elsevier.

Plastics & Sheet Forming Machinery & Materials Market. 276p. 1984. 1400.00 (ISBN 0-86621-550-6, E626). Frost & Sullivan.

Plastics Chemistry & Technology. Walter E. Driver. LC 78-24011. 1979. 33.95 (ISBN 0-442-22156-8). Van Nos Reinhold.

Plastics Common Object. Date not set. 37.00 (ISBN 0-317-57790-5). T-C Pubns CA.

Plastics Conference Proceedings, 1982. Business Communications Staff. 1983. 125.00 (ISBN 0-686-84693-1). BCC.

Plastics Conference Proceedings, 1983. Business Communications Staff. 1984. 125.00 (ISBN 0-89336-376-6). BCC.

Plastics: Designs & Materials. Sylvia Katz. (Illus.). 1979. 42.50 (ISBN 0-289-70783-8, Pub. by Studio Vista Bks England). Eastview.

Plastics Desk-Top Data Bank. 190.00 (ISBN 0-686-48183-6, 0306). T-C Pubns CA.

Plastics Eightyfive, Imagination, Quality, Innovation: ANTEC 85 Conference Proceedings Sponsored by SPE. 1378p. 1985. pap. 95.00 (ISBN 0-87762-409-7). Technomic.

Plastics EMI Shielding. Business Communications Staff. 297p. 1985. pap. 1950.00 (ISBN 0-89336-409-6, GB-066R). BCC.

Plastics Engineering. 2nd ed. R. J. Crawford. 400p. 1987. text ed. 69.00 (ISBN 0-08-032627-7, PBL); pap. text ed. 32.00 (ISBN 0-08-032626-9, PBL). Pergamon.

Plastics Engineering Handbook of the SPI. 4th ed. Joel Frados. 1976. 57.95 (ISBN 0-442-22469-9). Van Nos Reinhold.

Plastics Engineering Handbook of the SPI. 4th ed. Ed. by Joel Frados. 909p. 1976. 62.00 (ISBN 0-686-48143-7, 0208). T-C Pubns CA.

Plastics-Engineering Today for Tomorrow's World: ANTEC 83, 41st Annual Technical Conference Proceedings, May 2-5, 1983, Hyatt Regency in Chicago. Society of Plastics Engineers. pap. 160.00 (ISBN 0-317-28683-8, 2020447). Bks Demand UMI.

Plastics Extrusion Engineering. Obrien. (Society of Plastics Engineers Monographs). 1988. write for info. (ISBN 0-471-80920-9). Wiley.

Plastics Extrusion, June 1978-Feb. 1983. 282p. 1983. pap. 85.00 (ISBN 0-686-48337-5, LS120). T-C Pubns CA.

Plastics Extrusion Technology. 2nd ed. Allan L. Griff. LC 75-45329. 364p. 1976. Repr. of 1968 ed. 25.00 (ISBN 0-88275-386-X). Krieger.

Plastics Extrusion Technology. Ed. by Friedhelm Hensen. (Illus.). 749p. 1988. 95.00x (ISBN 0-02-947771-9, Pub. by Hanser International). Macmillan.

Plastics Extrusion Technology: Applications & Lay-out of Extrusion Lines. F. Hensen. (Illus.). 750p. 1988. price not set (ISBN 0-19-520760-2). Oxford U Pr.

Plastics Extrusion Technology Handbook. Sidney Levy. (Illus.). 316p. 1981. 37.00 (ISBN 0-686-48164-X, 1202). T-C Pubns CA.

Plastics, Fibres, Rubbers, Resins; Starting & Auxillary Materials, Degradation Products see Atlas of Polymer & Plastics Analysis.

Plastics Films. 2nd ed. Brison. 1986. 59.95 (ISBN 0-470-20430-3). Halsted Pr.

Plastics Finishing & Decoration. D. Satas. 500p. 1986. 70.00. T-C Pubns CA.

Plastics Finishing & Decoration. Donatas Satas. LC 85-15654. (Illus.). 528p. 1986. 58.95 (ISBN 0-442-28062-9). Van Nos Reinhold.

Plastics for Electronics. M. T. Goosey. 368p. 1985. 92.00 (ISBN 0-85334-338-1, Pub. by Elsevier Applied Sci England). Elsevier.

Plastics for External Car Components. Ed. by VDI Staff. 190p. 1980. 46.00 (ISBN 3-18-404059-3, Pub. by VDI W Germany). IPS.

Plastics for Large Automotive Parts. Business Communications Staff. 262p. 1987. pap. 2450.00 (ISBN 0-89336-603-X, P-104). BCC.

Plastics for Tomorrow's Medical Needs: Technical Papers; Regional Technical Conference, September 23-24, 1986, Hyatt Cherry Hill, Cherry Hill, NJ. Society of Plastics Engineers Staff. (Illus.). pap. 77.50 (ISBN 0-317-58184-8, 2029711). Bks Demand UMI.

Plastics in a World Economy: ANTEC 1984, 42nd Technical Conference Exhibition. Society of Plastics Engineers Staff. pap. 160.00 (ISBN 0-317-41784-3, 2023008). Bks Demand UMI.

Plastics in a World Economy: ANTEC 84 Conference Proceedings Sponsored by SPE. 1105p. 1984. pap. 95.00 (ISBN 0-87762-353-8). Technomic.

Plastics in a World Economy: ANTEC '84, 42nd Technical Conference & Exhibition. Society of Plastics Engineers. pap. 160.00 (ISBN 0-317-19848-3, 2023008). Bks Demand UMI.

Plastics in Agriculture. P. Dubois & C. A. Brighton. (Illus.). xiii, 176p. 1978. text ed. 39.75 (ISBN 0-85334-776-X, Pub. by Elsevier Applied Sci England). Elsevier.

Plastics in Architecture. Montella. (Plastics Engineering Ser.). 280p. 1985. 55.00 (ISBN 0-8247-7396-9). Dekker.

Plastics in Automobiles (U. S.) 1985. write for info. (ISBN 0-86621-325-2, A1408). Frost & Sullivan.

Plastics in Business Machines. Business Communications Staff. (Illus.). 215p. 1986. pap. 2000.00 (ISBN 0-89336-443-6, P-064R). BCC.

Plastics in Electronics 1986-1987: Proceedings. Business Communications Staff. 1987. pap. 150.00 (ISBN 0-89336-592-0). BCC.

Plastics in ESD Applications. Business Communications Staff. 192p. 1987. 2250.00 (ISBN 0-89336-575-0, P-099). BCC.

Plastics in Furniture. Ed. by D. N. Buttrey. (Illus.). 183p. 1976. 39.75 (ISBN 0-85334-647-X, Pub. by Elsevier Applied Sci England). Elsevier.

Plastics in Medicine, Science & Law: Subject Survey Analysis with Research Bibliography. Roy R. Zimmerman. LC 85-478711. 150p. 1987. 34.50 (ISBN 0-88164-414-5); pap. 26.50 (ISBN 0-88164-415-3). ABBE Pubs Assn.

Plastics in the Electrical Industry: Technical Papers, Regional Technical Conference, March 3-4, 1980, Milwaukee, Wisconsin. Society of Plastics Engineers. (Illus.). pap. 57.30 (ISBN 0-317-08863-7, 2012018). Bks Demand UMI.

Plastics Industrial Parts. Business Communications Staff. 1988. 2450.00 (ISBN 0-89336-683-8, P-113). BCC.

Plastics Industry in Western Europe: Facts & Figures. Ed. by Wolfgang W. Glenz. (Hanser Publications). (Illus.). 158p. 1984. 25.95 (ISBN 0-19-520751-3). Oxford U Pr.

Plastics Industry Safety Handbook. Society of the Plastics Industry. 328p. 1973. 21.95 (ISBN 0-8436-1207-X). Van Nos Reinhold.

Plastics Laboratory Procedures. Harry L. Hess. LC 78-26948. 1980. pap. 18.76 scp (ISBN 0-672-97138-0); pap. 3.67 scp answer key (ISBN 0-672-97268-9). Bobbs.

Plastics Materials. Arthur W. Birley & Martyn J. Scott. 1982. (Pub. by Chapman & Hall); pap. 25.00x (ISBN 0-412-00221-3, NO. 5022). Routledge Chapman & Hall.

Plastics Materials. 4th ed. J. A. Brydson. 864p. 1982. text ed. 105.00 (ISBN 0-408-00538-6). Butterworth.

Plastics Materials & Processes. Seymour Schwartz & Sid Goodman. (Illus.). 965p. 1982. 99.00 (ISBN 0-686-48123-2, 0209). T-C Pubns CA.

Plastics Materials: Properties & Applications. A. W. Birley et al. 208p. 1988. text ed. 82.50 (ISBN 0-412-01771-7, Pub. by Chapman & Hall England); pap. text ed. 36.95 (ISBN 0-412-01781-4, Pub. by Chapman & Hall England). Routledge Chapman & Hall.

Plastics Mold Design Engineering Handbook. 4th ed. J. Harry DuBois & Wayne I. Pribble. (Illus.). 704p. 1987. 59.95 (ISBN 0-442-21897-4). Van Nos Reinhold.

Plastics Molding: Equipment, Processes, & Materials. Ed. by J. S. Robinson. LC 81-90745. x, 299p. 1981. pap. 42.00 (ISBN 0-942378-00-8). Polymers & Plastics Tech Pub Hse.

Plastics Packaging for Food, Beverages & Pharmaceuticals. Ed. by G. C. Corfield & C. Jukes. 320p. 1988. 79.95 (ISBN 0-317-67259-2). Van Nos Reinhold.

Plastics-Pioneering the Twenty-First Century: ANTEC 87: Conference Proceedings 45th Annual Technical Conference & Exhibit, Los Angeles, May 4-7, 1987. Society of Plastics Engineers Staff. (Society of Plastics Engineers, Technical Papers: Vol. 33). 1598p. pap. 160.00 (2029973). Bks Demand UMI.

Plastics: Pioneering the 21st Century: ANTEC 87. 1600p. 1987. pap. 100.00 (ISBN 0-87762-524-7). Technomic.

Plastics Piping Manual. 130p. 1-12 copies 15.00 ea. (1321); 12 members 10.00 ea.; 12 copies or more 10.00 ea.; members 7.50 (ISBN 0-318-16596-1). Soc Plastic Ind.

Plastics Planning Conference: Proceedings. Business Communications Staff. 1987. 175.00 (ISBN 0-89336-646-3). BCC.

Plastics Planning Conference: Proceedings 1984. 1985. pap. 150.00 (ISBN 0-89336-427-4). BCC.

Plastics Planning Conference, 1986: Proceedings. Business Communication Staff. 1986. 150.00 (ISBN 0-89336-586-6). BCC.

Plastics Pneumatic Conveying & Bulk Storage. Ed. by Gordon Butters. (Illus.). 296p. 1981. 75.75 (ISBN 0-85334-983-5, Pub. by Elsevier Applied Sci England). Elsevier.

Plastics Polymer Science & Technology. Ed. by M. D. Baijal. (SPE Monograph). (Illus.). 945p. 1982. 205.00 (ISBN 0-686-48131-3, 0815). T-C Pubns CA.

Plastics Polymer Science & Technology, Vol. 1. Ed. by Mahendra D. Baijal. LC 81-13066. (Society of Plastics Engineers Monographs). 945p. 1982. 204.00x (ISBN 0-471-04044-4, Pub. by Wiley-Interscience). Wiley.

Plastics Processing Engineering. Throne. 1979. 135.00 (ISBN 0-8247-6700-4). Dekker.

Plastics Processing: Technology & Health Effects. Radian Corporation Staff. LC 86-17976. (Illus.). 413p. 1987. 39.00 (ISBN 0-8155-1091-8). Noyes.

Plastics Product Design Engineering Handbook. 2nd ed. Sidney Levy & J. Harry DuBois. (Illus.). 332p. 1985. text ed. 39.50 (ISBN 0-412-00511-5, 9006, Pub. by Chapman & Hall England); pap. text ed. 22.50 (ISBN 0-412-00521-2, 9007, Pub. by Chapman & Hall England). Routledge Chapman & Hall.

Plastics Products Design Handbook, Part A. Miller. (Mechanical Engineering Ser.: Vol. 10). 624p. 1981. 79.75 (ISBN 0-8247-1339-7). Dekker.

Plastics Products Design: Technical Papers, Regional Technical Conference, 1984. Society of Plastics Engineers. pap. 44.30 (ISBN 0-317-27172-5, 2024727). Bks Demand UMI.

Plastics Recycling As a Future Business Opportunity. Ed. by Plastics Institute of America, Inc. Staff. LC 86-51296. 148p. 1986. pap. 37.50 (ISBN 0-87762-510-7). Technomic.

Plastics Recycling As a Future Business Opportunity: Recyclingplas II Conference. LC 87-51225. 292p. 1987. pap. 39.00 (ISBN 0-87762-575-1). Technomic.

Plastics South: The SPI-SPE Connection... Filling a Real Need: Conference Proceedings, Georgia World Congress Center, Atlanta, GA, October 8-10, 1986. Society of Plastics Engineers Staff. (Illus.). pap. 98.60 (ISBN 0-317-58183-X, 2029710). Bks demand UMI.

Plastics: Space Applications. 163p. 1982. pap. 85.00 (ISBN 0-686-48320-0, LS134). T-C Pubns CA.

Plastics: Space Applications. 133p. 1982. pap. 85.00 (ISBN 0-686-48323-5, LS135). T-C Pubns CA.

Plastics: Surface & Finish. Ed. by S. H. Pinner & W. G. Simpson. (Illus.). 1971. 16.00 (ISBN 0-8088-0062-0). Davey.

Plastics Technical Dictionary, 3 vols. Ed. by A. M. Wittfoht. (Hanser Publications). (Illus.). 1602p. 1983. Set. 115.00 (ISBN 0-19-520733-5). Oxford U Pr.

Plastics Technical Dictionary: Alphabetical Dictionary, Pt. I. A. M. Wittfoht. LC 81-47456. (Hanser Publications). (Illus.). 550p. (Eng. & Ger.). 1981. 45.00 (ISBN 0-19-520736-X). Oxford U Pr.

Plastics Technical Dictionary: Alphabetical Dictionary, Pt. 2. Ed. by A. M. Wittfoht. LC 81-47456. (Hanser Publications). (Illus.). 534p. (Ger. & Eng.). 1983. 45.00 (ISBN 0-19-520734-3). Oxford U Pr.

Plastics Technical Dictionary: Reference Volume - Illustrated Systemactic Groups, Pt. 3. Ed. by A. M. Wittfoht. LC 81-47456. (Hanser Publications). (Illus.). 518p. (Eng. & Ger.). 1978. 45.00 (ISBN 0-19-520735-1). Oxford U Pr.

Plastics Technology. Robert V. Milby. (Illus.). 576p. 1973. text ed. 45.95 (ISBN 0-07-041918-3). McGraw.

Plastics: The/World's Harvest Ser. Jacqueline Dineen. 32p. (gr. 4-8). 1988. lib. bdg. 9.95 (ISBN 0-89490-221-0). Enslow Pubs.

Plastics-Thermoplastics & Thermosets. 1986. 175.00. Data Inc.

Plastics Used As Building or Construction Materials, 1975-May 1983. 201p. 1983. pap. 85.00 (ISBN 0-686-48319-7, LS136). T-C Pubns CA.

Plastics Uses in Cars & Commercial Vehicles. Ed. by VDI Staff. 1982. 59.00 (ISBN 3-18-404095-X, Pub. by VDI W Germany). IPS.

Plastics UV Stability. Business Communications Staff. 187p. 1984. 1750.00 (ISBN 0-89336-402-9, P-080). BCC.

Plastics: Volume 08.01, Plastics (I) C 177 to D 1600. 808p. 1986. 50.00 (ISBN 0-8031-0888-5). ASTM.

Plastics: Volume 08.02, Plastics (II) D 1601 to D 3099. 890p. 1986. 55.00 (ISBN 0-8031-0889-3). ASTM.

Plastics: Volume 08.03, Plastics (III) D 3100 to Latest. 938p. 1986. 61.00 (ISBN 0-8031-0890-7). ASTM.

Plastics: Volume 08.04, Plastic Pipe & Building Products. 1440p. 1986. 82.00 (ISBN 0-8031-0891-5). ASTM.

Plastics vs. Corrosives. Raymond B. Seymour. LC 81-21996. (Society of Plastics Engineers Monographs). 285p. 1982. 57.50x (ISBN 0-471-08182-5, Pub. by Wiley-Interscience). Wiley.

Plastics vs. Corrosives. Raymond B. Seymour. 285p. 58.00 (ISBN 0-686-48130-5, 0807). T-C Pubns CA.

Plastics Waste. Leidner. (Plastics Engineering Ser.: Vol. 1). 328p. 1981. 55.00 (ISBN 0-8247-1381-8). Dekker.

Plastics West Directory & Buyer's Guide. pap. 32.00 (ISBN 0-686-48120-8, 2101). T-C Pubns CA.

Plastidaere Mosaikgene: Struktur und Funktion des Chloroplasten-Gens fuer die Trnalys aus Sinapsis Alba L. Heike Neuhaus. (Dissertationes Botanicae Ser.: Vol. 115). (Illus.). 110p. (Ger.). 1988. pap. 39.50 (ISBN 3-443-64027-3). Lubrecht & Cramer.

Plastids: Their Chemistry, Structure, Growth & Inheritance. J. T. Kirk & R. A. Tilney-Basset. 960p. 1979. 279.00 (ISBN 0-444-80022-0, Biomedical Pr). Elsevier.

Plastique, Nos. 1-5. Ed. by Hans Arp et al. LC 74-91379. (Contemporary Art Ser). Repr. of 1939 ed. 16.00 (ISBN 0-405-00725-6). Ayer Co Pubs.

Plastisols & Organosols. Harold A. Sarvetnick. LC 83-105. 248p. 1983. Repr. of 1972 ed. text ed. 22.00 (ISBN 0-89874-614-0). Krieger.

Plastov. S. Kuznetsov. (Masters of Soviet Painting Ser.). 1974. 30.00x (ISBN 0-317-14315-8, Pub. by Collets (UK)). State Mutual Bk.

Platanos. (Productos Latinoamericanos Incluidos En el Sistema Generalizado De Preferencias De los Estados Unidos Ser.). 16p. 1978. pap. text ed. 3.00 (ISBN 0-8270-3455-5). OAS.

Plate Collecting. (Orig.). 1983. pap. 2.95 (ISBN 0-440-06981-5). Dell.

Plate Inspection Programme, PISC: November, 1979. OECD & Nuclear Energy Agency. (Illus.). 78p. (Orig.). 1980. pap. text ed. 7.50x (ISBN 92-64-12028-9, 66 80 02 1). OECD.

Plate Mounting on the Offset Press. 28p. 1985. 16.00 (ISBN 0-88362-043-X, 0631). Graphic Arts Tech Found.

Plate Number Coils. Ken Lawrence. 168p. Date not set. pap. 7.95 (ISBN 0-940403-09-9). Linns Stamp News.

Plate of Hot Toast. Jeanette Lockerbie. (Quiet Time Bks.). 128p. (Orig.). 1971. pap. 3.50 (ISBN 0-8024-6625-7). Moody.

Plate Reconstruction from Paleozoic Paleomagnetism. Ed. by R. Van der Voo et al. (Geodynamics Ser.: Vol. 12). 136p. 1984. 20.00. Am Geophysical.

Plate Tectonics. rev. ed. Ed. by John Bird. (Illus.). 986p. 1980. pap. 25.00 (ISBN 0-87590-223-5). Am Geophysical.

Plate Tectonics. Ed. by James H. Shea. (Benchmark Papers in Geology: Vol. 89). (Illus.). 368p. 1985. 55.95 (ISBN 0-442-28239-7). Van Nos Reinhold.

Plate Tectonics & Crustal Evolution. 2nd ed. Ed. by Kent C. Condie. (Illus.). 350p. 1982. text ed. 100.00 (ISBN 0-08-028076-5); pap. text ed. 42.50 (ISBN 0-08-028075-7). Pergamon.

Plate Tectonics: How It Works. Allan Cox & Brian R. Hart. LC 86-6138. (Illus.). 400p. 1986. pap. text ed. 29.95 (ISBN 0-86542-313-X). Blackwell Pubns.

Plateau Uplift: The Rhenish Shield-a Case History. Ed. by K. Fuchs et al. (Illus.). 420p. 1983. 59.00 (ISBN 0-387-12577-9). Springer-Verlag.

Plateauing Trap: How to Avoid It in Your Career... & Your Life. Judith M. Bardwick. LC 86-47583. 224p. 1987. 17.95 (ISBN 0-8144-5871-8). AMACOM.

Plateauing Trap: How to Avoid It In Your Career...In Your Life. Judith M. Bardwick. LC 87-47806. 224p. 1988. pap. 8.95 (ISBN 0-553-34496-X). Bantam.

Plateaus & the Curve of Learning in Motor Skill see Studies in Clinical Psychology.

Plated Structures: Stability & Strength. Ed. by R. Narayanan. (Illus.). 272p. 1984. 72.00 (ISBN 0-85334-218-0, I-340-83, Pub. by Elsevier Applied Sci England). Elsevier.

Platee see Oeuvres Completes De Jean-Philippe Rameau.

Platee, ou Junon Jalouse. Jean-Philippe Rameau. Ed. by Charles Poisot. (Chefs-d'oeuvre classiques de l'opera francais Ser.: Vol. 35). (Illus.). 316p. (Fr.). 1972. pap. 27.50x (ISBN 0-8450-1135-9). Broude.

Plateglass Universities. Michael Beloff. LC 70-88559. 208p. 1970. 18.50 (ISBN 0-8386-7550-6). Fairleigh Dickinson.

Platelet-Activating Factor & Cell Immunology. Ed. by P. Braquet. (New Trends in Lipid Mediators Research Ser.: Vol. 1). viii, 180p. 1988. 112.00 (ISBN 3-8055-4684-X). S Karger.

Platelet-Activating Factor & Related Lipid Mediators. Ed. by Fred Snyder. LC 87-14198. (Illus.). 492p. 1987. 79.50x (ISBN 0-306-42516-5, Plenum Pr). Plenum Pub.

Platelet-Activating Factor & Structurally Related Ether-Lipids. J. Benveniste & X. B. Arnou. (Inserm Symposium Ser.: Vol. 23). 1984. 114.25 (ISBN 0-444-80552-4, I-193-84). Elsevier.

Platelet Activation. Ed. by Hiroh Yamazaki & J. Fraser Mustard. 277p. 1988. 40.00 (ISBN 0-12-768260-0). Acad Pr.

Platelet Aggregation & Drugs. Ed. by Luciano Caprino. 1975. 76.00 (ISBN 0-12-158950-1). Acad Pr.

Platelet & Its Disorders. B. G. Firkin. 350p. 1984. 49.50 (ISBN 0-85200-704-3, Pub. by MTP Pr England). Kluwer Academic.

Platelet Function: Laboratory Evaluation & Clinical Application. Ed. by Douglas A. Triplett. LC 77-93630. (Illus.). 317p. 1978. text ed. 20.00 (ISBN 0-89189-037-8, 45-5-005-00). Am Soc Clinical.

Platelet Immunology. Ed. by C. Kaplan et al. (Current Studies in Hematology & Blood Tranfusion: No. 55). (Illus.). viii, 188p. 1988. 110.00 (ISBN 3-8055-4693-9). S Karger.

Platelet Immunology. Thomas J. Kunicki & James N. George. LC 65-10374. (Illus.). 496p. 1988. price not set (ISBN 0-397-50872-7, Lippincott Medical). Lippincott.

Platelet Kinetics & Imaging. Ed. by Anthon D. Heyns et al. Incl. Vol. I. Techniques & Normal Platelet Kinetics. 184p. 85.00 (ISBN 0-8493-5441-2, 5441FD); Vol. II. Clinical Applications. 128p. 69.00 (ISBN 0-8493-5442-0, 5442FD). 1985. CRC Pr.

Platelet Membrane Glycoproteins. Ed. by James N. George et al. LC 85-3498. 438p. 1985. 65.00x (ISBN 0-306-41857-6, Plenum Pr). Plenum Pub.

Platelet Membrane in Transfusion Medicine. Ed. by F. Decary & G. Rock. (Current Studies in Hematology & Blood-transfusion: No. 54). (Illus.). viii, 156p. 1988. 96.75 (ISBN 3-8055-4657-2). S Karger.

Platelet Responses & Metabolism, 3 Vols. Holm Holmsen. 728p. 1987. Set. 530.00 (ISBN 0-8493-5896-5). CRC Pr.

Platelet Serology. Ed. by Francine Decary & Gail A. Rock. (Current Studies in Hematology & Blood Transfusion: No. 52). (Illus.). vii, 124p. 1986. 65.50 (ISBN 3-8055-4208-9). S Karger.

Platelet-Vessel Wall Interaction. R. M. Pittilo & S. J. Machin. (Bloomsbury Series in Clinical Science). (Illus.). 195p. 1988. 79.50 (ISBN 0-387-17488-5). Springer-Verlag.

Platelets. Ed. by Gesina L. Longenecker. 1985. 75.00 (ISBN 0-12-455555-1). Acad Pr.

Platelets. Ed. by Dennis M. Smith, Jr. & Stephanie Summers. 1988. text ed. price not set (ISBN 0-915355-57-4). Am Assn Blood.

Platelets: A Multidisciplinary Approach. Ed. by Giovanni De Gaetano & Silvio Garattini. LC 78-66352. (Monographs of the Mario Negri Institute for Pharmacological Research). 501p. 1978. 78.50 (ISBN 0-89004-252-7). Raven.

Platelets, Analgesics & Asthma. Schmitz-Schumann et al. (Agents & Actions Supplements Ser.: No. 21). 206p. 1987. 47.00 (ISBN 0-8176-1806-6). Birkhauser.

Platelets & Prostaglandins in Cardiovascular Disease. Ed. by Jawahar Mehta & Paulette Mehta. LC 80-70422. (Illus.). 438p. 1981. 47.50 (ISBN 0-87993-089-6). Futura Pub.

Platelets, Cellular Response Mechanisms & Their Biological Significance: Proceedings. A. Rotman et al. LC 80-4127. 327p. 1980. 94.95 (ISBN 0-471-27896-3, Pub. by Wiley-Interscience). Wiley.

Platelets, Cellular Response Mechanisms & Their Biological Significance: Proceedings of the Embo Workshops on Patelets, Cellular Response Mechanisms & Their Biological Significance, 1980. Weizman Institute of Science Staff. Ed. by A. Rotman & F. A. Meyer. LC 80-41257. (Wiley-Interscience Publication). pap. 87.30 (ISBN 0-317-27728-6, 2052095). Bks Demand UMI.

Platelets, Drugs & Thrombosis: Proceedings. Symposium, Hamilton, Ont., Oct. 1972. Ed. by J. F. Cade et al. 320p. 1975. 65.50 (ISBN 3-8055-1745-9). S Karger.

Platelets in Biology & Pathology. Ed. by J. L. Gordon. (Research Monographs in Cell & Tissue Physiology: Vol. 1). 1977. 73.25 (ISBN 0-7204-0601-3, North-Holland). Elsevier.

Platelets in Biology & Pathology, Vol. 2. Ed. by J. L. Gordon. (Research Monographs in Cell & Tissue Physiology: Vol. 5). 512p. 1981. 92.00 (ISBN 0-444-80308-4, Biomedical Pr). Elsevier.

Platelets in Biology & Pathology, III. Ed. by D. E. MacIntyre & J. L. Gordon. (Research Monographs in Cell & Tissue Physiology: Vol. 13). 628p. 1987. 223.75 (ISBN 0-444-80820-5). Elsevier.

Platelets: Pathophysiology & Antiplatelet Drug Therapy. Ed. by Harvey J. Weiss. LC 82-13106. 178p. 1982. 25.00 (ISBN 0-8451-0217-6). A R Liss.

Platelets: Production, Function, Transfusion, & Storage. Ed. by Mario Baldini & Shirley Ebbe. LC 74-8749. (Illus.). 418p. 1974. 99.50 (ISBN 0-8089-0845-6, 790378). Grune.

Platelets, Prostaglandins & the Cardiovascular System. Ed. by Gian G. Serneri et al. (Advances in Prostaglandin, Thromboxane, & Leukotriene Research Ser.: Vol. 13). (Illus.). 422p. 1985. text ed. 37.50 (ISBN 0-88167-062-6). Raven.

Plateo's Big Race: A Tiny Dinos Story about Learning. Guy Gilchrist. LC 88-40026. (Tiny Dinos Ser.). (Illus.). 24p. (ps-2). 1988. bds. 4.95 (ISBN 1-55782-073-2). Warner Bks.

Platero & I. Juan R. Jimenez. Tr. by Eloise Roach from Span. (Illus.). 228p. 1957. pap. 6.95 (ISBN 0-292-76479-0). U of Tex Pr.

Platero & I. Juan R. Jimenez. Tr. by Antonio T. De Nicolas from Span. LC 85-23922. (Illus.). 179p. (Orig.). 1986. pap. 9.95 (ISBN 0-913729-06-X). Paragon Hse.

Plates & Shells with Cracks: A Collection of Stress Intensity Factor Solutions for Cracks in Plates & Shells. Ed. by G. C. Sih. (Mechanics of Fracture Ser.: No. 3). 352p. 1976. 62.50x (ISBN 90-286-0146-5, Pub. by Sijthoff & Noordhoff). Kluwer Academic.

Plates Illustrative of the Vocabulary for the Deaf & Dumb. Harvey Darton. 69.95 (ISBN 0-8490-0841-7). Gordon Pr.

Platform for Change. Stafford Beer. LC 73-10741. 457p. 1975. pap. 65.95x (ISBN 0-471-06189-1, Pub. by Wiley-Interscience). Wiley.

Platform: Its Rise & Progress, 2 vols. Henry Jephson. 1968. Repr. of 1829 ed. 75.00x set (ISBN 0-7146-2264-8, F Cass Co). Biblio Dist.

Platform: Its Rise & Progress, 2 vols. Henry Jephson. LC 68-133957. 1968. Repr. of 1892 ed. Set. 87.50x (ISBN 0-678-05180-1). Kelley.

Platform Margin & Deep Water Carbonates. Harry E. Cook, III & Albert C. Hine. (Short Course Notes Ser.: No. 12). 573p. 1983. pap. 33.00 (ISBN 0-918985-22-6). SEPM.

Platform Sutra of the Sixth Patriarch. Tr. by Philip B. Yampolsky. LC 67-11847. (Records of Civilization, Studies & Sources: No. 76). 1967. pap. 15.00x (ISBN 0-231-08361-0). Columbia U Pr.

Platform to the Stars. Clifford C. Cawley. LC 86-51458. 120p. (Orig.). 1987. pap. 6.00 (ISBN 0-916383-13-X, Univ Edtns). Aegina Pr.

Platforms on the Prairies: A Public Speaker's Odyssey from Southside Gym to St. Louis & Beyond. R. Galen Hanson. 47p. 1984. 5.50 (ISBN 0-682-40147-1). Exposition-Phoenix.

Plath's Incarnations: Women & Creative Process. Lynda K. Bundtzen. (Women & Culture Ser.). 240p. 1983. text ed. 27.50x (ISBN 0-472-10033-5). U of Mich Pr.

Platicas: Conversational Spanish. Marta Andrews et al. LC 80-84024. 304p. 1980. pap. text ed. 18.50 (ISBN 0-8403-2328-X). Kendall-Hunt.

Plating Waste Treatment. Kenneth F. Cherry. LC 81-68033. 324p. 1982. 59.95 (ISBN 0-250-40417-6). Butterworth.

Platinotype Instruction Manual. Thomas J. Shillea. (Illus.). 64p. (Orig.). 1986. pap. text ed. 12.95 (ISBN 0-9616925-0-2). T J Shillea.

Platinum & Other Metal Coordination Compounds in Cancer Chemotherapy. Ed. by Marino Nicolini. (Developments in Oncology Ser.). 1988. lib. bdg. 165.00 (ISBN 0-89838-358-7, Pub. by M Nijhoff Boston MA). Kluwer Academic.

Platinum Coordination Complexes in Cancer Chemotherapy. Ed. by T. A. Connors & J. J. Roberts. (Recent Results in Cancer Research Ser.: Vol. 48). (Illus.). 220p. 1974. 52.00 (ISBN 0-387-06793-0). Springer-Verlag.

Platinum Coordination Complexes in Cancer Chemotherapy. Ed. by Miles P. Hacker et al. (Developments in Oncology Ser.). 1984. lib. bdg. 45.00 (ISBN 0-89838-619-5, Pub. by Martinus Nijhoff Netherlands). Kluwer Academic.

Platinum Crime: Memoirs of America's Top Private Investigator of Big Bucks, White Collar Crime. Marvin Wolf & Armand Grant. 288p. 1988. pap. 3.95 (ISBN 0-671-63878-5). PB.

Platinum, Gold, & Other Metal Chemotherapeutic Agents. Ed. by Stephen J. Lippard. LC 82-24333. (Symposium Ser.: No. 209). 453p. 1983. lib. bdg. 59.95 (ISBN 0-8412-0758-5). Am Chemical.

Platinum-Group Element Exploration. D. L. Buchanan. (Developments in Economic Geology: Vol. 26). 200p. 1981. 79.00 (ISBN 0-444-42958-1). Elsevier.

Platinum-Iridium Reforming Catalysts. J. C. Rasse. 230p. (Orig.). 1977. pap. 34.00x (ISBN 90-6275-005-2, Pub. by Delft Univ Pr). Coronet Bks.

Platinum Man. Borden Deal. Date not set. cancelled (ISBN 0-88282-023-0). New Horizon NJ.

Platinum Print. John Hafey & Tom Shillea. LC 79-55710. (Illus.). 119p. (Orig.). 1979. pap. 14.95 (ISBN 0-89938-000-X). Tech & Ed Ctr Graph Arts RIT.

Platinum Rainbow. 6th, rev. ed. Bob Monaco & James Riordan. Ed. by Patricia Monaco. 193p. (Orig.). 1980. pap. 9.95. Swordsman Pr.

Platinum Rainbow: How to Succeed in the Music Business Without Selling Your Soul. Bob Monaco & James Riordan. (Swordsman Press Bk.). 280p. 9.95 (ISBN 0-940018-00-4). Contemp Bks.

Platinum Rainbow: How to Succeed in the Music Business Without Selling Your Soul. Bob Monaco & James Riordan. 260p. 1988. pap. 9.95 (ISBN 0-8092-4813-1). Contemp Bks.

Platitudes. Trey Ellis. Ed. by Erroll McDonald. LC 87-40109. (Vintage Contemporaries Ser.). 160p. 1988. pap. 6.95 (ISBN 0-394-75439-5, Vin). Random.

Platkops Children. Pauline Smith. 224p. 1981. text ed. 23.00 (ISBN 0-86961-131-3, Pub. by A A Balkema). Brookfield Pub Co.

Plato, 3 vols. Ed. by Paul Friedlander. Tr. by Hans Meyerhoff. Incl. Vol. 1. An Introduction. 2nd ed. 1970. 49.50x (ISBN 0-691-09812-3); pap. 14.50x (ISBN 0-691-01795-6). (Bollingen Ser.: Vol. 59). Princeton U Pr.

Plato. Robert W. Hall. (Political Thinkers Ser.). 1981. text ed. 24.95x (ISBN 0-04-320145-8); pap. text ed. 9.95x (ISBN 0-04-320146-6). Unwin Hyman.

Plato. R. M. Hare. (Past Masters Ser.). 96p. 1982. 13.95x (ISBN 0-19-287586-8); pap. 4.95 (ISBN 0-19-287585-X). Oxford U Pr.

PLATO. Harold F. Rahmlow et al. Ed. by Danny G. Langdon. LC 79-26395. (Instructional Design Library). 112p. 1980. 23.95 (ISBN 0-87778-150-8). Educ Tech Pubns.

Plato. Christopher Rowe. LC 84-13327. 228p. 1984. 25.00 (ISBN 0-312-61502-7). St Martin.

Plato. Christopher Rowe. 236p. pap. cancelled (ISBN 0-312-61503-5). St Martin.

Plato. facsimile ed. Alfred E. Taylor. LC 71-160995. (Select Bibliographies Reprint Ser.). Repr. of 1911 ed. 15.00 (ISBN 0-8369-5863-2). Ayer Co Pubs.

Plato. Eric Voegelin. LC 57-11670. x, 280p. 1966. pap. text ed. 8.95 (ISBN 0-8071-0102-8). La State U Pr.

Plato see Mind of Plato.

Plato & Aristotle see Order & History.

Plato & Aristotle on Poetry. Gerald F. Else. Ed. by Peter Burian. LC 86-1475. xxii, 221p. 1987. 27.00x (ISBN 0-8078-1708-2). U of NC Pr.

Plato & Augustine: Taken from Vol. 1 of the Great Philosophers. Karl Jaspers. Tr. by Karl Manheim. LC 67-38117. Orig. Title: Great Philosophers, Vol. 1 (Pt. 2) 1966. pap. 4.95 (ISBN 0-15-672035-3, Harv). HarBraceJ.

Plato & Freud: Two Theories of Love. Gerasimos Santas. 256p. 1988. 24.95 (ISBN 0-631-15914-2). Basil Blackwell.

Plato & Heidegger: In Search of Selfhood. Henry G. Wolz. LC 79-19974. 312p. 1981. 27.50 (ISBN 0-8387-5003-6). Bucknell U Pr.

Plato & His Contemporaries. Guy C. Field. LC 74-30008. (Studies in Philosophy, No. 40). 1974. lib. bdg. 75.00 (ISBN 0-8383-1992-0). Haskell.

Plato & Platonism. Walter H. Pater. 1970. Repr. of 1910 ed. lib. bdg. 25.00 (ISBN 0-8371-1151-X, PAPP). Greenwood.

Plato & Platonism. Walter H. Pater. Repr. of 1910 ed. 39.00 (ISBN 0-8274-3139-2). R West.

Plato & the Epinomis. A. E. Taylor. (Studies in Philosophy, No. 40). 1977. lib. bdg. 25.95x (ISBN 0-8383-0119-3). Haskell.

Plato & the Metaphysics of the State. Allan Rightridge. (Most Meaningful Classics in World Culture). (Illus.). 168p. 1981. 117.75 (ISBN 0-89266-297-2). Am Classical Coll Pr.

Plato & Vedic Idealism. Swami Paramananda. (Orig.). 1924. 4.50 (ISBN 0-911564-15-2). Vedanta Ctr.

Plato: Apology. Ed. by James J. Helm. (Bolchazy-Carducci Textbooks). (Illus., Orig.). pap. 10.00 (ISBN 0-86516-005-8). Bolchazy-Carducci.

Plato, Apology. M. C. Stokes. (BC-AP Classical Texts Ser.). 250p. 1986. text ed. 29.00x (ISBN 0-86516-168-2); pap. 16.50x (ISBN 0-86516-169-0). Bolchazy-Carducci.

Plato: Apology. Ed. by M. C. Stokes. (Classical Texts-Greek Texts Ser.). 1989. text ed. 37.50 (ISBN 0-317-59406-0, Pub. by Aris & Phillips); pap. text ed. 16.50 (ISBN 0-317-59407-9, Pub. by Aris & Phillips). Humanities.

Plato: Arguments of the Philosophers. J. C. Gosling. 319p. 1984. pap. 9.95 (ISBN 0-7102-0018-8). Routledge Chapman & Hall.

Plato, Aristotle & Pre-Aristotelian Philosophers: A Critical View, 2 vols. W. Austin Christ. 217p. 1987. Repr. of 1905 ed. Set. 177.50 (ISBN 0-89901-325-2). Found Class Reprints.

Plato, Aristotle & the Conflicting Effort for Truth. Anselm V. Hyde. (Illus.). 188p. 1988. 117.00 (ISBN 0-89266-624-2). Am Classical Coll Pr.

Plato As an Introduction to Modern Criticism of Life. Emil Reich. LC 74-101051. 1969. Repr. of 1906 ed. 26.50x (ISBN 0-8046-0716-8, Pub. by Kennikat). Assoc Faculty Pr.

Plato: Cratylus, Phaedo, Parmenides, Timaeus, & Critias. new ed. Tr. by Thomas Taylor. LC 73-84046. (Secret Doctrine Reference Ser). 460p. 1975. Repr. of 1793 ed. limited ed. o.p. 32.00x (ISBN 0-913510-09-2); lib. bdg. 27.00 (ISBN 0-913510-21-1). Wizards.

Plato, Derrida, & Writing. Jasper Neel. 256p. 1988. text ed. 19.95x (ISBN 0-8093-1440-1). S Ill U Pr.

Plato: Dramatist of the Life of Reason. John Randall. LC 71-106565. 288p. pap. 72.00 (ISBN 0-317-30468-2, 2024826). Bks Demand UMI.

Plato: Euthyphro, Apology, Crito. F. J. Church & Robert D. Cummings. 1956. pap. text ed. write for info. (ISBN 0-02-322410-X). Macmillan.

Plato for Beginners. Robert Cavalier. 1988. pap. 7.95 (ISBN 0-86316-039-5). Writers & Readers.

Plato for the Modern Age. Robert S. Brumbaugh. LC 78-13271. (Illus.). 1979. Repr. of 1962 ed. lib. bdg. 35.00x (ISBN 0-313-20630-9, BRPF). Greenwood.

Plato: Moral & Political Ideals. Adam Kensington & Adela M. Kensington. 1978. Repr. of 1913 ed. lib. bdg. 25.00 (ISBN 0-8495-0135-0). Arden Lib.

Plato, Nietzsche & the Insuperability of the Totalitarian State. William A. Muhlenberg. (Great Currents of History Library Book). (Illus.). 135p. 1981. 117.75 (ISBN 0-89266-307-3). Am Classical Coll Pr.

Plato on Beauty, Wisdom & the Arts. Ed. by Julius Moravcsik & Phillip Temko. LC 81-23434. (American Philosophical Quarterly Library of Philosophy). 160p. 1982. 33.50x (ISBN 0-8476-7030-9). Rowman.

Plato on Justice & Power: Reading Book I of Plato's Republic. Kimon Lycos. LC 86-19166. (SUNY Series in Philosophy). 224p. 1987. 49.50 (ISBN 0-88706-415-9); pap. 16.95x (ISBN 0-88706-416-7). State U NY Pr.

Plato on Knowledge & Reality. Nicholas P. White. LC 76-10993. 272p. 1976. 32.50 (ISBN 0-915144-21-2); pap. 16.50 (ISBN 0-915144-22-0). Hackett Pub.

Plato on Knowledge & Reality see Examination of Plato's Doctrines.

Plato on Man & Society see Examination of Plato's Doctrines.

Plato on Punishment. Mary M. Mackenzie. LC 80-6065. 272p. 1981. pap. 10.95x (ISBN 0-520-05624-8). U. of Cal Pr.

Plato on the Trial & Death of Socrates: Euthyphro, Apology, Crito, Phaedo. Tr. by Lane Cooper. (Paperback Ser.). 214p. 1967. 5.95x (ISBN 0-8014-9049-9). Cornell U Pr.

Plato One: Metaphysics & Epistemology; a Collection of Critical Essays. Ed. by Gregory Vlastos. LC 77-19103. (Modern Studies in Philosophy). 1978. pap. text ed. 10.95 (ISBN 0-268-01529-5). U. of Notre Dame Pr.

Plato: Phaedrus. Ed. by C. J. Rowe. (Classical Texts-Greek Texts Ser.). 232p. 1986. text ed. 48.00 (ISBN 0-85668-313-2, Pub. by Aris & Phillips UK); pap. text ed. 16.50 (ISBN 0-85668-314-0, Pub. by Aris & Phillips UK). Humanities.

Plato: Phaedrus. Ed. by R. J. Rowe. (BC-AP Classical Texts Ser.). 250p. (Gr. & Eng.). 1986. text ed. 49.00x (ISBN 0-86516-145-3); pap. 16.50x (ISBN 0-86516-144-5). Bolchazy-Carducci.

Plato, Prehistorian: 10000 to 5000 B.C. in Myth & Archaeology. Mary Settegast. LC 86-61988. (Illus.). 334p. 1987. 36.00 (ISBN 0-9617333-1-4). Rotenberg Pr.

Plato: Protagoras. Plato. Tr. by C. C. Taylor. (Clarendon Plato Ser.). 1976. 29.50x (ISBN 0-19-872045-9); pap. 12.95x (ISBN 0-19-872088-2). Oxford U Pr.

Plato Reader. Plato. Ed. by Ronald B. Levinson. (YA) (gr. 9 up). 1967. pap. 6.95 (ISBN 0-395-05197-5, RivEd). HM.

Plato: Republic, Bk. I. Ed. by D. J. Allen. (Classical Texts Ser.). 142p. pap. 9.95x (ISBN 0-631-13884-6). Basil Blackwell.

Plato: Republic, Bk. X. Ed. by John Ferguson. (Classical Texts Ser.). 192p. pap. 9.95x (ISBN 0-904679-14-4). Basil Blackwell.

Plato: Republic Book Ten. Ed. by F. S. Halliwell. (Classical Texts - Greek Texts). 1988. text ed. 49.95 (ISBN 0-85668-405-8, Pub. by Aris & Phillips UK); pap. text ed. 16.50 (ISBN 0-85668-406-6, Pub. by Aris & Phillips UK). Humanities.

Plato: The Man & His Work. A. E. Taylor. 1960. pap. 16.95x (ISBN 0-416-67590-5, NO. 6444). Routledge Chapman & Hall.

Plato: The Martyrdom of Socrates. F. Doherty. 112p. 1982. Repr. of 1923 ed. 12.25 (ISBN 0-906515-96-3, Pub. by Bristol Classical UK). Focus Info Gr.

Plato: The Midwife's Apprentice. I. M. Crombie. LC 81-6812. viii, 195p. 1981. Repr. of 1965 ed. lib. bdg. 35.00x (ISBN 0-313-23243-1, CRPL). Greenwood.

Plato: The Statesman. J. B. Skemp. 244p. 1987. Repr. of 1952 ed. 18.25 (ISBN 0-86292-191-0, Pub. by Bristol Classical UK). Focus Info Gr.

Plato: The Story of Atlantis. Christopher Gill. 120p. 1980. 12.25 (ISBN 0-906515-59-9, Pub. by Bristol Classical Pr). Focus Info Gr.

Plato: Theaetetus. (Clarendon Plato Ser.). 1974. pap. 13.95x (ISBN 0-19-872083-1). Oxford U Pr.

Plato to Machiavelli see Masters of Political Thought.

Plato Two: Ethics, Politics, & Philosophy of Art & Religion; a Collection of Critical Essays. Ed. by Gregory Vlastos. LC 77-19103. (Modern Studies in Philosophy). 1978. text ed. 18.95 (ISBN 0-268-01530-9); pap. text ed. 8.95x (ISBN 0-268-01531-7). U of Notre Dame Pr.

Platon, 3 vols. Paul Friedlaender. Incl. Vol. 1. Seinswahrheit und Lebenswirklichkeit. 3rd rev. & enl ed. (Illus.). x, 438p. 1964 (ISBN 3-11-000137-3); Vol. 2. Platonischen Schriften: Erste Periode. 3rd rev. ed. vi, 358p. 1964 (ISBN 3-11-000138-1); Vol. 3. Die Platonischen Shriften: Tweite und Periode. 1975. (Ger.). 29.60x ea. De Gruyter.

Platon: Sein Leben, Seine Schriften, Seine Lehre, 2 vols. facsimile ed. Constantin Ritter. LC 75-13291. (History of Ideas in Ancient Greece Ser.). (Ger.). 1976. Repr. Set. 92.50x (ISBN 0-405-07333-X); 46.50x ea. Vol. 1 (ISBN 0-405-07334-8). Vol. 2 (ISBN 0-405-07335-6). Ayer Co Pubs.

Platon und die Schriftlichkeit der Philosophie: Interpretationen zu den Fruehen und Mittleren Dialogen. Thomas A. Szlezak. x, 446p. (Ger.). 1985. 125.00x (ISBN 3-11-010272-2). De Gruyter.

Platonic Bearings in Rabindranath. Bhaktivenode Chakraborty. 1986. 9.00x (ISBN 0-8364-1580-9, Pub. by KP Bagchi India). South Asia Bks.

Platonic Blow & My Epitaph. W. H. Auden. LC 85-339. 8p. 1985. pap. 5.00 (ISBN 0-914061-04-6). Orchises Pr.

Platonic Epistles. facsimile ed. Plato. Tr. by J. Harward. LC 75-13287. (History of Ideas in Ancient Greece Ser.). 1976. Repr. of 1932 ed. 19.00x (ISBN 0-405-07330-5). Ayer Co Pubs.

Platonic Ideas in Spenser. Mohinimohana Bhattacharya. LC 72-187921. 1935. lib. bdg. 29.00 (ISBN 0-8414-1643-5). Folcroft.

Platonic Investigations. Ed. by Dominic J. O'Meara. LC 84-23906. (Studies in Philosophy & the History of Philosophy: Vol. 13). 320p. 1985. 31.95 (ISBN 0-8132-0608-1). Cath U Pr.

Platonic Love. Thomas Gould. LC 81-6881. vii, 216p. 1981. Repr. of 1963 ed. lib. bdg. 35.00x (ISBN 0-313-22520-6, GOPT). Greenwood.

Platonic Myth & Platonic Writing. Robert Zaslavsky. LC 80-5563. 306p. 1981. lib. bdg. 30.50 (ISBN 0-8191-1382-4); pap. text ed. 15.00 (ISBN 0-8191-1381-6). U Pr of Amer.

Platonic Quest. Edward J. Urwick. xxxiv, 264p. (Orig.). 1983. pap. 15.50 (ISBN 0-88695-001-5). Concord Grove.

Platonic Renaissance in England. Ernst Cassirer. LC 71-128186. 207p. 1970. Repr. of 1954 ed. 25.00x (ISBN 0-87752-128-X). Gordian.

Platonic Scripts. Donald Justice. (Poets on Poetry Ser.). 216p. 1984. pap. 8.95 (ISBN 0-472-06352-9). U of Mich Pr.

Platonic Studies of Greek Philosophy: Form, Arts, Gadgets, & Hemlock. Robert S. Brumbaugh. (Philosophy Ser.). 320p. (Orig.). 1989. text ed. 54.50x (ISBN 0-88706-897-9); pap. 17.95x (ISBN 0-88706-898-7). State U NY Pr.

Platonic Theology, Vol. II: Bks IV-VI. rev. ed. Proclus. Ed. by Robert Navon. Tr. by Thomas Taylor from Gr. LC 84-52789. (Great Works of Philosophy: Vol. II). 292p. 1986. text ed. 35.00 (ISBN 0-933601-05-0); pap. text ed. 22.50 (ISBN 0-933601-06-9). Selene Bks.

Platonic Theology: Vol. 1 - Books I-III. Rev. ed. Proclus. Ed. by Robert Navon. Tr. by Thomas Taylor from Gr. (Great Works of Philosophy Ser.: Vol. I). xxvi, 222p. 1985. text ed. 35.00 (ISBN 0-9609866-7-7); pap. text ed. 22.50 (ISBN 0-9609866-6-9). Selene Bks.

Platonic Tradition in English Religious Thought. William R. Inge. LC 77-8095. 1977. Repr. of 1926 ed. lib. bdg. 25.00 (ISBN 0-8414-5055-2). Folcroft.

Platonic Writings - Platonic Readings. Ed. by Charles L. Griswold, Jr. 320p. 1988. text ed. 39.50x (ISBN 0-7102-1565-7); pap. text ed. 13.95x (ISBN 0-7102-1566-5). Routledge Chapman & Hall.

Platonis Opera Omnia, 14 vols. G. Stallbaum. (Ancient Philosophy Ser.). 1982. lib. bdg. 804.00 Set. Garland Pub.

Platonis Sophista: Recentsuit, Prolegomenis et Commentariis Instruxit. Otto Apelt. Ed. by Leonardo Taran. LC 78-66612. (Ancent Philosophy Ser.: Vol. 1). 225p. lib. bdg. 26.00 (ISBN 0-8240-9611-8). Garland Pub.

Platonis Theaetetus. Martinus Wohlrab. LC 78-66603. (Ancient Philosophy Ser.). 248p. 1982. lib. bdg. 29.00 (ISBN 0-8240-9570-7). Garland Pub.

Platonische Aufsatze. facsimile ed. Otto Apelt. LC 75-13251. (History of Ideas in Ancient Greece Ser.). (Ger.). 1976. Repr. of 1912 ed. 19.00x (ISBN 0-405-07288-0). Ayer Co Pubs.

Platonische Staat. facsimile ed. August A. Krohn. LC 75-13277. (History of Ideas in Ancient Greece Ser.). (Ger.). 1976. Repr. of 1876 ed. 24.50x (ISBN 0-405-07317-8). Ayer Co Pubs.

Platonische Studien. facsimile ed. Eduard Zeller. LC 75-13301. (History of Ideas in Ancient Greece Ser.). (Ger.). 1976. Repr. of 1839 ed. 19.00x (ISBN 0-405-07344-5). Ayer Co Pubs.

Platonischen Schriften: Erste Periode see Platon.

Platonism. John Burnet. LC 83-1503. (Sather Classical Lectures Ser.: Vol. 5). 130p. 1983. Repr. of 1928 ed. lib. bdg. 35.00x (ISBN 0-313-23699-2, BUPL). Greenwood.

Platonism. 3rd ed. Paul E. More. LC 77-98631. Repr. of 1931 ed. 12.75 (ISBN 0-404-04417-4). AMS Pr.

Platonism & Cartesianism in the Philosophy of Ralph Cudworth. Lydia Gysi. 163p. 1962. 14.35 (ISBN 3-261-00648-X). P Lang Pubs.

Platonism in English Poetry of the Sixteenth & Seventeenth Centuries. John S. Harrison. LC 80-11587. (Columbia University Studies in Comparative Literature). xi, 235p. 1980. Repr. of 1903 ed. lib. bdg. 35.00x (ISBN 0-313-22374-2, HAPL). Greenwood.

Platonism of Aristotle. G. E. Owen. (Dawes Hicks Lectures on Philosophy). 1965. pap. 5.50 (ISBN 0-85672-272-3, Pub. by British Acad). Longwood Pub Group.

Platonism of Gregory of Nyssa. Harold F. Cherniss. 1971. Repr. of 1930 ed. lib. bdg. 18.50 (ISBN 0-8337-0556-3). B Franklin.

Platonism of Marsilio Ficino: A Study of His Phaedrus Commentary, Its Sources & Genesis. Michael J. Allen. LC 83-18187. (Center for Medieval & Renaissance Studies UCLA: No. 21). 290p. 1984. text ed. 37.50x (ISBN 0-520-05152-1). U of Cal Pr.

Playfair: Everybody's Guide to Noncompetitive Play. Matt Weinstein & Joel Goodman. LC 80-12591. 248p. (Orig.). 1980. pap. 9.95 (ISBN 0-915166-50-X). Impact Pubs Cal.

Playfair Hours: A Late Fifteenth Century Illuminated Manuscript from Rouen. Rowan Watson. 1985. pap. 29.95 slipcased (ISBN 0-905209-98-2). Faber & Faber.

Playful Fictions & Fictional Players: Game, Sport & Survival in Contemporary American Fiction. Neil D. Berman. (National University Publications, Literary Criticism Ser.). 125p. 1981. 17.50x (ISBN 0-8046-9265-3, Pub. by Kennikat). Assoc Faculty Pr.

Playful Gourmet: For Ladies Only. Stephen Cornwell & Debbie Cornwell. (Illus.). 64p. (Orig.). 1987. pap. 4.95 (ISBN 0-943678-21-8). Wellton Enter.

Playful Gourmet: For Lovers Only. Stephen Cornwell & Debbie Cornwell. (Illus.). 64p. (Orig.). 1987. pap. 4.95 (ISBN 0-943678-24-2). Wellton Enter.

Playful Gourmet: For Men Only. Stephen Cornwell & Debbie Cornwell. (Illus.). 64p. (Orig.). 1987. pap. 4.95 (ISBN 0-943678-22-6). Wellton Enter.

Playful Gourmet: For Red Hot Lovers. Stephen Cornwell & Debbie Cornwell. (Illus.). 64p. 1987. pap. 4.95 (ISBN 0-943678-19-6). Wellton Enter.

Playful Gourmet: For Red Hot Lovers. Stephen Cornwell & Debbie Cornwell. (Illus.). 64p. 1987. 4.95 (ISBN 0-317-61429-0). Wellton Enter.

Playful Gourmet: Just Married. Stephen Cornwell & Debbie Cornwell. (Illus.). 64p. 1987. 4.95 (ISBN 0-943678-20-X). Wellton Enter.

Playful Gourmet: Quickies. Stephen Cornwell & Debbie Cornwell. (Illus.). 64p. (Orig.). 1987. pap. 4.95 (ISBN 0-943678-23-4). Wellton Enter.

Playful Kittens. Nobuo Honda. (Cat Album Ser.). 1985. pap. 4.95 (ISBN 0-89346-255-1). Heian Intl.

Playful Lady Penelope. Kasey Michaels. 192p. 1988. pap. 2.95 (ISBN 0-380-75297-2). Avon.

Playful Learning: An Alternate Approach to Preschool. Anne Engelhardt & Cheryl Sullivan. LC 86-82265. (Illus.). 1986. pap. 14.95 (ISBN 0-912500-30-1). La Leche.

Playful Perception: Choosing How to Experience Your World. Herbert L. Leff. LC 83-19876. (Illus.). 172p. (Orig.). 1984. 15.95 (ISBN 0-914525-01-8); pap. 9.95 (ISBN 0-914525-00-X). Waterfront Bks.

Playful Pets. (Moving Eye Board Bks.). (Illus.). (ps). bds. 1.98 (ISBN 0-517-47117-5). Outlet Bk Co.

Playful Pirate's Cookbook. Carole Marsh. (Of All the Gaul Ser.). 250p. (Orig.). 1987. 17.95 (ISBN 1-55609-002-1). Gallopade Pub Group.

Playful Pups. Ed. by Jill Wolf. (Illus.). 24p. (gr. 2-6). 1985. pap. 1.95 (ISBN 0-89954-294-8). Antioch Pub Co.

Playfulness in Japanese Art. Nobuo Tsuji. (Franklin D. Murphy Lectures VII). (Illus.). 104p. 1986. 12.00 (ISBN 0-913689-23-8). Spencer Muse Art.

Playgirl Love & Sex Adviser. Ed. by Playgirl Editors. 1984. pap. 5.95 (ISBN 0-671-50133-X, Fireside). S&S.

Playgirl's Guide: How to Meet Men. Ellen Sklarz & Playgirl Editors. 160p. (Orig.). 1984. pap. 6.95 (ISBN 0-671-47613-0, Wallaby). S&S.

Playgoer's Handbook to Restoration Drama. Malcolm Elwin. LC 74-22296. 1974. Repr. of 1928 ed. lib. bdg. 35.00 (ISBN 0-8414-3923-0). Folcroft.

Playgoer's Handbook to Restoration Drama. Malcom Elwin. 1978. Repr. of 1928 ed. lib. bdg. 42.50 (ISBN 0-8495-1312-X). Arden Lib.

Playgoer's Handbook to the English Renaissance Drama. Agnes M. Mackenzie. LC 75-145871. 1971. Repr. of 1927 ed. 20.00x (ISBN 0-8154-0373-9). Cooper Sq.

Playgoer's Wanderings. H. M. Walbrook. 1975. Repr. of 1926 ed. 25.00 (ISBN 0-8274-4059-6). R West.

Playgoing: An Essay. James Agate. LC 72-83870. Repr. of 1937 ed. 16.00 (ISBN 0-405-08191-X, Pub. by Blom). Ayer Co Pubs.

Playgoing in Shakespeare's London. Andrew Gurr. (Illus.). 299p. 1987. 49.50 (ISBN 0-521-25336-5). Cambridge U Pr.

Playground. James Broughton. (Illus.). 1949. 7.50 (ISBN 0-685-79022-3). Small Pr Dist.

Playground. Kate Duke. LC 84-73141. (Guinea Pig Board Bks.). (Illus.). 12p. (ps). 1986. bds. 2.95 (ISBN 0-525-44206-5). Dutton.

Playground. H. V. Elkin. 1979. pap. 2.25 (ISBN 0-505-51423-0, Pub. by Tower Bks). Leisure NY.

Playground. Illus. by Kaye Quinn. (Hidden Pictures Coloring Bks.). (Illus.). 48p. (ps-2). 1988. pap. 2.95 (ISBN 0-8431-2249-8). Price Stern.

Playground. T. M. Wright. 320p. 1982. pap. 2.95 (ISBN 0-523-48046-6, Dist. by Warner Pub. Services & St. Martin's Press). Tor Bks.

Playground. T. M. Wright. 320p. 1988. pap. 3.95 (ISBN 0-8125-2748-8). Tor Bks.

Playground Design: Outdoor Environments for Learning & Development. Aase Eriksen. (Illus.). 164p. 1985. 26.95 (ISBN 0-442-22257-2). Van Nos Reinhold.

Playground Director. Jack Rudman. (Career Examination Ser.: C-590). (Cloth bdg. avail. on request). pap. 16.00 (ISBN 0-8373-0590-X). Natl Learning.

Playground Equipment: Do-It-Yourself, Indestructible, Practically Free. Lloyd Marston. LC 83-25565. (Illus.). 160p. 1984. pap. 14.95x (ISBN 0-89950-104-4). McFarland & Co.

Playground Fun. Sharon Gordon. LC 86-30854. (Illus.). 32p. (gr. k-2). 1987. lib. bdg. 5.41 (ISBN 0-8167-0990-4); pap. text ed. 1.50 (ISBN 0-8167-0991-2). Troll Assocs.

Playground Poems. Yvonne L. Rusiniak. Ed. by Gary S. Skeens. 87p. 1981. pap. 5.50 (ISBN 0-934040-05-2). Quality Ohio.

Playgrounds. Alan Gelb. 304p. 1987. 18.95 (ISBN 0-399-13277-5, Putnam). Putnam Pub Group.

Playgrounds. Gail Gibbons. LC 84-19285. (Illus.). 32p. (ps-3). 1985. reinforced bdg. 12.95 (ISBN 0-8234-0553-2). Holiday.

Playgrounds. Peter Heseltine & John Holborn. 224p. 1987. 49.50 (ISBN 0-89397-278-9). Nichols Pub.

Playgrounds. Merilyn Mohr. 1988. 21.00 (ISBN 0-8446-6316-6). Peter Smith.

Playgrounds (Health Education) Men. Jack Rudman. (Teachers License Examination Ser.: T-47a). (Cloth bdg. avail. on request). pap. 13.95 (ISBN 0-8373-8047-2). Natl Learning.

Playgrounds (Health Education) Women. Jack Rudman. (Teachers License Examination Ser.: T-47b). (Cloth bdg. avail. on request). pap. 13.95. Natl Learning.

Playgrounds (Kindergarten) Jack Rudman. (Teachers License Examination Ser.: T-48). (Cloth bdg. avail. on request). pap. 13.95 (ISBN 0-8373-8048-0). Natl Learning.

Playgrounds of Our Minds. John Barell. LC 79-27084. 185p. 1980. pap. text ed. 12.95x (ISBN 0-8077-2580-3). Tchrs Coll.

Playgrounds of the (San Francisco) Peninsula: The Player's Guide. Ava Z. Everett. (Illus.). 102p. 1988. pap. 6.95 (ISBN 0-935382-62-3). Tioga Pub Co.

Playgrounds (Swimming) Jack Rudman. (Teachers License Examination Ser.: T-49). (Cloth bdg. avail. on request). pap. 13.95 (ISBN 0-8373-8049-9). Natl Learning.

Playgroup. Nancy Weber. 288p. 1982. 13.95 (ISBN 0-312-61562-0, Pub. by Marek). St Martin.

Playgroup. Nancy Weber. 272p. 1984. pap. 3.50 (ISBN 0-441-67070-9). Ace Bks.

Playgroup Handbook. Laura P. Broad & Nancy T. Butterworth. LC 73-87399. (Griffin Ser.). (Illus.). 1974. pap. 8.95 (ISBN 0-312-61600-7). St Martin.

Playgroups: From Eighteen Months to Kindergarten - A Complete Guide for Parents. Sheila Wolper & Beth Levine. 1988. pap. 6.95 (ISBN 0-671-64397-5). PB.

Playhouse. Diane Alexander. LC 84-70527. (Illus.). 237p. 1984. 19.95 (ISBN 0-916329-00-3). Dorleac-MacLeish.

Playhouse. Richard Levinson & William Link. 224p. 1985. pap. 3.50 (ISBN 0-441-67071-7). Ace Bks.

Playhouse. Ada M. Zimmerman. 32p. 1980. 2.45 (ISBN 0-686-30763-1). Rod & Staff.

Playhouse & Cosmos: Shakespearean Theater As Metaphor. Kent Van Den Berg. LC 82-49308. (Illus.). 256p. 1985. 25.00 (ISBN 0-87413-244-4). U Delaware Pr.

Playhouse & the Play. Percy Mackaye. LC 9-10640. (Library of Literature, Drama & Criticism). Repr. of 1909 ed. 14.00 (ISBN 0-384-34860-2). Johnson Repr.

Playhouse Architecture: A Selected Bibliography. Anthony G. White. (Architecture Ser.: A 1721). 12p. 1986. 3.75 (ISBN 1-55590-111-5). Vance Biblios.

Playhouse for Monster. Virginia Mueller. Ed. by Ann Fay. (Illus.). 24p. (ps-1). 1985. PLB 9.95 (ISBN 0-8075-6541-5). A Whitman.

Playhouse for Monster. Virginia Mueller. (Illus.). (ps-1). 1988. pap. 3.95 (ISBN 0-14-050877-5, Puffin Bks). Penguin.

Playhouse Impressions. A. B. Walkley. LC 82-49102. (Degeneration & Regeneration Ser.). 269p. 1984. lib. bdg. 35.00 (ISBN 0-8240-5565-9). Garland Pub.

Playhouse of the Sixteenth Century. Ben Jonson. LC 73-18287. 1905. Repr. lib. bdg. 17.00 (ISBN 0-8414-5279-2). Folcroft.

Playing. Helen Oxenbury. (Oxenbury Board Bks.). (Illus.). 14p. (ps-k). 1981. bds. 3.50 (ISBN 0-671-42109-3, Little Simon). S&S.

Playing after Dark. Barbara L. Ascher. LC 87-45019. 160p. 1987. pap. 6.95 (ISBN 0-06-097112-6, PL/7112, PL). Har-Row.

Playing: An Introduction to Acting. Paul Kuritz. 250p. 1982. write for info. (ISBN 0-13-682906-6). P-H.

Playing & Coaching Wheelchair Basketball. Ed Owen. LC 81-10456. (Illus.). 320p. 1982. pap. 16.95 (ISBN 0-252-00867-7). U of Ill Pr.

Playing & Exploring: Education Through the Discovery of Order. R. A. Hodgkin. 180p. 1985. text ed. 29.00 (ISBN 0-416-40180-5, 9628); pap. text ed. 12.95 (ISBN 0-416-40300-X, 9629). Routledge Chapman & Hall.

Playing & Reality. Donald W. Winnicott. 1982. (Pub. by Tavistock England); pap. 10.95x (ISBN 0-422-78310-2, NO. 3741). Routledge Chapman & Hall.

Playing & Teaching Stringed Instruments, Pt. I. Ralph Matesky & Ralph E. Rush. (Orig.). 1963. pap. text ed. write for info. (ISBN 0-13-683789-1). P-H.

Playing & Teaching the Strings. Vincent Oddo. 189p. 1979. Spiralbound. text ed. write for info. (ISBN 0-534-00614-0). Wadsworth Pub.

Playing Away. Caryl Phillips. (Illus.). 80p. 1987. pap. 7.95 (ISBN 0-571-14583-3). Faber & Faber.

Playing Away: Roman Holidays & Other Mediterranean Excursions. Michael Mewshaw. 256p. 1988. 18.95 (ISBN 0-689-12006-0). Atheneum.

Playing Ball on Running Water: Living Morita Psychotherapy - The Japanese Way to Building a Better Life. David K. Reynolds. LC 84-8399. 160p. 1984. pap. 7.95 (ISBN 0-688-03913-8, Quill NY). Morrow.

Playing Beatie Bow. Ruth Park. LC 81-8097. 204p. (gr. 5-9). 1980. 12.95 (ISBN 0-689-30889-2, Atheneum Childrens Bks). Macmillan.

Playing Beatie Bow. Ruth Park. (Puffin Story Bks.). 200p. (gr. 5-9). 1984. pap. 3.95 (ISBN 0-14-031460-1, Puffin). Penguin.

Playing Blackjack As a Business. rev. ed. 1977. 15.00 (ISBN 0-686-67834-6); pap. 9.95 (ISBN 0-8184-0063-3). Paul Mann.

Playing Blackjack As a Business: 1977 Edition. Lawrence Revere. (Illus.). 1977. 15.00 (ISBN 0-686-67857-5); pap. 14.95 (ISBN 0-8184-0064-1). Lyle Stuart.

Playing by Different Rules: The General Mills-Parker Brothers Merger. Ellen Wojahn. 224p. 1988. 21.95 (ISBN 0-8144-5861-0). AMACOM.

Playing by the Rules. D. Stuart Briscoe. 192p. 1986. 9.95 (ISBN 0-8007-1489-X). Revell.

Playing Cards Around the World. Sid Sackson. (Illus.). (gr. 5 up). 1981. 9.95 (ISBN 0-13-683003-X). P-H.

Playing Cards: Fournier Musuem. Felix A. Fournier. (Illus.). 344p. 1982. 45.00 (ISBN 0-88079-026-1). US Games Syst.

Playing Cards of the World. Kathleen Wowk. (Illus.). 160p. 1982. 25.00 (ISBN 0-7188-2408-3). US Games Syst.

Playing Catch-Up. A. B. Guthrie, Jr. 183p. 1985. 13.95 (ISBN 0-395-35633-4). HM.

Playing Catch-Up. A. B. Guthrie, Jr. 176p. 1987. pap. 2.95 (ISBN 0-553-26720-5). Bantam.

Playing Chess. Robert Wade. (Illus.). 144p. 1984. pap. 8.95 (ISBN 0-02-011980-1, Collier). Macmillan.

Playing Consequences. Niel Micklem. 1985. 10.00x (ISBN 0-317-62253-6, Guild of Pastoral Psych). State Mutual Bk.

Playing Dirty. M. E. Cooper. (Couples Ser.: No. 32). 192p. (YA) (gr. 7 up). 1988. pap. 2.50 (ISBN 0-590-41267-1). Scholastic Inc.

Playing Dirty: The Secret War Against Beliefs. Omar V. Garrison. cancelled. Church of Scient Info.

Playing Dirty: The Secret War Against Beliefs. Omar V. Garrison. LC 80-51315. (Illus.). 288p. 1980. 10.50; pap. 4.95 (ISBN 0-931116-05-8). Ralston-Pilot.

Playing Doctor: Television, Storytelling, & Medical Power. Joseph Turow. (Illus.). 368p. 1988. 24.95 (ISBN 0-19-504490-8). Oxford U Pr.

Playing Fast & Loose with Time & Space. P. S. Mueller. 1989. 4.95 (ISBN 0-671-67740-3). Meadowbrook.

Playing Favorites. James Knudsen. 128p. 1987. pap. 2.50 (ISBN 0-380-89736-9, Flare). Avon.

Playing Flag Football. John M. Ferrell. 32p. (gr. 1-6). 1983. pap. 2.00x (ISBN 0-88035-052-0, Pub. by YMCA USA). Human Kinetics.

Playing for High Stakes: The Men, Money & Power of Corporate Wives. Elaine Denholtz. LC 86-2020. 210p. 1985. 16.95 (ISBN 0-88191-030-9). Freundlich.

Playing for Keeps. 356p. 1989. pap. price not set. Tor Bks.

Playing for Keeps. Janice Stevens. (Sweet Dreams Ser.: No. 104). 176p. (Orig.). 1986. pap. 2.25 (ISBN 0-553-25428-6). Bantam.

Playing for Keeps. Jane Waterhouse. 320p. 1987. 18.95 (ISBN 0-02-624310-5). Macmillan.

Playing for Life: Sports Stories for Young Teens. Nathan Aaseng. LC 87-18837. (Augsburg Young Teens Ser). (Illus.). 112p. (Orig.). (YA) (gr. 7-10). 1988. pap. 4.50 (ISBN 0-8066-2279-2, 10-4997). Augsburg.

Playing from an Orchestral Score. Eric Taylor. (YA) (gr. 9 up). 1967. pap. 5.75 (ISBN 0-19-321730-9). Oxford U Pr.

Playing Games. Jana Ellis. LC 88-12389. (Merivale Mall Ser.). 160p. (YA) (gr. 7 up). 1988. pap. text ed. 2.50 (ISBN 0-8167-1358-8). Troll Assocs.

Playing Games. (Sweet Dreams Ser.: No. 110). 176p. (gr. 5-6). 1986. pap. 2.25 (ISBN 0-553-25642-4). Bantam.

Playing Games. Jody T. Sorenson. (Cheerleaders Ser.: No. 9). 192p. (Orig.). (gr. 7up). 1985. pap. 2.25 (ISBN 0-590-33705-X). Scholastic Inc.

Playing God in the Nursery. Jeff Lyon. 368p. 1986. pap. 9.95 (ISBN 0-393-30309-8). Norton.

Playing God in Yellowstone: The Destruction of America's First National Park. Alston Chase. 1987. pap. 10.95 (ISBN 0-15-672036-1, Harv). HarBraceJ.

Playing God: The New World of Medical Choices. Thomas Scully & Colin Scully. 432p. 1988. 19.95 (ISBN 0-671-60144-X). S&S.

Playing Grown-up Is Serious Business: Breaking Free of Addictive Family Patterns. Barry Weinhold. 256p. (Orig.). 1988. pap. 10.95 (ISBN 0-913299-51-0). Stillpoint.

Playing Hardball: The Dynamics of Baseball Folk Speech. Lawrence Frank. LC 83-48834. 150p. (Orig.). 1984. text ed. 9.60 (ISBN 0-8204-0061-0). P Lang Pubs.

Playing Hardball with Soft Skills. Steven J. Bennett. LC 85-47796. 256p. 1986. pap. 8.95 (ISBN 0-553-34233-9). Bantam.

Playing Hooky. Francine Pascal. (Sweet Valley Twins Ser.: No. 20). (YA) (gr. 6 up). pap. 2.50. Bantam.

Playing in the Band: An Oral & Visual Portrait of the Grateful Dead. David Gans & Peter Simon. LC 84-52537. (Illus.). 192p. 1985. pap. 14.95 (ISBN 0-312-61630-9). St Martin.

Playing in the Gospel: Spirtual & Pastoral Models. Thomas E. Clarke. LC 86-63282. 192p. (Orig.). 1986. pap. 8.95 (ISBN 1-55612-013-3). Sheed & Ward MO.

Playing in the Rain. Barbara E. Harmeyer. (Book Friends Ser.). (ps-k). 1987. 4.95 (ISBN 0-312-00778-7). St Martin.

Playing Inside & Out: How to Promote Social Growth & Learning in Young Children Including the Developmentally Delayed Child. Thomas D. Yawkey et al. LC 85-51121. 189p. 1986. 25.00 (ISBN 0-87762-419-4). Technomic.

Playing It Straight: A Practical Discussion of the Ethical Principles of the American Society of Newspaper Editors (ASNE) John L. Hulteng. LC 81-65984. 96p. (Orig.). 1981. pap. 5.95 (ISBN 0-87106-955-5). Globe Pequot.

Playing Joan: Actresses on the Challenge of Shaw's Saint Joan. Holly Hill. LC 87-10051. 272p. (Orig.). 1987. pap. 10.95 (ISBN 0-930452-64-X). Theatre Comm.

Playing, Living, Learning: A Worldwide Perspective on Children's Opportunities to Play. Cor Westland & Jane Knight. LC 81-69902. (Illus.). 211p. (Orig.). 1982. pap. 13.95x (ISBN 0-910251-02-9). Venture Pub PA.

Playing Marbles. Julie Brinckloe. (ps-3). 1988. 12.95 (ISBN 0-688-07143-0). Morrow.

Playing Marbles with Diamonds: And Other Messages for America. Vance Havner. 80p. 1985. text ed. 7.95 (ISBN 0-8010-4290-9). Baker Bk.

Playing Murder. Sandra Scoppettone. LC 83-47707. 224p. (YA) (gr. 7 up). 1985. 11.70i (ISBN 0-06-025283-9); PLB 11.89g (ISBN 0-06-025284-7). HarpJ.

Playing Murder. Sandra Scoppettone. LC 83-47707. 224p. (YA) (gr. 7 up). 1987. pap. 2.75 (ISBN 0-694-05609-X, Harper Keypoint). HarpJ.

Playing My Part. Frida Leider. Tr. by Charles Osborne. LC 77-26171. (Music Reprint Ser., 1978). (Illus.). 1978. Repr. of 1959 ed. lib. bdg. 32.50 (ISBN 0-306-77535-2). Da Capo.

Playing on the Playground. Dorothy Chlad. LC 87-5197. (Safety Town Ser.). (Illus.). 32p. (ps-2). 1987. PLB 11.93 (ISBN 0-516-01989-9). Childrens.

Playing on Words: A Guide to Luciano Berio's Sinfonia. David Osmond-Smith. 104p. 1987. 24.95x (ISBN 0-947854-00-2, Pub. by Royal Musical Assn UK). U of Chicago Pr.

Playing Period Plays. Lyn Oxenford. (Illus.). 1984. 15.00x; pap. 9.50x (ISBN 0-85343-549-9). Coach Hse.

Playing Politics. Michael Laver. (Pelican Ser.). 1981. pap. 4.95 (ISBN 0-14-022228-6, Pelican). Penguin.

Playing Ponies for Profit. Ted Mathias. Ed. & illus. by T. M. Piukkula. 68p. (Orig.). 1988. pap. 5.95 (ISBN 0-9620450-0-4). Profit Pub.

Playing Rhymes. (Tiny Tots Rhymes Ser.). 2.95 (ISBN 0-86112-086-8, Brimax Bks). Borden.

Playing Safe. Eileen Dewhurst. LC 86-19714. (Crime Club Ser.). 192p. 1987. 12.95 (ISBN 0-385-23557-7). Doubleday.

Playing Sardines. Beverly Major. LC 87-9621. (Illus.). 32p. (ps-2). 1988. 12.95 (ISBN 0-590-41153-5, Scholastic Hardcover). Scholastic Inc.

Playing Shakespeare. John Barton. 208p. 1984. pap. 10.95 (ISBN 0-413-54790-6, NO. 9041); 22.00 (ISBN 0-413-54780-9, NO. 9040). Heinemann Ed.

Playing Soccer. Ken Laitin & Steve Laitin. (gr. 3-7). pap. 1.95 (ISBN 0-590-32156-0). Scholastic Inc.

Playing Tahoe. Sandra Hochman. 1981. 13.95 (ISBN 0-671-25358-1, Wyndham Bks). S&S.

Playing Tennis. Sue Barker. LC 79-66012. (Illus.). 134p. 1982. pap. 5.95 (ISBN 0-8008-6322-4). Taplinger.

Playing the Bass Guitar. Verdine White & Louis Satterfield. Ed. by Norman Schwartz. (Illus.). 100p. (Orig.). 1978. pap. 6.95 (ISBN 0-89705-011-8). Almo Pubns.

Playing the Cards: Developing Competence at the Bridge Table. Norma Sands. 1984. pap. 5.95. Rocky Mtn Bks.

Playing the Changes. Thulani Davis. viii, 64p. 1985. 17.00 (ISBN 0-8195-1120-X); pap. 8.95 (ISBN 0-8195-2119-1). Wesleyan U Pr.

Playing the Chord Organ & Learning to Read Music. Albert De Vito. (Illus.). 1974. 4.95 (ISBN 0-934286-08-6). Kenyon.

Playing the Field. Mamie Van Doren & Art Aveilhe. 1988. pap. 3.95. Berkley Pub.

Playing the Field, No. 133. Eileen Hehl. (Sweet Dreams Ser.). 192p. 1987. pap. 2.50 (ISBN 0-553-26864-3, Sweet Dreams). Bantam.

Playing the Field: My Story. Mamie Van Doren & Art Aveilhe. (Illus.). 288p. 1987. 18.95 (ISBN 0-399-13240-6, Putnam). Putnam Pub Group.

Playing the Field: Why Defense Is the Most Fascinating Art in Major League Baseball. Jim Kaplan. (Illus.). 200p. 1987. pap. 13.95 (ISBN 0-912697-36-9). Algonquin Bks.

Playing the Game. Raymond Blank. (Ace Business Library Ser.). 224p. 1982. pap. 2.95 (ISBN 0-441-67075-X). Ace Bks.

Playing the Game. I. Strelkova. 246p. 1983. 6.95 (ISBN 0-8285-2578-1, Pub. by Raduga Pubs USSR). Imported Pubns.

Playing the Game: Sport & the Physical Emancipation of English Women, 1870-1914. Kathleen E. McCrone. LC 87-32038. (Illus.). 336p. 1988. 35.00 (ISBN 0-8131-1641-4). U Pr of Ky.

Playing the Guitar. 3rd ed. Frederick M. Noad. LC 80-5494. (Illus.). 1981. pap. 10.95 (ISBN 0-02-871990-5). Schirmer Bks.

Playing the Harpsichord: With Revised Introduction. Howard Schott. LC 78-11951. 1979. pap. 5.95 (ISBN 0-312-61636-8). St Martin.

Playing the Jack. Mary Brown. 584p. 1985. 16.95 (ISBN 0-671-54252-4). S&S.

Playing the Jack. Mary Brown. (Paperback Ser.). 704p. 1986. pap. text ed. 4.95 (ISBN 0-07-008295-2). McGraw.

Playing the Mischief. John W. De Forest. Ed. by Joseph J. Rubin. (Monument Edition Ser.). 24.50x (ISBN 0-271-00320-0). Pa St U Pr.

Playing the Mischief. John W. De Forest. (Collected Works of John W. De Forest). 1988. Repr. of 1875 ed. lib. bdg. 59.00x. Am Biog Serv.

Playing the Mischief see Collected Works.

Playing the Numbers. Myron Turner. 55p. (Orig.). 1986. pap. 5.00x (ISBN 0-940237-00-8). ND Qtr Pr.

Playing the Palace: A Westminister Collection. Ed. by James Naughtie. 1986. 49.75x (ISBN 0-906391-73-3, Pub. by Mainstream Scotland). State Mutual Bk.

Playing the Piano. Phyllis Irwin. 198p. 1988. Spiralbound. text ed. write for info. (ISBN 0-534-08769-8). Wadsworth Pub.

Playing the Piano for Pleasure. Charles Cooke. 1960. pap. 6.95 (ISBN 0-671-57801-4, Fireside). S&S.

Playing the Private College Admissions Game. rev. ed. Richard Moll. 260p. 1986. pap. 7.95 (ISBN 0-14-009385-0). Penguin.

Playing the Scottish Card: The Franco-Jacobite Invasion of 1708. John S. Gibson. 200p. 1988. 27.50x (ISBN 0-85224-567-X, Pub. by Edinburgh U Pr Scotland). Columbia U Pr.

Playing the Stock & Bond Markets with Your Personal Computer. L. R. Schmeltz. 308p. 1981. pap. 10.25 (ISBN 0-8306-1251-3, 1251). TAB Bks.

Playing the String Game: Strategies for Teaching Cello & Strings. Phyllis Young. (Illus.). 114p. 1978. pap. text ed. 11.95 (ISBN 0-292-73815-3). U of Tex Pr.

Playing the Viola: Conversations with William Primrose. David Dalton. (Illus.). 272p. 1988. 34.50 (ISBN 0-19-318514-8). Oxford U Pr.

Playing Their Game Our Way: Using the Political Process to Meet Community Needs. Greg L. Speeter. LC 79-106542. (Illus., Orig.). 1978. pap. 7.00 (ISBN 0-934210-06-3). Devlp Commy.

Playing to Win. James Plaskett. (Chess Library). 1988. pap. 9.95 (ISBN 0-02-044711-6, Collier). Macmillan.

Playing to Win: Fran Tarkenton's Strategies for Business Success. Fran Tarkenton. LC 83-48390. 192p. 1984. 12.45i (ISBN 0-06-015242-7, HarpT). Har-Row.

Playing Urban Games: The Systems Approach to Planning. Martin Kuenzlen. LC 75-189032. 1978. 16.50x (ISBN 0-262-11069-5); pap. 6.95x (ISBN 0-262-61028-0). MIT Pr.

Playing with Energy. Ed. by Helen Carey. 106p. (Orig.). 1981. pap. 5.00 (ISBN 0-87355-020-X). Natl Sci Tchrs.

Playing with Fire. (Sweet Valley High Ser.: No. 3). 149p. (YA) (gr. 7-12). 1983. pap. 2.75 (ISBN 0-553-26627-6). Bantam.

Playing with Fire see Plays from the Cynical Life.

Playing with Fire: Dungeons & Dragons, Tunnels & Trolls, Chivalry & Sorcery & Other Fantasy Games. John Weldon & James Bjornstad. (Orig.). 1984. pap. 4.95 (ISBN 0-8024-0425-1). Moody.

Playing with Form: Children Draw in Six Countries. Alexander Alland, Jr. LC 82-25269. (Illus.). 224p. 1983. 35.00x (ISBN 0-231-05608-7); pap. 17.50x (ISBN 0-231-05609-5). Columbia U Pr.

Playing with Grown Ups. Fritz A. Callies. 1978. pap. 6.95 (ISBN 0-8100-0007-5, 11N0623). Northwest Pub.

Playing with Infinity: Mathematical Explorations & Excursions. Rozsa Peter. LC 75-26467. 288p. 1976. pap. text ed. 4.95 (ISBN 0-486-23265-4). Dover.

Playing with Logic. Mark Schoenfield & Jeanette Rosenblatt. (gr. 3-5). 1985. pap. 6.95 (ISBN 0-8224-5310-X). D S Lake Pubs.

Playing with Shadows: Stories. Gloria Whelan. LC 87-35690. (Illinois Short Fiction Ser.). 120p. 1988. 11.95 (ISBN 0-252-01524-X). U of Ill Pr.

Playing with Water: Passion & Solitude on a Philippine Island. James Hamilton-Paterson. 288p. 1987. 19.95 (ISBN 0-941533-10-7). New Amsterdam Bks.

Playland. Tom Zigal. 1979. 10.00 (ISBN 0-914476-91-2). Thorp Springs.

Playmaker. Thomas Keneally. 352p. 1987. 18.95 (ISBN 0-671-49343-4). S&S.

Playmaker. Thomas Keneally. LC 88-45036. 352p. 1988. pap. 8.95 (ISBN 0-06-097189-4, PL 7189, PL). Har-Row.

Playmaster. John Dalmas & Rod Martin. pap. 3.50. PB.

Playmasters. Rod Martin & John Dalmas. 1987. 3.50 (ISBN 0-671-65610-4). Baen Bks.

Playmates. Janet Ahlberg & Allan Ahlberg. LC 84-40123. (Slot Bks.). 20p. (ps-3). 1985. pap. 7.95 (ISBN 0-670-55988-1, Viking Kestrel). Viking.

Playmates. Barbara J. Crane. (Crane Reading System-English Ser.). (Illus.). (gr. k-2). 1977. pap. text ed. 3.86 (ISBN 0-89075-096-3). Crane Pub Co.

Playmates. Andrew Neiderman. 336p. (Orig.). 1987. pap. 3.95 (ISBN 0-425-09898-2). Berkley Pub.

Playmates. J. N. Williamson. 304p. 1986. pap. 3.50 (ISBN 0-8439-2362-8, Leisure Bks). Leisure NY.

Playoff: Professional Football's Great Championship Games. Howard Liss. LC 66-10675. (Illus.). (gr. 7 up). 1966. pap. 4.50 (ISBN 0-440-06939-4). Delacorte.

Playreadings. Louise Frankenstein. 132p. 1933. 5.00 (ISBN 0-573-60074-0). French.

Playrights of the New American Theatre. Thomas H. Dickinson. 1981. Repr. lib. bdg. 30.00 (ISBN 0-403-00943-X). Scholarly.

Playroom. Gloria Murphy. LC 87-45108. 256p. 1988. 17.95 (ISBN 1-55611-043-X). D I Fine.

Plays. Harley G. Barker. Ed. by Dennis Kennedy. (British & American Playrights, 1750-1920 Ser.). (Illus.). 288p. 1987. 42.50 (ISBN 0-521-30642-6); pap. 14.95 (ISBN 0-521-31407-0). Cambridge U Pr.

Plays. Dion Boucicault. Ed. by Peter Thomson. LC 83-7856. (British & American Playwrights Series, 1750 to 1920). (Illus.). 230p. 1984. 52.50 (ISBN 0-521-23997-4); pap. 17.95 (ISBN 0-521-28395-7). Cambridge U Pr.

Plays. Anton Chekhov. Tr. by Elisaveta Fen. Incl. Ivanov; Seagull; Uncle Vanya; Three Sisters; Cherry Orchard; Bear; The Marriage Proposal; Jubilee. (Classics Ser.). 1959. pap. 3.95 (ISBN 0-14-044096-8). Penguin.

Plays. Augustine Daly. Ed. by Don B. Wilmeth & Rosemary Cullen. LC 83-18929. (British & American Playwrights Series, 1750 to 1920). (Illus.). 250p. 1984. 49.50 (ISBN 0-521-24090-5); pap. 16.95 (ISBN 0-521-28432-5). Cambridge U Pr.

Plays. Samuel Foote & Arthur Murphy. Ed. by George Taylor. LC 83-18930. (British & American Playwrights Ser.). 220p. 1984. 49.50 (ISBN 0-521-24132-4); pap. 15.95 (ISBN 0-521-28467-8). Cambridge U Pr.

Plays. William S. Gilbert. Ed. by George Rowell. LC 81-12248. (British & American Playwrights 1750-1920 Ser.). (Illus.). 250p. 1982. 39.50 (ISBN 0-521-23589-8); pap. 13.95 (ISBN 0-521-28056-7). Cambridge U Pr.

Plays. William H. Gillette. Ed. by Rosemary Cullen & Don B. Wilmeth. LC 82-14692. (British & American Playwrights Ser.: 1750 - 1920). (Illus.). 250p. 1983. 39.50 (ISBN 0-521-24089-1); pap. 13.95 (ISBN 0-521-28431-7). Cambridge U Pr.

Plays. Susan Glaspell. Ed. by C. W. Bigsby. (British & American Playwrights 1750-1920 Ser.). (Illus.). 176p. 1987. 42.50 (ISBN 0-521-30945-X); pap. 14.95 (ISBN 0-521-31204-3). Cambridge U Pr.

Plays. Richard Morris. 1973. pap. 2.50 (ISBN 0-685-37099-2). Twowindows Pr.

Plays. Alexander Ostrovsky. Ed. by George R. Noyes. LC 70-98632. Repr. of 1917 ed. 24.00 (ISBN 0-404-04837-4). AMS Pr.

Plays. A. W. Pinero. Ed. by G. Rowell. (British & American Playwrights 1750-1920 Ser.). (Illus.). 315p. 1986. 47.50 (ISBN 0-521-24103-0); pap. 17.95 (ISBN 0-521-28440-6). Cambridge U Pr.

Plays. James R. Planche. Ed. by D. Roy. (British & American Playwrights 1750-1920 Ser.). 241p. 1986. 47.50 (ISBN 0-521-24111-1); pap. 17.95 (ISBN 0-521-28441-4). Cambridge U Pr.

Plays. Charles Reade. Ed. by Michael Hammet. (British & American Playwrights 1750-1920 Ser.). (Illus.). 200p. 1986. 47.50 (ISBN 0-521-24361-0); pap. 14.95 (ISBN 0-521-28627-1). Cambridge U Pr.

Plays. William Shakespeare. Ed. by John P. Collier. LC 72-175850. Repr. of 1853 ed. 32.50 (ISBN 0-404-01615-4). AMS Pr.

Plays, 8 vols. William Shakespeare. Ed. by Samuel Johnson. LC 68-59595. Repr. of 1765 ed. Set. 375.00 (ISBN 0-404-05810-8). AMS Pr.

Plays. George Bernard Shaw. pap. 4.95 (ISBN 0-451-51786-5, CE1786, Sig Classics). NAL.

Plays. Tom Taylor. Ed. by Martin Banham. (British & American Playwrights 1750-1920 Ser.). (Illus.). 243p. 1985. 47.50 (ISBN 0-521-24102-2); pap. 17.95 (ISBN 0-521-28439-2). Cambridge U Pr.

Plays. Heinrich Von Kleist. Ed. by Walter Hinderer. LC 81-22060. (German Library: Vol. 25). 340p. 1982. 27.50x (ISBN 0-8264-0253-4); pap. 8.95 (ISBN 0-8264-0263-1). Continuum.

Plays, Vol. 3. Edward Albee. Incl. Seascape; Counting the Ways & Listening; All Over. 1982. pap. 9.95 (ISBN 0-689-70615-4). Atheneum.

Plays About the Theatre in England, Seventeen Thirty-Seven to Eighteen Hundred or, the Self-Conscious Stage from Foote to Sheridan. Dane F. Smith & M. L. Lawhon. LC 77-74409. 288p. 1979. 25.00 (ISBN 0-8387-2074-9). Bucknell U Pr.

Plays, Acting & Music: A Book of Theory. Arthur Symons. 1978. Repr. of 1928 ed. lib. bdg. 29.00 (ISBN 0-8492-8077-X). R West.

Plays: An Enemy of the People, the Wild Duck, Rosmersholm. Henrik Ibsen. Ed. by J. W. McFarlane. (Oxford Paperbacks Ser.: No. 254). 1971. pap. 9.95x (ISBN 0-19-281109-6). Oxford U Pr.

Plays & Essays. Friedrich Durrenmatt. Ed. by Volkmar Sander. LC 81-22184. (German Library: Vol. 89). 315p. 1982. 27.50x (ISBN 0-8264-0257-7); pap. 10.95 (ISBN 0-8264-0267-4). Continuum.

Plays & Fragments: Menander. Tr. by Norma Miller. 274p. 1988. pap. 6.95 (ISBN 0-14-044501-3). Penguin.

Plays & Novels of Peter Handke. June Schlueter. LC 81-50242. (Critical Essays in Modern Literature Ser.). 226p. 1981. 21.95x (ISBN 0-8229-3443-4); pap. 10.95x (ISBN 0-8229-5330-7). U of Pittsburgh Pr.

Plays & Players in Modern Italy. Addison McLeod. LC 79-102848. 1970. Repr. of 1912 ed. 26.50x (ISBN 0-8046-0758-3, Pub. by Kennikat). Assoc Faculty Pr.

Plays & Players: Thirty Years of British Theatre 1953-1968, Vol. 1. Ed. by Peter Roberts. (Illus.). 256p. (Orig.). 35.00x (ISBN 0-413-52960-6, 9385); pap. 15.95x (ISBN 0-413-52970-3, 9372). Heinemann Ed.

Plays & Players: Thirty Years of British Theatre 1969-1983, Vol. 2. Ed. by Peter Roberts. (Illus.). 256p. (Orig.). 1985. 35.00x (ISBN 0-413-53720-X, 9386); pap. 15.95x (ISBN 0-413-53730-7, 9373). Heinemann Ed.

Plays & Players: Thirty Years of British Theatre 1953-1983 Vol. Two 1969-1983. Peter Roberts. (Illus.). 256p. 1987. lib. bdg. 35.00x (ISBN 0-317-61820-2); pap. 15.95x (ISBN 0-317-61821-0). Routledge Chapman & Hall.

Plays & Players: Thirty Years of British Theatre 1953-1983, Vol. One-1953-1968. Ed. by Peter Roberts. (Illus.). 256p. 1987. lib. bdg. 35.00x (ISBN 0-317-61817-2); pap. 15.95x (ISBN 0-317-61818-0). Routledge Chapman & Hall.

Plays & Playhouses in Imperial Decadence. Ed. by Anthony N. Zahareas. (Series Towards a Social History of Hispanic & Luso-Brazilian Literatures). 118p. (Orig.). 1987. pap. text ed. 6.95 (ISBN 0-910235-15-5). Prisma Bks.

Plays & Playwrights. Ed. by Andrew Delaplaine. (Orig.). 1986. pap. 29.95 (ISBN 0-934131-01-5). Inter Soc Drama.

Plays & Poems, 2 vols. George H. Boker. Repr. of 1856 ed. Set. 67.50 (ISBN 0-404-00930-1). AMS Pr.

Plays & Poems, 2 vols. Robert Greene. Ed. by John C. Collins. LC 79-130985. Repr. of 1905 ed. Set. 37.00 (ISBN 0-404-01634-0). Vol. 1 (ISBN 0-404-01635-9). Vol. 2 (ISBN 0-404-01636-7). AMS Pr.

Plays & Poems, 21 vols. William Shakespeare. Ed. by James Boswell. LC 68-59049. Repr. of 1821 ed. Set. 985.00 (ISBN 0-404-05870-1). AMS Pr.

Plays & Poems, 10 vols. William Shakespeare. Ed. by Edmond Malone. LC 68-59049. Repr. of 1790 ed. Set. 595.00 (ISBN 0-404-05850-7). AMS Pr.

Plays & Poems of Cyril Tourneur, 2 vols. Cyril Tourneur. LC 77-38370. (Select Bibliographies Reprint Ser). Repr. of 1878 ed. 34.50 (ISBN 0-8369-6787-9). Ayer Co Pubs.

Plays & Poems of Mercy Otis Warren. Mercy Otis Warren. LC 80-16625. 1980. 60.00x (ISBN 0-8201-1344-1). Schol Facsimiles.

Plays & Poems of Philip Massinger, 5 vols. Philip Massinger. Ed. by Philip Edwards & Colin Gibson. (Oxford English Texts Ser). 1976. 198.00x set (ISBN 0-19-811894-5). Oxford U Pr.

Plays & Poems of Robert Greene, 2 Vols. facs. ed. Robert Greene. Ed. by J. Churton Collins. LC 79-119957. (Select Bibliographies Reprint Ser). 1905. Set. 36.00 (ISBN 0-8369-5400-9). Ayer Co Pubs.

Plays & Poems, 1948-58. Elder Olson. LC 58-11951. (Midway Reprint Ser.). x, 170p. 1975. pap. text ed. 5.95x (ISBN 0-226-62896-5). U of Chicago Pr.

Plays & Puppets et Cetera. Courtaney Brooks. LC 81-68933. (Illus.). 100p. (Orig.). (gr. k up). 1981. pap. 11.95x (ISBN 0-941274-00-4). Belnice Bks.

Plays & Stories. Arthur Schnitzler. Ed. by Egon Schwartz. LC 82-18263. (German Library: Vol. 55). 320p. 1983. 27.50x (ISBN 0-8264-0270-4); pap. 10.95 (ISBN 0-8264-0271-2). Continuum.

Plays As Experience: One-Act Plays for the Secondary Schools. rev. ed. Ed. by Irwin J. Zachar. LC 62-13411. 1962. pap. 10.83 scp (ISBN 0-672-73228-9). Odyssey Pr.

Plays: Babes in the Wood, the Lancashire Lass, Our Boys & the Gaeity Gulliver. H. J. Byron & Jim Davis. LC 83-7852. (British & American Playwrights Series, 1750-1920). (Illus.). 220p. 1984. 47.50 (ISBN 0-521-24175-8). Cambridge U Pr.

Plays by American Women: Nineteen Hundred to Nineteen Thirty. rev. ed. Ed. by Judith Barlow. LC 84-24606. 304p. 1985. 24.95 (ISBN 1-55783-007-X); pap. 8.95 (ISBN 1-55783-008-8). Applause Theatre Bk Pubs.

Plays by American Women: The Early Years see Plays by American Women: 1900-1930.

Plays by American Women: 1900-1930. rev. ed. Ed. by Judith Barlow. Orig. Title: Plays by American Women: The Early Years. 265p. 1987. 24.95 (ISBN 0-317-65859-X); pap. 8.95 (ISBN 0-317-65860-3). Applause Theatre Bk Pubs.

Plays by & About Woman: An Anthology. Ed. by Victoria Sullivan & James Hatch. 1973. pap. 6.95 (ISBN 0-394-71896-8, Vin). Random.

Plays by David Garrick & George Colman the Elder. David Garrick & George Colman. Ed. by E. R. Wood. LC 81-17079. (British & American Playwrights 1750-1920 Ser.). 200p. 1982. 39.50 (ISBN 0-521-23590-1); pap. 14.95 (ISBN 0-521-28057-5). Cambridge U Pr.

Plays by George Colman the Younger & Thomas Morton: Inkle & Yarico; The Surrender of Calis; The Children in the Wood, Blue Beard & Speed the Plough. George Colman & Thomas Morton. Ed. by Barry Sutcliffe. LC 83-5156. (British & American Playwrights Ser.: 1750-1920). (Illus.). 246p. 1983. 47.50 (ISBN 0-521-24019-0); pap. 14.95 (ISBN 0-521-28400-7). Cambridge U Pr.

Plays by Leonid Andreyeff: The Life of Man, the Black Maskers, the Sabine Women. Leonid N. Andreev. Tr. by Clarence L. Meader & Fred N. Scott. LC 80-2885. (BCL Ser.: I & II). Repr. of 1915 ed. AMS Pr.

Plays by Tom Robertson. Tom Robertson. Ed. by William Tydeman. LC 81-10249. (British & American Playwrights 1750-1920 Ser.). (Illus.). 256p. 1982. 39.50 (ISBN 0-521-23386-0); pap. 13.95 (ISBN 0-521-29939-X). Cambridge U Pr.

Plays by Webster & Ford. John Webster. LC 75-41291. Repr. of 1933 ed. 19.50 (ISBN 0-404-14628-7). AMS Pr.

Plays by Women. Selected by & intro. by Mary Remnant. (Methuen Theatrescript Ser.). 200p. 1988. pap. 13.95 (ISBN 0-413-14080-6). Heinemann Ed.

Plays by Women, Vol. 1. Ed. by Michelene Wandor. 128p. 1982. pap. 8.50 (ISBN 0-413-50020-9, NO. 3634). Heinemann Ed.

Plays by Women, Vol. 2. Ed. by Michelene Wandor. 128p. 1983. pap. 8.50 (ISBN 0-413-51030-1, NO. 3804). Heinemann Ed.

Plays by Women, Vol. 3. Ed. by Michelene Wandor. 128p. 1984. pap. 8.50 (ISBN 0-413-54300-5, NO. 3994). Heinemann Ed.

Plays by Women, Vol. 4. Michelene Wandor. (Theatrefiles Ser.). 128p. 1985. pap. 8.95 (ISBN 0-413-56740-0, 9163). Heinemann Ed.

Plays by Women, Vol. 5. Ed. by Mary Remnant. (Methuen Theatrefile Ser.). 160p. 1986. pap. 8.95 (ISBN 0-413-41570-8, 9993). Heinemann Ed.

Plays Children Love, Vol. II. Coleman A. Jennings & Aurand Harris. 512p. 1988. 19.95x (ISBN 0-312-01490-2). St Martin.

Plays Children Love: A Treasury of Contemporary & Classic Plays for Children. Aurand Harris & Coleman Jennings. LC 80-2412. (Illus.). 678p. (gr. k-12). 1981. pap. 16.95 (ISBN 0-385-17096-3). Doubleday.

Plays Confuted in Five Actions. Stephen Gosson. 128p. Repr. of 1582 ed. 22.00 (ISBN 0-384-19335-8). Johnson Repr.

Plays, Dreams & Imitation in Childhood. Jean Piaget. 1988. 17.00 (ISBN 0-8446-6320-4). Peter Smith.

Plays: Five. Noel Coward. 432p. 1983. pap. 9.95 (ISBN 0-394-62456-4, B486, BC). Grove.

Plays for a New Theatre: Playbook 2. Incl. Long Night of Medea. Corrado Alvaro; Methusalem or the Eternal Bourgeois. Ivan Goll; Assault Upon Charles Sumner. Robert Hivnor; Wax Museum. John Hawkes; Knackery for All. Boris Vian. LC 66-17821. (Orig.). 7.50 (ISBN 0-8112-0245-3); pap. 2.95 (ISBN 0-8112-0000-0, NDP216). New Directions.

Plays for a Nuclear Age. Ed. by Dieke et al. 1988. pap. text ed. 11.95 (ISBN 0-948553-15-4, Playwrights Pr). Routledge Chapman & Hall.

Plays for Assembly. Peter M. Allen. (Illus.). 143p. 1987. 49.00x (ISBN 0-7217-3019-1, Pub. by Schofield & Sims UK). State Mutual Bk.

Plays for Pagans. Colin C. Clements. LC 77-94337. (One-Act Plays in Reprint Ser.). 1978. Repr. of 1924 ed. 18.75x (ISBN 0-8486-2035-6). Roth Pub Inc.

Plays for Players. Alun Richards. 367p. 1985. 35.50x (ISBN 0-85088-290-7, Pub. by Gomer Pr). State Mutual Bk.

Plays for Poet-Mimes. Alfred Kreymborg. LC 76-40388. (One-Act Plays in Reprint Ser.). 1976. Repr. of 1918 ed. 16.50x (ISBN 0-8486-2004-6). Roth Pub Inc.

Plays for the Children's Hour: An American Childhood Presentation. Ed. by Carolyn S. Bailey. LC 77-94332. (One-Act Plays in Reprint Ser.). 1978. Repr. of 1931 ed. 21.50x (ISBN 0-8486-2032-1). Roth Pub Inc.

Plays for the Poor Theatre: Five Short Plays (the Saliva Milkshake, Christie in Love, Heads, Skinny Spew, Gum & Goo) Howard Brenton. 104p. 1980. pap. 7.95 (ISBN 0-413-47080-6, NO. 2115). Heinemann Ed.

Plays for the Special Education Classroom. Charlotte Gibberman. 56p. 1986. pap. text ed. 5.95x (ISBN 0-8134-2612-X). Inter Print Pubs.

Plays: Four. Noel Coward. 512p. (Orig.). 1981. pap. 9.95 (ISBN 0-394-17943-9, B-462, BC). Grove.

Plays Friedrich Schiller. Ed. by Walter Hinderer. LC 83-7741. (German Library: Vol. 15). 346p. 1983. 27.50x (ISBN 0-8264-0274-7); pap. 10.95 (ISBN 0-8264-0275-5). Continuum.

Plays from Famous Stories & Fairy Tales. Adele Thane. (gr. 4-7). 1983. pap. 12.95 (ISBN 0-8238-0262-0). Plays.

Plays from Far & Wide. Merna Cichon. 56p. (Orig.). 1985. pap. 4.95 (ISBN 0-86417-023-8, Pub. by Kangaroo Pr). Intl Spec Bk.

Plays from Favorite Folk Tales. Ed. by Sylvia E. Kamerman. (Orig.). (gr. 2 up). 1987. pap. 13.95 (ISBN 0-8238-0280-9). Plays.

Plays from Padua Hills, 1982. Ed. by Murray Mednick. 1983. pap. 7.00 (ISBN 0-9611066-0-3). PAJ Pubns.

Plays from the Contemporary American Theater. Ed. by Brooks McNamara. 1988. pap. 4.95 (ISBN 0-451-62580-3, Mentor). NAL.

Plays from the Cynical Life. August Strindberg. Tr. by Walter Johnson from Swedish. Incl. Debit & Credit; Facing Death; First Warning; Mother Love; Pariah; Playing with Fire; Simoon. LC 82-13581. (Illus.). 144p. 1983. 25.00x (ISBN 0-295-95980-0). U of Wash Pr.

Plays in Review: 1956-1980. Ed. by Gareth Evans & Barbara L. Evans. 256p. 1985. 17.95 (ISBN 0-416-01171-3, 9684). Routledge Chapman & Hall.

Plays Introduction One. 352p. (Orig.). 1984. pap. 9.95 (ISBN 0-571-13038-0). Faber & Faber.

Plays Modelled on the Noh (1916) Ezra Pound. Ed. by Donald C. Gallup. (Illus.). 38p. 1987. pap. 17.00x (ISBN 0-918160-02-2). Friends Univ Toledo.

Plays of Aaron Hill. Aaron Hill. Ed. by Calhoun Winton. (Eighteenth Century English Drama Ser.). 1981. lib. bdg. 73.00 (ISBN 0-8240-3593-3). Garland Pub.

Plays of Anton Chekhov. Anton Chekhov. 19.95 (ISBN 0-89190-432-8, Pub. by Am Repr). Amereon Ltd.

Plays of Arthur Murphy, 4 vols. Arthur Murphy. Ed. by Paula R. Backscheider. LC 78-66610. (Eighteenth-Century English Drama Ser.: Vol. 30). 1980. Set. lib. bdg. 290.00 (ISBN 0-8240-3604-2); lib. bdg. 50.00 ea. Garland Pub.

Plays of Beaumont & Fletcher. Ernest H. Oliphant. LC 73-126657. Repr. of 1927 ed. 12.50 (ISBN 0-404-04814-5). AMS Pr.

Plays of Beaumont & Fletcher. Ernest H. Oliphant. LC 70-93250. 968p. 1970. Repr. of 1927 ed. 65.00x (ISBN 0-87753-030-0). Phaeton.

Plays of Beaumont & Fletcher: An Attempt to Determine Their Respective Shares & the Shares of Others. Ernest H. Oliphant. 1971. Repr. of 1927 ed. 10.00x (ISBN 0-403-01138-8). Scholarly.

Plays of Ben Jonson: A Reference Guide. Walter D. Lehrman & Dolores J. Sarafinski. 1980. lib. bdg. 41.50 (ISBN 0-8161-8112-8, Hall Reference). G K Hall.

Plays of Black Americans. Ed. by Sylvia E. Kamerman. LC 87-12207. (Orig.). (gr. 2-9). 1987. pap. 10.95 (ISBN 0-8238-0279-5). Plays.

Plays of Charles Gildon. Charles Gildon. Ed. by Paula R. Backscheider. LC 78-66609. (Eighteenth-Century English Drama Ser.: Vol. 17). 1979. lib. bdg. 73.00 (ISBN 0-8240-3591-7). Garland Pub.

Plays of Colley Cibber, 2 vols. Colley Cibber. Ed. by Rodney Hayley. LC 78-66634. (Eighteenth Century English Drama Ser.). 1980. Set. lib. bdg. 145.00 (ISBN 0-8240-3582-8). Garland Pub.

Plays of Confession & Therapy: To Damascus I, to Damascus II, & to Damascus III. August Strindberg. Tr. by Walter Johnson from Swedish. LC 78-20962. (Illus.). 260p. 1979. 25.00x (ISBN 0-295-95567-8). U of Wash Pr.

Plays of Cyril Tourneur. Ed. by G. Parfitt. LC 77-77014. (Plays by Renaissance & Restoration Dramatists Ser.). 1978. 37.50 (ISBN 0-521-21697-4); pap. 10.95 (ISBN 0-521-29235-2). Cambridge U Pr.

Plays of David Garrick, 4 vols. David Garrick. Ed. by Gerald Berkowitz. (Eighteenth Century English Drama Ser.). 1981. lib. bdg. 290.00 (ISBN 0-8240-3590-9). Garland Pub.

Plays of David Garrick, Vol. 1: Garrick's Own Plays, 1740-1766. Ed. by Harry W. Pedicord & Fredrick L. Bergmann. LC 79-28443. (Plays of David Garrick). (Illus.). 480p. 1980. 35.00x (ISBN 0-8093-0862-2). S Ill U Pr.

Plays of David Garrick, Vol. 2: Garrick's Own Plays, 1767-1775. Ed. by Harry W. Pedicord & Fredrick L. Bergmann. LC 79-28443. (Illus.). 444p. 1980. 35.00x (ISBN 0-8093-0863-0). S Ill U Pr.

Plays of David Garrick, Vol. 3: Garrick's Adaptations of Shakespeare, 1744-1756. Ed. by Harry W. Pedicord & Fredrick L. Bergmann. LC 79-28443. (Illus.). 496p. 1981. 50.00x (ISBN 0-8093-0968-8). S Ill U Pr.

Plays of David Garrick, Vol. 4: Garrick's Adaptions of Shakespeare, 1759-1773. Ed. by Harry W. Pedicord & Fredrick L. Bergmann. LC 79-28443. (Illus.). 1981. 50.00x (ISBN 0-8093-0969-6). S Ill U Pr.

Plays of David Garrick, Vol. 5: Garrick's Alterations of Others, 1742-1750. Ed. by Harry W. Pedicord & Fredrick L. Bergmann. LC 79-28443. 485p. 1982. 50.00x (ISBN 0-8093-0993-9). S Ill U Pr.

Plays of David Garrick, Vol. 6: Garrick's Alterations of Others, 1751-1756. Ed. by Harry W. Pedicord & Fredrick L. Bergmann. LC 79-28443. 453p. 1982. 50.00x (ISBN 0-8093-0994-7). S Ill U Pr.

Plays of David Garrick, Vol. 7: Garrick's Alterations of Others, 1757-1773. Ed. by Harry W. Pedicord & Fredrick L. Bergmann. LC 79-28443. 399p. 1982. 50.00x (ISBN 0-8093-1051-1). S Ill U Pr.

Plays of David Mallet. David Mallet. Ed. by Felicity Nussbaum. LC 78-66605. (Eighteenth-Century English Drama Ser.: Vol. 28). 1980. lib. bdg. 73.00 (ISBN 0-8240-3602-6). Garland Pub.

Plays of David Storey: A Thematic Study. William Hutchings. LC 87-35985. 256p. 1988. text ed. 25.95x (ISBN 0-8093-1461-4). S Ill U Pr.

Plays of Democracy. Ed. by Margaret Mayorga. 310p. 1981. Repr. of 1944 ed. lib. bdg. 39.50 (ISBN 0-89987-598-X). Darby Bks.

Plays of Edward Bond. Richard Scharine. 302p. Date not set. 24.50 (ISBN 0-8387-1538-9). Bucknell U Pr.

Plays of Edward Moore. Ed. by J. Paul Hunter. LC 78-66606. (Eighteenth Century English Drama Ser.). 1982. lib. bdg. 73.00 (ISBN 0-8240-3603-4). Garland Pub.

Plays of Edward Thompson. Edward Thompson. Ed. by P. R. Backsheider & Catherine N. Parke. LC 81-66631. (Eighteenth Century English Drama Ser.). lib. bdg. 73.00 (ISBN 0-8240-3608-5). Garland Pub.

Plays of Eliza Haywood. Valerie C. Rudolph. LC 78-66619. (Eighteenth Century English Drama Ser.). 1982. lib. bdg. 73.00 (ISBN 0-8240-3592-5). Garland Pub.

Plays of Elizabeth Inchbald, 2 Vols. Elizabeth Inchbald. Ed. by Paula R. Backscheider. LC 78-66648. (Eighteenth Century English Drama Ser.). lib. bdg. 145.00 (ISBN 0-8240-3597-6). Garland Pub.

Plays of Eugene O'Neill, 3 vols. Eugene O'Neill. 1941. boxed set o.p. 30.00 (ISBN 0-394-40654-0). Random.

Plays of Eugene O'Neill, 3 vols. Eugene O'Neill. LC 83-42952. 1982. 10.95 ea. Vol. I (ISBN 0-394-60805-4). Vol. II (ISBN 0-394-60806-2). Vol. III (ISBN 0-394-60807-0). Modern Lib.

Plays of Eugene O'Neill: A New Assessment. Virginia Floyd. (Literature & Life Ser.). (Illus.). 350p. 1984. pap. 24.50x (ISBN 0-8044-2206-0). Ungar.

Plays of Eugene O'Neill: A New Assessment. Virginia Floyd. (Illus.). 640p. 1987. pap. 15.95 (ISBN 0-8044-6153-8). Ungar.

Plays of Frances Sheridan. Ed. by Robert Hogan & Jerry C. Beasley. LC 82-49304. (Illus.). 216p. 1984. 27.50 (ISBN 0-87413-243-6). U Delaware Pr.

Plays of Frederick Reynolds, 3 vols. Ed. by Stanley W. Lindberg. LC 78-66625. (Eighteenth Century English Drama Ser.). 1982. lib. bdg. 218.00 Set (ISBN 0-8240-3607-7). Garland Pub.

Plays of Georg Buchner. Georg Buchner. Tr. by Victor Price. 1971. pap. 5.95x (ISBN 0-19-281120-7). Oxford U Pr.

Plays of George Chapman: The Comedies. Allan Holaday. 1982. 90.00 (ISBN 0-85991-266-3, Pub. by Boydell & Brewer). Longwood Pub Group.

Plays of George Chapman: Tragedies. Ed. by Alan Holaday et al. (The Tragedies, with Sir Gyles Goosecappe - A Critical Edition). 1987. 108.00 (ISBN 0-85991-243-4, Pub. by Boydell & Brewer). Longwood Pub Group.

Plays of George Colman, The Elder, 6 vols. Ed. by Kalman Burnim. LC 78-66618. (Eighteenth Century English Drama Ser.). 1982. lib. bdg. 436.00 Set (ISBN 0-8240-3584-4). Garland Pub.

Plays of George Colman, the Younger. George the Younger Colman. Ed. by Peter A. Tasch. (Eighteenth Century English Drama Ser.). 1981. lib. bdg. 145.00 (ISBN 0-8240-3585-2). Garland Pub.

Plays of George Fitzmaurice: Folkplays, Vol. 2. George Fitzmaurice. 1970. 12.95 (ISBN 0-85105-013-1). Dufour.

Plays of George Fitzmaurice: Realistic Plays, Vol. 3. George Fitzmaurice. Ed. by Howard K. Slaughter. 1970. 12.95 (ISBN 0-85105-174-X). Dufour.

Plays of George Lillo, 2 Vols. George Lillo. Ed. by Trudy Drucker. LC 78-66658. (Eighteenth-Century English Drama Ser.: Vol. 27). 1980. lib. bdg. 145.00 (ISBN 0-8240-3601-8). Garland Pub.

Plays of Gods & Men. Lord Dunsany. 1979. Repr. of 1917 ed. lib. bdg. 30.00 (ISBN 0-8495-1102-X). Arden Lib.

Plays of Gods & Men. Lord Dunsany. LC 77-70355. (One-Act Plays in Reprint Ser.). 1977. Repr. of 1917 ed. 16.50x (ISBN 0-8486-2015-1). Roth Pub Inc.

Plays of Grillparzer. G. A. Wells. 1969. 21.00 (ISBN 0-08-012950-1); pap. 10.25 (ISBN 0-08-012949-8). Pergamon.

Plays of Hannah Cowley, 2 vols. Hannah Cowley. Ed. by Frederick M. Link. LC 78-66646. (Eighteenth-Century English Drama Ser.: Vol. 12). 1980. Set. lib. bdg. 145.00 (ISBN 0-8240-3586-0); lib. bdg. 50.00 ea. Garland Pub.

Plays of Henry Carey. Henry Carey. Ed. by Samuel C. Macey. LC 78-66613. (Eighteenth Century English Drama Ser.). 1980. lib. bdg. 73.00 (ISBN 0-8240-3580-1). Garland Pub.

Plays of Henry Medwall. Henry Medwall. Ed. by Alan H. Nelson. (Tudor Interludes Ser.: No. II). 245p. 1981. 42.00 (ISBN 0-85991-054-7, Pub. by Boydell & Brewer). Longwood Pub Group.

Plays of Henry Medwall: A Critical Edition. M. E. Moeslein. LC 79-54353. (Renaissance Drama Ser.). 400p. 1982. lib. bdg. 53.00 (ISBN 0-8240-4470-3). Garland Pub.

Plays of Honore De Balzac, 2 vols. in 1. Honore De Balzac. 1976. Repr. of 1901 ed. 40.00x (ISBN 0-86527-291-3). Fertig.

Plays of Hrotswitha of Gandersheim. Tr. by Larissa Bonfante & Alexandra Bonfante-Warren. 1986. pap. 16.50 (ISBN 0-86516-178-X). Bolchazy-Carducci.

Plays of Hugh Kelly. Hugh Kelly. Ed. by Larry Carver. LC 78-66653. (Eighteenth Century English Drama Ser.). 1980. lib. bdg. 73.00 (ISBN 0-8240-3600-X). Garland Pub.

Plays of Ibsen, Vol. IV. Henrik Ibsen. 1986. pap. 4.95 (ISBN 0-671-60767-7). WSP.

Plays of Ibsen, Vol. I. Henrik Ibsen. 1986. pap. 4.95 (ISBN 0-671-60764-2). WSP.

Plays of Ibsen, Vol. II. Henrik Ibsen. 1986. pap. 4.95 (ISBN 0-671-60765-0). WSP.

Plays of Ibsen, Vol. III. Henrik Ibsen. 1986. pap. 4.95 (ISBN 0-671-60766-9). WSP.

Plays of Ibsen, Vols. III, IV. Tr. by Michael Meyer. pap. 4.95 (ISBN 0-317-43114-5). PB.

Plays of Impasse: Contemporary Drama Set in Confining Institutions. Carol Rosen. LC 82-61381. (Illus.). 304p. 1983. 28.50x (ISBN 0-691-06565-9). Princeton U Pr.

Plays of Isaac Bickerstaff, 3 vols. Issac Bickerstaff. Ed. by Peter A. Tasch. (Eighteenth Century English Drama Ser.). 1981. lib. bdg. 218.00 (ISBN 0-8240-3578-X). Garland Pub.

Plays of James Boaden. James Boaden. Ed. by P. R. Backscheider & Steven Cohan. LC 78-66608. (Eighteenth Century English Drama Ser.). lib. bdg. 73.00 (ISBN 0-8240-3579-8). Garland Pub.

Plays of James Thomson. James Thomson. Ed. by Paula R. Backscheider. LC 78-66637. (Eighteenth-Century English Drama Ser.: Vol. 35). 1980. lib. bdg. 73.00 (ISBN 0-8240-3609-3). Garland Pub.

Plays of Jewish Interest on the American Stage. Edward D. Coleman. 59.95 (ISBN 0-8490-0842-5). Gordon Pr.

Plays of John Dennis. John Dennis. Ed. by Paula R. Backscheider. LC 78-66657. (Eighteenth-Century English Drama Ser.: Vol. 14). 1980. lib. bdg. 73.00 (ISBN 0-8240-3588-7). Garland Pub.

Plays of John Galsworthy. John Galsworthy. 1150p. 1980. Repr. of 1929 ed. lib. bdg. 42.50 (ISBN 0-8492-4960-0). R West.

Plays of John Galsworthy. 1149p. 1983. Repr. of 1929 ed. lib. bdg. 57.50. Century Bookbindery.

Plays of John Gay, 2 vols. John Gay. LC 78-14747. 1978. Repr. of 1923 ed. Set. lib. bdg. 59.00 (ISBN 0-8414-2026-2). Folcroft.

Plays of John Home. Ed. by James S. Malek & Paula R. Backscheider. LC 78-66641. (Eighteenth-Century English Drama Ser.: Vol. 22). 1980. lib. bdg. 73.00 (ISBN 0-8240-3596-8). Garland Pub.

Plays of John Hoole. John Hoole. Ed. by Donald T. Siebert & Paula R. Backscheider. LC 78-66635. (Eighteenth-Century English Drama Ser.: Vol. 21). 1980. lib. bdg. 73.00 (ISBN 0-8240-3595-X). Garland Pub.

Plays of John Lyly. Ed. by Carter A. Daniel. LC 87-47849. 384p. 1988. 45.00x (ISBN 0-8387-5119-9). Bucknell U Pr.

Plays of John Marston, 3 vols. John Marston. Ed. by H. Harvey Wood. 1978. Repr. of 1934 ed. lib. bdg. 250.00 set (ISBN 0-8495-3747-9). Arden Lib.

Plays of John Marston, 3 vols. John Marston. Repr. of 1934 ed. 225.00x (ISBN 0-403-04206-2). Somerset Pub.

Plays of John Marston, 3 vols. John Marston. 1988. Repr. of 1934 ed. Set. lib. bdg. 290.00x. Am Biog Serv.

Plays of John O'Keefe, 4 vols. John O'Keefe. Ed. by Frederick M. Link. (Eighteenth Century English Drama Ser.). 1981. lib. bdg. 290.00 (ISBN 0-8240-3605-0). Garland Pub.

Plays of Leo Tolstoy. Leo Tolstoy. Tr. by N. H. Dole from Rus. xvi, 485p. Repr. of 1923 ed. lib. bdg. cancelled (ISBN 0-86527-375-8). Fertig.

Plays of Mary Pix & Catherine Trotter, 2 Vols. Mary Pix & Catherine Trotter. Ed. by Edna L. Steeves & P. R. Backscheider. LC 78-66620. (Eighteenth Century English Drama Ser.). Set. lib. bdg. 145.00 (ISBN 0-8240-3606-9). Garland Pub.

Plays of Max Frisch. Michael Butler. LC 84-17906. 144p. 1985. 25.00 (ISBN 0-312-61680-5). St Martin.

Plays of Negro Life: A Sourcebook of Native American Drama. Alain L. Locke. LC 77-132077. Repr. of 1927 ed. 32.50x (ISBN 0-8371-5037-X, IPN&). Greenwood.

Plays of Old Japan. Leo Duran. LC 73-476. 1973. lib. bdg. 33.50 (ISBN 0-8414-1487-4). Folcroft.

Plays of Old Japan. Ed. by Leo Duran. LC 77-94339. (One-Act Plays in Reprint Ser.). 1978. Repr. of 1921 ed. 16.50x (ISBN 0-8486-2037-2). Roth Pub Inc.

Plays of Oscar Wilde. Oscar Wilde. LC 87-40358. 368p. 1988. pap. 9.95 (ISBN 0-394-75788-2, Vin). Random.

Plays of Our Forefathers & Some of the Traditions upon Which They Were Founded. Charles M. Gayley. LC 68-25810. (Illus.). 1968. Repr. of 1907 ed. 15.00 (ISBN 0-8196-0209-4). Biblo.

Plays of Our Time. Ed. by Bennett Cerf. 1967. 22.95 (ISBN 0-394-40661-3, BYR). Random.

Plays of Philip Massinger, 4 Vols. 2nd ed. Philip Massinger. Ed. by William Gifford. LC 12-36722. Repr. of 1813 ed. Set. 160.00 (ISBN 0-404-04280-5); 40.00 ea. Vol. 1 (ISBN 0-404-04281-3). Vol. 2 (ISBN 0-404-04282-1). Vol. 3 (ISBN 0-404-04283-X). Vol. 4 (ISBN 0-404-04284-8). AMS Pr.

Plays of Protest. Upton Sinclair. LC 75-115275. 1970. Repr. of 1912 ed. 39.00x (ISBN 0-403-00293-1). Scholarly.

Plays of Richard Brinsley Sheridan. 455p. 1983. Repr. lib. bdg. 65.00 (ISBN 0-89984-616-5). Century Bookbindery.

Plays of Richard Cumberland: Eighteenth Century English Drama Ser, 3 Vols. Richard Cumberland. Ed. by Roberta F. Borkat. LC 78-66651. lib. bdg. 436.00 (ISBN 0-8240-3587-9). Garland Pub.

Plays of Richard Steele. Richard Steele. Ed. by Shirley S. Kenny. 1971. 63.00x (ISBN 0-19-812414-7). Oxford U Pr.

Plays of Robert Bolt. Maria Garstenauer. Ed. by James Hogg. (Poetic Drama & Poetic Theory ser.). (Orig.). 1985. pap. 15.00 (ISBN 3-7052-0840-3, Pub. by Salzburg Studies). Longwood Pub Group.

Plays of Robert Browning. Thomas J. Collins & Richard J. Shroyer. (Reference Library of the Humanities). 552p. 1988. lib. bdg. 74.00 (ISBN 0-8240-6693-6). Garland Pub.

Plays of Robert Jephson. Robert Jephson. Ed. by Temple Maynard & Paula R. Backscheider. LC 78-66647. (Eighteenth-Century English Drama Ser.: Vol. 24). 1980. lib. bdg. 73.00 (ISBN 0-8240-3598-4). Garland Pub.

Plays of Roswitha. Roswitha. Tr. by Christopher St John. LC 65-20048. Repr. of 1923 ed. 12.00 (ISBN 0-405-08900-7). Ayer Co Pubs.

Plays of Samuel Beckett. Eugene Webb. LC 72-2901. (Washington Paperback Ser., No. 71). 160p. 1972. 15.00x (ISBN 0-295-95202-4); pap. 5.95x (ISBN 0-295-95314-4). U of Wash Pr.

Plays of Samuel Foote, 3 vols. Ed. by Paula R. Backscheider. LC 78-66659. (Eighteenth Century English Drama Ser.). 1982. Set. lib. bdg. 218.00 (ISBN 0-8240-3589-5). Garland Pub.

Plays of Samuel Johnson of Cheshire. Samuel Johnson. Ed. by P. R. Backscheider & Valerie C. Rudolph. LC 78-66642. (Eighteenth Century English Drama Ser.). lib. bdg. 73.00 (ISBN 0-8240-3599-2). Garland Pub.

Plays of Sir George Etherege. George Etherege. Ed. by Michael Cordner. LC 82-1180. (Plays by Renaissance & Restoration Dramatists Ser.). (Illus.). 384p. 1982. 44.50 (ISBN 0-521-24654-7); pap. 16.95 (ISBN 0-521-28879-7). Cambridge U Pr.

Plays of Sophokles. Valdis Leinieks. vi, 215p. (Orig.). 1982. pap. 32.00x (ISBN 90-6032-226-6, Pub. by B R Gruener Netherlands). Benjamins North Am.

Plays of Susanna Centlivre, 3 vols. Susanna Centlivre. Ed. by Richard C. Frushell. LC 78-66629. (Eighteenth Century English Drama Ser.). 1437p. 1982. lib. bdg. 218.00 (ISBN 0-8240-3581-X). Garland Pub.

Plays of Tehophilus & Susanna Cibber. Tehophilus Cibber & Susanna Cibber. Ed. by David Mann. (Eighteen Century English Drama Ser.). 1981. lib. bdg. 73.00 (ISBN 0-8240-3583-6). Garland Pub.

Plays of the Eyes. Elias Canetti. Tr. by Ralph Manheim from Ital. 336p. 1981. pap. 9.95 (ISBN 0-374-52075-5). FS&G.

Plays of the Holocaust: An International Collection. Ed. by Elinor Fuchs. LC 87-9997. (Orig.). 1987. pap. 12.95 (ISBN 0-930452-63-1); 24.95 (ISBN 0-930452-67-4). Theatre Comm.

Plays of the Irish Renaissance, 1880-1930. Ed. by Curtis Canfield. LC 73-4881. (Play Anthology Reprint Ser.). Repr. of 1929 ed. 31.00 (ISBN 0-8369-8248-7). Ayer Co Pubs.

Plays of the Italian Theatre. Giovanni Verga et al. Tr. by Isaac Goldberg. LC 76-40394. (One-Act Plays in Reprint Ser.). 1976. Repr. of 1906 ed. 19.00x (ISBN 0-8486-2009-7). Roth Pub Inc.

Plays of the Natural & Supernatural. Theodore Dreiser. LC 73-97893. 1969. Repr. of 1916 ed. 18.00 (ISBN 0-404-02179-4). AMS Pr.

Plays of the Natural & the Supernatural. Theodore Dreiser. LC 74-131690. Repr. of 1916 ed. 49.00x (ISBN 0-403-00577-9). Scholarly.

Plays of the Pioneers: A Book of Historical Pageant Plays. Constance D. Mackay. LC 76-40389. (One-Act Plays in Reprint Ser.). 1976. Repr. of 1915 ed. 17.75x (ISBN 0-8486-2005-4). Roth Pub Inc.

Plays of the Present. John B. Clapp & Edwin F. Edgett. LC 73-83498. 1902. 22.00 (ISBN 0-405-08361-0, Blom Pubns). Ayer Co Pubs.

Plays of the Southern Americas. Stanford University Dramatists' Alliance. LC 74-173626. (Play Anthology Reprint Ser). Repr. of 1942 ed. 20.25 (ISBN 0-8369-8231-2). Ayer Co Pubs.

Plays of Thomas Holcroft, 2 vols. Thomas Holcroft. Ed. by Joseph Rosenblum. LC 78-66630. (Eighteenth Century English Drama Ser.). 1980. Set. lib. bdg. 145.00 (ISBN 0-8240-3594-1). Garland Pub.

Please Dear God Open the Door. Leslie A. Reed. 60p. 1988. 6.95 (ISBN 1-55523-152-7). Winston-Derek.
Please Dr., I'd Rather Do It Myself with Herbs. LaDean Griffin. 1979. pap. 4.95 (ISBN 0-89036-058-8). Hawkes Pub Inc.
Please Don't Ask Me to Sing in the Choir. Thomas L. Are. 120p. (Orig.). 1985. pap. 5.95 (ISBN 0-916642-28-3, 905). Hope Pub.
Please Don't Eat the Daisies. Jean Kerr. 1979. pap. 1.95 (ISBN 0-449-24099-1, Crest). Fawcett.
Please Don't Get There Before Your Time. Marie L. Davidson. LC 88-70287. 270p. (Orig.). 1988. pap. 11.00 (ISBN 1-55618-037-3). Brunswick Pub.
Please Don't Hurt Me. Grant Martin. 180p. 1987. pap. 6.95 (ISBN 0-89693-743-7). Victor Bks.
Please Don't Kiss Me Now. Merrill J. Gerber. 176p. (YA) (gr. 7 up). 1982. pap. 1.95 (ISBN 0-451-11575-9, Sig Vista). NAL.
Please Don't Say Hello: Living with Childhood Autism. Phyllis Gold. LC 74-13185. (Illus.). 48p. (gr. 6-10). 1975. 14.95 (ISBN 0-87705-211-5); pap. 5.95 (ISBN 0-89885-199-8). Human Sci Pr.
Please Don't Shoot My Dog. Jackie Cooper & Dick Kleiner. 1984. pap. 3.95 (ISBN 0-425-07483-8). Berkley Pub.
Please Don't Sit on the Kids: Alternatives to Punitive Discipline. Clare Cherry. LC 82-81981. (ps-3). 1982. pap. 9.95 (ISBN 0-8224-5474-2). D S Lake Pubs.
Please Don't Smoke in Our House. Jack Trop. LC 75-43454. (Illus.). 128p. (Orig.). 1976. pap. 2.50 (ISBN 0-914532-11-1). Natural Hygiene.
Please Don't Squeeze the Christian. Scott Sernau. LC 87-3155. 150p. (Orig.). 1987. pap. 5.95 (ISBN 0-87784-571-9). Inter Varsity.
Please Don't Step on Me. Elly-Kree George. (Illus.). 20p. (gr. 1-3). 1981. 3.00 (ISBN 0-935741-07-0). Cherokee Pubns.
Please Don't Tease Me. Jane M. Madsen et al. 32p. (gr. 3-4). 1980. pap. 2.95 (ISBN 0-8170-0876-4). Judson.
Please Excuse Jasper. Nathan Zimelman. 32p. (gr. k-4). 1987. 10.95 (ISBN 0-687-31643-X). Abingdon.
Please Explain. Isaac Asimov. LC 73-7908. (Illus.). 224p. (gr. 7 up). 1973. 5.95 (ISBN 0-395-17517-8). HM.
Please Give a Devotion. Amy Bolding. 1963. pap. 4.95 (ISBN 0-8010-0819-0). Baker Bk.
Please Give a Devotion for Active Teens. Amy Bolding. (Direction Bks). 1974. pap. 3.95 (ISBN 0-8010-0827-1). Baker Bk.
Please Give a Devotion for All Occasions. Amy Bolding. 1967. pap. 4.95 (ISBN 0-8010-0519-1). Baker Bk.
Please Give a Devotion for Church Groups. Amy Bolding. (Paperback Program Ser.). pap. 4.95 (ISBN 0-8010-0623-6). Baker Bk.
Please Give a Devotion: For Women's Groups. Amy Bolding. (Paperback Program Ser.). 108p. 1976. pap. 4.95 (ISBN 0-8010-0583-3). Baker Bk.
Please God. Gordon Stowell. (Little Fish Books About You & Me: III). 14p. (gr. 1-5). 1984. mini-bk 0.59 (ISBN 0-8307-0954-1, 5608381). Regal.
Please, God: Prayers for Young Children. Ron Klug & Lyn Klug. LC 80-67799. 32p. (Orig.). (ps-1). 1981. pap. 4.95 (ISBN 0-8066-1861-2, 10-4999). Augsburg.
Please God Take Care of the Mule. Lini M. De Vries. 127p. 1975. pap. 3.00 (ISBN 0-912434-19-8). Ocelot Pr.
Please Let Me Die. James D. Mackey & I. E. Stanley. LC 76-14099. (Illus.). 1976. pap. 1.95 (ISBN 0-917268-00-8). Damas Pub.
Please, Lord, Don't Put Me on Hold! Jane Graver. 1979. pap. 2.50 (ISBN 0-570-03790-5, 12-2753). Concordia.
Please, Lord, Untie My Tongue. K. Erickson. LC 12-2816. 1983. pap. 2.75 (ISBN 0-570-03881-2). Concordia.
Please Love Me. Keith Miller. 1983. pap. 3.95 (ISBN 0-671-54149-8). PB.
Please Love Me. Keith Miller. 316p. 1985. pap. 8.95 (ISBN 0-8499-3021-9, 3021-9). Word Bks.
Please Make Me Cry! Cookie Rodriguez. 1974. pap. 2.95 (ISBN 0-88368-042-4). Whitaker Hse.
Please Miss. A. C. Griffiths. 1987. 21.00x (ISBN 0-7223-2176-7, Pub. by A H Stockwell). State Mutual Bk.
Please Pass the Salt: A Manual for Low Salt Eaters. Roger H. Wilson & Nancy L. Wilson. LC 82-61761. (Illus.). 182p. 1983. 14.95 (ISBN 0-89313-027-3). G F Stickley.
Please Plan a Program. Amy Bolding. (Paperback Program Ser). (Orig.). 1971. pap. 3.95 (ISBN 0-8010-0527-2). Baker Bk.
Please Quote Me: Selected Poems. Alice G. Gaydos. 64p. 1980. 5.00 (ISBN 0-682-49626-X). Exposition-Phoenix.
Please Read This for Me. 1988. 15.45. Morrow.
Please Read This for Me: How to Tell the Man You Love Things You Can't Put into Words. Neil Chesanow & Gareth L. Esersky. 170p. 1988. 15.95 (ISBN 1-55710-016-0, Arbor Hse). Morrow.
Please See My Need. A. Jann Davis. (Illus.). 1981. pap. 6.95x (ISBN 0-9609184-0-X). Satellite Cont.
Please Send Junk Food. Susan Schneider. 160p. (Orig.). (gr. 5 up). 1985. pap. 2.25 (ISBN 0-448-47740-8). Putnam Pub Group.
Please Send Junk Food: A Camp Survival Guide. Susan Schneider. 100p. 1987. pap. 2.50 (ISBN 0-425-09596-7, Pub. by Berkley-Pacer). Berkley Pub.
Please Spend These Last Few Precious Moments with Me. Beba Papakyriakou. 1986. 10.95 (ISBN 0-533-06736-7). Vantage.
Please Stand by-Your Mother's Missing. Shirley B. Tallman & Nancy P. Gilsenan. LC 78-61590. 1980. 7.95 (ISBN 0-87212-097-X). Libra.
Please Take Your Dead Bird Home Today: Portrait of an Alternative School. Rita K. Mitchell. LC 77-79578. 1978. 7.95 (ISBN 0-87212-094-5). Libra.
Please Talk to Me, God! Donald Deffner. (Continued Applied Christianity). 1983. pap. 2.08 (ISBN 0-570-03899-5, 12-2981). Concordia.
Please Tell Me a Story see Stories to Tell in Children's Church.
Please Tell Me How You Feel. Marion Stroud. LC 83-22410. 160p. 1984. pap. 5.95 (ISBN 0-87123-427-0, 210427). Bethany Hse.
Please? Thanks! I'm Sorry. Jane B. Moncure. LC 85-11664. (New Values Ser.). (Illus.). 32p. (gr. k-2). 1985. PLB 7.95 (ISBN 0-89565-331-1). Childs World.
Please Touch: How to Stimulate Your Child's Creative Development. Susan Striker. (Illus.). 347p. 1986. 17.95 (ISBN 0-671-60593-3, Fireside); pap. 9.95 (ISBN 0-671-49648-4). S&S.
Please Try to Remember the First of Octember. Theo Lesieg. (Beginner Book & Cassette Library). (Illus.). 40p. (ps-1). 1988. pap. 5.95 bk. & cassette pkg. (ISBN 0-394-89779-X, BYR). Random.
Please Try to Remember the First of Octember. Theodore Le Sieg. LC 77-4504. (Illus.). 48p. (gr. 1-4). 1977. lib. bdg. 6.99 (ISBN 0-394-93563-2). Beginner.
Please Understand Me: Character & Temperament Types. David Keirsey & Marilyn Bates. 207p. 1978. pap. 9.95 (ISBN 0-9606954-0-0). Prometheus Nemesis.
Please, Wind? Carol Greene. LC 82-4548. (Rookie Readers Ser.). (Illus.). (ps-2). 1982. PLB 9.93 (ISBN 0-516-02033-1); pap. 2.50 (ISBN 0-516-42033-X). Childrens.
Please Write: A Beginning Composition Text for Students of ESL. Patricia Ackert. (Illus.). 208p. 1986. pap. text ed. write for info. (ISBN 0-13-683418-3). P-H.
Please Write for Details. John D. MacDonald. 288p. 1986. pap. 3.50 (GM). Fawcett.
Please Write: How to Improve Your Handwriting for Business & Pleasure in Ten Quick & Easy Lessons. Wolf Von Eckardt. (Illus.). 192p. 1988. 18.95. Atheneum.
Pleasers: Women Who Can't Say No & the Men Who Control Them. Kevin Leman. 320p. 1987. 14.95 (ISBN 0-8007-1551-9). Revell.
Pleasers (Women Who Can't Say No & the Men Who Control Them) Kevin Leman. 1988. pap. 4.50 (ISBN 0-440-20169-1). Dell.
Pleasing God. David Hocking. 144p. 1985. pap. 5.95 (ISBN 0-89840-101-1). Heres Life.
Pleasing God. David L. Hocking. LC 84-47802. 144p. 1984. Heres Life.
Pleasing God. R. C. Sproul. 224p. 1988. 10.95 (ISBN 0-8423-4968-5, 60-4968-5). Tyndale.
Pleasing Instructor. Ed. by Thomas Slack. (Children's Books from the Past: Vol. 6). 368p. (YA) 1973. Repr. of 1785 ed. 45.70 (ISBN 3-261-01008-8). P Lang Pubs.
Pleasurable Instruction: Form & Convention in Eighteenth-Century Travel Literature. Charles L. Batten, Jr. LC 76-14316. 1978. 27.50x (ISBN 0-520-03260-8). U of Cal Pr.
Pleasure: A Creative Approach to Life. Alexander Lowen. 1975. pap. 6.95 (ISBN 0-14-004033-1). Penguin.
Pleasure & Being: Hedonism from a Psychoanalytic Point of View. Moustafa Safouan. Tr. by Martin Thom. LC 82-16819. 150p. 1983. 21.95x (ISBN 0-312-61700-3). St Martin.
Pleasure & Business in Western Pennsylvania: The Journal of Joshua Gilpin, 1809. Ed. by Joseph E. Walker. LC 75-623536. (Illus.). 156p. 1975. 9.00 (ISBN 0-911124-78-0). Pa Hist & Mus.
Pleasure & Danger: Exploring Female Sexuality. Ed. by Carole Vance. 350p. 1984. cloth 25.00X (ISBN 0-7100-9974-6); pap. 11.95 (ISBN 0-7102-0248-2). Routledge Chapman & Hall.
Pleasure & Frustration: A Resynthesis of Clinical & Theoretical Psychoanalysis. Leon Wallace. LC 84-3787. xiv, 193p. 1984. text ed. 20.00x (ISBN 0-8236-4161-9). Intl Univs Pr.
Pleasure & Pain. J. L. Cowan. LC 68-13019. 1969. 22.50 (ISBN 0-312-61705-4). St Martin.
Pleasure & Repentance. T. Hands. 1976. pap. text ed. 4.40 flexi-cover (ISBN 0-08-018216-X). Pergamon.
Pleasure Areas: A New Theory of Behavior. H. J. Campbell. 288p. 1973. pap. 8.95 (ISBN 0-440-07226-3). Delacorte.
Pleasure Boats & Yachts Valued Under 15,000 Dollars. (Latin American Products Included in the U. S. General System of Preferences Ser.). 1978. pap. text ed. 3.00 (ISBN 0-8270-3375-3). OAS.
Pleasure Book. 2nd ed. Ed. by Rodema De Rohan & Raymond. (Illus.). 190p. (Orig.). 1982. pap. 5.00 (ISBN 0-943228-00-X). Raymonds Quiet Pr.
Pleasure Book. Russ Rueger. (Orig.). Date not set. pap. 9.95 (ISBN 0-671-50493-2, Wallaby). PB.
Pleasure Bound. 1988. pap. 3.95 (ISBN 0-8216-5005-X). Blue Moon Bks.
Pleasure Bound: Three Erotic Novels. LC 81-48540. 368p. 1982. pap. 4.95 (ISBN 0-394-17977-3, B-470, BC). Grove.
Pleasure Class. Aline Thompson. 320p. (Orig.). 1988. pap. 3.95 (ISBN 0-8439-2615-5, Pub. by Leisure Bks CT). Leisure NY.
Pleasure Connection: How Endorphins Affect Our Health & Happiness. Deva Beck & James Beck. LC 87-60379. 235p. (Orig.). 1987. pap. 9.95 (ISBN 0-318-22829-7). Synthesis Pr.
Pleasure Dome. Judith Liederman. 1983. pap. 3.75 (ISBN 0-8217-1134-2). Zebra.
Pleasure Dome: On Reading Modern Poetry. Lloyd Frankenberg. LC 68-57701. 384p. 1968. Repr. of 1949 ed. 40.00x (ISBN 0-87752-038-0). Gordian.
Pleasure Garden: An Illustrated History of English Gardening. Anne Scott-James & Osbert Lancaster. LC 77-84332. (Illus.). 1978. 5.95 (Pub. by Gambit); pap. 7.95 (Pub. by Gambit). Harvard Common Pr.
Pleasure Ground: A Miscellany of English Writing. Malcolm Elwin. 1947. 25.00 (ISBN 0-89984-037-X). Century Bookbindery.
Pleasure Handbook. J. J. Randall. 140p. 1986. pap. 14.95 (ISBN 0-938023-05-5). Wind River Bks.
Pleasure in Words. Eugene T. Maleska. 448p. 1982. pap. 9.95 (ISBN 0-671-44775-0, Fireside). S&S.
Pleasure Is Our Business. Jack Sandberg. 1977. pap. 1.75 (ISBN 0-685-78226-3, Leisure Bks). Leisure NY.
Pleasure Island. Nick Carter. (Nick Carter Ser.). 256p. (Orig.). 1981. pap. 2.50 (ISBN 0-441-67081-4). Ace Bks.
Pleasure of Being Oneself. Cyril E. Joad. LC 74-111841. (Essay Index Reprint Ser.). 1951. 18.00 (ISBN 0-8369-1665-4). Ayer Co Pubs.
Pleasure of Flowers. Victoria S. Roberts. LC 76-47181. (Illus., Orig.). 1977. pap. 5.95 (ISBN 0-89407-001-0). Strawberry Hill.
Pleasure of God's Company. Patrica G. Opatz. 96p. 1985. pap. 3.95 (ISBN 0-8146-1437-X). Liturgical Pr.
Pleasure of Herbs: A Month-By-Month Guide to Growing, Using, & Enjoying Herbs. Phyllis V. Shaudys. LC 86-14856. (Illus.). 280p. (Orig.). 1986. 22.50 (ISBN 0-88266-430-1); pap. 12.95 (ISBN 0-88266-423-9, Garden Way Pub). Storey Comm Inc.
Pleasure of Herbs Gift Pack. Phyllis V. Shaudys. LC 86-45003. (Illus.). 280p. 1988. 19.95 (ISBN 0-88266-484-0); 8 seeds packets incl. Storey Comm Inc.
Pleasure of Lolotte. (Red Stripe Ser.). 1988. pap. 4.50 (ISBN 0-8216-5054-8, Univ Bks). Lyle Stuart.
Pleasure of Miss Pym. Charles Burkhart. (Illus.). 140p. 1987. text ed. 17.95x (ISBN 0-292-76496-0); pap. 8.95 (ISBN 0-292-76501-0). U of Tex Pr.
Pleasure of Poetry with & by Children: A Handbook. Vardine Moore. LC 80-29015. 143p. 1981. 15.00 (ISBN 0-8108-1399-8). Scarecrow.
Pleasure of the Text. Roland Barthes. Tr. by Richard Miller from Fr. 80p. 1975. 8.95 (ISBN 0-8090-7722-1); pap. 5.95 (ISBN 0-8090-1380-0). Hill & Wang.
Pleasure of Their Company. Alister Kershaw. LC 85-22603. (Illus.). 199p. 1987. 19.50 (ISBN 0-7022-1987-8). U of Queensland Pr.
Pleasure of Your Company: A Socio-Psychological Analysis of Modern Sociability. Emile J. Pin & Jamie Turndorf. 304p. 1985. 35.00 (ISBN 0-275-91755-X, C1755). Praeger.
Pleasure Packing. Robert Wood. (Encore Edition). 1972. pap. 1.95 encore ed. (ISBN 0-684-16934-7, SL577, ScribT). Scribner.
Pleasure Packing for the Eighties. 2nd rev. ed. Robert S. Wood. (Illus.). 256p. 1981. pap. 6.95 (ISBN 0-89815-035-3). Ten Speed Pr.
Pleasure Palace. Joan Lee. (Orig.). 1987. pap. 3.95 (ISBN 0-440-16950-X). Dell.
Pleasure, Preference & Value: Studies in Philosophical Aesthetics. Ed. by Eva Schaper. LC 82-14775. 180p. 1983. 44.50 (ISBN 0-521-25101-X). Cambridge U Pr.
Pleasure, Preference & Value: Studies in Philosophical Aesthetics. Ed. by Eva Schaper. 192p. 1987. pap. 12.95 (ISBN 0-521-34967-2). Cambridge U Pr.
Pleasure Principle. Peter McCurtin. 1974. pap. 1.25 (ISBN 0-8439-0213-2, Leisure Bks). Leisure NY.
Pleasure Principle Diet: How to Lose Weight Permanently, Eating the Foods That Made You Fat. Robert E. Willner. LC 84-29121. 225p. 1985. 18.95; pap. 7.95. P-H.
Pleasure, Profit, Proslytism: British Culture & Sport at Home & Abroad 1700-1914. Ed. by J. A. Mangan. 250p. 1986. 27.50x (ISBN 0-7146-3289-9, F Cass Co); pap. 12.95x (ISBN 0-7146-4050-6, F Cass Co). Biblio Dist.
Pleasure Steamers. Andrew Motion. 58p. 1978. pap. 5.95 (ISBN 0-85635-247-0). Carcanet.
Pleasure Trove. facs. ed. Edward V. Lucas. LC 68-57329. (Essay Index Reprint Ser.). 1935. 17.00 (ISBN 0-8369-0631-4). Ayer Co Pubs.
Pleasure Within. Robert Carter. 96p. 1988. 13.95 (ISBN 0-689-11998-4). Macmillan.
Pleasure Within. Robert Carter. 1988. 15.95. Atheneum.
Pleasures & Days: & Other Writings. Marcel Proust. Tr. by L. Varese et al from Fr. LC 78-2432. 1978. Repr. of 1957 ed. 24.50x (ISBN 0-86527-293-X). Fertig.
Pleasures & Pains: A Theory of Qualitative Hedonism. Rem B. Edwards. LC 79-4168. 160p. 1979. 24.50x (ISBN 0-8014-1241-2). Cornell U Pr.
Pleasures & Pains of Modern Capitalism. George J. Stigler. (Institute of Economic Affairs, Occasional Papers Ser.: No. 64). pap. 4.25 technical (ISBN 0-255-36157-2). Transatl Arts.
Pleasures & Palaces. facs. ed. Frances L. Warner & Gertrude C. Warner. LC 68-58817. (Essay Index Reprint Ser). 1933. 15.00 (ISBN 0-8369-0132-0). Ayer Co Pubs.
Pleasures & Regrets. Marcel Proust. Tr. by Louise Varese from Fr. LC 84-6120. (Neglected Books of the 20th Century Ser.). 221p. 1984. pap. 7.50 (ISBN 0-88001-063-0). Ecco Pr.
Pleasures & Regrets. Marcel Proust. 236p. 1986. Repr. of 1948 ed. 21.00 (ISBN 0-7206-0655-1). Dufour.
Pleasures & Speculations. facsimile ed. Walter J. De La Mare. LC 76-90630. (Essay Index Reprint Ser). 1940. 19.50 (ISBN 0-8369-1255-1). Ayer Co Pubs.
Pleasures Forevermore: The Theology of C. S. Lewis. John R. Willis. 157p. 1983. 12.95 (ISBN 0-8294-0446-5). Loyola.
Pleasure's Mistress. 160p. 1987. pap. 3.95 (ISBN 0-88184-366-0). Carroll & Graf.
Pleasures of Afternoon Tea. Angela Hynes. LC 87-275. 160p. 1987. 17.95 (ISBN 0-89586-579-3). Price Stern.
Pleasures of an Absentee Landlord: And Other Essays. Samuel M. Crothers. LC 72-1326. (Essay Index Reprint Ser.). Repr. of 1916 ed. 18.00 (ISBN 0-8369-2844-X). Ayer Co Pubs.
Pleasures of Anthropology. Ed. by Morris Freilich. 464p. 1983. pap. 4.95 (ISBN 0-451-62240-5, Ment). NAL.
Pleasures of Chinese Cooking. Grace Z. Chu. (Illus.). 239p. 1975. pap. 3.95 (ISBN 0-671-22181-7, Fireside). S&S.
Pleasures of Colonial Cooking. Miller-Cory House Museum & the New Jersey Historical Society Staff. (Illus.). xviii, 168p. 1982. pap. text ed. 7.95 (ISBN 0-911020-06-3). NJ Hist Soc.
Pleasures of Entomology: Portraits of Insects & the People Who Study Them. Howard E. Evans. LC 84-600318. (Illus.). 238p. 1985. pap. 14.95 (ISBN 0-87474-421-0, EVPEP). Smithsonian.
Pleasures of Exile. George Lamming. 232p. 1984. 14.95 (ISBN 0-8052-8193-2, Pub. by Allison & Busby England); pap. 6.95 (ISBN 0-8052-8194-0). Schocken.
Pleasures of Gaelic Literature. Ed. by John Jordan. 120p. 1977. pap. 7.95 (ISBN 0-85342-492-6, Pub. by Mercier Pr Ireland). Irish Bks Media.
Pleasures of Helen. Lawrence Sanders. 256p. 1987. pap. 3.95 (ISBN 0-425-10168-1). Berkley Pub.
Pleasures of Ignorance. Robert Lynd. LC 75-108702. (Essay & General Literature Index Reprint Ser). 1970. Repr. of 1921 ed. 23.00x (ISBN 0-8046-0923-3). Assoc Faculty Pr.
Pleasures of Irish Nature Poetry. Ed. by Malachi McCormick. 32p. 1984. 5.95 (ISBN 0-943984-18-1). Stone St Pr.
Pleasures of Japanese Literature. Donald Keene. (Companions to Asian Studies). (Illus.). 120p. 1988. 20.00x (ISBN 0-231-06736-4). Columbia U Pr.
Pleasures of Life after Forty. Rex Curtis & James T. Pendergrast. 96p. (Orig.). 1985. pap. 2.95 (ISBN 0-345-32990-2). Ballantine.
Pleasures of Loving: The Erotic Fantasies & Experiences of Fifty-Two French Women. Francoise Ducout. Tr. by Nicholas Courtin from Fr. 192p. 1986. 13.95 (ISBN 0-312-61745-3). St Martin.
Pleasures of Manhood: Stories. Robley Wilson, Jr. LC 77-24216. (Illinois Short Fiction Ser.). 180p. 1977. 11.95 (ISBN 0-252-00665-8); pap. 8.95 (ISBN 0-252-00670-4). U of Ill Pr.
Pleasures of Music: An Anthology of Writings About Music & Musicians from Cellini to Bernard Shaw. abr. ed. Ed. by Jacques Barzun. 1977. 15.00x (ISBN 0-226-03856-4); pap. 10.95x (ISBN 0-226-03854-8, P727, Phoen). U of Chicago Pr.
Pleasures of Paris: A Gastronomic Companion. Michael Bond. 1988. 9.95 (ISBN 0-317-67725-X, C N Potter Bks). Crown.
Pleasures of Paris: A Gastronomic Guide. Michael Bond. (Illus.). 208p. 1988. pap. 9.95 (ISBN 0-517-56692-3, 566923, C N Potter Bks). Crown.
Pleasures of Philosophy. Will Durant. pap. 14.95 (ISBN 0-671-58110-4, Touchstone Bks). S&S.
Pleasures of Psychology. Ed. by Daniel Coleman. David Heller. 512p. 1986. pap. 4.95 (ISBN 0-451-62524-2, Ment). NAL.
Pleasures of Sketching Outdoors. rev. ed. Clayton Hoagland. (Illus.). 179p. 1970. pap. 5.95 (ISBN 0-486-22229-2). Dover.
Pleasures of Sociology. Lewis A. Coser. (Orig.). 1980. pap. 4.50 (ISBN 0-451-62264-2, ME2264, Ment). NAL.
Pleasures of the Belle-Epoque: Entertainment & Festivity in Turn-of-the-Century France. Charles Rearick. LC 85-40468. (Illus.). 240p. 1986. 32.50x (ISBN 0-300-03230-7). Yale U Pr.

Pleasures of the Belle Epoque: Entertainment & Festivity in Turn-of-the-Century France. Charles Rearick. LC 85-40468. 240p. 1988. Repr. of 1985 ed. 17.95 (ISBN 0-300-04381-3). Yale U Pr.

Pleasures of the Garden: Images from the Metropolitan Museum of Art. Mac Griswold. (Illus.). 160p. 1987. 29.95 (ISBN 0-8109-0997-9). Abrams.

Pleasures of the Palate. Harris Golden. Ed. by Candice Miles. LC 88-81018. (Illus.). 235p. 1988. text ed. write for info. (ISBN 0-9620669-0-7). Goldens Kitchen.

Pleasures of the Table. G. H. Ellwanger. 59.95 (ISBN 0-8490-0843-3). Gordon Pr.

Pleasures of the Table. Compiled by Theodora Fitzgibbon. (Small Oxford Books). (Illus.). 1981. 9.95 (ISBN 0-19-214120-1). Oxford U Pr.

Pleasures of Walking. Ed. by Edwin V. Mitchell. LC 48-11993. (Illus.). 1979. 8.95 (ISBN 0-8149-0825-X). Vanguard.

Pleasures of Watching Birds. Lola Oberman. 1986. 17.95 (ISBN 0-13-681305-4). P-H.

Pleasures of Your Food Processor. Norene Gilletz. 368p. 1984. pap. 9.95 (ISBN 0-446-37952-2). Warner Bks.

Pleasures: Women Write Erotica. Lonnie Barbach. LC 85-42550. 304p. 1985. pap. 7.95 (ISBN 0-06-097002-2, PL 7002, PL). Har-Row.

Pleasuring of Rory Malone. Charles Panati. LC 81-16715. 260p. 1982. 11.95 (ISBN 0-312-61731-3). St Martin.

Pleasuring of Rory Malone. Charles Panati. 320p. 1986. pap. 3.95 (ISBN 0-441-67087-3, Pub. by Charter Bks). Ace Bks.

Plebejer Proben Den Aufstand. Gunter Grass. Ed. by H. F. Brookes & C. E. Fraenkel. (Ger.). 1971. pap. text ed. 6.50x (ISBN 0-435-38372-8). Heinemann Ed.

Plebiscites & Sovereignty: The Crisis of Political Illegitimacy. Lawrence T. Farley. 224p. 1986. 25.00 (ISBN 0-8133-7217-8). Westview.

Plebs & Princeps. Zvi Yavetz. 192p. 1987. 29.95 (ISBN 0-88738-154-5). Transaction Bks.

Pledge. Howard Fast. 320p. 1988. 18.95 (ISBN 0-395-48308-5). HM.

Pledge Handbook. 52p. 1985. 2.00 (ISBN 0-318-14922-2). Mu Phi Ep.

Pledge of Allegiance in Signing Exact English. Margaret Oliver. (Written in Sutton Sign Writing). 3.00x (ISBN 0-914336-54-1). Ctr Sutton Movement.

Pledged Account Mortgage (PAM; see Graduated Payment Mortgage (GPM) The Pledged Account Mortgage (PAM), the FLIP Mortgage.

Plehve: Repression & Reform in Imperial Russia, 1902 to 1904. Edward H. Judge. 312p. 1983. text ed. 35.00x (ISBN 0-8156-2295-3). Syracuse U Pr.

Pleiades Stones. Raven Hail. LC 87-61690. 200p. (Author's Name Is Hail-Do Not Change to Hall). 1987. pap. 4.50 (ISBN 0-9617696-4-5). Raven Hail Bks.

Pleiads. Arthur De Gobineau. Tr. by J. F. Scanlan from Fr. 359p. 1981. Repr. of 1928 ed. lib. bdg. 30.00 (ISBN 0-89984-234-8). Century Bookbindery.

Pleiads. Arthur De Gobineau. Tr. by J. F. Scanlon from Fr. LC 76-50036. 1978. Repr. of 1928 ed. 35.00x (ISBN 0-86527-332-4). Fertig.

Pleiku: The Dawn of Helicopter Warfare in Vietnam. J. D. Coleman. (Illus.). 352p. 1988. 19.95 (ISBN 0-312-01807-X). St Martin.

Plein Air Painters of California: The North. Ruth Westphal. LC 86-50631. (Illus.). 216p. 1986. 79.00 (ISBN 0-9610520-1-5). Westphal Pub.

Plein Air Painters of California: The Southland. Lilly & Westphal. (Illus.). 220p. sewn bdg. 79.00 (ISBN 0-317-54895-6). Apollo.

Plein Air Painters of California: The Southland. Ruth Westphal. LC 82-90314. (Illus.). 228p. 1982. 79.00 (ISBN 0-9610520-0-7). Westphal Pub.

Plein Vol. Josette Smetana & Marie-Rose Myron. 528p. 1987. pap. text ed. write for info. (ISBN 0-03-070258-5). HR&W.

Pleiocene Fossils of South Carolina. Michael Tuomey & Francis S. Holmes. (Illus.). 1974. Repr. of 1857 ed. 10.00 (ISBN 0-87710-365-8). Paleo Res.

Pleistocene. Nilsson. 1982. lib. bdg. 115.00 (ISBN 90-277-1466-5, Pub. by Reidel Holland). Kluwer Academic.

Pleistocene & Holocene Carbonate Environments on San Salvador Island, Bahamas. R. J. Bain et al. 164p. 1985. pap. text ed. 20.00 (ISBN 0-935909-14-1). CCFL Bahamian.

Pleistocene & Recent Faunas from the Brynjulfson Caves, Missouri. Paul W. Parmalee & Ronald D. Oesch. (Reports of Investigations Ser.: No. 25). (Illus.). 52p. 1972. pap. 2.00x (ISBN 0-89792-049-X). Ill St Museum.

Pleistocene & Recent Vertebrate Faunas from Crankshaft Cave, Missouri. Paul W. Parmalee et al. (Reports of Investigations Ser.: No.14). (Illus.). 37p. 1969. pap. 1.00x (ISBN 0-89792-036-8). Ill St Museum.

Pleistocene Bovidae. S. H. Reynolds. Repr. of 1939 ed. 12.00 (ISBN 0-384-50400-0). Johnson Repr.

Pleistocene Geology of the Bulletin Area, Central Minnesota. Allan F. Schneider. LC 61-63788. (Bulletin: No. 40). 1961. 4.25x (ISBN 0-8166-0244-1). Minn Geol Survey.

Pleistocene Giant Deer & Errata, 2 vols. S. H. Reynolds. Repr. of 1929 ed. Set. 17.00 (ISBN 0-384-50410-8). Johnson Repr.

Pleistocene Hippopotamus. S. H. Reynolds. Repr. of 1922 ed. 14.00 (ISBN 0-384-50420-5). Johnson Repr.

Pleistocene History of the Middle Thames Valley. P. L. Gibbard. 160p. 1986. 72.50 (ISBN 0-521-26578-9). Cambridge U Pr.

Pleistocene Mammals of Florida. Ed. by Sawney D. Webb. LC 74-3115. 280p. pap. 72.80 (2030011). Bks Demand UMI.

Pleistocene Mammals of North America. Bjorn Kurten & Elaine Anderson. LC 79-26679. 1980. 60.00x (ISBN 0-231-03733-3). Columbia U Pr.

Pleistocene Man at San Diego. George F. Carter. LC 77-74811. Repr. of 1957 ed. 37.00 (ISBN 0-404-14885-9). AMS Pr.

Pleistocene Mustelidae. S. H. Reynolds. Repr. of 1912 ed. 16.00 (ISBN 0-384-50426-4). Johnson Repr.

Pleistocene Old World: Regional Perspectives. Ed. by Olga Soffer. LC 87-12329. (Interdisciplinary Contributions to Archaelogy Ser.). 402p. 1987. 39.50x (ISBN 0-306-42438-X, Plenum Pr). Plenum Pub.

Pleistocene Ovibos. S. H. Reynolds. pap. 10.00 (ISBN 0-384-50430-2). Johnson Repr.

Pleistocene Red Deer, Reindeer & Roe. S. H. Reynolds. pap. 10.00 (ISBN 0-384-50440-X). Johnson Repr.

Pleistocene Sequence in Southeastern Part of the Puget Sound Lowland, Washington. D. R. Crandall et al. (Reprint Ser.: No. 2). (Illus.). 14p. 1958. 0.25 (ISBN 0-686-36910-6). WA Div Geol.

Pleistocene Shoreline & Shelf Deposits at Fort Funston & Their Relation to Sea-Level Changes; Latest Cretaceous & Early Tertiary Depositional Systems of the Northern Diablo Range, California; Depositional Facies of Sedimentary Serpentinite: Selected Examples from the Coast Ranges, California. Ralph E. Hunter et al. (Guidebook Ser.: No. 3). 125p. 1984. pap. 19.00 (ISBN 0-918985-45-5). SEPM.

Pleistocene Vertebrate Faunas of Hungary. D. Janossy. (Developments in Palaeontology & Stratigraphy Ser.: No. 8). 205p. 1986. 78.00 (ISBN 0-444-99526-9). Elsevier.

Plekhanov, the Father of Russian Marxism. Samuel H. Baron. (Illus.). 1963. 39.50x (ISBN 0-8047-0104-0). Stanford U Pr.

Ple'Ma Spot? Eric Hill. 1985. 30.00x (ISBN 1-85022-004-2, Pub. by Dyllansow & Truran). State Mutual Bk.

Plena Ilustrita Vortaro De Esperanto. 2nd ed. Ed. by Gaston Waringhien. (Illus.). xxxvii, 1230p. (Esperanto.). 1970. 74.50x (ISBN 0-685-71608-2, 1069). Esperanto League North Am.

Plenary Meetings, 1985, Vol. II. 275p. 1987. pap. 21.00. UN.

Plenary Meetings, 1986, Vol. Two: Summary Records of the Plenary Meetings Held During the Second Regular Session of 1986. 163p. 1988. pap. 17.00. UN.

Plenary Papers: World Congress of Rehabilitation International, 14th, Winnipeg, Canada, 1980. 55p. 10.00 (ISBN 0-686-94883-1). Rehab Intl.

Pleneurethic: A New Approach to Life & Health. R. B. Collier. Ed. by Iris Myers. (Illus.). 1974. text ed. 4.50 (ISBN 0-533-01143-4, Pub. by Vantage). Pleneurethic Intl.

Pleneurethic: A World Class Philosophy. Richard B. Collier. (Illus.). 368p. 1981. 20.00 (ISBN 0-682-49753-3). Exposition-Phoenix.

Pleneurethic & the Brain. R. B. Collier. LC 65-81608. 2.50 (ISBN 0-686-17437-2). Pleneurethic Intl.

Pleneurethic: Its Evolution & Scientific Basis. Richard B. Collier. 318p. 1980. 15.00 (ISBN 0-682-49623-5). Exposition-Phoenix.

Plenty. David Hare. 1985. pap. 7.95 (ISBN 0-452-25956-8, Plume). NAL.

Plenty & Want. John Burnett. 1979. pap. 7.95 (ISBN 0-85967-462-2). Scolar.

Plenty & Want: A Social History of Diet in England from 1815 to the Present Day. John Burnett. 388p. (Orig.). 1985. pap. 10.95 (ISBN 0-85967-461-4, NO. 9344). Routledge Chapman & Hall.

Plenty-Coups: Chief of the Crows. Frank B. Linderman. LC 30-11369. (Illus.). x, 325p. 1962. pap. 7.95 (ISBN 0-8032-5121-1, BB 128, Bison). U of Nebr Pr.

Plenty for Everyone. Corrie TenBoom. 1967. pap. 2.95 (ISBN 0-87508-023-5). Chr Lit.

Plenty of Pelly & Peak. Sally Wittman. LC 79-3675. (Harper I Can Read Bks.). (Illus.). 64p. (gr. k-3). 1980. PLB 9.89 (ISBN 0-06-026564-7). HarpJ.

Plenty of Puppets to Make. Robyn Supraner & Lauren Supraner. LC 80-23785. (Illus.). 48p. (gr. 2-5). 1981. PLB 9.49 (ISBN 0-89375-432-3); pap. 1.95 (ISBN 0-89375-433-1). Troll Assocs.

Plenty of Room & Air. Dan Cushman. LC 75-20626. 1975. 14.95 (ISBN 0-911436-04-9). Stay Away.

Pleomorphic Fungi: The Diversity & Its Taxonomic Implications. Ed. by J. Sugiyama. 325p. 1987. 122.00 (ISBN 0-444-98966-8). Elsevier.

Pleroma Trinitatis: Die Trinitaetstheologie bei Matthias Joseph Scheeben. Karl-Heinz Minz. (Disputationes Theologicae Ser.: Vol. 10). 404p. 1982. 40.55 (ISBN 3-8204-6182-5). P Lang Pubs.

Plesiosaurus: The Swimming Reptile. Elizabeth Sandell. Ed. by Marjorie Oelerich & Howard Schroeder. LC 88-962. (Dinosaur Discovery Era Ser.). (Illus.). 32p. (gr. k-5). 1988. PLB 9.95 (ISBN 0-944280-04-8); pap. 4.95 (ISBN 0-944280-10-2). BSP Pub Inc.

Plessy Case: A Legal-Historical Interpretation. Charles A. Lofgren. LC 86-16264. 288p. 1987. 29.95x (ISBN 0-19-503852-5). Oxford U Pr.

Plessy Case: A Legal-Historical Interpretation. Charles A. Lofgren. 288p. 1988. pap. 9.95 (ISBN 0-19-505684-1). Oxford U Pr.

Plesteds: (A Family History) Dolores Plested. (Illus.). 205p. (Orig.). 1982. pap. 10.00. Bear Canon Bks.

Pletzl of Paris: Jewish Immigrant Workers in the Belle Epoque. Nancy L Green. 278p. 1985. 39.55 (ISBN 0-8419-0995-4). Holmes & Meier.

Pleuara in Health & Disease. Chretien. (Lung Biology in Health & Disease Ser.). 904p. 1986. 140.00 (ISBN 0-8247-7380-2). Dekker.

Pleural Effusion. Adrian O. Vladutiu. (Illus.). 440p. 1986. monograph 66.00 (ISBN 0-87993-285-6). Futura Pub.

Pleure pas P'tit Bonhomme. Rene Coulet-du-Gard. 320p. (Fr.). Repr. of 1977 ed. 18.00 (ISBN 0-939586-08-8). Edns Des Deux Mondes.

Plexus. Henry Miller. (Orig.). 1965. pap. 6.95 (ISBN 0-394-17431-3, B100, BC). Grove.

Plexus. Henry Miller. 640p. 1987. pap. 9.95 (ISBN 0-394-62370-3). Grove.

Plexus see Rosy Crucifixion.

Plexus Anesthesia: Perivascular Techniques of Brachial Plexus Block, Vol. 1. Alon P. Winnie. (Illus.). 272p. 1984. 83.00 (ISBN 0-7216-1172-9). Saunders.

Pleyel As Music Publisher. Rita Benton. Ed. by Jeanne Halley. (Annotated Reference Tools in Music Ser.: No. 3). 400p. 1989. lib. bdg. 65.00 (ISBN 0-918728-61-4). Pendragon NY.

Pleyn Delit: Medieval Cookery for Modern Cooks. rev ed. Constance B. Hieatt & Sharon Butler. LC 76-29734. (Illus.). 1976. 12.95; pap. 11.95 (ISBN 0-8020-6366-7). U of Toronto Pr.

Pleyto y Querella de los Guajolotes: Un Estudio. Gerardo Saenz. LC 87-81915. (Cuba y Sus Jueces). 122p. (Orig., Span.). 1988. pap. 16.00 (ISBN 0-89729-454-8). Ediciones.

Plight. Cid Corman. 1970. 5.00 (ISBN 0-685-00995-5). Elizabeth Pr.

Plight of a Sorcerer. Georges Dumezil et al. Ed. by Jaan Puhvel & David Weeks. 168p. 1986. text ed. 25.00x (ISBN 0-520-05534-9). U of Cal Pr.

Plight of Crime Victims in Modern Society. Ed. by Ezzat A. Fattah. 300p. 1987. 29.95 (ISBN 0-312-61758-5). St Martin.

Plight of Haitian Refugees. Jake C. Miller. LC 83-25209. 1984. 35.00 (ISBN 0-275-91230-2, C1230). Praeger.

Plight of Man & the Power of God. D. Martyn Lloyd-Jones. (Summit Bks.). 96p. 1982. pap. 2.95 (ISBN 0-8010-5621-7). Baker Bk.

Plight of Pamela Pollworth. Margaret SeBastian. 224p. (Orig.). 1980. pap. 1.75 (ISBN 0-449-50119-1, Coventry). Fawcett.

Plight of the Lesser Sawyer's Cricket: Plays, Prose & Poems. Curtis Zahn. Ed. & intro. by Clark Branson. 224p. (Orig.). 1987. 12.95 (ISBN 0-88496-262-8); pap. 7.95 (ISBN 0-88496-264-4). Capra Pr.

Plight of the Textile Industry: A Selective Bibliography. Alva W. Stewart. (Public Administration Ser.: P 2036). 12p. 1986. 3.75 (ISBN 1-55590-056-9). Vance Biblios.

Plight of the Thrift Institutions. Andrew S. Carron. LC 81-71434. (Studies in the Regulation of Economic Activity). 96p. 1982. 18.95 (ISBN 0-8157-1300-2); pap. 8.95 (ISBN 0-8157-1299-5). Brookings.

Plimpton Papers: Law & Diplomacy. Compiled by Pauline A. Plimpton & Kenneth W. Thompson. (Credibility of Institutions, Policies & Leadership Ser.: Vol. 8). 178p. (Orig.). 1985. lib. bdg. 19.75 (ISBN 0-8191-4783-4, Co-pub. by White Miller Center); pap. text ed. 11.50 (ISBN 0-8191-4784-2). U Pr of Amer.

Plins Pouvoirs. Jean Giraudoux. pap. 9.95 (ISBN 0-685-33923-8). French & Eur.

Pliny. Pliny. Tr. by C. Greig from Lat. LC 77-91088. (Illus.). 1979. 4.95x (ISBN 0-521-21978-7). Cambridge U Pr.

Pliny: Epistles Book X. Ed. by W. Williams. (Classical Texts-Latin Texts Ser.). 1990. text ed. 49.95 (ISBN 0-85668-407-4, Pub. by Aris & Phillips UK); pap. text ed. 16.50 (ISBN 0-85668-408-2, Pub. by Aris & Phillips UK). Humanities.

Pliocene Companion. Julian May. LC 84-9124. 219p. 1984. 13.95 (ISBN 0-395-36516-3). HM.

Pliocene Companion. Julian May. 1985. pap. 3.50 (ISBN 0-345-32290-8, Del Rey). Ballantine.

Pliocene Mollusca, 8 Nos. F. W. Harmer. 1914-24. Set. 128.00 (ISBN 0-384-21390-1). Johnson Repr.

PLO. Jillian Becker. (Illus.). 336p. 1985. pap. 9.95 (ISBN 0-312-59380-5). St Martin.

PLO--the Struggle Within: Towards an Independent Palestinian State. Alain Gresh. LC 88-3791. 320p. 1987. text ed. 49.95 (ISBN 0-86232-754-7, Pub. by Zed Pr); pap. text ed. 15.00 (ISBN 0-86232-755-5, Pub. by Zed Pr). Humanities.

P.L.O. after the Lebanon War. Emile Sahliyeh. 210p. 1985. 37.50x (ISBN 0-8133-0116-5). Westview.

PLO after Tripoli. Shireen Hunter. LC 84-9555. (Significant Issues Ser.: Vol. 6, No. 10). 26p. 1984. 6.95 (ISBN 0-89206-060-3). CSI Studies.

PLO after Tripoli. Ed. by Shireen Hunter. (Significant Issues Ser.: Vol. VI, No. 10). 34p. (Orig.). 1984. pap. text ed. 6.95 (ISBN 0-8191-5929-8, Pub. by CSIS). U Pr of Amer.

PLO & Palestine. Abdallah Frangi. (Illus.). 260p. 1983. 27.50x (ISBN 0-86232-194-8, Pub. by Zed Pr); pap. 9.955 (ISBN 0-86232-195-6, Pub. by Zed Pr). Humanities.

PLO & World Politics: Study of the Mobilisation of Support for the Palestinian Cause. Kemal Kirisci. 230p. 1987. 32.50 (ISBN 0-312-00382-X). St Martin.

PLO in Lebanon: Selected Documents. Ed. by Raphael Israeli. (Illus.). 316p. 1983. 25.00 (ISBN 0-312-59381-3). St Martin.

PLO: Politics of Survival. A. Miller. 1983. pap. 9.95 (ISBN 0-275-91583-2, B1583). Praeger.

PLO Strategy & Tactics. Aryeh Yodfat & Yuval Arnon-Ohanna. 1981. 25.00 (ISBN 0-312-61761-5). St Martin.

PLO: The Rise & Fall of the Palestine Liberation Organization. Jillian Becker. LC 84-40120. 288p. 1984. 19.95 (ISBN 0-312-59379-1). St Martin.

PLO under Arafat: Between Gun & Olive Branch. Shaul Mishal. LC 86-9140. 224p. 1986. 21.00x (ISBN 0-300-03709-0). Yale U Pr.

Plodding Princes of the Palouse. Nona Hengen. (Illus.). xi, 184p. (Orig.). 1984. pap. 14.95 (ISBN 0-931474-29-9). TBW Bks.

Plodmey: The Got-Me Pothole. Diane Ague. (Illus.). 21p. (gr. 1-3). 1987. 5.95 (ISBN 0-533-06905-X). Vantage.

Plop! Plop! Date not set. 3.95 (ISBN 0-8351-1245-4). China Bks.

Plosives. Joanne D. Subtelney & Ann K. Lieberth. (Speech & Auditory Training Ser.). 1985. text ed. 39.00 manual & cards (ISBN 0-88450-924-9). Communication Skill.

Plot. Ansen Dibell. 176p. 1988. 12.95 (ISBN 0-89879-303-3). Writers Digest.

Plot. Elizabeth Dipple. (Critical Idiom Ser.: Vol. 12). 1970. pap. 5.50x (ISBN 0-416-19780-9, NO. 2165). Routledge Chapman & Hall.

Plot. Irving Wallace. 1984. pap. 5.95 (ISBN 0-671-52523-9). PB.

Plot Against Christianity. Elizabeth Dilling. 310p. 12.00 (ISBN 0-913022-33-0). Angriff Pr.

Plot Against Christianity: A Study of the Talmud. E. Dilling. 1982. lib. bdg. 69.95 (ISBN 0-87700-359-9). Revisionist Pr.

Plot Against Mexico. L. J. De Bekker. 1976. lib. bdg. 59.95 (ISBN 0-8490-0844-1). Gordon Pr.

Plot Against Roger Rider. Julian Symons. 192p. 1975. pap. 3.95 (ISBN 0-14-003949-X). Penguin.

Plot Against the Catholic Church: Communism, Free Masonry & the Jewish Fifth Column in the Clergy. M. Pinay. 1979. lib. bdg. 69.95 (ISBN 0-8490-2984-8). Gordon Pr.

Plot Against the Church. Maurice Pinay. 1978. 15.00x (ISBN 0-911038-39-6). Noontide.

Plot Against the Pom-Pom Queen. Ellen Lenroe. (gr. 7 up). 1985. 12.95 (ISBN 0-525-67161-7, 01258-430). Lodestar Bks.

Plot Against the Pom-Pom Queen. Ellen Leroe. 144p. (YA) 1986. pap. 2.50 (ISBN 0-425-08867-7, Pub. by Berkley-Pacer). Berkley Pub.

Plot & Its Construction in Eighteenth Century Criticism of French Comedy: A Study of the Theory with Relation to the Practice of Beaumarchais. Edna C. Fredrick. LC 72-82001. 132p. 1973. Repr. of 1934 ed. lib. bdg. 21.00 (ISBN 0-8337-4118-7). B Franklin.

Plot-It-Yourself Adventure: Goonies Cavern of Horror. William Rotsler. Ed. by Diane Arico. 128p. (Orig.). (gr. 3-7). 1985. pap. 3.95 (ISBN 0-671-60135-0). Wanderer Bks.

Plot It Yourself Horror Stories, No. 8: Dungeon Demons. Hilary Milton. Ed. by Diane Arico. (Illus.). 128p. (gr. 3-7). 1985. pap. 2.95 (ISBN 0-671-54448-9). Wanderer Bks.

Plot of the Mice & Aesop's Forest. Robert Coover & Brian Swann. Incl. Aesop's Forest. (Back-to-Back Ser.). (Illus.). 96p. (Orig.). 1986. pap. 7.50 (ISBN 0-88496-252-0). Capra Pr.

Plot of the Short Story. Henry A. Phillips. LC 73-4412. 1973. lib. bdg. 25.50 (ISBN 0-8414-2465-9). Folcroft.

Plot or Politics: The Garrison Case & Its Cast. Rosemary James & Jack Wardlaw. (Illus.). 1967. pap. 2.95 (ISBN 0-911116-11-7). Pelican.

Plot Outlines of One Hundred Famous Plays. Ed. by Van H. Cartmell. 11.25 (ISBN 0-8446-0539-5). Peter Smith.

Plot Pak: Precalculus Tutorials with Computer Graphics. John Mowbray. (Software Ser.). 208p. 1986. pap. text ed. 29.95 pub net (ISBN 0-534-07542-8); disk incl. Brooks-Cole.

Plot, Story, & the Novel: From Dickens & Poe to the Modern Period. Robert L. Caserio. LC 79-4321. 1979. 34.00x (ISBN 0-691-06382-6). Princeton U Pr.

Plot-Your-Own-Adventure: Distress Call. William Rotsler. Ed. by Wendy Barish. (Star Trek II). (Illus., Orig.). (gr. 3-7). 1982. pap. 2.95 (ISBN 0-671-46389-6). Wanderer Bks.

Plot-Your-Own Horror Stories: Craven House Horrors, No. 1. Hilary Milton. Ed. by Meg Schneider. LC 82-7020. (Illus.). 128p. (Orig.). (gr. 3-7). 1982. pap. 2.95 (ISBN 0-671-45631-8). Wanderer Bks.

Plotin & l'Occident: Firmicus Maternus, Marius Victorinus, Saint Augustin, et Macrobe. P. Henry. (Classical Studies Ser.). (Fr.). Repr. of 1934 ed. lib. bdg. 39.50x (ISBN 0-697-00039-7). Irvington.

Plotinus. G. R. Mead. 1983. pap. 5.95 (ISBN 0-916411-01-X, Pub. by Alexandrian Pr). Holmes Pub.

Plotinus: Essay on the Beautiful. Plotinus. Tr. by Thomas Taylor. 1984. pap. 6.95 (ISBN 0-916411-86-9, Pub. by Alexandrian Pr). Holmes Pub.

Plotinus on Sense-Perception: A Philosophical Study. Eyjolfur K. Emilsson. 200p. 1988. 37.50 (ISBN 0-521-32988-4). Cambridge U Pr.

Plotinus: The Road to Reality. J. M. Rist. 1977. 39.50 (ISBN 0-521-06085-0); pap. 14.95 (ISBN 0-521-29202-6). Cambridge U Pr.

Plotonic Mr. P., the Unwritten Tales of Edgar Allan Poe: A Nineteenth Century Artist Who Might Have Been a Twentieth. Katrina Bachinger. Ed. by James Hogg. (Romantic Reassessment Ser.). 144p. (Orig.). 1980. pap. 15.00 (ISBN 3-7052-0554-4, Pub. by Salzburg Studies). Longwood Pub Group.

Plots. Jerome McDonough. 24p. (Orig.). 1981. pap. 1.50 (ISBN 0-88680-154-0). I E Clark.

Plots Against Presidents. 2nd ed. John M. Potter. 1969. 14.95 (ISBN 0-8392-1178-3). Astor-Honor.

Plots & Characters in Classic French Fiction. Ed. by Benjamin E. Hicks. LC 81-1709. (Plots & Characters Ser.). 253p. 1981. 27.50 (ISBN 0-208-01703-8, Archon). Shoe String.

Plots & Characters in Major Russian Fiction, Vol. 1: Pushkin, Lermontov, Turgenev, & Tolstoy. Thomas E. Berry. LC 76-58458. (Plots & Characters Ser.). xiv, 226p. 1977. 25.00 (ISBN 0-208-01584-1, Archon). Shoe String.

Plots & Characters in the Fiction of Eighteenth-Century English Authors, Vol. 1: Swift, Defoe & Richardson. Ed. by Clifford Johnson. LC 77-2572. xx, 270p. 1977. 27.50 (ISBN 0-208-01498-5, Archon). Shoe String.

Plots & Characters in the Fiction of Eighteenth-Century English Authors, Volume II: Stern, Fielding, Smollett, Goldsmith, & Johnson. Ed. by Clifford Johnson. (Plots & Characters Ser.). xxv, 243p. 1978. 27.50 (ISBN 0-208-01602-3, Archon). Shoe String.

Plots & Characters in the Fiction of Jane Austen, the Brontes & George Eliot. John Halperin & Janet Kunert. LC 76-14451. (Plots & Characters Ser.). x, 282p. 1976. 27.50 (ISBN 0-208-01460-8, Archon). Shoe String.

Plots & Characters in the Fiction of James Fenimore Cooper. Ed. by Warren S. Walker. LC 78-9469. (Plots & Characters Ser.). xii, 346p. 1978. 29.50 (ISBN 0-208-01497-7, Archon). Shoe String.

Plots & Characters in the Fiction of William Dean Howells. George C. Carrington, Jr. & Ildiko Carrington. LC 75-45257. (Plots & Characters Ser.). xxiii, 306p. 1976. 27.50 (ISBN 0-208-01461-6, Archon). Shoe String.

Plots & Conspiracies. Andrew Shirley. LC 75-27686. (Illus.). 142p. 1975. Repr. of 1957 ed. lib. bdg. 35.00x (ISBN 0-8371-8459-2, SHPC). Greenwood.

Plots & Personalities: A New Method of Testing & Training the Creative Imagination. Edwin E. Slosson & J. Downey. 1922. Repr. 20.00 (ISBN 0-8274-3145-7). R West.

Plots of Some of the Most Famous Old English Plays. Henry Grey. LC 72-13684. 1973. lib. bdg. 17.00 (ISBN 0-8414-1265-0). Folcroft.

Plots, Transformation & Regression: An Introduction to Graphical Methods of Diagnostic Regression Analysis. A. C. Atkinson. (Statistical Science Ser.). (Illus.). 296p. 1987. pap. 32.50 (ISBN 0-19-853371-3). Oxford U Pr.

Plots, Transformations & Regression: Introduction to Graphical Methods of Diagnostic Regression Analysis. A. C. Atkinson. (Oxford Statistical Science Ser.). (Illus.). 296p. 1985. 45.00x (ISBN 0-19-853359-4). Oxford U Pr.

Plotters & Patterns of American Land Surveying. 232p. (Orig.). 1986. pap. 16.00 (ISBN 0-317-59952-6, 974). Landmark Ent.

Plotters & Patterns of American Land Surveying. Date not set. price not set (S283). Am Congrs Survey.

Plotting America's Past: Fenimore Cooper & the Leatherstocking Tales. William P. Kelly. LC 83-4779. 208p. 1984. 19.95x (ISBN 0-8093-1144-5). S Ill U Pr.

Plotting Directions: An Activist's Guide. Chris Robinson. LC 82-80105. (Illus.). 68p. 1982. pap. 4.00. Recon Pubns.

Plotting the Golden West: American Literature & the Rhetoric of the California Trail. Stephen Fender. LC 81-6077. (Illus.). 200p. 1982. 27.95 (ISBN 0-521-23924-9). Cambridge U Pr.

Plough & the Swastika: The NSDAP & Agriculture in Germany 1928-45. John E. Farquharson. LC 74-31570. (Sage Studies in 20th Century History Ser.: Vol. 5). pap. 80.00 (ISBN 0-317-29682-5, 2021897). Bks Demand UMI.

Plough & the Sword. Carl T. Schmidt. LC 38-3030. Repr. of 1938 ed. 16.50 (ISBN 0-404-05608-3). AMS Pr.

Plough in Field Arable: Western Agribusiness in Third World Agriculture. Sarah P. Voll. LC 80-50490. (Illus.). 223p. 1980. 20.00x (ISBN 0-87451-186-0). U Pr of New Eng.

Plough Woman. Rachel Katznelson-Shazar. 1975. 7.95 (ISBN 0-685-82599-X); soft bdg. 3.95 (ISBN 0-685-82600-7). Herzl Pr.

Plough Women: Records of the Pioneer Women of Palestine. Ed. by Rachel Rubashow-Katznelson. LC 75-6441. (Rise of Jewish Nationalism & the Middle East Ser.). 306p. 1975. Repr. 27.50 (ISBN 0-88355-328-7). Hyperion Conn.

Ploughboy's Glory. Michael Dawney. 58p. (Orig.). 1977. pap. 9.95 (ISBN 0-85418-117-2). Princeton Bk Co.

Ploughman's Lunch. Ian McEwan. (Illus.). 72p. 1985. pap. 8.50 (ISBN 0-413-58420-8, 9653). Heinemann Ed.

Ploughs & Politicks: Charles Read of New Jersey & His Notes on Agriculture, 1715-1744. Carl R. Woodward. LC 73-16351. (Perspectives in American History Ser.: No. 24). (Illus.). 468p. 1974. Repr. of 1941 ed. lib. bdg. 37.50x (ISBN 0-87991-338-X). Porcupine Pr.

Ploughshare Village: Culture & Context in Taiwan. Stevan Harrell. LC 82-8333. (Publications of the School of International Studies on Asia: No. 35). (Illus.). 248p. 1982. 25.00x (ISBN 0-295-95946-0). U of Wash Pr.

Ploughshares into Swords: Josiah Gorgas & Confederate Ordinance. Frank E. Vandiver. (Austin Reprints Ser.). pap. 90.80 (2026979). Bks Demand UMI.

Ploughshares Poetry Reader. Ed. by Joyce Peseroff. 1987. pap. 9.95 (ISBN 0-452-00846-8, Mer). NAL.

Ploughshares Poetry Reader. Ed. & intro. by Joyce Peseroff. LC 86-6319. 336p. 25.00 (ISBN 0-933277-02-4). Ploughshares Bks.

Ploughshares Reader: New Fiction for the 80's. Ed. by DeWitt Henry. 1985. 24.95 (ISBN 0-916366-30-8). Pushcart Pr.

Ploughshares Reader: New Fiction for the Eighties. Ed. by DeWitt Henry. 112p. 1986. pap. 9.95 (ISBN 0-452-25824-3, Plume). NAL.

Plovers, Sandpipers, & Snipes of the World. Paul A. Johnsgard. LC 80-22712. (Illus.). xviii, 541p. 1981. 45.00 (ISBN 0-8032-2553-9). U of Nebr Pr.

Plow a New Furrow. Emma Hedman. 176p. (Orig.). 1985. pap. 8.95 (ISBN 0-934318-47-6). Falcon Pr MT.

Plow-Horse Cavalry: The Carey Creek Boys of the Thirty-Fourth Texas. Robert S. Weddle. LC 74-75208. 1974. 12.00 (ISBN 0-89052-004-6). Madrona Pr.

Plow, the Hammer, & the Knout: An Economic History of Eighteenth-Century Russia. Arcadius Kahan. Ed. by Richard Hellie. LC 84-16338. (Illus.). xii, 400p. 1985. 65.00x (ISBN 0-226-42253-4). U. of Chicago Pr.

Plow Women Rather Than Reapers: An Intellectual History of Feminism in the United States. Sarah S. Schramm. LC 78-10907. 451p. 1979. lib. bdg. 25.00 (ISBN 0-8108-1183-9). Scarecrow.

Plowboys, Cowboys & Slanted Pigs: A Collection. Jerry Flemmons. LC 84-2421. (Illus.). 230p. 1984. 15.95 (ISBN 0-912646-90-X); pap. 8.95 (ISBN 0-912646-95-0). Tex Christian.

Plowing My Own Furrow. Howard W. Moore. LC 84-22610. (Illus.). 1985. 12.95 (ISBN 0-393-01977-2). Norton.

Plowing the Wind. Betty Andrews. 50p. 1985. pap. 15.00 (ISBN 0-9614597-2-7). Ninja Pr.

Plowman from Bohemia. Johannes Saaz. Tr. by Alexander Henderson & Elizabeth Henderson. LC 66-16315. pap. 6.95x (ISBN 0-8044-6786-2). Ungar.

Plowman's Folly & a Second Look. Edward H. Faulkner. (Conservation Classics Ser.). 370p. 1987. 29.95 (ISBN 0-933280-51-3); pap. 19.95 (ISBN 0-933280-43-2). Island CA.

Plowshares: A Contemporary Fable of Peace & War. Sonia Ralston. LC 86-2443. 80p. 1986. pap. 4.95 (ISBN 0-8091-2788-1). Paulist Pr.

Plowshares into Swords: Arms Races in International Politics. Grant T. Hammond. (Westview Special Studies in International Relations: No. 14). 240p. 1988. 35.00 (ISBN 0-8133-7561-4). Westview.

Plowshares: Poems for Nuclear Disarmament & a Play. Jocelyn Hollis. LC 87-31912. 80p. 1988. lib. bdg. 14.95 (ISBN 0-930933-06-0); text ed. 14.95 (ISBN 0-930933-07-9); pap. text ed. 7.95 (ISBN 0-930933-08-7). Am Poetry & Lit.

Plowshares to Printouts. Hiram R. Drache. (Illus.). 263p. 1985. 14.95 (ISBN 0-8134-2459-3, 2459). Inter Print Pubs.

Plowzone Archeology: Contributions to Theory & Technique. Ed. by Michael J. O'Brien & Dennis E. Lewarch. (Publications in Anthropology: No.27). 214p. 1981. 12.15 (ISBN 0-935462-18-X). Vanderbilt Pubns.

Ploymer Physics. (Advances in Polymer Science Ser.: Vol. 85). (Illus.). 150p. 1987. 65.50 (ISBN 0-387-18484-8). Springer-Verlag.

Pluck. Jonathan Webb. 336p. 1986. pap. 3.95 (ISBN 0-7704-2009-5). Bantam.

Pluck & Luck. Robert Benchley. 296p. Repr. of 1925 ed. lib. bdg. 18.95x (ISBN 0-88411-308-6, Pub. by Aeonian Pr). Amereon Ltd.

Plucked Chickens. James Magorian. LC 80-68263. 32p. (gr. 4-6). 1981. 5.00 (ISBN 0-930674-04-9). Black Oak.

Plug-In Drug. rev. ed. Marie Winn. 304p. 1985. 17.95 (ISBN 0-670-80378-2). Viking.

Plug-In Drug: Television, Children & the Family. Marie Winn. (Penguin Nonfiction Ser.). 288p. 1985. pap. 6.95 (ISBN 0-14-007698-0). Penguin.

Plugged Nickel. Robert Campbell. 1987. pap. 3.50 (ISBN 0-671-64363-0). PB.

Plugging into Canada: Prospects for U. S. - Canadian Electricity Trade. Dina W. Kruger. 74p. (Orig.). 1988. pap. 50.00 (ISBN 0-931035-26-0). IRRC Inc DC.

Plugs, Receptacles, & Cable Connectors of the Pin & Sleeve Type for Industrial Use. 1983. 10.00 (ISBN 0-318-18029-4, PR 4-1983). Natl Elec Mfrs.

Plugs, Receptacles, & Connectors of the Pin & Sleeve Type for Hazardous Locations. 1983. 15.00 (ISBN 0-318-18028-6, PB 2.2-1983). Natl Elec Mfrs.

Pluie et le Beau Temps. Jacques Prevert. (Folio Ser.: No. 90). 256p. 1955. 6.95 (ISBN 0-686-54916-3). Schoenhof.

Plum Blossom. Li Ch'ing Chao. Tr. by James Cryer from Chinese. (Illus.). 90p. (Orig.). 1984. pap. 5.00 (ISBN 0-932112-18-8). Carolina Wren.

Plum Blossoms in the Mist. Rochelle Holt. 1977. 1.95 (ISBN 0-934536-09-0). Merging Media.

Plum Bun: A Novel Without a Moral. Jessie Fauset. 400p. 1985. 15.95 (ISBN 0-86358-057-2, Pandora Pr); pap. 8.95 (ISBN 0-86358-044-0, Pandora Pr). Routledge Chapman & Hall.

Plum Crazy, a Book about Beach Plums. Elizabeth P. Mirel. 160p. 1986. pap. 6.95 (ISBN 0-940160-34-X). Parnassus Imprints.

Plum Creek Story of Laura Ingalls Wilder. William Anderson. (Illus.). 50p. 1987. pap. 5.95 (ISBN 0-9610088-7-3). Anderson MI.

Plum Jelly & Stained Glass & Other Prayers. Jo Carr & Imogene Sorley. 1981. pap. 2.50 (ISBN 0-687-31660-X, Festival). Abingdon.

Plum Plum Pickers. 2nd ed. Raymond Barrio. LC 84-70568. 232p. 1984. pap. 12.00x (ISBN 0-916950-51-4). Biling Rev-Pr.

Plum Poems. Ross Feld. LC 79-137210. (Illus.). 1971. pap. 5.00 (ISBN 0-912330-06-6, Dist. by Inland Bk). Jargon Soc.

Plum Thicket. Janice H. Giles. 1978. pap. 1.95 (ISBN 0-449-23767-2, Crest). Fawcett.

Plum Tree. David G. Phillips. (Collected Works of David G. Phillips). 1988. Repr. of 1981 ed. lib. bdg. 59.00x. Am Biog Serv.

Plum Tree. David G. Phillips. LC 68-57547. (Muckrakers Ser.). (Illus.). 389p. Repr. of 1905 ed. lib. bdg. 17.50 (ISBN 0-8398-1566-2). Irvington.

Plum Tree. David G. Phillips. (American Author Ser.). 1981. Repr. lib. bdg. 19.00 (ISBN 0-686-71938-7). Scholarly.

Plum Tree. David G. Phillips. (Muckrakers Ser.). (Illus.). 389p. 1986. pap. text ed. 9.95x (ISBN 0-8290-1884-0). Irvington.

Plum Tree Lane. Lodwick Hartley. LC 78-53759. (Illus.). 204p. 1978. 5.95 (ISBN 0-87844-042-9). Sandlapper Pub Co.

Plumage of the Sun. Margaret K. Biggs. (Illus.). 92p. 1986. 12.00 (ISBN 0-942544-10-2). Negative Capability Pr.

Plumas Estelares De Puerto Rico, Bk. 2: Siglo XX. Cesareo Rosa Nieves. 6.25 (ISBN 0-8477-3148-0). U of PR Pr.

Plumas Sketches. Jane B. Little. LC 83-50356. (Illus.). 112p. (Orig.). 1983. 12.95 (ISBN 0-9611886-1-8); pap. 7.95 (ISBN 0-9611886-0-X). Wolf Creek Pr.

Plumbate: A Mesoamerican Trade Ware. Anna O. Shepard. LC 77-11522. (Carnegie Institution of Washington. Publication: No. 573). Repr. of 1948 ed. 23.00 (ISBN 0-404-16289-4). AMS Pr.

Plumber. Jack Rudman. (Career Examination Ser.: C-591). (Cloth bdg. avail. on request). pap. 14.00 (ISBN 0-8373-0591-8). Natl Learning.

Plumber-Steam Fitter. 4th ed. Sparandaro. 224p. 1987. pap. 10.95 (ISBN 0-13-683475-2). Arco.

Plumbers. Robert Stewart. LC 88-70064. 64p. 1988. 8.50 (ISBN 0-933532-68-7). BkMk.

Plumbers & Pipe Fitters Library, 3 vols. 3rd, rev. ed. Charles McConnell & Tom Philbin. Incl. Vol. 1. Materials, Tools, Roughing-In (ISBN 0-672-23385-1); Vol. 2. Welding, Heating, Air Conditioning (ISBN 0-672-23386-X); Vol. 3. Water Supply, Drainage, Calcuations (ISBN 0-672-23387-8). LC 83-6384. (Illus.). 1983. Set. 34.95 (ISBN 0-672-23384-3, Pub. by Audel); 11.95 ea. Macmillan.

Plumber's & Pipefitter's Handbook. William J. Hornung. (Illus.). 256p. 1984. 29.00 (ISBN 0-13-683912-6). P-H.

Plumbers & Pipefitters Library, 3 vols. Charles N. McConnell. Incl. Vol. I. Materials, Tools, Roughing-In. 19.95 (ISBN 0-02-582911-4); Vol. II. Welding, Heating, Air Conditioning. 19.95 (ISBN 0-02-582912-2); Vol. III. Water Supply, Drainage, Calculations. 19.95 (ISBN 0-02-582913-0). 1988. Set. 59.95 (ISBN 0-02-582914-9). Macmillan.

Plumber's Apprentice see Groves of Academe.

Plumber's Exam Preparation Guide. Howard C. Massey. LC 85-19050. 320p. (Orig.). 1985. pap. 21.00 (ISBN 0-934041-04-0). Craftsman.

Plumbers' Handbook. 7th ed. Joseph P. Almond. LC 82-1342. (Illus.). 1985. pap. 10.95 (ISBN 0-672-23419-X, Pub. by Audel). Macmillan.

Plumbers' Handbook. 6th ed. Joseph P. Almond, Sr. LC 82-1342. 1982. 9.95 (ISBN 0-672-23370-3). Bobbs.

Plumbers Handbook. rev. ed. Howard C. Massey. LC 85-9668. (Illus.). 240p. 1985. pap. 18.00 (ISBN 0-910460-49-3). Craftsman.

Plumber's Helper. Jack Rudman. (Career Examination Ser.: C-592). (Cloth bdg. avail. on request). pap. 12.00. Natl Learning.

Plumber's Toolbox Manual. Louis J. Mahiau. (On-the-Job Reference Ser.): 352p. 1989. pap. 9.95 (ISBN 0-13-683806-5). P-H.

Plumbing. 3rd ed. Harold E. Babbitt. 1959. text ed. 66.50 (ISBN 0-07-002688-2). McGraw.

Plumbing. G. J. Blower. (Illus.). 208p. 1982. pap. text ed. 19.95x (ISBN 0-7121-1750-4). Trans-Atl Phila.

Plumbing. (Illus.). 40p. (gr. 6-12). 1965. pap. 1.25x (ISBN 0-8395-3386-1, 3386). BSA.

Plumbing. (Home Repair & Improvement Ser.). (Illus.). 1976. 12.95 (ISBN 0-8094-2366-9). Time-Life.

Plumbing. Jack Rudman. (Occupational Competency Examination Ser.: OCE-29). (Cloth bdg. avail. on request). pap. 13.95 (ISBN 0-8373-5729-2). Natl Learning.

Plumbing. Ed. by Time Life Books. LC 76-46139. (Home Repair & Improvement Ser.). (Illus.). (gr. 7 up). 1976. lib. bdg. 15.94 (ISBN 0-8094-2367-7, Pub. by Time-Life). Silver.

Plumbing - Pipe Fitting Occupations: Equipment Planning Guides for Vocational & Technical Training. 2nd ed. (Technical Training & Education Programme: No. 6). 1981. pap. 28.00 (ISBN 92-2-101893-8, ILO1043, ILO). UNIPUB.

Plumbing & Heating. William J. Hornung. (Illus.). 224p. 1982. 28.00 (ISBN 0-13-683920-7). P-H.

Plumbing Design & Installation Reference Guide. Tyler G. Hicks. 368p. 1986. text ed. 42.00 (ISBN 0-07-028788-0). McGraw.

Plumbing Engineer. Jack Rudman. (Career Examination Ser.: C-2713). (Cloth bdg. avail. on request). 1988. pap. 16.00 (ISBN 0-8373-2713-X). Natl Learning.

Plumbing Fixtures & Fittings. 1987. 750.00 (ISBN 0-318-04397-1). Busn Trend.

Plumbing for Dummies. Don Fredrikson. 1985. pap. 10.95 (ISBN 0-02-081250-7, Collier). Macmillan.

Plumbing for Dummies: A Guide to the Maintenance & Repair of Everything Including the Kitchen Sink. Don Fredriksson. LC 82-17790. (Illus.). 256p. 1983. pap. 10.95 (ISBN 0-672-52738-3). Bobbs.

Plumbing for Old & New Houses. 2nd ed. Jay Hedden. Ed. by Shirley M. Horowitz. LC 81-67297. (Illus.). 160p. (Orig.). 1980. 22.95 (ISBN 0-932944-45-0); pap. 7.95 (ISBN 0-932944-46-9). Creative Homeowner.

Plumbing Fundamentals. James L. Thiesse. (Contemporary Construction Ser.). (Illus.). 192p. (gr. 10-12). 1981. text ed. 29.96 (ISBN 0-07-064191-9). McGraw.

Plumbing Inspector. Jack Rudman. (Career Examination Ser.: C-593). (Cloth bdg. avail. on request). pap. 16.00 (ISBN 0-8373-0593-4). Natl Learning.

Plumbing: Installation & Design. Thomas Philbin. 227p. 1988. text ed. 19.00 net (ISBN 0-15-570675-6). HarBraceJ.

Plumbing Installation & Design. 2nd ed. L. V. Ripka. (Illus.). 360p. 1987. 23.96 (ISBN 0-8269-0606-0). Am Technical.

Plumbing: Installation & Design. James A. Sullivan. (Illus.). 480p. 1980. text ed. 31.00 (ISBN 0-8359-5552-4, Reston); instr's. manual avail. (ISBN 0-8359-5553-2). P-H.

Plumbing Materials & Drinking Water Quality. Thomas J. Sorg & Frank A. Bell, Jr. LC 85-25840. (Pollution Technology Review Ser.: No. 128). (Illus.). 182p. 1986. 36.00 (ISBN 0-8155-1066-7). Noyes.

Plumbing Repairs Simplified. rev. ed. Donald R. Brann. LC 67-27691. 1976. lib. bdg. 5.95 (ISBN 0-87733-750-0). Easi-Bild.

Plumbing Repairs Simplified. Donald R. Brann. LC 82-70274. 1983. pap. 9.95 (ISBN 0-87733-875-2). Easi-Bild.

Plumbing Supervisor. Jack Rudman. (Career Examination Ser.: C-2583). (Cloth bdg. avail. on request). pap. 16.00 (ISBN 0-8373-2583-8). Natl Learning.

Plumbing Workbook. Jack Rudman. (Workbook Ser.: No. 3160). (Cloth bdg. avail. on request). 1988. pap. 13.95 (ISBN 0-8373-6805-7). Natl Learning.

Plume Rise. G. A. Briggs. LC 77-603261. (AEC Critical Review Ser.). 81p. 1969. pap. 10.00 (ISBN 0-87079-304-7, TID-25075); microfiche 6.50 (ISBN 0-87079-305-5, TID-25075). DOE.

Plumed Serpent. D. H. Lawrence. Ed. by L. D. Clark. (Cambridge Edition of the Works of D. H. Lawrence). 624p. 1987. 79.50 (ISBN 0-521-22262-1); pap. 24.95 (ISBN 0-521-29422-3). Cambridge U Pr.

Plumed Serpent. David H. Lawrence. 1955. pap. 6.95 (ISBN 0-394-70023-6, Vin). Random.

Plumes in the Dust: The Love Affair of Edgar Allen Poe & Fanny Osgood. John E. Walsh. LC 79-27534. (Illus.). 168p. 1980. 17.95 (ISBN 0-88229-683-3). Nelson-Hall.

Plymouth County, 1685. Cynthia H. Krusell. (Illus.). 64p. (Orig.). 1986. pap. 9.95 (ISBN 0-940628-43-0). Pilgrim Soc.

Plymouth Court Records, 16 vols. Ed. by David T. Konig. LC 78-62076. 1980. Set. 895.00 (ISBN 0-89453-096-8). M Glazier.

Plymouth in the Nineteenth Century. Laurence R. Pizer. (Pilgrim Society Notes Ser.: No. 31). 1983. 2.00 (ISBN 0-940628-48-1). Pilgrim Soc.

Plymouth Muscle Cars 1966-71. R. M. Clarke. (Illus.). 100p. (Orig.). 1983. pap. 13.95 (ISBN 0-946489-05-X, Pub. by Brooklands Bks England). Motorbooks Intl.

Plymouth Patents. Paul C. Reardon. (Pilgrim Society Notes Ser.: No. 27). 2.00 (ISBN 0-940628-35-X). Pilgrim Soc.

Plymouth Pilgrims: A History of the Eighty-Fifth New York Volunteer Infantry in the Civil War. Wayne Mahood. Ed. by David G. Martin. (Illus.). 1988. price not set (ISBN 0-944413-09-9). Longstreet Hse.

Plymouth Rock: History & Significance. Rose T. Briggs. 1968. 1.50 (ISBN 0-940628-03-1). Pilgrim Soc.

Plymouth 1968-1976. LC 76-9517. 256p. 1986. 13.95 (ISBN 0-8019-6552-7). Chilton.

Plyometrics. Will Freeman & Evelyn Freeman. 54p. (Orig.). 1984. pap. 5.95 (ISBN 0-89279-068-7). Championship Bks.

Plyometrics: Explosive Power Training. 2nd ed. James C. Radcliffe & Robert C. Farentinos. LC 85-14409. 136p. 1985. pap. text ed. 11.00x (ISBN 0-87322-024-2, BRAD0024). Human Kinetics.

Plywood & Adhesive Technology. Sellers. 840p. 1985. 110.00 (ISBN 0-8247-7407-8). Dekker.

Plywood, Fibreboard & Particle Board. (Terminology Bulletins: No. 30). 162p. (Eng., Fr., Ital., Ger. & Span.). 1976. pap. 11.25 (F1218, FAO). UNIPUB.

Plywood Headers for Residential Construction, Vol. 5. (Research Report Ser.). 48p. 1983. pap. 8.00 (ISBN 0-86718-200-8). Nat Assn H Build.

Plywood Manufacturing Practices. 2nd rev. ed. Richard F. Baldwin. LC 80-84894. (Forest Industries Bk.). (Illus.). 344p. 1981. 42.50 (ISBN 0-87930-092-2). Miller Freeman.

PM-AM: New & Selected Poems. Linda Pastan. 128p. 1982. pap. 6.95 (ISBN 0-393-30055-2). Norton.

PM in the AM. Jerry Burns. 1966. pap. 1.00 (ISBN 0-686-14905-X). Goliards Pr.

PMEF Oil Heat Technician's Manual. 534p. 1979. 40.00 (ISBN 0-318-17602-5, F-5). Petro Mktg Ed Found.

PMO Theory of Organic Chemistry. Michael J. Dewar & Ralph C. Dougherty. LC 74-12196. (Illus.). 576p. 1975. 79.50x (ISBN 0-306-30779-0, Plenum Pr); pap. 25.00x (ISBN 0-306-20010-4). Plenum Pub.

PMS: An Infobook for Teenage Women, Their Friends & Families. Gilda Berger. LC 85-14473. (Illus.). 96p. (gr. 7-12). 1985. pap. 6.95 (ISBN 0-89793-035-5). Hunter Hse.

PMS & Alcoholism. Therese Casey. 20p. (Orig.). 1984. pap. 0.95 (ISBN 0-89486-247-2). Hazelden.

PMS & You. Elizabeth K. White et al. (Illus.). 40p. 1986. pap. 2.00 (ISBN 0-317-59865-1). Budlong.

P.M.S. Attacks & Other Inconveniences of Life. Steven Phillips. (Illus.). 112p. 1988. pap. 4.95 (ISBN 0-89815-239-9). Ten Speed Pr.

PMS Diet Cookbook: With an Overview of Premenstrual Syndrome Plus Self-Help Recommendations for Every Woman. Sharon A. Heinz. 69p. (Orig.). 1987. pap. 6.50 (ISBN 0-9619495-0-3). Heinz Pr.

PMS: Pre-Menstrual Syndrome. Ronald V. Norris & Colleen Sullivan. 50p. 1987. pap. 4.50 (ISBN 0-425-10332-3). Berkley Pub.

PMS: Premenstrual Syndrome. Gilda Berger. (Impact Bks.). 128p. (gr. 7-12). 1984. lib. bdg. 12.90 (ISBN 0-531-04857-8). Watts.

PMS: Premenstrual Syndrome, an Infobook for Teenage Women & Their Friends & Families. Gilda Berger. LC 85-28012. 85p. 1985. Repr. lib. bdg. 19.95x (ISBN 0-89370-574-8). Borgo Pr.

PMS: Premenstrual Syndrome & You-Next Month Can be Different. Niels H. Lauersen & Eileen Stukane. LC 83-11359. (Illus.). 224p. (Orig.). 1983. 8.95 (ISBN 0-671-47242-9, Fireside). S&S.

PMS-Premenstrual Syndrome: The Cause & Cure of the Syndrome That Affects 5,000,000 American Women. Ronald V. Norris & Colleen Sullivan. LC 82-42700. 331p. 1983. 15.95 (ISBN 0-89256-238-2). Rawson Assocs.

PMS Solution: A Nutritional Approach to Premenstrual Syndrome. Ann Nazzaro et al. 156p. (Orig.). 1985. pap. 7.95 (ISBN 0-86683-793-0, AY8554, HarpR). Har-Row.

PMS Solution-Premenstrual Syndrome: The Nutritional Approach. Ann Nazzaro et al. 160p. (Orig.). 1985. pap. 9.95 (ISBN 0-920792-16-2). Eden Pr.

PMS: The Premenstrual Syndrome. Compiled by Lorna Peterson. 76p. 1985. pap. 16.00 (ISBN 0-89774-205-2). Oryx Pr.

PMS: What It Is & What You Can Do about It. Joe S. McIlhaney, Jr. & Sharon M. Sneed. 160p. (Orig.). 1988. pap. 6.95 (ISBN 0-8010-8290-0). Baker Bk.

PN Junction Diode. Gerold W. Neudeck. LC 81-14979. (Modular Series on Solid State Devices: No. 2). (Illus.). 120p. 1983. pap. write for info. (ISBN 0-201-05321-7). Addison-Wesley.

PN Junction Diode. 2nd ed. Gerold W. Neudeck. (Modular Series on Solid State Devices). (Illus.). 160p. 1988. pap. text ed. price not set (ISBN 0-201-12296-0). Addison-Wesley.

PNA: A Centennial History of the Polish National Alliance of the U. S. A. Donald Pienkos. 485p. 1984. 37.50x (ISBN 0-88033-060-0). East Eur Quarterly.

Pnat Molluscicides. Ed. by Kenneth E. Mott. LC 86-19045. 320p. 1987. pap. 75.00 (ISBN 0-471-91228-X). Wiley.

Pnaumatic Steelmaking Series: Tuyre Design. Work for Hire Staff. 120p. 1988. pap. 70.00 (ISBN 0-932897-38-X). Iron & Steel.

Pneumatic & Hydraulic Conveying of Solids. Williams. (Chemical Industries Ser.). 328p. 1983. 59.75 (ISBN 0-8247-1855-0). Dekker.

Pneumatic Circuits & Low Cost Automation. J. R. Fawcett. 150p. 1969. 30.00x (ISBN 0-85461-029-4, Pub. by Trade & Tech England). Brookfield Pub Co.

Pneumatic Controls for Industrial Application: A Practical & Comprehensive Presentation of Pneumatic Control System Fundamentals, Control Devices, Associated Facilities, & Application Circuitry for Manual, Semiautomatic, & Automatic Industrial Operations. American Society of Tool & Manufacturing Engineers Staff. Ed. by Frank W. Wilson. LC 65-13379. (Manufacturing Data Ser.). pap. 43.50 (ISBN 0-317-27763-4, 2024178). Bks Demand UMI.

Pneumatic Conveying. 2nd ed. H. A. Stoess, Jr. LC 83-6915. 277p. 1983. 46.95x (ISBN 0-471-86935-X, Pub. by Wiley-Interscience). Wiley.

Pneumatic Conveying of Bulk Materials. Milton N. Kraus & Chemical Engineering Magazine Editors. (Chemical Engineering Bks.). 352p. 1980. text ed. 48.00 (ISBN 0-07-010724-6). McGraw.

Pneumatic Conveying Systems for Handling Combustible Materials. National Fire Protection Association Staff. 1984. 10.50 (ISBN 0-317-63491-7, 650-84). Natl Fire Prot.

Pneumatic Conveying Systems for Handling Feed, Flour, Grain & Other Agricultural Dusts. (Sixty Ser). 1973. pap. 2.00 (ISBN 0-685-58068-7, 66). Natl Fire Prot.

Pneumatic Data, Vol. 2. Institute for Power System. 130p. 1979. 50.00x (ISBN 0-686-65623-7). State Mutual Bk.

Pneumatic Data, Vol. 3. Institute for Power System. 100p. 1979. 50.00x (ISBN 0-686-65624-5). State Mutual Bk.

Pneumatic Engineering Calculations. Institute for Power System. 120p. 1979. 50.00x (ISBN 0-686-65625-3). State Mutual Bk.

Pneumatic Engineering Calculations. Trade & Technical Press Editors. 120p. 1969. 26.00x (ISBN 0-85461-038-3, Pub by Trade & Tech England). Brookfield Pub Co.

Pneumatic Handbook. 5th ed. Institute for Power System. 700p. 1979. 150.00x (ISBN 0-85461-068-5). State Mutual Bk.

Pneumatic Handbook. 6th ed. Trade & Technical Press Editors. 700p. 1984. 128.00x (ISBN 0-85461-090-1, Pub by Trade & Tech England). Brookfield Pub Co.

Pneumatic Handbook. 6th ed. R. H. Warring. LC 82-82850. 448p. 1982. 75.00x (ISBN 0-87201-726-5). Gulf Pub.

Pneumatic Measurement & Control Applications, 3 vol. set. E. M. Eacho et al. (Illus.). 1981. Set. lib. bdg. 195.00x (ISBN 0-87683-010-6); Vol. 1, 400 p. text ed. 79.50x looseleaf (ISBN 0-87683-011-4); Vol. 2, 160p. looseleaf 79.50x (ISBN 0-87683-013-0); Vol. 3, 160p. lab manual solutions looseleaf 79.50x; lesson plans, looseleaf 595.00x (ISBN 0-87683-014-9). GP Pub.

Pneumatic Power Glossary. Institute for Power System. 80p. 1979. 30.00x (ISBN 0-686-65626-1). State Mutual Bk.

Pneumatics & Hydraulics. 4th, rev. ed. Harry L. Stewart. Ed. by Tom Philbin. LC 75-36658. (Illus.). 1976. 19.95 (ISBN 0-672-23412-2, 23237, Pub. by Audel). Macmillan.

Pneumatics Explained. Leo Rizzo. LC 84-730253. 1984. wkbk. 11.00 (ISBN 0-317-43492-6, 530); audio visual pkg. 239.00. Bergwall.

Pneumatikos-Psychikos Terminology in First Corinthians. Birger A. Pearson. LC 73-92202. (Society of Biblical Literature. Dissertation Ser.). 1975. pap. 8.95 (ISBN 0-88414-034-2, 060112). Scholars Pr GA.

Pneumo-Pelvigraphy: Examination of the Female Genital Organs by a Radiological Method. K. Richter et al. (Illus.). 122p. 1974. cancelled (ISBN 0-685-50593-6). Adlers Foreign Bks.

Pneumococcus & the Pneumococcal Vaccine. Paul G. Quie & Edward H. Kass. LC 81-71847. (Studies in Infectious Diseases Research). 420p. 1982. lib. bdg. 35.00x (ISBN 0-226-69932-3). U of Chicago Pr.

Pneumocystis Carinii Pneumonia: Pathogenesis-Diagnosis-Treatment. Lowell S. Young. (Lung Biology in Health & Diseases Ser.). 272p. 1983. 57.50 (ISBN 0-8247-7077-3). Dekker.

Pneumonia. Roderick Heffron. Incl. Biology of the Pneumococcus. Benjamin White. LC 78-10453. LC 78-10579. (Commonwealth Fund Ser.). (Illus.). 1979. Set. text ed. 75.00x (ISBN 0-674-67444-8). Harvard U Pr.

Pneumonia & Pneumococcal Infections. Ed. by H. P. Lambert & A. D. Caldwell. (International Congress & Symposium Ser.: No. 27). 117p. 1980. pap. 18.00 (ISBN 1-85315-031-2, Pub. by Royal Society of Medicine Services Ltd). Longwood Pub Group.

Pneumonia: Medical Subject Analysis, Reference & Research Guidebook. Dominic L. Stannic. LC 87-47637. 160p. 1987. 34.50 (ISBN 0-88164-592-3); pap. 26.50 (ISBN 0-88164-593-1). ABBE Pubs Assn.

Pneumonias. Matthew E. Levison. (Illus.). 592p. 1984. text ed. 50.00 (ISBN 0-7236-7020-X). PSG Pub Co.

Pneumonias. Hobart A. Reimann. LC 78-166458. (Illus.). 224p. 1971. 12.50 (ISBN 0-87527-119-7). Green.

Pneumonias. Weinstein. (Seminars in Infections Disease Ser.: Vol. 5). 1983. 57.95 (ISBN 0-86577-091-3). Thieme Med Pubs.

Pneumorhythm: Relief from Stress through Breathing. Oscar Ichazo. (Illus.). 32p. 1979. pap. 20.00 (ISBN 0-916554-10-4). Arica Inst Pr.

Pneumotransport Bibliography. Ed. by Wendy A. Thorton. 1972. text ed. 26.00x (ISBN 0-900983-17-5, Dist. by Air Science Co.). BHRA Fluid.

Pneumotransport Five: Proceedings. (International Conference on Pneumatic Transport of Solids in Pipes Ser.). (Illus.). 467p. 1980. pap. 87.00x (ISBN 0-686-77573-2, Dist. by Air Science Co.). BHRA Fluid.

Pnin. Vladimir Nabokov. Tr. by G. Barabtarlo from Eng. 175p. (Rus.). 1983. 25.00 (ISBN 0-88233-737-8); pap. 12.50 (ISBN 0-88233-738-6). Ardis Pubs.

Pnin. Vladimir Nabokov. 1982. pap. 3.50 (ISBN 0-380-00819-X, 62182-7, Bard). Avon.

Pnin. Vladimir Nabokov. LC 82-1208. 192p. 1982. Repr. of 1957 ed. 12.50 (ISBN 0-8376-0465-6). Bentley.

Pnin. Vladimir Nabokov. LC 83-22437. 192p. 1984. pap. 6.95 (ISBN 0-385-19116-2, Anch). Doubleday.

Po: Beyond Yes & No. Edward De Bono. Date not set. price not set. Intl Ctr Creat Think.

Po Hu T'Ung: The Comprehensive Discussions in the White Tiger Hall, 2 vols. Pan Ku. Tr. by Tjan Tjoe Som. (China Studies: from Confucius to Mao Ser.). 1988. Repr. of 1949 ed. Vol. 1. 27.50; Vol. 2. 27.50. Hyperion Conn.

Po Obe Storony Steny. Victor Nekrasov. LC 84-81387. (Povesti i Rasskazy Ser.). 216p. (Rus.). 1985. 12.50 (ISBN 0-911971-12-2). Effect Pub.

Po Obye Storoni Orgasma. Mikhail Armalinsky. 150p. (Rus.). 1988. pap. 23.00 (ISBN 0-916201-04-X). M I P Co.

Po Pai Mo: The Search for White Buffalo Woman. Robert Boissiere. LC 83-4668. (Illus.). 96p. (Orig.). 1983. pap. 8.95 (ISBN 0-86534-024-2). Sunstone Pr.

Po' White Trash & Other One-Act Dramas. Evelyn G. Sutherland. LC 77-70363. (One-Act Plays in Reprint Ser.). 1977. Repr. of 1900 ed. 16.75x (ISBN 0-8486-2023-2). Roth Pub Inc.

Poacher. H. E. Bates. 1985. 13.95 (ISBN 0-317-53146-8, Large Print Bks). G K Hall.

Poacher. Stephen Lewandowski. 1986. 4.00 (ISBN 0-934834-66-0). White Pine.

Poacher's Companion. E. G. Walsh. (Illus.). 286p. 1983. 22.00 (ISBN 0-85115-177-9, Pub. by Boydell & Brewer). Longwood Pub Group.

Poacher's Son. Rachel Anderson. 144p. (YA) (gr. 7 up). 1987. 13.95 (ISBN 0-19-271468-6). Oxford U Pr.

Poamorio. Dario Canton. Tr. by Drew M. Stroud. LC 84-51027. 160p. (Orig.). 1984. pap. text ed. 6.95 (ISBN 0-935086-01-3). Saru.

Pobabilisitic Models in Engineering Sciences: Random Variables & Stochastic Processes see Probabilistic Models in Engineering Sciences.

Pobedonostsev: His Life & Thought. Robert F. Byrnes. LC 68-14598. Repr. of 1968 ed. 96.80 (ISBN 0-8357-9231-5, 2013022). Bks Demand UMI.

Poblacion: Una Opcion Int. see People: An International Choice.

Poca. Charlott L. Motter. (Illus.). 27p. 1988. 5.95 (ISBN 0-533-07661-7). Vantage.

Pocahantas, Indian Princess. Patricia Adams. (Orig.). (gr. k-6). 1987. pap. 2.95 (ISBN 0-440-47067-6, YB). Dell.

Pocahontas. Ingri D'Aulaire & Edgar P. D'Aulaire. (Illus.). 48p. (gr. 1-4). 1985. pap. 9.95 (ISBN 0-385-07454-9). Doubleday.

Pocahontas. Jan Gleiter & Kathleen Thompson. LC 84-9819. (Stories Clippers Ser.). (Illus.). 34p. (gr. k-4). 1984. PLB 15.33 (ISBN 0-8172-2118-2); PLB 27.99 incl. cassette (ISBN 0-8172-2240-5); pap. 9.27 (ISBN 0-8172-2261-8); pap. 23.95 (ISBN 0-8172-2271-5); cassette 14.00. Raintree Pubs.

Pocahontas. Laurence Santrey. LC 84-8443. (Illus.). 32p. (gr. 3-6). 1985. PLB 8.45 (ISBN 0-8167-0276-4); pap. text ed. 1.95 (ISBN 0-8167-0277-2). Troll Assocs.

Pocahontas. Grace S. Woodward. LC 68-15687. (Civilization of the American Indian Ser.: No. 93). (Illus.). 1976. pap. 7.95 (ISBN 0-8061-1642-0). U of Okla Pr.

Pocahontas Alias Matoaka: And Her Descendants Through Her Marriage at Jamestown, Virginia in April, 1614, with John Rolfe, Gentleman. Wyndham Robertson & Robert A. Brock. LC 61-49177. 84p. 1982. Repr. of 1887 ed. 8.50 (ISBN 0-8063-0615-7). Genealog Pub.

Pocahontas & Co: The Fictorial American Indian Woman in Nineteenth Century Literature: A Study of Method. Asebrit Sundquist. LC 86-7997. 350p. 1986. 39.95 (ISBN 0-391-03447-2). Humanities.

Pocahontas & the Strangers. Clyde R. Bulla. (Illus.). 176p. (gr. 2-6). 1988. pap. 2.50 (ISBN 0-590-41711-8). Scholastic Inc.

Pocahontas, Child-Princess. Dorothy F. Richards. LC 78-7719. (Illus.). (gr. k-4). 1978. PLB 7.95 (ISBN 0-89565-035-5). Childs World.

Pocahontas County Cooking Yesterday & Today. Betsy Edgar. 1979. Repr. of 1973 ed. 3.75 (ISBN 0-87012-175-8). McClain.

Pocahontas' Descendants. Stuart E. Brown, Jr. et al. (Illus.). 451p. 1985. 49.50 (ISBN 0-317-40516-0). VA Bk.

Pocahontas, Girl of Jamestown. Kate Jassem. LC 78-18045. (Illus.). 48p. (gr. 4-6). 1979. PLB 9.59 (ISBN 0-89375-152-9); pap. 1.95 (ISBN 0-89375-142-1). Troll Assocs.

Pocahontas: Indian Princess. Katharine E. Wilkie. LC 69-10375. (Indians Ser.). (Illus.). 80p. (gr. 2-5). 1969. PLB 6.69 (ISBN 0-8116-6605-0). Garrard.

Pocahontas's Daughters: Gender & Ethnicity in American Culture. Mary V. Dearborn. 240p. 1986. 24.95x (ISBN 0-19-503632-8). Oxford U Pr.

Pocahontas's Daughters: Gender & Ethnicity in America Culture. Mary V. Dearborn. 288p. 1987. pap. 10.95 (ISBN 0-19-505182-3). Oxford U Pr.

Pochemu Ia Stal Simvolistom. Andrei Belyi. 120p. 1982. 20.00 (ISBN 0-88233-664-9); pap. 6.50 (ISBN 0-88233-665-7). Ardis Pubs.

Pochkhanawala, The Banker. N. J. Nanporia. (Illus.). 230p. 1982. text ed. 22.50x (ISBN 0-210-40638-0, Pub. by Jaisingh & Mehta India). Apt Bks.

Pocho. Jose A. Villarreal. LC 71-11196. 1970. pap. 4.95 (ISBN 0-385-06118-8, Anch). Doubleday.

Pocket. John B. Springs, III. 1985. pap. 2.50 (ISBN 0-87067-267-3, BH267). Holloway.

Pocket Aquinas. St. Thomas Aquinas. Ed. by V. Bourke. pap. 3.95 (ISBN 0-671-47354-9). WSP.

Pocket Architecture: A Walking Tour Guide to the Architecture of Downtown Minneapolis & St. Paul. rev., 2nd ed. Bernard Jacob & Carol Morphew. (Illus.). 140p. 1987. pap. 7.95 (ISBN 0-945056-00-1). AIA MN Soc.

Pocket Aristotle. Aristotle. Ed. by Justin Kaplan. 400p. 1983. pap. 5.95 (ISBN 0-671-46377-2). WSP.

Pocket Astrologer, Eastern Time, 1989. Jim Maynard. 2.95 (ISBN 0-930356-62-4). Quicksilver Prod.

Pocket Astrologer, Pacific Time, 1989. Jim Maynard. 2.95 (ISBN 0-930356-63-2). Quicksilver Prod.

Pocket Atlas of Anatomy. 3rd ed. Victor Pauchet & S. Dupret. (Illus.). 1937. pap. 14.95x (ISBN 0-19-263131-4). Oxford U Pr.

Pocket Atlas of Arrhythmias. Neville Conway. (Illus.). 1975. pap. 21.00 (ISBN 0-8151-5950-1). Year Bk Med.

Pocket Atlas of Cranial Magnetic Resonance Imaging. Victor M. Haughton & David L. Daniels. (Illus.). 64p. 1986. pap. text ed. 13.50 (ISBN 0-88167-171-1). Raven.

Pocket Atlas of Dermatology. Steigleder. (Flexi-Bk.). 1984. 18.50 (ISBN 0-86577-092-1). Thieme Med Pubs.

Pocket Atlas of Hematology. Harald Theml. Tr. by Gerhard S. Sharon. (Illus.). 184p. 1985. pap. 17.00 (ISBN 0-86577-210-X). Thieme Med Pubs.

Pocket Atlas of Human Anatomy. Heinz Feneis & Hans E. Kaiser. (Illus.). 480p. 1985. pap. text ed. 17.00 (ISBN 0-86577-167-7). Thieme Med Pubs.

Pocket Atlas of Human Histology. Robert Meadows. (Illus.). 1980. pap. text ed. 18.95x (ISBN 0-19-261177-1). Oxford U Pr.

Pocket Atlas of MRI Body Anatomy. Thomas H. Berquist et al. (Illus.). 112p. 1987. pap. text ed. 13.50 (ISBN 0-88167-282-3). Raven.

Pocket Atlas of Normal CT Anatomy. James B. Weinstein et al. (Illus.). 88p. 1985. pap. text ed. 13.50 (ISBN 0-88167-070-7). Raven.

Pocket Atlas of Normal Ultrasound Anatomy. Matthew D. Rifkin & Larry Waldroup. (Illus.). 72p. 1985. pap. text ed. 13.50 (ISBN 0-88167-163-0). Raven.

Pocket Atlas of Ophthalmology. Fritz Hollwich. Tr. by Frederick Blodi. (Illus.). 192p. 1981. pap. 17.00 (ISBN 0-86577-195-2). Thieme Med Pubs.

Pocket Atlas of Rheumatology. Dieter Wessinghage. Tr. by Gottfied Stiasny. (Illus.). 256p. 1986. pap. 17.00 (ISBN 0-317-53465-3). Thieme Med Pubs.

Pocket Bartender's Guide. Michael Jackson. 144p. 1984. pap. 7.95 (ISBN 0-671-25081-7). S&S.

Pocket Beatles. Ed. by Milton Okun. (Pocket Guitar Ser.). 253p. (Orig.). 1980. pap. 4.95 (ISBN 0-89524-126-9, 1323). Cherry Lane.

Pocket Bible Commentary. William Neil. LC 63-7607. 544p. 1975. pap. 7.95 (ISBN 0-06-066090-2, RD 92, HarpR). Har-Row.

Pocket Bible Ready Reference for Personal Workers. Ernest A. Clevenger, Jr. (Bible Ready Reference Ser.). 24p. (Orig.). 1982. pap. 0.50 (ISBN 0-88428-011-X). Parchment Pr.

Pocket Billiards: As It Should Be Learned & Played. 2nd ed. Beverly D. Wilson. (Illus.). 96p. 1984. pap. text ed. 7.75 (ISBN 0-8403-3321-8, 40318501). Kendall-Hunt.

Pocket Book Crossword, No. 11. Margaret Farrar. Date not set. pap. 2.50 (ISBN 0-671-55151-5). PB.

Pocket Book Crossword, No. 12. Margaret Farrar. Date not set. pap. 2.50 (ISBN 0-671-55152-3). PB.

Pocket Book of Bible Prayers. David E. Rosage. 224p. (Orig.). 1987. compact ed. 5.95 (ISBN 0-89283-320-3). Servant.

Pocket Book of British Ceramic Marks. 3rd ed. J. P. Cushion. LC 83-16527. (Illus.). 432p. (Orig.). 1984. pap. 8.95 (ISBN 0-571-13108-5). Faber & Faber.

Pocket Book of O. Henry Short Stories. O. Henry. Ed. by Harry Hansen. 256p. pap. 3.95 (ISBN 0-671-45360-2). WSP.

Pocket Book of Ogden Nash. Ogden Nash. 1983. pap. 3.95. PB.

Pocket Book of Ogden Nash. Ogden Nash. 200p. pap. 3.95. WSP.

Pocket Book of Prayers. M. Basil Pennington. LC 85-12936. 192p. 1986. pap. 4.95 (ISBN 0-385-23298-5, Im). Doubleday.

Pocket Book of Prayers. gift ed. M. Basil Pennington. LC 85-12936. 208p. 1987. pap. 14.95 (ISBN 0-385-24378-2, Im). Doubleday.

Pocket Book of Puzzles. Nancy Hite. 1979. 5.95 (ISBN 0-916456-47-1, GA98). Good Apple.

Pocket Book of Quotations. Ed. by Henry Davidoff. 1983. pap. 4.50 (ISBN 0-671-60386-8). PB.

Pocket Book of Short Stories. Ed. by Edmund M. Speare. (Orig.). (gr. 9 up). pap. 3.95 (ISBN 0-671-50982-9). WSP.

Pocket Books Guide to National Parks. William W. Wallace. 384p. (Orig.). 1984. pap. 3.95 (ISBN 0-671-50382-0). PB.

Pocket Bread Potpourri: Meals in Minutes. Madelain Farah & Leila Habib. 112p. 1984. spiral bdg. 8.95 (ISBN 0-9603050-3-3). Lebanese Cuisine.

Pocket Calculator. John Lewis. (Computer Handbooks). (gr. 5-9). 1982. 8.95 (ISBN 0-86020-634-3, Usborne-Hayes); PLB 12.96 (ISBN 0-88110-009-9); pap. 5.95 (ISBN 0-86020-633-5). EDC.

Pocket Calculator Boom. Francisco J. James. (Orig.). 1978. pap. 60.00 o.p (ISBN 0-933836-01-5); 6.25x (ISBN 0-933836-08-2). Simtek.

Pocket Calculators: How to Use & Enjoy Them. Arnold Madison & David L. Drotar. LC 78-707. (Illus.). (gr. 7 up). 1978. 8.95 (ISBN 0-525-66580-3). Lodestar Bks.

Pocket Catholic Catechism. John J. Hardon. 1988. pap. 5.95 (ISBN 0-385-24293-X). Doubleday.

Pocket Catholic Dictionary. John A. Hardon. LC 85-5790. 528p. 1985. pap. 7.95 (ISBN 0-385-23238-1, Im). Doubleday.

Pocket Computer Primer. Hank Librach. LC 82-80270. 96p. (Orig.). 1982. pap. 9.95 (ISBN 0-942412-00-1); pre-recorded cassette 8.95 (ISBN 0-686-87024-7). Micro Text Pubns.

Pocket Computer Program Writing Workbook. Jim Cole. 96p. 1983. 4.95 (ISBN 0-86668-817-X). ARCsoft.

Pocket Computer Programming Made Easy. Jim Cole. (Illus.). 128p. (Orig.). 1982. pap. 8.95 (ISBN 0-86668-009-8). ARCsoft.

Pocket Computer Programs for Astronomers. Fred Klein. 100p. (Orig.). 1983. pap. 12.95 (ISBN 0-913051-01-2). F Klein Pubns.

Pocket Computers in Agrometeorology. R. A. Gommes. (Plant Production & Protection Papers: No. 45). 149p. 1983. pap. 10.00 (ISBN 92-5-101336-5, F2449, FAO). UNIPUB.

Pocket Concise Chinese-English Dictionary. 620p. (Chinese & Eng.). 1978. pap. 9.95 (ISBN 0-686-92467-3, M-9182). French & Eur.

Pocket Concordance to the New Testament. Charles J. Hazelton. 1984. leather flex 5.95 (ISBN 0-8407-5824-3). Nelson.

Pocket Consultant: A Compendium of Differential Diagnosis & Annotated References. Anne A. Louis. 1988. pap. price not set (ISBN 0-471-87123-0). Churchill.

Pocket Cruisers for the Backyard Builder: 30 Small Sailboats You Can Build for Less Than 12,000. Dave Gerr. (Illus.). 144p. 1987. pap. 17.95 (ISBN 0-87742-240-0). Intl Marine.

Pocket Data Book U. S. A., 1979. 401p. (Orig.). 1980. pap. 7.50 (ISBN 0-318-11746-0, S/N 003-024-02682-1). USGPO.

Pocket Dicionary of Ukulele Chords. Charles Allen. pap. 1.50 (ISBN 0-934286-24-8). Kenyon.

Pocket Dictionary. rev. ed. Ed. by Houghton Mifflin Company Staff. LC 78-13455. (Illus.). 256p. 1978. pap. text ed. 2.95 (ISBN 0-395-27224-6). HM.

Pocket Dictionary. LC 78-13455. 1978. pap. 2.25 (ISBN 0-395-26661-0). HM.

Pocket Dictionary of Art Terms. Ed. by Julia M. Ehresmann. LC 74-143464. (Illus.). 1971. pap. 6.95 (ISBN 0-8212-0748-2, 712019). NYGS.

Pocket Dictionary of Automotive Technology. H. D. Junge. 232p. (Eng.). 1987. pap. 28.00 (ISBN 3-433-02815-X). VCH Pubs.

Pocket Dictionary of Banjo Chords. Neil Lambard. pap. 1.50 (ISBN 0-934286-19-1). Kenyon.

Pocket Dictionary of Baritone Ukulele Chords. Charles Allen. pap. 1.50 (ISBN 0-934286-21-3). Kenyon.

Pocket Dictionary of Chords. Albert DeVito. pap. 1.50 (ISBN 0-934286-18-3). Kenyon.

Pocket Dictionary of Horseman's Terms in English, German, French & Spanish. Hanns Muller. (Fr.). 1971. 7.50 (ISBN 0-685-00343-4). Transatl Arts.

Pocket Dictionary of Irish Myth & Legend. Ronan Coghlan. (Pocket Bk.). (Illus.). 96p. (Orig.). 1985. pap. 5.95 (ISBN 0-86281-152-X, Pub. by Appletree Pr). Irish Bks Media.

Pocket Dictionary of Laboratory Equipment: English-German. Hans-Dieter Junge. 201p. 1987. pap. text ed. 28.00 (ISBN 0-89573-596-2). VCH Pubs.

Pocket Dictionary of Mandolin Chords. Charles Allen. pap. 1.50 (ISBN 0-934286-23-X). Kenyon.

Pocket Dictionary of Music Terms. Albert De Vito. LC 65-8450. 1965. 1.95 (ISBN 0-934286-09-4). Kenyon.

Pocket Dictionary of Saints. John J. Delaney. LC 82-45479. 528p. 1983. pap. 7.50 (ISBN 0-385-18274-0, Im). Doubleday.

Pocket Dictionary of Signing. Rod R. Butterworth & Mickey Flodin. (Illus.). 192p. 1987. pap. 4.95 (ISBN 0-399-51347-7, Perigee). Putnam Pub Group.

Pocket Dictionary of Synonyms & Antonyms. 1960. pap. 2.95 (ISBN 0-394-51933-7). Random.

Pocket Dictionary of Tenor Banjo Chords. Charles Allen. pap. 1.50 (ISBN 0-934286-20-5). Kenyon.

Pocket Dictionary of the German & English Languages. K. Wichmann. (Ger. & Eng.). 1952. 12.00 (ISBN 0-7100-2290-5). Routledge Chapman & Hall.

Pocket Dictionary of the Spoken Arabic of Cairo: English-Arabic. Virginia Stevens & Maurice Salib. 226p. 1987. pap. 12.95 (ISBN 977-424-157-6, Pub. by Univ Cairo Pr). Columbia U Pr.

Pocket Diesel & Electric Guide: A Quick Reference Handbook to Locomotives in Service. LC 74-80803. (Illus.). 1974. wirebound 5.00 (ISBN 0-913556-11-4); pap. 4.00 (ISBN 0-913556-12-2). Spec Pr NJ.

Pocket Digital Multimeter Techniques. Homer L. Davidson. (Illus.). 320p. 1986. 22.95 (ISBN 0-8306-0887-7, 1887); pap. 14.95 (ISBN 0-8306-1887-2, 1887P). Tab Bks.

Pocket Directory of the California Legislature: 1986. Compiled by Capitol Enquiry Staff. 64p. (Orig.). 1986. Annual. text ed. 0.00; pap. 5.95 (ISBN 0-917982-32-0). Capitol Enquiry.

Pocket Directory of the California Legislature 1987. 56p. 1987. pap. 6.95 (ISBN 0-917872-33-9). Capitol Enquiry.

Pocket Directory of the California Legislature 1988. 64p. 1988. pap. 6.95 (ISBN 0-917982-34-7). Capitol Enquiry.

Pocket Doctor: A Carry-Along Guide for Healthy, Safe Traveling. Stephen Bezruchka. (Illus.). 80p. (Orig.). 1988. pap. 2.95 (ISBN 0-89886-165-9). Mountaineers.

Pocket Dramas. Jane Hixon. (New Alaskan Poets Ser.). 64p. (Orig.). 1987. pap. 5.95 (ISBN 0-914221-07-8). Fireweed Pr AK.

Pocket Drawing Book: On to the Basics. R. R. Dvorak. (Illus.). 162p. (Orig.). Date not set. pap. 9.95 (ISBN 0-945625-00-6). Inkwell Pr.

Pocket Economist. 2nd ed. Rupert Pennant-Rea & Bill Emmott. 224p. 1988. 24.95 (ISBN 0-631-15589-9); pap. 9.95 (ISBN 0-631-15591-0). Basil Blackwell.

Pocket Economist. Rupert Pennant-Rea & William Emmott. LC 83-15054. (Illus.). 194p. 1984. 18.95 (ISBN 0-521-26070-1). Cambridge U Pr.

Pocket Edition see Lutheran Book of Worship.

Pocket Employer. Derek Torrington & Jill Earnshaw. (Economist Pocket Guides). (Illus.). 220p. text ed. 44.95 (ISBN 0-631-15389-6). Basil Blackwell.

Pocket Encyclopedia. Adrienne Jack. LC 88-4462. (Illus.). 288p. (Orig.). (gr. 3-7). 1988. pap. 7.95 (ISBN 0-394-89993-8, BYR). Random.

Pocket Encyclopedia of American Wine, East of the Rockies. William I. Kaufman. 144p. 1986. pap. 5.95 (ISBN 0-932664-41-5). Wine Appreciation.

Pocket Encyclopedia of Cacti in Color. Edgar Lamb & Brian Lamp. (Illus.). 217p. 1980. 12.95 (ISBN 0-7137-1197-3, Pub. by Blandford Pr England). Sterling.

Pocket Encyclopedia of California Wine & Other Western States. William I. Kaufman. 336p. 1988. pap. 6.95 (ISBN 0-932664-42-3). Wine Appreciation.

Pocket Encyclopedia of California Wine & Other Western States. William I. Kaufman. 336p. 1985. pap. 5.95 (ISBN 0-932664-40-7). Wine Appreciation.

Pocket Encyclopedia of California Wine. William I. Kaufman. Ed. by Maurice T. Sullivan. 148p. (Orig.). 1980. 4.95 (ISBN 0-932664-09-1). Wine Appreciation.

Pocket Encyclopedia of California Wine. William I. Kaufman. 158p. 1982. pap. 4.95 (ISBN 0-932664-22-9). Wine Appreciation.

Pocket Encyclopedia of California Wine. William I. Kaufman. 212p. 1983. pap. 4.95 (ISBN 0-932664-24-5). Wine Appreciation.

Pocket Encyclopedia of California Wines. Bob Thompson. 1985. 8.95 (ISBN 0-671-52324-4). S&S.

Pocket Encyclopedia of California Wines. Robert Thompson. 1980. 4.95 (ISBN 0-671-41791-6). S&S.

Pocket Encyclopedia of Calories & Nutrition. Arnold Bender & Tony Nash. 1979. pap. 4.95 (ISBN 0-671-24839-1). S&S.

Pocket Encyclopedia of Nutrition. Jo-Ann Heslin & Annette Natow. Date not set. pap. 5.95 (ISBN 0-671-61278-6). PB.

Pocket Encyclopedia of Real Estate. 288p. (Orig.). 1982. pap. 7.95 (ISBN 0-8092-5671-1). Contemp Bks.

Pocket English-Chinese Dictionary. (Eng. & Chinese.). 1980. pap. 5.95 (ISBN 0-8351-0727-2). China Bks.

Pocket English-Chinese Dictionary. 451p. (Eng. & Chinese.). 1980. pap. text ed. 9.95 (ISBN 0-686-92473-8, M-9580). French & Eur.

Pocket English-Chinese (Pinyin) Dictionary. Ed. by Wang Liangbi & Zhu Yuan. 271p. 1983. pap. 5.95 (ISBN 0-88727-023-9, Pub by Commercial Pr HK). Cheng & Tsui.

Pocket English-Hungarian Dictionary. I. Orszagh. (Eng. & Hungarian.). 1980. 20.00x (ISBN 0-569-00408-X, Pub. by Collets (UK)). State Mutual Bk.

Pocket Estate & Gift Tax Calculator. Alfred G. Yates, Jr. 110p. (Orig.). 1983. pap. 5.65 (ISBN 0-87218-420-X). Natl Underwriter.

Pocket Estimator. 22nd ed. LC 82-2546. pap. cancelled. Nat Assn H Build.

Pocket Etymology of Medical Terms. D. Anderson & R. Buxton. 52p. 1981. 6.50 (ISBN 0-86292-015-9, Pub. by Bristol Classical UK). Focus Info Gr.

Pocket Examiner in Medicine. Alexander Lawrence & Zachary Johnson. LC 83-2381. 372p. (Orig.). 1986. pap. text ed. 12.50 (ISBN 0-443-03863-5). Churchill.

Pocket Flora of the Redwood Forest. Rudolf W. Becking. (Illus.). 262p. (Orig.). 1982. pap. 15.95x (ISBN 0-933280-02-5). Island CA.

Pocket for Corduroy. Don Freeman. (Illus.). (gr. 3-5). 1978. 10.95 (ISBN 0-670-56172-X). Viking.

Pocket for Corduroy. Don Freeman. (Illus.). (gr. k-3). 1982. incl. cass. 19.95 (ISBN 0-941078-17-5); pap. 12.95 incl. cass. (ISBN 0-941078-15-9); user's guide incl. 4 pbs. & cass. 27.95 (ISBN 0-941078-16-7). Live Oak Media.

Pocket for Corduroy. Don Freeman. 32p. (gr. k-3). pap. 2.25 (ISBN 0-590-31970-1). Scholastic Inc.

Pocket for Corduroy. Illus. by Don Freeman. (Illus.). (ps). 1980. pap. 3.95 (ISBN 0-14-050352-8, Puffin). Penguin.

Pocket Full of Miracles. Wallace Heflin & Harold McDougal. (Illus.). 164p. 1987. 9.95 (ISBN 0-914903-23-3); pap. 5.95. Destiny Image.

Pocket Full of Rye. Agatha Christie. 1986. pap. 3.50 (ISBN 0-671-55796-3). PB.

Pocket Full of Rye. L. G. Layberry. Ed. by Kathleen Morley-Clarke. 176p. 1986. 35.00x (ISBN 0-85936-251-5, Pub. by Spellmount Ltd Pubs). State Mutual Bk.

Pocket Games. Elaine Hardt. 1986. pap. 2.95 (ISBN 0-8423-4934-0). Tyndale.

Pocket Gems. Nelson Mink. 128p. 1985. pap. 2.95 (ISBN 0-8423-4927-8). Tyndale.

Pocket Gopher & Other Poems from the Gopher State. Gary De Young. (Illus.). 31p. pap. 7.50 (ISBN 0-936128-00-3). De Young Pr.

Pocket Gophers (Genus Thomomys) of Utah. Stephen D. Durrant. (Museum Ser.: Vol. 1, No. 1). 82p. 1946. pap. 4.25 (ISBN 0-686-80277-2). U of KS Mus Nat Hist.

Pocket Gourmet Instant Menu Translator: France, Italy, Germany, Spain. Ed. by Foulsham, W., & Co. Staff. 128p. (Orig.). 1982. pap. 8.95x (ISBN 0-572-01164-4). Trans-Atl Phila.

Pocket Guide for Medical-Surgical Nursing. Carol Neel & Mark Wallerstein. (Illus.). 448p. 1985. pap. text ed. 16.95 (ISBN 0-89303-772-9). Appleton & Lange.

Pocket Guide for the Church Choir Member. Kenneth W. Osbeck. 48p. 1984. pap. 1.25 (ISBN 0-8254-3408-4); Per Dozen. pap. 12.95 (ISBN 0-8254-3417-3). Kregel.

Pocket Guide for the Movies on Video. Alan S. Pedersen. 132p. (Orig.). 1987. pap. 3.95 (ISBN 0-9619856-0-7). Video Pr.

Pocket Guide to Antimicrobial Therapy in Otolaryngology Head & Neck Surgery. 4th ed. American Academy Otolaryngology - Head & Neck Surgery Foundation. 60p. 2.50; members 2.00. Am Acad Otolary.

Pocket Guide to Aquarium Fishes. Gwynne Vevers. 1980. 8.95 (ISBN 0-671-25451-0). S&S.

Pocket Guide to Astronomy. Patrick Moore. 1980. pap. 7.95 (ISBN 0-671-25309-3, 25309). S&S.

Pocket Guide to Babysitting. 68p. 1982. pap. 4.50 (ISBN 0-318-11815-7, S/N 017-091-00236-3). USGPO.

Pocket Guide to Beer. Michael Jackson. 144p. 1982. pap. 5.95 (ISBN 0-399-50578-4, Perigee). Putnam Pub Group.

Pocket Guide to Cheese. Barbara Ensrud. 144p. 1981. pap. 4.95 (ISBN 0-399-50518-0, Perigee). Putnam Pub Group.

Pocket Guide to Chess Engames: Basic Level. David Hooper. 205p. 1987. pap. 10.95 (ISBN 0-7134-5643-4, Pub. by Batsford England). David & Charles.

Pocket Guide to Choosing Woody Ornamentals. Gerd Krussman. Tr. by Michael Epp from Ger. LC 82-13690. Orig. Title: Taschenbuch Der Geholzverwendung. (Illus.). 140p. 1982. pap. 12.95 (ISBN 0-917304-24-1). Timber.

Pocket Guide to Clinical Nursing: Process for the Adult Medical-Surgical Client. Cynthia M. Loxley & Sheila S. Cress. 1985. pap. 7.95 (ISBN 0-671-55637-1). S&S.

Pocket Guide to Clinical Nursing: Process for the Pediatric Client. Cynthia M. Loxley & Sheila S. Cress. 1985. pap. 7.95 (ISBN 0-671-55638-X). S&S.

Pocket Guide to Coffees & Teas. Kenneth Anderson. (Illus.). 144p. 1982. pap. 5.95 (ISBN 0-399-50600-4, Perigee); pap. 59.50 10-copy counter prepack (ISBN 0-399-50630-6). Putnam Pub Group.

Pocket Guide to Color Reproduction. Miles Southworth. LC 79-53546. (Illus.). 109p. (Orig.). 1979. pap. 6.95 (ISBN 0-933600-01-1). Tech & Ed Ctr Graph Arts RIT.

Pocket Guide to Colorado. 2nd ed. Ed. by Karl Kocivar. (Illus.). 176p. 1985. pap. 6.95 (ISBN 0-939396-01-7). Colorado Expr.

Pocket Guide to Correct English. Michael Temple. 64p. 1981. pap. text ed. 3.50 (ISBN 0-8120-2425-7). Barron.

Pocket Guide to Correct Grammar. Hopper. 1984. pap. 3.50 (ISBN 0-8120-2849-X). Barron.

Pocket Guide to Correct Punctuation. Robert Brittain. 96p. 1982. pap. 3.50 (ISBN 0-8120-2599-7). Barron.

Pocket Guide to Correct Spelling. Francis Griffith. 256p. (gr. 6-12). 1982. pap. 3.50 (ISBN 0-8120-2620-9). Barron.

Pocket Guide to Depression Glass. 6th, rev. ed. Gene Florence. (Illus.). 160p. 1988. pap. 9.95 (ISBN 0-89145-381-4). Collector Bks.

Pocket Guide to Differential Diagnosis. 2nd ed. R. D. Eastham. 532p. 1985. pap. 19.00 (ISBN 0-7236-0844-X). PSG Pub Co.

Pocket Guide to Doll Marks & Makers. P. Fellows. LC 85-50106. 138p. 1985. pap. 5.95 (ISBN 0-87069-450-2). Wallace-Homestead.

Pocket Guide to Electrical Equipment & Instrumentation. R. R. Lee. LC 84-25340. (Illus.). 320p. (Orig.). 1985. 19.00x (ISBN 0-87201-246-8). Gulf Pub.

Pocket Guide to Flanges, Fittings, & Piping Data. R. R. Lee. LC 84-669. 96p. (Orig.). 1984. pap. 18.00x (ISBN 0-87201-704-4). Gulf Pub.

Pocket Guide to French Food & Wine. Tessa Youell & George Kimball. 1986. pap. 5.95 (ISBN 0-671-62205-6, Fireside). S&S.

Pocket Guide to Gambling. David Spanier. 1980. 6.95 (ISBN 0-671-25515-0). S&S.

Pocket Guide to Health Assessment. Karen Berger & Willa Fields. (Illus.). 1980. pap. text ed. 15.95 (ISBN 0-8359-5582-6). Appleton & Lange.

Pocket Guide to Indoor Plants. George Seddon. (Illus.). 1980. pap. 4.95 (ISBN 0-671-25249-6). S&S.

Pocket Guide to Injectable Drugs. 3rd ed. Lawrence A. Trissel. vi, 209p. 1987. pap. text ed. 15.00 (ISBN 0-930530-72-1). Am Soc Hosp Pharm.

Pocket Guide to Irish Family Names. Ida Grehan. (Pocket Bk.). (Illus.). 96p. (Orig.). (YA) 1985. pap. 5.95 (ISBN 0-86281-133-3, Pub. by Appletree Pr). Irish Bks Media.

Pocket Guide to Irish First Names. Ronan Coghlan. (Pocket Bk.). 72p. (Orig.). 1985. pap. 5.95 (ISBN 0-86281-153-8, Pub. by Appletree Pr). Irish Bks Media.

Pocket Guide to Irish Genealogy. Compiled by Brian S. Mitchell. 103p. (Orig.). 1988. pap. text ed. 7.95 (ISBN 1-55856-000-9). Closson Pr.

Pocket Guide to Irish Place Names. rev. ed. P. W. Joyce. (Illus.). 96p. (Orig.). 1984. pap. 5.95 (ISBN 0-86281-127-9, Pub. by Appletree Pr). Irish Bks Media.

Pocket Guide to Irish Traditional Music. Ciaran Carson. 72p. 1986. pap. 5.95 (ISBN 0-86281-168-6, Pub. by Appletree Pr). Irish Bks Media.

Pocket Guide to Irish Wild Flowers. Ruth I. Ross. (Illus.). 72p. (Orig.). 1987. pap. 8.95 (ISBN 0-86281-192-9, Pub. by Appletree Pr). Irish Bks Media.

Pocket Guide to Italian Food & Wine. Spike Hughes & Charmian Hughes. 1987. pap. 5.95 (ISBN 0-671-63877-7, Fireside). S&S.

Pocket Guide to Job Interviewing. rev. ed. A. Mendelsohn. Ed. by Joseph Chavez. 45p. (gr. 8 up). 1981. text ed. 1.50 (ISBN 0-918443-00-8, AJDBI101). Job Data.

Pocket Guide to Literature & Language Terms. Benjamin Griffeth. 176p. 1985. pap. 3.50 (ISBN 0-8120-2512-1). Barron.

Pocket Guide to London Theatre. George Kimball. 162p. 1988. 9.95 (ISBN 0-88162-287-7). Salem Hse Pubs.

Pocket Guide to Maryland's Chesapeake Bay. Howard A. Chatterton. (Illus.). 48p. (Orig.). 1984. pap. 4.95 (ISBN 0-933852-46-0). Nautical & Aviation.

Pocket Guide to Music Forms & Styles. Wendy Munro. 64p. 1988. pap. 5.95 (ISBN 0-550-18033-8). Cambridge U Pr.

Pocket Guide to Northern & Central Europe. Ed. by Philippe Gloaguen & Pierre Josse. (Collier World Traveler Ser.). (Illus.). 192p. 1985. pap. 6.95 (ISBN 0-02-097030-7, Collier). Macmillan.
Pocket Guide to Nursing Diagnoses. 2nd ed. Mi Ja Kim et al. (Illus.). 336p. 1987. 13.95 (ISBN 0-8016-2677-3). Mosby.
Pocket Guide to Nutrition & Diet Therapy. Moore. (Illus.). 384p. 1988. spiral bdg. 15.95 (ISBN 0-8016-3483-0). Mosby.
Pocket Guide to Organic Chemistry: A Tool Kit. Stuart Rosenfeld. 120p. 1989. pap. 7.95 (ISBN 0-15-601654-0). HarBraceJ.
Pocket Guide to Pediatric Fractures. John Ogden. 246p. 1987. 26.95 (ISBN 0-683-06637-4). Williams & Wilkins.
Pocket Guide to Perfect Photographs: Your Can Take Better Pictures Instantly. Richard L. Morris. (Illus.). 89p. (Orig.). Date not set. pap. price not set. Morris Pubns.
Pocket Guide to Reading Katakana. Carl Shaad. (Illus.). 102p. 9.95 (ISBN 0-8348-0219-8). Weatherhill.
Pocket Guide to Recommended World Restaurants. A. G. Small. LC 83-91446. (Orig.). 1984. pap. 6.95 (ISBN 0-915457-00-8). A G Small Pubns.
Pocket Guide to Safe Travel. Steven Sloan. 1986. pap. 3.25 (ISBN 0-8092-4830-1). Contemp Bks.
Pocket Guide to Spirits & Liqueurs: A Connoisseur's International Guide. Emanuel Greenburg & Madeline Greenburg. LC 82-20532. (Illus.). 144p. 1983. pap. 5.95 (ISBN 0-399-50730-2, Perigee). Putnam Pub Group.
Pocket Guide to Supervising in the Oilfield. A. Lee Hunt. 36p. (Orig.). 1983. pap. 6.00x (ISBN 0-87201-714-1). Gulf Pub.
Pocket Guide to the Animals of Ireland. Gordon D'Arcy. (Illus.). 72p. (Orig.). 1987. 8.95 (ISBN 0-86281-199-6, Pub. by Appletree Pr). Irish Bks Media.
Pocket Guide to the Bible. Cyril Bridgland & Francis Foulkes. LC 88-1389. (Illus.). 400p. 1988. text ed. 12.95 (ISBN 0-8308-1401-9). Inter-Varsity.
Pocket Guide to the Birds of Ireland. Gordon D'Arcy. (Illus.). 72p. 1986. 8.95 (ISBN 0-86281-162-7, Pub. by Appletree Pr). Irish Bks Media.
Pocket Guide to the Cliffs of Moher. Tony Whilde. (Illus.). 72p. (Orig.). 1987. pap. 5.95 (ISBN 0-86281-196-1, Pub. by Appletree Pr). Irish Bks Media.
Pocket Guide to the Common Wildflowers of Connecticut. John E. Klimas, Jr. LC 74-31928. (Illus.). 60p. 1984. 8.95 (ISBN 0-8027-0488-3). Walker & Co.
Pocket Guide to the G. E. D. Robert S. Boone. 384p. 1988. pap. 6.95 (ISBN 0-15-600593-X, BFP). HarBraceJ.
Pocket Guide to the G. E. D. Writing Skills Test. Robert S. Boone. 192p. 1988. pap. 6.95 (ISBN 0-15-600594-8, BFP). HarBraceJ.
Pocket Guide to the Language of Music. Wendy Munro. 64p. 1988. pap. 5.95 (ISBN 0-550-18032-X). Cambridge U Pr.
Pocket Guide to the National Electrical Code. Marvin J. Fischer. 288p. 1984. 9.95 (ISBN 0-13-683995-9). P-H.
Pocket Guide to the National Electrical Code. 1987 ed. Marvin J. Fischer. 288p. 1987. pap. text ed. 10.95 (ISBN 0-13-684606-8). P-H.
Pocket Guide to the Operating Room. Maxine Goldman. (Illus.). 500p. (Orig.). 1988. pap. text ed. 15.00 (ISBN 0-8036-4174-5). Davis Co.
Pocket Guide to the SAT. Weber. 224p. 1988. pap. 5.95 (ISBN 0-15-672186-4). HarBraceJ.
Pocket Guide to the Southeast Aegean. Rod Heikell & Mike Harper. 105p. 1986. 39.00x (ISBN 0-85288-101-0, Pub. by Imray Laurie Norie & Wilson England). State Mutual Bk.
Pocket Guide to the Wines of Burgundy. Serena Sutcliffe. 1986. pap. 7.95 (ISBN 0-671-61695-1, Fireside). S&S.
Pocket Guide to Treasure Signs. Thomas P. Terry. (Illus.). 24p. (Orig.). 1977. pap. 0.75 (ISBN 0-939850-08-7). Spec Pub.
Pocket Guide to Trees. Keith Rushforth. 1981. 7.95 (ISBN 0-686-73804-7). S&S.
Pocket Guide to Ultrasound Measurements. Craig. LC 65-10523. (Illus.). 150p. 1988. pap. 17.50 (ISBN 0-397-50887-5, Lippincott Medical). Lippincott.
Pocket Guide to Vocabulary. Brownstein & Weiner. 1984. pap. 3.50 (ISBN 0-8120-2814-7). Barron.
Pocket Guide to Wine: A Discriminating Guide to Good Wine. rev. ed. Barbara Ensrud. (Illus.). 144p. (Orig.). 1985. pap. 7.95 (ISBN 0-399-51145-8, Perigee). Putnam Pub Group.
Pocket Guide to WordStar. Anthony Bove & Cheryl Rhodes. (Micro Computer Ser.). 1983. pap. write for info. (ISBN 0-201-07754-X). Addison-Wesley.
Pocket Guitar. Ed. by Milton Okun & Dan Fox. (Pocket Guitar Ser.). (Orig.). 1980. pap. 3.95 (ISBN 0-89524-113-7, 8801). Cherry Lane.
Pocket Gynaecology. 10th ed. Stanley Clayton & John R. Newton. (Illus.). 1983. pap. text ed. 9.75 (ISBN 0-443-02402-2). Churchill.
Pocket Handbook for Hi-Tensile Fencing. Michael L. Hanson. (Illus.). 58p. (Orig.). 1982. write for info. Agri-Fence.
Pocket Handbook for Solid-Liquid Separations. Nicholas P. Cheremisinoff. LC 84-8970. 160p. 1984. 26.00x (ISBN 0-87201-830-X). Gulf Pub.
Pocket Handbook of Common Cardiac Arrythmias: Recognition & Treatment. Anne E. Garrett & Virginia Adams. (Illus.). 194p. 1985. pap. text ed. 13.75 (ISBN 0-397-54530-4, Lippincott Nursing). Lippincott.
Pocket Handbook of Infectious Agents & Their Treatments. Nancy Hartman & Daniel Shapiro. 1987. pap. text ed. 20.00x (ISBN 0-89529-354-4). Avery Pub.
Pocket Hawaiian Dictionary: With a Concise Hawaiian Grammar. Mary K. Pukui et al. LC 74-78865. 286p. (Hawaiian.). 1975. pap. 2.95 (ISBN 0-8248-0307-8). UH Pr.
Pocket Highway Atlas. Rev. ed. 64p. 1984. 1.25 (ISBN 0-88098-057-5). H M Gousha.
Pocket History of the United States. Allan Nevins & Henry S. Commager. (gr. 10 up). 1983. pap. 4.95. PB.
Pocket History of the United States. 2nd, rev. ed. Allan Nevins & Henry S. Commager. 688p. 1982. pap. 4.95. WSP.
Pocket Hungarian-English Dictionary. I. Orszagh. (Hungarian & Eng.). 1980. 20.00x (ISBN 0-569-00344-X, Pub. by Collets (UK)). State Mutual Bk.
Pocket I-Ching. Gary G. Melyan & Wen-kuang Chu. LC 88-50327. (Illus.). 182p. 1988. pap. 5.95 (ISBN 0-8048-1566-6). C E Tuttle.
Pocket Interlinear Bible: Numerically Coded to Strong's Exhaustive Concordance, 4 vols. Ed. by Jay P. Green. 1988. Set. pap. 37.80 (ISBN 0-8010-3828-6); Pocket Interlinear Old Testament, 3 vols. pap. 29.95 (ISBN 0-8010-3827-8); Pocket Interlinear New Testament, 1 vol. pap. 9.95 (ISBN 0-8010-3825-1). Baker Bk.
Pocket Interlinear New Testament. Ed. by Jay P. Green. 1981. pap. 5.95 (ISBN 0-8010-3777-8). Baker Bk.
Pocket Interlinear Old Testament, 3 vols. Jay P. Green, Sr. 2216p. 1987. pap. 34.95 (ISBN 0-913573-51-5). Hendrickson MA.
Pocket Irish Atlas. (Illus.). 48p. (Orig.). 1987. pap. 8.95 (ISBN 0-86281-191-0, Pub. by Appletree Pr). Irish Bks Media.
Pocket Irish Dictionary. Tr. by Seosamh Watson. (Pocket Bk.). 72p. (Orig.). 1985. pap. 5.95 (ISBN 0-86281-150-3, Pub. by Appletree Pub). Irish Bks Media.
Pocket Irish Phrase Book. Paul Dorris. 71p. (Orig.). 1983. pap. 5.95 (ISBN 0-86281-010-8, Pub. by Appletree Pr). Irish Bks Media.
Pocket John Denver for Guitar. John Denver. Ed. by Milton Okun. (Pocket Guitar Ser.). 224p. 1982. pap. 3.95 (ISBN 0-89524-155-2). Cherry Lane.
Pocket Knives. (Orig.). 1983. pap. 2.95 (ISBN 0-440-06982-3). Dell.
Pocket Lexicon & Concordance to the Temple Shakespeare. Marian Edwardes. LC 74-164759. Repr. of 1909 ed. 21.50 (ISBN 0-404-02261-8). AMS Pr.
Pocket Lexicon of Freemasonry. 4.00 (ISBN 0-685-19495-7). Powner.
Pocket Lexicon to the Greek New Testament. Ed. by Alexander Souter. 1916. 17.95x (ISBN 0-19-864203-2). Oxford U Pr.
Pocket Mad. (Mad Ser.). (Illus.). 1974. pap. 1.75 (ISBN 0-446-94594-3). Warner Bks.
Pocket Magic: Graphic Games for the Pocket Computer. Bill L. Behrendt. LC 82-80271. (Illus.). 96p. (Orig.). (YA) 1982. 17.95; pap. 9.95 (ISBN 0-942412-01-X); pre-recorded cassette 8.95 (ISBN 0-686-87025-5). Micro Text Pubns.
Pocket Manual of Basic Surgical Skills. Van Way & Buerk. 1986. 16.00 (ISBN 0-8016-5231-6). Mosby.
Pocket Manual of Critical Care. Cerra. (Illus.). 500p. 1986. pap. 29.95 (ISBN 0-8016-1010-9). Mosby.
Pocket Manual of Differential Diagnosis. 2nd ed. Stephen N. Adler et al. 1982. pap. text ed. 13.00 (ISBN 0-316-01106-1). Little.
Pocket Manual of Emergency Trauma Procedures. Moore et al. (Illus.). 300p. 1988. pap. 20.00 (ISBN 0-8016-3582-9). Mosby.
Pocket Manual of Surgical Nutrition. Cerra. (Illus.). 350p. 1984. pap. 17.95 (ISBN 0-8016-0937-2). Mosby.
Pocket Medical Encyclopedia & First Aid Guide. Mitchell Beazly Pub. Ltd. 1979. pap. 4.95 (ISBN 0-671-24671-2). S&S.
Pocket Mirror: Poems. Janet Frame. LC 67-18210. 1967. 4.95 (ISBN 0-8076-0408-9). Braziller.
Pocket Mnemonics for Practitioners. abr. ed. Robert Bloomfield & Ted Chandler. 1983. pap. 4.95 (ISBN 0-9612242-2-3). Harbinger Med Pr NC.
Pocket Money. Frank Endersby. (Choices Ser.). (ps). 1984. 3.50 (ISBN 0-85953-190-2, Child's Play England). Playspaces.
Pocket Notes for Personal Success: It's As Easy As ABC. King J. Bogardus, Jr. (Illus.). 44p. 1977. pap. 1.00 (ISBN 0-918176-01-8). P & K Ent.
Pocket Nurse Guide to Assessment in Critical Care. Talbot & Marquardt. (Illus.). 250p. 1988. 18.95 (ISBN 0-8016-4987-0). Mosby.
Pocket Nurse Guide to Drugs. Clark et al. (Illus.). 300p. 1986. pap. 19.95 spiral bound (ISBN 0-8016-1013-3). Mosby.
Pocket Nurse Guide to Electrocardiography. Conover. 1985. pap. 16.95 (ISBN 0-8016-1049-4). Mosby.
Pocket Nurse Guide to Fetal Monitoring. Tucker. (Illus.). 160p. 1988. spiral bdg. 16.95 (ISBN 0-8016-5145-X). Mosby.
Pocket Nurse Guide to Fluids & Electrolytes. Horne & Swearingen. (Illus.). 375p. 1988. 16.95 (ISBN 0-8016-5188-3). Mosby.
Pocket Nurse Guide to Intravenous Therapy. Larocca & Otto. (Illus.). 384p. 1988. spiral bdg. 16.96 (ISBN 0-8016-5189-1). Mosby.
Pocket Nurse Guide to Laboratory-Diagnostic Tests. Pagana. 1986. pap. 18.95 (ISBN 0-8016-3760-0). Mosby.
Pocket Nurse Guide to Nutrition. Williams. 1986. 14.95 (ISBN 0-8016-4645-6). Mosby.
Pocket Nurse Guide to Pediatric Assessment. Engel. 300p. 1988. spiral bdg. 14.95 (ISBN 0-8016-1795-2). Mosby.
Pocket Nurse Guide to Physical Assessment. Potter. 1985. pap. 16.95 (ISBN 0-8016-3962-X). Mosby.
Pocket Nurse Guide to Psychiatric Nursing. Stuart & Sundeen. 1986. 15.95 (ISBN 0-8016-4856-4). Mosby.
Pocket of Trouble. Ron Betts. 1982. 15.00x (ISBN 0-86319-006-5, Pub. by New Playwrights Network). State Mutual Bk.
Pocket Oxford Dictionary of Current English. 7th ed. R. E. Allen. 900p. 1984. 13.95 (ISBN 0-19-861133-1). Oxford U Pr.
Pocket Oxford English-Russian Dictionary. N. A. Rankin. (Eng. & Rus.). 1981. text ed. 11.95x (ISBN 0-19-864127-3). Oxford U Pr.
Pocket Oxford German Dictionary, 2 vols. in 1. Compiled by M. L. Barker & H. Homeyer. Incl. Pt. 1. German-English. 3rd ed. (Eng. & Ger.). 1975; Pt. 2. English-German. Compiled by C. T. Carr. (Eng. & Ger.). 1975. 712p. (Ger.). pap. 6.95 (ISBN 0-19-864138-9). Oxford U Pr.
Pocket Oxford Guide to Sailing Terms. Ian Dear. LC 86-21787. 1987. 23.95x (ISBN 0-19-211663-0); pap. 9.95 (ISBN 0-19-282012-5). Oxford U Pr.
Pocket Oxford Russian Dictionary: Russian-English - English-Russian. Ed. by Jessie Coulson et al. 844p. (Rus. & Eng.). 1981. pap. 12.95x (ISBN 0-19-864122-2). Oxford U Pr.
Pocket Oxford Russian-English Dictionary. Ed. by J. Coulson. (Rus. & Eng.). 1975. 12.95x (ISBN 0-19-864113-3). Oxford U Pr.
Pocket Parables. Carl G. Carlozzi & Ellen Parkes. 80p. (Orig.). 1985. pap. 2.95 (ISBN 0-8423-4919-7). Tyndale.
Pocket Pearls. Nelson G. Mink. 128p. (Orig.). 1987. pap. 2.95 (ISBN 0-8423-4930-8). Tyndale.
Pocket Photo Edition of the Directory of the California Legislative 1988. 80p. pap. 9.95 (ISBN 0-917982-35-5). Capitol Enquiry.
Pocket Picture Guide in Limb Injuries. Burge. LC 65-40108. (Illus.). 1988. text ed. price not set (ISBN 0-397-44576-8, Lippincott Medical). Lippincott.
Pocket Picture Guide to AIDS. Ian V. Weller & Adrian Mindel. (Gower Bk.). (Illus.). 96p. 1989. text ed. price not set (ISBN 0-397-44578-4, Lippincott MedicaL). Lippincott.
Pocket Picture Guide to Gastroenterology. Neil I. McNeil. LC 65-40223. (Gower Bk.). 1987. 9.95 (ISBN 0-397-44561-X, Lippincott Medical). Lippincott.
Pocket Picture Guide to Head Injuries. Teddy & Anslow. LC 65-40322. 1988. text ed. price not set (ISBN 0-397-44569-5, Lippincott Medical). Lippincott.
Pocket Picture Guide to Oral Medicine. Philip-John Lamey & Michael A. Lewis. LC 65-50165. (Illus.). 78p. 1988. 9.95 (ISBN 0-397-44575-X, Lippincott Medical). Lippincott.
Pocket Picture Guide to Skin Signs of Systemic Diseases. Denis E. Sharvill. LC 65-40298. (Illus.). 96p. 1988. 9.95 (ISBN 0-397-44574-1, Lippincott Medical). Lippincott.
Pocket Picture Guide to Spine Injuries. Houghton. LC 65-40157. (Illus.). 1988. text ed. price not set (ISBN 0-397-44577-6, Lippincott Medical). Lippincott.
Pocket Picture Guides for Nurses. J. Bingham. 100p. 1984. text ed. 9.95 (ISBN 0-683-00916-8). Williams & Wilkins.
Pocket Planner for Jewelry Show Exhibitors. 44p. 1983. pap. 4.75 (ISBN 0-931744-08-3). Jewelers Bk Club.
Pocket Poems: Selected for a Journey. Ed. by Paul B. Janeczko. LC 84-21537. 160p. (gr. 6 up). 1985. pap. 8.95 (ISBN 0-02-747820-3). Bradbury Pr.
Pocket Poets Series, 4 vols. LC 73-12817. (Illus.). 1964p. 1973. Repr. of 1971 ed. Set. 188.00 (ISBN 0-527-71600-6). Kraus Repr.
Pocket Power, No. 1: Medical. Joseph M. Leonard. 48p. (Orig.). 1988. pap. 2.95 (ISBN 0-945893-00-0). Pocket Power.
Pocket Power, No. 2: Taxes. Lois L. Leonard. Ed. by Joseph M. Leonard. 48p. (Orig.). 1988. pap. text ed. 2.95 (ISBN 0-945893-01-9). Pocket Power.
Pocket Power, No. 3: Legal. Douglas A. Stoodt. Ed. by Joseph M. Leonard. 48p. (Orig.). 1988. pap. 2.95 (ISBN 0-945893-02-7). Pocket Power.
Pocket Power, No. 4: Dental. Wayne A. Brannon & Joseph M. Leonard. 48p. (Orig.). 1988. pap. 2.95 (ISBN 0-945893-03-5). Pocket Power.
Pocket Power, No. 5: Veterinary. John L. Augustine & Joseph M. Leonard. 48p. (Orig.). 1988. pap. 2.95 (ISBN 0-945893-04-3). Pocket Power.
Pocket Power, No. 6: Travel. Allyson C. Burnette. Ed. by Joseph M. Leonard. 48p. (Orig.). 1988. pap. 2.95 (ISBN 0-945893-05-1). Pocket Power.
Pocket Praise. Robert C. Savage. (Pocket Ser.). 176p. 1985. pap. 2.95 (ISBN 0-8423-4931-6). Tyndale.
Pocket Prayers: Seven Hundred & Seventy-Seven Bible Ways to Pray. Robert C. Savage. 1982. pap. 3.50 (ISBN 0-8423-4849-2). Tyndale.
Pocket Price Guide & Checklist for World War II U. S. Military Patches. Robert Swope, Jr. (Illus.). 69p. (Orig.). 1986. pap. text ed. 5.95 (ISBN 0-936441-01-1). Heritage PA.
Pocket Primer of Parliamentary Procedure. 5th ed. Fred G. Stevenson. 1973. pap. 6.95 (ISBN 0-395-14088-9). HM.
Pocket Programmable Calculators in Biochemistry. John E. Barnes & Alan J. Waring. LC 79-2547. 363p. 1980. (Pub. by Wiley-Interscience); pap. 31.50 (ISBN 0-471-04713-9). Wiley.
Pocket Programmable Calculators in Biochemistry. John E. Barnes & Alan J. Waring. LC 79-2547. pap. 96.30 (2026809). Bks Demand UMI.
Pocket Promise Book. gift ed. David Wilkerson. LC 72-86208. 96p. 1981. imitation leather 4.95 (ISBN 0-8307-0789-1, 5007953). Regal.
Pocket Proverbs. David Wilkerson. LC 83-3405. (Orig.). 1983. pocket-sized 2.95 (ISBN 0-8307-0893-6, 5018103). Regal.
Pocket Quips: Seven Hundred Seventy Seven Quotables. Robert C. Savage. LC 83-51245. 160p. (Orig.). 1984. pap. 2.95 (ISBN 0-8423-4904-9). Tyndale.
Pocket R. L. S. Robert Louis Stevenson. 1903. Repr. 20.00 (ISBN 0-8274-3147-3). R West.
Pocket Reference for Medical Intensive Care. Barbara Phillips. 432p. 1986. 28.50 (ISBN 0-87189-283-9). Aspen Pub.
Pocket Reference to Displaywrite 4. Gail Todd. 128p. 1988. pap. text ed. 5.95 (ISBN 0-07-881380-8). Osborne-McGraw.
Pocket Reference to Health Disorders. Linda C. Fritschle & Susan R. Rudnick. (Nursing Ser.). 132p. 1983. pap. 6.95x (ISBN 0-86598-126-4, Rowman & Allanheld). Rowman.
Pocket Reference to Hypertalk & the External Commands. David A. Gewirtz. 70p. 1988. spiral bdg. 11.95 (ISBN 0-945266-00-6). Hyperpress Pub.
Pocket Rhyming Dictionary. 1960. pap. 2.95 (ISBN 0-394-40062-3). Random.
Pocket Sayings. Edythe Draper. (Tyndale House Pocket Ser.). 128p. (Orig.). (YA) (gr. 7 up). 1987. pap. 2.95 (ISBN 0-8423-4941-3). Tyndale.
Pocket Size Carpenter's Helper. Robert F. Bailey. (Illus.). 104p. (Orig.). 1986. pap. 8.95 (ISBN 0-937635-00-6). R S Wood.
Pocket Size Teddy Bears. Date not set. pap. 4.98 (ISBN 0-317-03199-6). Gick.
Pocket Smiles: Seven Hundred Seventy Seven Moldy Oldies. Robert C. Savage. 144p. 1984. 2.95 (ISBN 0-8423-4906-5). Tyndale.
Pocket Sundial. Lisa Zeidner. LC 88-40196. 90p. (Orig.). 1988. text ed. 12.50 (ISBN 0-299-11920-3); pap. text ed. 7.95 (ISBN 0-299-11924-6). U of Wis Pr.
Pocket Thackeray. Alfred H. Hyatt. 1906. 20.00 (ISBN 0-8274-3148-1). R West.
Pocket Tin Whistle Book. Francis McPeake. 72p. 1983. pap. 5.95 (ISBN 0-86281-112-0, Pub. by Appletree Pr). Irish Bks Media.
Pocket V-Speeds. Waltmann & Buckner Staff. 76p. (Orig.). 1985. pap. 5.95 (ISBN 0-934191-00-X). Waltman & Buckner Pub.
Pocket Watch Price Guide, Book 3: Foreign and American. Roy Erhardt. (Illus.). 1976. plastic ring bdg. 10.00 (ISBN 0-913902-16-0). Heart Am Pr.
Pocket Watch Price Indicator. Roy Ehrhardt. (Illus.). 1980. plastic ring bdg. 12.00 (ISBN 0-913902-32-2). Heart Am Pr.
Pocket Watch Price Indicator, 1976. Roy Ehrhardt. (Illus.). 1975. Repr. plastic ring bdg. 5.00 (ISBN 0-913902-15-2). Heart Am Pr.
Pocket Watch Price Indicator, 1977. Roy Ehrhardt. (Illus.). 1976. plastic ring bdg. 7.00 (ISBN 0-913902-21-7). Heart Am Pr.
Pocket Watch Price Indicator, 1978. Roy Ehrhardt. (Illus.). 1978. plastic ring bdg. 10.00 (ISBN 0-913902-26-8). Heart Am Pr.
Pocket Watch Price Indicator,1979. Roy Ehrhardt. (Illus.). 1979. plastic ring bdg. 10.00 (ISBN 0-913902-29-2). Heart Am Pr.
Pocket Watches. Reinhard Meis. (Illus.). 316p. 1987. 50.00 (ISBN 0-88740-084-1). Schiffer.
Pocket Weather Forecaster. 1977. 3.95 (ISBN 0-8120-0957-6). Barron.
Pocket Wisdom: Seven Hundred Seventy Seven Golden Nuggets. Robert C. Savage. LC 83-51246. 160p. (Orig.). 1984. pap. 3.50 (ISBN 0-8423-4905-7). Tyndale.
Pocketax, 1986. Commerce Clearing House, Inc. 32p. 1985. 1.50 (ISBN 0-317-30588-3, 4396). Commerce.
Pocketax, 1987. Commerce Clearing House, Inc. 32p. 1985. 1.50 (ISBN 0-317-47511-8, 4397). Commerce.
Pocketax, 1987. 32p. 1987. pap. 1.50 (ISBN 0-317-44617-7, 4397). Commerce.
Pocketax, 1988. 32p. (Orig.). 1987. pap. 1.50 (4398). Commerce.
Pocketax, 1989. Clark. 32p. Date not set. pap. 2.00 (4399). Commerce.

Pocketbook for Technical & Professional Writers. Earl G. Bingham. 283p. 1982. pap. text ed. write for info. (ISBN 0-534-01004-0). Wadsworth Pub.

Pocketbook of Porcelain & Pottery Marks. Peter Darty. 1974. 15.00 (ISBN 0-685-53252-6). ARS Ceramica.

Pocketbook of Statistical Distribution. Ed. by R. Odeh et al. (Statistics: Textbooks & Monographs: Vol. 22). 1977. 29.75 (ISBN 0-8247-6515-X). Dekker.

Pocketful of Cricket. Rebecca Caudill. LC 64-12617. (Illus.). 48p. (gr. k-2). 1964. reinforced bdg. 7.95 (ISBN 0-03-089752-1); pap. 2.95 (ISBN 0-03-086619-7). H Holt & Co.

Pocketful of Dreams. Mary A. VanderWeele. (Illus.). 256p. 1987. 13.95 (ISBN 0-943273-01-3); pap. 9.49 (ISBN 0-943273-00-5). Bolton Pub.

Pocketful of Goobers: A Story about George Washington Carver. Barbara Mitchell. (Creative Minds Ser.). (Illus.). 64p. (gr. 3-6). 1986. PLB 9.95 (ISBN 0-87614-292-7). Carolrhoda Bks.

Pocketful of Goobers: A Story about George Washington Carver. Barbara Mitchell. (Creative Minds Bks.). (Illus.). (gr. 3-6). 1987. pap. 4.95 (ISBN 0-87614-474-1, First Ave Edns). Lerner Pubns.

Pocketful of Hope. Mary C. Crowley. 352p. 1981. 12.50 (ISBN 0-8007-1272-2). Revell.

Pocketful of Miracles Holiday: Filefolder Games, Patterns & Directions. Connie Eisenhart & Ruth Bell. 1985. pap. 7.95 (ISBN 0-933212-24-0). Partner Pr.

Pocketful of Miracles Set I: Filefolder Games, Patterns & Directions. Connie Eisenhart. 1984. pap. 6.95 (ISBN 0-318-11994-3) (ISBN 0-318-11995-1). Partner Pr.

Pocketful of Pets. Jane B. Moncure. LC 87-11748. (Magic Castle Reader's Ser.). (Illus.). 32p. (ps-2). 1987. PLB 7.75 (ISBN 0-89565-370-2). Childs World.

Pocketful of Pets. Jane B. Moncure. (Magic Castle Readers Ser.). (Illus.). 32p. (ps-2). 1987. 11.93 (ISBN 0-516-05738-3). Childrens.

Pocketful of Poems. Babe Hart et al. LC 85-73259. 68p. (Orig.). 1985. pap. 4.95 (ISBN 0-9615829-0-1). Baja Bks.

Pocketful of Puppets: Mother Goose Rhymes. Tamara Hunt & Nancy Renfro. Ed. by Ann Schwalb. (Puppetry in Education Ser.). (Illus.). 80p. (Orig.). 1982. 13.50; pap. 9.50 (ISBN 0-931044-06-5). Renfro Studios.

Pocketful of Puppets: "Never Pick a Python for a Pet" & Other Animal Poems. Tamara Hunt. Ed. by Celeste Cromack. (Puppetry in Education Ser.). (Illus.). 80p. (Orig.). 1985. 13.50; pap. 9.50 (ISBN 0-931044-14-6). Renfro Studios.

Pocketful of Puppets: Poems for Church School. Lynn Irving. Ed. by Merily H. Keller. (Puppetry in Education ser.). (Illus.). 48p. (Orig.). 1982. 12.50; pap. 8.50 (ISBN 0-931044-05-7). Renfro Studios.

Pocketful of Puppets: Three Plump Fish & Other Short Stories. Yvonne Winer. Ed. by Merily H. Keller. (Puppetry in Education Ser.). (Illus.). 48p. (Orig.). 1982. 12.50; pap. 8.50 (ISBN 0-931044-08-1). Renfro Studios.

Pocketful of Rainbows. Clarice Burrell. 1967. 2.50 (ISBN 0-87511-014-2); pap. 1.50 (ISBN 0-87511-013-4). Claitors.

Pocketful of Smiles. Earl W. Engleman. (Illus.). 1979. pap. 4.50 (ISBN 0-933992-03-3). Coffee Break.

Pocketful of Word Finds. Pamela A. Klawitter. (Pretzel Ser.). (Illus.). 64p. (Orig.). (gr. 4-6). 1981. pap. 1.95 (ISBN 0-590-40980-8). Scholastic Inc.

Pocketguide to Health & Health Problems in School Physical Activities. LC 81-66886. 1981. pap. 4.50 (ISBN 0-917160-13-4). Am Sch Health.

Pocketguide to the Art Institute of Chicago. Ed. by Robert Sharp. (Illus.). 64p. (Orig.). 1983. pap. 1.25 (ISBN 0-86559-054-0). Art Inst Chi.

Pocketknives-Markings, Manufacturers & Dealers. 2nd ed. John E. Goins. LC 82-83511. (Illus.). 280p. (Orig.). 1982. pap. 8.95 (ISBN 0-940362-06-6). Knife World.

Pockets of Love. Russell Marano. 58p. 1984. 5.00x (ISBN 0-318-03893-5). Back Fork Bks.

Pockets of Time. Anita L. Hamm. 1982. 6.95 (ISBN 0-935513-04-3). Samara Pubns.

Poco. Garry Smith & Vesta Smith. LC 75-17874. (Illus.). 40p. (Eng. & Span.). (gr. k-3). 1975. 5.95 (ISBN 0-88468-006-1). Ethridge.

Poco a Poco: Spanish for Proficiency. James M. Hendrickson. 492p. 1986. 32.50 (ISBN 0-8384-1350-1); wkbk. 16.75 (ISBN 0-8384-1352-8). Heinle & Heinle.

Pocoangelini: A Fantography & Other Poems. Lewis Turco. 1971. pap. 4.95 (ISBN 0-912952-07-5). Mathom.

Poconos: An Illustrated Natural History Guide. Carl S. Oplinger & J. Robert Halma. (Illus.). 280p. 1988. text ed. 30.00 (ISBN 0-8135-1293-X); pap. 12.95 (ISBN 0-8135-1294-8). Rutgers U Pr.

Pocumtuck Housewife: A Guide to Domestic Cookery. Deerfield Parish Guild Staff. 55p. 1985. pap. 2.95 (ISBN 0-9612876-4-0). Pocumtuck Valley Mem.

Pod of Gray Whales. Francois Gohier. (Illus.). 40p. (Orig.). 1987. pap. 4.95 (ISBN 0-918303-14-1). Blake Print Pub.

Pod Sztandarem Z Gwiazd. Halina Bonikowska. LC 85-61376. 112p. (Orig., Pol.). 1985. pap. text ed. 8.00 (ISBN 0-930401-01-8). Artex Pr.

Pod Znakom Chetyrekh. Ludmila Shtern. 208p. 1984. pap. text ed. 8.50 (ISBN 0-938920-49-9). Hermitage.

Podal V. Drevnem Kieve. K. N. Gupalo. 128p. (Orig.). 1982. 29.00x (ISBN 0-317-40874-7, Pub. by Collets (UK)). State Mutual Bk.

Poder de la Oracion Tenaz. Juan Bisagno. Tr. by Olivia S. De Lerin from Eng. Orig. Title: Power of Positive Praying. 96p. (Span.). 1986. pap. 2.75 (ISBN 0-311-40029-9). Casa Bautista.

Poder del las Affirmaciones. Jerry Fankhauser. 56p. 1979. pap. 8.00 (ISBN 0-317-61721-4). J Fankhauser.

Poder del las Afirmaciones. Jerry Fankhauser. Tr. by Edith B. Rodas-Carroll from Eng. (Illus.). 24p. (Orig., Span.). pap. 3.50 (ISBN 0-9617006-3-7). J Fankhauser.

Poder para Vencer. Michael Harper. 1982. 2.95 (ISBN 0-88113-245-4). Edit Betania.

Poder Sanador de la Gracia. William P. Wilson & Kathryn Slattery. Ed. by Mario Llerena. Tr. by Luis Bernal from Span. Orig. Title: Grace to Grow. 176p. 1985. pap. text ed. 2.95 (ISBN 0-8297-0744-1). Life Pubs Intl.

Poder Sovietico y la Situacion Del Campesinado. V. I. Lenin. 113p. (Span.). 1979. pap. 1.45 (ISBN 0-8285-1487-9, Pub. by Progress Pubs USSR). Imported Pubns.

Poder y Derecho: Estrategias de Mujeres del Tercer Mundo. Ed. by Margaret Schuler. Tr. by Guillermo Delgado from Eng. LC 87-62631. 550p. 1988. pap. 15.00 (ISBN 0-912917-17-2). OEF Intl.

Poderes Tecnologicos y la Persona. 370p. 1984. pap. cancelled (ISBN 0-935372-16-4). Pope John Ctr.

Podiatric Dermatology. Daniel J. McCarthy. (Illus.). 300p. 1985. text ed. 51.95 (ISBN 0-683-05750-2). Williams & Wilkins.

Podiatric Marketing & Practice Management. Barry H. Block. 300p. 1988. 32.50 (ISBN 0-683-00852-8). Williams & Wilkins.

Podiatric Sports Medicine. Steven I. Subotnick. LC 74-82021. (Podiatric Medicine & Surgery Ser.: Vol. 4). 203p. 1975. 24.50 (ISBN 0-87993-044-6). Futura Pub.

Podiatric Sports Medicine of the Lower Extremity. 2nd ed. Steven I. Subotnick. 400p. 1986. 39.95 (ISBN 0-89116-315-8). Hemisphere Pub.

Podiatric Surgical Dissection: Fundamental Skills. O. A. Mercado. (Illus.). 67p. 1976. pap. text ed. 16.50 (ISBN 0-940542-01-3). Carolando.

Podiatry for the Assistant. 2nd ed. Irvin Donick. 260p. 1988. 27.00 (ISBN 0-683-02614-3). Williams & Wilkins.

Podiatry Manpower, U. S. 1970. Hugo Koch & Hazel Phillips. LC 74-2091. (Data on Health Resources: Manpower & Facilities Ser. 14: No. 14). 1974. pap. text ed. 1.50 (ISBN 0-8406-0005-4). Natl Ctr Health Stats.

Podiatry Workforce: A General Profile, United States, 1974. Ed. by Audrey Shipp. (Ser. 14: No. 18). 1977. pap. text ed. 1.75 (ISBN 0-8406-0095-X). Natl Ctr Health Stats.

Podiatry Workforce: Characteristics of the Provision of Patient Care: United States, 1974. P. Hannah et al. Ed. by Audurey Shipp. (Ser. 14: No. 22). 1978. pap. text ed. 1.75 (ISBN 0-8406-0152-2). Natl Ctr Health Stats.

Podium Humor: A Raconteur's Treasury of Witty & Humorous Stories. James C. Humes. LC 74-15832. 352p. 1975. 14.45i (ISBN 0-06-011999-3, HarpT). Har-Row.

Podium Humor: A Raconteur's Treasury of Witty & Humorous Stories. James C. Humes. LC 85-42572. 320p. 1985. pap. 6.95 (ISBN 0-06-091303-7, PL 1303, PL). Har-Row.

Podium Pointers. James P. King. 1986. pap. text ed. 7.50 (ISBN 0-936895-02-0). Brown House.

Podkayne of Mars. Robert A. Heinlein. 1987. pap. 2.95 (ISBN 0-441-67402-X, Pub. by Ace Science Fiction). Ace Bks.

Podopediatrics. 2nd ed. Herman R. Tax. (Illus.). 678p. 1985. text ed. 68.95 (ISBN 0-683-08118-7). Williams & Wilkins.

Podreczny Slownik Polsko-Niemiecki (Manual Dictionary Polish-German) A. Bzdega et al. 1018p. (Pol. & Ger.). 1977. leatherette 19.95 (ISBN 0-686-87194-4, M-0129). French & Eur.

Pods: Wildflowers & Weeds in Their Final Beauty. Jane Emberton. 1984. 20.00 (ISBN 0-8446-6117-1). Peter Smith.

Pods: Wildflowers & Weeds in Their Final Beauty. Jane Embertson. (Illus.). 1979. pap. 14.95 (ISBN 0-684-15543-5, ScribT). Scribner.

Podzol-Forming Process. A. A. Rode. 392p. 1970. text ed. 79.50x (ISBN 0-7065-1011-9, Pub. by Keter Pub Jerusalem). Coronet Bks.

Poe. Edgar Allan Poe. Ed. by Jean L. Scrocco. (Illus.). 164p. (gr. 7 up). 1986. 16.95 (ISBN 0-88101-057-X). Unicorn Pub.

Poe: A Collection of Critical Essays. Ed. by Robert Regan. 1967. 15.95 (ISBN 0-13-684936-9, Spec). P-H.

Poe & Chivers. Landon C. Bell. LC 73-9500. Repr. of 1931 ed. lib. bdg. 12.50 (ISBN 0-8414-3133-7). Folcroft.

Poe & His Poetry. Lewis N. Chase. LC 72-120973. (Poetry & Life Ser.). Repr. of 1913 ed. 7.25 (ISBN 0-404-52506-7). AMS Pr.

Poe & His Poetry. Lewis N. Chase. lib. bdg. 22.00 (ISBN 0-8414-3453-0). Folcroft.

Poe & His Poetry. Lewis N. Chase. LC 75-38649. (Studies in Poe, No. 23). 1976. Repr. of 1924 ed. lib. bdg. 75.00x (ISBN 0-8383-2112-7). Haskell.

Poe & Our Times: Influences & Affinities. Ed. & intro. by Benjamin F. Fisher, IV. 156p. Date not set. 18.00x (ISBN 0-9616449-0-7). Poe Soc Baltimore.

Poe & Pog. Norma M. Bracy. (Illus.). 22p. (gr. k-12). 1986. pap. text ed. 2.00 (ISBN 0-915783-02-9). Book Binder.

Poe & the British Magazine Tradition. Michael Allen. 1978. Repr. of 1969 ed. lib. bdg. 35.00 (ISBN 0-8495-0100-8). Arden Lib.

Poe & the Southern Literary Messenger. D. K. Jackson. LC 71-95432. (Studies in Poe, No. 23). 1970. Repr. of 1934 ed. lib. bdg. 39.95x (ISBN 0-8383-0983-6). Haskell.

Poe Cult & Other Poe Papers. Eugene L. Didier. LC 72-190662. 1909. lib. bdg. 33.00 (ISBN 0-8414-0808-4). Folcroft.

Poe, Death, & the Life of Writing. J. Gerald Kennedy. 256p. 1987. text ed. 19.50 (ISBN 0-300-03773-2). Yale U Pr.

Poe in Foreign Lands & Tongues. John C. French. LC 73-1694. 1973. lib. bdg. 25.00 (ISBN 0-8414-1954-X). Folcroft.

Poe in Northlight: The Scandinavian Response to His Life & Work. Carl L. Anderson. LC 72-88734. 1973. 22.95 (ISBN 0-8223-0275-6). Duke.

Poe: Journalist & Critic. Robert D. Jacobs. LC 70-80042. (Southern Literary Studies). xiv, 464p. 1969. 42.50 (ISBN 0-8071-0846-4). La State U Pr.

Poe Log: A Documentary Life of Edgar Allan Poe. Dwight Thomas & David K. Jackson. (Reference Bks.). (Illus.). 880p. 1987. lib. bdg. 75.00x (ISBN 0-8161-8734-7). G K Hall.

Poe! Poe! Poe! Kathryn S. Miller. (Illus.). 24p. (gr. 4-12). 1984. pap. 2.25 (ISBN 0-88680-224-5). I E Clark.

Poe Poe Poe Poe Poe Poe Poe. Daniel Hoffman. 1985. pap. 5.95 (ISBN 0-394-72908-0, Vin). Random.

Poe-Pourri: A North Carolina Cavalcade. Clarence Poe & Charles A. Poe. LC 87-90549. (Illus.). 157p. 1987. 11.95 (ISBN 0-9618716-0-1). Charles Poe.

Poe: The Rationale of the Uncanny. Sybil Wuletich-Brinberg. (Studies in Romantic & Modern Literature: Vol. 2). 235p. 1988. 42.50 (ISBN 0-8204-0669-4). P Lang Pubs.

Poem. Francis Neilson. 59.95 (ISBN 0-87700-066-2). Revisionist Pr.

Poem About Music. Anthony Barnett. (Burning Deck Poetry Ser.). 1974. 15.00 (ISBN 0-930900-00-6); pap. 4.00 (ISBN 0-930900-01-4). Burning Deck.

Poem: An Anthology. 2nd ed. Ed. by Stanley B. Greenfield & A. Kingsley Weatherhead. LC 68-15582. (Orig.). 1972. pap. text ed. write for info. (ISBN 0-13-684431-6). P-H.

Poem & the Book: Interpreting Collections of Romantic Poetry. Neil Fraistat. LC 84-10381. (Illus.). xiii, 241p. 1985. 22.50x (ISBN 0-8078-1615-9). U of NC Pr.

Poem As a Plant: A Biological View of Goethe's Faust. Salm Peter. LC 71-141461. pap. 42.30 (ISBN 0-317-08241-8, 2003259). Bks Demand UMI.

Poem As Green Girdle: Commercium in Sir Gawain & the Green Knight. R. A. Shoaf. LC 84-2285. (University of Florida Humanities Monographs: No. 55). 116p. 1984. pap. 13.50x (ISBN 0-8130-0766-6). U Presses Fla.

Poem As Initiation. Charles Tomlinson. LC 68-56436. 1968. 8.00x (ISBN 0-912568-03-8). Colgate U Pr.

Poem As Plant: A Biological View of Goethe's Faust. Peter Salm. LC 71-141461. (Illus.). 1971. 12.00 (ISBN 0-8295-0204-1). UPB.

Poem As Utterance. R. A. York. 210p. 1986. text ed. 36.95 (ISBN 0-416-42250-0, 9795); pap. text ed. 13.95 (ISBN 0-416-42260-8, 9806). Routledge Chapman & Hall.

Poem Beyond My Reach. Selma Stefanile. (Vagrom Chap Bk.: No. 19). (Illus.). 56p. (Orig.). 1982. pap. 4.00x (ISBN 0-935552-03-0). Sparrow Pr.

Poem for Executives: New Model Business Strategies. Andres Steinmetz. (Business of Business Ser.). (Illus.). 100p. (Orig.). 1989. 17.95; pap. 9.95 (ISBN 0-943920-50-7). Metamorphous Pr.

Poem from a Single Pallet. Fanny Howe. 1980. 4.50 (ISBN 0-932716-10-5). Kelsey St Pr.

Poem in Progress. John Logan. (Illus.). 1975. pap. 6.95 (ISBN 0-931848-09-1). Dryad Pr.

Poem in Question. Robert E. Bourdette, Jr. & Michael Cohen. 485p. 1983. pap. text ed. 13.00 net (ISBN 0-15-570654-3, HC). HarBraceJ.

Poem in Your Eye: An Introductory to the Art of Seeing, Through Poetry. E. B. Weinstock. LC 78-56918. 1978. pap. text ed. 9.75 (ISBN 0-8191-0523-6). U Pr of Amer.

Poem Itself. Stanley Burnshaw. 1989. 10.95 (Touchstone Bks). S&S.

Poem Itself. Ed. by Stanley Burnshaw. 380p. 1980. pap. 7.95 (ISBN 0-8180-1128-9). Horizon.

Poem of Job: A Literary Study with a New Translation. W. B. Stevenson. (British Academy, London, Schweich Lectures on Biblical Archaeology Series, 1943). pap. 19.00 (ISBN 0-8115-1285-1). Kraus Repr.

Poem of My Cid, 1207 (Poem de Mio Cid) Ed. by Peter Such & John Hodgkinson. (Hispanic Classics--Medieval Ser.). 242p. (Eng. & Span.). 1987. text ed. 49.95 (ISBN 0-85668-321-3, Pub. by Aris & Phillips UK); pap. text ed. 16.50 (ISBN 0-85668-322-1, Pub. by Aris & Phillips UK). Humanities.

Poem of the Cid. Tr. by R. Hamilton & J. Perry. (Classics Ser.). 256p. 1985. pap. 5.95 (ISBN 0-14-044446-7). Penguin.

Poem of the Cid. Tr. by W. S. Merwin. 1975. pap. 7.95 (ISBN 0-452-00790-9, Mer). NAL.

Poem of the Cid. Tr. by Lesley B. Simpson. (YA) (gr. 9 up). 1957. pap. 6.95 (ISBN 0-520-01176-7). U of Cal Pr.

Poem of the Deep Song. Federico Garcia Lorca. Tr. by Carlos Bauer from Span. (Orig.). 1987. 12.95 (ISBN 0-317-60500-3); pap. 6.95 (ISBN 0-87286-205-4). City Lights.

Poem Paintings. Melinda Takeuchi. 32p. 1977. 35.00x (ISBN 0-317-68979-7, Pub. by Han-Shan Tang Ltd). State Mutual Bk.

Poem Stew. Ed. by William Cole. LC 81-47106. (Illus.). 96p. (gr. 3-6). 1981. o. p. 10.10i (ISBN 0-397-31963-0, Lipp Jr Bks); PLB 11.89 (ISBN 0-397-31964-9). HarpJ.

Poem Stew. Ed. by William Cole. LC 81-47106. (Trophy I Can Read Bks.). (Illus.). 96p. (gr. 1-7). 1983. pap. 4.95 (ISBN 0-06-440136-7, Trophy). HarpJ.

Poem to Poets. Richard Eberhart. (Illus.). 40p. 1975. signed ed. 50.00 (ISBN 0-915778-04-1). Penmaen Pr.

Poem to Walt Disney. Stephen Kessler. 1977. pap. 1.00 (ISBN 0-686-18925-6); signed ed. 3.00 (ISBN 0-686-28598-0). Man-Root.

Poem You Asked For. Marianne Wolfe. Ed. by Morty Sklar. (Outstanding Author Ser.: No. 2). (Illus.). 1977. 1.35 (ISBN 0-930370-01-5). Spirit That Moves.

Poema De Jose: A Transcription & Comparison of the Extant Manuscripts. William W. Johnson. LC 73-93265. (Romance Monograph: No. 6). 1974. 18.00x (ISBN 84-399-1996-4); pap. 13.00x (ISBN 0-686-31730-0). Romance.

Poema en Veinte Surcos. Julia De Burgos. LC 83-82116. (Illus.). 72p. (Orig.). 1983. pap. 5.95 (ISBN 0-940238-23-3). Ediciones Huracan.

Poema Mio 1920-1944. Engenio Florit. 503p. (Span.). 4.50 (ISBN 0-318-14300-3). Hispanic Inst.

Poemas. Jennicel Velez. LC 83-3526. (UPREX Literatura Infantil Ser.: No. 63). xvi, 56p. (Span.). (gr. 3-7). 1983. pap. 2.00 (ISBN 0-8477-0063-1). U of PR Pr.

Poemas de Israel. Israel Rodriguez. LC 80-51403. 100p. 1980. pap. 12.00 (ISBN 0-89295-016-1). Society Sp & Sp-Am.

Poemas de la Nieve Negra. Juan M. Rivera. LC 84-62597. (Serie de Poesia Guampara: No. 3). 96p. (Orig., Span.). 1985. pap. text ed. 5.95 (ISBN 0-910235-09-0). Prisma Bks.

Poemas de Tierra Santa. Alfonso Lockward. 136p. 1983. pap. 3.50 (ISBN 0-89922-185-8). Edit Caribe.

Poemas de un Cristiano Ausente. Alfonso Lockward. 192p. (Span.). 1981. pap. 3.50 (ISBN 0-89922-214-5). Edit Caribe.

Poemas del Hombre y las Desolaciones. Odon Betanzos-Palacios. 1986. pap. 3.00 (ISBN 0-317-64201-4). Edit Mensaje.

Poemas en Prosa. Carmela V. De Rodriguez. 2.50 (ISBN 84-399-8110-4). Edit Mensaje.

Poemas y Cuentos. Ramona L. De Bryant. LC 84-52378. (Senda Poetica Ser.). 120p. (Orig., Span.). 1985. pap. 6.95 (ISBN 0-918454-44-1). Senda Nueva.

Poeme Babylonien de la Creation. Enuma Elish. LC 78-72734. (Ancient Mesopotamian Texts & Studies). Repr. of 1935 ed. 24.50 (ISBN 0-404-18173-2). AMS Pr.

Poeme Bourguignon du XIVe Siecle. Girard De Rousillon. LC 72-1634. (Yale Romanic Studies: No. 16). (Fr.). Repr. of 1939 ed. 42.00 (ISBN 0-404-53216-0). AMS Pr.

Poeme de Versailles. Andre Maurois. pap. 9.50 (ISBN 0-685-36952-8). French & Eur.

Poemes. Jean Genet. pap. 19.95 (ISBN 0-685-33953-X). French & Eur.

Poemes. Pierre de Ronsard. Ed. by Andre Barbier. (French Texts Ser.). 260p. (Fr.). 1951. pap. text ed. 9.95X (ISBN 0-631-00530-7). Basil Blackwell.

Poemes. Leopold S. Senghor. 256p. 1974. 9.95 (ISBN 0-686-55010-2). French & Eur.

Poemes. Alfred de Vigny. Ed. by Jean Chuzeville. 276p. 1953. 13.95 (ISBN 0-686-55715-8). French & Eur.

Poemes Antiques et Modernes: Avec: Les Destinees. Alfred de Vigny. (POesie Ser.). 320p. 1973. 8.95 (ISBN 0-686-55716-6). Schoenhof.

Poemes (Chants d'Ombre, Hosties Noires, Nocturnes, Ethopiques, Ballade Toucoulore de Samba-Foul, Ballade Khassonkaise du Dioudi. Leopold S. Senghor. 19.95 (ISBN 0-685-35641-8). French & Eur.

Poemes Choisis. Alphonse Lamartine. Ed. by J. L. Barbier. (Modern French Text Ser.). (Fr.). 1921. pap. 10.00 (ISBN 0-7190-0147-1, Pub. by Manchester Univ Pr). St Martin.

Poemes d'amour de Baudelaire: Avec des documents nouveaux. Charles P. Baudelaire. LC 77-10249. (Illus.). Repr. of 1927 ed. 20.50 (ISBN 0-404-16305-X). AMS Pr.

Poemes de Renee Vivien, 2 vols. in 1. Renee Vivien. LC 75-12354. (Homosexuality). (Fr.). 1975. Repr. 37.50x (ISBN 0-405-07397-6). Ayer Co Pubs.

Poemes d'Edgar Poe. Edgar Allan Poe. Tr. by Stephane Mallarme. LC 77-11473. (Illus., Fr.). Repr. of 1889 ed. 34.50 (ISBN 0-404-16335-1). AMS Pr.

Poemes - Discours des Miseres de Ce Temps see Oeuvres.

Poemes et Paroles Durant la Guerre De Trente Ans. Paul Claudel. 216p. 1945. 8.95 (ISBN 0-686-54417-X). French & Eur.

Poemes et Prose Choisis. Rene Char. 320p. 1957. 8.95 (ISBN 0-686-54167-7). French & Eur.

Poemes, Lyrick, & Pastorall. Michael Drayton. (Spencer Soc.: No. 4). 1605. 26.00 (ISBN 0-8337-0914-3). B Franklin.

Poemes Lyriques. Emile Zola. 6.95 (ISBN 0-686-55797-2). French & Eur.

Poemes, Pieces, Prose: Introduction a l'analyse De textes litteraires francais. Ed. by Peter Schofer et al. (Illus., Fr.). 1973. pap. text ed. 21.00x (ISBN 0-19-501643-2). Oxford U Pr.

Poemes Politiques. Paul Eluard. 60p. 1948. 8.95 (ISBN 0-686-55977-0). French & Eur.

Poemes Pour le Cours Avance - Nineteen Eighty-Five to Nineteen Eighty-Six. rev. ed. Andre O. Hurtgen. 148p. (gr. 9-12). 1981. pap. text ed. 6.95x (ISBN 0-686-81150-X). Ind Sch Pr.

Poemes pour Tous. 2nd ed. Paul Eluard. 246p. 1953. 12.50 (ISBN 0-686-55978-9). French & Eur.

Poemes Saturniens: Avec: Confessions. Paul Verlaine & Jean Gaudon. 375p. 1977. 4.50 (ISBN 0-686-55154-0). French & Eur.

Poemes: 34 Poems. Rene Tavernier. Tr. by John B. Gerald. 100p. (Orig.). 1984. pap. 7.00 (ISBN 0-941917-07-X). Gerald & Maas.

Poems. Aimeric De Peguilhan. LC 70-128941. Repr. of 1950 ed. 28.00 (ISBN 0-404-50724-7). AMS Pr.

Poems. Anna Akhmatova. Tr. by Lyn Coffin from Rus. 1983. 15.50 (ISBN 0-393-01567-X); pap. 7.95 (ISBN 0-393-30014-5). Norton.

Poems. William Allingham. LC 78-148741. Repr. of 1850 ed. 11.00 (ISBN 0-404-00345-1). AMS Pr.

Poems. Syed Amanuddin. 1984. text ed. 27.50x (ISBN 0-86590-317-4, Pub. by Sterling Pubs India). Apt Bks.

Poems. Matthew Arnold. 1965. 12.95x (ISBN 0-460-00334-8, Evman). Biblio Dist.

Poems, 2 Vols. Ausonius. (Loeb Classical Library: No. 96, 115). 13.95x ea. Vol. 1 (ISBN 0-674-99107-9). Vol. 2 (ISBN 0-674-99127-3). Harvard U Pr.

Poems. George Bannatyne. LC 78-144411. (Bannatyne Club, Edinburgh. Publications: No. 4a). Repr. of 1824 ed. 12.50 (ISBN 0-404-52705-1). AMS Pr.

Poems. John E. Barlas. 34.95 (ISBN 0-8490-0845-X). Gordon Pr.

Poems. Richard Bartholomew. (Writers Workshop Redbird Ser.). 1975. 8.00 (ISBN 0-88253-610-9); pap. text ed. 4.00 (ISBN 0-88253-609-5). Ind-US Inc.

Poems. Joachim Du Bellay. Ed. by H. W. Lawton. (French Texts Ser.). 206p. 1972. pap. text ed. 9.95x (ISBN 0-631-00600-1). Basil Blackwell.

Poems. 2nd ed. M. R. Bhagavan. (Redbird Bk.). 1976. lib. bdg. 8.00 (ISBN 0-89253-125-8); flexible bdg. 4.80 (ISBN 0-89253-139-8). Ind-US Inc.

Poems. facsimile ed. Eloise Bibb. LC 71-173601. (Black Heritage Library Collection). Repr. of 1895 ed. 12.50 (ISBN 0-8369-8897-3). Ayer Co Pubs.

Poems. Stefan Brecht. LC 78-2411. (Pocket Poets Ser.: No. 36). 1978. pap. 3.00 (ISBN 0-87286-099-X). City Lights.

Poems, 2 Vols. Alexander Brome. Ed. by Roman R. Dubinski. 560p. 1982. 75.00x set (ISBN 0-8020-5535-4). U of Toronto Pr.

Poems, 2 vols. William Browne. 1988. Repr. of 1894 ed. Set. lib. bdg. 99.00x. Am Biog Serv.

Poems, 2 Vols. William T. Browne. 1971. Repr. of 1894 ed. Set. 69.00x (ISBN 0-403-00846-8). Scholarly.

Poems. William E. Channing. LC 72-4955. (Romantic Tradition in American Literature Ser.). 162p. 1972. Repr. of 1843 ed. 20.00 (ISBN 0-405-04627-8). Ayer Co Pubs.

Poems. Sukanta Chaudhuri. 8.00 (ISBN 0-89253-500-8); flexible cloth 4.00 (ISBN 0-89253-501-6). Ind-US Inc.

Poems, 2 Vols. Claudian. (Loeb Classical Library: No. 135, 136). 13.95x ea. Vol. 1 (ISBN 0-674-99150-8). Vol. 2 (ISBN 0-674-99151-6). Harvard U Pr.

Poems. Evan T. Cole. 1985. 5.95 (ISBN 0-533-06090-7). Vantage.

Poems. Samuel Taylor Coleridge. Ed. by John Beer. 1974. 12.95x (ISBN 0-460-00043-8, Evman); pap. 4.50x (ISBN 0-460-01043-3, Evman). Biblio Dist.

Poems. facsimile ed. W. Collins. Ed. by Walter C. Bronson. 135p. Repr. of 1898 ed. cancelled (ISBN 3-4870-4665-2). Adlers Foreign Bks.

Poems. Tristan Corbiere. Tr. by Walter McElroy from Fr. LC 77-10257. 80p. Repr. of 1947 ed. 16.50 (ISBN 0-404-16312-2). AMS Pr.

Poems. Gerald Costanzo et al. 62p. 1973. pap. 3.00 (ISBN 0-915596-03-2). West Coast.

Poems, 3 vols. George Crabbe. Ed. by Adolphus W. Ward. LC 75-41067. (BCL Ser. II). Repr. of 1907 ed. 135.00 set (ISBN 0-404-14860-3). AMS Pr.

Poems. Richard C. Craven. 1987. 4.00 (ISBN 0-932526-15-2). Nexus Pr.

Poems. Roque Dalton. Tr. by Richard Schaaf from Span. 88p. (Orig.). 1984. 13.50 (ISBN 0-915306-45-X); pap. 7.50 (ISBN 0-915306-43-3). Curbstone.

Poems. Jatin Das. (Redbird Bk.). 1976. 8.00 (ISBN 0-89253-537-7); flexible bdg. 4.00 (ISBN 0-89253-098-7). Ind-US Inc.

Poems. John Davies. Ed. by Robert Krueger. (Oxford English Texts Ser). (Illus.). 1974. 74.00x (ISBN 0-19-812716-2). Oxford U Pr.

Poems. Richard Dehmel. 59.95 (ISBN 0-8490-0846-8). Gordon Pr.

Poems. John Donne. Ed. by Herbert J. Grierson. (Oxford Standard Authors Ser.). 1933. 35.00 (ISBN 0-19-254123-4); pap. 11.95x (ISBN 0-19-281113-4). Oxford U Pr.

Poems, 2 vols. Michael Drayton. (Spencer Soc.: Nos. 45-46). 1966. Repr. of 1888 ed. 52.00 (ISBN 0-8337-0915-1). B Franklin.

Poems. William Drummond. Ed. by Thomas Maitland. LC 77-144419. (Maitland Club. Glasgow. Publications: No. 18). Repr. of 1832 ed. 35.00 (ISBN 0-404-52956-9). AMS Pr.

Poems. William Drummond. LC 76-6156. (English Experience Ser.: No. 83). 128p. 1969. Repr. of 1616 ed. 16.00 (ISBN 90-221-0083-9). Walter J Johnson.

Poems, 3 vols. William Dunbar. Ed. by John Small. Repr. of 1893 ed. Set. cancelled (ISBN 3-4870-4650-4). Adlers Foreign Bks.

Poems. William Dunbar. 1979. Repr. of 1890 ed. lib. bdg. 50.00 (ISBN 0-8495-1110-0). Arden Lib.

Poems. Mary Baker Eddy. 14.95 (ISBN 0-87952-090-6). First Church.

Poems. Mihail Eminescu. 69.95 (ISBN 0-87968-466-6). Gordon Pr.

Poems. Carl A. Faber. LC 59-4760. 1974. 4.95 (ISBN 0-918026-01-6). Perseus Pr.

Poems. John Fowles. LC 72-96853. 100p. 1973. 7.50 (ISBN 0-912946-03-2). Ecco Pr.

Poems. M. C. Gabriel. 8.00 (ISBN 0-89253-479-6); flexible cloth 4.00 (ISBN 0-89253-480-X). Ind-US Inc.

Poems. Mario Garca. (Eng. & Span.). 1976. pap. 4.95. El Renacimiento.

Poems. Bertha Goodall. 28p. (Orig.). 1982. pap. 2.00 saddle-stitched (ISBN 0-911826-38-6, 5120). Am Atheist.

Poems, 4 vols. Thomas Gray. 1778. Set. 200.00 (ISBN 0-686-17753-3). Ridgeway Bks.

Poems. Daniel Haberman. LC 76-56618. (Illus.). 1977. 7.50 (ISBN 0-910158-24-X). Art Dir.

Poems. Frances E. Harper. LC 73-18576. Repr. of 1871 ed. 6.50 (ISBN 0-404-11387-7). AMS Pr.

Poems. Paul H. Hayne. LC 74-101918. (Illus.). Repr. of 1882 ed. 26.00 (ISBN 0-404-03167-6). AMS Pr.

Poems. Helen Jackson. LC 72-4966. (Romantic Tradition in American Literature Ser.). (Illus.). 326p. 1972. Repr. of 1892 ed. 31.00 (ISBN 0-405-04637-5). Ayer Co Pubs.

Poems. Anthony Johnson. Ed. by James Hogg. (Poetic Drama & Poetic Theory Ser.). (Orig.). 1984. pap. 15.00 (ISBN 3-7052-0901-9, Pub. by Salzburg Studies). Longwood Pub Group.

Poems. Samuel Johnson. Ed. by E. L. McAdam, Jr. & George Milne. (Works of Samuel Johnson Ser.: Vol. 6). (Illus.). 1965. 50.00t (ISBN 0-300-00734-5). Yale U Pr.

Poems. Ben Jonson. Ed. by Ian Donaldson. (Oxford Standard Authors Ser.). 1975. 29.95 (ISBN 0-19-254166-8). Oxford U Pr.

Poems. Francis S. Key. LC 79-104503. Repr. of 1857 ed. lib. bdg. 34.50 (ISBN 0-8398-1053-9). Irvington.

Poems. Anne Killigrew. LC 67-10177. 1967. Repr. of 1686 ed. 30.00x (ISBN 0-8201-1030-2). Schol Facsimiles.

Poems. Charles Kingsley. 341p. 1980. Repr. of 1907 ed. lib. bdg. 30.00 (ISBN 0-89984-301-8). Century Bookbindery.

Poems. facsimile ed. A. M. Klein. LC 74-27993. (Modern Jewish Experience Ser.). 1975. Repr. of 1944 ed. 13.00 (ISBN 0-405-06720-8). Ayer Co Pubs.

Poems. Jan Kochanowski. Tr. by Dorothea P. Radin et al from Pol. LC 76-29471. (Eng.). Repr. of 1928 ed. 15.50 (ISBN 0-404-15313-5). AMS Pr.

Poems. C. S. Lewis. Ed. by Walter Hooper. LC 77-4733. 142p. 1977. pap. 4.95 (ISBN 0-15-672248-8, Harv). HarBraceJ.

Poems. Dierdre Lichtenberg. (Illus.). 60p. (Orig.). pap. 5.00 (ISBN 0-9617811-0-6). Chandrabala Pr.

Poems. Henry Wadsworth Longfellow. 1983. Repr. of 1978 ed. 14.95x (ISBN 0-460-10382-2, Evman). Biblio Dist.

Poems. A. Madhavan. 8.00 (ISBN 0-89253-772-8); flexible cloth 4.00 (ISBN 0-89253-773-6). Ind-US Inc.

Poems. 4th ed. Ed. by C. F. Main & Peter J. Seng. 490p. 1978. pap. text ed. write for info. (ISBN 0-534-00541-1). Wadsworth Pub.

Poems. Stephane Mallarme. Tr. by Roger Fry from Fr. & Eng. LC 77-10279. 320p. Repr. of 1937 ed. 32.00 (ISBN 0-404-16330-0). AMS Pr.

Poems. Christopher Marlowe. Ed. by Millar Maclure. (Revels Plays Ser.). 207p. 1968. 50.00 (ISBN 0-7190-1506-5, Pub. by Manchester Univ Pr). St Martin.

Poems. V. Mayakovsky. 302p. 1976. 6.45 (ISBN 0-8285-1013-X, Pub. by Progress Pubs USSR). Imported Pubns.

Poems. Eduard Morike. Ed. by Lionel Thomas. (German Text Ser.). 152p. 1960. pap. 9.95x (ISBN 0-631-01660-0). Basil Blackwell.

Poems. David Murray. LC 70-144428. (Bannatyne Club, Edinburgh. Publications: No. 2). Repr. of 1823 ed. 15.00 (ISBN 0-404-52702-7). AMS Pr.

Poems. Suniti Namjoshi. 5.00 (ISBN 0-89253-704-3); flexible cloth 4.00 (ISBN 0-89253-705-1). Ind-US Inc.

Poems. Marcia Nardi. LC 79-179816. (New Poetry Ser.). Repr. of 1956 ed. 16.00 (ISBN 0-404-56016-4). AMS Pr.

Poems. Francis Neilson. 59.95 (ISBN 0-87700-006-9). Revisionist Pr.

Poems. Nikolai A. Nekrasov. Tr. by Juliet Soskice from Rus. LC 76-23889. (Classics of Russian Literature). 1977. 15.00 (ISBN 0-88355-503-4); pap. 10.00 (ISBN 0-88355-504-2). Hyperion Conn.

Poems. Leslie De Noronha. (Redbird). 1976. flexible bdg. 4.80 (ISBN 0-89253-141-X). Ind-US Inc.

Poems. James Oppenheimer. 69.95 (ISBN 0-8490-0847-6). Gordon Pr.

Poems. Oppian. Bd. with Poems. Colluthus; Poems. Tryphiodorus. (Loeb Classical Library: No. 219). 13.95x (ISBN 0-674-99241-5). Harvard U Pr.

Poems. Sultan Padamsee. (Redbird Bk.). 1976. 9.00 (ISBN 0-89253-123-1); flexible bdg. 6.75 (ISBN 0-89253-138-X). Ind-US Inc.

Poems. Thomas Parnell. Ed. by Lennox Robinson. 52p. 1971. Repr. of 1927 ed. 15.00x (ISBN 0-7165-1365-X, BBA 02076, Pub. by Cuala Press Ireland). Biblio Dist.

Poems. Edward C. Pinkney. LC 72-4970. (Romantic Tradition in American Literature Ser.). 76p. 1972. Repr. of 1838 ed. 19.00 (ISBN 0-405-04640-5). Ayer Co Pubs.

Poems. Nick Piombino. 88p. (Orig.). 1988. pap. 8.95 (ISBN 0-317-68144-3). Sun & Moon CA.

Poems. Propertius. Tr. by W. G. Shepherd. (Penguin Classics Ser.). 240p. 1986. pap. 5.95 (ISBN 0-14-044464-5). Penguin.

Poems. J. H. Prynne. (Agneau 2 Paperbook Ser.: 1). 320p. (Orig.). 1982. pap. 15.00 (ISBN 0-907954-01-4, Pub. by Allardyce & Barnett). Small Pr Dist.

Poems. Rakshat Puri. 8.00 (ISBN 0-89253-718-3); flexible cloth 4.80 (ISBN 0-89253-719-1). Ind-US Inc.

Poems. Raghavendra Rao. 8.00 (ISBN 0-89253-722-1); flexible cloth 4.00 (ISBN 0-89253-723-X). Ind-US Inc.

Poems. Aram Saroyan. 47p. (Orig.). 1986. pap. 4.00 (ISBN 0-9606772-5-9). Blackberry Bks.

Poems. Alexander Scott. Ed. by James Cranstoon. Repr. of 1896 ed. 24.00 (ISBN 0-384-54440-1). Johnson Repr.

Poems. William B. Scott. LC 77-140034. (Illus.). Repr. of 1875 ed. 19.00 (ISBN 0-404-05647-4). AMS Pr.

Poems. George Seferis. Tr. by Rex Warner from Gr. LC 78-74248. 1979. pap. 5.95 (ISBN 0-87923-281-1, Nonpareil Bks). Godine.

Poems. William Shakespeare. Ed. by Arthur Quiller-Couch et al. (New Shakespeare Ser). 1969. pap. 5.95x (ISBN 0-521-09493-3). Cambridge U Pr.

Poems. 3rd ed. William Shakespeare. Ed. by F. T. Prince. (Arden Shakespeare Ser.). 1969. 37.00x (ISBN 0-416-47610-4, NO. 2488); pap. 8.95 (ISBN 0-416-27870-1, NO. 2489). Routledge Chapman & Hall.

Poems. William Shakespeare. (Classics Ser.). 1988. pap. 4.95 (ISBN 0-553-21309-1, Bantam Classics). Bantam.

Poems. Virginia Sheahen. LC 87-81640. 72p. (Orig.). 1987. pap. 4.95 (ISBN 0-910725-04-7). Gain Pubns.

Poems. John Skelton. Ed. by Richard Hughes. LC 73-13596. 1974. Repr. of 1924 ed. lib. bdg. 47.50 (ISBN 0-8414-7637-3). Folcroft.

Poems, 2 vols. Robert Louis Stevenson. Ed. by George S. Hellman. LC 76-17043. 1979. Repr. of 1916 ed. lib. bdg. 60.00 set (ISBN 0-8414-8007-9). Folcroft.

Poems. Charles W. Stoddard. Ed. by Ina Coolbrith. LC 79-144690. Repr. of 1917 ed. 12.00 (ISBN 0-404-06279-2). AMS Pr.

Poems. John Theobald. 8.00 (ISBN 0-89253-741-8); flexible cloth 4.80 (ISBN 0-89253-742-6). Ind-US Inc.

Poems. Ioanna Tsatsos. Tr. by Jean Demos from Gr. 200p. 1984. 20.00 (ISBN 0-935476-15-6). Nostos Bks.

Poems. Paul M. Verlaine. Tr. by Jacques Leclercq. LC 77-13574. (Illus.). 1977. Repr. of 1961 ed. lib. bdg. 35.00 (ISBN 0-8371-9859-3, VEPO). Greenwood.

Poems. Gautam Vohra. (Writers Workshop Redbird Ser.). 1975. 9.00 (ISBN 0-88253-612-5); pap. text ed. 4.80 (ISBN 0-88253-611-7). Ind-US Inc.

Poems. Edmund Waller. Ed. by G. Thorn Drury. Repr. of 1893 ed. lib. bdg. 35.00x (ISBN 0-8371-0735-0, WAEW). Greenwood.

Poems. Henrik A. Wergeland. Tr. by Geoffrey M. Gathorne-Hardy et al. Repr. of 1929 ed. lib. bdg. 35.00x (ISBN 0-8371-3159-6, WEPO). Greenwood.

Poems. Nathaniel P. Willis. LC 72-144703. Repr. of 1891 ed. 17.00 (ISBN 0-404-06989-4). AMS Pr.

Poems. William Wordsworth. Ed. by George M. Harper. 1979. Repr. of 1923 ed. lib. bdg. 20.00 (ISBN 0-8495-5704-6). Arden Lib.

Poems, Vol. 1. Prudentius. LC 63-5499. (Fathers of the Church Ser: Vol. 43). 343p. 1962. 16.95x (ISBN 0-8132-0043-1). Cath U Pr.

Poems, Vol. 2. Prudentius. LC 63-5499. (Fathers of the Church Ser: Vol. 52). 224p. 1965. 15.95x (ISBN 0-8132-0052-0). Cath U Pr.

Poems see Poems.

Poems a Lou. Guillaume Apollinaire. Ed. by Decaudin. Bd. with Il y a. (Poesie Ser.). pap. 5.95 (ISBN 0-685-37174-3). Schoenhof.

Poems: A Selection. John C. Powys. Ed. by Kenneth Hopkins. 1964. 16.00x (ISBN 0-912568-00-3). Colgate U Pr.

Poems: A Selection of Forty-Five Poems. Ed. & tr. by N. J. Pok. 162p. 1952. 30.00x (ISBN 0-317-39137-2, Pub. by Luzac & Co Ltd). State Mutual Bk.

Poems About Birds from the Middle Ages to the Present. H. J. Massingham. 1977. Repr. 20.00 (ISBN 0-89984-059-0). Century Bookbindery.

Poems About Fur & Feather Friends. Ed. by Leland B. Jacobs. LC 79-157847. (Garrard Venture Ser.). (Illus.). 40p. (gr. k-3). 1971. PLB 6.69 (ISBN 0-8116-6713-8); pap. 1.19 (9021). Garrard.

Poems about Life. David Thompson. 64p. 1984. 3.95 (ISBN 0-89697-182-1). Intl Univ Pr.

Poems-Ackerman, Bolz & Steele. Diane Ackerman et al. 1973. wrappers 1.00 (ISBN 0-685-37096-8). Stone-Marrow Pr.

Poems After Martial. Philip Murray. LC 67-24109. 1967. 17.00x (ISBN 0-8195-3083-2). Wesleyan U Pr.

Poems Against Death. Karl Krolow. Tr. by Herman Salinger. LC 71-82716. 1980. 7.50 (ISBN 0-910350-07-8). Charioteer.

Poems: American Themes. Wilbert J. Levy. (gr. 11-12). 1979. pap. text ed. 11.92 (ISBN 0-87720-386-5). AMSCO Sch.

Poems & a Defence of Ryme. Samuel Daniel. Ed. by Arthur C. Sprague. 1965. pap. 2.95x (ISBN 0-226-13609-4, P200, Phoen). U of Chicago Pr.

Poems & Amyntas of Thomas Randolph. Thomas Randolph. Ed. by John J. Parry. 1917. 59.50x (ISBN 0-686-83704-5). Elliots Bks.

Poems & Ballads & Atalanta in Calydon. Algernon C. Swinburne. Ed. by Morse Peckham. LC 79-117333. (Library of Literature Ser). 1970. 10.25 (ISBN 0-672-51119-3). Bobbs.

Poems & Carols. Selwyn Image. 1987. pap. 7.50 (ISBN 0-89979-051-8). British Am Bks.

Poems & Contradictions. 2nd, rev. ed. Rex Warner. LC 83-45483. 1945. 18.00 (ISBN 0-404-20281-0, PR6045). AMS Pr.

Poems & Days. Michael Hannon. (Orig.). 1986. pap. 7.95 (ISBN 0-931037-03-4). Isis Pr CA.

Poems & Dramas of Fulke Greville First Lord Brooke, 2 vols. Fulke G. Brooke. Repr. of 1939 ed. 49.00 (ISBN 0-403-04210-0). Somerset Pub.

Poems & Epigrams. Richard O'Connell. pap. 25.00 (ISBN 0-87556-227-2). Saifer.

Poems & Epistles. John Fuller. LC 74-81511. 128p. 1973. 12.95 (ISBN 0-87923-103-3); pap. 5.95 (ISBN 0-87923-116-5). Godine.

Poems & Essays. Edgar Allan Poe. 1975. (Evman); pap. 4.50x (ISBN 0-460-01791-8, Evman). Biblio Dist.

Poems & Essays, London 1860. William C. Roscoe. Ed. by Fredeman et al. (Victorian Muse Ser.). 539p. 1986. lib. bdg. 65.00 (ISBN 0-8240-8616-3). Garland Pub.

Poems & Essays: With a Biographical Sketch by James Freeman Clarke. Jones Very. LC 72-4980. (Romantic Tradition in American Literature Ser.). 558p. 1972. Repr. of 1886 ed. 42.00 (ISBN 0-405-04649-9). Ayer Co Pubs.

Poems & Fragments. F. Holderlin. Tr. by M. Hamburger from Ger. LC 79-41382. 704p. 1980. o. p. 62.50 (ISBN 0-521-23051-9); pap. 18.95 o. p. (ISBN 0-521-29788-5). Cambridge U Pr.

Poems & Glyphs. Charles Stein. (Illus.). 100p. (Orig.). 1973. pap. 7.50 (ISBN 0-913028-18-5). North Atlantic.

Poems & Hymn Tunes As Songs: Metrical Partners. Joseph Jones. 84p. 1983. with 2 audio cassettes 24.50, (ISBN 0-88432-119-3, S1560). J Norton Pubs.

Poems & Letters, 2 Vols. Sidonius. (Loeb Classical Library, Nos. 296, 420: No. 296, 420). 13.95x ea. Vol. 1 (ISBN 0-674-99327-6). Vol. 2 (ISBN 0-674-99462-0). Harvard U Pr.

Poems & Letters of Andrew Marvell, 2 vols. 3rd ed. Andrew Marvell. Ed. by H. M. Margoliouth et al. (Oxford English Texts Ser). (Illus.). 1971. 98.00x set (ISBN 0-19-811853-8). Oxford U Pr.

Poems & Lyrics of Life. James M. Bryant. LC 74-77292. 1974. pap. 5.50 (ISBN 0-686-18745-8). J M Bryant.

Poems & Lyrics of Life. James M. Bryant. pap. 5.50 (ISBN 0-318-18287-4). Rocket Pub Co.

Poems & Other Stuff. Paul Bickford. (Illus.). 37p. 1982. pap. 4.95x (ISBN 0-910303-00-2). Writers Pub Serv.

Poems & Philosophical Satire. Harold O. Monroe. Ed. by Diane E. Randol. 95p. (Orig.). 1988. pap. 5.95 (ISBN 0-945674-00-7). New Endeavors Pub.

Poems from the Xenia Hotel. R. B. Weber. 80p. (Orig.). 1979. pap. 5.00 (ISBN 0-935252-21-5). Street Pr.

Poems from Three Decades. Richard Lattimore. LC 80-39709. xiv, 274p. 1981. pap. 14.00x (ISBN 0-226-46946-8). U of Chicago Pr.

Poems: Giacomo Leopardi. St. David's University Press. Tr. by Arturo Vivante. 1988. lib. bdg. 29.95x. E Mellen.

Poems Given. Joan D. Shambaugh. (Illus.). 1976. pap. 1.00 (ISBN 0-686-20049-7). Chthon Pr.

Poems in Contempt of Progress by Jerome Tichenor. Ed. by Joel W. Hedgpeth. 1974. pap. 2.95 (ISBN 0-910286-36-1). Boxwood.

Poems in English. Samuel Beckett. 1964. pap. 2.95 (ISBN 0-394-17196-9, E379, Ever). Grove.

Poems in English, 2 Vols. John Milton. LC 27-273. (Illus.). 1968. Repr. of 1926 ed. 79.00x (ISBN 0-403-00349-0). Scholarly.

Poems in Many Voices. Mary Hampden-Jackson. 70p. 1984. 19.00x (ISBN 0-7212-0557-7, Pub. by Regency Pr). State Mutual Bk.

Poems in One Part Harmony. T. J. Reddy. 60p. 1980. pap. 4.00 (ISBN 0-932112-07-2). Carolina Wren.

Poems in Praise of Practically Nothing. Samuel Hoffenstein. LC 83-46023. (Classics of Modern American Humor Ser.). Date not set. Repr. of 1928 ed. 30.00 (ISBN 0-404-19934-8). AMS Pr.

Poems in Praise of the Man. Francesca Guli. 1980. 6.50 (ISBN 0-8233-0309-8). Golden Quill.

Poems In Prose: In Russian & English. Ivan S. Turgenev & S. Konovalov. Tr. by Constance Garnett & Roger Rees. 219p. 1951. pap. 22.50x (ISBN 0-8236-4140-6). Intl Univs Pr.

Poems in the Key of Life. Leanett L. Smith. Ed. by Eugene W. Smith. 40p. (Orig.). Date not set. pap. price not set (ISBN 0-939403-00-5). Smith Slogans.

Poems in the Lap of Death: English & Spanish. Isabel Fraire. Tr. by Thomas Hoeksema. LC 81-3724. (Discoveries Ser.). 99p. 1980. pap. 8.50 (ISBN 0-935480-04-8). Lat Am Lit Rev Pr.

Poems in Their Place: The Intertextuality & Order of Poetic Collections. Ed. by Neil Fraistat. LC 85-28926. vii, 344p. 1987. 32.50x (ISBN 0-8078-1695-7). U of NC Pr.

Poems, in Two Volumes & Other Poems, 1800-1807. William Wordsworth. Ed. by Jared Curtis. LC 81-3124. 760p. 1982. 99.50x (ISBN 0-8014-1445-8). Cornell U Pr.

Poems: Including the Saint's Tragedy, Andromeda, Songs, Ballads. Charles Kingsley. 1979. Repr. of 1872 ed. lib. bdg. 25.00 (ISBN 0-8495-3030-X). Arden Lib.

Poems Inspired by Certain Pictures at the Art Treasures Exhibition. John B. Waring. (Victorian Muse Ser.). 108p. 1986. lib. bdg. 25.00 (ISBN 0-8240-8624-4). Garland Pub.

Poems: Jules Laforgue. Ed. by J. A. Hiddleston. 296p. 1975. pap. 9.95x (ISBN 0-631-15940-1). Basil Blackwell.

Poems, Letters & Essays. Thomas Gray. 1970. Repr. of 1912 ed. 14.95x (ISBN 0-460-00628-2, Evman). Biblio Dist.

Poems Made & Remade. Howard Meroney. 1966. pap. 6.00 (ISBN 0-685-62615-6). Atlantis Edns.

Poems: Maya Angelou, 4 bks. Maya Angelou. 1986. pap. 3.95 (ISBN 0-553-25576-2). Bantam.

Poems: Medley & Palestina. John W. DeForest. 1902. 16.50x (ISBN 0-685-89770-2). Elliots Bks.

Poems: Medley & Palestina. John W. De Forest. (Collected Works of John W. De Forest). 1988. Repr. of 1902 ed. lib. bdg. 59.00x. Am Biog Serv.

Poems: Medley & Palestina see Collected Works.

Poems, New & Old. John Freeman. 319p. 1920. Repr. 39.00x (ISBN 0-403-01761-0). Scholarly.

Poems: New & Selected. Frederick Morgan. LC 86-30844. (Poetry from Illinois Ser.). 280p. 1987. 24.95 (ISBN 0-252-01433-2); pap. 12.95 (ISBN 0-252-01434-0). U of Ill Pr.

Poems New & Selected. Jon Silkin. LC 66-14661. (Wesleyan Poetry Program Ser.: Vol. 30). 79p. (Orig.). 1966. 17.00x (ISBN 0-8195-2030-6). Wesleyan U Pr.

Poems, New & Selected: Nineteen Thirty-Five to Nineteen Seventy-Five. Gordon LeClaire. LC 75-28559. 272p. 1975. 8.00 (ISBN 0-8233-0234-2). Golden Quill.

Poems: Nineteen Eleven to Nineteen Thirty-One. Herbert E. Read. LC 78-64052. (Des Imagistes: Literature of the Imagist Movement). Repr. of 1935 ed. 18.00 (ISBN 0-404-17092-7). AMS Pr.

Poems, Nineteen Fifty - Nineteen Seventy-Four. Dunstan Thompson. 366p. 1984. 29.50 (ISBN 0-9506104-8-8). Archival Facsimiles.

Poems, Nineteen Fifty-Eight to Nineteen Eighty. Pentti N. Saarikoski. Tr. by Anselm Hollo from Finnish. LC 83-4778. 120p. (Orig.). 1984. 40.00 (ISBN 0-915124-78-5, Pub. by Toothpaste); pap. 10.00. Coffee Hse.

Poems, Nineteen Fifty-Five to Nineteen Eighty-Seven. Roy Fisher. 240p. 1988. pap. 13.95 (ISBN 0-19-282230-6). Oxford U Pr.

Poems, Nineteen Fifty-Five to Nineteen Eighty. Roy Fisher. 1980. 27.95x (ISBN 0-19-211935-4). Oxford U Pr.

Poems Nineteen Fifty Five to Nineteen Seventy Three. Ronald Bottrall. 1974. 10.00 (ISBN 0-685-78875-X, Pub. by Anvil Pr); sewn in wrappers 6.95 (ISBN 0-685-78876-8). Small Pr Dist.

Poems, Nineteen Fifty-Nine to Nineteen Seventy-Five. Yves Bonnefoy. Tr. by Richard Pevear. 1985. 7.95 (ISBN 0-394-73956-6, Vin). Random.

Poems, Nineteen Fifty-Seven to Nineteen Sixty-Seven. James Dickey. LC 67-15230. 1978. 18.95; pap. 12.95 (ISBN 0-8195-6055-3). Wesleyan U Pr.

Poems, Nineteen Fifty-Six to Nineteen Seventy-Three. Thomas Kinsella. LC 79-63668. 192p. 1979. pap. 7.95 (ISBN 0-916390-11-X). Wake Forest.

Poems, Nineteen Seventy-Eight to Nineteen Eighty-Three. Ed. by Robert Fox. LC 83-13163. 176p. (Orig.). 1983. pap. 6.00x (ISBN 0-913335-00-2). OH Arts Council.

Poems: Nineteen Sixty-Five to Nineteen Seventy-Five. Seamus Heaney. LC 80-68753. 228p. 1980. 12.95 (ISBN 0-374-23496-5); pap. 7.95 (ISBN 0-374-51652-9). FS&G.

Poems, Nineteen Sixty-Four to Nineteen Eighty. M. L. Rosenthal. (Illus.). 1981. 19.95x (ISBN 0-19-502996-8). Oxford U Pr.

Poems, Nineteen Sixty-Three to Nineteen Eighty-Three. Michael Longley. LC 87-50675. 206p. 1987. pap. 7.95 (ISBN 0-916390-28-4). Wake Forest.

Poems, Nineteen Sixty-Three to Nineteen Eighty-Three. C. K. Williams. 256p. 1988. 19.95 (ISBN 0-374-13465-0). FS&G.

Poems, Nineteen Sixty-Three to Nineteen Eighty-Three. C. K. Williams. 1988. pap. 19.95 (ISBN 0-374-23516-3). FS&G.

Poems, Nineteen Sixty to Nineteen Sixty-Seven: Including Jacob's Ladder, O Taste & See, & The Sorrow Dance. Denise Levertov. LC 82-2263. 256p. 1983. pap. 7.95 (ISBN 0-8112-0859-1, NDP549). New Directions.

Poems, Nineteen Sixty-Two to Nineteen Seventy-Eight. Derek Mahon. (Orig.). 1979. pap. 9.95x (ISBN 0-19-211897-8). Oxford U Pr.

Poems, Nineteen Thirty-Eight to Nineteen Forty-Five. Robert Graves. 58p. 1946. 4.95 (ISBN 0-374-23472-8). FS&G.

Poems, Nineteen Thirty-Four to Nineteen Sixty-Nine. David Ignatow. LC 79-105500. 1970. pap. 12.95 (ISBN 0-8195-6059-6). Wesleyan U Pr.

Poems, Nineteen Twelve-Nineteen Twenty-Six. Rainer M. Rilke. Tr. by Michael Hamburger. (Austrian-German Culture Ser.). 117p. 1982. 17.50 (ISBN 0-933806-17-5). Black Swan CT.

Poems: Nineteen Twelve to Nineteen Forty-Four. Eugene O'Neill. Ed. by Donald Gallup. 1980. 9.95 (ISBN 0-89919-007-3, Ticknor & Fields). HM.

Poems: Nineteen Twenty-Three to Nineteen Fifty-Four. e. e. Cummings. LC 54-9724. 468p. 1954. 15.95 (ISBN 0-15-172245-5). HarBraceJ.

Poems Now. Joseph A. Stepka. (Contemporary Poets of Dorrance Ser.). 32p. 1983. 3.95 (ISBN 0-8059-2890-1). Dorrance.

Poems of A. C. Benson. A. C. Benson. 1979. Repr. of 1909 ed. lib. bdg. 20.00 (ISBN 0-8492-3733-5). R West.

Poems of a Country Lady. B. Burchell. 1985. 35.00x (ISBN 0-317-54310-5, Pub. by J Richardson UK); pap. 20.00x. State Mutual Bk.

Poems of a Yosemite Packer. William D. Fouts. LC 87-91031. (Illus.). 89p. (Orig.). 1987. pap. text ed. 6.95 (ISBN 0-944798-00-4). Spurs Pub.

Poems of Akhamatova. Tr. by Stanley Kunitz & Max Hayward. 1973. (Pub. by Atlantic Monthly Pr); pap. 10.95 (ISBN 0-316-50699-0, Pub. by Atlantic Monthly Pr). Little.

Poems of al-Mutanabbi: A Selection with Introduction, Translations & Notes. Al-Mutanabbi & Abu al-Tayyib Ahmad ibn al-Husan. Tr. by A. J. Arberry. LC 66-17060. pap. 40.30 (ISBN 0-317-09928-0, 2051447). Bks Demand UMI.

Poems of Alan Dugan. Alan Dugan. LC 79-144761. (Yale Series of Younger Poets: No. 57). Repr. of 1961 ed. 18.00 (ISBN 0-404-53857-6). AMS Pr.

Poems of Alan Seeger. Alan Seeger. LC 72-1678. Repr. of 1916 ed. 17.00 (ISBN 0-404-08498-2). AMS Pr.

Poems of Alexander Pope: A One-Vol. Ed. of the Twickenham Text with Selected Annotations. Alexander Pope. Ed. by John Butt. (Illus.). 1963. pap. 15.95x 1966 (ISBN 0-300-00030-8, Y163). Yale U Pr.

Poems of Alexander Scott. Alexander Scott. Ed. by A. K. Donald. (ETS ES: No. 85). Repr. of 1902 ed. 25.00 (ISBN 0-527-00288-7). Kraus Repr.

Poems of Alfred Starr Hamilton. Alfred S. Hamilton. LC 77-76735. 1969. 12.00 (ISBN 0-912330-14-7, Dist. by Inland Bk); pap. 7.50 (ISBN 0-912330-15-5). Jargon Soc.

Poems of Algernon Charles Swinburne, 6 Vols. Algernon C. Swinburne. LC 77-148312. Repr. of 1905 ed. Set. 265.00 (ISBN 0-404-08930-5). AMS Pr.

Poems of Alice Meynell. Alice C. Meynell. Ed. by Frederick Page. LC 78-59032. 1979. Repr. of 1940 ed. 18.50 (ISBN 0-88355-704-5). Hyperion Conn.

Poems of Allan Ramsay, 2 Vols. Allan Ramsay. LC 71-144498. Repr. of 1877 ed. Set. 80.00 (ISBN 0-404-08584-9). Vol. 1 (ISBN 0-404-08585-7). Vol. 2 (ISBN 0-404-08586-5). AMS Pr.

Poems of American History. Ed. by Burton E. Stevenson. LC 72-116416. (Granger Index Reprint Ser). 1922. 35.00 (ISBN 0-8369-6159-5). Ayer Co Pubs.

Poems of American Patriotism. Ed. by Frederic L. Knowles. LC 76-109142. (Granger Index Reprint Ser). 1898. 17.00 (ISBN 0-8369-6126-9). Ayer Co Pubs.

Poems of American Patriotism. Brander Matthews. 1882. 27.00 (ISBN 0-8274-3150-3). R West.

Poems of American Patriotism. facs. ed. Ed. by Brander Matthews. LC 70-133072. (Granger Index Reprint Ser). 1881. 17.00 (ISBN 0-8369-6202-8). Ayer Co Pubs.

Poems of Ancient Tamil: Their Milieu & Their Sanskrit Counterparts. George L. Hart, III. LC 73-91667. (Center for South & Southeast Asia Studies, UC Berkeley: No. 21). 300p. 1975. 45.00x (ISBN 0-520-02672-1). U of Cal Pr.

Poems of Andre Breton: A Bilingual Anthology. Andre Breton. Tr. by Jean-Pierre Cauvin & Mary A. Caws. 298p. 1982. text ed. 27.50x (ISBN 0-292-76476-6); pap. 14.95 (ISBN 0-292-76477-4). U of Tex Pr.

Poems of Andrew Marvell. Andrew Marvell. Ed. by Hugh MacDonald. (Muses' Library). 206p. 1969. pap. 5.95 (ISBN 0-7100-4920-X). Routledge Chapman & Hall.

Poems of Anne Bronte: A New Text & Commentary. Edward Chitham. 217p. 1979. 23.50x (ISBN 0-8476-6100-8). Rowman.

Poems of Anne, Countess of Winchelsea. Anne K. Finch. Ed. & intro. by Myra Reynolds. Repr. of 1903 ed. 49.50 (ISBN 0-404-56856-4). AMS Pr.

Poems of Arthur Henry Hallam. Arthur H. Hallam. Ed. by Richard Le Gallienne. LC 75-148794. Repr. of 1893 ed. 16.00 (ISBN 0-404-08825-2). AMS Pr.

Poems of Arthur Hugh Clough. 2nd ed. Arthur H. Clough. Ed. by F. L. Mulhauser. (Oxford English Texts Ser). 1974. 89.00x (ISBN 0-19-811898-8). Oxford U Pr.

Poems of Arthur Hugh Clough. Ed. by A. L. Norrington. Clough Hugh. 340p. 1986. pap. 18.95x (ISBN 0-19-812343-4). Oxford U Pr.

Poems of Arthur O'Shaughnessy. Arthur E. O'Shaughnessy. Ed. by William A. Percy. LC 78-13947. 1979. Repr. of 1923 ed. lib. bdg. 35.00 (ISBN 0-313-21101-9, OSPO). Greenwood.

Poems of Attila Jozef. Tr. & intro. by Anton N. Nyerges. (Illus.). 224p. 1987. pap. text ed. 12.00 (ISBN 0-8191-6566-2, Pub. by Atlantic Rseh & Pubns Inc). U Pr of Amer.

Poems of Ben Johnson. Ed. by Bernard H. Newdigate. 420p. 1980. Repr. lib. bdg. 85.00 (ISBN 0-89987-602-1). Darby Bks.

Poems of Bishop Henry King. Ed. by James H. Baker. LC 60-8067. 138p. 1960. 5.95x (ISBN 0-8040-0249-5, Pub. by Swallow); (Pub. by Swallow). Ohio U Pr.

Poems of Bishop Henry King. Henry King. Ed. by John Sparrow. LC 72-10145. 1974. lib. bdg. 42.50 (ISBN 0-8414-0645-6). Folcroft.

Poems of Black Africa. Ed. by Wole Soyinka. 384p. 1975. 12.95 (ISBN 0-8090-7747-7). Hill & Wang.

Poems of Boris Pasternak. Tr. by Lydia Pasternak from Rus. 96p. (Orig.). 1984. pap. 6.95x (ISBN 0-04-891052-X). Unwin Hyman.

Poems of Byron Vazakas see Nostalgias for a House of Cards: Poems.

Poems of Cabin & Field. Paul L. Dunbar. LC 74-164803. (Illus.). Repr. of 1899 ed. 12.50 (ISBN 0-404-00041-X). AMS Pr.

Poems of Cabin & Field. facs. ed. Paul L. Dunbar. LC 72-83917. (Black Heritage Library Collection Ser). (Illus.). 1899. 12.00 (ISBN 0-8369-8564-8). Ayer Co Pubs.

Poems of Catullus. Catullus. Tr. by Peter Whigham from Lat. (Classics Ser.). 1980. pap. 5.95 (ISBN 0-14-044180-8). Penguin.

Poems of Catullus: A Bilingual Edition. Catullus. Tr. by Peter Whigham. 1983. Repr. text ed. 32.00x (ISBN 0-520-05082-7). U of Cal Pr.

Poems of Catullus: A Teaching Text. Phyllis Y. Forsyth. 580p. 1986. 39.50 (ISBN 0-8191-5150-5, Pub. by Classical Assn Atlantic); pap. text ed. 24.75 (ISBN 0-8191-5151-3). U Pr of Amer.

Poems of Charles Baudelaire. Charles P. Baudelaire. Tr. by F. P. Sturm. LC 77-10250. 192p. Repr. of 1906 ed. 27.50 (ISBN 0-404-16306-8). AMS Pr.

Poems of Charles Fenno Hoffman. Charles F. Hoffman. Ed. by Edward F. Hoffman. LC 72-80627. Repr. of 1873 ed. 19.50 (ISBN 0-404-03299-0). AMS Pr.

Poems of Charles Kingsley. Charles Kingsley. LC 78-131762. 1970. Repr. of 1927 ed. 39.00x (ISBN 0-403-00649-X). Scholarly.

Poems of Charles Sackville, Sixth Earl of Dorset. Brice Harris. LC 78-61562. 1979. lib. bdg. 33.00 (ISBN 0-8240-9753-X). Garland Pub.

Poems of Charlotte Bronte. Victor A. Neufeldt. LC 84-48884. 200p. 1985. lib. bdg. 27.00 (ISBN 0-8240-8742-9). Garland Pub.

Poems of Charlotte Bronte. Ed. by Tom Winnifrith. 464p. 1984. 39.95x (ISBN 0-631-12563-9). Basil Blackwell.

Poems of Childhood. Eugene Field. (Airmont Classics Ser.). (Illus.). (gr. 4 up). 1969. pap. 1.95 (ISBN 0-8049-0211-9, CL-211). Airmont.

Poems of Christmas. Ed. by Myra C. Livingston. LC 80-13627. 132p. (gr. 5 up). 1980. 12.95 (ISBN 0-689-50180-3, M K McElderry). Macmillan.

Poems of Cicero. William W. Ewbank. Ed. by Steele Commager. LC 77-70814. (Latin Poetry Ser.). 1978. lib. bdg. 34.00 (ISBN 0-8240-2955-0). Garland Pub.

Poems of Cloister & Jungle, a Buddhist Anthology. Rhys Davids. 59.95 (ISBN 0-8490-0849-2). Gordon Pr.

Poems of Cuthbert Shaw & Thomas Russell. facs. ed. Ed. by Eric Partridge. LC 74-117908. (Select Bibliographies Reprint Ser). 1925. 17.00 (ISBN 0-8369-5360-6). Ayer Co Pubs.

Poems of Dagny Juel Przybyszewska. Tr. by Hanne Bramness from Norwegian. (Illus.). 24p. (Orig.). 1988. pap. 10.00 (ISBN 0-9615784-2-4). Branch Redd.

Poems of Daniel Whitehead Hicky. Daniel W. Hicky. LC 75-16360. 128p. 1975. bds. 7.50 (ISBN 0-87797-032-7). Cherokee.

Poems of Death. Ed. by Phoebe Pool. (Poetry Library). 120p. 1985. Repr. of 1945 ed. 17.75x (ISBN 0-89609-255-0). Roth Pub Inc.

Poems of Devotion & Inspiration, Bk. I. Nona K. Duffy. 55p. 1985. 3.25 (ISBN 0-89697-237-2). Intl Univ Pr.

Poems of Devotion & Inspiration, Bk. II: Doors Will Open. Nona K. Duffy. 57p. 1985. 3.25 (ISBN 0-89697-238-0). Intl Univ Pr.

Poems of Digby Mackworth Dolben. Digby M. Dolben. Ed. & memoir by Robert Bridges. 1915. 25.00 (ISBN 0-8274-3152-X). R West.

Poems of Dylan Thomas. rev. ed. Dylan Thomas. Ed. by Daniel Jones. LC 79-145935. 1971. 14.00 (ISBN 0-8112-0398-0). New Directions.

Poems of Ebonized Meditation. Thomas P. Hill. 36p. 1986. 5.95 (ISBN 0-533-06756-1). Vantage.

Poems of Edgar Allan Poe. Ed. by Thomas D. Mabbott. (Harvard Paperbacks: No. 166). 512p. 1980. pap. 8.95 (ISBN 0-674-67780-3). Harvard U Pr.

Poems of Edgar Allan Poe. Edgar Allan Poe. Ed. by Floyd Stovall. LC 65-23455. 1977. 20.00x (ISBN 0-8139-0194-4). U Pr of Va.

Poems of Egan O'Rahilly: To Which Are Added Miscellaneous Pieces Illustrating Their Subjects & Language. Egan O'Rahilly. Ed. by Patrick S. Dinneen. LC 75-28837. Repr. of 1900 ed. 30.00 (ISBN 0-404-13826-8). AMS Pr.

Poems of Elizabethan Age. Ed. by G. G. Hiller. 1977. pap. 10.95x (ISBN 0-416-83210-5, NO. 2754). Routledge Chapman & Hall.

Poems of Emerson: Selected Criticism from the Coming Age & the Arena, 1899-1905. Charles Malloy. LC 80-2539. 1981. 32.50 (ISBN 0-404-19265-3). AMS Pr.

Poems of Emily Dickinson, 3 Vols. Emily Dickinson. Ed. by Thomas H. Johnson. (Illus.). 1350p. (Incl. Variant Readings Critically Compared with All Known Manuscripts). 1955. Set. boxed 75.00 (ISBN 0-674-67600-9, Belknap Pr). Harvard U Pr.

Poems of Emily Dickinson. Ed. by Helen Plotz. LC 64-12111. (Crowell Poets Ser.). (Illus.). 158p. (YA) (gr. 7 up). 1988. PLB 12.89 (ISBN 0-690-63366-1, Crowell Jr Bks). HarpJ.

Poems of Endre Ady. Endre Ady. LC 74-75423. (Literature Ser.). (Illus.). 491p. 1969. 24.00 (ISBN 0-914648-00-4). Hungarian Cultural.

Poems of Endre Ady. Tr. by Anton N. Nyerges & Anton N. Nyerges. (Illus.). 500p. 1987. Repr. of 1969 ed. lib. bdg. 32.50 (ISBN 0-8191-6568-9, Pub. by Atlantic Rseh & Pubns Inc). U Pr of Amer.

Poems of Fernando Pessoa. Ed. by Edwin Honig & Susan M. Brown. (Modern European Poets Ser.). 215p. 1988. pap. 10.50 (ISBN 0-88001-123-8). Ecco Pr.

Poems of Fernando Pessoa. Fernando Pessoa. Tr. by Joan M. Brown & Edwin Honig. (Modern European Poets Ser.). 217p. 1986. 19.95 (ISBN 0-88001-091-6). Ecco Pr.

Poems of Flowers. (Illus.). 20p. 1986. 4.00 (ISBN 0-930061-11-X). Interspace Bks.

Poems of Frances E. W. Harper. facs. ed. Frances E. Harper. LC 74-133155. (Black Heritage Library Collection). 1895. 10.75 (ISBN 0-8369-8710-1). Ayer Co Pubs.

Poems of Francis Thompson. rev. ed. Francis Thompson. Ed. by Terence L. Connolly. LC 78-10371. 1979. Repr. of 1941 ed. lib. bdg. 45.50x (ISBN 0-313-21003-9, THFT). Greenwood.

Poems of Francois Villon. Francois Villon. Ed. by Galway Kinnell. LC 81-71907. 270p. (Orig.). 1982. pap. 10.95x (ISBN 0-87451-236-0). U Pr of New Eng.

Poems of George Crabbe: A Literary & Historical Study. John H. Evans. 20.25 (ISBN 0-8369-7108-6, 7942). Ayer Co Pubs.

Poems of George Herbert. George Herbert. LC 75-41132. (Illus.). Repr. of 1907 ed. 24.50 (ISBN 0-404-14553-1). AMS Pr.

Poems of George Marion M'Clellan. facs. ed. George M. McClellan. LC 79-133159. (Black Heritage Library Collection). 1895. 12.00 (ISBN 0-8369-8714-4). Ayer Co Pubs.

Poems of George Meredith. George Meredith. Ed. by Phyllis B. Bartlett. LC 73-77142. 1978. Set. 150.00x (ISBN 0-300-01283-7). Yale U Pr.

Poems of Gerard Manley Hopkins. 4th ed. Gerard Manley Hopkins. Ed. by W. H. Gardner & N. H. MacKenzie. 1967. 35.00 (ISBN 0-19-500164-8); pap. 8.95x (ISBN 0-19-281094-4). Oxford U Pr.

Poems of the Hundred Names: A Short Introduction to Chinese Poetry, Together with 208 Original Translations. 3rd ed. Ed. by Henry H. Hart. LC 68-23295. (Illus.). 1968. Repr. of 1954 ed. lib. bdg. cancelled (ISBN 0-8371-0098-4, HACP). Greenwood.

Poems of the Inner World see Gallery Series: Poets.

Poems of the Irish Revolutionary Brotherhood. Thomas P. MacDonagh et al. Ed. by Padraic Colum & Edward J. O'Brien. 1978. Repr. of 1916 ed. lib. bdg. 15.00 (ISBN 0-89341-477-8). Longwood Pub Group.

Poems of the Late T'ang. Tr. by A. C. Graham. (Classics Ser.). 1977. pap. 4.95 (ISBN 0-14-044157-3). Penguin.

Poems of the Later Years. Irving Wilner. 64p. 1981. pap. 4.50 (ISBN 0-931848-31-8). Dryad Pr.

Poems of the Law. J. Greenbag Croke. (Legal Recreations Ser.). 311p. 1986. Repr. of 1885 ed. lib. bdg. 35.00 (ISBN 0-89941-447-8). W S Hein.

Poems of the Morning & Poems of the Storm. Wyatt. 1973. 6.00 (ISBN 0-685-36817-3); pap. 2.50 (ISBN 0-685-36818-1). Oyez.

Poems of the Old West. facs. ed. Ed. by Levette J. Davidson. LC 68-58824. (Granger Index Reprint Ser). 1951. 16.00 (ISBN 0-8369-6012-2). Ayer Co Pubs.

Poems of the Palliser Triangle. Alfred D. Highgate. 64p. 1986. 6.95 (ISBN 0-8062-2988-8). Carlton.

Poems of the Pearl Manuscript. Ed. by Malcolm Andrew & Ronald Waldron. LC 78-64464. (York Medieval Texts, Second Ser.). 1979. 55.00x (ISBN 0-520-03794-4); pap. 12.95x (ISBN 0-520-04631-5). U of Cal Pr.

Poems of the Scottish Minor Poets. Ed. by George B. Douglas. LC 73-144505. Repr. of 1891 ed. 26.00 (ISBN 0-404-08634-9). AMS Pr.

Poems of the Soul & the Sprit. Roxanne M. Collyer. 40p. 1986. 5.75 (ISBN 0-8062-2796-6). Carlton.

Poems of the Spirit, Vol. 2. Irene J. Burnell. 64p. 1988. 10.95 (ISBN 0-8062-3278-1). Carlton.

Poems of the Tarot. Malcolm K. Smith. 84p. 1984. 4.10 (ISBN 0-89697-218-6). Intl Univ Pr.

Poems of the Troubadour De Born Bertran. Bertran De Born et al. Ed. by Tilde Sankovitch & Patricia Stablein. LC 81-2393. 528p. 1984. text ed. 70.00x (ISBN 0-520-04297-2). U of Cal Pr.

Poems of the Troubadour Raimbaut de Vaqueiras. Raimbaut de Vaqueiras. Ed. by Joseph Linskill. LC 80-2190. Date not set. Repr. of 1964 ed. 45.00 (ISBN 0-404-19014-6). AMS Pr.

Poems of the Two Worlds. Frederick Morgan. LC 76-51907. 132p. 1977. 11.95 (ISBN 0-252-00604-6); pap. 8.95 (ISBN 0-252-00605-4). U of Ill Pr.

Poems of the Vietnam War. rev. ed. Jocelyn Hollis. LC 86-28776. 51p. 1987. lib. bdg. 13.95 (ISBN 0-933486-68-5); text ed. 13.95 (ISBN 0-933486-67-7); pap. 6.95 (ISBN 0-933486-69-3). Am Poetry & Lit.

Poems of the Vikings. Ed. by Patricia Terry. 1969. pap. text ed. write for info. (ISBN 0-02-419810-2). Macmillan.

Poems of the Vikings: The Elder Edda. Ed. by Patricia Terry. LC 69-16528. (Library of Liberal Arts). 1969. pap. 13.24 scp (ISBN 0-672-60332-2, LLA128). Bobbs.

Poems of the War. George H. Boker. LC 72-4949. (Romantic Tradition in American Literature Ser.). 204p. 1972. Repr. of 1864 ed. 25.50 (ISBN 0-405-04623-5). Ayer Co Pubs.

Poems of Thirty Years. Edwin Morgan. 442p. 1982. 21.00 (ISBN 0-85635-365-5). Carcanet.

Poems of This War by Younger Poets. Ed. by Patricia Leonard & Colin Strong. LC 42-23186. (Granger Poetry Library). 1976. Repr. of 1942 ed. 16.75x (ISBN 0-89609-023-X). Roth Pub Inc.

Poems of Thomas Bailey Aldrich. Thomas B. Aldrich. 1977. Repr. of 1908 ed. lib. bdg. 27.50 (ISBN 0-8495-0016-8). Arden Lib.

Poems of Thomas Blacklock. 3rd ed. Thomas Blacklock. Repr. of 1756 ed. 13.50 (ISBN 0-404-08553-9). AMS Pr.

Poems of Thomas Carew. Thomas Carew. Ed. by Arthur Vincent. LC 76-38343. (Selected Bibliographies Reprint Ser.). 1899. 17.00 (ISBN 0-8369-6760-7). Ayer Co Pubs.

Poems of Thomas Gordon Hake. Thomas G. Hake. LC 75-131504. Repr. of 1894 ed. 15.75 (ISBN 0-404-03026-2). AMS Pr.

Poems of Thomas Gray. Thomas Gray. 1814. Repr. lib. bdg. 35.00 (ISBN 0-8414-4673-3). Folcroft.

Poems of Thomas Washbourne. Thomas Washbourne. LC 73-21068. (Fuller Worthies' Library). 240p. 1983. Repr. of 1868 ed. 50.00 (ISBN 0-404-11498-9). AMS Pr.

Poems of Tibullus. Tibullus. Tr. by Philip Dunlop. (Classics Ser.). 176p. 1972. pap. 5.95 (ISBN 0-14-044266-9). Penguin.

Poems of Tibullus. Albius Tibullus. Tr. by Constance Carrier. LC 68-14614. (Greek & Latin Classics Series Midland Bks.: No. 116). Repr. of 1968 ed. 32.00 (ISBN 0-8357-9232-3, 2013014). Bks Demand UMI.

Poems of To-Day: First & Second Series. Ed. by English Association Staff. LC 77-88079. (Granger Poetry Library). 1976. Repr. of 1915 ed. 27.50x (ISBN 0-89609-036-1). Roth Pub Inc.

Poems of Trumbull Stickney. Trumbull Stickney. LC 72-4975. (Romantic Tradition in American Literature Ser.). 336p. 1972. Repr. of 1905 ed. 29.00 (ISBN 0-405-04645-6). Ayer Co Pubs.

Poems of Tukarama. Ed. by J. Nelson Fraser & K. B. Marathe. Tr. by J. Nelson Fraser & K. B. Marathe. 1981. Repr. of 1909 ed. 15.00x (ISBN 0-8364-0747-4, Pub. by Motilal Banarsidass). South Asia Bks.

Poems of W. B. Yeats. William B. Yeats. Ed. by Richard J. Finneran. LC 83-17567. 640p. 1983. 24.95 (ISBN 0-02-632940-9). Macmillan.

Poems of W. S. Landor. W. S. Landor. Ed. by F. Grigson. 1985. pap. 25.00x (ISBN 0-900000-74-0, Pub. by Centaur Bks). State Mutual Bk.

Poems of Wang-Wei. Wang-Wei. Tr. by G. W. Robinson. (Classics Ser.). 1974. pap. 5.95 (ISBN 0-14-044296-0). Penguin.

Poems of Washington Irving. Washington Irving. Ed. by William R. Langfeld. LC 74-22225. 1974. Repr. of 1931 ed. lib. bdg. 22.00 (ISBN 0-8414-5688-7). Folcroft.

Poems of Washington Irving. Washington Irving. 19p. 1980. Repr. of 1931 ed. lib. bdg. 17.00 (ISBN 0-8492-1631-1). R West.

Poems of Wilfrid Owen. Ed. by Jon Stallworthy. 1986. 19.95 (ISBN 0-393-02364-8); pap. 9.95 (ISBN 0-393-30385-3). Norton.

Poems of William B. Greene. William B. Greene. 1977. lib. bdg. 59.95 (ISBN 0-8490-2447-1). Gordon Pr.

Poems of William Barnes, 2 vols. William Barnes. 1985. Set. 125.00x (ISBN 0-900000-46-5, Pub. by Centaur Bks). State Mutual Bk.

Poems of William Blake. William Blake. Ed. by William B. Yeats. 277p. 1905. pap. 9.95 (ISBN 0-7100-0174-6). Routledge Chapman & Hall.

Poems of William Collins. Edmund Blunden. LC 73-11422. 1929. lib. bdg. 30.00 (ISBN 0-8414-3214-7). Folcroft.

Poems of William Collins. William Collins. Ed. by Walter C. Bronson. 170p. Repr. of 1898 ed. lib. bdg. 39.50x (ISBN 3-487-04665-2, Pub. by G. Olms BRD). Coronet Bks.

Poems of William Cowper, Vol. I: 1748 - 1782. William Cowper. Ed. by John D. Baird & Charles Ryskamp. (Oxford English Texts Ser.). (Illus.). 1980. text ed. 85.00x (ISBN 0-19-811875-9). Oxford U Pr.

Poems of William Drummond of Hawthornden. William Drummond. Repr. of 1832 ed. 46.00 (ISBN 0-384-13070-4). Johnson Repr.

Poems of William Drummond of Hawthornden, 2 vols. William Drummond. Ed. by William C. Ward. 1894. 65.00 set (ISBN 0-8274-3157-0). R West.

Poems of William Dunbar. William Dunbar. Ed. by James Kinsley. (Oxford English Texts Ser.). 1979. 95.00x (ISBN 0-19-811888-0). Oxford U Pr.

Poems of William Dunbar. William Dunbar. LC 70-161970. Repr. of 1950 ed. 29.00x (ISBN 0-403-01321-6). Scholarly.

Poems of William Dunbar: From the Obsolete. William Dunbar. Ed. by William Mackean. 1890. 35.00 (ISBN 0-8274-3158-9). R West.

Poems of William of Shoreham. William of Shoreham. Ed. by M. Konrath. (EETS, ES Ser.: No. 86). Repr. of 1902 ed. 35.00 (ISBN 0-527-00289-5). Kraus Repr.

Poems of William Smith. Ed. by Lawrence A. Sasek. LC 78-108203. (University Studies, Humanities Ser.: No. 20). 108p. 1970. 16.95 (ISBN 0-8071-0926-6). La State U Pr.

Poems of William Wordsworth, 3 vols. Nowell C. Smith. 616p. 1983. Repr. of 1908 ed. Set. lib. bdg. 200.00 (ISBN 0-89984-617-3). Century Bookbindery.

Poems of Wisdom & Learning in Old English. T. A. Shippey. 152p. 1976. 33.00 (ISBN 0-85991-014-8, Pub. by Boydell & Brewer). Longwood Pub Group.

Poems of Z. Paul Hyland. 1982. pap. 8.50 (ISBN 0-906427-44-4, Pub. by Bloodaxe Bks). Dufour.

Poems Old & New: 1918-1978. Janet Lewis. LC 80-26209. xvi, 112p. 1981. 15.95x (ISBN 0-8040-0371-8, Pub. by Swallow); pap. 8.95 (ISBN 0-8040-0372-6, Pub. by Swallow). Ohio U Pr.

Poems on a Boy's Paintings. 1981. pap. 5.95 (ISBN 0-8351-0880-5). China Bks.

Poems on a White Page. Frank Cady. (Flowering Quince Poetry Ser.: No. 4). (Illus.). 24p. (Orig.). 1982. pap. 7.50 (ISBN 0-940592-13-4). Heyeck Pr.

Poems on Affairs of State: Augustan Satirical Verse 1660-1714, Vol. 1, 1669-1678. Ed. by George D. Lord. (Illus.). 1963. 57.00t (ISBN 0-300-00726-4). Yale U Pr.

Poems on Affairs of State: Augustan Satirical Verse, 1660-1714, Vol. 3, 1682-1685. Ed. by Howard H. Schless. (Illus.). 1968. 62.00t (ISBN 0-300-00886-4). Yale U Pr.

Poems on Affairs of State: Augustan Satirical Verse 1660-1714, Vol. 4 1685-1688. Ed. by Galbraith M. Crump. LC 63-7938. (Illus.). 1968. 52.00x (ISBN 0-300-00389-7). Yale U Pr.

Poems on Affairs of State: Augustan Satirical Verse, 1660-1714, Vol. 6, 1697-1704. Ed. by Frank H. Ellis. (Illus.). 1970. 70.00x (ISBN 0-300-01194-6). Yale U Pr.

Poems on Affairs of State: Augustan Satirical Verse 1660-1714, Vol. 5 1688-1697. Ed. by William J. Cameron. LC 63-7983. (Illus.). 1972. 60.00x (ISBN 0-300-01190-3). Yale U Pr.

Poems on Affairs of State-Augustan Satirical Verse, 1660-1714, Vol. 7: 1704-1714. Ed. by Frank H. Ellis. LC 63-7938. (Illus.). 760p. 1975. 70.00x (ISBN 0-300-01772-3). Yale U Pr.

Poems on Love & Life. Frederick D. Harper. LC 84-73550. 125p. 1985. pap. 8.95 (ISBN 0-935392-05-X); 12.95 (ISBN 0-935392-06-8). Douglass Pubs.

Poems on Miscellaneous Subjects. 2nd ed. Frances E. Harper. 1854. 18.00 (ISBN 0-8115-3025-6). Kraus Repr.

Poems on Poetry: Literary Criticism by Yuan Hao-wen; 1190-1257. John T. Wixted. xvi, 482p. (Orig.). 1982. pap. text ed. 48.50x (ISBN 3-515-03914-7, Pub. by Franz Steiner). Coronet Bks.

Poems on Several Occasions. Sarah F. Egerton. LC 86-31375. 1987. 50.00x (ISBN 0-8201-1423-5). Schol Facsimiles.

Poems on the Abolition of the Slave Trade. facs. ed. James Montgomery et al. LC 79-149871. (Black Heritage Library Collection). 1809. 17.00 (ISBN 0-8369-8751-9). Ayer Co Pubs.

Poems on the Edge of Day. John Brandi. 1984. 4.50 (ISBN 0-934834-37-7). White Pine.

Poems on the Rising Glory of America see Millennium in America: From the Puritan Migration to the Civil War.

Poems on Various Subjects, Religious & Moral. Phillis Wheatley. LC 75-177828. Repr. of 1786 ed. 14.50 (ISBN 0-404-00126-2). AMS Pr.

Poems: On Writing Poetry. John Travers Moore. LC 79-181366. 1971. 5.00 (ISBN 0-87212-025-2). Libra.

Poems, Original & Translated. Charles T. Brooks. Ed. by W. P. Andrews. LC 72-4952. (Romantic Tradition in American Literature Ser.). 256p. 1972. Repr. of 1885 ed. 19.00 (ISBN 0-405-04624-3). Ayer Co Pubs.

Poems Out of a Hat. Walter Leuba. 1947. 2.75 (ISBN 0-911090-13-4). Pacific Bk Supply.

Poems: Partly Medical. Benjamin F. Miller. 9.95 (ISBN 0-686-23786-2). F A Countway.

Poems Plain & Fancy. Dick Higgins. LC 85-17237. 144p. (Orig.). 1986. pap. 7.95 (ISBN 0-88268-022-6). Station Hill Pr.

Poems, Plays & Other Remains of Sir John Suckling, 2 vols. facsimile ed. John Suckling. Ed. by W. Carew Hazlitt. LC 71-103669. (Select Bibliographies Reprint Ser.). 1892. 40.00 (ISBN 0-8369-5169-7). Ayer Co Pubs.

Poems, Prayers & Logics. Delbert L. Tibbs. LC 84-80264. (Illus.). 80p. (Orig.). 1984. pap. 6.00 (ISBN 0-915867-02-8). ENAAQ Pubns.

Poems, Prayers & Projects. Carole MacKenthum. (Helping Hand Ser.). (Illus.). 48p. (YA) (gr. 3-7). 1984. wkbk 5.95 (ISBN 0-86653-177-7). Good Apple.

Poems, Prayers & Promises. Charles E. Cravey. (Illus.). 120p. (Orig.). 1988. pap. 5.00 (ISBN 0-938645-02-1). Upper Rm Pub.

Poems: Reinvestigations & Descent from the Cross. Kostas Kindinis. Tr. by Kimon Friar from Gr. (Modern Greek History & Culture Ser.). 1980. 10.00 (ISBN 0-935476-05-9). Nostos Bks.

Poems Retrieved. Frank O'Hara. Ed. by Donald Allen. LC 77-554. 258p. 1977. 12.00 (ISBN 0-912516-18-6); pap. 5.00 (ISBN 0-912516-19-4). Grey Fox.

Poems, Sacred, Passionate, & Humorous, of Nathaniel Parker Willis. Nathaniel P. Willis. LC 72-4983. (Romantic Tradition in American Literature Ser.). 388p. 1972. Repr. of 1868 ed. 30.00 (ISBN 0-405-04652-9). Ayer Co Pubs.

Poems: Scots & English. John Buchan. 105p. 1981. Repr. lib. bdg. 20.00. Darby Bks.

Poems: Selected & New. Tony Curtis. Ed. by Robert McDowell & Mark Jarman. LC 86-60368. (Poetry Ser.). 80p. (Orig.). 1986. 15.00x (ISBN 0-934257-07-8); pap. 8.00 (ISBN 0-934257-06-X). Story Line.

Poems Seventy. Wyn Binding. 90p. 1985. 15.00x (ISBN 0-85088-455-1, Pub. by Gomer Pr). State Mutual Bk.

Poems Seventy-Eight. Graham Allen. 94p. 1985. 15.00x (ISBN 0-85088-660-0, Pub. by Gomer Pr). State Mutual Bk.

Poems Seventy-Four. Peter E. Lewis. 146p. 1985. 15.00x (ISBN 0-85088-264-8, Pub. by Gomer Pr). State Mutual Bk.

Poems Seventy-One. Jeremy Hooker. 117p. 1985. 15.00x (ISBN 0-317-54066-1, Pub. by Gomer Pr). State Mutual Bk.

Poems Seventy-Six. Glyn Jones. 89p. 1985. 15.00x (ISBN 0-85088-460-8, Pub. by Gomer Pr). State Mutual Bk.

Poems Seventy-Three. Gwyn Ramage. 105p. 1985. 15.00x (ISBN 0-85088-214-1, Pub. by Gomer Pr). State Mutual Bk.

Poems Seventy-Two. John Ackerman. 92p. 1985. 15.00x (ISBN 0-85088-149-8, Pub. by Gomer Pr). State Mutual Bk.

Poems, Short Stories & Plays for Youth. Bessie Frazier. 80p. 1980. 6.00 (ISBN 0-682-49591-3). Exposition-Phoenix.

Poems Sixty-Nine. John S. Williams. 85p. 1985. 15.00x (ISBN 0-85088-445-4, Pub. by Gomer Pr). State Mutual Bk.

Poems Teachers Ask for: Bks I & II. Ed. by Normal Instructor-Primary Plans Magazine Staff. LC 78-73496. (Granger Poetry Library). 1979. Repr. of 1925 ed. 19.25 ea.; Bk. I. (ISBN 0-89609-122-8); Bk. II. (ISBN 0-89609-123-6). Roth Pub Inc.

Poems That Every Child Should Know: A Selection of the Best Poems of All Times for Young People. Mary E. Burt. (gr. k up). 1904. 35.00 (ISBN 0-8274-3160-0). R West.

Poems That Every Child Should Know: A Selection of the Best Poems of All Times for Young People. facsimile ed. Ed. by Mary E. Burt. LC 71-168776. (Granger Index Reprint Ser.). Repr. of 1904 ed. 26.50 (ISBN 0-8369-6296-6). Ayer Co Pubs.

Poems That Live Forever. Ed. by Hazel Felleman. LC 65-13987. 1965. pap. 16.95 (ISBN 0-385-00358-7). Doubleday.

Poems That Tell Me Who I Am. Margaret L. McWhorter. LC 80-51481. (Illus.). 57p. 1978. pap. 4.95 (ISBN 0-9604342-0-8). Ransom Hill.

Poems That Touch the Heart. rev. & enl. ed. Compiled by A. L. Alexander. LC 56-11498. 1956. pap. 15.95 (ISBN 0-385-04401-1). Doubleday.

Poems: The Location of Things. Barbara Guest. 1962. 10.95 (ISBN 0-911660-06-2). Yankee Peddler.

Poems: The Pedlar, Tintern Abbey, The Two-Part Prelude, Vol. 1. William Wordsworth. Ed. by Jonathan Wordsworth. 80p. 1985. pap. 7.95 (ISBN 0-521-31937-4). Cambridge U Pr.

Poems: The Ruined Cottage, The Brothers, Michael, Vol. II. William Wordsworth. Ed. by Jonathan Wordsworth. 88p. 1985. pap. 7.95 (ISBN 0-521-31936-6). Cambridge U Pr.

Poems: The Sixteen Forty-Five Edition. John Milton. Bd. with Essays in Analysis. Cleanth Brooks & John E. Hardy. LC 68-24444. 369p. 1968. Repr. of 1952 ed. 35.00x (ISBN 0-87752-075-5). Gordian.

Poems to Be Read Aloud: A Victorian Drawing Room Entertainment. Tom Atkinson. 116p. 1986. 11.00x (ISBN 0-946487-00-6, Pub. by Luath Pr UK). State Mutual Bk.

Poems to Keep. Phillip Corwin. 42p. 1985. 4.95 (ISBN 0-9615475-0-2). Catnip Pr.

Poems to Ponder. Lawrence P. Montague. LC 85-2651. 48p. 1985. pap. 6.50 (ISBN 0-86534-068-4, Sundial Bks). Sunstone Pr.

Poems to Read to the Very Young. Ed. by Josette Frank. LC 82-518. (Illus.). 48p. (ps-3). 1982. lib. bdg. 8.99 (ISBN 0-394-95188-3); pap. 6.95 (ISBN 0-394-85188-9). Random.

Poems to Read to the Very Young. Ed. by Josette Frank. LC 87-23234. (Picturebacks Ser.). (Illus.). 32p. (ps-1). 1988. lib. bdg. 5.99 (ISBN 0-394-99768-9, BYR); pap. 1.95 (ISBN 0-394-89768-4). Random.

Poems to the Child-God: Structures & Strategies in the Poetry of Surdas. Kenneth E. Bryant. LC 77-80467. (Center for South & Southeast Asia Studies, UC Berkeley: No. 27). 1978. 37.50x (ISBN 0-520-03540-2). U of Cal Pr.

Poems Toward the Twenty-First Century. Holly Chetta. LC 84-90189. 58p. 1985. 6.95 (ISBN 0-533-06246-2). Vantage.

Poems, Transcripts, Letters: Facsimiles of Woodhouse's Scrapbook Materials in the Pierpoint Morgan Library, Vol. IV. John Keats. Ed. by Jack Stillinger. LC 83-49279. (Manuscripts of the Younger Romantics & the Bodleian Shelley Manuscripts Ser.). 330p. 1984. lib. bdg. 75.00 (ISBN 0-8240-6257-4). Garland Pub.

Poems Twice Told: Containing the Boatman & Welcoming Disaster. Jay Macpherson. 1981. 10.95 (ISBN 0-19-540379-7). Oxford U Pr.

Poems Two. B. S. Johnson. 1972. 7.00 (ISBN 0-685-27785-2, Pub. by Trigram Pr); signed ed. 15.00 (ISBN 0-685-27786-0); pap. 4.00 (ISBN 0-685-27787-9). Small Pr Dist.

Poem's Two Bodies: The Poetics of the 1590 Faerie Queene. David L. Miller. 304p. 1988. 29.50 (ISBN 0-691-06744-9). Princeton U Pr.

Poems West from Ballina. Gerald J. Shea. 50p. (Orig.). 1987. pap. 3.00 (ISBN 0-9618637-0-6). Oak St Bks.

Poems: With Elegies on the Author's Death. John Donne. LC 72-191. (English Experience Ser.: No. 240). 408p. 1970. Repr. of 1633 ed. 50.00 (ISBN 90-221-0240-8). Walter J Johnson.

Poems within Season. Mehdi Nakosteen. LC 74-75757. 142p. 1974. 14.95. Iran Bks.

Poems Written & Published During the American Revolutionary War. Philip M. Freneau. Intro. by Lewis Leary. LC 76-11754. 616p. 1976. Repr. of 1809 ed. lib. bdg. 90.00x (ISBN 0-8201-1173-2). Schol Facsimiles.

Poems Written Between the Years 1768 & 1794. Philip Freneau. 59.95 (ISBN 0-8490-0852-2). Gordon Pr.

Poems Written Between the Years 1768 & 1794. Philip M. Freneau. LC 76-11752. 480p. 1976. Repr. of 1795 ed. lib. bdg. 70.00x (ISBN 0-8201-1172-4). Schol Facsimiles.

Poems Written for Sbek's Mummies, Marie Menken & Other Important Persons, Places & Things. Anne Paolucci. Intro. by Glauco Cambon. pap. 9.95 (ISBN 0-918680-03-4). Griffon Hse.

Poems Written in Early Youth. T. S. Eliot. LC 67-18781. 1967. pap. 4.95 (ISBN 0-374-50708-2). FS&G.

Poems: You & I. Ralph De Toledano. LC 77-17944. 72p. 1978. 5.95 (ISBN 0-88289-173-1). Pelican.

Poet Dreaming in the Artist's House. Ed. by Emilie Buchwald & Ruth Roston. LC 83-73502. (Illus.). 144p. 1984. 13.95 (ISBN 0-915943-00-X); pap. 7.95 (ISBN 0-915943-01-8). Milkweed Ed.
Poet Errant: A Biography of Ruben Dario. Charles D. Watland. LC 64-21467. 1965. 5.95 (ISBN 0-8022-1817-2). Philos Lib.
Poet I Palach (Nekrasov I Murav'ev) Kornei Chukovsky. (Rus.). 1976. 10.00 (ISBN 0-88233-258-9); pap. 3.00 (ISBN 0-88233-259-7). Ardis Pubs.
Poet in America: Winfield Townley Scott. Scott Donaldson. (Illus.). 414p. 1972. 22.50x (ISBN 0-292-76400-6). U of Tex Pr.
Poet in Exile. Antonina Vallentin. LC 72-113327. 1970. Repr. of 1934 ed. 22.50x (ISBN 0-8046-1003-7, Pub. bu Kennikat). Assoc Faculty PR.
Poet in New York. Federico Garcia Lorca. 1981. pap. 4.95 (ISBN 0-394-17205-1, E54, Ever). Grove.
Poet in New York. Federico Garcia Lorca. Ed. by Christopher Maurer. Tr. by Greg Simon & Steven White. (Illus.). 320p. 1987. 22.50 (ISBN 0-374-23539-2); pap. 9.95 (ISBN 0-374-52083-6). FS&G.
Poet in Peru: Alienation & the Quest for a Super-Reality. James Higgins. (Liverpool Monographs in Hispanic Studies: No. 1). 166p. 1982. text ed. 28.00 (ISBN 0-905205-10-3, Pub. by F Cairns). Longwood Pub Group.
Poet in Pomfret, Poems by Maxim Konecky. Maxim Konecky. (Illus.). 68p. 1968. pap. 5.00 (ISBN 0-87423-004-7). Westburg.
Poet in the Desert. Charles E. Wood. 69.95 (ISBN 0-8490-0854-9). Gordon Pr.
Poet in the Poem. George T. Wright. LC 74-2404. 167p. 1974. Repr. of 1960 ed. 15.00x (ISBN 0-87752-169-7). Gordian.
Poet in the Theatre. Ronald Peacock. LC 86-22749. 211p. 1986. Repr. of 1961 ed. lib. bdg. 41.50x (ISBN 0-313-25220-3, PPOE). Greenwood.
Poet in the World. Denise Levertov. LC 73-78785. 288p. 1973. pap. 7.95 (ISBN 0-8112-0493-6, NDP363). New Directions.
Poet L'a Dit. Charles Peguy. pap. 5.95 (ISBN 0-685-37045-3). French & Eur.
Poet Li Po. Teng C. Yung. Ed. by John DeFrancis. LC 77-189614. (Pali Language Texts - Chinese). (Illus.). 80p. (Orig.). 1975. pap. text ed. 2.50x (ISBN 0-8248-0224-1). UH Pr.
Poet of Exile: A Study of Milton's Poetry. Louis L. Martz. LC 79-64079. 1980. 37.00t (ISBN 0-300-02393-6). Yale U Pr.
Poet of Home Life: Centenary Memories of William Cowper. Andrew J. Symington. 1900. 30.00 (ISBN 0-8274-3162-7). R West.
Poet of Malta. Dun Karm. Ed. by Arthur J. Arberry & P. Grech. (University of Cambridge Oriental Pubns.). 1961. 39.50 (ISBN 0-521-04040-X). Cambridge U Pr.
Poet on Painters: Essays on the Art of Painting by Twentieth-Century Poets. Ed. by J. D. McClatchy. (Illus.). 228p. 1987. 25.00 (ISBN 0-520-05777-5). U of Cal Pr.
Poet Philosophers. Goldie L. Morales. (Illus.). 48p. (Orig.). 1983. pap. 3.00 (ISBN 0-910083-16-9). Heritage Trails.
Poet Philosophers of the Rig Veda. C. Kunhan Raja. (Sanskrit & eng.). 10.00 (ISBN 0-89744-121-4, Pub. by Ganesh & Co. India). Auromere.
Poet-Physician: Keats & Medical Science. Donald C. Goellnicht. LC 83-47618. 304p. 1984. 31.95x (ISBN 0-8229-3807-3). U of Pittsburgh Pr.
Poet Physicians: An Anthology of Medical Poetry Written by Physicians. Ed. by Mary Lou McDonough. LC 78-74819. (Granger Poetry Library). 1979. Repr. of 1945 ed. 23.75x (ISBN 0-89609-138-4). Roth Pub Inc.
Poet President of Texas. new ed. Stanley Siegel. 1977. 12.50 (ISBN 0-8363-0153-6). Jenkins.
Poet Reclining. Ken Smith. 1982. (Pub. by Bloodaxe Bks); pap. 12.95 (ISBN 0-906427-51-7, Pub. by Bloodaxe Bks). Dufour.
Poet Robert Browning & His Kinsfolk by His Cousin Cyrus Mason. Ed. by W. Craig Turner. LC 81-86286. (Illus.). 240p. 1983. 24.00 (ISBN 0-918954-38-X). Baylor Univ Pr.
Poet Sa'di: A Persian Humanist. John D. Yohannan. (Persian Studies: No. 11). 162p. (Orig.). 1987. lib. bdg. 24.50 (ISBN 0-8191-5739-2, Pub. by Persian Heritage Foundation); pap. text ed. 11.75 (ISBN 0-8191-5740-6, Pub. by Persian Heritage Foundation). U Pr of Amer.
Poet Shen Yueh (441-513) The Reticent Marquis. Richard B. Mather. (Illus.). 192p. 1988. text ed. 42.50 (ISBN 0-691-06734-1). Princeton U Pr.
Poet to His Beloved: The Early Love Poems of W. B. Yeats. William B. Yeats. 64p. 1985. 8.95 (ISBN 0-312-61986-3). St Martin.
Poet to Poet: A Treasury of Golden Criticism. Ed. by Houston Peterson & William S. Lynch. 368p. 1983. Repr. of 1945 ed. lib. bdg. 40.00 (ISBN 0-8495-4421-1). Arden Lib.
Poet Toilers in Many Fields. Mrs. Robert A. Watson. LC 72-8528. (Essay Index Reprint Ser.). 1972. Repr. of 1884 ed. 21.00 (ISBN 0-8369-7336-4). Ayer Co Pubs.
Poet Under Saturn: The Tragedy of Verlaine. Marcel Coulon. Tr. by Edgell Rickwood. LC 77-103176. 1970. Repr. of 1932 ed. 21.50x (ISBN 0-8046-0813-X, Pub. by Kennikat). Assoc Faculty Pr.
Poet Wordsworth. W. Tuckwell. LC 76-26103. 1901. lib. bdg. 18.00 (ISBN 0-8414-8617-4). Folcroft.
Poeta Creator: Studien zu einer Figur der' antiken Dichtung. Godo Lieberg. ix, 179p. (Orig., Ger.). 1982. pap. 33.00x (ISBN 90-70265-53-2, Pub. by Gieben Amsterdam). Benjamins North Am.
Poeta y la Escultura: La Espana Que Huntington Conocio. Jose Garcia-Mazas. (Illus.). 1962. 2.50 (ISBN 0-87535-097-6). Hispanic Soc.
Poetae Comici Graeci, Vol. IV. Ed. by R. Kassel & C. Austin. 367p. (Ger.). 1983. 102.00 (ISBN 3-11-002405-5). De Gruyter.
Poetae Comici Graeci: Damoxenus - Magnes, Band V. Ed. by R. Kassel & C. Austin. xxxii, 640p. 1987. lib. bdg. 212.00 (ISBN 3-11-010922-0). De Gruyter.
Poetae Latini Minores, Leipzig, 1879-1883, 5 vols. Aemilius Bae Hrens. Ed. by Steele Commager. LC 77-70775. (Latin Poetry Ser.). 1979. Set. lib. bdg. 206.00 (ISBN 0-8240-2950-X). Garland Pub.
Poetae Melici Graeci. Ed. by Denys L. Page. 1962. 62.00x (ISBN 0-19-814333-8). Oxford U Pr.
Poetarum Melicorum Graecorum Fragmenta: Alcman, Stesichorus, Ibycus, Vol. I. Ed. by Malcolm Davies. 304p. (Lat. & Gr.). 1988. 95.00 (ISBN 0-19-814046-0). Oxford U Pr.
Poetas Cubanos: Los Vidaurreta. Ed. by Antolin G. Del Valle & Luis G. Del Valle. 180p. 1988. pap. 10.00 (ISBN 0-89295-056-0). Society Sp & Sp-Am.
Poetaster. Ben Jonson. Ed. by Josiah H. Penniman. Bd. with Stairomastix. Thomas Dekker. 456p. 1985. Repr. of 1913 ed. lib. bdg. 50.00 (ISBN 0-8414-3759-9). Folcroft.
Poetaster. Ed. by Josiah Penniman. Incl. Vol. 1 by Ben Jonson; Vol. 2, Satiromastix, by Thomas Dekker. 1913. 30.00 set (ISBN 0-8495-6287-2). Arden Lib.
Poetaster: From Quarto of 1602. Ben Jonson. Ed. by H. De Vocht. (Material for the Study of the Old English Drama Ser.: No. 2, Vol. 9). pap. 16.00 (ISBN 0-8115-0302-X). Kraus Repr.
Poetaster's Scrapbook. Lewis E. Walton. LC 84-90087. 85p. 1985. 6.95 (ISBN 0-533-06165-2). Vantage.
Poete Assassine. Guillaume Apollinaire. 12.50 (ISBN 0-685-37175-1). French & Eur.
Poete et le Shamisen: Avec: Le Poete et le Vase d'Encens, Jules ou l'Homme-aux-deux-cravates. Paul Claudel. 368p. 1970. 30.00 (ISBN 0-686-54419-6). French & Eur.
Poete Noir et Autres Textes. Antonin Artaud. 64p. 1966. 9.95 (ISBN 0-686-53835-8). French & Eur.
Poete Regarde la Croix. Paul Claudel. 290p. 1938. 8.95 (ISBN 0-686-54420-X). French & Eur.
Poetes Du XVI Siecle: Marot, Sceve, Louise Labe, J. du Bellay, Belleau, J. de Sponde, etc. 1120p. 9.95 (ISBN 0-686-56552-5). French & Eur.
Poetes Maudits. Paul M. Verlaine. LC 77-11495. (Symbolists Ser.). (Illus., Fr.). Repr. of 1888 ed. 16.50 (ISBN 0-404-16354-8). AMS Pr.
Poetess. Helen Ruggieri. LC 79-18883. 1980. 8.00 (ISBN 0-931588-09-X); pap. 3.50 (ISBN 0-931588-10-3). Allegany Mtn Pr.
Poetic Achievement of Ezra Pound. Michael Alexander. LC 78-59449. 1979. 38.00x (ISBN 0-520-03739-1); pap. 8.95 (ISBN 0-520-04507-6). U of Cal Pr.
Poetic & Legal Fiction in the Aristotelian Tradition. Kathy Eden. 240p. 1986. text ed. 28.00x (ISBN 0-691-06697-3). Princeton U Pr.
Poetic & Verse-Criticism in the Reign of Elizabeth. Felix E. Schelling. (English Literature Ser., No. 33). 1970. pap. 29.95x (ISBN 0-8383-0068-5). Haskell.
Poetic Approach to Language with Special Reference to the History of English. V. K. Gokak. LC 76-26145. 1952. 32.00 (ISBN 0-8414-4526-5). Folcroft.
Poetic Art. Paul Claudel. LC 73-86004. 1969. Repr. of 1948 ed. 21.00x (ISBN 0-8046-0607-2, Pub. by Kennikat). Assoc Faculty Pr.
Poetic Art: A Translation of Horace's "Ars Poetica". Horace. Ed. by C. H. Sission. 56p. 1975. pap. 9.50 (ISBN 0-85635-114-8). Carcanet.
Poetic Art of A. E. Housman: Theory & Practice. B. J. Leggett. LC 77-15792. xii, 161p. 1978. 15.50x (ISBN 0-8032-0969-X). U of Nebr Pr.
Poetic Artifice: A Theory of Twentieth Century Poetry. Veronica Forrest-Thompson. 1979. 26.00 (ISBN 0-312-61798-4). St Martin.
Poetic Authority: Spenser, Milton, & Literary History. John Guillory. 224p. 1983. 26.50x (ISBN 0-231-05540-4); pap. 14.00x (ISBN 0-231-05541-2). Columbia U Pr.
Poetic Avant-Garde in Poland, 1918-1939. Bogdana Carpenter. LC 83-1126. (Publications on Russia & Eastern Europe of the School of International Studies: No. 11). (Illus.). 254p. 1983. 22.50x (ISBN 0-295-95996-7). U of Wash Pr.
Poetic Closure: A Study of How Poems End. Barbara H. Smith. LC 68-15034. 1971. pap. 12.95x (ISBN 0-226-76343-9, P381, Phoen). U of Chicago Pr.
Poetic Craft in the Early Greek Elegists. A. W. H. Adkins. LC 84-16203. 250p. 1985. lib. bdg. 35.00x (ISBN 0-226-00725-1). U of Chicago Pr.
Poetic Creation: Inspiration or Craft. Carl Fehrman. Tr. by Karin Petherick from Swedish. 1980. 20.00x (ISBN 0-8166-0899-7). U of Minn Pr.
Poetic Debussy: A Collection of His Song Texts & Selected Letters. Ed. by Margaret G. Cobb. LC 81-19010. (Illus.). 340p. 1982. text ed. 22.95x (ISBN 0-930350-28-6). NE U Pr.
Poetic Dewdrops for Children. Mabel G. Haldeman. (Illus.). 304p. 1986. 12.95 (ISBN 0-9617506-0-X). Inc Trustees Gospel Worker Soc.
Poetic Dialect of Sappho & Alcaeus. rev ed. Angus M. Bowie. Ed. by W. R. Connor. LC 80-2641. (Monographs in Classical Studies). 1981. lib. bdg. 22.00 (ISBN 0-405-14029-0). Ayer Co Pubs.
Poetic Diction: A Study in Meaning. 3rd ed. Owen Barfield. LC 72-10631. 232p. 1973. pap. 12.95 (ISBN 0-8195-6026-X). Wesleyan U Pr.
Poetic Diction: A Study in Meaning. Owen Barfield. 230p. 1982. Repr. of 1975 ed. lib. bdg. 47.00 (ISBN 0-8495-0630-1). Arden Lib.
Poetic Diction: A Study of Eighteenth Century Verse. Thomas Quayle. 212p. 1980. Repr. of 1924 ed. lib. bdg. 35.50 (ISBN 0-8495-4430-0). Arden Lib.
Poetic Diction: A Study of Eighteenth Century Verse. Thomas Quayle. LC 74-13197. 1924. lib. bdg. 55.00 (ISBN 0-8414-6910-5). Folcroft.
Poetic Diction in the English Renaissance from Skelton Through Spenser. Vere L. Rubel. (MLA RFS). 1941. 39.00 (ISBN 0-527-77600-9). Kraus Repr.
Poetic Diction of Old English Meters of Boethius. Allan A. Metcalf. LC 72-94487. (De Proprietatibus Litterarum, Ser. Practica: No. 50). 164p. 1973. pap. text ed. 16.80x (ISBN 90-2792-537-2). Mouton.
Poetic Discourse: An Exercise in Stylistic Analysis. S. D. Chibber. 1987. text ed. 30.00x (ISBN 81-207-0693-5, Pub. by Sterling Pubs India). Apt Bks.
Poetic Drama. Glenda Leeming. (Modern Dramatists Ser.). 175p. 1987. 19.95 (ISBN 0-312-00858-9). St Martin.
Poetic Drama Interviews Robert Speaight, E. Martin Browne, & W. H. Auden. William B. Wahl. Ed. by James Hogg. (Poetic Drama & Poetic Theory Ser.). 107p. (Orig.). 1976. pap. 15.00 (ISBN 3-7052-0851-9, Pub. by Salzburg Studies). Longwood Pub Group.
Poetic Drama of Paul Claudel. Joseph Chiari. LC 71-90365. 1969. Repr. of 1954 ed. 25.00x (ISBN 0-87752-018-6). Gordian.
Poetic Edda. rev. ed. Tr. by Lee M. Hollander from Norse. 375p. 1986. pap. 12.95 (ISBN 0-292-76499-5). U of Tex Pr.
Poetic Edda in the Light of Archaeology. Birger Nerman. LC 76-43954. (Viking Society for Northern Research: Extra Ser.: Vol. 4). (Illus.). Repr. of 1931 ed. 30.00 (ISBN 0-404-60024-7). AMS Pr.
Poetic Edda Vol. 1: Heroic Poems. Ed. by Ursula Dronke. 1969. 39.95x (ISBN 0-19-811497-4). Oxford U Pr.
Poetic Equation: Conversations Between Nikki Giovanni & Margaret Walker. Nikki Giovanni & Margaret Walker. LC 73-85494. (Illus.). 135p. 1974. 9.95 (ISBN 0-88258-003-5). Howard U Pr.
Poetic Equation: Conversations Between Nikki Giovanni & Margaret Walker. 1983. pap. 6.95 (ISBN 0-88258-088-4). Howard U Pr.
Poetic Experience. Thomas Gilby. LC 77-15970. 1934. lib. bdg. 27.00 (ISBN 0-8414-4438-2). Folcroft.
Poetic Experience. Thomas Gilby. 114p. 1980. Repr. of 1934 ed. lib. bdg. 25.00 (ISBN 0-8492-4976-7). R West.
Poetic Experience. Joanne Harris. 1987. 5.95 (ISBN 0-533-07084-8). Vantage.
Poetic Fantasias. John A. McKinley. LC 73-151820. 192p. 1971. 9.50 (ISBN 0-87527-061-1). Green.
Poetic Fiction of Jose 'Lezama Lima. Raymond D. Souza. LC 83-1056. 192p. 1983. text ed. 20.00x (ISBN 0-8262-0406-6). U of Mo Pr.
Poetic Form & British Romanticism. Stuart Curran. 320p. 1986. 29.95x (ISBN 0-19-504019-8). Oxford U Pr.
Poetic Form in Blake's Milton. Susan Fox. LC 75-33417. 260p. 1976. 26.00x (ISBN 0-686-86666-5). Princeton U Pr.
Poetic Freedom & Poetic Truth: Chaucer, Shakespeare, Marlowe & Milton. Harriett Hawkins. 1976. 29.95x (ISBN 0-19-812071-0). Oxford U Pr.
Poetic Genius of Sri Aurobindo. K. D. Sethna. 141p. 1974. pap. 4.50 (ISBN 0-89071-285-9, Pub. by Sri Aurobindo Ashram India). Aurobindo Assn.
Poetic Heritage. John Press. 1977. Repr. of 1957 ed. 7.50. Century Bookbindery.
Poetic Identity in Guillaume de Mauchaut. Kevin Brownlee. LC 83-14498. 280p. 1984. text ed. 30.00x (ISBN 0-299-09200-3). U of Wis Pr.
Poetic Image. Cecil Day-Lewis. LC 83-45427. Repr. of 1947 ed. 22.00 (ISBN 0-404-20075-3). AMS Pr.
Poetic Image. G. C. Uhlenbeck. 67p. 1987. 70.00x (ISBN 0-317-69735-8, Pub. by Han-Shan Tang Ltd). State Mutual Bk.
Poetic Image in Six Genres. David Madden. LC 76-76189. 271p. 1969. 11.95x (ISBN 0-8093-0393-0). S Ill U Pr.
Poetic Image in Six Genres. David Madden. LC 76-76189. (Arcturus Books Paperbacks). 271p. 1969. pap. 7.95x (ISBN 0-8093-0394-9). S Ill U Pr.
Poetic Image: The Creative Power of the Visual World. C. Day Lewis. LC 84-55. 168p. 1984. pap. 4.95 (ISBN 0-87477-316-4). J P Tarcher.
Poetic Injury: The Surrealist Legacy in Post Modern Photography. Alternative Museum Staff. LC 87-72918. (Orig.). 1987. pap. 7.00 (ISBN 0-932075-17-7). Alternative Mus.
Poetic Interpretation of Nature. J. C. Shairp. LC 72-187951. 1878. lib. bdg. 25.50 (ISBN 0-8414-0570-0). Folcroft.
Poetic Justice. Amanda Cross. (YA) (gr. 7 up). 1979. pap. 2.95 (ISBN 0-380-44222-1, 82388-8). Avon.
Poetic Justice. L. A. Taylor. 1988. 16.95 (ISBN 0-8027-5701-4). Walker & Co.
Poetic Justice: A Memoir of My Father Roy Campbell. Anna C. Lyle. 156p. 60.00x (ISBN 0-930126-17-3). Typographeum.
Poetic Justice: The Funniest, Meanest Things Ever Said About Lawyers. Jonathan Roth & Edward Roth. LC 87-63575. 140p. (Orig.). 1988. pap. 8.95 (ISBN 0-87337-072-4). Nolo Pr.
Poetic Landscape: The Art & Experience of Sandford R. Gifford. Ila Weiss. LC 84-40805. (American Art Ser.). (Illus.). 384p. 1987. 75.00x (ISBN 0-87413-199-5). U Delaware Pr.
Poetic License: Authority & Authorship in Medieval & Renaissance Contexts. Jacqueline T. Miller. 192p. 1987. 24.95x (ISBN 0-19-504103-8). Oxford U Pr.
Poetic Light: Kavya Prakasha of Mammata, Vol. 1. 2nd rev. ed. Tr. by R. C. Dwivedi. 1977. pap. 11.95 (ISBN 0-89684-290-8). Orient Bk Dist.
Poetic Living. Sunnie D. Kidd & James W. Kidd. 45p. (Orig.). 1982. pap. text ed. 3.50 (ISBN 0-910727-03-1). Golden Phoenix.
Poetic Localities: Photographs of the Adironacks, Cambridge, Crete, Italy & Athens. William J. Stillman. Ed. by Anne Ehrenkranz & Linda S. Ferber. (Illus.). 128p. 1988. 29.95 (ISBN 0-89381-316-8). Aperture.
Poetic Maturing of William Morris: From the Earthly Paradise to the Pilgrim's Hope. Jessie Kocmanova. LC 72-190712. 1964. lib. bdg. 35.00 (ISBN 0-8414-5600-3). Folcroft.
Poetic Meditations. Roland R. Daneault. 64p. 1982. 4.00 (ISBN 0-682-49883-1). Exposition-Phoenix.
Poetic Memoirs of Lady Daibu. Tr. by Phillip T. Harries from Japanese. LC 79-65519. 336p. 1980. 25.00x (ISBN 0-8047-1077-5). Stanford U Pr.
Poetic Metaphysics. rev. ed. Tony Rizzo. 64p. 1983. pap. write for info. (ISBN 0-9611330-1-5). T Rizzo.
Poetic Meter & Poetic Form. rev. ed. Paul Fussell, Jr. 1979. pap. text ed. 10.50 (ISBN 0-394-32120-0, RanC). Random.
Poetic Mind. Frederick C. Prescott. LC 83-1547. xx, 308p. 1983. Repr. of 1922 ed. lib. bdg. 45.50x (ISBN 0-313-23925-8, PRPO). Greenwood.
Poetic New-World. facs. ed. Ed. by Lucy H. Humphrey. LC 75-149105. (Granger Index Reprint Ser.). 1910. 29.00 (ISBN 0-8369-6230-3). Ayer Co Pubs.
Poetic Old World. Ed. by Lucy H. Humphrey. LC 77-20395. (Granger Poetry Library Ser.). 1978. Repr. of 1908 ed. 29.50x (ISBN 0-89609-067-1). Roth Pub Inc.
Poetic Patterns in Rutebeuf: A Study in Noncourtly Poetic Modes of the Thirteenth Century. Nancy F. Regalado. LC 70-104620. (Yale Romanitc Series, Second Ser.: No. 21). pap. 96.00 (ISBN 0-317-29720-1, 2022033). Bks Demand UMI.
Poetic Pilgrimage. B. C. Diltz. LC 73-105780. 1970. Repr. of 1942 ed. 23.00x (ISBN 0-8046-0949-7, Pub. by Kennikat). Assoc Faculty Pr.
Poetic Potentials in Information of Astronomy. Polish Academy of Science. 1976. pap. 1.95 (ISBN 0-934982-05-8). Primary Pr.
Poetic Powers of Repetition. K. Lea. (Warton Lectures on English Petry). 1969. pap. 5.50 (ISBN 0-85672-350-9, Pub. by British Acad). Longwood Pub Group.
Poetic Presence & Illusion: Essays in Critical History & Theory. Murray Krieger. LC 79-14598. 1980. text ed. 35.00x (ISBN 0-8018-2199-1). Johns Hopkins.
Poetic Principles & Practice: Occasional Papers on Baudelaire, Mallarme, & Valery. Lloyd Austin. (Illus.). 350p. 1987. 49.50 (ISBN 0-521-32737-7). Cambridge U Pr.
Poetic Privilege. S. L. McKinney-Ludd. 52p. 1986. 5.95 (ISBN 0-533-06838-X). Vantage.
Poetic Process. George Whalley. LC 73-5274. 256p. 1973. Repr. of 1953 ed. lib. bdg. 35.00x (ISBN 0-8371-6878-3, WHPP). Greenwood.
Poetic Prophecy in Western Literature. Jan Wojcik & Raymond-Jean Frontain. LC 83-49339. 224p. 1984. 29.50 (ISBN 0-8386-3191-6). Fairleigh Dickinson.
Poetic Reflections. D. A. Pattie. LC 87-72042. 58p. (Orig.). 1987. pap. 1.95x (ISBN 0-911789-02-2). Pattie Prop Inc.
Poetic Remaking: The Art of Browning, Yeats, & Pound. George Bornstein. LC 87-25789. 176p. 1988. lib. bdg. 19.75x (ISBN 0-271-00620-X). Pa St U Pr.
Poetic Resemblance. Barbara Broughel. (Illus.). 24p. (Orig.). 1986. pap. write for info. (ISBN 0-936739-00-2). Hallwalls Inc.
Poetic Revolution of the Nineteen Twenties. B. B. Paliwal. 232p. 1974. text ed. 20.00x. Coronet Bks.
Poetic Romancers After Eighteen Fifty. Oliver Elton. LC 74-12473. 1914. lib. bdg. 15.00 (ISBN 0-8414-3966-4). Folcroft.

Poetic Shapes. Trina Gerson. (Illus.). 52p. (ps-7). 1981. pap. text ed. 2.95 (ISBN 0-9605878-0-2). Anirt Pr.

Poetic Statement & Critical Dogma. Gerald Graff. LC 80-14318. 208p. 1980. pap. 7.00x (ISBN 0-226-30601-1). U of Chicago Pr.

Poetic Structure of Change: A Study of the Surrealist Work of Benjamin Peret. Julia F. Costich. (Studies in the Romance Languages & Literatures: No.206). 1979. pap. 12.50x (ISBN 0-8078-9206-8). U of NC Pr.

Poetic Style of Erich Kaestner. John Winkleman. LC 57-63699. (Nebraska University Ser.: No. 13). pap. 20.00 (ISBN 0-317-08244-2, 2002886). Bks Demand UMI.

Poetic Techniques & Conceptual Elements in Ibn Zaydun's Love Poetry. Sieglinde Lug. LC 81-43813. 184p. (Orig.). 1982. lib. bdg. 30.50 (ISBN 0-8191-2515-6); pap. text ed. 12.25 (ISBN 0-8191-2516-4). U Pr of Amer.

Poetic Theology of Love: Cupid in Medieval & Renaissance Literature. Thomas Hyde. LC 84-40368. (Illus.). 216p. 1986. 29.50x (ISBN 0-87413-273-8). U Delaware Pr.

Poetic Theory & Practice of T. S. Eliot. LC 87-80659. 1987. write for info. (ISBN 0-938719-24-6). Envoy Press.

Poetic Theory of Pierre Reverdy. Robert W. Greene. LC 68-63065. 108p. 1983. Repr. of 1967 ed. lib. bdg. 19.95x (ISBN 0-89370-758-9). Borgo Pr.

Poetic Theory-Poetic Practice. Ed. by Robert Scholes. (Papers of the Midwest Modern Language Association Ser.: No. 1). viii, 174p. (Orig.). 1969. pap. 16.50x (ISBN 0-87352-170-6, MM68). Modern Lang.

Poetic Thinking: An Approach to Heidegger. David Halliburton. LC 81-7542. 1982. lib. bdg. 22.50x (ISBN 0-226-31372-7). U of Chicago Pr.

Poetic Traditions of the English Renaissance. Ed. by Maynard Mack & George D. Lord. LC 82-1941. 336p. 1982. 30.00x (ISBN 0-300-02785-0). Yale U Pr.

Poetic Truth. Robin Skelton. LC 78-57849. 131p. 1978. text ed. 26.50x (ISBN 0-06-496253-9). B&N Imports.

Poetic Truth & Transvluation in Nietzsche's Zarathustra: A Hermeneutic Study. Ernest Joos. (American University Studies V: Philosophy: Vol. 31). 172p. 1987. text ed. 28.00 (ISBN 0-8204-0432-2). P Lang Pubs.

Poetic Unreason & Other Studies. Robert Graves. LC 68-59244. 1968. Repr. of 1925 ed. 18.00 (ISBN 0-8196-0227-2). Biblo.

Poetic Values. E. A. Lamborn. 1973. lib. bdg. 25.50 (ISBN 0-8414-5765-4). Folcroft.

Poetic Values: A Guide to the Appreciation of the Golden Treasury. E. A. Lamborn. 226p. 1982. Repr. of 1928 ed. lib. bdg. 25.00 (ISBN 0-89984-805-2). Century Bookbindery.

Poetic Vision of Muriel Rukeyser. Louise Kertesz. LC 79-1131. (Illus.). xxii, 416p. 1979. text ed. 37.50 (ISBN 0-8071-0552-X). La State U Pr.

Poetic Vision of Robert Penn Warren. Victor H. Strandberg. LC 76-9503. 304p. 1977. 27.00 (ISBN 0-8131-1347-4). U Pr of Ky.

Poetic Voice of Charles Cros: A Centennial Study of His Songs. Robert L. Mitchell. LC 76-24891. (Romance Monograph: No. 21). 1976. 22.00x (ISBN 84-399-5835-8). Romance.

Poetic Workmanship of Alexander Pope. Rebecca P. Parkin. 1968. lib. bdg. 18.50x (ISBN 0-374-96270-7, Octagon). Hippocrene Bks.

Poetic Works of Flavien Ranaivo: L'Ombre et le Vent, Mes Chansons de Tourjours, Le Retour au Bercail. Flavien Ranaivo. 1962. Three works in one unit. 18.00 (ISBN 0-8115-2980-0). Kraus Repr.

Poetic Works of Pilar E. Barrios: Piel Negra, Mis Cantos, Campo Afuera. Pilar E. Barrios. 1959. Three works in one unit. 42.00 (ISBN 0-8115-2976-2). Kraus Repr.

Poetic World of Boris Pasternak. Olga R. Hughes. LC 73-2467. (Princeton Essays in Literature). 196p. 1974. 26.00x (ISBN 0-691-06262-5). Princeton U Pr.

Poetic World of William Carlos Williams. Alan Ostrom. LC 65-16536. (Crosscurrents-Modern Critiques Ser.). 191p. 1966. 6.95x (ISBN 0-8093-0217-9). S Ill U Pr.

Poetic Writings of Thomas Cradock, 1718-1770. Ed. by David C. Skaggs. LC 81-72059. (Illus.). 312p. 1983. 32.50 (ISBN 0-87413-206-1). U Delaware Pr.

Poetica de la Poblacion Marginal: Fundamentos Materialistas para una Historiografia. Hernan Vidal. (Literature & Human Rights Ser.: No. 1). 224p. (Orig., Span.). 1988. pap. 12.95 (ISBN 0-910235-19-8). Prisma Bks.

Poetica de la Poblacion Marginal: Sensibilidades Determinantes. Ed. by James V. Romano. (Literature & Human Rights Ser.: No. 2). 488p. (Orig., Span.). 1988. pap. 14.95 (ISBN 0-910235-20-1). Prisma Bks.

Poetica de la Poblacion Marginal: Teatro Poblacional, 1978-1985 (Antologia Critica) Diego Munoz. (Literature & Human Rights Ser.: No. 3). 488p. (Orig., Span.). 1988. pap. 14.95 (ISBN 0-910235-22-8). Prisma Bks.

Poetica Erotica. Ronne R. Gleason. Ed. by Bob Lewanski. (Illus.). 167p. (Orig.). 1985. 3.50 (ISBN 0-9608030-1-7). Taoist Pubs.

Poetica Erotica. Normajean MacLeod. LC 87-73493. (Illus.). v, 65p. 1988. pap. 6.00 (ISBN 0-934996-47-4). American Studies Pr.

Poetical Alphabet. Benjamin P. Blood. (Surrealist Research & Development Monograph). 24p. 1972. pap. 3.50. Black Swan Pr.

Poetical & Dramatic Works, 2 Vols. Charles Sedley. Ed. by V. De Sola Pinto. LC 70-85905. 1969. Repr. of 1928 ed. 40.00 (ISBN 0-404-05692-X). AMS Pr.

Poetical & Dramatic Works of Sir Charles Sidley, 2 vols. De Sola V. Pinto. 597p. 1980. Repr. of 1702 ed. lib. bdg. 250.00 set (ISBN 0-89984-383-2). Century Bookbindery.

Poetical & Dramatic Works of Thomas Randolph, 2 Vols. Thomas Randolph. Ed. by William C. Hazlitt. LC 68-57192. Repr. of 1875 ed. 44.00 (ISBN 0-405-08874-4). Ayer Co Pubs.

Poetical Books see Oxford Illustrated Old Testament: With Drawings by Contemporary Artists.

Poetical Career of Alexander Pope. Robert K. Root. 12.00 (ISBN 0-8446-1392-4). Peter Smith.

Poetical Dialogue of Solomon & Saturn. Solomon & Saturn. Ed. by Robert J. Menner. LC 73-12784. (MLA MS). xl, 176p. 1973. Repr. of 1941 ed. 20.00 (ISBN 0-527-84500-0). Kraus Repr.

Poetical, Dramatic, & Miscellaneous Works, 6 Vols. John Gay. LC 73-137415. Repr. of 1795 ed. Set. 180.00 (ISBN 0-404-02790-3); 30.00 ea. Vol. 1 (ISBN 0-404-02791-1). Vol. 2 (ISBN 0-404-02792-X). Vol. 3 (ISBN 0-404-02793-8). Vol. 4 (ISBN 0-404-02794-6). Vol. 5 (ISBN 0-404-02795-4). Vol. 6 (ISBN 0-404-02796-2). AMS Pr.

Poetical Expression. Edwin A. Boardman. 1973. Repr. of 1934 ed. 10.00 (ISBN 0-8274-1463-3). R West.

Poetical Favorites. Warren Snyder. 1977. Repr. of 1911 ed. 15.00. Century Bookbindery.

Poetical Favorites: Yours & Mine. facsimile ed. Compiled by Warren Snyder. LC 79-167482. (Granger Index Reprint Ser.). Repr. of 1910 ed. 24.50 (ISBN 0-8369-6287-7). Ayer Co Pubs.

Poetical Histories, Repr. Of 1671 Ed. Pierre Gautruche. Tr. by Marius D'Assigny. Bd. with Appendix De Diis et Heroibus Poeticis. Joseph de Jouvency. Repr. of 1705 ed. LC 75-27877. (Renaissance & the Gods Ser.: Vol. 32). (Illus.). 1976. lib. bdg. 88.00 (ISBN 0-8240-2081-2). Garland Pub.

Poetical Manuscripts of Mark Akenside. Mark Akenside. (Illus.). 32p. (Orig.). 1988. pap. 15.00x (ISBN 0-943184-02-9). Amherst Coll Pr.

Poetical Part in Lao-TSI. Bernhard Karlgren. 45p. 1932. pap. 210.00x (ISBN 0-317-68487-6, Pub. by Han-Shan Tang Ltd). State Mutual Bk.

Poetical Pursuit of Food: Japanese Recipes for American Cooks. Sonoko Kondo & Lou Stouman. 17.95 (ISBN 0-517-55653-7, C N Potter Bks). Crown.

Poetical Quotations from Chaucer to Tennyson. Samuel Allibone. 59.95 (ISBN 0-8490-0855-7). Gordon Pr.

Poetical Theory in Republican Rome. Lawrence Richardson. Ed. by Steele Commager. LC 77-70825. (Latin Poetry Ser.). 1978. lib. bdg. 26.00 (ISBN 0-8240-2977-1). Garland Pub.

Poetical Tributes to the Memory of Abraham Lincoln. Ed. by J. N. Plotts. 1972. Repr. of 1865 ed. lib. bdg. 20.00 (ISBN 0-8422-8105-3). Irvington.

Poetical Vagaries, Repr. Of 1812 Ed. George Colman. Bd. with Vagaries Vindicated: Or, Hypocritick Hypocriticks: a Poem Addressed to the Reviewers. Repr. of 1813 ed. LC 75-31182. (Romantic Context: Poetry 1789-1830 Ser.: Vol. 34). 1976. lib. bdg. 52.00 (ISBN 0-8240-2133-9). Garland Pub.

Poetical Works. James Beattie. LC 72-25. (Select Bibliographies Reprint Ser). 1972. Repr. of 1854 ed. 17.00 (ISBN 0-8369-9953-3). Ayer Co Pubs.

Poetical Works. James M. Bell. Ed. by Bishop Arnett. LC 70-39423. Repr. of 1901 ed. 11.00 (ISBN 0-404-00005-3). AMS Pr.

Poetical Works. William Blake. Ed. by William M. Rosetti. LC 79-13496. Repr. of 1914 ed. 21.50 (ISBN 0-404-07259-3). AMS Pr.

Poetical Works. Robert Burns. 702p. 1982. 50.00x (ISBN 0-317-39522-X, Pub. by Collets UK). State Mutual Bk.

Poetical Works. rev. ed. George Gordon Byron. Ed. by Frederick Page & John Jump. (Oxford Standard Author Ser.). (Illus.). 1979. Leatherbound o.p. 60.00 (ISBN 0-19-192822-4); pap. text ed. 11.95x (ISBN 0-19-281068-5). Oxford U Pr.

Poetical Works. Thomas Campbell. Ed. by Alfred Hill. LC 73-39665. (Select Bibliographies Reprint Ser). 1972. Repr. of 1875 ed. 19.75 (ISBN 0-8369-9932-0). Ayer Co Pubs.

Poetical Works. Charles Churchill. Ed. by Douglas Grant. 1956. 57.00x (ISBN 0-19-811316-1). Oxford U Pr.

Poetical Works. Austin Dobson. 1988. Repr. lib. bdg. 75.00x. Am Biog Serv.

Poetical Works. Ernest C. Dowson. 1980. Repr. of 1934 ed. 29.00x (ISBN 0-403-00948-0). Scholarly.

Poetical Works. Ernest C. Dowson. 1988. Repr. of 1934 ed. lib. bdg. 49.00x. Am Biog Serv.

Poetical Works, 2 vols. Ebenezer Elliott. 836p. Repr. of 1876 ed. cancelled (ISBN 3-4870-5326-8). Adlers Foreign Bks.

Poetical Works, 2 vols. Giles Fletcher & Phineas Fletcher. 1981. Repr. Set. lib. bdg. 49.00x (ISBN 0-403-00091-2). Scholarly.

Poetical Works. Patrick Hannay. (Illus.). 1875. 40.00 (ISBN 0-384-21325-1). Johnson Repr.

Poetical Works, 2 vols. John Milton. Ed. by Helen Darbishire. Incl. Vol. 1. Paradise Lost. 1952. 49.00x (ISBN 0-19-811819-8); Vol. 2. Paradise Regained, Samson Agonistes, Poems Upon Several Occasions. 1955. 49.00x (ISBN 0-19-811820-1). (Oxford English Texts Ser). Oxford U Pr.

Poetical Works. Thomas Parnell. LC 70-39664. (Select Bibliographies Reprint Ser). 1972. Repr. of 1833 ed. 17.25 (ISBN 0-8369-9942-8). Ayer Co Pubs.

Poetical Works. Alexander Pope. Ed. by Herbert Davis. (Oxford Paperback Ser.). 1966. 35.00 (ISBN 0-19-254155-2); pap. 10.95x (ISBN 0-19-281246-7). Oxford U Pr.

Poetical Works, 2 Vols. George Sandys. Ed. by R. Hooper. 1968. Repr. of 1872 ed. Set. cancelled (ISBN 0-685-05273-7). Adlers Foreign Bks.

Poetical Works. Percy Bysshe Shelley. Ed. by Thomas Hutchinson & G. M. Matthews. (Oxford Standard Authors Ser). 1971. 32.50x (ISBN 0-19-254143-9); leather bd. 75.00. Oxford U Pr.

Poetical Works. William Shenstone. 1854. Repr. 15.00x (ISBN 0-403-00124-2). Scholarly.

Poetical Works. Edmund Spenser. Ed. by J. C. Smith & Ernest De Selincourt. (Oxford Paperback Ser.). pap. 12.95x (ISBN 0-19-281070-7). Oxford U Pr.

Poetical Works. Jonathan Swift. Ed. by Herbert Davis. (Oxford Standard Authors Ser). 1967. 37.50 (ISBN 0-19-254161-7). Oxford U Pr.

Poetical Works, 2 Vols. John Trumbull. LC 30-20909. 1968. Repr. of 1820 ed. Set. 59.00x (ISBN 0-403-00049-1). Scholarly.

Poetical Works. John Trumbull. 1988. Repr. of 1820 ed. lib. bdg. 59.00x. Am Biog Serv.

Poetical Works, 5 vols. William Wordsworth. Ed. by Ernest De Selincourt & Helen Darbishire. Incl. Vol. 1. 1940. (ISBN 0-19-811827-9); Vol. 2. 2nd ed. 1952. (ISBN 0-19-811828-7); Vol. 3. 2nd ed. 1954. (ISBN 0-19-811829-5); Vol. 4. 1947. 67.00x (ISBN 0-19-811830-9); Vol. 5. 1949. 67.00x (ISBN 0-19-811831-7). (Oxford English Texts Ser.). Oxford U Pr.

Poetical Works, 2 vols. Edward Young. 1970. Vol. 2. lib. bdg. 18.75 (ISBN 0-8371-2923-0, YOPY). Greenwood.

Poetical Works & Other Writings of John Keats, 8 Vols. rev. & enl. ed. John Keats. Ed. by H. Buxton Forman & Maurice B. Forman. LC 79-114094. 2520p. (Facsimile Reprint of the Hampstead Edition). 1970. Repr. of 1938 ed. Set. text ed. 225.00x (ISBN 0-87753-047-5). Phaeton.

Poetical Works: Definitive Edition, 2 vols. John Payne. LC 73-128418. Repr. of 1902 ed. Set. 75.00 (ISBN 0-404-04946-X). Vol. 1 (ISBN 0-404-04947-8). Vol. 2 (ISBN 0-404-04948-6). AMS Pr.

Poetical Works Eighteen Thirty-Three to Eighteen Sixty-Four. Robert Browning. Ed. by Ian Jack. (Oxford Standard Authors Ser.). 1970. Repr. of 1970 ed. 29.95 (ISBN 0-19-254165-X, OPB 355). Oxford U Pr.

Poetical Works, Eighteen Thirty-Three to Eighteen Sixty-Four: Blue Morocco Edition. Robert Browning. Ed. by Ian Jack. (Standard Authors Ser.). 968p. 1987. 125.00 (ISBN 0-19-194002-X). Oxford U Pr.

Poetical Works of Ann Radcliffe, 2 vols. Ann Radcliffe. LC 70-37714. Repr. of 1834 ed. 85.00 set (ISBN 0-404-56805-X); 42.50 ea. (ISBN 0-686-57611-X). AMS Pr.

Poetical Works of Anna Seward: With Extracts from Her Literary Correspondence, 3 vols. Anna Seward. Ed. by Walter Scott. LC 70-37722. (Women of Letters). Repr. of 1810 ed. Set. 120.00 (ISBN 0-404-56850-5). AMS Pr.

Poetical Works of Arthur Hugh Clough: With a Memoir. Francis T. Palgrave. 1979. Repr. lib. bdg. 25.00 (ISBN 0-8492-2158-7). R West.

Poetical Works of Beattie, Blair, & Falconer. James Beattie. Ed. by George Gilfillian. LC 73-144580. Repr. of 1854 ed. 13.50 (ISBN 0-404-08552-0). AMS Pr.

Poetical Works of Bowles, Lamb & Hartley Coleridge. Hartley Coleridge. Ed. by William Tirebuck. 1887. 20.00 (ISBN 0-8274-3170-8). R West.

Poetical Works of Bowles, Lamb, & Hartley Coleridge. Ed. by William Tirebuck. 1978. lib. bdg. 20.00 (ISBN 0-8495-5120-X). Arden Lib.

Poetical Works of Bret Harte. Bret Harte. 1912. 25.00 (ISBN 0-932062-77-6). Sharon Hill.

Poetical Works of Burns. Robert Burns. (Cambridge Editions Ser.). 1974. 25.00 (ISBN 0-395-18486-X). HM.

Poetical Works of Byron. George Gordon Byron. Intro. by Robert F. Gleckner. LC 75-4909. (Cambridge Editions Ser.). 1975. 29.50 (ISBN 0-395-20431-3). HM.

Poetical Works of Charles Mackay. Charles Mackay. LC 70-144452. Repr. of 1876 ed. 25.00 (ISBN 0-404-08564-4). AMS Pr.

Poetical Works of Christina Georgina Rossetti. LC 77-3038. 1977. Repr. of 1904 ed. lib. bdg. 97.50 (ISBN 0-8414-7204-1). Folcroft.

Poetical Works of Christopher Smart: A Translation of the Psalms of David, Vol. III. Christopher Smart. Ed. by Marcus Walsh. 388p. 1988. 92.00 (ISBN 0-19-812771-5). Oxford U Pr.

Poetical Works of Christopher Smart, Volume I: Jubilate Agno. Christopher Smart. Ed. by Karina Williamson. (English Texts Ser.). (Illus.). 1980. 47.00x (ISBN 0-19-811869-4). Oxford U Pr.

Poetical Works of Christopher Smart, Vol. IV: Miscellaneous Poems, English & Latin. Ed. by Karina Williamson. (Illus.). 496p. 1987. 92.00 (ISBN 0-19-812768-5). Oxford U Pr.

Poetical Works of Christopher Smart: Vol. II: Religious Poetry, 1763-1771. Christopher Smart. Ed. by Karina Williamson & Marcus Walsh. LC 79-41319. (Oxford English Texts Ser.). 1983. 67.00x (ISBN 0-19-812767-7). Oxford U Pr.

Poetical Works of Dante Gabriel Rossetti. Dante G. Rossetti. LC 77-8806. Repr. of 1903 ed. lib. bdg. 79.50 (ISBN 0-8414-7312-9). Folcroft.

Poetical Works of David Garrick, 2 Vols. David Garrick. LC 68-21214. 1968. Repr. of 1785 ed. Set. 33.00 (ISBN 0-405-08553-2); 22.00 ea. Vol. 1 (ISBN 0-405-08554-0). Vol. 2 (ISBN 0-405-08555-9). Ayer Co Pubs.

Poetical Works of Edward Rowland Sill. 423p. 1981. Repr. of 1867 ed. lib. bdg. 20.00 (ISBN 0-89984-413-8). Century Bookbindery.

Poetical Works of Edward Rowland Sill. Edward R. Sill. LC 72-4972. (Romantic Tradition in American Literature Ser.). 462p. 1972. Repr. of 1906 ed. 35.50 (ISBN 0-405-04642-1). Ayer Co Pubs.

Poetical Works of Edward Rowland Sill. Edward R. Sill. 1978. Repr. of 1867 ed. lib. bdg. 27.50 (ISBN 0-8492-8058-3). R West.

Poetical Works of Edward Taylor. Edward Taylor. Ed. by Thomas H. Johnson. 1944. pap. 12.50x (ISBN 0-691-01275-X). Princeton U Pr.

Poetical Works of Elizabeth Barrett Browning. Elizabeth Barrett Browning. (Cambridge Editions Ser.). 1974. 22.95 (ISBN 0-395-18012-0). HM.

Poetical Works of Elizabeth Margaret Chandler. facs. ed. Elizabeth M. Chandler. LC 71-83930. (Black Heritage Library Collection Ser). 1836. 12.25 (ISBN 0-8369-8534-6). Ayer Co Pubs.

Poetical Works of Fitz-Green Halleck. J. G. Wilson. 59.95 (ISBN 0-8490-0856-5). Gordon Pr.

Poetical Works of Gavin Douglas, Bishop of Dunkeld, 4 vols. Gavin Douglas. Ed. by J. Small. (Illus.). 1970. Repr. of 1874 ed. Set. cancelled (ISBN 3-4870-3095-0). Adlers Foreign Bks.

Poetical Works of Geoffrey Chaucer, 6 Vols. Geoffrey Chaucer. Ed. by Harris Nicolas. LC 72-971. Repr. of 1845 ed. Set. 210.00 (ISBN 0-404-01560-3); 35.00 ea. AMS Pr.

Poetical Works of Geoffrey Chaucer, 6 vols. Ed. by Richard Morris. Repr. of 1891 ed. Set. lib. bdg. 150.00 (ISBN 0-8492-6845-1). R West.

Poetical Works of Geoffrey Chaucer: A Facsimile of Cambridge Library MS GG.4.27. Minor Poems, Troilus & Criseyde, the Canterbury Tales, the Legend of Good Women, 3 vols. set. Geoffrey Chaucer. 1980. Set. 550.00x (ISBN 0-85991-070-9). Pilgrim Bks OK.

Poetical Works of George Crabbe. George Crabbe. Ed. by A. J. Caryle & R. M. Caryle. LC 33-27214. 1971. Repr. of 1932 ed. 79.00x (ISBN 0-403-00908-1). Scholarly.

Poetical Works of Hector Macneill, 2 Vols. Hector Macneill. LC 74-144453. Repr. of 1806 ed. Set. 13.50 (ISBN 0-404-08565-2); 7.00 ea. Vol. 1 (ISBN 0-404-08566-0). Vol. 2 (ISBN 0-404-08567-9). AMS Pr.

Poetical Works of Henry Howard, Earl of Surry, Minor Contemporaneous Poets & Thomas Sackville, Lord Buckhurst. Henry Howard. Ed. by Robert Bell. Repr. 45.00 (ISBN 0-8274-3171-6). R West.

Poetical Works of James Madison Bell. facs. ed. James M. Bell. LC 78-133148. (Black Heritage Library Collection). 1901. 14.75 (ISBN 0-8369-8704-7). Ayer Co Pubs.

Poetical Works of James Russell Lowell. James R. Lowell. Rev. by Marjorie Kaufman. (Cambridge Edns.). 15.00 (ISBN 0-395-25726-3). HM.

Poetical Works of James Thomson. John Thomson. LC 73-145328. 1971. Repr. 49.00x (ISBN 0-403-01239-2). Scholarly.

Poetical Works of John Greenleaf Whittier. Ed. by W. Garrett Horder. 598p. 1986. Repr. of 1905 ed. lib. bdg. 59.50 (ISBN 0-8495-5929-4). Arden Lib.

Poetical Works of John Greenleaf Whittier with Notes, Index of First Lines & Chronological List. Ed. by W. Garrett Horder. 598p. 1986. Repr. of 1920 ed. lib. bdg. 65.00 (ISBN 0-89987-416-9). Darby Bks.

Poetical Works of John Keats. John Keats. Ed. by Heathcote W. Garrod. (Oxford Standard Authors Ser.). 1956. o.p 27.50x (ISBN 0-19-254132-3); leatherbound 60.00 (ISBN 0-19-192832-1); pap. 8.95x (ISBN 0-19-281067-7). Oxford U Pr.

Poetical Works of John Keats. 2nd ed. John Keats. Ed. by Heathcote W. Garrod. (Oxford English Texts Ser). 1958. 56.00x (ISBN 0-19-811815-5). Oxford U Pr.

Poetical Works of John Milton, 6 Vols. John Milton. Ed. by Egerton Brydges. LC 75-172735. (Illus.). Repr. of 1835 ed. Set. 195.00 (ISBN 0-404-04380-1); 32.50 ea. Vol. 1 (ISBN 0-404-04381-X). Vol. 2 (ISBN 0-404-04382-8). Vol. 3 (ISBN 0-404-04383-6). Vol. 4 (ISBN 0-404-04384-4). Vol. 5 (ISBN 0-404-04385-2). Vol. 6 (ISBN 0-404-04386-0). AMS Pr.

Poetical Works of John Milton - with Notes of Various Authors 7 Vols. 2nd ed. John Milton. LC 71-115361. Repr. of 1909 ed. Set. 315.00 (ISBN 0-404-04370-4); 45.00 ea. AMS Pr.

Poetical Works of John Milton, with the Principal Notes of Various Commentators, 6 Vols. John Milton. LC 72-1734. (Illus.). Repr. of 1801 ed. Set. 182.00 (ISBN 0-404-04390-9); 26.00 ea. AMS Pr.

Poetical Works of John Skelton, 2 Vols. John Skelton. Ed. by Alexander Dyce. LC 75-133856. Repr. of 1843 ed. 120.00 (ISBN 0-404-06105-2). AMS Pr.

Poetical Works of John Townsend Trowbridge. John T. Trowbridge. LC 72-4978. (Romantic Tradition in American Literature Ser.). 372p. 1972. Repr. of 1903 ed. 29.00 (ISBN 0-405-04647-2). Ayer Co Pubs.

Poetical Works of Keats. John Keats. Intro. by Paul D. Sheats. LC 74-26951. (Cambridge Editions Ser.). 512p. 1975. 25.00 (ISBN 0-395-18015-5). HM.

Poetical Works of Leigh Hunt. Leigh Hunt. Ed. by H. S. Milford. LC 75-41147. Repr. of 1923 ed. 44.50 (ISBN 0-404-14556-6). AMS Pr.

Poetical Works of Lionel Johnson. Lionel P. Johnson. LC 75-28820. Repr. of 1915 ed. 31.25 (ISBN 0-404-13812-8). AMS Pr.

Poetical Works of Longfellow. rev. new ed. Henry Wadsworth Longfellow. Intro. by George Monteiro. (Cambridge Editions Ser.). 1975. 25.00 (ISBN 0-395-18487-8). HM.

Poetical Works of Marcus Garvey. Ed. by Tony Martin. LC 83-61114. (New Marcus Garvey Library: No. 2). (Illus.). viii, 123p. 1983. 17.95 (ISBN 0-912469-02-1); pap. 4.95 (ISBN 0-912469-03-X). Majority Pr.

Poetical Works of Mark Akenside. Mark Akenside. Ed. by Alexander Dyce. LC 71-94924. Repr. of 1845 ed. 15.00 (ISBN 0-404-00299-4). AMS Pr.

Poetical Works of Matthew Arnold. Matthew Arnold. 1978. Repr. of 1893 ed. lib. bdg. 30.00 (ISBN 0-8495-0018-4). Arden Lib.

Poetical Works of Oliver Wendell Holmes. Oliver W. Holmes. Intro. by Eleanor M. Tilton. LC 74-30148. (Cambridge Editions Ser.). 496p. 1975. 12.50 (ISBN 0-395-18497-5). HM.

Poetical Works of Oliver Wendell Holmes. 426p. 1981. Repr. of 1899 ed. lib. bdg. 35.00 (ISBN 0-89987-380-4). Darby Bks.

Poetical Works of Patrick Hannay. Patrick Hannay. LC 68-21217. 1968. Repr. of 1875 ed. 20.00 (ISBN 0-405-08596-6, Blom Pubns). Ayer Co Pubs.

Poetical Works of Robert Bridges, Excluding the Eight Dramas. 2nd ed. Robert S. Bridges. LC 75-41036. (BCL Ser. II). Repr. of 1936 ed. 28.00 (ISBN 0-404-14511-6). AMS Pr.

Poetical Works of Robert Bridges: Excluding the Eight Dramas. 472p. 1983. Repr. of 1912 ed. lib. bdg. 49.00 (ISBN 0-89987-956-X). Darby Bks.

Poetical Works of Robert Browning. Robert Browning. (Cambridge Editions Ser.). 1974. 35.00 (ISBN 0-395-18485-1). HM.

Poetical Works of Robert Browning, 2 Vols. Robert Browning. Ed. by Margaret Smith & Ian Jack. (Oxford English Texts Ser.). 1982. Vol. 1. 92.00x (ISBN 0-19-811893-7); Vol. 2. 95.00x (ISBN 0-19-812317-5). Oxford U Pr.

Poetical Works of Robert Browning, Vol. III: Bells & Pomegranates I-VI (Including Pippa Passes & Dramatic Lyrics) Robert Browning. Ed. by Ian Jack & Rowena Fowler. (English Texts Ser.). 560p. 1988. 115.00 (ISBN 0-19-812762-6). Oxford U Pr.

Poetical Works of Robert Southey, 10 vols. in 5. Robert Southey. LC 76-7328. Repr. of 1884 ed. 225.00 set (ISBN 0-404-15180-9). AMS Pr.

Poetical Works of Rupert Brooke. Brooke. 15.95 (ISBN 0-8488-0351-5). Amereon Ltd.

Poetical Works of Rupert Brooke. Rupert Brooke. 216p. 1970. pap. 6.95 (ISBN 0-571-04704-1). Faber & Faber.

Poetical Works of Samuel Butler, 2 vols. 1980. Repr. lib. bdg. 40.00 ea. Vol.1, 278p. Vol. 2, 302p. Century Bookbindery.

Poetical Works of Samuel Taylor Coleridge, 2 vols. Samuel Taylor Coleridge. Ed. by T. Ashe. 1890. 50.00 set (ISBN 0-8274-3172-4). R West.

Poetical Works of Shelley. rev. ed. Percy Bysshe Shelley. Intro. by Newell F. Ford. LC 74-11133. (Cambridge Editions Ser.). 704p. 1975. 16.95 (ISBN 0-395-18461-4). HM.

Poetical Works of Sir John Denham. 2nd ed. John Denham. Ed. by Theodore H. Banks. xviii, 362p. 1969. 35.00 (ISBN 0-208-00155-7, Archon). Shoe String.

Poetical Works of Sir Thomas Wyatt. facs. ed. Thomas Wyatt. LC 76-119967. (Select Bibliographies Reprint Ser). 1854. 21.50 (ISBN 0-8369-5410-6). Ayer Co Pubs.

Poetical Works of Taras Shevchenko. Tr. by C. H. Andrusyshen & Watson Kirkconnell. LC 66-2188. (Illus.). 1964. 25.00x (ISBN 0-8020-3114-5). U of Toronto Pr.

Poetical Works of Tennyson. Alfred Tennyson. LC 74-1151. (Cambridge Editions Ser.). 736p. 1974. 25.00 (ISBN 0-395-18014-7). HM.

Poetical Works of Thomas Chatterton, 2 Vols. Thomas Chatterton. Ed. by W. W. Skeat. LC 68-59008. (BCL Ser.: No. I). Repr. of 1875 ed. Set. 75.00 (ISBN 0-404-01484-4). AMS Pr.

Poetical Works of Thomas Hood (The Lansdowne Poets) Thomas Hood. 615p. 1986. Repr. lib. bdg. 35.00 (ISBN 0-8492-5357-8). R West.

Poetical Works of Thomas MacDonagh. Thomas MacDonagh. LC 75-28822. Repr. of 1916 ed. 20.00 (ISBN 0-404-13814-4). AMS Pr.

Poetical Works of Thomas Moore. Thomas Moore. Ed. by A. D. Godley. LC 75-41197. Repr. of 1929 ed. 42.50 (ISBN 0-404-14688-0). AMS Pr.

Poetical Works of Thomas Moore, 10 vols. Thomas Moore. 1980. Repr. of 1840 ed. lib. bdg. 300.00 (ISBN 0-89987-599-8). Century Bookbindery.

Poetical Works of Whittier. rev. ed. John Greenleaf Whittier. Ed. & intro. by Hyatt H. Waggoner. (Cambridge Editions Ser.). 1975. 29.95 (ISBN 0-395-21599-4). HM.

Poetical Works of Wilfrid Scawen Blunt, 2 Vols. Wilfrid S. Blunt. LC 14-22324. 1968. Repr. of 1914 ed. Set. 59.00 (ISBN 0-403-00110-2). Scholarly.

Poetical Works of William Blake. John Sampson. LC 77-20904. 1977. Repr. of 1905 ed. lib. bdg. 40.00 (ISBN 0-89341-198-1). Longwood Pub Group.

Poetical Works of William Blake. John Sampson. 384p. 1978. Repr. of 1905 ed. 22.50 (ISBN 0-87928-099-9). Corner Hse.

Poetical Works of William Blake, Vols. 1 & 2. Ed. by Edwin J. Ellis. 1980. Repr. of 1906 ed. lib. bdg. 175.00 set (ISBN 0-8495-1342-1). Arden Lib.

Poetical Works of William Cowper. 4th ed. William Cowper. Ed. by H. S. Milford. LC 75-41066. (BCL Ser. II). Repr. of 1934 ed. 42.50 (ISBN 0-404-14525-6). AMS Pr.

Poetical Works of William Cullen Bryant. William C. Bryant. LC 79-85192. 1969. Repr. of 1903 ed. 42.50 (ISBN 0-404-01143-8). AMS Pr.

Poetical Works of William Drummond of Hawthornden, 2 Vols. W. Drummond. Ed. by L. E. Kastner. LC 68-24906. (Studies in Poetry, No. 38). 1969. Repr. of 1913 ed. lib. bdg. 89.95x (ISBN 0-8383-0157-6). Haskell.

Poetical Works of William Wordsworth, 8 vols. William Wordsworth. Ed. by William Knight. 1882. 300.00 set (ISBN 0-8274-3173-2). R West.

Poetical Works of Wordsworth. rev. ed. Ed. by Paul D. Sheats. (Cambridge Edition Ser.). 992p. 1982. 25.00 (ISBN 0-395-18496-7). HM.

Poetical Works with Introduction & Notes. new rev ed. William Wordsworth. Ed. by Thomas Hutchinson & Ernest De Selincourt. (Oxford Standard Authors Ser.). 1950. pap. 35.00 (ISBN 0-19-254152-8); pap. 11.50x (ISBN 0-19-281052-9, OPB). Oxford U Pr.

Poetical Works: With Memoir & Notes by William Michael Rossetti. Christina Rossetti. 1904. 85.00 (ISBN 0-686-17757-6). Ridgeway Bks.

Poetical Writings of Fitz-Greene Halleck with Extracts from Those of Joseph Rodman Drake. Fitz-Greene Halleck. Ed. by James G. Wilson. LC 70-80010. Repr. of 1869 ed. 28.00 (ISBN 0-404-03047-5). AMS Pr.

Poetics. Aristotle. 1978. Repr. of 1963 ed. 8.95x (ISBN 0-460-00901-X, Evman). Biblio Dist.

Poetics. Aristotle. Bd. with On the Sublime. Longinus; On Style. Demetrius. (Loeb Classical Library: No. 199). 12.50x (ISBN 0-674-99219-9). Harvard U Pr.

Poetics. Aristotle. 1968. 19.95x (ISBN 0-19-814024-X). Oxford U Pr.

Poetics. Aristotle. Tr. by Gerald F. Else. LC 67-11980. 1967. pap. 8.95 (ISBN 0-472-06166-6). U of Mich Pr.

Poetics. Aristotle. 1970. pap. 8.95 (166, AA). U of Mich Pr.

Poetics. Aristotle. Tr. by Richard Janko from Greek. (HPC Philosophical Classics Ser.). 268p. 1987. lib. bdg. 27.50 (ISBN 0-87220-034-5); pap. 6.95 (ISBN 0-87220-033-7). Hackett Pub.

Poetics. Eneas S. Dallas. 294p. 1980. Repr. of 1852 ed. lib. bdg. 40.00 (ISBN 0-8495-1118-6). Arden Lib.

Poetics. Rostam Keyan. LC 77-9221. 130p. 1979. 8.95 (ISBN 0-8022-2216-1). Philos Lib.

Poetics: An Essay on Poetry. E. S. Dallas. LC 72-13006. 1973. Repr. of 1852 ed. lib. bdg. 45.00 (ISBN 0-8414-1037-2). Folcroft.

Poetics: An Essay on Poetry. Eneas S. Dallas. (Classics in Art & Literary Criticism, House Ser.). Repr. of 1852 ed. 27.00 (ISBN 0-384-11435-0). Johnson Repr.

Poetics: An Essay on Poetry, London 1852. Eneas S. Dallas. Ed. by Fredeman et al. (Victoria Muse Ser.). 302p. 1986. lib. bdg. 40.00 (ISBN 0-8240-8603-1). Garland Pub.

Poetics & Dramaturgy: Some Concepts of Alamkara-Sastra. 2nd ed. V. Raghavan. 1973. 8.00 (ISBN 0-8356-7298-0). Theos Pub Hse.

Poetics of a Fictional Historian: A Synchronic-Diachronic Approach with a Focus on Alexandros Kotzias in the Context of European Fiction. Christos S. Romanos. LC 73-49255. (American University Studies III (Comparative Literature): Vol. 7). 202p. 1984. text ed. 28.00 (ISBN 0-8204-0088-2). P Lang Pubs.

Poetics of Ariosto. Marianne Shapiro. LC 87-25307. 279p. 1988. 32.50x (ISBN 0-8143-1894-0). Wayne St U Pr.

Poetics of Aristotle. Aristotle. Tr. by Preston H. Epps. xii, 70p. 1967. pap. 4.95x (ISBN 0-8078-4017-3). U of NC Pr.

Poetics of Aristotle. Lane Cooper. LC 63-10307. (Our Debt to Greece & Rome Ser). 157p. 1963. Repr. of 1930 ed. 18.50x (ISBN 0-8154-0053-5). Cooper Sq.

Poetics of Aristotle in England. Marvin J. Herrick. LC 76-12455. 206p. 1976. 19.50x (ISBN 0-87753-061-0). Phaeton.

Poetics of Aristotle: Translation & Commentary. Aristotle & Stephen Halliwell. 206p. 1987. 29.95X (ISBN 0-8078-1763-5); pap. 8.95X (ISBN 0-8078-4203-6). U of NC Pr.

Poetics of Ascent: Theories of Language in a Rabbinic Ascent Text. Naomi Janowitz. Ed. by Michael Fishbane et al. (Judaica - Hermeneutics, Mysticism & Religion Ser.). 176p. 1988. 39.50 (ISBN 0-88706-636-4); pap. 12.95x (ISBN 0-88706-637-2). State U NY Pr.

Poetics of Belief: Studies in Coleridge, Arnold, Pater, Santayana, Stevens & Heidegger. Nathan A. Scott. LC 84-20801. (Studies in Religion). 210p. 1985. 26.00x (ISBN 0-8078-1633-7). U of NC Pr.

Poetics of Biblical Narrative. Robert W. Funk. (Foundations & Facets Ser.). 288p. 1988. pap. 19.95 (ISBN 0-944344-04-6). Polebridge Pr.

Poetics of Biblical Narrative. Meir Sternberg. (Literary Biblical Ser.). 380p. cancelled (ISBN 0-8245-0640-5). Crossroad NY.

Poetics of Biblical Narrative: Ideological Literature & the Drama of Reading. Meir Sternberg. LC 85-42752. (Indiana Studies in Biblical Literature). 596p. 1985. 57.50x (ISBN 0-253-34521-9); pap. 15.00x (ISBN 0-253-20453-4). Ind U Pr.

Poetics of Byron's Comedy in 'Don Juan' John Cunningham & James Hogg. (Romantic Reassessment ser.). 242p. (Orig.). 1982. pap. 15.00 (ISBN 3-7052-0582-X, Pub. by Salzburg Studies). Longwood Pub Group.

Poetics of Cavafy: Textuality, Eroticism, History. Gregory Jusdanis. LC 87-3390. 200p. 1987. text ed. 29.00 (ISBN 0-691-06720-1). Princeton U Pr.

Poetics of Change: The New Spanish-American Narrative. Julio Ortega. Tr. by Galen D. Greaser. (Texas Pan American Ser.). 200p. 1984. text ed. 20.00x (ISBN 0-292-76488-X). U of Tex Pr.

Poetics of Change: The New Spanish-American Narrative. Julio Ortega. Tr. by Galen D. Greaser. 200p. 1988. pap. 8.95 (ISBN 0-292-76508-8). U of Tex Pr.

Poetics of Children's Literature. Zohar Shavit. LC 85-1110. 232p. 1986. 25.00x (ISBN 0-8203-0790-4). U of Ga Pr.

Poetics of Composition: The Structure of the Poetic Text & Typology of a Compositional Form. Boris Uspensky. Tr. by Valentina Zavarin & Susan Wittig. 199p. 1973. pap. 10.95x (ISBN 0-520-04788-5). U of Cal Pr.

Poetics of Conversion: Number Symbolism & Alchemy in Gottfried's "Tristan". Susan L. Clark & Julian N. Wasserman. (Utah Studies in Literature & Linguistics: Vol. 7). 168p. 1977. pap. 20.90 (ISBN 3-261-02085-7). P Lang Pubs.

Poetics of Disguise: The Autobiography of the Work in Homer, Dante, & Shakespeare. Franco Ferrucci. Tr. by Ann Dunnigan from Ital. LC 80-11242. 178p. 1980. 24.50x (ISBN 0-8014-1262-5). Cornell U Pr.

Poetics of Ecstasy. Willis Barnstone. 331p. 1983. 45.00 (ISBN 0-8419-0814-1); pap. 17.50 (ISBN 0-8419-0849-4). Holmes & Meier.

Poetics of Epiphany: Nineteenth Century Origins of the Modern Literary Moment. Ashton Nichols. LC 86-16042. 288p. 1987. 29.95 (ISBN 0-8173-0327-8). U of Ala Pr.

Poetics of Experiment: A Study of the Work of George Perec. Warren F. Jr. Motte. LC 83-81599. (French Forum Monographs: 51). 163p. (Orig.). 1984. pap. 12.95x (ISBN 0-917058-51-8). French Forum.

Poetics of Expressiveness: A Theory & Application. Yuri Shcheglov & Alexander Zholkovsky. LC 86-3572. (Linguistic & Literary Studies in Eastern Europe: Vol. 18). x, 362p. 1987. 74.00x (ISBN 90-272-1522-7). Benjamins North Am.

Poetics of Gardens. William Mitchell et al. (Illus.). 288p. 1988. 35.00 (ISBN 0-262-13231-1). MIT Pr.

Poetics of Gender. Ed. & intro. by Nancy K. Miller. LC 85-29904. 272p. 1986. 29.00 (ISBN 0-231-06310-5). Columbia U Pr.

Poetics of Gender. Ed. by Nancy K. Miller. LC 85-29904. (Gender & Culture Ser.). (Illus.). 303p. 1987. pap. text ed. 12.50 (ISBN 0-231-06311-3). Columbia U Pr.

Poetics of Greek Tragedy. Malcolm Heath. LC 86-63248. 250p. 1987. text ed. 32.50x (ISBN 0-8047-1398-7). Stanford U Pr.

Poetics of Impersonality: T. S. Eliot & Ezra Pound. Maud Ellmann. LC 87-7422. 224p. 1987. text ed. 22.50x (ISBN 0-674-67858-3). Harvard U Pr.

Poetics of Indeterminacy. Majorie Perloff. pap. 14.95 (ISBN 0-8101-0661-2). Northwestern U Pr.

Poetics of Indeterminacy: Rimbaud to Cage. Marjorie Perloff. LC 80-8569. (Illus.). 360p. 1981. 31.00x (ISBN 0-691-06462-8). Princeton U Pr.

Poetics of Influence: New & Selected Criticism of Harold Bloom. Harold Bloom. Ed. & intro. by John Hollander. 500p. Date not set. price not set (ISBN 0-939681-00-5); pap. 19.95 (ISBN 0-939681-01-3). H R Schwab.

Poetics of Jacobean Drama. Coburn Freer. LC 81-47599. 288p. 1982. text ed. 29.50x (ISBN 0-8018-2545-8). Johns Hopkins.

Poetics of Love: Meditations with John of the Cross. Mary E. Giles. (American University Studies VII-Theology & Religion). 177p. 1987. text ed. 28.00 (ISBN 0-8204-0321-0). P Lang Pubs.

Poetics of Manhood: Contest & Identity in Cretan Mountain Village. Michael Herzfeld. LC 84-26530. (Illus.). 330p. 1985. 39.50x (ISBN 0-691-09410-1); pap. 15.50 (ISBN 0-691-10244-9). Princeton U Pr.

Poetics of Murder: Detective Fiction & Literary Theory. Ed. by Glenn W. Most & William W. Stowe. LC 82-23429. 416p. 1983. 22.95 (ISBN 0-15-172280-3). HarBraceJ.

Poetics of Murder: Detective Fiction & Literary Theory. Ed. by Glenn W. Most & William W. Stowe. LC 82-23429. 416p. 1983. pap. 9.95 (ISBN --15-672312-3, Harv). HarBraceJ.

Poetics of Music in the Form of Six Lessons. Igor Stravinsky. LC 79-99520. (Charles Eliot Norton Lectures Ser: 1939-1940). (Fr. & Eng.). 1970. pap. 6.95 (ISBN 0-674-67856-7). Harvard U Pr.

Poetics of Nikki Bungaku: A Comparison of the Traditions, Conventions & Structure of Heian Diary Literature with Western Autobiographical Writing. Marilyn J. Miller. LC 84-48371. (Comparative Literature Ser.). 403p. 1985. lib. bdg. 55.00 (ISBN 0-8240-6704-5). Garland Pub.

Poetics of Plot: The Case of English Renaissance Drama. Thomas G. Pavel. LC 84-15663. (Theory & History of Literature Ser.: Vol. 18). 192p. 1985. 29.50x (ISBN 0-8166-1374-5); pap. 12.95 (ISBN 0-8166-1375-3). U of Minn Pr.

Poetics of Postmodernism: History, Theory & Fiction. Linda Hutcheon. 300p. 1988. text ed. 45.00 (ISBN 0-415-00705-4); pap. text ed. 14.95 (ISBN 0-415-00706-2). Routledge Chapman & Hall.

Poetics of Prose. Tzvetan Todorov. Tr. by Richard Howard. LC 76-28124. 272p. 1977. 32.50x (ISBN 0-8014-0857-1); pap. 9.95x (ISBN 0-8014-9165-7). Cornell U Pr.

Poetics of Protest: Literary Form & Political Implication in the Victim-of-Society Novel. George Goodin. 232p. 1985. text ed. 19.95x (ISBN 0-8093-1173-9). S Ill U Pr.

Poetics of Quotation in the European Novel. Herman Meyer. Tr. by Y. Ziolkowski & T. Ziolkowski. LC 65-17152. 1968. 34.00x (ISBN 0-691-06094-0). Princeton U Pr.

Poetics of Reading: Approaches to the Novel. Inge C. Wimmers. 168p. 1988. 28.95 (ISBN 0-691-06742-2); pap. 15.50 (ISBN 0-691-01447-7). Princeton U Pr.

Poetics of Reverie: Childhood, Language & the Cosmos. Gaston Bachelard. 1971. pap. 9.95x (ISBN 0-8070-6413-0, BP375). Beacon Pr.

Poetics of Roman Ingarden. Eugene H. Falk. LC 79-29655. xxi, 213p. 1981. 25.00x (ISBN 0-8078-1436-9); pap. 11.00x o. p. (ISBN 0-8078-4068-8). U of NC Pr.

Poetics of Sexual Myth: Gender & Ideology in the Verse of Swift & Pope. Ellen Pollak. LC 84-28125. (Women in Culture & Society Ser.). 1985. lib. bdg. 18.95x (ISBN 0-226-67345-6). U of Chicago Pr.

Poetics of Site. Steven Holl. (Illus.). 148p. (Orig.). 1988. pap. 25.00 (ISBN 0-910413-19-3). Princeton Arch.

Poetics of Space. Gaston Bachelard. Tr. by Maria Jolas. 1969. pap. 9.95 (ISBN 0-8070-6439-4, BP330). Beacon Pr.

Poetics of the Elements in the Human Condition: The Sea. Ed. by Anna-Teresa Tymieniecka. 1985. lib. bdg. 89.00 (ISBN 90-277-1906-3, Pub. by Reidel Holland). Kluwer Academic.

Poetics of the Holy: A Reading of "Paradise Lost". Michael Lieb. LC 80-29159. xxi, 442p. 1981. 35.00x (ISBN 0-8078-1479-2). U of NC Pr.

Poetics of the New American Poetry. Ed. by Donald M. Allen & Warren Taliman. LC 73-6222. 1973. pap. 12.50 (ISBN 0-394-17801-7, E609, Ever). Grove.

Poetics of the New Poetries. Ed. by Richard Kostelanetz & Benjamin Hrushovski. 256p. 1983. pap. 8.00 (ISBN 0-317-17979-9). RK Edns.

Poetics of the Ramakian. Theodora H. Bofman. (Northern Illnois University Special Report Ser.: No. 21). 258p. (Orig.). 1984. pap. 15.00x (ISBN 0-318-03064-0). Cellar.

Poetics of Translatio Studii & Conjointure: Chretien de Troyes's Cliges. Michelle A. Freeman. LC 78-54262. (French Forum Monographs: No. 12). 199p. (Orig.). 1979. pap. 12.95x (ISBN 0-917058-11-9). French Forum.

Poetry Connoisseur's Fifty Prizewinning Poems. Ed. by Robert Travis. 60p. (Orig.). 1986. pap. 5.95 ltd. ed. (ISBN 0-934673-00-4). Aesthetics.

Poetry Corner. Arnold Cheyney. 1982. pap. 11.95 (ISBN 0-673-16461-6). Scott F.

Poetry Cure: Anthology. Robert Schauffler. Repr. of 1932 ed. 35.00 (ISBN 0-686-18784-9). Scholars Ref Lib.

Poetry: Direct & Oblique. E. M. Tillyard. 1979. Repr. of 1956 ed. lib. bdg. 20.00 (ISBN 0-8495-5134-X). Arden Lib.

Poetry Experience: Teaching & Writing Poetry in Secondary Schools. S. Tunnicliffe. (Teaching Secondary English Ser.). 272p. (Orig.). 1984. text ed. 25.00 (ISBN 0-416-34600-6, 9217); pap. text ed. 10.95 (ISBN 0-416-34610-3, 9218). Routledge Chapman & Hall.

Poetry Explication: A Checklist of Interpretation Since 1925 of British and American Poems Past and Present. Nancy C. Martinez & Joseph M. Kuntz. 1980. lib. bdg. 46.00 (ISBN 0-8161-8313-9, Hall Reference). G K Hall.

Poetry for Children. facsimile ed. Ed. by Samuel Eliot. LC 76-160905. (Granger Index Reprint Ser.). Repr. of 1879 ed. 21.00 (ISBN 0-8369-6268-0). Ayer Co Pubs.

Poetry for Chuckles & Grins. Ed. by Leland B. Jacobs. LC 68-16162. (Garrard Poetry Ser.). (Illus.). 64p. (gr. 2-5). 1968. PLB 6.69 (ISBN 0-8116-4101-5). Garrard.

Poetry for Crazy Cowboys & Zen Monks. Raymond Coffin. (Illus.). 72p. 1980. pap. 4.95 (ISBN 0-915520-26-5). Ross-Erikson.

Poetry for Everyday People. Ruben J. Smoke. 32p. 1986. 5.95 (ISBN 0-89962-497-9). Todd & Honeywell.

Poetry for Holidays. Ed. by Nancy Larrick. LC 66-10724. (Garrard Poetry Ser.). (gr. 2-5). 1966. PLB 6.69 (ISBN 0-8116-4100-7). Garrard.

Poetry for Home & School. facsimile ed. Anna C. Brackett & Ida M. Eliot. LC 79-38593. (Granger Index Reprint Ser.). Repr. of 1876 ed. 19.00 (ISBN 0-8369-6325-3). Ayer Co Pubs.

Poetry for Men to Speak Chorally. Marion Robinson & Rozetta L. Thurston. 148p. 3.00 (ISBN 0-686-15465-7). Expression.

Poetry for My Valentine. Flavia E. Logie & Leander Barnhill. (Illus.). 20p. 1988. pap. 1.50. F E Logie & L D Barnhill.

Poetry for People, Vol. I. Clifton A. Wiles. LC 85-60785. (Illus.). 64p. (Orig.). 1985. pap. 5.95 (ISBN 0-9614593-0-1). Hell Box.

Poetry for People, Vol. II. Clifton A. Wiles. LC 85-60785. 55p. (Orig.). 1986. pap. 5.95 (ISBN 0-9614593-2-8). Hell Box.

Poetry for People, Vol. III. Clifton A. Wiles. LC 85-60785. 53p. (Orig.). 1988. pap. 5.95 (ISBN 0-9614593-3-6). Hell Box.

Poetry for Poetry's Sake. A. C. Bradley. LC 73-15728. 1901. lib. bdg. 15.00 (ISBN 0-8414-3306-2). Folcroft.

Poetry for School Reading. facsimile ed. Ed. by Marcus White. LC 72-160912. (Granger Index Reprint Ser.). Repr. of 1899 ed. 17.00 (ISBN 0-8369-6277-X). Ayer Co Pubs.

Poetry for the Peace Movement. A. C. Doyle. 17p. 1984. pap. text ed. 2.00 (ISBN 0-913597-56-2, Pub. by Alpha Pyramis). Prosperity & Profits.

Poetry for Wee Folks. Charlotte M. Hill. Ed. by Fred D. Hill. LC 88-70281. (Illus.). 31p. (gr. k-3). 1988. 8.95x (ISBN 0-9620182-0-1). Charill Pubs.

Poetry from Angola: Ao Som das Marimbas, Poemes Africians. Geraldo Bessa Victor. 1967. Two works in one unit. 21.00 (ISBN 0-8115-3041-8). Kraus Repr.

Poetry from Leeds. Ed. by J. J. Healy & R. Parthasarathy. 16p. 1968. 8.00 (ISBN 0-88253-614-1); flexible cloth 4.00 (ISBN 0-88253-613-3). Ind-US Inc.

Poetry from Literature for Our Time. Ed. by Harlow O. Waite & Benjamin P. Atkinson. LC 72-108589. (Granger Index Reprint Ser). 1958. 16.00 (ISBN 0-8369-6117-X). Ayer Co Pubs.

Poetry from the Bible. Ed. by Lincoln MacVeagh. 180p. 1981. Repr. of 1925 ed. lib. bdg. 30.00 (ISBN 0-8495-3531-X). Arden Lib.

Poetry from the Land of Sheba. Ali Luqman. Ed. by Wijdan Luqman. 112p. 1981. pap. 4.00 (ISBN 0-933180-29-2). Spoon Riv Poetry.

Poetry, Gongorism, & a Thousand Years. Robinson Jeffers. LC 74-14682. 1974. Repr. of 1949 ed. lib. bdg. 20.00 (ISBN 0-8414-5312-8). Folcroft.

Poetry Handbook: A Dictionary of Terms. 4th ed. Babette Deutsch. 224p. 1982. pap. 8.95 (ISBN 0-06-463548-1, EH 548, B&N Bks). Har-Row.

Poetry Hawaii: A Contemporary Anthology. Ed. by Frank Stewart & John Unterecker. LC 79-63338. (Illus.). 172p. (Orig.). 1979. pap. 5.95 (ISBN 0-8248-0642-5). UH Pr.

Poetry Hunter, No. 1. Ed. by Barbara Fisher & Richard Spiegel. (Illus.). 92p. (Orig.). (gr. k-6). 1981. pap. 2.00 (ISBN 0-934830-21-5). Ten Penny.

Poetry in a Divided World: The Clark Lectures, 1985. Henry Gifford. 120p. 1986. 23.95 (ISBN 0-521-30944-1). Cambridge U Pr.

Poetry in America: Expression & Its Values in the Times of Bryant, Whitman, & Pound. Bernard I. Duffey. LC 77-81281. 372p. pap. 96.80 (2052236). Bks Demand UMI.

Poetry in East Germany: Adjustments, Visions & Provocations 1945-1970. John Flores. LC 77-115368. (Yale Germanic Studies: No. 5). Repr. of 1971 ed. 70.00 (ISBN 0-8357-9442-3, 2016777). Bks Demand UMI.

Poetry in English: An Anthology. Ed. by M. L. Rosenthal. (Illus.). 1234p. 1987. pap. text ed. 19.95 (ISBN 0-19-520539-1). Oxford U Pr.

Poetry in English: An Introduction. Charles Barber. LC 82-23099. 220p. 1983. 21.95 (ISBN 0-312-61888-3). St Martin.

Poetry in France & England. Jean Stewart. LC 73-15819. 1973. lib. bdg. 25.00 (ISBN 0-8414-7687-X). Folcroft.

Poetry in Modern Ireland. Austin Clarke. 1978. Repr. of 1951 ed. lib. bdg. 29.00 (ISBN 0-8495-0904-1). Arden Lib.

Poetry in Modern Ireland. Austin Clarke. LC 74-12114. 1973. lib. bdg. 17.00 (ISBN 0-8414-3363-1). Folcroft.

Poetry in Motion. Zach M. Gunn. 30p. (Orig.). 1986. pap. 5.95 (ISBN 0-933865-11-2). Doris Pubns.

Poetry in Motion: Poems & Activities for Moving & Learning with Young Children. Rae Pica. Ed. by Frank Alexander. (Illus.). 94p. 1986. tchr's. ed. 7.95 (ISBN 0-915256-19-3, 118). Front Row.

Poetry in Mythology & Folklore. Thomas L. Hakes. 25p. 1985. pap. 3.95x (ISBN 0-915020-56-4). Bardic.

Poetry in Nature. S. Maeda. cancelled (ISBN 0-685-05018-1, 0-911156-28-7). Bern Porter.

Poetry in Prose. Walter De La Mare. LC 76-25537. 1935. lib. bdg. 15.00 (ISBN 0-8414-3738-6). Folcroft.

Poetry in Prose. Walter De La Mare. 1978. 42.50 (ISBN 0-685-87741-8). Bern Porter.

Poetry in Prose. T. S. Eliot et al. LC 78-64019. (Des Imagistes: Literature of the Imagist Movement). Repr. of 1921 ed. 11.00 (ISBN 0-404-17090-0). AMS Pr.

Poetry in the Age of Democracy: The Literary Criticism of Matthew Arnold. Mary W. Schneider. 208p. 1988. 22.50 (ISBN 0-7006-0380-8). U Pr of Ks.

Poetry in the Classroom. Ed. by Linda Wyman. 1984. pap. 5.95 (ISBN 0-8141-3606-0). NCTE.

Poetry in the Dark Ages. H. Waddell. (Studies in Poetry, No. 38). 1948. pap. 39.95x (ISBN 0-8383-0079-0). Haskell.

Poetry in the Dark Ages. Helen Waddell. LC 73-15992. 1974. Repr. of 1948 ed. lib. bdg. 25.00 (ISBN 0-8414-9483-5). Folcroft.

Poetry in the Making. Ted Hughes. 124p. 1967. pap. 4.95 (ISBN 0-571-09076-1). Faber & Faber.

Poetry in the Red Book of Hergest. Ed. by John G. Evans. LC 78-72676. (Series of Old Welsh Texts: Vol. 11A). Repr. of 1911 ed. 32.50 (ISBN 0-404-60594-X). AMS Pr.

Poetry in the Wars. Edna Longley. LC 86-25069. 264p. 1987. 29.50x (ISBN 0-87413-322-X). U Delaware Pr.

Poetry Index Annual, 1982. Granger Book Company, Editorial Board Staff. 372p. 1982. 54.99x (ISBN 0-89609-223-2). Roth Pub Inc.

Poetry Index Annual, 1983. Ed. by Granger Book Company, Editorial Board Staff. LC 83-641946. 337p. 1983. 54.99x (ISBN 0-89609-237-2). Roth Pub Inc.

Poetry Index Annual, 1984. Granger Book Company, Editorial Board Staff. 1984. 54.99x (ISBN 0-89609-240-2). Roth Pub Inc.

Poetry Index Annual, 1985. Granger Book Company, Editorial Board Staff. 680p. 1985. 54.99x (ISBN 0-89609-259-3). Roth Pub Inc.

Poetry Index Annual, 1986. Roth Publishing Editorial Board Staff. 470p. 1987. 54.99 (ISBN 0-89609-264-X). Roth Pub Inc.

Poetry Index Annual 1987. Ed. by Roth Publishing, Inc. Editorial Board. 400p. 1988. 54.99x (ISBN 0-89609-269-0). Roth Pub Inc.

Poetry into Drama: Early Tragedy & the Greek Poetic Tradition. John Herington. (Sather Classical Lectures: Vol. 49). (Illus.). 350p. 1985. 35.00x (ISBN 0-520-05100-9). U of Cal Pr.

Poetry Introduction, No. 6. Susannah Amoore et al. LC 70-424610. 112p. (Orig.). 1985. pap. 7.95 (ISBN 0-571-13543-9). Faber & Faber.

Poetry Is Soul. Elbert P. Green. 32p. 1988. 6.75 (ISBN 0-8062-3181-5). Carlton.

Poetry, Its Appreciation & Enjoyment. Louis Untermeyer & Carter Davidson. 530p. 1987. Repr. of 1934 ed. lib. bdg. 65.00 (ISBN 0-89987-919-5). Darby Bks.

Poetry: Its Music & Meaning. L. Abercrombie. 1979. 42.50 (ISBN 0-685-94339-9). Bern Porter.

Poetry: Its Music & Meaning. Lascelles Abercrombie. 1978. Repr. of 1932 ed. lib. bdg. 17.00 (ISBN 0-8495-0124-5). Arden Lib.

Poetry: Its Music & Meaning. Lascelles Abercrombie. LC 72-194362. 1932. lib. bdg. 9.50. Folcroft.

Poetry, Language & Politics. John Barrell. LC 88-1434. (Cultural Politics Ser.). 192p. 1988. 39.95 (ISBN 0-7190-2441-2, Pub. by Manchester Univ Pr); pap. 11.95 (ISBN 0-7190-2442-0, Pub. by Manchester Univ Pr). St Martin.

Poetry, Language, Thought. Martin Heidegger. Tr. by Albert Hofstadter from Ger. 1975. pap. 7.95 (ISBN 0-06-090430-5, CN430, PL). Har-Row.

Poetry London: Feb. 1939 to Winter 1951, 5 vols. Ed. by Tambimutta. (Illus.). 1328p. 1970. Repr. 285.00x (ISBN 0-7146-2112-9, F Cass Co). Biblio Dist.

Poetry: Lyrical, Narrative, & Satirical of the Civil War. Ed. by Richard G. White. LC 72-4981. (Romantic Tradition in American Literature Ser.). 360p. 1972. Repr. of 1866 ed. 27.50 (ISBN 0-405-04650-2). Ayer Co Pubs.

Poetry Nineteen Forty-Five to Nineteen Eighty. Anthony Thwaite & John Mole. (English Ser.). 224p. (Orig.). 1983. pap. text ed. 7.95 (ISBN 0-582-35148-0). Longman.

Poetry, Nineteen Forty-Five to Nineteen Fifty. Alan Ross. 1979. Repr. of 1951 ed. lib. bdg. 10.00 (ISBN 0-8492-7719-1). R West.

Poetry: Nineteen Forty-Five to Nineteen Fifty. Alan S. Ross. LC 74-16065. 1974. Repr. of 1951 ed. lib. bdg. 20.50 (ISBN 0-8414-7360-9). Folcroft.

Poetry Notebooks of Ralph Waldo Emerson. Ed. by Ralph H. Orth et al. LC 84-2184. 1024p. 1986. text ed. 65.00x (ISBN 0-8262-0444-9). U of Mo Pr.

Poetry of a Pensive Lady. Evelyn J. Buchler. 32p. 1986. cancelled (ISBN 0-8062-2053-8). Carlton.

Poetry of Abraham Cowley. David Trotter. LC 78-31613. 162p. 1979. 23.50x (ISBN 0-8476-6157-1). Rowman.

Poetry of Alfonso X, El Sabio: A Critical Bibliography. Joseph Snow. (Research Bibliographies & Checklists Ser.: No. 19). 140p. (Orig.). 1977. pap. 11.95 (ISBN 0-7293-0042-0, Pub. by Grant & Cutler). Longwood Pub Group.

Poetry of Alfred de Musset: Styles & Genres. Lloyd Bishop. (Studies in the Humanities: Vol. 6). 197p. 1987. text ed. 37.00 (ISBN 0-8204-0357-1). P Lang Pubs.

Poetry of Alfred Tennyson. C. H. Scaife. LC 76-56394. 1930. lib. bdg. 20.50 (ISBN 0-8414-7552-0). Folcroft.

Poetry of American Wit & Humor. Frederic L. Knowles. LC 78-98082. (Granger Index Reprint Ser). 1899. 21.00 (ISBN 0-8369-6079-3). Ayer Co Pubs.

Poetry of Andrew Lang. James Ormerod. LC 74-28468. 1943. lib. bdg. 17.50 (ISBN 0-8414-6502-9). Folcroft.

Poetry of Architecture. John Ruskin. LC 74-148294. Repr. of 1893 ed. 15.00 (ISBN 0-404-05463-3). AMS Pr.

Poetry of Architecture. John Ruskin. LC 78-115265. (Illus.). 274p. 1972. Repr. of 1893 ed. 13.00x (ISBN 0-403-00305-9). Scholarly.

Poetry of Architecture: Or, the Architecture of the Nations of Europe. John Ruskin. 59.95 (ISBN 0-8490-0859-X). Gordon Pr.

Poetry of Arnaut Daniel. Ed. & tr. by James J. Wilhelm. LC 80-8955. (Garland Library of Medieval Literature). 186p. 1981. lib. bdg. 31.00 (ISBN 0-8240-9446-8). Garland Pub.

Poetry of Asia: Five Millenniums of Verse from Thirty Three Languages. Ed. by Keith Bosley. 320p. 1979. 17.50 (ISBN 0-8348-0139-6). Weatherhill.

Poetry of Austin Clarke. Gregory Schirmer. LC 82-40376. 208p. 1983. 17.95 (ISBN 0-268-01549-X). U of Notre Dame Pr.

Poetry of Baruch: A Reconstruction & Analysis of the Original Hebrew Text of Baruch 3: 9-5: 9. Ed. by David G. Burke. LC 80-10271. (Society of Biblical Literature, Septuagint & Cognate Studies: No. 10). 1982. pap. 15.95 (ISBN 0-89130-382-0, 06-04-10). Scholars Pr GA.

Poetry of Beverly Taylor. Beverly Taylor. 43p. 1988. 6.95 (ISBN 0-533-07632-3). Vantage.

Poetry of Black America: Anthology of the Twentieth Century. Ed. by Arnold Adoff. LC 72-76518. 576p. (YA) (gr. 7 up). 1973. 24.70i (ISBN 0-06-020089-8); PLB 24.89 (ISBN 0-06-020090-1). HarpJ.

Poetry of Byron. Harold Nicolson. LC 77-4993. 1943. lib. bdg. 20.50 (ISBN 0-8414-6297-6). Folcroft.

Poetry of Byron. Harold G. Nicolson. 10p. 1980. Repr. of 1943 ed. lib. bdg. 15.00 (ISBN 0-8492-1972-8). R West.

Poetry of Caedmon. C. L. Wrenn. 1979. 42.50 (ISBN 0-685-94340-2). Bern Porter.

Poetry of Caedmon. Charles L. Wrenn. LC 77-24540. 1947. lib. bdg. 18.00 (ISBN 0-8414-9398-7). Folcroft.

Poetry of Cercamon & Jaufre Rudel. Ed. by George Wolf & Roy Rosenstein. (Garland Library of Medieval Literature). 1981. lib. bdg. 29.00 (ISBN 0-8240-9443-3). Garland Pub.

Poetry of Charles Olson: A Primer. Thomas F. Merrill. LC 81-40341. 224p. 1982. 26.50 (ISBN 0-87413-196-0). U Delaware Pr.

Poetry of Charles Potts. Hugh Fox. (American Dust Ser.: No. 12). 1979. pap. 2.95 (ISBN 0-913218-44-8). Dustbooks.

Poetry of Chaucer. John C. Gardner. LC 76-22713. 445p. 1978. pap. 15.95x (ISBN 0-8093-0871-1). S Ill U Pr.

Poetry of Chaucer. Robert K. Root. 59.95 (ISBN 0-8490-0860-3). Gordon Pr.

Poetry of Chaucer: A Guide to Its Study & Appreciation. rev. ed. Robert K. Root. 11.25 (ISBN 0-8446-1391-6). Peter Smith.

Poetry of Chess. Ed. by Andrew Waterman. 160p. (Orig.). 1981. pap. 9.95 (ISBN 0-85646-067-2, Pub. by Anvil Pr Poetry). Longwood Pub Group.

Poetry of Christian Hofmann von Hofmannswaldau: A New Reading. Fritz G. Cohen. LC 85-72042. (Studies in German Literature, Linguistics, & Culture: Vol. 22). (Illus.). 180p. 1985. 28.00x (ISBN 0-938100-38-6). Camden Hse.

Poetry of Cino da Pistoia. Ed. by Christopher Kleinhenz. LC 83-48059. (Publications in Medieval Studies). 420p. 1986. lib. bdg. 40.00 (ISBN 0-8240-9411-5). Garland Pub.

Poetry of Civic Virtue: Eliot, Malraux, Auden. Nathan A Scott. LC 76-7871. pap. 44.00 (2026896). Bks Demand UMI.

Poetry of Civilization: Mythopoeic Displacement in the Verse of Milton, Dryden, Pope, & Johnson. Sanford Budick. LC 73-86887. pap. 48.80 (ISBN 0-317-29590-X, 2021984). Bks Demand UMI.

Poetry of Clough. Walter E. Houghton. 1979. Repr. of 1963 ed. lib. bdg. 18.50x (ISBN 0-374-93982-9, Octagon). Hippocrene Bks.

Poetry of Commitment in South Africa. Jacques Alvarez-Pereyre. Tr. by Clive Wake from Fr. (Studies in African Literature). x, 278p. (Orig.). 1985. pap. text ed. 17.50x (ISBN 0-435-91056-6). Heinemann Ed.

Poetry of Conrad Ferdinand Meyer. Heinrich Henel. LC 54-8534. pap. 86.80 (ISBN 0-317-08223-X, 2005476). Bks Demand UMI.

Poetry of D. H. Lawrence: Texts & Contexts. Ross C. Murfin. LC 82-10940. xvi, 263p. 1983. 22.50x (ISBN 0-8032-3080-X). U of Nebr Pr.

Poetry of Dada & Surrealism: Aragon, Breton, Tzars, Eluard & Desnos. Mary A. Caws. LC 68-56304. pap. 59.00 (ISBN 0-317-42017-8, 2025687). Bks Demand UMI.

Poetry of Dante. Benedetto Croce. 319p. Repr. of 1922 ed. 10.00x (ISBN 0-911858-12-1). Appel.

Poetry of Dante G. Rossetti: A Critical Reading & Source Study. Florence S. Boos. (Studies in English Literature: No. 104). 1976. text ed. 32.00x (ISBN 90-2793-471-1). Mouton.

Poetry of Dante Gabriel Rossetti: Modes of Self Expression. Joan Rees. 150p. 1981. 42.50 (ISBN 0-521-23537-5). Cambridge U Pr.

Poetry of Dino Frescobaldi: Romance Language & Literature. Joseph Alessia. LC 83-5482. (American University Studies II: Vol. 2). 158p. (Orig.). 1983. pap. text ed. 15.80 (ISBN 0-8204-0008-4). P Lang Pubs.

Poetry of Discovery: The Spanish Generation of 1956-1971. Andrew P. Debicki. LC 82-40171. 248p. 1982. 22.00x (ISBN 0-8131-1461-6). U Pr of Ky.

Poetry of Dorothy Wordsworth. Dorothy Wordsworth. Ed. by Hyman Eigerman. 1970. Repr. of 1940 ed. lib. bdg. 35.00 (ISBN 0-8371-3436-6, WOPO). Greenwood.

Poetry of Duke William IX of Aguitaine (Guilhem of Poitiers) Ed. by Gerald A. Bond. (Garland Library of Medieval Literature). 1981. lib. bdg. 44.00 (ISBN 0-8240-9441-7). Garland Pub.

Poetry of Dylan Thomas. Elder Olson. LC 54-9580. 1961. pap. 1.75 (ISBN 0-226-62917-1, P72, Phoen). U of Chicago Pr.

Poetry of Edwin Arlington Robinson. L. Morris. LC 73-92976. (Studies in Poetry, No. 38). 1969. Repr. of 1923 ed. lib. bdg. 39.95x (ISBN 0-8383-0996-8). Haskell.

Poetry of Edwin Arlington Robinson. Lloyd Morris. LC 70-99664. (Select Bibliographies Reprint Ser). 1923. 18.00 (ISBN 0-8369-5093-3). Ayer Co Pubs.

Poetry of Edwin Arlington Robinson: An Essay in Appreciation. Lloyd Morris. LC 73-86047. 1969. Repr. of 1923 ed. 18.50x (ISBN 0-8046-0630-7, Pub. by Kennikat). Assoc Faculty Pr.

Poetry of Edwin Arlington Robinson: An Essay in Appreciation. Lloyd Morris & W. Van Whitall. LC 70-99664. (Select Bibliographies Reprint Ser.). 116p. Repr. of 1923 ed. 13.50 (ISBN 0-8290-0486-6). Irvington.

Poetry of Elizabeth Singer Rowe (1674-1737) Madeleine F. Marshall. LC 87-24399. (Studies in Women & Religion: Vol. 25). (Illus.). 380p. 1987. lib. bdg. 59.95x (ISBN 0-88946-524-X). E Mellen.

Poetry of Encounter: Three Indo-Anglian Poets, Dom Moraes, A. K. Ramanujan, & Nissim Ezekiel. Emmanuel N. Lall. 120p. 1984. 14.00 (ISBN 0-86578-221-0). Ind-US Inc.

Poetry of Enlightenment: Poems of Ancient Ch'an Masters. Tr. & intro. by Sheng-Yen Chang. 94p. (Orig.). 1987. pap. 5.95x (ISBN 0-9609854-1-7). Dharma Drum Pubs.

Poetry of Erica Jong. Erica Jong. 1976. pap. 11.95 (ISBN 0-03-018321-9). H Holt & Co.

Poetry of Ernest Dowson. Ed. by Desmond Flower. LC 75-88560. 165p. 1970. 24.50 (ISBN 0-8386-7551-4, 8386-7551-4). Fairleigh Dickinson.

Poetry of Events: Daniel Webster's Rhetoric of the American Dream. Paul D. Erickson. LC 86-18104. 224p. 1987. 32.00 (ISBN 0-8147-2170-2). NYU Pr.

Poetry of Experience: The Dramatic Monologue in Modern Literary Tradition. Robert Langbaum. LC 85-14861. 252p. 1986. pap. 9.95x (ISBN 0-226-46872-0). U of Chicago Pr.

Poetry of Ezra Pound. Hugh Kenner. LC 85-8622. xiv, 342p. 1985. pap. 8.95 (ISBN 0-8032-7756-3, BB 927, Bison). U of Nebr Pr.

Poetry of the Victorian Period. 3rd ed. Jerome H. Buckley & George B. Woods. 1965. text ed. write for info. (ISBN 0-673-05630-9). Scott F.

Poetry of the Victorian Period. George B. Woods. 1977. Repr. lib. bdg. 30.00 (ISBN 0-8492-2854-9). R West.

Poetry of Thomas Gray: A Lecture. David Cecil. Repr. of 1945 ed. lib. bdg. 12.50 (ISBN 0-8414-3620-7). Folcroft.

Poetry of Thomas Gray: Versions of the Self. R. Lonsdale. (Chatterton Lectures on an English Poet). 1973. pap. 5.50 (ISBN 0-85672-076-3, Pub. by British Acad). Longwood Pub Group.

Poetry of Thomas Hardy. Ed. by Patricia Clements & Juliet Grindle. (Critical Studies Ser.). 194p. 1980. 28.50x (ISBN 0-389-20057-3). B&N Imports.

Poetry of Thomas Hardy. 1978. 42.50 (ISBN 0-685-85867-7). Bern Porter.

Poetry of Thomas Hardy, 2 vols. Birjadish Prasad. Ed. by James Hogg. (Romantic Reassessment Ser.). 412p. (Orig.). 1977. Set. pap. 30.00 (ISBN 3-7052-0512-9, Pub. by Salzburg Studies). Longwood Pub Group.

Poetry of Thomas Hardy: A Study in Art & Ideas. William E. Buckler. (Illus.). 296p. 1983. 42.50x (ISBN 0-8147-1046-8). NYU Pr.

Poetry of Thomas Hardy in Four Studies. Archibald Strong. 1973. Repr. of 1932 ed. 17.50 (ISBN 0-8274-0420-4). R West.

Poetry of Thomas Hardy's Novel. Usha Walters. Ed. by Jomes Hogg. (Roamntic Reassessment ser.). 176p. (Orig.). 1980. pap. 15.00 (ISBN 3-7052-0562-5, Pub. by Salzburg Studies). Longwood Pub Group.

Poetry of To-Day. Ed. by Rosa M. Mikels & Grace Shoup. LC 78-73491. (Granger Poetry Library). 1979. Repr. of 1927 ed. 25.00x (ISBN 0-89609-117-1). Roth Pub Inc.

Poetry of Toil. Dorothy Wooldridge. 1977. Repr. of 1926 ed. 20.00. Century Bookbindery.

Poetry of Travelling in the United States. Caroline Gilman. LC 71-104465. 430p. 1977. Repr. of 1838 ed. lib. bdg. 29.00 (ISBN 0-8398-0660-4). Irvington.

Poetry of Travelling in the United States. Caroline Gilman. 430p. 1986. pap. text ed. 8.95x (ISBN 0-8290-1885-9). Irvington.

Poetry of Vachel Lindsay, Vol. 1. Vachel Lindsay. Ed. by Dennis Camp. 1984. 24.95 (ISBN 0-933180-45-4). Spoon Riv Poetry.

Poetry of Vachel Lindsay, Vol. 2. Vachel Lindsay. Ed. by Dennis Camp. 1984. 24.95 (ISBN 0-933180-67-5). Spoon Riv Poetry.

Poetry of Vachel Lindsay, Vol. 3. Ed. by Dennis Camp. 190p. 1986. 14.95 (ISBN 0-933180-77-2). Spoon Riv Poetry.

Poetry of Vachel Lindsay, Vol. 3. Vachel Lindsay. Ed. by Dennis Camp. 1986. 14.95 (ISBN 0-933180-83-7). Spoon Riv Poetry.

Poetry of Villon. John Fox. 174p. 1981. Repr. of 1962 ed. lib. bdg. 35.00 (ISBN 0-8495-1728-1). Arden Lib.

Poetry of W. B. Yeats. Louis MacNeice. LC 79-17894. 1979. Repr. of 1941 ed. lib. bdg. 35.00 (ISBN 0-313-22102-2, MAPO). Greenwood.

Poetry of Wallace Stevens. Robert Rehder. 272p. 1987. 32.50 (ISBN 0-312-00860-0); pap. 12.95 (ISBN 0-312-00861-9). St Martin.

Poetry of Wickedness & Other Poems. Lyn Coffin. LC 81-20085. 65p. (Orig.). 1981. pap. 4.00 (ISBN 0-87886-116-5). Greenfld Rev Pr.

Poetry of William Butler Yeats: An Introduction. William H. O'Donnell. (Literature & Life Ser.). 208p. 1986. 16.95x (ISBN 0-8044-2671-6). Ungar.

Poetry of William Collins. A. Johnston. (Warton Lectures on English Poetry). 1973. pap. 2.25 (ISBN 0-85672-097-6, Pub. by British Acad). Longwood Pub Group.

Poetry of William Cowper. Bill Hutchings. 246p. 1983. 29.95 (ISBN 0-7099-1249-8, Pub. by Croom Helm Ltd). Routledge Chapman & Hall.

Poetry of William Gilmore Simms: An Introduction & Bibliography. James E. Kibler, Jr. Ed. by James B. Meriwether. LC 78-15365. (South Caroliniana Ser.: Bibliographical & Textual: No. 3). (Illus.). 1979. 20.00 (ISBN 0-87152-276-4). Reprint.

Poetry of Witches, Elves & Goblins. Ed. by Leland B. Jacobs. LC 70-99767. (Garrard Poetry Ser.). (Illus.). (gr. 2-5). 1970. PLB 6.69 (ISBN 0-8116-4105-8). Garrard.

Poetry of Wordsworth in Lectures on Literature. W. S. McCormick. 1889. Repr. 30.00 (ISBN 0-8274-3179-1). R West.

Poetry of Yevgeny Yevtushenko. bilingual ed. Yevgeny Yevtushenko. 312p. 1981. pap. 8.95 (ISBN 0-7145-0482-3, Dist by Scribner). M Boyars Pubs.

Poetry of Yevgeny Yevtushenko. rev & enl. ed. Yevgeny Yevtushenko. 1964. 10.00 (ISBN 0-8079-0105-9). October.

Poetry on the Stage: William Poel, Producer of Verse Drama. Bernice Larson Webb. Ed. by James Hogg. (Poetic Drama & Poetic Theory). 280p. (Orig.). 1979. pap. 15.00 (ISBN 3-7052-0877-2, Pub. by Salzburg Studies). Longwood Pub Group.

Poetry Party. Linda Spellman. (Learning Works Creative Writing Ser.). 48p. (gr. 4-6). 1981. 4.95 (ISBN 0-88160-038-5, LW 223). Learning Wks.

Poetry Past & Present. Ed. by Frank Brady & Martin Price. 527p. (Orig.). 1974. pap. text ed. 13.00 net (ISBN 0-15-570662-9, HC). HarBraceJ.

Poetry Peddlers: Two from Music City Country. Craig Deitschmann et al. 128p. (Orig.). 1984. pap. 6.95 (ISBN 0-939298-46-5, 465). J M Prods.

Poetry, Politics & the English Tradition. L. C. Knights. LC 73-12771. 1954. Repr. lib. bdg. 18.50 (ISBN 0-8414-5452-3). Folcroft.

Poetry Power. 72p. 9.95 (ISBN 0-932269-36-2). Interspace Bks.

Poetry Project Four. Ed. by Joel Rudinger. (Poetry Projects Ser.). 104p. (Orig.). 1985. pap. 7.00 (ISBN 0-918342-22-8). Cambric.

Poetry Project One: American Anthology. 1981. pap. 5.50x (ISBN 0-932436-02-1). Cykx.

Poetry Project Three: Cambridge Poetry Projects. Joel Rudinger. (Orig.). 1983. pap. 7.95. Cambridge U Pr.

Poetry Project Three CPP-3. Ed. by Joel Rudinger. 128p. (Orig.). 1983. pap. 7.95 (ISBN 0-918342-16-3). Cambric.

Poetry Project Two: Poets of the World. 1981. pap. 5.50x (ISBN 0-932436-05-6). Cykx.

Poetry Quintet. Georgina Hammick et al. (Gollancz Poets Ser.). 1977. pap. 7.50 (ISBN 0-575-02156-X). Transatl Arts.

Poetry Reading: A Contemporary Compendium on Language & Performance. Intro. by Stephen Vincent & Ellen Zweig. 352p. 1981. 25.00 (ISBN 0-917672-11-9); pap. 9.95 (ISBN 0-917672-10-0). Momos.

Poetry Reading Series, 1982: An Anthology. 24p. 1983. ltd. ed. 3.00 (ISBN 0-943018-06-4). Backstreet.

Poetry Realized in Nature: Samuel Taylor Coleridge & Early Nineteenth-Century Science. Trevor H. Levere. LC 81-1930. 272p. 1981. 49.50 (ISBN 0-521-23920-6). Cambridge U Pr.

Poetry References in the Junior High School. Lucy Kangley. LC 75-176927. (Columbia University. Teachers College. Contributions to Education: No. 758). Repr. of 1938 ed. 22.50 (ISBN 0-404-55758-9). AMS Pr.

Poetry Reviews of Allen Tate, 1924-1944. Allen Tate. Ed. by Ashley Brown & Frances N. Cheney. LC 82-12687. (Southern Literary Studies). xii, 214p. 1983. 25.00 (ISBN 0-8071-1057-4). La State U Pr.

Poetry Ritual for Grammar Schools. Robert McGovern. 42p. 1974. pap. 1.50 (ISBN 0-912592-23-0). Ashland Poetry.

Poetry Room. Lewis MacAdams, Jr. LC 73-123978. 65p. 1970. 10.00 (ISBN 0-89366-104-X). Ultramarine Pub.

Poetry Self-Taught. Barbara Fischer. 40p. (Orig.). 1974. 12.95x (ISBN 0-912658-63-0). J Mark Pr.

Poetry Series. Charles J. Fitti. LC 76-181333. 1972. 5.00 (ISBN 0-8022-2079-7). Philos Lib.

Poetry Short Takes, Pt. II. Thomas L. Hakes. Date not set. pap. 1.95 (ISBN 0-915020-39-4). Bardic.

Poetry Short-Takes. Ed. by Thomas L. Hakes. (Illus.). 6p. (Orig.). 1984. pap. 2.00 (ISBN 0-915020-31-9). Bardic.

Poetry: Sight & Insight. James W. Kirkland & F. David Sanders. 456p. 1982. pap. text ed. write for info (ISBN 0-394-32353-X, RanC). Random.

Poetry Since Nineteen Thirty-Nine. S. Spender. LC 74-7038. (Studies in Poetry, No. 38). 1974. lib. bdg. 75.00x (ISBN 0-8383-1930-0). Haskell.

Poetry Since Nineteen Thirty Nine. Stephen Spender. LC 74-13198. 1939. lib. bdg. 20.00 (ISBN 0-8414-7794-9). Folcroft.

Poetry Since Nineteen Thirty-Nine. Stephen Spender. 1979. 42.50 (ISBN 0-685-94341-0). Bern Porter.

Poetry Since the Liberation. (YFS Ser.: No. 21). Repr. of 1958 ed. 16.00 (ISBN 0-527-01727-2). Kraus Repr.

Poetry Society of America Anthology. facsimile ed. Ed. by Amy Bonner et al. LC 76-75709. (Granger Index Reprint Ser). 1946. 20.00 (ISBN 0-8369-6003-3). Ayer Co Pubs.

Poetry: The Ecology of the Soul. Joel Oppenheimer. Ed. by David Landrey & Dennis Maloney. 1983. signed ed. 25.00; pap. 7.50 (ISBN 0-934834-36-9). White Pine.

Poetry: The Golden Anniversary Issue. Ed. by Henry Rago. LC 67-30352. 1967. pap. 1.95 (ISBN 0-226-70308-8, PP10, Phoen). U of Chicago Pr.

Poetry Themes: A Bibliographical Index to Subject Anthologies & Related Criticisms in the English Language, 1875-1975. Peter Marcan. LC 77-22483. xvi, 301p. 1978. 29.50 (ISBN 0-208-01545-0, Linnet). Shoe String.

Poetry Therapy for Modern Life. Bernard Brome. 1987. 7.95 (ISBN 0-533-07205-0). Vantage.

Poetry To-Day. Elizabeth Jennings. LC 76-47460. 1961. lib. bdg. 19.00 (ISBN 0-8414-5336-5). Folcroft.

Poetry To-day. Geoffrey Moore. LC 77-8853. 1977. lib. bdg. 17.50 (ISBN 0-8414-6069-8). Folcroft.

Poetry To-Day. Geoffrey Moore. 79p. 1980. Repr. of 1958 ed. lib. bdg. 15.00 (ISBN 0-8492-6829-X). R West.

Poetry To-Day. I. A. Williams. 1972. Repr. of 1927 ed. lib. bdg. 25.00 (ISBN 0-8414-9735-4). Folcroft.

Poetry To-Day. Iola A. Williams. 138p. 1984. Repr. of 1927 ed. lib. bdg. 30.00 (ISBN 0-89987-883-0). Darby Bks.

Poetry to Read Alone at Night. Laura B. Lynch. Ed. by Janice E. Cook. (Illus.). 20p. (Orig.). 1982. pap. 4.95 (ISBN 0-943190-00-2). Artefact Co.

Poetry to Read Aloud: Thistle Worth. Carole Marsh. (Illus.). 50p. (Orig.), (gr. 2-12). 1986. pap. 7.95 (ISBN 0-935326-60-X). Gallopade Pub Group.

Poetry Today: A Critical Guide to British Poetry 1960-1984. rev. ed. Anthony Thwaite. 128p. 1985. pap. text ed. 11.95 (ISBN 0-582-49419-2). Longman.

Poetry Unfolding. Incl. Some Things That Fly There Be. 0.00 (ISBN 0-915291-06-1); Fire & Ice. 0.00 (ISBN 0-915291-07-X); Ballad Singer. 0.00 (ISBN 0-915291-08-8); Sonnet Eighteen. 0.00 (ISBN 0-915291-10-X); Dream Variations. 0.00 (ISBN 0-915291-09-6); Eagle. 0.00 (ISBN 0-915291-11-8); In Time's A Noble Mercy of Proportion. 0.00 (ISBN 0-915291-12-6); Outdistanced. 0.00 (ISBN 0-915291-13-4); Ozymandias. 0.00 (ISBN 0-915291-14-2); Slumber Did My Spirit Seal. 0.00 (ISBN 0-915291-15-0); After Long Silence. 0.00 (ISBN 0-915291-16-9); Guide to Poetry Unfolding Film-Strip. 0.00 (ISBN 0-915291-17-7); Introduction & Manual for Teachers. 0.00 (ISBN 0-915291-18-5); Student's Guide for Independent Study. 0.00 (ISBN 0-915291-19-3); Index of Poetic Features. 0.00 (ISBN 0-915291-20-7). 1983. 0.00. Know Unltd.

Poetry Unfolding Basic Kit. Ed. by Asher E. Rivlin & Nancy Gimmestad. (Poetry Unfolding Ser.). 450p. (gr. 4-12). 1983. pap. 130.00 (ISBN 0-915291-05-3). Know Unltd.

Poetry Unfolding Expanded. Asher E Rivlin & Nancy Gimmestead. (Poetry Unfolding Ser.). 700p. 1983. Repr. of 1977 ed. tchr's ed. 180.00. Know Unltd.

Poetry Ventured, Four Years of PV's Best Poems: A Poetry Anthology. Ed. by Marjorie Schuck & George Garrott. 172p. 1972. pap. 3.00 (ISBN 0-912760-00-1). Valkyrie Pub Hse.

Poetry Video Learning Project: Student Workbook. Laura N. Vural. 48p. (Orig.). (YA) (gr. 6 up). 1987. pap. 3.50 (ISBN 0-944978-00-2). Rise & Shine Prodns.

Poetry with a Purpose. Barbara Malley & Frances Allen. 128p. (gr. 4-7). 1987. pap. 8.95 (ISBN 0-86653-415-6). Good Apple.

Poetry with a Purpose: Biblical Poetics & Interpretation. Harold Fisch. LC 87-45338. (Studies in Biblical Literature). (Illus.). 224p. 1988. 37.50x (ISBN 0-253-34557-X). Ind U Pr.

Poetry, Word-Play, & Word-War in Wallace Stevens. Eleanor Cook. 320p. 1988. 37.50 (ISBN 0-691-06747-3). Princeton U Pr.

Poetry World One, March 1986. Ed. by Daniel Weissbort. 160p. (Orig.). 1986. pap. 10.95 (ISBN 0-85646-171-7, Pub. by Anvil Pr Poetry). Longwood Pub Group.

Poetry World Two. Daniel Weissbort. 160p. 1987. pap. 10.95 (ISBN 0-85646-184-9, Pub. by Anvil Pr Poetry). Longwood Pub Group.

Poetry Worth Remembering. Ed. by Roy W. Watson. LC 86-72744. 235p. 1987. 22.95 (ISBN 1-55618-011-X); pap. 12.95 (ISBN 1-55618-010-1). Brunswick Pub.

Poetry Writing Self-Taught. Pauline D. Robertson. (Illus.). 208p. 1988. 12.95 (ISBN 0-942376-10-2). Paramount TX.

Poetry's Plea for Animals. Frances E. Clarke. 1977. Repr. of 1927 ed. 30.00. Century Bookbindery.

Poetry's Plea for Animals. Francis E. Clarke. 1927. 30.00 (ISBN 0-686-17675-8). Quaker City.

Poetry's Voice, Society's Song: Ottoman Lyric Poetry. Walter G. Andrews. LC 84-7351. (Publications on the Near East Ser.: No. 1). 1985. 25.00x (ISBN 0-295-96153-8). U of Wash Pr.

Poets & Artist in Greece. Ernest A. Gardner. 1975. Repr. of 1934 ed. 25.00 (ISBN 0-8274-4048-0). R West.

Poets & Dramatists of Ireland see Gallery of Irish Writers: The Irish Writers of the Seventeenth Century.

Poets & Dreamers: Studies & Translations from the Irish. Lady Gregory. LC 73-17133. (Studies in Irish Literature, No. 16). 1974. lib. bdg. 51.95x (ISBN 0-8383-1725-1). Haskell.

Poets & Dreamers: Studies & Translations from the Irish by Lady Gregory, Including Nine Plays by Douglas Hyde. 5th ed. Isabella A. Gregory. (Coole Edition of the Collected Works of Lady Gregory Ser.). 1974. text ed. 27.00x (ISBN 0-19-519790-9). Oxford U Pr.

Poets & Murder. Robert Van Gulik. (Judge Dee Mysteries). 1979. pap. 2.95 rack size (ISBN 0-684-16180-X, ScribT). Scribner.

Poets & Music. Edward W. Naylor. LC 80-16489. (Music Reprint Ser.). 1980. Repr. of 1928 ed. 29.50 (ISBN 0-306-76038-X). Da Capo.

Poets & Music. Edward W. Naylor. LC 78-66913. (Encore Music Editions Ser.). (Illus.). 1979. Repr. of 1929 ed. 20.75 (ISBN 0-88355-753-3). Hyperion Conn.

Poets & Mystics. facs. ed. Edward I. Watkin. LC 68-55862. (Essay Index Reprint Ser). 1953. 19.00 (ISBN 0-8369-0979-8). Ayer Co Pubs.

Poets & Nature. Phil Robinson. 1973. Repr. of 1893 ed. 30.00 (ISBN 0-8274-1632-6). R West.

Poets & Painters. David Shapiro. LC 79-55555. (Illus.). 80p. (Orig.). 1979. pap. 6.00 (ISBN 0-914738-17-8). Denver Art Mus.

Poets & Players. Ed. & tr. by Ann B. Krooth. 1976. pap. 4.00 (ISBN 0-939074-01-X). Harvest Pubns.

Poets & Poems. Lafcadio Hearn. 297p. 1980. Repr. of 1926 ed. lib. bdg. 39.50 (ISBN 0-8495-2272-2). Arden Lib.

Poets & Poems. Lafcadio Hearn. Ed. by R. Tanabe. LC 72-7217. 1926. lib. bdg. 46.00 (ISBN 0-8414-0275-2). Folcroft.

Poets & Poetry: Being Articles Reprinted from the Literary Supplement of 'The Times' facs. ed. John C. Bailey. LC 67-30196. (Essay Index Reprint Ser). 1911. 16.00 (ISBN 0-8369-0170-3). Ayer Co Pubs.

Poets & Poetry of America. Rufus W. Griswold. 1973. Repr. of 1855 ed. 22.00 (ISBN 0-8274-0639-8). R West.

Poets & Poetry of Europe: With Introductions & Biographical Notices. Henry Wadsworth Longfellow. 915p. 1982. Repr. of 1871 ed. lib. bdg. 150.00 (ISBN 0-8495-3342-2). Arden Lib.

Poets & Poetry of Munster: A Selection of Irish Songs by the Poets of the Last Century. 5th ed. Tr. by James C. Mangan. LC 75-28824. Repr. of 1909 ed. 34.50 (ISBN 0-404-13816-0). AMS Pr.

Poets & Poetry of Scotland, 4 vols. James G. Wilson. 1977. Repr. 95.00. Century Bookbindery.

Poets & Poetry of the West: With Biographical & Critical Notices. facsimile ed. William T. Coggeshall. LC 75-92. (Mid-American Frontier Ser.). 1975. Repr. of 1860 ed. 52.00x (ISBN 0-405-06859-X). Ayer Co Pubs.

Poets & Princepleasers: Literature & the English Court in the Late Middle Ages. Richard F. Green. 1980. 32.50x (ISBN 0-8020-5409-9). U of Toronto Pr.

Poets & Problems: Tennyson, Ruskin, Browning. George W. Cooke. LC 72-196438. 1886. lib. bdg. 32.00 (ISBN 0-8414-2385-7). Folcroft.

Poets & Prophets of Israel. Charles W. Conn. 1981. 5.25 (ISBN 0-87148-707-1); pap. 4.25 (ISBN 0-87148-708-X). Pathway Pr.

Poets & Prophets of Israel Instructor's Guide. 1981. pap. 7.95 (ISBN 0-87148-709-8). Pathway Pr.

Poets & Pundits: Essays & Addresses. Hugh L. Fausset. LC 67-25261. Repr. of 1947 ed. 26.75x (ISBN 0-8046-0139-9, Pub. by Kennikat). Assoc Faculty Pr.

Poets & Puritans. T. R. Glover. 1979. Repr. of 1915 ed. lib. bdg. 35.00 (ISBN 0-8414-4629-6). Folcroft.

Poets & Puritans. T. R. Glover. 1973. Repr. of 1915 ed. 29.00 (ISBN 0-8274-1572-9). R West.

Poets & Statesmen: Their Homes & Memorials in the Neighborhood of Windsor & Elton-Milton, Cowley, Denham, Waller, Pope. William Dowling. 1973. Repr. of 1856 ed. 50.00 (ISBN 0-8274-1698-9). R West.

Poets & Story-Tellers. David Cecil. 201p. 1980. Repr. of 1968 ed. lib. bdg. 30.00 (ISBN 0-8495-0852-5). Arden Lib.

Poets & the Poetry of the Century: Frederick Tennyson to Arthur Hugh Clough. Alfred H. Miles. 1977. 20.00 (ISBN 0-89984-145-7). Century Bookbindery.

Poets & the Poetry of the Century: Humor, Society, Parody & Occasional Verse. Alfred H. Miles. 1977. 20.00. Century Bookbindery.

Poets & the Poetry of the Century: Robert Bridges & Contemporary Poets. Alfred H. Miles. 1977. 20.00. Century Bookbindery.

Poets & the Poetry of the Century: Robert Southey to Percy Bysshe Shelley. Alfred H. Miles. 1977. 20.00. Century Bookbindery.

Poets & the Poetry of the Century: William Morris to Robert Buchanan. Alfred H. Miles. 1977. 20.00. Century Bookbindery.

Poets & the Poetry of the Nineteenth Century, 12 Vols. rev. ed. Ed. by Alfred H. Miles. LC 16-2291. Repr. of 1907 ed. Set. 510.00 (ISBN 0-404-05120-0); 42.50 ea. AMS Pr.

Poets & Their Critics: Langland & Milton. R. W. Chambers. 1942. lib. bdg. 15.00 (ISBN 0-685-10478-8). Folcroft.

Poet's Art. M. L. Rosenthal. 1987. 14.95 (ISBN 0-393-02432-6). Norton.

Poets at Play: Anthology of Paradies & Light Verse. Stephen Miall. lib. bdg. 10.00 (ISBN 0-8495-3702-9). Arden Lib.

Poets at Play: Irony & Parody in the Harley Lyrics. Daniel J. Ransom. LC 85-544. 160p. 1985. 31.95 (ISBN 0-937664-67-7). Pilgrim Bks OK.

Poets at Prayer. facs. ed. Sr. Mary J. Power. LC 68-29239. (Essay Index Reprint Ser). 1938. 18.00 (ISBN 0-8369-0797-3). Ayer Co Pubs.

Poet's Bazaar: A Journey to Greece, Turkey & up the Danube. Hans Christian Andersen. Tr. by Grace Thornton from Danish. LC 87-30993. (Illus.). 208p. 1987. 21.95 (ISBN 0-935576-23-1). Kesend Pub Ltd.

Poets' Beasts. Phil Robinson. 1973. Repr. of 1885 ed. 30.00 (ISBN 0-8274-1625-3). R West.

Poets Behind Barbed Wire. Keiho Soga & Taisanboku Mori. Ed. by Jiro Nakano & Kay Nakano. LC 83-71474. 64p. 1983. pap. 5.00 (ISBN 0-910043-05-1). Bamboo Ridge Pr.

Poet's Calling in the English Ode. Paul H. Fry. LC 79-20554. 1980. 32.50x (ISBN 0-300-02400-2). Yale U Pr.

Poet's Cat. facsimile ed. Ed. by Mona Gooden. LC 74-75711. (Granger Index Reprint Ser). 1946. 14.00 (ISBN 0-8369-6017-3). Ayer Co Pubs.

Poets Chantry. Katherine Bregy. LC 70-105766. 1970. Repr. of 1912 ed. 21.50x (ISBN 0-8046-1043-6, Pub. by Kennikat). Assoc Faculty Pr.

Poet's Choice: One Hundred American Poets' Favorite Poems. Ed. by George E. Murphy, Jr. 176p. 1980. 12.95 (ISBN 0-937504-01-7); pap. 5.95 (ISBN 0-937504-00-9). Tendril.

Poet's Circuits. Padraic Colum. 1984. pap. 14.95 (Pub. by Colin Smythe Ltd Britain). Dufour.

Poet's Corner. Max Beerbohm. 1978. Repr. of 1943 ed. lib. bdg. 20.50 (ISBN 0-8495-0388-4). Arden Lib.

Poet's Corner: A Manual for Students in English Poetry. J. C. Bellew. 1979. Repr. of 1884 ed. lib. bdg. 50.00 (ISBN 0-8495-0506-2). Arden Lib.

Poet's Corner or Haunts & Homes of the Poets. Alice Corkran. Repr. 35.00 (ISBN 0-8274-3163-5). R West.

Poet's Craft. Ed. by Helen F. Daringer & Anne T. Eaton. LC 72-8284. (Granger Index Reprint Ser). (Illus.). 1972. Repr. of 1935 ed. 21.00 (ISBN 0-8369-6385-7). Ayer Co Pubs.

Poet's Craft: An Outline of English Verse Composition for Schools. F. W. Felkin. LC 77-18843. 1973. Repr. of 1916 ed. 17.00 (ISBN 0-8492-0824-6). R West.

Poet's Craft: Interviews from The New York Quarterly. 2nd ed. Ed. by William Packard. LC 86-22643. 359p. 1987. 21.95 (ISBN 0-913729-30-2); pap. 10.95 (ISBN 0-913729-55-8). Paragon Hse.

Poets, Critics, Mystics: A Selection of Criticisms Written Between 1919 & 1955. John M. Murry. LC 78-83668. (Crosscurrents-Modern Critiques Ser.). 190p. 1970. 6.95x (ISBN 0-8093-0414-7). S Ill U Pr.

Poet's Defense. Jacob Bronowski. LC 78-14105. 1985. Repr. of 1939 ed. 25.00 (ISBN 0-88355-778-9). Hyperion Conn.

Poets Encyclopedia. John Cage et al. (Illus.). 1980. pap. 9.95 (ISBN 0-934450-03-X). Unmuzzled Ox.

Poets' Encyclopedia. John Cage et al. Ed. by Michael Andre & Erika Rothenberg. (Illus.). 1979. 14.95 (ISBN 0-934450-02-1). Unmuzzled Ox.

Poet's Eye. Violet Paget. LC 74-22116. 1974. lib. bdg. 25.50 (ISBN 0-8414-5663-1). Folcroft.

Poets' Fellowship. T. M. Pearce. LC 84-90445. 80p. 1984. 6.50 (ISBN 0-8233-0395-0). Golden Quill.

Poets for Africa. Ed. by Susann Flammang. 1987. 19.95 (ISBN 0-932873-73-1); pap. 8.95 (ISBN 0-932873-72-3). Family God.

Poets from the North of Ireland. Seamus Heaney et al. Ed. by Frank Ormsby. 244p. (Orig.). 1979. 8.95 (ISBN 0-85640-135-8, Pub. by Blackstaff Pr); pap. 8.95 (Pub. by Blackstaff Pr). Longwood Pub Group.

Poet's Guide to Freelance Selling. Kathleen Gilbert. (Illus.). 27p. 1983. pap. 3.00 (ISBN 0-915913-00-3). Violetta Bks.

Poet's Handbook. Judson Jerome. LC 80-17270. 224p. 1986. pap. 9.95 (ISBN 0-89879-219-3). Writers Digest.

Poet's Harvest Home. William B. Scott. LC 79-148298. Repr. of 1893 ed. 16.00 (ISBN 0-404-05648-2). AMS Pr.

Poets Historical: Dynastic Epic in the Renaissance. Andrew Fichter. LC 81-19795. 237p. 1982. text ed. 27.50t (ISBN 0-300-02721-4). Yale U Pr.

Poet's Homes: Pen & Pencil Sketches of American Poets & Their Homes, 2 vols. in 1. R. H. Stoddard. 1977. Repr. of 1879 ed. 25.00. Century Bookbindery.

Poet's Homes: Pen & Pencil Sketches of American Poets & Their Homes. R. H. Stoddard et al. 286p. 1983. Repr. of 1877 ed. lib. bdg. 75.00 (ISBN 0-89987-796-6). Darby Bks.

Poets' Homes: Pen & Pencil Sketches of American Poets & Their Homes, 2 vols. in 1. Richard H. Stoddard et al. LC 72-3491. (Essay Index Reprint Ser.). Repr. of 1879 ed. 44.00 (ISBN 0-8369-2926-8). Ayer Co Pubs.

Poets in Motion. Louis R. Rivera et al. (Illus., Orig.). 1976. pap. text ed. 3.00x (ISBN 0-917886-00-3). Shamal Bks.

Poets in the Flesh: Yeats, Tagore & Dunsany. R. F. Rattray. 1973. 17.00 (ISBN 0-8274-1072-7). R West.

Poets in the Nursery. Charles Powell. 79p. (ps up). Repr. of 1920 ed. PLB 25.00 (ISBN 0-8492-4221-5). R West.

Poets in Their Time: Essays on Poetry from Donne to Larkin. Ed. by Barbara Everett. 200p. 1986. 25.00 (ISBN 0-571-13978-7). Faber & Faber.

Poets in their Youth: A Memoir. Eileen Simpson. LC 81-48295. 256p. 1982. 15.00 (ISBN 0-394-52317-2). Random.

Poets in Their Youth: A Memoir. Eileen Simpson. LC 82-40429. (Illus.). 288p. 1983. pap. 5.95 (ISBN 0-394-71382-6, Vin). Random.

Poet's Job: To Go Too Far. Ed. by Margaret Honton. LC 85-50605. (Illus.). 244p. (Orig.). 1985. pap. 10.00 (ISBN 0-933981-05-8); pap. 13.00 velo-binding (ISBN 0-933981-04-X). Sophia Bks.

Poets Journal: A Personal Journal with Quotes. (Illus.). 96p. 1986. lib. bdg. 15.90 (ISBN 0-89471-463-5); pap. 5.95 (ISBN 0-89471-462-7). Running Pr.

Poet's Journal: Days of 1945-1951. George Seferis. Tr. by Athan Anagnostopoulos from Gr. LC 73-92634. 208p. 1974. (Belknap Pr); pap. 5.95 (ISBN 0-674-68041-3). Harvard U Pr.

Poet's Kitchen: A Collector's Work of Original, Creative Entertaining - It's About Time. Monika T. Clark. 152p. (Orig.). 1984. pap. 16.95 (ISBN 0-9613068-0-7). M T C Pub Co.

Poets Laureate. Kenneth Hopkins. LC 66-22838. 296p. 1966. pap. 3.45x (ISBN 0-8093-0223-3). S Ill U Pr.

Poets Laureate in England: Being a History of the Office. Walter Hamilton. 1970. Repr. of 1879 ed. 18.50 (ISBN 0-8337-1560-7). B Franklin.

Poets Laureate of England. W. Forbes Gray. 1914. Repr. 25.00 (ISBN 0-8274-3180-5). R West.

Poets Laureate of England. Walter Hamilton. LC 68-30621. 336p. 1968. Repr. of 1879 ed. 40.00x (ISBN 0-8103-3150-0). Gale.

Poets Laureate of England. Walter Hamilton. 1973. Repr. of 1879 ed. 35.00 (ISBN 0-8274-0189-2). R West.

Poets Laureate of England: From Earliest Times to the Present. John C. Wright. LC 72-194989. 1898. lib. bdg. 17.50 (ISBN 0-8414-9326-X). Folcroft.

Poet's Life. Harriet Monroe. LC 71-93777. Repr. of 1938 ed. 17.50 (ISBN 0-404-04349-6). AMS Pr.

Poets' Life of Christ. Norman Ault. 30.00 (ISBN 0-686-17669-3). Quaker City.

Poet's Madness: A Reading of George Trakl. Francis M. Sharp. (Illus.). 364p. 1981. 29.95x (ISBN 0-8014-1297-8). Cornell U Pr.

Poet's Manual & Rhyming Dictionary. Frances Stillman & Jane S. Whitfield. LC 65-11650. 1965. 15.45i (ISBN 0-690-64572-4). T Y Crowell.

Poet's Market '89. 4th ed. Ed. by Judson Jerome. (Illus.). 480p. 1988. 17.95 (ISBN 0-89879-334-3). Writers Digest.

Poet's Mind: L6. James A. Emanuel. Ed. by Jean McConochie. (Regents Readers Ser.). pap. text ed. 3.25 (ISBN 0-13-683962-2, 20975). Prentice ESL.

Poet's New England. Helen A. Clarke. 1911. Repr. 30.00 (ISBN 0-8274-3165-1). R West.

Poet's Notebook. Edith Sitwell. LC 71-152605. xviii, 276p. Repr. of 1950 ed. lib. bdg. 35.00x (ISBN 0-8371-6040-5, SIPN). Greenwood.

Poets of Action. G. Wilson Knight. LC 81-43479. 320p. 1982. lib. bdg. 31.50 (ISBN 0-8191-2073-1); pap. text ed. 15.25 (ISBN 0-8191-2074-X). U Pr of Amer.

Poets of America. Ed. by John Keese. 59.95 (ISBN 0-8490-0866-2). Gordon Pr.

Poets of America. Edmund C. Stedman. 1973. lib. bdg. 25.25 (ISBN 0-8414-7954-2). Folcroft.

Poets of America. Edmund C. Stedman. LC 18-13421. (Biography & Library of Literature, Drama & Criticism). Repr. of 1885 ed. 26.00 (ISBN 0-384-57750-4). Johnson Repr.

Poets of America. Edmund C. Stedman. LC 18-13421. 13.00x (ISBN 0-403-00058-0). Scholarly.

Poets of America. Edmund C. Stedman. 1988. Repr. of 1898 ed. lib. bdg. 49.00x. Am Biog Serv.

Poets of Bulgaria. Ed. by William Meredith. Tr. by Denise Levertov et al from Bulgarian. 150p. 1985. 25.00 (ISBN 0-87775-189-7); pap. 10.00 (ISBN 0-87775-190-0). Unicorn Pr.

Poets of Chile: A Bilingual Anthology, 1965-1985. Ed. by Steven F. White. LC 85-16479. (Illus.). 283p. (Orig.). 1986. 25.00 (ISBN 0-87775-179-X); pap. 12.50 (ISBN 0-87775-180-3). Unicorn Pr.

Poets of Darkness. James B. Goode. LC 80-29653. (Center for the Study of Southern Culture Ser.). 1981. 7.95 (ISBN 0-87805-133-3). U Pr of Miss.

Poets of Great Britain & Ireland, 1945-1960. Ed. by Vincent Sherry. (Dictionary of Literary Biography Ser.: Vol. 27). 416p. 1984. 95.00x (ISBN 0-8103-1705-2). Gale.

Poets of Greece. Edwin Arnold. LC 70-39680. (Essay Index Reprint Ser.). Repr. of 1869 ed. 16.00 (ISBN 0-8369-2738-9). Ayer Co Pubs.

Poets of Haiti. Ed. by Edna W. Underwood. 1977. lib. bdg. 34.95 (ISBN 0-8490-2449-8). Gordon Pr.

Poets of Harrow School. John Gawsworth. 1934. 12.50 (ISBN 0-932062-62-8). Sharon Hill.

Poets of Harrow School (Byron) An Anthology. John Gawsworth. 224p. 1982. Repr. of 1934 ed. lib. bdg. 30.00 (ISBN 0-89984-007-8). Century Bookbindery.

Poets of Ireland. D. J. O'Donoghue. 59.95 (ISBN 0-8490-0867-0). Gordon Pr.

Poets of Ireland. David J. O'Donoghue. LC 68-30622. 242p. 1968. Repr. of 1912 ed. 47.00x (ISBN 0-8103-3152-7). Gale.

Poets of Ireland: A Biographical & Bibliographical Dictionary of Irish Writers of English Verse. David J. O'Donoghue. (Library of Literature, Drama & Criticism). 1970. Repr. of 1912 ed. 42.00 (ISBN 0-384-42975-0). Johnson Repr.

Poets of Modern France. Ludwig Lewisohn. LC 78-103231. 1970. Repr. of 1918 ed. 23.00x (ISBN 0-8046-0868-7, Pub. by Kennikat). Assoc Faculty Pr.

Poets of Modern Russia. Peter France. LC 82-4264. (Cambridge Studies in Russian Literature). 256p. 1983. 42.50 (ISBN 0-521-23490-5); pap. 15.95 (ISBN 0-521-28000-1). Cambridge U Pr.

Poets of Munster. Ed. by Sean Dunne. 224p. 1985. 19.95 (ISBN 0-85646-121-0, Pub. by Anvil Pr Poetry); pap. 10.95 (ISBN 0-85646-122-9). Longwood Pub Group.

Poets of Nicaragua: A Bilingual Anthology 1918-1979. Ed. by Steven F. White. 1982. 20.00 (ISBN 0-686-91915-7); pap. 10.00 (ISBN 0-87775-133-1). Unicorn Pr.

Poets of Our Time: An Anthology. Compiled by F. E. S. Finn. 160p. 1976. pap. 7.95 (ISBN 0-7195-3243-4). Transatl Arts.

Poets of Poets: The Love Verse from the Minor Poems. Alexander B. Grosart. 1893. Repr. 15.00 (ISBN 0-8274-3181-3). R West.

Poets of Sensibility & the Sublime. Intro. by Harold Bloom. (Modern Critical Views Ser.). 324p. 1986. 29.50 (ISBN 0-87754-679-7). Chelsea Hse.

Poets of the Church. Edwin F. Hatfield. LC 77-91533. 1977. Repr. of 1884 ed. lib. bdg. 45.00 (ISBN 0-89341-195-7). Longwood Pub Group.

Poets of the Church: A Series of Biographical Sketches of Hymn-Writers, with Notes on Their Hymns. Edwin F. Hatfield. 728p. 1979. Repr. of 1884 ed. 110.00x (ISBN 0-8103-4291-X). Gale.

Poets of the Democracy. G. C. Martin. LC 79-113342. 1970. Repr. of 1917 ed. 16.50x (ISBN 0-8046-1048-7, Pub. by Kennikat). Assoc Faculty Pr.

Poets of the Early Seventeenth Century. Ed. by Bernard Davis & Elizabeth Davis. (Boutledge English Texts). 1967. pap. 5.95x (ISBN 0-7100-4512-3). Routledge Chapman & Hall.

Poets of the English Language, Vol. 4: Romantic Poets. Ed. by W. H. Auden & Norman H. Pearson. (Viking Portable Library: No. 52). 1977. pap. 8.95 (ISBN 0-14-015052-8, P52). Penguin.

Poets of the Insurrection. LC 75-28840. Repr. of 1918 ed. 20.00 (ISBN 0-404-13832-2). AMS Pr.

Poets of the New York School. Ed. by John B. Myers. (Illus.). 1969. 8.50 (ISBN 0-910664-14-5). Gotham.

Poets of the Nineties. Derek Stanford. 1973. lib. bdg. 37.00 (ISBN 0-8414-7950-X). Folcroft.

Poets of the Pacific: Second Series. facs. ed. Ed. by Yvor Winters. LC 68-57068. (Granger Index Reprint Ser). 1949. 12.00 (ISBN 0-8369-6049-1). Ayer Co Pubs.

Poets of the Pacific: Second Series. Ed. by Yvor Winters. LC 49-9205. pap. 30.00 (ISBN 0-317-29831-3, 2051957). Bks Demand UMI.

Poets of the South. facs. ed. Franklin V. Painter. LC 68-57064. (Granger Index Reprint Ser). 1903. 14.00 (ISBN 0-8369-6037-8). Ayer Co Pubs.

Poets of the Tamil Anthologies. George L. Hart. LC 79-83993. (Princeton Library of Asian Translations). 1979. 28.00x (ISBN 0-691-06406-7). Princeton U Pr.

Poets of the Younger Generation. William Archer. LC 76-120572. (BCL: Series I). Repr. of 1902 ed. 12.50 (ISBN 0-404-00367-2). AMS Pr.

Poets of the Younger Generation. William Archer. LC 72-8574. 564p. 1902. Repr. 12.00 (ISBN 0-403-00240-0). Scholarly.

Poets of Transcendentalism: An Anthology. George W. Cooke. 59.95 (ISBN 0-8490-0868-9). Gordon Pr.

Poets of Transcendentalism: An Anthology. Ed. by George W. Cooke. LC 72-126410. (Literature & Criticism Ser). 1971. Repr. of 1903 ed. lib. bdg. 21.00 (ISBN 0-8337-0652-7). B Franklin.

Poets on Christmas. Ed. by William Knight. Repr. of 1907 ed. lib. bdg. 25.00 (ISBN 0-8495-3016-4). Arden Lib.

Poets on Photography. Ed. by Mark Melnicove. LC 80-68860. (Illus.). 108p. (Orig.). 1981. pap. 20.00 (ISBN 0-937966-04-5). Dog Ear.

Poets on Stage: The Some Symposium on Poetry Readings. Ed. by Alan Ziegler et al. 1978. 7.95 (ISBN 0-913722-18-9, Pub. by Release); perfect bound in wrappers 3.50 (ISBN 0-913722-17-0). Small Pr Dist.

Poets on the Classics: An Anthology. Ed. by Stuart Gillespie. 256p. 1988. text ed. 35.00 (ISBN 0-415-00328-8). Routledge Chapman & Hall.

Poets on the Platform. Ed. by Robert McGovern & Richard Snyder. 40p. 1970. pap. 1.95 (ISBN 0-912592-01-X). Ashland Poetry.

Poet's Other Voice: Conversations on Translation Poetry. Edwin Honig. LC 84-28066. (Illus.). 232p. 1985. lib. bdg. 25.00x (ISBN 0-87023-476-5); pap. 11.95 (ISBN 0-87023-477-3). U of Mass Pr.

Poet's Parents: The Courtship Letters of Emily Norcross & Edward Dickinson. Ed. by Vivian R. Pollak. LC 87-35868. (Illus.). 320p. 1988. 27.50x (ISBN 0-8078-1797-X). U of NC Pr.

Poets, Patriots, & Lovers (Scott, Carlyle, Browning, Burns, Stevenson, Barrie, Dr. John Brown) Flora Masson. 1973. lib. bdg. 17.00 (ISBN 0-8414-6498-7). Folcroft.

Poets, Patrons & Professors. J. A. Dorsten. (Publications of Sir Thomas Brown Institute Ser: No. 2). 1962. lib. bdg. 24.00 (ISBN 90-6021-060-3, Pub. by Leiden Univ. Holland). Kluwer Academic.

Poets, Poems, Movements. Thomas Parkinson. Ed. by A. Walton Litz. LC 86-30910. (Studies in Modern Literature: No. 64). 340p. 1987. 44.95 (ISBN 0-8357-1783-6); pap. write for info. (ISBN 0-8357-1897-2). UMI Res Pr.

Poet's Poet. Elizabeth Atkins. LC 74-9902. 1922. lib. bdg. 25.00 (ISBN 0-8414-2981-2). Folcroft.

Poet's Poet & Other Essays: Robert Burns, Shakespeare, Eliot. William A. Quayle. 351p. 1981. Repr. of 1897 ed. lib. bdg. 30.00 (ISBN 0-8495-4433-5). Arden Lib.

Poets, Prophets & Pragmatists: A New Challenge to Religious Life. Evelyn Woodward. LC 86-72375. 248p. (Orig.). 1987. pap. 6.95 (ISBN 0-87793-349-9). Ave Maria.

Poets, Prophets & Revolutionaries: The Literary Avant-Garde from Rimbaud Through Postmodernism. Charles Russell. 305p. 1985. 29.95x (ISBN 0-19-503550-X). Oxford U Pr.

Poets, Prophets, & Revolutionaries: The Literary Avant-Garde from Rimbaud Through Postmodernism. Charles Russell. 320p. 1987. pap. 10.95 (ISBN 0-19-505078-9). Oxford U Pr.

Poets, Prophets, & Sages: Essays in Biblical Interpretation. Robert Gordis. LC 79-98984. pap. 111.50 (ISBN 0-317-37273-4, 2055498). Bks Demand UMI.

Poet's Prose: The Crisis in American Verse. Stephen Fredman. LC 83-7549. (Cambridge Studies in American Literature & Culture). 176p. 1983. 24.95 (ISBN 0-521-25722-0). Cambridge U Pr.

Poets Respond to AIDS. Ed. by Michael Klein. Date not set. price not set. Crown.

Poet's Riddles: Essays in Seventeenth Century Explication. Edward LeComte. LC 74-77656. 1975. 22.50x (ISBN 0-8046-9065-0, Natl U). Assoc Faculty Pr.

Poet's Tarot. 2nd ed. Jesse Cougar. (Illus., Orig.). 1987. pap. 14.95 (ISBN 0-9615129-7-0). Tough Dove.

Poet's Task. C. Day Lewis. LC 74-16140. 1951. lib. bdg. 17.00 (ISBN 0-8414-5745-X). Folcroft.

Poet's Testament: Poems & Two Plays. George Santayana. LC 75-3339. Repr. of 1953 ed. 22.00 (ISBN 0-404-59424-7). AMS Pr.

Poet's Third Eye. Gordon E. Bigelow. LC 76-15706. 159p. 1976. 8.95 (ISBN 0-8022-2188-2). Philos Lib.

Poet's Time: Politics & Religion in the Work of Andrew Marvell. Warren L. Chernaik. LC 82-4395. 250p. 1983. 37.50 (ISBN 0-521-24773-X). Cambridge U Pr.

Poets to the People. Ed. by Barry Feinberg. (African Writers Ser.). (Orig.). 1980. pap. text ed. 7.00 (ISBN 0-435-90230-X). Heinemann Ed.

Poets to the People: South African Freedom Poems. Ed. by Barry Feinberg. 82p. 1974. 4.50 (ISBN 0-317-36672-6). Africa Fund.

Poets Tongue. W. H. Auden & Garrett Auden. 1988. Repr. of 1935 ed. lib. bdg. 49.00x. Am Biog Serv.

Poet's Tongue. Ed. by W. H. Auden & John Garrett. LC 75-161942. 222p. 1935. Repr. 29.00x (ISBN 0-403-01326-7). Scholarly.

Poet's Translation Series, 2 vols. Ed. by Richard Aldington. Incl. Series One. LC 78-64005 (ISBN 0-404-17101-X); Series Two. LC 78-64016 (ISBN 0-404-17102-8). (Des Imagistes: Literature of the Imagist Movement). Repr. of 1920 ed. Set. 49.00 (ISBN 0-404-17100-1); 25.00 ea. AMS Pr.

Poet's Vision of History. Pratap Singh. Ed. by James Hogg. (Romantic Reassessment ser.). 106p. (Orig.). 1981. pap. 15.00 (ISBN 3-7052-0576-5, Pub. by Salzburg Studies). Longwood Pub Group.

Poets Walk In. Anna P. Broomell. 1954. pap. 2.50x (ISBN 0-87574-077-4, 077). Pendle Hill.

Poets West: An Anthology of Contemporary Poems from the Eleven Western States. Ed. by Lawrence P. Spingarn. LC 73-79233. 182p. 1976. pap. 11.95 (ISBN 0-912288-05-1). Perivale Pr.

Poetspeak: In Their Work About Their Work. Ed. by Paul B. Janeczko. LC 83-2715. 256p. (YA) (gr. 7 up). 1983. 12.95 (ISBN 0-02-747770-3). Bradbury Pr.

Poets's Life of Christ. Norman Ault. LC 72-2513. (Select Bibliographies Reprint Ser). 1972. Repr. of 1922 ed. 22.00 (ISBN 0-8369-6847-6). Ayer Co Pubs.

Pofessional Qualifications for Fire Inspector, Fire Investigator, & Fire Prevention Education Officer: NFPA 1031. National Fire Protection Association Staff. 1982. 10.50 (ISBN 0-317-46518-X, B7-NFPA-1031). Natl Fire Prot.

Poff the Cat, or When We Care. Hartmut Von Hentig. Tr. by Joel Agee from Ger. LC 83-82754. 56p. (Orig.). 1984. 3.98 (ISBN 0-940242-09-5). Fjord Pr.

Poganuc People. Fords et al. (Illus.). 416p. 1977. pap. 7.95 (ISBN 0-317-35972-X). Stowe-Day.

Poganuc People: Their Loves & Lives. Harriet Beecher Stowe. LC 76-56587. (Illus.). 1977. pap. 7.95 (ISBN 0-917482-06-9). Stowe-Day.

Pogo a la Sundae. Walt Kelly. 128p. 1977. 15.00 (ISBN 0-8398-2392-4). Ultramarine Pub.

Pogo: Even Better. Ed. by Kelly & Bill Crouch, Jr. (Illus.). 224p. (Orig.). 1984. pap. 9.95 (ISBN 0-671-50473-8, Fireside). S&S.

Pogo Papers. Walt Kelly. 200p. 1977. 15.00 (ISBN 0-8398-2386-X). Ultramarine Pub.

Pogo Peek-a-Book. Walt Kelly. 96p. 1977. 15.00 (ISBN 0-8398-2389-4). Ultramarine Pub.

Pogo: Romances Recaptured. Walt Kelly. (Illus.). 320p. (YA) 1975. pap. 9.95 (ISBN 0-671-22184-1, Fireside). S&S.

Pogo Stepmother Goose. Walt Kelly. 96p. 1977. 15.00 (ISBN 0-8398-2390-8). Ultramarine Pub.

Pogo User's Manual, General Aids to Graphic Programming. J. E. Rieber & V. R. Lamb. LC 70-131898. 191p. 1970. 25.00 (ISBN 0-403-04531-2). Scholarly.

Pogo: We Have Met the Enemy & He Is Us. Walt Kelly. 1972. pap. 7.95 (ISBN 0-671-21260-5, Fireside). S&S.

Pogo Will Be That Was. 1987. pap. 9.95 (ISBN 0-671-24854-5, Fireside). S&S.

Pogo's Body Politic. Walt Kelly. Ed. by Selby Kelly. 1976. pap. 2.95 (ISBN 0-671-22302-X, Fireside). S&S.

Pogo's Double Sundae, 2 vols. in 1. Walt Kelly. 1978. pap. 9.95 (ISBN 0-671-24139-7, Fireside). S&S.

Pohlstars. Frederik Pohl. 272p. 1984. pap. 2.95 (ISBN 0-345-31545-6, Del Rey). Ballantine.

Poiesis: Structure & Thought. H. D. Kitto. (Sather Classical Lectures: No. 36). 1966. 32.00x (ISBN 0-520-00651-8). U of Cal Pr.

Poil de Carotte. Renard. (EMC Easy Readers: Series A). (YA) (gr. 7-12). pap. 3.95 (ISBN 0-88436-046-6, 40264). EMC.

Poil de Carotte see Oeuvres.

Poimandres As Myth: Scholarly Theory & Gnostic Meaning. Robert A. Segal. (Religion & Reason Ser.: No. 33). 216p. 1986. lib. bdg. 63.50 (ISBN 0-89925-146-3). Mouton.

Poinciana. Phyllis A. Whitney. 1984. pap. 3.25 (ISBN 0-449-20439-1, Crest). Fawcett.

Poindexter of Washington: A Study in Progressive Politics. Howard W. Allen. LC 80-20123. 352p. 1981. 28.95x (ISBN 0-8093-0952-1). S Ill U Pr.

Poingdestre-Pendexter Family. G. T. Ridlon. LC 73-133877. (Saco Valley Settlements Ser). 1970. pap. 4.00 (ISBN 0-8048-0823-6). C E Tuttle.

Poinsett County Arkansas Census 1850. Courtney York & Gerlene York. 54p. (Orig.). pap. 12.00x (ISBN 0-916660-05-2). Hse of York.

Poinsettia & Her Family. Felicia Bond. LC 81-43035. (Illus.). 32p. (ps-3). 1981. 12.70 (ISBN 0-690-04144-6, Crowell Jr Bks); PLB 12.89 (ISBN 0-690-04145-4). HarpJ.

Poinsettia & Her Family. Felicia Bond. LC 81-43035. (Trophy Picture Bks.). (Illus.). 32p. (ps-3). 1985. pap. 2.95i (ISBN 0-06-443076-6, Trophy). HarpJ.

Poinsettia & the Firefighters. Felicia Bond. LC 83-46169. (Illus.). 32p. (ps-3). 1984. 12.70 (ISBN 0-690-04400-3, Crowell Jr Bks); PLB 12.89 (ISBN 0-690-04401-1). HarpJ.

Poinsettia & the Firefighters. Felicia Bond. LC 83-46169. (Trophy Picture Book). (Illus.). 32p. (ps-3). 1988. pap. 3.95 (ISBN 0-06-443160-6, Trophy). HarpJ.

Point After: Advice from God's Athletes. Elliot Johnson. 128p. 1987. pap. 5.95 (ISBN 0-310-26171-6, 12416P). Zondervan.

Point & Figure Method of Anticipating Stock Price Movements. Victor De Villiers. 1973. pap. 15.00 (ISBN 0-685-42039-6). Windsor.

Point & Line to Plane. Wassily Kandinsky. LC 79-50616. (Illus.). 1979. pap. text ed. 4.50 (ISBN 0-486-23808-3). Dover.

Point Beyond Silence: A Book of Poetry. Thomas A. Phelan. LC 87-50788. 100p. 1987. text ed. 9.95x (ISBN 0-317-67978-3); pap. text ed. 4.95x (ISBN 1-55605-013-5). Wyndham Hall.

Point Blank. (S.O.B. Ser.: No. 17). Date not set. pap. 2.50 (Pub. by Worldwide). Harlequin Bks.

Point Blank. Richard Stark. 160p. 1984. 13.95 (ISBN 0-8052-8199-1, Pub. by Allison & Busby England). Schocken.

Point Blank. Don L. Wulffson. 272p. 1987. pap. 3.95 (ISBN 0-451-14920-3, Sig). NAL.

Point Bonita to Point Reyes: Outdoors in Marin. Dick Murdock. (Illus.). 144p. (Orig.). 1989. pap. 7.95 (ISBN 0-932916-14-7). May Murdock.

Point Count Bidding. rev. ed. Charles H. Goren. 1958. pap. 5.95 (ISBN 0-671-59230-0, Fireside). S&S.

Point Counter Point. Aldous Huxley. 1965. pap. 4.95 (ISBN 0-06-083048-4, P3048, PL). Har-Row.

Point Counterpoint: Discussion & Persuasion Techniques. George W. Pifer & Nancy W. Mutoh. 200p. 1988. pap. text ed. 11.50 (ISBN 0-06-632403-3). Newbury Hse.

Point Counterpoint: Eight Cases for Composition. Thayle K. Anderson & Kent Forrester. 501p. 1987. pap. text ed. 13.00 (ISBN 0-15-570703-5). HarBraceJ.

Point-Counterpoint: Readings in American Government. 2nd ed. Herbert M. Levine. 1983. pap. text ed. write for info. (ISBN 0-673-15625-7). Scott F.

Point Defect in Metals II: Dynamical Properties & Diffusion Controlled Reactions. P. H. Dederichs & R. Zeller. (Springer Tracts in Modern Physics: Vol. 87). 1980. 45.00 (ISBN 0-387-09623-X). Springer-Verlag.

Point Defects & Defect Interactions in Metals: Proceedings of the Fifth Yamada Congerence on Point Defects & Defect Interactions in Metals. Ed. by J. Takamura et al. 1983. 160.75 (ISBN 0-444-86529-2, I-139-83, North-Holland). Elsevier.

Point Defects & Diffusion in Strained Metals. L. A. Girifalco & D. O. Welch. 180p. (Orig.). 1967. 82.00 (ISBN 0-677-01400-7). Gordon & Breach.

Point Defects in Crystals. R. K. Watts. LC 76-43013. Repr. of 1977 ed. 62.00 (ISBN 0-8357-9956-5, 2013522). Bks Demand UMI.

Point Defects in Materials. F. Agullo-Lopez & C. R. Catlow. 450p. 1988. price not set. Acad Pr.

Point Defects in Metals. A. C. Damask & G. J. Dienes. 328p. 1963. 95.00 (ISBN 0-677-00190-8). Gordon & Breach.

Point Defects in Minerals, Mineral Physics 1. Ed. by R. N. Schock. (Geophysical Monograph Ser.: Vol. 31). 240p. 1985. 25.00 (ISBN 0-87590-056-9). Am Geophysical.

Point Defects in Semiconductors I. M. Lannoo & J. Bourgoin. (Springer Ser. in Solid-State Sciences: Vol. 22). (Illus.). 260p. 1981. 39.00 (ISBN 0-387-10518-2). Springer-Verlag.

Point Defects in Semiconductors II: Experimental Aspects. J. Bourgoin & M. Lannoo. (Springer Series in Solid-State Sciences: Vol. 35). (Illus.). 295p. 1983. 41.00 (ISBN 0-387-11515-3). Springer-Verlag.

Point du Jour. Andre Breton. (Idees Ser.). 7.95 (ISBN 0-685-37237-5); pap. 3.95 (ISBN 0-686-66856-1). Schoenhof.

Point Elliott Treaty, Eighteen Fifty-Five. Lynn Kickingbird & Curtis Berkey. (Treaty Manuscripts Ser.: No. 9). 28p. 9.00 (ISBN 0-944253-31-8). Inst Dev Indian Law.

Point Four, Near East & Africa: A Selected Bibliography of Studies on Economically Underdeveloped Countries. U. S. Department of State-Division of Library & Reference Services. LC 65-55124. (Illus.). 1969. Repr. of 1951 ed. lib. bdg. 35.00x (ISBN 0-8371-1732-1, ROFO). Greenwood.

Point Group Symmetry Applications: Methods & Tables. Philip H. Butler. LC 80-17947. 578p. 1981. 85.00x (ISBN 0-306-40523-7, Plenum Pr). Plenum Pub.

Point Hope, an Eskimo Village in Transition. James W. Vanstone. LC 84-45530. (American Ethnological Society Monographs: No. 35). 1988. Repr. of 1962 ed. 31.50 (ISBN 0-404-62934-2). AMS Pr.

Point: Instant of Time. John A. Ebe. (Fundamentals of Mechanics Ser.: Vol. 1). 60p. lib. bdg. write for info. Ebe.

Point Lace & Diamonds. facsimile ed. George A. Baker, Jr. LC 74-103080. (Granger Index Reprint Ser.). 1875. 14.00 (ISBN 0-8369-6095-5). Ayer Co Pubs.

Point, Line, Plane & Solid: A Basic Text Workbook for Engineering Graphics. 3rd ed. Lawrence E. Kundis et al. 384p. 1983. pap. 26.95 (ISBN 0-8403-3185-1). Kendall-Hunt.

Point Lobos: An Illustrated Walker's Handbook. Frances Thompson. LC 80-82176. (Illus.). 112p. 1980. pap. 7.00 (ISBN 0-9604542-0-9). Inkstone Books.

Point Loma Community in California, 1897-1942: A Theosophical Experiment. Emmett A. Greenwalt. LC 76-42802. Repr. of 1955 ed. 26.00 (ISBN 0-404-60068-9). AMS Pr.

Point Loma Theosophical Society: A List of Publications, 1898 - 1942. Loren R. Brown. LC 81-187499. (Illus.). 136p. 1977. pap. 10.00 (ISBN 0-913510-46-7). Wizards.

Point Lookout Prison Camp for Confederates. LC 72-85750. 217p. 1983. 20.00 (ISBN 0-686-24148-7). E W Beitzell.

Point-No-Point Treaty, Eighteen Fifty-five. Lynn Kickingbird & Curtis Berkey. (Treaty Maunuscrips Ser.: No. 10). 29p. 9.00 (ISBN 0-944253-32-6). Inst Dev Indian Law.

Point of Attack: A Season with the New York Giants. Harry Carson & Jim Smith. (Illus.). 224p. 1987. text ed. 16.95 (ISBN 0-07-010227-9). McGraw.

Point of Attack: The Defense Strikes Back. Harry Carson & Jim Smith. 192p. 1988. pap. text ed. 4.95 (ISBN 0-07-010231-7). McGraw.

Point of Christology. Schubert M. Ogden. LC 81-47842. 224p. 1982. 15.45 (ISBN 0-06-066352-9, HarpR). Har-Row.

Point of Departure. James Cameron. 318p. 1986. 17.95 (ISBN 0-85362-175-6, Oriel). Routledge Chapman & Hall.

Point of Departure. Robert S. Gold. (gr. 7-12). 1981. pap. 2.75 (LE). Dell.

Point of Departure: Nineteen Stories of Youth & Discovery. Ed. by Robert S. Gold. 192p. (Orig.). (gr. 7 up). 1967. pap. 3.25 (ISBN 0-440-96983-2, LFL). Dell.

Point of Departure: The Autobiography of Jean Devanny. Jean Devanny. Ed. by Carole Ferrier. LC 86-7068. (Illus.). 332p. 1987. text ed. 34.50x (ISBN 0-7022-1979-7). U of Queensland Pr.

Point of Entry: A Study of Client Reception in the Social Services. Anthony S. Hall. 1974. 30.00x (ISBN 0-317-05811-8, Pub. by Natl Inst Social Work). State Mutual Bk.

Point of Murder. Margaret Yorke. 172p. 1987. pap. 4.95 (ISBN 0-89733-255-5). Academy Chi Pubs.

Point of No Return. John P. Marquand. 559p. 1985. pap. 11.95 (ISBN 0-89733-174-5). Academy Chi Pubs.

Point of No Return. Carole Mortimer. 192p. 1982. pap. 1.75 (ISBN 0-373-10479-0). Harlequin Bks.

Point of No Return. Peter Wenger. 1986. 13.95 (ISBN 0-533-06875-4). Vantage.

Point of Order: A Profile of Senator Joe McCarthy. Robert P. Ingalls. (Illus.). 1981. 9.95 (ISBN 0-399-20827-5, Putnam). Putnam Pub Group.

Point of Purchase Design. Ed. by Robert B. Konikow. LC 84-19036. (Illus.). 256p. 1984. 49.95 (ISBN 0-86636-003-4). PBC Intl Inc.

Point of Reference. Richard Russell. 1979. pap. 1.50 (ISBN 0-505-51394-3, Pub. by Tower Bks). Leisure NY.

Point-of-Sale: Current Trends & Beyond. 300p. 1986. pap. 65.00 (ISBN 0-317-65513-2, 30-5073). Natl Ret Merch.

Point of View. Rick Preston. LC 87-40205. (Illus.). 112p. 1988. 60.00 (ISBN 0-912383-51-8); ltd. ed. 350.00 (ISBN 0-317-61180-1). Van der Marck.

Point of View see Lady Barbarina.

Point of View in the Cinema: A Theory of Narration & Subjectivity in Classical Film. Edward Branigan. (Approaches to Semiotics Ser.: No. 66). xvi, 246p. 1984. 49.95x (ISBN 90-279-3079-1); pap. 19.95 (ISBN 90-279-3139-9). Mouton.

Point of View: Talks on Education. Edward H. Levi. LC 49-11213. 1970. 4.50x (ISBN 0-226-47412-7). U of Chicago Pr.

Point of Words: Children's Understanding of Metaphor & Irony. Ellen Winner. LC 87-21092. 256p. 1988. 22.50 (ISBN 0-674-68125-8). Harvard U Pr.

Point One: Smart Art. Ed. by Joseph Masheck. (Illus., Orig.). 1984. pap. 7.95 (ISBN 0-930279-01-8). Willis Locker & Owens.

Point Park College: The First 25 Years; An Oral History. Albert F. McLean. 1985. write for info. Point Park.

Point Pattern Analysis. Barry N. Boots & Arthur Getis. (Scientific Geography Ser.: Vol. 8). 96p. 1988. text ed. 16.95 (ISBN 0-8039-2245-0); pap. text ed. 7.95 (ISBN 0-8039-2588-3). Sage.

Point Process Models of Cavity Radiation & Detection: A Statistical Treatment of Photon Population Point Processes. S. K. Srinivasan. (Charles Griffin Book Ser.). (Illus.). 192p. 1988. 39.95 (ISBN 0-19-520636-3). Oxford U Pr.

Point Process Models: With Applications to Safety & Reliability. W. A. Thompson. 250p. 1988. text ed. 39.95 (ISBN 0-412-01481-5, Pub. by Chapman & Hall England). Routledge Chapman & Hall.

Point Process Queuing Problems. P. Bartfai & J. Tomko. (Colloquia Mathematics Ser.: Vol. 24). 426p. 1981. 105.25 (ISBN 0-444-85432-0). Elsevier.

Point Processes. D. R. Cox & V. Isham. 1980. 19.95 (ISBN 0-412-21910-7, NO. 2962, Pub. by Chapman & Hall England). Routledge Chapman & Hall.

Point Processes & Queues: Martingale Dynamics. P. Bremaud. (Springer Series in Statistics). (Illus.). 352p. 1981. 53.50 (ISBN 0-387-90536-7). Springer-Verlag.

Point Processes & Their Statistical Inference. Karr. (Probability Ser.: Pure & Applied). 608p. 1986. 95.00 (ISBN 0-8247-7513-9). Dekker.

Point Reyes. 2nd, rev. ed. Dorothy Whitnah. LC 85-51088. (Illus.). 114p. 1985. pap. 9.95 (ISBN 0-89997-056-7). Wilderness Pr.

Point Reyes: Secret Places & Magic Moments. rev. ed. Phil Arnot. LC 88-50274. (Illus.). 256p. (Orig.). 1988. pap. 9.95 (ISBN 0-933174-57-8). Wide World-Tetra.

Point System for Title 24 Residential Energy Code: Chapter 5 of ABAG Energy Conservation Handbook. 200p. 1985. 17.00 (ISBN 0-318-22697-9). Assn Bay Area.

Point Team. J. B. Hadley. 228p. (Orig.). 1984. pap. 2.95 (ISBN 0-446-30930-3). Warner Bks.

Point Team No. 3: Cobra Strike. J. B. Hadley. 258p. (Orig.). 1986. pap. 2.95 (ISBN 0-446-32782-4). Warner Bks.

Point the Sun Tomorrow. Gertrude M. Lutz. 1956. 2.50 (ISBN 0-8233-0061-7). Golden Quill.

Point-to-Set Maps & Mathematical Programming. Ed. by P. Huard. LC 78-23304. (Mathemartical Programming Studies: Vol. 10). 190p. 1979. 42.00 (ISBN 0-444-85243-3, North Holland). Elsevier.

Point Virtue. Anne T. Brooks. 1979. pap. 2.25 (ISBN 0-505-51370-6, Pub. by Tower Bks). Leisure NY.

Point Where Lovers Meet. Jesse Zimmerman. 160p. 1972. 4.95 (ISBN 0-87141-047-8). Manyland.

Point Where Teaching & Writing Intersect. Ed. by Nancy Larson Shapiro & Ron Padgett. 145p. 1983. pap. 6.00 (ISBN 0-915924-33-1). Tchrs & Writers Coll.

Point 045 Automatic. (Weaponry Ser.). 1986. lib. bdg. 79.95 (ISBN 0-8490-3853-7). Gordon Pr.

Pointed Sky. Rudy White. 8.95 (ISBN 0-533-06109-1). Vantage.

Pointed Tales. William C. Dixon. LC 80-81102. 98p. (Orig.). (gr. 1-4). 1980. pap. 5.95 (ISBN 0-8192-1270-9). Morehouse.

Pointed To. Skip Anderson. 44p. (Orig.). 1986. pap. 3.00 (ISBN 0-932662-57-9). St Andrews NC.

Pointer Champions: 1889-1980. Jan L. Pata. (Illus.). 108p. 1981. pap. 29.95 (ISBN 0-940808-00-5). Camino E E & B.

Pointer Champions: 1981-1986. Camino E. E. & B. Co. Staff. (Illus.). 145p. 1987. pap. 24.95 (ISBN 0-940808-43-9). Camino E E & B.

Pointers from Nisargadatta Maharaj. Ramesh s. Balsekar. LC 82-71505. xiv, 223p. 1983. Repr. of 1984 ed. 13.50 (ISBN 0-89386-004-2). Acorn NC.

Pointers in Punjab. Madan Gaur. 1985. 18.50x (ISBN 0-8364-1367-9, Pub. by Press & PR Serv). South Asia Bks.

Pointers to Cancer Prognosis. Ed. by Basil A. Stoll. (Developments in Oncology Ser.). 1987. lib. bdg. 106.00 (ISBN 0-89838-841-4, Pub. by Martinus Nijhoff Netherlands); pap. text ed. 39.95 (ISBN 0-89838-876-7, Pub. by Martinus Nijhoff Netherlands). Kluwer Academic.

Pointing the Way. facs. ed. Martin Buber. LC 77-134063. (Essay Index Reprint Ser). 1957. 16.00 (ISBN 0-8369-2149-6). Ayer Co Pubs.

Pointing the Way. Sutton E. Griggs. LC 75-144622. Repr. of 1908 ed. 12.50 (ISBN 0-404-00167-X). AMS Pr.

Pointing the Way with Puppets. Pat Zabriskie. LC 81-81240. 80p. 1981. pap. 3.95 (ISBN 0-88243-574-4, 02-0574). Gospel Pub.

Pointlike Structures Inside & Outside Hadrons. Ed. by Antonio Zichichi. LC 80-25632. (Subnuclear Ser.: Vol. 17). 748p. 1982. 120.00x (ISBN 0-306-40568-7, Plenum Pr). Plenum Pub.

Points & Lines. Seicho Matsumoto. LC 72-117385. 160p. 1986. pap. 4.95 (ISBN 0-87011-456-5). Kodansha.

Points at Issue, & Some Other Points. facs. ed. Henry A. Beers. LC 67-22055. (Essay Index Reprint Ser). 1904. 17.00 (ISBN 0-8369-0183-5). Ayer Co Pubs.

Points Discount Disclosure Tables. Financial Publishing Co. Staff. 256p. 1981. pap. 10.75 (ISBN 0-87600-654-3). Finan Pub.

Points for a Compass Rose. Evan S. Connell. LC 85-60864. 256p. 1985. pap. 12.50 (ISBN 0-86547-205-X). N Point Pr.

Points for a Diet. Virginia Stucky. 96p. (Orig.). 1984. pap. 3.95 (ISBN 0-941040-01-1). Diet Teach Progs.

Points for a Good Life Nutrition: Diet Manual. Virginia Stucky. LC 81-68748. (Illus.). 192p. (Orig.). 1981. pap. text ed. 11.95 (ISBN 0-941040-00-3). Diet Teach Progs.

Points for Emphasis. William J. Fallis. (Orig.). 1989. pap. 2.95 (ISBN 0-8054-1566-1). Broadman.

Points for Emphasis, Nineteen Eighty-Eight to Nineteen Eighty-Nine. William J. Fallis. (Orig.). 1988. pap. 3.95 (ISBN 0-8054-1565-3). Broadman.

Points for Parents Perplexed about Drugs. David C. Hancock. 16p. (Orig.). 1975. pap. 0.75 (ISBN 0-89486-031-3). Hazelden.

Points: Guide to Frequent Traveler Bonus Programs. Susan Michaels & Taylor Milsal. (Illus.). 204p. (Orig.). 1987. pap. 6.95 (ISBN 0-87052-375-9). Hippocrene Bks.

Points in a Journey. Keith Harrison. LC 67-28706. 1967. 10.00 (ISBN 0-8023-1130-X). Dufour.

Points in Time. Paul Bowles. LC 83-16571. 96p. 1984. 12.50 (ISBN 0-88001-044-4). Ecco Pr.

Points, Lines & Walls: In Liquid Crystals, Magnetic Systems & Various Ordered Media. M. Klemen. LC 81-21976. 322p. 1982. 97.95 (ISBN 0-471-10194-X, Pub. by Wiley-Interscience). Wiley.

Points of Chinese Acupuncture. J. Lavier. Tr. by Philip Chancellor from Fr. 115p. 1974. text ed. 10.95x (ISBN 0-8464-1038-9). Beekman Pubs.

Points of Chinese Acupuncture. J. Lavier. 1980. 15.00x (ISBN 0-85032-168-9, Pub. by Daniel Co England). State Mutual Bk.

Points of Departure. Dan Pagis. Ed. by Allen Mandelbaum & Yehuda Amichai. Tr. by Stephen Mitchel from Hebrew. (Jewish Poetry Ser.). 160p. 1982. 12.95 (ISBN 0-8276-0200-6); pap. 8.95 (ISBN 0-8276-0201-4). JPS Phila.

Points of Departure: An Anthology of Nonfiction. Ed. by James Moffett. 1985. pap. 4.95 (ISBN 0-451-62380-0, Ment). NAL.

Points of Departure: An Introduction to the Systematic Study of Public Policy. Benjamin Most. 360p. cancelled (ISBN 0-87073-305-2); pap. 11.95 (ISBN 0-87073-319-2). Schenkman Bks Inc.

Points of Departure: Essays & Stories for College English. facsimile ed. Ed. by Arthur J. Carr & William R. Steinhoff. LC 74-167324. (Essay Index Reprint Ser). Repr. of 1960 ed. 35.50 (ISBN 0-8369-2449-5). Ayer Co Pubs.

Points of Eighteenth-Century Verse. I. A. Williams. LC 72-6575. 1934. lib. bdg. 30.00 (ISBN 0-8414-0158-6). Folcroft.

Points of Entry. Ed. by Mildred Schell. (Orig.). 1973. pap. 1.35 (ISBN 0-377-80301-4). Friendship Pr.

Points of Friction. facs. ed. Agnes Repplier. LC 77-121505. (Essay Index Reprint Ser). 1920. 21.50 (ISBN 0-8369-2027-9). Ayer Co Pubs.

Points of Honor. Thomas A. Boyd. LC 72-5859. (Short Story Index Reprint Ser.). 1972. Repr. of 1925 ed. 22.00 (ISBN 0-8369-4192-6). Ayer Co Pubs.

Points of Issue: A Compendium of Points of Issue of Books by 20th Century Authors. 2nd ed. Ed. by William M. McBride. 104p. pap. 6.00x. McBride Pub.

Points of Light. Linda G. Sexton. 288p. 1988. 16.95 (ISBN 0-316-78200-9). Little.

Points of Modern English Syntax. P. A. Erades. Ed. by N. J. Robat. (Contributions to English Studies). 260p. 1975. pap. text ed. 22.00 (ISBN 90-265-0184-6, Pub. by Swets Pub Serv Holland). Swets North Am.

Points of View, 2 Vols. facsimile ed. Frederick E. Birkenhead. LC 77-111815. (Essay Index Reprint Ser.). 1923. 36.50 (ISBN 0-8369-1594-1). Ayer Co Pubs.

Points of View. 3rd ed. Robert Diclerico & Allan Hammock. 352p. 1986. pap. text ed. write for info (ISBN 0-394-35408-7, RanC). Random.

Points of View. Thomas S. Eliot. Ed. by John Hayward. LC 78-14116. 1981. Repr. of 1941 ed. 15.00 (ISBN 0-88355-788-6). Hyperion Conn.

Poland After Solidarity: Social Movements versus the State. Ed. by Bronislaw Misztal. 1985. 19.95 (ISBN 0-88738-049-2). Transaction Bks.

Poland: An Annotated Bibliography of Books. Ed. by Gerald A. Kanka. (Reference Library of the Humanities). 1988. lib. bdg. 45.00 (ISBN 0-8240-8492-6). Garland Pub.

Poland & the Minority Races. Arthur L. Goodhart. LC 71-135809. (Eastern Europe Collection Ser). 1970. Repr. of 1920 ed. 14.00x (ISBN 0-405-02751-6). Ayer Co Pubs.

Poland: Behind the Crisis. Sam Marcy. 168p. 1982. pap. 3.95 (ISBN 0-89567-076-3). World View Forum.

Poland Between the Superpowers: Security Versus Economic Recovery. Arthur R. Rachwald. LC 83-6758. (Replica Edition Ser.). 154p. 1984. pap. 24.50x (ISBN 0-86531-975-8). Westview.

Poland Challenges a Divided World. John Rensenbrink. LC 88-1393. 256p. 1988. 19.95 (ISBN 0-8071-1446-4). La State U Pr.

Poland: Communism, Nationalism, Anti-Semitism. Michael Checinski. 320p. 1982. text ed. 22.95x (ISBN 0-918294-18-5). Karz-Cohl Pub.

Poland: Genesis of a Revolution. Ed. by Abraham Brumberg. LC 82-40137. 367p. 1983. 19.45 (ISBN 0-394-52323-7, Vin); pap. 7.95 (ISBN 0-394-71025-8). Random.

Poland in the British Parliament: Documentary Material Relating to the Cause of Poland During World War Two, 3 vols. Pilsudski Institute of America. Ed. by Waclaw Jedrzejewicz. 1834p. Vol. 1. (ISBN 0-940962-25-X). Vol. 2 (ISBN 0-940962-26-8). Vol. 3 (ISBN 0-940962-27-6). Set. 25.00 (ISBN 0-940962-28-4). Polish Inst Art & Sci.

Poland in the Second World War. Josef Garlinski. (Illus.). 390p. 1987. pap. 14.95 (ISBN 0-87052-372-4). Hippocrene Bks.

Poland in the Twentieth Century. M. K. Dziewanowski. LC 76-51216. (Illus.). 1977. pap. 17.00x (ISBN 0-231-08372-6). Columbia U Pr.

Poland: Land of Freedom Fighters. Christine Pfeiffer. LC 83-15025. (Discovering Our Heritage Ser.). (Illus.). 175p. (gr. 5 up). 1984. PLB 12.95 (ISBN 0-87518-254-2). Dillon.

Poland, Nineteen Forty-Four to Nineteen Sixty-Two: The Sovietization of a Captive People. Richard F. Staar. LC 75-1297. (Illus.). 300p. 1975. Repr. of 1962 ed. lib. bdg. 38.50x (ISBN 0-8371-8008-2, STPO). Greenwood.

Poland, Nineteen Thirty-Nine to Nineteen Forty-Seven. John Coutouvidis & Jaime Reynolds. Ed. by Geoffrey Warner & David M. Ellwood. (Politics of Liberation Ser.). (Illus.). 393p. 1986. 59.50 (ISBN 0-8419-1093-6). Holmes & Meier.

Poland, Nineteen Thirty-One. Jerome Rothenberg. LC 74-8646. (Illus.). 160p. 1974. 7.50 (ISBN 0-8112-0541-X); pap. 3.25 (ISBN 0-8112-0542-8, NDP379). New Directions.

Poland Past & Present: Select Bibliography of Works in English. Norman Davies. (Illus.). 175p. 1976. lib. bdg. 26.00 (ISBN 0-89250-010-7). Orient Res Partners.

Poland: Penal Code of the Polish People's Republic. (American Series of Foreign Penal Codes: Vol. 19). xiii, 139p. 1973. 17.50x (ISBN 0-8377-0039-6). Rothman.

Poland: Politics, Economics & Society. G. Kolankiewicz. (Marxist Regimes Ser.). 220p. 1987. 35.00 (ISBN 0-317-61006-6, Pub. by Pinter Pubs UK); pap. 12.50 (ISBN 0-86187-437-4). Columbia U Pr.

Poland Since Nineteen Fifty-Six: Readings & Essays on Polish Government & Politics. Ed. by Tadeusz N. Cieplak. LC 79-125262. 482p. 1972. text ed. 39.50x (ISBN 0-8290-0193-X); pap. text ed. 16.50x (ISBN 0-8290-0374-6). Irvington.

Poland: Socialist State, Rebellious Nation. Ray Taras. 178p. 1986. 27.50 (ISBN 0-8133-0181-5). Westview.

Poland, Solidarity, Walesa. Michael Dobbs et al. (Illus.). 128p. 1981. 23.00 (ISBN 0-08-028147-8). McGraw.

Poland Statistical Data, 1979. cancelled (ISBN 0-8002-2328-4). Intl Pubns Serv.

Poland, the Captive Satellite: A Study in National Psychology. Joseph W. Zurawski. (Illus.). 1962. 4.75 (ISBN 0-685-09286-0). Endurance.

Poland: The Protracted Crisis. Adam Bromke. 264p. (Orig.). 1986. (Pub. by Mosaic Canada); pap. 13.95 (ISBN 0-88962-194-2). Riverrun NY.

Poland: The Role of the Press in Political Change. Madeleine K. Albright. LC 83-16144. (Washington Papers). 168p. 1983. pap. 9.95 (ISBN 0-275-91559-X, B1559). Praeger.

Poland, the United States, & the Stabilizaton of Europe, 1919-1933. Neal Pease. 224p. 1986. 24.95x (ISBN 0-19-504050-3). Oxford U Pr.

Poland: Three Years after-A Report on Human Rights in Poland. 1983. 10.00 (ISBN 0-934143-11-0). Lawyers Comm Intl.

Poland Today: The State of the Republic. Compiled by Experience & the Future Discussion Group Staff. Tr. by Michel Vale et al from Pol. LC 81-8782. 256p. 1981. 29.95 (ISBN 0-87332-201-0). M E Sharpe.

Poland Travel Guide. Marc Heine. 1987. pap. 8.95 (ISBN 0-87052-380-5). Hippocrene Bks.

Poland under Black Light. Janusz Anderman. Tr. by Andrew Short & Nina Taylor. (Readers International Ser.). 150p. 1985. 12.50 (ISBN 0-930523-13-X, Dist. by Consortium). Readers Intl.

Poland under Black Light. Janusz Anderman. Tr. by Nina Taylor & Andrew Short. (Readers International Ser.). 155p. (Orig.). 1988. pap. 6.95 (ISBN 0-930523-14-8, Dist. by Consortium). Readers Intl.

Poland under Martial Law: A Report by the Polish Helsinki Watch Committee. Helsinki Watch Staff. 352p. 1983. 6.00 (ISBN 0-938579-94-0). Fund Free Expression.

Poland's Caribbean Tragedy. Jan Pachonski & Reuel K. Wilson. 352p. 1986. 35.00 (ISBN 0-88033-093-7). East Eur Quarterly.

Poland's Caribbean Tragedy: A Study of Polish Legions in the Haitian War of Independence 1802-1803. Jan Pachonski & Reuel K. Wilson. (East European Monographs). (Illus.). 386p. 35.00 (ISBN 0-317-57824-3). Columbia U Pr.

Poland's Commitment to Its Past: A Report on Two Study Tours. Krystyna Puc. LC 85-21716. (Illus.). 48p. (Orig.). 1985. pap. 4.50 (ISBN 0-941182-16-9). Partners Livable.

Poland's Ghettos at War. Alfred Katz. LC 78-120535. 1978. 34.50 (ISBN 0-8290-0194-8); pap. text ed. 12.95x (ISBN 0-8290-0195-6). Irvington.

Poland's International Affairs 1919-1960. Stephan Horak. LC 64-63009. (Indiana University Russian & East European Ser.: Vol. 31). Repr. of 1964 ed. 51.00 (ISBN 0-8357-9233-1, 2015455). Bks Demand UMI.

Poland's Millenium of Christianity. Canadian Polish Millenium Fund Staff. 50p. (Eng. & Fr.). 1966. 1.00 (ISBN 0-940962-29-2). Polish Inst Art & Sci.

Poland's Place in Europe: General Sikorski & the Origin of the Oder-Neisse Line, 1939-1943. S. M. Terry. 1982. 50.50x (ISBN 0-691-07643-X); pap. 19.50 (ISBN 0-691-10136-1). Princeton U Pr.

Poland's Politicized Army: Communists in Uniform. George C. Malcher. LC 84-6894. 272p. 1984. 36.95 (ISBN 0-275-91221-3, C1221). Praeger.

Poland's Politics: Idealism vs. Realism. Adam Bromke. LC 66-21331. (Harvard University, Russian Research Center Studies: Vol. 51). pap. 82.50 (ISBN 0-317-08918-8, 2017754). Bks Demand UMI.

Poland's Self-Limiting Revolution. Jadwiga Staniszkis. Ed. by Jan T. Gross. LC 82-61387. 328p. 1984. 29.50x (ISBN 0-691-09403-9). Princeton U Pr.

Polanski. Barbara Leaming. 1983. pap. 6.95 (ISBN 0-671-24986-X, Touchstone Bks). S&S.

Polanski: Three Film Scripts, Knife in the Water, Repulsion, Cul-de-Sac. Roman Polanski. LC 74-24656. (Illus.). 214p. 1975. 17.95 (ISBN 0-06-438425-X). Boulevard.

Polanyian Meditations: In Search of a Post-Critical Logic. William H. Poteat. LC 85-20429. x, 330p. 1985. 39.50 (ISBN 0-8223-0542-9). Duke.

Polar & Magnetospheric Substorms. S. I. Akasofu. (Astrophysics & Space Science Library: No.11). 280p. 1968. lib. bdg. 37.00 (ISBN 90-277-0108-3, Pub. by Reidel Holland). Kluwer Academic.

Polar Animals. N. S. Barrett. Ed. by FS Staff. (Picture Library). (Illus.). 32p. (gr. 1-6). 1988. 10.90 (ISBN 0-531-10531-8). Watts.

Polar Bear. Mark Ahlstrom. Ed. by Howard Schroeder. LC 85-30900. (Wildlife (Habits & Habitat) Ser.). (Illus.). 48p. (gr. 4-5). 1986. PLB 10.95 (ISBN 0-89686-268-2). Crestwood Hse.

Polar Bear Cat. Nicola Bayley. LC 83-23744. (Copycats Ser.). (Illus.). 24p. (gr. k up). 1984. 3.95 (ISBN 0-394-86501-4). Knopf.

Polar Bear Express. Edward Packard. (Choose Your Own Adventure Ser.: No. 23). 64p. (Orig.). 1984. pap. 2.25 (ISBN 0-553-15409-5). Bantam.

Polar Bear Leaps. Derek Hall. LC 84-29734. (Sierra Club's Growing up Bks.). (Illus.). 24p. (ps-2). 1985. 4.95 (ISBN 0-394-86531-6). Knopf.

Polar Bears. Tara Moore. (Endangered Species Ser.). (Illus.). 48p. (gr. 4-8). 1982. PLB 8.95 (ISBN 0-8116-2901-5). Garrard.

Polar Bears. Ian Stirling & Dan Guravich. (Illus.). 1988. 39.50 (ISBN 0-472-10100-5). U of Mich Pr.

Polar Bears. Wildlife Education, Ltd. Staff. (Illus.). 20p. (Orig.). (gr. k-12). 1985. pap. 1.95 (ISBN 0-937934-36-4). Wildlife Educ.

Polar Convalense. Ed. by R. T. Sanderson. 1983. 25.00 (ISBN 0-12-618080-6). Acad Pr.

Polar Cusp. Ed. by Jan Anstein Holtet & Alv Egeland. (NATO ASI C: Mathematical & Physical Sciences Ser.). 1985. lib. bdg. 55.00 (ISBN 90-277-1923-3, Pub. by Reidel Holland). Kluwer Academic.

Polar Deserts & Modern Man. Ed. by Terah L. Smiley & James H. Zumberge. LC 73-85722. 173p. 1974. 22.50x (ISBN 0-8165-0383-4). U of Ariz Pr.

Polar Diaries. Y. Fedorov. 344p. 1983. 9.95 (ISBN 0-8285-2682-6, Pub. by Progress Pubs USSR). Imported Pubns.

Polar Dielectrics & Their Applications. Jack C. Burfoot & George W. Taylor. LC 78-62835. 1979. 75.00x (ISBN 0-520-03749-9). U of Cal Pr.

Polar Ecology. B. Stonehouse. (Tertiary Level Biology Ser.). (Illus.). 1988. text ed. 69.50 (ISBN 0-412-01701-6, Pub. by Chapman & Hall England); pap. text ed. 35.00 (ISBN 0-412-01711-3, Pub. by Chapman & Hall England). Routledge Chapman & Hall.

Polar Express. Chris Van Allsburg. LC 85-10907. (Illus.). 32p. (gr. 2 up). 1985. 15.95 (ISBN 0-395-38949-6). HM.

Polar Ionosphere & Magnetospheric Processes. Ed. by G. Skovli. 358p. 1970. 119.00 (ISBN 0-677-13930-6). Gordon & Breach.

Polar Night see Ten Top Stories.

Polar Regions. David Lambert. (Our World Ser.). (Illus.). 48p. (gr. 5-8). 1987. PLB 12.96 (ISBN 0-382-09502-2). Silver.

Polar Regions. John Richardson. LC 74-5869. Repr. of 1861 ed. 25.00 (ISBN 0-404-11676-0). AMS Pr.

Polar Structures in the Book of Qohelet. Jamer A. Loader. (Beihefte aur Zeitschrift fuer die alttestamentliche Wissenschaft). 150p. 1979. text ed. 32.75x (ISBN 3-11-007636-5). De Gruyter.

Polar Sun. Sandi Piccione. LC 79-4685. 1979. pap. 4.00 (ISBN 0-918366-12-7). Slow Loris.

Polar Wandering & Continental Drift. Ed. by Arthur C. Munyan. LC 64-6318. (Society of Economic Paleontologists & Mineralogists, Special Publication: No. 10). pap. 43.80 (ISBN 0-317-27161-X, 2024736). Bks Demand UMI.

Polaris. Sheldon Perkins. 1979. pap. 1.75 (ISBN 0-505-51386-2, Pub. by Tower Bks). Leisure NY.

Polaris System Development: Bureaucratic & Programmatic Success in Government. Harvey Sapolsky. LC 72-79311. (Illus.). 1972. 18.50x (ISBN 0-674-68225-4). Harvard U Pr.

Polarites, Transitions et Geneses dans une Epistemologie des Structures see Cahiers de l'Institut de Science Economique Appliquee.

Polarities of Marriage: Narrowing the Intimacy Gap. Donald M. Hull. 1988. 13.95 (ISBN 0-533-07812-1). Vantage.

Polariton - Mediated Light Scattering & Electronic Structure of Noble Metals. B. Bendow & B. Langeler. (Springer Tracts in Modern Physics Ser.: Vol. 82). (Illus.). 1978. 33.00 (ISBN 0-387-08814-8). Springer-Verlag.

Polaritons: Proceedings, Taormina Research Conference on the Structure of Matter, 1st, Taormina, Italy, Oct, 1972. Ed. by Elias Burstein & Francesco De Martini. LC 73-12845. 1975. 69.00 (ISBN 0-08-017825-1). Pergamon.

Polarity & War: The Changing Structure of International Conflict. Ed. by Alan N. Sabrosky. (Westview Special Studies in International Relations). 225p. 1985. pap. 26.50 (ISBN 0-8133-7000-0). Westview.

Polarity, Dialectic, & Organicity. Archie J. Bahm. LC 77-81834. 293p. 1977. pap. 10.00 (ISBN 0-911714-09-X, World Bks). Bahm.

Polarity of Mexican Thought. Michael A. Weinstein. LC 76-23159. 1977. 21.50x (ISBN 0-271-01232-3). Pa St U Pr.

Polarity Sensitivity As Inherent Scope Relations. William A. Ladusaw & Jorge Hankamer. LC 79-6614. (Outstanding Dissertations in Linguistics Ser.). 236p. 1985. lib. bdg. 35.00 (ISBN 0-8240-4555-6). Garland Pub.

Polarity Therapy: The Complete Collected Works, Vol. 1. Randolph Stone. LC 84-71548. (Illus.). 330p. (Orig.). 1986. sewn 25.00 (ISBN 0-916360-48-2). CRCS Pubns CA.

Polarity Therapy: The Complete Collected Works, Vol. 2. Randolph Stone. LC 84-71548. (Illus.). 240p. (Orig.). 1987. lib. bdg. 25.00 (ISBN 0-916360-25-3). CRCS Pubns CA.

Polarity Therapy: The Power That Heals. Alan Siegel. pap. 12.95 (ISBN 0-317-64636-2, Pub. by Prism Pr). Avery Pub.

Polarization & Intensity of Light in the Atmosphere. Kinsell L. Coulson. 600p. 1988. 57.00 (ISBN 0-937194-12-3). A Deepak Pub.

Polarization Considerations for Optical Systems. Ed. by Chipman. 1988. 50.00 (ISBN 0-89252-926-1, 891). SPIE.

Polarization in Antennas & Radar. Harold Mott. LC 86-1349. 297p. 1986. 43.95 (ISBN 0-471-01167-3). Wiley.

Polarization Interferometers: Applications in Microscopy & Macroscopy. Maurice Francon & S. Mallick. LC 75-147194. (Wiley Ser. in Pure & Appied Optics). pap. 43.00 (ISBN 0-317-29330-3, 2024021). Bks Demand UMI.

Polarization Method of Seismic Studies. E. I. Galperin. 1983. lib. bdg. 58.00 (ISBN 90-277-1555-6, Pub. by Reidel Holland). Kluwer Academic.

Polarization Phenomena in Nuclear Physics, 1980: Fifth International Symposium, Santa Fe. Ed. by G. G. Ohlsen et al. (AIP Conference Proceedings: No. 69). 1536p. 1981. lib. bdg. 84.00 (ISBN 0-88318-168-1). Am Inst Physics.

Polarization Phenomena in Nuclear Reactions: Proceedings. Symposium - 3rd - Madison - 1970. Ed. by Henry H. Barschall & Willy Haeberli. LC 71-143762. 960p. 1971. text ed. 60.00x (ISBN 0-299-05890-5). U of Wis Pr.

Polarized Beams at SCC & Polarized Antiprotons. Ed. by A. D. Krisch et al. LC 86-71343. (AIP Conference Proceedings Ser.: No.145). 270p. 1986. lib. bdg. 51.50 (ISBN 0-88318-344-7). Am Inst Physics.

Polarized Development & Regional Policies. Ed. by Antoni Kuklinski. 518p. 1981. 73.50x (ISBN 90-279-3099-6). Mouton.

Polarized Electrons. 2nd ed. J. Kessler. (Springer Series on Atoms & Plasmas: Vol. 1). (Illus.). 310p. 1985. 42.00 (ISBN 0-387-15736-0). Springer-Verlag.

Polarized Electrons at Surfaces. J. M. Kirschner. (Springer Tracts in Modern Physics Ser.: Vol. 106). (Illus.). 175p. 1985. 29.50 (ISBN 0-387-15003-X). Springer-Verlag.

Polarized Electrons in Surface Physics, Vol. 1. Ed. by R. Feder. (Advanced Series in Surface Science). 600p. 1986. 76.00 (ISBN 9971-978-49-0); pap. 36.00 (ISBN 9971-50-978-4). World Scientific Pub.

Polarized Law (with an English Translation of the Hague Conventions on Private International Law) Three Lectures on Conflicts of Law, Delivered at the University of London. T. Baty. (Legal Reprint Ser.). xv, 210p. 1986. Repr. of 1914 ed. lib. bdg. 25.00x (ISBN 0-421-35520-4). Rothman.

Polarized Light. Ed. by William Swindell. LC 74-26881. (Benchmark Papers in Optics Ser: No. 1). 418p. 1975. 78.00 (ISBN 0-12-787498-4). Acad Pr.

Polarized Light in Nature. G. P. Konnen. 172p. 1985. 37.50 (ISBN 0-521-25862-6). Cambridge U Pr.

Polarized Light: Production & Use. William A. Shurcliff. LC 62-11405. pap. 54.50 (ISBN 0-317-08051-2, 2051980). Bks Demand UMI.

Polarized Neutrons. W. Gavin Williams. (Studies in Neutron Scattering & Condensed Matter Science: No. 1). (Illus.). 320p. 1988. 65.00 (ISBN 0-19-851005-5). Oxford U Pr.

Polarized Proton Ion Sources: Ann Arbor, 1981. Ed. by A. D. Krisch & A. T. M. Lin. LC 82-71025. (AIP Conference Proceedings: No. 80). 214p. 1982. lib. bdg. 30.00 (ISBN 0-88318-179-7). Am Inst Physics.

Polarized Proton Ion Sources: Conference Proceedings, TRIUMF, Vancouver, 1983. Ed. by G. Roy & P. Schmor. LC 84-71235. (AIP Conference Proceedings Ser.: No. 117). 209p. 1984. lib. bdg. 37.00 (ISBN 0-88318-316-1). Am Inst Physics.

Polarografia. (Serie De Quimica: No. 13). (Span.). 1974. pap. 3.50 (ISBN 0-8270-6385-7). OAS.

Polarographic Oxygen Sensor: Its Theory of Operation & Its Application in Biology, Medicine & Technology. Irving Fatt. LC 82-6581. 290p. (Orig.). 1982. Repr. of 1976 ed. 59.95 (ISBN 0-89874-511-X). Krieger.

Polarographic Oxygen Sensors: Aquatic & Physiological Applications. Ed. by E. Gnaiger & H. Forstner. (Illus.). 370p. 1983. 69.00 (ISBN 0-387-11654-0). Springer-Verlag.

Polarographic Techniques. 2nd ed. Louis Meites. LC 65-19735. (Electrochemical Data Ser.). (Illus.). 752p. 1965. 90.00x (ISBN 0-470-59205-2, Pub. by Wiley-Interscience). Wiley.

Polarography of Molecules of Biological Significance. Ed. by W. Franklin Smyth. 1979. 86.00 (ISBN 0-12-653050-5). Acad Pr.

Polaroid Black & White Land Films. Polaroid Corporation Staff. (Illus.). 68p. (Orig.). 1983. pap. 9.95 (ISBN 0-240-51705-9). Focal Pr.

Polaroid Color Films. Polaroid Corporation Staff. (Illus.). 56p. pap. cancelled (ISBN 0-240-51706-7). Focal Pr.

Polaroid Corporation's Tuition Assistance Plan. Kathleen Knox. (Tuition Aid Case Study Ser.). 40p. (Orig.). 1979. pap. text ed. 8.00 (ISBN 0-86510-023-3). Natl Inst Work.

Polaroid Materials & Processes. Morgan & Morgan Staff. Ed. by Liliane De Cock. (Illus.). 104p. 1987. pap. 10.95 (ISBN 0-87100-255-8, 2255). Morgan.

Polarons & Excitons in Polar Semiconductors & Ionic Crystals. Ed. by J. T. Devreese & F. Peeters. (NATO ASI Series B, Physics: Vol. 108). 490p. 1984. 82.50x (ISBN 0-306-41498-8, Plenum Pr). Plenum Pub.

Polarons in Ionic Crystals & Polar Semiconductors: Proceedings of the 1971 Antwerp Advanced Study Institute. Ed. by J. T. Devreese. 1976. 94.75 (ISBN 0-444-10409-7, North-Holland). Elsevier.

Polchius & the Prodigal. Sisters of the Community of Jesus Staff. (See & Believe Children's Bible Stories). (Illus.). 75p. (Orig.). (gr. k-4). 1987. pap. text ed. 8.95 (ISBN 0-941478-57-2). Paraclete Pr.

Polden' I Polnoch' Aleksandr Glezer. LC 83-63004. (Russica Poetry Ser.: No. 7). 120p. (Rus.). 1986. pap. 7.95 (ISBN 0-89830-076-2). Russica Pubs.

Pole & Post Buildings. 48p. 3.50 (ISBN 0-317-59377-3, NRAES-1). NE Agri Engineer.

Pole Shift. 3rd ed. John White. (Illus.). 413p. 1985. pap. 5.95 (ISBN 0-87604-162-4). ARE Pr.

Polec: Dictionary of Politics & Economics. 2nd, rev. & enl. ed. Ed. by Harry Back et al. (Ger., Eng. & Fr.). 1967. 37.50x (ISBN 3-11-000892-0). De Gruyter.

Polecat Bench. Allen G. Richardson. LC 82-84447. (Illus.). 220p. 1983. 12.95 (ISBN 0-936204-40-0); pap. 7.95 (ISBN 0-936204-39-7). Jelm Mtn.

Polemaischen Munz-und Rechnugswerte. F. Hultsch. 66p. (Ger.). 15.00 (ISBN 0-916710-81-5). Obol Intl.

Polemic Character, 1640-1661. Benjamin Boyce. 1969. lib. bdg. 18.00x (ISBN 0-374-90893-1, Octagon). Hippocrene Bks.

Polemic on the General Line of the International Communist Movement: Hung Ch'i. LC 71-38078. Repr. of 1965 ed. 30.00 (ISBN 0-404-56942-0). AMS Pr.

Police in America: An Introduction. Samuel Walker. (Illus.). 368p. 1983. pap. 22.95 (ISBN 0-07-067854-5). McGraw.
Police in American Society. Edward F. Dolan. Ed. by Henry Rasof. (Illus.). 160p. (YA) (gr. 7-12). 1988. 13.90 (ISBN 0-531-10608-X). Watts.
Police in Changing India. Ajay K. Mehra. 1985. 18.00x (ISBN 0-8364-1414-4, Pub. by Usha). South Asia Bks.
Police in Ferment. S. K. Ghosh. 140p. 1981. 17.95 (ISBN 0-317-12335-1, Pub. by Lights & Life Pubs India). Asia Bk Corp.
Police in Great Britain, 6 vols. Ed. by Robert M. Fogelson. 1971. Repr. Set. 281.00 (ISBN 0-405-03405-9). Ayer Co Pubs.
Police in New York City: An Investigation. Board of Aldermen Staff. LC 79-154565. (Police in America Ser). 1971. Repr. of 1913 ed. 27.00 (ISBN 0-405-03382-6). Ayer Co Pubs.
Police in Urban America, Eighteen Hundred Sixty to Nineteen Hundred Twenty. Eric Monkkonen. LC 80-16762. (Interdisciplinary Perspectives on Modern History Ser.). (Illus.). 256p. 1981. 32.50 (ISBN 0-521-23454-9). Cambridge U Pr.
Police Informant Management. Jack Morris. LC 83-63214. (Illus.). 90p. 1983. pap. 12.95 (ISBN 0-912479-02-7). Palmer Ent.
Police Integrity: The Role of Psychological Screening of Applicants. Allen E. Shealy. (Criminal Justice Center Monographs). 1978. pap. text ed. 1.00x. John Jay Pr.
Police Intelligence Files. Jack Morris. (Illus.). 104p. 1983. pap. 12.95 (ISBN 0-912479-00-0). Palmer Ent.
Police Intelligence Reports. Charles Frost & Jack Morris. LC 83-62701. (Illus.). 135p. 1985. pap. 11.95 (ISBN 0-912479-03-5). Palmer Ent.
Police Intelligence System. John B. Wolf. (Criminal Justice Center Monographs). 1978. pap. text ed. 3.00x (ISBN 0-89444-048-9). John Jay Pr.
Police Intelligence Systems in Crime Control: Maintaining a Delicate Balance in a Liberal Democracy. Justin J. Dintino & Frederick T. Martens. (Illus.). 176p. 1983. 21.75x (ISBN 0-398-04830-4). C C Thomas.
Police Intelligence: The Operations of an Investigative Unit. Anthony J. Bouza. LC 75-8667. (Studies in Criminal Justice: No. 2). 1976. 32.50 (ISBN 0-404-13138-7). AMS Pr.
Police Interrogation & Confessions: Essays in Law & Policy. Yale Kamisar. 1980. 19.95x (ISBN 0-472-09318-5). U of Mich Pr.
Police Investigation & Prosecution. K. Krishnamurthi. 900p. 1986. 45.95. Asia Bk Corp.
Police Ju Jitsu. J. McCauslin Moynahan, Jr. (Illus.). 132p. 1962. 9.75 (ISBN 0-398-01366-7). C C Thomas.
Police Know Everything: And Other Maine Stories. Sanford Phippen. Ed. by Constance Hunting. 149p. (Orig.). 1982. pap. 6.95 (ISBN 0-913006-27-0). Puckerbrush.
Police Lab. Melvin Berger. LC 75-33198. (Illus.). (gr. 4-6). 1976. PLB 12.89 (ISBN 0-381-99620-4, Crowell Jr Books). HarpJ.
Police Leadership. Arthur R. Pell. (Illus.). 152p. 1967. 21.75x (ISBN 0-398-01471-X). C C Thomas.
Police Leadership in America: Crisis & Opportunity. William A. Geller. LC 85-6284. 1985. 44.95 (ISBN 0-275-90205-6, C0205); pap. 20.95 (ISBN 0-275-91672-3, B1672). Praeger.
Police Lieutenant. Jack Rudman. (Career Examination Ser.: C-2802). (Cloth bdg. avail. on request). 1988. pap. 16.00 (ISBN 0-8373-2802-0). Natl Learning.
Police Management. A. J. Butler. LC 84-10343. 224p. (Orig.). 1984. pap. text ed. 21.95x (ISBN 0-566-00646-4). Gower Pub Co.
Police Management & Organizational Behavior: A Contingency Approach. Roy R. Roberg. (Criminal Justice Ser.). (Illus.). 348p. 1979. text ed. 37.00 (ISBN 0-8299-0275-9); instrs.' manual avail. (ISBN 0-8299-0599-5). West Pub.
Police Management Today: Issues & Case Studies. Ed. by James J. Fyfe. LC 85-155. (Practical Management Ser.). 214p. (Orig.). 1985. pap. text ed. 21.00 (ISBN 0-87326-044-9). Intl City Mgt.
Police Manager. 3rd ed. Ronald C. Lynch. 320p. 1986. text ed. write for info (ISBN 0-394-34717-X, RanC). Random.
Police Managerial Use of Psychology & Psychologists. Harry W. More & Peter C. Unsinger. (Illus.). 202p. 1987. 34.50 (ISBN 0-398-05293-X). C C Thomas.
Police Meet the Press. Gerald W. Garner. 292p. 1984. 32.75x (ISBN 0-398-04916-5). C C Thomas.
Police, Military, & Ethnicity. Cynthia Enloe. LC 79-64569. 179p. 1980. text ed. 19.95 (ISBN 0-87855-302-9). Transaction Bks.
Police-Minority Community Relations: The Control & Structuring of Police Discretion. Spring Hill Center Staff. Ed. by Donna Hoel & John Ziegenhagen. 1978. pap. text ed. 2.50 (ISBN 0-932676-04-9). Spring Hill.
Police Misconduct: Law & Litigation. 2nd ed. Michael Avery & David Rudovsky. LC 80-23165. 1980. looseleaf 75.00 (ISBN 0-87632-112-0). Clark Boardman.
Police Misconduct: Scope of the Problems & Remedies. William A. Geller. (American Bar Foundation Research Reporter Ser.: No.23). pap. 20.00 (ISBN 0-317-30476-3, 2024819). Bks Demand UMI.
Police Nonlethal Force Manual: Your Choices This Side of Deadly. Bill Clede. LC 87-6458. (Illus.). 128p. 1987. 15.95 (ISBN 0-8117-1300-8). Stackpole.
Police of France. Phillip J. Stead. 1983. 19.95 (ISBN 0-02-930820-8). Free Pr.
Police of Paris, 1718-1789. Alan Williams. LC 78-24189. 416p. 1979. 37.50 (ISBN 0-8071-0491-4). La State U Pr.
Police Officer. Francis Burkhardt et al. Date not set. write for info. S&S.
Police Officer. 9th ed. LC 84-12376. 1985. 8.95 (ISBN 0-668-05872-2). Arco.
Police Officer. Jack Rudman. (Career Examination Ser.: C-1939). (Cloth bdg. avail. on request). 1988. pap. 12.00 (ISBN 0-8373-1939-0). Natl Learning.
Police Officer - Los Angeles Police Department (LAPD) Jack Rudman. (Career Examination Ser.: C-2441). (Cloth bdg. avail. on request). pap. 14.00 (ISBN 0-8373-2441-6). Natl Learning.
Police Officer - Nassau County Police Dept. (NCPD) Jack Rudman. (Career Examination Ser.: C-1755). (Cloth bdg. avail. on request). pap. 14.00 (ISBN 0-8373-1755-X). Natl Learning.
Police Officer - New York Police Dept. (NYPD) Jack Rudman. (Career Examination Ser.: C-1739). (Cloth bdg. avail. on request). 1988. pap. 14.00 (ISBN 0-8373-1739-8). Natl Learning.
Police Officer - Suffolk County Police Dept. (SCPD) Jack Rudman. (Career Examination Ser.: C-1741). (Cloth bdg. avail. on request). 1988. pap. 14.00 (ISBN 0-8373-1741-X). Natl Learning.
Police Officer in Court. R. David Petersen. (Illus.). 192p. 1975. 22.50x (ISBN 0-398-03321-8). C C Thomas.
Police Officer Jones. Harry Bornstein. (Signed English Ser.). 18p. 1976. pap. 3.50 (ISBN 0-913580-53-8, Clerc Bks). Gallaudet Univ Pr.
Police Officers: A to Z. Jean Johnson. (Walker's Community Helpers Ser.). (Illus.). 48p. (gr. k-3). 1986. 11.95 (ISBN 0-8027-6614-5); lib. bdg. 11.85 (ISBN 0-8027-6615-3). Walker & Co.
Police Officer's Dilemma: Balancing Peace, Order & Individual Rights. Jay S. Albanese. LC 87-81602. 174p. (Orig.). 1988. pap. 12.95 (ISBN 0-944461-00-X). Great Bks Pub.
Police Officer's Guide to Better Communication. T. Richard Cheatham & Keith Erickson. (PROCOM Ser.). 1984. pap. 9.95 (ISBN 0-673-15556-0). Scott F.
Police Officer's Hand Book. Mahendra Singh. 611p. 1977. 150.00x (ISBN 0-317-57680-1, Pub. by Eastern Bk India). State Mutual Bk.
Police Officers Universal Log. write for info. Looseleaf Law.
Police Operation CSS. write for info. Looseleaf Law.
Police Operational Intelligence. rev. ed. D. O. Schultz & L. A. Norton. (Illus.). 244p. 1973. 27.00 (ISBN 0-398-02832-X). C C Thomas.
Police Operations. Gwynne Peirson. LC 75-44334. (Justice Administration Ser.). 180p. 1976. 22.95x (ISBN 0-911012-86-9). Nelson-Hall.
Police Operations - Tactical Approaches to Crimes in Progress. Andrew P. Sutor. LC 76-16911. (Criminal Justice Ser.). 1976. 19.95; pap. text ed. write for info. (ISBN 0-8299-0609-6); instrs.' manual avail. (ISBN 0-8299-0611-8). West Pub.
Police Operations Aide. (Career Examination Ser.: C-3402). Date not set. pap. 12.00 (ISBN 0-8373-3402-0). Natl Learning.
Police Operations: Policies & Procedures: Four Hundred Field Situations with Solutions. 2nd ed. John P. Kenney & John B. Williams. (Illus.). 224p. 1973. 28.50x (ISBN 0-398-01004-8). C C Thomas.
Police: Organisation & Command. R. S. Bunyard. (Illus.). 400p. 1978. 29.95x (ISBN 0-7121-1671-0, Pub. by Macdonald & Evans England). Trans-Atl Phila.
Police Organization & Administration. Sam S. Souryal. 150p. 1985. write for info. (ISBN 0-932930-69-7). Pilgrimage Inc.
Police Organization & Management. 7th ed. V. A. Leonard & Harry W. More. (Police Science Ser.). 568p. 1986. text ed. 26.95 (ISBN 0-88277-344-5). Foundation Pr.
Police Organization & Management. 6th ed. Ed. by V. A. Leonard & Harry W. More, Jr. LC 82-8436. (Police Science Ser.). 663p. 1982. text ed. 22.00 (ISBN 0-88277-049-7). Foundation Pr.
Police Passages. John G. Stratton. (Illus.). 350p. 1984. text ed. 24.95 (ISBN 0-317-11361-5). Glennon Pub.
Police Patrol: Operations & Management. Charles D. Hale. LC 80-36814. 328p. 1981. text ed. 32.95 (ISBN 0-471-03291-3); Avail. tchr's manual (ISBN 0-471-08901-X). Wiley.
Police Patrol: Tactics & Techniques. T. Adams. LC 71-138484. (Essential of Law Enforcements Ser). 1971. ref. ed. 24.95. P-H.
Police Patrol Techniques & Tactics. Vern L. Folley. 192p. 1974. photocopy ed. 22.75x (ISBN 0-398-02842-7). C C Thomas.
Police Patrolman. Jack Rudman. (Career Examination Ser.: C-595). (Cloth bdg. avail. on request). pap. 12.00 (ISBN 0-8373-0595-0). Natl Learning.
Police Personal Behavior & Human Relations: For Police, Deputy, Jail, Corrections & Security Personnel. Priss Dufford. (Illus.). 160p. 1986. 24.75x (ISBN 0-398-05223-9). C C Thomas.
Police Personnel System. Calvin J. Swank & James A. Conser. LC 82-13523. 392p. 1983. 29.95 (ISBN 0-471-06106-9). Wiley.
Police Photography: Law Enforcement Handbook. 2nd ed. Sam J. Sansone. 203p. 1987. pap. text ed. 25.95 (ISBN 0-87084-773-2). Anderson Pub Co.
Police Planning. 2nd ed. O. W. Wilson. (Illus.). 562p. 1977. 64.75 (ISBN 0-398-02081-7). C C Thomas.
Police Policy Manual - Operations. Harry W. More & O. R. Shipley. 288p. 1987. 38.50 (ISBN 0-398-05324-3). C C Thomas.
Police Policy Manual-Personnel. Harry W. More & O. R. Shipley. (Illus.). 268p. 1987. 36.50x (ISBN 0-398-05360-X). C C Thomas.
Police, Politics & Race: The New York City Referendum on Civilian Review. David W. Abbott et al. 1969. pap. 3.00x (ISBN 0-674-68321-8). Harvard U Pr.
Police Power & Colonial Rule, Madras, 1859-1947. David Arnold. LC 86-900007. 277p. 1987. 26.00x (ISBN 0-19-561893-9). Oxford U Pr.
Police Power: Public Policy & Constitutional Rights. Ernst Freund. LC 75-17223. (Social Problems & Social Policy Ser.). 1976. Repr. of 1904 ed. 67.50x (ISBN 0-405-07493-X). Ayer Co Pubs.
Police Power: Public Policy & Constitutional Rights. Ed. by Ernst Freund & R. H. Helmholz, Jr. LC 80-84868. (Historical Writings in Law & Jurisprudence Ser.: Title No. 22, Bk. 32). 918p. 1981. Repr. of 1904 ed. lib. bdg. 48.00 (ISBN 0-89941-084-7). W S Hein.
Police Powers & Accountability. J. L. Lambert. LC 85-21282. 1985. 29.00 (ISBN 0-7099-1660-4, Pub. by Croom Helm Ltd). Routledge Chapman & Hall.
Police Powers & Duties: A Practical Guide to the Police & Criminal Evidence Act 1984. John Marston & Robin W. Nottridge. 168p. 1985. 80.00x (ISBN 0-906840-82-1, Pub. by Fourmat England). State Mutual Bk.
Police Powers & the Individual. John Robilliard & Jenny McEwan. pap. 24.95x (ISBN 0-317-59083-9). Basil Blackwell.
Police Powers & the Individual. St. John Robilliard & Jenny McEwan. 256p. 1986. text ed. 49.95 (ISBN 0-631-13995-8). Basil Blackwell.
Police: Powers, Procedures & Proprieties. John Benyon & C. J. Bourn. LC 85-29783. 1986. text ed. 41.00 (ISBN 0-08-032697-8, PBL); pap. text ed. 19.25 (ISBN 0-08-032696-X). Pergamon.
Police Practices. Ed. by John C. Weistart. LC 73-7932. (Library of Law and Contemporary Problems). 160p. 1974. lib. bdg. 10.00x (ISBN 0-379-11517-4). Oceana.
Police Practices & the Law: Essays from the Michigan Law Review. Michigan Law Review. LC 82-2612. 450p. 1981. text ed. 24.50x (ISBN 0-472-10015-7). U of Mich Pr.
Police, Prison, & Punishment. Ed. by Kermit L. Hall. (United States Constitutional & Legal History Ser.). 752p. 1987. lib. bdg. 85.00 (ISBN 0-8240-0143-5). Garland Pub.
Police Procedural. George N. Dove. LC 81-84214. 1982. 20.95 (ISBN 0-87972-188-X); pap. 10.95 (ISBN 0-87972-189-8). Bowling Green Univ.
Police Procedures & Defense Tactics Training Manual. Harry Aziz. Ed. by Sydney S. Halet. (Illus.). 1979. 20.95 (ISBN 0-87040-451-2). Japan Pubns USA.
Police Professionalism: The Renaissance of American Law Enforcement. Thomas J. Deakin. 340p. 1988. 43.50 (ISBN 0-398-05471-1). C C Thomas.
Police Promotion Course. Jack Rudman. (Career Examination Ser.: CS-18). (Cloth bdg. avail. on request). pap. 16.00 (ISBN 0-8373-3718-6). Natl Learning.
Police Promotion Examinations. Hugh E. O'Neil. LC 83-8770. 288p. 1983. pap. 12.95 (ISBN 0-668-05604-5, 5604). Arco.
Police Promotion Manual. write for info. Looseleaf Law.
Police Psychology: Collected Papers. Martin Reiser. LC 81-82247. 1982. 24.95 (ISBN 0-934486-01-8). LEHI Pub Co.
Police, Public Order & Civil Liberties: Legacies of Miners' Strike. Ed. by Sarah McCabe et al. 256p. 1988. lib. bdg. 45.00 (ISBN 0-422-60950-1). Routledge Chapman & Hall.
Police, Public Order & the State. John D. Brewer et al. LC 87-23474. 241p. 1988. 49.95 (ISBN 0-312-01565-8). St Martin.
Police Pursuit Driving Handbook. Donald O. Schultz. LC 79-50244. 96p. (Orig.). 1979. pap. 9.00x (ISBN 0-87201-771-0). Gulf Pub.
Police Radar: A Guide to Basic Understanding. Robert E. Nichols, Jr. 76p. 1982. 15.25x (ISBN 0-398-04573-9). C C Thomas.
Police Radar: How to Beat It. Edward F. Urquhart. LC 83-90835. (Illus.). 52p. (Orig.). 1983. pap. 7.99 (ISBN 0-9611618-0-9). E Urquhart.
Police Reading Comprehension. Jack Rudman. (Career Examination Ser.: CS-23). (Cloth bdg. avail. on request). 1988. pap. 14.00 (ISBN 0-8373-3723-2). Natl Learning.
Police Records Administration. William H. Hewitt. LC 67-26022. 941p. write for info. Lawyers Co-Op.
Police Records & Recollections or Boston by Daylight & Gaslight for Two Hundred & Forty Years. Edward H. Savage. LC 74-154048. (Criminology, Law Enforcement, & Social Problems Ser.: No. 123). (Illus., With intro. & index added). 1970. Repr. of 1873 ed. 15.00x (ISBN 0-87585-123-1). Patterson Smith.
Police Records System. V. A. Leonard. (Illus.). 104p. 1977. 17.50x (ISBN 0-398-01104-4). C C Thomas.
Police Referral to Drug Treatment. 1986. lib. bdg. 79.95 (ISBN 0-8490-3516-3). Gordon Pr.
Police Reform in the United States: The Era of August Vollmer, 1905-1932. Gene E. Carte & Elaine A. Carte. LC 73-87248. 390p. 1976. 30.00x (ISBN 0-520-02599-7). U of Cal Pr.
Police Rights: Civil Remedies for Law Enforcement Officers. 2nd ed. Charles E. Friend. LC 87-17901. 192p. 1987. pap. 14.95 (ISBN 0-8366-0000-2). Callaghan.
Police Role in Alcohol-Related Crises. Gerald W. Garner. 168p. 1979. 19.25x. C C Thomas.
Police Science Fundamentals. 1973 ed. Henry J. Mulhearn. 220p. pap. 7.50 (ISBN 0-87526-160-4). Gould.
Police Selection: A Case Study. Ed. by Suzanne O. Hazlett. (Center for Responsive Psychology Monograph). 14p. (Orig.). 1985. pap. 4.00 (ISBN 0-318-19260-8). Ctr Respon Psych.
Police Selection & Evaluation: Issues & Techniques. Charles D. Spielberger. LC 78-9958. (Praeger Special Studies). 328p. 1979. 44.95 (ISBN 0-275-90428-8, C0428). Praeger.
Police Selection & Training. Ed. by John C. Yuille. 1986. lib. bdg. 97.00 (ISBN 90-247-3369-3, Pub. by Martinus Nijhoff Netherlands). Kluwer Academic.
Police Shootings & the Prosecutor in Los Angeles County: An Evaluation of Operation Rollout. Craig D. Uchida et al. LC 81-85315. (Illus.). Date not set. price not set. Police Found.
Police Shotgun Manual. photocopy ed. Roger H. Robinson. (Illus.). 168p. 1973. 21.75 (ISBN 0-398-02630-0). C C Thomas.
Police Shotgun Manual: How to Survive Against All Odds. Bill Clede. (Illus.). 128p. 1986. 13.95 (ISBN 0-8117-1350-4). Stackpole.
Police Sous Louis XIV. Pierre Clement. 492p. (Fr.). Repr. of 1866 ed. lib. bdg. 87.50x. Coronet Bks.
Police State: Could It Happen Here? Jules Archer. LC 76-58720. 192p. (YA) (gr. 7 up). 1977. PLB 12.89 (ISBN 0-06-020154-1). HarpJ.
Police: Streetcorner Politicians. William K. Muir, Jr. LC 76-8085. (Illus.). 1977. pap. 11.00x (ISBN 0-226-54633-0, P825, Phoen). U of Chicago Pr.
Police Supervision. Henry J. Mulhearn. 150p. 1976. pap. 7.50 (ISBN 0-87526-226-0). Gould.
Police Supervision: A Common Sense Approach. Gerald W. Garner. 264p. 1981. 30.25x (ISBN 0-398-04127-X). C C Thomas.
Police Supervision: Theory & Practice. 2nd ed. P. M. Whisenand. (Illus.). 576p. 1976. 35.00 (ISBN 0-13-686311-6). P-H.
Police Surgeon. Jack Rudman. (Career Examination Ser.: C-596). (Cloth bdg. avail. on request). pap. 27.95 (ISBN 0-8373-0596-9). Natl Learning.
Police Systems of Europe: A Survey of Selected Police Organizations. 2nd ed. Harold K. Becker. (Illus.). 256p. 1980. pap. 18.50x spiral (ISBN 0-398-04023-0). C C Thomas.
Police Tactics in Armed Operations: A Guide for Law Enforcement Officers. C. Greenwood. 1986. lib. bdg. 79.95 (ISBN 0-8490-3651-8). Gordon Pr.
Police Team. rev. ed. Educational Research Council of America Staff. Ed. by Theodore N. Ferris & John P. Marchak. (Real People at Work Ser.: B). (Illus.). 36p. 1976. pap. text ed. 2.70 (ISBN 0-89247-018-6, 9218). Changing Times.
Police: The Constitution & the Community. Ed. by John Baxter & Lawrence Koffman. 274p. 1985. 20.00x (ISBN 0-317-54892-1, Pub. by NCCL UK). State Mutual Bk.
Police: The Exercise of Power. Don Campbell. 128p. 1978. 27.50x (ISBN 0-7121-1678-8, Pub. by Macdonald & Evans England). Trans-Atl Phila.
Police: The Investigation of Violence. Keith Simpson. (Illus.). 240p. 1978. 29.95x (ISBN 0-7121-1689-3, Pub. by Macdonald & Evans England). Trans-Atl Phila.
Police Today. Sankar Sen. 1986. 19.00X (ISBN 81-7024-047-6, Pub. by Ashish India). South Asia Bks.
Police Traffic Control Function. 4th ed. Paul B. Weston. (Illus.). 420p. 1978. 28.50 (ISBN 0-398-03764-7). C C Thomas.
Police Trainee. Jack Rudman. (Career Examination Ser.: C-597). (Cloth bdg. avail. on request). pap. 12.00 (ISBN 0-8373-0597-7). Natl Learning.
Police Training: A Bibliography. Mary Vance. (Public Administration Ser.: P 2139). 22p. 1987. 6.25 (ISBN 1-55590-279-0). Vance Biblios.
Police Training for Tough Calls: Discretionary Situations. Frank J. Vandall. 130p. 1976. pap. 15.00x (ISBN 0-8046-9312-9, Pub. by Kennikat). Assoc Faculty Pr.
Police Training Officer. David A. Hansen & Thomas R. Culley. (Illus.). 244p. 1973. 30.25x (ISBN 0-398-02493-6). C C Thomas.
Police Transportation Management. G. Ray Wynne. (Illus.). 1965. pap. 9.50 (ISBN 0-910390-03-7). Auto Bk.

Policy & Police: The Enforcement of the Reformation in the Age of Thomas Cromwell. G. R. Elton. 458p. 1985. pap. 14.95 (ISBN 0-521-31309-0). Cambridge U Pr.

Policy & Politics in Britain: The Limits of Consensus. Douglas E. Ashford. (Policy & Politics in Industrial States Ser.). 330p. 1980. 34.95 (ISBN 0-87722-194-4); pap. text ed. 12.95 (ISBN 0-87722-195-2). Temple U Pr.

Policy & Politics in Contemporary Poland. Jean Woodall. LC 81-47980. 288p. 1982. 25.00x (ISBN 0-312-61999-5). St Martin.

Policy & Politics in Contemporary Poland: Reform, Failure & Crisis. Ed. by Jean Woodall. 200p. 1982. pap. 16.00 (ISBN 0-86187-222-3, Pub. by Frances Pinter). Longwood Pub Group.

Policy & Politics in France: Living with Uncertainty. Douglas E. Ashford. LC 82-5771. (Policy & Politics in Industrial States Ser.). 365p. 1982. 34.95 (ISBN 0-87722-261-4); pap. text ed. 12.95x (ISBN 0-87722-262-2). Temple U Pr.

Policy & Politics in Japan: Creative Conservatism. T. J. Pempel. (Policy & Politics in Industrial States Ser.). 330p. 1982. 34.95 (ISBN 0-87722-249-5); pap. 12.95 (ISBN 0-87722-250-9). Temple U Pr.

Policy & Politics in Sweden: Principled Pragmatism. Hugh Heclo & Henrik Madsen. (Policy & Politics in Industrial States). 352p. 1986. 34.95 (ISBN 0-87722-265-7); pap. 14.95 (ISBN 0-87722-266-5). Temple U Pr.

Policy & Politics in the Federal Republic of Germany. Ed. by Klaus Von Beyme & Manfred G. Schmidt. LC 84-40651. 257p. 1985. 29.95 (ISBN 0-312-62006-3). St Martin.

Policy & Politics in the United States: The Limits of Localism. E. W. Kelley. (Policy & Politics in Industrial States Ser.). 416p. 1987. 34.95 (ISBN 0-87722-267-3); pap. 16.95 (ISBN 0-87722-268-1). Temple U Pr.

Policy & Politics in West Germany. Peter V. Katzenstein. (Policy & Politics in Industrial States Ser.). 464p. 1987. 34.94 (ISBN 0-87722-263-0); pap. 16.95 (ISBN 0-87722-264-9). Temple U Pr.

Policy & Power: Two Centuries of American Foreign Relations. Ruhl J. Bartlett. LC 79-25201. (American Century Ser.). (Illus.). 303p. 1980. Repr. of 1963 ed. lib. bdg. 27.50x (ISBN 0-313-22217-7, BAPN). Greenwood.

Policy & Practice: Essays in Memory of Sir John Crawford. Ed. by L. T. Evans & J. D. Miller. (Illus.). 226p. 1987. text ed. 22.45 (ISBN 0-08-034390-2, ANUP). Pergamon.

Policy & Practice in Bibliographic Control of Nonbook Media. Ed. by Sheila Intner & Richard Smiraglia. LC 87-1849. 208p. 1987. pap. text ed. 24.95x (ISBN 0-8389-0468-8). ALA.

Policy & Practice in Rural Development. Ed. by Guy Hunter et al. LC 76-15078. 520p. 1976. text ed. 21.50x (ISBN 0-86598-002-0, Pub. by Allanheld). Rowman.

Policy & Procedure Manual for Church & Synagogue Libraries: A Do-It-Yourself Guide. Martin Ruoss. LC 79-28676. (Guide Ser.: No. 9). 14p. 1983. pap. 3.95 (ISBN 0-915324-17-2); pap. 3.00 members. CSLA.

Policy & Procedure Training Manual for the Environmental Health Services Department. 2nd ed. Charles B. Miller. LC 83-26129. 1984. pap. 12.00 (ISBN 0-87125-092-6). Cath Health.

Policy & Program Planning: A Developmental Perspective. Robert R. Mayer. (Illus.). 224p. 1985. text ed. write for info. (ISBN 0-13-684473-1). P-H.

Policy & Provision for the Single Homeless: Research Paper. Madeline Drake & Tony Biebuych. 1977. 22.00x (ISBN 0-317-05797-9, Pub. by Natl Inst Social Work). State Mutual Bk.

Policy & Trade Issues of the Japanese Economy: American & Japanese Perspectives. Ed. by Kozo Yamamura. LC 82-15918. (Publications of the School of International Studies on Asia: No. 36). 348p. 1983. 25.00x (ISBN 0-295-95900-2). U of Wash Pr.

Policy Arguments in Judicial Decisions. John Bell. LC 83-4207. 1983. 49.95x (ISBN 0-19-825397-4); pap. 17.95x (ISBN 0-19-825522-5). Oxford U Pr.

Policy Aspects of Climate Forecasting. Ed. by Richard Krasnow. 176p. 1986. 11.50. Resources Future.

Policy Choices in Vocational Education. Gregory Schmid. 68p. 1979. 7.50 (ISBN 0-318-14417-4, R48A). Inst Future.

Policy Conflicts in Post-Mao China: A Documentary Survey with Analysis. John P. Burns & Stanley Rosen. 280p. 1986. 39.95 (ISBN 0-87332-337-8); pap. 14.95 (ISBN 0-87332-338-6). M E Sharpe.

Policy Consequences of John Maynard Keynes. Harold L. Wattel. LC 84-23542. 35.00 (ISBN 0-87332-316-5); pap. 15.95 (ISBN 0-87332-317-3). M E Sharpe.

Policy Controversies in Higher Education. Ed. by Samuel K. Gove & Thomas M. Stauffer. LC 86-4646. (Contributions to the Study of Education Ser.: No. 19). 285p. 1986. lib. bdg. 38.95 (ISBN 0-313-25381-1, GPC/). Greenwood.

Policy Decision Making in Education: An Introduction to Calculation & Control. Dale Mann. LC 74-13962. 1975. text ed. 13.95x (ISBN 0-8077-2440-8). Tchrs Coll.

Policy Design & the Politics of Implementation: The Case of Child Health Care in the American States. Malcolm L. Goggin. LC 86-11333. 312p. 1987. text ed. 29.95x (ISBN 0-87049-513-5). U of Tenn Pr.

Policy Development & Planning in State Government. Jack Brizius et al. Date not set. price not set. CSPA.

Policy Development in Sport Management. Harold J. VanderZwaag. LC 86-71385. (Illus.). 400p. 1988. text ed. 32.95 (ISBN 0-936157-09-7). Benchmark Pr.

Policy Dilemma: Federal Crime Policy & the Law Enforcement Assistance Administration. Malcolm M. Feeley & Austin Sarat. 1981. 19.50x (ISBN 0-8166-0901-2); pap. 8.95 (ISBN 0-8166-0904-7). U of Minn Pr.

Policy Dilemmas & the Struggle for Power in Kremlin: The Andropov Period. Ilya Zemtsov. 300p. 1985. pap. 19.95 (ISBN 0-915979-10-1). Hero Books.

Policy Directions for U. S. Agriculture: Long-Range Choices in Farming & Rural Living. Marion Clawson. LC 68-16163. pap. 104.00 (ISBN 0-317-09637-0, 2020958). Bks Demand UMI.

Policy Dynamics. Brian Hogwood & Guy Peters. LC 82-10330. 304p. 1983. 27.50x (ISBN 0-312-62014-4). St Martin.

Policy Economics. Tony Killick. (Orig.). 1981. pap. text ed. 17.50x (ISBN 0-435-97373-8). Heinemann Ed.

Policy Evaluation for Local Government. Ed. by Terry Busson & Philip Coulter. (Orig.). 1983. pap. 8.00 (ISBN 0-918592-69-0). Policy Studies.

Policy Evaluation: Making Optimum Decisions. Stuart S. Nagel. LC 81-12123. 352p. 1982. 42.95 (ISBN 0-275-90866-6, C0866). Praeger.

Policy Evalution for Local Government. Ed. by Terry Busson & Phillip Coulter. LC 87-7532. (Contributions in Political Science Ser.: No. 182). 288p. 1987. lib. bdg. 39.95 (ISBN 0-313-25953-4, BEV/). Greenwood.

Policy Experience of Twelve Less Developed Countries, 1973-1978. Bela Balassa. (Working Paper: No. 449). 36p. 1981. pap. 3.50 (ISBN 0-686-39745-2, WP-0449). World Bank.

Policy Exploration Through Microanalytic Simulation. Guy H. Orcutt et al. 370p. 1976. 29.95x (ISBN 0-87766-170-7, 15100); pap. 12.95x (ISBN 0-87766-169-3, 15300). Urban Inst.

Policy Factor: Agricultural Performance in Kenya & Tanzania. Michael F. Lofchie. (Food in Africa Ser.). 275p. 1988. lib. bdg. 30.00 (ISBN 1-55587-136-4). Lynne Rienner.

Policy for Agricultural Research. Ed. by Vernon W. Ruttan & Carl Pray. (Special Studies in Agriculture Science & Policy). 200p. 1987. 36.50 (ISBN 0-8133-7369-7). Westview.

Policy for Fuel. Colin Robinson. (Institute of Economic Affairs, Occasional Papers Ser.: No. 31). pap. 2.50 technical (ISBN 0-255-27607-9). Transatl Arts.

Policy for School Boards. Linda Leopardi. (School Board Library Ser.). 68p. (Orig.). 1983. pap. 9.95 (ISBN 0-912337-03-6). NJ Schl Bds.

Policy for the Social Work Practitioner. Dean Pierce. LC 83-22179. 256p. 1984. pap. text ed. 18.95 (ISBN 0-582-28403-1). Longman.

Policy Formation in the European Communities: A Bibliographic Guide to Community Documentation 1958-1978. Michael Hopkins. 360p. 1981. 56.00x (ISBN 0-7201-1597-3). Mansell.

Policy Formulation & Administration: A Casebook of Top-Management Problems in Business. 9th ed. C. Roland Christensen et al. 1985. 39.95x (ISBN 0-256-03012-X). Irwin.

Policy Formulation & Strategy Management: Text & Cases. 2nd ed. Robert E. Schellenberger & Glenn Boseman. LC 81-14739. (Management Ser.). 760p. 1982. 38.00 (ISBN 0-471-08215-5); tchrs'. ed. (ISBN 0-471-86332-7). Wiley.

Policy Game: How Special Interests & Ideologues Are Stealing America. Peter Navarro. LC 84-13012. (Wiley Management Series on Problem Solving, Decision Making & Strategic Thinking). 340p. 1984. 18.95 (ISBN 0-471-81169-6, Pub by Wiley-Interscience). Wiley.

Policy Game: How Special Interests & Ideologues Are Stealing America. Peter Navarro. 360p. (Orig.). 1986. pap. text ed. 12.95x (ISBN 0-669-14112-7). Lexington Bks.

Policy Grants Directory. Ed. by Stuart Nagel & Marian Neef. 1977. pap. 8.00 (ISBN 0-918592-25-9). Policy Studies.

Policy Guidelines for Bail: An Experiment in Court Reform. John S. Goldkamp & Michael R. Gottfredson. LC 84-26798. 307p. 1985. 34.95 (ISBN 0-87722-381-5). Temple U Pr.

Policy Handbook for Flood Control. T. V. Hromadka, II et al. (Illus.). 94p. Date not set. 19.50 (ISBN 0-914055-08-9). Lighthouse Pubns.

Policy Impact of Universities in Developing Countries. Ed. by Fred Lazin et al. LC 88-1387. (Policy Studies Organization Ser.). 256p. 1988. 45.00 (ISBN 0-312-01698-0). St Martin.

Policy Implementation & Bureaucracy. 2nd ed. Randall B. Ripley & Grace A. Franklin. 249p. 1986. 15.00x (ISBN 0-256-03393-5). Dorsey.

Policy Implementation & PL. 99-457: Planning for Young Children with Special Needs. Ed. by James J. Gallagher et al. 300p. 1989. pap. text ed. 28.00 (ISBN 1-55766-013-1). P H Brookes.

Policy Implementation & Social Welfare in the 1980s: Israel & the United States. Frederick A. Lazin. 224p. (Orig.). 1986. 29.95 (ISBN 0-88738-084-0). Transaction Bks.

Policy Implementation in Federal & Unitary Systems: Questions of Analysis & Design. Ed. by Kenneth Hanf & A. J. Toonen. 1985. lib. bdg. 49.50 (ISBN 90-247-3137-2, Pub. by Martinus Nijhoff Netherlands). Kluwer Academic.

Policy Implementation in Post-Mao China. Ed. by David M. Lampton. LC 85-23218. (Studies in China: No. 6). 439p. 1987. 48.00x (ISBN 0-520-05706-6). U of Cal Pr.

Policy Implications of Data Network Developments in the OECD Area. OECD. (Information Computer Communications Policy: No. 3). (Illus.). 206p. (Orig., Fr.). 1980. pap. 12.50x (ISBN 92-64-12005-X, 93-79-02-1). OECD.

Policy in Evolution: The U. S. Role in China's Reunification. Martin L. Lasater. (Special Studies on China & East Asia). 176p. 1988. pap. 22.00 (ISBN 0-8133-7595-9). Westview.

Policy Indicators: Links Between Social Science & Public Debate. Duncan MacRae, Jr. LC 84-17294. (Urban & Regional Policy & Development Studies). xvi, 414p. 37.50x (ISBN 0-8078-1628-0). U of NC Pr.

Policy Interventions for Technological Innovation in Developing Countries. Charles Cooper. (Working Paper: No. 441). 59p. 1980. 5.00 (ISBN 0-686-36148-2, WP-0441). World Bank.

Policy Is Personal: Sex, Gender & Informal Care. Claire Ungerson. 180p. 1987. lib. bdg. 45.00x (ISBN 0-422-78500-8, Pub. by Routledge UK); pap. 19.95x (ISBN 0-422-78510-5, Pub. by Routledge UK). Routledge Chapman & Hall.

Policy Issues in Residential Care: Discussion Paper. 1978. 10.00x (ISBN 0-317-05796-0, Pub. by Natl Soc Work). State Mutual Bk.

Policy Issues in Small Business Research. Allan Gibb & Terry Webb. 224p. 1980. text ed. 37.95x (ISBN 0-566-00312-0). Gower Pub Co.

Policy Issues in Work & Retirement. Herbert S. Parnes. LC 83-4950. 1983. text ed. 20.95 (ISBN 0-88099-011-2); pap. text ed. 13.95 (ISBN 0-88099-010-4). W E Upjohn.

Policy Makers & Critics: Conflicting Theories of American Foreign Poilicy. rev. ed. Cecil V. Crabb, Jr. LC 86-16901. 311p. 1986. lib. bdg. 40.95 (ISBN 0-275-92209-X, C2209); pap. 15.95 (ISBN 0-275-92210-3, B2210). Praeger.

Policy Making & Effective Leadership: A National Study of Academic Management. J. Victor Baldridge et al. LC 77-82909. (Higher Education Ser.). 1978. text ed. 27.95x (ISBN 0-87589-351-1). Jossey-Bass.

Policy-Making & Planning in the Health Sector. Kenneth Lee & Anne Mills. (Illus.). 208p. 1982. 30.00 (ISBN 0-85664-965-1, Pub. by Croom Helm). Routledge Chapman & Hall.

Policy Making for American Education. Roald F. Campbell & Donald H. Layton. 1969. pap. 4.00 (ISBN 0-931080-03-7). U Chicago Midwest Admin.

Policy Making in a Disorderly World Economy. G. Eliasson et al. 418p. (Orig.). 1983. pap. 38.50x (ISBN 91-7204-166-8, Pub. by Almqvist & Wiksell). Coronet Bks.

Policy-Making in a New State: Papua New Guinea 1972-77. Ed. by J. A. Ballard. (Illus.). 331p. 1981. text ed. 37.50x (ISBN 0-7022-1529-5). U of Queensland Pr.

Policy Making in a Three-Party System Committees, Coalitions & Parliament. Ian Marsh. 256p. 1986. text ed. 55.00 (ISBN 0-416-92090-X, 1021). Routledge Chapman & Hall.

Policy Making in China: Leaders, Structures, & Processes. Kenneth Lieberthal & Michel Oksenberg. (Illus.). 456p. 1988. 45.00 (ISBN 0-691-05668-4). Princeton U Pr.

Policy Making in Communist Party States. Gary K. Bertsch. (CISE Learning Package Ser.: No. 10). (Illus.). 114p. (Orig.). 1975. pap. text ed. 4.00x (ISBN 0-936876-25-5). LRIS.

Policy Making in Education. Ed. by Ann Lieberman & Milbrey McLaughlin. LC 81-85130. (National Society for the Study of Education 81st Yearbook, Part 1). 300p. 1982. lib. bdg. 15.00x (ISBN 0-226-60132-3). U of Chicago Pr.

Policy Making in Education: The Breakdown of Consensus. Ed. by I. McNay & J. Ozga. 346p. 1985. text ed. 39.00 (ISBN 0-08-032671-4, M110, M115, Pub. by PPL); pap. text ed. 18.25 (ISBN 0-08-032670-6). Pergamon.

Policy Making in India: An Approach to Optimisation. Krishan Saigal. 1983. text ed. 20.00x (ISBN 0-7069-2274-3, Pub. by Vikas India). Advent NY.

Policy-Making in the Federal Executive Branch. Ed. by Randall B. Ripley & Grace A. Franklin. LC 74-33093. (Illus.). 1975. 20.95 (ISBN 0-02-926490-1). Free Pr.

Policy Making in the German Democratic Republic. Ed. by Klaus Von Beyme. LC 82-5544. 220p. 1984. 27.50x (ISBN 0-312-62032-2). St Martin.

Policy Making Process. 2nd ed. Charles E. Lindblom. 1980. pap. write for info. (ISBN 0-13-686543-7). P-H.

Policy Management in the Human Services. John E. Tropman. LC 83-19029. 296p. 1984. 35.00x (ISBN 0-231-05614-1). Columbia U Pr.

Policy of Keeping the World on Edge. B. Dmitriev. 280p. 1987. pap. 3.95 (ISBN 0-8285-3725-9, Pub. by Progress Pubs USSR). Imported Pubns.

Policy of Public Works under the Fascist Regime. G. G. Baraveli. 1976. lib. bdg. 59.95 (ISBN 0-8490-2450-1). Gordon Pr.

Policy of the Entente: Essays of the Determinants of British Foreign Policy 1904-1914. Keith M. Wilson. 224p. 1985. 39.50 (ISBN 0-521-30195-5). Cambridge U Pr.

Policy of the United States As Regards Intervention. Charles E. Martin. LC 21-3655. (Columbia University. Studies in the Social Sciences: No. 211). Repr. of 1921 ed. 16.50 (ISBN 0-404-51211-9). AMS Pr.

Policy of the United States Toward Maritime Commerce in War, 2 Vols. Carlton Savage. LC 34-28033. 1969. Repr. of 1936 ed. Set. 48.00 (ISBN 0-527-79000-1). Kraus Repr.

Policy of the United States Toward the Neutrals, 1917-1918. Thomas A. Bailey. 1972. 40.00 (ISBN 0-405-10578-9). Ayer Co Pubs.

Policy of the United States Towards Industrial Monopoly. Oswald W. Knauth. LC 68-56664. (Columbia University. Studies in the Social Sciences: No. 138). Repr. of 1914 ed. 20.00 (ISBN 0-404-51138-4). AMS Pr.

Policy of the United States Towards the Neutrals, 1917-1918. Thomas A. Bailey. 12.75 (ISBN 0-8446-1036-4). Peter Smith.

Policy of Tomorrow. Mirrit B. Ghali. Tr. by Ismail R. El Faruqi. LC 54-837. viii, 139p. 1971. pap. 3.50x (ISBN 0-87950-263-0). Spoken Lang Serv.

Policy on Land Use & Source Control Aspects of Traffic Noise Attenuation. 1980. 1.00 (ISBN 0-686-29469-6). AASHTO.

Policy Options for Preschool Programs. Lawrence J. Schweinhart & Jeffrey Koshel. 30p. 1986. pap. 5.00 (ISBN 0-931114-38-1). High-Scope.

Policy Options for Quality Education. 1984. 4.00 (ISBN 0-318-18979-8). NASBE.

Policy Options for the Singapore Economy. Lim C. Yah. 512p. 1988. price not set (ISBN 0-07-099133-2). McGraw.

Policy Options in Long-Term Care. Ed. by Judith Meltzer et al. LC 81-10445. 1982. lib. bdg. 28.00x (ISBN 0-226-51973-2); pap. 12.50x (ISBN 0-226-51974-0). U of Chicago Pr.

Policy Organization. Ed. by Aronold J. Meltsner & Christopher Bellavita. (Managing Information Ser.: Vol. 5). (Illus.). 224p. 1983. 28.00 (ISBN 0-8039-1912-3); pap. 14.00 (ISBN 0-8039-1913-1). Sage.

Policy Paradox & Political Reason. Deborah A. Stone. (Orig.). 1988. pap. text ed. write for info. (ISBN 0-673-39751-3). Scott F.

Policy Perspectives. Henry M. Wriston. LC 64-17776. (Brown University Bicentennial Publications: Studies in the Fields of General Scholarship). pap. 47.00 (ISBN 0-317-41780-0, 2023229). Bks Demand UMI.

Policy Planning & Local Government. Robin Hambleton. LC 78-73593. (Landmark Study). (Illus.). 384p. 1979. Repr. of 1978 ed. text ed. 22.00x (ISBN 0-916672-92-1, Pub. by Allanheld). Rowman.

Policy, Planning & Management in Technical & Vocational Education: A Comparative Study. (Trends & Issues in Technical & Vocational Education: No. 3). 158p. 1985. pap. 8.00 (ISBN 92-3-102169-9, U1465 6011, UNESCO). UNIPUB.

Policy Planning Organizations: Elite Agendas & America's Rightward Turn. Joseph G. Peschek. 296p. 1987. 24.95 (ISBN 0-87722-468-4). Temple U Pr.

Policy, Politics, Health & Medicine Series, 6 vols. Ed. by Vicente Navarro. (Orig.). 1983. Set. pap. text ed. 55.00x (ISBN 0-89503-026-8). Vol. 1: 160 pgs. Vol. 2: 160 pgs. Vol. 3: 288 pgs. Vol. 4: 264 pgs. Vol. 5: 312 pgs. Vol. 5: 288 pgs. Baywood Pub.

Policy, Power & Order: The Persistence of Economic Problems. Kerry Schott. LC 84-40187. 216p. 1988. Repr. of 1984 ed. 11.95 (ISBN 0-300-04276-0). Yale U Pr.

Policy, Power & Order: The Persistence of Economic Problems in Capitalist States. Kerry Schott. LC 84-40187. 288p. 1984. 23.00x (ISBN 0-300-03237-4). Yale U Pr.

Policy, Procedures, & People. Philip G. Schrag. (Special Studies in National Security & Defense Policy). 160p. 1989. pap. 31.00 (ISBN 0-8133-7702-1). Westview.

Policy Process in the Modern Capitalist State. Christopher Ham & Michael J. Hill. LC 83-23110. 256p. 1984. 29.95 (ISBN 0-312-62018-7). St Martin.

Policy Process in the Modern Capitalist State. Christopher Ham & Michael J. Hill. 256p. pap. cancelled (ISBN 0-312-62017-9). St Martin.

Policy Readings in Individual Taxation. Philip F. Postlewaite. 459p. 1980. text ed. 90.00 (ISBN 0-07-050543-8); pap. 23.00 (ISBN 0-07-050538-1). Shepards-McGraw.

Polish Marriage Applicants, St. Joseph County, Indiana, 1905-1915. Gene Szymarek & G. Lucky Ladewski. vi, 212p. (Orig.). 1988. pap. 13.50 (ISBN 1-55613-094-5). Heritage Bk.

Polish Memoirs of William John Rose. William J. Rose. Ed. by Daniel Stone. LC 74-79986. pap. 68.50 (ISBN 0-317-41778-9, 2023673). Bks Demand UMI.

Polish Museums: Anglo-Saxon & Later Medieval British Coins. Andrzej Mikolajczyk. (Sylloge of Coins of the British Isles Ser.: Vol. 37). (Illus.). 88p. 1988. 49.95 (ISBN 0-19-726063-2). Oxford U Pr.

Polish National Liberation Struggles & the Genesis of the Modern Nation. Emanuel Halicz. (Odense Studies in History & Social Sciences: No. 73). 197p. (Orig.). 1982. pap. 26.50x (ISBN 87-7492-374-9, Pub. by Odense Universitets Forlag (Odense Denmark)). Coronet Bks.

Polish Ordeal: The View from Within. LC 82-132725. 154p. 1982. 17.50 (ISBN 0-686-39800-9). Hippocrene Bks.

Polish Orders, Medals, Badges & Insignia, 1705-1985. Zdzislaw P. Wesolowski. LC 86-90004. (Military & Civilian Ser.). (Illus.). 400p. (Orig.). 1986. 35.50x (ISBN 0-937527-02-5); lib. bdg. 35.50x (ISBN 0-937527-01-7); text ed. 35.50x (ISBN 0-937527-03-3); pap. 29.50x (ISBN 0-937527-00-9); pap. text ed. 29.50x (ISBN 0-937527-04-1). Z P Wesolowski.

Polish Painting, Fifteenth to Twentieth Centuries. Agnieszka Morawinska. 1984. 175.00x (ISBN 0-317-61351-0, Pub. by Collets (UK)). State Mutual Bk.

Polish Painting from the Englightenment to Recent Times. Tadeusz Dobrowolski. 1981. 150.00x (ISBN 0-317-57338-1, Pub. by Collets UK). State Mutual Bk.

Polish Painting from the Enlightenment to Recent Times. Tadeusz Dobrowolski. 1981. 116.00x (ISBN 0-317-61354-5, Pub. by Collets (UK)). State Mutual Bk.

Polish Paradox: Communism & National Renewal. William E. Schaufele. (Headline Series 256). (Illus.). 72p. (gr. 11-12). 1981. pap. 4.00 (ISBN 0-87124-071-8). Foreign Policy.

Polish Parish Records of the Roman Catholic Church, Their Use & Understanding in Genealogical Research. rev. ed. Gerald A. Ortell. (Illus.). 86p. 1984. pap. 10.00 (ISBN 0-912811-03-X). Genun Pubs.

Polish Peasant in Europe & America. abr. ed. William I. Thomas & Florian Znaniecki. Ed. by Eli Zaretsky. LC 83-6500. 320p. 1984. 29.95 (ISBN 0-252-01090-6); pap. 9.95 (ISBN 0-252-01092-2). U of Ill Pr.

Polish People in Canada: A Visual History. William Makowski. (Illus.). 300p. 1987. 45.00 (ISBN 0-88776-170-4, Dist. by U of Toronto Pr); pap. 25.00 (ISBN 0-88776-189-5). Tundra Bks.

Polish People's Republic. James F. Morrison. LC 68-10209. (Integration & Community Building in Eastern Europe Ser.: No. 2). pap. 46.00 (ISBN 0-317-09029-1, 2002280). Bks Demand UMI.

Polish Phrase Book. Magdalena Hall & Jill Norman. 224p. 1976. pap. 4.95 (ISBN 0-14-003561-3). Penguin.

Polish Plays in English Translations: A Bibliography. Boleslaw Taborski. 74p. 1968. pap. 3.50 (ISBN 0-940962-34-9). Polish Inst Art & Sci.

Polish Pocket Dictionary. Stanislawski & Jaslan. 712p. (Eng. & Pol.). 1985. 19.50x (ISBN 83-214-0363-8, P555). Vanous.

Polish Political Science Yearbook 1982. 310p. 1982. 50.00x (Pub. by Collets (UK)). State Mutual BK.

Polish Politics & National Reform, 1775-1788. Daniel Stone. (East European Monographs: No. 22). 122p. 1976. 20.00x (ISBN 0-914710-15-X). East Eur Quarterly.

Polish Politics: Edge of the Abyss. Ed. by Jack Bielasiak. LC 83-24759. 384p. 1984. 42.95 (ISBN 0-275-91128-4, C1128). Praeger.

Polish Politics in Transition: The Camp of National Unity & the Struggle for Power, 1935-1939. Edward D. Wynot. LC 73-85024. pap. 81.20 (2031064). Bks Demand UMI.

Polish Practical Dictionary (English-Polish) J. Stanislawski & K. Billip. 1983. 22.00x (ISBN 83-214-0245-3, P-533). Vanous.

Polish Press in America. Jan Kowalik. LC 77-90363. 1978. soft cover 10.95 (ISBN 0-88247-498-7). R & E Pubs.

Polish Problem at the Paris Peace Conference: A Study of the Great Powers & the Poles, 1918-1919. Kay Lundgreen-Nielsen. (Odense Studies in History & Social Sciences: No. 59). 603p. (Orig.). 1979. pap. 42.50x (ISBN 87-7492-261-0, Pub. by Odense Universitets Forlag (Odense Denmark)). Coronet Bks.

Polish Prose & Verse. J. Pietrkiewicz. (London East European Ser.). 205p. 1956. 28.50 (ISBN 0-485-17502-9, Pub. by Athlone Pr UK). Humanities.

Polish Question in the Russian State Duma. Edward Chmielewski. LC 77-100411. pap. 49.00 (ISBN 0-317-29722-8, 2022213). Bks Demand UMI.

Polish Radio Broadcasting in the United States. Joseph Migala. 320p. 1987. text ed. 25.00 (ISBN 0-88033-112-7, 216). East Eur Quarterly.

Polish Reference Grammar. Maria Z. Brooks. LC 74-78500. (Slavistic Printings & Reprintings Textbook Ser.: No. 2). 580p. 1976. text ed. 64.00x (ISBN 90-2793-313-8). Mouton.

Polish Renaissance in Its European Context. Ed. by Samuel Fiszman. LC 88-1717. (Illus.). 450p. 1988. 50.00 (ISBN 0-253-34627-4). Ind U Pr.

Polish Review. (J). avail., quarterly; back issues avail. Polish Inst Art & Sci.

Polish Review: Index: 1956-1966. Ed. by Irene Sokol & Ludwik Krzyzanowski. 66p. 1967. 2.00 (ISBN 0-940962-06-3). Polish Inst Art & Sci.

Polish Review: Index 1969-1970. Ed. by Irene Sokel. 39p. 1971. 1.00. Polish Inst Art & Sci.

Polish Revolution: Solidarity. Timothy G. Ash. 384p. 1984. 17.95 (ISBN 0-684-18114-2, ScribT). Scribner.

Polish Revolution: Solidarity. Timothy G. Ash. 1985. 10.95 (ISBN 0-394-72907-2, Vin). Random.

Polish Romantic Drama: Three Plays in English Translation. Ed. by Harold B. Segel. LC 76-50264. (Illus.). 304p. 1977. 32.50x (ISBN 0-8014-0871-7). Cornell U Pr.

Polish Romantic Literature. facs. ed. Julian Krzyzanowski. LC 68-22922. (Essay Index Reprint Ser). 1931. 18.00 (ISBN 0-8369-0602-0). Ayer Co Pubs.

Polish-Russian Dictionary of Economics. M. N. Osmowej. 494p. (Pol. & Rus.). 1977. leatherette 35.00 (ISBN 0-686-92093-7, M-9121). French & Eur.

Polish-Russian, Russian-Polish Dictionary. I. Nitronowa et al. 575p. (Pol. & Rus.). 1980. leatherette 9.95 (ISBN 0-686-97442-5, M-9102). French & Eur.

Polish, Say It In. M. Grala & R. Retman. 110p. 1982. pap. 12.50x (ISBN 83-01-03922-1, P-542). Vanous.

Polish Science & Technology Dictionary: English-Polish. 6th ed. S. Czerni & M. Skrzynska. 910p. 1982. 50.00x (ISBN 83-204-0763-X, P536). Vanous.

Polish Second Corps & the Italian Campaign. Ed. by W. Victor Madej. LC 84-81892. (Illus.). 186p. 1984. 13.95 (ISBN 0-941052-51-6, 51); pap. 9.95 (ISBN 0-941052-34-6, 1). Valor Pub.

Polish Solution of the Enigma: Breakthrough '32. C. A. Deavours. 90p. (Orig.). 1988. pap. text ed. 48.80 (ISBN 0-89412-152-9). Aegean Park Pr.

Polish-Soviet Relations, Nineteen Thirty-Two to Nineteen Thirty-Nine. Bohdan B. Budurowycz. LC 63-7509. (East-Central Studies of the Russian Institute). 229p. 1963. 28.00x (ISBN 0-231-02593-9). Columbia U Pr.

Polish Texans. T. Lindsay Baker. (Illus.). 120p. 1982. 8.95 (ISBN 0-933164-98-X); pap. 5.95 (ISBN 0-933164-99-8). U of Tex Inst Tex Culture.

Polish: Textbook of the Polish Language for English-Speaking People. Joseph Wira. LC 87-91220. (Illus.). 672p. 1987. text ed. 25.00 (ISBN 0-9618215-0-7). Belweder Pr.

Polish Trivia. Claire Bielawa. (Illus.). 182p. 1987. pap. 7.95 (ISBN 0-933341-73-3). Quinlan Pr.

Polish Trivia Book. John M. Vraniak. LC 87-71341. 169p. 1988. 5.95 (ISBN 0-910977-03-8). Avenue Pub.

Polish Underground State. Stefan Korbonski. 288p. 1981. pap. 10.00 (ISBN 0-88254-517-5). Hippocrene Bks.

Polish-U. S. Industrial Cooperation in the 1980's: Findings of a Joint Research Project. Ed. by Paul Marer & Eugeniusz Tabaczynski. LC 81-47884. (Illus.). 448p. 1982. 25.00x (ISBN 0-253-34529-4). Ind U Pr.

Polish Way. Adam Zamoyski. 1988. 24.95 (ISBN 0-531-15069-0). Watts.

Polish Worker: Study of a Social Stratum. Feliks Gross. LC 77-87525. Repr. of 1945 ed. 22.00 (ISBN 0-404-16602-4). AMS Pr.

Polish Wycinanki Designs. Frances Drwal. (International Design Library). (Illus.). 48p. (Orig.). 1984. pap. 5.95 (ISBN 0-88045-058-4). Stemmer Hse.

Polished Ebony. Octavus R. Cohen. LC 74-128725. (Short Story Index Reprint Ser). (Illus.). 1919. 19.00 (ISBN 0-8369-3616-7). Ayer Co Pubs.

Polished Stone Articles Used by the New York Aborigines Before & During European Occupation. William M. Beauchamp. LC 74-7930. Repr. of 1897 ed. 17.50 (ISBN 0-404-11816-X). AMS Pr.

Polishing & Plating of Metals. Hawkins. 1987. pap. 11.95. Lindsay Pubns.

Polishing & Waxing Compositions: Recent Developments. Ed. by M. G. Halpern. LC 82-7691. (Chemical Technology Rev. 213). (Illus.). 301p. 1983. 36.00 (ISBN 0-8155-0916-2). Noyes.

Polishing up the Brass: Honest Observations on Modern Military Life. Michele McCormick. LC 87-16021. 160p. (Orig.). 1988. pap. 8.95 (ISBN 0-8117-2257-0). Stackpole.

Polishing Your Professional Image. Bobbi Linkemer. LC 86-47814. (Successful Office Skills Ser.). 1987. pap. 3.50 (ISBN 0-8144-7670-8). AMACOM.

Politburo: Demographic Trends, Gorbachev & The Future. Roy D. Laird. 203p. 1986. pap. 25.00 (ISBN 0-8133-7198-8). Westview.

Polite Academy. 3rd ed. Ed. by Linda Sibbald. (Children's Books from the Past: Vol. 2). 181p. 1973. Repr. of 1765 ed. 41.10. P Lang Pubs.

Polite Americans: A Wide-Angle View of Our More or Less Good Manners over 300 Years. Gerald Carson. LC 80-11824. (Illus.). xvi, 346p. 1980. Repr. of 1966 ed. lib. bdg. 35.00x (ISBN 0-313-22417-X, CAPO). Greenwood.

Polite Conversations. Jonathan Swift. LC 75-33790. 1975. Repr. of 1738 ed. lib. bdg. 30.00 (ISBN 0-8414-7547-4). Folcroft.

Polite Escape: On the Myth of Secularization. Harry J. Ausmus. LC 81-16924. xii, 189p. 1982. lib. bdg. 22.95x (ISBN 0-8214-0650-7). Ohio U Pr.

Polite Essays. facs. ed. Ezra L. Pound. LC 67-22111. (Essay Index Reprint Ser). 1937. 20.00 (ISBN 0-8369-0796-5). Ayer Co Pubs.

Polite Farces for the Drawing Room. (Collected Works of Arnold Bennett: Vol. 66). 1976. Repr. of 1900 ed. 15.75 (ISBN 0-685-72140-X, 19147). Ayer Co Pubs.

Polite Marriage. facs. ed. Joyce M. Tompkins. LC 77-80403. (Essay Index Reprint Ser). 1938. 16.50 (ISBN 0-8369-1053-2). Ayer Co Pubs.

Polite Satires. Clifford Bax. LC 76-40385. (One-Act Plays in Reprint Ser.). 1976. Repr. of 1922 ed. 15.00x (ISBN 0-8486-2001-1). Roth Pub Inc.

Politely Tell a Gardener: Spanish-English Gardening Instructions. rev. ed. Linda Wolf. 30p. 1982. pap. 3.50 (ISBN 0-945651-02-3). Tell Maid.

Politely Tell a Maid: Spanish-English Housekeeping Instructions. rev. ed. Linda Wolf. 30p. 1981. pap. 3.50 (ISBN 0-945651-00-7). Tell Maid.

Politeness: Some Universals in Language Usage. Penelope Brown & Stephen C. Levinson. (Illus.). 300p. 1987. 39.50 (ISBN 0-521-30862-3); pap. 12.95 (ISBN 0-521-31355-4). Cambridge U Pr.

Politica. Aristotle. Ed. by W. David Ross. (Oxford Classical Texts). 1957. 19.95x (ISBN 0-19-814515-2). Oxford U Pr.

Politica Cientifica en American Latina. (No. 3). pap. 7.50 (U344, UNESCO). UNIPUB.

Politica de los EE.UU. en la Cuenca del Caribe. N. Poiarkova. 142p. 1986. pap. 2.95 (ISBN 0-8285-3249-4, Pub. by Progress Pubs USSR). Imported Pubns.

Politica Espanola en Puerto Rico Durante el Siglo XIX. Maria A. Garcia Ochoa. LC 78-14035. 1979. 14.00 (ISBN 0-8477-0854-3); pap. 12.00 (ISBN 0-8477-0855-1). U of PR Pr.

Politica Methodice Digesta of Johannes Althusius. Johannes Althusius. Ed. by J. P. Mayer. LC 78-67326. (European Political Thought Ser.). 1979. Repr. of 1932 ed. lib. bdg. 39.00x (ISBN 0-405-11673-X). Ayer Co Pubs.

Politica Puertorriquena y el Nuevo Trato. Thomas Mathews. Tr. by Antonio J. Colorado. 5.00 (ISBN 0-8477-0831-4); pap. 3.75 (ISBN 0-8477-0832-2). U of PR Pr.

Politica Tributaria como Instrumento del Desarrolo: Documentos y Conclusiones de la III Conferencia Interamericana Sobre Tributacion. 554p. (Span.). 1973. 25.00 (ISBN 0-8270-3785-6). OAS.

Political. Seligman. 1986. 12.95 (ISBN 0-471-77563-0). Wiley.

Political Action for Patient Advocacy. Ed. by Barbara B. Minckley & Sandra N. Funk. LC 82-12610. 60p. (Orig.). 1982. pap. 9.50 (ISBN 0-942146-02-6). Midwest Alliance Nursing.

Political Action Handbook for Nurses. Diana J. Mason & Susan Talbott. 550p. 1986. pap. text ed. write for info. (ISBN 0-201-16368-3, Hlth-Sci). Addison-Wesley.

Political Action: Mass Participation in Five Western Democracies. Samuel H. Barnes & Max Kasse. LC 78-19649. (Illus.). 607p. 1979. 35.00 (ISBN 0-8039-0956-X). Sage.

Political Action: The Key to Understanding Politics. George Beam & Dick Simpson. LC 84-5976. xiii, 253p. 1984. 19.95x (ISBN 0-8040-0834-5, Swallow); pap. 9.95 (ISBN 0-8040-0835-3, Swallow). Ohio U Pr.

Political Activities of Philip Freneau. Samuel E. Forman. LC 77-125693. (American Journalists Ser). 1970. Repr. of 1902 ed. 14.00 (ISBN 0-405-01670-0). Ayer Co Pubs.

Political Activities of Phillip Freneau. Samuel E. Forman. LC 78-63891. (Johns Hopkins University. Studies in the Social Sciences. Twentieth Ser. 1902: 9-10). Repr. of 1902 ed. 11.50 (ISBN 0-404-61145-1). AMS Pr.

Political Activities of the Baptists & the Fifth Monarchy Men in England During the Interregnum. Louise F. Brown. 1964. Repr. of 1911 ed. 20.50 (ISBN 0-8337-0399-4). B Franklin.

Political Adaptation in Sa'udi Arabia: A Study of the Council of Ministers. Summer S. Huyette. (Westview Special Studies on the Middle East). 175p. 1985. softcover 26.50x (ISBN 0-8133-0203-X). Westview.

Political Advancement in the South Pacific: A Comparative Study of Colonial Practice in Fiji, Tahiti & American Samoa. Francis J. West. LC 84-6745. xi, 188p. 1984. Repr. of 1961 ed. lib. bdg. 35.00 (ISBN 0-313-24533-9, WPSP). Greenwood.

Political Advocacy & Cultural Communication: Organizing the Nation's Public Diplomacy. Gifford D. Malone. (Rhetoric & Political Discourse Ser.: Vol. 11). 178p. (Orig.). 1988. lib. bdg. 21.50 (ISBN 0-8191-6619-7, Co-pub. by White Miller Center); pap. text ed. 10.75 (ISBN 0-317-64811-X). U Pr of Amer.

Political Alienation. Robert Lamb et al. 192p. (Orig.). 1975. pap. write for info. (ISBN 0-312-62055-1). St Martin.

Political Analysis & American Medical Care. Theodore R. Marmor. LC 83-1904. 304p. 1983. pap. 15.95 (ISBN 0-521-28352-3). Cambridge U Pr.

Political Analysis of Deviance. Ed. by Pat Lauderdale. (Illus.). 1980. 22.50x (ISBN 0-8166-0931-4). U of Minn Pr.

Political Analysis of European History at the End of the 19th Century. Gabriel Hanotaux. (Illus.). 167p. 1984. 87.85x (ISBN 0-86722-079-1). Inst Econ Pol.

Political Analysis: Shifting Trends & Questionable Assumptions. John Pulparampil. LC 76-904610. 1976. 8.50x (ISBN 0-88386-804-0). South Asia Bks.

Political Analysis: Technique & Practice. Louise G. White & Robert P. Clark. LC 82-22827. (Political Science Ser.). 300p. 1983. pap. text ed. 15.25 pub net (ISBN 0-534-01284-1). Brooks-Cole.

Political Analysis Through the Prince System. William D. Coplin & Michael K. O'Leary. (Learning Packages in the Policy Sciences Ser.: No. 23). (Illus.). 100p. (Orig.). 1983. pap. text ed. 5.50x (ISBN 0-936826-18-5). PS Assocs Croton.

Political Anatomy of Ireland. W. Petty. 260p. 1970. Repr. of 1691 ed. 32.50x (ISBN 0-7165-0093-0, BBA 03502, Pub. by Irish Academic Pr Ireland). Biblio Dist.

Political Anatomy of the Body: Medical Knowledge in Britain in the Twentieth Century. David Armstrong. LC 82-9546. 176p. 1983. 34.50 (ISBN 0-521-24746-2). Cambridge U Pr.

Political & Administrative Development. Ed. by Ralph J. Braibanti. LC 75-79965. (Commonwealth Studies Center: No. 36). xii, 700p. 1969. 40.95 (ISBN 0-8223-0022-2). Duke.

Political & Civil History of the United States of America from the Year 1763 to the Close of the Administration of President Washington in March, 1797, 2 Vols. Timothy Pitkin. LC 79-109613. (Ear of the American Revolution Ser). 1970. Repr. of 1823 ed. Set. lib. bdg. 135.00 (ISBN 0-306-71908-8). Da Capo.

Political & Commercial Geology & the World's Mineral Resources. Ed. by Josia E. Spurr. LC 82-48322. (World Economy Ser.). 562p. 1982. lib. bdg. 66.00 (ISBN 0-8240-5378-8). Garland Pub.

Political & Constitutional Ideas of the Court Whigs. Reed Browning. LC 81-19372. 290p. 1982. text ed. 32.50 (ISBN 0-8071-0980-0). La State U Pr.

Political & Cultural History of the Ancient World: A Syllabus with Suggested Readings. Martin R. McGuire. pap. 54.50 (ISBN 0-317-09243-X, 2005215). Bks DEmand UMI.

Political & Diplomatic Documents of the State of Israel, December, 1947-May, 1948, 2 vols. Ed. by Gedalia Yogev. (Documents on the Foreign Policy of Israel Ser.). 1980. Set. 69.95 (ISBN 0-87855-368-1) (ISBN 0-87855-389-4). Transaction Bks.

Political & Ecclesiastical Allegory of First Book of the Faerie Queen. Frederick M. Padelford. 1911. lib. bdg. 18.50 (ISBN 0-8414-9237-9). Folcroft.

Political & Ecclesiastical Allegory of the First Book of the Fairie Queen. Frederick M. Padelford. LC 70-111785. Repr. of 1911 ed. 5.00 (ISBN 0-404-04856-0). AMS Pr.

Political & Economic Activities of the Jesuits in the Plata Region. Magnus Morner. 1976. lib. bdg. 59.95 (ISBN 0-8490-2451-X). Gordon Pr.

Political & Economic Development of Pakistan. Omar Noman. 260p. 1988. lib. bdg. 55.00 (ISBN 0-7103-0211-8, Kegan Paul). Routledge Chapman & Hall.

Political & Economic Development of Modern Turkey. William Hale. 1981. 32.50 (ISBN 0-312-62059-4). St Martin.

Political & Economic Doctrines of John Marshall. John Marshall & John E. Oster. 1914. 22.50 (ISBN 0-8337-2636-6). B Franklin.

Political & Economic Migrants in America: Cubans & Mexicans. Silvia Pedraza-Bailey. LC 84-19648. 252p. 1985. text ed. 30.00x (ISBN 0-292-76492-8). U of Tex pr.

Political & Economic Structures. Bela Hubbard. LC 56-7403. 1964. 4.00 (ISBN 0-87004-067-7). Caxton.

Political & Economic Trends in the Middle East: Implications for U. S. Policy. Shireen Hunter. 1985. pap. 21.50x (ISBN 0-8133-0311-7). Westview.

Political & Economic Writings. A. R. Orage. 59.95 (ISBN 0-8490-0872-7). Gordon Pr.

Political & Economic Writings from the New English Weekly, 1932-1934. facs. ed. Alfred R. Orage. LC 67-28762. (Essay Index Reprint Ser). 1936. 17.00 (ISBN 0-8369-0753-1). Ayer Co Pubs.

Political & Electoral Handbook for Wales: 1959-1979. Denis Balsom & Martin Burch. 208p. 1980. text ed. 44.50x (ISBN 0-566-00236-1). Gower Pub Co.

Political & Historical Significance of the Major European Wars of the 19th Century, 2 vols. Harold Murdock. (Illus.). 437p. 1987. 247.50 (ISBN 0-86722-163-1). Inst Econ Pol.

Political & Historical Theories Suggested by the Rise & Fall of the Venetian Empire, 2 vols. R. R. Holmes. (Illus.). 257p. 1987. Set. 187.75 (ISBN 0-86722-154-2). Inst Econ Pol.

Political Change in Underdeveloped Countries: Nationalism & Communism. Ed. by John H. Kautsky. LC 76-17658. 364p. 1976. Repr. of 1962 ed. text ed. 18.50 (ISBN 0-88275-436-X). Krieger.
Political Chaos of the World & the Violent Leadership Role of Communist Russia. Rudolph D. Douhait. (Illus.). 127p. 1983. 77.45x (ISBN 0-86722-033-3). Inst Econ Pol.
Political Character of Adolescence: The Influence of Families & Schools. M. Kent Jennings & Richard G. Niemi. LC 73-16779. 1974. 45.00x (ISBN 0-691-09362-8); pap. 9.95x o.p (ISBN 0-691-02816-8). Princeton U Pr.
Political Character of the Japanese Press. Jung Bock Lee. (Institute of Social Sciences International Studies: No. 6). 214p. 1985. text ed. 20.00x (ISBN 0-8248-1094-5, Pub. by Seoul U Pr). UH Pr.
Political China Observed: A Western Perspective. Peter Harris. LC 80-10363. 320p. 1980. 28.00 (ISBN 0-312-62212-0). St Martin.
Political Choice in Canada. H. Clarke et al. 1979. text ed. 24.95 (ISBN 0-07-082783-4). McGraw.
Political Clientalism, Patronage & Development. Lemarchand Eisenstadt. (Illus.). 344p. 1981. pap. 14.95 (ISBN 0-8039-9795-7). Sage.
Political Clubs of New York City. Roy V. Peel. LC 68-18356. (Empire State Historical Publications: No. 48). (Illus.). 1968. Repr. of 1935 ed. 17.50 (ISBN 0-8046-8048-5, Ira J Friedman). Assoc Faculty Pr.
Political Cognition. Ed. by Richard R. Lau & David O. Sears. (Carnegie Symposium on Cognition Ser., 19th Annual). 424p. 1986. text ed. 39.95 (ISBN 0-89859-652-1). L Erlbaum Assocs.
Political Communication. Ed. by Steven H. Chaffee. LC 75-14629. (Sage Annual Reviews of Communication Research Ser.: Vol. 4). 319p. 1975. 35.00 (ISBN 0-8039-0505-X); pap. 16.95 (ISBN 0-8039-0507-6). Sage.
Political Communication & Information: A Selected Bibliography. Robert Goehlert. (Public Administration Ser.: P 1688). 18p. 1985. 3.00 (ISBN 0-89028-418-0). Vance Biblios.
Political Communication & Public Opinion in America. Dan Nimmo. LC 77-13143. (Illus.). 1978. text ed. write for info. (ISBN 0-673-16269-9); pap. text ed. write for info. (ISBN 0-673-16270-2). Scott F.
Political Communication in America. Robert E. Denton, Jr. & Gary C. Woodward. 384p. 1985. 46.95 (ISBN 0-275-90085-1, C0085); pap. 17.95 (ISBN 0-275-91639-1, B1639). Praeger.
Political Communication Research: Approaches, Studies, Assessments. David Paletz. Ed. by Melvin J. Voigt. LC 86-17475. (Communication & Information Science Ser.). 288p. 1987. text ed. 39.50 (ISBN 0-89391-329-4). Ablex Pub.
Political Communication Yearbook, 1984. Ed. by Keith R. Sanders et al. 304p. 1985. text ed. 30.00x (ISBN 0-8093-1183-6). S Ill U Pr.
Political Communications: The General Election Campaign of 1983. Ivor Crewe & Martin Harrop. (Illus.). 336p. 1986. 47.50 (ISBN 0-521-30425-3). Cambridge U Pr.
Political Community & the North Atlantic Area: International Organization in the Light of Historical Experience. Karl W. Deutsch et al. LC 69-13882. 1969. Repr. of 1957 ed. lib. bdg. 35.00 (ISBN 0-8371-1054-8, DEPO). Greenwood.
Political Concepts: A Reconstruction. Felix E. Oppenheim. LC 80-23846. 240p. 1981. pap. 5.50X (ISBN 0-226-63185-0, Phoen). U of Chicago Pr.
Political Conflict & Economic Change in Nigeria. Henry Bienen. 192p. 1985. 29.50x (ISBN 0-7146-3266-X, F Cass Co). Biblio Dist.
Political Conflict in Thailand: Reform, Reaction, Revolution. David Morell & Chai-Anan Samudavanija. LC 81-3926. 380p. 1981. text ed. 35.00 (ISBN 0-89946-044-5); 15.00 (ISBN 0-89946-169-7). Oelgeschlager.
Political Conflict on the Horn of Africa. Robert F. Gorman. LC 81-5183. 256p. 1981. 40.95 (ISBN 0-275-90636-1, C0636). Praeger.
Political Conflicts of True & Real Interests: Black-Race & White-Ethic Kith & Kinship Ties & Binds (of & - or the Jesse Jackson Faction in the Democratic Race & the Republican Religious Faction, Vol. II. (American University Studies Ser.: No. X). 511p. (Orig.). 1988. text ed. 70.00 (ISBN 0-8204-0528-0). P Lang Pubs.
Political Consciousness & American Democracy. James F. Lea. LC 81-13133. 304p. 1982. pap. 9.95 (ISBN 0-87805-151-1). U Pr of Miss.
Political Consciousness in the U. S. A. Traditions & Evolution. Yu. Zamoshkin & Ya. Balatov. 334p. 1984. 8.95 (ISBN 0-8285-2867-5, Pub. by Progress Pubs USSR). Imported Pubns.
Political Consequences of Electoral Laws. Douglas W. Rae. LC 67-24511. pap. 56.80 (ISBN 0-317-09417-3, 2010565). Bks Demand UMI.
Political Consequences of Modernization. John H. Kautsky. LC 80-16087. 286p. 1980. pap. 12.50 (ISBN 0-89874-215-3). Krieger.
Political Constructions: Defoe, Richardson, & Sterne in Relation to Hobbes, Hume, & Burke. Carol Kay. LC 88-3741. 288p. 1988. 29.95x (ISBN 0-8014-2043-1). Cornell U Pr.
Political Context of Law. Ed. by Richard Eales & David Sullivan. 184p. 1987. 35.00 (ISBN 0-907628-84-2). Hambledon Press.
Political Context of Sociology. Leon Bramson. 1961. pap. 10.50x (ISBN 0-691-02804-4). Princeton U Pr.
Political Control: A Selected Bibliography. Robert Goehlert. (Public Administration Ser.: P 1814). 19p. 1985. 3.00 (ISBN 0-89028-644-2). Vance Biblios.
Political Control of the Economy. Edward R. Tufte. LC 77-85570. 184p. 1980. pap. 8.95x (ISBN 0-691-02180-5). Princeton U Pr.
Political Correspondence & Public Papers of Aaron Burr, 2 vols. Ed. by Mary-Jo Kline & Joanne W. Ryan. LC 82-61396. (Illus.). 1118p. Set. 155.00x (ISBN 0-691-04685-9). Princeton U Pr.
Political Corruption: A Handbook. 2nd, rev. ed. Ed. by Arnold J. Heidenheimer et al. 1010p. 1988. 69.95x (ISBN 0-88738-163-4). Transaction Bks.
Political Corruption: A Selected Bibliography. Robert Goehlert. (Public Administration Ser.: P 1816). 19p. 1985. 3.00 (ISBN 0-89028-646-9). Vance Biblios.
Political Corruption in Africa. Robert Williams. 251p. 1987. text ed. 39.95 (ISBN 0-566-00794-0, Pub. by Gower Pub England). Gower Pub Co.
Political Corruption: Power, Money, & Sex. John C. Bollens & Henry J. Schmandt. LC 79-88114. 1979. pap. 8.95 (ISBN 0-913530-18-2). Palisades Pub.
Political Corruption: Readings in Comparative Analysis. Arnold J. Heidenheimer. LC 77-10874. 582p. 1978. pap. text ed. 16.95x (ISBN 0-87855-636-2). Transaction Bks.
Political Corruption: The Ghana Case. Victor T. Le Vine. LC 74-13629. (Publications Ser.: No. 138). 169p. 1975. 8.95x (ISBN 0-8179-1381-5). Hoover Inst Pr.
Political Crime. facs. ed. A. M. Gibson. LC 69-16851. (Select Bibliographies Reprint Ser). 1885. 21.50 (ISBN 0-8369-5007-0). Ayer Co Pubs.
Political Crime. Louis Proal. LC 70-172565. (Criminology, Law Enforcement, & Social Problems Ser.: No. 146). (With intro. & index added). 1973. Repr. of 1898 ed. 20.00x (ISBN 0-87585-146-0). Patterson Smith.
Political Crime in Europe: A Comparative Study of France, Germany, & England. Barton Ingraham. LC 77-83103. 1979. 45.00x (ISBN 0-520-03562-3). U of Cal Pr.
Political Crimes & Offenses: Monographs. Mary Vance. (Public Administration Ser.: P 2164). 40p. 1987. pap. 10.00 (ISBN 1-55590-324-X). Vance Biblios.
Political Criminal. Stephen Schafer. LC 73-10700. 1974. 8.95 (ISBN 0-02-927820-1). Free Pr.
Political Criminality: Policing & Social Conflict. Austin T. Turk. (Sage Library of Social Research: Vol. 136). 250p. 1982. 35.00 (ISBN 0-8039-1772-4); pap. 16.95 (ISBN 0-8039-1773-2). Sage.
Political Crisis-Fiscal Crisis: The Collapse & Revival of New York City. Martin Shefter. LC 84-45315. 336p. 1985. 21.95 (ISBN 0-465-05875-2). Basic.
Political Crisis-Fiscal Crisis: The Collapse & Revival of New York City. Martin Shefter. LC 84-45315. 288p. 1987. pap. 9.95 (ISBN 0-465-05876-0, PL 5176). Basic.
Political Crisis of the Enterprise System. Richard Eells. LC 79-48016. (Studies of the Modern Corporation Ser.). 1980. 10.00 (ISBN 0-02-909250-7). Free Pr.
Political Crisis of the 1850's. Michael F. Holt. 352p. 1983. 8.95x (ISBN 0-393-95370-X). Norton.
Political Culture & Behavior of Latin America. Louis K. Harris & Victor Alba. LC 74-79151. 250p. 1974. 10.00x (ISBN 0-87338-154-8); pap. text ed. 5.50x (ISBN 0-87338-155-6). Kent St U Pr.
Political Culture & Communist Studies. Ed. by Archie Brown. LC 84-20314. 256p. (Orig.). 1984. 37.50 (ISBN 0-87332-309-2); pap. 16.95 (ISBN 0-87332-310-6). M E Sharpe.
Political Culture & Judicial Behavior, Volume 1: Political Culture & Judicial Elites, a Comparative Analysis. Glendon Schubert. (Illus.). 308p. (Orig.). 1985. lib. bdg. 33.25 (ISBN 0-8191-4521-1); pap. text ed. 16.50 (ISBN 0-8191-4522-X). U Pr of Amer.
Political Culture & Judicial Behavior, Volume 2: Subcultural Analysis of Judicial Behavior, a Direct Observational Study. Glendon Schubert. (Illus.). 352p. (Orig.). 1985. lib. bdg. 33.25 (ISBN 0-8191-4501-7); pap. text ed. 16.50 (ISBN 0-8191-4502-5). U Pr of Amer.
Political Culture & Leadership in Soviet Russia: From Lenin to Gorbachev. Robert C. Tucker. LC 87-11025. 1987. 22.50 (ISBN 0-393-02489-X). Norton.
Political Culture & Political Change in Communist States. 2nd, rev. ed. Ed. by Archie Brown & Jack Gray. LC 76-41832. 375p. 1979. 35.00x (ISBN 0-8419-0508-8); pap. 18.00x (ISBN 0-8419-0509-6). Holmes & Meier.
Political Culture & Soviet Politics. Stephen White. 1980. 29.95 (ISBN 0-312-62249-X). St Martin.
Political Culture, Foreign Policy & Conflict: The Palestine Area Conflict System. Basheer Meibar. LC 81-427. (Contributions in Political Science Ser.: No. 63). (Illus.). 352p. 1982. lib. bdg. 35.00 (ISBN 0-313-22941-4, MEP/). Greenwood.
Political Culture in Israel: Cleavage & Integration among Israeli Jews. Eva Etzioni-Halevy & Rina Shapira. LC 76-24350. (Special Studies). 1977. 44.95 (ISBN 0-275-90263-3, C0263). Praeger.
Political Culture of Japan. Bradley Richardson. (Center for Japanese Studies, UC Berkeley: No. 11). 1974. pap. 11.95x (ISBN 0-520-03049-4). U of Cal Pr.
Political Culture of the American Whigs. Daniel W. Howe. LC 79-12576. 1980. lib. bdg. 25.00x (ISBN 0-226-35478-4). U of Chicago Pr.
Political Culture of the American Whigs. Daniel W. Howe. LC 79-12576. x, 404p. 1984. pap. 14.00x (ISBN 0-226-35479-2). U of Chicago Pr.
Political Culture, Public Policy, & the American States. Ed. by John Kincaid. LC 82-889. 250p. 1982. text ed. 16.50 (ISBN 0-89727-035-5); pap. text ed. 9.95 (ISBN 0-89727-041-X). ISHI PA.
Political Cultures in Transition. Warren E. Miller & M. Kent Jennings. LC 86-6771. 250p. 1986. text ed. 22.95 (ISBN 0-87154-602-7). Russell Sage.
Political Cultures of Massachusetts. Edgar Litt. 1965. 25.00x (ISBN 0-262-12021-6). MIT Pr.
Political Decadence in Imperial Germany: Personnel-Political Aspects of the German Government Crisis, 1894-97. Ekkehard-Teja P. Wilke. LC 76-3591. (Illinois Studies in Social Sciences: No. 59). 280p. 1976. 24.95 (ISBN 0-252-00571-6). U of Ill Pr.
Political Deliverance: The Mormon Quest for Utah Statehood. Edward L. Lyman. LC 85-1204. (Illus.). 352p. 1986. 22.95 (ISBN 0-252-01239-9). U of Ill Pr.
Political Development & Change. Ed. by Garry D. Brewer & Ronald D. Brunner. LC 74-482. (Illus.). 1975. 28.00 (ISBN 0-02-904710-2). Free Pr.
Political Development & Constitutional Change. Amal Ray & S. K. Chatterjee. 117p. 1983. text ed. 15.00x (ISBN 0-7069-1778-2, Pub. by Vikas England). Advent NY.
Political Development & Democracy in Peru: Continuity in Change & Crisis. Raul P. Saba. LC 87-14733. 180p. 1987. pap. 19.95 (ISBN 0-8133-7435-9). Westview.
Political Development & Social Change. 2nd ed. Jason L. Finkle & Richard W. Gable. LC 72-149769. pap. 160.00 (ISBN 0-317-19822-X, 2023215). Bks Demand UMI.
Political Development in Modern Japan. Ed. by Robert E. Ward. (Studies in the Modernization of Japan). 1968. pap. 19.50x (ISBN 0-691-00017-4). Princeton U Pr.
Political Development in Singapore, 1945-1955. Kim W. Yeo. 320p. 1973. 18.00x (ISBN 0-8214-0486-5, Pub. by Singapore U Pr). Ohio U Pr.
Political Development in South Asia. Permanand. 304p. 1988. text ed. 40.00x (ISBN 81-207-0767-2, Pub. by Sterling Pubs India). Apt Bks.
Political Development of Tanganyika. J. Clagett Taylor. 1963. 25.00x (ISBN 0-8047-0147-4). Stanford U Pr.
Political Development of Uganda Nineteen Hundred to Nineteen Eighty-Six. T. V. Sathyamurthy. 700p. 1986. text ed. 75.50 (ISBN 0-566-05247-4, Pub. by Gower Pub England). Gower Pub Co.
Political Dictionary of the Arab World. Yaacov Shimoni. LC 87-12392. 520p. 1988. 50.00 (ISBN 0-02-916422-2). Macmillan.
Political Dilemma of Popular Education: An African Case. David B. Abernethy. LC 69-13175. 1969. 35.00x (ISBN 0-8047-0703-0). Stanford U Pr.
Political Dilemmas of Military Regimes. Ed. by Christopher Clapham et al. LC 84-18414. 294p. 1985. 29.50x (ISBN 0-389-20533-8, 08095). B&N Imports.
Political Dimension of Labor-Management Relations: National Trends & State Level Developments in Massachusetts, 1946-1960. Phillip Saunders. Ed. by Stuart Bruchey. (American Business History Ser.). 1027p. 1986. lib. bdg. 125.00 (ISBN 0-8240-8369-5). Garland Pub.
Political Dimensions of India - U. S. S. R. Relations. S. P. Singh. 302p. 1987. 37.95. Asia Bk Corp.
Political Dimensions of Land Reforms in India. P. Eashvaraish. 1985. 18.00x (ISBN 0-8364-1382-2, Pub. by Ashish India). South Asia Bks.
Political Disaffection among British University Students: Concepts, Measurement, & Causes. Jack Citrin & David J. Elkins. LC 75-620051. (Research Ser.: No. 23). 80p. 1975. pap. 2.00x (ISBN 0-87725-123-1). U of Cal Intl St.
Political Discourse: A Case Study of the Watergate Affair. L. H. Larue. LC 87-13279. 184p. 1988. 20.00x (ISBN 0-8203-0980-X); pap. 10.00x (ISBN 0-8203-1027-1). U of GA Pr.
Political Disintegration of Europe & the Cultural Collapse of the Human Race. Robert W. Bransonnard. (Illus.). 139p. 1986. 175.50 (ISBN 0-86722-127-5). Inst Econ Pol.
Political Disquisitions, 3 Vols. James Burgh. LC 78-146144. (American Constitutional & Legal History Ser). 1971. Repr. of 1775 ed. Set. lib. bdg. 175.00 (ISBN 0-306-70101-4). Da Capo.
Political Doctrine of Ali-Baqillani. Yusuf Ibish. 1966. 19.95x (ISBN 0-8156-6029-4, Am U Beirut). Syracuse U Pr.
Political Doctrine of the Isma'ilis. Abu Al-Fawaris. Ed. by Sami N. Makarim. LC 77-16600. 156p. 1977. 25.00x (ISBN 0-88206-016-3). Caravan Bks.
Political Doctrines of Sun Yat-Sen. Paul Linebarger. LC 73-3926. 278p. 1973. Repr. of 1937 ed. lib. bdg. 35.00x (ISBN 0-8371-6855-4, LISY). Greenwood.
Political Doctrines of Sun Yat-Sen: An Exposition of the San Min Chu I. Paul M. Linebarger. LC 78-64293. (Johns Hopkins University. Studies in the Social Sciences. Extra Volumes: 24). Repr. of 1937 ed. 13.00 (ISBN 0-404-61393-4). AMS Pr.
Political Doctrines of Sun Yat-Sen: An Exposition of the San Min Chu-I. Paul M. Linebarger. LC 73-889. (China Studies: From Confucius to Mao Ser). xiv, 278p. 1973. Repr. of 1937 ed. 21.45 (ISBN 0-88355-082-2). Hyperion Conn.
Political Dogmatic. Jens Glebe-Moller. LC 86-46428. 192p. 1987. pap. 10.95 (ISBN 0-8006-2053-4). Fortress.
Political Domination in Africa: Reflections on the Limits of Power. Ed. by Patrick Chabal. (African Studies Ser.: No. 50). 240p. 1986. 42.50 (ISBN 0-521-32297-9); pap. 13.95 (ISBN 0-521-31148-9). Cambridge U Pr.
Political Dynamic in Taiwan: Continuity & Change in a Party-State, P-378. Tien Hung-mao. 336p. 1989. text ed. 35.95 (ISBN 0-8179-8781-9); pap. text ed. 22.95 (ISBN 0-8179-8782-7). Hoover Inst Pr.
Political Dynamics & Crisis in Punjab. Paul Wallace & Surendra Chopra. 1988. 28.00x (ISBN 0-8364-2286-4, Pub. by Nanak Dev Univ India). South Asia Bks.
Political Dynamics in the Middle East. Ed. by Paul Y. Hammond et al. LC 71-161688. (Middle East Ser.: Economic & Political Problems & Prospects). pap. 160.00 (ISBN 0-317-08143-8, 2007640). Bks Demand UMI.
Political Dynamics of Direct Foreign Investment. Veenaskay Sahar & Mukassa Sahar. 150p. 1985. 30.00 (ISBN 0-944025-02-1). Advance Research.
Political Dynamics of European Economic Integration. Leon N. Lindberg. LC 63-14129. pap. 29.90 (2030976). Bks Demand UMI.
Political Dynamics of Japan. Jun-ichi Kyogoku. Tr. by Nobutaka Ike from Japanese. 240p. 1987. 24.50 (ISBN 0-86008-409-4, Pub. by U of Tokyo Japan). Columbia U Pr.
Political Dynamics of Punjab. Ed. by Paul Wallace & Surendra Chopra. 1982. 18.50x (ISBN 0-8364-0915-9, Pub. by Nanak Dev Univ India). South Asia Bks.
Political Ecology of Disease in Tanzania. Meredeith Turshen. 224p. 1984. text ed. 27.00 (ISBN 0-8135-1030-9). Rutgers U Pr.
Political, Economic & Labor Climate in Brazil. rev. ed. Luis F. Andrade et al. (Multinational Industrial Relations Ser.: No. 4). (Illus.). 300p. 1986. pap. write for info. (ISBN 0-89546-057-2). Indus Res Unit-Wharton.
Political, Economic, & Labor Climate in Argentina. David R. Decker. Frwd. by Herbert R. Northrup. LC 83-81084. (Multinational Industrial Relations Ser.: No. 4f). 131p. (Orig.). 1983. pap. 20.00 (ISBN 0-89546-041-6). Indus Res Unit-Wharton.
Political, Economic, & Labor Climate in Colombia. David R. Decker & Ignacio Duran. LC 82-82996. (Multinational Industrial Relations Ser.: No. 4e). 1982. pap. 18.00 (ISBN 0-89546-025-4). Indus Res Unit-Wharton.
Political Economic, & Labor Climate in Peru. Nancy R. Johnson. LC 78-56286. (Multinational Industrial Relations Ser.: No. 4c). (Illus.). 223p. 1979. pap. 15.00 (ISBN 0-89546-018-1). Indus Res Unit-Wharton.
Political, Economic, & Labor Climate in Mexico. rev. ed. James L. Schlagheck et al. LC 79-92307. (Multinational Industrial Relations Ser.: Latin American Studies No.4b). (Illus.). 186p. 1980. pap. 15.00 (ISBN 0-89546-019-X). Indus Res Unit-Wharton.
Political, Economic, & Labor Climate in Tunisia. Anwar Shabon. (Multinational Industrial Relations Ser.: No. 9b). 109p. (Orig.). 1985. pap. text ed. 15.00 (ISBN 0-89546-059-9). Indus Res Unit-Wharton.
Political, Economic & Labor Climate in Turkey. Anwar M. Shabon & Isik U. Zeytinoglu. Ed. by Kate C. Bradford. 277p. (Orig.). 1985. pap. text ed. 22.00 (ISBN 0-89546-052-1). Indus Res Unit-Wharton.
Political, Economic, & Labor Climate in Venezuela. Cecilia M. Valente. LC 78-24665. (Multinational Industrial Relations Ser.: No. 4d). 280p. 1979. pap. 12.00 (ISBN 0-89546-011-4). Indus Res Unit-Wharton.
Political, Economic, & Labor Climate in India. Viswanathan Venkatachalam & Rajiva K. Singh. LC 82-80931. (Multinational Industrial Relations Ser.: No. 8b). 147p. 1982. pap. 18.00 (ISBN 0-89546-030-0). Indus Res Unit-Wharton.
Political, Economic, & Labor Climate in the Countries of the Arabian Peninsula, No. 9a. Anwar Shabon. LC 81-81928. (Multinational Industrial Relations Ser.). 325p. 1981. pap. 20.00 (ISBN 0-89546-032-7). Indus Res Unit-Wharton.
Political, Economic, & Labor Climate in the Philippines. Jaime T. Infante. LC 80-53988. (Multinational Industrial Relations Ser.: No. 8a). (Illus.). 147p. 1980. pap. 15.00 (ISBN 0-89546-024-6). Indus Res Unit-Wharton.
Political, Economic, & Labor in Spain. Mario Gobbo. LC 81-52617. (Multinational Industrial Relations Ser.: No. 10a). 134p. pap. 18.00 (ISBN 0-89546-034-3). Indus Res Unit-Wharton.

Political Economy of Iran under the Shah. M. M. Malek. 288p. 1987. 34.50 (ISBN 0-7099-3519-6, Pub. by Croom Helm UK). Routledge Chapman & Hall.

Political Economy of Iran under the Shah. M. M. Malek. 288p. 1988. text ed. 42.00 (ISBN 0-415-00472-1). Routledge Chapman & Hall.

Political Economy of Israel. Ira Sharkansky. 224p. 1986. 29.95 (ISBN 0-88738-117-0). Transaction Bks.

Political Economy of Japan, Vol. 2: The Changing International Context. Ed. by Takashi Inoguchi & Daniel I. Okimoto. LC 86-30037. 592p. 1988. text ed. 37.50 (ISBN 0-8047-1448-7). Stanford U Pr.

Political Economy of Japan, Vol. 2: The Changing International Context. Ed. by Takashi Inoguchi & Daniel I. Okimoto. LC 86-30037. 592p. 1988. pap. 12.95 (ISBN 0-8047-1481-9). Stanford U Pr.

Political Economy of Japan, Volume 1: The Domestic Transformation. Ed. by Kozo Yamamura & Yasukichi Yasuba. LC 86-30037. 696p. 1987. text ed. 37.50x (ISBN 0-8047-1380-4); pap. 12.95 (ISBN 0-8047-1381-2, SP-193). Stanford U Pr.

Political Economy of Kenya. Ed. by Michael G. Schatzberg. 253p. 1988. lib. bdg. 42.95 (ISBN 0-275-92672-9, C2672). Praeger.

Political Economy of Land Reforms. G. Thimmaiah. 1984. 14.00x (ISBN 0-8364-1145-5, Pub. by Ashish India). South Asia Bks.

Political Economy of Land: The State & Urban Development in Venezuela. Alan Gilbert & Patsy Healey. 200p. 1985. text ed. 36.95 (ISBN 0-566-05007-2). Gower Pub Co.

Political Economy of Latin American Defense Spending: Case Studies of Venezuela & Argentina. Robert E. Looney. LC 85-46043. 352p. 1986. 39.00x (ISBN 0-669-12928-3). Lexington Bks.

Political Economy of Latin American Development: Seven Exercises in Retrospection. Albert O. Hirschman. (Copublications Ser.: No. 3). 57p. (Orig.). 1986. pap. 5.00 (ISBN 0-935391-64-9). Ctr Mex Studies.

Political Economy of Law: A Third World Reader. Ed. by Y. Ghai & R. Luckham. cancelled. Intl Ctr Law.

Political Economy of Law: A Third World Reader. Ed. by Yash Ghai et al. 838p. 1988. 48.00 (ISBN 0-19-561991-9). Oxford U Pr.

Political Economy of Malaysia. Ed. by E. K. Fisk & Osman Rani. 1982. 59.00x (ISBN 0-19-582501-2). Oxford U Pr.

Political Economy of Manufacturing Protection. Ed. by Ross Garnaut & Christopher Findlay. 320p. (Orig.). 1987. pap. text ed. 24.95x (ISBN 0-04-330378-1). Unwin Hyman.

Political Economy of Marx. 2nd ed. Ed. by M. C. Howard & J. E. King. 280p. 1988. 35.00 (ISBN 0-8147-3452-9); pap. 15.00 (ISBN 0-8147-3453-7). NYU Pr.

Political Economy of Mechanization in U. S. Agriculture. Barry L. Price. LC 83-10412. (Replica Edition Ser.). 108p. 1983. pap. 22.50x (ISBN 0-86531-976-6). Westview.

Political Economy of Medicine: Great Britain & the United States. J. Rogers Hollingsworth. LC 86-2720. 352p. 1986. text ed. 37.50x (ISBN 0-8018-3262-4). Johns Hopkins.

Political Economy of Mexico: Two Studies. William P. Glade, Jr. & Charles W. Anderson. LC 63-10531. 256p. 1968. pap. 8.95x (ISBN 0-299-02894-1). U of Wis Pr.

Political Economy of Mexico under de la Madrid: The Crisis Deepens, 1985-1986. Wayne A. Cornelius. (Research Report Ser.: No. 43). 50p. (Orig.). 1986. pap. 6.50 (ISBN 0-935391-65-7). Ctr Mex Studies.

Political Economy of Modern Iran: Despotism & Pseudo-Modernism, 1926-1979. Homa Katouzian. 448p. 1981. 50.00x (ISBN 0-8147-4577-6); pap. 20.00x (ISBN 0-8147-4578-4). NYU Pr.

Political Economy of Modern South Africa. Alf Stadler. LC 86-20235. 205p. 1987. 35.00 (ISBN 0-312-74700-4). St Martin.

Political Economy of Modern Spain: Policy-Making in an Authoritarian System. Charles W. Anderson. LC 72-106036. (Illus.). 298p. 1970. 27.50x (ISBN 0-299-05611-2); pap. 11.95x (ISBN 0-299-05614-7). U of Wis Pr.

Political Economy of Morocco: A SAIS Study on Africa. Ed. by I. William Zartman. LC 87-6953. 288p. 1987. lib. bdg. 39.95 (ISBN 0-275-92593-5, C2593). Praeger.

Political Economy of Mubarak's Egypt. Robert Springborg. 350p. 1988. 38.50 (ISBN 0-8133-7643-2). Westview.

Political Economy of Namibia: An Annotated Critical Bibliography. Torre L. Eriksen & Richard Moorsom. 423p. 1987. 39.50 (ISBN 0-8419-9789-6). Holmes & Meier.

Political Economy of National Defense. William J. Weida & Frank L. Gertcher. 256p. 1986. 36.00 (ISBN 0-8133-0432-6). Westview.

Political Economy of Nationalism. Dudley Seers. (Library of Political Economy). (Illus.). 1983. 29.95x (ISBN 0-19-828456-X); pap. 12.50x (ISBN 0-19-828473-X). Oxford U Pr.

Political Economy of Natural Gas. Ferdinand Banks. 224p. 1987. lib. bdg. 72.50x (ISBN 0-7099-3940-X, Pub. by Croom Helm UK). Routledge Chapman & Hall.

Political Economy of Nicaragua. Rose J. Spalding. (Thematic Studies in Latin America). 256p. 1986. text ed. 39.95x (ISBN 0-04-497014-5); pap. text ed. 13.95x (ISBN 0-04-497015-3). Unwin Hyman.

Political Economy of Nigeria. Ed. by Claude Ake. 192p. (Orig.). 1986. pap. text ed. 14.95 (ISBN 0-582-64448-8). Longman.

Political Economy of Nigeria. Ed. by I. William Zartman. 298p. 1983. 40.95 (ISBN 0-275-91818-1, C1818); pap. 15.95 (ISBN 0-275-91595-6, B1595). Praeger.

Political Economy of Northern Ireland. Bob Rowthorn & Naomi Wayne. (Aspects of Political Economy Ser.). 200p. 1988. 45.00 (ISBN 0-8133-0825-9). Westview.

Political Economy of Numbers. Ed. by William Alonso & Paul Starr. LC 86-10060. 480p. 1987. text ed. 34.90 (ISBN 0-87154-015-0). Russell Sage.

Political Economy of Organizational Change: Urban Institutional Response to War on Poverty. Bruce Jacobs. (Quantitative Studies in Social Relations). 1981. 32.50 (ISBN 0-12-379660-1). Acad Pr.

Political Economy of Pan African Nationalism: Historical Origins & Contemporary Forms. Linus A. Hoskins. (International Affairs Ser.). 57p. (Orig.). 1987. pap. 4.95 (ISBN 0-939841-00-2). Pyramid MD.

Political Economy of Participation in Local Development Programs: Short-Term Impasse & Long-Term Change in South Asia & the United States from the 1950s to the 1970s. Harry W. Blair. (Monograph Ser.). 180p. (Orig.). 1981. pap. text ed. 10.65 (ISBN 0-86731-055-3). Cornell CIS RDC.

Political Economy of Peru, Nineteen Fifty-Six to Nineteen Seventy-Eight: Economic Development & the Restructuring of Capital. Edmund Fitzgerald. LC 78-72086. pap. 96.80 (2031649). Bks Demand UMI.

Political Economy of Policy-Making: Essays in Honor of Will E. Mason. Ed. by Michael P. Dooley et al. LC 78-25960. (Comparative Political Economy & Public Policy Ser.: Vol. 4). (Illus.). pap. 62.00 (ISBN 0-317-09719-9, 2021889). Bks Demand UMI.

Political Economy of Pondoland, Eighteen Sixty to Nineteen Thirty: Production, Labour, Migrancy & Chiefs in Rural South Africa. William Beinart. LC 81-21619. (Afican Studies: No. 33). (Illus.). 232p. 1982. 44.50 (ISBN 0-521-24393-9). Cambridge U Pr.

Political Economy of Post-War Britain. Bob Jessop. 280p. Date not set. 29.95 (ISBN 0-85520-549-0); pap. 10.95 (ISBN 0-85520-550-4). Basil Blackwell.

Political Economy of Prosperity. Arthur M. Okun. LC 76-108835. 122p. 1970. 14.95 (ISBN 0-8157-6478-2). Brookings.

Political Economy of Protection in Belgium. P. K. Tharakan. (Working Paper: No. 431). 22p. 1980. pap. 3.50 (ISBN 0-686-39771-1, WP-0431). World Bank.

Political Economy of Protection in Italy: Some Empirical Evidence. Enzo Grilli & Mauro La Noce. (Working Paper: No. 567). 48p. 1983. 5.00 (ISBN 0-8213-0197-7, WP 0567). World Bank.

Political Economy of Public Choice: An Introduction to Welfare Economics. Robert Sugden. LC 81-10333. 217p. 1981. 37.95x (ISBN 0-470-27201-5). Halsted Pr.

Political Economy of Public Policy. Alan Stone. (Sage Yearbooks in Politics & Public Policy: Vol. 10). 256p. 1982. 35.00 (ISBN 0-8039-1795-3); pap. 16.95 (ISBN 0-8039-1796-1). Sage.

Political Economy of Race & Class in South Africa. Bernard Magubane. LC 78-13917. 364p. 1980. pap. 9.00 (ISBN 0-85345-506-6). Monthly Rev.

Political Economy of Reaganomics: A Critique. Stephen Rousseas. LC 82-10659. 160p. 1982. pap. 10.95 (ISBN 0-87332-239-8). M E Sharpe.

Political Economy of Reform in Post-Mao China. Intro. by Elisabeth J. Perry & Christine Wong. (Harvard Contemporary China Ser.: No. 2). 325p. 1985. pap. text ed. 14.00x (ISBN 0-674-68590-3, Pub. by Coun East Asian Stud). Harvard U Pr.

Political Economy of Regionalism in Africa: The Case of the Economic Community of West African States. S. K. Asante. LC 85-16740. 286p. 1985. 40.95 (ISBN 0-275-90194-7, C0194). Praeger.

Political Economy of Regulation: The Case of Insurance. Kenneth J. Meier. (Public Administration Ser.). (Illus.). 272p. 1988. 49.50 (ISBN 0-88706-731-X); pap. 14.95x (ISBN 0-88706-732-8). State U NY Pr.

Political Economy of Rent Seeking. Ed. by Charles Rowley & Robert D. Tollison. 1988. lib. bdg. 85.00 (ISBN 0-89838-241-6). Kluwer Academic.

Political Economy of Risk & Choice in Senegal. Ed. by Mark Gersovitz & John Waterbury. 350p. 1986. 47.50x (ISBN 0-7146-3297-X, F Cass Co). Biblio Dist.

Political Economy of Rural Development. J. S. Brava. 1983. 15.00x (ISBN 0-8364-1012-2, Pub. by Allied India). South Asia Bks.

Political Economy of Rural Development. Ed. by Rosemary E. Galli. LC 81-1741. 270p. 1981. 59.50 (ISBN 0-87395-484-X); pap. 19.95x (ISBN 0-87395-485-8). State U NY Pr.

Political Economy of Sanctions Against Apartheid. Ali K. Haider. 130p. 1988. lib. bdg. 18.50 (ISBN 1-55587-145-3). Lynne Rienner.

Political Economy of Science & Technology. Norman Clark. 300p. 1985. 39.95x (ISBN 0-631-14293-2); pap. 14.95x (ISBN 0-631-14294-0). Basil Blackwell.

Political Economy of Slavery: Studies in Economy & Society of the Slave South. Eugene D. Genovese. 1967. pap. 3.96 (ISBN 0-394-70400-2, V400, Vin). Random.

Political Economy of Social Policy. A. J. Culyer. 1980. 32.50 (ISBN 0-312-62242-2). St Martin.

Political Economy of Socialism: A Marxist View. Branko Horvat. LC 81-9430. 660p. 1983. pap. 19.95 (ISBN 0-87332-256-8). M E Sharpe.

Political Economy of Soil Erosion in Developing Countries. Piers Blaikie. 184p. 1986. pap. 16.95 (ISBN 0-470-20419-2, Co-Pub. with Longman). Wiley.

Political Economy of Soviet Defence Spending. R. T. Maddock. LC 87-25075. 272p. 1988. 49.95 (ISBN 0-312-01579-8). St Martin.

Political Economy of Taxation. Ed. by Alan Peacock & Frances Forte. 1981. 32.50x (ISBN 0-312-62256-2). St Martin.

Political Economy of Thatcherism. John Gaster. 224p. 1984. cancelled (ISBN 0-85520-792-2); pap. cancelled (ISBN 0-85520-793-0). Basil Blackwell.

Political Economy of the African Crisis. Bade Onimode. 304p. 1988. text ed. 60.00 (ISBN 0-86232-373-8, Pub. by Zed Pr UK); pap. text ed. 19.95 (ISBN 0-86232-374-6, Pub. by Zed Pr UK). Humanities.

Political Economy of the Black Ghetto. William K. Tabb. LC 70-124347. 1971. 8.95x (ISBN 0-393-05426-8); pap. text ed. 5.95x (ISBN 0-393-09930-X). Norton.

Political Economy of the Brazilian State, 1889-1930. Steven Topik. LC 87-5835. (Latin American Monographs: No. 71). (Illus.). 255p. 1987. text ed. 25.00x (ISBN 0-292-76500-2). U of Tex Pr.

Political Economy of the Cotton South. Ed. by Gavin Wright. 1978. pap. 7.95x (ISBN 0-393-09038-8). Norton.

Political Economy of the Educational Process. Richard B. McKenzie. (Studies in Public Choice: Vol. 2). 1979. lib. bdg. 26.95 (ISBN 0-89838-012-X, Martinus Nijhoff Pubs). Kluwer Academic.

Political Economy of the Ivory Coast: An SAIS Study on Africa. Ed. by William I. Zartman & Christopher L. Delgado. LC 84-1998. 268p. 1984. 35.00 (ISBN 0-275-91295-7, C1295). Praeger.

Political Economy of the Latin American Motor Vehicle Industry. Ed. by Richard Kronish & Kenneth S. Mericle. 336p. 1984. text ed. 37.50x (ISBN 0-262-11089-X). MIT Pr.

Political Economy of the New Asian Industrialism. Ed. by Frederic C. Deyo. LC 86-29103. (Studies in Political Economy). (Illus.). 288p. 1987. 29.95x (ISBN 0-8014-1948-4); pap. 12.95x (ISBN 0-8014-9449-4). Cornell U Pr.

Political Economy of the New Left: An Outsider's View. 2nd ed. Assar Lindbeck. 1977. pap. text ed. 17.95 scp (ISBN 0-06-044009-0, HarpC). Harrow.

Political Economy of the Space Program. Mary A. Holman. LC 79-180902. (Science & Technology Management Ser., No. 1). (Illus.). 1974. 24.95x (ISBN 0-87015-199-1). Pacific Bks.

Political Economy of the State. Ed. by Dimitrios I. Roussopoulos. 200p. 1973. 16.95 (ISBN 0-919618-02-2, Dist. by U of Toronto Pr); pap. 6.95 (ISBN 0-919618-01-4, Dist. by U of Toronto Pr). Black Rose Bks.

Political Economy of the Third Sector: Co-Operation & Participation. Ed. by Alasdair Clayre. 1980. 29.95x (ISBN 0-19-877137-1). Oxford U Pr.

Political Economy of the Third World Countries. Ed. by Devendra Thakur. 212p. 1987. 34.95. Asia Bk Corp.

Political Economy of the United States. Ed. by C. Stoffaes. 576p. 1982. 158.00 (ISBN 0-444-86342-7, I-40-82, North-Holland). Elsevier.

Political Economy of the Urban Ghetto. Daniel R. Fusfeld & Timothy Bates. LC 83-20424. (Political & Social Economy Ser.). 304p. 1984. 17.95x (ISBN 0-8093-1157-7); pap. text ed. 16.95x (ISBN 0-8093-1158-5). S Ill U Pr.

Political Economy of the Welfare State. Ian Gough. (Critical Texts in Social Work & the Welfare State Ser.). 1979. pap. text ed. 15.00x (ISBN 0-333-21599-0). Humanities.

Political Economy of the Welfare State. Thomas Wilson & Dorothy J. Wilson. (Studies in Economics: No. 19). 240p. 1982. text ed. 39.95x (ISBN 0-04-336077-7); pap. text ed. 14.95x (ISBN 0-04-336078-5). Unwin Hyman.

Political Economy of Tolerable Survival. Ed. by Maxwell Gaskin. (Illus.). 220p. 1981. 30.00 (ISBN 0-7099-0266-2, Pub. by Croom Helm Ltd). Routledge Chapman & Hall.

Political Economy of Trade & Development: Comparative Advantage & Growth, Vol. 1. H. Davids Evans. LC 87-16370. 335p. 1988. 45.00 (ISBN 0-312-00955-0). St Martin.

Political Economy of Underdevelopment: Dependence in Senegal. Ed. by Rita C. O'Brien. LC 78-27183. (Sage Ser. on African Modernization & Development: Vol. 3). 277p. 1979. 29.95 (ISBN 0-8039-1222-6); pap. 14.95 (ISBN 0-8039-1223-4). Sage.

Political Economy of Underdevelopment in Northern Rhodesia, 1918-1960: A Case Study of Customs Tariff & Railway Freight Policies. Ackson M. Kanduza. LC 85-29835. (Dalhousie African Studies: No.5). (Illus.). 346p. (Orig.). 1986. lib. bdg. 27.25 (ISBN 0-8191-5189-0, Pub.by Dalhousie Univ Pr); pap. text ed. 16.75 (ISBN 0-8191-5190-4). U Pr of Amer.

Political Economy of Underdevelopment. Amiya K. Bagchi. LC 81-10237. (Modern Cambridge Economics Ser.). 304p. 1982. 44.50 (ISBN 0-521-24024-7); pap. 16.95 (ISBN 0-521-28404-X). Cambridge U Pr.

Political Economy of Underdevelopment. S. B. De Silva. (International Library of Sociology). 640p. 1982. 50.00x (ISBN 0-7100-0469-9). Routledge Chapman & Hall.

Political Economy of Underdevelopment. S. B. DeSilva. (International Library of Sociology). 645p. 1984. pap. 23.95x (ISBN 0-7102-0273-3). Routledge Chapman & Hall.

Political Economy of Underdevelopment. Tamas Szentes. 426p. 1983. 143.75x (Pub. by Collets (UK)). State Mutual Bk.

Political Economy of U. S. Import Policy. Robert E. Baldwin. 172p. 1986. text ed. 25.00x (ISBN 0-262-02232-X). MIT Pr.

Political Economy of U. S. Policy Toward South Africa. Kevin Danaher. (Westview Special Studies on Africa). 300p. 1985. pap. 19.85x (ISBN 0-8133-0115-7). Westview.

Political Economy of U. S. Tariffs: An Empirical Analysis. Ed. by Real P. Lavergne. (Economic Theory, Econometrics, Mathematical Economics Ser.). 1983. 24.95 (ISBN 0-12-438740-3). Acad Pr.

Political Economy of Urban Poverty. Charles Sackrey. 172p. 1972. pap. 4.95x (ISBN 0-393-09410-3, NortonC). Norton.

Political Economy of Urban Schools. Martin C. Katzman. LC 70-139723. (Joint Center for Urban Studies Publications). 1971. 18.50x (ISBN 0-674-68576-8). Harvard U Pr.

Political Economy of Urban Transportation. Delbert A. Taebel & James V. Cornehls. LC 77-23150. (National University Publications Interdisciplinary Urban Ser). (Illus.). 1977. 23.50 (ISBN 0-8046-9178-9, Pub. by Kennikat). Assoc Faculty Pr.

Political Economy of Uruguay since 1870. M. H. Finch. LC 80-21047. 1981. 29.95x (ISBN 0-312-62244-9). St Martin.

Political Economy of West African Agriculture. Keith Hart. LC 81-18174. (Cambridge Studies in Social Anthropology: No. 43). (Illus.). 256p. 1982. 42.50 (ISBN 0-521-24073-5); pap. 16.95 (ISBN 0-521-28423-6). Cambridge U Pr.

Political Economy of West Germany: Modell Deutschland. Ed. by Andrei S. Markovits. LC 81-20996. 240p. 1982. 36.95 (ISBN 0-275-90854-2, C0854). Praeger.

Political Economy of West Germany, 1945-1985: An Introduction. Jeremy Leaman. 256p. 1987. 39.95 (ISBN 0-312-00541-5). St Martin.

Political Economy: Public Policies in the United States & Britain. Ed. by Jerold L. Waltman & Donley T. Studlar. LC 87-10425. 285p. 1987. 25.00x (ISBN 0-87805-313-1); pap. text ed. 12.95 (ISBN 0-87805-314-X). U Pr of Miss.

Political Economy, Radical Economics, Law & War, Vol. 20. Compiled by Edward Tower. 200p. 1985. 14.00 (ISBN 0-88024-220-5). Eno River Pr.

Political Economy: Readings in the Politics & Economics of American Public Economy. Ed. by Thomas Ferguson & Joel Rogers. 380p. 1984. 35.00x (ISBN 0-87332-276-2); pap. 14.95x (ISBN 0-87332-272-X). M E Sharpe.

Political Economy: Socialism. Ed. by G. A. Kozlov. 493p. 1977. 5.95 (ISBN 0-8285-0373-7, Pub. by Progress Pubs USSR). Imported Pubns.

Political Econonmy of Romanian Socialism. William E. Crowther. 216p. 1988. lib. bdg. 49.95 (ISBN 0-275-92840-3, C2840). Praeger.

Political Education. Robert Brownhill & Patricia Smart. 224p. 1988. lib. bdg. 33.00x (ISBN 0-7099-3972-8, Pub. by Croom Helm UK). Routledge Chapman & Hall.

Political Education: A Washington Memoir. Harry McPherson. (Illus.). 416p. 1988. pap. 11.95 (ISBN 0-395-48899-0). HM.

Political Education & Stability: Elite Responses to Political Conflict. Edward Tapper. LC 75-30817. pap. 69.30 (ISBN 0-317-29384-2, 2024286). Bks Demand UMI.

Political Education in Britain. Ed. by Clive Harber. 200p. 1987. 38.00x (ISBN 1-85000-285-1, Falmer Pr); pap. 19.00x (ISBN 1-85000-286-X). Taylor & Francis.

Political Education in the Southern Farmers Alliance, 1887-1900. Theodore Mitchell. LC 87-40141. (Illus.). 192p. 1987. text ed. 39.50x (ISBN 0-299-11470-8); pap. text ed. 16.50x (ISBN 0-299-11474-0). U of Wis Pr.

Political Education of Servants of the State. Ed. by Roger Fieldhouse. LC 87-36686. 224p. 1988. 45.00 (ISBN 0-7190-2343-2, Pub. by Manchester Univ Pr). St Martin.

Political Education of Soldiers, Vol. XI. Ed. by Morris Janowitz & Stephen D. Wesbrook. (War, Revolution & Peacekeeping Ser.). 328p. 1983. 28.00 (ISBN 0-8039-1020-7). Seven Locks Pr.

Political Ideologies of Organized Labor: The New Deal Era. Ruth L. Horowitz. LC 76-58229. 260p. 1978. text ed. 27.95 (ISBN 0-87855-208-1). Transaction Bks.

Political Ideologies: Their Origins & Impact. 2nd ed. Leon P. Baradat. (Illus.). 384p. 1984. pap. 23.33 (ISBN 0-13-684365-4). P-H.

Political Ideologies: Their Origins & Impact. 3rd ed. Leon P. Baradat. (Illus.). 1988. pap. text ed. 23.33 (ISBN 0-13-684390-5). P-H.

Political Ideology & Educational Reform in Chile, 1964-1976. Kathleen B. Fischer. LC 79-620018. (Latin American Studies: Vol. 46). 1979. 14.95x (ISBN 0-87903-046-1). UCLA Lat Am Ctr.

Political Ideology & Voting: An Exploratory Study. Elinor Scarbrough. (Illus.). 257p. 1984. 39.95x (ISBN 0-19-827469-6). Oxford U Pr.

Political Ideology in Malaysia: Reality & the Beliefs of an Elite. James C. Scott. LC 68-27766. (Yale Southwest Asia Studies: No. 3). pap. 79.00 (ISBN 0-317-09395-9, 2016803). Bks Demand UMI.

Political Image Merchants: Strategies for the Seventies. rev. ed. Ed. by Ray E. Hiebert et al. LC 74-30619. 312p. 1975. 9.95 (ISBN 0-87491-143-5); pap. 6.95 (ISBN 0-87491-144-3). Acropolis.

Political Impact of Colonial Administration. Arthur J. Vidich. Ed. by Harriet Zuckerman & Robert K. Merton. LC 79-9036. (Dissertations on Sociology Ser.). 1980. lib. bdg. 33.50x (ISBN 0-405-13003-1). Ayer Co Pubs.

Political India Eighteen Thirty-Two to Nineteen Thirty-Two: A Cooperative Survey of a Century. Ed. by John G. Cumming. 332p. 1968. text ed. 20.00x. Coronet Bks.

Political India, 1935-42: Anatomy of Indian Politics. Ramji Lal. 308p. 1986. 28.00X (ISBN 81-202-0160-4, Pub. by Ajanta). South Asia Bks.

Political Influence. Edward C. Banfield. LC 60-12182. 1965. pap. text ed. 12.95 (ISBN 0-02-901590-1). Free Pr.

Political Innovation & Conceptual Change. Ed. by Terence Ball et al. (Ideas in Context Ser.). 352p. Date not set. price not set (ISBN 0-521-35190-1); pap. price not set (ISBN 0-521-35978-3). Cambridge U Pr.

Political Innovation in America. Nelson W. Polsby. LC 83-14749. 200p. 1985. pap. 8.95x (ISBN 0-300-03428-8, Y-538). Yale U Pr.

Political Innovation in America: The Politics of Policy Initation. Nelson W. Polsby. LC 83-14749. 200p. 1984. 25.00x (ISBN 0-300-03089-4). Yale U Pr.

Political Institutionalization: A Political Study of Two Sardinian Communities. Francesco Kjellberg. LC 74-20693. pap. 40.00 (ISBN 0-317-09618-4, 2016161). Bks Demand UMI.

Political Institutions & Issues in Britain. James Cable. 192p. 1987. text ed. 39.95x (ISBN 0-333-40540-4, Pub. by Macmillan London); pap. text ed. 18.50x (ISBN 0-333-40541-2, Pub. by Macmillan London). Sheridan.

Political Institutions of the German Revolution, 1918-1919. Ed. by Charles B. Burdick & Ralph H. Lutz. LC 66-13464. (Publications Ser.: No. 40). 305p. 1966. 10.95x (ISBN 0-8179-1401-3). Hoover Inst Pr.

Political Integration & Disintegration in the British Isles. Anthony H. Birch. 1977. pap. text ed. 10.95x (ISBN 0-04-320124-5). Unwin Hyman.

Political Integration in French-Speaking Africa. Abdul A. Jalloh. LC 73-620178. (Research Ser.: No. 20). 225p. 1973. pap. 3.50x (ISBN 0-87725-120-7). U of Cal Intl St.

Political Integration of Women: Roles, Socialization, & Politics. Virginia Sapiro. LC 82-2672. 216p. 1984. pap. 7.95 (ISBN 0-252-01141-4). U of Ill Pr.

Political Intelligence for America's Future. Ed. by Bertram M. Gross & Richard D. Lambert. LC 78-112787. (Annals of the American Academy of Political & Social Science: No. 388). 1970. 15.00 (ISBN 0-87761-126-2); pap. 7.95 (ISBN 0-87761-125-4). Am Acad Pol Soc Sci.

Political Interpretations of Educational Administration. David K. Wiles. 288p. 1977. text ed. 29.50x (ISBN 0-8422-5267-3); pap. text ed. 12.95x (ISBN 0-8422-0557-8). Irvington.

Political Intrigue in the Establishment of the Identity of Jesus & Mary. James H. Boykin. LC 86-90957. 286p. 1986. pap. 15.00x (ISBN 0-9603342-6-2). Boykin.

Political Investments in Food Production. Ed. by Barbara Huddleston & Jon McLin. LC 79-5025. (Illus.). 256p. pap. 66.60 (2056424). Bks Demand UMI.

Political Involvement of Adolescents. Roberta S. Sigel & Marilyn B. Hoskin. 320p. 1981. 35.00 (ISBN 0-8135-0897-5). Rutgers U Pr.

Political Issues Debated: An Introduction to Politics. Herbert M. Levine. (Illus.). 352p. 1982. pap. write for info. (ISBN 0-13-685032-4). P-H.

Political Issues Debated: An Introduction to Politics. 2nd ed. Herbert M. Levine. 336p. 1987. pap. text ed. write for info. (ISBN 0-13-685009-X). P-H.

Political Issues in America Today. Ed. by Philip J. Davies & Fredric A. Waldstein. (Politics Today Ser.). 240p. 1988. 29.95 (ISBN 0-7190-1490-5, Pub. by Manchester Univ Pr); pap. 8.95 (ISBN 0-7190-1496-4). St Martin.

Political Issues in Britain Today. 2nd ed. Ed. by Bill Jones. (Politics Today Ser.). 192p. 1987. 27.00 (ISBN 0-7190-2465-X, Pub. by Manchester Univ Pr); pap. 8.00 (ISBN 0-7190-2466-8, Pub. by Manchester Univ Pr). St Martin.

Political Issues in Luke-Acts. Ed. by Richard J. Cassidy & Philip J. Scharper. LC 82-19060. 192p. (Orig.). 1983. 16.95 (ISBN 0-88344-390-2); pap. 9.95 (ISBN 0-88344-385-6). Orbis Bks.

Political Issues in Nursing: Past, Present & Future, Vol. 1. Ed. by Rosemary White. 156p. 1986. pap. 18.95 (ISBN 0-471-90800-2). Wiley.

Political Issues in Nursing: Past, Present & Future, Vol. 2. Ed. by Rosemary White. (Developments in Nursing Research Ser.). 1986. pap. 19.95 (ISBN 0-471-90913-0). Wiley.

Political Jokes from Leningrad. Arie Zand. (Illus.). 80p. 1984. pap. 4.50 (ISBN 0-941432-01-7). Silvergirl Inc.

Political Judgement. Ronald Beiner. LC 83-50829. 1984. lib. bdg. 20.00x (ISBN 0-226-04164-6); pap. 9.50x (ISBN 0-226-04165-4). U of Chicago Pr.

Political Judges & the Rule of Law. R. Dworkin. (Maccabaean Lectures in Jurisprudence). 1977. pap. 5.50 (ISBN 0-85672-182-4, Pub. by British Acad). Longwood Pub Group.

Political Justice. William Godwin. 59.95 (ISBN 0-8490-0873-5). Gordon Pr.

Political Justice in a Republic: James Fenimore Cooper's America. John P. McWilliams, Jr. LC 75-182283. 1973. 35.00x (ISBN 0-520-02175-4). U of Cal Pr.

Political Justice in the Soviet Union: Dissent & Repression in Lithuania, 1969-1987. Thomas Oleszczuk. (East European Monographs: No. 247). 240p. 1988. 30.00 (ISBN 0-88033-144-5). East Eur Quarterly.

Political Kidnapping. E. L. Cassidy. (Law Enforcement Ser.). 1986. lib. bdg. 79.95 (ISBN 0-8490-3852-9). Gordon Pr.

Political Kidnapping. William L. Cassidy. 70p. 1978. pap. 6.00 (ISBN 0-87364-141-8). Paladin Pr.

Political Killings by Governments. Intro. by Theodore Van Boven. 144p. 1983. pap. 4.95 (ISBN 0-86210-051-8). Amnesty Intl USA.

Political Kingdom in Uganda: A Study in Bureaucratic Nationalism. 2nd ed. LC 67-18831. (Illus.). pap. 132.00 (ISBN 0-317-11316-X, 2051599). Bks Demand UMI.

Political Kingdoms of the Temne: Temne Government in Sierra Leone, 1825-1900. Kenneth Wylie. LC 77-1067. 300p. 1977. 45.00 (ISBN 0-8419-0149-X, Africana). Holmes & Meier.

Political Language & Oratory in Traditional Society. Ed. by Maurice Bloch. 1975. 55.50 (ISBN 0-12-106850-1). Acad Pr.

Political Language & Rhetoric. Paul E. Corcoran. LC 79-63529. 234p. 1979. text ed. 20.00x (ISBN 0-292-76458-8). U of Tex Pr.

Political Language of Film & the Avant-Garde. Dana B. Polan. Ed. by Diane Kirkpatrick. LC 84-24062. (Studies in Cinema: No. 30). 152p. 1985. 39.95 (ISBN 0-8357-1604-X). UMI Res Pr.

Political Language of Islam. Bernard Lewis. (Illus.). x, 168p. 1988. 14.95 (ISBN 0-226-47692-8). U of Chicago Pr.

Political Languages: Words That Succeed & Policies That Fail. M. Edelman. (Institute for Research on Poverty Monograph). 1977. pap. 14.95 (ISBN 0-12-230662-7). Acad Pr.

Political Leaders of Provincial Pennsylvania. facsimile ed. Isaac Sharpless. LC 75-169774. (Select Bibliographies Reprint Ser.). Repr. of 1919 ed. 19.00 (ISBN 0-8369-5994-9). Ayer Co Pubs.

Political Leaders of Upper Canada. facs. ed. William Smith. LC 68-26475. (Essay Index Reprint Ser.). 1931. 20.00 (ISBN 0-8369-0886-4). Ayer Co Pubs.

Political Leadership. Glenn Paige. LC 76-169237. 1972. 18.00 (ISBN 0-02-923610-X). Free Pr.

Political Leadership: A Source Book. Barbara Kellerman. LC 85-26436. (Pitt Series in Policy & Institutional Studies). 478p. 39.95x (ISBN 0-8229-3534-1); pap. 16.95x (ISBN 0-8229-5382-X). U of Pittsburgh Pr.

Political Leadership among Swat Pathans. Fredrik Barth. (London School of Economics Monographs on Social Anthropology: No. 19). 144p. 1965. pap. 16.50 (ISBN 0-485-19619-0, Pub. by Athlone Pr UK). Humanities.

Political Leadership & Nihilism: A Study of Weber & Nietzsche. Robert Eden. LC 83-17075. 348p. 1984. 34.00x (ISBN 0-8130-0758-5). U Presses Fla.

Political Leadership in Africa. John R. Cartwright. LC 82-23151. 310p. 1983. 27.50 (ISBN 0-312-62314-3). St Martin.

Political Leadership in Africa. Victor T. Le Vine. LC 67-25788. (Studies Ser.: No. 18). 114p. 1967. pap. 5.95x (ISBN 0-8179-3182-1). Hoover Inst Pr.

Political Leadership in Jefferson's Virginia. Daniel P. Jordan. LC 82-23867. 274p. 1983. 24.95x (ISBN 0-8139-0967-8). U Pr of Va.

Political Leadership in Korea. Ed. by Dae-Sook Suh & Chae-Jin Lee. LC 76-5480. (Publications on Asia of the Institute for Comparative & Foreign Area Studies: No. 27). 276p. 1976. 25.00x (ISBN 0-295-95437-X). U of Wash Pr.

Political Leadership in Sierra Leone. John R. Cartwright. LC 79-300056. pap. 77.00 (ISBN 0-317-26934-8, 2023602). Bks Demand UMI.

Political Leadership in the Bahamas: Interviews with the Prime Minister of the Commonwealth of the Bahamas & with the Leader of the Opposition. Dean W. Collinwood & Steve Dodge. 32p. (Orig.). 1987. pap. 3.00 (ISBN 0-932265-05-7). White Sound.

Political Leadership: Jawaharlal Nehru. Akhileshwar Singh. 1986. 27.50 (ISBN 0-8364-1906-5, Pub. by Deep). South Asia Bks.

Political Legitimacy: A Bibliography. Robert Goehlert. (Public Administration Ser.: P 1783). 13p. 1985. 2.00 (ISBN 0-89028-583-7). Vance Biblios.

Political Legitimization in Communist States. T. H. Rigby & Ferenc Feher. LC 81-9066. 1982. 25.00 (ISBN 0-312-62318-6). St Martin.

Political Liberalization in an Authoritarian Regime. Kevin J. Middlebrook. (Research Report Ser.: No. 41). 36p. (Orig.). 1985. pap. 6.00 (ISBN 0-935391-40-1, RR-41). Ctr Mex Studies.

Political Liberalization in Brazil. Ed. by Wayne A. Selcher. (WVSS on Latin America & the Carribean Ser.). 315p. 1985. pap. 27.95x (ISBN 0-8133-0263-3). Westview.

Political Liberty. Alexander J. Carlyle. 220p. 1963. 26.00x (ISBN 0-7146-1551-X, F Cass Co). Biblio Dist.

Political Liberty: A History of the Conception in the Middle Ages & Modern Times. Alexander J. Carlyle. LC 80-18967. viii, 220p. 1980. Repr. of 1963 ed. lib. bdg. 35.00x (ISBN 0-313-21482-4, CAPL). Greenwood.

Political Life. Robert E. Lane. LC 58-6485. 1965. pap. text ed. 3.00 (ISBN 0-02-917870-3). Free Pr.

Political Life in Assam During the 19th Century. B. B. Hazarika. 1987. 19.50x (ISBN 81-212-0069-5, Pub. by Gian Pub Hse India). South Asia Bks.

Political Life in Eighteenth Century Virginia. Jack P. Greene. (Foundations of America Ser.). (Illus.). 56p. (Orig.). 1987. pap. 5.95 (ISBN 0-87935-116-0). Williamsburg.

Political Life in Washington: Governing the Evergreen State. Ed. by Thor Swanson et al. (Illus.). 224p. 1985. pap. 14.95 (ISBN 0-87422-018-1). Wash St U Pr.

Political Life of American Jewish Women. Susan Welch & Fred Ullrich. 90p. (Orig.). 1984. pap. 5.00 (ISBN 0-9602036-9-9). Biblio NY.

Political Life of Children. Robert Coles. Ed. by Peter Davison. LC 85-22821. (Illus.). 342p. 1986. 19.95 (ISBN 0-87113-035-1). Atlantic Monthly.

Political Life of Children. Robert Coles. (Illus.). 352p. 1987. pap. 10.95 (ISBN 0-395-43152-2). HM.

Political Life of the American States: American Political Parties & Elections. Ed. by Gerald M. Pomper & Alan Rosenthal. LC 83-17756. 344p. 1984. pap. 14.95 (ISBN 0-275-91630-8, B1630). Praeger.

Political Literature of the Progressive Era. Ed. by George L. Groman. xxii, 287p. 1967. 6.50 (ISBN 0-87013-107-9). Mich St U Pr.

Political Machine: What It Is, How It Works. Gerald Kurland. (Topics of Our Times Ser.: No. 9). 32p. lib. bdg. 3.75 incl. catalog cards (ISBN 0-87157-810-7); pap. 2.50 vinyl laminated covers (ISBN 0-87157-310-5). SamHar Pr.

Political Man. Robert E. Lane. LC 75-158930. (Illus.). 1972. 14.95 (ISBN 0-02-917800-2); pap. text ed. 4.50 (ISBN 0-02-917810-X). Free Pr.

Political Man: The Social Bases of Politics. Seymour M. Lipset. LC 80-8867. 608p. 1981. pap. text ed. 12.00x (ISBN 0-8018-2522-9). Johns Hopkins.

Political Management: Redefining the Public Sphere. H. T. Wilson. LC 84-17608. (Studies in Organization: No. 2). x, 316p. 1984. 49.95 (ISBN 3-11-009902-0). De Gruyter.

Political Manipulation & Administrative Power: A Comparative Study. Eva Etzioni-Halevy. (International Library of Sociology). 1980. 26.95x (ISBN 0-7100-0352-8). Routledge Chapman & Hall.

Political Marketing: An Approach to Campaign Strategy. Gary A. Mauser. Ed. by Steven E. Permut. (Praeger Series in Public & Nonprofit Sector Marketing). 320p. 1983. 36.95 (ISBN 0-275-91721-5, C1721). Praeger.

Political Marketing: Readings & Annotated Bibliography. Ed. by Bruce I. Newman & Jagdish N. Sheth. LC 85-26866. (Reading Ser.). 259p. (Orig.). 1986. pap. text ed. 29.00 (ISBN 0-87757-180-5). Am Mktg.

Political Memoirs, 1914-17. Nicholas, Prince of Greece. LC 72-1274. (Select Bibliographies Reprint Ser.). 1972. Repr. of 1927 ed. 31.00 (ISBN 0-8369-6833-6). Ayer Co Pubs.

Political Memoranda of Francis Fifth Duke of Leeds. Francis O. Leeds. Ed. by O. Browning. Repr. of 1884 ed. 27.00 (ISBN 0-384-32055-4). Johnson Repr.

Political Memoranda: Revision of Instructions to Political Officers on Subjects Chiefly Political & Administrative, 1913-1918. 3rd rev. ed. Frederick J. Lugard. 480p. 1970. 35.00x (ISBN 0-7146-1693-1, F Cass Co). Biblio Dist.

Political Messianism: The Romantic Phase. J. L. Talmon. (Encore Edition Ser.). 608p. 1985. Repr. of 1960 ed. soft cover 49.00x (ISBN 0-8133-0166-1). Westview.

Political-Military Applications of Bayesian Analysis: Methodological Issues. Douglas E. Hunter. (Replica Edition Ser.). 275p. 1984. 38.00x (ISBN 0-86531-954-5). Westview.

Political Miscellany: Essays in Memory of Professor Ramesh Chandra Ghosh. 1986. 22.00 (Pub. by KP Bagchi India). South Asia Bks.

Political Mobilization & Economic Extraction: Chinese Communist Agrarian Policies During the Kiangi Period. Hsu King-Yi. LC 78-74335. (Modern Chinese Economy Ser.). 400p. 1980. lib. bdg. 53.00 (ISBN 0-8240-4275-1). Garland Pub.

Political Mobilization & Industry in Libya. Maja Naur. (Illus.). 268p. (Orig.). 1986. pap. text ed. 43.50x (ISBN 0-317-65573-6). Coronet Bks.

Political Mobilization of the Venezuelan Peasant. John D. Powell. LC 70-134947. (Center for International Affairs Ser). (Illus.). 1971. 18.50x (ISBN 0-674-68626-8). Harvard U Pr.

Political Modernization: A Selected Bibliography. Robert Goehlert. (Public Administration Ser.: P 1815). 23p. 1985. 3.75 (ISBN 0-89028-645-0). Vance Biblios.

Political Modernization in Three Guatemalan Indian Communities see Community Culture & National Change.

Political Money: A Strategy for Campaign Financing in America. 2nd ed. David W. Adamany & George E. Agree. LC 75-11351. 254p. 1980. pap. text ed. 8.95x (ISBN 0-8018-2377-3). Johns Hopkins.

Political Money: A Strategy for Companion Financing in America. David W. Adamany & George E. Agree. LC 75-11352. pap. 63.50 (ISBN 0-317-39630-7, 2025820). Bks Demand UMI.

Political Morality of the International Monetary Fund. Ed. by Robert S. Browne. (Ethics in Foreign Policy Ser.: Vol. 3). 164p. 1987. 24.95 (ISBN 0-88738-143-X); pap. 14.95 (ISBN 0-88738-674-1). Transaction Bks.

Political Morality of the International Monetary Fund. Ed. by Robert J. Myers. (Ethics & Foreigh Policy Ser.: Vol. 3). 164p. 1987. write for info.; pap. text ed. 14.95. Carnegie Ethics & Intl Affairs.

Political Murder: From Tyrannicide to Terrorism. Franklin L. Ford. LC 85-5837. (Illus.). 456p. 1985. 31.50 (ISBN 0-674-68635-7). Harvard U Pr.

Political Murder: From Tyrannicide to Terrorism. Franklin L. Ford. (Illus.). 456p. 1987. pap. 9.95 (ISBN 0-674-68636-5). Harvard U Pr.

Political Murder in Central America: Death Squads & U. S. Policies. Ed. by Gary E. McCuen. (Ideas in Conflict Ser.). (Illus.). 136p. 1985. lib. bdg. 10.95 (ISBN 0-86596-050-X). G E McCuen Pubns.

Political Myth & Epic. Gilbert M. Cuthbertson. xxi, 234p. 1975. 10.00x (ISBN 0-87013-185-0). Mich St U Pr.

Political Mythology & Popular Fiction. Ed. by Ernest J. Yanarella & Lee Sigelman. LC 87-17802. (Contributions in Political Science Ser.: No. 197). 200p. 1988. lib. bdg. 37.95 (ISBN 0-313-25976-3, SYT/). Greenwood.

Political Mythology of Apartheid. Leonard Thompson. LC 85-3195. (Illus.). 310p. 1985. 27.00t (ISBN 0-300-03368-0). Yale U Pr.

Political Mythology of Apartheid. Leonard Thompson. LC 85-3195. 310p. 1986. pap. 10.95 (ISBN 0-300-03512-8). Yale U Pr.

Political Myths & Economic Realities. Francis Delaisi. LC 70-137938. (Economic Thought, History & Challenge Ser). 1971. Repr. of 1927 ed. 39.50x (ISBN 0-8046-1442-3, Pub. by Kennikat). Assoc Faculty Pr.

Political Nativism in New York State. Louis D. Scisco. LC 79-76668. (Columbia University. Studies in the Social Sciences: No. 35). 1968. Repr. of 1901 ed. 16.50 (ISBN 0-404-51035-3). AMS Pr.

Political Nature of a Ruling Class Capital & Ideology in South Africa, 1890-1933. Belinda Bozzoli. (International Library of Sociology). 356p. 1981. 40.00x (ISBN 0-7100-0722-1). Routledge Chapman & Hall.

Political Networks & the Chinese Policy Process. John W. Lewis. (Occasional Paper of the Northeast Asia-United States Forum on International Policy at Stanford University). 32p. (Orig.). pap. 6.00 (ISBN 0-935371-15-X). ISIS.

Political Novel. Joseph L. Blotner. LC 78-9868. 1979. Repr. of 1955 ed. lib. bdg. 35.00x (ISBN 0-313-21228-7, BLPN). Greenwood.

Political Nursery: 1897-1901, Vols. 1-4. Ed. by John J. Chapman. LC 75-309. (Radical Tradition in America Ser). 1975. Repr. of 1897 ed. Set. 27.50 (ISBN 0-88355-213-2). Hyperion Conn.

Political Obligation in Its Historical Context. John Dunn. LC 80-40037. (Illus.). 360p. 1980. 42.50 (ISBN 0-521-22890-5). Cambridge U Pr.

Political Offence Exception to Extradition. Christine Van den Wijngaert. 270p. 1980. lib. bdg. 48.00 (ISBN 90-26-8118-53, Pub. by Kluwer Law & Taxation). Kluwer Academic.

Political Operas 1: Satire & Allegory. Ed. by Walter H. Rubsamen. (Ballad Opera Ser.). 1974. lib. bdg. 61.00 (ISBN 0-8240-0919-3). Garland Pub.

Political Operas 2: Attack upon Excise. Ed. by Walter H. Rubsamen. (Ballad Opera Ser.). 1974. lib. bdg. 61.00 (ISBN 0-8240-0920-7). Garland Pub.

Political Opinion in Massachusetts During Civil War & Reconstruction. Edith E. Ware. LC 77-76697. (Columbia University. Studies in the Social Sciences: No. 175). Repr. of 1916 ed. 18.00 (ISBN 0-404-51175-9). AMS Pr.

Political Opinion Polling: An International Review. Ed. by Robert M. Worcester. LC 82-21438. 260p. 1983. 25.00 (ISBN 0-312-62321-6). St Martin.

Political Opposition & Foreign Policy in Comparative Perspective. Joe D. Hagan. 190p. 1989. 28.50x (ISBN 0-317-59230-0). Lynne Rienner.

Political Opposition & Local Politics in Japan. Ed. by Kurt Steiner et al. LC 80-7555. 480p. 1980. 55.50x (ISBN 0-691-07625-1); pap. 19.50x (ISBN 0-691-10109-4). Princeton U Pr.

Political Opposition in Korea, 1945-1960. Chi-Young Pak. (Institute of Social Sciences Korean Studies: No. 2). 251p. 1980. text ed. 18.00x (ISBN 0-8248-0932-7). UH Pr.

Political Opposition in Post-Confucian Society. Peter R. Moody, Jr. 1988. price not set (ISBN 0-275-93063-7, C3063). Praeger.

Political Oppositions in Western Democracies. Ed. by Robert A. Dahl. LC 65-22315. pap. 120.00 (ISBN 0-317-09366-5, 2016758). Bks Demand UMI.

Political Order in Changing Societies. Samuel P. Huntington. (Henry L. Stimson Lectures). 1969. pap. 11.95x (ISBN 0-300-01171-7). Yale U Pr.

Political Order: Philosophical Anthropology, Modernity, & the Challenge of Ideology. David J. Levy. LC 87-13456. 208p. 1988. text ed. 22.50 (ISBN 0-8071-1389-1). La State U Pr.

Political Organization Approach to Transnational Terrorism. Kent L. Oots. LC 85-17030. (Contributions to Political Science Ser.: No. 141). (Illus.). 184p. 1986. lib. bdg. 35.00 (ISBN 0-313-25105-3, OPO/). Greenwood.

Political Organization of Attica. John S. Traill. LC 74-17324. (Hesperia Ser.: Supplement 14). 1975. pap. 12.50x (ISBN 0-87661-514-0). Am Sch Athens.

Political Organization of Space. E. W. Soja. LC 70-135471. (CCG Resource Papers Ser.: No. 8). (Illus.). 1971. pap. text ed. 5.00 (ISBN 0-89291-055-0). Assn Am Geographers.

Political Organization of the Plains Indians: With Special Reference to the Council. Maurice G. Smith. LC 76-43837. (Nebraska Univ. Studies: Vol. 24, Nos. 1 & 2). Repr. of 1924 ed. 15.00 (ISBN 0-404-15691-6). AMS Pr.

Political Organization of Unyamwezi. R. G. Abrahams. LC 67-12842. (Cambridge Studies in Social Anthropology: No. 1). pap. 57.00 (2027274). Bks Demand UMI.

Political Organizations & Law-Ways of the Comanche Indians. E. A. Hoebel. LC 42-13539. (American Anthro. Association Memoirs). 1940. 13.00 (ISBN 0-527-00553-3). Kraus Repr.

Political Organizations in Socialist Yugoslavia. James H. Seroka & Rados Smiljkovic. LC 86-4446. (DPPS Ser.). xxvi, 322p. 1986. text ed. 49.50 (ISBN 0-8223-0570-4). Duke.

Political Organizations in the Soviet Armed Forces: The Role of the Party & Komsomol. Sergei Zamascikov. Ed. by Barbara Dash. (Orig.). Date not set. pap. text ed. 35.00 (ISBN 1-55831-057-6). Delphic Associates.

Political Orientation of People in Rural India. A. K. Singh. 1987. 24.00 (ISBN 81-7099-025-4, Pub. by Mittal). South Asia Bks.

Political Origins of the U. S. Income Tax. JeroldL. Waltman. LC 84-13100. 1985. 12.50x (ISBN 0-87805-245-3). U Pr of Miss.

Political Outsiders: Blacks & Indians in a Rural Oklahoma County. Brian F. Rader. LC 77-94282. 1978. pap. 13.95 perfect bdg. (ISBN 0-88247-517-7). R & E Pubs.

Political Paintings of Merlyn Evans, 1930-1950. Intro. by David F. Jenkins. (Illus.). 48p. 1985. pap. 6.95 (ISBN 0-946590-22-2). Salem Hse Pubs.

Political Palate: A Feminist Vegetarian Cookbook. Bloodroot Collective Staff. LC 80-53521. (Illus.). 325p. (Orig.). 1980. pap. 10.95 (ISBN 0-9605210-0-3). Sanguinaria.

Political Pamphlets. A. F. Pollard. 1973. Repr. of 1897 ed. 45.00 (ISBN 0-8274-1636-9). R West.

Political Participation. Herbert A. Asher et al. 243p. (Orig.). 1984. pap. text ed. 15.00 (ISBN 0-317-28641-2, Pub. by Campus Verlag W. Germany). Transnatl Pubs.

Political Participation & Change in South Asia: In the Context of Nepal. Ed. by M. D. Dharamdasani. 1985. 22.00x (ISBN 0-8364-1363-6, Pub. by Shalimar). South Asia Bks.

Political Participation & Learning. Kenneth P. Langton. 1980. 10.95 (ISBN 0-8158-0382-6). Chris Mass.

Political Participation: How & Why Do People Get Involved in Politics? Lester W. Milbrath & M. I. Goel. (Illus.). 236p. 1982. pap. text ed. 12.00 (ISBN 0-8191-2647-0). U Pr of Amer.

Political Participation in a Non-Electoral Setting: The Urban Poor in Lima, Peru. Henry A. Dietz & Richard J. Moore. LC 79-14218. (Papers in International Studies: Latin America Ser.: No. 6). 1979. pap. 9.00x (ISBN 0-89680-085-7, Ohio U Ctr Intl). Ohio U Pr.

Political Participation in America, 1967. Sidney Verba & Norman Nie. LC 75-43068. 1976. codebk. write for info. (ISBN 0-89138-152-X). ICPSR.

Political Participation in Communist China. James R. Townsend. (Center for Chinese Studies, UC Berkeley: No. 1). 1967. 40.00x (ISBN 0-520-01279-8); pap. 11.95x (ISBN 0-520-01416-2). U of Cal Pr.

Political Participation in Communist Systems. Donald E. Schulz. (Pergamon Policy Studies). 1981. 54.00 (ISBN 0-08-024665-6). Pergamon.

Political Participation in Latin America: Citizen & State, Vol. 1. Ed. by John A. Booth & Mitchell A. Seligson. LC 77-16666. 260p. 1978. 34.50x (ISBN 0-8419-0334-4); pap. 14.00x (ISBN 0-8419-0376-X). Holmes & Meier.

Political Participation in Modern Indonesia. Ed. by R. William Liddle et al. LC 73-89521. (Monograph Ser.: No. 19). (Illus.). 206p. 1973. 9.50x (ISBN 0-938692-11-9). Yale U SE Asia.

Political Participation in Rural China. John P. Burns. 1988. 35.00 (ISBN 0-520-06005-9). U of Cal Pr.

Political Participation in the U. S. C. Q. Press Staff & M. Margaret Conway. LC 85-15186. 170p. 1985. pap. 12.95 (ISBN 0-87187-331-1). Congr Quarterly.

Political Participation of Women in the United States: A Selected Bibliography, 1950-1976. Kathy Stanwick & Christine Li. LC 77-23036. 169p. 1977. 19.00 (ISBN 0-8108-1075-1). Scarecrow.

Political Participation, Public Investment, & Support for the System: A Comparative Study of Rural Communities in Mexico. Carlos Salinas. Tr. by Ricardo Anzaldua from Span. (Research Report Ser.: No. 35). 45p. (Orig.). 1982. pap. 5.50 (ISBN 0-935391-34-7, RR-35). Ctr Mex Studies.

Political Parties. Ed. by William E. Leuchtenburg. LC 76-54572. (Great Contemporary Issues Ser.). 1977. lib. bdg. 35.00x (ISBN 0-405-09866-9). Ayer Co Pubs.

Political Parties. Robert Michels. LC 61-18564. 1966. pap. text ed. 12.95 (ISBN 0-02-921250-2). Free Pr.

Political Parties: A Cross-National Survey. Kenneth Janda. LC 80-15430. (Illus.). 1980. 125.00 (ISBN 0-02-916120-7). Free Pr.

Political Parties: A Sociological Study of the Oligarchical Tendencies of Modern Democracy. Robert Michels. 1960. 13.25 (ISBN 0-8446-2582-5). Peter Smith.

Political Parties & Civic Action Groups. Edward L. Schapsmeier & Frederick H. Schapsmeier. LC 80-1714. (Encyclopedia of American Institutions Ser.: No. 4). (Illus.). xxxiii, 554p. 1981. lib. bdg. 67.95 (ISBN 0-313-21442-5, SPC/). Greenwood.

Political Parties & Coalitional Behavior in Italy: An Interpretive Study. Geoffrey Pridham. 256p. 1988. lib. bdg. 65.00x (ISBN 0-415-00503-5, Pub. by Croom Helm UK). Routledge Chapman & Hall.

Political Parties & Elections in Austria. Melanie Sully. 1981. 26.00 (ISBN 0-312-62325-9). St Martin.

Political Parties & Elections in Latin America. R. H. McDonald & J. Mark Ruhl. 300p. 1988. 35.00 (ISBN 0-8133-0431-8); pap. 18.95 (ISBN 0-8133-0483-0). Westview.

Political Parties & Elections in the French 5th Republic. J. R. Frears. LC 77-82043. 1978. 25.00 (ISBN 0-312-62331-3). St Martin.

Political Parties & Elections in the United States. Jose Marti. Ed. by Philip S. Foner. Tr. by Elinor Randall from Span. 208p. 1989. 24.95 (ISBN 0-87722-604-0). Temple U Pr.

Political Parties & Elections in West Germany: The Search for a New Stability. Stephen Padgett & Tony Burkett. LC 86-20436. 320p. 1986. 32.50 (ISBN 0-312-00099-5); pap. 14.95 (ISBN 0-312-00100-2). St Martin.

Political Parties & Elections on American State. 3rd ed. Malcolm Jewell & David Olson. 1987. pap. text ed. 15.00 (ISBN 0-256-06074-6). Dorsey.

Political Parties & Linkage: A Comparative Perspective. Ed. by Kay Lawson. LC 79-26751. 1980. text ed. 54.00t (ISBN 0-300-02331-6); pap. 13.95x (ISBN 0-300-02610-2). Yale U Pr.

Political Parties & Political Development. Ed. by Joseph La Palombara & M. Weiner. (Studies in Political Development, Vol. 6). 1966. pap. 15.50x (ISBN 0-691-02163-5). Princeton U Pr.

Political Parties & Public Policy, 1982-1987. Dale E. Casper. (Public Administration Ser.: P 2301). 13p. 1987. 3.75 (ISBN 1-55590-601-X). Vance Biblios.

Political Parties & the Modern State. Ed. by Richard L. McCormick. 150p. 1984. text ed. 25.00 (ISBN 0-8135-1027-9). Rutgers U Pr.

Political Parties & the Party System in Britain: A Symposium. Ed. by Sydney D. Bailey. LC 78-14099. 1979. Repr. of 1952 ed. 21.75 (ISBN 0-88355-773-8). Hyperion Conn.

Political Parties Before the Constitution. Jackson T. Main. (Illus.). 512p. 1974. pap. 4.95x (ISBN 0-393-00718-9). Norton.

Political Parties Before the Constitution. Jackson T. Main. LC 71-184228. (Institute of Early American History & Culture Ser.). (Illus.). xx, 481p. 1973. 35.00x (ISBN 0-8078-1194-7). U of NC Pr.

Political Parties: Development & Decay. Ed. by Louis Meisel & Joseph Cooper. LC 76-46782. (Sage Electoral Studies Yearbook: Vol. 4). pap. 86.00 (ISBN 0-317-08816-5, 2021927). Bks Demand UMI.

Political Parties: Electoral Change & Structural Response. Ed. by Alan Ware. 258p. 1987. text ed. 45.00 (ISBN 0-631-14758-6); pap. text ed. 16.95 (ISBN 0-631-14759-4). Basil Blackwell.

Political Parties in America. 2nd ed. Robert J. Huckshorn. LC 83-14299. (Political Science Ser.). 425p. 1983. text ed. 19.50 pub net (ISBN 0-534-02885-3). Brooks-Cole.

Political Parties in American History. Keith I. Polakoff. 480p. 1981. pap. text ed. write for info (ISBN 0-394-34201-1, RanC). Random.

Political Parties in American Society. Samuel J. Eldersveld. LC 81-68790. 1982. 22.95x (ISBN 0-465-05935-X). Basic.

Political Parties in China. Jermyn Chi-Mung Lynn. (Studies in Chinese Government & Law). 255p. 1977. Repr. of 1930 ed. 19.50 (ISBN 0-89093-069-4). U Pubns Amer.

Political Parties in Europe. Theo Stamm. 1981. 42.50x (ISBN 0-930466-28-4). Meckler Corp.

Political Parties in India. 2nd rev. & ext. ed. Horst Hartmann. 1977. 11.50x (ISBN 0-88386-976-4). South Asia Bks.

Political Parties in India. Horst Hartmann. 1983. 17.50x (ISBN 0-8364-1068-8, Meenakshi). South Asia Bks.

Political Parties in Local Areas. Ed. by William Crotty. LC 86-7093. 272p. text ed. 27.95x (ISBN 0-87049-511-9). U of Tenn Pr.

Political Parties in Puerto Rico, 1897-1976. Ed. by Raoul Gordon. 1976. lib. bdg. 59.95 (ISBN 0-8490-0874-3). Gordon Pr.

Political Parties in Revolutionary Massachusetts. Stephen E. Patterson. LC 72-7991. 312p. 1973. 35.00x (ISBN 0-299-06260-0). U of Wis Pr.

Political Parties in the American Mold. Leon Epstein. LC 86-40050. 448p. 1986. text ed. 27.50x (ISBN 0-299-10700-0). U of Wis Pr.

Political Parties in the Eighties. Ed. by Robert A. Goldwin. 152p. 1980. 20.75 (ISBN 0-8447-3382-2); pap. 11.00 (ISBN 0-8447-3377-6). Am Enterprise.

Political Parties in the Irish Free State. Warner Moss. LC 68-58610. (Columbia University. Studies in the Social Sciences: No. 382). Repr. of 1933 ed. 20.00 (ISBN 0-404-51382-4). AMS Pr.

Political Parties in the Irish Republic. Michael Gallagher. LC 84-17161. 174p. 1985. 25.00 (ISBN 0-7190-1742-4, Pub. by Manchester Univ Pr); pap. 14.00 (ISBN 0-7190-1797-1). St Martin.

Political Parties in the Third World. Ed. by Vicky Randall. (One-Off Ser.). 256p. 1988. text ed. 39.95 (ISBN 0-8039-8143-0); pap. text ed. 16.50 (ISBN 0-8039-8144-9). Sage.

Political Parties in the United States, 1846-1861. Jesse Macy. LC 73-19160. (Politics & People Ser.). 344p. 1974. Repr. 24.50x (ISBN 0-405-05882-9). Ayer Co Pubs.

Political Parties in the West Bank under the Jordanian Regime (1949-1967) Amnon Cohen. 344p. 1983. 29.95x (ISBN 0-8014-1321-4). Cornell U Pr.

Political Parties in Turkey: The Role of Islam. Mehmet Y. Geyikdaqi. LC 83-24470. 177p. 1984. 35.00 (ISBN 0-275-91167-5, C1167). Praeger.

Political Parties in Western Democracies. Klaus Von Beyme. LC 84-18171. 444p. 1985. 39.95 (ISBN 0-312-62375-5). St Martin.

Political Parties, Interest Groups & Public Policy: Group Iinluence in American Politics. Dennis S. Ippolito & Thomas G. Walker. 431p. 1980. text ed. write for info. (ISBN 0-13-684357-3). P-H.

Political Parties of Asia & the Pacific, 2 vols. Haruhiro Fukui. Ed. by Colin A. Hughes et al. LC 84-19252. (Historical Encyclopedia of the World's Political Parties Ser.). (Illus.). xviii, 1328p. 1985. Vol. 1. lib. bdg. 95.00 (ISBN 0-313-25143-6, FUA/01); Vol. 2. lib. bdg. 95.00 (ISBN 0-313-25144-4, FUA/02). Greenwood.

Political Parties of Europe, 2 vols. Ed. by Vincent McHale & Sharon Skowronski. LC 82-15408. (Greenwood Encyclopedia of the World's Political Parties). (Illus.). 1400p. 1983. Set. lib. bdg. 125.00 (ISBN 0-313-21405-0, MPP/); Vol. I: xix, 700p. lib. bdg. 85.00 (ISBN 0-313-23804-9, MPP/01); Vol. II: 1297p. lib. bdg. 65.00 (ISBN 0-313-23805-7, MPP/02). Greenwood.

Political Parties of the Americas: Canada, Latin America, & the West Indies, 2 vols. Ed. by Robert J. Alexander. LC 81-6952. (Greenwood Historical Encyclopedia of the World's Political Parties Ser.). (Illus.). xxviii, 1274p. 1982. lib. bdg. 95.00x (ISBN 0-313-21474-3, APA/); lib. bdg. 50.00 ea. (ISBN 0-313-23753-0, APA/01) (ISBN 0-313-23754-9, APA/02). Greenwood.

Political Parties of the World. Compiled by Alan J. Day & Henry W. Degenhardt. LC 80-83467. 432p. 1984. 90.00x (ISBN 0-582-90252-5, Pub. by Longman). Gale.

Political Parties of to-Day: A Study in Republican & Democratic Politics. Arthur N. Holcombe. LC 73-19153. (Politics & People Ser.). 410p. 1974. Repr. 27.50x (ISBN 0-405-05875-6). Ayer Co Pubs.

Political Parties: Organisation & Power. Angelo Panebianco. Tr. by Marc Silver. (Cambridge Studies in Modern Political Economies). (Illus.). 360p. 1988. 54.50 (ISBN 0-521-30627-2); pap. 16.95 (ISBN 0-521-31401-1). Cambridge U Pr.

Political Parties: Their Organization & Activity in the Modern State. 3rd rev. ed. Maurice Duverger. Tr. by Barbara North & Robert North. 1964. pap. 13.95x (ISBN 0-416-68320-7, NO. 2173). Routledge Chapman & Hall.

Political Party As a Social Process. Viva B. Boothe. LC 73-19131. (Politics & People Ser.). (Illus.). 130p. 1974. Repr. 11.00 (ISBN 0-405-05856-X). Ayer Co Pubs.

Political Party Organizations: A Bibliography. Robert Goehlert. (Public Administration Ser.: P 1785). 21p. 1985. 3.00 (ISBN 0-89028-585-3). Vance Biblios.

Political Passages: The Journey of Two Decades in America, 1968-1988. Ed. by John H. Bunzel. 320p. 1988. 21.95 (ISBN 0-02-904921-0). Free Pr.

Political Patronage & Control over the Sangha. Somboon Suksamran. 57p. (Orig.). 1981. pap. text ed. 9.50x (ISBN 9971-902-37-0, Pub. by Inst Southeast Asian Stud). Gower Pub Co.

Political Perceptions of the Palestinians on the West Bank & the Gaza Strip. Ann M. Lesch. LC 80-81807. (Middle East Institute Special Study: No. 3). (Illus.). pap. 29.80 (ISBN 0-317-09280-4, 2022763). Bks Demand UMI.

Political Personality of Islam. Fida E. Islam. 280p. 1985. pap. 6.95 (ISBN 0-940368-37-4). Tahrike Tarsile Quran.

Political Perspectives on the Muslim World. Asaf Hussain. LC 82-24029. 220p. 1984. 27.50 (ISBN 0-312-62382-8). St Martin.

Political Persuasion in Presidential Campaigns. Ed. by L. Patrick Develin. 275p. (Orig.). 1986. 29.95 (ISBN 0-88738-078-6). Transaction Bks.

Political Philosophy. Gerald C. MacCallum. 192p. 1987. pap. text ed. 15.00 (ISBN 0-13-684689-0). P-H.

Political Philosophy. Ed. by Anthony Quinton. (Oxford Readings in Philosophy). (Orig.). 1967. pap. 7.95x (ISBN 0-19-875002-1). Oxford U Pr.

Political Philosophy: A History of the Search for Order. reference ed. James L. Wiser. 400p. 1983. 33.33 (ISBN 0-13-684845-1). P-H.

Political Philosophy & Rhetoric: A Study of the Origins of American Party Politics. John Zvesper. LC 76-11097. (Cambridge Studies in the History & Theory of Politics). pap. 61.50 (ISBN 0-317-09148-4, 2022480). Bks Demand UMI.

Political Philosophy & the Issues of Politics. Joseph Cropsey. LC 76-22960. 1977. lib. bdg. 22.00x (ISBN 0-226-12123-2). U of Chicago Pr.

Political Philosophy & the Issues of Politics. Joseph Cropsey. LC 76-22960. 1980. pap. 7.50x (ISBN 0-226-12124-0, 864, Phoen). U of Chicago Pr.

Political Philosophy & the Open Society. Dante Germino. LC 81-14312. 180p. 1982. text ed. 22.50 (ISBN 0-8071-0974-6). La State U Pr.

Political Philosophy & Time: Plato & the Origins of Political Vision. John G. Gunnell. LC 86-25012. xx, 314p. 1987. pap. 12.95 (ISBN 0-226-31079-5). U of Chicago Pr.

Political Philosophy As Therapy: Marcuse Reconsidered. Gertrude A. Steuernagel. LC 77-94747. (Contributions in Political Science Ser.: No. 11). 1979. lib. bdg. 46.95x (ISBN 0-313-20315-6, SPP/). Greenwood.

Political Philosophy of Bakunin. Mikhail A. Bakunin. Ed. by G. P. Maximoff. 1964. pap. text ed. 14.95 (ISBN 0-02-901210-4). Free Pr.

Political Philosophy of Burke. John MacCunn. LC 65-18817. 1965. Repr. of 1913 ed. 8.00x (ISBN 0-8462-0616-1). Russell.

Political Philosophy of Hobbes: Its Basis & Its Genesis. Leo Strauss. Tr. by Elsa M. Sinclair. LC 52-9720. 1984. pap. 10.00x (ISBN 0-226-77705-7). U of Chicago Pr.

Political Philosophy of Luis De Molina, S. J. Frank B. Costello. 1974. pap. 18.00 (ISBN 88-7041-338-1). Jesuit Hist.

Political Philosophy of Mao Tse-Tung. Manoranjan Mohanty. 1978. 14.00x (ISBN 0-8364-0266-9). South Asia Bks.

Political Philosophy of Martin Luther King Jr. Hanes Walton, Jr. LC 76-111260. (Contributions in Afro-American & African Studies: No. 10). 137p. 1976. (Pub. by Negro U Pr); pap. 4.95 (ISBN 0-8371-8931-4, WMK/). Greenwood.

Political Philosophy of Modern Shinto: A Study of the State Religion of Japan. Daniel C. Holtom. LC 84-3072. (BCC Ser.). 338p. 1984. Repr. of 1922 ed. 37.50 (ISBN 0-404-15937-0). AMS Pr.

Political Philosophy of Niccolo' Macchiavelli As It Applies to Politics, the Management of the Firm & the Science of Living. Fritz L. Mervil. (Illus.). 167p. 1981. 127.75 (ISBN 0-89266-270-0). Am Classical Coll Pr.

Political Philosophy of Plato & Hegel. Michael B. Foster. LC 83-48506. (Philosophy of Hegel Ser.). 220p. 1984. lib. bdg. 30.00 (ISBN 0-8240-5629-9). Garland Pub.

Political Philosophy of Robert M. LaFollette. Ed. by Ellen Torelle. LC 75-348. (Radical Tradition in America Ser). (Illus.). 426p. 1975. Repr. of 1920 ed. 31.35 (ISBN 0-88355-252-3). Hyperion Conn.

Political Philosophy of Rousseau. Roger D. Masters. 1976. 55.50x (ISBN 0-691-07515-8); pap. 13.50x (ISBN 0-691-01989-4). Princeton U Pr.

Political Philosophy of Spinoza. Robert J. McShea. LC 68-17553. pap. 56.00 (ISBN 0-317-07751-1, 2007204). Bks Demand UMI.

Political Philosophy of Sri Aurobindo. 2nd rev. ed. V. P. Varma. 1976. 18.00 (ISBN 0-8426-0873-7). Orient Bk Dist.

Political Philosophy of Swami Vevekawada. A. Rathna Reddy. 210p. 1984. text ed. 22.50x (ISBN 0-86590-281-X, Sterling Pubs India). Apt Bks.

Political Philosophy of the Frankfurt School. George Friedman. LC 80-66890. 320p. 1981. 36.50x (ISBN 0-8014-1279-X). Cornell U Pr.

Political Philosophy of the Great de Medici As Revealed by Their Correspondence, 2 vols. Cosimo Giovanni & Lorenzo De Medici. (Illus.). 1985. Set. 227.50 (ISBN 0-86722-106-2). Inst Econ Pol.

Political Philosophy of the Orthodox Church. Apostolos Makrakis. Ed. by Orthodox Christian Educational Society. Tr. by Denver Cummings from Hellenic. Orig. Title: Orthodox Definition of Political Science. 163p. (Orig.). 1965. pap. 4.00x (ISBN 0-938366-11-4). Orthodox Chr.

Political Pilgrims: Travels of Western Intellectuals to the Soviet Union, China, & Cuba 1928-1978. Paul Hollander. LC 80-29417. 1981. 27.50x (ISBN 0-19-502937-2). Oxford U Pr.

Political Plans of Mexico. Thomas B. Davis & Amado Ricon. LC 87-10568. 704p. 1987. lib. bdg. 38.50 (ISBN 0-8191-6426-7). U Pr of Amer.

Political Plays for Children: The Grips Theater of Berlin. Ed. & tr. by Jack Zipes. LC 76-17461. (gr. 5-7). 1976. pap. 5.00 (ISBN 0-914386-16-6). Telos Pr.

Political Poems & Songs Relating to English History, Composed During the Period from the Accession of Edward III to That of Richard III, 2 vols. Ed. by Thomas Wright. (Rolls Ser.: No. 14). Repr. of 1861 ed. 88.00 (ISBN 0-8115-1019-0). Kraus Repr.

Political Poetry & Ideology of F. I. Tiutchev. Roger Conant. (Ardis Essay Ser.: No. 6). 1983. 10.00 (ISBN 0-88233-624-X). Ardis Pubs.

Political Police in Britain. Tony Bunyan. LC 75-45815. (Illus.). 304p. 1976. 22.50 (ISBN 0-312-62405-0). St Martin.

Political Policing in Wales. Ed. by John Davies et al. 1984. 20.00x (ISBN 0-317-54898-0, Pub. by NCCL UK). State Mutual Bk.

Political Portraits. Charles Whibley. LC 70-112821. 1970. Repr. of 1917 ed. 26.50x (ISBN 0-8046-1088-6, Pub. by Kennikat). Assoc Faculty Pr.

Political Portraits First Series. facs. ed. Charles Whibley. LC 74-105050. (Essay Index Reprint Ser.). 1917. Repr. of 1917 ed. 20.00 (ISBN 0-8369-1586-0). Ayer Co Pubs.

Political Portraits, Second Series. Charles Whibley. LC 76-117859. (Essay Index Reprint Ser). 1923. 19.00 (ISBN 0-8369-1734-0). Ayer Co Pubs.

Political Power. Gilbert M. Cuthbertson. LC 68-5794. (Rice University Studies: Vol. 54, No. 1). 72p. 1968. pap. 10.00x (ISBN 0-89263-195-3). Rice Univ.

Political Power & Communications in Indonesia. Ed. by Karl D. Jackson & Lucian W. Pye. LC 76-19976. 1978. pap. 11.95x (ISBN 0-520-04205-0). U of Cal Pr.

Political Power & Social Theory, Vol. 1. Ed. by Maurice Zeitlin. 1980. lib. bdg. 52.50 (ISBN 0-89232-115-6). Jai Pr.

Political Power & Social Theory, Vol. 2. Maurice Zeitlin. 375p. (Orig.). 1981. 52.50 (ISBN 0-89232-143-1). Jai Pr.

Political Power & Social Theory, Vol. 3. Ed. by Maurice Zeitlin. 375p. 1981. 52.50 (ISBN 0-89232-204-7). Jai Pr.

Political Power & Social Theory, Vol. 4. Ed. by Howard Kimeldorf & Maurice Zeitlin. 302p. 1984. 52.50 (ISBN 0-89232-330-2). Jai Pr.

Political Power & Social Theory, Vol. 5. Maurice Zeitlin. 1985. 52.50 (ISBN 0-89232-523-2). Jai Pr.

Political Power & Social Theory, Vol. 6. Maurice Zeitlin. 1987. 56.50 (ISBN 0-89232-709-X). Jai Pr.

Political Power & the Arab Oil Weapon: The Netherlands, Great Britain, Canada, Japan & the United States. Roy Licklider. 320p. 1988. 37.50x (ISBN 0-520-06243-4). U of Cal Pr.

Political Power & the Governmental Process. Karl Lowenstein. LC 65-8901. (Chicago University Charles R. Walgreen Foundation for the Study of American Institutions, Lecture Ser.). pap. 118.50 (ISBN 0-317-09811-X, 2020109). Bks Demand UMI.

Political Power in Birmingham, 1871-1921. Carl V. Harris. LC 77-1110. (Twentieth Century America Ser.). (Illus.). 336p. 1977. 29.95x (ISBN 0-87049-211-X). U of Tenn Pr.

Political Power in Ecuador. Osvaldo Hurtado. Tr. by Nick Mills, Jr. 432p. 1985. pap. 36.50x (ISBN 0-8133-0264-1). Westview.

Political Power in Poor Neighborhoods. Curt Lamb. 320p. 1975. pap. 11.95 (ISBN 0-87073-247-1). Schenkman Bks Inc.

Political Power in the Soviet Union: A Study of Decision-Making in Stalingrad. Philip D. Stewart. LC 68-17706. 1968. pap. 6.55 scp (ISBN 0-672-60764-6). Bobbs.

Political Power in the Soviet Union: A Study of Decision-Making in Stalingrad. Philip D. Stewart. LC 68-17706. 1968. 39.50x (ISBN 0-672-51163-0). Irvington.

Political Power in the U. S. S. R., 1917-1947. Julian Towster. LC 74-27729. (Illus.). 443p. 1975. Repr. lib. bdg. 48.50x (ISBN 0-8371-7913-0, TOPP). Greenwood.

Political Prairie Fire: The Nonpartisan League, 1915-1922. Robert L. Morlan. LC 74-9275. (Illus.). 408p. 1974. Repr. of 1955 ed. lib. bdg. 35.00 (ISBN 0-8371-7639-5, MOPF). Greenwood.

Political Prairie Fire: The Nonpartisan League, 1915-1922. Robert L. Morlan. LC 85-18792. (Borealis Books Reprint). xxviii, 410p. 1985. pap. 10.95 (ISBN 0-87351-186-7). Minn Hist.

Political Presidency: Practice of Leadership from Kennedy to Reagan. Barbara Kellerman. 300p. 1984. 22.50x (ISBN 0-19-503457-0). Oxford U Pr.

Political Presidency: Practice of Leadership from Kennedy Through Reagan. Barbara Kellerman. 300p. 1986. pap. 10.95x (ISBN 0-19-504037-6). Oxford U Pr.

Political Principles of Mencius. Cho-Min Wei. LC 77-72187. (Studies in Chinese Government & Law). 99p. 1977. Repr. of 1916 ed. 11.50 (ISBN 0-89093-063-5). U Pubns Amer.

Political Principles of Mencius. Francis C. Wei. 1977. lib. bdg. 59.95 (ISBN 0-8490-2452-8). Gordon Pr.

Political Principles of Some Notable Prime Ministers of the Nineteenth Century. Ed. by Fossey J. Hearnshaw. LC 74-107710. (Essay Index Reprint Ser.). 1926. 21.50 (ISBN 0-8369-1512-7). Ayer Co Pubs.

Political Prints in the Age of Hogarth: A Study of the Ideographic Representation of Politics. Herbert M. Atherton. (Illus.). 1974. 65.00x (ISBN 0-19-827188-3). Oxford U Pr.

Political Prisoner. Cesare Pavese. Tr. by W. J. Strachan. 237p. 1986. Repr. of 1955 ed. 19.95 (ISBN 0-7206-6202-8). Dufour.

Political Prisoners in Zaire: An Amnesty International Special Briefing. LC 83-195344. 16p. 1983. pap. 3.00. Amnesty Intl USA.

Political Process. David Cohen. (Task Force on the Eighties Ser.). 34p. 1981. pap. 2.50 (ISBN 0-87495-040-6). Am Jewish Comm.

Political Process & Economic Change. Ed. by Kristen R. Monroe. LC 83-11866. 250p. 1983. 24.50x (ISBN 0-87586-063-X); pap. 15.00x (ISBN 0-87586-062-1). Agathon.

Political Process & Foreign Policy: The Making of the Japanese Peace Settlement. Bernard C. Cohen. LC 80-19832. x, 293p. 1980. Repr. of 1957 ed. lib. bdg. 45.50x (ISBN 0-313-22715-2, COPF). Greenwood.

Political Process & the Development of Black Insurgency, 1930 to 1970. Doug McAdam. LC 82-2712. (Illus.). viii, 304p. 1985. lib. bdg. 27.50x (ISBN 0-226-55551-8); pap. 11.95 (ISBN 0-226-55552-6). U of Chicago Pr.

Political Processes & Regional Development Planning in Nigeria. Bola Ayeni & Akin L. Mobogunje. (Working Papers Ser.: No. 82-7). 33p. 1982. pap. 7.50 (ISBN 0-686-43301-7, CRD144, UNCRD). UNIPUB.

Political Profiles of Black College Students in the South: Socio-Political Attitudes, Preferences, Personality & Characteristics. J. Dudley McClain. LC 77-82709. 1977. 14.95 (ISBN 0-89583-002-7); pap. 7.95 (ISBN 0-89583-003-5). Resurgens Pubns.

Political Profiles of College Students in Southern Appalachia: Socio-Political Attitudes, Preferences, Personality & Characteristics. J. Dudley McClain. LC 77-84178. 1978. 14.95 (ISBN 0-89583-006-X); pap. 7.95 (ISBN 0-89583-007-8). Resurgens Pubns.

Political Profiles of College Students in the South: Socio-Political Attitudes, Preferences, Personality & Characteristics. J. Dudley McClain. LC 77-82715. 1977. 14.95 (ISBN 0-89583-000-0); pap. 9.95 (ISBN 0-89583-001-9). Resurgens Pubns.

Political Profiles of Female College Students in the South: Socio-Political Attitudes, Preferences, Personality & Characteristics. J. Dudley McClain. LC 77-84179. 1978. 14.95 (ISBN 0-89583-008-6); pap. 9.95 (ISBN 0-89583-009-4). Resurgens Pubns.

Political Profiles of Male College Students in the South: Socio-Political Attitudes, Preferences, Personality & Characteristics. J. Dudley McClain. LC 79-65787. 1979. 14.95 (ISBN 0-89583-012-4); pap. 9.95 (ISBN 0-89583-013-2). Resurgens Pubns.

Political Profiles of White College Students in the South: Socio-Political Attitudes, Preferences, Personality & Characteristics. J. Dudley McClain. LC 77-84177. 1977. 14.95 (ISBN 0-89583-004-3); pap. 9.95 (ISBN 0-89583-005-1). Resurgens Pubns.

Political Profiles Series, 5 vols. 1982. Set. 225.00x (ISBN 0-686-94230-2). Facts on File.

Political Propaganda. F. C. Bartlett. 158p. 1973. Repr. of 1940 ed. lib. bdg. 18.00x (ISBN 0-374-90425-1, Octagon). Hippocrene Bks.

Political Prophecy in England. Rupert Taylor. LC 11-23809. Repr. of 1911 ed. 16.00 (ISBN 0-404-06357-8). AMS Pr.

Political Protest & Social Control in Prewar Japan: The Origins of Buraku Liberation. Ian Neary. LC 87-4209. (Studies on East Asia). 192p. 1989. text ed. 35.00 (ISBN 0-391-03495-2). Humanities.

Political Protest in the Congo: The Parti Solidaire Africain During the Independence Struggle. Herbert F. Weiss. LC 66-14316. 1967. 42.00x (ISBN 0-691-03048-0). Princeton U Pr.

Political Psychology: Contemporary Problems & Issues. Ed. by Margaret G. Hermann. LC 85-45905. (Social & Behavioral Science Ser.). 1986. text ed. 45.00x (ISBN 0-87589-682-0). Jossey-Bass.

Political Psychology of Appeasement: Finlandization & Other Unpopular Essays on World Affairs. Walter Laqueur. LC 79-6854. 283p. 1980. text ed. 27.95 (ISBN 0-87855-336-3). Transaction Bks.

Political Pulpit. Roderick P. Hart. LC 76-12290. 160p. 1977. 7.95 (ISBN 0-911198-44-X). Purdue U Pr.

Political Questions in the Courts: A Judicial Function in Democracies - Israel & the United States. Yaacov S. Zemach. LC 76-14392. 257p. 1976. 25.00x (ISBN 0-8143-1566-6). Wayne St U Pr.

Political Questions: Political Philosophy from Plato to Rawls. Larry Arnhart. 545p. 1987. text ed. write for info. (ISBN 0-02-304130-7). Macmillan.

Political Radicalism in Late Imperial Vienna: Origins of the Christian Social Movement, 1848-1897. John W. Boyer. LC 80-17302. (Illus.). 1981. lib. bdg. 40.00x (ISBN 0-226-06957-5). U of Chicago Pr.

Political Re-Education of Germany & Her Allies after World War II. Ed. by Nicholas Pronay & Keith Wilson. LC 84-24359. 270p. 1985. 22.50x (ISBN 0-389-20546-X, BNB-08107). B&N Imports.

Political Realism & International Morality: Ethics in the Nuclear Age. Ed. by Kenneth Kipnis & Diana T. Meyers. 288p. 1987. 35.00 (ISBN 0-8133-0457-1); pap. 19.50 (ISBN 0-8133-0456-3). Westview.

Political Realism & the Crisis of World Politics: An American Approach to Foreign Policy. Kenneth W. Thompson. LC 82-45061. 270p. 1982. pap. text ed. 12.50 (ISBN 0-8191-2352-8). U Pr of Amer.

Political Realism in American Thought. John W. Coffey. 217p. 1978. 20.00 (ISBN 0-8387-1903-1). Bucknell U Pr.

Political Reality & Political Consciousness. V. Mshvenieradze. 444p. 1985. pap. 5.95 (ISBN 0-8285-3370-9, Pub. by Progress Pubs USSR). Imported Pubns.

Political Reasoning. Evert Vedung. (Illus.). 224p. 1982. 29.95 (ISBN 0-8039-1815-1). Sage.

Political Reasoning & Cognition: A Piagetian View. Shawn Rosenberg et al. 193p. 1989. lib. bdg. 32.50 (ISBN 0-8223-0856-8). Duke.

Political Recollections 1840-1872. facs. ed. George W. Julian. LC 78-83885. (Black Heritage Library Collection Ser). 1884. 18.00 (ISBN 0-8369-8615-6). Ayer Co Pubs.

Political Reconstruction of China. Eu-Yang Kwang. LC 76-55089. (Studies in Chinese Government & Law). 190p. 1977. Repr. of 1922 ed. 18.50 (ISBN 0-89093-058-9). U Pubns Amer.

Political Redistricting & Geographic Theory. Richard L. Morrill. Ed. by C. Gregory Knight. LC 81-69235. (Resource Publications in Geography Ser.). (Orig.). 1981. pap. 6.00 (ISBN 0-89291-159-X). Assn Am Geographers.

Political Reflections on the Finances & Commerce of France. Charles Dutot. LC 76-146461. 1974. Repr. of 1739 ed. lib. bdg. 49.50x (ISBN 0-678-00842-6). Kelley.

Political Reform in Wisconsin: A Historical Review of the Subjects of Primary Election, Taxation & Railway Regulation. Emanuel L. Philipp. Ed. by Stanley P. Caine & Roger Wyman. LC 73-620042. (Illus.). 197p. 1973. Repr. of 1910 ed. 12.00 (ISBN 0-87020-123-9). State Hist Soc Wis.

Political Refugees: Monographs. Mary Vance. (Public Administration Ser.: P 2190). 40p. 1987. 10.00 (ISBN 1-55590-370-3). Vance Biblios.

Political Regime & Public Policy in the Philippines: A Comparison of Bacolod & Iloilo Cities. Howard M. Leichter. (Northern Illinois Univ. CSeas Special Report Ser.: No. 11). 1975. wrps. 4.00 (ISBN 0-686-09458-1). Cellar.

Political Register, Setting Forth the Principles of the Whig & Locofoco Parties in the United States, with the Life & Public Services of Henry Clay. William G. Brownlow. LC 73-23063. 348p. 1974. Repr. of 1844 ed. 25.00 (ISBN 0-87152-153-9). Reprint.

Political Reliability of the Warsaw Pact Armies: The Southern Tier. Ivan Volgyes. LC 82-12984. (Duke Press Policy Studies). xii, 116p. 27.50 (ISBN 0-8223-0509-7). Duke.

Political Religions. Eric Voegelin. LC 85-28524. (Toronto Studies in Theology: Vol 23). 1986. lib. bdg. 49.95x (ISBN 0-88946-767-6). E Mellen.

Political, Religious & Historiographical Ideas of Juan Francisco Masdeu, S. J. (1744-1817) Roberto Mantelli. Ed. by Maurice Cranston. (Political Theory & Political Philosophy Ser.). 600p. 1987. lib. bdg. 85.00 (ISBN 0-8240-0824-3). Garland Pub.

Political, Religious, & Love Poems. Ed. by F. J. Furnival. (EETS OS Ser.: Vol. 15). Repr. of 1866 ed. 25.00 (ISBN 0-8115-3346-8). Kraus Repr.

Political, Religious & Love Poems. Ed. by Frederick J. Furnivall. 348p. 1981. Repr. of 1866 ed. lib. bdg. 75.00 (ISBN 0-89987-276-X). Darby Bks.

Political Reorientation of Japan 1945-1948, 2 vols. Supreme Commander for Allied Powers. 1968. Set. 75.00x (ISBN 0-403-00028-9). Scholarly.

Political Report of the CPSU Central Committee to the 27th Congress of the Communist Party of the Soviet Union. Mikhail Gorbachov. 160p. 1986. pap. 1.95 (ISBN 0-8285-3179-X, Pub. by Novosti Pr USSR). Imported Pubns.

Political Representation in England & the Origins of the American Republic. J. R. Pole. 1969. 27.50 (ISBN 0-312-62440-9). St Martin.

Political Representation in England & the Origins of the American Republic. J. R. Pole. 1971. pap. 10.95x (ISBN 0-520-01903-2). U of Cal Pr.

Political Representation in France. Philip E. Converse & Roy Pierce. LC 85-15789. (Illus.). 1040p. 1986. 55.00x (ISBN 0-674-68660-8, Belknap Pr). Harvard U Pr.

Political Repression in Modern America: 1870 to the Present. 2nd ed. Robert J. Goldstein. 704p. pap. text ed. cancelled (ISBN 0-87047-013-2); cancelled (ISBN 0-87047-012-4). Schenkman Bks Inc.

Political Repression in Nineteenth Century Europe. Robert J. Goldstein. LC 83-10541. 416p. 1983. 28.50x (ISBN 0-389-20419-6, 07305). B&N Imports.

Political Research: A Methodological Sampler. Betty Zisk. 352p. 1981. pap. text ed. 13.50 (ISBN 0-669-02338-8). Heath.

Political Research & Knowledge: A Bibliography. Robert Goehlert. (Public Administration Ser.: P 1782). 15p. 1985. 2.25 (ISBN 0-89028-582-9). Vance Biblios.

Political Research & Political Theory. Ed. by Oliver Garceau. LC 68-28693. (Illus.). 1968. 19.50x (ISBN 0-674-68700-0). Harvard U Pr.

Political Resource Directory: National Edition 1988-1989. Ed. by Carol Hess. 480p. pap. text ed. 95.00 (ISBN 0-944320-00-7). C Hess Assocs.

Political Resource Directory, 1986-1987: New York Metro Edition. Intro. by Carol Hess. 160p. (Orig.). 1986. pap. 17.95 (ISBN 0-8115-0002-0). Kraus Repr.

Political Responsibility: Choices for the Future. rev. ed. United States Catholic Conference Administrative Board. Tr. by Marina Herrera. 40p. (Orig., Eng. & Span.). 1988. pap. 1.00 (ISBN 1-55586-186-5). US Catholic.

Political Responsibility of the Critic. Jim Merod. LC 86-47977. 288p. 1987. 24.95x (ISBN 0-8014-1976-X). Cornell U Pr.

Political Rights for European Citizens. Guido V. Berghe. 256p. (Orig.). 1982. text ed. 38.00 (ISBN 0-566-00524-7). Gower Pub Co.

Political Risk. William H. Overholt. (Euromoney Ser.). 152p. (Orig.). 1982. pap. 115.00 (ISBN 0-903121-33-6, Pub. by Woodhead-Faulkner). Longwood Pub Group.

Political Risk Assessment: An Annotated Bibliography. Ed. by David A. Jodice. LC 84-19784. (Bibliographies & Indexes in Law & Political Science Ser.: No. 3). xii, 279p. 1985. lib. bdg. 36.95 (ISBN 0-313-24444-8, JOP/). Greenwood.

Political Risk in the International Oil & Gas Industry. Howard L. Lax. LC 82-83329. (Illus.). 195p. 1983. lib. bdg. 36.00x (ISBN 0-934634-20-3). Intl Human Res.

Political Risk in Thirty-Five Countries. 1984. cancelled 150.00x (ISBN 0-8002-3172-4). Intl Pubns Serv.

Political Risk in Thirty-Five Countries: Nineteen Eighty-Three Edition. 160p. 1983. 185.00x (ISBN 0-8002-3409-X). Intl Pubns Serv.

Political Risk Management: International Lending & Investing under Environmental Uncertainty. Charles R. Kennedy, Jr. LC 86-25588. 177p. 1987. lib. bdg. 35.00 (ISBN 0-89930-157-6, KPK/, Quorum Bks). Greenwood.

Political Risks in International Business: New Directions for Research, Management & Public Policy. Ed. by Thomas L. Brewer. 384p. 1985. 40.95 (ISBN 0-275-90066-5, C0066). Praeger.

Political Role of International Trade Unions. G. K. Busch. LC 82-16818. 320p. 1983. 30.00 (ISBN 0-312-62447-6). St Martin.

Political Role of Labor in Developing Countries. Bruce H. Millen. LC 79-29735. x, 148p. 1980. Repr. of 1963 ed. lib. bdg. 35.00x (ISBN 0-313-22286-X, MIPO). Greenwood.

Political Role of Law Courts in Modern Democracies. Jerold L. Waldman & Kenneth M. Holland. LC 86-24822. 256p. 1987. 35.00 (ISBN 0-312-00383-8). St Martin.

Political Role of Minority Groups in the Middle East. Ed. by R. D. McLaurin. LC 79-20588. (Praeger Special Studies). 328p. 1979. 42.95 (ISBN 0-275-90393-1, C0393). Praeger.

Political Role of Mongol Buddhism. Larry W. Moses. LC 81-622859. (Indiana University Uralic & Altaic Ser.: Vol. 133). x, 299p. 1977. 15.00 (ISBN 0-933070-01-2). Ind U Res Inst.

Political Role of Religion in the U. S. Ed. by Stephen D. Johnson, Jr. & Joseph B. Tamney. (Special Study Ser.). 300p. 1986. pap. text ed. 33.50x (ISBN 0-8133-7030-2). Westview.

Political Role of the General Assembly. Henry F. Haviland. LC 78-2808. (Carnegie Endowment for International Peace, United Nation Studies: No. 7). 1978. Repr. of 1951 ed. lib. bdg. 22.50x (ISBN 0-313-20334-2, HAPG). Greenwood.

Political Theory: An Introduction to Interpretation. Elizabeth M. James. LC 81-40791. 104p. 1982. pap. text ed. 9.75 (ISBN 0-8191-2008-1). U Pr of Amer.

Political Theory & Institutions of the Khawarij. Elie A. Salem. LC 78-64226. (Johns Hopkins University. Studies in the Social Sciences. Seventy-Fourth Ser. 1956: 2). Repr. of 1956 ed. 15.50 (ISBN 0-404-61328-4). AMS Pr.

Political Theory & International Relations. Charles R. Beitz. LC 79-83976. 212p. 1979. 28.00x (ISBN 0-691-07614-6); pap. 9.50x (ISBN 0-691-02192-9). Princeton U Pr.

Political Theory & Modernity. William E. Connolly. 224p. text ed. 45.00. Basil Blackwell.

Political Theory & Political Education. Ed. by Melvin Richter. LC 79-17833. 1980. 26.00x (ISBN 0-691-07612-X). Princeton U Pr.

Political Theory & Praxis: New Perspectives. Ed. by Terence Ball. LC 77-73320. 1977. 16.75x (ISBN 0-8166-0816-4). U of Minn Pr.

Political Theory & Public Policy. Robert E. Goodin. LC 81-23120. 1982. lib. bdg. 27.50x (ISBN 0-226-30296-2). U of Chicago Pr.

Political Theory & Public Policy. Robert E. Goodin. LC 81-23120. 286p. 1983. pap. 12.95x (ISBN 0-226-30297-0). U of Chicago Pr.

Political Theory & Social Policy. Albert Weale. LC 83-42846. 240p. 1983. 24.95 (ISBN 0-312-62553-7). St Martin.

Political Theory As Public Confession. Peter D. Bathory. LC 80-15667. 180p. 1981. 24.95 (ISBN 0-87855-405-X). Transaction Bks.

Political Theory of a Compound Republic: Designing the American Experiment. 2nd ed. Vincent Ostrom. LC 86-7063. xxx, 240p. 1987. 22.50x (ISBN 0-8032-3554-2); pap. 8.95x (ISBN 0-8032-8600-7). U of Nebr Pr.

Political Theory of Arthur J. Penty. Asa D. Sokolow. 1940. pap. 39.50x (ISBN 0-686-83707-X). Elliots Bks.

Political Theory of Beatrice Webb. Barbara E Nolan, Sr. LC 87-12592. (Studies in Social History: No. 7). 1988. 47.50 (ISBN 0-404-61607-0). AMS Pr.

Political Theory of Eric Voegelin. Barry Cooper. LC 86-23517. (Toronto Studies in Theology: Vol. 27). 256p. 1986. lib. bdg. 49.95x (ISBN 0-88946-771-4). E Mellen.

Political Theory of Islam. A. A. Maududi. pap. 1.00 (ISBN 0-686-18547-1). Kazi Pubns.

Political Theory of John C. Calhoun. August O. Spain. LC 68-27336. 1968. Repr. of 1951 ed. lib. bdg. 20.50x (ISBN 0-374-97524-8, Octagon). Hippocrene Bks.

Political Theory of John Taylor of Caroline. C. William Hill, Jr. LC 75-39115. 343p. 1977. 27.50 (ISBN 0-8386-1902-9). Fairleigh Dickinson.

Political Theory of John Wyclif. Lowrie J. Daly. LC 62-20515. (Jesuit Studies). 1962. 4.95 (ISBN 0-8294-0020-6). Loyola.

Political Theory of Liberal Democracy. Paul Wilkinson. 300p. 1985. 24.95x (ISBN 0-85520-763-9). Basil Blackwell.

Political Theory of Local Government. W. Hardy Wickwar. LC 71-95258. xii, 118p. 1970. 19.95x (ISBN 0-87249-174-9). U of SC Pr.

Political Theory of Painting from Reynolds to Hazlitt: The Body of the Public. John Barrell. LC 86-50362. 352p. 1986. text ed. 30.00x (ISBN 0-300-03720-1). Yale U Pr.

Political Theory of Possessive Individualism: Hobbes to Locke. Crawford B. Macpherson. (Oxford Paperbacks Ser). 1962. pap. 7.95x (ISBN 0-19-881084-9). Oxford U Pr.

Political Theory of the Ancient Empires & Reasons for Their Catastrophic End. Wilfred Gillette. (Illus.). 301p. 1986. 257.15 (ISBN 0-86722-136-4). Inst Econ Pol.

Political Theory of "The Federalist". David F. Epstein. LC 83-17858. x, 234p. 1986. lib. bdg. 25.00x (ISBN 0-226-21299-8); pap. 9.95 (ISBN 0-226-21300-5). U of Chicago Pr.

Political Theory of the Growth of Contemporary France, 2 vols. Gabriel Hanotaux. (Illus.). 317p. 1986. Set. 237.50 (ISBN 0-89901-262-0). Found Class Reprints.

Political Theory of the Huguenots of the Dispersion. Guy H. Dodge. LC 79-159178. ix, 287p. 1971. Repr. of 1947 ed. lib. bdg. 20.00x (ISBN 0-374-92213-6, Octagon). Hippocrene Bks.

Political Theory of the Italian, the Irish, & the Jewish Mafia, 2 vols. in one. Edward Bramanti. (Illus.). 200p. 1976. 127.75 (ISBN 0-913314-78-1). Am Classical Coll Pr.

Political Theory: The Foundations of Twentieth Century Political Thought. Arnold Brecht. LC 59-5591. pap. 115.40 (ISBN 0-317-09452-1, 2015011). Bks Demand UMI.

Political Theory: Tradition & Interpretation. John G. Gunnell. (Illus.). 192p. 1987. pap. text ed. 8.75 (ISBN 0-8191-5954-9). U Pr of Amer.

Political Thinkers. Ed. by David Muschamp. LC 85-26074. 353p. 1986. 29.95x (ISBN 0-312-62558-8). St Martin.

Political Thinking of Indonesian Chinese, 1900-1977. Leo Suryadinata. 270p. 1980. 18.00x (ISBN 0-8214-0548-9, Pub. by Singapore U Pr); pap. 11.00x (ISBN 0-8214-0549-7). Ohio U Pr.

Political Thinking: The Perennial Questions. 4th ed. Glenn Tinder. 1986. pap. text ed. write for info. (ISBN 0-673-39484-0). Scott F.

Political Thought. Jacob Mayer et al. LC 72-134114. (Essay Index Reprint Ser.). 1939. 26.50 (ISBN 0-8369-1932-7). Ayer Co Pubs.

Political Thought from Plato to NATO. Brian Redhead. 228p. (Orig.). 1987. pap. text ed. 10.00 (ISBN 0-256-06461-X). Dorsey.

Political Thought: From Plato to the Present. Mont J. Harmon. (Political Science Ser.). 1964. text ed. 42.95 (ISBN 0-07-026625-5). McGraw.

Political Thought in America: An Anthology. 2nd ed. Michael B. Levy. 700p. 1987. pap. text ed. 22.00 (ISBN 0-256-06073-8). Dorsey.

Political Thought in Early Meiji Japan, 1868-1889: 1868-1889. Joseph Pittau. LC 65-22065. (Harvard East Asian Ser.: No. 24). pap. 65.30 (ISBN 0-317-09172-7, 2003781). Bks Demand UMI.

Political Thought in England, Eighteen Forty-Eight to Nineteen Fourteen. 2nd ed. Ernest Barker. LC 80-19766. (Home University Library of Modern Knowledge: 104). 256p. 1980. Repr. of 1928 ed. lib. bdg. 35.00x (ISBN 0-313-22216-9, BAPL). Greenwood.

Political Thought in England from Bacon to Halifax. George P. Gooch. LC 75-41115. Repr. of 1955 ed. 18.00 (ISBN 0-404-14754-2). AMS Pr.

Political Thought in France. J. P. Mayer. LC 78-67367. (European Political Thought Ser.). 1979. Repr. of 1943 ed. lib. bdg. 14.00x (ISBN 0-405-11718-3). Ayer Co Pubs.

Political Thought in Hellenistic Times. G. J. Aalders. vi, 132p. (Orig.). 1975. pap. text ed. 32.50x (ISBN 0-317-54492-6, Pub. by A. M. Hakkert). Coronet Bks.

Political Thought in Medieval Islam: An Introductory Outline. Erwin I. Rosenthal. LC 85-21909. ix, 345p. 1985. Repr. of 1958 ed. lib. bdg. 52.50x (ISBN 0-313-25094-4, ROPTH). Greenwood.

Political Thought in Medieval Times. John B. Morrall. (Medieval Academy Reprints for Teaching Ser.). 1980. pap. 5.95c (ISBN 0-8020-6413-2). U of Toronto Pr.

Political Thought of Abraham Lincoln. Richard N. Current. LC 67-30069. 1967. pap. write for info. (ISBN 0-02-326420-9, AHS46). Macmillan.

Political Thought of American Statesmen: Selected Writings & Speeches. Ed. by Morton J. Frisch & Richard G. Stevens. LC 72-89723. 374p. 1973. pap. text ed. 16.95 (ISBN 0-87581-142-6). Peacock Pubs.

Political Thought of Baldus de Ubaldis. (Cambridge Studies in Medieval Life & Thought: Fourth Series: No. 6). 320p. 1987. 49.50 (ISBN 0-521-32521-8). Cambridge U Pr.

Political Thought of G. W. Hegel. Henry Paolucci. 1978. pap. 3.00 (ISBN 0-918680-06-9). Griffon Hse.

Political Thought of Harold J. Laski. G. N. Sarma. 158p. 1984. text ed. 16.95x (ISBN 0-86590-266-6, Sterling Pubs India). Apt Bks.

Political Thought of Ibn Tamiyyah. Qamar-ud-Din Khan. 19.95 (ISBN 0-317-60646-8). Kazi Pubns.

Political Thought of John Locke: An Historical Account of the Argument of the 'Two Treatises of Government' John Dunn. 306p. 1983. pap. 16.95 (ISBN 0-521-27139-8). Cambridge U Pr.

Political Thought of Lord Durham. Janet Ajzenstat. 1988. text ed. 22.95x (ISBN 0-7735-0637-3). McGill-Queens U Pr.

Political Thought of Lord Salisbury, 1854-1868. Michael Pinto-Duschinsky. LC 67-102643. 214p. 1967. 22.50 (ISBN 0-208-00757-1, Archon). Shoe String.

Political Thought of Martin Luther. W. D. Cargill-Thompson. Ed. by Philip Broadhead. LC 83-27521. 204p. 1984. 27.50x (ISBN 0-389-20468-4, 08029). B&N Imports.

Political Thought of Max Weber: In Quest of Statesmanship. Ilse Dronberger. LC 70-133904. (Orig.). 1971. 46.00 (ISBN 0-89197-349-4); pap. text ed. 14.95x (ISBN 0-89197-350-8). Irvington.

Political Thought of Pierre D'Ailly. Francis Oakley. (Yale Historical Pubs. Miscellany Ser.: No. 81). 1964. 75.00x (ISBN 0-685-69849-1). Elliots Bks.

Political Thought of Pierre-Joseph Proudhon. Alan Ritter. LC 80-19558. (Illus.). xii, 222p. 1980. Repr. of 1969 ed. lib. bdg. 29.75x (ISBN 0-313-22719-5, RIPT). Greenwood.

Political Thought of Plato & Aristotle. Ernest Barker. 1959. pap. 9.95 (ISBN 0-486-20521-5). Dover.

Political Thought of Plato & Aristotle. Ernest Barker. 16.25 (ISBN 0-8446-1594-3). Peter Smith.

Political Thought of Samuel Taylor Coleridge. Reginald J. White. LC 78-28086. 1938. lib. bdg. 42.00 (ISBN 0-8414-9706-0). Folcroft.

Political Thought of Thomas G. Masaryk. Roman Szporluk. (East European Monograph: No. 85). 224p. 1981. 24.00x (ISBN 0-914710-79-6). East Eur Quarterly.

Political Thought of William of Ockham. A. S. McGrade. LC 73-86044. (Studies in Medieval Life & Thought). 264p. 1974. Cambridge U Pr.

Political Thought of Woodrow Wilson, 1875-1910. Niels A. Thorsen. (Papers of Woodrow Wilson, Supplementary Volume). 365p. 1988. text ed. 34.50 (ISBN 0-691-04751-0). Princeton U Pr.

Political Thought of Yu. F. Samarin, 1840-1864. Loren D. Calder. Ed. by William H. McNeill & Barbara Jelavich. (Modern European History Ser.). 351p. 1987. lib. bdg. 55.00 (ISBN 0-8240-8052-1). Garland Pub.

Political Tolerance & American Democracy. John L. Sullivan et al. LC 81-16406. 256p. 1982. lib. bdg. 27.50x (ISBN 0-226-77990-4). U of Chicago Pr.

Political Tolerance in Context: Support for Unpopular Minorities in Israel, New Zealand & the United States. Ed. by John L. Sullivan et al. (Replica Edition-Softcover Ser.). 190p. 1985. pap. 27.50x (ISBN 0-86531-851-4). Westview.

Political Tracts of Wordsworth, Coleridge, & Shelly. R. J. White. 1978. Repr. of 1953 ed. lib. bdg. 39.00 (ISBN 0-8492-3038-1). R West.

Political Tracts of Wordsworth, Coleridge & Shelly. Reginald J. White. LC 74-31033. 1953. lib. bdg. 42.00 (ISBN 0-8414-9591-2). Folcroft.

Political Tracts Seventeen Eleven to Seventeen Thirteen. Jonathan Swift. Ed. by Herbert Davis & L. Landa. (Prose Writings of Jonathan Swift Ser.). 248p. 1986. text ed. 60.00x (ISBN 0-631-00230-8). Basil Blackwell.

Political Tracts Seventeen Thirteen to Seventeen Nineteen. Jonathan Swift. Ed. by Herbert Davis & L. Landa. (Prose Writings of Jonathan Swift Ser.). 248p. 1986. text ed. 60.00x (ISBN 0-631-00250-2). Basil Blackwell.

Political Tradition of the West: A Study in the Development of Modern Liberalism. Frederick M. Watkins. LC 82-9157. xiv, 368p. 1982. Repr. of 1948 ed. lib. bdg. 38.50x (ISBN 0-313-23368-3, WAPT). Greenwood.

Political Transformation of Spain after Franco. John F. Coverdale. LC 78-19777. (Praeger Special Studies). 176p. 1979. 40.95 (ISBN 0-275-90343-5, C0343). Praeger.

Political Transformation of the Brazilian Catholic Church. Thomas C. Bruneau. LC 73-79318. (Perspective on Development Ser.: Vol. 2). (gr. 4-7). pap. 71.00 (ISBN 0-317-28009-0, 2025579). Bks Demand UMI.

Political Transitions & Foreign Affairs in Britain & France: Their Relevance for the United States. Don K. Price & Robert H. Evans. Ed. & intro. by Frederick C. Mosher. (Papers on Presidential Transitions in Foreign Policy Ser.: Vol III). 100p. (Orig.). 1986. lib. bdg. 17.50 (ISBN 0-8191-5313-3, Co-pub. by White Miller Center); pap. text ed. 8.25. U Pr of Amer.

Political Trashing. Victor Santoro. LC 87-81102. 160p. (Orig.). 1987. pap. 9.95 (ISBN 0-915179-64-4). Loompanics.

Political Trends in the Arab World: The Role of Ideas & Ideals in Politics. Majid Khadduri. LC 83-12729. xi, 298p. 1983. Repr. of 1970 ed. lib. bdg. 38.50x (ISBN 0-313-24181-3, KHP0). Greenwood.

Political Trends in the Arab World: The Role of Ideas & Ideals in Politics. Majid Khadduri. LC 79-112361. Repr. of 1972 ed. 59.30 (ISBN 0-8357-9281-1, 2016574). Bks Demand UMI.

Political Trials: Gordian Knots in the Law. Ronald S. Christenson. 252p. (Orig.). 1985. 29.95 (ISBN 0-88738-076-X). Transaction Bks.

Political Trials in Poland: Nineteen Eighty-One to Nineteen Eighty-Six. Andrezej Swidlicki. 432p. 1988. lib. bdg. 52.50 (ISBN 0-7099-4444-6, Pub. by Croom Helm UK). Routledge Chapman & Hall.

Political Unconscious: Narrative As a Socially Symbolic Act. Fredric Jameson. LC 80-21459. (Paperback Ser.). 320p. 1982. pap. 9.95x (ISBN 0-8014-9222-X). Cornell U Pr.

Political Unification: A Comparitive Study of Leaders & Forces. Amitai Etzioni. LC 74-12176. 366p. 1974. Repr. of 1965 ed. 18.50 (ISBN 0-88275-196-4). Krieger.

Political Unrest in Upper Canada, 1815-1836. Aileen Dunham. LC 74-3751. 210p. 1975. Repr. of 1927 ed. lib. bdg. 35.00x (ISBN 0-8371-7474-0, DUPU). Greenwood.

Political Untouchables: The Tories & the '45. Eveline Cruickshanks. LC 79-10340. (Illus.). 166p. 1979. 45.00 (ISBN 0-8419-0511-8). Holmes & Meier.

Political Use of the Radio. Thomas Grandin. LC 73-161178. (History of Broadcasting: Radio to Television Ser). 1971. Repr. of 1939 ed. 15.00 (ISBN 0-405-03584-5). Ayer Co Pubs.

Political Uses of International Law. Ann-Sofie Nilsson. 194p. (Orig.). 1987. pap. 34.00x (ISBN 91-7504-083-2, Pub. by Dialogos Sweden). Coronet Bks.

Political Uses of Photography in the Third French Republic, 1871-1914. Donald E. English. Ed. by Diane Kirkpatrick. LC 83-24239. (Studies in Photography: No. 3). 278p. 1984. 42.95 (ISBN 0-8357-1473-X). UMI Res Pr.

Political Uses of Sea Power. Edward N. Luttwak. LC 74-8219. (Washington Center of Foreign Policy Research. Studies in International Affairs: No. 23). pap. 22.50 (2026324). Bks Demand UMI.

Political Uses of Symbols. Charles D. Elder & Roger W. Cobb. Ed. by Irving Rockwood. LC 82-12722. (Professional Studies in Political Communication). (Illus.). 192p. 1983. pap. text ed. 14.95 (ISBN 0-582-28393-0). Longman.

Political Utopianism: Some Philosophical Problems. Amitava Ray. 1979. 11.00x (ISBN 0-8364-0499-8, Minerva India). South Asia Bks.

Political Values & the Educated Class in Africa. Ali A. Mazrui. LC 76-19999. 1978. 42.00x (ISBN 0-520-03292-6). U of Cal Pr.

Political Verse & Song from Britain & Ireland. Mary Asbraf. 1976. 9.95x (ISBN 0-8464-0731-0). Beekman Pubs.

Political Violence. Ted Honderich. LC 76-12816. 128p. 1977. 17.95x (ISBN 0-8014-1017-7). Cornell U Pr.

Political Violence & Terror: Motifs & Motivations. Ed. by Peter H. Merkl. LC 85-24505. 400p. 1986. 37.50x (ISBN 0-520-05605-1). U of Cal Pr.

Political Violence & the Rise of Nazism: The Storm Troopers in Eastern Germany 1925-1934. Richard Bessel. LC 83-40477. 256p. 1984. 24.00x (ISBN 0-300-03171-8). Yale U Pr.

Political Violence, Crisis, & Revolution: Theories & Research. Ekkart Zimmerman. 792p. 1983. pap. text ed. 19.95x (ISBN 0-87073-894-1). Schenkman Bks Inc.

Political Violence in Drama: Classical Models, Contemporary Variations. Mary K. Dahl. Ed. by Oscar Brockett. LC 86-19246. (Theater & Dramatic Studies: No. 36). 174p. 1986. 39.95 (ISBN 0-8357-1754-2); pap. write for info. (ISBN 0-8357-1920-0). UMI Res Pr.

Political Violence in Ireland: Government & Resistance since 1848. Charles Townshend. 445p. 1984. 45.00x (ISBN 0-19-821753-6); pap. 14.95x (ISBN 0-19-820084-6). Oxford U Pr.

Political Violence in the United States, 1875-1974: A Bibliography. Jarol B. Manheim & Melanie Wallace. LC 74-34143. (Reference Library of Social Science: No. 8). 118p. 1974. lib. bdg. 25.00 (ISBN 0-8240-1093-0). Garland Pub.

Political Violence under the Swastika: 581 Early Nazis. Peter H. Merkl. 1975. 80.00x (ISBN 0-691-07561-1); pap. 28.00x (ISBN 0-691-10028-4). Princeton U Pr.

Political Vision of the Divine Comedy. Joan M. Ferrante. LC 82-26906. 400p. 1984. text ed. 39.00x (ISBN 0-691-06603-5). Princeton U pr.

Political Voice: Citizen Demand for Urban Public Services. Philip B. Coulter. LC 86-14617. (Institute for Social Science Research Monographs). (Illus.). 105p. 1988. pap. 14.95 (ISBN 0-8173-0338-3). U of Ala Pr.

Political Voices, No. 1: Interviews with Prominent American Politicians. Jeffrey M. Elliot. LC 81-21643. (Borgo Bioviews Ser.: Vol. 2). 96p. Date not set. lib. bdg. 14.95x (ISBN 0-89370-154-8); pap. text ed. 6.95x (ISBN 0-89370-254-4). Borgo Pr.

Political Women, 2 Vols. Elizabeth Stone. LC 78-112815. 1970. Repr. of 1878 ed. Set. 55.00x (ISBN 0-8046-1082-7, Pub. by Kennikat). Assoc Faculty Pr.

Political Women: Current Roles in State & Local Government. Janet A. Flammang. LC 84-6922. (Yearbooks in Women's Policy Studies: Vol. 8). 320p. 1984. 35.00 (ISBN 0-8039-2139-X); pap. 16.95 (ISBN 0-8039-2140-3). Sage.

Political Women in Japan: The Search for a Place in Political Life. Susan J. Pharr. LC 80-12984. 275p. 1981. 35.00x (ISBN 0-520-04071-6); pap. 8.95x (ISBN 0-520-04453-3). U of Cal Pr.

Political Works of Concealed Authorship: Relating to the United States 1789-1810. 3rd ed. Pierce W. Gaines. LC 76-178861. xx, 226p. 1972. 25.00 (ISBN 0-208-01241-9, Archon). Shoe String.

Political Works of James Harrington. Ed. by J. G. Pocock. LC 75-41712. (Studies in the History and Theory of Politics: No. 27). 1977. 100.00 (ISBN 0-521-21161-1). Cambridge U Pr.

Political World of American Zionism. LC 61-10126. pap. 112.30 (ISBN 0-317-08433-X, 2001332). Bks Demand UMI.

Political Writings. Benjamin Constant. Ed. by Biancamaria Fontana. (Cambridge Texts in the History of Political Thought Ser.). 300p. Date not set. price not set (ISBN 0-521-30336-2); pap. price not set (ISBN 0-521-31632-4). Cambridge U Pr.

Political Writings. Dennis Fonvizin. Tr. by Walter Gleason from Rus. 170p. 1985. 22.50 (ISBN 0-88233-799-8). Ardis Pubs.

Political Writings. George W. Hegel. LC 83-48510. (Philosophy of Hegel Ser.). 342p. 1984. lib. bdg. 40.00 (ISBN 0-8240-5633-7). Garland Pub.

Political Writings. G. W. Leibniz. Ed. by Patrick Riley. (Cambridge Texts in the History of Political Thought Ser.). 214p. Date not set. price not set (ISBN 0-521-35380-7); pap. price not set (ISBN 0-521-35899-X). Cambridge U Pr.

Political Writings, 2 vols. Karl Marx. Ed. by David Fernbach. Incl. Vol. 1. The Revolutions of 1848; Vol. 2. Surveys from Exile. pap. 3.95 (ISBN 0-394-72003-2). 1974. pap. (Vin). Random.

Political Writings. William Morris. Ed. by A. L. Morton. 248p. (Orig.). 1973. pap. 1.95 (ISBN 0-7178-0333-3). Intl Pubs Co.

Political Writings of James Harrington: Representative Selections. James Harrington. Ed. by Charles Blitzer. LC 80-21163. (Library of Liberal Arts: No. 38). xiii, 165p. 1980. Repr. of 1955 ed. lib. bdg. 35.00x (ISBN 0-313-22670-9, HAWR). Greenwood.

TITLE INDEX POLITICS & HEALTH CARE

Political Writings of Joel Barlow with a Bibliographical List Prepared by the Library of Congress, 2 vols. in 1. Joel Barlow. LC 70-135175. 324p. 1972. Repr. of 1796 ed. lib. bdg. 21.00 (ISBN 0-8337-0166-5). B Franklin.
Political Writings of John Adams. John Adams. Ed. by George A. Peek, Jr. LC 54-4998. 1954. pap. 7.87 scp (ISBN 0-672-60010-2). Bobbs.
Political Writings of John Dickinson, 1764-1774. John Dickinson. Ed. by P. L. Ford. LC 70-119061. (Era of the American Revolution). 1970. Repr. of 1895 ed. lib. bdg. 49.50 (ISBN 0-306-71950-9). Da Capo.
Political Writings of John Knox: The First Blast of the Trumpet Against the Monstrous Regiment of Women & Other Selected Works. Ed. by Marvin Breslow. LC 84-47549. 160p. 1985. 23.50 (ISBN 0-918016-75-4). Folger Bks.
Political Writings of Leibniz. G. W. Leibniz. Ed. by Patrick Riley. LC 78-171681. (Cambridge Studies in the History & Theory of Politics). 214p. 1981. pap. 16.95 (ISBN 0-521-28585-2). Cambridge U Pr.
Political Writings of Percy Bysshe Shelley. Percy Bysshe Shelley. Ed. by Roland A. Duerksen. LC 75-102035. (Crofts Classic Ser.). 1970. pap. text ed. 1.95x (ISBN 0-88295-089-4). Harlan Davidson.
Political Writings of Richard Cobden. Richard Cobden. 59.95 (ISBN 0-8490-0875-1). Gordon Pr.
Political Writings of Richard Cobden, 2 Vols in 1. 4th ed. Richard Cobden. LC 4-8568. 1969. Repr. of 1903 ed. 48.00 (ISBN 0-527-18200-1). Kraus Repr.
Political Writings of St. Augustine. Saint Augustine. Ed. by Henry Paolucci. 358p. pap. 9.95 (ISBN 0-89526-941-4). Regnery Gateway.
Political Writings of Thomas Jefferson. Thomas Jefferson. Ed. by Edward Dumbauld. LC 55-2881. 1955. pap. 7.87 scp (ISBN 0-672-60012-9, AHS9). Bobbs.
Political Writings of Viscount Bolingbroke. Bolingbroke. Ed. by Isaac Kramnick. LC 78-91459. (Crofts Classics Ser.). 1970. pap. text ed. 1.25x (ISBN 0-88295-015-0). Harlan Davidson.
Political Writings: The Works of Samuel Johnson, Vol. 10. Samuel Johnson. Ed. by Donald J. Greene. LC 57-11918. (Illus.). 1977. 52.00t (ISBN 0-300-01593-3). Yale U Pr.
Politicalisation of Agricultural Workers in Kerala. Jose George. 1985. 11.50x (ISBN 0-8364-1400-4, Pub. by KP Bagchi India). South Asia Bks.
Politically Mad. Lou Silverstone & Jack Rickard. (Illus.). 1982. pap. 1.95 (ISBN 0-446-30479-4). Warner Bks.
Politically Speaking: Cross-Cultural Studies of Rhetoric. Ed. by Robert Paine. LC 80-25411. 232p. 1981. text ed. 19.95x (ISBN 0-89727-017-7). ISHI PA.
Politician. Robert Welch. LC 64-8456. 6.00 (ISBN 0-686-79638-1); pap. 2.00. Western Islands.
Politician: His Habits. James H. Wallis. LC 73-19183. (Politics & People Ser.). (Illus.). 368p. 1974. Repr. 25.50x (ISBN 0-405-05904-3). Ayer Co Pubs.
Politician, Party & People. Henry C. Emery. 1913. 39.50x (ISBN 0-685-89771-0). Elliots Bks.
Politician: The Life & Times of Lyndon Johnson. Ronnie Dugger. (Illus.). 544p. 1982. 18.95 (ISBN 0-393-01598-X). Norton.
Politicians & Moralists of the Nineteenth Century. facs. ed. Emile Faguet. LC 75-128239. (Essay Index Reprint Ser.). 1928. 19.00 (ISBN 0-8369-1828-2). Ayer Co Pubs.
Politicians & Other Scoundrels. Ferdinand Lundberg. 160p. 1988. pap. 6.95 (ISBN 0-8184-0483-3). Lyle Stuart.
Politicians & Soldiers in Ghana, 1966-1972. Ed. by Dennis Austin & Robin Lucuham. (Studies in Commonwealth Politics & History: No. 3). 332p. 1975. 32.50x (ISBN 0-7146-3049-7, F Cass Co); pap. 9.95x (ISBN 0-7146-4019-0, F Cass Co). Biblio Dist.
Politicians & the War, 1914-1916. Lord W. M. Beaverbrook. LC 68-7857. (Illus.). 556p. 1968. Repr. of 1928 ed. 42.50 (ISBN 0-208-00718-0, Archon). Shoe String.
Politicians & Virtuosi: Essays in Early Modern History. H. G. Koenigsberger. 288p. 1986. 35.00 (ISBN 0-907628-65-6). Hambledon Press.
Politicians, Bureaucrats & the Development Process. Rajinder S. Bakshi. xii, 246p. 1986. text ed. 25.00x (ISBN 81-7027-094-4, Pub. by Radiant Pubs India). Advent NY.
Politicians in Business: A History of Liquor Control System in Montana. Larry D. Quinn. 7.50 (ISBN 0-318-00811-4); pap. 4.95 (ISBN 0-318-00812-2). U of MT Pubns Hist.
Politicians, Judges & City Schools: Reforming School Finance in New York. Joel S. Berke et al. LC 84-60265. 228p. 1985. 25.00x (ISBN 0-87154-108-4). Russell Sage.
Politicians, Judges, & the People: A Study in Citizens' Participation. Charles H. Sheldon & Frank P. Weaver. LC 79-7472. (Contributions in Political Science Ser.: No. 36). 1980. lib. bdg. 35.00x (ISBN 0-313-21492-1, SPJ/). Greenwood.
Politicians, Legislation, & the Economy: An Inquiry into the Interest-Group Theory of Government. Robert E. McCormick & Robert D. Tollison. (Rochester Economics & Public Policy Issue Studies). 160p. 1981. lib. bdg. 20.00 (ISBN 0-89838-058-8, Pub. by Martinus Nijhoff). Kluwer Academic.
Politicians, Planters & Plain Folk: Courthouse & Statehouse in the Upper South, 1850-1860. Ralph A. Wooster. LC 74-32339. pap. 55.00 (ISBN 0-317-29303-6, 2022224). Bks Demand UMI.
Politicians, Poets, & Con Men: Emotional History in Late Victorian America. Burton Raffel. LC 86-1178. xi, 220p. 1986. 24.50 (ISBN 0-208-02067-5, Archon). Shoe String.
Politicisation of Business in Western Europe. Ed. by M. Van Schendelen. R. Jackson. 208p. 1987. lib. bdg. 59.95x (ISBN 0-7099-2632-4, Pub. by Croom Helm UK). Routledge Chapman & Hall.
Politicization of Society. Ed. by Templeton. LC 78-17491. 1979. 10.00 (ISBN 0-913966-48-7, Liberty Pr); pap. 4.50 (ISBN 0-913966-49-5). Liberty Fund.
Politicized Economy. 2nd ed. Michael H. Best & William E. Connolly. 224p. 1982. pap. 11.50 (ISBN 0-669-04005-3). Heath.
Politicized Market Economy: Alcohol in Brazil's Energy Strategy. Michael Barzelay. LC 85-8612. (Studies in International Political Economy: Vol. 14). 1986. text ed. 35.00x (ISBN 0-520-05382-6). U of Cal Pr.
Politico Honesto. Elliot S. Glass. 157p. (Orig.). 1981. 10.00x. SDSU Press.
Politico-Legal India, 5 vols. Shiv Lal. 1986. Set. 1950.00x (ISBN 81-7051-000-7, Pub. by Archives Pubs). State Mutual Bk.
Politicos. Matthew Josephson. LC 38-27301. 760p. 1963. pap. 5.95 (ISBN 0-15-672799-4, Harv). HarBraceJ.
Politics. Aristotle. (Loeb Classical Library: No. 264). 1932. 13.95x (ISBN 0-674-99291-1). Harvard U Pr.
Politics. Aristotle. Tr. by Ernest Barker. (YA) (gr. 9 up). 1946. pap. 8.95x (ISBN 0-19-500306-3). Oxford U Pr.
Politics. Aristotle. Tr. by Carnes Lord from Gr. LC 84-215. (Illus.). vi, 284p. 1984. lib. bdg. 35.00x (ISBN 0-226-02667-1); pap. 10.95 (ISBN 0-226-02669-8). U of Chicago Pr.
Politics. Aristotle. Tr. by William Ellis. LC 86-70378. 250p. 1986. pap. text ed. 4.95 (ISBN 0-87975-346-3). Prometheus Bks.
Politics. Aristotle. Ed. by Stephen Everson. (Cambridge Texts in the History of Political Thought Ser.). 200p. Date not set. price not set (ISBN 0-521-35449-8); pap. price not set (ISBN 0-521-35731-4). Cambridge U Pr.
Politics. Edward I. Koch. 336p. 1986. pap. 4.50 (ISBN 0-446-32300-4). Warner Bks.
Politics. Edward I. Koch & William Rauch. (Illus.). 256p. 1986. 17.95 (ISBN 0-671-53296-0). S&S.
Politics. Roberto M. Unger. write for info. Cambridge U Pr.
Politics, 2 vols. Heinrich G. Von Treitschke. LC 72-970. Repr. of 1916 ed. Set. 60.00 (ISBN 0-404-13141-7). AMS Pr.
Politics, Vols. 1-6, No. 1. 1969. Repr. of 1944 ed. Vol. 1. lib. bdg. 28.00 (ISBN 0-313-21857-9, PL01); Vol. 2. lib. bdg. 28.00 (ISBN 0-313-21858-7, PL02); Vol. 3. lib. bdg. 28.00 (ISBN 0-313-21859-5, PL03); Vols. 4-6. lib. bdg. 28.00 (ISBN 0-313-21860-9, PL04). Greenwood.
Politics: A Handbook for Students. Robert Weissberg. 422p. 1985. pap. text ed. 12.00x net (ISBN 0-15-570740-X, HC). HarBraceJ.
Politics Against Markets: The Social Democratic Road to Power. Gosta Esping-Andersen. 366p. 1988. pap. text ed. 14.95 (ISBN 0-691-02842-7). Princeton U Pr.
Politics against Markets: The Social Democratic Road to Power. Gosta Esping Mandersen. LC 84-42882. 376p. 1985. text ed. 45.00x (ISBN 0-691-09408-X). Princeton U Pr.
Politics among Nations. 6th, rev. ed. Hans J. Morgenthau. Ed. by Kenneth W. Thompson. 688p. 1985. text ed. 23.00 (ISBN 0-394-33564-3, KnopfC). Knopf.
Politics among Nations: The Struggle for Power & Peace. 5th, rev. ed. Hans J. Morgenthau. 1978. text ed. 20.00 (ISBN 0-394-32193-6). Knopf.
Politics among Nations: The Struggle for Power & Peace. Hans J. Morgenthau & Kenneth W. Thompson. Ed. by Ashbel Green. 1985. 37.45 (ISBN 0-394-54101-4). Knopf.
Politics & Administration in Nigeria. Ladipo Adamolekum. 192p. (Orig.). 1986. pap. 10.95 (ISBN 0-09-158091-9, Pub. by Hutchinson Educ). Longwood Pub Group.
Politics & Administration: Woodrow Wilson & American Public Administration. Jack Rabin & James S. Bowman. LC 83-20875. (Public Administration & Public Policy Ser.: No. 21). 1984. 35.00 (ISBN 0-8247-7068-4). Dekker.
Politics & Ambiguity. William Connolly. LC 86-15819. (Rhetoric of the Human Sciences Ser.). 184p. 1987. text ed. 25.00x (ISBN 0-299-10990-9). U of Wis Pr.
Politics & Biomedicine: Subject Analysis & Research Index with Bibliography. John C. Bartone. LC 83-48714. 155p. 1984. 34.50 (ISBN 0-88164-078-6); pap. 26.50 (ISBN 0-88164-079-4). ABBE Pubs Assn.
Politics & Biotechnology: A Checklist of Materials. Lorna Peterson. (Public Administration Ser.: P 2293). 15p. 1987. 3.75 (ISBN 1-55590-573-0). Vance Biblios.
Politics & Budgeting in the World Health Organization. Francis W. Hoole. LC 76-19. (Studies in Development: No. 11). pap. 60.00 (2056230). Bks Demand UMI.
Politics & Change in Al-Karak, Jordan. Peter Gubser. (Westview Encore Edition Ser.). (Illus.). 200p. 1985. pap. 30.50x (ISBN 0-8133-0281-1). Westview.
Politics & Change in Developing Countries: Studies in the Theory & Practice of Development. Ed. by Colin Leys. pap. 75.30 (ISBN 0-317-09390-8, 2051389). Bks Demand UMI.
Politics & Change in Spain. Ed. by Thomas D. Lancaster & Gary Prevost. LC 84-18107. 240p. 1985. 35.00 (ISBN 0-275-90133-5, C0133). Praeger.
Politics & Change in the Middle East: Sources of Conflict & Accommodation. 2nd ed. Roy R. Anderson et al. (Illus.). 336p. 1987. pap. text ed. write for info. (ISBN 0-13-685207-6). P-H.
Politics & Christianity in Malawi 1875-1940. J. McCracken. LC 76-27905. (Cambridge Commonwealth Ser.). (Illus.). 1977. 49.50 (ISBN 0-521-21444-0). Cambridge U Pr.
Politics & Cinema. Andrew Sarris. LC 78-16334. 1978. 27.00x (ISBN 0-231-04034-2). Columbia U Pr.
Politics & Class. N. Woodhead. 1985. 32.00x (ISBN 0-905777-23-9, Pub. by Hesketh UK). State Mutual Bk.
Politics & Class Analysis. Barry Hindess. 192p. (Orig.). Date not set. text ed. 45.00 (ISBN 0-631-15066-8); pap. text ed. 15.95 (ISBN 0-631-15067-6). Basil Blackwell.
Politics & Class Formation in Uganda. Mahmood Mamdani. LC 75-15348. 337p. 1976. 16.50 (ISBN 0-85345-378-0). Monthly Rev.
Politics & Class in Zaire: Bureaucracy, Business, & Beer in Lisala. Michael C. Schatzberg. LC 79-11852. (Illus.). 228p. 1980. 35.00 (ISBN 0-8419-0438-3, Africana). Holmes & Meier.
Politics & Constitution in the History of the United States, 3 vols. W. W. Crosskey & William Jeffrey, Jr. 2040p. 1981. lib. bdg. 140.00x (ISBN 0-226-12134-8). U of Chicago Pr.
Politics & Criminal Prosecution. Raymond Moley. LC 73-19161. (Politics & People Ser.). 256p. 1974. Repr. 18.00x (ISBN 0-405-05883-7). Ayer Co Pubs.
Politics & Cultural Values. Toshio Yatsushiro. Ed. by Roger Daniels. LC 78-54848. (Asian Experience in North America Ser.). 1979. lib. bdg. 46.00x (ISBN 0-405-11299-8). Ayer Co Pubs.
Politics & Culture in Early Modern Europe: Essays in Honour of H. G. Koenigsberger. Ed. by Phyllis Mack & Margaret C. Jacob. (Illus.). 319p. 1987. 49.50 (ISBN 0-521-30197-1). Cambridge U Pr.
Politics & Culture in Renaissance Naples. Jerry H. Bently. (Illus.). 336p. 1987. text ed. 39.50 (ISBN 0-691-05498-3). Princeton U Pr.
Politics & Culture in Wartime Japan. Ben-Ami Shillony. 1981. text ed. 37.00x (ISBN 0-19-821573-8). Oxford U Pr.
Politics & Dependency in the Third World: The Case of Latin America. Ronaldo Munck. (Latin America Ser.). (Illus.). 384p. 1984. 35.50x (ISBN 0-86232-165-4, Pub. by Zed Pr England); pap. 13.95 (ISBN 0-86232-166-2, Pub. by Zed Pr England). Humanities.
Politics & Development. Ed. by Brian Head. 280p. 1987. text ed. 34.95x (ISBN 0-86861-811-X). Unwin Hyman.
Politics & Development of the Federal Income Tax. John F. Witte. LC 84-40506. (Illus.). 464p. 1985. pap. text ed. 25.00x (ISBN 0-299-10200-9); pap. 12.50 (ISBN 0-299-10204-1). U of Wis Pr.
Politics & Economic Growth. Graham Hutton. (Institute of Economic Affairs, Occasional Papers Ser.: No. 23). pap. 2.50 technical (ISBN 0-685-20614-9). Transatl Arts.
Politics & Economic Policy: A Checklist of Current Journal Articles. Dale E. Casper. (Public Administration Ser.: P 2026). 11p. 1986. 3.75 (ISBN 1-55590-046-1). Vance Biblios.
Politics & Economic Policy in the U. K. since 1964: The Jekyll & Hyde Years. Michael Stewart. 1978. pap. text ed. 18.75 (ISBN 0-08-022469-5). Pergamon.
Politics & Economics in Contemporary Japan: Eleven Essays in Structure & Function. Ed. by Hyoe Murakami & Johannes Hirschmeier. LC 83-80228. (Illus.). 244p. 1983. pap. 6.50 (ISBN 0-87011-612-6). Kodansha.
Politics & Economics of Appeasement: British Foreign Policy in the 1930's. Gustav Schmidt. LC 85-32109. 464p. 1986. 37.50x (ISBN 0-312-62617-7). St Martin.
Politics & Economics of Columbia River Water. Ed. by Charles F. Broches & Michael S. Spranger. LC 85-11506. (Orig.). 1985. pap. 10.00 (ISBN 0-934539-02-2, WSG-WO). Wash Sea Grant.
Politics & Economics of External Debt Crisis: The Latin American Experience. Miguel S. Wionczek. 300p. 1985. pap. 49.00x (ISBN 0-86531-797-6). Westview.
Politics & Economics of Organized Crime. Herbert E. Alexander & Gerald E. Caiden. LC 84-48376. 192p. 1984. 27.00x (ISBN 0-669-09342-4). Lexington Bks.
Politics & Economics of Public Policy: An Introductory Analysis: with Cases. Grover Starling. LC 78-60557. (Dorsey Series in Political Science). pap. 160.00 (ISBN 0-317-27986-6, 2055814). Bks Demand UMI.
Politics & Economics Policy: From Hoover to Reagan. William Withers. 1986. 10.95 (ISBN 0-8062-2722-2). Carlton.
Politics & Economics, 1982-1986. Dale E. Casper. (Public Administration Ser.: P 2243). 10p. 1987. 3.00 (ISBN 1-55590-483-1). Vance Biblios.
Politics & Education: Cases from Eleven Nations. Ed. by R. Murray Thomas. 330p. 1983. text ed. 52.00 (ISBN 0-08-028905-3); pap. text ed. 22.00 (ISBN 0-08-028904-5). Pergamon.
Politics & Ethics: Machiavelli to Niebuhr. Erwin A. Gaede. LC 83-19751. 168p. (Orig.). 1984. lib. bdg. 25.50 (ISBN 0-8191-3603-4); pap. text ed. 11.25 (ISBN 0-8191-3604-2). U Pr of Amer.
Politics & Ethics of Evaluation. Ed. by Clem Adelman. LC 83-40173. 160p. 1984. 22.50 (ISBN 0-312-62619-3). St Martin.
Politics & Ethics of Fieldwork. Maurice Punch. (Qualitative Research Methodology Ser.: No. 3). 96p. 1985. text ed. 12.50 (ISBN 0-8039-2562-X); pap. text ed. 6.00 (ISBN 0-8039-2517-4). Sage.
Politics & Ethnicity on the Rio Yaqui: Potam Revisited. Thomas R. McGuire. (PROFMEX Ser.). 186p. 1986. 19.95x (ISBN 0-8165-0893-3). U of Ariz Pr.
Politics & Exegesis: Origen & the Two Swords. Gerard E. Caspary. LC 77-71058. 1979. 42.00x (ISBN 0-520-03445-7). U of Cal Pr.
Politics & Experience: Essays Presented to Professor Michael Oakeshott on the Occasion of His Retirement. Ed. by Preston T. King & B. C. Parekh. LC 68-24482. pap. 108.50 (ISBN 0-317-27557-7, 2024509). Bks Demand UMI.
Politics & Finance in the Eighteenth Century. Lucy Sutherland. 550p. 1984. 45.00 (ISBN 0-907628-46-X). Hambledon Press.
Politics & Force Levels: The Strategic Missile Program of the Kennedy Administration. Desmond J. Ball. LC 78-57302. 400p. 1981. 45.00x (ISBN 0-520-03698-0). U of Cal Pr.
Politics & Foreign Policy in Australia: The Impact of Vietnam & Conscription. Henry S. Albinski. LC 76-101128. Repr. of 1970 ed. 45.60 (ISBN 0-8357-9114-9, 2017878). Bks Demand UMI.
Politics & Freedom: Human Will & Action in the Thought of Hannah Arendt. Gabriel M. Tlaba. 224p. (Orig.). 1987. lib. bdg. 24.75 (ISBN 0-8191-6468-2); pap. text ed. 12.75 (ISBN 0-8191-6469-0). U Pr of Amer.
Politics & Government: A Brief Introduction to the United States, Great Britain, Canada, France, Germany, U. S. S. R., Yugoslavia, China, Japan, Mexico, & the Third World. 2nd ed. Alex N. Dragnich et al. LC 87-7990. 256p. 1987. pap. 12.95x (ISBN 0-934540-43-8). Chatham Hse Pubs.
Politics & Government: How People Decide Their Fate. 3rd ed. Karl W. Deutsch. LC 79-90262. (Illus.). 1980. text ed. 39.96 (ISBN 0-395-28486-4); instr's. manual 2.00 (ISBN 0-395-28487-2). HM.
Politics & Government in African States. Peter Duignan & Robert H. Jackson. 442p. 1987. text ed. 36.95 (ISBN 0-8179-8481-X, Co-Pub. by Croom Helm); pap. 20.95 (ISBN 0-8179-8482-8, Co-Pub. by Croom Helm). Hoover Inst Pr.
Politics & Government in Britain. 2nd ed. Tom Brennan. LC 82-4145. (Illus.). 352p. 1982. pap. 16.95 (ISBN 0-521-28600-X). Cambridge U Pr.
Politics & Government in California. 11th ed. Bernard L. Hyink et al. 256p. 1985. pap. text ed. 17.95 scp (ISBN 0-06-043041-9, HarpC). Har-Row.
Politics & Government in Japan. 3rd ed. Theodore McNelly. (Illus.). 284p. 1985. pap. text ed. 10.25 (ISBN 0-8191-4359-6). U Pr of Amer.
Politics & Government in the Federal Republic of Germany: Basic Documents. Ed. by Carl-Christof Schweitzer et al. LC 83-40293. 444p. 1984. pap. 15.95 (ISBN 0-907582-13-3, Pub. by Berg Pubs). St Martin.
Politics & Government in the Federal Republic of Germany: Basic Documents. Ed. by Carl-Christof Schweitzer et al. LC 83-40293. 464p. 1984. 37.50 (ISBN 0-312-62622-3). St Martin.
Politics & Government in Turkey. Clement H. Dodd. LC 78-85453. 351p. pap. 91.30 (2029951). Bks Demand UMI.
Politics & Grass: The Administration of Grazing on the Public Domain. Phillip O. Foss. LC 75-90508. (Illus.). ix, 236p. 1970. Repr. of 1960 ed. lib. bdg. 35.00 (ISBN 0-8371-2136-1, FOPG). Greenwood.
Politics & Health Care. Ed. by John B. McKinlay. (Milbank Readers Ser.: No. 6). 368p. 1982. pap. text ed. 13.95x (ISBN 0-262-63082-6). MIT Pr.
Politics & Health Care Organization: HMOS's Federal Policy. Lawrence D. Brown. LC 81-70466. 540p. 1983. 36.95 (ISBN 0-8157-1158-1); pap. 16.95 (ISBN 0-8157-1157-3). Brookings.

Politics & History. Raymond Aron. Ed. by Miriam B. Conant. 304p. 1984. pap. 14.95 (ISBN 0-87855-944-2). Transaction Bks.

Politics & History in Band Societies. Ed. by Eleanor B. Leacock & Richard B. Lee. (Illus.). 368p. 1982. pap. 20.95 (ISBN 0-521-28412-0). Cambridge U Pr.

Politics & History: Selected Essays. Raymond Aron. Ed. by Miriam B. Conant. LC 78-54122. 1978. 24.95 (ISBN 0-02-901000-4). Free Pr.

Politics & Human Nature. Ian Forbes & Steve Smith. LC 83-42531. 250p. 1983. 29.95 (ISBN 0-312-62625-8). St Martin.

Politics & Ideology. James Donald & Stuart Hall. 288p. 1985. 65.00x (ISBN 0-335-15099-3, Open Univ Pr); pap. 21.00x (ISBN 0-335-15098-5). Taylor & Francis.

Politics & Ideology in England, 1603-1640. Johann P. Sommerville. 254p. (Orig.). 1986. pap. text ed. 13.95 (ISBN 0-582-49432-X). Longman.

Politics & Ideology in the Age of the Civil War. Eric Foner. LC 80-13024. 1980. 22.95x (ISBN 0-19-502781-7). Oxford U Pr.

Politics & Ideology in the Age of the Civil War. Eric Foner. 1980. pap. 8.95x (ISBN 0-19-502926-7). Oxford U Pr.

Politics & Innocence: A Humanistic Debate. Rollo May et al. LC 85-155385. 223p. 1986. 15.95 (ISBN 0-933071-00-0, Dist. by W. W. Norton). Saybrook Pub Co.

Politics & Intergovernmental Relations in Brazil--1964-1982. A. C. De Medeiros. (Outstanding Theses from the London School of Economics & Political Science Ser.). 475p. 1987. lib. bdg. 75.00 (ISBN 0-8240-1927-X). Garland Pub.

Politics & Jewish Purpose. Michael Selzer. 45p. 1972. pap. 2.50 (ISBN 0-934676-12-7). Greenlf Bks.

Politics & Jurisprudence. Paul Woelfl. LC 65-26035. (Orig.). 1966. pap. 2.95 (ISBN 0-8294-0083-4). Loyola.

Politics & Language in Dryden's Poetry. Steven N. Zwicker. LC 84-4255. (Illus.). 265p. 1984. text ed. 28.00x (ISBN 0-691-06618-3). Princeton U Pr.

Politics & Language: Spanish & English in the United States. Ed. by D. J. Bruckner. (Orig.). 1980. pap. 4.00x (ISBN 0-686-28732-0). U Chi Ctr Policy.

Politics & Law in South Africa: Essays on Race Relations. Julius Lewin. pap. 29.00 (ISBN 0-317-11029-2, 2001695). Bks Demand UMI.

Politics & Letters. T. H. Escott. 1973. Repr. of 1886 ed. 35.00 (ISBN 0-8274-1682-2). R West.

Politics & Literature. G. D. Cole. LC 73-1577. 1973. Repr. of 1929 ed. lib. bdg. 17.00 (ISBN 0-8414-1806-3). Folcroft.

Politics & Literature. Jean-Paul Sartre. 12.95 (ISBN 0-7145-0823-3). Riverrun NY.

Politics & Management of Restraint in Government. Peter Aucoin. 254p. 1981. pap. text ed. 17.95x (ISBN 0-920380-32-8, Pub. by Inst Res Pub Canada). Brookfield Pub Co.

Politics & Markets: The World's Political-Economic Systems. Charles E. Lindblom. LC 77-75250. 403p. 1980. pap. 12.95x (ISBN 0-465-05958-9, TB-5045). Basic.

Politics & Media. Renata Adler. 224p. 1988. 16.95 (ISBN 0-312-01817-7). St Martin.

Politics & Method: Contrasting Studies in Industrial Geography. Ed. by Doreen Massey & Richard Meegan. 200p. pap. 13.95 (ISBN 0-317-19448-8, 9123). Routledge Chapman & Hall.

Politics & Modernization in South & Southeast Asia. Ed. by Robert N. Kearney. LC 74-13637. (States & Societies of the Third World Ser.). 277p. 1975. 16.50x (ISBN 0-470-46232-9). Halsted Pr.

Politics & Nationalist Awakening in South India, 1852-1891. R. Suntharalingam. LC 73-93408. (Association for Asian Studies Monograph: No. 27). 396p. 1974. 7.95x (ISBN 0-8165-0447-4). U of Ariz Pr.

Politics & Nuclear Power: Energy Policy in Western Europe. Michael T. Hatch. LC 85-29545. 232p. 1986. 22.00x (ISBN 0-8131-1583-3). U Pr of Ky.

Politics & Oil: Moscow in the Middle East. Lincoln Landis. LC 72-148702. (Illus.). 350p. 1973. 22.95x (ISBN 0-8046-7029-3, Pub. by Kennikat). Assoc Faculty Pr.

Politics & Paradigms: Changing Theories of Change in Social Science. Andrew C. Janos. 200p. 1986. 28.50x (ISBN 0-8047-1332-4); pap. 10.95x (ISBN 0-8047-1333-2). Stanford U Pr.

Politics & Parentela in Paraiba: A Case Study of Family-Based Oligarchy in Brazil. Linda Lewin. LC 86-42850. (Illus.). 392p. 1987. text ed. 52.50 (ISBN 0-691-07719-3). Princeton U Pr.

Politics & Participation under Communist Rule. Ed. by Peter J. Potichnyj et al. LC 82-15082. 304p. 1983. 38.95 (ISBN 0-275-91060-1, C1060). Praeger.

Politics & Patronage in the Gilded Age: The Correspondence of James A. Garfield & Charles E. Henry. Ed. by James D. Norris & Arthur H. Shaffer. LC 70-629850. (Illus.). 304p. 1970. 15.00 (ISBN 0-87020-107-7). State Hist Soc Wis.

Politics & People, 58 bks. Ed. by Leon Stein. 1974. 1483.50x set (ISBN 0-405-05850-0). Ayer Co Pubs.

Politics & People in Revolutionary England: Essays in Honor of Ivan Roots. Ed. by Colin Jones et al. 320p. 1986. text ed. 49.95 (ISBN 0-631-14613-X). Basil Blackwell.

Politics & Personalities, with Other Essays. facs. ed. George W. E. Russell. (Essay Index Reprint Ser). 1917. 20.00 (ISBN 0-8369-0844-9). Ayer Co Pubs.

Politics & Personality Seventeen Sixty to Eighteen Twenty-Seven. Ed. by Michael J. Barnes. LC 68-97214. (Selections from History Today Ser.: No. 6). (Illus.). 1967. 10.95 (ISBN 0-686-85915-4); pap. 7.95 (ISBN 0-05-001535-4). Dufour.

Politics & Philosophy in the Thought of Destutt de Tracy. Brian W. Head. Ed. by Maurice Cranston. (Political Theory & Political Philosophy Ser.). 450p. 1987. lib. bdg. 65.00 (ISBN 0-8240-0819-7). Garland Pub.

Politics & Philosophy of Economics: Marxians, Keynesians, & Austrians. T. W. Hutchinson. 240p. 1981. 40.00x (ISBN 0-8147-3416-2); pap. 15.00x (ISBN 0-8147-3423-5). NYU Pr.

Politics & Planners: Economic Development Policy in Central America. Gary W. Wynia. 240p. 1972. 27.50x (ISBN 0-299-06210-4). U of Wis Pr.

Politics & Planning: A National Study of American Planners. Michael L. Vasu. LC 78-10440. (Institute for Research in Social Science Ser.). xv, 236p. 1979. 22.50x (ISBN 0-8078-1342-7). U of NC Pr.

Politics & Poetic Value. Ed. by Robert Von Hallberg. 360p. 1987. 35.00x (ISBN 0-226-86495-2); pap. 14.95 (ISBN 0-226-86496-0). U of Chicago Pr.

Politics & Poetics of Transgression. Peter Stallybrass & Allon White. LC 85-48241. (Paperback Ser.). 224p. 1986. 29.95x (ISBN 0-8014-1893-3); pap. 12.95x (ISBN 0-8014-9382-X). Cornell U Pr.

Politics & Poetry. Tarquinio Vallese. 1979. Repr. of 1927 ed. lib. bdg. 29.50 (ISBN 0-8495-5526-4). Arden Lib.

Politics & Poetry in Restoration England: The Case of Dryden's Annus Mirabilis. Michael McKeon. 322p. 1975. text ed. 24.50x (ISBN 0-674-68755-8). Harvard U Pr.

Politics & Poetry (Political Influence on English Poetry) Tarquinio Vallese. LC 76-40951. 1974. Repr. of 1937 ed. lib. bdg. 29.50 (ISBN 0-8414-9177-1). Folcroft.

Politics & Policies in Divided Korea: Regimes in Contest, 1845-1983. Young Whan Kihl. 330p. 1983. 42.50x (ISBN 0-86531-700-3); pap. text ed. 18.95x (ISBN 0-86531-701-1). Westview.

Politics & Policy. Erwin C Hargrove & Michael Nelson. 320p. 1984. pap. text ed. 11.00 (ISBN 0-394-33006-4). Knopf.

Politics & Policy Implementation in the Third World. Ed. by Merilee S. Grindle. LC 79-3213. 1980. pap. 10.95x (ISBN 0-691-02195-3). Princeton U Pr.

Politics & Policy in States & Communities. 2nd ed. John J. Harrigan. 1984. text ed. write for info. (ISBN 0-673-39443-3). Scott F.

Politics & Policy in States & Communities. 3rd ed. John J. Harrigan. 1988. text ed. write for info. (ISBN 0-673-39725-4). Scott F.

Politics & Policy in the European Community. Stephen George. LC 84-27315. 1985. 27.95x (ISBN 0-19-876164-3); pap. 12.95x (ISBN 0-19-876165-1). Oxford U Pr.

Politics & Policy in Traditional Korea, 1864-1876. James B. Palais. (East Asian Monographs). 288p. 1976. text ed. 21.00x (ISBN 0-674-19058-0). Harvard U Pr.

Politics & Policy-Making in Finland: A Study of a Small Democracy in a West European Outpost. David Arter. LC 87-9575. 267p. 1987. 45.00 (ISBN 0-312-00901-1). St Martin.

Politics & Policy: The Eisenhower, Kennedy, & Johnson Years. James L. Sundquist. LC 68-31837. 560p. 1968. 28.95 (ISBN 0-8157-8222-5). Brookings.

Politics & Policy: The Genesis & Theology of Social Statements in the Lutheran Church in America. Ed. by Christa Klein. LC 88-45242. 224p. 1989. 19.95 (ISBN 0-8006-0898-4). Fortress.

Politics & Political Leadership in Goa. Sarto Esteves. 1987. text ed. 27.50x (ISBN 81-207-0602-1, Pub. by Sterling Pubs India). Apt Bks.

Politics & Poverty: Modernization & Response in Five Poor Neighborhoods. Stanley B. Greenberg. LC 73-10273. (Wiley Series in Urban Research). pap. 75.30 (ISBN 0-317-09220-0, 2051329). Bks Demand UMI.

Politics & Power in a Slave Society: Alabama, 1800-1860. J. Mills Thornton. LC 77-4296. (Illus.). xxiv, 492p. 1978. 40.00 (ISBN 0-8071-0259-8); pap. 12.95x (ISBN 0-8071-0891-X). La State U Pr.

Politics & Primary Medical Care: Dehumanization & Overutilization. Zeev Ben-Sira. 232p. 1988. text ed. 44.40 (ISBN 0-566-05566-X, Pub. by Gower Pub England). Gower Pub Co.

Politics & Privilege in a Mexican City. Richard R. Fagen & William S. Tuohy. xiv, 210p. 1972. 7.95x (ISBN 0-8047-0809-6). Stanford U Pr.

Politics & Process in the Specialized Agencies of the United Nations. Houshang Ameri. 304p. 1982. text ed. 48.00x (ISBN 0-566-00538-7). Gower Pub Co.

Politics & Process of American Government. Getz & Feigert. 608p. 1982. text ed. write for info. (ISBN 0-697-06798-X); instr's. manual avail. (ISBN 0-697-06799-8). Wm C Brown.

Politics & Progress: The Rise of Urban Progressivism in Baltimore, 1895 to 1911. James B. Crooks. LC 68-21805. pap. 70.30 (ISBN 0-317-30010-5, 2051877). Bks Demand UMI.

Politics & Protestant Theology: An Interpretation of Tillich, Barth, Bonhoeffer, & Brunner. Rene De Visme Williamson. LC 76-20817. x, 180p. 1976. 22.50 (ISBN 0-8071-0193-1). La State U Pr.

Politics & Public Administration in Hungary. Ed. by Gyorgy Szoboszlai. Tr. by Eva Ernold et al from Hungarian. 496p. 1985. 39.95x (ISBN 963-05-4205-6, Pub. by Akademiai Kaido Hungary). Humanities.

Politics & Public Policy. Van Horn et al. 350p. 1988. price not set (ISBN 0-87187-481-4). Congr Quarterly.

Politics & Public Policy in Indiana. William P. Hojnacki. 216p. 1983. pap. text ed. 15.75 (ISBN 0-8403-2974-1). Kendall-Hunt.

Politics & Public Policy in Kenya & Tanzania. rev. ed. Ed. by Joel D. Barkan & John J. Okumu. 394p. 1984. 38.95 (ISBN 0-275-91124-1, C1124); pap. 15.95 (ISBN 0-275-91599-9, B1599). Praeger.

Politics & Public Policy in Latin America. Steven W. Hughes & Kenneth J. Mijeski. 240p. 1985. 39.50x (ISBN 0-8133-0040-1); pap. text ed. 17.95x (ISBN 0-8133-0041-X). Westview.

Politics & Punishment: The History of the Louisiana State Penal System. Mark T. Carleton. LC 78-165067. xii, 216p. 1971. pap. 14.95x (ISBN 0-8071-1219-4). La State U Pr.

Politics & Purges in China: Rectification & the Decline of Party Norms, 1950-1965. Frederick Teiwes. LC 79-51182. Repr. of 1979 ed. 160.00 (2027625). Bks Demand UMI.

Politics & Religious Consciousness in America. George A. Kelly. LC 83-9284. 312p. 1983. 34.95 (ISBN 0-87855-484-X). Transaction Bks.

Politics & Remembrance: Republican Themes in Machiavelli, Burke, Tocqueville. Bruce J. Smith. Ed. by Marshall Cohen. LC 84-15946. 288p. 1985. text ed. 30.50x (ISBN 0-691-07681-2). Princeton U Pr.

Politics & Rhetoric of Scientific Method. Ed. by John A. Schuster & Richard R. Yeo. 1986. lib. bdg. 64.50 (ISBN 90-277-2152-1, Pub. by Reidel Holland). Kluwer Academic.

Politics & Ritual in Early Medieval Europe. Janet L. Nelson. 440p. 1986. 40.00 (ISBN 0-907628-59-1). Hambledon Press.

Politics & Rural Society: The Southern Massif Central, c. 1750-1880. Peter Jones. 388p. 1985. 54.50 (ISBN 0-521-25797-2). Cambridge U Pr.

Politics & Security in the Southern Region of the Atlantic Alliance. Ed. by Douglas T. Stuart. LC 86-21081. 256p. 1988. text ed. 29.50x (ISBN 0-8018-3483-X). Johns Hopkins.

Politics & Sexual Equality: The Comparative Position of Women in Western Democracies. Pippa Norris. LC 87-9465. 176p. 1987. lib. bdg. 25.00x (ISBN 1-55587-072-4). Lynne Rienner.

Politics & Sinology: The Case of Naito Konan (1866-1934) Joshua A. Fogel. (Harvard East Asian Monographs: No. 114). 1984. text ed. 20.00x (ISBN 0-674-68790-6). Harvard U Pr.

Politics & Social Change in East Germany: An Evaluation of Socialist Democracy. C. Bradley Scharf. (Westview Special Studies on the Soviet Union & Eastern Europe). 215p. 1984. 35.50x (ISBN 0-89158-945-7); pap. text ed. 16.95x (ISBN 0-86531-451-9). Westview.

Politics & Social Change in Latin America: The Distinct Tradition. 2nd, rev. ed. Ed. by Howard J. Wiarda. LC 81-16022. 384p. pap. text ed. 12.95x (ISBN 0-87023-333-5). U of Mass Pr.

Politics & Social Change in Modern Britain. P. J. Waller. LC 87-14014. 256p. 1987. 29.95 (ISBN 0-312-01251-9). St Martin.

Politics & Social Conflict in South India: The Non-Brahman Movement & Tamil Separatism, 1916-1929. Eugene F. Irschick. LC 69-31595. (Center for South & Southeast Asia Studies, UC Berkeley: No. 3). (Illus.). 1969. 40.00x (ISBN 0-520-00596-1). U of Cal Pr.

Politics & Social Forces in Chilean Development. James Petras. 1969. 37.50x (ISBN 0-520-01463-4). U of Cal Pr.

Politics & Social Structure in Latin America. James Petras. LC 73-122737. 384p. 1970. pap. 5.95 (ISBN 0-85345-195-8). Monthly Rev.

Politics & Social Theory. Ed. by Peter Lassman. 240p. 1988. pap. text ed. 15.95 (ISBN 0-415-01799-8). Routledge Chapman & Hall.

Politics & Social Welfare Policy in the United States. Robert X Browning. LC 85-17837. 220p. 1986. text ed. 18.95x (ISBN 0-87049-486-4). U of Tenn Pr.

Politics & Society in Britain: An Introduction. Michael Moran. LC 85-11718. 272p. 1985. 27.50 (ISBN 0-312-62629-0). St Martin.

Politics & Society in Contemporary France. Ed. by Ezra N. Suleiman. 186p. (Orig.). 1977. pap. text ed. 4.00x (ISBN 0-87855-679-6). Transaction Bks.

Politics & Society in Early Modern Iraq. Tom Nieuwenhuis. 1982. lib. bdg. 33.00 (ISBN 90-247-2576-3, Pub. by Martinus Nijhoff Netherlands). Kluwer Academic.

Politics & Society in Eastern Europe. Joni Lovenduski & Jean Woodall. LC 87-3682. (Illus.). 488p. 1987. 45.00x (ISBN 0-253-34546-4); pap. 14.50x (ISBN 0-253-28603-4). Ind U Pr.

Politics & Society in Israel. Ed. by Ernest Krausz. (Studies of Israeli Society: Vol. III). 400p. 1984. text ed. 29.95x (ISBN 0-88738-012-3); pap. text ed. 9.95x. Transaction Bks.

Politics & Society in Post-war Naples. P. A. Allum. LC 75-174259. pap. 106.50 (ISBN 0-317-26136-3, 2024408). Bks Demand UMI.

Politics & Society in Reformation Europe. Ed. by Tom Scott & E. I. Kouri. 500p. 1987. 45.00 (ISBN 0-312-00537-7). St Martin.

Politics & Society in the South. Earl Black & Merle Black. LC 86-18421. (Illus.). 384p. 1987. text ed. 25.00x (ISBN 0-674-68958-5). Harvard U Pr.

Politics & Society in the Third World. Jean-Yves Calvez. Tr. by Matthew J. OConnell from Fr. LC 72-85792. 256p. (Orig.). 1973. pap. 3.48 (ISBN 0-88344-389-9). Orbis Bks.

Politics & Society in Twentieth Century Spain. Stanley G. Payne. LC 75-38923. (Modern Scholarship on European History Ser.). 1976. pap. text ed. 8.95 (ISBN 0-531-05588-4, Dist. by M & B Fulfillment). Wiener Pub Inc.

Politics & Society in Western Europe. Jan-Erik Lane & Svante Ersson. 352p. 1987. text ed. 39.95 (ISBN 0-8039-8008-6); pap. text ed. 16.50 (ISBN 0-8039-8009-4). Sage.

Politics & Society on Colonial America. 2nd ed. Michael G. Kammen. LC 78-13376. 160p. 1978. pap. text ed. 6.50 (ISBN 0-88275-747-4). Krieger.

Politics & Sociology in the Thought of Max Weber. Anthony Giddens. (Studies in Sociology). 64p. 1972. pap. 8.50x (ISBN 0-333-13436-2). Humanities.

Politics & Statecraft in the Kingdom of Greece. John A. Petropulos. LC 66-21837. 1968. 50.00x (ISBN 0-691-05144-5). Princeton U Pr.

Politics & Statesmanship: Essays on the American Whig Party. Thomas Brown. LC 84-15601. 328p. 1985. 36.00x (ISBN 0-231-05602-8). Columbia U Pr.

Politics & Strategy in the Second World War: Germany, Great Britain, Japan, the Soviet Union & the United States. Ed. by Arthur L. Funk. 113p. 1976. pap. text ed. 4.50x (ISBN 0-89126-024-2). MA-AH Pub.

Politics & Structure: Essentials of America National Government. 4th ed. Thomas G. Ingersoll & Robert E. O'Connor. LC 85-20939. (Government Ser.). 200p. 1985. pap. 10.50 pub net (ISBN 0-534-05844-2). Brooks-Cole.

Politics & Technology in the Soviet Union. Bruce Parrott. 440p. 1985. pap. text ed. 12.50x (ISBN 0-262-66054-7). MIT Pr.

Politics & Television Re-Viewed. Ed. by Kurt Lang & Gladys E. Lang. LC 84-11637. 223p. 1984. 28.00 (ISBN 0-8039-2345-7); pap. 14.00 (ISBN 0-8039-2346-5). Sage.

Politics & Territory: The Sociology of Regional Persistence in Canada. Mildred A. Schwartz. 360p. 1974. 32.95x (ISBN 0-7735-0166-5). McGill-Queens U Pr.

Politics & the Academy: Arnold Toynbee & the Koraes Chair. Richard Clogg. 128p. 1986. 30.00x (ISBN 0-7146-3290-2, F Cass Co). Biblio Dist.

Politics & the American Future. John J. Harrigan. (Illus.). 608p. 1984. pap. text ed. write for info (ISBN 0-394-34946-6, RanC); write for info (ISBN 0-394-34948-2). Random.

Politics & the American Future. 2nd ed. John J. Harrigan. 612p. 1987. pap. text ed. write for info. (ISBN 0-394-36148-2, RanC). Random.

Politics & the Appointment of Justices of the Peace: 1675-1720. Lionel K. Glassey. (Historical Monographs). 1979. 37.00x (ISBN 0-19-821875-3). Oxford U Pr.

Politics & the Arts: Letter to M. D'Alembert on the Theatre. Jean-Jacques Rousseau. Tr. by Allan Bloom. (Agora Paperback Ed.). 196p. 1968. pap. 8.95x (ISBN 0-8014-9071-5). Cornell U Pr.

Politics & the Biblical Drama. Richard J. Mouw. 1983. pap. 5.95 (ISBN 0-8010-6153-9). Baker Bk.

Politics & the Budget: The Struggle Between the President & the Congress. Howard E. Shuman. (Illus.). 320p. 1984. pap. text ed. 24.00 (ISBN 0-13-684341-7). P-H.

Politics & the Budget: The Struggle Between the President & the Congress. 2nd ed. Howard E. Shuman. (Illus.). 352p. 1988. pap. text ed. 22.67 (ISBN 0-13-684416-2). P-H.

Politics & the Bureaucracy: Policy Making in the Fourth Branch of Government. 2nd ed. Kenneth J. Meier. LC 86-1437. (Political Science Ser.). 225p. 1986. pap. text ed. 10.50 (ISBN 0-534-06990-8). Brooks-Cole.

Politics & the Christian Vision. Clifford. Date not set. pap. 10.95 (Pub. by SCM Pr England). Fortress.

Politics & the Churches in Great Britain 1869 to 1921. G. I. Machin. LC 87-1620. 400p. 1987. 72.00 (ISBN 0-19-820106-0). Oxford U Pr.

Politics & the Churches in Great Britain, 1832-1868. G. I. Machin. 1977. 57.00x (ISBN 0-19-826436-4). Oxford U Pr.

Politics & the Constitution in the History of the United States: Vol. III, The Political Background of the Federal Convention. William W. Crosskey & William Jeffrey, Jr. LC 53-7433. 1981. lib. bdg. 35.00x (ISBN 0-226-12138-0). U of Chicago Pr.

Politics in the First World War. A. J. Taylor. (Raleigh Lectures on History). 1959. pap. 5.50 (ISBN 0-85672-135-2, Pub. by British Acad). Longwood Pub Group.

Politics in the Gilded Age, in New York State & Rockland County: A Biography of Clarence Lexow. Isabelle K. Savell. (Illus.). 1984. 12.50. Rockland County Hist.

Politics in the Golden State: The California Connection. 2nd ed. Terry Christensen & Larry N. Gerston. 1988. pap. text ed. write for info. (ISBN 0-673-39713-0). Scott F.

Politics in the Media Age. R. Berkman & L. Kitch. 400p. 1986. pap. text ed. 21.95 (ISBN 0-07-004882-7). McGraw.

Politics in the Middle East. 2nd ed. James A. Bill et al. 1983. write for info. (ISBN 0-673-39423-9). Scott F.

Politics in the Poetry of Coleridge. Carl R. Woodring. LC 61-11643. Repr. of 1961 ed. 68.00 (ISBN 0-8357-9778-3, 2015374). Bks Demand UMI.

Politics in the Post Welfare State: Responses to the New Individualism. Ed. by M. Donald Hancock & Gideon Sjoberg. LC 79-165181. 335p. 1972. 35.00x (ISBN 0-231-03127-0). Columbia U Pr.

Politics in the Reign of Charles II. K. H. Haley. (Historical Association Studies). 96p. 1985. pap. 6.95x (ISBN 0-631-13928-1). Basil Blackwell.

Politics in the Semi-Periphery: Early Parliamentarism & Late Industrialization in the Balkans & Latin America. Nicos P. Mouzelis. LC 84-27738. 320p. 1986. 32.50 (ISBN 0-312-62886-2). St Martin.

Politics in the Soviet Union: From Brezhnev to Gorbachev. (Chambers Political Spotlights Ser.). 138p. 1988. pap. 8.95 (ISBN 0-550-20745-7, Pub. by W & R Chambers). Cambridge U Pr.

Politics in the Tokugawa Bakufu, 1600-1843. Conrad Totman. LC 67-22873. (East Asian Ser.: No. 30). (Illus.). 1967. 17.50x (ISBN 0-674-68800-7). Harvard U Pr.

Politics in the Tokugawa Bakufu, 1600-1843. Conrad Totman. 368p. (Orig.). 1988. pap. 12.95 (ISBN 0-520-06313-9). U of Cal Pr.

Politics in the Twentieth Century, 3 vols. Hans J. Morgenthau. Incl. Vol. 1. The Decline of Democratic Politics. pap. 110.80 (ISBN 0-317-10505-1); Vol. 2. The Impasse of American Foreign Policy. pap. 80.00 (ISBN 0-317-10506-X); Vol. 3. The Restoration of American Politics. 100.30 (ISBN 0-317-10507-8). LC 62-18111. pap. (2020126). Bks Demand UMI.

Politics in the Twentieth Century. abr. ed. Hans W. Morgenthau. LC 70-148581. 1971. pap. 4.95x (ISBN 0-226-53825-7, P425, Phoen). U of Chicago Pr.

Politics in the U. S. A. 3rd ed. M. J. Vile. (Illus.). 288p. 1984. pap. 10.95 (ISBN 0-09-151571-8, Pub. by Hutchinson Educ). Longwood Pub Group.

Politics in the United Nations: A Study of United States Influence in the General Assembly. Robert E. Riggs. LC 83-20164. vi, 207p. 1984. Repr. of 1958 ed. 38.50x (ISBN 0-313-24298-4, RIP0). Greenwood.

Politics in the United Nations: A Study of United States Influence in the General Assembly. Robert E. Riggs. (Social Studies Ser.: No. 41). 216p. 1958. 19.95 (ISBN 0-252-72609-X). U of Ill Pr.

Politics in the United Nations System after Forty Years. Ed. by Lawrence S. Finkelstein. LC 87-27240. xvi, 503p. 1988. lib. bdg. 65.00 (ISBN 0-8223-0804-5); pap. text ed. 22.50 (ISBN 0-8223-0820-7). Duke.

Politics in the United States: From Carter to Reagan. (Chambers Political Spotlights Ser.). 138p. 1988. pap. 8.95 (ISBN 0-550-20741-4, Pub. by W & R Chambers). Cambridge U Pr.

Politics in the U. S. S. R. 3rd ed. Frederick C. Barghoorn & Thomas Remington. 1986. pap. text ed. write for info. (ISBN 0-673-39420-4). Scott F.

Politics in Three Worlds: An Introduction to Political Science. P. Best & K. Rai. 475p. 1985. write for info. (ISBN 0-02-309190-8); write for info. tchr's manual (ISBN 0-02-309240-8). Macmillan.

Politics in War: The Bases of Political Community in South Vietnam. Allan E. Goodman. LC 72-96629. 328p. 1973. 22.50x (ISBN 0-674-68825-2). Harvard U Pr.

Politics in West Africa. William A. Lewis. LC 81-13317. (Whidden Lectures for 1965 Ser.). 90p. 1982. Repr. of 1970 ed. lib. bdg. 35.00x (ISBN 0-313-23202-4, LEPW). Greenwood.

Politics in West German. Russell J. Dalton. 1989. pap. text ed. price not set (ISBN 0-673-39887-0). Scott F.

Politics in West Germany: From Schmidt to Kohl. (Chambers Political Spotlights Ser.). 138p. 1988. pap. 8.95 (ISBN 0-550-20740-6, Pub. by W & R Chambers). Cambridge U Pr.

Politics in Western Europe. Ed. by Gerald Dorfman & Peter Duignan. 1988. pap. 16.95 (ISBN 0-8179-8602-2). Hoover Inst Pr.

Politics in Western Europe: A Comparative Analysis. 4th ed. Gordon R. Smith. 350p. 1984. 35.50 (ISBN 0-8419-0964-4); pap. 18.50x (ISBN 0-8419-0965-2). Holmes & Meier.

Politics in Western Europe: France, Germany, Italy, Sweden & the United Kingdom. M. Donald Hancock. (Illus.). 384p. 1989. pap. text ed. 14.95x (ISBN 0-934540-30-6). Chatham Hse Pubs.

Politics in Wisconsin. Leon D. Epstein. 233p. 1958. 21.50x (ISBN 0-299-01730-3). U of Wis Pr.

Politics: Individual & State. Robert G. Wesson. 336p. 1988. text ed. price not set (ISBN 0-13-684309-3). P-H.

Politics Is a Funny Business. Joel Rothman. (Illus.). 78p. 1985. pap. 2.95 (ISBN 0-86051-233-9). Parkwest Pubns.

Politics Is Adjourned see Woodrow Wilson & the War Congress, 1916-18.

Politics Is for People. Shirley Williams. LC 81-80916. 224p. 1981. 17.50x (ISBN 0-674-68910-0). Harvard U Pr.

Politics Is My Parish: An Autobiography. Brooks Hays. LC 80-29144. (Illus.). 291p. 1981. 30.00 (ISBN 0-8071-0798-0). La State U Pr.

Politics, Language, & Thought: The Somali Experience. David D Laitin. LC 76-22958. (Illus.). 1977. lib. bdg. 23.00x (ISBN 0-226-46791-0). U of Chicago Pr.

Politics, Law & Ritual in Tribal Society. Max Gluckman. (Illus.). 376p. 1965. pap. 14.95 (ISBN 0-631-08750-8). Basil Blackwell.

Politics, Law, & Social Change: Selected Essays. Otto Kircheimer. Ed. by Frederic S. Burin & Kurt L. Shell. LC 69-16955. (Records of Civilization Ser.). 483p. 1969. 35.00x (ISBN 0-231-03191-2). Columbia U Pr.

Politics Mainly Indian. W. H. Morris-Jones. 1978. 18.00x (ISBN 0-8364-0161-1). South Asia Bks.

Politics Mainly Indian. W. H. Morris-Jones. 392p. 1978. 19.95. Asia Bk Corp.

Politics, Minerals, & Survival. Ed. by Ralph W. Marsden. LC 74-27310. 104p. 1975. 17.50x (ISBN 0-299-06810-2); pap. 9.95x (ISBN 0-299-06814-5). U of Wis Pr.

Politics: National & International. Prem Bhasin. 1970. 13.50 (ISBN 0-686-20285-6). Intl Bk Dist.

Politics of a Colonial Career: Jose Baquijano & the Audiencia of Lime. Mark A. Burkholder. LC 80-52279. pap. 51.30 (ISBN 0-317-55622-3, 2029322). Bks Demand UMI.

Politics of a Literary Man: William Gilmore Simms. Jon L. Wakelyn. LC 72-845. (Contributions in American Studies: No. 5). 256p. 1973. lib. bdg. 35.00 (ISBN 0-8371-6414-1, WPL/). Greenwood.

Politics of a Prison Riot. Adolph Saenz. (Illus.). 190p. (Orig.). 1986. pap. 8.50 (ISBN 0-936455-00-4). Rhombus Pub.

Politics of Abortion. Raymond Tatalovich et al. 1981. 38.95 (ISBN 0-275-90730-9, C0730). Praeger.

Politics of Accommodation: German Social Democracy & the Catholic Church, 1945-1959. Paul R. Waibel. (European University Studies: No. 31, Vol. 35). 161p. 1983. pap. 23.15 (ISBN 3-8204-7270-3). P Lang Pubs.

Politics of Administrative Alienation in India's Rural Development Programme. James W. Bjorkman. 1979. 14.00x (ISBN 0-8364-0341-X). South Asia Bks.

Politics of Adoption. Mary K. Benet. LC 76-14287. 1976. 14.95 (ISBN 0-02-902500-1). Free Pr.

Politics of Afghanistan. Richard S. Newell. Ed. by Richard L. Park. LC 78-176487. 254p. 1972. 32.50x (ISBN 0-8014-0688-9). Cornell U Pr.

Politics of African & Middle Eastern States: An Annotated Bibliography. Anne G. Drabek & Wilfred Knapp. LC 76-26649. 1977. 34.00 (ISBN 0-08-020584-4); pap. 16.25 (ISBN 0-08-020583-6). Pergamon.

Politics of Africa's Economic Stagnation. Richard Sandbrook & Judith Barker. (African Society Today Ser.). 208p. 1985. 34.50 (ISBN 0-521-26587-8); pap. 11.95 (ISBN 0-521-31961-7). Cambridge U Pr.

Politics of Aging among Elder Hispanics. Fernando M. Torres-Gil. LC 82-16067. 230p. (Orig.). 1983. pap. text ed. 13.25 (ISBN 0-8191-2757-4). U Pr of Amer.

Politics of Aging: Power & Policy. John B. Williamson et al. (Illus.). 350p. 1982. 38.25 (ISBN 0-398-04608-5). C C Thomas.

Politics of Agricultural Mechanization in China. Benedict Stavis. LC 77-90916. (Illus.). 320p. 1978. 32.50x (ISBN 0-8014-1087-8). Cornell U Pr.

Politics of Agricultural Policy-making in Canada. Grace D. Skogstad. 229p. 1987. 30.00 (ISBN 0-8020-5728-4). U of Toronto Pr.

Politics of Agricultural Research. Don F. Hadwiger. LC 81-24077. x, 230p. 1982. 21.00x (ISBN 0-8032-2322-6). U of Nebr Pr.

Politics of Agriculture in Tropical Africa. Jonathan Barker. LC 84-2013. (Sage Series on African Modernization & Development: Vol. 9). 1984. 29.95 (ISBN 0-8039-2295-7). Sage.

Politics of Airline Deregulation. Anthony E. Brown. LC 86-25125. 240p. 1987. lib. bdg. 22.95x (ISBN 0-87049-532-1). U of Tenn Pr.

Politics of Alcoholism: Building An Arena Around a Social Problem. Carolyn Wiener. LC 79-66450. 310p. 1981. 25.95 (ISBN 0-87855-379-7). Transaction Bks.

Politics of Alienation in Assam. Bhawani Singh. 1985. 11.50x (ISBN 0-8364-1521-3, Pub. by Ajanta). South Asia Bks.

Politics of Alternative Technology. David Dickson. LC 75-7919. 224p. 1975. pap. 8.00x (ISBN 0-87663-224-X). Universe.

Politics of Alternative Technology. David Dickson. LC 75-7919. 1977. pap. 4.50x (ISBN 0-87663-917-1). Universe.

Politics of American Cities: Private Power & Public Policy. 2nd ed. Dennis R. Judd. 1984. pap. text ed. 17.50 (ISBN 0-673-39453-0). Scott F.

Politics of American Cities: Private Power & Public Policy. 3rd ed. Dennis R. Judd. 1988. pap. text ed. write for info. (ISBN 0-673-39730-0). Scott F.

Politics of American Democracy. 7th ed. Marion D. Irish et al. (Illus.). 544p. 1981. text ed. write for info. (ISBN 0-13-685156-8). P-H.

Politics of American Economic Policy Making. Ed. by Paul Peretz. 480p. 1987. text ed. 37.50 (ISBN 0-87332-406-4); pap. text ed. 14.95 (ISBN 0-87332-407-2). M E Sharpe.

Politics of American English. David Simpson. 256p. 1986. 27.00x (ISBN 0-19-503724-3). Oxford U Pr.

Politics of American English, 1776-1850. David Simpson. 256p. 1988. pap. 10.95 (ISBN 0-19-505643-4). Oxford U Pr.

Politics of American Foreign Policy. James Dull. (Illus.). 1985. pap. text ed. 26.00 (ISBN 0-13-684291-7). P-H.

Politics of American Foreign Policy: The Social Contexts of Decisions. M. Berkowitz et al. (Illus.). 1977. pap. text ed. write for info. (ISBN 0-13-685073-1). P-H.

Politics of American Individualism: Herbert Hoover in Transition, 1918-1921. Gary D. Best. LC 75-16960. 202p. 1975. lib. bdg. 35.00 (ISBN 0-8371-8160-7, BPA/). Greenwood.

Politics of American National Government. 5th ed. David C. Saffell. 1983. pap. text ed. write for info. (ISBN 0-673-39477-8); tchr's. manual avail.; study guide avail. (ISBN 0-673-39478-6). Scott F.

Politics of American Naval Rearmament, 1930-1938. Ed. by Frank Feidel & Ernest May. (Harvard Dissertations in American History & Political Science Ser.). 496p. 1988. lib. bdg. 80.00 (ISBN 0-8240-5135-1). Garland Pub.

Politics of American Science: 1939 to the Present. rev. ed. Ed. by James L. Penick et al. 480p. 1972. pap. 6.95x (ISBN 0-262-66014-8). MIT Pr.

Politics of an Emerging Profession: The American Library Association, 1876-1917. Wayne A. Wiegand. LC 85-12679. (Contributions in Librarianship & Information Science Ser.: No. 56). (Illus.). 332p. 1986. lib. bdg. 40.95 (ISBN 0-313-25022-7, WPD/). Greenwood.

Politics of An Erasmian Lawyer: Vasco de Quiroga. Ross Dealy. (Humana Civilitas Ser.: Vol.3). 34p. 1976. pap. 3.90x (ISBN 0-89003-015-4). Undena Pubns.

Politics of Annexation: Oligarchic Power in a Southern City. John V. Moeser & Rutledge M. Dennis. 232p. 1982. 18.95 (ISBN 0-87073-501-2); pap. 11.95 (ISBN 0-87073-502-0). Schenkman Bks Inc.

Politics of Anthropology: From Colonialism & Sexism Toward a View from Below. Ed. by Gerrit Huizer & Bruce Mannheim. (World Anthropology Ser.). xii, 520p. 1979. text ed. 61.50 (ISBN 90-279-7750-X). Mouton.

Politics of Antipolitics: The Military in Latin America. Ed. by Brian Loveman & Thomas M. Davies, Jr. LC 77-25256. x, 309p. 1978. pap. 7.50x (ISBN 0-8032-7900-0, BB 672, Bison). U of Nebr Pr.

Politics of Anxiety: Sellafield's Cancer-Link Controversy. Sally MacGill. 209p. 1987. text ed. 28.95x (ISBN 0-85086-127-6, Pub. by Pion England). Routledge Chapman & Hall.

Politics of Aristocratic Empires. John H. Kautsky. LC 81-12983. xvi, 416p. 1982. 32.50x (ISBN 0-8078-1502-0). U of NC Pr.

Politics of Aristotle, 4 vols. Aristotle. LC 72-9297. (Philosophy of Plato & Aristotle Ser.). (Gr. & Eng.). Repr. of 1902 ed. Set. 154.00 (ISBN 0-405-04848-3); 38.50 ea. Vol.1 (ISBN 0-405-04849-1). Vol.2 (ISBN 0-405-04850-5). Vol.3 (ISBN 0-405-04851-3). Vol.4 (ISBN 0-405-04852-1). Ayer Co Pubs.

Politics of Aristotle. facsimile ed. Aristotle. LC 75-13363. (History of Ideas in Ancient Greece Ser.: Bks. 1-5). (Gr. & Eng.). 1976. Repr. of 1894 ed. 39.00x set (ISBN 0-405-07291-0). Ayer Co Pubs.

Politics of Arms Control: The Role & Effectiveness of the U. S. Arms Control & Disarmament Agency. Duncan L. Clarke. LC 79-1955. 1979. 22.95 (ISBN 0-02-905700-0). Free Pr.

Politics of ASEAN Economic Co-operation: The Case of ASEAN Industrial Projects. Marjorie L. Suriyamongkol. (Illus.). 368p. 1988. 39.95 (ISBN 0-19-588874-X). Oxford U Pr.

Politics of Assimilation: Hegemony & Its Aftermath. Charles F. Doran. LC 77-148241. pap. 59.30 (ISBN 0-317-20650-8, 2024137). Bks Demand UMI.

Politics of Assimilation: The French Jewish Community at the Time of the Dreyfus Affair. Michael R. Marrus. (Illus.). 1980. pap. 19.95x (ISBN 0-19-822591-1). Oxford U Pr.

Politics of Association in Europe. John N. Kinnas. 122p. 1982. 14.95x (ISBN 3-593-32371-0). Irvington.

Politics of Attraction: Four Middle Powers & the United States. Annette B. Fox. LC 76-27291. (Institute of War & Peace Studies). 371p. 1977. 31.00x (ISBN 0-231-04116-0). Columbia U Pr.

Politics of Baby Foods: Successful Challenges to International Marketing Strategies. Andrew Chetley. LC 85-303000063. 200p. 1986. 27.50 (ISBN 0-312-62633-9). St Martin.

Politics of Backwardness in Hungary, 1825-1945. A. C. Janos. 1981. 38.00x (ISBN 0-691-07633-2); pap. 17.50x (ISBN 0-691-10123-X). Princeton U Pr.

Politics of Balanced Interdependence: Nepal & SAARC. Lok Raj Baral. 148p. 1988. text ed. 22.50x (ISBN 81-207-0784-2, Pub. by Sterling Pubs India). Apt Bks.

Politics of Banking. George S. Eccles. Ed. by Sidney Hyman. 320p. 1982. pap. 13.00 (ISBN 0-87480-209-1). U of Utah Pr.

Politics of Banking: The Strange Case of Competition & Credit Control. Michael Moran. LC 83-16068. 256p. 1984. 27.50 (ISBN 0-312-62635-5). St Martin.

Politics of "Basic Needs" Urban Aspects of Assaulting Poverty in Africa. Richard Sandbrook. 320p. 1982. 30.00x (ISBN 0-8020-2428-9); pap. 12.95c (ISBN 0-8020-6439-6). U of Toronto Pr.

Politics of Being Mortal. Alfred G. Killilea. 188p. 1988. 21.00 (ISBN 0-8131-1643-0). U Pr of Ky.

Politics of Belgium: Crisis & Compromise in a Plural Society. John Fitzmaurice. LC 82-24056. 300p. 1983. 25.00x (ISBN 0-312-62639-8). St Martin.

Politics of Belief in Nineteenth-Century France. Philip Spencer. LC 77-80592. 284p. 1973. Repr. of 1954 ed. 29.50x (ISBN 0-86527-156-9). Fertig.

Politics of Benevolence: Revival Religion & American Voting Behavior. John L. Hammond. LC 78-16050. 256p. 1979. 39.50x (ISBN 0-89391-013-9). Ablex Pub.

Politics of Bhutan. Leo E. Rose. LC 77-4792. 304p. 1977. 35.00x (ISBN 0-8014-0909-8). Cornell U Pr.

Politics of Black Migration: Gold Mining & the State in Southern Africa, 1920-1987. Jonathan Crush et al. (African Modernization & Development Ser.). 240p. 1988. pap. 31.50 (ISBN 0-8133-7417-0). Westview.

Politics of Bonaire. A. Klomp. Tr. by D. H. van der Elst from Dutch. 240p. 1986. pap. 17.50 (ISBN 90-232-2181-8, Pub. by Van Gorcum Holland). Longwood Pub Group.

Politics of Brazilian Development, 1930-1954. John D. Wirth. 1970. 27.50x (ISBN 0-8047-0710-3). Stanford U Pr.

Politics of British Foreign Policy in the Era of Disraeli & Gladstone. Marvin Swartz. LC 84-17696. 220p. 1985. 27.50 (ISBN 0-312-62645-2). St Martin.

Politics of Broadcast Regulation. 3rd ed. Erwin G. Krasnow & Lawrence D. Longley. LC 81-51850. 304p. 1982. pap. text ed. write for info. (ISBN 0-312-62654-1). St Martin.

Politics of Broadcasting: An International Survey. Ed. by Raymond Kuhn. LC 84-15996. 224p. 1985. 25.00 (ISBN 0-312-62660-6). St Martin.

Politics of Bureaucracy. Gordon Tullock. 1964. 6.00 (ISBN 0-8183-0192-9). Pub Aff Pr.

Politics of Bureaucracy. Gordon Tullock. 232p. 1987. pap. text ed. 11.75 (ISBN 0-8191-5814-3, Pub. by G Mason U Pr). U Pr of Amer.

Politics of Bureaucracy: A Comparative Analysis. B. Guy Peters. LC 77-24584. (Comparative Studies of Political Life). (Illus.). 1983. text ed. 33.95 (ISBN 0-582-28317-5); pap. text ed. 17.95 (ISBN 0-582-28316-7). Longman.

Politics of Bureaucratic Reform: The Case of the California State Employment Service. Michael B. Preston. LC 83-6980. 216p. 1984. 16.95 (ISBN 0-252-01048-5). U of Ill Pr.

Politics of Business in California, 1890-1920. Mansel G. Blackford. LC 76-27319. 235p. 1977. 12.50x (ISBN 0-8142-0259-4). Ohio St U Pr.

Politics of California Coastal Legislation: The Crucial Year, 1976. Peverill Squire & Stanley Scott. LC 84-715. 104p. 1984. pap. 3.95 (ISBN 0-87772-298-6). UCB IGS.

Politics of Canadian Airport Development: Lessons for Federalism. Elliot J. Feldman & Jerome Milch. LC 82-18343. (Duke Press Policy Studies, Commonwealth & Comparative Studies: No. 47). xix, 261p. 1983. 29.95 (ISBN 0-8223-0479-1). Duke.

Politics of Canadian Broadcasting, 1920-1951. Frank W. Peers. LC 78-430275. pap. 118.50 (ISBN 0-317-55707-6, 2029342). Bks Demand UMI.

Politics of Canadian Foreign Policy. Kim R. Nossal. 224p. 1985. pap. text ed. write for info. (ISBN 0-13-684325-5). P-H.

Politics of Canadian Public Policy. Ed. by Michael M. Atkinson & Marsha A. Chandler. 296p. 1983. 30.00x (ISBN 0-8020-2485-8); pap. 14.95c (ISBN 0-8020-6517-1). U of Toronto Pr.

Politics of Capital Investment: The Case of Philadelphia. Carolyn T. Adams. (Urban Public Policy Ser.). 1988. 39.50 (ISBN 0-88706-847-2); pap. 12.95 (ISBN 0-88706-848-0). State U NY Pr.

Politics of Caring. Susan B. Foster. 176p. 1987. 36.00x (ISBN 1-85000-233-9, Pub. by Falmer Pr); pap. 16.00x (ISBN 1-85000-232-0). Taylor & Francis.

Politics of Change: A Jamaican Testament. Michael Manley. LC 74-34066. 1975. 11.95 (ISBN 0-88258-049-3); pap. 6.95 (ISBN 0-88258-060-4). Howard U Pr.

Politics of Change & Leadership Development: New Leaders in India & Africa. Ed. by Anthony DeSouza. 1978. 15.00x (ISBN 0-8364-0192-1). South Asia Bks.

Politics of Change in a Zambian Community. George C. Bond. LC 75-12228. (Illus.). 232p. 1976. lib. bdg. 18.00x (ISBN 0-226-06408-5). U of Chicago Pr.

Politics of Change in Venezuela, 3 vols. Frank Bonilla & Jose A. Silva-Michelena. Incl. Vol. 1. Strategy for Research on Social Policy. 1967; Vol. 2. Failure of Elites. 1970. 35.00x (ISBN 0-262-02058-0); Vol. 3. Illusion of Democracy in Dependent Nations. 1971. 32.50x (ISBN 0-262-19069-9). MIT Pr.

Politics of Chicano Liberation. Ed. by Olga Rodriguez. 1977. 16.00 (ISBN 0-87348-513-0); pap. 5.95 (ISBN 0-87348-514-9). Path Pr NY.

Politics of Child Abuse. Nigel Parton. LC 84-26276. 288p. 1985. 29.95 (ISBN 0-312-62675-4). St Martin.

Politics of Chinese Communism: Kiangi under Soviet Rule. Ilpyong Kim. LC 73-76101. (Center for Chinese Studies: No. 12). 1974. 35.00x (ISBN 0-520-02438-9). U of Cal Pr.

Politics of City-County Merger: The Lexington-Fayette County Experience. W. E. Lyons. LC 77-73706. (Illus.). 192p. 1977. 17.00x (ISBN 0-8131-1363-6). U Pr of Ky.

Politics of City Revenue. Arnold J. Meltsner. LC 70-129610. (Oakland Project Ser.). 1971. 33.00x (ISBN 0-520-01812-5); pap. 10.95x (ISBN 0-520-02773-6). U of Cal Pr.

Politics of Civil Rights in the Truman Administration. William C. Berman. LC 70-114736. 273p. 1970. 8.00 (ISBN 0-8142-0142-3). Ohio St U Pr.

Politics of Clean Air: EPA Standards for Coal Burning Power Plants. Elizabeth H. Haskell. LC 81-13863. 224p. 1982. 35.00 (ISBN 0-275-90816-X, C0816). Praeger.

Politics of Coalition Rule in Colombia. Jonathan Hartlyn. (Cambridge Latin American Studies: No. 66). (Illus.). 352p. Date not set. 42.50 (ISBN 0-521-34055-1). Cambridge U Pr.

Politics of Colombia. Robert H. Dix. LC 86-21168. 265p. 1986. lib. bdg. 38.95 (ISBN 0-275-92315-0, C2315). Praeger.

Politics of Command in the American Revolution. Jonathan G. Rossie. 272p. 1975. 16.95x (ISBN 0-8156-0112-3). Syracuse U Pr.

Politics of Communication. Claus Mueller. 1973. 19.95x (ISBN 0-19-501720-X). Oxford U Pr.

Politics of Community Action. Jan O'Malley. 180p. 40.00x (ISBN 0-85124-184-0, Pub. by Bertrand Russell Hse); pap. 16.25x (ISBN 0-85124-183-2). State Mutual Bk.

Politics of Community Conflict: The Fluoridation Decision. Robert L. Crain et al. LC 68-31777. 1969. pap. text ed. 3.95x (ISBN 0-672-60840-5). Irvington.

Politics of Community: Migration & Politics in Antebellum Ohio. Kenneth J. Winkle. (Interdisciplinary Perspective on Modern History Ser.). (Illus.). 200p. 1988. 32.50 (ISBN 0-521-34372-0). Cambridge U Pr.

Politics of Compassion: A Biblical Perspective on World Hunger, the Arms Race & U. S. Policy in Central America. Jack Nelson-Pallmeyer. LC 85-25809. 128p. (Orig.). 1986. pap. 8.95 (ISBN 0-88344-356-2). Orbis Bks.

Politics of Compassion & Transformation. Dick Simpson. 350p. 1988. text ed. 29.95x (ISBN 0-8040-0903-1); pap. 15.95x (ISBN 0-8040-0904-X). Ohio U Pr.

Politics of Comprehensive Manpower Legislation. Roger H. Davidson. LC 72-10874. (Policy Studies in Employment & Welfare: No. 15). pap. 32.00 (ISBN 0-317-19878-5, 2023092). Bks Demand UMI.

Politics of Compromise: State & Religion in Israel. Ervin Birnbaum. LC 70-92557. 348p. 1970. 27.50 (ISBN 0-8386-7567-0). Fairleigh Dickinson.

Politics of Confrontation. Ed. by Samuel Hendel. LC 75-148865. 1971. pap. text ed. 12.95x (ISBN 0-89197-893-3). Irvington.

Politics of Congo-Brazzaville. Rene Gauze. Tr. by Virginia Thompson & Richard Adloff. LC 73-75886. (Publications Ser.: No. 129). (Illus.). 283p. 1973. 10.95x (ISBN 0-8179-6291-3). Hoover Inst Pr.

Politics of Congress. 5th ed. David J. Vogler. 348p. 1988. pap. text ed. write for info. (ISBN 0-697-06813-7). Wm C Brown.

Politics of Congressional Elections. 2nd ed. Gary C. Jacobson. 1987. pap. text ed. 12.00 (ISBN 0-673-39449-2). Scott F.

Politics of Conscience. Albert N. Keim & Grant M. Stoltzfus. 192p. (Orig.). 1987. pap. 14.95 (ISBN 0-8361-1295-4). Herald Pr.

Politics of Conscience: T. H. Green & His Age. Melvin Richter. LC 83-3509. (Illus.). 425p. 1983. pap. text ed. 17.75 (ISBN 0-8191-2685-3). U Pr of Amer.

Politics of Consent. Francis Pym. 256p. 1984. 20.95 (ISBN 0-241-11351-2, Pub. by Hamish Hamilton England). David & Charles.

Politics of Consumer Protection. Mark Nadel. LC 78-170712. (Policy Analysis Ser.). 1971. pap. 9.08 scp (ISBN 0-672-61223-2). Bobbs.

Politics of Continuity: Maryland Political Parties from 1858 to 1870. Jean H. Baker. LC 72-12354. (Goucher College Ser.). (Illus.). 254p. 1973. 27.50x (ISBN 0-8018-1418-9). Johns Hopkins.

Politics of Contraception: Birth Control in the Year 2001. Carl Djerassi. LC 81-5460. (Illus.). 282p. 1981. pap. 13.95 (ISBN 0-7167-1342-X). W H Freeman.

Politics of Corruption: Organized Crime in an American City. John A. Gardiner. LC 79-107958. 130p. 1970. 12.50x (ISBN 0-87154-299-4). Russell Sage.

Politics of Cotton Textiles in Kuomintang China, 1927-1937: China During the Interregnum 1911-1949, the Economy & Society. Richard C. Bush. Ed. by Ramon H. Myers. LC 80-8836. 360p. 1982. lib. bdg. 36.00 (ISBN 0-8240-4691-9). Garland Pub.

Politics of Crime & Conflict: A Comparative History of Four Cities. Ted R. Gurr et al. LC 76-45429. pap. 160.00 (ISBN 0-317-29676-0, 2021910). Bks Demand UMI.

Politics of Crime & Criminal Justice. Erika Fairchild & Vincent J. Webb. LC 84-27590. 1985. 25.00 (ISBN 0-8039-2423-2); pap. 12.95 (ISBN 0-8039-2424-0). Sage.

Politics of Crisis Reporting: Learning to Be a Foreign Correspondent. John C. Pollock. LC 81-15350. (Praeger Special Studies). 240p. 1981. 38.95 (ISBN 0-275-90703-1, C0703). Praeger.

Politics of Critique. Dick Howard. 224p. (Orig.). 1988. 35.00x (ISBN 0-8166-1681-7); pap. 14.95 (ISBN 0-8166-1682-5). U of Minn Pr.

Politics of Cultural Despair: A Study in the Rise of the Germanic Ideology. Fritz R. Stern. 1961. 38.50x (ISBN 0-520-02643-8); pap. 10.95x (ISBN 0-520-02626-8). U of Cal Pr.

Politics of Cultural Nationalism in South India. M. R. Barnett. 1976. 47.00x (ISBN 0-691-07577-8). Princeton U Pr.

Politics of Cultural Pluralism. Crawford Young. LC 74-27318. (Illus.). .574p. 1976. 35.00x (ISBN 0-299-06740-8); pap. 13.50x (ISBN 0-299-06744-0). U of Wis Pr.

Politics of Culture. George Buchanan. 1977. 4.00 (ISBN 0-685-04167-0, Pub. by Menard Pr). Small Pr Dist.

Politics of Culture & Other Essays. Roger Scruton. 245p. 1981. 17.50 (ISBN 0-85635-362-0). Carcanet.

Politics of Culture: Proceedings, Vol. 5. Pacific Coast Council on Latin American Studies, 1976. Ed. by Robert Smetherman. LC 77-83497. 191p. (Orig.). 1977. pap. 10.00 (ISBN 0-916304-28-0). SDSU Press.

Politics of Daylight Time. Fred W. Zuercher. 1966. 1.00 (ISBN 1-55614-081-9). U of SD Gov Res Bur.

Politics of De-Industrialisation: The Contraction of the West European Shipbuilding Industry. Bo Strath. 320p. 1987. lib. bdg. 57.50x (ISBN 0-7099-5401-8, Pub. by Croom Helm UK). Routledge Chapman & Hall.

Politics of Decolonization: Kenya Europeans & the Land Issue, 1960-1965. Gary Wasserman. LC 75-2735. (African Studies Ser.: No. 17). 235p. pap. 61.10 (2030628). Bks Demand UMI.

Politics of Defeat: Campaigning for Congress. Robert J. Huckshorn & Robert C. Spencer. LC 71-123538. 272p. 1971. 20.00x (ISBN 0-87023-082-4); pap. 10.95x (ISBN 0-87023-078-6). U of Mass Pr.

Politics of Defense Budgeting: A Study of Organisation & Resource Allocations in the United Kindom & the United States. Michael P. Hobkirk. LC 83-600596. (Illus.). 179p. 1983. pap. 5.50 (S/N 008-020-00968-7). USGPO.

Politics of Defense Contracting: The Iron Triangle. Gordon Adams. 465p. 1981. pap. 15.00 (ISBN 0-87871-012-4). CEP.

Politics of Democracy. Pendleton Herring. (Illus.). 1965. pap. 2.95x (ISBN 0-393-00306-X, Norton Lib). Norton.

Politics of Democracy: American Parties in Action. P. Herring. (Illus.). 11.25 (ISBN 0-8446-2246-X). Peter Smith.

Politics of Democratic Socialism. Evan F. Durbin. LC 71-83799. 1969. Repr. of 1940 ed. 39.50x (ISBN 0-678-06513-6). Kelley.

Politics of Dependency: Urban Reform in Istanbul. Steven T. Rosenthal. LC 79-7588. (Contributions in Comparative Colonial Studies: No. 3). (Illus.). 1980. lib. bdg. 56.95 (ISBN 0-313-20927-8, RPO/). Greenwood.

Politics of Depression in France, Nineteen Thirty-Two to Nineteen Thirty-Six. Julian Jackson. 336p. 1985. 44.50 (ISBN 0-521-26559-2). Cambridge U Pr.

Politics of Deregulation. Martha Derthick & Paul J. Quirk. LC 85-16602. 265p. 1985. 28.95 (ISBN 0-8157-1818-7); pap. 10.95 (ISBN 0-8157-1817-9). Brookings.

Politics of Deterrence: American & Soviet Defense Policies Compared, 1960-1964. Paul M. Kozar. LC 87-42512. 175p. 1987. lib. bdg. 24.95x (ISBN 0-89950-274-1). McFarland & Co.

Politics of Developed Socialism: The Soviet Union As a Post-Industrial State. Donald R. Kelley. LC 85-30562. (Contributions in Political Science Ser.: No. 149). (Illus.). 226p. 1986. lib. bdg. 40.92 (ISBN 0-313-25243-2, KPD/). Greenwood.

Politics of Development: An Introduction to Global Issues. John L. Seitz. (Illus.). 220p. (Orig.). Date not set. text ed. 45.00 (ISBN 0-631-15746-8); pap. text ed. 17.95 (ISBN 0-631-15801-4). Basil Blackwell.

Politics of Development: Forests, Mines & Hydro-Electro Power in Ontario, 1849-1941. H. V. Nelles. LC 74-4038. xiii, 514p. 1974. 45.00 (ISBN 0-208-01450-0, Archon). Shoe String.

Politics of Development in Botswana: A Model for Success? Louis A. Picard. LC 87-31331. 300p. 1987. lib. bdg. 32.00x (ISBN 0-931477-95-6). Lynne Rienner.

Politics of Development: Transportation Policy in Nepal. Aran Schloss. LC 83-6807. (Monographs: No. 22). (Illus.). 198p. (Orig.). 1983. lib. bdg. 28.50 (ISBN 0-8191-3250-0, Co-pub. by Ctr S&SE Asia Stud); pap. text ed. 12.50 (ISBN 0-8191-3251-9). U Pr of Amer.

Politics of Discontent. Ed. by Ramsay Cook. LC 23-16213. (Canadian Historical Readings Ser.: No. 4). 1967. pap. 4.95x (ISBN 0-8020-1453-4). U of Toronto Pr.

Politics of Discourse: The Literature & History of Seventeenth-Century England. Ed. by Kevin Sharpe & Steven N. Zwicker. LC 86-19153. (Illus.). 370p. 1987. 49.95x (ISBN 0-520-05829-1); pap. 14.95x (ISBN 0-520-06070-9). U of Cal Pr.

Politics of Discretion. Leonard Krieger. LC 65-14428. 1965. 18.00x (ISBN 0-226-45359-6). U of Chicago Pr.

Politics of Displacement: Racial & Ethnic Transition in Three American Cities. Peter K. Eisinger. LC 80-12927. (Institute for Research on Poverty Monograph Ser.). 1980. 27.95 (ISBN 0-12-235560-1). Acad Pr.

Politics of Diversity: Essays in the History of Colonial New York. Milton M. Klein. LC 74-77647. (National University Publications Ser.). 212p. 1974. 22.50x (ISBN 0-8046-9081-2, Pub. by Kennikat). Assoc Faculty Pr.

Politics of Divination. Eugene L. Mendonsa. LC 81-16400. (Illus.). 320p. 1982. 34.00x (ISBN 0-520-04594-7). U of Cal Pr.

Politics of Domesticity: Women, Evangelism, & Temperance in Nineteenth-Century America. Barbara L. Epstein. LC 80-16671. 188p. 1981. 19.50x (ISBN 0-8195-5050-7). Wesleyan U Pr.

Politics of Domesticity: Women, Evangelism, & Temperance in Nineteenth-Century America. Barbara L. Epstein. xii, 188p. 1986. pap. 12.95 (ISBN 0-8195-6184-3). Wesleyan U Pr.

Politics of Early Old English Sound Change. Thomas E. Toon. (Quantitative Analyses of Linguistic Structure Ser.). 1983. 19.95 (ISBN 0-12-694980-8). Acad Pr.

Politics of East-West Communication in Europe. Karl E. Birnbaum. 182p. 1979. text ed. 37.95x (ISBN 0-566-00254-X). Gower Pub Co.

Politics of East-West Trade. Ed. by Gordon B. Smith. 280p. 1984. 42.50x (ISBN 0-86531-713-5). Westview.

Politics of Eastern Cape Separatism, 1820-1854. Basil A. Le Cordeur. (Illus.). 1981. 45.00x (ISBN 0-19-570196-8). Oxford U Pr.

Politics of Economic Crisis: Lessons from Western Europe. E. Damgaard et al. 1988. text ed. 50.00 (ISBN 0-566-05517-1, Pub. by Gower Pub England). Gower Pub Co.

Politics of Economic Despair: Shopkeepers & German Politics, 1890-1914. Robert Gellately. LC 74-81024. (Sage Studies in 20th Century History Ser.: Vol. 1). pap. 83.50 (ISBN 0-317-29677-9, 2021905). Bks Demand UMI.

Politics of Economic Interdependence. Edmund Dell. LC 86-31345. 352p. 1987. 37.50 (ISBN 0-312-00526-1). St Martin.

Politics of Economic Modernization in the Soviet Union. Erik P. Hoffmann & Robbin F. Laird. LC 81-70716. 224p. 1982. 29.50x (ISBN 0-8014-1448-2). Cornell U Pr.

Politics of Economic Policy. Lauber. 366p. 1983. pap. 9.95 (ISBN 0-275-91579-4, B1579). Praeger.

Politics of Economic Power in Southern Africa. Ronald T. Libby. (Illus.). 384p. 1987. text ed. 45.00 (ISBN 0-691-07723-1); pap. text ed. 14.50 (ISBN 0-691-02256-9). Princeton U Pr.

Politics of Education: Conflict & Consensus on Capitol Hill. John Brademas & Lynne P. Brown. LC 86-40526. (Julian J Rothbaum Distinguished Lecture Ser.: Vol. 1). 144p. 1987. 14.95 (ISBN 0-8061-2058-4). U of Okla Pr.

Politics of Education: Culture, Power, & Liberation. Paulo Freire. Tr. by Donaldo Macedo from Port. LC 84-18572. (Critical Studies in Education Ser.). 240p. text ed. 29.95 (ISBN 0-89789-042-6); pap. text ed. 10.95 (ISBN 0-89789-043-4). Bergin & Garvey.

Politics of Education in Colonial Algeria & Kenya. Elsa M. Harik & Donald C. Schilling. LC 83-11422. (Papers in International Studies Africa Ser.: No. 43 A). 102p. 1984. pap. 11.50x monograph (ISBN 0-89680-117-9). Ohio U Pr.

Politics of Education in the States. Harmon Zeigler & Karl F. Johnson. LC 70-175225. 1972. 34.50x (ISBN 0-697-00221-7). Irvington.

Politics of Education: 76th Yearbook, Part 2. Ed. by Jay Scribner. LC 74-44918. (National Society for the Study of Education Ser.). 1976. pap. 7.50x (ISBN 0-226-60104-8). U of Chicago Pr.

Politics of Educational Innovation. Ernest R. House. LC 74-12822. 324p. 1974. 16.50x (ISBN 0-8211-0754-2); pap. text ed. 14.50x 10 or more copies. McCutchan.

Politics of Educational Reform in France, 1918-1940. John E. Talbott. 1969. 37.50x (ISBN 0-691-05173-9). Princeton U Pr.

Politics of Educational Reform 1920-1940. Brian Simon. (Studies History of Education: No. 3). 400p. 1974. 29.95 (ISBN 0-8464-0732-9); pap. 16.95 (ISBN 0-8464-0733-7). Beekman Pubs.

Politics of Efficiency: Municipal Administration & Reform in America, 1880-1920. Martin Schiesl. LC 75-17285. 1977. 36.50x (ISBN 0-520-03067-2); pap. 10.95x (ISBN 0-520-04086-4). U of Cal Pr.

Politics of Elite Culture: Explorations in the Dramaturgy of Power in a Modern African Society. Abner Cohen. LC 80-5469. 200p. 1981. 35.00x (ISBN 0-520-04120-8); pap. 11.95x (ISBN 0-520-04275-1). U of Cal Pr.

Politics of Energy Conservation. Pietro S. Nivola. LC 85-48265. 294p. 1986. 32.95 (ISBN 0-8157-6088-4); pap. 12.95 (ISBN 0-8157-6087-6). Brookings.

Politics of Energy Forecasting: A Comparative Study of Energy Forecasting in Western Europe & North America. Thomas Baumgartner & Atle Midttun. LC 86-23885. 328p. 1987. 67.00 (ISBN 0-19-828547-7). Oxford U Pr.

Politics of Energy Policy Change in Sweden. Robert C. Sahr. 222p. 1985. text ed. 19.95x (ISBN 0-472-10058-0). U of Mich Pr.

Politics of Energy Research & Development. Ed. by John Byren & Daniel Rich. (Energy Policy Studies: Vol. 3). 170p. 1986. pap. 14.95 (ISBN 0-88738-653-9). Transaction Bks.

Politics of Environmental Mediation. Douglas J. Amy. 288p. 1987. 30.00 (ISBN 0-231-06424-1). Columbia U Pr.

Politics of Environmental Policy. Ed. by Lester W. Milbrath et al. LC 75-27013. (Sage Contemporary Social Science Issues Ser.: No. 18). pap. 34.00 (ISBN 0-317-09728-8, 2021932). Bks Demand UMI.

Politics of Environmental Reform: Controlling Kentucky Strip Mining. Marc K. Landy. LC 76-15907. (RFF Working Paper Ser.: PD-2). (Illus.). 414p. pap. 107.70 (2030208). Bks Demand UMI.

Politics of Envy. Lester H. Hunt. 16p. 1983. pap. text ed. 3.95x (ISBN 0-88738-639-3). Transaction Bks.

Politics of Erasmus: A Pacifist Intellectual & His Political Milieu. James D. Tracy. LC 77-20697. (Erasmus Studies). 1978. 22.50x (ISBN 0-8020-5393-9). U of Toronto Pr.

Politics of Ernest Hemingway. Stephen Cooper. Ed. by A. Walton Litz. LC 87-5872. (Studies in Modern Literature: No. 71). 174p. 1987. 34.95 (ISBN 0-8357-1799-2). UMI Res Pr.

Politics of Ethnic Survival: Germans in Prague, 1861-1914. Gary B. Cohen. LC 81-47119. (Illus.). 316p. 1981. 41.00x (ISBN 0-691-05332-4). Princeton U Pr.

Politics of Ethnicity. Michael Walzer & E. Kantowicz. (Dimensions in Ethnicity Ser.). 160p. 1982. pap. text ed. 6.95x (ISBN 0-674-68753-1). Harvard U Pr.

Politics of Ethnicity in Eastern Europe. Ed. by George Klein & Milan J. Reban. (ASN Series in Issues Studies: No. 93). 279p. 1981. 25.00x (ISBN 0-914710-87-7). East Eur Quarterly.

Politics of Eurocommunism: Socialism in Transition. Ed. by Carl Boggs & David Plotke. LC 79-66993. 479p. 1980. 20.00 (ISBN 0-89608-052-8); pap. 10.00 (ISBN 0-89608-051-X). South End Pr.

Politics of European Defense Cooperation. David Garnham. 264p. 1988. 29.95 (ISBN 0-88730-302-1). Ballinger Pub.

Politics of Excellence & Choice: 1987 Yearbook of the Politics of Education Association. Ed. by William L. Boyd & Charles T. Kerchner. (Education Policy & Perspectives Ser.: Vol. 2, No. 5). 248p. 1988. 49.00x (ISBN 1-85000-397-1, Falmer Pr); pap. 22.00x (ISBN 1-85000-398-X, Falmer Pr). Taylor & Francis.

Politics of Exclusion. Michael N. Danielson. LC 76-7609. 443p. 1976. 40.00x (ISBN 0-231-03697-3); pap. 18.00x (ISBN 0-231-08342-4). Columbia U Pr.

Politics of Experience. R. D. Laing. 1983. 4.95 (ISBN 0-394-71475-X). Pantheon.

Politics of Expertise. 2nd ed. Guy Benveniste. LC 77-9200. 1977. text ed. 18.75x (ISBN 0-87835-067-5); pap. text ed. 9.95x (ISBN 0-87835-060-8). Boyd & Fraser.

Politics of External Influence in the Dominican Republic. Michael J. Kryzanek & Howard J. Wiarda. LC 87-38481. (Politics in Latin America Ser.). (Illus.). 208p. 1988. lib. bdg. 39.95 (ISBN 0-275-92992-2, C2992). Praeger.

Politics of Faction: Christian Democratic Rule in Italy. Alan S. Zuckerman. 1979. text ed. 30.00t (ISBN 0-300-02285-9). Yale U Pr.

Politics of Family Planning Policy: Thailand - A Case of Successful Implementation. Ronald L. Krannick & Caryl R. Krannick. (Monographs: No. 19). (Illus.). 122p. 1983. pap. text ed. 11.00 (ISBN 0-8191-3131-8, Co-pub. by Ctr S SE Asia). U Pr of Amer.

Politics of Fantasy: C. S. Lewis & J. R. R. Tolkien. Lee D. Rossi. Ed. by Robert Scholes. LC 84-16116. (Studies in Speculative Fiction: No. 10). 154p. 1984. 37.95 (ISBN 0-8357-1597-3). UMI Res Pr.

Politics of Fear: Joseph R. McCarthy & the Senate. 2nd ed. Robert Griffith. LC 87-13766. 392p. 1987. pap. 11.95 (ISBN 0-87023-555-9). U of Mass Pr.

Politics of Federal Aid to Education in 1965: A Study in Political Innovation. Philip Meranto. LC 67-16846. (Orig.). 1967. pap. 4.95x (ISBN 0-8156-2107-8). Syracuse U Pr.

Politics of Federal Reorganization: Creating the U. S. Department of Education. B. A. Radin & W. D. Howley. LC 87-6972. (Illus.). 250p. 1988. 32.50 (ISBN 0-08-033978-6); pap. 14.95 (ISBN 0-08-033977-8). Pergamon.

Politics of Federalism: Ontario's Relations with the Federal Government 1867-1942. Christopher Armstrong. (Ontario Historical Studies). 316p. 1981. 18.95x (ISBN 0-8020-2434-3). U of Toronto Pr.

Politics of Financial Liberalisation in Japan: The Case of Foreign Banking. Louis W. Pauly. (Cornell University East Asia Papers: No. 45). 82p. (Orig.). 1987. pap. 5.00 (ISBN 0-939657-45-7). Cornell East Asia Pgm.

Politics of Fishing in Britain & France. Michael Shackleton. 400p. 1986. text ed. 55.95 (ISBN 0-566-05161-3, Pub. by Gower Pub England). Gower Pub Co.

Politics of Food. Joel Solkoff. LC 85-2119. 256p. 1985. 17.95 (ISBN 0-87156-846-2). Sierra.

Politics of Force: Bargaining During International Crises. Oran R. Young. LC 68-27408. (Center of International Studies). Repr. of 1968 ed. 85.50 (ISBN 0-8357-9509-8, 2016020). Bks Demand UMI.

Politics of Foreign Aid. John A. White. LC 74-77769. 320p. 1974. 27.50 (ISBN 0-312-62685-1). St Martin.

Politics of Foreign Aid in the Brazilian Northeast. Riordan Roett. LC 73-166403. (Illus.). 1972. 12.95x (ISBN 0-8265-1177-5). Vanderbilt U Pr.

Politics of Foreign Aid: U. S. Foreign Assistance & Aid to Israel. Mohamed Rabie. 1988. 36.85 (ISBN 0-275-93000-9, C3000). Praeger.

Politics of Formosan Nationalism. Douglas Mendel. LC 78-94982. (Illus.). 1970. 37.95x (ISBN 0-520-01557-6). U of Cal Pr.

Politics of Frustration: Harry Midgley & the Failure of Labour in Northern Ireland. Graham S. Walker. LC 85-10684. (Illus.). 256p. 1985. 45.00 (ISBN 0-7190-1821-8, Pub. by Manchester Univ Pr). St Martin.

Politics of Genocide: The Holocaust in Hungary, 2 vols. Randolph L. Braham. LC 80-11096. (Illus.). 1116p. 1980. Set. 112.00x (ISBN 0-231-04496-8). Columbia U Pr.

Politics of Glamour: Ideology & Democracy in the Screen Guild. David F. Prindle. LC 88-40194. (Illus.). 240p. 1988. 24.50 (ISBN 0-299-11810-X). U of Wis Pr.

Politics of Global Economics Relations. 3rd ed. David H. Blake & Robert H. Walters. (Illus.). 256p. 1987. pap. text ed. write for info. (ISBN 0-13-685298-X). P-H.

Politics of Global Resources: Energy, Environment, Population, & Food. Ed. by James E. Harf & B. Thomas Trout. LC 86-4481. (Illus.). xviii, 316p. (Orig.). 1986. text ed. 42.50 (ISBN 0-8223-0583-6); pap. 14.95 (ISBN 0-8223-0623-9). Duke.

Politics of God. 2nd ed. Hugh J. Schonfield. LC 78-9024. (Illus.). 264p. 1978. pap. 9.95 (ISBN 0-916438-14-7). Univ of Trees.

Politics of Governing America. Roger Hilsman. LC 84-11604. (Illus.). 432p. 1985. pap. text ed. write for info. (ISBN 0-13-684622-X). P-H.

Politics of Government Growth: Early Victorian Attitudes Towards State Intervention, 1833-1848. William C. Lubenow. LC 70-26511. (Library of Politics & Society Ser.). 237p. 1971. 26.00 (ISBN 0-208-01227-3, Archon). Shoe String.

Politics of Grandeur. Phillip G. Cerny. LC 79-50232. 1980. Cambridge U Pr.

Politics of Grandeur: Ideological Aspects of De Gaulle's Foreign Policy. Philip G. Cerny. LC 83-23725. 319p. 1984. pap. 12.00 (ISBN 0-86187-360-2, Pub. by Frances Pinter). Longwood Pub Group.

Politics of Greed: The New Right & the Welfare State. Martin Loney. 192p. 1986. pap. 9.50 (ISBN 0-7453-0145-2, Pub. by Pluto Pr). Longwood Pub Group.

Politics of Gulliver's Travels. F. P. Lock. 1980. text ed. 29.95x (ISBN 0-19-812656-5). Oxford U Pr.

Politics of Harmony: Civil Service, & Social Reform in Baden, 1800-1850. Lloyd E. Lee. LC 77-92569. 272p. 1980. 27.50 (ISBN 0-87413-143-X). U Delaware Pr.

Politics of Hazardous Waste Management. Ed. by James P. Lester & Ann Bowman. (Duke Press Policy Studies). x, 317p. (Orig.). 1984. text ed. 37.50 (ISBN 0-8223-0507-0); pap. text ed. 13.95 (ISBN 0-8223-0523-2). Duke.

Politics of Health & Safety. G. K. Wilson. 1985. text ed. 25.95x (ISBN 0-19-827468-8). Oxford U Pr.

Politics of Health in India. Roger Jeffery. (Comparative Studies of Health Systems & Medical Care: Vol. 21). 1988. 39.95x (ISBN 0-520-05938-7). U of CaL Pr.

Politics of Health Legislation: An Economic Perspective. Paul J. Feldstein. LC 88-582. 314p. 1988. pap. 25.00x (ISBN 0-910701-35-0, 0874). Health Admin Pr.

Politics of Heaven & Hell: Christian Themes from Classical, Medieval & Modern Political Philosophy. James V. Schall. LC 84-7409. 360p. (Orig.). 1984. lib. bdg. 27.50 (ISBN 0-8191-3991-2); pap. text ed. 14.25 (ISBN 0-8191-3992-0). U Pr of Amer.

Politics of Heresy: The Modernist Crisis in Roman Catholicism. Lester R. Kurtz. LC 85-1179. 256p. 1986. text ed. 37.50x (ISBN 0-520-05537-3). U of Cal Pr.

Politics of History: Writing the History of the American Revolution, 1783-1815. Arthur H. Shaffer. LC 75-7865. 228p. 1975. 16.95. Precedent Pub.

Politics of History: Writing the History of the American Revolution 1775-1815. Arthur H. Shaffer. 228p. 1975. 16.95. Transaction Bks.

Politics of Hope. Bernard P. Dauenhauer. (Critical Social Thought Ser.). 200p. 1986. 45.00 (ISBN 0-7102-0823-5, 08235, Pub. by Routledge UK). Routledge Chapman & Hall.

Politics of Hostility: Castro's Revolution & United States Policy. Lynn D. Bender. Ed. by John Zebrowski et al. LC 74-78314. 160p. 1974. 7.95 (ISBN 0-913480-24-X). Inter Am U Pr.

Politics of Housing in Britain & France. Roger H. Duclaud-Williams. LC 78-323819. (Centre for Environmental Studies Ser.). 1978. text ed. 28.50x (ISBN 0-435-85222-1). Gower Pub Co.

Politics of Human Nature. Thomas Fleming. 276p. 1988. 29.95 (ISBN 0-88738-189-8). Transaction Bks.

Politics of Human Rights. Ed. by Paula R. Newberg. LC 79-1998. (UNA-USA Bk.). 1981. 35.00x (ISBN 0-8147-5754-5); pap. 15.00x (ISBN 0-8147-5755-3). NYU Pr.

Politics of Human Rights. Andrei Sakharov et al. 6.00 (ISBN 0-318-03636-3). Trilateral Comm.

Politics of Human Rights & Civil Liberties. Attar Chand. 377p. 1985. 59.95x (ISBN 0-317-39866-0, Pub. by UDH Pubs India). Asia Bk Corp.

Politics of Human Services: A Radical Alternative to the Welfare State. Steven Wineman. LC 84-50938. 250p. (Orig.). 1984. 20.00 (ISBN 0-89608-234-2); pap. 9.00 (ISBN 0-89608-233-4). South End Pr.

Politics of Hunger: The Allied Blockade of Germany, 1915-1919. C. Paul Vincent. LC 85-11572. (Illus.). 191p. 1986. text ed. 19.95x (ISBN 0-8214-0820-8). Ohio U Pr.

Politics of Hunger: The Allied Blockade of Germany, 1915-1919. C. Paul Vincent. 191p. 1986. pap. 9.95x (ISBN 0-8214-0831-3). Ohio U Pr.

Politics of Hunger: The Global Food System. John W. Warnock. LC 87-1659. 288p. 1988. pap. text ed. 13.95 (ISBN 0-458-80630-7). Routledge Chapman & Hall.

Politics of Hunting. Richard H. Thomas. 313p. 1983. text ed. 34.50x (ISBN 0-566-00614-6). Gower Pub Co.

Politics of Hysteria: The Sources of Twentieth-Century Conflict. Edmund O. Stillman & William Pfaff. LC 81-4630. x, 273p. 1981. Repr. of 1964 ed. lib. bdg. 35.00x (ISBN 0-313-22973-2, STPOH). Greenwood.

Politics of Ideas. Lawrence J. Herson. 376p. 1984. 19.00x (ISBN 0-256-03111-8). Dorsey.

Politics of Identity. Peter Dupreez. 1980. 26.00 (ISBN 0-312-62697-5). St Martin.

Politics of Identity: Liberation & the Natural Community. Kenneth R. Hoover. LC 75-8797. 179p. 1975. 15.95 (ISBN 0-252-00436-1). U of Ill Pr.

Politics of Illusion & Empire: German Occupation Policy in the Soviet Union, Nineteen Forty-Two to Nineteen Forty Three. Timothy P. Mulligan. 220p. 1988. lib. bdg. 39.95 (ISBN 0-275-92837-3, C2837). Praeger.

Politics of Imagination in Coleridge's Critical Thought. Nigel Leask. LC 88-3265. 220p. 1988. 35.00 (ISBN 0-312-02041-4). St Martin.

Politics of Inclusion. Thomas H. Kean. 256p. 1988. 17.95 (ISBN 0-02-918341-3). Free Pr.

Politics of Indecision: Origins & Implications of American Involvement with the Palestine Problem. Daniel Tschirgi. LC 82-15115. 368p. 1983. 36.95 (ISBN 0-275-91092-X, C1092). Praeger.

Politics of Independence: A Study of a Scottish Town. Frank W. Bealey & John Sewel. 280p. 1981. 30.00 (ISBN 0-08-025736-4). Pergamon.

Politics of Independent Kenya, 1963-8. Cherry J. Gertzel. LC 73-124293. pap. 48.00 (ISBN 0-317-11320-8, 2015296). Bks Demand UMI.

Politics of Indian Removal: Creek Government & Society in Crisis. Michael D. Green. LC 81-14670. xvi, 237p. 1982. 22.50x (ISBN 0-8032-2109-6). U of Nebr Pr.

Politics of Indian Removal: Creek Government & Society in Crisis. Michael D. Green. LC 81-14670. xvi, 237p. 1985. pap. 5.95x (ISBN 0-8032-7015-1). U of Nebr Pr.

Politics of Individualism: Parties & the American Character in the Jacksonian Era. Lawrence F. Kohl. 304p. 1988. 27.95 (ISBN 0-19-505374-5). Oxford U Pr.

Politics of Industrial Change: Railway Policy in North America. R. Kent Weaver. LC 85-24274. 291p. 1985. 31.95 (ISBN 0-8157-9260-3); pap. 11.95 (ISBN 0-8157-9259-X). Brookings.

Politics of Industrial Closure. Ed. by Tony Dickson & David Judge. 201p. 1987. 49.00x (ISBN 0-333-40492-0, Pub. by Macmillan Pr Ltd). Intl Spec Bk.

Politics of Industrial Mobilization in Russia, 1915-1917: A Study of the War-Industries Committees. Lewis H. Siegelbaum. LC 82-23036. 332p. 1984. 27.50 (ISBN 0-312-62699-1). St Martin.

Politics of Industrial Policy. Ed. by Claude E. Barfield & William A. Schambra. 344p. 1986. 22.50 (ISBN 0-8447-2262-6); pap. 13.50 (ISBN 0-8447-2261-8). Am Enterprise.

Politics of Industrial Restructuring: Canadian Textiles. Rianne Mahon. (State & Economic Life Ser.: No. 7). xii, 204p. 1984. 25.00x (ISBN 0-8020-2538-2); pap. 12.50 (ISBN 0-8020-6546-5). U of Toronto Pr.

Politics of Inequality: Competition & Control in An Indian Village. Miriam Sharma. LC 78-5526. (Asian Studies at Hawaii: No. 22). 279p. 1978. pap. text ed. 10.50x (ISBN 0-8248-0569-0). UH Pr.

Politics of Inflation & Economic Stagnation. Ed. by Leon N. Lindberg & Charles S. Maier. LC 84-23263. 612p. 1985. 39.95 (ISBN 0-8157-5264-4); pap. 18.95 (ISBN 0-8157-5263-6). Brookings.

Politics of Influence: British Ex-Servicemen, Cabinet Decisions & Cultural Change, 1917-1957. Graham Wootton. LC 63-5612. (Illus.). 1963. 24.50x (ISBN 0-674-68900-3). Harvard U Pr.

Politics of Informal Justice: The American Experience, Vol. 1. Richard Abel. LC 81-14920. (Studies on Law & Social Control Ser.). 352p. 1981. 32.50 (ISBN 0-12-041501-1). Acad Pr.

Politics of Informal Justice: Vol. 2, Comparative Studies. Ed. by Richard Abel. LC 81-14920. (Studies on Law & Social Control Ser.). 1981. 32.50 (ISBN 0-12-041502-X). Acad Pr.

Politics of Insurgency: The Farm Worker Movement in the 1960's. J. Craig Jenkins. LC 84-27509. 320p. 1985. 35.00x (ISBN 0-231-05692-3). Columbia U Pr.

Politics of International Credit: Private Finance & Foreign Policy in Germany & Japan. Andrew J. Spindler. LC 84-73394. 220p. 1984. 31.95 (ISBN 0-8157-8070-2); pap. 11.95 (ISBN 0-8157-8069-9). Brookings.

Politics of International Debt. Ed. by Miles Kahler. LC 85-48243. (Studies in Political Economy). 272p. 1986. 29.95x (ISBN 0-8014-1911-5); pap. 10.95x (ISBN 0-8014-9385-4). Cornell U Pr.

Politics of International Economic Relations. Ramashray Roy. 234p. 1982. 24.95. Asia Bk Corp.

Politics of International Economic Relations. Ed. by Ramashray Roy. 1982. 21.50x (ISBN 0-8364-0885-3, Pub. by Ajanta). South Asia Bks.

Politics of International Economic Relations. 3rd ed. Joan E. Spero. LC 84-51139. 400p. 1985. pap. text ed. write for info. (ISBN 0-312-62706-8). St Martin.

Politics of International Investment. Earl H. Fry. 224p. 1983. text ed. 29.95 (ISBN 0-07-022610-5). McGraw.

Politics of International Standards: France & the Color TV War. Rhonda J. Crane. LC 79-4231. (Communication & Information Science Ser.). 1979. 29.50x (ISBN 0-89391-019-8). Ablex Pub.

Politics of International Telecommunication Regulation. James G. Savage. 208p. 1988. pap. 25.00 (ISBN 0-8133-7682-3). Westview.

Politics of Interpretation. rev. ed. Ed. by W. J. T. Mitchell. LC 83-3581. 1983. 25.00x (ISBN 0-226-53219-4); pap. 9.95x (ISBN 0-226-53220-8). U of Chicago Pr.

Politics of Interpretation: Alterity & Ideology in Old Yiddish Studies. Jerold C. Frakes. 320p. (Orig.). 1988. text ed. 49.50 (ISBN 0-88706-845-6); pap. text ed. 16.95 (ISBN 0-88706-846-4). State U NY Pr.

Politics of Intervention: The United States in Central Amer.ca. Ed. by Roger Burbach & Patricia Flynn. LC 83-42526. 272p. 1984. 25.00 (ISBN 0-85345-634-8); pap. 10.00 (ISBN 0-85345-635-6). Monthly Rev.

Politics of Irish Freedom. Gerry Adams. 192p. 1987. pap. 7.95 (ISBN 0-86322-084-3, Pub. by Brandon Bks). Longwood Pub Group.

Politics of Islamic Reassertion. Mohammed Ayoob. LC 81-4353. 1981. 29.95 (ISBN 0-312-62707-6). St Martin.

Politics of Islamic Revivalism: Diversity & Unity. Ed. by Shireen T. Hunter. LC 87-21380. (Illus.). 320p. 1988. 35.00x (ISBN 0-253-34549-9); pap. 12.95 (ISBN 0-253-20466-6). Ind U Pr.

Politics of Jacksonian Finance. John M. McFaul. LC 72-4635. 245p. 1972. 24.95x (ISBN 0-8014-0738-9). Cornell U Pr.

Politics of Jesus. John H. Yoder. 176p. 1972. pap. 7.95 (ISBN 0-8028-1485-9). Eerdmans.

Politics of John Dewey. Gary Bullert. LC 83-62872. 219p. 1983. 26.95 (ISBN 0-87975-208-4). Prometheus Bks.

Politics of Judicial Interpretation: The Federal Courts, Department of Justice & Civil Rights, 1866-1876. Robert J. Kaczorowski. LC 85-2894. (New York University School of Law-Linden Studies in Legal History). 241p. 1985. lib. bdg. 32.50 (ISBN 0-379-20818-0). Oceana.

Politics of Judicial Modernization: The Case of the Tennessee Court System. Ed. by John M. Scheb, II & Stephen J. Rechichar. (Studies in Tennessee Politics). 100p. 1986. pap. 3.50 (ISBN 0-914079-15-8). Bureau Pub Admin U Tenn.

Politics of Justice: A Study in Law, Social Science & Public Policy. William C. Louthan. (National University Pubns. Legal Series). 1979. 21.95 (ISBN 0-8046-9218-1, Pub. by Kennikat). Assoc Faculty Pr.

Politics of Justice: Lower Federal Judicial Selection & the Second Party System, 1829-1861. Kermit L. Hall. LC 79-9238. xx, 268p. 1979. 23.95x (ISBN 0-8032-2302-1). U of Nebr Pr.

Politics of Juvenile Crime. John Pitts. (Contemporary Criminology Ser.: Vol. 2). 192p. 1988. text ed. 39.95 (ISBN 0-8039-8132-5); pap. text ed. 16.50 (ISBN 0-8039-8133-3). Sage.

Politics of King Lear. E. Muir. LC 76-99171. (Studies in Shakespeare, No. 24). 1970. Repr. of 1947 ed. lib. bdg. 49.95x (ISBN 0-8383-0331-5). Haskell.

Politics of King Lear. Edwin Muir. LC 77-8457. 1947. lib. bdg. 16.50 (ISBN 0-8414-6092-2). Folcroft.

Politics of King Lear. Edwin Muir. 59.95 (ISBN 0-87968-032-6). Gordon Pr.

Politics of Labor Legislation in Japan: National-International Interaction. Ehud Harari. LC 72-78945. (Center for Japanese Studies, UC Berkeley: No. 8). 1973. 34.95x (ISBN 0-520-02264-5). U of Cal Pr.

Politics of Land Reform in Chile, 1950-1970. Robert R. Kaufman. LC 72-75407. (Center for International Affairs Ser.). 1972. 24.50x (ISBN 0-674-68920-8). Harvard U Pr.

Politics of Land-Use Reform. Frank Popper. 338p. 1981. 29.50x (ISBN 0-299-08530-9); pap. text ed. 12.50x (ISBN 0-299-08534-1). U of Wis Pr.

Politics of Landscape: Rural Scenery & Society in English Poetry, 1630-1660. James G. Turner. LC 78-11027. (Illus.). 1979. text ed. 18.50x (ISBN 0-674-68930-5). Harvard U Pr.

Politics of Language: Liberalism as Word & Symbol. Ronald D. Rotunda. 148p. 1986. 14.95 (ISBN 0-87745-139-7, 85-24548). U of Iowa Pr.

Politics of Language, Seventeen Ninety-One to Eighteen Nineteen. Olivia Smith. 1985. 29.95x (ISBN 0-19-812817-7). Oxford U Pr.

Politics of Language, 1791-1819. Olivia Smith. 288p. 1986. pap. 15.95x (ISBN 0-19-812878-9). Oxford U Pr.

Politics of Latin American Development. 2nd ed. Gary W. Wynia. LC 83-15156. 304p. 1984. 47.50 (ISBN 0-521-26120-1); pap. 13.95 (ISBN 0-521-27842-2). Cambridge U Pr.

Politics of Laurence Sterne. Lewis P. Curtis. 1978. Repr. of 1929 ed. lib. bdg. 22.50 (ISBN 0-8495-0742-1). Arden Lib.

Politics of Laurence Sterne. Lewis P. Curtis. LC 73-6822. Repr. of 1929 ed. lib. bdg. 35.50 (ISBN 0-8414-3365-8). Folcroft.

Politics of Law: A Progressive Critique. Kairys David. 1982. pap. 7.00. Natl Lawyers Guild.

Politics of Law: A Progressive Critique. Ed. by David Kairys. 1982. 22.00 (ISBN 0-394-51981-7); pap. 10.95 (ISBN 0-394-71110-6). Pantheon.

Politics of Law & Order: A History of the Bavarian Einwohnerwehr, 1918-1921. David C. Large. LC 79-54273. (Transactions Ser.: Vol. 70, Pt. 2). 1980. 10.00 (ISBN 0-87169-702-5). Am Philos.

Politics of Law & Order: Street Crime & Public Policy. Stuart A. Scheingold. LC 83-16212. (Professional Studies in Law & Public Policy). 1984. pap. 16.95 (ISBN 0-582-28416-3). Longman.

Politics of Law & the Courts in Nineteenth-Century Egypt. Byron Cannon. 312p. 1988. 30.00x (ISBN 0-87480-279-2). U of Utah Pr.

Politics of Letters. Richard Ohmann. (Illus.). xiv, 322p. 1988. pap. 14.95 (ISBN 0-8195-6213-0). Wesleyan U Pr.

Politics of Letters. Richard M. Ohmann. 258p. 1987. 25.95 (ISBN 0-8195-5175-9); pap. 12.95. Wesleyan U Pr.

Politics of Liberation. John M. Swomley, Jr. 128p. (Orig.). 1984. pap. 7.95 (ISBN 0-87178-712-1). Brethren.

Politics of Liberation Theology: Views from Latin America & the United States. Intro. by Richard L. Rubenstein & John K. Roth. 368p. 1988. text ed. 24.95x (ISBN 0-88702-039-9); pap. text ed. 14.95x (ISBN 0-88702-040-2). Washington Inst Pr.

Politics of Linguistics. Frederick J. Newmeyer. LC 86-11225. 192p. 1986. lib. bdg. 23.95x (ISBN 0-226-57720-1). U of Chicago Pr.

Politics of Linguistics. Frederick J. Newmeyer. viii, 172p. 1988. pap. 9.95 (ISBN 0-226-57722-8). U of Chicago Pr.

Politics of Literacy. Ed. by Martin Hoyles. (Education Ser.). 216p. 1980. 14.00 (ISBN 0-904613-47-X); pap. 5.95 (ISBN 0-904613-28-3). Writers & Readers.

Politics of Literary Expression: A Study of Major Black Writers. Donald B. Gibson. LC 80-27284. (Contributions in Afro-American & African Studies: No. 63). 240p. 1981. lib. bdg. 35.00 (ISBN 0-313-21271-6, GPE/). Greenwood.

Politics of Local Government. Barrie Houlihan. (Topics in British Politics Ser.). 64p. (Orig.). 1986. pap. text ed. 9.95 (ISBN 0-582-33198-6). Longman.

Politics of Local Government Finance. Tony Travers. Ed. by P. G. Richards. LC 86-3331. (New Local Government Ser.: No. 27). 250p. 1987. text ed. 44.95x (ISBN 0-04-352215-7); pap. text ed. 17.95x (ISBN 0-04-352235-1). Unwin Hyman.

Politics of Local Government in the United Kingdom. Alan Alexander. LC 81-20872. pap. 38.30 (ISBN 0-317-27719-7, 2025222). Bks Demand UMI.

Politics of Local Socialism. John Gyford. (Local Government Briefings Ser.). 170p. 1985. text ed. 29.95x (ISBN 0-04-352213-0); pap. text ed. 11.95x (ISBN 0-04-352214-9). Unwin Hyman.

Politics of Local Spending. Arthur Midwinter. 1986. 62.50x (ISBN 0-906391-55-5, Pub. by Mainstream Scotland). State Mutual Bk.

Politics of Location. A. Kirby. (Illus.). 1982. 28.00 (ISBN 0-416-33900-X, NO.3726); pap. 14.95x (ISBN 0-416-33910-7, NO.3727). Routledge Chapman & Hall.

Politics of Locke's Philosophy: A Social Study of "An Essay Concerning Human Understanding". Neal Wood. 1983. 33.00x (ISBN 0-520-04457-6). U of Cal Pr.

Politics of Loyalty. Alan D. Harper. LC 73-95509. (Contributions in American History: No. 2). (Illus.). 1969. lib. bdg. 35.00 (ISBN 0-8371-2343-7, HAL/). Greenwood.

Politics of Management. Philip B. Heymann. LC 86-51340. 264p. 1987. 22.50x (ISBN 0-300-03777-5). Yale U Pr.

Politics of Management. Andrew Kakabadse. LC 83-20702. 174p. 1984. 29.50 (ISBN 0-89397-182-0). Nichols Pub.

Politics of Management Consulting. Gerald L. Moore. LC 83-19231. 176p. 1984. 35.00 (ISBN 0-275-91743-6, C1743). Praeger.

Politics of Management: Exploring the Inner Workings of Public & Private Organizations. Douglas Yates, Jr. LC 85-45067. (Management Ser.). 1985. text ed. 23.95x (ISBN 0-87589-671-5). Jossey-Bass.

Politics of Manpower Planning: Graduate Unemployment & the Planning of Higher Education in India. Trilok N. Dhar. LC 75-905987. 1974. 13.00x (ISBN 0-88386-475-4). South Asia Bks.

Politics of Manpower, 1914-18. Keith Grieves. LC 87-20511. 256p. 1987. 45.00 (ISBN 0-312-01320-5). St Martin.

Politics of Marriage in Contemporary China. Elisabeth Croll. LC 80-40586. (Contemporary China Institute Publications Ser.). (Illus.). 224p. 1981. 44.50 (ISBN 0-521-23345-3). Cambridge U Pr.

Politics of Mass Housing in Britain, 1945-1975: A Study of Corporate Power & Professional Influence in the Welfare State. Patrick Dunleavy. (Illus.). 1981. 49.95x (ISBN 0-19-827426-2). Oxford U Pr.

Politics of Massacre: Political Processes in South Vietnam. Charles A. Joiner. LC 72-95882. 362p. 1974. 19.95 (ISBN 0-87722-060-3). Temple U Pr.

Politics of Meaning: Power & Explanation in the Construction of Social Reality. Peter C. Sederberg. LC 84-2739. 294p. 1984. 22.50x (ISBN 0-8165-0860-7). U of Ariz Pr.

Politics of Medicare. Theodore R. Marmor. LC 76-169517. 1973. 29.95x (ISBN 0-202-24036-3); pap. 16.95x (ISBN 0-202-24037-1). Aldine de Gruyter.

Politics of Mental Health Legislation. Clive Unsworth. LC 86-26813. 384p. 1987. 69.00 (ISBN 0-19-825512-8). Oxford U Pr.

Politics of Mental Health: Organizing Community Mental Health in Metropolitan Areas. Robert H. Connery et al. LC 68-28396. (Illus.). 595p. 1968. 45.00x (ISBN 0-231-03029-0). Columbia U Pr.

Politics of Mercantilism. Philip W. Buck. 1964. lib. bdg. 20.00x (ISBN 0-374-91083-9, Octagon). Hippocrene Bks.

Politics of Mexican Development. Roger D. Hansen. LC 77-134300. (Illus.). 298p. 1971. 32.00x (ISBN 0-8018-1193-7); pap. 10.95x (ISBN 0-8018-1651-3). Johns Hopkins.

Politics of Michigan 1865-1878. Harriette M. Dilla. (Columbia University Studies in the Social Sciences: No. 118). Repr. of 1912 ed. 21.50 (ISBN 0-404-51118-X). AMS Pr.

Politics of Migration Policies. 2nd ed. Ed. by Daniel Kubat. LC 77-93185. (Illus.). Date not set. 12.95 (ISBN 0-913256-34-X, 2.3). Ctr Migration.

Politics of Military Revolution in Korea. Se-Jin Kim. LC 71-123101. (Illus.). xv, 239p. 1971. 22.50 (ISBN 0-8078-1168-8). U of NC Pr.

Politics of Military Rule in Brazil, 1964-85. Thomas E. Skidmore. (Illus.). 432p. 1988. 29.95 (ISBN 0-19-503898-3). Oxford U Pr.

Politics of Military Unification: A Study of Conflict & the Policy Process. Ed. by Demetrios Caraley. LC 66-15762. (Institute of War & Peace Studies). 345p. 1966. 35.00x (ISBN 0-231-02885-7). Columbia U Pr.

Politics of Milton's Prose Style. Keith M. Stavely. LC 74-20086. (Yale Studies in English: Vol. 185). pap. 36.50 (ISBN 0-317-09388-6, 2022042). Bks Demand UMI.

Politics of Mineral Resource Development in Antarctica: Alternative Regimes for the Future. William E. Westermeyer. LC 83-10167. 1983. 31.50x (ISBN 0-86531-972-3). Westview.

Politics of Minorities. Moin Shakir. 1980. 16.00x (ISBN 0-8364-0622-2, Pub. by Ajanta). South Asia Bks.

Politics of Mirth: Jonson, Herrick, Milton, Marvell, & the Defense of Old Holiday Pastimes. Leah S. Marcus. LC 86-7133. (Illus.). 328p. 1986. lib. bdg. 29.00x (ISBN 0-226-50451-4). U of Chicago Pr.

Politics of Miseducation: The Booker Washington Institute of Liberia, 1929-1984. Donald Spivey. LC 86-13163. 192p. 1986. 18.00 (ISBN 0-8131-1598-1). U Pr of Ky.

Politics of Mistrust: Estimating American Oil & Gas Resources. Aaron Wildavsky & Ellen Tenenbaum. LC 80-29049. (Managing Information Ser.: Vol. 1). (Illus.). 364p. 1981. 29.95 (ISBN 0-8039-1582-9). Sage.

Politics of Mistrust: Estimating American Oil & Gas Resources. Aaron Wildavsky & Ellen Tenenbaum. LC 80-29049. (Managing Information Ser.: Vol. 1). (Illus.). 364p. 1981. pap. 14.95 (ISBN 0-8039-1583-7). Sage.

Politics of Moderation: An Interpretation of Plato's "Republic". John F. Wilson. LC 84-10442. 242p. (Orig.). 1984. lib. bdg. 25.75 (ISBN 0-8191-4017-1); pap. text ed. 13.00 (ISBN 0-8191-4018-X). U Pr of Amer.

Politics of Monetarism: Its Historical & Institutional Development. George Macesich. LC 83-24766. 170p. 1984. 28.50x (ISBN 0-8476-7344-8, Rowman & Allanheld); pap. cancelled (ISBN 0-8476-7345-6). Rowman.

Politics of Motherhood: Child & Maternal Welfare in England, 1900-1939. Jane Lewis. 240p. 1980. 32.95x (ISBN 0-7735-0521-0). McGill-Queens U Pr.

Politics of Multinationals. M. K. Saini. 342p. 1981. 32.95. Asia Bk Corp.

Politics of Multiracial Education. Madan Sarup. (Education Bks.). 160p. (Orig.). 1986. pap. text ed. 9.95 (ISBN 0-7102-0570-8). Routledge Chapman & Hall.

Politics of National Despair: French Royalism in the Post-Reformation Era. George D. Balsama. 1977. pap. text ed. 10.00 (ISBN 0-8191-0142-7). U Pr of Amer.

Politics of National Health Insurance: An Interdisciplinary Research Study. Charles J. Austin. LC 75-14975. (Trinity Univ. Health Services Research Ser.). 109p. 1975. 7.50 (ISBN 0-911536-60-4). Trinity U Pr.

Politics of National Party Conventions. rev. ed. Paul T. David et al. 394p. 1984. pap. text ed. 13.25 (ISBN 0-8191-4002-3). U Pr of Amer.

Politics of National Security. Marcus G. Raskin. LC 78-55935. (Issues in Contemporary Civilization). 320p. 1979. 27.95x (ISBN 0-87855-239-1); pap. text ed. 14.95x (ISBN 0-87855-662-1). Transaction Bks.

Politics of Nationalism & Devolution. Henry M. Drucker & Gordon Brown. LC 79-41025. pap. 36.00 (ISBN 0-317-27702-2, 2025219). Bks Demand UMI.

Politics of Neglect: Urban Aid from Model Cities to Revenue Sharing. Bernard J. Frieden & Marshall Kaplan. LC 75-6792. (MIT-Harvard Joint Center for Urban Studies). 386p. 1975. pap. 9.95x (ISBN 0-262-56016-X). MIT Pr.

Politics of Neo-Corporatism in France: Farmers, the State, & Agricultural Policymaking in the Fifth Republic. John T. Keeler. LC 86-5172. 384p. 1987. 39.95 (ISBN 0-19-504078-3). Oxford U Pr.

Politics of Non-Alignment. M. M. Rahman. 1969. 16.50 (ISBN 0-686-20286-4). Intl Bk Dist.

Politics of Nonviolent Action, 3 pts. Gene Sharp. Ed. by Marina Finkelstein. Incl. Pt. 1. Power & Struggle. 144p. pap. 3.95 (ISBN 0-87558-070-X); Pt. 2. Methods of Nonviolent Action. 368p. pap. 4.95 (ISBN 0-87558-071-8); Pt. 3. Dynamics of Nonviolent Action. 480p. pap. 5.95 (ISBN 0-87558-072-6). LC 72-95483. (Extending Horizons Ser). 1974. pap. Porter Sargent.

Politics of Northern Ireland. Raymond Mullan. (Topics in British Politics Ser.). 64p. 1986. pap. text ed. 9.95 (ISBN 0-582-34316-X). Longman.

Politics of Nostalgia: Racism & the Extreme Right in New Zealand. Paul Spoonley. 313p. (Orig.). 1987. pap. 38.00 (ISBN 0-86469-063-0, Pub. by Dunmore NZ). Intl Spec Bk.

Politics of Nuclear Balance: Ambiguity & Continuity in Strategic Policies. William H. Baugh. LC 82-24995. 320p. 1983. 33.95 (ISBN 0-582-28214-4). Longman.

Politics of Nuclear Consultation in NATO: 1965-1980. Paul Buteux. LC 82-22016. (International Studies). 256p. 1983. 47.50 (ISBN 0-521-24798-5). Cambridge U Pr.

Politics of Nuclear Defence: A Comprehensive Introduction. Greville Rumble. 280p. 1986. text ed. 34.95x (ISBN 0-7456-0194-4); pap. text ed. 14.95x (ISBN 0-7456-0195-2). Basil Blackwell.

Politics of Nuclear Proliferation. George H. Quester. LC 73-8119. pap. 66.00 (ISBN 0-317-20467-X, 2023002). Bks Demand UMI.

Politics of Nuclear Waste: Social, Political & Institutional Issues. Ed. by E. W. Colglazier. (Pergamon Policy Studies on Energy). (Illus.). 275p. 1982. 41.00 (ISBN 0-08-026323-2). Pergamon.

Politics of Obedience. Etienne De La Boetie. 1984. lib. bdg. 79.95 (ISBN 0-87700-648-2). Revisionist Pr.

Politics of Obedience: The Discourse of Voluntary Servitude. Etienne La Boetie. Tr. by Harry Kurz from Fr. 88p. 1975. 19.95 (ISBN 0-919618-58-8, Dist. by U of Toronto Pr); pap. 9.95 (ISBN 0-919618-57-X, Dist. by U of Toronto Pr). Black Rose Bks.

Politics of Offshore Oil. Joan Goldstein. LC 82-7697. 208p. 1982. 35.00 (ISBN 0-275-90805-4, C0805). Praeger.

Politics of Oil: A Study of Private Power & Democratic Directions. 2nd ed. Robert Engler. LC 61-17192. 1976. pap. 5.95 (ISBN 0-226-20947-4, P284, Phoen). U of Chicago Pr.

Politics of Oil & Revolution in Iran. Shaul B. Bakhash. LC 82-72116. 37p. 1982. pap. 6.95 (ISBN 0-8157-0781-9). Brookings.

Politics of Oil in Indonesia: Foreign Company-Host Government Relations. Khong Cho Oon. (LSE Monographs in International Studies). 253p. 1986. 42.50 (ISBN 0-521-30901-8). Cambridge U Pr.

Politics of Oil in Venezuela. Franklin Tugwell. LC 74-25930. xvi, 216p. 1975. 19.50x (ISBN 0-8047-0881-9). Stanford U Pr.

Politics of Organizational Change. Iain Mangham. LC 79-23. (Contributions in Economics & Economic History: No. 26). 1979. lib. bdg. 35.00 (ISBN 0-313-20981-2, MPC/). Greenwood.

Politics of Palestinian Nationalism. William B. Quandt et al. (Rand Corporation Research Study). 1973. 30.00x (ISBN 0-520-02336-6); pap. 9.95x (ISBN 0-520-02372-2). U of Cal Pr.

Politics of Park Design: A History of Urban Parks in America. Galen Cranz. (Illus.). 352p. 1982. 37.50x (ISBN 0-262-03086-1). MIT Pr.

Politics of Parliamentary Reform. David Judge. LC 83-25378. 220p. 1984. 27.50 (ISBN 0-8386-3221-1). Fairleigh Dickinson.

Politics of Passion: Structure & Strategy in Sikh Society. Harry Izmirlian. 1979. 14.00x (ISBN 0-8364-0551-X). South Asia Bks.

Politics of Peace: An Evaluation of Arms Control. John H. Barton. LC 79-67776. xii, 257p. 1981. 25.00x (ISBN 0-8047-1081-3). Stanford U Pr.

Politics of Penury: Debts & Taxes in Mexico, 1821-1856. Barbara Tenenbaum. LC 86-16027. 268p. 1986. 32.50x (ISBN 0-8263-0890-2). U of NM Pr.

Politics of People's Action: The Communist Party in the '72 Elections. Henry Winston. 48p. 1972. pap. 0.50 (ISBN 0-87898-077-6). New Outlook.

Politics of Persuasion: British Policy & French African Neutrality, 1940-1942. Desmond Dinan. LC 88-10690. 320p. (Orig.). 1988. lib. bdg. 32.50 (ISBN 0-8191-6982-X); pap. text ed. 16.25 (ISBN 0-8191-6983-8). U Pr of Amer.

Politics of Philanthropy: Abraham Flexner & Medical Education. Steven C. Wheatley. LC 88-40199. (History of American Thought & Culture Ser.). 256p. (Orig.). 1988. text ed. 37.50x (ISBN 0-299-11750-2); pap. text ed. 14.95x (ISBN 0-299-11754-5). U of Wis Pr.

Politics of Philo Judaeus. Erwin R. Goodenough & H. L. Goodhart. 1938. 85.00x (ISBN 0-685-69822-X). Elliots Bks.

Politics of Planning. Francis Gladstone. 1977. 15.00 (ISBN 0-85117-106-0). Transatl Arts.

Politics of Planning & Development. Anthony J. Catanese. LC 84-8334. (Sage Library of Social Research: Vol. 156). 231p. 1984. 29.95 (ISBN 0-8039-2314-7); pap. 14.95 (ISBN 0-8039-2315-5). Sage.

Politics of Pluralism: A Comparative Study of Lebanon & Ghana. David R. Smock & Audrey C. Smock. LC 75-8278. pap. 94.80 (2026265). Bks Demand UMI.

Politics of Policy Implementation. Robert T. Nakamura & Frank Smallwood. 201p. 1980. pap. text ed. write for info. (ISBN 0-312-62780-7). St Martin.

Politics of Policy in Local Government. John Dearlove. LC 73-77179. (Illus.). 300p. 1973. 34.50 (ISBN 0-521-20244-2). Cambridge U Pr.

Politics of Policy Making & Pressure Groups. Christopher Barnes. 160p. 1987. text ed. 30.00x (ISBN 0-566-05202-4, Pub. by Gower Pub England). Gower Pub Co.

Politics of Policy Making in Defense & Foreign Affairs: Conceptual Models & Bureaucratic Politics. Roger Hilsman. 320p. 1987. pap. text ed. 22.00 (ISBN 0-13-685173-8). P-H.

Politics of Population Control. Thomas B. Littlewood. LC 76-51619. 1979. pap. text ed. 8.95x (ISBN 0-268-01532-5). U of Notre Dame Pr.

Politics of Population Control. Thomas B Littlewood. LC 76-51619. 1977. text ed. 19.95 (ISBN 0-268-01523-6). U of Notre Dame Pr.

Politics of Population in Brazil: Elite Ambivalence & Public Demand. Peter McDonough & Amaury DeSouza. (Texas Pan American Ser). 190p. 1981. text ed. 22.50x (ISBN 0-292-76466-9). U of Tex Pr.

Politics of Positive Discrimination: An Evaluation of the Urban Programme, 1967-1977. John Edwards & Richard Batley. 1978. 27.00x (ISBN 0-422-76660-7, NO. 2176, Pub. by Tavistock). Routledge Chapman & Hall.

Politics of Poverty. R. N. Hadimani. 1985. 19.00x (ISBN 0-8364-1329-6, Pub. by Ashish India). South Asia Bks.

Politics of Power: A Critical Introduction to American Government. 3rd ed. Ira Katznelson & Mark Kesselman. 427p. 1987. pap. text ed. 13.00 net (ISBN 0-15-570735-3, HC). HarBraceJ.

Politics of Prejudice: The Anti-Japanese Movement in California & The Struggle for Japanese Exclusion. Roger Daniels. LC 62-63248. 1968. pap. text ed. 3.95x (ISBN 0-689-70059-8, 116). Atheneum.

Politics of Prejudice: The Anti-Japanese Movement in California & The Struggle for Japanese Exclusion. Roger Daniels. 1978. 32.50x (ISBN 0-520-03412-0); pap. 7.95x (ISBN 0-520-03411-2). U of Cal Pr.

Politics of Presidential Appointments. G. Calvin Mackenzie. LC 80-1029. (Illus.). 1980. 24.95 (ISBN 0-02-919670-1). Free Pr.

Politics of Presidential Commissions: A Public Policy Perspective. David Flitner, Jr. 260p. 1986. lib. bdg. 35.00 avail. (ISBN 0-941320-42-1). Transnatl Pubs.

Politics of Pressure: American Arms & Israeli Policy Since the Six Day War. David Pollock. LC 81-23720. (Contributions in Political Science Ser.: No. 79). 328p. 1982. lib. bdg. 36.95 (ISBN 0-313-22113-8, POP/). Greenwood.

Politics of Privacy, Computers, & Criminal Justice Records: Controlling the Social Costs of Technological Change. Donald A. Marchand. LC 80-80675. xvi, 433p. 1980. text ed. 34.95 (ISBN 0-87815-030-7). Info Resources.

Politics of Privacy: Planning for Pesonal Data Systems As Powerful Technologies. Rule & McAdam. 27.95 (ISBN 0-444-99074-7, RPP/, Pub. by Elsevier). Greenwood.

Politics of Privatisation: Contracting out Public Services. Kate Ascher. LC 86-17647. 320p. 1987. 35.00 (ISBN 0-312-62713-0). St Martin.

Politics of Procrustes: Contradictions of Enforced Equality. Antony Flew. 216p. 1981. text ed. 22.95 (ISBN 0-87975-150-9). Prometheus Bks.

Politics of Professional Knowledge: Strategies of Change in Medicine & Planning. Lily M. Hoffman. (Sociology of Work Ser.). 304p. 1989. text ed. 54.50x (ISBN 0-88706-948-7); pap. 17.95x (ISBN 0-88706-949-5). State U NY Pr.

Politics of Professionalism, Opportunity, Employment & Gender. Ed. by Sarah Slavin. LC 86-29491. (Women & Politics Ser.). 144p. 1987. text ed. 19.95 (ISBN 0-86656-626-0). Haworth Pr.

Politics of Program Evaluation. Ed. by Dennis J. Palumbo. 304p. 1987. text ed. 35.00 (ISBN 0-8039-2736-3); pap. text ed. 16.95 (ISBN 0-8039-2737-1). Sage.

Politics of Progress. Richard Cooper & Ryland Crary. (YA) (gr. 7-12). 1982. 9.95 (ISBN 0-931992-42-7). Penns Valley.

Politics of Progress: The Origins & Development of the Commercial Republic, 1600-1835. Hiram Caton. 1988. 49.00x (ISBN 0-8130-0847-6). U Presses Fla.

Politics of Projects. Bob Block. (Illus.). 160p. 1983. pap. 19.95 (ISBN 0-917072-35-9, Yourdon). P-H.

Politics of Propaganda: The Office of War Information, 1942-1945. Allan M. Winkler. LC 77-21746. (Historical Publications Ser.: No. 118). 1978. 26.00x (ISBN 0-300-02148-8). Yale U Pr.

Politics of Prose: Essay on Sartre. Denis Hollier. Tr. by Jeffrey Mehlman from Fr. LC 86-11205. (Theory & History of Literature Ser.: Vol. 35). 242p. 1987. 29.50x (ISBN 0-8166-1509-8); pap. 14.95 (ISBN 0-8166-1510-1). U of Minn Pr.

Politics of Prosecution: Jim Thompson, Richard Nixon, Marje Everett, & the Trial of Otto Kerner. Hank Messick. LC 77-15915. (Illus.). 253p. 1978. 10.95 (ISBN 0-916054-64-0, Dist. by Kampmann). Green Hill.

Politics of Protection: The United States Secret Service in the Terrorist Age. Philip H. Melanson. LC 84-11606. 1984. 35.00 (ISBN 0-275-91229-9, C1229). Praeger.

Politics of Provincialism: The Democratic Party in Transition, 1918 to 1932. David Burner. LC 81-6542. (Illus.). 1981. Repr. of 1968 ed. lib. bdg. 35.00x (ISBN 0-313-22926-0, BUPP). Greenwood.

Politics of Provincialism: The Democratic Party in Transition, 1918-1932. David Burner. 320p. 1986. pap. text ed. 9.95x (ISBN 0-674-68940-2). Harvard U Pr.

Politics of Provocation: Participation & Protest in Israel. Gadi Wolfsfeld. (SUNY Series in Israeli Studies). (Illus.). 240p. 1988. 44.50x (ISBN 0-88706-768-9); pap. 14.95x (ISBN 0-88706-769-7). State U NY Pr.

Politics of Psychoanalysis. Steven Frosh. LC 86-51354. 288p. 1987. 27.50x (ISBN 0-300-03801-1). Yale U Pr.

Politics of Public Enterprise: Oil & the French State. Harvey B. Feigenbaum. LC 84-42883. 184p. 1985. 28.00x (ISBN 0-691-07677-4); pap. 9.95x (ISBN 0-691-02229-1). Princeton U Pr.

Politics of Public-Facility Planning. John E. Seley. LC 82-47802. (Politics of Planning Ser.). (Illus.). 256p. 1983. 32.00x (ISBN 0-669-05642-1). Lexington Bks.

Politics of Public Librarianship. David Shavit. LC 86-7573. (New Directions in Information Management Ser.: No. 12). (Illus.). 170p. 1986. lib. bdg. 35.00 (ISBN 0-313-24816-8, SVP/). Greenwood.

Politics of Public Sector Labor Relations: Some Predictions. George H. Questoer. (IPE Monographs: No. 1). 32p. 1973. pap. 2.25 (ISBN 0-87546-237-5). ILR Pr.

Politics of Public Utility Regulation. William T. Gormley, Jr. LC 82-42756. 281p. 1983. 29.95x (ISBN 0-8229-3479-5); pap. 12.95x (ISBN 0-8229-5351-X). U of Pittsburgh Pr.

Politics of Puerto Rican University Students. Arthur Liebman. (Latin American Monographs No. 20). 217p. 1970. 12.50x (ISBN 0-292-70046-6). U of Tex Pr.

Politics of Race & Gender in Therapy. Ed. by Lenora Fulani. LC 88-657. (Women & Therapy Ser.: Vol. 6, No. 4). 130p. 1988. text ed. 12.95 (ISBN 0-86656-723-2). Haworth Pr.

Politics of Race, Class & Nationalism in Twentieth Century South Africa. Shula Marks & Stanley Trapido. LC 86-27554. (Illus.). 1987. pap. text ed. 21.95 (ISBN 0-582-64490-9). Longman.

Politics of Race, Class, & Nationalism in 20th Century South Africa. Marks & Trapido. 462p. (Orig.). 1987. pap. text ed. 19.95 (ISBN 0-317-64742-3). Longman.

Politics of Race in Britain. Zig Layton-Henry. LC 84-6265. 208p. 1984. text ed. 39.95x (ISBN 0-04-323026-1); pap. text ed. 14.95x (ISBN 0-04-323027-X). Unwin Hyman.

Politics of Race in New York: The Struggle for Black Suffrage in the Civil War Era. Phyllis F. Field. 256p. 1982. 24.95x (ISBN 0-8014-1408-3). Cornell U Pr.

Politics of Racial Inequality: A Systematic Comparative Macro-Analysis from the Colonial Period to 1970. J. Owens Smith. LC 87-225. (Contributions in Ethnic Studies: No. 22). 224p. 1987. lib. bdg. 37.95 (ISBN 0-313-25731-0, SHQ/). Greenwood.

Politics of Railroad Coordination, 1933-1936. Earl Latham. LC 59-9279. 1959. 24.50x (ISBN 0-674-68951-8). Harvard U Pr.

Politics of Rapid Urbanization: Government & Growth in Modern Turkey. (Illus.). 304p. 1985. 34.95x (ISBN 0-8419-0951-2); pap. 19.50x (ISBN 0-8419-0952-0). Holmes & Meier.

Politics of Rational Man. Robert E. Goodin. LC 75-35616. pap. 54.50 (ISBN 0-317-07750-3, 2022401). Bks Demand UMI.

Politics of Reading: Power, Opportunity, & Prospects for Change in America's Public Schools. Jo M. Fraatz. 256p. 1987. 29.95x (ISBN 0-8077-2887-X); pap. text ed. 17.85x (ISBN 0-8077-2886-1). Tchrs Coll.

Politics of Realignment: Party Changes in the Mountain West. Ed. by Peter F. Galderisi et al. (Special Studies in American Government & Politics). 235p. 1986. pap. 26.50 (ISBN 0-8133-7251-8). Westview.

Politics of Reality: Essays in Feminist Theory. Marilyn Frye. LC 83-2082. 176p. 1983. 21.95 (ISBN 0-89594-100-7); pap. 8.95 (ISBN 0-89594-099-X). Crossing Pr.

Politics of Reapportionment. Ed. by Malcolm E. Jewell. LC 82-18695. (Atherton Press Political Science Ser.). xii, 334p. 1982. Repr. of 1962 ed. lib. bdg. 41.50x (ISBN 0-313-23317-9, JERA). Greenwood.

Politics of Reappraisal: Nineteen Eighteen to Nineteen Thirty-Nine. Ed. by Gillian Peele & Christopher Cook. LC 75-13591. 250p. 1975. 26.00 (ISBN 0-312-62720-3). St Martin.

Politics of Reconstruction: 1863-1867. David Donald. 128p. 1984. pap. text ed. 5.95x (ISBN 0-674-68953-4). Harvard U Pr.

Politics of Reconstruction, 1863-1867. David H. Donald. LC 82-1015. (Walter Lynnwood Fleming Lectures in Southern History). 105p. 1982. Repr. of 1967 ed. lib. bdg. 35.00x (ISBN 0-313-23481-7, DONP). Greenwood.

Politics of Recovery: Roosevelt's New Deal. Albert U. Romasco. LC 82-14499. 1983. 24.95 (ISBN 0-19-503248-9). Oxford U Pr.

Politics of Reflexivity: Narrative & the Constitutive Poetics of Culture. Robert Siegle. LC 86-2700. 288p. 1986. text ed. 29.50x (ISBN 0-8018-3334-5). Johns Hopkins.

Politics of Reform in Peru: The Aprista & Other Mass Parties of Latin America. Grant Hilliker. LC 76-128763. (Illus.). pap. 55.30 (ISBN 0-317-41673-1, 2025850). Bks Demand UMI.

Politics of Reform in Thailand: Education in the Reign of King Chulalongkorn. David K. Wyatt. LC 77-81435. (Yale Southeast Asia Studies: No. 4). pap. 111.50 (ISBN 0-317-29702-3, 2022055). Bks Demand UMI.

Politics of Regional Integration in East Africa. Z. M. Khan. 215p. 1985. 30.00 (ISBN 0-944025-03-X). Advance Research.

Politics of Regional Integration: The Central American Case, Vol. 12. James D. Cochrane. LC 79-12590. 1969. 11.00 (ISBN 0-930598-11-3). Tulane Stud Pol.

Politics of Regional Policy in Japan: Localities Incorporated? Richard J. Samuels. LC 83-42575. 312p. 1983. 41.00x (ISBN 0-691-07657-X); pap. 17.50x (ISBN 0-691-10152-3). Princeton U Pr.

Politics of Regions: The Economics & Politics of Territory. Ann R. Markusen. LC 87-4359. 400p. 1987. 37.50 (ISBN 0-8476-7394-4). Rowman.

Politics of Regulation. James Q. Wilson. 1982. pap. 14.95x (ISBN 0-465-05968-6, TB-5089). Basic.

Politics of Relationships. Barbara Ruth. (Poetry Chapbooks: No. 1). 32p. 1979. pap. 2.50 (ISBN 0-913282-14-6). Seven Woods Pr.

Politics of Religion & Social Change. Ed. by Jeffrey T. Hadden & Anson Shupe. 428p. 1988. 24.95 (Pub. by New Era Bks); pap. 12.95 (Pub. by New Era Bks). Paragon Hse.

Politics of Representation: Continuities in Theory & Research. Heinz Eulau & John C. Wahlke. LC 78-17128. pap. 78.00 (ISBN 0-317-29687-6, 2021894). Bks Demand UMI.

Politics of Representation: Writing Practices in Biography, Photography, & Political Analysis. Michael J. Shapiro. LC 87-40373. (Rhetoric of the Human Sciences Ser.). (Illus.). 256p. 1988. text ed. 27.50x (ISBN 0-299-11630-1). U of Wis Pr.

Politics of Reproduction. Mary O'Brien. 1983. pap. 10.95 (ISBN 0-7100-9498-1). Routledge Chapman & Hall.

Politics of Reproductive Ritual. Karen E. Paige & Jeffrey M. Paige. 392p. 1981. 35.00x (ISBN 0-520-03071-0); pap. 10.95x (ISBN 0-520-04782-6). U of Cal Pr.

Politics of Rescue. Henry L. Feingold. LC 80-81713. (Illus.). 432p. (Orig.). 1970. pap. 12.95 (ISBN 0-89604-019-4). Holocaust Pubns.

Politics of Rescue: The Roosevelt Administration & the Holocaust, 1938-1945. Henry L. Feingold. LC 75-127049. 1970. 45.00 (ISBN 0-8135-0664-6). Rutgers U Pr.

Politics of Rescue: The Roosevelt Administration & the Holocaust, 1938 to 1945. expanded & updated ed. Henry L. Feingold. LC 80-81713. 432p. 1980. pap. 12.95 (ISBN 0-8052-5019-0, Pub. by Holocaust Library). Schocken.

Politics of Rescue: The Roosevelt Administration & the Holocaust, 1938-1945. Henry L. Feingold. 432p. pap. 7.95 (ISBN 0-686-95080-1). ADL.

Politics of Research. Richard J. Barber. 9.50 (ISBN 0-8183-0194-5). Pub Aff Pr.

Politics of Resistance in France, 1940-1944: A History of the Mouvements Unis de la Resistance. John F. Sweets. LC 75-15014. (Illus.). 260p. 1976. 20.00 (ISBN 0-87580-061-0). N Ill U Pr.

Politics of Resource Allocation in the U. S. Department of Defense. Alex Mintz. 145p. 1988. pap. 18.50x (ISBN 0-86531-809-3). Westview.

Politics of Return: International Return Migration in Europe. Ed. by Daniel Kubat. LC 84-9477. (Immigration Theory & Policy Ser.). 369p. 1984. pap. 14.95 (ISBN 0-913256-68-4). Ctr Migration.

Politics of Revenue Sharing. Paul R. Dommel. LC 74-376. (Illus.). Repr. of 1974 ed. 55.80 (ISBN 0-8357-9235-8, 2017617). Bks Demand UMI.

Politics of Rights: Lawyers, Public Policy & Political Change. Stuart A. Scheingold. LC 74-79972. 240p. 1974. 26.00x (ISBN 0-300-01783-9); pap. 10.95x (ISBN 0-300-01811-8). Yale U Pr.

Politics of Riot Behavior. L. Alex Swan. LC 79-5510. 1980. pap. text ed. 13.50 (ISBN 0-8191-0905-3). U Pr of Amer.

Politics of Rock Music. John Orman. LC 84-4846. (Illus.). 224p. 1984. lib. bdg. 23.95x (ISBN 0-8304-1025-2); pap. 11.95x (ISBN 0-8304-1119-4). Nelson-Hall.

Politics of Rural Russia, 1905-1914. Ed. by Leopold H. Haimson. LC 78-62420. (Studies of the Russian Institute, Columbia University). 319p. pap. 83.00 (2056422). Bks Demand UMI.

Politics of Salvation: The Hegelian Idea of the State. Paul Lakeland. LC 83-17875. (Hegelian Studies). 197p. 1985. 59.50 (ISBN 0-87395-846-2); pap. 19.95x (ISBN 0-87395-847-0). State U NY Pr.

Politics of San Antonio: Community, Progress, & Power. Ed. by David R. Johnson et al. LC 83-5766. (Illus.). xiv, 248p. 1983. 24.50x (ISBN 0-8032-1178-3); pap. 10.95 (ISBN 0-8032-6068-7, BB 861, Bison). U of Nebr Pr.

Politics of Scandal: Power & Process in Liberal Democracies. Ed. by Andrei S. Markovitz & Mark Silverstein. 300p. 1988. 44.50x (ISBN 0-8419-1097-9); pap. 19.95 (ISBN 0-8419-1098-7). Holmes & Meier.

Politics of Scarcity: Public Pressure & Political Response in India. Myron Weiner. LC 62-15047. pap. 67.80 (ISBN 0-317-11131-0, 2020177). Bks Demand UMI.

Politics of Scarcity: Water in the Middle East. Ed. by Joyce R. Starr & Daniel C. Stoll. (Special Studies on the Middle East). 128p. 1988. pap. 18.50 (ISBN 0-8133-7285-2). Westview.

Politics of School Accountibility. Edward Wynne. LC 74-190055. 300p. 1972. 25.25x (ISBN 0-8211-2250-9); text ed. 22.50x 10 or more copies (ISBN 0-685-24960-3). McCutchan.

Politics of School Desegregation: Comparative Case Studies of Community Structure & Policy-Making. Robert L. Crain. LC 67-27390. (NORC Monographs in Social Research Ser.: No. 14). (Illus.). 1968. 9.95x (ISBN 0-202-30033-1). NORC.

Politics of School Desegregation: The Metropolitan Remedy in Delaware. Jeffrey A. Raffel. 312p. 1980. 34.95 (ISBN 0-87722-176-6). Temple U Pr.

Politics of School Government. Ed. by G. Baron. LC 80-40913. (International Studies in Education & Social Change). 304p. 1981. 64.00 (ISBN 0-08-025213-3). Pergamon.

Politics of School Management. Eric Hoyle. (Studies in Teaching & Learning). 188p. (Orig.). 1986. pap. text ed. 20.95 (ISBN 0-340-38993-1). Princeton Bk Co.

Politics of School Reform, 1870-1940. Paul E. Peterson. LC 85-1042. x, 242p. 1985. lib. bdg. 27.50x o.s.i (ISBN 0-226-66294-2); pap. 11.95 (ISBN 0-226-66295-0). U of Chicago Pr.

Politics of Secrecy. James Michael. 1979. 20.00x (ISBN 0-901108-80-4, Pub. by NCCL UK). State Mutual Bk.

Politics of Security in the Nordic Area see Security & Politics in the Nordic Area.

Politics of Self-Esteem. Ed. by Nancy P. Greenleaf. LC 78-55202. 84p. 1978. pap. text ed. 25.95 (ISBN 0-913654-48-5). Aspen Pub.

Politics of Self-Sufficiency. Michael Allaby & Peter Bunyard. 1980. 32.00x (ISBN 0-19-217695-1). Oxford U Pr.

Politics of Sentiment: Churches & Foreign Investment in South Africa. Richard E. Sincere, Jr. Frwd. by Lucy Mvubelo. LC 84-28642. 176p. (Orig.). 1984. pap. 11.75 (ISBN 0-89633-088-5); 23.50. Ethics & Public Policy.

Politics of Sex & Religion: A Case History in the Development of Doctrine, 1962-1984. Robert B. Kaiser. LC 84-82552. 200p. (Orig.). 1985. pap. 10.95 (ISBN 0-934134-16-2, Leaven Pr). Sheed & Ward MO.

Politics of Shared Power. 2nd ed. Louis Fisher. 241p. 1987. pap. 11.95 (ISBN 0-87187-410-5). Congr Quarterly.

Politics of Sikhs. Jitender Kaur. 280p. 1986. 24.00x (ISBN 0-8364-1795-X, Pub. by Manohar India). South Asia Bks.

Politics of Sino-Indian Confrontation. Mohan Ram. 1973. 9.00 (ISBN 0-7069-0266-1). Intl Bk Dist.

Politics of SinoIndian Confrontation. M. Ram. 1973. 11.25 (ISBN 0-89684-554-0). Orient Bk Dist.

Politics of Size: Representation in the United States, 1776-1850. Rosemarie Zagarri. LC 87-47609. (Illus.). 192p. 1987. 23.50x (ISBN 0-8014-2019-9). Cornell U Pr.

Politics of Small Business. Harmon Zeigler. Ed. by Stuart Bruchey & Vincent P. Carosso. LC 78-18154. (Small Business Enterprise in America Ser.). 1979. Repr. of 1961 ed. lib. bdg. 14.00x (ISBN 0-405-11511-3). Ayer Co Pubs.

Politics of Social Change in the Middle East & North Africa. Manfred Halpern. (Rand Corporation Research Studies). 1963. pap. 15.50x (ISBN 0-691-00006-9). Princeton U Pr.

Politics of Social Knowledge. Larry D. Spence. LC 77-10543. 1978. 28.75x (ISBN 0-271-00521-1). Pa St U Pr.

Politics of Social Policy in the United States. Ed. by Margaret Weir et al. (Studies from the Project on the Federal Social Role). (Illus.). 500p. 1988. text ed. 52.00 (ISBN 0-691-09436-5); pap. text ed. 14.50 (ISBN 0-691-02841-9). Princeton U Pr.

Politics of Social Security in Brazil. James M. Malloy. LC 78-53994. (Pitt Latin American Ser.). (Illus.). 1979. 22.95x (ISBN 0-8229-3385-3). U of Pittsburgh Pr.

Politics of Social Theory: Habermas, Freud, & the Critique of Positivism. Russell Keat. LC 81-40532. 256p. 1981. 25.00x (ISBN 0-226-42875-3); pap. 9.00x (ISBN 0-226-42876-1). U of Chicago Pr.

Politics of Socialism: An Essay in Political Theory. John Dunn. (Themes in the Social Sciences Ser.). 140p. 1984. 37.50 (ISBN 0-521-26736-6); pap. 11.95 (ISBN 0-521-31840-8). Cambridge U Pr.

Politics of Sociology in the Soviet Union. Vladimir Shlapentokh. (Delphic Monograph). 200p. 1987. pap. 19.95 (ISBN 0-8133-7259-3). Westview.

Politics of Soft Coal: The Bituminous Industry from World War I through the New Deal. James P. Johnson. LC 78-31555. 280p. 1979. 24.95 (ISBN 0-252-00739-5). U of Ill Pr.

Politics of Solzhenitsyn. Stephen Carter. LC 76-28346. 161p. 1977. 19.75x (ISBN 0-8419-0244-5). Holmes & Meier.

Politics of South Africa. Howard Brotz. LC 76-49406. (Illus.). 1977. 19.95x (ISBN 0-19-215671-3). Oxford U Pr.

Politics of South India, 1920-1937. Christopher J. Baker. LC 75-2716. (Cambridge South Asian Studies: 17). pap. 96.80 (2027279). Bks Demand UMI.

Politics of Southwestern Water. Ryan J. Barilleaux. (Southwestern Studies: No. 73). (Illus.). 48p. 1984. pap. 5.00 (ISBN 0-87404-149-X). Tex Western.

Politics of Soviet Agriculture: 1960-1970. Werner G. Hahn. LC 72-151. 320p. 1972. 34.50x (ISBN 0-8018-1359-X). Johns Hopkins.

Politics of Soviet Culture: Anatolii Lunacharskii. Timothy E. O'Connor. Ed. by Stephen Foster. LC 83-18231. (Studies in the Fine Arts: The Avant-Garde: No. 42). 212p. 1983. 42.95 (ISBN 0-8357-1468-3). UMI Res Pr.

Politics of Soviet Education. Ed. by George Z. Bereday & Jaan Pennar. LC 75-28662. 217p. 1976. Repr. of 1960 ed. lib. bdg. 59.50x (ISBN 0-8371-8477-0, BEPS). Greenwood.

Politics of Space: A Comparison of the Soviet & American Space Programs. William H. Schauer. LC 74-84657. 317p. 1976. 42.50x (ISBN 0-8419-0185-6). Holmes & Meier.

Politics of Special Educational Needs. Len Barton. 200p. 1988. 33.00 (ISBN 1-85000-370-X, Falmer Pr); pap. 17.00 (ISBN 1-85000-371-8, Falmer Pr). Taylor & Francis.

Politics of Spencer's 'Complaints' & Sidney's Philisides Poems. Dennis Moore. Ed. by James Hogg. (Elizabethan & Renaissance Studies). 196p. (Orig.). 1982. pap. 15.00 (ISBN 3-7052-0768-7, Pub. by Salzburg Studies). Longwood Pub Group.

Politics of Spirituality. William Stringfellow. LC 84-10434. (Spirituality & the Christian Life Ser.: Vol. 4). 90p. 1984. pap. 7.95 (ISBN 0-664-24633-8). Westminster John Knox.

Politics of Sport. Lincoln Allison. LC 88-2359. 240p. 1988. pap. 14.95 (ISBN 0-7190-2334-3, Pub. by Manchester Univ Pr). St Martin.

Politics of State & City Administration: Public Administration in the 1980s. Glenn Abney & Thomas P. Lauth. LC 85-14873. 260p. (Orig.). 1986. 54.50 (ISBN 0-88706-255-5); pap. 16.95x (ISBN 0-88706-256-3). State U NY Pr.

Politics of State & Local Government. 3rd ed. Dunne Lockard. 288p. 1983. pap. text ed. write for info. (ISBN 0-02-371530-8). Macmillan.

Politics of State & Local Government Debated. Herbert M. Levine. LC 84-11691. 384p. 1985. pap. text ed. write for info. (ISBN 0-13-684333-6). P-H.

Politics of Steel: Western Europe & the Steel Industry in the Crisis Years (1974-1984) Ed. by Yves Meny & Vincent Wright. (European University Institute Series C: Political & Social Sciences: No. 7). x, 812p. 1986. lib. bdg. 193.00 (ISBN 3-11-010517-9). De Gruyter.

Politics of Story in Victorian Social Fiction. Rosemarie Bodenheimer. LC 87-17313. 264p. 1988. 24.95x (ISBN 0-8014-2099-7). Cornell U Pr.

Politics of Subnational Governance. Ed. by Dierdre A. Zimmerman & Joseph F. Zimmerman. LC 83-14581. 412p. (Orig.). 1983. lib. bdg. 38.25 (ISBN 0-8191-3437-6); pap. text ed. 16.50 (ISBN 0-8191-3438-4). U Pr of Amer.

Politics of Surrealism. Helena Lewis. LC 87-16986. (Illus.). 229p. 1988. 25.95 (ISBN 0-913729-44-2); pap. 12.95 (ISBN 0-913729-91-4). Paragon Hse.

Politics of T. V. Violence: Policy Uses of Communication Research. Willard D. Rowland, Jr. (People & Communication Ser.: Vol. 16). (Illus.). 320p. 1983. pap. 16.95 (ISBN 0-8039-1953-0). Sage.

Politics of Taxation. Thomas J. Reese. LC 79-8413. (Illus.). xxv, 237p. 1980. lib. bdg. 36.95 (ISBN 0-89930-003-0, RPT/, Quorum). Greenwood.

Politics of Taxation: Revenue Without Representation. Susan B. Hansen. LC 83-4043. 304p. 1983. 38.95 (ISBN 0-275-90996-4, C0996). Praeger.

Politics of Teacher Unionism: International Perspectives. Ed. by Martin Lawn. LC 85-4176. 302p. 1985. 31.00 (ISBN 0-7099-1696-5, Pub. by Croom Helm Ltd). Routledge Chapman & Hall.

Politics of Technology Transfer in Mexico. Van R. Whiting, Jr. (Reseach Report Ser.: No. 37). 61p. (Orig.). 1984. pap. 7.50 (ISBN 0-935391-36-3, RR-37). Ctr Mex Studies.

Politics of Terror: The Macedonian Liberation Movements, 1893-1903. Duncan M. Perry. (Illus.). 1988. lib. bdg. 29.75 (ISBN 0-8223-0813-4). Duke.

Politics of Terrorism. 3rd, rev. & enl. ed. Stohl. (Public Administration & Public Policy Ser.). 640p. 1988. 45.00 (ISBN 0-8247-7814-6). Dekker.

Politics of the American Civil Liberties Union. William A. Donohue. 390p. 1985. 29.95 (ISBN 0-88738-021-2); pap. 14.95 (ISBN 0-87855-983-3). Transaction Bks.

Politics of the Anglo-American Economic Special Relationship, 1940-1987. Alan P. Dobson. LC 87-35618. 286p. 1988. 45.00 (ISBN 0-312-01892-4). St Martin.

Politics of the Budgetary Process. 4th ed. Aaron Wildavsky. 1983. pap. text ed. write for info. (ISBN 0-673-39491-3). Scott F.

Politics of the Caribbean Community, 1961-79: Regional Integration Among New States. A. J. Payne. LC 80-10500. 1980. 27.50 (ISBN 0-312-62874-9). St Martin.

Politics of the Chaco Peace Conference, 1935-1939. Leslie B. Rout, Jr. (Latin American Monographs: No. 19). (Illus.). 286p. 1970. 12.50x (ISBN 0-292-70049-0). U of Tex Pr.

Politics of the Chinese Cultural Revolution: A Case Study. Hong Y. Lee. LC 76-19993. (Center for Chinese Studies, UC Berkeley: No. 17). 1978. pap. 12.95x (ISBN 0-520-04065-1). U of Cal Pr.

Politics, Prices & Petroleum: The Political Economy of Energy. David Glasner. LC 84-19134. (Illus.). 297p. 1985. 34.95 (ISBN 0-88410-953-4); pap. 12.95 (ISBN 0-88410-954-2). PRIPP.

Politics, Professionalism & Urban Services: The Police. Peter F. Nardulli & Jeffrey M. Stonecash. LC 80-27169. 224p. 1981. text ed. 30.00 (ISBN 0-89946-076-3). Oelgeschlager.

Politics, Programs, & Bureaucrats. William P. Browne. (National University Publications, Political Science Ser.). 184p. 1980. 22.95x (ISBN 0-8046-9263-7, Pub. by Kennikat). Assoc Faculty Pr.

Politics, Projects, & People: Institutional Development in Haiti. Ed. by Derick W. Brinkerhoff & Jean-claude Garcia-Zamor. LC 85-16979. 304p. 1985. 35.00 (ISBN 0-275-90035-5, C0035). Praeger.

Politics, Psychology & Art: Proceedings, Supplementary Vol. 23. Aristotelian Society for the Systematic Study of Philosophy Staff. pap. 9.00 (ISBN 0-384-47123-4). Johnson Repr.

Politics, Public Enterprise & the Industrial Development Agency: Industrialisation Policies & Practices. N. S. Carey-Jones et al. 248p. 1975. 22.50x (ISBN 0-8419-5500-X). Holmes & Meier.

Politics, Science, & Dread Disease: A Short History of the United States Medical Research Policy. Stephen P. Strickland. LC 72-78427. (Commonwealth Fund Publications Ser). 472p. 1972. 24.50x (ISBN 0-674-68955-0). Harvard U Pr.

Politics, Security & Development in Small States. Ed. by Colin Clarke & Tony Payne. LC 87-1199. 238p. 1987. 34.95 (ISBN 0-04-320203-9). Unwin Hyman.

Politics, Self, & Society: A Theme & Variations. Heinz Eulau. (Illus.). 592p. 1986. text ed. 39.95x (ISBN 0-674-68760-4). Harvard U Pr.

Politics, Society & Civil War in Warwickshire, 1620-1660. Ann Hughes. (Cambridge Studies in Early Modern British History). (Illus.). 320p. 1987. 49.50 (ISBN 0-521-33252-4). Cambridge U Pr.

Politics, Society, & Nationality in Gorbachev's Soviet Union. Ed. by Seweryn Bialer. 172p. 1988. 25.00 (ISBN 0-8133-0752-X). Westview.

Politics, Society, & Nationality in Gorbachev's Soviet Union. Ed. by Seweryn Bialer. 172p. 1988. pap. 12.95 (ISBN 0-8133-0753-8). Westview.

Politics, Technology & the Environment: Technology, Assessment & Nuclear Energy. William T. Keating. Ed. by Stuart Bruchey. LC 78-22691. (Energy in the American Economy Ser.). 1979. lib. bdg. 30.00x (ISBN 0-405-11994-1). Ayer Co Pubs.

Politics: The Citizen's Business. William A. White. LC 73-19186. (Politics & People Ser.). 338p. 1974. Repr. 23.50x (ISBN 0-405-05906-X). Ayer Co Pubs.

Politics, the Constitution & the Warren Court. Philip B. Kurland. LC 74-124734. 1970. 15.00x (ISBN 0-226-46408-3). U of Chicago Pr.

Politics the Japanese Way. Jon Woronoff. LC 87-20679. 450p. 1987. 45.00 (ISBN 0-312-01332-9). St Martin.

Politics Thro' the Looking Glass. Stan Windass. (Illus.). 188p. (Orig.). 1981. pap. 3.75x (ISBN 0-907650-00-7). LRIS.

Politics Through a Looking-Glass: Understanding Political Cultures Through a Structuralist Interpretation of Narratives. Eloise A. Buker. LC 87-8671. (Contributions in Political Science Ser.: No. 184). 264p. 1987. lib. bdg. 37.95 (ISBN 0-313-25662-4, BPK/). Greenwood.

Politics, Values, & Public Policy. Frank Fischer. (Westview Special Study Ser.). 275p. 1980. lib. bdg. 38.50x (ISBN 0-89158-799-3); pap. 16.95x (ISBN 0-86531-214-1). Westview.

Politics vs. Economics in World Steel Trade. Kent A. Jones. (World Industry Ser.). 250p. 1986. text ed. 34.95x (ISBN 0-04-338118-9). Unwin Hyman.

Politics: Who Gets What, When & How. Harold D. Lasswell. 12.50 (ISBN 0-8446-1277-4). Peter Smith.

Politics Within: A Primer in Political Attitudes & Behavior. 2nd ed. Jarol B. Manheim. LC 81-12320. (Illus.). 192p. 1982. 14.95 (ISBN 0-582-28283-7). Longman.

Politics Without Democracy: Great Britain, 1815-1914 Perception & Preoccupation in British Government. Michael Bentley. LC 84-21676. (Illus.). 446p. 1985. 28.50x (ISBN 0-389-20542-7, BNB-08104). B&N Imports.

Politics Without Parliaments, 1629-1640. Esther S. Cope. 256p. 1987. text ed. 34.95x (ISBN 0-04-941020-2). Unwin Hyman.

Politics, Work, & Daily Life in the U. S. S. R. A Survey of Former Soviet Citizens. Ed. by James R. Millar. (Illus.). 400p. 1987. 49.50 (ISBN 0-521-33476-4); pap. 16.95 (ISBN 0-521-34890-0). Cambridge U Pr.

Politics, Writing, Mutilation: The Cases of Bataille, Blanchot, Roussel, Leiris, & Ponge. Allan Stoekl. LC 85-8594. xix, 161p. 1985. 25.00x (ISBN 0-8166-1299-4); pap. 11.95 (ISBN 0-8166-1300-1). U of Minn Pr.

Polities & Partitions: Human Boundaries & the Growth of Complex Societies. Ed. & intro. by Kathryn M. Trinkaus. LC 87-70155. (Arizona State University Anthropological Research Papers: No. 37). (Illus.). 255p. (Orig.). 1987. pap. 17.50 (ISBN 0-936249-00-5). AZ Univ ARP.

Polities & Power: An Economic & Political History of the Western Pubelo. Steadman Upham. (Studies in Archaeology). 1982. 19.95 (ISBN 0-12-709180-7). Acad Pr.

Politik in Suedkorea Zwischen Tradition und Fortschritt: Krisensequenzen in einem Schwellenland. Jong-Min Kim. (European University Studies: No. 31, Vol. 31). 301p. (Ger.). 1983. 35.80 (ISBN 3-8204-5992-8). P Lang Pubs.

Politik, Wirtschaft, Offentliches Leben see International Biographical Dictionary of Central European Emigres: 1933-1945.

Politikos: Selected Papers of the American Chapter of the Society for Greek Political Thought. Ed. by Kent Moors. 200p. 1989. text ed. 32.50x (ISBN 0-8207-0204-8). Duquesne.

Politique de l'Imaginaire. Dominique Guerin. (Archontes Ser.: No. 1). 140p. (Fr.). 1975. pap. text ed. 15.20x (ISBN 90-2797-795-X). Mouton.

Politique Des Grands Travaux En France: 1929-1939. Pierre Saly. Ed. by Stuart Bruchey. LC 77-77184. (Dissertations in European Economic History Ser.). (Fr.). 1977. lib. bdg. 36.50 (ISBN 0-405-10797-8). Ayer Co Pubs.

Politique des Prix et Equilibre des Productions de Lait et de Viande see Cahiers de l'Institut de Science Economique Appliquee.

Politique et Morale see Cahiers de l'Institut de Science Economique Appliquee.

Politique Financiere des Jacobins. George Mallet. 449p. (Fr.). 1972. Repr. of 1913 ed. lib. bdg. 29.00 (ISBN 0-8337-2196-8). B Franklin.

Politique Morale de John Locke. Raymond Polin. LC 83-48575. (Philosophy of John Locke Ser.). 320p. 1984. lib. bdg. 40.00 (ISBN 0-8240-5610-8). Garland Pub.

Politique Urbaine Dans la Region Lyonnaise, 1945-1972. Jean Lojkine. (La Recherche Urbaine: No. 7). 1974. pap. 11.20x (ISBN 90-2797-310-5). Mouton.

Politique Urbaine Dans la Region Parisienne, 1945-1972. Jean Lojkine. (La Recherche Urbaine: No. 1). 1976. pap. 11.20x (ISBN 90-2797-583-3). Mouton.

Politiques de l'ecriture. Jean-Michel Heimonet. (Studies in Romance Languages & Literatures: No. 229). 231p. 1987. 17.50X (ISBN 0-8078-9233-5). U of NC Pr.

Politiques Economiques, Croissance, et Equilibre Exterieur Dans les Pays du Maghreb: Symposium Tenue en Tunisie, Organise par L'Institut de Financement du Developpement du Maghreb Arabse, la Banque Centrale de Tunisie, et le Fonds Monetaire International. 386p. 1988. pap. 18.00 (ISBN 1-55775-010-6). Intl Monetary.

Politische Geschichte see Aufstieg und Niedergang der romischen Welt: Section 1, von den Anfangen Roms bis zum Ausgang der Republik.

Politische Lied Im Schulischen Musikunterricht der DDR. Erich Neitmann. (European University Studies: No. 11, Vol. 132). 246p. (Ger.). 1982. 30.55 (ISBN 3-8204-7042-5). P Lang Pubs.

Politische Philosophus. C. A. Heumann. 1973. Repr. of 1724 ed. 50.00 (ISBN 0-384-22778-3). Johnson Repr.

Politische Schlagworter Aus der Zeit Des Peloponnesischen Krieges. Gustav Grosmann. LC 72-7893. (Greek History Ser.). (Ger.). Repr. of 1950 ed. 18.00 (ISBN 0-405-04789-4). Ayer Co Pubs.

Politische und theologische schriften, monucleus aureus see Saemtliche Schriften.

Politisches Woerterbuch. Siegfried Landshut. (Ger.). 1958. pap. 75.00 (ISBN 3-16-811742-0, M-7589, Pub. by Hochschule Fuer Wirtschaft U. Politik). French & Eur.

Politization of Architecture: A Guide to Albert Speer, Fascism, Communism, & Architecture, 1980-1985. Coppa & Avery Consultants Staff. (Architecture Ser.: A 1761). 7p. 1987. 3.00 (ISBN 1-55590-191-3). Vance Biblios.

Politocal Economy of Botswana: A Study of Growth & Distribution. Christopher Colclough & Stephen McCarthy. (Illus.). 1980. 45.00x (ISBN 0-19-877136-3). Oxford U Pr.

Polity. Norton E. Long. (Reprints in Sociology Ser.). lib. bdg. 24.50x (ISBN 0-685-70258-8); pap. 9.95x (ISBN 0-685-70259-6). Irvington.

Polity & Praxis: A Program for American Practical Theology. Dennis P. McCann & Charles R. Strain. 176p. 1985. 15.95 (ISBN 0-86683-986-0, AY8571, HarpR). Har-Row.

Polity & Theatre in Historical Perspective. Karen Hermassi. LC 76-19971. 1977. 30.00x (ISBN 0-520-03294-2). U of Cal Pr.

Polity Law Lost Art: Law Arithmetic. abr. ed. Luanna C. Blagrove. (Illus.). 237p. 1988. 29.95 (ISBN 0-939776-46-4). Blagrove Pubns.

Polity: The Journal of the Northeastern Political Science Association. Ed. by Jerome M. Mileur. (Illus.). 200p. individuals 20.00 (0032-3497); lib. bdg. 35.00 institutions; agency price 32.00. NE Poli Sci.

Polk & the Presidency. Charles A. McCoy. LC 72-10451. (American Biography Ser., No. 32). 1973. Repr. of 1960 ed. lib. bdg. 75.00x (ISBN 0-8383-1686-7). Haskell.

Polk County Arkansas Census 1850. Courtney York & Gerlene York. (Orig.). 1969. pap. 12.00x (ISBN 0-916660-06-0). Hse of York.

Polk County Courthouse Facilities Project, Des Moines, Iowa. National Center for State Courts Staff. 233p. 1979. manuscript 13.98 (NCRO-010). Natl Ctr St Courts.

Polk County Folks, Vol. 1. Don Hendrix. LC 84-80314. 167p. (Orig.). 1984. pap. 15.95 (ISBN 0-911317-30-9). Ericson Bks.

Polk County Judicial Facilities Master Plan Project. National Center for State Courts Staff. 360p. 1979. manuscript 21.60 (NCRO-027). Natl Ctr St Courts.

Polka. Earl Atkinson. (Ballroom Dance Ser.). 1986. lib. bdg. 79.95 (ISBN 0-8490-3637-2). Gordon Pr.

Polka-Dot Puppy. Jane B. Moncure. (Magic Castle Readers Ser.). (Illus.). 32p. (ps-2). 1987. 11.93 (ISBN 0-516-05729-4). Childrens.

Polka-Dot Puppy. Jane B. Moncure. LC 87-15813. (Magic Castle Readers Ser.). (Illus.). 32p. (ps-2). 1987. PLB 7.75 (ISBN 0-89565-407-5). Childs World.

Polka-Dot Puppy's Birthday: A Book about Colors. Diane D. Suire. LC 88-10937. (Polka-Dot Puppy Bks.). (Illus.). 32p. (ps-2). 1988. PLB 7.95 (ISBN 0-89565-381-8). Childs World.

Polka-Dot Puppy's New House: A Book about Counting. Janet McDonnell. LC 88-11941. (Polka-Dot Puppy Bks.). (Illus.). 32p. (ps-2). 1988. PLB 7.95 (ISBN 0-89565-380-X). Childs World.

Polka-Dot Puppy's Visitor: A Book about Opposites. Janet Riehecky. LC 88-10935. (Polka-Dot Puppy Bks.). (Illus.). 32p. (ps-2). 1988. PLB 7.95 (ISBN 0-89565-378-8). Childs World.

Polka-Dot Puppy's Walk: A Book about Sequences. Janet Riehecky. LC 88-10934. (Polka-Dot Puppy Bks.). (Illus.). 32p. (ps-2). 1988. PLB 7.95 (ISBN 0-89565-379-6). Childs World.

Polka Dot Twins. Augusto Lunel. LC 64-23162. (Illus., Eng. & Fr.). (gr. 4-6). 1964. 2.50 (ISBN 0-8076-0271-X). Braziller.

Polka Dots, Checks, & Stripes. Carol Cornelius. LC 78-983. (Illus.). (ps-4). 1978. PLB 7.45 (ISBN 0-89565-017-7). Childs World.

Polka Dotted Pals, Pt. 1. Sheila Jenkins et al. 100p. (gr. k-1). 1980. pap. 8.95 (ISBN 0-932970-13-3). Prinit Pr.

Polka Dotted Pals, Pt. 2. Sheila Jenkins. Ed. by Irene Goodwin & Rath Silvers. LC 80-84112. (Orig.). (gr. k). 1980. pap. 8.95 (ISBN 0-932970-20-6). Prinit Pr.

Polka Dotted Pencil Pushers: Comprehension. Irene Goodwin & Ruth Silvers. 142p. 1980. pap. 8.95 (ISBN 0-932970-12-5). Prinit Pr.

Polka Dotted Pencil Pushers: Math. Irene Goodwin & Ruth Silvers. LC 79-63129. (Illus.). 156p. (Orig.). 1979. pap. 8.95 tchr's. guide (ISBN 0-932970-08-7). Prinit Pr.

Polka-Dotted Pencil Pushers: Story Starters. Irene Goodwin & Ruth Silvers. LC 79-63129. 1979. pap. 8.95 (ISBN 0-932970-06-0). Prinit Pr.

Polka Party Dances. Valerie Plezia. (Ethnic Dance Bk. Ser.: No.280). 130p. (Orig.). 1982. 8.95x (ISBN 0-9609368-0-7). V Plezia.

Polka Party Dances. Valerie Plezia. (Ballroom Dance Ser.). 1985. lib. bdg. 60.00 (ISBN 0-87700-687-3). Revisionist Pr.

Polka Party Dances. Valerie Plezia. (Ballroom Dance Ser.). 1986. lib. bdg. 79.95 (ISBN 0-8490-3344-6). Gordon Pr.

Polkas, Galoppe, Maersche see Werke fuer Pianoforte.

Polk's Bluebook of Model Ships. (Blue Book of Hobbies Ser.). (Illus.). 135p. write for info. Polk.

Polks Dots & Friendship. Dorothy Rodgers. 1988. 5.95 (ISBN 0-533-07728-1). Vantage.

Pollack & After: The Critical Debate. Intro. by Francis Frascina. LC 84-48596. (Illus.). 320p. 1985. 19.50 (ISBN 0-06-433126-1, Icon Edns); pap. 10.95 (IN-147, Icon Edns). Har-Row.

Pollard: The Spy's Story. Bernard R. Henderson. 1988. 19.95 (ISBN 0-317-67509-5). Alpha Bks.

Pollard: the Spy's Story: An American Dreyfus Affair? Bernard R. Henderson. 206p. 1988. 19.95 (ISBN 0-944392-00-8). Alpha NY.

Pollbooks: How Victorians Voted. John R. Vincent. LC 67-10160. pap. 51.50 (ISBN 0-317-27091-5, 2024555). Bks Demand UMI.

Pollen. Y. Iwanami et al. 200p. 1988. 72.50 (ISBN 0-387-18833-9). Springer-Verlag.

Pollen & Spores: Form & Function. S. Blackmore & I. K. Ferguson. (Linnean Society Symposium Ser.: No. 12). 1986. 92.50 (ISBN 0-12-103460-7). Acad Pr.

Pollen & Spores of Chile: Modern Types of The Pteridophyta, Gymnospermae, & Angiospermae. Calvin J. Heusser. LC 75-114322. pap. 45.00 (2056210). Bks Demand UMI.

Pollen: Biology & Implications of Plant Breeding. Ed. by D. L. Mulcahy & E. Ottaviano. 1983. 84.50 (ISBN 0-444-00738-5, Biomedical Pr). Elsevier.

Pollen-Collecting Bees of the Anthidiini of California: Hymenoptera: Megachilidae. Albert A. Grigarick & L. A. Stange. LC 68-64309. (Bulletin of the California Insect Survey Ser.: No. 9). (Illus.). 119p. pap. 31.00 (2030305). Bks Demand UMI.

Pollen Development in Copper Deficient Cereals. University of London. 22p. 1983. write for info. Intl Copper.

Pollen Flora of Argentina: Modern Pollen & Spore Types of Pteridophyta, Gymnospermae, & Angiospermae. Vera Markgraf & Hector L. D'Antoni. LC 78-3770. 208p. 1978. pap. 19.95x (ISBN 0-8165-0649-3). U of Ariz Pr.

Pollen Flora of the Gangetic Plain. A. R. Rao & Priti Shukla. (Indian Pollen Spore Flora Ser.: Vol. I). 140p. 1977. 15.00 (ISBN 0-88065-179-2, Pub. by Messers Today & Tomorrows Printers & Publishers India). Scholarly Pubns.

Pollen Grains: Their Structure, Identification, & Significance in Science & Medicine. Roger P. Wodehouse. LC 59-15783. pap. 147.50 (ISBN 0-317-29159-9, 2055596). Bks Demand UMI.

Pollen Identification for Beekeepers. Rex Sawyer. (Illus.). 111p. (Orig.). 1981. pap. 10.50 (ISBN 0-906449-29-4, Pub. by UC Cardiff Pr). Longwood Pub Group.

Pollen Papers: The Privately Circulated Printed Works of Arthur Hungerford Pollen, 1901-1916. Jon T. Sumida. 69.00x (ISBN 0-317-44212-0, Pub. by Navy Rec Soc). State Mutual Bk.

Pollen Path: A Collection of Navajo Myths. Retold by Margaret S. Link. LC 56-7272. (Illus.). 1956. 19.50x (ISBN 0-8047-0473-2). Stanford U Pr.

Pollen Pie. Louise Argiroff. LC 87-3462. (Illus.). 32p. (gr. 1-4). 1988. 13.95 (ISBN 0-689-31359-4, Atheneum Childrens Bks). Macmillan.

Pollen Records of Late-Quaternary North American Sediments. Ed. by Vaughn M. Bryant, Jr. & Richard G. Holloway. LC 85-71610. (Illus.). 440p. 1985. 35.00 (ISBN 0-931871-01-8). Am Assn Strat.

Pollenanalytische und Stratigraphische Untersuchungen im Sewensee. Ein Beitrag Zur Spaet- und Postglazealen Vegetations-Geschichte der Suedvogesen. S. Schloss. (Dissertationes Botanica 52 Ser.). (Illus., Ger.). 1980. lib. bdg. 28.50x (ISBN 3-7682-1240-8). Lubrecht & Cramer.

Pollination. B. J. D. Meeuse. Ed. by John J. Head. LC 83-71165. (Carolina Biology Readers Ser.). (Illus.). 16p. (gr. 10 up). 1984. pap. 1.65 (ISBN 0-89278-333-8, 45-9733). Carolina Biological.

Pollination Biology. Ed. by Leslie A. Real. LC 83-11873. 1983. 49.95 (ISBN 0-12-583980-4); pap. 21.50 (ISBN 0-12-583982-0). Acad Pr.

Pollination Biology: An Analysis. Ed. by R. P. Kapil. (Illus.). xxviii, 300p. 1986. text ed. 50.00x (ISBN 81-210-0048-3, Pub. by Inter India Pubns N Delhi). Apt Bks.

Pollination Mechanisms, Reproduction & Plant Breeding. R. Frankel & E. Galun. (Monographs on Theoretical & Applied Genetics: Vol. 2). 1977. 39.00 (ISBN 0-387-07934-3). Springer-Verlag.

Polling & the Public: What Every Citizen Should Know. Herb Asher. 168p. 1988. pap. 11.95 (ISBN 0-87187-402-4). Congr Quarterly.

Polling on the Issues. Ed. by Albert H. Cantril et al. Jack Germond & Irving Grespi. LC 80-23439. 224p. 1980. pap. 7.95 (ISBN 0-932020-03-8). Seven Locks Pr.

Pollitiaue Plott, for the Honour of the Prince. Robert Hitchcock. LC 77-38110. (English Experience Ser.: No. 388). 54p. 1971. Repr. of 1580 ed. 8.00 (ISBN 90-221-0388-9). Walter J Johnson.

Pollito Pequenito Cuenta hasta diez. Margaret Friskey. Tr. by Lada Kratky from Eng. (Spanish Easy Reading Bks.). (Illus.). 32p. (Span.). (gr. k-3). 1984. lib. bdg. 11.93 (ISBN 0-516-33431-X); pap. 2.95 (ISBN 0-516-53431-9). Childrens.

Pollock Painting. Hans Namuth. Ed. by Barbara Rose. LC 79-57621. (Illus.). 112p. 1980. 25.00 (ISBN 0-9601068-6-3); pap. 14.95 (ISBN 0-9601068-5-5). Agrinde Pubns.

Pollock Personal Shorthand: A Primer. John Pollock. 1972. 3.50 (ISBN 0-682-47360-X). Exposition-Phoenix.

Polls & Public Opinion. Ed. by Norman G. Meier & Harold W. Saunders. LC 49-11509. 1949. text ed. 4.50 (ISBN 0-911090-16-9). Pacific Bk Supply.

Polls & Surveys: Understanding What They Tell Us. Norman M. Bradburn & Seymour Sudman. LC 88-42778. 1988. 22.95x (ISBN 1-55542-098-2). Jossey-Bass.

Polls & the Awareness of Public Opinion. Leo Bogart. 250p. 1985. pap. 16.95 (ISBN 0-88738-620-2). Transaction Bks.

Polls, Politics & Populism. John Clemens. 208p. 1983. text ed. 35.50x (ISBN 0-566-00602-2). Gower Pub Co.

Polluntants in Porous Media: The Unsaturated Zone Between Soil Surface & Groundwater. Ed. by B. Yaron et al. (Ecological Studies, Analysis & Synthesis: Vol. 47). (Illus.). 330p. 1984. 73.50 (ISBN 0-387-13179-5). Springer-Verlag.

Pollutant Studies in Marine Animals. Ed. by C. S. Giam. 224p. 1987. 110.00 (ISBN 0-8493-5407-2). CRC Pr.

Pollutant Transfer & Transport in the Sea, 2 vols. Gunnar Kullemberg. 1982. Vol. I, 240p. 89.00 (ISBN 0-8493-5601-6); Vol. II, 248. 89.00 (ISBN 0-8493-5602-4). CRC Pr.

Polo for the Pony Club. British Horse Society & Pony Club Staff & Faudel. LC 76-54905. 1977. pap. 4.95 (ISBN 0-8120-0785-9). Barron.

Polo Solo. Kennealy. 1988. pap. 2.95 (ISBN 0-312-91074-6). St Martin.

Polo Solo. Jerry Kennealy. 192p. 1987. 13.95 (ISBN 0-312-00671-3). St Martin.

Polo: The Manual for Coach & Player. Ed. by Peter Cutino & Dennis Bledsoe. LC 75-20710. (Illus.). 225p. 1975. pap. 13.45 (ISBN 0-685-56491-6). Swimming.

Polonaise. Jane A. Hodge. 1988. pap. 3.95 (ISBN 0-449-21455-9, Crest). Fawcett.

Polo's Ponies. Jerry Kennealy. 176p. 1988. 14.95 (ISBN 0-312-02267-0). St Martin.

Polpop: Politics & Popular Culture in America. James Combs. LC 83-73574. 1984. 24.95 (ISBN 0-87972-276-2); pap. 9.95 (ISBN 0-87972-277-0). Bowling Green Univ.

Polsinney Harbour. Pearce. 1988. pap. 3.95 (ISBN 0-312-90502-5). St Martin.

Polski Instytut Naukowy w Ameryce w Trzydziesta Rocznice 1942-1972. Ed. by Damian Wandycz. 80p. 1974. 4.00 (ISBN 0-940962-35-7). Polish Inst Art & Sci.

Polsku Mowimy Po: A Beginners Course. W. Bisko & S. Karolak. 327p. 1979. pap. 15.00x (ISBN 83-214-0089-2, P519); 3 Cassettes 35.00x (ISBN 0-89918-518-5, P518). Vanous.

Poltava Museum of Art. K. G. Skalatskii. (Illus.). 1982. 62.00x (ISBN 0-317-39525-4, Pub. by Collets UK). State Mutual Bk.

Poltergeist. James Kahn. 304p. (Orig.). 1982. pap. 2.95 (ISBN 0-446-30222-8). Warner Bks.

Poltergeist! Colin Wilson. 382p. 1983. pap. 6.95 (ISBN 0-399-50732-9, Perigee). Putnam Pub Group.

Poltergeist II: The Other Side. James Kahn. 192p. (Orig.). 1986. pap. 3.50 (ISBN 0-345-33382-9). Ballantine.

Poltergeists. Alan Gauld & A. D. Cornell. (Illus.). 1979. 26.95 (ISBN 0-7100-0185-1). Routledge Chapman & Hall.

Poltergeists - Fact or Fiction? Sacheverell Sitwell. 256p. 1988. 16.95 (ISBN 0-88029-165-6). Dorset Pr.

Poltergeists: An Annotated Bibliography of Works in English, Circa 1880-1975. Compiled by Michael Goss. LC 78-11492. 389p. 1979. 22.50 (ISBN 0-8108-1181-2). Scarecrow.

Poltergeists, Ghosts & Other Weird Stuff. R. G. Austin. (Which Way Bks.: No. 14). (Illus.). 128p. (Orig.). (gr. 3-6). 1984. pap. 1.95 (ISBN 0-671-46977-0). Archway.

Poltergeists: Opposing Viewpoints. Peter Roop & Connie Roop. LC 87-7572. (Great Mysteries Ser.). (Illus.). 96p. (gr. 3-10). 1987. lib. bdg. 12.95 (ISBN 0-89908-052-9). Greenhaven.

Polvo del Camino. Rima Vallbona. 132p. (Span.). 1985. 7.50 (ISBN 0-317-06981-0). Arte Publico.

Polvos De Arroz see Rice Powder.

Poly (N-Vinylcarbazole) J. M. Pearson & M. Stolka. (Polymer Monographs: Vol. 6). 184p. 1981. 84.00 (ISBN 0-677-05520-X). Gordon & Breach.

Poly: New Speculative Writing. Ed. by Lee Ballentine. (Illus.). 200p. 1987. 19.95 (ISBN 0-938075-05-5). Ocean View Bks.

Poly-Olbion: A Chronologic Description of Great Britain, 3 Vols. in One. Michael Drayton. (Spencer Soc.: Nos. 1-3). (Illus.). 1966. 78.50 (ISBN 0-8337-0921-6). B Franklin.

Poly (Tetrahydrofuran) P. Dreyfuss. (Polymer Monographs: Vol., 8). 320p. 1982. 78.00 (ISBN 0-677-03330-3). Gordon & Breach.

Poly (y-Benzyl-L-Glutamate) H. Block. (Polymer Monographs: Vol. 9). 215p. 1983. 59.00 (ISBN 0-677-05680-X). Gordon & Breach.

Polya Picture Album. Ed. by Gerald Alexanderson. 140p. 1987. 35.00 (ISBN 0-8176-3352-9). Birkhauser.

Polyacetal Resins. Marshall Sittig. LC 63-1271. 152p. 1963. 6.95x (ISBN 0-87201-722-2). Gulf Pub.

Polyacetylene: Chemistry, Physics, & Material Science. James C. Chien. LC 83-7237. 1984. 98.00 (ISBN 0-12-172460-3). Acad Pr.

Polyaldehydes: Papers Presented at the...Winter Meeting of the American Chemical Society. Symposium on Polymerization of Aldehydes & Structure of Polyaldehydes, 1966, Phoenix, Arizona. Ed. by O. Vogl. LC 67-18891. pap. 36.80 (2027108). Bks Demand UMI.

Polyamines As Biochemical Markers of Normal & Malignant Growth. D. H. Russell & G. M. Durie. LC 75-43340. (Progress in Cancer Research & Therapy Ser.: Vol. 8). 192p. 1978. 40.00 (ISBN 0-89004-116-4). Raven.

Polyamines: Basic & Clinical Aspects: Proceedings of a Satellite Symposium of the 3rd International Congress on Cell Biology, Japan, 1984. Ed. by K. Imahori et al. 544p. 1985. lib. bdg. 135.00x (ISBN 90-6764-042-5). Coronet Bks.

Polyamines in Biology & Medicine. Morris & Marton. (Biochemistry of Disease Ser.: Vol. 8). 512p. 1981. 75.00 (ISBN 0-8247-1342-7). Dekker.

Polyamines in Normal & Neoplastic Growth. Ed. by Diane H. Russell. LC 72-96336. (Illus.). 441p. 1973. 64.50 (ISBN 0-911216-44-8). Raven.

Polyamines in Plants. Ed. by Arthur W. Galston & Terence A. Smith. (Advances in Agricultural Biotechnology Ser.). 1986. lib. bdg. 52.50 (ISBN 90-247-3245-X, Pub. by Martinus Nijhoff Netherlands). Kluwer-Academic.

Polyamino Acids, Polypeptides & Proteins: Proceedings of an International Symposium Held at the University of Wisconsin, 1961. Ed. by Mark A. Stahmann. LC 62-12893. pap. 104.00 (ISBN 0-317-29055-X, 2021149). Bks Demand UMI.

Polyandry in Ancient India. Sarva D. Singh. 1987. 21.50x (ISBN 81-208-0487-2, Pub. by Motilal Banarsidass). South Asia Bks.

Polyandry in India. M. K. Raha. 1987. 61.00x (ISBN 81-212-0105-5, Pub. by Gian Pub Hse India). South Asia Bks.

Polyarchy: Participation & Opposition. Robert A. Dahl. LC 70-140534. 1971. pap. 11.95x (ISBN 0-300-01565-8, Y254). Yale U Pr.

Polyatomic Molecules. Ed. by Robert Mulliken & W. C. Ermler. LC 80-2764. 1981. 68.50 (ISBN 0-12-509860-X). Acad Pr.

Polybenzine Hydrocarbons & their Derivatives see Rodd's Chemistry of Carbon Compounds.

Polybius on Roman Imperialism. Polybius. Ed. by Alvin H. Bernstein. Tr. by Evelyn S. Shuckburgh. LC 79-66479. 540p. (Orig.). 1980. pap. text ed. 10.95 (ISBN 0-89526-902-3). Regnery Gateway.

Polycarbonate-Workshop Amsterdam, September 1985. Ed. by L. W. Henderson et al. (Journal: Blood Purification: Vol. 4, No. 1-3, 1986). (Illus.). 184p. 1986. pap. 98.00 (ISBN 3-8055-4352-2). S Karger.

Polycave to the Monocotyledonous Families of the World. C. K. Rao & R. J. Pankhurst. (Illus.). 62p. 1986. pap. text ed. 45.00x (ISBN 0-565-00999-0, Pub. by Brit Mus Nat Hist England). Sabbot-Natural Hist Bks.

Polychaeta Errantia of Antarctica. Ed. by O. Hartman. LC 64-60091. (Antarctic Research Ser.: Vol. 3). (Illus.). 131p. 1964. 12.00 (ISBN 0-87590-103-4). Am Geophysical.

Polychaeta from Hawaii. M. Holly. (BMB). pap. 10.00 (ISBN 0-527-02235-7). Kraus Repr.

Polychaeta Myzostomidae & Sedentaria of Antarctica. Ed. by O. Hartman. LC 66-61601. (Antarctic Research Ser.: Vol. 7). (Illus.). 158p. 1966. 13.00 (ISBN 0-87590-107-7). Am Geophysical.

Polychaete Worms, Definitions & Keys to the Orders, Families & Genera. Kristian Fauchald. (Science Ser.: No. 28). (Illus.). 188p. 1977. 8.00 (ISBN 0-938644-08-4). Nat Hist Mus.

Polychlorinated Biphenyls. National Research Council Staff. 1979. pap. 8.75x (ISBN 0-309-02885-X). Natl Acad Pr.

Polychlorinated Biphinyls (PCBS) Mammalian & Environmental Toxicology. S. Safe. (Environmental Tonin Ser.: Vol. 1). 160p. 1987. 59.50 (ISBN 0-387-15550-3). Springer-Verlag.

Polychromatic Assembly for Woodturning. rev. ed. Emmett E. Brown & Cyril Brown. Ed. by R. Sorsky. (Illus.). 120p. 1982. pap. 8.95 (ISBN 0-941936-05-8). Linden Pub Fresno.

Polychromatic Screen Printing. Joy Stocksdale. (Illus.). 128p. (Orig.). 1984. pap. 8.95 (ISBN 0-9613331-0-3). Oreg Street Pr.

Polychrome Historical Haggadah. Meir Ai-Nai-Yim. (Illus.). 40.00 (ISBN 0-686-10317-3). J Freedman Liturgy.

Polychronicon Ranulphi Higden, Monachi Cestrensis, Together with the English Translation of John of Trevisa & of an Unknown Writer in the 15th Century, 9 vols. Ed. by Churchill Babington & Joseph R. Lumby. (Rolls Ser.: No. 41). Repr. of 1886 ed. Set. 396.00 (ISBN 0-8115-1100-6). Kraus Repr.

Polycrystalline & Amorphous Thin Films & Devices. Ed. by Lawrence L. Kazmerski. LC 79-8860. (Materials Science & Technology Ser.). 1980. 56.50 (ISBN 0-12-403880-8). Acad Pr.

Polycrystalline Semiconductors. Ed. by G. Harbeke. (Springer Series in Solid-State Sciences: Vol. 57). (Illus.). viii, 245p. 1985. 35.00 (ISBN 0-387-15143-5). Springer-Verlag.

Polycrystalline Silicon for Integrated Circuit Applications. Ted Kamins. 1988. lib. bdg. 55.00 (ISBN 0-89838-259-9). Kluwer Academic.

Polycyclic Aromatic Hydrocarbon Carcinogenesis: Structure-Activity Relationships. Ed. by Shen K. Yang & B. D. Silverman. 1988. 125.00. Vol. I, 256 pgs (ISBN 0-8493-6730-1, 6730). Vol. II, 256 pgs (ISBN 0-8493-6731-X, 6731). CRC Pr.

Polycyclic Aromatic Hydrocarbons & Astrophysics. Ed. by A. Leger et al. 1986. lib. bdg. 74.50 (ISBN 90-277-2361-3, Pub. by Reidel Holland). Kluwer Academic.

Polycyclic Aromatic Hydrocarbons in the Aquatic Environment: Sources, Fates & Biological Effects. Jerry M. Neff. (Illus.). 262p. 1979. 72.00 (ISBN 0-85334-832-4, Pub. by Elsevier Applied Sci England). Elsevier.

Polycyclic Aromatic Hydrocarbons in Water Systems. David J. Futoma et al. 200p. 1981. 79.00 (ISBN 0-8493-6255-5). CRC Pr.

Polycyclic Aromatic Hydrocarbons VDI 358. VDI Editors. 1979. 104.00 (ISBN 3-18-090358-9, Pub. by VDI W Germany). IPS.

Polycyclic Compounds Excluding Steroids see Rodd's Chemistry of Carbon Compounds.

Polycyclic Groups. Daniel Segal. LC 82-9476. (Cambridge Tracts in Mathematics Ser.: No. 82). 200p. 1983. 54.50 (ISBN 0-521-24146-4). Cambridge U Pr.

Polycyclic Hydrocarbons & Cancer, 3 vols. Ed. by Harry V. Gelboin. Incl. Vol. 1. Environment, Chemistry & Metabolism. 1978. 70.00 (ISBN 0-12-279201-7); Vol. 2. Molecular & Cell Biology. 1979. 70.00 (ISBN 0-12-279202-5). 1978. Acad Pr.

Polycyclic Hydrocarbons & Carcinogens. Ronald G. Harvey. (ACS Symposium Ser.: No. 283). 406p. 1985. lib. bdg. 74.95 (ISBN 0-8412-0924-3). Am Chemical.

Polycyclic Hydrocardons & Cancer, Vol. 3. Ed. by Harry Gelboin & Paul O. Ts'O. LC 78-17706. 1981. 85.00 (ISBN 0-12-279203-3). Acad Pr.

Polycystic Ovarian Disease. W. Futterweit. (Clinical Perspectives in Obstetrics & Gynecology Ser.). (Illus.). 155p. 1984. 59.00 (ISBN 0-387-90981-8). Springer-Verlag.

Polydiacetylenes. Ed. by H. J. Cantow. (Advances in Polymer Science: Fortschritte der Hochpolymeren-Forschung: Vol. 63). (Illus.). 160p. 1984. 49.00 (ISBN 0-387-13414-X). Springer-Verlag.

Polydiacetylenes: Synthesis, Structure & Electronic Properties. Ed. by D. Bloor & R. R. Chance. 1985. lib. bdg. 67.00 (ISBN 90-247-3251-4, Pub. by Martinus Nijhoff Netherlands). Kluwer Academic.

Polydiagnostic Approach in Psychiatry. Ed. by G. Lenz & G. Pakesch. (Journal: Psychopathology: Vol. 19, No. 5, 1986). (Illus.). 76p. 1987. pap. 32.00 (ISBN 3-8055-4540-1). S Karger.

Polydore Vergil's English History, from an Early Translation. Polydorus Vergilius. Ed. by Henry Ellis. (Camden Society, London. Publications, First Ser.: No. 36). Repr. of 1846 ed. 37.00 (ISBN 0-404-50136-2). AMS Pr.

Polydori Virgilii De Rerum Inventoribus. Polidorus Vergilius. Tr. by John Langley. LC 76-171513. (Research & Source Works Ser.: No. 820). 1971. Repr. of 1868 ed. lib. bdg. 23.00 (ISBN 0-8337-1563-1). B Franklin.

Polydoxy: Explorations in a Philosophy of Liberal Religion. Alvin J. Reines. LC 87-2259. 219p. 1987. 22.95x (ISBN 0-87975-399-4). Prometheus Bks.

Polydrug Abuse: The Results of a National Collaborative Study. Ed. by Donald R. Wesson & Kenneth Adams. 1978. 24.95 (ISBN 0-12-745250-8). Acad Pr.

Polyedergeometrie in n-dimensionalen Raeumen konstanter Kruemmung. J. Boehm & E. Hertel. (LMW-MA Ser.: No. 70). 288p. 1980. 51.95x (ISBN 0-8176-1160-6). Birkhauser.

Polyelectrolytes. Kurt C. Frisch et al. LC 76-177446. (Illus.). 1976. 35.00 (ISBN 0-87762-076-8). Technomic.

Polyelectrolytes. Fumio Oosawa. LC 70-134786. (Illus.). pap. 31.80 (ISBN 0-317-07976-X, 2055010). Bks Demand UMI.

Polyelectrolytes: Aids to Better Water Quality. (AWWA Handbooks-Proceedings). (Illus.). 128p. 1972. pap. text ed. 6.00 (ISBN 0-89867-037-3). Am Water Wks Assn.

Polyelectrolytes for Water & Wastewater Treatment. Ed. by William L. Schwoyer. 288p. 1981. 99.00 (ISBN 0-8493-5439-0). CRC Pr.

Polyester & Fiberglass. 8th ed. Maurice Lannon. 1969. 6.00 (ISBN 0-685-11725-1). Gem-O-Lite.

Polyester Growth Markets. Business Communications Staff. (Illus.). 123p. 1983. 1250.00 (ISBN 0-89336-100-3, P-047R). BCC.

Polyester Molding Compounds. Burns. (Plastics Engineering Ser.: Vol. 2). 304p. 1982. 69.75 (ISBN 0-8247-1280-3). Dekker.

Polyether Antibiotics: Vol. 1, Carboxylic Acid Ionospheres. Westley. 1982. 85.00 (ISBN 0-8247-1655-8). Dekker.

Polyether Antibiotics: Vol. 2, Naturally Occuring Acid, Ionophores. Westly. 392p. 1983. 75.00 (ISBN 0-8247-1888-7). Dekker.

Polyethnicity & National Unity in World History. William H. McNeill. 14.95x (ISBN 0-8020-5730-6); pap. 7.95 (ISBN 0-8020-6643-7). U of Toronto Pr.

Polyeucte. Pierre Corneille. Ed. by R. A. Sayce. (French Text Ser.). 112p. 1962. pap. 9.95x (ISBN 0-631-00480-7). Basil Blackwell.

Polyeucte. Pierre Corneille. 1965. pap. 5.95 (ISBN 0-685-11500-3). French & Eur.

Polyeuctus, the Liar, Nicomedes. Pierre Corneille. Tr. by John Cairncross from Fr. (Penguin Classics). 1980. pap. 4.95 (ISBN 0-14-044349-5). Penguin.

Polygamy in Islamic Law. G. A. Badawi. pap. 1.00 (ISBN 0-686-18440-8). Kazi Pubns.

Polygamy Was Better Than Monotony: To My Grandfathers & Their Plural Wives. Paul Bailey. LC 72-83538. (Illus.). 9.25 (ISBN 0-87026-027-8). Westernlore.

Polyglot. Alfred Natho. 96p. 1986. 8.95 (ISBN 0-89962-562-2). Todd & Honeywell.

Polyglot Dictionary of Musical Terms. 798p. 1978. 195.00 (ISBN 0-686-92096-1, M-9436). French & Eur.

Polyglot Dictionary of Plant Names. Erevan University Press Staff. 180p. 1981. pap. 40.00x (ISBN 0-686-82330-3, Pub. by Collets (UK)). State Mutual Bk.

Polyglot Dictionary of Plant Names. 180p. (Armenian, Lat., Rus., Eng., Fr. & Ger.). 1981. 32.00x (ISBN 0-686-44741-7, Pub. by Collets (UK)). State Mutual Bk.

Polyglot of Foreign Proverbs. Henry G. Bohn. LC 68-55796. (Bohn's Antiquarian Library Ser.). Repr. of 1857 ed. 12.50 (ISBN 0-404-50004-8). AMS Pr.

Polyglot of Foreign Proverbs - with English Translations. Ed. by Henry G. Bohn. LC 67-23915. (Polyglot Ser.). 590p. 1968. Repr. of 1857 ed. 40.00x (ISBN 0-8103-3197-7). Gale.

Polyglot of Foreign Proverbs: Comprising French, Italian, German, Dutch, Spanish, Portuguese & Danish with English Translations. Henry G. Bohn. 579p. 1983. Repr. of 1889 ed. lib. bdg. 85.00 (ISBN 0-8495-0613-1). Arden Lib.

Polygonum Section Echinocaulon (Polygonaceae) C. Park. (Memoirs of the New York Botanical Garden Ser.: Vol. 47). 1988. pap. text ed. write for info. (ISBN 0-89327-329-5). NY Botanical.

Polygraph Defeats. John J. Williams & Laurie Williams. 54p. (Orig.). 1986. pap. 20.00 (ISBN 0-934274-12-6). Consumertronics.

Polygraph Handbook for Attorneys. Stanley Abrams. LC 77-6074. (Illus.). 1977. 33.00x (ISBN 0-669-01598-9). Lexington Bks.

Polygraph in Court. Robert J. Ferguson, Jr. & Allan L. Miller. (Illus.). 372p. 1973. photocopy ed. 31.75x (ISBN 0-398-02679-3). C C Thomas.

Polygraph in Private Industry. Robert J. Ferguson, Jr. (Illus.). 352p. 1966. 31.75x (ISBN 0-398-00557-5). C C Thomas.

Polygraph: Issues & Answers. Joseph P. Buckley. 1987. 2.00. Am Polygraph.

Polygraph Profession. Norman Ansley & Stanley Abrams. pap. 20.00 (ISBN 0-317-27137-7, 2024681). Bks Demand UMI.

Polygraph Test: Lies, Truth & Science. Ed. by Anthony Gale. 256p. 1988. text ed. 35.00 (ISBN 0-8039-8122-8). Sage.

Polyharmonic Functions. N. Aronszajn & T. M. Creese. (Mathematical Monographs). 1983. 59.00x (ISBN 0-19-853906-1). Oxford U Pr.

Polyhedral Boranes. Earl L. Muetterties & Walter H. Knoth. LC 68-11437. pap. 51.30 (2027109). Bks Demand UMI.

Polyhedral Combinatorics, Vol. 8. M. L. Balinski & A. J. Hoffman. 234p. 1978. pap. 39.50 (ISBN 0-444-85196-8). Elsevier.

Polyhedron Models. Magnus J. Wenninger. LC 69-10200. (Illus.). 1971. pap. 18.95 (ISBN 0-521-09859-9). Cambridge U Pr.

Polyhedron Models for the Classroom. 2nd ed. Magnus J. Wenninger. (Illus.). 80p. 1975. pap. 6.00 (ISBN 0-87353-083-7). NCTM.

Polyhistor: A Critical Edition. William of Malmesbury. Ed. & intro. by Helen T. Ouellette. LC 81-18918. (Medieval & Renaissance Texts & Studies: Vol. 10). 176p. (Lat.). 1982. 25.00 (ISBN 0-86698-017-2). Medieval & Renaissance NY.

Polyimides: A New Class of Heat-Resistant Polymers. N. A. Adrova et al. 168p. 1969. text ed. 36.00x (ISBN 0-7065-0617-0, Pub. by Keter Pub Jerusalem). Coronet Bks.

Polyimides: Synthesis, Characterization & Applications, 2 vols. Ed. by K. L. Mittal. 1984. Set. 165.00x (Plenum Pr); Vol. 1, 586p. 95.00x (ISBN 0-306-41670-0, Plenum Pr); Vol. 2, 564p. 95.00x (ISBN 0-306-41673-5, Plenum Pr). Plenum Pub.

Polyimides: Synthesis, Characterization & Application: Proceedings of Second International Conference on Polyimides, the Nevele Country Club, Ellenville, NY, October 30-November 1985. International Conference on Polyimides. pap. 160.00 (2027694). Bks Demand UMI.

Polyimides: Thermally Stable Polymers. M. I. Bessonov et al. Ed. by W. W. Wright. Tr. by L. V. Backinowsky & M. A. Chlenov. (Macromolecular Compounds Ser.). 318p. 1987. 69.50x (ISBN 0-306-10993-X, Consultants). Plenum Pub.

Polylogarithms & Associated Functions. Leonard Lewin. 360p. 1981. 89.50 (ISBN 0-444-00550-1, North-Holland). Elsevier.

Polymer Additives. Ed. by J. E. Kresta. (Polymer Science & Technology Ser.: Vol. 26). 418p. 1984. 79.50x (ISBN 0-306-41807-X, Plenum Pr). Plenum Pub.

Polymer Adsorption & Dispersion Stability. Ed. by E. D. Goddard & B. Vincent. LC 83-25787. (ACS Symposium Ser.: No. 240). 477p. 1984. lib. bdg. 79.95 (ISBN 0-8412-0820-4). Am Chemical.

Polymer Alloys I: Blends, Blocks, Grafts, & Interpenetrating Networks. Ed. by Daniel Klempner & Kurt C. Frisch. LC 77-21559. (Polymer Science & Technology Ser.: Vol. 10). 502p. 1977. 85.00x (ISBN 0-306-36410-7, Plenum Pr). Plenum Pub.

Polymer Alloys II: Blends, Blocks, Grafts, & Interpenetrating Networks. Ed. by Daniel Klempner & Kurt C. Frisch. LC 79-28487. (Polymer Science & Technology Ser.: Vol. 11). 290p. 1980. 59.50x (ISBN 0-306-40346-3, Plenum Pr). Plenum Pub.

Polymer Alloys III: Blends, Blocks, Grafts, & Interpenetrating Networks. Ed. by Daniel Klempner & Kurt C. Frisch. 312p. 1983. 59.50x (ISBN 0-306-41138-5, Plenum Pr). Plenum Pub.

Polymeric Reagents & Catalysts. Ed. by Warren T. Ford. LC 86-3521. (ACS Symposium Ser.: No. 308). (Illus.). viii, 295p. 1986. 54.95 (ISBN 0-8412-0972-3). Am Chemical.
Polymeric Separation Media. Ed. by Anthony R. Cooper. LC 82-3668. (Polymer Science & Technology Ser.: Vol. 16). 286p. 1982. 59.50x (ISBN 0-306-40902-X, Plenum Pr). Plenum Pub.
Polymeric Stabilization of Colloidal Dispersions, Vol. 1. Don H. Napper. (Colloid Science Ser.). 1984. 68.00 (ISBN 0-12-513980-2). Acad Pr.
Polymeric Surfaces for Sports & Recreation. G. Tipp & V. J. Watson. (Illus.). x, 402p. 1982. 77.50 (ISBN 0-85334-980-0, Pub. by Elsevier Applied Sci England). Elsevier.
Polymerization at Advanced Degrees of Conversion. G. P. Gladyshev & K. M. Gibov. 128p. 1970. text ed. 32.00x (ISBN 0-7065-1003-8, Pub. by Keter Pub Jerusalem). Coronet Bks.
Polymerization by Organometallic Compounds. Leo Reich & A. Schindler. LC 65-14732. (Polymer Rev. Ser.: Vol.12). pap. 160.00 (ISBN 0-317-08659-6, 2011965). Bks Demand UMI.
Polymerization in Biological Systems. Ciba Foundation Staff. LC 72-86558. (Ciba Foundation Symposium: New Ser.: No. 7). pap. 80.50 (ISBN 0-317-28314-6, 2022139). Bks Demand UMI.
Polymerization of Heterocyclics: Papers Presented at the XXIII IUPAC Congress. Ed. by Otto Vogl & Junji Furukawa. LC 73-76028. pap. 56.80 (ISBN 0-317-08378-3, 2055023). Bks Demand UMI.
Polymerization of Organized Systems. Elias. (Midland Macromolecular Monographs). 240p. 1977. 77.00 (ISBN 0-677-15930-7). Gordon & Breach.
Polymerization Processes. Ed. by H. J. Cantow et al. (Advances in Polymer Sciences Ser.: Vol. 38). (Illus.). 180p. 1981. 48.00 (ISBN 0-387-10217-5). Springer-Verlag.
Polymerization Processes see High Polymers.
Polymerization Reactions. Ed. by H. J. Cantow et al. LC 61-642. (Advances in Polymer Science: Vol. 28). (Illus.). 1978. 51.00 (ISBN 0-387-08885-7). Springer-Verlag.
Polymerization Reactors & Processes. Ed. by J. Neil Henderson & Thomas Bouton. LC 79-12519. (ACS Symposium Ser.: No. 104). 1979. 34.95 (ISBN 0-8412-0506-X). Am Chemical.
Polymerizations & Polymer Properties. Ed. by H. Cantow. (Advances in Polymer Science Ser.: Vol. 43). (Illus.). 240p. 1982. 56.00 (ISBN 0-387-11048-8). Springer-Verlag.
Polymerized Liposomes: Unique Carriers of Drugs, Catalysts, Other Agents. 150p. 1988. spiral bound 900.00. Tech Insights.
Polymers & Their Properties: Fundamentals of Structured Mechanics, Vol. 1. J. S. Hearle. LC 81-13316. 385p. 1982. 124.00 (ISBN 0-470-27302-X). Halsted Pr.
Polymers As Aids in Organic Chemistry. N. K. Mathur et al. LC 79-52789. 1980. 39.50 (ISBN 0-12-479850-0). Acad Pr.
Polymers As Biomaterials. Ed. by Shalaby W. Shalaby et al. 400p. 1985. 69.50x (ISBN 0-306-41886-X, Plenum Pr). Plenum Pub.
Polymers As Materials for Packaging. Jiri Stepek. (Polymer Science & Technology Ser.). 480p. 1988. 79.95 (ISBN 0-470-20720-5). Wiley.
Polymers at Surfaces & Colloid Stability. E. Eisenreighler & P. Pincus. (Advanced Series in Surface Science: Vol. 2). 220p. 1988. 32.00 (ISBN 9971-50-234-8). World Scientific Pub.
Polymers: Chemistry & Physics of Modern Materials. J. M. Cowie. (Illus.). 1973. pap. text ed. 24.00x (ISBN 0-7002-0222-6). Trans-Atl Phila.
Polymers for Advanced Technologies: IUPAC International Symposium. Menachem Lewin. 950p. 1988. lib. bdg. 125.00 (ISBN 0-89573-293-9). VCH Pubs.
Polymers for Engineering Applications. 200p. 1987. 53.00 (ISBN 0-87170-247-9). ASM.
Polymers For High Technology: Electronics & Photonics. Ed. by Murrae J. Bowden & Richard S. Turner. LC 87-14573. (ACS Symposium Ser.: No. 346). x, 631p. 1987. 109.95 (ISBN 0-8412-1406-9). Am Chemical.
Polymers in Concrete. American Concrete Institute Staff. LC 73-86176. (American Concrete Institute Publication Ser.: No. SP-40). (Illus.). pap. 92.00 (ISBN 0-317-10006-8, 2004294). Bks Demand UMI.
Polymers in Concrete. 92p. 1977. 22.95 (ISBN 0-317-32083-1, 548R-77). ACI.
Polymers in Concrete: International Symposium. American Concrete Institute Staff. LC 78-73077. (American Concrete Institute Publication Ser.: SP-58). pap. 106.50 (ISBN 0-317-27232-2, 2025082). Bks Demand UMI.
Polymers in Controlled Drug Delivery. L. Illum & S. S. Davis. (Illus.). 216p. 1988. 83.00 (ISBN 0-7236-0573-4). PSG Pub Co.
Polymers in Electronics. Ed. by Theodore Davidson. LC 83-25782. (ACS Symposium Ser.: No. 242). 605p. 1984. lib. bdg. 79.95x (ISBN 0-8412-0823-9). Am Chemical.
Polymers in Friction Assemblies of Machines & Devices: A Handbook. Ed. by A. V. Chichinadze. xii, 280p. 1984. 68.50 (ISBN 0-89864-010-5). Allerton Pr.
Polymers in Injection Molding. Piaras V. De Cleir. LC 85-51316. 176p. 1985. 48.00 (ISBN 0-938648-25-X). T-C Pubns CA.
Polymers in Medicine. J. Drobnik et al. (Advances in Polymer Science Ser.: Vol. 57). (Illus.). 190p. 1984. 54.00 (ISBN 0-387-12796-8). Springer-Verlag.
Polymers in Medicine & Surgery. Ed. by Richard L. Kronenthal et al. LC 75-33684. (Polymer Science & Technology Ser.: Vol. 8). 346p. 1975. 65.00x (ISBN 0-306-36408-5, Plenum Pr). Plenum Pub.
Polymers in Medicine I: Biomedical & Pharmacological Applications. Ed. by E. Chiellini & P. Giusti. 425p. 1983. 67.50x (ISBN 0-306-41360-4, Plenum Pr). Plenum Pub.
Polymers in Medicine II: Biomedical & Pharmaceutical Applications. Ed. by E. Chiellini et al. (Polymer Science & Technology Ser.: Vol. 34). 440p. 1986. 79.50x (ISBN 0-306-42390-1, Plenum Pr.). Plenum Pub.
Polymers in Nature. Ed. by A. MacGregor & C. T. Greenwood. LC 79-41787. 391p. 1981. 100.00 (ISBN 0-471-27762-2, Pub. by Wiley-Interscience); pap. text ed. write for info. (ISBN 0-471-27794-0). Wiley.
Polymers in Solar Energy Utilization. Ed. by Charles G. Gebelein & David J. Williams. LC 83-6367. (Symposium Ser.: No. 220). 519p. 1983. lib. bdg. 59.95 (ISBN 0-8412-0776-3). Am Chemical.
Polymers in Solution: Theoretical Considerations & Newer Methods of Characterization. Ed. by William C. Forsman. 298p. 1986. 52.50x (ISBN 0-306-42146-1, Plenum Pr). Plenum Pub.
Polymers, Laminations & Coatings Conference: 1984 Proceedings, Books 1 & 2. Technical Association of the Pulp & Paper Industry. Book 1. pap. 89.30 (ISBN 0-317-27227-6, 2024779); Book 2. pap. 87.50 (ISBN 0-317-27228-4). Bks Demand UMI.
Polymers, Laminations & Coatings Conference, 1986: Proceedings of TAPPI, Opryland Hotel, Nashville, TN, September 15-17, Bks. 1 & 2. Technical Association of the Pulp & Paper Industry. Bk. 1. pap. 46.80 (ISBN 0-317-55753-X, 2029281); Bk. 2. pap. 98.30 (ISBN 0-317-55754-8). Bks Demand UMI.
Polymers, Liquid Crystals & Low-Dimensional Solids. Ed. by Norman March & Mario Tosi. (Physics of Solids & Liquids Ser.). 622p. 1984. 95.00x (ISBN 0-306-41641-7, Plenum Pr). Plenum Pub.
Polymers or Fibers & Elastomers. Ed. by Jett C. Arthur, Jr. LC 84-14635. (Symposium Ser.: No. 260). 434p. 1984. lib. bdg. 69.95x (ISBN 0-8412-0859-X). Am Chemical.
Polymers, Paint, Colour Yearbook, 1988. Ed. by Portcullis Press Ltd. Staff. 1985. 150.00x (Pub. by Portcullis Pr UK). State Mutual Bk.
Polymers, Structures, & Spectra see Atlas of Polymer & Plastics Analysis.
Polymers: Syntheses, Reactivities, Properties. H. J. Cantow et al. (Advances in Poymer Science: Vol. 32). (Illus.). 1979. 56.00 (ISBN 0-387-09442-3). Springer-Verlag.
Polymers: The Origins & Growth of a Science. Herbert Morawetz. LC 84-26996. 306p. 1985. 51.95 (ISBN 0-471-89638-1). Wiley.
Polymers with Unusual Properties. Ed. by Allen. 1984. pap. write for info. (ISBN 0-471-88172-4). Wiley.
Polymetis. Joseph Spence. LC 75-27886. (Renaissance & the Gods Ser.: Vol. 41). (Illus.). 1976. Repr. of 1747 ed. lib. bdg. 88.00 (ISBN 0-8240-2090-1). Garland Pub.
Polymorphic Programming Languages: Design & Implementation. D. M. Harland. (Computers & Their Applications Ser.). 251p. 1984. 52.95 (ISBN 0-470-20029-4). Halsted Pr.
Polymorphisms & Fertility. Ed. by M. Adinolfi. (Journal: Experimental & Clinical Immunogenetics: Vol. 2; No. 2). (Illus.). 88p. 1985. pap. 26.75 (ISBN 3-8055-4066-3). S Karger.
Polymyositis & Dermatomyositis. Marinos Dalakas. (Illus.). 352p. 1988. text ed. 59.95 (ISBN 0-409-95191-9). Butterworth.
Polynesian & American Linguistic Connections. Mary R. Key. LC 85-101. (Edward Sapir Monograph Series in Language, Culture & Cognition: No. 12). xii, 80p. (Orig.). 1984. pap. 8.00x (ISBN 0-933104-17-0). Jupiter Pr.
Polynesian Botanical Bibliography, 1773-1935. E. D. Merrill. (BPBMB Ser.). 1937. 26.00 (ISBN 0-527-02252-7). Kraus Repr.
Polynesian Canoes & Navigation. Judi Thompson & Alan Taylor. (Pamphlets Polynesia Ser.: No. 2). 32p. pap. 3.50 (ISBN 0-939154-15-3). Inst Polynesian.
Polynesian Crafts. June Sasaki. (Illus.). 1978. pap. 3.95 (ISBN 0-912180-33-1). Petroglyph.
Polynesian Cultural Center Fun Book. 2nd ed. Lawrence Lau. 1982. 3.75 (ISBN 0-939154-12-9). Inst Polynesian.
Polynesian Culture History: Essays in Honor of Kenneth P. Emory. Ed. by Genevieve A. Highland & Roland W. Force. LC 67-29172. (Bernice P. Bishop Museum Special Publication Ser.: No. 56). (Illus.). 614p. pap. 159.70 (2030320). Bks Demand UMI.
Polynesian Decorative Designs. R. H. Greiner. (BMB). Repr. of 1923 ed. 28.00 (ISBN 0-527-02110-5). Kraus Repr.
Polynesian Family System in Kau, Hawaii. E. S. Handy & Mary K. Pukui. LC 75-171998. 1972. pap. 9.95 (ISBN 0-8048-1031-1). C E Tuttle.
Polynesian Journal of Henry Byam Martin. Henry B. Martin. Ed. by Edward Dodd. (Illus.). 200p. 1981. 16.95 (ISBN 0-87577-060-6). Peabody Mus Salem.
Polynesian Languages: A Guide, Vol. 5. Viktor Krupa. (Languages of Asia & Africa Ser.). 200p. (Orig., Pol.). 1982. pap. 17.95x (ISBN 0-7100-9075-7). Routledge Chapman & Hall.
Polynesian Languages: A Survey of Research. Viktor Krupa. (Janua Linguarum, Series Critica: No. 11). 1973. pap. text ed. 12.80x (ISBN 90-2792-423-6). Mouton.
Polynesian Music. Ed. by Viking Seven Seas Ltd. 85p. 1966. pap. 3.25 (ISBN 0-85467-052-1, Pub. by Viking New Zealand). Intl Spec Bk.
Polynesian Mythology & Ancient Traditional History of the New Zealanders As Furnished by Their Priests & Chiefs. George Grey. LC 75-35253. Repr. of 1906 ed. 20.50 (ISBN 0-404-14425-X). AMS Pr.
Polynesian Religion. E. S. Handy. (Bayard Dominick Expedition Publication Ser: No. 12). Repr. of 1927 ed. 56.00 (ISBN 0-527-02137-7). Kraus Repr.
Polynesian Researches: Hawaii. William Ellis. LC 69-19607. 1969. pap. 6.75 (ISBN 0-8048-0476-1). C E Tuttle.
Polynesian Researches: Polynesia. William Ellis. LC 69-19601. (Illus.). 1978. pap. 4.50 (ISBN 0-8048-0475-3). C E Tuttle.
Polynesian Seafaring & Navigation: Ocean Travel in Anutan Culture & Society. Richard Feinberg. LC 87-22572. (Illus.). 222p. 1988. 30.00x (ISBN 0-87338-352-4). Kent St U Pr.
Polynesian Species of Hedyotis. F. R. Fosberg. Repr. of 1943 ed. 13.00 (ISBN 0-527-02282-9, BMB). Kraus Repr.
Polynesian Tattooing. Alan Taylor. (Pamphlets Polynesia Ser.: No. 3). pap. 3.50 (ISBN 0-939154-21-8). Inst Polynesian.
Polynesian Voyagers see Maori Canoe.
Polynesian Wanderings. William Churchill. LC 75-35186. Repr. of 1911 ed. 45.00 (ISBN 0-404-14215-X). AMS Pr.
Polynesians: Prehistory of an Island People. Peter Bellwood. LC 78-55086. (Ancient Peoples & Places Ser.). (Illus.). 176p. 1987. pap. 10.95 (ISBN 0-500-27450-9). Thames Hudson.
Polynesiens: Leur origine, leurs migrations, leur langage, 4 vols. Pierre A. Lesson. LC 75-35201. Repr. of 1884 ed. Set. 162.50 (ISBN 0-404-14270-2). AMS Pr.
Polynesiens orientaux au contact de la civilisation. Auguste C. Caillot. LC 75-35184. Repr. of 1909 ed. 29.00 (ISBN 0-404-14211-7). AMS Pr.
Polyneuropathies Associated with Plasma Cell Dyscrasias. John J. Kelly et al. (Topics in the Neurosciences Ser.). 1987. lib. bdg. 50.00 (ISBN 0-89838-884-8, Pub. by Martinus Nijhoff Netherlands). Kluwer Academic.
Polynj Pravoslavnyj Bogoslavskij Enciklopediceskij. Ed. by Variorum. 1240p. 1971. 75.00x (ISBN 0-902089-08-0). State Mutual Bk.
Polynomes Arithmetiques et Methode des Polyedres en Combinatoire. E. Ehrhart. (International Series of Numerical Mathematics: No. 35). 169p. (Ger.). 1977. pap. 27.95x (ISBN 0-8176-0872-9). Birkhauser.
Polynomes Orthogonaux et Applications. Ed. by C. Brezinski et al. (Lecture Notes in Mathematics Ser.: Vol. 1171). 584p. (Fr. & Ger.). 1985. 46.00 (ISBN 0-387-16059-0). Springer-Verlag.
Polynomial & Spline Approximation. Ed. by Badri N. Sahney. (NATO Advanced Study Institutes Ser.: No. C-49). 1979. lib. bdg. 37.00 (ISBN 90-277-0984-X, Pub. by Reidel Holland). Kluwer Academic.
Polynomial Expansions of Analytic Functions. 2nd ed. R. P. Boas, Jr. & R. C. Buck. (Ergebnisse der Mathematik und Ihrer Grenzgebiete: Vol. 19). (Illus.). 1964. 23.10 (ISBN 0-387-03123-5). Springer-Verlag.
Polynomial Identities in Ring Theory. Louis H. Rowen. (Pure & Applied Mathematics Ser.). 1980. 68.50 (ISBN 0-12-599850-3). Acad Pr.
Polynomial Linear Control Systems. Barnett. (Pure & Applied Mathematics Ser.: Vol. 77). 1983. 65.00 (ISBN 0-8247-1898-4). Dekker.
Polynomial Representations of GLN. J. A. Green. (Lecture Notes in Mathematics: Vol. 830). 118p. 1980. pap. 13.00 (ISBN 0-387-10258-2). Springer-Verlag.
Polynomial Rings & Affine Spaces. M. Nagata. LC 78-8264. (Conference Board of the Mathematical Sciences Ser.: No. 37). 1980. Repr. of 1978 ed. 12.00 (ISBN 0-8218-1687-X, CBMS 37). Am Math.
Polynomials in Several Variables & Fractional Equations. rev. ed. Mervin Keedy & Marvin Bittinger. (Algebra, a Modern Introduction Ser.). (gr. 7-9). 1981. pap. text ed. write for info. (ISBN 0-201-03987-7). Addison-Wesley.
Polynomials Orthogonal over a Region & Bieberbach Polynomials: Proceedings. Steklov Institute of Mathematics, Academy of Sciences, U. S. S. R., No. 100 & P. K. Suetin. (Proceedings of the Steklov Institute of Mathematics: No. 100). 1974. 39.00 (ISBN 0-8218-3000-7, STEKLO-100). Am Math.
Polynuclear Aromatic Hydrocarbons. International Symposium on Analysis, Chemistry, & Biology. Ed. by Peter W. Jones & Ralph I. Freudenthal. LC 77-87456. (Carcinogenesis-A Comprehensive Survey Ser.: Vol. 3). 507p. 1978. 90.00 (ISBN 0-89004-241-1). Raven.
Polynuclear Aromatic Hydrocarbons: A Decade of Progress. Ed. by Marcus Cooke & Anthony J. Dennis. LC 79-642622. (Proceedings of the Tenth Polynuclear Aromatic Hydrocarbons International Symposiums Ser.). 912p. 1987. text ed. 75.00 (ISBN 0-935470-34-4). Battelle.
Polynuclear Aromatic Hydrocarbons: Chemical Analysis & Biological Fate. Ed. by Marcus Cooke & Anthony J. Dennis. LC 81-3669. (Fifth International Symposium on Polynuclear Aromatic Hydrocarbons Ser.). 770p. 1981. 65.00 (ISBN 0-935470-09-3). Battelle.
Polynuclear Aromatic Hydrocarbons: Chemistry & Biological Effects. Ed. by Alf Bjorseth & Anthony J. Dennis. LC 80-17877. (Fourth International Symposium on Polynuclear Aromatic Hydrocarbons Ser.). (Illus.). 1097p. 1980. 65.00 (ISBN 0-935470-05-0). Battelle.
Polynuclear Aromatic Hydrocarbons: Chemistry, Characterization & Carcinogenesis. M. Cooke & A. J. Dennis. LC 86-18430. (Ninth International Symposium on Polynuclear Aromatic Hydrocarbons Ser.). 987p. 1986. 75.00 (ISBN 0-935470-25-5). Battelle.
Polynuclear Aromatic Hydrocarbons: Formation, Metabolism & Measurement. Marcus Cooke & Anthony J. Dennis. LC 83-12734. (Seventh International Poynuclear Aromatic Symposium on Hydrocarbons). 1301p. 1983. 65.00 (ISBN 0-935470-16-6). Battelle.
Polynuclear Aromatic Hydrocarbons: Mechanisms, Methods & Metabolism. Marcus Cooke & Anthony J. Dennis. LC 84-24254. (Eighth International Symposium on Polynuclear Aromatic Hydrocarbons Ser.). 1504p. 1984. 75.00 (ISBN 0-935470-22-0). Battelle.
Polynuclear Aromatic Hydrocarbons: Physical & Biological Chemistry. Ed. by Marcus Cooke & Anthony J. Dennis. (Sixth International Symposium on Polynuclear Aromatic Hydrocarbons). 947p. 1982. 65.00 (ISBN 0-935470-13-1). Battelle.
Polyol Paradigm & Complications of Diabetes. M. P. Cohen. (Illus.). xii, 143p. 1986. 39.50 (ISBN 0-387-96418-5). Springer-Verlag.
Polyol Pathway & its Role in Diabetic Complications: Proceedings of the International Symposium, Kashikojima, Japan,28-30 Oct., 1986. Ed. by N. Sakamoto et al. (International Congress Ser.: No. 760). 584p. 1988. 197.25 (ISBN 0-444-80925-2, Excerpta Medica). Elsevier.
Polyolefins IV: Technical Papers, Regional Technical Conference, 1984. Society of Plastics Engineers. pap. 115.00 (ISBN 0-317-27179-2, 2024729). Bks Demand UMI.
Polyolefins: Modification of Structure & Properties. A. G. Sirota. 124p. 1971. text ed. 30.00x (ISBN 0-7065-1111-5, Pub. by Keter Pub Jerusalem). Coronet Bks.
Polyoma Virus. B. E. Eddy. Bd. with Rubella Virus. E. Norrby. (Virology Monographs: Vol. 7). (Illus.). iv, 174p. 1969. 34.00 (ISBN 0-387-80934-1). Springer-Verlag.
Polyomaviruses & Human Neurological Disease. Ed. by John L. Sever & David Madden. LC 82-22945. (Progress in Clinical & Biological Research Ser.: Vol. 105). 398p. 1983. 73.00 (ISBN 0-8451-0105-6). A R Liss.
Poly(One-Butene) Its Preparation & Properties. Isaac D. Rubin. LC 67-28233. (Polymer Monographs). (Illus.). 138p. 1968. 52.00 (ISBN 0-677-01270-5). Gordon & Breach.
Polypeptide & Protein Structure. A. G. Walton. 1981. 57.00 (ISBN 0-444-00407-6). Elsevier.
Polypeptide Hormone Receptors. Posner. (Receptors & Ligands in Intercellular Communications Ser.). 648p. 1985. 99.75 (ISBN 0-8247-7110-9). Dekker.
Polypeptide Hormones. Miles International Symposium, 12th. Ed. by Roland F. Beers, Jr. & Edward Bassett. 544p. 1980. text ed. 103.50 (ISBN 0-89004-462-7). Raven.
Polypeptide Hormones: Molecular & Cellular Aspects. Ciba Foundation Staff. (CIBA Foundation Symposium Ser.: No. 41). 1976. 54.25 (ISBN 0-444-15207-5, Excerpta Medica). Elsevier.
Polypeptide Hormones: Molecular & Cellular Aspects. Ciba Foundation Staff. LC 76-2666. (Ciba Foundation Symposium, New Ser.: 41). pap. 100.00 (ISBN 0-317-29787-2, 2022169). Bks Demand UMI.
Polyphase Motors: A Direct Approach to Their Design. Enrico Levi. LC 83-16850. 438p. 1984. 52.95x (ISBN 0-471-89866-X, Pub. by Wiley-Interscience). Wiley.
Polyphemes: Strange Adventures among Strange Beings. F. Hernaman Johnson. LC 74-15981. (Science Fiction Ser.). 318p. 1975. Repr. of 1906 ed. 24.50x (ISBN 0-405-06297-4). Ayer Co Pubs.
Polyphemus. Michael Shea. (Illus.). 256p. 1987. 16.95 (ISBN 0-87054-155-2). Arkham.

Pond Life. Alexander L. Crosby. LC 64-12627. (E. G. Junior Science Ser.). (Illus.). (gr. 2-5). 1964. PLB 6.69 (ISBN 0-8116-6169-5). Garrard.

Pond Life. George K. Reid. Ed. by Herbert S. Zim. (Golden Guide Ser.). (Illus.). (gr. 7 up). 1967. pap. 3.95 (ISBN 0-307-24017-7, Golden Pr). Western Pub.

Pond Life. Lynn M. Stone. LC 83-7311. (New True Bks.). (Illus.). 48p. (gr. k-4). 1983. PLB 12.60 (ISBN 0-516-01705-5); pap. 3.95 (ISBN 0-516-41705-3). Childrens.

Pond Water. 2nd ed. Elementary Science Study Staff. 1975. tchr's guide 16.16 (ISBN 0-07-018586-7). McGraw.

Ponder Heart. Eudora Welty. LC 77-92140. 158p. 1967. pap. 3.95 (ISBN 0-15-672915-6, Harv). HarBraceJ.

Ponder on This: A Compilation. Alice A Bailey. 1987. pap. 9.00 (ISBN 0-85330-131-X). Lucis.

Ponderables. Jay Hall. LC 82-83907. 93p. 1982. pap. text ed. 9.95 (ISBN 0-937932-02-7). Teleometrics.

Ponderables: Essays on Managerial Choice - Past & Future. Jay Hall. 1988. pap. 9.95. Woodstead Pr.

Pondering the Proverbs. Donald Hunt. (Bible Study Textbook Ser.). (Illus.). 1974. 15.95 (ISBN 0-89900-018-5). College Pr Pub.

Ponderings. Kenneth Grant. 48p. 1986. 6.95 (ISBN 0-8378-5087-8). Gibson.

Ponderings. Fran Parker. 50p. 1976. pap. 3.50 (ISBN 0-686-40981-7). TarPar.

Ponderings of a Citizen of the Milky Way. Alexander F. Horn. (Orig.). 1987. pap. 9.95 (ISBN 1-85230-000-0, Pub. by Element Bks UK). Tempest Brookline.

Ponderosa Country: A Scenic & Historic Guide to Reno & Vicinity. Stanley W. Paher. LC 72-87135. (Illus.). 1972. 7.50 (ISBN 0-913814-02-4). Nevada Pubns.

Ponds & Pools - Oases in the Landscape. K. Kabisch & J. Hemmerling. 262p. 1982. 63.00x (Pub. by Collets (UK)). State Mutual Bk.

Ponds & Streams. Judith Court. (Action Science Ser.). 32p. (gr. 1-8). 1985. PLB 11.90 (ISBN 0-531-04952-3). Watts.

Ponds & Water Gardens. rev. ed. Bill Heritage. (Illus.). 168p. (Orig.). 1987. pap. 12.95 (ISBN 0-7137-1861-7, Pub. by Blandford Pr England). Sterling.

Ponies. Nancy Robison. Ed. by Howard Schroeder. LC 83-7833. (Horses (Pasture to Paddock) Ser.). (Illus.). 48p. (gr. 4 up). 1983. PLB 9.95 (ISBN 0-89686-229-1). Crestwood Hse.

Ponies, Patriots & Powder Monkeys: A History of Children in America's Armed Forces, 1776-1916. Eleanor C. Bishop. (Illus.). 180p. 1983. 12.95 (ISBN 0-911329-00-5). Bishop Pr.

Ponkapog Papers. facs. ed. Thomas B. Aldrich. LC 70-84293. (Essay Index Reprint Ser). 1903. 12.25 (ISBN 0-8369-1073-7). Ayer Co Pubs.

PONS (Profile of Nonverbal Sensitivity) Test Manual. Robert Rosenthal et al. (Illus.). 1979. pap. text ed. 12.95x (ISBN 0-89197-647-7); audio cassette 11.00x (ISBN 0-8290-0753-9). Irvington.

Pons Schoffler Weis English-German, German-English Dictionary. E. Weis et al. 1060p. (Eng. & Ger.). 1979. 45.00 (ISBN 3-12-517120-2, M-9361). French & Eur.

Ponsonby Post. Bernice Rubens. 224p. 1986. pap. 4.50 (ISBN 0-446-32902-9). Warner Bks.

Pont de la Riviere Kwai. Pierre Boulle. 9.95 (ISBN 0-686-54111-1). French & Eur.

Pont de Londres. Louis-Ferdinand D. Celine. (Folio Ser.: No. 230). 1964. 13.95 (ISBN 0-686-51953-1); pap. 8.95 (ISBN 0-686-51954-X). Schoenhof.

Pont-De-Montvert: Social Structure & Politics in a French Village 1700-1914. Patrice L. Higonnet. LC 70-133209. (Historical Studies: No. 85). (Illus.). 1971. 15.00x (ISBN 0-674-68960-7). Harvard U Pr.

Pont-St-Pierre, 1398-1789: Lordship, Community & Capitalism in Early Modern France. Jonathan Dewald. (Studies on the History of Society & Culture: No. 3). 344p. 1987. 35.00x (ISBN 0-520-05673-6). U of Cal Pr.

Ponteach: The Savages of America. Robert Rogers. LC 72-153037. (Theatre & Drama Ser.: No. 20). 1971. Repr. of 1914 ed. lib. bdg. 20.50 (ISBN 0-8337-3044-4). B Franklin.

Pontiac. William L. Johnston. Ed. by Robert Benson. (Chapbook Ser.: No. 8). 21p. 1981. pap. 3.00 (ISBN 0-932884-07-5). Red Herring.

Pontiac. (Popular Mechanics-Motor Car Care Guide Ser.). (Illus.). 192p. pap. 6.95 (ISBN 0-87851-945-9). Hearst Bks.

Pontiac. Marie Tolbert. (Illus.). 116p. (Orig.). 1984. pap. 8.00 (ISBN 0-935787-00-3). Freedom Pubs.

Pontiac & the Indian Uprising. 2nd ed. Howard H. Peckham. LC 70-102528. (Illus.). 1970. Repr. of 1961 ed. 17.00x (ISBN 0-8462-1502-0). Russell.

Pontiac, Chief of the Ottawas. Jane Fleischer. LC 78-18050. (Illus.). 48p. (gr. 4-6). 1979. PLB 9.59 (ISBN 0-89375-156-1); pap. 1.95 (ISBN 0-89375-146-4); cassette avail. Troll Assocs.

Pontiac Fiero: 1984-85. Chilton Automotives Editorial Staff. LC 84-45478. 224p. (Orig.). 1985. pap. 13.95 (ISBN 0-8019-7571-9). Chilton.

Pontiac Fiero, 1984-88. R. M. Clarke. (Brooklands Ser.). (Illus.). 100p. 1988. pap. 13.95 (ISBN 1-87064-201-5, Pub. by Brooklands Bks England). Motorbooks Intl.

Pontiac Firebird, 1967 to 1973. R. M. Clarke. (Brooklands Bks.). (Illus.). 100p. (Orig.). 1982. pap. 13.95 (ISBN 0-907073-30-1, Pub. by Brooklands Bks England). Motorbooks Intl.

Pontiac Firebird 1970-1981 Shop Manual. (Illus., Orig.). pap. text ed. 14.95 (ISBN 0-89287-306-X, A235). Clymer Pub.

Pontiac GTO: 1964-1970. R. M. Clarke. (Brooklands Bks Ser.). (Illus.). 100p. (Orig.). 1980. pap. 13.95 (ISBN 0-907073-02-6, Brooklands Bks). Motorbooks Intl.

Pontiac: Mighty Ottawa Chief. Virginia F. Voight. LC 76-25244. (Indians Ser.). (Illus.). 80p. (gr. 2-5). 1977. PLB 6.69 (ISBN 0-8116-6613-1). Garrard.

Pontiac Shop Manual, 1966-76. Ed. by M. Schechter. (Illus.). 220p. 1986. pap. 18.95 (ISBN 0-87938-234-1). Motorbooks Intl.

Pontiac Show Cars: Experimentals & Special Editions. Dale Sass. (Illus.). 96p. 1986. pap. 9.95 (ISBN 0-934780-83-8). Bookman Pub.

Pontiac: The Complete History, 1926-1986. Thomas E. Bonsall. LC 79-56550. (Illus.). 352p. 1985. 29.95 (ISBN 0-934780-79-X). Bookman Pub.

Pontiac: The Performance Years, Vol. 3. Martyn Schorr. (Illus.). 84p. 1984. pap. 4.95 (ISBN 0-940346-24-9, Pub. by Quicksilver). Motorbooks Intl.

Pontifes de L'Ancienne Rome: Etudes Historique sur les Institutions Religieuses de Rome. facsimile ed. Auguste Bouche-Leclercq. LC 75-10630. (Ancient Religion & Mythology Ser.). (Fr.). 1976. Repr. of 1871 ed. 33.00x (ISBN 0-405-07006-3). Ayer Co Pubs.

Pontius Pilate. Paul L. Maier. 1981. pap. 4.50 (ISBN 0-8423-4852-2). Tyndale.

Pontius Pilate: 20B.C.-A.D.36. Adrian Johns. 199p. 1988. 30.00x (ISBN 0-7223-1960-6, Pub. by A H Stockwell England). State Mutual Bk.

Pontormo's Diary. Rosemary Mayer. (Illus.). 200p. 1983. 26.95 (ISBN 0-915570-17-3); pap. 16.95 (ISBN 0-686-86541-3). Oolp Pr.

Pontos Essenciais Do Portugues Comercial. Jose I. Suarez. 112p. (Orig.). 1987. pap. text ed. 15.00x (ISBN 0-917129-06-7). Slusa.

Pontryagin Duality of Compact O-Dimensional Semilattices & Its Applications. K. H. Hofmann & M. Mislove. (Lecture Notes in Mathematics: Vol. 396). xvi, 122p. 1974. pap. 18.00 (ISBN 0-387-06807-4). Springer-Verlag.

Pony Called Lightning. Miriam E. Mason. LC 48-9570. (Illus.). 144p. (gr. 2-4). 1971. pap. 3.95 (ISBN 0-02-044700-0, Collier). Macmillan.

Pony Club, No. 1. Ed. by Harrap Ltd. 1986. 24.75X (ISBN 0-901366-02-1, Pub. by Harrap Ltd England). State Mutual Bk.

Pony Club Quiz Book. Ed. by Harrap Limited Staff. 1986. pap. 12.50X (Pub. by Harrap Ltd England). State Mutual Bk.

Pony Engine. (gr. k-3). 0.79 (ISBN 0-8431-4152-2). Wonder.

Pony Express. Fred Reinfeld. LC 64-21330. (Illus.). 127p. 1973. pap. 4.95 (ISBN 0-8032-5786-4, BB 572, Bison). U of Nebr Pr.

Pony Express: A Thrilling & Truthful History. William L. Visscher. Ed. by William R. Jones. (Illus.). 64p. 1980. pap. 3.95 (ISBN 0-89646-062-2). Outbooks.

Pony Express Guidebook. Jamison Station Press Staff. (Desert Rat Guidebook Ser.: No. 3). (Illus.). 57p. 1984. 2.95. Jamison Stn.

Pony Express: The Reader of Romantic Adventure in Business. Arthur Chapman. LC 70-164522. (Illus.). 320p. 1971. Repr. of 1932 ed. 23.50. (ISBN 0-8154-0391-7). Cooper Sq.

Pony Express '76' Joan Covey. 14.00 (ISBN 0-686-37636-6). Snohomish Pub.

Pony for the Winter. Helen Kay. (gr. 2-3). pap. 1.75 (ISBN 0-590-08082-2). Scholastic Inc.

Pony Madness. Rita Lyttle. (Illus.). 176p. (gr. 5-7). 1988. 15.95 (ISBN 0-340-41127-9, Pub. by Hodder & Stoughton UK). David & Charles.

Pony Problem. Barbara Holland. (gr. 4-7). 1977. 6.95 (ISBN 0-525-37345-4). Dutton.

Pony Riders Book. George Wheatley. 1970. 10.00x (ISBN 0-87556-407-0). Saifer.

Pony That Nobody Wanted. Lurlene McDaniel. (Illus.). 96p. (gr. 2-5). 1982. 2.25 (ISBN 0-87406-074-5). Willowisp Pr.

Pony to Keep. Betty Roberts. 88p. (Orig.). 1985. pap. 4.95 (ISBN 0-86417-020-3, Pub. by Kangaroo Pr). Intl Spec Bk.

Pony Tracks. Frederic Remington. 17.95 (ISBN 0-89190-780-7, Pub. by Am Repr). Amereon Ltd.

Pony Tracks. Frederick Remington. (Golden West Ser.). (Illus.). 1977. pap. 1.25 (ISBN 0-8439-0457-7, Leisure Bks). Leisure NY.

Pony Tracks. Frederick Remington. (Western Frontier Library: No. 19). (Illus.). 1983. pap. 6.95 (ISBN 0-8061-1248-4). U of Okla Pr.

Pony Trails in Wyoming: Hoofprints of a Cowboy & U. S. Ranger. John K. Rollinson. 1988. pap. 11.95 (ISBN 0-8032-8932-4). U of Nebr Pr.

Pony Trekking. Glenda Spooner. (Illus.). pap. 2.95 (ISBN 0-85131-246-2, NL51, Pub. by J A Allen U K). S R Smith Sporting Bks.

Pony's Tale: A Year in the Life of a Foal. Jane Burton & Michael Allaby. LC 87-17606. (Illus.). 128p. 1987. 16.95 (ISBN 0-939481-02-2). Half Halt Pr.

Ponywise. Susan McBane. 1988. 39.00x (ISBN 0-901366-94-3, Pub. by Harrap Ltd England). State Mutual Bk.

Poochie. Phillip C. Snyder. (Illus.). 28p. (Orig.). (ps). 1982. pap. 3.95 (ISBN 0-940560-04-6). Custom Hse.

Poodle. Anna K. Nicholas. (Illus.). 288p. 1984. text ed. 16.95 (ISBN 0-86622-033-X, PS-814). TFH Pubns.

Poodle Owners' Medical Manual. Robert M. Brown. LC 87-71345. 350p. (Orig.). 1988. pap. 13.95 (ISBN 0-938681-02-8). Breed Manual Pubns.

Poodle Who Barked at the Wind. Charlotte Zolotow. LC 86-42992. (Illus.). 32p. (ps-3). 1987. 11.70i (ISBN 0-06-026965-0); PLB 11.89 (ISBN 0-06-026966-9). HarpJ.

Poodles. Kerry Donnelly. (Illus.). 1979. 9.95 (ISBN 0-87666-699-3, KW-010). TFH Pubns.

Poodles. (Illus.). 80p. 1984. pap. text ed. 5.95 (ISBN 0-86622-234-0, PB-122). TFH Pubns.

Poodles. Ullmann & Ullmann. (Pet Care Ser.). 1984. pap. 3.95 (ISBN 0-8120-2812-0). Barron.

Poof - The Aerosol Game. Elaine Peterson. 64p. 1988. 7.95 (ISBN 0-8062-3256-0). Carlton.

Pooh & Some Bees. A. A. Milne. (Illus.). 10p. (ps up). 1987. 6.95 (ISBN 0-525-44339-8, 0674-210). Dutton.

Pooh Birthday Book. A. A. Milne. (Illus.). 128p. (ps up). 1985. 5.95 (ISBN 0-525-44212-X). Dutton.

Pooh Goes Visiting. A. A. Milne. (Illus.). 10p. (ps up). 1987. 6.95 (ISBN 0-525-44337-1, 0674-210). Dutton.

Pooh Perplex: A Freshman Casebook. Frederick C. Crews. (Illus.). 1965. pap. 5.95 (ISBN 0-525-47160-X). Dutton.

Pooh Sketchbook. Brian Sibley. (Illus.). 96p. (gr. 5up). 1984. 11.95 (ISBN 0-525-44084-4). Dutton.

Pooh Song Book. A. A. Milne & H. Fraser-Simon. LC 61-1021. (Illus.). 154p. 1985. pap. 8.95 (ISBN 0-87923-557-8). Godine.

Pooh Sticker Books, 4 vols. A. A. Milne. (Illus.). 18p. (ps-4). 1986. pap. 2.98 ea. Dutton.

Pooh Story Book. A. A. Milne. (Illus.). (gr. k-4). 1965. 11.95 (ISBN 0-525-37546-5). Dutton.

Pooh's Adventures with Eeyore & Tigger. A. A. Milne. (Pooh Sticker Bks.). (ps-4). 1986. 2.98 (ISBN 0-525-44263-4). Dutton.

Pooh's Adventures with Piglet. A. A. Milne. (Pooh Sticker Bks.). 18p. (ps-4). 1986. 2.98 (ISBN 0-525-44264-2). Dutton.

Pooh's Bedtime Book. A. A. Milne & Shepard. (Illus.). 48p. (ps-3). 1980. 8.95 (ISBN 0-525-37373-X). Dutton.

Pooh's Library, 4 bks. A. A. Milne. (Illus.). (ps up). 1988. Set. 39.95 (ISBN 0-525-44451-3, 03875-1200). Dutton.

Pooh's Pot O'Honey, 4 vols. A. A. Milne. (Illus.). (ps up). 1968. Boxed Set. 8.95 (ISBN 0-525-37518-X). Dutton.

Pooh's Workout Book. Ethan Mordden. (Illus.). 160p. 1984. 10.95 (ISBN 0-525-24276-7). Dutton.

Pooh's Workout Book. Ethan Mordden. 180p. 1985. pap. 5.95 (ISBN 0-14-008304-9). Penguin.

Pookins Gets Her Way. Helen Lester. (Illus.). (ps-3). 1987. 12.95 (ISBN 0-395-42636-7). HM.

Pool & Irving Villages: A Study of Hopewell Occupation in the Illinois River Valley. John C. McGregor. LC 58-5605. (Illus.). Repr. of 1958 ed. 61.00 (ISBN 0-8357-9694-9, 2015864). Bks Demand UMI.

Pool & Waterside Gardening. Peter Robinson. (Illus.). 128p. 1987. 7.95 (ISBN 0-88192-038-X). Timber.

Pool Checkers: Spanish Fool. Theodore P. Hines. 1970. pap. 5.00 (ISBN 0-685-04929-9). Univ Place.

Pool in the Desert. Sara J. Duncan. (Fiction Ser.). 224p. 1985. pap. 6.95 (ISBN 0-14-007457-0). Penguin.

Pool of Fire. John Christopher. LC 68-23062. 178p. (gr. 5-7). 1968. 12.95 (ISBN 0-02-718350-5); pap. 3.95 (ISBN 0-02-042720-4, Collier). Macmillan.

Pool of Fire. 2nd ed. John Christopher. LC 88-16117. (Tripods Trilogy Ser.). 224p. (YA) (gr. 7 up). Date not set. pap. 3.95 (ISBN 0-02-042721-2, Collier). Macmillan.

Pool of Fire see Tripods Trilogy.

Pool of St Branok. Philippa Carr. 400p. 1987. 19.95 (ISBN 0-399-13257-0, Putnam). Putnam Pub Group.

Pool Players Bible. Ray Langley. (Illus.). 1981. 6.00 (ISBN 0-686-29667-2). Langley.

Pool Playing Techniques. Ray S. Lindenmeyer. (Illus.). 112p. 1986. 9.95 (ISBN 0-89962-531-2). Todd & Honeywell.

Poole Collection. Kurt E. Schon. LC 52-932. (Illus.). 116p. 1980. 18.00 (ISBN 0-9603880-0-1). K E Schon.

Poole: Harbour, Health & Islands. R. M. Bloomfield. 108p. 1984. 30.00x (ISBN 0-7212-0664-6, Pub. by Regency Pr). State Mutual Bk.

Poole Potteries. Jennifer Hawkins. (Illus.). 224p. 1989. 55.00 (Pub. by Century Hutchinson). David & Charles.

Poole's Index to Periodical Literature, Author Index. Ed. by C. Edward Wall. LC 77-143237. (Cumulative Author Index Ser.: No. 1). 1971. 110.00 (ISBN 0-87650-006-8). Pierian.

Poole's Index to Periodical Literature. Incl. Vol. 1. 1802-1881, 2 pts. Pt. I, A-J; Pt. 2, K-Z (ISBN 0-8446-1353-3); Vol. 2. 1882-1887 (1st Suppl. (ISBN 0-8446-1354-1); Vol. 3. 1887-1892 (2nd Suppl. (ISBN 0-8446-1355-X); Vol. 4. 1892-1896 (3rd Suppl. (ISBN 0-8446-1356-8); Vol. 5. 1897-1902 (4th Suppl. (ISBN 0-8446-1357-6); Vol. 6. 1902-1906 (5th Suppl. (ISBN 0-8446-1358-4). 36.00 ea.; Set. 252.00 (ISBN 0-8446-5695-X). Peter Smith.

Pools of Lodging for the Moon: Strategy for a Positive Life-style. David K. Reynolds. 192p. (Orig.). 1989. pap. 6.95 (ISBN 0-688-08156-8, Quill). Morrow.

Pools of Water, Pillars of Fire: The Literature of Ibuse Masuji. John W. Treat. (Illus.). 328p. 1988. 30.00 (ISBN 0-295-96625-4). U of Wash Pr.

Pools Winners. Stephen Smith & Peter Razzell. 245p. 1975. 16.50 (ISBN 0-904573-00-1, Pub. by Caliban Bks); pap. 8.50 (ISBN 0-904573-01-X). Longwood Pub Group.

Poona in the Eighteenth Century: An Urban History. Balkrishna G. Gokhale. (Illus.). 237p. 1988. 19.95 (ISBN 0-19-562137-9). Oxford U Pr.

Poor - The Church's First Priority: Latin American Bishops' Conference, Puebla. CIIR Staff. 1979. 2.00x (ISBN 0-904393-35-6, Pub. by CIIR). State Mutual Bk.

Poor Americans: How the White Poor Live. Ed. by Marc Pilisuk & Phyllis Pilisuk. 192p. 1971. 3.05; pap. text ed. 11.95x. Transaction Bks.

Poor among Us: Jewish Tradition & Social Policy. Gary Rubin et al. LC 86-72482. 63p. (Orig.). 1986. pap. 7.50 (ISBN 0-87495-084-8). Am Jewish Comm.

Poor & Minority Health Care. Ed. by Gary McCuen. LC 87-91953. (Ideas in Conflict Ser.). (Illus.). 202p. 1988. lib. bdg. 12.95 (ISBN 0-86596-065-8). G E McCuen Pubns.

Poor & the Church in Latin America. Gustavo Gutierrez. 28p. 1984. 3.00x (ISBN 0-946848-10-6, Pub. by CIIR). State Mutual Bk.

Poor & the City: The English Poor Law in its Urban Context 1834-1914. Ed. by Michael E. Rose. LC 85-2139. (Themes in Urban History Ser.). (Illus.). 192p. 1985. 29.95 (ISBN 0-312-56897-5). St Martin.

Poor & the Hard-Core Unemployed: Recommendations for New Approaches. Ed. by Wil J. Smith. LC 77-632182. 1970. pap. text ed. 5.00x (ISBN 0-87736-311-0). U of Mich Inst Labor.

Poor & the Poorest: Some Interim Findings. Michael Lipton. (World Bank Discussion Paper Ser.: No. 25). 76p. 1988. 6.50 (ISBN 0-8213-1034-8, DP0025). World Bank.

Poor & the Powerless: Economic Policy & Change in the Caribbean. Clive Y. Thomas. 416p. 1988. 28.00 (ISBN 0-85345-743-3); pap. 12.00 (ISBN 0-85345-744-1). Monthly Rev.

Poor, Black & in Real Trouble. Jerome D. Wright. 1979. pap. 2.25 (ISBN 0-87067-001-8, BH001). Holloway.

Poor Bloody Infantry, 1939-1945. Charles Whiting. (Illus.). 278p. 1988. 34.95 (ISBN 0-09-172380-9, Pub. by Century Hutchinson). David & Charles.

Poor Boy. Robert Brissenden. 224p. 1988. 15.95 (ISBN 0-312-01808-8). St Martin.

Poor Boy. limited ed. E. M. Schorb. LC 74-25863. (Living Poets' Library Ser.). (Illus.). 1975. pap. 2.50 (ISBN 0-686-10403-X). Dragons Teeth.

Poor Boy & a Long Way from Home. James Sherburne. 1984. 13.95 (ISBN 0-395-35400-5). HM.

Poor Boy, Rich Boy. Clyde R. Bulla. LC 79-2685. (Harper I Can Read Bks.). (Illus.). 64p. (gr. k-3). 1982. 9.70i (ISBN 0-06-020896-1); PLB 10.89g (ISBN 0-06-020897-X). HarpJ.

Poor Boy's Guide to Marrying a Rich Girl. Brian R. Duffy. (Illus.). 1987. pap. 6.95 (ISBN 0-14-009721-X). Penguin.

Poor Boy's Guide to Marrying a Rich Girl. Brian R. Duffy. 192p. 1987. pap. 69.50 (ISBN 0-14-778201-5). Penguin.

Poor Britain. Joanna Mack & Stewart Lansley. 280p. 1985. text ed. 34.95x (ISBN 0-04-336082-3); pap. text ed. 12.95x (ISBN 0-04-336083-1). Unwin Hyman.

Poor Carolina: Politics & Society in Colonial North Carolina, 1729-1776. A. Roger Ekirch. LC 80-39889. (Illus.). xix, 305p. 1981. 27.50x (ISBN 0-8078-1475-X). U of NC Pr.

Poor Caroline. Winifred Holtby. (Virago Modern Classics Ser.). 272p. 1986. pap. 6.95 (ISBN 0-14-016125-2). Penguin.

Poor Caroline, the Indiaman's Daughter: All's Well That Ends Well. Alexander L. Stimson. LC 72-2037. (Black Heritage Library Collection Ser.). Repr. of 1845 ed. 14.75 (ISBN 0-8369-9066-8). Ayer Co Pubs.

Poor Christ of Bomba. Mongo Beti. (African Writers Ser.). 1971. pap. text ed. 7.00 (ISBN 0-435-90088-9). Heinemann Ed.

Poor Countries & Authoritarian Rule. Maurice F. Neufeld. LC 65-63408. (International Report Ser.: No. 6). 256p. 1965. 5.00 (ISBN 0-87546-010-0). ILR Pr.

Popcorn. Gary Provost & Gail Levine-Provost. LC 84-20444. 160p. (gr. 6-8). 1985. 11.95 (ISBN 0-02-774960-6). Bradbury Pr.

Popcorn. Gary Provost & Gail Levine-Provost. 160p. 1986. pap. 2.50 (ISBN 0-425-08884-7, Pub. by Berkley-Pacer). Berkley Pub.

Popcorn & Firecrackers. Ann Averitt-Taylor. (Illus.). 64p. 1985. 6.95 (ISBN 0-89962-477-4). Todd & Honeywell.

Popcorn Book. Tomie De Paola. LC 77-21456. (Illus.). 32p. (gr. k-3). 1978. reinforced bdg. 12.95 (ISBN 0-8234-0314-9). Holiday.

Popcorn Book. Tomie DePaola. (gr. k-3). 1979. pap. 2.50. Scholastic Inc.

Popcorn Book. Tomie DePaola. LC 77-21456. (Illus.). 32p. (gr. k-3). 1984. pap. 5.95 (ISBN 0-8234-0533-8). Holiday.

Popcorn Commodity Exchange Encyclopaedia. Ed. by Barter Publishing Staff. 1984. pap. text ed. 1.95 (ISBN 0-911617-06-X, Pub. by Barter Pub). Prosperity & Profits.

Popcorn Crochet Bedspread Designs. Ed. by Rita Weiss. (Knitting, Crocheting, Tatting, Lace Making Ser.). 48p. 1985. pap. 2.95 (ISBN 0-486-24862-3). Dover.

Popcorn Days & Buttermilk Nights. Gary Paulsen. 160p. (gr. 7 up). 1983. 10.95 (ISBN 0-525-66770-9, 01063-320). Lodestar Bks.

Popcorn Girl. Richard Dankleff. LC 79-17681. 64p. 1979. pap. 4.95 (ISBN 0-87071-334-5). Oreg St U Pr.

Popcorn Lover's Book. Sue Spitler & Nao Hauser. (Illus.). 96p. (Orig.). 1983. pap. 5.95 (ISBN 0-8092-5542-1). Contemp Bks.

Popcorn Magic. (Beginning to Read Ser.). (gr. 2 up). 1988. PLB 5.95 (ISBN 0-8136-5195-6); pap. 2.95 (ISBN 0-8136-5695-8). Modern Curr.

Popcorn-Plus Diet. Joel Herskowitz. 224p. 1988. pap. 3.50 (ISBN 1-55817-065-0). Windsor NY.

Popcorn Use As Food, Crafts, Ornaments, Etc. & More with Select Recipes. Carrol, Frieda, Research Division Staff. 1984. pap. text ed. 3.95 (ISBN 0-318-04342-4). Prosperity & Profits.

Pope. Brean Hammond. (Harvester New Readings Ser.). 220p. 1986. text ed. 25.00x (ISBN 0-391-03421-9). Humanities.

Pope. John Mackail. 59.95 (ISBN 0-8490-0877-8). Gordon Pr.

Pope. John W. Mackail. LC 73-7628. 1973. lib. bdg. 15.50 (ISBN 0-8414-5939-8). Folcroft.

Pope. Leslie Stephen. Ed. by John Morley. LC 68-58397. (English Men of Letters Ser). Repr. of 1888 ed. lib. bdg. 18.00 (ISBN 0-404-51730-7). AMS Pr.

Pope. Lytton Strachey. LC 76-28504. 1974. Repr. of 1925 ed. lib. bdg. 17.00 (ISBN 0-8414-7742-6). Folcroft.

Pope Alexander III & the Council of Tours (1163) A Study of Ecclesiastical Politics & Institutions in the Twelfth Century. Robert Somerville. (Center for Medieval & Renaissance Studies, UCLA: Publications No. 12). 1978. 30.00x (ISBN 0-520-03184-9). U of Cal Pr.

Pope Alexander the Seventh & the College of Cardinals. John Bargrave. Ed. by James C. Robertson. LC 78-160001. (Camden Society, London. Publications, First Ser.: No. 92). Repr. of 1867 ed. 19.00 (ISBN 0-404-50192-3). AMS Pr.

Pope Alexander the Seventh & the College of Cardinals. John Bargrave. 19.00 (ISBN 0-384-03435-7). Johnson Repr.

Pope: An Analysis of the Office of the Pope & the Roman Church & City. Jean Carrere. 1977. lib. bdg. 59.95 (ISBN 0-8490-2453-6). Gordon Pr.

Pope & Bishops: A Study of the Papal Monarchy in the Twelfth & Thirteenth Centuries. Kenneth Pennington. LC 83-21799. (Middle Ages Ser.). 227p. 1984. 35.95x (ISBN 0-8122-7918-2). U of Pa Pr.

Pope & Bolingbroke: A Study of Friendship & Influence. Brean S. Hammond. LC 83-1068. 200p. 1984. text ed. 25.00x (ISBN 0-8262-0404-X). U of Mo Pr.

Pope & Dulness. E. Jones. (Chatterton Lectures on an English Poet Ser.). 1968. pap. 2.25 (ISBN 0-85672-260-X, Pub. by British Acad). Longwood Pub Group.

Pope & His Contemporaries. Ed. by James L. Clifford & Louis A. Landa. LC 83-45420. Repr. of 1949 ed. AMS Pr.

Pope & His Contemporaries: Essays Presented to George Sherburn. Ed. by J. L. Clifford & L. Landa. 1978. Repr. of 1949 ed. lib. bdg. 24.00x (ISBN 0-374-91700-0, Octagon). Hippocrene Bks.

Pope & His Critics. Wilbert L. MacDonald. LC 78-17391. lib. bdg. 29.50 (ISBN 0-8495-3516-6). Arden Lib.

Pope & His Critics. Wilbert L. MacDonald. LC 76-17901. 1976. lib. bdg. 35.00 (ISBN 0-8414-6033-7). Folcroft.

Pope & His Critics. Wilbert L. MacDonald. LC 74-30369. (English Literature Ser., No. 33). 1974. lib. bdg. 57.95x (ISBN 0-8383-1990-4). Haskell.

Pope & His Poetry. Edward W. Edmunds. LC 77-120969. (Poetry & Life Ser.). Repr. of 1913 ed. 7.25 (ISBN 0-404-52510-5). AMS Pr.

Pope & His Poetry. Edward W. Edmunds. LC 74-7051. 1921. lib. bdg. 27.50 (ISBN 0-8414-3934-6). Folcroft.

Pope & His Poetry. Edward W. Edmunds. LC 73-18098. (English Biography Ser., No. 31). 1974. lib. bdg. 49.95x (ISBN 0-8383-1735-9). Haskell.

Pope & Horace: Studies in Imitation. Frank Stack. 350p. 1985. 42.50 (ISBN 0-521-26695-5). Cambridge U PR.

Pope & Revolution: John Paul II Confronts Liberation Theology. Ed. by Quentin L. Quade. LC 82-4971. 205p. 1982. pap. 11.50 (ISBN 0-89633-054-0). Ethics & Public Policy.

Pope & the Augustan Stage. Malcolm Goldstein. LC 72-1632. (Stanford University. Stanford Studies in Language & Literature: No. 17). Repr. of 1958 ed. 20.00 (ISBN 0-404-51827-3). AMS Pr.

Pope & the Context of Controversy: The Manipulation of Ideas in an Essay on Man. Douglas H. White. LC 70-120009. 1970. 15.00x (ISBN 0-226-89494-0). U of Chicago Pr.

Pope & the Duce. Peter Kent. 1981. 26.00 (ISBN 0-312-63024-7). St Martin.

Pope & the Heroic Tradition: A Critical Study of His Iliad. Douglas Knight. LC 69-15686. (Yale Studies in English: No. 117). viii, 123p. 1969. Repr. of 1951 ed. 19.50 (ISBN 0-208-00775-X, Archon). Shoe String.

Pope & the Italian Jackal. Joseph McCabe. 31p. pap. cancelled (ISBN 0-911826-88-2). Am Atheist.

Pope & the Mavericks. Louis Baldwin. 221p. 1988. 19.95 (ISBN 0-87975-466-4). Prometheus Bks.

Pope & the Neo-Classicists. Alexander Pope. (Plain Texts of the Poets Ser). 1968. pap. 2.50x (ISBN 0-7022-0646-6). U of Queensland Pr.

Pope & the New Apocalypse: The Holy War Against Family Planning. Stephen D. Mumford. (Illus.). 82p. (Orig.). 1986. 6.95 (ISBN 0-937307-00-9); pap. 3.95 (ISBN 0-937307-01-7). CRPS.

Pope Anthology: Selections from the English Poets. Edward Arber. 1901. Repr. 20.00 (ISBN 0-8274-3184-8). R West.

Pope Chronology. Reginald Berry. 192p. 1988. lib. bdg. 35.00x (ISBN 0-8161-8951-X, Hall Reference). G K Hall.

Pope: Considered in His Relations with the Church, Temporal Sovereignties, Separated Churches, & the Cause of Civilization. Joseph De Maistre. Tr. by A. McD. Dawson from Fr. LC 75-5690. (Illus.). 370p. 1975. Repr. of 1850 ed. 35.00 (ISBN 0-685-53977-6). Fertig.

Pope from the Ghetto: The Legend of the Family of Pier Leone. Gertrud Von Le Fort. Tr. by Conrad R. Bonacina. 330p. 1981. Repr. of 1935 ed. lib. bdg. 15.00. Century Bookbindery.

Pope Gregory XI: The Failure of Tradition. Paul R. Thibault. 252p. 1986. lib. bdg. 28.00 (ISBN 0-8191-5462-8); pap. text ed. 13.50 (ISBN 0-8191-5463-6). U Pr of Amer.

Pope Helps Hitler to World Power. Joseph McCabe. 35p. 1988. pap. cancelled (ISBN 0-911826-87-4). Am Atheist.

Pope, His Banker & Venice. Felix Gilbert. LC 80-13062. (Illus.). 167p. 1980. text ed. 13.95x (ISBN 0-674-68975-5). Harvard U Pr.

Pope: His Descent & Family Connections. Joseph Hunter. LC 73-565. 1973. lib. bdg. 16.00 (ISBN 0-8414-1570-6). Folcroft.

Pope: His Friends & His Poetry. C. W. Brodribb. LC 73-4440. 1973. lib. bdg. 15.00 (ISBN 0-8414-1555-2). Folcroft.

Pope Innocent III. H. Tillmann. (Europe in the Middle Ages Selected Studies: Vol. 12). 374p. 1980. 84.25 (ISBN 0-444-85137-2, North-Holland). Elsevier.

Pope Joan. Lawrence Durrell. LC 82-81088. (Tusk Bks.). 176p. 1984. 22.50 (ISBN 0-87951-963-0); pap. 8.95 (ISBN 0-87951-964-9). Overlook Pr.

Pope John Paul II. Mary Craig. (Profiles Ser.). (Illus.). 64p. (gr. 3-6). 1982. 9.95 (ISBN 0-241-10711-3, Pub. by Hamish Hamilton England). David & Charles.

Pope John Paul II & the Catholic Restoration. Paul Johnson. 224p. 1982. 11.95 (ISBN 0-312-63032-8). St Martin.

Pope John Paul II & the Family & Text. Pope Paul II. LC 82-13308. 416p. 1983. 15.00 (ISBN 0-8199-0851-7). Franciscan Herald.

Pope John Paul II: Bringing Love to a Troubled World. Anthony DiFranco. LC 82-23618. (Taking Part Ser.). (Illus.). 48p. (gr. 3 up). 1983. PLB 9.95 (ISBN 0-87518-241-0). Dillon.

Pope John Paul II: Building up the Body of Christ: A Pastoral Visit to the United States. Ed. by National Catholic News Service Staff. LC 87-82683. 225p. 1987. 19.95 (ISBN 0-89870-178-3). Ignatius Pr.

Pope John Paul II Catechest: Commentary on Catechesi Trandendae - the New Charter for Religious Education in Our Time. John Paul II. LC 80-26792. 243p. 1980. 4.50 (ISBN 0-8199-0815-0). Franciscan Herald.

Pope John Paul II: Catechist. 1980. 4.50 (ISBN 0-317-46877-4). Franciscan Herald.

Pope John Paul II: He Came to Us As a Father. (Illus.). 1979. gift edition 14.95 (ISBN 0-8198-0628-5). Dghtrs St Paul.

Pope John Paul II in America. Lucius Annese. LC 79-56497. 1980. 50.00 (ISBN 0-933402-10-4). Charisma Pr.

Pope John Paul II: On Jews & Judiasm, 1979-1986. Pope John Paul II. (Orig.). 1987. pap. 3.95 (ISBN 1-55586-151-2). US Catholic.

Pope John Paul II: Pilgrim of Peace. Pope John Paul II. 1987. 25.00 (ISBN 0-517-56423-8, Harmony). Crown.

Pope John Paul II: The People's Pope. George Sullivan. LC 83-40395. (Illus.). 120p. (gr. 7 up). 1984. 11.95 (ISBN 0-8027-6523-8). Walker & Co.

Pope John the Twenty-Third & Master John Hus of Bohemia. Eustace J. Kitts. LC 77-84726. Repr. of 1910 ed. 47.00 (ISBN 0-404-16127-8). AMS Pr.

Pope John Twenty-Third: A Clever, Pastoral Leader. Bernard R. Bonnot. LC 79-1770. 1980. 9.95 (ISBN 0-8189-0388-0). Alba.

Pope John XXIII. Timothy Walch. (World Leaders--Past & Present Ser.). (Illus.). 112p. 1987. lib. bdg. 16.95 (ISBN 0-87754-535-9). Chelsea Hse.

Pope John XXIII: Shepherd of the Modern World. Peter Hebblethwaite. (Illus.). 552p. 1987. pap. 10.95 (ISBN 0-385-23537-2, Im). Doubleday.

Pope-Leighey House. Ed. by National Trust for Historic Preservation Staff. LC 74-105251. (Illus.). 120p. 1969. pap. 5.95 (ISBN 0-89133-003-8). Preservation Pr.

Pope Must Die. Frank Norwood. 320p. 1985. pap. 3.50 (ISBN 0-441-67421-6, Pub. by Charter Bks). Ace Bks.

Pope of AntiSemitism: The Career & Legacy of Edouard-Adolphe Drumont. Frederick Busi. 242p. (Orig.). 1986. text ed. 28.00 (ISBN 0-8191-5594-2); pap. text ed. 13.25 (ISBN 0-8191-5595-0). U Pr of Amer.

Pope of Greenwich Village. Vincent Patrick. 1984. pap. 3.50 (ISBN 0-671-52578-6). PB.

Pope, or President? Startling Disclosures of Romanism As Revealed by Its Own Writers: Facts for Americans. Ed. by Gerald Grob. LC 76-46094. (Anti-Movements in America). 1977. lib. bdg. 27.50x (ISBN 0-405-09967-3). Ayer Co Pubs.

Pope: Poems: An Essay on Criticism; the Rape of the Lock; an Essay on Man; Epistle to Dr. Arbuthnot; the Dunciad (Variorum) Intro. by Geoffrey Day. 480p. 1988. text ed. 120.00 (ISBN 0-85967-752-4, Pub. by Scolar Pr). Gower Pub Co.

Pope: Poems & Prose. Alexander Pope. (Poetry Library). 192p. 1985. pap. 4.95 (ISBN 0-14-058508-7). Penguin.

Pope: Poetry & Prose with Essays by Johnson, Coleridge, Hazlitt, Etc. Ed. by H. V. Dyson. 1977. Repr. of 1933 ed. lib. bdg. 20.00 (ISBN 0-8414-1852-7). Folcroft.

Pope: Recent Essays by Several Hands. Ed. by Maynard Mack & James A. Winn. LC 79-26345. (Essential Articles Ser.). iv, 768p. 1979. 39.50 (ISBN 0-208-01769-0, Archon). Shoe String.

Pope St. Pius X. F. A. Forbes. LC 87-51072. 125p. 1987. pap. 4.50 (ISBN 0-89555-328-7). TAN Bks Pubs.

Pope Speaks: Teachings of Pius XII on Purity. Nazareno Camilleri. 1985. pap. 1.95 (ISBN 0-317-40933-6). AMI Pr.

Pope, the Council, & the Mass. James Likoudis & K. D. Whitehead. 1981. 13.95 (ISBN 0-8158-0400-8). Chris Mass.

Pope: The Critical Heritage. Ed. by John Barnard. (Critical Heritage Ser.). 550p. 1973. 42.00x (ISBN 0-7100-7390-9); pap. 15.00 (ISBN 0-7102-0516-3). Routledge Chapman & Hall.

Pope, the Protestants, & the Irish: Papal Aggression & Anti-Catholicism in Mid-Nineteenth Century England. Robert J. Klaus. Ed. by William H. McNeill & Peter Stansky. (Modern European History Ser.). 400p. 1987. lib. bdg. 60.00 (ISBN 0-8240-7820-9). Garland Pub.

Popeiana, 25 vols. Incl. Vol. 1. Early Criticism, Seventeen Eleven to Seventeen Sixteen (ISBN 0-8240-1239-9); Vol. 2. Pope's Homer, One (ISBN 0-8240-1240-2); Vol. 3. Pope's Homer, Two; Vol. 4. On Literary Farces (ISBN 0-8240-1242-9); Vol. 5. Pope's Shakespeare. O.s.i. (ISBN 0-8240-1243-7); Vol. 6. Dunciad, One. Repr. of 1728 ed (ISBN 0-8240-1244-5); Vol. 7. Dunciad, Two. Repr. of 1728 ed (ISBN 0-8240-1245-3); Vol. 8. Dunciad, Three. Repr. of 1729 ed (ISBN 0-8240-1246-1); Vol. 9. Attack of Thomas Cooke (ISBN 0-8240-1247-X); Vol. 10. Dunciad & Other Matters. Repr. of 1730 ed (ISBN 0-8240-1248-8); Vol. 11. On Taste, Seventeen Thirty-Two to Seventeen Thirty-Five (ISBN 0-8240-1249-6); Vol. 12. Essay on Man, Crousaz (ISBN 0-8240-1250-X); Vol. 13. Essay on Man, Crousaz Two (ISBN 0-8240-1251-8); Vol. 14. Essay on Man, Warburton, Etc (ISBN 0-8240-1252-6); Vol. 15. Cibber & the Dunciad (ISBN 0-8240-1253-4); Vol. 16. Dunciad. Repr. of 1742 ed (ISBN 0-8240-1254-2); Vol. 17. Pope's Death & the Critical Aftermath. O.s.i. (ISBN 0-8240-1255-0); Vols. 18-19. Warton on Pope, 2 vols (ISBN 0-8240-1256-9); Vols. 20-21. Biography (ISBN 0-8240-1257-7); Vol. 22. Biography (ISBN 0-8240-1258-5); Vol. 23. Biography (ISBN 0-8240-1259-3); Vol. 24. Biography (ISBN 0-8240-1260-7); Vol. 25. Folio Verse: Attacks, Defences, & Imitations (ISBN 0-8240-1261-5). (Life & Times of Seven Major British Writers Ser). 1974. lib. bdg. 61.00 ea. Garland Pub.

Popes & European Revolution. Owen Chadwick. (Oxford History of the Christian Church Ser.). 1981. 86.00x (ISBN 0-19-826919-6). Oxford U Pr.

Popes & Heresy in the Thirteenth Century. Albert C. Shannon. LC 78-63192. (Heresies of the Early Christian & Medieval Era: Second Ser.). Repr. of 1949 ed. 31.00 (ISBN 0-404-16228-2). AMS Pr.

Popes & Princes Fourteen Seventeen to Fifteen Seventeen: Politics & Polity in Late Medieval Church. J. A. Thomson. (Early Modern Europe Today Ser.). 256p. 1980. text ed. 14.95 (ISBN 0-04-901027-1). Unwin Hyman.

Popes & Science. James J. Walsh. 1977. lib. bdg. 59.95 (ISBN 0-8490-2454-4). Gordon Pr.

Pope's Confessor & Other Stories. Denis Murphy. 115p. (Orig.). 1985. pap. 8.25x (ISBN 971-10-0188-8, Pub. by New Day Philippines). Cellar.

Pope's Death & the Critical Aftermath see Popeiana.

Pope's Divisions. Peter Nichols. 16.95 (ISBN 0-03-047576-7). Brown Bk.

Pope's Dunciad, a Study of Its Meaning. Aubrey L. Williams. (Illus.). ix, 162p. 1968. Repr. of 1955 ed. 22.00 (ISBN 0-208-00136-0, Archon). Shoe String.

Pope's Dunciad & the Queen of Night: A Study in Emotional Jacobitism. Douglas Brooks-Davies. 200p. (Orig.). 1986. 40.00 (ISBN 0-7190-1735-1, Pub. by Manchester Univ Pr); pap. 14.00 (ISBN 0-7190-1828-5). St Martin.

Pope's Essay on Man. A. D. Nuttall. LC 83-22298. (Unwin Critical Library). 250p. 1984. text ed. 37.95x (ISBN 0-04-800017-5). Unwin Hyman.

Pope's Homer, One see Popeiana.

Pope's Homer, Two see Popeiana.

Pope's Iliad: A Selection with Commentary. F. Rosslyn. 256p. 1985. 20.00 (ISBN 0-86292-049-3, Pub. by Bristol Classical UK). Focus Info Gr.

Pope's Iliad: Homer in the Age of Passion. Steven Shankman. LC 82-61384. 176p. 1983. 27.50x (ISBN 0-691-06566-7). Princeton U Pr.

Pope's Imagination. David Fairer. LC 84-832. 208p. 1984. 67.50 (ISBN 0-7190-1080-2, Pub. by Manchester Univ Pr). St Martin.

Pope's Jews. Sam Waagenaar. (Illus.). 500p. 1974. 9.95 (ISBN 0-912050-49-7, Library Pr). Open Court.

Popes, Monks & Crusaders. H. E. Cowdrey. 400p. 1983. 45.00 (ISBN 0-907628-34-6). Hambledon Press.

Popes of the 20th Century. 2.50 (ISBN 0-8198-5811-0); 1.50 (ISBN 0-8198-5812-9). Dghtrs St Paul.

Popes of Vatican Council II. Peter Wigginton. 329p. 1983. 15.00 (ISBN 0-8199-0828-2). Franciscan Herald.

Pope's Once & Future Kings: Satire & Politics in the Early Career. John M. Aden. LC 78-16618. 1978. 22.95x (ISBN 0-87049-252-7). U of Tenn Pr.

Pope's Own Miscellany: Being A Reprint of Poems on Several Occasions 1717 Containing New Poems by Alexander Pope & Others. Norman Ault. LC 73-1492. 1973. lib. bdg. 25.00 (ISBN 0-8414-1710-5). Folcroft.

Pope's Plan for Social Reconstruction. Charles P. Bruehl. 10.00 (ISBN 0-8159-6507-9). Devin.

Pope's Poetical Manuscripts. J. Butt. (Warton Lectures on English Poetry). 1954. pap. 5.50 (ISBN 0-902732-28-5, Pub by British Acad). Longwood Pub Group.

Pope's Poetical Manuscripts. John Butt. LC 74-3370. 1954. lib. bdg. 15.00 (ISBN 0-8414-3113-2). Folcroft.

Pope's Shakespeare see Popeiana.

Pope's Taste in Shakespeare. John Butt. LC 74-100736. 1970. Repr. of 1936 ed. 39.95x (ISBN 0-8383-0011-1). Haskell.

Pope's Taste in Shakespeare. John E. Butt. LC 75-17694. 1975. Repr. of 1936 ed. lib. bdg. 15.00 (ISBN 0-8414-3226-0). Folcroft.

Pope's Wedding. Edward Bond. 111p. 1971. pap. 6.95 (ISBN 0-416-09210-1, NO. 2983). Routledge Chapman & Hall.

Popessa. Paul I. Murphy & R. Rene Arlington. LC 82-61880. (Illus.). 296p. (Orig.). 1983. 16.50 (ISBN 0-446-51258-3). Warner Bks.

Popessa. Paul I. Murphy & R. Rene Arlington. 432p. 1985. pap. 4.95 (ISBN 0-446-32817-0). Warner Bks.

Popeye, No. 1. Bud Sagendorf. 128p. 1984. pap. 1.95 (ISBN 0-441-67472-0). Ace Bks.

Popeye, No. 2. Bud Sagendorf. 128p. 1984. pap. 1.95 (ISBN 0-441-67473-9). Ace Bks.

Popeye: A Photo-Storybook Based on the Movie. Adapted by Stephanie Spinner. LC 80-623. (Movie Storybooks Ser.). (Illus.). 64p. (gr. 6-9). 1981. pap. 5.95 boards o.p. (ISBN 0-394-84668-0). Random.

Popeye & the Haunted House. (gr. k-3). 1980. 0.79 (ISBN 0-8431-4132-8). Wonder.

Popeye Climbs a Mountain. (gr. k-3). 1980. 0.79 (ISBN 0-8431-4129-8). Wonder.

Popeye Goes Fishing. (gr. k-3). 1980. 0.79 (ISBN 0-8431-4130-1). Wonder.

Popeye Goes on a Picnic. (gr. k-3). 0.79 (ISBN 0-8431-4131-X). Wonder.

Popeye: The First Fifty Years. Bud Sagendorf. LC 78-65820. (Illus.). 144p. 1979. pap. 9.95 (ISBN 0-89480-065-5). Workman Pub.

Popeye the Sailor, No. 2. Sagendorf. 1.50 (ISBN 0-523-49091-7, Dist. by Warner Pub Services & Saint Martin's Press). Tor Bks.

Popeye's Big Surprise. (gr. k-3). 0.79 (ISBN 0-8431-4128-X). Wonder.

Popham. Edward Oubre. (Free Range Ser.). 184p. (Orig.). 1985. pap. 5.00 (ISBN 0-9613873-2-7). E P Oubre.

Popinjay Stairs: An Historical Adventure about Samuel Pepys. Geoffrey Trease. LC 74-30873. 192p. (gr. 3-6). 1982. 12.95 (ISBN 0-8149-0758-X). Vanguard.

Popish Kingdom: Reign of Antichrist Written in Latin Verse. Thomas Neogeorgus. Tr. by B. Googe. 190p. 1972. Repr. of 1570 ed. 30.00 (ISBN 0-384-40840-0). Johnson Repr.

Popism: The Warhol Sixties. Andy Warhol & Pat Hackett. LC 83-47574. (Illus.). 320p. 1983. pap. 12.95 (ISBN 0-06-091062-3, CN1062, PL). Har-Row.

Poplars & Willows. (Forestry Ser.: No. 10). 360p. 1980. 41.25 (ISBN 92-5-100500-1, F2046, FAO). UNIPUB.

Poplollies & Bellibones. Susan K. Sperling. (Illus.). 1979. pap. 6.95 (ISBN 0-14-005190-2). Penguin.

Popo: The Adventures of a Mexican Donkey. William R. Streiber & Flora M. Rizzoto. LC 70-146604. (Illus.). (gr. 1-4). 1971. 3.75 (ISBN 0-8356-0420-9, Quest). Theos Pub Hse.

Popol Vuh: Mythic & Heroic Sagas of the Kiches of Central America. Lewis Spence. LC 75-139178. (Popular Studies in Mythology, Romance & Folklore: No. 16). Repr. of 1908 ed. 5.50 (ISBN 0-404-53516-X). AMS Pr.

Popol Vuh: The Definitive Edition of the Mayan Book of the Dawn of Life and the Glories of Gods & Kings. Tr. & photos by Dennis Tedlock. (Illus.). 1985. 19.95 (ISBN 0-671-45241-X). S&S.

Popol Vuh: The Definitive of the Mayan Book of the Dawn of Life & the Glories Gods & Kings. Dennis Tedlock. 416p. 1986. pap. 9.95 (ISBN 0-671-61771-0, Touchstone). S&S.

Popol Vuh: The Sacred Book of the Ancient Quiche Maya: Spanish Version of the Original Maya. Tr. by Adrian Recinos & Delia Goetz. (Civilization of the American Indian Ser.: No. 29). (Eng). 1983. Repr. of 1950 ed. 16.95 (ISBN 0-8061-0205-5). U of Okla Pr.

Poppa John. Larry Woiwode. 204p. 1981. 10.95 (ISBN 0-374-23630-5). FS&G.

Popper & after: Four Modern Irrationalists. David Stove. 192p. 1982. text ed. 24.50 (ISBN 0-08-026792-0); pap. 16.00 (ISBN 0-08-026791-2). Pergamon.

Popper & the Human Sciences. Ed. by Gregory Currie & Alan Musgrave. 1985. lib. bdg. 41.50 (ISBN 90-247-2998-X, Pub. by Martinus Nijhoff Netherlands); pap. text ed. 14.95 (ISBN 90-247-3141-0, Pub. by Martinus Nijhoff Netherlands). Kluwer Academic.

Popper Selections. Karl Popper. Ed. by David Miller. LC 83-43084. 480p. 1985. pap. 36.50x (ISBN 0-691-07287-6); pap. 10.95x (ISBN 0-691-02031-0). Princeton U Pr.

Poppie Nongena. Elsa Joubert. 1986. 15.95 (ISBN 0-393-02242-0). Norton.

Poppie Nongena: A Novel of South Africa. Elsa Joubert. 1987. pap. 8.95 (ISBN 0-8050-0230-8). H Holt & Co.

Poppies. Noel Greig. 45p. (Orig.). 1983. pap. 3.50 (ISBN 0-907040-27-6, Pub. by GMP England). Alyson Pubns.

Poppies. Judith Harris. LC 81-50428. (VI Ser.). 50p. (Orig.). 1981. pap. text ed. 4.00 (ISBN 0-931846-19-6). Wash Writers Pub.

Poppies & Mandragora. Edgar Saltus. LC 74-182710. Repr. of 1926 ed. 17.50 (ISBN 0-404-05553-2). AMS Pr.

Poppies in the Wind. Louise O'Flaherty. 448p. (Orig.). 1981. pap. 2.95 (ISBN 0-345-29201-4). Ballantine.

Poppies: Odyssey of an Opium Eater. Eric Detzer. LC 87-28746. 170p. 1988. pap. 8.95 (ISBN 0-916515-30-3). Mercury Hse Inc.

Poppies, Pipes, & People: Opium & Its Use in Laos. Joseph Westermeyer. LC 81-21995. (Illus.). 360p. 1982. 35.00x (ISBN 0-520-04622-6). U of Cal Pr.

Popple in Your Pocket & Other Funny Poems. Ed. by Bobbi Katz. LC 85-43342. (Illus.). 32p. (gr. k-5). 1986. 4.95 (ISBN 0-394-88042-0). Random.

Popple Opposites. Peggy Kahn. LC 85-63459. (Chunky Bks.). (Illus.). 28p. (ps). 1986. 2.95 (ISBN 0-394-88266-0, BYR). Random.

Popple Peeking. Nicole Lorian. (Lift-the-flaps Storybooks). (Illus.). 24p. (ps-1). 5.95 (ISBN 0-394-88040-4). Random.

Popples & King Most. Peggy Kahn. LC 85-19414. (Illus.). 32p. (gr. k-5). 1986. 4.95 (ISBN 0-394-88148-6). Random.

Popples & the Kitchen Caper. Michael Gerver. LC 85-63793. (Mini-Storybooks Ser.). (Illus.). 32p. (ps-3). 1986. pap. 1.25 (ISBN 0-394-88351-9, BYR). Random.

Popples & the Puppy. Gail George. LC 85-63821. (Mini-Storybooks Ser.). (Illus.). 32p. (ps-3). 1986. pap. 1.25 (ISBN 0-394-88304-7, BYR). Random.

Popples' Book of Jokes & Riddles. Barbara George. LC 86-62222. (Mini-Storybooks Ser.). (Illus.). 32p. (ps-3). 1987. pap. 1.25 (ISBN 0-394-88757-3, BYR). Random.

Popples' Pajama Party. Gail George. LC 85-19403. (Picturebacks Ser.). (Illus.). 32p. (ps-3). 1986. pap. 1.95 (ISBN 0-394-88041-2). Random.

Popples' Vacation. Peggy Kahn. LC 86-62220. (Mini-Storybooks). (Illus.). 32p. (ps-3). 1987. pap. 1.25 (ISBN 0-394-88758-1, BYR). Random.

Poppy. Linda Dubreuil. 1976. pap. 1.50 (ISBN 0-685-69146-2, LB357ZK, Leisure Bks). Leisure NY.

Poppy. Barbara Larriva. 1987. 10.95 (ISBN 0-345-34308-5, Pub. by Ballantine Epiphany). Ballantine.

Poppy. Peter Nichols. 70p. 1982. pap. 6.95 (ISBN 0-413-49490-X, NO. 3633). Heinemann Ed.

Poppy. Leonard Rogers. 1984. 15.00x (ISBN 0-86319-018-9, Pub. by New Playwrights Network). State Mutual Bk.

Poppy. Jennie Tremaine, pseud. 1982. pap. 2.95 (ISBN 0-440-16969-0). Dell.

Poppy & the Outdoors Cat. Dorothy Haas. Ed. by Kathleen Tucker. LC 80-19140. (Illus.). 128p. (gr. 2-5). 1982. PLB 8.95 (ISBN 0-8075-6621-7). A Whitman.

Poppy & the Outdoors Cat. Dorothy Haas. (Illus.). 128p. (gr. 2-5). 1985. pap. 2.25 (ISBN 0-590-33567-7, Lucky Star). Scholastic Inc.

Poppy & the Outdoors Cat. Dorothy Haas. (Illus.). 128p. (ps-3). 1988. pap. 2.50 (ISBN 0-590-41569-7). Scholastic Inc.

Poppy Flower: A Journey thru Addiction. Penny Jones. Ed. by Barbara McCaig. (Illus.). 40p. (Orig.). 1987. pap. text ed. 4.95 (ISBN 0-935201-18-1). Affordable Adven.

Poppy Seeds, Too: A Twisted Tale for Shabbat. Deborah U. Miller. LC 82-84021. (Illus.). 48p. (ps-3). 1982. pap. 4.95 (ISBN 0-930494-17-2). Kar Ben.

Poppy the Panda. Dick Gackenbach. LC 84-4952. (Illus.). 32p. (ps-3). 1984. PLB 11.95 (ISBN 0-89919-276-9, Clarion). HM.

Poppy the Panda. Dick Gackenbach. (Illus.). (ps-3). 1987. pap. 4.95 (ISBN 0-317-56436-6, Pub. by Clarion). Ticknor & Fields.

Pops. Romulus Linney. 65p. 1987. pap. 3.50 (ISBN 0-317-59789-2). Dramatists Play.

Pops Foster: The Autobiography of a New Orleans Jazzman. George M. Foster. As told to Tom Stoddard. LC 75-132414. 1971. pap. 6.95 (ISBN 0-520-02355-2). U of Cal Pr.

Pops: Paul Whiteman, King of Jazz. Thomas A. Delong. LC 83-19291. (Illus.). 352p. 1983. 17.95 (ISBN 0-8329-0264-0). New Century.

Pop's Secret. Maryann Townsend. LC 84-40773. 1980. 8.70i (ISBN 0-201-07707-8, Lipp Jr Bks). HarpJ.

Popsicles Are Cold: Storybook for Young Children in Sign Languages. Sue Johnson. (Talking Fingers Bks.). (Illus.). 30p. (Orig.). (ps-3). pap. 4.25x (ISBN 0-916708-12-8). Modern Signs.

Popski's Private Army. Vladimir Peniakoff. 368p. 1980. pap. 3.95 (ISBN 0-553-27170-9). Bantam.

Populace in Shakespeare. Brents Stirling. LC 71-176445. Repr. of 1949 ed. 14.00 (ISBN 0-404-06277-6). AMS Pr.

Popular Abstracts. Ray B. Browne. 1978. 12.95 (ISBN 0-87972-166-9); pap. 6.95 (ISBN 0-87972-165-0). Bowling Green Univ.

Popular Amusements. Richard H. Edwards. LC 75-22812. (America in Two Centuries Ser). 1976. Repr. of 1915 ed. 18.00x (ISBN 0-405-07686-X). Ayer Co Pubs.

Popular Amusements in Horse & Buggy America. William L. Slout. LC 84-12310. (Clipper Studies in the American Theater: No. 2). 144p. (Orig.). 1988. lib. bdg. 19.95x (ISBN 0-89370-361-3); pap. text ed. 9.95x (ISBN 0-89370-461-X). Borgo Pr.

Popular & Polite Art in the Age of Hogarth & Fielding. Ronald Paulson. LC 79-63358. (Ward-Phillips Lectures in English Language & Literature Ser.: No. 10). 1979. text ed. 29.95 (ISBN 0-268-01534-1). U of Notre Dame Pr.

Popular & Traditional Songs of Puerto Rico, Cuba, Mexico & Spain. Ed. by Allena Luce. (Latin American Music Ser.). 1979. lib. bdg. 59.95 (ISBN 0-8490-2985-6). Gordon Pr.

Popular Annuals of Eastern North America, 1865-1914. Peggy C. Newcomb. LC 84-1674. (Illus.). 208p. (Orig.). 1985. pap. 15.00x (ISBN 0-88402-138-6). Dumbarton Oaks.

Popular Antiques Yearbook. Huon Mallalia. (Illus.). 240p. 1985. 14.95 (ISBN 0-7148-8023-X). Salem Hse Pubs.

Popular Antiques Yearbook. Ed. by Huon Mallalieu. (Illus.). 240p. 14.95 (ISBN 0-317-55013-6). Apollo.

Popular Antiques Yearbook: Trends & Prices of Everyday Antiques of 1987. Ed. by Huon Mallalieu. (Illus.). 240p. 1988. 19.95 (ISBN 0-7148-8049-3, Pub. by Salem House-Phaidon). Salem Hse Pubs.

Popular Antiques Yearbook, Vol. 2: Current Trends & Prices of Everyday Antiques. Huon Mallalieu. (Illus.). 240p. 1987. 19.95 (ISBN 0-7148-8035-3). Salem Hse Pubs.

Popular Appeal in English Drama to Eighteen Fifty. Peter Davison. LC 79-55528. 234p. 1982. text ed. 28.50x (ISBN 0-389-20231-2). B&N Imports.

Popular Arts in America: A Reader. 2nd ed. Ed. by William M. Hammel. 501p. (Orig.). 1977. pap. text ed. 12.00 net (ISBN 0-15-570742-6, HC). HarBraceJ.

Popular Ballad. Francis B. Gummere. 69.95 (ISBN 0-87968-285-X). Gordon Pr.

Popular Beliefs & Folklore Tradition in Siberia. Ed. by V. Dioszegi. (Uralic & Altaic Ser.: No. 57). 1968. text ed. 40.80x (ISBN 0-686-22621-6). Mouton.

Popular Beliefs & Superstitions: A Compendium of American Folklore, 3 vols. Compiled by Newbell N. Puckett. 1903p. 1981. Set. lib. bdg. 125.50 (ISBN 0-8161-8585-9, Hall Reference). G K Hall.

Popular Beliefs & Superstitions from North Carolina, Pt. 2 see Frank C. Brown Collection of North Carolina Folklore.

Popular Beliefs & Superstitions from Utah. Ed. by Anthon S. Cannon et al. 526p. 1984. 45.00x (ISBN 0-87480-236-9). U of Utah Pr.

Popular Book: A History of America's Literary Taste. James D. Hart. 1950. pap. 6.95 (ISBN 0-520-00538-4). U of Cal Pr.

Popular Buddhism in China. Shao-ch'Ang Li. lib. bdg. 79.95 (ISBN 0-87968-539-5). Krishna Pr.

Popular Capitalism. John Redwood. 208p. 1988. lib. bdg. 49.95 (ISBN 0-415-00114-5). Routledge Chapman & Hall.

Popular Card Tricks. Walter B. Gibson. pap. 5.00 (ISBN 0-87505-249-5). Borden.

Popular Card Tricks. Walter B. Gibson. (Illus.). 47p. 1981. pap. 3.50 (ISBN 0-915926-05-9). Magic Ltd.

Popular Careers. (Skyview Ser.). (gr. 4-7). 3.95 (ISBN 0-317-42454-8). Learning Well.

Popular Catholicism in Nineteenth-Century Germany. Johnathan Sperber. LC 84-42559. 552p. 1984. text ed. 50.00x (ISBN 0-691-05432-0). Princeton U Pr.

Popular Chinese Literature & Performing Arts in the People's Republic of China, 1949-1979. Ed. by Bonnie S. McDougall. LC 82-21942. (Studies on China: Vol. 2). 450p. 1984. lib. bdg. 45.00x (ISBN 0-520-04852-0). U of Cal Pr.

Popular Christianity. Catherine Booth. (Writings of Catherine Booth Ser.). 1986. Repr. of 1888 ed. deluxe ed. 4.95 (ISBN 0-86544-035-2). Salvation Army.

Popular Circuits Ready-Reference. John Markus. 160p. 1982. pap. text ed. 19.95 (ISBN 0-07-040458-5). McGraw.

Popular Classics. Ed. by Reader's Digest Editors. (Illus.). 252p. 1988. 25.95 (ISBN 0-89577-274-4, Dist by Random). Rd Assn.

Popular Commencement Book. Effa E. Preston. LC 70-175776. 434p. 1975. Repr. of 1931 ed. 45.00x (ISBN 0-8103-4034-8). Gale.

Popular Commentary of the Bible, 4 Vols. 2 Pts. Paul E. Kretzmann. Set. 74.95 (ISBN 0-570-06735-9, 15-1201). Concordia.

Popular Crafts Guide to Pottery. Bridgewater. LC 86-47616. 160p. 1986. pap. 10.95 (ISBN 0-8019-7722-3). Chilton.

Popular Cuban Music. Emilio Grenet. (Ballroom Dance Ser.). 1985. lib. bdg. 79.95 (ISBN 0-87700-679-2). Revisionist Pr.

Popular Cuban Music. Emilio Grenet. (Ballroom Dance Ser.). 1986. lib. bdg. 79.95 (ISBN 0-8490-3352-7). Gordon Pr.

Popular Culture & American Life: Selected Topics in the Study of Twentieth Century American Popular Culture. Martin W. Laforse & James A. Drake. LC 80-27809. 264p. 1981. text ed. 23.95x (ISBN 0-88229-577-2); pap. text ed. 11.95x (ISBN 0-88229-778-3). Nelson-Hall.

Popular Culture & Critical Pedagogy: Schooling & the Language of Everyday Life. Henry A. Giroux et al. (Critical Studies in Education). 256p. (Orig.). 1989. lib. bdg. 39.95 (ISBN 0-89789-187-2); pap. text ed. 14.95 (ISBN 0-89789-186-4). Bergin & Garvey.

Popular Culture & Curricula. rev. ed. Ed. by Ray B. Browne. 101p. pap. 5.95 (ISBN 0-87972-002-6). Bowling Green Univ.

Popular Culture & Custom in Nineteenth-Century England. Ed. by Robert D. Storch. LC 82-3302. 232p. 1982. 27.50x (ISBN 0-312-63033-6). St Martin.

Popular Culture & Elite Culture in France, 1400-1750. Robert Muchembled. Tr. by Lydia Cochrane from Fr. LC 84-25078. 326p. 1985. text ed. 32.50 (ISBN 0-8071-1218-6). La State U Pr.

Popular Culture & High Culture: An Analysis & Evaluation of Taste. Herbert J. Gans. LC 74-79287. 1975. pap. 8.50x (ISBN 0-465-09717-0, TB-5061). Basic.

Popular Culture & Media Events. Ed. by Vincent Mosco & Janet Wasko. LC 82-11592. (Critical Communications Review Ser.: Vol. 3). 344p. 1985. inst. ed. 45.00 (ISBN 0-89391-279-4); pers. ed. 27.50. Ablex Pub.

Popular Culture & Popular Movements in Reformation Germany. R. W. Scribner. 1988. 40.00 (ISBN 0-907628-81-8). Hambledon Press.

Popular Culture & Popular Protest in Late Medieval & Early Modern Europe. Michael Mullett. 256p. 1987. lib. bdg. 49.95x (ISBN 0-7099-3566-8, Pub. by Croom Helm UK). Routledge Chapman & Hall.

Popular Culture & Social Relations. Tony Bennett et al. 224p. 1986. 65.00x (ISBN 0-335-15108-6, Open Univ Pr); pap. 24.00x (ISBN 0-335-15107-8). Taylor & Francis.

Popular Culture in America. Ed. by Paul Buhle. LC 86-7117. (Illus.). 298p. 1987. 29.50x (ISBN 0-8166-1408-3); pap. 12.95 (ISBN 0-8166-1409-1). U of Minn Pr.

Popular Culture in America: 1800-1925, 27 vols. David M. White. 1975. Set. 540.00 (ISBN 0-405-06360-1). Ayer Co Pubs.

Popular Culture in Early Modern Europe. Peter Burke. 1978. pap. 8.95x (ISBN 0-06-131928-7, TB 1928, Torch). Har-Row.

Popular Culture in Early Modern Europe. Peter Burke. LC 78-52051. 400p. 1978. 20.00x, UKE (ISBN 0-8147-1011-5). NYU Pr.

Popular Culture in Early Modern Europe. Peter Burke. 377p. 1988. pap. text ed. 20.00 (ISBN 0-7045-0596-7, Pub. by Wildwood Hse Bks). Gower Pub Co.

Popular Culture in Late Imperial China. D. Johnson et al. 466p. 1987. pap. 70.00x (Pub. by Han-Shan Tang Ltd). State Mutual Bk.

Popular Culture in Late Imperial China. Ed. by David Johnson et al. LC 83-18012. (Studies on China: Vol. 4). 424p. 1985. 48.00x (ISBN 0-520-05120-3). U of Cal Pr.

Popular Culture in Late Imperial China. Ed. by David Johnson et al. (Asian Studies). 466p. 1987. pap. 12.95 (ISBN 0-520-06172-1). U of Cal Pr.

Popular Culture in Libraries. Frank W. Hoffmann. LC 84-17165. xviii, 312p. 1985. lib. bdg. 29.50 (ISBN 0-208-01981-2, Lib Prof Pubns); pap. text ed. 18.50x (ISBN 0-208-01983-9, Lib Prof Pubns). Shoe String.

Popular Culture in Seventeenth Century England. Ed. by Barry Reay. LC 85-2496. 319p. 1985. 29.95 (ISBN 0-312-63036-0). St Martin.

Popular Culture in the Middle Ages. Josie P. Campbell. LC 86-71408. 157p. 1986. 19.95 (ISBN 0-87972-339-4); pap. 9.95 (ISBN 0-87972-340-8). Bowling Green Univ.

Popular Culture, Leisure & Social Order. Susan Easton et al. 220p. 1986. text ed. 33.00 (ISBN 0-566-05123-0). Gower Pub Co.

Popular Culture: Past & Present. Ed. by Bernard Waites et al. 326p. 1982. pap. 12.00 (ISBN 0-7099-1909-3, Pub. by Croom Helm Ltd). Routledge Chapman & Hall.

Popular Culture Reader. 3rd ed. Christopher Geist & Jack Nachbar. LC 78-61077. 1983. pap. text ed. 35.00 (ISBN 0-87972-273-8); pap. 11.95 (ISBN 0-87972-274-6). Bowling Green Univ.

Popular Culture Reader. Jack Nachbar. LC 78-61077. 1978. 14.95 (ISBN 0-87972-095-6); pap. 7.95 (ISBN 0-87972-094-8). Bowling Green Univ.

Popular Culture: The Metropolitan Experience. Iain Chambers. (Studies in Communication). (Illus.). 180p. 1986. 29.95 (ISBN 0-416-37670-3, 1040); pap. 9.95 (ISBN 0-416-37680-0, 1022). Routledge Chapman & Hall.

Popular Dances Made Easy. A. Levine. (Ballroom Dancing Ser.). 1984. lib. bdg. 79.95 (ISBN 0-87700-503-6). Revisionist Pr.

Popular Dances Made Easy. (Ballroom Dance Ser.). 1985. lib. bdg. 79.00 (ISBN 0-87700-822-1). Revisionist Pr.

Popular Dances Made Easy. (Ballroom Dance Ser.). 1986. lib. bdg. 79.95 (ISBN 0-8490-3277-6). Gordon Pr.

Popular Devotionals. Leslie Brandt. Incl. Psalms-Now. 222p; Epistles-Now. 187p (ISBN 0-570-04427-8); Jesus-Now. 216p (ISBN 0-570-04428-6); Prophets-Now. 136p (ISBN 0-570-04429-4). pap. 5.95 ea.; slipcase set 19.95 (ISBN 0-570-04425-1); audio cass. 14.95 (ISBN 0-570-09051-2). Concordia.

Popular Dictionary of Buddhism. Christmas Humphreys. 224p. 1988. pap. 39.00x (Pub. by Curzon Pr Ltd UK). State Mutual Bk.

Popular Dictionary of Christian Mysticism. Georg Feuerstein. (World Windows Ser.). (Illus.). 144p. (Orig.). Date not set. pap. 7.50. Integral Pub.

Popular Dictionary of Judaism. Hugh J. Schonfield. 1966. pap. 1.75 (ISBN 0-8065-0075-1, 232, Pub. by Citadel Pr). Lyle Stuart.

Popular Dictionary of Tantra. Georg Feuerstein. (World Windows Ser.). (Illus.). 144p. (Orig.). Date not set. pap. 7.50. Integral Pub.

Popular Dictionary of Yoga. Georg Feuerstein. (World Windows Ser.). (Illus.). 144p. (Orig.). Date not set. pap. 7.50. Integral Pub.

Popular Diplomacy & War. Sisley Huddleston. 9.00 (ISBN 0-8159-6508-7). Devin.

Popular Disturbances & Public Order in Regency England. Frank O. Darvall. LC 68-58973. 1969. Repr. of 1934 ed. lib. bdg. 37.50x (ISBN 0-678-00458-7). Kelley.

Popular Education & Democratic Thought in America. Rush Welter. LC 62-19909. 1963. 49.50x (ISBN 0-231-02560-2). Columbia U Pr.

Popular Education in Eighteenth Century England: A Study in the Origins of the Mass Reading Public. Victor E. Neuberg. 210p. 1971. 25.00x (ISBN 0-7130-0000-7, Pub. by Woburn Pr England). Biblio Dist.

Popular Election of United States Senators. J. Haynes. Bd. with Local Government in the South & Southwest. E. W. Bemis. 1973. Repr. of 1893 ed. 13.00. Johnson Repr.

Popular Election of United States Senators. John Haynes. LC 78-63825. (Johns Hopkins University. Studies in the Social Sciences. Eleventh Ser. 1893: 12). Repr. of 1893 ed. 11.50 (ISBN 0-404-61086-2). AMS Pr.

Popular Election of United States Senators see Local Government in the South & Southwest.

Popular Enamelling. Erika Speel. (Illus.). 128p. 1984. 24.95 (ISBN 0-7134-4193-3, Pub. by Batsford England). David & Charles.

Popular Encyclopedia of Plants. Ed. by V. H. Heywood & S. R. Chant. LC 81-21713. (Illus.). 1982. 39.50 (ISBN 0-521-24611-3). Cambridge U Pr.

Popular English Ballads, Vol. 1. facsimile ed. Ed. by R. Brimley Johnson. LC 72-152151. (Granger Index Reprint Ser.). (Illus.). Repr. of 1894 ed. 22.00 (ISBN 0-8369-6257-5). Ayer Co Pubs.

Popular English Ballads, Vol. 2. facsimile ed. Ed. by R. Brimley Johnson. LC 72-152151. (Granger Index Reprint Ser.). (Illus.). Repr. of 1894 ed. 22.00 (ISBN 0-8369-6258-3). Ayer Co Pubs.

Popular English Ballads, Vol. 3. facsimile ed. Ed. by R. Brimley Johnson. LC 72-152151. (Granger Index Reprint Ser.). (Illus.). Repr. of 1894 ed. 20.00 (ISBN 0-8369-6259-1). Ayer Co Pubs.

Popular English Ballads, Vol. 4. facsimile ed. Ed. by R. Brimley Johnson. LC 72-152151. (Granger Index Reprint Ser.). (Illus.). Repr. of 1894 ed. 20.00 (ISBN 0-8369-6260-5). Ayer Co Pubs.

Popular Entertainment, Class & Politics in Munich, 1900-1923. Robert E. Sackett. 208p. 1982. text ed. 24.50x (ISBN 0-674-68985-2). Harvard U Pr.

Popular Entertainments Through the Ages. Samuel McKechnie. LC 78-79998. (Illus.). Repr. of 1931 ed. 20.00 (ISBN 0-405-08768-3). Ayer Co Pubs.

Popular Epics of the Middle Ages of the Norse-German & Carlovingian Cycles, 2 vols. John M. Ludlow. 1976. lib. bdg. 200.00 (ISBN 0-8490-2455-2). Gordon Pr.

Popular Epics of the Middle Ages of the Norse German & Carlovingian Cycles, 2 vols. John M. Ludlow. LC 77-94598. 1979. Repr. of 1865 ed. Set. lib. bdg. 95.00 (ISBN 0-89341-186-8). Longwood Pub Group.

Popular Ethics in Ancient Greece. Lionel Pearson. 1962. 25.00x (ISBN 0-8047-0102-4). Stanford U Pr.

Popular Fallacies, a Book of Common Errors: Explained & Corrected with Copious References to Authorities. 4th ed. A. S. Ackermann. LC 79-121184. 862p. 1970. Repr. of 1950 ed. 74.00x (ISBN 0-8103-3295-7). Gale.

Popular Fiction. James Sherry. LC 85-61017. 86p. (Orig.). 1985. pap. text ed. 6.00 (ISBN 0-937804-15-0). Segue NYC.

Popular Fiction & Social Change. Ed. by Christopher Pawling. LC 83-40588. 256p. 1984. 25.00 (ISBN 0-312-63034-4). St Martin.

Popular Fiction: Technology, Ideology, Production, Reading. Ed. by Tony Bennet. 400p. 1988. text ed. 45.00 (ISBN 0-415-02518-4); pap. text ed. 15.95 (ISBN 0-415-02517-6). Routledge Chapman & Hall.

Popular Fictions: Essays in Literature & History. Ed. by Peter Humm & Paul Stigant. (New Accents Ser.). 224p. 1987. 24.50 (ISBN 0-416-90040-2, 9902); pap. 12.95 (ISBN 0-416-90050-X, 9945). Routledge Chapman & Hall.

Popular Film Culture in Facist Italy: The Passing of the Rex. James Hay. 1987. 37.50x (ISBN 0-253-36107-9); 14.95x (ISBN 0-253-20432-1). Ind U Pr.

Popular Financial Delusions. Robert L. Smitley. LC 63-18275. 1963. Repr. of 1933 ed. flexible cover 16.00 (ISBN 0-87034-004-2). Fraser Pub Co.

Popular Fly Patterns. Terry Hellekson. LC 76-49452. (Illus.). 250p. 1975. pap. 14.95 (ISBN 0-87905-065-9, Peregrine Smith). Gibbs Smith Pub.

Popular Freethought in America, 1825-1850. Albert Post. LC 73-20002. 258p. 1974. Repr. of 1943 ed. lib. bdg. 18.00x (ISBN 0-374-96531-5, Octagon). Hippocrene Bks.

Popular French Romanticism: Authors, Readers, & Books in the 19th Century. James S. Allen. LC 80-27129. (Illus.). 320p. 1980. 20.00x (ISBN 0-8156-2232-5). Syracuse U Pr.

Popular Front in Europe. Ed. by Helen Graham & Paul Preston. 250p. 1987. 32.50 (ISBN 0-312-63043-3). St Martin.

Popular Front in France: Defending Democracy, 1934-1938. Julian Jackson. (Illus.). 388p. 1988. 54.50 (ISBN 0-521-32088-7). Cambridge U Pr.

Popular Gardening, 4 vols. D. T. Fish. 1974. lib. bdg. 600.00 (ISBN 0-685-51357-2). Revisionist Pr.

Popular German Stories. Ed. by F. W. Lieder. (Orig., Ger.). pap. text ed. 6.95x (ISBN 0-89197-351-6). Irvington.

Popular Girls. Joan Oviatt. LC 87-82116. 176p. 1987. 9.95 (ISBN 0-88290-297-0). Horizon Utah.

Popular Government. Henry S. Maine. LC 76-26329. 1977. 7.95 (ISBN 0-913966-14-2, Liberty Clas). Liberty Fund.

Popular Government in an African Town: Kita, Mali. Nicholas S. Hopkins. LC 70-162528. 1972. 25.00x (ISBN 0-226-35173-4). U of Chicago Pr.

Popular Government: Its Essence, Its Permanence, Its Perils. William H. Taft. Repr. of 1913 ed. 21.00 (ISBN 0-527-88612-2). Kraus Repr.

Popular Government: Its Essence, Its Performance, Its Perils. William H. Taft. 1913. 20.00x (ISBN 0-686-83709-6). Elliots Bks.

Popular Guide to Government Publications. 4th ed. W. Philip Leidy. LC 76-17803. 440p. 1976. 45.00x (ISBN 0-231-04019-9). Columbia U Pr.

Popular Guide to New Testament Criticism. H. P. Hamann. 1977. pap. 4.75 (ISBN 0-570-03760-3, 12-2671). Concordia.

Popular Guide to Puppy Rearing. Olwen Gwynne-Jones. (Popular Dog Ser.). (Illus.). 107p. 1988. pap. 9.95 (ISBN 0-09-143701-6, Pub. by Century Hutchinson). David & Charles.

Popular Guitar Music. Barry Pollack. 256p. 1985. 16.95 (ISBN 0-13-685629-2); pap. 12.95 (ISBN 0-13-685611-X). P-H.

Popular Handbook of British Birds. 4th ed. P. A. Hollom. (Illus.). 1975. 27.95 (ISBN 0-8464-0735-3). Beekman Pubs.

Popular Herbs: Their History, Growth & Use. Dawn Macleod. (Illus.). 191p. 1981. pap. 10.00 (ISBN 0-7156-1526-2, Pub. by Duckworth London). Longwood Pub Group.

Popular Hinduism & Hindu Mythology: An Annotated Bibliography. Compiled by Barron Holland. LC 79-7188. 1979. lib. bdg. 46.95 (ISBN 0-313-21358-5, HPH/). Greenwood.

Popular Hinduism: The Religion of the Masses. Lewis S. O'Malley. LC 70-142072. 1971. Repr. of 1935 ed. 24.00 (ISBN 0-384-43305-7). Johnson Repr.

Popular History of American Invention, 2 vols. Ed. by Waldemar B. Kaempffert. LC 74-9385. (Illus.). Repr. of 1924 ed. Set. 125.00 (ISBN 0-404-11921-2); Vol. 1. (ISBN 0-404-11922-0); Vol. 2. (ISBN 0-404-11923-9). AMS Pr.

Popular History of Astronomy in the Nineteenth Century. Agnes M. Clerke. LC 70-166614. 1908. Repr. 39.00 (ISBN 0-403-01492-1). Scholarly.

Popular History of Comets. Yeomans. (Science Editions Ser.). 1989. price not set (ISBN 0-471-61011-9). Wiley.

Popular History of English Poetry. T. Earle Welby. 1973. lib. bdg. 25.50 (ISBN 0-8414-9664-1). Folcroft.

Popular History of Philosophy. Teodoro De la Torre. 411p. 1988. 18.95 (ISBN 0-912414-48-0). Lumen Christi.

Popular History of the Archdiocese of New York. Florence D. Cohalan. LC 82-84246. (USCHS Monograph: Vol. 37). (Illus.). xviii, 354p. 1983. 15.00x (ISBN 0-930060-17-2). US Cath Hist.

Popular History of the Art of Music from the Earliest Times until the Present. rev. ed. William S. Mathews. LC 74-173058. Repr. of 1915 ed. 37.50 (ISBN 0-404-07212-7). AMS Pr.

Popular History of Two Revolutions: Guatemala & Nicaragua. Guillermo T. Garrido. Tr. by Rebecca Schwaner from Span. 60p. (Orig.). 1985. pap. 3.95 (ISBN 0-89935-055-0). Synthesis Pubns.

Popular Images of American Presidents. Ed. by William C. Spragens. 1988. 125.85 (ISBN 0-317-65580-9). Greenwood.

Popular Images of American Presidents. Ed. by William C. Spragens. LC 87-24944. 640p. 1988. lib. bdg. 95.00 (ISBN 0-313-22899-X, SAP/). Greenwood.

Popular Influence upon Public Policy: Petitioning in Eighteenth-Century Virginia. Raymond C. Bailey. LC 78-73792. (Contributions in Legal Studies Ser.: No. 10). (Illus.). xii, 203p. 1979. lib. bdg. 46.95 (ISBN 0-313-20892-1, BPP/). Greenwood.

Popular Interset in Psychiatric Remedies: A Study in Social Control. Egon Bittner. Ed. by Harriet Zuckerman & Robert K. Merton. LC 79-8977. (Dissertations on Sociology). 1980. lib. bdg. 24.50x (ISBN 0-405-12953-X). Ayer Co Pubs.

Popular Islam South of the Sahara. Ed. by J. D. Peel & Charles C. Stewart. (African Studies). 128p. 1986. pap. 16.00 (ISBN 0-7190-1975-3, Pub. by Manchester Univ Pr). St Martin.

Popular Italian Madrigals of the Sixteenth Century. Ed. by Alec Harman. 1977. pap. 14.95x (ISBN 0-19-343646-9). Oxford U Pr.

Popular Justice: A History of American Criminal Justice. Samuel E. Walker. 1980. pap. text ed. 10.95x (ISBN 0-19-502654-3). Oxford U Pr.

Popular Leadership & Collective Behavior in the Late Roman Republic (ca. 80 - 50 B.C. Paul J. Vanderbroeck. (Dutch Monographs on Ancient History & Archaeology: Vol. III). 281p. 1987. 52.00x (ISBN 90-5063-001-4, Pub. by Gieben Amsterdam). Benjamins North Am.

Popular Literature: A History & Guide. Victor E. Neuburg. (Illus.). 302p. 1977. 23.50x (ISBN 0-7130-0158-5, Pub. by Woburn Pr England). Biblio Dist.

Popular Literature in Ancient Egypt. A. Wiedemann. LC 77-8347. 1973. lib. bdg. 35.50 (ISBN 0-8414-9611-0). Folcroft.

Popular Literature in Victorian Scotland: Language, Fiction & the Press. Ed. by William Donaldson. (Illus.). 176p. 1986. text ed. 23.95 (ISBN 0-08-034513-1, AUP); pap. text ed. 14.75 (ISBN 0-08-034515-8). Pergamon.

Popular Literature of Medieval England. Ed. by Thomas J. Heffernan. LC 84-26959. (Tennessee Studies in Literature: Vol. 28). 368p. 1986. 32.95x (ISBN 0-87049-453-8). U of Tenn Pr.

Popular Literature: Poe's Not So Soon Forgotten Lore. J. Lasley Dameron. Ed. by Averil J. Kadis. 1980. pap. 2.50 (ISBN 0-910556-16-4). Enoch Pratt.

Popular Manual of English Literature, 2 vols. Maude G. Phillips. 1973. Repr. of 1895 ed. 50.00 set (ISBN 0-8274-1137-5). R West.

Popular Marine Fish for Your Aquarium. Martyn Haywood. (Illus.). 112p. (Orig.). 1984. pap. 11.50 (ISBN 0-8306-0621-1, 1621P). TAB Bks.

Popular Media in China: Shaping New Cultural Patterns. Ed. by Godwin C. Chu. LC 78-13282. 273p. 1978. text ed. 14.00x (ISBN 0-8248-0622-0, Eastwest Ctr). UH Pr.

Popular Medicine in Puntarenas, Costa Rica: Urban & Societal Features see Community Culture & National Change.

Popular Medicine in Seventeenth-Century England. Doreen E. Nagy. LC 88-70523. 140p. 1988. text ed. 25.95 (ISBN 0-87972-435-8); pap. text ed. 12.95 (ISBN 0-87972-436-6). Bowling Green Univ.

Popular Model Railroads You Can Build. Model Railroader Staff. Ed. by Donnette Dolzall. LC 77-20736. (Illus.). 1977. pap. 7.95 (ISBN 0-89024-530-4). Kalmbach.

Popular Mood of Pre-Civil War America. Lewis O. Saum. LC 79-8281. (Contributions in American History: No. 46). xxiv, 336p. 1980. lib. bdg. 35.00 (ISBN 0-313-21056-X, SPM/). Greenwood.

Popular Movements & Secret Societies in China, 1840-1950. Ed. by Jean Chesneaux. LC 70-153816. 342p. 1972. 35.00x (ISBN 0-8047-0790-1). Stanford U Pr.

Popular Music: A Reference Guide. Roman Iwaschkin. LC 85-45140. (Reference Library of the Humanities: Vol. 642). 672p. 1986. 80.00 (ISBN 0-8240-8680-5). Garland Pub.

Popular Music: A Teacher's Guide. Graham Vulliamy & Edward Lee. (Routledge Popular Music Ser.). (Orig.). 1982. pap. 12.95x (ISBN 0-7100-0895-3). Routledge Chapman & Hall.

Popular Music: An Annotated Guide to Recordings. Dean Tudor. LC 84-18749. 669p. 1984. lib. bdg. 65.00 (ISBN 0-87287-395-1). Libs Unl.

Popular Music: An Annotated Index of Popular Songs. Ed. by Nat Shapiro. Incl. Vol. 8, 1975-1979 (ISBN 0-8103-0846-0); Vol. 9, 1980-1984. 350p. 1986. 66.00x (ISBN 0-8103-0848-7); Vol. 10, 1986. 350p. 44.00x (ISBN 0-8103-0849-5). (Popular Music Ser.). (350 pages per vol.). 66.00x ea. Vol. 1, 1950-1959 (ISBN 0-8103-0839-8). Vol. 2, 1940-1949 (ISBN 0-8103-0840-1). Vol. 3, 1960-1964 (ISBN 0-8103-0841-X). Vol. 4, 1930-1939 (ISBN 0-8103-0842-8). Vol. 5, 1920-1929 (ISBN 0-8103-0843-6). Vol. 6, 1965-1969 (ISBN 0-8103-0844-4). Vol. 7, 1970-74 (ISBN 0-8103-0845-2). Vol. 8, 1975-1979. Gale.

Popular Music & Communication: Social & Cultural Perspectives. Ed. by James Lull. (Focus Editions Ser.: Vol. 89). 320p. 1987. text ed. 35.00 (ISBN 0-8039-2825-4); pap. text ed. 16.95 (ISBN 0-8039-2826-2). Sage.

Popular Music Handbook: A Resource for Teacher's, Librarians, & Media Specialists. B. Lee Cooper. LC 84-19448. 441p. 1984. lib. bdg. 37.50 (ISBN 0-87287-393-5). Libs Unl.

Popular Music in England, 1840-1914: A Social Hisotry. Dave Russell. 336p. 1987. 35.00x (ISBN 0-7735-0541-5). McGill-Queens U Pr.

Popular Music in Mexico. Claes Geijerstam. LC 75-17373. pap. 52.30 (ISBN 0-317-20583-8, 2024677). Bks Demand UMI.

Popular Music, Nineteen Eighty-Seven, Vol. 12. annotated ed. Ed. by Nat Shapiro. Bruce Pollock. 350p. 1988. 48.00x. Gale.

Popular Music, Nineteen Twenty to Nineteen Seventy-Nine, 3 vols. Ed. by Bruce Pollock. 2839p. 1985. Set. 230.00x (ISBN 0-8103-0847-9). Gale.

Popular Music since Nineteen Fifty-Five: A Critical Guide to the Literature. Paul Taylor. 549p. 1985. lib. bdg. 41.50 (ISBN 0-8161-8784-3). G K Hall.

Popular Music 1986: An Annotated Index of American Popular Songs, Vol. 11. Ed. by Nat Shapiro & Bruce Pollock. (Popular Music Ser.). 179p. 1987. 44.00x (ISBN 0-8103-1809-1). Gale.

Popular Music, 1987, Vol. 12. Ed. by Bruce Pollock. 175p. 1988. 48.00 (ISBN 0-8103-1810-5). Gale.

Popular Musics of the Non-Western World: An Introductory Survey. Peter Manuel. (Illus.). 304p. 1988. 24.95 (ISBN 0-19-505342-7). Oxford U Pr.

Popular Names of U. S. Government Reports: A Catalog. 4th ed. Ed. by Bernard A. Bernier, Jr. & Karen A. Wood. x, 272p. 1984. 13.00 (ISBN 0-317-59997-6). Lib Congress.

Popular Narrative Ballads of Modern Egypt. Pierre Cachia. 384p. 1988. 59.00 (ISBN 0-19-826545-X). Oxford U Pr.

Popular Nineteenth Century European Painting. (Illus.). 1987. 92.00. Editions Pub.

Popular Nineteenth Century Painting. Philip Hook & Mark Poltimore. (Illus.). 632p. 1986. 89.50 (ISBN 1-85149-011-6). Antique Collect.

Popular Novel in England, 1770-1800. J. M. Tompkins. LC 32-24699. x, 389p. 1961. pap. 6.95x (ISBN 0-8032-5201-3, BB 121, Bison). U of Nebr Pr.

Popular Novel in England 1770-1800. Joyce Tompkins. LC 76-174. 388p. 1976. Repr. of 1961 ed. lib. bdg. 35.00x (ISBN 0-8371-8656-0, TOPN). Greenwood.

Popular Nursery Rhymes. Ed. by Jennifer Mulherin. (Illus.). (ps-1). 1983. 8.95 (ISBN 0-448-01346-0, G&D). Putnam Pub Group.

Popular Nutritional Practices. Jack Z. Yetic. (Orig.). 1988. pap. 4.95 (ISBN 0-440-20046-6). Dell.

Popular Nutritional Practices: A Scientific Appraisal. Jack Z. Yetiv. LC 86-23243. (Illus.). 320p. (Orig.). 1986. 23.95 (ISBN 0-936575-30-1); pap. 12.95 (ISBN 0-936575-29-8). Popular Med Pr.

Popular Opinion & Political Dissent in the Third Reich: Bavaria 1933-1945. Ian Kershaw. (Illus.). 1983. pap. 18.95x (ISBN 0-19-821971-7). Oxford U Pr.

Popular Opposition to the Eighteen Thirty-Four Poor Law. J. Knott. 192p. cancelled (ISBN 0-7099-1532-2, Pub. by Croom Helm Ltd). Routledge Chapman & Hall.

Popular Opposition to the Eighteen Thirty-Four Poor Law. J. Knott. LC 85-19577. 297p. 1986. 27.50 (ISBN 0-312-63056-5). St Martin.

Popular Orchids. Brian Rittershausen & Wilma Rittershausen. 224p. 1982. 35.00x (ISBN 0-7223-0940-6, Pub. by A H Stockwell England). State Mutual Bk.

Popular Organ Classics. Albert De Vito. 1964. pap. 3.25 (ISBN 0-934286-43-4). Kenyon.

Popular Parrots. Matthew M. Vriends. LC 83-10832. (Illus.). 240p. 1983. 17.95 (ISBN 0-87605-819-5). Howell Bk.

Popular Participation in Decision Making for Development. pap. 5.00 (ISBN 92-1-130080-0, E.75.IV.10). UN.

Popular Participation in Planning for Basic Needs: Concept, Methods & Practices. Franklyn Lisk. LC 85-18436. 286p. 1986. 29.95 (ISBN 0-312-63060-3). St Martin.

Popular Participation in Selected Upgrading Programmes in Urban Areas. 62p. 1987. pap. 8.50 (ISBN 92-1-130115-7, E.86.IV.8). UN.

Popular Participation in Social Change: Cooperatives, Collectives, & Nationalized Industry. Ed. by June Nash et al. (World Anthropology Ser.). xviii, 622p. 1976. 61.50 (ISBN 90-279-7849-2). Mouton.

Popular Participation Policies As Methods for Advancing Social Integration. 51p. 1987. 7.00 (ISBN 92-1-130123-8, E.87.IV.3). UN.

Popular Piano Classics. Albert De Vito. 1964. pap. 3.25 (ISBN 0-934286-51-5). Kenyon.

Popular Piano Self Taught. 3rd ed. Win Stormen. LC 81-12762. 144p. 1982. 11.95 (ISBN 0-668-05371-2, 5371); pap. 6.95 (ISBN 0-668-05386-0). Arco.

Popular Plant Manager. Water Pollution Control Federation Staff. (Manual of Practice Ser.: MSM6). 92p. 1986. pap. 24.00 (ISBN 0-943244-70-6). Water Pollution.

Popular Poetic Pearls & Biographies of Poets. Frank McAlpine. LC 74-15745. (Popular Culture in America Ser.). (Illus.). 384p. 1975. Repr. of 1885 ed. 30.00x (ISBN 0-405-06380-6). Ayer Co Pubs.

Popular Poetry in Puerto Rico: Origins & Themes. Maria C. De Martinez. (Puerto Rico Ser.). 1979. lib. bdg. 69.95 (ISBN 0-8490-2986-4). Gordon Pr.

Popular Poetry in Soviet Russia. George Z. Patrick. LC 74-174378. Repr. of 1929 ed. 20.75 (ISBN 0-405-08841-8, Pub. by Blom). Ayer Co Pubs.

Popular Poetry of the Finns. Charles J. Billson. (Popular Studies in Mythology, Romance & Folklore: No. 5). Repr. of 1900 ed. 5.50 (ISBN 0-404-53505-4). AMS Pr.

Popular Political Economy. Thomas Hodgskin. LC 66-19688. Repr. of 1827 ed. 39.50x (ISBN 0-678-00150-2). Kelley.

Popular Politics & Society in Late Victorian Britain. Henry Pelling. LC 68-29377. 1969. 22.50 (ISBN 0-312-63070-0). St Martin.

Popular Politics & the American Revolution in England: Petitions, the Crown, & Public Opinion. James E. Bradley. LC 86-5180. 320p. 1986. 34.95 (ISBN 0-86554-181-7, MUP/H170). Mercer Univ Pr.

Popular Pottery. Shirley Bates. (Illus.). 128p. 1982. 16.95 (ISBN 0-7134-4168-2, Pub. by Batsford England). David & Charles.

Popular Practice of Fraud. T. Swann Harding. LC 75-39246. (Getting & Spending: the Consumer's Dilemma). 1976. Repr. of 1935 ed. 29.00x (ISBN 0-405-08020-4). Ayer Co Pubs.

Popular Press Companion to Popular Literature. Victor Neuberg. LC 82-74162. 1983. 19.95 (ISBN 0-87972-233-9). Bowling Green Univ.

Popular Protest & Public Order: Six Studies in British History, 1790-1920. Ed. by R. Quinault & J. Stevenson. LC 74-26213. 256p. 1975. 26.00 (ISBN 0-312-63105-7). St Martin.

Popular Psychological Fallacies. James G. Taylor. 275p. 1981. Repr. of 1938 ed. lib. bdg. 40.00 (ISBN 0-89984-457-X). Century Bookbindery.

Popular Quotations for All Uses. Lewis Copeland. 31.95 (ISBN 0-89190-474-3, Pub. by Am Repr). Amereon Ltd.

Popular Radicalism: The Working Class Experience. Wright. (Studies in Modern History Ser.). 211p. 1988. pap. text ed. 13.95 (ISBN 0-582-49440-0). Longman.

Popular Reading for Children: A Collection of the Booklist Columns. Barbara Elleman. LC 81-144124. pap. 20.00 (ISBN 0-317-41821-1, 2025608). Bks Demand UMI.

Popular Reading for Children II: A Collection of Booklist Columns. Ed. by Barbara Elleman. LC 86-3385. 86p. 1986. pap. 6.00x (ISBN 0-8389-3330-0). ALA.

Popular Religion. Ed. by Norbert Greinacher & Norbert Mette. (Concilium Nineteen Eighty-Six Ser.). 120p. 1986. pap. 14.95 (ISBN 0-567-30066-8, Pub. by T & T Clark Ltd UK). Fortress.

Popular Religion in Restoration England. C. John Sommerville. LC 77-7618. (University of Florida Social Sciences Monographs: No. 59). 1977. pap. 10.00x (ISBN 0-8130-0564-7). U Presses Fla.

Popular Religion in the Middle Ages. Rosalind Brooke & Christopher Brooke. (Illus.). 1985. pap. 10.95 (ISBN 0-500-27381-2). Thames Hudson.

Popular Religion: Inspirational Books in America. Louis Schneider & Sanford M. Dornbusch. LC 58-11958. (Midway Reprint Ser.). pap. 46.50 (2026741). Bks Demand UMI.

Popular Rhymes & Nursery Tales. James O. Halliwell-Phillipps. LC 78-67715. (Folktale). Repr. of 1849 ed. 25.00 (ISBN 0-404-16092-1). AMS Pr.

Popular Rhymes & Nursery Tales. James O. Halliwell-Phillipps. LC 68-23470. 288p. 1968. Repr. of 1849 ed. 34.00x (ISBN 0-8103-3484-4). Gale.

Popular Rhymes & Nursery Tales. J. O. Halliwell-Phillips. 59.95 (ISBN 0-8490-0878-6). Gordon Pr.

Popular Rhymes of Scotland. R. Chambers. 59.95 (ISBN 0-8490-0879-4). Gordon Pr.

Popular Rhymes of Scotland. Robert Chambers. LC 68-58902. 404p. 1969. Repr. of 1870 ed. 40.00x (ISBN 0-8103-3828-9). Gale.

Popular Rhymes of Scotland. Robert Chambers. 1870. 27.50 (ISBN 0-686-17672-3). Quaker City.

Popular Rhymes, Sayings, & Proverbs of the County of Berwick. G. Henderson. LC 77-1079. 1977. Repr. of 1856 ed. lib. bdg. 35.00 (ISBN 0-8414-4946-5). Folcroft.

Popular Romances of the Middle Ages. G. E. Cox & E. H. Jones. 1976. lib. bdg. 69.95 (ISBN 0-8490-2456-0). Gordon Pr.

Popular Romances of the West of England. Robert Hunt. 1881. Repr. 47.50 (ISBN 0-8274-3185-6). R West.

Popular Romances of the West of England. Ed. by Robert Hunt. LC 68-56495. 1968. Repr. of 1916 ed. 27.50 (ISBN 0-405-08643-1, Blom Pubns). Ayer Co Pubs.

Popular School. Ed. by Terence P. Logan & Denzell S. Smith. LC 74-81364. (Survey & Bibliography of Recent Studies in English Renaissance Drama Ser.). xiv, 299p. 1975. 26.00x (ISBN 0-8032-0844-8). U of Nebr Pr.

Popular Science Book of Home Heating & Cooling. Evan Powell & Ernest V. Hern. (Illus.). 380p. 1983. 28.95 (ISBN 0-8359-5564-8, Reston). P-H.

Popular Science Do-It-Yourself Yearbook 2. Popular Science Books Editors. 1983. 19.95 (ISBN 0-442-27489-0). Van Nos Reinhold.

Popular Scientific Lectures. Ernst Mach. LC 85-10640. 415p. 1986. pap. 9.95 (ISBN 0-87548-440-9). Open Court.

Popular Smithsonian. Alborn et al. 1976. pap. 0.95 (ISBN 0-87972-080-8). Bowling Green Univ.

Popular Song Index. Patricia P. Havlice. LC 75-9896. 933p. 1975. 57.50 (ISBN 0-8108-0820-X). Scarecrow.

Popular Song Index: First Supplement. Patricia P. Havlice. LC 77-25219. 386p. 1978. 32.50 (ISBN 0-8108-1099-9). Scarecrow.

Popular Song Index: Second Supplement. Patricia P. Havlice. LC 83-7692. 534p. 1984. 37.50 (ISBN 0-8108-1642-3). Scarecrow.

Popular Songs & Ballads of Han China. Anne Birrell. 370p. 1988. 39.95 (ISBN 0-04-895028-9). Unwin Hyman.

Popular Songs, Illustrative of the French Invasions of Ireland. Ed. by Thomas C. Croker. Repr. of 1845 ed. 32.00 (ISBN 0-384-10205-0). Johnson Repr.

Popular Songs of Bruce Kingery. Ed. by John E. Westburg. 56p. pap. 3.00 (ISBN 0-87423-014-4). Westburg.

Popular Songs of Nineteenth Century America: Complete Original Sheet Music for 64 Songs. Richard Jackson. 17.25 (ISBN 0-8446-5456-6). Peter Smith.

Popular Songs of Nineteenth Century America. Ed. by Richard Jackson. 320p. 1976. pap. 9.95 (ISBN 0-486-23270-0). Dover.

Popular Songs That Will Live Forever. Ed. by Reader's Digest Editors. LC 81-84487. (Illus.). 252p. 1982. Lie-flat spiral bdg. 26.95 (ISBN 0-89577-104-7, Pub. by RD Assn). Random.

Popular Sources of Political Authority: Documents on the Massachusetts Constitution of 1780. Ed. by Oscar Handlin & Mary F. Handlin. LC 66-18247. (Center for the Study of the History of Liberty in America Ser.). 1966. 40.00x (ISBN 0-674-69000-1, Belknap Pr). Harvard U Pr.

Popular Struggles for Democracy in Africa. Ed. by Peter A. Nyong'o. (Studies in African Political Economy). 304p. 1987. 49.95 (ISBN 0-86232-736-9, Pub. by Zed); pap. 15.95 (ISBN 0-86232-737-7, Pub. by Zed). Humanities.

Popular Studies in Mythology, Romance & Folklore, 15 vols. Repr. of 1908 ed. write for info. (ISBN 0-404-53500-3). AMS Pr.

Popular Studies of Nineteenth Century Poets. J. Marshall Mather. LC 72-192050. 1892. lib. bdg. 29.50 (ISBN 0-8414-6454-5). Folcroft.

Popular Superstitions. Charles Platt. LC 70-167114. 246p. 1973. Repr. of 1925 ed. 46.00x (ISBN 0-8103-3170-5). Gale.

Popular Superstitions & Festive Amusements of the Highlanders of Scotland. W. Grant Stewart. 1978. Repr. of 1851 ed. lib. bdg. 45.50 (ISBN 0-8492-8007-9). R West.

Popular Survey of the Old Testament. Norman L. Geisler. LC 77-78578. 1977. pap. 8.95 (ISBN 0-8010-3684-4). Baker Bk.

Popular Tales. Charles Perrault. Ed. by Richard M. Dorson. LC 77-70607. (International Folklore Ser.). (Illus.). 1977. Repr. of 1888 ed. lib. bdg. 20.00 (ISBN 0-405-10118-X). Ayer Co Pubs.

Popular Tales & Fictions, Their Migrations & Transformations, 2 Vols. William A. Clouston. LC 67-23920. 512p. 1968. Repr. of 1887 ed. Set. 95.00x (ISBN 0-8103-3460-7). Gale.

Popular Tales from the Norse: With an Introductory Essay on the Origin & Diffusion of Popular Tales. 3rd ed. George W. Dasent. LC 74-136733. clii, 598p. 1971. Repr. of 1888 ed. 43.00x (ISBN 0-8103-3796-7). Gale.

Popular Tales of the West Highlands, 4 Vols. John F. Campbell. LC 67-23921. 1892p. 1969. Repr. of 1890 ed. 150.00x (ISBN 0-8103-3458-5). Gale.

Popular Technology, 2 vols. Edward Hazen. 275p. cloth 7.75 (ISBN 0-317-64495-5). Early Am Indus.

Popular Television & Film. Ed. by Tony Bennett et al. (Illus.). 320p. 1981. 21.95 (ISBN 0-85170-115-9, Pub. by British Film Inst England); pap. 15.95 (ISBN 0-85170-116-7, Pub. by British Film Inst England). U of Ill Pr.

Popular Theater for Social Change in Latin America: Essays in Spanish & English. Gerardo Luzuriaga. LC 77-620071. (Latin American Studies: Vol. 41). 1978. 16.50x (ISBN 0-87903-041-0). UCLA Lat Am Ctr.

Popular Theatre. George J. Nathan. LC 75-120099. 236p. 1971. 20.00 (ISBN 0-8386-7945-5). Fairleigh Dickinson.

Popular Titles & Subtitles of Musical Compositions. 2nd ed. Freda P. Berkowitz. LC 75-4751. 217p. 1975. 17.50 (ISBN 0-8108-0806-4). Scarecrow.

Popular Traditions & Learned Culture in France, 17th-20th Centuries. Ed. by Marc Bertrand. (Stanford French & Italian Studies: Vol. 35). (Illus.). 350p. 1986. pap. 34.50 (ISBN 0-915838-02-8). Anma Libri.

Popular Tribunals, 2 vols. Hubert H. Bancroft. LC 67-29422. (Works of Hubert Howe Bancroft Ser.). 1967. Repr. of 1888 ed. 60.00x (ISBN 0-914888-39-0). Bancroft Pr.

Popular Tropical Fish for Your Aquarium. Cliff Harrison. (Illus.). 104p. (Orig.). 1984. pap. 11.50 (ISBN 0-8306-1631-4, 1631P). TAB Bks.

Popular Uprisings in the Philippines, 1840-1940. David R. Sturtevant. LC 75-36521. (Illus.). 344p. 1976. 34.50x (ISBN 0-8014-0877-6). Cornell U Pr.

Popular Variations in Ballroom Dancing. Alex Moore. (Ballroom Dancing Ser.). 1984. lib. bdg. 79.95 (ISBN 0-87700-508-7). Revisionist Pr.

Popular Variations in Ballroom Dancing. Alex Moore. (Ballroom Dance Ser.). 1986. lib. bdg. 79.95 (ISBN 0-8490-3310-1). Gordon Pr.

Popular Variations in Latin-American Dancing. Ed. by Elizabeth Romain. 1984. lib. bdg. 79.95 (ISBN 0-87700-514-1). Revisionist Pr.

Popular View of the Doctrines of Charles Fourier. 2nd ed. Parke Godwin. LC 72-2951. Repr. of 1844 ed. 19.50 (ISBN 0-404-10716-8). AMS Pr.

Popular View of the Doctrines of Charles Fourier. Parke Godwin. Bd. with Democracy, Constructive & Pacific. 55p. LC 77-187451. (American Utopian Adventure Ser.). 175p. 1973. Repr. of 1844 ed. lib. bdg. 22.50x (ISBN 0-87991-006-2). Porcupine Pr.

Popular West: American Illustrators 1900-1940. Phoenix Art Museum. (Illus.). 55p. (Orig.). pap. 8.00 (ISBN 0-910407-08-8). Phoenix Art.

Popular Witchcraft. John Fritscher. 224p. 1973. 6.95 (ISBN 0-8065-0380-7, Pub. by Citadel Pr). Lyle Stuart.

Popular World Fiction 1900-Present, Vols. 1-4. Ed. by Walton Beacham. 1842p. 1987. Set. lib. bdg. 249.00 (ISBN 0-933833-08-3). Beacham Pub.

Popular Writing. Harold Stolerman & Helen O'Connor. 432p. 1986. pap. text ed. 15.95 (ISBN 0-03-071117-7, HoltC). HR&W.

Popular Writing in America: The Interaction of Style & Audience. 3rd ed. Ed. by Donald McQuade & Robert Atwan. (Illus.). 696p. 1985. pap. text ed. 16.95x (ISBN 0-19-503589-5); tchr's. manual avail. (ISBN 0-19-503603-4). Oxford U Pr.

Popular Writing in America: The Interaction of Style & Audience. 4th ed. Ed. by Donald McQuade & Robert Atwan. (Illus.). 784p. 1988. pap. text ed. 19.95 (ISBN 0-19-505323-0). Oxford U Pr.

Popular Yoga Asanas. Swami Kuvalayananda. LC 76-130420. (Illus.). (YA) (gr. 9 up). 1972. Repr. of 1931 ed. 12.50 (ISBN 0-8048-0673-X). C E Tuttle.

Populare Schriften see Ludwig Boltzmann: Theoretical Physics & Philosophical Problems, Selected Writings.

Popularity of Middle English Romance. Velma Richmond. LC 75-21576. 1975. 13.95 (ISBN 0-87972-114-6). Bowling Green Univ.

Popularity Plan. Rosemary Vernon. (Teenage Romance Ser.). 1981. pap. 2.50 (ISBN 0-553-26614-4). Bantam.

Popularity Summer. Rosemary Vernon. (Sweet Dreams Ser.: No. 20). 160p. 1984. pap. 2.25 (ISBN 0-553-24466-3). Bantam.

Popularity Trap: The Fabulous Five, No. 3. Betsy Haynes. (gr. 4-7). 1988. pap. 2.75 (ISBN 0-553-15634-9, Skylark). Bantam.

Population. Colin Clark. 30p. 1974. pap. 0.50 (ISBN 0-912414-19-7). Lumen Christi.

Population. David Killingray. Ed. by Edmund O'Connor. (World History Ser.). (Illus.). 32p. (gr. 6-11). 1980. lib. bdg. 6.95 (ISBN 0-89908-141-X); pap. text ed. 2.45 (ISBN 0-89908-116-9). Greenhaven.

Population. George Mosby, Jr. 1983. pap. 7.00 (ISBN 0-914610-35-X). Hanging Loose.

Population, 25 vols. (British Parliamentary Papers). 1971. Set. 3109.00x (ISBN 0-7165-1497-4, Pub. by Irish Academic Pr Ireland). Biblio Dist.

Population, Vol. 1, (incl. 1972-1974 Supplements) Ed. by Eleanor C. Goldstein. (Social Issues Resources Ser.). 1975. 75.00 (ISBN 0-89777-001-3). Soc Issues.

Population, Vol. 2 (incl. 1975-1979 Supplements) Ed. by Eleanor C. Goldstein. (Social Issues Resources Ser.). 1980. 75.00 (ISBN 0-89777-033-1). Soc Issues.

Population, Vol. 3 (incl. 1980-1984 Supplements) Ed. by Eleanor C. Goldstein. (Social Issues Resources Ser.). 1985. 75.00 (ISBN 0-89777-065-X). Soc Issues.

Population see Human Reproduction: Lectures in Physiology, Population, & Family Planning.

Population: A Basic Orientation. 2nd ed. Charles B. Nam & Susan G. Philliber. (Illus.). 400p. 1984. write for info. (ISBN 0-13-687210-7). P-H.

Population: A Study in Malthusianism. Warren S. Thompson. LC 74-76699. (Columbia University Studies in the Social Sciences: No. 153). Repr. of 1915 ed. 18.50 (ISBN 0-404-51153-8). AMS Pr.

Population Active Feminine et Travail Professionel de la Femme Mariee en France Depuis la Premiere Guerre Mondiale see Cahiers de l'Institut de Science Economique Appliquee.

Population Aging in Australia: Implications for Social & Economic Policy. Graeme Hugo. Ed. by Sandra E. Ward. (Papers of the East-West Population Institute: No. 98). (Illus.). viii, 47p. (Orig.). 1986. pap. 3.00 (ISBN 0-86638-078-7). EW Ctr HI.

Population Ahead. Roy G. Francis. LC 58-7927. pap. 42.50 (ISBN 0-317-41773-8, 2055869). Bks Demand UMI.

Population Alternative: A New Look at Competition & the Species. Jacques Ruffie. Tr. by Laurence Garvey from Fr. LC 85-19085. 342p. 1986. 24.45 (ISBN 0-394-54452-8). Pantheon.

Population: An International Directory of Organizations & Information Resources. Thaddeus C. Trzyna & Joan D. Smith. LC 76-4269. (Who's Doing What Ser.: No. 3). 160p. (Orig.). 1976. pap. 18.75x (ISBN 0-912102-22-5). Cal Inst Public.

Population: An Introduction. Johannes Overbeeke. LC 82-81687. 278p. 1982. text ed. 15.00 net (ISBN 0-15-543488-8, HC). HarBraceJ.

Population: An Introduction to Concepts & Issues. 3rd ed. John R. Weeks. 525p. 1986. text ed. write for info. (ISBN 0-534-06138-9). Wadsworth Pub.

Population: An Introduction to Concepts & Issues. 4th ed. John R. Weeks. Date not set. text ed. write for info. (ISBN 0-534-10122-4). Wadsworth Pub.

Population: An Introduction to Social Demography. Paul Zopf. 501p. 1984. text ed. 29.95 (ISBN 0-87484-715-X). Mayfield Pub.

Population & Agricultural Development - Selected Relationships & Possible Planning Uses, No. 8: Demographic Variables in Relation to Planning for Agricultural Development. (Development Documents: No. 54). 28p. 1978. pap. 6.25 (ISBN 0-686-92872-5, F1640, FAO). UNIPUB.

Population & Agricultural Development: Selected Relationships & Possible Planning Uses. (Economic & Social Development Papers: No. 4). (Illus., Eng., Fr. & Span., 3rd Printing 1979). 1977. pap. 9.50 (ISBN 92-5-100490-0, F1337, FAO). UNIPUB.

Population & Agricultural Development: Selected Relationships & Possible Planning Uses, No. 1: Population & Socio-Economic Change in Peasant Societies - The Historical Record of Hungary, 1700 to the Present. (Development Documents: No. 47). 127p. 1978. pap. 8.25 (ISBN 0-686-92843-1, F2052, FAO). UNIPUB.

Population & Agricultural Development: Selected Relationships & Possible Planning Uses, No. 2: The Population Problem & the Development Solution. (Development Documents: No. 48). 144p. 1978. pap. 8.25 (ISBN 0-686-92847-4, F1644, FAO). UNIPUB.

Population & Agricultural Development: Selected Relationships & Possible Planning Uses, No. 4: Economic-Demographic Simulation Models - A Review of Their Usefulness for Policy Analysis. (Development Documents: No. 50). 167p. 1978. pap. 11.25 (ISBN 0-686-92851-2, F1646, FAO). UNIPUB.

Population & Agricultural Development: Selected Relationships & Possible Planning Uses, No. 5: Population Growth & Agricultural Development - A Case Study of Kerala. (Development Documents: No. 51). 99p. 1978. pap. 7.50 (ISBN 0-686-92855-5, F1643, FAO). UNIPUB.

Population & Agricultural Development: Selected Relationships & Possible Planning Uses, No. 6: Economic-Demographic Interactions in Agricultural Development - The Case of Rural-to-Urban Migration. (Development Documents: No. 52). 171p. 1978. pap. 7.50 (ISBN 0-686-92861-X, F1642, FAO). UNIPUB.

Population & Agricultural Development: Selected Relationships & Possible Planning Uses, No. 7: Productivity, Wages & Nutrition in the Context of Less Developed Countries. (Development Documents: No. 53). 45p. 1978. pap. 6.25 (ISBN 0-686-92867-9, F1641, FAO). UNIPUB.

Population & Agriculture in the Developing Countries. J. Cairncross. (Economic & Social Development Papers: No. 15). 52p. (Eng., Fr. & Span.). 1981. pap. 7.50 (ISBN 92-5-100885-X, F2117, FAO). UNIPUB.

Population & Community Ecology: Principles & Methods. new ed. E. C. Pielou. LC 72-86334. (Illus.). 432p. 1974. 88.00 (ISBN 0-677-03580-2). Gordon & Breach.

Population & Demography: Annotated Bibliography. 1976. pap. 7.50 (ISBN 0-685-66316-7, F963, FAO). UNIPUB.

Population & Development. Ed. by Geoffrey Hawthorn. 210p. 1978. 30.00x (ISBN 0-7146-3102-7, F Cass Co). Biblio Dist.

Population & Development. P. D. Malgavkar & V. A. Panandiker. 1982. 18.50x (ISBN 0-8364-0923-X, Pub. by Somaiya). South Asia Bks.

Population & Development in Kenya. Ed. by S. H. Ominde. ix, 129p. 1984. text ed. 45.00x (ISBN 0-435-95761-9). Heinemann Ed.

Population & Development in Rural Egypt. Allen C. Kelley et al. LC 82-2425. (Duke Press Policy Studies & Studies in Social & Economic Demography: No. 5). xvii, 278p. 1982. 32.50 (ISBN 0-8223-0475-9). Duke.

Population & Development in the Third World. Allan Findlay & Anne Findlay. (Methuen Introductions to Development Ser.). (Illus.). 140p. 1987. pap. 9.95 (ISBN 0-416-91950-2). Routledge Chapman & Hall.

Population & Development Modeling: Proceedings of the United Nations-UNFPA Expert Group Meeting, Geneva, 24-28 September 1979. (Population Studies: No.73). 129p. 1981. pap. 12.00 (ISBN 0-686-79014-6, E.81.XIII.2). UN.

Population & Development Planning. Ed. & pref. by Warren C. Robinson. LC 74-84573. 263p. (Orig.). 1975. pap. text ed. 4.50 (ISBN 0-87834-024-6). Population Coun.

Population & Development: Projects in Africa. Ed. by John I. Clarke et al. 336p. 1985. 54.50 (ISBN 0-521-30527-6). Cambridge U Pr.

Population & Development: The Search for Selective Interventions. Ronald G. Ridker. LC 76-16806. (Resources for the Future Ser.). (Illus.). 488p. 1977. 45.00x. Johns Hopkins.

Population & Development: The Search for Selective Interventions. Ed. by Ronald G. Ridker. 488p. 1977. 37.50 (ISBN 0-8018-1884-2). Resources Future.

Population & Economic Change in Developing Countries. Richard A. Easterlin. LC 79-12569. (NBER Universities-National Bureau Conference Ser.). x, 582p. 1987. pap. text ed. 32.00 (ISBN 0-226-18027-1). U of Chicago Pr.

Population & Economic Development in Brazil: Eighteen Hundred to the Present. Thomas W. Merrick & Douglas H. Graham. LC 78-20523. 408p. 1979. text ed. 45.00x (ISBN 0-8018-2182-7). Johns Hopkins.

Population & Economic Growth Theory. Julian L. Simon. 250p. 1985. 24.95x (ISBN 0-631-14427-7). Basil Blackwell.

Population & Economy: From the Traditional to the Modern World. Ed. by Robert Rotberg et al. (Studies in Interdisciplinary History). (Illus.). 220p. 1986. 37.50 (ISBN 0-521-32540-4); pap. 12.95 (ISBN 0-521-31055-5). Cambridge U Pr.

Population & Emigration in Nineteenth Century Britain. D. V. Glass & P. A. Taylor. (Government & Society in 19th. Century Britain Ser.). 132p. 1976. 30.00x (ISBN 0-7165-2219-5, BBA 02037, Pub. by Irish Academic Pr Ireland). Biblio Dist.

Population & Employment in Developing Countries. Ghazi M. Farooq. (Background Paper for Training in Population, Human Resources & Development Planning: No. 1). vii, 75p. (Orig.). 1985. pap. 10.50 (ISBN 92-2-100515-1). Intl Labour Office.

Population & Energy: A Systems Analysis of Resource Utilization in the Dominican Republic. Gustavo A. Antonini et al. LC 75-2495. (University of Florida Latin American Monographs: No. 14). 166p. 1975. 15.00 (ISBN 0-8130-0502-7). U Presses Fla.

Population & Family Education. 5.00 (ISBN 0-685-27881-6, UB51, UB). UNIPUB.

Population & Family in the Low Countries, No. 1. Ed. by H. G. Moors et al. 1976. pap. 21.00 (ISBN 90-247-1859-7, Pub. by Martinus Nijhoff Netherlands). Kluwer Academic.

Population & Family in the Low Countries, No. 2. Ed. by H. G. Moors et al. (Publication of NIDI & CBGS: Vol. 6). 1978. pap. 17.00 (ISBN 90-207-0687-X, Pub. by Martinus Nijhoff Netherlands). Kluwer Academic.

Population & Family Planning in Bangladesh: A Study of the Research. Mohammad Alauddin & Rashid Faruqee. (Working Paper: No. 557). 176p. 1983. 8.00 (ISBN 0-8213-0150-0, WP 0557). World Bank.

Population & Family Planning in India. G. C. Kendadamath. 1986. 20.00x (ISBN 0-8364-1557-4, Pub. by Indian Doc Serv India). South Asia Bks.

Population & Family Planning Programs: A Compendium of Data Through 1983. 12th ed. Dorothy Nortman. (Orig.). 1985. pap. 7.00 (ISBN 0-87834-053-X). Population Coun.

Population & Frustration. Ira S. Steinberg. LC 73-22397. (Boyd H. Bode Memorial Lecture New Ser.: No. 1). 27p. (Orig.). 1974. pap. 1.50 (ISBN 0-8142-0211-X). Ohio St U Pr.

Population & Health Policy in the Peoples Republic of China. Peter Chan. 150p. 1978. pap. 6.00 (ISBN 0-686-76148-0). Neo Pr.

Population & History. E. A. Wrigley. (Illus., Orig.). 1969. pap. text ed. 3.95 (ISBN 0-07-072115-7). McGraw.

Population & International Migration. Gurushri Swamy. (Working Paper: No. 689). 100p. 1985. 5.00 (ISBN 0-8213-0606-5, WP 0689). World Bank.

Population & Its Problems. George V. Zito. LC 79-581. 283p. 1979. text ed. 39.95 (ISBN 0-87705-396-0); pap. text ed. 19.95 (ISBN 0-87705-414-2). Human Sci Pr.

Population & Marketing Settlements in Ch'ing China. Gilbert Rozman. LC 81-17961. (Illus.). 192p. 1982. 39.50 (ISBN 0-521-23556-1). Cambridge U Pr.

Population & Metropolis: The Demography of London, 1580-1650. Roger A. Finlay. LC 78-20956. (Cambridge Geographical Studies: No. 12). 224p. 1981. 52.50 (ISBN 0-521-22535-3). Cambridge U Pr.

Population & Peace in the Pacific. Warren S. Thompson. LC 79-1151. (Essay Index Reprint Ser.). Repr. of 1946 ed. 24.50 (ISBN 0-8369-2867-9). Ayer Co Pubs.

Population & Planning in Developing Nations: A Review of Sixty Development Plans for the 1970s. B. Maxwell Stamper. LC 77-24209. 265p. (Orig.). 1977. pap. text ed. 5.95 (ISBN 0-87834-026-2). Population Coun.

Population & Political Systems in Tropical Africa. Robert F. Stevenson. LC 68-11435. (Illus.). 306p. 1968. 32.00x (ISBN 0-231-03052-5). Columbia U Pr.

Population & Population Policy in Hungary. Ed. by David Biro et al. 232p. 1984. 67.50x (ISBN 0-317-53870-5, Pub. by Collets (UK)). State Mutual Bk.

Population & Poverty in the Developing World. Nancy Birdsall. (Working Paper: No. 404). 96p. 1980. 5.00 (ISBN 0-686-36200-4, WP-0404). World Bank.

Population & Progress in the Far East. Warren S. Thompson. LC 59-10428. pap. 113.30 (ISBN 0-317-42272-3, 2025793). Bks Demand UMI.

Population & Related Organizations: International Address List. Ruth Sandor & Jane Vanderlin. LC 84-6302. (APLIC Special Publication Ser.: No. 5). 87p. (Orig.). 1984. pap. 45.00. APLIC Intl.

Population & Related Organizations: International Address List. Ruth Sandor & Jane Vanderlin. 87p. 1984. 45.00 (LC 84-6302); members 30.00 (ISBN 0-318-03481-6). Assn Pop Lib.

Population & Resources. Harry Robinson. 1982. 24.95x (ISBN 0-312-63120-0). St Martin.

Population & Retail Services in Nonmetropolitan America. Kenneth M. Johnson. (Rural Studies). 350p. 1985. pap. 32.50x (ISBN 0-86531-584-1). Westview.

Population & Revenue in the Towns of Palestine in the Sixteenth Century. Amnon Cohen & Bernard Lewis. LC 78-51160. (Illus.). 1978. 38.00x (ISBN 0-691-09375-X). Princeton U Pr.

Population & Settlement in U. P. A Geographical Analysis. Alok Kumar Singh. (Illus.). xx, 231p. 1986. text ed. 40.00x (ISBN 81-210-0023-8, Pub. by Inter India Pubns N Delhi). Apt Bks.

Population & Social Development Communication Documentation Service Catalog. PSD Doc Service. 180p. (Orig.). 1982. pap. text ed. 3.50 (ISBN 0-89836-033-1). Comm & Family.

Population & Social Organization. Ed. by Moni Nag. (World Anthropology Ser.). x, 368p. 1975. 29.75 (ISBN 90-279-7589-2). Mouton.

Population & Society. 4th ed. Dennis H. Wrong. 1977. pap. text ed. write for info (ISBN 0-394-31250-3, RanC). Random.

Population & Society: A Sociological Perspective. Carl F. Grindstaff. 192p. 1981. pap. 8.95 (ISBN 0-8158-0397-4). Chris Mass.

Population & Society in Britain, 1850-1980. Ed. by Theo Barker & Michael Drake. 240p. 1982. 35.00x (ISBN 0-8147-1043-3). NYU Pr.

Population & Society in India. B. Kuppuswamy. 136p. 1975. 14.95. Asia Bk Corp.

Population & Society in Norway, 1735-1865. Michael Drake. LC 69-14393. (Cambridge Studies in Economic History). pap. 69.00 (ISBN 0-317-26008-1, 2024445). Bks Demand UMI.

Population & Society in Twentieth Century France. Colin Dyer. LC 77-2908. (Illus.). 256p. 1978. 39.50x (ISBN 0-8419-0308-5); pap. 13.50x (ISBN 0-8419-6209-X). Holmes & Meier.

Population & Society Seventeen Fifty to Nineteen Forty. N. L. Tranter. (Themes in British Social History Ser.). 1985. pap. text ed. 13.95 (ISBN 0-582-49224-6). Longman.

Population & Socio-Economic Development. D. Valenti et al. 187p. 1986. 6.95 (ISBN 0-8285-3239-7, Pub. by Progress Pubs USSR). Imported Pubns.

Population & Technological Change: A Study of Long-Term Trends. Ester Boserup. LC 80-21116. (Illus.). 256p. 1983. pap. 9.00x (ISBN 0-226-06674-6). U of Chicago Pr.

Population & the Labor Force in Rural Economics. (FAO Economic & Social Development Paper Ser.: No. 59). (Illus.). 169p. (Orig.). 1986. pap. text ed. 13.25 (ISBN 92-5-102364-6, F2919, FAO). UNIPUB.

Population & the Population Explosion: A Bibliography for 1970. Stephen H. Goode. LC 72-87106. xxv, 361p. 1973. 17.00x (ISBN 0-87875-032-0). Whitston Pub.

Population & the Population Explosion: A Bibliography for 1976. 1980. 38.50x (ISBN 0-87875-129-7). Whitston Pub.

Population & the Population Explosion: A Bibliography for 1973. Charles W. Triche & Diane S. Triche. LC 72-87106. 1975. 13.00x (ISBN 0-87875-059-2). Whitston Pub.

Population & the Population Explosion: A Bibliography for 1975. Charles W. Triche & Diane S. Triche. LC 72-87106. 1976. 18.00x (ISBN 0-87875-098-3). Whitston Pub.

Population & the Social System. Francesco S. Nitti. LC 75-38140. (Demography Ser.). (Illus.). 1976. Repr. of 1894 ed. 17.00x (ISBN 0-405-07993-1). Ayer Co Pubs.

Population & the Urban Future. Philip M. Hauser et al. LC 82-5529. 187p. 1983. 59.50 (ISBN 0-87395-591-9); pap. 18.95 (ISBN 0-87395-592-7). State U NY Pr.

Population & the World Economy in the 21st Century. Just Faaland. LC 82-10579. 272p. 1982. 35.00 (ISBN 0-312-63123-5). St Martin.

Population & Utilization of Land & Sea in Hawaii. J. W. Coulter. (BMB Ser.). pap. 10.00 (ISBN 0-527-02194-6). Kraus Repr.

Population & Vital Statistics: Local & Health Authority Area Summary, 1985. (OPCS Reference Ser.). 90p. (Orig.). 1987. pap. text ed. 13.50 (ISBN 0-11-691186-7, HM484, Pub. by Her Maj Station Ofc). UNIPUB.

Population & World Politics. Ed. by Philip Hauser. LC 58-9400. 1958. 11.95 (ISBN 0-02-914250-4). Free Pr.

Population & World Politics. M. Leroy. (Publications of the Netherlands Inter-University Demographic Institute (NIDI) & the Population & Family Study Centre (CBGS): Vol. 4). 1979. 22.00 (ISBN 90-207-0744-2, Pub. by Martinus Nijhoff Netherlands). Kluwer Academic.

Population Atlas of China. Ed. by The Population Census Office of the State Council of the People's Republic of China & The Institute of Geography of the Chinese Academy of Sciences. LC 87-675262. (Illus.). 242p. 1987. 250.00 (ISBN 0-19-584092-5). Oxford U Pr.

Population-Based Medicine. Ed. by Mack Lipkin, Jr. & William A. Lybrand. LC 81-21116. 220p. 1982. 36.95 (ISBN 0-275-91370-8, C1370). Praeger.

Population Biology. Ed. by H. I. Freedman & C. Strobeck. (Lecture Notes in Biomathematics Ser.: Vol. 52). 440p. pap. 31.00 (ISBN 0-387-12677-5). Springer-Verlag.

Population Biology. Ed. by Simon Levin. LC 83-21389. (Proceedings of Symposia in Applied Mathematics: Vol. 30). 102p. 1984. 27.00 (ISBN 0-8218-0083-3, PSAPM 30); pap. 24.00. Am Math.

Population Biology & Evolution. Ed. by K. Woehrmann & V. Loschcke. (Proceedings in Life Sciences Ser.). (Illus.). 300p. 1984. 62.00 (ISBN 0-387-13278-3). Springer Verlag.

Population Biology & Evolution of Clonal Organisms. Jeremy B. Jackson. Ed. by Leo W. Buss & Robert E. Cook. LC 85-14186. 608p. 1986. text ed. 63.00 (ISBN 0-300-03379-6); pap. 30.00x (ISBN 0-300-03650-7, Y0580). Yale U Pr.

Population Biology of Infectious Diseases: Berlin, 1982. Ed. by R. C. Anderson & R. M. May. (Dahlem Workshop Reports: Vol. 25). (Illus.). 320p. 1982. 23.00 (ISBN 0-387-11650-8). Springer-Verlag.

Population Biology of Plants. J. L. Harper. 1977. 91.00 (ISBN 0-12-325850-2). Acad Pr.

Population Biology of Plants. J. L. Harper. LC 76-16973. 1981. pap. 30.00 (ISBN 0-12-325852-9). Acad Pr.

Population Biology of Tropical Insects. Allen M. Young. LC 82-7562. 524p. 1982. 79.50x (ISBN 0-306-40843-0, Plenum Pr). Plenum Pub.

Population Biology: Progress & Problems of Studies on Natural Populations. A. V. Yakovlev. 303p. 1986. 12.95 (ISBN 0-8285-3446-2, Pub. by Mir Pubs USSR). Imported Pubns.

Population Biology: Retrospect & Prospect. Charles E. King & Peter S. Dawson. 240p. 1983. 34.00 (ISBN 0-231-05252-9). Columbia U Pr.

Population Biology: The Evolution & Ecology of Populations. Philip W. Hedrick. 464p. 1984. text ed. 27.50 (ISBN 0-86720-043-X). Jones & Bartlett.

Population Bomb. rev. ed. Paul R. Ehrlich. 201p. 1975. lib. bdg. 18.95 (ISBN 0-89190-861-7, Pub. by River City Pr). Amereon Ltd.

Population Bomb. new rev. ed. Paul R. Ehrlich. (Orig.). 1976. pap. 3.50 (ISBN 0-345-33834-0). Ballantine.

Population Bulletin of the United Nations, No. 17-1984. 93p. 1985. pap. 11.00 (ISBN 92-1-151105-4, E.84.XIII.13). UN.

Population Bulletin of the United Nations, No. 21-22. 1987. pap. 10.00 (ISBN 92-1-151166-6, E.87.XIII.5). UN.

Population Bulletin of the United Nations, 1986: A Special Issue in Commemoration of the 40th Anniversary of the Population Commission, Nos.19-20. 167p. 1987. 16.50 (ISBN 92-1-151162-3, E.87.XIII.2). UN.

Population Challenge: A Handbook for Non-Specialists. Johannes Overbeek. LC 76-5328. (Contributions in Sociology Ser.: No. 19). (Illus.). 224p. 1976. lib. bdg. 35.00 (ISBN 0-8371-8896-2, OPC/). Greenwood.

Population Change - Public Policy Relationship. Raymond K. Oldakowski. (Public Administration Ser.: P 2186). 17p. 1987. 5.00 (ISBN 1-55590-366-5). Vance Biblios.

Population Change & Agricultural Development in 19th Century France. William Henry Newell. Ed. by Stuart Bruchey. LC 77-77783. (Dissertations in European Economic History Ser.). (Illus.). 1977. lib. bdg. 26.50x (ISBN 0-405-10796-X). Ayer Co Pubs.

Population Change & Crime Change. Deborah Caulfield. 15p. (Orig.). 1982. pap. 1.50 (ISBN 1-55719-040-2). U NE Ctr Applied Urban Rsch.

Population Change & Economic Development. World Bank Staff. (Illus.). 1985. pap. 9.95x (ISBN 0-19-520484-0). Oxford U Pr.

Population Change & Social Continuity: Ten Years in a Coal Town. Harold W. Annand. LC 85-40506. (Illus.). 144p. 1986. 24.50x (ISBN 0-941664-14-7, Pub. by Susquehanna U Pr). Susquehanna U Pr.

Population Change & Social Policy. Nathan Keyfitz. 1982. text ed. 31.50 (ISBN 0-89011-568-0); pap. 17.75. Abt Bks.

Population Change & Social Policy. Nathan Keyfitz. (Illus.). 286p. 1984. lib. bdg. 32.75 (ISBN 0-8191-4072-4); pap. text ed. 18.75 (ISBN 0-8191-4073-2). U Pr of Amer.

Population Change & the Economy. Andrew M. Isserman. 1985. lib. bdg. 42.50 (ISBN 0-89838-140-1, Pub. by Kluwer-Nijhoff (Netherlands)). Kluwer Academic.

Population Change: Asia & Oceania, Proceedings of the Sydney Conference, Australia, 1967. International Union for the Scientific Study of Population. Ed. by W. D. Borrie & Morag Cameron. LC 73-168088. pap. 54.00 (ISBN 0-317-26213-0, 2052119). Bks Demand UMI.

Population Change in North-Western Europe, 1750-1850. Michael Anderson. (Studies in Economic & Social History). 96p. 1988. pap. text ed. 9.95 (ISBN 0-333-34386-7, Pub. by Macmillan UK). Humanities.

Population Change in Southeast Asia. Ed. by Wilfredo F. Arce & Gabrqel C. Alvarez. 499p. 1984. text ed. 58.50x (ISBN 9971-902-56-7, Pub. by Inst Southeast Asian Stud). Gower Pub Co.

Population Change, Labor Supply, & Agriculture in Ausburg, 1480-1618: A Study of Early Demographic-Economic Interactions. Martha W. Paas. Ed. by Stuart Bruchey. LC 80-2821. (Dissertations in European Economic History II). (Illus.). 1981. lib. bdg. 26.50x (ISBN 0-405-14005-3). Ayer Co Pubs.

Population Change, Natural Resources & Regionalism. Ed. by Ann C. Reid. (Breaking New Ground Ser.: No. 1). 104p. 1986. pap. 15.00 (ISBN 0-938549-00-6). Grey Towers Pr.

Population Changes in Omaha-Council Bluffs YMCA Branch Office Areas. Rebecca S. Fahrlander. 10p. (Orig.). 1981. pap. 1.00 (ISBN 1-55719-058-5). U NE Ctr Applied Urban Rsch.

Population Concepts in Agricultural Cooperative Training Courses. (Economic & Social Development Papers: No. 23). 60p. (Eng. , Fr. & Span.). 1981. pap. 7.50 (ISBN 92-5-101165-6, F2289, FAO). UNIPUB.

Population Concepts in Agricultural Training Curricula. 1979. pap. 7.50 (ISBN 92-5-100600-8, F1516, FAO). UNIPUB.

Population Concepts in Farm Management Courses. 32p. 1978. pap. 7.50 (ISBN 92-5-100471-4, F1333, FAO). UNIPUB.

Population Concepts in Home Management Courses. 36p. 1979. pap. 8.50 (ISBN 92-5-100847-7, F1965, FAO). UNIPUB.

Population, Contact & Climate in the New Mexican Pueblos. Ezra B. Zubrow. LC 73-86447. (Anthropological Papers of the University of Arizona: No. 24). pap. 23.80 (ISBN 0-317-26793-0, 2024324). Bks Demand UMI.

Population Control for Zero Growth in Singapore. Swee-Hock Saw. (Oxford in Asia Current Affairs Ser.). 1980. 33.00x (ISBN 0-19-580430-9). Oxford U Pr.

Population Control in China: Theory & Applications. Song Jian & Chi-Hsien Tuan. 310p. 1985. 46.95 (ISBN 0-275-90166-1, C0166). Praeger.

Population Control Politics: Women, Sterilization & Reproductive Choice. Thomas M. Shapiro. (Health, Society, & Policy Ser.). 256p. 1985. 24.95 (ISBN 0-87722-365-3). Temple U Pr.

Population Council: A Chronicle of the First Twenty-Five Years, 1952-1977. LC 78-21678. 210p. 1978. text ed. avail. (ISBN 0-87834-037-8). Population Coun.

Population Crisis & Moral Responsibility. Ed. by Philip J. Wogaman. 1973. 15.00 (ISBN 0-8183-0146-5). Pub Aff Pr.

Population Crisis in India. K. P. Bahadur. 180p. 1977. 15.95. Asia Bk Corp.

Population de la France de 1700 a 1959. J. C. Toutain. (Economies et Societes Serie AF: No. 3). 1963. pap. 26.00 (ISBN 0-8115-0627-4). Kraus Repr.

Population Decline in Europe: Implications of a Declining or Stationary Population. Ed. by Council of Europe Staff. LC 78-3106. (Illus.). 1978. 37.50x (ISBN 0-312-63125-1). St Martin.

Population: Demography & Policy. Robert H. Weller & Leon F. Bouvier. 384p. 1981. text ed. write for info. (ISBN 0-312-63114-6); instr's. manual avail. St Martin.

Population Density & Concentration in England & Wales, 1971 & 1981. J. Craig. (Studies on Medical & Population Subjects: No. 52). 47p. 1988. pap. 18.00 (ISBN 0-11-691224-3, HM3416, Pub. by Her Maj Station Ofc). UNIPUB.

Population, Development & Income Distribution: A Modeling Approach. R. Scott Moreland. LC 83-23105. 224p. 1984. 27.50 (ISBN 0-312-63131-6). St Martin.

Population Dilemma. Ed. by Philip M. Hauser. LC 73-96967. 1963. 3.95 (ISBN 0-13-685677-2); pap. 2.45. Am Assembly.

Population, Disease & Land in Early Japan, 645-900. William W. Farris. (Harvard-Yenching Institute Monograph Ser.: No. 24). (Illus.). 400p. 1984. text ed. 20.00x (ISBN 0-674-69031-1). Harvard U Pr.

Population Dispersal from Major Metropolitan Regions: An International Comparison. Daniel R. Vining, Jr. & Thomas Kontuly. (Discussion Paper Ser.: No. 100). 1977. pap. 5.50 (ISBN 0-686-32266-5). Regional Sci Res Inst.

Population Distribution in Colonial America. Stella H. Sutherland. LC 70-182725. Repr. of 1936 ed. 24.50 (ISBN 0-404-06306-3). AMS Pr.

Population Dose Evaluation & Standards for Man & His Environment. (Illus.). 646p. (Orig.). 1975. pap. 49.00 (ISBN 92-0-020374-4, ISP375, IAEA). UNIPUB.

Population Dynamics: Alternative Models. Bertram G. Murray, Jr. (Physiological Ecology Ser.). 1979. 19.95 (ISBN 0-12-511750-7). Acad Pr.

Population Dynamics & Family Planning. Date not set. 4.40. Coun Soc Wk Ed.

Population Dynamics & Infectious Disease. Roy M. Anderson. (Illus.). 376p. 1982. 45.00x (ISBN 0-412-21610-8, NO. 6655, Pub. by Chapman & Hall). Routledge Chapman & Hall.

Population: Dynamics, Ethics & Policy. Ed. by Priscilla Reining & Irene Tinker. LC 75-4498. (Science Compendium Ser.: Vol. 3). 184p. 1975. casebound 10.00 (ISBN 0-87168-214-1); pap. 3.50 (ISBN 0-87168-225-7). AAAS.

Population: Dynamics, Ethics & Policy. Ed. by Priscilla Reining & Irene Tinker. 1975. 32.50 (ISBN 0-12-586750-6); pap. 19.00 (ISBN 0-12-586751-4). Acad Pr.

Population Dynamics of Four Confined Populations of the Continental Vole: Microtus Arvalis Pallas. 1960. pap. 5.00 (ISBN 90-220-0052-4, PDC157, PUDOC). UNIPUB.

Population Dynamics of Nepal. Judith Banister & Shyam Thapa. 120p. 1981. 12.00 (ISBN 0-318-04181-2). Am-Nepal Ed.

Population Dynamics of Rabies in Wildlife. Ed. by Philip J. Bacon. 1985. 64.50 (ISBN 0-12-071350-0); pap. 32.50 (ISBN 0-12-071351-9). Acad Pr.

Population Dynamics of the Waterbuck, Kobus Ellipsiprymnus (Ogilby, 1833), in the Sabi-Sand Wildtuin. Harry J. Herbert. (Mammalia Depicta Ser.: Vol. 7). (Illus.). 68p. (Orig.). 1972. pap. text ed. 20.00 (ISBN 3-4900-2518-0). Parey Sci Pubs.

Population Dynamics, Reproduction, & Activities of the Kangaroo Rat, Dipodomys ordii, in Western Texas. Herschel W. Garner. (Graduate Studies: No. 7). (Illus.). 28p. 1974. pap. 2.00 (ISBN 0-89672-014-4). Tex Tech Univ Pr.

Population Ecology: A Unified Study of Animals & Plants. 2nd, rev. ed. Michael Begon & Martin Mortimer. LC 85-27712. (Illus.). 216p. (Orig.). 1986. text ed. cancelled (ISBN 0-87893-064-7); pap. text ed. 19.95x (ISBN 0-87893-065-5). Sinauer Assocs.

Population, Ecology, & Social Evolution. Ed. by Steven Polgar. (World Anthropology Ser.). (Illus.). x, 354p. 1975. 29.75 (ISBN 90-279-7599-X). Mouton.

Population Ecology of Cycles in Small Mammals: Mathematical Theory & Biological Fact. James P. Finerty. LC 79-23774. (Illus.). 1981. text ed. 29.00t (ISBN 0-300-02382-0). Yale U Pr.

Population Ecology of Individuals. Adam Lomnicki. Ed. by Robert M. May. (Monographs in Population Biology: No. 25). 220p. 1988. text ed. 45.00 (ISBN 0-691-08471-8); pap. text ed. 13.95 (ISBN 0-691-08462-9). Princeton U Pr.

Population Ecology of Raptors. Ian Newton. LC 79-50279. (Illus.). 1979. 35.00 (ISBN 0-931130-03-4). Buteo.

Population Ecology of the Bobwhite. John L. Roseberry & Willard D. Klimstra. LC 83-2481. (Illus.). 282p. 1983. 25.00x (ISBN 0-8093-1116-X). S Ill U Pr.

Population Ecology of the Cooperatively Breeding Acorn Woodpecker. Walter D. Koenig & Ronald L. Mumme. (Monographs in Population Biology: No. 24). (Illus.). 496p. 1987. text ed. 55.00 (ISBN 0-691-08422-X); pap. text ed. 16.95 (ISBN 0-691-08464-5). Princeton U Pr.

Population Ecology of the Gray Bat (Myotis Grisescens) Factors Influencing Early Growth & Development. Merlin D. Tuttle. (Occasional Papers: No. 36). 24p. 1975. pap. 1.50 (ISBN 0-317-04951-8). U of KS Mus Nat Hist.

Population Ecology of the Gray Bat (Myotis Grisescens) Philopatry, Timing & Patterns of Movement, Weight Loss During Migration, & Seasonal Adaptive Strategies. Merlin D. Tuttle. (Occasional Papers: No. 54). 38p. 1976. pap. 2.25 (ISBN 0-317-04955-0). U of KS Mus Nat Hist.

Population Ecology of the Little Brown Bat, Myotis Lucifugus, in Indiana and Northcentral Kentucky. Stephen R. Humphrey & James B. Cope. (ASM Special Publication Ser.: No. 4). (Illus.). vii, 81p. 1976. 7.50 (ISBN 0-943612-03-9). Am Soc Mammalogists.

Population Economics. T. Paul Schulz. LC 80-36830. (Perspectives in Economics Ser.). 224p. 1981. pap. text ed. write for info. (ISBN 0-201-08371-X). Addison-Wesley.

Population Economics: Selected Essays of Joseph J. Spengler. Joseph J. Spengler. LC 78-72019. (Illus.). vii, 536p. 1972. 42.50 (ISBN 0-8223-0286-1). Duke.

Population Education: A Contemporary Concern: International Study of the Conceptualization and Methodology of Population Education (ISCOMPE) (Educational Studies & Documents: No. 28). 120p. 1978. pap. 5.00 (ISBN 92-3-101553-2, U825, UNESCO). UNIPUB.

Population Education: A Guide to Curriculum & Teacher Education. D. Gopal Rao. xii, 136p. 1974. 6.75x (ISBN 0-88386-470-3). South Asia Bks.

Population Education: A Knowledge Base. Willard J. Jacobson. LC 78-13398. 1979. text ed. 18.95x (ISBN 0-8077-2533-1). Tchrs Coll.

Population Education for Developing Countries. K. R. Salkar. 288p. 1986. text ed. 27.50x (ISBN 81-207-0116-X, Pub. by Sterling Pubs India). Apt Bks.

Population Education for Nepal. Daniel Taylor & Hem B. Hamal. 81p. 1974. pap. 4.00 (ISBN 0-89055-110-3). Carolina Pop Ctr.

Population Education in Asia: A Source Book. (Illus.). 303p. 1975. pap. 29.95 (ISBN 0-685-55210-1, UB50, UB). UNIPUB.

Population Education Sourcebook for Sub-Saharan Africa. Ed. by Reuben K. Udo. 1980. pap. text ed. 25.00x (ISBN 0-435-95917-4). Heinemann Ed.

Population Energy Relationships of the Agrimi (Capra Aegagrus Cretica) on Theodorou Island, Greece. Nikolaos Papageorgiou. (Mammalia Depicta Ser.: Vol. 11). (Illus.). 56p. (Orig.). pap. text ed. 14.00 (ISBN 3-490-21518-4). Parey Sci Pubs.

Population, Environment & Resources, & Third World Development. Ed. by Pradip K. Ghosh. LC 83-26430. (International Development Resource Bks.: No. 5). (Illus.). xx, 634p. 1984. lib. bdg. 56.95 (ISBN 0-313-24141-4, GPL/). Greenwood.

Population, Environment, & the Quality of Life. Intro. by Parker G. Marden & Dennis Hodgson. LC 74-579. (Studies in Modern Society: Political & Social Issues: No. 6). 1975. 32.50 (ISBN 0-404-10536-X). AMS Pr.

Population Environment Relations in Tropical Islands: The Case of Eastern Fiji. H. Brookfield. (MAB Technical Notes: No. 13). (Illus.). 233p. (Based on the Findings of the UNESCO-UNFPA Pilot Project "Studies on Population-Environment, relationships in the Eastern Islands of Fiji"). 1981. pap. 10.50 (ISBN 92-3-101821-3, U1054, UNESCO). UNIPUB.

Population Estimates by Age Nineteen Seventy-Seven. Vicki S. Stepp. (Nebraska Economic & Business Report: No. 20). 1978. 5.00 (ISBN 0-686-28410-0). Bur Busn Res U Nebr.

Population Estimates: Methods for Small Area Analysis. Everett S. Lee & Harold F. Goldsmith. (Illus.). 200p. 1982. 29.95 (ISBN 0-8039-1812-7). Sage.

Population Estimation Methods, Canada. 1987. pap. text ed. 26.50 (ISBN 0-317-64540-4, SSC242, Pub. by State Canada). UNIPUB.

Population Factor in African Studies: Proceedings of the African Studies Association of the United Kingdom, Sept. 1972. African Studies Association of the United Kingdom Staff. Ed. by R. P. Moss & R. J. Rathbone. 209p. 1972. 17.00 (ISBN 0-8419-6200-6, Africana). Holmes & Meier.

Population Factors in Development Planning in the Middle East. Ed. by F. C. Shorter & Huda Zurayk. 208p. 1985. pap. write for info. (ISBN 0-87834-054-8). Population Coun.

Population Family & Culture. R. N. Pati. 1987. 31.95. Asia Bk Corp.

Population, Family & Culture. RN Pati. 1987. 25.00x (ISBN 81-7024-151-0, Pub. by Ashish India). South Asia Bks.

Population Genetics & Evolution. G. De Jong. (Illus.). 305p. 1988. 89.50 (ISBN 0-387-18452-X). Springer-Verlag.

Population Genetics & Evolution. 2nd ed. Lawrence E. Mettler et al. (Illus.). 448p. 1988. text ed. 24.00 (ISBN 0-13-685678-0). P-H.

Population Genetics & Fishery Management. Ed. by Nils Ryman & Fred Utter. LC 86-19042. 488p. 1987. 35.00 (ISBN 0-295-96435-9, Pub. by Wash Sea Grant); pap. 17.50 (ISBN 0-295-96436-7). U of Wash Pr.

Population Genetics & Molecular Evolution. Ed. by T. Ohta & K. Aoki. 400p. 1985. 53.50 (ISBN 0-387-15584-8). Springer-Verlag.

Population Genetics: Basic Principles. D. P. Doolittle. (Advanced Series in Agricultural Sciences: Vol. 16). (Illus.). 300p. 1987. pap. 35.00 (ISBN 0-387-17326-9). Springer-Verlag.

Population Genetics in Animal Breeding. 2nd ed. Franz Pirchner. Tr. by D. L. Frape from Ger. LC 83-2164. 424p. 1983. 65.00x (ISBN 0-306-41201-2, Plenum Pr.). Plenum Pub.

Population Genetics in Forestry. Ed. by H. R. Gregorius. (Lecture Notes in Biomathematics Ser.: Vol. 60). vi, 287p. 1985. pap. 21.50 (ISBN 0-387-15980-0). Springer-Verlag.

Population Genetics: Outline Studies in Biology. L. M. Cook. 1976. pap. 8.50 (ISBN 0-412-13930-8, NO. 6064, Pub. by Chapman & Hall). Routledge Chapman & Hall.

Population Geography. 2nd ed. J. I. Clarke. LC 70-183339. 187p. 1972. text ed. 27.00 (ISBN 0-08-016853-1); pap. text ed. 11.50 (ISBN 0-08-016854-X). Pergamon.

Population Geography & Developing Countries. J. I. Clarke. 1972. text ed. 27.00 (ISBN 0-08-016445-5); pap. text ed. 14.75 (ISBN 0-08-016446-3). Pergamon.

Population Geography: Problems, Concepts, & Prospects. 2nd ed. Gary L. Peters & Robert P. Larkin. 336p. 1983. pap. text ed. 21.95 (ISBN 0-8403-2925-3, 40292501). Kendall-Hunt.

Population Geography: Progress & Prospects. Ed. by Michael Pacione. (Progress in Geography Ser.). 336p. 1986. 43.00 (ISBN 0-7099-4045-9, Pub. by Croom Helm Ltd). Routledge Chapman & Hall.

Population Growth. Eric McGraw. (World Issues Ser.). (Illus.). 48p. (gr. 5 up). 1987. PLB 58.40 set (ISBN 0-317-60380-9); PLB 14.60 (ISBN 0-86592-276-4). Rourke Corp.

Population Growth: A Problem-Solving Approach. Darlene Southworth & Thomas M. Hursh. (gr. 11-12). 1979. pap. text ed. 6.95x (ISBN 0-933694-01-6). COMPress.

Population Growth & Agrarian Change. David B. Grigg. LC 79-4237. (Cambridge Geographical Studies: No. 13). 368p. 1981. 59.50 (ISBN 0-521-22760-7); pap. 22.95 (ISBN 0-521-29635-8). Cambridge U Pr.

Population Growth & Balance, Joni Keating. 60p. tchr's. ed. 9.95 (ISBN 0-89824-179-0). Trillium Pr.

Population Growth & Economic Development in Africa. Ed. by S. H. Ominde & C. N. Ejiogu. 1972. 35.00x (ISBN 0-435-97470-X). Heinemann Ed.

Population Growth & Economic Development: Issues & Evidence. Ed. by D. Gale Johnson & Ronald D. Lee. LC 86-40447. (Social Demography Ser.). 800p. 1987. text ed. 45.00x (ISBN 0-299-11130-X). U of Wis Pr.

Population Growth & Economic Development. National Research Council. 120p. (Orig.). 1986. pap. text ed. 10.00x (ISBN 0-309-03641-0). Natl Acad Pr.

Population Growth & Employment Opportunities in Nepal. Y. P. Pant. 1985. 12.50x (ISBN 0-8364-1277-X, Pub. by Oxford IBH). South Asia Bks.

Population Growth & Its Demands upon Land for Housing in Evanston, Illinois. Albert G. Hinman. LC 73-2904. (Metropolitan America Ser.). (Illus.). 132p. 1974. Repr. 14.00x (ISBN 0-405-05395-9). Ayer Co Pubs.

Population Growth & Labor Absorption in the Developing World: 1960-2000. Ed. by Paul Demeny & W. Parker Mauldin. Date not set. write for info. Population Coun.

Population Growth & Planning Policy: Housing & Employment Location in the West Midlands. David E. Eversley et al. (Illus.). 88p. 1965. 24.00x (ISBN 0-7146-1583-8, F Cass Co). Biblio Dist.

Population Growth & Policies in Sub-Saharan Africa. 120p. (Eng. & Fr.). 1986. Eng. 7.50 (BK0773); Fr. 7.50 (ISBN 0-8213-0833-5, BK0833). World Bank.

Population Growth & Savings in Developing Countries: A Survey. Jeffrey S. Hammer. (Working Paper: No. 687). 46p. 1985. 3.50 (ISBN 0-8213-0518-2, WP 0687). World Bank.

Population Growth & Social Complexity: An Examination of Settlement & Environment in the Central Maya Lowlands. Anabel Ford. LC 85-52430. (Arizona State University Anthropological Research Papers: No. 35). (Illus.). xiii, 200p. (Orig.). 1986. pap. 12.50 (ISBN 0-9611932-5-5). AZ Univ ARP.

Population Growth & Socioeconomic Change in West Africa. Ed. by John C. Caldwell et al. LC 74-17409. 763p. (Orig.). 1975. text ed. write for info. Population Coun.

Population Growth & Socioeconomic Change in West Africa. Ed. by John C. Caldwell et al. LC 74-17409. 736p. 1975. 60.00x (ISBN 0-231-03732-5). Columbia U Pr.

Population Growth & Socioeconomic Progress in Less Developed Countries: Determinants of Fertility Transition. Peter N. Hess. 192p. 1988. 39.95 (ISBN 0-275-92979-5, C2979). Praeger.

Population Growth & Umemployment in India. N. R. Prabhakara & M. N. Usha. 1986. 15.00x (ISBN 81-7024-041-7, Pub. by Ashish India). South Asia Bks.

Population Growth & Urban Systems Development. G. A. Van Der Knaap. (Studies in Applied Regional Science: Vol. 18). 245p. 1980. lib. bdg. 16.00 (ISBN 0-89838-024-3, Pub. by Martinus Nijhoff Netherlands). Kluwer Academic.

Population Growth & Urbanization in Latin America. Ed. by John M. Hunter et al. 310p. 1983. 18.95 (ISBN 0-87073-225-0); pap. 11.95 (ISBN 0-87073-226-9). Schenkman Bks Inc.

Population Growth & Urbanization in South & Southeast Asia. S. B. Mukherjee. 176p. 1988. text ed. 25.00x (ISBN 81-207-0844-X, Pub. by Sterling Pubs India). Apt Bks.

Population Growth Control: The Next Move Is America's. Stephen D. Mumford. LC 76-51004. (Illus.). 181p. 1977. 8.95 (ISBN 0-8022-2200-5). Philos Lib.

Population Growth, Economic Development & Social Change in Bavaria: 1750-1850. W. R. Lee. Ed. by Stuart Bruchey. LC 77-77194. (Dissertations in European Economic History Ser.). (Illus.). 1977. lib. bdg. 43.00x (ISBN 0-405-10806-0). Ayer Co Pubs.

Population Growth, Employment, & Economic-Demographic Interactions in Kenya: Bachue, Kenya. Richard Anker & James C. Knowles. LC 83-3444. 754p. 1983. 50.00x (ISBN 0-312-63146-4). St Martin.

Population Growth Estimation: A Handbook of Vital Statistics Measurement. Eli S. Marks et al. LC 73-79791. 481p. 1974. text ed. 9.95 (ISBN 0-87834-018-1). Population Coun.

Population Growth in Latin America & U. S. National Security. Ed. by John Saunders. 224p. 1986. text ed. 37.95x (ISBN 0-04-497002-1). Unwin Hyman.

Population Growth of Indonesia: An Analysis of Fertility & Mortality Based on the 1971 Population Census. Lee-Jay Cho et al. 135p. 1980. text ed. 16.00x (ISBN 0-8248-0691-3, Pub. by Ctr Southeast Asian Studies Kyoto Univ Japan); pap. text ed. 10.00x (ISBN 0-8248-0696-4). UH Pr.

Population Growth, Society & Culture: An Inventory of Cross-Culturally Tested Causal Hypotheses. Richard G. Sipes. LC 80-81242. (Comparative Studies Ser.). 134p. 1980. 14.50x (ISBN 0-87536-337-7); pap. 7.00 (ISBN 0-87536-338-5). HRAFP.

Population Growth: The Human Dilemma, An NSTA Environmental Materials Guide. Kathryn M. Fowler. 104p. 1977. pap. 1.00 (ISBN 0-87355-008-0). Natl Sci Tchrs.

Population Handbook. 2nd ed. Arthur Haupt & Thomas T. Kane. 72p. 1985. 5.00 (ISBN 0-917136-09-8). Population Ref.

Population, Health & Nutrition in the Sahel: Issues in the Welfare of Selected West African Communities. Allan G. Hill. 394p. 29.95x (ISBN 0-7103-0099-9). Routledge Chapman & Hall.

Population History of England 1541-1871: A Reconstruction. E. A. Wrigley & R. S. Schofield. LC 81-5010. (Studies in Social & Demographic History). (Illus.). 779p. 1982. text ed. 75.00x (ISBN 0-674-69007-9). Harvard U Pr.

Population History of England, 1541-1871. E. A. Wrigley & R. S. Schofield. (Illus.). 796p. Date not set. price not set (ISBN 0-521-35688-1). Cambridge U Pr.

Population History of New York City. Ira Rosenwaike. LC 75-39829. (New York State Studies). (Illus.). 274p. 1972. 14.95x (ISBN 0-8156-2155-8). Syracuse U Pr.

Population in an Interacting World. Ed. by William Alonso. LC 86-20133. (Illus.). 320p. 1987. text ed. 32.50x (ISBN 0-674-69008-7). Harvard U Pr.

Population in Development Planning: Background & Bibliography. Richard E. Bilsborrow. 1976. pap. 5.00 (ISBN 0-89055-048-4). Carolina Pop Ctr.

Population in India: A Study of Inter-State Variations. P. J. Bhattacharjee & G. N. Shastri. 1976. 9.00 (ISBN 0-7069-0426-5). Intl Bk Dist.

Population in India's Development, 1947-2000. A. Bose et al. 1974. 18.00 (ISBN 0-686-20289-9). Intl Bk Dist.

Population in Modern China. Ta Chen. 1973. lib. bdg. 14.50x (ISBN 0-374-91467-2, Octagon). Hippocrene Bks.

Population in the Countryside: Growth & Stagnation in the Cotswolds. Valerie J. Jackson. (Illus.). 176p. 1968. 27.50x (ISBN 0-7146-1584-6, F Cass Co). Biblio Dist.

Population in the Global Arena. Parker G. Marden et al. Ed. by James E. Harf & B. Thomas Trout. LC 81-7211. (Global Issues Ser.). 168p. 1982. pap. text ed. 9.95 (ISBN 0-03-060061-8). HR&W.

Population in the Global Arena: Actors, Values, Policies, & Futures. Parker G. Marden. LC 81-7211. (Duke Press Global Issues Ser.). xvii, 146p. pap. 10.95 (ISBN 0-8223-0584-4). Duke.

Population Increases into Alta California in the Spanish Period, 1769-1821: Thesis. Alexander Avilez. LC 74-76499. 1974. Repr. of 1955 ed. soft bdg. 10.95 (ISBN 0-88247-268-2). R & E Pubs.

Population Information in Nineteenth Century Census Volumes. Suzanne Schulze. LC 83-17380. (Illus.). 456p. 1983. lib. bdg. 82.00 (ISBN 0-89774-122-6). Oryx Pr.

Population Information in Twentieth Century Census Volumes: 1900-1940. Suzanne Schulze. LC 84-42813. (Illus.). 288p. 1985. lib. bdg. 82.00 (ISBN 0-89774-164-1). Oryx Pr.

Population Information: Resources & Activities in the Asia & the Pacific Region. LC 80-39639. 1980. pap. 8.00 (ISBN 0-933438-04-4, SP 4). APLIC Intl.

Population Issues see Social Science Skills: Activities for the Secondary Classroom, Grades 9-12.

Population, Labor Force & Long Swings in Economic Growth: The American Experience. Richard A. Easterlin. (General Ser: No. 86). (Illus.). 318p. 1968. 19.00 (ISBN 0-87014-474-X, Dist. by Columbia U Pr). Natl Bur Econ Res.

Population, Labour & Migration in 19th & 20th-Century Germany. Ed. by Klaus J. Bade. LC 86-24470. 208p. 1987. 35.00 (ISBN 0-85496-503-3, Pub. by Berg Pubs). St Martin.

Population, Land Values & Government: Studies of Growth & Population & Land Values & Problems of Government, Vol. 4. (Metropolitan America Ser.). 326p. 1974. 19.00x (ISBN 0-405-05417-3). Ayer Co Pubs.

Population Law & Policy: Source Materials & Issues. Stephen L. Isaacs. LC 80-24549. 431p. 1981. text ed. 49.95x (ISBN 0-89885-000-2). Human Sci Pr.

Population Mobility & Economic Development in Eastern India. Kailash Mahto. (Illus.). 273p. 1985. text ed. 75.00x (ISBN 0-86590-586-X, Inter India Pubns Delhi). Apt Bks.

Population Mobility & Productive Relations: Demographic Links & Policy Evolution. Guy Standing. (Working Paper: No. 695). 64p. 1984. 5.00 (ISBN 0-8213-0455-0, WP 0695). World Bank.

Population Mobility & Residential Change. W. A. Clark & Eric G. Moore. (Studies in Geography: No. 25). 1978. pap. 10.95 (ISBN 0-8101-0523-3). Northwestern U Pr.

Population Mobility & Wealth Transfers in Indonesia & Other 3rd World Societies. Graeme J. Hugo. LC 83-14008. (Papers of the East-West Population Institute: No. 87). v, 50p. (Orig.). 1983. pap. text ed. 1.75 (ISBN 0-86638-045-0). EW Ctr HI.

Population Mobility in the People's Republic of China. Sidney Goldstein & Alice Goldstein. (Papers of the East-West Population Institute: No. 95). 52p. (Orig.). 1985. pap. 3.00 (ISBN 0-86638-069-8). EW Ctr Hi.

Population Mobility in West Java. Graeme J. Hugo & Gadjah Mada. (Illus.). xvi, 335p. 1981. pap. 11.95x (ISBN 0-8214-0773-2). Ohio U Pr.

Population Movement in Wet Rice Communities. Ida B. Mantra & Gadjah Mada. LC 82-95065. (Illus.). x, 210p. 1981. pap. 9.95x (ISBN 0-8214-0774-0). Ohio U Pr.

Population Movements in the Caribbean. Malcolm J. Proudfoot. LC 75-109359. 1970. Repr. of 1950 ed. 35.00x (ISBN 0-8371-3634-2, PCA&). Greenwood.

Population, Nineteen Sixty, Vol. 1. U. S. Bureau of the Census. LC 75-22863. (America in Two Centuries Ser). (Illus.). 1976. Repr. of 1964 ed. 85.00x (ISBN 0-405-07729-7). Ayer Co Pubs.

Population of Athens in the Fifth & Fourth Centuries B. C. Arnold W. Gomme. LC 86-18344. 96p. 1987. Repr. of 1967 ed. lib. bdg. 35.00x (ISBN 0-313-22001-8, GOPL). Greenwood.

Population of Burma: An Analysis of the 1973 Census. M. Ismael Khin Maung. Ed. by Sandra E. Ward. (Papers of the East-West Population Institute: No. 97). (Illus.). viii, 32p. 1986. pap. 3.00 (ISBN 0-86638-077-9). EW Ctr HI.

Population of Central Mexico in the Sixteenth Century. Sherburne F. Cook & Lesley B. Simpson. LC 76-29408. (Ibero-Americana: 31). Repr. of 1948 ed. 31.50 (ISBN 0-404-15333-X). AMS Pr.

Population of Indochina: Some Preliminary Observations. Hg S. Meng. 126p. (Orig.). 1974. pap. text ed. 10.00x (ISBN 0-566-04006-9, Pub. by Inst Southeast Asian Stud). Gower Pub Co.

Population of Ireland, 1750-1845. Kenneth H. Connell. LC 74-9165. 293p. 1975. Repr. of 1950 ed. lib. bdg. 35.00x (ISBN 0-8371-7620-4, COPI). Greenwood.

Population of Jamaica. George W. Roberts. LC 78-23974. 1979. Repr. of 1957 ed. lib. bdg. 40.00 (ISBN 0-527-75865-5). Kraus Repr.

Population of Kalamazoo County, Michigan: Estimates As of July 1, 1973 & Projections to 2000. Rodger S. Lawson. 63p. 1975. pap. 2.95 (ISBN 0-911558-47-0). W E Upjohn.

Population of Latin America. Nicolas Sanchez-Albornoz. Tr. by W. A. Richardson. 1974. 46.50x (ISBN 0-520-01766-8); pap. 11.95x (ISBN 0-520-02745-0). U of Cal Pr.

Population of Mexico: Trends, Issues, & Policies. Francisco Alba. LC 81-1432. (Illus.). 150p. 1981. 24.95 (ISBN 0-87855-359-2). Transaction Bks.

Population of Palestine: Population History & Statistics of the Late Ottoman Period & Mandate. Justin McCarthy. 350p. Date not set. price not set (ISBN 0-88728-157-5); pap. text ed. price not set (ISBN 0-88728-158-3). Inst Palestine.

Population of Thailand: Its Growth & Welfare. Susan Hill Cochran. (Working Paper: No. 337). iv, 73p. 1979. 5.00 (ISBN 0-686-36201-2, WP-0337). World Bank.

Population of the British Colonies in America Before 1776: A Survey of Census Data. Robert V. Wells. LC 75-3483. 380p. 1975. 44.00x (ISBN 0-691-04616-6). Princeton U Pr.

Population of the California Indians 1769-1970. Sherburne F. Cook. LC 74-27287. 1976. 37.50x (ISBN 0-520-02923-2). U of Cal Pr.

Population of the South: Structure & Change in Social Demographic Context. Ed. by Dudley L. Poston, Jr. & Robert H. Weller. 317p. 1981. text ed. 25.00x (ISBN 0-292-76467-7). U of Tex Pr.

Population of the Soviet Union: History & Prospects. Frank Lorimer. LC 76-29424. Repr. of 1946 ed. 37.50 (ISBN 0-404-15339-9). AMS Pr.

Population of the United Nations, No. 18. 76p. 1986. 9.50 (ISBN 92-1-151153-4, E.85.XIII.6). UN.

Population of the United States: Historical Trends & Future Projections. Rev. ed. Donald J. Bogue. LC 84-18688. 704p. 1985. 100.00x (ISBN 0-02-904700-5). Free Pr.

Population of Virginia: Past, Present & Future. William J. Serow. LC 77-10340. 322p. 1978. 20.00x (ISBN 0-8139-0659-8). U Pr of Va.

Population-Oriented Psychology. Gerald Caplan. 232p. 1988. 34.95x (ISBN 0-89885-418-0). Human Sci Pr.

Population: Patterns, Dynamics & Prospects. James L. Newman & Gordon E. Matzke. (Illus.). 368p. 1984. write for info. (ISBN 0-13-687566-1). P-H.

Population Patterns of Southwestern Michigan. Charles F. Heller et al. 1974. 5.00 (ISBN 0-932826-10-5). New Issues MI.

Population Perspectives on Organizations. Howard Aldrich et al. 110p. (Orig.). 1986. pap. text ed. 20.00x (ISBN 91-554-1909-7, Pub. by Uppsala Univ Acta Univ Uppsaliensis (Uppsala Sweden)). Coronet Bks.

Population Planning. Leslie Corsa & Deborah Oakley. (Illus.). 1979. text ed. 22.50x (ISBN 0-472-08243-4). U of Mich Pr.

Population Policies & Movements in Europe. David V. Glass. LC 67-19728. 1967. Repr. of 1940 ed. 39.50x (ISBN 0-678-05049-X). Kelley.

Population Policies & Movements in Europe. P. V. Glass. 490p. 1967. 37.50x (ISBN 0-7146-1580-3, F Cass Co). Biblio Dist.

Population Policies for a New Economic Era. Lester R. Brown. LC 83-60702. (Worldwatch Papers). 1983. pap. text ed. 4.00 (ISBN 0-916468-52-6). Worldwatch Inst.

Population Policy. new ed. Ed. by Michael Kraft & Mark Schneider. 1977. pap. 8.00 (ISBN 0-918592-23-2). Policy Studies.

Population Policy Analysis: Issues in American Politics. Michael E. Kraft & Mark Schneider. (Illus.). 224p. 1985. Repr. of 1978 ed. lib. bdg. 20.75 (ISBN 0-8191-5146-7, Pub. by Policy Studies). U Pr of Amer.

Population Policy & Development Planning: Aspects of Technical Cooperation. (Population Studies: No. 73). 54p. 1981. pap. 6.00 (ISBN 92-1-104117-1, E.81.11.A.1). UN.

Population Policy & Ethics: The American Experience. Ed. by Robert M. Veatch. 507p. pap. text ed. cancelled (ISBN 0-8290-1045-9). Irvington.

Population Policy & the U. S. Constitution. Larry D. Barnett. (Studies in Human Issues). 1982. lib. bdg. 25.00 (ISBN 0-89838-082-0, Pub. by Kluwer-Nijhoff (Netherlands)). Kluwer Academic.

Population Policy: Directions for the Future. Carmen Miro & Joseph Potter. 1981. 19.95 (ISBN 0-312-63158-8). St Martin.

Population Policy in Developed Countries. Ed. by Bernard Berelson. LC 73-18368. 793p. 1974. write for info. Population Coun.

Population Policy in Western Europe: Responses to Low Fertility in France, Sweden, & West Germany. C. Alison McIntosh. LC 82-5840. (Illus.). 300p. 1983. 40.00 (ISBN 0-87332-226-6). M E Sharpe.

Population, Politics, & the Future of Southern Asia. Ed. by W. Howard Wriggins & James F. Guyot. LC 73-8673. 400p. 1973. 40.00x (ISBN 0-231-03756-2); pap. 18.00x (ISBN 0-231-03757-0). Columbia U Pr.

Population Pressure & Cultural Adjustment. Virginia Abernethy. LC 78-11676. 189p. 1979. 29.95 (ISBN 0-87705-329-4). Human Sci Pr.

Population Pressure & Human Fertility Response: Ohio, 1810-1860. Don R. Leet. LC 77-14754. (Dissertations in American Economic History Ser.). 1978. 30.00 (ISBN 0-405-11046-4). Ayer Co Pubs.

Population Pressure & Peasant Occupations in Rural Central Java: Occasional Paper, Centre of Se Asian Studies, University of Kent at Canterbury. Masami Mizuno. (No. 4). iv, 71p. (Orig.). 1985. pap. 4.50x (ISBN 0-318-18412-5, Ctr SE Asian Stud). Cellar.

Population Pressures: Emigration & Government in Late Nineteenth-Century Britain. Howard Malchow. 1979. write for info. Sposs.

Population Pressures: Emigration & Government in Late Nineteenth-Century Britain. Howard L. Malchow. LC 79-64166. (Illus.). 335p. 1979. 18.00x (ISBN 0-930664-02-7). SPOSS.

Population Primer. Francis Frech. Date not set. price not set (ISBN 0-913631-00-0). Anastasia VA.

Population Problem. G. A. Cevasco. (Topics of Our Times Ser.: No. 8). 32p. lib. bdg. 3.75 incl. catalog cards (ISBN 0-87157-809-3); pap. 2.50 vinyl laminated covers (ISBN 0-87157-309-1). SamHar Pr.

Population Problem: A Study in Human Evolution. A. M. Carr-Saunders. LC 73-14150. (Perspectives in Social Inquiry Ser.). 520p. 1974. Repr. 27.00x (ISBN 0-405-05496-3). Ayer Co Pubs.

Population Problems of the Age of Malthus. 2nd ed. Talbot Griffith. (Illus.). 280p. 1967. Repr. of 1926 ed. 35.00x (ISBN 0-7146-1155-7, BHA-01155, F Cass Co). Biblio Dist.

Population Problems of the Pacific. Stephen H. Roberts. LC 71-99884. Repr. of 1927 ed. 29.50 (ISBN 0-404-00599-3). AMS Pr.

Population Profile of the United States: 1984-85. 11th ed. (Current Population Reports Series P-23, Special Studies: No. 150). (Illus.). 56p. 1987. pap. 2.75 (ISBN 0-318-22934-X, S/N 803-005-10003-1). USGPO.

Population Projections. 48p. (Orig.). 1987. pap. text ed. 24.00 (ISBN 0-11-691207-3, HM1637, Pub. by Her Maj Station Ofc). UNIPUB.

Population Projections for Singapore 1980-2070. Saw Swee-Hock. 36p. (Orig.). 1984. pap. text ed. 5.95x (ISBN 9971-902-68-0, Pub. by Inst Southeast Asian Stud). Gower Pub Co.

Population Projections: Methodology of the United Nations. (Population Studies: No. 83). 85p. (Orig.). 1984. pap. 11.00 (ISBN 92-1-151032-5, E.83.XIII.7). UN.

Population, Prosperity, & Poverty. Polly Hill. LC 77-23167. (Illus.). 1977. 39.50 (ISBN 0-521-21511-0). Cambridge U Pr.

Population Redistribution & Development in South Asia. Ed. by Leszek Kosinski & Maudood K. Elahi. 1985. lib. bdg. 44.00 (ISBN 90-277-1938-1, Pub. by Reidel Holland). Kluwer Academic.

Population Redistribution & Economic Growth: United States, 1870-1950. Simon S. Kuznets et al. LC 57-10071. (American Philosophical Society, Memoirs: Vol. 51). pap. 76.30 (ISBN 0-317-28303-0, 2019711). Bks Demand UMI.

Population Redistribution in the U. S. S. R. Its Impact on Society 1897-1977. Robert A. Lewis & Richard H. Rowland. LC 79-18076. (Praeger Special Studies Ser.). 510p. 1979. 56.95 (ISBN 0-275-90382-6, C0382). Praeger.

Population Reference Bureau's Population Handbook, in Arabic. Arthur Haupt & Thomas T. Kane. (Illus.). 80p. (Orig., Arabic.). 1980. pap. 5.00 (ISBN 0-917136-07-1). Population Ref.

Population Reference Bureau's Population Handbook: International Edition. 2nd ed. Arthur Haupt & Thomas T. Kane. (Illus.). 76p. 1986. pap. 5.00 (ISBN 0-917136-10-1). Population Ref.

Population Research in Latin America & the Caribbean: A Reference Bibliography. Barry Edmonston. LC 79-14653. (Monograph Publishing; Sponsor Ser.). pap. 44.30 (ISBN 0-317-28153-4, 2022594). Bks Demand UMI.

Population Research, Policy & Related Studies in Puerto Rico: An Inventory. Kent C. Earnhardt. LC 77-16466. (Planning Ser: S-6). 1984. pap. 8.00 (ISBN 0-8477-2447-6). U of PR Pr.

Population, Resources, Environment & Development: Proceedings of the Expert Group, Geneva, 25-29 April 1983. (Population Studies: No.90). 534p. 1985. 37.00 (ISBN 92-1-151103-8, E.84.XIII.12). UN.

Population-Sample Decomposition Method. A. M. Wesselman. 1987. lib. bdg. 47.50 (ISBN 90-247-3603-X). Kluwer Academic.

Population Settlements: Development & Planning. K. M. Lal. 1988. 32.00x (ISBN 81-85076-48-0, Pub. by Chugh Pubns India). South Asia Bks.

Population, Society & Agricultural Planning. Alain Marcoux. 163p. 1987. pap. text ed. 10.25 (ISBN 92-5-102225-9, F3094, FAO). UNIPUB.

Population Statistics: A Review of U. K. Sources. Bernard Benjamin. 328p. 1989. text ed. 70.00 (ISBN 0-566-05731-X, Pub. by Gower Pub England). Gower Pub Co.

Population Statistics in India. Ed. by Ashish Bose et al. 1986. text ed. 32.50x (ISBN 0-7069-2961-6, Pub. by Vikas India). Advent NY.

Population Structure & Genetic Disorders: Proceedings of the 7th Sigfred Juselius Foundation Symposia. Ed. by A. W. Eriksson et al. LC 80-40143. 1981. 170.00 (ISBN 0-12-241450-0). Acad Pr.

Population Structure & Human Variation. Ed. by G. A. Harrison. LC 76-22987. (International Biological Programme Ser.: No. 11). (Illus.). 1977. 82.50 (ISBN 0-521-21399-1). Cambridge U Pr.

Population Structure of Indian Cities. Ram D. Singh. (Illus.). 173p. 1985. text ed. 37.50x (ISBN 0-86590-710-2, Pub. by Inter Pubns N. Delhi). Apt Bks.

Population Structure of Indian Cities. Ram D. Singh. 173p. 1985. 39.95. Asia Bk Corp.

Population Structure of Vegetation. Ed. by J. White. (Handbook of Vegetation Science). 1985. lib. bdg. 97.50 (ISBN 90-6193-184-3, Pub. by Junk Pubs Netherlands). Kluwer-Academic.

Population Structures & Models: Developments in Spatial Demography. Ed. by Robert I. Woods & Philip H. Rees. 400p. text ed. 70.00x (ISBN 0-04-301200-0). Unwin Hyman.

Population Studies of European Sparrows in North America. Ted R. Anderson. (Occasional Papers: No. 70). 58p. 1978. pap. 3.25 (ISBN 0-317-04581-4). U of KS Mus Nat Hist.

Population Study of the Prairie Vole (Microtus Ochrogaster) Northeastern Kansas. Edwin P. Martin. (Museum Ser.: Vol. 8, No. 6). 56p. 1956. pap. 3.00 (ISBN 0-317-04886-4). U of KS Mus Nat Hist.

Population System Control. J. Song & J. Yu. (Illus.). 290p. 1987. 83.70 (ISBN 0-387-18288-8). Springer-Verlag.

Population Systems: A General Introduction. Alan A. Berryman. LC 80-26167. 238p. 1981. 24.95x (ISBN 0-306-40589-X, Plenum Pr). Plenum Pub.

Population Technology & Develepment. Priyatosh Maitra. 200p. 1986. text ed. 42.00 (ISBN 0-566-05205-9, Pub. by Gower Pub England). Gower Pub Co.

Population, Technology & Resources. pap. 5.50 (ISBN 0-660-00405-4, SSC88, SSC). UNIPUB.

Population Terminology. 32p. 1986. 6.50 (BK0762). World Bank.

Population: The First Essay. Thomas R. Malthus. 1959. pap. 5.95 (ISBN 0-472-06031-7, 31, AA). U of Mich Pr.

Population: The Growth of Metropolitan Districts in the United States, 1900-1940. Warren S. Thompson. LC 75-21958. (America in Two Centuries Ser). 1976. Repr. of 1947 ed. 11.00x (ISBN 0-405-07736-X). Ayer Co Pubs.

Population: The UNFPA Experience. Ed. by Nafis Sadik. 224p. 1984. pap. 13.50x (ISBN 0-8147-8171-3). NYU Pr.

Population Theory in China. Ed. by H. Yuan Tien. LC 79-57159. 144p. 1980. 30.00 (ISBN 0-87332-174-X). M E Sharpe.

Population Thought in the Age of the Demographic Revolution. James C. Riley. LC 83-70312. (Illus.). 240p. 1985. lib. bdg. 24.75 (ISBN 0-89089-257-1). Carolina Acad Pr.

Population Trends & Implications. Ed. by Douglas N. Ross. LC 77-93928. (Report Ser.: No. 735). 85p. 1977. pap. 15.00 (ISBN 0-8237-0171-9). Conference Bd.

Population Trends in Indonesia. Nitisastro Widjojo. LC 71-106356. Orig. Title: Past & Future. 288p. 1970. 42.50x (ISBN 0-8014-0555-6). Cornell U Pr.

Population Trends in Majority Black Counties in Eleven Southern States: 1900 to 1980. Brimah K. Farouk & Richard A. Hudlin. 1981. 1.00 (ISBN 0-686-38018-5). Voter Ed Proj.

Population Trends in the United States. W. S. Thompson & P. K. Whelpton. (Demographic Monographs). 428p. 1969. 92.00 (ISBN 0-677-02370-7). Gordon & Breach.

Population Trends in the United States. W. S. Thompson & P. K. Whelpton. 1933. 32.00 (ISBN 0-527-89780-9). Kraus Repr.

Population, Urbanization, & Settlement in Ghana: A Bibliographic Survey. Joseph A. Sarfoh. LC 87-19627. (African Special Bibliographic Ser.: No. 8). 124p. 1987. lib. bdg. 35.00 (ISBN 0-313-26073-7, SPX/). Greenwood.

Population Validity & College Entrance Measures. Hunter M. Breland. LC 79-51738. (Research Monograph: No. 8). 104p. (Orig.). 1979. pap. 7.50 (ISBN 0-87447-110-9, 270501). College Bd.

Population, Vol. 4 (incl. 1985-1987 Supplement) Ed. by Eleanor C. Goldstein. (Social Issues Resources Ser.). 1988. 45.00 (ISBN 0-89777-119-2). Soc Issues.

Populations De L'est-Aquitain Au Debut De L'epoque Contempoaine: Recherche Sur une Region Moins Developpee, 1845-1871. Andre Armengaud. (Societe, Mouvements Sociaux et Ideologis, Etudes: No. 3). 1961. pap. 34.80x (ISBN 90-2796-236-7). Mouton.

Populations of the Middle East & North Africa: A Geographical Approach. J. I. Clarke & W. B. Fisher. LC 72-80410. 432p. 1972. 44.50x (ISBN 0-8419-0125-2). Holmes & Meier.

Populations Ouvrieres et les Industries de la France, 2 Vols. 2nd ed. Armand Audiganne. (Research & Source Works Ser., History, Economics & Social Science). 1971. Repr. of 1860 ed. lib. bdg. 48.00 (ISBN 0-8337-0124-X). B Franklin.

Populations, Species, & Evolution: An Abridgment of Animal Species & Evolution. abr. ed. Ernst Mayr. LC 79-111486. 1970. 25.00x (ISBN 0-674-69010-9, Belknap Pr); pap. 9.95x (ISBN 0-674-69013-3). Harvard U Pr.

Populism & Elitism. Revilo P. Oliver. 1984. lib. bdg. 79.95 (ISBN 0-87700-592-3). Revisionist Pr.

Populism in Peru: The Emergence of the Masses & the Politics of Social Control. Steve Stein. LC 79-5415. (Illus.). 320p. 1980. 29.50x (ISBN 0-299-07990-2). U of Wis Pr.

Populism in the Mountain West. Robert W. Larson. LC 86-16160. (Illus.). 220p. 1986. 27.50x (ISBN 0-8263-0900-3). U of NM Pr.

Populism: Its Past, Present & Future. Vladmir Khoros. Tr. by Nadezhda Burov. 294p. 1984. pap. 8.95 (Pub. by Progress Pubns USSR). Imported Pubns.

Populism: Its Past, Present & Future. Vladmir Khoros. 294p. 1984. 24.75x (ISBN 0-317-53777-6, Pub. by Collets (UK)). State Mutual Bk.

Populism, Progressivism, & the Transformation of Nebraska Politics, 1885-1915. Robert W. Cherny. LC 80-11151. (Illus.). xviii, 227p. 1981. 21.50x (ISBN 0-8032-1407-3). U of Nebr Pr.

Populism: Reaction or Reform? Ed. by Theodore Saloutos. LC 77-15587. (American Problem Studies). 128p. 1978. pap. text ed. 6.50 (ISBN 0-88275-638-9). Krieger.

Populism to Progressivism in Alabama. Sheldon Hackney. LC 68-56311. 1969. 45.00x (ISBN 0-691-04591-7). Princeton U Pr.

Populist Assault: Sarah E. Van de Vort Emery on American Democracy 1862-1895. Pauline Adams & Emma S. Thornton. LC 82-60665. (Illus.). 146p. 1982. 13.95 (ISBN 0-87972-203-7); pap. 6.95 (ISBN 0-87972-204-5). Bowling Green Univ.

Populist Challenge: Argentine Electoral Behavior in the Postwar Era. Lars Schoultz. LC 82-24831. (James Sprunt Studies in History & Political Science: Vol. 58). xii, 141p. (Orig.). 1983. pap. 10.95x (ISBN 0-8078-5059-4). U of NC Pr.

Populist Context: Rural Versus Urban Power on a Great Plains Frontier. Stanley B. Parsons. LC 72-824. (Contributions in American History Ser.: No. 22). (Illus.). xviii, 205p. 1973. lib. bdg. 35.00 (ISBN 0-8371-6392-7, PAC/). Greenwood.

Populist Manifestos. Lawrence Ferlinghetti. LC 80-22105. 56p. 1981. pap. 3.95 (ISBN 0-912516-52-6). Grey Fox.

Populist Moment: A Short History of the Agrarian Revolt in America. Lawrence Goodwyn. 1978. 25.00x (ISBN 0-19-502416-8). Oxford U Pr.

Populist Moment: A Short History of the Agrarian Revolt in America. Lawrence Goodwyn. 1978. pap. 9.95 (ISBN 0-19-502417-6). Oxford U Pr.

Populist Movement in Georgia: A View of the Agrarian Crusade in the Light of Solid-South Politics. Alex M. Arnett. LC 74-158272. (Columbia University Studies in the Social Sciences: No. 235). Repr. of 1922 ed. 20.00 (ISBN 0-404-51235-6). AMS Pr.

Populist Nationalism in Pre-War Japan: A Biography of Nakano Seigo. Leslie Oates. 135p. 1985. text ed. 29.95x (ISBN 0-86861-111-5). Unwin Hyman.

Populist Reader: Selections from the Works of American Populist Leaders. Ed. by George B. Tindall. 11.25 (ISBN 0-8446-3075-6). Peter Smith.

Populist Religion & Left-Wing Politics in France, 1830-1852. Edward Berenson. LC 83-42548. 345p. 1984. 41.00x (ISBN 0-691-05396-0). Princeton U Pr.

Populist Response to Industrial America. Norman Pollack. 1976. pap. 5.95x (ISBN 0-674-69051-6). Harvard U Pr.

Populist Revolt: A History of the Farmer's Alliance & the People's Party. John D. Hicks. LC 81-3236. (Illus.). xii, 473p. 1981. Repr. of 1961 ed. lib. bdg. 38.50x (ISBN 0-313-22567-2, HIPR). Greenwood.

Populist Vanguard: A History of the Southern Farmers' Alliance. Robert C. McMath, Jr. 1977. pap. 3.95x (ISBN 0-393-00869-X, N869, Norton Lib). Norton.

Populist Vanguard: A History of the Southern Farmer's Alliance. Robert C. McMath, Jr. LC 75-9751. xiii, 221p. 1975. 25.00x (ISBN 0-8078-1251-X). U of NC Pr.

Populists & Patricians: Essays in Modern German History. David Blackbourn. 304p. 1987. text ed. 49.95 (ISBN 0-04-943047-5). Unwin Hyman.

Populists, Plungers, & Progressives: A Social History of Stock & Commodity Speculation. Cedric B. Cowing. LC 65-12988. (Orig.). 1965. 38.00x (ISBN 0-691-04555-0); pap. 11.95x (ISBN 0-691-00563-X). Princeton U Pr.

Populuxe. Thomas Hine. 1986. 29.95 (ISBN 0-394-54593-1). Knopf.

Populuxe. Thomas Hine. LC 86-45270. (Illus.). Date not set. pap. 16.95 (ISBN 0-394-74014-9). Knopf.

Por Amor al Pueblo (Not Guilty) The Trial of the Winooski 44. Ed. by Ben Bradley et al. LC 86-82607. 176p. (Orig.). 1986. pap. 8.95 (ISBN 0-9617504-0-5). Front Porch Pub.

Por Aqui. Jose Escribano. tchrs. guide & cassettes 79.00 (ISBN 0-686-82067-3, 70033); student textbook 8.95 (ISBN 0-88436-911-0, 70277); 3.00 (ISBN 0-88436-912-9, 70814). EMC.

Por Fronteras Culturales. Anthony Papalia & Jose A. Mendoza. (Orig.). (gr. 11). 1976. pap. text ed. 11.00 (ISBN 0-87720-518-3). AMSCO Sch.

Por Hispanoamerica: Conversando, Conociendo, Gozando. Emilita Stone & Clara I. Berkeley. 324p. (Span.). 1987. pap. write for info. (ISBN 0-02-417800-4). Macmillan.

Por la Acera de la Sombra (Cuentos Cubanos) Pancho Vives. LC 81-69538. (Coleccion Caniqui). (Orig.). pap. 7.95 (ISBN 0-89729-300-2). Ediciones.

Por la Salud de Nuestros Ninos. M. Studenikin. 255p. (Span.). 1976. 5.45 (ISBN 0-8285-1697-9, Pub. by Mir Pubs USSR). Imported Pubns.

Por la Union Latino Americana. University of Latin American Workers Staff. (Coleccion CLAT Ser.). 300p. (Orig., Span.). 1987. pap. 10.00 (ISBN 0-917049-14-4). Saeta.

Por Que Esperar Hasta el Matrimonio? Evelyn M. Duval. Tr. by Pablo A. Deiros from Eng. Orig. Title: Why Wait till Marriage? 160p. 1982. pap. 3.75 (ISBN 0-311-46044-5, Edit Mundo). Casa Bautista.

Por Que Guardamos el Domingo? Domingo Fernandez. 87p. 1984. pap. 2.50 (ISBN 0-311-05603-2). Casa Bautista.

Port Arthur: A Place of Misery. Maggie Weidenhofer. (Illus.). 1981. 34.95x (ISBN 0-19-554323-8). Oxford U Pr.
Port Authority. Walter Griffin. (Illus.). 1976. pap. 3.95 (ISBN 0-917838-00-9). Brevity.
Port Authority Poetry Review, Vol. II. Mary Y. Sampson & Maurice Hart. Ed. by Mary Bertschmann. 100p. (Orig.). 1986. pap. 6.00 (ISBN 0-935505-01-6). Bank St Pr.
Port Authority Poetry Review, Vol. III. Mary Y. Sampson & Maurice Hart. Ed. by Mary Bertschmann. 96p. (Orig.). 1986. pap. 6.00 (ISBN 0-935505-02-4). Bank St Pr.
Port Authority Poetry Review, Vol. IV. Mary Y. Sampson & Maurice Hart. Ed. by Mary Bertschmann. 100p. (Orig.). 1987. pap. 6.00 (ISBN 0-935505-03-2). Bank St Pr.
Port Authority Poetry Review, Vol. 1. Maurice Hart et al. 100p. (Orig.). 1985. pap. 6.00 (ISBN 0-935505-00-8). Bank St Pr.
Port Development: A Handbood for Planners in Developing Countries. The Secretariat of UNCTAD. 227p. 1985. 23.00 (ISBN 92-1-112160-4, E.84.II.D.1). UN.
Port Economics. Jan Owen Jansson & Dan Shneerson. (Transportation Studies). (Illus.). 208p. 1982. 40.00x (ISBN 0-262-10025-8). MIT Pr.
Port Engineering. 3rd ed. Per Bruun. LC 81-603. 800p. 1981. 89.00x (ISBN 0-87201-739-7). Gulf Pub.
Port Engineering & Operation: Proceedings of a Conference Organized by the Institution of Civil Engineers. 235p. 1985. 33.00 (ISBN 0-7277-0244-0, Pub. by T Telford UK). Am Soc Civil Eng.
Port Engineering Seminar. Ed. by Cargo Systems Staff. 1986. 195.00x (ISBN 0-907499-54-6, Pub. by Cargo Systs UK). State Mutual Bk.
Port Eternity. C. J. Cherryh. 192p. 1987. pap. 2.95 (ISBN 0-88677-206-0). DAW Bks.
Port Hudson, Confederate Bastion on the Mississippi. Lawrence L. Hewitt. LC 87-3198. (Illus.). 232p. 1987. 19.95 (ISBN 0-8071-1351-4). La State U Pr.
Port Jervis Diamond Jubilee Journal History, 1982. Orange County Genealogical Society. 140p. 1986. 5.00 (ISBN 0-937135-16-X). Orange county Genealog.
Port Jervis Industrial Record, 1902. Orange County Genealogical Society. 42p. 1986. 4.00 (ISBN 0-937135-17-8, 86-47). Orange County Genealog.
Port of Bellingham: 1919-1979. Hitchman. (Occasional Papers: No. 1). WWU CPNS.
Port of Derry Ship List. Derry Youth & Community Workshop Ltd. of Northern Ireland. 107p. 1984. perfect bdg. 9.95 (ISBN 0-933227-44-2). Closson Pr.
Port of Dover: Two Centuries of Shipping on the Cochecho. Robert A. Whitehouse & Cathleen C. Beaudoin. (Portsmouth Marine Society Ser.: No. 11). (Illus.). 1987. 24.95 (ISBN 0-915819-10-4). Portsmouth Marine Soc.
Port of Eureka, California: Ship Registries & Enrollments, 1864-1940. Federal Writers Project. (Ship Registries of the United States: No. 1). 100p. 1988. lib. bdg. 19.95x (ISBN 0-8095-2902-5); pap. text ed. 9.95x (ISBN 0-8095-3902-0). Borgo Pr.
Port of Light. David Serafin. 208p. 1987. 14.95 (ISBN 0-312-01077-X). St Martin.
Port of Marshfield, Oregon: Ship Registries & Enrollments, 1873-1941. Federal Writers Project. (Ship Registries of the United States Ser.: No. 2). 96p. Date not set. lib. bdg. 19.95x (ISBN 0-8095-2901-7); pap. text ed. 9.95x (ISBN 0-8095-3901-2). Borgo Pr.
Port of Milwaukee. Edward Hamming. LC 55-3708. (Augustana College Library Publication Ser.: No. 25). 162p. 1953. pap. 4.00x (ISBN 0-910182-20-5). Augustana Coll.
Port of Milwaukee: An Economic Review. Eric Schenker. LC 67-13553. pap. 57.00 (ISBN 0-317-41772-X, 2023715). Bks Demand UMI.
Port of Missing Men. Meredith Nicholson. 1975. lib. bdg. 17.25x (ISBN 0-89966-143-2). Buccaneer Bks.
Port of Nagoya Development & the Role of Government. Akio Ogo. (Working Papers Ser.: No. 73-3). 64p. 1973. pap. 6.00 (ISBN 0-686-78494-4, CRD076, UNCRD). UNIPUB.
Port of New York: A History of the Rail & Terminal System from the Beginnings to Pennsylvania Station, Vol. 1. Carl W. Condit. LC 79-16850. (Illus.). 1980. lib. bdg. 40.00x (ISBN 0-226-11460-0). U of Chicago Pr.
Port of New York: A History of the Rail & Terminal System from the Grand Central Electrification to the Present, Vol. 2. Carl W. Condit. LC 79-16850. 384p. 40.00x (ISBN 0-226-11461-9). U of Chicago Pr.
Port of New York Authority. Erwin W. Bard. LC 68-58547. (Columbia University Studies in the Social Sciences: No. 468). Repr. of 1942 ed. 24.50 (ISBN 0-404-51468-5). AMS Pr.
Port of New York: Essays on Fourteen American Moderns. Paul Rosenfeld. LC 61-6536. (Illus.). 367p. 1961. pap. 10.95 (ISBN 0-252-72611-1). U of Ill Pr.
Port of Portland, Oregon: Ship Registries & Enrollments, 1869-1941. Federal Writers Project. (Ship Registries of the United States Ser.: No. 3). 144p. Date not set. lib. bdg. 24.95x (ISBN 0-8095-2900-9); pap. text ed. 14.95x (ISBN 0-8095-3900-4). Borgo Pr.
Port of Portsmouth Ships & the Cotton Trade, 1783-1829. Ray Brighton. (Portsmouth Marine Society Ser: No. 10). (Illus.). 236p. 1985. 24.95 (ISBN 0-915819-09-0). Portsmouth Marine Soc.
Port of Roman London. Gustav Milne. (Illus.). 176p. 1986. 45.00 (ISBN 0-7134-4364-2, Pub. by Batsford England); pap. 24.95 (ISBN 0-7134-4365-0). David & Charles.
Port of Saints. William S. Burroughs. LC 80-10309. 1980. 24.95 (ISBN 0-912652-64-0); signed, numbered & boxed 49.95x (ISBN 0-912652-66-7); pap. 9.95 (ISBN 0-912652-65-9). Blue Wind.
Port Planning & Development. Ernst G. Frankel. 848p. 1987. 95.00 (ISBN 0-471-83708-3). Wiley.
Port Pricing & Investment Policy for Developing Countries. Esra Bennathan & Alan A. Walters. 1979. 27.50x (ISBN 0-19-520092-6); pap. 12.50x (ISBN 0-19-520093-4). Oxford U Pr.
Port-Royal. Henry De Montherlant. (Fr.). 1960. write for info. French & Eur.
Port-Royal, 3 tomes. Charles-Augustin De Sainte-Beuve. (Pleiade Ser.). 1953-1955. Set. 79.95 (ISBN 0-685-11502-X); Vol. 1. 45.95; Vol. 2. 47.95; Vol. 3. 43.95. Schoenhof.
Port-Royal. Henry de Montherlant. Ed. by Richard Griffiths. (French Texts Ser.). 200p. 1976. pap. text ed. 9.95x (ISBN 0-631-00730-X). Basil Blackwell.
Port Royal: Avec: Notes de Theatre sur le Maitre de Santiago et Port-Royal. Henry de Montherlant. (Folio Ser.: No. 253). 192p. 1972. 5.95 (ISBN 0-686-55529-5). Schoenhof.
Port Royal, Jamaica. Michael Pawson & David Buisseret. (Illus.). 1975. 49.95x (ISBN 0-19-821556-8). Oxford U Pr.
Port Tarascon: The Last Adventures of the Illustrious Tartarin. Alphonse Daudet. Ed. by Henry James. (Illus.). 359p. 1986. Repr. of 1891 ed. PLB 50.00 (ISBN 0-8495-1065-1). Arden Lib.
Port Tropique. Barry Gifford. 160p. 1986. pap. 3.95 (ISBN 0-88739-012-9, Pub. by Black Lizard). Creative Arts Bk.
Port Valdez, Alaska: Environmental Studies, Nineteen Seventy-Six to Nineteen Seventy-Nine. Ed. by J. M. Colonell & H. K. Stockholm. (Occasional Publications Ser.: No. 5). (Illus.). 373p. 1980. 20.00. U of AK Inst Marine.
Port Wine Stain: Partick Boyle's Best Short Stroies. Patrick Boyle. Ed. by Peter Fallon. (Classic Irish Fiction Ser.). 236p. 1983. 13.75. Devin.
Portability & Style in Ada. J. C. Nissen & P. J. Wallis. LC 83-26237. (Ada Companion Ser.). 255p. 1984. 27.95 (ISBN 0-521-26482-0). Cambridge U Pr.
Portability & the C Language. Rex Jaeschke. (Illus.). 400p. (Orig.). 1988. pap. 24.95 (ISBN 0-672-48428-5). Sams.
Portability Guide: Data Management, Vol. 5. 3rd ed. 1988. pap. 30.00 (ISBN 0-13-685876-7). P-H.
Portability Guide: Networking, Vol. 6. 3rd ed. 1988. pap. 30.00 (ISBN 0-13-685884-8). P-H.
Portability Guide: Operating Systems, Vol. 7. 3rd ed. 1988. pap. 30.00 (ISBN 0-13-685892-9). P-H.
Portability Guide: Programming Languages, Vol. 4. 3rd ed. 1988. pap. 30.00 (ISBN 0-13-685868-6). P-H.
Portability Guide: System V Specification Calls & Libraries, Vol. 2. 3rd ed. 1988. pap. 30.00 (ISBN 0-13-685843-0). P-H.
Portability Guide: System V Specification Commands & Utilities, Vol. 1. 3rd ed. 1988. pap. 30.00 (ISBN 0-13-685835-X). P-H.
Portability Guide: System V Specification Definition, Vol. 3. 3rd ed. 1988. pap. 30.00 (ISBN 0-13-685850-3). P-H.
Portability of Numerical Software: Proceedings. Ed. by W. Crowell. LC 77-13623. (Lecture Notes in Computer Science: Vol. 57). 1977. pap. text ed. 28.00 (ISBN 0-387-08446-0). Springer-Verlag.
Portable Arthur Miller. Arthur Miller. Ed. by Harold Clurman. LC 77-119777. (Viking Portable Library: No. 71). 1977. pap. 7.95 (ISBN 0-14-015071-4). Penguin.
Portable Back School. Ray C. Mulry & Arthur H. White. LC 81-3960. (Illus.). 53p. 1981. pap. text ed. 13.95 (ISBN 0-8016-3597-7). Mosby.
Portable Barbara Baynton. Barbara Baynton. Ed. by Sally Krimmer & Alan Lawson. (UQP Australian Authors Ser.). 340p. 1981. text ed. 32.50 (ISBN 0-7022-1377-2); pap. 12.00. U of Queensland Pr.
Portable BASIC: Programming the TRS-80 Model 100 & NEC PC-8201A Computers. D. Thomas. 352p. 1985. pap. text ed. 9.95 (ISBN 0-07-064260-5). McGraw.
Portable Bernard Shaw. George Bernard Shaw. Ed. by Stanley Weintraub. (Viking Portable Library: P90). 1977. pap. 7.95 (ISBN 0-14-015090-0). Penguin.
Portable Blake. William Blake. Ed. by Alfred Kazin. (Portable Library: No. 26). 1977. pap. 7.95 (ISBN 0-14-015026-9, P26). Penguin.
Portable C & UNIX Systems Programming. J. E. Lapin. 208p. 1986. pap. 27.95 (ISBN 0-13-686494-5). P-H.
Portable Cervantes. Miguel de Cervantes Saavedra. Tr. by Samuel Putnam. (Viking Portable Library: P57). 1976. pap. 8.95 (ISBN 0-14-015057-9). Penguin.
Portable Charles Dickens. Charles Dickens. Ed. by Angus Wilson. 800p. 1983. pap. 7.95 (ISBN 0-14-015099-4). Penguin.
Portable Charles Lamb. Charles Lamb. Ed. by John M. Brown. (Viking Portable Library). 43p. 1980. pap. 7.95 (ISBN 0-14-015043-9). Penguin.
Portable Chaucer. rev. ed. Geoffrey Chaucer. Ed. by Theodore Morrison. LC 75-2224. (Viking Portable Library: P 81). 1977. pap. 7.95 (ISBN 0-14-015081-1). Penguin.
Portable Chekhov. Anton Chekhov. Ed. by Avrahm Yarmolinsky. (Viking Portable Library: P 35). 1977. pap. 8.95 (ISBN 0-14-015035-8). Penguin.
Portable Circular Sawing Machine Techniques. Roger W. Cliffe. LC 87-33673. (Illus.). 352p. (Orig.). 1988. pap. 14.95 (ISBN 0-8069-6552-5). Sterling.
Portable City. Don Austin. 149p. (Orig.). 1983. pap. 7.95 (ISBN 0-317-14859-1). Left Bank.
Portable Coleridge. Samuel Taylor Coleridge. Ed. by Ivor A. Richards. (Viking Portable Library: No. 48). (gr. 10 up). 1977. pap. 7.95 (ISBN 0-14-015048-X, P48). Penguin.
Portable Computer Book. James E. Balmer & Matthijs Moes. 400p. 1984. 19.95 (ISBN 0-912003-36-7). Bk Co.
Portable Computer Buyer's Guide. Tony Webster. (Illus.). 151p. 1985. pap. text ed. 11.95 (ISBN 0-07-068969-5). McGraw.
Portable Computer Market. 238p. 1985. 1725.00 (ISBN 0-86621-303-1, A1381). Frost & Sullivan.
Portable Computer Markets. Market Intelligence Research Company Staff. Ed. by W. Hammrsley. 256p. (Orig.). 1987. pap. text ed. 995.00x (ISBN 0-916483-27-4). Market Res Co.
Portable Computer Markets, 1984-1990. Market Intelligence Research Company Staff. 250p. 1985. pap. text ed. 795.00 (ISBN 0-317-19551-4). Market Res Co.
Portable Computers. Frost & Sullivan, Inc. Staff. 227p. 1986. 1875.00 (ISBN 0-86621-766-5, A1583). Frost & Sullivan.
Portable Conrad. rev. ed. Joseph Conrad. Ed. by Morton D. Zabel & Frederick R. Karl. (Viking Portable Library: No. 33). 1976. pap. 7.95 (ISBN 0-14-015033-1, P33). Penguin.
Portable Conservative Reader. Ed. by Russell Kirk. 1982. pap. 8.95 (ISBN 0-14-015095-1). Penguin.
Portable Curmudgeon. Jon Winokur. 1987. 15.95 (ISBN 0-453-00565-9). NAL.
Portable D. H. Lawrence. D. H. Lawrence. Ed. by Diana Trilling. (Viking Portable Library: No. 28). 1977. pap. 7.95 (ISBN 0-14-015028-5, P28). Penguin.
Portable Dante. rev. ed. Dante Alighieri. Ed. by Paolo Milano. (Viking Portable Library: No. 32). 1977. pap. 8.95 (ISBN 0-14-015032-3, P32). Penguin.
Portable Data Recorder Market. Frost & Sullivan, Inc. Staff. 198p. 1985. 1800.00 (ISBN 0-86621-480-1, A1553). Frost & Sullivan.
Portable Dictionary of Real Estate Terminology. Irving Marcus. 120p. 1983. pap. 6.00 (ISBN 0-8283-1739-9). Branden Pub Co.
Portable Dr. Zarg. Joe Pumilia. (Orig.). 1982. pap. 2.00 (ISBN 0-934646-11-2). TX S & S Pr.
Portable Dorothy Parker. rev ed. Dorothy R. Parker. (Viking Portable Library: No. 74). 1976. pap. 8.95 (ISBN 0-14-015074-9). Penguin.
Portable Dorothy Parker. (Viking Portable Library). 1985. 6.98 (ISBN 0-517-47855-2). Outlet Bk Co.
Portable Dragon: The Western Man's Guide to the I Ching. R. G. Siu. LC 68-18242. 1968. pap. 12.50 (ISBN 0-262-69030-6). MIT Pr.
Portable Edmund Wilson. Edmund Wilson. Ed. by Lewis M. Dabney. 704p. 1983. pap. 7.95 (ISBN 0-14-015098-6). Penguin.
Portable Emerson. Ralph Waldo Emerson. Ed. by Carl Bode & Malcolm Cowley. 664p. 1981. pap. 7.95 (ISBN 0-14-015094-3). Penguin.
Portable Engineer - Any Motive Power Except Steam (AMPES) Jack Rudman. (Career Examination Ser.: C-599). (Cloth bdg. avail. on request). pap. 16.00 (ISBN 0-8373-0599-3). Natl Learning.
Portable Engineer (Steam) Jack Rudman. (Career Examination Ser.: C-600). (Cloth bdg. avail. on request). pap. 14.00 (ISBN 0-8373-0600-0). Natl Learning.
Portable English Handbook. 3rd ed. William Herman. 464p. 1986. pap. text ed. 12.95 (ISBN 0-03-002137-5, HoltC). HR&W.
Portable English Handbook: An Index to Grammar, Usage, & the Research Paper. 2nd ed. William Herman. 1982. pap. text ed. 11.95 (ISBN 0-03-059121-X). HR&W.
Portable English Workbook. William Herman. 1982. pap. text ed. 11.95 (ISBN 0-03-059423-5). HR&W.
Portable Faulkner. rev. ed. William Faulkner. Ed. by Malcolm Cowley. (Viking Portable Library: No. 18). (gr. 10 up). 1977. pap. 8.95 (ISBN 0-14-015018-8). Penguin.
Portable Feast. rev. ed. Diane MacMillan. (Illus.). 192p. 1984. pap. 7.95 (ISBN 0-89286-226-2). One Hund One Prods.
Portable Fire Extinguishers. National Fire Protection Association Staff. 48p. 1984. 12.00 (ISBN 0-317-63040-7, 10-84). Natl Fire Prot.
Portable Furniture: A Practical Guide to Space-Saving Furnishings. Vicki Brooks. LC 86-8730. (Illus.). 192p. (Orig.). 1986. 20.00 (ISBN 0-915590-88-3); pap. 9.95 (ISBN 0-915590-87-5). Main Street.
Portable Graham Greene. Graham Greene. Ed. by Philip Stratford. LC 76-55791. 1977. pap. 8.95 (ISBN 0-14-015075-7). Penguin.
Portable Greek Historians. Ed. by M. I. Finley. (Viking Portable Library: No. 65). 1977. pap. 7.95 (ISBN 0-14-015065-X). Penguin.
Portable Greek Reader. Ed. by W. H. Auden. (Viking Portable Library: No. 39). 1977. pap. 7.95 (ISBN 0-14-015039-0, P39). Penguin.
Portable Hal Porter. Hal Porter. Ed. by Mary Lord. (Illus.). 408p. 1980. 32.50x (ISBN 0-7022-1465-5); pap. 12.95x (ISBN 0-7022-1466-3). U of Queensland Pr.
Portable Hawthorne. rev. ed. Nathaniel Hawthorne. Ed. by Malcolm Cowley. (Viking Portable Library: No. 38). 1977. pap. 7.95 (ISBN 0-14-015038-2, P38). Penguin.
Portable Henry James. rev. ed. Henry James. Ed. by Morton D. Zabel. (Viking Portable Library: No. 55). 1977. pap. 8.95 (ISBN 0-14-015055-2). Penguin.
Portable Henry Kingsley. Henry Kingsley. Ed. by J. S. Mellick. LC 81-19990. (UQP Australian Authors Ser.). 603p. (YA) 1982. text ed. 34.50; pap. 14.95 (ISBN 0-7022-1760-3). U of Queensland Pr.
Portable Henry Lawson. Ed. by Brian Kiernan. (UQP Australia Authors Ser.). 394p. 1977. 32.50x (ISBN 0-7022-1230-X); pap. 12.95x (ISBN 0-7022-1231-8). U of Queensland Pr.
Portable Home Valuation Guide. Guy V. Smith. 1982. 59.50 (ISBN 0-13-686428-7). Exec Reports.
Portable James Joyce. James Joyce. (Viking Portable Library: No. 30). 1976. pap. 8.95 (ISBN 0-14-015030-7). Penguin.
Portable Joseph Furphy. Joseph Furphy. Ed. by John Barnes. (UQP Australian Authors Ser.). (Illus.). xxv, 439p. 1982. text ed. 32.50 (ISBN 0-7022-1611-9); pap. 12.95 (ISBN 0-7022-1612-7). U of Queensland Pr.
Portable Jung. C. G. Jung. Ed. by Joseph Campbell. (Viking Portable Library: No. 70). 1976. pap. 7.95 (ISBN 0-14-015070-6). Penguin.
Portable Karl Marx. Karl Marx. Ed. by Eugene Kamenka. 704p. 1983. pap. 8.95 (ISBN 0-14-015096-X). Penguin.
Portable Machiavelli. Tr. by Peter Bondanella & Mark Musa. (Viking Portable Library: No. 92). (Orig.). 1979. pap. 8.95 (ISBN 0-14-015092-7). Penguin.
Portable Mad. William M. Gaines. pap. 1.25 (ISBN 0-451-06742-8, Y6742, Sig). NAL.
Portable Mad. (Mad Ser. No. 28). (Illus.). 1977. pap. 1.95 (ISBN 0-446-90596-8). Warner Bks.
Portable Marcus Clarke. Ed. by Michael Wilding. (Portable Austrailian Authors Ser.). 690p. 1977. 34.50x (ISBN 0-7022-1171-0); pap. 12.95 (ISBN 0-7022-1181-8). U of Queensland Pr.
Portable Mark Twain. (Viking Portable Library). 1985. 6.98 (ISBN 0-517-47856-0). Outlet Bk Co.
Portable Mark Twain. Mark Twain. Ed. by Bernard De Voto. (Viking Portable Library: No. 20). 1977. pap. 7.95 (ISBN 0-14-015020-X). Penguin.
Portable Medieval Reader. Ed. by James B. Ross & Mary M. McLaughlin. (Viking Portable Library: No. 46). 1977. pap. 9.95 (ISBN 0-14-015046-3). Penguin.
Portable Milton. John Milton. Ed. by Douglas Bush. (Viking Portable Library: No. 44). 1976. pap. 7.95 (ISBN 0-14-015044-7). Penguin.
Portable Mother Goose & Grimm. Mike Peters. (Orig.). (gr. k-12). 1987. pap. 5.95 (ISBN 0-440-55860-3, LE). Dell.
Portable Nathaniel Hawthorne. (Viking Portable Library). 1985. 6.98 (ISBN 0-517-47857-9). Outlet Bk Co.
Portable Needlepoint Boutique. Joyce Aiken. LC 76-53870. (Illus.). 1977. 10.95 (ISBN 0-8008-6416-6). Taplinger.
Portable Nietzsche. Friedrich Nietzsche. Ed. by Walter Kaufmann. (Viking Portable Library: No. 62). 1977. pap. 7.95 (ISBN 0-14-015062-5). Penguin.
Portable North American Indian Reader. Ed. by Frederick W. Turner, 3rd. LC 72-12545. (Viking Portable Library: No. 77). 1977. pap. 8.95 (ISBN 0-14-015077-3). Penguin.
Portable Office: Take Your Office on the Road. Jefferson D. Bates & Stuart Crump, Jr. (Illus.). 180p. 1987. 16.95 (ISBN 0-87491-841-3). Acropolis.
Portable Oscar Wilde. Oscar Wilde. Ed. by Stanley Weintraub & Richard Aldington. 704p. 1981. pap. 7.95 (ISBN 0-14-015093-5). Penguin.
Portable Pensions. Jozetta H. Srb. (Key Issues Ser.: No. 4). 40p. 1969. pap. 2.00 (ISBN 0-87546-245-6). ILR Pr.
Portable Personal Self-Defense Products. 203p. 1985. 985.00x (ISBN 0-88694-681-6). Intl Res Dev.
Portable Pet. Barbara Nicholas. LC 83-22689. (Other Dog Bks.). 80p. 1983. pap. 5.95 (ISBN 0-87714-117-7). Denlingers.
Portable Pet: How to Travel Anywhere with Your Dog or Cat. Barbara Nicholas. LC 83-22689. 96p. 1984. 12.95 (ISBN 0-916782-50-6); pap. 5.95 (ISBN 0-916782-49-2). Harvard Common Pr.
Portable Plato. Plato. Ed. by Scott Buchanan. (Viking Portable Library: No. 40). 1977. pap. 7.95 (ISBN 0-14-015040-4). Penguin.

Portland's Forest Park: One City's Wilderness. Marcy C. Houle. (Illus.). 120p. (Orig.). 1988. pap. 6.95 (ISBN 0-87595-187-2). Oregon Hist.

Portland's Public Art: A Guide & History. Norma C. Gleason & Chet Orloff. (Illus.). 82p. (Orig.). 1984. pap. 4.95 (ISBN 0-87595-059-0). Oregon Hist.

Portmanteau Plays. Stuart Walker. Ed. & intro. by Edward Hale Bierstadt. LC 77-70364. (One-Act Plays in Reprint Ser.). 1977. Repr. of 1917 ed. 17.50x (ISBN 0-8486-2024-0). Roth Pub Inc.

Portnoy's Complaint. Philip Roth. LC 69-16414. 1969. 14.50 (ISBN 0-394-44198-2). Random.

Portnoy's Complaint. Philip Roth. LC 83-42950. 288p. 1982. 6.95 (ISBN 0-394-60810-0). Modern Lib.

Portnoy's Complaint. Philip Roth. 320p. 1984. pap. 4.95 (ISBN 0-449-20291-7, Crest). Fawcett.

Porto Rico, Past & Present: The Island after Thirty Years of American Rule. Cuesta J. Enamorado. LC 74-14231. (Puerto Rican Experience Ser). (Illus.). 180p. 1975. Repr. 12.00x (ISBN 0-405-06220-6). Ayer Co Pubs.

Portofino PTA. Gerald Green. 1976. Repr. of 1962 ed. lib. bdg. 15.95x (ISBN 0-89190-124-8, Pub. by River City Pr). Amereon Ltd.

Portolan Charts: Carte Nautiche Italiane. P. Frabetti. (Illus.). 1983. pap. 65.00 (ISBN 0-87556-599-9). Saifer.

Portorium: Etude Sur L'organisation Douaniere Chez les Romains, Surtout a L'epoque Du Haut-Empire. Siegfried J. De Laet. LC 75-7312. (Roman History Ser.). (Fr.). 1975. Repr. 38.50x (ISBN 0-405-07194-9). Ayer Co Pubs.

Portrait Album of Four RI Leaders. Marguerite Appleton. 1978. 8.95 (ISBN 0-932840-00-0). RI Hist Soc.

Portrait & Biographical Record of Lancaster County, Pa. rev. ed. Ed. by William L. Iscrupe & Shirley G. Iscrupe. (Illus.). 608p. 1988. Repr. of 1894 ed. 39.95 (ISBN 0-944128-00-9). SW PA Geneal Servs.

Portrait & Story: Dramaturgical Approaches to the Study of Persons. Larry Cochran. LC 85-12708. (Contributions in Psychology Ser.: No. 7). 210p. 1986. lib. bdg. 36.95 (ISBN 0-313-24966-0, CPS/). Greenwood.

Portrait Bust, Renaissance to Enlightenment. Brown University, Department of Art Staff. (Illus.). 1969. 1.00 (ISBN 0-911517-30-8). Mus of Art RI.

Portrait Cast in Steel: Buckeye International & Columbus, Ohio, 1881-1980. Mansel G. Blackford. LC 82-6114. (Contributions in Economics & Economic History Ser.: No. 49). (Illus.). xviii, 225p. 1982. lib. bdg. 36.95 (ISBN 0-313-23393-4, BPC/). Greenwood.

Portrait De Sophie. Carole Mortimer. (Harlequin Romantique Ser.). 192p. 1983. pap. 1.95 (ISBN 0-373-41225-8). Harlequin Bks.

Portrait Drawing. Wendon Blake. (Artist's Painting Library). (Illus.). 80p. (Orig.). 1981. pap. 8.95 (ISBN 0-8230-4094-1). Watson-Guptill.

Portrait d'un Ami qui s'appelait Moi. Andre Maurois. (Coll. Les Auteurs Juges par leurs Oeuvres). pap. 17.50 (ISBN 0-685-36953-6). French & Eur.

Portrait d'Un Espion du Dix-Septieme Siecle. Safa F. Shimi. (Fr.). 1980. 10.00x (ISBN 0-936968-00-1). Intl Bk Ctr.

Portrait d'un Inconnu. Nathalie Sarraute. (Folio Ser.: No. 942). 1964. pap. 6.95 (ISBN 0-685-11504-6). Schoenhof.

Portrait d'un Inconnu. Nathalie Sarraute. 1964. write for info. French & Eur.

Portrait d'une Amitie et d'Autres Morts Memorables. Vercors. 184p. 1954. 3.95 (ISBN 0-686-55131-1). French & Eur.

Portrait for Posterity: Lincoln & His Biographers. Benjamin P. Thomas. LC 72-38318. (Biography Index Reprint Ser). (Illus.). Repr. of 1947 ed. 18.25 (ISBN 0-8369-8130-8). Ayer Co Pubs.

Portrait Game: The Game Played with Imaginary Sketches. Ivan S. Turgenev. (Illus.). 151p. 1973. 5.95 (ISBN 0-8180-1002-9). Horizon.

Portrait in a Mirror. Charles Morgan. 284p. 1982. Repr. of 1932 ed. lib. bdg. 20.00 (ISBN 0-8495-3900-5). Arden Lib.

Portrait in Art. Ed. by Stephen Longstreet. (Master Draughtsman Ser.). (Illus., Orig.). treasure trove bdg. 10.95x (ISBN 0-87505-046-8); pap. 4.95 (ISBN 0-87505-199-5). Borden.

Portrait in Blood. Mary Kirchoff. LC 85-50142. (Amazing Bks.). 220p. (Orig.). 1985. pap. 2.95 (ISBN 0-88038-258-9). TSR Inc.

Portrait in Britain & America with a Dictionary of Portrait Painters, 1680-1914. Robin Simon. 256p. 1987. lib. bdg. 50.00x (ISBN 0-8161-8795-9, Hall Reference). G K Hall.

Portrait in Brownstone. Louis Auchincloss. (Paperbacks Ser.). 320p. 1987. pap. text ed. 4.95 (ISBN 0-07-002441-3). McGraw.

Portrait in Murder & Gay Colors. H. Paul Jeffers. LC 85-4275. 288p. (Orig.). 1985. pap. 7.95 (ISBN 0-915175-09-6). Knights Pr.

Portrait in Shadows. John Wainwright. 192p. 1986. 12.95 (ISBN 0-312-63174-X). St Martin.

Portrait in Shadows. John Wainwright. 286p. 1987. pap. 3.50 (ISBN 1-55547-196-X). Critics Choice Paper.

Portrait in the Renaissance. John Pope-Hennessy. (Bollingen Ser.: Vol. 35). (Illus., A. W. Mellon Lecture, No. 12). 1967. 66.00x (ISBN 0-691-09795-X). Princeton U Pr.

Portrait in Twelfth Century French Literature: An Example of the Stylistic Originality of Chretien de Troyes. A. M. Colby. 206p. (Orig.). 1965. pap. text ed. 18.00x (ISBN 0-317-56025-5, Pub. by Droz Switzerland). Coronet Bks.

Portrait Life of Lincoln. facsimile ed. Francis T. Miller. LC 76-133528. (Select Bibliographies Reprint Ser). Repr. of 1910 ed. 25.50 (ISBN 0-8369-5560-9). Ayer Co Pubs.

Portrait Miniatures from the Collection of the Russian Museum. K. Mikhailov & G. Smirnov. (Seventeenth to Early Twentieth Centuries Ser.). 1979. 39.00x (ISBN 0-317-14316-6, Pub. by Collets (UK)). State Mutual Bk.

Portrait' Miniatures in Early American History: 1750-1840. Norton (R. W.) Art Gallery. LC 76-11634. 1976. pap. 3.50x (ISBN 0-913060-09-7). Norton Art.

Portrait Miniatures in the National Museum of American Art. Robin Bolton-Smith. LC 84-2692. (CVL Ser.: No. 46). (Illus.). 88p. 1984. pap. 60.00 (ISBN 0-226-68857-7). U of Chicago Pr.

Portrait of a Banker, James Stillman. Anna R. Burr. 33.00 (ISBN 0-405-06950-2, 19126). Ayer Co Pubs.

Portrait of a Banker: James Stillman, 1850-1918. Anna R. Burr. 370p. 1982. Repr. of 1927 ed. lib. bdg. 35.00 (ISBN 0-686-91747-2). Darby Bks.

Portrait of a Builder: William A. McIntyre. Clarence W. Hall. 1983. pap. 5.95 (ISBN 0-86544-020-4). Salv Army Suppl South.

Portrait of a Chef. Helen Morris. (Midway Reprint Ser.). (Illus.). xii, 222p. 1975. pap. text ed. 7.95x (ISBN 0-226-54000-6). U of Chicago Pr.

Portrait of a Chinese Diplomat of the Last Manchu Emperors: Sir Chentung Liang Cheng. Walter M. Whitehill. (Robert Charles Billings Fund Pamphlet Ser.: No.3). (Illus.). 18p. (Orig.). 1974. pap. 1.50 (ISBN 0-934552-29-0). Boston Athenaeum.

Portrait of a Chinese Lady. Lady Hosie. 404p. 1929. 105.00x (Pub. by Han-Shan Tang Ltd). State Mutual Bk.

Portrait of a Community: Ojai Yesterday & Today. Ellen M. James. (Illus.). 96p. (Orig.). 1984. pap. 7.95 (ISBN 0-9610188-0-1). O V N Pubns.

Portrait of a Country Artist: C. F. Tunnicliffe. Ian Niall. (Illus.). 224p. 1985. pap. 15.95 (ISBN 0-575-03694-X, Pub. by Gollancz England). David & Charles.

Portrait of a Country Artist: Charles Tunnicliffe R. A. 1901-1979. Ian Niall. 1980. 29.95 (ISBN 0-575-02868-8, Pub. by Gollancz England). David & Charles.

Portrait of a Crack. V. Finkel. Tr. by Y. Nadler. 166p. 1985. pap. 3.95 (ISBN 0-8285-3030-0, Pub. by Mir Pubs USSR). Imported Pubns.

Portrait of a Crack. V. Finkel. 166p. 1985. 40.00x (ISBN 0-317-46683-6, Pub. by Collets (UK)); pap. 14.00. State Mutual Bk.

Portrait of a Dalai Lama: The Life & Times of the Great Thirteenth. Charles Bell. (Wisdom Tibet Books - Yellow Ser.). (Illus.). 464p. 1987. pap. 22.95 (ISBN 0-86171-055-X). Wisdom MA.

Portrait of a Decade: London Life, 1945-1955. Douglas Sutherland. 1988. 49.00x (Pub. by Harrap Ltd England). State Mutual Bk.

Portrait of a Decade: Roy Stryker & the Development of Documentary Photography in the Thirties. F. Jack Hurley & Robert Doherty. LC 76-51427. (Quality Paperbacks Ser.). 1977. pap. 6.95 (ISBN 0-306-80058-6). Da Capo.

Portrait of a Decade: The Nineteen Sixties. Trevor Fisher. (Illus.). 72p. (YA) (gr. 7-9). 1988. 19.95 (ISBN 0-7134-5603-5, Pub. by Batsford England). David & Charles.

Portrait of a Director: Satyajit Ray. Marie Seton. 350p. 1981. 60.00x (ISBN 0-234-72127-8, Pub. by Dobson Bks England). State Mutual Bk.

Portrait of a Father. Robert Penn Warren. 96p. 1988. 12.00 (ISBN 0-8131-1655-4). U Pr of Ky.

Portrait of a Friend. Gwen Watkins. 226p. 1983. 45.00x (ISBN 0-85088-847-6, Pub. by Gomer Pr). State Mutual Bk.

Portrait of a Golfaholic. Mark Oman. (Illus.). 96p. (Orig.). 1984. pap. 6.95 (ISBN 0-8092-5335-6). Contemp Bks.

Portrait of a Hill Town: A History of Washington, N. H., 1876-1976. Ronald Jager & Grace Jager. LC 76-62912. (Illus.). 1977. 22.00 (ISBN 0-686-22158-3). Wash Hist Comm.

Portrait of a Lady. Henry James. (Airmont Classics Ser.). (gr. 11 up). pap. 2.50 (ISBN 0-8049-0098-1, CL-98). Airmont.

Portrait of a Lady. Henry James. Ed. by Leon Edel. LC 56-13883. (YA) (gr. 9 up). 1956. pap. 6.50 (ISBN 0-395-05106-1, RivEd). HM.

Portrait of a Lady. Henry James. (Modern Library College Editions Ser.). 1966. pap. write for info (ISBN 0-394-30947-2, T47, RanC). Random.

Portrait of a Lady. Henry James. (Orig.). pap. 3.50 (ISBN 0-451-51605-2, CE1605, Sig Classics). NAL.

Portrait of a Lady. Henry James. Ed. by Robert D. Bamberg. (Norton Critical Edition Ser.). 1975. pap. text ed. 12.95x (ISBN 0-393-09259-3). Norton.

Portrait of a Lady. rev. ed. Henry James. Ed. by Robert J. Dixson. (American Classics Ser.: Bk. 7). (gr. 9 up). 1974. pap. text ed. 4.75 (ISBN 0-13-024571-2, 18126); cassettes 55.00 (ISBN 0-13-024746-4, 58229). Prentice ESL.

Portrait of a Lady. Henry James. (World's Classics Ser.). 1981. pap. 3.95 (ISBN 0-19-281514-8). Oxford U Pr.

Portrait of a Lady. Henry James. LC 82-42867. 8.95 (ISBN 0-394-60432-6). Modern Lib.

Portrait of a Lady. Henry James. 598p. 1983. pap. 4.95x (ISBN 0-460-01320-3, Pub. by Evman England). Biblio Dist.

Portrait of a Lady. Henry James. 544p. 1983. pap. 3.50 (ISBN 0-553-21127-7, Bantam Classics). Bantam.

Portrait of a Lady. Henry James. Ed. by Geoffrey Moore. (English Library). 688p. 1984. pap. 3.95 (ISBN 0-14-043223-X). Penguin.

Portrait of a Lady, Vol. 1. Henry James. LC 72-158782. (Novels & Tales of Henry James: Vol. 3). Repr. of 1908 ed. lib. bdg. 28.75x (ISBN 0-678-02803-6). Kelley.

Portrait of a Lady, Vol. 2. Henry James. LC 72-158782. (Novels & Tales of Henry James: Vol. 4). Repr. of 1908 ed. lib. bdg. 28.75x (ISBN 0-678-02804-4). Kelley.

Portrait of a Lady see Novels Eighteen Eighty-One to Eighteen Eighty-Six.

Portrait of a Lady Notes. James L. Roberts. (Orig.). 1965. pap. 3.50 (ISBN 0-8220-1066-6). Cliffs.

Portrait of a Market: Photographs of Seattle's Pike Place Market. John Stamets. (Illus.). 96p. (Orig.). 1987. pap. 14.95 (ISBN 0-941104-17-6). Real Comet.

Portrait of a Marriage. Nigel Nicolson. LC 79-25497. 1973. 10.00 (ISBN 0-689-10574-6, 257); pap. 9.95 (ISBN 0-689-70597-2, 257). Atheneum.

Portrait of a Married Woman. Sally Mandel. 320p. 1986. 15.95 (ISBN 0-553-05079-6). Bantam.

Portrait of a Married Woman. Sally Mandel. 304p. (Orig.). 1987. pap. 4.50 (ISBN 0-553-25837-0). Bantam.

Portrait of a Nude Woman As Cleopatra. Barbara Chase-Riboud. Ed. by Pat Golbitz. LC 86-81220. 80p. 1987. 15.95 (ISBN 0-688-06403-5); pap. 8.95 (ISBN 0-317-54469-1). Morrow.

Portrait of a Party: The Origins & Development of the Whig Persuasion in New York State. Ed. by Frank Feidel & Ernest May. (Harvard Dissertations in American History & Political Science Ser.). 510p. 1988. lib. bdg. 85.00 (ISBN 0-8240-5113-0). Garland Pub.

Portrait of a Patriot: Selected Writings by Mohammad Hatta. Mohammed Hatta. 1972. text ed. 44.80x (ISBN 0-686-22529-5). Mouton.

Portrait of a People. Eli Weinberg. (Illus.). 200p. 1982. pap. 8.95 (ISBN 0-88208-201-9, Pub. by Intl Defence England). Chicago Review.

Portrait of a Pioneer: The Letters of Sidney Turner from South Africa. Ed. by Daphne Child. (Illus.). 144p. 1982. 19.95x (ISBN 0-86954-095-5, Pub. by Macmillan S Africa). Intl Spec Bk.

Portrait of a Place: San Luis Obispo. Barbara Seymour. (Illus.). 120p. (Orig.). 1986. pap. 12.95 (ISBN 0-9617522-0-3). Garden Creek Pubns.

Portrait of a Place, Some American Landscape Painters in Gloucester. Intro. by James F. O'Gorman. (Illus.). 1973. 8.95 (ISBN 0-930352-03-3). Nelson B Robinson.

Portrait of a Port. L. G. Taylor. 71p. 1978. 10.95x (ISBN 0-85174-312-9). Sheridan.

Portrait of a Port: Boston, 1852-1914. William H. Bunting. LC 77-145893. (Illus.). 1971. 27.50 (ISBN 0-674-69075-3, Belknap Pr). Harvard U Pr.

Portrait of a Preacher. John Fletcher. 8.95 (ISBN 0-686-12902-4). Schmul Pub Co.

Portrait of a Professional: The Nat the Bush Doctor Story. Nathaniel Mathis. As told to Jim Link. LC 86-90782. (Illus.). 112p. (Orig.). 1986. pap. text ed. 5.95 (ISBN 0-9616389-0-7). N Mathis.

Portrait of a Progressive: The Political Career of Christopher, Viscount Addison. Kenneth Morgan & Jane Morgan. (Illus.). 1980. 47.00x (ISBN 0-19-822494-X). Oxford U Pr.

Portrait of a Quaker. Donald McNichols. LC 80-66654. (Illus.). 180p. 1980. 12.50 (ISBN 0-913342-24-6). Barclay Pr.

Portrait of a Romantic. Steven Millhauser. pap. 6.95 (ISBN 0-317-56014-X). PB.

Portrait of a Scholar, & Other Essays Written in Macedonia, 1916-1918. facs. ed. Robert W. Chapman. LC 68-29197. (Essay Index Reprint Ser). 1968. Repr. of 1920 ed. 15.00 (ISBN 0-8369-0291-2). Ayer Co Pubs.

Portrait of a Ship, the Benj. F. Packard. Paul C. Morris. LC 87-80164. (Illus.). 200p. 1987. 30.00 (ISBN 0-936972-09-2). Lower Cape.

Portrait of a Silver Lady: The Train They Called the California Zephyr. Bruce MacGregor & Ted Benson. LC 77-3053. (Illus.). 1977. 39.95 (ISBN 0-87108-509-7). Pruett.

Portrait of a Symbolist Hero. Robert R. Champigny. 1954. 20.00 (ISBN 0-527-16100-4). Kraus Repr.

Portrait of a Tortoise. Gilbert White. 64p. 1982. pap. 2.50 (ISBN 0-380-58123-X, 58123-X, Discus). Avon.

Portrait of a Village. facsimile ed. Francis B. Young. LC 73-163050. (Short Story Index Reprint Ser.). (Illus.). Repr. of 1938 ed. 17.00 (ISBN 0-8369-3964-6). Ayer Co Pubs.

Portrait of a Virus: AIDS in the Body of America. L. G. Foster. LC 87-70904. (Illus.). 300p. Date not set. pap. price not set (ISBN 0-942691-00-8). Beta Bks.

Portrait of a Waldorf School. A. C. Harwood. (Illus.). 24p. 1977. pap. 1.50 (ISBN 0-913098-06-X). Myrin Institute.

Portrait of a Woman. Herbert O'Driscoll. 96p. (Orig.). 1981. pap. 4.95 (ISBN 0-8164-2332-6, HarpR). Har-Row.

Portrait of a Woman Down East: Selected Writings of Mary Bolte. Ed. by Charles Bolte. 1981. 7.95 (ISBN 0-89272-129-4). Down East.

Portrait of Alison. Francis Durbridge. 1988. 30.00x (ISBN 0-86025-246-9, Pub. by Ian Henry Pubns England). State Mutual Bk.

Portrait of Ambrose Bierce. Adolph de Castro. LC 74-610. (Illus.). 1974. Repr. 18.50x (ISBN 0-8464-0737-X). Beekman Pubs.

Portrait of America, Vols. 1 & 2. 4th ed. Stephen B. Oates. LC 86-81446. 1987. Vol. 1. pap. text ed. 17.56 (ISBN 0-395-35954-6); Vol. 2. pap. text ed. 17.56 (ISBN 0-395-36934-7). HM.

Portrait of American Mothers & Daughters. Photos by Raisa Fastman. (Illus.). 128p. 1987. text ed. 30.00x (ISBN 0-939165-03-1); pap. 22.95x (ISBN 0-939165-04-X); ltd ed. 60.00 (ISBN 0-939165-05-8). NewSage Press.

Portrait of an Age. 2nd ed. G. M. Young. 1988. pap. 9.95 (ISBN 0-19-281005-7). Oxford U Pr.

Portrait of an American City: The Novelists' New York. Joan Zlotnick. (Interdisplinary Urban Studies). 256p. 1982. 24.95x (ISBN 0-8046-9310-2, Pub. by Kennikat). Assoc Faculty Pr.

Portrait of an American Romantic. Steven Millhauser. 1987. 6.95 (ISBN 0-317-56560-5). WSP.

Portrait of an Artist: A Biography of Georgia O'Keefe. Laurie Lisle. 486p. 1987. pap. 5.95 (ISBN 0-671-60040-0). WSP.

Portrait of an Artist: A Biography of Georgia O'Keeffe. rev. & enl. ed. Laurie Lisle. LC 86-16061. (Illus.). 418p. 1986. 29.95 (ISBN 0-8263-0907-0). U of NM Pr.

Portrait of an Artist: A Biography of Georgia O'Keefe. Laurie Lisle. 1987. pap. 5.95 (ISBN 0-317-56918-X). PB.

Portrait of an Artist with Twenty-Six Horses. William Eastlake. LC 80-52282. (Zia Books Ser.). 230p. 1980. pap. 8.95 (ISBN 0-8263-0558-X). U of NM Pr.

Portrait of an Early American Family: The Shippens of Pennsylvania Across Five Generations. Randolph S. Klein. LC 75-10128. (Illus.). 1975. 26.95x (ISBN 0-8122-7700-7). U of Pa Pr.

Portrait of an Estuary. Verle Barnes. Ed. by Aubrey R. McKinney. LC 86-81736. (Adventures in Science Ser.). (Illus.). 220p. 1986. 24.95 (ISBN 0-914587-04-8). Helix Pr.

Portrait of an Expatriate: William Gardner Smith, Writer. Leroy S. Hodges, Jr. LC 85-934. (Contributions in Afro-American & African Studies: No. 91). xvi, 130p. 1985. lib. bdg. 35.00 (ISBN 0-313-24882-6, HPO/). Greenwood.

Portrait of an Explorer: Hiram Bingham, Discoverer of Machu Picchu. Alfred M. Bingham. 288p. 1988. 24.95t (ISBN 0-8138-0136-2). Iowa St U Pr.

Portrait of an Independent: Moorfield Storey, 1845-1929. facsimile ed. Mark A. Howe. LC 76-37346. (Select Bibliographies Reprint Ser). Repr. of 1932 ed. 24.50 (ISBN 0-8369-6693-7). Ayer Co Pubs.

Portrait of an Invisible Man: The Working Life of Stewart McAllister, Film Editor. Dai Vaughan. (British Film Institute Bks.). 209p. 1983. pap. 15.95 (ISBN 0-85170-147-7, Pub. by British Film Inst England). U of Ill Pr.

Portrait of an Island. John Teal & Mildred Teal. LC 81-7631. (Brown Thrasher Bks.). (Illus.). 184p. 1981. pap. 7.50 (ISBN 0-8203-0581-2). U of Ga Pr.

Portrait of an Old Lady: Turmoil At the Bank of England. Stephen Fay. 208p. 1988. 17.95 (ISBN 0-670-81934-4). Viking.

Portrait of an Unknown Gentleman. Sarah Francis. 1985. 24.95x (ISBN 0-7090-1647-6, Pub. by R Hale Ltd UK). State Mutual Bk.

Portrait of Andre Gide. Justin O'Brien. 390p. 1976. Repr. of 1953 ed. lib. bdg. 29.00x (ISBN 0-374-96139-5, Octagon). Hippocrene Bks.

Portrait of Antarctica. Photos by Launcelot Fleming et al. (Illus.). 168p. 1983. 19.95 (ISBN 0-540-01075-8, Pub. by G Philip). Sheridan.

Portrait of Aphasia. David Knox. LC 85-8958. 128p. (Orig.). 1985. pap. 8.95x (ISBN 0-8143-1800-2). Wayne St U Pr.

Portrait of Appalachia. Kenneth Murray. 1985. pap. 7.95 (ISBN 0-913239-39-9). Appalach Consortium.

Portrait of Aristotle. Marjorie Grene. LC 63-5566. 1979. pap. text ed. 14.00x (ISBN 0-226-30822-7, Midway Reprint). U of Chicago Pr.

Portrait of Barrie. Cynthia Asquith. 1973. Repr. of 1954 ed. 20.00 (ISBN 0-8274-1702-0). R West.

Portrait of Bethany. Anne Weale. (Harlequin Presents Ser.). 192p. 1982. pap. 1.75 (ISBN 0-373-10541-X). Harlequin Bks.

Portraits: Goldsmith, Johnson, Garrick. 1952. Repr. 35.00 (ISBN 0-8274-3189-9). R West.

Portraits in American Sanctity. Ed. by Joseph N. Tylenda. 1983. 18.00 (ISBN 0-8199-0846-0). Franciscan Herald.

Portraits in British History. Ronald Pollitt & Herbert F. Curry. LC 74-24454. (Dorsey Series in History). pap. 85.00 (ISBN 0-317-29614-0, 2021664). Bks Demand UMI.

Portraits in Life & Death. Peter Hujar. LC 75-46627. 1976. 27.50 (ISBN 0-306-70755-1); pap. 8.95 (ISBN 0-306-80038-1). Da Capo.

Portraits in Miniature & Other Essays by Lytton Strachey. Giles L. Strachey. LC 77-10347. 1977. Repr. of 1931 ed. lib. bdg. 35.00x (ISBN 0-8371-9823-2, STPM). Greenwood.

Portraits in Music I. David Jenkins & Mark Visocchi. 1980. 6.00 (ISBN 0-19-321400-8). Oxford U Pr.

Portraits in Music 2. David Jenkins & Mark Visocchi. 1982. 6.00 (ISBN 0-19-321401-6). Oxford U Pr.

Portraits in Oil. Wendon Blake. (Artist's Painting Library). (Illus.). 80p. (Orig.). 1980. pap. 8.95 (ISBN 0-8230-4105-0). Watson-Guptill.

Portraits in Oil the Van Wyk Way. Helen Van Wyk. Ed. by Herbert Rogoff. (Illus.). 128p. (Orig.). 1986. pap. text ed. 26.00. Art Instr Assocs.

Portraits in Pottery. A. Lee. LC 78-57428. (Illus.). 1979. write for info. (ISBN 0-89344-026-4). ARS Ceramica.

Portraits in Prose. Hugh MacDonald. Repr. of 1946 ed. lib. bdg. 22.50 (ISBN 0-8414-6396-4). Folcroft.

Portraits in Prose. Hugh MacDonald. Repr. of 1946 ed. 20.00 (ISBN 0-686-18787-3). Scholars Ref Lib.

Portraits in Prose. Ed. by Hugh Macdonald. LC 71-101830. (Biography Index Reprint Ser.). 1946. 27.50 (ISBN 0-8369-8004-2). Ayer Co Pubs.

Portraits in Prose: A Collection of Characters. Hugh MacDonald. 1946. 18.50x (ISBN 0-685-89772-9). Elliots Bks.

Portraits in Satire. Kenneth Hopkins. LC 71-161941. 290p. 1958. Repr. 39.00x (ISBN 0-403-01330-5). Scholarly.

Portraits in Silicon. Robert Slater. 350p. 1987. 24.95 (ISBN 0-262-19262-4). MIT Pr.

Portraits in the Collection of the Virginia Historical Society: A Catalogue. Virginius C. Hall, Jr. LC 80-14079. 283p. 1981. 50.00 (ISBN 0-8139-0813-2). U Pr of Va.

Portraits in the Massachusetts Historical Society. Andrew Oliver et al. (Illus.). 163p. 1988. 50.00x (ISBN 0-934909-26-1). Mass Hist Soc.

Portraits in the Wild: Animal Behavior in East Africa. 2nd ed. Cynthia Moss. LC 81-23092. (Illus.). 1982. 28.00x (ISBN 0-226-54232-7); pap. 14.95 (ISBN 0-226-54233-5). U of Chicago Pr.

Portraits: O Those I Love. Daniel Berrigan. (Crossroad Paperback Ser.). 160p. 1982. pap. 8.95 (ISBN 0-8245-0416-X). Crossroad NY.

Portraits of a Changing World. Wendell K. Babcock. 1987. 12.95 (ISBN 0-533-07142-9). Vantage.

Portraits of American Presidents-The Eisenhower Presidency: Eleven Intimate Perspectives of Dwight D. Eisenhower, Vol. III. Ed. by Kenneth W. Thompson. LC 84-7368. 268p. (Orig.). 1984. lib. bdg. 26.25 (ISBN 0-8191-3985-8, Co-pub. by White Miller Center); pap. text ed. 11.25 (ISBN 0-8191-3986-6, Co-pub. by White Miller Center). U Pr of Amer.

Portraits of Artists: Reflexivity in Gidean Fiction, 1902-1936. Arthur E. Babcock. 127p. 1981. 14.95 (ISBN 0-917786-26-2). Summa Pubns.

Portraits of Bible Men. George Matheson. LC 86-7428. (First Series (Adam to Job)). Orig. Title: Representative Men of the Bible. 384p. 1986. pap. 8.95 (ISBN 0-8254-3251-0). Kregel.

Portraits of Bible Men. George Matheson. LC 86-27221. (Ishmael to David, Second Ser.). 368p. 1987. pap. 8.95 (ISBN 0-8254-3252-9). Kregel.

Portraits of Bible Men. George Matheson. LC 86-27220. (John the Baptist to Paul, Third Ser.). 384p. 1987. pap. 8.95 (ISBN 0-8254-3253-7). Kregel.

Portraits of Bible Women. George Matheson. LC 86-7429. Orig. Title: Representative Women of the Bible (Eve to Mary Magdalene) 264p. 1986. pap. 7.95 (ISBN 0-8254-3250-2). Kregel.

Portraits of Celebrated Men. C. A. Sainte-Beuve. 59.95 (ISBN 0-8490-0882-4). Gordon Pr.

Portraits of Celebrated Women. C. A. Sainte-Beuve. 59.95 (ISBN 0-8490-0883-2). Gordon Pr.

Portraits of Charles V of France, 1338-1380. Claire R. Sherman. LC 69-18286. (College Art Association Monograph Ser.: Vol. 20). (Illus.). 168p. 1985. Repr. of 1969 ed. 30.00x (ISBN 0-271-00407-X). Pa St U Pr.

Portraits of Chinese Women in Revolution. Agnes Smedley. Ed. by Jan MacKinnon & Steve MacKinnon. (Illus.). 208p. 1976. pap. 10.95 (ISBN 0-912670-44-4). Feminist Pr.

Portraits of Christ. Ernst Kitzinger & Elizabeth Senior. (Illus.). 62p. 1983. Repr. of 1940 ed. lib. bdg. 25.00 (ISBN 0-89987-459-2). Darby Bks.

Portraits of Christ in Scripture. Robert W. Wingard. LC 87-71667. 80p. 1987. pap. 4.95 (ISBN 0-88177-047-7, DR047B). Discipleship Res.

Portraits of Conflict: A Photographic History of Arkansas in the Civil War. Bobby Roberts & Carl Moneyhon. LC 87-5869. (Illus.). 224p. (YA) (gr. 4-12). 1987. 34.95 (ISBN 0-938626-83-3); pap. 19.95 (ISBN 0-938626-84-1). U of Ark Pr.

Portraits of Courageous Women. Ardis O. Higgins. (Illus.). (gr. 5-8). 1978. pap. text ed. 4.00x (ISBN 0-912256-12-5). Halls of Ivy.

Portraits of Customs & Carols. Norma Leary. 1983. pap. 3.25 (ISBN 0-937172-54-5). JLJ Pubs.

Portraits of Discipleship. Daniel Mueller. 1987. pap. 5.95 (ISBN 0-937172-67-7). JLJ Pubs.

Portraits of Dutch Painters & Other Artists of the Low Countries: Specime of an Iconography, Reportorium. H. Van Hall. 432p. 1963. text ed. 92.00 (ISBN 90-265-0027-0, Pub. by Swets Pub Serv Holland). Swets North Am.

Portraits of Early Russian Liberals: A Study of the Thought of T. N. Granovsky, V. P. Botkin, P. V. Annenkov, A. V. Druzhinin, & K. D. Kavelin. Derek Offord. (Cambridge Studies in Russian Literature). 306p. 1985. 44.50 (ISBN 0-521-30550-0). Cambridge U Pr.

Portraits of Earth. Freeman Patterson. LC 87-4795. (Illus.). 180p. 1987. text ed. 35.00 (ISBN 0-87156-717-2). Sierra.

Portraits of Earth. Freeman Patterson. (Illus.). 1987. 40.00 (ISBN 1-55013-030-7, Pub. by Key Porter Canada). U of Toronto Pr.

Portraits of Faith. Albert J. Lown. 155p. (Orig.). 1981. pap. 3.95 (ISBN 0-8341-0695-7). Beacon Hill.

Portraits of Faith: A Pictorial History of Religions in North Carolina. (Illus.). 254p. 1987. 25.00 (ISBN 0-89865-454-8). Donning Co.

Portraits of Friends & Acquaintances. (Illus.). 96p. 1987. spiral bdg. 25.00 (ISBN 0-318-23155-7). Man Mtn Pub.

Portraits of Garden Bedfellows: The Gardeners Guide to Plants that Go - & Grow - Well Together. Elise Laurenzi & Gerald B. Levinson. LC 86-92069. (Illus.). 24p. 1987. pap. 5.95 (ISBN 0-9617942-0-8). Corydalis Pr.

Portraits of God: Word Pictures of the Deity from the Earliest Times Through Today. Louis Baldwin. LC 85-43571. 192p. 1986. lib. bdg. 18.95x (ISBN 0-89950-198-2). McFarland & Co.

Portraits of High School. Ed. by Vito Perrone. LC 85-12809. 658p. 1985. pap. text ed. 22.50 (ISBN 0-931050-27-8). Carnegie Found.

Portraits of His Children. George R. Martin. 1987. 18.95 (ISBN 0-913165-19-0). Dark Harvest.

Portraits of Homoeopathic Medicines: Psychophysical Analyses of Select Constitutional Types. Catherine R. Coulter. 500p. 1985. 25.00 (ISBN 0-938190-61-X). North Atlantic.

Portraits of Homoeopathic Medicines, Vol. Two: Psychophysical Analyses of Selected Constitutional Types. Catherine R. Coulter. 400p. 1988. 25.00 (ISBN 1-55643-036-1). North Atlantic.

Portraits of Jews by Gilbert Stuart & Other Early American Artists. Hannah R. London. LC 69-19613. (Illus.). 1969. Repr. 13.75 (ISBN 0-8048-0459-1). C E Tuttle.

Portraits of John & Abigail Adams. Andrew Oliver. (Adams Papers, Ser. 4, Adams Family Portraits). (Illus.). 1967. 22.50x (ISBN 0-674-69150-4). Harvard U Pr.

Portraits of John Marshall. Andrew Oliver. LC 76-13648. (Illus.). 209p. 1977. 16.95x (ISBN 0-8139-0633-4, Institute of Early American History & Culture). U Pr of Va.

Portraits of John Quincy Adams & His Wife. Andrew Oliver. LC 70-128349. (Adams Papers, Series 4, Adams Family Portraits Ser.). (Illus.). 1970. 29.95x (ISBN 0-674-69152-0). Harvard U Pr.

Portraits of Linguists, 2 vols. Ed. by Thomas A. Sebeok. LC 75-45352. (Indiana University Studies in the History 2nd Theory of Linguistics, 1746-1963). 1976. Repr. of 1966 ed. Vol. 1. lib. bdg. 42.50 (ISBN 0-8371-8819-9, SEPLA). Greenwood.

Portraits of Marriage in Literature. Ed. by Anne C. Hargrove & Maurine Magliocco. (Essays in Literature Bk.). 189p. 1984. pap. 8.00 (ISBN 0-934312-05-2). WIU Essays Lit.

Portraits of Men. Charles A. Sainte-Beuve. Tr. by Forsyth Edereain. LC 72-4650. (Essay Index Reprint Ser.). Repr. of 1891 ed. 17.00 (ISBN 0-8369-2972-1). Ayer Co Pubs.

Portraits of Mexican Birds: Fifty Selected Paintings. George M. Sutton. LC 74-15911. (Illus.). 18p. 1980. pap. 17.95 (ISBN 0-8061-1685-4). U of Okla Pr.

Portraits of Nathaniel Hawthorne: An Iconography. Rita K. Gollin. LC 83-12155. 122p. 1984. 30.00 (ISBN 0-87580-087-4). N Ill U Pr.

Portraits of Nature: Paintings by Robert Bateman. Stanwyn G. Shetler. LC 86-22102. (Illus.). 160p. (Orig.). 1987. pap. 17.50 (ISBN 0-87474-839-9). Smithsonian.

Portraits of Nature: Paintings by Robert Bateman. Stanwyn G. Shetler. (Illus.). 1987. pap. 17.50 (ISBN 0-14-010068-7). Penguin.

Portraits of New Orleans Jazz. Raymond J. Martinez. 63p. 1971. pap. 3.95 (ISBN 0-911116-93-1). Pelican.

Portraits of Places. Henry James. LC 72-3300. (Essay Index Reprint Ser.). Repr. of 1883 ed. 19.50 (ISBN 0-8369-2910-1). Ayer Co Pubs.

Portraits of Places. Henry James. 376p. Repr. of 1884 ed. lib. bdg. 50.00 (ISBN 0-686-47013-3). Arden Lib.

Portraits of Places. Henry James. 376p. 1984. Repr. of 1883 ed. lib. bdg. 52.50 (ISBN 0-89984-719-6). Century Bookbindery.

Portraits of Plants by Jacques le Moyne de Morgues. Jacques Le Moyne De Morgues. (Illus.). 64p. 1984. pap. 13.95 (ISBN 0-905209-52-4, Pub. by Victoria & Albert Mus UK). Faber & Faber.

Portraits of Poets. Christopher Barker. Ed. by Sebastian Barker. (Illus.). 127p. 1986. pap. 16.95 (ISBN 0-85635-651-4). Carcanet.

Portraits of Power. Norman D. Greenwald. LC 73-101828. (Biography Index Reprint Ser.). 1961. 18.00 (ISBN 0-8369-8001-8). Ayer Co Pubs.

Portraits of Septimius Severus. A. M. McCann. (Memoirs: No. 30). (Illus.). 222p. 1968. 37.00 (ISBN 0-318-12328-2). Am Acad Rome.

Portraits of Septimus Severus, A.D. 193-211. A. M. McCann. 222p. 1968. 48.00x (ISBN 0-271-00452-5). Pa St U Pr.

Portraits of Success: Impressions of Silicon Valley Pioneers. Carolyn Caddes. LC 86-40032. (Illus.). 138p. 1986. 45.00 (ISBN 0-935382-56-9). Tioga Pub Co.

Portraits of Temperament. David Keirsey. 124p. 1987. pap. 9.95 (ISBN 0-317-61639-0). Prometheus Nemesis.

Portraits of Thai Politics. Jayanta Kumar Ray. 1972. 22.00x (ISBN 0-8046-8825-7, Pub. by Kennikat). Assoc Faculty Pr.

Portraits of the Artist in Contemporary Fiction. Lee T. Lemon. LC 84-22005. xx, 261p. 1985. 22.50x (ISBN 0-8032-2868-6). U of Nebr Pr.

Portraits of the Artist in Exile: Recollections of James Joyce by Europeans. Ed. by Willard Potts. LC 78-4367. (Illus.). 320p. 1979. 20.00x (ISBN 0-295-95614-3). U of Wash Pr.

Portraits of the Artist in Exile: Recollections of James Joyce by Europeans. Ed. by Willard Potts. (Illus.). 320p. 1986. pap. 7.95 (ISBN 0-15-672980-6, Harv). HarBraceJ.

Portraits of the Artist: Psychoanalysis of Creativity & Its Vicissitudes. John E. Gedo. LC 83-1693. 1983. 30.00 (ISBN 0-89862-629-3, 2629). Guilford Pr.

Portraits of the British Cinema: Sixty Glorious Years. John R. Taylor & John Kobal. (Illus.). 160p. 1985. 22.95 (ISBN 0-88162-151-X). Salem Hse Pubs.

Portraits of the Eighties. Horace G. Hutchinson. LC 74-13913. 1974. Repr. of 1920 ed. lib. bdg. 35.00 (ISBN 0-8414-4854-X). Folcroft.

Portraits of the Eighties. Horatio G. Hutchinson. LC 72-105020. (Essay Index Reprint Ser.). 1920. 26.50 (ISBN 0-8369-1441-4). Ayer Co Pubs.

Portraits of the Fifties: The Photographs of Sanford Roth. Sanford Roth & Beulah Roth. LC 87-12152. (Illus.). 128p. (Orig.). 1987. pap. 19.95 (ISBN 0-916515-29-X). Mercury Hse Inc.

Portraits of the Greeks. G. M. Richter. Ed. by R. R. Smith. LC 83-73222. (Illus.). 272p. 1984. 42.50x (ISBN 0-8014-1683-3). Cornell U Pr.

Portraits of the Irish. Elgy Gillespie. (Illus.). 96p. 1985. 27.95 (ISBN 0-86281-159-7, Pub. by Appletree Pr). Irish Bks Media.

Portraits of the Later Plantagenets. Frederick Hepburn. (Illus.). 224p. 1986. 72.00 (ISBN 0-85115-422-0, Pub. by Boydell & Brewer). Longwood Pub Group.

Portraits of the Members & Candidates for Membership of the Polit-Bureau of the Central Committee of the Communist Party of the Soviet Union. 1983. 60.00x (ISBN 0-317-57413-2, Pub. by Collets UK). State Mutual Bk.

Portraits of the New Century. Edward R. Thompson. LC 74-117853. (Essay Index Reprint Ser). 1928. 19.00 (ISBN 0-8369-1685-9). Ayer Co Pubs.

Portraits of the Nineties. Edward R. Thompson. LC 78-117854. (Essay Index Reprint Ser). 1921. 19.50 (ISBN 0-8369-1686-7). Ayer Co Pubs.

Portraits of the Nineties (George Meredith, Oscar Wilde, Aubrey Beardsley, Hardy) E. T. Raymond. 1973. lib. bdg. 35.50 (ISBN 0-8414-7412-5). Folcroft.

Portraits of the Passion. Paul G. Hansen. 1983. 6.25 (ISBN 0-89536-582-0, 1624). CSS of Ohio.

Portraits of the Seventeenth Century, Historic & Literary, 2 vols. C. A. Sainte-Beuve. Set. lib. bdg. 200.00 (ISBN 0-8490-0884-0). Gordon Pr.

Portraits of the Seventies. George W. E. Russell. LC 73-117834. (Essay Index Reprint Ser). 1916. 22.00 (ISBN 0-8369-1717-0). Ayer Co Pubs.

Portraits of the Sixties. facsimile ed. Justin McCarthy. LC 79-142661. (Essay Index Reprint Ser). Repr. of 1903 ed. 23.00 (ISBN 0-8369-2061-9). Ayer Co Pubs.

Portraits of the Sixties. Justin McCarthy. 1973. Repr. of 1903 ed. 25.00 (ISBN 0-8274-0752-1). R West.

Portraits of the Spruggins Family Arranged by Richard Sucklethumkin Spruggins Esq. Frances Countess & Walter Sneyd. (English Heritage Ser.). (Illus.). 128p. 1987. Repr. of 1829 ed. 39.00 (ISBN 0-948285-05-2). Archival Facsimiles.

Portraits of the U. S. A. U. S. A. Today Staff. (Illus.). 141p. 1986. 37.95 (ISBN 0-87491-815-4). Acropolis.

Portraits of the Whiteman. Keith H. Basso. LC 78-31535. 1979. o. p. 21.95 (ISBN 0-521-22640-6); pap. 10.95 (ISBN 0-521-29593-9). Cambridge U Pr.

Portraits of Viruses: A History of Virology. Ed. by F. Fenner & A. Gibbs. (Illus.). viii, 344p. 1988. 98.00 (ISBN 3-8055-4819-2). S Karger.

Portraits of White Racism. Ed. by D. T. Wellman. LC 76-47187. 1977. 42.50 (ISBN 0-521-21514-5); pap. 13.95 (ISBN 0-521-29179-8). Cambridge U Pr.

Portraits of Women. facsimile ed. Gamaliel Bradford. LC 75-90611. (Essay Index Reprint Ser). 1916. 18.00 (ISBN 0-8369-1247-0). Ayer Co Pubs.

Portraits of Women. facsimile ed. Gamaliel Bradford. LC 75-90611. (Essay Index Reprint Ser.). (Illus.). 202p. Repr. of 1916 ed. lib. bdg. 17.00 (ISBN 0-8290-0469-6). Irvington.

Portraits of Wordsworth. Frances Blanshard. (Illus.). 208p. 1981. Repr. of 1959 ed. lib. bdg. 30.00 (ISBN 0-89987-077-5). Darby Bks.

Portraits of Wordsworth. Frances Blanshard. 208p. 1983. Repr. of 1959 ed. lib. bdg. 45.00 (ISBN 0-8495-0616-6). Arden Lib.

Portraits of Yaroslavl. I. Fedorova & S. Iamshchikov. 1984. 145.00x (ISBN 0-317-61355-3, Pub. by Collets (UK)). State Mutual Bk.

Portraits, Political & Personal. Leon Trotsky. Ed. by George Breitman & George Saunders. LC 77-50342. (Illus.). 1977. 23.00 (ISBN 0-87348-503-3); pap. 7.95 (ISBN 0-87348-504-1). Path Pr NY.

Portraits, Prints & Writings of John Milton. John Milton. LC 73-15855. 1908. lib. bdg. 27.50 (ISBN 0-8414-6060-4). Folcroft.

Portraits: Real & Imaginary. Ernest A. Boyd. LC 77-126702. (BCL Ser. I). Repr. of 1924 ed. 9.50 (ISBN 0-404-00965-4). AMS Pr.

Portraits: Real & Imaginary. Ernest A. Boyd. LC 71-131641. 1970. Repr. of 1924 ed. 8.00x (ISBN 0-403-00528-0). Scholarly.

Portraits Souvenir: 1900-1914. Jean Cocteau. (Illus.). 216p. 1977. 22.95 (ISBN 0-686-54553-2). French & Eur.

Portraits, Tableaux, Dessins. Romaine Brooks. LC 75-12306. (Homosexuality Ser.). (Illus.). 1975. Repr. of 1952 ed. 11.00x (ISBN 0-405-07396-8). Ayer Co Pubs.

Portraits U. S. A. 1776-1976. Harold E. Dickson. (Illus.). 133p. 1976. pap. 10.00 exhibition catalogue (ISBN 0-911209-07-7). Penn St Art.

Portraits: Wooden Houses of Key West. Rev. ed. Sharon Wells. LC 79-620056. (Illus.). 64p. 1982. pap. 10.95 (ISBN 0-943528-02-X). Hist Fl Keys.

Portraiture in Prints. Constance Harris. LC 85-43579. 349p. 1987. lib. bdg. 39.95x (ISBN 0-89950-207-5). McFarland & Co.

Portraiture of Domestic Slavery in the United States. Jesse Torrey. LC 70-92446. (Illus.). 1970. Repr. of 1817 ed. 29.00x (ISBN 0-403-00184-6). Scholarly.

Portraiture of Gaius & Lucius Caesar. John Pollini. LC 87-80111. (Illus.). xvi, 133p. 1987. 75.00x (ISBN 0-8232-1127-4). Fordham.

Portraiture of Shakerism. Mary Marshall. LC 70-134420. Repr. of 1822 ed. 32.50 (ISBN 0-404-08461-3). AMS Pr.

Portrayal of the Child in Children's Literature: Proceedings of the 6th Conference of the IRSCL Bordeaux, 1983. International Research Society on Children's Literature. Ed. by Denise Escarpit. (Illus.). 392p. (Eng. & Fr.). 1985. lib. bdg. 46.00 (ISBN 3-598-10581-9). K G Saur.

Portraying Analogy. James F. Ross. LC 81-15463. (Cambridge Studies in Philosophy). (Illus.). 280p. 1982. 37.50 (ISBN 0-521-23805-6). Cambridge U Pr.

Portraying the President: The White House & the News Media. Michael B. Grossman & Martha J. Kumar. LC 80-24634. 368p. pap. 95.70 (2029914). Bks Demand UMI.

Portraying the Self: Sean O'Casey & the Art of Autobiography. Michael Kenneally. (Irish Literary Studies: No. 26). 425p. 1987. 28.50 (ISBN 0-389-20714-4). B&N Imports.

Portreath: Some Chapters in Its History. Michael Tangye. 1985. 8.00x (ISBN 0-907566-88-X, Pub. by Dyllansow & Truran). State Mutual Bk.

Ports & Harbours of Great Britain. William Finden & Edward Finden. (Illus.). 1975. Repr. of 1836 ed. 29.00 (ISBN 0-8464-0738-8). Beekman Pubs.

Ports Designated in Applications of the International Health Regulations 1969: Situation As at 1 January 1974. 1974. 1.60 (ISBN 92-4-058003-4). World Health.

Ports in the West. Ed. by Benjamin F. Gilbert & K. Jack Bauer. (Illus.). 100p. (Orig.). 1982. pap. text ed. 9.95x (ISBN 0-89745-022-1). Sunflower U Pr.

Ports, Inland Waterways & Civil Aviation. R. E. Baxter & C. Phillips. Ed. by W. F. Maunder. 1979. 85.00 (ISBN 0-08-022460-1). Pergamon.

Ports, Nineteen Eighty-Six. Ed. by Paul H. Sorenson. (Conference Proceedings Ser.). 1062p. 1986. 93.00x (ISBN 0-87262-538-9). Am Soc Civil Eng.

Ports of Call: A Study of the American Nautical Novel. Gordon Milne. (Illus.). 132p. 1987. lib. bdg. 19.75 (ISBN 0-8191-5673-6); pap. text ed. 9.75 (ISBN 0-8191-5674-4). U Pr of Amer.

Ports of Entry: Ethnic Impressions. Abelle Mason. 139p. 1984. pap. text ed. 8.00 net (ISBN 0-15-570748-5, HC). HarBraceJ.

Ports of Entry: Scientific Concerns. Abelle Mason. 208p. 1986. pap. text ed. 9.95 (ISBN 0-15-570752-3, Pub. by HC). HarBraceJ.

Ports of Entry: Social Concerns. Abelle Mason. 186p. 1985. pap. text ed. 8.00x net (ISBN 0-15-570749-3, HC). HarBraceJ.

Ports of Piscataqua. William G. Saltonstall. (Illus.). 244p. 1987. pap. 16.50 (ISBN 1-55613-040-6). Heritage Bk.

Ports '77, 2 Vols. Compiled by American Society of Civil Engineers Staff. 416p. 1977. pap. 36.00x (ISBN 0-87262-084-0). Am Soc Civil Eng.

Ports '80. Ed. by John Mascenik. LC 80-65719. 848p. 1980. pap. 50.00x (ISBN 0-87262-108-1). Am Soc Civil Eng.

Ports '83. Ed. by Kong Wong. 842p. 1983. pap. 60.00x (ISBN 0-87262-352-1). Am Soc Civil Eng.

Portsea Island Churches. Rodney Hubbuck. 1969. 39.00x (ISBN 0-317-43678-3, Pub. by City of Portsmouth). State Mutual Bk.

Portsmouth - As Others Have Seen It: Part II - 1790-1900. Margaret J. Hoad. 1973. 42.00 (ISBN 0-317-43707-0, Pub. by City of Portsmouth). State Mutual Bk.

Portsmouth: A French Gibraltar? A. Temple Patterson. 1970. 39.00x (ISBN 0-317-43680-5, Pub. by City of Portsmouth). State Mutual Bk.

Portsmouth & Sheet Turnpike Commissioners' Minute Book, 1711-1754. W. Albert & P. D. Harvey. 1974. 49.00x (ISBN 0-317-43806-9, Pub. by City of Portsmouth). State Mutual Bk.

Portsmouth & the Crimean War. Margaret J. Hoad & A. Temple Patterson. 1973. 42.00x (ISBN 0-317-43703-8, Pub. by City of Portsmouth). State Mutual Bk.

Portsmouth & the Fall of the Puritan Republic. D. Dymond. 1979. Repr. of 1971 ed. 39.00x (ISBN 0-317-43683-X, Pub. by City of Portsmouth). State Mutual Bk.

Portsmouth & the Piscataqua. Peter Randall. LC 81-66563. (Illus., Orig.). 1982. pap. 8.95 (ISBN 0-89272-087-5). Down East.

Portsmouth: Architecture in an Ohio River Town. Sergio Sanabria & Edna C. Southard. LC 82-82114. (Illus., Orig.). 1982. pap. 7.50 (ISBN 0-940784-01-7). Miami Univ Art.

Portsmouth-As Others Have Seen It: Part I-1540-1790. Margaret J. Hoad. 1972. 39.00x (ISBN 0-317-43691-0, Pub. by City of Portsmouth). State Mutual Bk.

Portsmouth at the Polls. Robert Cook. 1987. 45.00x (Pub. by K A F Brewin Bks UK); pap. 30.00x (Pub. by K A F Brewin Bks UK). State Mutual Bk.

Portsmouth Borough Gaol in the Nineteenth Century. Pat Thompson. 1980. 42.00x (ISBN 0-317-43753-4, Pub. by City of Portsmouth). State Mutual Bk.

Portsmouth-Built: Submarines of the Portsmouth Naval Shipyard. Richard E. Winslow, III. LC 84-18127. (Portsmouth Marine Society Ser.: No. 6). (Illus.). 248p. 1985. 19.95 (ISBN 0-915819-04-X). Portsmouth Marine Soc.

Portsmouth-Built Warships Fourteen Ninety-Seven to Nineteen Sixty-Seven. James Goss. 112p. 1987. 39.00x (ISBN 0-85937-278-2, Pub. by K Mason Pubns Ltd UK). State Mutual Bk.

Portsmouth During the Great French Wars, 1770-1800. Alastair Geddes. 1980. Repr. of 1970 ed. 39.00x (ISBN 0-317-43679-1, Pub. by City of Portsmouth). State Mutual Bk.

Portsmouth Emporium. Ron Brown. (Down Memory Lane, Old Hampshire Ser.). (Illus.). 80p. (Orig.). 1987. pap. 5.95 (ISBN 0-903852-43-8, Pub. by Milestone Pubns UK). Seven Hills Bks.

Portsmouth Free Mart Fair: The Last Phase, 1800-1847. John Webb. 1982. 42.00x (ISBN 0-317-43758-5, Pub. by City of Portsmouth). State Mutual Bk.

Portsmouth Guidebook: An Historical Guide for Visitors. (Illus.). 64p. 1987. pap. 3.50 (ISBN 0-903852-58-6, Pub. by Milestone Pubns UK). Seven Hills Bks.

Portsmouth (NH) Records, 1645-1656: A Transcript of the First Thirty-Five Pages of the Earliest Town Book. Frank W. Hackett. 76p. 1985. pap. 8.75 (ISBN 0-935207-17-1). DanBury Hse Bks.

Portsmouth Nineteenth-Century Literary Figures. A. Temple Patterson. 1972. 39.00x (ISBN 0-317-43689-9, Pub. by City of Portsmouth). State Mutual Bk.

Portsmouth Past & Present. Anthony Triggs. (Illus.). 95p. 1987. 9.95 (ISBN 0-903852-61-6, Pub. by Milestone Pubns UK). Seven Hills Bks.

Portsmouth Point: British Navy in Fiction, 1793-1815. C. Northcote Parkinson. 12.50 (ISBN 0-87556-509-3). Saifer.

Portsmouth Project: A Documentary View of Portsmouth, 1740-1760. Charles E. Clark & Charles W. Eastman. LC 74-18701. (Illus.). 100p. 1974. pap. 10.00x (ISBN 0-912274-46-8). NH Pub Co.

Portsmouth Railways. Edwin Course. 1972. 39.00x (ISBN 0-317-43674-0, Pub. by City of Portsmouth). State Mutual Bk.

Portsmouth: Then & Now. Anthony Triggs. (Illus.). 96p. 1987. 8.95 (ISBN 0-903852-66-7, Pub. by Milestone Pubns UK). Seven Hills Bks.

Portsmouth to Southampton. Vic Mitchell & Keith Smith. 1986. 34.75x (ISBN 0-906520-31-2, Pub. by Middleton Pr UK). State Mutual Bk.

Portsmouth's Pictorial Past. Ron Brown. (Illus.). 96p. 1987. 13.95 (ISBN 0-903852-63-2, Pub. by Milestone Pubns UK). Seven Hills Bks.

Portsmouth's Political Patterns, 1885-1945. G. J. Ashworth. 1976. 42.00x (ISBN 0-317-43719-4, Pub. by City of Portsmouth). State Mutual Bk.

Portsmouth's Water Supply, 1800-1860. Mary Hallett. 1971. 39.00x (ISBN 0-317-43685-6, Pub. by City of Portsmouth). State Mutual Bk.

Portugais Sans Peine. Albert O. Cherel. 24.95 (ISBN 0-685-11505-4); Three cassettes. 125.00. French & Eur.

Portugal. Esther Cross & Wilbur Cross. LC 85-26991. (Enchantment of the World Ser.). (Illus.). 127p. (gr. 5-6). 1986. PLB 22.60 (ISBN 0-516-02778-6). Childrens.

Portugal. David Evans. (Cadogan Guides). (Illus.). 1989. pap. price not set (ISBN 0-87106-682-3). Globe Pequot.

Portugal. Jean Giraudoux. Bd. with Combat Avec l'Image. pap. 9.50 (ISBN 0-685-33924-6). French & Eur.

Portugal. (Panorama Bks.). (Illus., Fr.). 3.95 (ISBN 0-685-11506-2). French & Eur.

Portugal. (Let's Visit Places & Peoples - - Nations, Dependencies, & Sovereignties of the World Ser.). (Illus.). (gr. 5 up). 1988. 12.95 (ISBN 0-222-01031-2). Chelsea Hse.

Portugal. 2nd, rev. ed. Ian Robertson. (Blue Guides Ser.). (Illus.). 1985. 16.95 (ISBN 0-393-30068-4). Norton.

Portugal. 3rd ed. Ian Robertson. (Blue Guides Ser.). (Illus.). 1988. pap. 18.95 (ISBN 0-393-30477-9). Norton.

Portugal. P. T. Unwin. (World Bibliography Ser.: No. 71). 269p. 1987. lib. bdg. 50.50 (ISBN 1-85109-016-9). ABC-Clio.

Portugal: A Hugo Phrase Book. (Hugo's Language Courses Ser.: No. 565). 1974. pap. 3.25 (ISBN 0-8226-0565-1). Littlefield.

Portugal & Africa, 1815-1910: A Study in Uneconomic Imperialism. R. J. Hammond. (Illus.). 1966. 37.50x (ISBN 0-8047-0296-9). Stanford U Pr.

Portugal & Galicia: Review of the Social & Political State of the Basque Provinces. 3rd ed. Henry J. Carnarvon. LC 77-87712. Repr. of 1848 ed. 27.50 (ISBN 0-404-16578-8). AMS Pr.

Portugal & Porcelain. Ilda Arez. (Illus.). 89p. 1984. pap. 105.00x (ISBN 0-317-69142-2, Pub. by Han-Shan Tang Ltd). State Mutual Bk.

Portugal & the East Through Embroidery: 16th to 18th Century Coverlets from the Museu Nacional De Arte Antiga, Lisbon. Maria H. Pinto et al. LC 81-83994. (Illus.). 40p. 1981. pap. 10.80 (ISBN 0-88397-038-4). Intl Exhibitions.

Portugal: Birth of a Democracy. Robert Harvey. LC 78-4507. 1978. 24.00x (ISBN 0-312-63184-7). St Martin.

Portugal: English Edition-Country, City & Regional Guides. (Michelin Green Guides). pap. 12.95 (ISBN 0-686-56388-3). French & Eur.

Portugal: French Edition-Country & City Guide. (Michelin Green Guides). pap. 10.95 (ISBN 0-686-56405-7). French & Eur.

Portugal in Revolution. Michael Harsgor. (Washington Papers: Vol. III, No. 32). 96p. (Orig.). 1976. pap. text ed. 7.95 (ISBN 0-8191-5987-5, Pub. by CSIS). U Pr of Amer.

Portugal in the Nineteen Eighties: Dilemmas of Democratic Consolidation. Ed. by Kenneth Maxwell. LC 85-9872. (Contributions in Political Science Ser.: No. 138). (Illus.). 268p. 1986. lib. bdg. 40.95 (ISBN 0-313-24889-3, MPG/). Greenwood.

Portugal: Message of Fatima. Pope John Paul II. 3.50 (ISBN 0-8198-5809-9); 2.50 (ISBN 0-8198-5810-2). Dghtrs St Paul.

Portugal of Salazar. Michael Derrick. (Select Bibliographies Reprint Ser). 1972. Repr. of 1938 ed. 12.50 (ISBN 0-8369-9959-2). Ayer Co Pubs.

Portugal of the Portuguese. A. F. Bell. 1976. lib. bdg. 69.95 (ISBN 0-8490-2458-7). Gordon Pr.

Portugal: Revolutionary Change in an Open Economy. Rodney J. Morrison. LC 81-2099. 184p. 1981. 26.95 (ISBN 0-86569-077-4). Auburn Hse.

Portugal Seventeen Fifteen to Eighteen Eight: Joanine, Pombaline & Rococo Portugal As Seen by British Diplomats & Traders. David Francis. (Serie A: Monagrafias, CVIII). (Illus.). 291p. 1985. 36.00 (ISBN 0-7293-0190-7, Pub. by Tamesis Bks Ltd). Longwood Pub Group.

Portugal: The Impossible Revolution. Phil Mailer. 400p. 1977. 19.95 (ISBN 0-919618-34-0, Dist. by U of Toronto Pr); pap. 9.95 (ISBN 0-919618-33-2, Dist. by U of Toronto Pr). Black Rose Bks.

Portugal: The Villages. Rosella Pace. 1977. saddlestitched in wrappers 2.00 (ISBN 0-88031-039-1). Invisible-Red Hill.

Portugal's Political Development: A Comparative Approach. Walter Opello. (Special Studies on European Politics & Society). 230p. 1985. softcover 33.00 (ISBN 0-8133-7020-5). Westview.

Portugal's Revolution: Ten Years On. Hugo G. Ferreira & Michael W. Marshall. (Illus.). 226p. 1986. 37.50 (ISBN 0-521-32204-9). Cambridge U Pr.

Portugese Americans & Spanish Americans: An Original Anthology. Ed. by Carlos E. Cortes. LC 79-6233. (Hispanics in the United States Ser.). 1981. lib. bdg. 28.50x (ISBN 0-405-13180-1). Ayer Co Pubs.

Portugese Pioneers in India: Spotlight on Medicine. P. D. Gaitonde. 1983. 27.00x (ISBN 0-8364-1052-1, Pub. by Popular Prakashan). South Asia Bks.

Portugiesisch Ohne Muhe. Albert O. Cherel. 24.95 (ISBN 0-685-11507-0); Three cassettes. 125.00. French & Eur.

Portugues Asia; Or, the History of the Discovery & Conquest of India by the Portugues. Manuel De Faria y Sousa. 1482p. Repr. of 1695 ed. text ed. 248.40x (ISBN 0-576-03499-1, Pub. by Gregg Intl Pubs England). Gregg Intl.

Portugues Contemporaneo, 2 vols. Maria I. Abreu & Clea Rameh. Incl. Vol. 1. 256p. pap. 7.95 (ISBN 0-87840-026-5); 11 cassettes 70.00 (ISBN 0-87840-048-6); 22 reel-to-reel tapes 120.00 (ISBN 0-87840-075-3); Vol. 2. 346p. pap. 7.95 (ISBN 0-87840-025-7); 10 cassettes 70.00 (ISBN 0-87840-049-4); 20 tapes 120.00 (ISBN 0-87840-076-1). LC 66-25520. 1971. Georgetown U Pr.

Portuguese. (Hugo's Phrasebooks). 128p. (Orig.). 1988. pap. 3.25 (ISBN 0-85285-092-1). Hunter Pub NY.

Portuguese: A Conversational Course. Emissora Nacional de Radiodifusao Staff. 1980. pap. text ed. 5.95 (ISBN 0-940630-09-5, T7089). Playette Corp.

Portuguese Africa & the West. William Minter. LC 73-8054. pap. 53.10 (2030763). Bks Demand UMI.

Portuguese Agriculture in Transition. Ed. by Scott R. Pearson et al. LC 86-29198. (Illus.). 288p. 1987. 27.50x (ISBN 0-8014-1954-9). Cornell U Pr.

Portuguese-American Cookbook. E. Donald Asselin. LC 66-20571. 1966. pap. 3.95 (ISBN 0-8048-0480-X). C E Tuttle.

Portuguese-Americans. Leo Pap. (Immigrant Heritage of America Ser.). 1981. lib. bdg. 17.95 (ISBN 0-8057-8417-9, Twayne). G K Hall.

Portuguese & Spanish Keyboard Music of the Eighteenth Century. Oswald Jonas. pap. 20.00 (ISBN 0-317-09732-6, 2003915). Bks Demand UMI.

Portuguese Armed Forces & the Revolution. Douglas Porch. (Publications Ser.: No. 188). (Illus.). 12.50x. Hoover Inst Pr.

Portuguese Bankers at the Court of Spain, 1626-1650. James C. Boyajian. 300p. 1983. 43.00 (ISBN 0-8135-0962-9). Rutgers U Pr.

Portuguese Brazil: The King's Plantation. James Lang. (Studies in Social Discontinuity). 1979. 24.95 (ISBN 0-12-436480-2). Acad Pr.

Portuguese Colonial in America: Belmira Nunes Lopes: The Autobiography of a Cape Verdean-American. Maria L. Nunes. Ed. by Yvette E. Miller. LC 82-6569. 215p. 1982. pap. 11.95 (ISBN 0-935480-07-2); 25.00 (ISBN 0-935480-08-0). Lat Am Lit Rev Pr.

Portuguese Country Inns & Pousadas. Karen Brown. 1988. pap. 12.95 (ISBN 0-446-38811-4, Pub. by Travel Pr). Warner Bks.

Portuguese Embassy to Japan (1644-1647) Charles R. Boxer. Bd. with Embassy of Captain Concalo de Siqueria de Souza to Japan in 1644-7. (Studies in Japanese History & Civilization). 172p. 22.00 (ISBN 0-89093-256-5). U Pubns Amer.

Portuguese-English Dictionary. Berlitz Editors. (Port. & Eng.). 1982. 5.95 (ISBN 0-02-964440-2, Berlitz). Macmillan.

Portuguese-English Dictionary. rev. ed. J. Albino Ferreira. Ed. by A. De Morais. (Port. & Eng.). 37.50 (ISBN 0-87559-029-2); thumb indexed 42.50 (ISBN 0-87559-030-6). Shalom.

Portuguese-English Dictionary. M. J. Martins. (Port. & Eng.). 25.00. Heinman.

Portuguese-English Dictionary. rev. ed. James L. Taylor. 1970. 32.50x (ISBN 0-8047-0480-5). Stanford U Pr.

Portuguese-English, English-Portuguese Dictionary. Antonio Houaics. 718p. (Orig.). 1987. pap. 9.95 (ISBN 0-87052-374-0). Hippocrene Bks.

Portuguese-English, English-Portuguese Dictionary. Antoio Houaiss & Ismael Cardim. 421p. 1988. 15.95 (ISBN 0-87052-440-2). Hippocrene Bks.

Portuguese-English, English-Portuguese Dictionary. Ed. by Porto. 15.00. Heinman.

Portuguese-English, English-Portuguese Illustrated Dictionary: The New Michaelis, 2 vols. Ed. by F. Pietzschke. (Port. & Eng.). Set. 130.00; Portuguese-English, 43rd Ed. 65.00 (ISBN 85-06-00078-5); English-Portuguese, 44th Ed. 65.00 (ISBN 85-06-00007-6). Heinman.

Portuguese-English, English-Portuguese Pocket Dictionary. 28th ed. Michaelis. pap. 17.50. Heinman.

Portuguese-English, English-Portuguese Technical Dictionary, 2 vols. Araujo A. De Pina. (Port. & Eng.). Set. 55.00; Portuguese-English. 27.50; English-Portuguese. 27.50. Heinman.

Portuguese Expedition to Abyssinia in 1541-1543. Ed. by R. S. Whiteway. Bd. with Some Contemporary Letters; Short Account of Bermudez; Correa: Extracts. (Halkuyt Society Work Series 2: Vol. 10). Repr. of 1902 ed. 60.00 (ISBN 0-8115-0332-1). Kraus Repr.

Portuguese Folk-Tales. Pederoso Consigleri. Tr. by H. Montfiro. Bd. with Researches Respecting the Books of Sindibad. Domenico Comparaetti. (Folk-Lore Society, London: vol. 9). pap. 14.00 (ISBN 0-8115-0503-0). Kraus Repr.

Portuguese Folk-Tales. Z. Consigliere-Pedroso. LC 68-57186. 1969. Repr. of 1882 ed. 10.00 (ISBN 0-405-08375-0, Blom Pubns). Ayer Co Pubs.

Portuguese for Travel Cassettepack. Berlitz Editors. 1983. 14.95 (ISBN 0-02-962790-7, Berlitz); cassette incl. Macmillan.

Portuguese Grammar. Raul D'Eca & Eric V. Greenfield. 1979. pap. 7.95 (ISBN 0-06-460185-4, CO 185, B&N Bks). Har-Row.

Portuguese-Hungarian Concise Dictionary. R. Kiraly. 728p. (Port. & Hungarian.). 1978. 49.95 (ISBN 963-05-1382-X, M-9326). French & Eur.

Portuguese in America, 590 BC-1974: A Chronology & Fact Book. Manoel D. Cardozo. LC 75-45203. (Ethnic Chronology Ser.: No. 22). 154p. 1976. lib. bdg. 8.50 (ISBN 0-379-00520-4). Oceana.

Portuguese in India, 2 Vols. Frederick C. Danvers. 1966. Set. lib. bdg. 72.00x (ISBN 0-374-92052-4, Octagon). Hippocrene Bks.

Portuguese in India, 2 vols. Frederick C. Danvers. 1986. Repr. Set. 84.00X (Pub. by Usha). South Asia Bks.

Portuguese in India, 2 vols. new ed. Frederik C. Danvers. (Illus.). 1966. 95.00x set (ISBN 0-7146-2005-X, F Cass Co). Biblio Dist.

Portuguese in India. M. N. Pearson. (New Cambridge History of India Ser.). 200p. 1988. 29.95 (ISBN 0-521-25713-1). Cambridge U Pr.

Portuguese in Rhode Island: A History. M. Rachel Cunha et al. Ed. by Patrick T. Conley. (Rhode Island Ethnic Heritage Ser.). (Illus.). 33p. (Orig.). 1985. pap. 2.75 (ISBN 0-917012-72-0). RI Pubns Soc.

Portuguese in the United States: A Bibliography. Leo Pap. LC 76-9270. (Bibliographies & Documentation Ser.). 1976. pap. 9.95 (ISBN 0-913256-21-8). Ctr Migration.

Portuguese in Three Months. Hugo. 160p. 1986. 39.95 (ISBN 0-935161-04-X); four-hour tape incl. Hunter Pub NY.

Portuguese in Three Months. (Hugo's Language Bks.). 192p. (Orig.). 1987. pap. 6.95 (ISBN 0-935161-87-2); pap. 29.95 bk. & 4 tapes. Hunter Pub NY.

Portuguese Language. J. Mattoso Camara, Jr. Tr. by Anthony J. Naro. LC 79-167939. (History & Structure of Language Ser). 208p. 1972. text ed. 22.00x (ISBN 0-226-51121-9). U of Chicago Pr.

Portuguese Letters: Love Letters of a Nun to a French Officer. 2nd ed. Donald E. Ericson. LC 86-71957. 78p. 1986. pap. 5.95 (ISBN 0-9617271-0-1). Bennett-Edwards.

Portuguese Needlework Rugs: The Time-Honored Art of Arraiolos Rugs Adapted for Modern Handcrafters. Patricia Stone. (Illus.). 128p. 1981. 22.95 (ISBN 0-914440-49-7). EPM Pubns.

Portuguese of the Arabian Coast. R. B. Serjeant. (Arab Background Ser.). 1968. 16.00x (ISBN 0-86685-027-9). Intl Bk Ctr.

Portuguese Pioneers. Edgar Prestage. xiv, 352p. 1985. Repr. of 1933 ed. lib. bdg. 49.00 (ISBN 0-932051-44-8, Pub. by Am Repr Serv). Am Biog Serv.

Portuguese Planters & British Humanitarians: The Case for S. Thome see Slavery in Portuguese Africa: Opposing Views.

Portuguese Princess & Other Stories. Tibor Dery. Tr. by Kathleen Szasz from Hungarian. 224p. 1987. pap. 9.95 (ISBN 0-8101-0766-X). Northwestern U Pr.

Portuguese Rule on the Gold Coast, 1469-1682. John Vogt. LC 77-18831. 278p. 1978. 23.00x (ISBN 0-8203-0443-3). U of Ga Pr.

Portuguese Trade with India in the 16th Century. K. S. Mathew. 1983. 24.00x (ISBN 0-8364-0996-5, Pub. by Manohar India). South Asia Bks.

Portuguese Verbs. (Hugo's Verbs Simplified Ser.). 96p. 1988. 3.95 (ISBN 0-85285-108-1). Hunter Pub NY.

Portuguese Voyages, 1498-1663. Charles D. Ley. 1977. lib. bdg. 59.95 (ISBN 0-8490-2459-5). Gordon Pr.

Portuguese Water Dog Champions, 1983-1986. Camino E. E. & B. Co. Staff & Dorothy L. Johnson. (Illus.). 49p. 1987. pap. 24.95 (ISBN 0-940808-40-4). Camino E E & B.

Portuguese Word-Formation with Suffixes. J. H. D. Allen. (LD Ser.). 1941. 13.00 (ISBN 0-527-00779-X). Kraus Repr.

Pos Activity Book. Art Fettig. LC 86-83237. (Illus.). 48p. 1984. pap. 5.95 (ISBN 0-9601334-5-3). Growth Unltd.

Pos Just Say "Yes" Activity Book. Art Fettig. LC 86-83236. (Illus.). 64p. 1987. pap. 5.95 (ISBN 0-916927-06-7). Growth Unltd.

Pos Parenting: A Guide to Greatness. Art Fettig. LC 85-80482. (Illus.). 80p. 1986. pap. 19.95 with cassette tape (ISBN 0-916927-01-6); pap. 6.95. Growth Unltd.

Posada: A Bilingual Christmas Service. 32p. (gr. 6). 1987. pap. 1.00 (ISBN 0-317-57837-5, 23-1690). Augsburg.

Posada's Mexico. Ed. by Ron Tyler. LC 79-22460. (Illus.). xii, 316p. 1979. pap. 18.00 (ISBN 0-8444-0315-6). Lib Congress.

Posada's Popular Mexican Prints. Jose G. Posada. Ed. by Robert Berdecio & Stanley Appelbaum. LC 77-178994. (Illus.). 192p. (Orig.). 1972. pap. 9.95 (ISBN 0-486-22854-1). Dover.

Pose of Happiness. Gail Mazur. LC 85-45963. 96p. 1986. 12.95 (ISBN 0-87923-615-9); pap. 8.95 (ISBN 0-87923-616-7). Godine.

Posedown! Muscletalk with the Champs. George Snyder & Rick Wayne. LC 86-30095. (Illus.). 160p. (Orig.). 1987. pap. 9.95 (ISBN 0-8069-6470-7). Sterling.

Poseidon, Apollo see Cults of the Greek States.

Posey Carpentier's Master Plan for Real Estate Selling Success. Posey Carpentier. (Illus.). 186p. 1984. 19.95 (ISBN 0-13-687716-8, Busn). P-H.

Posidonius: Vol. 1, The Fragments. Ed. by L. Edelstein & I. G. Kidd. LC 77-145609. (Classical Texts & Commentaries Ser., No. 13). 352p. 1972. 59.00 (ISBN 0-521-08046-0). Cambridge U Pr.

Posie, Positive History: Reference Guide. Compiled by A. C. Doyle. 1983. pap. 6.95 (ISBN 0-317-00636-3, Pub. by Biblio Pr GA). Prosperity & Profits.

Posie the Positive Train: Illustrated Edition. A. C. Doyle. 60p. 1983. pap. 9.95 (ISBN 0-939476-96-7, Pub. by Biblio Pr GA). Prosperity & Profits.

Posie the Positive Train: Story Edition. Bibliotheca Press Staff. Date not set. 6.95 (ISBN 0-939476-27-4, Pub. by Biblio Pr GA); pap. 4.95 (ISBN 0-939476-28-2, Pub. by Biblio Pr GA). Prosperity & Profits.

Posies of G. Gascoigne, Corrected & Augmented. George Gascoigne. LC 79-84110. (English Experience Ser.: No. 929). 532p. 1979. Repr. of 1575 ed. lib. bdg. 50.00 (ISBN 90-221-0929-1). Walter J Johnson.

Posing Techniques for Photographers & Models. Cheyenne Staff. (Illus.). 160p. 1983. 27.50 (ISBN 0-8174-4525-0, Amphoto); pap. 18.95 (ISBN 0-8174-5544-2). Watson-Guptill.

Posing: The Art of Hardcore Physique Display. Robert Kennedy. (Illus.). 128p. (Orig.). 1988. pap. 7.95 (ISBN 0-8069-6420-0). Sterling.

Position & Change. Lars Lindahl. Tr. by Paul Needham from Swedish. (Synthese Library: No. 112). 1977. lib. bdg. 45.00 (ISBN 90-277-0787-1, Pub. by Reidel Holland). Kluwer Academic.

Position & Rights of a Bona Fide Purchaser for Value of Goods Improperly Obtained. J. Walter Jones. 128p. 1987. Repr. of 1921 ed. lib. bdg. 25.00x (ISBN 0-8377-2303-5). Rothman.

Position & the Nature of Personhood: An Approach to the Understanding of Persons. Larry Cochran. LC 84-12852. (Contributions in Psychology Ser.: No. 5). xiv, 191p. 1985. lib. bdg. 35.00 (ISBN 0-313-24633-5, CPN/). Greenwood.

Position at Noon. Eric Linklater. 1983. 30.00x (ISBN 0-904265-38-2, Pub. by Macdonald Pub UK). State Mutual Bk.

Position Classification Specialist. Jack Rudman. (Career Examination Ser.: C-601). (Cloth bdg. avail. on request). pap. 16.00 (ISBN 0-8373-0601-9). Natl Learning.

Position Descriptions in Special Libraries: A Collection of Examples. Ed. by Barbara Ivantcho. LC 83-10168. 160p. 1983. 16.75 (ISBN 0-87111-303-1). SLA.

Position Etudes. Shinichi Suzuki. (Suzuki Violin School Ser.). 32p. (Japanese.). (gr. k-12). 1973. pap. text ed. 5.95 (ISBN 0-87487-096-8, Suzuki Method). Birch Tree Gr.

Position in Law of Women: A Concise & Comprehensive Treatise on the Position of Women at Common Law as Modified by the Doctrines of Equity & by Recent Legislation, Together with the Married Women's Property Acts, 1870, 1874, 1882: The Rules of the Supreme Court, 1883, Relating to Taking Acknowledgments & the Postal Regulations, 1883, Affecting Married Women. Thomas Barrett-Lennard. xxviii, 181p. 1983. Repr. of 1883 ed. lib. bdg. 25.00x (ISBN 0-8377-0336-0). Rothman.

Position of African Countries Regarding the Ratification & Implementation of International Labour Standards: Report of the Director General, Pt. 2. 1983. pap. text ed. 8.75 (ISBN 92-2-103527-1, ILO271, ILO). UNIPUB.

Position of America & Other Essays. facs. ed. Alfonso Reyes. Tr. by Harriet De Onis. LC 77-142690. (Essay Index Reprint Ser). 1950. 17.00 (ISBN 0-8369-2067-8). Ayer Co Pubs.

Position of Bernard Shaw in European Drama & Philosophy. Martin Ellehauge. LC 68-853. 1970. Repr. of 1931 ed. 75.00x (ISBN 0-8383-0659-4). Haskell.

Position of Christianity in the United States, in Its Relations with Our Political Institutions, & Specially with Reference to Religious Instruction in the Public Schools. Stephen Colwell. LC 78-38444. (Religion in America, Ser. 2). 180p. 1972. Repr. of 1854 ed. 17.00 (ISBN 0-405-04063-6). Ayer Co Pubs.

Position of Duchamp's Glass in the Development of His Art. Lawrence D. Steefel, Jr. LC 76-23647. (Outstanding Dissertations in the Fine Arts Ser.). 489p. 1977. lib. bdg. 76.00 (ISBN 0-8240-2730-2). Garland Pub.

Position of Foreign Corporations in American Constitutional Law: A Contribution to the History & Theory of Juristic Persons in Anglo-American Law. Gerard C. Henderson. LC 18-12331. (Harvard Studies in Jurisprudence Ser.: Vol.2). xix, 199p. 1979. Repr. of 1918 ed. lib. bdg. 40.00 (ISBN 0-89941-137-1). W S Hein.

Position of Foreign States Before National Courts, Chiefly in Continental Europe. E. W. Allen. LC 33-31666. Repr. of 1933 ed. 32.00 (ISBN 0-527-01200-9). Kraus Repr.

Position of Man & the Growth of the Age of Reason in Europe, 2 vols. William c. Davenport. (Illus.). 1986. Set. 227.50 (ISBN 0-89266-549-1). Am Classical Coll Pr.

Position of Modern Science on the Beginning of Human Life. Scientists for Life. 45p. (Orig.). 1983. pap. 1.25 (ISBN 0-937930-02-4). Sun Life.

Position of Pobindolol: A New Betw-Blocker, No. 106. Ed. by P. A. Van Zwieten. (Proceedings of a Round-Table Discussion). 1987. pap. 37.50 (ISBN 0-905958-36-5, Pub. by Royal Society of Medicine Services Ltd). Longwood Pub Group.

Position of Possessive & Demonstrative Adjectives in the Noctes Atticae of Aulus Gellius. Edward Yoder. (LD). 1928. pap. 16.00 (ISBN 0-527-00748-X). Kraus Repr.

Position of Romani in Indo-Aryan. Ralph L. Turner. 1977. lib. bdg. 59.95 (ISBN 0-8490-2460-9). Gordon Pr.

Position of the Body. Richard Stern. 195p. 1986. 29.95x (ISBN 0-8101-0730-9); pap. 12.95 (ISBN 0-8101-0731-7). Northwestern U Pr.

Position of the Charleston Dialect see Vocabulary of Marble Playing.

Position of the Laborer in a System of Nationalism. Edgar S. Furniss. LC 58-3121. 1957. Repr. of 1920 ed. 29.50x (ISBN 0-678-00093-X). Kelley.

Position of the Polynesian Languages within the (Austronesian Malayo-Polynesian) Language Family. George W. Grace. LC 59-7612. (Indiana University Publications in Anthropology & Linguistics Memoir: No. 16). pap. 21.30 (ISBN 0-317-27811-8, 2015201). Bks Demand UMI.

Position of the "Roode En Witte Roos" in the Saga of "King Richard Third". Lambert Van Den Bos. Ed. by Oscar J. Campbell. LC 72-131494. Repr. of 1919 ed. 16.50 (ISBN 0-404-01375-9). AMS Pr.

Position of Trust. Roy Hart. 336p. 1985. 15.95 (ISBN 0-312-63186-3). St Martin.

Position of Trust. Roy Hart. 208p. 1987. pap. 3.95 (ISBN 0-380-70278-9). Avon.

Position of Trust. Roy Hart. 240p. 1985. 24.95x (ISBN 0-7090-2178-X, Pub. by R Hale Ltd UK). State Mutual Bk.

Position of Woman in Early China: According to the Lieh Nu Chuan, "The Biographies of Eminent Chinese Women". Albert R. O'Hara. LC 79-2949. 301p. 1984. Repr. of 1945 ed. 22.75 (ISBN 0-8305-0112-6). Hyperion Conn.

Position of Women As Considered by Representative American Authors Since 1800. C. B. Guest. 59.95 (ISBN 0-8490-0885-9). Gordon Pr.

Position of Women in Contemporary France. Francis I. Clark. LC 79-5210. 250p. 1982. Repr. of 1937 ed. 21.60 (ISBN 0-8305-0101-0). Hyperion Conn.

Position of Women in Hindu Civilization. A. S. Altekar. 1978. 16.95 (ISBN 0-89684-273-8); pap. 11.95 (ISBN 0-89684-485-4). Orient Bk Dist.

Position of Women in Hindu Civilization. A. S. Altekar. 384p. 1978. 17.95. Asia Bk Corp.

Position of Women in Hindu Law. Dwarka Mitter. 707p. 1984. Repr. of 1913 ed. text ed. 60.00x (ISBN 0-86590-285-2, Pub. by Inter India Pubns India). Apt Bks.

Position of Women in Labor & Social Security Law, Vol. 111. International Society of Labor Law & Social Security. 38.00 (0429). BNA.

Position of Women in the U. S. S. R. facs. ed. George N. Serebrennikov. LC 72-137384. (Select Bibliographies Reprint Ser.). 1937. 16.00 (ISBN 0-8369-5585-4). Ayer Co Pubs.

Position Politique Du Surrealisme. Andre Breton. (La Bibliotheque Volante). pap. 9.95 (ISBN 0-685-37238-3). French & Eur.

Position-Sensitive Detection of Thermal Neutrons. Ed. by Pierre Convert & J. Bruce Forsyth. 1984. 52.50 (ISBN 0-12-186180-5). Acad Pr.

Position Sensors & Automation Aids Market. 211p. 1984. 1550.00 (ISBN 0-86621-241-8, A1311). Frost & Sullivan.

Position Sensors Market. Frost & Sullivan, Inc. Staff. 255p. 1986. 2300.00 (ISBN 0-86621-748-7, E818). Frost & Sullivan.

Positional Astronomy & Astro-Navigation Made Easy: A New Approach Using the Pocket Calculator. H. R. Mills. LC 77-13142. 267p. 1978. 44.95x (ISBN 0-470-99324-3). Halsted Pr.

Positional Chess. Shaun Talbot. (Illus.). 102p. 1983. 12.50 (ISBN 0-04-794017-4). Unwin Hyman.

Positional Controls in Plant Development. Ed. by P. W. Barlow & D. J. Carr. LC 83-7393. 350p. 1984. 90.00 (ISBN 0-521-25406-X). Cambridge U Pr.

Positional Welding. Richard Hunter. (Series 904B). (Orig.). 1977. pap. 7.00 wkbk. (ISBN 0-8064-0375-6, 904B); audio visual pkg. 279.00 (ISBN 0-8064-0376-4). Bergwall.

Positioneering. Charles N. Aronson. (Illus.). 347p. 1969. 20.00 (ISBN 0-915736-01-2). C N Aronson.

Positioning in Anesthesia & Surgery. John T. Martin. LC 77-16972. 1978. text ed. write for info. (ISBN 0-7216-6133-5). Saunders.

Positioning in Anesthesia & Surgery. 2nd ed. John T. Martin. (Illus.). 368p. 1987. 46.95 (ISBN 0-03-012797-1). Saunders.

Positioning: The Battle for Your Mind. Al Ries & Jack Trout. 224p. 1981. text ed. 19.95 (ISBN 0-07-065263-5). McGraw.

Positioning: The Battle for Your Mind. Jack Trout & Al Ries. 256p. 1986. pap. 4.50 (ISBN 0-446-32897-9). Warner Bks.

Positioning: The Battle for Your Mind. rev. ed. Jack Trout & Al Ries. Date not set. pap. 4.95 (ISBN 0-446-34794-9). Warner Bks.

Positioning the Client with Central Nervous System Deficits: The Wheelchair & Other Adapted Equipment. 2nd, rev ed. Adrienne F. Bergen & Cheryl Colangelo. (Illus.). 1985. pap. text ed. 29.95x (ISBN 0-911681-02-7). Valhalla Rehab.

Positioning the Handicapped Child for Function: A Guide to Evaluate & Prescribe Equipment for the Child with Central Nervous System Dysfunction. 2nd, rev. ed. Diane E. Ward. (Illus.). 137p. (Orig.). 1984. pap. text ed. 20.00 (ISBN 0-9614029-0-3). Phoenix Chicago.

Positioning the Surgical Patient. J. M. Anderton et al. (Illus.). 128p. 1988. pap. text ed. 19.95 (ISBN 0-407-01220-6). Butterworth.

Positioning the Surgical Patient: Assessment & Evaluation. (Modular Independent Learning System Ser.). 1987. 15.00 (ISBN 0-939583-25-9). Assn Oper Rm Nurses.

Positioning to Win: Planning & Executing the Superior Proposal. J. M. Beveridge & E. J. Velton. LC 81-66638. (Illus.). 256p. 1982. 29.95 (ISBN 0-8019-7112-8). Chilton.

Positions. Jacques Derrida. Tr. by Alan Bass from Fr. LC 80-17620. 1981. 11.95x (ISBN 0-226-14332-5); pap. 5.00x (ISBN 0-226-14331-7). U of Chicago Pr.

Positions see Let's Learn Set.

Positions & Presuppositions in Science Fiction. Darko Suvin. LC 87-18352. 300p. 1988. 26.00x (ISBN 0-87338-356-7). Kent St U Pr.

Positions et Propositions, 2 vols. Paul Claudel. 1928. Vol. 1. pap. 8.95 (ISBN 0-686-54422-6); Vol. 2. pap. 5.95 (ISBN 0-686-54423-4). French & Eur.

Positions: Under, on, Beside, in, Behind. Janet Dellosa et al. (Let's Learn Ser.). (Illus.). 32p. (ps-1). 1983. pap. 1.98 (ISBN 0-88724-007-0, CD-7008). Carson-Dellos.

Positions Wherein Those Circumstances Be Examined Necessarie for the Training up of Children. Richard Mulcaster. LC 70-26207. (English Experience Ser.: No. 339). 304p. 1971. Repr. of 1581 ed. 35.00 (ISBN 90-221-0339-0). Walter J Johnson.

Positions with White Roses. Ursule Molinaro. LC 82-24916. 104p. 1983. 9.95 (ISBN 0-914232-58-4); ltd. ed. 25.00 (ISBN 0-914232-59-2). McPherson & Co.

Positive Accounting Theory. Ross L. Watts & Jerold L. Zimmerman. (Illus.). 432p. 1986. text ed. write for info. (ISBN 0-13-686171-7). P-H.

Positive Action for Women. Paddy Stamp & Sadie Robarts. 1986. 20.00x (ISBN 0-946088-25-X, Pub. by NCCL UK). State Mutual Bk.

Positive Addiction. William Glasser. LC 75-15305. (Illus.). 176p. 1976. 12.45i (ISBN 0-06-011558-0, HarpT). Har-Row.

Positive Addiction. William Glasser. LC 84-48643. 176p. 1985. pap. 7.95 (ISBN 0-06-091249-9, CN 1249, PL). Har-Row.

Positive Adjustment in Manpower & Social Policies. OECD Staff. 88p. (Orig.). 1984. pap. 15.00x (ISBN 92-64-12564-7). OECD.

Positive Adjustment Policies in the Dairy Sector. OECD. (Agricultural Products & Markets Ser.). 104p. (Orig.). 1984. pap. 11.00x (ISBN 92-64-12515-9). OECD.

Positive Adjustment Policies: Managing Structural Change. OECD Staff. 116p. (Orig.). 1983. pap. 12.50x (ISBN 92-64-12402-0). OECD.

Positive Analysis of Social Phenomena. August Comte. (The Essential Library of the Great Philosophers). (Illus.). 129p. (Fr.). 1981. 127.75 (ISBN 0-89901-027-X). Found Class Reprints.

Positive Analysis of Social Phenomena. August Comte. (Illus.). 117p. 1983. 154.50 (ISBN 0-89266-426-6). Am Classical Coll Pr.

Positive & Negative Symptoms in Psychosis Description, Research & Futute Directions. Ed. by Philip D. Harvey & Elaine Walker. 352p. 1987. text ed. 29.95 (ISBN 0-89859-880-X). L Erlbaum Assocs.

Positive & the Preventive Check: A Study of the Rate of Growth of Pre-Industrial Populations. Per G. Ohlin. Ed. by Stuart Bruchey. LC 80-2819. (Dissertations in European Economic History II). (Illus.). 1981. lib. bdg. 49.50x (ISBN 0-405-14003-7). Ayer Co Pubs.

Positive Application of Racial Qualities: Color As a Growth Factor. Robert E. Birdsong. (Aquarian Academy Monograph: Ser. F, No. 6). 1980. pap. 1.50 (ISBN 0-917108-31-0). Sirius Bks.

Positive Approach to Golf. Carol Johnson & Ann C. Johnstone. (Illus.). 170p. 1975. pap. text ed. write for info (ISBN 0-394-34889-3, RanC). Random.

Positive Approach to Head Injury: Guidelines for Professionals & Families. Beverly Slater. LC 86-42635. 200p. 1987. 24.95 (ISBN 0-943432-85-5). Slack Inc.

Positive Approach to the International Economic Order, 2 Pts. Incl. Pt. 2. Nontrade Issues. Alasdair MacBean & V. N. Balasubramanyam. 1980. 5.00 (ISBN 0-902594-37-0); Trade & Structural Adjustment. 82p. 1978. 3.00 (ISBN 0-902594-33-8). (British North American Committee Ser.). Natl Planning.

Positive Approaches to Classroom Discipline. Betty B. Martin & Joan Quilling. 1981. 4.00 (ISBN 0-911365-19-2, A261-08452). Home Econ Educ.

Positive Approaches to Living with End Stage Renal Disease: Psychosocial & Thanatalogic Aspects. Ed. by Michael A. Hardy. LC 85-28334. 239p. 1986. 40.95 (ISBN 0-275-92019-4, C2019). Praeger.

Positive Attitudes for the Physically Challenged. Hoyt Anderson. 20p. (Orig.). 1986. pap. 3.95 (ISBN 0-937743-00-3). Successful Living.

Positive Awareness (Experiential Extension), Purposeful Relaxation, & (Differentiated Psychophysiological) "Feeling" States, Set-PA. Russell E. Mason. 1975. pap. 30.00x tape (ISBN 0-89533-012-1); tape-1a, t-3, t-4 incl., Notes, Brief Outlines 2, Feeling Training. F I Comm.

Positive Background of Hindu Sociology, 2 vols. Benoy K. Sarkar. LC 73-3807. (Sacred Books of the Hindus: Nos. 16 & 25). Repr. of 1926 ed. Set. 74.50 (ISBN 0-404-57839-X). AMS Pr.

Positive Background of Hindu Sociology: Introduction to Hindu Positivism. Benny K. Sarkar. 697p. 1986. 36.00 (ISBN 0-89581-819-1, Pub. by Motilal Banarsidass). South Asia Bks.

Positive Background of Hindu Sociology: Introduction to Hindu Positivism. Benoy K. Sarkar. LC 74-17338. (Sacred Books of the Hindus: 32). Repr. of 1937 ed. 74.50 (ISBN 0-404-57850-0). AMS Pr.

Positive Behavior Management: A Manual for Teachers. P. L. Cheesman & P. E. Watts. 140p. 1985. 23.50 (ISBN 0-89397-227-4); pap. 14.50 (ISBN 0-89397-228-2). Nichols Pub.

Positive Behavior Patterns. Robert E. Birdsong. (Aquarian Academy Monography: Suppl. Lecture No. 2). 1978. pap. text ed. 1.00 (ISBN 0-917108-21-3). Sirius Bks.

Positive Career Paths: A Self-Directed Career Counseling Guide. Marc Landy. LC 86-91285. 252p. 1987. pap. 14.95 (ISBN 0-9617077-0-4). Landy Assocs.

Positive Christian Living. J. J. Turner. pap. 4.25 (ISBN 0-89137-316-0). Quality Pubns.

Positive Classroom Discipline. Fredric H. Jones. 384p. 1987. text ed. 22.95 (ISBN 0-07-032782-3). McGraw.

Positive Criminology. Ed. by Michael R. Gottfredson & Travis Hirschi. 192p. 1987. text ed. 29.95 (ISBN 0-8039-2911-0). Sage.

Positive Declarer's Play. Terence Reese & Julian Pottage. (Master Bridge Ser.). 128p. 1986. 18.95 (ISBN 0-575-03838-1, Pub. by Gollancz England); pap. 12.95 (ISBN 0-575-03839-X, Pub. by Gollancz England). David & Charles.

Positive Defence. Terence Reese & Julian Pottage. (Master Bridge Ser.). 128p. 1985. 18.95 (ISBN 0-575-03562-5, Pub. by Gollancz England); (Pub. by Gollancz England). David & Charles.

Positive Definite Kernels, Continuous Tensor Products, & Central Limit Theorems of Probability Theory. K. R. Parthasarathy & K. Schmidt. LC 72-85400. (Lecture Notes in Mathematics: Vol. 272). 107p. 1972. pap. 13.00 (ISBN 0-387-05908-3). Springer-Verlag.

Positive Discipline. Didactic Systems Staff. (Study Units Ser.). 1978. pap. 9.00 (ISBN 0-89401-122-7). Didactic Syst.

Positive Discipline. Jane Nelsen. 1987. pap. 6.95 (ISBN 0-345-34856-7). Ballantine.

Positive Discipline: A Pocketful of Ideas. William W. Purkey & David B. Strahan. 49p. 1986. 6.00 (ISBN 0-317-61699-4). Natl Middle Schl.

Positive Discipline: Teaching Children Self-Discipline, Responsibility, Cooperation & Problem-Solving Skills. 2nd ed. Jane Nelsen. LC 85-63354. (Illus.). 196p. 1985. pap. 7.95 (ISBN 0-9606896-1-3). Sunrise Pr.

Positive Discrimination & Social Justice. John Edwards. 220p. 1987. pap. text ed. 18.95 (ISBN 0-422-78990-9, 1156, Pub. by Tavistock England). Routledge Chapman & Hall.

Positive Egocentricity: Aquarian Academy Monograph. Robert E. Birdsong. (Aquarian Academy Monograph). 1978. pap. 1.25x (ISBN 0-917108-23-X). Sirius Bks.

Positive Evolution of Religion. facs. ed. Frederic Harrison. LC 74-142641. (Essay Index Reprint Ser). 1913. 18.00 (ISBN 0-8369-2053-8). Ayer Co Pubs.

Positive Experiences in Constructing & Operating Nuclear Power Plants Worldwide. Atomic Industrial Forum Staff. (Technical & Economic Reports: Construction). 76p. 1984. 100.00 (ISBN 0-318-02250-8). US Coun Energy Awareness.

Positive Family. Arvella Schuller. 1983. pap. 2.75 (ISBN 0-8007-8474-X, Spire Bks). Revell.

Positive Family. Arvella Schuller. 144p. 1984. pap. 2.95 (ISBN 0-515-08091-8). Jove Pubns.

Positive Family Therapy. N. Peseschkian. Tr. by R. Rohlfing from Ger. 340p. 1985. pap. 14.00 (ISBN 0-387-15768-9). Springer-Verlag.

Positive Feedback in Natural Systems. D. L. Deangelis et al. (Biomathematics Ser.: Vol. 15). (Illus.). 305p. 1986. 63.00 (ISBN 0-387-15942-8). Springer-Verlag.

Positive Film Make-Up. cancelled (ISBN 0-318-02628-7). Print Indus Am.

Positive Flying. William Guinther & Richard L. Taylor. 1983. 18.95 (ISBN 0-02-546570-8). Macmillan.

Positive Health. Ed. by Paul A. Lawrence. Jim Moody. LC 84-90564. (Illus.). 84p. 1984. pap. 5.95 (ISBN 0-938034-08-1). Pal Pr.

Possibilities & Limits of Regulation in Transport Policy. OECD Staff. (ECMT Round Table Ser.: No. 62). 120p. 1984. pap. 12.00 (ISBN 92-821-1087-7). OECD.
Possibilities Lifestyle Total Employee Wellness Program. Date not set. Lifestyle Possibility Sampler. 795.00; Trainer Sampler. 375.00; Self Help Sampler. 150.00. Human Res Dev Pr.
Possibilities of Charting Modern Life. S. Erixon. 1970. 42.00 (ISBN 0-08-013308-8). Pergamon.
Possibilities of Order: Cleanth Brooks & His Work. Lewis P. Simpson. LC 75-18046. xxiv, 254p. 1976. 30.00 (ISBN 0-8071-0165-6). La State U Pr.
Possibilities of Organization. Barry Oshry. 178p. (Orig.). 1986. pap. text ed. 18.95 (ISBN 0-910411-10-7). Power & Sys.
Possibilities of Prayer. E. M. Bounds. (Direction Bks). 1979. pap. 3.95 (ISBN 0-8010-0757-7). Baker Bk.
Possibilities of Processing & Marketing of Products Made From Antartic Krill. E. Budzinski et al. (FAO Fisheries Technical Paper: No. 268). (Illus.). 46p. (Orig.). 1986. pap. text ed. 7.50 (ISBN 92-5-102344-1, F2872, FAO). UNIPUB.
Possibilities of the Improvement of Nitrogen Fertilizer Efficiency in Rice Production. D. H. Parish. (IFDC Paper Sers. P-1). 1980. 4.00 (ISBN 0-88090-061-X). Intl Fertilizer.
Possibilities of the Negro in Symposium. facsimile ed. LC 75-173610. (Black Heritage Library Collection). Repr. of 1904 ed. 14.00 (ISBN 0-8369-8902-3). Ayer Co Pubs.
Possibility. Scott M. Buchanan. (Midway Reprint Ser). vi, 198p. 1975. pap. text ed. 5.45x (ISBN 0-226-07822-1). U of Chicago Pr.
Possibility & Necessity, Vols. I & II. Jean Piaget. Tr. by Feider from Fr. LC 86-7052. 1987. 50.00 set (ISBN 0-8166-1368-0); Vol. I. 25.00 (ISBN 0-8166-1370-2); Vol. II. 25.00 (ISBN 0-8166-1372-9). U of Minn Pr.
Possibility: Lectures. University Of California Philosophical Union - 1933. (Publications in Philosophy: Vol. 17). 1933. 20.00 (ISBN 0-384-07100-7). Johnson Repr.
Possibility of a Universal Language see Needed Words.
Possibility of Altruism. Thomas Nagel. LC 78-4323. 1979. 18.00x (ISBN 0-691-07231-0); pap. 9.50x (ISBN 0-691-02002-7). Princeton U Pr.
Possibility of an All-Knowing God. Jonathan L. Kvanvig. LC 86-6465. 224p. 1986. 27.50 (ISBN 0-312-63195-2). St Martin.
Possibility of Being: Selected Poems. Rainer M. Rilke. Tr. by J. B. Leishman from Ger. LC 77-4656. 1977. pap. 4.95 (ISBN 0-8112-0651-3, NDP436). New Directions.
Possibility of Cooperation. rev. ed. Michael Taylor. (Studies in Rationality & Social Change). 180p. 1987. 39.50 (ISBN 0-521-32793-8); pap. 12.95 (ISBN 0-521-33990-1). Cambridge U Pr.
Possibility of God. James F. Drane. (Quality Paperback Ser.: No. 321). 194p. 1976. pap. 5.95 (ISBN 0-8226-0321-7). Littlefield.
Possibility of Knowledge: Nozick & His Critics. Ed. by Steven Luper-Foy. 352p. 1987. 35.95 (ISBN 0-8476-7446-0); pap. 14.95 (ISBN 0-8476-7447-9). Rowman.
Possibility of Politics: A Study in the Political Economy of the Welfare State. Stein Ringen. 316p. 1987. 59.00 (ISBN 0-19-828574-4). Oxford U Pr.
Possibility of Prediction. D. H. Mellor. (Philosophical Lectures (Henriette Hertz Trust)). 1979. pap. 5.50 (ISBN 0-85672-200-6, Pub. by British Acad). Longwood Pub Group.
Possibility of the Aesthetic Experience. Ed. by M. H. Mitias. 1986. lib. bdg. 47.50 (ISBN 90-247-3278-6, Pub. by Martinus Nijhoff Netherlands). Kluwer Academic.
Possibility of Universal Moral Judgement in Existential Ethics: A Critical Analysis of the Phenomenology of Moral Experience According to Jean-Paul Sartre. Joseph Kariuki. (European University Studies: Series 20, Philosophy: Vol. 87). 363p. 1981. 37.95 (ISBN 3-261-04962-6). P Lang Pubs.
Possibility of Weakness of Will. Robert Dunn. LC 85-24784. 192p. 1986. lib. bdg. 25.00 (ISBN 0-915145-99-5); pap. 14.50 (ISBN 0-915145-98-7). Hackett Pub.
Possibility Theory: An Approach to Computerized Processing of Uncertainty. D. Dubois & H. Prade. LC 87-32179. (Illus.). 280p. 1988. 39.50x (ISBN 0-306-42520-3, Plenum Pr). Plenum Pub.
Possible & the Actual. Francois Jacob. 1982. pap. 3.96 (ISBN 0-394-70671-4). Pantheon.
Possible & the Actual. Francois Jacob. LC 81-16452. (Jessie & John Danz Lecture Ser.). 80p. 1982. 10.00x (ISBN 0-295-95888-X). U of Wash Pr.
Possible & the Actual: Readings in the Metaphysics of Modality. Intro. by Michael J. Loux. LC 79-7618. 336p. 1979. 39.95x (ISBN 0-8014-1238-2); pap. 10.95x (ISBN 0-8014-9178-9). Cornell U Pr.
Possible Begetter of the Old English Beowulf & Widsith. Albert S. Cook. (Beowulf & Literature of the Anlgo-Saxons Ser., No. 2). 1970. pap. 22.95x (ISBN 0-8383-0018-9). Haskell.
Possible Cinema: The Films of Alain Tanner. Jim Leach. LC 84-10610. 220p. 1984. 16.50 (ISBN 0-8108-1714-4). Scarecrow.
Possible Death on the Highway: Attempted Murder or an Accident, Example of a Logical Map. (Analysis Ser.: No. 11). 1983. pap. 12.50 (ISBN 0-686-42847-1, 0686428463). Inst Analysis.
Possible Dream. Paul Conn. 1982. pap. 3.50 (ISBN 0-425-10566-0). Berkley Pub.
Possible Dream: Toward Understanding the Black Experience. Peter A. Angeles. (Orig.). 1971. pap. 1.95 (ISBN 0-377-01211-4). Friendship Pr.
Possible Future Oil Provinces of the United States & Canada: Proceedings of the American Association of Petroleum Geologists, 26th, Houston, 1941. American Association of Petroleum Geologists Staff. Ed. by A. I. Levorsen. LC 41-23448. pap. 40.00 (ISBN 0-317-29056-8, 2023744). Bks Demand UMI.
Possible Human: A Course in Extending Your Physical, Mental, & Creative Abilities. Jean Houston. LC 82-17070. (Illus.). 272p. 1982. 16.95 (ISBN 0-87477-219-2); pap. 10.95 (ISBN 0-87477-218-4). J P Tarcher.
Possible Influence of Montaigne's Essais on Descartes' Treatise on the Passions. Michael G. Paulson. 138p. (Orig.). 1988. lib. bdg. 22.50 (ISBN 0-8191-7027-5); pap. text ed. 10.25 (ISBN 0-8191-7028-3). U Pr of Amer.
Possible She. Susan Jacoby. 160p. 1980. pap. 2.50 (ISBN 0-345-28735-5). Ballantine.
Possible She. Susan Jacoby. 208p. 1979. 8.95 (ISBN 0-374-23645-3). FS&G.
Possible Solution of the Number Series on Pages Fifty-One to Fifty-Eight of the Dresden Codex. C. E. Guthe. (Harvard University Peabody Museum of Archaeology & Ethnology Papers). pap. 15.00 (ISBN 0-527-01207-6). Kraus Repr.
Possible Solutions. Krzysztof Ostaszewski. Tr. by Wojtek Stelmaszynski from Pol. (Translation Ser.: Vol. 1). 80p. (Orig.). 1987. pap. 8.00 (ISBN 0-936993-16-2, 87-11-X). Europa Media.
Possible Vision: Holistic New Age Education. George A. Jones. LC 80-52612. 104p. 1981. pap. 5.00 (ISBN 0-917610-02-4). Peacehaven.
Possible Worlds: An Introduction to Logic & Its Philosophy. Raymond Bradley & Norman Swartz. LC 79-51037. (Illus.). 424p. 1979. lib. bdg. 30.00 (ISBN 0-915144-60-3); pap. text ed. 14.50 (ISBN 0-915144-59-X). Hackett Pub.
Possible Worlds & Other Essays. J. B. Haldane. 1927. 35.00 (ISBN 0-8274-4214-9). R West.
Possible Worlds: And Other Papers. facsimile ed. John B. Haldane. LC 75-167351. (Essay Index Reprint Ser). Repr. of 1928 ed. 18.00 (ISBN 0-8369-2452-5). Ayer Co Pubs.
Posson Jone & Pere Raphael see Collected Works.
Possum & Ole Ez in the Public Eye: Contemporaries & Peers on T. S. Eliot & Ezra Pound. Ed. by Burton Raffel. LC 84-24593. 143p. 1985. 21.50 (ISBN 0-208-02057-8, Archon). Shoe String.
Possum, & Other Receits for the Recovery of "Southern" Being. Marion Montgomery. LC 86-19309. (Mercer University Lamar Memorial Lectures). 176p. 1987. 16.00x (ISBN 0-8203-0926-5). U of Ga Pr.
Possum Crest's Greatest Christmas Show. Marilyn Walton. LC 83-7354. (Celebration Bks.). (Illus.). 32p. (gr. k-4). 1983. PLB 14.25 (ISBN 0-940742-19-5). Raintree Pubs.
'Possum Hunter & the Tar Heels: A Historical Novel of Post Civil War Days. James S. Willoughby. LC 87-72027. 450p. (Orig.). 1988. 17.95 (ISBN 0-944161-01-4); pap. 9.95 (ISBN 0-944161-00-6). Tall Timber Pub.
Possum Huts. Helga Tacreiter & Walter Hankinson. LC 84-70691. (Illus.). 68p. 1984. pap. 6.95 (ISBN 0-916949-01-X). Amaya Pub.
Possum in the House. Kiersten Jensen. Ed. by Rhoda Sherwood. LC 88-42910. (Illus.). 32p. (ps-1). 1988. PLB 11.25 (ISBN 1-55532-933-0). Stevens Inc.
Possum Magic. Mem Fox. 32p. (ps-3). 1987. 11.95 (ISBN 0-687-31732-0). Abingdon.
Post- to Neo: The Art World of the 1980s. Calvin Tomkins. LC 88-4481. 1988. 19.95 (ISBN 0-8050-0663-X). H Holt & Co.
Post Accident Debris Cooling: Proceedings of the Fifth Post Accident Heat Removal Information Exchange Meeting, 1982, Nuclear Research Center Karlsruhe. Ed. by U. Mueller & C. Guenther. (Illus.). 364p. (Orig.). 1983. text ed. 30.00x (ISBN 3-7650-2034-6). Sheridan.
Post Accident Heat Removal. V. Coen & H. Holtbecker. (European Applied Research Reports Special Topics Ser.). 402p. 1980. pap. text ed. 165.00 (ISBN 3-7186-0025-0). Harwood Academic.
Post-Accident Procedures for Chemicals & Propellants. Deborah K. Shaver & Robert L. Berkowitz. LC 84-4123. (Pollution Technology Review Ser.: No. 109). (Illus.). 236p. 1984. 32.00 (ISBN 0-8155-0986-3). Noyes.
Post-Adjudication Procedures in the Allegheny County (PA) Court of Common Pleas: Report of Findings, Vol. 5. National Center for State Courts Staff. 112p. 1982. manuscript 6.72 (NERO-114). Natl Ctr St Courts.
Post-Adjudication Procedures in the Delaware County (PA) Court of Common Pleas: Report of Findings, Vol. 6. National Center for State Courts Staff. 81p. 1982. manuscript 4.86 (NERO-116). Natl Ctr St Courts.
Post-Adjudication Procedures in the Dauphin County (PA) Court of Common Pleas: Report of Findings, Vol. 8. National Center for State Courts Staff. 81p. 1982. manuscript 4.86 (NERO-110). Natl Ctr St Courts.
Post-Adjudication Procedures in the Forest-Warren County (PA) Court of Common Pleas: Report of Findings, Vol. 10. National Center for State Courts Staff. 80p. 1982. manuscript 4.80 (NERO-115). Natl Ctr St Courts.
Post-Adjudication Procedures in the Lycoming County (PA) Court of Common Pleas: Report of Findings, Vol. 9. National Center for State Courts Staff. 75p. 1982. manuscript 4.50 (NERO-106). Natl Ctr St Courts.
Post-Adjudication Procedures in the Pennsylvania Courts of Common Pleas: Report of Findings, Vol. I. National Center for State Courts Staff. 172p. 1982. manuscript 10.32 (NERO-117). Natl Ctr St Courts.
Post-Adjudication Procedures in the Pennsylvania Court of Common Pleas: Report of Statewide Findings, Vol. 2. National Center for State Courts Staff. 152p. 1982. manuscript 9.12 (NERO-113). Natl Ctr St Courts.
Post-Adjudication Procedures in the Philadelphia (PA) Court of Common Pleas: Report of Findings, Vol. 4. National Center for State Courts Staff. 145p. 1982. manuscript 8.70 (NERO-112). Natl Ctr St Courts.
Post-Adjudication Procedures in the Susquehanna County (PA) Court of Common Pleas: Report of Findings, Vol. 11. National Center for State Courts Staff. 66p. 1982. manuscript 3.96 (NERO-108). Natl Ctr St Courts.
Post-Adjudication Procedures in the York County (PA) Court of Common Pleas: Report of Findings, Vol. 7. National Center for State Courts Staff. 84p. 1982. manuscript 5.04 (NERO-107). Natl Ctr St Courts.
Post Age: Newspapering in a Small Town. David L. Roberts. (Illus.). 200p. (Orig.). 1986. pap. 9.95 (ISBN 0-914767-06-2). Skyline West Pr.
Post-Analytic Philosophy. Ed. by John Rajchman & Cornel West. LC 85-377. 304p. 1985. 37.00 (ISBN 0-231-06066-1); pap. 15.50 (ISBN 0-231-06067-X). Columbia U Pr.
Post-Anasthetic Recovery. R. Eltringham et al. Ed. by M. Durkin & S. Andrewes. (Illus.). 130p. 1983. pap. 21.00 (ISBN 0-387-12631-7). Springer-Verlag.
Post Apollo Space Exploration, 2 Vols. American Astronautical Society Staff. (Advances in Astronautical Ser.: Vol. 20). 1966. Set. 85.00x (ISBN 0-87703-022-7, Pub. by Am Astronaut). Univelt Inc.
Post-Augustan Poetry. Harold E. Butler. (Latin Poetry Ser.: Vol. 15). (LC 77-070766). 1977. Repr. of 1909 ed. lib. bdg. 40.00 (ISBN 0-8240-2964-X). Garland Pub.
Post-Augustan Poetry from Seneca to Juvenal. H. E. Butler. 1909. 25.00 (ISBN 0-89984-036-1). Century Bookbindery.
Post-Augustan Poetry from Seneca to Juvenal. facsimile ed. Harold E. Butler. LC 70-99656. (Select Bibliographies Reprint Ser). 1909. 27.50 (ISBN 0-8369-5085-2). Ayer Co Pubs.
Post-Augustan Satire: Charles Churchill & Satirical Poetry, 1750-1800. Thomas Lockwood. LC 78-4366. 208p. 1979. 25.00x (ISBN 0-295-95612-7). U of Wash Pr.
Post-Avant-Garde - Painting in the Eighties. (Art & Design Profiles Ser.). (Illus.). 80p. 1988. 19.95x (ISBN 0-312-01283-7). St Martin.
Post-Biblical Hebrew Literature: An Anthology, 2 vols. B. Halper. 251p. 1984. Repr. of 1921 ed. lib. bdg. 100.00 set (ISBN 0-8495-2402-4). Arden Lib.
Post-Brezhnev Era. Silviu Brucan. LC 83-16158. 144p. 1983. 35.00 (ISBN 0-275-90953-0, C0953). Praeger.
Post-Buckling of Elastic Structures: Proceedings of the EUROMECH Colloquium No. 200, Matrafured, Hungary, October 5-7, 1985. Ed. by J. Szabo et al. (Developments in Civil Engineering Ser.: No. 17). 350p. 1987. 142.00 (ISBN 0-444-98978-1). Elsevier.
Post-Byzantine Ecclesiastical Personalities. Ed. by Nomikos M. Vaporis. LC 78-11037. 111p. 1978. pap. 3.95 (ISBN 0-916586-30-8). Holy Cross Orthodox.
Post Card: From Socrates to Freud & Beyond. Jacques Derrida. Tr. by Alan Bass. LC 86-27259. (Illus.). 552p. 1987. text ed. 46.00x (ISBN 0-226-14320-1); pap. text ed. 18.95x (ISBN 0-226-14322-8). U of Chicago Pr.
Post Card Views & Other Souvenirs. Marcia M. Miller. (Illus.). 64p. 1973. pap. 2.95 (ISBN 0-913270-24-5). Sunstone Pr.
Post Cards from Old Kansas City. Mrs. Sam Ray. LC 80-84468. (Illus.). 48p. 1980. pap. 9.50. Hist Kansas City.
Post Charismatic Experience: The New Wave of the Spirit. Robert Wild. 136p. (Orig.). 1984. pap. text ed. 4.50 (ISBN 0-914544-50-0). Living Flame Pr.
Post-Civil War Spanish Social Poets. Santiago Daydi-Tolson. (World Authors Ser.). 1983. lib. bdg. 22.95 (ISBN 0-8057-6533-6, Twayne). G K Hall.
Post Communication: Rhetorical Analysis & Evaluation. Robert Cathcart. LC 80-36842. (Speech Communication Ser.). 144p. 1981. pap. text ed. 8.40 scp (ISBN 0-672-61520-7). Bobbs.
Post-Communication: Rhetorical Analysis & Evaluation. 2nd ed. Robert Cathcart. 144p. 1980. pap. text ed. write for info. (ISBN 0-02-319690-4). Macmillan.
Post-Compulsory Education II: The Way Ahead. Edmund J. King & Christine H. Moor. LC 74-3157. (Sage Studies in Social & Educational Change: Vol. 2). pap. 49.50 (ISBN 0-317-08785-1, 2021917). Bks Demand UMI.
Post-Conservative America: People, Politics, & Ideology in a Time of Crisis. Kevin P. Phillips. LC 82-48898. 288p. 1983. pap. 7.95 (ISBN 0-394-71438-5, Vin). Random.
Post-Consonantal W in Indo-European. Francis A. Wood. (LM). 1926. pap. 16.00 (ISBN 0-527-00807-9). Kraus Repr.
Post-Conviction Remedies. Daniel E. Manville. 600p. Date not set. lib. bdg. 35.00 (ISBN 0-379-20778-8); pap. 16.50 (ISBN 0-379-20779-6). Oceana.
Post-Conviction Remedies. Robert Popper. (Nutshell Ser.). 360p. 1978. 7.95 (ISBN 0-317-00018-7). West Pub.
Post Conviction Remedies: Cases & Materials. Ira P. Robbins. LC 82-2557. (American Casebook Ser.). 506p. 1982. text ed. 22.95 (ISBN 0-314-64851-8). West Pub.
Post-Coup Chilean Poetry: A Bilingual Anthology. Silverio Munoz. Tr. by Mary E. Acevedo & Jocelyn Paska. LC 86-80932. (Illus.). 88p. 1986. pap. text ed. 7.50 (ISBN 0-937985-01-5). Ediciones Arauco.
Post-Cranial Skeletal Characters of Bison & Bos. S. J. Olsen. (Harvard University Peabody Museum of Archaeology & Ethnology Papers). Repr. of 1960 ed. 15.00 (ISBN 0-527-01291-2). Kraus Repr.
Post Darwinian Controversies. J. R. Moore. LC 77-94372. 1979. 65.00 (ISBN 0-521-21989-2); pap. 24.95 (ISBN 0-521-28517-8). Cambridge U Pr.
Post-Digital Electronics. F. R. Pettit. (Electrical & Electronic Engineering Ser.). 176p. 1982. 59.95x (ISBN 0-470-27334-8). Halsted Pr.
Post-Education Society: Recognising Adults As Learners. Norman Evans. LC 84-12750. (Radical Forum on Adult Education Ser.). 160p. 1984. 26.00 (ISBN 0-7099-0919-5, Pub. by Croom Helm Ltd); pap. 11.95 (ISBN 0-7099-0948-9). Routledge Chapman & Hall.
Post Exilic Prophecy. Eileen Schuller. (Message Biblical Spirituality Ser.: Vol. 4). 1988. 12.95 (ISBN 0-89453-554-4); pap. 8.95 (ISBN 0-89453-570-6). M Glazier.
Post for Divers Partes of the World, to Travaile from One Notable Citie unto an Other, 2 pts. Richard Rowlands. LC 77-7422. (English Experience Ser.: No. 889). 1977. Repr. of 1576 ed. 13.00 (ISBN 90-221-0889-9). Walter J Johnson.
Post-Glacial Vegetation of Canada. J. C. Ritchie. (Illus.). 240p. 1987. 70.00 (ISBN 0-521-30868-2). Cambridge U Pr.
Post-Graduate Education in the 1980s. OECD. 82p. (Orig.). 1987. pap. 13.00x (ISBN 92-64-12980-4). OECD.
Post-Harvest Pathology of Fruits & Vegatables. Ed. by Colin Dennis. (Food Science & Technology Ser.). 1983. 57.50 (ISBN 0-12-210680-6). Acad Pr.
Post-Harvest Physiology & Crop Preservation. Ed. by Morris Lieberman. LC 82-3645. (NATO ASI Series A, Life Sciences: Vol. 46). 586p. 1983. 95.00x (ISBN 0-306-40984-4, Plenum Pr). Plenum Pub.
Post-Harvest Physiology of Food Crops. W. G. Burton. (Illus.). 320p. 1982. 37.95x (ISBN 0-582-46038-7). Wiley.
Post Harvest Physiology of Food Crops. W. G. Burton. 320p. 1986. 38.95 (ISBN 0-470-20433-8, Co-Pub. with Longman). Wiley.
Post Harvest Physiology of Vegetables. Weichmann. (Food Science Ser.). 568p. 1987. 150.50 (ISBN 0-8247-7601-1). Dekker.
Post-Herzalian Period: 1904-1914. Ed. by Isaiah Friedman & Howard M. Sachar. (Rise of Israel Ser.). 440p. 1987. lib. bdg. 85.00 (ISBN 0-8240-4902-0). Garland Pub.
Post-Holocaust Dialogues: Critcal Studies in Modern Jewish Thought. Steven T. Katz. 416p. 1983. 45.00x (ISBN 0-8147-4583-0). NYU Pr.
Post-Holocaust Dialogues: Critical Studies in Modern Jewish Thought. Steven T. Katz. 1985. pap. 15.00x (ISBN 0-8147-4587-3). NYU Pr.
Post-Hospital Care Arrangements for the Functionally Disabled Elderly. Francis G. Caro. 19p. 1983. pap. 2.25 (ISBN 0-88156-016-2). Comm Serv Soc NY.
Post Hypnotic Instructions. Arnold Furst. pap. 5.00 (ISBN 0-87980-119-0). Wilshire.
Post Imperial Presidency. Ed. by Vincent Davis. LC 79-67064. 202p. 1980. 36.95 (ISBN 0-275-90466-0, C0466). Praeger.
Post-Imperial Presidency. Ed. by Vincent Davis. LC 79-67064. 190p. 1980. pap. text ed. 12.95x (ISBN 0-87855-747-4). Transaction Bks.
Post-Impressionism: From Van Gogh to Gauguin. 3rd, rev. ed. John Rewald. LC 77-77286. (Illus.). 584p. 1978. 60.00 (ISBN 0-87070-532-6, 714674, Pub. by Museum of Modern Art). NYGS.
Post-Impressionist Group Exhibitions. Ed. by Theodore Reff. (Modern Art in Paris Ser.). 302p. 1981. lib. bdg. 48.00 (ISBN 0-8240-4728-1). Garland Pub.

Post War Baby Austins. Barney Sharratt. (Illus.). 200p. 1988. 39.95 (ISBN 0-85045-710-6, Pub. by Osprey England). Motorbooks Intl.

Post-War Britain. C. M. Woodhouse. LC 67-15646. 1967. 10.95 (ISBN 0-8023-1122-9). Dufour.

Post-War Britain: A Political History. Alan Sked & Chris Cook. (Penguin Nonfiction Ser.). 480p. 1985. pap. 7.95 (ISBN 0-14-022594-3). Penguin.

Post-War Britain: A Political History. Alan Sked & Chris Cooke. LC 79-312. 394p. 1979. 26.50x (ISBN 0-06-496322-5). B&N Imports.

Post-War British Theatre. rev. ed. John Elsom. (Illus.). 1979. pap. 9.50 (ISBN 0-7100-0168-1). Routledge Chapman & Hall.

Post War Discoveries of T'ang & Sung Kiln Sites. Koyama Fujio. 1962. 15.00x (ISBN 0-317-44160-4, Pub. by Han-Shan Tang Ltd). State Mutual Bk.

Post War Economic Development of Japan. B. P. Shreshtha. 93p. 1988. text ed. 15.95x (ISBN 0-89891-029-3, Pub. by Himalaya Pub India). Advent NY.

Post-War Economic Growth Revisited, Lectures in Economics: Theory Institutions, Policy, Vol. 8. G. Bombach. 150p. 1985. pap. 42.00 (ISBN 0-444-87729-0, North Holland). Elsevier.

Post-War Friends. Peter Samuelson. 47p. (Orig.). 1987. pap. 13.95 (ISBN 0-85449-075-2, Pub. by GMP England). Alyson Pubns.

Post-War History of the Stock Market. A. G. Ellinger & T. H. Stewart. 80p. 1984. 15.00 (ISBN 0-85941-153-2, Pub. by Woodhead-Faulkner). Longwood Pub Group.

Post-War Integration in Europe. Ed. by Richard Vaughan. LC 76-14513. (Documents of Modern History Ser.). 1976. 25.00 (ISBN 0-312-63245-2). St Martin.

Post War International Money Crisis: An Analysis. Victor Argy. 472p. (Orig.). 1981. pap. text ed. 19.95x (ISBN 0-04-332076-7). Unwin Hyman.

Post-War Japanese Resource Policies & Strategies: The Case of Southeast Asia. Shoko Tanaka. (East Asia Papers: No. 43). 130p. (Orig.). 1986. pap. 5.00 (ISBN 0-939657-43-0). Cornell East Asia Pgm.

Post-War Jets. (Aircraft Archive Ser.: Vol. 1). (Illus.). 96p. (Orig.). 1988. pap. 16.95 (ISBN 0-85242-940-1, Pub. by Argus Pub UK). Motorbooks Intl.

Post-War Mind of Germany & Other European Studies. C. H. Herford. Repr. of 1927 ed. lib. bdg. 32.00 (ISBN 0-8414-5046-3). Folcroft.

Post War Progress in Child Welfare. J. Prentice Murphy. LC 30-24228. 1971. Repr. of 1930 ed. 25.00 (ISBN 0-384-01053-9). Johnson Repr.

Post-World War Two Fighters, 1945-1973. Marcelle S. Knaack. (Reference Ser.). Orig. Title: Encyclopedia of U. S. Air Force Aircraft & Missile Systems. (Illus.). 358p. 1986. Repr. of 1978 ed. write for info. (ISBN 0-912799-19-6). Off Air Force.

Post-Yield Fracture Mechanics. 2nd ed. Ed. by D. G. Latzko et al. (Illus.). 512p. 1985. 133.25 (ISBN 0-85334-276-8, Pub. by Elsevier Applied Sci England). Elsevier.

Postage Stamp Catalogue of the People's Republic of China, 1949-1980. China National Stamp Corp. Staff. 132p. (Orig.). 1983. pap. 15.00 (ISBN 0-88727-020-4, Pub. by People's Posts CC). Cheng & Tsui.

Postage Stamp Garden Book: How to Grow All the Food You Can Eat in Very Little Space. Duane G. Newcomb. LC 74-23021. (Illus.). 150p. 1975. pap. 7.95 (ISBN 0-87477-035-1). J P Tarcher.

Postage Stamp Recycling As Fundraising, Crafts & a Hobby. Carrol, Frieda, Research Division Staff. 1984. pap. text ed. 8.95 (ISBN 0-318-04346-7, Pub. by F. Carrol). Prosperity & Profits.

Postage Stamps & Freemasonry. C. L. Murphy. 432p. 1986. 20.95 (ISBN 0-8062-2966-7). Carlton.

Postage Stamps & Postal History of Canada. Winthrop S. Boggs. LC 74-79893. (Illus.). 896p. 1974. Repr. of 1945 ed. 60.00x (ISBN 0-88000-042-2). Quarterman.

Postage Stamps of Japan & Dependencies. Alphonse M. Woodward. LC 73-86773. (Illus.). 768p. 1976. Repr. of 1928 ed. 65.00x (ISBN 0-88000-020-1). Quarterman.

Postage Stamps of Lithuania. Lithuanian Philatelic Societies of New York & Toronto. 237p. 1979. 18.00x (ISBN 0-912574-33-X). Collectors.

Postage Stamps of Mexico, 1856-1868. Samuel Chapman. LC 75-40501. (Illus.). 1976. Repr. 40.00x (ISBN 0-88000-079-1). Quarterman.

Postage Stamps of New Brunswick Nova Scotia. Nicholas Argenti. LC 76-19723. 1976. 35.00x (ISBN 0-88000-088-0). Quarterman.

Postal Arithmetic. Jack Rudman. (Career Examination Ser.: CS-20). (Cloth bdg. avail. on request). pap. 14.00 (ISBN 0-8373-3770-4). Natl Learning.

Postal Clerk-Carrier & Mail Handler Exams. 4th ed. Harry W. Koch. 1981. 8.00 (ISBN 0-913164-89-5). Ken-Bks.

Postal Communication in China & Its Modernization, 1860-1896. Ying-Wan Cheng. LC 70-120316. (East Asian Monographs Ser: No. 34). (Illus.). xii, 150p. 1970. pap. 11.00x (ISBN 0-674-69320-5). Harvard U Pr.

Postal History & Postage Stamps of Serbia, 1841-1921. Mirko R. Rasic. (Illus.). 276p. 1979. 18.00x (ISBN 0-912574-25-9). Collectors.

Postal History Cancellation Study of the U. S. Pacific Islands: Including the Trust Territories. Robert T. Murphy. 361p. 1983. 46.00 (ISBN 0-933580-11-8). Am Philatelic Society.

Postal History of American Prisoners of War: World War II, Korea, Vietnam. Norman Gruenzner. LC 79-50817. (APS Handbook Ser.). 1979. 12.50 (ISBN 0-933580-00-2). Am Philatelic Society.

Postal History of Indiana, 2 vols. J. David Baker. Ed. by Leonard H. Hartmann. LC 76-10531. (Illus.). 1100p. 1976. 75.00 (ISBN 0-917528-03-4); microfiche incl. L H Hartmann.

Postal History of Newfoundland. Robert H. Pratt. (Illus.). 910p. 1985. 140.00 (ISBN 0-912574-34-8). Collectors.

Postal History of Sioux City. Inez E. Kirkpatrick. (Illus.). 1977. lib. bdg. 13.50 (ISBN 0-916170-07-1). J-B Pub.

Postal History of the Forwarding Agents. Kenneth Rowe. Ed. by Leonard H. Hartmann. LC 84-80011. (Illus.). 296p. 1984. 35.00 (ISBN 0-917528-06-9). L H Hartmann.

Postal History of Yukon Territory, Canada. Robert G. Woodall. LC 76-15747. 1976. 35.00x (ISBN 0-88000-086-4). Quarterman.

Postal Inspector (U. S. P. S.) Jack Rudman. (Career Examination Ser.: C-602). (Cloth bdg. avail. on request). pap. 16.00 (ISBN 0-8373-0602-7). Natl Learning.

Postal Machines Mechanic (USPS) (Career Examination Ser.: C-3366). Date not set. pap. 18.00 (ISBN 0-8373-3366-0). Natl Learning.

Postal Markings. Harry M. Konwiser. LC 76-27964. 768p. 1980. lib. bdg. 60.00x (ISBN 0-88000-089-9). Quarterman.

Postal Markings of England, London & Wales, 1661-1900. Oliver R. Sanford, Jr. (Illus.). 76p. (Orig.). 1986. pap. 6.50 (ISBN 0-938139-00-2). Lord Byron Stamps.

Postal Monopoly: An Assessment of the Private Express Statutes. John Haldi. 1974. pap. 7.00 (ISBN 0-8447-3123-4). Am Enterprise.

Postal Powers of Congress: A Study in Constitutional Expansion. Lindsay Rogers. LC 78-63956. (Johns Hopkins University. Studies in the Social Sciences. Thirty-Fourth 1916: 2). Repr. of 1916 ed. 19.00 (ISBN 0-404-61204-0). AMS Pr.

Postal Precipice: Can the U. S. Postal Service Be Saved. Kathleen Conkey. 515p. 1983. pap. text ed. 30.00 (ISBN 0-936758-09-0). Ctr Responsive Law.

Postal Service: Competition or Monopoly? Ian Senior. (Institute Of Economic Affairs, Background Memoranda Ser.: No. 3). pap. 2.50 technical (ISBN 0-686-89190-2). Transatl Arts.

Postal Service Guide to U. S. Stamps. 12th ed. Ed. by Kathleen Ineman. (Illus.). 312p. pap. 3.50 (ISBN 0-9604756-5-6). USPS.

Postal Service Guide to U. S. Stamps. 14th ed. Mobium Corporation for Design & Communication Staff. LC 87-656545. (Illus.). 320p. 1987. 5.00 (ISBN 0-9604756-6-4). Mobium Pr.

Postal Service in Boston, 1639-1893. Carl W. Ernst. 1975. 3.00 (ISBN 0-89073-004-0). Boston Public Lib.

Postal Supervisor (U. S. P. S.) Jack Rudman. (Career Examination Ser.: C-603). (Cloth bdg. avail. on request). pap. 16.00 (ISBN 0-8373-0603-5). Natl Learning.

Postal System Examiner (U. S. P. S.) Jack Rudman. (Career Examination Ser.: C-2079). (Cloth bdg. avail. on request). 1988. pap. 18.00 (ISBN 0-8373-2079-8). Natl Learning.

Postal Technology & Management. Husain Mustafa. LC 73-165579. (Illus.). 240p. 1971. 23.50 (ISBN 0-912338-01-6); microfiche 9.50 (ISBN 0-912338-02-4). Lomond.

Postal Transportation Clerk (U. S. P. S.) Jack Rudman. (Career Examination Ser.: C-604). (Cloth bdg. avail. on request). pap. 14.00 (ISBN 0-8373-0604-3). Natl Learning.

Postal Workers: A to Z. 48p. (gr. 1-3). 1987. 11.95 (ISBN 0-8027-6663-3); PLB 12.85 (ISBN 0-8027-6664-1). Walker & Co.

Postan, Michael Moissey (Eighteen Ninety-Nine to Nineteen Eighty-One) Edward Miller. (Memoirs of the Fellows of the British Academy Ser.). (Illus.). 1985. pap. 5.50 (ISBN 0-85672-502-1, Pub. by British Acad). Longwood Pub Group.

Postattack Recovery Strategies. William M. Brown & Doris Yokelson. 178p. 1980. 20.00 (ISBN 0-318-14352-6, HI3100RR). Hudson Inst.

Postbasic & Graduate Education for Nurses. (EURO Reports & Studies: No. 99). 38p. 1985. pap. 3.60 (ISBN 92-890-1265-X). World Health.

Postcard Books: Cats in Art. 1988. pap. 5.95 (ISBN 0-449-90315-X). Fawcett.

Postcard Books: Flower Paintings. 1988. pap. 5.95 (ISBN 0-449-90316-8). Fawcett.

Postcard Books: Renaissance Artists. 1988. pap. 5.95 (ISBN 0-449-90314-1). Fawcett.

Postcard Books: The Impressionists. 1989. pap. 5.95 (ISBN 0-449-90313-3). Fawcett.

Postcard Collector's Handbook. Jack H. Smith. (New Ser.). 512p. 1988. text ed. 29.95 (ISBN 0-87069-519-3). Wallace-Homestead.

Postcard from Rome. David Helwig. LC 87-51352. 256p. Date not set. 17.95 (ISBN 0-670-82137-3). Viking.

Postcard Paint Book. (gr. k-3). 5.25 (ISBN 0-87497-099-7, 19475). Merrimack.

Postcards. C. S. Giscombe. LC 77-13756. 57p. 1977. 3.50 (ISBN 0-87886-089-4). Greenfld Rev Pr.

Postcards from Maine. Tim Sample. (Illus., Orig.). 1988. pap. 8.95 (ISBN 0-88448-050-X). Harpswell Pr.

Postcards from Old Kansas City. Mrs. Sam Ray. LC 80-84468. 48p. 1980. pap. 9.50. Lowell Pr.

Postcards from Surfers. Helen Garper. 112p. 1986. pap. 4.95 (ISBN 0-14-008462-2). Penguin.

Postcards from the Edge. Carrie Fisher. 1987. 15.95 (ISBN 0-671-62441-5). S&S.

Postcards from the Edge. Carrie Fisher. 288p. 1988. pap. 4.50 (ISBN 0-671-66218-X). PB.

Postcards from the End of the World: Child Abuse in Freud's Vienna. Larry Wolff. 288p. 1988. 18.95 (ISBN 0-689-11883-X). Atheneum.

Postcards of Bucks County As Printed by the Arnold Bros. Bertha Davis et al. (Illus.). 80p. pap. 4.95 (ISBN 0-9610608-0-8). Wash Cross Card.

Postcards of Falkland Islands: A Catalogue, 1900-1950. Henry Heyburn & Frances Heyburn. (Illus.). 256p. 1987. 105.00x (ISBN 0-902633-99-6, Pub. by Picton UK). State Mutual Bk.

Postcards Please. Wilfred Harrison. 1984. 15.00x (ISBN 0-86319-046-4, Pub. by New Playwrights Network). State Mutual Bk.

Postclassic & Early Colonial Mixtec Houses in the Nochixtlan Valley, Oaxaca, Mexico. Michael Lind. (Publications in Anthropology: No. 23). 79p. 1979. 6.25 (ISBN 0-935462-12-0). Vanderbilt Pubns.

Postconviction Remedies, Vol. I. Larry W. Yackle. 1981. 74.50 (ISBN 0-686-31140-X); Suppl. 1987. 33.00; Suppl. 1988. 36.00. Lawyers Co Op.

Postdeath Tax Elections. 83p. 1987. pap. 20.00 (ES-49018). Cal Cont Ed Bar.

Postdoctoral Appointments & Disappointments. National Research Council. 1981. pap. text ed. 15.75x (ISBN 0-309-03132-X). Natl Acad Pr.

Poster: A Worldwide Survey & History. Alain Weill. (Reference Publications in Art). 1985. lib. bdg. 39.00 (ISBN 0-8161-8746-0). G K Hall.

Poster Catalogue. Vicki Wray. Ed. by Nancy McGaw. (Illus.). 447p. 1985. 40.00 (ISBN 0-9613932-0-3). B McGaw Graphics.

Poster Ideas & Bulletin Board Techniques. 2nd ed. Kate Coplan. LC 80-24971. 248p. 1981. lib. bdg. 25.00 (ISBN 0-379-20333-2). Oceana.

Posterior Analytics. Aristotle. Ed. by Jonathan Barnes. (Clarendon Aristotle Ser.). 1975. pap. 19.95x (ISBN 0-19-872067-X). Oxford U Pr.

Posterior Analytics, Bks. 1 & 2. Aristotle. Bd. with Topica, Bks. 1-8. (Loeb Classical Library: No. 391). (Gr. & Eng.). 13.95x (ISBN 0-674-99430-2). Harvard U Pr.

Posterior-Chamber Lens Implant Surgery. H. Kell Yang & Oram R. Kline, Jr. (Illus.). 120p. 1983. text ed. 38.00 (ISBN 0-89004-787-1). Raven.

Posterior Fossa, Spinal Cord & Peripheral Nerve Disease see Operative Neurosurgery.

Posterior Pituitary: Hormone Secretion in Health & Disease. Baylis & Padfield. (Basic & Clinical Endocrinology Ser.). 528p. 1985. 85.00 (ISBN 0-8247-7359-4). Dekker.

Postern of Fate. Agatha Christie. (HC Collection Ser.). 1974. pap. 3.50 (ISBN 0-553-25493-6). Bantam.

Posters. Maurice Sendak. (Illus.). 48p. 1986. 45.00 (ISBN 0-517-56343-6, Harmony); pap. 19.95 (ISBN 0-517-56344-4, Harmony). Crown.

Posters: A Concise History. John Barnicoat. (World of Art Ser.). (Illus.). 288p. 1985. pap. 11.95 (ISBN 0-500-20118-8). Thames Hudson.

Posters of Jules Cheret. Jules Cheret & Lucy Broido. (Illus.). 128p. (Orig.). 1980. pap. 9.95 (ISBN 0-486-24010-X). Dover.

Posters of Jules Cheret. Jules Cheret & Lucy Broido. (Illus.). 19.00 (ISBN 0-8446-5742-5). Peter Smith.

Posters of Mucha: A Collection of Posters by Alphonse Mucha. Alphonse Mucha. (Illus.). 48p. 1975. pap. 9.95 (ISBN 0-517-52043-5, Harmony). Crown.

Posters of World War I & World War II in George C. Marshall Research Foundation. Ed. by Anthony R. Crawford. LC 79-9852. (Illus.). xi, 128p. 1979. 13.95x (ISBN 0-8139-0778-0). U Pr of Va.

Posters of WPA. Chris DeNoon. (Illus.). 176p. 1987. 39.95 (ISBN 0-295-96543-6). U of Wash Pr.

Postgastrectomy & Postvagatomy Syndromes. H. D. Becker & W. F. Caspary. (Illus.). 500p. 1980. 85.00 (ISBN 0-387-09445-8). Springer-Verlag.

Postgraduate Education & Training in Public Health: Report. WHO Expert Committee. Geneva, 1973. (Technical Report Ser.: No. 533). (Also avail. in French & Spanish). 1973. pap. 2.00 (ISBN 92-4-120533-4). World Health.

Postgraduate Education for Medical Personnel in the U. S. S. R. Report Prepared by the Participants in a Study Tour Organized by the World Health Organization. (Public Health Papers: No. 39). 52p. 1970. pap. 2.00 (ISBN 92-4-130039-6, 558). World Health.

Postgraduate Nephrology. 3rd ed. Roger Gabriel. (Illus.). 272p. 1986. pap. text ed. 34.95 (ISBN 0-407-36116-2). Butterworth.

Postgraduate Nephrology. Ed. by Frank P. Marsh. (Illus.). 656p. text ed. 95.00x (ISBN 0-433-20332-3, Pub. by W Heinemann Med Bks). Sheridan.

Postgraduate Obestetrics & Gynacology. Ed. by M. K. Menon & P. K. Devi. xiii, 504p. 1982. text ed. 30.00x (ISBN 0-86131-303-8, Pub. by Orient Longman Ltd India). Apt Bks.

Postgraduate Textbook of Clinical Orthopaedics. N. H. Harris. (Illus.). 1048p. 1983. 175.00 (ISBN 0-7236-0638-2). PSG Pub Co.

Postharvest Biology of Horticultural Crops. Saltveit et al. 1988. write for info. (ISBN 0-471-86531-1). Wiley.

Postharvest Biotechnology of Cereals. Ed. by D. K. Salunkhe et al. (Postharvest Biotechnology Ser.). 224p. 1985. 79.00 (ISBN 0-8493-6288-1). CRC Pr.

Postharvest Biotechnology of Food Legumes. Ed. by D. K. Salunkhe et al. (Postharvest Biotechnology Ser.). 176p. 1985. 79.00 (ISBN 0-8493-6287-3). CRC Pr.

Postharvest Biotechnology of Fruits, 2 vols. D. K. Salunkhe & B. B. Desai. LC 83-7770. (Postharvest Biotechnology Ser.). 1984. Vol. I, 184p. 79.00 (ISBN 0-8493-6121-4); Vol. II, 168p. 79.00 (ISBN 0-8493-6122-2). CRC Pr.

Postharvest Biotechnology of Oilseeds. D. K. Salunkhe & B. B. Desai. 288p. 1986. 99.00 (ISBN 0-8493-6289-X). CRC Pr.

Postharvest Biotechnology of Sugar Crops. D. K. Salunkhe. 224p. 1988. 119.00 (ISBN 0-8493-4578-2, 4578). CRC Pr.

Postharvest Biotechnology of Vegetables. D. K. Salunkhe & B. B. Desai. (Postharvest Biotechnology Ser.). 1984. 85.00 ea. Vol. I, 224 p (ISBN 0-8493-6123-0). Vol. II, 216 p (ISBN 0-8493-6124-9). CRC Pr.

Postharvest Losses, Technology, & Employment: The Case of Rice in Bangladesh. Martin Greeley. (Special Studies in Social, Political, & Economic Development). 350p. 1987. pap. 35.00 (ISBN 0-8133-7371-9). Westview.

Postharvest Technology of Horticultural Crops. Ed. by Adel A. Kader. LC 85-70729. (Illus.). 212p. (Orig.). 1985. pap. 20.00x (ISBN 0-931876-72-9, 3311). ANR Pubns CA.

Posthumes. Bradford Morrow. 52p. 1982. o. p. signed ltd. ed. 20.00 (ISBN 0-932274-26-9); pap. 5.00 (ISBN 0-932274-25-0). Cadmus Eds.

Posthumous see Richard Wagner's Prose Works.

Posthumous Confession. Marcellus Emants. 194p. 1987. pap. 8.95 (ISBN 0-7043-0023-0, Pub. by Quartet Bks). Salem Hse Pubs.

Posthumous Essays of John Churton Collins. John C. Collins. Ed. by L. C. Collins. 1912. lib. bdg. 30.00 (ISBN 0-8414-0946-3). Folcroft.

Posthumous Humanity. Adolphe D'Assier. Ed. & tr. by H. S. Olcott. LC 81-50204. (Secret Doctrine Reference Ser.). 384p. 1981. Repr. of 1887 ed. 17.00 (ISBN 0-913510-36-X). Wizards.

Posthumous Life of Plato. Frantisek Novotny. Ed. by Ludvik Svoboda & J. L. Barton. Tr. by Jana Fabryova 1978. lib. bdg. 53.00 (ISBN 90-247-2060-5, Pub. by Martinus Nijhoff Netherlands). Kluwer Academic.

Posthumous Meditations: A Dialogue in Three Acts. W. A. McMullen. LC 82-916. (HPC Dialogue Ser.). 84p. 1982. pap. text ed. 3.95 (ISBN 0-915145-35-9). Hackett Pub.

Posthumous Papers of a Living Author. Robert Musil. Tr. by Peter Wortsman from Ger. 149p. 1988. 21.00 (ISBN 0-941419-00-2); pap. 12.00 (ISBN 0-941419-01-0). Eridanos Pr.

Posthumous Papers of the Pickwick Club. George Davis. LC 72-3167. (Studies in Dickens, No. 52). 1972. Repr. of 1928 ed. lib. bdg. 29.95x (ISBN 0-8383-1533-X). Haskell.

Posthumous Papers of the Pickwick Club. George W. Davis. LC 73-14971. 1928. lib. bdg. 17.00 (ISBN 0-8414-3681-9). Folcroft.

Posthumous Papers of the Pickwick Club see Oxford Illustrated Dickens.

Posthumous Poems. Algernon C. Swinburne et al. 14.00 (ISBN 0-8369-6993-6, 7870). Ayer Co Pubs.

Posthumous Theological Works, 2 vols. Emanuel Swedenborg. student ed. 12.00 ea. Vol. 1. Vol. 2. Set. 24.00. Swedenborg.

Posthumous Works. Ann E. Bleecker. LC 70-104419. 375p. Repr. of 1793 ed. lib. bdg. 29.00 (ISBN 0-8398-0167-X). Irvington.

Posthumous Works. Ann E. Bleeker. 375p. 1986. pap. text ed. 7.95x (ISBN 0-8290-1888-3). Irvington.

Posthumous Works. Robert Hooke. (Illus.). 518p. 1971. Repr. of 1775 ed. 65.00x (ISBN 0-7146-1600-1, F Cass Co). Biblio Dist.

Posthumous Works. Robert Hooke. (Sources of Science Ser., No. 73). 1969. Repr. of 1705 ed. 40.00 (ISBN 0-384-24165-4). Johnson Repr.

Posthumous Works of Thomas DeQuincey, 2 vols. in 1. Thomas DeQuincey. Ed. by Alexander H. Japp. 608p. Repr. of 1891 ed. lib. bdg. 77.50x (ISBN 3-487-05658-5, Pub. by G. Olms BRD). Coronet Bks.

Posthumous Writings. Gottlob Frege. Ed. by Hans Hermes et al. Tr. by Roger White & Peter Long. LC 79-10986. 1979. Repr. lib. bdg. 35.00x (ISBN 0-226-26199-9). U of Chicago Pr.

Postimperialism: International Capitalism & Development in the Late Twentieth Century. David G. Becker et al. LC 87-4455. 250p. 1987. lib. bdg. 32.50x (ISBN 1-55587-046-5); pap. text ed. 14.95x (ISBN 1-55587-047-3). Lynne Rienner.

Postwar World: The USA since 1945. Elizabeth Campling. (Postwar World Ser.). (Illus.). 64p. (YA) (gr. 7-9). 1988. 19.95 (ISBN 0-7134-5756-2, Pub. by Batsford England). David & Charles.

Posviashchenie. I. C. Sokolov-Mitkitov. 158p. 1982. 29.00x (Pub. by Collets UK). State Mutual Bk.

Posy. Charlotte Pomerantz. LC 83-1452. (Illus.). 48p. (gr. 1-3). 1983. PLB 10.88 (ISBN 0-688-02299-5). Greenwillow.

Posy of a Ring: A Cycle of Poems. Francis K. Weaver. LC 86-71489. (Living Poets Ser.: No. 36). (Illus.). 103p. 1986. pap. 10.00 ltd. ed. (ISBN 0-934218-36-6). Dragons Teeth.

Posy Ring. facs. ed. Ed. by Kate D. Wiggin & Nora A. Smith. LC 70-128164. (Granger Index Reprint Ser). 1903. 16.00 (ISBN 0-8369-6193-5). Ayer Co Pubs.

Pot: A Guide for Young People. 1984. pap. 0.25 (ISBN 0-89230-162-7). Do it Now.

Pot: A Handbook of Marijuana. John Rosevear. 2.25 (ISBN 0-8065-0204-5, Pub. by Citadel Pr). Lyle Stuart.

Pot au Feu. Theodore P. Fraser & Alan L. Whipple. (Illus.). 218p. (gr. 7-10). 1975. pap. text ed. 6.50x (ISBN 0-88334-068-2). Ind Sch Pr.

Pot Boiler. Alice Gerstenberg. 24p. 1983. pap. 1.25 (ISBN 0-88680-206-7). I E Clark.

Pot-Bouille. Emile Zola. (Coll. Diamant). 12.95 (ISBN 0-685-23949-7). French & Eur.

Pot-Bouille. Emile Zola. Ed. by Colette Becker. 4.95 (ISBN 0-686-55798-0). French & Eur.

Pot Likker, Pulley Bones, & Pea Vine Hay. Faye Brown. (Illus.). 226p. (Orig.). 1987. pap. 7.50 (ISBN 0-943487-02-1). Sevgo Pr.

Pot Luck: Potato Recipes from Ireland. Nell Donnelly. (Illus.). 96p. (Orig.). 1987. pap. 7.95 (ISBN 0-86327-119-7, Pub. by Wolfhound Pr Ireland). Irish Bks Media.

Pot of Gold see Amphitryon.

Pot of Gold see Clouds.

Pot of Gold: A Juvenile Fantasy Novel. John Wiessner, Jr. (Illus.). 160p. (gr. 5-8). 1981. 5.95 (ISBN 0-8059-2769-7). Dorrance.

Pot of Gold & Other Plays. Plautus. Tr. by E. F. Watling. Incl. Brothers Menaechmus; Prisoner; Swaggering Soldier; Pseudolus. (Clasics Ser.). (Orig.). 1965. pap. 4.95 (ISBN 0-14-044149-2). Penguin.

Pot of Gold & Other Stories. Mary E. Wilkins Freeman. LC 74-113661. (Short Story Index Reprint Ser.). 1892. 19.50 (ISBN 0-8369-3390-7). Ayer Co Pubs.

Pot of Paint. John K. Rothenstein. LC 70-128303. (Essay Index Reprint Ser). 1929. 18.00 (ISBN 0-8369-1847-9). Ayer Co Pubs.

Pot Pourri. Dianne Draze. (Illus.). (gr. 3-8). 1978. pap. 7.00 (ISBN 0-931724-01-5). Dandy Lion.

Pot Pourri: A Practical Guide. Mary Lane. 100p. 1985. 30.00x (Pub. by Bishopsgate Pr. Ltd); pap. 21.00x. State Mutual Bk.

Pot Safari: A Visit to the Top Marijuana Researchers in the U. S. Rev. ed. Peggy Mann. LC 82-91050. 131p. (Orig.). (YA) (gr. 9-12). 1987. pap. 6.95 (ISBN 0-942493-01-X). Woodmere Press.

Pot Shots at Poetry. Robert Francis. (Poets on Poetry Ser.). 1980. pap. 8.95 (ISBN 0-472-06318-9). U of Mich Pr.

Pot: What It Is, What It Does. Ann Tobias. LC 78-10817. (Greenwillow Read-Alone Bks.). (Illus.). 48p. (gr. 3-4). 1979. PLB 12.88 (ISBN 0-688-84200-3). Greenwillow.

Pot: Why Not: Your Questions Answered by a National Expert. Peggy Mann. (Illus.). 64p. (Orig.). (gr. 4-6). 1988. pap. 4.95 (ISBN 0-942493-03-6). Woodmere Press.

Potable Gold see New Arts.

Potala of Tibet. Richard Kemp. LC 86-14486. (Illus.). 187p. 1988. 29.95 (ISBN 0-905743-48-2, Pub. by Stacey Intl). Humanities.

Potala Palace of Tibet. Cultural Relics Administration Staff. (Illus.). 128p. 1982. 175.00x (ISBN 0-317-69146-5, Pub. by Han-Shan Tang Ltd). State Mutual Bk.

Potala Palace of Tibet. Date not set. 34.95 (ISBN 962-04-0196-4, POPATI). China Bks.

Potash & Perlmutter: Their Co-Partnership Ventures & Adventures. facsimile ed. Montagu Glass. LC 74-27988. (Modern Jewish Experience Ser.). (Illus.). 1975. Repr. of 1909 ed. 35.50x (ISBN 0-405-06715-1). Ayer Co Pubs.

Potash Mining Processing Transportation: Proceedings of the International Potash Technology Conference, Saskatoon, Saskatchewan, Canada, October 3-5, 1983. Ed. by R. M. McKercher. (Illus.). 887p. 1983. 230.00 (ISBN 0-08-025401-2). Pergamon.

Potassium. I. M. Korenman. (Analytical Chemistry of the Elements Ser.). 280p. 1970. text ed. 55.00x (ISBN 0-7065-0751-7, Pub. by Keter Pub Jerusalem). Coronet Bks.

Potassium, Calcium, & Magnesium in the Tropics & Subtropics. Robert D. Munson. Ed. by J. C. Brosheer. LC 82-11944. (Technical Bulletins Ser.: T-23). (Illus.). 70p. (Orig.). 1982. pap. text ed. 8.00 (ISBN 0-88090-041-5). Intl Fertilizer.

Potassium: Its Biologic Significance. Robert Whang. 176p. 1983. 65.00 (ISBN 0-8493-5872-8). CRC Pr.

Potassium, the Heart & Hypertension: A Symposium Sponsored by the Italian Society of Cardiology. Ed. by Bruno Magnani and Lennart Hansson. LC 82-51013. (Illus.). 200p. 1982. write for info. (ISBN 0-88137-000-2). TransMedica.

Potato. Ed. by Y. P. Bajaj. (Biotechnology in Agriculture & Forestry: Vol. 3). (Illus.). 535p. 1987. 198.80 (ISBN 0-387-17966-6). Springer-Verlag.

Potato & Its Wild Relatives: Section Tuberarium of the Genus Solanum. Donovan S. Correll. (Illus.). 606p. 1962. lib. bdg. 20.00x (ISBN 0-934454-93-0). Lubrecht & Cramer.

Potato Beetles: The Genus Leptinotarsa in North America. Richard L. Jacques, Jr. LC 87-15095. (Flora & Fauna Handbook Ser.: No. 3). (Illus.). 144p. 1988. pap. text ed. 19.95 (ISBN 0-916846-40-7). Flora & Fauna.

Potato Breeding - Problems & Perspectives. Hans Ross & W. Hunnius. (Advances in Plant Breeding Ser.: No. 13). (Illus.). 160p. (Orig.). 1986. pap. text ed. 38.00x (ISBN 3-489-61110-1). Parey Sci Pubs.

Potato Chips & a Slice of Moon. Lee B. Hopkins & Misha Arenstein. 96p. (gr. 4-6). pap. 2.25 (ISBN 0-590-40213-7). Scholastic Inc.

Potato Chips for Breakfast. Cynthia G. Scales. 150p. (Orig.). 1986. 13.95 (ISBN 0-934391-04-1); pap. 8.95 (ISBN 0-934391-05-X). Quotidian.

Potato Crop: The Scientific Basis for Improvement. Ed. by P. M. Harris. 1978. 88.00x (ISBN 0-412-12830-6, NO. 6143, Pub. by Chapman & Hall). Routledge Chapman & Hall.

Potato Diseases. Avery E. Rich. LC 82-24290. (Monograph Ser.). 1983. 49.95 (ISBN 0-12-587420-0). Acad Pr.

Potato Experience. Lisa Tanner. LC 85-27922. (Illus.). 240p. (Orig.). 1986. pap. 9.95 (ISBN 0-89815-159-7). Ten Speed Pr.

Potato Famine & the Irish Emigrants. P. F. Speed. Ed. by Marjorie Reeves. (Then & There Ser.). (Illus.). 96p. (Orig.). (gr. 7-12). 1976. pap. text ed. 4.75 (ISBN 0-582-21721-0). Longman.

Potato in the Human Diet. J. A. Woolfe. 200p. 1987. 32.50 (ISBN 0-521-32669-9). Cambridge U Pr.

Potato Jokes. Paul McMahon. (Orig.). 1984. pap. 3.95 (ISBN 0-671-54280-X, Long Shadow Bks). PB.

Potato Man. Sophia Marcus. Ed. by Gerald Wheeler. (Banner Ser.). 128p. (Orig.). 1986. pap. 6.95 (ISBN 0-8280-0309-2). Review & Herald.

Potato Mechanisation & Storage. C. F. Bishop & W. F. Maunder. (Illus.). 256p. 23.95 (ISBN 0-85236-109-2, Pub. by Farming Pr UK). Diamond Farm Bk.

Potato Pancakes All Around: A Hanukkah Tale. Marilyn Hirsh. (Illus.). 34p. (gr. 4-8). 1982. pap. 5.95 (ISBN 0-8276-0217-0, 604). JPS Phila.

Potato Physiology. Paul H. Li. 1985. 91.50 (ISBN 0-12-447660-0); pap. 49.95 (ISBN 0-12-447661-9). Acad Pr.

Potato Printing. Helen R. Haddad. LC 80-2458. (Illus.). 64p. (gr. 3-6). 1981. (Crowell Jr Bks); PLB 13.89 (ISBN 0-690-04089-X). HarpJ.

Potato Processing. 4th ed. Talburt. 1987. 83.95 (ISBN 0-442-28315-6). Van Nos Reinhold.

Potato Research of Tomorrow - Drought Tolerance, Virus Resistance & Analytic Breeding Methods: Proceedings - International Seminar, Wageningen, Neth 30-31 October, 1985. Pref. by Lidwine Dellaert. (Illus.). 170p. (Orig.). 1986. pap. text ed. 30.00 (ISBN 90-220-0904-1, PDC306, Pub. by PUDOC). UNIPUB.

Potato: Uses for the Whole Potato. Recycling Consortium. 1984. pap. text ed. 1.95 (Pub. by Recycling Consort). Prosperity & Profits.

Potatoes. Sylvia A. Johnson. (Lerner Natural Science Bks.). (Illus.). 48p. (gr. 4-10). 1984. lib. bdg. 12.95 (ISBN 0-8225-1459-1). Lerner Pubns.

Potatoes. Kathleen Pohl. (Nature Close-Ups Ser.). (Illus.). 32p. (gr. 3-4). 1986. PLB 15.33 (ISBN 0-8172-2723-7); pap. text ed. 9.27 (ISBN 0-8172-2741-5). Raintree Pubs.

Potatoes of Bolivia: Their Breeding Value & Evolutionary Relationships. J. G. Hawkes & J. P. Hjerting. (Illus.). 480p. 1988. 110.00 (ISBN 0-19-854220-8). Oxford U Pr.

Potatoes, Potatoes. Anita Lobel. LC 67-16231. (Illus.). 48p. (gr. k-3). 1984. 12.25i (ISBN 0-06-023927-1); PLB 11.89g (ISBN 0-06-023928-X). HarpJ.

Potatoes: Production, Marketing & Programs in Developing Countries. Douglas E. Horton. (Winrock Development Oriented Literature Ser.). 260p. 1987. 29.85 (ISBN 0-8133-7197-X). Westview.

Potawatomi. James A. Clifton. (Indians of North America Ser.). (Illus.). 104p. (gr. 5 up). 1988. lib. bdg. 16.95x (ISBN 1-55546-725-3). Chelsea Hse.

Potawatomis: Keepers of the Fire. David Edmunds. LC 78-5628. (Civilization of the American Indian Ser.: Vol. 145). (Illus.). 374p. 1987. pap. 12.95 (ISBN 0-8061-2069-X). U of Okla Pr.

Potawatomis: Keepers of the Fire. R. David Edmunds. LC 78-5628. (Civilization of the American Indian Ser: No. 145). (Illus.). 384p. 1980. 22.95 (ISBN 0-8061-1478-9). U of Okla Pr.

Potboilers. Gaylon Duke. 64p. 1980. pap. text ed. 15.00 (ISBN 0-87879-251-1). Acad Therapy.

Potboilers: Three Black Comedies. Charles Marowitz. 192p. (Orig.). 1987. (Dist. by Kampmann & Co); pap. 11.95 (ISBN 0-7145-2862-5). M Boyars Pubs.

Potemkin. George Soloveytchik. LC 72-7192. (Select Bibliographies Reprint Ser.). 1972. Repr. of 1938 ed. 32.00 (ISBN 0-8369-6954-5). Ayer Co Pubs.

Potent Prayers. Harriete Curtiss & F. Homer. 1976p. pap. 1.00 (ISBN 0-87516-362-9). DeVorss.

Potent Self: The Dynamics of the Body & the Mind. Moshe Feldenkrais. LC 84-48217. 224p. 1985. 17.95 (ISBN 0-06-250320-0, HarpR). Har-Row.

Potential Benefits of Reducing Occupational Radiation Exposure (AIF-NESP-010R) rev. ed. NES Division of Science Applications, Inc. (National Environment Studies Project: NESP Reports). 60p. 1979. 45.00 (ISBN 0-318-13589-2); to NESP sponsors 15.00 (ISBN 0-318-13590-6). US Coun Energy Awareness.

Potential Carcinogenicity of Nitrosatable Drugs. Ed. by Frederick Coulston & John F. Dunne. LC 79-16498. (Illus.). 1980. 35.00x (ISBN 0-89391-022-8). Ablex Pub.

Potential Economies in the Reorganization of Local School Attendance Units. Harry A. Little. LC 72-177900. (Columbia University. Teachers College. Contributions to Education: No. 628). Repr. of 1934 ed. 22.50 (ISBN 0-404-55628-0). AMS Pr.

Potential Effects of Income Redistribution on Selected Growth Constraints: A Case Study of Kenya. Osman S. Ahmed. LC 80-6093. (Illus.). 368p. (Orig.). 1982. lib. bdg. 34.00 (ISBN 0-8191-2112-6); pap. text ed. 16.75 (ISBN 0-8191-2113-4). U Pr of Amer.

Potential Energy. M. Kenward. LC 75-36174. (Illus.). 256p. 1976. pap. 12.95 o. p. (ISBN 0-521-29056-2). Cambridge U Pr.

Potential Energy Functions in Conformational Analysis. K. Rasmussen. (Lecture Notes in Chemistry Ser.: Vol. 37). xiii, 231p. 1985. pap. 24.00 (ISBN 0-387-13906-0). Springer-Verlag.

Potential Energy Hypersurfaces. P. G. Mezey. (Studies in Physical & Theoretical Chemistry: Vol. 53). 538p. 1988. 156.00 (ISBN 0-444-42887-9). Elsevier.

Potential Energy Surfaces. D. M. Hirst. 248p. 1985. 53.00x (ISBN 0-85066-275-3). Taylor & Francis.

Potential Energy Surfaces. Ed. by K. P. Lawley. LC 81-466015. pap. 154.50 (ISBN 0-317-26346-3, 2025196). Bks Demand UMI.

Potential Energy Surfaces, Vol. 42. Ed. by K. P. Lawley. (Advances in Chemical Physics Ser.). 610p. 1980. 174.00 (ISBN 0-471-27633-2, Pub. by Wiley-Interscience). Wiley.

Potential Energy Surfaces & Dynamics Calculations for Chemical Reactions & Molecular Energy Transfer. Ed. by D. G. Truhlar. LC 81-8666. 878p. 1981. 125.00x (ISBN 0-306-40755-8, Plenum Pr). Plenum Pub.

Potential Fields & Their Transformations in Applied Geophysics. Wladimir Baranov. (Geoexploration Monographs: Series 1, No. 6). (Illus.). 121p. 1975. lib. bdg. 38.50x (ISBN 3-4431-3008-9). Lubrecht & Cramer.

Potential for Energy Efficiency in the Fertilizer Industry. Roger Heath et al. (Technical Paper: No. 35). 126p. 1985. 5.00 (ISBN 0-8213-0525-5, BK 0525). World Bank.

Potential for Field Beans-Phaseolus Vulgaris L.-In West & North Africa. Centro Internacional de Agricultura Tropical Staff. 143p. (Orig.). 1985. pap. text ed. 14.95x (ISBN 84-89206-45-7, Pub. by CIAT Colombia). Agribookstore.

Potential for Liquid Fuels from Agriculture & Forestry in Australia. G. A. Stewart et al. 147p. 1980. pap. 6.00 (ISBN 0-643-00353-3, Pub. by CSIRO Australia). Intl Spec Bk.

Potential for Production of 'Hydrocarbon' Fuels from Crops in Australia. G. A. Stewart et al. (Illus.). 86p. (Orig.). 1983. pap. 6.00 (ISBN 0-643-02931-1, Pub. by CSIRO Australia). Intl Spec Bk.

Potential for Reform of Criminal Justice. Ed. by Herbert Jacob. LC 73-77871. (Sage Criminal Justice System Annuals Ser.: Vol. 3). pap. 88.00 (ISBN 0-317-08942-0, 2021915). Bks Demand UMI.

Potential Fulfilled, Vol. VI. Priscilla Gilbert. 105p. 1976. 4.50 (ISBN 0-86690-105-1, 1145-01). Am Fed Astrologers.

Potential Fulfilled - What Saved Them, Vol. 2. Priscilla Gilbert. LC 76-26745. 104p. 1976. 4.50 (ISBN 0-86690-106-X). Am Fed Astrologers.

Potential Health & Safety Impacts of High-BTU Coal Gasification: Occupational. Flow Resources Corporation Staff. 200p. 1978. pap. 3.50 (ISBN 0-318-12669-9, F00687). Am Gas Assn.

Potential Health Effects in the Human from Exposure to Polychlorinated Biphenyls (PCBs) & Related Impurities see PCB Health Effects.

Potential Impact of Changes in Fertility on Infant, Child & Maternal Mortality. James Trussell & Anne R. Pebley. (Working Paper: No. 698). 60p. 1985. 5.00 (ISBN 0-8213-0453-4, WP 0698). World Bank.

Potential Industrial Carcinogens & Mutagens. L. Fishbein. (Studies in Environmental Science: Vol. 4). 534p. 1979. 147.50 (ISBN 0-444-41777-X). Elsevier.

Potential Is Within You. Roy E. Davis. 176p. 1982. 7.95 (ISBN 0-317-20867-5). CSA Pr.

Potential Leaders. Costa Deir. Ed. by Dick Myhre & Bob Briggs. (Principles of Leadership Ser.). (Orig.). 1988. pap. 3.95 (ISBN 0-939159-12-0). Cityhill Pub.

Potential Liabilities of Probation & Parole Officers. rev. ed. Rolando V. Del Carmen. LC 86-211793. 202p. 1986. 18.95 (ISBN 0-87084-184-X). Anderson Pub Co.

Potential Liabilities of Probation & Parole Officers. rev. ed. Rolando V. Del Carmen. Ed. by Melvin T. Axilbund. 220p. 1985. pap. 11.00 (027-000-01274-4). USGPO.

Potential Low-Grade Iron Ore & Hydraulic-Fracturing Sand in Cambrian Sandstones, Northwestern Llano Region, Texas. V. E. Barnes & D. A. Schofield. (Report of Investigations Ser.: RI 53). (Illus.). 58p. 1964. 2.00 (ISBN 0-686-29335-5). Bur Econ Geology.

Potential Market Demand for Two-Way Information Services to the Home, 1970-1990. Paul Baran. 139p. 1971. 10.50 (ISBN 0-318-14418-2, R26). Inst Future.

Potential Methods in the Theory of Elasticity. V. D. Kupradze. 352p. 1965. text ed. 70.00x (ISBN 0-7065-0549-2, Pub. by Keter Pub Jerusalem). Coronet Bks.

Potential of Earth-Shelter & Underground Space: Today's Resource for Tomorrow's Space & Energy Viability: Proceedings of the Underground Space Conference & Exposition, Kansas City, MO, June 8-10, 1981. Ed. by T. Lance Holthusen. (Illus.). 501p. 1981. 92.00 (ISBN 0-08-028050-1). Pergamon.

Potential of Fantasy & Imagination. A. A. Sheikh & John T. Shaffer. LC 79-88092. 1979. lib. bdg. 25.00 (ISBN 0-913412-31-7). Brandon Hse.

Potential of Herbs As a Cash Crop. Richard A. Miller. 230p. 1985. pap. 13.20 (ISBN 0-911311-10-6). Halcyon Hse.

Potential of the Traditional Birth Attendant. Ed. by A. Mangay Maglacas & J. Simons. (WHO Offset Publication: No. 95). 105p. 1986. pap. 9.60 (ISBN 92-4-170095-5). World Health.

Potential Pattern Recognition in Chemical & Medical Decision Making. D. Coomans & I. Broeckaert. LC 86-625. (Chemometrics Research Studies). 256p. 1986. 59.95 (ISBN 0-471-91009-0). Wiley.

Potential Population Supporting Capacities of Lands in the Developing World: Land Resources for Populations of the Future. Rev. ed. G. M. Higgins & A. H. Kassam. (Technical Report of Project: No. INT/75/P13). (Illus.). 139p. 1985. pap. 47.00 (ISBN 92-5-101411-6, F2663, FAO). UNIPUB.

Potential Principal see Como Vivir al Maximo.

Potential Principle. Edwin L. Cole. 144p. (Orig.). 1984. pap. 3.95 (ISBN 0-88368-144-7). Whitaker Hse.

Potential Principle Study Guide. Ed Cole. pap. 4.95 (ISBN 0-317-40154-8). Harrison Hse.

Potential Private Revenue & Public Benefits from Alternative Agriculture. The National Conference of State Legislatures Staff. (State Legislative Report: Vol. 11, No. 4). pap. 5.00 (ISBN 1-55516-160-X). Natl Conf State Legis.

Potential Products for Export. (Productivity Ser.: No. 18). 75p. 1985. pap. 9.00 (ISBN 92-833-1708-4, APO164, APO). UNIPUB.

Potential Role of Oil Shale in the U. S. Energy Mix: Questions of Development & Policy Formulation in an Environment Age. Theodore J. Ellis. Ed. by Stuart Bruchey. LC 78-22677. (Energy in the American Economy Ser.). (Illus.). 1979. lib. bdg. 23.00x (ISBN 0-405-11980-1). Ayer Co Pubs.

Potential Role of T-Cells in Cancer Therapy. Ed. by Alexander Fefer & Allan Goldstein. (Progress in Cancer Research & Therapy Ser.: Vol. 22). 311p. 1982. text ed. 67.00 (ISBN 0-89004-747-2). Raven.

Potential Scattering in Atomic Physics. P. G. Burke. LC 76-28965. (Illus.). 138p. 1977. 32.50x (ISBN 0-306-30933-5, Plenum Pr). Plenum Pub.

Potential: The Name Analysis Book. Paul Rice & Valeta Rice. 160p. (Orig.). 1987. pap. 8.95 (ISBN 0-87728-632-9). Weiser.

Potential Theory. J. Bliedtner. (Universitext Ser.). xiv, 435p. 1986. pap. 40.00 (ISBN 0-387-16396-4). Springer-Verlag.

Potential Theory. Ed. by J. Kral et al. (Illus.). 376p. 1988. 75.00x (ISBN 0-306-42838-5, Plenum Pr). Plenum Pub.

Potential Theory & Function Theory for Irregular Regions. Iurii D. Burago & V. G. Mazya. LC 69-15004. (Seminars in Mathematics Ser.: Vol. 3). pap. 20.00 (ISBN 0-317-08891-2, 2020695). Bks Demand UMI.

Potential Theory Copenhagen Nineteen Seventy-Nine: Proceedings. Ed. by C. Berg et al. (Lecture Notes in Mathematics: Vol. 787). 319p. 1980. pap. text ed. 23.00 (ISBN 0-387-09967-0). Springer-Verlag.

Potential Theory in Modern Function Theory. 2nd ed. Masatugu Tsuji. LC 74-4297. 600p. 1975. text ed. 29.50 (ISBN 0-8284-0281-7). Chelsea Pub.

Potential Theory of Unsteady Supersonic Flow. John W. Miles. LC 59-564. (Cambridge Monographs on Mechanics & Mathematics). pap. 58.50 (ISBN 0-317-10245-1, 2050772). Bks Demand UMI.

Potential Theory on Harmonic Spaces. C. Constantinescu & A. Cornea. LC 72-86117. (Grundlehren der Mathematischen Wissenschaften: Vol. 158). 1972. 69.00 (ISBN 0-387-05916-4). Springer-Verlag.

Potts Village Site (39C019), Oahe Reservoir, North Central South Dakota. Robert L. Stephenson. Ed. by Robert T. Bray. (Missouri Archaeologist Ser.: Vol. 33). (Illus.). 140p. (Orig.). 1971. pap. 3.00 (ISBN 0-943414-50-4). MO Arch Soc.

Potty Time. Anne Civardi. (Illus.). 24p. (ps). 1988. 6.95 (ISBN 0-671-65896-4, Little Simon). S&S.

Potty Time! Yellow Ladder Books for Toddlers Through 4 Years. Illus. by Betty Reichmeier. (Learning Ladders Ser.). (Illus.). 10p. Date not set. vinyl 5.95 (ISBN 0-394-89403-0, BYR). Random.

Potty Training Your Baby: Early Potty Training for Babies & Toddlers. Katie Van Pelt. (Illus.). 144p. 1988. pap. 6.95 (ISBN 0-89529-398-6). Avery Pub.

Potwin Place: Its History & Traditions. 4.95 (ISBN 0-686-79880-5, 45). Shawnee County Hist.

Pouce par Pouce. Leo Lionni. (Illus., Fr.). (gr. k-1). 1961. 10.95 (ISBN 0-8392-3028-1). Astor-Honor.

Poudre Aux Yeux. Eugene Labiche. 9.95 (ISBN 0-686-54250-9). French & Eur.

Poul Anderson - Myth-Maker & Wonder-Weaver: An Interim Bibliography (1947-1985) 4th ed. Ed. by Gordon Benson, Jr. 46p. 1982. pap. 3.50 (ISBN 0-912613-03-3). Galactic Central.

Poul Jorgenson's Book of Fly Tying: A Guide to Fly for All Game Fish. Poul Jorgenson. 1988. 34.95 (ISBN 1-55566-002-9); pap. 19.95 (ISBN 1-55566-004-5). Johnson Bks.

Poulains de Corinthe. Ravel. 1980. 80.00. Ares.

"Poulains" de Corinthe. O. E. Ravel. (Illus.). 1979. text ed. 80.00 (ISBN 0-916710-47-5). Obol Intl.

Poular, Dielecte Peul Du Fouta Senegalais II: Lexique Poular-Francais. Henri Gaden. 280p. Repr. text ed. 62.10x (ISBN 0-576-11603-3, Pub. by Gregg Intl Pubs England). Gregg Intl.

Poulet: A Rooster Who Laid Eggs. Robin Fox. (Illus., Fr.). 3.50 (ISBN 0-685-11509-7). French & Eur.

Pouliuli. Albert Wendt. LC 80-15158. (Pacific Classics Ser.: No. 8). 147p. 1980. pap. text ed. 5.95x (ISBN 0-8248-0728-6). UH Pr.

Poulou et Sebastien see Paul & Sebastian.

Poultry. Bon Appetit Magazine Editors. LC 83-24867. (Cooking with Bon Appetit Ser.). (Illus.). 1984. 12.95 (ISBN 0-89535-134-X). Knapp Pr.

Poultry. LC 78-13802. (Good Cook Ser.). (Illus.). (gr. 7 up). 1979. lib. bdg. 22.60 (ISBN 0-8094-2851-2, Pub. by Time-Life). Silver.

Poultry. Ed. by Time-Life Books. (Good Cook Ser.). (Illus.). 1979. 14.95 (ISBN 0-8094-2850-4). Time-Life.

Poultry see Cooking with Bon Appetit.

Poultry: A Guide to Management. Carol Twinch. (Illus.). 1985. 12.95 (ISBN 0-946284-32-6, Pub. by Crowood Pr). Longwood Pub Group.

Poultry & Egg Statistics, 1960-85. Allen Baker & Eunice Armstrong. (Statistical Bulletin Ser.: No. 747). 1986. pap. 4.25 (ISBN 0-318-22425-9, S/N 001-019-00495-9). USGPO.

Poultry & Small Game. (Illus.). 210p. 1987. pap. 695.00 (ISBN 0-318-04171-5). Busn Trend.

Poultry As a Hobby. Michael Baumeister & Heinz Meyer. (Illus.). 221p. 1987. 19.95 (ISBN 0-86622-935-3, PS-214). TFH Pubns.

Poultry Diseases. 2nd ed. R. F. Gordon & F. T. Jordan. (Illus.). 416p. 1982. 58.00 (ISBN 0-7216-0779-9, Bailliere-Tindall). Saunders.

Poultry Egg & Meat Production. C. R. Parkhurst & G. J. Mountney. (Illus.). 300p. 1987. 39.95 (ISBN 0-442-27497-1). Van Nos Reinhold.

Poultry Health & Management. 2nd ed. David Sainsbury. (Illus.). 195p. 1984. pap. text ed. 19.50x (ISBN 0-246-12355-9, Pub. by Granada England). Sheridan.

Poultry Inspection: The Basis for a Risk-Assessment Approach. National Research Council Staff. 177p. 1987. pap. text ed. 14.95x (ISBN 0-309-03743-3). Natl Acad Pr.

Poultry on the Farm. Cliff Moon. LC 83-71631. (Down on the Farm Bks.). (Illus.). 33p. (ps-2). 1983. PLB 9.40 (ISBN 0-531-04697-4). Watts.

Poultry Production. 12th ed. Malden C. Nesheim et al. LC 78-31386. (Illus.). 399p. 1979. text ed. 17.50 (ISBN 0-8121-0665-2). Lea & Febiger.

Poultry Recipes. Better Homes & Gardens Editors. (Illus.). 48p. 1988. pap. 2.95 (ISBN 0-696-01831-4). BH&G.

Poultry Science. 2nd ed. M. E. Ensminger. (Illus.). (gr. 9-12). 1980. 38.60 (ISBN 0-8134-2087-3, 2087); text ed. 28.95x. Inter Print Pubs.

Poultry Science & Production. Robert Moreng & John Avens. 1984. text ed. 37.00 (ISBN 0-8359-5559-1, Reston); instr's. manual avail. (ISBN 0-8359-5562-1). P-H.

Pounamu, Pounamu: Short Stories. Witi Ihimaera. 132p. (Orig.). 1983. pap. 4.95x (ISBN 0-86863-675-4, Pub. by Heinemann Pub New Zealand). Intl Spec Bk.

Pound - Joyce: Letters & Essays. Ezra Pound. LC 66-27616. 1970. pap. 10.95 (ISBN 0-8112-0159-7, NDP296). New Directions.

Pound As Wuz: Essays & Lectures on Ezra Pound. James Laughlin. (Illus.). 270p. (Orig.). 1987. 17.00 (ISBN 1-55597-097-4); pap. 9.50 (ISBN 1-55597-098-2). Graywolf.

Pound Conference: Perspectives on Justice in the Future. Ed. by Leo A. Levin & Russell R. Wheeler. LC 80-14618. 368p. 1980. text ed. 25.00 (ISBN 0-8299-2096-X). West Pub.

Pound Era. Hugh Kenner. LC 72-138349. 1971. 37.50x (ISBN 0-520-01860-5); pap. 12.95x (ISBN 0-520-02427-3). U of Cal Pr.

Pound-Ford: The Story of a Literary Friendship. Ezra Pound & Ford Madox Ford. Ed. by Brita L. Seyersted. LC 82-2255. 384p. 1982. 22.95 (ISBN 0-8112-0833-8). New Directions.

Pound-Lewis: The Letters of Ezra Pound & Wyndham Lewis. Ezra Pound & Wyndham Lewis. Ed. by Timothy Materer. LC 85-3007. 384p. 1985. 37.50 (ISBN 0-8112-0932-6). New Directions.

Pound Puppies in Lost & Found. Teddy Slater. LC 87-81748. (Golden Look-Look Bks.). (Illus.). 24p. (ps-3). 1988. pap. 1.50 (ISBN 0-307-11812-6, Pub. by Golden Bks). Western Pub.

Pound Puppies in Public Nuisance. Justine Korman. LC 87-81749. (Golden Look-Look Bks.). (Illus.). 24p. (ps-3). 1988. pap. 1.50 (ISBN 0-307-11811-8, Pub. by Golden Bks). Western Pub.

Pound Puppies in the Puppy Nobody Wanted. Larry Weinberg. LC 85-81578. (Big Little Golden Bks.). (Illus.). (gr. k-3). 1986. write for info. (ISBN 0-307-10270-X, Pub. by Golden Bks.). Western Pub.

Pound Revised. Paul Smith. (Illus.). 192p. 1983. 29.25 (ISBN 0-7099-2346-5, Pub. by Croom Helm Ltd). Routledge Chapman & Hall.

Pound Sterling. Imre Devegh. Ed. by Mira Wilkins. LC 78-3908. (International Finance Ser.). 1978. Repr. of 1939 ed. lib. bdg. 14.00x (ISBN 0-405-11213-0). Ayer Co Pubs.

Pound the Little Review: The Letters of Ezra Pound to Margaret Anderson. Ezra Pound & Margaret Anderson. Ed. by Thomas L. Scott et al. LC 88-3410. (Correspondence of Ezra Pound Ser.: Vol. 6). 384p. 1988. 37.50 (ISBN 0-8112-1059-6). New Directions.

Pound Wise. facsimile ed. Osbert Sitwell. LC 74-134136. (Essay Index Reprint Ser.). Repr. of 1963 ed. 21.00 (ISBN 0-8369-2429-0). Ayer Co Pubs.

Pound, Yeats, Eliot & the Modernist Movement. C. K. Stead. 300p. 1985. text ed. 27.50 (ISBN 0-8135-1075-9). Rutgers U Pr.

Pounder's Marine Diesel Engines. 6th ed. C. Wilbur & D. Wight. 475p. 1984. text ed. 52.95 (ISBN 0-408-01136-X). Butterworth.

Pounding Hooves. Dorothy G. Johnston. LC 75-18645. (Horse Stories Gift Set Ser.). (Illus.). 256p. (gr. 6-8). 1976. pap. 2.95 (ISBN 0-912692-77-4). Cook.

Pound's Artists: Ezra Pound & the Visual Arts in London, Paris, & Italy. Richard Humphreys & John Alexander. (Illus.). 176p. 1986. pap. 14.95 (ISBN 0-946590-26-5, Pub. by Tate Gall Pubns). Salem Hse Pubs.

Pound's Cantos. Peter Makin. Ed. by Claude Rawson. (Unwin Critical Library). 368p. 1985. text ed. 39.95x (ISBN 0-04-811001-9); pap. text ed. 14.95x (ISBN 0-04-811002-7). Unwin Hyman.

Pound's Cantos Declassified. Philip Furia. LC 83-43227. 160p. 1984. 20.00x (ISBN 0-271-00373-1). Pa St U Pr.

Pound's Cavalcanti: An Edition of the Translations, Notes & Essays. D. Anderson. 1982. 31.50x (ISBN 0-691-06519-5). Princeton U Pr.

Pounds Off. Prevention Magazine Editors. Ed. by Sharon Faelten. 96p. 1987. pap. 4.95 (ISBN 0-87857-706-8). Rodale Pr Inc.

Poupee. Jacques Audiberti. 112p. 1969. 9.95 (ISBN 0-686-54500-1). French & Eur.

Poupliniere et la Musique de Chambre Au XVIII Siecle. G. Cucuel. LC 70-158961. (Music Ser). (Fr.). 1971. Repr. of 1913 ed. lib. bdg. 55.00 (ISBN 0-306-70186-3). Da Capo.

Pour & Separate Models see D.A.E Project: Instructional Materials for Dental Health Professions.

Pour et le Contre: Correspondance Polemique sur le Respect de la Posterite. Pline et les Anciens Auteurs qui ont Parle de Peinture et de Sculpture. Denis Diderot et al. (Illus.). 384p. 1958. 12.95 (ISBN 0-686-56025-6). French & Eur.

Pour et le Contre: Lettres Sur la Posterite. Denis Diderot et al. 384p. 1958. 9.95 (ISBN 0-686-56024-8). French & Eur.

Pour Finir Encore. Samuel Beckett. Bd. with Immobile et Autres Foirades. 1976. pap. 8.95 (ISBN 0-686-52220-6). French & Eur.

Pour It On! A Complete Guide to Quick & Healthy Sauces. Marcia Mills. (Illus.). 96p. (Orig.). Date not set. pap. 7.95 (ISBN 0-942267-13-3). Profile Press.

Pour la Paix - Notes et Documents. Frederick Passy. LC 70-147451. (Library of War & Peace; Problems of the Organized Peace Movement: Selected Documents). lib. bdg. 46.00 (ISBN 0-8240-0243-1). Garland Pub.

Pour la Patrie see For My Country.

Pour la Revolution Africaine. Frantz Fanon. (Petite Coll. Maspero). pap. 9.95 (ISBN 0-685-35634-5). French & Eur.

Pour le Communisme: Questions de Theorie. Nicola Badaloni. (Archontes: No. 9). 262p. (Orig.). 1976. pap. text ed. 22.40x (ISBN 90-2797-533-7). Mouton.

Pour l'Effort (Aout 62-Dec. 65; see Discours et Messages.

Pour l'Honneur de l'Esprit: Correspondance, 1898-1914. Charles Peguy & Jean Basstaire. 352p. 1973. 11.95 (ISBN 0-686-54864-7). French & Eur.

Pour l'Honneur de l'Esprit: Correspondance (1898-1914) Romain Rolland & Charles Peguy. (Illus.). 352p. 1973. 12.95 (ISBN 0-686-55265-2). French & Eur.

Pour Lucrece. Jean Giraudoux. pap. 11.50 (ISBN 0-685-33925-4). French & Eur.

Pour Moi...Mais Oui: Watercolors & Verse. Clair E. Krizov. LC 85-71664. (Illus.). 50p. 1985. pap. 14.95 (ISBN 0-934857-30-X). Bear Pub Co.

Pour Oublier un Reve. Charlotte Lamb. (Collection Harlequin). 192p. 1983. pap. 1.95 (ISBN 0-373-49321-5). Harlequin Bks.

Pour Parler: Manual De Conversation Francaise. 2nd ed. Anne-Marie Bryan & Jean Duche. (Illus.). 1977. text ed. write for info. (ISBN 0-13-686386-8); tapes 180.00 (ISBN 0-13-686378-7). P-H.

Pour Piano Seul. Andre Maurois. pap. 19.50 (ISBN 0-685-36954-4). French & Eur.

Pour Prendre Conge. Vercors. 4.95 (ISBN 0-686-55132-X). French & Eur.

Pour preparer un oeuf dur see Theatre.

Pour Quelques Boucles D'or. Sondra Stanford. (Harlequin Romantique Ser.). 192p. 1983. pap. 1.95 (ISBN 0-373-41199-5). Harlequin Bks.

Pour Raison Garder, 3 vols. Jules Romains. 1963-67. Vol. 1. pap. 4.95 (ISBN 0-686-55285-7); Vol. 2. pap. 7.95 (ISBN 0-686-55286-5); Vol. 3. pap. 7.95 (ISBN 0-686-55287-3). French & Eur.

Pour Saluer Melville. Jean Giono. (Idees Ser.). 184p. 1941. 5.95 (ISBN 0-686-53982-6). Schoenhof.

Pour Sganarelle. Romain Gary. 480p. 1965. 11.95 (ISBN 0-686-55884-7). French & Eur.

Pour Sganarelle Recherche d'un Personnage et d'un Roman see Frere Ocean.

Pour un Nouveau Roman: Critique litteraire. Alain Robbe-Grillet. 1963. pap. 6.95 (ISBN 0-685-11510-0). French & Eur.

Pour un Nouvel Ordre Economique International see Towards a New International Economic Order.

Pour une Histoire du Quotidien au XIXe Siecle en Nivernais. 1977. 12.80x (ISBN 90-279-7883-2). Mouton.

Pour une Morale de l'Ambiguite, Pyrrhus et Cineas. Simone De Beauvoir. (Idees Ser.). pap. 8.95 (ISBN 0-685-37190-5). Schoenhof.

Pour une Philosophie de l'Education. Jacques Maritain. 254p. 1960. 9.95 (ISBN 0-686-56364-6). French & Eur.

Pour une Relecture Africaine de Marx et d'Engels. Leopold S. Senghor. 67p. 1976. 9.95 (ISBN 0-686-55011-0). French & Eur.

Pour une Seule Valse. Julia Carole. (Collection Colombine). 192p. 1983. pap. 1.95 (ISBN 0-373-48057-1). Harlequin Bks.

Pour une Sociologie Scientifiques: Epsitemlogie Compare de le Analyse Conceptuelle. Antonio Piaser. (Interaction - l'Homme et Son Environment Social: No. 9). (Fr.). 1976. pap. text ed. 29.60x (ISBN 90-2797-563-9). Mouton.

Pourboire Sixteen: Peter Kaplan's Book. Peter Kaplan et al. (Pourboire Ser.). 1979. pap. 5.00 (ISBN 0-930900-59-6). Burning Deck.

Pourin It All Out. Jay Saporita. (Illus.). 224p. 1980. 10.00 (ISBN 0-8065-0696-2, Pub. by Citadel Pr); pap. 5.95 (ISBN 0-8065-0729-2). Lyle Stuart.

Pouring for Profit: A Guide to Bar & Beverage Management. Katsigris. 1988. pap. price not set (ISBN 0-471-84293-1). Wiley.

Pouring for Profit: A Guide to Bar & Beverage Management. Costas Katsigris & Mary Porter. LC 83-5887. 433p. 1983. pap. 19.95 (ISBN 0-471-88900-8). Wiley.

Pourpre et de Soleil. Kate Bowes. (Harlequin Seduction Ser.). 332p. 1983. pap. 3.25 (ISBN 0-373-45021-4). Harlequin Bks.

Pourquoi Pas Toujours? Yvonne Whittal. (Harlequin Romantique Ser.). 192p. 1984. pap. 1.95 (ISBN 0-373-41242-8). Harlequin Bks.

Pourrais Tu Arreter Joseqhine. Stephane Poulin. (Fr.). 1988. 12.95 (ISBN 0-88776-217-4). Tundra Bks.

Poursuite Inattendue. Christiane Szeps-Fralin. (Illus.). 56p. (Fr.). 1983. pap. 3.25 (ISBN 0-8219-0021-8, 40291); wkbk 1.75 (ISBN 0-8219-0022-6, 40653). EMC.

Pousadas of Portugal: Unique Lodgings in State-Owned Castles, Palaces, Mansions, & Hotels. rev. ed. Sam Ballard & Jane Ballard. LC 86-351. (Companion to Paradores of Spain). (Illus.). 176p. 1986. pap. 8.95 (ISBN 0-916782-77-8). Harvard Common Pr.

Poussin - The Early Years in Rome: The Origins of French Classicism. Konrad Oberhuber. (Illus.). 360p. 1988. 65.00. Hudson Hills.

Poussin Paintings: A Catalogue Raisonne. Christopher Wright. (Illus.). 303p. 1985. 60.00 (ISBN 0-87052-218-3). Hippocrene Bks.

Poussin: The Early Years in Rome: The Origins of French Classicism. Konrad Oberhuber. (Illus.). 360p. 1988. 65.00; pap. 35.00. Hudson Hills.

Poustinia. Catherine D. Doherty. LC 74-19961. 216p. 1975. pap. 3.95 (ISBN 0-87793-083-X). Ave Maria.

Pouvoir & les Groupes de Pression: Etude de la Structure Politique du Capitalisme. rev. ed. Stanislaw Ehrlich. (Societe, Mouvements Sociaux & Ideologies, Etudes: No. 9). 1971. pap. 14.00x (ISBN 90-2796-903-5). Mouton.

Pouvoir aux Enfants. Pierre Daninos. 8.95 (ISBN 0-686-55570-8). French & Eur.

Pouvoir Enfin T'Aimer. Marjorie Lewty. (Collection Harlequin Ser.). 192p. 1983. pap. 1.95 (ISBN 0-373-49360-6). Harlequin Bks.

Poverello: St. Francis of Assisi. Mark Hegener. pap. 2.00 (ISBN 0-8199-0358-2). Franciscan Herald.

Poverty. Bill Dudley. (Opposing Viewpoints Ser.). (Illus.). (YA) (gr. 10 up). 1988. lib. bdg. 13.95 (ISBN 0-89908-432-X); pap. text ed. 6.95 (ISBN 0-89908-407-9). Greenhaven.

Poverty. A. Dures & K. Dures. (History in Focus Ser.). (Illus.). 72p. (gr. 7-12). 1984. 17.95 (ISBN 0-7134-4349-9, Pub. by Batsford England). David & Charles.

Poverty: A Study of Town Life. 2nd ed. B. Seebohm Rountree. LC 79-56969. (English Working Class Ser.). 1980. lib. bdg. 51.00 (ISBN 0-8240-0120-6). Garland Pub.

Poverty, Agriculture & Economic Growth. B. M. Bhatia. 1977. 15.00x (ISBN 0-7069-0524-5). Intl Bk Dist.

Poverty Amid Plenty: A Political & Economic Analysis. Harrell R. Rodgers, Jr. (Political Science Ser.). (Illus.). 240p. 1979. text ed. 9.75 (ISBN 0-394-34937-7, RanC). Random.

Poverty: An Interdisciplinary Approach. Sarveswara Rao. 1982. 24.00x (ISBN 0-8364-0902-7, Pub. by Somaiya). South Asia Bks.

Poverty & Aid. Ed. by J. R. Parkinson. LC 83-9780. 280p. 1983. 32.50 (ISBN 0-312-63302-5). St Martin.

Poverty & Basic Needs: Evidence from Guyana & the Philippines. Guy Standing & Richard Szal. (WEP Study Ser.). viii, 154p. 1979. pap. 10.50 (ISBN 92-2-102034-7, ILO117, ILO). UNIPUB.

Poverty & Charity in Aix-en-Provence, 1640-1789. Cissie C. Fairchilds. LC 75-36930. (Studies in Historical & Political Science Ninety-Fourth Ser.: No. 1 (1976)). (Illus.). 216p. 1976. 25.00x (ISBN 0-8018-1677-7). Johns Hopkins.

Poverty & Discrimination. Lester C. Thurow. LC 69-18825. (Studies in Social Economics). pap. 57.00 (ISBN 0-317-28349-9, 2022557). Bks Demand UMI.

Poverty & Economic Justice: A Philosophical Approach. Ed. by Robert H. Hartman. 1984. pap. 10.95 (ISBN 0-8091-2597-8). Paulist Pr.

Poverty & Famines: An Essay on Entitlement & Deprivation. Amartya Sen. 1981. pap. 10.95x (ISBN 0-19-828463-2). Oxford U Pr.

Poverty & Growth in Kenya. Paul Collier & Deepak Lal. (Working Paper: No. 389). 76p. 1980. 5.00 (ISBN 0-686-36149-0, WP-0389). World Bank.

Poverty & Human Development. The World Bank. (Illus.). 1980. pap. text ed. 7.95x (ISBN 0-19-520389-5). Oxford U Pr.

Poverty & Hunger: Issues & Options for Food Security in Developing Countries. (World Bank Policy Study). 82p. (Eng. , Fr. & Span.). 1986. 7.50 (ISBN 0-8213-0678-2, BK0678). World Bank.

Poverty & Ill-Health in a Third World City. CIIR Staff. 8p. 1984. 3.00x (ISBN 0-946848-65-3, Pub. by CIIR). State Mutual Bk.

Poverty & Incentives: The Economics of Social Security. Richard Hemming. LC 83-13468. 1984. 32.50x (ISBN 0-19-877164-9). Oxford U Pr.

Poverty & Its Vicious Circles. Jamison B. Hurry. LC 73-14158. (Perspectives in Social Inquiry Ser.). 196p. 1974. Repr. 11.00x (ISBN 0-405-05504-8). Ayer Co Pubs.

Poverty & Living Standards in Asia: An Overview of the Main Results & Lessons of Selected Household Surveys. Pravin Visaria & Shyamalendu Pal. (LSMS Working Paper: No. 2). 248p. 10.00 (ISBN 0-317-59148-7, BK 0030). World Bank.

Poverty & Malnutrition in Latin America: Early Childhood Intervention Programs. Ernesto Pollitt. LC 80-18811. 150p. 1980. 36.95 (ISBN 0-275-90538-1, C0538). Praeger.

Poverty & Mobility in India. Shekjar Mukherji. 1983. 15.00x (ISBN 0-686-43913-9, Pub. by P Prajana India). South Asia Bks.

Poverty & Piety in an English Village: Terling, 1525-1700. Keith Wrightson & David Levine. LC 78-1102. (Studies in Social Discontinuity Ser.). 1979. 19.95 (ISBN 0-12-765950-1). Acad Pr.

Poverty & Planning. C. N. Vakil. LC 73-19310. 357p. 1974. Repr. of 1963 ed. lib. bdg. 35.00x (ISBN 0-8371-7320-5, VAPP). Greenwood.

Poverty & Policy in American History: Monograph. Ed. by Michael B. Katz. (Studies in Social Discontinuity). 226p. 1983. 24.95 (ISBN 0-12-401760-6); pap. 14.95 (ISBN 0-12-401762-2). Acad Pr.

Poverty & Politics in Harlem. Alphonso Pinkney & Roger R. Woock. 1970. 12.95x (ISBN 0-8084-0249-8); pap. 8.95x (ISBN 0-8084-0250-1). New Coll U Pr.

Poverty & Politics: The Urban Poor in Brazil, 1870-1920. June E. Hahner. LC 86-1258. (Illus.). 431p. 1986. 32.50x (ISBN 0-8263-0878-3). U of NM Pr.

Poverty & Population. Titmuss. (English Workers Ser.). 1985. lib. bdg. 44.00 (ISBN 0-8240-7631-1). Garland Pub.

Poverty & Population: Approaches & Evidence. Gerry Rodgers. (WEP Study). 213p. 1984. pap. 19.25 (ISBN 92-2-103803-3). Intl Labour Office.

Poverty & Population Control. Lars Bondestam & Staffan Bergstrom. LC 79-40945. 1980. 55.50 (ISBN 0-12-114250-7); pap. 30.50 (ISBN 0-12-114252-3). Acad Pr.

Poverty & Power: The Case for a Political Approach to Development. Rachel Heatley. 96p. (Orig.). 1981. pap. 5.95x (ISBN 0-905762-52-5, Pub. by Zed Pr). Humanities.

Poverty & Problem-Solving under Military Rule: The Urban Poor in Lima, Peru. Henry A. Dietz. LC 79-620013. (Latin American Monographs: No. 51). (Illus.). 300p. 1980. text ed. 22.50x (ISBN 0-292-76460-X). U of Tex Pr.

Poverty & Progress. Rowntree. (English Workers Ser.). 1985. lib. bdg. 66.00 (ISBN 0-8240-7628-1). Garland Pub.

Poverty & Progress in Britain, 1953-1973: A Statistical Study of Low Income Households. Guy Fiegehen et al. LC 77-2143. (NIESR, Occasional Paper: No. 29). (Illus.). 1977. 32.50 (ISBN 0-521-21683-4). Cambridge U Pr.

Poverty & Progress: Social Mobility in a Nineteenth Century City. Stephan Thernstrom. LC 64-21793. (Joint Center for Urban Studies Publications). 1964. 22.50x (ISBN 0-674-69500-3); pap. 8.95x (ISBN 0-674-69501-1). Harvard U Pr.

Poverty & Prostitution. Frances Finnegan. LC 78-68123. (Illus.). 1979. 42.50 (ISBN 0-521-22447-0). Cambridge U Pr.

Poverty & Public Health. G. C. M'Gonigle & J. Kirby. (English Workers & the Coming of the Welfare State Ser., 1918-1945). 278p. 1985. lib. bdg. 39.00 (ISBN 0-8240-7620-6). Garland Pub.

Poverty & Public Policy: An Analysis of Federal Intervention Efforts. Michael Morris & John B. Williamson. LC 86-398. (Studies in Social Welfare Policies & Programs: No. 3). 248p. 1986. 36.95 (ISBN 0-313-24942-3, MPV/). Greenwood.

Poverty & Public Policy: An Evaluation of Social Science Research. Ed. by Vincent Covello. 288p. 1980. pap. text ed. 13.95x (ISBN 0-87073-889-5). Schenkman Bks Inc.

Poverty & Social Change. Kirsten Gronbjerg et al. LC 78-876. viii, 248p. 1980. pap. 9.00x (ISBN 0-226-30963-0). U of Chicago Pr.

Poverty & Social Change: With a Reappraisal. 2nd ed. Tarlok Singh. LC 74-33899. 352p. 1975. Repr. of 1969 ed. lib. bdg. 35.00x (ISBN 0-8371-8000-7, SIPO). Greenwood.

Poverty & Social Justice: Critical Perspectives. Tr. by Jimenez Francisco. 160p. 1987. 18.00x (ISBN 0-916950-75-1); pap. 10.00 (ISBN 0-916950-76-X). Biling Rev-Pr.

Poverty & Social Security. Tony Novak. 104p. 1984. pap. 6.75 (ISBN 0-86104-646-3, Pub. by Pluto Pr). Longwood Pub Group.

Poverty & Social Security in Britain since 1961. Wilfred Beckerman & Stephen Clark. 1982. 29.95x (ISBN 0-19-829004-7). Oxford U Pr.

Poverty & Social Welfare in the United States. Roy Lubove. LC 73-160032. (American Problem Studies). 128p. 1972. pap. text ed. 5.95 (ISBN 0-685-72300-3, Pub. by HR&W). Krieger.

Poverty & Social Welfare in the United States: Current Research Perspectives. Ed. by Donald Tomaskovic-Devey. 190p. 1987. pap. 23.50 (ISBN 0-8133-7458-8). Westview.

Poverty & Society: The Growth of the American Welfare State in International Comparison. Daniel Levine. 368p. 1988. text ed. 40.00 (ISBN 0-8135-1337-5); pap. text ed. 15.00 (ISBN 0-8135-1353-7). Rutgers U Pr.

Poverty & State Support. Peter Alcock & Chris Harrison. 232p. 1987. pap. 14.95 (ISBN 0-582-29652-8). Longman.

Poverty & the Development of Anti-Poverty Policy in the U. K. Richard Berthoud & Joan C. Brown. (Policy Studies Institute Ser.). 288p. 1981. text ed. 27.50x (ISBN 0-435-83102-X). Gower Pub Co.

Poverty & the Development of Human Resources: Regional Perspective. Willem Bussink & David Davies. (Working Paper: No. 406). iii, 193p. 1980. 10.00 (ISBN 0-686-36133-4, WP-0406). World Bank.

Poverty & the Impact of Income Maintenance Programmes in Four Developed Countries: Case Studies of Australia, Belgium, Norway & Great Britain. Wilfred Beckerman et al. (Illus.). 90p. (Orig.). 1979. 19.25 (ISBN 9-22-102063-0); pap. 12.25 (ISBN 92-2-102064-9). Intl Labour Office.

Poverty & the Impact of Income Maintenance Programmes in Four Developed Countries. 1979. pap. 10.00 (ISBN 92-2-102064-9, ILO133, ILO). UNIPUB.

Poverty & the Minimum Wage. Donald O. Parsons. 1980. pap. 7.00 (ISBN 0-8447-3409-8). Am Enterprise.

Poverty & the State: An Historical Sociology. Tony Novak. 192p. 1988. 59.00 (ISBN 0-335-15545-6, Open Univ Pr); pap. 21.00 (ISBN 0-335-15540-5). Taylor & Francis.

Poverty & Transfers In-Kind: A Re-Evaluation of Poverty in the United States. Morton Paglin. LC 79-88586. (Publication: No. 219). 108p. 1980. pap. 6.95x (ISBN 0-8179-7192-0). Hoover Inst Pr.

Poverty & Unemployment in India: An Analysis of Recent Evidence. Pravin Visaria. (Working Paper: No. 417). 42p. 1980. 5.00 (ISBN 0-8213-9322-7, WP 0417). World Bank.

Poverty & Wealth in James. Pedrito U. Maynard-Reid. LC 86-23506. 128p. (Orig.). 1987. pap. 8.95 (ISBN 0-88344-417-8). Orbis Bks.

Poverty & Wealth: The Christian Debate over Capitalism. Ronald H. Nash. LC 86-70291. 256p. (Orig.). 1986. pap. 8.95 (ISBN 0-89107-402-3, Crossway Bks). Good News.

Poverty & Welfare in Hapsburg Spain: The Example of Toledo. Linda Martz. LC 82-19725. (Cambridge Iberian & Latin American Studies). (Illus.). 300p. 1983. 57.50 (ISBN 0-521-23952-4). Cambridge U Pr.

Poverty & Welfare in Scotland, 1890-1948. Ian Levitt. 200p. 1988. 45.00 (ISBN 0-85224-558-0, Pub. by Edinburgh U Pr Scotland). Columbia U Pr.

Poverty & Women's Work: A Study of Sweeper Women in Delhi. Malavika Karlekar. 165p. 1982. text ed. 22.50x (ISBN 0-7069-1968-8, Pub. by Vikas India). Advent NY.

Poverty Bay. Earl W. Emerson. 256p. 1985. pap. 3.50 (ISBN 0-380-89647-8). Avon.

Poverty Before Politics. (Institue of Economic Affairs Hobart Papers Ser.: No. 73). 1977. pap. 5.95 technical (ISBN 0-255-36094-0). Transatl Arts.

Poverty Curtain: Choices for the Third World. Haq Mahbub Ul. LC 76-7470. 247p. 1976. pap. 15.00x (ISBN 0-231-04063-6). Columbia U Pr.

Poverty, Development & Exchange Relations. Arun Majumdar. 175p. 1987. text ed. 15.95x (ISBN 81-7027-108-8, Pub. by Radiant Pubs India). Advent NY.

Poverty, Development & Food. Ed. by Edward Clay & John Shaw. 258p. 1987. 53.00x (ISBN 0-333-43325-4, Pub. by Macmillan Pr Ltd). Intl Spec Bk.

Poverty: Explanations of Social Deprivation. Robert Holman. LC 78-576. 1978. 26.00x (ISBN 0-312-63296-7). St Martin.

Poverty in a Land of Plenty: Tenancy in Eighteenth-Century Maryland. Gregory A. Stiverson. LC 77-4554. (Maryland Bicentennial Studies). (Illus.). 1978. text ed. 22.50x (ISBN 0-8018-1966-0). Johns Hopkins.

Poverty in America. Conference on Poverty in America. Ed. by M. S. Gordon. (New Reprints in Essays & General Literature Index Ser.). 1975. Repr. of 1965 ed. 31.00 (ISBN 0-518-10197-5, 10197). Ayer Co Pubs.

Poverty in America. Milton Meltzer. LC 85-31963. 122p. (gr. 7 up). 1986. 11.95 (ISBN 0-688-05911-2, Morrow Junior Books). Morrow.

Poverty in America - the Impact of Changing Attitudes & Public Policies on the Poor: Proceedings of the National Assembly & the National Conference on Social Welfare, May 22, 1984. 72p. 10.00 (ISBN 0-317-42938-8). Natl Conf Soc Welfare.

Poverty in America: A Book of Readings. rev. ed. Ed. by Louis A. Ferman et al. LC 68-29261. 1968. 12.50 (ISBN 0-472-31281-2). U of Mich Pr.

Poverty in America: The Welfare Dilemma. Ralph Segalman & Asoke Basu. LC 79-6568. (Contributions in Sociology Ser.: No. 39). (Illus.). xvi, 418p. 1981. lib. bdg. 36.95 (ISBN 0-313-20751-8, BPO/). Greenwood.

Poverty in Britain & the Reform of Social Security. Anthony B. Atkinson. LC 76-85711. (University of Cambridge, Dept. of Applied Economics, Occasional Paper: 18). pap. 56.00 (ISBN 0-317-26110-X, 2024402). Bks Demand UMI.

Poverty in Cambridgeshire. Michael J. Murphy. (Cambridge Town, Gown & County Ser.: Vol. 23). (Illus.). 1978. pap. 4.50 (ISBN 0-900891-29-7). Oleander Pr.

Poverty in India. V. M. Dandekar. 159p. 1971. 8.95. Asia Bk Corp.

Poverty in Indonesia: A Profile. Dov Chernichovsky & Oey A. Meesook. (Working Paper: No. 671). 74p. 1984. 5.00 (ISBN 0-8213-0419-4, WP 0671). World Bank.

Poverty in Latin America: The Impact of Depression. 28p. 1986. 3.50 (ISBN 0-8213-0836-X, BK 0836). World Bank.

Poverty in Metropolitan Cities. S. Manzoor Alam & Fatima Alikhan. 1987. 28.50 (ISBN 0-8364-2255-4, Pub. by Concept India). South Asia Bks.

Poverty in New York City: 1980-1985. Terry J. Rosenberg. LC 88-116988. 45p. 1987. pap. text ed. 6.50 (ISBN 0-88156-061-8). Comm Serv Soc NY.

Poverty in New York, 1783-1825. Raymond A. Mohl. (Urban Life in America Ser). 1971. 19.95x (ISBN 0-19-501367-0). Oxford U Pr.

Poverty in Rural America: A Case Study. Janet M. Fitchen. (Special Studies in Contemporary Social Issues). 266p. (Orig.). 1981. pap. text ed. 16.95x (ISBN 0-89158-901-5). Westview.

Poverty in the American Dream: Women & Children First. Karin Stallard et al. (Politics & Economics Ser.). (Illus.). 64p. (Orig.). 1983. pap. 4.75 (ISBN 0-89608-197-4). South End Pr.

Poverty in the Dual Economy. Tussing. 1975. write for info. (ISBN 0-312-63315-7). St Martin.

Poverty in the Soviet Union. Mervyn Matthews. (Illus.). 260p. 1986. 39.50 (ISBN 0-521-32544-7); pap. 13.95 (ISBN 0-521-31059-8). Cambridge U Pr.

Poverty in the United Kingdom: A Survey of Household Resoures & Standards of Living. Peter Townsend. 1979. 55.00x (ISBN 0-520-03871-1); pap. 18.95x (ISBN 0-520-03976-9). U of Cal Pr.

Poverty, Inequality & Class Structure. Ed. by Dorothy Wedderburn. LC 73-80479. (Illus.). 232p. 1974. pap. 12.95 (ISBN 0-521-09823-8). Cambridge U Pr.

Poverty, Inequality, & Development. Gary S. Fields. LC 79-21017. (Illus.). 256p. 1980. pap. 14.95 (ISBN 0-521-29852-0). Cambridge U Pr.

Poverty, Inequality & the Law: Cases, Commentary & Analyses. Barbara E. Brudno. 934p. 1976. write for info. West Pub.

Poverty: Its Illegal Causes & Legal Cure. L. Spooner. LC 78-156804. (Studies in American History & Government Ser.). 108p. 1971. Repr. of 1846 ed. lib. bdg. 19.50 (ISBN 0-306-70207-X). Da Capo.

Poverty, Justice, & the Law: New Essays on Needs, Rights, & Obligations. Ed. by George R. Lucas, Jr. LC 86-24604. 172p. 1987. lib. bdg. 24.75 (ISBN 0-8191-5716-3); pap. text ed. 12.75 (ISBN 0-8191-5717-1). U Pr of Amer.

Poverty of a Rich Society. John F. Gardner. 32p. 1976. pap. 1.50 (ISBN 0-913098-09-4). Myrin Institute.

Poverty of Abundance: Hoover, the Nation, the Depression. Albert U. Romasco. LC 65-26565. 1965. pap. 7.95 (ISBN 0-19-500760-3). Oxford U Pr.

Poverty of Affluence: A Psychological Analysis of Life in the Consumer Society. Paul L. Wachtel. LC 83-47655. 320p. 1983. 19.95 (ISBN 0-02-933540-X). Free Pr.

Poverty of Affluence: A Psychological Portrait of the American Way of Life. Paul L. Wachtel. 336p. 1988. pap. 12.95 (ISBN 0-86571-151-8). New Soc Pubs.

Poverty of Communism. Nick Eberstadt. 224p. 1987. 24.95 (ISBN 0-88738-188-X). Transaction Bks.

Poverty of "Development Economics". Lal Deepak. (Hobart Paperbacks: No. 16). 1983. pap. 10.95 technical (ISBN 0-255-36163-7, Pub. by Inst Econ Affairs). Transatl Arts.

Poverty of "Development Economics". Deepak Lal. (Illus.). 144p. 1985. text ed. 18.50x (ISBN 0-674-69470-8); pap. text ed. 7.95x (ISBN 0-674-69471-6). Harvard U Pr.

Poverty of Historicism. Karl Popper. 166p. 1988. pap. text ed. 8.95 (ISBN 0-7448-0052-8, Pub. by Ark Paperbks). Routledge Chapman & Hall.

Poverty of Liberalism. Robert P. Wolff. LC 68-29314. 1969. pap. 11.95x (ISBN 0-8070-0583-5, BPA10, Pub. by Ariadne Bks.). Beacon Pr.

Poverty of Nations: A Global Perspective of Mass Poverty in the Third World. Jayantanuja Bandyopadhyaya. 1988. 28.50x (ISBN 0-8364-2302-X, Pub. by Allied India). South Asia Bks.

Poverty of Nations & New Economic Order. Usha Garg & Jagdish Vibhakar. 246p. 1985. 20.95x (ISBN 0-317-39868-7, Pub. by UDH Pubs India). Asia Bk Corp.

Poverty of Nations: The Political Economy of Hunger & Population. William W. Murdoch. LC 80-16201. 400p. 1981. text ed. 39.50x (ISBN 0-8018-2313-7); pap. 12.95x (ISBN 0-8018-2462-1). Johns Hopkins.

Poverty of Objects: The Prose Poem & the Politics of Genre. Jonathan Monroe. LC 86-24026. 352p. 1987. 29.95x (ISBN 0-8014-1967-0). Cornell U Pr.

Poverty of Philosophy. Karl Marx. 205p. 1973. 5.95 (ISBN 0-8285-0047-9, Pub. by Progress Pubs USSR). Imported Pubns.

Poverty of Philosophy. Karl Marx. LC 63-10632. 356p. 1963. pap. 3.50 (ISBN 0-7178-0163-2). Intl Pubs Co.

Poverty of Progress-Changing Ways of Life in Industrial Societies: Selected Proceedings of Two International Conferences on Alternative Ways of Life', Cartigny, Switzerland, 1978, & Trappeto, Sicily, 1979. Ed. by I. Miles & J. Irvine. (Illus.). 275p. 1982. text ed. 55.00 (ISBN 0-08-028906-1, K110); pap. text ed. 21.00 (ISBN 0-08-027935-X). Pergamon.

Poverty of Progress: Latin America in the Nineteenth Century. E. Bradford Burns. LC 80-51236. 224p. 1980. 25.00x (ISBN 0-520-04160-7); pap. 10.95x (ISBN 0-520-05078-9, CAMPUS 312). U of Cal Pr.

Poverty of Revolution: The State & the Urban Poor in Mexico. S. Eckstein. 388p. 1977. 39.00x (ISBN 0-691-09367-9); pap. 15.95 (ISBN 0-691-02282-8). Princeton U Pr.

Poverty of Spirit. Johannes B. Metz. LC 68-31045. 56p. 1968. 2.95 (ISBN 0-8091-1924-2). Paulist Pr.

Poverty of Statism: A Debate. N. Bukharin et al. 1984. lib. bdg. 79.95 (ISBN 0-87700-632-6). Revisionist Pr.

Poverty of Statism: Anarchism vs. Marxism. Nikolai Bukharin et al. 93p. (Orig.). 1981. pap. 3.50 (ISBN 0-904564-28-2). Left Bank.

Poverty, Participating, Protest, & Black Americans: A Selected Bibliography for Use in Social Work Education. Compiled by Charlotte Dunmore. Date not set. 3.00 (70-382-02). Coun Soc WK Ed.

Poverty, Policy, & Food Security in Southern Africa. Ed. by Coralie Bryant. LC 87-32243. 280p. 1988. lib. bdg. 30.00x (ISBN 1-55587-092-9). Lynne Rienner.

Poverty Policy & Poverty Research: The Great Society & the Social Sciences. Robert H. Haveman. LC 86-40453. 320p. 1987. text ed. 37.50x (ISBN 0-299-11150-4). U of Wis Pr.

Poverty, Revolution & the Church. Wilkes M. Paget. 142p. (Orig.). 1982. pap. text ed. 13.50 (ISBN 0-85364-285-0). Attic Pr.

Poverty, Society & Philanthropy in the Late Mediaeval Greek World: From the Fourth Crusade Through the Fall. Demetrios J. Constantelos. (Studies in the Social and Religious History of the Mediaeval Greek World: Vol. II). 352p. Date not set. lib. bdg. 50.00 (ISBN 0-89241-401-4). Caratzas.

Poverty Survival Handbook. Pat B. O'Grady. LC 86-62681. (Illus.). 72p. (Orig.). 1986. pap. 5.00 (ISBN 0-9601846-3-5). PM Ent.

Poverty: The Forgotten Englishmen. Ken Coates & Richard Siburn. 282p. 77.50x (Pub. by Bertrand Russell Hse); pap. 20.00x. State Mutual Bk.

Poverty U. S. A., the Historical Record, 44 vols. Ed. by David J. Rothman. 1971. Repr. 1064.50 (ISBN 0-405-03090-8). Ayer Co Pubs.

Poverty, Undernutrition & Hunger. Michael Lipton. (Working Paper: No. 597). 120p. 1983. 5.00 (ISBN 0-8213-0204-3, WP 0597). World Bank.

Poverty Warriors: The Human Experience of Planned Social Intervention. Louis A. Zurcher, Jr. (Hogg Foundation Research Ser). 468p. 1970. 22.50x (ISBN 0-292-70051-2). U of Tex Pr.

Poverty: Wealth of Mankind. Albert Tevoedjre. 1979. 39.00 (ISBN 0-08-023367-8); pap. 18.75 (ISBN 0-08-023366-X). Pergamon.

Povest' o Stikhakh. Iurii Ivask. LC 85-62144. 150p. (Orig.). 1987. pap. 13.00 (ISBN 0-89830-102-5). Russica Pubs.

Povest' OB Ugolovnom Rozyske. Nagornyi et al. 512p. 1984. 59.00x (ISBN 0-317-42704-0, Pub. by Collets (UK)). State Mutual Bk.

Povest'O Varlaame I Ioasafe. O. V. Tvorogov. 296p. (Rus.). 1985. 39.00x (ISBN 0-317-42815-2, Pub by Collets (UK)). State Mutual BK.

Povratak Suncu. Milos Acin-Kosta. LC 82-50490. 145p. (Serbo-Croatian.). 1982. pap. 10.00 (ISBN 0-931931-12-6). Ravnogorski.

Pow-Wows. G. Hohman. 4.00x (ISBN 0-685-22072-9). Wehman.

Powder & Bulk Solids & Handling & Processing: Ninth Annual Proceedings of the Technical Program. International Powder & Bulk Solids Conference Exhibition (1984: Rosemont, IL) pap. 160.00 (ISBN 0-317-41770-3, 2023188). Bks Demand UMI.

Powder & Bulk Solids Handling. Iinoya et al. (Chemical Industries Ser.). 296p. 1988. 85.00 (ISBN 0-8247-7971-1). Dekker.

Powder & Bulk Solids Handling & Processing: Proceedings of the Technical Program-May 7-9, 1985, Rosemont, IL. Powder & Bulk Solids Handling & Processing (10th: 1985: Rosemont, IL) pap. 160.00 (ISBN 0-317-26157-6, 2025192). Bks Demand UMI.

Powder & Bulk Solids Handling & Processing: Proceedings of the Technical Program: May 12-14, 1987. Powder & Bulk Solids Handling & Processing (12th: 1987: Rosemont, IL) Staff. (Illus.). 716p. pap. 160.00 (2030234). Bks Demand UMI.

Powder Coating. David D. Taft. LC 76-359611. pap. 77.80 (ISBN 0-317-42095-X, 2052168). Bks Demand UMI.

Powder Coatings Market. 220p. 1985. 1750.00 (ISBN 0-86621-333-3, A1416). Frost & Sullivan.

Powder Coatings Markets. 303p. 1984. 1800.00 (ISBN 0-86621-636-7, E708). Frost & Sullivan.

Powder Coatings: Recent Developments. Ed. by M. T. Gillies. LC 80-26426. (Chemical Tech. Rev.: 183). (Illus.). 326p. 1981. 48.00 (ISBN 0-8155-0836-0). Noyes.

Powder Magazine at Fort Michilimackinac: Excavation Report. Donald P. Heldman & William L. Minnerly. Ed. by David A. Armour. (Reports in Mackinac History & Archaeology Ser.: No. 6). (Illus., Orig.). 1977. pap. 3.00 (ISBN 0-911872-22-1). Mackinac Island.

Powder Metal Parts. 1983. 35.00 (ISBN 0-89883-306-X, SP535). Soc Auto Engineers.

Powder Metallurgy. Business Communications Staff. 164p. 1987. pap. 1950.00 (ISBN 0-89336-596-3, GB-041N). BCC.

Powder Metallurgy Alloys: Proceedings of the Symposium on Powder Metallurgy Alloys Held at I. I. T. Bombay on 11th October, 1980. Ed. by P. Ramakrishnan. 124p. 1982. text ed. 24.50 (ISBN 90-6191-406-X, Pub. by A A Balkema). Brookfield Pub Co.

Powder Metallurgy: Applications, Advantages & Limitations. Ed. by Erhard Klare. 1983. 59.00 (ISBN 0-87170-154-5). ASM.

Powder Metallurgy Equipment Manual. 3rd ed. Ed. by Samuel Bradbury, III. 199p. pap. 45.00 (ISBN 0-918404-68-1). Metal Powder.

Powder Metallurgy in Defense Technology, 3 Vols. Incl. Vol. 3. 1977. 37.50 (ISBN 0-918404-42-8); Vol. 4. 1978. 24.00 (ISBN 0-918404-46-0); Vol. 5. Yuma Arizona. 1979 (ISBN 0-918404-50-9). (Defense Technology Seminar). Metal Powder.

Powder Metallurgy of Superalloys. G. H. Gessinger. (Monographs in Materials). 330p. 1984. text ed. 75.00 (ISBN 0-408-11033-3). Butterworth.

Powder Metallurgy of Titanium Alloys: Proceedings of a Symposium (109th: Las Vegas, NV: 1980) The Metallurgy Society of AIME. Ed. by F. H. Froes & John E. Smugenesky. LC 80-83013. pap. 79.80 (ISBN 0-317-42396-7, 2056069). Bks Demand UMI.

Powder Metallurgy Opportunity for Engineering Industries. Ed. by P. Ramakrishnan. 1987. 18.00x (ISBN 81-204-0173-5, Pub. by Oxford IBH). South Asia Bks.

Powder Metallurgy: Principles & Applications. Fritz V. Lenel. LC 80-81830. (Illus.). 608p. 1980. 55.00 (ISBN 0-918404-48-7). Metal Powder.

Powder Metallurgy Processing: New Techniques & Analyses. Ed. by Howard A. Kuhn & Alan Lawley. 1978. 61.00 (ISBN 0-12-428450-7). Acad Pr.

Powder Metallurgy Science. LC 84-60862. 279p. 1984. 35.00 (ISBN 0-918404-60-6). Metal Powder.

Powder, Profit & Privateers: A Documentary History of the Virgin Islands During the Era of the American Revolution. George F. Tyson, Jr. (Illus.). 114p. 1977. 15.00 (ISBN 0-318-14617-7). Isl Resources.

Powder Puff. Vivian F. Lewis. 144p. 1988. 10.95 (ISBN 0-89962-635-1). Todd & Honeywell.

Powder Puff Puzzle. Patricia R. Giff. (Polka Dot Private Eye Ser.: No. 4). (Orig.). (gr. k-6). 1987. pap. 2.50 (ISBN 0-440-47180-X, YB). Dell.

Powder River. Gary McCarthy. 384p. (Orig.). 1985. pap. 3.50 (ISBN 0-345-30435-7). Ballantine.

Powder River Country. Ed. by Margaret B. Hanson. (Illus.). 510p. 1981. 21.95 (ISBN 0-9605834-0-8). Hanson.

Powder River: Let'er Buck. Struthers M. Burt. LC 73-144923. (Illus.). 1971. Repr. of 1938 ed. 39.00x (ISBN 0-403-00886-7). Scholarly.

Powder Surface Area & Porosity. 2nd ed. S. Lowell & J. E. Shields. (Powder Technology Ser.). 230p. 1984. 55.00 (ISBN 0-412-25240-6, NO. 9012, Pub. by Chapman & Hall England). Routledge Chapman & Hall.

Powder Technology: Proceedings. International Symposium on Powder Technology, Sept. 27- Oct. 1981, Kyoto, Japan. Ed. by Koichi Iinoya & J. Keith Beddow. LC 83-18641. (Illus.). 823p. 1984. 125.00 (ISBN 0-89116-285-2). Hemisphere Pub.

Powder Testing Guide: Methods of Measuring the Physical Properties of Bulk Powders. L. Svarovsky. 142p. 1987. 54.00 (ISBN 1-85166-137-9, Pub. by Elsevier Applied Sci England). Elsevier.

Powdered & Particulate Rubber Technology. C. W. Evans. (Illus.). 107p. 1978. 34.25 (ISBN 0-85334-773-5, Pub. by Elsevier Applied Sci England). Elsevier.

Powdered Eggs. Charles Simmons. 224p. 1973. pap. 6.95 (ISBN 0-14-003201-0). Penguin.

Powderhorn Passage: Sequel to Where the Pirates Are. Tom Townsend. Ed. by Melissa Roberts. (Vol. 3). (gr. 4-7). 1988. 8.95 (ISBN 0-89015-642-5). Eakin Pr.

Powdersmoke Lawyer. Lee Floren. (Gunsmoke Western Ser.). 176p. 1988. text ed. 12.95x (ISBN 0-85997-856-7, Pub. by Firecrest Pub Ltd). Prescott Pr NH.

Powdersmoke Payoff. Al Cody. 1980. pap. 1.75 (ISBN 0-8439-0834-3, Leisure Bks). Leisure NY.

Powell & the Anthropology of Canyon Country. John W. Powell. (Illus.). 30p. pap. 1.50 (ISBN 0-938216-26-0). GCNHA.

Powell on Real Property, 15 vols. Richard R. Powell & Patrick J. Rohan. 1949. Set. looseleaf 620.00 (550); Updates 1985, updates avail. 428.50; Updates 1986. 499.00. Bender.

Powell's Army, No. 1: Unchained Lightning. Terence Duncan. 224p. 1987. pap. 2.50 (ISBN 0-8217-1994-7). Zebra.

Powell's Army, No. 2: Apache Raiders. 05/1987 ed. Terence Duncan. 224p. pap. 2.50 (ISBN 0-8217-2073-2). Zebra.

Powell's Army, No. 5: Rocky Mountain Showdown. Terence Duncan. 256p. 1988. pap. 2.95 (ISBN 0-8217-2383-9). Zebra.

Powell's Army, No. 6: Red River Desperadoes. Terence Duncan. 256p. 1988. pap. 2.95 (ISBN 0-8217-2515-7). Zebra.

Powell's Canyon Voyage. W. L. Rusho. LC 70-64908. (Wild & Woolly West Ser., No. 11). (Illus., Orig.). 1969. avail.; pap. 2.00 (ISBN 0-910584-12-5). Filter.

Powenz Pack. Ernst Penzoldt. Tr. by John E. Woods from Ger. LC 81-22169. (Illus.). 272p. 1982. 13.95 (ISBN 0-88064-002-2). Fromm Intl Pub.

Power. Judd Biasiotto. 80p. (Orig.). 1988. pap. 6.00 (ISBN 0-933079-07-9). World Class Enterprises.

Power. Ed. by John R. Champlin. (Controversy Ser). 194p. 1971. 12.95x (ISBN 0-202-24048-7); pap. 6.95x (ISBN 0-202-24049-5). Lieber-Atherton.

Power. Howard E. Goldfluss. LC 87-46269. 1988. 18.95 (ISBN 1-55611-087-1). D I Fine.

Power. Betsy Haynes. (Twilight Ser.: No. 2). (Orig.). (gr. 5 up). 1982. pap. 1.95 (ISBN 0-440-97164-0, LFL). Dell.

Power. Ronald S. Joseph. 464p. (Orig.). 1980. pap. 3.50 (ISBN 0-446-36161-5). Warner Bks.

Power. Ed. by Steven Lukes. LC 86-8511. 256p. 1986. 30.00x (ISBN 0-8147-5030-3); pap. 15.00x (ISBN 0-8147-5031-1). NYU Pr.

Power: A Philosophical Analysis. Peter Morriss. LC 87-9837. 350p. 1987. 35.00 (ISBN 0-312-00943-7). St Martin.

Power: A Radical Review. Steven Lukes. (Studies in Sociology). 64p. 1974. pap. 8.50 (ISBN 0-333-16672-8, Pub. by Macmillan UK). Humanities.

Power: A Repossession Manual--Organizing Strategies for Citizens. Greg L. Speeter. LC 79-624732. (Illus., Orig.). 1978. pap. 10.00 (ISBN 0-934210-00-4). Devlp Commy.

Power Accountants Handbook. John Harrington & Michael Patrick. 96p. 1988. 9.95 (ISBN 0-89962-716-1). Todd & Honeywell.

Power, Action & Belief: A New Sociology of Knowledge? Ed. by John Law. (Sociological Review Monograph: No. 32). 300p. (Orig.). 1986. pap. text ed. 18.95 (ISBN 0-7102-0802-2). Routledge Chapman & Hall.

Power Adaptations & Changing Cultures. Thorne Deuel. (Scientific Papers Ser.: Vol. XV). (Illus.). 114p. 1976. pap. 4.00x (ISBN 0-89792-063-5). Ill St Museum.

Power & Authority in Adolescence: The Origins & Resolutions of Intergenerational Conflict, Vol. 10. GAP Committee on Adolescence. LC 78-55380. (Publication: No. 101). 1978. pap. 8.95 (ISBN 0-87318-138-7, Pub. by GAP). Brunner-Mazel.

Power & Authority in the Catholic Church: Cardinal Cody in Chicago. Charles Dahm & Robert Ghelardi. LC 81-40453. 334p. 1982. text ed. 26.95 (ISBN 0-268-01546-5). U of Notre Dame Pr.

Power & Authority: Transformation of Campus Governace. Ed. by Harold L. Hodgkinson & L. Richard Meeth. LC 74-132821. (Jossey-Bass Ser. in Higher Education). pap. 57.80 (2027755). Bks Demand UMI.

Power & Bulk Solids Handling & Processing: Proceedings of the Technical Program: 11th, O'Hare Exposition Center, Rosemont, IL, May 13-15, 1986. Powder & Bulk Solids Handlings & Processing. pap. 160.00 (ISBN 0-317-55767-X, 2029367). Bks Demand UMI.

Power & Choice: An Introduction to Politics. W. Phillips Shively. 336p. 1986. pap. text ed. write for info. (ISBN 0-394-35271-8, RanC). Random.

Power & Civility: The Civilizing Process, Vol. II. Norbert Elias. Tr. by Edmund Jephcott. LC 82-8157. 376p. 1982. 22.00 (ISBN 0-394-52769-0). Pantheon.

Power & Class in Africa: An Introduction to Change & Conflict in African Politics. Irving L. Markowitz. 1977. pap. text ed. write for info. (ISBN 0-13-686642-5). P-H.

Power & Class: The Italian American Experience Today. Ed. by Francis X. Femminella. 1971. 9.95 (ISBN 0-934675-04-X). Am Italian.

Power & Communication. Andrew King. 153p. (Orig.). 1987. pap. text ed. 8.95x (ISBN 0-88133-283-6). Waveland Pr.

Power & Conflict in the University: Research in the Sociology of Complex Organizations. J. V. Baldridge. LC 70-140548. Repr. of 1971 ed. 48.30 (ISBN 0-8357-9957-3, 2013113). Bks Demand UMI.

Power & Criminality (India) Rao S. Venugopala. 1977. 10.00x (ISBN 0-88386-994-2). South Asia Bks.

Power & Criticism: Post-Structural Investigations in Education. Cleo Cherryholmes. (Advances in Contemporary Educational Thought Ser.). 240p. 1988. text ed. 22.95x (ISBN 0-8077-2927-2). Tchrs Coll.

Power & Culture. Herbert Gutman. Ed. by Ira Berlin. LC 87-43018. 416p. 1987. 29.95 (ISBN 0-394-56026-4). Pantheon.

Power & Culture: The Japanese-American War, 1941-1945. Akira Iriye. LC 80-23536. (Illus.). 336p. 1982. text ed. 27.00x (ISBN 0-674-69580-1); pap. text ed. 9.95x (ISBN 0-674-69582-8). Harvard U Pr.

Power & Democracy in America. Peter F. Drucker et al. Ed. by William V. D'Antonio & Howard J. Ehrlich. LC 79-28576. xviii, 181p. 1980. Repr. of 1961 ed. lib. bdg. 35.00x (ISBN 0-313-22319-X, PDAM). Greenwood.

Power & Display in the Seventeenth Century: The Arts & Their Patrons in Modena & Ferrara. Janet Southorn. (Cambridge Studies in the History of Art). (Illus.). 264p. Date not set. price not set (ISBN 0-521-34563-4). Cambridge U Pr.

Power & Economic Change: The Response to Emancipation in Jamaica & British Guiana, 1840-1865. (South American & Latin American Economic History Ser.). 271p. 1987. lib. bdg. 40.00 (ISBN 0-8240-1366-2). Garland Pub.

Power & Elusiveness in Shelley. Oscar Firkins. LC 70-120253. 1970. Repr. lib. bdg. 17.00x (ISBN 0-374-92745-6, Octagon). Hippocrene Bks.

Power & Empowerment. Lynn PhD Atkinson. LC 88-80073. 1988. pap. 7.95 (ISBN 0-941404-77-3). Falcon PR AZ.

Power & Empowerment in Higher Education: Studies in Honor of Louis Smith. Ed. by D. B. Robertson. LC 77-76333. 168p. 1978. 15.00 (ISBN 0-8131-1373-3). U Pr of Ky.

Power & Energy in Alternating-Current Circuits. Heinz Rieger. (Siemens Programmed Instruction Ser.: No. 14). pap. 20.00 (ISBN 0-317-27750-2, 2052090). Bks Demand UMI.

Power & Faction in Louis XIV's France. Roger Mettam. 280p. 1987. text ed. 45.00 (ISBN 0-631-15667-4). Basil Blackwell.

Power & Family Therapy: A Special Issue of Contemporary Family Therapy. William C. Nichols. 75p. 1988. pap. 9.95 (ISBN 0-89885-430-X). Human Sci Pr.

Power & Form of Emerson's Thought. Jeffrey L. Duncan. LC 73-85043. xiv, 105p. 1974. 12.95x (ISBN 0-8139-0510-9). U Pr of Va.

Power & Glory, the Life of Boies Penrose. Walter Davenport. LC 77-100525. (BCL Ser. I). (Illus.). Repr. of 1931 ed. 11.50 (ISBN 0-404-01938-2). AMS Pr.

Power & Gold. Susan Rodgers. 369p. 1985. 134.00x (ISBN 0-317-68616-X, Pub. by Han-Shan Tang Ltd). State Mutual Bk.

Power & Humanism. Lucien Goldman. 64p. 20.00x (ISBN 0-85124-085-2, Pub by Bertrand Russell Hse). State Mutual Bk.

Power & Ideas: Milton Friedman & the Big U-Turn, 2 Vols. William Frazer. LC 87-82665. (Illus.). 1988. Set. 75.00 (ISBN 0-9619206-0-2); Vol. I. 37.50 (ISBN 0-9619206-1-0); Vol. II. 37.50 (ISBN 0-9619206-2-9). Gulf Atlan Pub.

Power & Identity: Tribalism in World Politics. Harold R. Isaacs. LC 79-55304. (Headline Ser.: No. 246). (Orig.). 1979. pap. 4.00 (ISBN 0-87124-057-2). Foreign Policy.

Power & Ideology in Brazil. Peter McDonough. LC 81-47147. 356p. 1981. 39.00x (ISBN 0-691-07628-6); pap. 12.95x (ISBN 0-691-02203-8). Princeton U Pr.

Power & Ideology in Education. Ed. by Jerome Karabel & A. H. Halsey. 1977. pap. text ed. 18.95x (ISBN 0-19-502139-8). Oxford U Pr.

Power & Illness: The Political Sociology of Health & Medical Care. Elliot A. Krause. LC 77-317. 384p. 1977. 32.00 (ISBN 0-444-99037-2); pap. 19.25 (ISBN 0-444-99056-9). Elsevier.

Power & Imagination: City-States in Renaissance Italy. Lauro Martines. LC 87-29843. (Illus.). 400p. 1988. pap. text ed. 12.95x (ISBN 0-8018-3643-3). Johns Hopkins.

Power & Immortality. Ramon R. Lopez-Reyes. LC 70-146911. 1971. 10.00 (ISBN 0-682-47247-6, University). Exposition-Phoenix.

Power & Influence: A Source Book for Nurses. Kathleen R. Stevens. LC 82-13397. 304p. 1983. pap. 15.95 (ISBN 0-471-08870-6, Pub. by Wiley Med). Wiley.

Power & Influence: Beyond Formal Authority. John P. Kotter. 212p. 1985. 19.95 (ISBN 0-02-918330-8). Free Pr.

Power & Innocence: A Search for the Sources of Violence. Rollo May. 288p. 1972. 14.95 (ISBN 0-393-01065-1). Norton.

Power & Interdependence. 2nd ed. Robert O. Keohane & Joseph S. Nye. 1988. pap. text ed. write for info. (ISBN 0-673-39891-9). Scott F.

Power & Interdependence: World Politics in Transition. Robert O. Keohane & Joseph S. Nye. 1977. pap. text ed. write for info. (ISBN 0-673-39454-9). Scott F.

Power & Justice: The State in Industrial Relations. E. A. Ramaswamy. 1985. 19.95x (ISBN 0-19-561662-6). Oxford U Pr.

Power & Knowledge: Anthropological & Sociological Approaches. Ed. by Richard Fardon. 216p. 1986. 19.95x (ISBN 0-7073-0443-1, Pub. by Scot Acad Pr). Smithsonian.

Power & Law: American Dilemma in World Affairs. Ed. by Charles A. Barker. LC 76-135660. (Illus.). 224p. 1971. 24.00x (ISBN 0-8018-1254-2). Johns Hopkins.

Power & Leadership in Pluralist Systems. Andrew S. McFarland. LC 68-26781. 1969. 27.50x (ISBN 0-8047-0677-8). Stanford U Pr.

Power & Light. Barry Hannah. LC 83-62166. 80p. 1983. 15.00 (ISBN 0-913773-04-2); specially bound, ltd. & signed issue 75.00 (ISBN 0-913773-05-0). S Wright.

Power & Light: Political Strategies for the Solar Transition. David Talbot & Richard E. Morgan. LC 81-10552. 160p. (Orig.). 1981. pap. 6.95 (ISBN 0-8298-0459-5). Pilgrim NY.

Power & Magic. Daniel Kane. 212p. (Orig.). 1987. pap. 9.95 (ISBN 0-85449-078-7, Pub. by GMP England). Alyson Pubns.

Power & Market: Government & the Economy. Murray N. Rothbard. LC 70-111536. (Studies in Economic Theory). 304p. 1977. 25.00x (ISBN 0-8362-0750-5). NYU Pr.

Power & Marxist Theory: A Realist View. Jeffrey C. Isaac. LC 87-6690. 248p. 1987. 24.95x (ISBN 0-8014-1934-4). Cornell U Pr.

Power & Money: Writings about Politics, 1971-1987. Thomas B. Edsall. 1988. 19.95 (ISBN 0-393-02571-3). Norton.

Power & Morality: American Business Ethics, 1840-1914. Saul Engelbourg. LC 79-8288. (Contributions in Economics & Economic History Ser.: No. 28). 1980. lib. bdg. 35.00 (ISBN 0-313-20871-9, ENP/). Greenwood.

Power & Morality in Global Transformation. Soedjatmoko. (First Morgenthau Memorial Lecture). 20p. 1982. pap. 4.00 (ISBN 0-87641-219-3). Carnegie Ethics & Intl Affairs.

Power & Opposition in Post-Revolutionary Societies. Ed. by Patrick Camiller & Jon Rothschild. Orig. Title: Potere e Opposizione Nelle Societa Post-rivoluzionare. 281p. 1979. 15.95 (ISBN 0-906133-18-1, Pub. by Ink Links Ltd.); pap. 6.95 (ISBN 0-906133-19-X). Longwood Pub Group.

Power & Order: Henry Adams & the Naturalist Tradition in American Fiction. Harold Kaplan. LC 80-23414. 1981. lib. bdg. 15.00x (ISBN 0-226-42424-3). U of Chicago Pr.

Power & Organization Development. Larry E. Greiner & Virginia E. Schein. (Organization Development Ser.). (Illus.). 176p. 1988. pap. text ed. 15.95x (ISBN 0-201-12185-9). Addison-Wesley.

Power & Paranoia: History, Narrative, & the American Cinema, 1940-1950. Dana Polan. LC 86-4144. 352p. 1986. 27.50x (ISBN 0-231-06284-2). Columbia U Pr.

Power & Pawn: The Female in Iberian Families, Societies & Cultures. Ann M. Pescatello. LC 75-35352. (Council on Intercultural & Comparative Studies: No. 1). 320p. 1976. lib. bdg. 35.00 (ISBN 0-8371-8583-1, PPP/). Greenwood.

Power & Peace in Prayer. R. A. Torrey. (One Evening Christmas Classic Ser.). 1976. pap. 2.50 (ISBN 0-89107-019-2). Good News.

Power & Penury: Government, Technology & Science in Philip II's Spain. David Goodmam. (Illus.). 250p. 1988. 44.50 (ISBN 0-521-30532-2). Cambridge U Pr.

Power & Performance in Organizations. Iain Mangham. 250p. 1985. 24.95x (ISBN 0-631-13083-7). Basil Blackwell.

Power & Persuasion: Fiestas & Social Control in Rural Mexico. Stanley Brandes. (Illus.). 224p. 1987. text ed. 27.95x (ISBN 0-8122-8077-6); pap. text ed. 14.95x (ISBN 0-8122-1253-3). U of Pa Pr.

Power & Pluralism in American Cities: Researching the Urban Laboratory. Robert J. Waste. LC 86-19381. (Contributions in Political Science Ser.: No. 165). (Illus.). 200p. 1987. lib. bdg. 32.95 (ISBN 0-313-25016-2, WPM). Greenwood.

Power & Policy. Thomas K. Finletter. LC 74-159718. 408p. 1972. Repr. of 1954 ed. lib. bdg. 35.00x (ISBN 0-8371-6189-4, FIPP). Greenwood.

Power & Policy in China. 2nd, enl. ed. Parris H. Chang. LC 78-50773. (Illus.). 1978. 24.50x (ISBN 0-271-00543-2); pap. text ed. 12.50x (ISBN 0-271-00544-0). Pa St U Pr.

Power & Policy in Communist Systems. 3rd ed. Gary K. Bertsch. LC 85-12122. 181p. 1985. pap. 12.95 (ISBN 0-471-82672-3). Wiley.

Power & Policy in Education: The Case of Independent Schooling. Brian Salter & Ted Tapper. (Issues in Education & Training Ser.: Vol. 6). 260p. 1985. 36.00x (ISBN 1-85000-062-X, Falmer Pr); pap. 20.00x (ISBN 1-85000-063-8, Falmer Pr). Taylor & Francis.

Power & Policy in Quest of the Law: Essays in Honor of Eugene Victor Rostow. Eugene V. Rostow et al. LC 83-26502. 1984. lib. bdg. 96.00 (ISBN 9-02-472911-4, Pub. by Martinus Nijhoff Netherlands). Kluwer Academic.

Power & Policy in the PRC. Yu-ming Shaw. (Westview Special Studies on East Asia). 450p. 1985. 42.50x (ISBN 0-8133-0135-1). Westview.

Power & Policy in the Third World. 3rd ed. Robert P. Clark. 1986. write for info. (ISBN 0-02-322670-6). Macmillan.

Power & Policy in the Third World. 3rd ed. Robert P. Clark. LC 85-12203. 176p. 1986. pap. 13.95 (ISBN 0-471-82669-3). Wiley.

Power & Policy in Transition: Essays Presented on the Tenth Anniversary of the National Committee on American Foreign Policy in Honor of Its Founder, Hans J. Morgenthau. Ed. by Vojtech Mastny. LC 84-15778. (Contributions in Political Science Ser.: No. 126). (Illus.). ix, 271p. 1984. lib. bdg. 36.95 (ISBN 0-313-24498-7, MAY/). Greenwood.

Power & Policy in Western European Democracies. 3rd ed. David M. Wood. 1986. write for info. (ISBN 0-02-429570-1). Macmillan.

Power & Political Theory: Some European Perspectives. Ed. by Brian M. Barry. LC 75-25556. 312p. pap. 81.20 (2030403). Bks Demand UMI.

Power & Politics in a Chicano Barrio: A Study of Mobilization Efforts & Community Power in El Paso. Benjamin Marquez. LC 85-3347. (Illus.). 276p. (Orig.). 1985. lib. bdg. 29.00 (ISBN 0-8191-4623-4); pap. text ed. 14.25 (ISBN 0-8191-4624-2). U Pr of Amer.

Power & Politics in America. 4th ed. Leonard Freedman. LC 82-12867. 496p. 1982. pap. text ed. 18.50 pub net (ISBN 0-534-01252-3). Brooks-Cole.

Power & Politics in California. 3rd ed. John H. Culver & John C. Syer. 366p. 1988. text ed. write for info. (ISBN 0-02-326321-0). Macmillan.

Power & Politics in Communist Systems. 3rd ed. Gary K. Bertsch. 1985. write for info. (ISBN 0-02-309120-7). Macmillan.

Power & Politics in Early Britain & Ireland. Ed. by S. T. Driscoll & M. R. Nieke. (Illus.). 200p. 1988. 35.00 (ISBN 0-85224-520-3, Pub. by Edinburgh U Pr Scotland); pap. 17.50 (ISBN 0-85224-521-1). Columbia U Pr.

Power & Politics in Late Imperial China: Yuan Shi-kai in Beijing & Tianjin, 1901-1908. Stephen R. MacKinnon. LC 80-15779. (Center for Chinese Studies, UC Berkeley: No. 24). (Illus.). 400p. 1981. 33.00x (ISBN 0-520-04025-2). U of Cal Pr.

Power Elites & Organizations. Ed. by G. William Domhoff & Thomas R. Dye. (Focus Editions Ser.: Vol. 82). 320p. (Orig.). 1987. text ed. 35.00 (ISBN 0-8039-2680-4); pap. text ed. 16.95 (ISBN 0-8039-2681-2). Sage.

Power, Empire Building, & Mergers. Stephen A. Rhoades. LC 82-49255. 176p. 1983. 27.00x (ISBN 0-669-06439-4). Lexington Bks.

Power Encounters: Stories of the Work of the Holy Spirit in the World Today. Ed. by Kevin Springer. LC 87-45724. (Illus.). 320p. (Orig.). 1988. pap. 10.95 (ISBN 0-06-069537-4, RD 715, HarpR). Har-Row.

Power Engineering & Technology: Energy Efficient Use of Working Fluids, Alternative Processes, Heat Pumps& Organic Rankine Cycle. Ed. by H. D. Baehr et al. 1984. 179.50 (ISBN 0-89116-436-7). Hemisphere Pub.

Power Engineering '84: Proceedings, IASTED Symposium, New Orleans, U. S. A., November 12-14, 1984. Ed. by M. H. Hamza. 86p. 1984. 45.00 (ISBN 0-88986-071-8, 081). Acta Pr.

Power English & Word Command, Bk. 1. Ed. by Margaret M. Bynum. 64p. (Orig.). (YA) (gr. 10-12). 1986. wkbk. 15.00 (ISBN 0-913286-97-4). Learn Inc.

Power English & Word Command, Bk. 2. Ed. by Margaret M. Bynum. 96p. (Orig.). (gr. 10-12). 1986. pap. 15.00 wkbk. (ISBN 0-913286-98-2). Learn Inc.

Power English & Word Command, Bk. 3. Margaret M. Bynum. 32p. (Orig.). (gr. 10-12). 1986. pap. 15.00 wkbk. (ISBN 0-913286-99-0). Learn Inc.

Power English & Word Command Total Program. Margaret M. Bynum. 192p. (Orig.). (gr. 10-12). 1986. Set of 3 books. pap. 69.95 wkbk. (ISBN 0-913286-96-6). Learn INC.

Power Evangelism. John Wimber & Kevin Springer. 224p. 1986. 13.45 (ISBN 0-06-069532-3). Har-Row.

Power FET Handbook. Pelly. 1987. write for info. (ISBN 0-471-82867-X). Wiley.

Power FETs & Their Applications. Ed Oxner. (Illus.). 336p. 1982. 43.00 (ISBN 0-13-686923-8). P-H.

Power Flex: Reading for Meaning, Flexibility, & Study. Walter Hill et al. 425p. 1988. pap. text ed. 20.50 (ISBN 0-06-042854-6, HarpC). Har-Row.

Power for a Finished Work. J. L. Shuler. LC 78-53212. (Stories That Win Ser.). 1978. pap. 0.50 (ISBN 0-8163-0208-1, 16416-0). Pacific Pr Pub Assn.

Power for Abundant Living. Victor P. Wierwille. LC 72-164674. 380p. 6.95 (ISBN 0-910068-01-1). Am Christian.

Power for Living. Horace Ward. (International Correspondence Program Ser.). (Orig.). 1986. pap. text ed. 6.95 (ISBN 0-87148-718-7). Pathway Pr.

Power for Positive Ageing. Douglas G. McKenzie. (Illus.). 64p. (Orig.). 1985. pap. 6.95 (ISBN 0-85819-501-1, Pub. by JBCE). ANZ Religious Pubns.

Power for Positive Living: Studies in Philippians & Colossians. Doris W. Greig. Ed. by Mary Beckwith. (Joy of Living Bible Study). 180p. 1988. pap. 5.95 (ISBN 0-8307-1286-0, 5419493). Regal.

Power for Service. Jessie Penn-Lewis. 1962. pap. 3.25 (ISBN 0-87508-951-8). Chr Lit.

Power for the Day: 108 Meditations from Matthew. John T. Seamands. LC 75-45044. Repr. of 1976 ed. 28.00 (ISBN 0-8357-9020-7, 2016391). Bks Demand UMI.

Power for the MTA. (Illus.). 90p. (B). 1977. 10.00 (ISBN 0-318-16374-8); members 7.00 (ISBN 0-318-16375-6). Regional Plan Assn.

Power for the People. Trevor Cairns. LC 76-30607. (Cambridge Introduction to World History Course: Bk. 8). (Illus.). 96p. (YA) (gr. 7 up). 1978. 7.95 (ISBN 0-521-20902-1). Cambridge U Pr.

Power for the People. Trevor Cairns. LC 79-2973. (Cambridge Introduction to History Ser.). (Illus.). (gr. 5 up). 1980. PLB 10.95 (ISBN 0-8225-0808-7). Lerner Pubns.

Power for the People: Montana's Cooperative Utilities. Frank J. Busch. 12.50 (ISBN 0-318-00809-2). U of MT Pubns Hist.

Power for the Use of Man. 127p. 1978. 20.00 (ISBN 0-7277-0067-7, Pub. by T Telford UK). Am Soc Civil Eng.

Power, Form & Mind. Arthur Berndtson. LC 80-65658. 296p. 1981. 27.50 (ISBN 0-8387-5010-9). Bucknell U Pr.

Power from Oil: The Life & Times of John Alstyne Secor - Inventor. William H. Higgins. LC 88-90912. (Illus.). 400p. 1988. 24.95 (ISBN 0-9620211-0-5). Power Bk Co.

Power from on High. Charles G. Finney. 1962. pap. 2.50 (ISBN 0-87508-190-8). Chr Lit.

Power from on High. L. D. Wilcox. 1.50 (ISBN 0-686-27776-7). Schmul Pub Co.

Power from Sea Waves. Brian Count. (Institute of Mathematics & Its Applications Conference Ser.). 1981. 91.00 (ISBN 0-12-193550-7). Acad Pr.

Power from the North. Robert Bourassa. Date not set. write for info. S&S.

Power from the People: Innovation, User Participation & Forest Energy Development. Matthew S. Gamser. 224p. (Orig.). 1988. pap. 19.50x (ISBN 0-946688-94-X, Pub. by Intermediate Tech England). Intermediate Tech.

Power from the Wind: A Bibliography. VITA Staff. 63p. 1982. 6.55 (ISBN 0-317-36532-0, 11069-BK) (ISBN 0-86619-163-1). Vols Tech Asst.

Power from Within: A Guide for Women to Discover Their Power & Express It in Creative, Caring Ways. Marguerite Craig et al. (Illus., Orig.). 1977. pap. 3.50x (ISBN 0-914158-27-9). ProActive Pr.

Power from Within: Cosmic Reality of a Poet. Annie Carpenter. 68p. (Orig.). 1983. pap. 7.95 (ISBN 0-934393-07-9). Rector Pr.

Power Game: An Examination of Decision-Making in Government. Jock Bruce-Gardyne & Nigel Lawson. LC 76-6971. (Illus.). 204p. 1976. 27.50 (ISBN 0-208-01598-1, Archon). Shoe String.

Power Game: How Washington Really Works. Hedrick Smith. LC 87-42669. 704p. 1987. 24.95 (ISBN 0-394-55447-7). Random.

Power Generation Calculations Reference Guide. Tyler G. Hicks. (Engineering Reference Ser.). 384p. 1987. text ed. 36.50 (ISBN 0-07-028800-3). McGraw.

Power Generation, Operation, & Control. Allen J. Wood & Bruce F. Wollenberg. LC 83-1172. 444p. 1983. text ed. write for info. (ISBN 0-471-09182-0). Wiley.

Power Generation: Resources, Hazards, Technology & Costs. Philip G. Hill. LC 76-54739. 1977. 40.00x (ISBN 0-262-08091-5). MIT Pr.

Power Golf. Ben Hogan. 1984. pap. 3.95 (ISBN 0-671-60258-6). PB.

Power Healing. John Wimber & Kevin Springer. LC 86-43025. (Illus.). 320p. 1987. 14.95 (ISBN 0-06-069533-1, HarpR). Har-Row.

Power House: Creative Youth Programs. Mark Boykin. LC 86-83180. (Illus.). 336p. 1987. 3 ring-binder 29.95 (ISBN 0-88243-852-2, 02-0852). Gospel Pub.

Power House Within You. M. Lawrence. pap. 3.95 (ISBN 0-937816-11-6). Tech Data.

Power: How to Get It, How to Use It. Michael Korda. 1976. pap. 3.95 (ISBN 0-345-34632-7). Ballantine.

Power! IBM PC Version. Shari Steiner. (Power User's Manual Ser.). 1983. pap. write for info. (ISBN 0-913733-01-6). Computing.

Power Ideas for a Happy Family. Robert H. Schuller. 1987. 8.95 (ISBN 0-8007-1528-4). Revell.

Power in a Trade Union: The Role of the District Committee in the AUEW. Larry James. LC 83-7673. (Management & Industrial Relations: No. 5). 150p. 1984. 29.95 (ISBN 0-521-25798-0). Cambridge U Pr.

Power in American State Legislatures, Vol. 11. Ed. by Alex B. Lacy, Jr. LC 74-216. 1966. 11.00 (ISBN 0-930598-10-5). Tulane Stud Pol.

Power in & Around Organizations. Henry Mintzberg. (Illus.). 704p. 1983. 39.00 (ISBN 0-13-686857-6). P-H.

Power in Britain: Sociological Readings. J. Urry & J. Wakeford. 1973. text ed. 32.00 (ISBN 0-435-82900-9); pap. text ed. 26.50x (ISBN 0-435-82901-7). Gower Pub Co.

Power in Capitalist Societies: Theory, Explanation & Cases. Andrew Cox et al. LC 85-8132. 224p. 1985. 27.50 (ISBN 0-312-63409-9). St Martin.

Power in Congress. 158p. 1987. pap. 9.95 (ISBN 0-87187-436-9). Congr Quarterly.

Power in Europe? Great Britain, France, Italy & Germany in a Postwar World, 1945-1950, Contributions to an International Colloquim at Augsburg, April 1984. Ed. by Josef Becker & Franz Knipping. viii, 583p. 1986. lib. bdg. 122.00 (ISBN 3-11-010608-6). De Gruyter.

Power in Management. John P. Kotter. 1979. 11.95 (ISBN 0-8144-5507-7). AMACOM.

Power in Management. John P. Kotter. LC 78-31558. pap. 29.30 (ISBN 0-317-42058-5, 2056090). Bks Demand UMI.

Power in Numbers: How to Manage for Profit. Brian Forst. 256p. 1987. 22.95 (ISBN 0-471-62809-3). Wiley.

Power in Numbers: The Political Strategy of Protest & Rebellion. James DeNardo. LC 84-42880. (Illus.). 240p. 1985. text ed. 28.00x (ISBN 0-691-07682-0). Princeton U Pr.

Power in Nursing. Ed. by Dalton E. McFarland & Nola Shiflett. LC 79-84506. 86p. 1979. pap. text ed. 24.75 (ISBN 0-913654-54-X). Aspen Pub.

Power in Organizations. Jeffrey Pfeffer. LC 80-29883. 391p. 1981. pap. text ed. 16.95x (ISBN 0-88730-199-1). Ballinger Pub.

Power in Organizations. Ed. by Mayer N. Zald. LC 71-91949. 1970. 14.95x (ISBN 0-8265-1147-3). Vanderbilt U Pr.

Power in Our Hands: A Curriculum on the History of Work & Workers in the United States. Norman Diamond & William Bigelow. 256p. (Orig.). (YA) (gr. 9-12). 1988. tchr's ed. 15.00 (ISBN 0-85345-753-0); wkbk. 5.00 (ISBN 0-85345-754-9). Monthly Rev.

Power in Penance. Michael Scanlan. 64p. 1972. pap. 0.95 (ISBN 0-87793-092-9). Ave Maria.

Power in Praise. Merlin R. Carothers. 143p. 1972. pap. 4.95 (ISBN 0-943026-01-6). Carothers.

Power in Psychotherapeutic Practice. David Heller. 192p. 1985. 24.95 (ISBN 0-89885-228-5). Human Sci Pr.

Power in the Blood: Popular Culture & Village Discourse in Early Modern Germany. David W. Sabean. (Illus.). 256p. 1988. pap. 10.95 (ISBN 0-521-34778-5). Cambridge U Pr.

Power in the Caribbean Basin: A Comparative Study of Political Economy. Carl Stone. LC 84-8985. (Inter-American Politics Ser.: Vol. 5). (Illus.). 180p. 1985. text ed. 29.95 (ISBN 0-89727-056-8). ISHI PA.

Power in the City: Decision Making in San Francisco. Frederick M. Wirt. LC 73-90662. (Institute of Governmental Studies, UC Berkeley: No. 5). 1975. 40.00x (ISBN 0-520-02654-3); pap. 8.95 (ISBN 0-520-03640-9). U of Cal Pr.

Power in the Helping Professions. Adolf Guggenbuhl-Craig. Tr. by Myron Gubitz from Ger. LC 86-17901. 155p. 1971. pap. 10.00 (ISBN 0-88214-304-2). Spring Pubns.

Power in the Isthmus: A Political History of Modern Central America. James Dunkerley. 600p. 1988. 37.50 (ISBN 0-86091-196-9, Pub. by Verso). Routledge Chapman & Hall.

Power in the Land. Fred Harrison. (Universe Press). 318p. 1983. 5.00. Schalkenbach.

Power in the Land: An Inquiry into Unemployment, the Profits Crisis & Land Speculation. Fred Harrison. LC 83-10576. (Illus.). 316p. 1983. text ed. 17.50x (ISBN 0-87663-424-2). Universe.

Power in the Organisation: The Discourse of Power in Managerial Praxis. Phillipe Daudi. 280p. 1986. text ed. 49.95 (ISBN 0-631-15086-2). Basil Blackwell.

Power in the Pacific: The Origins of Naval Arms Limitation, 1914-1922. Roger Dingman. LC 75-36402. 1976. lib. bdg. 22.50x (ISBN 0-226-15331-2). U of Chicago Pr.

Power in the People. F. Morley. (Humane Studies). 293p. 1980. text ed. 10.50x (ISBN 0-8402-1296-8); pap. text ed. 4.95x. Humanities.

Power in Verse: Metaphor & Metonymy in the Renaissance Lyric. Jane Hedley. LC 87-43120. 210p. 1988. lib. bdg. 22.50 (ISBN 0-271-00623-4). Pa St U Pr.

Power in Weakness: New Hearing for Gospel Stories of Healing & Discipleship. Frederick H. Borsh. LC 82-15997. 160p. 1983. pap. 8.95 (ISBN 0-8006-1703-7, 1-1703). Fortress.

Power in World Politics. Ed. by Richard Stoll & Michael Ward. 275p. 1989. lib. bdg. 30.00 (ISBN 1-55587-125-9). Lynne Rienner.

Power in You: Ten Secret Ingredients for Inner Strength. Wally Amos & Gregory Amos. 1988. 16.95. D I Fine.

Power Index Method for Profitable Futures Trading. Harold Goldberg. 1986. 50.00 (ISBN 0-930233-09-3). Windsor.

Power, Inequality, & Democratic Politics: Essays in Honor of Robert Dahl. Ed. by Ian Shapiro & Grant Reeher. 313p. 1988. 50.00 (ISBN 0-8133-0762-7). Westview.

Power, Influence, & Authority: The Hazards of Carrying a Sword. Morgan W. McCall, Jr. (Technical Report Ser.: No. 10). 39p. 1978. pap. 10.00 (ISBN 0-912879-09-2). Ctr Creat Leader.

Power-Integrated Circuits: Physics, Design & Applications. P. Antognetti. 544p. 1986. text ed. 43.95 (ISBN 0-07-002129-5). McGraw.

Power, Intimacy, & the Life Story: Personological Inquiries into Identity. Dan P. McAdams. 1988. write for info. (ISBN 0-89862-506-8). Guilford Pr.

Power Is You. Bernie Fass & Rosemary Caggiano. 48p. (gr. 2-12). 1979. pap. 8.95 (ISBN 0-86704-005-X). Clarus Music.

Power: Its Forms, Bases, & Uses. Dennis Wrong. xii, 326p. 1988. pap. 12.95 (ISBN 0-226-91067-9). U of Chicago Pr.

Power: Its Nature, Its Uses & Its Limits. Ed. by Donald W. Harward. 210p. 1982. pap. text ed. 11.95 (ISBN 0-87073-895-X). Schenkman Bks Inc.

Power-Knowledge: Selected Interviews & Other Writings, 1972-1977. Michel Foucault. 1981. 12.95 (ISBN 0-394-51357-6); pap. 8.95 (ISBN 0-394-73954-X). Pantheon.

Power, Labor & Livelihood: Processes of Change in Rural Java. Gillian Hart. 1986. 35.00x (ISBN 0-520-05499-7). U of Cal Pr.

Power Lasers. Eloy. (Electrical & Electronic Engineering Ser.). 160p. 1987. 39.95 (ISBN 0-470-20851-1). Halsted Pr.

Power Lasers & Their Applications. Ed. by V. S. Letokhov & N. D. Ustinov. 136p. 1983. 55.00 (ISBN 3-7186-0166-4). Harwood Academic.

Power Lawn Mowers: An Unreasonably Dangerous Product. Sevart & Hall. (Illus.). 207p. 1982. 39.95 (ISBN 0-938830-01-5). Inst Product.

Power Line Radiation. Kikuchi. 1983. lib. bdg. 41.50 (ISBN 90-277-1541-6, Pub. by Reidel Holland). Kluwer Academic.

Power Lines. Robert L. Burgers. pap. 4.75 (ISBN 0-89137-317-9). Quality Pubns.

Power Lines & the Environment. Robert Goodland. LC 73-89356. (Illus.). 1973. pap. 5.00x (ISBN 0-89327-050-4). NY Botanical.

Power Look. Egon Von Furstenberg. 1979. pap. 5.95 (ISBN 0-449-90009-6, Columbine). Fawcett.

Power, Love & Wisdom. Friedhelm Hardy. 350p. 1988. 39.95 (ISBN 0-04-440118-3). Unwin Hyman.

Power Lunching. E. Melvin Pinsel & Ligita Dienhart. (Illus.). 220p. 1985. pap. 6.95. Turnbull & Willoughby.

Power Maintainer - Group A. Jack Rudman. (Career Examination Ser.: C-607). (Cloth bdg. avail. on request). pap. 12.00 (ISBN 0-8373-0607-8). Natl Learning.

Power Maintainer - Group B. Jack Rudman. (Career Examination Ser.: C-608). (Cloth bdg. avail. on request). pap. 12.00. Natl Learning.

Power Maintainer - Group C. Jack Rudman. (Career Examination Ser.: C-609). (Cloth bdg. avail. on request). pap. 12.00 (ISBN 0-8373-0609-4). Natl Learning.

Power Makers: The Inside Story of America's Biggest Business...& Its Struggle to Control Tomorrow's Electricity. Richard Munson. 272p. 1985. 16.95 (ISBN 0-87857-550-2). Rodale Pr Inc.

Power Management: A Three Step Program for Successful Leadership. James H. Brewer et al. (Illus.). 166p. 1984. 15.95 (ISBN 0-13-687682-X); pap. 8.95 (ISBN 0-13-687674-9). P-H.

Power Mechanics. P. H. Atteberry. 1986. 7.20 (ISBN 0-87006-557-2). Goodheart.

Power Mechanics. McKnight Staff Members & Wilbur R. Miller. LC 78-53394. (Basic Industrial Arts Ser.). (Illus.). 1978. softbound 6.60 (ISBN 0-02-672870-2). Glencoe Bennett & McKnight.

Power: Mechanics of Energy Control. 2nd ed. Bohm & MacDonald. 1983. 21.32 (ISBN 0-02-672460-X); instr's. guide 5.88 (ISBN 0-02-672470-7). Glencoe Bennett & McKnight.

Power, Modernity & Sociology: Selected Sociological Writings. Raymond Aron. Ed. by Dominique Schnapper. 1988. text ed. 50.00 (ISBN 1-85278-030-4, Pub. by Gower Pub England). Gower Pub Co.

Power Money. Tom J. Fatjor, Jr. & J. Keith Miller. 180p. 16.95 (ISBN 0-89015-651-4). Eakin Pr.

Power, Money, & the People: The Making of Modern Austin. Anthony M. Orum. (Illus.). 400p. 1987. cancelled (ISBN 0-87719-081-X); pap. 16.95 (ISBN 0-87719-092-5). Texas Month Pr.

Power, Morals & the Founding Fathers: Essays in the Interpretation of the American Enlightenment. Adrienne Koch. (Paperback Ser.). 169p. 1961. pap. 7.95x (ISBN 0-8014-9019-7, CP19). Cornell U Pr.

Power Motive. David G. Winter. LC 72-92869. 1973. 19.95 (ISBN 0-02-935460-9). Free Pr.

Power Negotiating Tactics & Techniques. David V. Lewis. LC 81-5164. 243p. 1981. 19.95 (ISBN 0-13-686808-8, Busn). P-H.

Power Negotiating Tactics & Techniques. David V. Lewis. 1984. pap. 5.95 (ISBN 0-13-687740-0, Busn). P-H.

Power Negotioting: Strategies for Winning in Life & Business. John Ilich. LC 79-12646. 1980. text ed. write for info. (ISBN 0-201-03149-3). Addison-Wesley.

Power: Nursing's Challenge for Change. 178p. 1979. 6.00 (ISBN 0-318-13337-7, G-135). ANA.

Power of Affirmation. Subramuniya. pap. 1.00 (ISBN 0-87516-357-2). DeVorss.

Power of Affirmations. Jerry Fankhauser. 56p. 1979. pap. 8.00 (ISBN 0-9617006-1-0). J Fankhauser.

Power of Affirming Touch. Wilson W. Grant. LC 86-10830. (Christian Growth Bks). 128p. (Orig.). 1986. pap. 6.95 (ISBN 0-8066-2210-5, 10-5028). Augsburg.

Power of Alpha Thinking. Jess Stearn. 1977. pap. 3.95 (ISBN 0-451-14191-1, Sig). NAL.

Power of an Idea. Ernest Holmes. Ed. by Willis H. Kinnear. 96p. 1965. pap. 4.50 (ISBN 0-911336-31-1). Sci of Mind.

Power of Apple Works. Robert E. Williams. (Illus.). 240p. 1984. 19.95 (ISBN 0-943518-16-4); 34.95, incl. diskette. MIS Press.

Power of Aries: Myth & Reality in Karen Blixen's Life. Anders Westenholtz. Tr. by Lise Kure-Jensen. LC 86-18534. 121p. 1987. text ed. 15.95 (ISBN 0-8071-1261-5). La State U Pr.

Power of Attitude. Patricia Metten. LC 81-50865. (Power Tales Ser.). (gr. k-7). pap. write for info. (ISBN 0-911712-91-7). Eagle Mktg Corp.

Power of Attorney Book. Denis Clifford. LC 85-61925. (Illus.). 248p. (Orig.). 1985. 15.95 (ISBN 0-917316-95-9). Nolo Pr.

Power of Attorney Book. 2nd ed. Denis Clifford. LC 85-61925. 250p. 1988. pap. 17.95 (ISBN 0-87337-068-6). Nolo Pr.

Power of Attorney Kit. 30p. 1987. 9.95 (ISBN 0-88908-664-8). ISC Pr.

Power of Auto-Suggestion & How to Master It for the Energizing of One's Life. Augustus Vienne' (Illus.). 121p. 1983. 117.75 (ISBN 0-89920-053-2). Am Inst Psych.

Power of Autosuggestion & How to Master It. Patrick L. Sackett. (Illus.). 1979. deluxe ed. 117.75 (ISBN 0-930582-61-6). Gloucester Art.

Power of Awareness. rev. ed. Darwin Gross & Neville Goddard. 144p. 1984. pap. 4.95 (ISBN 0-931689-00-7). SOS Pub OR.

Power of Babel: A Study of Logophilia. Michel Pierssens. Tr. by Carl R. Lovitt from Fr. Orig. Title: Tour De Babil. 144p. 1980. Repr. of 1976 ed. 21.95x (ISBN 0-7100-0373-0). Routledge Chapman & Hall.

Power of Balance: The Rolfing Process. Brain W. Fahey. (Health Reference Ser.). (Illus.). 224p. 1988. 17.95 (ISBN 0-943920-52-3); pap. cancelled. Metamorphous Pr.

Power of Being a Woman. Anita Canfield. 108p. 1985. 7.95 (ISBN 0-934126-62-3). Randall Bk Co.

Power of Being Debt-Free. Robert H. Schuller & Paul D. Dunn. LC 84-29453. 240p. 1985. 14.95 (ISBN 0-8407-5461-2). Nelson.

Power of Being Industrious. Virginia Swenson. LC 81-50662. (Power Tales Ser.). (gr. k-7). pap. write for info. (ISBN 0-911712-88-7). Eagle Mktg Corp.

Power of Blackness. Jack Williamson. LC 75-29508. 1976. 20.00 (ISBN 0-399-11467-X). Ultramarine Pub.

Power of Blackness: Hawthorne, Poe, Melville. Harry Levin. LC 80-83221. xxii, 263p. 1980. pap. 6.95x (ISBN 0-8214-0581-0). Ohio U Pr.

Power of CalcResult For the Commodore 64. Robert Williams. (Power Ser.). 1983. pap. 14.95. P-H.

Power of Calculus. 3rd ed. Kenneth L. Whipkey & Mary N. Whipkey. LC 78-24067. 373p. 1979. 33.50 (ISBN 0-471-03140-2); tchr's. manual avail. (ISBN 0-471-05500-X). Wiley.

Power of Calculus. 4th ed. Kenneth L. Whipkey & Mary N. Whipkey. LC 85-13022. 474p. 1986. write for info. (ISBN 0-471-06382-7). Wiley.

Power of Caring. Phyllia Colonna & Ana M. Phillips. LC 81-50388. (Power Tales Ser.). (gr. k-7). pap. write for info. (ISBN 0-911712-87-9). Eagle Mktg Corp.

Power of Cheerfulness. Phyllis Colonna & Della M. Rasmussen. LC 80-85337. (Power Tales Ser.). (gr. k-7). pap. write for info. Eagle Mktg Corp.

Power of Children. Ashley Bronson. 122p. 1989. write for info. (ISBN 0-9616807-1-7). Bestsell Pubns.

Power of Choice. Robert Fritz & Brian R. Smith. (Illus.). 21p. 1982. pap. 4.95 (ISBN 0-943290-00-7). Fainshaw Pr.

Power of Choice: A Guide to Personal & Professional Self-Management. Ted Willey. 252p. 1988. 19.95 (ISBN 0-929376-92-7). Berwick Hse.

Power of Clothes. Elizabeth B. Hurlock. 144p. 1988. 9.95 (ISBN 0-8062-3322-2). Carlton.

Power of Commitment. Jerry White. 1987. pap. 5.95 (ISBN 0-317-56192-8). NavPress.

Power of Communication. Kenneth A. Erickson. 112p. (Orig.). 1986. pap. 4.95 (ISBN 0-570-04435-9, 12-3053). Concordia.

Power of Community Education. W. Fred Totten. LC 73-123592. 168p. 1970. 13.20 (ISBN 0-87812-011-4). Pendell Pub.

Power of Compassion. James McNamara. 1984. pap. 4.95 (ISBN 0-8091-2567-6). Paulist Pr.

Power of Concentration. Theron Dumont. 8.00 (ISBN 0-911662-39-1). Yoga.

Power of Congress. Robert LeFevre. Ed. by R. S. Radford. LC 76-12211. 1976. pap. text ed. 6.95 (ISBN 0-932196-03-9). Pine Tree Pr.

Power of Congress. Robert Lefevre. Ed. by Robert Radford. 174p. pap. 9.50x (ISBN 0-318-16582-1). Soc Libertarian Life.

Power of Construction Management Using Lotus 1-2-3. Jay Compton. (Illus.). 300p. 1984. pap. 29.95 (ISBN 0-943518-17-2); pap. 44.95, incl. disk (ISBN 0-317-11824-2). MIS Press.

Power of Construction Management Using Multiplan. Jay Compton. (Illus.). 300p. 1984. 29.95 (ISBN 0-943518-18-0); 44.95, incl. disk (ISBN 0-317-11827-7). MIS Press.

Power of Consultative Selling. Bryce Webster. (Illus.). 228p. 1987. 19.95 (ISBN 0-13-685918-6); pap. 9.95. P-H.

Power of Courage. Phyllis Colonna & Della M. Ramussen. LC 80-85338. (Power Tales Ser.). (gr. k-7). write for info. Eagle Mktg Corp.

Power of Creativity. Patricia Metten. LC 81-50863. (Power Tales Ser.). (gr. k-7). pap. write for info. (ISBN 0-911712-89-5). Eagle Mktg Corp.

Power of Darkness. Doris Sutcliffe Adams. 1978. pap. 1.95 (ISBN 0-8439-0567-0, Leisure Bks). Leisure NY.

Power of Darkness. Durwood Buchheim. 1985. 6.95 (ISBN 0-89536-746-7, 5852). CSS of Ohio.

Power of David's Key. Vincent M. Walsh. 192p. (Orig.). 1981. pap. 5.00 (ISBN 0-943374-03-0). Key of David.

Power of Determination. Phyllis Colonna & Della M. Rasmussen. LC 80-85339. (Power Tales Ser.). (gr. k-7). pap. write for info. Eagle Mktg Corp.

Power of Effective Speech. Augusta I. Barrick. (Orig.). 1959. 14.95x; pap. 10.95x (ISBN 0-8084-0251-X). New Coll U Pr.

Power of Eloquence: Magic Key to Success in Public Speaking. Thomas Montalbo. LC 83-11078. 278p. 1983. 19.95 (ISBN 0-13-687657-9, Busn); pap. 6.95 (ISBN 0-13-687640-4). P-H.

Power of Encouragement. Jeanne Doering. 176p. (Orig.). 1983. pap. 6.95 (ISBN 0-8024-0146-5). Moody.

Power of Enthusiasm. Phyllis Colonna & Della M. Rasmussen. LC 81-50864. (Power Tales Ser.). (gr. k-7). pap. write for info. Eagle Mktg Corp.

Power of Ethical Management: Why the Ethical Way Is the Profitable Way - in Your Life & in Your Business. Kenneth Blanchard & Norman V. Peale. 136p. 1987. 15.95 (ISBN 0-688-07062-0). Morrow.

Power of Eureka: One Hundred Twenty-Five Applications. Neil J. Salkind. 256p. 1988. 19.95 (ISBN 0-673-38592-2). Scott F.

Power of Example. Leslie Horan. (Illus.). 24p. 1987. pap. 10.00 (ISBN 0-944290-01-9). Light Speed.

Power of Faith Exemplified in the Life & Writings of the Late Mrs. Isabella Graham. Joanna Bethune. Ed. by Carolyn G. De Swarte & Donald Dayton. (Women in American Protestant Religion Series 1800-1930). 440p. 1987. lib. bdg. 65.00 (ISBN 0-8240-0659-3). Garland Pub.

Power of Faith: Hebrews 11, 1 - 12, 4. John MacArthur, Jr. (John MacArthur Bible Studies). 1987. pap. 4.95 (ISBN 0-8024-5353-8). Moody.

Power of Family. Patricia Metten. LC 81-50867. (Power Tales Ser.). (gr. k-7). pap. write for info. (ISBN 0-911712-93-3). Eagle Mktg Corp.

Power of Fantasy: Where Our Daydreams Come from, & How They Can Harm or Help Us. Lucy Freeman & Kristin Kupfermann. 212p. 1988. 16.95 (ISBN 0-8264-0410-3). Continuum.

Power of Food. pap. 8.25 (F1280, FAO). UNIPUB.

Power of Form. Gilbert J. Rose. LC 79-53592. (Psychological Issues, Monograph: No.49, Vol. 13, No. 1). (Illus.). 234p. 1980. text ed. 27.50x (ISBN 0-8236-4171-6). Intl Univs Pr.

Power of Frameworks. Robert E. Williams. (Illus.). 200p. 1984. 14.95 (ISBN 0-943518-22-9). MIS Press.

Power of Gems & Charms. George H. Bratley. 198p. 1988. Repr. lib. bdg. 24.95x (ISBN 0-8095-6132-8). Borgo Pr.

Power of Gems & Charms. George H. Bratley. 198p. (Orig.). 1988. pap. 9.95 (ISBN 0-87877-132-8). Newcastle Pub.

Power of Genre. Aden Rosmarin. LC 85-8630. 200p. 1986. 25.00x (ISBN 0-8166-1395-8); pap. 11.95 (ISBN 0-8166-1396-6). U of Minn Pr.

Power of Geography: How Territory Shapes Social Life. Ed. by Jennifer R. Wolch & M. J. Dear. 352p. 1988. text ed. 45.00 (ISBN 0-04-445056-7); pap. 19.95 (ISBN 0-04-445228-4). Unwin Hyman.

Power of God. Dom G. Dix. 96p. 1984. pap. 5.95 (ISBN 0-8192-1334-9). Morehouse.

Power of God. Daniel L. Migliore. LC 82-20037. (Library of Living Faith Ser.: Vol. 8). 116p. (Orig.). 1983. pap. 5.95 (ISBN 0-664-24454-8). Westminster John Knox.

Power of God's Character. Don Clowers. 230p. (Orig.). 1983. pap. text ed. 10.95 (ISBN 0-914307-14-2). Word Faith.

Power of Goodness. Cesare Zappulli. 1980. 3.00 (ISBN 0-8198-5800-5); pap. 2.00 (ISBN 0-8198-5801-3). Dghtrs St Paul.

Power of Historical Knowledge: Narrating the Past in Hawthorne, James, & Dreiser. Susan L. Mizruchi. 336p. 1988. text ed. 32.50 (ISBN 0-691-06725-2). Princeton U Pr.

Power of Holistic Aromatherapy. Christine Stead. 128p. (Orig.). 1987. pap. 5.95 (ISBN 0-7137-1675-4, Pub. by Javelin England). Sterling.

Power of Human Imagination. Ed. by Kenneth S. Singer & Jerome L. Pope. LC 78-15392. (Emotions, Personality, & Psychotherapy Ser.). (Illus.). 426p. 1978. 42.50x (ISBN 0-306-31140-2, Plenum Pr). Plenum Pub.

Power of Human Needs in World Society. Ed. by Roger A. Coate & Jerel Rosati. LC 87-32225. 300p. 1988. lib. bdg. 35.00x (ISBN 1-55587-091-0). Lynne Rienner.

Power of Ice. Ruth Radlauer & Lisa S. Gitkin. LC 85-5714. (Radlauer Geo Bks.). (Illus.). 48p. (gr. 3-6). 1985. PLB 13.27 (ISBN 0-516-07839-9); pap. 3.95 (ISBN 0-516-47839-7). Childrens.

Power of Ideals in American History. Ephraim D. Adams. LC 75-98025. (BCL Ser.: No. II). Repr. of 1913 ed. 14.50 (ISBN 0-404-00285-4). AMS Pr.

Power of Ideology: The Quest for Technological Autonomy in Argentina and Brazil. Emanuel Adler. LC 85-2084. (Studies in International Political Economy: Vol. 16). 520p. 1987. 45.00x (ISBN 0-520-05485-7). U of Cal PR.

Power of Images in the Age of Augustus. Paul Zanker. 1988. text ed. 30.00 (ISBN 0-472-10101-3). U of Mich Pr.

Power of Intecession. Peter Grant. 108p. (Orig.). 1984. pap. 5.95 (ISBN 0-89283-132-4). Servant.

Power of Integrity. Phyllis Colonna & Della M. Rasmussen. LC 81-50390. (Power Tales Ser.). (gr. k-7). pap. write for info. (ISBN 0-911712-85-2). Eagle Mktg Corp.

Power of Intuition. Joyce Keane & Robert A. Butterworth. (Illus.). 150p. (Orig.). 1988. pap. 12.95 (ISBN 0-938257-04-8). Omni Lrn Inst.

Power of Jewelry. Nancy Schiffer. (Illus.). 256p. 1988. 75.00 (ISBN 0-88740-135-X). Schiffer.

Power of Kindness. Harry M. Tippett. (Uplook Ser.). 32p. 1955. pap. 0.99 (ISBN 0-8163-0076-3, 16415-2). Pacific Pr Pub Assn.

Power of Knowing Who I Am in Christ. J. R. Reinhart. LC 82-73254. 220p. 1983. pap. 8.95 (ISBN 0-918060-04-4). Burn-Hart.

Power of Life or Death. Michael V. Disalle. LC 82-45662. (Capital Punishment Ser.). Date not set. Repr. of 1965 ed. 28.50 (ISBN 0-404-62411-1). AMS Pr.

Power of Light. Isaac Bashevis Singer. 80p. (gr. 4 up). 1987. pap. 2.50 (ISBN 0-380-60103-6, Camelot). Avon.

Power of Light: Eight Stories for Hanukkah. Isaac Bashevis Singer. LC 80-20263. (Illus.). 87p. (ps-3). 1980. 12.95 (ISBN 0-374-36099-5). FS&G.

Power of Limits: Proportional Harmonies in Nature, Art, & Architecture. Gyorgy Doczi. LC 77-90883. (Illus.). 224p. 1981. pap. 15.95 (ISBN 0-87773-193-4). Shambhala Pubns.

Power of Limits: Proportional Harmonies in Nature, Art & Architecture. Gyorgy Doczi. pap. 17.95 (ISBN 0-394-73580-3). Shambhala Pubns.

Power of Little Words: Some Ideas to Improve Your Writing. John L. Beckley. (Illus.). 128p. 1984. 14.95 (ISBN 0-910187-02-9). Economics Pr.

Power Of: Lotus 1-2-3 Complete Reference Guide. Robert E. Williams. (Power of Ser.). 294p. (Orig.). 1986. pap. 19.95 (ISBN 0-943518-65-2). MIS Press.

Power Of: Lotus 1-2-3 Release 2 for Business Applications. Robert E. Williams. (Power of Ser.). 314p. (Orig.). 1986. pap. 19.95 (ISBN 0-943518-64-4); incl. diskette 34.95. MIS Press.

Power of Mac MultiPlan. Robert E. Williams. (Illus.). 200p. cancelled (ISBN 0-943518-24-5). MIS Press.

Power Of: Microsoft Word 4.0 Including Style Sheets & Desktop Publishing. 2nd ed. Timothy Perrin. Ed. by Kim Thomas. 475p. 1987. pap. 21.95 (ISBN 0-943518-31-8). MIS Press.

Power of Minorities. Gabriel Mugny. (European Monographs in Social Psychology: No. 31). 1982. 43.50 (ISBN 0-12-509720-4). Acad Pr.

Power of Modern Greek: Basic Course I. Strati Demertzis. 136p. (Orig.). (YA) (gr. 7-12). 1986. pap. text ed. 11.00 (ISBN 0-9618466-0-7). Expressway Pubs.

Power of Modern Greek: Basic Course II. Strati Demertzis. 164p. (Orig.). (YA) (gr. 7-12). 1986. pap. text ed. 12.00 (ISBN 0-9618466-1-5). Expressway Pubs.

Power of Money. Henry L. Bretton. LC 79-23484. 418p. 1980. 54.50 (ISBN 0-87395-425-4); pap. 19.95x (ISBN 0-87395-426-2). State U NY Pr.

Power of Money Dynamics. Venita VanCaspel. 1982. text ed. 22.00 (ISBN 0-8359-5570-2, Reston). P-H.

Power of Money Dynamics. Venita Van Caspel. 1985. 19.95 (ISBN 0-671-61436-3). S&S.

Power of Money in American Politics. Gus Tyler et al. 50p. (Orig.). 1982. pap. text ed. 5.00 (ISBN 0-8191-5879-8, Pub. by Aspen Inst for Humanistic Studies). U Pr of Amer.

Power of Movement in Plants. 2nd ed. Charles Darwin. LC 65-23402. 1966. Repr. of 1881 ed. lib. bdg. 55.00 (ISBN 0-306-70921-X). Da Capo.

Power of Movement in Plants. Charles Darwin. 1892. 49.00 (ISBN 0-8274-3193-7). R West.

Power of Movement in Plants. 3rd ed. Charles Darwin. LC 72-3901. (Illus.). x, 592p. 1972. 42.50 (ISBN 0-404-08415-X). AMS Pr.

Power Of: Multiplan. Robert E. Williams. (Illus.). 169p. 1982. pap. 14.95 (ISBN 0-943518-05-9); pap. 28.95, incl. diskette. MIS Press.

Power of Myth. Joseph Campbell & Bill Moyers. LC 88-4218. 1988. 27.50 (ISBN 0-385-24773-7); pap. 19.95 (ISBN 0-385-24774-5). Doubleday.

Power of Negative Thinking. Woodie Hall. Ed. by Arlene A. Wright. 104p. (Orig.). 1985. pap. 5.95 (ISBN 0-940156-49-0). Wright Group.

Power of Nonviolence. 3rd ed. Richard B. Gregg. 192p. (Orig.). 1984. pap. 9.50 (ISBN 0-934676-70-4). Greenlf Bks.

Power of Numbers. Mary Valla. 1972. pap. 5.95 (ISBN 0-87516-108-1). DeVorss.

Power of One. 40p. 5.95 (ISBN 0-318-23891-8). Future Home.

Power of Ordinary Christians: Witnessing in a New Age. Margaret Wold. LC 88-10507. 128p. (Orig.). 1988. pap. 6.95 (ISBN 0-8066-2374-8, 10-5036). Augsburg.

Power of OS-2: A Comprehensive User's Manual. Judi Fernandez & Ruth Ashley. 1988. pap. 19.95 (ISBN 0-8306-2993-9, 2993). TAB Bks.

Power of Overcoming. Virginia Swenson. LC 81-50866. (Power Tales Ser.). (gr. k-7). pap. write for info. (ISBN 0-911712-92-5). Eagle Mktg Corp.

Power of Pascal. Larry Leff. 1986. 29.95 (ISBN 0-13-687450-9, Busn). P-H.

Power of Pasta. Olwen Woodier. LC 84-48812. (Illus.). 154p. 1985. pap. 6.95 (ISBN 0-88266-384-4). Storey Comm Inc.

Power of Patriotism. DeLynn Decker. LC 81-50387. (Power Tales Ser.). (gr. k-7). pap. write for info. (ISBN 0-911712-84-4). Eagle Mktg Corp.

Power of PC Works. Gia L. Rozells. 1988. pap. 19.95 (ISBN 0-673-38145-5). Scott F.

Power of Peonage. Robert L. Glass. 1979. 9.00 (ISBN 0-686-23742-0). Computing Trends.

Power of People Skills: A Manager's Guide to Assessing & Developing Your Organization's Greatest Resource. Douglas Stewart. LC 85-31529. 288p. 1986. 14.95 (ISBN 0-471-85038-1); pap. 17.95 (ISBN 0-471-01187-8). Wiley.

Power of Perception. Marcus Bach. LC 73-5535. 156p. 1983. pap. 5.95 (ISBN 0-87516-523-0). DeVorss.

Power of Persuasion: Giving up Control on the Way to Power. Ray G. Funkhouser. LC 86-5730. (Illus.). 288p. 1986. 18.95 (ISBN 0-8129-1318-3). Times Bks.

Power of Persuasive Parenting. Harold J. Sala. 11lp. (Orig.). 1982. pap. 5.75x (ISBN 0-686-37686-2, Pub. by New Day Philippines). Cellar.

Power of Pluto: The Complete Book. Arlene Robertson & Margaret Wilson. 270p. 1979. pap. 7.95 perfect bdg. (ISBN 0-930706-02-1). Seek-It Pubns.

Power of Poetry. Sterling W. Sill. LC 83-83267. 141p. 1984. 7.95 (ISBN 0-88290-238-5). Horizon Utah.

Power of Positive Evangelism: How to Hold a Revival. John R. Bisagno. LC 68-26912. 1968. pap. 4.95 (ISBN 0-8054-2503-9). Broadman.

Power of Positive Giving. John R. Bisagno. LC 88-315. (Orig.). 1988. pap. 3.50 (ISBN 0-8054-6407-7). Broadman.

Power of Positive Handwriting. Elayne V. Lindberg & Gary Lindberg. (Illus.). 224p. (Orig.). 1987. pap. 9.95 (ISBN 0-934860-49-1). Adventure Pubns.

Power of Positive Living. John R. Bisagno. LC 70-93913. (Orig.). 1970. pap. 3.95 (ISBN 0-8054-1910-1). Broadman.

Power of Positive Parenting. T. Jefferson Research Center Staff. 1987. incl. six audio tapes 29.95 (ISBN 0-938308-16-5). T Jefferson Res Ctr.

Power of Positive Persuasion: A Professional's Guide to Communications. Francis A. Acquaviva & Robert A. Malone. 96p. pap. 9.95 (RAMSCO 00200). Ramsco Pub.

Power of Positive Praying. John Bisagno. 1965. pap. 3.95 (ISBN 0-310-21212-X, 9238P). Zondervan.

Power of Positive Praying see Poder de la Oracion Tenaz.

Power of Positive Reinforcement: A Handbook of Behavior Modification. Judith E. Favell. (Illus.). 288p. 1977. 23.00 (ISBN 0-398-03620-9). C C Thomas.

Power of Positive Resistance. Roy H. Hicks. 128p. 1983. pap. 2.95 (ISBN 0-89274-294-1). Harrison Hse.

Power of Positive Self Image. Baird. 1983. 5.95 (ISBN 0-88207-316-8). Victor Bks.

Power of Positive Shrinking: Appetite - Weight Control by Hypnosis & Behavior Modification. Richard U. Gunderson. 54p. (Orig.). 1981. 12.95 (ISBN 0-686-36697-2). Gunderson.

Power of Positive Students. H. William Mitchell & Charles P. Conn. 192p. 1986. pap. 3.95 (ISBN 0-553-26110-X). Bantam.

Power of Positive Students. William Mitchell & Charles P. Conn. LC 84-27233. 1985. 12.95 (ISBN 0-688-04492-1). Morrow.

Power of Positive Thinking. Norman V. Peale. 1954. pap. 9.95 (ISBN 0-13-686402-3). P-H.

Power of Positive Thinking. Norman V. Peale. 552p. 1985. pap. 15.95 large print ed. (ISBN 0-8027-2465-5). Walker & Co.

Power of Positive Thinking: Thirty-Fifth Anniversary Edition. rev. ed. Norman Vincent Peale. 304p. 1987. pap. 13.95 (ISBN 0-13-686445-7). P-H.

Power of Power Politics: A Critique. John A. Vasquez. (Illus.). 300p. 1983. 35.00x (ISBN 0-8135-0919-X). Rutgers U Pr.

Power of Praise. Henry G. Bosch. 1987. pap. 1.50x (ISBN 0-8010-0872-7). Baker Bk.

Power of Praise. Kenneth Erickson. 1984. pap. 4.95 (ISBN 0-570-03925-8, 12-2859). Concordia.

Power of Praise & Worship. Terry Law. (Illus.). 256p. (Orig.). 1985. pap. 6.95 (ISBN 0-932081-01-0). Victory Hse.

Power of Prayer. R. A. Torrey. 1987. pap. 6.95 (ISBN 0-310-33311-3, 10909P). Zondervan.

Power of Prayer. Reuben A. Torrey. 192p. 1971. pap. 6.95 (10909P). Zondervan.

Power of Prayer & Fasting. Marlin A. Hoffman. 2.50 (ISBN 0-89137-535-X). Quality Pubns.

Power of Prayer: The Inspired Words of Yogi Bhajan. Harbhajan Singh Khalsa. 95p. 1988. Repr. lib. bdg. 19.95x (ISBN 0-89370-896-8). Borgo Pr.

Power of Prevention: Reduce Your Risk of Cancer Through Diet & Nutrition. Oliver Alabaster. 432p. 1986. pap. 7.95 (ISBN 0-671-62798-8, Fireside). S&S.

Power of Professional Management. George S. Dively. LC 77-151052. 1971. 12.95 (ISBN 0-8144-5188-8). AMACOM.

Power of Professional Management. George S. Dively. LC 77-151052. pap. 47.80 (ISBN 0-317-28127-5, 2055740). Bks Demand UMI.

Power of Prosperous Thinking: A Practical & Inspirational Guide to Making, Managing, & Multiplying Your Money. Jack Johnstad & Lois Johnstad. (Illus.). 256p. 1982. 12.95 (ISBN 0-312-63431-5); pap. 5.95 (ISBN 0-312-63432-3). St Martin.

Power of Psychiatry. Ed. by Peter Miller & Nikolas Rose. 288p. 1986. text ed. 49.95 (ISBN 0-7456-0235-5); pap. text ed. 16.95 (ISBN 0-7456-0236-3). Basil Blackwell.

Power of Public Ideas. Ed. by Robert B. Reich. LC 87-1371. 264p. 1987. 20.45 (ISBN 0-88730-128-2). Ballinger Pub.

Power of Public Relations. Joseph F. Awad. LC 85-6258. 176p. 1985. 35.00 (ISBN 0-275-90054-1, C0054). Praeger.

Power of Purpose. Richard J. Leider. 192p. 1985. pap. 2.95 (ISBN 0-449-12840-7, GM). Fawcett.

Power Of: Q & A, Version 2. Paul Dlug. (Power of Ser.). 300p. (Orig.). 1987. pap. cancelled (ISBN 0-943518-70-9). MIS Press.

Power of Quattro: Business User's Guide. Neil Salkind. 1988. pap. 18.95 (ISBN 0-471-61407-6). Wiley.

Power Of: RBase 5000. Robert E. Williams. 330p. 1985. 19.95 (ISBN 0-943518-62-8); incl. diskett 34.95. MIS Press.
Power of Real Estate Syndication. Greg James. 128p. (Orig.). pap. 29.95 (ISBN 0-910019-25-8). Regency Bks.
Power of Reason - 1988: An Autobiography. Lyndon H. LaRouche, Jr. LC 87-7894. (Illus.). 331p. (Orig.). 1987. pap. 10.00 (ISBN 0-943235-00-6). Exec Intel Review.
Power of Receiving. Landon B. Saunders. (Twentieth Century Sermons Ser.). 1979. 11.95 (ISBN 0-89112-312-1). Abilene Christ U.
Power of Reflex Plus. William B. Sanders. 256p. 1988. pap. 19.95 (ISBN 0-673-38593-0). Scott F.
Power of Relevant Mathematics: The Basic Concept. Mary N. Whipkey et al. (Illus.). 1977. text ed. write for info. (ISBN 0-13-687202-6). P-H.
Power of Resurrection: Bible Stories That Live. Margaret Graham. LC 87-45703. 160p. 1988. 13.45 (ISBN 0-06-063382-4, HarpR). Har-Row.
Power of Rhetoric: Hugo's Metaphor & Poetics. Wendy N. Greenberg. (American University Studies II: Romance Languages & Literature: Vol. 35). 143p. 1985. text ed. 27.00 (ISBN 0-8204-0254-0). P Lang Pubs.
Power of Running PC DOS. Carl Siechert & Chris Wood. (Power Of Ser.). 386p. (Orig.). 1986. pap. 22.95 (ISBN 0-943518-74-1). MIS Press.
Power of Sexual Surrender. Marie N. Robinson. pap. 1.50 (ISBN 0-451-06921-8, W6921, Sig). NAL.
Power of Shame: A Rational Perspective. Agnes Heller. 352p. 1985. 42.50x (ISBN 0-7100-9922-3). Routledge Chapman & Hall.
Power of Silence: Further Lessons of Don Juan. Carlos Castaneda. 368p. 1987. 17.95 (ISBN 0-671-50067-8). S&S.
Power of Sportsmanship. Phyllis Colonna & Della M. Rasmussen. LC 81-50868. (Power Tales Ser.). (gr. k-7). pap. write for info. (ISBN 0-911712-94-1). Eagle Mktg Corp.
Power of Steam: An Illustrated History of the World's Steam Age. Asa Briggs. LC 82-40321. (Illus.). 208p. 1983. 22.50x (ISBN 0-226-07495-1); pap. 10.00 (ISBN 0-226-07497-8). U of Chicago Pr.
Power Of: Step-by-Step Through LOGO Turtle Graphics. Ann Rose. (Illus.). 47p. 1983. pap. 6.95 (ISBN 0-943518-11-3). MIS Press.
Power of Surrender. 2nd ed. Tom Johnson. 1984. pap. 3.00 (ISBN 0-941992-12-8). Los Arboles Pub.
Power of Symbols in Religion & Culture. F. W. Dillistone. 176p. 1986. 16.95 (ISBN 0-8245-0784-3). Crossroad NY.
Power of Sympathy. William H. Brown. Bd. with Coquette. Hannah Foster. Ed. by William S. Osborne. (Masterworks of Literature Ser.). 1970. 11.95x (ISBN 0-8084-0345-1); pap. 7.95x (ISBN 0-8084-0346-X). New Coll U Pr.
Power of Symphony. Robert E. Williams. (Illus.). 200p. 1984. 14.95 (ISBN 0-943518-23-7); 29.95, incl. diskette. MIS Press.
Power of Television: A Critical Appraisal. Conrad Lodziak. LC 86-17706. 233p. 1986. 27.50 (ISBN 0-312-63397-1). St Martin.
Power of the Aleph Beth, Vol. II. Philip S. Berg. 224p. 1988. 15.95 (ISBN 0-943688-56-6); pap. 10.95 (ISBN 0-943688-57-4). Res Ctr Kabbalah.
Power of the Aleph Beth, Vol. 1. Philip S. Berg. 288p. 1988. 15.95 (ISBN 0-943688-11-6); pap. 10.95 (ISBN 0-943688-10-8). Res Ctr Kabbalah.
Power of the Blood. Andrew Murray. 1984. pap. 3.50 (ISBN 0-87508-428-1). Chr Lit.
Power of the Blood. H. A. Whyte. 1973. pap. 2.95 (ISBN 0-88368-027-0). Whitaker Hse.
Power of the Blood of Jesus. Andrew Murray. 144p. 1987. pap. 5.95 (ISBN 0-310-29701-X, 10369P). Zondervan.
Power of the Center: The New Version. Rudolf Arnheim. (Illus.). 256p. 1988. 32.50 (ISBN 0-520-06241-8); pap. 12.95 (ISBN 0-520-06242-6). U of Cal Pr.
Power of the Charlatan. Grete de Francesco. Tr. by Miriam Beard from Ger. LC 79-8609. Repr. of 1939 ed. 31.50 (ISBN 0-404-18471-5). AMS Pr.
Power of the Dog. Thomas Savage. LC 82-13705. 276p. 1983. pap. 5.95x (ISBN 0-941324-01-X). Van Vactor & Goodheart.
Power of the Dog: Moments in History & Anti-History. Howard Barker. (Playscript: No. 109). 48p. (Orig.). 1985. pap. 3.95 (ISBN 0-7145-4066-8). Riverrun NY.
Power of the Early Tudor Nobility: A Study of the Fourth & Fifth Earls of Shrewsbury. G. W. Bernard. LC 84-16757. 240p. 1985. 27.50x (ISBN 0-389-20525-7, 08087). B&N Imports.
Power of the Eyes. Patricia Webbink. 240p. 1986. text ed. 23.95 (ISBN 0-8261-2670-7). Springer Pub.
Power of the Family: Mastering the Hidden Dance of Family Relationships. Michael P. Nichols. 432p. 1988. 21.95 (ISBN 0-671-67189-8, Fireside); pap. 9.95 (ISBN 0-671-64408-4, Fireside). S&S.
Power of the Holy Spirit, Vol. III. 3rd ed. Don Dewelt. 1972. pap. 3.95 (ISBN 0-89900-125-4). College Pr Pub.
Power of the Holy Spirit, Vol. IV. 2nd ed. Don DeWelt. (Orig.). 1976. pap. 6.95 (ISBN 0-89900-126-2). College Pr Pub.
Power of the Holy Spirit, Vol. II. 5th ed. Don DeWelt. (Orig.). 1971. pap. 3.95 (ISBN 0-89900-124-6). College Pr Pub.
Power of the Holy Spirit, Vol. I. 8th ed. Don DeWelt. (Orig.). 1963. pap. 3.95 (ISBN 0-89900-123-8). College Pr Pub.
Power of the Image: Essays on Representation & Sexuality. Annette Kuhn. (Illus.). 176p. 1985. 19.95s (ISBN 0-7102-0625-9); pap. 9.95 (ISBN 0-7100-9731-X). Routledge Chapman & Hall.
Power of the Mind & How to Fortify One's Will. Frank C. Haddock. (Illus.). 109p. 1982. 157.75 (ISBN 0-89920-036-2). Am Inst Psych.
Power of the Past: Essays for Eric Hobsbawm. Ed. by Pat Thane et al. 304p. 1984. 54.50 (ISBN 0-521-25525-2). Cambridge U Pr.
Power of the Pendulum. T. C. Lethbridge. (Illus.). 160p. 1984. pap. 5.95 (ISBN 1-85063-003-8, Ark Paperbks). Routledge Chapman & Hall.
Power of the People: Active Nonviolence in the United States. rev. & updated ed. Ed. by Robert Cooney & Helen Michalowski. (Illus.). 272p. 1987. lib. bdg. 39.95 (ISBN 0-86571-089-9); pap. 18.95 (ISBN 0-86571-090-2). New Soc Pubs.
Power of the Plus Factor. Norman V. Peale. 1987. 14.95 (ISBN 0-8007-1526-8). Revell.
Power of the Plus Factor. Norman V. Peale. 1988. pap. 3.95 (ISBN 0-449-21600-4, Crest). Fawcett.
Power of the Poor in History. Gustavo Gutierrez. Tr. by Robert R. Barr from Span. LC 82-22252. Orig. Title: Fuerza Historica de los Pobres. 256p. (Orig.). 1983. pap. 10.95 (ISBN 0-88344-388-0). Orbis Bks.
Power of the Powerless. Jurgen Moltmann. 176p. 1983. 13.45 (ISBN 0-06-065907-6, HarpT). Har-Row.
Power of the Powerless: A Brother's Lesson. Christopher De Vinck. LC 87-19838. (Illus.). 144p. 1988. 14.95 (ISBN 0-385-24138-0). Doubleday.
Power of the Powerless: Citizens against the State in Central Eastern Europe. Vaclav Havel et al. Ed. by John Keane. Tr. by Paul Wilson & A. G. Brain. 232p. 1986. 35.00 (ISBN 0-87332-370-X). M E Sharpe.
Power of the Presidency. James L. Fisher. 240p. 1984. 17.95 (ISBN 0-02-910520-X, 2016). Macmillan.
Power of the Presidency: Concepts & Controversy. 3rd ed. Ed. by Robert S. Hirschfield. 1982. 37.95x (ISBN 0-202-24159-9); pap. 18.95x (ISBN 0-202-24160-2). Aldine de Gruyter.
Power of the Press: The Birth of American Political Reporting. Thomas C. Leonard. (Illus.). 288p. 1987. pap. 7.95 (ISBN 0-19-505184-X). Oxford U Pr.
Power of the Press: The Birth of American Political Reporting. Thomas G. Leonard. (Illus.). 282p. 1986. 22.50 (ISBN 0-19-503719-7). Oxford U Pr.
Power of the Professional Person. Ed. by Robert W. Clarke & Robert P. Lawry. LC 88-840. 250p. (Orig.). 1988. lib. bdg. 28.50 (ISBN 0-8191-6955-2, Pub. by CWRU CPE); pap. text ed. 12.50 (ISBN 0-8191-6956-0, Pub. by CWRU CPE). U Pr of Amer.
Power of the Prophetic. Elbert A. Denyssey. 1988. pap. 15.00 (ISBN 0-8309-0512-X). Herald Hse.
Power of the Pulpit. Gardiner Spring. 244p. 1986. Repr. of 1848 ed. 12.95 (ISBN 0-85151-492-8). Banner of Truth.
Power of the Purse: A History of American Public Finance. E. James Ferguson. LC 61-325. (Institute of Early American History & Culture Ser.). xvii, 358p. Repr. of 1961 ed. 32.50x (ISBN 0-8078-0804-0). U of NC Pr.
Power of the Rays. S. G. Ouseley. 104p. 1981. pap. 4.95 (ISBN 0-85243-063-9). Ariel OH.
Power of the Rellard. Carolyn F. Logan. LC 87-22592. 288p. (gr. 4-7). 1988. 13.95 (ISBN 0-689-50445-4, M K McElderry). Macmillan.
Power of the Spirit. William Law. Ed. by Andrew Murray. LC 76-57110. (Classics of Devotions Ser). 224p. 1977. pap. 4.95 (ISBN 0-87123-463-7, 200463). Bethany Hse.
Power of the Spirit. William Law. Ed. by D. Hunt. 1971. pap. 2.95 (ISBN 0-87508-247-5). Chr Lit.
Power of the Spoken Word. Florence S. Shinn. Ed. by Christine Schneider. 1978. pap. 3.50 (ISBN 0-87516-260-6). DeVorss.
Power of the Sword. Wilbur Smith. 1986. 19.95 (ISBN 0-316-80171-2). Little.
Power of the Sword. Wilbur Smith. 602p. 1987. pap. 4.95 (ISBN 0-449-21414-1, Crest). Fawcett.
Power of the Tongue. Perry A. Gaspard. 1983. pap. 2.00 (ISBN 0-931867-04-5). Abundant Life Pubns.
Power of the Visible. Robert Dana. LC 79-171877. 71p. 1971. 8.95 (ISBN 0-8040-0551-6, Pub. by Swallow); pap. 4.95 (ISBN 0-8040-0646-6, Pub. by Swallow). Ohio U Pr.
Power of the White Wolf. Trish Reinius. (Illus.). 160p. 1985. pap. 8.00 (ISBN 0-932987-01-X). Iris IO.
Power of the Word: Holy Scripture in Orthodox Interpretation, Confession & Celebration. John Breck. LC 86-24773. 237p. 1987. pap. 8.95 (ISBN 0-88141-043-8). St Vladimirs.
Power of Three. Diana W. Jones. 208p. 1984. pap. 2.25 (ISBN 0-441-67630-8). Ace Bks.
Power of Total Living. Marcus Bach. 1981. pap. 2.50 (ISBN 0-449-23747-8, Crest). Fawcett.
Power of Total Living: A Holistic Approach to the Coming of the New Person for the New Age. Marcus Bach. (Illus.). 224p. 1984. pap. 7.95 (ISBN 0-396-08351-X). Dodd.
Power of Truth. Herrymon Maurer. 1950. pap. 2.50x (ISBN 0-87574-053-7, 053). Pendle Hill.
Power of Trying Again. Phyllis Colonna & Della M. Rasmussen. LC 81-50389. (Power Tales Ser.). (gr. k-7). pap. write for info. (ISBN 0-911712-86-0). Eagle Mktg Corp.
Power of Turbo Basic: Programming with Applications. Leon A. Wortman. (Illus.). 290p. 1988. 25.95 (ISBN 0-8306-1697-7, 2997); pap. 17.95 (ISBN 0-8306-2997-1). TAB Bks.
Power of Turbo Pascal. Philippe Kahn & Sanjiva Nath. 320p. 1986. pap. 19.95 (ISBN 0-89303-791-5); incl. disk & book 39.95 (ISBN 0-89303-794-X). P-H.
Power of Turbo Prolog: The Natural Language of Artificial Intelligence. Ralph Roberts. (Illus.). 256p. 1987. 22.95 (ISBN 0-8306-0782-X, 2782); pap. 14.95 (ISBN 0-8306-2782-0). TAB Bks.
Power of Ula. Miles Sheldon-Williams. Ed. by R. Reginald & Douglas Melville. LC 77-84276. (Lost Race & Adult Fantasy Ser.). 1978. Repr. of 1906 ed. lib. bdg. 25.50x (ISBN 0-405-11014-6). Ayer Co Pubs.
Power of Welsh Witchcraft: Psychic Development & the Old Religion. Rhuddlwm Gawr. LC 85-73762. (Illus.). 144p. (Orig.). Date not set. pap. 12.95 (ISBN 0-931760-39-9, CP 10117); text ed. 10.95 (ISBN 0-931760-17-8). Camelot GA.
Power of Will. Frank C. Haddock. 10.95 (ISBN 0-912576-17-0). R Collier.
Power Of: Word Perfect, Version 4.2. Robert Krumm. (Power of Ser.). 449p. (Orig.). 1987. pap. 19.95 (ISBN 0-943518-69-5). MIS Press.
Power of Words. Stuart Chase & Marian T Chase. LC 54-5980. 308p. 1954. 9.95 (ISBN 0-15-173487-9). HarBraceJ.
Power of Your Other Hand: A Course in Channelling the Inner Wisdom of the Right Brain. Lucia Capacchione. 196p. 1988. Repr. lib. bdg. 24.95x (ISBN 0-8095-6130-1). Borgo Pr.
Power of Your Other Hand: A Course in Channelling the Inner Wisdom of the Right Brain. Lucia Capacchione. 196p. (Orig.). 1988. pap. 9.95 (ISBN 0-87877-130-1). Newcastle Pub.
Power of Your Perceptions. William V. Arnold. LC 83-26089. (Potentials: Guides for Productive Living Ser.: Vol. 6). 118p. (Orig.). 1984. pap. 7.95 (ISBN 0-664-24524-2). Westminster John Knox.
Power of Your Subconscious Mind. Joseph Murphy. 1963. pap. 5.95 (Reward) (ISBN 0-13-685925-9). P-H.
Power of Your Subconscious Mind. Joseph Murphy. 224p. 1985. pap. 4.50 (ISBN 0-553-23399-8). Bantam.
Power of Your Subconscious Mind. Joseph Murphy. 1982. pap. 4.50 (ISBN 0-553-27043-5). Bantam.
Power of Your Subconscious Mind. Joseph Murphy. 224p. 1988. pap. 6.95 (ISBN 0-13-687972-1). P-H.
Power of Your Supermind. Vernon Howard. 1979. pap. 7.00 (ISBN 0-87516-375-0). DeVorss.
Power of Your Thoughts. James Allen. Ed. by Charles Chickadel. 48p. 1988. write for info. Meridian Learn Systs.
Power of 3: Patients & Partners in Hospital Care. Mary D. Scheller. 242p. 1988. pap. 7.95 (ISBN 0-933071-22-1, Dist. by W. W. Norton). Saybrook Pub Co.
Power on Display: The Politics of Shakespeare's Genres. Leonard Tennenhouse. 220p. 1986. text ed. 33.00 (ISBN 0-416-01271-X, 9211); pap. text ed. 12.95 (ISBN 0-416-01281-7, 9212). Routledge Chapman & Hall.
Power on Ice. Denis Potvin & Stan Fischler. LC 76-9198. (Illus.). (YA) 1977. 12.45i (ISBN 0-06-013387-2, HarpT). Har-Row.
Power on the Right. William Turner. LC 72-158916. 220p. 1971. lib. bdg. 7.95 (ISBN 0-87867-003-3). Ramparts.
Power over People. Louise B. Young. LC 72-91020. (Illus.). 1973. pap. 3.95 (ISBN 0-19-501830-3). Oxford U Pr.
Power over Power: What Power Means in Ordinary Life, How it is Related to Acting Freely, & What it Can Contribute to a Renovated Ethics of Education. David Nyberg. LC 81-67053. 224p. 1981. 19.95x (ISBN 0-8014-1414-8). Cornell U Pr.
Power over Power: What Power Means in Ordinary Life, How It Is Related to Acting Freely, & What It Can Contribute to a Renovated Ethics of Education. David Nyberg. LC 81-67053. 208p. 1988. pap. 15.95x (ISBN 0-8014-9497-4). Cornell U Pr.
Power over Your Pain Without Drugs. Neal H. Olshan. 256p. 1983. pap. 7.95 (ISBN 0-8253-0114-9). Beaufort Bks NY.
Power Pack. Bob Bartlett. LC 85-16841. 100p. 1985. pap. 4.95 (ISBN 0-89221-124-5). New Leaf.
Power Pak for Preschool Programs. Claudette Gronski & Judith Meeker. LC 83-83187. (Illus.). 240p. (ps-1). 1984. pap. text ed. 12.95 (ISBN 0-86530-025-9, IP 25-9). Incentive Pubns.
Power Paradigms in the Social Sciences. Charles R. Spruill. (Illus.). 196p. (Orig.). 1983. lib. bdg. 28.50 (ISBN 0-8191-3287-X); pap. text ed. 13.00 (ISBN 0-8191-3288-8). U Pr of Amer.
Power Paragraphs: Building Blocks for Eloquent Essays. Robinson. 72p. (Orig.). 1987. WKBK 9.95x (ISBN 0-88725-081-5). Hunter Textbks.
Power, Passions & Purpose: Prospects for North-South Negotiations. Ed. by Jagdish N. Bhagwati & John Gerald Ruggie. (Illus.). 360p. (Orig.). 1984. text ed. 35.00x (ISBN 0-262-02201-X); pap. text ed. 14.95x (ISBN 0-262-52091-5). MIT Pr.
Power, Pathology, Paradox: The Dynamics of Evil & Good. Marguerite Shuster. 352p. 1987. 22.95 (ISBN 0-310-39750-2, 18398). Zondervan.
Power Pattern Offenses for Winning Basketball. Jack Nagle. LC 85-32072. 185p. 1986. 19.95 (ISBN 0-13-687708-7, Parker). P-H.
Power Persuaders. 55p. 1978. 1.00 (ISBN 0-914389-08-4). Common Cause.
Power Persuasion: A Surefire System to Get Ahead in Business. William D. Coplin et al. LC 85-11159. 224p. 1985. write for info. (ISBN 0-201-11201-9). Addison-Wesley.
Power Phrases. Richard Cash. 300p. (Orig.). 1988. pap. 8.95 (ISBN 0-9601194-4-2, Phrasebks); pap. text ed. 8.95 (Phrasebks). Manderino Bks.
Power Picture. Estelle McCarthy & Charles McCarthy. (Orig.). 1973. pap. 1.95 (ISBN 0-377-03031-7). Friendship Pr.
Power Piping Data. Technical Association of the Pulp & Paper Industry. Ed. by Frank M. Tenore. pap. 20.00 (ISBN 0-317-26877-5, 2025295). Bks Demand UMI.
Power-Places of Central Tibet. Keith Dowman. 320p. 1988. pap. 56.00x (Pub. by Han-Shan Tang Ltd). State Mutual Bk.
Power-Places of Central Tibet: A Pilgrim's Guide. Keith Dowman. 320p. 1988. pap. text ed. 15.95 (ISBN 0-7102-1370-0, Pub. by Routledge UK). Routledge Chapman & HAll.
Power Plant Chemistry. Center for Occupational Research & Development Staff. (EUTEC Environmental & Chemical Analysis Curriculum Ser.). (Illus.). 291p. 1985. pap. text ed. 29.00 (ISBN 1-55502-200-6). Ctr Res & Dev.
Power Plant Engineering Opportunities. James R. Crape. LC 82-61199. (Illus.). 52p. (Orig.). 1982. pap. 4.95 (ISBN 0-916367-01-0). J R C Pub.
Power Plant Engineers Guide. 3rd ed. Frank Graham & Charles Buffinghon. LC 83-17779. (Illus.). 816p. 1984. 27.50 (ISBN 0-672-23329-0, Pub. by Audel). Macmillan.
Power Plant Evaluation & Design Reference Guide. Tyler G. Hicks. 400p. 1986. text ed. 44.50 (ISBN 0-07-028794-5). McGraw.
Power Plant Fans Specification Guidelines. 32p. 1977. 30.00 (ISBN 0-318-22009-1, #801); member 20.00. Air Mvmt & Cont.
Power Plant Fitting & Testing, 2 vols. W. Atherton et al. (Illus.). 492p. 1981. Repr. of 1981 ed. spiral 89.95x. Trans-Atl Phila.
Power Plant Fitting & Testing, 2 vols. 1982. 50.00x (Pub. by Engineering Ind). State Mutual Bk.
Power Plant Fundamentals & Systems I. Center for Occupational Research & Development Staff. (EUTEC Instrumentation & Control Curriculum Ser.). (Illus.). 160p. Date not set. pap. text ed. 22.00 (ISBN 1-55502-180-8). Ctr Res & Dev.
Power Plant Fundamentals & Systems II. Center for Occupational Research & Development Staff. (EUTEC Instrumentation & Control Curriculum Ser.). (Illus.). 186p. 1985. pap. text ed. 22.00 (ISBN 1-55502-181-6). Ctr Res & Dev.
Power Plant Instrumentation for Measurement of High-Purity Water Quality - STP 742. Ed. by R. W. Lane & G. Otten. 235p. 1981. 26.50 (ISBN 0-8031-0798-6, 04-742000-16). ASTM.
Power Plant Noise Control. Richard K. Miller. (Illus.). 130p. pap. text ed. cancelled (ISBN 0-89671-019-X). SEAI Tech Pubns.
Power Plant Operator. Jack Rudman. (Career Examination Ser.: C-1395). (Cloth bdg. avail. on request). pap. 14.00 (ISBN 0-8373-1395-3). Natl Learning.
Power Plant Operator Level I. Center for Occupational Research & Development Staff. (EUTEC Power Plant Operator Curriculum Ser.). (Illus.). 884p. 1985. pap. text ed. 90.00 (ISBN 1-55502-192-1). Ctr Res & Dev.
Power Plant Operator Level II. Center for Occupational Research & Development Staff. (EUTEC Power Plant Operator Curriculum Ser.). (Illus.). 698p. 1985. pap. text ed. 77.00 (ISBN 1-55502-193-X). Ctr Res & Dev.
Power Plant Operator Level III. Center for Occupational Research & Development Staff. (EUTEC Power Plant Operator Curriculum Ser.). (Illus.). 236p. 1985. pap. text ed. 26.00 (ISBN 1-55502-196-4). Ctr Res & Dev.
Power Plant Performance. A. B. Gill. 624p. 1984. text ed. 125.00 (ISBN 0-408-01427-X). Butterworth.
Power Plant Performance: Nuclear & Coal Capacity Factors & Economics. CEP Staff & Charles Komanoff. Ed. by Fred Armentrout. LC 76-50521. 1976. pap. 2.50 (ISBN 0-87871-004-3). CEP.
Power Plant Simulation, 1988. Ed. by David Hetrick. (Illus.). 112p. (Orig.). 1988. pap. 28.00X (ISBN 0-911801-27-8). Soc Computer Sim.
Power Plant System Design. Kam W. Li & A. Paul Priddy. LC 84-22177. 641p. 1985. write for info. (ISBN 0-471-88847-8). Wiley.

Power Systems Analysis & Planning. Ed. by A. H. El Abiad. LC 82-6228. (Arab School on Science & Technology Ser.). (Illus.). 350p. 1982. text ed. 89.95 (ISBN 0-89116-272-0). Hemisphere Pub.

Power Systems & Power Plant Control: Proceedings of the IFAC Symposium, Beijing, China 12-15 August 1986. Ed. by Wang Pingyang. (IFAC Publication). (Illus.). 430p. 1987. 135.00 (ISBN 0-08-034077-6). Pergamon.

Power Systems for Space Flight, PAAS11. Ed. by M A. Zipkin & R. N. Edwards. LC 63-13306. (Illus.). 943p. 89.50 (ISBN 0-317-36826-5). AIAA.

Power Systems in Communications Engineering: Principles, Pt. 1. Hans Gumhalter. LC 83-13666. 230p. 1984. pap. 61.95x (ISBN 0-471-90290-X). Wiley.

Power Tactics of Jesus Christ, & Other Essays. 2nd ed. Jay Haley. 160p. 1986. 14.95 (ISBN 0-931513-04-9, Dist. by W. W. Norton, Inc). Triang Pr.

Power Talk: How to Use Theater Techniques to Win Your Audience. Niki Flacks & Robert W. Rasberry. LC 81-69632. 256p. 1982. text ed. 19.95 (ISBN 0-02-910390-8). Free Pr.

Power Technology. 4th ed. George E. Stephenson. 544p. 1986. text ed. 24.95 (ISBN 0-8273-2446-4); Student activity guide, 96 pp. pap. 8.95 (ISBN 0-8273-2424-3); instr's. guide 7.00 (ISBN 0-8273-2447-2). Delmar.

Power That Preserves. Stephen R. Donaldson. 1979. pap. 4.95 (ISBN 0-345-34867-2, Del Rey Bks.). Ballantine.

Power That Preserves see Chronicles of Thomas Covenant.

Power That Worketh in Us. F. Henry Edwards. 1987. pap. 16.00 (ISBN 0-8309-0481-6). Herald Hse.

Power: The Inner Experience. David C. McClelland. LC 75-35603. (Illus.). 441p. 1979. 39.50x (ISBN 0-8290-0686-9); pap. text ed. 15.95x (ISBN 0-8290-0101-8). Irvington.

Power Through Bureaucracy: Urban Political Analysis in Brazil. Richard Batley. LC 82-16872. 240p. 1983. 27.50x (ISBN 0-312-63437-4). St Martin.

Power Through Constructive Thinking. Emmet Fox. 1940. 13.45 (ISBN 0-06-062930-4, HarpR). Har-Row.

Power Through Discourse. Leah Kedar. LC 86-32029. 192p. 1987. text ed. 29.50 (ISBN 0-89391-328-6). Ablex Pub.

Power Through Prayer. E. M. Bounds. (Direction Bks). 1972. pap. 3.95 (ISBN 0-8010-0584-1). Baker Bk.

Power Through Prayer. E. M. Bounds. pap. 3.95 (ISBN 0-310-21612-5, 9237P). Zondervan.

Power Through Prayer. E. M. Bounds. 112p. 1983. pap. text ed. 2.95 (ISBN 0-88368-117-X). Whitaker Hse.

Power Through Prayer. E. M. Bounds. (Moody Classics Ser.). 1985. pap. text ed. 3.50 (ISBN 0-8024-6729-6). Moody.

Power Through Release. Ruth Stapleton. pap. 0.50 (ISBN 0-910924-39-2); 3 for 1.00 (ISBN 0-685-04195-6). Macalester.

Power Through Subversion. Lawrence W. Beilenson. 1972. 12.00 (ISBN 0-8183-0195-3). Pub Aff Pr.

Power Thyristor Physics. A. Blicher. (Applied Physics & Engineering Ser.: Vol. 12). 1976. 63.00 (ISBN 0-387-90173-6). Springer-Verlag.

Power to Be. Thomas Olbricht. LC 79-67136. (Journey Bks.). 1979. pap. 3.50 (ISBN 0-8344-0108-8, Sweet). Worthy TX.

Power to Become: The Person God Wants You to Be. Gynnath Ford. 128p. 1988. pap. 4.95 (ISBN 0-89225-306-1). Gospel Advocate.

Power to Change: Family Case Studies in Treatment of Alcoholism. Edward Kaufman. 356p. 1984. 27.95 (ISBN 0-89876-091-7). Gardner Pr.

Power to Change Geography. Diane O'Hehir. LC 78-13323. (Contemporary Poets Ser). 70p. 1979. 15.00x (ISBN 0-691-06385-0); pap. 8.95 (ISBN 0-691-01354-3). Princeton U Pr.

Power to Change: How to Stay Slim, Sober, & Smokeless. Harold Hill & Liz Rogers. 319p. (Orig.). 1987. pap. 4.95 (ISBN 0-88270-625-X). Bridge Pub.

Power to Communicate: Gender Differences As Barriers. Deborah Borisoff & Lisa Merrill. 100p. (Orig.). 1985. pap. text ed. 5.95x (ISBN 0-88133-130-9). Waveland Pr.

Power to Dancers: Self-Actualization for Women Through Dancing. Beverly Kalinin. (For Women by Women Ser.). (Illus.). 224p. (Orig.). 1988. 17.95 (ISBN 0-943920-43-4); pap. 14.95 (ISBN 0-943920-44-2). Metamorphous Pr.

Power to Die. Robert H. Long. (CSU Poetry Ser.: Vol. XXIV). 108p. (Orig.). 1987. pap. 6.00 (ISBN 0-914946-63-3). Cleveland St Univ Poetry Ctr.

Power to Dissolve: Lawyers & Marriages in the Courts of the Roman Curia. John T. Noonan, Jr. LC 75-176044. (Illus.). 464p. 1972. 32.00x (ISBN 0-674-69575-5, Belknap Pr). Harvard U Pr.

Power to Elect: The Case for Proportional Representation. Enid Lakeman. 178p. 1982. 22.50 (ISBN 0-8419-6108-5). Holmes & Meier.

Power to Excel. Hubert E. Dobson. LC 81-90553. 273p. 1982. 10.95 (ISBN 0-9607256-0-1); pap. 4.95 (ISBN 0-9607256-1-X). Rich Pub Co.

Power to Fly. Devon Francis. (Illus.). 106p. 1986. pap. 24.95 (ISBN 0-8168-7632-0, NO. 27632, TAB-Aero). TAB Bks.

Power to Get Wealth. Albert E. Moehring. LC 86-83408. (Orig.). 1988. pap. 10.00 (ISBN 0-89896-221-8). Larksdale.

Power to Govern. W. H. Hamilton & D. Adair. LC 77-37759. (American Constitutional & Legal History Ser). 252p. 1972. Repr. of 1937 ed. lib. bdg. 32.50 (ISBN 0-306-70433-1). Da Capo.

Power to Govern, Vol. 34, No. 2. LC 81-68573. 1981. 7.50 (ISBN 0-318-01787-3). Acad Poli Sci.

Power to Grow Beyond Yourself. Robert A. Schuller. (Illus.). 224p. 1987. 14.95 (ISBN 0-8007-1541-1). Revell.

Power to Heal. Francis MacNutt. LC 77-77845. 256p. 1977. pap. 4.95 (ISBN 0-87793-133-X). Ave Maria.

Power to Influence People see People Power.

Power to Keep Peace, Today & in a World Without War. Lincoln P. Bloomfield. pap. 2.95 (ISBN 0-912018-12-7). World Without War Pubns.

Power to Lead: The Crisis of the American Presidency. James M. Burns. 273p. 1984. 16.45 (ISBN 0-671-42731-8). S&S.

Power to Live Through Nutrition. James W. McAfee. LC 80-82331. (Illus.). 196p. (Orig.). 1980. pap. 6.95 (ISBN 0-9604592-0-0). Image Awareness.

Power to Make Things New: Messages by Bruce Larson, Lloyd John Ogilvie... Bruce Larson. 160p. 1986. pap. 9.95 (ISBN 0-8499-3022-7). Word Bks.

Power to Persuade: A Rhetoric Reader for Argumentative Writing. Sally D. Spurgin. (Illus.). 352p. 1985. pap. text ed. write for info. (ISBN 0-13-688052-5). P-H.

Power to Punish: A Social Inquiry into Coercion & Control in Urban Schools. Stanley W. Rothstein. 188p. (Orig.). 1984. lib. bdg. 24.50 (ISBN 0-8191-3731-6); pap. text ed. 11.25 (ISBN 0-8191-3732-4). U Pr of Amer.

Power to Tax. G. Brennan & J. Buchanan. LC 79-56862. (Illus.). 300p. 1980. 37.50 (ISBN 0-521-23329-1). Cambridge U Pr.

Power to the People: South Africa in Struggle, a Pictorial History, Pt. 1. Peder Gouwenius. (Illus.). 96p. (Orig.). 1981. (Pub. by Zed Pr); pap. 7.95 (ISBN 0-905762-66-5, Pub. by Zed Pr). Humanities.

Power Tool Maintenance. D. Irvin. 1971. text ed. 45.95 (ISBN 0-07-032050-0). McGraw.

Power Tool Safety & Operation. rev. ed. Thomas Hoerner & Mervin Bettis. (Illus.). 94p. 1986. pap. 6.75x (ISBN 0-913163-20-1). Hobar Pubns.

Power Tool Woodworking for Everyone. rev. ed. R. J. DeCristoforo. LC 83-22995. (Illus.). 360p. 1984. 31.95 (ISBN 0-8359-5567-2). Shopsmith.

Power Tools Care & Use. William Veasey. (Illus.). 64p. 1985. pap. 7.95 (ISBN 0-88740-047-7). Schiffer.

Power Training in Kung-Fu & Karate. Ron Marchini & Leo Fong. Ed. by John Cocoran & John Scurra. LC 74-14128. (Specialties Ser.). (Illus.). 1974. pap. text ed. 10.50x (ISBN 0-89750-047-4, 400, Dist. by Wehman). Ohara Pubns.

Power Trains: Compact Equipment. Deere & Company Staff. (Fundamentals of Service Compact Equipment Ser.). (Illus.). 104p. 1983. pap. text ed. 9.70 (ISBN 0-86691-030-1); wkbk. 6.95 (ISBN 0-86691-033-6); tchr's guide 6.95 (ISBN 0-86691-040-9); slide set 89.25. Deere & Co.

Power Transformer Handbook. Bernard Hochart. (Illus.). 272p. 1987. text ed. 95.00 (ISBN 0-408-02590-5). Butterworth.

Power Transformers of the Oil Immersed Sealed Type. EEMUA Staff. 1982. 75.00x (ISBN 0-85931-048-5, Pub. by EEMUA). State Mutual Bk.

Power Transformers of the Oil Immersed Sealed Type. Oil Companies Materials Association (OCMA) Staff. (OCMA Ser.). 1974. pap. 24.95 (ISBN 0-471-25934-9, Wiley Heyden). Wiley.

Power-Transistor & TTL Integrated-Circuit Applications. Texas Instruments, Inc. (Texas Instruments Ser.). (Illus.). 1977. text ed. 43.95 (ISBN 0-07-063754-7). McGraw.

Power Transistor Data Book-1984. Texas Instruments Engineering Staff. LC 83-51812. 600p. (Orig.). 1983. pap. text ed. 13.95 (ISBN 0-89512-150-6, SLPD001). Tex Instr Inc.

Power Transistors: Device Design & Applications. Ed. by B. J. Baliga & D. Y. Chen. LC 84-19747. 400p. 1985. 57.80 (ISBN 0-87942-181-9, PC01750). Inst Electrical.

Power Transmission & Automation for Ships & Submersibles. I. Mortimer Datz. (Illus.). 190p. 45.00 (ISBN 0-85238-074-7, FN23, FNB). UNIPUB.

Power Transmission by Direct Current. y. M. Chervonenkis. 104p. 1983. 25.00x (ISBN 0-7065-0275-2, Pub. by Keter Pub Jerusalem). Coronet Bks.

Power Transmission by Direct Current. E. Uhlmann. LC 75-8920. (Illus.). 400p. 1975. 105.10 (ISBN 0-387-07122-9). Springer-Verlag.

Power Transmission over Distances of 1500 to 3000 KM. V. K. Shcherbakov. 344p. 1968. text ed. 68.00x (ISBN 0-7065-0642-1, Pub. by Keter PUb Jerusalem). Coronet Bks.

Power Trio. Mae Wilson-Ludlam. 152p. 1981. Repr. of 1976 ed. soft cover 6.95 (ISBN 0-88053-765-5, A-316). Macoy Pub.

Power Trio: Mars, Jupiter, Saturn. Wilson-Ludlam. 156p. 1976. 6.95 (ISBN 0-86690-331-3, 1537-03). Am Fed Astrologers.

Power Unlimited: The Corruption of Union Leadership. Sylvester Petro. LC 79-4432. (McClellan Committee Hearings). 1979. Repr. of 1959 ed. lib. bdg. 35.00x (ISBN 0-313-20898-0, PEPU). Greenwood.

Power Up for the Recovery: Industrial Power Conference 1983. Ed. by F. M. Rhodes. 104p. 1983. pap. text ed. 25.00 (ISBN 0-317-02641-0, I00159). ASME.

Power User's Guide to Hard Disk Management. Jonathan Kamin. 315p. (Orig.). 1987. pap. 21.95 (ISBN 0-89588-401-1). Sybex.

Power User's Guide to 1-2-3. Pete Antoniak. 368p. (Orig.). 1987. pap. 19.95 (ISBN 0-89588-421-6). Sybex.

Power User's Manual: Over 1000 Hints & Tips for the Macintosh. Randal L Kottwitz. Ed. by Steven T. Birchall. LC 86-62172. (Illus.). 176p. 1987. spiral bound 17.95 (ISBN 0-9617462-0-3). MacUser Pubns.

Power, Values & Society: An Introduction to Sociology. C. Michael Otten. LC 80-29411. 1981. pap. text ed. write for info (ISBN 0-394-33295-4, RanC). Random.

Power Vested. Harry Krenek. (Illus.). 1980. collectors special 40.00 (ISBN 0-935978-09-7). Presidial.

Power Volleyball. 3rd ed. Thomas Slaymaker et al. 107p. 1983. pap. text ed. write for info. (ISBN 0-697-06308-9). Wm C Brown.

Power Volleyball for Girls & Women. 2nd ed. Janet Thigpen. 158p. 1974. pap. text ed. write for info. (ISBN 0-697-07317-3). Wm C Brown.

Power Volleyball: The Woman's Game. Andy Banachowski. LC 82-74326. (Illus.). 104p. (Orig.). 1983. pap. text ed. 7.95 (ISBN 0-87670-068-7). Athletic Inst.

Power vs. Profit: Multinational Corporation-Nation State Interaction. Reza Bassiry. Ed. by Stuart Bruchey. LC 80-566. (Multinational Corporations Ser.). 1980. lib. bdg. 28.50x (ISBN 0-405-13363-4). Ayer Co Pubs.

Power Windows. Jim Heid. 304p. 1988. pap. 19.95 (ISBN 1-55615-008-3). Microsoft.

Power with People. James K. Van Fleet. 1970. 16.95 (ISBN 0-13-686956-4, Reward); pap. 4.95 (ISBN 0-13-686964-5). P-H.

Power with Purpose. John Sims. 1985. text ed. 8.95 (ISBN 0-87148-717-9); pap. text ed. 7.95 (ISBN 0-87148-716-0). Pathway Pr.

Power Within Henry Washe. William G. Dallavo. (Illus.). 51p. 1983. pap. 6.00 (ISBN 0-942494-74-1). Coleman Pub.

Power Within: Living with Your Full Potential. Jerald H. Reckner & Jeni F. Norton. (Illus., Orig.). 1987. pap. 8.95 (ISBN 0-943889-00-6). Assoc Beta Cos.

Power Within Us. facs. ed. Charles Baudouin. LC 68-16905. (Essay Index Reprint Ser). 1923. 15.00 (ISBN 0-8369-0176-2). Ayer Co Pubs.

Power Within You. John-Roger. 1984. pap. 8.00 (ISBN 0-914829-24-6). Mandeville LA.

Power Words for Prosperous Living! 120p. 1984. pap. 4.95 (ISBN 0-9602166-1-8). Golden Key.

Power Writing. rev. ed. Robert R. Max & Sarah P. Cerny. 167p. 1988. Repr. of 1979 ed. incl. 4 tapes 99.95 (ISBN 1-55678-006-0); tchr's. guide 75.00 (ISBN 1-55678-008-7). Learn Inc.

Power Writing: Ten Steps to Results. J. E. Sparks & Tony Larson. 176p. (Orig.). 1988. pap. 10.95 (ISBN 0-937359-39-4). HDL Pubs.

Power Writng for Executive Women. Patricia H. Westheimer. 1988. text ed. 14.95 (ISBN 0-673-38100-5). Scott F.

Power Yachts. Rosemary Mudie & Colin Mudie. (Illus.). 1977. 39.95x (ISBN 0-8464-1298-5). Beekman Pubs.

Powerboat Maintenance. (Illus.). 288p. pap. 9.95 (ISBN 0-89287-069-9). Western Marine Ent.

Powercise: The Elaine Powers Total Body Workout. (Illus.). 128p. 1983. 9.95 (ISBN 0-671-49428-7, Fireside). S&S.

Powereading, 3 vols. rev. ed. Barry M. Smith et al. (Powereading Program Ser.: Bk. 1). (Illus.). 1986. Set Of 3 Bks. pap. text ed. 28.50x; tchr's ed. 18.95. Book 1 (ISBN 0-89702-050-2). Book 2 (ISBN 0-89702-051-0). Book 3 (ISBN 0-89702-052-9). PAR Inc.

Powered Industrial Trucks, Including Type Designations, Areas of Use, Maintenance, & Operation. National Fire Protection Association Staff. 33p. 1982. 12.00 (ISBN 0-317-63480-1, 505-82). Natl Fire Prot.

Powered Lift System-JVX Program. 1983. 38.00 (ISBN 0-89883-326-4, SP555). Soc Auto Engineers.

Powered Ultralight Flying. Dennis Pagen. (Illus.). 183p. (Orig.). 1983. pap. 11.95 (ISBN 0-936310-06-5). Black Mntn.

Powered Ultralight Training Course. Dennis Pagen. (Illus.). 110p. 1981. pap. 9.95. Black Mntn.

Powerful! Churches Alive, Inc. Staff. (God in You Study Ser.). (Illus.). 1986. wkbk. 3.95 (ISBN 0-89109-095-9). Churches Alive.

Powerful Ideas for Text Processing. Gary F. Simons. LC 83-51795. 200p. (Orig.). 1984. pap. 10.00x (ISBN 0-88312-930-2); program disk 12.50. microfiche (3) 6.00 (ISBN 0-88312-984-1). Summer Inst Ling.

Powerful Images: A Women's Guide to Audiovisual Resources. (Illus.). 210p. 1987. pap. 12.00 (ISBN 0-942317-00-9). ISIS Intl.

Powerful, Impressive Art of Diego Rodriguez de Silva Velasquez. Edward W. Kimball. (Art Library of the Great Masters of the World). (Illus.). 103p. 1983. 137.45 (ISBN 0-86650-049-9). Gloucester Art.

Powerful Peacemaking: A Strategy for a Living Revolution. rev. ed. George Lakey. 266p. 1987. 29.95 (ISBN 0-86571-096-1); pap. 9.95 (ISBN 0-86571-097-X). New Soc Pubs.

Powerful Petite Prayers. 3rd ed. Anna Cook. LC 85-52398. (Illus.). 112p. 1986. pap. 4.95 (ISBN 0-936029-02-1). Western Bk Journ.

Powerful Points for Preaching. John R. Terry. 150p. 1982. pap. 4.95 (ISBN 0-933704-44-5). Dawn Pr.

Powerholders. David Kipnis. LC 75-43230. (Illus.). 1976. 15.00x (ISBN 0-226-43731-0). U of Chicago Pr.

Powerholders. David Kipnis. LC 75-43230. (Illus.). 1979. pap. 8.00x (ISBN 0-226-43732-9, P820, Phoen). U of Chicago Pr.

Powerhouse. Robert L. Sumner. 1978. pap. 3.95 (ISBN 0-914012-18-5). Sword of Lord.

Powerhouse for God: Sacred Speech, Chant & Song in an Appalachian Baptist Church. Jeff T. Titon. (American Folklore Recordings Ser.). 26p. 1982. pap. 22.00x incl. records (ISBN 0-8078-4084-X). U of NC Pr.

Powerhouse for God: Speech, Chant, & Song in an Appalachian Baptist Church. Jeff T. Titon. (Illus.). 568p. 1988. 35.00 (ISBN 0-292-76485-5). U of Tex Pr.

Powerhouse of the Atom. K. Gladkov. (Illus.). 303p. 1972. 19.95x (ISBN 0-8464-0741-8). Beekman Pubs.

Powerhouse of the Atom. K. Gladkov. 1980. 15.00x (ISBN 0-89875-003-2, Pub. by U Pr Pacific). Intl Spec Bk.

Powering Civilization: The Complete Energy Reader. Ed. by James Ridgeway. LC 82-47878. 416p. 1983. pap. 10.36 (ISBN 0-394-71129-7). Pantheon.

Powerless Position: The Commanding General of the Army of the United States, 1864-1903. Robert F. Stohlman, Jr. 184p. 1975. pap. text ed. 18.50x (ISBN 0-89126-022-6). MA-AH Pub.

Powerlifters Manual. John Lear. 64p. 1982. 25.00x (ISBN 0-686-44639-9, Pub. by EP Pub England). State Mutual Bk.

Powerlifting: A Scientific Approach. Frederick C. Hatfield. (Illus.). 1981. pap. 9.95 (ISBN 0-8092-7001-3). Contemp Bks.

Powerline: The First Battle of America's Energy War. Barry M. Casper & Paul D. Wellstone. LC 80-25903. (Illus.). 328p. 1981. lib. bdg. 22.50x (ISBN 0-87023-320-3); pap. 11.95x (ISBN 0-87023-321-1). U of Mass Pr.

Powermates, Vol. 1. Barbara O'Rear. (gr. 6-12). 1981. pap. text ed. 4.95 (ISBN 0-86703-037-2); 6.95 (ISBN 0-86703-039-9). Opportunities Learn.

Powermates, Vol. 2. Barbara O'Rear. (gr. 6-12). 1981. pap. text ed. 4.95 (ISBN 0-86703-038-0); 6.95 (ISBN 0-86703-040-2). Opportunities Learn.

Powermatics: A Discursive Critique of New Technology. Marike Finlay. (International Library of Phenomenology & Moral Sciences). 376p. 1987. lib. bdg. 69.95x (ISBN 0-7102-0761-1, Pub. by Routledge UK). Routledge Chapman & Hall.

Powerplant Mechanic. Dale Crane. (Capstan Guide: Fast-Track Method Ser.). (Illus.). 176p. 1987. pap. text ed. 8.95 (ISBN 0-914565-28-1, 28-1). Av Suppl & Acad.

Powerplant Technology. M. M. El-Wakil. 1984. text ed. 52.95 (ISBN 0-07-019288-X). McGraw.

Powerplants for Aerospace Vehicles see Aircraft Powerplants.

Powerplay: What Really Happened at Bendix. Mary Cunningham & Fran Schumer. 320p. 1984. 15.45 (ISBN 0-671-47563-0, Linden Pr). S&S.

Powerplays: Trevor Griffiths in Television. Mike Poole & John Wyver. (Illus.). 200p. 1984. 28.95 (ISBN 0-85170-152-3, Pub. by British Film Inst England); pap. 17.95 (ISBN 0-85170-153-1, Pub. by British Film Inst England). U of Ill Pr.

Powers & Duties of Police Officers & Coroners. Robert H. Vickers. LC 74-156034. (Foundations of Criminal Justice Ser.). Repr. of 1889 ed. 18.00 (ISBN 0-404-09136-9). AMS Pr.

Powers & Jurisdiction of Criminal Courts & Criminal Trials. 1034p. 1973. 105.00x (ISBN 0-317-54735-6, Pub. by Eastern Bk India). State Mutual Bk.

Powers & Liberties: The Causes & Consequences of the Rise of the West. John A. Hall. 272p. 1986. 25.00x (ISBN 0-520-05778-3). U of Cal Pr.

Powers & the Middle East: The Ultimate Strategic Arena. Ed. by Bernard Reich. LC 86-21266. 361p. 1986. lib. bdg. 46.95 (ISBN 0-275-92304-5, C2304). Praeger.

Powers at Play. Bliss Perry. LC 74-110209. (Short Story Index Review Ser.). 1899. 18.00 (ISBN 0-8369-3360-5). Ayer Co Pubs.

Powers, Duties & Operations of State Attorneys General, 5 pts. (Illus.). 404p. 1977. 10.00 (ISBN 0-318-15221-5). Natl Attys General.

Powers, Duties, Liabilities of Corporate Officers & Directors. 32p. 1983. 2.00x (ISBN 0-686-89213-5, 68687-3). P-H.

Powers of Attorney. Andrew Long. 150p. 1987. 26.25 (ISBN 0-902197-50-9, Pub. by Woodhead-Faulkner). Longwood Pub Group.

Powers of Attorney & Other Instruments Conferring Authority. Andrew Long. LC 87-3777. 1987. 75.00 (ISBN 0-317-59079-0, Pub. by ISCA Pub UK). State Mutual Bk.

Powers of Charlotte. Jane Lazarre. LC 87-15736. 350p. 1987. 18.95 (ISBN 0-89594-249-6). Crossing Pr.

Powers of Charlotte. Jane Lazarre. 350p. (Orig.). 1988. pap. 8.95 (ISBN 0-89594-329-8). Crossing Pr.

Powers of Congress. 2nd ed. Congressional Quarterly, Inc. Staff. LC 82-14331. 380p. 1982. pap. 9.95 (ISBN 0-87187-242-0). Congr Quarterly.

Powers of Desire: The Politics of Sexuality. Ed. by Ann Snitow et al. LC 82-48037. (New Feminist Library). 448p. 1983. 25.00 (ISBN 0-85345-609-7); pap. 12.50 (ISBN 0-85345-610-0). Monthly Rev.

Powers of Horror: An Essay on Abjection. Julia Kristeva. Tr. by Leon Roudiez from Fr. LC 82-4481. (European Perspectives Ser.). 248p. 1984. pap. 14.00x (ISBN 0-231-05347-9). Columbia U Pr.

Powers of Imagining: Ignatius de Loyola: A Philosophical Hermeneutic of Imagining through the Collected Works of Ignatius de Loyola with a Translation of These Works. Antonio De Nicolas. LC 85-2739. 390p. 1986. 59.50 (ISBN 0-88706-109-5); pap. 19.95x (ISBN 0-88706-110-9). State U NY Pr.

Powers of Mind. Adam Smith. 448p. 1982. pap. 8.95 (ISBN 0-671-44797-1). Summit Bks.

Powers of Nature. Ed. by Donald J. Crump. LC 76-57002. (Special Publications: Series 12, No. 4). (Illus.). 1978. 7.95 (ISBN 0-87044-234-1); lib. bdg. 9.50 (ISBN 0-87044-239-2). Natl Geog.

Powers of Presence: Consciousness, Myth, & Affecting Presence. Robert P. Armstrong. LC 81-51136. (Illus.). 224p. 1981. 30.95 (ISBN 0-8122-7804-6). U of Pa Pr.

Powers of Prophecy: The Cedar of Lebanon Vision from the Mongol Onslaught to the Dawn of the Enlightenment. Robert E. Lerner. LC 82-4824. 256p. 1983. text ed. 42.00x (ISBN 0-520-04461-4). U of Cal Pr.

Powers of Ten. Morrison & Eames. LC 82-5504. (Scientific American Library). (Illus.). 164p. 1985. 32.95; pap. 19.95. W H Freeman.

Powers of the President As Commander-in-Chief of the Army & Navy of the United States. Dorothy Schaffter & Dorothy Mathews. LC 76-172099. (American Constitution & Legal History Ser.). xi, 145p. 1974. Repr. of 1974 ed. lib. bdg. 22.50 (ISBN 0-306-70615-6). Da Capo.

Powers of the President During Crises. John Malcolm Smith & Cornelius P. Cotter. LC 71-39371. (American Constitutional & Legal History Ser). 1972. Repr. of 1960 ed. lib. bdg. 22.50 (ISBN 0-306-70462-5). Da Capo.

Powers of the President During National Crises. Cornelius Cotter. 1960. 8.50 (ISBN 0-8183-0196-1). Pub Aff Pr.

Powers of the Press: Twelve of the World's Influential Newspapers. Martin Walker. LC 83-2211. 416p. 1983. 20.00 (ISBN 0-8298-0659-8). Pilgrim NY.

Powers of the Press: Twelve of the World's Influential Newspapers. Martin Walker. LC 84-10975. 416p. 1984. pap. 12.95 (ISBN 0-915361-10-8, Dist. by Watts). Adama Pubs Inc.

Powers of the Psalms. Anna Riva. 128p. (Orig.). 1982. pap. 4.95 (ISBN 0-943832-07-1). Intl Imports.

Powers of Theory: Capitalism, the State & Democracy. Robert R. Alford & Roger Friedland. 544p. 1985. 54.50 (ISBN 0-521-30349-4); pap. 15.95 (ISBN 0-521-31635-9). Cambridge U Pr.

Powers of Thirteen. John Hollander. LC 82-73010. 96p. (Orig.). 1983. 13.95 (ISBN 0-689-11371-4); pap. 6.95 (ISBN 0-689-11372-2). Atheneum.

Powers of Thought. Omraam M. Aivanhov. (Izvor Collection Ser.: Vol. 224). 230p. (Orig.). 1988. pap. 7.95 (ISBN 2-85566-436-5, Pub by Prosveta France). Prosveta USA.

Powers, Plumes & Piglets: Phenomena of Melanesian Religion. Ed. by Norman C. Habrel. (Special Studies in Religions: No. 3). 240p. (Orig.). 1979. pap. 13.95 (ISBN 0-908083-07-6, Pub. by AASR Australia). ANZ Religious Pubns.

Powers: Testing the Psychic & Supernatural. Danny Korem. 216p. (Orig.). 1988. pap. 7.95 (ISBN 0-8308-1277-6). Inter-Varsity.

Powers That Be. David Halberstam. 1072p. 1986. pap. 6.95 (ISBN 0-440-36997-5, LE). Dell.

Powers That Be. David Halberstam. LC 78-20605. 1979. 17.95 (ISBN 0-394-50381-3). Knopf.

Powers That Be: Earthly Rulers & Demonic Powers in Romans, Chapter 13, 1-7. Clinton D. Morrison. LC 60-4219. (Studies in Biblical Theology: No. 29). 1960. pap. 10.00x (ISBN 0-8401-3029-5). A R Allenson.

Powers That Be: Process of Ruling Class Domination in America. G. William Domhoff. LC 78-55633. 1979. pap. 6.95 (ISBN 0-394-72649-9, Vin). Random.

Powers That Make Us Human: The Foundations of Medical Ethics. Ed. by Kenneth Vaux. LC 84-28028. 152p. 1986. 16.95 (ISBN 0-252-01187-2). U of Ill Pr.

Powerspeak: The Complete Guide to Persuasive Public Speaking & Presenting. Dorothy Leeds. 240p. 1988. 17.95 (ISBN 0-13-686866-5). Prentice Hall Pr.

Powerticians: Politics & Social Life in Jersey City. Thomas F. Smith. (Illus.). 256p. 1982. 15.00 (ISBN 0-8184-0328-4). Lyle Stuart.

Powertrain. Philip F. Lynch. LC 80-16504. (Primer in Drilling & Production Equipment Ser.: Vol. 1). (Illus.). 165p. (Orig.). 1980. pap. 21.00x (ISBN 0-87201-198-4). Gulf Pub.

Powerwalking. Steve Reeves & James A. Peterson. LC 81-18184. 1982. pap. 8.95 (ISBN 0-672-52713-8). Bobbs.

Powhatan County Marriages, Seventeen Seventy-Seven to Eighteen Thirty. Catherine L. Knorr. 110p. 1982. Repr. of 1937 ed. 15.00 (ISBN 0-89308-258-9, VA 21). Southern Hist Pr.

Powhatan County Marriages, Seventeen Seventy-Seven to Eighteen Fifty. John Vogt & T. William Kethley, Jr. (Virginia Historic Marriage Register Ser.). (Illus.). viii, 143p. (Orig.). 1985. pap. 11.00 (ISBN 0-935931-12-0). Iberian Pub.

Powhatan County Marriages, Seventeen Seventy-Seven to Eighteen Fifty. John Vogt & T. William Kethley, Jr. (Virginia Historic Marriage Register Ser.). 143p. 1988. Repr. lib. bdg. 26.95x (ISBN 0-8095-8226-0). Borgo Pr.

Powhatan Tribes: Middle Atlantic. Ed. by Frank W. Porter. (Indians of North America Ser.). (Illus.). (gr. 5 up). 1989. 16.95 (ISBN 1-55546-726-1). Chelsea Hse.

POWTECH Eighty-Five: Proceedings of the International Symposium on Particle Technology, Birmingham, U. K., March 5-7, 1985. Ed. by Institution of Chemical Engineers. (Institution of Chemical Engineers Symposium Ser.: Vol. 91). 270p. 1985. 26.00 (ISBN 0-08-031443-0). Pergamon.

POWTECH Seventy-Five: Proceedings of the Third International Powder Technology & Bulk Solids Conference. 3rd ed. International Powder Technology & Bulk Solids Conference, 1975. (Powder Technology Publication Ser.: No. 6). pap. 23.50 (ISBN 0-317-26490-7, 2024038). Bks Demand UMI.

POWTECH Seventy-One: Proceedings of POWTECH '71. International Powder Technology & Bulk Solids Conference (1st: 1971: Harrogate, Eng) Ed. by A. S. Goldberg. (Powder Technology Publication Ser.: No. 1). pap. 69.30 (ISBN 0-317-26655-1, 2024036). Bks Demand UMI.

POWTECH Seventy-Three Papers-Particulate Matter: Special POWTECH 73 Issue. International Powder Technology & Bulk Solids Exhibition & Conference (1973: Harrogate, Eng.) Ed. by A. S. Goldberg. (Powder Technology Publication Ser.: No. 2). pap. 27.50 (ISBN 0-317-26663-2, 2024037). Bks Demand UMI.

Powwow. June Behrens. LC 83-7274. (Ethnic & Traditional Holidays Ser.). (Illus.). 32p. (gr. k-4). 1983. PLB 12.60 (ISBN 0-516-02387-X). Childrens.

Powys Brothers. Kenneth Hopkins. LC 68-10855. 275p. 1967. 20.00 (ISBN 0-8386-6754-6). Fairleigh Dickinson.

Powys Family. Littleton C. Powys. LC 74-7023. (English Biography Ser., No. 31). 1974. lib. bdg. 29.95x (ISBN 0-8383-1995-5). Haskell.

Powys to Eric the Red: Letters of John Cowper Powys. Cedric Hentschel. 112p. 1983. text ed. 18.50x (ISBN 0-900821-50-7). Humanities.

Powys to Knight: The Letters of John Cowper Powys to G. R. Wilson Knight. Robert Blackmore. 144p. 1983. text ed. 18.50x (ISBN 0-900821-48-5). Humanities.

Pozieres, Nineteen Sixteen: The Australians on the Somme. Peter Charlton. (Illus.). 256p. 1987. 39.95 (ISBN 0-436-09580-7, Pub. by Secker & Warburg UK). David & Charles.

PPO Handbook. Barger et al. 202p. 1984. 43.50 (ISBN 0-89443-569-8). Aspen Pub.

PPOs: An Executive's Guide. Samuel J. Tibbitts & Allen J. Manzano. LC 83-62497. 296p. 1984. text ed. 32.95 (ISBN 0-931028-40-X). Pluribus Pr.

PQR: Prescription for a Quality Relationship. Allen Fay. 242p. (Orig.). Date not set. pap. 9.95 (ISBN 0-929110-00-5). Multimodal Pr.

PR for Pennies: Low-Cost Library Public Relations. Virginia Van W. Baeckler. LC 77-90578. (Illus.). 1978. pap. 4.00x (ISBN 0-9603232-0-1). Sources.

PR 101: The Funniest Course in College. Jim Weakley. LC 77-85116. (Illus.). 1977. pap. 3.95 (ISBN 0-912760-54-0). Valkyrie Pub Hse.

Prabhakara School of Purva Mimamsa. 2nd, rev. ed. Ganganatha Jha. 1978. 12.50 (ISBN 0-89684-016-6, Pub. by Motilal Banarsidass India). Orient Bk Dist.

Prabhodacandrodaya of Krsnamisra. Tr. by S. K. Nambiar. 1971. 6.50 (ISBN 0-89684-293-2). Orient Bk Dist.

Prabhupada. Satsvarupa Das Goswami. (Illus.). 387p. 1983. pap. 2.95 (ISBN 0-89213-127-6). Bhaktivedanta.

Prabhupada: He Built a House in Which the Whole World Could Live. Satsvarupa Das Goswami. 7.95 (ISBN 0-89213-133-0). Bhaktivedanta.

Prabhupada Nectar, Bk. 2. Satsvarupa Das Goswami. Ed. by Bimala Dasi. 145p. pap. 3.95 (ISBN 0-911233-23-7). Gita Nagari.

Prabhupada Nectar, Vol. 3. Satvarupa Dasa Goswami. Ed. by Bimala dasi. 160p. 1985. pap. text ed. 3.95 (ISBN 0-911233-24-5). Gita Nagari.

Prabhupada Nectar, Vol. 4. Satsvarupa Das Goswami. Ed. by Bimala dasi. 160p. 1985. pap. text ed. 3.95 (ISBN 0-911233-29-6). Gita Nagari.

Prabhupada Nectar, Vol. 5. Satsvarupa Das Goswami. Ed. by Bimala dasi. 160p. 1986. pap. text ed. 3.95 (ISBN 0-911233-31-8). Gita Nagari.

Praca Caput Regni. Collet's Staff. (Czech., Rus., Ger., Fr. & Eng.). 1985. 32.00x (ISBN 0-317-57304-7, Pub. by Collets UK). State Mutual Bk.

Prace: Pisma Ksiedza Biskupa Franciszka Hodura, Tom Drug, 2 vols. Jozef L. Zawistowski. 145p. (Orig., Pol.). 1986. Set. pap. 20.00 (ISBN 0-944497-03-9). Polish Natl Cath Ch.

Practial Design of Masonry Structures. 396p. 1987. 72.00 (ISBN 0-317-65952-9, Pub. by T Telford UK). Am Soc Civil Eng.

Practica de Jesus see Practice of Jesus.

Practica de la Terapia de Realidad. Norman Matlin. Tr. by Domingo Luiggi & Hilda Luiggi. LC 81-68708. (Coleccion Semilla Ser.). 174p. 1981. pap. 6.95 (ISBN 0-940238-47-0). Ediciones Hura.

Practica Della Mercatura. F. Balducci Pegolotti. Ed. by Allan Evans. (MAA.P). 1936. 36.00 (ISBN 0-527-01695-0). Kraus Repr.

Practica Forense Federal. (Span.). 1987. write for info. Equity Pub NH.

Practica Musica: A Music Fundamentals Textbook & Software fo the Macintosh. Jeffrey Evans. LC 88-71355. 200p. 1988. pap. text ed. 125.00 (ISBN 0-929444-00-0). Ars Nova SW.

Practica Musice. Franchinus Gafurius. (Monuments of Music & Music Literature in Facsimile, Ser. II: Vol. 99). 1979. Repr. of 1496 ed. 42.50 (ISBN 0-8450-2299-7). Broude.

Practicable Socialism: Essays on Social Reform. Samuel A. Barnett & Henrietta O. Barnett. LC 72-3394. (Essay Index Reprint Ser.). Repr. of 1888 ed. 15.00 (ISBN 0-8369-2891-1). Ayer Co Pubs.

Practical Absorption Spectrometry. Ed. by A. Knowles & C. Burgess. (Techniques in Ultraviolet Spectrometry Ser.: Vol. 3). 300p. 1984. 42.00x (ISBN 0-412-24390-3, NO. 6850). Routledge Chapman & Hall.

Practical Account of General Paralysis, Its Mental & Physical Symptoms, Statistics, Causes, Seat, & Treatment. Thomas J. Austin. LC 75-16681. (Classics in Psychiatry Ser.). 1976. Repr. of 1859 ed. 18.00x (ISBN 0-405-07413-1). Ayer Co Pubs.

Practical Accounting. 3rd ed. John G. Black & Delmar S. Stanley. LC 75-40983. 1980. pap. text ed. write for info. (ISBN 0-673-16133-1). Scott F.

Practical Accounting Cost-Keeping for Contractors. 9th. ed. Ed. by Brisbane Brown & Susan Powers. (Illus.). 250p. 1982. 22.95 (ISBN 0-911592-09-1). F R Walker.

Practical Accounting for Business Studies. V. N. Newcomb. LC 82-11103. pap. 95.00 (ISBN 0-317-41955-2, 2025984). Bks Demand UMI.

Practical Accounting Procedures. 2nd ed. Jeffrey Slater. (Illus.). 544p. 1984. write for info. (ISBN 0-13-688143-2); write for info. practice set (ISBN 0-13-688169-6). P-H.

Practical Advertising & Publicity: Effective Promotion of Products & Services to Industry & Commerce. Norman Hart. (Illus.). 300p. 1988. pap. 14.95 (ISBN 0-07-707079-8). McGraw.

Practical Aerobic Conditioning. D. Ray Collins & Patrick B. Hodges. 1986. pap. text ed. 10.95 (ISBN 0-89917-491-4). TIS Inc.

Practical Agitation. John J. Chapman. LC 1581. (American Studies). 1970. Repr. of 1900 ed. 14.00 (ISBN 0-384-08505-9). Johnson Repr.

Practical Alchemist: Showing the Way an Ordinary House Cat My Be Transformed into True Gold. Christopher Manson. (Illus.). 96p. 1988. pap. 7.95 (ISBN 0-8050-0455-6). H Holt & Co.

Practical Algebra. Peter H. Selby. LC 73-18336. 326p. 1974. pap. text ed. 10.95x (ISBN 0-471-77557-6). Wiley.

Practical Allergy & Immunology. William B. Klaustermeyer. LC 82-17416. (Family Practice Today - A Comprehensive Postgraduate Library). 217p. 1983. 40.00x (ISBN 0-471-09564-8, Pub. by Wiley Med); 14.95. Wiley.

Practical Ampelography: Grapevine Indentification. Pierre Galet. Tr. by Lucie Morton. LC 78-59631. (Comstock Bk). (Illus.). 248p. 1979. 39.95x (ISBN 0-8014-1240-4). Cornell U Pr.

Practical Anaesthesia for Surgical Emergencies. Ed. by Peter W. Jackson. 128p. (Orig.). 1985. pap. text ed. 17.95x (ISBN 0-433-16980-X, Pub. by W Heinemann Med Bks). Sheridan Med Bks.

Practical Analysis of Advanced Electronic Circuits Through Experimentation. 2nd ed. Lorne MacDonald. 384p. 1984. pap. 16.50x (ISBN 0-911908-18-8). Tech Ed Pr.

Practical Analysis of Amplifier Circuits Through Experimentation. 3rd ed. Lorne MacDonald. 432p. 1981. pap. 16.50x (ISBN 0-911908-14-5). Tech Ed Pr.

Practical Analytical Electron Microscopy in Materials Science. David B. Williams. (Illus.). 180p. 1984. pap. 32.00 (ISBN 0-9612934-0-3). Electron Optics Pub Grp.

Practical Analytical Electron Microscopy in Materials Science. David B. Williams. 153p. 1984. text ed. 38.00x (ISBN 0-89573-307-2). VCH Pubs.

Practical & Critical Grammar of the English Language. Noble Butler. 1874. 15.00 (ISBN 0-8274-3194-5). R West.

Practical & Decorative Woodworking Joints. John E. Bairstow. LC 84-51838. (Illus.). 128p. 1985. pap. 11.95 (ISBN 0-8069-7948-8). Sterling.

Practical & Legal Considerations in the International Licensing of Technology, Folio 8. 2nd ed. Marcus B. Finnegan. Ed. by Walter S. Surrey & Don Wallace, Jr. (Lawyer's Guide International Business Transactions Ser.: Part III). 51p. 1981. pap. text ed. 8.00 (ISBN 0-686-32429-3). Am Law Inst.

Practical & Perplexing Questions Answered see Preguntas Practicas y Dificiles Contestadas.

Practical & Simple Guide to a Home Mortgage: A Step-by-Step Guide to Finding & Financing Your Next House. Gary J. Bass. LC 87-82025. 66p. (Orig.). 1987. pap. text ed. 6.95 (ISBN 0-944319-00-9). G & P Pub.

Practical & Theoretical Aspects of Psychoanalysis. rev. ed. Lawrence S. Kubie. LC 74-6433. 361p. 1975. text ed. 37.50x (ISBN 0-8236-4181-3); pap. text ed. 17.95 (ISBN 0-8236-8193-9, 24180). Intl Univs Pr.

Practical Anesthetic Pharmacology. 2nd ed. Rafik R. Attia et al. 416p. 1986. 55.00 (ISBN 0-8385-7912-4). Appleton & Lange.

Practical Animal Husbandry. T. K. Ewer. (Illus.). 272p. 1982. text ed. 28.00 (ISBN 0-85608-026-8). PSG Pub Co.

Practical Answers to Common Questions about Sex in Marriage. Tim LaHaye & Beverly LaHaye. 72p. (Orig.). 1984. pap. 1.95 (ISBN 0-310-27042-1, 18340P). Zondervan.

Practical Anthropology. Georges Olivier. Tr. by M. A. MacConaill. (Illus.). 344p. 1969. 39.25 (ISBN 0-398-01424-8). C C Thomas.

Practical Anthropometry. 2nd ed. Ales Hrdlicka. LC 71-137243. Repr. of 1939 ed. 20.00 (ISBN 0-404-03372-5). AMS Pr.

Practical Application of Azolla for Rice Production. Ed. by W. S. Silver & E. C. Schroder. (Development in Plant & Soil Sciences). 1984. lib. bdg. 35.00 (ISBN 90-247-3068-6, Pub. by Martinus Nijhoff Netherlands). Kluwer-Academic.

Practical Application of Expert Systems. Susan Lindsay. 224p. 1988. 34.50 (ISBN 0-89435-235-0). QED Info Sci.

Practical Application of Individual Supervisory - Management Styles. Rex P. Gatto. (Illus.). 219p. 1987. teacher's ed. 110.00 (ISBN 0-945997-05-1); wrkbk. 85.00 (ISBN 0-945997-04-3). GATTO Training Assocs.

Practical Application of Remote Sensing in Forestry. Ed. by Sune Sohlberg & Viatcheslav E. Sokolov. (Forestry Sciences Ser.). 1986. lib. bdg. 45.90 (ISBN 90-247-3392-8, Pub. by Martinus Nijhoff Netherlands). Kluwer Academic.

Practical Application of Science of Mind. Ernest Holmes & Willis Kinnear. 96p. 1958. pap. 4.50 (ISBN 0-911336-24-9). Sci of Mind.

Practical Application of Solar Energy to Wood Processing. 85p. 1977. 7.00 (ISBN 0-935018-15-8). Forest Prod.

Practical Application of Statistical Analysis in the Industrial Process. Earl W. Ramsdell. 81p. 1981. soft cover 44.95 (ISBN 0-89852-390-7, 01-01-R090). TAPPI.

Practical Application of the Gas Laws to Pulmonary Physiology. Joan Abramson. 97p. (Orig.). 1981. pap. text ed. 10.00x (ISBN 0-89787-107-3). Gorsuch Scarisbrick.

Practical Applications in Basic Auto Body Repair. Duane Ballweber. (Illus.). 288p. 1983. text ed. 14.00 (ISBN 0-13-689216-7). P-H.

Practical Applications of Accounting Standards: A Decade of Comment on Accounting & Auditing Problems. Carman G. Blough. Ed. by Richard P. Brief. LC 80-1472. (Dimensions of Accounting Theory & Practice Ser.). 1981. Repr. of 1957 ed. lib. bdg. 45.00x (ISBN 0-405-13502-5). Ayer Co Pubs.

Practical Applications of Business Mathematics. Jake D. Tedder. (Illus.). 1978. text ed. write for info. (ISBN 0-87909-652-7, Reston). P-H.

Practical Applications of Dynamic Symmetry. Jay Hambidge. 1965. 9.50 (ISBN 0-8159-6509-5). Devin.

Practical Applications of Management Principles in the Pulp & Paper Industry Staff: May 23-24 Atlanta Hilton, Atlanta, GA. Technical Association of the Pulp & Paper Industry. pap. 85.50 (ISBN 0-317-28029-5, 2025566). Bks Demand UMI.

Practical Applications of Neutron Radiography & Gaging - STP 586. 330p. 1976. 25.50 (ISBN 0-8031-0535-5, 04-586000-22). ASTM.

Practical Applications of Psychology. 3rd ed. Anthony F. Grasha. 1987. pap. text ed. write for info. (ISBN 0-673-39511-1). Scott F.

Practical Applications of Quantitative Metallography - STP 839. Ed. by J. L. McCall & J. H. Steele, Jr. LC 83-73230. 190p. 1984. text ed. 34.00 (ISBN 0-8031-0220-8, 04-839000-28). ASTM.

Practical Appraisal of Industrial Projects-Application of Social Cost-Benefit Analysis in Pakistan. 181p. 1980. pap. 13.00 (ISBN 92-1-106100-8, E.79.11.B.5). UN.

Practical Approach to Angiography. 2nd ed. Irwin S. Johnsrude & Dunnick. 565p. 1987. 85.00 (ISBN 0-316-46981-5, Little Med Div). Little.

Practical Approach to Angiography. 2nd ed. Irwin S. Johnsrude & Donald C. Jackson. 1987. text ed. 75.00. Little.

Practical Approach to Bank Lending. 2nd ed. L. S. Dyer. 232p. 1980. 54.00x (ISBN 0-85297-084-6, Pub. Inst of Bankers). State Mutual Bk.

Practical Approach to Business Presentations. Stephen P. Morse. 144p. 1985. 60.00x (ISBN 0-946679-15-0, Pub. by Mgmt Update UK); pap. 39.00x (ISBN 0-946679-16-9). State Mutual Bk.

Practical Approach to Costume Design & Construction: Design & Construction, Vol. II. Beverly J. Thomas. 322p. 1981. pap. 36.95 (ISBN 0-205-07367-0, Pub. by Longwood Div.). Allyn.

Practical Approach to Dealing with Children's Misbehavior. Lawrence Zuckerman & Fred Gladish. 23p. (Orig.). 1979. pap. 3.00 (ISBN 0-918560-23-3). A Adler Inst.

Practical Approach to Eighteenth Century Counterpoint. Robert Gauldin. 300p. 1988. text ed. price not set (ISBN 0-13-693615-6). P-H.

Practical Approach to Emergency Medicine. Ed. by Robert Stine & Robert Marcus. 1987. pap. 29.50 (Little Med Div). Little.

Practical Approach to Emergency Medicine. Robert J. Stine & Robert H. Marcus. 736p. 1987. pap. text ed. 35.00 (ISBN 0-316-81619-1). Little.

Practical Approach to Human Behavior in Business. Allen Appell. 384p. 1984. text ed. 31.95 (ISBN 0-675-20087-3). Merrill.

Practical Approach to Industrial Relations for Line Supervisors. R. M. Bielstein. 109p. 1965. 9.00x (ISBN 0-87201-381-2). Gulf Pub.

Practical Approach to International Operations. Michael Gendron. 1988. price not set (ISBN 0-89930-252-1, GNO/, Quorum Bks). Greenwood.

Practical Approach to Investing. Robert W. Kolb. 1988. text ed. price not set (ISBN 0-673-18749-7). Scott F.

Practical Approach to Liens on Real Estate. Pennsylvania Bar Institute Staff. 1985. 50.00 (ISBN 0-318-19068-0, 324). PA Bar Inst.

Practical Approach to Modern Imaging Equipment. 2nd ed. Thomas T. Thompson. 1978. text ed. 27.50 (ISBN 0-316-84194-3). Little.

Practical Approach to Operating Systems. Malcolm Lane & James Mooney. 672p. 1988. 40.00 (ISBN 0-87835-300-3). Boyd & Fraser.

Practical Approach to Quality Control. 4th ed. R. H. Caplen. 326p. 1983. pap. text ed. 17.00x (ISBN 0-09-147451-5, Pub. by Busn Bks England). Brookfield Pub Co.

Practical Approach to Sedimentology. Roy Lindholm. (Illus.). 192p. 1987. text ed. 45.00x (ISBN 0-04-551131-4); pap. text ed. 17.95x (ISBN 0-04-551132-2). Unwin Hyman.

Practical Approach to Serials Cataloging. Lynn S. Smith. Ed. by Robert W. Stueart. LC 76-5645. (Foundations in Library & Information Science: Vol. 2). 424p. 1978. lib. bdg. 52.50 (ISBN 0-89232-007-9). Jai Pr.

Practical Approach to Sixteenth Century Counterpoint. Robert Gauldin. (Illus.). 304p. 1985. text ed. 35.00 (ISBN 0-13-689258-2). P-H.

Practical Approach to Skills Analysis. E. J. Singer & J. Ramsden. (Illus.). 1970. 9.00 (ISBN 0-8088-4211-0). Davey.

Practical Approach to Teaching Physical Education. David L. Kizer et al. 1984. text ed. 14.95 (ISBN 0-932392-18-0). Mouvement Pubns.

Practical Approach to Teaching Reading. Dorothy Rubin. 1982. text ed. 29.95 (ISBN 0-03-059103-1). HR&W.

Practical Approach to the Study of Form in Music. Peter Spencer & Peter M. Temko. (Illus.). 320p. 1988. text ed. price not set (ISBN 0-13-689050-4). P-H.

Practical Approach to Writing Business Letters. Kenneth Durr & Ralph White. 1984. pap. 17.50 (ISBN 0-8403-3295-5, 40329501). Kendall Hunt.

Practical Approaches to Alcoholism Psychotherapy. 2nd ed. Ed. by Sheldon Zimberg et al. LC 84-24922. 432p. 1985. 26.50x (ISBN 0-306-41762-6, Plenum Pr). Plenum Pub.

Practical Approaches to Development Planning: Korea's Second Five-Year Plan. Ed. by Irma Adelman. LC 69-19467. 320p. 1969. 32.50x (ISBN 0-8018-1061-2). Johns Hopkins.

Practical Approaches to Earthquake Prediction & Warning. Ed. by C. Kisslinger & T. Rikitake. 1986. lib. bdg. 89.00 (ISBN 90-277-2168-8, Pub. by Reidel Holland). Kluwer Academic.

Practical Approaches to Fire Fighting, No. 1. 1985. pap. 9.45 (ISBN 0-912212-10-1). Fire Eng.

Practical Approaches to Impromptu Speaking: Social & Business. Isaacson & Saperstein. 64p. 1987. pap. text ed. 8.95 (ISBN 0-8403-4653-0). Kendall-Hunt.

Practical Approaches to Legal Research. Intros. by Kent Olson & Robert C. Berring. LC 88-6800. (Legal Reference Services Quarterly Ser.: Supp. 1). 150p. 1988. text ed. 29.95 (ISBN 0-86656-253-2); pap. text ed. 14.95 (ISBN 0-86656-853-0). Haworth Pr.

Practical Approaches to Pediatric Radiology. Andrew K. Poznanski. LC 75-16022. pap. 119.50 (ISBN 0-317-28230-1, 2022728). Bks Demand UMI.

Practical Approaches to Speech Coding. Panos Papamichalis. 368p. 1986. 39.95 (ISBN 0-13-689019-9). P-H.

Practical Approval Plan Management. Jennifer S. Cargill & Brian Alley. 104p. 1979. lib. bdg. 33.00x (ISBN 0-912700-52-1). Oryx Pr.

Practical Arabic. George Scott. 14.00x (ISBN 0-86685-050-3). Intl Bk Ctr.

Practical Archaeologist. Jane McIntosh. (Illus.). 192p. 1986. 21.95 (ISBN 0-8160-1400-0). Facts on File.

Practical Archaeologist. Jane McIntosh. (Illus.). 192p. 1988. pap. 12.95 (ISBN 0-8160-1814-6). Facts on File.

Practical Archaeology: An Introduction to Archaeological Field Work Excavations. Graham Webster. LC 74-82133. 1975. 25.00 (ISBN 0-312-63455-2). St Martin.

Practical Archaeology: Field & Laboratory Techniques & Archaeological Logistics. Ed. by Brian D. Dillon. (Archaeological Research Tools: 2). 125p. 1982. pap. 8.50x (ISBN 0-917956-42-7). UCLA Arch.

Practical Architecture. William Halfpenny & John Halfpenny. LC 68-8317. (Illus.). 1968. Repr. of 1730 ed. 17.00 (ISBN 0-405-08590-7, Blom Pubns). Ayer Co Pubs.

Practical Area Navigation. Paul Garrison. pap. 7.95 (ISBN 0-8306-2286-1, 2286). TAB Bks.

Practical Arithmetic: The Third "R". C. Johnson. (Illus.). 1977. write for info. (ISBN 0-13-689273-6). P-H.

Practical Art of Diagnostic Interviewing. Gerald R. Pascal. LC 82-72867. (Dorsey Professional Bks.). 132p. 1983. 21.00 (ISBN 0-256-36700-0). Dorsey.

Practical Aspects of Blood Administration. Ed. by Alice W. Reynolds & Del Steckler. LC 86-17470. 1986. text ed. 19.00 (ISBN 0-915355-30-2). Am Assn Blood.

Practical Aspects of Data Communications. Paul S. Kreager. (Illus.). 256p. 1983. text ed. 38.95 (ISBN 0-07-035429-4). McGraw.

Practical Aspects of Drug Utilization Review: A Multidisciplinary Approach. Ed. by Byron Breedlove et al. LC 86-70098. (Practical Aspects of Drug Utilization Review Ser.). (Illus.). 275p. 1986. pap. 79.00x (ISBN 0-9603332-7-4). Am Health Consults.

Practical Aspects of Gas Chromotography-Mass Spectrometry. Gordon M. Message. LC 83-23475. 351p. 1984. 73.00x (ISBN 0-471-06277-4, Pub. by Wiley-Interscience). Wiley.

Practical Aspects of Ground Water Modeling. 2nd ed. LC 85-29755. 1985. 31.25 (ISBN 0-318-23021-6). Natl Water Well.

Practical Aspects of Gynecourology. Ed. by A. Tanko et al. (Illus.). xiv, 470p. 1986. 68.00 (ISBN 963-05-4440-7, Pub. by Akademiai Kiado Budapest). Stillman Pubs.

Practical Aspects of Homicide Investigation: Tactics, Procedures & Forensic Techniques. V. J. Geberth. (Elsevier Series in Practical Aspects of Criminal & Forensic Investigations: Vol. 1). 488p. 1982. 26.50 (ISBN 0-444-00712-1). Elsevier.

Practical Aspects of Intravenous Therapy Techniques for the Practicing Nurse, Pharmacist, Physician. Richard D. Leff & Robert J. Roberts. 112p. 1985. pap. 12.00 (ISBN 0-930530-54-3). Am Soc Hosp Pharm.

Practical Aspects of Magnetic Resonance Imaging. Keeler et al. (Advances in Diagnostic Imaging & Research Ser.). 1988. price not set (ISBN 0-471-63581-2). Churchill.

Practical Aspects of Ophthalmic Optics. 3rd ed. Margaret Dowaliby. (Illus.). 250p. 1988. text ed. 33.00 (ISBN 0-87873-081-8). Prof Pr Bks NYC.

Practical Aspects of Pressing & Drying Seminar: 1984 Notes. Technical Association of the Pulp & Paper Industry. pap. 50.00 (ISBN 0-317-20565-X, 2022798). Bks Demand UMI.

Practical Aspects of Pressing & Drying Seminar, 1985: Notes of TAPPI, the Waverly, Atlanta, GA March 18-22. Technical Association of the Pulp & Paper Industry. pap. 58.50 (ISBN 0-317-26843-0, 2025284). Bks Demand UMI.

Practical Aspects of Pressing & Drying Seminar, 1986: Notes of TAPPI, the Waverly Hotel, Atlanta, GA, March 17-21. Technical Association of the Pulp & Paper Industry. pap. 66.30 (ISBN 0-317-55385-2, 2029178). Bks Demand UMI.

Practical Aspects of Pressing & Drying Seminar, 1987: Notes of TAPPI, Intercontinental Hotel, Geneva, Switzerland, March 16-20. Technical Association of the Pulp & Paper Industry Staff. (Illus.). 267p. pap. 69.50 (2029985). Bks Demand UMI.

Practical Aspects of Rape Investigation: A Multidisciplinary Approach. Robert R. Hazelwood & Ann Wolbert Burgess. LC 86-29326. (Practical Aspects of Criminal & Forensic Investigations Ser.). 589p. 1987. 34.95 (ISBN 0-444-01144-7). Elsevier.

Practical Aspects of Subcontracting under a Government Contract. 255p. 1981. spiral 40.00 (ISBN 0-686-48226-3). Amer Bar Assn.

Practical Aspects of Urinary Incontinence. Ed. by F. M. Debruyne & E. V. Van Kerrebroeck. (Developments in Surgery Ser.). 1986. lib. bdg. 96.90 (ISBN 0-89838-752-3, Pub. by Martinus Nijhoff Netherlands). Kluwer Academic.

Practical Astrologer. Nicholas Campion. (Illus.). 240p. 1987. 24.95 (ISBN 0-8109-1492-1); pap. 14.95 (ISBN 0-8109-2354-8). Abrams.

Practical Astrology. A. Leo. 228p. Date not set. 9.95. Asia Bk Corp.

Practical Astronomy: Lectures on Time, Place & Space. David H. DeVorkin. LC 86-42648. (Illus.). 160p. (Orig.). 1986. pap. 12.95 (ISBN 0-87474-359-1, DEPAP). Smithsonian.

Practical Astronomy with Your Calculator. 2nd ed. Peter Duffett-Smith. LC 81-6191. 200p. 1981. pap. 17.95 (ISBN 0-521-28411-2). Cambridge U Pr.

Practical Astronomy with Your Calculator. 3rd ed. Peter J. Duffett-Smith. (Illus.). 200p. Date not set. price not set (ISBN 0-521-35629-6); spiral bdg. 19.95 (ISBN 0-521-35699-7). Cambridge U Pr.

Practical Atomic Absorption Spectrometry. J. M. Ottaway & A. M. Ure. 1989. text ed. 30.01 (ISBN 0-08-023800-9, PBL). Pergamon.

Practical AV-Video Budgeting. Richard E. Van Deusen. LC 84-17079. (Video Bookshelf Ser.). (Illus.). 168p. 1984. professional 39.95 (ISBN 0-86729-100-1). Knowledge Indus.

Practical Baking. 4th ed. William J. Sultan. (Illus.). 1986. 37.95 (ISBN 0-87055-489-1). AVI.

Practical Baking Manual. William J. Sultan. 175p. 1976. pap. 14.95 (ISBN 0-87055-563-4). AVI.

Practical Band Instrument Repair Manual. 3rd ed. Clayton H. Tiede. 160p. 1976. write for info. wire coil (ISBN 0-697-03678-2). Wm C Brown.

Practical Bank Operation, 2 vols. L. H. Langston. Ed. by Stuart Bruchey. LC 80-1159. (Rise of Commercial Banking Ser.). (Illus.). 1981. Repr. of 1921 ed. Set. lib. bdg. 65.00x (ISBN 0-405-13666-8). Ayer Co Pubs.

Practical Banking. Albert S. Bolles. Ed. by Stuart Bruchey. LC 80-1136. (Rise of Commercial Banking Ser.). 1981. Repr. of 1884 ed. lib. bdg. 28.00x. Ayer Co Pubs.

Practical Bar Management. H. L. Grossman. 23.50x (ISBN 0-911202-26-9). Radio City.

Practical Bar Management. Harold J. Grossman. LC 59-9744. 1959. 9.95 (ISBN 0-317-39762-1). Brown Bk.

Practical BASIC for Teachers. Jim Thompson. 200p. 1985. 21.95 (ISBN 0-675-20340-6). Merrill.

Practical BASIC Programs. Ed. by Lon Poole. 171p. (Orig.). 1980. pap. 16.95 (ISBN 0-931988-38-1). Osborne-McGraw.

Practical Bazar Medicines with over 200 Useful Prescriptions. G. T. Birdwood. 220p. 1986. Repr. 15.00X (ISBN 0-8364-1768-2, Pub. by Manohar India). South Asia Bks.

Practical Beauty Culture Workbook. Milady Editors. (Illus.). 1985. 11.30 (ISBN 0-87350-406-2). Milady Pub.

Practical Bee-Keeping. Herbert Mace. (Illus.). 96p. 1988. pap. 11.95 (ISBN 0-7063-6420-1, Pub. by Ward Lock). David & Charles.

Practical Beekeeping. Roger Griffith & Enoch Tompkins. LC 76-51401. (Illus.). 224p. 1977. o. p. 9.95 (ISBN 0-88266-092-6, Garden Way Pub); pap. 8.95 (ISBN 0-88266-091-8). Storey Comm Inc.

Practical Beginning Theory. 6th ed. Bruce Benward & Barbara G. Jackson. 336p. 1987. pap. text ed. write for info. (ISBN 0-697-00611-5); write for info. instr's. manual (ISBN 0-697-00609-3); write for info. three cassettes (ISBN 0-697-00610-7). Wm C Brown.

Practical Bible Doctrine. Keith L. Brooks. (Teach Yourself the Bible Ser.). 1962. pap. 2.95 (ISBN 0-8024-6733-4). Moody.

Practical Bilingual Special Education Guide. Bertha E. Segal et al. 55p. (Span., Eng.). 1984. tchr's ed. 8.50 (ISBN 0-938395-08-4). B Segal.

Practical Biochemistry for Medical Students. G. Rajagopal & S. Ramakrishnan. (Illus.). 80p. (Orig.). 1983. pap. text ed. 8.95x (ISBN 0-86131-415-8, Pub by Orient Longman Ltd India). Apt Bks.

Practical Blacksmithing & Metalworking. 2nd ed. Percy W. Blandford. (Illus.). 368p. 1988. 24.95 (ISBN 0-8306-0394-8); pap. 16.95 (ISBN 0-8306-2894-0). TAB Bks.

Practical Boat Buying. Practical Sailor Editors. Intro. by Sue Weller. LC 83-83347. (Illus.). 224p. (Orig.). 1984. pap. 22.95 (ISBN 0-9613139-0-0). Eng Communi Inc.

Practical Boiler Water Treatment: Including Air-Conditioning Systems. Leo I. Pincus. LC 80-29604. 284p. 1981. Repr. of 1962 ed. lib. bdg. 23.50 (ISBN 0-89874-255-2). Krieger.

Practical Bonsai for Beginners. Kenji Murata. LC 64-7611. (Illus.). 1977. pap. 7.95 (ISBN 0-87040-230-7). Japan Pubns USA.

Practical Book of American Antiques. Harold D. Eberlein & Abbot McClure. (Paperback Ser.). (Illus.). 1977. pap. 7.95 (ISBN 0-306-80062-4). Da Capo.

Practical Book of Greenhouse Gardening. Ronald H. Menage. 168p. 1983. 7.95 (ISBN 0-312-63461-7). St Martin.

Practical Book of Knives. Ken Warner. (Illus.). 192p. pap. 10.95 (ISBN 0-88317-025-6). Stoeger Pub Co.

Practical Bookkeeping for the Small Business. Mary L. Dyer. LC 75-32968. (Illus.). 240p. 1976. pap. 14.95 (ISBN 0-8092-8206-2). Contemp Bks.

Practical Borehole Logging Procedures for Mineral Exploration, With Emphasis Uranium. (Technical Reports Ser.: No. 259). (Illus.). 44p. (Orig.). 1986. pap. text ed. 15.50 (ISBN 92-0-145086-9, IDC259, IAEA). UNIPUB.

Practical Botany. Peter Kaufman et al. 1983. text ed. 31.00 (ISBN 0-8359-5580-X, Reston); instr's. manual avail. (ISBN 0-8359-5581-8). P-H.

Practical Bronchoscopy. Doty et al. 1986. 27.75 (ISBN 0-8016-1366-3). Mosby.

Practical Building Conservation: English Heritage Technical Handbook. John Ashurst & Nicola Ashurst. 1988. Vol. 1, Stone Masonry, 112p. 31.95 (ISBN 0-470-21104-0); Vol. 2, Brick Terracotta & Earthstone, 138p. 33.95 (ISBN 0-470-21105-9); Vol. 3, Mortars Plasters & Renders, 98p. 29.95 (ISBN 0-470-21106-7); Vol. 4, Metals, 176p. 36.95 (ISBN 0-470-21107-5); Vol. 5, Glass & Resins,144p. 33.95 (ISBN 0-470-21108-3). Wiley.

Practical Business & Tax Guide for the Craftsperson. rev. ed. James E. Norris & Fred Bair. (Illus.). 100p. 1986. pap. 16.00x (ISBN 0-942280-23-7). Pub Horizons.

Practical Business Communications. Robert Nixon. 594p. 1984. text ed. 26.00 net (ISBN 0-15-570875-9, HC); write for info. instr's manual (ISBN 0-15-570876-7). HarBraceJ.

Practical Business Communications. Robert Nixon. 1986. text ed. 23.00 (ISBN 0-12-519990-2); instr's. manual 2.50 (ISBN 0-12-519991-0). Acad Pr.

Practical Business Forecasting. J. Saunders et al. 250p. 1986. text ed. 59.95 (ISBN 0-566-02516-7, Pub. by Gower Pub England). Gower Pub Co.

Practical Business Forecasting with Your Micro: The Box-Jenkins Approach. C. Beaumont. (Illus.). 230p. 1987. 20.00 (ISBN 0-85626-459-8). Abacus Pr.

Practical Business Law. John J. Moran. (Illus.). 640p. 1985. text ed. write for info. (ISBN 0-13-689027-X); write for info. (ISBN 0-13-689043-1). P-H.

Practical Business Math: A Performance Approach. 4th ed. Michael D. Tuttle. 560p. 1987. pap. text ed. write for info. (ISBN 0-697-00620-4); write for info. instr's. ed. (ISBN 0-697-00704-9). Wm C Brown.

Practical Business Math Procedures. 2nd ed. Slater. 1986. 29.95 (ISBN 0-256-03654-3). Irwin.

Practical Business Mathematics. Lloyd D. Brooks. 464p. 1984. text ed. write for info. (ISBN 0-574-20725-2, 13-3725); write for info. tchr's ed. (ISBN 0-574-20728-7, 13-3728); wkbk. resource manual avail. (ISBN 0-574-20729-5, 13-3729). SRA.

Practical Business Writing. Arn Tibbetts. 1987. pap. text ed. write for info. (ISBN 0-673-39315-1). Scott F.

Practical Calculations for Business Studies: Problems & Applications for Students in Africa. V. N. Newcomb. LC 80-42019. 152p. 1981. 48.95x (ISBN 0-471-27966-8, Pub. by Wiley-Interscience). Wiley.

Practical Calculations for Business Studies: Problems & Applications for Students in Africa. V. N. Newcomb. LC 80-42019. pap. 42.70 (2031760). Bks Demand UMI.

Practical Candle-Burning Rituals. Raymond Buckland. (Illus.). 189p. 1984. pap. 5.95 (ISBN 0-87542-048-6). Llewellyn Pubns.

Practical Cardiac Pacing. Ed. by Paul C. Gillette. (Cardiology Surgery Ser.). 288p. 1986. pap. 39.50 (ISBN 0-683-03526-6). Williams & Wilkins.

Practical Cardiology. C. V. Shah. (Illus.). 246p. 1985. 23.50. Asia Bk Corp.

Practical Cardiovascular Diagnosis. John B. Kostis et al. (Focus On Clinical Diagnosis Ser.: Vol. 2). 1984. text ed. 52.75 (ISBN 0-87488-174-9). Med Exam.

Practical Care of the Ambulatory Patient. Stults & Dere. 560p. Date not set. price not set (ISBN 0-7216-2474-X). Saunders.

Practical Casting. Tim McCreight. LC 85-73045. 128p. 1986. 10.95 (ISBN 0-9615984-0-9). Brynmorgen.

Practical Cataloguing. W. Dent. 1966. 6.95 (ISBN 0-8022-0382-5). Philos Lib.

Practical Catalytic Hydrogenation: Techniques & Applications. Morris Freifelder. LC 76-123740. 1971. 42.50 (ISBN 0-471-27800-9, Pub. by Wiley-Interscience). Wiley.

Practical Catechism, 3 Vols. Henry Hammond. LC 79-168238. (Library of Anglo-Catholic Theology: No. 8). Repr. of 1850 ed. Set. 87.50 (ISBN 0-404-52090-1). AMS Pr.

Practical Celestial. rev. ed. Susan P. Howell. Ed. by Donald Treworgy. (Illus.). 272p. 1987. pap. 19.95. Mystic Sea Mus.

Practical Celtic Magic. Murry Hope. (Illus.). 256p. (Orig.). 1988. pap. 9.99 (ISBN 0-85030-624-8, Pub. by Aquarian Pr England). Sterling.

Practical Cheese Making. G. H. Wilster. 1980. pap. text ed. 29.95x (ISBN 0-88246-127-3). Oreg St U Bkstrs.

Practical Chemistry in the Twelfth Century. Muhammad Ibn Zakariya. Ed. by Robert R. Steele. Tr. by Gerard Of Cremona. LC 79-8590. Repr. of 1929 ed. 19.50 (ISBN 0-404-18444-8). AMS Pr.

Practical Chess Endings. Irving Chernev. LC 69-15362. (Illus.). 1969. pap. 5.95 (ISBN 0-486-22208-X). Dover.

Practical Chess Endings. Paul Keres. (Illus.). 272p. 1983. pap. 16.95 (ISBN 0-7134-4210-7, Pub. by Batsford England). David & Charles.
Practical Chess Endings. LC 75-36974. 1976. pap. 10.95 (ISBN 0-89058-028-6). R H M Pr.
Practical Chess Openings. Reuben Fine. 1979. pap. 8.95 (ISBN 0-679-14031-X, Tartan). McKay.
Practical Chess Playing. Raymond Edwards. (Routledge Chess Handbooks Ser.). 128p. (Orig.). 1984. pap. 7.95 (ISBN 0-7100-9653-4). Routledge Chapman & Hall.
Practical Chinese Reader, Bk. 1. 551p. 1981. pap. 8.95 (ISBN 0-8351-0915-1). China Bks.
Practical Chinese Reader, Bk. 2. 506p. 1981. pap. 8.95 (ISBN 0-8351-0916-X). China Bks.
Practical Chinese Reader: Elementary Course Book, Vol. 1. Beijing Language Institute Staff. 551p. 1981. pap. 8.95 (ISBN 0-917056-48-5, Pub. by Commercial Pr China). Cheng & Tsui.
Practical Chinese Reader: Elementary Course Book, Vol. 2. Beijing Language Institute Staff. 506p. 1981. pap. 8.95 (ISBN 0-917056-49-3, Pub. by Commercial Pr China). Cheng & Tsui.
Practical Chinese Reader: Elementary Course Book, Vol. 3. Beijing Language Institute Staff. 1986. 8.95 (ISBN 0-88727-078-6, Pub. by Commercial Pr China). Cheng & Tsui.
Practical Chinese Reader III. Li Xun et al. (Illus.). 393p. 1986. pap. 8.95 (ISBN 0-8351-1788-X). China Bks.
Practical Chinese Reader IV. Liu Xun et al. (Illus.). 381p. (Orig.). 1987. pap. 12.95 (ISBN 0-8351-1814-2). China Bks.
Practical Christian Socialism. Adin Ballou. LC 72-2936. (Communal Societies in America Ser.). Repr. of 1854 ed. 45.50 (ISBN 0-404-10702-8). AMS Pr.
Practical Christian Socialism, 2 vols. Adin Ballou. 655p. 1985. Repr. of 1854 ed. Set. lib. bdg. 79.00 (ISBN 0-932051-86-3, Pub. by Am Repr Serv). Am Biog Serv.
Practical Christianity. 500p. 1987. 14.95 (ISBN 0-8423-4957-X). Tyndale.
Practical Christianity of Malcolm Muggeridge. David Porter. LC 83-26442. 132p. 1984. pap. 4.95 (ISBN 0-87784-971-4). Inter-Varsity.
Practical Christianity: Studies in the Book of James. David L. Roper. 148p. (Orig.). 1987. pap. 3.59 (ISBN 0-89225-291-X). Gospel Advocate.
Practical Church Financing. Frederick Harrison. 128p. 1970. pap. 5.95 (ISBN 0-912522-58-5). Aero Medical.
Practical Classroom Organization in the Primary School. Michael Bassey. (Ward Lock Educational Ser.). 29.00x (ISBN 0-7062-3665-3, Pub. by Ward Lock Educ Co Ltd). State Mutual Bk.
Practical Clinical Cytology. photocopy ed. Virginia A. LiVolsi. (Illus.). 352p. 1980. 42.50x (ISBN 0-398-03927-5). C C Thomas.
Practical Clinical Enzymology: Techniques & Interpretations & Biochemical Profiling. Paul L. Wolf et al. LC 80-12468. 592p. 1982. Repr. of 1973 ed. lib. bdg. 36.50 (ISBN 0-89874-162-9). Krieger.
Practical Clinical Psychopharmacology. 3rd ed. William Appleton. 200p. 1988. pap. 26.95 (ISBN 0-683-00239-2). Williams & Wilkins.
Practical Clock Repairing. Don DeCarle. 21.95x (ISBN 0-685-22074-5). Wehman.
Practical Coaching Techniques for the Sprints & Relays, 10 bks. Mel Rosen et al. (Orig.). 1980. Set. pap. 27.95 (ISBN 0-317-14596-7). Championship Bks.
Practical Coal Mine Management. Scott G. Britton. LC 81-11426. 233p. 1981. 37.50 (Pub. by Wiley-Interscience). Wiley.
Practical Coal Mine Management. Scott G. Britton. LC 81-11426. 248p. 1981. 37.50 (ISBN 0-471-09035-2, (JW)). Krieger.
Practical COBOL for Microcomputers. Kevin Sullivan. 204p. 1984. 15.00 (ISBN 0-905104-60-9, Pub. by Sigma Pr UK). Bk Clearing Hse.
Practical Cogitator: The Thinker's Anthology. Charles P. Curtis, Jr. & Ferris Greenslet. 1983. pap. 9.95 (ISBN 0-395-34635-5); pap. 53.70 6-copy prepack (ISBN 0-395-34931-1). HM.
Practical Color Magick. Raymond Buckland. Ed. by Carl L. Weschcke. LC 83-80173. (Practical Magic Ser.). (Illus.). 1985. pap. 5.95 (ISBN 0-87542-047-8). Llewellyn Pubns.
Practical Composition in Photography. Axel Bruck. LC 80-40759. (Practical Photography Ser.). (Illus.). 192p. 1981. 30.95 (ISBN 0-240-51060-7). Focal Pr.
Practical Comprehensive Treatment of Anorexia Nervosa & Bulimia. Arnold E. Andersen. LC 84-47958. (Series in Contemporary Medicine & Public Health). 224p. 1985. text ed. 28.50X (ISBN 0-8018-2442-7). Johns Hopkins.
Practical Computer Applications in Radionuclide Imaging. Ed. by Arvis G. Williams, Jr. & Christopher G. Eckel. (Contemporary Issues in Nuclear Imaging Ser.: Vol. 3). (Illus.). 291p. 1986. text ed. 52.00 (ISBN 0-443-08465-3). Churchill.
Practical Computer Cost Accounting. Kenneth M. Sullivan. (Illus.). 320p. 1983. 33.95 (ISBN 0-442-27961-2). Van Nos Reinhold.
Practical Computer Data Communications. William J. Barksdale. (Applications of Communications Theory Ser.). 450p. 1986. 59.50x (ISBN 0-306-42323-5, Plenum Pr.). Plenum Pub.
Practical Computing for Experimental Scientists. John D. Beasley. (Illus.). 248p. 1988. 55.00 (ISBN 0-19-853728-X); pap. 27.95 (ISBN 0-19-853754-9). Oxford U Pr.
Practical Concerns about Siblings: Bridging the Research-Practice Gap. Ed. by Frances F. Schachter & Richard K. Stone. LC 87-31095. (Journal of Children in Contemporary Society Ser.). (Illus.). 210p. 1988. text ed. 24.95 (ISBN 0-86656-647-3). Haworth Pr.
Practical Conservation in English 2. Eugene Hall. 158p. (gr. 9-12). 1981. pap. text ed. 4.75 (ISBN 0-88345-439-4, 20064); cassettes 45.00 (ISBN 0-686-86691-6, 40028). Prentice ESL.
Practical Construction Equipment Maintenance Reference Guide. Lindley R. Higgins. (Engineering Reference Guide). 512p. 1987. write for info. McGraw.
Practical Construction Science. Brian J. Smith. LC 79-40562. (Longman Technician Ser.: Construction & Civil Engineering). pap. 87.00 (ISBN 0-317-27785-5, 2025235). Bks Demand UMI.
Practical Contemporary Home Plans. Ed. by National Plan Service, Inc. Staff. (Illus.). 32p. (Orig.). Date not set. pap. 3.95 (ISBN 0-934039-09-7, A52). Natl Plan Serv.
Practical Contraception. Saroja Ramaswamy & Tony Smith. (Illus.). 149p. 1977. text ed. 9.00x (ISBN 0-89313-004-4). G F Stickley Co.
Practical Control of Indoor Air Problems: Proceedings of IAQ 87 Conference in Washington. 400p. Date not set. 55.00 (ISBN 0-910110-51-4). Am Heat Ref & Air Eng.
Practical Conversation in English 1. Eugene Hall. (Practical Conversations in English Ser.). (gr. 9-12). 1981. pap. text ed. 6.00 (ISBN 0-13-689142-X, 20052). Prentice ESL.
Practical Cookery: A Compilation of Principles of Cookery & Recipes. 24th ed. Kansas State University Staff. LC 20-21946. 281p. 1976. text ed. 33.95x (ISBN 0-471-45641-1). Wiley.
Practical Cooking & Baking for Schools & Institutions. Joseph Amendola & James M. Berrini. LC 79-179954. 1971. 8.50x (ISBN 0-317-39775-3). Brown Bk.
Practical Corrosion Control Methods for Gas Utility Piping. LC 76-5317. (Illus.). 141p. 1970. 10.00 (ISBN 0-915567-81-4). Natl Corrosion Eng.
Practical Cost Estimating for Metal Fabrication. Richard Budzik & George Kuprianczyk. 1988. 49.95 (ISBN 0-912914-32-7). Practical Pubns.
Practical Counseling in the Schools. 2nd ed. Gary S. Belkin. 544p. 1981. pap. text ed. write for info. (ISBN 0-697-06055-1); instr's. manual avail. (ISBN 0-697-06039-X). Wm C Brown.
Practical Course in Modern Locksmithing. Whitcomb Crichton. 222p. 1943. 16.95 (ISBN 0-911012-06-0). Nelson-Hall.
Practical Course in Modern Shoe Repairing. Ralph Sarlette. Orig. Title: Shoe Repairing Course. 1956. 16.95 (ISBN 0-911012-44-3). Nelson-Hall.
Practical Course into Spanish, Italian, French & Egyptian Pottery. M. S. Lockwood. (Illus.). 136p. 1983. 137.45 (ISBN 0-86650-075-8). Gloucester Art.
Practical Craft: Readings for Business & Technical Writers. W. Keats Sparrow & Donald H. Cunningham. LC 77-93967. (Illus.). 1978. pap. text ed. 21.50 (ISBN 0-395-25590-2). HM.
Practical Criticism, a Study of Literary Judgment. Ivor A. Richards. LC 56-13740. 362p. 1956. pap. 7.95 (ISBN 0-15-673626-8, Harv). HarBraceJ.
Practical CT Technology & Techniques. Lincoln L. Berland. (Illus.). 288p. 1987. pap. text ed. 31.00 (ISBN 0-88167-261-0). Raven.
Practical Current Awareness Services from Libraries. Ed. by Tom Whitehall. 120p. 1986. text ed. 33.95 (ISBN 0-566-03519-7, Gower Pub UK). Gower Pub Co.
Practical Curriculum Study. Douglas Barnes. (Rutledge Education Bks.). 160p. 1983. pap. 19.95x (ISBN 0-7100-0979-8). Routledge Chapman & Hall.
Practical Cutaneous Cryosurgery. Douglas Torre et al. Date not set. text ed. 49.95 (ISBN 0-8385-7870-5). Appleton & Lange.
Practical Dental Management: Patients & Practice. John H. Manhold & Cecelia Black. 300p. (Orig.). 1984. pap. 19.50 (ISBN 0-912791-04-7). Ishiyaku Euro.
Practical Dermatology of the Genital Region. G. W. Korting. 190p. 1981. text ed. 68.00 (ISBN 0-7216-5498-3). Saunders.
Practical Descriptive Geometry. 2nd ed. Hiram E. Grant. LC 65-16867. pap. 72.00 (ISBN 0-317-08784-3, 2004354). Bks Demand UMI.
Practical Descriptive Geometry. Samuel E. Rusinoff. LC 47-24789. pap. 67.00 (ISBN 0-317-12987-2, 2004562). Bks Demand UMI.
Practical Design of Reinforced & Prestressed Concrete Structures. 36p. 1984. 25.00 (ISBN 0-7277-0214-9, Pub. by T Telford UK). Am Soc Civil Eng.
Practical Design of Reinforced Concrete. Russell S. Fling. LC 86-11158. 516p. 1987. write for info. (ISBN 0-471-80827-X). Wiley.
Practical Designs for Wood Turning. Roland Seale. LC 79-65084. (Home Craftsman Bk.). (Illus.). 152p. 1979. pap. 7.95 (ISBN 0-8069-8874-6). Sterling.
Practical Detail of the Cotton Manufacture of the U. S. James Montgomery. LC 70-127191. (Research & Source Work Ser: No. 491). 1970. Repr. of 1840 ed. 18.50 (ISBN 0-8337-2442-8). B Franklin.
Practical Detail of the Cotton Manufacture of the United States of America. James Montgomery. LC 68-56266. 1969. Repr. of 1840 ed. 29.50x (ISBN 0-678-00572-9). Kelley.
Practical Developments in Inherited Metabolic Diseases. Ed. by G. M. Addison et al. 1986. lib. bdg. 80.75 (ISBN 0-85200-690-X, Pub. by MTP Pr England). Kluwer Academic.
Practical Dictionary of Music Composers. Sandy Feldstein. (An Alfred Handy Guide). (Illus.). 64p. 1984. pap. 2.95 (ISBN 0-88284-332-X, 2240). Alfred Pub.
Practical Dictionary of Shipping Business: Japanese-English; English-Japanese. 236p. (Japanese & Eng.). 1978. 59.95 (ISBN 0-686-92099-6, M-9340). French & Eur.
Practical Digital Data & Data Communication... With LSI Applications. Paul Bates. (Illus.). 1987. write for info. P-H.
Practical Digital Design Using ICs. 2nd ed. Joseph D. Greenfield. LC 82-10931. (Electronic Technology Ser.). 717p. 1983. write for info. (ISBN 0-471-05791-6). Wiley.
Practical Directions for Portrait Painting. M. Merrifield. (Library of the Arts Ser.). (Illus.). 1977. 77.75 (ISBN 0-89266-069-4). Am Classical Coll Pr.
Practical Dissector & Textbook of Human Anatomy: Emphasizing the Musculoskeletal System. Donald J. Hobart. (Allied Health Bks.: Vol. I). 1984. pap. text ed. 30.00 (ISBN 0-87488-425-X). Med Exam.
Practical Distiller. Monzert. 1987. pap. 7.95 (ISBN 0-917914-58-9). Lindsay Pubns.
Practical Divinity: Theology in the Wesleyan Tradition. Thomas A. Langford. 304p. (Orig.). 1983. pap. 9.95 (ISBN 0-687-33326-1). Abingdon.
Practical Dog Breeding & Genetics. Eleanor Frankling. (Popular Dog Ser.). (Illus.). 212p. 1988. 34.95 (ISBN 0-09-171540-7, Pub. by Century Hutchinson). David & Charles.
Practical Dope on the Big Bores. F. C. Ness. (Library Classics Ser.). (Illus.). 436p. 1984. Repr. deluxe ed. 42.00 (ISBN 0-935632-16-6). Wolfe Pub CO.
Practical DOS. Ruth Schmitz. 272p. 1989. pap. text ed. price not set (ISBN 0-394-39485-2). Knopf.
Practical Drafting for the HVAC Trades. 2nd ed. John E. Traister. (Illus.). 272p. 1984. pap. text ed. 26.00 (ISBN 0-13-689308-2). P-H.
Practical Dreamer: Israel Friedlaender & the Shaping of American Judaism. Baila R. Shargel. (Illus.). 1985. text ed. 20.00 (ISBN 0-87334-025-6, Pub. by Jewish Theol Seminary). Ktav.
Practical Dreamer: Israel Friedlander & the Shaping of American Judaism. Baila R. Shargel. (Moreshet Ser.: No. X). 1985. 20.00 (ISBN 0-87334-027-2). Jewish Sem.
Practical Dressage for Amateur Trainers. Janice M. Ladendorf. LC 73-149. 192p. 1973. 8.95 (ISBN 0-498-01285-9). A S Barnes.
Practical Drilling & Production Design. Douglas Byrum. 528p. 1982. 54.95 (ISBN 0-87814-180-4, P-4256). Pennwell Bks.
Practical Ear Training. Janet M. McGaughey. 1977. pap. 11.95 (ISBN 0-8008-6472-7, Crescendo). Taplinger.
Practical Ear Training Workbook. Janet M. McGaughey. 1977. pap. 7.95 (ISBN 0-8008-6473-5, Crescendo). Taplinger.
Practical Echocardiology. Jos Roelandt. LC 77-1619. (Ultrasound in Biomedicine Ser.). 306p. 1980. pap. 69.95x (ISBN 0-471-27891-2, Pub. by Res Stud Pr). Wiley.
Practical Ecology for Geography & Biology: Survey, Mapping & Data Analysis. David Gilbertson et al. (Illus.). 350p. (Orig.). 1985. pap. 12.95 (ISBN 0-09-162651-X, Pub. by Hutchinson Educ). Longwood Pub Group.
Practical Economics for the Real Economist. P. Bowbrick. 1988. lib. bdg. 66.50 (ISBN 1-85333-076-0, Pub. by Graham & Trotman UK). Kluwer Academic.
Practical Education, 2 vols. Maria Edgeworth & Richard L. Edgeworth. Ed. by Gina Luria. (Feminist Controversy in England, 1788-1810 Ser.). 1974. Set. lib. bdg. 121.00 (ISBN 0-8240-0857-X). Garland Pub.
Practical Education in the Diagnosis of Rheumatic Disorders. T. P. Torralba. 58p. 1986. pap. text ed. 12.90 (ISBN 0-920887-06-6, Pub. by Hans Huber). Hogrefe Intl.
Practical Education Program for the Diabetic Client Within the Rehabilitation Setting. Nancy Dyer & Pat Homeyer. 151p. 1979. pap. 5.00 (ISBN 0-89128-970-4, PRP970). Am Foun Blind.
Practical Egyptian Magic. Murry Hope. 192p. 1986. pap. 7.95 (ISBN 0-312-63474-9). St Martin.
Practical Electrical Project Engineering. L. B. Roe. 1978. text ed. 39.95 (ISBN 0-07-053392-X). McGraw.
Practical Electrical Safety: Occupational Safety & Health. Winburn. 288p. 1988. 49.75 (ISBN 0-8247-7948-7). Dekker.
Practical Electrical Wiring. 14th ed. Herbert P. Richter & W. Creighton Schwan. (Illus.). 688p. 1987. text ed. 32.95 (ISBN 0-07-052391-6). McGraw.
Practical Electrical Wiring: Residential, Farm & Industrial. 8th ed. Herbert P. Richter. 1972. text ed. 12.50 (ISBN 0-07-052385-1). McGraw.
Practical Electricity. 4th ed. Robert Middleton & L. Donald Meyers. LC 82-20642. (Illus.). 1983. 14.95 (ISBN 0-672-23375-4, Pub. by Audel). Macmillan.
Practical Electricity. 5th ed. Robert G. Middleton. 1988. 19.95 (ISBN 0-02-584561-6, Pub. by Audel). Macmillan.
Practical Electrocardiography. 7th ed. Henry J. Marriott. (Illus.). 496p. 1983. text ed. 24.95 (ISBN 0-683-05574-7). Williams & Wilkins.
Practical Electron Microscopy: A Beginners Illustrated Guide. Elaine E. Hunter. LC 83-17778. 112p. 1984. text ed. 29.95 (ISBN 0-275-91435-6, C1435). Praeger.
Practical Electron Microscopy for Biologists. 2nd ed. Geoffrey A. Meek. LC 75-4955. 528p. 1978. text ed. 48.95 (ISBN 0-471-59031-2). Wiley.
Practical Electron Microscopy for Biologists. 2nd ed. Geoffrey A. Meek. LC 75-4955. pap. 143.00 (2052242). Bks Demand UMI.
Practical Electronic Projects for Model Railroaders. Peter J. Thorne. LC 74-82041. (Illus.). 80p. (Orig.). 1974. pap. 7.50 (ISBN 0-89024-523-1). Kalmbach.
Practical Electronics Troubleshooting. James Perozzo. LC 84-28626. 256p. 1985. pap. text ed. 19.95 (ISBN 0-8273-2433-2); instr's. guide 6.00 (ISBN 0-8273-2434-0). Delmar.
Practical Elments of Thorough-Bass. Wolfgang A. Mozart. LC 76-27136. 1976. pap. 3.00 (ISBN 0-915282-04-6). J Patelson Mus.
Practical Embryology. C. H. Barnett. 124p. 1969. 14.95 (ISBN 0-8464-1326-4). Beekman Pubs.
Practical Encyclopedia of Natural Healing. rev. ed. Mark Bricklin. (Illus.). 592p. 1983. 21.95 (ISBN 0-87857-480-8). Rodale Pr Inc.
Practical Encyclopedia of Pet Birds for Home & Garden: Featuring Two Hundred Birds from Around the World. Don Harper. (Illus.). 208p. 1987. 17.95 (ISBN 0-517-56546-3, Harmony). Crown.
Practical Endgame Lessons. Edmar Mednis. pap. 7.95 (ISBN 0-679-14102-2). McKay.
Practical Endocrinology. 4th ed. Nelson B. Watts & Joseph H. Keffer. (Illus.). 210p. 1989. pap. text ed. price not set (ISBN 0-8121-1179-6). Lea & Febiger.
Practical Engineering Project Management. Milton D. Rosenau, Jr. (Illus.). 280p. 25.00 (Lifetime Learn). Van Nos Reinhold.
Practical English. Carol Pemberton. 1988. pap. text ed. price not set (ISBN 0-673-39824-2). Scott F.
Practical English, 2 vols. Madeline Semmelmeyer. 1968. Set. 29.95 (ISBN 0-911744-02-9). Career Pub IL.
Practical English-Cantonese Dictionary. Chiang Ker-Chiu. (Eng. & Chinese.). 25.00x (ISBN 0-686-00881-2). Colton Bk.
Practical English-Chinese Dictionary. 1674p. (Eng. & Chinese.). 1979. leatherette 29.95 (ISBN 0-686-97443-3, M-9291). French & Eur.
Practical English-Chinese Pronouncing Dictionary. Janey Chen. LC 78-77122. (Eng. & Chinese.). 1970. 26.50 (ISBN 0-8048-0663-2). C E Tuttle.
Practical English Grammar. English Language Services Staff. 1968. pap. 7.95 (ISBN 0-02-971830-9); wkbk. 7.95 (ISBN 0-02-971840-6, 97184). Macmillan.
Practical English Handbook. 7th ed. Floyd C. Watkins & William B. Dillingham. LC 85-81206. 416p. 1985. pap. text ed. 15.96 (ISBN 0-395-35745-4). Third ed. wkbk 13.56 (ISBN 0-395-36401-9); instr's manual-wkbk. 2.36 (ISBN 0-395-36402-7). HM.
Practical English Handbook. 8th ed. Floyd C. Watkins & William B. Dillingham. LC 88-81366. 1989. price not set (ISBN 0-395-43243-X); annot. instr's. ed., wkbk. avail.; instr's. manual for wkbk., tests avail. HM.
Practical English: One Thousand Most Effective Words. Norman W. Schur. (Orig.). 1983. pap. 2.95 (ISBN 0-345-31038-1). Ballantine.
Practical English-Polish Dictionary. J. Stanislawski et al. 913p. (Eng. & Pol.). 1976. leatherette 35.00 (ISBN 0-686-92102-X, M-9328). French & Eur.
Practical English Structure, Vol. 1. Marcia Beth Bordman et al. LC 80-85299. (Practical English Structure Ser.). (Illus.). xii, 200p. 1981. text ed. 15.95x (ISBN 0-913580-66-X, Clerc Bks). Gallaudet Univ Pr.
Practical English Structure, Vol. 2. Marcia B. Bordman et al. LC 80-85299. (Practical English Structure Ser.). (Illus.). xii, 224p. 1981. text ed. 15.95x (ISBN 0-913580-67-8, Clerc Bks). Gallaudet Univ Pr.
Practical English Structure, Vol. 3. Marcia B. Bordman et al. LC 80-85299. (Practical English Structure Ser.). (Illus.). xii, 220p. 1981. text ed. 15.95x (ISBN 0-913580-68-6, Clerc Bks). Gallaudet Univ Pr.
Practical English Structure, Vol. 4. Marcia B. Bordman et al. LC 80-85299. (Practical English Structure Ser.). (Illus.). xiv, 218p. 1981. text ed. 15.95x (ISBN 0-913580-69-4, Clerc Bks). Gallaudet Univ Pr.

Practical English Structure, Vol. 5. Marcia B. Bordman et al. LC 80-85299. (Practical English Structure Ser.). (Illus.). xii, 340p. 1982. text ed. 15.95x (ISBN 0-913580-70-8, Clerc Bks). Gallaudet Univ Pr.

Practical English Three. Tim Harris. (Illus.). 292p. 1981. pap. text ed. 5.75 (ISBN 0-15-570906-2, HC); instr's. manual avail. (ISBN 0-15-570907-0); cassette tapes 45.00 (ISBN 0-15-570911-9); Writing Practical English 3 2.98 (ISBN 0-15-570908-9). HarBraceJ.

Practical English Two. Tim Harris. (Illus.). 240p. 1980. pap. text ed. 4.98 (ISBN 0-15-570902-X, HC); instr's. manual avail. (ISBN 0-15-570903-8); cassettes avail. 35.00 (ISBN 0-15-570910-0); Writing Practical English 2 2.98 (ISBN 0-15-570905-4). HarBraceJ.

Practical English Usage. Michael Swan. (Orig.). 1980. pap. 9.95x (ISBN 0-19-431185-6). Oxford U Pr.

Practical English Workbook Form B. 2nd ed. Floyd C. Watkins et al. 312p. 1983. 11.95 (ISBN 0-395-33187-0); instr's. manual 2.00 (ISBN 0-395-33186-2). HM.

Practical English 1. 2nd ed. Tim Harris & Allan Rowe. 1986. pap. text ed. write for info. (ISBN 0-15-570912-7, Pub. by HC); instr's. manual avail. (ISBN 0-15-570918-6); 3 cassette tapes 30.00 (ISBN 0-15-570919-4). HarBraceJ.

Practical English 1A. 2nd ed. Tim Harris & Rowe. 1986. pap. text ed. 4.00 net (ISBN 0-15-570913-5, Pub. by HC). HarBraceJ.

Practical English 1B. 2nd ed. Tim Harris & Rowe. 1986. pap. text ed. write for info. (Pub. by HC). HarBraceJ.

Practical English 2. 2nd ed. Tim Harris & Allan Rowe. 292p. 1987. pap. text ed. 7.00 (ISBN 0-15-570920-8); write for info. tchr's. ed. (ISBN 0-15-570926-7); Cassette tapes. write for info. (ISBN 0-15-570927-5). HarBraceJ.

Practical English 2A. 2nd ed. Tim Harris & Allan Rowe. 143p. 1987. pap. text ed. 3.75 (ISBN 0-15-570921-6). HarBraceJ.

Practical English 2B. 2nd ed. Tim Harris & Allan Rowe. 290p. 1987. pap. text ed. 3.75 (ISBN 0-15-570922-4). HarBraceJ.

Practical English 3A. 2nd ed. Tim Harris & Rowe. Date not set. pap. text ed. price not set (ISBN 0-15-570929-1). HarBraceJ.

Practical English 3B. 2nd ed. Tim Harris & Rowe. Date not set. pap. text ed. price not set (ISBN 0-15-570930-5). HarBraceJ.

Practical Enzymology of the Sphingolipidoses. Ed. by Robert H. Glew & Stephen P. Peters. LC 77-15819. (Laboratory & Research Methods in Biology & Medicine: Vol. 1). 322p. 1977. 52.00 (ISBN 0-8451-1650-9). A R Liss.

Practical Essays. Alexander Bain. LC 72-4533. (Essay Index Reprint Ser.). Repr. of 1884 ed. 19.00 (ISBN 0-8369-2935-7). Ayer Co Pubs.

Practical Essays on American Government. Albert B. Hart. LC 73-19152. (Politics & People Ser.). 320p. 1974. Repr. 21.00x (ISBN 0-405-05874-8). Ayer Co Pubs.

Practical Estuarine Chemistry: A Handbook. Ed. by P. C. Head. (Estuarine & Brackish-Water Sciences Association Handbook). 350p. 1985. 62.50 (ISBN 0-521-30165-3). Cambridge U Pr.

Practical Ethics. Peter Singer. LC 79-52328. 1980. 39.50 (ISBN 0-521-22920-0); pap. 11.95 (ISBN 0-521-29720-6). Cambridge U Pr.

Practical Ethics: A Collection of Addresses & Essays. Henry Sidgwick. 13.75 (ISBN 0-8369-7122-1, 7956). Ayer Co Pubs.

Practical Evaluation. Michael Q. Patton. (Illus.). 320p. 1982. 29.95 (ISBN 0-8039-1904-2); pap. 14.95 (ISBN 0-8039-1905-0). Sage.

Practical Eventing. Sally O'Connor. LC 80-51298. 165p. 1987. pap. 8.00 (ISBN 0-9617826-1-7). USCTA.

Practical Evidence Primer for the Practitioner & Judge. Hamline University, Advanced Legal Education Staff. LC 84-183852. 244p. 1984. 37.10. Hamline Law.

Practical Exercises in Probability & Statistics. N. A. Rahman. 1973. 20.75x (ISBN 0-02-850790-8). Hafner.

Practical Exercises in Probability & Statistics: With Answers & Hints on Solutions. N. A. Rahman. 1972. 26.95 (ISBN 0-85264-217-2). Lubrecht & Cramer.

Practical Experience of Machine Translation. V. Lawson. 200p. 1982. 63.25 (ISBN 0-444-86381-8, North-Holland). Elsevier.

Practical Experience with Shipboard Automation: A Joint Conference Held on March 6, 1974. (Illus.). 58p. 1975. pap. 15.00x (ISBN 0-900976-40-3, Pub. by Inst Marine Eng). Intl Spec Bk.

Practical Experiences of Control & Automation in Wastewater Treatment & Water Resources Management, Vol. 13,8-12. S. H. Jenkins et al. 1982. pap. 180.00 flexi-cover (ISBN 0-08-029086-8). Pergamon.

Practical Experiences with Flow-Induced Vibrations: Symposium Proceedings. Ed. by E. Naudascher & D. Rockwell. (International Association for Hydraulic Research - International Union of Theoretical & Applied Mechanics). (Illus.). 850p. 1980. 82.60 (ISBN 0-387-10314-7). Springer-Verlag.

Practical Experiment Designs for Engineers & Scientists. William J. Diamond. 348p. 1981. text ed. 33.50x (Lifetime Learn). Van Nos Reinhold.

Practical Experiment Designs for Engineers & Scientists. William J. Diamond. 348p. 1981. 41.95 (ISBN 0-534-97992-0). Van Nos Reinhold.

Practical Experimental Design & Optimization Methods for Chemists. C. K. Bayne & I. B. Rubin. (Illus.). 205p. 1986. lib. bdg. 43.00 (ISBN 0-89573-136-3). VCH Pubs.

Practical Export Trade Finance & International Business Credit Management. Eugene W. Perry. 475p. 1988. 50.00 (ISBN 0-317-67955-4). Dow Jones-Irwin.

Practical Farm Buildings: A Text & Handbook. 2nd ed. James S. Boyd. LC 78-179872. 1979. 21.25 (ISBN 0-8134-2054-7, 2054); text ed. 15.95x. Inter Print Pubs.

Practical Farmer: Being a New & Compendious System of Husbandry, Adapted to the Different Soils & Climates of America. John Spurrier. LC 72-89091. (Rural America Ser.). 1973. Repr. of 1793 ed. 32.00 (ISBN 0-8420-1499-3). Scholarly Res Inc.

Practical Fiberoptic Bronchoscopy. 2nd ed. Kenkichi Oho. LC 84-3836. (Illus.). 240p. 1984. 65.00 (ISBN 0-89640-103-0). Igaku-Shoin.

Practical Fiberoptic Colonoscopy. Yoshihiro Sakai. LC 81-80101. (Illus.). 162p. 1981. 46.00 (ISBN 0-89640-053-0). Igaku-Shoin.

Practical Fiberoptic Esophagoscopy. Yoshiya Kumagai. LC 87-4094. (Illus.). 126p. 1987. 65.00 (ISBN 0-89640-129-4). Igaku-Shoin.

Practical Finance on the TRS-80 Model 100. Diane Burns & Sharyn Venit. 1984. pap. 15.95 (ISBN 0-452-25576-7, Plume). NAL.

Practical Financial Management. Richard Dobbins & Stephen Witt. (Illus.). 256p. 1988. text ed. 75.00x (ISBN 0-631-14095-6); pap. text ed. 24.95x (ISBN 0-631-14096-4). Basil Blackwell.

Practical Financial Management: New Techniques for Local Government. Ed. by John Matzer, Jr. (Practical Management Ser.). (Illus.). 207p. 1984. pap. text ed. 21.00 (ISBN 0-87326-043-0). Intl City Mgt.

Practical Financial Manager: Maximizing Cash Flows in Investment & Capital Markets Transactions. 1988. 49.50 (ISBN 0-317-66805-6). Prentice Hall Pr.

Practical Fire & Arson Investigation. J. J. O'Connor. (Elsevier Series in Practical Aspects of Criminal & Forensic Investigation). 400p. 1986. 34.95 (ISBN 0-444-00874-8). Elsevier.

Practical Fishing Knots. Lefty Kreh & Mark Sosin. write for info. (ISBN 0-8329-0246-2). N Lyons Bks.

Practical Flow Cytometry. 2nd ed. Howard M. Shapiro. LC 88-9486. 370p. 1988. 59.50 (ISBN 0-8451-4254-2, 4254). A R Liss.

Practical Fluorescence: Theory, Methods, & Techniques. G. G. Guilbault. 680p. 1973. 115.00 (ISBN 0-8247-1263-3). Dekker.

Practical Fly Fisherman. A. J. McClane. 240p. 1983. pap. 7.95 (ISBN 0-13-689380-5, Reward). P-H.

Practical Folk Medicine of Hawaii. L. R. McBride. (Illus.). 1975. pap. 6.95 (ISBN 0-912180-27-7). Petroglyph.

Practical Food Microbiology & Technology. 3rd ed. G. Mountney. 1987. 59.95 (ISBN 0-442-22688-8). Van Nos Reinhold.

Practical Food Service Spreadsheets with Lotus 1-2-3. Joel Chaban. (Professional Book Ser.). (Illus.). 192p. 1987. 26.95 (ISBN 0-442-21798-6). Van Nos Reinhold.

Practical Forensic Pathology. Charles V. Wetli. LC 87-35275. (Illus.). 160p. 1988. 35.00 (ISBN 0-89640-144-8). Igaku Shoin.

Practical Formulas for Hobby or Profit. Henry Goldschmiedt. (Illus.). 1973. 17.00 (ISBN 0-8206-0235-3). Chem Pub.

Practical Formwork & Mould Construction. 2nd ed. Ed. by J. G. Richardson. (Illus.). xv, 294p. 1976. 52.00 (ISBN 0-85334-629-1, Pub. by Elsevier Applied Sci England). Elsevier.

Practical Four-Shaft Weaving. Vera Miles. (Illus.). 50p. 1979. pap. 5.95 (ISBN 0-85219-128-6, Pub. by Batsford England). David & Charles.

Practical French-English, English-French Dictionary. Rosalind Williams. (Practical Language Dictionaries Ser.). 400p. (Orig., Eng. & Fr.). 1983. pap. 6.95 (ISBN 0-88254-815-8). Hippocrene Bks.

Practical Fungal Physiology. Peter M. Robinson. LC 78-4243. 123p. 1978. pap. 24.95 (ISBN 0-471-99656-4, Pub. by Wiley-Interscience). Wiley.

Practical Fungal Physiology. Peter M. Robinson. LC 78-4243. 131p. pap. 34.10 (2030473). Bks Demand UMI.

Practical Gastroenterology. John R. Bennett. 325p. 1988. pap. text ed. 55.00 (ISBN 0-02-308201-1). Macmillan.

Practical Gemmology. Robert Webster. 216p. 1987. 50.00x (ISBN 0-7198-0131-1, Pub. by E Bruton Assocs Ltd UK). State Mutual Bk.

Practical General Practice. A. Khot & A. Polmear. 320p. 1988. pap. text ed. 39.95 (ISBN 0-407-00473-4). Butterworth.

Practical Genetic Counselling. 2nd ed. Peter S. Harper. (Illus.). 338p. 1984. 34.00 (ISBN 0-7236-0737-0). PSG Pub Co.

Practical Genetics. Ed. by P. M. Sheppard. LC 73-9709. 337p. 1974. text ed. 68.95x (ISBN 0-470-78360-5). Halsted Pr.

Practical Geometry & Engineering Graphics. 8th ed. W. Abbot. (Illus.). 1971. pap. text ed. 23.50x (ISBN 0-216-89450-6). Trans-Atl Phila.

Practical Geometry in the High Middle Ages: "Artis cuiuslibet consummatio" & the "Pratike de geometrie". Stephen K. Victor. LC 78-73170. (Memoirs Ser.: Vol. 134). 1979. 12.00 (ISBN 0-87169-134-5). Am Philos.

Practical Geostatistics. Isobel Clark. (Illus.). 129p. 1979. 38.00 (ISBN 0-85334-843-X, Pub. by Elsevier Applied Sci England). Elsevier.

Practical Geriatric Medicine. Ed. by A. Norman Exton-Smith. Marc E. Weksler. LC 84-21439. (Illus.). 475p. 1985. text ed. 50.00 (ISBN 0-443-02702-1). Churchill.

Practical Geriatric Therapeutics. Sloan. 352p. 1986. pap. 29.95 (ISBN 0-87489-369-0). Med Economics.

Practical Geriatric Therapeutics. Richard W. Sloan. 336p. 1986. 24.95. Soc Tchrs Fam Med.

Practical Geriatrics. Ed. by H. P. Hahn. (Illus.). 448p. 1975. 21.50 (ISBN 3-8055-1768-8). S Karger.

Practical German-English, English-German Dictionary. Stephen Jones. (Practical Language Dictionaries Ser.). 400p. (Orig., Eng. & Ger.). 1983. pap. 6.95 (ISBN 0-88254-813-1). Hippocrene Bks.

Practical German for the Tourist. Cathrine O. Gekker. 1976. perf. bnd. 5.00 (ISBN 0-686-00543-0). Huffman Pr.

Practical Goat-Keeping. John Halliday & Jill Halliday. (Illus.). 104p. 1982. 12.95x (ISBN 0-8464-1290-X). Beekman Pubs.

Practical Goat-Keeping. John Halliday & Jill Halliday. (Illus.). 104p. 1988. pap. 11.95 (ISBN 0-7063-6486-4, Pub. by Ward Lock). David & Charles.

Practical Golf. John Jacobs & Ken Bowden. LC 82-73277. 192p. 1983. pap. 13.95 (ISBN 0-689-70634-0). Atheneum.

Practical Grammar. Betty Pasta. 256p. 1985. pap. text ed. 14.95 (ISBN 0-8403-3721-3). Kendall-Hunt.

Practical Grammar for Classical Hebrew. 2nd ed. Jacob Weingreen. 1959. 15.95x (ISBN 0-19-815422-4). Oxford U Pr.

Practical Grammar of the Arabic Language. F. El-Shidiac. 160p. 1987. pap. 50.00x (ISBN 1-85077-187-1, Pub. by Darf Pubs Ltd). State Mutual Bk.

Practical Grammar of the English Language. Thomas W. Harvey. 1987. 50.00x (ISBN 0-8201-1427-8). Schol Facsimiles.

Practical Grammar: The No-Frills Basics. Peter Hartley. 45p. 1983. pap. 4.98 (ISBN 0-9611790-1-5). Devco Pr.

Practical Greek Magic. Murray Hope. 176p. (Orig.). 1987. pap. 7.99 (ISBN 0-85030-430-X, Pub. by Aquarian Pr England). Sterling.

Practical Guidance for Parents of the Visually Handicapped Preschooler. Patricia L. Maloney. (Illus.). 88p. 1981. spiral bdg. 14.25x (ISBN 0-398-04583-6). C C Thomas.

Practical Guide for Advanced Writers in English As a Second Language. Munsell & Martha Clough. 1984. text ed. write for info. (ISBN 0-02-384910-X). Macmillan.

Practical Guide for Employer & Employee to the Industrial Relations Act, 1971. Alan Pardoe. xx, 319p. 1972. pap. text ed. 6.50x (ISBN 0-85308-024-0). Rothman.

Practical Guide for Foreign Visitors. Ed. by Barbara C. Connotillo. 49p. 1979. 3.50 (ISBN 0-87206-096-9). Inst Intl Educ.

Practical Guide for Handling Drug Crises. Jonathan W. Lehrman et al. 134p. 1980. pap. 15.25x spiral (ISBN 0-398-04100-8). C C Thomas.

Practical Guide for Improving Your Sheet Metal Shop Layout with Easy to Use Suggestions & Aids. Richard S. Budzik. 1988. 29.95 (ISBN 0-912914-23-8). Practical Pubns.

Practical Guide for Instructional Supervision: A tool for Adminstrators & Supervisors. Ed. by Curriculum & Instruction Leaders Committee. 1987. pap. 15.00 (ISBN 0-943397-05-7). Assn Calif Sch Admin.

Practical Guide for Making Decisions. Daniel D. Wheeler & Irving L. Janis. LC 79-6766. 1980. 12.95 (ISBN 0-02-934460-3). Free Pr.

Practical Guide for Mariners English-Italian. F. Picchi. 319p. (Eng. & Ital.). 1980. pap. 29.95 (ISBN 0-686-97444-1, M-9193). French & Eur.

Practical Guide for Notaries Public in Pennsylvania. 20th ed. LC 63-11110. 1985. pap. write for info. Penn Assoc Not.

Practical Guide for Private Investigators. E. R. Smith. 1986. lib. bdg. 79.95 (ISBN 0-8490-3650-X). Gordon Pr.

Practical Guide for Private Investigators. Edward R. Smith. 144p. 1982. pap. 12.00 (ISBN 0-87364-255-4). Paladin Pr.

Practical Guide for Royal Arch Chapter Officers & Companions. rev. ed. Elmer T. Reid. (Illus.). 92p. 1980. Repr. of 1970 ed. softcover 5.50 (ISBN 0-88053-015-4, M-063). Macoy Pub.

Practical Guide for Supervisory Training & Development. 2nd ed. David L. Kirkpatrick. (Illus.). 224p. 1983. text ed. write for info. (ISBN 0-201-13435-7). Addison-Wesley.

Practical Guide for Teachers of Elementary Japanese. Mutsuko E. Simon. LC 83-21075. (Illus.). xvi, 101p. (Orig.). 1984. pap. text ed. 7.00 (ISBN 0-939512-16-5). U MI Japan.

Practical Guide for Teaching & Training Adults. W. Franklin Spikes et al. 1989. lib. bdg. write for info. (ISBN 0-89464-273-1). Krieger.

Practical Guide for the Bilingual Classroom. Berty Segal, Inc. Staff. 80p. 1986. 8.50 (ISBN 0-317-58894-X). B Segal.

Practical Guide for the Bilingual Classroom. 2nd rev., ed. Bertha E. Segal. 80p. (Span. & Eng.). 1987. 8.95 (ISBN 0-938395-07-6). B Segal.

Practical Guide for the Genealogist in England. 2nd ed. Rachael Mellen. (Illus.). viii, 140p. (Orig.). 1987. pap. write for info. (ISBN 1-55613-050-3). Heritage Bk.

Practical Guide for Writing Goals & Objectives. rev. 1981 ed. Fran S. Gelb. LC 73-88787. 112p. 1973. pap. 6.00x (ISBN 0-87879-274-0). Acad Therapy.

Practical Guide in the Use & Implementation of Bibliotherapy. Jacquelyn W. Stephens. 64p. 1981. PLB 6.95 (ISBN 0-89962-045-0). Todd & Honeywell.

Practical Guide to Airplane Performance & Design. Donald R. Crawford. (Illus.). 1981. pap. 18.95 (Pub. by D R Crawford). Aviation.

Practical Guide to Airplane Performance & Design. rev. ed. Donald R. Crawford. LC 81-67801. (Illus.). 222p. 1981. pap. 18.95 (ISBN 0-9603934-0-4). Crawford Aviation.

Practical Guide to Arabic for the Businessman. Atallah & Shilling. 1978. 100.00 (ISBN 0-916400-08-5). Inter Crescent.

Practical Guide to Behavioral Research. 2nd ed. Robert Sommer & Barbara B. Sommer. (Illus.). 1986. text ed. 24.95x (ISBN 0-19-503977-7); pap. text ed. 15.95x (ISBN 0-19-503978-5). Oxford U Pr.

Practical Guide to Better Concentration. Melvin Powers. (Orig.). pap. 3.00 (ISBN 0-87980-120-4). Wilshire.

Practical Guide to Bills of Lading. C. F. Powers. LC 66-29850. 283p. 1966. 20.00 (ISBN 0-379-00329-5). Oceana.

Practical Guide to Book Repair & Conservation. Arthur Johnson. (Illus.). 1988. pap. 14.95 (ISBN 0-500-27518-1). Thames Hudson.

Practical Guide to Box-Jenkins Forecasting. John C. Hoff. (Research Methods Ser.). (Illus.). 316p. 1983. 30.00 (Lifetime Learn). Van Nos Reinhold.

Practical Guide to Box-Jenkins Forecasting. John C. Hoff. 316p. 1983. 36.95 (ISBN 0-534-02719-9). Van Nos Reinhold.

Practical Guide to Breastfeeding. Jan Riordan. LC 82-8225. (Illus.). 384p. 1983. pap. text ed. 22.95 (ISBN 0-8016-4230-2). Mosby.

Practical Guide to Calligraphy. Rosemary Sassoon. (Illus.). 1982. pap. 9.25f (ISBN 0-500-27251-4). Thames Hudson.

Practical Guide to Canvas Work from the Victoria & Albert Museum. Ed. by Linda Parry. LC 87-13990. (Illus.). 72p. 1987. 12.95 (ISBN 1-55562-033-7). Main Street.

Practical Guide to Cardiac Pacing. 2nd ed. H. Weston Moses & George J. Taylor. 149p. 1987. pap. text ed. 17.50 (ISBN 0-316-58556-4). Little.

Practical Guide to Cataract & Lens Implant Surgery. R. S. Bartholomew. (Illus.). 72p. 1987. text ed. 40.00 (ISBN 0-443-03637-3). Churchill.

Practical Guide to Catching More Crappie. Buck Taylor. (Illus.). 238p. (Orig.). 1983. pap. 9.95 (ISBN 0-940022-02-8). Outdoor Skills.

Practical Guide to Christian Living. Michael Scrogin. 144p. 1985. pap. 6.95 (ISBN 0-8170-1053-X). Judson.

Practical Guide to Cleft Lip & Palate Birth Defects: Helpful, Practical Information & Answers for Parents, Physicians, Nurses & Other Professionals. Ed. by Sidney K. Wynn & Alfred L. Miller. (Illus.). 144p. 1984. 20.50 (ISBN 0-398-05024-4). C C Thomas.

Practical Guide to Commercial Credit & Collection. Robert Thompson. Date not set. pap. price not set. (ISBN 0-941161-18-8). PES Inc WI.

Practical Guide to Computer Applications in Neurosciences. Jan Bures & Ivan Krekule. 398p. 1983. 82.95 (ISBN 0-471-10012-9, Pub. by Wiley-Interscience). Wiley.

Practical Guide to Computer Communications & Networking. 2nd ed. R. J. Deasington. LC 84-4617. (Computers & Their Applications Ser.: 1-403). 126p. 1984. pap. text ed. 26.95x (ISBN 0-470-20078-2). Halsted Pr.

Practical Guide to Computer Methods for Engineers. T. Shoup. 1979. 43.00 (ISBN 0-13-690651-6). P-H.

Practical Guide to Computer Programming Management, Vol. 2. Auerbach. pap. 14.95 (ISBN 0-317-64241-3). Van Nos Reinhold.

Practical Guide to Computer Shopping Before You Buy a Computer. Dona Z. Meilach. LC 82-18281. 1983. o. p. 15.95 (ISBN 0-517-54732-5); pap. 8.95 (ISBN 0-517-54733-3). Crown.

Practical Guide to Computer Uses in the English-Language Arts Classroom. William Wresch. (Illus.). 192p. 1987. pap. text ed. 18.00 (ISBN 0-13-690660-5). P-H.

Practical Guide to Conducting Empirical Methods. R. Barker Bausell. 1986. pap. text ed. 22.95 (ISBN 0-06-040542-2, HarpC). Har-Row.

Practical Guide to Construction Lending. Richard Ridloff. LC 84-11833. 1985. 38.95 (ISBN 0-442-28225-7). Van Nos Reinhold.

Practical Guide to Contracts of Affreightment & Hybrid Contracts. Lars Gordon & Rolf Ihre. 1986. 55.00 (ISBN 0-907432-81-6). Lloyds London Pr.

Practical Guide to Counseling the Gifted in a School Setting. Ed. by Joyce VanTassel-Baska. 59p. 1983. pap. 8.00 (ISBN 0-86586-146-3). Coun Exc Child.

Practical Guide to CP-M. Carl Townsend. Ed. by Tim Barry. (CP-M Ser.: No. 2). 250p. 1983. pap. 5.95 (ISBN 0-88056-077-0). Weber Systems.

Practical Guide to Craft Bookbinding. Arthur W. Johnson. LC 84-51825. (Illus.). 125p. 1985. pap. 9.95f (ISBN 0-500-27360-X). Thames Hudson.

Practical Guide to Creative Senility. Donovan Bess. Ed. by Paul M. Clemens. LC 88-9551. (Illus.). 160p. (Orig.). 1988. pap. 9.95 (ISBN 0-931892-16-3). B Dolphin Pub.

Practical Guide to Customer Service Management & Operation. E. Patricia Birsner & Ronald D. Balsley. 224p. 1982. 19.95 (ISBN 0-8144-5673-1). AMACOM.

Practical Guide to Customer Service Management & Operations. E. Patricia Birsner & Ronald D. Balsley. LC 81-69366. pap. 56.00 (ISBN 0-317-26242-4, 2052140). Bks Demand UMI.

Practical Guide to Data Base Management, Vol. 4. Auerbach. pap. 14.95 (ISBN 0-317-64242-1). Van Nos Reinhold.

Practical Guide to Data Center Operations Management, Vol. 6. Auerbach. pap. 14.95 (ISBN 0-317-64243-X). Van Nos Reinhold.

Practical Guide to Data Processing Management, Vol. 1. Auerbach. pap. 14.95 (ISBN 0-317-64244-8). Van Nos Reinhold.

Practical Guide to DBMS Selection. Lindsay Peat. 340p. 1982. 67.50x (ISBN 3-11-008167-9). De Gruyter.

Practical Guide to Death & Dying: Conquer Fear & Anxiety Through a Program of Personal Action. 2nd ed. John White. LC 88-40134. 226p. 1988. pap. 7.50 (ISBN 0-8356-0633-3). Theos Pub Hse.

Practical Guide to Designing Expert Systems. Sholom M. Weiss & Casimir A. Kulikowski. (Illus.). 186p. 1984. text ed. 29.95x (ISBN 0-86598-108-6, Rowman & Allanheld). Rowman.

Practical Guide to Digital Integrated Circuits. 2nd ed. Alfred W. Barber. LC 83-21208. (Illus.). 1984. 24.95 (ISBN 0-13-690751-2, Busn). P-H.

Practical Guide to Discrimination Law. Michael Malone. 292p. 1980. 40.00x (ISBN 0-86360-002-6, Pub. by R Anderson Pubns Ltd). State Mutual Bk.

Practical Guide to Distributed Processing Management, Vol. 8. Auerbach. pap. 14.95 (ISBN 0-317-64245-6). Van Nos Reinhold.

Practical Guide to Divorce in Hawaii. Peter J. Herman. LC 85-20125. 160p. 1986. pap. 7.95 (ISBN 0-8248-1016-3). Uh Pr.

Practical Guide to Document Authentication: Legalization of Notarized & Certified Documents. John P. Sinnott. One binder 100.00. Oceana.

Practical Guide to Document Authentication: Legalization of Notarized & Certified Documents. John P. Sinnott. LC 83-22023. 1984. 1 bdr. looseleaf 100.00 (ISBN 0-379-20832-6). Oceana.

Practical Guide to Early Childhood Curriculum. 3rd ed. Claudia Eliason & Loa Jenkins. 425p. 1986. pap. text ed. 23.95 (ISBN 0-675-20572-7). Merrill.

Practical Guide to Edible & Useful Plants. Delena Tull. LC 86-30076. (Illus.). 400p. 1987. 23.95 (ISBN 0-87719-022-4). Texas Month Pr.

Practical Guide to EDP Auditing Managment, Vol. 7. Auerbach. pap. 14.95 (ISBN 0-317-64246-4). Van Nos Reinhold.

Practical Guide to Educational Research. Ward M. Cates. (Illus.). 224p. 1985. pap. text ed. 18.25 (ISBN 0-13-690678-8). P-H.

Practical Guide to Environmental Law. Ed. by Frank B. Friedman & David Sive. 425p. 1987. 65.00 (ISBN 0-8318-0520-X, B520). Am Law Inst.

Practical Guide to Enzymology. Clarence H. Suelter. (Biochemistry Ser.). (Illus.). 1985. 45.00 (ISBN 0-471-86431-5). Wiley.

Practical Guide to Equal Employment Opportunity, 2 vols. Walter B. Connolly, Jr. & Michael J. Connolly. 1100p. 1979. Set. looseleaf 95.00 (ISBN 0-318-20278-6, 00527). NY Law Pub.

Practical Guide to Equal Employment Opportunity, 2 vols. Walter B. Connolly, Jr. & Michael J. Connolly. 1100p. 1979. 95.00. NY Law Pub.

Practical Guide to Etching & Other Intaglio Printmaking Techniques. Manly Banister. 128p. 1986. pap. 5.95 (ISBN 0-486-25165-9). Dover.

Practical Guide to Etching & Other Intaglio Printmaking Techniques. Manly Banister. 15.75 (ISBN 0-8446-6281-X). Peter Smith.

Practical Guide to European Travel. M. N. Polfen. 200p. 1981. pap. 7.95 (ISBN 0-934036-07-1). PMF Research.

Practical Guide to Financial Management of the Clinical Laboratory. 2nd ed. Janice Sattler & S. Alice Smith. 176p. 1986. pap. text ed. 27.95 (ISBN 0-87489-415-8). Med Economics.

Practical Guide to Financial Management: Tips & Techniques for the Non-Financial Manager. Michael M. Coltman. 160p. 1984. pap. 6.95 (ISBN 0-88908-600-1, 9531). ISC Pr.

Practical Guide to Finding & Using Your Spiritual Gifts. Tim Blanchard. 1983. pap. 6.95 (ISBN 0-8423-4898-0). Tyndale.

Practical Guide to Fluid Inclusion Studies. T. J. Shepherd et al. (Illus.). 224p. 1985. 59.95 (ISBN 0-412-00601-4, 9023). Routledge Chapman & Hall.

Practical Guide to Foster Family Care. Bert L. Kaplan & Martin Seitz. 112p. 1980. 14.25 (ISBN 0-398-04033-8). C C Thomas.

Practical Guide to Fourth Generation Programming Languages. Jeff Bernknopf. (Illus.). 320p. 1988. 39.95 (ISBN 0-07-004960-2). McGraw.

Practical Guide to Free Tissue Transfer. Martin H. Webster & David S. Soutar. (Illus.). 144p. 1986. text ed. 49.95 (ISBN 0-407-00243-X). Butterworth.

Practical Guide to French Pronunciation. H. S. McKellar. pap. 39.30 (2026531). Bks Demand UMI.

Practical Guide to Graduate Research. M. Stock. 176p. 1985. text ed. 14.95 (ISBN 0-07-061583-7). McGraw.

Practical Guide to Grand Opera. M. N. Polfen. 200p. (Orig.). 1981. pap. 7.95 (ISBN 0-934036-08-X). PMF Research.

Practical Guide to Handling IRS Income Tax Audits. Ralph L. Guyette. LC 86-4905. Date not set. 39.95 (ISBN 0-13-690876-4). P-H.

Practical Guide to Health Assessment. Hogstel. 1988. pap. write for info. (ISBN 0-471-60722-3). Wiley.

Practical Guide to Hearing Aid Usage. Alfred L. Miller. (Illus.). 88p. 1988. text ed. 19.75x (ISBN 0-398-05430-4). C C Thomas.

Practical Guide to Helping Children with Speech & Language Problems: For Parents & Teachers Only. Carol G. Rousey. 100p. 1984. 20.50 (ISBN 0-398-04947-5). C C Thomas.

Practical Guide to High-Risk Pregnancy & Delivery. Arias. (Illus.). 520p. 1989. 35.95 (ISBN 0-8016-0057-X). Mosby.

Practical Guide to Holistic Health. Swami Rama. 152p. pap. 6.95 (ISBN 0-89389-065-0). Himalayan Pubs.

Practical Guide to Home Landscaping. Reader's Digest Editors. LC 72-157525. (Illus.). 479p. 1972. 23.95 (ISBN 0-89577-005-9, Pub. by RD Assn). Random.

Practical Guide to Horseshoeing. pap. 5.00 (ISBN 0-87980-239-1). Wilshire.

Practical Guide to Import-Export. Arthur C. Simon. LC 78-55996. (Illus.). 1978. softcover 12.95 (ISBN 0-930490-14-2). Future Shop.

Practical Guide to In-Service Teacher Training in Africa: Establishment, Execution and Control of Training Programmes. 81p. (Orig.). 1970. pap. 5.00 (ISBN 92-3-100812-9, U475, UNESCO). UNIPUB.

Practical Guide to Independent Living for Older People. Alice H. Phillips & Caryl K. Roman. LC 84-95150. (Illus.). 140p. (Orig.). 1984. pap. 6.95 (ISBN 0-914718-92-4). Pacific Search.

Practical Guide to Integral Yoga. 7th ed. Sri Aurobindo. Ed. by Manibhai. 1979. pap. 9.00 (ISBN 0-89744-942-8). Auromere.

Practical Guide to Integral Yoga. Sri Aurobindo. (Illus.). 1985. (ISBN 0-89071-217-4); pap. 6.50. Aurobindo Assn.

Practical Guide to Integrated Circuits. 2nd ed. Alfred W. Barber. write for info. P-H.

Practical Guide to Interactive Video Design. Nicholas V. Iuppa. LC 84-7872. (Video Bookshelf Ser.). 135p. 1984. professional 39.95 (ISBN 0-86729-041-2). Knowledge Indus.

Practical Guide to Introducing Evidence: Basic Foundations & Objections. Harold W. Potter, Jr. & Paul E. Troy. LC 86-72608. 203p. 1987. looseleaf 50.00 (ISBN 0-944490-02-6). Mass CLE.

Practical Guide to Japanese Signs: Especially for Newcomers. Tae Moriyama. LC 86-45788. 200p. (Orig.). 1987. pap. 9.95 (ISBN 0-87011-790-4). Kodansha.

Practical Guide to Japanese Signs: Making Life Easier. 2nd part ed. Tae Moriyama. LC 86-45788. 200p. (Orig.). 1987. pap. 9.95 (ISBN 0-87011-791-2). Kodansha.

Practical Guide to Kashruth. 1982. 8.95 (ISBN 0-686-76247-9); pap. 6.95. Feldheim.

Practical Guide to Language Testing. Grant Henning. 200p. 1987. pap. text ed. 18.50 (ISBN 0-06-632277-4). Newbury Hse.

Practical Guide to Legal Issues Affecting College Teachers. Patricia A. Hollander. Ed. by D. Parker Young & Donald D. Gehring. LC 85-16644. (Higher Education Administration Ser.). 41p. (Orig.). 1985. pap. 4.95 (ISBN 0-912557-02-8). Coll Admin Pubns.

Practical Guide to Legal Malpractice: When the Client Sues the Lawyer. Hilton L. Stein. 150p. 1988. 29.95 (ISBN 0-945163-00-2). Legal Malpractice.

Practical Guide to Legal Writing & Legal Method. John C. Dernbach & Richard V. Singleton, II. xviii, 246p. 1981. pap. text ed. 12.50x (ISBN 0-8377-0513-4). Rothman.

Practical Guide to Lettering & Applied Calligraphy. Rosemary Sassoon. LC 84-52181. (Illus.). 150p. (Orig.). 1986. pap. 10.95f (ISBN 0-500-27366-9). Thames Hudson.

Practical Guide to Living & Travel in the Arab World. N. A. Shilling. LC 78-70799. 1978. 35.00 (ISBN 0-916400-03-4). Inter-Crescent.

Practical Guide to Local Area Networks. Rowland Archer. (Illus.). 250p. (Orig.). 1986. pap. text ed. 21.95 (ISBN 0-07-881190-2). Osborne-Mcgraw.

Practical Guide to Management of the Painful Neck & Back: Diagnosis, Manipulation, Exercises, Prevention. James W. Fisk. (Illus.). 248p. 1977. photocopy ed. 32.50x (ISBN 0-398-03640-3). C C Thomas.

Practical Guide to Marbling Paper. Anne Chambers. LC 86-70729. (Illus.). 96p. (Orig.). 1986. pap. 14.95 (ISBN 0-500-27421-5). Thames Hudson.

Practical Guide to Market Research. Bank Administration Institute Staff. 52p. 1983. 42.00 (ISBN 0-317-36436-7, 356). Bank Admin Inst.

Practical Guide to Michigan Law. Fred S. Steingold. LC 82-10965. (Illus.). 184p. 1983. pap. 12.95 (ISBN 0-472-06341-3). U of Mich Pr.

Practical Guide to Microbial & Parasitic Diseases. Gerhard H. Schwebach. (Illus.). 256p. 1980. spiral bdg. 28.25 (ISBN 0-398-03980-1). C C Thomas.

Practical Guide to Molecular Cloning. Bernard Perbal. 554p. 1984. 64.50x (ISBN 0-471-87652-6, Pub. by Wiley-Interscience); pap. 39.50x (ISBN 0-471-87653-4). Wiley.

Practical Guide to Molecular Cloning. 2nd ed. Bernard Prebal. 1988. 800p. 99.50, (ISBN 0-471-85071-3); pap. 49.50, 811p. (ISBN 0-471-85070-5). Wiley.

Practical Guide to Newsletter Editing & Design: Instructions for Printing by Mimeograph or Offset for the Inexperienced Editor. 2nd ed. LaRae H. Wales. LC 76-1753. (Illus.). 52p. pap. 20.00 (2029778). Bks Demand UMI.

Practical Guide to Obtaining Permanent Residence in Australia. 2nd ed. Adrian Joel. vii, 91p. 1986. pap. text ed. 14.50 (ISBN 0-949553-13-1, Pub by Legal Bks.). W W Gaunt.

Practical Guide to Open Shop Construction. 71p. 1982. 9.00 (ISBN 0-318-17988-1). Assn Gen Con.

Practical Guide to Owning Your Own Horse. Steven D. Price. pap. 3.00. Borden.

Practical Guide to Owning Your Own Horse. Steven D. Price. 1974. pap. 3.00 (ISBN 0-87980-292-8). Wilshire.

Practical Guide to Package Holiday Law & Contracts. John Nelson-Jones & Peter Stewart. 1987. 120.00x (ISBN 1-85190-041-1, Pub. by Fourmat England). State Mutual Bk.

Practical Guide to Parliamentary Procedure. 2nd ed. Edward Strother & David Shepard. 68p. 1983. pap. text ed. 7.95x (ISBN 0-89917-380-2). Tichenor Pub.

Practical Guide to Past-Life Regression. Florence W. McClain. LC 85-45285. (Psi-Tech Ser.). 176p. (Orig.). 1986. pap. 7.95 (ISBN 0-87542-510-0, L-510). Llewellyn Pubns.

Practical Guide to Patchwork from the Victoria & Albert Museum. Ed. by Linda Parry. LC 87-14163. (Illus.). 72p. 1987. 12.95 (ISBN 1-55562-032-9). Main Street.

Practical Guide to Patent Law. Brian C. Reid. 1987. 125.00x (Pub. by ESC Ltd UK); pap. 95.00x (ISBN 0-906214-15-7, Pub. by ESC Ltd UK). State Mutual Bk.

Practical Guide to Pediatric Intensive Care. 2nd ed. Ed. by Daniel L. Levin & Frances C. Morriss. (Illus.). 569p. 1984. pap. 38.95 (ISBN 0-8016-3010-X). Mosby.

Practical Guide to Performance-Based Instruction: How to Develop the Skills of Attaining Classroom Objectives. new ed. Paul Kahn. LC 75-3717. (Patterns of Teacher Competency Ser: Structure & Modern Classroom: Vol.1). (Illus.). 80p. 1975. wkbk. 4.95 (ISBN 0-914394-02-9). Microbim.

Practical Guide to Photographing American Wildlife. Joe McDonald. (Illus.). 170p. 1983. pap. 6.36 cancelled (ISBN 0-9613246-0-0). Foxy Owl Pubns.

Practical Guide to Photographing American Wildlife. 2nd ed. Joe McDonald. LC 84-128754. (Illus.). 190p. 1984. pap. 9.95x (ISBN 0-9613246-1-9). Foxy Owl Pubns.

Practical Guide to Physican-Sponsored HMO Development. Eric R. Wagner & Valerie J. Hackenberg. 64p. 1986. 15.00 (ISBN 0-317-47278-X). Am Soc Intern Med.

Practical Guide to Planning a Family Reunion. Emma J. Wisdom. LC 88-90539. (Illus., Orig.). 1988. pap. 8.95x (ISBN 0-9620115-0-9). Post Oak Pubns.

Practical Guide to Plant Environmental Audits. Blakeslee. 1985. 38.95 (ISBN 0-442-21421-9). Van Nos Reinhold.

Practical Guide to Police Report Writing. Tom E. Kakonis & Donald Hanzek. 1977. pap. 29.95 (ISBN 0-07-033246-0). McGraw.

Practical Guide to Positive Reinforcement: How to Develop the Skills of Behavior Modification in the Classroom. new ed. Paul Kahn. LC 75-14951. (Patterns of Teacher Competency Ser.: Structure & the Modern Classroom: Vol. 2). (Illus.). 80p. 1975. wkbk. 4.95 (ISBN 0-914394-03-7). Microbim.

Practical Guide to Preventing Legal Malpractice. Duke Stern et al. 436p. 1983. text ed. 90.00 (ISBN 0-07-061192-0). Shepards-McGraw.

Practical Guide to Prize Winning Photography. David Davenport. (Practical Photography Ser.: No. 2). (Illus.). 160p. 1987. 29.95 (Oxford Ill Pr). Haynes Pubns.

Practical Guide to Productivity Measurement. Leon Greenberg. LC 73-75981. pap. 20.00 (2026794). Bks Demand UMI.

Practical Guide to Program Planning: A Teaching Models Approach. Adrianne Bank et al. LC 81-959. (Orig.). 1981. pap. 16.95x (ISBN 0-8077-2641-9). Tchrs Coll.

Practical Guide to Psychodiagnostic Testing. Lawrence Katz. 216p. 1985. 27.00x (ISBN 0-398-05118-6). C C Thomas.

Practical Guide to Public Speaking. Maurice Forley. pap. 5.00 (ISBN 0-87980-121-2). Wilshire.

Practical Guide to Qabalistic Symbolism. Gareth Knight. 1978. 25.00 (ISBN 0-87728-397-4). Weiser.

Practical Guide to Real-Time Office Sonography in Obstetrics & Gynecology. Robert V. Giglia et al. LC 85-12033. 236p. 1986. spiral bound 45.00x (ISBN 0-306-41865-7, Plenum Pr). Plenum Pub.

Practical Guide to Remics. rev. ed. Kenneth G. Lore & Kyllikki Kusma. (Illus.). 246p. 1988. pap. 48.00 (ISBN 0-945359-50-0). Mortgage Bankers.

Practical Guide to Research Methods. 3rd ed. Gerhard Lang & George D. Heiss. LC 83-23343. 206p. (Orig.). 1984. lib. bdg. 32.25 (ISBN 0-8191-3725-1); pap. text ed. 18.75 (ISBN 0-8191-3726-X). U Pr of Amer.

Practical Guide to Research Papers. James P. Farrelly & Lorraine M. Murphy. 280p. 1988. pap. text ed. 8.00 (ISBN 0-15-571033-8). HarBraceJ.

Practical Guide to Respirator Usage in Industry. David S. Blackwell & G. S. Rajhans. (Illus.). 144p. 1985. pap. text ed. 27.95 (ISBN 0-250-40477-X). Butterworth.

Practical Guide to Screen Printing. Merrill Green. LC 84-71004. (Illus.). 96p. 1984. write for info. (ISBN 0-9613500-0-8). Adv Group.

Practical Guide to Selecting Small Business Computers. Philip M. Wolfe et al. 1982. pap. text ed. 16.00 (ISBN 0-89806-033-8). Inst Indus Eng.

Practical Guide to Self-Hypnosis. Melvin Powers. (Orig.). 1960. pap. 3.00 (ISBN 0-87980-122-0). Wilshire.

Practical Guide to Sermon Preparation. Jerry Vines. 1985. 11.95 (ISBN 0-8024-6744-X). Moody.

Practical Guide to Small Computers for Business & Professional Use. rev. ed. Robert M. Rinder. 288p. 1983. pap. 11.95 (ISBN 0-671-47091-4). Monarch Pr.

Practical Guide to Solving Preschool Behavior Problems. Eva Essa. LC 82-70426. (Illus.). 288p. (Orig.). 1983. pap. text ed. 14.95 (ISBN 0-8273-2082-5). Delmar.

Practical Guide to Soul Winning. Charles Crane. LC 87-72712. 248p. 1988. pap. 6.95 (ISBN 0-89900-220-X). College Pr Pub.

Practical Guide to Spiritual Reading. Susan Muto. 9.95 (ISBN 0-87193-046-3). Dimension Bks.

Practical Guide to Splines. C. De Boor. (Applied Mathematical Sciences Ser.: Vol. 27). (Illus.). 1978. pap. 32.00 (ISBN 0-387-90356-9). Springer-Verlag.

Practical Guide to Statistical Intervals. Hahn. (Probability & Mathematical Statistics Ser.). 1988. write for info. (ISBN 0-471-88769-2). Wiley.

Practical Guide to Structured Systems Design. Meilir Page-Jones. LC 79-67259. (Illus.). 368p. (Orig.). 1980. pap. 29.95 (ISBN 0-917072-17-0, Yourdon). P-H.

Practical Guide to Structured Systems Design. 2nd ed. Meilir Page-Jones. (Illus.). 384p. 1988. pap. text ed. 35.00 (ISBN 0-13-690769-5). P-H.

Practical Guide to Successful Interviewing. Philip Hodgson. 104p. 1987. pap. text ed. 8.95 (ISBN 0-07-084941-2). McGraw.

Practical Guide to Systems Development Management, Vol. 5. Auerbach. pap. 14.95 (ISBN 0-317-64247-2). Van Nos Reinhold.

Practical Guide to Tax Shelter Litigation. Edward Brodsky. 1982. looseleaf 70.00 (ISBN 0-318-20292-1, 00577). NY Law Pub.

Practical Guide to Tax Shelter Litigation. Edward Brodsky. 600p. 1985. looseleaf 70.00 (ISBN 0-318-21434-2, 00577). NY Law Pub.

Practical Guide to Teaching in Four Dimensions: How to Develop the Skills of Reaching the Whole Child. Paul Kahn. LC 85-30222. (Patterns of Teacher Competency Ser.: Structure of the Modern Classroom: Vol.3). (Illus.). 80p. 1975. wkbk 4.95 (ISBN 0-914394-04-5). Microbim.

Practical Guide to Teletraffic Engineering & Administration. Robert W. Lawson. 128p. 20.00 (ISBN 0-317-06282-4). Intertec IL.

Practical Guide to the Anatomy & Physiology of Pacific Salmon. (Illus.). 14p. 1975. pap. 5.00 (SSC69, SSC). UNIPUB.

Practical Guide to the Basics of Physical Evidence: A Reference Text for the Criminalist, Investigator, Student & Attorney. Claude W. Cook. (Illus.). 288p. 1984. 32.75x (ISBN 0-398-04933-5). C C Thomas.

Practical Guide to the BPI Accounting System. Dale N. Flanagan. (Illus.). 224p. 1986. 21.95 (ISBN 0-8306-0396-4, 2696). TAB Bks.

Practical Guide to the Cable Communications Policy Act of 1984. Practising Law Institute Staff & George R.. Dorsari. LC 85-196289. (Patents, Copyrights, Trademarks, & Literary Property Course Handbooks: No. 200). 1985. 15.00 (G43771). PLI.

Practical Guide to the Care of the Medical Patient. Ferri. (Illus.). 450p. 1987. 21.95 (ISBN 0-8016-1661-1). Mosby.

Practical Guide to the Care of the Surgical Patient. 3rd ed. McEntyre. 1989. spiral bdg. 21.00. Mosby.

Practical Guide to the Care of the Surgical Patient. 2nd ed. Robert L. McEntyre. (Illus.). 290p. 1984. pap. 22.00 (ISBN 0-8016-3211-0). Mosby.

Practical Guide to the Child Behavior Checklist & Related Materials. Stephanie H. McConaughy & Thomas H. Achenbach. LC 87-73078. (Illus.). 140p. (Orig.). 1988. pap. 14.30 (ISBN 0-938565-03-6). U of VT Psych.

Practical Guide to the Comprehensive Crime Control Act of 1984. B. James George. 1985. 55.00 (ISBN 0-317-29417-2, #H43864, Pub. by Law & Business). HarBraceJ.

Practical Guide to the IBM Personal Computer AT. Dennis L. Foster. LC 85-1249. 1985. write for info. (ISBN 0-201-12040-2). Addison-Wesley.

Practical Guide to the Law of Secured Lending. Eric M. Holmes & Peter J. Shedd. LC 85-25568. 1986. 59.95 (ISBN 0-13-690942-6, Busn). P-H.

Practical Guide to the Legal & Appraisal Aspects of Condemnation. Ed. by Sidney Z. Searles. 485p. 1969. pap. 3.00 (ISBN 0-317-30758-4, B251). Am Law Inst.

Practical Guide to the MMPI: An Introduction for Psychologists, Physicians, Social Workers, & Other Professionals. Patricia K. Good & John Brantner. 1974. 10.95 (ISBN 0-8166-0706-0). U of Minn Pr.

Practical Guide to the New York Equitable Distribution Divorce Law. Ed. by Henry H. Foster, Jr. 771p. 1980. 35.00 (ISBN 0-686-89094-9, C00566, Law & Business). HarBraceJ.

Practical Guide to the Occupational Safety & Health Act. Walter B. Connolly, Jr. & Donald R. Crowell. 650p. 1982. 60.00 (00578). NY Law Pub.

Practical Guide to the Persian Alphabet. Ahmad Jabbari. LC 83-50569. (Illus.). 74p. (Orig.). 1983. pap. text ed. 6.50 (ISBN 0-939214-12-1). Mazda Pubs.

Practical Guide to the Proposed OID Regulations. David C. Garlock. LC 87-6990. Date not set. price not set (ISBN 0-15-004431-3). P-H.

Practical Guide to the Structure of English for the English Teacher. Joe E. Pierce. LC 87-80359. 100p. (Orig.). 1987. pap. 7.95 (ISBN 0-913244-67-8). Hapi Pr.

Practical Guide to the Tax Act of 1984. Ed. by Law & Business Inc. Staff. LC 84-27795. 243p. 1985. 60.00 (ISBN 0-15-004375-9, Law & Business). HarBraceJ.

Practical Guide to the Teaching of English As a Foreign Language. Robert J. Dixson. 1975. pap. text ed. 4.25 (ISBN 0-13-691032-7, 18132). Prentice ESL.

Practical Guide to the Teaching of English: As a Second or Foreign Language. Wilga M. Rivers & Mary S. Temperley. 1978. pap. 10.95x (ISBN 0-19-502210-6). Oxford U Pr.

Practical Guide to the Teaching of French. Wilga Rivers. 1975. pap. text ed. 9.95x (ISBN 0-19-501911-3). Oxford U Pr.

Practical Guide to the Teaching of German. Wilga Rivers et al. 1975. pap. text ed. 9.95x (ISBN 0-19-501910-5). Oxford U Pr.

Practical Guide to the Understanding of Architecture. J. C. Squire. (Illus.). 221p. 1986. 137.15 (ISBN 0-86650-198-3). Gloucester Art.

Practical Guide to the UNIX System. Mark G. Sobell. 1984. 25.95 (ISBN 0-8053-8910-5, 38910). Benjamin-Cummings.

Practical Guide to the UNIX System V. Mark G. Sobell. 1985. 30.25 (ISBN 0-8053-8915-6). Benjamin Cummings.

Practical Guide to Timetabling. Roger Simper. 176p. 30.00x (ISBN 0-7062-4064-2, Pub. by Ward Lock Educ Co Ltd). State Mutual Bk.

Practical Guide to Trade Marks. Amanda M. Barrister. 216p. 1982. 39.00x (ISBN 0-686-97894-3, Pub. by ESC Pub England). State Mutual Bk.

Practical Guide to Trade Marks. Amanda Michaels. 1987. 125.00x (ISBN 0-906214-12-2, Pub. by ESC Ltd UK); pap. 95.00x (ISBN 0-906214-09-2, Pub. by ESC Ltd UK). State Mutual Bk.

Practical Guide to Travel Photography. Philip Dunn. (Illus.). 144p. 1986. 29.95 (ISBN 0-946609-26-8, Pub. by Oxford Ill Pr). Haynes Pubns.

Practical Guide to Ultrasound in Obstetrics & Gynecology. Eric E. Sauerbrei et al. (Illus.). 200p. 1987. pap. text ed. 28.00 (ISBN 0-88167-268-8). Raven.

Practical Guide to UNIX. 2nd ed. Mark G. Sobell. (Illus.). 550p. 1988. text ed. 27.95 (ISBN 0-8053-0243-3). Benjamin-Cummings.

Practical Guide to Urban & Environmental Movies: Educational Orientation, No. 780. rev. ed. Ed. by Ambrose Klain & Dennis M. Phelan. 1975. 5.00 (ISBN 0-686-20349-6). CPL Biblios.

Practical Guide to Voice Mail. Martin F. Parker. (Illus.). 250p. 1986. pap. text ed. 24.95 (ISBN 0-07-881243-7). Osborne-McGraw.

Practical Guide to Working in an Equipment Rental Business. Dick Detmer. 114p. 1986. pap. 15.00. Am Rent Assn.

Practical Guide to Writing. 5th ed. Sylvan Barnet & Marcia Stubbs. 1986. pap. text ed. write for info. (ISBN 0-673-39189-2). Scott F.

Practical Guide to Writing & Publishing Professional Books: Business, Technical, Scientific, Scholarly. Daniel N. Fischel. 300p. 1984. 33.95 (ISBN 0-442-22482-6). Van Nos Reinhold.

Practical Guide to Writing with Additional Readings. 5th ed. Sylvan Barnet & Marcia Stubbs. 1986. pap. text ed. write for info.; 0.00. Scott F.

Practical Guide to Your Unemployment Insurance Rates. Howard Dressman. 76p. 1984. pap. 4.95 (ISBN 0-317-70028-6). H Dressman.

Practical Guidelines for Better Living. Don Nedd. 58p. 1983. pap. 3.00 (ISBN 0-317-20877-2). CSA Pr.

Practical Guidelines for Statistical Monitoring of Fisheries in Manpower Limited Situations. J. F. Caddy & G. P. Bazigos. (Fisheries Technical Papers: No. 257). 86p. 1985. pap. 7.50 (ISBN 92-5-102256-9, F2784 6011, FAO). UNIPUB.

Practical Guidelines for the Selection, Design & Installation of Piles: Committee on Deep Foundations of the Geotechnical Engineering Division. 105p. 1984. 13.00x (ISBN 0-87262-403-X). Am Soc Civil Eng.

Practical Guidelines for Understanding, Management & Treatment of Eating & Mood Disorders. Felix Larocca. 250p. 1989. 27.50 (ISBN 0-912791-53-5). Ishiyaku Euro.

Practical Gynerologic Oncology. Jonathan Berek. 640p. 1988. 60.00 (ISBN 0-683-00598-7). Williams & Wilkins.

Practical Handbook & Guide to Focus Group Research. Thomas L. Greenbaum. LC 86-45946. 208p. 1987. 39.95x (ISBN 0-669-14775-3). Lexington Bks.

Practical Handbook for College Teachers. Babara S. Fuhrmann & Anthony F. Grasha. 315p. 1983. text ed. 30.75; pap. text ed. 14.25 (ISBN 0-673-39151-5). Scott F.

Practical Handbook for Software Development. N. D. Birrell & M. A. Ould. (Illus.). 259p. 1988. pap. 22.95 (ISBN 0-521-34792-0). Cambridge U Pr.

Practical Handbook for the Treatment of Depression. D. Kelly. (Illus.). 250p. 1987. 45.00 (ISBN 0-940813-12-2). Parthenon NJ.

Practical Handbook for Underground Rock Mechanics. T. R. Stacey & C. H. Page. (Series on Rock & Soil Mechanics: Vol. 12). 150p. 1986. text ed. 24.00x (ISBN 0-87849-056-6, Trans Tech Germany). Trans Tech.

Practical Handbook of Amateur Radio FM & Repeaters. Bill Pasternak. (Illus., Orig.). 1980. pap. 12.95 (ISBN 0-8306-1212-2, 1212). TAB Bks.

Practical Handbook of Basic Letter, Memo & Report Formats. Peter Hartley. (Illus.). 136p. 1982. pap. 24.95 (ISBN 0-9611790-0-7). Devco Pr.

Practical Handbook of British Beetles. N. H. Joy. 622p. 1932. 65.00x (ISBN 0-317-07170-X, Pub. by FW Classey Uk). State Mutual Bk.

Practical Handbook of Ceramic Art with Important Technological Notes. Wiley J. Granville. (Illus.). 149p. 1980. 117.75 (ISBN 0-930582-85-3). Gloucester Art.

Practical Handbook of Distribution-Customer Service. Warren Blanding. Ed. by Leslie Harps. (Illus.). 584p. 1985. 40.00 (ISBN 0-87408-033-9). Intl Thom Trans Pr.

Practical Handbook of Industrial Traffic Management. 6th ed. Leon W. Morse. LC 77-9240. 532p. 1980. text ed. 32.50 (ISBN 0-87408-020-7). Intl Thom Trans Pr.

Practical Handbook of Joint Fluid Analysis. Robert A. Gatter. LC 83-18704. (Illus.). 1984. text ed. 22.50 (ISBN 0-8121-0902-3). Lea & Febiger.

Practical Handbook of Modern Library Cataloging. William W. Bishop. (Library Science Ser.). 1980. lib. bdg. 59.95 (ISBN 0-8490-3179-6). Gordon Pr.

Practical Handbook of Plant Alchemy: How to Prepare Medicinal Essences, Tinctures & Elixirs. Manfred M. Junius. (Illus.). 272p. (Orig.). 1985. pap. 12.95 (ISBN 0-89281-060-2). Inner Tradit.

Practical Handbook of Private Trucking. Colin Barrett. LC 83-50039. 208p. 1983. 26.00 (ISBN 0-87408-026-6). Intl Thom Trans Pr.

Practical Handbook of Quebec & Acadian French. Sinclair Robinson & Donald Smith. 256p. (Orig.). 1984. pap. 14.95 (ISBN 0-88784-137-6, Pub. by Hse Anansi Pr Canada). U of Toronto Pr.

Practical Handbook of Seawater Analysis. 2nd ed. pap. 18.75 (SSC70, SSC). UNIPUB.

Practical Handbook of Solid State Troubleshooting. Robert C. Genn. (Illus.). 1984. pap. 12.95 (ISBN 0-13-691295-8, Busn). P-H.

Practical Handbook of Solid State Troubleshooting. Robert C. Genn, Jr. LC 80-23897. 256p. 1981. 12.95 (ISBN 0-13-691303-2, Parker). P-H.

Practical Handbook of Spanish Commercial Correspondence. Fletcher R. Wickham. LC 43-12208. 1943. text ed. 3.50x (ISBN 0-911090-27-4). Pacific Bk Supply.

Practical Handbook of Stage Lighting & Sound. W. Edmund Hood. LC 85-19730. 304p. 1988. Repr. of 1981 ed. lib. bdg. write for info. (ISBN 0-89874-901-8). Krieger.

Practical Handbook of Warehousing. 2nd ed. Kenneth B. Ackerman. 1985. 40.00 (ISBN 0-87408-036-3). Intl Thom Trans Pr.

Practical Handbook on Stress in the Russian Language. V. Klepko. 1985. 9.50 (ISBN 0-87557-072-0). Saphrograph.

Practical Handgun Ballistics. photocopy ed. M. Williams. (Illus.). 232p. 1980. 25.25 (ISBN 0-398-04032-X). C C Thomas.

Practical Hardware Details for 8080, 8085, Z80, & 6800 Microprocessor Systems. James W. Coffron. (Illus.). 352p. 1981. text ed. 39.00 (ISBN 0-13-691089-0). P-H.

Practical Harmonics. Delphine Jay. LC 83-70793. 104p. 1983. 9.00 (ISBN 0-86690-237-6, 2304-01). Am Fed Astrologers.

Practical Harmonist at the Harpsichord. Francesco Gasparini. Ed. by David L. Burrows. Tr. by Frank S. Stillings from Ital. LC 79-26854. (Music Reprint Ser.: 1980). (Illus.). 1980. Repr. of 1963 ed. lib. bdg. 27.50 (ISBN 0-306-76017-7). Da Capo.

Practical Hematology. William G. Hocking. LC 82-20087. (Family Practice Today: A Comprehensive Postgraduate Library). 294p. 1983. 35.00 (ISBN 0-471-09563-X, Pub. by Wiley Med). Krieger.

Practical Hermeneutics: A Revised Agenda for the Ministry. Charles E. Winquist. LC 79-22848. (Scholars Press General Ser.: No. 1). 94p. 1980. 12.95 (ISBN 0-89130-363-4, 00 03 01); pap. 9.75 (ISBN 0-89130-364-2). Scholars Pr GA.

Practical Heterocyclic Chemistry. A. O. Fitton & R. K. Smalley. LC 68-19255. 1968. 40.00 (ISBN 0-12-257850-3). Acad Pr.

Practical High Performance Liquid Chromatography Method Development. Joseph Glajch et al. LC 88-238. 1988. write for info. (ISBN 0-471-62782-8). Wiley.

Practical High Performance Liquid Chromatography. Ed. by Colin F. Simpson. pap. 81.80 (ISBN 0-317-28972-1, 2052065). Bks Demand UMI.

Practical Hindi-English Dictionary. Mahendra Chaturvedi & Nath T. Bhola. 700p. (Hindi & Eng.). 1974. 16.00x (ISBN 0-88386-380-4). South Asia Bks.

Practical Histochemistry. Joseph Chayen et al. LC 72-8596. 285p. pap. 74.10 (2030495). Bks Demand UMI.

Practical Holiness: A Second Look. David K. Bernard. LC 86-119761. 336p. (Orig.). 1985. pap. 6.95 (ISBN 0-912315-91-1). Word Aflame.

Practical Holography, No. II. Ed. by Jeong. 157p. 1987. 43.00 (ISBN 0-89252-782-X, 747). SPIE.

Practical Holography, No. I. Ed. by Jeong & Ludman. 140p. 1986. 43.00 (ISBN 0-89252-650-5, 615). SPIE.

Practical Holography. Graham Saxby. 560p. 1988. text ed. 45.00 (ISBN 0-13-693797-7). P-H.

Practical Home Maintenance. Robert Tattersall. (Illus.). 256p. (Orig.). 1986. pap. 21.95x (ISBN 0-356-12314-6, Pub. by MacD & Co). Trans-Atl Phila.

Practical Homecraft Handbook: How to Do It Manual. H. Barrie. 22.00 (ISBN 0-87559-108-6). Shalom.

Practical Homicide Investigation. Edward A. Dieckmann. 96p. 1961. 17.50X (ISBN 0-398-00450-1). C C Thomas.

Practical Hooked Rugs. Stella Hay Rex. (Illus.). 1975. 12.95 (ISBN 0-89166-004-6); pap. 9.00 (ISBN 0-89166-003-8). Cobblesmith.

Practical Horse Psychology. pap. 5.00 (ISBN 0-87980-247-2). Wilshire.

Practical Horseman's Book of Horsekeeping. Ed. by M. A. Stoneridge. LC 82-45150. (Illus.). 320p. 1983. pap. 27.95 (ISBN 0-385-17788-7). Doubleday.

Practical Horseman's Book of Riding, Training & Showing Hunters, & Jumpers. Ed. by M. A. Stoneridge. 1989. 29.95 (ISBN 0-385-19691-1). Doubleday.

Practical Horticulture: A Guide to Growing Indoor & Outdoor Plants. Robert Rice & Laura Rice. 1985. text ed. 32.00 (ISBN 0-8359-5771-3, Reston); tchr's ed. avail. (ISBN 0-8359-5772-1). P-H.

Practical House Carpenter. Asher Benjamin. 119p. Repr. of 1830 ed. 49.00 (ISBN 0-318-04471-4, Pub. by Am Repr Serv). Am Biog Serv.

Practical House Carpenter: Being a Complete Development of the Grecian Orders of Architecture. Asher Benjamin. 1976. Repr. of 1830 ed. 49.00x (ISBN 0-403-06633-6, Regency). Scholarly.

Practical House Carpenter: 1830 see Works of Asher Benjamin: Boston, 1806-1843.

Practical Housebuilding for Practically Everyone. Frank Jackson. (Illus.). 272p. 1984. text ed. 22.95 (ISBN 0-07-032035-7); pap. text ed. 12.95 (ISBN 0-07-032038-1). McGraw.

Practical HPLC. Veronika R. Meyer. LC 87-37136. 208p. 1988. write for info. (ISBN 0-471-91140-2). Wiley.

Practical Human Biology. J. S. Weiner & J. A. Lourie. LC 81-66372. 1981. 42.00 (ISBN 0-12-741960-8). Acad Pr.

Practical Hunter's Handbook. Anthony J. Acerrano. LC 83-60291. (Illus.). 1981. 13.95 (ISBN 0-8329-3427-5, Pub. by Winchester Pr). New Century.

Practical Hydraulics. 3rd ed. Andrew Simon. LC 85-20273. 493p. 1986. write for info. (ISBN 0-471-88488-X). Wiley.

Practical Hydraulics. 2nd ed. Andrew L. Simon. LC 79-27270. 403p. 1981. 30.95 (ISBN 0-471-05381-3); tchrs.' ed. avail. (ISBN 0-471-07783-6). Wiley.

Practical Hymnology. Hubert M. Poteat. LC 72-1693. Repr. of 1921 ed. 14.50 (ISBN 0-404-09912-2). AMS Pr.

Practical Hypnotism. Philip Magonet. pap. 3.00 (ISBN 0-87980-123-9). Wilshire.

Practical IBM Personal Computer Programs for Beginners. Michael Fox. 96p. 1984. 8.95 (ISBN 0-86668-045-4). ARCsoft.

Practical Ice Carving. Joseph F. Durocher. 112p. 1983. pap. 15.95 (ISBN 0-8436-2206-7). Van Nos Reinhold.

Practical Ideas for Metalworking Operations, Tooling & Maintenance. American Machinist Magazine Staff. 352p. 1985. text ed. 37.50 (ISBN 0-07-001551-1). McGraw.

Practical Ideas for the Design, Operation, & Maintenance of Plant Energy Systems. Thomas C. Elliott. LC 84-7161. (Illus.). 304p. 1985. text ed. 31.50 (ISBN 0-07-050583-7). McGraw.

Practical Ideas...for Metalworking Operations, Tooling, & Maintenance. Ed. by American Machinist & Automated Manufacturing Magazine Staff. (Illus.). 330p. Date not set. Repr. of 1984 ed. 18.75 (ISBN 0-932905-05-6). Penton Pub.

Practical Identification of Wood Pulp Fibers. Russell A. Parham & Richard L. Gray. 212p. 1982. 34.95 (ISBN 0-89852-400-8, 01 01R0100). TAPPI.

Practical Identification of Wood Pulp Fibers. Russell A. Parham & Richard L. Gray. LC 82-50114. pap. 55.00 (ISBN 0-317-20555-2, 2022820). Bks Demand UMI.

Practical Ideology & Symbolic Community: An Ethnography of Schools of Choice. Robert B. Everhart. 200p. 1988. 55.00x (ISBN 1-85000-355-6, Falmer Pr); pap. 24.00x (ISBN 1-85000-356-4, Falmer Pr). Taylor & Francis.

Practical Illustrations of Rhetorical Gesture & Action. Henry Siddons. LC 67-18425. (Illus.). 1968. Repr. of 1822 ed. 27.50 (ISBN 0-405-08971-6). Ayer Co Pubs.

Practical Imagination. Compact ed. Northrop Frye et al. 1445p. 1987. pap. text ed. 24.50 scp (ISBN 0-06-042223-8, HarpC). Har-Row.

Practical Immunisation. G. Dick. 1986. lib. bdg. 32.00 (ISBN 0-85200-925-9, Pub. by MTP Pr England). Kluwer-Academic.

Practical Immunoassay. Butt. (Clinical & Biochemical Analysis Ser.). 360p. 1984. 65.00 (ISBN 0-8247-7094-3). Dekker.

Practical Implications of Calvinism. Albert N. Martin. 1979. pap. 1.00 (ISBN 0-85151-296-8). Banner of Truth.

Practical Inferences. D. S. Clarke, Jr. (International Library of Philosophy). 192p. 1985. 32.50x (ISBN 0-7102-0415-9). Routledge Chapman & Hall.

Practical Inorganic Chemistry. V. I. Spitsyn. 304p. 1986. 12.95 (ISBN 0-8285-3321-0, Pub. by Mir Pubs USSR). Imported Pubns.

Practical Inorganic Chemistry: Preparations, Reactions & Instrumental Methods. 2nd ed. G. Pass & H. Sutcliffe. 256p. 1979. pap. 12.95x (ISBN 0-412-16150-8, NO. 6214, Pub. by Chapman & Hall England). Routledge Chapman & Hall.

Practical Insect Pest Management. 2nd ed. M. Curtis Wilson et al. LC 79-57132. (Insects of Livestock & Agronomic Crops Ser.: No. 2). (Illus.). 208p. 1980. pap. text ed. 11.95x (ISBN 0-917974-39-5). Waveland Pr.

Practical Insect Pest Management: Fundamentals of Applied Entomology, No. 1. 2nd ed. M. Curtis Wilson et al. (Illus.). 1984. pap. text ed. 11.95x (ISBN 0-88133-031-0). Waveland Pr.

Practical Insect Pest Management: Insects of Ornamental Plants, No. 4. 2nd ed. M. C. Wilson & D. L. Schuder. LC 82-50792. (Illus.). 150p. 1982. pap. text ed. 9.95x (ISBN 0-917974-93-X). Waveland Pr.

Practical Insect Pest Management: Insects of Vegetables & Fruit, Vol. 3. 2nd ed. M. Curtis Wilson et al. LC 81-70506. (Illus.). 144p. 1982. pap. text ed. 9.95x (ISBN 0-917974-65-4). Waveland Pr.

Practical Insights in the Use of Statistics. Hahn. (Probability & Mathematical Statistics Ser.). 1987. write for info. (ISBN 0-471-09237-1). Wiley.

Practical Instruction in Animal Magnetism. Ed. by Jean P. Deleuze. Tr. by Thomas Hartshorn from Fr. (Hypnosis & Altered States of Consciousness Ser.). 1982. Repr. of 1843 ed. lib. bdg. 45.00 (ISBN 0-306-76074-6). Da Capo.

Practical Intelligence: Origins of Competence in the Everyday World. Ed. by Robert J. Sternberg & Richard K. Wagner. (Illus.). 240p. 1986. 54.50 (ISBN 0-521-30253-6); pap. 17.95 (ISBN 0-521-31797-5). Cambridge U Pr.

Practical Intelligence: Working Smarter in Business & Everyday Life. Roger Peters. LC 86-46096. 288p. 1987. 17.95i (ISBN 0-06-015681-3, HarpT). Har-Row.

Practical Interfacing Projects with the Commodore Computers. Robert H. Luetzow. (Illus.). 256p. (Orig.). 1986. pap. 16.95 (ISBN 0-8306-1983-6). Tab Bks.

Practical Interfacing Techniques for Microprocessor Systems. James W. Coffron & William E. Long. (Illus.). 432p. 1983. 38.00 (ISBN 0-13-691394-6). P-H.

Practical International Tax Planning 1986-1987. Marshall J. Langer. 1985. 125.00 (JI-1461); looseleaf compression binder 125.00. PLI.

Practical Introduction to Borehole Geophysics. James A. Labo. Ed. by Samuel H. Mentemeier & Gerald H. Gardner. LC 87-60425. (Geophysical Reference Ser.: No. 2). (Illus.). 336p. 1987. text ed. 56.00 (ISBN 0-931830-39-7). Soc Expl Geophys.

Practical Introduction to Business. 4th ed. Harold Koontz & Robert M. Fulmer. 1984. 32.95 (ISBN 0-256-03030-8). Irwin.

Practical Introduction to Computer Graphics. Ian O. Angell. LC 81-11361. (Computers & Their Applications Ser.). 143p. 1981. pap. 23.95x (ISBN 0-470-27251-1). Halsted Pr.

Practical Introduction to Denotational Semantics. L. Allison. (Cambridge Computer Science Texts Ser.: No. 23). (Illus.). 154p. 1987. 34.50 (ISBN 0-521-30689-2); pap. 10.95 (ISBN 0-521-31423-2). Cambridge U Pr.

Practical Introduction to Electric Circuits. M. H. Jones. LC 76-11083. (Illus.). 1977. pap. 16.95x o. p. (ISBN 0-521-29087-2). Cambridge U Pr.

Practical Introduction to Electronic Circuits. 2nd ed. M. H. Jones. 275p. 1985. 54.50 (ISBN 0-521-30785-6); pap. 17.95 (ISBN 0-521-31312-0). Cambridge U Pr.

Practical Introduction to Greek Accentuation. rev. 2nd ed. H. W. Chandler. (College Classical Ser.). xxxiii, 292p. 1981. Repr. of 1881 ed. lib. bdg. 40.00x (ISBN 0-89241-112-0). Caratzas.

Practical Introduction to Impedence Matching. Robert L. Thomas. LC 75-31378. pap. 43.80 (ISBN 0-317-42078-X, 2056085). Bks Demand UMI.

Practical Introduction to Optical Mineralogy. C. D. Gribble & A. J. Hall. (Illus.). 200p. 1985. text ed. 39.95x (ISBN 0-04-549007-4); pap. text ed. 18.95x (ISBN 0-04-549008-2). Unwin Hyman.

Practical Introduction to Pascal. 2nd ed. I. R. Wilson & A. M. Addyman. 236p. 1982. pap. 17.95 (ISBN 0-387-91210-X, BSI 6192). Springer-Verlag.

Practical Introduction to Phonetics. J. C. Catford. (Illus.). 256p. 1988. 55.00 (ISBN 0-19-824218-2); pap. text ed. 17.95 (ISBN 0-19-824217-4). Oxford U Pr.

Practical Introduction to Standard PASCAL. I. D. Chivers. (Computers & Their Applications Ser.). 276p. 1986. 33.95 (ISBN 0-470-20359-5). Halsted Pr.

Practical Introduction to the New Logic Symbols. 2nd ed. Ian Kampel. (Illus.). 176p. 1986. text ed. 21.95 (ISBN 0-408-03010-0). Butterworth.

Practical Introduction to Trade Marks. Brian C. Reid. (Illus.). 192p. 1984. 29.00 (ISBN 0-08-039170-2). Pergamon.

Practical Issues of This Life. Watchman Nee. Tr. by Stephen Kaung. 1975. pap. 3.25 (ISBN 0-935008-29-2). Christian Fellow Pubs.

Practical Italian-English, English-Italian Dictionary. Peter Ross. (Practical Language Dictionaries Ser.). 400p. (Orig., Eng. & Ital.). 1983. pap. 6.95 (ISBN 0-88254-816-6). Hippocrene Bks.

Practical IV Therapy. Julie Steele. 300p. 1988. pap. 15.95 spiral (ISBN 0-87434-131-0). Springhouse Pub.

Practical Japanese Cooking: Easy & Elegant. Shizuo Tsuji & Koichioro Hata. LC 85-45706. (Illus.). 152p. 1986. 22.50 (ISBN 0-87011-762-9). Kodansha.

Practical Japanese Cuisine. Chen Shiu-Lee. 104p. 1988. pap. 15.95 (ISBN 0-941676-19-6). Wei-Chuan's Cooking.

Practical Japanese Made Simple. Iwaki. pap. 4.95 (ISBN 0-87505-147-2). Borden.

Practical Jewellery Repair. James E. Hickling. 198p. 1987. 50.00x (ISBN 0-7198-0082-X, Pub. by E Bruton Assocs Ltd UK). State Mutual Bk.

Practical Jung: Nuts & Bolts of Jungian Psychotherapy. Harry A. Wilmer. LC 87-18233. 279p. 1987. 27.95 (ISBN 0-933029-24-1); pap. 14.95 (ISBN 0-933029-16-0). Chiron Pubns.

Practical Jurisprudence: A Comment on Austin. E. C. Clark. xii, 403p. 1980. Repr. of 1883 ed. lib. bdg. 30.00x (ISBN 0-8377-0427-8). Rothman.

Practical Justice of the Peace & Parish-Officer, of His Majesty's Province of South Carolina. William Simpson. LC 70-37985. (American Law Ser.: The Formative Years). 288p. 1972. Repr. of 1761 ed. 21.00 (ISBN 0-405-04028-8). Ayer Co Pubs.

Practical Karate, 6 vols. Donn F. Draeger & Masatoshi Nakayama. LC 63-11828. (Illus.). 1963-65. Vol. 1. pap. 7.50 (ISBN 0-8048-0481-8); Vol. 2. pap. 5.95 (ISBN 0-8048-0482-6); Vol. 3. pap. 5.95 (ISBN 0-8048-0483-4); Vol. 4. pap. 5.95 (ISBN 0-8048-0484-2); Vol. 5. pap. 7.50 (ISBN 0-8048-0485-0); Vol. 6. pap. 7.50 (ISBN 0-8048-0486-9). C E Tuttle.

Practical Key to the Kannada Language. F. Ziegler. 112p. 1986. Repr. of 1953 ed. 22.00x (ISBN 0-8364-1844-1, Pub. by Usha). South Asia Bks.

Practical Knots & Ropework. Percy W. Blandford. (Illus., Orig.). 1980. pap. 10.95 (ISBN 0-8306-1237-8, 1237). TAB Bks.

Practical Knowledge for a Private Security Officer. John L. Coleman. (Illus.). 202p. 1986. 27.25x (ISBN 0-398-05203-4). C C Thomas.

Practical Knowledge, Tradition & Technique. Ed. by J. C. Nyiri & Barry Smith. 224p. 1987. lib. bdg. 45.00x (ISBN 0-7099-4477-2, Pub. by Croom Helm UK). Routledge Chapman & Hall.

Practical Korean Cooking. Chin-hwa Noh. (Illus.). 192p. 1985. 28.50x (ISBN 0-930878-37-X). Hollym Intl.

Practical Labor Relations. Kenneth A. Kovach. LC 86-9288. 380p. 1987. pap. text ed. 17.50 (ISBN 0-8191-5419-9). U Pr of Amer.

Practical Labor Relations: A Collection of Readings. Ed. by Paul E. Hoffner et al. LC 80-5525. 183p. 1980. pap. text ed. 11.00 (ISBN 0-8191-1119-8). U Pr of Amer.

Practical Laboratory Parasitology. Elmer W. Koneman et al. LC 78-21673. (Illus.). 142p. 1979. pap. text ed. 9.95 (ISBN 0-88275-804-7). Krieger.

Practical Laparoscopy. G. Berci & A. Cuschieri. (Illus.). 192p. 1986. 38.95 (ISBN 0-7020-1132-0, Bailliere-Tindall). Saunders.

Practical Laser Technology. Hrand Muncheryan. 400p. 1986. pap. cancelled (ISBN 0-672-22487-9, 22487). Sams.

Practical Law Enforcement Guide to Writing Field Reports, Grant Proposals, Memos, & Resumes. T. J. Agnos & S. Schatt. (Illus.). 136p. 1980. spiral bdg. 17.50x (ISBN 0-398-04042-7). C C Thomas.

Practical Law for Jail & Prison Personnel: A Resource Manual & Training Curriculum. 255p. 1987. 20.00; Instructor's manual. write for info. Am Correctional.

Practical Laws of Islam. Imam Khomeini. LC 83-50077. 1983. pap. 9.00 (ISBN 0-940368-25-0). Tahrike Tarsile Quran.

Practical Lawyer Storage Album. vinyl binder 10.00 (ISBN 0-317-55934-6, F101). Am Law Inst.

Practical Lawyer's Cumulative Index. 92p. 1976. pap. 4.00 (ISBN 0-317-30756-8, F103). Am Law Inst.

Practical Lawyer's Insurance Manual, No. 1. 184p. 1975. pap. 10.00 (ISBN 0-317-30718-5, F120). Am Law Inst.

Practical Lawyer's Law Office Management Manual, No. 3. 178p. 1972. pap. 10.00 (ISBN 0-317-65897-2, F108). Am Law Inst.

Practical Lawyer's Law Office Management Manual, No. 4. 163p. 1974. pap. 10.00 (ISBN 0-317-30729-0, F109). Am Law Inst.

Practical Lawyer's Law Office Management Manual, No. 5. ALI-ABA Committee on Continuing Professional Education. 218p. 1984. pap. 15.00 (ISBN 0-317-12707-1, F125). Am Law Inst.

Practical Lawyer's Law Office Manual, No. 1. 158p. 1956. pap. 10.00 (ISBN 0-317-65900-6, F104). Am Law Inst.

Practical Lawyer's Law Office Manual, No. 2. 119p. 1959. pap. 12.00 (ISBN 0-317-30736-3, F106). Am Law Inst.

Practical Lawyer's Manual for Automatic Law Office Typing & Word Processing. 116p. 1979. pap. 10.00 (ISBN 0-317-30702-9, F113). Am Law Inst.

Practical Lawyer's Manual of Business Forms & Check Lists. ALI-ABA Committee on Continuing Professional Education. LC 84-71224. (Illus.). 230p. 1984. pap. 15.00 (F129). Am Law Inst.

Practical Lawyer's Manual of Law Office Training for Associates. Theodore Voorhees. 118p. 1969. pap. 10.00 (ISBN 0-317-30739-8, F116). Am Law Inst.

Practical Lawyer's Manual of Pretrial Discovery. 152p. 1973. pap. 10.00 (ISBN 0-317-30745-2, F122). Am Law Inst.

Practical Lawyer's Manual of Trial & Appellate Practice, No. 1. 178p. 1973. pap. 10.00 (ISBN 0-317-65906-5, F114). Am Law Inst.

Practical Lawyer's Manual of Trial & Appellate Practice, No. 2. 190p. 1979. pap. 10.00 (ISBN 0-317-30749-5, F115). Am Law Inst.

Practical Lawyer's Manual of Trial & Appellate Practice, No.3. 171p. 1986. pap. 15.00 (ISBN 0-317-65907-3, F135). Am Law Inst.

Practical Lawyer's Manual on Criminal Law & Procedure. ALI-ABA Committee on Continuing Professional Education & Mark T. Carroll. LC 84-7303. (Illus.). viii, 220p. 1984. pap. 15.00 (F130). Am Law Inst.

Practical Lawyer's Manual on Divorce & Separation. LC 85-72055. 173p. 1985. pap. 15.00 (F128). Am Law Inst.

Practical Lawyer's Manual on Labor Law. LC 82-74526. 216p. 1983. pap. 15.00 (ISBN 0-686-40800-4, F124). Am Law Inst.

Practical Lawyer's Manual on Labor Law, No. 2. LC 82-74526. 204p. 1988. pap. 20.00 (F137). Am Law Inst.

Practical Lawyer's Manual on Lawyer-Client Relations. ALI-ABA Committee on Continuing Professional Education. 197p. 1983. pap. 15.00 (ISBN 0-317-12708-X, F127). Am Law Inst.

Practical Lawyer's Manual on Legal Research, Writing & Indexing. F. Trowbridge Vom Baur. (Illus.). 103p. 1979. pap. 10.00 (ISBN 0-317-30740-1, F121). Am Law Inst.

Practical Lawyer's Manual on Pretrial Preparation. 169p. 1985. pap. 15.00 (ISBN 0-317-55933-8, F132). Am Law Inst.

Practical Lawyer's Manual on Pretrial Preparation, No. 2. 188p. 1986. pap. 15.00 (ISBN 0-317-65909-X, F134). Am Law Inst.

Practical Lawyer's Manual on Real Property Law, No. 2. ALI-ABA Committee on Continuing Professional Education. 209p. 1983. pap. 15.00 (ISBN 0-317-12709-8, F126). Am Law Inst.

Practical Lawyer's Manual on Trade Regulation. Michael G. Walsh. LC 85-72345. 210p. 1985. pap. 15.00 (F133). Am Law Inst.

Practical Lawyer's Manual on Wills & Probate, No. 1. 188p. 1974. pap. 10.00 (ISBN 0-317-30752-5, F118). Am Law Inst.

Practical Lawyer's Negligence Law Manual, No. 1. 136p. 1964. pap. 10.00 (ISBN 0-317-65911-1, F110). Am Law Inst.

Practical Lawyer's Negligence Law Manual, No. 2. 163p. 1973. pap. 10.00 (ISBN 0-317-30743-6, F111). Am Law Inst.

Practical Lawyer's Real Property Law Manual, No. 1. 189p. 1974. pap. 10.00 (ISBN 0-317-65904-9, F119). Am Law Inst.

Practical Lawyer's Real Property Law Manual, No.2. 209p. 1983. pap. 15.00 (ISBN 0-317-55938-9, F126). Am Law Inst.

Practical LCP: A Direct Approach to Structured Programming. Albert C. Gardner. (Illus.). 256p. 1982. 32.50x (ISBN 0-07-084561-1). McGraw.

Practical Leadership Skills: Accident-Incident Investigation. Ed. by M. Douglas Clark. 1986. 3-ring binder 125.00 (ISBN 0-88061-056-5). Institute Pr.

Practical Leadership Skills: Causes & Effects of Loss. Ed. by M. Douglas Clark. 1986. 3-ring Binder 125.00 (ISBN 0-88061-055-7). Institute Pr.

Practical Leadership Skills: Group Meetings. Ed. by M. Douglas Clark. 1986. 3-Ring Binder 125.00 (ISBN 0-88061-060-3). Institute Pr.

Practical Leadership Skills: Job Pride Development. Ed. by M. Douglas Clark. 1986. 3-ring binder 125.00 (ISBN 0-88061-074-3). Institute Pr.

Practical Leadership Skills: Job-Task Analysis & Procedures. Ed. by M. Douglas Clark. 1986. 3-Ring Binder 125.00 (ISBN 0-88061-059-X). Institute Pr.

Practical Leadership Skills: Management Control. Ed. by M. Douglas Clark. 1986. 3-ring binder 125.00 (ISBN 0-88061-075-1). Institute Pr.

Practical Leadership Skills: Personal Communications. Ed. by M. Douglas Clark. 1986. 3-Ring Binder 125.00 (ISBN 0-88061-061-1). Institute Pr.

Practical Leadership Skills: Planned Inspections. Ed. by M. Douglas Clark. 1986. 3-Ring Binder 125.00 (ISBN 0-88061-057-3). Institute Pr.

Practical Leadership Skills: Planned Job-Task Observation. Ed. by M. Douglas Clark. 1986. 3-Ring Binder 125.00 (ISBN 0-88061-058-1). Institute Pr.

Practical Leather Technology. 3rd ed. Thomas C. Thorstensen. LC 83-19557. 340p. 1985. lib. bdg. 28.50 (ISBN 0-89874-692-2). Krieger.

Practical Liquid Chromatography. S. G. Perry et al. LC 75-179760. 230p. 1972. 39.50x (ISBN 0-306-30548-8, Plenum Pr); pap. 14.95x (ISBN 0-306-20002-3). Plenum Pub.

Practical Lisp on a Microcomputer. Kevin Sullivan. 200p. 1985. 40.00x (ISBN 0-317-43566-3, Pub. by Sigma Pr). State Mutual Bk.

Practical Lithographic Printmaking. Manly Banister. (Illus.). 128p. 1988. pap. 5.95 (ISBN 0-486-25568-9). Dover.

Practical Logic. 3rd ed. Vincent E. Barry & Douglas J. Soccio. (Illus.). 528p. 1988. text ed. price not set (ISBN 0-03-012693-2). HR&W.

Practical Logic. Monroe C. Beardsley. 1950. text ed. write for info. (ISBN 0-13-692111-6). P-H.

Practical Logic: With the Appendix on Deontic Logic. Zygmunt Ziembinski. Tr. by Leon Ter-Oganian. LC 75-45254. 1976. lib. bdg. 43.00 (ISBN 90-277-0557-7, Pub. by Reidel Holland). Kluwer Academic.

Practical Loss Control Leadership. F. E. Bird, Jr. & George L. Germain. (Illus.). 446p. 1986. pap. text ed. 35.00 (ISBN 0-88061-054-9). Institute Pr.

Practical Machine Vision. Julie Pingry. 140p. Date not set. wkbk. 77.00 (ISBN 0-943779-00-6). Cutter Information.

Practical Machinery Management for Process Plants, Vol. 1: Omproving Machinery Reliability. 2nd ed. Heinz P. Bloch. (Illus.). 465p. 1988. 64.00 (ISBN 0-87201-455-X). Gulf Pub.

Practical Macromolecular Organic Chemistry. Ed. by Braun et al. (MMI Press Polymer Monographs). 344p. 1984. text ed. 105.00 (ISBN 3-7186-0059-5). Harwood Academic.

Practical Magic: A Translation of Basic Neuro-Linguistic Programming into Clinical Psychotherapy. Stephen Lankton. LC 80-50148. 1980. 12.95 (ISBN 0-916990-08-7). Meta Pubns.

Practical Magic & the Western Mystery Tradition. Date not set. price not set (ISBN 0-85030-411-3, Pub. by Thorsons UK). Weiser.

Practical Magic: Poems. Carl Bode. LC 80-17597. viii, 54p. 1981. 11.95x (ISBN 0-8040-0362-9, Pub. by Swallow); pap. 6.95 (ISBN 0-8040-0373-4, Pub. by Swallow). Ohio U Pr.

Practical Magnetic Resonance Imaging: A Case Study Approach. Wilson Wong et al. 451p. 1986. 95.00 (ISBN 0-87189-600-1). Aspen Pub.

Practical Management Communication. Vickie J. Stout & Edward A. Perkins. 1987. text ed. write for info. (ISBN 0-538-05560-X, E56). SW Pub.

Practical Management of Asthma. T. Clark & J. Rees. (Practical Problems in Medicine Ser.). (Illus.). 174p. 1985. lib. bdg. 45.00 (ISBN 0-906348-74-9, Pub. by Martin Dunitz Ltd UK). VCH Pubs.

Practical Management of Asthma. Arthur Dawson & Ronald Simon. 288p. 1983. text ed. 45.50 (ISBN 0-8089-1595-9, 791008). Grune.

Practical Management of Diabetic Retinopathy. Peter H. Morse. (Illus.). 256p. 1985. 55.00 (ISBN 0-8385-7872-1). Appleton & Lange.

Practical Management of Emotional Problems in Medicine. 2nd ed. Hugh J. Lurie. 272p. 1982. text ed. 40.00 (ISBN 0-89004-707-3); pap. 25.50 (ISBN 0-89004-849-5). Raven.

Practical Management of Pain. Raj. 1986. 148.00 (ISBN 0-8151-7013-0). Year Bk Med.

Practical Management of Stroke. Graham P. Mulley. 174p. 1985. pap. 24.50 (ISBN 0-87489-613-4). Med Economics.

Practical Management Skills for Engineers & Scientists. William C. Giegold. (Engineering Ser.). (Illus.). 430p. 1982. 32.95 (ISBN 0-534-97961-0, Lifetime Learn); leader's skills 14.95 (ISBN 0-534-03008-4). Van Nos Reinhold.

Practical Management Skills: Leader's Guide. Giegold. pap. 14.95 (ISBN 0-317-64248-0). Van Nos Reinhold.

Practical Manager's Guide to Excellence in Management. Ronald Brown. LC 79-11883. pap. 32.00 (ISBN 0-317-26946-1, 2023587). Bks Demand UMI.

Practical Mangement of the Dermatologic Patient. Arthur Rook et al. (Illus.). 304p. 1986. text ed. 49.50 (ISBN 0-397-50590-6, Lippincott Medical). Lippincott.

Practical Manual of Obstetric Care: A Pocket Reference for Those Who Treat the Pregnant Patient. Frederick P. Zuspan & Edward J. Quilligan. LC 81-14050. (Illus.). 414p. 1981. pap. text ed. 21.95 (ISBN 0-8016-4064-4). Mosby.

Practical Manual of Screen Playwriting for Theater & Television Films. Lewis Herman. pap. 8.95 (ISBN 0-452-00746-1, Mer). NAL.

Practical Manual of Site Development. B. Colley. 256p. 1985. text ed. 42.00 (ISBN 0-07-011803-5). Mcgraw.

Practical Marine Electrical Knowledge. Dennis T. Hall. 132p. 1984. 144.00 (ISBN 0-900886-87-0, Pub. by Witherby & Co England). State Mutual Bk.

Practical Marketing in Australia. Peter November. 1985. pap. 25.95 (ISBN 0-471-33396-4). Wiley.

Practical Marketing Research. Jeffrey L. Pope. 304p. 1981. 34.95 (ISBN 0-8144-5651-0). AMACOM.

Practical Mass Spectrometry: A Contemporary Introduction. Ed. by Brian S. Middleditch. LC 79-351. 404p. 1979. 39.50x (ISBN 0-306-40230-0, Plenum Pr). Plenum Pub.

Practical Math for Business. 4th ed. Alan R. Curtis. Date not set. text ed. 30.76 (ISBN 0-395-35649-0); transparencies 101.56 (ISBN 0-395-42401-1). HM.

Practical Math for Electricity & Electronics. Paul Calter. 1984. pap. text ed. 9.95 (ISBN 0-07-009652-X). McGraw.

Practical Math Handbook for the Building Trades. Paul Calter. (Illus.). 288p. 1983. pap. 11.95 (ISBN 0-13-692228-7). P-H.

Practical Mathematics. 3rd ed. G. M. Hobbs & J. McKinney. (Illus.). 591p. 1972. pap. 15.48 (ISBN 0-8269-2242-2). Am Technical.

Practical Mathematics. 7th ed. Claude I. Palmer & L. A. Mrachek. 560p. 1985. text ed. 32.95 (ISBN 0-07-048254-3). McGraw.

Practical Mathematics. 6th ed. Claude I. Palmer et al. (Illus.). (gr. 10 up). 1977. text ed. 43.95 (ISBN 0-07-048253-5). McGraw.

Practical Mathematics. 2nd ed. Russell Person & Vernon Person. LC 83-3480. 633p. 1984. 29.95 (ISBN 0-471-86079-4); tchr's manual avail. Wiley.

Practical Mathematics for Metalworking Trainees. rev. ed. William E. Hardman. 272p. 1982. pap. text ed. 16.75 cat. no. 5012 (ISBN 0-910399-03-4); instr's. guide cat. no. 5112 14.95 (ISBN 0-910399-19-0). Natl Tool & Mach.

Practical Measurement of Physical Performance. Helen M. Eckert. LC 73-16292. (Health Education, Physical Education, & Recreation Ser.). pap. 76.80 (2056185). Bks Demand UMI.

Practical Meat Cut Beef, Vol. 1. 3rd ed. Fabbricante. 1987. pap. 22.95 (ISBN 0-442-22495-8). Van Nos Reinhold.

Practical Meat Cutting & Merchandising, Vol. 1: Beef. 3rd ed. Thomas Fabbricante & William J. Sultan. (Illus.). 1987. 21.50 (ISBN 0-317-52350-3). AVI.

Practical Meat Cutting & Merchandising, Vol. 2: Pork, Lamb, & Veal. Thomas Fabbricante & William J. Sultan. (Illus.). 1975. pap. 22.95 (ISBN 0-87055-177-9). AVI.

Practical Meditator. Harry C. Meserve. LC 80-15631. 137p. 1981. 24.95 (ISBN 0-87705-506-8); professional o.p. 16.95. Human Sci Pr.

Practical Mental Magic. Theodore Annemann. (Illus.). 310p. (Orig.). 1983. pap. 6.95 (ISBN 0-486-24426-1). Dover.

Practical Merchandising Math for Everyday Use. 700p. pap. text ed. 22.00 (ISBN 0-87102-013-0, 45-9476). Natl Ret Merch.

Practical Metallurgy & Materials of Industry. 2nd ed. John E. Neely. 406p. 1984. write for info. (ISBN 0-471-86461-7); tchr's. manual avail. (ISBN 0-471-80125-9). Wiley.

Practical Methods in Choral Speaking. Marguerite E. DeWitt et al. 1973. text ed. 2.50 (ISBN 0-686-09411-5). Expression.

Practical Methods in Electron Microscopy, Vols. 1-8. A. M. Glauert. (Biomedical Pr); Vol. 2, 1974. 120.00 (ISBN 0-444-10644-8); Vol. 3, 1975. 120.00 (ISBN 0-444-10665-0); Vol. 4, 1975. 59.50 (ISBN 0-444-10807-6); Vol. 5, 1977. 161.00 (ISBN 0-7204-0605-6); Vol. 6, 1978. 143.25 (ISBN 0-7204-0636-6); Vol. 7, 1979. 109.50 (ISBN 0-7204-0665-X); Vol. 8, 1980. 109.50. Elsevier.

Practical Methods in Molecular Biology. R. F. Schleif & P. C. Wensink. (Illus.). 220p. 1981. 44.00 (ISBN 0-387-90603-7). Springer-Verlag.

Practical Methods of Optimization. 2nd ed. R. Fletcher. LC 87-8126. 1988. 49.95 (ISBN 0-471-91547-5). Wiley.

Practical Microprocessor Interfacing. S. A. Money. LC 87-23204. 247p. 1987. 31.95 (ISBN 0-471-63788-2). Wiley.

Practical Microscopic Hematology. 3rd ed. Fritz Heckner et al. (Illus.). 140p. 1987. pap. 24.50 (ISBN 0-8067-0813-1). Urban & S.

Practical Microwave Oven Repair. Homer L. Davidson. (Illus.). 364p. (Orig.). 1984. pap. 14.95 (ISBN 0-8306-1667-5). TAB Bks.

Practical Microwaves. Thomas S. Laverghetta. LC 83-51119. 39.95 (ISBN 0-672-21945-X, 21945). Sams.

Practical Mind Reading. William W. Atkinson. pap. 2.00 (ISBN 0-911662-43-X). Yoga.

Practical Mineralogy. Meurig P. Jones. (Illus.). 250p. 1986. 79.00 (ISBN 0-86010-510-5); pap. 35.00 (ISBN 0-86010-511-3). Graham & Trotman.

Practical Mock Scene Manual. Tim Perry. 60p. 1986. manual 59.95 (ISBN 0-915837-02-1). Palladium Pubns.

Practical Modern Basketball. 3rd ed. John R. Wooden. 441p. 1988. text ed. write for info. (ISBN 0-02-429470-5). Macmillan.

Practical Modern Knitting. Rita Weiss. 1986. pap. cancelled (ISBN 0-442-29265-1). Van Nos Reinhold.

Practical, Moral, & Political Economy. Thomas R. Edmonds. LC 68-55706. 1969. Repr. of 1828 ed. 39.50x (ISBN 0-678-00564-8). Kelley.

Practical Motivation Handbook. Kenneth Carlisle & Sheila Murphy. LC 86-11043. 376p. 1986. pap. 34.95 (ISBN 0-471-84497-7). Wiley.

Practical Musical Criticism. Oscar Thompson. (Music Reprint Ser.: 1979). 1979. Repr. of 1934 ed. lib. bdg. 29.50 (ISBN 0-306-79514-0). Da Capo.

Practical Muskrat Raising. E. J. Dailey. (Illus.). 136p. pap. 3.50 (ISBN 0-936622-17-2). A R Harding Pub.

Practical MVS JCL for Today's Programmer. James G. Janossy. LC 86-33951. 452p. 1987. pap. 29.95 (ISBN 0-471-83648-6). Wiley.

Practical Mysticism. Evelyn Underhill. 160p. 1986. pap. 5.95 (ISBN 0-89804-143-0). Ariel OH.

Practical Natural Gas Engineering. R. V. Smith. LC 82-24684. 248p. 1983. 54.95 (ISBN 0-87814-225-8, P-4331). Pennwell Bks.

Practical Nature Cure. 13th ed. K. Lakshmana Sarma. 743p. Date not set. 37.95. Asia Bk Corp.

Practical Navigation for Second Mates. 5th ed. A. Frost. 281p. 1981. 25.00x (ISBN 0-85174-397-8). Sheridan.

Practical Negotiations of Government Contracts: Course Manual. Timothy Sullivan. LC 86-213796. Date not set. price not set. Fed Pubns Inc.

Practical Negotiator. I. William Zartman & Maureen Berman. LC 81-40435. 264p. 1982. 30.00x (ISBN 0-300-02523-8). Yale U Pr.

Practical Negotiator. I. William Zartman & Maureen Burman. LC 81-40435. 263p. 1983. pap. 11.95x (ISBN 0-300-03097-5, Y-467). Yale U Pr.

Practical Neonatal Respiratory Care. Ed. by Richard L. Schreiner & Jeffrey A. Kisling. 482p. 1982. text ed. 75.00 (ISBN 0-89004-559-3). Raven.

Practical Neurology for the Primary Care Physician. William H. Olson et al. (Illus.). 456p. 1981. spiral bdg. 31.50x (ISBN 0-398-04135-0). C C Thomas.

Practical News Assignments for Student Reporters. 5th ed. James L. Julian. 256p. 1980. write for info. wire coil (ISBN 0-697-04336-3); instructor's manual avail. (ISBN 0-697-04337-1). Wm C Brown.

Practical NMR Spectroscopy. Maryvonne L. Martin et al. pap. 123.00 (ISBN 0-317-26326-9, 2025202). Bks Demand UMI.

Practical Noninvasive Vascular Diagnosis. 2nd ed. Richard F. Kempczinski. (Illus.). 431p. 1987. text ed. 60.50 (ISBN 0-8151-5019-9). Year Bk Med.

Practical Nonparametric Statistics. 2nd ed. W. J. Conover. LC 80-301. (Probability & Mathematical Statistics Ser.). 493p. 1980. write for info. (ISBN 0-471-02867-3). Wiley.

Practical Nuclear Medicine. Ed. by Fued Ashkar. LC 73-13794. 217p. 1974. 25.00 (ISBN 0-8463-0126-1, Pub. by W & W). Krieger.

Practical Nuclear Power Plant Technology, 2 vols. R. W. Deutsch et al. (Illus.). 1973. Set. looseleaf 149.50x (ISBN 0-87683-295-8); Vol. 1; 368p. looseleaf o.p. 79.95x (ISBN 0-87683-296-6); Vol. 2; 320pp. looseleaf o.p. 79.95x (ISBN 0-87683-297-4). GP Pub.

Practical Numerical Methods: Algorithms & Programs. Michael C. Kohn. 352p. 1987. 34.95 (ISBN 0-02-948760-9). Macmillan.

Practical Nurse. Dorothy Deming. Ed. by Susan Reverby. LC 83-49138. (History of American Nursing Ser.). 370p. 1984. Repr. of 1947 ed. lib. bdg. 45.00 (ISBN 0-8240-6509-3). Garland Pub.

Practical Nurse. Jack Rudman. (Career Examination Ser.: C-642). (Cloth bdg. avail. on request). pap. 14.00 (ISBN 0-8373-0642-6). Natl Learning.

Practical Nurse & Today's Family. 2nd ed. Doris Hasler. 1972. pap. text ed. write for info. (ISBN 0-02-351700-X). Macmillan.

Practical Nursing. 13th ed. M. Clarke. (Illus.). 416p. 1983. pap. 10.95 (ISBN 0-7216-0932-5, Bailliere-Tindall). Saunders.

Practical Nursing: PreTest Self-Assessment & Review. 210p. 1979. 13.95 (ISBN 0-07-051571-9). McGraw-Pretest.

Practical Nutritional Support. S. J. Karran & K. G. Alberti. LC 79-56645. 364p. 1980. 45.00 (ISBN 0-471-08024-1, JW). Krieger.

Practical Observations on the Small Claims Court. National Center for State Courts Staff. 56p. (On loan through the NCSC Library). 1979. pap. write for info. (ISBN 0-89656-039-2, R-047). Natl Ctr St Courts.

Practical Obstetrical Ultrasound. John W. Seeds & Robert C. Cefalo. 200p. 1986. 37.00 (ISBN 0-87189-273-1). Aspen Pub.

Practical Obstetrics & Gynaecology. 3rd ed. Bikash C. Basu. 1982. 59.00x (ISBN 0-317-39557-2, Pub. by Current Dist). State Mutual Bk.

Practical Obstetrics & Gynecology: Manual of Selected Procedures & Treatments. Vaclav Insler & Roy Homburg. (Illus.). 1979. bookblock 54.75 (ISBN 3-8055-2945-7). S Karger.

Practical Occultism. 3rd ed. Helena P. Blavatsky. 1967. 2.50 (ISBN 0-8356-7124-0). Theos Pub Hse.

Practical Occultism: From the Private Letters of William Q. Judge. William Q. Judge. LC 78-63320. 1979. 11.00 (ISBN 0-911500-29-4); pap. 7.50 (ISBN 0-911500-30-8). Theos U Pr.

Practical Oil-Field Metallurgy. Bruce Craig. LC 83-4060. 200p. 1983. 54.95 (ISBN 0-87814-232-0, P-4328). Pennwell Bks.

Practical on-the-Job Training. (Study Units Ser.). 1977. pap. 9.00 (ISBN 0-89401-114-6). Didactic Syst.

Practical Operations & Management of a Bank. 2nd ed. Marshall C. Corns. LC 68-17247. (Illus.). 979p. pap. 160.00 (2052227). Bks Demand UMI.

Practical Operations Mangement. Mike Hayes & Anne Tomes. 256p. 1988. text ed. 49.95 (ISBN 0-86003-558-1, Pub. by Philip Allan); pap. text ed. 19.95 (ISBN 0-86003-658-8). Humanities.

Practical Ophthalmic Microsurgery. A. Lim Siew Ming. (Illus.). 1980. 26.00 (ISBN 3-8055-3036-6). S Karger.

Practical Ophthalmic Problems for Allied Health Professionals. Wayne F. March. (Allied Health Professions Monograph Ser.). 148p. 1984. 12.50 (ISBN 0-87527-329-7). Green.

Practical Optics. William P. Ewald & W. Arthur Young. Ed. by Richard H. Roberts. (Illus.). 280p. 1983. pap. text ed. 45.00 (ISBN 0-911705-00-7). Image Makers.

Practical Optics. Ernest Zebrowski, Jr. (Illus.). 30p. (Orig.). 1982. pap. text ed. 2.95 (ISBN 0-943908-00-0). ITEC.

Practical Optics see Optics & Optical Instruments.

Practical Optimization. Margaret Wright. LC 81-66366. 1982. 29.50 (ISBN 0-12-283952-8). Acad Pr.

Practical Oral Surgery. 3rd ed. Henry B. Clark. LC 65-19426. pap. 95.60 (ISBN 0-317-28180-1, 2014534). Bks Demand UMI.

Practical Organic Mass Spectrometry. J. R. Chapman. LC 84-27132. 197p. 1985. 47.95 (ISBN 0-471-90696-4). Wiley.

Practical Orthography of African Languages. rev. ed. International African Institute Staff. (International Institute of African Languages & Cultures Memorandum Ser.: No. 1). pap. 20.00 (ISBN 0-317-09374-6, 2052040). Bks Demand UMI.

Practical Orthopaedic Medicine. Brian Corrigan & G. D. Maitland. 436p. 1985. pap. text ed. 45.00 (ISBN 0-407-00440-8). Butterworth.

Practical Orthopedics. 2nd ed. L. R. Mercier. 1986. 51.00 (ISBN 0-8151-5864-5). Year Bk Med.

Practical Oscilloscope Handbook. John Douglas-Young. (Illus.). 1979. 14.95 (ISBN 0-13-693549-4, Parker). P-H.

Practical Paediatric Endocrinology. C. G. Brook. 152p. 1978. 29.50 (ISBN 0-8089-1084-1, 790683). Grune.

Practical Paediatrics. Ed. by M. J. Robinson. LC 85-14945. (Illus.). 625p. (Orig.). 1986. text ed. 49.00 (ISBN 0-443-02817-6). Churchill.

Practical Palmistry: A Positive Approach from a Modern Perspective. David Brandon-Jones. LC 86-24485. (Illus.). 264p. (Orig.). 1986. pap. 8.95 (ISBN 0-916360-35-0). CRCS Pubns CA.

Practical Paper Patched Bullet. Paul Matthews. (Illus.). 96p. 1986. 9.50 (ISBN 0-935632-41-7). Wolfe Pub Co.

Practical Paradox: Applications & Programming Techniques. Ken Knecht. (Illus.). 288p. 1986. 27.95 (ISBN 0-8306-0243-7); pap. 18.95 (ISBN 0-8306-2743-X, NO. 2743). TAB Bks.

Practical Parasitology - General Laboratory Techniques & Parasitic Protozoa: Animal Husbandry - Notes for Students. pap. 7.50 (F329, FAO). UNIPUB.

Practical Parenting Tips. Vicki Lansky. (Illus.). 1982. pap. 4.95 (ISBN 0-686-87039-5). Macmillan.

Practical Parenting Tips for the School Age Years. Vicki Lansky. 192p. (Orig.). 1985. pap. 5.95 (ISBN 0-553-34187-1). Bantam.

Practical Partners: Microcomputers & the Industrial Engineer. Gary E. Whitehouse. 1985. 34.95 (ISBN 0-89806-068-0). Inst Indus Eng.

Practical Pascal for Microcomputers. Roger Graham. LC 83-10213. 230p. 1984. pap. 14.95 (ISBN 0-471-88234-8, Pub. by Wiley Pr). Wiley.

Practical Passive Solar Design: A Guide to Homebuilding & Land Development. J. S. Crowley & L. Z. Zimmerman. 256p. 1983. text ed. 43.00 (ISBN 0-07-014769-8). McGraw.

Practical Pattern Manual for Woodcarving & Other Crafts. Art McKellips. LC 81-21254. 120p. (Orig.). 1981. pap. 12.95 (ISBN 0-917304-67-5). Timber.

Practical PC-2-PC-1500 Pocket Computer Programs. Jim Cole. 96p. 1983. 7.95 (ISBN 0-86668-028-4). Arcsoft.

Practical Pediatric & Adolescent Gynecology. Dewhurst. (Reproductive Medicine Ser.: Vol. 1). 288p. 1980. 55.00 (ISBN 0-8247-6978-3). Dekker.

Practical Pediatric Dermatology. William L. Weston. 1985. text ed. 47.00 (ISBN 0-316-93167-5). Little.

Practical Pediatric Gastroenterology. J. A. Walker-Smith & J. R. Hamilton. 368p. 1983. text ed. 49.95 (ISBN 0-407-00204-9). Butterworth.

Practical Pediatric Imaging. Donald Kirks. 811p. 1984. text ed. 99.00 (ISBN 0-316-49471-2). Little.

Practical Pediatric Nutrition. E. M. Poskitt. (Illus.). 304p. 1988. pap. text ed. 49.95 (ISBN 0-407-00408-4). Butterworth.

Practical Pediatric Radiology. Saskia Hilton et al. (Illus.). 619p. 1984. 78.00 (ISBN 0-7216-4682-4). Saunders.

Practical Pediatric Therapy. Eichenwald & Stroder. 1985. 64.95 (ISBN 0-8016-1543-7). Mosby.

Practical Pediatrics in Less-Developed Countries. Karen Olness. 1980. pap. 9.95 (ISBN 0-9602790-2-4). The Garden.

Practical Pedology. Stuart G. McRae. 300p. 1988. 49.95 (ISBN 0-470-21062-1). Wiley.

Practical Pendulum Book. D. Jurriaanse. LC 85-45051. (Illus.). 64p. 1986. pap. 5.95 (ISBN 0-87728-517-9). Weiser.

Practical Performance Appraisal. V. Stewart & A. Stewart. 182p. 1978. text ed. 37.95x (ISBN 0-566-02081-5). Gower Pub Co.

Practical Perioteneal Dialysis. S. F. Beardsworth. (Illus.). 112p. 1984. 27.00 (ISBN 0-7236-0756-7). PSG Pub Co.

Practical Personnel Policies for Small Business. Cohn. 1983. 30.95 (ISBN 0-442-21699-8). Van Nos Reinhold.

Practical Petroleum Engineers' Handbook. 5th ed. Joseph Zaba & W. T. Doherty. LC 58-12306. 948p. 1970. 59.00x (ISBN 0-87201-744-3). Gulf Pub.

Practical Petroleum Engineer's Handbook. 6th ed. Joseph Zaba & W. T. Doherty. Ed. by William C. Lyons. 1400p. 1988. 175.00 (ISBN 0-87201-718-4). Gulf Pub.

Practical Petroleum Geology. Jeff Morris et al. Ed. by Jodie Leecraft. (Illus.). 234p. (Orig.). 1985. pap. text ed. 14.00 (ISBN 0-88698-097-6, 1.00210). PETEX.

Practical Pharmaceutical Chemistry, Part II. 4th, rev. ed. A. H. Beckett & J. B. Stenlake. LC 87-14470. 560p. 1987. 75.00 (ISBN 0-485-11323-6, Pub. by Athlone Pr). Humanities.

Practical Pharmaceutical Chemistry, Part I. 4th, Rev., ed. A. H. Beckett & J. B. Stenlake. LC 87-14470. 382p. 1987. text ed. 55.00 (ISBN 0-485-11322-8, Pub. by Athlone Pr UK). Humanities.

Practical Phonetics for Students of African Languages. D. Westermann & Ida C. Ward. (Published in Association with the International Frican Institute Ser.). 169p. 1988. pap. 15.95 (ISBN 0-7103-0295-9, Pub. by Kegan Paul). Routledge Chapman & Hall.

Practical Photovoltaics: Electricity from Solar Cells. 2nd ed. Richard J. Komp. LC 84-72363. (Illus.). 216p. 1984. pap. 16.95x (ISBN 0-937948-06-3). AATEC Pubns.

Practical Physical Chemistry. 3rd ed. Arthur M. James & F. E. Prichard. LC 73-85687. pap. 89.50 (ISBN 0-317-27847-9, 2025254). Bks Demand UMI.

Practical Physical Geology: Problems & Solutions. John A. Ciciarelli. 274p. 1986. text ed. 65.00 (ISBN 2-88124-098-4); pap. text ed. 25.00 (ISBN 2-88124-065-8). Gordon & Breach.

Practical Physics. 3rd ed. G. L. Squires. 200p. 1985. 49.50 (ISBN 0-521-24952-X); pap. 19.95 (ISBN 0-521-27095-2). Cambridge U Pr.

Practical Physics. Jerry D. Wilson. 560p. 1986. text ed. 37.25 (ISBN 0-03-063512-8). SCP.

Practical Physics. Ernest Zebrowski, Jr. (Illus.). 1980. text ed. 33.95 (ISBN 0-07-072788-0). McGraw.

Practical Physics: How Things Work. David Lazarus & Manfred Raether. (Illus.). 1984. pap. text ed. 13.80x (ISBN 0-87563-167-3). Stipes.

Practical Piano Skills. 3rd ed. William Starr & Constance Starr. 192p. 1984. write for info plastic comb. (ISBN 0-697-03640-5). Wm C Brown.

Practical Piano Skills. 4th ed. William Starr & Constance Starr. 224p. 1988. write for info. plastic comb. bdg. (ISBN 0-697-03661-8). Wm C Brown.

Practical Pig Nutrition. 2nd ed. C. T. Whittemore & F. W. Esley. (Illus.). 190p. Repr. of 1976 ed. 19.95 (ISBN 0-85236-074-6, Pub. by Farming Pr UK). Diamond Farm Bk.

Practical Pig Production. 3rd ed. Keith Thornton. (Illus.). 225p. 1981. Repr. of 1973 ed. 19.95 (ISBN 0-85236-115-7, Pub. by Farming Pr UK). Diamond Farm Bk.

Practical Pilot: Coastal Navigation by Eye, Intuition, Common Sense, & Cunning. Leonard Eyges. (Illus.). 192p. 1988. pap. 19.95 (ISBN 0-87742-969-3). Intl Marine.

Practical Piloting. Tom Bottomley. (Illus.). 182p. (Orig.). 1983. pap. 10.25 (ISBN 0-8306-0619-X, 1619). TAB Bks.

Practical Piping Handbook. Otto Mendel. 340p. 1981. 59.95 (ISBN 0-87814-169-3, P-4270). Pennwell Bks.

Practical PL-I. Gordon R. Clarke et al. (British Computer Society Monographs in Informatics). (Illus.). 229p. 1986. pap. 24.95 (ISBN 0-521-31768-1). Cambridge U Pr.

Practical Planning: A How-To Guide for Solos & Small Law Firms. Henry W. Ewalt. 1985. 36.95 (ISBN 0-89707-196-4). Amer Bar Assn.

Practical Planning Law: A Handbook for Planners, Architects & Surveyors. J. F. Garner. 246p. 1981. pap. 11.50 (ISBN 0-7099-1107-6, Pub. by Croom Helm Ltd); 31.50 (ISBN 0-7099-1106-8). Routledge Chapman & Hall.

Practical Planning Techniques for Personnel Managers. Stephen D. Bruce. 1986. pap. 24.95 (ISBN 1-55645-508-9). Busn Legal Reports.

Practical Plant Layout. Richard Muther. 1956. text ed. 49.95 (ISBN 0-07-044156-1). McGraw.

Practical Plant Physiology. J. Roberts & D. G. Whitehouse. LC 75-46566. pap. 42.80 (ISBN 0-317-27666-2, 2025213). Bks Demand UMI.

Practical Plumbing Design Guide. James C. Church. LC 78-18823. (Illus.). 1979. text ed. 47.50 (ISBN 0-07-010832-3). McGraw.

Practical Pointers for Training Your Child. Lloy A. Kniss. 1975. pap. 2.75 (ISBN 0-87813-509-X). Christian Light.

Practical Points in Anesthesiology. 3rd ed. Robert Stark et al. Ed. by Hilda Pederson. (Practical Points Ser.: Vol. 1). 1985. pap. text ed. 28.25 (ISBN 0-87488-480-2). Med Exam.

Practical Points in Gynecology. Donald P. Swartz. (Practical Points Ser.: Vol. 3). 1984. pap. 26.50 (ISBN 0-87488-706-2). Med Exam.

Practical Points in Pediatrics. 4th ed. Raymond Russo et al. (Practical Points Ser.: Vol. 10). 1985. pap. text ed. 30.00 (ISBN 0-87488-618-X). Med Exam.

Practical Points in Pulmonary Diseases. 2nd ed. Daniel Stone et al. (Practical Points Ser.: Vol. 6). 1984. text ed. 29.95 (ISBN 0-87488-747-X); pap. text ed. 22.50 (ISBN 0-87488-724-0). Med Exam.

Practical Pole Building Construction. Leigh Seddon. Ed. by Susan Williamson. (Illus.). 176p. 1985. pap. 9.95 (ISBN 0-913589-16-0). Williamson Pub Co.

Practical Polish-English Dictionary. J. Stanislawski. 1030p. (Pol. & Eng.). 1978. Leatherette 19.95 (ISBN 0-686-92364-2, M-9134). French & Eur.

Practical Polish-English, English-Polish Dictionary. rev. ed. Iwo C. Pogonowski. (Practical Dictionaries Ser.). 400p. 1988. pap. 7.95 (ISBN 0-87052-550-6). Hippocrene Bks.

Practical Politics: Social Work & Political Responsibility. Ed. by Maryann Mahaffey & John Hanks. 1982. text ed. 19.95x (ISBN 0-87101-099-2); pap. text ed. 16.95x (ISBN 0-87101-093-3). Natl Assn Soc Wkrs.

Practical Politics: Twentieth-Century Views on Politics & Economics. George Bernard Shaw. Ed. by Lloyd Hubenka. LC 75-3571. xxviii, 266p. 1976. 24.50x (ISBN 0-8032-0856-1). U of Nebr Pr.

Practical Polo. W. G. Vickers. (Illus.). pap. 5.50 (ISBN 0-85131-186-5, NL51, Pub. by J A Allen U K). S R Smith Sporting Bks.

Practical Power-Control Techniques. Irving M. Gottlieb. 248p. 1986. pap. 14.95 (ISBN 0-672-22493-3). Sams.

Practical PR for School Library Media Centers. Marian S. Edsall. LC 83-4086. 165p. 1984. 27.95 (ISBN 0-918212-77-4). Neal-Schuman.

Practical Pre-Retirement Planning. Sanford J. Schlesinger & Paul G. Hoffman. LC 86-60315. (Tax Law & Estate Planning Ser.). 320p. 1986. 45.00 (D4-4186). PLI.

Practical Pregnancy. Maxine G. Wolfe & Margot Goldsmith. LC 79-22003. (Illus.). 320p. (Orig.). 1980. 12.50 (ISBN 0-446-51204-4); pap. 9.95 (ISBN 0-446-38273-6). Warner Bks.

Practical Prescribing. Ed. by Martin J. Brodie & P. Ian Harrison. LC 85-20926. (Illus.). 295p. 1986. pap. text ed. 25.50 (ISBN 0-443-03304-8). Churchill.

Practical Primary Drama. Geoff Davies. vii, 63p. 1983. pap. text ed. 7.50x (ISBN 0-435-18236-6). Heinemann Ed.

Practical Primary Science: A Source Book for Teachers. Romola Showell. (Ward Lock Educational Ser.). 29.00x (ISBN 0-7062-4240-8, Pub. by Ward Lock Educ Co Ltd). State Mutual Bk.

Practical Principles of Ion-Exchange Water Treatment. Dean L. Owens. 320p. 1985. 45.00x (ISBN 0-927188-00-7). Tall Oaks Pub.

Practical Sermons: New York, 1858. Nathaniel W. Taylor. Ed. by Bruce Kuklick. (American Religious Thought of the 18th & 19th Centuries Ser.). 455p. 1987. lib. bdg. 60.00 (ISBN 0-8240-6959-5). Garland Pub.

Practical Sermons That Motivate. J. J. Turner. pap. 2.95 (ISBN 0-89315-211-0). Lambert Bk.

Practical Sex Crime Investigation. O'Reilly. Date not set. price not set (ISBN 0-444-00872-1). Elsevier.

Practical Sheet Metal Projects-130 Graded Projects with Drawings, Forming Information & Sequences. 2nd ed. Richard S. Budzik. LC 79-93132. (Illus.). (gr. 7-12). 1979. 29.95 (ISBN 0-912914-28-9). Practical Pubns.

Practical Shellfish Farming. Phil Schwind. LC 77-84167. pap. 25.30 (ISBN 0-317-42105-0, 2026225). Bks Demand UMI.

Practical Ship Handling. M. C. Armstrong. 112p. 1980. 19.50x (ISBN 0-85174-387-0). Sheridan.

Practical Shipbuilding, 2 vols. A. C. Holms. LC 76-49170. 1977. lib. bdg. 200.00 (ISBN 0-8490-2461-7). Gordon Pr.

Practical Shop Mathematics. Thomas C. Power. (Illus.). 1979. pap. 29.95 (ISBN 0-07-050591-8). McGraw.

Practical Shop Mathematics. 200p. 1988. 30.00 (ISBN 0-933931-09-3). Hitchcock Pub.

Practical Shop Mathematics, Vol. 1: Elementary. 4th ed. John H. Wolfe & E. R. Phelps. 1958. text ed. 25.20 (ISBN 0-07-071358-8). McGraw.

Practical Shoulder Surgery. Ed. by Michael Watson. (Illus.). 288p. 1985. 56.50 (ISBN 0-8089-1702-1, 794755). Grune.

Practical Sign Shop Operation. Bob Fitzgerald. (Illus.). 1982. 26.95 (ISBN 0-911380-58-2). Signs of Times.

Practical Simulation of Radar Antennas & Radomes. Hebert L. Hirsch & Douglas C. Grove. 300p. 1988. text ed. 66.00 (ISBN 0-89006-237-4). Artech Hse.

Practical Small Boat Designs. John Atkin. LC 82-48618. (Illus.). 192p. 1983. pap. 16.95 (ISBN 0-87742-160-9, P577). Intl Marine.

Practical Soccer Tactics. Larry Maisner. LC 78-64382. (Illus.). 144p. 1979. pap. 4.95 (ISBN 0-89037-157-1). Anderson World.

Practical Soccer Tactics. Larry Maisner. 1985. 7.95 (ISBN 0-02-028790-9). Macmillan.

Practical Socialism for Britain. Hugh Dalton. (English Workers & The Coming of the Welfare State Ser.). 401p. 1985. lib. bdg. 55.00 (ISBN 0-8240-7609-5). Garland Pub.

Practical Soil Science. N. N. Nikol'skil. 248p. 1963. text ed. 54.00x (ISBN 0-7065-0252-3, Pub. by Keter Pub Jerusalem). Coronet Bks.

Practical Solar Energy Technology. Martin L. Greenwald & Thomas K. McHugh. LC 84-23721. (Illus.). 256p. 1985. text ed. 34.00 (ISBN 0-13-693979-1). P-H.

Practical Solutions to Problems in Experimental Mechanics, 1940-1985. Given A. Brewer. 1987. 16.95 (ISBN 0-533-07224-7). Vantage.

Practical Space Applications. Ed. by L. L. Kavanau. (Advances in the Astronautical Sciences Ser.: Vol. 21). 1967. 40.00x (ISBN 0-87703-024-3, Pub. by Am Astronaut). Univelt Inc.

Practical Spanish Dictionary & Phrasebook. Marguerite D. Bomse. (Span.). 1978. pap. text ed. 11.50 (ISBN 0-08-023020-2). Pergamon.

Practical Spanish-English, English-Spanish Dictionary. Arthur Butterfield. (Practical Language Dictionaries Ser.). 400p. (Orig., Eng. & Span.). 1983. pap. 6.95 (ISBN 0-88254-814-X). Hippocrene Bks.

Practical Spanish for Medical & Hospital Personnel. 2nd ed. Marguerite D. Bomse & Julian H. Alfaro. 1978. pap. text ed. 10.00 (ISBN 0-08-023001-6). Pergamon.

Practical Spanish for Public Safety Personnel. Moreno & Hayden. 1987. 10.95 (ISBN 0-317-67667-9). Davis Pub Co.

Practical Spanish for School Personnel, Firemen, Policemen & Community Agencies. 2nd ed. Marguerite D. Bomse & Julian H. Alfaro. 1978. pap. text ed. 10.00 (ISBN 0-08-023002-4). Pergamon.

Practical Spanish Grammar. Marguerite D. Bomse. 1978. pap. text ed. 11.50 (ISBN 0-08-021859-8). Pergamon.

Practical Spanish Grammar. Marcial Prado. (Self-Teaching Ser.). 360p. 1983. pap. text ed. 10.95 (ISBN 0-471-89894-5, 1-581, Pub. by Wiley Pr). Wiley.

Practical Specifier: A Manual of Construction Documentation for Architects. W. Rosenfeld. 194p. 1985. text ed. 34.50 (ISBN 0-07-053779-8). McGraw.

Practical Speech for Modern Business. Robert C. Martin et al. LC 63-7333. 1963. 29.50x (ISBN 0-89197-353-2). Irvington.

Practical Spirituality. John R. Price. 160p. (Orig.). 1985. pap. 6.95 (ISBN 0-942082-06-0). Quartus Bks.

Practical Spirituality for Lay People. Dolores R. Leckey. LC 86-63342. 112p. (Orig.). 1987. pap. 6.95 (ISBN 0-934134-80-4). Sheed & Ward MO.

Practical Spoken Spanish. 7th ed. F. M. Kercheville. LC 35-4432. 160p. 1985. pap. 7.95 (ISBN 0-8263-0059-6). U of NM Pr.

Practical Stable Management. Christine Hughes & Robert Oliver. (Illus.). 208p. Date not set. 22.95 (ISBN 0-7207-1759-0, Pub. by Michael Joseph). Viking.

Practical Statistician: Simplified Handbook of Statistics. Marigold Linton & Phillip S. Gallo, Jr. LC 73-91423. (Illus.). 1975. pap. text ed. 16.00 pub net (ISBN 0-8185-0127-8). Brooks-Cole.

Practical Statistics. S. S. Cohen. (Illus.). 224p. (Orig.). 1988. pap. text ed. 17.95 (ISBN 0-7131-3648-0, Pub. by E Arnold UK). Routledge Chapman & Hall.

Practical Statistics & Probability. Robert Loveday. 256p. 1974. pap. text ed. 8.95x (ISBN 0-521-20291-4). Cambridge U Pr.

Practical Statistics for Analytical Chemists. Robert L. Anderson. (Illus.). 352p. 1987. 39.95 (ISBN 0-442-20973-8). Van Nos Reinhold.

Practical Statistics for Engineers & Scientists. Nicholas P. Cheremisinoff. LC 86-72352. 224p. 1987. 35.00 (ISBN 0-87762-505-0); DATA-FIT software disc (supp. to text) 69.00 (ISBN 0-317-55594-4). Technomic.

Practical Statistics for Experimental Biologists. A. C. Wardlaw. LC 85-3147. 1985. 49.95 (ISBN 0-471-90737-5); pap. 30.80 (ISBN 0-471-90738-3). Wiley.

Practical Statistics Simply Explained. 2nd ed. Russell A. Langley. 1971. pap. 6.95 (ISBN 0-486-22729-4). Dover.

Practical Steps to Quality Printing. Ed. by Eastman Kodak Co. 24p. 1977. pap. 5.00 (ISBN 0-87985-209-7, Q-72). Eastman Kodak.

Practical Stereology. John C. Russ. 194p. 1986. 29.50x (ISBN 0-306-42460-6, Plenum Pr). Plenum Pub.

Practical Stock & Inventory Techniques. C. L. Hohenstein. 192p. 1982. 27.95 (ISBN 0-442-23609-3). Van Nos Reinhold.

Practical Stonemasonry Made Easy. Stephen M. Kennedy. (Illus.). 256p. 1987. 24.95 (ISBN 0-8306-1115-0, 2915H); pap. 16.95 (ISBN 0-8306-2915-7, 2915P). Tab Bks.

Practical Strategic Planning: A Guide & Manual for Line Managers. William P. Anthony. LC 85-9489. (Illus.). xii, 217p. 1985. lib. bdg. 40.95 (ISBN 0-89930-102-9, ANT/). Greenwood.

Practical Strategies for Taming the Paper & People Problems in Teaching. Anne W. Dodd. (Illus.). 176p. 1987. text ed. 24.75x (ISBN 0-398-05386-3). C C Thomas.

Practical Strategies for the Teaching of Thinking. Beyer. 1987. 32.95 (ISBN 0-205-10544-0, Pub. by Longwood Div). Allyn.

Practical Strategies in Outpatient Medicine. Brendan M. Reilly. (Illus.). 806p. 1984. pap. 63.00 (ISBN 0-7216-7539-5). Saunders.

Practical Strategist: Business & Corporate Strategy in the 90s. Robert J. Allio. 240p. 1988. 29.95 (ISBN 0-88730-319-6). Ballinger Pub.

Practical Stress Analysis in Engineering Design. Alexander Blake. (Mechanical Engineering Ser.: Vol. 12). (Illus.). 680p. 1982. 55.00 (ISBN 0-8247-1370-2). Dekker.

Practical Structural Analysis for Architectural Engineering. August E. Komendant. (Illus.). 160p. 1987. text ed. 43.00 (ISBN 0-13-693961-9). P-H.

Practical Studies in Systematic Design. V. Hubka et al. 216p. 1988. text ed. 39.95 (ISBN 0-408-01420-2). Butterworth.

Practical Study of Argument. 2nd ed. Trudy Govier. 376p. 1988. pap. text ed. write for info. (ISBN 0-534-08262-9). Wadsworth Pub.

Practical Study of the Use of the Natural Vegetable Dyes in New Mexico. Mela S. Brewster. LC 38-28365. 1982. lib. bdg. 19.95x (ISBN 0-89370-726-0). Borgo Pr.

Practical Stylist Canadian. 2nd ed. Sheridan Baker. 288p. 1985. pap. text ed. 13.50 (ISBN 0-06-040468-X, HarpC). Har-Row.

Practical Stylist: With Readings. 6th ed. Sheridan Baker & Robert Yarber. 528p. 1985. pap. text ed. 21.95 scp (ISBN 0-06-040444-2, HarpC). Har-Row.

Practical Suggestions for the Learning of an African Language in the Field. Ida C. Ward. (International African Institute Memorandum: Vol. 14). pap. 20.00 (ISBN 0-317-10181-1, 2055390). Bks Demand UMI.

Practical Sun Power. David A. Wilson & William H. Rankins. (Illus.). 56p. (Orig.). 1974. pap. 6.00 (ISBN 0-934852-13-8). Lorien Hse.

Practical Supervision: How to Organize for Effectiveness. Anthony M. Micolo. Ed. by Stephen E. Bruce. 332p. 1987. looseleaf 59.95 (ISBN 1-55645-427-9). Busn Legal Reports.

Practical Surface Analysis by Auger & Photo-Electron Spectoscopy. D. Briggs & M. P. Seah. 533p. 1983. 127.95x (ISBN 0-471-26279-X, Pub. by Wiley-Interscience). Wiley.

Practical Surgical Pathology. Ed. by Zeynel A. Karcioglu. Ayten Someren. LC 83-72632. (Illus.). 1024p. 1984. 150.00 (ISBN 0-669-07499-3, Collamore). Heath.

Practical Tax Guide for the Horse Owner, 1986 Edition. John Talbott. (Illus.). 97p. 1986. pap. 15.00x (ISBN 0-317-40030-4). Pub Horizons.

Practical Taxidermy. 2nd ed. John W. Moyer. 146p. 1984. pap. 12.95 (ISBN 0-471-80356-1). Wiley.

Practical Techniques for the Recording Engineer. 2nd ed. Sherman Keene. LC 81-148444. (Illus.). 1981. text ed. 34.95 (ISBN 0-942080-00-9); pap. text ed. 24.95 (ISBN 0-942080-08-4); tchr's manual 45.00 (ISBN 0-942080-03-3); students wkbk. o.p. 7.75 (ISBN 0-942080-04-1); tchr's answer key (ISBN 0-942080-05-X). SKE Pub.

Practical Techniques of Astral Projection. Douglas Baker. (Illus.). 96p. (Orig.). 1977. pap. 6.95 (ISBN 0-85030-141-6, Pub. by Thorsons Pub). Weiser.

Practical Techniques of Business Forecasting: Fundamentals & Applications for Marketing, Production, & Finacial Managers. George Kress. LC 85-6361. (Illus.). xvi, 257p. 1985. lib. bdg. 40.95 (ISBN 0-89930-107-X, KSU/, Quorum). Greenwood.

Practical Techniques of Electronic Circuit Design. 2nd ed. Robert L. Bonebreak. LC 86-23382. 431p. 1987. 46.50 (ISBN 0-471-85244-9). Wiley.

Practical Techniques of Psychic Self-Defense. Murry Hope. 96p. 1985. pap. 5.95 (ISBN 0-312-63552-4). St Martin.

Practical Teratology. Pamela Taylor. 1986. 29.50 (ISBN 0-12-683860-7). Acad Pr.

Practical Thai Cooking. Puangkram C. Schmitz & Michael J. Worman. LC 85-40060. (Illus.). 176p. 1985. 19.95 (ISBN 0-87011-727-0). Kodansha.

Practical Theology of Spirituality. Lawrence O. Richards. 288p. 1987. 18.95 (ISBN 0-310-39140-7, 18301). Zondervan.

Practical Theology: The Emerging Field in Theology, Church & World. Ed. by Don S. Browning. LC 82-47739. 128p. (Orig.). 1982. pap. 8.95 (ISBN 0-06-061153-7, RD-410, HarpR). Har-Row.

Practical Theorist: The Life & Work of Kurt Lewin. Alfred J. Marrow. LC 77-1400. pap. 79.80 (ISBN 0-317-28352-9, 2022551). Bks Demand UMI.

Practical Thermoforming: Principles & Applications. Florian. (Plastics Engineering Ser.). 424p. 1987. 79.75 (ISBN 0-8247-7662-3). Dekker.

Practical Things to Do with a Microcomputer. Tatchell & N. Cutter. (Computer & Electronics Ser.). (Illus.). 48p. (gr. 6 up). 1983. pap. 2.95 (ISBN 0-86020-731-5); lib. bdg. 9.96 (ISBN 0-88110-140-0). EDC.

Practical Thinking. Edward De Bono. Date not set. price not set. Intl Ctr Creat Think.

Practical Thirteen CNMR Spectroscopy: A Textbook for the Chemist. Cheng. 1988. write for info. (ISBN 0-471-85773-4). Wiley.

Practical Time Management. Marion E. Haynes. 136p. 1984. 29.95 (ISBN 0-87814-273-8, P-4380). PennWell Bks.

Practical Time Management - How to Get More Done in Less Time. Bradley C. McRae. 160p. 1988. pap. 6.95 (ISBN 0-88908-673-7, 9559). TAB Bks.

Practical Timex-Sinclair Computer Programs for Beginners. Edward Page. 96p. 1983. 7.95 (ISBN 0-86668-027-6). Arcsoft.

Practical Tips on How to Study. rev ed. Ed. by Clyde E. Noble. LC 72-82234. 85p. 1974. pap. text ed. 4.95 (ISBN 0-87842-056-8). Mountain Pr.

Practical Tissue Culture Applications. Ed. by Karl Maramorosh & Hiroyuki Hirumi. LC 79-12068. 1979. 29.95 (ISBN 0-12-470285-6). Acad Pr.

Practical Tools & Techniques for Managing Time. Myrna Lebov. 1981. pap. 5.95 (ISBN 0-917386-38-8). Exec Ent Pubns.

Practical Tourist; or, Sketches of the State of the Useful Arts, & of Society, Scenery in Great Britain, France & Holland, 2 vols. in 1. Zachariah Allen. LC 73-38258. (Evolution of Capitalism Ser.). 896p. 1972. Repr. of 1832 ed. 52.00x (ISBN 0-405-04111-X). Ayer Co Pubs.

Practical Training in Thought. Rudolf Steiner. 1968. pap. 2.95 (ISBN 0-910142-29-7). Anthroposophic.

Practical Transistor Circuit Design & Analysis. Gerald E. Williams. (Illus.). 420p. 1973. text ed. 44.95 (ISBN 0-07-070398-1). McGraw.

Practical Transistors & Linear Integrated Circuits. Joseph D. Greenfield. LC 87-21708. 686p. 1988. write for info. (ISBN 0-471-89097-9). Wiley.

Practical Transistors & Linear Integrated Circuits, Experiments. Joseph D. Greenfield. 132p. (Orig.). 1988. pap. price not set (ISBN 0-471-63830-7). Wiley.

Practical Treatise of Cast & Wrought Iron Bridges & Girders: As Applied to Railway Structures & to Buildings Generally. William Humber. (Industrial Antiquites Ser.). (Illus.). 236p. 1987. Repr. of 1857 ed. 180.00 (ISBN 1-85297-018-9). Archival Facsimiles.

Practical Treatise on Business. Edwin T. Freedley. LC 73-2508. (Big Business; Economic Power in a Free Society Ser.). Repr. of 1853 ed. 23.50 (ISBN 0-405-05089-5). Ayer Co Pubs.

Practical Treatise on Coal, Petroleum & Other Distilled Oils. 2nd ed. Abraham Gesner. Ed. by George W. Gesner. LC 67-29511. 1968. Repr. of 1865 ed. 29.50x (ISBN 0-678-00440-4). Kelley.

Practical Treatise on Engine Crankshaft Torsional Vibration Control. 44p. (Orig.). 1979. pap. 15.00 (ISBN 0-89883-216-0, SP445). Soc Auto Engineers.

Practical Treatise on Japanese Ink Painting. Osaki Okiyama. (Illus.). 161p. 1986. 127.75 (ISBN 0-86650-189-4). Gloucester Art.

Practical Treatise on Military Surgery. Frank H. Hamilton. LC 88-60873. (American Civil War Surgery Ser.). 240p. 1988. price not set (ISBN 0-930405-05-6). Norman SF.

Practical Treatise on Nervous Exhaustion (Neurasthenia) Its Symptoms, Nature, Sequences, Treatment. 5th enl. ed. G. M. Beard. Ed. by A. D. Rockwell. Repr. of 1905 ed. 29.00 (ISBN 0-527-06340-1). Kraus Repr.

Practical Treatise on Organ - Building. F. E. Robertson. (Illus.). 370p. Set. pap. 50.00x (ISBN 0-913746-04-5). Organ Lit.

Practical Treatise on the Domestic Management & Most Important Diseases of Advanced Life. George E. Day. Ed. by Robert Kastenbaum. LC 78-22198. (Aging & Old Age Ser.). 1979. Repr. of 1849 ed. lib. bdg. 17.00x (ISBN 0-405-11815-5). Ayer Co Pubs.

Practical Treatise on the Use of the Microscope. John Quekett. (History of Microscopy Ser.). 512p. 1987. Repr. of 1848 ed. write for info. (ISBN 0-940095-05-X). Sci Heritage Pr.

Practical Treatise upon the Law of Railways. 2nd ed. Isaac F. Redfield. LC 70-37982. (American Law Ser.: The Formative Years). 850p. 1972. Repr. of 1858 ed. 48.50 (ISBN 0-405-04025-3). Ayer Co Pubs.

Practical Treatise upon the Law of Railways. 2nd ed. Isaac F. Redfield. Repr. of 1858 ed. 60.00. Johnson Repr.

Practical Treatment of Backache & Sciatica. D. N Golding & J. Barrett. 1984. lib. bdg. 26.75 (ISBN 0-85200-773-6, Pub. by MTP Pr England). Kluwer Academic.

Practical Troubleshooting for Microprocessors. James W. Coffron. (Illus.). 256p. 1981. text ed. 39.00 (ISBN 0-13-694273-3). P-H.

Practical Troubleshooting with Modern Electronic Test Instruments. Robert L. Goodman. (Illus.). 1979. pap. 9.95 (ISBN 0-8306-1177-0, 1177). TAB Bks.

Practical Truth Series, 6 Vols. Alfred Edersheim et al. Incl. Elisha; Jonah; Thessalonians; Pastoral Epistles; Israel's Wanderings; Judges. 1940p. 1986. Set. 74.70 (ISBN 0-8254-3529-3). Kregel.

Practical Truths from Elisha. Alfred Edersheim. LC 82-18702. 368p. 1983. 14.95 (ISBN 0-8254-2511-5). Kregel.

Practical Truths from First Thessalonians. F. E. Marsh. LC 86-2742. Orig. Title: Flashes from the Lighthouse of Truth. 272p. 1986. Repr. 12.95 (ISBN 0-8254-3234-0). Kregel.

Practical Truths from Israel's Wanderings. George Wagner. LC 82-18706. 384p. 1983. 14.95 (ISBN 0-8254-4017-3). Kregel.

Practical Truths from Jonah. Joseph S. Exell. LC 82-18671. 240p. 1983. 11.95 (ISBN 0-8254-2525-5). Kregel.

Practical Truths From Judges. Luke H. Wiseman. LC 85-8096. 354p. 1985. 14.95 (ISBN 0-8254-4034-3). Kregel.

Practical Truths from the Pastoral Epistles. Eugene Stock. LC 83-6113. 352p. 1983. 14.95 (ISBN 0-8254-3746-6). Kregel.

Practical TSO-ISPF for Today's Programmers. James G. Janossy. LC 88-95. 1988. 29.95 (ISBN 0-471-63357-7). Wiley.

Practical Tutor. Emily Myer & Louise Z. Smith. (Illus.). 368p. 1987. 32.50 (ISBN 0-19-504109-7); pap. text ed. 14.95 (ISBN 0-19-503865-7). Oxford U Pr.

Practical Typography from A to Z. Frank Romano. 176p. 19.95 (ISBN 0-318-03257-0). Print Indus Am.

Practical Urologic Endoscopy. Makoto Miki. LC 83-13037. (Illus.). 96p. 1983. text ed. 44.00 (ISBN 0-89640-090-5). Igaku-Shoin.

Practical Use of Antibiotics: An Update for the 1980's. W. Lee Hand et al. 88p. 1984. Boxed Set. incl. 8 Cassettes, text & self-assessment exam 250.00 (ISBN 0-918473-06-3). Sci-Thru-Media.

Practical Use of the Microscope. George H. Needham. (Illus.). 520p. 1977. 57.75 (ISBN 0-398-03645-4). C C Thomas.

Practical Use of Theory in Fluid Flow, Bk. 1: Inertial Flows. S. W. Churchill. 155p. 1988. text ed. 34.95 (ISBN 0-317-68869-3). Butterworth.

Practical Uses of Speech Communication. 6th ed. Harold Barrett. 416p. 1987. pap. text ed. write for info. (ISBN 0-03-003272-5). HR&W.

Practical Vedanta. Swami Vivekananda. pap. 1.50 (ISBN 0-87481-124-4). Vedanta Pr.

Practical Vedic Dictionary. Suryakanta. 1981. 49.95x (ISBN 0-19-561298-1). Oxford U Pr.

Practical Vibration Primer. Charles Jackson. LC 79-50249. (Illus.). 120p. 1979. 37.00x (ISBN 0-87201-891-1). Gulf Pub.

Practical View of the Present State of Slavery in the West Indies. facs. ed. Alexander Barclay. LC 74-83955. (Black Heritage Library Collection Ser.). 1828. 22.50 (ISBN 0-8369-8508-7). Ayer Co Pubs.

Practical Virology for Medical Students & Practitioners in Tropical Countries. D. Metselaar & D. I. Simpson. (Illus.). 1982. pap. text ed. 25.00x (ISBN 0-19-261317-0). Oxford U Pr.

Practical Vision of Christian Unity. Jean C. Lyles. LC 81-15032. (Into Our Third Century Ser.). 96p. (Orig.). 1982. pap. 3.95 (ISBN 0-687-33330-X). Abingdon.

Practice Issues in Social Welfare Administration, Policy & Planning. Ed. by Milton M. Lebowitz. LC 82-6269. (Administration in Social Work Ser.: Vol. 6, Nos. 2-3). 157p. 1982. text ed. 32.95 (ISBN 0-86656-142-0, B142); pap. text ed. 14.95 (ISBN 0-86656-166-8). Haworth Pr.

Practice Makes Perfect. Jahnna Beecham. (Sweet Dreams Ser.: No. 149). 176p. (Orig.). 1988. pap. 2.50 (ISBN 0-553-27276-4). Bantam.

Practice Makes Perfect. Edward Vernon. (Lythway Ser.). 1987. lib. bdg. 17.50x (ISBN 0-7451-0596-3, Pub. by Chivers Pr UK). G K Hall.

Practice Management for Physicians. Donald L. Donohugh. (Illus.). 365p. 1986. pap. 30.95 (ISBN 0-7216-1889-8). Saunders.

Practice Manual for Child Abuse & Neglect Cases in the District of Columbia. Justine A. Dunlap et al. 510p. (Orig.). 1988. pap. text ed. 45.00 (ISBN 0-940259-00-1). Council Ct Excell.

Practice Manual for Microvascular Surgery. 2nd ed. Acland. 132p. 1988. 23.00 (ISBN 0-8016-0006-5). Mosby.

Practice Manual for Social Security Claims: 1983 Supplement. Dennis M. Sweeney & James J. Lyko. 89p. 1983. pap. 15.00 (ISBN 0-686-82489-X, C5-1175). PLI.

Practice of Advertising. Norman A. Hart & James O'Connor. 224p. 1984. pap. 20.95 (ISBN 0-434-90716-2, Pub. by W Heinemann Ltd). David & Charles.

Practice of Anaesthesia & Resuscitation. P. K. Gupta. 1985. 59.00x (ISBN 0-317-38791-X, Pub. by Current Dist). State Mutual Bk.

Practice of Anesthesia for Infants & Children. Ed. by John F. Ryan et al. LC 79-3619. 352p. 1986. 69.50 (ISBN 0-8089-1732-3, 793691). Grune.

Practice of Architecture: 1833 see Works of Asher Benjamin: Boston, 1806-1843.

Practice of Aromatherapy: Holistic Health & the Essential Oils of Flowers & Herbs. Jean Valnet. LC 82-4968. (Illus.). 279p. 1982. pap. 8.95 (ISBN 0-89281-026-2, Destiny Bks). Inner Tradit.

Practice of Arthroscopic Surgery. 3rd ed. Johnson. 1986. 360.00 (ISBN 0-8016-2591-2). Mosby.

Practice of Astrology. Dane Rudhyar. LC 77-90881. 1978. pap. 6.95 (ISBN 0-87773-125-X). Shambhala Pubns.

Practice of Autosuggestion by the Method of Emile Coue. C. Harry Brooks. 120p. 1981. pap. 7.00 (ISBN 0-89540-076-6, SB-076). Sun Pub.

Practice of Banking in England, Vol. 1. J. E. Kelly. 528p. (Orig.). 1984. pap. text ed. 27.50x (ISBN 0-318-04636-9). Trans-Atl Phila.

Practice of Banking in England, Vol. 2. D. G. Wild & J. R. Marsh. 352p. (Orig.). 1985. pap. text ed. 27.50x (ISBN 0-7121-1680-X). Trans-Atl Phila.

Practice of Banking: Quiz Book, No. 1. Ed. by The Institute of Bankers Staff. 1985. 35.00x (ISBN 0-85297-131-1, Pub. by Inst of Bankers). State Mutual BK.

Practice of Banking 1. Michael Marsden. 225p. 1985. 31.00 (ISBN 0-86010-580-6); pap. 24.00 (ISBN 0-86010-563-6); Vol. 5 of B & F Series Manual; 150p. manual 16.50 (ISBN 0-86010-588-1). Graham & Trotman.

Practice of Behavior Therapy. 3rd ed. Joseph Wolpe. (Illus.). 425p. 1982. pap. text ed. 19.50 (ISBN 0-08-027164-2). Pergamon.

Practice of Behavioural Medicine. Ed. by Shirley Pearce & Jane Wardle. 320p. 1988. 65.00 (ISBN 0-19-261691-9); pap. 35.00 (ISBN 0-19-261689-7). Oxford U Pr.

Practice of Cardiac Pacing. Seymour Furman et al. (Illus.). 496p. 1986. monograph 59.50 (ISBN 0-87993-271-6). Futura Pub.

Practice of Cardiology. Ed. by Robert A. Johnson et al. 1980. text ed. 82.00 (ISBN 0-316-46945-9). Little.

Practice of Cardiothoracic Surgery. M. P. Holden. (Illus.). 448p. 1982. text ed. 63.00 (ISBN 0-7236-0626-9). PSG Pub Co.

Practice of Child Therapy. Ed. by Richard J. Morris & Thomas R. Kratochwill. (Pergamon General Psychology Ser.: No. 124). (Illus.). 360p. 1983. text ed. 68.00 (ISBN 0-08-028033-1); pap. text ed. 23.00 (ISBN 0-08-028032-3). Pergamon.

Practice of Chinese Buddhism, 1900-1950. Holmes H. Welch. LC 67-13256. pap. 10.95x (ISBN 0-674-69701-4). Harvard U Pr.

Practice of Clinical Child Psychology. Alan O. Ross. LC 59-9399. (Illus.). 288p. 1959. 49.50 (ISBN 0-8089-0390-X, 793662). Grune.

Practice of Clinical Engineering. Ed. by C. A. Caceres. 1977. 89.00 (ISBN 0-12-153860-5). Acad Pr.

Practice of Clinical Health Psychology. Cynthia D. Belar et al. (Psychology Practitioner Guidebooks Ser.). 160p. 1987. text ed. 22.50 (ISBN 0-08-034678-2, PBI); pap. text ed. 12.95 (ISBN 0-08-034677-4, PBI). Pergamon.

Practice of Clinical Research: The Single Case Method. John H. Behling & Esther S. Merves. LC 84-13179. (Illus.). 122p. (Orig.). 1984. lib. bdg. 22.00 (ISBN 0-8191-4183-6); pap. text ed. 8.75 (ISBN 0-8191-4184-4). U Pr of Amer.

Practice of Clinical Sociology. L. Alex Swan. 160p. 1983. 18.95 (ISBN 0-87073-618-3); pap. 11.95 (ISBN 0-87073-619-1). Schenkman Bks Inc.

Practice of Collage. Brian French & Anne Butler. (Illus.). 87p. 1976. 12.50 (ISBN 0-263-05711-9). Transatl Arts.

Practice of Collective Bargaining. 8th ed. Begin & Beal. 1989. 37.95 (ISBN 0-256-07116-0). Irwin.

Practice of Collective Bargaining. 7th ed. Jame P. Begin & Edwin F. Beal. 1985. 34.95 (ISBN 0-256-03214-9). Irwin.

Practice of Collective Bargaining: An Experiential Approach. Luis R. Gomez-Mejia & Kathleen J. Powers. 1985. 17.95x (ISBN 0-256-03158-4). Business Pubns.

Practice of Conjoint Therapy: Combining Individual & Group Treatment. Louis Ormont & Herbert S. Strean. LC 77-17079. 231p. 1978. text ed. 29.95 (ISBN 0-87705-355-3). Human Sci Pr.

Practice of Construction Management. Barry Fryer. (Illus.). 225p. 1985. pap. text ed. 22.50x (ISBN 0-00-383030-6, Pub. by Collins England). Sheridan.

Practice of Continuing Education in Nursing. Signe S. Cooper. LC 82-13872. 340p. 1983. 45.50 (ISBN 0-89443-664-3). Aspen Pub.

Practice of Coronary Angioplasty. T. Ischinger. (Illus.). 320p. 1985. 79.00 (ISBN 0-387-15949-5). Springer-Verlag.

Practice of Coronary Artery Bypass Surgery. D. W. Miller. LC 77-10975. (Topics in Cardiovascular Disease Ser.). (Illus.). 254p. 1977. 45.00x (ISBN 0-306-31065-1, Plenum Med. Bk.). Plenum Pub.

Practice of Critical Care Pharmacy. Thomas C. Majerus & Joseph F. Dasta. 315p. 1984. 52.95 (ISBN 0-89443-571-X). Aspen Pub.

Practice of Criticism: A Comparative Analysis of W. B. Yeats among School Children. Abraham Verhoeff. LC 72-187524. 1925. lib. bdg. 25.50 (ISBN 0-8414-9193-3). Folcroft.

Practice of Dermatology. Richard L. Dobson. (Illus.). 350p. 1985. pap. text ed. 34.50 (ISBN 0-06-140697-X, Harper Medical). Lippincott.

Practice of Diabetes Mellitus. Ed. by M. M. Ahuja. text ed. 32.50x (ISBN 0-7069-2183-6, Pub. by Vikas India). Advent NY.

Practice of Digital Electronics. Pierre Pelloso. LC 85-15524. 219p. 1986. pap. 22.95 (ISBN 0-471-90733-2). Wiley.

Practice of Electrocardiography. 2nd ed. Thomas M. Blake. 1985. pap. text ed. 20.00 (ISBN 0-87488-897-2). Elsevier.

Practice of Emergency Care. 2nd ed. James H. Cosgriff, Jr. & Diann L. Anderson. (Illus.). 652p. 1984. text ed. 39.95 (ISBN 0-397-54357-3, 64-02994, Lippincott Nursing). Lippincott.

Practice of English Fundamentals: V. Form. A. Bachelor & J. Haley. 1945. pap. text ed. 12.95. P-H.

Practice of English Language Teaching. Jeremy Harmer. (Handbooks for Language Teachers Ser.). 252p. (Orig.). 1985. pap. text ed. 13.95 (ISBN 0-582-74612-4). Longman.

Practice of Entrepreneurship. G. Meredith et al. ix, 196p. 1982. text ed. 21.00 (ISBN 92-2-102839-9); pap. text ed. 14.00 (ISBN 92-2-102846-1). Intl Labour Office.

Practice of Entrepreneurship. Robert E. Nelson & Geoffrey G. Meredith. 196p. 1982. pap. 14.00 (ISBN 92-2-102846-1, ILO198, ILO) (ISBN 92-2-102839-9). UNIPUB.

Practice of Entrepreneurship, 1982. 196p. 19.95x (ISBN 92-2-102839-9). Intl Pubns Serv.

Practice of Everyday Life. Michel De Certeau. Tr. by Steven F. Rendall from Fr. LC 83-18070. 260p. 1984. 30.00x (ISBN 0-520-04750-8). U of Cal Pr.

Practice of Extraordinary Remedies: Habeas Corpus & Other Common Law Writs, Vols. 1-2. Chester J. Antieau. LC 87-5668. 844p. 1987. lib. bdg. 175.00 set (ISBN 0-379-20791-5). Oceana.

Practice of Faith: A Handbook of Contemporary Spirituality. Karl Rahner. 354p. 1983. 19.50 (ISBN 0-8245-0603-0); pap. 16.95. Crossroad NY.

Practice of Faith: A Handbook of Contemporary Spirituality. rev. ed. Karl Rahner. 336p. 1986. pap. 16.95 (ISBN 0-8245-0779-7). Crossroad NY.

Practice of Fiction in America: Writers from Hawthorne to the Present. Jerome Klinkowitz. 140p. (gr. 9-12). 1980. text ed. 10.95x (ISBN 0-8138-1420-0). Iowa St U Pr.

Practice of Field Instruction in Social Work Theory & Process. Marion Bogo & Elaine Vayda. 176p. pap. text ed. 9.95c (ISBN 0-8020-6689-5). U of Toronto PR.

Practice of Fortification: Wherein Is Shewed the Manner of Fortifying in All Sorts of Scituations, with the Considerations to Be Used in Dealing, & Makeing of Royal Frontiers, Skonces, & Renforcing of Ould Walled Townes. Paul Ive. 44p. Repr. text ed. 24.84x (ISBN 0-576-15157-2, Pub. by Gregg Intl Pubs England). Gregg Intl.

Practice of Freedom. Banerjea Benoyendranath. 1983. 9.00x (ISBN 0-8364-0918-3, Pub. by Minerva India). South Asia Bks.

Practice of Geography. Anne Buttimer. LC 82-13091. (Illus.). 1984. text ed. 31.95 (ISBN 0-582-30087-8). Longman.

Practice of Geriatric Medicine. Evan Calkins. (Illus.). 617p. 1986. 79.00 (ISBN 0-7216-2329-8). Saunders.

Practice of Geriatric Psychiatry. A. Comfort. 1980. 34.75 (ISBN 0-444-00360-6, Biomedical Pr). Elsevier.

Practice of Godliness. Jerry Bridges. LC 83-61499. 272p. 1983. pap. 4.50 (ISBN 0-89109-497-0). NavPress.

Practice of Group Therapy. Ed. by S. R. Slavson. 272p. 1965. text ed. 32.50x (ISBN 0-8236-4200-3). Intl Univs Pr.

Practice of Group Work. Ed. by William Schwartz & Serapio R. Zalba. LC 75-127101. 1971. 30.00x (ISBN 0-231-03241-2); pap. 14.00x (ISBN 0-231-08674-1). Columbia U Pr.

Practice of Harmony. Peter Spencer. (Illus.). 336p. 1983. pap. 33.00 (ISBN 0-13-694489-2). P-H.

Practice of High Performance Liquid Chromatography. Ed. by H. Engelhardt. (Illus.). 480p. 1985. 79.00 (ISBN 0-387-12589-2). Springer-Verlag.

Practice of Hospitality Management II: Profitability in a Changing Environment. Robert C. Lewis et al. (Illus.). 553p. 1986. 48.95 (ISBN 0-87055-515-4). AVI.

Practice of Humility. Pope Leo. Tr. by John F. O'Connor. 1976. lib. bdg. 59.95 (ISBN 0-8490-2462-5). Gordon Pr.

Practice of Humility. Pope Leo. Tr. by John F. O'Connor. 1980. lib. bdg. 59.95 (ISBN 0-8490-3177-X). Gordon Pr.

Practice of Hypnotherapy see Medical Hypnosis.

Practice of Inpatient Behavior Therapy: A Clinical Guide. Ed. by Michel Hersen. 304p. 1985. 39.50 (ISBN 0-8089-1715-3, 791976). Grune.

Practice of Intramedullary Nailing. Gerhard Kuntscher. (Illus.). 388p. 1967. photocopy ed. 39.50x (ISBN 0-398-01067-6). C C Thomas.

Practice of Ion Chromatography. Frank C. Smith & Richard C. Chang. LC 82-23914. 218p. 1983. 68.00x (ISBN 0-471-05517-4, Pub. by Wiley-Interscience). Wiley.

Practice of Japan in International Law, 1961-1970. Ed. by Shigeru Oda et al. 470p. 1982. 62.50 (ISBN 0-86008-301-2, Pub. by U of Tokyo Japan). Columbia U Pr.

Practice of Jesus. Hugo Echegaray. Tr. by Matthew J. O'Connell from Span. LC 83-19341. Orig. Title: Practica de Jesus. 176p. (Orig.). 1984. pap. 7.95 (ISBN 0-88344-397-X). Orbis Bks.

Practice of Journalism: A Guide to Reporting & Writing the News. Timothy Ferris & Bruce Porter. (Illus.). 448p. 1988. pap. text ed. price not set (ISBN 0-13-693706-3). P-H.

Practice of Karma Yoga. Swami Sivananda. 1974. 7.95 (ISBN 0-8426-0675-0). Orient Bk Dist.

Practice of Large Animal Surgery, 2 Vols. Paul B. Jennings, Jr. (Illus.). 1335p. 1984. Vol. 1. 85.00 (ISBN 0-7216-1347-0); Vol. 2. 85.00 (ISBN 0-7216-1348-9); Two Vol. Set. 160.00 (ISBN 0-7216-5118-6). Saunders.

Practice of Local Government Planning. 2nd ed. Ed. by Frank S. So & Judith Getzels. (Municipal Management Ser.). 500p. 1988. text ed. 38.95 (ISBN 0-87326-077-5). Intl City Mgt.

Practice of Local Government Planning. 5th ed. Ed. by Frank S. So et al. 700p. 1979. 37.00 (ISBN 0-318-17101-5); members & PAS subscribers 35.00 (ISBN 0-318-17102-3). Am Plan Assn.

Practice of Local Government Planning. Ed. by Frank S. So et al. LC 79-21380. (Municipal Management Ser.). (Illus.). 676p. 1979. text ed. 38.95 (ISBN 0-87326-020-1). Intl City Mgt.

Practice of M-Mode & Two-Dimensional Echocardiagraphy. J. Roelandt. 1983. 59.00 (ISBN 90-247-2745-6, Pub. by Martinus Nijhoff Netherlands). Kluwer Academic.

Practice of Magical Evocation. 4th ed. Franz Bardon. Tr. by Peter Dimai from Ger. (Illus.). 435p. 1984. 27.00 (ISBN 0-914732-11-0). Bro Life Inc.

Practice of Management. Peter F. Drucker. LC 54-8946. 1954. 18.45i (ISBN 0-06-011095-3, HarpT). Har-Row.

Practice of Management. Peter F. Drucker. LC 85-45189. 416p. 1986. pap. 10.95 (ISBN 0-06-091316-9, PL 1316, PL). Har-Row.

Practice of Management Development. Ed. by Sidney Mailick et al. 1988. 42.85 (ISBN 0-275-92357-6, C2357). Praeger.

Practice of Management for Health Care Professionals. Rita E. Numerof. 608p. 1982. 29.95 (ISBN 0-8144-5735-5). AMACOM.

Practice of Management Science. Martin K. Starr & Irving Stein. (Illus.). 208p. 1976. 26.00 (ISBN 0-13-693630-X). P-H.

Practice of Management: Text, Readings & Cases. John Miner et al. 832p. 1985. 35.95 (ISBN 0-675-20388-0); study guide 15.95 (ISBN 0-675-20391-0); additional supplements avail. Merrill.

Practice of Managerial Psychology. Andrew J. Du Brin. 1975. 31.00 (ISBN 0-08-016764-0); pap. 19.25 (ISBN 0-08-018126-0). Pergamon.

Practice of Marketing Management: Analysis, Planning & Implementation. William Cohen. 1065p. 1987. text ed. write for info. (ISBN 0-02-323150-5). Macmillan.

Practice of Mass Communication: Some Lessons from Research. Y. V. Lakshmana Rao. LC 72-79892. (Reports & Papers on Mass Communication Ser.: No. 65). 52p. (Orig.). 1972. pap. 5.00 (ISBN 92-3-100946-X, U476, UNESCO). UNIPUB.

Practice of Medical Radiesthesia. Vernon D. Wethered. 150p. 1977. 9.15x (ISBN 0-8464-1040-0). Beekman Pubs.

Practice of Medical Radiesthesia. Vernon D. Wethered. 1980. 29.50x (ISBN 0-85207-139-6, Pub. by Daniel Co England). State Mutual Bk.

Practice of Medicine: A Self-Assessment Guide. 4th ed. Simeon Margolis. 1988. pap. 29.95 (ISBN 0-317-67312-2). Appleton & Lange.

Practice of Medicine: A Self Assessment Guide. 3rd ed. Ed. by Simeon Margolis. (Illus.). 352p. 1984. pap. 29.95 (ISBN 0-8385-7873-X). Appleton & Lange.

Practice of Medicine among the Burmese. Keith N. MacDonald. LC 77-87505. Repr. of 1879 ed. 35.00 (ISBN 0-404-16837-X). AMS Pr.

Practice of Meditation 1971. rev. ed. Charles Bowness. (Paths to Inner Power Ser.). 1979. pap. 3.95 (ISBN 0-85030-182-3, Pub. by Thorsons UK). Weiser.

Practice of Mental Health Consultation. Fortune Mannino. 1975. 24.95 (ISBN 0-89876-082-8). Gardner Pr.

Practice of Modern Internal Auditing. 2nd rev. & enl. ed. Larry B. Sawyer. Ed. by Ceel Pasternak. LC 81-810325. 912p. 1981. text ed. 63.00 (ISBN 0-89413-092-7). Inst Inter Aud.

Practice of Multimodule Therapy. Arnold A. Lazarus. (Illus.). 256p. 1981. text ed. 31.50 (ISBN 0-07-036813-9). McGraw.

Practice of Multinational Banking: Macro-Policy Issues & Key International Concepts. Dara M. Khambata. LC 85-31253. 281p. 1986. 40.95 (ISBN 0-89930-139-8, KPB/, Quorum Bks). Greenwood.

Practice of Municipal Administration. Lent D. Upson. LC 73-11912. (Metropolitan America Ser.). 604p. 1974. Repr. 37.50x (ISBN 0-405-05432-7). Ayer Co Pubs.

Practice of Newpaper Management. W. Parkman Rankin. LC 85-28099. 176p. 1986. 35.00 (ISBN 0-275-92051-8, C2051). Praeger.

Practice of NMR Spectroscopy: With Spectra-Structure Correlations for Hydrogen-One. Nugent F. Chamberlain. LC 74-11479. (Illus.). 424p. 1974. 65.00x (ISBN 0-306-30766-9, Plenum Pr). Plenum Pub.

Practice of Nursing Research: Conduct, Critique, & Utilization. Nancy Burns & Susan K. Grove. (Illus.). 816p. 1987. 29.95 (ISBN 0-7216-1095-1); instr's. manual avail. (ISBN 0-03-013427-7). Saunders.

Practice of Obstetrics & Gynaecology: A Primer for the DRCOG. 2nd ed. Geoffrey Chamberlain & John Dewhurst. LC 85-12109. 197p. (Orig.). 1986. pap. text ed. 29.00 (ISBN 0-443-03684-5). Churchill.

Practice of Obstetrics & Gynecology. Geoffrey Chamberlain & C. J. Dewhurst. (Illus.). 271p. 1977. 27.95 (ISBN 0-8464-1120-2). Beekman Pubs.

Practice of Ocean Rescue. R. E. Sanders. 1977. lib. bdg. 75.00 (ISBN 0-8490-2463-3). Gordon Pr.

Practice of Ocean Rescue. R. E. Sanders. 260p. 1977. 13.50x (ISBN 0-85174-294-7). Sheridan.

Practice of Osteosynthesis: An Accident Surgery Atlas--Ligaments, Joints, Bones. 2nd rev. ed. Frank Schauwecker. (Illus.). 313p. 1982. 84.95 (ISBN 0-86577-054-9). Thieme Med Pubs.

Practice of Palmistry. C. De Saint-Germain. 410p. 1973. pap. 7.95 (ISBN 0-87877-019-4, P-19). Newcastle Pub.

Practice of Palmistry for Professional Purposes. Comte De Saint-Germain. LC 80-23774. 416p. 1980. Repr. of 1973 ed. lib. bdg. 19.95x (ISBN 0-89370-619-1). Borgo Pr.

Practice of Peptide Synthesis. M. Bodanszky et al. (Reactivity & Structure, Concepts in Organic Chemistry Ser.: Vol. 21). 240p. 1984. 69.00 (ISBN 0-387-13471-9). Springer-Verlag.

Practice of Pharmacy: Institutional & Ambulatory Pharmaceutical Services. Ed. by Donald C. McLeod & William A. Miller. LC 81-51777. (Illus.). 502p. 1981. text ed. 34.50 (ISBN 0-9606488-0-1). H W Bks.

Practice of Philosophy: A Handbook for Beginners. 2nd ed. Jay Rosenberg. 128p. 1984. pap. text ed. write for info. (ISBN 0-13-687467-3). P-H.

Practice of Photography. 2nd ed. Philip H. Delamotte. LC 72-9193. (Literature of Photography Ser.). Repr. of 1855 ed. 15.00 (ISBN 0-405-04903-X). Ayer Co Pubs.

Practice of Physical Medicine. Paul E. Kaplan. (Illus.). 574p. 1984. 53.50x (ISBN 0-398-04963-7). C C Thomas.

Practice of Piety: Directing a Christian How to Walk, That He May Please God. Lewis Bayly. LC 75-31081. Repr. of 1718 ed. 34.50 (ISBN 0-404-13500-5). AMS Pr.

Practice of Piety: Puritan Devotional Disciplines in Seventeenth-Century New England. Charles E. Hambrick-Stowe. LC 81-19806. (Institute of Early American History & Culture Ser.). (Illus.). xvi, 298p. 1982. 30.00x (ISBN 0-8078-1518-7). U of NC Pr.

Practice of Piety: Puritan Devotional Disciplines in Seventeenth Century New England. Charles E. Hambrick-Stowe. LC 81-19806. (Published for the Institute of Early American History & Culture, Williamsburg, Virginia Ser.). xvi, 298p. 1986. pap. 11.95x (ISBN 0-8078-4145-5). U of Nc Pr.

Practice of Policy Evaluation. Ed. by David Nachmias. 478p. 1980. text ed. write for info. (ISBN 0-312-63537-0); pap. text ed. write for info. (ISBN 0-312-63538-9). St Martin.

Practices & Procedures under the Taylor Law: A Practical Guide in Narrative Form. Grace S. Aboud & Robert E. Doherty. 84p. 1974. pap. 2.00 (ISBN 0-87546-203-0). ILR Pr.

Practices in Veterinary Public Health & Preventive Medicine in the United States. Ed. by George T. Woods. 348p. 1986. text ed. 37.50x (ISBN 0-8138-1441-3). Iowa St U Pr.

Practices that Improve Teaching Evaluation. Ed. by Grace French-Lazovik. LC 81-48584. (Teaching & Learning Ser.: No. 11). 1982. 12.95x (ISBN 0-87589-925-0). Jossey-Bass.

Practicing. Jamie MacInnis. 88p. (Orig.). 1980. pap. 5.00 (ISBN 0-939180-13-8). Tombouctou.

Practicing American English. Grant Taylor. (Saxon Series in English As a Second Language). (gr. 9-12). 1960. text ed. 5.40 (ISBN 0-07-062943-9). McGraw.

Practicing Attorneys Guide to Law Office Automation. Ayres. (Trial Practice Library). 1989. price not set (ISBN 0-471-61385-1). Wiley.

Practicing Before the International Trade Commission, Vol. 284. Practising Law Institute. 549p. 1985. pap. 15.00 (ISBN 0-317-27617-4, #H4-4971). PLI.

Practicing California Judicial Arbitration. Norman Harris & William A. Robinson. 243p. 1986. 60.00 (CP-30660); December '85 supp. 20.00; December '86 supp. 22.00. Cal Cont Ed Bar.

Practicing California Judicial Arbitration. LC 82-74525. 243p. 1983. 60.00 (ISBN 0-88124-104-0). Cal Cont Ed Bar.

Practicing Christianity. Margaret R. Miles. 256p. 1988. 17.95 (ISBN 0-8245-0904-8). Crossroad NY.

Practicing Church. Donald L. Roberts. LC 1-67318. 100p. (Orig.). 1981. pap. 2.95 (ISBN 0-87509-303-5). Chr Pubns.

Practicing Compassion for the Stranger. Nancy Alexander. 1986. pap. 2.50x (ISBN 0-87574-271-8). Pendle Hill.

Practicing Development Anthropology. Edward C. Green. (Special Studies in Applied Anthropology). 283p. 1986. pap. 29.00 (ISBN 0-8133-7256-9). Westview.

Practicing Educational Psychology. Margaret M. Clifford. (Illus.). 752p. 1981. text ed. 30.95 (ISBN 0-395-29921-7); pap. text ed. 27.95 (ISBN 0-395-29922-5); instr's manual 1.50 (ISBN 0-395-29923-3); test bank 3.50 (ISBN 0-395-29925-X). HM.

Practicing Enlightenment: Hume & the Formation of a Literary Career. Jerome Christensen. LC 86-40048. 336p. 1986. 40.00x (ISBN 0-299-10750-7); pap. 17.50x (ISBN 0-299-10754-X). U of Wis Pr.

Practicing Environmental Archaeology: Methods & Interpretations. Roger W. Moeller. LC 82-73087. (Occasional Papers No. 3). (Illus.). 112p. 1982. pap. text ed. 10.00 (ISBN 0-936322-00-4). Am Indian Arch.

Practicing Family Therapy in Diverse Settings: New Approaches to the Connections Among Families, Therapists, & Treatment Settings. Michael Berger et al. LC 83-49256. (Social & Behavioral Science Ser.). 1984. text ed. 25.95x (ISBN 0-87589-591-3). Jossey-Bass.

Practicing Health for All. Ed. by David Morley et al. Jon E. Rohde & Glen Williams. (Illus.). 1983. pap. 8.95x (ISBN 0-19-261445-2). Oxford U Pr.

Practicing His Presence. 3rd ed. Brother Lawrence & Frank Laubach. Ed. by Gene Edwards. 1973. pap. 6.95 (ISBN 0-940232-01-4). Christian Bks.

Practicing History: Selected Essays. Barbara Tuchman. LC 81-47509. 320p. 1981. 16.50 (ISBN 0-394-52086-6). Knopf.

Practicing History: Selected Essays. Barbara Tuchman. 1982. pap. 8.95 (ISBN 0-345-30363-6). Ballantine.

Practicing Insanity. Alfred E. Bruey. (Orig.). 1987. pap. 4.00 (ISBN 0-317-66651-7). Pudding Hse Pubns.

Practicing Law & Managing People: How to Be Successful. Heller & Hunt. 1988. price not set (ISBN 0-88063-171-6). Butterworth Legal Pubs.

Practicing Law in New York City. Ed. by Council of New York Law Associates Staff et al. 195p. 1975. pap. 3.75 (ISBN 0-318-03111-6). Coun NY Law.

Practicing Marriage. William E. Hulme & Lucy V. Hulme. LC 86-45916. 112p. 1987. pap. text ed. 4.95 (ISBN 0-8006-1957-9, 1-1957). Fortress.

Practicing Mind Models. John Chrisci. LC 84-90982. 115p. (Orig.). 1985. 12.00 (ISBN 0-317-37279-3). Pison River Hse.

Practicing Our Sighs: The Collected Poems of Richard Snyder. Richard Snyder. Ed. by Mary Snyder & Robert McGovern. 1988. 35.00 (ISBN 0-912592-26-5); pap. write for info. (ISBN 0-912592-27-3). Ashland Poetry.

Practicing Peace: Ten Spiritual Exercises That Heal. W. Glyn Evans. 160p. 1987. pap. 6.95 (ISBN 0-310-29381-2, 10463P). Zondervan.

Practicing Physician's Approach to Headache. 4th ed. Diamond & Dalessio. LC 85-20339. (Illus.). 260p. 1986. 39.50 (ISBN 0-683-02505-8). Williams & Wilkins.

Practicing Plant Parenthood. Maggie Baylis. LC 75-22361. (Illus.). 192p. (Orig.). 1975. 4.95 (ISBN 0-912238-62-3); pap. 4.95. One Hund One Prods.

Practicing Psychotherapy: Basic Techniques & Practical Issues. Edmund C. Neuhaus & William Astwood. LC 79-25464. 208p. 1980. text ed. 29.95 (ISBN 0-87705-467-3); pap. 16.95 (ISBN 0-89885-230-7). Human Sci Pr.

Practicing Public Management: A Casebook. C. Kenneth Meyer et al. LC 82-60473. 275p. 1983. pap. text ed. write for info. (ISBN 0-312-63549-4). St Martin.

Practicing Sentence Options. William Strong. 1984. pap. text ed. write for info (ISBN 0-394-33613-5, RanC). Random.

Practicing Texas Politics. 7th ed. Eugene Jones et al. LC 88-81337. 1989. pap. text ed. price not set (ISBN 0-395-38007-3); study guide, tests avail.; instr's. manual with test items avail.; transparencies avail. HM.

Practicing Texas Politics. 6th ed. Eugene W. Jones et al. LC 85-60779. 576p. 1986. pap. text ed. 23.56 (ISBN 0-395-35941-4); instr's manual 3.16 (ISBN 0-395-40017-1); study guide 12.76 (ISBN 0-395-39213-6); computer-assisted programming avail. HM.

Practicing Texas Politics: A Brief Survey. Eugene W. Jones et al. LC 83-81616. 256p. 1984. pap. text ed. 18.50 (ISBN 0-395-34935-4); instr's manual 3.00 (ISBN 0-395-35125-1). HM.

Practicing Texas Politics: A Brief Survey. 2nd ed. Eugene W. Jones et al. LC 86-81541. 272p. 1987. pap. text ed. 21.96 (ISBN 0-395-42324-4); instr's manual with test items 3.16 (ISBN 0-395-42325-2). HM.

Practicing the Prayer of Presence. Adrian van Kaam & Susan Muto. 7.95 (ISBN 0-87193-174-5). Dimension Bks.

Practicing the Presence. Joel S. Goldsmith. LC 58-7474. 1958. 12.45 (ISBN 0-06-063250-X, HarpR). Har-Row.

Practicing the Process: A Basic Text. Marlene Martin. 1988. pap. text ed. price not set (ISBN 0-673-18759-4). Scott F.

Practicing to Be a Woman: New & Selected Poems. Rochelle Ratner. Ed. by Robert B. Peters. LC 81-21472. (Poets Now Ser.: No. 2: No. 2). 152p. 1982. 13.50 (ISBN 0-8108-1510-9). Scarecrow.

Practicing to Take the GRE Biology Test. (Orig.). 1983. pap. 6.95 (ISBN 0-88685-001-0). Educ Testing Serv.

Practicing to Take the GRE Chemistry Test. (Orig.). 1983. pap. 6.95 (ISBN 0-88685-002-9). Educ Testing Serv.

Practicing to Take the GRE Computer Science Test. 56p. (Orig.). 1986. pap. text ed. 6.95 (ISBN 0-446-38455-0). Educ Testing Serv.

Practicing to Take the GRE Economics Test. 44p. 1986. pap. text ed. 6.95 (ISBN 0-446-38457-7). Educ Testing Serv.

Practicing to Take the GRE Education Test. (Orig.). 1983. pap. 6.95 (ISBN 0-88685-003-7). Educ Testing Serv.

Practicing to Take the GRE Engineering Test. (Orig.). 1983. pap. 6.95 (ISBN 0-88685-004-5). Educ Testing Serv.

Practicing to Take the GRE General Test. Educational Testing Service Staff. (No. 3). 1986. pap. 7.95 (ISBN 0-446-38441-0). Warner Bks.

Practicing to Take the GRE General Test. (Orig.). 1983. pap. 7.95 (ISBN 0-88685-000-2). Educ Testing Serv.

Practicing to Take the GRE General Test. 2nd ed. 170p. (Orig.). 1984. pap. text ed. 7.95 (ISBN 0-88685-023-1). Educ Testing Serv.

Practicing to Take the GRE General Test, No. 4. 168p. (Orig.). 1986. pap. text ed. 7.95 (ISBN 0-446-38439-9). Educ Testing Serv.

Practicing to Take the GRE General Test, No. 5. Educational Testing Service Staff. Date not set. pap. 7.95 (ISBN 0-446-38594-8). Warner Bks.

Practicing to Take the GRE General Test, No. 6. 1988. pap. 7.95 (ISBN 0-446-35307-8). Warner Bks.

Practicing to Take the GRE General Test, No. 4: APPLE Software Edition. Educational Testing Service Staff. 1986. Software, Manual & Preparing to Take the GRE General Test. casebound 55.00 (ISBN 0-446-38443-7). Warner Bks.

Practicing to Take the GRE General Test, No. 4: IBM Software Edition. Educational Testing Service Staff. 1986. Software, Manual & Preparing to Take the GRE General Test. casebound 55.00 (ISBN 0-446-38445-3). Warner Bks.

Practicing to Take the GRE Geology Test. Educational Testing Service Staff. Date not set. pap. 6.95 (ISBN 0-446-38596-4). Warner Bks.

Practicing to Take the GRE History Test. 48p. 1986. pap. text ed. 6.95. Educ Testing Serv.

Practicing to Take the GRE Literature in English Test. (Orig.). 1983. pap. 6.95 (ISBN 0-88685-005-3). Educ Testing Serv.

Practicing to Take the GRE Mathematics Test. Educational Testing Service Staff. Date not set. pap. 6.95 (ISBN 0-446-38598-0). Warner Bks.

Practicing to Take the GRE Music Test. 1988. pap. 6.95 (ISBN 0-446-35308-6). Warner Bks.

Practicing to Take the GRE Physics Test. 40p. (Orig.). 1986. pap. text ed. 6.95 (ISBN 0-446-38467-4). Educ Testing Serv.

Practicing to Take the GRE Political Science Test. 1988. pap. 6.95 (ISBN 0-446-35310-8). Warner Bks.

Practicing to Take the GRE Psychology Test. (Orig.). 1983. pap. 6.95 (ISBN 0-88685-006-1). Educ Testing Serv.

Practicing to Take the GRE Sociology Test. Educational Testing Service Staff. Date not set. pap. 6.95 (ISBN 0-446-38652-9). Warner Bks.

Practicing Vivaldi. Mary Shumway. (W.N.J. Ser.: No. 15). 1981. signed ed. o.p. 20.00 (ISBN 0-686-79771-X); pap. 6.00 (ISBN 1-55780-064-2). Juniper Pr WI.

Practicing Writer. Arthur Bell & Thomas Klammer. LC 82-83411. 224p. 1983. 21.16 (ISBN 0-395-32564-1); instr's. manual 2.36 (ISBN 0-395-32565-X). HM.

Practioner's Guide to Ada. R. H. Wallace. 320p. 1986. text ed. 39.95 (ISBN 0-07-067922-3). McGraw.

Practique de la Fiscalite en Europe 1982. 412p. (Eng., Fr. & Ital.). pap. 34.00 (ISBN 0-686-41013-0). Kluwer Academic.

Practiquemos la Visitacion. J. T. Sisemore. Ed. by Ananias Gonzalez. Tr. by Josue Grijalva. Orig. Title: Ministry of Visitation. 1981. Repr. of 1979 ed. 2.95 (ISBN 0-311-11034-7). Casa Bautista.

Practise of Chymicall, & Hermeticall Physicke, for the Preservation of Health. Joseph Du Chesne. Tr. by T. Timme from Lat. LC 74-28847. (English Experience Ser.: No. 728). 1975. Repr. of 1605 ed. 35.00 (ISBN 90-221-0728-0). Walter J Johnson.

Practising Angels: A Contemporary Anthology of San Francisco Bay Area Poetry. Ed. by Michael Mayo. LC 86-60764. 211p. (Orig.). 1986. pap. 9.95 (ISBN 0-932977-31-6). Seismograph Pubns.

Practising Before the U. S. Court of Appeals for the Federal Court, Vol. 282. Practising Law Institute. 250p. 1985. pap. 15.00 (ISBN 0-317-27602-6, #H4-4970). PLI.

Practising Dentistry. K. Kimmel & R. O. Walker. (Illus.). 258p. 1972. 32.00 (ISBN 0-931386-67-5). Quint Pub Co.

Practising Prevention. British Medical Journal Staff. 112p. 1983. pap. 13.00x (ISBN 0-7279-0155-9, Pub. by British Med Assoc UK). Taylor & Francis.

Practising Translation in Renaissance France: The Example of Etienne Dolet. Valerie Worth. (Modern Languages & Literature Monographs). 326p. 1988. 65.00 (ISBN 0-19-815818-1). Oxford U Pr.

Practitioner Manual for Introductory Patterns of Neuro Linguistic Programming. Maryann Reese & Carol L Yancar. 245p. 1986. write for info. (ISBN 0-9615502-1-X). Southern Inst Pr.

Practitioner-Teacher Role: Practice What You Teach. Lorraine Machan. LC 80-80814. 185p. 1980. pap. text ed. 32.85 (ISBN 0-913654-65-5). Aspen Pub.

Practitioner's Blueprint for Logical & Physical Data Base Design. Eric G. Vesely. (Illus.). 240p. 1986. text ed. 38.00 (ISBN 0-13-694267-9). P-H.

Practitioners Guide to Alcoholism & the Law. David G. Evans. 93p. 1983. 7.95 (ISBN 0-89486-177-8). Hazelden.

Practitioners' Guide to Econometrics. Semoon Chang. (Illus.). 190p. (Orig.). 1984. pap. text ed. 12.50 (ISBN 0-8191-3693-X). U Pr of Amer.

Practitioner's Guide to Liquor Liability Litigation. Ed. by Ronald S. Beitman. 175p. 1987. 55.00 (ISBN 0-8318-0556-0, B556). Am Law Inst.

Practitioner's Guide to Managing Attention Disorders in Children. Goldstein. (Personality Processes Ser.). 1990. price not set (ISBN 0-471-61137-9). Wiley.

Practitioner's Guide to Planning, Managing & Controlling Computer Systems. Atre. 1988. price not set (ISBN 0-471-86827-2). Wiley.

Practitioner's Guide to Psychoactive Drugs. 2nd ed. Ed. by Ellen L. Bassuk & Alan J. Gelenberg. LC 82-22468. (Topics In General Psychiatry Ser.). 454p. 1983. 29.50x (ISBN 0-306-41093-1, Plenum Pr). Plenum Pub.

Practitioner's Guide to Public Sector Productivity Improvement. Elaine Morley. LC 87-19388. 272p. 1988. Repr. of 1986 ed. lib. bdg. 29.50 (ISBN 0-89464-252-9). Krieger.

Practitioner's Guide to Public Sector Productivity Improvement. Elaine J. Morley. (Illus.). 272p. 1985. 35.95 (ISBN 0-442-26323-6). Van Nos Reinhold.

Practitioner's Guide to Rational-Emotive Therapy. Susan R. Walen et al. 1980. pap. 12.95x (ISBN 0-19-502668-3). Oxford U Pr.

Practitioner's Guide to Reflexology. Kevin Kunz & Barbara Kunz. 1985. 17.95 (ISBN 0-13-694324-1); pap. 9.95 (ISBN 0-13-694316-0). P-H.

Practitioner's Guide to Residential Real Estate Transactions: Tennessee Edition. Brian L. Smith & C. Philip Owens. write for info. M Lee Smith.

Practitioner's Guide to the Edwards Personal Preference Schedule. Janet E. Helms. (Illus.). 268p. 1983. 32.75x (ISBN 0-398-04740-5). C C Thomas.

Practitioner's Handbook of Ambulatory OB-GYN. Jean D. Neeson & Connie R. Stockdale. LC 80-26151. 394p. 1981. 26.00x (ISBN 0-471-05670-7). Wiley.

Practitioner's Handbook on the Modelling of Dynamic Change on Ecosystems: SCOPE 34. Jeffers. (SCOPE Ser.). 508p. 1988. write for info. (ISBN 0-471-10519-8). Wiley.

Practitioners' Probate Manual. 22nd ed. Ed. by R. F. Yeldham & A. Plumb. (Waterlow Practitioners Library). 320p. 1985. 29.00 (ISBN 0-08-039242-3, Pub by Waterlow). Pergamon.

Practitioners Shell Model. G. Bertsche. 1972. 24.50 (ISBN 0-444-10348-1). Elsevier.

Pradeeps Standard Oxford Dictionary: English to English, Panjabi & Hindi. 1983. 16.50x (ISBN 0-8364-0991-4, Pub. by Pradeep Co). South Asia Bks.

Prader-Willi Syndrome. Ed. by M. L. Caldwell & R. L. Taylor. (Illus.). 120p. 1988. 42.50 (ISBN 0-387-96699-4). Springer-Verlag.

Prader-Willi Syndrome: A Handbook for Parents. Shirley Neason. 51p. 3.50 (ISBN 0-318-16187-7); members 2.50 (ISBN 0-318-16188-5). Prader-Willi.

Prado. Alfonso E. Sanches. Ed. by Antonio Da Urbina. (Illus.). 256p. 1987. 29.95 (ISBN 0-935748-75-X). Scala Books.

Prado de Valencia. Gasper Mercader. Repr. of 1907 ed. 31.00 (ISBN 0-384-38150-2). Johnson Repr.

Prado de Valencia. Francisco A. Tarrega. (Serie B: Textos: Vol. XXVI). 210p. (Span.). 1986. pap. 19.95 (ISBN 0-7293-0214-8, Pub. by Tamesis Bks Ltd). Longwood Pub Group.

Prados of Sao Paulo, Brazil: An Elite Family & Social Change, 1840-1930. Darrell E. Levi. LC 86-30826. 304p. 1987. 32.00x (ISBN 0-8203-0944-3). U of Ga Pr.

Prae-Italic Dialects, 3 Vols. Robert S. Conway et al. 1967. Repr. of 1933 ed. Set. cancelled (ISBN 3-4870-1889-6). Adlers Foreign Bks.

Praeraphaelite Diaries & Letters. Ed. by William M. Rossetti. LC 70-148293. Repr. of 1900 ed. 14.00 (ISBN 0-404-08898-8). AMS Pr.

Praesidium of Archive. Jefferson P. Swycaffer. 197p. 1986. pap. 2.95 (ISBN 0-380-89663-X). Avon.

Praeterita: The Autobiography of John Ruskin. John Ruskin. 1978. pap. 9.95x (ISBN 0-19-281253-X). Oxford U Pr.

Praeventive Aspekte in der Paediatrie. Ed. by G. Stalder & C. P. Fliegel. (Paediatrische Fortbildungskurse fuer die Praxis: Vol. 52). (Illus.). vi, 182p. 1981. 49.50 (ISBN 3-8055-1980-X). S Karger.

Pragmalinguistics: East European Approaches. Jan Prucha. (Pragmatics & Beyond An Interdisciplinary Series of Language Studies: Vol. IV, No. 5). v, 103p. (Orig.). 1983. pap. 26.00x (ISBN 0-915027-28-3). Benjamins North Am.

Pragmalinguistics: Theory & Practice. Ed. by Jacob L. Mey. (Janua Linguarum, Series Maior: No. 85). 1979. text ed. 41.00 (ISBN 90-279-7757-7). Mouton.

Pragmatic a Priori. S. Rosenthal. LC 75-41707. 104p. 1975. 10.00. Green.

Pragmatic a Priori. Sandra Rosenthal. LC 75-41707. 104p. 1975. 10.00 (ISBN 0-87527-142-1). Fireside Bks.

Pragmatic Aspects of English Text Structure. Larry B. Jones. LC 81-84506. (Publications in Linguistics: No. 67). 150p. (Orig.). 1983. pap. 12.00x (ISBN 0-88312-088-7); microfiche (2) 4.00 (ISBN 0-88312-983-3). Summer Inst Ling.

Pragmatic Aspects of Human Communication. Ed. by Colin Cherry. LC 73-91427. (Theory & Decision Library: No. 4). 176p. 1974. lib. bdg. 31.50 (ISBN 90-277-0432-5, Pub. by Reidel Holland); pap. 21.00 (ISBN 90-277-0520-8, Pub. by Reidel Holland). Kluwer Academic.

Pragmatic Assessment & Intervention Issues in Language. Ed. by Tanya M. Gallagher & Carol A. Prutting. LC 82-17752. (Illus.). 286p. 1983. pap. 31.00 (ISBN 0-316-30284-8). College-Hill.

Pragmatic Basis of Aphasia: A Neurolinguistic Study of Morphosyntax among Bilinguals. Marc L. Schnitzer. 225p. 1988. price not set (ISBN 0-8058-0190-1). L Erlbaum Assocs.

Pragmatic Choral Procedures. Russell A. Hammar. LC 84-5332. 377p. 1984. 27.50 (ISBN 0-8108-1698-9). Scarecrow.

Pragmatic Federalism: An Intergovernmental View of American Government. 2nd ed. Parris N. Glendening & Mavis M. Reeves. LC 83-62328. (Illus.). 1984. pap. 12.95 (ISBN 0-913530-36-0). Palisades Pub.

Pragmatic Humanism of F. C. S. Schiller. Reuben Abel. LC 70-158220. Repr. of 1955 ed. 18.50 (ISBN 0-404-00275-7). AMS Pr.

Pragmatic Imagination: A History of the Wharton School 1881-1981. Steven A. Sass. 1983. 30.95x (ISBN 0-8122-7814-3). U of Pa Pr.

Pragmatic Logic for Commands. Melvin J. Adler. (Pragmatics & Beyond Ser.: No.3). viii, 131p. 1980. pap. 20.00 (ISBN 90-272-2501-X). Benjamins North Am.

Pragmatic Meaning of God. Robert O. Johann. (Aquinas Lecture). 1966. 7.95 (ISBN 0-87462-131-3). Marquette.

Pragmatic Naturalism: An Introduction. S. Morris Eames. LC 76-58441. 256p. 1977. pap. 8.95x (ISBN 0-8093-0803-7). S Ill U Pr.

Pragmatic Perspective: Selected Papers from the 1985 International Pragmatics Conference. Ed. by Jef Verschueren & Marcella Bertuccelli-Papi. LC 87-18409. (Pragmatics & Beyond Companion Ser.: No. 5). xiii, 836p. 1987. 130.00x (ISBN 1-55619-011-5). Benjamins North Am.

Prairie Liberalism: The Liberal Party in Saskatchewan, 1905-1971. David E. Smith. LC 74-78676. 1975. pap. 9.50 (ISBN 0-8020-6290-3). U of Toronto Pr.

Prairie Mosaic: An Ethnic Atlas of Rural North Dakota. William C. Sherman. LC 82-61305. (Illus.). 152p. 1983. 12.85 (ISBN 0-911042-27-X). N Dak Inst.

Prairie Night Before Christmas. rev. ed. James Rice. (gr. 1-6). 1986. 10.95 (ISBN 0-88289-630-X). Pelican.

Prairie Paradise. Emma Harrington, pseud. 512p. 1988. pap. 3.95 (ISBN 0-8217-2504-1). Zebra.

Prairie Peninsula, Proceedings: In the "Shadow" of Transeau. North American Prairie Conference, 6th, Ohio State Univ., Columbus, Ohio, Aug. 12-17, 1978. Ed. by Ronald L. Stuckey & Karen J. Reese. LC 81-82059. (Illus.). 1982. text ed. 12.50 (ISBN 0-86727-090-X). Ohio Bio Survey.

Prairie People: Continuity & Change in Potawatomi Indian Culture, 1665-1965. James A. Clifton. LC 76-51774. xx, 532p. 1977. 35.00x (ISBN 0-7006-0155-4). U Pr of KS.

Prairie Politics: Kay Orr vs. Helen Boosalis, the Historic 1986 Gubernatorial Race. John B. Barrette. (Illus.). 196p. 1987. pap. 9.95 (ISBN 0-939644-26-6). Media Prods & Mktg.

Prairie Print Makers. 2nd ed. Barbara T. O'Neil & George C. Foreman. Ed. by Howard W. Ellington. (Illus.). 60p. 1984. pap. 10.00x (ISBN 0-9614307-0-2). Gallery Ellington.

Prairie Provinces. Ed. by P. J. Smith. (Studies in Canadian Geography). 1972. pap. 6.00x (ISBN 0-8020-6161-3). U of Toronto Pr.

Prairie Rose. Lela DeMille. 205p. (Orig.). 1987. pap. 3.95 (ISBN 0-89367-125-8). Light & Life.

Prairie Rose & Rosebud. Lela DeMille. (Prairie Rose Ser.). 175p. 1988. pap. 4.50 (ISBN 0-89367-140-1). Light & Life.

Prairie School. Lois Lenski. LC 51-11169. (Illus.). 204p. (gr. 4-7). 1951. PLB 13.89 (ISBN 0-397-30194-4, Lipp Jr Bks). HarpJ.

Prairie School Architecture: Studies from the Western Architect. Ed. by H. Allen Brooks. 352p. 1983. pap. 26.95 (ISBN 0-442-21309-3). Van Nos Reinhold.

Prairie School Architecture: Studies from "The Western Architect". Ed. by Harold A. Brooks. LC 73-91567. pap. 87.80 (ISBN 0-317-28690-0, 2020459). Bks Demand UMI.

Prairie School: Frank Lloyd Wright & His Midwest Contemporaries. H. Allen Brooks. (Illus.). 400p. 1976. pap. 14.95 (ISBN 0-393-00811-8, N811). Norton.

Prairie School: Frank Lloyd Wright & His Midwest Contemporaries. Harold A. Brooks. LC 72-151363. pap. 99.50 (2026419). Bks Demand UMI.

Prairie School in Iowa. Richard G. Wilson & Sidney K. Robinson. (Iowa Heritage Collection). (Illus.). 128p. 1987. pap. 5.95 (ISBN 0-8138-0914-2). Iowa St U Pr.

Prairie Smoke. Melvin R. Gilmore. LC 78-168148. (Illus.). Repr. of 1929 ed. 18.00 (ISBN 0-404-02776-8). AMS Pr.

Prairie Smoke. Melvin R. Gilmore. LC 86-31205. (Borealis Books Reprint). xxviii, 225p. (gr. 4-12). 1987. pap. 6.95 (ISBN 0-87351-207-3). Minn Hist.

Prairie Song & Western Story. facsimile ed. Hamlin Garland. LC 73-163026. (Short Story Index Reprint Ser.). (Illus.). Repr. of 1928 ed. 20.00 (ISBN 0-8369-3940-9). Ayer Co Pubs.

Prairie Songs. Pam Conrad. LC 85-42633. (Trophy Bks.). (Illus.). 176p. (gr. 5 up). 1987. pap. 3.50 (ISBN 0-06-440206-1, Trophy). HarpJ.

Prairie Songs. Pamela Conrad. LC 85-42633. (Illus.). 176p. (gr. 5 up). 1985. 12.95i (ISBN 0-06-021336-1); PLB 12.89g (ISBN 0-06-021337-X). HarpJ.

Prairie Songs. Hamlin Garland. (Collected Works of Hamlin Garland). 1988. Repr. of 1893 ed. lib. bdg. 59.00x. Am Biog Serv.

Prairie Songs see Collected Works.

Prairie Songs, Being Chants Rhymed & Unihymed of the Level Lands of the Great West. Hamlin Garland. 164p. Repr. of 1898 ed. lib. bdg. 49.50 (ISBN 0-317-16156-3). Folcroft.

Prairie Star: Journal of Kansas First Literary Society (1857) Compiled by John W. Ripley. 140p. pap. 5.95 (ISBN 0-916934-02-0). Shawnee County Hist.

Prairie Stationmaster: The Story of One Man's Railroading Career in Nebraska 1917-1963. Barbara B. Clayburn. LC 78-78305. (Illus.). 128p. 1979. 6.50 (ISBN 0-8187-0034-3). Harlo Pr.

Prairie: The Legend of Charles Burton Irwin & the Y6 Ranch. Anna L. Waldo. 1216p. 1987. pap. 5.95 (ISBN 0-441-67640-5, Pub. by Charter Bks). Ace Bks.

Prairie: The Legends of Charles Burton Irwin & the Y6 Ranch. Anna L. Waldo. 1987. 24.95 (ISBN 0-425-10401-X). Berkley Pub.

Prairie-Town Boy. Carl Sandburg. LC 77-4647. (Illus.). 179p. (gr. 7 up). 1977. pap. 1.75 (ISBN 0-15-673700-0, VoyB). HarBraceJ.

Prairie Trails & Cow Towns. Floyd B. Streeter. (Illus.). 1963. 12.95 (ISBN 0-8159-6510-9). Devin.

Prairie Traveler. Randolph B. Marcy. (Illus.). 356p. 1968. Repr. of 1859 ed. 21.00 (ISBN 0-87928-001-8). Corner Hse.

Prairie Traveler. Randolph B. Marcy. 256p. 1988. pap. 10.95 (ISBN 0-918222-89-3). Applewood.

Prairie Tree. Marilyn G. Komechak. LC 87-91064. (Illus.). 80p. (Orig.). 1987. pap. 7.00 (ISBN 0-9619277-0-4). Clear Fork Cafe.

Prairie Vengeance. M. L. Warren. 208p. 1985. pap. 2.25 (ISBN 0-8439-2244-3, Leisure Bks). Leisure NY.

Prairie Visions. Robert Gard. 288p. 1987. 14.95 (ISBN 0-942802-54-3). Northword.

Prairie West: Historical Readings. Ed. by R. Douglas Francis & Howard Palmer. xiv, 660p. 1985. pap. text ed. 21.00x (ISBN 0-88864-048-X, Pub. by Univ of Alta Pr Canada). U of Nebr Pr.

Prairie Wetland Drainage Regulations: Discussion & Annotated Bibliography. Jay A. Leitch & David M. Saxowsky. LC 82-623103. 10p. Date not set. price not set. U ND Pr.

Prairie Wife. Arthur Stringer. 1976. lib. bdg. 14.85x (ISBN 0-89968-122-0). Lightyear.

Prairie Wildflowers. Dee Strickler. LC 86-90566. (Illus.). 80p. (Orig.). 1986. pap. 6.95 (ISBN 0-934318-99-9). Falcon Pr MT.

Prairie Wings. Edgar M. Queeny. (Illus.). 256p. 1979. Repr. of 1946 ed. 50.00 (ISBN 0-916838-21-8). Schiffer.

Prairie Wings: The Classic Illustrated Study of American Wildfowl in Flight. Edgar Queeny. (Nature Ser.). 256p. 1984. pap. 12.50 (ISBN 0-486-24544-6). Dover.

Prairie Women: Images in American & Canadian Fiction. Carol Fairbanks. LC 85-22616. 320p. 1986. 22.00x (ISBN 0-300-03374-5). Yale U Pr.

Prairie World. David F. Costello. (Illus.). 1980. pap. 9.95 (ISBN 0-8166-0938-1). U of Minn Pr.

Prairies & Grasslands. James P. Rowan. LC 83-7310. (New True Bks.). (Illus.). 48p. (gr. k-4). 1983. PLB 12.60 (ISBN 0-516-01706-3). Childrens.

Prairies & the Pampas: Agrarian Policy in Canada & Argentina, 1880-1930. Carl E. Solberg. LC 86-27854. (Comparative Studies in History, Institutions & Public Policy). 320p. 1987. text ed. 39.50x (ISBN 0-8047-1346-4). Stanford U Pr.

Prairies, Prayers & Promises: An Illustrated History of Galesburg. Jean C. Lee. LC 87-10453. 128p. 1987. 22.95 (ISBN 0-89781-194-1). Windsor Pubns Inc.

Prairies Within: The Tragic Trilogy of Ole Rolvaag. Harold P. Simonson. LC 85-32294. 112p. 1987. 15.00 (ISBN 0-295-96388-3). U of Wash Pr.

Prairiescapes. Photos by Larry Kanfer. LC 87-14807. (Illus.). 120p. 1987. 29.95 (ISBN 0-252-01482-0). U of Ill Pr.

Praise. Robert Hass. LC 78-16016. (American Poetry Ser.: No. 17). 1980. pap. 8.95 (ISBN 0-912946-62-8). Ecco Pr.

Praise: A Door to God's Presence. Warren Myers & Ruth Myers. (Orig.). 1987. pap. 6.95 (ISBN 0-89109-144-0). NavPress.

Praise: A Matter of Life & Breath. R. Allen. Tr. by Silas Chan. 204p. (Chinese.). 1982. pap. write for info. (ISBN 0-941598-04-7). Living Spring Pubns.

Praise & Lament in the Psalms. rev. enl. ed. Claus Westermann. Tr. by Keith Crim & Richard Soulen. LC 65-10553. 1981. 12.95 (ISBN 0-8042-1791-2, John Knox); pap. 9.95 (ISBN 0-8042-1792-0). Westminster John Knox.

Praise & Paradox: Merchants & Craftsmen in Elizabethan Popular Literature. Laura C. Stevenson. (Past & Present Publications). 236p. 1985. 39.50 (ISBN 0-521-26506-1). Cambridge U Pr.

Praise & Prayer. Gary P. Colton. 1978. 7.95 (ISBN 0-8198-0593-9). Dghtrs St Paul.

Praise & Thanksgiving. James Weekley. 1986. 6.95 (ISBN 0-89536-792-0, 6810). CSS of Ohio.

Praise & Thanksgiving: Full Music Edition. 1987. 40.00x (ISBN 0-317-58599-1, Pub. by Gresham England). State Mutual Bk.

Praise Avenue. Don Gossett. 128p. 1976. pap. 2.95 (ISBN 0-88368-059-9). Whitaker Hse.

Praise Book. Compiled by Dale Dieleman. 1984. pap. 5.95 (ISBN 0-8010-2947-3). Baker Bk.

Praise Classic I. 1988. 13.95 (ISBN 0-943026-14-8). Carothers.

Praise Faith in Action. Charles Trombley. (Orig.). 1976. pap. 3.95 (ISBN 0-89350-009-7). Fountain Pr.

Praise God: Common Prayer at Taize. Ed. by Members of Community at Taize, France. LC 76-47437. 1977. 16.95x (ISBN 0-19-519915-4). Oxford U Pr.

Praise Him! A Prayerbook for Today's Christian. William G. Storey. 224p. (Orig.). 1973. pap. 2.95 (ISBN 0-87793-056-2). Ave Maria.

Praise Him, Praise Him! Jennie Davis. (ps-3). 1982. pap. text ed. 5.95 (ISBN 0-89693-208-7, Sonflower Bks). SP Pubns.

Praise Him! Praise Him! Jennie Davis. LC 82-7238. (Illus.). 32p. (ps-k). 1982. lib. bdg. 4.95. Dandelion Hse.

Praise in St. Augustine: Readings & Reflections. John M. Quinn. 220p. pap. 8.95 (ISBN 0-8158-0430-X). Chris Mass.

Praise in "The Faerie Queene". Thomas H. Cain. LC 78-8962. (Illus.). xvi, 229p. 1978. 21.00x (ISBN 0-8032-1405-7). U of Nebr Pr.

Praise of Folly. Erasmus. Tr. by Betty Radice. (Classics Ser.). 252p. 1971. pap. 5.95 (ISBN 0-14-044240-5). Penguin.

Praise of Folly. Desiderius Erasmus. Ed. by Leonard F. Dean. 182p. 1983. pap. 5.95 (ISBN 0-87532-105-4). Hendricks House.

Praise of Folly. Desiderius Erasmus. Ed. by Harvey Gross. Tr. by John Wilson. LC 79-65739. (Mind of Man Ser.). (Illus.). 160p. 1979. limited ed. 25.00 (ISBN 0-934710-01-5). J Simon.

Praise of Folly. Desiderius Erasmus. Tr. by Hoyt H. Hudson. 1941. pap. 7.95x (ISBN 0-691-01969-X). Princeton U Pr.

Praise of Folly. Desiderius Erasmus. 1958. pap. 6.95 (ISBN 0-472-06023-6, 23, AA). U of Mich Pr.

Praise of Folly. Desiderius Erasmus. Intro. by Clarence H. Miller. LC 78-13575. 1979. pap. 9.95x (ISBN 0-300-02373-1). Yale U Pr.

Praise of Folly. Desiderius Erasmus. 327p. cancelled (ISBN 0-317-32351-2). Am Atheist.

Praise of Folly & Other Writings: (Norton Critical Edition) Desiderius Erasmus & Robert M. Adams. 1988. pap. price not set (ISBN 0-393-95749-7). Norton.

Praise of Lincoln. Ed. by A. Dallas Williams. LC 77-108590. (Granger Index Reprint Ser). 1911. 19.00 (ISBN 0-8369-6118-8). Ayer Co Pubs.

Praise of Musicke. John Case. 162p. Repr. of 1586 ed. lib. bdg. 37.50X (ISBN 3-487-06704-8, Pub. by G. Olms BRD). Coronet Bks.

Praise Poems: The Katherine White Collection. Pamela McClusky. (Illus.). 122p. 1984. 40.00 (ISBN 0-932216-16-1, Dist. by U. of Chicago Press.); pap. 20.00 (ISBN 0-932216-15-3). Seattle Art.

Praise Poems: The Katherine White Collection. Pamela McClusky. LC 83-51840. (Illus.). xiv, 122p. 1985. lib. bdg. 45.00X (ISBN 0-317-14122-8, 73445-5, Distributed for Seattle Art Museum); pap. 20.00 (ISBN 0-317-14123-6, 73446-3). U of Chicago Pr.

Praise Releases Faith. Terry Law. 252p. 1987. pap. 6.95 (ISBN 0-932081-15-0). Victory Hse.

Praise Singer. Mary Renault. LC 78-53495. 1978. 12.95 (ISBN 0-394-50273-6). Pantheon.

Praise Singer. Mary Renault. LC 86-46176. 304p. 1988. pap. 6.95 (ISBN 0-394-75102-7, Vin). Random.

Praise Songs. Dianne Tittle-deLaet. (Praise Songs Ser.: Vol. I). 80p. (Orig.). 1987. pap. text ed. price not set. Arete.

Praise! Songs & Poems from the Bible Retold for Children. A. J. McCallen. (Illus.). 96p. (gr. 3-8). 1986. 6.95 (ISBN 0-318-23286-3, Collins Liturgical). HarpR.

Praise the Bridge That Carries You Over: The Life of Joseph Sutton. Shepard Krech, 3rd. 238p. 1981. pap. text ed. 13.95 (ISBN 0-87073-650-7). Schenkman Bks Inc.

Praise the High Grass. Peter Carlos. 1977. 1.50 (ISBN 0-918476-01-1). Cornerstone Pr.

Praise the Human Season. Don Robertson. 544p. 1983. pap. 3.95 (ISBN 0-345-29528-5). Ballantine.

Praise the Lord! James E. Haas. LC 74-80388. 1974. pap. 3.95 (ISBN 0-8192-1176-1). Morehouse.

Praise the Lord & Rub It Out. Ralph Gross. (Illus.). 30p. (Orig.). 1981. pap. 5.00 (ISBN 0-686-32010-7). Karma Pub.

Praise the Lord Anyway. Frances Hunter. 1978. pap. 3.95 (ISBN 0-87162-131-2). Hunter Bks.

Praise the Lord with Psalms: Metrical Paraphrases of Selected Psalms. Laura B. Lane. 1986. 5.95 (ISBN 0-533-06823-1). Vantage.

Praise to the Morning Koel. Deepak Dubey. 8.00 (ISBN 0-89253-477-X); flexible cloth 4.00 (ISBN 0-89253-478-8). Ind-US Inc.

Praise with Understanding. David Wright & Jill Wright. 64p. 1983. pap. 4.95 (ISBN 0-85364-355-5, Pub. by Paternoster UK). Attic Pr.

Praise Works. Merlin R. Carothers. 161p. (Orig.). 1973. pap. 4.95. Carothers.

Praise Ye the Lord: Haiku Written to Psalm 148. Lesley Einer. 15p. (Orig.). 1988. pap. 3.50. Sage Shadow Pr.

Praises & Dispraises: Poetry & Politics, the 20th Century. Terrence Des Pres. LC 87-40540. 288p. 1988. 18.95 (ISBN 0-670-80406-1). Viking.

Praises We Sing. Elmina Yoder & Lula Miller. 1980. 5.45 (ISBN 0-87813-515-4). Christian Light.

Praisesong for the Widow. Paule Marshall. Date not set. pap. 7.95 (ISBN 0-525-48303-9, Obelisk). Dutton.

Praising & Knowing God. Daniel W. Hardy & David F. Ford. LC 84-25756. 226p. (Orig.). 1985. pap. 12.95 (ISBN 0-664-24624-9). Westminster John Knox.

Praising the Sand. William Vernon. 12p. 1983. pap. 1.00 (ISBN 0-686-46857-0). Samisdat.

Prajapati's Rise to Higher Rank. J. Gonda. (Orientalia Rheno-Traiectina: Vol. 29). x, 208p. 1986. 66.00 (ISBN 90-04-07734-0, Pub. by E J Brill). Heinman.

Prakrit Dhammapada. Suttapitaka. LC 78-70127. Repr. of 1921 ed. 31.50 (ISBN 0-404-17386-1). AMS Pr.

Prakrita Grammarians. L. Nitti-Dolci. Tr. by Prabhakara Jha. 1972. 14.50 (ISBN 0-89684-295-9). Orient Bk Dist.

Prakrita-Prakasa of Vararuchi see Grammar of Prakrit Language.

Prakruti: Your Ayurvedic Constitution. Robert E. Svoboda. (Illus.). 206p. (Orig.). 1988. pap. 11.00 (ISBN 0-945669-00-3). Geocom Ltd.

Praktische Andrologie. 2nd ed. C. Schirren. (Illus.). 1982. pap. 26.75 (ISBN 3-8055-3474-4). S Karger.

Praktische Anleitung Zur Interpretation Von Dichtung. Doris F. Merrifield. LC 81-40127. 246p. (Orig.). 1982. pap. text ed. 12.50 (ISBN 0-8191-2054-5). U Pr of Amer.

Praktische Aspekte der Onkologie. Ed. by U. R. Kleeberg. (Journal: Onkologie: Vol. 7, Suppl. 1). (Illus.). 64p. 1984. pap. 13.50 (ISBN 3-8055-3918-5). S Karger.

Praktische Lexikon der Naturheilkunde. Ernst Meyer-Camberg. (Ger.). 1977. pap. 45.95 (ISBN 3-570-06579-0, M-7594, Pub. by Mosaik/VVA). French & Eur.

Praktische Neonatologie. Ed. by E. Bossi. (Paediatrische Fortbildungskurse fuer die Praxis: Vol. 57). (Illus.). xii, 208p. 1983. pap. 65.50 (ISBN 3-8055-3657-7). S Karger.

Praktische Theologie nach den Grundsatzen. Friedrich Schleiermacher. 845p. (Ger.). 1983. 96.00 (ISBN 3-11-009699-4). De Gruyter.

Pralekhan aur Abhivechan (The Art of Conveyancing & Pleading in Hindi) Murli Manohar. 314p. 1979. 37.50x (ISBN 0-317-54572-8, Pub. by Eastern Bk India). State Mutual Bk.

Pranayama: The Yoga of Breathing. Andre Van Lysebeth. (Unwin Paperbacks). (Illus.). 1979. pap. 14.95 (ISBN 0-04-149050-9). Unwin Hyman.

Prancing Nigger. Ronald Firbank. 77p. 1977. pap. 6.75 (ISBN 0-7156-1098-8, Pub. by Duckworth London). Longwood Pub Group.

Prancing Nigger see Five Novels.

Prank. Kathryn Lasky. LC 83-23677. 276p. (gr. 7 up). 1984. 12.95 (ISBN 0-02-751690-3). Macmillan.

Prank. Kathryn Lasky. (gr. 6 up). 1986. pap. 2.75 (ISBN 0-440-97144-6, LFL). Dell.

Pranks. Dennis Higman. 432p. 1987. pap. 3.95 (ISBN 0-8439-2526-4). Leisure NY.

Pranks. Dennis J. Higman. 432p. (Orig.). 1983. pap. 3.50 (ISBN 0-8439-1154-9, Leisure Bks). Leisure NY.

Pranks, Tricks & Practical Jokes: 100 Harmless Ways to Fool Your Friends. Gyles Brandreth. LC 79-65291. (Illus.). 128p. (gr. 3 up). 1986. pap. 3.95 (ISBN 0-8069-6376-X). Sterling.

Prapanchasara Tantra. Ed. by Arthur Avalon, pseud. 617p. (Sanskrit.). 1982. text ed. 48.00 (ISBN 0-89744-239-3). Auromere.

Prarie Fire. rev. ed. Kent White, Jr. 256p. 1988. pap. 3.50 (ISBN 1-55785-062-3). Bart Books.

Prarie Logbooks: Dragoon Campaigns to the Pawnee Villages in 1844, & to the Rocky Mountains in 1845. J. Henry Carleton. Ed. by Louis Pelzer. xviii, 295p. 1983. 25.95x (ISBN 0-8032-1422-7); pap. 7.50 (ISBN 0-8032-6314-7, BB 845, Bison). U of Nebr Pr.

Prasna Upanishad. Tr. by Swami Gambhirananda from Sanskrit. (Upanishads with Shankara's Commentary Ser.). 104p. 1980. pap. 1.50 (ISBN 0-87481-204-6). Vedanta Pr.

Prasnopanisad. Tr. by Swami Sarvananda. (Sanskrit & English). pap. 1.00 (ISBN 0-87481-459-6). Vedanta Pr.

Prater Violet. Christopher Isherwood. 1985. pap. 2.75 (ISBN 0-380-01836-5, 63016-8, Bard). Avon.

Prater Violet. Christopher Isherwood. (Michael Di Capua Books). 128p. 1987. pap. 5.95 (ISBN 0-374-52053-4). FS&G.

Praters in Wiltshire, 1480-1670, Vol. I. John W. Prather, Jr. (Prater-Prather Family History & Genealogy). (Illus.). 215p. 1987. Set. 30.00 (ISBN 0-9619434-0-8); (ISBN 0-9619434-1-6). J W Prather.

Pratfall. T. A. Schock. 240p. 1986. pap. 2.95 (ISBN 0-8439-5002-1, Leisure Bks). Leisure NY.

Pratidanam, Indian, Iranian & Indo-European Studies Presented to Franciscus Bernardus Jacobus Kuiper on His 60th Birthday. J. C. Heesterman et al. (Janua Linguarum, Ser. Major: No. 34). 1968. text ed. 89.60x (ISBN 90-2790-686-6). Mouton.

Pratidwandi. Sunil Gangopadhyay. Tr. by Enakshi Chatterjee from Bengali. LC 74-900546. 1974. lib. bdg. 4.50x (ISBN 0-8364-0447-5). South Asia Bks.

Pratique, Vol. I. Dominique E. Secretan. 208p. (Fr.). 1975. pap. text ed. 16.00 (ISBN 0-7190-0447-0, Pub. by Manchester Univ Pr). St Martin.

Pratique De la Construction Des Batiments: Aide-Memoire Encyclopedique a L'usage Des Ingenieurs, Architectes et Entrepreneurs. M. Mittag. 352p. (Fr.). 1977. 95.00 (ISBN 0-686-57052-9, M-6415). French & Eur.

Pratique de la grammaire see Basic French.

Pratique de l'Allemand. (Assimil Ser.). 24.95 (ISBN 0-685-36084-9). French & Eur.

Pratique de l'Anglais. (Assimil Ser.). 24.95 (ISBN 0-685-36083-0). French & Eur.

Pratique de l'Espagnol. (Assimil Ser.). 24.95 (ISBN 0-685-35941-7). French & Eur.

Pratique du Francais, Vol. II. Dominique E. Secretan. 190p. (Fr.). 1972. pap. 16.00 (ISBN 0-7190-0490-X, Pub. by Manchester Univ Pr). St Martin.

Pratique du Francais Parle. Leon-Francois Hoffmann. LC 72-7530. 93p. (Fr.). 1973. pap. text ed. write for info. (ISBN 0-02-355630-7, Pub. by Scribner). Macmillan.

Pratiques Culturelles, Vol. 3. Bernadette Bucher et al. Ed. by Jean Carduner. LC 81-50963. (Michigan Romance Studies). 209p. (Orig.). 1983. pap. 8.00 (ISBN 0-939730-02-2). Mich Romance.

Pratsia Uchytelia. 2nd ed. A. Vivcharuk. 32p. (Ukrainian.). 1945. pap. 1.00 (ISBN 0-686-48395-2). Slavia Lib.

Pratt Journal of Architecture. Pratt Institute Staff. 92p. Vol. 2: 1988. 10.00 (ISBN 0-8478-5455-8). Rizzoli Intl.

Pratt Library Album: Baltimore Neighborhoods in Focus. Jacques Kelly. LC 86-11522. 1986. pap. 15.00 (ISBN 0-910556-23-7). Enoch Pratt.

Pratt Portraits. Anna Fuller. LC 79-94725. (Short Story Index Reprint Ser.). 1897. 19.00 (ISBN 0-8369-3104-1). Ayer Co Pubs.

Pratt Ware 1780-1840. J. G. Lewis. (Illus.). 304p. 1984. 69.50 (ISBN 0-907462-56-1). Antique Collect.

Pratt's Guide to Venture Capital Sources. 12th ed. Stanley E. Pratt & Jane K. Morris. 704p. 1988. 125.00 (ISBN 0-914470-23-X). Oryx Pr.

Pratt's Guide to Venture Capital Sources. 11th ed. Ed. by Stanley E. Pratt & Jane K. Morris. 744p. 1987. 95.00 (ISBN 0-914470-19-1). Venture Econ Inc.

Pratt's Guide to Venture Capital Sources. 11th ed. Ed. by Stanley E. Pratt & Jane K. Morris. 704p. 1987. 95.00 (ISBN 0-914470-15-9). Oryx Pr.

Prauda O Revoliutsiii Grazhdanskoy Voine: Truth about Russian Revolution & Civil War. S. L. Sofronoff. (Illus.). 140p. (Orig., Rus.). 1983. pap. 10.00 (ISBN 0-88669-061-7). Globus Pubs.

Pravda. H. Brenton & D. Hare. (Modern Plays Ser.). 96p. (Orig.). 1985. pap. 6.95 (ISBN 0-413-58480-1, 9481). Heinemann Ed.

Pravda: Inside the Soviet News Machine. Angus Roxburgh. LC 87-11707. (Illus.). 290p. 1987. 19.95 (ISBN 0-8076-1186-7). Braziller.

Pravda o Russkoj Tserkvi na Rodinje i za Rubjezhom. George Grabbe. 216p. 1961. pap. 8.00 (ISBN 0-317-30359-7). Holy Trinity.

Pravda ob Ubijstvje Tsarskoj Semji. P. Paganuzzi. LC 80-84594. 234p. 1981. 15.00 (ISBN 0-317-29234-X); pap. 10.00 (ISBN 0-317-29235-8). Holy Trinity.

Pravo na Ostrov. Vasily Aksenov. LC 83-8924. 180p. (Orig.). 1983. pap. 7.00 (ISBN 0-938920-34-0). Hermitage.

Pravosavnoje Dogmaticheskoje Bogoslovije. Protopresbyter Michael Pomazansky. 280p. 1963. pap. text ed. 20.00 (ISBN 0-317-29309-5). Holy Trinity.

Pravoslavije i Inoslavnija Khristianskija Ispovjedanija. Metropolitan Panteleimon. 1950. pap. 0.55 (ISBN 0-317-30259-0). Holy Trinity.

Pravoslavije, Rimo-Katolichestvo, Protenstatizm i Sektantstvo. Mitrophan Znoskovo-Borovsky. 156p. 1972. pap. text ed. 5.00 (ISBN 0-317-30254-X). Holy Trinity.

Pravoslavno-Khristijanskaja Apologetika. I. M. Andreyev. 92p. 1965. pap. text ed. 5.00 (ISBN 0-317-30249-3). Holy Trinity.

Pravoslavno-Khristijanskoe Nravstvennoje Bogoslovije. I. M. Andreyev. 148p. 1966. pap. text ed. 5.00 (ISBN 0-317-30264-7). Holy Trinity.

Prawn Ascot: A Pawn in Aspic. Charles E. Gould, Jr. (Illus.). 8p. (Orig.). 1987. pap. write for info. (ISBN 0-9618531-0-7). C E Gould Jr.

Praxedes: Wife, Mother, Widow, & Lay Dominican. Martin-Maria Olive. LC 87-50548. 203p. 1987. pap. 4.50 (ISBN 0-89555-309-0). TAN Bks Pubs.

Praxeology: An Anthology. Ed. by Gunnar Skirbekk. 180p. (Orig.). 1984. pap. 20.00x (ISBN 82-00-06659-2). Oxford U Pr.

Praxiological Studies. Wojciech Gasparski. 1983. lib. bdg. 78.00 (ISBN 90-277-1258-1, Pub. by Reidel Holland). Kluwer Academic.

Praxis. Ed. by Mihailo Markovic & Gajo Petrovic. (Boston Studies in the Philosophy of Science: No. XXXVI; Synthese Library, No. 134). 1979. lib. bdg. 55.00 (ISBN 90-277-0727-8, Pub. by Reidel Holland); pap. 23.50 (ISBN 90-277-0968-8, Pub. by Reidel Holland). Kluwer Academic.

Praxis & Action: Contemporary Philosophies of Human Activity. Richard J. Bernstein. LC 77-157048. 360p. 1971. 15.50 (ISBN 0-8122-1016-6). U of Pa Pr.

Praxis & Reason: Studies in the Philosophy of Nicholas Rescher. Ed. by Robert Almeder. LC 81-43602. (Nicholas Rescher Ser.). 276p. (Orig.). 1982. lib. bdg. 33.75 (ISBN 0-8191-2648-9); pap. text ed. 14.50 (ISBN 0-8191-2649-7). U Pr of Amer.

Praxis: Marxist Criticism & Dissent in Socialist Yugoslavia. Gerson S. Sher. LC 77-72193. pap. 95.00 (ISBN 0-317-27863-0, 2056059). Bks Demand UMI.

Praxis of My System see Chess Praxis.

Praxis of Suffering: An Interpretation of Liberation & Political Theologies. Rebecca S. Chopp. LC 86-824. 192p. (Orig.). 1986. pap. 12.95 (ISBN 0-88344-256-6). Orbis Bks.

Praxis, Truth & Liberation: Essays on Gadamer, Taylor, Polanyi, Habermas, Guterrez, & Ricoeur. Terry Hoy. 134p. (Orig.). 1988. pap. text ed. 10.25 (ISBN 0-8191-7072-0). U Pr of Amer.

Pray All Ways. Edward Hays. LC 81-69329. (Illus.). 164p. (Orig.). 1981. pap. 7.95 (ISBN 0-939516-01-2). Forest Peace.

Pray Always. James Alberione. 1966. 4.00 (ISBN 0-8198-0126-7); pap. 3.00 (ISBN 0-8198-0127-5). Dghtrs St Paul.

Pray: An Introduction to the Spiritual Life for Busy People. Richard J. Huelsmann. LC 76-24449. (Participants Handbook). 136p. 1976. pap. 4.95 (ISBN 0-8091-1976-5). Paulist Pr.

Pray & Grow: Evangelism Prayer Ministries. Terry Teykl. LC 88-70272. 48p. (Orig.). 1988. pap. 5.95 (ISBN 0-88177-055-8, DR055B). Discipleship Res.

Pray Continually. Saint Aphraates et al. pap. 0.95 (ISBN 0-317-60812-6). Eastern Orthodox.

Pray for a Brave Heart. Helen MacInnes. 1985. pap. 3.95 (ISBN 0-449-21013-8, Crest). Fawcett.

Pray for Ricky Foster. Jane Johnston. 200p. 1985. 12.95 (ISBN 0-312-63555-9). St Martin.

Pray: God Is Listening. enl. ed. Richard DeHaan. 96p. 1988. pap. 4.95 (ISBN 0-310-23541-3, Pub. by Daybreak). Zondervan.

Pray in the Spirit. Arthur Wallis. 1970. pap. 2.95 (ISBN 0-87508-561-X). Chr Lit.

Pray in This Way. Dorothy F. Richards. LC 83-7342. (Illus.). 32p. (gr. 3-4). 1983. PLB 4.95 (ISBN 0-89693-215-X). Dandelion Hse.

Pray It Again, Sam. Kenneth J. Roberts. Ed. by Anna Marie Ruskin. LC 83-61243. 116p. (Orig.). 1983. pap. 3.95 (ISBN 0-9610984-0-6). Pax Tapes.

Pray: Moderator's Manual: An Introduction to the Spiritual Life for Busy People. Huelsman. LC 76-2449. 168p. 1976. pap. 7.95 (ISBN 0-8091-1975-7). Paulist Pr.

Pray the Rosary. J. M. Lelen. (Illus., Purse-Size). blue bdg. 0.60 (ISBN 0-89942-040-0, 40/05). Catholic Bk Pub.

Pray to Win! A Blueprint for Success. Alfred A. Montapert. LC 86-73037. 235p. 1986. perfect bdg. 4.95 (ISBN 0-9603174-4-9). Bks of Value.

Pray to Win: A Blueprint for Success. Alfred A. Montapert. pap. 4.95 (Pub. by Bks of Value). Borden.

Pray to Your Father in Secret. Jean Lafrance. 1988. pap. 8.00 (ISBN 0-317-67463-3, SP0562). Dghtrs St Paul.

Pray Today's Gospel: Reflections on the Day's Good News. Bernard C. Mischke & Fritz Mischke. LC 80-14186. 358p. (Orig.). 1980. pap. 9.95 (ISBN 0-8189-0403-8). Alba.

Pray with Your Eyes Open. Richard L. Pratt, Jr. LC 87-2762. 224p. 1987. pap. 10.95 (ISBN 0-87552-377-3). Presby & Reformed.

Pray with Your Eyes Open: Looking at God, Ourselves, & Our Prayers. Richard L. Pratt, Jr. 193p. (Orig.). 1988. pap. 10.95 (ISBN 0-8010-7104-6). Baker Bk.

Pray Your Way Through It. Joseph Murphy. 171p. 1973. pap. 6.00 (ISBN 0-87516-190-1). DeVorss.

Prayer. Abhishiktananda. LC 73-600. 88p. 1973. pap. 4.95 (ISBN 0-664-24973-6). Westminster John Knox.

Prayer. Saint Aphraates. 1975. pap. 0.50 (ISBN 0-686-10940-6). Eastern Orthodox.

Prayer. Saint Aphraates. pap. 0.50 (ISBN 0-317-60813-4). Eastern Orthodox.

Prayer. 2nd ed. Karl Barth. Ed. by Don E. Saliers. Tr. by Sara F. Terrien from Ger. LC 84-25782. 96p. 1985. pap. 7.95 (ISBN 0-664-24626-5). Westminster John Knox.

Prayer. O. Hallesby. LC 75-2846. 176p. 1959. pap. 4.50 (ISBN 0-8066-1473-0, 10-5067). Augsburg.

Prayer. Karen D. Merrell. 23p. (ps-2). pap. 4.95 (ISBN 0-87747-562-8). Deseret Bk.

Prayer. Rudolf Steiner. 1966. pap. 2.95 (ISBN 0-910142-30-0). Anthroposophic.

Prayer. Hans U. Von Balthasar. Tr. by Graham Harrison from Ger. LC 85-82172. Orig. Title: Das Betrachtende Gebet. 311p. 1986. pap. 10.95 (ISBN 0-89870-074-4). Ignatius Pr.

Prayer. John White. 1984. pap. 0.75 (ISBN 0-87784-067-9). Inter-Varsity.

Prayer, a Baha'i Approach. Incl. Part I. Man's Link with God. William Hellaby; Part II. Prayer as a Living Reality. William Hellaby & Madeline Hellaby. 1985. 9.95 (ISBN 0-85398-212-0); pap. 4.95 (ISBN 0-85398-213-9). G Ronald Pub.

Prayer: A Discovery of Life. Alexandra Kovats. (Nazareth Bks). 128p. 1983. pap. 4.95 (ISBN 0-86683-714-0, AY8361, HarpR). Har-Row.

Prayer: A Guide When Troubled. Martin C. Helldorfer. LC 85-13561. (Illus.). 88p. (Orig.). 1985. pap. 7.95 (ISBN 0-89571-024-2). Affirmation.

Prayer: A New Encounter. Martin Thornton. LC 87-30337. 186p. (Orig.). 1988. pap. 8.95 (ISBN 0-936384-54-9). Cowley Pubns.

Prayer after Nine Rainy Days & Other Family Prayers. Pat C. Hinton. 1978. pap. 4.95 (ISBN 0-86683-626-8, HarpR). Har-Row.

Prayer: An Adventure in Living. B. C. Butler. LC 82-84591. (Ways of Prayer Ser.: Vol. 10). 8.95 (ISBN 0-89453-431-9); pap. 4.95 (ISBN 0-89453-302-9). M Glazier.

Prayer: An Invitation from God. Charles Nieman. 140p. (Orig.). 1983. pap. text ed. 4.95 (ISBN 0-914307-03-7, Dist. by Harrison Hse). Word Faith.

Prayer & Community: The Havurah Movement in American Judaism. Riv-Ellen Prell. (Illus.). 300p. 1988. 27.50x (ISBN 0-8143-1934-3); pap. 14.95x (ISBN 0-8143-1935-1). Wayne St U Pr.

Prayer & Evangelism. Jessie Penn-Lewis. 1962. pap. 2.95 (ISBN 0-87508-952-6). Chr Lit.

Prayer & Faith, Oma Ellis Talks About. Oma Ellis & Georgia Smelser. Ed. by David Bernard. LC 87-13306. (Illus.). 160p. (Orig.). 1987. pap. 5.95 (ISBN 0-932581-16-1). Word Aflame.

Prayer & Fasting. Gordon Lindsay. (School of Prayer Ser.). 1.75 (ISBN 0-89985-076-6). Christ Nations.

Prayer & Meditation. Intro. by Elizabeth C. Prophet. LC 76-28086. (Illus.). 360p. (Orig.). 1978. pap. 9.95 (ISBN 0-916766-19-5). Summit Univ.

Prayer & Meditation for Middle School Kids. John B. Hesch. 144p. (Orig.). 1985. pap. 7.95 (ISBN 0-8091-2723-7). Paulist Pr.

Prayer & Modern Man. Jacques Ellul. Tr. by C. Edward Hopkins from Fr. 192p. 1973. pap. 6.95 (ISBN 0-8164-2081-5, HarpR). Har-Row.

Prayer & Our Bodies. Flora S. Wuellner. 144p. (Orig.). 1987. pap. 6.95 (ISBN 0-8358-0568-9). Upper Room.

Prayer & Our Children: Passing on the Tradition. M. Terese Donze. LC 87-71000. 96p. (Orig.). 1987. pap. 3.95 (ISBN 0-87793-365-0). Ave Maria.

Prayer & Peanut Butter. Shirley Lueth. (Illus.). 147p. (Orig.). 1986. pap. 5.95 (ISBN 0-937911-01-1). Lueth Hse Pub.

Prayer & Peanut Butter: Talking Book. Shirley Lueth. (Illus.). 147p. 1983. pap. 4.85 (ISBN 0-8300-2129-9). Aurora News Reg.

Prayer & Personal Religion. John B. Coburn. LC 85-10477. 160p. 1985. pap. 8.95 (ISBN 0-8027-2509-0). Walker & Co.

Prayer & Poetry: Contribution to Poetical Theory. Henri Bremond. LC 72-188148. 1927. lib. bdg. 25.00 (ISBN 0-8414-9825-3). Folcroft.

Prayer & Power in the Capital: With Prayers of the Presidents. Ed. by Pauline Innis. LC 82-156801. (Illus.). 120p. 1982. 7.50 (ISBN 0-941402-02-9). Devon Pub.

Prayer & Praying Men. E. M. Bounds. (Direction Bks). 1977. pap. 3.95 (ISBN 0-8010-0721-6). Baker Bk.

Prayer & Revival. Wim Malgo. 4.95 (ISBN 0-937422-12-6). Midnight Call.

Prayer & Temperament: Different Prayer Forms for Different Personality Types. Kodansha Ltd. & Marie C. Norrisey. 192p. (Orig.). 1984. pap. 5.95 (ISBN 0-940136-01-5). Open Door Inc.

Prayer & the Christian Life: C-4 Devotional Journal II. Ed. by Steve Clapp. (C-4 Journals Ser.). 126p. (Orig.). 1982. pap. 6.00 (ISBN 0-317-11522-7). C-Four Res.

Prayer & the Christian's Devotional Life. G. Raymond Carlson. LC 80-83522. (Radiant Life Ser.). 128p. (Orig.). 1981. 2.50 (ISBN 0-88243-878-6, 02-0878); teacher's guide 3.95 (ISBN 0-88243-190-0, 32-0190). Gospel Pub.

Prayer & the Common Life. Thomas Langford. LC 83-51396. 96p. (Orig.). 1984. pap. 3.95 (ISBN 0-8358-0473-9). Upper Room.

Prayer & the Press see From Resentment to Gratitude.

Prayer & the Will of God. Hubert Van Zeller. 1978. 4.95 (ISBN 0-87243-084-7). Templegate.

Prayer & Worship. Douglas V. Steere. LC 78-70480. 1978. pap. 4.95 (ISBN 0-944350-01-1). Friends United.

Prayer & You: A Journey with the Lord. Michael Pennock. LC 85-70162. (High School Religion Text Program Ser.). (Illus., Orig.). (YA) (gr. 9-12). 1985. pap. text ed. 5.50 student ed., 160 pg. (ISBN 0-87793-284-0); tchr's. manual, 144 pg. 7.95 (ISBN 0-87793-285-9). Ave Maria.

Prayer Answered. Dorothy Martin. (Peggy Ser.: No. 10). (gr. 7). 1985. pap. 3.50 (ISBN 0-8024-8310-0). Moody.

Prayer at the Ruins of Jerusalem. C. B. Chavel. 32p. 1978. pap. 2.50 (ISBN 0-88328-031-0). Shilo Pub Hse.

Prayer Attitude in the Eastern Church. Gabriele Winkler. 1978. pap. 1.45 (ISBN 0-937032-01-8). Light&Life Pub Co MN.

Prayer Beyond the Beginnings: Exploring Contemplative Prayer. Barbara Pursey. 40p. 1984. 2.95x (ISBN 0-934421-05-6). Presby Renewal Pubns.

Prayer Book. Tr. by Ben Z. Bokser from Hebrew. 430p. 1983. 10.00 (ISBN 0-87441-368-0); pap. 11.95 (ISBN 0-87441-372-9). Behrman.

Prayer Book. 368p. (Orig.). 1979. 10.00 (ISBN 0-317-30304-X). Holy Trinity.

Prayer Book. Ed. by Anna Riva et al. 128p. (Orig.). 1984. pap. 4.95 (ISBN 0-943832-09-8). Intl Imports.

Prayer Book. S. Singer. Repr. of 1962 ed. 10.95x (ISBN 0-8197-0057-6). Bloch.

Prayer Book & the Lord's Prayer. Frederick D. Maurice. 416p. 1977. Repr. of 1880 ed. 14.00 (ISBN 0-87921-038-9). Attic Pr.

Prayer Book for Elders. Ron Potter. 79p. (Orig.). 1985. pap. 9.95 (ISBN 0-85819-504-6, Pub. by Uniting Church). ANZ Religious Pubns.

Prayer Book for Summer Camps. Morris Silverman & Hillel Silverman. (gr. 3-12). 8.95x (ISBN 0-87677-060-X); pap. 6.95x (ISBN 0-87677-061-8). Prayer Bk.

Prayer Book for Young Catholics. Robert J. Fox. LC 82-81318. 168p. (gr. 4-8). 1982. pap. 5.50 Leatherette (ISBN 0-87973-370-5, 370). Our Sunday Visitor.

Prayer Book Guide to Christian Education. Episcopal Church. 224p. 1983. pap. 9.95 (ISBN 0-8164-2422-5, HarpR). Har-Row.

Prayer Book of Michelino Da Besozzo. Colin Eisler & Patricia Corbett. LC 81-68186. (Illus.). 1981. 50.00 (ISBN 0-8076-1016-X). Braziller.

Prayer Book of the Bible: Reflection on the Old Testament. Peter M. Stravinskas. LC 83-63171. 160p. 1984. pap. 5.95 (ISBN 0-87973-606-2, 606). Our Sunday Visitor.

Prayer Book of the Saints. Charles Dollen. LC 84-60749. 1984. pap. 6.95 (ISBN 0-87973-717-4, 717). Our Sunday Visitor.

Prayer Book Office. Ed. by Howard Galley. 800p. 1980. 39.95 (ISBN 0-8164-0370-8, HarpR). Har-Row.

Prayer Can Change Your Life. William R. Parker & Elaine St. Johns. 270p. 1983. pap. 6.95 (ISBN 0-13-694786-7, Reward). P-H.

Prayer Can Change Your Marriage. Ron Auch. Ed. by Cliff Dudley. LC 84-61916. 120p. (Orig.). 1985. pap. 5.95 (ISBN 0-89221-118-0). New Leaf.

Prayer Changes My Life. large print ed. Pearl Brians. 23p. 1985. pap. 4.00 (ISBN 0-914009-35-4). VHI Library.

Prayer Course for Healing Life's Hurts: Book. Matthew Linn & Dennis Linn. 128p. 1983. pap. 5.95 (ISBN 0-8091-2522-6). Paulist Pr.

Prayer Factor. Sammy Tippit. 1988. pap. 5.95 (ISBN 0-8024-2594-1). Moody.

Prayer Flags: The Spiritual Life & Songs of Jigten Sumgon. Khenpo K. Gyalsten. 96p. (Orig.). 1986. pap. 6.95 (ISBN 0-937938-37-8). Snow Lion.

Prayer for a Child. Rachel Field. LC 44-47191. (Illus.). 32p. (ps-1). 1968. 8.95 (ISBN 0-02-735190-4). Macmillan.

Prayer for a Child. Rachel Field. LC 84-70991. (Illus.). 32p. (ps-1). 1984. 3.95 (ISBN 0-02-043070-1, Aladdin Bks). Macmillan.

Prayer for All Times. Pierre Charles. Tr. by Robin Waterfield from Fr. 157p. 1983. pap. 5.95 (ISBN 0-87061-090-2). Chr Classics.

Prayer for Fair Weather. John Broderick. LC 83-6341. 192p. 1984. 13.95 (ISBN 0-7145-2796-3, Dist. by Kampmann & Co). M Boyars Pubs.

Prayer for Guidance. Elbert Willis. 1977. 1.25 (ISBN 0-89858-012-9). Fill the Gap.

Prayer for Katerina Horovitzova. Arnost Lustig. Tr. by Jeanne Nemcova. LC 84-25593. 176p. 1987. 15.95 (ISBN 0-87951-998-3); pap. 9.95 (ISBN 0-87951-223-7). Overlook Pr.

Prayer for Our Day. E. Lee Phillips. LC 81-82349. 156p. 1982. pap. 7.95 (ISBN 0-8042-2583-4, John Knox). Westminster John Knox.

Prayer for Patient Waiting. Elbert Willis. 1977. 1.25 (ISBN 0-89858-002-1). Fill the Gap.

Prayer for Pilgrims: A Book about Prayer for Ordinary People. Sheila A. Cassidy. (Crossroad Paperback Ser.). 192p. 1982. pap. 6.95 (ISBN 0-8245-0420-8). Crossroad NY.

Prayer for Relief: The Constitutional Infirmities of the Military Academies' Conduct, Honor, & Ethics Systems. Michael T. Rose. vii, 194p. (Orig.). 1973. pap. text ed. 7.50x (ISBN 0-8377-1025-1). Rothman.

Prayer for the Dying. Jack Higgins. 1987. pap. 3.95 (ISBN 0-451-14994-7, Sig). NAL.

Prayer for Today's People: Sermons on Prayer by Carl Michalson (1915-1965) Ed. by Edward J. Wynne, Jr. & Henry O. Thompson. LC 82-17583. 88p. (Orig.). 1983. lib. bdg. 24.75 (ISBN 0-8191-2771-X); pap. text ed. 9.25 (ISBN 0-8191-2772-8). U Pr of Amer.

Prayer Forms: Twenty-two Prayer Forms for Classrooms & Youth Groups. The Christian Brothers. LC 86-51541. 64p. 1987. pap. 6.95 (ISBN 0-89622-330-2). Twenty-Third.

Prayer: God's Time & Ours! Warren F. Groff. 144p. (Orig.). 1984. pap. 6.95 (ISBN 0-87178-714-8). Brethren.

Prayer: How to Talk to God. (BMC Teaching Bks.). (Illus.). (gr. 1-8). 1970. pap. text ed. 3.50 (ISBN 0-86508-153-0). BCM Pubn.

Prayer, Humility & Compassion. Samuel Dresner. 4.95 (ISBN 0-87677-006-5). Hartmore.

Prayer-Hymns: A New & Different Hymnal for Church & Home. W. Armstrong. LC 73-101347. pap. write for info. (ISBN 0-686-08988-X). Gonzaga U Pr.

Prayer in Baptist Life. Charles W. Deweese. LC 85-21301. 1986. pap. 4.95 (ISBN 0-8054-6941-9). Broadman.

Prayer in Practice. Simon Tugwell. 1980. pap. 7.95 (ISBN 0-87243-099-5). Templegate.

Prayer in Sixteenth Century England. Faye L. Kelly. LC 66-64090. (U of Fla. Humanities Monographs: No. 22). 1966. pap. 6.00x (ISBN 0-8130-0127-7). U Presses Fla.

Prayer in the Black Tradition. O. R. Bowyer et al. 112p. 1986. pap. 5.95 (ISBN 0-8358-0538-7, ICN 609100, Dist. by Abingdon Press). Upper Room.

Prayer in the Contemporary World. Douglas V. Steere. LC 80-82942. 32p. pap. 2.50x (ISBN 0-87574-907-0). Pendle Hill.

Prayer in the Home. Ed. by David M. Thomas. LC 81-69503. (Marriage & Family Living in Depth Bk.). 1981. pap. 2.45 (ISBN 0-87029-180-7, 20250-7). Abbey.

Prayer in the Life of Jesus. Paris Donehoo. (Orig.). 1984. pap. 3.95 (ISBN 0-8054-5101-3). Broadman.

Prayer in the New Age. White Eagle. 1957. 4.50 (ISBN 0-85487-041-5). DeVorss.

Prayer in the New Age. White Eagle. 112p. 1984. Repr. of 1957 ed. 5.95 (ISBN 0-85487-064-4, Pub. by White Eagle Pub). DeVorss.

Prayer in the Religious Traditions of Africa. Aylward Shorter. 1975. pap. 7.95 (ISBN 0-19-519848-4). Oxford U Pr.

Prayer in the Talmud: Forms & Patterns. Joseph Heinemann. (Studia Judaica: Vol. 9). 1977. 61.00 (ISBN 3-11-004289-4). De Gruyter.

Prayer Is... Furn F. Kelling. (Illus.). (gr. k-3). 1979. 5.95 (ISBN 0-8054-4256-1, 4242-56). Broadman.

Prayer Is a Hunger. Edward Farrell. 4.95 (ISBN 0-87193-031-5). Dimension Bks.

Prayer Is Invading the Impossible. Jack Hayford. (Epiphany Bks.). 160p. 1983. pap. 2.95. Ballantine.

Prayer Is Invading the Impossible. Jack W. Hayford. LC 77-71684. 150p. 1977. pap. 5.95 (ISBN 0-88270-218-1). Bridge Pub.

Prayer Is Invading the Impossible see Oracion Invade Lo Imposible.

Prayer Is Reaching. Howard Bogot & Daniel Syme. (Illus.). 32p. (ps). 1982. text ed. 4.00 (ISBN 0-8074-0172-2, 101230). UAHC.

Prayer Is the Answer. Joseph Murphy. 190p. 1973. pap. 5.00 (ISBN 0-87516-189-8). DeVorss.

Prayer: Its Nature & Technique. 4th ed. Kirpal Singh. LC 81-50727. (Illus.). 149p. 1982. pap. 6.50 (ISBN 0-918224-10-1). Sawan Kirpal Pubns.

Prayer, Its Significance & Benefits. A. Rahman. pap. 12.50 (ISBN 0-317-46106-0). Kazi Pubns.

Prayer: Key to Revival. Paul Y. Cho & R. Whitney Manzano. 224p. 1984. 9.95 (ISBN 0-8499-0453-6, 0453-6). Word Bks.

Prayer: Learning How to Talk to God. J. L. Groth. LC 56-1395. (Concept Books for Children: Series Four). (gr. 1 up). 1983. pap. 3.95 (ISBN 0-570-07799-0). Concordia.

Prayer Life. Agape Ministries Staff. (Orig.). 1984. pap. 3.50 (ISBN 0-89274-346-8). Harrison Hse.

Prayer Life. Andrew Murray. (Andrew Murray Ser.). pap. 3.95 (ISBN 0-8024-6806-3). Moody.

Prayer Life. Andrew Murray. 160p. 1981. pap. 2.95 (ISBN 0-88368-102-1). Whitaker Hse.

Prayer Life. Charles H. Usher. 1967. pap. 1.50 (ISBN 0-87508-545-8). Chr Lit.

Prayer Life: A Guide to the Inner Chamber. Andrew Murray. 128p. 1987. pap. 3.95 (ISBN 0-310-55072-6, 19007P). Zondervan.

Prayer Life of Jesus. Harold D. Vaughan. 96p. (Orig.). 1987. pap. 3.50 (ISBN 0-942889-00-2). Christ Life Pubns.

Prayer: Life's Limitless Reach. Jack R. Taylor. LC 77-73984. 1977. 8.95 (ISBN 0-8054-5258-3). Broadman.

Prayer: Living with God. Simon Tugwell. 1980. pap. 7.95 (ISBN 0-87243-100-2). Templegate.

Prayer Meeting at Our House. large print ed. Pearl Brians. 25p. 1985. pap. 4.00 (ISBN 0-914009-33-8). VHI Library.

Prayer Meetings. Harry Doty. LC 78-10622. 1979. pap. 6.00 (ISBN 0-8309-0228-7). Herald Hse.

Prayer Ministry of the Church. Watchman Nee. Tr. by Stephen Kaung. 1973. pap. 2.75 (ISBN 0-935008-30-6). Christian Fellow Pubs.

Prayer: More Than Words. LeRoy Eims. LC 82-61301. 162p. 1983. pap. 3.95 (ISBN 0-89109-493-8). NavPress.

Prayer Movements: An International Directory. International Partners in Prayer Staff. 20p. Date not set. pap. 3.00 (ISBN 0-917593-00-6, Pub. by Intl Partners). Prosperity & Profits.

Prayer of Catholic Educators. Robert J. Kealey. 152p. 1987. 8.30. Natl Cath Educ.

Prayer of Cosa: Praying in the Way of Francis of Assisi. Cornelia Jessey. (Orig.). 1985. pap. 5.95 (ISBN 0-86683-936-4, AY8512, HarpR). Har-Row.

Prayer of Faith. Leonard S. Boase. 1985. Repr. 5.95 (ISBN 0-8294-0493-7). Loyola.

Prayer of Faith. Ed. by J. O. Fraser & Mary E. Allbutt. pap. 1.00 (ISBN 0-85363-106-9). OMF Bks.

Prayer of Faith. Quentin Hakenewerth. 76p. (Orig.). 1969. pap. 1.75 (ISBN 0-9608124-3-1). Marianist Com Ctr.

Prayer of Love: The Art of Aspiration. Venard Poslusney. 128p. (Orig.). 1975. pap. 2.95. Living Flame Pr.

Prayer of Recollection: St. Teresa of Avila. 1983. 1.95 (ISBN 0-87193-208-3). Dimension Bks.

Prayer of St. Patrick. pap. 1.00 (ISBN 0-686-18721-0). Eastern Orthodox.

Prayer of the Faithful: Understanding & Creatively Using the Prayer of the Church. Walter Huffman. 80p. (Orig.). 1986. pap. 6.95 (ISBN 0-8066-2230-X, 10-5079). Augsburg.

Prayer of the Heart. George A. Maloney. LC 80-69095. 208p. (Orig.). 1981. pap. 3.95 (ISBN 0-87793-216-6). Ave Maria.

Prayer on Target. George E. Vandeman. (Outreach Ser.). 46p. 1987. pap. 1.25 (ISBN 0-8163-0772-5). Pacific Pr Pub Assn.

Prayer Partners. Arnold Prater. 128p. 1987. 10.95 (ISBN 0-687-33480-2). Abingdon.

Prayer, Patronage, & Power: The Abbey of la Trinite, Vendome, 1032-1187. Penelope Johnson. (Illus.). 224p. 1981. 35.00x (ISBN 0-8147-4162-2). NYU Pr.

Prayer: Personal & Liturgical. Agnes Cunningham. LC 84-48853. (Message of the Fathers of the Church Ser.: Vol. 16). 1985. 12.95 (ISBN 0-89453-356-8); pap. 8.95 (ISBN 0-89453-327-4). M Glazier.

Prayer Perspectives. Ed. by Edward Carter. LC 86-28675. 108p. (Orig.). 1987. pap. 5.95 (ISBN 0-8189-0513-1). Alba.

Prayer Pilgrimage Through Scripture. Rea McDonnell. LC 83-82025. (Orig.). 1984. pap. 6.95 (ISBN 0-8091-2601-X). Paulist Pr.

Prayer Pilgrimage with Paul. Rea McDonnell. 112p. 1986. pap. 4.95 (ISBN 0-8091-2746-6). Paulist Pr.

Prayer Poems. facsimile ed. Ed. by O. V. Armstrong & Helen Armstrong. LC 72-86793. (Granger Index Reprint Ser). 1942. 16.00 (ISBN 0-8369-6094-7). Ayer Co Pubs.

Prayer, Politics, & Power. Joel C. Hunter. 192p. (Orig.). 1988. pap. 5.95 (ISBN 0-8423-4973-1, 75-4973-1). Tyndale.

Prayer Power & Stress Management. Stewart Bedford. pap. 6.95 (ISBN 0-935930-05-1). A & S Pr.

Prayer Power Unlimited. J. Oswald Sanders. (Moody Press Electives Ser.). (Orig.). 1984. pap. 3.95 (ISBN 0-8024-6677-X); pap. 2.50 leader's guide (ISBN 0-8024-6676-1). Moody.

Prayer Primer. Nancy Cook. 1987. pap. 5.95 (ISBN 0-937462-06-3). Net Pr.

Prayer Primer. Erwin Kolb. 1982. pap. 4.25 (ISBN 0-570-03843-X, 12-2946). Concordia.

Prayer Primer: A Philosophy Book. Patty Jo Cornish. Ed. by Roberto Quintero. LC 84-81741. 68p. (Orig.). pap. 5.95 (ISBN 0-9613717-0-6). Hilltop Hse.

Prayer, Principles & Power. John R. Price. 116p. (Orig.). 1987. pap. 3.95 (ISBN 0-942082-10-9). Quartus Bks.

Prayer, Responding to God. Robert B. Hall & Marjorie W. Hall. 1985. pap. 6.95 (ISBN 0-318-04676-8). Episcopal Ctr.

Prayer Room Counselor's Handbook. Cathy Jakobcic. 47p. 1983. pap. 2.25 (ISBN 0-88144-015-9). Christian Pub.

Prayer Rugs. Richard Ettinghausen et al. LC 74-15703. (Illus.). 139p. 1974. pap. 18.50 (ISBN 0-87405-004-9). Textile Mus.

Prayer Rugs from Private Collections. Patricia Fiske. (Illus.). 139p. 1974. pap. 2.50 (ISBN 0-87405-003-0). Textile Mus.

Prayer, Saints, Scripture & Ourselves. Chuck Gallagher & Oliver Crilly. LC 83-60189. 162p. (Orig.). 1983. pap. text ed. 6.95 (ISBN 0-911905-03-0). Past & Mat Rene Ctr.

Prayer Secrets. 2nd ed. Kenneth E. Hagin. 1983. pap. 1.00 (ISBN 0-89276-005-2). Hagin Ministries.

Prayer: Selections from the Writings of the Holy Fathers. pap. 2.95 (ISBN 0-317-11391-7). Eastern Orthodox.

Prayer Seminar-Workshop Workbook. International Partners in Prayer. 11p. 1984. pap. 2.50 (ISBN 0-917593-02-2, Pub. by Intl Partners). Prosperity & Profits.

Prayer Services for Parish Meetings. Debra T. Hintz. LC 83-70620. (Illus.). 96p. (Orig.). 1983. pap. 9.95 (ISBN 0-89622-170-9). Twenty-Third.

Prayer, Stress & Our Inner Wounds. Flora S. Wuellner. 94p. (Orig.). 1985. pap. 4.95 (ISBN 0-8358-0501-8). Upper Room.

Prayer-Talk: Casual Conversations with God. William V. Coleman. LC 82-74085. 112p. (Orig.). 1983. pap. 3.95 (ISBN 0-87793-265-4). Ave Maria.

Prayer That Heals. Francis MacNutt. LC 80-69770. 120p. (Orig.). 1981. pap. 2.95 (ISBN 0-87793-219-0). Ave Maria.

Prayer That Heals Our Emotions. rev. ed. Eddie Ensley. LC 88-45134. 144p. 1988. pap. 8.95 (ISBN 0-06-062253-9, HarpR). Har-Row.

Prayer That Moves Mountains. Gordon Lindsay. (School of Prayer Ser.). 2.50 (ISBN 0-89985-078-2). Christ Nations.

Prayer That Spans the World. Helmut Thielicke. Tr. by J. W. Doberstein from Ger. 160p. 1978. Repr. 17.95 (ISBN 0-227-67671-8). Attic Pr.

Prayer: The Compulsive Word. Gladys A. Reichard. LC 84-45512. (American Ethnological Society Monographs: No. 7). 1988. Repr. of 1944 ed. 24.50 (ISBN 0-404-62907-5). AMS Pr.

Prayer: The Cornerstone. Helen G. Hole. LC 62-19073. (Orig.). 1962. pap. 2.50x (ISBN 0-87574-123-1). Pendle Hill.

Prayer: The Divine Dialog. Carroll E. Simcox. LC 84-28930. 108p. (Orig.). 1985. pap. 5.95 (ISBN 0-87784-527-1). Inter-Varsity.

Prayer: The Eastern Tradition. Andrew Ryder. (Orig.). 1983. pap. 2.95 (ISBN 0-914544-47-0). Living Flame Pr.

Prayer: The Great Conversation-Straight Answers to Tough Questions about Prayer. Peter Kreeft. 164p. (Orig.). 1985. pap. 6.95 (ISBN 0-89283-218-5). Servant.

Prayer-the Key to Salvation. Michael Muller. LC 85-52207. 226p. 1985. pap. 6.00 (ISBN 0-89555-287-6). Tan Bks Pubs.

Prayer: The Master Key. James D. Freeman. 1975. 5.95 (ISBN 0-87159-128-6). Unity School.

Prayer: The Vital Link. William J. Krutza. 96p. 1983. pap. 3.95 (ISBN 0-8170-0986-8). Judson.

Prayer Times for Primary Grades. Marilyn Brokamp. 1987. pap. 4.95 (ISBN 0-317-57175-3). St Anthony Mess Pr.

Prayer to Fish. James Iody. 15p. 1983. pap. 2.00 (ISBN 0-941720-11-X). Slough Pr TX.

Prayer Transparencies. Stuart Kelman. 32p. (Orig.). 1982. 29.95x (ISBN 0-686-81835-0). Arbit.

Prayer Works! Robert Collier. 4.95 (ISBN 0-912576-01-4). R Collier.

Prayerable a Day. Irene B. Harrell. (Orig.). 1988. pap. 7.00 (ISBN 0-915541-15-7). Star Bks Inc.

Prayerbook. Tr. by Laurence Mancuso from Slavic & Gr. (New Skete). (Illus.). 720p. 1976. 35.00x (ISBN 0-9607924-3-0). Monks of New Skete.

Prayerbook for Catholics. Robert J. Fox. 112p. (Orig.). 1982. 6.95 (ISBN 0-931888-08-5); pap. 3.95. Christendom Coll Pr.

Prayerbook (for Hospitals) Alphonse Coan. 48p. 1950. pap. 0.30 (ISBN 0-8199-0503-8). Franciscan Herald.

Prayerbook Hebrew Teacher's Guide. Joseph Anderson. Ed. by Ethelyn Simon & Victoria Kelman. (Orig.). 1985. pap. text ed. 4.95 (ISBN 0-939144-10-7). EKS Pub Co.

Prayerbook Hebrew the Easy Way. 2nd ed. Joseph Anderson et al. Ed. by Ethelyn Simon. 1985. pap. text ed. 14.95 (ISBN 0-939144-12-3). EKS Pub Co.

Prayerbook of Favorite Litanies: 116 Favorite Catholic Litanies & Responsory Prayers. Compiled by Albert Hebert. LC 84-51818. 192p. 1985. pap. 8.50 (ISBN 0-89555-252-3). Tan Bks Pubs.

Prayerbook Reform in Europe: The Liturgy of European Liberal & Reform Judaism. Jakob J. Petuchowski. LC 68-8262. (Illus.). 1969. 13.50 (ISBN 0-8074-0091-2, 387580, Pub. by World Union). UAHC.

Prayerbook: Service of the Heart. (Home Study Program Ser.: No. 302). 6.00 (ISBN 0-686-96123-4). United Syn Bk.

Prayerful Heart. Charles L. Allen & Helen S. Rice. 160p. (Orig.). 1981. pap. 5.95 (ISBN 0-8007-5073-X, Power Bks). Revell.

Prayerful Pauses with Jesus & Mary. Bill Peffley. LC 85-50690. (Illus.). 96p. (Orig.). 1985. pap. 5.95 (ISBN 0-89622-251-9). Twenty-Third.

Prayerfully. Helen S. Rice. 32p. 1971. 6.95 (ISBN 0-8007-0475-4). Revell.

Prayerfully Sinning. Bryan A. Floyd. LC 83-63239. 92p. 1984. text ed. 16.95 (ISBN 0-932966-49-7). Permanent Pr.

Prayerfully Sinning. Bryan A. Floyd. LC 83-63239. 92p. 1985. pap. 8.95 (ISBN 0-932966-48-9). Permanent Pr.

Prayerpath. Jack Hayford. 80p. (Orig.). 1987. mass 2.95, (ISBN 0-8423-4964-2). Tyndale.

Prayers. Theodore P. Ferris. 1981. 6.95 (ISBN 0-8164-0483-6, HarpR). Har-Row.

Prayers. Michel Quoist. LC 63-17141. 179p. 1985. pap. 6.95 (ISBN 0-934134-46-4). Sheed & Ward MO.

Prayers Alleged to Be Jewish: An Examination of the Constitutiones Apostolorum. David A. Fiensy. (Brown Judaic Studies). 1985. 29.95 (ISBN 0-89130-795-8, 14-00-65); pap. 21.95 (ISBN 0-89130-796-6). Scholars Pr GA.

Prayers & Blessings for Daily Life in Christ. Michael Scanlan & John Bertolucci. 48p. (Orig.). 1983. pap. 2.00 (ISBN 0-940535-00-9, UP100). Franciscan U Pr.

Prayers & Devotions from Pope John Paul II. Ed. by Peter C. Van Lierde. 472p. 1984. 10.95 (ISBN 0-89526-601-6). Regnery Gateway.

Prayers & Graces. Alice J. Davidson. (Alice in Bibleland Ser.). 32p. (ps-3). 1986. 4.95 (ISBN 0-8378-5078-9). Gibson.

Prayers & Inspiration for Senior Children of God. Anne Kunath & Lillian Riegert. 1979. pap. 1.75. DeVorss.

Prayers & Meditation for Healing. 2nd ed. Charles Toye. 96p. 1988. pap. 6.95 (ISBN 0-9619732-0-X). Send Your Spirit Pub.

Prayers & Meditations. rev. ed. Tr. by Aurobindo from Fr. 380p. (Orig.). 1979. pap. 16.00 (ISBN 0-89744-998-3, Sri Aurobindo Ashram Trust India); text ed. 21.00 (ISBN 0-89744-219-9). Auromere.

Prayers & Meditations. Baha'u'llah. Tr. by Shoghi Effendi. LC 53-10767. 1938. 14.95 (ISBN 0-87743-024-1, 103-010). Baha'i.

Prayers & Meditations. Baha'u'llah. Tr. by Shoghi Effendi. 1978. 21.95 (ISBN 0-900125-39-X). Baha'i.

Prayers & Meditations. Bahaullah. Tr. by Shoghi Effendi. 1987. pocket-size 6.50 (ISBN 0-87743-209-0). Baha'i.

Prayers & Meditations: An Anthology of the Spiritual Writings of Karl Rahner. Karl Rahner. Ed. by John Griffiths. 128p. 1980. pap. 4.95 (ISBN 0-8245-0053-9). Crossroad NY.

Prayers & Meditations: Imre Lev. Hester Rothschild. 544p. Date not set. 5.00 (ISBN 0-88482-120-X). Hebrew Pub.

Prayers & Meditations of St. Anselm. Tr. by Benedicta Ward. (Classics Ser.). 1979. pap. 5.95 (ISBN 0-14-044278-2). Penguin.

Prayers & Others Pieces of Thomas Becon, Chaplain to Archbishop Cranmer. Thomas Becon. Repr. of 1844 ed. 55.00 (ISBN 0-384-03730-5). Johnson Repr.

Prayers & Praises. Nathaniel Micklem. 1982. pap. 3.95x (ISBN 0-7152-0541-2). Outlook.

Prayers & Promises for Every Day from the Living Bible. Corrie Ten Boom. 272p. 1985. pap. 9.95 (ISBN 0-8027-2505-8). Walker & Co.

Prayers & Promises for Every Day: With Corrie Ten Boom. Corrie Ten Boom. Ed. by Luci Shaw. LC 77-92352. (Day Star Devotional). 144p. 1977. pap. 3.50 (ISBN 0-87788-689-X). Shaw Pubs.

Prayers & Reading for Worship. Ed. by Judy Judd. 1987. pap. 12.50 (ISBN 0-8309-0478-6). Herald Hse.

Prayers & Recommended Practices. 2nd ed. Jerome F. Coniker. LC 78-66374. (Living Meditation & Prayerbook Ser.). (Illus.). 91p. pap. text ed. 3.00 (ISBN 0-932406-01-7). AFC.

Prayers at Meals. Michael Kwatera & Dietrich Reinhart. 48p. 1983. pap. 0.50 (ISBN 0-8146-1318-7). Liturgical Pr.

Prayers at Midnight. Charles Angoff. 1971. 2.00 (ISBN 0-87141-036-2). Manyland.

Prayers at Midpoint: Conversations with God for Those in Life's Second Half. William A. Miller. LC 83-72110. 96p. 1984. pap. 6.50 (ISBN 0-8066-2054-4, 10-5081). Augsburg.

Prayers Before & after Communion. Paschal Botz et al. 24p. 1981. pap. 0.50 (ISBN 0-8146-1213-X). Liturgical Pr.

Prayers for a Lifetime. Karl Rahner. 256p. 1986. pap. 9.95 (ISBN 0-317-42453-X). Crossroad NY.

Prayers for a Small Child. LC 83-16050. (Knee-High Bks.). (Illus.). 24p. (ps-1). 1984. 4.95 (ISBN 0-394-86281-3, BYR). Random.

Prayers for All Occasions. Andrew W. Blackwood. (Pocket Pulpit Library). pap. 3.95 (ISBN 0-8010-0923-5). Baker Bk.

Prayers for All Occasions. Ed. by Francis Evans. 160p. (Orig.). 1988. pap. 3.75 (ISBN 0-89942-917-3, 917/09). Catholic Bk Pub.

Prayers for All Occasions. Stuart R. Oglesby. 180p. 1983. pap. 5.95 (ISBN 0-8042-2485-4, John Knox). Westminster John Knox.

Prayers for All Occasions. 1951. 1.00 (ISBN 0-88028-006-9). Forward Movement.

Prayers, for All People, for All Occasions. Leander M. Zimmerman. pap. 20.00 (2027877). Bks Demand UMI.

Prayers for All Reasons. Roy D. Fauth. 1980. 3.50 (ISBN 0-89536-448-4, 1642). CSS of Ohio.

Prayers for Boys. Herman C. Alleman. LC 81-142145. (gr. 4-9). pap. 4.95 (ISBN 0-8407-5241-5). Nelson.

Prayers for Boys. Ruth Odor. (gr. 3-6). 1985. pap. 0.69 pocket size (ISBN 0-87239-825-0, 2815). Standard Pub.

Prayers for Boys & Prayers for Girls. Herman Alleman & Elizabeth R. Scovil. (gr. 5-7). 3.95x. Nelson.

Prayers for Children. 32p. (gr. k-5). 1981. pap. 3.95 (ISBN 0-8249-8023-9). Ideals.

Prayers for Contemporary Worship. Church of Scotland - Committee on Public Worship & Aids to Devotion. 1977. pap. 4.95x (ISBN 0-7152-0351-7). Outlook.

Prayers: For Daily & Occasional Use. Victor Hoagland. pap. 1.45 (ISBN 0-8091-5158-8). Paulist Pr.

Prayers for Dark People. W. E. B. Du Bois. Ed. by Herbert Aptheker. LC 80-12234. 88p. 1980. pap. 6.95 (ISBN 0-87023-303-3). U of Mass Pr.

Prayers for Every Need. William H. Kadel. pap. 5.95 (ISBN 0-8042-2496-X, John Knox). Westminster John Knox.

Prayers for Every Occasion. Ed. by Frank Colquhoun. Orig. Title: Parish Prayers. 445p. 1974. Repr. of 1967 ed. kivar 14.95 (ISBN 0-8192-1280-6). Morehouse.

Prayers for Everyone. (Illus.). 16p. (gr. k-3). 1982. pap. 0.99 (ISBN 0-86683-653-5, AY8232, HarpR). Har-Row.

Prayers for Girls. Herman C. Alleman. (gr. 4-8). 4.95 (ISBN 0-8407-5242-3). Nelson.

Prayers for Girls. Ruth Odor. (gr. 3-6). 1985. pap. 0.69 pocket size (ISBN 0-87239-826-9, 2816). Standard Pub.

Prayers for God's People. Thomas B. Roberts. Ed. by Michael L. Sherer. (Orig.). 1988. pap. 5.95 (ISBN 1-55673-025-X, 8810). CSS of Ohio.

Prayers for Healing. William H. Hull. 122p. (Orig.). 1987. pap. text ed. 6.95 (ISBN 0-939330-02-4). W H Hull.

Prayers for Holy Communion. Holy Transfiguration Monastery Staff. 120p. (Orig.). 1986. pap. 3.00x (ISBN 0-913026-60-3, Holy Transfiguration). St Nectarios.

Prayers for Home & School. (Illus.). 16p. 1982. pap. 0.99 (ISBN 0-86683-652-7, AY8231, HarpR). Har-Row.

Prayers for Impossible Days. Paul Geres. Tr. by Ingalill H. Hjelm from Fr. LC 75-36442. 64p. 1976. pap. 3.95 (ISBN 0-8006-1214-0, 1-1214). Fortress.

Prayers for Inner Strength. Ed. by John Beilenson. (Illus.). 64p. 1986. 5.95 (ISBN 0-88088-468-1, 884681). Peter Pauper.

Prayers for Inner Strength: In Times of Bereavement: A Book-Greeting Card. Ed. by John Beilenson. 1986. 2.50 (ISBN 0-88088-882-2, 888822). Peter Pauper.

Pre-Columbian Architecture, Art, & Artifacts Slide Catalog. H. L. Murvin. 99p. 1983. pap. 3.95 (ISBN 0-9608498-2-3). H L Murvin.

Pre-Columbian Architecture of Mesoamerica. rev. ed. Doris Heyden & Paul Gendrop. LC 87-43257. (History of World Architecture Ser.). (Illus.). 224p. 1988. pap. 25.00 (ISBN 0-8478-0917-X). Rizzoli Intl.

Pre-Columbian Art. Dumbarton Oaks Collection Staff. Ed. by Elizabeth P. Benson. LC 76-8176. 1976. 25.00 (ISBN 0-226-68981-6, Chicago Visual Lib); 1 colorfiche incl. U of Chicago Pr.

Pre-Columbian Art. Jose A. Franch. (Illus.). 618p. 1983. 125.00 (ISBN 0-8109-0645-7). Abrams.

Pre-Columbian Art. Lee A. Parsons. LC 80-7593. (Icon Editions). (Illus.). 336p. 1980. 40.00i (ISBN 0-06-437000-3, HarpT). Har-Row.

Pre-Columbian Art from the Land Collection. Alana Cordy-Collins & H. B. Nicholson. Ed. by L. K. Land. (Illus.). 272p. (Orig.). 1979. pap. 25.00 (ISBN 0-940228-03-3). Calif Acad Sci.

Pre-Columbian Art from the Land Collection. H. B. Nicholson & Alana Cordy-Collins. Ed. by L. K. Land. LC 78-78330. (Illus.). 280p. (Orig.). 1981. pap. 24.95 (ISBN 0-295-95809-X, Pub. by Calif Acad Sci). U of Wash Pr.

Pre-Columbian Art History. rev. ed. Alana Cordy-Collins. (Illus.). 400p. 1982. pap. text ed. 16.95 (ISBN 0-917962-71-0). T H Peek.

Pre-Columbian Art of Mexico & Central America. George A. Kubler. 1988. 22.95 (ISBN 0-89467-039-5). Yale Art Gallery.

Pre-Columbian Collections in European Museums. Ed. by Anne-Marie Hocquednghem et al. 1987. text ed. 55.00 (ISBN 963-05-4730-9, Pub. by Akademiai Kiado Hungary). Humanities.

Pre-Columbian Designs from Panama: 591 Illustrations of Cocle Pottery. Samuel K. Lothrop. LC 75-17177. (Pictorial Archive Ser.). (Illus.). 112p. (Orig.). 1976. pap. 6.50 (ISBN 0-486-23232-8). Dover.

Pre-Columbian Designs from Panama: 591 Illustrations of Cocle Pottery. Samuel K. Lothrop. 14.00 (ISBN 0-8446-5508-2). Peter Smith.

Pre-Columbian Literatures of Mexico. Miguel Leon-Portilla. Tr. by Grace Lobanov. LC 85-40941. (Civilization of the American Indian Ser.: Vol. 92). (Illus.). 256p. (Orig.). 1986. pap. 7.95 (ISBN 0-8061-1974-8). U of Okla Pr.

Pre-Columbian Man Finds Central America. Doris Stone. LC 72-801668. (Peabody Museum Press Ser.). (Illus.). 1976. 25.00x (ISBN 0-87365-803-5); pap. 15.00x (ISBN 0-87365-776-4). Peabody Harvard.

Pre-Columbian Man in Costa Rica. Doris Stone. LC 77-86538. (Peabody Museum Press Ser.). (Illus.). 1977. pap. 15.00x (ISBN 0-87365-792-6). Peabody Harvard.

Pre-Columbian Metallurgy of South-America, Proceedings: A Conference at Dumbarton Oaks, October 18 & 19, 1975. Ed. by Elizabeth P. Benson. LC 79-49261. (Illus.). 107p. 1979. 20.00x (ISBN 0-88402-094-0). Dumbarton Oaks.

Pre-Columbian Plant Migration from Lowland South America to Mesoamerica. Ed. by Doris Stone. (Peabody Museum Papers: Vol. 76). (Illus.). 220p. (Orig.). 1984. pap. text ed. 30.00x (ISBN 0-87365-202-9). Harvard U Pr.

Pre-Columbian Shell Engravings from the Craig Mound at Spiro, Oklahoma, 6 vols. Philip Phillips & James A. Brown. LC 74-77557. (Illus.). 1983. lib. bdg. 360.00x ltd. ed. (ISBN 0-87365-777-2). Peabody Harvard.

Pre-Columbian Shell Engravings from the Craig Mound at Spiro, Oklahoma, Pt. 1. Philip Phillips & James A. Brown. LC 78-56050. (Illus.). 1978. pap. 35.00x (ISBN 0-87365-795-0). Peabody Harvard.

Pre-Columbian Shell Engravings from the Craig Mound at Spiro, Oklahoma, Pt. 2. Philip Phillips & James A. Brown. LC 78-56050. (Illus.). 600p. 1983. pap. 35.00x (ISBN 0-87365-802-7). Peabody Harvard.

Pre-Conceptions: What You Can Do Before Pregnancy to Help You Have a Healthy Baby. Norra Tannenhaus. 224p. (Orig.). 1988. pap. 7.95 (ISBN 0-8092-4679-1). Contemp Bks.

Pre-Confederation Premiers: Ontario Government Leaders 1841 to 1867. Ed. by J. M. Careless. (Ontario Historical Studies). 368p. 1985. 15.95 (ISBN 0-8020-6590-2). U of Toronto Pr.

Pre-Confederation Premiers: Ontario Government Leaders, 1841-1867. Ed. by James M. Careless. LC 80-501684. (Ontario Historical Studies Ser.). pap. 89.50 (2056119). Bks Demand UMI.

Pre-Conquest Boroughs of England. C. A. Raleigh-Radford. (Mortimer Wheeler Archaeological Lectures). 1978. pap. 5.50 (ISBN 0-85672-173-5, Pub. by British Acad). Longwood Pub Group.

Pre-Conquest Church in England. 2nd ed. Margaret Deanesly. (Ecclesiastical History of England Ser.). 376p. 1963. text ed. 30.00x (ISBN 0-06-491638-3). B&N Imports.

Pre-Conquest English Prayer-Book: BL MSS Cotton Galba A.xiv & Nero A.ii. Bernard J. Muir. (Publications of the Henry Bradshaw Society Ser. CIII (103)). 1987. 45.00 (ISBN 0-9501009-5-1, Pub. by Boydell & Brewer). Longwood Pub Group.

Pre-Contract Practice for Architects & Quantity Surveyors. 7th ed. The AQUA Group Staff. (Illus.). 110p. 1986. pap. text ed. 19.95x (ISBN 0-00-383254-6, Pub. by Collins England). Sheridan.

Pre-Dressing Skills. Marsha L. Dunn. (Skill Starters for Motor Development Ser.). 100p. 1983. pap. text ed. 14.95 (ISBN 0-88450-868-4, 4689-B). Communication Skill.

Pre-Earthly Deeds of Christ. Rudolf Steiner. 16p. 1976. pap. 2.95 (ISBN 0-919924-01-8, Pub. by Steiner Book Centre Canada). Anthroposophic.

Pre-Eclampsia: The Hypertensive Disease of Pregnancy. Ian MacGillivray. (Illus.). 400p. 1983. write for info. (ISBN 0-7216-1195-8). Saunders.

Pre-Eighteen Hundred Architectural Monographs in the Collection of the Thomas Fisher Rare Book Library, University of Toronto. John Rossini. (Architecture Ser.: A 1968). 9p. 1988. 3.00 (ISBN 1-55590-618-4). Vance Biblios.

Pre-Election Polling: Sources of Accuracy & Error. Irving Crespi. 208p. Date not set. 17.50. Russell Sage.

Pre-Emergency Planning. William F. Jenaway. (Illus.). 164p. 1986. pap. text ed. 21.87 (ISBN 0-9615990-2-2). Intl Soc Fire Serv.

Pre-Employment Counselor. Jack Rudman. (Career Examination Ser.: C-1396). (Cloth bdg. avail. on request). pap. 14.00 (ISBN 0-8373-1396-1). Natl Learning.

Pre-Established Harmony vs. Constant Conjunction: A Reconsideration of the Distinction Between Rationalism & Empiricism. Hide Ishiguro. (Dawes Hicks Lectures on Philosophy). 1977. pap. 5.50 (ISBN 0-85672-159-X, Pub. by British Acad). Longwood Pub Group.

Pre-Eternal Rest. Frank E. Stranges. 12p. 1985. pap. text ed. 2.00 (ISBN 0-933470-07-X). Intl Evang.

Pre Exilic Prophecy. Richard J. Sklba. (Message Biblical Spirituality Ser.: Vol. 3). 1988. 12.95 (ISBN 0-89453-553-6); pap. 8.95 (ISBN 0-89453-569-2). M Glazier.

Pre-Faces & Other Writings. Jerome Rothenberg. LC 80-24031. 224p. 1981. 14.95 (ISBN 0-8112-0785-4); pap. 6.95 (ISBN 0-8112-0786-2, NDP511). New Directions.

Pre-Fascist Italy: The Rise & Fall of the Parliamentary Regime. Margot Hentze. LC 70-120628. 1970. Repr. of 1939 ed. lib. bdg. 26.00x (ISBN 0-374-93809-1, Octagon). Hippocrene Bks.

Pre-Flight Planning. Ron Fowler. (Illus.). 320p. 1983. 17.95 (ISBN 0-02-540300-1). Macmillan.

Pre-GED Program in Language Skills. Ed. by Cambridge Staff & Dennis Mendyk. (Pre-GED Ser.). 224p. 1983. pap. text ed. 4.95 (ISBN 0-8428-9318-0); student wkbk. 3.25 (ISBN 0-8428-9323-7). Cambridge Bk.

Pre-GED Program in Math Skills: 1984 Edition. Ed. by Cambridge Staff. (Pre-GED Ser.). 288p. 1984. pap. text ed. 4.95 (ISBN 0-8428-9325-3); student wkbk. 3.25 (ISBN 0-8428-9322-9). Cambridge Bk.

Pre-GED Program in Reading Skills. Ed. by Cambridge Staff & Dennis Mendyk. (Pre-GED Ser.). 224p. 1983. pap. text ed. 4.95 (ISBN 0-8428-9320-2); wkbk. 3.25 (ISBN 0-8428-9324-5). Cambridge Bk.

Pre-Hispanic Mexican Stamp Designs. Frederick V. Field. (Illus.). 12.00 (ISBN 0-8446-5031-5). Peter Smith.

Pre-Hispanic Occupance in the Valley of Sonora, Mexico: Archaeological Confirmations of Early Spanish Reports. William E. Doolittle. LC 87-30040. (Anthropological Papers: No. 48). 88p. 1988. pap. 24.95x (ISBN 0-8165-1010-5). U of Ariz Pr.

Pre-Historic Archaelogy of Madhya Pradesh. Pandeez. 1987. 62.50 (ISBN 81-85067-04-X, Pub. by Sundeep). South Asia Bks.

Pre-Historic Art in India. H. D. Sankalia. LC 78-54435. (Centers of Civilization Ser.). (Illus.). 121p. 1978. 24.75 (ISBN 0-89089-091-9). Carolina Acad Pr.

Pre-Historic Nations. John D. Baldwin. (Works of John D. Baldwin). vii, 411p. Repr. of 1872 ed. lib. bdg. 59.00 (ISBN 0-932051-07-3, Pub. by Am Repr Serv). Am Biog Serv.

Pre-Historic Times. facsimile ed. John Lubbock. LC 74-169771. (Select Bibliographies Reprint Ser). Repr. of 1890 ed. 38.50 (ISBN 0-8369-5991-4). Ayer Co Pubs.

Pre-Historic Times. Louis R. Nougier. LC 80-54635. (Silver Burdett Picture Histories Ser.). (Illus.). 64p. (gr. 5 up). PLB 14.96 (ISBN 0-382-06522-0); pap. 8.95 (ISBN 0-382-06924-2). Silver.

Pre-History of Germanic Europe. Herbert Schutz. LC 83-40000. (Illus.). 400p. 1983. 57.00x (ISBN 0-300-02863-6). Yale U Pr.

Pre-History of the Armenian People. LC 83-15429. 1985. 50.00x (ISBN 0-88206-039-2). Caravan Bks.

Pre-History of the Burnt Bluff Area. Ed. by James E. Fitting. (Anthropological Papers: No. 34). 1968. pap. 3.00x (ISBN 0-932206-32-8). U Mich Mus Anthro.

Pre-Hospital Emergency Care. S. Mather & David Edbrooke. 320p. 1986. pap. 16.00 (ISBN 0-7236-0701-X). PSG Pub Co.

Pre-Hospital Emergency Care by Ambulance Services. Dorothy J. Douglas & Julian A. Roth. 300p. 1988. text ed. 39.50x (ISBN 0-8290-2391-7). Irvington.

Pre-Hospital Trauma Life Support. National Association of EMT's Pre-Hospital Life Support Committee et al. Ed. by Alexander M. Butman et al. 220p. 1986. pap. text ed. 18.50 (ISBN 0-940432-06-4). Educ Direction.

Pre-Imperial Coinage of Roman Antioch. Edward F. Newell. 45p. 1980. pap. 5.00 (ISBN 0-916710-66-1). Obol Intl.

Pre-Industrial Economic Growth: Social Organization & Technological Progress. Gunnar Persson. 208p. Date not set. text ed. 45.00 (ISBN 0-631-14963-5). Basil Blackwell.

Pre-Industrial Population Changes. Ed. by Tommy Bengtsson et al. 420p. 1984. text ed. 62.50x (ISBN 91-22-00741-5, Pub. by Almqvist & Wiksell). Coronet Bks.

Pre-Inferno Period. August Strindberg. Tr. by Evert Sprinchorn from Swedish. LC 85-8742. (Selected Plays Ser.: Vol. 1). (Orig.). 1986. pap. 10.95 (ISBN 0-8166-1338-9). U of Minn Pr.

Pre-Inferno Plays: The Father, Lady Julie, Creditors, the Stronger, the Bond. August Strindberg. Tr. & intros by Walter Johnson. 1976. pap. 6.95 (ISBN 0-393-00834-7, Norton Lib). Norton.

Pre-Inferno Plays: The Father, Lady Julie, Creditors, The Stronger, The Bond. August Strindberg. Tr. by Walter Johnson from Swedish. LC 79-117735. (Illus.). 255p. 1971. 20.00x (ISBN 0-295-95084-6). U of Wash Pr.

Pre-Invasion Bombing Strategy: General Eisenhower's Decision of March 25, 1944. W. W. Rostow. (Ideas & Action Ser.: No. 1). 180p. 1981. text ed. 18.95x (ISBN 0-292-76470-7); pap. 8.95 (ISBN 0-292-76471-5). U of Tex Pr.

Pre-Kushana Art of Mathura. Vasudeva Agrawala. 1986. 11.00x (ISBN 0-8364-1534-5, Pub. by Prithiva Prakashan). South Asia Bks.

Pre-Law Equivalency Examination (PL) Jack Rudman. (Admission Test Ser.: ATS-40). (Cloth bdg. avail. on request). pap. 13.95 (ISBN 0-8373-5040-9). Natl Learning.

Pre-Llano Cultures of the Americas: Paradoxes & Possibilities. Robert L. Humphrey & Dennis Stanford. (Anthropological Society of Washington Ser.). (Illus.). 150p. 1984. pap. 9.95x (ISBN 0-87474-523-3, HUPLP). Smithsonian.

Pre-Malthusian Doctrines of Population. Charles E. Stangeland. LC 5-7910. (Columbia University. Studies in the Social Sciences: No. 56). Repr. of 1904 ed. 10.00 (ISBN 0-404-51056-6). AMS Pr.

Pre-Malthusian Doctrines of Population. Charles E. Stangeland. LC 66-21372. 1966. Repr. of 1904 ed. 39.50x (ISBN 0-678-00159-6). Kelley.

Pre-Marital Assessment Skills Training Program Leader Guide. Kenneth Metz & John Trokan. 144p. 1986. pap. 9.95 (ISBN 0-8091-2809-8). Paulist Pr.

Pre-Marital Assessment Skills Training Program: Team Couple Workbook. Kenneth Metz & John Trokan. 96p. 1986. pap. 9.95 (ISBN 0-8091-2810-1). Paulist Pr.

Pre-Med Handbook. Howard Levitin. 336p. (Orig.). 1986. pap. 12.95 (ISBN 0-446-38291-4). Warner Bks.

Pre-Menstrual Syndrome: Proceedings of a Round-Table Discussion, September 1986, No. 119. Ed. by H. W. Fisher. 1988. pap. 8.00 (ISBN 0-905958-51-9, Pub. by Royal Society of Medicine Services Ltd). Longwood Pub Group.

Pre-Modern Art of Vienna, 1848-1898. Ed. by Leon Botstein & Linda Weintraub. LC 87-27929. (Illus.). 160p. 1987. 39.95x (ISBN 0-8143-1959-9). Wayne St U Pr.

Pre-Nursing Reviews in Arithmetic. 2nd ed. Mary E. Stehman. 33p. 1961. pap. 3.95 (ISBN 0-8036-8140-2). Davis Co.

Pre Pack Care & Feeding of Southern Men. Claudia Greco. (Illus.). 144p. 1987. 69.50 (ISBN 0-912697-75-X). Algonquin Bks.

Pre-Paid Long-Term Care Health Plans: A Policy Option for California's Medi-Cal Program. Charlene Harrington et al. 94p. 1983. pap. 5.50 (ISBN 0-317-00868-4). UCB IGS.

Pre-Pleiade Poetry. Ed. by Jerry C. Nash. LC 84-81851. (French Forum Monographs: No. 57). 148p. (Orig.). 1985. pap. 12.95x (ISBN 0-917058-57-7). French Forum.

Pre-Pregnancy Planner. Josleen Wilson. LC 85-30737. (Illus.). 288p. 1986. pap. 9.95 (ISBN 0-385-23174-1). Doubleday.

Pre-Professional Skills Test (PPST) (Admission Test Ser.: ATS-95). Date not set. pap. 13.95 (ISBN 0-8373-5095-6). Natl Learning.

Pre-Prosthetic Surgery: A Self-Instructional Guide, Bk. 7. 3rd, rev. ed. James R. Hooley & Robert J. Whitacre. (Illus.). 58p. 1983. pap. 5.95x (ISBN 0-89939-071-4). Stoma Pr.

Pre-Raphaelite, & Other Poets. facs. ed. Lafcadio Hearn. Ed. by J. Erskine. LC 68-22096. (Essay Index Reprint Ser). 1922. 20.00 (ISBN 0-8369-0526-1). Ayer Co Pubs.

Pre-Raphaelite Camera: Images of Victorian Photography. Michael Bartram. LC 85-40023. 1985. 34.00 (ISBN 0-8212-1595-7, 717592). NYGS.

Pre-Raphaelite Drawings of Edward Burne-Jones. Edward Burne-Jones. (Dover Art Library). (Illus.). 48p. (Orig.). 1981. pap. 3.50 (ISBN 0-486-24113-0). Dover.

Pre-Raphaelite Dream. William Gaunt. 1943. Repr. 39.00 (ISBN 0-8274-3197-X). R West.

Pre-Raphaelite Friendship: The Correspondence of William Holman Hunt & John Lucas Tupper. Ed. by James H. Coombs et al. LC 86-1486. (Nineteenth-Century Studies). 358p. 1986. 39.95 (ISBN 0-8357-1745-3). UMI Res Pr.

Pre-Raphaelite Imagination, 1848-1900. John D. Hunt. LC 69-13334. (Landmark Ed.). (Illus.). xvi, 262p. 1969. 22.50x (ISBN 0-8032-0083-8). U of Nebr Pr.

Pre-Raphaelite Influence on Victorian Jewellery Design. Charlotte Gere & Geoffrey Munn. (Illus.). 200p. 1988. cancelled. Antique Collect.

Pre-Raphaelite Paintings: From the Manchester City Art Gallery. Julian Treuherz. (Illus.). 152p. 1980. pap. 25.00x (ISBN 0-85331-432-2, Pub. by Lund Humphries Pubs England). Humanities.

Pre-Raphaelite Papers. Ed. by Leslie Parris. (Illus.). 272p. 1985. pap. 12.95 (ISBN 0-946590-02-8). Salem Hse Pubs.

Pre-Raphaelite Photography. Ed. by Graham Ovenden. (Illus.). 84p. 1984. pap. 14.95 (ISBN 0-312-63736-5). St Martin.

Pre-Raphaelite Poets. Intro. by Harold Bloom. (Modern Critical Views Ser.). 1986. 29.50 (ISBN 0-87754-667-3). Chelsea Hse.

Pre-Raphaelite Poets. Lionel Stevenson. 336p. 1974. pap. 3.95x (ISBN 0-393-00720-0, Norton Lib). Norton.

Pre-Raphaelite Sisterhood. Jan Marsh. (Illus.). 416p. 1985. 21.95 (ISBN 0-312-63738-1). St Martin.

Pre-Raphaelite Twilight: The Story of Charles Augustus Howell. Helen R. Angeli. LC 72-158494. (Illus.). 1971. Repr. of 1954 ed. 25.00 (ISBN 0-403-01312-7). Scholarly.

Pre-Raphaelite Twilight: The Story of Charles Augustus Howell. Helen R. Angeli. 1988. Repr. of 1954 ed. lib. bdg. 49.00x. Am Biog Serv.

Pre-Raphaelite Women: Images of Femininity. Jan Marsh. (Illus.). 160p. 1988. 30.00 (ISBN 0-517-56799-7, Harmony). Crown.

Pre-Raphaelite Writing. Ed. by Derek Stanford. (Illus.). 246p. 1984. pap. 5.95x (ISBN 0-460-11033-0, DEL-05073, Pub. by Evman England). Biblio Dist.

Pre-Raphaelites. Timothy Hilton. (World of Art Ser.). (Illus.). 216p. 1985. pap. 11.95 (ISBN 0-500-20102-1). Thames Hudson.

Pre-Raphaelites. Andrew Rose. (Phaidon Color Library). (Illus.). 84p. 1983. pap. 17.95 (ISBN 0-7148-2166-7). Salem Hse Pubs.

Pre-Raphaelites: An Anthololgy. Ed. by Jerome Buckley. 503p. 1986. pap. 10.95 (ISBN 0-89733-237-7). Academy Chi Pubs.

Pre-Raphaelites & Oxford. J. E. Alden. LC 74-1477. 1948. lib. bdg. 10.00. Folcroft.

Pre-Raphaelites & Their Circle. 2nd, rev. ed. Cecil Y. Lang. LC 75-12233. xxix, 592p. 1975. pap. 15.00x (ISBN 0-226-46866-6, P651, Phoen). U of Chicago Pr.

Pre-Raphaelites in Literature & Art. facs. ed. Ed. by D. S. Welland. LC 72-76949. (Granger Index Reprint Ser). 1953. 15.00 (ISBN 0-8369-6046-7). Ayer Co Pubs.

Pre-Raphaelites in Love. Gay Daly. 1989. 24.95 (ISBN 0-89919-450-8). Ticknor & Fields.

Pre-Raphaelitism: A Collection of Critical Essays. Intro. by James Sambrook. LC 73-89790. 1976. pap. 4.95x (ISBN 0-226-73453-6, PLC12, Phoen); pap. text ed. 17.50X (ISBN 0-226-73452-8). U of Chicago Pr.

Pre-Raphaelitism & the Pre-Raphaelite Brotherhood, 2 Vols. William H. Hunt. LC 5-40801. Repr. of 1906 ed. 62.50 (ISBN 0-404-03437-3). AMS Pr.

Pre-Reform Coinage of Diocletian. Percy H. Webb. (Illus.). 1977. 3.50 (ISBN 0-915018-29-2). Attic Bks.

Pre-Reformation England. H. Maymard Smith. 1979. Repr. of 1938 ed. lib. bdg. 50.00 (ISBN 0-8495-4934-5). Arden Lib.

Pre-Reformation English Spirituality. Ed. by James Walsh. LC 65-12885. 1966. 25.00 (ISBN 0-8232-0655-6). Fordham.

Pre-Reformation Scholars in Scotland in the 16th Century: With a Bibliography & a List of Graduates from 1500 to 1560. William Forbes-Leith. LC 76-150158. 1975. Repr. of 1915 ed. 14.50 (ISBN 0-8337-1173-3). B Franklin.

Pre-Republican Rome: An Analysis of the Cultural & Chronological Relations, 1000-500 B.C. Jorgen C. Meyer. (Analecta Romana Ser.: Suppl XI). 210p. (Orig.). 1983. pap. 23.00x (ISBN 87-7492-434-6, Pub. by Odense Universitets Forlag (Odense Denmark)). Coronet Bks.

Pre-Requisites for the Study of Jacob Boehme. C. J. Barker. 1987. pap. 4.95 (ISBN 1-55818-104-0). Sure Fire.

Pre-Restoration Stage Studies. William J. Lawrence. LC 67-23857. 1967. Repr. of 1927 ed. 27.50 (ISBN 0-405-08738-1, Pub. by Blom). Ayer Co Pubs.

Pre-Retirement Planner. Hunnisett. LC 79-90485. 1979. 39.95 (ISBN 0-534-97991-2, Lifetime Learn). Van Nos Reinhold.

Pre-Revolutionary Caracas: Politics, Economy & Society 1777-1811. P. Michael McKinley. (Cambridge Latin American Studies: No. 56). (Illus.). 232p. 1986. 42.50 (ISBN 0-521-30450-4). Cambridge U Pr.

Preaching the Great Themes of the Bible. Chevis F. Horne. (Orig.). 1986. pap. 7.95 (ISBN 0-8054-2262-5). Broadman.

Preaching the Lectionary: The Word of God for the Church Today. rev. ed. Reginald H. Fuller. 672p. 1984. pap. 16.95 (ISBN 0-8146-1351-9). Liturgical Pr.

Preaching the New Common Lectionary. Fred B. Craddock et al. 176p. (Orig.). 1984. pap. 8.50 (ISBN 0-687-33845-X). Abingdon.

Preaching the New Common Lectionary: Year B: Lent, Holy Week, Easter, 2 vols. Fred B. Craddock et al. 256p. (Orig.). 1984. Vol. 2, 256 pgs. pap. 9.95 (ISBN 0-687-33846-8); Vol. 3, 304 pgs. pap. 11.95 (ISBN 0-687-33847-6). Abingdon.

Preaching the New Common Lectionary: Year C-Advent, Christmas, Epiphany. Fred B. Craddock et al. 176p. (Orig.). 1985. pap. 9.50 (ISBN 0-687-33848-4). Abingdon.

Preaching the New Common Lectionary: Year C, Lent, Holy Week, Easter. Ed. by Fred B. Craddock et al. 240p. (Orig.). 1986. pap. 9.95 (ISBN 0-687-33849-2). Abingdon.

Preaching the New Testament. Archibald M. Hunter. LC 81-19482. pap. 39.00 (ISBN 0-317-30145-4, 2025328). Bks Demand UMI.

Preaching the Parables: Series B. John Brokhoff. (Orig.). 1987. pap. 7.25 (ISBN 0-89536-880-3, 7866). CSS of Ohio.

Preaching: The Sacrament of the Word. Donald Coggan. 160p. 1988. 12.95 (ISBN 0-8245-0854-8). Crossroad NY.

Preaching the Saints As Models. David Q. Liptak. 1983. pap. 8.95 (ISBN 0-941850-10-2). Liturgical Pubns.

Preaching the Story. Edmund A. Steimle et al. LC 78-14675. 208p. 1980. 9.95 (ISBN 0-8006-0538-1, 1-538). Fortress.

Preaching the Sunday & Holy Day Scriptures. Thomas J. Higgins. (Cycle A Ser.). 164p. (Orig.). 1987. pap. 9.95 (ISBN 0-941850-19-6). Liturgical Pubns.

Preaching the Sunday & Holy Day Scriptures. Thomas J. Higgins. 151p. 1988. pap. 9.95 (ISBN 0-940169-02-9). Liturgical Pubns.

Preaching the Word. Thomas K. Carroll. LC 83-81840. (Message of the Fathers of the Church Ser.: Vol. 11). 15.95 (ISBN 0-89453-351-7); pap. 9.95 (ISBN 0-89453-322-3). M Glazier.

Preaching the Word of God. Anthony Coniaris. 137p. 1983. pap. 7.95. Holy Cross Orthodox.

Preaching Through the Bible, 14 vols. Joseph Parker. 295.00 (ISBN 0-8010-7032-5). Baker Bk.

Preaching Through the Life of Christ. D. W. Cleverly. Ed. by Herbert Lambert. LC 85-19002. 112p. 1986. pap. 7.95 (ISBN 0-8272-2930-5). CBP.

Preaching Through the Prophets. John B. Taylor. LC 84-23773. 110p. 1985. pap. 7.95 (ISBN 0-8272-2929-1). CBP.

Preaching Through the Saints. James A. Wallace. LC 82-7745. 80p. 1982. pap. 2.50 (ISBN 0-8146-1271-7). Liturgical Pr.

Preaching Through the Year. David Steel. LC 80-82191. 168p. 1980. pap. 1.79 (ISBN 0-8042-1801-3, John Knox). Westminster John Knox.

Preaching to Convince. James D. Berkley. 192p. 1986. 9.95 (ISBN 0-8499-0577-X). Word Bks.

Preaching to Convince. Ed. by Jim Berkley. (Leadership Library). 175p. 1986. 9.95 (ISBN 0-917463-11-0). Chr Today.

Preaching to Modern Man. Frank Pack & Prentice A. Meador, Jr. Ed. by J. D. Thomas. LC 73-75928. 1969. 10.95 (ISBN 0-89112-060-2). Abilene Christ U.

Preaching to Sufferers: God & the Problem of Pain. Kent Richmond. 160p. 1988. pap. 9.95 (ISBN 0-687-33873-5). Abingdon.

Preaching to the Spirits in Prison. W. Kelly. pap. 4.75 (ISBN 0-88172-105-0). Believers Bkshelf.

Preaching Tradition: A Brief History. DeWitte T. Holland. LC 80-16339. (Abingdon Preacher's Library). 128p. (Orig.). 1980. pap. 7.95 (ISBN 0-687-33875-1). Abingdon.

Preaching with Power. Edward Fudge. pap. 2.00 (ISBN 0-686-12680-7). E Fudge.

Preaching with Purpose. Jay E. Adams. 1983. pap. 6.95 (ISBN 0-87552-078-2). Presby & Reformed.

Preaching with Purpose & Power: Selected E. Y. Mullins Lectures on Preaching. Ed. by Don Aycock. LC 81-22388. vi, 314p. 1982. 15.95 (ISBN 0-86554-027-6, MUP-H27). Mercer Univ Pr.

Preaching with Purpose: The Urgent Task of Homiletics. Jay E. Adams. (Jay Adams Library). 160p. 1986. pap. 6.95 (ISBN 0-310-51091-0, 12121P). Zondervan.

Preachings of Islam. T. W. Arnold. 467p. 1984. Repr. of 1913 ed. text ed. 50.00x (ISBN 0-86590-250-X, Pub. by Renaissance New Delhi). Apt Bks.

Prealgebra. rev. ed. CMSP Projects. (Illus.). 101p. (YA) pap. text ed. write for info. (ISBN 0-942851-00-5). CMSP Projects.

Prealgebra. Charles P. McKeague. 462p. 1987. pap. text ed. write for info. (ISBN 0-534-07596-7). Wadsworth Pub.

Preanesthetic Assessment One. Elizabeth Frost. 320p. 1988. 34.50 (ISBN 0-8176-3376-6). Birkhauser.

Preble County, Ohio, 1850 Census. Rose Shilt. 1974. 14.00 (ISBN 0-935057-02-1). OH Genealogical.

Precalculus. Anton. 1988. write for info. (ISBN 0-471-88682-3). Wiley.

Precalculus. Dennis Bila & Donald Ross. 480p. (gr. 12). 1986. 18.36 (ISBN 0-935115-00-5). Instruct Tech.

Precalculus. David Cohen. (Illus.). 627p. 1984. text ed. 35.00 (ISBN 0-314-77871-3); instrs.' manual avail. (ISBN 0-314-79135-3). West Pub.

Precalculus. 2nd ed. David Cohen. (Illus.). 725p. 1987. text ed. 37.75 (ISBN 0-314-26209-1); instr's. manual avail. (ISBN 0-314-34724-0); test bank avail. (ISBN 0-314-34728-3). West Pub.

Precalculus. John R. Durbin. LC 85-26493. 691p. 1986. write for info. (ISBN 0-471-88603-3). Wiley.

Precalculus. Joseph Elich & Lawrence O. Cannon. 1989. text ed. price not set (ISBN 0-673-18831-0). Scott F.

Precalculus. Bodh Gulati & Helen Bass. 759p. 1988. text ed. write for info. (ISBN 0-697-06763-7); write for info. Instructor's Manual (ISBN 0-697-06994-X). Wm C Brown.

Precalculus. Jerome E. Kaufmann. 640p. 1988. text ed. 29.50 (ISBN 0-534-92007-1). PWS Kent Pub.

Precalculus. 2nd ed. Larson. 736p. 1988. text ed. 28.00 (ISBN 0-669-16277-9); solutions guide 9.00 (ISBN 0-669-16280-9); study & solutions guide 7.00 (ISBN 0-669-17345-2); instr's. guide 2.00 (ISBN 0-669-16278-7); transparencies 60.00 (ISBN 0-669-17346-0). Heath.

Precalculus. Roland E. Larson & Robert P. Hostetler. LC 84-80507. 525p. 1985. text ed. 28.00 (ISBN 0-669-08617-7); instr's guide 2.00 (ISBN 0-669-08618-5); solns. manual 7.00 (ISBN 0-669-12000-6); Archive testing prog. Apple 150.00 (ISBN 0-669-13028-1). Heath.

Precalculus. Margaret L. Lial & Charles D. Miller. 1988. text ed. write for info. (ISBN 0-673-15872-1). Scott F.

Precalculus. Steven Roman. 587p. 1987. text ed. 28.00 (ISBN 0-15-571052-4); student solution manual 12.00 (ISBN 0-15-571054-0). HarBraceJ.

Precalculus. 2nd ed. Saturnino L. Salas & Charles G. Salas. LC 78-23236. 356p. 1979. text ed. 28.45 (ISBN 0-471-03124-0). Wiley.

Precalculus. Mailyn Studer. 1981. text ed. cancelled (ISBN 0-8162-8540-3); study guide. Holden-Day.

Precalculus: A Functional Approach to Algebra & Trigonometry. Peter Evanovich & Martin Kerner. 1981. text ed. 28.95x (ISBN 0-8162-2715-2); study guide & instr's manual avail. Holden-Day.

Precalculus Algebra & Trigonometry. 2nd ed. M. N. Manougian. 1987. 31.50 (ISBN 0-931541-07-7). Bk Pubs.

Precalculus & Mathematics: Algebra & Trigonometry. Steven Bryant & Daniel Saltz. (Illus.). 1980. text ed. write for info. (ISBN 0-673-16242-7). Scott F.

Precalculus: Functions & Graphs. Bernard Kolman & Arnold Shapiro. 1984. 25.00 (ISBN 0-12-417894-4); instr's manual 5.00 (ISBN 0-12-417895-2); test bank 50.00 (ISBN 0-12-417896-0). Acad Pr.

Precalculus: Functions & Graphs. 4th ed. M. Munen & James P. Yizze. (Illus.). 1985. text ed. 31.95x (ISBN 0-87901-258-7); study guide 8.95x (ISBN 0-87901-259-5). Worth.

Precalculus Functions & Graphs. 5th ed. Swokowski. 1987. text ed. 29.50 (ISBN 0-87150-060-4, 33L4350, Prindle). PWS Kent Pub.

Precalculus Mathematics. 3rd ed. Daniel D. Benice. (Illus.). 544p. 1986. pap. text ed. write for info. (ISBN 0-13-695503-7). P-H.

Precalculus Mathematics. 2nd ed. Harley Flanders & Justin J. Price. 1981. text ed. 40.00 (ISBN 0-03-057723-3, CBS C); instr's manual 15.50 (ISBN 0-03-058251-2); study guide 16.00 (ISBN 0-03-058253-9). SCP.

Precalculus Mathematics. Walter Fleming & Dale E. Varberg. (Illus.). 480p. 1984. write for info. (ISBN 0-13-694851-0). P-H.

Precalculus Mathematics. 2nd ed. Walter Fleming & Dale E. Varberg. (Illus.). 465p. 1988. text ed. write for info. (ISBN 0-13-695008-6). P-H.

Precalculus Mathematics. Vivian Groza & Susanne Shelley. LC 76-158479. 1972. text ed. 22.95x (ISBN 0-03-077670-8). Irvington.

Precalculus Mathematics. 2nd ed. Thomas W. Hungerford & Richard Mercer. 688p. 1985. text ed. 40.00 (ISBN 0-03-000843-3, CBS C). SCP.

Precalculus Mathematics. Thomason. LC 86-18957. 811p. 1987. write for info. (ISBN 0-471-01153-3). Wiley.

Precalculus Mathematics: A Functional Approach. 2nd ed. James F. Connelly & Robert A. Fratangelo. (Illus.). 1980. text ed. write for info. (ISBN 0-02-324400-3); write for info. study guide (ISBN 0-02-324420-8). Macmillan.

Precalculus Mathematics: A Functional Approach. 3rd ed. Karl J. Smith. LC 85-14678. (Mathematics Ser.). 550p. 1985. text ed. 26.50 pub net (ISBN 0-534-05232-0). Brooks-Cole.

Precalculus Mathematics: A Functions Approach. Floyd F. Helton & Margaret L. Lial. 1983. text ed. write for info. (ISBN 0-673-15507-2). Scott F.

Precalculus Mathematics: A Short Course. Russell E. Thompson. LC 82-13366. 200p. (Orig.). 1982. pap. text ed. 12.25 (ISBN 0-8191-2634-9). U Pr of Amer.

Precalculus Mathematics: Algebra, Trigonometry, & Analytic Geometry. Harvey Braverman. LC 83-11298. 546p. 1983. Repr. of 1975 ed. text ed. 31.50 (ISBN 0-89874-653-1). Krieger.

Precalculus Mathematics for Technical Students. P. D. Mavrommatis & P. F. Reichmeider. (Technical Mathematics Ser.). (Illus.). 416p. 1976. write for info. (ISBN 0-13-695163-5). P-H.

Precalculus Mathematics in a Nutshell. 119p. 1987. pap. 7.95 (ISBN 0-939765-13-6, GK109). Janson Pubns.

Precalculus Mathematics: New Impressions. Michael Payne. (Illus.). 1978. text ed. 30.95 (ISBN 0-7216-7126-8). HR&W.

Precalculus with Calculator Applications. Joseph Elich & Carletta J. Elich. (Math-Mallion Ser.). (Illus.). 576p. 1982. instr's. manual o.p. 3.00 (ISBN 0-201-13346-6); write for info. student solution bk. (ISBN 0-201-13348-2); answer bk.o.p. 2.50 (ISBN 0-201-13347-4). Addison-Wesley.

Precambrian Banded Iron Formations: Physicochemical Conditions of Formations. Ed. by Y. P. Melnik. (Developments in Precambrian Geology Ser.: Vol. 5). 310p. 1982. 100.00 (ISBN 0-444-41934-9). Elsevier.

Precambrian Geochronology of North America: An Annotated Bibliography,1951-1977. R. G. Vugrinovich. LC 80-68063. (Microform Publication: No. 11). 1980. 3.20 (ISBN 0-8137-6011-9). Geol Soc.

Precambrian Geology & Geochronology of Minnesota. Samuel S. Goldich et al. LC 61-8016. (Bulletin: No. 41). (Illus.). 1961. 4.00x (ISBN 0-8166-0224-7). Minn Geol Survey.

Precambrian Geology of India. A. Mahmood Naqvi. (Oxford Monographs on Geology & Geophysics). (Illus.). 240p. 1987. 50.00 (ISBN 0-19-503653-0). Oxford U Pr.

Precambrian Geology of North Snowy Block, Beartooth Mountains, Montana. Rolland R. Reid & William J. McMannis. LC 74-28529. (Geological Society of America SpecialPaper: No. 157). pap. 47.00 (ISBN 0-317-28367-7, 2025470). Bks Demand UMI.

Precambrian Geology: Proceedings of the 27th International Geological Congress, Vol. 5. International Geological Congress Staff. 362p. 1984. lib. bdg. 97.50x (ISBN 90-6764-014-X). Coronet Bks.

Precambrian in Younger Fold Belts. V. Zoubek. (International Geological Correlation Programme Ser.). 300p. 1988. 275.00 (ISBN 0-471-91226-3). Wiley.

Precambrian of the Northern Hemisphere. L. J. Salop. (Developments in Paleontology & Stratigraphy Ser.: Vol. 3). 382p. 1977. 129.00 (ISBN 0-444-41510-6). Elsevier.

Precambrian of the Southern Hemisphere. Ed. by D. R. Hunter. (Developments in Precambrian Geology Ser.: Vol. 2). 882p. 1981. 200.00 (ISBN 0-444-41862-8). Elsevier.

Precambrian Plate Tectonics. Ed. by A. Kroner. (Developments in Precambrian Geology Ser.: Vol. 4). 782p. 1981. 210.75 (ISBN 0-444-41910-1). Elsevier.

Precambrian Symposium: The Relationship of Mineralization to Precambrian Stratigraphy in Certain Mining Areas of Ontario & Quebec. Geological Association of Canada. LC 68-43. (Geological Association of Canada. Special Paper: No. 3). pap. 36.00 (2027838). Bks Demand UMI.

Precambrian Tectonics Illustrated: International Union of Geological Sciences, Commission on Tectonics, Subcommission on Precambrian Structural Type Regions, Final Report. Ed. by A. Kroener & R. Greiling. (Illus.). 419p. 1984. lib. bdg. 114.70x (ISBN 3-510-65118-9). Lubrecht & Cramer.

Precancerous Lesions of the Gastrointestinal Tract. Morson & Jass. 1985. 41.95 (ISBN 0-7020-1053-7, Bailliere-Tindall). Saunders.

Precancerous Lesions of the Gastrointestinal Tract. Basil C. Morson & Jeremy R. Jass. (Illus.). 175p. 1985. 41.95 (ISBN 0-7216-0977-5, Bailliere-Tindall). Saunders.

Precancerous Lesions of the Gastrointestinal Tract. Ed. by Paul Sherlock et al. 344p. 1983. text ed. 66.00 (ISBN 0-89004-883-5). Raven.

Precancerous States. Richard L. Carter. (Illus.). 1984. 63.00x (ISBN 0-19-261279-4). Oxford U Pr.

Precario-Precarious. Bi-lingual ed. Cecilia Vicuna. Tr. by Ann Twitty. (Illus.). 80p. (Orig., Span. & Eng.). 1983. 12.95 (ISBN 0-934378-45-2); pap. 5.95 (ISBN 0-934378-46-0). Tanam Pr.

Precarious Balance: State & Society in Africa. Ed. by Donald Rothchild & Naomi Chazan. (Special Studies on Africa). 320p. 1987. text ed. 32.50 (ISBN 0-86531-738-0). Westview.

Precarious Enchantment: A Reading of Meredith's Poetry. Carol L. Bernstein. LC 79-744. 202p. 1979. 17.50x (ISBN 0-8132-0543-3). Cath U Pr.

Precarious Organisation: Sociological Explorations of the Church's Mission & Structure. Mady A. Thung. (Religion & Society Ser.: No. 5). 1976. text ed. 22.00 (ISBN 0-686-22627-5). Mouton.

Precarious Republic: Political Modernization in Lebanon. Michael C. Hudson. (Westview Encore Edition-Softcover Ser.). 366p. 1985. pap. 42.50x (ISBN 0-8133-0105-X). Westview.

Precarious Truce: Anglo-Soviet Relations, 1924-27. Gabriel Gorodetsky. LC 76-2279. (Soviet & East European Studies). 303p. pap. 78.80 (2030598). Bks Demand UMI.

Precariously Privileged. Zuzana Shonfield. (Illus.). 320p. 1987. 34.00 (ISBN 0-19-212265-7). Oxford U Pr.

Precast & Prestressed Concrete for Justice Facilities. 56p. 1985. pap. 30.00 (ISBN 0-318-19722-7, MK-6-85). Prestressed Concrete.

Precast Concrete Connection Details: Part 1-Structural Design manual. Beton Staff. 1981. 87.00 (ISBN 3-7640-0112-7, Pub. by Beton Bks W Germany). IPS.

Precast Concrete Connection Details: Part 2-Floor Connections. Beton Staff. 1978. 71.00 (ISBN 3-7640-0143-7, Pub. by Beton Bks W Germany). IPS.

Precast Concrete: Design & Applications. A. M. Haas. (Illus.). 160p. 1983. 72.00 (ISBN 0-85334-197-4, I-342-83, Pub. by Elsevier Applied Sci England). Elsevier.

Precast Concrete: Handling & Erection. Joseph J. Waddell. (Monograph: No. 8). 1974. 31.75 (ISBN 0-685-85142-7, M-8) (ISBN 0-685-85143-5). ACI.

Precast Concrete in Efficient Passive Solar Designs. (PCI Journal Reprints Ser.). 36p. pap. 9.00 (ISBN 0-318-19799-5, JR288). Prestressed Concrete.

Precast Concrete: Materials, Manufacture, Properties & Usage. Ed. by M. Levitt. (Illus.). ix, 233p. 1982. 63.00 (ISBN 0-85334-994-0, Pub. by Elsevier Applied Sci England). Elsevier.

Precast Concrete Piles. 44p. 1985. 28.80 (ISBN 0-7277-0217-3, Pub. by T Telford UK). Am Soc Civil Eng.

Precast Concrete Production. J. G. Richardson. 1977. pap. 35.00 (ISBN 0-7210-0912-3, Pub. by C & CA London). Scholium Intl.

Precast Piling Practice. Bengt B. Broms. 132p. 1981. 19.00 (ISBN 0-7277-0121-5, Pub. by T Telford UK). Am Soc Civil Eng.

Precast, Prestressed Box Beams: A State-of-the-Art Report. (PCI Journal Reprints Ser.). 25p. 1985. pap. 5.00 (ISBN 0-318-19740-5, JR71). Prestressed Concrete.

Precast Prestressed Clinker Storage Silo Saves Time & Money. (PCI Journal Reprints Ser.). 20p. pap. 5.00 (ISBN 0-686-40089-5, JR168). Prestressed Concrete.

Precast Prestressed Concrete Bridges for Low Volume Roads. 16p. 1985. pap. 5.00 (ISBN 0-318-19725-1, JR-206). Prestressed Concrete.

Precast Prestressed Concrete Industry Code of Standard Practice for Precast Concrete. 19p. pap. 6.00 (ISBN 0-686-39952-8, JR-195). Prestressed Concrete.

Precast Prestressed Concrete Short Span Bridges: Spans to 100 Feet. 2nd ed. 40p. 1985. pap. 10.00 (ISBN 0-318-19723-5, SSB-1-81). Prestressed Concrete.

Precast Prestressed "Space Mountain" Highlights Walt Disney World. (PCI Journal Reprints Ser.). 16p. pap. 5.00 (ISBN 0-686-40085-2, JR165). Prestressed Concrete.

Precast Prestressed System Provides Solutions for Stadium Expansion. (PCI Journal Reprints Ser.). 16p. pap. 5.00 (ISBN 0-686-40124-7, JR216). Prestressed Concrete.

Precast Prestressed Wall System Used for Water Storage Reservoir. (PCI Journal Reprints Ser.). 12p. 1985. pap. 5.00 (ISBN 0-318-19762-6, JR229). Prestressed Concrete.

Precast Reinforced Concrete. P. Dyachenko & S. Mirotvorsky. (Russian Monographs). 240p. 1969. 85.00 (ISBN 0-677-20780-8). Gordon & Breach.

Precast Trapezoidal Girders Spliced with Post-Tensioning for Highway Underpass. Prestressed Concrete Institute Staff. (PCI Journal Reprints Ser.). 4p. pap. 3.00 (ISBN 0-318-19863-0, JR219). Prestressed Concrete.

Precaution, 2 vols. James Fenimore Cooper. LC 73-1898. (BCL Ser.: No. I). Repr. of 1820 ed. Set. 47.50 (ISBN 0-404-01707-X). AMS Pr.

Precaution. James Fenimore Cooper. LC 6-29686. Repr. of 1820 ed. 11.00x (ISBN 0-403-00101-3). Scholarly.

Precautions for Explosive Materials. Center for Occupational Research & Development Staff. (Job Safety & Health Instructional Materials Ser.). (Illus.). 26p. 1981. pap. text ed. 2.00 (ISBN 1-55502-098-4). Ctr Res & Dev.

Precautions in the Management of Patients Who Have Received Therapeutic Amounts of Radionuclides. LC 76-125343. (NCRP Reports Ser.: No. 37). 1970. 12.00 (ISBN 0-913392-19-7). NCRP Pubns.

Precedence. Rae Armantrout. 48p. 1985. 15.00 (ISBN 0-930901-23-1); pap. 5.00 (ISBN 0-930901-24-X). Burning Deck.

Precedence & Arrow Networking Techniques for Construction. Robert B. Harris. LC 78-5786. 429p. 1978. text ed. 49.50 (ISBN 0-471-04123-8). Wiley.

Precedence in England & Wales. George D. Squibb. 1981. 37.50x (ISBN 0-19-825389-3). Oxford U Pr.

Precedence Networks for Project Planning & Control. P. J. Burman. 1980. 20.00x (ISBN 0-9606344-0-1). Blitz Pub Co.

Precedent in English Law. 3rd. ed. Rupert Cross. 1977. pap. text ed. 17.95x (ISBN 0-19-876073-6). Oxford U Pr.

Precedent in English Law & Other Essays. J. L. Montrose. 374p. 1968. 32.50x (ISBN 0-7165-0503-7, BBA 02204, Pub. by Irish Academic Pr Ireland). Biblio Dist.

Precision Sheet Metal Shop Practice. Richard S. Budzik. LC 78-97566. (Illus.). 96p. 1969. 15.95 (ISBN 0-912914-17-3); tchrs' materials 26.95 (ISBN 0-912914-19-X); wkbk 21.95 (ISBN 0-912914-18-1). Practical Pubns.

Precision Sheet Metal Shop Theory. 2nd ed. Richard S. Budzik. LC 79-77566. (Illus.). 450p. 1988. 49.95 (ISBN 0-912914-25-4); tchrs' materials 49.95 (ISBN 0-912914-10-6); wkbk 21.95 (ISBN 0-912914-09-2). Practical Pubns.

Precision Signal Handling & Converter-Microprocessor Interface: A Tutorial Presentation. Donald J. Travers. 90p. 1984. pap. text ed. 29.95x (ISBN 0-87664-803-0). Instru Soc.

Precision Site Surveying & Setting Out. Tomalin. cancelled (ISBN 0-85274-058-1, Pub. by A Hilger U. K.). Taylor & Francis.

Precision Summary. C. C. Wei. 10p. (Orig.). folder 1.00 (ISBN 0-87643-040-X). M Lisa Precision.

Precision System of Contract Bridge Bidding. rev. ed. Charles H. Goren. 224p. 1984. pap. 6.95 (ISBN 0-671-53232-4, Fireside). S&S.

Precision Valley: The Machine Tool Companies of Springfield, Vermont. Wayne G. Broehl, Jr. LC 75-41748. (Companies & Men: Business Enterprises in America). (Illus.). 1976. Repr. of 1959 ed. 29.00x (ISBN 0-405-08065-4). Ayer Co Pubs.

Precision's One Club Complete. Katherine Wei & Judi Radin. 169p. (Orig.). 1981. pap. 7.95 (ISBN 0-87643-042-6). M Lisa Precision.

Precision's One Club Complete. Kathie Wei & Judi Radin. 169p. 1981. 7.95. Barclay Bridge.

Preclassic Maya Pottery at Cuello, Belize. Laura J. Kosakowsky. LC 87-16249. (Anthropological Papers: No. 47). 101p. 1987. monograph 29.95x (ISBN 0-8165-1017-2). U of Ariz Pr.

Preclassical Monetary Theories. Thomas Guggenheim. (Graduate Institute of International Studies Ser.). 200p. 1989. 39.00x (ISBN 0-86187-958-9, Pub. by Pinter Pubs UK). Columbia U Pr.

Preclinical Hyperthermia. Ed. by W. Hinkelbein et al. (Recent Results in Cancer Research Ser.). (Illus.). 295p. 1988. 98.00 (ISBN 0-387-18487-2). Springer-Verlag.

Preclinical Psychopharmacology, Pt. 1. D. G. Grahame-Smith & P. J. Cowen. (Psychopharmacology Ser.: Vol. 2). xxi, 490p. 1985. 173.25 (ISBN 0-444-90350-X). Elsevier.

Preclinical Safety of Biotechnology Products Intended for Human Use. Ed. by Charles E. Graham. LC 87-4130. (Progress in Clinical & Biological Research Ser.: Vol. 235). 230p. 1987. 36.00 (ISBN 0-8451-5085-5, 5085). A R Liss.

Preclinical Teaching of Psychiatry, Vol. 5. GAP Committee on Medical Education. (Report: No. 54). 1962. pap. 5.00 (ISBN 0-87318-073-9, Pub. by GAP). Brunner-Mazel.

Precollege Programs for Blind & Visually Handicapped Students. Ed. by Susan J. Spungin. 30p. 1975. pap. text ed. 1.80 (ISBN 0-89128-096-0, PEP096). Am Foun Blind.

Precolonial African History. Philip D. Curtin. LC 73-93606. (AHA Pamphlets: No. 501). (Illus.). 60p. 1974. pap. text ed. 1.50 (ISBN 0-87229-017-4). Am Hist Assn.

Precolonial Black Africa. Cheikh A. Diop. 252p. 1987. 8.95 (ISBN 0-86543-070-5, Co-pub. by Lawrence Hill & Co.). Africa World.

Preconcentration & Drinking of Food Materials: Thijssen Memorial Symposium - Proceedings of the International Symposium, Eindhoven, the Netherlands, Nov. 5-6, 1987. Ed. by S. Bruin. (Process Technology Proceedings Ser.: No. 5). 354p. 1988. 102.75 (ISBN 0-444-42968-9). Elsevier.

Preconception Gender Diet. Sally Langendoen & William Proctor. LC 82-1470. 168p. 1982. 10.95 (ISBN 0-87131-372-3). M Evans.

Preconceptional Health Promotion: A Practical Guide. Robert C. Cefalo & Merry-K. Moos. 300p. 1988. price not set. Aspen Pub.

Preconditioning Methods: Analysis & Application. Ed. by David J. Evans. (Topics in Computer Mathematics Ser.: Vol. 1). 568p. 1983. 85.00 (ISBN 0-677-16320-7). Gordon & Breach.

Preconditions of Revolution in Early Modern Europe. Ed. by Robert Forster & Jack P. Greene. LC 76-122010. (Johns Hopkins Symposia in History Ser.). pap. 56.00 (ISBN 0-317-29826-7, 2019820). Bks Demand UMI.

Preconscious Processing. Norman F. Dixon. LC 80-42012. 313p. 1981. 59.95x (ISBN 0-471-27982-X). Wiley.

Preconscious Stimulation in Dreams, Associations & Images: Classical Studies. Otto Potzl et al. (Psychological Issues Monograph: No. 7, Vol. 2, No. 3). 156p. (Orig.). 1961. text ed. 20.00x (ISBN 0-8236-4260-7). Intl Univs Pr.

Precurseur D'Adam Smith en France: J. J. L. Graslin (1727-1790) J. Desmars. LC 77-159696. 257p. (Fr.). 1973. Repr. of 1900 ed. 20.50 (ISBN 0-8337-0840-6). B Franklin.

Precursors of Early Speech. Ed. by Bjorn Lindblom & Rolf Zetterstrom. LC 86-1897. (Wenner-Gren Center International Symposium Ser.: Vol. 44). 300p. 1986. 100.00x (ISBN 0-943818-95-8, Stockton Pr). Groves Dict Music.

Precursors of Gastric Cancer. Ed. by Si-Chun Ming. LC 83-27025. 350p. 1984. 56.95 (ISBN 0-275-91444-5, C1444). Praeger.

Precursors of Modern Management: An Original Anthology. Ed. by Alfred D. Chandler. LC 79-7527. (History of Management Thought & Practice Ser.). 1980. lib. bdg. 28.50x (ISBN 0-405-12311-6). Ayer Co Pubs.

Predaceous Nematodes of Oregon. Harold J. Jensen & Roland H. Mulvey. LC 68-63023. (Studies in Zoology: No. 12). (Illus.). 64p. (Orig.). 1968. pap. 4.95x (ISBN 0-87071-112-1). Oreg St U Pr.

Predation. R. J. Taylor. (Population & Community Biology Ser.). (Illus.). 176p. 1984. text ed. 39.95 (ISBN 0-412-25060-8, 6770, Pub. by Chapman & Hall England); pap. text ed. 19.95 (ISBN 0-412-26120-0, 6771). Routledge Chapman & Hall.

Predation: Direct & Indirect Impacts on Aquatic Communities. Ed. by W. Charles Kerfoot & Andrew Sih. LC 86-40113. (Illus.). 394p. 1987. 60.00x (ISBN 0-87451-376-6). U Pr of New Eng.

Predator. Anthony John. 352p. (Orig.). 1983. pap. 3.50 (ISBN 0-345-29888-8). Ballantine.

Predator. Paul Monette. Date not set. pap. 3.50 (ISBN 0-515-09002-6). Jove Pubns.

Predator Caller's Companion. Gerry Blair. LC 81-497. 280p. 1981. 18.95 (ISBN 0-8329-3362-7, Pub. by Winchester Pr). New Century.

Predator Control & the Sheep Industry: The Role of Science in Formation of Policy. Frederic H. Wagner. (Contemporary Issues in Natural Resources & Environmental Policy Ser.: No. 1). 240p. 1988. text ed. 21.95x (ISBN 0-941690-26-1); pap. text ed. 11.95x (ISBN 0-941690-27-X). Regina Bks.

Predator-Prey Model: Do We Live in a Volterra World? Ed. by Collet's Holdings, Ltd. Staff. 1986. 105.00x (ISBN 0-317-46689-5, Pub. by Collets (UK)). State Mutual Bk.

Predator-Prey Model: Do We Live in a Volterra World? M. Peschel & W. Mende. (Illus.). 260p. 1986. 22.00 (ISBN 0-387-81848-0). Springer-Verlag.

Predator Prey Puppets & Toys: Eight Paper Animal Projects to Make. Ronald Mah. (Illus.). 32p. (ps-3). 1986. pap. 3.95 (ISBN 0-9615903-1-9). Symbiosis Bks.

Predator-Prey Relationships: Perspectives & Approaches from the Study of Lower Vertebrates. Ed. by Martin E. Feder & George V. Lauder. LC 85-24709. (Illus.). x, 198p. 1986. 26.00x (ISBN 0-226-23945-4); pap. 11.95x (ISBN 0-226-23946-2). U of Chicago Pr.

Predators. Mark Rosenthal. LC 83-7512. (New True Bks.). (Illus.). 48p. (gr. k-4). 1983. PLB 12.60 (ISBN 0-516-01707-1); pap. 3.95 (ISBN 0-516-41707-X). Childrens.

Predators. Eric Sauter. 352p. 1987. pap. 3.95 (ISBN 0-671-61719-2). PB.

Predators & Prey. Noel Simon. (Dent Wildlife Bks.). (Illus.). 46p. (gr. 4 up). 1985. 8.50x (ISBN 0-460-06893-8, BKA 05285, Pub. by J M Dent England). Biblio Dist.

Predators & Their Prey. F. W. Jenkins. LC 87-71716. 121p. (Orig.). 1987. pap. 5.95 (ISBN 0-916383-33-4). Aegina Pr.

Predator's Ball: How the Junk Bond Machine Staked the Corporate Raiders. Connie Bruck. 1988. 19.95 (ISBN 0-671-61780-X). S&S.

Predators in Our Pulpits: A Compelling Call to Follow Christ with Unswerving Sacrifice. W. Phillip Keller. LC 87-83692. 160p. (Orig.). 1988. pap. 6.95 (ISBN 0-89081-674-3). Harvest Hse.

Predators of Southern Africa. Hans Grobler et al. (Illus.). 134p. 14.95 (ISBN 0-86954-194-3, Pub. by Macmillan S Africa). Intl Spec Bk.

Predatory Behavior among Wild Chimpanzees. Geza Teleki. LC 70-124442. (Illus.). 232p. 1973. 28.50 (ISBN 0-8387-7747-3). Bucknell U Pr.

Predatory Dinosaurs of the World: A Complete Illustrated Guide. Gregory S. Paul. (Illus.). 300p. 1988. 19.95 (ISBN 0-671-61946-2). S&S.

Predatory Female. Lawrence Shannon. 171p. (Orig.). 1986. pap. 4.95 (ISBN 0-9615938-0-6). Banner Bks.

Predatory Kinship & the Creation of Norman Power, 840-1066. Eleanor Searle. 275p. 1988. text ed. 32.00x (ISBN 0-520-06276-0). U of Cal Pr.

Predatory Pricing in a Market Economy. Roland H. Koller, II. LC 77-14781. (Dissertations in American Economic History Ser.). 1978. 37.50 (ISBN 0-405-11043-X). Ayer Co Pubs.

Predecessors of Shakespeare. Ed. by Terence P. Logan & Denzell S. Smith. LC 72-75344. (A Survey & Bibliography of Recent Studies in English Renaissance Drama Ser). xiv, 348p. 1973. 30.00x (ISBN 0-8032-0775-1). U of Nebr Pr.

Predecisional Process in Educational Administration: A Philosophical Analysis. Ellis A. Joseph. LC 74-17065. iv, 105p. 1975. 9.95 (ISBN 0-88280-017-5); pap. 5.95 (ISBN 0-88280-018-3). ETC Pubns.

Predestination. Gordon H. Clark. LC 87-16815. 224p. (Orig.). 1987. pap. 7.95 (ISBN 0-87552-169-X). Presby & Reformed.

Predestination. George Fletcher. pap. 0.50 (ISBN 0-686-64389-5). Reiner.

Predestination & Free Will. David Basinger & Randall Basinger. LC 85-23887. 180p. 1986. pap. 8.95 (ISBN 0-87784-567-0). Inter-Varsity.

Predestination, God's Foreknowledge & Future Contingents. 2nd ed. William of Ockham. Tr. by Norman Kretzmann & Marilyn M. Adams. LC 82-23317. 146p. 1983. 22.50 (ISBN 0-915144-14-X); pap. text ed. 4.95 (ISBN 0-915144-13-1). Hackett Pub.

Predestination Primer. John H. Gerstner. 1981. pap. 2.50 (ISBN 0-88469-145-4). BMH Bks.

Predestined: A Novel of New York Life. Stephen F. Whitman. LC 74-8672. (Lost American Fiction Ser). 486p. 1974. Repr. of 1910 ed. 8.95 (ISBN 0-8093-0701-4). S Ill U Pr.

Predestined Love. Dick Sutphen. 256p. 1988. pap. 3.95 (ISBN 0-671-64613-3). PB.

Predicacion Biblica para el Mundo Actual. Lloyd M. Perry. Tr. by Angel A. Carrodeguas from Eng. Orig. Title: Biblical Preaching for Today's World. 176p. (Span.). 1986. pap. 4.95 (ISBN 0-8297-0957-6). Life Pubs Intl.

Predicacion Expositiva. D. M. White. Tr. by Francisco E. Estrello. Orig. Title: Excellence of Exposition. 160p. 1982. Repr. of 1980 ed. 3.75 (ISBN 0-311-42061-3). Casa Bautista.

Predicador: Platicas a Mis Estudiantes. Alejandro Trevino. 155p. 1984. pap. 2.95 (ISBN 0-311-42016-8). Casa Bautista.

Predicament. Ronald H. Morrieson. 248p. 1987. pap. 4.95 (ISBN 0-14-008841-5). Penguin.

Predicament of Culture: Twentieth-Century Ethnography, Literature, & Art. James Clifford. LC 87-24173. (Illus.). 384p. 1988. text ed. 30.00 (ISBN 0-674-69842-8); pap. text ed. 15.95 (ISBN 0-674-69843-6). Harvard U Pr.

Predicament of Democratic Man. Edmond N. Cahn. LC 78-16399. 1979. Repr. of 1961 ed. lib. bdg. 35.00x (ISBN 0-313-20597-3, CAPR). Greenwood.

Predicament of the Prosperous. Bruce C. Birch & Larry L. Rasmussen. LC 78-18412. (Biblical Perspectives on Current Issues). 212p. 1978. pap. 8.95 (ISBN 0-664-24211-1). Westminster John Knox.

Predicaments. facs. ed. Louis E. Shipman. LC 71-142276. (Short Story Index Reprint Ser). (Illus.). 1899. 14.00 (ISBN 0-8369-3760-0). Ayer Co Pubs.

Predicaments, or Music & the Future: An Essay in Constructive Criticism. Cecil Gray. LC 79-103652. (Select Bibliographies Reprint Ser). 1936. 24.50 (ISBN 0-8369-5152-2). Ayer Co Pubs.

Predicar Al Corazon-Bosquejos Selectos. Jay E. Adams & Lyle A. Thompson. Tr. by Angel A. Carrodeguas from Eng. 175p. (Span.). 1986. pap. 2.95 (ISBN 0-8297-0699-2). Life Pubs Intl.

Predicate & Argument of Rengao Grammar. Kenneth Gregerson. (Sil Publications in Linguistics Ser.: No. 61). 141p. (Orig.). 1979. pap. 6.50x (ISBN 0-88312-075-5); microfiche (2) 4.00 (ISBN 0-88312-485-8). Summer Inst Ling.

Predicate Formation in the Verbal System of Modern Hebrew. J. Junger. (Functional Grammar Ser.). vi, 182p. 1988. pap. write for info. (ISBN 90-6765-368-3). Foris Pubns.

Predicates & Terms In Functional Grammar. Ed. by A. M. Bolkestein et al. (Functional Grammar Ser.: No. 2). 304p. 1985. pap. 24.90 (ISBN 9-067-65104-4). Foris Pubns.

Predication: A Study of Its Development. Carol Wall. LC 74-76119. (Janua Linguarum, Ser. Minor: No. 201). 1974. pap. 16.80 (ISBN 90-279-2665-4). Mouton.

Predication & Expression of Functional Grammar. A. M. Bolkestein et al. LC 81-68966. 1982. 64.00 (ISBN 0-12-111350-7). Acad Pr.

Predication Theory: A Case-Study for Indexing Theory. Donna J. Napoli. (Cambridge Studies in Linguistics: No. 50). (Illus.). 400p. Date not set. price not set (ISBN 0-521-35298-3); pap. price not set (ISBN 0-521-36820-0). Cambridge U Pr.

Prediccative Arithmetic. Edward Nelson. (Mathematical Notes: No. 32). (Illus.). 199p. 1987. text ed. 21.00 (ISBN 0-691-08455-6). Princeton U Pr.

Predictability, Correlation, & Contiguity. Ed. by Peter Harzem & Michael D. Zeiler. LC 80-40843. (Advances in Analysis of Behaviour Ser.: No. 2). (Illus.). 431p. pap. 112.10 (2030507). Bks Demand UMI.

Predictability, Correlation & Contiguity, Vol. 2. Ed. by Peter Harzem & Michael D. Zeiler. LC 80-40843. (Advances in Analysis of Behavior Ser.). 432p. 1981. 84.95 (ISBN 0-471-27847-5, Pub. by Wiley-Interscience). Wiley.

Predictability in Science & Society. Ed. by John Mason et al. (Illus.). 145p. 1986. pap. text ed. 33.00x (ISBN 0-85403-284-3, Pub. by Royal Soc London). Scholium Intl.

Predictability of Corporate Failure. R. A. I. Van Frederikslust. 1978. lib. bdg. 26.00 (ISBN 90-207-0736-1, Pub. by Martinus Nijhoff Netherlands). Kluwer Academic.

Predictability of Fluid Motions: AIP Conference Proccedings, La Jolla Institute, 1983, No. 106. Ed. by Greg Holloway & Bruce J. West. LC 83-73661. 60p. 1984. lib. bdg. 48.50 (ISBN 0-88318-305-6). Am Inst Physics.

Predicting Achievement: A Ten-Year Follow-Up of Black & White Adolescents. Joseph Lowman et al. LC 80-17139. (IRSS Research Reports Ser.). (Illus.). 101p. (Orig.). 1980. pap. text ed. 7.00 (ISBN 0-89143-100-4). U NC Inst Res Soc Sci.

Predicting Adolescent Drug Use: Utility Structure & Marijuana. Karl E. Bauman. LC 79-22736. 192p. 1980. 40.95 (ISBN 0-275-90450-4, C0450). Praeger.

Predicting Adult Stature for Individuals. Ed. by A. F. Roche. (Monographs in Paediatrics: Vol. 3). 1975. 32.75 (ISBN 3-8055-1843-9). S Karger.

Predicting & Deciding. D. Pears. (Philosophical Lectures (Henriette Hertz Trust)). 1964. pap. 5.50 (ISBN 0-85672-304-5, Pub. by British Acad). Longwood Pub Group.

Predicting & Designing for Natural & Man-Made Hazards. Compiled by American Society of Civil Engineers Staff. 297p. 1979. pap. 30.00x (ISBN 0-87262-187-1). Am Soc Civil Eng.

Predicting & Measuring Fugitive Dust. Howard E. Hesketh & Mohammad S. El-Shobokshy. LC 84-51877. 131p. 1985. pap. 24.50 (ISBN 0-87762-375-9). Technomic.

Predicting Criminality: Forecasting Behavior on Parole. Ferris F. Laune. LC 73-10851. 163p. 1974. Repr. of 1936 ed. lib. bdg. 22.50x (ISBN 0-8371-7041-9, LAPC). Greenwood.

Predicting Ecology & Fish Yields in African Reservoirs from Preimpoundment Physico-Chemical Data. B. E. Marshall. (CIFA Technical Papers: No. 12). 35p. (Eng. & Fr.). 1985. pap. 7.50 (ISBN 92-5-002155-0, F2706, FAO). UNIPUB.

Predicting Effects of Power Plant On-Through Cooling on Aquatic Systems: A State-of-the-Art Report of IHP Working Group 6.2 on the Effects of Thermal Discharges. Ed. by W. Majewski & D. Miller. (Technical Papers in Hydrology: No. 20). (Illus.). 171p. 1979. pap. 9.50 (ISBN 92-3-101704-7, U939, UNESCO). UNIPUB.

Predicting Executive Success: What It Takes to Make It into Senior Management. Melvin Sorcher. LC 85-3293. 280p. 1986. 19.95 (ISBN 0-471-81565-9). Wiley.

Predicting Feed Intake of Major Food-Producing Animals. National Research Council. 96p. 1986. pap. text ed. 15.95x (ISBN 0-309-03695-X). Natl Acad Pr.

Predicting First Grade Reading Achievement: A Study in Reading Readiness. Erby C. Deputy. LC 77-176705. (Columbia University. Teachers College. Contributions to Education: No. 426). Repr. of 1930 ed. 22.50 (ISBN 0-404-55426-1). AMS Pr.

Predicting Intercity Freight Flows. P. T. Harker. (Topics in Transportation Ser.). 270p. 1987. lib. bdg. 88.50x (ISBN 90-6764-064-6). Coronet Bks.

Predicting Oklahoma Elections: An Inexpensive & Accurate Method. Kenneth J. Meier. 57p. 1979. 3.50 (ISBN 0-686-32071-9). Univ OK Gov Res.

Predicting Outcomes. Sheldon L. Tilkin & Judith Conoway. (Horizons E Ser.). (Illus.). 24p. (gr. 3-4). 1980. wkbk. 2.50 (ISBN 0-89403-575-4). EDC.

Predicting Outcomes. Sheldon L. Tilkin & Judith Conoway. (Horizons F Ser.). (Illus.). 24p. (gr. 4-5). 1980. wkbk. 2.50 (ISBN 0-89403-585-1). EDC.

Predicting Photosynthesis for Ecosystem Models, 2 vols. John D. Hesketh & J. W. Jones. 1980. Vol. 1, 288p. 99.00 (ISBN 0-8493-5335-1); Vol. 2, 304p. 99.00 (ISBN 0-8493-5336-X). CRC Pr.

Predicting Social Maladjustment. J. Sarnecki & S. Sollenhag. 158p. (Orig.). 1985. pap. text ed. 19.50x (ISBN 91-38-08877-0, Pub. by Almqvist & Wiksell). Coronet Bks.

Predicting Sociocultural Change. Ed. by Susan Abbott & John Van Willigen. LC 79-10193. (Southern Anthropological Society Proceedings Ser.: No. 13). 158p. 1980. 14.00x (ISBN 0-8203-0477-8); pap. 7.00x (ISBN 0-8203-0484-0). U of Ga Pr.

Predicting Temperature Rise in Fire Protected Structural Steel Beams. David C. Jeanes. 7.50 (ISBN 0-318-03818-8, TR84-4). Society Fire Protect.

Predicting the Behavior of the Educational System. Thomas Green et al. (Illus.). 224p. 1980. 15.95x (ISBN 0-8156-2223-6); pap. 8.95x (ISBN 0-8156-2224-4). Syracuse U Pr.

Predicting the Productivity of Sitka Spruce on Upland Sites in Northern Britain. R. Worrell. 12p. (Orig.). 1987. pap. 5.00 (ISBN 0-11-710253-9, HM1474, Pub. by Her Maj Station Ofc). UNIPUB.

Predicting the Properties of Mixtures. Lawrence E. Nielsen. 1978. 39.75 (ISBN 0-8247-6690-3). Dekker.

Predicting the Quality of Sand & Gravel Deposits in Area of Fluvioglacial Deposition. D. Chester. (Department of Geography, Research Paper: No. 10). 84p. 1982. pap. text ed. 7.95x (ISBN 0-85323-414-0, Pub. by Liverpool U Pr). Humanities.

Predicting the Quality of Teaching: The Predictive Value of Certain Traits for Effectiveness in Teaching. Arthur L. Odenweller. LC 72-177130. (Columbia University. Teachers College. Contributions to Education: No. 676). Repr. of 1936 ed. 22.50 (ISBN 0-404-55676-0). AMS Pr.

Predicting Tillage Effects on Soil Physical Properties & Processes. Ed. by P. W. Unger & J. M. Van Doren, Jr. (ASA Special Publication Ser.). 198p. 1982. pap. 10.00 (ISBN 0-89118-069-9). Am Soc Agron.

Predicting Your Future. The Diagram Group. 128p. 1983. pap. 7.95 (ISBN 0-345-33579-1). Ballantine.

Prediction & Assessment of Antibiotic Clinical Efficacy. F. O'Grady. (Beecham Colloquia Ser.). 203p. 1987. 45.00 (ISBN 0-12-524755-9). Acad Pr.

Preface to Social Economics. John M. Clark. LC 67-28453. 1967. Repr. of 1936 ed. 45.00x (ISBN 0-678-00333-5). Kelley.
Preface to T. S. Eliot. Ron Tamplin. (Preface Bks.). 192p. Date not set. pap. text ed. 10.95 (ISBN 0-582-35191-X). Longman.
Preface to the Magic Flute. E. M. Batley. 176p. 1981. 35.00x (ISBN 0-234-77205-0, Pub. by Dobson Bks England). State Mutual Bk.
Preface to the 'Nibelungenlied' Theodore M. Andersson. LC 86-28064. 320p. 1987. 35.00x (ISBN 0-8047-1362-6). Stanford U Pr.
Preface to the Nibelungenlied. Theodore M. Andersson. 1987. 35.00. Stanford U Pr.
Preface to Urban Economics. Wilbur Thompson. LC 68-4313. pap. 107.80 (ISBN 0-317-20607-9, 2024148). Bks Demand UMI.
Preface to Well Being. Joseph R. Narot. pap. 1.00 (ISBN 0-686-15806-7). Rostrum Bks.
Preface to Wills, Trusts & Administration. Paul G. Haskell. (University Textbook Ser.). 308p. 1987. text ed. 17.95 (ISBN 0-88277-561-8). Foundation Pr.
Preface to Wordsworth. 2nd ed. John Purkis. (Preface Bks). (Illus.). 1986. pap. text ed. 10.95 (ISBN 0-582-35482-X). Longman.
Prefaces. J. Frank Dobie. 212p. 1982. pap. 7.95 (ISBN 0-292-76461-8). U of Tex Pr.
Prefaces & Essays. George E. Saintsbury. LC 72-99722. (Essay Index Reprint Ser). 1933. 25.00 (ISBN 0-8369-1377-9). Ayer Co Pubs.
Prefaces by Bernard Shaw. George Bernard Shaw. LC 71-145294. 1971. Repr. of 1934 ed. 95.00x (ISBN 0-403-00785-2). Scholarly.
Prefaces by Bernard Shaw. George Bernard Shaw. 1988. Repr. of 1934 ed. lib. bdg. 150.00x. Am Biog Serv.
Prefaces by Leigh Hunt, Mainly to His Periodicals. Leigh Hunt. Ed. by R. B. Johnson. LC 67-27610. 1967. Repr. of 1927 ed. 21.00x (ISBN 0-8046-0230-1, Pub. by Kennikat). Assoc Faculty Pr.
Prefaces by Leigh Hunt: Mainly to His Periodicals. Ed. by R. B. Johnson. 147p. 1982. Repr. of 1927 ed. lib. bdg. 50.00 (ISBN 0-89987-432-0). Darby Bks.
Prefaces, Introductions & Other Uncollected Papers. Anatole France. LC 74-108698. (Essay & General Literature Index Reprint Ser). 1970. Repr. of 1927 ed. 23.00x (ISBN 0-8046-0919-5, Pub. by Kennikat). Assoc Faculty Pr.
Prefaces to Byron. Leslie A. Marchand. 131p. 1980. Repr. of 1979 ed. lib. bdg. 39.00 (ISBN 0-8414-5876-6). Folcroft.
Prefaces to Contemporaries, 1882-1920. William D. Howells. LC 57-6416. 1978. Repr. 40.00x (ISBN 0-8201-1238-0). Schol Facsimiles.
Prefaces to Liberty: Selected Writings of John Stuart Mill. Ed. by Bernard Wishy. LC 83-6527. 380p. 1983. pap. text ed. 15.00 (ISBN 0-8191-3189-X). U Pr of Amer.
Prefaces to Shakespeare. Harley Granville-Barker. Incl. Vol. 1. Hamlet, King Lear, the Merchant of Venice, Anthony & Cleopatra, Cymbeline. pap. 16.95x (ISBN 0-691-01350-0); Vol. 2. Othello, Coriolanus, Julius Caesar, Romeo & Juliet, Love's Labor Lost. pap. 11.50x (ISBN 0-691-01351-9). Princeton U Pr.
Prefaces to Shakespeare: Caesar, Anthony & Cleopatra. Harley Granville-Barker. 160p. 1982. pap. 14.95 (ISBN 0-7134-4511-4, Pub. by Batsford England). David & Charles.
Prefaces to Shakespeare: Coriolanus. Harley Granville-Barker. 160p. 1982. pap. 14.95 (ISBN 0-7134-4328-6, Pub. by Batsford England). David & Charles.
Prefaces to Shakespeare: Cymbeline - The Winter's Tale. Harley Granville-Barker. (Prefaces to Shakespeare Ser.). 104p. 1985. pap. 14.95 (ISBN 0-7134-4836-9, Pub. by Batsford England). David & Charles.
Prefaces to Shakespeare: King Lear & Macbeth. Harley Granville-Barker. 160p. 1982. pap. 14.95 (ISBN 0-7134-4512-2, Pub. by Batsford England). David & Charles.
Prefaces to Shakespeare: Love's Labour's Lost, The Merchant of Venice, Romeo & Juliet. Harley Granville-Barker. 160p. 1982. pap. 14.95 (ISBN 0-7134-4330-8, Pub. by Batsford England). David & Charles.
Prefaces to Shakespeare: Vol. 6, a Winter's Tale, Twelfth Night, Midsummer Night's Dream, Macbeth, from Henry V to Hamlet. Harley Granville-Barker. 176p. 1974. pap. 14.95 (ISBN 0-7134-2791-4, Pub. by Batsford England). David & Charles.
Prefaces to Shakespeare's Plays. A. L. Rowse. 256p. 1986. 18.95 (ISBN 0-85613-653-0). Salem Hse Pubs.
Prefaces to the Experience of Literature. Lionel Trilling. LC 79-1850. 352p. 1981. 12.95 (ISBN 0-15-173915-3); pap. 8.95. HarBraceJ.
Prefaces to the Waverley Novels. Walter Scott. Ed. by Mark A. Weinstein. LC 78-2710. xviii, 269p. 1978. 23.95x (ISBN 0-8032-4700-1). U of Nebr Pr.
Prefaces Without Books: Prefaces & Introductions to Thirty Books. Christopher Morley. Ed. by Herman Abromson. LC 76-14891. (Illus.). 1970. 7.50 (ISBN 0-87959-062-9). U of Tex H Ransom Ctr.
Prefatory Epistles of Jacques Lefevre d'Etaples & Related Texts. Eugene F. Rice, Jr. LC 71-123577. 480p. 1972. 50.00x (ISBN 0-231-03163-7). Columbia U Pr.
Prefect in French Public Administration. Howard Machin. LC 76-27185. 1977. 26.00x (ISBN 0-312-63805-1). St Martin.
Preference Laws for Syllable Structure & the Explanation of Sound Change: With Special Reference to German, Germanic, Italian, & Latin. Theo Vennemann. 96p. 1988. pap. text ed. 8.25 (ISBN 0-89925-411-X). De Gruyter.
Preference Modelling. M. Roubens & P. Vincke. (Lecture Notes in Economics & Mathematical Sciences Ser.: Vol. 250). (Illus.). viii, 94p. 1985. pap. 13.50 (ISBN 0-387-15685-2). Springer-Verlag.
Preference, Production & Capital: Selected Papers of Hirofumi Uzawa. Hirofumi Uzawa. (Illus.). 319p. Date not set. price not set (ISBN 0-521-36174-5). Cambridge U Pr.
Preference Reversals. Paul Slovic. (Working Papers on Risk & Rationality). Date not set. 2.50 (RR2). IPPP.
Preferences. Julien Gracq. 256p. 1961. 27.50 (ISBN 0-686-54024-7). French & Eur.
Preferences, Uncertainty, & Optimality. John S. Chipman et al. 288p. 1988. 55.00 (ISBN 0-8133-0723-6). Westview.
Preferential Tax Treatment of Fringe Benefits & the Form of Employee Compensation. Robert W. Turner. Date not set. price not set. Intl Found Employ.
Preferential Treatment in Public Employment & Equality of Opportunity. S. S. Gupta. 242p. 1979. 90.00x (ISBN 0-317-54692-9, Pub. by Eastern Bk India). State Mutual Bk.
Preferential Treatment of the Actual Settler in the Primary Disposition of the Vacant Lands in the United States to 1841. Henry W. Tatter. Ed. by Stuart Bruchey. LC 78-53568. (Development of Public Land Law in the U. S. Ser.). 1979. lib. bdg. 32.50x (ISBN 0-405-11367-6). Ayer Co Pubs.
Preferred Accounting Practices for State Governments. 240p. 1983. pap. 14.95 (ISBN 0-87292-035-6, C-5). Coun State Govts.
Preferred Dwelling Plan. 2nd ed. 1987. pap. 24.95 (ISBN 0-85139-246-6). Van Nos Reinhold.
Preferred Orientation in Deformed Materials. Ed. by Hans Rudolf Wenk. 1985. 70.50 (ISBN 0-12-744020-8). Acad Pr.
Preferred Provider Organizations & Alternative Health Care Delivery Systems. 167p. 1984. 45.00 (ISBN 0-318-03926-5, 275). PA Bar Inst.
Preferred Provider Organizations: Planning, Structure & Operation. Dale H. Cowan. 320p. 1984. 50.95 (ISBN 0-89443-593-0). Aspen Pub.
Preferred Resources. (Illus.). 288p. 1989. pap. 14.95. QED Pubns.
Preferred Risk. Frederik Pohl. pap. 1.95 (ISBN 0-345-28575-1, Del Rey). Ballantine.
Preferred Wisdom of Elementary Schools. 52p. 4.00 (ISBN 0-318-17474-X); members 2.00 (ISBN 0-318-17475-8). Mid St Coll & Schl.
Prefiguration. Frank Samperi. 1971. 15.00 (ISBN 0-685-78985-3, Pub. by Mushinsha Bks). Small Pr Dist.
Prefiguration et structure romanesque dans A la recherche du temps perdu. Marcel Muller. LC 78-73096. (French Forum Monographs: 14). (Illus.). 95p. (Orig.). 1979. pap. 9.95x (ISBN 0-917058-13-5). French Forum.
Prefigurations in Meistergesang. Clarence W. Friedman. LC 75-140020. (Catholic University of America Studies in German Ser.: No. 18). Repr. of 1943 ed. 22.00 (ISBN 0-404-50238-5). AMS Pr.
Prefigurative Imagination of John Keats: A Study of the Beauty-Truth Identification & Its Implications. Newell F. Ford. LC 74-24643. (Stanford University. Stanford Studies in Language & Literature: No. 2). Repr. of 1951 ed. 18.00 (ISBN 0-404-51818-4). AMS Pr.
Prefixes & Other Word-Initial Elements of English. Ed. by Christine N. Donohue & Laurence Urdang. LC 83-20662. 536p. 1983. 80.00x (ISBN 0-8103-1548-3). Gale.
Prefixes, Bases, & Suffixes. Barbara Gregorich. (Horizons II Ser.). (Illus.). 24p. (gr. 3-4). 1980. wkbk. 2.50 (ISBN 0-89403-600-9). EDC.
Prefrontal Cortex: Anatomy, Physiology, & Neuropsychology of the Frontal Lobe. 2nd ed. Joaquin M. Fuster. 320p. 1988. text ed. price not set (ISBN 0-88167-466-4). Raven.
Preg-Not: A Guide for Modern Women. rev. ed. pap. 1.50 (ISBN 0-89230-179-1). Do it Now.
Pregare in Certosa Oggi. Mario Giacometti. Ed. by James Hogg. (Analecta Cartusiana Ser.: No. 97). 141p. (Orig.). 1980. pap. 25.00 (ISBN 3-7052-0168-9, Pub. by Salzburg Studies). Longwood Pub Group.
Pregnancy: A Psychological & Social Study. Ed. by Stephen Wolkind & Eva Zajicek. 228p. 1981. 35.50 (ISBN 0-8089-1411-1, 794897). Grune.
Pregnancy: A Time for Caring. Ed. by John Gallagher. (Illus.). 150p. (Orig.). 1988. 6.95. St Marys Hospt.
Pregnancy after Thirty. Mary Anderson. 128p. (Orig.). 1984. pap. 7.95 (ISBN 0-571-13355-X). Faber & Faber.
Pregnancy after Thirty-Five. Carole S. McCauley. 1983. pap. 3.95 (ISBN 0-671-49704-9). PB.
Pregnancy after Thirty-Five. Carole S. McCauley. 224p. 1987. pap. 3.95 (ISBN 0-317-59883-X). PB.
Pregnancy after Thirty Workbook: A Program for Safe Childbearing-No Matter What Your Age. Ed. by Gail S. Brewer. (Illus.). 1978. pap. 11.95 (ISBN 0-87857-215-5). Rodale Pr Inc.
Pregnancy & Abortion in Adolescence: Report. WHO Meeting. Geneva, 1974. (Technical Report Ser.: No. 583). (Also avail. in French & Spanish). 1975. pap. 2.40 (ISBN 92-4-120583-0). World Health.
Pregnancy & Birth. Ed. by Dale C. Garell & Solomon H. Snyder. (Encyclopedia of Health Ser.). (Illus.). (YA) (gr. 7-12). 1989. 17.95 (ISBN 0-7910-0040-0). Chelsea Hse.
Pregnancy & Childbearing During Adolescence: Research Priorities for the 1980's. Elizabeth R. McAnarney & Gabriel Stickle. LC 81-11756. (Birth Defects: Original Article Ser.: Vol. 17, No. 3). 186p. 1981. 31.00 (ISBN 0-8451-1043-8). A R Liss.
Pregnancy & Childbirth. Tracy Hotchner. 720p. 1984. pap. 7.95 (ISBN 0-380-43083-5). Avon.
Pregnancy & Childbirth: As They Grow. Parents Magazine Editors. (Orig.). 1986. pap. 6.95 (ISBN 0-345-32170-7). Ballantine.
Pregnancy & Childbirth: The Complete Guide for a New Life. Tracy Hotchner. 736p. (Orig.). 1988. pap. 10.95 (ISBN 0-380-87635-3). Avon.
Pregnancy & Employment. 210p. 1987. 65.00 (ISBN 0-87179-936-7). BNA.
Pregnancy & Life-Style Habits. Peter Fried. LC 83-2650. 240p. 1983. 9.95 (ISBN 0-8253-0151-3). Beaufort Bks NY.
Pregnancy & Motherhood Diary: Planning the First Year of Your Second Career. Susan S. Stautberg. 1987. pap. 12.95 (ISBN 0-942361-00-8, Dist. by Kampmann). MasterMedia Ltd.
Pregnancy & Nutrition: The Complete D.I.E.T. Guide see D. I. E. T. During Pregnancy: The Complete Guide & Calendar.
Pregnancy & Parenting. Phyllis M. Stern. (Health Care for Women International Ser.). 200p. 1988. 29.95 (ISBN 0-89116-846-X). Hemisphere Pub.
Pregnancy & Parenting Program. Kathy M. Johnson. (Illus.). 423p. 1987. teacher's manual 250.00 (ISBN 0-9616488-2-1). Alef Bet Comns.
Pregnancy & Sports Fitness. Lynne Pirie & Lindsay Curtis. 1987. 12.95 (ISBN 1-55561-001-3). Fisher Bks.
Pregnancy & Work. Jean G. Fitzpatrick. 256p. 1984. pap. 7.95 (ISBN 0-380-88666-9, 88666-9). Avon.
Pregnancy As a Disease: The Pill in Society. Donald H. Merkin. 1976. 18.95x (ISBN 0-8046-9138-X, Pub. by Kennikat). Assoc Faculty Pr.
Pregnancy as Healing see Cesarean Birth: Risk & Culture.
Pregnancy As Healing: Holistic Philosophy for Prenatal Care, Vol. 1. Gayle Peterson & Lewis Mehl. (Mind & Matter Ser.). (Illus.). 318p. 1984. pap. 12.95 (ISBN 0-939508-04-4). Mindbody.
Pregnancy at Work. Noreen Burrows. (Medico-Legal Issue Ser.: Vol. 4). 1989. text ed. 40.00x (ISBN 0-566-05362-4, Pub. by Gower Pub England). Gower Pub Co.
Pregnancy, Birth & Family Planning. Alan F. Guttmacher. 1984. pap. 9.95 (ISBN 0-452-25536-8, Plume). NAL.
Pregnancy, Birth & Family Planning. Alan F. Guttmacher. Rev. by Irwin H. Kaiser. 1986. 18.95 (ISBN 0-525-24420-4). Dutton.
Pregnancy, Birth & Family Planning. rev. ed. Alan F. Guttmacher. 1986. pap. 9.95 (ISBN 0-452-25827-8, Plume). NAL.
Pregnancy, Birth & Family Planning. Alan F. Guttmacher & Irwin H. Kaiser. 1987. pap. 4.95 (ISBN 0-451-14762-6, Sig). NAL.
Pregnancy, Birth, & Parenthood: Adaptations of Mothers, Fathers, & Infants. Frances K. Grossman et al. LC 80-16518. (Social & Behavioral Science Ser.). 1980. text ed. 32.95x (ISBN 0-87589-465-8). Jossey-Bass.
Pregnancy, Birth & the Early Months: A Complete Guide. Richard I. Feinbloom & Betty Yetta Forman. LC 87-1758. (Illus.). 384p. 1987. write for info. (ISBN 0-201-10805-4); pap. 9.95 (ISBN 0-201-10925-5). Addison-Wesley.
Pregnancy Book for Today's Woman. Shapiro. (Illus.). 462p. 1988. write for info. (ISBN 0-06-055083-X, Lippincott Medical); pap. 12.95 (ISBN 0-06-091059-3, Lippincott Medical). Lippincott.
Pregnancy Book for Today's Woman: An Obstetrician Answers All Your Questions about Pregnancy & Childbirth & Some You May Not Have Considered. Howard I. Shapiro. LC 80-7916. (Illus.). 448p. 1983. 17.45i (ISBN 0-06-181766-X, HarpT). Har-Row.
Pregnancy Book for Today's Woman: An Obstetrician Answers All Your Questions about Pregnancy & Childbirth & Some You May Not Have Considered. Howard I. Shapiro. LC 80-7916. (Illus.). 448p. 1983. pap. 12.95 (CN1059, PL). Har-Row.
Pregnancy Care. rev. ed. Gloria M. Bertacchi. 84p. 1988. pap. text ed. 4.95 (ISBN 0-945753-05-5). Natl Med Seminars.
Pregnancy Care for the 1980's: Based on Conference Held at the Royal Society of Medicine. Ed. by Luke Zander & Geoffrey Chamberlain. (Illus.). 295p. 1984. pap. text ed. 19.95x (ISBN 0-333-33346-2). Sheridan Med Bks.
Pregnancy, Childbirth & Parenthood. P. Ahmed. (Coping with Medical Issues Ser.: Vol. 2). 414p. 1981. 57.25 (ISBN 0-444-00558-7, Biomedical Pr). Elsevier.
Pregnancy, Childbirth, & the Newborn. Penny Simkin et al. Ed. by Tom Grady. LC 83-21941. (Illus.). 288p. (Orig.). 1984. pap. 9.95 (ISBN 0-671-54498-5). Meadowbrook.
Pregnancy, Children, & the Vegan Diet. Michael Klaper. Ed. by Cynthia Klaper. 1988. write for info. (ISBN 0-9614248-2-6). Gentle World.
Pregnancy Day-by-Day Book. Colleen Darragh. (Illus.). 192p. 1983. 10.45i (ISBN 0-06-015152-8, HarpT). Har-Row.
Pregnancy, Diabetes & Birth: A Management Guide. Dorothy R. Hollingsworth. 192p. 1984. lib. bdg. 39.95 (ISBN 0-683-04102-9). Williams & Wilkins.
Pregnancy Exercise Book. Barbara Dale & Johanna Roeber. 1982. pap. 7.95 (ISBN 0-394-71119-X). Pantheon.
Pregnancy Hypertension: A Systematic Evaluation of Clinical Diagnostic Criteria. E. A. Friedman & R. K. Neff. LC 76-45951. 268p. 1977. 36.00 (ISBN 0-88416-185-4). PSG Pub Co.
Pregnancy in the Executive Suite. Valerie Lee. LC 87-61045. 224p. 1988. 19.95 (ISBN 0-944315-00-3). Success Pubns.
Pregnancy Journal. Marcy Jackson & Mark Brokering. 1985. 9.95 (ISBN 0-394-54361-0). Random.
Pregnancy Loss: Medical Therapeutics & Practical Considerations. James Woods & Jenifer Esposite. (Illus.). 392p. 1987. 29.95 (ISBN 0-683-09256-1). Williams & Wilkins.
Pregnancy Metabolism, Diabetes & the Fetus. Symposium on Pregnancy Metabolism, Diabetes, & the Fetus (1978: London, England) LC 78-32046. (Ciba Foundation Symposium New Ser.: No. 63). pap. 83.50 (2014648). Bks Demand UMI.
Pregnancy Nine to Five. Susan Strautberg. 1985. pap. 7.95 (ISBN 0-671-52413-5, Pub. by Fireside). S&S.
Pregnancy Nutrition. Joyce Sorenson & Nancy Murray. (Menus for Better Health Ser.). 36p. (Orig.). 1982. pap. cancelled (ISBN 0-911638-12-1). Witkower.
Pregnancy Organizer. Arlene Eisenberg et al. 192p. 1986. 25.00 (ISBN 0-89480-058-2). Workman Pub.
Pregnancy Planner: What You Have to Know, Remember, & Track Each Week of Your Pregnancy. Barbara C. Costa & Judith S. Ron. 112p. (Orig.). 1986. pap. 8.95 (ISBN 0-688-05839-6, Quill). Morrow.
Pregnancy Proteins: Biology, Chemistry & Clinical Application (Australia) Ed. by J. B. Grudzinskas & M. Seppala. 474p. 1982. 72.50 (ISBN 0-12-304850-8). Acad Pr.
Pregnancy Proteins in Animals: Proceedings of the International Meeting, Copenhagen, Denmark, April 22-24, 1985. Ed. by Jann Hau. (Illus.). xi, 536p. 1986. lib. bdg. 181.00 (ISBN 0-89925-213-3). De Gruyter.
Pregnancy Testing. David J. Gerrick. (Illus.). 1978. 20.00 (ISBN 0-916750-46-9). Dayton Labs.
Pregnancy: The Best State of the Union. Waldo L. Fielding. LC 76-2152. (Illus.). 184p. 1976. pap. 6.95 (ISBN 0-87027-147-4). Cumberland Pr.
Pregnancy Workbook. Ellen K. Anderson. (Illus.). 96p. (Orig.). 1983. pap. 8.95 (ISBN 0-939374-01-3). Homefront Graphics.
Pregnant Adolescent: Problems of Premature Parenthood. Frank G. Bolton, Jr. LC 79-27082. (Sage Library of Social Research: Vol. 100). (Illus.). 247p. 1980. 35.00 (ISBN 0-8039-1433-4); pap. 16.95 (ISBN 0-8039-1434-2). Sage.
Pregnant & Beautiful. Lindsay Curtis et al. LC 84-62550. 240p. 1985. pap. 8.95 (ISBN 0-89586-366-9). Price Stern.
Pregnant & Lovin' It. Lindsay R. Curtis & Yvonne Coroles. LC 77-82012. (Illus.). 1977. pap. 6.95 (ISBN 0-912656-82-4). Price Stern.
Pregnant & Lovin' It. rev. ed. Lindsay R. Curtis & Yvonne Coroles. (Illus.). 228p. 1988. pap. 6.95 (ISBN 0-89586-763-X). Price Stern.
Pregnant & Prepared: A Guide to Preparing for Childbirth. Susan O'Halloran. (Avery's Childbirth Education Ser.). (Illus.). 144p. 1984. pap. text ed. 7.95 plastic comb (ISBN 0-89529-250-5). Avery Pub.
Pregnant by Mistake: The Stories of Seventeen Women. Katrina Maxtone-Graham. 456p. 1988. 21.95; pap. 12.95. Remi Bks.
Pregnant Fathers: Making the Best of the Father's Role Before, During, & after Childbirth. Jack Heinowitz. LC 81-21147. (Transformation Ser.). 126p. 1982. (Spec); pap. 6.95 (ISBN 0-13-694927-4, Spec). P-H.
Pregnant Feelings. Rahima Baldwin & Terra Palmarini. LC 85-62305. (Illus.). 208p. (Orig.). 1986. pap. 10.95 (ISBN 0-89087-423-9). Celestial Arts.
Pregnant Is Beautiful. Ronald M. Caplan. (Orig.). 1985. pap. 3.95 (ISBN 0-671-53259-6). PB.
Pregnant Pause or Love's Labor Lost. Georges Feydeau. Tr. by Norman R. Shapiro from Fr. (Tour De Farce Ser.: Vol. 1). 96p. (Orig.). 1987. pap. 5.95 (ISBN 0-936839-58-9). Applause Theatre Bk Pubs.
Pregnant Surgical Patient. Ed. by Jeffrey M. Baden & Jay B. Brodsky. (Illus.). 272p. 1985. monograph 36.00 (ISBN 0-87993-238-4). Futura Pub.

Prehistoric Monsters Did the Strangest Things. Leonora Hornblow & Arthur Hornblow. LC 73-9348. (Illus.). 72p. 1974. 5.95 (ISBN 0-394-82051-7, BYR); lib. bdg. 8.99 (ISBN 0-394-92051-1). Random.

Prehistoric Native American Art of Mud Glyph Cave. Ed. by Charles H. Faulkner. LC 86-1697. (Illus.). 136p. 1986. 12.95 (ISBN 0-87049-505-4). U of Tenn Pr.

Prehistoric New Mexico: Background for Survey. David E. Stuart & Rory P. Gauthier. (Illus.). 472p. 1988. pap. 19.95 (ISBN 0-8263-1066-4). U of NM Pr.

Prehistoric Occupation of Chavin de Huantar, Peru. Richard L. Burger. LC 83-1389. (UC Publications in Anthropology: Vol. 14). 436p. 1984. pap. 33.00x (ISBN 0-520-09667-3). U of Cal Pr.

Prehistoric Occupation Patterns in Southwest Wyoming & Cultural Relationships with the Great Basin & Plains Culture Areas. Floyd W. Sharrock. (Utah Anthropological Papers: No. 77). Repr. of 1966 ed. 24.00 (ISBN 0-404-60677-6). AMS Pr.

Prehistoric Occupation Patterns in Southwest Wyoming & Cultural Relationships in the Great Basin & Plains Culture Areas. Floyd W. Sharrock. (University of Utah Anthropological Papers: No. 77). 1966. pap. 15.00x (ISBN 0-87480-144-3). U of Utah Pr.

Prehistoric Patterns of Human Behavior: A Case Study in the Mississippi Valley. Bruce D. Smith. (Studies in Archeology Ser.). 1978. 24.95 (ISBN 0-12-650650-7). Acad Pr.

Prehistoric People. Laurence Santrey. LC 84-8464. (Illus.). 32p. (gr. 3-6). 1985. PLB 8.45 (ISBN 0-8167-0242-X); pap. text ed. 1.95 (ISBN 0-8167-0243-8). Troll Assocs.

Prehistoric People. Ovid Wong. (True Bks.). (gr. 5-9). 1988. pap. 3.95 (ISBN 0-317-69618-1). Childrens.

Prehistoric Peoples of Maine. Ed. by William H. Soule. (Illus.). 66p. 1970. looseleaf tchrs' ed. 2.00 (ISBN 0-913764-02-7). Maine St Mus.

Prehistoric Peoples of Minnesota. rev. ed. Elden Johnson. LC 87-32663. (Illus.). 35p. (YA) (gr. 9-12). 1988. pap. 3.95 (ISBN 0-87351-223-5). Minn Hist.

Prehistoric Peoples of Scotland. Ed. by Stuart Piggott. LC 80-27371. (Studies in Ancient History & Archaeology). (Illus.). ix, 165p. 1981. Repr. of 1962 ed. lib. bdg. 35.00x (ISBN 0-313-22916-3, PIPR). Greenwood.

Prehistoric Peoples of Southern Illinois. James S. Penny, Jr. (Illus.). ix, 70p. (Orig.). 1986. pap. 3.50 (ISBN 0-88104-062-2). Center Archaeo.

Prehistoric Period in South Africa. J. P. Johnson. 1977. lib. bdg. 59.95 (ISBN 0-8490-2468-4). Gordon Pr.

Prehistoric Pinkerton. Steven Kellogg. LC 86-2201. (Illus.). 32p. (ps-3). 1987. 12.95 (ISBN 0-8037-0322-8, 01258-370); PLB 12.89 (ISBN 0-8037-0323-6). Dial Bks Young.

Prehistoric Political Dynamics: A Case Study From the American Southwest. Kent G. Lightfoot. LC 83-25079. 193p. 1984. 25.00 (ISBN 0-87580-097-1). N Ill U Pr.

Prehistoric Pottery Analysis & the Ceramics of Barton Ramie in the Belize Valley. James C. Gifford. LC 75-40772. (Peabody Museum Memoirs: Vol. 18). 1976. pap. 35.00x (ISBN 0-87365-691-1). Peabody Harvard.

Prehistoric Pottery in China. G. D. Wu. 180p. 1939. 665.00x (ISBN 0-317-45184-7, Pub. by Han-Shan Tang Ltd). State Mutual Bk.

Prehistoric Pottery in the Collection from El Acebuchal: Site near Carmona, Province of Sevilla. A. W. Frothingham. (Illus.). 1953. pap. 0.60 (ISBN 0-87535-075-5). Hispanic Soc.

Prehistoric Production & Exchange: The Aegean & Eastern Mediterranean. Ed. by A. Bernard Knapp & Tamara Stech. (Monograph xxv). (Illus.). 133p. (Orig.). 1985. pap. 13.00x (ISBN 0-917956-49-4). UCLA Arch.

Prehistoric Pueblo Settlement Patterns: The Arroyo Hondo, New Mexico, Site Survey. D. Bruce Dickson. LC 79-21542. (Arroyo Hondo Archaeological Ser.: Vol. 2). (Illus.). 151p. 1980. pap. 10.00 (ISBN 0-933452-02-0). Schol Am Res.

Prehistoric Quarries & Lithic Production. Ed. by Jonathon E. Ericson & Barbara A. Purdy. LC 83-18822. (New Directions in Archaeology Ser.). (Illus.). 170p. 1984. 44.50 (ISBN 0-521-25622-4). Cambridge U Pr.

Prehistoric Relics. facs. ed. Warren K. Moorehead. (Shorey Historical Ser.). (Illus.). 165p. pap. 10.95 (ISBN 0-8466-0157-5, S157). Shorey.

Prehistoric Religion in Greece. J. V. Leuven. (Illus.). 280p. 1987. lib. bdg. 84.00x (ISBN 0-317-54494-2, Pub. by A. M. Hakkert). Coronet Bks.

Prehistoric Reptiles of the Sea & Air: Text Editions. Joseph Gabriele. (Illus.). 32p. (gr. 1-3). 1985. pap. 1.95 (ISBN 0-911211-58-6, Pub. by Know & Show Bks). Penny Lane Pubns.

Prehistoric Rock Art of Nevada & Eastern California. Robert F. Heizer & Martin A. Baumhoff. LC 62-13074. (Illus.). 430p. 1976. 60.00x (ISBN 0-520-02911-9); pap. 16.95 (ISBN 0-520-05324-9). U of Cal Pr.

Prehistoric Rock Pictures in Europe & Africa. Leo Frobenius & Douglas C. Fox. LC 74-169302. (The Museum of Modern Art Publications in Reprint from Arno Press). (Illus.). 80p. 1972. Repr. of 1937 ed. 17.00 (ISBN 0-405-01561-5). Ayer Co Pubs.

Prehistoric Ruins of Copan, Honduras: A Preliminary Report of the Explorations by Museum, 1891-1895. G. B. Gordon. (HU PMM). Repr. of 1896 ed. 34.00 (ISBN 0-527-01150-9). Kraus Repr.

Prehistoric Ruins of Tikal, Guatemala see Explorations in the Department of Peten, Guatemala.

Prehistoric Sea Life: An Educational Coloring Book. Spizzirri Publishing Co. Staff. Ed. by Linda Spizzirri. (Illus.). 32p. (gr. 1-8). 1981. pap. 1.49 (ISBN 0-86545-020-X). Spizzirri.

Prehistoric Settlement & Physical Environment in the Mesa Verde Area. Joyce Herold. (Utah Anthropological Papers: No. 53). Repr. of 1961 ed. 38.00 (ISBN 0-404-60653-9). AMS Pr.

Prehistoric Settlement & Trade Models in the Santa Clara Valley, California. Judith C. Bergthold. x, 328p. 1985. pap. text ed. 22.00x (ISBN 1-55567-017-2). Coyote Press.

Prehistoric Settlement Patterns: Essays in Honor of Gordon R. Willey. Ed. by Evon Z. Vogt & Richard M. Leventhal. LC 83-1342. (Illus.). 543p. 1983. 42.50x (ISBN 0-8263-0691-8). U of NM Pr.

Prehistoric Settlement Patterns in Clay County, Mississippi. John T. Sparks. (Mississippi Department of Archives & History Archaeological Reports). (Illus.). 65p. (Orig.). 1987. pap. 5.00 (ISBN 0-938896-52-0). Mississippi Archives.

Prehistoric Settlement Patterns in the New World. Gordon R. Wiley. LC 81-13233. (Viking Fund Publications in Anthropology Ser.: No. 23). viii, 202p. 1982. Repr. of 1956 ed. lib. bdg. 35.00 (ISBN 0-313-23223-7, WIPE). Greenwood.

Prehistoric Settlement Patterns in the Libyan Desert. James J. Hester & Philip M. Hobler. (Nubian Ser.: No. 4). Repr. of 1969 ed. 44.00 (ISBN 0-404-60692-X, UAP NO. 92). AMS Pr.

Prehistoric Settlement Patterns in the Southern Valley of Mexico: The Chalco-Xochimilco Report. Jeffrey R. Parsons et al. (Memoir Ser.: No. 14). (Orig.). 1982. pap. 16.00x (ISBN 0-932206-88-3). U Mich Mus Anthro.

Prehistoric Settlement Patterns in the Texcoco Region, Mexico. Jeffrey R. Parsons. (Memoirs Ser.: No. 3). (Illus.). 1971. pap. 8.00x (ISBN 0-932206-65-4). U Mich Mus Anthro.

Prehistoric Settlement-Subsistence Relationships in the Fishing River Drainage Western Missouri. Terrell L. Martin. Ed. by Robert T. Bray. (Missouri Archaeologist Ser.: Vol. 37). (Illus.). 170p. (Orig.). 1976. pap. 6.00 (ISBN 0-943414-54-7). MO Arch Soc.

Prehistoric Slavic Contraction. Jiri Marvan. Tr. by Wilson Gray. LC 78-23498. (Illus.). 1979. text ed. 24.95x (ISBN 0-271-00210-7). Pa St U Pr.

Prehistoric Social, Political, & Economic Development in the Area of the Tehuacan Valley: Some Results of the Palo Blanco Project. Ed. by Robert D. Drennan. (Technical Reports Ser.: No. 11; Contribution 6 in Research Reports in Archaeology). (Illus., Orig.). 1979. pap. 6.50x (ISBN 0-932206-82-4). U Mich Mus Anthro.

Prehistoric Southern Ozark Marginality: A Myth Exposed. James A. Brown. Ed. by W. Raymond Wood. LC 83-63187. (Special Publications Ser.: No. 6). (Illus.). 85p. (Orig.). 1984. pap. 5.00 (ISBN 0-943414-18-0). MO Arch Soc.

Prehistoric Southwestern Craft Arts. Clara L. Tanner. LC 75-19865. (Illus.). 226p. 1976. 27.50 (ISBN 0-8165-0582-9). U of Ariz Pr.

Prehistoric Southwesterners from Basketmaker to Pueblo. Charles A. Amsden. LC 76-43642. Repr. of 1949 ed. 25.00 (ISBN 0-404-15477-8). AMS Pr.

Prehistoric Southwesterners from Basketmaker to Pueblo. Charles A. Amsden. xiv, 163p. 1976. pap. 5.00 (ISBN 0-916561-57-7). Southwest Mus.

Prehistoric Stone Implements of Northeastern Arizona. R. B. Woodbury. (HU PMP). (Illus.). 1954. 32.00 (ISBN 0-527-01286-6). Kraus Repr.

Prehistoric Stone Technology on Northern Black Mesa, Arizona. William J. Parry & Andrew L. Christenson. LC 87-72676. (Occasional Paper Ser.: No. 12). (Illus.). 328p. (Orig.). 1987. pap. 23.00 (ISBN 0-88104-052-5). Center Archaeo.

Prehistoric Subsistence & Population Change along the Lower Agua Fria River, Arizona: A Model Simulation. Donald E. Dove. (No. 32). (Illus.). viii, 139p. 1984. 10.00 (ISBN 9-9951512-5-1). AZ Univ ARP.

Prehistoric Technology. S. A. Semenov. Tr. by M. W. Thompson. (Illus.). 181p. 1986. pap. 22.50x (ISBN 0-389-20571-0). B&N Imports.

Prehistoric Textiles of the Southwest. Kate P. Kent. LC 82-20313. (School of American Research Southwest Indian Arts Ser.). (Illus.). 335p. 1982. 50.00x (ISBN 0-8263-0591-1). U of NM Pr.

Prehistoric Thessaly. Alan J. Wace. LC 75-41286. Repr. of 1912 ed. 42.50 (ISBN 0-404-14734-8). AMS Pr.

Prehistoric Times. Brian M. Fagan. LC 82-24235. (Scientific American Readers Ser.). (Illus.). 320p. 1983. pap. text ed. 16.95 (ISBN 0-7167-1491-4). W H Freeman.

Prehistoric Trails of Atacama: Archaeology of Northern Chile. Ed. by Clement W. Meighan & D. L. True. (Monumenta Archaeologica: 7). (Illus.). 228p. 1980. 33.00x (ISBN 0-917956-10-9). UCLA Arch.

Prehistoric Tuberculosis in the Americas. Ed. by Jane E. Buikstra. LC 80-28660. (Scientific Papers Ser.: No.5). (Illus.). 194p. (Orig.). 1981. pap. 14.50 (ISBN 0-942118-10-3). Ctr Amer Arche.

Prehistoric Villages Castles & Towers of Southwestern Colorado. Jesse W. Fewkes. Repr. of 1919 ed. 29.00x (ISBN 0-403-03690-9). Scholarly.

Prehistoric Weapons in the Southwest. Stewart Peckham. (Illus.). 1965. pap. 1.50 (ISBN 0-89013-017-5). Museum NM Pr.

Prehistoric World. Michael Benton. (Illustrated Encyclopedia Ser.). (Illus.). 128p. (gr. 5-9). 1988. PLB 14.95 (ISBN 0-671-64492-0, Little Simon). S&S.

Prehistorical Site & the Black Earthern-Wares in Lian-Chu District, Hangchow. He Tianxing. 20p. 1937. 60.00x (ISBN 0-317-44171-X, Pub. by Han-Shan Tang Ltd). State Mutual Bk.

Prehistory. Jean-Jacques Barloy. (Focus on Science Ser.). (Illus.). 80p. 1987. pap. 4.95 (ISBN 0-8120-3835-5). Barron.

Prehistory. Keith Branigan. LC 84-50696. (History As Evidence Ser.). (Illus.). 40p. (gr. 4-9). 1986. lib. bdg. 12.40 (ISBN 0-531-03745-2). Watts.

Prehistory: An Introduction. Derek Roe. LC 70-81799. 1972. pap. 6.95 (ISBN 0-520-02252-1). U of Cal Pr.

Prehistory & Human Ecology of the Valley of Oaxaca: Memoirs, 1 vol, No. 10. Ed. by Kent V. Flannery & Richard Blanton. Incl. Part 1. Vegetational History of the Oaxaca Valley. C. Earle Smith; Part 2. Zapotec Plant Knowledge: Classification, Uses & Communication About Plants in Mitla, Oaxaca, Mexico. Ellen Messer. (Illus.). 1978. pap. 8.00x (ISBN 0-932206-72-7). U Mich Mus Anthro.

Prehistory & Palaeogeography of the Great Indian Desert. Ed. by Bridget Allchin et al. 1978. 106.00. Acad Pr.

Prehistory & Paleoecology of Guadalupe Ruin, New Mexico. Lonnie C. Pippin. (Anthropological Papers: No. 112). (Illus.). 272p. (Orig.). 1987. pap. text ed. 25.00x. U of Utah Pr.

Prehistory & Paleoenvironments in the Central Negev, Israel, Vol. II: The Avdat-Aqev, Pt. 2 & the Har Harif. Ed. by Anthony E. Marks. LC 75-40116. (Institute for the Study of Earth & Man: Reports of Investigations Ser.: No. 2). (Illus.). x, 368p. 1977. pap. 25.00x (ISBN 0-89643-000-6). SMU Press.

Prehistory & Paleoenvironments in the Central Negev, Israel, Vol. III: The Advat-Aqev Area, Pt.3. Ed. by Anthony E. Marks. LC 75-40116. (Institute for the Study of Earth & Man: Reports of Investigations Ser.: No. 2). (Illus.). xvi, 368p. 1983. pap. 35.00x (ISBN 0-89643-113-4). SMU Press.

Prehistory & Paleoenvironments in the Central Negev, Israel, Vol. 1: The Avdat-Aqev, Area, Part 1. Ed. by Anthony E. Marks. LC 75-40116. (Institute for the Study of Earth & Man - Reports of Investigations Ser.: No. 2). (Illus.). 392p. 1976. pap. 27.50x (ISBN 0-87074-153-5). SMU Press.

Prehistory & Prohistory of Eastern India. Ahmad Hasan Dani. 1981. 28.00x (ISBN 0-8364-0734-2, Pub. by Mukhopadhyay). South Asia Bks.

Prehistory & Protohistory to Eleven Hundred B.C. Ed. by George A. Christopoulos & John C. Bastias. Tr. by Philip Sherrard. LC 75-18610. (History of the Hellenic World Ser.: Vol. 1). (Illus.). 420p. 1975. 56.50 (ISBN 0-271-01199-8). Pa St U Pr.

Prehistory at Cambridge & Beyond. Grahame Clarke. (Illus.). 200p. Date not set. price not set (ISBN 0-521-35031-X). Cambridge U Pr.

Prehistory in Haiti: A Study in Method. Irving Rouse. LC 64-21834. (Yale University Publications in Anthropology Reprints Ser.: No. 21). 202p. 1964. pap. 15.00x (ISBN 0-87536-504-3). HRAFP.

Prehistory in the Navajo Reservoir District, 2 pts. Frank W. Eddy. (Illus.). 1966. pap. 8.95 ea. Pt. 1 (ISBN 0-89013-023-X). Pt. 2 (ISBN 0-89013-024-8). Museum NM Pr.

Prehistory in the Pacific Islands. J. Terrell. 1988. pap. 19.95 (ISBN 0-521-36956-8). Cambridge U Pr.

Prehistory in the Pacific Islands: A Study of Variation in Language, Customs & Human Biology. John E. Terrell. (New Studies in Archaeology). (Illus.). 300p. 1986. 47.50 (ISBN 0-521-30604-3). Cambridge U Pr.

Prehistory of Arid North Africa: Essays in Honor of Fred Wendorf. Ed. by Angela E. Close. LC 86-31510. (Illus.). 374p. 1987. 39.95x (ISBN 0-87074-222-1); pap. 19.95x (ISBN 0-87074-223-X). SMU Press.

Prehistory of Australia, New Guinea & Sahul: International Edition. Ed. by J. P. White & J. F. O'Connell. LC 81-71781. 1983. 24.95 (ISBN 0-12-746750-5). Acad Pr.

Prehistory of Chalchuapa, El Salvador, 3 vols. Ed. by Robert Sharer. LC 74-31606. (Orig.). 1978. Set. pap. 59.95 (ISBN 0-8122-7692-2). Vol. 1 (ISBN 0-8122-7689-2). Vol. 2 (ISBN 0-8122-7690-6). Vol. 3 (ISBN 0-8122-7691-4). U of Pa Pr.

Prehistory of Chalchuapa, El Salvador, 3 Vols. Ed. by Robert J. Sharer. (University Museum Monographs: No. 36). 1978. Set. pap. 45.00 (ISBN 0-318-01017-8); per volume 17.00 (ISBN 0-318-01018-6). Vol. 1: xv, 194 pp. Vol. 2: xx, 211 pp. Vol. 3: xvii, 226 pp. Univ Mus of U PA.

Prehistory of Denmark. Jorgen Jenson. LC 82-24885. 331p. 1983. 39.95x (ISBN 0-416-34190-X, NO. 3839); pap. 19.95x (ISBN 0-416-34200-0, NO. 3838). Routledge Chapman & Hall.

Prehistory of Dickson Mounds: The Dickson Excavation. rev. ed. Alan D. Harn. (Reports of Investigations Ser.: No. 35). (Illus.). 146p. 1980. pap. 6.00x (ISBN 0-89792-085-6). Ill St Museum.

Prehistory of Fishtrap, Kentucky. R. C. Dunnell. LC 72-90078. (Publications in Anthropology: No. 75). 1972. pap. 7.00 (ISBN 0-913516-08-2). Yale U Anthro.

Prehistory of Flight. Clive Hart. LC 84-8677. (Illus.). 279p. 1985. 40.00x (ISBN 0-520-05213-7). U of Cal Pr.

Prehistory of India. H. D. Sankalia. LC 77-906557. (Illus.). 1977. 16.50x (ISBN 0-89684-444-7). Orient Bk Dist.

Prehistory of Japan. C. Melvin Aikens & Takayasu Higuchi. LC 80-70596. (Studies in Archaeology). 1981. 39.50 (ISBN 0-12-045280-4). Acad Pr.

Prehistory of Japan. facsimile ed. Gerard J. Groot. Ed. by Bertram S. Kraus. LC 79-37884. (Select Bibliographies Reprint Ser). Repr. of 1951 ed. 36.00 (ISBN 0-8369-6721-6). Ayer Co Pubs.

Prehistory of Korea. Jeong-Hak Kim. Tr. by Richard J. Pearson & Kazue Pearson. LC 77-28056. 272p. 1979. text ed. 20.00x (ISBN 0-8248-0552-6). UH Pr.

Prehistory of Languages. Mary R. Haas. LC 76-75689. (Janua Linguarum, Ser. Minor: No. 57). 1978. pap. text ed. 15.75 (ISBN 90-279-0681-5). Mouton.

Prehistory of Metallurgy in the British Isles. R. F. Tylecote. 250p. 1986. text ed. 34.95x (ISBN 0-904357-72-4, Pub. by Inst Metals). Brookfield Pub Co.

Prehistory of Northern North America As Seen from the Yukon. Frederica De Laguna. LC 76-43687. (Society for American Archaeology Memoirs.: No. 3). Repr. of 1947 ed. 54.50 (ISBN 0-404-15520-0). AMS Pr.

Prehistory of Nubia, 2 Vols. Ed. by Fred Wendorf. LC 68-18382. (Contributions in Anthropology: No. 2). (Illus.). 1094p. 1968. Set with separate atlas 72.00x (ISBN 0-87074-125-X). SMU Press.

Prehistory of Oklahoma. Ed. by Robert E. Bell. LC 83-12321. (New World Archaeological Record Ser.). 1983. 39.95 (ISBN 0-12-085180-6). Acad Pr.

Prehistory of Orkney. Ed. by Colin Renfrew. 304p. 1985. 30.00x (ISBN 0-85224-456-8, Pub. by Edinburgh U Pr Scotland). Columbia U Pr.

Prehistory of Orkney: 4000 B.C. to 1000 A.D. Ed. by Colin Renfrew. (Illus.). 310p. 1987. pap. 15.00 (ISBN 0-85224-506-8, Pub. by Edinburgh U Pr). Columbia U Pr.

Prehistory of Photography: Original Anthology. Ed. by Robert A. Sobieszek. LC 76-23040. (Sources of Modern Photography Ser.). (Illus.). 1979. lib. bdg. 34.50x (ISBN 0-405-09661-5). Ayer Co Pubs.

Prehistory of Salts Cave, Kentucky. Patty J. Watson. (Reports of Investigations Ser.: No. 16). (Illus.). 86p. 1969. pap. 2.50x (ISBN 0-89792-037-6). Ill St Museum.

Prehistory of the Americas. Stuart J. Fiedel. (Illus.). 408p. 1987. 49.50 (ISBN 0-521-32773-3); pap. 14.95 (ISBN 0-521-33979-0). Cambridge U Pr.

Prehistory of the Ayacucho Basin, Peru, Vol. II: Excavations & Chronology. Richard S. MacNeish et al. LC 80-13960. (Illus.). 368p. 1981. text ed. 45.00x (ISBN 0-472-04907-0). U of Mich Pr.

Prehistory of the Ayacucho Basin, Peru: Vol. III: Nonceramic Artifacts. Richard S. MacNeish et al. (Illus.). 360p. 45.00x (ISBN 0-472-02707-7). U of Mich Pr.

Prehistory of the Ayacucho Basin, Peru, Vol. IV: The Preceramic Way of Life. Richard S. MacNeish et al. (Illus.). 312p. 1983. text ed. 45.00x (ISBN 0-472-04967-4). U of Mich Pr.

Prehistory of the Burnt Bluff Area. James E. Fitting. (Anthropological Papers: No. 34). (Illus.). 140p. 1968. pap. 3.00. U Mich Mus Anthro.

Prehistory of the Eastern Arctic. Maxwell. (New World Archaelogical Record Ser.). 1985. 39.95 (ISBN 0-12-481270-8). Acad Pr.

Prehistory of the Eastern Highlands of New Guinea. Virginia D. Watson & J. David Cole. LC 76-49166. (Anthropological Studies in the Eastern Highlands of New Guinea: No. 3). (Illus.). 243p. 1978. 35.00x (ISBN 0-295-95541-4). U of Wash Pr.

Prehistory of the Eastern Sahara. Fred Wendorf & Romauld Schild. LC 79-8865. (Studies in Archaeology). 1980. 29.95 (ISBN 0-12-743960-9). Acad Pr.

Prehistory of the Far West: Homes of Vanished Peoples. Luther S. Cressman. LC 75-30153. (Illus.). 1976. 19.95 (ISBN 0-87480-113-3). U of Utah Pr.

Prehistory of the Indo-Malaysian Archipelago. P. S. Bellwood. 1986. 58.00 (ISBN 0-12-085370-1); pap. 34.50 (ISBN 0-12-085371-X). Acad Pr.

Preliminary Report Concerning Explorations & Surveys Principally in Nevada & Arizona. facs. ed. George M. Wheeler. LC 70-137389. (Select Bibliographies Reprint). 1872. 21.00 (ISBN 0-8369-5590-0). Ayer Co Pubs.

Preliminary Report: Education of the Royal Commission on Bilingualism & Biculturalism, 3 vols. in one. Royal Commission on Bilingualism & Biculturalism. Ed. by Francesco Cordasco. LC 77-17707. (Bilingual-Bicultural Education in the U. S. Ser.). 1978. Repr. of 1968 ed. lib. bdg. 64.00x (ISBN 0-405-11109-6). Ayer Co Pubs.

Preliminary Report of the Committee on General Welfare in the Matter of a Request of the Conference of Organized Labor Relative to Educational Facilities. Meeting of June 26, 1917. New York City. Board of Aldermen. Committee on General Welfare. LC 73-11924. (Metropolitan America Ser.). 350p. 1974. Repr. 25.50x (ISBN 0-405-05407-6). Ayer Co Pubs.

Preliminary Report of the Inland Waterways Commission Message from the President of the United States. United States Inland Waterways Commission. LC 72-2844. (Use & Abuse of America's Natural Resources Ser). 714p. 1972. Repr. of 1908 ed. 39.00 (ISBN 0-405-04529-8). Ayer Co Pubs.

Preliminary Report on Archaeological Research in Kansu. J. G. Andersson. 56p. 1925. pap. 168.00x (ISBN 0-317-68980-0, Pub. by Han-Shan Tang Ltd). State Mutual Bk.

Preliminary Report on Fish Distribution & Marketing in Sicily. G. Bombace. (General Fisheries Council of the Mediterranean (GFCM): Studies & Reviews: No. 28). 28p. (Eng. & Fr.). 1966. pap. 7.50 (ISBN 92-5-101946-0, F1789, FAO). UNIPUB.

Preliminary Report on Manuscript Materials in the British Archives Relating to the American Revolution in the West Indian Islands. George E. Tyson, Jr. & Carolyn Tyson. LC 76-51512. 1978. pap. 15.00 (ISBN 0-527-91440-1). Kraus Repr.

Preliminary Report on Mongolian Studies. Junpei Hagiwara. 51p. 1977. 40.00x (ISBN 0-317-68983-5, Pub. by Han-Shan Tang Ltd). State Mutual Bk.

Preliminary Report on Petroleum & Natural Gas in Washington. Sheldon L. Glover. (Report of Investigations Ser.: No. 4). (Illus.). 24p. 1936. 0.25 (ISBN 0-686-34727-7). WA Div Geol.

Preliminary Report on the Mill Creek Area of Andrew County, Missouri. Francis L. Stubbs. Ed. by Carl H. Chapman. (Missouri Archaeologist Ser.: Vol. 12, No. 1). (Illus.). 43p. (Orig.). 1950. pap. 1.00 (ISBN 0-943414-29-6). MO Arch Soc.

Preliminary Report on the Synagogue at Dura-Europos. H. F. Pearson et al. (Illus.). 1936. pap. 49.50x (ISBN 0-686-51290-1). Elliots Bks.

Preliminary Report on Two Scientific Expeditions in Nepal. Giuseppe Tucci. 153p. 1956. pap. 80.00x (ISBN 0-317-68448-5, Pub. by Han-Shan Tang Ltd). State Mutual Bk.

Preliminary Reports of ASOR-Sponsored Excavations 1981-83. Ed. by Walter E. Rast. LC 85-12851. (Bulletin of the American Schools of Oriental Research, Supplement Ser.: No. 23). 135p. 1985. pap. 17.50x (ISBN 0-89757-323-4, Dist. by Eisenbrauns). Am Sch Orient Res.

Preliminary Reports of ASOR-Sponsored Excavations 1980-84. Ed. by Walter E. Rast. LC 86-11482. (BASOR Supplements Ser.: No. 24). 164p. 1986. pap. text ed. 20.00x (ISBN 0-89757-324-2, Dist. by Eisenbrauns). Am Sch Orient Res.

Preliminary Reports on Precast Trapezoidal Box Girders, Spliced 1 Girders. (PCI Journal Reprints Ser.). 36p. pap. 6.00 (ISBN 0-686-40028-3, JR96). Prestressed Concrete.

Preliminary Research in the Triassic Chinle Formation. Ralph W. Wyckoff et al. (Bulletin Ser.). 23p. 1973. 1.50 (BS-47). Mus Northern Ariz.

Preliminary Review of the Allegheny County Court of Common Pleas Criminal Division's Individual Calendar Program. National Center for State Courts Staff. 16p. 1982. manuscript 0.96 (NERO, T/A-513). Natl Ctr St Courts.

Preliminary Salvage Archaeology in the Pomme de Terre Reservoir Area, Missouri. Carl H. Chapman. (Missouri Archaeologist Ser.: Vol. 16, No. 3 & 4). (Illus.). 116p. (Orig.). 1954. pap. 2.00 (ISBN 0-943414-34-2). MO Arch Soc.

Preliminary Scholastic Aptitude Test: National Merit Scholarship Qualifying Test (PSAT-NMSQT) 7th ed. Eve P. Steinberg. 336p. (Orig.). 1985. pap. 7.95 (ISBN 0-668-06100-6). Arco.

Preliminary Stray-Current Tests HVDC Power Transmission: The Dallas-Los Angeles. Ebasco Services Inc. 500p. 1969. 10.00 (ISBN 0-318-12671-0, L19720). Am Gas Assn.

Preliminary Study of Angas Phonology. D. A. Burquest. (Language Data, African Ser.: No. 1). 52p. 1971. pap. 2.85x (ISBN 0-88312-601-X); microfiche 2.00 (ISBN 0-88312-701-6). Summer Inst Ling.

Preliminary Study of the Homeless in Omaha-Douglas County. Jeff Luke. 43p. (Orig.). 1986. pap. 3.50 (ISBN 1-55719-020-8). U NE Ctr Applied Urban Rsch.

Preliminary Study of the Interpretation of Bodily Expression. William H. Blake. LC 75-176568. (Columbia University. Teachers College. Contributions to Education: No. 574). Repr. of 1933 ed. 22.50 (ISBN 0-404-55574-8). AMS Pr.

Preliminary Study of the Prehistoric Ruins of Nakum, Guatemala. A. M. Tozzer. (HU PMM). Repr. of 1913 ed. 29.00 (ISBN 0-527-01167-3). Kraus Repr.

Preliminary Study of the Pueblo of Taos, New Mexico. Merton L. Miller. LC 74-7992. Repr. of 1898 ed. 10.00 (ISBN 0-404-11879-8). AMS Pr.

Preliminary Study of the Ruins of Coba, Quintana Roo, Mexico. John E. Thompson et al. LC 77-11526. (Carnegie Institution of Washington. Publication: No. 424). Repr. of 1932 ed. 33.00 (ISBN 0-404-16285-1). AMS Pr.

Preliminary Study of the Ruins of Xcaret, Quintana Roo, Mexico, with Notes on Other Archaeological Remains on the Central East Coast of the Yucatan Peninsula. E. Wyllys Andrews, IV & Anthony P. Andrews. (Illus.). xii, 117p. 1975. 17.50 (ISBN 0-939238-46-2). Tulane MARI.

Preliminary Study of Underglaze Blue & White Ch'ing Hua. Yu-Kuan Lee. 37p. 1971. 45.00x (ISBN 0-317-44174-4, Pub. by Han-Shan Tang Ltd); Supp. 60.00 (ISBN 0-317-44175-2, Pub. by Han-Shan Tang Ltd.). State Mutual Bk.

Preliminary Suggestions see Monitoring the Outcome of Social Services.

Preliminary Survey of the Fontenelle Reservoir, Wyoming. David S. Dibble & C. Day Kent. (Upper Colorado Ser: No. 7). Repr. of 1962 ed. 18.00 (ISBN 0-685-91138-1). AMS Pr.

Preliminary Survey of the Vocabulary of White Alabamians. Virginia O. Foscue. (Publications of the American Dialect Society Ser., No. 56). 48p. 1971. pap. 3.10 (ISBN 0-8173-0656-0, Am Dialect Soc). U of Ala Pr.

Preliminary Survey on Methods of Teaching & Writing, Pt. 1: Survey of Theories & Practices (UNESCO) William S. Gray. (Education Studies & Documents: No. 5). pap. 13.00 (ISBN 0-8115-1329-7). Kraus Repr.

Preliminary Treatise on Evidence at Common Law. James B. Thayer. LC 74-96340. 1969. Repr. of 1898 ed. 49.50x (ISBN 0-678-04531-3). Kelley.

Preliminary Treatise on Evidence at Common Law. James B. Thayer. 636p. 1970. Repr. of 1898 ed. text ed. 37.50x (ISBN 0-8377-2625-5). Rothman.

Preliminary Treatment for Wastewater Facilities ('80) Manual of Practice, Operation & Maintenance-2, No. 2. Water Pollution Control Federation Staff. 52p. 1980. pap. 9.00 (ISBN 0-943244-22-6, MOM2). Water Pollution.

Preliminary Union List of Materials on Chinese Law: With a List of Chinese Studies & Translations of Foreign Law. Harvard University, Law School Library Staff. (Studies in Chinese Law: No. 6). 1967. 40.00x (ISBN 0-674-70070-8). Harvard U Pr.

Prelinguistic Communication in Infancy. Alan Ziajka. LC 81-379. 192p. 1981. 35.00 (ISBN 0-275-90747-3, C0747). Praeger.

Prelis. Karl G. Joreskog & Dag Sorbom. looseleaf binder 17.00 (ISBN 0-89498-011-4). Sci Ware.

Prelude. Marie Joseph. 256p. 1985. 14.95 (ISBN 0-312-63634-2). St Martin.

Prelude: A Parallel Text. William Wordsworth. Ed. by J. C. Maxwell. (Poets Ser.). 1977. pap. 8.95 (ISBN 0-14-042214-5). Penguin.

Prelude: A Poem. Conrad Aiken. 1978. lib. bdg. 29.00 (ISBN 0-8495-0037-0). Arden Lib.

Prelude: A Poem. Conrad Aiken. LC 73-4435. 1973. lib. bdg. 25.00 (ISBN 0-8414-1728-8). Folcroft.

Prelude Notes. Paul Warren. 72p. (Orig.). 1964. pap. 2.95 (ISBN 0-8220-1075-5). Cliffs.

Prelude, or, Growth of a Poet's Mind. new ed. William Wordsworth. (Oxford Paperbacks Ser). 1970. pap. 6.95x (ISBN 0-19-281074-X). Oxford U Pr.

Prelude: Seventeen Ninety-Nine, Eighteen Hundred & Five, Eighteen Fifty. William Wordsworth. Ed. by Jonathan Wordsworth et al. (Norton Critical Editions). 1979. pap. text ed. 14.95x (ISBN 0-393-09071-X). Norton.

Prelude to a Certain Midnight. Gerald Kersh. (Detective Stories Ser.). 192p. 1983. pap. 3.95 (ISBN 0-486-24536-5). Dover.

Prelude to a Song. Margaret Pargeter. (Harlequin Presents Ser.). 192p. 1983. pap. 1.75 (ISBN 0-373-10572-X). Harlequin Bks.

Prelude to a Woman. Barbara Nightingale. Ed. by Barbara Holley. (Earth Poetry Ser.). (Illus.). 52p. (Orig.). 1986. pap. 4.50 (ISBN 0-933494-27-0). Earthwise Pubns.

Prelude to Appeasement: East European Central Diplomacy in the Early 1930's. Lisanne Radice. (East European Quarterly Ser.: No. 80). 218p. 1981. 20.00x (ISBN 0-914710-74-5). East Eur Quarterly.

Prelude to Balfour Declaration see Letters & Papers of Chaim Weizmann.

Prelude to Bolshevism. Alexander Kerensky. LC 72-740. (World History Ser., No. 48). 1972. Repr. of 1919 ed. lib. bdg. 75.00x (ISBN 0-8383-1422-8). Haskell.

Prelude to Chaos. Edward Llewellyn. 256p. 1986. pap. 2.95 (ISBN 0-88677-008-4). DAW Bks.

Prelude to Chemistry: An Outline of Alchemy, Its Literature & Relationships. John Read. LC 79-8622. (Illus.). Repr. of 1937 ed. 48.00 (ISBN 0-404-18488-X). AMS Pr.

Prelude to Civil War: The Nullification Controversy in South Carolina, 1816-1836. William Freehling. (Illus.). 1968. pap. 8.95x (ISBN 0-06-131359-9, TB1359, Torch). Har-Row.

Prelude to Delilah see Samson.

Prelude to Disaster: The Course of Indian-White Relations Which Led to the Black Hawk War of 1832. Anthony F. Wallace. 1970. 2.50 (ISBN 0-912226-11-0). Ill St Hist Soc.

Prelude to Empire. John A. Brinkman. (Occasional Publications of the Babylonian Fund: No. 7 OPBF 7). xiii, 159p. 1984. 25.00x (ISBN 0-934718-62-8). Univ Mus of U PA.

Prelude to Empire: Portugal Overseas Before Henry the Navigator. Bailey W. Diffie. 11.25 (ISBN 0-8446-5705-0). Peter Smith.

Prelude to Empire: Portugal Overseas Before Henry the Navigator. Bailey W. Diffie. LC 60-14301. (Illus.). xii, 129p. 1960. pap. 3.25x (ISBN 0-8032-5049-5). U of Nebr Pr.

Prelude to Fame: Crawford Long's Discovery of Anaesthesia. Ruby L. Radford. LC 74-81776. (gr. 7 up). 1969. 4.95 (ISBN 0-87672-104-8). Geron-X.

Prelude to Foundation. Isaac Asimov. LC 87-33086. 1988. 18.95 (ISBN 0-385-23313-2); ltd. ed. 175.00 (ISBN 0-385-24585-8). Doubleday.

Prelude to Genocide: Nazi Ideology & the Struggle for Power. Simon Taylor. LC 85-16854. 228p. 1985. 35.00 (ISBN 0-312-63636-9). St Martin.

Prelude to Glory. Herbert Krause & Gary D. Olson. LC 74-80769. (Illus.). 279p. (Orig.). 1974. 19.95 (ISBN 0-88498-018-9); ltd. lea. ed. 75.00 (ISBN 0-685-50460-3); pap. 10.95 (ISBN 0-88498-019-7). Brevet Pr.

Prelude to Glory Practical Christianity. Wayne D. Leeper. 238p. (Orig.). 1987. pap. 9.95 (ISBN 0-89225-293-6). Gospel Advocate.

Prelude to Greatness: Lincoln in the 1850's. Don E. Fehrenbacher. 1962. 20.00x (ISBN 0-8047-0119-9); pap. 7.95x (ISBN 0-8047-0120-2). Stanford U Pr.

Prelude to Icaros. John W. Andrews. 1966. pap. 6.00 (ISBN 0-8283-1227-3). Branden Pub Co.

Prelude to Independence: The Newspaper War on Britain 1764-1776. Arthur M. Schlesinger, Jr. LC 80-22830. 349p. 1980. pap. 9.95x (ISBN 0-930350-13-8). NE U Pr.

Prelude to Infamy. Gordon Brooke-Shepherd. 1962. 12.95 (ISBN 0-8392-1086-8). Astor-Honor.

Prelude to Israel: An Analysis of Zionist Diplomacy, 1897-1947. rev. ed. Alan Taylor. 126p. 1970. Repr. of 1961 ed. 3.50 (ISBN 0-88728-093-5). Inst Palestine.

Prelude to Literacy: A Preschool Child's Encounter with Picture & Story. Maureen Crago & Hugh Crago. LC 82-19235. (Illus.). 320p. 1983. 18.95x (ISBN 0-8093-1077-5). S Ill U Pr.

Prelude to Mathematics. W. W. Sawyer. (Popular Science Ser.). 224p. 1983. pap. 4.50 (ISBN 0-486-24401-6). Dover.

Prelude to Paradise. Daphne Hamilton. (Superromances Ser.). 384p. 1983. pap. 2.50 (ISBN 0-373-70048-2, Pub. by Worldwide). Harlequin Bks.

Prelude to Parnassus: Scenes from the Life of Alexander Sergeyvich Pushkin 1799-1847. James Cleugh. 1973. Repr. of 1936 ed. 20.00 (ISBN 0-8274-1775-6). R West.

Prelude to Partition: The Indian Muslims & the Imperia; System of Control, 1920-32. David Page. 1982. 28.00x (ISBN 0-19-561303-1). Oxford U Pr.

Prelude to Physics. Clifford Swartz. LC 82-16037. 202p. 1983. pap. 20.95 (ISBN 0-471-06028-3). Wiley.

Prelude to Poetry. Ed. by Ernest Rhys. 1970. Repr. of 1927 ed. 14.95x (ISBN 0-460-00789-0, Evman). Biblio Dist.

Prelude to Point Four: American Technical Missions Overseas 1838 to 1938. Merle E. Curti & Kendall Birr. LC 78-4874. 284p. 1978. Repr. of 1954 ed. lib. bdg. 35.00x (ISBN 0-313-20397-0, CUPP). Greenwood.

Prelude to Power: The Parisian Radical Press, 1789-1791. Jack R. Censer. LC 76-7968. pap. 51.50 (ISBN 0-317-41652-9, 2025841). Bks Demand UMI.

Prelude to Programming: Problem Solving & Algorithms. William Mitchell. 1984. text ed. 30.00 (ISBN 0-8359-5614-8, Reston); pap. text ed. write for info. (ISBN 0-8359-5627-X). P-H.

Prelude to Protectorate in Morocco: Precolonial Protest & Resistance, 1860-1912. Edmund Burke. LC 75-43228. (Illus.). 1977. lib. bdg. 25.00x (ISBN 0-226-08075-7). U of Chicago Pr.

Prelude to Quebec's Quiet Revolution: Liberalism vs. Neo-Nationalism, 1945-1960. Michael D. Behiels. 384p. 1985. 15.95x (ISBN 0-7735-0424-9). McGill-Queens U Pr.

Prelude to Revolution: The Petrograd Bolsheviks & the July 1917 Uprising. Alexander Rabinowitch. LC 68-10278. Repr. of 1968 ed. 59.90 (ISBN 0-8357-9236-6, 2055224). Bks Demand UMI.

Prelude to Solidarity: Poland & the Politics of the Gierek Regime. Keith J. Lepak. 320p. 1988. 35.00x (ISBN 0-231-06608-2). Columbia U Pr.

Prelude to Space. Arthur C. Clarke. 192p. 1976. pap. 2.95 (ISBN 0-345-34102-3). Ballantine.

Prelude to Terror: The Constituent Assembly & the Failure of Consensus, 1789-91. 288p. text ed. 40.00 (ISBN 0-631-15237-7). Basil Blackwell.

Prelude to the Cold War: The Tsarist, Soviet, & U. S. Armies in the Two World Wars. Jonathan R. Adelman. LC 88-2048. 260p. 1988. lib. bdg. 30.00 (ISBN 1-55587-123-2). Lynne Rienner.

Prelude to the Enlightenment: French Literature, 1690-1740. Geoffroy Atkinson & Abraham C. Keller. LC 70-114416. 221p. 1971. 20.00x (ISBN 0-295-95082-X). U of Wash Pr.

Prelude to the Migraine Attack. Amery & Wauquier. 1987. 41.95 (ISBN 0-7020-1152-5, Bailliere-Tindall). Saunders.

Prelude to the Monsoon: Assignment in Sumatra. G. F. Jacobs. LC 81-16183. 280p. 1982. Repr. of 1965 ed. 24.95 (ISBN 0-8122-7838-0). U of Pa Pr.

Prelude to the Presidency: The Political Character & Legislative Leadership Style of Governor Jimmy Carter. Gary M. Fink. LC 79-7725. (Contributions in Political Science: No. 40). (Illus.). 1980. lib. bdg. 35.00 (ISBN 0-313-22055-7, FPP/). Greenwood.

Prelude to the Reformation: A Study of English Church Life from the Age of Wycliffe to the Breach with Rome. Richard S. Arrowsmith. LC 83-45573. Date not set. Repr. of 1923 ed. 30.00 (ISBN 0-404-19891-0). AMS Pr.

Prelude to the Russian Campaign: From the Moscow Pact (August 21st 1939) to the Opening of Hostilities in Russia (June 22nd 1941) Grigore Gafencu. LC 79-5207. 348p. 1981. Repr. of 1945 ed. 29.00 (ISBN 0-8305-0072-3). Hyperion Conn.

Prelude to the Space Age: The Rocket Societies: 1924-1940. Frank H. Winter. LC 81-607883. (Illus.). 222p. (Orig.). 1983. pap. text ed. 19.95 (ISBN 0-87474-963-8, WIPSP). Smithsonian.

Prelude to the Total Force: The Air National Guard, 1943-1969. Charles J. Gross. LC 84-7432. (United States Air Force General Histories). (Illus.). 267p. 1985. 17.00 (ISBN 0-318-18817-1, S/N 008-070-00556-5). USGPO.

Prelude to the Truman Doctrine: British Policy in Greece, 1944-47. G. M. Alexander. 1982. 49.95x (ISBN 0-19-822653-5). Oxford U Pr.

Prelude to Victory of the Ten Hour Movement: 1844. LC 72-2536. (British Labour Struggles Before 1850 Ser). (4 pamphlets). 1972. 18.00 (ISBN 0-405-04429-1). Ayer Co Pubs.

Prelude to War. Robert Elson. (World War II Ser.). (Illus.). 1976. 14.95 (ISBN 0-8094-2450-9). Time-Life.

Prelude to War: The Chinese Student Rebellion of 1935-1936. Hubert Freyn. LC 75-39026. (China Studies: from Confucius to Mao). 122p. 1977. Repr. of 1939 ed. 17.60 (ISBN 0-88355-382-1). Hyperion Conn.

Prelude to War: The International Repercussion of the Spanish Civil War. P. van Der Esch. 1976. lib. bdg. 59.95 (ISBN 0-8490-2469-2). Gordon Pr.

Prelude, 1798-1799. Ed. by Stephen M. Parrish. (Wordsworth Ser.). (Illus.). 324p. 1977. 49.50x (ISBN 0-8014-0854-7). Cornell U Pr.

Prelude: 1799, 1789, 1805, 1850. William Wordsworth. Ed. by Jonathan Wordsworth et al. (Norton Critical Editions Ser.). 1980. 22.95x (ISBN 0-393-04496-3). Norton.

Preludes. Maurits I. Boas. LC 78-855. 1978. 9.95 (ISBN 0-8119-0305-2). Fell.

Preludes & Studies. Alan Dent. LC 75-105778. 1970. Repr. of 1942 ed. 23.00x (ISBN 0-8046-0948-9, Pub. by Kennikat). Assoc Faculty Pr.

Preludes for Piano. Harold Zabrack. 1979. pap. 5.00 (ISBN 0-934286-10-8). Kenyon.

Preludes to Genetics. Ed. by Gloria Robinson. 15.00x (ISBN 0-87291-127-6). Coronado Pr.

Preludes to Growth: An Experiential Approach. Richard Katz. LC 72-94013. 1973. pap. text ed. 7.95 (ISBN 0-02-917190-3). Free Pr.

Preludes to My Autobiography. J. L. Moreno. 8.00 (ISBN 0-685-52594-5). Beacon Hse.

Preludes to Vision: The Epic Venture in Blake, Keats, Wordsworth, & Hart Crane. Thomas A. Vogler. LC 70-107662. (No. 22). 1971. 32.50x (ISBN 0-520-01687-4). U of Cal Pr.

Premachine Planning & Tool Presetting. Ed. by Robert R. Runck. LC 67-28208. (American Society of Tool & Manufacturing Engineers Ser.). pap. 20.50 (ISBN 0-317-10932-4, 2016005). Bks Demand UMI.

Premarital Agreements: When, Why, & How to Write Them. Joseph P. Zwack. LC 86-46113. 1987. 17.45i (ISBN 0-06-055072-4). Har-Row.

Premarital Agreements: When, Why, & How to Write Them. Joseph P. Zwack. LC 86-46113. 1987. pap. 7.95 (ISBN 0-06-096181-3, PL6181, PL). Har-Row.

Premarital Counseling. rev. ed. H. Norman Wright. LC 77-2355. 1981. 14.95 (ISBN 0-8024-6812-8). Moody.

Premarital Counseling: A Manual for Clergy & Counselors. John L. Mitman. 128p. (Orig.). 1984. pap. 6.95 (ISBN 0-86683-879-1, 7874, HarpR). Har-Row.

Premarital Counseling Handbook for Ministers. Theodore K. Pitt. 192p. 1985. pap. 9.95 (ISBN 0-8170-1071-8). Judson.

Premarital Guide for Couples & Their Counselors. David A. Thompson. 80p. 1979. pap. 4.95 (ISBN 0-87123-465-3, 210465). Bethany Hse.

Premarital Intercourse & Interpersonal Relationships: A Research Study of Interpersonal Relationships Based on Case Histories of 668 Premarital Intercourse Experiences Reported by 200 College Level Males. Lester A. Kirkendall. LC 85-22576. xvii, 302p. 1984. Repr. of 1961 ed. lib. bdg. 38.50x (ISBN 0-313-24293-3, KIPR). Greenwood.

Premarital Sexual Standards in America. Ira L. Reiss. LC 60-7095. 1960. 14.95 (ISBN 0-02-926190-2). Free Pr.

Premarital Sexuality: Attitudes, Relationships, Behavior. John DeLamater & Patricia MacCorquodale. LC 78-65019. 314p. 1979. 35.00x (ISBN 0-299-07840-X). U of Wis Pr.

Premarric. Susan Howatch. 1984. pap. 3.95 (ISBN 0-449-20622-X, Crest). Fawcett.

Premartial Counseling: The Professional's Handbook. Robert F. Stahmann & William J. Hiebert. 288p. 1987. 29.95x (ISBN 0-669-13925-4). Lexington Bks.

Premature Adolescent Pregnancy & Parenthood. Elizabeth McAnarney. 418p. 1983. 49.50 (ISBN 0-8089-1518-5, 792819). Grune.

Premature Antifascists: North American Volunteers in the Spanish Civil War 1936-1939. John Gerassi. 304p. 1986. 44.95 (ISBN 0-275-92062-3, C2062); pap. 14.95 (ISBN 0-275-92067-4, B2067). Praeger.

Premature Babies. W. H. Kitchen et al. (Illus.). 96p. 1985. pap. 6.95 (ISBN 0-87857-557-X). Rodale Pr Inc.

Premature Babies: A Different Beginning. William A. Sammons & Jennifer M. Lewis. 1985. pap. 16.95 (ISBN 0-8016-4305-8). Mosby.

Premature Babies: A Handbook for Parents by Parents. Sherri Nance. 320p. 1984. pap. 3.50 (ISBN 0-425-07256-8). Berkley Pub.

Premature Baby Book: A Parents Guide to Coping & Caring in the First Years. Helen Harrison & Ann Kositsky. (Illus.). 320p. 1983. 24.95 (ISBN 0-312-63648-2); pap. text ed. 15.95 (ISBN 0-312-63649-0). St Martin.

Premature Chromosome Condensation: Application in Basic, Clinical & Mutation Research. Ed. by Potu Rao et al. (Cell Biology Ser.). 1982. 65.50 (ISBN 0-12-580450-4). Acad Pr.

Premature in Context. Max Sugar. 141p. 1982. text ed. 20.00 (ISBN 0-88331-183-6). Luce.

Premature Labour Handbook: Successfully Sustaining Your High-Risk Pregnancy. Patricia Robertson & Peggy H. Berlin. LC 85-10170. (Illus.). 240p. 1986. pap. 9.95 (ISBN 0-385-19924-4). Doubleday.

Premature Reformation: Wycliffite Texts & Lollard History. 560p. 1988. 96.00 (ISBN 0-19-822762-0). Oxford U Pr.

Prematurely Saved. John Garvey. 1986. pap. 8.95 (ISBN 0-87243-150-9). Templegate.

Prematurely Yours. Kim Bryant & Becky Meloan. Ed. by Cheryl Quaintance. (Illus.). 40p. 1985. 20.00 (ISBN 0-9614786-0-8). Sunrise Publ.

Premcand Eighteen Eighty to Nineteen Thirty-Six. Usha Tripathi. (Illus.). 21p. (Orig.). 1980. pap. 2.25 (ISBN 0-903359-28-6, Pub. by British Lib). Longwood Pub Group.

Premchand: A Western Appraisal. S. A. Schulz. 1983. 4.50x (ISBN 0-8364-1023-8, Pub. by Allied India). South Asia Bks.

Premchand: His Life & Work. V. S. Naravane. 280p. 1980. text ed. 22.50x (ISBN 0-7069-1091-5, Pub. by Vikas India). Advent NY.

Premedical Planning Guide to Allopathic (M.D.), Osteopathic (D.O.) & Podiatric Medical Schools. Jane D. Crawford. 248p. (Orig.). 1985. pap. 12.50 (ISBN 0-941406-06-7). Betz Pub Co Inc.

Premeditated Success Through Hypnotism. Carl W. Bordas. 168p. (Orig.). 1981. pap. 4.50x (ISBN 0-935648-07-0). Halldin Pub.

Premenopause. Muriel C. Clausen. 53p. 1979. pap. 6.25 (ISBN 0-9603664-0-7). M C Clausen.

Premenstrual Syndrome. Jane Chihal. LC 84-71600. 1985. 8.65 (ISBN 0-917634-15-2). Creative Infomatics.

Premenstrual Syndrome. Keye. Date not set. price not set (ISBN 0-8089-1898-2). Grune.

Premenstrual Syndrome. Keye. 208p. 1988. 29.95 (ISBN 0-7216-2560-6). Saunders.

Premenstrual Syndrome. Ed. by Pieter A. Van Keep. 1981. lib. bdg. 19.95 (ISBN 0-85200-387-0, Pub. by MTP Pr England). Kluwer Academic.

Premenstrual Syndrome: A Guide for Young Women. 2nd ed. Gilda Berger. 96p. 1988. pap. 6.95 (ISBN 0-89793-048-7). Hunter Hse.

Premenstrual Syndrome: A Nutritional Approach. Louise Tenney. (Todays Health Ser.: Vol. 3). Date not set. pap. 3.95 (ISBN 0-913923-30-3). Woodland UT.

Premenstrual Syndrome: A Self Help Guide. Wendy Van Biert Rappoport. (Illus.). 96p. (Orig.). 1984. pap. 4.95 (ISBN 0-936320-19-2). Compact Bks.

Premenstrual Syndrome & Dysmenorrhea. Ed. by M. Yusoff Dawood et al. LC 84-7571. (Illus.). 247p. 1984. text ed. 36.50 (ISBN 0-8067-0411-X). Urban & S.

Premenstrual Syndrome & Progesterone Therapy. 2nd ed. Dalton. 1984. 35.50 (ISBN 0-8151-2266-7). Year Bk Med.

Premenstrual Syndrome: Current Findings & Future Directions. Howard J. Osofsky & Susan J. Blumenthal. LC 85-6100. (Progress in Psychiatry Ser.). 112p. 1985. text ed. 17.95X (ISBN 0-88048-071-8, 48-071-8). Am Psychiatric.

Premenstrual Syndrome: Depression, PMT, Weight Gain, Aggression. Caroline Shreeve. 144p. Date not set. pap. 7.99 (ISBN 0-7225-0829-8, Pub. by Thorsons (England)). Sterling.

Premenstrual Syndrome: Ethical & Legal Implications in a Biomedical Perspective. Ed. by Benson E. Ginsburg & Bonnie F. Carter. LC 86-30562. 452p. 1987. 55.00x (ISBN 0-306-42498-3, Plenum Pr). Plenum Pub.

Premenstrual Syndrome: Index of Modern Information. Jacob L. Liehaus. LC 88-47618. 150p. 1988. 34.50 (ISBN 0-88164-868-X); pap. 26.50 (ISBN 0-88164-869-8). ABBE Pubs Assn.

Premenstrual Syndrome Self Help Book. Susan Lark. 1984. 12.95 (ISBN 0-936614-03-X). PMS Self Help.

Premenstrual Syndrome: The Curse That Can Be Cured. Caroline Shreeve. LC 86-18833. 143p. 1986. lib. bdg. 19.95x (ISBN 0-8095-7017-3). Borgo Pr.

Premenstrual Syndromes: New Findings & Controversies. Gise. (Volume 2, CIOG). 1987. 39.00 (ISBN 0-443-08537-4). Churchill.

Premenstrual Tension: A Multidisciplinary Approach. Ed. by Charles M. Debrovner. LC 81-6659. 111p. 1982. 24.95x (ISBN 0-89885-019-3). Human Sci Pr.

Premerger Notification Practice Manual. LC 85-73087. 153p. 1985. pap. 40.00 (ISBN 0-89707-206-5, 503-0058-01). Amer Bar Assn.

Premices Philosophiques. Pierre Duhem. Ed. by Stanley L. Jaki. (Brill's Studies in Intellectual History: No. 3). 260p. 1987. 43.25 (ISBN 90-04-08117-8, Pub. by E J Brill). Heinman.

Premier Amour. Samuel Beckett. pap. 8.95 (ISBN 0-685-37200-6). French & Eur.

Premier Amour. Marcel Pagnol. 214p. 1974. 11.95 (ISBN 0-686-54839-6). French & Eur.

Premier Book of Major Poets. Ed. by Anita Dore. 1988. pap. 4.95 (ISBN 0-449-44507-0, Crest). Fawcett.

Premier Fascicule des Melanges see Maitres Musiciens de la Renaissance Francaise.

Premier Fascicule des 150 Psaumes see Maitres Musiciens de la Renaissance Francaise.

Premier Hotels of Great Britain. William McMinnies. 406p. 1988. pap. 12.95 (ISBN 0-88289-691-1). Pelican.

Premier Livre Des Amours De Pierre De Ronsard, (I-XIX) see Monuments de la musique francaise au temps de la Renaissance.

Premier livre des Amours de Pierre de Ronsard, (XX-XXXV) see Monuments de la musique francaise au temps de la Renaissance.

Premier livre des Octonaires de la vanite du Monde see Monuments de la musique francaise au temps de la Renaissance.

Premier Peaks of the World. Takehide Kazami. 96p. 1988. 28.95 (ISBN 4-7661-0472-2, Pub. by Graphic Sha Japan). Bks Nippan.

Premier Resorts Edition. (Illus.). Date not set. price not set. Am Map.

Premier Voyage du Sieur de la Courbe Fait a la Coste d'Afrique en 1685. P. Cultru. (Fr.). 1913. 36.00 (ISBN 0-8115-3079-5). Kraus Repr.

Premiere Education Sentimentale. Gustave Flaubert. 1963. 14.95 (ISBN 0-686-55987-8). French & Eur.

Premiere Enquete De Maigret. Georges Simenon. pap. 3.95 (ISBN 0-685-11513-5). French & Eur.

Premiere Formation d'une Chaine de Postes entre le Fleuve Saint-Laurent et le Golfe du Mexique (1683-1724) see Decouvertes et Establissements des francais dans l'ouest et dans le sud de l'Amerique septentrional: 1614-1754.

Premiere Internationale en Espagne. M. Nettlau. Rev. by Renee Lamberet. (Illus.). 683p. (Fr.). 1969. lib. bdg. 97.50 (ISBN 90-277-0103-2). Kluwer Academic.

Premiere Partie Des Mocedades Del Cid De Don Guillen De Castro. Guillem De Castro Y Bellius. Repr. of 1890 ed. 28.00 (ISBN 0-384-07870-2). Johnson Repr.

Premiere Planete a Droite En Sortant Parla Voie Lactee. Pierre Daninos. 1975. 13.95 (ISBN 0-686-55571-6); pap. 3.95 (ISBN 0-686-55572-4). French & Eur.

Premiere Promenade de Spot (Spot's First Walk) (Fr.). (ps-1). 1986. 9.95 (ISBN 0-399-21274-4). Putnam Pub Group.

Premieres Etapes du Machinisme see Histoire Generale des Techniques.

Premieres Lectures Economiques de Karl Marx (II) see Cahiers de l'Institut de Science Economique Appliquee.

Premieres of the Year. Jacob T. Grein. LC 77-93162. Repr. of 1900 ed. 15.00 (ISBN 0-405-08581-8, Blom Pubns). Ayer Co Pubs.

Premieres Poesies 1829-1835. Alfred de Musset. Ed. by Maurice Allem. 338p. 1958. 7.95 (ISBN 0-686-55556-2). French & Eur.

Premiers Capetiens 987-1137. Achille Luchaire. 439p. Repr. of 1903 ed. lib. bdg. 87.50x. Coronet Bks.

Premiers Empires see First Empires.

Premiers of Western Australia 1890-1982. G. S. Reid & M. R. Oliver. (Illus.). viii, 122p. 1983. 15.65x (ISBN 0-85564-214-9, Pub. by U of W Austral Pr). Intl Spec Bk.

Premiers Pas de L'Univers. Jules Supervielle. 240p. 1950. 4.95 (ISBN 0-686-55102-8). French & Eur.

Premiers Poemes. Gustave Kahn. LC 78-64037. (Des Imagistes: Literature of the Imagist Movement). Repr. of 1897 ed. 27.50 (ISBN 0-404-17118-4). AMS Pr.

Premiers Poemes. Ruth P. Weinreb. (gr. 8-10). 1982. pap. text ed. 5.95x (ISBN 0-88334-156-5). Ind Sch Pr.

Premiers Textes Litteraires. 2nd ed. Eve M. Stadler. Ed. by Doris-Jean Gourevitch. LC 74-83346. 244p. 1975. pap. text ed. 17.00x (ISBN 0-471-00811-7). Wiley.

Premises & Motifs in Renaissance Thought & Literature. C. A. Patrides. LC 81-47940. (Illus.). 256p. 1982. 28.00x (ISBN 0-691-06505-5). Princeton U Pr.

Premises for Propaganda. Leo Bogart. LC 75-18007. 1976. 12.95 (ISBN 0-02-904390-5). Free Pr.

Premises of Political Economy. Simon. Patten. LC 68-30540. 1968. Repr. of 1885 ed. 35.00x (ISBN 0-678-00446-3). Kelley.

Premises Security Practice Manual. Dombroff. (Trial Practice Library). 1988. write for info. (ISBN 0-471-83120-4). Wiley.

Premium Adult Desserts. Ed. by Peter Allen. 250p. 1988. 1250.00 (ISBN 0-941285-18-9). FIND-SVP.

Premium Auditing Applications, 2 vols. 2nd ed. Robert J. Gibbons et al. LC 84-82306. 681p. 1984. Vol. 1. 22.00 (ISBN 0-89462-019-3, APA 92); Vol. 2. 22.00. IIA.

Premium Calculation in Insurance. Ed. by F. De Vylder et al. 1984. lib. bdg. 76.00 (ISBN 90-277-1732-X, Pub. by Reidel Holland). Kluwer Academic.

Premium on Death. Roy Lewis. 208p. 1988. pap. 2.95 (ISBN 1-55547-260-5). Critics Choice Paper.

Premium on Death: An Eric Ward Novel. Roy Lewis. 208p. 1987. 13.95 (ISBN 0-312-00019-7). St Martin.

Premiums, Gifts & Competitions. J. J. Boddewyn. 78p. 1978. pap. 15.00 non-members (ISBN 0-318-14496-4); members 7.50. Intl Advertising Assn.

Premodern China: A Bibliographical Introduction. Chun-shu Chang. (Michigan Monographs in Chinese Studies: No. 11). 183p. 1971. pap. 6.00 (ISBN 0-89264-011-1). U of Mich Ctr Chinese.

Premodern Financial Systems: A Historical Comparative Study. Raymond W. Goldsmith. (Illus.). 352p. 1987. 49.50 (ISBN 0-521-32947-7). Cambridge U Pr.

Premonition. J. N. Williamson. 288p. pap. 3.50 (ISBN 0-8439-2334-2, Leisure Bks). Leisure NY.

Premonitions. Frank Bonham. LC 84-3844. 176p. (gr. 4 up). 1984. 11.95 (ISBN 0-03-071306-4). H Holt & Co.

Premonitions of an Uneasy Guest. Carolyne Wright. 69p. (Orig.). 1983. pap. 5.95x (ISBN 0-910075-01-8); pap. text ed. 5.95 (ISBN 0-910075-02-6). Hardin-Simmons.

Prenatal & Paranatal Factors in the Development of Childhood Reading Disorders. A. A. Kawi & B. Pasamanick. (SRCD M). 1959. 15.00 (ISBN 0-527-01580-6). Kraus Repr.

Prenatal & Perinatal Biology & Medicine, Vols. 1 & 2. Ed. by Norman Kretchmer et al. 1987. Set. 112.00 (ISBN 3-7186-0359-4); 70.00 (ISBN 3-7186-0344-6); 70.00 (ISBN 3-7186-0345-4). Harwood Academic.

Prenatal & Perinatal Infections. (EURO Reports & Studies: No. 93). 147p. 1985. pap. 7.20 (ISBN 92-890-1259-5). World Health.

Prenatal Antecedents of Postnatal Growth. Stanley Garn. (Illus.). 224p. Date not set. text ed. 25.00x (ISBN 0-472-10074-2). U of Mich Pr.

Prenatal Care. 108p. 1983. pap. 2.50 (ISBN 0-318-11817-3, S/N 017-091-00237-1). USGPO.

Prenatal Care: United States, 1969-1975. Selma Taffel. Ed. by Taloria Stevenson. (Ser. 21: No. 33). 1978. pap. text ed. 1.75 (ISBN 0-8406-0144-1). Natl Ctr Health Stats.

Prenatal Culture: How to Create the Perfect Baby. R. Swinburne Clymer. 144p. 1950. 4.95 (ISBN 0-932785-50-6). Philos Pub.

Prenatal Determinants of Abnormal Behavior: A Primer of Behavioral Mutagenesis & Teratogenesis. E. L. Abel. (Illus.). 345p. Date not set. price not set (ISBN 0-306-43053-3, Plenum Pr). Plenum Pub.

Prenatal Diagnosis. 1987. write for info. Wiley.

Prenatal Diagnosis & Mechanisms of Teratogenesis: Pt. A of Annual Review of Birth Defects, 1981. Ed. by William L. Nyhan & Kenneth L. Jones. LC 82-9992. (Birth Defects; Original Article Ser.: Vol. 18, No. 3A). 232p. 1982. 40.00 (ISBN 0-8451-1047-0). A R Liss.

Prenatal Diagnosis & Selective Abortion. Harry Harris. LC 75-3847. 112p. 1975. text ed. 9.95x (ISBN 0-674-70080-5). Harvard U Pr.

Prenatal Diagnosis of Congenital Anomalies. Roberto Romero et al. 400p. 1987. 79.95 (ISBN 0-8385-7921-3, Dist. by Prentice-Hall). Appleton & Lange.

Prenatal Diagnosis of Heritable Skin Diseases. Ed. by T. Gedde-Dahl & K. D. Wuepper. (Current Problems in Dermatology: Vol. 16). (Illus.). viii, 216p. 1987. 145.50 (ISBN 3-8055-4397-2). S Karger.

Prenatal Diagnosis of Thalassemia & the Hemoglobinopathies. Ed. by Dimitris Loukopoulos. 272p. 1988. 125.00 (ISBN 0-8493-5972-4, 5972). CRC Pr.

Prenatal Diagnosis: Past, Present, & Future: Report of an International Workshop Held at Val David, Quebec, November 4-8, 1979. Ed. by John L. Hamerton & Nancy E. Simpson. (Prenatal Diagnosis, December 1980, Special Issue Ser.). pap. 20.00 (ISBN 0-317-55677-0, 2029269). Bks Demand UMI.

Prenatal Drug Exposure: Kinetics & Dynamics. Ed. by C. Nora Chiang & Charles C. Lee. (NIDA Research Monograph: No. 60). (Illus.). 159p. (Orig.). 1985. pap. 3.50 (ISBN 0-318-18818-X, S/N 017-024-01257-2). USGPO.

Prenatal Gliogenesis in the Neopallium of the Rat. M. Rickmann & J. R. Wolff. (Advances in Anatomy, Embryology & Cell Biology Ser.: Vol. 93). (Illus.). 100p. 1985. pap. 29.00 (ISBN 0-387-13849-8). Springer-Verlag.

Prenatal Life: Biological & Clinical Perspectives, Proceedings. Symposium on the Physiology & Pathology of Human Reproduction (3rd: 1967, Detroit) Ed. by Harold C. Mack. LC 73-91873. Repr. of 1970 ed. 62.30 (2027609). Bks Demand UMI.

Prenatal Screening, Policies, & Values: The Example of Neural Tube Defects. Ed. by Elena O. Nightingale & Susan B. Meister. (Illus.). 160p. 1987. pap. text ed. 10.95x (ISBN 0-674-70075-9). Harvard U Pr.

Prenatal Tests: What They Are, Their Benefits & Risks, & How to Decide Whether to Have Them or Not. Robin Blatt. LC 87-40546. (Illus.). 288p. (Orig.). 1988. pap. 9.95 (ISBN 0-394-75887-0, Vin). Random.

Prenatal Ultrasound: A Color Atlas with Anatomic & Pathologic Correlations. Beverly A. Spirt et al. Ed. by Lawrence P. Gordon & Michael Oliphant. (Illus.). 148p. 1987. text ed. 70.00 (ISBN 0-443-08455-6). Churchill.

Prenatal Yoga & Natural Birth. rev. ed. Jeannine Parvati. (Illus.). 64p. 1986. pap. 7.95 (ISBN 0-938190-89-X). North Atlantic.

Prenatal Yoga & Natural Birth. Jeannine Parvati & O'Brien Medvin. LC 74-19553. (Illus.). 1978. pap. text ed. 5.00 (ISBN 0-913512-52-4). Freestone Pub Co.

Prende le large: Big Jim Cote pecheur. Julien Olivier. (Oral History Ser.). (Illus.). 107p. (Fr.). (gr. 9-10). 1981. pap. 2.50 (ISBN 0-911409-08-4). Natl Mat Dev.

Prenegotiation Planning Book. William F. Morrison. LC 85-9289. 260p. 1985. 24.95 (ISBN 0-471-82276-0). Wiley.

Prenn Drifting. Jozsef Lengyel. 293p. 1966. 14.95 (ISBN 0-8464-0747-7). Beekman Pubs.

Prensa de Guatemala y la question de limites con Honduras. 248p. (Span.). 1932. 4.75 (ISBN 0-318-14571-5). Intl Guatemala.

Prentice Alvin. Orson S. Card. 1989. price not set; pap. price not set. Tor Bks.

Prentice-Hall American World Atlas. Ed. by Bill Willett. LC 84-67206. 224p. 1984. 39.95 (ISBN 0-13-695024-8). P-H.

Prentice-Hall Author's Guide. 5th ed. 1975. pap. 15.00 (ISBN 0-13-695015-9). P-H.

Prentice-Hall Business Tax Deduction Master Guide. Updated & expanded ed. Tax Reduction Institute, Washington D. C. Staff. 300p. 1986. 29.95 (ISBN 0-13-108242-6); pap. 16.95 (ISBN 0-13-108234-5). P-H.

Prentice-Hall Complete Secretarial Letter Book. Mary A. DeVries. (Illus.). 1978. 19.95 (ISBN 0-13-695494-4, Busn); pap. 7.95 (ISBN 0-13-696682-9). P-H.

Prentice-Hall Dictionary of Business, Finance & Law. Michael D. Rice. LC 83-3022. 362p. 1983. 39.95 (ISBN 0-13-696583-0). P-H.

Prentice-Hall Dictionary of Nutrition & Health. Kenneth Anderson & Lois Harmo. LC 84-11590. 257p. 1985. 21.95 (ISBN 0-13-695610-6); pap. 9.95 (ISBN 0-13-695602-5). P-H.

Prentice-Hall Encyclopedia of Information Technology. Robert Edmunds. 640p. 1987. 67.50 (ISBN 0-13-695214-3, Busn). P-H.

Prentice-Hall Encyclopedia of Mathematics. Ellen Griesbach & Jerry Taylor. Ed. by Louis Taylor. (Illus., Orig.). (YA) (gr. 6 up). 1982. 39.50 (ISBN 0-13-696013-8). P-H.

Prentice-Hall Encyclopedia of World Proverbs: A Treasury of Wit & Wisdom. Wolfgang Mieder. Date not set. write for info. S&S.

Prentice-Hall Federal Tax Course. Prentice-Hall Editorial Staff. Ed. by A. Rubin. 1981. student's ed. 21.00; pap. 7.95 study guide. P-H.

Prentice-Hall Federal Tax Course, 1987, Student Edition. Ed. by Al Rubin. 1440p. 1986. text ed. write for info. (ISBN 0-13-312992-6). P-H.

Prentice-Hall Federal Tax Course 1984: Student Guide. Dale Bandy. (Illus.). 368p. 1983. pap. 10.95 (ISBN 0-13-312736-2). P-H.

Prentice-Hall Federal Tax Course 1986: Student Guide. Dale Bandy. (Illus.). 352p. 1985. 11.95 (ISBN 0-13-312802-4). P-H.

Prentice-Hall Federal Tax Course, 1983 Edition. Dale Bandy. (Illus.). 368p. 1982. pap. text ed. 9.95 Student Guide (ISBN 0-13-312637-4). P-H.

Prentice-Hall Federal Tax Course 1986. Ed. by A. Rubin. 1440p. 1985. text ed. 34.95 student's ed. (ISBN 0-13-312794-X). P-H.

Prentice Hall Federal Tax Course: 1988 Edition. Alan Rubin. (Illus.). 1440p. 1987. text ed. write for info. (ISBN 0-13-313040-1). P-H.

Prentice-Hall Federal Tax Treaties, 2 vols. Prentice-Hall Editorial Staff. LC 58-1169. (Federal Taxes Ser.). Date not set. Set. price not set, looseleaf. P-H.

Prentice-Hall Great International Atlas. George P. Raintree. 416p. 1981. 75.00 (ISBN 0-13-695833-8). P-H.

Prentice Hall Guide to Expert Systems. Robert A. Edmunds. 448p. 1988. 39.95 (ISBN 0-13-703241-2, Busn). P-H.

Prentice-Hall Handbook for Writers. 9th ed. Glenn H. Leggett et al. (Illus.). 576p. 1985. text ed. write for info. (ISBN 0-13-695206-2). P-H.

Prentice-Hall Handbook for Writers. Glenn H. Leggett et al. (Illus.). 608p. 1988. text ed. price not set (ISBN 0-13-695271-2). P-H.

Prentice-Hall Illustrated Atlas of the World. George P. Raintree. (Illus.). 208p. 1982. 29.95 (ISBN 0-13-696542-3). P-H.

Prentice Hall Illustrated Handbook of Advanced Manufacturing Methods. Jerome H. Fuchs. 784p. 1988. 69.95 (ISBN 0-13-698318-9, Busn). P-H.

Prentice-Hall Inheritance Taxes. Prentice-Hall Editorial Staff. LC 83-134068. (Illus.). Date not set. price not set. P-H.

Prentice-Hall Miracle Sales Guide. Prentice-Hall Editorial Staff. 288p. 1987. pap. 12.95 (ISBN 0-13-693813-2). P-H.

Prentice-Hall Modern Home Atlas. 1986. 6.95 (ISBN 0-13-695107-4). P-H.

Prentice-Hall Nineteen Eighty-Seven. Dale Bandy. (Illus.). 352p. 1986. student ed. 11.95 (ISBN 0-317-46064-1). P-H.

Prentice-Hall Pocket Atlas of the World. George P. Raintree. 24p. 1983. pap. 2.95 (ISBN 0-13-697045-1). P-H.

Prentice-Hall Reader. George Miller. (Illus.). 576p. 1986. pap. text ed. write for info. (ISBN 0-13-699935-2). P-H.

Prentice Hall Real Estate Appraisal Deskbook. Frank J. Blankenship. 320p. 1986. 39.95 (ISBN 0-13-696378-1). P-H.

Prentice-Hall R.N. Review Manual for State Board Examinations. 2nd ed. Ellen McMorrow & Louise Malarkey. (Illus.). 512p. 1983. 22.95 (ISBN 0-13-696567-9). P-H.

Prentice-Hall Standard Glossary of Computer Terminology. Robert A. Edmunds. LC 84-4765. 1984. 29.95 (ISBN 0-13-698234-4); pap. 19.95 (ISBN 0-13-698226-3). P-H.

Prentice-Hall Students Edition of the Concise Webster's New World Dictionary of the American Language. World Pub. Co. 1971. 7.80 (ISBN 0-13-944561-7). P-H.

Prentice-Hall Textbook of Cosmetology. 2nd ed. Olive P. Scott et al. (Illus.). 496p. 1984. pap. 12.00 (ISBN 0-13-696716-7). P-H.

Prentice Hall TOEFL Prep Book. Linford Lougheed. 448p. 1986. pap. 10.25 (ISBN 0-13-696600-4). P-H.

Prentice-Hall Universal Atlas. George P. Raintree. 408p. 1983. 34.95 (ISBN 0-13-697094-X). P-H.

Prentice-Hall University Atlas. Ed. by Harold Fullard et al. LC 84-675201. (Illus.). 144p. 1984. 27.50 (ISBN 0-13-698259-X). P-H.

Prentice Hall Word Book. Louis C. Nanassy & William Selden. 1984. pap. 7.95 (ISBN 0-13-697029-X). P-H.

Prentice-Hall Workbook for Writers. 3rd ed. Melinda G. Kramer & Donald C. Rigg. 320p. 1983. P-H.

Prentice-Hall Workbook for Writers. Melinda G. Kramer et al. 352p. 1983. pap. text ed. write for info. (ISBN 0-13-696591-1). P-H.

Prentice-Hall Workbook for Writers. 4th ed. Melinda G. Kramer et al. 384p. 1985. pap. text ed. write for info. (ISBN 0-13-696055-3). P-H.

Prentice-Hall 1985 Federal Tax Course. 1985 ed. Dale Bandy. (Illus.). 368p. 1984. 11.95 (ISBN 0-13-312778-8). P-H.

Prentice-Hall's Complete Guide to T & E Deductions & Business Car Writeoffs. Kenneth Soderman & Robert Trinz. 1987. write for info. Am Inst CPA.

Prentice-Hall's Corporation Library. write for info. P-H.

Prentice Hall's Daily Sales Planner, 1988. Herbert F. Holtje. 432p. 1987. 32.50 (ISBN 0-13-695686-6, Busn). P-H.

Prentice-Hall's Explanation of the Tax Reform Act of 1986: As Passed by the House of Representatives (September 25, 1986) & Sent to the Senate. LC 86-222025. Date not set. price not set (ISBN 0-13-695123-6). P-H.

Prentice Hall's Guide to Sales & Use Taxes. Prentice Hall Editorial Staff. 720p. 1989. pap. 37.95 (ISBN 0-13-705881-0, Busn). P-H.

Prentice-Hall's Guide to Tax Court Practice & Procedure. LC 86-190810. Date not set. 20.00 (ISBN 0-13-695826-5). P-H.

Prentice Hall's IRS Practice & Procedure Handbook. 280p. write for info. P-H.

Prentice-Hall's Practice Test for the TOEFL. Roberta Steinberg. (Illus.). 180p. 1987. pap. 7.50 (ISBN 0-13-696386-2). P-H.

Prenticeana: Or, Wit & Humor in Paragraphs. George D. Prentice. 306p. 1981. Repr. of 1871 ed. lib. bdg. 30.00 (ISBN 0-8495-4400-9). Arden Lib.

Preobrazhenie Mira. M. Gor'kii. 398p. 1980. 39.00x (ISBN 0-317-40728-7, Pub. by Collets UK). State Mutual Bk.

Preobrazhenie Gospodnje. Ed. by Moscow Synod. Staff. 128p. pap. 6.00 (ISBN 0-317-29169-6). Holy Trinity.

Preoccupations: Selected Prose 1968-1978. Seamus Heaney. 224p. 1980. 15.00 (ISBN 0-374-23703-4); pap. 7.95 (ISBN 0-374-51650-2). FS&G.

Preocular Tear Film: In Health, Disease, & Contact Lens Wear. Ed. by Frank J. Holly. 1986. 150.00 (ISBN 0-9616938-0-0). Dry Eye Inst.

Preoedipal Origin & Psychoanalytic Therapy of Sexual Perversions. Charles W. Socarides. 1988. text ed. 60.00x (ISBN 0-8236-4287-9). Intl Univs Pr.

Preology: The Scientific Study of the Planning of Human Development. Norman Barraclough. LC 80-40600. 265p. 1981. pap. 19.00 (ISBN 0-08-026083-7). Pergamon.

Preoperative (Neoadjuvant) Chemotherapy. Ed. by J. Ragaz et al. (Recent Results in Cancer Research Ser.: Vol. 103). (Illus.). 196p. 1986. pap. 47.00 (ISBN 0-387-16129-5). Springer-Verlag.

Preoperative Sensory Preparation to Promote Recovery Rate. Ed. by Jo Anne Horsley. (Using Research to Improve Nursing Prectice Ser.). 1981. 15.50 (ISBN 0-8089-1327-1, 792067). Grune.

Prep Chem. John Strohl. 536p. 1982. pap. text ed. 27.50 scp (ISBN 0-06-046466-6, HarpC). Har-Row.

Prep: For Better Reading. 3rd ed. W. Royce Adams. LC 87-8562. 384p. 1988. pap. text ed. price not set (ISBN 0-03-013324-6). HR&W.

PREP for Effective Family Living. Don Dinkmeyer, Sr. et al. (YA) (gr. 7 up). 1985. 83.50 (ISBN 0-88671-225-4). Am Guidance.

PREP for Effective Family Living: Student Handbook. Don Dinkmeyer, Sr. et al. (PREP Ser.). 1985. pap. 8.75 (ISBN 0-88671-226-2); pap. text ed. 17.00 (ISBN 0-88671-227-0); tchr's. ed. 29.75 (ISBN 0-88671-229-7); activity bk 4.50 (ISBN 0-88671-228-9). Am Guidance.

Prepaid-Group Legal Service Plan: What They Are, How they Work. 1.50 (ISBN 0-317-40258-7, 2-007). Am Prepaid.

Prepaid-Group Legal Service Plans: What They Are & How They Work. American Prepaid Legal Services Institute. 26p. 1979. pap. 1.50 (ISBN 0-317-63642-1, 716-0044-01). Amer Bar Assn.

Prepaid Group Legal Service Plans: What They Are & How They Work. American Prepaid Legal Services Institute. 26p. 1979. pap. 1.50. Amer Bar Assn.

Prepaid Legal Service Plans in Profile. 72p. 1984. 20.00 (ISBN 0-317-40252-8, 2-014). Am Prepaid.

Prepaid Legal Services. Roger D. Billings, Jr. LC 79-92375. 1981. 79.50 (ISBN 0-686-35941-0); Suppl. 1987. 27.50. Lawyers Co-Op.

Prepaid Legal Services: Opportunities & Challenges for Lawyers. ABA, Special Commission on Prepaid Legal Services. 8p. 1985. pap. 5.00. Amer Bar Assn.

Prepaid Ticketing. Barbara A. Krygel. (Ticketing Ser.: No. 3). (Illus.). 23p. 1983. 12.95x (ISBN 0-917063-02-3); of 3 bks. 24.95x set. Travel Text.

Preparacion de Sermones Biblicos. A. W. Blackwood. Tr. by Santiago D. Crane. 255p. (Span.). 1985. pap. 3.95 (ISBN 0-311-42030-3). Casa Bautista.

Preparacion para el Examen de Cartero. Serran-Pagan. 192p. 1987. pap. 8.95 (ISBN 0-668-06551-6). Arco.

Preparacion para el Examen de Ciudadania. Carlos F. Paz. LC 83-6407. (Illus.). 144p. (Orig.). 1983. pap. 4.95 (ISBN 0-668-05677-0, 5677). Arco.

Preparacion para el Examen de Ciudadania. 2nd, rev. ed. Carlos F. Paz. 208p. 1988. pap. 7.95 (ISBN 0-13-705063-1). S&S.

Preparacion Para el Examen de Equivalencia de la Escuela Superior. 3rd ed. Susan Lanzano & Rosendo Abreu. Ed. by Martin Ringel & William K. Banks. LC 80-17685. 368p. (Span.). 1981. pap. 6.95 (ISBN 0-668-05095-0, 50950). Arco.

Preparation & Characterisation of Mammalian Plasma Membranes. W. H. Evans. (Techniques in Biochemistry & Molecular Biology Ser.: Vol. 7, Pt. 1). 1978. pap. 28.00 (ISBN 0-7204-4222-2, 7:1). Elsevier.

Preparation & Characterization of Materials. Ed. by J. M. Honig & C. N. Rao. LC 81-20510. 1982. 69.50 (ISBN 0-12-355040-8). Acad Pr.

Preparation & Control of Radiopharmaceuticals in Hospitals. (Technical Reports Ser.: No. 194). (Illus.). 119p. 1980. pap. 21.00 (ISBN 92-0-145279-9, IDC194, IAEA). UNIPUB.

Preparation & Crystal Growth of Materials with Layered Structures. Ed. by Ronald M. Lieth. (Physics & Chemistry of Materials with Layered Structures: Vol. I). 200p. 1978. lib. bdg. 50.00 (ISBN 90-277-0638-7, Pub. by Reidel Holland). Kluwer Academic.

Preparation & Presentation of the Show Dog. 2nd, rev. ed. Jeff Brucker & Betty Brucker. LC 82-7427. (Other Dog Bks.). (Illus.). 96p. 1982. 17.95 (ISBN 0-87714-099-5); pap. 12.95 (ISBN 0-87714-105-3). Denlingers.

Preparation & Properties of Solid State Materials: Aspects of Crystal Growth, Vol. 1. Ed. by Robert A. Lefever. LC 78-155744. (Illus.). pap. 73.00 (ISBN 0-317-08022-9, 2017856). Bks Demand UMI.

Preparation & Pursuance of Civil Litigation. Leon Rock. LC 76-24398. (Illus.). ix, 753p. 1983. 37.50. Natl Ctr PT.

Preparation & Restoration of the Multi-Rooted Tooth with Furcation Involvement. Daniel P. Casullo & Francis S. Matarazzo. Ed. by D. Walter Cohen. (Continuing Dental Education Series). 108p. 1980. 20.00 (ISBN 0-931386-20-9). Quint Pub Co.

Preparation & Testing of Reagent Water in the Clinical Laboratory: Proposed Guideline, Vol. 5. 2nd ed. National Committee for Clinical Laboratory Standards. 1985. 20.00 (ISBN 0-318-19370-1, C3-P2). Natl Comm Clin Lab Stds.

Preparation & Trial of a Civil Commitment Case: A Practice Manual. 87p. 1979. pap. 5.00 (ISBN 0-686-48108-9). Amer Bar Assn.

Preparation & Trial of a Complex Toxic Chemical or Hazardous Waste Case 1986, Vol. 316. Practising Law Institute. 480p. 1986. pap. 45.00 (ISBN 0-317-27563-1, H4-5006). PLI.

Preparation & Trial of Medical Malpractice Cases. Richard E. Shandell. 350p. 1985. Repr. of 1981 ed. casebound 55.00 (ISBN 0-318-21439-3, 00564). NY Law Pub.

Preparation & Use of Checklists. (Fossil Power Plant Startup Training Ser.). (Illus.). 59p. 1983. spiral bdg. 17.50 (ISBN 0-87683-360-1). GP Pub.

Preparation & Work of Alabama High School Teachers. Henry C. Pannell. LC 77-177142. (Columbia University. Teachers College. Contributions to Education: No. 551). Repr. of 1933 ed. 22.50 (ISBN 0-404-55551-9). AMS Pr.

Preparation De le Reforme De L'ecriture En Republique Populaire De Chine 1949-1954. Constantin Milsky. (Materiaux pour l'Etude de l'Extreme-Orient Moderne et Contemporian Travaux Ser.: No. 7). 504p. (Fr.). 1975. pap. text ed. 42.00x (ISBN 90-2797-319-9). Mouton.

Preparation for Apprenticeship Through CETA, Vol. I. Kenneth W. Tolo. 130p. 1980. pap. 4.95 (ISBN 0-89940-800-1). LBJ Sch Pub Aff.

Preparation for Birth: The Complete Guide to the Lamaze Method. Beverly Savage & Diana Simkin. 224p. (Orig.). 1987. pap. 10.95 (ISBN 0-345-31230-9, Pub. by Ballantine Trade). Ballantine.

Preparation for Calculus. 3rd ed. S. L. Salas & C. G. Salas. LC 84-21003. 477p. 1985. write for info. (ISBN 0-471-87386-1); sol. manual avail. (ISBN 0-471-81894-1). Wiley.

Preparation for Childbearing. 4th, rev. ed. (Illus.). 48p. 1985. 2.00 (ISBN 0-912758-01-5); bulk prices avail. Maternity Ctr.

Preparation for Childbirth. Donna Ewy & Rodger Ewy. 224p. 1974. pap. 3.95 (ISBN 0-451-11921-5, AE1921, Sig). NAL.

Preparation for Childbirth. 3rd, rev. ed. Donna Ewy & Rodger Ewy. LC 81-15879. (Illus.). 180p. 1982. pap. 9.95 (ISBN 0-87108-602-6). Pruett.

Preparation for Civil Service. Leonard S. Bennett et al. pap. 4.95 (ISBN 0-87738-019-8). Youth Ed.

Preparation for Cosmetology Licensing Examinations. Susan Macdonald & Maxine Mottram. LC 79-27911. 160p. (Orig.). 1980. pap. 7.95 (ISBN 0-668-04756-9). Arco.

Preparation for Covenant Life. Frank R. Keller. LC 79-53522. 1979. pap. 4.95x (ISBN 0-87303-018-4). Faith & Life.

Preparation for Death. abr. ed. Alphonsus Liguori. LC 82-50596. 1982. pap. 5.00 (ISBN 0-89555-174-8). TAN Bks Pubs.

Preparation for General Chemistry. H. Wight & D. Williamson. 1974. text ed. 34.95 (ISBN 0-07-070165-2). McGraw.

Preparation for Life Curriculum. Brian Wilcox et al. LC 84-12749. 260p. 1984. 29.00 (ISBN 0-7099-3604-4, Pub. by Croom Helm Ltd). Routledge Chapman & Hall.

Preparation for Life? The Paradox of Education in the Late Twentieth Century. Joan N. Burstyn. 200p. 1986. 36.00x (ISBN 1-85000-102-2, Falmer Pr); pap. 17.00x (ISBN 1-85000-103-0, Falmer Pr). Taylor & Francis.

Preparation for MRCP, Part II. P. Siklos & S. A. Olczak. 200p. 1983. text ed. write for info. (ISBN 0-85200-703-5, Pub. by MTP Pr England). Kluwer Academic.

Preparation for NCLEX-RN: Saunders Nursing Review & Practice Tests. 4th ed. Dee A. Gillies. 416p. 1987. pap. 21.95 (ISBN 0-7216-1454-X). Saunders.

Preparation for Ordination. Herman Hersey. 1981. pap. 1.95 (ISBN 0-89265-069-9). Randall Hse.

Preparation for Parenthood. Donna Gray. 240p. 1986. pap. 3.50 (ISBN 0-451-14567-4, Sig). NAL.

Preparation for Parenthood: How to Create a Nurturing Family. Donna Ewy. 208p. 1985. 6.95 (ISBN 0-452-25691-7, Plume). NAL.

Preparation for Pesticide Certification Examinations: Questions & Answers for Commercial Pesticide Applicators. Austin M. Frishman. LC 79-18406. 176p. (Orig.). 1980. pap. 10.00 (ISBN 0-668-04761-5). Arco.

Preparation for Problem-Solving in Science & Mathematics. Aftab Hassan. 200p. (Orig.). 1989. pap. 20.00 (ISBN 0-941406-12-1). Betz Pub Co Inc.

Preparation for the ACT. William Gladstone. 352p. (Orig.). 1985. pap. 8.95 (ISBN 0-671-50220-4, Dist by S&S). Monarch Pr.

Preparation for the Armed Forces Test (ASVAB) Texe W. Marrs. 384p. pap. 9.95 (ISBN 0-671-55517-0, Pub. by Monarch Pr). S&S.

Preparation for the Final Crisis. Fernando Chaij. LC 66-29118. 1966. pap. 7.95 (ISBN 0-8163-0137-9, 16510-0). Pacific Pr Pub Assn.

Preparation for the GED High School Equivalency Examination. 10th ed. Seymour Barasch et al. (Illus.). 512p. (Orig.). pap. text ed. 7.95 (ISBN 0-668-06485-4). P-H.

Preparation for the Gospel, 2 vols. Eusebius. Tr. by Edwin H. Gifford from Gr. (Twin Brooks Ser.). 948p. 1982. pap. 24.95 (ISBN 0-8010-3369-1). Baker Bk.

Preparation for the Landing. Ruth Norman. (Illus.). 500p. 1987. 16.95 (ISBN 0-935097-07-4). Unarius Pubns.

Preparation for the Landing. Ruth Norman. 460p. 1988. 17.95 (ISBN 0-317-66614-2). Unarius Pubns.

Preparation for the Law School Admission Test: LSAT. Edward C. Gruber & Gary R. Gruber. (Exam Prep. Ser.). 1982. pap. 8.95. Monarch Pr.

Preparation for the Professional Engineering (P. E.) Examination. Leopold DeMarinis. (Illus.). 400p. 1986. pap. 14.95 (ISBN 0-668-06570-2). P-H.

Preparation for the PSAT-NMSQT: Preliminary Scholastic Aptitude Test-National Merit Scholarship Qualifying Test. 8th ed. Eve P. Steinberg et al. (ARCO Academic Test Preparation Ser.). 1988. pap. 9.95 (ISBN 0-13-731829-4). S&S.

Preparation for the S. A. T. Mathematics Examination. 2nd ed. Daniel J. Svenconis. 254p. (Orig.). (gr. 10-12). 1978. pap. 11.45 (ISBN 0-930124-02-2). Transemantics.

Preparation for the S. A. T. Verbal Examination. 2nd 1983 ed. Daniel J. Svenconis. 400p. (Orig.). (gr. 10-12). 1981. pap. 11.45 (ISBN 0-930124-03-0). Transemantics.

Preparation for the SAT: Scholastic Aptitude Test. 6th ed. Ed. by Edward J. Deptula. 1986. pap. 7.95 (ISBN 0-668-06323-8). P-H.

Preparation for the Scholastic Aptitude Test (SAT) Edward Deptula. (Academic Test Preparation Ser.). 688p. 1987. pap. 9.95 (ISBN 0-13-700865-1). Arco.

Preparation for the Standard Written English Test. Gary R. Gruber. (Exam Prep Ser.). 176p. (Orig.). 1982. pap. 6.75 (ISBN 0-671-45884-1). Monarch Pr.

Preparation for the Study of Medicine: Proceedings. Conference on the Optimal Preparation for the Study of Medicine, (1967: University of Chicago) Ed. by Robert G. Page & Mary H. Littlemeyer. LC 69-19280. pap. 73.80 (ISBN 0-317-20632-X, 2024123). Bks Demand UMI.

Preparation for Total Consecration. pap. 2.00 (ISBN 0-910984-10-7). Montfort Pubns.

Preparation for Trial. Hubert Hickam & Thomas M. Scanlon. 295p. 1963. 2.00 (ISBN 0-317-30868-8, B110). Am Law Inst.

Preparation for Writing: Grammar. Milton Wohl. LC 78-647. 208p. 1978. pap. text ed. 11.50 (ISBN 0-88377-106-3). Newbury Hse.

Preparation Handbook: A Guide to CPCU-IIA Study. Rev. ed. 1985. 3.00 (ISBN 0-686-95937-X). IIA.

Preparation of a Product Liability Case. Scott Baldwin et al. 1054p. 1981. 80.00 (ISBN 0-316-07925-1). Little.

Preparation of a Rubella IgM Antibody Reference Material: Proposed Guideline, Vol. 5. National Committee for Clinical Laboratory Standards. 1985. 20.00 (ISBN 0-318-19407-4, I-LA8-P). Natl Comm Clin Lab Stds.

Preparation of Annual Disclosure Documents, 1987. (Corporate Law & Practice Ser.). 1987. 45.00. PLI.

Preparation of Annual Disclosure Documents, 1988. (Corporate Law & Practice Ser.). 882p. 1988. 45.00 (B4-6816). PLI.

Preparation of Archaeological Reports. 2nd ed. Leslie Grinsell & Phillip Rantz. LC 74-82135. 1974. 27.50 (ISBN 0-312-63945-7). St Martin.

Preparation of Archival Copies of Theses & Dissertations. Jane Boyd & Don Etherington. LC 85-28939. 1986. pap. 3.95x (ISBN 0-8389-0449-1). ALA.

Preparation of Biological Specimens for Scanning Electron Microscopy. Ed. by Godfried M. Roomans. Judith A. Murphy. (Illus.). 352p. (Orig.). 1984. pap. text ed. 32.00 (ISBN 0-931288-33-9). Scanning Microscopy.

Preparation of Catalysts II: Scientific Basis for the Preparation of Heterogeneous Catalysts; Proceedings. International Symposium, Louvain, Sept., 1978. Ed. by B. Delmon et al. (Studies in Surface Science & Catalysts: Vol. 3). 762p. 1979. 173.75 (ISBN 0-444-41733-8). Elsevier.

Preparing for High Technology: CAD-CAM Programs. Robert E. Abram et al. 79p. 1983. 6.50 (ISBN 0-318-22175-6, RD234). Natl Ctr Res Voc Ed.
Preparing for High Technology: Model Programs in the U. S. A. Charles R. Doty. 100p. 1985. 8.00 (ISBN 0-318-20416-9, RD258). Natl Ctr Res Voc Ed.
Preparing for High Technology: Robotics Programs. William L. Ashley et al. 57p. 1983. 5.75 (ISBN 0-318-22176-4, RD233). Natl Ctr Res Voc Ed.
Preparing for High Technology: Successful Co-op Strategies. Stephen J. Franchak & O. Michael Smith. 124p. 10.50 (ISBN 0-318-22177-2, RD263). Natl Ctr Res Voc Ed.
Preparing for High Technology: Thirty Steps to Implementation. Robert E. Abram et al. 49p. 1983. 6.50 (ISBN 0-318-22178-0, RD232). Natl Ctr Res Voc Ed.
Preparing for Liturgy: A Theology & Sprituality. Austin H. Fleming. (Orig.). 1985. pap. 6.95 (ISBN 0-912405-16-3). Pastoral Pr.
Preparing for Marriage. Larry Hard & Mark P. Watts. 1984. 2.95 (ISBN 0-89536-673-8, 1638). CSS of Ohio.
Preparing for Marriage Handbook. Ed. by Jean M. Hiesberger. LC 80-80386. (Paths of Life Ser.). 112p. 1980. 2.95 (ISBN 0-8091-2260-X). Paulist Pr.
Preparing for Medical School: A Guide to Requirements, Admission, Financial Aid, & More. Brice W. Corder. LC 83-71087. (Illus.). 200p. (Orig.). 1983. pap. 8.95 (ISBN 0-913011-00-2). Ambleside.
Preparing for Paradise. George Fuller. 52p. 1986. 10.95 (ISBN 0-937310-27-1); pap. 5.95 (ISBN 0-937310-26-3). Jazz Pr.
Preparing for Planning. John Kraus & Robert E. Engel. 43p. 1978. 5.00 (ISBN 0-911696-31-8). Assn Am Coll.
Preparing for Power: America's Elite Boarding Schools. Peter W. Cookson, Jr. & Carolina H. Persell. LC 85-47559. 288p. 1985. 19.95 (ISBN 0-465-06268-7). Basic.
Preparing for Power: America's Elite Boarding Schools. Peter W. Cookson, Jr. & Caroline H. Persell. LC 85-47559. 27.2p. 1987. pap. 9.95 (ISBN 0-465-06269-5, PL 5196). Basic.
Preparing for Sabbath Fiction. Nessa Rapoport. 300p. 1988. pap. 10.95 (ISBN 0-930395-05-0). Biblio NY.
Preparing for Spiritual Direction. Jean LaPlace. 196p. 1975. 6.95 (ISBN 0-8199-0558-5). Franciscan Herald.
Preparing for Teletex. S. G. Price. 140p. 1983. pap. 14.20 (ISBN 0-471-88999-7). Wiley.
Preparing for the CRM Examination: A Handbook. 131p. 1985. 25.00 (ISBN 0-933887-07-8). Assn Recs Mgrs & Admin.
Preparing for the Drug (Free) Years: A Family Activity Book. 2nd ed. Developmental Research & Programs, Inc. Staff & Roberts, Fitzmahan & Associates Staff. 142p. (Orig.). 1987. pap. 10.95. Comprehen Health Educ.
Preparing for the Engineer-In-Training Examination. Irving J. Levinson. LC 82-18251. 242p. 1983. pap. 14.95 (ISBN 0-910554-40-4). Engineering.
Preparing for the FCC License Exam. Donald Middleton. (Illus.). 411p. 1982. 21.95 (ISBN 0-13-697219-5); pap. 16.95 (ISBN 0-13-697201-2). P-H.
Preparing for the Foodservice Industry: An Introductory Approach. Earl R. Palan & Judith A. Stadler. 1986. pap. 26.95 (ISBN 0-87055-521-9). AVI.
Preparing for the Foodservice Industry Workbook. Palan. 1987. pap. 12.95 (ISBN 0-87055-548-0). Van Nos Reinhold.
Preparing for the Future. 80p. 1983. 3.00 (ISBN 0-317-36793-5, 611-83306). Assn Supervision.
Preparing for the Future: An Essay on the Rights Future Generations. John Ahrens. 44p. 1983. pap. 5.95. Transaction Bks.
Preparing for the Future: An Essay on the Rights of Future Generations. John Ahrens. (Studies in Social Philosophy & Policy: No. 2). 44p. (Orig.). 1983. pap. 4.00. Soc Phil Pol.
Preparing for the Greatest Two Years of Your Life. Mark A. Dennison. pap. 3.95 (ISBN 0-89036-128-2). Hawkes Pub Inc.
Preparing for the Messiah. Doris Williams & Patricia Griggs. (Griggs Educational Resources Ser.). 1979. pap. 5.95 (ISBN 0-687-33920-0). Abingdon.
Preparing for the Next War: American Plans for Postwar Defense, 1941-45. Michael S. Sherry. LC 76-27853. (Illus.). 1977. 30.00x (ISBN 0-300-02031-7). Yale U Pr.
Preparing for the Sacrament of Marriage. Anthony Del Vecchio & Mary Del Vecchio. LC 80-67721. (Illus.). 144p. (Orig.). 1980. pap. 4.95 (ISBN 0-87793-208-5). Ave Maria.
Preparing for the Science RCT. Lorraine Godlewski et al. (WPCO's Science Ser.). (Illus., Orig.). 1987. wkbk. 3.45 (ISBN 0-937323-08-X). United Pub Co.
Preparing for the Sixth Epoch. Rudolf Steiner. Orig. Title: How Anthroposophic Groups Prepare for the Sixth Epoch. 1976. pap. 2.95 (ISBN 0-910142-72-6). Anthroposophic.
Preparing for the Storm. Kenneth D. Barney. LC 74-21021. 96p. 1975. pap. 1.25 (ISBN 0-88243-576-0, 02-0576). Gospel Pub.
Preparing for the Test of Standard Written English. Franklin G. Meyers & Joyce N. French. 80p. (gr. 10-12). 1985. pap. text ed. 5.95 (ISBN 0-89026-070-2); tchr's. ed. 6.95 (ISBN 0-89026-071-0). College Skills.
Preparing for the Twenty-First Century: Proceeding of the Mountain Plains Library Association Academic Library Section Research Fourm. Ed. & intro. by V. Sue Hatfield. 104p. (Orig.). 1986. pap. 7.50 (ISBN 0-934068-03-8). Memorial Union.
Preparing for Tomorrow: Successfully Integrating People & Technology for the Profitable Practice of Law. International Conference on Law Office Economics & Management & Canadian Bar Association Staff. LC 86-160596. x, 375p. Date not set. 45.00. Amer Bar Assn.
Preparing for Ulysses: Politics & Veterans During World War Two. Davis R. Ross. LC 78-94513. (Contemporary American History Ser.). 1969. 37.50x (ISBN 0-231-03222-6). Columbia U Pr.
Preparing for Work: The Induction Pack. Sue Carroll & Patricia McQuade. 176p. 1987. 170.00x (ISBN 1-85008-005-4, Pub. by Framework UK). State Mutual Bk.
Preparing for Your Marriage. William J. McRae. 160p. (Orig.). 1980. pap. 7.95 (ISBN 0-310-42761-4, 9366P). Zondervan.
Preparing for Your Retirement Years. Rev. ed. Frank Corrick. LC 70-160362. 59p. (Orig.). 1979. pap. 2.50 (ISBN 0-87576-036-8). Pilot Bks.
Preparing Humanists for Work: A National Study of Undergraduate Internships in the Humanities. 99p. 1985. 13.00 (ISBN 0-937883-03-4). NSIEE.
Preparing Instructional Objectives. 2nd, rev. ed. Robert F. Mager. LC 83-60503. 1984. pap. 11.95 (ISBN 0-8224-4341-4). D S Lake Pubs.
Preparing Managers for Planning. Rochelle O'Connor. (Report Ser.: No. 781). (Illus.). 55p. (Orig.). 1980. pap. 22.50 (ISBN 0-8237-0217-0). Conference Bd.
Preparing Matrimonial Agreements. Stanley Plesent. (Basic Practice Skills Ser.). 175p. 1988. 50.00 (Q1-3003). PLI.
Preparing Missionaries for Intercultural Communication. Lyman E. Reed. LC 84-23060. (Illus.). 204p. (Orig.). 1985. pap. text ed. 6.95x (ISBN 0-87808-438-X). William Carey Lib.
Preparing Multi-Media Teaching Materials: A Source Book. (Illus.). 41p. (Orig.). 1986. pap. text ed. 7.50 (ISBN 0-317-53610-9, UB222, UB). UNIPUB.
Preparing Multiple-Image Impositions (Step & Repeat) 40p. 1981. 16.00 (ISBN 0-88362-037-5, 0461). Graphic Arts Tech Found.
Preparing Now for the New Immigration Law: Representing Employers or Aliens. 207p. 1986. pap. 27.00 (MI-49106). Cal Cont Ed Bar.
Preparing Preschoolers: An Easy-to-Use Nursery School Program with Lesson Plans & Teaching Aids forParents & Professionals. Susan W. Allen & Karen H. Talbot. LC 80-83029. 150p. (Orig.). 1981. pap. 14.95 (ISBN 0-88290-160-5, 2047). Horizon Utah.
Preparing Products Liability Cases. Terrence F. Kiely. LC 85-22458. (Trial Practice Library). 307p. 1986. 95.00 (ISBN 0-471-80638-2). Wiley.
Preparing Products Liability Cases: 1988 Supplement. Kiely. (Trial Practice Library). 1988. pap. 35.00 (ISBN 0-471-60181-0). Wiley.
Preparing Professional Women for the Future: Resources for Teachers & Trainers. Ed. by V. Jean Ramsey. (Michigan Business Papers: No. 67). 1985. pap. text ed. 10.00 (ISBN 0-87712-239-3). UMI Div Res GSBA.
Preparing School Leaders for Educational Improvement. Ed. by K. A. Leithwood et al. (Croom Helm Series on Education Management). 224p. 1986. 34.95 (ISBN 0-7099-4123-4, Pub. by Croom Helm UK). Routledge Chapman & Hall.
Preparing Students for Mainstreaming. Sharon Bunting. 80p. (Orig.). 1982. pap. 8.90 (ISBN 0-936326-02-6). Cedars Pr.
Preparing Teachers for Lifelong Education. Ed. by L. H. Goad. (Advances in Lifelong Education Ser.: Vol. 8). (Illus.). 200p. 1984. text ed. 34.00 (ISBN 0-08-026786-6); pap. text ed. 15.75 (ISBN 0-08-026787-4). Pergamon.
Preparing Teachers for Urban Schools. Martin Haberman. LC 88-60075. (Fastback Ser.: No. 267). 50p. (Orig.). 1988. pap. 0.90 (ISBN 0-87367-267-4). Phi Delta Kappa.
Preparing the Ground. Gary Gach. 48p. (Orig.). 1975. pap. text ed. 4.95 (ISBN 0-915970-02-3). Heirs Intl.
Preparing the Pharmacy for a Joint Commission Survey. 2nd ed. Charles P. Coe. 171p. 1987. pap. text ed. 30.00 (ISBN 0-930530-82-9). Am Soc Hosp Pharm.
Preparing Theses & Other Typed Manuscripts. Roy O. Billett. (Quality Paperback Ser.: No. 63). (Orig.). 1968. pap. 3.95 (ISBN 0-8226-0063-3). Littlefield.
Preparing to be Happy. Alan Broughton. LC 87-71456. (Poetry Ser). 1988. 14.95 (ISBN 0-88748-060-8); pap. 7.95 (ISBN 0-88748-061-6). Carnegie Mellon.
Preparing to Enter Dental School. Shailer A. Peterson. 1979. text ed. 13.95 (ISBN 0-13-697326-4, Spec); (Spec). P-H.
Preparing to Enter Medical School. Shailer A. Peterson. 1980. text ed. 14.95 (ISBN 0-13-697342-6, Spec). P-H.
Preparing to Leave. Phoebe Hesketh. 1977. signed, specially bd 10.00 (ISBN 0-685-84029-8, Pub. by Enitharmon Pr); wrappers 3.50 (ISBN 0-685-84030-1); 4.75 (ISBN 0-685-84031-X). Small Pr Dist.
Preparing to Receive Holy Communion. Tom Avramis. 1986. pap. 1.95 (ISBN 0-937032-43-3). Light&Life Pub Co MN.
Preparing to Receive Jesus Christ. Daughters of St. Paul. (Way, Truth & Life Ser.). 1978. 1.75 (ISBN 0-8198-0548-3); tchr's manual 3.50 (ISBN 0-8198-0549-1); activity book 1.00 (ISBN 0-8198-0550-5). Dghtrs St Paul.
Preparing to Serve As a God Parent. William S. Chiganos. 1986. pap. 1.25 (ISBN 0-937032-44-1). Light&Life Pub Co MN.
Preparing to Study. Ed. by Michael Richardson et al. 72p. 1979. pap. 11.00x (ISBN 0-335-00255-2, Pub. by Open Univ Pr). Taylor & Francis.
Preparing to Take the GRE General Test, No. 4. Educational Testing Service Staff. 1986. pap. 7.95 (ISBN 0-317-56825-6). Warner Bks.
Preparing to Teach Economics: Approaches & Resources. rev. & exp. ed. Suzanne W. Helburn & James E. Davis. LC 82-5474. 112p. 1982. pap. 9.95 (ISBN 0-89994-268-7). Soc Sci Ed.
Preparing to Teach God's Word. G. Raymond Carlson. LC 75-5221. (Sunday School Staff Training Ser.). (Illus.). 128p. 1975. pap. 1.25 (ISBN 0-88243-579-5, 02-0579). Gospel Pub.
Preparing to Teach Writing. James D. Williams. Date not set. pap. text ed. write for info. (ISBN 0-534-10026-0). Wadsworth Pub.
Preparing Written Material. Jack Rudman. (Career Examination Ser.: CS-37). (Cloth bdg. avail. on request). pap. 12.00 (ISBN 0-8373-3737-2). Natl Learning.
Preparing Young Children for Math: A Book of Games. Claudia Zaslavsky. LC 79-12552. (Illus.). 160p. 1986. pap. 7.95 (ISBN 0-8052-0796-1). Schocken.
Preparing Young Children for Science: A Book of Games. Lois B. Arnold. LC 79-26119. (Illus.). 128p. (Orig.). 1980. text ed. 11.95x (ISBN 0-8052-3740-2); pap. 7.95 (ISBN 0-8052-0641-8). Schocken.
Preparing Your Body to Fly, Vol. 1. Millicent Linden. (Tx 112-882). 1977. pap. 7.00 (ISBN 0-912628-05-7). M Linden NY.
Preparing Your Business Budget with SYMPHONY. Dennis P. Curtin & William R. Osgood. (Illus.). 160p. 1985. pap. 27.95 (ISBN 0-13-698804-0). P-H.
Preparing Your Business Plan: Multiplan on the DEC Rainbow. William R. Osgood & J. David Maupin. (DEC Bks.). 170p. (Orig.). 1985. pap. 25.00 (ISBN 0-932376-75-4, EY-00047-DP). Digital Pr.
Preparing Your Business Plan with Excel. William Fletcher et al. (Illus.). 225p. (Orig.). 1986. pap. text ed. 17.95 (ISBN 0-07-881226-7). Osborne-McGraw.
Preparing Your Business Plan with LOTUS 1-2-3. William R. Osgood & Dennis P. Curtin. (Illus.). 176p. 1985. pap. 27.95 (ISBN 0-13-698424-X); pap. 44.95 (ISBN 0-13-698432-0); disk incl. P-H.
Preparing Your Business Plan with MULTIPLAN. William R. Osgood & Dennis P. Curtin. 44.95. P-H.
Preparing Your Business Plan with SYMPHONY. William R. Osgood & Dennis P. Curtin. 27.95. P-H.
Preparing Your Children for Greatness. Jessie R. Sandberg. (Joyful Living Ser.). 1987. pap. 1.50 (ISBN 0-912623-05-5). Joyful Woman.
Preparing Your Church for Ministry to Alcoholics & Their Families. Thomas H. Cairns. 136p. 1986. 21.75 (ISBN 0-398-05230-1). C C Thomas.
Preparing Your Curriculum Guide. Marilyn Winters. (Illus.). 19p. 1980. 8.50 (611-80208). Assn Supervision.
Preparing Your Design for Print. Lynn John. 1988. 27.95 (ISBN 0-89134-257-5). Writers Digest.
Preparing Your Manuscript. Elizabeth Preston et al. (Orig.). 1986. pap. 8.95 (ISBN 0-87116-144-3). Writer.
Preparing Your Own Chapel Talks for Children. Dolores E. Hermann. 1987. pap. 3.95 (ISBN 0-570-04466-9, 12-3082). Concordia.
Preparing Your Preschooler for Reading: A Book of Games. Brandon Sparkman & Jane Saul. LC 77-75284. (Illus.). 128p. 1986. pap. 7.95 (ISBN 0-8052-0799-6). Schocken.
Preparing Your Research Paper. J. Harris Nierman. (Illus.). 23p. (Orig.). (gr. 10 up). 1979. pap. 1.95 (ISBN 0-935770-00-3). Creative Res & Educ.
Preparing Youth for Dating, Courtship & Marriage-Teacher's Guide. Norman Wright & Marvin Inmon. LC 78-56879. (Orig.). 1978. pap. 9.95 (ISBN 0-89081-147-4); transparencies & repro masters incl. Harvest Hse.
Prepartion for the New GED High School Equivalency Examination. 11th ed. Seymour Barasch et al. (Arco Academic Test Preparation Ser.). 608p. 1988. pap. 9.95 (ISBN 0-13-698789-3). Arco.
Prepayment Mortgage Value Tables, No. 438. 944p. 1982. 29.95 (ISBN 0-87600-438-9). Finan Pub.
Prepayment Mortgage Yield Table for Monthly Payment Mortgages. 7th ed. Financial Publishing Company Staff. 960p. 1980. pap. 29.95 (ISBN 0-87600-435-4). Finan Pub.
Prepayment Mortgage Yield Table: Incorporated Eighth Rates. rev. ed. Ed. by Financial Publishing Co. Staff. 464p. 1986. text ed. 25.00 (ISBN 0-87600-159-2). Finan Pub.
Prepodobny Feodor, Igumen Studiisky, 2 vols. in 1. Andreevich Dobrovol'skii. LC 80-2355. Repr. of 1913 ed. 115.50 (ISBN 0-404-18907-5). AMS Pr.
Prepoetics of William Carlos Williams: "Kora in Hell". Roy Miki. Ed. by A. Walton Litz. LC 83-15551. (Studies in Modern Literature: No. 32). 224p. 1983. 42.95 (ISBN 0-8357-1476-4). UMI Res Pr.
Preponderance Espagnole 1559-1660. Henri Hauser. (Nouvelle Introduction Par Pierre Chaunu Reeditions Ser.: No. 11). 1973. 34.40 (ISBN 90-2797-225-7); pap. 31.20x (ISBN 0-686-21234-7). Mouton.
Prepositional Phrases & Prepositional Verbs: A Study in Grammatical Function. T. Vestergaard. (Janua Linguarum, Series Minor: No. 161). 1977. 18.40x (ISBN 90-279-7616-3). Mouton.
Prepositions. Alice C. Pack. (Dyad Learning Program Ser.). 1977. pap. text ed. 10.50 (ISBN 0-88377-076-8); avail. tchr's. edition (ISBN 0-88377-078-4). Newbury Hse.
Prepositions: An Analytical Bibliography. Claude Guimier. (Library & Information Sources in Linguistics Ser.: No. 8). viii, 244p. 1981. 32.00x (ISBN 90-272-3734-4). Benjamins North Am.
Prepositions & Conjunctions. Barbara Gregorich. (Horizons II Ser.). (Illus.). 24p. (gr. 3-4). 1980. wkbk. 2.50 (ISBN 0-89403-597-5). EDC.
Prepositions: The Collected Critical Essays of Louis Zukofsky. expanded ed. Louis Zukofsky. 200p. 1981. 28.00x (ISBN 0-520-03224-1); pap. 8.95 (ISBN 0-520-04361-8). U of Cal Pr.
Prepositions Through Pictures. Harris Winitz. (Language Through Pictures Ser.). (Illus.). 31p. (gr. 2-12). 1982. pap. 3.95 (ISBN 0-939990-35-0). Intl Linguistics.
Preppie Murder Trial. Bryna Taubman. 1988. pap. 3.95. St Martin.
Preppy Cat. J. C. Suares et al. pap. 3.95 (ISBN 0-425-05724-0). Berkley Pub.
Preppy Chef. rev. ed. Karen B. Riggs. LC 82-960707. (Illus.). 229p. 1982. Repr. 7.00 (ISBN 0-686-39718-5). Riggs.
Preppy Problem. Stephanie Austin. 1984. pap. 1.95 (ISBN 0-449-70036-4, Juniper). Fawcett.
Prepreg Composition, Processing, & Applications, 1973-1984. 160p. 1984. pap. 85.00 (ISBN 0-686-48278-6, LS109). T-C Pubns CA.
Preprints of Papers for the Physics & Chemistry of the Silver Halide Crystal: An International Colloquium at the University of Montreal. Society of Photographic Scientists & Engineers. LC 72-170666. pap. 83.50 (ISBN 0-317-42044-5, 2025699). Bks Demand UMI.
Prereading Activities for Content Area Reading & Learning. David W. Moore & John E. Readence. (Reading Aids Ser.). 72p. (Orig.). 1982. pap. 5.00 (ISBN 0-87207-228-2). Intl Reading.
Prerecorded & Blank Audio & Video Tapes. 1985. 595.00. Busn Trend.
Prerequisite Algebra. Charles P. McKeague. 556p. 1988. text ed. 26.00 (ISBN 0-15-571093-1, HC). HarBraceJ.
Prerequisite Algebra: Instructor's Resource Manual. Charles P. McKeague. 129p. 1988. pap. text ed. 4.00 net (ISBN 0-15-571094-X). HarBraceJ.
Prerequisites for Community Wellbeing. Brown et al. 1972. pap. 1.50 (ISBN 0-910420-20-3). Comm Serv OH.
Prerequisites for Good Planning Sessions in Team Teaching see Team Teaching Modules.
Prerequisites for Peace. Norman M. Thomas. LC 78-13967. 1979. Repr. of 1959 ed. lib. bdg. 35.00x (ISBN 0-313-20732-1, THPP). Greenwood.
Prerequisites for Winning Government R&D Contracts. rev. ed. Robert Guyton et al. LC 81-52984. (Project-Contract Acquisition & Management Ser.). 170p. 1983. pap. 28.00 (ISBN 0-912426-08-X). Univ Tech.
Preretirement Planning: Individual, Institutional, & Social Perspectives. Carl I. Brahce. 49p. 1983. 4.95 (ISBN 0-318-17789-7, IN264). Natl Ctr Res Voc Ed.
Prerogativa Regis: Tertia Lectura Roberti Constable De Lyncolnis Inne. Robert Constable. Ed. by Samuel E. Thorne. 1949. 65.00x (ISBN 0-685-69876-9). Elliots Bks.
Prerogative of Asylumdom: Social, Cultural, & Administrative Aspects of the Institutional Treatment of the Insane in Nineteenth Century Britain. D. J. Mellett. Ed. by Peter Stansky & Leslie Hume. LC 81-48363. (Modern British Ser.). 290p. 1982. lib. bdg. 40.00 (ISBN 0-8240-5159-9). Garland Pub.

Presence of Ford Madox Ford. Ed. by Sondra Stang. (Illus.). 1981. 33.95x (ISBN 0-8122-7794-5). U of Pa Pr.

Presence of God. Roland Murphy et al. LC 78-107214. (Concilium Ser.: Vol. 50). 215p. 7.95 (ISBN 0-8091-0116-5). Paulist Pr.

Presence of Grace. facs. ed. James F. Powers. LC 77-85694. (Short Story Index Reprint Ser). 1956. 17.00 (ISBN 0-8369-3037-1). Ayer Co Pubs.

Presence of Grace & Other Book Reviews by Flannery O'Connor. Flannery O'Conner. Ed. by Carter W. Martin. LC 82-20064. 200p. 1983. 16.00x (ISBN 0-8203-0663-0). U of Ga Pr.

Presence of Hawthorne. Hyatt H. Waggoner. LC 79-14573. xvi, 170p. 1979. text ed. 22.50 (ISBN 0-8071-0576-7). La State U Pr.

Presence of Milton. Ed. by B. Rajan. LC 69-12335. (Milton Studies Ser: Vol. XI). (Illus.). 1978. 32.95x (ISBN 0-8229-3373-X). U of Pittsburgh Pr.

Presence of Other Worlds. Wilson Van Dusen. LC 73-18684. 240p. pap. 5.95 (ISBN 0-87785-166-2). Swedenborg.

Presence of Rene Char. Mary Ann Caws. LC 75-30188. 1976. 44.00x (ISBN 0-691-06305-2). Princeton U Pr.

Presence of Siva. Stella Kramrisch. LC 80-8558. (Illus.). 550p. 1981. 55.00x (ISBN 0-691-03964-X); pap. 19.95x (ISBN 0-691-10115-9). Princeton U Pr.

Presence of Stoicism in Medieval Thought. Gerard Verbeke. LC 82-4134. 109p. 1982. pap. 6.95 (ISBN 0-8132-0573-5). Cath U Pr.

Presence of the Actor. Joseph Chaikin. LC 70-175287. (Illus.). 1972. pap. text ed. 8.95x (ISBN 0-689-70338-4, 194). Atheneum.

Presence of the Past: A History of the Preservation Movement in the U. S. Before Williamsburg. Charles B. Hosmer. LC 65-13292. 386p. 14.95 (ISBN 0-89133-085-2). Preservation Pr.

Presence of the Past: Essays on Modern British & American Poetry. Jeremy Hooker. LC 87-60975. 228p. 1987. 31.00 (ISBN 0-907476-71-6, Pub. by Poetry Wales Pr UK). Dufour.

Presence of the Past: John Dewey & Alfred Schutz on the Genesis & Organization of Experience. Rodman B. Webb. LC 76-25461. (University of Florida Social Sciences Monographs: No. 57). 1976. pap. 9.00x (ISBN 0-8130-0560-4). U Presses Fla.

Presence of the Past: Morphic Resonance & the Memory of Nature. Rupert Sheldrake. LC 87-40200. (Illus.). 320p. 1988. 19.95 (ISBN 0-8129-1666-2). Times Bks.

Presence of the Past: T.S. Eliot's Victorian Inheritance. David N. Tobin. Ed. by A. Walton Litz. LC 83-5733. (Studies in Modern Literature: No. 8). 192p. 1983. 37.95 (ISBN 0-8357-1413-6). UMI Res Pr.

Presence of the Word: Some Prolegomena for Cultural & Religious History. Walter J. Ong. LC 81-3017. xvi, 360p. 1981. pap. 12.95 (ISBN 0-8166-1043-6). U of Minn Pr.

Presence of Thought: Introspective Accounts of Reading & Writing. Marilyn Sternglass. Ed. by Roy O. Freedle. (Advances in Discourse Processes Ser.: Vol. 34). 240p. 1988. text ed. 32.50 (ISBN 0-89391-516-5). Ablex Pub.

Presence of Walker Evans. Isabelle Storey & Alan Trachtenberg. (Illus.). 1978. 5.00 (ISBN 0-910663-13-0). ICA Inc.

Presence of Walt Whitman see Selected Papers from the English Institute.

Presence: Poems 1984-87. Kathleen Raine. 80p. 1988. 14.95 (ISBN 0-89281-082-3, Lindusfarne Pr). Inner Tradit.

Presence, Power, Praise; Documents on Charismatic Renewal: International Documents, Vol. 3. Ed. by Kilian McDonnell. LC 79-26080. 306p. 1980. 15.00 (ISBN 0-8146-1065-X). Liturgical Pr.

Presence, Power, Praise: Documents on Charismatic Renewal: National Documents, Vol. 1. Ed. by Kilian McDonnell. LC 79-26080. 696p. 1980. 20.00 (ISBN 0-8146-1066-8). Liturgical Pr.

Presence, Power, Praise: Documents on Charismatic Renewal: National Documents, Vol. 2. Kilian McDonnell. LC 79-26080. 568p. 1980. 20.00 (ISBN 0-8146-1189-3). Liturgical Pr.

Presence: The God Who Delivers & Guides. Bruce Larson. LC 87-46214. 128p. 1988. 14.45 (ISBN 0-317-67185-5, HarpR). Har-Row.

Presence, the Transco Tower. Ann Holmes. (Illus.). 112p. 1985. 50.00 (ISBN 0-917001-03-6). Herring Pr.

Presence Through the Word. Evelyn Ann Schumacher, Sr. 144p. (Orig.). 1983. pap. 2.95 (ISBN 0-914544-46-2). Living Flame Pr.

Presences Contemporaines: Auteurs Francais du XXe Siecle. Brodin. 9.95 (ISBN 0-685-37147-6). French & Eur.

Presences of Jesus. 2nd ed. Carl J. Pfeifer. LC 84-50163. 112p. 1984. pap. 4.95 (ISBN 0-89622-193-8). Twenty-Third.

Presences of Nature: British Landscape 1780-1830. Louis Hawes. LC 82-50608. (Center for British Art Publication Ser.). (Illus.). 224p. 1982. text ed. 50.00t (ISBN 0-300-02930-6); pap. 18.95 (ISBN 0-300-02931-4). Yale U Pr.

Presencia de Antonio Machado en la Poesia Espanola de Posguerra. Jose O. Jimenez. LC 82-51174. 230p. 1983. pap. 25.00 (ISBN 0-89295-024-2). Society Sp & Sp-Am.

Present Age. Soren Kierkegaard. Ed. & tr. by Alexander Dru. pap. 6.95x (ISBN 0-06-130094-2, TB94, Torch). Har-Row.

Present Age after Nineteen Hundred & Twenty. David Daiches. 376p. 1986. Repr. of 1940 ed. lib. bdg. 45.00. Arden Lib.

Present Age: Progress & Anarchy in Modern America. Robert Nisbet. LC 87-46158. 192p. 1988. 18.45 (ISBN 0-06-015902-2, HarpT). Har-Row.

Present & Future Automotive Fuels: Performance & Exhaust Clarification. Ed. by Osamu Hirao & Richard K. Pefley. LC 87-6234. 400p. 1988. 70.00 (ISBN 0-471-80259-X). Wiley.

Present & Future of Counseling Psychology. John M. Whiteley & Bruce R. Fretz. 1980. 7.25 (ISBN 1-55620-019-6, 71005C). Am Assn Coun Dev.

Present & Future Security Problems of Korea. Lee K. Baek. (Significant Issues Ser. Vol. 9, No. 9). 12p. (Orig.). 1987. pap. 6.95 (ISBN 0-89206-108-1). CSI Studies.

Present & Past. Ivy Compton-Burnett. 1986. pap. 6.95 (ISBN 0-14-003347-5). Penguin.

Present & Past in Middle Life. Ed. by Dorothy Eichorn et al. LC 80-70589. 1982. 44.00 (ISBN 0-12-233680-1). Acad Pr.

Present & Projected Business Utilization of International Telecommunications: 1985. Ronald S. Eward. (National Telecommunications & Informational Administration Contractor Reports: No. 85-35). (Illus.). 90p. (Orig.). 1985. pap. 3.50 (ISBN 0-318-18819-8, S/N 003-000-00642-5). USGPO.

Present & the Past. Ivy Compton-Burnett. 1953. 16.95 (ISBN 0-575-01416-4, Pub by Gollancz England). David & Charles.

Present Appearances: Aspects of Poetic Structure in Rimbaud's "Illuminations". Nathaniel Wing. LC 74-7380. (Romance Monographs: No. 9). 1974. pap. 15.00x (ISBN 84-399-2424-0). Romance.

Present As History: Essays & Reviews of Capitalism & Socialism. Paul M. Sweezy. LC 53-12728. pap. 96.00 (ISBN 0-8357-9443-1, 2016446). Bks Demand UMI.

Present at the Creation: My Years in the State Department. Dean Acheson. (Illus.). 848p. 1987. pap. 12.95 (ISBN 0-393-30412-4). Norton.

Present at the Creation: My Years in the State Department. Dean Acheson. (Illus.). 1987. 29.95 (ISBN 0-393-07448-X). Norton.

Present Christ. John Main. 128p. (Orig.). 1986. pap. 7.95 (ISBN 0-8245-0740-1). Crossroad NY.

Present Company. M. Gleason. 1978. 5.00 (ISBN 0-8233-0278-4). Golden Quill.

Present Concerns. C. S. Lewis. 1987. 14.95 (ISBN 0-15-173948-X, Harv); pap. 4.95 (ISBN 0-15-673840-6, Harv). HarBraceJ.

Present Danger. William J. Buchanan. 256p. 1986. 16.95 (ISBN 0-02-517970-5). Macmillan.

Present Danger. William J. Buchanan. 256p. 1987. pap. 3.95 (ISBN 0-7701-0512-2). PaperJacks US.

Present Danger. Norman Podhoretz. 1980. (Touchstone Bks); pap. 3.95 (ISBN 0-671-41328-7). S&S.

Present Danger: Do We Have the Will to Reverse the Decline of American Power. Norman Podhoretz. 112p. 1986. pap. 6.95 (ISBN 0-671-62866-6, Touchstone Bks). S&S.

Present-Day Christological Debate. Klaus Runia. Ed. by I. Howard Marshall. LC 84-6554. (Issues in Contemporary Theology Ser.). 120p. 1984. pap. 8.95 (ISBN 0-87784-937-4). Inter-Varsity.

Present Day Ethnic Processes in the U. S. S. R. J. V. Bromley et al. 277p. 1982. 7.95 (ISBN 0-8285-2327-4, Pub. by Progress Pubs U. S. S. R.). Imported Pubns.

Present Day Gemorphological Processes. Ed. by A. Pissart & J. H. Terwindt. (Annals of Gemorphology Supplement Ser.: No. 49). (Illus.). 207p. (Orig.). 1984. pap. text ed. 78.50x (ISBN 3-443-21049-X, Pub. by Gebruder Borntraeger). Coronet Bks.

Present Day Impressions of Japan. W. H. Morton-Cameron. 931p. 1919. 2275.00x (ISBN 0-317-68986-X, Pub. by Han-Shan Tang Ltd). State Mutual Bk.

Present-Day Law Schools in the United States & Canada. Alfred Z. Reed. LC 75-22836. (America in Two Centuries Ser). 1976. Repr. of 1928 ed. 46.50x (ISBN 0-405-07707-6). Ayer Co Pubs.

Present-Day Law Schools in the United States & Canada. Alfred Z. Reed. (Historical Writings in Law & Jurisprudence. Second Ser.: No. 12). xv, 508p. 1987. Repr. of 1928 ed. lib. bdg. 38.50 (ISBN 0-89941-546-6, 305100). W S Hein.

Present-Day Ministry of Jesus Christ. 2nd ed. Kenneth E. Hagin. 1983. pap. 1.00 (ISBN 0-89276-014-1). Hagin Ministries.

Present-Day Non-Marxist Political Economy. A. G. Nileikovsky et al. 575p. 1981. 9.50 (ISBN 0-8285-2152-2, Pub. by Progress Pubs USSR). Imported Pubns.

Present Day Problems: A Collection of Addresses Delivered on Various Occasions. facs. ed. William H. Taft. LC 67-26788. (Essay Index Reprint Ser). 1908. 19.00 (ISBN 0-8369-0922-4). Ayer Co Pubs.

Present-Day Relevance of 18th Century Thought. Ed. by Roger P. McCutcheon. LC 56-12885. viii, 86p. 1971. pap. 2.00x (ISBN 0-87950-278-9). Spoken Lang Serv.

Present Day Rock Garden. Sampson Clay. LC 76-1833. (Illus.). 1976. Repr. of 1937 ed. 25.00 (ISBN 0-913728-09-8). Theophrastus.

Present Day Russian Psychology. Ed. by N. O'Connor. 1967. pap. 17.00 (ISBN 0-08-012098-9). Pergamon.

Present Day Spanish. 2nd ed. J. R. Scarr. 1976. pap. text ed. 6.30 (ISBN 0-08-020716-2). Pergamon.

Present Day Truths. 4th ed. Dick Iverson. 252p. 1975. 7.95 (ISBN 0-914936-11-5). Bible Temple.

Present for Charles Dickens. Seon Manley. LC 82-24862. (Illus.). 124p. (gr. 5 up). 1983. 12.95 (ISBN 0-664-32706-0). Westminster John Knox.

Present for Jessica. Teddi Doleski. (Illus.). 48p. (Orig.). 1986. pap. 2.50 (ISBN 0-8091-6557-0). Paulist Pr.

Present for Santa. James Burke. 304p. 1986. 16.95 (Thomas Dunne Bks). St Martin.

Present for Servants from Their Ministers, Masters & Other Friends. LC 83-48608. (Marriage, Sex & the Family in England Ser.). 158p. 1985. lib. bdg. 28.00 (ISBN 0-8240-5934-4). Garland Pub.

Present: Guide to English Literature. Ed. by Boris Ford. 640p. (Orig.). 1984. pap. 7.95 (ISBN 0-14-022271-5, Pelican). Penguin.

Present History: On Nuclear War, Detente & Other Controversies. Theodore Draper. 1984. pap. 9.95 (ISBN 0-394-72371-6, Vin). Random.

Present Indicative: An Autobiography. Noel Coward. LC 79-29681. (Illus.). 1980. pap. 9.95 (ISBN 0-306-80112-4). Da Capo.

Present Knowledge in Nutrition: Nutrition Reviews. 5th ed. 900p. 1984. 18.00 (ISBN 0-935368-40-X). Nutrition Found.

Present Passe, Passe Present. Eugene Ionesco. (Idees Ser.). 1976. 7.95 (ISBN 0-686-54198-7). Schoenhof.

Present, Past & Future Property Estimation Techniques. 20p. 1968. pap. 22.00 (ISBN 0-8169-0036-1, M-5). Am Inst Chem Eng.

Present Past, Past Present. Eugene Ionesco. Tr. by Helen R. Lane from Fr. LC 70-139253. 192p. 1971. pap. 1.95 (ISBN 0-394-17783-5, E589, Ever). Grove.

Present Philosophical Tendencies. Ralph B. Perry. LC 68-21318. 1968. Repr. of 1955 ed. lib. bdg. 35.00x (ISBN 0-8371-0191-3, PEPT). Greenwood.

Present Position & Prospects of the British Trade with China. James Matheson. 1836. worn half-leather 1050.00x (Pub. by Han-Shan Tang Ltd). State Mutual Bk.

Present Position of the Khazar Problem. A. Landau. 1978. lib. bdg. 59.95 (ISBN 0-685-62304-1). Revisionist Pr.

Present State & Future Needs in General Practice. J. Fry. 150p. 1983. text ed. write for info. (ISBN 0-85200-708-6, Pub. by MTP Pr England). Kluwer Academic.

Present State of Australia. Robert Dawson. (Discovery of the Pacific & Australia Ser.). (Illus.). 488p. 1987. Repr. of 1830 ed. 100.00 (ISBN 1-85297-003-0). Archival Facsimiles.

Present State of Consumer Theory. Timothy P. Roth. LC 86-24619. 176p. (Orig.). 1987. lib. bdg. 28.00 (ISBN 0-8191-5708-2); pap. text ed. 13.75 (ISBN 0-8191-5709-0). U Pr of Amer.

Present State of Egypt; Or, a New Relation of a Late Voyage into That Kingdom Performed in the Years 1672 & 1673. Johann Vansleb. 266p. Repr. of 1678 ed. text ed. 62.10x (ISBN 0-576-17124-7, Pub. by Gregg Intl Pubs England). Gregg Intl.

Present State of England in Regard to Agriculture, Trade & Finance. 2nd ed. Joseph Lowe. LC 66-21682. 1967. Repr. of 1823 ed. 49.50x (ISBN 0-678-00320-3). Kelley.

Present State of French Studies: A Collection of Research Reviews. Charles B. Osburn. LC 78-149990. 995p. 1971. 42.50 (ISBN 0-8108-0373-9). Scarecrow.

Present State of Hayti (Saint Domingo) James Franklin. 412p. 1972. Repr. of 1828 ed. 35.00x (ISBN 0-7146-2707-0, F Cass Co). Biblio Dist.

Present State of Leptospirosis Diagnosis & Control. Ed. by W. A. Ellis & T. W. Little. (Current Topics in Veterinary Medicine & Animal Science Ser.). 1986. lib. bdg. 49.50 (ISBN 0-89838-777-9, Pub. by Martinus Nijhoff Netherlands). Kluwer-Academic.

Present State of Music in France & Italy. 2nd corr. ed. Charles Burney. LC 74-24263. 1976. Repr. of 1773 ed. 27.50 (ISBN 0-404-12875-0). AMS Pr.

Present State of New England. Cotton Mather. LC 68-24989. (American History & Americana Ser., No. 47). 1969. Repr. of 1690 ed. lib. bdg. 49.95x (ISBN 0-8383-0214-9). Haskell.

Present State of Physics: Proceedings of the American Advancement of Science, New York, 1949. facsimile ed. American Association for the Advancement of Science Staff. Ed. by Frederick S. Brackett. LC 75-99617. (Essay Index Reprint Ser.). 1954. 27.50 (ISBN 0-8369-1542-9). Ayer Co Pubs.

Present State of Regional Development in Japan. 117p. 1975. pap. 6.00 (ISBN 0-686-78248-8, CRD069, UNCRD). UNIPUB.

Present State of Russia, 2 Vols. Friedrich C. Weber. (Russia Through European Eyes Ser.). 1968. Repr. of 1723 ed. Set. lib. bdg. 89.50 (ISBN 0-306-77022-9). Da Capo.

Present State of Scholarship in Fourteenth Century Literature. Ed. by Thomas D. Cooke. (Illus.). 352p. 1983. 32.00x (ISBN 0-8262-0379-5). U of MO Pr.

Present State of Scholarship in Historical & Contemporary Rhetoric. Ed. by Winifred B. Horner. LC 82-20002. 240p. 1983. text ed. 25.00x (ISBN 0-8262-0398-1); pap. 10.00x (ISBN 0-8262-0467-8). U of Mo Pr.

Present State of Scholarship in Sixteenth-Century Literature. Ed. by William M. Jones. LC 78-50810. 272p. 1978. text ed. 25.00x (ISBN 0-8262-0253-5). U of Mo Pr.

Present State of the Cape of Good-Hope: Or, a Particular Account of the Several Nations of the Hottentots, 2 vols. Peter Kolb. (Anthropology Ser.). 1969. Repr. of 1731 ed. Vol. 1. 35.00 (ISBN 0-384-30100-2); Vol. 2. 42.00 (ISBN 0-685-13553-5). Johnson Repr.

Present State of the Empire of Morocco, 2 Vols. in 1. Louis De Chenier. 1788. 52.00 (ISBN 0-384-08620-9). Johnson Repr.

Present State of the European Settlements on the Mississippi: With a Geographical Description of That River Illustrated by Plans & Draughts. Philip Pittman. Intro. by Robert R. Rea. LC 73-2821. (Floridiana Facsimile & Reprint Ser.). (Illus.). 156p. 1973. Repr. of 1770 ed. 10.00 (ISBN 0-8130-0368-7). U Presses Fla.

Present State of the Greek & Armenian Churches. Paul Rycaut. LC 75-13321. Repr. of 1679 ed. 32.50 (ISBN 0-404-05476-5). AMS Pr.

Present State of the Greek Church in Russia. Platon. LC 75-131031. Repr. of 1815 ed. 21.50 (ISBN 0-404-05059-X). AMS Pr.

Present State of the Ottoman Empire. Paul Rycaut. LC 76-135845. (Eastern Europe Collection Ser). 1970. Repr. of 1668 ed. 14.00 (ISBN 0-405-02787-7). Ayer Co Pubs.

Present State of Thoracic Surgery. Ed. by J. A. Dyde & R. E. Smih. 300p. 1981. text ed. 54.00 (ISBN 0-8464-1218-7). Beekman Pubs.

Present State of Turkish Language. Geoffrey Lewis. 1985. pap. 5.50 (ISBN 0-85672-537-4, Pub. by British Acad). Longwood Pub Group.

Present State of Virginia. Hugh Jones. LC 75-31095. Repr. of 1865 ed. 29.50 (ISBN 0-404-13512-9). AMS Pr.

Present Status of Computer Support in Ambulatory Care. Ed. by P. L. Reichertz & R. Engelbrecht. (Lecture Notes in Medical Informatics Ser.: Vol. 30). 241p. 1987. pap. 32.20 (ISBN 0-387-17672-1). Springer-Verlag.

Present Status of Fisheries & Assessment of Potential Resources of the Indian Ocean & Adjacent Seas. IPCP Group of Experts on the Indian Ocean, Rome, 1967. (Fisheries Reports: No. 54). 33p. 1967. pap. 7.50 (ISBN 0-686-92888-1, F1679, FAO). UNIPUB.

Present Status of Non-Toxic Concepts in Cancer. Ed. by K. F. Klippel & E. Macher. (Illus.). xii, 288p. 1987. pap. 47.50 (ISBN 3-8055-4437-5). S Karger.

Present Status of the Philosophy of Law & of Rights. William E. Hocking. viii, 97p. 1986. Repr. of 1926 ed. lib. bdg. 22.50x (ISBN 0-8377-2234-9). Rothman.

Present System of Trade & Payment Versus Full Employment & Welfare State. Eprime Eshag. LC 76-1515. 1966. 8.50x (ISBN 0-678-06278-1). Kelley.

Present Takers. Aidan Chambers. LC 83-48470. (Charlotte Zolotow Bks.). 160p. (gr. 5 up). 1984. 12.70i (ISBN 0-06-021251-9); PLB 12.89 (ISBN 0-06-021252-7). HarpJ.

Present: Teddy Horsley Celebrates Epiphany. Leslie J. Francis & Nicola M. Slee. (Teddy Horsley Books for Young Christians). (Illus.). 24p. (ps-2). 1986. pap. 1.25 (ISBN 0-00-599867-0, Collins Liturgical). HarpR.

Present Tense & Personal Effects: A Pair of Comedies. John McNamara. 60p. 1986. pap. 3.50x (ISBN 0-317-44296-1). Dramatists Play.

Present to the Newborn: A Book for Parents & All Whose Lives Touch the Lives of Children. Emily H. Slingluff. 112p. (Orig.). (YA) (gr. 7 up). 1988. pap. 7.95 (ISBN 0-87491-918-5). Acropolis.

Present Value Approach for the Determination of the Accounting Income & Wealth of the Firm. Evangelina Vives-Amengual. pap. 5.00 (ISBN 0-8477-2621-5). U of PR Pr.

Present Value of Debt Settlements. 5p. 1979. pap. 40.00 (ISBN 0-939050-37-4). Credit Res NYS.

Present Your Sale. John Nemec. LC 87-90713. 50p. (Orig.). 1987. side 2.95 (ISBN 0-9618998-1-6). Nemec Pub.

Present Yourself! Captivate Your Audience with Great Presentation Skills. Michael J. Gelb. Ed. by Bradley L. Winch. LC 88-80768. (Right Brain - Whole Brain Learning Ser.). (Illus.). 128p. (Orig.). 1988. 18.95 (ISBN 0-915190-50-8, JP9050-8); pap. 9.95 (ISBN 0-915190-51-6, JP9051-6). Jalmar Pr.

Present Yourself with Impact. Caryl Winter. pap. 2.95 (ISBN 0-345-30338-5). Ballantine.

Preserving Traditional Arts: A Toolkit for Native American Communities. Susan Dyal. (American Indian Manuals & Handbook Ser.). 205p. 1985. vinyl 20.00 (ISBN 0-935626-30-1). U Cal AISC.

Preserving Valves Through Reading Children's Literature. Althea S. Southwick. 76p. (Orig.). 1987. pap. 6.95 (ISBN 0-9614058-3-X). Southco.

Preserving Wilderness in Our National Parks. Ed. by Jack H. Bryan. cancelled (ISBN 0-940091-02-X); pap. cancelled (ISBN 0-940091-01-1). Natl Parks & Cons.

Preserving Wilderness in Our National Parks. Ed. by Anthony W. Smith. 1986. cancelled (ISBN 0-940091-00-3). Natl Parks & Cons.

Preserving Your American Heritage: A Guide to Family & Local History Research. 2nd, rev. ed. Norman E. Wright. LC 80-27934. (Illus.). 1981. pap. text ed. 9.95 (ISBN 0-8425-1863-0). Brigham.

Presidencies of Grover Cleveland. Richard E. Welch, Jr. LC 88-268. (American Presidency Ser.). xviii, 246p. 1988. 25.00x (ISBN 0-7006-0355-7). U Pr of KS.

Presidencies of James A. Garfield & Chester A. Arthur. Justus D. Doenecke. LC 80-18957. (American Presidency Ser.). xiv, 230p. 1981. 22.50x (ISBN 0-7006-0208-9). U Pr of KS.

Presidencies of Zachary Taylor & Millard Fillmore. Elbert B. Smith. LC 88-5722. (American Presidency Ser.). x, 262p. 1988. 25.00x (ISBN 0-7006-0362-X). U Pr of KS.

Presidency. Marcus Cunliffe. 1986. 19.95 (ISBN 0-8281-1217-7, Am Heritage); pap. 10.95 (ISBN 0-8281-1202-9, Am Heritage). HM.

Presidency. new ed. George E. Reedy. LC 74-77691. (Great Contemporary Issues Ser.). (Illus.). 1975. 35.00 (ISBN 0-405-04169-1, Co Pub by New York Times). Ayer Co Pubs.

Presidency. Christine Sciabine. (Know Your Government Ser.). (Illus.). 96p. 1988. lib. bdg. 12.95 (ISBN 1-55546-118-2). Chelsea Hse.

Presidency: A Research Guide. Robert U. Goehlert & Fenton S. Martin. LC 84-6425. 341p. 1985. lib. bdg. 30.00 (ISBN 0-87436-373-X). ABC-Clio.

Presidency & Black Civil Rights: Eisenhower to Nixon. Allan Wolk. LC 70-135029. 276p. 1971. 24.50 (ISBN 0-8386-7805-X). Fairleigh Dickinson.

Presidency & Information Policy. Harold C. Relyea et al. 216p. (Orig.). 1981. 10.00 (ISBN 0-938204-03-3); pap. 7.00 (ISBN 0-938204-04-1). Ctr Study Presidency.

Presidency & National Security Policy, Vol. V. R. Gordon Hoxie et al. 502p. 1984. 20.00 (ISBN 0-938204-05-X); pap. 12.00 (ISBN 0-938204-06-8). Ctr Study Presidency.

Presidency & Public Policy Making. Ed. by George C. Edwards, III et al. LC 85-40337. (Pitt Series in Policy & Institutional Studies). (Illus.). 1985. 26.95x (ISBN 0-8229-3522-8); pap. text ed. 11.95x (ISBN 0-8229-5373-0). U of Pittsburgh Pr.

Presidency & Public Policy: The Four Arenas of Presidential Power. Robert J. Spitzer. LC 81-19802. (Illus.). 224p. 1983. text ed. 18.75 (ISBN 0-8173-0109-7). U of Ala Pr.

Presidency & Science Advising, Vol. IV. Kenneth W. Thompson. LC 87-8206. 90p. (Orig.). 1988. lib. bdg. 17.50 (ISBN 0-8191-6670-7, Co-pub. by White Miller Center); pap. 8.25 (ISBN 0-8191-6671-5). U Pr of Amer.

Presidency & Science Advising. Ed. by Kenneth W. Thompson. (Tenth Anniversary Series of the White Burkett Miller Center of Public Affairs). 94p. (Orig.). 1986. lib. bdg. 17.50 (ISBN 0-8191-5311-7, Co-pub. by White Miller Center); pap. text ed. 8.25 (ISBN 0-8191-5312-5, Co-Pub. by White Miller Center). U Pr of Amer.

Presidency & Science Advising, Vol. II. Ed. by Kenneth W. Thompson. LC 86-4132. 88p. (Orig.). 1987. lib. bdg. 16.50 (ISBN 0-8191-6344-9, Co-pub. by White Miller Center); pap. text ed. 6.75 (ISBN 0-8191-6345-7, White Miller Center). U Pr of Amer.

Presidency & Science Advising, Vol. III. Ed. by Kenneth W. Thompson. LC 87-8206. 142p. (Orig.). 1987. lib. bdg. 21.50 (ISBN 0-8191-6458-5, Co-Pub. by White Miller Center); pap. text ed. 9.75 (ISBN 0-8191-6459-3). U Pr of Amer.

Presidency & Science Advising, Vol. V. Ed. by Kenneth W. Thompson. LC 86-4132. 124p. (Orig.). 1988. lib. bdg. 19.50 (ISBN 0-8191-6957-9, Co-pub. by White Miller Center); pap. text ed. 9.75 (ISBN 0-8191-6958-7, Co-pub. by White Miller Center). U Pr of Amer.

Presidency & the Congress: A Shifting Balance of Power? Ed. by William S. Livingston et al. 450p. 1979. pap. 8.95 (ISBN 0-89940-407-3). LBJ Sch Pub Aff.

Presidency & the Political System. 2nd ed. Ed. by Michael Nelson. 498p. 1988. pap. 17.95 (ISBN 0-87187-438-5). Congr Quarterly.

Presidency & the Press. Ed. by Hoyt Purvis. (Symposia Ser.). 120p. 1976. pap. 3.50 (ISBN 0-89940-405-7). LBJ Sch Pub Aff.

Presidency & the Quality of American Life. Louis W. Keonig. 1971. 1.00 (ISBN 1-55614-089-4). U of SD Gov Res Bur.

Presidency: Crisis & Regeneration. Herman Finer. 1974. pap. 2.95x (ISBN 0-226-24970-0, P588, Phoen). U of Chicago Pr.

Presidency in Flux. George Reedy. LC 73-2580. 200p. 1973. 20.00x (ISBN 0-231-03736-8). Columbia U Pr.

Presidency in the Constitutional Order. Ed. by Joseph M. Bessette & Jeffrey Tulis. LC 80-14250. xvi, 349p. 1981. text ed. 37.50 (ISBN 0-8071-0774-3); pap. text ed. 10.95 (ISBN 0-8071-0781-6). La State U Pr.

Presidency in the Courts. Glendon A. Schubert. LC 72-8122. (American Constitutional & Legal History Ser). 408p. 1973. Repr. of 1957 ed. lib. bdg. 39.50 (ISBN 0-306-70529-X). Da Capo.

Presidency in Transition. Ed. by Rankin. 1949. pap. 7.50 (ISBN 0-317-27710-3). Kallman.

Presidency: Its Duties, Its Powers, Its Opportunities & Its Limitations. William H. Taft. 145p. Repr. of 1916 ed. 23.00 (ISBN 0-384-59440-9). Johnson Repr.

Presidency of Andrew Johnson. Albert Castel. LC 79-11050. (American Presidency Ser.). x, 262p. 1979. 25.00x (ISBN 0-7006-0190-2). U Pr of KS.

Presidency of Benjamin Harrison. Homer E. Socolofsky & Allan Spetter. (American Presidency Ser.). 250p. 1987. 25.00x (ISBN 0-7006-0320-4). U Pr of KS.

Presidency of Dwight D. Eisenhower. Elmo Richardson. LC 78-17923. (American Presidency Ser.). xii, 220p. 1979. 22.50x (ISBN 0-7006-0183-X); pap. 9.95 (ISBN 0-7006-0267-4). U Pr of KS.

Presidency of George Washington. Forrest McDonald. LC 73-11344. (American Presidency Ser.). xiv, 210p. 1974. 19.95x (ISBN 0-7006-0110-4). U Pr of KS.

Presidency of George Washington. Forrest McDonald. LC 73-11344. xiv, 210p. 1988. pap. 9.95 (ISBN 0-7006-0359-X). U Pr of KS.

Presidency of Harry S. Truman. Donald R. McCoy. (American Presidency Ser.). xii, 356p. 1984. 25.00x (ISBN 0-7006-0252-6); pap. 14.95 (ISBN 0-7006-0255-0). U Pr of Ks.

Presidency of Herbert C. Hoover. Martin L. Fausold. LC 84-17252. (American Presidency Ser.). xii, 292p. 1985. 25.00x (ISBN 0-7006-0259-3). U Pr of KS.

Presidency of Herbert C. Hoover. Martin L. Fausold. 304p. 1988. pap. 12.95 (ISBN 0-7006-0358-1). U Pr of KS.

Presidency of James Buchanan. Elbert B. Smith. LC 74-31220. (American Presidency Ser.). xvi, 228p. 1975. 25.00x (ISBN 0-7006-0132-5). U Pr of KS.

Presidency of James K. Polk. Paul H. Bergeron. (American Presidency Ser.). 300p. 1987. 25.00x (ISBN 0-7006-0319-0). U Pr of KS.

Presidency of John Adams. Ralph A. Brown. LC 75-5526. (American Presidency Ser). xii, 248p. 1975. 22.50x (ISBN 0-7006-0134-1). U Pr of Ks.

Presidency of John Quincy Adams. Mary W. Hargreaves. LC 85-11147. (American Presidency Ser.). xvi, 400p. 1985. 25.00x (ISBN 0-7006-0272-0). U Pr of KS.

Presidency of Lyndon B. Johnson. Vaughn D. Bornet. LC 83-12560. (American Presidency Ser.). xvi, 416p. 1983. 25.00x (ISBN 0-7006-0237-2); pap. 14.95 (ISBN 0-7006-0242-9). U Pr of KS.

Presidency of Martin Van Buren. Major L. Wilson. LC 83-17871. (American Presidency Ser.). xiv, 258p. 1984. 25.00x (ISBN 0-7006-0238-0). U Pr of KS.

Presidency of Rutherford B. Hayes. Kenneth E. Davison. LC 79-176289. (Contributions in American Studies: No. 3). 1972. lib. bdg. 29.95 (ISBN 0-8371-6275-0, DPH/). Greenwood.

Presidency of Rutherford B. Hayes. Ari Hoogenboom. LC 88-5709. (American Presidency Ser). 288p. 1988. 25.00 (ISBN 0-7006-0338-7). U Pr of Ks.

Presidency of the Continental Congress 1774-89: A Study in American Institutional History. Jennings B. Sanders. 11.25 (ISBN 0-8446-0889-0). Peter Smith.

Presidency of the Council of Ministers of the European Communities: An Insight. Guy De Bassompierre. (CSIS Washington Papers). 1988. write for info. Praeger.

Presidency of the European Council of Ministers: Impact & Implications for National Government. Collin Onuallain. LC 84-23123. 280p. 1985. 34.50 (ISBN 0-7099-0946-2, Pub. by Croom Helm Ltd). Routledge Chapman & Hall.

Presidency of the 1970's. R. Gordon Hoxie. LC 73-75234. 196p. 10.00 (ISBN 0-317-39575-0). Ctr Study Presidency.

Presidency of Thomas Jefferson. Forrest McDonald. LC 76-803. (American Presidency Ser.). xii, 204p. 1976. 22.50x (ISBN 0-7006-0147-3); pap. 9.95 (ISBN 0-7006-0330-1). U Pr of KS.

Presidency of Warren G. Harding. Eugene P. Trani & David L. Wilson. LC 76-26110. (American Presidency Ser.). xii, 232p. 1977. 22.50x (ISBN 0-7006-0152-X). U Pr of KS.

Presidency of William Howard Taft. Paolo E. Coletta. LC 72-92564. (American Presidency Ser.). xii, 308p. 1973. 25.00x (ISBN 0-7006-0096-5). U Pr of KS.

Presidency of William McKinley. Lewis L. Gould. LC 80-16022. (American Presidency Ser.). xiv, 294p. 1981. 25.00x (ISBN 0-7006-0206-2). U Pr of KS.

Presidency of Woodrow Wilson. Leon H. Canfield. LC 66-24796. (Illus.). 299p. 1968. 28.50 (ISBN 0-8386-6744-9). Fairleigh Dickinson.

Presidency of Yuan Shih-K'ai: Liberalism & Dictatorship in Early Republican China. Ernest P. Young. LC 75-31057. (Michigan Studies on China). (Illus.). 1976. text ed. 17.50x (ISBN 0-472-08995-1). U of Mich Pr.

Presidency on Trial: Robert Kennedy's 1968 Campaign & Afterwards. Stuart G. Brown. 1972. 10.00x (ISBN 0-8248-0202-0). UH Pr.

Presidency, The Congress & The Supreme Court. Richard Bernstein & Jerome Agel. (Into the Third Century Ser.). (YA) (gr. 7 up). Date not set. 13.95. Walker & Co.

President. Keith Brandt. LC 84-2652. (Illus.). 32p. (gr. 3-6). 1985. PLB 8.45 (ISBN 0-8167-0268-3); pap. text ed. 1.95 (ISBN 0-8167-0269-1). Troll Assocs.

President see Eisenhower.

President & Civil Rights: Policy-Making by Executive Order. Ruth P. Morgan. LC 87-13327. 1987. pap. 9.75 (ISBN 0-8191-6475-5). U Pr of Amer.

President & Congress. Rowland Egger & Joseph P. Harris. LC 88-2329. (Foundations of American Government & Political Science Ser.). 136p. 1988. Repr. of 1963 ed. lib. bdg. 35.00x (ISBN 0-313-24217-8, EGPC). Greenwood.

President & Congress. Louise Fisher. LC 78-142362. 1972. 17.00 (ISBN 0-02-910320-7); pap. text ed. 4.95 (ISBN 0-02-910340-1). Free Pr.

President & Congress: Assessing Reagan's First Year. Ed. by Norman J. Ornstein. 1982. pap. 11.00 (ISBN 0-8447-2237-5). Am Enterprise.

President & Economic Policy. Ed. by James P. Pfiffner. LC 84-19746. 283p. 1986. text ed. 35.00 (ISBN 0-89727-063-0); pap. text ed. 14.95 (ISBN 0-89727-064-9). ISHI PA.

President & Eve of Retirement: Two Plays. Thomas Bernhard. Tr. by Gitta Honegger. LC 82-80615. 1982. 16.95 (ISBN 0-933826-24-9); pap. 6.95 (ISBN 0-933826-25-7). PAJ Pubns.

President & Foreign Affairs: Evaluation, Performance & Power. Ryan J. Barilleaux. LC 84-26282. 224p. 1985. 36.95 (ISBN 0-275-90057-6, C0057). Praeger.

President & Her Sweet Old Ladies: A Chronicle of the Burton Senior Citizens. limited ed. Patricia W. Simmons. LC 75-17144. (Illus.). 100p. 1976. 25.00 (ISBN 0-8283-1637-6). Branden Pub Co.

President & His Powers. William H. Taft. LC 38-32819. 1967. pap. 15.00x (ISBN 0-231-08574-5). Columbia U Pr.

President & Parliament: A Short History of the French Presidency. Leslie Derfler. LC 82-16133. x, 286p. 1984. 24.00x (ISBN 0-8130-0733-X). U Presses Fla.

President & Power in Nigeria: The Life of Shehu Shagari. David Williams. (Illus.). 302p. 1982. text ed. 25.00x (ISBN 0-7146-3182-5, F Cass Co). Biblio Dist.

President & Protest: Hoover, Conspiracy & the Bonus Riot. Donald J. Lisio. LC 73-89489. 368p. 1974. 24.00x (ISBN 0-8262-0158-X). U of Mo Pr.

President & Public Opinion: Leadership in Foreign Affairs. Manfred Landecker. 1968. 8.00 (ISBN 0-8183-0197-X). Pub Aff Pr.

President & the Council of Economic Advisors: Interviews with the CEA Chairmen. Ed. by Erwin C. Hargrove & Samuel A. Morley. LC 84-51229. (Replica Edition Ser.). 530p. 1984. 38.50x (ISBN 0-86531-866-2). Westview.

President & the Executive Director in Girl Scouting. rev. ed. 32p. 1984. pap. 5.50 (ISBN 0-88441-452-3, 26-173). Girl Scouts USA.

President & the Indian Constitution. Valmiki Chaudhary. 379p. 1985. 32.95. Asia Bk Corp.

President & the Public. Ed. by Doris A. Graber. LC 82-3032. 324p. 1982. text ed. 19.95 (ISBN 0-89727-038-X); pap. text ed. 9.95 (ISBN 0-89727-042-8). ISHI PA.

President & the Public Philosophy. Kenneth W. Thompson. LC 80-26165. (Miller Center Series on the American Presidency). x, 214p. 1981. 24.00 (ISBN 0-8071-0795-6). La State U Pr.

President & the Public: Rhetoric & National Leadership. Ed. by Craig A. Smith & Kathy B. Smith. LC 85-20299. (Credibility of Institutions, Policies, & Leadership Ser.: Vol. 7). 340p. (Orig.). 1986. lib. bdg. 31.50 (ISBN 0-8191-4722-2, Co-Pub. by White Miller Center); pap. text ed. 10.25 (ISBN 0-8191-4723-0). U Pr of Amer.

President As Chief Administrator. A. J. Wann. 8.00 (ISBN 0-8183-0199-6). Pub Aff Pr.

President As Policymaker: Jimmy Carter & Welfare Reform. Laurence E. Lynn, Jr. & David def. Whitman. 351p. 1981. 34.95 (ISBN 0-87722-223-1); pap. 12.95 (ISBN 0-87722-238-X). Temple U Pr.

President Castello Branco: Brazilian Reformer. John W. Dulles. LC 79-5281. (Illus.). 568p. 1981. 34.50x (ISBN 0-89096-092-5). Tex A&M Univ Pr.

President Charles Bradlaugh, MP. David Tribe. LC 70-27779. 391p. 1971. 37.50 (ISBN 0-208-01155-2, Archon). Shoe String.

President, Congress & Legislation. Lawrence H. Chamberlain. LC 72-181927. (Columbia University Studies in the Social Sciences: No. 523). Repr. of 1946 ed. 24.50 (ISBN 0-404-51523-1). AMS Pr.

President, Congress & the Constitution: Power & Legitimacy in American Politics. Ed. by Christopher H. Pyle & Richard M. Pious. LC 83-48643. 448p. 1984. pap. 15.95x (ISBN 0-02-925380-2). Free Pr.

President Edvard Benes, Between East & West: 1938-1948. Edward Taborsky. LC 80-83829. (Publication Ser.: No. 246). (Illus.). 312p. 1981. 19.95x (ISBN 0-8179-7461-X). Hoover Inst Pr.

President from Texas: Lyndon Baines Johnson. Dudley Lynch. LC 74-26817. (Illus.). 192p. (gr. 6 up). 1975. 12.70 (ISBN 0-690-00627-6, Crowell Jr Bks). HarpJ.

President Harry Truman & the Independent Regulatory Commissions, 1945-1952. Gale E. Peterson. (Modern American History Ser.). 618p. 1985. lib. bdg. 60.00 (ISBN 0-8240-5676-0). Garland Pub.

President in the Twentieth Century, Vol. I: The Ascendant President: From William McKinley to Lyndon B. Johnson. Ed. by Louis Filler. 424p. lib. bdg. 24.95x (ISBN 0-89198-127-6); pap. text ed. 13.95x (ISBN 0-89198-128-4). Ozer.

President Is a Lot Smarter Than You Think. G. B. Trudeau. LC 72-78133. (Illus.). 128p. (YA) 1973. pap. 3.95 (ISBN 0-03-091406-X). H Holt & Co.

President Is Coming to Lunch. Nan Lyons & Ivan Lyons. 216p. 1988. 16.95 (ISBN 0-385-19916-3). Doubleday.

President Is Stuck in the Mud. Stephen A. Bly. (Making Choices Ser.: No. 4). (Orig.). (gr. 3-8). 1982. pap. 3.50 (ISBN 0-89191-661-X, 56614). Cook.

President Jackson Case. Ray Broekel. LC 79-52406. (Carolrhoda Mini-Mysteries Ser.). (Illus.). (gr. 1-4). 1980. PLB 5.95g (ISBN 0-87614-112-2). Carolrhoda Bks.

President James Buchanan: A Biography. Philip S. Klein. LC 62-12623. (Illus.). 1962. 28.50x (ISBN 0-271-73093-5). Pa St U Pr.

President John Smith: The Story of a Peaceful Revolution. Frederick U. Adams. LC 72-154428. (Utopian Literature Ser). (Illus.). 1971. Repr. of 1897 ed. 23.50 (ISBN 0-405-03511-X). Ayer Co Pubs.

President Johnson's War on Poverty: Rhetoric & History. David Zarefsky. LC 84-24098. 280p. 1986. 24.50 (ISBN 0-8173-0266-2). U of Ala Pr.

President Kennedy's Policy toward the Arab States & Israel. Mordechai Gazit. 134p. (Orig.). 1983. pap. text ed. 9.95x (ISBN 0-8156-7051-6, Pub. by Shiloah Ctr Mid East & African Studies Israel). Syracuse U Pr.

President Kimball Speaks Out. Spencer W. Kimball. LC 81-68861. 103p. 1981. 5.95 (ISBN 0-87747-881-3). Deseret Bk.

President Lincoln's Attitude Toward Slavery & Emancipation. Henry W. Wilbur. 1914. 15.00 (ISBN 0-8196-0267-1). Biblo.

President Masaryk. facs. ed. Cecil J. Street. LC 74-119945. (Select Bibliographies Reprint Ser). 1930. 19.00 (ISBN 0-8369-5388-6). Ayer Co Pubs.

President Masaryk Tells His Story. Karel Capek. LC 71-135797. (Eastern Europe Collection Ser). 1970. Repr. of 1935 ed. 25.50 (ISBN 0-405-02739-7). Ayer Co Pubs.

President Needs Help: Proceedings of a Conference Held on January 15, 1987. Ed. by Frederick C. Mosher. (Miller Center Tenth Anniversary Commemorative Publications 1975-1985). 98p. (Orig.). 1988. lib. bdg. 17.50 (ISBN 0-8191-6780-0, Co-pub. by White Miller Center); pap. text ed. 7.75 (ISBN 0-8191-6781-9). U Pr of Amer.

President of a Small College. Peter Sammartino. 162p. 1982. 9.95 (ISBN 0-8453-4757-8, Cornwall Bks). Assoc Univ Prs.

President: Office & Powers. 5th, rev. ed. Edward S. Corwin. Ed. by Randall W. Bland et al. 600p. 1984. 50.00x (ISBN 0-8147-1390-4); pap. 22.50x (ISBN 0-8147-1391-2). NYU Pr.

President: Preacher, Teacher, Salesman-Selected Presidential Speeches, 1933-1983. Ed. by Thomas T. Lyons. LC 84-51315. (Illus.). 206p. (Orig.). 1985. lib. bdg. 15.95 (ISBN 0-9608014-9-9); pap. text ed. 11.95 (ISBN 0-9608014-4-8). World Eagle.

President Ron's Appointment Book. Morton Mintz & Margaret Mintz. 64p. 1988. pap. 4.95 (ISBN 0-312-01663-8). St Martin.

President Roosevelt & the Origins of the 1939 War. David L. Hoggan. 1983. lib. bdg. 79.95 (ISBN 0-87700-469-2). Revisionist Pr.

President Roosevelt's Campaign to Incite War in Europe: The Secret Documents. Mark Weber. 1983. lib. bdg. 79.95 (ISBN 0-87700-468-4). Revisionist Pr.

President, the Congress, & Foreign Policy: A Joint Project of the Association of Former Members of Congress & the Atlantic Council of the United States. Kenneth Rush et al. LC 86-1634. 1986. 27.50 (ISBN 0-8191-5283-8); pap. 15.00 (ISBN 0-8191-5284-6). U Pr of Amer.

President vs. Congress: Does the Separation of Powers Still Work? Henry O. Brandon & Lloyd Cutler. 1981. pap. 5.00 (ISBN 0-8447-2206-5). Am Enterprise.

President Washington's Indian War: The Struggle for the Old Northwest, 1790-1795. Wiley Sword. LC 85-40481. (Illus.). 432p. 1985. 24.95 (ISBN 0-8061-1864-4). U of Okla Pr.

President Who Failed: Carter Out of Control. Clark R. Mollenhoff. LC 79-6767. 1980. 10.95 (ISBN 0-02-921750-4). Macmillan.

Presidential Quiz Book. E. H. Thomas. 176p. (Orig.). 1988. pap. 7.95 (ISBN 0-87052-551-4). Hippocrene Bks.

Presidential Quiz Book. Fred L. Worth. 368p. 7.98 (ISBN 0-517-65571-3, Pub. by Bell Publishing Co). Crown.

Presidential Reflections upon U. S. -Soviet Summitry. Ian Brzezinski. (Significant Issues Ser.: Vol. VII, No. 8). 22p. 1985. 6.95 (ISBN 0-89206-089-1). CSI Studies.

Presidential Rhetoric, Nineteen Sixty-One to the Present. 4th ed. Theodore Windt. LC 83-81606. x, 400p. 1987. pap. 19.95 (ISBN 0-8403-4430-9, 40308401). Kendall-Hunt.

Presidential Saints & Sinners. Thomas A. Bailey. 288p. 1981. 17.95 (ISBN 0-02-901330-5). Free Pr.

Presidential Search. John W. Nason. 92p. 1982. 18.00 (ISBN 0-318-17380-8). Assn Gov Bds.

Presidential Secrecy & Deception: Beyond the Power to Persuade. John M. Orman. LC 79-8410. (Contributions in Political Science Ser.: No. 43). (Illus.). xv, 239p. 1980. lib. bdg. 35.00x (ISBN 0-313-22036-0, OPS/). Greenwood.

Presidential Seizure in Labor Disputes. John L. Blackman. LC 67-20871. (Wertheim Publications in Industrial Relations). 367p. 1967. 24.50x (ISBN 0-674-70201-8). Harvard U Pr.

Presidential Selection. Ed. by Alexander Heard & Michael Nelson. LC 87-9164. x, 413p. 1987. lib. bdg. 50.00 (ISBN 0-8223-0750-2); pap. text ed. 17.95 (ISBN 0-8223-0785-5). Duke.

Presidential Selection. LC 82-71080. 150p. 1982. pap. 8.00 (ISBN 0-686-47958-0). Amer Bar Assn.

Presidential Selection: Theory & Development. James W. Ceaser. LC 78-70282. 1979. 39.00x (ISBN 0-691-07602-2); pap. 10.95x (ISBN 0-691-02188-0). Princeton U Pr.

Presidential Spending Power. Louis Fisher. LC 75-4408. 300p. 1975. 44.50x (ISBN 0-691-07575-1); pap. 10.95x (ISBN 0-691-02173-2). Princeton U Pr.

Presidential Succession. Ruth C. Silva. LC 68-54437. (Illus.). 1968. Repr. of 1951 ed. lib. bdg. 35.00x (ISBN 0-8371-0229-4, SIPS). Greenwood.

Presidential System: A Better Alternative. J. B. Mehta. (Illus.). 79p. 1979. 5.95. Asia Bk Corp.

Presidential Team: Perspectives on the Role of the Spouse. Vaughan, George B., & Associates Staff. 1987. 14.95 (1060). Am Assn Comm Jr Coll.

Presidential Transitions & Foreign Affairs. Frederick C. Mosher et al. LC 86-21087. (Miller Center Series on the American Presidency). 280p. 1987. text ed. 25.00 (ISBN 0-8071-1356-5). La State U Pr.

Presidential Transitions: Eisenhower Through Reagan. Carl M. Brauer. LC 85-30983. 320p. 1986. 22.95 (ISBN 0-19-504051-1). Oxford U Pr.

Presidential Transitions: Eisenhower Through Reagan. Carl M. Brauer. 336p. 1988. pap. 8.95 (ISBN 0-19-505655-8). Oxford U Pr.

Presidential Veto. Robert J. Spitzer. (Leadership Studies). 176p. 1988. 34.50x (ISBN 0-88706-802-2); pap. 10.95x (ISBN 0-88706-803-0). State U NY Pr.

Presidential Vote, 1896-1932. Edgar E. Robinson. LC 71-120658. 1970. Repr. of 1934 ed. lib. bdg. 29.00x (ISBN 0-374-96882-9, Octagon). Hippocrene Bks.

Presidential Wives. Paul F. Boller, Jr. 554p. 1988. 19.95 (ISBN 0-19-503763-4). Oxford U Pr.

Presidentialism in Commonwealth Africa. B. O. Nwabueze. LC 74-76990. 480p. 1975. 35.00 (ISBN 0-312-64120-6). St Martin.

Presidents. Jerry Aten. 160p. (gr. 4-8). 1985. wkbk. 10.95 (ISBN 0-86653-281-1). Good Apple.

Presidents. Harold Coy. (First Bks.). (Illus.). (gr. 4-6). 1977. PLB 10.40 s&l (ISBN 0-531-02906-9). Watts.

Presidents. Carol Greene. LC 84-7719. (New True Bks.). (Illus.). 48p. (gr. k-4). 1984. lib. bdg. 12.60 (ISBN 0-516-01928-7); pap. 3.95 (ISBN 0-516-41928-5). Childrens.

Presidents see Tesla Speaks.

Presidents - Birthplaces Homes & Burial Sites. Rachel M. Kochmann. 156p. 12.95 (ISBN 0-9616666-0-9). Osage Pub.

Presidents: A Reference History. Henry F. Graff. LC 83-20225. 700p. 1984. lib. bdg. 65.00 (ISBN 0-684-17607-6, ScribR). Scribner.

Presidents above Party: The First American Presidency, 1789 to 1829. Ralph Ketcham. LC 83-12517. (Institute of Early American History & Culture Ser.). xiv, 269p. 1984. 27.50x (ISBN 0-8078-1582-9). U of NC Pr.

Presidents above Party: The First American Presidency, 1789-1829. Ralph Ketcham. LC 83-12517. (Published for the Institute of Early American History & Culture, Williamsburg, VA, Ser.). xiv, 269p. 1987. pap. 9.95x (ISBN 0-8078-4179-X). U of NC Pr.

President's Agenda: Domestic Policy Choice from Kennedy to Carter with Notes on Ronald Reagan. Paul C. Light. LC 81-47607. 256p. 1983. 28.00X (ISBN 0-8018-2657-8); pap. 8.95x (ISBN 0-8018-2658-6). Johns Hopkins.

Presidents & Chancellors. Intro. by Dale Parnell. 132p. (Orig.). 1982. pap. 15.00 (ISBN 0-87117-113-9). Am Assn Comm Jr Coll.

Presidents & Civil Disorder. Bennett M. Rich. LC 79-26839. (Institute for Government Research of the Brookings Institution, Studies in Administration Ser.: No. 42). x, 235p. 1980. Repr. of 1941 ed. lib. bdg. 35.00x (ISBN 0-313-22299-1, RIPD). Greenwood.

Presidents & Foreign Policy Making: From FDR to Reagan. Cecil V. Crabb, Jr. & Kevin V. Mulcahy. LC 86-7508. (Political Traditions in Foreign Policy Ser.). 359p. 1986. text ed. 37.50 (ISBN 0-8071-1329-8); pap. text ed. 15.95 (ISBN 0-8071-1365-4). La State U Pr.

Presidents & Politics: The Limits of Power. Charles Funderburk. 1982. pub net 14.50 (ISBN 0-534-01086-5, 81-15444). Brooks-Cole.

Presidents & Prime Mininsters. Ed. by Richard Rose et al. 347p. 1980. pap. 15.75 (ISBN 0-8447-3386-5). Am Enterprise.

Presidents & Promises: From Campaign Pledge to Presidential Performance. Jeff Fishel & C Q Press Staff. LC 84-23782. 226p. 1985. pap. 11.95 (ISBN 0-87187-336-2); 18.95 (ISBN 0-87187-344-3). Congr Quarterly.

Presidents & the Press. James E. Pollard. LC 73-10262. xiii, 866p. 1973. Repr. of 1947 ed. lib. bdg. 52.00x (ISBN 0-374-96514-5, Octagon). Hippocrene Bks.

Presidents & the Press: The Nixon Legacy. Joseph C. Spear. 384p. 1986. pap. 9.95 (ISBN 0-262-69100-0). MIT Pr.

Presidents & the Press: Truman to Johnson. James E. Pollard. 1964. pap. 2.50 (ISBN 0-8183-0201-1). Pub Aff Pr.

Presidents Are People Too. Frank Cormier. 1966. 11.00 (ISBN 0-8183-0198-8). Pub Aff Pr.

Presidents, Bureaucrats, & Foreign Policy: The Politics of Organizational Reform. I. M. Destler. LC 77-166368. 362p. 1972. pap. 16.50x (ISBN 0-691-02169-4). Princeton U Pr.

President's Cabinet: Studies in the Origin, Formation & Structure of an American Institution. Henry B. Learned. LC 72-80393. xii, 471p. 1972. Repr. of 1912 ed. lib. bdg. 26.00 (ISBN 0-8337-4644-8). B Franklin.

Presidents Can't Punt: The OU Football Tradition. George L. Cross. LC 77-8867. (Illus.). 1978. 18.95 (ISBN 0-8061-1419-3). U of Okla Pr.

President's Car. Nancy W. Parker. LC 79-7898. (Illus.). 64p. (gr. 3-5). 1981. 11.70i (ISBN 0-690-03963-8, Crowell Jr Bks); PLB 11.89 (ISBN 0-690-03964-6). HarpJ.

President's Child Safety Partnership: Final Report. William W. McConnell. 196p. 1987. pap. 5.50 (ISBN 0-318-23756-3, 027-000-01281-7). USGPO.

President's Commissions. Frank Popper. LC 73-12304. (Twentieth Century Fund Ser.). 74p. 1973. pap. 15.00 (ISBN 0-527-71960-9). Kraus Repr.

Presidents Confront Reality: From Edifice Complex to University Without Walls. Lyman A. Glenny et al. LC 75-24014. (Carnegie Council Ser.). pap. 67.80 (ISBN 0-317-41807-6, 2025654). Bks Demand UMI.

President's Control of Foreign Relations. Edward S. Corwin. (Political Science Ser.). 1970. Repr. of 1917 ed. 19.00 (ISBN 0-384-09880-0, P540). Johnson Repr.

President's Council on Physical Fitness & Sports, 1985: National School Population Fitness Survey. Guy G. Reiff. (Illus.). 107p. 1986. pap. 5.00 (ISBN 0-318-23441-6, S/N 017-001-00463-4). USGPO.

President's Daughter. Nan Britton. 27.50 (ISBN 0-8369-7132-9, 7966). Ayer Co Pubs.

President's Daughter. Ellen E. White. 304p. 1984. pap. 2.95 (ISBN 0-380-88740-1, 88740, Flare). Avon.

Presidents Day. Jack Winder. Ed. by Alton Jordan. (ARO Holidays Ser.). (Illus.). (gr. k-3). 1977. PLB 3.95 (ISBN 0-89868-028-X, Read Res); pap. text ed. 1.75 (ISBN 0-89868-061-1). ARO Pub.

President's Grass Is Missing. Patricia Breen-Bond. (Orig.). 1980. pap. text ed. 1.75 (ISBN 0-505-51546-6, Pub. by Tower Bks). Leisure NY.

President's Guide to Attracting & Developing Top-Caliber Employees. Norman Sanders. 1981. 89.50 (ISBN 0-13-697532-1). Exec Reports.

President's Guide to People: Power Strategies. H. W. Koch. 1982. 89.50 (ISBN 0-13-697557-7). Exec Reports.

President's House: A History, 2 vols. (Illus.). 1306p. 1986. Set. 39.95. Natl Geog.

President's House: A History, 2 vols. William Seale. (Illus.). 1304p. 1986. 39.95 (ISBN 0-912308-28-1); Limited, Numbered Edition. 1000.00 (ISBN 0-912308-29-X). White House Hist.

President's House: A History. William Seale. 1987. 39.95 (ISBN 0-8109-1490-5). Abrams.

Presidents I've Known & Two Near Presidents. Charles W. Thompson. LC 71-93383. (Essay Index Reprint Ser). 1929. 24.50 (ISBN 0-8369-1728-6). Ayer Co Pubs.

President's Lady. Irving Stone. 320p. 1968. pap. 3.95 (ISBN 0-451-13990-9, AE2849, Sig). NAL.

Presidents Leadership Manual. 81p. 1.50 (ISBN 0-318-15189-8, 111-833). Natl Assoc Realtors.

President's Letter Book. John R. Taylor & Elise D. Bigger. 288p. 1986. 39.95 (ISBN 0-13-700493-1). P-H.

President's Man. Nicholas Guild. 364p. 1982. 13.95 (ISBN 0-312-64128-1). St Martin.

Presidents, Management, & Regulation. Edward P. Fuchs. (Illus.). 176p. 1988. pap. text ed. price not set (ISBN 0-13-699813-X). P-H.

President's Odyssey. Merriman Smith. LC 74-28759. 272p. 1975. Repr. of 1961 ed. lib. bdg. 35.00x (ISBN 0-8371-7921-1, SMPR). Greenwood.

Presidents of India. A. B. Kohli. xii, 108p. 1986. text ed. 20.00x (ISBN 81-7018-284-0, Pub. by B R Pub Corp Delhi). Apt Bks.

Presidents of the Church. Ed. by Leonard J. Arrington. LC 85-31117. 468p. 1986. 15.95 (ISBN 0-87579-026-7). Deseret Bk.

Presidents of the Republic of Texas: Chronology-Documents-Bibliography. George Lankevich. LC 78-23995. (Presidential Chronology Ser.). 230p. 1979. lib. bdg. 15.00 (ISBN 0-379-12085-2). Oceana.

Presidents of the U. S. 2.85 (ISBN 0-936672-21-8). Aerial Photo.

Presidents of the United Nations General Assembly: Speak Out. 15.00 (ISBN 92-1-157090-5, E.86.XV.CR/27). UN.

Presidents of the United States. Frank Freidel. LC 81-81182. 87p. 1981. 8.00 (ISBN 0-318-11819-X, S/N 066-000-00007-9). USGPO.

Presidents of the United States & Their Administrations from Washington to the Present. 7th ed. Maxim Armbruster. (Illus.). 400p. 1981. 15.95 (ISBN 0-8180-0812-1). Horizon.

Presidents of the United States of America. 87p. 1985. 4.50 (ISBN 0-912308-25-7); pap. 3.25 (ISBN 0-912308-24-9). White House Hist.

Presidents of the United States: Portraits & Biographies. August Dietz, Sr. 2.00 (ISBN 0-87517-014-5). Dietz.

Presidents, Pitchers, & Passers. John A. Hurst. LC 87-2291. ("And so the Story Goes.." Ser.: No. 2). 80p. (Orig.). 1987. pap. 7.95 (ISBN 0-89196-133-X, 31698). Quality Bks IL.

Presidents, Pitchers & Passers see And Hereby Hangs the Tale Series: Little Known Facts about Well-Known People, Places or Things.

Presidents, Politics & Policy. Erwin C. Hargrove & Michael Nelson. LC 84-47959. 1984. text ed. 32.50x (ISBN 0-8018-3243-8). Johns Hopkins.

Presidents, Prime Ministers & the Press. Ed. by Kenneth W. Thompson. (White House Press on the Presidency Ser.: Vol.6). 98p. (Orig.). 1986. lib. bdg. 16.75 (ISBN 0-8191-5437-7, Co-pub. by White Miller Center); pap. text ed. 8.25 (ISBN 0-8191-5438-5, Co-pub by White Miller Center). U Pr of Amer.

Presidents, Professors, & Trustees: The Evolution of American Academic Government. W. H. Cowley. Ed. by Donald T. Williams, Jr. LC 79-92461. (Higher Education Ser.). 1980. text ed. 27.95x (ISBN 0-87589-448-8). Jossey-Bass.

Presidents, Public Opinion & Power: Headline Ser. Terry L. Deibel. LC 87-80536. (No. 280). (Orig.). 1986. pap. 4.00 (ISBN 0-87124-112-9). Foreign Policy.

President's Rule in India. Shriman Maheshwari. 1977. 12.50x (ISBN 0-88386-985-3). South Asia Bks.

President's Secret Wars: CIA & Pentagon Covert Operations Since World War II. John Prados. LC 86-12854. 576p. 1986. 22.95 (ISBN 0-688-05384-X). Morrow.

Presidents' Secret Wars: CIA & Pentagon Covert Operations since World War II Through Iranscam. John Prados. LC 87-30440. 480p. 1988. pap. 9.95 (ISBN 0-688-07759-5, Quill). Morrow.

President's Son. Krandall Kraus. 299p. (Orig.). 1986. pap. 7.95 (ISBN 0-932870-83-X). Alyson Pubns.

Presidents' Sons: The Prestige of Name in a Democracy. facs. ed. Joseph J. Perling. LC 70-148226. (Biography Index Reprint Ser.). 1947. 26.50 (ISBN 0-8369-8073-5). Ayer Co Pubs.

President's Tax Proposals to the Congress for Fairness, Growth & Simplicity. 509p. (Orig.). 1985. pap. 18.00 (ISBN 0-318-11748-7, S/N 048-000-00373-7). USGPO.

Presidents: Tidbits & Trivia. rev. ed. Sid Frank & Arden Melick. LC 79-47990. (Illus.). 160p. (YA) (gr. 5-8). 1982. pap. 9.95 (ISBN 0-8437-3350-0). Hammond Inc.

President's Women. June F. Singer. 1988. 19.95 (ISBN 0-517-57028-9). Crown.

Presiding Ideas in Wordsworth's Poetry. Melvin M. Rader. LC 68-8341. 94p. 1968. Repr. of 1931 ed. 15.00x (ISBN 0-87752-090-9). Gordian.

Presidio. Mike Cogan. 1988. pap. 3.50 (ISBN 0-671-66876-5). PB.

Presidio & Militia on the Northern Frontier of New Spain: A Documentary History - 1570-1700, Vol. I. Thomas H. Naylor & Charles W. Polzer. LC 86-13283. 756p. 1986. 50.00x (ISBN 0-8165-0903-4). U of Ariz Pr.

Presley Arrangement. Monte W. Nicholson. LC 86-91710. 210p. 1987. 12.95 (ISBN 0-533-07380-4). Vantage.

Presley: Entertainer of the Century. Antony James. 1976. pap. 1.95 (ISBN 0-505-51239-4, Pub. by Tower Bks). Leisure NY.

Preso Sin Nombre, Celda Sin Numero see Prisoner Without a Name, Cell Without a Number.

Presocratic Philosophers. Rev. ed. Jonathan Barnes. (Arguments of the Philosophers Ser.). 680p. 1982. pap. 19.95 (ISBN 0-7100-9200-8). Routledge Chapman & Hall.

Presocratic Philosphers: A Critical History with a Selections of Texts. 2nd ed. G. S. Kirk et al. LC 82-23505. 500p. 1984. 70.00 (ISBN 0-521-25444-2); pap. 20.95 (ISBN 0-521-27455-9). Cambridge U Pr.

Presocratics. Hudson River ed. Edward Hussey. LC 72-4126. 168p. 1973. 20.00 (ISBN 0-684-17601-7). Scribner.

Presocratics. Edward Hussey. (Classical Life & Letters Ser.). 168p. 1972. 40.50 (ISBN 0-7156-0630-1, Pub. by Duckworth London); pap. 13.50 (ISBN 0-7156-0824-X). Longwood Pub Group.

Presocratics. Philip Wheelwright. 1966. pap. text ed. write for info. (ISBN 0-02-426640-X). Macmillan.

Presocratics. Ed. & tr. by Philip Wheelwright. LC 66-12944. (Orig.). 1966. pap. 10.28 scp (ISBN 0-672-63091-5). Odyssey Pr.

Presocratics: The Main Fragments. M. R. Wright. 214p. 1985. 15.25 (ISBN 0-86292-079-5, Pub. by Bristol Classical UK). Focus Info Gr.

Presque Isle. Daniel Morris. (Illus.). 102p. (Orig.). 1988. pap. price not set. Osage Pr.

Presqu'ile: Avec: La Route, Le Roi Cophetua. Julien Gracq. 256p. 1970. 29.95 (ISBN 0-686-54025-5). French & Eur.

Press. A. J. Liebling. 1981. pap. 6.95 (ISBN 0-394-74849-2). Pantheon.

Press: A Handbook of Elementary Classroom Ideas to Motivate Teaching Through the Use of the Newspaper. (Spice Ser.). 1978. 8.95 (ISBN 0-89273-126-5). Educ Serv.

Press: A Neglected Factor in the Economic History of the Twentieth Century. Harold A. Innis. LC 76-29440. 1977. Repr. of 1949 ed. 11.50 (ISBN 0-404-15310-0). AMS Pr.

Press & America: An Interpretive History of the Mass Media. 5th ed. Edwin Emery & Michael Emery. (Illus.). 624p. 1984. text ed. 42.00 (ISBN 0-13-697988-2). P-H.

Press & America: An Interpretive History of the Mass Media. 6th ed. Michael Emery & Edwin Emery. (Illus.). 784p. 1988. text ed. 37.25 (ISBN 0-13-699059-2). P-H.

Press & Apartheid: Repression & Propaganda in South Africa. William Hachten & C. Anthony Giffard. LC 84-40150. 352p. 1984. text ed. 22.50x (ISBN 0-299-09940-7). U of Wis Pr.

Press & Foreign Policy. Bernard C. Cohen. LC 83-12989. ix, 288p. 1983. Repr. of 1963 ed. lib. bdg. 45.50x (ISBN 0-313-24215-1, CPFP). Greenwood.

Press & Media Access to the Criminal Courtroom. Warren Freedman. LC 88-4039. 144p. 1988. lib. bdg. 39.95 (ISBN 0-89930-328-5, FPB/, Quorum Bks). Greenwood.

Press & Poetry of Modern Persia. Edward G. Browne. (Illus.). xi, 357p. 1983. Repr. of 1914 ed. 35.00 (ISBN 0-933770-39-1). Kalimat.

Press & Political Dissent: A Question of Censorship. Mark Hollingsworth. Ed. by Neil Middleton. 288p. (Orig.). 1986. pap. 13.25 (ISBN 0-7453-0139-8, Pub. by Pluto Pr). Longwood Pub Group.

Press & Politics in British Western Punjab, 1836-1947. Emmett Davis. 1985. 22.00x (ISBN 0-8364-1261-3, Pub. by Academic India). South Asia Bks.

Press & Politics in Pre-Revolutionary France. Jack C. Censer & Jeremy Popkin. LC 85-23220. 300p. 1987. text ed. 30.00x (ISBN 0-520-05672-8). U of Cal Pr.

Press & Politics: Monographs. Mary Vance. (Public Administration Ser.: P 1781). 15p. 1985. 2.25 (ISBN 0-89028-581-0). Vance Biblios.

Press & Public: Who Reads What, Where, & Why in American Newspapers. Leo Bogart. LC 80-18357. 304p. 1981. text ed. 29.95 (ISBN 0-89859-077-9). L Erlbaum Assocs.

Press & Society. R. D. Parikh. 154p. 1965. 9.95. Asia Bk Corp.

Press & the American Revolution. Ed. by Bernard Bailyn & John B. Hench. LC 81-14207. 383p. 1980. text ed. 27.95x (ISBN 0-930350-32-4); pap. 9.95x (ISBN 0-930350-30-8). NE U Pr.

Press & the Carter Presidency. Mark J. Rozell. 230p. 1988. 28.00. Westview.

Press & the Cold War. rev. ed. Jim Aronson. Ed. by Joanne Dolinar. 350p. 1988. pap. text ed. 14.00x (ISBN 0-8038-9312-4, Dist by Kampmann & Co.). Hastings.

Press & the Decline of Democracy: The Democratic Socialist Response in Public Policy. Robert G. Picard. LC 85-5583. (Contributions to the Study of Mass Media & Communications Ser.: No. 4). (Illus.). xii, 176p. 1985. lib. bdg. 35.00 (ISBN 0-313-24915-6, PPD/). Greenwood.

Press & the Origins of the Cold War, 1944-1947. Louis Liebovich. LC 87-38478. 192p. 1988. lib. bdg. 39.95 (ISBN 0-275-92999-X, C2999). Praeger.

Press & the Presidency. John W. Tebbel & Sarah M. Watts. LC 85-4887. write for info. Amer Bar Assn.

Press & the Presidency: From George Washington to Ronald Reagan. John Tebbel & Sarah M. Watts. 1985. 29.95 (ISBN 0-19-503628-X). Oxford U Pr.

Press & the Public Interest. Ed. by Warren K. Agee. 1968. 9.00 (ISBN 0-8183-0200-3). Pub Aff Pr.

Press & the Public: The Story of the British Press Council. George Murray. LC 72-173462. (New Horizons in Journalism Ser). 256p. 1972. 8.95x (ISBN 0-8093-0542-9). S Ill U Pr.

Press & the Rebirth of Iberian Democracy. Ed. by Kenneth Maxwell. LC 82-24201. (Contributions in Political Science Ser.: No. 99). (Illus.). xvi, 198p. 1983. lib. bdg. 35.00 (ISBN 0-313-23100-1, MPI/). Greenwood.

Press & the State: Sociohistorical & Contemporary Interpretations. Walter M. Brasch & Dana R. Ulloth. LC 86-15855. 826p. (Orig.). 1987. lib. bdg. 50.00 (ISBN 0-8191-5502-0); pap. text ed. 26.25 (ISBN 0-8191-5272-2). U Pr of Amer.

Press & the Suburbs: The Daily Newspapers of New Jersey. David Sachsman & Warren Sloat. 224p. (Orig.). 1986. pap. text ed. 10.95x (ISBN 0-88285-108-X). Transaction Bks.

Press & World Affairs. Robert W. Desmond. LC 72-4665. (International Propaganda & Communications Ser.). (Illus.). 449p. 1972. Repr. of 1937 ed. 25.00 (ISBN 0-405-04746-0). Ayer Co Pubs.

Press As an Ally in Collecting Folk Speech see American Dialect Society: A Historical Sketch.

Press Beyond Calcutta-North & East. Katharine S. Diehl. (Printers & Printing in the East Indies to 1850 Ser.: Vol. VI). Date not set. write for info. (ISBN 0-89241-395-6). Caratzas.

Press Box: Red Smith's Favorite Sport Stories. Ed. by Red Smith. 192p. pap. 2.95 (ISBN 0-380-63685-9, 63685-9, Discus). Avon.

Press Boycott of Aesthetic Realism: Documentation. Ed. by Martha Baird & Ellen Reiss. LC 77-80498. 1978. pap. 2.50 (ISBN 0-910492-30-1). Definition.

Press Concentration & Monopoly. Robert G. Picard et al. Ed. by Brenda Dervin. LC 87-33328. (Communication & Information Science Ser.). 288p. 1988. text ed. 39.50 (ISBN 0-89391-464-9). Ablex Pub.

Press Conference. 1985. 39.00x (ISBN 0-317-39105-4, Pub. by Norbury Pubns Ltd). State Mutual Bk.

Press Control Around the World. Jane L. Curry. LC 82-9837. 304p. 1982. 36.95 (ISBN 0-275-90775-9, C0775). Praeger.

Press Council: A Self Regulatory Mechanism for the Indian Press. N. K. Trikha. 1987. 26.00x (ISBN 81-7039-112-1, Pub. by Somaiya). South Asia Bks.

Press Coverage of the Falklands Conflict. J. Laurence Day. LC 83-198373. (UFSI Reports Ser.: No. 47). U Field Staff Intl.

Press Cuttings. George Bernard Shaw. LC 76-40393. (One-Act Plays in Reprint Ser.). 1976. Repr. of 1919 ed. 15.00x (ISBN 0-8486-2008-9). Roth Pub Inc.

Press Cuttings see Getting Married.

Press During the Hungarian Revolution. Domokos Kosary. 520p. 1986. 45.00 (ISBN 0-88033-091-0). East Eur Quarterly.

Press, Film, Radio, 5 vols. in 3. UNESCO. LC 72-4683. (International Propaganda & Communications Ser.). 2114p. 1972. Repr. of 1951 ed. Set. 106.00 (ISBN 0-405-04767-3); 35.50 ea. Vols. 1 & 2 (ISBN 0-405-04772-X). Vols. 3 & 4 (ISBN 0-405-04773-8). Vol. 5 (ISBN 0-405-04774-6). Ayer Co Pubs.

Press: Free & Responsible? (Symposia Ser.). 114p. 1982. 7.95 (ISBN 0-89940-411-1). LBJ Sch Pub Aff.

Press Freedom & Political Stress in Nepal. Subhadra Belbase. 28p. 1981. pap. 2.00 (ISBN 0-318-23184-0). Am-Nepal Ed.

Press Freedoms: A Descriptive Calender of Concepts, Interpretations, Events & Court Actions, from 4000 BC to the Present. Louis E. Ingelhart. LC 86-31834. 449p. 1987. lib. bdg. 45.00 (ISBN 0-313-25636-5, IPF/). Greenwood.

Press Freedoms under Pressure. Report of the Twentieth Century Fund Task Force on the Government & the Press & Fred Graham. LC 72-80586. 1972. pap. free (ISBN 0-87078-125-1). Priority Pr Pubns.

Press in Authoritarian Countries see International Press Institute Surveys.

Press in Chains. Zamir Niazi. 252p. 1987. 27.50x (ISBN 81-202-0182-5, Pub. by Ajanta). South Asia Bks.

Press in English Society from the Seventeenth to the Nineteenth Centuries. Ed. by Michael Harris & Alan J. Lee. LC 85-45535. (Illus.). 264p. 1986. 35.00x (ISBN 0-8386-3272-6). Fairleigh Dickinson.

Press in India. R. C. Sarkar. 320p. 1984. 32.95. Asia Bk Corp.

Press in Perspective. Ed. by Ralph D. Casey. LC 63-16657. pap. 58.80 (ISBN 0-317-30011-3, 2051876). Bks Demand UMI.

Press in the French Revolution. Ed. by W. Gilchrist & W. J. Murray. LC 77-150256. 1971. 64.50x (ISBN 0-89197-596-9). Irvington.

Press Law & Press Freedom for High School Publications: Court Cases & Related Decisions Discussing Free Expression Guarantees & Limitations for High School Students & Journalists. Louis E. Ingelhart. LC 85-24807. (Contributions to the Study of Mass Media & Communications Ser.: No. 6). 178p. 1986. lib. bdg. 35.00 (ISBN 0-313-25154-1, IPL/). Greenwood.

Press Law in Modern Democracies: A Comparative Study. Pnina Lahav. LC 83-19595. (Annenberg-Longman Communication Bks.). 1984. 40.95 (ISBN 0-582-28478-3). Longman.

Press of Africa: Persecution & Perseverence. Frank Barton. LC 78-7363. 304p. 1979. 44.50 (ISBN 0-8419-0393-X, Africana). Holmes & Meier.

Press of Battle. Jack E. Pulwers. 400p. 1988. pap. 24.95 (ISBN 0-915979-09-8). Hero Books.

Press of Latin America: A Tentative & Selected Bibliography in Spanish & Portuguese. Mary A. Gardner. LC 72-619723. (Guides & Bibliographies Ser.: No. 4). pap. 20.00 (2027330). Bks Demand UMI.

Press On! Further Adventures in the Good Life. Chuck Yeager & Charles Leerhsen. LC 88-47756. 208p. 1988. 17.95 (ISBN 0-553-05333-7). Bantam.

Press On: I'll Meet You at the Gate. Jo Ann Fox. (Illus.). 480p. (Orig.). 1987. pap. 11.95 (ISBN 0-944039-03-0). Van Winkle Pr.

Press Operator. Jack Rudman. (Career Examination Ser.: C-3190). (Cloth bdg. avail. on request). 1988. pap. 14.00 (ISBN 0-8373-3190-0). Natl Learning.

Press, Party, & Presidency. Richard L. Rubin. 1981. pap. text ed. 6.95x (ISBN 0-393-95206-1). Norton.

Press, Politics, & Power: Egypt's Heikal & Al-Ahram. Munir K. Nasser. 1979. pap. text ed. 9.50x (ISBN 0-8138-1290-9). Iowa St U Pr.

Press Politics & Public Opinion in India. B. M. Sankhdher. 1986. 34.00x (ISBN 0-8364-1547-7, Pub. by Deep). South Asia Bks.

Press Time. 3rd ed. Julian Adams & Kenneth Stratton. 1975. text ed. 21.80 (ISBN 0-13-699041-X). P-H.

Press Tool Making. 1982. 50.00x (Pub. by Engineering Ind). State Mutual Bk.

Press Toolmaking. 2nd ed. Ed. by F. Ballard et al. (Engineering Craftsmen: No. H21). (Illus.). 1972. spiral bdg. 39.95x. Trans-Atl Phila.

Press Tools & Presswork. John A. Waller. 454p. 1985. 95.00x (ISBN 0-86108-168-4, Pub. by Portcullis Pr UK). State Mutual Bk.

Press Versus the Government. D. R. Mankekar. 187p. 1978. 14.95. Asia Bk Corp.

Press View the FBI Raid. (Illus.). pap. cancelled (ISBN 0-915598-17-5). Church of Scient Info.

Press vs. Government: Constitutional Issues. Donald J. Rogers. LC 86-8369. (Illus.). 160p. (gr. 5-9). 1987. 10.29 (ISBN 0-671-61105-4). Messner.

Press Watch: A Provocative Look at How Newspapers Report the News. David Shaw. 288p. 1984. 15.95 (ISBN 0-02-610030-4). MacMillan.

Presse: A Reader & Workbook. Klaus A. Mueller & Susanne Hoppmann-Liecty. 192p. 1975. pap. text ed. 14.00 (ISBN 0-669-92536-5). Heath.

Presse der Stadt Dortmund und der Ehemaligen Grafschaft Mark: Bibliographie, Standortnachweis, Archivalien, und Literatur. Gert Hagelweide. (Dortmunder Beitrage Ser.: Vol. 44). 238p. 1988. pap. text ed. 20.00 (ISBN 3-598-21301-8). K G Saur.

Presse Deux. 2nd ed. Brian N. Morton & Jacqueline Morton. 1977. pap. text ed. 14.50 (ISBN 0-669-01636-5). Heath.

Presse et le Mouvement National Chez les Musulmans De Russie Avant 1920 see Mouvements Nationaux Chez les Musulmans De Russie.

Presse Franco-Americaine et la Politique: L'oeuvre de Charles-Roger Daoust. Robert B. Perreault. (Illus.). 102p. (Fr.). 1980. pap. text ed. 3.50 (ISBN 0-911409-39-4). Natl Mat Dev.

Presse und Geschichte II: Neue Beitrage zur historischen Kommunikations Forschung. Ed. by Hartwig Gebhardt et al. (Deutsche Presseforschung: Vol. 26). 426p. (Ger.). 1987. lib. bdg. 45.00 (ISBN 3-598-21627-0). K G Saur.

Presse und Rundfunkarchive vol. 8: Partner von Redaktion, Produktion und Program: Protokoll der 47. Tagung der Fachgruppe der Archivare an Presse, Rundfunk und Filmarchiven im Verein deutscher Archivare. Compiled by Marianne Englert & Eckhard Lange. (Presse, Rundfunk, und Filmarchive, Mediendokumentation). 207p. (Ger.). 1987. text ed. 35.00 (ISBN 3-598-20338-1). K G Saur.

Pressed Flowers. Cathy Bossi. (Illus.). Date not set. 15.95. Saifer.

Pressed Flowers & Flower Pictures. Margaret K. Scott. (Illus.). 128p. 1988. 24.95 (ISBN 0-7134-5245-5, Pub. by Batsford England). David & Charles.

Pressed Flowers Through the Seasons. Margaret K. Scott & Mary Beazley. (Illus.). 120p. 1983. 22.95 (ISBN 0-7134-4039-2, Pub. by Batsford England). David & Charles.

Pressed Glass: Eighteen Twenty-Five to Nineteen Twenty-Five. Corning Museum of Glass Staff. (Antiques Ser.). 48p. (Orig.). 1983. pap. 6.00 (ISBN 0-486-24510-1). Dover.

Pressed Glass in America: Encyclopedia of the First Hundred Years, 1825-1925. John Welker & Elizabeth Welker. LC 85-73252. (Illus.). 512p. 1986. 49.00x (ISBN 0-9615861-0-9). Antique Acres.

Pressed Glass: 1825-1925. LC 82-73854. (Illus.). 48p. 1983. 6.00 (ISBN 0-87290-107-6). Corning.

Pressed Wild Flowers Pictures. Mary Beazley. (Illus.). 120p. 1986. 22.95 (ISBN 0-7134-4614-5, Pub. by Batsford England). David & Charles.

Presser. Jack Rudman. (Career Examination Ser.: C-1397). (Cloth bdg. avail. on request). pap. 14.00 (ISBN 0-8373-1397-X). Natl Learning.

Presses. Society of Manufacturing Engineers. (Productivity Equipment Ser.). 704p. 1985. 44.00. SME.

Pressing Business: An Organizational Manual for Independent Publishers. Volunteer Lawyers for the Arts & Barbara S. Taylor. LC 85-8876. 59p. 1984. 7.95 (ISBN 0-917103-01-7). Vol Lawyers Arts.

Pressing on When You'd Rather Turn Back: Philippians. rev. ed. Gene A. Getz. (Biblical Renewal Ser.). 200p. 1985. pap. 6.95 (ISBN 0-8307-1089-2, 5418561). Regal.

Pressing Toward the Mark. Ed. by Robert Fisher. LC 83-63384. 176p. 1983. pap. text ed. 8.95 (ISBN 0-87148-714-4). Pathway Pr.

Pressrom Manager's Guidebook. 2nd ed. Frank Drazan. (Illus.). 112p. 1986. pap. 20.00 (ISBN 0-318-21788-0). F Drazan.

Pressroom Managers Training Guide. 165p. spiral 250.00 (ISBN 0-318-23319-3). F Drazan.

Pressure. (Tops Cards Ser.: No. 16). 1978. pap. 8.80 (ISBN 0-941008-16-9). Tops Learning.

Pressure. Sam Rutigliano. 1988. pap. 14.95 (ISBN 0-8407-9087-2). Oliver-Nelson.

Pressure Analysis Methods. (SPE Reprint Ser). 256p. 1967. 25.00x (ISBN 0-317-32931-6, 30509). Soc Petrol Engineers.

Pressure Boys: The Inside Story of Lobbying in America. Kenneth G. Crawford. LC 73-19139. (Politics & People Ser.). 320p. 1974. Repr. 21.00x (ISBN 0-405-05864-0). Ayer Co Pubs.

Pressure Buildup & Flow Tests in Wells. C. S. Matthews & D. G. Russell. 163p. 1967. 30.00x (ISBN 0-89520-200-X, 30401). Soc Petrol Engineers.

Pressure Change Testing see Leak Testing Question & Answer Books H.

Pressure Cooker. Don Biggs. (Illus.). 1979. 14.95 (ISBN 0-393-08815-4). Norton.

Pressure Cycled Ventilators. Deborah B. Clark & Debra Bradford. (Illus.). 208p. 1984. text ed. 24.95 (ISBN 0-13-699090-8). P-H.

Pressure Diecasting: Metals-Machines-Furnaces, Pt. 1. B. Upton. (Materials Engineering Practice Ser.). (Illus.). 165p. 1982. text ed. 34.00 (ISBN 0-08-027621-0); pap. text ed. 16.00 (ISBN 0-08-027622-9). Pergamon.

Pressure Diecasting: The Technology of the Casting & the Die, Pt. 2. D. F. Allsop & D. Kennedy. (Materials Engineering Practice Ser.). (Illus.). 186p. 1983. text ed. 36.00 (ISBN 0-08-027615-6); pap. text ed. 17.00 (ISBN 0-08-027614-8). Pergamon.

Pressure Enthalpy Charts. Byron Short et al. LC 70-11431. (Orig.). 1970. pap. 18.00x (ISBN 0-87201-105-4). Gulf Pub.

Pressure, Flow & Level Instrumentation Market. 260p. 1984. 1575.00 (ISBN 0-86621-260-4, A1332). Frost & Sullivan.

Pressure for the Poor: The Poverty Lobby & Policy Making. Paul Whiteley & Stephen Winyard. 250p. 1988. lib. bdg. 60.00x (ISBN 0-416-36370-9). Routledge Chapman & Hall.

Pressure Gauge Handbook. United States Ametek Gauge Staff. (Mechanical Engineering Ser.). 304p. 1985. 49.75 (ISBN 0-8247-7433-7). Dekker.

Pressure Gauges. EEMUA Staff. 1972. 75.00x (Pub. by EEMUA). State Mutual Bk.

Pressure Groups among "Small Businessmen". Roger S. Pepper. Ed. by Stuart Bruchey & Vincent P. Carosso. LC 78-18973. (Small Business Enterprise in America Ser.). 1979. lib. bdg. 12.00x (ISBN 0-405-11476-1). Ayer Co Pubs.

Pressure Groups & Foreign Policy. Oladapo O. Fafowora. 1986. 12.95 (ISBN 0-533-06103-2). Vantage.

Pressure Groups & Politics in Antebellum Tariffs. J. J. Pincus. LC 76-51733. 1977. 29.50x (ISBN 0-231-03963-8). Columbia U Pr.

Pressure Groups in Britain 1720-1970: An Essay in Interpretation with Original Documents. Graham Wootton. LC 74-23832. x, 375p. (Orig.). 1975. 35.00 (ISBN 0-208-01500-0, Archon). Shoe String.

Pressure Groups in the Global System. Peter Willetts. LC 81-47979. 280p. 1982. 25.00x (ISBN 0-312-64162-1). St Martin.

Pressure Groups in the Global System. Ed. by Peter Willetts. (Global Politics Ser.). 226p. 1982. pap. 16.00 (ISBN 0-86187-224-X, Pub. by Frances Pinter). Longwood Pub Group.

Pressure Losses in Ducted Flows. A. Ward Smith. (Illus.). 1971. 18.25 (ISBN 0-8088-7015-7). Davey.

Pressure Point. Hank Bostrom. (Gabriel's Flight Ser.: No. 2). 368p. (Orig.). 1988. pap. 3.95 (ISBN 1-55802-086-1). Lynx Bks.

Pressure Points: Do It Yourself Acupuncture Without Needles. Keith Kenyon. LC 77-7291. (Illus.). 1977. lib. bdg. 8.95 o. p. (ISBN 0-668-04329-6); pap. 5.95 (ISBN 0-668-04333-4). Arco.

Pressure Points: How To Deal with Stress. Don Osgood. pap. 2.95 (ISBN 0-345-33064-1). Ballantine.

Pressure Politics in Industrial Societies: A Comparative Introduction. Alan R. Ball & Frances Millard. LC 86-18930. 324p. 1986. text ed. 39.95 (ISBN 0-391-03485-5); pap. text ed. 12.50 (ISBN 0-391-03486-3). Humanities.

Pressure Rating, Vol. B. rev. ed. Ed. by Shirley C. Seal. (Fluid Power Standards 1987 Ser.). (Illus.). 262p. 1987. 56.25 (ISBN 0-942220-83-8). Natl Fluid Power.

Pressure Sensitive Adhesives Market. 287p. 1984. 1800.00 (ISBN 0-86621-619-7, E691). Frost & Sullivan.

Pressure-Sensitive Papers. Jack Weiner & Lillian Roth. LC 65-29030. (Bibliographic Ser.: No. 222, Suppl. 3). 1973. pap. 19.00 (ISBN 0-87010-018-1). Inst Paper Chem.

Pressure-Sensitive Papers. Jack Weiner & Lillian Roth. (Bibliographic Ser.: No. 222). 79p. 1965. 8.00 (ISBN 0-317-34418-8). Inst Paper Chem.

Pressure Sensitive: Popular Musicians under Stress. Geoff Wills & Cary L. Cooper. (Communications in Society Ser.). 160p. 1988. text ed. 42.75 (ISBN 0-8039-8141-4); pap. text ed. 16.95 (ISBN 0-8039-8142-2). Sage.

Pressure Sores. Betty Garee. 32p. (Orig.). 1987. pap. 3.50 (ISBN 0-915708-20-5). Cheever Pub.

Pressure Sores: Aetiology, Treatment & Prevention. Colin Torrance. (Illus.). 128p. (Orig.). 1983. pap. text ed. 16.50x (ISBN 0-7099-2418-6, Pub. by Croom Helm England). Sheridan.

Pressure Transient Testing Methods. (SPE Reprint Ser.). 345p. 1980. 24.00x (ISBN 0-317-36507-X, 30514). Soc Petrol Engineers.

Pressure Ulcers: Principles & Techniques of Management. Ed. by Mark B. Constantian. 320p. 1980. text ed. 50.00 (ISBN 0-316-15330-3). Little.

Pressure under Grace. William Greenway. LC 82-1284. 45p. 1982. pap. 5.95 (ISBN 0-932576-10-9); limited, signed o.s.i. 50.00. Breitenbush Bks.

Pressure Vessel Analysis. David Burgreen. LC 79-51160. 1979. 27.00 (ISBN 0-9600452-3-6). C P Pr.

Pressure Vessel Analysis. David Burgreen. 363p. 48.00 (ISBN 0-916877-05-1). Arcturus Pubs.

Pressure Vessel & Piping 1972 Computer Programs Verification: An Aid to Developers & Users. Ed. by I. S. Tuba & W. B. Wright. LC 72-94235. (Illus.). pap. 49.80 (ISBN 0-317-08488-7, 2016906). Bks Demand UMI.

Pressure Vessel Codes & Standards. Ed. by R. W. Nichols. 312p. 1987. 79.25 (ISBN 1-85166-048-8, Pub. by Elsevier Applied Sci England). Elsevier.

Pressure Vessel Codes: Their Application to Nuclear Reactor Systems. (Technical Reports Ser.: No. 56). (Illus.). 32p. 1966. pap. 9.00 (ISBN 92-0-155066-9, IDC56, IAEA). UNIPUB.

Pressure Vessel Design. Ed. by G. E. O. Widera. (PVP: Vol. 57). 217p. 1982. 44.00 (H00214). ASME.

Pressure Vessel Design Handbook. 2nd ed. Henry H. Bednar. (Illus.). 448p. 1985. 51.95 (ISBN 0-442-21385-9). Van Nos Reinhold.

Pressure Vessel Design Manual: Illustrated Procedures for Solving Every Major Pressure Vessel Design Problem. Dennis R. Moss. LC 87-360. (Illus.). 300p. 1987. 79.00 (ISBN 0-87201-719-2). Gulf Pub.

Pressure Vessel Design: 36 Miscellaneous Computer Programs. B. Fred Forman & Technical Research Service, Inc. Staff. 495.00 (ISBN 0-914458-13-2). Pressure.

Pressure Vessel Engineering Technology. Ed. by R. W. Nichols. (Illus.). 603p. 1970. 108.00 (ISBN 0-444-20061-4, Pub. by Elsevier Applied Sci England). Elsevier.

Pressure Vessel Handbook. 7th ed. Ed. by Eugene F. Megyesy. (Illus.). 1986. 38.00 (ISBN 0-914458-12-4). Pressure.

Pressure Vessel Inspection Safety Code. (Institute of Petroleum Model Code of Safety Practice in the Petroleum Industry Ser.: Pt. 12). 1977. 11.00 (ISBN 0-85501-302-8). Wiley.

Pressure Vessel Technology: Proceedings of the International Conference, 6th, Beijing, People's Republic of China, 11-15 September 1988, 2 vols. Ed. by Cengdian Liu & R. W. Nichols. (Illus.). 1750p. 1989. 395.01 (ISBN 0-08-035896-9); prepub. 240.01 (ISBN 0-08-035897-7). Pergamon.

Pressure Vessel Technology 1985. Ed. by H. L. Stark. 95p. 1985. pap. text ed. 15.00 (ISBN 0-85825-260-0, Pub. by Inst Engineering Australia). Brookfield Pub Co.

Pressure Vessels: A Workbook for Engineers. American Society of Mechanical Engineers Staff. Ed. by E. J. Hicks. LC 81-111549. pap. 20.00 (ISBN 0-317-29757-0, 2017372). Bks Demand UMI.

Pressure Vessels & Piping Computer Program Evaluation & Qualification: Presented at the Energy Technology Conference, Houston TX, Sept. 18-23, 1977. Energy Technology Conference. Ed. by D. E. Dietrich. LC 77-82203. pap. 31.80 (2056306). Bks Demand UMI.

Pressure Vessels & Piping: Design & Analysis - A Decade of Progress, 4 vols. Ed. by G. J. Bohm & R. L. Cloud. Incl. Vol. 1. Analysis. 780p; Vol. 2. Components & Structural Dynamics. 812p. 1972. 35.00 ea. (G00019, G00020). ASME.

Pressure Vessels & Piping: Design & Analysis - A Decade of Progress: Quality Assurance - Applications - Components, Vol. 4. Ed. by H. H. Waite. 1976. text ed. 50.00 (ISBN 0-685-72346-1, G00101). ASME.

Pressure Vessels & Piping: Design Technology, 1982-A Decade of Progress. Ed. by S. Y. Zamrik & D. Dietrich. 647p. 1982. 85.00 (G00213). ASME.

Pressure Vessels & Piping: Verification & Qualification of Inelastic Analysis Computer Programs. National Congress on Pressure Vessels & Piping (2nd: 1975: San Francisco. Ed. by J. M. Corum & W. B. Wright. LC 75-8090. (Illus.). pap. 29.30 (ISBN 0-317-08401-1, 2016813). Bks Demand UMI.

Pressure Vessels: The ASME Code Simplified. 6th ed. R. Chuse & S. M. Eber. 1984. text ed. 42.50 (ISBN 0-07-010874-9). McGraw.

Pressure Without Sanctions: The Influence of World Jewry on Israeli Policy. Charles S. Liebman. LC 75-18242. 304p. 1976. 27.50 (ISBN 0-8386-1791-3). Fairleigh Dickinson.

Pressuremeter & Foundation Engineering. F. Baguelin et al. (Rock & Soil Mechanics Ser.). (Illus.). 1978. 58.00x (ISBN 0-87849-019-1). Trans Tech.

Pressuremeter & Its Marine Applications: Second International Symposium, STP 950. Ed. by Louis J. Briaud & M. E. Audibert. LC 86-3337. (Special Technical Publications). (Illus.). 505p. 1986. text ed. 64.00 (ISBN 0-8031-0454-5, 04-950000-38). ASTM.

Pressuremeter & Its Marine Applications. Institut Francais du Petrole Laboratoires des Ponts et Chaussees. 430p. (Orig.). 1983. pap. 95.00x (ISBN 0-87201-735-4). Gulf pub.

Pressuremeter Testing: Methods & Interpretation. R. J. Mair & D. M. Wood. (Illus.). 160p. 1987. text ed. 29.95 (ISBN 0-408-02434-8). Butterworth.

Pressures of the Hand: Expressionist Impulses in Recent American Art. Carter Ratcliff. (Illus.). 36p. 1984. pap. 12.50 (ISBN 0-942746-05-8). SUNYP R Gibson.

Pressures on the Countryside. Derrick Golland. (Considering Conservation Ser.). (Illus.). 48p. (YA) (gr. 7-12). 1986. 17.95 (ISBN 0-85219-625-3, Pub. by Batsford England). David & Charles.

Pressures on the Legislature of New Jersey. Dayton D. McKean. LC 66-27121. 1967. Repr. of 1938 ed. 8.00x (ISBN 0-8462-0850-4). Russell.

Pressurized Fluidized Bed Combustion Technology. W. F. Podolski et al. LC 83-13215. (Energy Tech. Rev. 87; Pollution Tech. Rev. 103). (Illus.). 429p. 1984. 45.00 (ISBN 0-8155-0960-X). Noyes.

Pressworking Aids for Designers & Diemakers. Daniel B. Dallas. LC 77-90988. (Manufacturing Data Ser.). 275p. 1978. 26.50x (ISBN 0-87263-042-0). SME.

Pressworking: Stampings & Dies. Ed. by Karl Keyes. LC 80-53009. (Manufacturing Update Ser.). (Illus.). 260p. 1980. 35.00 (ISBN 0-87263-061-7). SME.

Prestel in the Library Context: Proceedings of Two Seminars. Ed. by Anna Sheldon. LC 83-151354. (LIR Report 6). (Illus.). 69p. (Orig.). 1983. pap. 12.00 (ISBN 0-7123-3009-7, Pub. by British Lib). Longwood Pub Group.

Prestel in the Public Library: Reaction of the General Public to Prestel & Its Potential for Conveying Local Information. Robin Yeates. LC 82-212860. (LIR Report 2). (Illus.). 143p. (Orig.). 1982. pap. 13.50 (ISBN 0-7123-3003-8, Pub. by British Lib). Longwood Pub Group.

Prester John. John Buchan. LC 75-131650. (Illus.). 1970. 49.00x (ISBN 0-403-00537-X). Scholarly.

Prester John. John Buchan. 1988. Repr. of 1970 ed. lib. bdg. 49.00x. Am Biog Serv.

Prester John of the Indies: A True Relation of the Lands of the Prester John, Being the Narrative. Francisco Alvares. Ed. by C. F. Beckingham & G. W. Huntingford. Tr. by Lord Stanley of Alderley. (Hakluyt Society Works Ser. II: Vols. 114-115). 95.00 (ISBN 0-8115-0404-2). Kraus Repr.

Prestige & Association in an Urban Community: An Analysis of an Urban Stratification System. Edward O. Laumann. LC 66-29709. 1966. cancelled (ISBN 0-672-51165-7). Irvington.

Prestige, Class & Mobility. Kaare Svalastoga. Ed. by Lewis A. Coser & Walter W. Powell. LC 79-7024. (Perennial Works in Sociology Ser.). (Illus.). 1979. Repr. of 1959 ed. lib. bdg. 38.00x (ISBN 0-405-12123-7). Ayer Co Pubs.

Prestige Label: A Discography. Compiled by Michel Ruppli. LC 79-8294. (Discographies Ser.: No. 3). 1980. lib. bdg. 35.00x (ISBN 0-313-22019-0, RPL/). Greenwood.

Prestige of Evil: The Murderer As Romantic Hero from Sade to Lacenaire. Laurence Senelick. Ed. by James J. Wilhelm & Richard Saez. (Harvard Dissertations in Comparative Literature Ser.). 427p. 1987. lib. bdg. 65.00 (ISBN 0-8240-8434-9). Garland Pub.

Prestige of Schiller in England, 1788-1859. Frederic Ewen. Repr. of 1932 ed. 22.50 (ISBN 0-404-02364-9). AMS Pr.

Prestige Press: A Comparative Study of Political Symbols. Ed. by Ithiel De Sola Pool. 1970. pap. 6.95x (ISBN 0-262-66022-9). MIT Pr.

Prestige Press & the Christmas Bombing, 1972: Images & Reality in Vietnam. Martin F. Herz & Leslie Rider. 120p. 1985. pap. text ed. 7.00 (ISBN 0-8191-4486-X). U Pr of Amer.

Presto! Roberta Smoodin. LC 81-69200. (Illus.). 288p. 1982. 13.95 (ISBN 0-689-11273-4). Atheneum.

Presto Change-O. Audrey Wood. (Child's Play Library). (Illus.). 32p. (ps-2). 1983. 5.50 (ISBN 0-85953-181-3, Child's Play England). Playspaces.

Presto! Magic for the Beginner. George Schindler. 1977. pap. 5.00 (ISBN 0-89515-000-X). Natl Paragon.

Preston Jones. Mark Busby. LC 82-74092. (Western Writers Ser.: No. 58). (Illus., Orig.). 1983. pap. 2.95x (ISBN 0-88430-032-3). Boise St Univ.

Preston Morton Collection of American Art. Ed. by Katherine H. Mead. LC 81-52029. (Illus.). 272p. (Orig.). 1981. pap. 19.95 (ISBN 0-295-96073-6). U of Wash Pr.

Preston Morton Collection of American Art. Ed. by Katherine H. Mead. LC 81-52029. (Illus.). 272p. (Orig.). 1981. pap. 12.00 (ISBN 0-89951-043-4). Santa Barb Mus Art.

Preston Smith: The Making of a Texas Governor. Jerry D. Conn. (Illus.). 173p. 8.50 (ISBN 0-8363-0078-5). Jenkins.

Preston Sturges: A Guide to References & Resources. Ray Cywinski. 1984. lib. bdg. 46.00 (ISBN 0-8161-8510-7, Hall Reference). G K Hall.

Prestons of Smithfield & Greenfield in Virginia. John F. Dorman. LC 80-2841. (Filson Club Publications, Second Ser.: No. 3). (Illus.). 441p. 1982. 28.75 (ISBN 0-9601072-1-5). Filson Club.

Prestressed Concrete. I. I. Graduck. 150p. 1970. 64.00 (ISBN 0-677-61730-5). Gordon & Breach.

Prestressed Concrete: Analysis & Design. Antoine E. Naaman. (Illus.). 736p. 1982. text ed. 47.95x (ISBN 0-07-045761-1). McGraw.

Prestressed Concrete Beams: Design & Logical Analysis. C. B. Wilby. (Illus.). 97p. 1969. 22.00 (ISBN 0-444-20037-1, Pub. by Elsevier Applied Sci England). Elsevier.

Prestressed Concrete Buildings. Ed. by T. Y. Lin & J. W. Kelly. (Illus.). 334p. 1962. 94.00 (ISBN 0-677-10310-7). Gordon & Breach.

Prestressed Concrete Column Behavior. 208p. Date not set. 30.00 (R&D3). Prestressed Concrete.

Prestressed Concrete Design. M. K. Hurst. 350p. 1988. text ed. 55.00 (ISBN 0-412-28960-1, Pub. by Chapman & Hall England). Routledge Chapman & Hall.

Prestressed Concrete-Design & Construction. 2nd rev. ed. F. Leonhardt. (Illus.). 74.95x (ISBN 3-433-00435-8). Adlers Foreign Bks.

Prestressed Concrete Design by Computer. R. Hulse & W. H. Mosley. (Illus.). 148p. 1987. text ed. 37.50x (ISBN 0-333-44549-X, Pub. by Macmillan England); pap. text ed. 25.50x (ISBN 0-333-44550-3, Pub. by Macmillan England). Scholium Intl.

Prestressed Concrete Designer's Handbook. 3rd ed. P W. Abeles & B K. Bardham Roy. (Illus.). 550p. 1981. text ed. 45.00 (ISBN 0-7210-1227-2, Pub. by Viewpoint). Scholium Intl.

Prestressed Concrete for Buildings. (PCI Journal Reprints Ser.). 48p. pap. 7.00 (JR177). Prestressed Concrete.

Prestressed Concrete for the Storage of Liquefied Gas. Ir A. Bruggeling. Tr. by C. Van Amerongen from Dutch. (Viewpoint Ser.). (Illus.). 111p. 1981. pap. text ed. 49.50x (ISBN 0-7210-1187-X, Pub. by C & CA London). Scholium Intl.

Prestressed Concrete Institute Journal: 25-Year Index, 1956-1981. 224p. 30.00 (ISBN 0-318-17395-6, JR-1-82). Prestressed Concrete.

Prestressed Concrete Pedestrian Bridges. 28p. 1985. pap. 6.00 (ISBN 0-318-19726-X, JR-199). Prestressed Concrete.

Prestressed Concrete Piles. (PCI Journal Reprints Ser.). 29p. 1985. pap. 6.00 (ISBN 0-318-19739-1, JR67). Prestressed Concrete.

Prestressed Concrete Piling Interaction Diagrams. (PCI Journal Reprints Ser.). 56p. 1985. pap. 30.00 (ISBN 0-318-19764-2, JR187A). Prestressed Concrete.

Prestressed Concrete Poles: State-of-the-Art. 52p. pap. 10.00 (ISBN 0-318-19813-4, JR302). Prestressed Concrete.

Prestressed Concrete Pressure Vessels. (Conference Proceedings Ser.). 770p. 1968. 68.00 (ISBN 0-901948-45-4, Pub. by T Telford UK). Am Soc Civil Eng.

Prestressed Concrete Saves Energy. (PCI Journal Reprints Ser.). 2p. pap. 3.00 (ISBN 0-686-40127-1, JR221). Prestressed Concrete.

Prestressing the CN Tower. (PCI Journal Reprints Ser.). 32p. 1985. pap. 6.00 (ISBN 0-318-19757-X, JR174). Prestressed Concrete.

Presumed Dead. Ritchie Perry. LC 86-19709. (Crime Club Ser.). 192p. 1987. 12.95 (ISBN 0-385-23558-5). Doubleday.

Presumed Innocent. Scott Turow. 1987. 18.95 (ISBN 0-374-23713-1). FS&G.

Presumed Innocent. Scott Turow. 1988. pap. 4.95 (ISBN 0-446-35098-2). Warner Bks.

Presumed Innocent, Vol. 1. Tracy Voigt et al. 1982. write for info. T Voigt.

Presumption of Guilt. Jeffrey Ashford. 192p. 1985. 13.95 (ISBN 0-8027-5619-0). Walker & Co.

Presumption of Guilt. Jeffrey Ashford. 192p. 1986. Walker & Co.

Presumptuous Dreamers: A Sociological History of the Life & Times of Abigail Scott Duniway, 1834-1871, Vol. I. Helen K. Smith. LC 74-79460. (Western Americana Book). (Orig.). 1974. 20.00 (ISBN 0-913626-11-2); pap. 15.00 (ISBN 0-913626-12-0). S S S Pub Co.

Presumptuous Dreamers: A Sociological History of the Life & Times of Abigail Scott Duniway, 1877-1912. Helen K. Smith & Harriet L Smith. LC 74-79460. (Western American Bk.: Vol. 3). (Illus., Orig.). 1987. pap. 15.00 (ISBN 0-913626-39-2). S S S Pub Co.

Presumptuous Dreamers: A Sociological History of the Life & Times of Abigail Scott Duniway, 1872-1876, Vol. 2. Helen K. Smith. LC 74-79460. (Western Americana Bk.). (Orig.). 1983. pap. 15.00 (ISBN 0-913626-27-9). S S S Pub Co.

Presuposiciones de Preguntas en el Quechua de Huanuco. Diana Weber. (Documentos del Trabajo (Peru) Ser.: No. 8). 14p. 1976. microfiche 2.00. Summer Inst Ling.

Presupposition. David E. Cooper. (Janua Linguarum, Ser. Minor: No. 203). 130p. 1974. pap. text ed. 13.60x (ISBN 90-2793-152-6). Mouton.

Presupposition see Syntax & Semantics.

Presupposition & the Delimitation of Semantics. Ruth M. Kempson. LC 74-25078. (Studies in Linguistics Monographs: No. 15). 260p. 1975. 44.50 (ISBN 0-521-20733-9); pap. 15.95 (ISBN 0-521-09938-2). Cambridge U Pr.

Presupposition & Transcendental Inference. Humphrey Palmer. LC 84-18384. 108p. 1985. 25.00 (ISBN 0-312-64173-7). St Martin.

Presurgical Evaluation of Epileptics. Ed. by H. G. Wieser & C. Elger. (Illus.). 415p. 1987. 162.30 (ISBN 0-387-16344-1). Springer-Verlag.

Presurgical Evaluation of Eyes with Opaque Media. Ed. by Dwain Fuller & William Hutton. 240p. 1982. 53.50 (ISBN 0-8089-1470-7, 791460). Grune.

Presynadtic Receptors: Proceedings of the Satellite Symposium, Paris, July 22-23 1978, 7th International Congress of Pharmacology. S. Z. Langer et al. (Illus.). 414p. 1979. 79.00 (ISBN 0-08-023190-X). Pergamon.

Presystemic Drug Elimination (BIMR Clinical Pharmacology & Therapeutics, Vol. 1) Charles F. George & Andrew G. Renwick. (International Medical Reviews Ser.). 320p. 1982. 59.95 (ISBN 0-407-02322-4). Butterworth.

Pret a Lire. Gustave W. Andrian & Jane Davies. 1980. pap. write for info. (ISBN 0-02-303440-8). Macmillan.

Pretence, the Vengeful Heart & My Heart's a Dancer. Roberta Leigh. (Harlequin Romances Ser.: 3 vols. in 1). 576p. 1983. pap. 3.95 (ISBN 0-373-20076-5). Harlequin Bks.

Pretend Indians: Images of Native Americans in the Movies. Ed. by Gretchen M. Bataille & Charles L. Silet. LC 79-27432. 232p. pap. 60.40 (2030317). Bks Demand UMI.

Pretend the World Is Funny & Forever: A Psychological Analysis of Comedians, Clowns, & Actors. Seymour Fisher & Rhoda L. Fisher. LC 80-7777. 288p. 1981. text ed. 29.95 (ISBN 0-89859-073-6). L Erlbaum Assocs.

Pretendant. Auguste de Villiers De L'Isle-Adam. 224p. 1965. 9.95 (ISBN 0-686-55724-7). French & Eur.

Pretender. Piers Anthony & Frances Hall. LC 79-317. (Illus.). 159p. 1979. lib. bdg. 17.95x (ISBN 0-89370-130-0); pap. 7.95x (ISBN 0-89370-230-7). Borgo Pr.

Pretender. Piers Anthony & Frances Hall. 288p. 1985. pap. 3.50 (ISBN 0-8125-3108-6, Dist. by Warner Pub Services & St. Martin's Press). Tor Bks.

Pretender. S. Mokashi-Punekar. 6.75 (ISBN 0-89253-702-7); flexible cloth 4.00 (ISBN 0-89253-703-5). Ind-US Inc.

Pretender to the Throne: The Further Adventures of Private Ivan Chonkin. Vladimir Voinovich. Tr. by Richard Lourie from Rus. LC 81-3137. 365p. 1981. 17.95 (ISBN 0-374-23715-8). FS&G.

Pretenders. Gwen Davis. Date not set. pap. 4.95 (ISBN 0-446-34563-6). Warner Bks.

Pretenders to the English Throne. Jeremy Potter. LC 86-26483. (Illus.). 224p. 1987. 25.00x (ISBN 0-389-20703-9). B&N Imports.

Pretending. Leslie Davis. (Cheerleaders Ser.: No. 44). 160p. (YA) (gr. 6-9). 1988. pap. 2.50 (ISBN 0-590-41638-3). Scholastic Inc.

Pretending. Shelagh McGee. (Little Library). (Illus.). 20p. (ps). 1988. 4.95 (ISBN 0-8120-5880-1). Barron.

Pretenses. Created by Francine Pascal. 160p. (Orig.). Date not set. pap. 2.95. Bantam.

Pretensions. Sally Rinard. 384p. 1985. 17.95 (ISBN 0-312-64181-8). St Martin.

Pretensions. Sally Rinard. 1988. pap. 4.50 (ISBN 0-312-90301-4). St Martin.

Preterm Birth & Psychological Development. Ed. by Sarah L. Friedman & Marian Sigman. LC 80-980. (Developmental Psychology Ser.). 1980. 65.00 (ISBN 0-12-267880-X). Acad Pr.

Preterm Labour & Its Consequences. Ed. by F. Sharp & P. Dunn. (Research in Perinatal Medicine Ser.: No. III). (Illus.). 403p. 1985. 68.50x (ISBN 0-916859-08-8). Perinatology.

PreTest for Physicians Preparing for the American Board of Internal Medicine Certifying Examination. 4th ed. PreTest Editors. (Illus.). 96p. 1982. pap. 34.00 (ISBN 0-07-079093-0). McGraw-Pretest.

PreTest for Physicians Preparing for the ECFMG Examination. 3rd ed. Pretest Editors. (Illus.). 61p. 1982. pap. 35.00 (ISBN 0-07-079108-2). McGraw-Pretest.

Pretest for Physicians Preparing for the Federation Licensing Examination (FLEX) 5th ed. PreTest Editors. 104p. 1987. 37.50 (ISBN 0-07-079157-0). McGraw-Pretest.

Pretest for Physicians Preparing for the Federation Licensing Examination: Flex. 4th ed. Pretest Series Editors. (Illus.). 1982. pap. 34.00. McGraw-Pretest.

PreTest for Physicians Preparing for the Federation Licensing Examination: FLEX. 4th ed. PreTest Service, Inc. 104p. 1982. 34.00. McGraw.

PreTest for Physicians Preparing for the Foreign Medical Graduate Examination in the Medical Sciences (FMGEMS) PreTest Editors. 96p. 1987. pap. 37.50 (ISBN 0-07-079159-7). McGraw-Pretest.

PreTest for Physicians Preparing for the VISA Qualifying Examination. 2nd ed. Pretest Editors. (Illus.). 135p. 1982. pap. 35.00 (ISBN 0-07-079109-0). McGraw-Pretest.

PreTest for Students Preparing for the National Board Examination. 5th ed. Pretest Editors. (Illus.). 1982. Pt. I. pap. 30.00 (ISBN 0-07-079037-X); Pt. II. pap. 30.00 (ISBN 0-07-079092-2). McGraw-Pretest.

Pretest for Students Preparing for the National Board Examination, Pt. II. 6th ed. PreTest Editors. 80p. 1986. 30.00 (ISBN 0-07-079155-4). McGraw-Pretest.

PreTest for Students Preparing for the National Board Examination, Pt. 1. 6th ed. PreTest Editors. 80p. 1986. 30.00 (ISBN 0-07-079154-6). McGraw-Pretest.

Pretest Sel-Assessment & Review. (Basic Science Ser.). 200p. 1988. 14.95. McGraw.

Pretextes et Nouveaux Pretextes. Andre Gide. 12.95 (ISBN 0-685-34153-4). French & Eur.

Pretre. Pierre Teilhard De Chardin. pap. 4.95 (ISBN 0-685-36600-6). French & Eur.

Pretreatment of Blast Furnace Molten Iron. 168p. 1987. pap. 20.00 (ISBN 0-932897-25-8). Iron & Steel.

Pretreatment of Condenser Tubing for Enhanced Corrosion Resistance. 54p. 1982. write for info. (284C). Intl Copper.

Pretrial Advocacy: Planning, Analysis & Strategy. Marilyn J. Berger et al. 800p. 1988. text ed. write for info. (ISBN 0-316-09162-6). Little.

Pretrial Delay: A Review & Bibliography. 96p. 1978. pap. 2.40 (ISBN 0-89656-024-4, R-036). Natl Ctr St Courts.

Pretrial Detention: A Bibliography. Mary E. Hulls. LC 85-233397. (Public Administration Bibliography Ser.). 1985. 2.00 (ISBN 0-89028-533-0). Vance Biblios.

Pretrial Discovery & the Adversary System. William A. Glaser. LC 68-54410. 300p. 1968. 27.50x (ISBN 0-87154-305-2). Russell Sage.

Pretrial Preparation. 15.00 (ISBN 0-317-39453-3, F132). Am Law Inst.

Pretrial Problems of the Prosecutor see Roles & Functions of the Prosecutor.

Pretrial Proceedings in Litigating Computer Contract Disputes. Michael D. Scott. (Computer Law Monograph Ser.). 44p. 1980. 10.00 (ISBN 0-935200-03-7). Ctr Comp Law.

Pretrial Proceedings; Trial & Post-Trial Motions: Unit 4. Bender's Editorial Staff. (California Civil Litigation Forms System Ser.). 1985. incl. disks 475.00 (ISBN 0-317-37652-7, 795). Bender.

Pretrial Reimbursement Program. National Center for State Courts. (Paul Reardon Ser.). 24p. 1982. manuscript 1.44 (PRS-036). Natl Ctr St Courts.

Pretrial Release in Durham, North Carolina. Stevens H. Clarke & Mariam S. Saxon. 71p. 1987. pap. 5.00. U of nC Inst Gov.

Pretrial Release Programming: Issues and Trends. Chris W. Eskridge. LC 82-24357. 223p. (Orig.). 1983. pap. 17.95 (ISBN 0-87632-323-9); student ed. 17.95. Clark Boardman.

Pretrial Services Training & Clearinghouse Project: Final Report. National Center for State Courts Staff. 158p. 1975. manuscript 9.48 (MAB-087). Natl Ctr St Courts.

Pretribulation Rapture & the Bible. Charles R. Taylor. (Illus.). 40p. (Orig.). 1980. pap. 1.50 (ISBN 0-937682-03-9). Today Bible.

Prettier Than the Black Pea Flower. Prithvindra Chakravarti. (Redbird Bk.). 1976. lib. bdg. 8.00 (ISBN 0-89253-092-8); flexible bdg. 4.80 (ISBN 0-89253-147-9). Ind-US Inc.

Prettiest Love Letters in the World: The Letters Between Lucrezia Borgia & Pietro Bembo. Tr. by Hugh Shankland. LC 87-81209. (Illus.). 112p. 1987. 25.00 (ISBN 0-87923-716-3); pre-Chistmas 25.00 (ISBN 0-317-62852-6). Godine.

Pretty As a Picture: A Guide to Manners, Poise & Appearance. Maria P. Everding. 138p. (Orig.). (gr. 4-7). 1986. pap. 14.95 (ISBN 0-9617665-0-6). GME Pub Co.

Pretty As a Picture: Fabric Frames. Pam Aulson. (Illus.). 24p. 1981. pap. 3.00 (ISBN 0-9601896-4-5). Patch As Patch.

Pretty Boy Dead: A Novel. rev. ed. Joseph Hansen. 208p. 1984. pap. 8.95 (ISBN 0-917342-48-8). Gay Sunshine.

Prevention & Control of Fires in Ships. Ed. by Royal Institution of Naval Architects & Institute of Marine Engineering. (Illus.). 1976. 15.00x (ISBN 0-89955-400-8, Pub. by Inst Marine Eng). Intl Spec Bk.

Prevention & Control of Intestinal Parasitic Infections. (Technical Report: No. 749). 86p. 1987. pap. 7.20 (ISBN 92-4-120749-3). World Health.

Prevention & Control of Iodine Deficiency Disorders. Ed. by B. S. Hetzel et al. (Major Health Issues Ser.: No. 2). 354p. 1987. 110.75 (ISBN 0-444-80874-4). Elsevier.

Prevention & Control of Juvenile Delinquency. Richard J. Lundman. LC 83-23772. 1984. 9.95x (ISBN 0-19-503451-1). Oxford U Pr.

Prevention & Control of Nosocomial Infections. Ed. by Richard P. Wenzel. (Infectious Disease Ser.). (Illus.). 640p. 1986. text ed. 67.95 (ISBN 0-683-08923-4). Williams & Wilkins.

Prevention & Control of Water-Caused Problems in Building Potable Water Systems (TPC-7) LC 80-85055. (Illus.). 58p. 1980. 20.00 (ISBN 0-317-36497-9). Natl Corrosion Eng.

Prevention & Control of Wildlife Damage. rev. ed. Ed. by Robert M. Timm. (Illus.). 640p. 1983. loose leaf 20.00 (ISBN 0-9613015-0-3). Coop Ext Serv Univ Nebraska.

Prevention & Control of Yellow Fever in Africa. 99p. 1986. pap. 10.20 (ISBN 92-4-156091-6). World Health.

Prevention & Correction of Reading Difficulties. Emmett A. Betts. 402p. 1984. Repr. of 1936 ed. lib. bdg. 47.50 (ISBN 0-89987-973-X). Darby Bks.

Prevention & Health: Directions for Policy & Practice. Ed. by Alfred Katz et al. LC 87-17634. (Prevention in Human Services). 140p. 1987. text ed. 29.95 (ISBN 0-86656-668-6). Haworth Pr.

Prevention & Prosecution of Computer & High Technology Crime, No. 095. Stanley S. Arkin. 85.00 (ISBN 0-317-67049-2). Bender.

Prevention & Settlement of Industrial Conflict in the Community Member States. Commission of the European Communities. 1984. 12.00 (ISBN 92-825-5009-5). Comm Europe Comm.

Prevention & Treatment of Contraceptive Failure. Ed. by Uta Landy & S. S. Ratnam. LC 86-25318. 256p. 1986. 49.50x (ISBN 0-306-42477-0, Plenum Pr.). Plenum Pub.

Prevention & Treatment of Coronary Heart Disease & Its Complications. Ed. by J. Lequime. (International Congress Ser.: Vol. 530). 168p. 1980. 57.50 (ISBN 0-444-90162-0, Excerpta Medica). Elsevier.

Prevention & Treatment of Diabetic Nephropathy. H. Keen & M. Legrain. 400p. 1983. lib. bdg. 48.00 (ISBN 0-85200-744-2, Pub. by MTP Pr Netherlands). Kluwer ACademic.

Prevention & Treatment of Running Injuries. Robert D'Ambrosia & D. Drez. LC 81-86239. 204p. 1982. 60.00 (ISBN 0-913590-86-X). Slack Inc.

Prevention & Treatment of Running Injuries. 2nd ed. Robert D'Ambrosia & David Drez. LC 86-42863. 230p. 1988. 39.95 (ISBN 0-943432-99-5). Slack Inc.

Prevention: Basic & Clinical Aspects. Ed. by G. Nikiforuk. (Understanding Dental Caries (Ltd. Vol. Ser.): Vol. 2). (Illus.). xiv, 290p. 1985. 29.00 (ISBN 3-8055-3905-3). S Karger.

Prevention in Clinical Practice. Ed. by D. H. Becker & L. Gardner. LC 88-12568. (Illus.). 468p. 1988. 49.50x (ISBN 0-306-42624-2, Plenum Med Bk). Plenum Pub.

Prevention in Family Services: Approaches to Family Wellness. Ed. by David R. Mace. (New Perspectives on Family Ser.). 256p. 1983. 29.95 (ISBN 0-8039-2154-3). Sage.

Prevention in Health Psychology. Ed. by James C. Rosen & Laura J. Solomon. LC 84-40594. (Primary Prevention of Psychopathology Ser.: No. 8). (Illus.). 456p. 1985. 40.00x (ISBN 0-87451-320-0); pap. text ed. 22.50x (ISBN 0-87451-344-8). U Pr of New Eng.

Prevention in Mental Health: Research, Policy, & Practice. Ed. by Richard H. Price et al. LC 80-14676. (Sage Annual Reviews of Community Mental Health Ser.: Vol. 1). (Illus.). 320p. 1981. 35.00 (ISBN 0-8039-1468-7). Sage.

Prevention Is Better: An A-Z of Common Illnesses & Problems & How to Prevent Them. Andrew Stanway. 406p. 1987. 30.95 (ISBN 0-7126-1211-4, Pub. by Century Hutchinson). David & Charles.

Prevention of Accidents Due to Explosions Underground in Coal Mines: ILO Code of Practice. 1974. 7.00 (ISBN 92-2-101062-7). Intl Labour Office.

Prevention of Alcohol Abuse. Ed. by Peter M. Miller & Ted D. Nirenberg. 536p. 1984. 69.50x (ISBN 0-306-41328-0, Plenum Pr). Plenum Pub.

Prevention of Baldness. 1p. pap. 2.00 (ISBN 0-317-52798-3). Truth Seeker.

Prevention of Black Alcoholism: Issues & Strategies. Roosevelt Wright, Jr. & Thomas D. Watts. (Illus.). 236p. 1985. 27.25 (ISBN 0-398-05139-9). C C Thomas.

Prevention of Blindness: Report. WHO Study Group. Geneva, 1972. (Technical Report Ser.: No. 518). (Also avail. in French & Spanish). 1973. pap. 1.20 (ISBN 0-686-16791-0). World Health.

Prevention of Breast Cancer. A. N. Papaioannou. 1988. 27.50 (ISBN 0-87527-227-4). Green.

Prevention of Cardiovascular Diseases: An Approach to Active Long Life: Proceedings of the International Symposium, Tokyo, Japan, October 26, 1985. Ed. by Y. Yamori & C. Lenfant. (International Congress Ser.: No. 727). 258p. 1987. 97.75 (ISBN 0-444-80881-7). Elsevier.

Prevention of Coronary Heart Disease. Hutchinson. 1985. 43.50 (ISBN 0-8151-4790-2). Year Bk Med.

Prevention of Coronary Heart Disease: Practical Management of Risk Factors. Norman M. Kaplan & Jeremiah Stamler. (Illus.). 232p. 1983. write for info. (ISBN 0-7216-5277-8). Saunders.

Prevention of Delinquent Behavior: Primary Prevention of Psychopathology, Vol. X. John D. Burchard & Sarah N. Burchard. LC 86-26095. 400p. 1987. 35.00 (ISBN 0-8039-2908-0). Sage.

Prevention of Dental Disease. John J. Murray. (Illus.). 1984. 47.50x (ISBN 0-19-261261-1); pap. 24.95x (ISBN 0-19-261550-5). Oxford U Pr.

Prevention of Developmental Disabilities: Strategies for the 80's. Ed. by Siegfried Pueschel & James Mulick. text ed. 34.95t (ISBN 0-938550-28-4). Acad Guild.

Prevention of Dust Explosions in Coal Preparation Plants. (Sixty Ser.). 1971. pap. 2.00 (ISBN 0-685-58072-5, 653). Natl Fire Prot.

Prevention of Dust Explosions in Confectionery Manufacturing Plants. (Sixty Ser.). 1967. pap. 2.00 (ISBN 0-685-58070-9, 657). Natl Fire Prot.

Prevention of Dust Explosions in the Plastic Industry. (Sixty Ser.). 51p. 1970. pap. 2.00 (ISBN 0-685-46073-8, 654). Natl Fire Prot.

Prevention of Dust Explosions in Woodworking & Wood Flour Manufacturing Plants. (Sixty Ser.). 1971. pap. 2.00 (ISBN 0-685-58069-5, 664). Natl Fire Prot.

Prevention of Dust Explosions, Pulverized Sugar & Cocoa. (Sixty Ser.). 1967. pap. 2.00 (ISBN 0-685-58076-8, 62). Natl Fire Prot.

Prevention of Dust Ignitions in Spice Grinding Plants. (Sixty Ser.). 1971. pap. 2.00 (ISBN 0-685-58045-8, 656). Natl Fire Prot.

Prevention of Failure in First Grade Reading by Means of Adjusted Instruction. Howard T. Dunklin. LC 71-176733. (Columbia University. Teachers College. Contributions to Education: No. 802). Repr. of 1940 ed. 22.50 (ISBN 0-404-55802-X). AMS Pr.

Prevention of Fire & Dust Explosions in Feed Mills. National Fire Protection Association Staff. 24p. 1984. 12.00 (61C-84). Natl Fire Prot.

Prevention of Fire & Dust Explosions in Facilities Manufacturing & Handling Starch. National Fire Protection Association Staff. 26p. 1984. 12.00 (ISBN 0-317-63207-8, 61A-84). Natl Fire Prot.

Prevention of Fire & Dust Explosions in Grain Elevators & Bulk Grain Handling Facilities. (Sixty Ser.). 1973. pap. 2.00 (ISBN 0-685-58080-6, 61B). Natl Fire Prot.

Prevention of Fire & Dust Explosions in the Chemical, Dye, Pharmaceutical, & Plastics Industries. National Fire Protection Association Staff. 34p. 1982. 12.00 (ISBN 0-317-63496-8, 654-82). Natl Fire Prot.

Prevention of Fire & Dust Explosions in the Milling of Agricultural Commodities for Human Consumption. National Fire Protection Association Staff. 24p. 1984. 12.00 (ISBN 0-317-63210-8, 61D-84). Natl Fire Prot.

Prevention of Fires & Explosions in Wood Processing & Woodworking Facilities. National Fire Protection Association Staff. 1981. 12.00 (ISBN 0-317-63498-4, 664-81). Natl Fire Prot.

Prevention of Food Adulteration Act. A. P. Mathur. 838p. 1983. 270.00x (ISBN 0-317-54566-3, Pub. Eastern Bk India). State Mutual Bk.

Prevention of Football Injuries: Protecting the Health of the Student Athlete. O. Charles Olson. LC 70-157472. Repr. of 1971 ed. 34.00 (ISBN 0-8357-9413-X, 2014569). Bks Demand UMI.

Prevention of Furnace Explosions in Fuel-Oil & Natural Gas-Fired Single Burner Boiler-Furnaces. National Fire Protection Association Staff. 36p. 1982. 12.00 (ISBN 0-317-63236-1, 85A-82). Natl Fire Prot.

Prevention of Furnace Explosions in Fuel-Oil & Natural Gas-Fired Watertube Boiler Furnaces with One Burner. (Eighty-Ninety Ser.). 68p. 1973. pap. 2.00 (ISBN 0-685-44149-0, 85). Natl Fire Prot.

Prevention of Furnace Explosions in Fuel Oil-Fired Multiple Burner Boiler-Furnaces. National Fire Protection Association Staff. 32p. 1984. 12.00 (ISBN 0-317-63270-1, 85D-84). Natl Fire Prot.

Prevention of Furnace Explosions in Fuel Oil-Fired Multiple Burner Boiler-Furnaces. (Eighty-Ninety Ser.). 84p. 1974. pap. 3.50 (ISBN 0-685-44131-8, 85D). Natl Fire Prot.

Prevention of Furnace Explosions in Natural Gas-Fired Multiple Burner Boiler-Furnaces. National Fire Protection Association Staff. 28p. 1984. 12.00 (ISBN 0-317-63268-X, 85B-84). Natl Fire Prot.

Prevention of Furnace Explosions in Natural Gas-Fired Multiple Burner Boiler-Furnaces. (Eighty-Ninety Ser.). 68p. 1973. pap. 3.50 (ISBN 0-685-44130-X, 85B). Natl Fire Prot.

Prevention of Furnace Explosions in Pulverized Coal-Fired Multiple Burner Boiler Furnaces. National Fire Protection Association Staff. 25p. 1985. 12.00 (ISBN 0-317-63274-4, 85E-85). Natl Fire Prot.

Prevention of Furnace Explosions in Pulverized Coal-Fired Multiple Burner Boiler-Furnaces. (Eighty-Ninety Ser.). 68p. 1974. pap. 3.50 (ISBN 0-685-44132-6, 85E). Natl Fire Prot.

Prevention of Furnace Implosions in Multiple Burner Boiler-Furnaces. National Fire Protection Association Staff. 22p. 1982. 12.00 (ISBN 0-317-63284-1, 85G-82). Natl Fire Prot.

Prevention of Genetic Disease & Mental Retardation. Aubrey Milunsky. LC 74-21015. (Illus.). Repr. of 1975 ed. 130.50 (ISBN 0-8357-9554-3, 2016674). Bks Demand UMI.

Prevention of Genocide. Leo Kuper. LC 85-40465. 293p. 1986. 25.00x (ISBN 0-300-03418-0). Yale U Pr.

Prevention of Ground Water Pollution from Oil & Gas Related Activities. Larry W. Canter & Deborah Fairchild. 500p. cancelled (ISBN 0-87371-067-3). Lewis Pubs Inc.

Prevention of Handicap Through Antenatal Care. Ed. by A. C. Turnbull & F. P. Woodford. (Institute for Research into Mental & Multiple Handicap, Review of Research & Practice Ser.: Vol. 18). 176p. 1976. 31.75 (ISBN 0-444-15210-5, Excerpta Medica). Elsevier.

Prevention of Head Injuries in Skiing. S. Oh. (Illus.). viii, 164p. 1985. pap. 32.75 (ISBN 3-8055-3978-9). S Karger.

Prevention of Hereditary Large Bowel Cancer. Ed. by John Ingall & Anthony J. Mastromarino. LC 82-24988. (Progress in Clinical & Biological Research Ser.: Vol. 115). 278p. 1983. 33.00 (ISBN 0-8451-0115-3). A R Liss.

Prevention of Incurable Disease. M. Bircher-Brenner. LC 78-61330. 1978. pap. 3.95 (ISBN 0-87983-186-3). Keats.

Prevention of Infant Mortality & Morbidity. Ed. by F. Falkner. (Child Health & Development: Vol. 4). (Illus.). viii, 176p. 1985. 59.50 (ISBN 3-8055-3989-4). S Karger.

Prevention of Kidney Disease & Long-Term Survival. Ed. by M. M. Avram. 354p. 1982. 59.50x (ISBN 0-306-40965-8, Plenum Med Bk). Plenum Pub.

Prevention of Mental Handicap: Proceedings of the British Institute of Mental Handicap. M. J. Griffiths et al. 63p. 1985. 29.00x (ISBN 0-906054-29-X, Pub. by British Inst Mental). State Mutual Bk.

Prevention of Mental Handicapp: A World View. Ed. by G. Hosking & G. Murphy. (International Congress & Symposium Ser.: No. 112). 1987. pap. write for info. (ISBN 0-905958-43-8, Pub. by Royal Society of Medicine Services Ltd). Longwood Pub Group.

Prevention of Mental Retardation & Other Developlmental Disabilities. Ed. by Michael K. McCormack. (Pediatric Habilitation Ser.: Vol. 1). (Illus.). 680p. 1980. 79.75 (ISBN 0-8247-6950-3). Dekker.

Prevention of Mycotoxins: Recommended Practices for the Prevention of Mycotoxins in Food, Feed & Their Products. (Food & Nutrition Papers: No. 10). 71p. (Eng., Fr. & Span.). 1979. pap. 7.50 (ISBN 92-5-100703-9, F1628, FAO). UNIPUB.

Prevention of Neurotoxic Illness in Working Populations. Johnson. 1987. 65.00 (ISBN 0-471-91625-0). Wiley.

Prevention of Nuclear War: A United Nations Perspective. William Epstein. LC 84-2248. 1984. 25.00 (ISBN 0-89946-184-0). Oelgeschlager.

Prevention of Nuclear War: An American Approach. William H. Lewis. 90p. 1986. text ed. 25.00 (ISBN 0-89946-206-5). Oelgeschlager.

Prevention of Nuclear War: Soviet Scientists' Viewpoints. A. N. Kaliadin & O. V. Bogdanov. 91p. 1983. text ed. 15.00 (ISBN 92-1-157038-7, E.83.XV.RR/31). UN.

Prevention of Nuclear War: Soviet Scientists' Viewpoints. A. N. Kaliadin et al. (Policy & Efficacy Studies Ser.). 91p. 1983. 15.00 (ISBN 0-318-02097-1, E.83.XV.RR/31). Unitar.

Prevention of Obstruction of Coronary & Vital Arteries. William Dock. LC 79-50185. 200p. 1983. 42.50 (ISBN 0-87527-202-9). Green.

Prevention of Occupational Cancer. Ed. by Charles R. Shaw. 256p. 1981. 69.95 (ISBN 0-8493-5625-3). CRC Pr.

Prevention of Occupational Cancer: International Symposium. (Occupational Safety & Health Ser.: No. 46). 600p. (Multilingual). 1981. pap. 27.10 (ISBN 92-2-002907-3, ILO216, ILO). UNIPUB.

Prevention of Occupational Cancer International Symposium: Proceedings of the International Symposium on the Prevention of Occupational Cancer, Helsinki, April 21-24. Institute of Occupational Health Staff et al. (Occupational Safety & Health Ser.: No. 46). viii, 658p. (Orig.). 1982. pap. 33.25 (ISBN 92-2-002907-3). Intl Labour Office.

Prevention of Occupational Cancer, 1982. 680p. 32.00x (ISBN 92-2-002907-3). Intl Pubns Serv.

Prevention of Occupational Skin Diseases. 56p. 1981. 3.00 (ISBN 0-318-16524-4). Soap & Detergent.

Prevention of Oil Pollution. Ed. by J. Wardley-Smith. 264p. 1979. 53.50 (ISBN 0-86010-129-0). Graham & Trotman.

Prevention of Perinatal Mortality & Morbidity. F. Falkner. (Child Health & Development: Vol. 3). (Illus.). vi, 182p. 1984. 49.50 (ISBN 3-8055-3854-5). S Karger.

Prevention of Perinatal Mortality & Morbidity: A Report. WHO Expert Committee, Geneva, 1970. (Technical Report Ser: No. 457). 60p. 1970. pap. 2.40 (ISBN 92-4-120457-5, 664). World Health.

Prevention of Perinatal Mortality & Morbidity: A Report. WHO Seminar, Tours, 1969. (Public Health Papers Ser: No. 42). 97p. 1972. pap. 2.80 (ISBN 92-4-130042-6, 668). World Health.

Prevention of Periodontal Disease. Carranza & Kenney. 1981. 32.00 (ISBN 0-931386-51-9). Quint Pub Co.

Prevention of Perioperative Infections. H. Schoenfeld. (Antibiotics & Chemotherapy: Vol. 33). (Illus.). viii, 208p. 1985. 99.50 (ISBN 3-8055-3936-3). S Karger.

Prevention of Physical & Mental Congenital Defects, Pt. A: The Scope of the Problem. Maurice Marois. (Progress in Clinical & Biological Research Ser.: Vol. 163A). 252p. 1985. 54.00 (ISBN 0-8451-0183-8). A R Liss.

Prevention of Physical & Mental Congenital Defects, Pt. B: Epidemiology, Early Detection & Therapy & Environmental Factors. Maurice Marois. (Progress in Clinical & Biological Research Ser.: Vol. 163B). 518p. 1985. 98.00 (ISBN 0-8451-0184-6). A R Liss.

Prevention of Physical & Mental Congenital Defects, Pt. C: Basic & Medical Science, Education & Future Strategies. Maurice Marois. (Progress in Clinical & Biological Research Ser.: Vol. 163C). 462p. 1985. 96.00 (ISBN 0-8451-0185-4). A R Liss.

Prevention of Post-Harvest Food Losses: A Training Manual. (FAO Training Ser.: No. 10). (Illus.). 120p. 1986. pap. text ed. 20.75 (ISBN 0-318-21526-8, F2921, FAO). UNIPUB.

Prevention of Problems in Childhood: Psychological Research & Applications. Ed. by Michael C. Roberts & Lizette Peterson. LC 84-7279. (Personality Processes Ser. (1-341)). 544p. 1984. text ed. 43.95x (ISBN 0-471-87444-2, Pub. by Wiley-Interscience). Wiley.

Prevention of Psychiatric Disorders in Children. Thomas Stapleton & Julian Katz. (International Lectures in Preventive Medicine Ser.). 244p. 1988. 26.75 (ISBN 0-87527-234-7). Green.

Prevention of Rh Sensitization: Report. WHO Scientific Group. Geneva, 1970. (Technical Report Ser.: No. 468). (Also avail. French & Spanish). 1971. pap. 2.00 (ISBN 92-4-120468-0). World Health.

Prevention of Sexual Disorders: Issues & Approaches. Ed. by C. Brandon Qualls et al. LC 78-1700. (Perspectives In Sexuality Ser.). 212p. 1978. 32.50x (ISBN 0-306-31118-6, Plenum Pr). Plenum Pub.

Prevention of Spillages Through Cargo Sea Valves. ICS Staff & OCIMF Staff. 1976. 36.00 (ISBN 0-317-61271-9, Pub. by Witherby & Co England). State Mutual Bk.

Prevention of Spina Bifida & Other Neural Tube Defects. Ed. by John Dobbing. 1983. 48.00 (ISBN 0-12-218860-8). Acad Pr.

Prevention of Structural Failures: The Role of NDT, Fracture Mechanics & Failure Analysis: Proceedings of Two Annual Forums, 19-22 June, 1977 & 14-16 June 1976, Tarpon Springs, Florida. American Society for Metals Staff. LC 78-15388. (Materials-Metalworking Technology Ser.). (Illus.). pap. 90.00 (ISBN 0-317-09726-1, 2019489). Bks Demand UMI.

Prevention of Suicide. (Public Health Papers Ser: No. 35). 84p. 1968. pap. 2.00 (ISBN 92-4-130035-3, 1493). World Health.

Prevention of Sulfur Fires & Explosions. National Fire Protection Association Staff. 1982. 12.00 (ISBN 0-317-63497-6, 655-82). Natl Fire Prot.

Prevention of Sulfur Fires & Explosions. (Sixty Ser.). 1971. pap. 2.00 (ISBN 0-685-58071-7, 655). Natl Fire Prot.

Prevention of Surgical Infection: Perioperative Techniques. Glenn W. Geelhoed. 1989. text ed. 60.00 (ISBN 0-912791-36-5). Ishiyaku Euro.

Prevention of Terrorism in British Law. Clive Walker. 288p. 1986. 47.50 (ISBN 0-7190-1782-3, Pub. by Manchester Univ Pr). St Martin.

Prevention of the Arms Race in Outer Space. 26p. 1986. pap. 4.00 (ISBN 92-9045-012-6, GV.E.86.O.2). UN.

Prevention of Type One Diabetes & Autoimmune Thyroid Disease. Ed. by S. Nagataki et al. (Current Clinical Practice Ser.: Vol. 49). 158p. 1988. 65.75. Elsevier.

Prevention of Youthful Crime: The Great Stumble Forward. James C. Hackler. 1979. pap. 12.00x (ISBN 0-416-60001-8, NO. 2825). Routledge Chapman & Hall.

Prevention-Oriented School Based Dental Health Program: Guidelines for Implementation. 4 copies 6.00 (ISBN 0-934510-23-7, W014). Am Dental.

Prevention, Permanence, & Family Support: A New Practice Context for Group Child Care. Ed. by Richard Small. write for info. (ISBN 0-87868-241-4, F-69, 2414). Child Welfare.

Price Guide to Collectable Clocks Eighteen Forty to Nineteen Forty. Shenton. (Illus.). 1977. 59.50 (ISBN 0-902028-71-5). Apollo.
Price Guide to Collectible Antiques. J. Mackey. (Illus.). 1975. 29.50 (ISBN 0-902028-08-1). Apollo.
Price Guide to Collectible Clocks 1840-1940. 2nd ed. Alan Shenton & Rita Shenton. (Illus.). 477p. 1985. 59.50 (ISBN 0-907462-66-9). Antique Collect.
Price Guide to Collectors' Records with New Revised Value Chart. 3rd ed. Julian M. Moses. 32p. 1976. pap. 9.95x (ISBN 0-914652-03-6). Am Record.
Price Guide to Crested China, 1989. Nicholas Pine. (Illus.). 384p. 1988. 29.95 (ISBN 1-85265-101-6, Pub. by Milestone Pubns UK). Seven Hills Bks.
Price Guide to Dolls. Constance E. King. (Price Guide Ser.). (Illus.). 483p. 1977. 29.50. Antique Collect.
Price Guide to Dolls, Antique & Modern. King. (Illus.). 1977. 29.50 (ISBN 0-902028-60-X). Apollo.
Price Guide to Jewelery: Three Thousand B.C. to Nineteen Fifty A.D. Michael Poynder. (Price Guide Ser.). (Illus.). 385p. 1976. 69.50 (ISBN 0-902028-50-2). Antique Collect.
Price Guide to Metal Toys. Gardiner & Morris. (Price Guide Ser.). (Illus.). 214p. 1986. pap. 29.50 (ISBN 1-85149-016-7). Antique Collect.
Price Guide to Metal Toys. G. Gardner & A. Morris. (Illus.). 1981. pap. 29.50 (ISBN 0-902028-92-8). Apollo.
Price Guide to Miniature Lamps Combining Book I & II. rev. ed. Ruth E. Smith & Hellen A. Feltner. 48p. 1987. pap. 10.00 (ISBN 0-88740-085-X). Schiffer.
Price Guide to More Collectible Antiques. Mackey. (Illus.). 1980. 25.50 (ISBN 0-902028-62-6). Apollo.
Price Guide to Nineteenth & Twentieth Century British Porcelain. Battie & Turner. (Illus.). 1980. 29.50 (ISBN 0-902028-38-3). Apollo.
Price Guide to Nineteenth & Twentieth Century British Pottery. Battie & Turner. (Illus.). 1979. 49.50. Apollo.
Price Guide to Nineteenth & Twentieth Century British Porcelain. David Battie & Michael Turner. (Price Guide Ser.). (Illus.). 486p. 1975. 29.50. Antique Collect.
Price Guide to Nineteenth & Twentieth Century British Pottery. 2nd ed. David Battie & Michael Turner. (Price Guide Ser.). (Illus.). 244p. 1987. 49.50 (ISBN 1-85149-009-4). Antique Collect.
Price Guide to Nineteenth Century European Furniture. Christopher Payne. (Illus.). 506p. 1985. 69.50 (ISBN 0-902028-91-X). Apollo.
Price Guide to Nippon Porcelain. John F. Hotchkiss. pap. 1.25 (ISBN 0-912220-10-4). Hotchkiss House.
Price Guide to Photographic Cards. H. A. James. 132p. 1985. 40.00x (ISBN 0-900873-50-7, Pub. by Bishopsgate Pr. Ltd.); pap. 25.00x (ISBN 0-900873-45-0). State Mutual Bk.
Price Guide to Pot-Lids & Other Underglaze Multicolour Prints on Ware. 2nd ed. A. Ball. (Price Guide Ser.). (Illus.). 320p. 1980. 49.50. Antique Collect.
Price Guide to Red Wing Potters & Their Wares. rev. ed. Gary T. Tefft & Bonnie J. Tefft. 1986. pap. 1.50 (ISBN 0-9606730-4-0). Locust Ent.
Price Guide to the Collector's Encyclopedia of Cloth Dolls. Carol G. Glassmire. 48p. 1985. pap. 4.95 (ISBN 0-87069-384-0). Wallace-Homestead.
Price Guide to the Decorated Tumbler. Hazel M. Weatherman. (Illus.). 128p. 1983. pap. 4.00 (ISBN 0-913074-19-5). Glassbooks MO.
Price Guide to the Models of W. H. Goss. Roland Ward. (Price Guide Ser.). (Illus.). 182p. 1980. 29.50 (ISBN 0-902028-20-0). Antique Collect.
Price Guide to the Twentieth Century Dolls Series. rev. ed. Carol G. Glassmire. 224p. 1983. pap. 9.95 (ISBN 0-87069-379-4). Wallace-Homestead.
Price Guide to Victorian, Edwardian & Nineteen Twenty Furniture. J. Andrews. (Illus.). 1980. 49.50. Apollo.
Price Guide to Victorian, Edwardian & 1920's Furniture. rev ed. John Andrews. (Price Guide Ser.). (Illus.). 218p. 1986. 49.50 (ISBN 1-85149-018-3). Antique Collect.
Price Guide to Wallace Nutting Pictures. 2nd ed. Michael Ivankovich. LC 85-73342. (Illus.). 64p. 1985. pap. 7.95 (ISBN 0-9615843-2-7). Diamond Pr PA.
Price Guide Update for Modern Collector Doll Series. Patricia Smith. 32p. 1984. pap. 5.95 (ISBN 0-89145-278-8). Collector Bks.
Price Index. S. N. Afriat. LC 77-2134. pap. 50.80 (ISBN 0-317-26069-3, 2024409). Bks Demand UMI.
Price Inflation in the Soviet Machine-Building & Metal Working Sector. Fyodor I. Kushnirsky. (Orig.). Date not set. pap. text ed. 35.00 (ISBN 1-55831-025-8). Delphic Associates.
Price Level Changes & Financial Statements: Case Studies of Four Companies. Ralph C. Jones. 179p. 3.00 (ISBN 0-86539-003-7). Am Accounting.
Price List of General Photographic Apparatus & Materials. Kodak Limited. Ed. by Peter C. Bunnell & Robert A. Sobieszek. LC 78-19590. (Sources of Modern Photography Ser.). (Illus.). 1979. Repr. of 1904 ed. lib. bdg. 51.50x (ISBN 0-405-09662-3). Ayer Co Pubs.
Price List of Joiners' Bench Planes & Moulding Tools, Greenfield Tool Co., 1854. Ed. by Kenneth D. Roberts. 30p. 1981. pap. 2.00 (ISBN 0-913602-43-4). K Roberts.
Price List of Rules, Planes, Gauges, etc. Manufactured by Hermon Chapin, July 1859. 12p. 1983. pap. 2.50 (ISBN 0-913602-58-2). K Roberts.
Price List of Stanley Rule & Level, 1867. 1973. Repr. 4.00 (ISBN 0-913602-03-5). K Roberts.
Price Making in a Democracy. Edwin G. Nourse. LC 75-39262. (Getting & Spending: the Consumer's Dilemma). 1976. Repr. of 1944 ed. 42.00x (ISBN 0-405-08035-2). Ayer Co Pubs.
Price of a Perfect Baby. Bruce Anderson. LC 83-22382. 192p. 1984. pap. 4.95 (ISBN 0-87123-426-2, 210426). Bethany Hse.
Price of Adventure: Mountain Rescue Stories from Four Continents. Hamish MacInnes. (Illus.). 192p. 1988. 15.95 (ISBN 0-89886-174-8). Mountaineers.
Price of Affluence: Dilemmas of Contemporary Japan. Rokuro Hidaka. Tr. by Gavan McCormack from Japanese. LC 83-48875. 176p. 1984. 14.95 (ISBN 0-87011-655-X). Kodansha.
Price of Blood. M. Cooper & A. J. Culyer. (Institute of Economic Affairs Hobart Papers Ser.: No. 41). 1977. pap. 2.50 technical (ISBN 0-255-69626-4). Transatl Arts.
Price of Equality. Sally K. Brocato. 48p. 1988. 6.95 (ISBN 0-8062-3334-6). Carlton.
Price of Free Land. Treva A. Strait. LC 78-24287. (Illus.). (gr. 4-6). 1979. 11.70i (ISBN 0-397-31836-7, Lipp Jr Bks); PLB 11.89 (ISBN 0-397-31883-9). HarpJ.
Price of Freedom: A Russian Doctor Immigrates to the United States. Vladimir Golyakhousky. 1986. 19.95 (ISBN 0-525-24449-2). Dutton.
Price of Freedom: Young Indochinese Refugees in Australia. Ed. by J. Krupinski & G. Burrows. 500p. 1986. text ed. 40.00 (ISBN 0-08-029884-2, Pub. by PPA). Pergamon.
Price of Genius. April Fitzlyon. (Orig.). 1981. pap. 5.95 (ISBN 0-7145-0488-2). Riverrun NY.
Price of Glory. FASA Staff. (Battletech Ser.). (Illus.). 380p. 1987. pap. 4.95 (ISBN 1-55560-038-7). FASA Corp.
Price of Glory: Verdun Nineteen Sixteen. Alistair Horne. (Illus.). 1979. pap. 6.95 (ISBN 0-14-002215-5). Penguin.
Price of Gold: A Problem of International Monetary Reform. Rudolf Frei. 75p. 1966. pap. text ed. 13.95x (Pub. by J. C. B. Mohr BRD). Coronet Bks.
Price of Health. Ed. by George J. Agich & Charles E. Begley. 1987. lib. bdg. 49.00 (ISBN 90-277-2285-4, Pub. by Reidel Holland). Kluwer Academic.
Price of Independence: A Realistic View of the Price of Independence; the American Revolution. Broadus Mitchell. 1974. 25.00x (ISBN 0-19-501735-8). Oxford U Pr.
Price of Industrial Labor: The Role of Wages in Business Cycles & Economic Growth. James E. Annable. LC 83-48131. 272p. 1984. 37.00x (ISBN 0-669-06952-3); pap. text ed. 15.00x (ISBN 0-669-09781-0). Lexington Bks.
Price of Justice. Howard Levenson. 1981. 20.00x (ISBN 0-900137-17-7, Pub. by NCCL UK). State Mutual Bk.
Price of Liberty. Alan Barth. LC 74-176486. (Civil Liberties in American History Ser.). 1972. Repr. of 1961 ed. lib. bdg. 29.50 (ISBN 0-306-70416-1). Da Capo.
Price of Liberty: Perspectives on Civil Liberties by Member of the A.C.L.U. Ed. by Alan Reitman. 1968. 6.95x (ISBN 0-393-05284-2, Norton Lib); pap. 1.95x, 1969 (ISBN 0-393-00505-4). Norton.
Price of Liberty: The Public Debt of the American Revolution. William G. Anderson. LC 82-17420. 1983. 20.00x (ISBN 0-8139-0975-9). U Pr of Va.
Price of Life. Jessica Sutton. (Bel Air General Ser.). 288p. 1987. pap. 3.50 (ISBN 0-8041-0026-8, Pub. by Ivy). Ballantine.
Price of Local Justice: A Cost of Operations of the Town & Village Courts in New York State. National Center for State Courts Staff. 45p. 1978. manuscript 2.70 (NERO-019). Natl Ctr St Courts.
Price of Love. Arnold Bennett. LC 74-17050. (Collected Works of Arnold Bennett: Vol. 68). 1976. Repr. of 1914 ed. 35.50 (ISBN 0-518-19149-4). Ayer Co Pubs.
Price of Money, Nineteen Forty-Six to Nineteen Sixty-Nine: An Analytical Study of U. S. & Foreign Interest Rates. Sidney Homer & Richard I. Johannesen. 1969. 30.00 (ISBN 0-8135-0607-7). Rutgers U Pr.
Price of Murder. John D. MacDonald. 1986. pap. 2.95 (ISBN 0-449-13045-2, GM). Fawcett.
Price of Nuclear Power. Colin Sweet. xiii, 107p. (Orig.). 1983. pap. text ed. 7.50x (ISBN 0-435-84831-3). Gower Pub Co.
Price of Paradise. Jane Arbor. (Harlequin Romances Ser.). 192p. 1982. pap. 1.50 (ISBN 0-373-02509-2). Harlequin Bks.
Price of Peace & Other Stories. Mary R. Zook. 1975. 8.50 (ISBN 0-686-11148-6). Rod & Staff.
Price of Phoenix. Sondra Marshak & Myrna Culbreath. (Star Trek Ser.). 192p. (Orig.). 1985. pap. 2.95 (ISBN 0-553-24635-6). Bantam.
Price of Power. W. W. Baldwin. LC 76-990. (FDR & the Era of the New Deal Ser.). 361p. 1976. Repr. of 1948 ed. lib. bdg. 39.50 (ISBN 0-306-70803-5). Da Capo.
Price of Power. Rose Estes. LC 86-51275. (Greyhawk Adventures Ser.: No. 4). 352p. (Orig.). 1987. pap. 3.95 (ISBN 0-88038-458-1). TSR Inc.
Price of Power: America Since Nineteen Forty-Five. Herbert Agar. LC 57-8575. (Chicago History of American Civilization Ser). xii, 200p. 1957. pap. 8.00x (ISBN 0-226-00937-8, CHAC1). U of Chicago Pr.
Price of Power: America since Nineteen Forty Five. Herbert Agar. LC 57-8575. (Chicago History of American Civilization Ser.). pap. 53.00 (ISBN 0-317-09974-4, 2020018). Bks Demand UMI.
Price of Power: Electric Utilities & the Environment. Council on Economic Priorities Staff. 376p. 1973. pap. 25.00x (ISBN 0-262-53024-4). MIT Pr.
Price of Power: Kissinger in the Nixon White House. Seymour Hersh. 480p. 1983. 19.95 (ISBN 0-671-44760-2). Summit Bks.
Price of Power: Kissinger in the Nixon White House. Seymour Hersh. 704p. 1984. pap. 9.95 (ISBN 0-671-50688-9). Summit Bks.
Price of Power Update: Electric Utilities & the Environment. CEP Staff & Ronald White. LC 77-92111. 1977. pap. 3.95 (ISBN 0-87871-007-8). CEP.
Price of Progress: Cobbett's England, Seventeen Eighty to Eighteen Thirty-Five. John Clarke. 1979. 24.95 (ISBN 0-8464-0098-7). Beekman Pubs.
Price of Prosperity. Chiaki Nishiyama. (Institute of Economic Affairs Hobart Papers Ser.: No. 58). 1977. pap. 4.25 technical (ISBN 0-255-36054-1). Transatl Arts.
Price of Reindeer. John Elsberg. (WEP Poetry Ser.: No. 2). 1979. pap. 2.00 (ISBN 0-917976-05-3, White Ewe Pr). Thunder Baas Pr.
Price of Salt. Claire Morgan. LC 75-12340. (Homosexuality Ser.). 1975. Repr. of 1952 ed. 17.00x (ISBN 0-405-07384-4). Ayer Co Pubs.
Price of Salt. Claire Morgan. 288p. 1984. pap. 8.95 (ISBN 0-930044-49-5). Naiad Pr.
Price of Silence. Hugh Pentecost. 224p. 1984. 12.95 (ISBN 0-396-08406-0). Dodd.
Price of Spiritual Power. Roberts Liardon. 47p. 1987. pap. 2.95 (ISBN 0-88144-090-6). Christian Pub.
Price of Stability...? Sydney Caine. (Institute of Economic Affairs, Hobart Papers: No. 97). pap. 5.95 technical (ISBN 0-255-36160-2). Transatl Arts.
Price of Stone & Earlier Poems. Richard Murphy. LC 85-51492. 200p. 1985. 14.95x (ISBN 0-916390-24-1); pap. 7.95 (ISBN 0-916390-23-3). Wake Forest.
Price of Success: An Autobiography. J. B. Phillips. 288p. (Orig.). 1985. pap. 7.95 (ISBN 0-87788-659-8). Shaw Pubs.
Price of the Ticket: Collected Nonfiction, 1948-1985. James Baldwin. 704p. 1985. 29.95 (ISBN 0-312-64306-3, Pub. by Marek); Ltd. signed ed. deluxe ed. 100.00 (ISBN 0-312-64307-1, Pub. by Marek). St Martin.
Price of Truth: The Story of Rare Earth Elements. D. N. Trifonov. Tr. by O. Gleboy & I. Polyuan. 132p. 1985. 3.95 (ISBN 0-8285-2880-2, Pub by Mir Pubs USSR). Imported Pubns.
Price of Truth: The Story of the Reuters Millions. John Lawrenson & Lionel Barber. 1986. 49.75x (ISBN 0-906391-82-2, Pub. by Mainstream Scotland). State Mutual Bk.
Price of Victory. Michael Charlton. LC 84-26512. (Illus.). 316p. 1985. 24.95 (ISBN 0-88186-328-9). Parkwest Pubns.
Price of War: British Policy on German Reparations 1941-1949. Alec Cairncross. 256p. 1986. text ed. 34.95 (ISBN 0-631-14919-8). Basil Blackwell.
Price of War: Urbanization in Vietnam, 1954-1985. Nigel Thrift & Dean Forbes. (Illus.). 224p. 1986. text ed. 37.95x (ISBN 0-04-301210-8). Unwin Hyman.
Price Policy. Ed. by Malcolm S. Adiseshiah. 1987. 26.00x (ISBN 81-7062-027-9, Pub. by Ashish Hse). South Asia Bks.
Price Portfolio: Forty-Six Reprints of Medical Papers of Dr. Weston A. Price. 1978. 35.00 (ISBN 0-916764-04-4). Price-Pottenger.
Price-Quality Interactions in Business Cycles. Frederick C. Mills. LC 75-19728. (National Bureau of Economic Research Ser.). (Illus.). 1975. Repr. 17.00x (ISBN 0-405-07606-1). Ayer Co Pubs.
Price She Paid. David C. Phillips. (Collected Works of David G. Phillips). 1988. Repr. of 1912 ed. lib. bdg. 59.00x. Am Biog Serv.
Price She Paid see Collected Works.
Price Sources: Index of Commercial & Economic Publications Currently Received in the Libraries of the Dept. of Commerce Which Contain Current Market Commodity Prices. U. S. Department of Commerce Library. (Research & Source Works Ser.: No. 195). 1968. Repr. of 1931 ed. 22.50 (ISBN 0-8337-0477-X). B Franklin.
Price System & Resource Allocation. 10th, rev. ed. Ross D. Eckert & Richard H. Leftwich. (Illus.). 672p. 1988. text ed. price not set (ISBN 0-03-012533-2); pap. text ed. price not set study guide (ISBN 0-03-012529-4). Dryden Pr.
Price System & Resource Allocation. 9th ed. Richard H. Leftwich & Ross D. Eckert. 656p. 1985. text ed. 32.95 (ISBN 0-03-071477-X). Dryden Pr.
Price Theory. Milton Friedman. LC 76-1397. 352p. 1976. 36.95x (ISBN 0-202-06074-8). Aldine de Gruyter.
Price Theory: An Intermediate Text. David D. Friedman. 1986. text ed. write for info. (ISBN 0-538-08050-7, H05). SW Pub.
Price Theory & Applications. 3rd ed. Jack Hirshleifer. (Illus.). 640p. 1984. text ed. write for info. (ISBN 0-13-699736-8). P-H.
Price Theory & Applications. 4th ed. Jack Hirshleifer. (Illus.). 624p. 1988. text ed. write for info. (ISBN 0-13-699752-X). P-H.
Price Theory & Applications. 3rd ed. Michael Sproul. (Illus.). 208p. 1984. write for info. (ISBN 0-13-699778-3). P-H.
Price Theory & Its Uses. 5th ed. Donald S. Watson & Malcolm Getz. LC 80-82461. (Illus.). 480p. 1981. text ed. 39.56 (ISBN 0-395-30056-8); instr's manual 1.56 (ISBN 0-395-30057-6). HM.
Price Theory in Action: A Book of Readings. 4th ed. Ed. by Donald S. Watson & Malcolm Getz. (Illus.). 443p. 1987. pap. text ed. 14.95x (ISBN 0-88133-263-1). Waveland Pr.
Price to Be Met. Jessica Steele. (Harlequin Presents). 192p. 1983. pap. text ed. 1.95 (ISBN 0-373-10596-7). Harlequin Bks.
Price to Pay. Veva Keeler. 214p. (Orig.). 1984. pap. 8.95 (ISBN 0-932334-70-9). Heart of the Lakes.
Price Trends. Hazel M. Weatherman. (Bk. 1). (Illus.). 144p. 1984. pap. 6.00. Glassbooks MO.
International Fuels Report: Supply/Price Trends & Forecasts 1988. Ed. by Christopher Swain. 138p. 1988. pap. 215.00 (ISBN 0-8133-0726-0). Westview.
Price Trends & Policies in India. A. B. Ghosh. 1974. 10.50x (ISBN 0-686-20291-0). Intl Bk Dist.
Price Was High: The Last Uncollected Stories of F. Scott Fitzgerald. Matthew J. Bruccoli. LC 78-14074. 785p. 1981. 19.95 (ISBN 0-15-174020-8). HarBraceJ.
Price Watch 1981. H. M. Weatherman. (Illus.). 152p. 1981. pap. 6.00. Weatherman.
Price, Waterhouse & Company in America: A History of a Public Accounting Firm. C. W. DeMond. Ed. by Richard P. Brief. LC 80-1485. (Dimensions of a Accounting Firm). 1981. Repr. of 1951 ed. lib. bdg. 40.00x (ISBN 0-405-13515-7). Ayer Co Pubs.
Price Waterhouse Guide to Personal Financial Planning. Stanley H. Breitbard & Donna S. Carpenter. LC 87-8493. 400p. 1988. 19.95 (ISBN 0-8050-0387-8). H Holt & Co.
Price Waterhouse Guide to the New Tax Law. 1986. pap. 3.95 (ISBN 0-553-26590-3). Bantam.
Price Waterhouse Guide to Your Child's Taxes. Price Waterhouse Staff & Donna S. Carpenter. 96p. 1988. pap. 5.95 (ISBN 0-553-34545-1). Bantam.
Price Waterhouse Personal Tax Advisor. Price Waterhouse Staff & Donna S. Carpenter. 256p. 1987. pap. 3.95 (ISBN 0-553-27203-9). Bantam.
Price We Pay for Love. Karen H. Barnes. 64p. 1987. 6.95 (ISBN 0-8062-3157-2). Carlton.
Priceless Ingredient. Eugene E. Whitworth. 50p. Date not set. 2.00. Grt Western Univ.
Priceless Love. Laurie Lykken. (Sweet Dreams Ser.: No. 144). 192p. (Orig.). (YA) (gr. 7 up). 1988. pap. 2.50 (ISBN 0-553-27174-1). Bantam.
Priceless Pearl. Ruhiyyih Rabbani. (Illus.). 1969. pap. 9.95 (ISBN 0-900125-03-9, 331-048). Baha'i.
Priceless Privilege. Lucy Conley. 1981. 7.75 (ISBN 0-686-30773-9). Rod & Staff.
Prices & Choices: Microeconomic Vignettes. rev. ed. David Hemenway. LC 77-2733. 280p. 1983. pap. text ed. 16.95x prof. ref (ISBN 0-88410-866-X). Ballinger Pub.
Prices & Choices: Microeconomic Vignettes. 2nd ed. David Hemenway. LC 87-17437. 336p. (Orig.). 1987. pap. text ed. 16.95x (ISBN 0-88730-242-4). Ballinger Pub.
Prices & Economic Fluctuations in India: 1861-1947. A. K. Ghosh. 1983. text ed. 22.00x. Coronet Bks.
Prices & Markets. 3rd, reference ed. Robert Dorfman. LC 77-26772. (Foundations of Modern Economics Ser.). 1978. pap. write for info. (ISBN 0-13-699611-6). P-H.
Prices & Markets: Intermediate Microeconomics. 2nd ed. Charles W. Baird. (Illus.). 386p. 1982. text ed. 34.25 (ISBN 0-314-63156-9). West Pub.
Prices & Production of Machinery in the Soviet Union 1928-1958. Richard Moorsteen. LC 62-7336. (Rand Corporation Research Studies). 1962. 32.50x (ISBN 0-674-70450-9). Harvard U Pr.
Prices & Profits in the Pharmaceutical Industry. M. H. Cooper. 1967. 33.00 (ISBN 0-08-012178-0); pap. 17.00 (ISBN 0-08-012177-2). Pergamon.
Prices & Purchasing Power Parties in Latin America 1960-1972. (Economics). 250p. 1978. 7.50 (ISBN 0-8270-3780-5). OAS.
Prices & Quantities: A Macroeconomic Analysis. Arthur M. Okun. LC 80-70076. 367p. 1981. 32.95 (ISBN 0-8157-6480-4); pap. 12.95 (ISBN 0-8157-6479-0). Brookings.
Prices, Competition & Equilibrium. Ed. by M. H. Peston & R. E. Quandt. LC 86-3549. 352p. 1986. 44.50x (ISBN 0-389-20626-1). B&N Imports.
Prices Go Up... Prices Go Down. David A. Adler. (Money Power Ser.). (Illus.). 32p. 1984. lib. bdg. 9.90 (ISBN 0-531-04628-1). Watts.

Pride of the Peacock. Stephanie S. Tolan. LC 85-40290. 192p. (gr. 7 up). 1986. 13.95 (ISBN 0-684-18489-3, Pub. by Scribner). Macmillan.

Pride of the Peacock. Stephanie S. Tolan. 176p. 1987. pap. 2.50 (ISBN 0-449-70207-3, Juniper). Fawcett.

Pride of the South: A Social History of Southern Architecture. Wayne Andrews. LC 78-3214. (Illus.). 1979. 20.00 (ISBN 0-689-10931-8); pap. 10.95 (ISBN 0-689-70579-4). Atheneum.

Pride of the Terrys: Family Saga. Marguerite Steen. LC 77-18754. (Illus.). 1978. Repr. of 1962 ed. lib. bdg. 45.50x (ISBN 0-313-20221-4, STPT). Greenwood.

Pride of Weaving. Bd. with Your Handbook of Weaving. (Illus.). 4.00 (ISBN 0-934182-00-0). 1979. 4.00 (ISBN 0-934182-01-9). Turtle Lodge.

Pride of Weaving see Your Handbook of Weaving.

Pride of Women: An Illustrated Book of Days. (Archives & Special Collections on Women in Medicine). (Illus.). 110p. (Orig.). 1987. 10.00 (ISBN 0-944542-02-6). Med Coll PA ASCWM.

Pride, Shame & Guilt: Emotions of Self-Assessment. Gabriele Taylor. 152p. 1985. 24.95x (ISBN 0-19-824620-X); pap. 14.95. Oxford U Pr.

Pride, Shame, & Guilt: Emotions of Self-Assessment. Gabrielle Taylor. 152p. 1987. pap. 14.95 (ISBN 0-317-66469-7). Oxford U Pr.

Pride's Captive. Mary R. Daheim. 352p. 1986. pap. 3.95 (ISBN 0-380-89849-7). Avon.

Pride's Passion. Linda P. Sandifer. 400p. 1986. pap. 3.95 (ISBN 0-380-75171-2). Avon.

Pride's Purge: Politics in the Puritan Revolution. David Underdown. 440p. 1985. pap. text ed. 16.95x (ISBN 0-04-822045-0). Unwin Hyman.

Priere aux Etoiles. Marcel Pagnol. 344p. 1974. 22.50 (ISBN 0-686-54840-X). French & Eur.

Prieres. Charles Peguy. 124p. 1934. 2.50 (ISBN 0-686-54866-3). French & Eur.

Prieres en Ancien Francais. Keith V. Sinclair. LC 78-137. 208p. 1978. 35.00 (ISBN 0-208-01741-0, Archon). Shoe String.

Priest. Joseph Caruso. 18.00 (ISBN 0-405-10821-4). Ayer Co Pubs.

Priest. William L. Sullivan. 22.00 (ISBN 0-405-10861-3, 11859). Ayer Co Pubs.

Priest: A Fiction. Michael P. Harding. LC 86-20766. 153p. 1987. 15.00 (ISBN 0-85640-366-0, Pub. by Blackstaff Pr); pap. 6.75 (ISBN 0-85640-367-9, Pub. by Blackstaff Pr). Longwood Pub Group.

Priest & a Dead Priestess Speaks. H. D., pseud. (Illus.). 38p. 1983. 90.00x (ISBN 0-914742-79-5). Copper Canyon.

Priest & Bishop. Raymond E. Brown. LC 78-139594. 96p. 1970. pap. 4.95 (ISBN 0-8091-1661-8). Paulist Pr.

Priest & Parish in Eighteenth-Century France. Timothy Tackett. LC 76-29801. 368p. 1986. 19.50x (ISBN 0-691-10199-X). Princeton U Pr.

Priest & Stress. 26p. 1982. pap. 2.25 (ISBN 1-55586-832-0). US Catholic.

Priest & the Policeman. Roger Boyes & John Moody. 1987. 17.95 (ISBN 0-671-61896-2). Summit Bks.

Priest & the Siren, & Other Literary Studies. William S. Jones. LC 76-50078. 1976. Repr. of 1953 ed. lib. bdg. 29.00 (ISBN 0-8414-5309-8). Folcroft.

Priest As a Person: A Philosophy of Priestly Existence. Robert E. Lauder. LC 81-3665. 144p. (Orig.). 1981. pap. 5.00 (ISBN 0-89571-013-7). Affirmation.

Priest As Type of Christ: The Leader of the Eucharist in Salvation History According to Cyprian of Carthage. John D. Laurance. LC 84-47539. (American University Studies VII (Theology & Religion): Vol. 5). 245p. (Orig.). 1984. 37.25 (ISBN 0-8204-0117-X). P Lang Pubs.

Priest for All Reason: William B. Faherty 50 Years a Jesuit. Ed. by Angela Harris & Dick Friedrich. LC 81-52127. (Illus., Orig.). 1981. pap. 6.95 (ISBN 0-933150-27-X). River City MO.

Priest for All Seasons: Masculine & Celibate. Conrad W. Baars. LC 72-87091. (Synthesis Ser). 1972. pap. 1.25 (ISBN 0-8199-0375-2). Franciscan Herald.

Priest Honen & Chion-in Temple. Kyoto National Museum Staff. 250p. 1982. pap. 250.00x (Pub. by Han-Shan Tang Ltd). State Mutual Bk.

Priest in Public Service: Francis J. Haas & the New Deal. Thomas E. Blantz. LC 81-40452. 384p. 1982. 29.95 (ISBN 0-268-01547-3). U of Notre Dame Pr.

Priest of Consciousness: Essays on Conrad Aiken. Ed. by Ted R. Spivey. (Georgia State Literary Studies: No. 6). 1988. 45.00 (ISBN 0-404-63206-8). AMS Pr.

Priest of Love: D. H. Lawrence. Harry T. Moore. 1981. pap. 6.95 (ISBN 0-14-005392-1). Penguin.

Priest the Man of God: His Dignity & Duties. St. Joseph Cafasso. Tr. by Patrick O'Connell from Ital. LC 79-112472. 1971. Repr. of 1892 ed. 7.00 (ISBN 0-89555-041-5). TAN Bks Pubs.

Priest, the Woman, & the Confessional. Charles Chiniquy. 144p. 1979. pap. 4.50 (ISBN 0-937958-03-4). Chick Pubns.

Priest to the World & Other Prose Works. Cesar T. Mella. 77p. (Orig.). 1984. pap. 5.50x (ISBN 971-10-0180-2, Pub. by New Day Philipines). Cellar.

Priestcraft & the Slaughterhouse Religion. Jack Lasley. 160p. 1987. 5.00 (ISBN 0-918757-01-0). NISGO Pubns.

Priester und Beamtentum der Altbabylonischen Kontrakte. Ernest Lindl. Repr. of 1913 ed. 37.00 (ISBN 0-384-32780-X). Johnson Repr.

Priester und Tempel Im Hellenistischen Agypten: Ein Beitrag Zur Kulturgeschichte Des Hellenismus, 2 vols. in 1. facsimile ed. Walter G. Otto. LC 75-10645. (Ancient Religion & Mythology Ser.). (Ger.). 1976. Repr. 62.00x (ISBN 0-405-07278-3). Ayer Co Pubs.

Priesterschrift von Numeri 1, 1 bis 10, 10: Literarkritisch und traditionsgeschichtlich untersucht. Diether Kellermann. (Beiheft 120 zur Zeitschrift fuer die alttestamentliche Wissenschaft). 168p. 1970. 23.60 (ISBN 3-11-006439-1). De Gruyter.

Priesthood. Spencer W. Kimball et al. LC 81-5394. 170p. 1981. 8.95 (ISBN 0-87747-859-7). Deseret Bk.

Priesthood. Wilhelm Stockums. 242p. 1982. pap. 8.50 (ISBN 0-89555-170-5). TAN Bks Pubs.

Priesthood Manual. rev. ed. Ed. by Clifford A. Cole. LC 81-7220. 1985. 15.00 (ISBN 0-8309-0420-4). Herald Hse.

Priesthood, Old & New. Edward Laity. 1980. 2.25 (ISBN 0-86544-012-3). Salv Army Suppl South.

Priesthoods & Apostasies of Pierce Connally: A Study of Victorian Conversion & Anticatholicism. D. G. Paz. LC 86-2487. (Studies in American Religion: Vol. 18). 418p. 1986. lib. bdg. 69.95x (ISBN 0-88946-662-9). E Mellen.

Priestley in America: Seventeen Hundred Ninety-Four to Eighteen Four. Edgar F. Smith. Ed. by I. Bernard Cohen. LC 79-8408. (Three Centuries of Science in America Ser.). 1980. Repr. of 1920 ed. lib. bdg. 16.00x (ISBN 0-405-12557-7). Ayer Co Pubs.

Priestly Celibacy: Recurrent Battle & Lasting Values. Albert J. Hebert. 198p. 1971. 6.00 (ISBN 0-912414-01-4). Lumen Christi.

Priestly Gift in Mishnah: A Study of Tractate Terumot. Alan Peck. LC 81-2764. (Brown BJS Ser.). 1981. pap. 16.50 (ISBN 0-89130-488-6, 140020). Scholars Pr GA.

Priestly Heart. James A. Griffin. LC 83-26611. 149p. (Orig.). 1984. pap. 6.95 (ISBN 0-8189-0460-7). Alba.

Priestly Kingdom: Social Ethics As Gospel. John H. Yoder. LC 84-40358. 208p. 1986. text ed. 18.95 (ISBN 0-268-01627-5); pap. text ed. 8.95 (ISBN 0-268-01628-3). U of Notre Dame Pr.

Priestly Murders. Joe Gash. (Crime Monthly Ser.). 176p. 1985. pap. 3.95 (ISBN 0-14-008223-9). Penguin.

Priestly People. Edward O'Donnell. 64p. 1982. pap. 1.50 (ISBN 0-89243-168-7). Liguori Pubns.

Priestness: The Life & Magic of Dion Fortune. Alan Richardson. 256p. 1987. pap. 15.50 (ISBN 0-85030-461-X, Pub. by Thorsons UK). Weiser.

Priests & Kings. H. F. Fleure & Harold Peake. (Corridors of Time Ser.: No. 4). 1927. 39.50x (ISBN 0-686-83710-X). Elliots Bks.

Priests & Kings see Corridors of Time: New Haven & London, 1927-1956.

Priests & Politicians: The Mafia of the Soul. Bhagwan S. Rajneesh. 112p. (Orig.). 1988. pap. text ed. 6.95 (ISBN 3-89338-000-0, Pub. by Rebel Hse BRD). Chidvilas Inc.

Priests & Power: The Case of the Dente Shrine in Nineteenth-Century Ghana. D. J. E. Maier. LC 82-48582. (Illus.). 272p. 1983. 22.50X (ISBN 0-253-34602-9). Ind U Pr.

Priest's Diary. Sigbjorn Obstfelder. Tr. & intro. by James McFarlane. LC 87-63149. (Series B: No. 1). 75p. (Orig.). 1988. pap. 11.95 (ISBN 1-870041-01-1, Pub. by Norvik Pr). Dufour.

Priest's Handbook: The Ceremonies of the Church. Dennis G. Michno. LC 81-84716. (Illus.). 304p. 1983. 32.50 (ISBN 0-8192-1300-4). Morehouse.

Priests: Images, Ideals, & Changing Roles. James A. Fischer. (Illus.). 272p. 1987. 17.95 (ISBN 0-396-08987-9). Dodd.

Priests in Working Class Blue: The History of the Worker-Priests, (1943-1954) Oscar L. Arnal. 248p. (Orig.). 1986. pap. 11.95 (ISBN 0-8091-2831-4). Paulist Pr.

Priests of Ancient Egypt. Serge Sauneron. LC 59-10792. (Illus.). 192p. 1980. pap. 3.50 (ISBN 0-394-17410-0, B433, BC). Grove.

Priests on Trial. Ed. by Alfred W. McCoy. 256p. 1985. pap. 6.95 (ISBN 0-14-007938-6). Penguin.

Priests, Philosophers & Prophets. Thomas Whittaker. LC 77-102589. 1970. Repr. of 1911 ed. 22.50x (ISBN 0-8046-0748-6, Pub. by Kennikat). Assoc Faculty Pr.

Priests to Each Other. Carlyle Marney. 125p. 1985. pap. 6.95 (ISBN 0-913029-06-8). Stevens Bk Pr.

Priests, Warriors & Cattle: A Study in the Ecology of Religions. Bruce Lincoln. LC 78-68826. (Hermeneutics: Studies in the History of Religions: No. 9). 240p. 1981. 40.00x (ISBN 0-520-03880-0). U of Cal Pr.

Prigione di Edimburgo & Excerpts from Un Dello Sotto Richelieu. Federico Ricci. (Italian Opera II Ser.). 375p. lib. bdg. 85.00 (ISBN 0-8240-6590-5). Garland Pub.

Prigionia Di un Artista: Il Romanzo Di Luigi Cherubini, 2 vols. Giulio Confalonieri. LC 80-2267. Repr. of 1948 ed. 78.00 (ISBN 0-404-18820-6). AMS Pr.

Priglashenie Na Kazn. Vladimir Nabokov. (Rus.). 1979. pap. 7.95 (ISBN 0-88233-430-1). Ardis Pubs.

Prigotovlenije k Ispovjedi i Blagogvejnomy Prithashcheniju Svijatikh Khristvikh Tajin. Archpriest Michael Bogoslovsky. 169p. pap. 8.00 (ISBN 0-317-29105-X). Holy Trinity.

Prima Della Rivoluzione. Michael A. Bernstein. LC 83-83108. (Poet's Ser.). 65p. 1984. 12.95x (ISBN 0-915032-41-4); pap. 4.95 (ISBN 0-915032-16-3). Natl Poet Foun.

Prima Diner. 2nd ed. Ed. by Mildred Petrie. (Illus.). 172p. (Orig.). 1984. 7.95 (ISBN 0-9605844-0-4, TX 727-394). Sarasota Opera.

Prima Donna. 252p. 1984. pap. 3.95 (ISBN 0-88184-088-2). Carroll & Graf.

Prima Donna: A History. Rubert Christansen. 384p. 1985. 19.95 (ISBN 0-670-80482-7). Viking.

Prima Donna: A History. Rupert Christiansen. (Illus.). 368p. 1987. pap. 6.95 (ISBN 0-14-008378-2). Penguin.

Prima Donna at Large. Barbara Paul. 304p. 1985. 15.95 (ISBN 0-312-64414-0). St Martin.

Prima Donna at Large. Barbara Paul. 256p. 1987. pap. 3.50 (ISBN 0-451-14816-9, Sig). NAL.

Prima Donna: Her History & Surroundings from the 17th to the 19th Century, 2 vols, Vol. 1. H. Sutherland Edwards. LC 77-17875. (Music Reprint Ser.). 1978. Repr. of 1888 ed. Set. lib. bdg. 75.00 (ISBN 0-306-77536-0). Da Capo.

Prima Facie: A Guide to Value Debate. Stephen Wood & John Midgley. 224p. 1987. pap. text ed. 16.95 (ISBN 0-8403-4209-8). Kendall Hunt.

Primacy of Caring: Stress & Coping in Health & Illness. Patricia Benner & Judith Wrubel. 1988. pap. write for info. (ISBN 0-201-12002-X). Addison-Wesley.

Primacy of Christ. Michael D. Meilach. 1964. 4.95 (ISBN 0-8199-0087-7, L38655). Franciscan Herald.

Primacy of Faith. Richard Kroner. LC 77-27184. (Gifford Lectures: 1939-40). Repr. of 1943 ed. 26.25 (ISBN 0-404-60497-8). AMS Pr.

Primacy of Freedom in Development, Vol. XX. Ambassador Soedjatmoko. Ed. by Anne E. Murase & Kenneth W. Thompson. LC 85-6062. (American Values Projected Abroad Ser.). 112p. (Orig.). 1985. lib. bdg. 21.50 (ISBN 0-8191-4672-2, Co-pub. by White Miller Center); pap. 7.25 (ISBN 0-8191-4673-0). U Pr of Amer.

Primacy of Perception. Maurice Merleau-Ponty. Ed. by James M. Edie. Tr. by William Cobb et al. (Studies in Phenomenology & Existential Philosophy Ser). 1964. 24.95 (ISBN 0-8101-0165-3); pap. 11.95 (ISBN 0-8101-0164-5). Northwestern U Pr.

Primacy of Perception: Towards a Neutral Monism. Ingmar Persson. 248p. 1985. pap. text ed. 27.50x (Pub. by Almqvist & Wiksell). Coronet Bks.

Primacy of the Southern Lands in the Commission of the Most Atrocious Crimes in History with the Complicity of the North, 2 vols. Alexandre Dumas. (Illus.). 317p. 1987. Set. 327.45 (ISBN 0-89901-322-8). Found Class Reprints.

Primacy of the Spoken Word: Redemptive Proclamation in a Complex World. Walter R. Wietzke. LC 88-3422. 176p. (Orig.). 1988. pap. 9.95 (ISBN 0-8066-2352-7, 10-5194). Augsburg.

Primacy or World Order: American Foreign Policy since the Cold War. Stanley Hoffmann. 1980. text ed. 27.50 (ISBN 0-07-029205-1). McGraw.

Primal Dream & Primal Crime: Orwell's Development As a Psychological Novelist. Richard I. Smyer. LC 79-4840. 200p. 1980. text ed. 22.00x (ISBN 0-8262-0282-9). U of Mo Pr.

Primal Mind: Vision & Reality in Indian America. Jamake Highwater. LC 80-8929. 256p. 1981. 13.45i (ISBN 0-06-014866-7). Har-Row.

Primal Mind: Vision & Reality in Indian America. Ed. by Jamake Highwater. LC 82-11392. 256p. 1982. pap. 7.95 (ISBN 0-452-00690-2, F690, Mer). NAL.

Primal Myths: Creating the World. Barbara C. Sproul. LC 78-4429. 1979. pap. 11.95 (ISBN 0-06-067501-2, HarpR, RD 230, HarpR). Har-Row.

Primal Place. Robert Finch. LC 82-22566. 213p. 1983. 15.00 (ISBN 0-393-01623-4). Norton.

Primal Place. Robert Finch. 256p. 1985. pap. 5.95 (ISBN 0-393-30228-8). Norton.

Primal Power in Man: The Kundalini Shakti Yoga. Swami Narayananda. 155p. 1971. pap. 11.95 (ISBN 0-88697-027-X). Life Science.

Primal Ripe. Bert Glick. (Illus.). 56p. (Orig.). 1981. pap. 3.00 (ISBN 0-931020-19-0). Crosscut Saw.

Primal Scene. Yale Kramer. 388p. 1989. 18.95 (ISBN 1-55710-025-X, Arbor Hse). Morrow.

Primal Scenes: Literature, Philosophy, Psychoanalysis. Ned Lukacher. LC 85-25513. 368p. 1986. 29.95x (ISBN 0-8014-1886-0). Cornell U Pr.

Primal Scenes: Literature, Philosophy, Psychoanalysis. Ned Lukacher. LC 85-25513. (Paperbacks Ser.). 344p. 1988. pap. 9.95x (ISBN 0-8014-9486-9). Cornell U Pr.

Primal Scream. Arthur Janov. 448p. 1981. pap. 9.95 (ISBN 0-399-50537-7, Perigee). Putnam Pub Group.

Primal Screen: How to Write, Sell & Produce Movies for Television. Bob Shanks. LC 85-8807. 1986. 16.95 (ISBN 0-393-01993-4). Norton.

Primal Screen: How to Write, Sell, & Produce Movies for Television. Bob Shanks. 416p. 1987. pap. 9.95 (ISBN 0-449-90229-3, Columbine). Fawcett.

Primal Vision. Gottfried Benn. Ed. by E. B. Ashton. LC 58-13434. 1971. pap. 8.95 (ISBN 0-8112-0008-6, NDP322). New Directions.

Primal Vision: Selected Writings. Gottfried Benn. Ed. by E. B. Ashton. Tr. by Michael Hamburger et al from Ger. 292p. 1985. Repr. 18.00 (ISBN 0-7145-2500-6, Dist. by Kampmann & Co). M Boyars Pubs.

Primality & Cryptography. Evangelos Kranakis. LC 85-29485. 235p. 1986. 49.95 (ISBN 0-471-90934-3). Wiley.

Primaquine: Pharmacokinetics, Metabolism, Toxicity & Activity. Ed. by Walter H. Wernsdorfer & Peter I. Trigg. 176p. 1987. 36.00 (ISBN 0-471-91182-8). Wiley.

Primarily Basic. 2nd ed. George L. Miller. 216p. (Orig.). 1984. pap. text ed. 14.95 (ISBN 0-8403-2620-3, 40262003). Kendall-Hunt.

Primarily LOGO. D. Beardon et al. 1984. pap. 13.95 (ISBN 0-8359-5677-6, Reston). P-H.

Primarily Me. Irene Hubbard & Lori Soderstrom. (gr. k-3). 1976. 9.50 (ISBN 0-916456-09-9, GA65). Good Apple.

Primarily Puppets. Mabel Duch. (Illus.). 64p. (ps-3). 1985. wkbk. 6.95 (ISBN 0-86653-312-5). Good Apple.

Primarily Time. Lori Soderstrom. (gr. k-3). 1978. 7.95 (ISBN 0-916456-28-5, GA92). Good Apple.

Primary Abilities at Mental Age Six. C. E. Meyers et al. 1962. pap. 14.00 SRCD Monos. (ISBN 0-527-01592-X). Kraus Repr.

Primary Acoustic Nuclei. Raphael Lorente de No. (Illus.). 189p. 1981. text ed. 58.00 (ISBN 0-89004-318-3). Raven.

Primary Acts in Radiation Chemical Processes: A Portion of Proceedings of the First All-Union Conference on Radiation Chemistry, Moscow, 1957 in English Translation. Consultants Bureau Staff. pap. 20.00 (ISBN 0-317-09397-5, 2020688). Bks Demand UMI.

Primary Aerobatic Flight Training: How to Fly Beginning & Advanced Aerobatics. 3rd. ed. Art Medore. pap. 9.95 (ISBN 0-911721-08-8). Aviation.

Primary Aeronautical Language Manual. Aviation Language School, Inc. Staff. 201p. 1980. pap. text ed. 29.95 (ISBN 0-941456-00-5). Aviation Lang Sch.

Primary Alphabet Soup: A Curriculum for Your First Week of School. Illus. by Pat Fellers. Kathy Gritzmacher. Ed. by Ron Marson. (Master Teacher Ser.). (Illus.). 112p. 1988. tchrs.' ed. 13.95 (ISBN 0-941008-64-9). Tops Learning.

Primary & Junior Child see Understanding the Pupil.

Primary & Secondary Brain Stem Lesions. G. Csecsei et al. (Illus.). 150p. 1988. 100.00 (ISBN 0-387-82025-6). Springer-Verlag.

Primary & Secondary Metabolism of Plant Cell Cultures. Ed. by K. H. Neumann et al. LC 85-17257. (Proceedings in Life Sciences Ser.). (Illus.). 400p. 1985. 84.00 (ISBN 0-387-15797-2). Springer-Verlag.

Primary & Secondary Prevention of Coronary Heart Disease: Results of New Trials. Ed. by H. Hofmann. (Illus.). 170p. 1985. pap. 44.50 (ISBN 0-387-15249-0). Springer-Verlag.

Primary & Team Health Care Education. Ed. by Troy L. Thompson & Richard L. Byny. 264p. 1983. 44.95 (ISBN 0-275-91416-X, C1416). Praeger.

Primary & Tertiary Structure of Nucleic Acids & Cancer Research. Ed. by M. Miwa & S. Nishimura. (Illus.). 325p. 1983. 49.50x (ISBN 4-7622-6343-5, Pub. by Japan Sci Soc Japan). Intl Spec Bk.

Primary Anesthesia. Maurice King. (Illus.). 288p. 1986. pap. 16.95 (ISBN 0-19-261592-0). Oxford U Pr.

Primary Battery, Vol. 1. Ed. by George W. Heise & N. Corey Cahoon. LC 73-121906. 500p. 1971. 45.00 (ISBN 0-471-36899-7, Pub. by Wiley). Krieger.

Primary Bone Cancer: the Multidiscipline Disease: Proceedings of the Annual West Coast Cancer Symposium, 10th, San Francisco, CA, September 1974. Annual West Coast Cancer Symposium Staff. Ed. by J. Vaeth. (Frontiers of Radiation Therapy & Oncology: Vol. 10). viii, 243p. 1975. 63.50 (ISBN 3-8055-2185-5). S Karger.

Primary Cardiology Quick Reference Guides to Cardiovascular Medicine. Ed. by Norman Brachfeld. (Illus.). 208p. 1986. 35.00 (ISBN 0-88722-000-2). PW Comm NJ.

Primary Care. Ed. by J. Fry. 560p. (Orig.). 1980. pap. 32.00x (ISBN 0-433-10918-1, Pub. by W Heinemann Med Bks). Sheridan Med Bks.

Primary Care: A Contemporary Nursing Perspective. Ed. by Ingeborg Mauksch. 172p. 1981. 19.50 (ISBN 0-8089-1392-1, 792813). Grune.

Primary Care & the Practice of Medicine. Ed. by John Noble. LC 75-41569. 1976. text ed. 28.00 (ISBN 0-316-61148-4). Little.

Primary Care by Nurses: Sphere of Responsibility & Accountability. 79p. 1977. pap. 3.00 (ISBN 0-686-21451-X, G-127). ANA.

Primary Synopsis of Universology & Alwato: The New Scientific Universal Language. Stephen P. Andrews. Ed. by Madeleine B. Stern. 1971. 12.50x (ISBN 0-87730-007-0). M&S Pr.
Primary Target. Max A. Collins. (Quarry Novel Ser.). 208p. 1987. 14.95 (ISBN 0-88150-098-4). Countryman.
Primary Teacher's Pet. Linda Schwartz. (Teacher Time-Savers Ser.). 192p. (gr. 1-3). 1984. 12.95 (ISBN 0-88160-110-1, LW 131). Learning Wks.
Primary Teacher's Ready-to-Use Activities Program. Prentice Hall Press Editorial Staff. 112p. 1988. pap. 11.95 (ISBN 0-87628-651-1, Busn). P-H.
Primary Trigonometric Ratios: Unit 3. Rudolph A. Zimmer. 48p. 1980. pap. text ed. 6.00 (ISBN 0-8403-2276-3). Kendall-Hunt.
Primary Writing Fun. Sandra Whiteside & Rita G. Whiteside. (Illus.). 80p. (gr. 1-3). 1983. wkbk. 7.95 (ISBN 0-86653-101-7, GA 461). Good Apple.
Primaryplots: A Book Talk Guide for Use with Readers Ages 5-7. Rebecca Thomas. 250p. 1989. text ed. 39.95 (ISBN 0-8352-2514-3). Bowker.
Primate Adaptation & Evolution. John G. Fleagle. 352p. 1988. price not set (ISBN 0-12-260340-0). Acad Pr.
Primate Aggression, Territoriality & Xenophobia: A Comparative Perspective. Ralph Holloway. 1974. 55.00 (ISBN 0-12-352850-X). Acad Pr.
Primate Atherosclerosis. G. A. Gresham. Ed. by D. Kritchevsky et al. (Monographs on Atherosclerosis: Vol. 7). 1976. 32.75 (ISBN 3-8055-2270-3). S Karger.
Primate Behavior. Ed. by James Fobes & James King. (Communication & Behavior Ser.). 385p. 1982. 46.00 (ISBN 0-12-261320-1). Acad Pr.
Primate Behavior & Social Ecology. (Illus.). 200p. 1984. pap. 25.00 (ISBN 0-412-23220-0, 6894, Pub. by Chapman & Hall England). Routledge Chapman & Hall.
Primate Behavior & Sociobiology: Selected Papers - Proceedings, Pt. B. Ed. by A. B. Chiarelli & R. S. Corruscini. (Proceedings in Life Sciences Ser.). (Illus.). 230p. 1981. 39.50 (ISBN 0-387-11024-0). Springer-Verlag.
Primate Brain. Ed. by C. R. Noback & W. Montagna. LC 73-95612. (Advances in Primatology: Vol. 1). pap. 83.50 (ISBN 0-317-26292-0, 2055692). Bks Demand UMI.
Primate Brain Evolution: Methods & Concepts. Ed. by Este Armstrong & Dean Falk. LC 81-21150. 346p. 1982. 60.00x (ISBN 0-306-40914-3, Plenum Pr). Plenum Pub.
Primate Communication. Ed. by Charles T. Snowdon et al. LC 82-1219. 472p. 1983. 54.50 (ISBN 0-521-24690-3). Cambridge U Pr.
Primate Conservation in the Tropical Rain Forest. Ed. by Clive W. Marsh & Russell A. Mittermeier. LC 85-10414. (Monographs in Primatology: Vol. 9). 384p. 1987. 90.00 (ISBN 0-8451-3408-6). A R Liss.
Primate Ecology & Conservation. Ed. by James G. Else & Phyllis C. Lee. (Selected Proceedings of the Tenth Congress of the International Primatological Society: No. 2). (Illus.). 400p. 1986. 59.50 (ISBN 0-521-32451-3); pap. 19.95 (ISBN 0-521-31012-1). Cambridge U Pr.
Primate Ecology & Social Organization. Alison F. Richard. Ed. by J. J. Head. LC 80-66617. (Carolina Biology Readers Ser.). (Illus.). 16p. (gr. 10 up). 1982. pap. 1.65 (ISBN 0-89278-308-7, 45-9708). Carolina Biological.
Primate Ecology: Problem Oriented Field Studies. Robert W. Sussman. LC 78-17828. 596p. 1979. text ed. 25.00 (ISBN 0-394-34409-X). Random.
Primate Ecology: Studies of Feeding & Ranging Behavior in Lemurs, Monkeys & Apes. Ed. by T. H. Clutton-Brock. 1977. 99.00 (ISBN 0-12-176850-3). Acad Pr.
Primate Evolution. Glenn Conroy. (Illus.). 1988. pap. write for info. (ISBN 0-393-95649-0). Norton.
Primate Evolution. Ed. by James G. Else & Phyllis C. Lee. (Selected Proceedings of the Tenth Congress of the International Primatological Society: No. 1). (Illus.). 350p. 1986. 65.00 (ISBN 0-521-32450-5); pap. 21.95 (ISBN 0-521-31011-3). Cambridge U Pr.
Primate Evolution & Human Origins. Ed. by Russell L. Ciochon & John G. Fleagle. (Foundations of Human Behavior Ser.). (Illus.). 416p. 1987. pap. text ed. 19.95x (ISBN 0-202-01175-5). Aldine de Gruyter.
Primate Evolutionary Biology: Selected Papers - Proceedings, Pt. A. Ed. by A. B. Chiarelli & R. S. Corruscini. (Illus.). 150p. 1981. 29.00 (ISBN 0-387-11023-2). Springer-Verlag.
Primate Functional Morphology & Evolution. Ed. by Russell H. Tuttle. (World Anthropology Ser.). (Illus.). xvi, 584p. 1975. 61.50 (ISBN 90-279-7689-9). Mouton.
Primate Locomotion. Ed. by Farish A. Jenkins. 1974. 80.50 (ISBN 0-12-384050-3). Acad Pr.
Primate Models for the Evolution of Human Behavior. Ed. by Warren G. Kinzey. (Primatology Ser.). 288p. (Orig.). 1986. 56.50 (ISBN 0-88706-267-9); pap. 18.95x (ISBN 0-88706-268-7). State U NY Pr.
Primate Models of Human Neurogenic Disorders. V. G. Startsev. 198p. 1976. text ed. 29.95x (ISBN 0-89859-305-0). L Erlbaum Assocs.
Primate Models of Neurological Disorders. Ed. by B. S. Meldrum & C. D. Marsden. LC 74-21980. (Advances in Neurology: Vol. 10). 378p. 1975. 60.00 (ISBN 0-89004-002-8). Raven.
Primate Ontogeny, Cognition & Social Behaviour. Ed. by James G. Else & Phyllis C. Lee. (Selected Proceedings of the Tenth Congress of the International Primatological Society: No. 3). (Illus.). 400p. 1986. 65.00 (ISBN 0-521-32452-1); pap. 21.95 (ISBN 0-521-31013-X). Cambridge U Pr.
Primate Ovary. Ed. by R. L. Stouffer. LC 88-2545. (Serono Symposia U. S. A. Ser.). (Illus.). 288p. 1988. 59.50x (ISBN 0-306-42824-5, Plenum Pr). Plenum Pub.
Primate Paradigms: Sex Roles & Social Bonds. Linda M. Fedigan. (Illus.). 1982. (ISBN 0-920792-03-0); pap. 18.95. Eden Pr.
Primate Paternalism. David Taub. (Behavioral Science Ser.). (Illus.). 464p. 1984. 52.95 (ISBN 0-442-27217-0). Van Nos Reinhold.
Primate Phylogeny. Ed. by E. E. Grine et al. 146p. (Orig.). 1988. pap. 15.95 (ISBN 0-12-303960-6). Acad Pr.
Primate Postcranial Remains from the Oligocene of Egypt. G. C. Conroy. (Contributions to Primatology: Vol.8). 140p. 1976. 42.00 (ISBN 3-8055-2333-5). S Karger.
Primate Postcranium: Studies in Adaptation & Evolution. Ed. by Elizabeth Strasser & Marian Dagosto. 208p. 1989. price not set (ISBN 0-12-673005-9). Acad Pr.
Primate Radiation: Evolutionary Biology of the African Guenons. Ed. by A. Gautier-Hion et al. (Illus.). 550p. Date not set. price not set (ISBN 0-521-33523-X). Cambridge U Pr.
Primate Social Relationships. Ed. by Robert A. Hinde. LC 83-12023. (Illus.). 400p. 1983. text ed. 47.50x (ISBN 0-87893-275-5); pap. text ed. 29.95x (ISBN 0-87893-276-3). Sinauer Assocs.
Primate Social Systems. Robin I. Dunbar. LC 87-47595. (Illus.). 300p. 1987. text ed. 49.50x (ISBN 0-8014-2087-3, Comstock Pub); pap. text ed. 24.95x (ISBN 0-8014-9412-5). Cornell U Pr.
Primate Societies. Ed. by Barbara B. Smuts et al. LC 86-7091. (Illus.). 608p. 1986. text ed. 70.00X (ISBN 0-226-76715-9); pap. text ed. 27.50X (ISBN 0-226-76716-7). U of Chicago Pr.
Primate Societies: Group Techniques of Ecological Adaptations. Hans Kummer. LC 78-140010. (Worlds of Man Ser.). 1971. pap. text ed. 10.95 (ISBN 0-88295-613-2). Harlan Davidson.
Primate Sociobiology. J. Patrick Gray. LC 85-60629. (Monograhs). 376p. (Orig.). 1985. pap. 21.00 (ISBN 0-87536-344-X). HRAFP.
Primates. Ed. by K. Benirschke. (Illus.). 1120p. 1986. 79.00 (ISBN 0-387-96270-0). Springer-Verlag.
Primates: An Annotated Bibliography. Linda D. Wolfe. (Garland Reference Library of Social Science). 298p. 1987. lib. bdg. 43.00 (ISBN 0-8240-8552-3). Garland Pub.
Primates: An Educational Coloring Book. Spizzirri Publishing Co. Staff. Ed. by Linda Spizzirri. (Illus.). 32p. (gr. 1-8). 1981. pap. 1.49 (ISBN 0-86545-030-7). Spizzirri.
Primates & the Tropical Forests. Ed. by Russell A. Mittermeier & Mark J. Plotkin. 54p. 1982. pap. 6.00 (ISBN 0-942635-01-9). Wrld Wldlife Fund.
Primates & Their Adaptations. rev. ed. J. R. Napier. Ed. by J. J. Head. LC 76-29380. (Carolina Biology Readers Ser.). (Illus.). 16p. (gr. 10 up). 1977. pap. 1.60 (ISBN 0-89278-228-5, 45-9628). Carolina Biological.
Primates in Nature. Alison F. Richard. LC 84-18802. (Illus.). 558p. 1985. 27.95 (ISBN 0-7167-1487-6); pap. 17.95 (ISBN 0-7167-1647-X). W H Freeman.
Primates in the Classroom: An Evolutionary Perspective on Children's Education. J. Gary Bernhard. LC 87-19153. 216p. (Orig.). 1988. lib. bdg. 27.50x (ISBN 0-87023-610-5); pap. 11.95 (ISBN 0-87023-611-3). U of Mass Pr.
Primates of Madagascar. Ian Tattersall. LC 81-15477. 448p. 1982. 57.00x (ISBN 0-231-04704-5). Columbia U Pr.
Primates of South Asia: Ecology, Sociobiology, & Behavior. M. L. Roonwal & S. M. Mohnot. 1977. 29.50x (ISBN 0-674-70485-1). Harvard U Pr.
Primates of the World: Distribution, Abundance & Conservation. Jaclyn H. Wolfheim. LC 82-13464. (Illus.). 854p. 1983. 57.50x (ISBN 0-295-95899-5). U of Wash Pr.
Primatology: Proceedings, 4 vols. International Congress of Primatology, 4th, August 1972, Portland. Ed. by W. Montagna. Incl. Vol 1. Precultural Primate Behavior. Ed. by E. W. Menzel. 200p. 76.75 (ISBN 3-8055-1494-8); Vol 2. Primate Reproductive Behavior. Ed. by C. H. Phoenix. 200p. 38.75 (ISBN 3-8055-1495-6); Vol 3. Craniofacial Biology of Primates. Ed. by M. R. Zingesel. 180p. 76.75 (ISBN 3-8055-1496-4); Vol. 4. Nonhuman Primates & Human Diseases. Ed. by W. P. McNulty, Jr. 180p. 45.50 (ISBN 3-8055-1497-2). 1973. Set. 213.50 (ISBN 3-8055-1498-0). S Karger.
Primatology: Proceedings, 3 vols. International Congress of Primatology, 3rd, Zurich, 1970. Incl. Vol. 1. Taxonomy, Anatomy, Reproduction. Ed. by J. Biegert & W. Leutenegger. (Illus.). xvi, 278p. 63.50 (ISBN 3-8055-1244-9); Vol. 2. Neurobiology, Immunology, Cytology. Ed. by J. Biegert & W. Leutenegger. (Illus.). x, 245p. 60.00 (ISBN 3-8055-1245-7); Vol. 3. Behavior. Ed. by H. Kummer. (Illus.). x, 191p. 46.75 (ISBN 3-8055-1246-5). 1971. Set. 170.00 (ISBN 3-8055-1247-3). S Karger.
Primavera. Marjorie David. (Orig.). 1981. pap. 2.50 (ISBN 0-671-83520-3). PB.
Primavera. David Miller. (Burning Deck Poetry Ser). 1979. pap. 10.00 signed ed (ISBN 0-930900-63-4). Burning Deck.
Primavera, Vol. VIII. Leslie A. Miller et al. Ed. by Rebecca H. Lewis & Karen Peterson. LC 76-647540. (Illus.). 112p. 1983. pap. 5.00 (ISBN 0-916980-07-3). Primavera.
Primavera. J. M. Parramon et al. (Four Seasons Ser.). (Span.). (ps). 1986. pap. 3.95 (ISBN 0-8120-3648-4). Barron.
Primavera, Vols. VI & VII. Harriet Susskind et al. Ed. by Janet R. Heller et al. LC 76-647540. (Illus.). 120p. (Orig.). 1981. pap. 5.00 (ISBN 0-916980-06-5). Primavera.
Primavera: An Introduction to Italian. Helen McFie et al. (Ital.). 1983. text ed. 29.95 (ISBN 0-03-061564-X); lab manual 13.95 (ISBN 0-03-062514-9); tapes avail. (ISBN 0-03-062516-5). HR&W.
Primavera, I: Women Writers & Artists Anthology. Ed. by Janet R. Heller. (Illus.). 90p. 1975. pap. 4.00 (ISBN 0-916980-00-6). Primavera.
Primavera, II. Ed. by Janet R. Heller et al. LC 76-647540. (Illus., Orig.). 1976. pap. 4.00 (ISBN 0-916980-02-2). Primavera.
Primavera, III. Ed. by Janet R. Heller et al. LC 76-647540. (Illus.). 1977. pap. 4.00 (ISBN 0-916980-03-0). Primavera.
Primavera, IV. Lisel Mueller et al. Ed. by Janet R. Heller et al. LC 76-647540. (Illus.). 1978. pap. 4.00 (ISBN 0-916980-04-9). Primavera.
Primavera: The Restoration of Botticelli's Masterpiece. Umberto Baldini. (Illus.). 120p. 1986. pap. 9.95 (ISBN 0-8109-2314-9). Abrams.
Primavera, V. Felicia Cotich et al. Ed. by Janet R. Heller et al. LC 76-647540. (Illus.). 1979. pap. 4.00 (ISBN 0-916980-05-7). Primavera.
Prime Cut: Livestock Raising & Meatpacking in the United States, 1607-1983. Jimmy M. Skaggs. LC 85-40742. (Illus.). 270p. 1986. 28.50x (ISBN 0-89096-249-9). Tex A&M Univ Pr.
Prime Cut: Total Fitness for Men Eighteen to Thirty-Four. Pete Broccoletti. (Illus.). 200p. 1984. 16.95 (ISBN 0-89651-604-0); wire bdg. 10.95 (ISBN 0-89651-605-9). B L Pub.
Prime Education et Morale De Classe. Luc Boltanski. (Cahiers Du Centre De Sociologie Europeenne: No. 5). 1969. pap. 8.40x (ISBN 90-2796-255-3). Mouton.
Prime Evil. Ed Kelleher & Harriette Vidal. 368p. (Orig.). 1988. pap. 3.95 (ISBN 0-8439-2669-4, Pub. by Leisure Bks CT). Leisure NY.
Prime Evil. Judith Kelman. 272p. 1986. pap. 3.50 (ISBN 0-425-09326-3). Berkley Pub.
Prime Evil: New Stories from the Masters of Modern Horror. Douglas Winter. LC 87-34722. 352p. 1988. 18.95 (ISBN 0-453-00572-1). NAL.
Prime Farmland in Georgia. James E. Kundell & Fred C. White. 49p. 1982. pap. 6.50 (ISBN 0-89854-081-X). U of GA Inst Govt.
Prime Farmland Restoration. Russell Boulding. Ed. by Pamela Mavrolas & Chuck Sheketoff. (Your Rights in the Coalfields Ser.). 1984. pap. 3.00 (ISBN 0-943724-06-6). Illinois South.
Prime Fathers. Frederick Manfred. LC 86-27847. 190p. 1988. 15.95 (ISBN 0-935704-36-1); pap. 9.95 (ISBN 0-935704-37-X). Howe Brothers.
Prime from Introduction to BASIC. Michael Outram & S. Joseph Haremza. 272p. 1985. pap. text ed. 15.50 (ISBN 0-8403-3683-7). Kendall-Hunt.
Prime Letture Italiane per Stranieri, 2 vols. A. Roncari. 1976. Vol. 1. 4.00x (ISBN 0-686-16884-4); Vol. 2. 4.50x (ISBN 0-686-16885-2). Intl Learn Syst.
Prime Minister. Anthony Trollope. Ed. by Jennifer Uglow. (World's Classics-Paperback Ser.). (Illus.). 1983. pap. 6.95 (ISBN 0-19-281590-3). Oxford U Pr.
Prime Minister Gyula Andrassy's Influence on Habsburg Foreign Policy. Janos Decsy. (East European Monographs: No. 52). 177p. 1979. 20.00x (ISBN 0-914710-44-3). East Eur Quarterly.
Prime Ministers & Diplomats: The Making of Australian Foreign Policy 1901-49. Peter G. Edwards. 1983. 49.95x (ISBN 0-19-554389-0). Oxford U Pr.
Prime Ministers & Some Others. George W. E. Russell. 1919. Repr. 20.00 (ISBN 0-8274-3203-8). R West.
Prime Minister's Brain. Gillian Cross. (Illus.). 192p. (ps up). 1987. 9.95 (ISBN 0-19-271489-9). Oxford U Pr.
Prime Ministers of Britain. Charles C. Mersey. LC 74-86772. (Essay Index Reprint Ser.). 1924. 33.00 (ISBN 0-8369-1422-8). Ayer Co Pubs.
Prime Ministers of Britain, 1721-1924. Clive Bigham. 1977. 59.95 (ISBN 0-8490-2470-6). Gordon Pr.
Prime Mover. Paul Mariani. Ed. by Robert Pack. LC 85-14838. (Poetry Ser.). 98p. 1985. 22.50 (ISBN 0-394-55015-3). Grove.
Prime Mover. Paul Mariani. Ed. by Robert Pack. LC 85-14838. (Poetry Ser.). 98p. 1985. pap. 7.95 (ISBN 0-394-62083-6, Ever). Grove.
Prime Mover, Opus III: The String Model Universe Where Strings Are Everything. 2nd ed. Rocky McCollum. (Illus.). 500p. 1988. pap. 10.00. Kiva Pub.
Prime Mover, Opus Three: The String Model Universe, Where Strings Are Everything. 3rd ed. Rocky McCollum. (Illus.). 500p. 1988. pap. 10.00. KIVA Pub.
Prime Movers: Engines, Motors, Turbines, Pumps, Blowers & Generators. Ed. by Water Pollution Control Federation Staff. LC 84-51933. (Manual of Practice Ser.: No. OM-5). (Illus.). 181p. (Orig.). 1984. pap. text ed. 40.00 (ISBN 0-943244-56-0, MOPOM5). Water Pollution.
Prime Movers: Role of the Individual in History. Madhu Limaye. xii, 448p. 1986. text ed. 45.00x (ISBN 81-7027-087-1, Pub. by Radiant Pubs India). Advent NY.
Prime Movers: The Makers of Modern Dance in America. Joseph H. Mazo. LC 82-62346. (Illus.). 322p. 1983. pap. text ed. 14.95 (ISBN 0-916622-27-4). Princeton Bk Co.
Prime Number: Seventeen Stories from Illinois Short Fiction. Ed. by Ann L. Weir. 320p. 1988. 19.95 (ISBN 0-252-01572-X); pap. 8.95 (ISBN 0-252-06032-6). U of Ill Pr.
Prime Numbers. William J. Ellison. 417p. 1985. Repr. 52.50 (ISBN 0-471-82653-7). Wiley.
Prime Numbers & Computer Method for Factorization. Hans Riesel. (Progress in Mathematics Ser.: No. 57). 1985. 52.00 (ISBN 0-8176-3291-3). Birkhauser.
Prime of Miss Jean Brodie. Muriel Spark. LC 84-6771. 192p. 1984. pap. 6.95 (ISBN 0-452-25589-9, Plume). NAL.
Prime of Your Life. Joe Michaels et al. LC 80-21205. pap. 91.50 (ISBN 0-317-26073-1, 2025159). Bks Demand UMI.
Prime Period Lengths. Samuel Yates. 525p. 1975. pap. 10.00 (ISBN 0-9608652-1-7). S Yates.
Prime Rib & Apple. Jill Briscoe. 1976. pap. 6.95 (ISBN 0-310-21811-X, 9257P). Zondervan.
Prime Spectra in Non-Communicative Algebra. F. Van Oystaeyen. LC 75-4877. (Lecture Notes in Mathematics Ser.: Vol. 444). v, 128p. 1975. pap. 13.00 (ISBN 0-387-07146-6). Springer-Verlag.
Prime Suspect. R. D. Brown. (Orig.). 1981. pap. 1.95 (ISBN 0-505-51685-3, Pub. by Tower Bks). Leisure NY.
Prime Suspects. Bill Pronzini & Martin H. Greenberg. 240p. (Orig.). 1987. pap. 2.95 (ISBN 0-8041-0125-6, Pub. by Ivy). Ballantine.
Prime Target. Martin Russell. (Lythway Ser.). 248p. 1988. lib. bdg. 19.50 (ISBN 0-7451-0639-0, Pub. by Chivers Pr UK). G K HAll.
Prime Time. Joan Collins. 1988. 19.95 (ISBN 0-671-61885-7). S&S.
Prime Time. James Kearney. 1977. pap. 1.95 (ISBN 0-8439-0499-2, Leisure Bks). Leisure NY.
Prime Time. Susan B. Pfeffer. (Make Me a Star Ser.). 192p. (Orig.). (gr. 5 up). 1985. 2.25 (ISBN 0-448-47736-X). Putnam Pub Group.
Prime Time. Susan B. Pfeffer. 176p. 1987. pap. 2.50 (ISBN 0-425-10035-9, Pub. by Berkley-Pacer). Berkley Pub.
Prime Time Aerobics: Workbook. Leslie Johnson & Charlene Schade. Orig. Title: Rhythmic Aerobex. (Illus.). 98p. 1985. 15.95 (ISBN 0-9610234-0-6). Prime Time Aerobics.
Prime-Time America: Life On & Behind the Television Screen. Robert Sklar. 1980. pap. 6.95 (ISBN 0-19-503046-X). Oxford U Pr.
Prime Time Attraction. Barbara Girion. (Going Places Ser.: No. 4). (Orig.). (gr. k-12). 1987. pap. 2.50 (ISBN 0-440-97179-9, LFL). Dell.
Prime Time Crime: Criminals & Law Enforcers in TV Entertainment. Linda Lichter & S. Robert Lichter. Ed. by Media Institute. LC 82-73726. (Illus.). 76p. (Orig.). 1983. pap. 5.00 (ISBN 0-937790-14-1). Media Inst.
Prime Time I, Pts. 1 & 2. Elizabeth Vierck. 200p. (Orig.). 1987. pap. 9.95 (ISBN 0-87491-849-9); 16.95 (ISBN 0-87491-881-2). Acropolis.
Prime Time I: Older Is Better. Elizabeth Vierck. (Prime Time Ser.). (Illus.). 164p. 1988. 11.95 (ISBN 0-317-66826-9); pap. 7.95 (ISBN 0-87491-894-4). Acropolis.
Prime Time II: Your Positive Guide to Health, Safety, & Well Being. Elizabeth Vierck. (Prime Time Ser.). (Illus.). 164p. 1988. 11.95 (ISBN 0-317-66828-5); pap. 7.95 (ISBN 0-87491-896-0). Acropolis.
Prime Time Law Enforcement: Crime Show Viewing & Attitudes Toward the Criminal Justice System. James M. Carlson. LC 85-9420. 238p. 1985. 36.95 (ISBN 0-275-90070-3, C0070). Praeger.
Prime Time Life Skills. Jerry Aten. (Illus.). 64p. (gr. 2-5). 1983. wkbk. 6.95 (ISBN 0-86653-126-2, GA 487). Good Apple.
Prime Time: Love, Life & Sex after Fifty. Mary A. Wollison. 240p. (Orig.). 1986. pap. 3.95 (ISBN 0-7701-0489-4). Paperjacks US.

Primer of Playwriting. 2nd ed. Kenneth Macgowen. LC 80-39768. 199p. 1981. Repr. of 1962 ed. lib. bdg. 25.00x (ISBN 0-313-22896-5, MACP). Greenwood.

Primer of Politics. James E. Combs & Dan Nimmo. 496p. 1984. pap. text ed. write for info. (ISBN 0-02-324100-4). Macmillan.

Primer of Population Biology. Edward O. Wilson & William H. Bossert. LC 73-155365. (Illus.). 192p. (Orig.). 1971. pap. text ed. 9.95x (ISBN 0-87893-926-1). Sinauer Assocs.

Primer of Population Genetics. 2nd, rev. ed. Daniel L. Hartl. LC 87-20530. (Illus.). 225p. 1987. pap. text ed. 15.95x (ISBN 0-87893-301-8). Sinauer Assocs.

Primer of Prayer Gesture. Kay Irwin. 43p. 1977. pap. 3.00 (ISBN 0-941500-21-7). Sharing Co.

Primer of Projective Techniques of Psychological Assessment. Ed. by James C. Crumbaugh. LC 87-92178. 1988. 20.00 (ISBN 0-87212-215-8). Libra.

Primer of Psychobiology. 2nd ed. Teyler. LC 83-20642. (Illus.). 181p. 1984. 15.95 (ISBN 0-7167-1459-0); pap. 9.95 (ISBN 0-7167-1460-4). W H Freeman.

Primer of Psychophysiology. James Hassett. LC 77-20913. (Psychology Ser.). (Illus.). 215p. 1978. pap. text ed. 13.95 (ISBN 0-7167-0037-9). W H Freeman.

Primer of Psychotherapy. Robert Langs. 300p. 1988. text ed. 29.95 (ISBN 0-89876-142-5). Gardner Pr.

Primer of Quantum Chemistry. Frank C. Goodrich. LC 80-11938. 244p. 1982. Repr. of 1972 ed. lib. bdg. 19.50 (ISBN 0-89874-149-1). Krieger.

Primer of Quantum Mechanics. Marvin Chester. 352p. 1987. 41.35 (ISBN 0-471-00914-8). Wiley.

Primer of Real Functions. 3rd ed. Ralph P. Boas, Jr. LC 81-82669. (Carus Monograph: No. 13). 232p. 1982. 21.00 (ISBN 0-88385-022-2). Math Assn.

Primer of Rotational Physics. Myrna M. Milani & Brian R. Smith. LC 84-13518. (Rational Physics Ser.). (Illus., Orig.). 1985. 15.00 (ISBN 0-943290-02-3); pap. 10.00 (ISBN 0-943290-01-5). Fainshaw Pr.

Primer of Scientific Management. 2nd ed. Frank B. Gilbreth. LC 72-9513. (Management History Ser.: No. 12). 116p. 1973. Repr. of 1914 ed. 15.00 (ISBN 0-87960-024-1). Hive Pub.

Primer of Scientific Management see Principles of Scientific Management: 1911.

Primer of Social Casework. Elizabeth Nicholds. LC 60-12810. 181p. 1960. 25.00x (ISBN 0-231-02406-1). Columbia U Pr.

Primer of Soto Zen: A Translation of Dogen's Shobogenzo Zuimonki. Dogen. Tr. by Reiho Masunaga from Japanese. LC 76-126044. 128p. 1975. pap. text ed. 5.95x (ISBN 0-8248-0357-4, Eastwest Ctr). UH Pr.

Primer of Structured Program Design. Gary L. Richardson et al. 1980. 19.95 (ISBN 0-89433-085-3); pap. 15.00 (ISBN 0-89433-110-8). Petrocelli.

Primer of Tennyson. W. MacNelle Dixon. LC 70-130255. (Studies in Tennyson, No. 27). 1971. Repr. of 1896 ed. lib. bdg. 45.95x (ISBN 0-8383-1147-4). Haskell.

Primer of the North American Fur Trade. James A. Crutchfield. 7.50 (ISBN 0-913150-52-5). Pioneer Pr.

Primer of the Novel. Vincent McHugh. xv, 308p. 1975. Repr. of 1950 ed. lib. bdg. 20.00x (ISBN 0-374-95515-8, Octagon). Hippocrene Bks.

Primer of the Novel: For Readers & Writers. David Madden. LC 79-21881. 466p. 1980. lib. bdg. 25.00 (ISBN 0-8108-1265-7). Scarecrow.

Primer of Towing. George H. Reid. LC 75-38648. (Illus.). 102p. 1975. pap. 7.50x (ISBN 0-87033-212-0). Cornell Maritime.

Primer of Transformational Grammar: For Rank Beginners. Suzette H. Elgin. 25p. 1975. pap. 3.75 (ISBN 0-8141-3693-1). NCTE.

Primer of Vectorcardiography. Travis Winsor. LC 76-146035. (Illus.). Repr. of 1972 ed. 79.80 (ISBN 0-8357-9415-6, 2014588). Bks Demand UMI.

Primer of Visual Literacy. Donis A. Dondis. 1973. pap. 7.95x (ISBN 0-262-54029-0). MIT Pr.

Primer of Water, Electrolyte & Acid-Base Syndromes. 7th ed. Emanuel Goldberger. LC 85-19909. (Illus.). 414p. 1986. pap. text ed. 19.50 (ISBN 0-8121-1015-3). Lea & Febiger.

Primer of Wordsworth. Laurie Magnus. LC 72-3170. (Studies in Wordsworth, No. 29). 1972. Repr. of 1897 ed. lib. bdg. 49.95x (ISBN 0-8383-1519-4). Haskell.

Primer on Aging. Richard M. Brett. 1988. 7.95 (ISBN 0-533-07827-X). Vantage.

Primer on American Labor Law. 2nd ed. William B. Gould. 272p. 1986. pap. text ed. 9.95x (ISBN 0-262-57063-7). MIT Pr.

Primer on Browning. F. Mary Wilson. LC 72-113351. 1970. Repr. of 1891 ed. 23.50x (ISBN 0-8046-1039-8, Pub. By Kennikat). Assoc Faculty Pr.

Primer on Business Finance. Ed. by Frank De Felice. LC 73-20489. 1974. 34.75x (ISBN 0-8422-5132-4). Irvington.

Primer on Composite Materials: Analysis Revised. J. C. Halpin. LC 84-50921. 187p. 1984. pap. 25.00 (ISBN 0-87762-349-X). Technomic.

Primer on Connective Tissue Biochemistry. Maxwell Schubert & David Hamerman. LC 68-25209. pap. 82.50 (ISBN 0-317-29249-8, 2055443). Bks Demand UMI.

Primer on Constitutional Law. Albert P. Melone & Carl Kalvelage. LC 81-83775. 116p. 1982. pap. 4.95x (ISBN 0-913530-27-1). Palisades Pub.

Primer on Data Communications. 20.00 (ISBN 0-318-02627-9). Print Indus Am.

Primer on Dental Practice Management. Leslie F. Gaskins. 1984. pap. text ed. 19.95 (ISBN 0-8359-5669-5). Appleton & Lange.

Primer on Determinism. John Earman. 1986. lib. bdg. 64.00 (ISBN 90-277-2240-4, Pub. by Reidel Holland); pap. 16.50 (ISBN 90-277-2241-2, Pub. by Reidel Holland). Kluwer Academic.

Primer on Dispensationalism. John H. Gerstner. 1982. pap. 1.75 (ISBN 0-87552-273-4). Presby & Reformed.

Primer on Educational Governance in the Catholic Church. CACE-NABE Governance Task Force. 64p. 1987. 6.50. Natl Cath Educ.

Primer on ERISA. 2nd ed. Barbara J. Coleman. 178p. 1987. pap. text ed. 23.00 (ISBN 0-87179-555-8, 0555). BNA.

Primer on Establishing & Financing a Business. S. E. Trotter. 1977. pap. text ed. 7.25 (ISBN 0-8191-0337-3). U Pr of Amer.

Primer on Ethnomethodology. Kenneth Leiter. 1980. pap. text ed. 9.95x (ISBN 0-19-502629-2). Oxford U Pr.

Primer on Foreign Exchange. Jon G. Taylor & F. John Mathis. LC 85-10561. (Illus.). 112p. (Orig.). 1985. pap. text ed. 21.00 (ISBN 0-936742-23-2). Robt Morris Assocs.

Primer on Free Will. John H. Gerstner. 1982. pap. 1.50 (ISBN 0-87552-272-6). Presby & Reformed.

Primer on Integrated Services Digital Networks (ISDN) Implications for Future Global Communications. 1983. 75.00 (ISBN 0-317-11976-1). Info Gatekeepers.

Primer on Justification. John H. Gerstner. 32p. 1983. pap. 1.50 (ISBN 0-87552-276-9). Presby & Reformed.

Primer on Linear Algebra. Israel N. Herstein. 518p. 1988. text ed. write for info. (ISBN 0-02-353953-4). Macmillan.

Primer on Medical Malpractice. Harry Rein. 400p. 1988. manual 100.00 (ISBN 0-318-23994-9, 132B). Natl Prac Inst.

Primer on Metapsychiatry. Jan Linthorst. 79p. 1987. pap. 7.00 (ISBN 0-913105-21-X). PAGL Pr.

Primer on Monopoly & Competition. Willard F. Mueller. 1970. pap. text ed. 6.00 (ISBN 0-394-30738-0). Random.

Primer on Museum Security. Caroline K. Keck. pap. 2.50 (ISBN 0-917334-08-6). Fenimore Bk.

Primer on Music for Non-Musician Educators. Margaret D. Merrion & Marilyn C. Vincent. LC 88-60072. (Fastback Ser.: No. 270). 50p. (Orig.). 1988. pap. 0.90 (ISBN 0-87367-270-4). Phi Delta Kappa.

Primer on Pensions. Hamline University, Advanced Legal Education Staff. 287p. 1986. 42.40 (ISBN 0-317-42997-3). Hamline Law.

Primer on Piaget. William Penrose. LC 78-61324. (Fastback Ser.: No. 128). 1979. pap. 0.90 (ISBN 0-87367-128-7). Phi Delta Kappa.

Primer on Prayer. W. T. Purkiser. (Christian Living Ser.). 32p. (Orig.). 1987. pap. 1.50 (ISBN 0-8341-1191-8). Beacon Hill.

Primer on Prayer. Paul R. Sponheim. LC 87-45903. 160p. 1988. pap. 10.95 (ISBN 0-8006-2083-6). Fortress.

Primer on Radical Christianity. Gene W. Marshall. LC 85-71566. 231p. 1985. 10.00 (ISBN 0-9611552-1-3). Realistic Living.

Primer on Refraction. Ernst H. Christman. (Illus.). 128p. 1972. photocopy ed. 18.50x (ISBN 0-398-02258-5). C C Thomas.

Primer on Riemann Surfaces. Alan Beardon. LC 82-4439. (London Mathematical Society Lecture Note Ser.: No. 78). 150p. 1984. pap. 24.95 (ISBN 0-521-27104-5). Cambridge U Pr.

Primer on School Law: A Guide for Board Members in Catholic Schools. Mary A. Shaughnessey. 48p. (Orig.). 1988. pap. 6.00 (ISBN 1-55833-000-3). Natl Cath Educ.

Primer on Soft Tissue Injuries. Harry Rein. 272p. 1988. manual 25.00 (ISBN 0-318-23993-0, 131B). Natl Prac Inst.

Primer on SQL. Ageloff. 208p. 1988. pap. 17.95 (ISBN 0-8016-0085-5). Mosby.

Primer on the Atonement. John H. Gerstner. LC 84-3467. 32p. 1984. pap. 1.50 (ISBN 0-87552-278-5). Presby & Reformed.

Primer on the Deity of Christ. John H. Gerstner. LC 84-1706. 40p. 1984. pap. 1.75 (ISBN 0-87552-277-7). Presby & Reformed.

Primer on the Economic History of Europe. Paul Hohenberg. LC 81-40794. 254p. 1981. pap. text ed. 11.25 (ISBN 0-8191-1804-4). U Pr of Amer.

Primer on Thermography. Harry Rein. 275p. 1988. 85.00 (ISBN 0-318-23992-2, 133B). Natl Prac Inst.

Primer on Wage & Hour Laws. Joseph E. Kalet. 214p. 1987. pap. text ed. 23.00 (ISBN 0-87179-564-7, 0564). BNA.

Primer on Workers' Compensation. Jeffrey V. Nackley. 240p. 1987. pap. text ed. 23.00 (ISBN 0-87179-541-8, 0541). BNA.

Primer on Year-Round Education. Don Glines. 96p. 1988. pap. 16.00 (ISBN 0-943397-06-5). Assn Calif Sch Admin.

Primer Paseo de Spot. Eric Hill. Orig. Title: Spot's First Walk. (Illus., Span.). (ps-2). 1983. pap. 9.95 (ISBN 0-399-21019-9, Putnam). Putnam Pub Group.

Primer Plano Anthology, 6 vols. Ed. by R. Gordon. 1976. lib. bdg. 999.95 (ISBN 0-8490-2471-4). Gordon Pr.

Primer: Preservation for the Property Owner. Ed. by Diana S. Waite & Frederick D. Cawley. (Illus.). 35p. (Orig.). 1978. pap. 3.00 (ISBN 0-942000-01-3). Pres League NYS.

Primer, Presses, & Composing Sticks: Women Printers of the Colonial Period. Richard L. Demeter. 1979. 7.50 (ISBN 0-682-49195-0, University). Exposition-Phoenix.

Primer Set Forth by the Kinges Maiestie & His Clergie (1545) LC 74-5335. 175p. 1974. Repr. of 1546 ed. 30.00x (ISBN 0-8201-1129-5). Schol Facsimiles.

Primer Simposio sobre Ecologia Islena-First Symposium on Island Ecological Systems: Papers of the Symposium Held at Inter American University, Oct. 28, 1983. Intro. by Herminio L. Lugo. 160p. (Orig., Eng. & Span.). 1984. pap. text ed. 5.95 (ISBN 0-913480-62-2). Inter Am U Pr.

Primera Epistola a los Corintios. Ernesto Trenchard. 348p. (Span.). 1970. 9.75 (ISBN 0-8254-1728-7); pap. 8.95 (ISBN 0-8254-1727-9). Kregel.

Primera Navidad de Spot. Eric Hill. (Illus., Span.). (ps-2). 1983. pap. 9.95 (ISBN 0-399-21024-5, Putnam). Putnam Pub Group.

Primera Pascua de Spot (Spot's First Easter) 32p. (Span.). (ps-1). 11.95 (ISBN 0-399-21551-4, Pub. by Putnam). Putnam Pub Group.

Primera y Segunda Pedro, Comentario Biblico Portavoz. Louis A. Barbieri. Orig. Title: First & Second Peter, Everyman's Bible Commentary. (Span.). 1981. pap. 3.95 (ISBN 0-8254-1051-7). Kregel.

Primera y Segunda Tesalonicenses (Comentario Biblico Portavoz) Charles C. Ryrie. Orig. Title: First & Second Thessalonians (Everyman's Bible Commentary) 104p. (Span.). 1981. pap. 3.95 (ISBN 0-8254-1634-5). Kregel.

Primera y Segunda Timoteo (Comentario Biblico Portavoz) Edmond Hiebert. (Span.). 1988. pap. 6.95 (ISBN 0-8254-1316-8). Kregel.

Primeras Lecturas en Espanol see Sequential Spanish Readers.

Primeros Encuentros-First Encounters. Sabine R. Ulibarri. LC 81-71732. ii, 87p. (Span. & Eng.). 1982. pap. 7.00x (ISBN 0-916950-27-1). Biling Rev-Pr.

Primeros Pasos: Una Bibliografia Para Empezar a Investigar la Historia de Puerto Rico. Maria de Los Angeles Castro Staff et al. LC 87-80623. (Semilla Ser.). 130p. (Span.). 1987. pap. 5.95 (ISBN 0-940238-88-8). Ediciones Huracan.

Primes & Their Neighbors: Ten Tales of Middle Georgia. Richard M. Johnston. LC 77-101285. (Short Story Index Reprint Ser.). 1891. 19.00 (ISBN 0-8369-3222-6). Ayer Co Pubs.

Primes Moves: Exercises for Mature Adults. Dianne Edwards. (Illus.). 120p. (Orig.). 1988. pap. 7.95 (ISBN 0-89529-394-3, Pub. by Prism Pr). Avery Pub.

Primetime: Network Television Programming. Richard A. Blum & Richard D. Lindheim. LC 87-328. (Illus.). 224p. (Orig.). 1987. pap. text ed. 19.95 (ISBN 0-240-51756-3). Focal Pr.

Primetime Presidency of Ronald Reagan: The Era of the Television Presidency. Robert E. Denton, Jr. LC 88-5910. 128p. 1988. lib. bdg. 29.95 (ISBN 0-275-92603-6, C2603). Praeger.

Primeval Universe. Jayant V. Narlikar. (Illus.). 256p. 1988. 29.95 (ISBN 0-19-219229-9). Oxford U Pr.

Primi Saggi di Logismografia Presentati, All' XI Congresso Degli Scienziati Italiani in Roma. Giuseppe Cerboni. Ed. by Richard P. Brief. LC 80-1477. (Dimensions of Accounting Theory & Practice Ser.). (Ital.). 1981. Repr. of 1873 ed. lib. bdg. 14.00x (ISBN 0-405-13507-6). Ayer Co Pubs.

Priming the German Economy: American Occupational Policies, 1945-1948. John H. Backer. LC 70-142289. pap. 55.50 (ISBN 0-317-28970-5, 2023758). Bks Demand UMI.

Primitiae: Essays in English Literature by Students of the University of Liverpool(Blake, Crabbe, Shelley, Hartley Coleridge, Morris, Humor in Romantic Period) LC 76-25525. 1973. lib. bdg. 47.00 (ISBN 0-8414-6731-5). Folcroft.

Primitiae Monographiae Rosarum: Meteriaux Pour Servir a L'Histoire Des Roses, 6 pts. in 1 vol. F. Crepin. 1972. Repr. of 1882 ed. 60.00x (ISBN 3-7682-0759-5). Lubrecht & Cramer.

Primitifs du XIIIe. Jacques Prevert & P. Guilbaud. 5.95 (ISBN 0-686-54917-1). French & Eur.

Primitive. George Oppen. 36p. 1979. 10.00 (ISBN 0-87685-415-3); pap. 3.00 (ISBN 0-87685-414-5). Black Sparrow.

Primitive American Armor: Including Armor, Shields, & Other Defensive Devices. Walter Hough. (Illus.). Repr. of 1897 ed. 14.95 (ISBN 0-8488-0033-8, Pub. by J M C & Co). Amereon Ltd.

Primitive & Folk Jewelry. Martin Gerlach. (Illus.). 1971. pap. 9.95 (ISBN 0-486-22747-2). Dover.

Primitive & Folk Jewelry. Martin Gerlach. (Illus.). 16.75 (ISBN 0-8446-0107-1). Peter Smith.

Primitive & Peasant Markets. Richard Hodges. (Illus.). 192p. text ed. 49.95 (ISBN 0-317-64820-9); pap. text ed. 24.95 (ISBN 0-317-64821-7). Basil Blackwell.

Primitive & Pioneer Sports for Recreation Today: Rope Spinning, Lariat Throwing, Tumblesticks, Whip Cracking, Boomerangs, Log Rolling, Boomabirds, Tomahawks, Darts, Blowguns, & Many Others. Bernard S. Mason. LC 76-162516. (Illus.). 352p. 1975. Repr. of 1937 ed. 43.00x (ISBN 0-8103-4029-1). Gale.

Primitive Architecture. Enrico Guidoni. LC 86-43188. (History of World Architecture Ser.). (Illus.). 224p. 1987. pap. 25.00 (ISBN 0-8478-0797-5). Rizzoli Intl.

Primitive Architecture: A Selected Bibliography. Anthony G. White. (Architecture Ser.: A 1363). 6p. 1985. 2.00 (ISBN 0-89028-353-2). Vance Biblios.

Primitive Art. Franz Boas. (Illus.). 1927. pap. 6.95 (ISBN 0-486-20025-6). Dover.

Primitive Art. Franz Boas. (Illus.). 1962. 15.50 (ISBN 0-8446-1695-8). Peter Smith.

Primitive Art: Its Traditions & Styles. Paul S. Wingert. (Illus.). 1965. pap. 9.95 (ISBN 0-452-00793-5, F545, Mer). NAL.

Primitive Art: Master Works. new ed. Museum of Primitive Art. (Illus.). 1974. pap. 6.75 (ISBN 0-685-56731-1). Am Fed Arts.

Primitive Art of the New Zealand Maori. Glen Pownall. 92p. 1980. 23.00 (ISBN 0-85467-013-0, Pub. by Viking Sevenseas). Intl Spec Bk.

Primitive Arts & Crafts. Roderick U. Sayce. (Illus.). 1963. Repr. of 1933 ed. 15.00 (ISBN 0-8196-0124-1). Biblo.

Primitive Athens As Described by Thucydides. J. Ellen Harrison. xii, 168p. 1976. 15.00 (ISBN 0-89005-104-6). Ares.

Primitive Baptist Hymns of the Blue Ridge. Brett Sutton. (American Folklore Recordings Ser.). 28p. 1982. pap. 16.00x incl. records (ISBN 0-8078-4083-1). U of NC Pr.

Primitive Baseball: The First Quarter-Century of the National Pastime. Harvey Frommer. (Illus.). 224p. 1988. 17.95 (ISBN 0-689-11567-9). Atheneum.

Primitive Behavior. William I. Thomas. (Reprints in Sociology Ser). (Illus.). lib. bdg. 49.50x (ISBN 0-697-00220-9). Irvington.

Primitive Beliefs in the North-East of Scotland. Joseph M. McPherson. Ed. by Richard M. Dorson. LC 77-70605. (International Folklore Ser.). 1977. Repr. of 1929 ed. lib. bdg. 24.50x (ISBN 0-405-10109-0). Ayer Co Pubs.

Primitive Christianity, 4 vols. Otto Pfleiderer. Ed. by W. D. Morrison. Tr. by W. Montgomery. LC 65-22085. (Library of Religious & Philosophical Thought). 1966. Repr. of 1906 ed. lib. bdg. 175.00x (ISBN 0-678-09954-5, Reference Bk Pubs). Kelley.

Primitive Christianity & Its Non-Jewish Sources. D. D. Clemen. 1977. lib. bdg. 59.95 (ISBN 0-8490-2472-2). Gordon Pr.

Primitive Christianity: In Its Contemporary Setting. Rudolf Bultmann. Tr. by Reginald H. Fuller from Ger. LC 80-8043. 256p. 1980. pap. 8.95 (ISBN 0-8006-1408-9, 1-1408). Fortress.

Primitive Church. D. I. Lanslots. LC 79-67862. 295p. 1980. pap. 7.00 (ISBN 0-89555-134-9). TAN Bks Pubs.

Primitive Church: Studies in the Origin of the Christian Ministry. B. H. Streeter. 1977. lib. bdg. 59.95 (ISBN 0-8490-2473-0). Gordon Pr.

Primitive Civilizations or Outlines of the History of Ownership in Archaic Communities, 2 vols. E. J. Simcox. 1977. lib. bdg. 200.00 (ISBN 0-8490-2474-9). Gordon Pr.

Primitive Classification. Emile Durkheim & Marcel Mauss. Tr. by Rodney Needham. LC 63-9737. 1967. pap. 7.00x (ISBN 0-226-17334-8, P273, Phoen). U of Chicago Pr.

Primitive Conceptions of Death & the Nether World in the Old Testament. Nicholas J. Tromp. (Biblica et Orientalia: Vol. 21). 1969. pap. 21.00 (ISBN 88-7653-321-4). Loyola.

Primitive Culture, 2 vols. E. Tylor. lib. bdg. 500.00 (ISBN 0-87968-091-1). Gordon Pr.

Primitive Culture in Italy. facsimile ed. Herbert J. Rose. LC 73-168503. (Select Bibliographies Reprint Ser). Repr. of 1926 ed. 19.00 (ISBN 0-8369-5948-5). Ayer Co Pubs.

Primitive Culture in Japan. Neil G. Munro. 212p. 1906. 750.00x (Pub. by Han-Shan Tang Ltd). State Mutual Bk.

Primitive Drinking: A Study of the Uses & Functions of Alcohol in Preliterate Societies. Chandler Washburne. 1961. 18.95x (ISBN 0-8084-0253-6). New Coll U Pr.

Primitive Family in Its Origin & Development. Carl N. Starcke. Ed. by Rodney Needham. LC 75-12232. 336p. pap. 14.00x (ISBN 0-226-77133-4, Midway). U of Chicago Pr.

Primitive Folk-Moots: Or, Open-Air Assemblies in Britain. George L. Gomme. LC 67-23899. 328p. 1968. Repr. of 1880 ed. 40.00x (ISBN 0-8103-3433-X). Gale.

Primitive Government. Lucy Mair. 12.00 (ISBN 0-8446-2513-2). Peter Smith.

Prince & the Pauper. Mark Twain. (Regents Illustrated Classics Ser.). (Illus.). 62p. (gr. 7-12). 1982. pap. text ed. 3.50 (ISBN 0-13-703027-4, 20494). Prentice ESL.

Prince & the Pauper. Mark Twain. Ed. by Victor Fischer & Lin Salamo. (Iowa-California Works of Mark Twain: Vol. 6). (Illus.). 1979. 35.00x (ISBN 0-520-03622-0). U of Cal Pr.

Prince & the Pauper. Mark Twain. 1982. Repr. lib. bdg. 16.95x (ISBN 0-89966-380-X). Buccaneer Bks.

Prince & the Pauper. Mark Twain. (Bantam Classics Ser.). 219p. (gr. 4-12). 1983. pap. 2.25 (ISBN 0-553-21256-7). Bantam.

Prince & the Pauper. Mark Twain. Bd. with Connecticut Yankee. 544p. 1982. pap. 3.50 (ISBN 0-451-51628-1, CE1628, Sig Classics). NAL.

Prince & the Pauper. Mark Twain. (Puffin Classics Ser.). 256p. (gr. 3-7). 1983. pap. 2.25 (ISBN 0-14-035017-9, Puffin). Penguin.

Prince & the Pauper. Mark Twain. LC 83-47882. (Mark Twain Library: No. 5). (Illus.). 324p. 1983. 22.50 (ISBN 0-520-05088-6); pap. 7.95 (ISBN 0-520-05108-4). U of Cal Pr.

Prince & the Pauper. Mark Twain. (Dent's Illustrated Children's Classics Ser.). (Illus.). (gr. 6 up). 11.00x (ISBN 0-460-05080-X, BKA 01628, Pub. by J. M. Dent, England). Biblio Dist.

Prince & the Pauper. Mark Twain. (gr. k-6). 1985. pap. 4.95 (ISBN 0-440-47186-9, Pub. by Yearling Classics). Dell.

Prince & the Pauper see Good Literature for Slow Readers.

Prince & the Pauper see New Method Supplementary Readers.

Prince & the Pauper see Writings of Mark Twain.

Prince & the Pauper: Christmas Program. Joyce Reynolds. 32p. (Orig.). 1979. 2.25 (ISBN 0-88243-102-1, 30-0102). Gospel Pub.

Prince & the Pauper Notes. L. David Allen. 77p. (Orig.). 1980. pap. text ed. 3.25 (ISBN 0-8220-1096-8). Cliffs.

Prince & the Pretender. Vincent Lardo. 206p. (Orig.). 1984. pap. 5.95 (ISBN 0-932870-53-8). Alyson Pubns.

Prince & the Pretender: A Study in the Writing of History. A J. Youngson. LC 84-29350. 270p. 1985. 29.00 (ISBN 0-7099-2912-9, Pub. by Croom Helm Ltd). Routledge Chapman & Hall.

Prince & the Princess. Norman King. 256p. 1983. pap. 5.95 (ISBN 0-671-45784-5, Wallaby); pap. 71.40 12-copy counter display (ISBN 0-671-93151-2). S&S.

Prince & the Quakeress, Vol. 4. Jean Plaidy. (Georian Suga Ser.: Vol. 4). 320p. 1986. 17.95 (ISBN 0-399-13191-4, Putnam). Putnam Pub Group.

Prince & the Three Beggars. R. Edward Miller. 33p. (Orig.). (YA) (gr. 12). 1975. pap. 2.00 (ISBN 0-945818-04-1). Peniel Pubns.

Prince Bertram the Bad. Arnold Lobel. LC 63-8741. (Illus.). (gr. k-3). 1963. PLB 12.89 (ISBN 0-06-023976-X). HarpJ.

Prince Bertram the Bad. Arnold Lobel. 32p. (gr. k-3). pap. 2.50 (ISBN 0-590-40265-X). Scholastic Inc.

Prince Boghole. Erik C. Haugaard. LC 86-61. (Illus.). (ps-3). 1987. 13.95 (ISBN 0-02-743440-0). Macmillan.

Prince Caspian. C. S. Lewis. LC 51-12799. (Illus.). 192p. (gr. 4 up). 1969. 11.95 (ISBN 0-02-758550-6); pap. 2.95 (ISBN 0-02-044240-8, Collier). Macmillan.

Prince Caspian. C. S. Lewis. (Chronicles of Narnia Ser.: Vol. 2). (Illus.). 249p. (gr. 4-8). 1986. lib. bdg. 13.95x (ISBN 0-8161-4090-1, Large Print Bks.). G K Hall.

Prince Caspian. C. S. Lewis. LC 85-18999. (Chronicles of Narnia Ser.). (Illus.). 192p. (gr. 4 up). 1986. pap. 5.95 (ISBN 0-02-044430-3, Collier). Macmillan.

Prince Caspian. C. S. Lewis. LC 51-12799. (Chronicles of Narnia Ser.). (Illus.). 192p. (gr. 4 up). 1988. 12.95 (ISBN 0-02-758580-8). Macmillan.

Prince Charles. Michelle Brown. (Illus.). 192p. 1980. 12.95 (ISBN 0-517-54019-3). Crown.

Prince Charles. Anthony Holden. LC 82-52176. (Illus.). 432p. 1983. pap. 10.95 (ISBN 0-689-70638-3, 287). Atheneum.

Prince Charles Edward. Andrew Lang. LC 1-25240. Repr. of 1900 ed. 55.00 (ISBN 0-404-03855-7). AMS Pr.

Prince Charles: England's Future King. Jean Nugent. LC 81-22183. (Taking Part Ser.). (Illus.). 48p. (gr. 3 up). 1982. PLB 9.95 (ISBN 0-87518-226-7). Dillon.

Prince Charles, Growing up in Buckingham Palace. Alma Gilleo. LC 78-18938. (Illus.). (gr. k-4). 1978. PLB 7.95 (ISBN 0-89565-029-0). Childs World.

Prince Charles: The Making of a Prince. Helen Cathcart. LC 77-73686. (Illus.). 1977. 8.50 (ISBN 0-8008-6555-3). Taplinger.

Prince Charles's Puritan Chaplain, John Preston. Irvonwy Morgan. LC 58-3992. 1957. 10.00x (ISBN 0-8401-1648-9). A R Allenson.

Prince Charming Replies. Sherryl Woods. (Second Chance at Love Ser.: No. 430). 192p. 1988. pap. 2.50 (ISBN 0-425-10604-7). Berkley Pub.

Prince Cinders. Babette Cole. (Illus.). (gr. 1-3). 1988. 12.95 (ISBN 0-399-21502-6). Putnam Pub Group.

Prince Dracula: Son of the Devil. Douglas Myles. 304p. 1988. 18.95 (ISBN 0-07-072176-9). McGraw.

Prince Edward County Marriages, 1754-1810. Catherine L. Knorr. 108p. 1982. Repr. of 1958 ed. 15.00 (ISBN 0-89308-263-5, VA 21). Southern Hist Pr.

Prince Eugene at War: Eighteen Hundred Nine. Robert M. Epstein. LC 84-81744. (Napoleon's Commanders Ser.). (Illus.). 160p. 1984. 24.95 (ISBN 0-913037-05-2). Empire Games Pr.

Prince Felix zu Schwarzenberg: Prime Minister of Austria, 1848-1852. Adolph Schwarzenberg. Repr. of 1946 ed. 16.00 (ISBN 0-404-05628-8). AMS Pr.

Prince Friedrich of Homburg. Heinrich Von Kleist. Tr. by Diana L. S. Peters & Frederick G. Peters. LC 78-6670. 1978. pap. 6.95 (ISBN 0-8112-0694-7, NDP462). New Directions.

Prince George County, Virginia, Vol. 6. Lindsay O. Duvall. (Virginia Colonial Abstracts, Series II). 80p. 1978. pap. 17.50 (ISBN 0-89308-067-5). Southern Hist Pr.

Prince George's County Land Records, 1696-1702, Vol. A. Ed. by Shirley Wilcox. 98p. 1976. 8.00 (ISBN 0-916805-00-X). Prince Georges County Gen Soc.

Prince George's Heritage. Louise J. Hienton. LC 72-86376. (Illus.). 1972. 12.50 (ISBN 0-938420-13-5). Md Hist.

Prince Hagen: A Phantasy. Upton Sinclair. Ed. by R. Reginald & Douglas Melville. LC 77-84267. (Lost Race & Adult Fantasy). 1978. Repr. of 1903 ed. lib. bdg. 20.00x (ISBN 0-405-11008-1). Ayer Co Pubs.

Prince Hall & His Followers. George W. Crawford. LC 74-144591. Repr. of 1914 ed. 16.00 (ISBN 0-404-00145-9). AMS Pr.

Prince Hall: Social Reformer. Ed. by Nathan I. Huggins. (Black Americans of Achievement Ser.). (Illus.). 1989. 16.95 (ISBN 1-55546-588-9). Chelsea Hse.

Prince Harry's First Quiz Book. Sean Hardie & John Lloyd. 96p. (Orig.). 1986. pap. 9.95 (ISBN 0-571-13558-7). Faber & Faber.

Prince Henry: Duke of Gloucester. Noble Frankland. (Illus.). 343p. 1980. 25.00x (ISBN 0-297-77705-X, GWN 03582, Pub. by Weidenfeld & Nicolson England). Biblio Dist.

Prince Henry of Prussia, Brother of Frederick the Great. Chester V. Easum. LC 75-113061. (Illus.). 403p. 1971. Repr. of 1942 ed. lib. bdg. 35.00x (ISBN 0-8371-4697-6, EAPH). Greenwood.

Prince Henry the Navigator, the Hero of Portugal & of Modern Discovery 1394-1460. Charles R. Beazley. LC 68-57121. (Research & Source Works Ser: No. 316). (Illus.). 1968. Repr. of 1911 ed. 21.50 (ISBN 0-8337-0210-6). B Franklin.

Prince in Waiting. John Christopher. LC 70-119838. 192p. (gr. 5-9). 1974. pap. 4.95 (ISBN 0-02-042400-0, Collier). Macmillan.

Prince in Waiting. John Christopher. (gr. 5-9). 1984. 13.50 (ISBN 0-8446-6157-0). Peter Smith.

Prince in Waiting see Sword of the Spirits Trilogy.

Prince Ishmael. Marianne Hauser. Date not set. price not set. Sun & Moon CA.

Prince Ito. Kengi Hamada. LC 79-65475. (Studies Injapanese History & Civilzation). 240p. 1979. Repr. of 1936 ed. 22.00 (ISBN 0-89093-267-0). U Pubns Amer.

Prince Library. 1870. 25.00 (ISBN 0-89073-023-7). Boston Public Lib.

Prince Lichnowsky & the Great War. Harry F. Young. LC 75-11448. pap. 76.70 (2031057). Bks Demand UMI.

Prince: Machaivelli. Ed. by James Atkinson. 1976. pap. text ed. write for info. (ISBN 0-02-304270-2). Macmillan.

Prince (Machiavelli) Ratliff. (Book Note Ser.). 1985. pap. 2.50 (ISBN 0-8120-3536-4). Barron.

Prince Marko: The Hero of South Slavic Epics. Tatyana Popovic. (Illus.). 280p. 1988. 32.00x (ISBN 0-8156-2444-1). Syracuse U Pr.

Prince Napoleon in America, 1861: Letters from His Aide-De-Camp. Camille F. Ferri-Pisani. Tr. by Georges J. Joyaux from Fr. LC 72-85279. (Illus.). 1973. Repr. of 1959 ed. 29.50x (ISBN 0-8046-1695-7, Pub. by Kennikat). Assoc Faculty Pr.

Prince Notes. Luisa Vergani. (Orig.). 1967. pap. 3.25 (ISBN 0-8220-1093-3). Cliffs.

Prince of a Guy. Kathleen Korbel. (Silhouette Desire Ser.). pap. 2.50 (ISBN 0-373-05389-4). Harlequin Bks.

Prince of Abissinia: A Tale, 1759, 2 vols. in 1. Samuel Johnson. Bd. with Candide; or, All for the Best, 1759. Voltaire. LC 74-17303. (Novel in England, 1700-1775 Ser). 1974. lib. bdg. 61.00 (ISBN 0-8240-1150-3). Garland Pub.

Prince of Ayodhya. Hansa Mehta. (Nehru Library for Children). (Illus.). (gr. 1-9). 1979. pap. 2.50 (ISBN 0-89744-178-8). Auromere.

Prince of Darkness. Barbara Michaels. 240p. 1988. pap. 3.50 (ISBN 0-425-10853-8). Berkley Pub.

Prince of Darkness. Jean Plaidy. 320p. 1982. pap. 2.95 (ISBN 0-449-24529-2, Crest). Fawcett.

Prince of Darkness: A Witchcraft Anthology. Gerald Verner et al. 1978. Repr. of 1946 ed. lib. bdg. 25.00 (ISBN 0-8492-2816-6). R West.

Prince of Darkness: Radical Evil & the Power of Good in History. Jeffrey B. Russell. LC 88-47744. (Illus.). 320p. 1988. 21.95 (ISBN 0-8014-2014-8). Cornell U Pr.

Prince of Fences: The Life & Crimes of Ikey Solomons. J. J. Tobias. (Illus.). 178p. 1974. 25.00x (ISBN 0-85303-174-6, Pub. by Vallentine Mitchell England). Biblio Dist.

Prince of Game Birds: The Bobwhite Quail. Charles Elliot. LC 74-24440. (Illus.). 204p. 1974. 14.95 (ISBN 0-87797-135-8). Cherokee.

Prince of Georgia, & Other Tales. facs. ed. Julian Ralph. LC 74-142274. (Short Story Index Reprint Ser.). 1899. 17.00 (ISBN 0-8369-3758-9). Ayer Co Pubs.

Prince of Gravas: A Story of the Past. Alfred C. Fleckenstein. Ed. by R. Reginald & Douglas Melville. LC 77-84233. (Lost Race & Adult Fantasy Ser.). (Illus.). 1978. Repr. of 1898 ed. lib. bdg. 24.50x (ISBN 0-405-10976-8). Ayer Co Pubs.

Prince of Judah & Other Stories of a Great Journey. 1962 ed. Rufus Learsi. LC 62-21985. (Illus.). (gr. 5-9). 7.95 (ISBN 0-88400-031-1). Shengold.

Prince of Martyrs: A Brief Account of Imam Husayn. A. Q. Faizi. 74p. 1977. pap. 4.00 (ISBN 0-85398-073-X). G Ronald Pub.

Prince of Mount Tahan. Ishak H. Muhammad. Tr. by Harry Aveling from Malay. (Orig.). 1981. pap. text ed. 5.00x (ISBN 0-686-72740-1, 00239). Heinemann Ed.

Prince of Our Disorder: The Life of T. E. Lawrence. John E. Mack. (Illus.). 1978. pap. 12.95 (ISBN 0-316-54229-6). Little.

Prince of Peace. James Carroll. 1985. pap. 4.95 (ISBN 0-451-13847-3, Sig). NAL.

Prince of Peace. Alban Goodier. 152p. 1982. 3.25 (ISBN 0-8198-5807-2, SP0585); pap. 2.25 (ISBN 0-8198-5808-0). Dghtrs St Paul.

Prince of Peace. Carl G. Nelson. LC 79-63954. (Illus., Ltd. ed-600copies). 1979. 10.00 (ISBN 0-930954-11-4). Tidal Pr.

Prince of Peace: Returns to Fulfill All Prophecy. Shirley Telford. (Illus.). 56p. (Orig.). 1984. 5.50 (ISBN 0-9600202-0-9); Audio-Video Cassette. 30.00 (ISBN 0-9613706-1-0). William & Rich.

Prince of Pirates: The Temenggongs & the Development of Johor & Singapore, 1784-1885. Carl A. Trocki. 272p. 1978. 15.00x (ISBN 0-8214-0506-3, Pub. by Singapore U Pr). Ohio U Pr.

Prince of Players: Edwin Booth. Eleanor Ruggles. 22.95 (ISBN 0-89190-565-0, Pub. by Am Repr). Amereon Ltd.

Prince of Publishers: A Biography of the Great Victorian Publisher, George Smith. Jennifer Glynn. 240p. 1987. 25.00 (ISBN 0-85031-697-9, Pub. by Allison & Busby England). Schocken.

Prince of Publishers: A Study of the Work & Career of Jacob Tonson. Harry M. Geduld. LC 68-64121. (Indiana University Humanities Ser.: No. 66). pap. 65.00 (ISBN 0-317-10301-6, 2005742). Bks Demand UMI.

Prince of Stars in the Cavern of Time. Ian Dennis. 1989. 17.95. Overlook Pr.

Prince of Storytellers: The Life of E. Phillips Oppenheim. Robert Standish. 1979. Repr. of 1957 ed. lib. bdg. 25.00 (ISBN 0-8495-4913-2). Arden Lib.

Prince of the City. Robert Daley. 352p. 1986. pap. 3.95 (ISBN 0-425-09789-7). Berkley Pub.

Prince of the Dolomites. Tomie De Paola. LC 79-18524. (Illus.). 48p. (ps-3). 1980. pap. 4.50 (ISBN 0-15-674432-5, VoyB). HarBraceJ.

Prince of the Ghetto. Maurice Samuel. LC 87-8191. (Brown Classics in Judaica Ser.). 306p. 1987. pap. text ed. 15.75 (ISBN 0-8191-5784-8). U Pr of Amer.

Prince of the Godborn. Geraldine Harris. LC 82-11999. (Seven Citadels Ser.: Pt. 1). 196p. (gr. 6 up). 1983. reinforced bdg. 10.25 (ISBN 0-688-01792-4). Greenwillow.

Prince of the Godborn. Geraldine Harris. (Seven Citadels Ser.: No. 1). (gr. k-12). 1987. pap. 2.50 (ISBN 0-440-95407-X, LFL). Dell.

Prince of the House of David. F. Ingraham & Eric Anderson. Orig. Title: Three Years in the Holy City. 363p. 1980. Repr. text ed. 15.95 (ISBN 0-89841-003-7). Zoe Pubns.

Prince of the House of David. J. H. Ingraham. LC 77-28640. 1897. lib. bdg. 42.00 (ISBN 0-8414-5076-5). Folcroft.

Prince of the House of David. Joseph H. Ingraham. 474p. 1980. Repr. of 1897 ed. lib. bdg. 47.50 (ISBN 0-8492-1223-5). R West.

Prince of the Rabbits. Felix Meroux. LC 84-81640. (Illus.). 40p. (Orig.). (ps-3). 1984. pap. 8.95 (ISBN 0-88138-030-X, Star & Elephant Bks.). Green Tiger Pr.

Prince of the Renaissance: The Life of Francois I. Desmond Seward. 1973. text ed. 26.50x (ISBN 0-09-457900-8, Pub. by Constable Pubs UK). Trans-Atl Phila.

Prince of Thieves. Chris Martindale. LC 88-90039. (Advanced Dungeons & Dragons Gamebook Ser.: No. 18). (Illus.). 192p. (Orig.). (gr. 5 up). 1988. pap. 2.95 (ISBN 0-88038-596-0). TSR Inc.

Prince of Tides. Pat Conroy. 1986. 19.95 (ISBN 0-395-35300-9). HM.

Prince of Tides. Pat Conroy. 704p. 1987. pap. 4.95 (ISBN 0-553-26888-0). Bantam.

Prince of Whales. R. L. Fisher. LC 84-28538. 160p. 1985. 12.95 (ISBN 0-88184-127-7). Carroll & Graf.

Prince of Whales. R. L. Fisher. (Illus.). 160p. (gr. 3 up). 1987. pap. 2.50 (ISBN 0-8125-6635-1). Tor Bks.

Prince of Whales. R. L. Fisher. 160p. 1988. pap. 2.95 (ISBN 0-8125-6637-8). Tor Bks.

Prince of Whales. R. L. Fisher. (gr. k-9). 1988. pap. 2.50. Scholastic Inc.

Prince of Whales: A Fantasy Adventure. R. L. Fischer. 160p. 1986. pap. 5.95 (ISBN 0-88184-256-7). Carroll & Graf.

Prince Ombra. Roderick Macleish. 1983. pap. 3.50 (ISBN 0-8125-4550-8, Dist. Warner Pub Services & St. Martin's Press). Tor Bks.

Prince Raynor. Henry Kuttner. Ed. by Gary Lovisi. (Illus.). 80p. 1987. 5.95 (ISBN 0-936071-06-0). Gryphon Pubns.

Prince Regent's Silver Bell. 256p. 1987. 16.95 (ISBN 0-8027-0954-0). Walker & Co.

Prince Ring: Icelandic Fairy Tale. Illus. by Heinz Edelman. (Creative's Collection of Fairy Tales). (Illus.). 32p. (gr. 6 up). 1986. 10.45 (ISBN 0-87191-951-6). Creative Ed.

Prince Rupert of the Rhine. Patrick Morrah. 1976. 28.50x (ISBN 0-09-460910-1, Pub. by Constable Pubs UK). Trans-Atl-Phila.

Prince Siddhartha. rev. ed. Jonathan Landaw & Janet Brooke. (Wisdom Children's Book). (Illus.). 144p. (gr. 1-8). 1984. 15.95 (ISBN 0-86171-016-9). Wisdom MA.

Prince Sihanouk: Cambodian Leader. Ed. by Arthur M. Schlesinger, Jr. (World Leaders - Past & Present Ser.). (Illus.). (gr. 5-12). 1989. 16.95 (ISBN 1-55546-851-9). Chelsea Hse.

Prince Singh. Florence Guerin. (Collection Colombine Ser.). 192p. 1983. pap. 1.95 (ISBN 0-373-48072-5). Harlequin Bks.

Prince Skippy's Quest. Gwen Hoelscher. (Illus.). 64p. (Orig.). (gr. 6 up). 1986. pap. 7.95 (ISBN 0-9617597-0-4). Wright Monday Pr.

Prince Star. Anne Dalton. (Illus.). 32p. (gr. k-3). 1985. 14.95 (ISBN 0-7182-2101-X, Pub. by Kaye & Ward). David & Charles.

Prince, the Architects & New Wave Architecture. Charles Jencks. (Illus.). 56p. 1988. pap. 14.95 (ISBN 0-8478-1010-0). Rizzoli intl.

Prince, the Fool & the Nunnery: The Religious Theme in the Early Poetry of Anna Akhmatova. Wendy Rosslyn. 264p. Repr. of 1984 ed. text ed. 35.50 (ISBN 0-566-05445-0, Pub. by Gower Pub England). Gower Pub Co.

Prince, the Princess, & the Twisted Path. Francis T. Gambatese. (gr. 3-5). 1987. 4.95 (ISBN 0-533-06818-5). Vantage.

Prince Valiant-An American Epic, Vol. I. Hal Foster. LC 82-17919. (Prince Valiant Ser.). 56p. 1982. 100.00 (ISBN 0-936414-04-9). Manuscript Pr.

Prince Valiant-An American Epic, Vol. 2. Hal Foster. Ed. by Rick Norwood. (Complete Prince Valiant Ser.: Bk. 2). (Illus.). 60p. (Orig.). 1984. pap. 100.00 (ISBN 0-936414-05-7). Manuscript Pr.

Prince Wen Hui's Cook. Bob Flaws & Honora L. Wolfe. 208p. (Orig.). 1985. pap. 12.95 (ISBN 0-912111-05-4). Paradigm Pubns.

Prince Who Became a Cuckoo: A Tale of Liberation. Lo-dro of Drepung. Tr. by Geshe Wangyal. (Bhaisajaguru Ser.). 1982. pap. 6.95 (ISBN 0-87830-574-2). Theatre Arts.

Prince Who Knew His Fate. Tr. by Lise Manniche. (Illus.). 40p. 1982. 10.95 (ISBN 0-399-20850-X, Philomel). Putnam Pub Group.

Prince William B. The Philosophical Conceptions of William Blake. Norman Nathan. (Studies in English Literature: No. 100). 164p. 1975. pap. text ed. 18.40x (ISBN 90-2793-117-8). Mouton.

Prince William, the Story of Its People & Its Places. Writers Program, Virginia. LC 73-3657. (American Guide Ser.). 1941. Repr. 10.50 (ISBN 0-404-57957-4). AMS Pr.

Prince Zaleski. M. P. Shiel. Repr. lib. bdg. 16.95 (ISBN 0-89190-486-7, Pub. by River City Pr). Amereon Ltd.

Prince Zaleski. Matthew P. Shiel. LC 75-32782. (Literature of Mystery & Detection Ser.). 1976. Repr. of 1895 ed. 14.00x (ISBN 0-405-07898-6). Ayer Co Pubs.

Prince Zaleski & Cummings King Monk. M. P. Shiel. LC 76-17993. 1977. 7.50 (ISBN 0-87054-007-6, Mycroft & Moran). Arkham.

Princely Feasts & Festivals: Five Centuries of Pageantry & Spectacle. Bryan Holme. LC 88-50132. (Illus.). 1988. 29.95 (ISBN 0-500-01451-5). Thames Hudson.

Princely Gardens: The Origins & Development of the French Formal Style. Kenneth Woodbridge. LC 85-19640. (Illus.). 280p. 1986. 45.00 (ISBN 0-8478-0684-7). Rizzoli Intl.

Princely Profits of Party Plan. 12th ed. Dean F. Du Vall. 84p. 1980. pap. 10.00 (ISBN 0-931232-08-2). Du Vall Financial.

Princely States of India: A Chronological Checklist of Their Rulers. David Henige. LC 87-810. (Stokvis Studies in Historical Chronology & Thought: No. 7). Date not set. lib. bdg. 24.95x (ISBN 0-89370-325-7); pap. 14.95x (ISBN 0-89370-425-3). Borgo Pr.

Principal Accountant. Jack Rudman. (Career Examination Ser.: C-654). (Cloth bdg. avail. on request). pap. 16.00 (ISBN 0-8373-0654-X). Natl Learning.

Principal Actions of ECMT in the Field of Road Safety: 1986 Edition. OECD. 444p. (Orig., Eng. & Fr.). 1986. pap. 40.00x (ISBN 92-821-0107-X). OECD.

Principal Actuarial Clerk. Jack Rudman. (Career Examination Ser.: C-2424). (Cloth bdg. avail. on request). pap. 16.00 (ISBN 0-8373-2424-6). Natl Learning.

Principal Actuary. Jack Rudman. (Career Examination Ser.: C-610). (Cloth bdg. avail. on request). pap. 20.00 (ISBN 0-8373-0610-8). Natl Learning.

Principal Addiction Specialist. Jack Rudman. (Career Examination Ser.: C-1398). (Cloth bdg. avail. on request). pap. 16.00 (ISBN 0-8373-1398-8). Natl Learning.

Principal Administrative Analyst. Jack Rudman. (Career Examination Ser.: C-2710). (Cloth bdg. avail. on request). 1988. pap. 16.00 (ISBN 0-8373-2710-5). Natl Learning.

Principal Administrative Associate. Jack Rudman. (Career Examination Ser.: C-2394). (Cloth bdg. avail. on request). pap. 16.00 (ISBN 0-8373-2394-0). Natl Learning.

Principal Administrative Associate-Administrative Assistant. 7th ed. Ed. by Hy Hammer. LC 83-8821. 240p. 1983. pap. 10.00 (ISBN 0-668-05617-7, 5617). Arco.

Principal Administrative Services Clerk. Jack Rudman. (Career Examination Ser.: C-2871). (Cloth bdg. avail. on request). pap. 16.00 (ISBN 0-8373-2871-3). Natl Learning.

Principal Admitting Clerk. Jack Rudman. (Career Examination Ser.: C-656). (Cloth bdg. avail. on request). pap. 16.00 (ISBN 0-8373-0656-6). Natl Learning.

Principal Affirmative Action Officer. Jack Rudman. (Career Examination Ser.: C-2689). (Cloth bdg. avail. on request). pap. 16.00 (ISBN 0-8373-2689-3). Natl Learning.

Principal Alcoholism Rehabilitaion Counselor. Jack Rudman. (Career Examination Ser.: C-2796). (Cloth bdg. avail. on request). 1988. pap. 16.00 (ISBN 0-8373-2796-2). Natl Learning.

Principal & Subsidiary Dialect Areas in the North-Central States. Albert H. Marckwardt. Bd. with English Loan Words in the Low German Dialect of Westphalia, Missouri. W. A. Willibrand. (Publications of the American Dialect Society: No. 27). 32p. 1957. pap. 2.35 (ISBN 0-8173-0627-7). U of Ala Pr.

Principal Attorney. Jack Rudman. (Career Examination Ser.: C-1913). (Cloth bdg. avail. on request). pap. 18.00 (ISBN 0-8373-1913-7). Natl Learning.

Principal Audit Clerk. Jack Rudman. (Career Examination Ser.: C-657). (Cloth bdg. avail. on request). pap. 16.00 (ISBN 0-8373-0657-4). Natl Learning.

Principal Auditor. Jack Rudman. (Career Examination Ser.: C-2405). (Cloth bdg. avail. on request). pap. 16.00 (ISBN 0-8373-2405-X). Natl Learning.

Principal Bank Examiner. Jack Rudman. (Career Examination Ser.: C-658). (Cloth bdg. avail. on request). pap. 16.00 (ISBN 0-8373-0658-2). Natl Learning.

Principal Bookkeeper. Jack Rudman. (Career Examination Ser.: C-1756). (Cloth bdg. avail. on request). 1988. pap. 16.00 (ISBN 0-8373-1756-8). Natl Learning.

Principal Budget Analyst. Jack Rudman. (Career Examination Ser.: C-2416). (Cloth bdg. avail. on request). pap. 16.00 (ISBN 0-8373-2416-5). Natl Learning.

Principal Budget Examiner. Jack Rudman. (Career Examination Ser.: C-1637). (Cloth bdg. avail. on request). 1988. pap. 16.00 (ISBN 0-8373-1637-5). Natl Learning.

Principal Budget Officer. Jack Rudman. (Career Examination Ser.: C-2685). (Cloth bdg. avail. on request). pap. 16.00. Natl Learning.

Principal Building Inspector. Jack Rudman. (Career Examination Ser.: C-2853). (Cloth bdg. avail. on request). 1988. pap. 18.00 (ISBN 0-8373-2853-5). Natl Learning.

Principal Buildings Manager. Jack Rudman. (Career Examination Ser.: C-2719). (Cloth bdg. avail. on request). pap. 16.00. Natl Learning.

Principal Buyer. (Career Examination Ser.: C-3419). Date not set. pap. 14.00 (ISBN 0-8373-3419-5). Natl Learning.

Principal Cashier. Jack Rudman. (Career Examination Ser.: C-1974). (Cloth bdg. avail. on request). pap. 14.00 (ISBN 0-8373-1974-9). Natl Learning.

Principal: Change-Agent in Desegregation. Turnage. LC 72-87658. pap. 2.75 (ISBN 0-912008-07-5). Equity & Excel.

Principal Characteristics of Sausages of the World Listed by Country of Origin. Donald M. Kinsman. 134p. (Orig.). 1983. pap. text ed. 11.95x (ISBN 0-89641-122-2). American Pr.

Principal Chemist. Jack Rudman. (Career Examination Ser.: C-2403). (Cloth bdg. avail. on request). pap. 18.00 (ISBN 0-8373-2403-3). Natl Learning.

Principal Children's Counselor. Jack Rudman. (Career Examination Ser.: C-1602). (Cloth bdg. avail. on request). pap. 16.00 (ISBN 0-8373-1602-2). Natl Learning.

Principal Civil Engineer. Jack Rudman. (Career Examination Ser.: C-318). 1988. pap. 18.00 (ISBN 0-8373-0318-4). Natl Learning.

Principal Clerk. Jack Rudman. (Career Examination Ser.: C-611). (Cloth bdg. avail. on request). pap. 14.00 (ISBN 0-8373-0611-6). Natl Learning.

Principal Clerk (Personnel) Jack Rudman. (Career Examination Ser.: C-1399). (Cloth bdg. avail. on request). pap. 16.00 (ISBN 0-8373-1399-6). Natl Learning.

Principal Clerk-Principal Stenographer. rev. ed. Hy Hammer. LC 82-11446. 256p. 1982. pap. 8.00 (ISBN 0-668-05536-7, 5536). Arco.

Principal Clerk-Stenographer. Jack Rudman. (Career Examination Ser.: C-3327). (Cloth bdg. avail. on request). 1987. pap. 16.00 (ISBN 0-8373-3327-X). Natl Learning.

Principal Clerk Surrogate. Jack Rudman. (Career Examination Ser.: C-2129). (Cloth bdg. avail. on request). 1988. pap. 16.00 (ISBN 0-8373-2129-8). Natl Learning.

Principal Commissary Clerk. Jack Rudman. (Career Examination Ser.: C-2049). (Cloth bdg. avail. on request). pap. 16.00 (ISBN 0-8373-2049-6). Natl Learning.

Principal Communications Technician. Jack Rudman. (Career Examination Ser.: C-2413). (Cloth bdg. avail. on request). pap. 16.00 (ISBN 0-8373-2413-0). Natl Learning.

Principal Component Analysis. I. T. Jolliffe. (Statistics Ser.). (Illus.). 290p. 1986. 39.00 (ISBN 0-387-96269-7). Springer-Verlag.

Principal Components & Curvature in Occupational Stratification. Alden D. Miller. (Working Papers in Methodology Ser.: No. 2). 152p. 1967. pap. text ed. 4.00 (ISBN 0-89143-026-1). U NC Inst Res Soc Sci.

Principal-Comprehensive High School. Jack Rudman. (Teachers License Examination Ser.: S-11). (Cloth bdg. avail. on request). pap. 19.95 (ISBN 0-8373-8111-8). Natl Learning.

Principal Computer Programmer. Jack Rudman. (Career Examination Ser.: C-1626). (Cloth bdg. avail. on request). pap. 16.00 (ISBN 0-8373-1626-X). Natl Learning.

Principal Construction Inspector. Jack Rudman. (Career Examination Ser.: C-1400). (Cloth bdg. avail. on request). pap. 18.00 (ISBN 0-8373-1400-3). Natl Learning.

Principal Consumer Affairs Inspector. Jack Rudman. (Career Examination Ser.: C-1658). (Cloth bdg. avail. on request). 1988. pap. 16.00 (ISBN 0-8373-1658-8). Natl Learning.

Principal Consumer Affairs Investigator. Jack Rudman. (Career Examination Ser.: C-2377). (Cloth bdg. avail. on request). pap. 16.00 (ISBN 0-8373-2377-0). Natl Learning.

Principal Contributions of Henry Walter Bates to a Knowledge of the Butterflies & Longicorn Beetles of the Amazon Valley: Original Anthology. Ed. by E. Gorton Linsley & Keir B. Sterling. LC 77-81106. (Biologists & Their World Ser.). (Illus.). 1978. lib. bdg. 66.00x (ISBN 0-405-10690-4). Ayer Co Pubs.

Principal Court Clerk. Jack Rudman. (Career Examination Ser.: C-2588). (Cloth bdg. avail. on request). pap. 16.00 (ISBN 0-8373-2588-9). Natl Learning.

Principal Custodial Foreman. Jack Rudman. (Career Examination Ser.: C-2560). (Cloth bdg. avail. on request). pap. 16.00 (ISBN 0-8373-2560-9). Natl Learning.

Principal Data Entry Machine Operator. Jack Rudman. (Career Examination Ser.: C-2866). (Cloth bdg. avail. on request). pap. 16.00 (ISBN 0-8373-2866-7). Natl Learning.

Principal Data Processing Control Clerk. Jack Rudman. (Career Examination Ser.: C-2485). (Cloth bdg. avail. on request). pap. 16.00 (ISBN 0-8373-2485-8). Natl Learning.

Principal Data Processing Equipment Operator. Jack Rudman. (Career Examination Ser.: C-2303). (Cloth bdg. avail. on request). 1988. pap. 16.00 (ISBN 0-8373-2303-7). Natl Learning.

Principal Developmental Specialist. Jack Rudman. (Career Examination Ser.: C-925). (Cloth bdg. avail. on request). pap. 16.00 (ISBN 0-8373-0925-5). Natl Learning.

Principal Diseases of Lower Vertebrates. H. Reichenbach-Klinke & E. Elkan. Incl. Book 1. Diseases of Fishes. (Illus.). pap. 19.95 (ISBN 0-87666-042-1, PS-205); Book 2. Diseases of Amphibians. pap. 19.95 (ISBN 0-87666-044-8, PS-206); Book 3. Diseases of Reptiles. o. p. 19.95 (ISBN 0-87666-045-6, PS-207). 1972. pap. TFH Pubns.

Principal Drafting Technician. Jack Rudman. (Career Examination Ser.: C-2680). (Cloth bdg. avail. on request). pap. 16.00 (ISBN 0-8373-2680-X). Natl Learning.

Principal Draftsman. Jack Rudman. (Career Examination Ser.: C-1576). (Cloth bdg. avail. on request). pap. 16.00 (ISBN 0-8373-1576-X). Natl Learning.

Principal Drug & Alcohol Counselor. Jack Rudman. (Career Examination Ser.: C-2743). (Cloth bdg. avail. on request). 1988. pap. 16.00 (ISBN 0-8373-2743-1). Natl Learning.

Principal Drugs: An Alphabetical Guide to Therapeutic Agents. 8th ed. s. J. Hopkins. 186p. 1985. pap. 4.95 (ISBN 0-571-13423-8). Faber & Faber.

Principal Ecclesiastical Judgments Delivered in the Court of Arches 1867 to 1875. Robert Phillimore. xiii, 420p. 1981. Repr. of 1876 ed. lib. bdg. 35.00x (ISBN 0-8377-2504-6). Rothman.

Principal Editorial Clerk. Jack Rudman. (Career Examination Ser.: C-2566). (Cloth bdg. avail. on request). pap. 16.00 (ISBN 0-8373-2566-8). Natl Learning.

Principal-Elementary School. Jack Rudman. (Teachers License Examination Ser.: S-3). (Cloth bdg. avail. on request). pap. 19.95 (ISBN 0-8373-8103-7). Natl Learning.

Principal Employment Security Clerk. Jack Rudman. (Career Examination Ser.: C-2352). (Cloth bdg. avail. on request). pap. 16.00 (ISBN 0-8373-2352-5). Natl Learning.

Principal Engineering Aide. Jack Rudman. (Career Examination Ser.: C-1561). (Cloth bdg. avail. on request). pap. 16.00 (ISBN 0-8373-1561-1). Natl Learning.

Principal Engineering Inspector. Jack Rudman. (Career Examination Ser.: C-911). (Cloth bdg. avail. on request). pap. 16.00 (ISBN 0-8373-0911-5). Natl Learning.

Principal Engineering Technician. Jack Rudman. (Career Examination Ser.: C-1425). (Cloth bdg. avail. on request). pap. 16.00 (ISBN 0-8373-1425-9). Natl Learning.

Principal Engineering Technician (Drafting) Jack Rudman. (Career Examination Ser.: C-1954). (Cloth bdg. avail. on request). pap. 16.00 (ISBN 0-8373-1954-4). Natl Learning.

Principal Engineering Technician: Environmental Quality. Jack Rudman. (Career Examination Ser.: C-3239). 1988. pap. 16.00 (ISBN 0-8373-3239-7). Natl Learning.

Principal Environmental Analyst. Jack Rudman. (Career Examination Ser.: C-2661). (Cloth bdg. avail. on request). pap. 16.00 (ISBN 0-8373-2661-3). Natl Learning.

Principal Environmental Planner. Jack Rudman. (Career Examination Ser.: C-2664). (Cloth bdg. avail. on request). pap. 16.00 (ISBN 0-8373-2664-8). Natl Learning.

Principal Evidence Technician. Jack Rudman. (Career Examination Ser.: C-2750). (Cloth bdg. avail. on request). 1988. pap. 16.00 (ISBN 0-8373-2750-4). Natl Learning.

Principal Examiner of Municipal Affairs. Jack Rudman. (Career Examination Ser.: C-2727). (Cloth bdg. avail. on request). 1988. pap. 18.00 (ISBN 0-8373-2727-X). Natl Learning.

Principal Executive Officer. Jack Rudman. (Career Examination Ser.: C-2827). (Cloth bdg. avail. on request). 1988. pap. 16.00 (ISBN 0-8373-2827-6). Natl Learning.

Principal Field Accountant. Jack Rudman. (Career Examination Ser.: C-1570). (Cloth bdg. avail. on request). pap. 16.00 (ISBN 0-8373-1570-0). Natl Learning.

Principal File Clerk. Jack Rudman. (Career Examination Ser.: C-659). (Cloth bdg. avail. on request). pap. 14.00 (ISBN 0-8373-0659-0). Natl Learning.

Principal Financial Analyst. Jack Rudman. (Career Examination Ser.: C-2644). (Cloth bdg. avail. on request). pap. 16.00 (ISBN 0-8373-2644-3). Natl Learning.

Principal Forestry Technician. Jack Rudman. (Career Examination Ser.: C-2716). (Cloth bdg. avail. on request). 1988. pap. 16.00. Natl Learning.

Principal Generaux: Tutorial Automatic Testing. Ed. by Network Staff. 1985. 95.00x (ISBN 0-907634-00-1, Pub. by Network Events Ltd). State Mutual Bk.

Principal Grants Analyst. Jack Rudman. (Career Examination Ser.: C-2835). (Cloth bdg. avail. on request). 1988. pap. 16.00 (ISBN 0-8373-2835-7). Natl Learning.

Principal Grounds & Maxims with an Analysis of the Laws of England. 3rd ed. William Noy. xxviii, 219p. 1980. Repr. of 1845 ed. lib. bdg. 25.00x (ISBN 0-8377-0906-7). Rothman.

Principal Groundskeeper. Jack Rudman. (Career Examination Ser.: C-1573). (Cloth bdg. avail. on request). pap. 14.00 (ISBN 0-8373-1573-5). Natl Learning.

Principal Home Economist. Jack Rudman. (Career Examination Ser.: C-1627). (Cloth bdg. avail. on request). pap. 16.00 (ISBN 0-8373-1627-8). Natl Learning.

Principal Hospital Care Investigator. Jack Rudman. (Career Examination Ser.: C-612). (Cloth bdg. avail. on request). pap. 16.00 (ISBN 0-8373-0612-4). Natl Learning.

Principal Housing Inspector. Jack Rudman. (Career Examination Ser.: C-1426). (Cloth bdg. avail. on request). 1988. pap. 16.00 (ISBN 0-8373-1426-7). Natl Learning.

Principal Human Resources Specialist. Jack Rudman. (Career Examination Ser.: C-974). (Cloth bdg. avail. on request). pap. 16.00 (ISBN 0-8373-0974-3). Natl Learning.

Principal Hydrological Features of the Pacific Ocean. A. M. Muromtsev. 424p. 1963. text ed. 85.00x (ISBN 0-7065-0216-7, Pub. by Keter Pub Jerusalem). Coronet Bks.

Principal Illustrator. Jack Rudman. (Career Examination Ser.: C-1713). (Cloth bdg. avail. on request). pap. 16.00 (ISBN 0-8373-1713-4). Natl Learning.

Principal in Metropolitan Schools. Ed. by Donald A. Erickson & Theodore L. Reller. LC 78-62641. (Contemporary Educational Issues Ser.). 347p. 1978. 26.50x (ISBN 0-8211-0417-9); text ed. 23.75x ten or more copies. McCutchan.

Principal Infectious Diseases of Childhood. Nelles Silverthorne & C. S. Anglin. LC 66-6101. pap. 36.50 (ISBN 0-317-28233-6, 2014411). Bks Demand UMI.

Principal Insurance Examiner. Jack Rudman. (Career Examination Ser.: C-2696). (Cloth bdg. avail. on request). pap. 16.00 (ISBN 0-8373-2696-6). Natl Learning.

Principal Investigator. Jack Rudman. (Career Examination Ser.: C-1791). (Cloth bdg. avail. on request). pap. 16.00 (ISBN 0-8373-1791-6). Natl Learning.

Principal-Junior High School. Jack Rudman. (Teachers License Examination Ser.: S-4). (Cloth bdg. avail. on request). 1988. pap. 19.95 (ISBN 0-8373-8104-5). Natl Learning.

Principal Juvenile Counselor. Jack Rudman. (Career Examination Ser.: C-422). (Cloth bdg. avail. on request). pap. 16.00 (ISBN 0-8373-0422-9). Natl Learning.

Principal Key Punch Operator. Jack Rudman. (Career Examination Ser.: C-2103). (Cloth bdg. avail. on request). 1977. pap. 14.00. Natl Learning.

Principal Labor-Management Practices Adjustor. Jack Rudman. (Career Examination Ser.: C-613). (Cloth bdg. avail. on request). pap. 18.00 (ISBN 0-8373-0613-2). Natl Learning.

Principal Labor Relations Analyst. Jack Rudman. (Career Examination Ser.: C-2231). (Cloth bdg. avail. on request). pap. 18.00 (ISBN 0-8373-2231-6). Natl Learning.

Principal Labor Specialist. Jack Rudman. (Career Examination Ser.: C-2670). (Cloth bdg. avail. on request). pap. 18.00 (ISBN 0-8373-2670-2). Natl Learning.

Principal Laboratory Technician. Jack Rudman. (Career Examination Ser.: C-3014). 1988. pap. 18.00 (ISBN 0-8373-3014-9). Natl Learning.

Principal Land Management Specialist. Jack Rudman. (Career Examination Ser.: C-2620). (Cloth bdg. avail. on request). pap. 16.00 (ISBN 0-8373-2620-6). Natl Learning.

Principal Librarian. Jack Rudman. (Career Examination Ser.: C-2915). (Cloth bdg. avail. on request). pap. 16.00 (ISBN 0-8373-2915-9). Natl Learning.

Principal Library Clerk. Jack Rudman. (Career Examination Ser.: C-1932). (Cloth bdg. avail. on request). pap. 14.00 (ISBN 0-8373-1932-3). Natl Learning.

Principal Mail & Supply Clerk. Jack Rudman. (Career Examination Ser.: C-975). (Cloth bdg. avail. on request). pap. 14.00 (ISBN 0-8373-0975-1). Natl Learning.

Principal Management Analyst. Jack Rudman. (Career Examination Ser.: C-1737). (Cloth bdg. avail. on request). pap. 16.00 (ISBN 0-8373-1737-1). Natl Learning.

Principal Management Technician. Jack Rudman. (Career Examination Ser.: C-2753). (Cloth bdg. avail. on request). 1988. pap. 14.00 (ISBN 0-8373-2753-9). Natl Learning.

Principal Manpower Development Specialist. Jack Rudman. (Career Examination Ser.: C-2819). (Cloth bdg. avail. on request). 1988. pap. 18.00 (ISBN 0-8373-2819-5). Natl Learning.

Principal Mechanical Engineer. Jack Rudman. (Career Examination Ser.: C-3249). 1988. pap. 16.00 (ISBN 0-8373-3249-4). Natl Learning.

Principal Methods Analyst. Jack Rudman. (Career Examination Ser.: C-1738). (Cloth bdg. avail. on request). pap. 16.00 (ISBN 0-8373-1738-X). Natl Learning.

Principal Museum Curator. Jack Rudman. (Career Examination Ser.: C-2375). (Cloth bdg. avail. on request). pap. 16.00 (ISBN 0-8373-2375-4). Natl Learning.

Principal Navigations, Voyages, Traffiques & Discoveries of the English Nation, 12 Vols. Richard Hakluyt. LC 76-181901. Repr. of 1905 ed. Set. 265.00 (ISBN 0-404-03030-0); 16.00 ea. AMS Pr.

Principal Occupational Analyst. Jack Rudman. (Career Examination Ser.: C-2535). (Cloth bdg. avail. on request). pap. 16.00 (ISBN 0-8373-2535-8). Natl Learning.

Principal Office Assistant. Jack Rudman. (Career Examination Ser.: C-2595). (cloth bdg. avail. on request). pap. 14.00 (ISBN 0-8373-2595-1). Natl Learning.

Principal Office Stenographer. (Career Examination Ser.: C-3377). Date not set. pap. 14.00 (ISBN 0-8373-3377-6). Natl Learning.

Principal Office Typist. (Career Examination Ser.: C-3375). Date not set. pap. 14.00 (ISBN 0-8373-3375-X). Natl Learning.

Principal Officers of Department of State & United States Chiefs of Missions, 1978-1986. (Department of State Publication). 168p. (Orig.). 1986. pap. 8.50 (ISBN 0-318-21646-9, S/N 044-000-02150-1). USGPO.

Principal Park Supervisor. Jack Rudman. (Career Examination Ser.: C-2355). (Cloth bdg. avail. on request). pap. 14.00 (ISBN 0-8373-2355-X). Natl Learning.

Principal Personnel Administrator. Jack Rudman. (Career Examination Ser.: C-2411). (Cloth bdg. avail. on request). pap. 16.00 (ISBN 0-8373-2411-4). Natl Learning.

Principal Personnel Analyst. Jack Rudman. (Career Examination Ser.: C-2346). (Cloth bdg. avail. on request). pap. 16.00 (ISBN 0-8373-2346-0). Natl Learning.

Principal Personnel Clerk. Jack Rudman. (Career Examination Ser.: C-2944). (Cloth bdg. avail. on request). pap. 16.00 (ISBN 0-8373-2944-2). Natl Learning.

Principal Personnel Examiner. Jack Rudman. (Career Examination Ser.: C-1915). (Cloth bdg. avail. on request). pap. 16.00 (ISBN 0-8373-1915-3). Natl Learning.

Principal Planner. Jack Rudman. (Career Examination Ser.: C-1764). (Cloth bdg. avail on request). 1988. pap. 14.00 (ISBN 0-8373-1764-9). Natl Learning.

Principal Planner (Education) Jack Rudman. (Career Examination Ser.: C-1669). (Cloth bdg. avail. on request). pap. 16.00 (ISBN 0-8373-1669-3). Natl Learning.

Principal Planner (Manpower) Jack Rudman. (Career Examination Ser.: C-1599). (Cloth bdg. avail. on request). pap. 18.00 (ISBN 0-8373-1599-9). Natl Learning.

Principal Probation Officer. Jack Rudman. (Career Examination Ser.: C-1427). (Cloth bdg. avail. on request). pap. 14.00 (ISBN 0-8373-1427-5). Natl Learning.

Principal Program Evaluation Specialist. Jack Rudman. (Career Examination Ser.: C-2701). (Cloth bdg. avail. on request). 1988. pap. 16.00 (ISBN 0-8373-2701-6). Natl Learning.

Principal Program Examiner. Jack Rudman. (Career Examination Ser.: C-2756). (Cloth bdg. avail. on request). 1988. pap. 18.00 (ISBN 0-8373-2756-3). Natl Learning.

Principal Program Research Analyst. Jack Rudman. (Career Examination Ser.: C-2218). (Cloth bdg. avail. on request). 1988. pap. 18.00 (ISBN 0-8373-2218-9). Natl Learning.

Principal Program Specialist. Jack Rudman. (Career Examination Ser.: C-2863). (Cloth bdg. avail. on request). 1988. pap. 16.00 (ISBN 0-8373-2863-2). Natl Learning.

Principal Program Specialist (Correction) Jack Rudman. (Career Examination Ser.: C-2259). (Cloth bdg. avail. on request). 1988. pap. 18.00 (ISBN 0-8373-2259-6). Natl Learning.

Principal Public Health Engineer. Jack Rudman. (Career Examination Ser.: C-3099). 1988. pap. 16.00 (ISBN 0-8373-3099-8). Natl Learning.

Principal Public Health Nutritionist. Jack Rudman. (Career Examination Ser.: C-1566). (Cloth bdg. avail. on request). pap. 16.00 (ISBN 0-8373-1566-2). Natl Learning.

Principal Public Health Representative. Jack Rudman. (Career Examination Ser.: C-3025). 1988. pap. 14.00 (ISBN 0-8373-3025-4). Natl Learning.

Principal Public Health Sanitarian. (Career Examination Ser.: C-3347). Date not set. pap. 16.00 (ISBN 0-8373-3347-4). Natl Learning.

Principal Purchase Inspector. Jack Rudman. (Career Examination Ser.: C-1747). (Cloth bdg. avail. on request). 1988. pap. 14.00 (ISBN 0-8373-1747-9). Natl Learning.

Principal Purchasing Agent. Jack Rudman. (Career Examination Ser.: C-912). (Cloth bdg. avail. on request). pap. 14.00 (ISBN 0-8373-0912-3). Natl Learning.

Principal Quantitative Analyst. Jack Rudman. (Career Examination Ser.: C-1715). (Cloth bdg. avail. on request). pap. 16.00 (ISBN 0-8373-1715-0). Natl Learning.

Principal Real Estate Manager. Jack Rudman. (Career Examination Ser.: C-1628). (Cloth bdg. avail. on request). pap. 16.00 (ISBN 0-8373-1628-6). Natl Learning.

Principal Records Center Assistant. Jack Rudman. (Career Examination Ser.: C-1914). (Cloth bdg. avail. on request). pap. 16.00 (ISBN 0-8373-1914-5). Natl Learning.

Principal Rent Examiner. Jack Rudman. (Career Examination Ser.: C-2093). (Cloth bdg. avail. on request). 1988. pap. 16.00 (ISBN 0-8373-2093-3). Natl Learning.

Principal Research Analyst. Jack Rudman. (Career Examination Ser.: C-2353). (Cloth bdg. avail. on request). pap. 16.00 (ISBN 0-8373-2353-3). Natl Learning.

Principal Right-Of-Way Aide. Jack Rudman. (Career Examination Ser.: C-2737). (Cloth bdg. avail. on request). 1988. pap. 16.00 (ISBN 0-8373-2737-7). Natl Learning.

Principal Safety Coordinator. Jack Rudman. (Career Examination Ser.: C-2669). (Cloth bdg. avail. on request). pap. 16.00 (ISBN 0-8373-2669-9). Natl Learning.

Principal Sanitary Engineer. Jack Rudman. (Career Examination Ser.: C-1819). (Cloth bdg. avail. on request). pap. 16.00 (ISBN 0-8373-1819-X). Natl Learning.

Principal Senior Citizens Program Coordinator. Jack Rudman. (Career Examination Ser.: C-2799). (Cloth bdg. avail. on request). 1988. pap. 16.00 (ISBN 0-8373-2799-7). Natl Learning.

Principal-Six Hundred School. Jack Rudman. (Teachers License Examination Ser.: S-7). (Cloth bdg. avail. on request). pap. 17.95 (ISBN 0-8373-8107-X). Natl Learning.

Principal Social Welfare Examiner. Jack Rudman. (Career Examination Ser.: C-2495). (Cloth bdg. avail. on request). pap. 16.00 (ISBN 0-8373-2495-5). Natl Learning.

Principal Solutions of Ordinary Differential Equations in the Complex Domain. Walter Strodt. LC 52-42839. (Memoirs: No. 26). 107p. 1972. pap. 14.00 (ISBN 0-8218-1226-2, MEMO-26). Am Math.

Principal Special Investigator. Jack Rudman. (Career Examination Ser.: C-1590). (Cloth bdg. avail. on request). pap. 16.00 (ISBN 0-8373-1590-5). Natl Learning.

Principal Special Officer. (Career Examination Ser.: C-3420). Date not set. pap. 14.00 (ISBN 0-8373-3420-9). Natl Learning.

Principal Staff Development Specialist. Jack Rudman. (Career Examimation Ser.: C-2703). (Cloth bdg. avail. on request). 1988. pap. 16.00 (ISBN 0-8373-2703-2). Natl Learning.

Principal Stationary Engineer. Jack Rudman. (Career Examination Ser.: C-1719). (Cloth bdg. avail. on request). pap. 16.00 (ISBN 0-8373-1719-3). Natl Learning.

Principal Statistician. Jack Rudman. (Career Examination Ser.: C-976). (Cloth bdg. avail. on request). pap. 16.00 (ISBN 0-8373-0976-X). Natl Learning.

Principal Statistics Clerk. Jack Rudman. (Career Examination Ser.: C-977). (Cloth bdg. avail. on request). pap. 14.00 (ISBN 0-8373-0977-8). Natl Learning.

Principal Stenographer. Jack Rudman. (Career Examination Ser.: C-614). (Cloth bdg. avail. on request). pap. 14.00 (ISBN 0-8373-0614-0). Natl Learning.

Principal Stenographer (Law) Jack Rudman. (Career Examination Ser.: C-3294). 1988. pap. 16.00 (ISBN 0-8373-3294-X). Natl Learning.

Principal Storekeeper. Jack Rudman. (Career Examination Ser.: C-3013). 1988. pap. 14.00 (ISBN 0-8373-3013-0). Natl Learning.

Principal Stores Clerk. Jack Rudman. (Career Examination Ser.: C-978). (Cloth bdg. avail. on request). pap. 14.00 (ISBN 0-8373-0978-6). Natl Learning.

Principal Systems Analyst. Jack Rudman. (Career Examination Ser.: C-2388). (Cloth bdg. avail. on request). pap. 16.00 (ISBN 0-8373-2388-6). Natl Learning.

Principal Tax Compliance Agent. Jack Rudman. (Career Examination Ser.: C-2954). (Cloth bdg. avail. on request). pap. 16.00 (ISBN 0-8373-2954-X). Natl Learning.

Principal Telephone Operator. Jack Rudman. (Career Examination Ser.: C-2493). (Cloth bdg. avail. on request). pap. 14.00 (ISBN 0-8373-2493-9). Natl Learning.

Principal Typist. Jack Rudman. (Career Examination Ser.: C-615). (Cloth bdg. avail. on request). pap. 14.00 (ISBN 0-8373-0615-9). Natl Learning.

Principal Unemployment Insurance Hearing Representative. Jack Rudman. (Career Examination Ser.: C-2730). (Cloth bdg. avail. on request). 1988. pap. 16.00 (ISBN 0-8373-2730-X). Natl Learning.

Principal Unemployment Insurance Investigator. Jack Rudman. (Career Examination Ser.: C-2831). (Cloth bdg. avail. on request). pap. 16.00 (ISBN 0-8373-2831-4). Natl Learning.

Principal, Vocational High School. Jack Rudman. (Teachers License Examination Ser.: S-6). 1988. pap. 19.95 (ISBN 0-8373-8106-1). Natl Learning.

Principal War Telegrams & Memo, 1940-1943, 7 Vols. Great Britain Cabinet Office Staff. 1976. lib. bdg. 450.00x (ISBN 0-527-35650-6). Kraus Intl.

Principal Water Plant Supervisor. Jack Rudman. (Career Examination Ser.: C-2960). 1988. pap. 16.00 (ISBN 0-8373-2960-4). Natl Learning.

Principal Winners Abroad of 1978. 10.00 (ISBN 0-936032-06-5). Blood-Horse.

Principal Winners Abroad of 1979. Ed. by Blood-Horse, Inc. Staff. (Annual Supplement, the Blood-Horse). (Orig.). 1980. pap. 10.00 (ISBN 0-936032-07-3). Blood-Horse.

Principal Winners Abroad of 1980. Ed. by Blood-Horse, Inc. Staff. (Annual Supplement of the Blood-Horse). (Orig.). 1981. pap. 10.00 (ISBN 0-936032-38-3). Blood-Horse.

Principal Winners Abroad of 1981. Ed. by Blood-Horse, Inc. Staff. (Blood-Horse Annual Supplement). 160p. (Orig.). 1982. pap. 10.00 (ISBN 0-936032-47-2). Blood-Horse.

Principal Winners Abroad of 1982. Ed. by Blood Horse Staff. (Blood-Horse Annual Supplement Ser.). 175p. 1983. pap. 10.00 (ISBN 0-936032-56-1). Blood-Horse.

Principal Winners Abroad of 1983. (Annual Supplement Ser.). 150p. 1984. pap. 11.50 (ISBN 0-936032-66-9). Blood Horse.

Principal Winners Abroad of 1984. (Annual Supplement Ser.). 150p. 1985. pap. 11.50 (ISBN 0-936032-78-2). Blood-Horse.

Principal Workers' Compensation Review Analyst. Jack Rudman. (Career Examination Ser.: C-310). (Cloth bdg. avail. on request). pap. 16.00 (ISBN 0-8373-0310-9). Natl Learning.

Principal Workmen's Compensation Examiner. Jack Rudman. (Career Examination Ser.: C-1548). (Cloth bdg. avail. on request). pap. 16.00 (ISBN 0-8373-1548-4). Natl Learning.

Principal Works of Simon Stevin, 5 vols. Incl. Vol. 1. General Introduction-Mechanism. Ed. by E. J. Dijksterhuis. 1955 (ISBN 90-265-0070-X); Vols. 2 A & B. Mathematics. Ed. by D. J. Struik. 973p. 1958 (ISBN 90-265-0071-8); Vol. 3. Astronomy & Navigation. Ed. by A. Pannekoek & E. Croone. 632p. 1961 (ISBN 90-265-0073-4); Vol. 4. Art of War. Ed. by W. H. Schukking. 525p. 1964 (ISBN 90-265-0074-2); Vol. 5. Engineering-Music-Civic Life. R. J. Forbes et al. 609p. 1967 (ISBN 90-265-0075-0). (Dutch & Eng.). text ed. 125.00 ea. (Pub. by Swets Pub Serv Holland). Swets North Am.

Principal X-Ray Technician. Jack Rudman. (Career Examination Ser.: C-979). (Cloth bdg. avail. on request). pap. 16.00 (ISBN 0-8373-0979-4). Natl Learning.

Principal, Youth & Adult Center. Jack Rudman. (Teachers License Examination Ser.: S-8). 1988. pap. 19.95 (ISBN 0-8373-8108-8). Natl Learning.

Principal Zoning Inspector. Jack Rudman. (Career Examination Ser.: C-2854). (Cloth bdg. avail. on request). 1988. pap. 16.00 (ISBN 0-8373-2854-3). Natl Learning.

Principalities & Powers. John W. Montgomery. LC 74-29081. 256p. 1981. pap. 7.95 (ISBN 0-87123-470-X, 210470). Bethany Hse.

Principalities & Powers in the New Testament. Heinrich Schlier. LC 79-8119. Repr. of 1961 ed. 18.00 (ISBN 0-404-18432-4). AMS Pr.

Principality of Wales in the Later Middle Ages: The Structure & Personnel of Government, Volume 1; South Wales 1277-1536. R. Griffiths. (History & Law Ser.: No. 26). 634p. 1972. text ed. 32.50x (ISBN 0-7083-0450-8, Pub. by U of Wales). Humanities.

Principall Navigations, Voyages, Traffiques & Discoveries of the English Nation, 12 Vols. 3rd ed. Richard Hakluyt. LC 70-75411. 1969. Repr. of 1903 ed. Set. 395.00x (ISBN 0-678-00488-9). Kelley.

Principals & Agents: The Structure of Business. Ed. by John W. Pratt & Richard J. Zeckhauser. LC 84-29039. 256p. 1985. 24.95 (ISBN 0-87584-164-3, Dist. by Harper & Row Pubs., Inc.). Harvard Busn.

Principal's Guide to High School Journalism. Benedict. 1.50 (ISBN 0-318-19221-7). Quill & Scroll.

Principal's Guide to Improving Reading Instruction. Robert L. Hillerich. 300p. 1983. 36.95 (ISBN 0-205-07820-6, 237820, Pub. by Longwood Div). Allyn.

Principal's Guide to the Educational Rights of Handicapped Students. T. Page Johnson. 68p. 1986. pap. 7.00 (ISBN 0-88210-179-X). Natl Assn Principals.

Principal's Handbook. Donald Helwig et al. 189p. 1984. three ring binder 23.95 (ISBN 0-938272-10-1). WELS Board.

Principal's Handbook. Thomas Jefferson Research Center Staff. 90p. (YA) (gr. 9 up). 1987. tchr's. ed. 49.95 (ISBN 0-938308-13-0). T Jefferson Res Ctr.

Principal's Handbook on the School Media Center. Betty Martin & Ben Carson. LC 81-801. 212p. 1981. pap. 21.00x (ISBN 0-208-01912-X, Lib Prof Pubns). Shoe String.

Principals in Action: The Reality of Managing Schools. Van C. Morris et al. 1984. 34.95 (ISBN 0-675-09790-8). Merrill.

Principals of Color. Rev. ed. Faber Birren. (Illus.). 96p. 1987. pap. 10.95 (ISBN 0-88740-103-1). Schiffer.

Principals of Electrodynamics. Melvin Schwartz. (Illus.). 352p. 1987. pap. text ed. 8.95 (ISBN 0-486-65493-1). Dover.

Principals' Survival Packets, Vols. I & II. 1987. Set. 39.00 (ISBN 0-87545-027-X, 415-14415) (ISBN 0-87545-025-3). Natl Sch PR.

Principalship. 3rd ed. Thelbert L. Drake & William H. Roe. vii, 604p. 1986. text ed. write for info. (ISBN 0-02-330420-0). Macmillan.

Principalship. Sergiovanni. 408p. pap. 37.95x (ISBN 0-205-08851-1, Pub. by Longwood Div). Allyn.

Principalship: New Perspectives. Paul B. Jacobson et al. 512p. 1973. 37.00 (ISBN 0-13-700856-2). P-H.

Principe. Niccolo Machiavelli. (Illus.). 189p. 1987. 127.75 (ISBN 0-89266-583-1). Am Classical Coll Pr.

Principe. billingual ed. Nicolas Maquiavelo. (Biblioteca De Cultura Basica Ser.). 1986. 9.95 (ISBN 0-8477-0710-5). U of PR Pr.

Principe (De Principatibus) Niccolo Machiavelli. Ed. by Brian Richardson & Kathleen Speight. 153p. (Ital.). 1979. pap. 10.95x (ISBN 0-7190-0742-9, Pub. by Manchester England). S F Vanni.

Principe D'une Theorie Mathematique De l'Echange. Leon Walras. 20.00 (ISBN 0-8337-3677-9). B Franklin.

Principe Que Ha de Venir. Robert Anderson. Orig. Title: Coming Prince. 288p. (Span.). 1980. pap. 6.95 (ISBN 0-8254-1021-5). Kregel.

Principes see Oeuvres.

Principes de la Philosophie, Vol. 1. 3rd ed. Rene Descartes. 158p. 1970. 9.95 (ISBN 0-686-55678-X). French & Eur.

Principes de Phonetique Francaise a l' Usage des Etudiants Anglo-Americains. Pierre Delattre. (Fr.). 1951. pap. 3.95x (ISBN 0-910408-01-7). Coll Store.

Principes d'Economique Politique, 2 vols. A. Marshall. 1156p. 1971. pap. 135.00 (ISBN 0-677-50535-3). Gordon & Breach.

Principes des Assurances de Personnes: Guide de l'Etudiante. Alexa M. Selph. (FLMI Insurance Education Program Ser.). 305p. (Fr.). 1985. wkbk. 10.00 (ISBN 0-915322-73-0). LOMA.

Principes des Assurances de Personnes. Gene Morton & Brian McGreevy. Tr. by Frenette, Boulanger, & Co. Staff. LC 83-83153. (FLMI Insurance Education Program Ser.). 358p. (Fr.). 1985. text ed. 30.00 (ISBN 0-915322-72-2). LOMA.

Principes des Mathematiques. Louis Coutrat. 318p. Repr. of 1905 ed. lib. bdg. 47.50X (Pub. by G. Olms BRD). Coronet Bks.

Principi di Architettura Civile. Francesco Milizia. Repr. of 1781 ed. 50.00 (ISBN 0-384-38875-2). Johnson Repr.

Principia Discordia. Malaclypse the Younger. 1978. pap. 5.95 (ISBN 0-686-23670-X). Loompanics.

Principia Discordia: or How I Found Goddess & What I Did to Her When I Found Her. Macalypse The Younger. 1976. lib. bdg. 59.95 (ISBN 0-685-75085-X). Revisionist Pr.

Principia Ethica. G. E. Moore. (Great Books in Philosophy). 260p. 1988. pap. text ed. 4.95 (ISBN 0-87975-498-2). Prometheus Bks.

Principia Ethica. George E. Moore. 1959. 37.50 (ISBN 0-521-05753-1); pap. 13.95 (ISBN 0-521-09114-4). Cambridge U Pr.

Principia Martindale. Edward Swift. Date not set. price not set (ISBN 0-670-57701-4). Viking.

Principia Mathematica, 3 Vols. Alfred N. Whitehead & Bertrand Russell. Set. 420.50 (ISBN 0-521-06791-X). Cambridge U Pr.

Principia Mathematica to Fifty-Six. 2nd ed. Alfred N. Whitehead & Bertrand Russell. 1925-27. pap. 37.50 (ISBN 0-521-09187-X). Cambridge U Pr.

Principia or Basis of Social Science: A Survey from the Moral & Theological, Yet Liberal & Progressive Standpoint. Robert J. Wright. LC 73-14190. (Perspectives in Social Inquiry Ser.). 528p. 1974. Repr. 33.00x (ISBN 0-405-05533-1). Ayer Co Pubs.

Principia: Or the First Principles of Natural Things, Vols. I & II. Emanuel Swedenborg. Tr. & intro. by Augustus Clissold. (Illus.). 1976. Repr. of 1846 ed. Set. 15.00 (ISBN 0-915221-20-9). Vol. I, 380p (ISBN 0-915221-37-3). Vol. II, 413p (ISBN 0-915221-38-1). Swedenborg Sci Assn.

Principia Philosophiae see Oeuvres.

Principio Company: Iron-Making in Colonial Maryland, 1720-1781. Michael W. Robbins. Ed. by Stuart Bruchey. (American Business History Ser.). 344p. 1986. lib. bdg. 40.00 (ISBN 0-8240-8367-9). Garland Pub.

Principios Basicos para la Ensenanza de la Biologia. rev. ed. (Serie De Biologia: No. 4). (Span.). 1976. pap. 1.25 (ISBN 0-8270-1385-X). OAS.

Principios de Electronica. 2nd ed. Albert P. Malvino. 1984. text ed. 5.95 (ISBN 0-07-039914-X). McGraw.

Principios Fundamentales de Evaluacion para Educadores. 4th ed. Harris F. Bunker. 5.00 (ISBN 0-8477-2730-0); pap. 3.75 (ISBN 0-8477-2702-5). U of PR Pr.

Principios Generales de Microbiologia: Serie de Biologia No. 7. 2nd ed. OAS Gerneral Secretariat Department of Scientific & Technological Affairs. (Biology Ser.: No. 7). 143p. 1980. text ed. 3.50 (ISBN 0-8270-1097-4). OAS.

Principios Rosacruces para el Hogar y los Negocios. 4th ed. H. Spencer Lewis. Tr. by AMORC Staff. 210p. (Orig., Span.). 1980. pap. 8.00 (ISBN 0-912057-76-9, GS-502). AMORC.

Principios y Alternativas de Trabajo Pastoral. Alberto Barrientos. 368p. (Orig.). 1982. pap. 8.95 (ISBN 0-89922-220-X). Edit Caribe.

Principito. Antoine De Saint-Exupery. Tr. by Bonifacio Del Carril from Fr. LC 73-5511. (Illus.). 113p. (Span.). 1973. pap. 3.95 (ISBN 0-15-628450-2, Harv). HarBraceJ.

Principito - The Little Prince. Antoine de Saint-Exupery. (Illus.). 88p. (gr. 4 up). Date not set. pap. 6.95 (ISBN 0-8442-7622-7, Passport Bks). Natl Textbk.

Principius de la Economia del Movimiento. (Span.). 1978. 5.00 (ISBN 0-940876-10-8). City Hope.

Principle. Kathryn S. Caldwell. 193p. 1983. 9.95 (ISBN 0-934126-39-9). Randall Bk Co.

Principle & Practicality: Essays in Neo-Confucianism & Practical Learning. Ed. by W. Theodore De Bary & Irene Bloom. LC 78-11530. (Neo-Confucian Series & Studies in Oriental Culture). 1979. 45.00x (ISBN 0-231-04612-X); pap. 22.50x (ISBN 0-231-04613-8). Columbia U Pr.

Principle & Practice of Mahayana Buddhism: An Interpretation of Professor Suzuki's Translation of Ashvaghosa's Awakening of Faith. Asvaghosa. Ed. by Dwight Goodard. LC 78-72373. Repr. of 1933 ed. 18.00 (ISBN 0-404-17223-7). AMS Pr.

Principle & Practice of Navigation. A. Frost. 319p. 1978. 29.50x (ISBN 0-85174-310-2). Sheridan.

Principle Aspects of Clinical Nutrition. Ed. by J. C. Somogyi. (Bibliotheca Nutritio et Dieta: No. 35). (Illus.). viii, 132p. 1985. 75.50 (ISBN 3-8055-3950-9). S Karger.

Principle in Art. Coventry Patmore. 274p. Repr. of 1898 ed. text ed. 41.40x (ISBN 0-576-02175-X, Pub. by Gregg Intl Pubs England). Gregg Intl.

Principle of Auditing: Canadian Edition. 3rd ed. Walter B. Meigs. 1987. 45.50x (ISBN 0-256-03580-6). Irwin.

Principle of Creation. Ed. by Chung H. Kwak. (Home Study Course Ser.). 60p. 1980. pap. 4.00. HSA Pubns.

Principle of Hope, 3 Vols. Ernst Bloch. Tr. by Neville Plaice et al. boxed set 95.00 (ISBN 0-317-46917-7). MIT Pr.

Principle of Individuality & Value. Bernard Bosanquet. LC 12-14490. (Gifford Lectures Ser.). 1968. Repr. of 1912 ed. 29.00 (ISBN 0-527-10036-6). Kraus Repr.

Principle of Inertia in the Middle Ages. Allan Franklin. LC 76-10515. 100p. (Orig.). 1976. pap. 8.95x (ISBN 0-87081-069-3). Colo Assoc.

Principle of Microeconomics. Paul Heyne. (Illus.). 400p. 1988. pap. text ed. write for info. (ISBN 0-574-19485-1, 13-2486); write for info. instr's. guide (ISBN 0-574-19486-X, 13-2486); write for info. study guide (ISBN 0-574-19487-8, 13-2487); write for info. software test generator (ISBN 0-574-21885-8, 13-4885); write for info. test bank bklt. (ISBN 0-574-19488-6, 13-2488). SRA.

Principle of Non-Resistance As Held by the Mennonite Church. John Horsch. Bd. with Hutterian Brethren, Fifteen Twenty-Eight to Nineteen Thirty-One. John Horsch. LC 74-147672. (Library of War & Peace; Relig. & Ethical Positions on War). lib. bdg. 46.00 (ISBN 0-8240-0430-2). Garland Pub.

Principle of Penetrants. 2nd ed. C. E. Betz. Ed. by F. S. Catlin. LC 76-95933. (Illus.). 34.00 (ISBN 0-686-21416-1). Magnaflux.

Principle of Poetic Justice Illustrated in Restoration Tragedy. John Dale Ebbs. Ed. by James Hogg. (Poetic Drama & Poetic Theory Ser.). 211p. (Orig.). 1973. pap. 15.00 (ISBN 3-7052-0828-4, Pub. by Salzburg Studies). Longwood Pub Group.

Principle of Protestantism: Chambersburg, PA 1845. Philip Schaff. Ed. by Bruce Kuklick. Bd. with What Is Church History? Philadelphia, PA 1846. 215p. (American Religious Thought of the 18th & 19th Centuries Ser.). 343p. 1987. lib. bdg. 50.00. Garland Pub.

Principle of Reincarnation. Walter J. Stein. 1986. pap. 2.50 (ISBN 0-916786-85-4). St George Bk Serv.

Principle of Relativity. Albert Einstein et al. 1924. pap. 4.50 (ISBN 0-486-60081-5). Dover.

Principle of Relativity in the Light of the Philosophy of Science. Paul Carus. LC 75-3109. Repr. of 1913 ed. 18.00 (ISBN 0-404-59105-1). AMS Pr.

Principle of Self-Determination in International Law. W. Ofuatey-Kodjoe. 250p. 1977. text ed. 26.50x (ISBN 0-8290-1569-8). Irvington.

Principle of Sovereignty Over Natural Resources. G. Elian. 250p. 1979. 42.50x (ISBN 90-286-0049-3, Pub. by Sijthoff & Noordhoff). Kluwer Academic.

Principle of Spiritual Economy. Rudolf Steiner. Tr. by Peter Mollenhauer. 220p. 1986. 20.00 (ISBN 0-88010-163-6); pap. 10.95 (ISBN 0-88010-162-8). Anthroposophic.

Principle of Stellar Structure, 2 Vols. Ed. by J. P. Cox. LC 68-26755. (Illus.). 1327p. 1968. Set. 440.00 (ISBN 0-677-01950-5). Gordon & Breach.

Principle of Sufficient Reason in Some Scholastic Systems, 1750-1900. John E. Gurr. 1959. 12.95 (ISBN 0-87462-411-8). Marquette.

Principle or Pragmatism: Interest Groups, PACs, & Campaign Contributions in 1984. Michael W. Rubinoff. Date not set. price not set. Free Congr Res.

Principle or Tien. Giancarlo Finazzo. 161p. 1980. 14.50 (ISBN 0-89955-145-9, Pub. by Mei Ya China). Intl Spec Bk.

Principles & a Philosophy For Vocational Education. Melvin D. Miller. 250p. 1985. 17.00 (ISBN 0-318-17790-0, SN48). Natl Ctr Res Voc Ed.

Principles & Acts of the Revolution in America. Hezekiah Niles. LC 74-153040. (Research & Source Works Ser.: No. 666). 1971. Repr. of 1822 ed. lib. bdg. 29.50 (ISBN 0-8337-2541-6). B Franklin.

Principles & Applications of Biomedical Magnetic Resonance Imaging. Ed. by F. Wehrli et al. 500p. 1988. lib. bdg. 95.00 (ISBN 0-89573-349-8). VCH Pubs.

Principles & Applications of Coal Petrology. Ed. by John Crelling & Russell R. Dutcher. (Short Course Notes Ser.: No. 8). 127p. 1980. 9.00 (ISBN 0-918985-40-4); members 7.00. SEPM.

Principles & Applications of Digital Devices. J. A. Llewellyn & R. Gilbert. 1983. Student's Guide 180p. pap. text ed. 24.50x (ISBN 0-87664-683-6); Instr's. Guide. pap. text ed. 10.00x (ISBN 0-87664-684-4); Slides (set of 89) 260.00 (1686-OSL); Pencilbox. 140.00x (1686-OPB); PADD Components. 27.50x (1686-OCP); Classroom pkg. (10 student texts, 10 pencilboxes, 1 instr. guide, 10 wkbks., 10 components, set slide) 1850.00x (ISBN 0-87664-686-0); pap. text ed. 22.50x. Instru Soc.

Principles & Applications of Digital Devices. J. A. Llewllyn & R. Gilbert. 1983. pap. 22.50 student wkbk. (ISBN 0-87664-685-2). Instru Soc.

Principles & Applications of Digital Electronics. Larry D. Jones. 576p. 1985. text ed. write for info. (ISBN 0-02-361320-3); write for info. lab manual (ISBN 0-02-360750-5). Macmillan.

Principles & Applications of Electrochemistry. 2nd ed. D. R. Crow. LC 79-75. (Chemistry Textbook Ser.). 238p. 1979. pap. 14.95x (ISBN 0-412-16020-X, NO. 6071, Pub. by Chapman & Hall England). Routledge Chapman & Hall.

Principles & Applications of Electrochemistry. D. R. Crow. (Illus.). 260p. 1988. pap. text ed. 25.00 (ISBN 0-412-30270-5, Pub. by Chapman & Hall England). Routledge Chapman & Hall.

Principles & Applications of Ferroelectrics & Related Materials. Malcom E. Lines & Alastair M. Glass. (International Series of Monographs on Physics). (Illus.). 1977. 89.00x (ISBN 0-19-851286-4); pap. 35.00x (ISBN 0-19-852003-4). Oxford U Pr.

Principles & Applications of High Energy Ion Microbeams. Ed. by G. W. Grime & F. Watt. 432p. 1987. 99.00x (ISBN 0-85274-517-6, Pub. by A Hilger UK). Taylor & Francis.

Principles & Applications of Homogeneous Catalysis. Akira Nakamura & Minoru Tsutsui. LC 79-24754. 216p. 1980. 60.00 (ISBN 0-471-02869-X, Pub. by Wiley-Interscience). Krieger.

Principles & Applications of Hydrochemistry. Erik Eriksson. 200p. 1985. 39.95 (ISBN 0-412-25040-3, 9671). Routledge Chapman & Hall.

Principles & Applications of Medicolegal Alcohol Determination. E. M. Widmark. LC 81-66542. Orig. Title: Die Theoretische Grundlagen und die Praktische Verwendbarkeit der Gerichtlich-Medizinischen Alkoholbestimmung (1932) (Illus.). 200p. 1981. text ed. 37.00 (ISBN 0-931890-07-1, Biomed Pubns). PSG Pub Co.

Principles & Applications of Organotransition Metal Chemistry. 2nd ed. Collman et al. (Illus.). 989p. 1987. text ed. 48.00 (ISBN 0-935702-51-2). Univ Sci Bks.

Principles & Applications of Photochemistry. Richard P. Wayne. (Illus.). 280p. 1988. text ed. 49.95 (ISBN 0-19-855234-3); pap. text ed. 24.95 (ISBN 0-19-855233-5). Oxford U Pr.

Principles & Applications of Photogeology. Pandey. 300p. 1986. 29.95 (ISBN 0-470-20126-6). Halsted Pr.

Principles & Applications of Polarography & Other Electroanalytical Processes. George W. Milner. LC 57-3248. pap. 160.00 (ISBN 0-317-09850-0, 2004947). Bks Demand UMI.

Principles & Applications of Resonance Ionisation Spectroscopy. G. S. Hurst & M. G. Payne. 440p. 1988. 162.00x (ISBN 0-85274-460-9, A Hilger UK). Taylor & Francis.

Principles & Applications of Room Acoustics, Vols. 1 & 2. Ed. by L. Cremer et al. Tr. by T. J. Shultz. (Illus.). 1982. Vol. 1: Geometrical, Statistical & Psychological Room Acoustics. 120.75 (ISBN 0-85334-113-3, Pub. by Elsevier Applied Sci England); Vol. 2: Wave Theoretical Room Acoustics. 80.00 (ISBN 0-85334-114-1). Elsevier.

Principles & Applications of Soil Geography. E. M. Bridges. 312p. 1982. pap. 15.95 (ISBN 0-470-20429-X, Co-Pub. with Longman). Wiley.

Principles & Applications of Stirling Engines. Colin D. West. (Illus.). 256p. 1986. 39.95x (ISBN 0-442-29273-2). Van Nos Reinhold.

Principles & Art of Cure by Homoeopathy. 1942. 14.95x (ISBN 0-85032-049-6, Pub. by C. W. Daniels). Formur Intl.

Principles & Art of Cure by Homoeopathy. Herbert A. Roberts. 286p. 1942. 14.95x (ISBN 0-8464-1042-7). Beekman Pubs.

Principles & Art of Cure by Homoeopathy. Herbert A. Roberts. 1980. 23.75 (ISBN 0-85032-181-6, Pub. by Daniel Co England). State Mutual Bk.

Principles & Art of Plastic Surgery, 2 Vols. Harold Gillies & D. Ralph Millard, Jr. 690p. 1966. Vol. 1. 96.00 (ISBN 0-316-31376-9); Vol. 2. 96.00 (ISBN 0-316-31377-7). Little.

Principles & Cases of the Law of Arrest, Search, & Seizure. Thomas J. Gardner & Maurice Victor. (Illus.). 552p. 1973. pap. 39.95 (ISBN 0-07-022837-X). McGraw.

Principles & Development of Jewish Law. Mendell Lewittes. LC 87-11778. 298p. (Orig.). 19.95x (ISBN 0-8197-0512-8); pap. 12.95x (ISBN 0-8197-0506-3). Bloch.

Principles & Elements of Thought Construction, Artificial Intelligence & Cognitive Robotics. Charles M. Bowling. LC 87-73448. (Illus.). 152p. 1987. 29.95 (ISBN 0-945541-00-7). CSY Pub Inc.

Principles & Issues in Nutrition. Y H. Hui. LC 84-27051. (Nursing Ser.). 700p. 1985. text ed. 35.00 (ISBN 0-534-04374-7). Jones & Bartlett.

Principles & Labs for Physical Fitness & Wellness. Werner Hoeger. (Illus.). 338p. 1988. pap. text ed. 18.95x (ISBN 0-89582-180-X). Morton Pub.

Principles & Law of Sales Tax. S. D. Singh. 1200p. 1973. 210.00x (ISBN 0-317-57701-8, Pub. by Eastern Bk India). State Mutual Bk.

Principles & Management of Adrenal Cancer. Ed. by N. Javadpour. 195p. 1987. 100.00 (ISBN 0-387-16210-0). Springer-Verlag.

Principles & Management of Human Reproduction. Duncan E. Reid et al. LC 70-118593. (Illus.). Repr. of 1972 ed. 120.00 (2016678). Bks Demand UMI.

Principles & Management of Testicular Cancer. Ed. by Nasser Javadpour. (Illus.). 384p. 1985. 85.00 (ISBN 0-86577-194-4). Thieme Med Pubs.

Principles & Method in the Study of English Literature. William Macpherson. 1978. Repr. of 1908 ed. lib. bdg. 12.50 (ISBN 0-8495-3502-6). Arden Lib.

Principles & Methods. S. Mandelbrojt. LC 75-170339. (Dirichlet Ser.). 166p. 1972. 26.00 (ISBN 90-277-0214-4, Pub. by Reidel Holland). Kluwer Academic.

Principles & Methods for Determining Ecological Criteria on Hydrobiocenoses. Ed. by R. Amavis & Commission of the European Communities. LC 76-14624. 1976. pap. 120.00 (ISBN 0-08-021233-6). Pergamon.

Principles & Methods for Historical Linguistics. Robert J. Jeffers & Ilse Lehiste. 1979. pap. text ed. 9.95x (ISBN 0-262-60011-0). MIT Pr.

Principles & Methods for the Assessment of Neurotoxicity Associated with Exposure to Chemicals. (Environmental Health Criteria Ser.: No. 60). 180p. 1986. pap. 9.60 (ISBN 92-4-154260-8). World Health.

Principles & Methods in Receptor Binding. Ed. by F. Cattabeni & S. Nicosia. LC 83-277248. (NATO ASI Series A, Life Sicences: Vol. 72). 276p. 1984. 52.50x (ISBN 0-306-41613-1, Plenum Pr). Plenum Pub.

Principles & Methods of Adapted Physical Education & Recreation. Auxter & Pyfer. (Illus.). 544p. 1988. 27.95 (ISBN 0-8016-0380-3). Mosby.

Principles & Methods of Adapted Physical Education & Recreation. 5th ed. David Auxter & Jean Pyfer. 1985. 29.95 (ISBN 0-8016-0378-1). Mosby.

Principles & Methods of Contemporary Structural Linguistics. Ju. D. Apresjan. Tr. by Dina B. Crockett from Dutch. LC 72-94441. (Janua Linguarum, Ser. Minor: No. 144). (Illus.). 349p. (Orig.). 1973. pap. text ed. 26.00x (ISBN 90-2792-386-8). Mouton.

Principles & Methods of Musical Criticism. M. D. Calvocoressi. LC 79-9864. (Music Reprint Ser.). 1979. Repr. of 1931 ed. 29.50 (ISBN 0-306-79557-4). Da Capo.

Principles & Methods of Musical Criticism. Michel D. Calvocoressi. LC 78-66887. (Encore Music Editions Ser.). (Illus.). 1979. Repr. of 1931 ed. 19.25 (ISBN 0-88355-729-0). Hyperion Conn.

Principles & Methods of Pharmacy Management. 3rd ed. Harry A. Smith. LC 86-7304. (Illus.). 468p. 1986. text ed. 32.50 (ISBN 0-8121-1040-4). Lea & Febiger.

Principles & Methods of Reclamation Science with Case Studies from the Arid Southwest. Ed. by Charles C. Reith & Loren D. Potter. LC 85-24645. (Illus.). 243p. 1986. 30.00x (ISBN 0-8263-0830-9); pap. 17.50x (ISBN 0-8263-0831-7). U of NM Pr.

Principles & Methods of Scheduling Reservations. 2nd ed. David W. Howell. (Illus.). 296p. (Orig.). 1983. pap. text ed. 23.95x (ISBN 0-935920-56-0). Natl Pub Black Hills.

Principles & Methods of Social Psychology. 4th ed. Edwin P. Hollander. (Illus.). 1981. text ed. 26.95x (ISBN 0-19-502822-8); instr's. manual avail. Oxford U Pr.

Principles & Methods of Sterilization in Health Sciences. 2nd ed. John J. Perkins. (Illus.). 580p. 1983. 34.00 (ISBN 0-398-01478-7). C C Thomas.

Principles & Methods of Temperature Measurement. Thomas D. McGee. LC 87-22926. 525p. 1988. 54.95 (ISBN 0-471-62767-4). Wiley.

Principles & Methods of Toxicology. 2nd ed. Ed. by A. Wallace Hayes. (Illus.). 1988. text ed. price not set (ISBN 0-88167-439-7). Raven.

Principles & Models of Biological Transport. M. H. Friedman. (Illus.). 280p. 1986. 39.00 (ISBN 0-387-16370-0). Springer-Verlag.

Principles & Patterns of Public Speaking. Richard A. Katula. 392p. 1987. pap. text ed. write for info. (ISBN 0-534-07656-4). Wadsworth Pub.

Principles & Performance in Diesel Engineering. Ed. by S. D. Haddad & N. Watson. (Mechanical Engineering Ser.: 1-476). 360p. 1984. text ed. 71.95x (ISBN 0-470-20075-8). Halsted Pr.

Principles & Persons: An Ethical Interpretation of Existentialism. Frederick A. Olafson. LC 67-16038. 272p. 1967. 28.50x (ISBN 0-8018-0497-3); pap. 9.95x (ISBN 0-8018-1213-5). Johns Hopkins.

Principles & Perspective in Drug Bioavailability. J. Blanchard et al. 1978. 65.50 (ISBN 3-8055-2440-4). S Karger.

Principles & Practice of Accident Insurance. W. A. Dinsdale. 268p. 1975. 68.00x (ISBN 0-948691-06-9, Pub. by Witherby & Co England). State Mutual Bk.

Principles & Practice of Acute Cardiac Care. Das Gupta. 1984. 79.00 (ISBN 0-8151-2279-9). Year Bk Med.

Principles & Practice of Ambulatory Pediatrics. S. Rajkumar & C. Toback. 830p. 1988. 125.00x (ISBN 0-306-42500-9, Plenum Med Bk). Plenum Pub.

Principles & Practice of Aquaculture. Pillay. 1989. price not set (ISBN 0-471-61296-0). Wiley.

Principles & Practice of Automatic Process Control. Carlos A. Smith & Armando B. Corripio. LC 84-21982. 614p. 1985. write for info. (ISBN 0-471-88346-8). Wiley.

Principles & Practice of Blood-Gas Analysis. 2nd ed. A. P. Adams & C. E. Hahn. LC 81-21709. (Illus.). 101p. 1982. pap. text ed. 36.00 (ISBN 0-443-02521-5). Churchill.

Principles & Practice of Child Psychiatry. 2nd ed. Stella Chess & Mahin Hassibi. 550p. 1986. 35.00x (ISBN 0-306-42167-4, Plenum Pr). Plenum Pub.

Principles & Practice of Clinical Cardiology. 2nd ed. Arthur Selzer. (Illus.). 588p. 1983. 46.95 (ISBN 0-7216-8064-X). Saunders.

Principles & Practice of Criticism: Hamlet, the Merry Wives, Othello. Allan H. Gilbert. LC 77-168145. Repr. of 1959 ed. 15.00 (ISBN 0-404-02758-X). AMS Pr.

Principles & Practice of Database Systems. S. M. Deem. (Computer Science Ser.). (Illus.). 404p. (Orig.). 1985. text ed. 42.50x (ISBN 0-333-37099-6, Pub. by Macmillan England); pap. text ed. 28.50x (ISBN 0-333-37100-3, Pub. by Macmillan England). Scholium Intl.

Principles & Practice of Dermatology. 2nd ed. W. E. Delauney & W. A. Land. 1984. text ed. 45.00 (ISBN 0-409-49331-7). Butterworth.

Principles & Practice of Electron Microscopy. Ian M. Watt. (Illus.). 250p. 1985. 52.50 (ISBN 0-521-25557-0). Cambridge U Pr.

Principles & Practice of Electron Microscope Operation. A. W. Agar et al. (Practical Methods in Electron Microscopy: Vol. 2). 1974. 76.50 (ISBN 0-7204-4254-0, Biomedical Pr); pap. 31.25 (ISBN 0-7204-4255-9). Elsevier.

Principles & Practice of Emergency Medicine, 2 vols. 2nd ed. George R. Schwartz et al. (Illus.). 1179p. 1986. Set. 125.00 (ISBN 0-03-013544-3); Vol. 1. 70.00 (ISBN 0-7216-8027-5); Vol. 2. 65.00 (ISBN 0-7216-8028-3). Saunders.

Principles & Practice of Emergency Medicine: The Essential Update. Schwartz. 250p. Date not set. price not set (ISBN 0-7216-2459-6). Saunders.

Principles & Practice of Endocrinology & Metabolism. Ed. by Kenneth L. Becker et al. LC 65-9236. (Illus.). 1500p. 1989. price not set (ISBN 0-397-50759-3, Lippincott Medical). Lippincott.

Principles & Practice of Export Marketing. E. P. Hibbert. (Illus.). 352p. 1985. pap. 30.95 (ISBN 0-434-90746-4, Pub. by W Heinemann Ltd). David & Charles.

Principles & Practice of Foot Roentgenology. Frank Weinstein. LC 73-11606. (Illus.). 300p. 1974. 32.50. Green.

Principles & Practice of Freedom of Speech. 2nd ed. Haig A. Bosmajian. LC 82-23739. 424p. 1983. pap. text ed. 18.75 (ISBN 0-8191-2962-3). U Pr of Amer.

Principles & Practice of Gynecologic Laser Surgery. Joseph H. Bellina & Gaetano Bandieramonte. LC 84-3434. 308p. 1984. 45.00x (ISBN 0-306-41543-7, Plenum Pr). Plenum Pub.

Principles & Practice of Health Visiting. R. Hale et al. 1968. text ed. 18.25 (ISBN 0-08-012700-2). Pergamon.

Principles & Practice of Hormone Therapy in Gynaecology & Obstetrics. Joachim Ufer. 1969. 29.00 (ISBN 3-11-000614-6). De Gruyter.

Principles & Practice of Human Physiology. Ed. by Otto Edholm & Joe Weiner. LC 80-40831. 1981. 74.50 (ISBN 0-12-231650-9). Acad Pr.

Principles & Practice of Impedance. 2nd ed. Rufus P. Turner & Stan Gibilisco. (Illus.). 224p. 1987. 21.95 (ISBN 0-8306-0725-0); pap. 14.95 (ISBN 0-8306-2725-1, NO. 2725). TAB Bks.

Principles & Practice of Indigenous Church Planting. Charles Brock. 1981. pap. 4.25 (ISBN 0-8054-6328-3). Broadman.

Principles & Practice of Information Theory. Richard E. Blahut. (Electrical & Computer Engineering Ser.). (Illus.). 448p. 1987. text ed. 48.50 (ISBN 0-201-10709-0). Addison-Wesley.

Principles & Practice of Interruption Insurance. G. J. Hickmott. 934p. 1981. 315.00 (ISBN 0-900886-56-0, Pub. By Witherby & Co England). State Mutual Bk.

Principles & Practice of Intravenous Therapy. 4th ed. Ada L. Plumer. 1987. pap. text ed. write for info. (ISBN 0-673-39403-4). Scott F.

Principles & Practice of Laser-Doppler Anemometry. 2nd ed. F. Durst et al. 1981. 88.00 (ISBN 0-12-225260-8). Acad Pr.

Principles & Practice of Laser Technology. Hrand M. Muncheryan. (Illus.). 294p. 1983. pap. 14.95 (ISBN 0-8306-1529-6, 1529). TAB Bks.

Principles & Values for College & University Administration. Earl V. Pullias & Leslie Wilbur. LC 84-4259. 103p. 1984. 10.00 (ISBN 0-8022-2443-1). Philos Lib.

Principles & Values in School & Society. James J. Jelinek. LC 74-156779. 1978. 15.00 (ISBN 0-931702-28-3). Far Western Phil.

Principles at Issue. Ed. by Americans for Due Process Staff. 40p. (Orig.). 1988. pap. 5.00 (ISBN 0-9617222-2-3). Amer Due Process.

Principles, Dialogues & Philosophical Correspondence. George Berkeley. Tr. by Colin M. Turbayne. LC 64-66065. 1965. pap. write for info. (ISBN 0-02-421600-3, LLA208). Macmillan.

Principles for a Catholic Morality. Timothy E. O'Connell. 1978. (HarpR); pap. 9.95 (ISBN 0-86683-885-6). Har-Row.

Principles for an Income Security System. John Palmer. 80p. 5.00 (ISBN 0-317-35046-3, 5813). Natl Conf Soc Welfare.

Principles for Developing Coastal Water Quality Criteria. (GESAMP Reports & Studies: No. 5). (Illus.). 23p. 1976. pap. 7.50 (ISBN 92-5-100078-6, F1072, FAO). UNIPUB.

Principles for Electric Power Policy. Technology Futures, Inc. Staff & Scientific Foresight, Inc. Staff. LC 84-4692. (Illus.). xx, 448p. 1984. lib. bdg. 50.95 (ISBN 0-89930-095-2, FRK/, Quorum). Greenwood.

Principles for Establishing Intervention Levels for the Protection of the Event of a Nuclear Accident or Radiological Emergency. (Safety Ser.: No. 72). 35p. 1986. pap. text ed. 9.00 (ISBN 92-0-623085-9, ISP708, IAEA). UNIPUB.

Principles for Evaluating Health Risks from Chemicals During Infancy & Early Childhood: The Need for a Special Approach. (Environmental Health Criteria Ser.: No. 59). 73p. 1986. pap. 5.40 (ISBN 92-4-154259-4). World Health.

Principles for Limiting Exposure of the Public to Natural Sources of Radiation. Ed. by F. D. Sowby. (ICRP Publication Ser.: No. 39). 20p. 1984. pap. 18.75 (ISBN 0-08-031503-8). Pergamon.

Principles for Limiting Release of Radioactive Effluents into the Environment. (IAEA Safety Guides, Safety Ser.: No. 77). (Illus.). 32p. (Orig.). 1986. pap. text ed. 13.50 (ISBN 92-0-123486-4, ISP728, IAEA). UNIPUB.

Principles for Principals. rev. ed. M. A. Nottingham. 220p. 1984. lib. bdg. 27.50 (ISBN 0-8191-3570-4); pap. text ed. 13.25 (ISBN 0-8191-3571-2). U Pr of Amer.

Principles for the Clinical Evaluation of Drugs: Report. WHO Scientific Group. Geneva, 1967. (Technical Report Ser.: No. 403). (Also avail. in French, Russian & Spanish). 1968. pap. 2.00 (ISBN 92-4-120403-6). World Health.

Principles for the Safety Assessment of Food Additives & Contaminants. (Environmental Health Criteria Ser.: No. 70). 174p. 1987. pap. 8.40 (ISBN 92-4-154270-5). World Health.

Principles for the Testing & Evaluation of Drugs for Carcinogenicity: Report. WHO Scientific Group. Geneva, 1968. (Technical Report Ser.: No. 426). (Also avail. in French & Spanish). 1969. pap. 1.20 (ISBN 92-4-120426-5). World Health.

Principles Fundamentaux de la Vie Chretienne. James A. Berg. (Fr.). 1987. pap. write for info. (ISBN 0-89084-393-7). Bob Jones Univ Pr.

Principles, Guidelines & Guarantees for the Protection of Persons Detained on Grounds of Mental Ill-Health or Suffering from Mental Disorder. 38p. 1986. 7.00 (ISBN 92-1-154056-9, E.85.XIV.9). UN.

Principles in General Pharmacology. R. J. Tallarida et al. (Pharmacologic Science Ser.). (Illus.). 250p. 1988. 69.00. Springer-Verlag.

Principles of Abnormal Psychology. Harry Munsinger. 672p. 1983. text ed. write for info. (ISBN 0-02-384870-7). Macmillan.

Principles of Accounting. K. A. Abdullah et al. 600p. (Arabic.). 1984. pap. 16.00 (ISBN 0-471-87222-9). Wiley.

Principles of Accounting. 4th ed. James J. Benjamin et al. LC 83-70550. 1007p. 1988. 38.95x (ISBN 0-87393-077-0); study guide 12.95x (ISBN 0-87393-078-9); Vol. I. working papers 9.95x; Vol. II. working papers 9.95x. Dame Pubns.

Principles of Accounting. John Cerepak & Donald H. Taylor. (Illus.). 1100p. 1987. text ed. 29.95 (ISBN 0-13-700956-9); By Hussein D. Emin. write for info. practice set one (ISBN 0-13-708520-6); write for info. practice set two (ISBN 0-13-708686-5). P-H.

Principles of Accounting. rev. ed. Thomas P. Edmonds et al. LC 83-72201. 1034p. 1987. 39.95x (ISBN 0-87393-043-6); study guide 11.95x (ISBN 0-87393-069-X); working papers, Vols. I & II 9.95x (ISBN 0-87393-068-1). Dame Pubns.

Principles of Accounting. 3rd ed. Helmkamp et al. 1989. price not set (ISBN 0-471-61245-6); College Hills Cycle Shop, Practice Set 1B. practice set avail. (ISBN 0-471-61952-3). Wiley.

Principles of Accounting. John G. Helmkamp et al. Incl. Workpapers I. 482p. pap. text ed. 13.45 (ISBN 0-471-86290-8); Principles of Accounting. Workpapers II: Active Entry. John G. Helmkamp et al. 482p. 1983. pap. text ed. 15.00 (ISBN 0-471-86288-6); Principles of Accounting: Practice Set 1A. 2nd ed. 72p. 1983. pap. text ed. 13.45 (ISBN 0-471-86292-4); Practice Set 1B. 136p. pap. text ed. 14.00 (ISBN 0-471-89353-6); Practice Set 2. 91p. pap. text ed. 13.45 (ISBN 0-471-86293-2); Practice Set 3. 30p. pap. text ed. 12.45 (ISBN 0-471-86294-0). LC 82-20124. 1150p. 1983. transparencies 483p. avail. (ISBN 0-471-86295-9); problem book 16.45 (ISBN 0-471-87859-6). Wiley.

Principles of Accounting. 2nd ed. John G. Helmkamp et al. LC 85-26357. 1264p. 1986. write for info. (ISBN 0-471-82018-0); Practice Set 1A. write for info (ISBN 0-471-84805-0); Working Papers 1. write for info. (ISBN 0-471-84014-9); Working Papers 1. write for info. (ISBN 0-471-84016-5); study guide 1 avail. (ISBN 0-471-83462-9); study guide 2 avail. (ISBN 0-471-83463-7); Practice Set 1B. write for info. (ISBN 0-471-84806-9); Practice Set 2B. write for info.; Practice Set III. write for info. (ISBN 0-471-00897-4). Wiley.

Principles of Accounting. 3rd ed. Belverd E. Needles et al. LC 86-80401. 1058p. 1987. text ed. 47.16; instr's. handbk. 5.96 (ISBN 0-395-42556-5); solutions manual 7.96 (ISBN 0-395-42555-7); study guide & select readings 17.56 (ISBN 0-395-42557-3); Achievement Tests A 9.56 (ISBN 0-395-42567-0); Achievement Tests B 9.56 (ISBN 0-395-42568-9); instr's manual 2.36 (ISBN 0-395-43145-X); Demonstrations problems bk. 14.36 (ISBN 0-395-43144-1); blank working papers, 159.96 ea., boxed transparencies (Chaps. 1-14), boxed transparencies (Chaps. 15-28) 17.56, 266.76 teaching transparencies, test bank, working papers 1A, working papers 1B, 17.56 ea., working papers 2A, working papers 2B. HM.

Principles of Accounting. 2nd ed. Loren A. Nikolai et al. 1240p. (gr. 11-12). 1986. text ed. 33.50 (ISBN 0-534-05124-3). PWS Kent Pub.

Principles of Accounting. William A. Paton & Russell A. Stevenson. LC 75-18479. (History of Accounting Ser.). 1976. Repr. 15.00x (ISBN 0-405-07561-8). Ayer Co Pubs.

Principles of Accounting. William A. Paton & Russell A. Stevenson. Ed. by Richard P. Brief. LC 77-87284. (Contemporary Accounting Thought Ser.). 1978. Repr. of 1918 ed. lib. bdg. 54.00x (ISBN 0-405-10912-1). Ayer Co Pubs.

Principles of Accounting. 3rd ed. Isaac N. Reynolds et al. 1056p. 1984. text ed. 33.95x (ISBN 0-03-063313-3); study guide 10.95x (ISBN 0-03-063321-4); instr.'s manual 19.95 (ISBN 0-03-063314-1); Working Papers I 12.95x (ISBN 0-03-063328-1); Working Papers II 12.95x (ISBN 0-03-063329-X); Practice Set A 13.95x (ISBN 0-03-063316-8); Practice Set B 13.95x (ISBN 0-03-063318-4); Practice Set C 13.95x (ISBN 0-03-063319-2); solutions manual 11.95 (ISBN 0-03-063322-2). Dryden Pr.

Principles of Accounting. Jack Topiol. 1976. pap. 8.95 working papers (ISBN 0-7216-8873-X). HR&W.

Principles of Accounting. William Ventolo & Sidney Davidson. 350p. (gr. 12). 1984. pap. text ed. 14.95 (ISBN 0-915777-00-2). Perf Progs TX.

Principles of Accounting. William L. Ventolo, Jr. Ed. by Sidney Davidson. (Illus.). 350p. (gr. 12). 1984. text ed. 19.95 (ISBN 0-686-28726-6). Perf Progs TX.

Principles of Accounting. 4th ed. Paul H. Walgenbach et al. 1146p. 1986. text ed. 34.95 (ISBN 0-15-571375-2); tchr's. ed. 11.50 (ISBN 0-15-571377-9); study guide 12.95 (ISBN 0-15-571376-0); working papers (I) 13.95 (ISBN 0-15-571379-5); working papers (II) 13.95 (ISBN 0-15-571380-9); solutions manual 23.00; teaching transparencies 40.00 (ISBN 0-15-571388-4); Practice Set C 6.95 (ISBN 0-15-571384-1); solutions manual transparencies 225.00 (ISBN 0-15-571389-2). HarBraceJ.

Principles of Accounting. 2nd ed. Rufus Wixon & Robert G. Cox. LC 69-14676. Repr. of 1969 ed. 120.00 (ISBN 0-8357-9959-X, 2055141). Bks Demand UMI.

Principles of Accounting I. Terry Campbell et al. LC 85-7657. 330p. 1988. pap. 10.95 (ISBN 0-15-600028-8, BFP). HarBraceJ.

Principles of Accounting I. Richard D. Mott. (The Academe Collections). 142p. 1987. 7.95 (ISBN 0-944554-00-8). Educ Images.

Principles of Accounting II. Mary A. Emery. 277p. 1988. pap. 10.95 (ISBN 0-15-600029-6, BFP). HarBraceJ.

Principles of Accounting: Practice Set II Runner's Shoe Corporation. Jim M. Weglin. 112p. 1985. pap. text ed. write for info. student manual (ISBN 0-201-11385-6). Addison-Wesley.

Principles of Accounting: Practice Set II Runners Shoe Corporation. Jim M. Weglin. 80p. 1985. write for info. solutions manual (ISBN 0-201-11429-1). Addison-Wesley.

Principles of Accounting: Practice Set 1A see Principles of Accounting.

Principles of Accounting: Practices Sets I-III. Kell et al. Date not set. Practice Set IA. pap. price not set (ISBN 0-471-82447-X); Practice Set IB. pap. price not set (ISBN 0-471-82445-3); Practice Set II. pap. price not set (ISBN 0-471-82446-1); Practice Set III. pap. price not set (ISBN 0-471-82444-5); Practice Set 2B. pap. 12.95 (ISBN 0-471-00896-6). Wiley.

Principles of Accounting. Workpapers II: Active Entry see Principles of Accounting.

Principles of Accounts. 7th ed. E. F. Castle & N. P. Owens. 401p. 1984. pap. text ed. 26.50x (ISBN 0-7121-1769-5). Trans-Atl Phila.

Principles of Acoustic Devices. Velimir M. Ristic. LC 82-20278. 359p. 1983. 51.95 (ISBN 0-471-09153-7). Wiley.

Principles of Active Network Synthesis & Design. Gobind Daryanani. LC 76-20659. 495p. 1976. write for info. (ISBN 0-471-19545-6). Wiley.

Principles of Administration Applied to Nursing Service. H. A. Goddard. (Monograph Ser.: No. 41). (Also avail. in French & Spanish). 1958. 4.80 (ISBN 92-4-140041-2). World Health.

Principles of Adolescent Medicine. Irwin. Date not set. price not set (ISBN 0-444-00863-2). Elsevier.

Principles of Adsorption & Adsorption Processes. D. M. Ruthven. LC 83-16904. 433p. 1984. 58.00x (ISBN 0-471-86606-7, Pub. by Wiley-Interscience). Wiley.

Principles of Adsorption Chromatography: The Separation of Nonionic Organic Compounds. Lloyd R. Snyder. LC 68-17426. (Chromatographic Science: Vol. 3). (Illus.). pap. 107.30 (ISBN 0-317-08018-0, 2017858). Bks Demand UMI.

Principles of Advanced Mathematical Physics, Vol. II. R. D. Richtmyer. (Texts & Monographs in Physics Ser.). (Illus.). 350p. 1981. 42.00 (ISBN 0-387-10772-X). Springer Verlag.

Principles of Advanced Mathematical Physics: Vol. 1. R. D. Richtmyer. (Texts & Monographs in Physics Ser.). (Illus.). 1978. 36.00 (ISBN 0-387-08873-3). Springer-Verlag.

Principles of Advertising. Daniel Starch. LC 84-46041. 1005p. 1985. lib. bdg. 100.00 (ISBN 0-8240-6735-5). Garland Pub.

Principles of Aeroelasticity. 2nd ed. Raymond L. Bisplinghoff & Holt Ashley. LC 74-20442. (Illus.). 527p. 1975. Repr. of 1962 ed. 10.00 (ISBN 0-486-61349-6). Dover.

Principles of Agribusiness Management. J. Beierlein et al. 1986. 32.00 (ISBN 0-8359-5599-0, Reston). P-H.

Principles of Agricultural Economics: Markets & Prices in Less Developed Countries. David Caman & Trevor Young. (Wye Studies in Agricultural & Rural Development). (Illus.). 300p. Date not set. price not set (ISBN 0-521-33430-6); pap. price not set (ISBN 0-521-33664-3). Cambridge U Pr.

Principles of Air Conditioning. 3rd ed. V. Paul Lang. LC 77-78900. (Air Conditioning, Refrigeration Ser.). 1979. instr.'s. guide 5.00 (ISBN 0-8273-1002-1). Delmar.

Principles of Air Conditioning. 4th ed. V. Paul Lang. LC 86-32988. 384p. 1987. pap. text ed. 21.95 (ISBN 0-8273-2759-5); instr's guide 6.00 (ISBN 0-8273-2760-9). Delmar.

Principles of Algebraic Geometry. Phillip Griffiths & Joseph Harris. LC 78-6993. (Pure & Applied Mathematics Ser.). 813p. 1978. 71.95x (ISBN 0-471-32792-1, Pub. by Wiley-Interscience). Wiley.

Principles of Ambulatory Medicine. 2nd ed. Barker et al. (Illus.). 1512p. 1986. 89.95 (ISBN 0-683-00436-0). Williams & Wilkins.

Principles of American Government. 10th ed. Albert B. Saye & John F. Allums. (Illus.). 400p. 1986. pap. text ed. write for info. (ISBN 0-13-701178-4). P-H.

Principles of American Government: A PSI Handbook. Theodore T. Hindson et al. 111p. 1978. pap. text ed. 3.95x (ISBN 0-89641-006-4). American Pr.

Principles of American Nuclear Chemistry: A Novel. Thomas McMahon. 224p. 1981. pap. 2.95 (ISBN 0-380-54122-X, 54122-X, Bard). Avon.

Principles of American Prosperity. Leighton A. Wilkie & Richard S. Rimanoczy. LC 75-5394. 256p. 1975. 10.00 (ISBN 0-8159-6512-5). Devin.

Principles of American Prosperity. Leighton A. Wilkie & Richard S. Rimanoczy. LC 81-66941. 100p. 1981. pap. 3.95 (ISBN 0-933028-18-0). Fisher Inst.

Principles of Analytical Electron Microscopy. Ed. by David C. Joy et al. 464p. 1986. 35.00x (ISBN 0-306-42387-1, Plenum Pr.). Plenum Pub.

Principles of Anatomy & Physiology. 5th ed. Gerard J. Tortora & Nicholas P. Anagnostakos. 764p. 1986. text ed. 48.95 scp (ISBN 0-06-046669-3, HarpC). Har-Row.

Principles of Anesthesiology. 3rd ed. Vincent J. Collins. (Illus.). 1850p. 1989. pap. text ed. price not set. Lea & Febiger.

Principles of Animal Agriculture. Charles E. Stufflebeam. (Illus.). 464p. 1983. 34.00 (ISBN 0-13-700948-8). P-H.

Principles of Animal Extrapolation. Edward J. Calabrese. LC 82-10972. (Environmental Science & Technology Ser.). 603p. 1983. 85.00 (ISBN 0-471-08762-9). Wiley.

Principles of Animal Learning & Motivation. Roger M. Tarpy. 1982. pap. text ed. write for info. (ISBN 0-673-15383-5). Scott F.

Principles of Animal Taxonomy. George G. Simpson. LC 60-13939. (Columbia Biological Ser.: No. 20). (Illus.). 1961. 40.00x (ISBN 0-231-02427-4). Columbia U Pr.

Principles of Antenna Theory. Kai Fong Lee. LC 83-7042. 324p. 1984. cloth 42.95X (ISBN 0-471-90167-9, Pub. by Wiley-Interscience). Wiley.

Principles of Antennas: Wire & Aperture. T. S. Maclean. (Illus.). 275p. 1986. 80.00 (ISBN 0-521-30668-X). Cambridge U Pr.

Principles of Anthropology & Sociology in Their Relations to Criminal Procedure. Maurice Parmelee. viii, 410p. 1980. Repr. of 1908 ed. 30.00x (ISBN 0-8377-1004-9). Rothman.

Principles of Aperture & Array System Design: Including Random & Adaptive Arrays. Bernard D. Steinberg. LC 75-30847. 356p. 1976. 53.95x (ISBN 0-471-82102-0, Pub. by Wiley-Interscience). Wiley.

Principles of Applied Biomedical Instrumentation. 2nd ed. L. A. Geddes & L. E. Baker. LC 74-34390. (Biomedical Engineering & Health Systems Ser.). 616p. 1975. 47.95x (ISBN 0-471-29496-9, Pub. by Wiley-Interscience). Wiley.

Principles of Applied Biomedical Instrumentation. 3rd ed. L. A. Geddes & L. E. Baker. 992p. 1988. price not set (ISBN 0-471-60899-8). Wiley.

Principles of Applied Clinical Chemistry: Chemical Background & Medical Applications, 2 vols. Ed. by Samuel Natelson & Ethan A. Natelson. Incl. Vol. 1, Maintenance of Fluid & Electrolyte Balance. 394p. 1975. 55.00x (ISBN 0-306-35231-1); Vol. 2, The Erythrocyte Chemical Composition, Normal & Aberrant Metabolism. 584p. 1978. 79.50x (ISBN 0-306-35232-X). LC 75-4798. (Illus., Plenum Pr). Plenum Pub.

Principles of Applied Clinical Chemistry, Vol. 3: Plasma Protein. Samuel Natelson & Ethan A. Natelson. (Illus.). 576p. 1980. 79.50x (ISBN 0-306-40276-9, Plenum Pr). Plenum Pub.

Principles of Applied Geophysics. 3rd ed. D. S. Parasnis. 1979. 32.00 (ISBN 0-412-15140-5, NO. 6304, Pub. by Chapman & Hall); pap. 15.95x (ISBN 0-412-15810-8, NO. 6387). Routledge Chapman & Hall.

Principles of Applied Geophysics. D. S. Parasnis. 450p. 1986. text ed. 69.95 (ISBN 0-412-28320-4, 9937, Pub. by Chapman & Hall England); pap. text ed. 29.95 (ISBN 0-412-28330-1, 9947, Pub. by Chapman & Hall England). Routledge Chapman & Hall.

Principles of Applied Mathematics. James Keener. 608p. 1988. 48.50 (ISBN 0-201-15674-1). Addison-Wesley.

Principles of Applied Statistics. Myron Melnyk. LC 73-7943. 1974. 36.00 (ISBN 0-08-017108-7). Pergamon.

Principles of Aquatic Chemistry. Francois M. Morel. 446p. 1983. 57.95x (ISBN 0-471-08683-5). Wiley.

Principles of Arable Crop Production. F. Harper. 352p. 1983. pap. 22.50x (ISBN 0-246-11741-9, Pub. by Granada England). Sheridan.

Principles of Archaeological Stratigraphy. Edward Harris. LC 79-41368. (Studies in Archaeological Science Ser.). 1980. 33.00 (ISBN 0-12-326650-5). Acad Pr.

Principles of Architectural History. Paul Frankl. Tr. by James F. O'Gorman. LC 68-18236. 1968. pap. 10.95x (ISBN 0-262-56013-5). MIT Pr.

Principles of Arithmeticke. Bernard Salignacus. Tr. by W. Bedwell. LC 70-26250. (English Experience Ser.: No. 130). 134p. 1969. Repr. of 1616 ed. 25.00 (ISBN 90-221-0130-4). Walter J Johnson.

Principles of Art. Robin G. Collingwood. 1958. pap. 9.95 (ISBN 0-19-500209-1). Oxford U Pr.

Principles of Art As Illustrated in the Ruskin Museum. William White. LC 78-16532. 1978. Repr. of 1895 ed. lib. bdg. 65.00 (ISBN 0-89341-355-0). Longwood Pub Group.

Principles of Art History: The Problem of the Development of Style in Later Art. Heinrich Wolfflin. (Illus.). pap. 5.95 (ISBN 0-486-20276-3). Dover.

Principles of Art History: The Problem of the Development of Style in Later Art. Heinrich Wolfflin. (Illus.). 14.75 (ISBN 0-8446-3205-8). Peter Smith.

Principles of Artificial Intelligence. Nils J. Nilsson. LC 86-2815. (Illus.). 476p. 1986. Repr. of 1980 ed. text ed. 34.95 (ISBN 0-934613-10-9). Morgan Kaufmann.

Principles of Aseptic Processing & Packaging. Philip E. Nelson et al. 120p. (Orig.). Date not set. pap. 60.00 (ISBN 0-937774-17-0). Food Processors.

Principles of Assembler Language Programming for the IBM 370. S. D. Stoddard. 656p. 1985. text ed. 37.95 (ISBN 0-07-061561-6). McGraw.

Principles of Association Management. rev. ed. Ed. by Henry Ernsthal & Vivian Jefferson. 256p. 1988. pap. text ed. 30.00 (ISBN 0-88034-008-8). Am Soc Assn Execs.

Principles of Association Management. 446p. (Orig.). 1975. pap. text ed. 30.00 (ISBN 0-88034-003-7). Am Soc Assn Execs.

Principles of Astrology. Charles E. Carter. LC 79-154829. 5.75 (ISBN 0-8356-0423-3, Quest). Theos Pub Hse.

TITLE INDEX PRINCIPLES OF CONTINUOUS SYSTEM

Principles of Astronomy. 3rd ed. Stanley P. Wyatt. 1977. text ed. 34.00 (ISBN 0-205-05679-2, 7356794); answer book avail. (ISBN 0-205-05680-6). Allyn.

Principles of Audiology: A Study Guide. Frederick Martin. LC 83-22477. (Illus.). 240p. 1984. pap. text ed. 17.00x (ISBN 0-8391-1873-2, 1312). Pro Ed.

Principles of Auditing. 21st ed. Leslie R. Howard. 407p. 1983. pap. text ed. 26.60x (ISBN 0-7121-1762-8). Trans-Atl Phila.

Principles of Auditing. 9th ed. Meigs et al. 1988. 42.95 (ISBN 0-256-06803-8). Irwin.

Principles of Auditing. 8th ed. Walter B. Meigs et al. 1985. 41.95x (ISBN 0-256-03176-2); study guide 13.95 (ISBN 0-256-03294-7). Irwin.

Principles of Auditing. F. R. Paula. LC 82-48360. (Accounting History & the Development of a Profession Ser.). 222p. 1984. lib. bdg. 30.00 (ISBN 0-8240-6322-8). Garland Pub.

Principles of Auto Body Repairing & Repainting. 4th ed. Andre G. Deroche & N. N. Hildebrand. (Illus.). 752p. 1987. text ed. 32.00 (ISBN 0-13-708173-1). P-H.

Principles of Automated Drafting. Daniel L. Ryan. (Mechanical Engineering Ser.: Vol. 28). (Illus.). 336p. 1984. 35.00 (ISBN 0-8247-7175-3). Dekker.

Principles of Automatic Process Control. rev. ed. (Illus.). 48p. pap. text ed. 8.00x (ISBN 0-87664-108-7). Instru Soc.

Principles of Automatic Transmissions. rev. & enl. ed. Jay Webster. LC 79-51618. (Illus.). 1980. pap. 6.95x (ISBN 0-911168-43-5). Prakken.

Principles of Banking. 3rd ed. Eric N. Compton. (Illus.). 385p. 1988. text ed. 33.00 (ISBN 0-89982-353-X). Am Bankers.

Principles of Behavior Therapy. G. Terence Wilson & K. Daniel O'Leary. (Social Learning Theory Ser.). (Illus.). 1980. text ed. write for info. (ISBN 0-13-701102-4). P-H.

Principles of Behavioral Neurology. Ed. by M-Marsel Mesulam. LC 84-28650. (Contemporary Neurology Ser.: Vol. 26). (Illus.). 405p. 1985. text ed. 62.00 (ISBN 0-8036-6151-7); Set of 5 booklets (Tests of Directed Attention & Memory for Principles of Behavioral Neurology) 10.00 (ISBN 0-8036-6152-5). Davis Co.

Principles of Benthic Marine Paleo-Ecology. Arthur Boucot. LC 79-8535. 1981. 49.95 (ISBN 0-12-118980-5). Acad Pr.

Principles of Biblical Hermeneutics. J. Edwin Hartill. 15.95 (ISBN 0-310-25900-2, 9774). Zondervan.

Principles of Biblical Interpretations in the Lutheran Confessions. rev. ed. Ralph A. Bohlmann. 192p. 1983. pap. 8.95 (ISBN 0-570-03910-X, 12-2991). Concordia.

Principles of Biblical Interpretation. Louis Berkhof. 1950. 9.95 (ISBN 0-8010-0549-3). Baker Bk.

Principles of Biochemical Toxicology. J. A. Timbrell. 240p. 1985. 55.00x (ISBN 0-85066-221-4); pap. text ed. 21.00x (ISBN 0-85066-319-9). Taylor & Francis.

Principles of Biochemistry. Albert L. Lehninger. (Illus.). 1011p. 1982. text ed. 42.95x (ISBN 0-87901-136-X); By Paul van Eikeren 544pp, 1984. guide & solutions manual 18.95x (ISBN 0-87901-178-5). Worth.

Principles of Biochemistry. 7th ed. Emil L. Smith & Robert L. Hill. Incl. General Aspects. 912p. 1983. text ed. 36.00 (ISBN 0-07-069762-0); Mammalian Biochemistry. 752p. 1982. text ed. 42.00 (ISBN 0-07-069763-9). (Illus.). 1983. McGraw.

Principles of Biography. Sidney Lee. LC 72-18678. 1973. lib. bdg. 17.00 (ISBN 0-8414-0356-2). Folcroft.

Principles of Bioinstrumentation. Richard A. Normann. 350p. 1988. write for info. (ISBN 0-471-60514-X). Wiley.

Principles of Biological Autonomy. F. J. Varela. (North Holland Ser. in General Systems Research: Vol. 2). 336p. 1979. 66.25 (ISBN 0-444-00321-5, North Holland). Elsevier.

Principles of Biological Chemistry. 2nd ed. David S. Page. LC 80-39968. 454p. 1981. text ed. 25.00 pub net (ISBN 0-87150-740-4, 31N4311); pub net study guide 7.75 (ISBN 0-87150-746-3, 31N4316). Brooks-Cole.

Principles of Biological Regulation: An Introduction to Feedback Systems. Richard W. Jones. 1973. 39.95 (ISBN 0-12-389950-8). Acad Pr.

Principles of Biology Laboratory Investigations & Lecture Supplements. John W. Thornton et al. 144p. 1984. pap. text ed. 9.95 (ISBN 0-8403-4073-7). Kendall-Hunt.

Principles of Biology: Laboratory Investigations. 3rd ed. Virginia G. Latta et al. (Illus.). 1982. lab manual 8.95x (ISBN 0-89459-177-0). Hunter Textbks.

Principles of Biology: Laboratory Investigations. 4th ed. Ed. by Virginia G. Latta et al. 1984. 9.95 (ISBN 0-88725-019-X). Hunter Textbks.

Principles of Biology Laboratory Manual. Laraine Unbehaun et al. 222p. (Orig.). 1980. pap. text ed. write for info. (ISBN 0-8087-2115-1). Burgess MN Intl.

Principles of Biomedical Ethics. 2nd ed. Tom L. Beauchamp & James F. Childress. 1983. 29.95x (ISBN 0-19-503285-3); pap. 16.95x (ISBN 0-19-503286-1). Oxford U Pr.

Principles of Biopsy: A Self-Instructional Guide, Bk. 8. 3rd, rev. ed. Thomas H. Morton, Jr. et al. (Illus.). 94p. 1983. pap. 14.95x (ISBN 0-89939-081-1). Stoma Pr.

Principles of Biosystematics. 2nd ed. Thomas R. Mertens & Judy L. Lines. (Programmed Biology Studies). (Illus.). 1978. pap. text ed. 6.95 (ISBN 0-88462-038-7, 3304-34, Ed Methods). Longman Finan.

Principles of Biotechnology. Ed. by A. Wiseman. (Illus.). 288p. 1988. pap. text ed. 47.50 (ISBN 0-412-01791-1, Pub. by Chapman & Hall England). Routledge Chapman & Hall.

Principles of Biotechnology. Ed. by Alan Wiseman. 192p. 1983. pap. 23.95 (ISBN 0-412-00261-2, NO. 5029). Routledge Chapman & Hall.

Principles of Black Political Economy. Lloyd Hogan. 224p. 1984. 19.95X (ISBN 0-7102-0177-X); pap. 8.95x (ISBN 0-7102-0241-5). Routledge Chapman & Hall.

Principles of Buddhist Psychology. David J. Kalupahana. LC 86-14583. (Buddhist Studies). 236p. 1987. 49.50 (ISBN 0-88706-404-3); pap. 16.95 (ISBN 0-88706-403-5). State U NY Pr.

Principles of Business Communication. Francis Weeks & D. A. Jameson. 1984. pap. 6.80x (ISBN 0-87563-256-4). Stipes.

Principles of Business Communications: A Comprehensive Approach. C. G. Pearce et al. LC 83-16888. (Business Communications Ser.: 1-573). 648p. 1984. text ed. write for info. (ISBN 0-471-86537-0). tchrs.' manual avail. (ISBN 0-471-88530-4). Wiley.

Principles of Business Communication: Theory Application & Technology. 1984. pap. write for info. (ISBN 0-471-82592-1). Wiley.

Principles of Business Data Processing. Edward L. Essick. 672p. 1986. text ed. write for info. (ISBN 0-574-21935-8, 13-4935); write for info. study guide (ISBN 0-574-21937-4, 13-4937); write for info. instr's guide (ISBN 0-574-21936-6, 13-4936). Sci Res Assoc Coll.

Principles of Business Law. 13th ed. Robert N. Corley et al. (Illus.). 1120p. 1986. text ed. write for info. (ISBN 0-13-701186-5). P-H.

Principles of Business Mathematics: Using the Electronic Calculator. Harry Huffman & Larry Fiber. (Illus.). 1978. text ed. 24.75 (ISBN 0-07-030890-X). McGraw.

Principles of Business Organization & Operation. 4th ed. Ralph C. Davis. LC 72-9522. (Management History Ser.: No. 16). (Illus.). 150p. 1973. Repr. of 1937 ed. 24.00 (ISBN 0-87960-019-5). Hive Pub.

Principles of Business Taxation. John Pointon & Derek Spratley. (Illus.). 352p. 1988. 59.00 (ISBN 0-19-877257-2). Oxford U Pr.

Principles of California Real Estate. 5th ed. Rockwell et al. (Illus.). 491p. 1988. pap. text ed. 29.95 (ISBN 0-915799-46-4). Natl Real Estate Inst.

Principles of California Real Estate. 4th, rev. ed. David L. Rockwell et al. (Illus.). 491p. 1987. pap. 29.95 (ISBN 0-915799-29-4). Natl Real Estate Inst.

Principles of Cancer Biotherapy. Ed. by Robert K. Oldham. (Illus.). 512p. 1988. text ed. 77.00 (ISBN 0-88167-364-1). Raven.

Principles of Cancer Treatment. Ed. by Stephen K. Carter et al. (Illus.). 976p. 1982. text ed. 110.00 (ISBN 0-07-010183-3). McGraw.

Principles of Canon Law. Hubert S. Box. LC 86-3163. 82p. 1986. Repr. of 1949 ed. 35.00x (ISBN 0-313-25204-1, BPRC). Greenwood.

Principles of Cartography. Erwin J. Raisz. (Geography Ser.). 1962. text ed. 33.00 (ISBN 0-07-051151-9, C). McGraw.

Principles of Catholic Moral Life. Ed. by William E. May. LC 80-10969. 456p. 1981. 10.50 (ISBN 0-8199-0794-4). Franciscan Herald.

Principles of Catholic Theology: A Synthesis of Dogma & Morals. Edward Gratsch et al. LC 80-26272. 401p. (Orig.). 1981. pap. 12.95 (ISBN 0-8189-0407-0). Alba.

Principles of Catholic Theology: Building Stones for Fundamental Theology. Joseph C. Ratzinger. Tr. by Mary F. McCarthy from Ger. LC 86-83133. 398p. (Orig.). 1986. 24.95 (ISBN 0-89870-133-3). Ignatius Pr.

Principles of Cell Biology. Lewis J. Kleinsmith & Valerie M. Kish. 796p. 1987. text ed. 45.95 (ISBN 0-06-043712-X, HarpC). Har-Row.

Principles of Cereal Science & Technology. R. Hoseney. LC 86-70292. 327p. 1986. 46.95x (ISBN 0-913250-43-0). Am Assn Cereal Chem.

Principles of Cerebral Dominance: The Evolutionary Significance of the Radical Deduplication of the Human Brain. Charles W. Needham. (Illus.). 192p. 1982. 27.25 (ISBN 0-398-04700-6). C C Thomas.

Principles of Charged Particle Acceleration. Stanley Humphries. LC 85-17792. 573p. 1986. 65.95 (ISBN 0-471-87878-2). Wiley.

Principles of Chemical Equilibrium. 4th ed. Kenneth G. Denbigh. (Illus.). 506p. 1981. 80.00 (ISBN 0-521-23682-7); pap. 27.95 (ISBN 0-521-28150-4). Cambridge U Pr.

Principles of Chemical Instrumentation. Gray T. Bender. (Illus.). 384p. 1987. 25.95 (ISBN 0-7216-1834-0). Saunders.

Principles of Chemical Kinetics. Gordon G. Hammes. 1978. 35.00 (ISBN 0-12-321950-7). Acad Pr.

Principles of Chemistry. Raymond E. Davis et al. LC 83-19271. 884p. 1984. text ed. 48.00 (ISBN 0-03-060458-3). SCP.

Principles of Chemistry. Frank E. Harris. (gr. 10-12). 1977. pap. text ed. 25.00 each incl. 8 texts (ISBN 0-8449-0400-7); tchrs' manual 6.00; test 8.00; Complete Course. 214.00. Learning Line.

Principles of Chemistry, 4 pts. in 2 vols. 3rd ed. D. I. Mendeleev. Ed. by Thomas H. Pope. Tr. by G. Kamensky. 1905. Set. 66.00 (ISBN 0-527-63100-0). Kraus Repr.

Principles of Chemistry. C. Stuart Patterson et al. LC 66-28993. (Illus.). 1967. 37.00x (ISBN 0-89197-530-6). Irvington.

Principles of Chemistry. Willard Roundy. 19.95 (ISBN 0-317-47207-0). Paladin Hse.

Principles of Chemistry Laboratory: Manual for CH 111A & 112A. H. W. Cain & R. L. Hunt. 1984. pap. text ed. 16.25 (ISBN 0-89917-431-0). Tichenor Pub.

Principles of Chemistry with other Treatises. Emanuel Swedenborg. Tr. & intro. by Charles E. Strutt. (Illus.). 253p. 1976. Repr. of 1847 ed. 8.00 (ISBN 0-915221-22-5). Swedenborg Sci Assn.

Principles of Chest Roentgenology: A Programed Text. Benjamin Felson et al. LC 65-23091. (Illus.). 1965. pap. 30.95 (ISBN 0-7216-3605-5). Saunders.

Principles of Chest X-Ray Diagnosis. 4th ed. G. Simon. 1978. 79.95 (ISBN 0-407-36323-8). Butterworth.

Principles of Chinese Bible Translation As Expressed in Five Selected Versions of the New Testament & Exemplified by Mathew 5.1 & Coloossians 1. Thor Strandenaes. 166p. (Orig.). 1987. pap. 28.50x (ISBN 91-22-00993-0, Pub. by Almqvist & Wiksell). Coronet Bks.

Principles of Chinese Painting. rev ed. G. Rowley. (Monographs in Art & Archaeology: No. 24). 1959. 44.00x (ISBN 0-691-03834-1); pap. 11.50x (ISBN 0-691-00300-9). Princeton U Pr.

Principles of Chinese Painting. George Rowley. 121p. 1947. 315.00x (ISBN 0-317-68892-8, Pub. by Han-Shan Tang Ltd). State Mutual Bk.

Principles of Christian Art. Percy Gardner. 1977. lib. bdg. 59.95 (ISBN 0-8490-2479-X). Gordon Pr.

Principles of Christian Faith. Harold McDougal. 264p. (Orig.). 1986. pap. 14.95 (ISBN 0-914903-18-7). Destiny Image.

Principles of Christian Morality. Joseph Ratzinger et al. Tr. by Graham Harrison from Ger. LC 85-82176. Orig. Title: Prinzipien Chrislicher Moral. 104p. (Orig.). 1986. pap. 6.95 (ISBN 0-89870-086-8). Ignatius Pr.

Principles of Christian Religion. Thomas Becon. LC 76-57355. (English Experience Ser.: No. 774). 1977. Repr. of 1552 ed. lib. bdg. 25.00 (ISBN 90-221-0774-4). Walter J Johnson.

Principles of Christian Theology. 2nd ed. John Macquarrie. LC 76-23182. 544p. 1977. pap. text ed. write for info. (ISBN 0-02-374510-X, Pub. by Scribner). Macmillan.

Principles of City Land Values. Richard M. Hurd. LC 78-112551. (Rise of Urban America). (Illus.). 1970. Repr. of 1924 ed. 14.00 (ISBN 0-405-02458-4). Ayer Co Pubs.

Principles of Classical Japanese Literature. Earl Miner. LC 84-42895. 272p. 1985. text ed. 33.50x (ISBN 0-691-06635-3). Princeton U Pr.

Principles of Classical Mechanics & Field Theory see Encyclopedia of Physics.

Principles of Clinical Chemistry. Kenneth E. Blick & Suzanne M. Liles. LC 85-3175. 697p. 1985. 30.00 (ISBN 0-471-88502-9). Wiley.

Principles of Clinical Electrocardiography. 12th ed. Mervin J. Goldman. (Illus.). 1986. 22.00 (ISBN 0-87041-084-9). Appleton & Lange.

Principles of Clinical Psychiatry. 2nd. ed. Arnold M. Ludwig. 672p. 1985. 37.50x (ISBN 0-02-919350-8). Free Pr.

Principles of Clinical Toxicology. Thomas A. Gossel & J. Douglas Bricker. (Illus.). 368p. 1984. text ed. 58.00 (ISBN 0-89004-951-3). Raven.

Principles of CMOS VLSI: A Systems Perspective. Neil Weste & Karman Eshraghian. LC 84-16738. 1985. text ed. 47.50 (ISBN 0-201-08222-5). Addison-Wesley.

Principles of Coaching Football. Mike Bobo & Jerry Moore. 320p. 1987. pap. text ed. write for info. (ISBN 0-697-00118-0). Wm C Brown.

Principles of Collage. Brian French. LC 78-67955. (Illus.). 1978. 12.95 (ISBN 0-87523-188-8). Emerson.

Principles of Color Design. Wucius Wong. (Illus.). 1986. pap. 14.95 (ISBN 0-442-29284-8). Van Nos Reinhold.

Principles of Color Reproduction, Applied to Photomechanical Reproduction, Color Photography, & the Ink, Paper, & Other Related Industries. John A. Yule. LC 66-26764. (Wiley Series on Photographic Science & Technology & the Graphic Arts). pap. 111.80 (2056153). Bks Demand UMI.

Principles of Color Technology. 2nd ed. Fred W. Billmeyer, Jr. & Max Saltzman. LC 80-21561. 240p. 1981. 43.50 (ISBN 0-471-03052-X). Wiley.

Principles of Combinatorics. Claude Berge. (Mathematics in Science & Engineering Ser.: Vol. 72). 1971. 49.50 (ISBN 0-12-089750-4). Acad Pr.

Principles of Combustion Engineering for Boilers. Ed. by Christopher J. Lawn. (Combustion Treatise Ser.). 628p. 1988. 110.00 (ISBN 0-12-439035-8). Acad Pr.

Principles of Comedy & Dramatic Effect. Percy Fitzgerald. LC 76-7982. 1973. Repr. of 1870 ed. lib. bdg. 32.50 (ISBN 0-8414-4221-5). Folcroft.

Principles of Command & Control. Ed. by Jon L. Boyes & Stephen J. Andriole. (AFCEA Signal Magazine C3I Ser.). (Illus.). 500p. 1987. 44.95 (ISBN 0-916159-12-4). AFCEA Intl Pr.

Principles of Communication & Networking Protocols. Simon S. Lam. (Tutorial Text Ser.). 528p. 1984. 36.00 (ISBN 0-8186-0582-0, EZ582). IEEE Comp Soc.

Principles of Communication Engineering. John M. Wozencraft & Irwin M. Jacobs. LC 65-16429. 720p. 1965. write for info. (ISBN 0-471-96240-6). Wiley.

Principles of Communication Systems. Herbert Taub & Donald L. Schilling. (Electronic & Electronic Engineering Ser.). 1970. text ed. 50.95 (ISBN 0-07-062923-4). McGraw.

Principles of Communication Systems. 2nd ed. Herbert Taub & Donald L. Schilling. (Electrical Engineering Ser.). 736p. 1986. text ed. 51.95 (ISBN 0-07-062955-2). McGraw.

Principles of Communications for Science & Technology. Leslie Olsen & Thomas Huchin. (Illus.). 432p. 1983. text ed. 27.95 (ISBN 0-07-047821-X). McGraw.

Principles of Communications: Systems, Modulations & Noise. 2nd ed. Rodger E. Ziemer & William Tranter. LC 84-81048. (Illus.). 640p. 1985. text ed. 53.36 (ISBN 0-395-35724-1); solution manual 9.16 (ISBN 0-395-36464-7). HM.

Principles of Communism see Communist Manifesto.

Principles of Community Health. 3rd ed. Jack Smolensky. 456p. 1982. text ed. write for info. (ISBN 0-697-06309-7). Wm C Brown.

Principles of Community Property. 2nd ed. William Q. De Funiak & Michael J. Vaughn. LC 72-101099. pap. 143.80 (ISBN 0-317-28651-X, 2055347). Bks Demand UMI.

Principles of Comparative Anatomy of Invertebrates, 2 Vols. V. N. Beklemishev. Ed. by Z. Kabata. Tr. by J. M. McLennan. LC 70-97749. 1970. Set. 60.00x (ISBN 0-226-04175-1). U of Chicago Pr.

Principles of Comparative Respiratory Physiology. 2nd ed. Ed. by Pierre Dejours. LC 74-25821. 251p. 1981. 51.00 (ISBN 0-444-80279-7, North-Holland). Elsevier.

Principles of Competitive Protein-Binding Assays. 2nd ed. Paul Frauchimont. Ed. by William D. Odell. LC 82-10941. 311p. 1982. 47.50 (ISBN 0-471-08924-9). Wiley.

Principles of Composition. Percy H. Boynton. Repr. of 1915 ed. 25.00 (ISBN 0-686-19877-8). Ridgeway Bks.

Principles of Computer-Aided Design. Joe Rooney & Philip Steadman. (Illus.). 352p. 1988. text ed. 40.00 (ISBN 0-13-709346-2). P-H.

Principles of Computer Communication Network Design. J. Seidler. LC 82-23248. 507p. 1983. 112.00 (ISBN 0-470-27405-0). Halsted Pr.

Principles of Computer Design. Leonard R. Marino. LC 84-23812. (Principles of Computer Science Ser.). 578p. 1986. text ed. 41.95 (ISBN 0-88175-064-6, Computer Sci Pr). W H Freeman.

Principles of Computer Hardware. Alan Clements. (Illus.). 1985. 49.95x (ISBN 0-19-853704-2); pap. 22.50x (ISBN 0-19-853703-4). Oxford U Pr.

Principles of Computer Operations. Stephen C. Kanski. LC 83-5087. 312p. 1983. pap. text ed. 22.95 (ISBN 0-471-86846-9). Wiley.

Principles of Computer Organization. G. Michael Schneider. LC 84-20853. 526p. 1985. text ed. write for info. (ISBN 0-471-88552-5). Wiley.

Principles of Computer Programming. Mills et al. 688p. 1987. pap. 36.67 (ISBN 0-205-07996-2). Wm C Brown.

Principles of Computer Science: Concepts, Algorithms, Data Structures, & Applications. M. Sandra Carberry et al. 636p. 1986. text ed. 36.95 (ISBN 0-914894-79-X, Computer Sci Pr); 20.00 (ISBN 0-88175-154-5). W H Freeman.

Principles of Computer Speech. Ian H. Witten. (Computer & People Ser.). 1983. 39.50 (ISBN 0-12-760760-9). Acad Pr.

Principles of Computerized Tomographic Imaging. A. C. Kak & M. Slaney. LC 87-22645. 344p. 1988. 51.95 (ISBN 0-87942-198-3, PC02071). Inst Electrical.

Principles of Conditioning in Human Goal Behavior see Differential Forecasts of Achievement & Their Use in Educational Counseling.

Principles of Constructing Linguistic Models. P. N. Denisov. LC 72-88205. (Janua Linguarum, Ser. Minor: No. 91). 173p. (Orig.). 1973. pap. text ed. 20.00x (ISBN 90-2792-376-0). Mouton.

Principles of Construction of Hot-Mix Asphalt Pavements. 300p. 1983. 15.00 (ISBN 0-318-17743-9, MS-22). Asphalt Inst.

Principles of Continuous System Simulation. W. K Giloi. (Illus.). 1976. pap. 20.95x (ISBN 3-519-02336-9). Adlers Foreign Bks.

Principles of Contract at Law & in Equity: A Treatise on the General Principles Concerning the Validity of Agreements in the Law of England & America. Frederick Pollock. cliv, 985p. 1988. Repr. of 1906 ed. lib. bdg. 95.00x (ISBN 0-8377-2516-X). Rothman.

Principles of Corporate Finance. 2nd ed. Richard Brealey & Stewart C. Myers. (Finance Ser.). 864p. 1984. text ed. 42.95x (ISBN 0-07-007383-X). McGraw.

Principles of Corporate Finance. Richard A. Brealey & Stewart C. Myers. (Finance Ser.). (Illus.). 1981. text ed. 39.95x (ISBN 0-07-007380-5). McGraw.

Principles of Corporate Finance. 3rd ed. Richard A. Brealey & Stewart C. Myers. 976p. 1988. text ed. 44.95 (ISBN 0-07-007386-4). McGraw.

Principles of Corporate Finance. Ward S. Curran. 742p. 1988. text ed. 34.00 (ISBN 0-15-571550-X, HC); instr's. manual 3.75 (ISBN 0-15-571551-8). HarBraceJ.

Principles of Corporate Finance: Test Book. Ward S. Curran. 133p. 1988. pap. text ed. 5.75 net (ISBN 0-15-571552-6). HarBraceJ.

Principles of Corporate Governance: Analysis & Recommendations. 331p. 1984. pap. 15.00 (ISBN 0-317-63193-4, 531-0044-01). Amer Bar Assn.

Principles of Corporate Governance: Analysis & Recommendations: Tentative Draft No. 1: Parts 1-4. 426p. 1982. write for info. Am Law Inst.

Principles of Corporate Governance: Analysis & Recommendations: Tentative Draft No. 2. 124p. 1984. write for info. Am law Inst.

Principles of Corporate Governance: Analysis & Recommendations: Tentative Draft No. 3. 271p. 1984. write for info. Am Law Inst.

Principles of Cost Accounting. 4th ed. Rayburn. 1989. 42.95 (ISBN 0-256-06827-5). Irwin.

Principles of Cost Accounting. 8th ed. Robert E. Schmiedicke et al. 512p. 1988. text ed. write for info. (ISBN 0-538-01680-9, A68). SW Pub.

Principles of Cost Accounting. 3rd ed. C. J. Walker. 352p. 1982. pap. text ed. 26.50x (ISBN 0-7121-1757-1). Trans-Atl Phila.

Principles of Cost Accounting: Questions & Answers. 3rd ed. C. J. Walker. 416p. (Orig.). 1982. pap. text ed. 28.50x (ISBN 0-7121-1758-X). Trans-Atl Phila.

Principles of Cost Accounting with Managerial Implications. 3rd ed. L. Gayle Rayburn. 1986. 41.95x (ISBN 0-256-03324-2); study guide 14.95x (ISBN 0-256-03457-5). Irwin.

Principles of County Jail Administration & Management. David B. Kalinich & Frederick J. Postill. (Illus.). 208p. 1981. photocopy ed. 26.25x (ISBN 0-398-04140-7). C C Thomas.

Principles of Course Design for Langauge Teaching. Janice Yalden. (New Directions in Language Teaching Ser.). 1987. 27.95 (ISBN 0-521-30989-1); pap. 9.95 (ISBN 0-521-31221-3). Cambridge U Pr.

Principles of Creative Selling. 3rd ed. Kenneth B. Haas & John Ernest. 1978. text ed. write for info. (ISBN 0-02-474980-X). Macmillan.

Principles of Credit Evaluation see Installment Credit Series.

Principles of Criminal Law. Wayne R. LaFave. (Criminal Justice Ser.). 656p. 1978. text ed. 37.00 (ISBN 0-8299-0215-5); instrs.' manual avail. (ISBN 0-8299-0595-2). West Pub.

Principles of Criminal Law (with Model Questions & Suggested Readings) O. P. Srivastava. 186p. 1985. 36.00x (ISBN 0-317-57729-8, Pub. by Eastern Bk India). State Mutual Bk.

Principles of Criminology. G. Avanesov. 344p. 1982. 7.95 (ISBN 0-8285-2511-0, 230065, Pub. by Progress Pubs USSR). Imported Pubns.

Principles of Critical Care. Janet K. Ihde et al. (Illus.). 456p. 1987. 25.95 (ISBN 0-7216-1802-2). Saunders.

Principles of Criticism. W. Basil Worsfold. LC 75-105857. 1970. Repr. of 1902 ed. 24.00x (ISBN 0-8046-0991-8, Pub. by Kennikat). Assoc Faculty Pr.

Principles of Crop Improvement. N. W. Simmonds. LC 78-40726. (Illus.). 1979. pap. text ed. 23.95x (ISBN 0-582-44630-9). Wiley.

Principles of Crop Improvement. N. W. Simmonds. 384p. 1979. pap. 39.95 (ISBN 0-470-20588-1, Co-Pub. with Longman). Wiley.

Principles of Cultivar Development, Vol. 1: Theory & Technique. Walter R. Fehr. 672p. 1987. 60.00x (ISBN 0-02-949920-8). Macmillan.

Principles of Cultivar Development, Vol. 2: Crop Species. Ed. by Walter R. Fehr. 768p. 1987. 60.00x (ISBN 0-02-949181-9). Macmillan.

Principles of Cultural Cooperation. Sulwyn Lewis. (Reports & Papers on Mass Communication: No. 61). 27p. (Orig.). 1971. pap. 5.00 (ISBN 92-3-100810-2, U482, UNESCO). UNIPUB.

Principles of Dairy Farming. 9th ed. Kenneth Russell & Ken Slater. (Illus.). 288p. 1981. 24.95 (ISBN 0-85236-116-5, Pub. by Farming Pr UK). Diamond Farm Bk.

Principles of Dairy Processing. 1976. 4.00 (ISBN 0-471-63915-X). Wiley.

Principles of Data Base Management. James Martin. (Illus.). 320p. 1976. Ref. Ed. 48.00 (ISBN 0-13-708917-1). P-H.

Principles of Data Communication. James Martin & Joe Leben. (Illus.). 384p. 1988. text ed. 44.00 (ISBN 0-13-709891-X). P-H.

Principles of Data Communications. Richard Dolphin. 1983. write for info. (ISBN 0-935506-15-2). Carnegie Pr.

Principles of Data Processing. 3rd ed. Steve L. Mandell. (Illus.). 172p. 1984. pap. text ed. 19.00 (ISBN 0-314-77923-X); tchrs.' manual avail. (ISBN 0-314-77924-8). West Pub.

Principles of Data Security. Ernst L. Leiss. LC 82-22272. (Foundations of Computer Science Ser.). 238p. 1982. 32.50x (ISBN 0-306-41098-2, Plenum Pr). Plenum Pub.

Principles of Data Structures & Algorithms with Pascal. Robert R. Korfhage & Norman E. Gibbs. 480p. 1987. text ed. write for info. (ISBN 0-697-00123-7); write for info. solutions manual (ISBN 0-697-00994-7). Wm C Brown.

Principles of Database Design: Logical Organizations, Vol. I. S. Bing Yao. (Illus.). 496p. 1985. text ed. 52.00 (ISBN 0-13-708876-0). P-H.

Principles of Database Systems. 2nd ed. Jeffrey D. Ullman. LC 82-2510. (Computer Software Engineering Ser.). 484p. 1982. text ed. 39.95 (ISBN 0-914894-36-6, Computer Sci Pr). W H Freeman.

Principles of DC & AC Circuits. 2nd ed. George J. Angerbauer. 750p. 1985. 33.50 (ISBN 0-534-04203-1, PWS-Kent Ser Tech); write for info. (ISBN 0-534-04206-6); study guide 13.75 (ISBN 0-534-04204-X, 77F6059); write for info. (ISBN 0-534-04205-8). PWS Kent Pub.

Principles of Deductive Logic. John T. Kearns. LC 86-23035. 480p. 1987. 49.50x (ISBN 0-88706-478-7); pap. 24.50 (ISBN 0-88706-479-5). State U NY Pr.

Principles of Democratic Supervision. John A. Rorer. LC 74-177207. (Columbia University. Teachers College. Contributions to Education: No. 858). Repr. of 1942 ed. 22.50 (ISBN 0-404-55858-5). AMS Pr.

Principles of Dental Public Health. James M. Dunning. LC 86-4632. (Illus.). 736p. 1986. text ed. 37.00x (ISBN 0-674-70550-5). Harvard U Pr.

Principles of Dental Treatment Planning. Robert B. Morris. LC 82-15370. (Illus.). 240p. 1983. text ed. 33.50 (ISBN 0-8121-0841-8). Lea & Febiger.

Principles of Dependency Phonology. John M. Anderson & Colin J. Ewen. (Cambridge Studies in Linguistics: No. 47). (Illus.). 347p. 1987. 49.50 (ISBN 0-521-32313-4). Cambridge U Pr.

Principles of Depreciation. Earl A. Saliers. Ed. by Richard P. Brief. LC 80-1576. (Dimensions of Accounting Theory & Practice Ser.). 1981. Repr. of 1915 ed. lib. bdg. 21.00x (ISBN 0-405-13542-4). Ayer Co Pubs.

Principles of Dermatologic Plastic Surgery. Ed. by Marwali Harahap. LC 85-14584. 336p. 1988. text ed. 75.00 (ISBN 0-89335-235-7). PMA Pub Corp.

Principles of Dermatology. Donald P. Lookingbill & James G. Marks. (Principles of Medicine Ser.). (Illus.). 257p. 1986. pap. 33.95 (ISBN 0-7216-1275-X). Saunders.

Principles of Desalination. 2nd ed. Ed. by K. S. Spiegler & A. D. Laird. 1980. Pt. A. 58.50 (ISBN 0-12-656701-8); Pt. B. 67.00 (ISBN 0-12-656702-6). Acad Pr.

Principles of Descartes' Philosophy. Benedictus De Spinoza. Tr. by Halbert H. Britan from Lat. LC 74-3096. 177p. 1961. pap. 2.95 (ISBN 0-87548-053-5). Open Court.

Principles of Descriptive Inorganic Chemistry. Gary Wulfsberg. (Illus.). 464p. 1987. text ed. 27.50 (ISBN 0-534-07494-4). Brooks-Cole.

Principles of Design Improvement for Light Water Reactors. Long Sun Tong. 393p. 1988. 79.50 (ISBN 0-89116-416-2). Hemisphere Pub.

Principles of Design in Architecture. K. W. Smithies. 88p. 1981. pap. 15.95 (ISBN 0-442-30442-0). Van Nos Reinhold.

Principles of Designing Control Systems for Water Resources & Irrigation Using Modern Techniques: Proceedings - Symposium 1981. 199p. 27.00 (ISBN 0-318-17921-0). US Comm Irrigation.

Principles of Development of Model Health Care Programmes. (EURO Reports & Studies: No. 96). 41p. 1985. pap. 3.60 (ISBN 92-890-1262-5). World Health.

Principles of Devotion. rev. ed. Charles Finney. Ed. by Louis Parkhurst. 288p. 1987. pap. 6.95 (ISBN 0-87123-872-1). Bethany Hse.

Principles of Diabetes Management. Ed. by M. Bergman. (Other Medical Bks.: Vol. 20). 500p. 1987. 29.25 (ISBN 0-444-01125-0). Med Exam.

Principles of Diachronic Syntax. D. W. Lightfoot. LC 78-54717. (Cambridge Studies in Linguistics Monograph: No. 23). (Illus.). 1979. pap. 29.95x (ISBN 0-521-29350-2). Cambridge U Pr.

Principles of Diary Science. Glen Schmidt & L. D. VanVleck. (Illus.). 512p. 1988. text ed. 38.00 (ISBN 0-13-709818-9). P-H.

Principles of Differential & Integral Equations. 2nd ed. Constantin Corduneanu. LC 77-2962. 1977. text ed. 15.95 (ISBN 0-8284-0295-7). Chelsea Pub.

Principles of Digital & Analog Communications. Jerry D. Gibson. 681p. 1989. write for info. (ISBN 0-02-341780-3). Macmillan.

Principles of Digital Audio. Ken C. Pohlmann. (Illus.). 1985. 19.95 (ISBN 0-672-22388-0, 22388-0). Sams.

Principles of Digital Audio. 2nd ed. Kenneth C. Pohlmann. 320p. 1988. pap. 29.95 (ISBN 0-672-22634-0). Sams.

Principles of Digital Communication. J. Das et al. LC 85-16347. 645p. 1986. 36.95 (ISBN 0-470-20240-8). Halsted Pr.

Principles of Digital Communication & Coding. Andrew J. Viterbi & James K. Omura. (Electrical Engineering Ser.). (Illus.). 1979. text ed. 58.95 (ISBN 0-07-067516-3). McGraw.

Principles of Digital Data Transmission. 2nd ed. A. P. Clark. LC 83-6710. 1983. 33.95x (ISBN 0-470-27458-1). Halsted Pr.

Principles of Direct Current Resistivity Prospecting. Geza Kunetz. Tr. by R. Van Nostrans from Fr. (Geoexploration Monographs: Ser. 1, No. 1). (Illus.). 103p. 1966. text ed. 22.00x (ISBN 3-4431-3001-1). Lubrecht & Cramer.

Principles of Discipleship. Debbie Crinzi. 102p. 1984. pap. text ed. 5.00 (ISBN 0-8309-0394-1). Herald Hse.

Principles of Discipleship. Charles Finney. Ed. by L. G. Parkhurst. (Principles...Ser.). 240p. (Orig.). 1988. pap. 6.95 (ISBN 0-87123-860-8). Bethany Hse.

Principles of Discrete Event Simulation. 2nd ed. Fishman. (Systems Engineering & Analysis Ser.). 1988. write for info. (ISBN 0-471-89054-5). Wiley.

Principles of Discrete Event Simulation. George S. Fishman. LC 78-17555. (Systems Engineering & Analysis Ser.). 514p. 1978. 52.95x (ISBN 0-471-04395-8, Pub. by Wiley-Interscience). Wiley.

Principles of Dispersal in Higher Plants. L. Van Der Pijl. (Illus.). 250p. 1982. 36.00 (ISBN 0-387-11280-4). Springer-Verlag.

Principles of Drilling Fluid Control. 12th ed. (Illus.). 232p. 1969. pap. text ed. 10.00 (ISBN 0-88698-118-2, 2.70120). PETEX.

Principles of Drug Action: The Basis of Pharmacology. 2nd ed. Avram Goldstein et al. LC 73-15871. 834p. 1974. 52.00x (ISBN 0-471-31260-6, Pub. by Wiley-Medical). Wiley.

Principles of Drug Information Services. Arthur S. Watanabe & Christopher S. Conner. LC 78-50219. 240p. 1978. 16.25 (ISBN 0-914768-31-X). Drug Intell Pubns.

Principles of Dynamic Programming, Pt. 1. Larson & Casti. (Control & Systems Theory Ser.: Vol. 7). 1978. 39.75 (ISBN 0-8247-6589-3). Dekker.

Principles of Dynamic Programming, Part Two. Robert E. Larson & John L. Casti. (Control & Systems Theory Ser.: Vol. 7). 1982. 45.00 (ISBN 0-8247-6590-7). Dekker.

Principles of Dynamics. 2nd ed. Donald T. Greenwood. (Illus.). 544p. 1988. text ed. 48.95 (ISBN 0-317-60135-0). P-H.

Principles of Dynamics. Ed. by Donald T. Greenwood & Y. C. Fung. 1965. text ed. 48.00 (ISBN 0-13-708974-0). P-H.

Principles of Ecology. Richard Brewer. LC 77-84666. (Illus.). 1979. pap. text ed. 18.95 (ISBN 0-7216-1988-6). HR&W.

Principles of Ecology. R. J. Putman & S. D. Wratten. LC 83-18028. 384p. 1984. lib. bdg. 42.00x (ISBN 0-520-05235-8); pap. 18.95x (ISBN 0-520-05254-4). U of Cal Pr.

Principles of Econometrics. Henri Theil. LC 78-118626. (Illus.). 736p. 1971. 47.95 (ISBN 0-471-85845-5). Wiley.

Principles of Economic Analysis, 2 vols. David Ricardo. 267p. 1987. Set. 227.75 (ISBN 0-86654-236-1). Inst Econ Finan.

Principles of Economic Appraisal in Health Care. M. F. Drummond. (Illus.). 1980. pap. 15.95x (ISBN 0-19-261273-5). Oxford U Pr.

Principles of Economic Justice: Reflections on the Bishop's Letter. Daniel L. Lowery. 32p. (Orig.). 1987. pap. 1.50 (ISBN 0-89243-277-2). Liguori Pubns.

Principles of Economic Science. B. N. Ghosh. 1983. text ed. 15.95x (ISBN 0-686-45575-4, Pub. by Vikas India). Advent NY.

Principles of Economics. 4th ed. Ryan Amacher & Holley Ulbrich. 928p. 1989. text ed. price not set (ISBN 0-538-80072-0, HB67DA-HB67DA2); Principles of Microeconomics. pap. text ed. price not set (ISBN 0-538-80074-7, HB67DA-HB67DA2); Principles of Macroeconomics. pap. text ed. price not set (ISBN 0-538-80076-3, HB67DA-HB67DA2). SW Pub.

Principles of Economics. 3rd ed. Ryan C. Amacher & Holley H. Ulbrich. 1986. text ed. write for info. (ISBN 0-538-08671-8, H67). SW Pub.

Principles of Economics. 2nd ed. Roger Chisholm & Marilu McCarty. 1981. text ed. write for info. (ISBN 0-673-15492-0). Scott F.

Principles of Economics. D. N. Dwivedi. 922p. 1985. pap. text ed. 25.00x (ISBN 0-7069-2716-8, Pub. by Vikas India). Advent NY.

Principles of Economics. Belton M. Fleisher et al. 824p. 1987. 40.00 (ISBN 0-205-11480-6, H1480-6); study guide avail. (ISBN 0-205-11482-2, H1482-2); instr's. manual avail. (ISBN 0-205-11481-4, H1481-4); transparencies avail. (ISBN 0-205-11483-0, H1483-0). Allyn.

Principles of Economics. William S. Jevons. LC 65-20926. Repr. of 1905 ed. 35.00x (ISBN 0-678-00109-X). Kelley.

Principles of Economics. 8th. ed. Alfred Marshall. (Illus.). xxxii, 731p. 1982. pap. 19.95x (ISBN 0-87991-051-8). Porcupine Pr.

Principles of Economics. Carl Menger. Tr. by James Dingwall & Bert F. Hoselitz. (Institute for Humane Studies Ser. in Economic Theory). 328p. 1981. pap. 12.50 (ISBN 0-8147-5381-7). NYU Pr.

Principles of Economics. H. Omar. 800p. (Arabic.). 1986. pap. 21.50 (ISBN 0-471-88323-9). Wiley.

Principles of Economics, 2 vols. 6th ed. Willis L. Peterson. 1986. pap. 21.95x macro (ISBN 0-256-03346-3); pap. 21.95x micro (ISBN 0-256-03348-X); pap. 9.95x study guide, macro (ISBN 0-256-03347-1); pap. 9.95x study guide, micro (ISBN 0-256-03349-8). Irwin.

Principles of Economics. Jack Rudman. (DANTES Ser.: No. 32). 1988. 25.95 (ISBN 0-8373-6682-8); pap. 13.95 (ISBN 0-8373-6632-1). Natl Learning.

Principles of Economics. 2nd ed. Roy Ruffin & Paul Gregory. 1986. write for info. (ISBN 0-673-18225-8); instr's. manual avail. Scott F.

Principles of Economics. 3rd ed. Roy Ruffin & Paul Gregory. 1987. text ed. write for info. (ISBN 0-673-18871-X). Scott F.

Principles of Economics. Truett. 960p. 1986. text ed. 42.95. Mosby.

Principles of Economics: Macro. 7th ed. Peterson. 1988. 16.95 (ISBN 0-256-06795-3). Irwin.

Principles of Economics, Macro: Personal Learning Aid. 4th ed. Reynolds & Michas. (Plaid Ser.). 1983. pap. 10.95 (ISBN 0-87094-430-4). Dow Jones-Irwin.

Principles of Economics: Macroeconomics. David E. Emery. LC 86-7653. 347p. 1988. pap. 10.95 (ISBN 0-15-601586-2, BFP). HarBraceJ.

Principles of Economics: Micro. 7th ed. Peterson. 1988. 16.95 (ISBN 0-256-06796-1). Irwin.

Principles of Economics, Micro: Personal Learning Aid. 4th ed. Reynolds & Michas. 1983. pap. 10.95 (ISBN 0-87094-429-0). Dow Jones-Irwin.

Principles of Economics: Microeconomics. E. David Emery. (College Outline Ser.). 319p. 1988. pap. 9.95 (ISBN 0-15-600053-9, BFP). HarBraceJ.

Principles of Economics: Student Guide. Iris F. Hartley. (FLMI Insurance Education Program Ser.). 1985. 7.00 (ISBN 0-915322-71-4). LOMA.

Principles of Education. J. C. Chapman et al. Ed. by Ellwood P. Cubberley. 645p. 1980. Repr. of 1924 ed. lib. bdg. 49.00 (ISBN 0-8495-0851-7). Arden Lib.

Principles of Educational & Psychological Measurement & Evaluation. 2nd ed. Gilbert Sax. 688p. 1980. text ed. write for info. (ISBN 0-534-00832-1). Wadsworth Pub.

Principles of Educational & Psychological Measurement & Evaluation. 3rd ed. Gilbert Sax. Date not set. text ed. write for info. (ISBN 0-534-09978-5). Wadsworth Pub.

Principles of Educational & Psychological Testing. 3rd ed. Frederick Brown. 1983. text ed. 32.95 (ISBN 0-03-060103-7). HR&W.

Principles of Educational Practice. Paul Klapper. 1979. Repr. of 1923 ed. lib. bdg. 25.00 (ISBN 0-8492-1485-8). R West.

Principles of Effective Insurance Agents. Didactic Systems Staff. (Didactic Simulation Game Ser). 1973. pap. 24.90 (ISBN 0-685-77372-8); pap. 21.50 for 2 or more (ISBN 0-686-57883-X); pap. 24.90 spanish ed.; pap. 21.50 for 2 or more (ISBN 0-686-57884-8); pap. 0.50 leader's guide (ISBN 0-685-77375-2). Didactic Syst.

Principles of Effective Salesmanship. J. S. Schiff et al. (Simulation Game Ser.). 1971. pap. 23.50 (ISBN 0-89401-075-1); pap. 21.50 two or more (ISBN 0-686-57905-4); pap. 24.90 spanish ed. (ISBN 0-685-79375-3); pap. 24.90 portuguese ed. (ISBN 0-685-79376-1); pap. 24.90 french ed. (ISBN 0-685-79377-X); pap. 21.50 two or more (ISBN 0-686-57906-2); pap. 0.50 leaders guide (ISBN 0-685-79379-6). Didactic Syst.

Principles of Effective School District Governance & Administration. 1984. 3.50 (ISBN 0-317-61184-4, 021-00136). Am Assn Sch Admin.

Principles of Egyptian Art. Heinrich Schafer. Ed. by Emma Brunner-Traut. Tr. by John Baines from Ger. (Illus.). 500p. 1986. text ed. 84.00 (ISBN 0-900416-52-1, Pub. by Aris & Phillips UK); pap. text ed. 52.00 (ISBN 0-900416-51-3, Pub. by Aris & Phillips UK). Humanities.

Principles of Electric Circuits. 2nd ed. Thomas L. Floyd. 864p. 1985. text ed. 40.95 (ISBN 0-675-20402-X). Additional supplements may be obtained from publisher. Merrill.

Principles of Electric Circuits. 3rd ed. Thomas L. Floyd. 1020p. 1988. 40.95 (ISBN 0-675-21062-3). Merrill.

Principles of Electric Machines & Power Electronics. P. C. Sen. LC 88-5725. 1988. pap. write for info. (ISBN 0-471-85084-5). Wiley.

Principles of Electricity for Students of Physics & Engineering. Eugene Key. (Orig.). 1967. pap. 8.95 (ISBN 0-06-460118-8, CO 118, B&N Bks). Har-Row.

Principles of Electroanalytical Methods. Tom Riley & Colin Tomlinson. Ed. by Arthur M. James. (Analytical Chemistry by Open Learning Ser.). 252p. 1987. pap. 19.95 (ISBN 0-471-91330-8). Wiley.

Principles of Electrochemical Engineering: Extended Version of a DECHEMA Experimental Course. Ewald Heitz & Gerhard Kreysa. 294p. 1986. pap. 43.00 (ISBN 0-89573-203-3). VCH Pubs.

TITLE INDEX PRINCIPLES OF FUNCTIONAL ANALYSIS

Principles of Electrochemical Reactor Analysis. T. Z. Fahidy. (Chemical Engineering Monographs: Vol. 18). 1985. 97.50 (ISBN 0-444-42451-2). Elsevier.
Principles of Electrochemistry. J. Koryta & H. Dvorak. LC 86-15686. 447p. 1987. 95.00 (ISBN 0-471-91211-5). Wiley.
Principles of Electrodynamics & Relativity see Encyclopedia of Physics.
Principles of Electrolocation & Jamming Avoidance in Electric Fish: A Neuroethological Approach. W. Heiligenberg. (Studies of Brain Functions: Vol. 1). (Illus.). 1977. pap. 19.00 (ISBN 0-387-08367-7). Springer-Verlag.
Principles of Electromagnetic Compatibility. B. J. Keiser. LC 79-12032. 1983. 66.00x (ISBN 0-89006-065-7). Artech Hse.
Principles of Electromagnetic Theory & Relativity. M. A. Tonnelat. Tr. by Arthur Knodel from Fr. 475p. 1966. lib. bdg. 47.50 (ISBN 90-277-0107-5, Pub. by Reidel Holland). Kluwer Academic.
Principles of Electromagnetism Theory & Relativity. Marie A. Tonnelat. 488p. 1966. 152.00 (ISBN 0-677-01220-9). Gordon & Breach.
Principles of Electromechanical-Energy Conversion. Jerome Meisel. LC 82-6540. 656p. 1984. Repr. of 1966 ed. lib. bdg. 46.50 (ISBN 0-89874-495-4). Krieger.
Principles of Electron Optics, Vol. 1. Ed. by P. W. Hawkes & E. Kaspar. 550p. 1988. 59.95 (ISBN 0-12-333351-2). Acad Pr.
Principles of Electron Optics, Vol. 2. P. W. Hawkes & E. Kaspar. 600p. 1988. write for info. (ISBN 0-12-333352-0). Acad Pr.
Principles of Electron Tunneling Spectroscopy. E. L. Wolf. (International Series of Monographs on Physics). (Illus.). 1985. 80.00x (ISBN 0-19-503417-1). Oxford U Pr.
Principles of Electronic Circuits. Stanley Burns & Paul Bond. LC 86-24706. (Illus.). 811p. 1986. text ed. 55.25 (ISBN 0-314-23505-1); solutions manual avail. (ISBN 0-314-34722-4). West Pub.
Principles of Electronic Data Processing Management. Alexander Gaydasch. 300p. 1982. text ed. 36.00 (ISBN 0-8359-5604-0, Reston); instr's. manual avail. P-H.
Principles of Electronic Instrumentation & Measurement. Howard M. Berlin & Frank C. Getz, Jr. 512p. 1988. case bound 36.95 (ISBN 0-675-20449-6); lab manual 15.95 (ISBN 0-675-20450-X); supplements avail. Merrill.
Principles of Electronic Instrumentation. A. Desa. LC 80-28240. 280p. 1981. pap. 37.95x (ISBN 0-470-27135-3). Halsted Pr.
Principles of Electronic Instrumentation. 2nd ed. James Diefenderfer. 1979. text ed. 58.75 (ISBN 0-7216-3076-6, CBS C). SCP.
Principles of Electronic Warfare. Robert J. Schlesinger et al. LC 61-15515. (Illus.). 1979. pap. 14.95 (ISBN 0-932146-01-5). Peninsula CA.
Principles of Electronics. M. F. Ahmad & M. K. Katib. 300p. (Arabic.). 1984. pap. 15.00 (ISBN 0-471-88556-8). Wiley.
Principles of Electronics: Analog & Digital. Lloyd R. Fortney. 1987. text ed. 39.00 net (ISBN 0-15-571630-1, HC); solutions manual net 5.75 (ISBN 0-15-571631-X). HarBraceJ.
Principles of Elementary Algebra with Applications. Harry L. Nustad & Terry H. Wesner. 608p. 1987. pap. text ed. write for info. (ISBN 0-697-00265-9); instr's. manual avail. (ISBN 0-697-01298-0); student study guide avail. (ISBN 0-697-01352-9); audiotapes avail. (ISBN 0-697-04488-2); videotapes avail. (ISBN 0-697-04489-0). Wm C Brown.
Principles of Elocution. Alexander M. Bell. (Works of Alexander Melville Bell). xvi, 240p. 1985. Repr. lib. bdg. 39.00 (ISBN 0-932051-80-4, Pub. by Am Repr Serv). Am Biog Serv.
Principles of Emendation in Shakespeare. Walter W. Greg. LC 72-195248. Repr. of 1928 ed. 17.00 (ISBN 0-8414-4523-0). Folcroft.
Principles of Emendation in Shakespeare. Walter W. Greg. 1971. Repr. of 1928 ed. 10.00x (ISBN 0-403-00613-9). Scholarly.
Principles of Emergency Medical Dispatch. Jeff J Clawson & Kate B. Dernccoeur. (Illus.). 352p. 1988. pap. text ed. 24.95 (ISBN 0-89303-796-6). P-H.
Principles of Emergent Realism. W. Preston Warren. LC 70-96993. 380p. 1970. 16.50 (ISBN 0-87527-083-2). Fireside Bks.
Principles of Emergent Realism: Philosophical Essays of Roy Wood Sellars. Ed. by W. Preston Warren. LC 70-96993. (Illus.). 380p. 1970. 16.50. Green.
Principles of Empirical or Inductive Logic. 2nd ed. John Venn. LC 77-165344. 604p. 1973. Repr. of 1907 ed. 33.50 (ISBN 0-8337-3625-6). B Franklin.
Principles of Empirical, or Inductive Logic see Principles of Inductive Logic.
Principles of Employment Psychology. rev. ed. Harold E. Burtt. LC 78-109286. (Illus.). xii, 568p. 1971. Repr. of 1942 ed. lib. bdg. 35.00x (ISBN 0-8371-3829-9, BUEP). Greenwood.
Principles of Endocrine Pharmacology. John A. Thomas & Edward J. Keenan. LC 85-28251. 310p. 1986. 39.50x (ISBN 0-306-42129-1, Plenum Med); pap. 22.50x (ISBN 0-306-42143-7, Plenum Med). Plenum Pub.
Principles of Endodontics. Mumford & Jedynakiewicz. 1988. pap. text ed. price not set (1569). Quint Pub Co.
Principles of Energetics. K. S. Spiegler. (Illus.). 175p. 1983. 39.50 (ISBN 0-387-12441-1). Springer-Verlag.
Principles of Energy Conversion. Archie W. Culp. (Illus.). 1979. text ed. 47.95 (ISBN 0-07-014892-9). McGraw.
Principles of Engineering. James Duderstadt et al. LC 81-10450. 574p. 1982. 42.50 (ISBN 0-471-08445-X, JW). Krieger.
Principles of Engineering. James J. Duderstadt et al. LC 87-21440. 574p. 1988. Repr. of 1982 ed. lib. bdg. price not set (ISBN 0-89464-251-0). Krieger.
Principles of Engineering Economic Analysis. 3rd ed. White et al. 1989. price not set (ISBN 0-471-61320-7). Wiley.
Principles of Engineering Economic Analysis. John A. White et al. LC 77-4663. 480p. 1977. text ed. 34.50 (ISBN 0-471-01773-6). Wiley.
Principles of Engineering Economic Analysis. 2nd ed. John A. White et al. LC 83-21586. 546p. 1984. text ed. write for info. (ISBN 0-471-08607-X); write for info (ISBN 0-471-88203-8). Wiley.
Principles of Engineering Economy. 7th ed. Eugene L. Grant et al. LC 81-10399. 687p. 1982. text ed. write for info. (ISBN 0-471-06436-X); tchr's. manual avail. (ISBN 0-471-08439-5). Wiley.
Principles of Engineering Economy. 7th ed. Eugene L. Grant et al. 700p. (Arabic.). 1985. pap. 18.50 (ISBN 0-471-87183-4). Wiley.
Principles of Engineering Geology. Peter Attwell & Ian Farmer. 1976. 105.00 (NO. 6016, Pub. by Chapman & Hall). Routledge Chapman & Hall.
Principles of Engineering Geology. Jerome V. DeGraff. 576p. 1988. pap. write for info. (ISBN 0-471-61275-8). Wiley.
Principles of Engineering Geology. Robert B. Johnson & Jerome V. DeGraff. LC 88-5510. 576p. 1988. price not set (ISBN 0-471-03436-3). Wiley.
Principles of Engineering Geology & Geotechnics. Dimitri P. Krynine & William R. Judd. (Soil Mechanics & Foundations Library). (Illus.). 1957. text ed. 51.95 (ISBN 0-07-035560-6). McGraw.
Principles of Engineering Materials. C. Barrett et al. 1973. 50.00 (ISBN 0-13-709394-2). P-H.
Principles of Engineering Mechanics. H. R. Harrison & T. Nettleton. (Illus.). 255p. 1984. pap. text ed. 24.00x (ISBN 0-7131-3378-3). Trans-Atl Phila.
Principles of Engineering Mechanics, Vol. 1: Kinematics-The Geometry of Motion. Millard F. Beatty. (Mathematical Concepts & Methods in Science & Engineering Ser.: Vol. 32). 414p. 1986. 49.50x (ISBN 0-306-42131-3, Plenum Pr). Plenum Pub.
Principles of Engineering Organization. S. H. Wearne. (Illus.). 1973. pap. text ed. 21.50x (ISBN 0-7131-3290-6). Trans-Atl Phila.
Principles of Engineering Thermodynamics. E. M. Goddger. 256p. 1984. 75.00x (ISBN 0-333-37150-X, Pub. by Macmillan Ed UK). State Mutual Bk.
Principles of English Etymology. Walter W. Skeat. 23.00 (ISBN 0-405-18884-6). Ayer Co Pubs.
Principles of English Grammar. Peter Bullions. LC 82-10418. (American Linguistics Ser.). 1983. 45.00x (ISBN 0-8201-1386-7). Schol Facsimiles.
Principles of English Metre. Egerton Smith. 1971. Repr. of 1923 ed. lib. bdg. 35.00x (ISBN 0-8371-4340-3, SMEM). Greenwood.
Principles of English Prosody, Pt. 1. Lascelles Abercrombie. LC 75-41000. (BCL Ser.: No. II). Repr. of 1923 ed. 15.00 (ISBN 0-404-14735-6). AMS Pr.
Principles of Environmental Sampling. Ed. by Lawrence H. Keith. LC 87-22975. (Illus.). xxiv, 480p. 1988. 59.95 (ISBN 0-8412-1173-6); pap. 39.95 (ISBN 0-8412-1437-9). Am Chemical.
Principles of Environmental Science & Technology. S. E. Jorgensen & I. Johnson. (Studies in Environmental Science: Vol. 14). 516p. 1981. 87.00 (ISBN 0-444-99721-0). Elsevier.
Principles of Enzymology for the Food Sciences. J. R. Whitaker. (Food Science Ser: Vol. 2). 656p. 1972. 69.75 (ISBN 0-8247-1780-5). Dekker.
Principles of Epidemiology: A Self Teaching Guide. Roth Lewis. 1982. 34.00 (ISBN 0-12-593180-8). Acad Pr.
Principles of Ethics. Borden P. Bowne. LC 75-3073. (Philosophy in America Ser.). Repr. of 1892 ed. 35.00 (ISBN 0-404-59074-8). AMS Pr.
Principles of Ethics, 2 vols. Herbert Spencer. LC 77-71453. 550p. 1980. Set. pap. 8.00 (ISBN 0-913966-34-7, Liberty Clas); Vol. I. pap. (ISBN 0-913966-77-0); Vol. II. pap. (ISBN 0-913966-75-4). Liberty Fund.
Principles of Ethics, 2 vols. Herbert Spencer. LC 77-71453. 1978. Repr. Set. 20.00 (ISBN 0-913966-33-9, Liberty Clas); Vol. I. (ISBN 0-913966-76-2); Vol. II. (ISBN 0-913966-74-6). Liberty Fund.
Principles of Ethics. Taylor. write for info. Watts.
Principles of Ethics: An Introduction. Paul W. Taylor. 234p. 1975. pap. text ed. write for info. (ISBN 0-8221-0142-4). Wadsworth Pub.
Principles of Everyday Behavior Analysis. 2nd ed. L. Keith Miller. LC 79-27797. 1980. text ed. 20.75 pub net (ISBN 0-8185-0373-4); instr's manual avail. (ISBN 0-534-02114-X). Brooks-Cole.
Principles of Evidence. Irving Younger & Michael Goldsmith. LC 84-61800. 1984. 38.50 (322B). Natl Prac Inst.
Principles of Evidence: 1987 Supplement. 181p. 1988. manual 14.95 (ISBN 0-318-23995-7, 322S). Natl Prac Inst.
Principles of Examining. J. M. Thyne. LC 74-4381. 278p. 1974. text ed. 24.95x (ISBN 0-470-86700-0). Halsted Pr.
Principles of Exercise Biochemistry. Ed. by J. R. Poortmans. (Medicine & Sport Science Ser.: Vol. 27). (Illus.). viii, 220p. 1988. 120.00 (ISBN 3-8055-4790-0). S Karger.
Principles of Exercise Testing & Interpretation. Karlman Wasserman et al. LC 86-86. (Illus.). 274p. 1987. text ed. 39.50 (ISBN 0-8121-1020-X). Lea & Febiger.
Principles of Experimental Psychology. Henri Pieron. 190p. 1983. Repr. of 1929 ed. lib. bdg. 85.00 (ISBN 0-8495-4418-1). Arden Lib.
Principles of Expression in Pianoforte Playing. Adolph Christiani. LC 74-1348. (Music Reprint Ser.). 303p. 1974. Repr. of 1886 ed. lib. bdg. 35.00 (ISBN 0-306-70623-7). Da Capo.
Principles of Extracorporeal Shock Wave Lithotripsy. Ed. by Robert A. Riehle, Jr. (Illus.). 256p. 1987. text ed. 50.00 (ISBN 0-443-08513-7). Churchill.
Principles of Extractive Metallurgy. 2nd ed. Terkel Rosenqvist. (Materials Science & Electronics Ser.). 608p. 1983. text ed. 52.95 (ISBN 0-07-053910-3). McGraw.
Principles of Faghr & Sufism. Shahmagsoud Sadegh Angha. 173p. (Persian.). 1974. 35.00 (ISBN 0-910735-10-7); pap. 29.00 (ISBN 0-317-68047-1). MTO Printing & Pubn Ctr.
Principles of Faith. rev. ed. Charles Finney. Ed. by L. G. Parkhurst. 240p. 1988. pap. 6.95 (ISBN 0-87123-993-0). Bethany Hse.
Principles of Faith (Rosh Amanah) Isaac Abravanal. (Littman Library of Jewish Civilization). 272p. 1982. 26.00x (ISBN 0-19-710045-7). Oxford U Pr.
Principles of Family Medicine. Robert F. Rakel. LC 76-41541. (Illus.). 1977. text ed. write for info. (ISBN 0-7216-7449-6). Saunders.
Principles of Family Systems in Family Medicine. Ed. by Sergio Henao & Nellie Grose. LC 85-5909. 438p. 1985. 45.00 (ISBN 0-87630-388-2). Brunner-Mazel.
Principles of Family Systems in Family Medicine. Ed. by Sergio Henao & Nellie P. Grose. 423p. 1985. 40.00. Soc Tchrs Fam Med.
Principles of Farm Irrigation System Design. Larry G. James. 543p. 1987. write for info. (ISBN 0-471-83954-X). Wiley.
Principles of Farm Machinery. 3rd ed. R. A. Kepner & Roy Bainer. (Illus.). 1978. text ed. 34.95 (ISBN 0-87055-252-X). AVI.
Principles of Federal Income Taxation. D. J. Gaffney & D. H. Skadden. 1982. text ed. 32.95 (ISBN 0-07-057781-1). McGraw.
Principles of Federal Pollution Control Law. David Luban. Date not set. 1.00. IPPP.
Principles of Feedback Control. George Biernson. LC 87-30539. 1040p. 1988. 69.96 (ISBN 0-471-82167-5). Wiley.
Principles of Fermentation Technology. P. F. Stanbury & A. Whitaker. (Illus.). 304p. 1984. text ed. 61.00 (ISBN 0-08-024400-9); pap. text ed. 24.00 (ISBN 0-08-024406-8). Pergamon.
Principles of Field Crop Production. John H. Martin et al. 1989. text ed. write for info. Macmillan.
Principles of Field Ionization & Field Desorption Mass Spectrometry. H. D. Beckey. LC 77-33014. 1971. 83.00 (ISBN 0-08-017557-0). Pergamon.
Principles of File Processing. Richard H. Austing & Lillian N. Cassel. 400p. 1988. text ed. 28.00 (ISBN 0-669-12375-7); Instr. Guide 2.00 (ISBN 0-669-12376-5). Heath.
Principles of Finance. Robert W. Kolb. 1988. text ed. write for info. (ISBN 0-673-18597-4). Scott F.
Principles of Financial & Managerial Accounting. Belverd E. Needles, Jr. et al. LC 87-80110. 950p. 1987. text ed. 45.96 (ISBN 0-395-43348-7); study guide 15.16 (ISBN 0-395-44715-1); instr's solns. manual 5.56 (ISBN 0-395-44721-6); Working papers two sets. instr's handbook 5.56 (ISBN 0-395-44720-8); 15.96 ea.; Transparencies two sets. 159.96 ea. HM.
Principles of Financial & Managerial Accounting. Carl S. Warren & Philip E. Fess. LC 85-61429. 1986. text ed. write for info. (ISBN 0-538-01202-1, A20). SW Pub.
Principles of Financial & Managerial Accounting. 2nd ed. Carl S. Warren et al. 1989. text ed. price not set (ISBN 0-538-80171-9, AB60BA). SW Pub.
Principles of Financial Management. 2nd ed. Benton E. Gup. 704p. 1987. 41.50 (ISBN 0-471-81203-X); study guide avail. (ISBN 0-471-83811-X); Sampler Advertisement & Text Set. write for info. (ISBN 0-471-85832-3). Wiley.
Principles of Financial Management. Burton Kolb. 1983. text ed. 36.95 (ISBN 0-256-02879-6); study guide 12.95 (ISBN 0-256-02880-X). Business Pubns.
Principles of Financial Management. 2nd ed. Burton Kolb & Demong. 1988. 39.95 (ISBN 0-256-03699-3); study guide 12.95. Business Pubns.
Principles of Financial Management. Haim Levy & Marshall Sarnat. (Illus.). 752p. 1988. text ed. 43.00 (ISBN 0-13-710054-X). P-H.
Principles of Fire Protection. Percy Bugbee. Ed. by Keith Tower & Amy Dean. LC 76-50848. 1978. text ed. 16.50 (ISBN 0-87765-084-5, TXT-4); instr. manual 3.50 (ISBN 0-87765-122-1, TXT-4A). Natl Fire Prot.
Principles of Fire Protection. Percy Bugbee. text ed. 29.50 (B7-TXT-4). Natl Fire Prot.
Principles of Fire Protection Chemistry: Instructor's Manual. Ed. by Keith Tower. LC 76-41622. 1976. pap. text ed. 3.50 (ISBN 0-87765-083-7). Natl Fire Prot.
Principles of Fire Protection Chemistry. Richard L. Tuve. Ed. by Keith Tower. LC 76-26781. 1976. pap. text ed. 27.00 (ISBN 0-87765-080-2, B7-TXT-2). Natl Fire Prot.
Principles of Fire Protection: Instructor's Manual. Ed. by Gordon P. McKinnon. LC 76-27198. 1976. pap. 3.50 (ISBN 0-685-73837-X, IM-FPM). Natl Fire Prot.
Principles of Firmware Engineering in Microprogram Control. Michael Andrews. LC 80-19386. (Digital Systems Design Ser.). (Illus.). 347p. 1980. 41.95 (ISBN 0-914894-63-3, Computer Sci Pr). W H Freeman.
Principles of Fishery Science. 2nd ed. W. Harry Everhart & William D. Youngs. (Illus.). 343p. 1981. 27.50x (ISBN 0-8014-1334-6). Cornell U Pr.
Principles of Flat Pattern Design. Nora M. McDonald & Ruth E. Weibel. (Illus.). 320p. 1988. pap. text ed. price not set. P-H.
Principles of Fluid Mechanics. Wen-Hsiung Li & Sau-Hai Lam. 1964. write for info. (ISBN 0-201-04240-1). Addison-Wesley.
Principles of Fluorescence Spectroscopy. Joseph R. Lakowicz. LC 85-28251. 510p. 1983. 35.00x (ISBN 0-306-41285-3, Plenum Pr). Plenum Pub.
Principles of Food Analysis for Filth, Decomposition & Foreign Matter. 2nd ed. Ed. by J. Richard Gorman. (FDA Technical Bulletin Ser.: No. 1). (Illus.). 286p. 1981. pap. 44.00. Assoc Official.
Principles of Food & Beverage Operations. Jack D. Ninemeier. Ed. by Timothy Eaton. LC 84-18766. (Illus.). 451p. 1984. text ed. 36.95 (ISBN 0-86612-017-3). Educ Inst Am Hotel.
Principles of Food, Beverage & Labor Cost. 3rd ed. Dittmer & Griffin. 1984. 26.95 (ISBN 0-442-21973-3). Van Nos Reinhold.
Principles of Food, Beverage & Labor Costs. P. Dittmer. 1983. write for info. (ISBN 0-8436-2202-4). Van Nos Reinhold.
Principles of Food Chemistry. rev. ed. J. M. DeMan. (Illus.). 1982. pap. 29.95 (ISBN 0-87055-419-0). AVI.
Principles of Food Packaging. 2nd ed. Stanley Sacharow & Roger C. Griffin. (Illus.). 1980. lib. bdg. 39.95 (ISBN 0-87055-347-X). AVI.
Principles of Food Preparation: A Laboratory Manual. 2nd ed. Jeanne H. Freeland-Grave. 377p. 1987. pap. write for info. (ISBN 0-02-339350-5). Macmillan.
Principles of Food Processing Sanitation. Food Processors Institute Staff. Ed. by Allen Katsuyama. LC 79-57624. 303p. (Orig.). 1980. pap. 40.00 (ISBN 0-937774-03-0). Food Processors.
Principles of Food Sanitation. Marriott. 37.95 (ISBN 0-317-64250-2). Van Nos Reinhold.
Principles of Food Sanitation. N. G. Marriott. (Food Science & Technology Ser.). (Illus.). 1985. 39.95 (ISBN 0-87055-485-9). AVI.
Principles of Food Science: Physical Methods of Food Preservation, Pt. 2. Owen Fennema. (Food Science Ser.: Vol. 4). 1975. 69.75 (ISBN 0-8247-6322-X); text ed. 29.75. Dekker.
Principles of Foreign Policy: The Civil State in Its World Setting. Roy E. Jones. LC 79-9835. 1979. 9.95x (ISBN 0-312-64561-9). St Martin.
Principles of Forensic Handwriting Identification & Testimony. Edward J. Smith. (Illus.). 138p. 1984. 27.25 (ISBN 0-398-04973-4). C C Thomas.
Principles of Forensic Medicine. 3rd rev. enl. ed. William A. Guy. LC 75-23715. (Illus.). Repr. of 1868 ed. 54.00 (ISBN 0-404-13268-5). AMS Pr.
Principles of Forest Entomology. Douglas C. Allen. LC 84-8509. (Illus.). 224p. 1984. lab manual 13.95x (ISBN 0-8156-2318-6). Syracuse U Pr.
Principles of Forest Entomology. 5th ed. Fred B. Knight & Herman J. Heikkenen. (Forestry Ser.). (Illus.). 480p. 1980. text ed. 48.95 (ISBN 0-07-035095-7). McGraw.
Principles of Forest Hydrology. John D. Hewlett. LC 81-16371. 192p. 1982. pap. 8.00x (ISBN 0-8203-0608-8). U of Ga Pr.
Principles of Formulating Polyvinyl Chloride. Wickson. 1988. price not set (ISBN 0-471-60182-9). Wiley.
Principles of FORTRAN 77 Programming. Jerrold L. Wagener. LC 79-17421. 370p. 1980. pap. text ed. 30.95 (ISBN 0-471-04474-1). Wiley.
Principles of Free Trade. 2nd ed. Condy Raguet. LC 68-56569. 1969. Repr. of 1840 ed. 45.00x (ISBN 0-678-00529-X). Kelley.
Principles of Freedom. Terence MacSwiney. LC 73-102616. (Irish Culture & History Ser). 1970. Repr. of 1921 ed. 23.00x (ISBN 0-8046-0793-1, Pub. by Kennikat). Assoc Faculty Pr.
Principles of Functional Analysis & Operator Methods in Quantum Mechanics. Martin Schechter. 383p. 1975. 44.50 (ISBN 0-12-622751-9). Acad Pr.

Principles of Functional Programming. Hankin et al. (Illus.). 288p. 1985. text ed. 36.00 (ISBN 0-13-709148-6). P-H.

Principles of Gardening. Hugh Johnson. 1981. 75.00x (ISBN 0-686-78771-4, Pub. by RHS Ent England). State Mutual Bk.

Principles of Gardening. Hugh Johnson. (Illus., Orig.). 1987. pap. 17.95 (ISBN 0-671-50805-9, Fireside). S&S.

Principles of Gardening for Australia. C. Bogue-Luffman. 96p. (Orig.). 1985. 12.95 (ISBN 0-86417-039-4, Pub. by Kangaroo Pr). Intl Spec Bk.

Principles of Gene Manipulation. 3rd ed. R. W. Old & S. B. Primrose. (Illus.). 414p. 1985. pap. text ed. 21.00x (ISBN 0-632-01318-4). Blackwell Pubns.

Principles of General Thermodynamics. George N. Hatsopoulos & Joseph H. Keenan. LC 80-25946. 830p. 1981. Repr. of 1965 ed. 47.50 (ISBN 0-89874-303-6). Krieger.

Principles of Genetic Counseling. Edmond A. Murphy & Gary A. Chase. LC 75-16020. pap. 102.30 (ISBN 0-317-26170-3, 2024267). Bks Demand UMI.

Principles of Genetic Epistemology. Jean Piaget. pap. 7.95 (ISBN 0-7100-8660-1). Routledge Chapman & Hall.

Principles of Genetic Toxicology. David Brusick. LC 80-16514. 300p. 1980. 32.50x (ISBN 0-306-40414-1, Plenum Pr). Plenum Pub.

Principles of Genetic Toxicology. 2nd ed. David Brusick. LC 87-17169. (Illus.). 302p. 1987. 35.00x (ISBN 0-306-42532-7, Plenum Pr). Plenum Pub.

Principles of Genetics. 2nd ed. James W. Fristrom & Michael T. Clegg. LC 85-61621. (Illus.). 700p. 1988. text ed. 34.95x (ISBN 0-913462-11-X). Chiron Pr.

Principles of Genetics. 7th ed. Eldon J. Gardner & D. Peter Snustad. LC 83-21798. 672p. 1984. write for info. (ISBN 0-471-87610-0). Wiley.

Principles of Geodynamics. 3rd, rev. ed. A. E. Scheidegger. (Illus.). 380p. 1982. 96.00 (ISBN 0-387-11323-1). Springer-Verlag.

Principles of Geographical Information Systems for Land Resources Assessment. P. A. Burrough. (Monographs on Soil & Resources Survey: No. 12). (Illus.). 220p. 1986. 75.00 (ISBN 0-19-854563-0); pap. 39.95 (ISBN 0-19-854592-4). Oxford U Pr.

Principles of Geology. 4th ed. James Gilluly et al. LC 74-23076. (Geology Ser.). (Illus.). 527p. 1975. text ed. 30.95 (ISBN 0-7167-0269-X). W H Freeman.

Principles of Geology, 3 vols. Charles Lyell. (Illus.). 1970. Repr. of 1833 ed. Set. text ed. 117.00x (ISBN 3-7682-0685-8). Lubrecht & Cramer.

Principles of Geometrie Gathered out of G. Henischius by F. Cooke. Georg Henisch. LC 71-25788. (English Experience Ser.: No. 321). 88p. 1971. Repr. of 1591 ed. 20.00 (ISBN 90-221-0321-8). Walter J Johnson.

Principles of Geomorphology. 2nd ed. William D. Thornbury. LC 68-8323. 594p. 1969. text ed. write for info. (ISBN 0-471-86197-9). Wiley.

Principles of Geotechnical Engineering. Braja M. Das. 1985. text ed. 41.00 (ISBN 0-534-03765-8, 21R4400, Pub. by PWS Engineering). PWS Kent Pub.

Principles of Geriatric Medicine. Ed. by R. Andres et al. (Illus.). 1100p. 1985. text ed. 85.00 (ISBN 0-07-001781-6). McGraw.

Principles of Gestalt Family Therapy. Walter Kempler. LC 74-26006. 1973. pap. 8.50 (ISBN 0-9600808-1-3). Kempler Inst.

Principles of Government: A Treatise on Free Institutions. Nathaniel Chipman. LC 76-99478. (American Constitutional & Legal History Ser.). 1970. Repr. of 1833 ed. 39.50 (ISBN 0-306-71851-0). Da Capo.

Principles of Government, a Treatise on Free Institutions, Including the Constitution of the U. S. Nathaniel Chipman. 1969. 20.50 (ISBN 0-8337-0562-8). B Franklin.

Principles of Government Purchasing. Arthur G. Thomas. (Brookings Institution Reprint Ser). Repr. of 1919 ed. lib. bdg. 29.50 (ISBN 0-697-00173-3). Irvington.

Principles of Grammar & Learning. William O'Grady. LC 86-11402. 248p. 1987. lib. bdg. 27.50x (ISBN 0-226-62074-3). U of Chicago Pr.

Principles of Group Solidarity. Michael Hechter. LC 87-5074. (California Series on Social Choice & Political Economy: Vol. 11). 288p. 1987. 28.50 (ISBN 0-520-06102-0). U of Cal Pr.

Principles of Group Solidarity. Michael Hechter. 234p. (Orig.). 1988. pap. text ed. 8.95x (ISBN 0-520-06462-3). U of Cal Pr.

Principles of Guidance. Jack Rudman. (DANTES Ser.: No. 33). 1988. 25.95 (ISBN 0-8373-6683-6); pap. 13.95 (ISBN 0-8373-6633-X). Natl Learning.

Principles of Gynaecological Surgery. Ed. by S. L. Stanton. (Illus.). 320p. 1987. 49.50 (ISBN 0-387-17485-0). Springer-Verlag.

Principles of Harmonic Analysis. Walter Piston. 1933. pap. 13.00 (ISBN 0-911318-05-4). E C Schirmer.

Principles of Harmonic Substitution. Dom Minasi. Ed. by Thomas Gambino. 48p. (Orig.). 1979. pap. 8.95 wkbk. (ISBN 0-936519-02-9). Sunrise Artistries.

Principles of Harmony & Contrast of Colors & Their Applications to the Arts. M. E. Chevreul. 256p. 49.50 (ISBN 0-88740-090-6). Schiffer.

Principles of Harmony & Contrast of Colors. M. E. Chevreul. 1981. pap. 27.95 (ISBN 0-442-21212-7). Van Nos Reinhold.

Principles of Hazardous Materials Management. Roger D. Griffin. (Illus.). 260p. 1988. 45.00 (ISBN 0-87371-145-9). Lewis Pubs Inc.

Principles of Health Insurance & Disability Income Insurance Selling. 3rd, rev. ed. 225p. 1987. pap. text ed. 18.95 (ISBN 0-88462-700-4, 5403-04). Longman Finan.

Principles of Health Maintenance. Paul R. Schnurrenberger. Ed. by Robert S. Sharman. LC 82-18067. 304p. 1983. 44.95 (ISBN 0-275-91413-5, C1413). Praeger.

Principles of Health Planning in the U. S. S. R. G. A. Popov. (Public Health Paper: No. 43). (Also avail. in French, Russian & Spanish). 1971. pap. 4.80 (ISBN 92-4-130043-4). World Health.

Principles of Health Risk Assessment. Ed. by Paolo F. Ricci. (Illus.). 432p. 1985. text ed. 37.33 (ISBN 0-13-709197-4). P-H.

Principles of Heat Treatment of Steel. George Krauss. 1980. 87.00 (ISBN 0-87170-100-6). ASM.

Principles of High Resolution NMR in Solids. M. Mehring. (Illus.). 342p. 1983. 99.00 (ISBN 0-387-11852-7). Springer-Verlag.

Principles of High-Resolution Radar. August W. Rihaczek. LC 85-63231. 505p. 1985. Repr. of 1977 ed. 38.95 (ISBN 0-932146-11-2). Peninsula CA.

Principles of Historical Linguistics. Hans H. Hock. (Trends in Linguistics, Studies & Monographs: No. 34). (Illus.). xiv, 706p. 1986. lib. bdg. 172.00x (ISBN 3-11-010600-0); pap. text ed. 29.95X (ISBN 3-11-011068-7). Mouton.

Principles of Holiness. Charles G. Finney. LC 83-25769. 274p. 1984. pap. 6.95 (ISBN 0-87123-403-3, 210403). Bethany Hse.

Principles of Holistic Skin Therapy With Herbal Essences. Dietrich Gumbel. Tr. by Ritva Abao from Ger. (Illus.). 247p. 1986. pap. text ed. 18.00 (ISBN 3-7760-0931-4, Pub. by K F Haug Pubs). Medicina Bio.

Principles of Holography. 2nd ed. Howard M. Smith. LC 75-5631. pap. 73.30 (2056155). Bks Demand UMI.

Principles of Horseshoeing II. Doug Butler. (Illus.). 567p. 1985. 49.95x (ISBN 0-916992-02-0). Doug Butler.

Principles of Horticultural Production. V. R. Gardner. 583p. 1966. text ed. 18.50x (ISBN 0-87013-095-1). Mich St U Pr.

Principles of Horticultural Taxonomy. Dehgan. 1988. write for info. (ISBN 0-471-84739-9). Wiley.

Principles of Horticulture. Charles Adams & Katherine Bamford. (Illus.). 264p. 1984. pap. 29.95 (ISBN 0-434-90008-7, Pub. by W Heinemann Ltd). David & Charles.

Principles of Horticulture. 2nd ed. Ervin L. Denisen. (Illus.). 1979. text ed. write for info. (ISBN 0-02-328380-7); write for info (ISBN 0-685-96773-5). Macmillan.

Principles of Hospital Business Office Management. Beaufort B. Longest, Jr. 1975. instr's manual o.p. 23.50 (ISBN 0-686-77078-1, 1448). Healthcare Fin Man Assn.

Principles of Host-Plant Resistance to Insect Pests. N. Panda. LC 78-59169. (Illus.). 406p. 1980. text ed. 38.50x (ISBN 0-916672-93-X, Pub. by Allanheld). Rowman.

Principles of Human Anatomy. 4th ed. Gerard Tortora. 816p. 1985. text ed. 44.95 scp (ISBN 0-06-046623-5, HarpC). Har-Row.

Principles of Human Anatomy. 5th ed. Gerard J. Tortora. 832p. 1988. text ed. 40.50t (ISBN 0-06-046685-5, HarpC). Har-Row.

Principles of Human Biochemical Genetics. 3rd ed. Ed. by H. Harris. LC 75-108280. (Frontiers of Biology Ser.: Vol. 19). 477p. 1981. 37.50 (ISBN 0-444-80264-9, Biomedical Pr); pap. 25.00 (ISBN 0-444-80256-8). Elsevier.

Principles of Human Knowledge see Empiricists.

Principles of Human Knowledge - Three Dialogues. George Berkeley. Ed. by Roger Woolhouse. 224p. 1988. pap. 5.95 (ISBN 0-14-043293-0). Penguin.

Principles of Human Knowledge & Three Dialogues Between Hylas & Philonous. George Berkeley. 12.00 (ISBN 0-8446-1667-2). Peter Smith.

Principles of Human Physiology. 2nd ed. Gerard Tortora & Ronald Evans. 704p. 1986. text ed. 47.50 scp (ISBN 0-06-046658-8, HarpC). Har-Row.

Principles of Hydrocarbon Reservoir Simulation. 2nd ed. Gordon W. Thomas. LC 81-82011. (Illus.). 207p. 1981. text ed. 52.00 (ISBN 0-934634-11-4). Intl Human Res.

Principles of Hydrometallurgical Extraction & Reclamation. Eric Jakson. 1986. 54.95 (ISBN 0-470-20314-5). Halsted Pr.

Principles of Hypnotherapy see Medical Hypnosis.

Principles of Ideal-Fluid Aerodynamics. K. Karamcheti. LC 79-26876. 654p. 1980. Repr. of 1966 ed. lib. bdg. 43.00 (ISBN 0-89874-113-0). Krieger.

Principles of Igneous Petrology. S. Maaloe. (Illus.). 415p. 1985. 55.00 (ISBN 0-387-13520-0). Springer-Verlag.

Principles of Immunology. 2nd ed. Ed. by Noel R. Rose & Felix Milgrom. (Illus.). 1979. pap. text ed. write for info. (ISBN 0-02-403610-2). Macmillan.

Principles of Immunology & Immunodiagnostics. Ralph M. Aloisi. LC 87-31150. (Illus.). 238p. 1988. pap. text ed. 22.50 (ISBN 0-8121-1133-8). Lea & Febiger.

Principles of Improvised Explosive Devices. (Illus.). 120p. (Orig.). 1984. pap. 12.00 (ISBN 0-87364-288-0). Paladin Pr.

Principles of Improvised Explosive Devices. 1986. lib. bdg. 79.95 (ISBN 0-8490-3656-9). Gordon Pr.

Principles of Induced Polarization for Geophysical Exploration. J. S. Sumner. (Developments in Economic Geology Ser.: Vol. 5). 278p. 1976. 71.00 (ISBN 0-444-41481-9). Elsevier.

Principles of Induction Melting. 96p. 1987. pap. 30.00 (ISBN 0-317-59859-7, TE7705). Am Foundrymen.

Principles of Inductive Logic. 2nd ed. John Venn. LC 72-119162. Orig. Title: Principles of Empirical, or Inductive Logic. 624p. 1973. 19.50 (ISBN 0-8284-0265-5). Chelsea Pub.

Principles of Industrial Chemistry. 2nd ed. Clausen. 1988. price not set (ISBN 0-471-62823-9). Wiley.

Principles of Industrial Chemistry. Chris A. Clausen, III & Guy C. Mattson. LC 78-9450. 412p. 1978. 50.00 (ISBN 0-471-02774-X). Wiley.

Principles of Industrial Engineering. Charles B. Going. LC 77-17900. (Management History Ser.: No. 45). 177p. Repr. of 1911 ed. 22.50 (ISBN 0-87960-049-7). Hive Pub.

Principles of Industrial Facility Planning. Howard A. Stafford. LC 80-26737. (Illus.). 289p. 1980. pap. 11.95 (ISBN 0-910436-08-8). Conway Data.

Principles of Industrial Measurement for Control Application. Ernest Smith. 452p. 1984. text ed. 52.50x (ISBN 0-87664-465-5). Instru Soc.

Principles of Industrial Measurement for Control Applications. Ernest Smith. (Illus.). 464p. 1985. text ed. 46.00 (ISBN 0-13-709213-X). P-H.

Principles of Industrial Therapy for the Mentally Ill. Bertram J. Black. LC 73-88017. 200p. 1970. 54.50 (ISBN 0-8089-0062-5, 790600). Grune.

Principles of Industrial Welding. Enrico P. Bongio. 1978. text ed. 6.50 (ISBN 0-686-24289-0); text ed. 5.85 (ISBN 0-686-26120-8). Lincoln Arc Weld.

Principles of Information Processing. 4th ed. Steven L. Mandell. 225p. 1988. pap. text ed. 20.50 (ISBN 0-314-68950-8). West Pub.

Principles of Information Processing. Donald Spencer. 250p. 1985. 25.95 (ISBN 0-675-20410-0). Additional supplements may be obtained from publisher. Merrill.

Principles of Information Storage & Retrieval. 34p. 1964. pap. 20.00 (ISBN 0-8169-0018-3, ED-3). Am Inst Chem Eng.

Principles of Information Systems. Burch. 1988. pap. write for info. (ISBN 0-471-85701-7). Wiley.

Principles of Information Systems Analysis & Design. Harlan D. Mills et al. 1986. 37.50 (ISBN 0-12-497545-3). Acad Pr.

Principles of Information Systems for Management. 2nd ed. Niv Ahituv & Seev Neumann. 624p. 1986. text ed. write for info. (ISBN 0-697-08267-9); write for info. solutions manual (ISBN 0-697-00884-3); write for info. test item file (ISBN 0-697-08421-3). Wm C Brown.

Principles of Insect Physiology. 7th ed. Vincent B. Wigglesworth. (Illus.). 1972. (Pub. by Chapman & Hall); pap. 35.00 (ISBN 0-412-24660-0, 6763). Routledge Chapman & Hall.

Principles of Instructional Design. 3rd ed. Robert M. Gagne et al. LC 87-18618. (Illus.). 384p. 1987. text ed. price not set (ISBN 0-03-011958-8). HR&W.

Principles of Instrumental Analysis. 3rd ed. Douglas A. Skoog & Donald M. West. 960p. 1985. text ed. 56.75x (ISBN 0-03-001229-5, CBS C); solns. manual 14.00 (ISBN 0-03-001232-5). SCP.

Principles of Insurance. 8th ed. Robert I. Mehr et al. 1985. 39.95x (ISBN 0-256-03008-1). Irwin.

Principles of Insurance. 2nd ed. George E. Rejda. 1986. text ed. write for info. (ISBN 0-673-18209-6). Scott F.

Principles of Insurance. 3rd ed. George E. Rejda. 1988. text ed. price not set (ISBN 0-673-38409-8). Scott F.

Principles of Insurance Law. Emeric Fischer & Peter N. Swisher. LC 86-71031. Date not set. price not set. Bender.

Principles of Insurance Production. 2nd ed. LC 80-80640. 685p. 1986. pap. text ed. 18.00 (ISBN 0-89462-027-4). IIA.

Principles of Integral Science of Religion. Georg Schmid. (Religion & Reason Ser.). 1979. text ed. 33.75 (ISBN 90-279-7864-6). Mouton.

Principles of Intensive Psychotherapy. Frieda Fromm-Reichmann. LC 50-9782. 1960. pap. 9.95 (ISBN 0-226-26599-4, P49, Phoen). U of Chicago Pr.

Principles of Interactive Computer Graphics. 2nd ed. William M. Newman & Robert F. Sproull. (Illus.). 1979. text ed. 48.95 (ISBN 0-07-046338-7). McGraw.

Principles of Interferometric Spectroscopy. John Chamberlain. LC 78-13206. 347p. 1979. 116.00 (ISBN 0-471-99719-6). Wiley.

Principles of Intermediate Algebra with Applications. Harry L. Nustad & Terry H. Wesner. 744p. 1985. pap. text ed. write for info. (ISBN 0-697-00270-5); instr's. manual avail. (ISBN 0-697-00598-4); student guide to exercises avail. (ISBN 0-697-00467-8); audio tapes avail. (ISBN 0-697-03138-1); video tapes avail. (ISBN 0-697-03137-3). Wm C Brown.

Principles of Intermediate Swimming. Joel A. Bloom. (Illus.). 111p. 1978. pap. text ed. 4.95x plastic comb bdg. (ISBN 0-89641-002-1); pap. text ed. 4.95x perfect bdg. (ISBN 0-89641-010-2). American Pr.

Principles of International Accounting. Samuel Fox & Norlin G. Rueschhoff. LC 85-80012. (Illus.). 170p. 1986. 35.00x (ISBN 0-914872-22-2); solution manual, 92p. 7.50. Austin Pr.

Principles of International Development Law: Progressive Development of the Principles of International Law Relating to the New International Economic Order. Milan Bulajic. LC 86-2515. 1986. lib. bdg. 76.50 (ISBN 9-02-473304-9, Pub. by Kluwer-Nijhoff (Netherlands)). Kluwer Academic.

Principles of International Economics. Miltiades Chacholiades. (Illus.). 656p. 1981. text ed. 42.95 (ISBN 0-07-010345-3). McGraw.

Principles of International Finance. Daniel R. Kane. 256p. 1987. lib. bdg. 49.95x (ISBN 0-7099-1584-5, Pub. by Croom Helm UK); pap. text ed. 14.95x (ISBN 0-7099-3134-4, Pub. by Croom Helm UK). Routledge Chapman & Hall.

Principles of International Law. T. J. Lawrence. xxi, 645p. 1987. Repr. of 1895 ed. lib. bdg. 57.50x (ISBN 0-8377-2405-8). Rothman.

Principles of International Law Concerning Friendly Relations & Cooperation. Ed. by Milan Sahovic. LC 73-8985. 470p. 1972. lib. bdg. 17.50 (ISBN 0-379-00020-2). Oceana.

Principles of Interpretation. Edward Goodwin Ballard. LC 83-4281. (Continental Thought Ser.: Vol. 5). xiv, 247p. 1983. text ed. 28.95x (ISBN 0-8214-0688-4); pap. 13.95x (ISBN 0-8214-0689-2). Ohio U Pr.

Principles of Interpretation. Steven T. Levy. LC 84-2808. 236p. 1984. 25.00x (ISBN 0-87668-705-2). Aronson.

Principles of Intuitionism. A. S. Troelstra. LC 74-88182. (Lecture Notes in Mathematics: Vol. 95). 1969. pap. 10.70 (ISBN 0-387-04614-3). Springer-Verlag.

Principles of Inventory & Materials Management. R. J. Tersine. 554p. 1987. 39.95 (ISBN 0-444-01162-5, North Holland). Elsevier.

Principles of Inventory & Materials Management. 2nd ed. Richard J. Tersine. 496p. 1981. 31.00 (ISBN 0-444-00641-9, North-Holland). Elsevier.

Principles of Inventory Materials Management. 3rd ed. Tersine. 500p. 1987. 39.95. Elsevier.

Principles of Inverter Circuits. B. D. Bedford & R. G. Hoft. LC 83-26789. 430p. 1985. Repr. of 1964 ed. lib. bdg. 42.50 (ISBN 0-89874-730-9). Krieger.

Principles of Inverter Circuits. Burnice D. Bedford & R. G. Hoft. LC 64-20078. 413p. 1964. 42.95x (ISBN 0-471-06134-4, Pub. by Wiley-Interscience). Wiley.

Principles of Inverter Circuits. Burnice D. Bedford & R. G. Hoft. LC 64-20078. pap. 107.30 (ISBN 0-317-09138-7, 2020596). Bks Demand UMI.

Principles of Investigation. John P. Kenney & Harry W. More, Jr. (Criminal Justice Ser.). (Illus.). 448p. 1979. text ed. 36.00 (ISBN 0-8299-0284-8); wkbk. 14.50 (ISBN 0-8299-0289-9); instrs. manual avail. (ISBN 0-8299-0592-8). West Pub.

Principles of Investment. 3rd ed. Frederick Amling. (Plaid Ser.). 198p. 1983. pap. 12.95 (ISBN 0-87094-336-7). Dow Jones-Irwin.

Principles of Investment. facsimile ed. Aaron M. Sakolski. LC 75-2665. (Wall Street & the Security Market Ser.). 1975. Repr. of 1925 ed. 38.50x (ISBN 0-405-06989-8). Ayer Co Pubs.

Principles of Ion-Selective Electrodes & of Membrane Transport. W. E. Morf. (Studies in Analytical Chemistry: Vol. 2). 434p. 1981. 105.25 (ISBN 0-444-99749-0). Elsevier.

Principles of Islamic Education. K. Ahmed. 1.00 (ISBN 0-686-18355-X). Kazi Pubns.

Principles of Isotope Geology. 2nd ed. Gunter Faure. LC 86-9147. 589p. 1986. 45.50 (ISBN 0-471-86412-9). Wiley.

Principles of Jewish Law. Ed. by Menachem Elon. 866p. 1975. 50.00 (ISBN 0-87855-188-3). Transaction Bks.

Principles of Joy: Studies in Philippians. David L. Hocking. pap. 5.95 (ISBN 0-88469-027-X). BMH Bks.

Principles of Judicial Administration. W. F. Willoughby. xxii, 662p. 1981. Repr. of 1929 ed. lib. bdg. 45.00x (ISBN 0-8377-1312-9). Rothman.

Principles of Jurisprudence & Legal Theory. V. D. Mahajan. 482p. 1980. 75.00x (ISBN 0-317-54877-8, Pub. by Eastern Bk India). State Mutual Bk.

Principles of Justice in Taxation. Stephen F. Weston. LC 68-56695. (Columbia University, Studies in Social Sciences Ser.: No. 45). 1968. Repr. of 1903 ed. 22.50 (ISBN 0-404-51045-0). AMS Pr.

Principles of Knitting: Methods & Techniques of Hand Knitting. June H. Hiatt. (Illus.). 448p. 1988. 24.95 (ISBN 0-671-55233-3). S&S.

Principles of Microsurgical Techniques in Infertility. Ed. by J. Victor Reyniak & Niels H. Lauersen. LC 81-3045. 310p. 1982. 49.50x (ISBN 0-306-40781-7, Plenum Med Bk). Plenum Pub.
Principles of Military Communication Systems. Don J. Torrieri. LC 81-67379. pap. 77.50 (2027160). Bks Demand UMI.
Principles of Mineral Behavior. A. Putnis & J. D. McConnell. (Geological Studies: Vol. 1). 258p. 1980. 41.00 (ISBN 0-444-00439-4); pap. 32.50 (ISBN 0-444-00444-0). Elsevier.
Principles of Mineral Flotation. Ed. by Jones & Woodcock. 335p. 1984. text ed. 45.00x (ISBN 0-909520-85-2, Pub. by Australian Inst M & M). Brookfield Pub Co.
Principles of Mineralogy. William H. Blackburn & William H. Dennen. 432p. 1988. text ed. write for info. (ISBN 0-697-01190-9). Wm C Brown.
Principles of Mini-Computer Operations, TI-990. Stewart Ferguson. (Illus.). 218p. 1986. pap. text ed. 12.95x (ISBN 0-935920-26-9). Natl Pub Black Hills.
Principles of Modern Biology. Armitage. (gr. 9-12). 1972. pap. text ed. 12.00 each incl. 9 texts (ISBN 0-8449-0450-3); tchrs' manual 4.00; test 3.00; complete biology course 150.00. Learning Line.
Principles of Modern Chemistry. David W. Oxtoby & Norman H. Nachtreib. 896p. 1986. text ed. 50.75 (ISBN 0-03-070653-X); student guide 15.00 (ISBN 0-03-070654-8). SCP.
Principles of Modern Immunobiology: Basic & Clinical. Byung H. Park & Robert A. Good. LC 73-13831. (Illus.). Repr. of 1974 ed. 119.20 (ISBN 0-8357-9416-4, 2014573). Bks Demand UMI.
Principles of Modern Mathematics. William E. Hartnett. LC 63-7108. pap. 108.00 (ISBN 0-317-09389-4, 2051870). Bks Demand UMI.
Principles of Modern Psychological Measurement: A Festschrift for Frederic M. Lord. Ed. by Howard Wainer & Samuel Messick. 416p. 1983. text ed. 39.95x (ISBN 0-89859-277-1). L Erlbaum Assocs.
Principles of Modern Radar. J. L. Eaves & E. K. Reedy. (Illus.). 672p. 1987. 62.95 (ISBN 0-442-22104-5). Van Nos Reinhold.
Principles of Modern Radar Systems. Michel H. Carpentier. (Radar Library). 350p. 1988. text ed. 66.00 (ISBN 0-89006-285-4). Artech hse.
Principles of Money, Banking, & Financial Markets. 5th ed. Lawernce S. Ritter & William L. Silber. LC 85-47560. 619p. 1986. text ed. 32.95x (HarpC). Har-Row.
Principles of Money, Banking, & Financial Markets. 5th ed. Lawrence S. Ritter & William L. Silber. LC 85-47560. (Illus.). 640p. 1986. 32.95x; tchr's ed. free (ISBN 0-465-06331-4); pap. 9.95x study guide. Basic.
Principles of Money, Banking & Financial Markets. 6th ed. Lawrence S. Ritter & William L. Silber. LC 88-47759. 672p. 1988. text ed. 36.95 (ISBN 0-465-06350-0); Study Guide by Gabriel A. Hawawini, 277p. pap. text ed. 34.95 (ISBN 0-465-06351-9). Basic.
Principles of Monitoring for the Radiation Protection of the Public. Ed. by F. D. Sowby. (ICRP Publication Ser.: No. 43). (Illus.). 20p. 1984. pap. 24.00 (ISBN 0-08-032335-9). Pergamon.
Principles of Moral & Political Philosophy. William Paley. Ed. by Rene Wellek. LC 75-11246. (British Philosophers & Theologians of the 17th & 18th Centuries Ser.: Vol. 45). 1977. Repr. of 1785 ed. lib. bdg. 51.00 (ISBN 0-8240-1797-8). Garland Pub.
Principles of Moral & Political Science, 2 Vols. Adam Ferguson. LC 71-147970. Repr. of 1792 ed. Set. 85.00 (ISBN 0-404-08222-X). AMS Pr.
Principles of Moral & Political Science, 2 vols. Adam Ferguson. Ed. by Rene Wellek. LC 75-11218. (British Philosophers & Theologians of the 17th & 18th Centuries Ser.: Vol. 21). 1978. Repr. of 1792 ed. Set. lib. bdg. 101.00 (ISBN 0-8240-1772-2). Garland Pub.
Principles of Morals & Legislation. Jeremy Bentham. LC 88-60151. (Great Books in Philosophy). 330p. 1988. pap. 5.95 (ISBN 0-87975-434-6). Prometheus Bks.
Principles of Mossbauer Spectroscopy. Terence C. Gibb. 254p. 1976. 43.00x (ISBN 0-412-13960-X, NO. 6123, Pub. by Chapman & Hall England); pap. 19.95x (ISBN 0-412-23060-7, NO. 6586, Pub. by Chapman & Hall England). Routledge Chapman & Hall.
Principles of Muhammadan Jurisprudence According to the Hanali, Maliki, Shafi'i & Hanbali Schools. Abdur Rahim. LC 79-2879. 443p. 1981. Repr. of 1911 ed. 34.50 (ISBN 0-8305-0047-2). Hyperion Conn.
Principles of Multivariate Analysis: A User's Perspective. W. J. Krzanowski. (Statistical Science Ser.: No. 3). (Illus.). 500p. 1988. 75.00 (ISBN 0-19-852211-8). Oxford U Pr.
Principles of Music & Visual Arts. Horton Presley. LC 86-1525. (Illus.). 144p. (Orig.). 1986. pap. text ed. 8.25 (ISBN 0-8191-5258-7). U Pr of Amer.
Principles of Musical Theory. Renee Longy-Miquelle. 1925. 9.50 (ISBN 0-911318-06-2). E C Schirmer.
Principles of Musik, in Singing & Setting. Charles Butler. LC 68-13273. (Music Ser.). 1970. Repr. of 1636 ed. lib. bdg. 23.50 (ISBN 0-306-70939-2). Da Capo.
Principles of Musik, in Singing & Setting. Charles Butler. LC 74-25439. (English Experience Ser.: No. 284). 136p. 1971. Repr. of 1636 ed. 14.00 (ISBN 90-221-0284-X). Walter J Johnson.
Principles of Natural & Politic Law. 5th ed. Jean J. Burlamaqui. Tr. by Thomas Nugent. LC 70-38249. (Evolution of Capitalism Ser.). 500p. 1972. Repr. of 1807 ed. 35.00 (ISBN 0-405-04114-4). Ayer Co Pubs.
Principles of Natural Theology. George H. Joyce. LC 79-170829. Repr. of 1923 ed. 37.45 (ISBN 0-404-03609-0). AMS Pr.
Principles of Nature. Elihu Palmer. LC 75-3301. Repr. of 1819 ed. 16.50 (ISBN 0-404-59286-4). AMS Pr.
Principles of Nature see Selected Writings of St. Thomas Aquinas.
Principles of Naval Weapons Systems. Ed. by David R. Frieden. (Illus.). 584p. 1985. 19.95 (ISBN 0-87021-537-X). Naval Inst Pr.
Principles of Naval Weapons Systems Workbook. 96p. 1985. 3-ring binder 8.50 (ISBN 0-87021-539-6). Naval Inst Pr.
Principles of Network Thermodynamics. L. Peusner. xv, 255p. 1987. 19.95 (ISBN 0-938876-21-X). Entropy Ltd.
Principles of Neural Development. Dale Purves & Jeff W. Lichtman. LC 84-10566. (Illus.). 375p. 1985. text ed. 34.95x (ISBN 0-87893-744-7). Sinauer Assocs.
Principles of Neural Science. 2nd ed. Ed. by E. R. Kandel & J. H. Schwartz. 1024p. 1985. 56.00 (ISBN 0-444-00944-2). Elsevier.
Principles of Neuroanatomy. Jay B. Angevine, Jr. & Carl W. Cotman. (Illus.). 1981. 36.95x (ISBN 0-19-502885-6); pap. 18.95x (ISBN 0-19-502886-4). Oxford U Pr.
Principles of Neurobiology. Nolte. 1990. 26.95 (ISBN 0-8016-3263-3); International ed. price not set. Mosby.
Principles of Neurology. 3rd ed. R. D. Adams & Maurice Victor. 1200p. 1985. text ed. 68.00 (ISBN 0-07-000296-7). McGraw.
Principles of New Testament Christianity. Charles E. Crouch. 1985. pap. 5.95 (ISBN 0-89137-546-5). Quality Pubns.
Principles of Non Impact Printing. Jerome L. Johnson. (Illus.). 372p. 1986. 225.00 (ISBN 0-9618005-0-X). Palatino Pr.
Principles of Non-Linear Analysis: Theory & Applications. Berger. 1987. write for info. (ISBN 0-471-83092-5). Wiley.
Principles of Nonlinear Optics. Y. R. Shen. LC 83-23259. (Pure & Applied Optics Ser.: 1-349). 563p. 1984. 53.95x (ISBN 0-471-88998-9). Wiley.
Principles of Nuclear Geology. U. Aswathanarayana. 410p. 1985. text ed. 40.00 (ISBN 90-6191-572-4, Pub. by A A Balkema). Brookfield Pub Co.
Principles of Nuclear Magnetic Resonance in One & Two Dimensions. Richard Ernst et al. (International Series of Monographs on Chemistry: No. 14). (Illus.). 640p. 1987. 110.00 (ISBN 0-19-855629-2). Oxford U Pr.
Principles of Nuclear Magnetism. A. Abragam. (International Series of Monographs on Physics). 1983. pap. 35.00x (ISBN 0-19-852014-X). Oxford U Pr.
Principles of Nuclear Science & Engineering. Harms. 1987. write for info. (ISBN 0-471-91628-5). Wiley.
Principles of Nucleic Acid Structure. W. Saenger. (Springer Advanced Texts in Chemistry). (Illus.). xx, 556p. 1983. 44.00 (ISBN 0-387-90762-9); pap. 34.00 (ISBN 0-387-90761-0). Springer-Verlag.
Principles of Numerical Control. 3rd ed. James J. Childs. LC 81-20296. (Illus.). 316p. 1982. 26.95x (ISBN 0-8311-1135-6). Indus Pr.
Principles of Nutrition. 4th ed. Eva D. Wilson et al. LC 78-11710. 607p. 1979. write for info. (ISBN 0-02-428330-4); write for info. tchr's manual (ISBN 0-02-428350-9). Macmillan.
Principles of Obstetrics. B. M. Hibbard. 800p. 1988. text ed. 125.00 (ISBN 0-407-00095-X). Butterworth.
Principles of Occult Healing. Mary W. Burnett. 135p. 1981. pap. 8.00 (ISBN 0-89540-072-3, SB-072). Sun Pub.
Principles of Occupational Health. Amdur et al. (Environmental Science & Technology Ser.). 1988. price not set (ISBN 0-471-09259-2). Wiley.
Principles of Ocean Physics. John R. Apel. (International Geophysics Ser.). 520p. 1987. 76.00 (ISBN 0-12-058865-X); pap. 39.00 (ISBN 0-12-058866-8). Acad Pr.
Principles of Oil Well Production. 2nd ed. T. E. Nind. (Illus.). 384p. 1981. text ed. 50.00 (ISBN 0-07-046576-2). McGraw.
Principles of Operating Systems. Sacha Krakowiok. 450p. 1988. 37.50x (ISBN 0-262-11122-5). MIT Pr.
Principles of Operations Research for Management. Frank S. Budnick et al. (Operations Management & Quant Methods Ser.). 1988. text ed. 42.95 (ISBN 0-256-02643-2). Irwin.
Principles of Operations Research with Applications to Managerial Decisions. 2nd ed. Harvey M. Wagner. (Illus.). 1088p. 1975. 46.00 (ISBN 0-13-709592-9). P-H.
Principles of Optical Disc Systems. G. Bouwhuis et al. Ed. by E. R. Pike. (Illus.). 283p. 1985. 88.00x (ISBN 0-85274-785-3, Pub. by A Hilger UK). Taylor & Francis.
Principles of Optical Fiber Measurements. D. Marcuse. LC 80-2339. 1981. 49.50 (ISBN 0-12-470980-X). Acad Pr.
Principles of Optics: Electromagnetic Theory of Propagation, Interference & Diffraction of Light. 6th ed. M. Born & E. Wolf. (Illus.). 808p. 1980. text ed. 79.50 (ISBN 0-08-026482-4); pap. text ed. 42.50 (ISBN 0-08-026481-6). Pergamon.
Principles of Optimal Control Theory. R. V. Gamkrelidze. LC 77-10742. (Mathematical Concepts & Methods In Science & Engineering Ser.: Vol. 7). 186p. 1977. 35.00x (ISBN 0-306-30977-7, Plenum Pr). Plenum Pub.
Principles of Optimal Design: Modeling & Computation. Panos Y. Papalambros & Douglass J. Wilde. (Illus.). 450p. 1988. 49.50 (ISBN 0-521-30674-4). Cambridge U Pr.
Principles of Oral Surgery. 3rd ed. Ed. by J. R. Moore & G. V. Gillbe. 254p. 1981. pap. text ed. 15.00 (ISBN 0-7190-0801-8, Pub. by Manchester Univ Pr). St Martin.
Principles of Orchestration. Nikolay Rimsky-Korsakov. 1922. pap. text ed. 9.95 (ISBN 0-486-21266-1). Dover.
Principles of Orchestration: With Musical Examples Drawn from His Own Works, 2 Vols. in 1. Nikolay Rimsky-Korsakov. Ed. by Maximilian Steinberg. 15.50 (ISBN 0-8446-2813-1). Peter Smith.
Principles of Organ Transplantation. M. Wayne Flye. (Illus.). 688p. 1988. 125.00 (ISBN 0-7216-1323-3). Saunders.
Principles of Organic Stereochemistry. Testa. (Studies in Organic Chemistry: Vol. 6). 1978. 38.75 (ISBN 0-8247-6758-6). Dekker.
Principles of Organic Synthesis. 2nd ed. R. O. Norman. 1978. pap. 29.95x (ISBN 0-412-15520-6, NO. 6210, Pub. by Chapman & Hall). Routledge Chapman & Hall.
Principles of Organization As Applied to Business. Henry P. Dutton. (Management History Ser.: No. 33). 325p. Repr. of 1931 ed. 22.50 (ISBN 0-87960-067-5). Hive Pub.
Principles of Organometallic Chemistry. G. E. Coates et al. 1968. 18.95 (ISBN 0-412-15350-5, NO. 6062, Pub. by Chapman & Hall). Routledge Chapman & Hall.
Principles of Organometallic Chemistry. Paul Powell. 384p. 1988. text ed. 39.95 (ISBN 0-412-27580-5, Pub. by Chapman & Hall England). Routledge Chapman & Hall.
Principles of Orthopedic Practice. Roger Dee et al. 2576p. 1988. text ed. 160.00 (ISBN 0-07-079996-2). McGraw.
Principles of Ostomy Care. Debra C. Broadwell & Bettie S. Jackson. LC 81-14073. (Illus.). 815p. 1981. 52.95 (ISBN 0-8016-2378-2). Mosby.
Principles of Package Development. 2nd ed. Roger C. Griffin, Jr. et al. (Illus.). 1985. 50.95 (ISBN 0-87055-465-4). AVI.
Principles of Paediatric Nursing. 2nd ed. Rosa M. Sacharin. LC 85-11685. (Illus.). 617p. (Orig.). 1986. pap. 36.00 (ISBN 0-443-03301-3). Churchill.
Principles of Paediatric Pharmacology. George M. Maxwell. 1984. 39.95x (ISBN 0-19-520447-6). Oxford U Pr.
Principles of Paleontology. 2nd ed. David M. Raup & Steven M. Stanley. LC 77-17443. (Illus.). 481p. 1978. text ed. 33.95x (ISBN 0-7167-0022-0). W H Freeman.
Principles of Paralled & Multi Processing. G. R. Desrochers. 450p. 1987. text ed. 49.50 (ISBN 0-07-016579-3). McGraw.
Principles of Parasitology. William C. Marquardt & Richard S. Demaree. 592p. 1985. text ed. write for info. (ISBN 0-02-376250-0). Macmillan.
Principles of Passive Solar Building Design: With Microcomputer Applications. C. Carter & J. De Villiers. 208p. 1987. 44.00 (ISBN 0-08-033637-X, PBI); pap. 29.00 (ISBN 0-08-033636-1). Pergamon.
Principles of Pasture Improvement & Range Management & Their Application in Somalia. Pierino Iannelli. (Pasture & Fodder Crop Studies: No. 9). 213p. 1985. pap. 17.50 (ISBN 92-5-102223-2, F2758 6011, FAO). UNIPUB.
Principles of Pathobiology. 3rd ed. Ed. by Rol la B. Hill & Mariano F. La Via. (Illus.). 1980. 24.95x (ISBN 0-19-502660-8); pap. 17.95x (ISBN 0-19-502661-6). Oxford U Pr.
Principles of Patristic Exegesis: Romans 9-11 in Origen, John Chrysostom & Augustine. Peter Gorday. LC 83-20588. (Studies in the Bible & Early Christianity: Vol. 4). 424p. 1984. lib. bdg. 69.95x (ISBN 0-88946-602-5). E Mellen.
Principles of Pavement Design. 2nd ed. E. J. Yoder & M. W. Witczak. LC 75-12555. 711p. 1975. 57.95x (ISBN 0-471-97780-2, Pub. by Wiley-Interscience). Wiley.
Principles of Peace. Thomas Hancock. 59.95 (ISBN 0-8490-0891-3). Gordon Pr.
Principles of Peace: Exemplified by the Conduct of the Society of Friends in Ireland, 1798. Thomas Hancock. LC 70-147620. (Library of War & Peace; Non-Resis. & Non-Vio.). lib. bdg. 46.00 (ISBN 0-8240-0377-2). Garland Pub.
Principles of Pediatric Fluid Therapy. 2nd ed. Robert W. Winters. 1982. pap. text ed. 21.00 (ISBN 0-316-94738-5). Little.
Principles of Pediatrics: PreTest Self Assessment & Review. Ed. by Robert A. Hoekelman. (Illus.). 260p. (Orig.). 1981. text ed. 35.00 (ISBN 0-07-051648-0). McGraw Pretest.
Principles of Penetrants: NDT: Penetrant Testing. 2nd ed. Carl E. Betz. 506p. 1960. 38.85 (ISBN 0-318-21488-1, 542). Am Soc Nondestructive.
Principles of Peptide Synthesis. M. Bodanszky. (Reactivity & Structure Ser.: Vol. 16). (Illus.). 240p. 1984. 59.00 (ISBN 0-387-12395-4). Springer-Verlag.
Principles of Perceptual Learning & Development. E. Gibson. 1969. 43.00 (ISBN 0-13-709618-6). P-H.
Principles of Persian Calligraphy. James R. Ballantyne. 1977. lib. bdg. 59.95 (ISBN 0-8490-2480-3). Gordon Pr.
Principles of Personal Defense. J. Cooper. 1986. lib. bdg. 79.95 (ISBN 0-8490-3720-4). Gordon Pr.
Principles of Personal Defense. Jeff Cooper. 30p. 1972. pap. 5.00 (ISBN 0-87364-001-2). Paladin Pr.
Principles of Personal Selling. 1st ed. 1968. pap. 10.83 scp (ISBN 0-672-96052-4); scp tchrs' manual 7.33 (ISBN 0-672-96053-2). Bobbs.
Principles of Personal Selling. Harry R. Tosdal. Ed. by Henry Assael. LC 78-322. (Century of Marketing Ser.). (Illus.). 1978. Repr. of 1925 ed. lib. bdg. 58.50x (ISBN 0-405-11184-3). Ayer Co Pubs.
Principles of Personality. Jerry S. Wiggins et al. LC 75-28729. (Illus.). 549p. 1976. text ed. 21.00 (ISBN 0-394-34784-6, RanC). Random.
Principles of Personnel Management. 5th, rev. ed. Edwin B. Flippo. (Illus.). 1979. text ed. 33.95 (ISBN 0-07-021319-4). McGraw.
Principles of Petroleum Legislation: The Case of a Developing Country. A. Al-Qasem. 245p. 1985. 88.50 (ISBN 0-86010-560-1). Graham & Trotman.
Principles of Pharmaceutical Marketing. 3rd ed. Ed. by Mickey C. Smith. LC 82-6624. (Illus.). 529p. 1983. text ed. 29.75 (ISBN 0-8121-0858-2). Lea & Febiger.
Principles of Phase Conjugation. B. Y. Zel'dovich et al. (Springer Series in Optical Sciences: Vol. 42). (Illus.). 270p. 1985. 55.00 (ISBN 0-387-13458-1). Springer-Verlag.
Principles of Phase Diagrams in Materials Systems. Paul Gordon. LC 82-14073. 248p. 1983. Repr. of 1968 ed. 21.50 (ISBN 0-89874-408-3). Krieger.
Principles of Philosophical Reasoning. Ed. by James H. Fetzer. LC 83-15985. (American Philosophical Quarterly Library of Philosophy). 304p. 1984. text ed. 34.50x (ISBN 0-8476-7158-5, Rowman & Allanheld). Rowman.
Principles of Philosophical Reasoning. Ed. by James H. Fetzer. LC 83-15985. 304p. 1984. pap. 18.95x (ISBN 0-8476-7341-3, Rowman & Allanheld). Rowman.
Principles of Philosophy. Rene Descartes. Tr. by Reese P. Miller & Valentine R. Miller. 1983. lib. bdg. 59.00 (ISBN 0-686-37924-1, Pub by Reidel Holland). Kluwer Academic.
Principles of Philosophy. Rene Descartes. Tr. by Valentine R. Miller & Resse P. Miller. (Orig.). 1984. pap. text ed. 19.50 (ISBN 90-277-1754-0, Pub. by Reidel Holland). Kluwer Academic.
Principles of Philosophy of Religion. H. G. Hubbeling. (Philosophia Religionis Ser.: Vol. 25). 280p. 1987. pap. 30.00 (ISBN 90-232-2272-5, Pub. by Van Gorcum Holland). Longwood Pub Group.
Principles of Photochemistry. J. A. Barltrop & J. D. Coyle. LC 78-16622. 213p. 1979. pap. 29.95x (ISBN 0-471-99687-4, Pub. by Wiley-Interscience). Wiley.
Principles of Photochemistry. J. A. Barltrop & J. D. Coyle. LC 78-16622. pap. 55.80 (ISBN 0-317-20842-X, 2024796). Bks Demand UMI.
Principles of Physical & Chemical Metallurgy. Giles F. Carter. LC 79-19184. pap. 111.80 (ISBN 0-317-20682-6, 2025146). Bks Demand UMI.
Principles of Physical Chemistry. E. Kirk Roberts. 1983. text ed. 45.00 (ISBN 0-205-08011-1, 688011); write for info. (ISBN 0-205-08012-X, 688012). Allyn.
Principles of Physical Chemistry with Applications to the Biological Sciences. 2nd ed. David Freifelder. 809p. 1985. text ed. 32.50 (ISBN 0-86720-046-4). Jones & Bartlett.
Principles of Physical Geology. 3rd ed. A. Holmes. 1978. pap. 41.95 (ISBN 0-442-30780-2). Van Nos Reinhold.
Principles of Physical Geology. John E. Sanders & R. Carola. LC 81-50125. 624p. 1981. write for info. (ISBN 0-471-08424-7); tchr's. manual avail. (ISBN 0-471-09378-5). Wiley.
Principles of Physical Geology Laboratory Manual. Eastern Kentucky University, Dept. of Geology. 80p. 1980. pap. text ed. 6.95 (ISBN 0-8403-3420-6). Kendall-Hunt.
Principles of Physical Medicine & Rehabilitation in the Musculoskeletal Diseases. Ed. by James C. Leek et al. 544p. 1986. 69.50 (ISBN 0-8089-1773-0, 792502). Grune.
Principles of Physical, Organic, & Biological Chemistry: An Introduction to the Molecular Basis of Life. John R. Holum. LC 68-9249. (Illus.). pap. 120.00 (ISBN 0-317-09458-0, 2055142). Bks Demand UMI.

Principles of Physical Security. Donald Schultz. LC 77-86192. 168p. 1978. 19.00x (ISBN 0-87201-748-6). Gulf Pub.

Principles of Physical Sedimentology. John R. Allen. (Illus.). 400p. 1985. text ed. 56.00x (ISBN 0-04-551095-4); pap. text ed. 29.95x (ISBN 0-04-551096-2). Unwin Hyman.

Principles of Physical Therapy. Peter Tsarfis. 384p. 1983. 85.50 (ISBN 0-8089-1428-6, 794648). Grune.

Principles of Physics. 4th ed. Frederick J. Bueche. (Illus.). 864p. 1982. text ed. 42.95x (ISBN 0-07-008867-5). McGraw.

Principles of Physics. 5th ed. Frederick J. Bueche. 896p. 1987. text ed. 43.95 (ISBN 0-07-008892-6); 12.95 (ISBN 0-07-008896-9). McGraw.

Principles of Physiological Measurement. Monograph ed. James N. Cameron. 1986. 59.50 (ISBN 0-12-156955-1); pap. 23.95 (ISBN 0-12-156956-X). Acad Pr.

Principles of Physiological Psychology, Vol. 1. W. M. Wundt. Repr. of 1910 ed. 29.00 (ISBN 0-527-98400-0). Kraus Repr.

Principles of Phytopathology. 2nd ed. Clare B. Kenaga. (Illus.). 402p. 1986. pap. text ed. 18.95x (ISBN 0-88133-268-2). Waveland Pr.

Principles of Pictorial Photography. John W. Gillies. LC 72-9201. (Literature of Photography Ser.). Repr. of 1923 ed. 20.00 (ISBN 0-405-04910-2). Ayer Co Pubs.

Principles of Piping Analysis. David Burgreen. LC 77-70079. 1977. text ed. 27.00 (ISBN 0-9600452-2-8). C P Pr.

Principles of Piping Analysis. David Burgreen. 483p. 48.00 (ISBN 0-916877-04-3). Arcturus Pubs.

Principles of Plant & Animal Pest Control, Vol. 1, Plant-Disease Development & Control. National Research Council. 1968. pap. 7.00x (ISBN 0-309-01596-0). Natl Acad Pr.

Principles of Plant & Animal Pest Control, Vol. 2, Weed Control. National Research Council. 1968. pap. 11.50x (ISBN 0-309-01597-9). Natl Acad Pr.

Principles of Plant & Animal Pest Control, Vol. 6: Effects of Pesticides on Fruit & Vegetable Physiology. National Research Council. 1968. pap. 5.95x (ISBN 0-309-01698-3). Natl Acad Pr.

Principles of Plant Biotechnology. S. H. Mantell et al. (Illus.). 200p. 1985. pap. text ed. 35.00x (ISBN 0-632-01215-3). Blackwell Pubns.

Principles of Plant Breeding. R. W. Allard. LC 60-14240. 485p. 1960. write for info. (ISBN 0-471-02310-8). Wiley.

Principles of Plant Disease Management. William E. Fry. 366p. 1982. 32.95 (ISBN 0-12-269180-6). Acad Pr.

Principles of Plant Infection. J. E. Van Der Plank. 1975. 48.50 (ISBN 0-12-711460-2). Acad Pr.

Principles of Plant Pathology. Couch. 1988. write for info. (ISBN 0-471-03147-X). Wiley.

Principles of Plant Pathology. J. G. Manners. LC 81-10186. (Illus.). 249p. 1982. pap. 19.95 (ISBN 0-521-28592-5). Cambridge U Pr.

Principles of Plant Pathology. E. C. Stakman & J. G. Harrar. LC 57-9298. (Illus.). Repr. of 1957 ed. 148.30 (ISBN 0-8357-9960-3, 2012439). Bks Demand UMI.

Principles of Plant-Teratology, 2 Vols. W. C. Worsdell. Repr. of 1916 ed. Set. 83.00 (ISBN 0-384-69263-X). Johnson Repr.

Principles of Plasma Diagnostics. I. H. Hutchinson. (Illus.). 448p. 1987. 65.00 (ISBN 0-521-32622-2). Cambridge U Pr.

Principles of Plasma Electrodynamics. A. F. Alexandrov et al. (Springer Series in Electrophysics: Vol. 9). (Illus.). 510p. 1984. 63.00 (ISBN 0-387-12613-9). Springer-Verlag.

Principles of Plasma Mechanics. 2nd ed. 1987. 5.00 (ISBN 0-471-63890-0). Wiley.

Principles of Plasma Physics. N. A. Krall & A. W. Trivelpiece. (Illus.). 1986. pap. 25.00 (ISBN 0-911302-58-1). San Francisco Pr.

Principles of Plastics Extrusion: A Teaching Programmer. Ed. by J. Brydson & D. G. Peacock. (Illus.). 108p. 1973. 23.50 (ISBN 0-85334-563-5, Pub. by Elsevier Applied Sci England). Elsevier.

Principles of Playmaking. Brander Matthews. LC 79-134113. (Essay Index Reprint Ser.). 1919. 21.00 (ISBN 0-8369-1989-0). Ayer Co Pubs.

Principles of Pleistocene Stratigraphy Applied to the Gulf of Mexico. Ed. by Nancy Healy-Williams. LC 84-6669. (Illus.). 236p. 1984. 39.00 (ISBN 0-934634-72-6). Intl Human Res.

Principles of Pneumatics. Trade & Technical Press Editors. 100p. 1967. 30.00x (ISBN 0-85461-010-3, Pub by Trade & Tech England). Brookfield Pub Co.

Principles of Police Patrol. N. F. Iannone. 1974. text ed. 39.95 (ISBN 0-07-031667-8). McGraw.

Principles of Political Economy, 3 Vols. Henry C. Carey. LC 65-16983. 1965. Repr. of 1837 ed. Set. 95.00x (ISBN 0-678-00071-9). Kelley.

Principles of Political Economy. Charles Gide. Tr. by Ernest F. Row from Fr. LC 78-126685. Repr. of 1924 ed. 18.50 (ISBN 0-404-02739-3). AMS Pr.

Principles of Political Economy. 5th ed. John R. McCulloch. LC 65-19651. 1965. Repr. of 1864 ed. 45.00x (ISBN 0-678-00097-2). Kelley.

Principles of Political Economy. 2nd ed. Thomas R. Malthus. LC 86-10606. 1986. Repr. of 1836 ed. 45.00x (ISBN 0-678-00038-7). Kelley.

Principles of Political Economy, 3 vols. James E. Meade. Incl. Vol. 1. The Stationary Economy. LC 65-26549. 1965; Vol. 2. The Growing Economy. LC 79-26549. 1968. 49.50 (ISBN 0-87395-203-0); Vol. 3. The Controlled Economy. LC 79-37998. 1972. 49.50 (ISBN 0-87395-204-9); Vol. 4. The Just Economy. LC 65-26549. 1976. 44.50 (ISBN 0-87395-205-7). State U NY Pr.

Principles of Political Economy. John S. Mill. Ed. by William J. Ashley. 1987. 49.50x (ISBN 0-678-00073-5); pap. 24.95x (ISBN 0-678-01453-1). Kelley.

Principles of Political Economy. John S. Mill. Ed. by Donald Winch. (Penguin Classics Ser.). 400p. 1986. pap. 6.95 (ISBN 0-14-043260-4). Penguin.

Principles of Political Economy. Simon Newcomb. LC 65-26372. 1966. Repr. of 1886 ed. 45.00x (ISBN 0-678-00156-1). Kelley.

Principles of Political Economy. William Roscher. LC 72-38255. (Evolution of Capitalism Ser.). 964p. 1972. Repr. of 1878 ed. 59.50 (ISBN 0-405-04136-5). Ayer Co Pubs.

Principles of Political Economy. George J. Scrope & G. J. Poulett. LC 68-58008. 1969. Repr. of 1833 ed. 45.00x (ISBN 0-678-00563-X). Kelley.

Principles of Political Economy. 3rd ed. Henry Sidgwick. LC 2-22640. 1968. Repr. of 1901 ed. 39.00 (ISBN 0-527-82836-X). Kraus Repr.

Principles of Political Economy. 2nd ed. Henry Vethake. LC 61-21698. 1971. Repr. of 1844 ed. 45.00x (ISBN 0-678-00301-7). Kelley.

Principles of Political Economy & Taxation. David Ricardo. 1978. (Evman); pap. 3.95x (ISBN 0-460-01590-7, Evman). Biblio Dist.

Principles of Political Economy, Applied to the Condition, the Resources, & the Institutions of the American People. Francis Bowen. (Neglected American Economists Ser.). 1974. lib. bdg. 61.00 (ISBN 0-8240-1011-6). Garland Pub.

Principles of Political Economy: Variorum Edition, 2 vols. T. R. Malthus. Ed. by John Pullen. Date not set. Set. price not set (ISBN 0-521-24775-6, VOL. 1 600 PP., VOL. 2 450 PP.). Cambridge U Pr.

Principles of Political Economy with Some of Their Applications to Social Philosophy. John S. Mill. Ed. by William Ashley. liii, 1013p. 1985. pap. 24.95x cancelled (ISBN 0-87991-251-0, Pub. by Orion Editions). Porcupine Pr.

Principles of Political Economy with Some of Their Applications to Social Philosphy, 2 vols. John S. Mill. 940p. 1986. Repr. of 1900 ed. text ed. 125.00 (ISBN 0-8495-3921-8). Arden Lib.

Principles of Politics. facsimile ed. Arthur R. Lord. LC 70-179637. (Select Bibliographies Reprint Ser.). Repr. of 1921 ed. 21.00 (ISBN 0-8369-6658-9). Ayer Co Pubs.

Principles of Politics. J. R. Lucas. 1985. pap. 15.95x (ISBN 0-19-824774-5). Oxford U Pr.

Principles of Politics: An Introduction. John J. Schrems. (Illus.). 416p. 1986. pap. text ed. write for info. (ISBN 0-13-701806-1). P-H.

Principles of Politics & Government. 3rd ed. Coulter. 324p. 1986. pap. text ed. write for info. (ISBN 0-205-10340-5); instr's. manual/TIF avail. (ISBN 0-697-06795-5). Wm C Brown.

Principles of Pollination Ecology. 2nd ed. K. Faegri & L. Van Der Pijl. 304p. 1979. pap. text ed. 26.00 (ISBN 0-08-023160-8). Pergamon.

Principles of Polymer Chemistry. Paul J. Flory. (George Fisher Baker Non-Resident Lectureship in Chemistry). (Illus.). 688p. 1953. 49.50x (ISBN 0-8014-0134-8). Cornell U Pr.

Principles of Polymer Composites. A. A. Berlin et al. (Polymers: Properties & Applications Ser.: Vol. 10). (Illus.). 150p. 1985. 57.00 (ISBN 0-387-15051-X). Springer-Verlag.

Principles of Polymer Engineering. N. G. McCrum et al. (Illus.). 408p. 1988. text ed. 49.95 (ISBN 0-19-856155-5); pap. text ed. 29.95 (ISBN 0-19-856152-0). Oxford U Pr.

Principles of Polymer Morphology. D. C. Bassett. (Cambrige Solid State Science Ser.). (Illus.). 220p. 1981. o. p. 67.50 (ISBN 0-521-23270-8); pap. 24.95 (ISBN 0-521-29886-5). Cambridge U Pr.

Principles of Polymer Processing. R. T. Fenner. 1980. 35.00 (ISBN 0-8206-0285-X). Chem Pub.

Principles of Polymer Processing. Zehev Tadmor & Costas G. Gogos. LC 78-17859. (SPE Monographs). 736p. 1979. 73.00x (ISBN 0-471-84320-2, Pub. by Wiley-Interscience). Wiley.

Principles of Polymer Systems. Rodriguez. 575p. 1982. 49.00 (ISBN 0-89116-503-7). Hemisphere Pub.

Principles of Polymerization. 3rd ed. Odian. 1990. price not set (ISBN 0-471-61020-8). Wiley.

Principles of Polymerization. 2nd ed. George Odian. LC 80-29226. 731p. 1981. 44.50x (ISBN 0-471-05146-2, Pub. by Wiley-Interscience). Wiley.

Principles of Polymerization Engineering. Joseph A. Biesenberger & Donald H. Sebastain. LC 82-23746. 744p. 1983. 59.50 (ISBN 0-471-08616-9). Wiley.

Principles of Population & Production. J. Weyland. (Development of Industrial Society Ser.). 336p. 1971. Repr. of 1816 ed. 32.50x (ISBN 0-7165-1777-9, BBA 02148, Pub. by Irish Academic Pr Ireland). Biblio Dist.

Principles of Population & Production. John Weyland. LC 68-58665. 1969. Repr. of 1816 ed. 45.00x (ISBN 0-678-00485-4). Kelley.

Principles of Population Genetics. Daniel L. Hartl. LC 79-28384. (Illus.). 225p. 1980. text ed. 32.95x (ISBN 0-87893-272-0). Sinauer Assocs.

Principles of Power: The Great Political Crises of History. Guglielmo Ferrero. Tr. by Theodore R. Jaeckel. LC 72-4274. (World Affairs Ser.: National & International Viewpoints). 346p. 1972. Repr. of 1942 ed. 22.50 (ISBN 0-405-04569-7). Ayer Co Pubs.

Principles of Practical Cost-Analysis. Robert Sugden & Alan Williams. (Illus.). 1978. pap. text ed. 14.50x (ISBN 0-19-877041-3). Oxford U Pr.

Principles of Practice Management. W. E. Fabb & J. Fry. 1984. lib. bdg. 40.00 (ISBN 0-85200-859-7, Pub. by MTP Pr England). Kluwer Academic.

Principles of Pragmatics. Geoffrey N. Leech. LC 82-22850. (Linguistics Library Ser.). 1983. pap. text ed. 15.95 (ISBN 0-582-55110-2). Longman.

Principles of Pragmatism: A Philosophical Interpretation of Experience. Henry H. Bawden. LC 75-3034. (Philosophy in America Ser.). 1976. Repr. of 1910 ed. 25.00 (ISBN 0-404-59042-X). AMS Pr.

Principles of Prayer. Charles G. Finney. Ed. by L. G. Parkhurst. LC 80-17856. 112p. (Orig.). 1980. pap. 4.95 (ISBN 0-87123-468-8, 210468). Bethany Hse.

Principles of Premium Auditing, 2 vols. 2nd ed. Ed. by Robert J. Gibbons et al. LC 86-80639. 668p. 1986. Vol. 1. 22.00 (APA 91); Vol. 2. 22.00 (ISBN 0-89462-029-0). IIA.

Principles of Productive Software Management. Michael W. Evans et al. 240p. 1983. 39.95x (ISBN 0-471-89796-5, Pub. by Wiley-Interscience). Wiley.

Principles of Program Design. M. A. Jackson. (Automatic Programming Information Centre Studies in Data Processing Ser.). 310p. 1975. 35.00 (ISBN 0-12-379050-6). Acad Pr.

Principles of Programming Languages. Bruce J. MacLennan. 1983. text ed. 38.95 (ISBN 0-03-061711-1). HR&W.

Principles of Programming Languages. 2nd ed. Bruce J. MacLennan. 544p. 1987. text ed. write for info. (ISBN 0-03-005163-0). HR&W.

Principles of Programming Languages. R. Tennent. 1981. 40.00 (ISBN 0-13-709873-1). P-H.

Principles of Project Formulation for Irrigation & Drainage Projects. Ed. by George R. Baumli. LC 82-73505. 144p. 1982. pap. 16.00x (ISBN 0-87262-345-9). Am Soc Civil Eng.

Principles of Property & Liability Underwriting. 3rd ed. J. J. Launie et al. LC 77-80641. 562p. 1977. text ed. 22.00 (ISBN 0-89462-030-4, UND 61). IIA.

Principles of Prosecution: A Guide for the Anatomic Pathologist. K. Kendall Pierson. LC 80-12400. 252p. Repr. of 1980 ed. 32.50 (ISBN 0-471-05811-4, JW). Krieger.

Principles of Psychoanalysis: Their Application to the Neuroses. Herman Nunberg. LC 55-11549. 382p. (Orig.). 1969. text ed. 45.00x (ISBN 0-8236-4300-X); pap. text ed. 19.95 (ISBN 0-8236-8198-X, 24300). Intl Univs Pr.

Principles of Psychoanalytic Psychotherapy: A Manual for Supportive-Expressive Treatment. Lester Luborsky. 304p. 1984. 22.95x (ISBN 0-465-06328-4, 83-54377). Basic.

Principles of Psychological Research. Joel A. Gold. 248p. 1984. pap. 21.00x (ISBN 0-256-02858-3). Dorsey.

Principles of Psychology, 2 Vols. William James. 1890. Vol. 1. pap. text ed. 9.95 (ISBN 0-486-20381-6); Vol. 2. pap. text ed. 9.95 (ISBN 0-486-20382-4). Dover.

Principles of Psychology, Vols. I & II. William James. LC 81-4194. (Works of William James). (Illus.). 1392p. 1981. text ed. 65.00x (ISBN 0-674-70559-9). Harvard U Pr.

Principles of Psychology, Vol. III. William James. LC 81-4194. (Works of William James). 480p. 1981. text ed. 27.50x (ISBN 0-674-70555-6). Harvard U Pr.

Principles of Psychology, 2 Vols. William James. Set. 33.50 (ISBN 0-8446-2310-5). Peter Smith.

Principles of Psychology. William James. 1312p. 1983. pap. 18.95 (ISBN 0-674-70625-0). Harvard U Pr.

Principles of Psychology, 2 Vols. J. R. Kantor. 1924-26. Set. 20.00 (ISBN 0-911188-44-4). Principia Pr.

Principles of Psychology. Richard H. Price et al. 1982. text ed. 33.95 (ISBN 0-03-048411-1); study guide 11.95 (ISBN 0-03-060069-3). HR&W.

Principles of Psychology. 2nd ed. Richard H. Price et al. 1987. text ed. write for info. (ISBN 0-673-18743-8). Scott F.

Principles of Psychology, 2 vols. Herbert Spencer. LC 77-13277. 1977. Repr. of 1881 ed. Set. lib. bdg. 70.00 (ISBN 0-89341-140-X). Longwood Pub Group.

Principles of Psychology. Herbert Spencer. 622p. Repr. of 1855 ed. text ed. 62.10x (ISBN 0-576-29155-2, Pub. by Gregg Intl Pubs England). Gregg Intl.

Principles of Psychology Today. Gordon H. Bower. 624p. 1987. text ed. write for info. (ISBN 0-394-37085-6, RanC); write for info. wkbk. (ISBN 0-394-37195-X, RanC). Random.

Principles of Psychophysiology: A Survey of Modern Scientific Psychology, 3 vols. Leonard T. Troland. LC 68-57643. (Illus.). 1970. Repr. of 1932 ed. Vol. 1. lib. bdg. 19.75 (ISBN 0-8371-1007-6, TRPT); Vol. 2. lib. bdg. 19.75 (ISBN 0-8371-1008-4, TRPU); Vol. 3. lib. bdg. 19.75 (ISBN 0-8371-1009-2, TRPV). Greenwood.

Principles of Psychotherapy. Pierre Janet. Tr. by H. M. Guthrie & E. R. Guthrie. 322p. 1980. Repr. of 1924 ed. lib. bdg. 40.00 (ISBN 0-8495-2760-0). Arden Lib.

Principles of Psychotherapy. facsimile ed. Pierre Janet. Tr. by H. M. Guthrie & E. R. Guthrie. (Select Bibliographies Reprint Ser.). Repr. of 1924 ed. 22.00 (ISBN 0-8369-5894-2). Ayer Co Pubs.

Principles of Psychotherapy. Irving B. Weiner. LC 74-26830. (Personality Processes Ser.). 332p. 1975. 45.00x (ISBN 0-471-92569-1, Pub. by Wiley-Interscience). Wiley.

Principles of Public International Law. 3rd ed. Ian Brownlie. 1979. pap. 32.00x (ISBN 0-19-876067-1). Oxford U Pr.

Principles of Public Utility Rates. 2nd ed. James C. Bonbright et al. 750p. 1988. 50.00 (ISBN 0-910325-23-5). Public Util.

Principles of Public Utility Regulation, 2 vols. A. J. Priest. 1969. Set. 75.00x (ISBN 0-87215-043-7). Michie Co.

Principles of Pulmonary Medicine. Steven E. Weinberger. (Principles of Medicine Ser.). (Illus.). 337p. 1985. pap. 27.95 (ISBN 0-7216-1559-7). Saunders.

Principles of Punishment as Applied in the Administration of the Criminal Law by Judges & Magistrates. Edward W. Cox. LC 83-49234. (Crime & Punishment in England, 1850-1922 Ser.). 226p. 1984. lib. bdg. 30.00 (ISBN 0-8240-6209-4). Garland Pub.

Principles of Pyrometallurgy. C. B. Alcock. 1977. 91.00 (ISBN 0-12-048950-3). Acad Pr.

Principles of Pyrometallurgy Extractive Metalurgy, Vol. 3. Fathi Habashi. (Pyrometallurgy Ser.). 450p. 1985. text ed. 95.00 (ISBN 2-88124-041-0). Gordon & Breach.

Principles of Quality Assurance & Cost Containment in Health Care: A Guide for Medical Students, Residents, & Other Health Professionals. John W. Williamson et al. LC 82-48072. (Higher Education Ser.). 1982. text ed. 24.95x (ISBN 0-87589-531-X). Jossey-Bass.

Principles of Quality Costs. Quality Costs Committee Staff. Ed. by John T. Hagan. (Illus.). 71p. (Orig.). 1986. pap. 17.95 (ISBN 0-87389-019-1, T166). ASQC Qual Pr.

Principles of Quantitative X-Ray Fluorescence. Tertian & Claiss. 404p. 1982. 92.95 (ISBN 0-471-26199-8). Wiley.

Principles of Quantum Electronics. D. Marcuse. LC 79-8857. 1980. 45.00 (ISBN 0-12-471050-6). Acad Pr.

Principles of Quantum Mechanics. 4th ed. P. A. Dirac. (International Series of Monographs on Physics). 1958. pap. text ed. 19.95x (ISBN 0-19-852011-5). Oxford U Pr.

Principles of Quantum Mechanics. R. Shankar. LC 79-24490. (Illus.). 630p. 1980. 35.00x (ISBN 0-306-40397-8, Plenum Pr). Plenum Pub.

Principles of Quick Kill. U. S. Army Infantry School Ft. Benning, Ga. (Illus.). 72p. 1967. pap. 8.00 (ISBN 0-87364-065-9). Paladin Pr.

Principles of Quick Kill: An Inside Look at the Army's Technique for Instinct Shooting. 1986. lib. bdg. 79.95 (ISBN 0-8490-3693-3). Gordon Pr.

Principles of R & D Management. Philip H. Francis. LC 77-24179. pap. 60.00 (ISBN 0-317-27075-3, 2023534). Bks Demand UMI.

Principles of Radiation Protection. K. Z. Morgan & J. E. Turner. LC 67-22415. 640p. 1973. Repr. of 1967 ed. 39.50 (ISBN 0-88275-128-X). Krieger.

Principles of Radiation Shielding. Arthur B. Chilton & Kenneth Shultis. (Illus.). 464p. 1984. 62.00 (ISBN 0-13-709907-X). P-H.

Principles of Radioisotope Methodology. 3rd ed. Grafton D. Chase & Joseph L. Rabinowitz. LC 66-19903. 1967. text ed. write for info. (ISBN 0-8087-0308-0). Burgess MN Intl.

Principles of Radiological Health. E. F. Gloyna & J. O. Ledbetter. (Environmental Health Engineering Textbk Ser: Vol. 1). 1969. 45.00 (ISBN 0-8247-1250-1). Dekker.

Principles of Radiological Physics. 2nd ed. Robin J. Wilks. LC 86-17526. (Illus.). 594p. (Orig.). 1987. pap. text ed. 42.00 (ISBN 0-443-03780-9). Churchill.

Principles of Radionuclide Emission Imaging. Ed. by D. E. Kuhl. 318p. 1983. 34.00 (ISBN 0-08-027093-X). Pergamon.

Principles of Radiopharmacology, Vol. III. Lelio G. Colombetti. 352p. 1979. 101.00 (ISBN 0-8493-5467-6). CRC Pr.

Principles of Radiopharmacology, 2 vols. Ed. by Lelio G. Columbetti. 1979. Vol. 1, 304p. 95.00 (ISBN 0-8493-5465-X); Vol. 2, 288p. 95.00 (ISBN 0-8493-5466-8). CRC Pr.

Principles of Radiopharmacology. Ed. by H. Deckhart & P. H. Cox. 1986. lib. bdg. 67.00 (ISBN 0-89838-774-4, Pub. by Martinus Nijhoff Netherlands). Kluwer Academic.

Principles of Random Variate Generation. John Dagpunar. (Illus.). 256p. 1988. 70.00 (ISBN 0-19-852202-9). Oxford U Pr.

Principles of Real Analysis. C. D. Aliprantis & O. Burkinshaw. 288p. 1981. 41.75 (ISBN 0-444-00448-3). Elsevier.

Principles of Real Analysis. rev. ed. 1987. 3.25 (ISBN 0-471-63880-3). Wiley.

Principles of Real Estate. Paul T. O'Donnell & Eugene L. Maleady. LC 75-14863. 610p. 1975. pap. text ed. 28.95 (ISBN 0-7216-6911-5). HR&W.

Principles of Real Estate Decisions. Donald R. Epley & Joseph Rabianski. LC 80-21354. 1981. text ed. write for info. (ISBN 0-201-03188-4); instrs' manual o.p. 9.95 (ISBN 0-201-03189-2). Addison-Wesley.

Principles of Real Estate Decisions. Donald R. Epley & Joseph Rabianski. 752p. 1986. pap. text ed. write for info. (ISBN 0-317-44720-3). P-H.

Principles of Real Estate Finance. Samuel K. Freshman. 1980. write for info. S K Freshman.

Principles of Real Estate Law. Paul G. Creteau. LC 76-52549. (Illus.). 1977. 22.00 (ISBN 0-9603372-0-2). Castle Pub Co.

Principles of Real Estate Management. 12th ed. James Downs, Jr. Ed. by Nancye J. Kirk. LC 79-92870. (Illus.). 386p. 1980. 26.95 (ISBN 0-912104-43-0, 852). Inst Real Estate.

Principles of Real-Time Sonography in Modern Obstetrics: A Handbook for the Practicing Physician. Nicola Perone. (Illus.). 176p. 1984. text ed. 52.00 (ISBN 0-89004-999-8). Raven.

Principles of Recepterology. Ed. by M. K. Agarwal. LC 83-15441. (Illus.). vii, 677p. 1983. 116.00x (ISBN 3-11-009558-0). De Gruyter.

Principles of Receptor Physiology see Handbook of Sensory Physiology.

Principles of Refrigeration. 2nd ed. Roy J. Dossat. LC 78-2938. 603p. 1978. text ed. write for info. (ISBN 0-471-03550-5); solutions manual 8.00 (ISBN 0-471-03771-0). Wiley.

Principles of Refrigeration. W. B. Gosney. LC 80-42210. (Illus.). 700p. 1982. 120.00 (ISBN 0-521-23671-1). Cambridge U Pr.

Principles of Refrigeration. C. T. Olivo & R. W. Marsh. LC 76-14089. 1979. 24.95 (ISBN 0-8273-3557-1); pap. 20.95. Delmar.

Principles of Regression Analysis. R. L. Plackett. LC 60-50875. pap. 46.00 (ISBN 0-317-09179-4, 2051613). Bks Demand UMI.

Principles of Reimbursement in Health Care. Donald Beck. LC 83-12300. 320p. 1983. 48.50 (ISBN 0-89443-887-5). Aspen Pub.

Principles of Relativity Physics. James L. Anderson. 1967. 44.50 (ISBN 0-12-058450-6). Acad Pr.

Principles of Relief. Edward T. Devine. LC 74-137162. (Poverty U. S. A. Historical Record Ser). 1971. Repr. of 1904 ed. 25.00 (ISBN 0-405-03132-7). Ayer Co Pubs.

Principles of Remote Sensing. P. J. Curran. 300p. 1985. 34.95 (ISBN 0-470-20393-5, Co-Pub. with Longman). Wiley.

Principles of Remote Sensing. Paul Curran. (Illus.). 260p. 1984. text ed. 24.95 (ISBN 0-582-30097-5). Wiley.

Principles of Renal Physiology. Homer W. Smith. LC 56-6992. pap. 61.80 (ISBN 0-317-29977-8, 2051761). Bks Demand UMI.

Principles of Renal Psysiology. 2nd ed. Christopher J. Lote. (Illus.). 192p. 1987. pap. text ed. 19.95x (ISBN 0-7099-4142-0, Pub. by Croom Helm UK). Sheridan Med Bks.

Principles of Revival. Rev. ed. Charles G. Finney. Ed. by L. G. Parkhurst. (Finney Principles Ser.). 192p. 1987. pap. 5.95 (ISBN 0-87123-929-9). Bethany Hse.

Principles of Rheology for Polymer Engineers. White. 1988. write for info. (ISBN 0-471-85362-3). Wiley.

Principles of Rhetoric. Adams S. Hill. 1973. Repr. of 1878 ed. 20.00 (ISBN 0-8274-1573-7). R West.

Principles of Rheumatic Diseases. Richard S. Panush. LC 81-1951. 492p. 1982. 50.00 (ISBN 0-471-05198-5, Pub. by Wiley Med). Wiley.

Principles of Riding. Ed. by Harrap Limited Staff. pap. 24.75X (ISBN 0-901366-31-5, Pub. by Harrap Ltd England). State Mutual Bk.

Principles of Riding: Official Instruction Handbook of the German National Equestrian Federation. Ed. by Jane Kidd. (Illus.). 224p. 1985. 11.95 (ISBN 0-668-06469-2); pap. 6.95 (ISBN 0-668-06393-9). Arco.

Principles of Right of Way. LC 72-85601. 224p. 20.00 (ISBN 0-318-22262-0). Intl Right Way.

Principles of Risk Management & Insurance (for CPCU 1) R. Robert Rackley. (CPCU Ser.). 1984. 155.00 (ISBN 0-88171-079-2). Insurance Achiev.

Principles of Risk Management & Insurance, 2 vols. 2nd ed. C. Arthur Williams, Jr. et al. LC 81-66112. 1981. 22.00 ea. (CPCU 1). Vol. 1 (ISBN 0-89463-022-9). Vol. 2 (ISBN 0-89463-023-7). Am Inst Property.

Principles of Rock Deformation. Adolphe Nicolas. 1987. lib. bdg. 59.00 (ISBN 90-277-2368-0, Pub. by Reidel Holland); pap. text ed. 32.50 (ISBN 90-277-2369-9, Pub. by Reidel Holland). Kluwer Academic.

Principles of Rock Drilling & Bit Wear, Pt. 1. George B. Clark. Ed. by Jon W. Raese. LC 82-1148. (Colorado School of Mines Quarterly Ser.: Vol. 77, No. 1). (Illus.). 118p. 1982. 12.00. Colo Sch Mines.

Principles of Rock Drilling & Bit Wear, Pt. 2. rev. ed. George B. Clark. Ed. by Jon W. Raese. LC 82-1148. (Colorado School of Mines Quarterly Ser.: Vol. 77 No. 2). (Illus.). 42p. 1982. pap. text ed. 10.00 (ISBN 0-686-79748-5). Colo Sch Mines.

Principles of Rock Fragmentation. George B. Clark. 1987. 59.95 (ISBN 0-471-88854-0). Wiley.

Principles of Rural-Urban Sociology. P. A. Sorokin & C. C. Zimmerman. Repr. of 1929 ed. 36.00 (ISBN 0-527-84822-0). Kraus Repr.

Principles of Safety in Physical Education & Sport. 1987. 12.95 (ISBN 0-88314-345-3). AAHPERD.

Principles of Sample Handling & Sampling Systems Design for Process Analysis. E. A. Houser. LC 72-85741. pap. 29.50 (ISBN 0-317-29907-7, 2017575). Bks Demand UMI.

Principles of Sanctification. rev. ed. Charles Finney & Louis Parkhurst. 240p. 1986. pap. 5.95 (ISBN 0-87123-859-4). Bethany Hse.

Principles of School Business Management. Ed. by R. Craig Wood. 675p. 1987. text ed. 39.95 (ISBN 0-910170-46-0). Assn Sch Busn.

Principles of School Supply Management. Robert B. Taylor. LC 71-177722. (Columbia University. Teachers College Contributions to Education Ser.: No. 228). Repr. of 1926 ed. 22.50 (ISBN 0-404-55228-5). AMS Pr.

Principles of Science. 2nd, rev. ed. W. S. Jevons. 1986. Repr. of 1877 ed. lib. bdg. 40.00x (ISBN 0-935005-47-1). Ibis Pub VA.

Principles of Scientific Botany. Mathias J. Schleiden. Tr. by E. Lankester. (Sources of Science Ser.: No. 40). Repr. of 1849 ed. 48.00 (ISBN 0-384-53950-5). Johnson Repr.

Principles of Scientific Botany: Or Botany As an Inductive Science. M. J. Schleiden. Tr. by Edwin Lankester. 1849. 38.00 (ISBN 0-527-80150-X). Kraus Repr.

Principles of Scientific Management: 1911. 2nd ed. Frederick W. Taylor & Frank B. Gilbreth. Bd. with Primer of Scientific Management. (Management History Ser.: No. 86). (Illus.). 250p. 1982. lib. bdg. 24.00 (ISBN 0-87960-117-5); pap. 16.95 (ISBN 0-87960-122-1). Hive Pub.

Principles of Scientific Socialism: A Primer on Marxism-Leninism. Phillip Sharnoff. LC 83-61351. 300p. 1983. pap. 6.95 (ISBN 0-87867-093-9). Ramparts.

Principles of Scientific Sociology. Walter L. Wallace. LC 83-11764. 1983. text ed. 34.95x (ISBN 0-202-30304-7). Aldine de Gruyter.

Principles of Scientific Thinking. Rom Harre. LC 78-126074. 1970. 22.50x (ISBN 0-226-31708-0). U of Chicago Pr.

Principles of Scottish Private Law, Vol. II. 4th ed. David M. Walker. 720p. 1988. 79.00 (ISBN 0-19-876216-X). Oxford U Pr.

Principles of Scottish Private Law, Vol. I. 4th ed. David M. Walker. 480p. 1988. 85.00 (ISBN 0-19-876215-1). Oxford U Pr.

Principles of Scottish Private Law, Vol. 1. 3rd ed. David M. Walker. 1982. 62.00x (ISBN 0-19-876132-5). Oxford U Pr.

Principles of Scottish Private Law, Vol. 2. 3rd ed. David M. Walker. 1983. 59.00x (ISBN 0-19-876133-3). Oxford U Pr.

Principles of Scottish Private Law, Vol. 3. 3rd ed. David M. Walker. 1983. 59.00x (ISBN 0-19-876134-1). Oxford U Pr.

Principles of Scottish Private Law, Vol. 4. David M. Walker. 1983. text ed. 55.00x (ISBN 0-19-876135-X). Oxford U Pr.

Principles of Secondary School Teaching, a Workbook. Walter E. Sistrunk. 288p. 1978. pap. 13.95 (ISBN 0-8403-0890-6). Kendall-Hunt.

Principles of Secure Communication Systems. Don J. Torrieri. 453p. 1985. text ed. 71.00 (ISBN 0-89006-139-4). Artech Hse.

Principles of Security: An Introduction. 2nd ed. Truett A. Ricks et al. LC 87-12159. (Criminal Justice Studies). 1987. 19.95 (ISBN 0-87084-745-7). Anderson Pub Co.

Principles of Security Management. 2nd ed. Richard J. Healy & Timothy J. Walsh. LC 81-81449. 274p. 1983. pap. text ed. 15.75 (ISBN 0-9605954-0-6). Prof Pubns.

Principles of Sedimentary Basin Analysis. A. D. Miall. (Illus.). 550p. 1984. 43.00 (ISBN 0-387-90941-9). Springer-Verlag.

Principles of Sedimentology. Gerald M. Friedman & John E. Sanders. LC 78-5355. 792p. 1978. text ed. write for info. (ISBN 0-471-75245-2). Wiley.

Principles of Seed Pathology, 2 vols. Vijendra K. Agarwal & James B. Sinclair. 352p. 1987. Set. 199.00 (ISBN 0-8493-4313-5). CRC Pr.

Principles of Selling. Jay Diamond & Gerald Pintel. (Illus.). 384p. 1985. text ed. write for info. (ISBN 0-13-709957-6). P-H.

Principles of Semiotic. D. S. Clarke, Jr. 160p. 1987. 25.00 (ISBN 0-7102-0981-9, Pub. by Routledge UK); pap. 13.95 (ISBN 0-7102-1136-8). Routledge Chapman & Hall.

Principles of Sensory Evaluation of Food. Maynard A. Amerine et al. (Food and Science Technology Monographs). 1965. 82.50 (ISBN 0-12-056150-6). Acad Pr.

Principles of Sentencing: The Sentencing Policy of the Court of Appeal, Criminal Division. 2nd ed. David A. Thomas. LC 79-315920. (Cambridge Studies in Criminology). 1979. pap. text ed. 24.00 (ISBN 0-435-82882-7). Gower Pub Co.

Principles of Shakespearian Production with Special Reference to the Tragedies. George W. Knight. Repr. of 1936 ed. 39.00x (ISBN 0-403-04222-4). Somerset Pub.

Principles of Shakespearian Production with Special Reference to Tragedies. George W. Knight. 1988. Repr. of 1936 ed. lib. bdg. 49.00x. Am Biog Serv.

Principles of Signals & Systems: Deterministic Signals. Bernard Picinbono. (Telecommunications Library). 200p. 1988. text ed. 60.00 (ISBN 0-89006-295-1). Artech Hse.

Principles of Singing. Kenneth E. Miller. (Illus.). 240p. 1983. write for info. (ISBN 0-13-710038-8); pap. 21.95 (ISBN 0-13-710020-5). P-H.

Principles of Small Business Management. W. N. MacFarlane. (Illus.). 1977. text ed. 37.75 (ISBN 0-07-044380-7). McGraw.

Principles of Social & Political Theory. Ernest Barker. LC 80-10811. viii, 284p. 1980. Repr. of 1961 ed. lib. bdg. cancelled (ISBN 0-313-22329-7, BAPRS). Greenwood.

Principles of Social Case Recording. Gordon Hamilton. LC 46-1911. 142p. 1946. 25.00 (ISBN 0-231-01541-0). Columbia U Pr.

Principles of Social Evolution. Christopher R. Hallpike. LC 86-5437. 412p. 1987. 59.00 (ISBN 0-19-827265-0). Oxford U Pr.

Principles of Social Order: Selected Essays of Lon L. Fuller. Ed. by Kenneth I. Winston. LC 80-68477. 313p. 1981. 31.50 (ISBN 0-8223-0448-1); pap. 13.95 (ISBN 0-8223-0477-5). Duke.

Principles of Social Organization in Southern Kurdistan. Fredrik Barth. LC 77-87641. Repr. of 1953 ed. 16.50 (ISBN 0-404-16423-4). AMS Pr.

Principles of Social Psychology. 3rd ed. Kelly G. Shaver. 656p. 1987. text ed. 29.95 (ISBN 0-89859-592-4). L Erlbaum Assocs.

Principles of Social Science, 3 Vols. Henry C. Carey. LC 63-22257. 1963. Repr. of 1859 ed. Set. 125.00x (ISBN 0-678-00013-1). Kelley.

Principles of Social Science Measurement. James L. Payne. LC 75-7177. 157p. (Orig.). 1975. pap. text ed. 7.95x (ISBN 0-915728-02-8). Lytton Pub.

Principles of Social Studies: The Why, What & How of Social Studies Instruction. 2nd ed. James L. Barth et al. 194p. 1984. pap. text ed. 14.00 (ISBN 0-8191-3724-3). U Pr of Amer.

Principles of Social Welfare: An Introduction to Thinking about the Welfare State. Paul Spicker. 224p. 1988. lib. bdg. 49.50 (ISBN 0-415-00630-9). Routledge Chapman & Hall.

Principles of Sociology. Franklin H. Gidding. 1911. 25.00 (ISBN 0-686-17698-7). Quality Lib.

Principles of Sociology: An Analysis of the Phenomena of Association & of Social Organization. Franklin H. Giddings. (American Studies). 1970. Repr. of 1926 ed. 32.00 (ISBN 0-384-18430-8). Johnson Repr.

Principles of Sociology: Selections. Herbert Spencer. Ed. by Stanislav Andreski. LC 73-6040. xxxvi, 821p. 1969. Repr. of 1868 ed. 59.50 (ISBN 0-208-00849-7, Archon). Shoe String.

Principles of Software Engineering & Design. Marvin V. Zelkowitz et al. LC 78-27315. (Illus.). 1979. text ed. 48.00 (ISBN 0-13-710202-X). P-H.

Principles of Software Engineering Management. Tom Gilb. (Illus.). 304p. 1988. pap. text ed. 34.50X (ISBN 0-201-19246-2). Addison-Wesley.

Principles of Soil Chemistry. Tan. (Books in Soil & the Environment). 304p. 1982. 39.75 (ISBN 0-8247-1336-2). Dekker.

Principles of Soil-Plant Interrelationships. V. V. Rendig & H. M. Taylor. 400p. 1988. 38.00 (ISBN 0-02-947792-1). Macmillan.

Principles of Solar Engineering. Kreith. 778p. 1978. 45.00 (ISBN 0-89116-495-2). Hemisphere Pub.

Principles of Solid State Chemistry. P. P. Budnikov & A. M. Ginstling. 468p. 1970. 155.00 (ISBN 0-677-61250-8). Gordon & Breach.

Principles of Solid State Chemistry. P. P. Budnikov & A. M. Ginstling. Tr. by K. Shaw. (Illus.). 454p. 1968. 52.00 (ISBN 0-85334-028-5, Pub. by Elsevier Applied Sci England). Elsevier.

Principles of Solid State Power Conversion. Ralph E. Tarter. 44.95 (ISBN 0-672-22018-0, 22018). Sams.

Principles of Solidification. Bruce Chalmers. LC 76-18772. 336p. 1977. Repr. of 1964 ed. 22.50 (ISBN 0-88275-446-7). Krieger.

Principles of Speech Audiometry. Ed. by Dan. F. Konkle & William F. Rintelmann. LC 82-13612. (Perspectives in Audiology Ser.). (Illus.). 432p. 1983. text ed. 26.00x (ISBN 0-8391-1767-1, 1306). Pro Ed.

Principles of Speech Communication. 9th ed. Douglas Ehninger & Bruce E. Gronbeck. 1984. pap. text ed. write for info. (ISBN 0-673-15877-2). Scott F.

Principles of Speech Communication: Brief Edition. 10th ed. Bruce E. Gronbeck et al. 1987. pap. text ed. write for info. (ISBN 0-673-18708-X). Scott F.

Principles of Speedwriting. (Landmark Ser.). 304p. 1977. text ed. 19.31 scp (ISBN 0-672-98001-0); scp tchr's. manual 7.33 (ISBN 0-672-98002-9); scp dictation & transcription text 25.35 (ISBN 0-672-98004-5); scp wkbk. 13.24 (ISBN 0-672-98003-7); scp theory tapes 270.99 (ISBN 0-672-98027-4); scp dictionary 16.88 (ISBN 0-672-98358-3); scp tchr's. manual 3.67 (ISBN 0-672-98005-3). Bobbs.

Principles of Speedwriting: College Edition. LC 76-41045. (Landmark Ser.). 1977. pap. text ed. 14.47 scp (ISBN 0-672-98048-7); scp tchr' s manual 3.67 (ISBN 0-672-98049-5); scp wkbk. 13.24 (ISBN 0-672-98050-9). Bobbs.

Principles of Speedwriting: Premier Edition. 373p. 1977. text ed. 28.24 scp (ISBN 0-672-98096-7); scp tchr's. ed. 7.43 (ISBN 0-672-98097-5); dictation & transcription text 21.79 (ISBN 0-672-98098-3); theory tapes 542.44 (ISBN 0-672-98142-4); dictionary 21.79 (ISBN 0-672-98100-9). Bobbs.

Principles of Speedwriting Shorthand: Regency Edition. Joe M. Pullis & Linda Bippen. (Speedwriting Shorthand Ser.). 304p. (gr. 10-12). 1984. text ed. 15.35 scp (ISBN 0-672-98501-2); scp instr's guide 7.33 (ISBN 0-672-98502-0); scp wkbk 7.64 (ISBN 0-672-98503-9). Bobbs.

Principles of Spiritual Science. Carl Unger. Tr. & intro. by Alan Howard. 1976. 3.95 (ISBN 0-910142-69-6). Anthroposophic.

Principles of Sports Medicine. W. N. Scott et al. 448p. 1984. 73.95 (ISBN 0-683-07615-9). Williams & Wilkins.

Principles of Sports Training. Dietrich Harre. 231p. 1982. 22.50 (ISBN 0-8285-2381-9, Pub. by Sportverlag Berlin GDR). Imported Pubns.

Principles of Stage Combat. Claude D. Kezer. (Illus.). 62p. 1983. pap. 12.50 (ISBN 0-88680-156-7). I E Clark.

Principles of State & Government. Muhammad Asad. 107p. (Orig.). 1980. pap. 9.95 (ISBN 0-317-52457-7, Pub. by Dar Al Andalus). New Era Pubns MI.

Principles of State Interference. facsimile ed. David G. Ritchie. LC 70-94282. (Select Bibliogrpahies Reprint Ser). 1902. 19.00 (ISBN 0-8369-5060-7). Ayer Co Pubs.

Principles of Statistical Mechanics. Richard C. Tolman. LC 79-52649. 1980. pap. text ed. 11.95 (ISBN 0-486-63896-0). Dover.

Principles of Statistical Mechanics: The Information Theory Approach. Amnon Katz. LC 67-12181. pap. 48.80 (ISBN 0-317-08729-0, 2055549). Bks Demand UMI.

Principles of Statistical Radiophysics, No. 2. S. M. Rytov et al. (Illus.). 240p. 1988. 79.00 (ISBN 0-387-16186-4). Springer-Verlag.

Principles of Statistical Radiophysics I. S. M. Rytov & Y. A. Kravtsov. (Illus.). 260p. 1987. 69.00 (ISBN 0-387-12562-0). Springer-Verlag.

Principles of Statistical Techniques. P. G. Moore. LC 75-85731. (Illus.). 280p. 1976. 34.50 (ISBN 0-521-07631-5); pap. 15.95 (ISBN 0-521-29055-4). Cambridge U Pr.

Principles of Statistics. M. G. Bulmer. LC 78-72991. 1979. pap. 5.95 (ISBN 0-486-63760-3). Dover.

Principles of Statistics. Paul A. Herzberg. LC 83-1283. 513p. 1983. text ed. 31.95 (ISBN 0-471-07989-8); tchr's. manual avail. (ISBN 0-471-87306-3); study guide 12.95 (ISBN 0-471-08237-6); text ed. 40.00 comp. (ISBN 0-471-87102-8). Wiley.

Principles of Steam Generation, 20 Modules. (Illus.). 1830p. 1982. Set. spiral bdg. 325.00x (ISBN 0-87683-250-8). lesson plans 325.00x (ISBN 0-87683-292-3). GP Pub.

Principles of Stellar Evolution & Nucleosynthesis. Donald D. Clayton. LC 83-5106. (Illus.). xii, 612p. 1984. 37.00x (ISBN 0-226-10952-6); pap. 20.00x (ISBN 0-226-10953-4). U of Chicago Pr.

Principles of String Theory. L. Brink & M. Henneaux. LC 87-29815. (Centro de Estudios Cientificos de Santiago Ser.). (Illus.). 302p. 1988. 62.50x (ISBN 0-306-42657-9, Plenum Pr). Plenum Pub.

Principles of Structural Equilibrium: A Study of Equilibrium Conditions by Graphic, Force-Moment & Virtual Displacement. George C. Ernst et al. LC 62-7876. pap. 42.50 (ISBN 0-317-10687-2, 2001977). Bks Demand UMI.

Principles of Structural Geology. John Suppe. (Illus.). 560p. 1985. text ed. write for info. (ISBN 0-13-710500-2). P-H.

Principles of Structural Linguistics. S. K. Saumjan. Tr. by James Miller. (Janua Linguarum, Ser. Major). 359p. 1971. text ed. 46.00x (ISBN 90-2791-658-6). Mouton.

Principles of Structural Stability Theory. Alexander Chajes. (Civil Engineering & Engineering Mechanics Ser.). (Illus.). 288p. 1974. 54.00 (ISBN 0-13-709964-9). P-H.

Principles of Structural Typology. B. Uspensky. LC 68-17893. (Janua Linguarum, Ser. Minor). (Orig.). 1968. pap. text ed. 10.00x (ISBN 90-2790-590-8). Mouton.

Principles of Style for the Business Writer. William C. Paxson. 160p. 1985. 14.95 (ISBN 0-396-08725-6); pap. 8.95 (ISBN 0-396-08734-5). Dodd.

Principles of Success in Literature. Fred N. Scott. Ed. by George H. Lewes. LC 78-7780. 1978. Repr. lib. bdg. 39.00 (ISBN 0-8414-0297-3). Folcroft.

Principles of Superconductive Devices & Circuits. Ed. by T. Van Duzer & O. Turner. 370p. 1981. 41.50 (ISBN 0-444-00411-4). Elsevier.

Printed Bygones. G. Potter. 88p. 1986. pap. 22.00x (ISBN 0-7212-0742-1, Pub. by Regency Pr). State Mutual Bk.
Printed Circuit Assembly Manufacturing. Kear. (Manufacturing Engineering Ser.). 336p. 1987. 79.75 (ISBN 0-8247-7675-5). Dekker.
Printed Circuit Board ATE Markets. Market Intelligence Research Company Staff. 125p. 1985. pap. text ed. 695.00 (ISBN 0-317-19567-0). Market Res Co.
Printed Circuit Board Basics. Ed. by Donna J. Esposito. 92p. (Orig.). 1986. 19.95 (ISBN 0-931463-00-9). PMS Indus.
Printed Circuit Board Industry: A Strategic Analysis. Business Communications Staff. 117p. 1985. pap. 1750.00 (ISBN 0-89336-451-7, GO67R). BCC.
Printed Circuit Board Market. Frost & Sullivan, Inc. Staff. 399p. 1986. 1800.00 (A1607). Frost & Sullivan.
Printed Circuit Board Market Opportunities. International Resource Development Staff. 151p. 1986. 985.00x (ISBN 0-88694-694-8). Intl Res Dev.
Printed Circuit Board Precision Artwork Generation & Manufacturing Methods. Bishop Graphics, Inc. Staff & Preben Lund. (Illus.). 458p. 1987. text ed. 42.67 (ISBN 0-13-709601-1). P-H.
Printed Circuit Board Precision Artwork Generation & Manufacturing Methods. Preben Lund. LC 85-73135. (Illus.). 432p. 1986. 39.95 (ISBN 0-9601748-7-7, 10011). Bishop Graphics.
Printed Circuit Board Specification System, SPESY-D. Preben Lund. Orig. Title: Danish. (Illus.). 48p. (Orig.). 1988. pap. 9.95 (ISBN 0-9601748-8-5, 10016). Bishop Graphics.
Printed Circuit Board Technologies for the 1990's. Business Communications Staff. 1988. 2250.00 (ISBN 0-89336-657-9, G-067N). BCC.
Printed Circuit Board Technology. 173p. 35.00 (ISBN 0-938648-09-8). T-C Pubns CA.
Printed Circuit Boards. Russell L. Heiserman. 146p. 1983. pap. 15.95 (ISBN 0-471-86177-4). Wiley.
Printed Circuit Troubleshooting. H. R. Shemilt. 105p. 1980. 150.00x (ISBN 0-901150-03-7, Pub. by Electrochemical Scotland). State Mutual Bk.
Printed Circuits Handbook. 2nd ed. Ed. by C. G. Coombes. 536p. 59.00 (ISBN 0-318-12558-7). Am Electro Surface.
Printed Circuits Handbook. Clyde F. Coombs. 1979. text ed. 64.95 (ISBN 0-07-012608-9). McGraw.
Printed Italian Vernacular Religious Books 1465-1550: A Finding List. A. J. Shutte. 484p. 1983. text ed. 65.00x (ISBN 0-317-56031-X, Pub. by Droz Switzerland). Coronet Bks.
Printed Maps of the British Isles 1650-1750. Rodney W. Shirley. (Illus.). 1987. 56.00 (ISBN 0-317-60076-1, Pub. by British Lib). Longwood Pub Group.
Printed Maps of Utah to 1900: An Annotated Cartobibliography. Riley M. Moffat. LC 81-659. (Western Association of Map Libraries: Occasional Paper: No. 8). (Illus.). 193p. (Orig.). 1981. pap. 10.00 (ISBN 0-939112-09-4). Western Assn Map.
Printed Note: Five Hundred Years of Music Printing & Engraving. A. Beverly Barksdale. LC 81-2100. (Music Ser.). (Illus.). 145p. 1981. Repr. of 1957 ed. lib. bdg. 29.50 (ISBN 0-306-76087-8). Da Capo.
Printed Propaganda under Louis XIV: Absolute Monarchy & Public Opinion. J. Klaits. 1976. 42.00x (ISBN 0-691-05238-7). Princeton U Pr.
Printed Reference Material. Ed. by Gavin Higgens. 560p. 1980. 50.00x (ISBN 0-8389-3257-6). ALA.
Printed Textiles: A Guide to Creative Design Fundamentals. Terry Gentille. LC 87-26098. 144p. (Orig.). 1988. pap. 14.95 (ISBN 0-937274-37-2, Dist. by Sterling). Lark Bks.
Printed Textiles: Seventeen Sixty to Eighteen Sixty. Gillian Moss. Ed. by Nancy Aakre. (Collection Handbk Ser.). (Illus.). 32p. (Orig.). 1987. pap. text ed. 3.95 (ISBN 0-910503-57-5). Cooper-Hewitt Museum.
Printed Wiring Circuit - Board, 2 vols. Ed. by Jerome H. Lieblich. 1253p. loose-leaf 229.95 (ISBN 0-912702-13-3, PW C/B). Global Eng.
Printed Writings of Jonathan Edwards 1703-1758: A Bibliography. Thomas H. Johnson. 1970. Repr. of 1940 ed. text ed. 21.50 (ISBN 0-8337-1854-1). B Franklin.
Printemps Au Parking. Christiane Rochefort. 270p. 1969. 10.95 (ISBN 0-686-55226-1); pap. 3.95 (ISBN 0-686-55227-X). French & Eur.
Printemps Romain: Avec: Choix de Lettres de Romain Rolland a sa Mere (1889-1890) Romain Rolland. 360p. 1954. 4.95 (ISBN 0-686-55266-0). French & Eur.
Printemps, Troisieme Fascicule see Maitres Musiciens de la Renaissance Francaise.
Printer. Larry McGurn. 68p. 1981. pap. 3.50 (ISBN 0-939391-00-7). B Woodley Pr.
Printer. Jack Rudman. (Career Examination Ser.: C-C16). (Cloth bdg. avail. on request). pap. 14.00 (ISBN 0-8373-0616-7). Natl Learning.
Printer & Plotter: Manual II. John J. Williams. Ed. by Laurie Williams. (Illus.). 60p. (Orig.). 1986. pap. 22.00 (ISBN 0-934274-15-0). Consumertronics.
Printer & the Pardoner. 1985. write for info. Lib Congress.
Printer Codes & Interfaces. Mindy Skelton. (Simplifier Ser.). 27p. (Orig.). 1985. pap. 5.00 (ISBN 0-935393-02-1). Write Protect.
Printer Connections Bible. House & Marble. 240p. 1985. 16.95 (ISBN 0-672-22406-2, 22406-2). Sams.
Printer in Eighteenth Century Williamsburg. Colonial Williamsburg Foundation Staff. (Williamsburg Craft Ser.). (Illus.). 34p. (Orig.). 1955. pap. 1.50 (ISBN 0-910412-20-0). Williamsburg.
Printer in Three Republics. 1981. 15.00 (ISBN 0-8363-0166-8). Jenkins.
Printer of Malgudi. R. K. Narayan. 276p. 1957. 6.00 (ISBN 0-87013-025-0). Mich St U Pr.
Printer of Shakespeare. Edwin W. Willoughby. LC 77-92993. (Studies in Shakespeare, No. 24). 1969. Repr. of 1934 ed. lib. bdg. 49.95x (ISBN 0-8383-1212-8). Haskell.
Printer-Proofreader. Jack Rudman. (Career Examination Ser.: C-617). (Cloth bdg. avail. on request). pap. 14.00 (ISBN 0-8373-0617-5). Natl Learning.
Printer Troubleshooting & Repair Guide. John Heilborn. 300p. 1988. 19.95 (ISBN 0-672-22543-3). Sams.
Printers. Leonard E. Fisher. LC 87-45461. (Colonial American Craftsmen Ser.). (Illus.). 48p. 1988. 11.95 (ISBN 0-87923-708-2); pap. 4.95 (ISBN 0-87923-709-0). Godine.
Printers: A Study in American Trade Unionism. George E. Barnett. 1977. lib. bdg. 59.95 (ISBN 0-8490-2481-1). Gordon Pr.
Printers & Press Freedom: The Ideology of Early American Journalism. Jeffery A. Smith. 248p. 1987. 24.95 (ISBN 0-19-505144-0). Oxford U Pr.
Printers & Printing. facsimile ed. David Pottinger. LC 70-175709. (Select Bibliographies Reprint Ser). Repr. of 1941 ed. 15.00 (ISBN 0-8369-6624-4). Ayer Co Pubs.
Printers & Printing in Philately. John Alden. 76p. 1987. 35.00x (ISBN 0-902633-29-5, Pub. by Picton UK). State Mutual Bk.
Printers & Printing in the East Indies to 1850, 9 vols. Katharine S. Diehl. 1988. Set. price not set (ISBN 0-89241-384-0). Caratzas.
Printers' & Publishers' Devices in England & Scotland, 1485-1640. Ronald B. McKerrow. (Bibliographical Society, Illustrated Monographs: Vol. 16). (Illus.). pap. 85.00 (ISBN 0-317-28612-9, 2055408). Bks Demand UMI.
Printer's Business Planning Manual. 350.00 (ISBN 0-318-02545-0). Print Indus Am.
Printer's Catch: An Artist's Guide to Pacific Coast Edible Marine Life. Christopher M. Dewees. LC 83-51816. (Illus.). 128p. 1984. 19.95 (ISBN 0-930118-10-3). Sea Chall.
Printer's Devil. Christian D. Stevens. 288p. 1987. 15.95 (ISBN 0-312-00176-2). St Martin.
Printer's Dozen. Philip Gallo. (Illus., Orig.). 1988. pap. 42.50x (ISBN 0-931460-28-X). Bieler.
Printers' Flowers. Paul Woodbine. (Illus.). 25p. 1988. 98.00 (ISBN 0-916258-17-3); portfolio 110.00 (ISBN 0-916258-18-1). Mercury Print.
Printers for Use with OCLC Workstations: Supplement to Small Computers in Libraries. James S. Hensinger. 1987. pap. text ed. 34.95x (ISBN 0-88736-180-3). Meckler Corp.
Printer's Guide: Or, an Introduction to the Art of Printing Including an Essay on Punctuation & Remarks on Orthography. Cornelius S. van Winkle. LC 78-74408. (Nineteenth Century Book Arts & Printing Ser.). 290p. 1980. lib. bdg. 33.00 (ISBN 0-8240-3892-4). Garland Pub.
Printers (London & South) Ed. by ICC Info. Group Staff. 1987. 695.00x (ISBN 1-85036-968-2, ICC Info Group Ltd UK). State Mutual Bk.
Printer's Manual, a Practical Guide for Compositors & Pressmen. Thomas Lynch. LC 78-74410. (Nineteenth Century Book Arts & Printing). 270p. 1980. lib. bdg. 33.00 (ISBN 0-8240-3894-0). Garland Pub.
Printer's Manual, an Abridgement of Stower's Grammar, Comprising All the Plans in That Work for Imposing Forms, Several Tables & Other Useful Articles. Caleb Stower. LC 78-74405. (Nineteenth Century Book Arts & Printing Ser.). 200p. 1980. lib. bdg. 26.00 (ISBN 0-8240-3891-6). Garland Pub.
Printers' Marks & Devices. Howard W. Winger. 1976. 20.00 (ISBN 0-940550-06-7). Caxton Club.
Printers (Midland & North) Ed. by ICC Information Group Ltd. Staff. 1987. 695.00x (ISBN 1-85036-973-9, ICC Info Group Ltd UK). State Mutual Bk.
Printers of the Modern Mind see New Arts.
Printers' Price List, a Manual for the Use of Clerks & Book-Keepers in Job Printing Offices. Theodore L. De Vinne. Ed. by John Bidwell. LC 78-74396. (Nineteenth-Century Book Arts & Printing History Ser.: Vol. 10). 1980. lib. bdg. 46.00 (ISBN 0-8240-3884-3). Garland Pub.
Printers, Stationers, & Book-Binders of Westminster & London from 1476 to 1535. E. Gordon Duff. LC 78-172540. (Illus.). Repr. of 1906 ed. 22.00 (ISBN 0-405-08467-6, Blom Pubns). Ayer Co Pubs.
Printers Supplies. Ed. by ICC Info. Group Staff. 1987. 695.00x (ISBN 1-85036-978-X, ICC Info Group Ltd UK). State Mutual Bk.
Printers' Vocabulary. Charles T. Jacobi. LC 68-30613. 176p. 1975. Repr. of 1888 ed. 35.00x (ISBN 0-8103-3309-0). Gale.
Printing. Hilary Devonshire. Ed. by FS-Ltd Staff. (Fresh Start Ser.). (Illus.). 32p. (gr. 1-6). 1988. 11.90 (ISBN 0-531-10555-5). Watts.
Printing & Computer Terminology. Harold C. Durbin. LC 80-65655. 206p. (Orig.). 1980. pap. 9.50 (ISBN 0-936786-00-0); pap. text ed. 8.50 (ISBN 0-936786-01-9). Durbin Assoc.
Printing & Embroidery. Mary Newland & Carol Walklin. 1977. 20.95 (ISBN 0-7134-0136-2, Pub. by Batsford England). David & Charles.
Printing & Graphic Arts Buyers Directory. 2nd ed. Edward L. Stern. 272p. 1986. pap. 75.00 (ISBN 0-934464-16-2). Hilary Hse Pubs.
Printing & Graphics Industry. (UNIDO Guides to Information Sources: No. 14). pap. 4.00 (ISBN 92-1-106148-2, 10/135). UN.
Printing & Patterns. Tony Hart. (Tony Hart Fun Bks.). (Illus.). 32p. (gr. 1-4). 1984. 5.95 (ISBN 0-7182-2953-3, Pub. by Kaye & Ward). David & Charles.
Printing & Production for Promotional Materials. Bob Woods & Herbert Holtje. (Illus.). 224p. 1986. 22.95 (ISBN 0-442-23108-3). Van Nos Reinhold.
Printing & Publishing Evidence: Thesauri for Use in Rare Book & Special Collections Cataloging. Association of College & Research Libraries, Rare Books & Manuscripts Staff. 28p. 1986. pap. text ed. 7.50x (ISBN 0-8389-7108-3). ALA.
Printing & Publishing in Fifteenth Century Venice. Leonardas V. Gerulaitis. 204p. 1976. 25.00x (ISBN 0-8389-0126-3). ALA.
Printing & Publishing in Medieval China. Denis Twitchett. LC 82-60317. (Illus.). 96p. 1983. pap. 14.95 (ISBN 0-913720-08-9). Beil.
Printing & Publishing: Printing & Publishing of Newspapers & Periodicals; General Printing & Publishing. W. D. McClelland. (Reviews of U. K. Statistical Sources Ser.: Vol. XXII). 210p. 1987. 59.00 (ISBN 0-08-034781-9). Pergamon.
Printing & Publishing Your Family History. Marilyn Lind. LC 86-8100. (Illus.). 63p. (Orig.). 1986. pap. text ed. 7.50 (ISBN 0-937463-10-8). Linden Tree.
Printing & Society in Early America. Ed. by William L. Joyce & David D. Hall. LC 83-6358. xii, 322p. 1983. text ed. 35.00 (ISBN 0-912296-55-0, Dist. by U Pr of VA). Am Antiquarian.
Printing & the Renaissance. John R. Slater. Ed. by Irving Lew. (Bibliographical Reprint Ser.). 1980. Repr. of 1921 ed. ltd. ed. 25.00 (ISBN 0-89782-006-1). Battery Pk.
Printing Arts in Texas. Al Lowman. (Illus.). 1975. 150.00 (ISBN 0-911796-03-7). Beacham.
Printing Arts in Texas. Al Lowman. (Illus.). 1981. 29.50 (ISBN 0-686-73811-X). Jenkins.
Printing Calculator: Student Guide. 2nd ed. Charlotte Butsch. 1971. pap. text ed. 3.85 (ISBN 0-89420-022-4, 126855); cassette recordings 50.20 (ISBN 0-89420-174-3, 156760). Natl Book.
Printing Color Negatives (E-66) rev. ed. Eastman Kodak Company Staff. (Illus.). 72p. 1982. pap. 8.95 (ISBN 0-87985-322-0). Eastman Kodak.
Printing Estimating. Gerald A. Silver. LC 70-112001. pap. 40.00 (ISBN 0-317-10639-2, 2011151). Bks Demand UMI.
Printing Estimating: Forms Book. Gerald A. Silver. pap. 20.00 (ISBN 0-317-10888-3, 2013558). Bks Demand UMI.
Printing Estimating: Principles & Practices. 2nd ed. Philip K. Ruggles. 358p. Date not set. 30.00 (ISBN 0-318-21972-7, XR102). NAPL.
Printing Estimating: Principles & Practices. 2nd ed. Philip K. Ruggles. LC 81-18070. 358p. 1985. text ed. 34.95 (ISBN 0-8273-2706-4). Delmar.
Printing Fundamentals. Ed. by Alex Glassman. 1985. write for info (ISBN 0-89852-045-2). TAPPI.
Printing Fundamentals. Ed. by Alex Glassman. LC 85-50986. pap. 102.30 (2027006). Bks Demand UMI.
Printing Handbook. 55.00 (ISBN 0-318-02615-5). Print Indus Am.
Printing in Colonial Spanish America. Lawrence S. Thompson & Hensley C. Woodbridge. LC 75-8384. 1976. 12.50x (ISBN 0-87875-076-2). Whitston Pub.
Printing in Dublin Prior to 1601. 2nd ed. Ernest R. Dix. LC 75-132674. 1971. Repr. of 1932 ed. lib. bdg. 14.50 (ISBN 0-8337-0874-0). B Franklin.
Printing in Spain, 1501-1520: With a Note on the Early Editions of the "Celestina". Frederick J. Norton. LC 65-19156. (Sandars Lectures Ser.: 1963). pap. 60.50 (ISBN 0-317-10580-9, 2022464). Bks Demand UMI.
Printing Industry. 40.45 (ISBN 0-318-02546-9). Print Indus Am.
Printing Industry Electro-Optical Output Devices. 1984. write for info. (ISBN 0-86621-543-3, E619). Frost & Sullivan.
Printing Ink Formulations. Ernest W. Flick. LC 84-22636. 184p. 1985. 36.00 (ISBN 0-8155-1014-4). Noyes.
Printing Ink Handbook. (Illus.). 112p. pap. 4.00 (ISBN 0-318-15106-5). NAPIM.
Printing Ink Manual. 3rd ed. Ed. by D. E. Bissett et al. R. H. Leach & C. H. Williams. (Illus.). 480p. 1979. 52.95 (ISBN 0-442-30600-8). Van Nos Reinhold.
Printing Ink Manual. Robert Leach. (Illus.). 896p. 1988. text ed. 82.95 (ISBN 0-7476-0000-7). Van Nos Reinhold.
Printing Inks: Developments Since 1975. J. I. Duffy. LC 79-16231. (Chemical Technology Review Ser.: No. 139). (Illus.). 336p. 1980. 42.00 (ISBN 0-8155-0772-0). Noyes.
Printing It. Clifford Burke. (Illus.). 128p. 1974. pap. 4.95 (ISBN 0-914728-03-2). Wingbow Pr.
Printing: Its Birth & Growth. William Jaggard. LC 77-94591. 1979. Repr. of 1908 ed. lib. bdg. 15.00 (ISBN 0-89341-184-1). Longwood Pub Group.
Printing of Books. Holbrook Jackson. LC 70-134100. (Essay Index Reprint Ser.). 1939. 24.50 (ISBN 0-8369-1931-9). Ayer Co Pubs.
Printing of Mathematics: Aids for Authors & Editions & Rules for Compositors & Readers at the University Press, Oxford. Theodore W. Chaundy et al. pap. 29.80 (ISBN 0-317-10261-3, 2051896). Bks Demand UMI.
Printing of Mayne's Plays. W. W. Gregg. Incl. Worcester College Library. C. H. Wilkinson. Repr. of 1927 ed. (Oxford Bibliographical Society Ser.: Vol. 1, Pt. 4). pap. 13.00 (ISBN 0-8115-1228-2). Kraus Repr.
Printing of the Bodleian Catalogue in 1604 & 1605 see Proof-Reading by English Authors of the Sixteenth & Seventeenth Centuries.
Printing of the First Folio of Shakespeare. Edwin E. Willoughby. 1979. Repr. of 1932 ed. lib. bdg. 27.00 (ISBN 0-8495-5717-8). Arden Lib.
Printing of the First Folio of Shakespeare. Edwin E. Willoughby. LC 72-192038. 1932. lib. bdg. 17.00 (ISBN 0-8414-9744-3). Folcroft.
Printing on Textiles by Direct & Transfer Techniques. Ed. by R. W. Lee. LC 81-38321. (Chem. Tech. Rev. 189). (Illus.). 418p. 1981. 48.00 (ISBN 0-8155-0850-6). Noyes.
Printing Poetry. Clifford Burke. LC 80-52171. 168p. 1980. 50.00 (ISBN 0-912962-01-1); unbound 37.50 (ISBN 0-912962-02-X). Scarab Pr.
Printing Postage Stamps by Line Engraving. James H. Baxter. LC 81-50924. Repr. of 1939 ed. lib. bdg. 30.00x (ISBN 0-88000-129-1). Quarterman.
Printing Practice. Linda Slawter. (Let's Learn Ser.). (Illus.). 32p. (ps-k). 1984. pap. 1.98 (ISBN 0-88724-071-2, CD-7014). Carson-Dellos.
Printing Practice see Let's Learn Set.
Printing Press As an Agent of Change, 2 vols. Elizabeth Eisenstein. LC 77-91083. 1979. Vol. 1. 67.50 (ISBN 0-521-21967-1); Vol. 2. 47.50 (ISBN 0-521-21969-8); Set. 120.00 (ISBN 0-521-22044-0). Cambridge U Pr.
Printing Press As an Agent of Change, 2 vols. in 1. Elizabeth Eisenstein. LC 77-91083. 852p. 1980. pap. 24.95 (ISBN 0-521-29955-1). Cambridge U Pr.
Printing Presses: History & Development from the Fifteenth Century to Modern Times. James Moran. (Illus.). 1973. 48.50x (ISBN 0-520-02245-9); pap. 10.95x (ISBN 0-520-02904-6). U of Cal Pr.
Printing Processes, Bk. 3. Judith Wilkinson. (Guide to Basic Print Production Ser.). 60p. (Orig.). 1985. pap. 7.50x (ISBN 0-946688-76-1, Pub. by Intermediate Tech England). Intermediate Tech.
Printing Revolution in Early Modern Europe. Elizabeth L. Eisenstein. LC 83-10145. 336p. 1984. 42.50 (ISBN 0-521-25858-8); pap. 9.95 (ISBN 0-521-27735-3). Cambridge U Pr.
Printing Shop Safety. William Levy. LC 79-730770. 1978. wkbk. 6.00 (ISBN 0-8064-0057-9, 310); audio visual pkg. 169.00 (ISBN 0-8064-0058-7). Bergwall.
Printing Technology. 2nd ed. J. Michael Adams & David D. Faux. LC 81-81070. 611p. 1982. text ed. 30.95 (ISBN 0-8273-2616-5); study guide 14.00 (ISBN 0-8273-2618-1). Delmar.
Printing Technology: A Medium of Visual Communications. J. Michael Adams & David D. Faux. 640p. 1987. text ed. 30.95 (ISBN 0-8273-2775-7); 8.00 (ISBN 0-8273-2776-5); study guide 14.00. Delmar.
Printing Technology, Letters, & Samuel Johnson. Alvin Kernan. (Illus.). 408p. 1987. text ed. 29.50 (ISBN 0-691-06692-2). Princeton U Pr.
Printing Trades Blue Book: 1986-1987 Northeastern Edition. rev. ed. 700p. pap. 70.00 (ISBN 0-910880-28-X). Lewis.
Printing Trades Blue Book, 1987-1988 Delaware Valley-Ohio Edition. 500p. 1987. pap. 70.00 (ISBN 0-910880-31-X). Lewis.
Printing Trades Blue Book, 1987-1988, Southeastern Edition. 700p. 1987. pap. 70.00 (ISBN 0-910880-32-8). Lewis.
Printing Trades Blue Book: 1988 New York Metropolitan Edition. 700p. 1988. pap. 70.00 (ISBN 0-910880-33-6). Lewis.
Printing Trades Directory 1988. 320p. 1988. pap. 135.00 (ISBN 0-86382-061-1, Pub. by Benn Pubns). Nichols Pub.
Printing Types: An Introduction. Alexander S. Lawson. LC 70-136232. 160p. 1974. pap. 7.95x (ISBN 0-8070-6659-1, BP474). Beacon Pr.
Printing with a Small Lithographic Offset Press. 48p. 1985. 16.00 (ISBN 0-88362-055-3, 0611). Graphic Arts Tech Found.
Printing with Peter Possum. Schaffer, Frank, Publications Staff. (Help Your Child Learn Ser.). (Illus.). 24p. (gr. k-2). 1978. wkbk. 2.50 (ISBN 0-86734-006-1, FS 3007). Schaffer Pubns.

Printing with Wood Blocks, Stencils & Engravings. Alan Bridgewater & Gill Bridgewater. LC 82-74506. (Illus.). 160p. 1983. 19.95 (ISBN 0-668-05839-0, 5839). Arco.

Printmakers: Currier & Ives; American on Stone; California on Stone. Harry T. Peters. 655.00 (ISBN 0-405-07705-X, 93). Ayer Co Pubs.

Printmaking. Don Bolognese & Elaine Raphael. (Illustrators Library). (Illus.). 64p. (gr. 4-9). 1987. PLB 9.90 (ISBN 0-531-10316-1). Watts.

Printmaking & Picture Printing: A Bibliographical Guide to Artistic & Industrial Techniques in Britain, 1750-1900. Gavin Bridson & Geoffrey Wakeman. 1984. 55.00 (ISBN 0-916271-00-5). BkPr Ltd.

Printmaking in France Eighteen Fifty to Nineteen Hundred. Marjorie H. Beebe. 1982. 3.00 (ISBN 0-915478-48-X). Galleries Coll.

Printmaking in the Service of Botany. G. D. Bridson & D. E. Wendel. (Illus.). 167p. 1986. pap. 20.00 softcover (ISBN 0-913196-49-5). Hunt Inst Botanical.

Printouts. Keith Rahmings. 36p. (Orig.). 1981. pap. 3.00 (ISBN 0-937013-06-4). Potes Poets.

Printrol: An Approach to Printing Management. 24.00 (ISBN 0-318-02602-3); GCA members 11.00; nonmembers 22.00. Print Indus Am.

Prints. Donald Karshan. Ed. by Brenda Gilchrist. LC 78-62726. (Smithsonian Illustrated Library of Antiques). (Illus.). 128p. (Orig.). 1980. 9.95 (ISBN 0-910503-28-1). Cooper-Hewitt Museum.

Prints & Books. William M. Ivins, Jr. LC 76-75295. (Graphic Art Ser). 1969. Repr. of 1927 ed. lib. bdg. 49.50 (ISBN 0-306-71288-1). Da Capo.

Prints & Drawings. Elizabeth Peak. (Illus.). 1982. pap. 5.00 (ISBN 0-916606-04-X). Bowdoin Coll.

Prints & Drawings of Kathe Kollwitz. Kathe Kollwitz. Ed. by Carl Zigrosser. LC 73-76286. 1969. pap. 9.95 (ISBN 0-486-22177-6). Dover.

Prints & Illustrated Books. Alan Wofsy. (Catalogue No. 4 Ser.). (Illus.). 1976. pap. 5.00 (ISBN 0-915346-13-3). A Wofsy Fine Arts.

Prints & Illustrated Books Six Centuries. Antiquarian Catalogues Staff. (Illus.). 56p. 1974. 7.50 (ISBN 0-915346-21-4). A Wofsy Fine Arts.

Prints & Patterns. (MacDonald Educational Ser.). (Illus., Arabic.). (gr. 5-12). 3.50x (ISBN 0-86685-219-0). Intl Bk Ctr.

Prints & People: A Social History of Printed Pictures. A. Hyatt Mayor. LC 80-7817. (Illus.). 496p. 1980. 64.50x (ISBN 0-691-03958-5); pap. 20.95 (ISBN 0-691-00326-2). Princeton U Pr.

Prints & Posters of Ben Shahn. Ben Shahn. 1983. 16.25 (ISBN 0-8446-5944-4). Peter Smith.

Prints & Printmakers of New York State, 1825-1940. Ed. by David Tatham. LC 86-3773. (New York State Studies). (Illus.). 296p. 1986. 34.95 (ISBN 0-8156-0204-9). Syracuse U Pr.

Prints & Printmaking: An Introduction to the History & Techniques. Antony Griffiths. 152p. 1981. text ed. 17.00 (ISBN 0-394-32673-3, KnopfC). Knopf.

Prints & Related Drawings by the Carracci Family. Diane D. Bohlin. LC 78-31551. (Illus.). pap. 8.00 (ISBN 0-89468-047-1). Natl Gallery Art.

Prints & the Print Markets: A Handbook for Buyers, Collectors, & Connoisseurs. Theodore B. Donson. LC 76-14487. (Illus.). 1977. 24.45i (ISBN 0-690-01160-1). T Y Crowell.

Prints & Visual Communication. William M. Ivins, Jr. LC 68-31583. (Graphic Art Ser). (Illus.). 1969. Repr. of 1953 ed. lib. bdg. 29.50 (ISBN 0-306-71159-1). Da Capo.

Prints & Visual Communication. William M. Ivins, Jr. 1969. pap. 9.95x (ISBN 0-262-59002-6). MIT Pr.

Prints at the Essex Institute. Bettina A. Norton. Ed. by Anne Farnam & Bryant F. Tolles, Jr. LC 78-19448. (E.I. Museum Booklet Ser.). (Illus.). 1978. pap. 4.95 (ISBN 0-88389-069-0). Essex Inst.

Print's First Kiss: A Rhetorical Investigation of the Implied Reader in the Fourth Gospel. Jeffrey L. Staley. LC 85-27724. (SBL-Dissertation Ser.). 146p. 1988. 16.95 (06-01-82); pap. 10.95. Scholars Pr GA.

Prints from Blocks: Gauguin to Now. Riva Castleman. (Illus.). 84p. 1983. pap. 8.95 (ISBN 0-87070-561-X). Museum Mod Art.

Prints from the Guggenheim Museum Collection. Linda Konheim. LC 78-59812. (Illus.). 1978. pap. 4.95 (ISBN 0-89207-015-3). S R Guggenheim.

Prints in the Public Library. Donald L. Foster. LC 72-13056. (Illus.). 1973. 15.00 (ISBN 0-8108-0579-0). Scarecrow.

Prints of Adolf Dehn: A Catalogue Raisonne. Compiled by Joycelyn P. Lumsdaine & Thomas O'Sullivan. LC 87-7776. (Illus.). 268p. 1987. 75.00 (ISBN 0-87351-203-0). Minn Hist.

Prints of Benton Murdoch Spruance: A Catalogue Raisonne. Ruth Fine. (Illus.). 360p. 1986. 57.95 (ISBN 0-8122-8004-0). U of PA Pr.

Prints of Don Freeman: A Catalogue Raisonne. Edith McCulloch. LC 87-8141. (Illus.). 192p. 1988. 45.00 (ISBN 0-8139-1135-4). U Pr of Va.

Prints of Edouard Manet. Jay M. Fisher. Ed. by B. J. Bradley. LC 85-80175. (Illus.). 128p. (Orig.). 1985. pap. 9.95 (ISBN 0-88397-083-X). Intl Exhibitions.

Prints of Edouard Manet. Jay. M. Fisher. LC 85-80175. (Illus.). 128p. 1987. pap. 14.95 (ISBN 0-295-96556-8). U of Wash Pr.

Prints of Edvard Munch: Mirror of His Life. Sarah G. Epstein. Ed. by Jane Van Nimmen. LC 82-62882. (Illus.). 210p. (Orig.). 1983. pap. 12.95 (ISBN 0-942946-02-2). Ober Coll Allen.

Prints of Ellsworth Kelly: A Catalogue Raisonne 1949-1985. Richard H. Axsom & Phylis Floyd. LC 87-3079. (Illus.). 200p. 1987. 50.00 (ISBN 0-933920-84-9, Dist. by Rizzoli); pap. 27.50 for museum distribution only (ISBN 0-933920-86-5). Hudson Hills.

Prints of Frank Stella: A Catalogue Raisonne. Richard Axsom et al. (Illus.). 192p. 1983. 50.00 (ISBN 0-912303-92-1); pap. 19.50 (ISBN 0-912303-25-5). Michigan Mus.

Prints of James Ensor. James Ensor. LC 76-184012. 1972. Repr. of 1952 ed. lib. bdg. 35.00 (ISBN 0-306-70439-0). Da Capo.

Prints of LeRoy Neiman: A Catalogue Raisonne of Serigraphs, Lithographs & Etchings. Ed. by Maury Leibovitz. (Illus.). 359p. 100.00 (ISBN 0-937608-00-9). Knoedler.

Prints of Lucas van Leyden & His Contemporaries. Ellen S. Jacobowitz & Stephanie L. Stepanek. (Illus.). 336p. 1983. 77.00x. Princeton U Pr.

Prints of Margaret Preston: A Catalogue Raisonne. Roger Butler. (Illus.). 348p. 1987. 145.00 (ISBN 0-19-554864-7). Oxford U Pr.

Prints of Marian Korn: A Catalogue Raisonne. Donald Richie & Tsuguo Yanai. (Illus.). 208p. 60.00 (ISBN 0-8348-0223-6). Weatherhill.

Prints of Martin Hardie. Ed. by Frank Hardie. (Illus.). 97p. (Orig.). 1975. pap. 6.00x (ISBN 0-900090-24-3, Pub. by Ashmolean Museum). State Mutual Bk.

Prints of Martin Hardie. Ed. by Frank Hardie. (Illus.). 97p. (Orig.). 1975. pap. 8.50 (ISBN 0-317-58647-5, Pub. by Ashmolean Mus). Longwood Pub Group.

Prints of Paul Jacoulet. Richard Miles. LC 82-81033. (Illus.). 140p. (Orig.). 1982. pap. 30.00 (ISBN 0-903697-13-0, Pub. by R G Sawers UK). C E Tuttle.

Prints of Reginald Marsh. Norman Sasowsky. 287p. 1976. 75.00 (ISBN 0-686-87740-3). A Wofsy Fine Arts.

Prints of Rockwell Kent. Dan B. Jones. 219p. 1975. 75.00 (ISBN 0-686-87739-X). A Wofsy Fine Arts.

Prints of Samuel Chamberlain N.A. Narcissa G. Chamberlain & Jane F. Kingsland. 1984. 75.00 (ISBN 0-317-13423-X). Boston Public Lib.

Prints of the American West: Papers Presented at the Ninth Annual North American Print Conference. Ed. by Ron Tyler. LC 83-70145. (Illus.). 142p. 1983. 16.95x (ISBN 0-88360-045-5). Amon Carter.

Prints of the High Museum: Image & Process. Irving L. Finkelstein. Ed. by Kelly Morris. LC 78-61741. (Illus.). 72p. (Orig.). 1978. pap. 4.00 (ISBN 0-939802-06-6). High Mus Art.

Prints of the Pont-Aven School: Gauguin & His Circle in Brittany. Caroline Boyle-Turner. (Illus.). 144p. 1987. 35.00 (ISBN 0-89659-742-3). Abbeville Pr.

Prints of the Twentieth Century: A History. Riva Castleman. LC 76-9219. (Illus.). 1976. pap. 10.95 (ISBN 0-19-519888-3). Oxford U Pr.

Prints of the Twentieth Century: A History. rev. ed. Riva Castleman. LC 87-51289. (Illus.). 192p. 1988. pap. 11.95 (ISBN 0-500-20228-1). Thames Hudson.

Printworld Directory of Contemporary Prints & Prices, 1988-89. Selma Smith. (Illus.). 760p. 1988. pap. 100.00 (ISBN 0-943606-03-9). Printworld.

Printworld Directory of Contemporary Prints & Prices, 1982. Selma L. Smith. 35.00 (ISBN 0-943606-00-4). Printworld.

Printworld Directory of Contemporary Prints & Prices, 1983-84. Selma L. Smith. 1983. 49.95 (ISBN 0-943606-01-2). Printworld.

Printworld Directory of Contemporary Prints & Prices, 1985-86. Selma L. Smith. 704p. 1985. 59.95 (ISBN 0-943606-02-0). Printworld.

Prinz Louis Ferdinand. Fanny Lewald. Tr. by Linda Rogols-Siegel from Ger. (Studies in German Thought & History: Vol. 6). 450p. 1988. lib. bdg. 69.95 (ISBN 0-88946-357-3). E Mellen.

Prinzip des Non-Refoulement. Walter Kaelin. (European University Studies: No. 2, Vol. 298). 393p. (Ger.). 1982. 36.25 (ISBN 3-261-05041-1). P Lang Pubs.

Prinzip Handlung in der Philosophie Kants. Friedrich Kaulbach. 1978. 50.80x (ISBN 3-11-007219-X). De Gruyter.

Prinzipien Chrislicher Moral see Principles of Christian Morality.

Prinzipien Der Literaturwissenschaft: Einfuhrung Von Herman Salinger und Alois Arnoldner, 2 Vols. in 1. Ernst Elster. 1972. 72.00 (ISBN 0-384-14280-X). Johnson Repr.

Prinzipienproblem in der Philosophie des Thomas von Aquin. Wilfried Kuehn. (Bochum Studies in Philosophy Ser.: No. 1). xxxviii, 555p. 1982. 50.00x (ISBN 90-6032-227-4, Pub by B R Gruener Amsterdam). Benjamins North Am.

Prions: Novel Infectious Pathogens Causing Scrapie & Greutzfeldt - Jakob Disease. Ed. by Stanley B. Prusiner. 540p. 1987. 65.00 (ISBN 0-12-566300-5). Acad Pr.

Prior Analytics. Aristotle. Ed. & tr. by Robin Smith. 336p. (Orig.). 1988. lib. bdg. 37.50 (ISBN 0-87220-065-5); pap. 12.50 (ISBN 0-87220-064-7). Hackett Pub.

Prior & Posterior Analytics. Aristotle. Tr. by John Warrington. 1964. 12.95x (ISBN 0-460-00450-6, Evman). Biblio Dist.

Prior Consent & Nuclear Cooperation. Myron B. Kratzer. (Technical & Economic Reports: Proliferation & Safeguards). 1983. 50.00 (ISBN 0-318-02239-7). US Coun Energy Awareness.

Prior Consultation in International Law. Frederic L. Kirgis. LC 82-17354. (Procedural Aspects of International Law Ser.: Vol. 16). 389p. 1983. 35.00x (ISBN 0-8139-0971-6). U Pr of Va.

Prior Information in Linear Models. Helge Toutenburg. LC 81-14653. (Series in Probabiliy & Mathematical Statistics-Tracts on Probability & Statistics Section). 192p. 1982. 61.95x (ISBN 0-471-09974-0, Pub. by Wiley-Interscience). Wiley.

Prior to Consciousness: Talks with Sri Nisargadatta Maharaj. Nisargadatta Maharaj. Ed. by Jean Dunn. LC 85-71544. ix, 159p. (Orig.). pap. 9.95 (ISBN 0-317-19710-X). Acorn NC.

Prioress' Prologue & Tale. Geoffrey Chaucer. Ed. by J. Winny. LC 74-19531. (Selected Tales from Chaucer Ser.). 64p. 1974. pap. text ed. 5.95 (ISBN 0-521-20744-4). Cambridge U Pr.

Prioress's Tale. Geoffrey Chaucer. Ed. by Beverly Boyd. LC 86-25064. (Variorum Edition of the Works of Geoffrey Chaucer: Vol. II, Pt. 20). (Illus.). 224p. 1987. 38.50x (ISBN 0-8061-2045-2). U of Okla Pr.

Prioress's Tale & Other Tales by Geoffrey Chaucer Done into Modern English by Prof. Skeat. Geoffrey Chaucer. Ed. by W. W. Skeat. 158p. Repr. of 1904 ed. lib. bdg. 32.50 (ISBN 0-8492-8214-4). R West.

Priori & World: European Contributions to Husserlian Phenomenology. Ed. by William McKenna et al. (Martinus Nijhoff Philosophy Texts Ser.: No. 2). 280p. 1981. 42.00 (ISBN 90-247-2375-2, Pub. by Martinus Nijhoff Netherlands). Kluwer Academic.

Priorities: A Handbook for Basic Writing. Betty Rizzo. 426p. 1984. pap. 18.95 (ISBN 0-06-045427-X, HarpC). Har-Row.

Priorities for Health Promotion & Disease Prevention. Gerald C. Hyner & Christopher L. Melby. 173p. 1987. pap. text ed. 14.95x (ISBN 0-912855-74-6). E Bowers Pub.

Priorities for Planning in Vocational Education: Alternatives for the 1970s. Leonard A. Lecht. LC 75-37419. 68p. 1975. 3.00 (ISBN 0-89068-006-X). Natl Planning.

Priorities for Postsecondary Education in the South. 2.00 (ISBN 0-686-22200-8). S Regional Ed.

Priorities for Science & Technology Research in Africa: Report of a Seminar Held at the University of Ife, Ile-Ife, Nigeria, 3-6 Dec. 1979. 32p. 1981. pap. 5.00 (ISBN 0-88936-279-3, IDRC162, IDRC). UNIPUB.

Priorities in Adult Education. David Rauch. LC 72-77273. (Illus.). 1972. 10.00 (ISBN 0-02-896750-X). Macmillan.

Priorities in Biomedical Ethics. James F. Childress. LC 81-3. 144p. 1981. pap. 8.95 (ISBN 0-664-24368-1). Westminster John Knox.

Priorities in Curriculum for the Gifted-Talented. Mary A. Awad et al. 1988. 21.25 (ISBN 0-318-23166-2). NSLTIGT.

Priorities in Death Education & Counseling. Ed. by Richard A. Pacholski & Charles A. Corr. viii, 282p. 1982. pap. 12.95 (ISBN 0-9607394-1-6). Assn Death Educ.

Priorities in Nuclear Technology: Program Prosperity & Decay in the U. S. Atomic Energy Commission, 1956-1971. Ed. by Frank Freidel & Ernest May. (Harvard Dissertations in American History & Political Science Ser.). 348p. 1988. lib. bdg. 65.00 (ISBN 0-8240-5117-3). Garland Pub.

Priorities in Planning. M. Gane. 1969. 30.00x (ISBN 0-85074-007-X, Pub. by For Lib Comm England). State Mutual Bk.

Priorities in Praying: Learning from the Lord's Prayer. Merlin Davies. 104p. (Orig.). 1984. pap. 5.95 (ISBN 0-86474-002-6, Pub. by Interface Press). ANZ Religious Pubns.

Priorities in Psychiatric Research. Ed. by Malcolm Lader. LC 80-40583. pap. 61.30 (ISBN 0-317-26111-8, 2024280). Bks Demand UMI.

Priorities in Research. J. Kendrew & J. Shelley. (International Congress Ser.: Vol. 615). 1984. 84.75 (ISBN 0-444-90333-X, I-181-84). Elsevier.

Priorities Within the Health Care System: A Delphi Survey. 53p. 1981. 6.00 (ISBN 0-686-40498-X, G-148). ANA.

Priority Concerns of Five Groups Involved in Experiential Education Programs. Lester F. Jipp & Richard J. Miguel. 81p. 1980. 5.50 (ISBN 0-318-15538-9, RD195). Natl Ctr Res Voc Ed.

Priority: Jesus' Life in Sixty Drawings. Annie Vallotton. (Illus.). 64p. (gr. k-4). 1969. pap. 0.95 (ISBN 0-8361-1901-0). Herald Pr.

Priority of John. John A. Robinson. 464p. 1987. pap. 19.95 (ISBN 0-940989-01-8). Meyer Stone Bks.

Priority of Labor: A Commentary on "Laborem Exercens", Encyclical Letter of Pope John Paul II. Gregory Baum. 112p. 1982. pap. 5.95 (ISBN 0-8091-2479-3). Paulist Pr.

Priority Planner. 3rd ed. Linda Dillow. 1986. plastic comb-bound 7.95 (ISBN 0-8407-3054-3). Nelson.

Priority Queues. N. K. Jaiswal. (Mathematics in Science & Engineering Ser.: Vol. 50). 1968. 77.00 (ISBN 0-12-380050-1). Acad Pr.

Priority Setting Skills see Productive Supervisor: A Program of Practical Managerial Skills.

Priory of St. Bernard: An Old English Tale. M Harley. Ed. by Devendra P. Varma. LC 77-2039. (Gothic Novels Ser. III). 1977. Repr. of 1789 ed. lib. bdg. 46.50x (ISBN 0-405-10138-4). Ayer Co Pubs.

Pris W-O Name-Span-Exp. Jacobo Timerman. LC 80-2715. (Span.). Date not set. pap. price not set (ISBN 0-394-70778-8). Knopf.

Priscilla. Colene Copeland. LC 81-80663. (Illus.). 212p. (Orig.). (gr. 3 up). 1981. 8.95 (ISBN 0-939810-01-8); pap. 3.95 (ISBN 0-939810-02-6). Jordan Valley.

Priscilla & Aquila: A Novel. Lois T. Henderson & Harold I. Smith. LC 84-48429. 288p. 1985. 13.45 (ISBN 0-06-063868-0, HarpR). Har-Row.

Priscilla & Aquila: A Novel. Lois T. Henderson & Harold I. Smith. LC 83-48429. 352p. 1986. pap. 7.95 (ISBN 0-06-063872-9, HarpR). Har-Row.

Priscilla, Elvis, & Me: In the Shadow of the King. Michael Edwards & Ellis Amburn. (Illus.). 288p. 1988. 18.95 (ISBN 0-312-02268-9). St Martin.

Priscilla Hauser's Folk Art Painting for Home Decoration. Priscilla Hauser. (Illus.). 160p. 1986. 14.95 (ISBN 0-13-710823-0); pap. 19.95 (ISBN 0-13-710831-1). P-H.

Priscillian of Avila: The Occult & the Charismatic in the Early Church. Henry Chadwick. 1976. 39.95x (ISBN 0-19-826643-X). Oxford U Pr.

Prise De Cordres et De Sebille. 1896. 38.00 (ISBN 0-384-47941-3); pap. 32.00 (ISBN 0-384-47931-6). Johnson Repr.

Prise De Defur & le Voyage D'Alexandre Au Paradis Terrestre. L. P. Peckham. (Elliott Monographs). (Fr). Repr. of 1935 ed. 20.00 (ISBN 0-527-02638-7). Kraus Repr.

Prision of Expectations: The Family in Victorian Culture. Steven Mintz. 232p. 1985. 40.00X (ISBN 0-8147-5388-4); pap. 15.00x (ISBN 0-8147-5391-4). NYU Pr.

Prism. Anna Lain. 384p. 1988. pap. 4.50 (ISBN 0-8217-2377-4). Zebra.

Prism. Valerie Taylor. 180p. (Orig.). 1981. pap. 6.95 (ISBN 0-930044-18-5). Naiad Pr.

Prism & Lens Making: A Textbook for Optical Glassworkers. 2nd, rev. ed. Frank Twyman. 680p. 1988. 68.00x (ISBN 0-85274-150-2, Pub. by A Hilger). Taylor & Francis.

Prism & the Pine Twig. John Taggart. 1977. bound in boards, slipcased 10.00 (ISBN 0-685-89009-0); in wraps 5.00 (ISBN 0-685-89010-4). Elizabeth Pr.

Prism: Andrea's World. Jonathan Bliss & Eugene Bliss. 1986. pap. 3.95 (ISBN 0-451-40004-6, Sig). NAL.

Prism of Science. Ed. by Edna Ullmann-Margalit. 1986. lib. bdg. 44.00 (ISBN 90-277-2160-2, Pub. by Reidel Holland); pap. 16.00 (ISBN 90-277-2161-0, Pub. by Reidel Holland). Kluwer Academic.

Prism of Scripture: Studies on History & Historicity in the Work of Jonathan Edwards, Vol. 1. Karl D. Pfisterer. (Anglo-American Forum Ser.: Vol. 1). 381p. 1975. pap. 31.55 (ISBN 3-261-00965-9). P Lang Pubs.

Prism of Sex: Essays in the Sociology of Knowledge. Ed. by Julia A. Sherman & Evelyn T. Beck. LC 79-3969. 320p. 1979. 25.00x (ISBN 0-299-08010-2). U of Wis Pr.

Prisma's Modern English-Swedish Dictionary. 400p. 1984. pap. 15.95 (ISBN 0-8166-1312-5). U of Minn Pr.

Prisma's Modern Swedish-English & English-Swedish Dictionary. LC 83-23375. 946p. 1984. combined ed 39.50x (ISBN 0-8166-1314-1). U of Minn Pr.

Prisma's Modern Swedish-English Dictionary. 400p. 1984. pap. 15.95. U of Minn Pr.

Prismatic Design Coloring Book. Peter Von Thenen. (Illus.). (gr. 5 up). pap. 2.75 (ISBN 0-486-23716-8). Dover.

Prisms. Theodor W. Adorno. Tr. by Samuel Weber & Shierry Weber. 272p. 1982. pap. 7.95 (ISBN 0-262-51025-1). MIT Pr.

Prison: A System in Trouble. Ann E. Weiss. 160p. (YA) (gr. 6-12). 1988. 14.95 (ISBN 0-89490-165-6). Enslow Pubs.

Prison Administration in India. B. V. Trivedi. 1987. 21.00x (ISBN 81-85024-13-8, Pub. by Uppal Pub Hse New Delhi). South Asia Bks.

Prison & Plantation: Crime, Justice, & Authority in Massachusetts & South Carolina, 1767-1878. Michael S. Hindus. LC 79-19493. (Studies in Legal History). (Illus.). xxviii, 285p. 1980. 27.50x (ISBN 0-8078-1417-2). U of NC Pr.

Prison Architecture. 1987. 145.95 (ISBN 0-85139-547-3). Van Nos Reinhold.

Prison Books & Their Authors. J. A. Langford. 59.95 (ISBN 0-8490-0892-1). Gordon Pr.

Prison-Breakers: A Book of Escapes from Captivity. Alban M. Phillip. LC 76-174093. (Illus.). 296p. 1971. Repr. of 1927 ed. 40.00x (ISBN 0-8103-3803-3). Gale.

Prison Chaplain: Memoirs of the Rev. John Clay with Selections from His Reports & Correspondence & a Sketch of Prison Discipline in England. Walter L. Clay. LC 69-16232. (Criminology, Law Enforcement, & Social Problems Ser.: No. 90). (Index added). 1969. Repr. of 1861 ed. 25.00 (ISBN 0-87585-090-1). Patterson Smith.

Prison Crowding: A Psychological Perspective. P. B. Paulus. (Research in Criminology Ser.). (Illus.). 105p. 1988. 43.00 (ISBN 0-387-96650-1). Springer-Verlag.

Prison Diary. Jayaprakash Narayan. Ed. by A. B. Shaw. LC 78-5471. 156p. 1979. 15.00x (ISBN 0-295-95613-5). U of Wash Pr.

Prison Discipline in America. Francis C. Gray. LC 77-172599. (Criminology, Law Enforcement, & Social Problems Ser.: No. 189). (With intro. & index added). 1973. Repr. of 1847 ed. 15.00x (ISBN 0-87585-189-4). Patterson Smith.

Prison Door Is Open: What Are You Still Doing Inside? Kenneth Hagin, Jr. 1982. pap. 0.50 mini bk (ISBN 0-89276-710-3). Hagin Ministries.

Prison Epistles: Praise from Prison. Bernard Rossier. 272p. 1987. 17.95 (ISBN 0-912981-18-0). Hse Bon Giovanni.

Prison et Paradis. Colette. 1973. pap. 28.95 (ISBN 0-686-54603-2). French & Eur.

Prison Experience: An Anthology. Ed. by Karl Weiss. LC 75-32920. 352p. (gr. 6 up). 1976. pap. 9.95 (ISBN 0-440-06017-6). Delacorte.

Prison Expose & Muldergate: A Case Study in Changing Government-Press Relations in South Africa. Gordon Jackson. (Graduate Student Paper Competition Ser.: No. 3). 25p. (Orig.). 1980. pap. text ed. 2.00 (ISBN 0-941934-31-4). Indiana Africa.

Prison Garden Book. Nancy Flinn. 56p. 1986. pap. 8.95 (ISBN 0-915873-05-2). Natl Gardening Assn.

Prison Guard. Jack Rudman. (Career Examination Ser.: C-618). (Cloth bdg. avail. on request). pap. 12.00 (ISBN 0-8373-0618-3). Natl Learning.

Prison Guards: The Culture & Perspective of an Occupational Group. G. L. Webb & David G. Morris. LC 78-72960. 1978. 5.95 (ISBN 0-933012-00-4). Coker Pub.

Prison Health Care. Richard Smith. 182p. 1984. pap. 17.60x (ISBN 0-7279-0151-6, Pub. by British Med Assoc UK). Taylor & Francis.

Prison Homosexuality: Myth & Reality. Alice M. Propper. LC 79-48003. 256p. 1981. 27.50x (ISBN 0-669-03628-5). Lexington Bks.

Prison-House of Language: A Critical Account of Structuralism & Russian Formalism. Fredric Jameson. LC 78-173757. (Princeton Essays in Literature Ser.). 228p. 1972. pap. 9.95x (ISBN 0-691-01316-0). Princeton U Pr.

Prison Labor & Convict Competition with Free Workers in Industrializing America, 1840-1890. Glen A. Gildemeister. Ed. by Harold Hyman & Stuart Bruchey. (American Legal & Constitutional History Ser.). 278p. 1987. lib. bdg. 35.00 (ISBN 0-8240-8269-9). Garland Pub.

Prison Letters. John Jenkins. Ed. by Rhondri Williams. 20.00X (ISBN 0-86243-010-0, Pub. by Y Lolfa Wales). State Mutual Bk.

Prison Librarianship: A Selective, Annotated, Classified Bibliography, 1945-1985. Fred R. Hartz et al. LC 86-43080. 125p. 1987. pap. 19.95x (ISBN 0-89950-258-X). McFarland & Co.

Prison Life & Human Worth. Paul W. Keve. LC 74-84252. 1974. 15.00x (ISBN 0-8166-0734-6). U of Minn Pr.

Prison Life & Reflections: Or, a Narrative of the Arrest, Trial of Work, Burr, & Thompson, 3 Pts. in 1 Vol. George Thompson. LC 79-138348. (Black Heritage Library Collection Ser.). 1847. 18.00 (ISBN 0-8369-8739-X). Ayer Co Pubs.

Prison Life in America. Anna Kosof. LC 84-7340. (Single Title Ser.). (Illus.). 128p. (gr. 6-10). 1984. PLB 11.90 (ISBN 0-531-04860-8). Watts.

Prison Literature in America: The Victim As Criminal & Artist. 3rd, rev. & enl. ed. H. Bruce Franklin. 400p. 1988. pap. 10.95 (ISBN 0-19-505358-3). Oxford U Pr.

Prison Memoirs of an Anarchist. Alexander Berkman. (Illus.). 540p. 1970. 8.50 (ISBN 0-686-05057-6); pap. 3.50 (ISBN 0-686-05058-4). Frontier Press Calif.

Prison Methods in New York State. Philip Klein. LC 79-78000. (Columbia University. Studies in the Social Sciences: No. 205). Repr. of 1920 ed. 28.00 (ISBN 0-404-51205-4). AMS Pr.

Prison Ministry Training Manual. Tay Wallace. (Illus.). 44p. (Orig.). 1981. pap. 3.00 (ISBN 0-933643-08-X). Grace World Outreach.

Prison Notebooks: Selections. Antonio Gramsci. Tr. by Quintin Hoare & Geoffrey N. Smith. LC 73-77646. 572p. 1971. pap. 7.25 (ISBN 0-7178-0397-X). Intl Pubs Co.

Prison Notes of an Anti-War Activist. Barbara Deming. 1966. lib. bdg. 22.95 (ISBN 0-88286-107-7); pap. 10.95. C H Kerr.

Prison of Love. Diego de San Pedro. Tr. by Keith Whinnom from Span. 105p. 1979. pap. 10.00x (ISBN 0-85224-380-4, Pub. by Edinburgh U Pr Scotland). Columbia U Pr.

Prison of Womanhood: Four Provincial Heroines in Nineteenth-Century Fiction. Elizabeth J. Sabiston. 176p. 1987. 27.50 (ISBN 0-312-00081-2). St Martin.

Prison Officers & Their World. Kelsey Kauffman. (Illus.). 320p. 1988. text ed. 27.50 (ISBN 0-674-70716-8). Harvard U Pr.

Prison or Paradise? The New Religious Cults? A. James Rudin & Marcia R. Rudin. LC 80-10210. 168p. 1980. pap. 4.95 (ISBN 0-8006-1937-4). Fortress.

Prison Ordeal. G. L. Webb. LC 83-72039. (Criminal Justice Ser.). v, 232p. 1984. 12.50 (ISBN 0-933012-06-3). Coker Pub.

Prison Overcrowding Emergency Powers Act: The Michigan Experience. (Innovations Reports). 8p. 1984. 4.00 (ISBN 0-317-45838-8, RM 734). Coun State Govts.

Prison Papers of Bozorg Alavi: A Literary Odyssey. Ed. & tr. by Donne Raffat. LC 85-8053. (Contemporary Issues in the Middle East Ser.). (Illus.). 256p. 1985. 28.00 (ISBN 0-8156-0195-6). Syracuse U Pr.

Prison Poems. Daniel Berrigan. LC 73-76683. 124p. (Orig.). 1982. pap. 6.00 (ISBN 0-87775-149-8). Unicorn Pr.

Prison: Policy & Practice. Gordon Hawkins. LC 75-20892. (Studies in Crime & Justice). 1977. pap. 8.00x (ISBN 0-226-32000-6, P749, Phoen). U of Chicago Pr.

Prison Reform. Charles R. Henderson. (Russell Sage Foundation Reprint Ser.). (Illus.). Repr. of 1910 ed. lib. bdg. 39.00x (ISBN 0-697-00206-3). Irvington.

Prison Reform in Lancashire, 1700-1850: A Study in Local Administration. Margaret DeLacy. LC 84-51714. 288p. 1986. 34.00x (ISBN 0-8047-1272-7). Stanford U Pr.

Prison Reform: Together with a Discussion of the Prison of the Future by Thomas M. Osborne. Corinne Bacon. LC 70-38659. Repr. of 1917 ed. 22.50 (ISBN 0-404-09147-4). AMS Pr.

Prison Secrets. A. R. MacDonald. LC 79-90185. (Mass Violence in America Ser.). Repr. of 1893 ed. 15.50 (ISBN 0-405-01327-2). Ayer Co Pubs.

Prison Sexual Violence. D. Lockwood. 168p. 1979. 24.50 (ISBN 0-444-99067-4). Elsevier.

Prison Solitary. Carolyn Baxter. LC 79-54299. 1979. 2.00 (ISBN 0-912678-41-0). Greenfld Rev Pr.

Prison Survival: A No-Nonsense Guide. Lou Gattis. (Illus.). 152p. (Orig.). 1986. pap. 9.00 (ISBN 0-936241-00-4). Cheetah Pub.

Prison Survival: The Inmate Self-Help Sourcebook. rev. ed. Lou Gattis. (Illus.). 200p. 1988. pap. 15.00 tchr's ed (ISBN 0-936241-04-7). Cheetah Pub.

Prison Survival, The Inmate Self-help Sourcebook. Lou Gattis. (Illus.). 254p. (Orig.). (YA) (gr. 10 up). 1987. pap. 15.00 (ISBN 0-936241-45-4). Cheetah Pub.

Prison Systems & Correctional Laws: Europe, the United States & Japan, a Comparative Analysis. 3rd ed. Gunther Kaiser. Orig. Title: Strafvollzug Im Europeaischen Vergleich. 250p. 1984. Repr. of 1974 ed. lib. bdg. 48.75 (ISBN 0-941320-12-X). Transnatl Pubs.

Prison Teacher. Kenneth Haroldson. 68p. (Orig.). 1987. pap. 3.95 (ISBN 0-317-57636-4). Unltd Pub.

Prison to Praise. Merlin R. Carothers. 106p. (Orig.). 1970. pap. 2.95 (ISBN 0-943026-02-4). Carothers.

Prison to Praise: Giant Print. Merlin R. Carothers. 106p. (Orig.). 1970. pap. 3.95 (ISBN 0-943026-08-3). Carothers.

Prison Victimization: A Gruesome Catalog of Unintended Punishment. Bowker. 232p. 1980. 20.75 (ISBN 0-444-99077-1); pap. 16.50 (ISBN 0-444-00551-X). Elsevier.

Prison Violence in America. Michael Braswell et al. LC 85-70120. (Criminal Justice Studies). 178p. 1985. 16.95 (ISBN 0-87084-092-4). Anderson Pub Co.

Prison vs. Probation in California: Implications for Crime & Offender Recidivism. Joan Petersilia et al. 63p. 1986. 7.50 (ISBN 0-8330-0738-6, R-3323-NIJ). Rand Corp.

Prison Window, Jerusalem Blue. Bruce Clements. LC 77-10081. 256p. (gr. 7 up). 1977. 10.95 (ISBN 0-374-36126-6). FS&G.

Prison Writings. Kim Dae Jung. Tr. by Choi Sung-Il & David R. McCann. 348p. (Korean.). 1987. 25.00 (ISBN 0-520-05482-2). U of Cal Pr.

Prisoner, Pt. 2. John Peel. Ed. by Hal Schuster. (Files Ser.). 60p. pap. 5.95 (ISBN 1-55698-004-3). Movie Pubs Servs.

Prisoner & Other Tales of Faith. 1980. pap. 5.95 (ISBN 0-87306-243-4). Feldheim.

Prisoner & Other Tales of Faith: Twenty-Six Heart Warming Stories. Solomon A. Halpern. (gr. 3-7). 6.95. Feldheim.

Prisoner & Yet. Corrie Ten Boom. 1964. pap. 3.50 (ISBN 0-87508-019-7). Chr Lit.

Prisoner at the Bar: Sidelights on the Administration of Criminal Justice. Arthur Train. LC 74-3858. (Criminal Justice in America Ser.). 1974. Repr. 27.50x (ISBN 0-405-06174-9). Ayer Co Pubs.

Prisoner in the American Revolution. Charles H. Metzger. LC 75-81744. 1971. pap. 6.35 (ISBN 0-8294-0175-X). Loyola.

Prisoner in the Caucasus. Leo Tolstoy. 173p. 1984. pap. 6.95 (ISBN 0-8285-2671-0, Pub. by Raduga Pubs USSR). Imported Pubns.

Prisoner in the Opal. A. E. Mason. 356p. 1986. pap. 3.95 (ISBN 0-88184-221-4). Carroll & Graf.

Prisoner Litigation. Thomas. 1988. text ed. 37.50 (ISBN 0-8476-7477-0). Rowman.

Prisoner of Desire. Jennifer Blake. (Orig.). 1986. pap. 7.95 (ISBN 0-449-90176-9, Pub. by Columbine). Fawcett.

Prisoner of Grace. Joyce Cary. 301p. 1976. Repr. of 1952 ed. lib. bdg. 18.95x (ISBN 0-88411-313-2, Pub. by Queens Hse). Amereon Ltd.

Prisoner of Grace. Joyce Cary. LC 85-10662. (Second Trilogy & The Revived Modern Classics Ser.: Bk. 1). 320p. 1985. pap. 7.95 (ISBN 0-8112-0964-4, NDP606). New Directions.

Prisoner of Martial Law: Camp Journal-Poland, 1981-1982. Jan Mur. Tr. by Lillian Vallee. (Illus.). 224p. 1984. 19.95 (ISBN 0-15-173088-1). HarBraceJ.

Prisoner of Nemesis. David Dewhurst. 169p. 1985. 35.00x (ISBN 0-901976-92-X, Pub. by United Writers Pubns England). State Mutual Bk.

Prisoner of Pineapple Place. Anne Lindbergh. LC 87-28815. 160p. (gr. 3-7). 1988. 13.95 (ISBN 0-15-263559-9, HJ). HarBraceJ.

Prisoner of Psi. Annabel Johnson & Edgar Johnson. LC 85-7450. 156p. (gr. 5 up). 1985. 12.95 (ISBN 0-689-31132-X, Atheneum Childrens Bks). Macmillan.

Prisoner of Second Avenue. Neil Simon. LC 72-2743. 1972. 9.45 (ISBN 0-394-48259-X). Random.

Prisoner of Sex. Norman Mailer. LC 85-80630. 240p. 1985. pap. 8.95 (ISBN 0-917657-59-4, Pub. by Primus Lib Contemp). D I Fine.

Prisoner of the Ant People. R. A. Montgomery. (Choose Your Own Adventure Ser.: No. 25). (Illus.). 115p. (gr. 4). 1983. pap. 2.25 (ISBN 0-553-25763-3). Bantam.

Prisoner of the Mind. David Hey. 56p. (Orig.). 1988. pap. 4.95. Little Warrior Pr.

Prisoner of the Ogpu. George Kitchin. LC 70-115551. (Russia Observed Ser., No. 1). 1970. Repr. of 1935 ed. 17.00 (ISBN 0-405-03038-X). Ayer Co Pubs.

Prisoner of the Soviet Union. Zoltan Toth. 208p. 1978. 15.95x (ISBN 0-905418-20-4, Pub. by Gresham England). State Mutual Bk.

Prisoner of Vampires. Nancy Garden. LC 84-47840. (Illus.). 213p. (gr. 5 up). 1985. 12.95 (ISBN 0-374-36129-0). FS&G.

Prisoner of Vampires. Nancy Garden. (gr. 2-6). 1986. pap. 2.95 (ISBN 0-440-47194-X, YB). Dell.

Prisoner of War. Kenneth W. Simmons. (War Ser.). 256p. (Orig.). 1988. pap. 3.95 (ISBN 0-553-26710-8). Bantam.

Prisoner of War Resistance. U. S. Army. (Illus.). 112p. 1985. pap. 12.00 (ISBN 0-87364-348-8). Paladin Pr.

Prisoner of War: Six Years in Hanoi. John M. McGrath. LC 75-11400. (Illus.). 128p. 1975. 14.95 (ISBN 0-87021-527-2); bulk rates avail. Naval Inst Pr.

Prisoner of War: The Inside Story of the POW from the Ancient World to Colditz & After. Pat Reid & Maurice Michael. (Illus.). 192p. 1986. 17.95 (ISBN 0-8253-0372-9). Beaufort Bks NY.

Prisoner of Zenda. Anthony Hope. (Airmont Classics Ser.). (Illus.). (gr. 8 up). pap. 1.25 (ISBN 0-8049-0139-2, CL-139). Airmont.

Prisoner of Zenda. Anthony Hope. lib. bdg. 17.95x (ISBN 0-89966-226-9). Buccaneer Bks.

Prisoner of Zenda. Anthony Hope. (Puffin Classics Ser.). 176p. (gr. 4-6). 1984. pap. 2.25 (ISBN 0-14-035032-2, Puffin). Penguin.

Prisoner of Zenda. Anthony Hope-Hawkins. Ed. by John C. Fago. (Now Age Illustrated IV Ser.). (Illus.). (gr. 4-12). 1978. text ed. 7.50 (ISBN 0-88301-330-4); pap. text ed. 2.95 (ISBN 0-88301-318-5); activity bk. 1.25 (ISBN 0-88301-342-8). Pendulum Pr.

Prisoner of Zenda. Ed. by S. E. Paces. 1985. 20.00x (ISBN 0-7062-4168-1, Pub. by Ward Lock Educ Co Ltd). State Mutual Bk.

Prisoner on Board the S. S. Beagle. Calvin Murry. (Prison Writing Ser.). spiral bdg 5.00 (ISBN 0-912678-53-4). Greenfld Rev Pr.

Prisoner Participation in Prison Power. J. E. Baker. LC 85-8363. 430p. 1985. 29.50 (ISBN 0-8108-1820-5). Scarecrow.

Prisoner Without a Name, Cell Without a Number. Jacobo Timerman. Tr. by Tony Talbot from Span. 176p. 1981. 12.00 (ISBN 0-394-51448-3). Knopf.

Prisoner Without a Name, Cell Without a Number. Jacobo Timerman. Tr. by Toby Talbot from Span. LC 81-52261. Orig. Title: Preso Sin Nombre, Celda Sin Numero. 176p. 1982. pap. 3.95 (ISBN 0-394-75131-0, Vin). Random.

Prisoner Wouldn't Cry. Edward White. (Anch ser.). 1985. pap. 7.95 (ISBN 0-8163-0588-9). Pacific Pr Pub Assn.

Prisoner 20-801: A French National in the Nazi Labor Camps. Aime Bonifas. Tr. by Claude R. Foster, Jr. & Mildred M. Van Sice. LC 87-2676. 184p. 1987. 18.95 (ISBN 0-8093-1392-8). S Ill U Pr.

Prisoners. Dorothy Bryant. LC 79-55170. (Orig.). 1980. 14.95 (ISBN 0-931688-04-3); pap. 7.95 (ISBN 0-931688-05-1). Ata Bks.

Prisoners. C. Chakraborty. Orig. Title: Lauha Kapat. 253p. 1976. pap. 3.25 (ISBN 0-89253-061-8). Ind-US Inc.

Prisoners. Bill Ripley. 208p. (Orig.). 1988. pap. 6.95 (ISBN 0-87113-207-9). Atlantic Monthly.

Prisoners see Three Plays.

Prisoners among Us: The Problem of Parole. David T. Stanley. LC 75-44506. 223p. pap. 58.00 (2030004). Bks Demand UMI.

Prisoners & Paupers: A Study of the Abnormal Increase of Criminals & the Public Burden of Pauperism in the United States; the Causes & Remedies. Henry M. Boies. LC 72-5478. (Select Bibliographies Reprint Ser.). 1972. Repr. of 1893 ed. 25.00 (ISBN 0-8369-6897-2). Ayer Co Pubs.

Prisoners & the Law. Ira P. Robbins. LC 85-16678. 1985. looseleaf 75.00 (ISBN 0-87632-478-2). Clark Boardman.

Prisoners Are People. Kenyon J. Scudder. LC 68-8072. (Illus.). 1968. Repr. of 1952 ed. lib. bdg. 35.00x (ISBN 0-8371-0651-6, SCPP). Greenwood.

Prisoners at Kota Cane. Leon Salim. Tr. by Audrey R. Kahin. (Translation Ser.). (Illus.). 112p. (Orig., Indonesian.). 1986. pap. 9.00 (ISBN 0-87763-032-1). Cornell Mod Indo.

Prisoners at the Bar: An Account of the Trials of the William Haywood Case, the Sacco-Vanzetti Case, the Loeb-Leopold Case, the Bruno Hauptmann Case. facs. ed. Francis X. Busch. LC 77-126319. (Biography Index Reprint Ser., Vol. 2). 1952. 18.00 (ISBN 0-8369-8025-5). Ayer Co Pubs.

Prisoners at the Kitchen Table. Barbara Holland. 160p. (gr. 4-7). 1979. 11.95 (ISBN 0-395-28969-6, Clarion). HM.

Prisoners Conference. Thomas Savile. LC 70-38222. (English Experience Ser.: No. 486). 120p. 1972. Repr. of 1605 ed. 8.00 (ISBN 90-221-0486-9). Walter J Johnson.

Prisoners de la Esperanza: Perpare Aur Hearts. Roberto Escamilla. 1983. pap. 3.00 (ISBN 0-8358-0438-0). Upper Room.

Prisoner's Dilemma. Richard Powers. LC 87-31824. 352p. 1988. 19.95 (ISBN 0-688-07350-6, Pub. by Beech Tree Bks). Morrow.

Prisoner's Dilemma. Anatol Rapoport & Albert M. Chammah. LC 65-11462. (Illus.). 1965. 9.95 (ISBN 0-472-75602-8). U of Mich Pr.

Prisoner's Dilemma. Anatol Rapoport & Albert M. Chammah. (Illus.). 1970. pap. 2.95 (ISBN 0-472-06165-8, 165, AA). U of Mich Pr.

Prisoner's Family: A Study of the Effects of Imprisonment on the Families of Prisoners. Donald P. Schneller. LC 75-38303. 1976. softbound 12.95 (ISBN 0-88247-407-3). R & E Pubs.

Prisoners: Health & Medical Subject Analysis with Reference Bibliography. Ira T. Reece. LC 85-48088. 150p. 1987. 34.50 (ISBN 0-88164-448-X); pap. 26.50 (ISBN 0-88164-449-8). ABBE Pubs Assn.

Prisoners in America: Perspectives on Our Correctional System. Ed. by Lloyd E. Ohlin. LC 73-1221. (American Assembly Guides). 224p. 1973. 6.95 (ISBN 0-13-710822-2); pap. 2.45 (ISBN 0-13-710814-1). Am Assembly.

Prisoners in Prison Societies. Ulla V. Bondeson. 356p. 1988. 34.95 (ISBN 0-88738-205-3). Transaction Bks.

Prisoners of Arionn. Brian Herbert. 416p. 1987. 17.95 (ISBN 0-87795-886-6). Morrow.

Prisoners of Childhood. Alice Miller. LC 80-50535. 1981. 13.95 (ISBN 0-465-06347-0). Basic.

Prisoners of Conscience in the U. S. S. R. Amnesty International. 1976. pap. 2.00 (ISBN 0-394-73173-5). Random.

Prisoners of Conscience in the U. S. S. R. Their Treatment & Conditions. Amnesty International Staff. (Illus.). 217p. (Orig.). 1980. pap. 5.95 (ISBN 0-86210-006-2, Pub. by Amnesty Intl Pubns UK). Amnesty Intl USA.

Prisoners of God: The Modern-Day Conflict of Arab & Jew. David Smith. (Illus.). 256p. 1988. 24.95 (ISBN 0-7043-2607-8, Pub. by Quartet Bks). Salem Hse Pubs.

Prisoners of Hate: The Story of Israelis in Syrian Jails. Yehezkel Hameiri. 261p. 1969. 24.95x (ISBN 0-87855-189-1). Transaction Bks.

Prisoners of Hope. John S. Carroll. LC 70-118407. 1971. Repr. of 1906 ed. 38.50x (ISBN 0-8046-1184-X, Pub. by Kennikat). Assoc Faculty Pr.

Prisoners of Hope. Mary Johnston. 1902. Repr. lib. bdg. 49.00 (ISBN 0-8414-5420-5). Folcroft.

Prisoners of Hope: A Tale of Colonial Virginia. Mary Johnston. 378p. 1982. Repr. of 1899 ed. lib. bdg. 45.00 (ISBN 0-89987-435-5). Darby Bks.

Prisoners of Hope: The Silver Age of the Italian Jews, 1924-1974. H. Stuart Hughes. 184p. 1983. text ed. 16.00x (ISBN 0-674-70727-3). Harvard U Pr.

Prisoners of Insecurity, Nuclear Deterrence, the Arms Race, & Arms Control. Bruce Russett. LC 82-15981. (Illus.). 204p. 1983. pap. text ed. 13.95 (ISBN 0-7167-1472-8). W H Freeman.

Prisoners of Isolation: Solitary Confinement in Canada. Michael Jackson. 352p. 1983. 35.00x (ISBN 0-8020-5620-2); pap. 15.95 (ISBN 0-8020-6514-7). U of Toronto Pr.

Prisoners of Liberation. 1981. 8.95 (ISBN 0-8351-0819-8). China Bks.

Prisoners of Paradise. Ronald A. Cross. 256p. 1988. 16.95 (ISBN 0-531-15083-6). Watts.

Prisoners of Pax Tharkas. Morris Simon. LC 84-91364. (Super Endless Quest Books Ser.). (Illus.). 192p. (gr. 5-7). 1985. pap. 2.50 (ISBN 0-394-73977-9). Random.

Private Civil War: Popular Thought During the Sectional Conflict. Randall C. Jimerson. (Illus.). 312p. 1988. 24.95 (ISBN 0-8071-1454-5). La State U Pr.

Private Collection. Junior League of Palo Alto. Ed. by Bonnie S. Mickelson. (Illus.). 1980. 13.95 (ISBN 0-9606324-0-9). Jr League Palo Alto.

Private Collection Two. Junior League of Palo Alto. Ed. by Bonnie S. Mickelson. (Illus.). 1984. 13.95 (ISBN 0-9606324-1-7). Jr League Palo Alto.

Private Collections: A Culinary Treasure. Janet E. Wurtzburger & Mac K. Griswold. (Illus.). 253p. 1983. write for info. (ISBN 0-911886-31-1). Walters Art.

Private Colleges & Universities, 2 vols. John F. Ohles & Shirley M. Ohles. LC 81-13238. (Encyclopedia of American Institutions Ser.: No. 6). x, 1619p. 1982. Set. lib. bdg. 125.00 (ISBN 0-313-21416-6, OHP/); lib. bdg. 75.00 (ISBN 0-313-23323-3, OHP/01); Vol. 2. lib. bdg. 75.00 (OHP/02). Greenwood.

Private Company in Germany: A Translation & Commentary. M. C. Oliver & M. A. Barrister. LC 85-23769. (International Corporate Law Ser.: No. 2). 1986. 35.00 (ISBN 9-06-544244-8, Pub. by Kluwer Netherlands). Kluwer Academic.

Private Company Secretary's Manual. Sidney Bunker. 1988. binder 135.00 (ISBN 0-902197-62-2, Pub. by Woodhead-Faulkner). Longwood Pub Group.

Private Company Secretary's Manual. H. M. Williams. 150p. 1988. 60.00x (ISBN 0-566-02734-8, Pub. by Gower Pub England). Gower Pub Co.

Private Connection. A Texas City Official's Guide for Contracting with the Private Sector. David W. Tees & Stanley E. Wilkes, Jr. 96p. (Orig.). 1982. pap. 10.00 (ISBN 0-936440-42-2). Inst Urban Studies.

Private Conscience & Public Law: The American Experience. Richard J. Regan. LC 72-77602. x, 245p. 1972. 25.00 (ISBN 0-8232-0945-8). Fordham.

Private Consultants & Municipalities: A Selected Checklist. Jamie W. Coniglio. (Public Administration Ser.: P 1774). 3p. 1985. 2.00 (ISBN 0-89028-574-8). Vance Biblios.

Private Consulting: How to Turn Experience into Employment Dollars. Barbara Johnson. (Illus.). 147p. 1982. pap. 7.95 (ISBN 0-13-710871-0). P-H.

Private Contentment. Reynolds Price. LC 83-45523. 160p. 1984. 12.95 (ISBN 0-689-11455-9). Atheneum.

Private Correspondence of Henry Clay. facsimile ed. Henry Clay. Ed. by Calvin Colton. LC 78-169756. (Select Bibliographies Reprint Ser). Repr. of 1855 ed. 35.50 (ISBN 0-8369-5976-0). Ayer Co Pubs.

Private Correspondence of Niccolo Machiavelli. Niccolo Machiavelli. Tr. by Oreste Ferrara. (Illus.). 127p. 1986. 117.85 (ISBN 0-89901-289-2). Found Class Reprints.

Private Correspondence of Sarah, Duchess of Marlborough, Illustrative of the Court & Times of Queen Anne. Sarah J. Marlborough. Ed. by Sarah J. Churchill. 1838. Repr. 51.00 (ISBN 0-527-61770-9). Kraus Repr.

Private Correspondence School Enrollee. Richard B. Kennan. LC 71-176934. (Columbia University. Teachers College. Contributions to Education: No. 796). Repr. of 1940 ed. 22.50 (ISBN 0-404-55796-1). AMS Pr.

Private Cosmos, No. 3. Philip Jose Farmer. (World of Tiers Ser.). 1981. 18.00 (ISBN 0-932096-10-7). Phantasia Pr.

Private Crisis, Public Cost: Policy Perspectives on Teenage Childbearing. Kristin A. Moore & Martha R. Burt. LC 82-60293. 166p. (Orig.). 1982. pap. text ed. 11.00 (ISBN 0-87766-314-9). Urban Inst.

Private Degas. Richard Thomson. LC 86-51297. (Illus.). 144p. 1987. 19.95 (ISBN 0-500-01408-6). Thames Hudson.

Private Demons: The Life of Shirley Jackson. Judy Oppenheimer. 304p. 1988. 19.95 (ISBN 0-399-13356-9). Putnam Pub Group.

Private Detective & Investigator Course. Max Dabbah. (Illus.). 380p. (Orig.). 1987. write for info. (ISBN 0-945406-00-2). Magnum Schl.

Private Devotions of Lancelot Andrewes. Lancelot Andrewes. Tr. & intro. by F. E. Brightman. 15.25 (ISBN 0-8446-1534-X). Peter Smith.

Private Diary of Ananda Ranga Pillai in 12 Volumes. Ananda R. Pillai et al. Ed. by J. F. Price & Rangachari. Tr. by Joseph F. Dupleix. 1986. Repr. per set 420.00X (PUb. by Abhinav by India). South Asia Bks.

Private Diary of Dr. John Dee & the Catalogue of His Library of Manuscripts. John Dee. Ed. by James O. Halliwell. (Camden Society, London. Publications, First Ser.: No. 19). Repr. of 1842 ed. 19.00 (ISBN 0-404-50119-2). AMS Pr.

Private Diary of Dr. John Dee & the Catalogue of His Library of Manuscripts. John Dee. 1842. 19.00 (ISBN 0-384-11180-7). Johnson Repr.

Private Die Match Stamps. Christopher West. LC 80-83685. (C. & S. Revenue Ser.). (Illus.). 288p. 44.95x (ISBN 0-9603498-2-0). Castenholz Sons.

Private Die Proprietary Medicine Stamps. (Medical Handbook Ser.). 80p. 4.00 (ISBN 0-318-13308-3). Am Topical Assn.

Private Diplomacy with the Soviet Union. Ed. & frwd. by David D. Newsom. LC 86-28926. 156p. (Orig.). 1987. lib. bdg. 22.50 (ISBN 0-934742-34-0, Inst Study Diplomacy); pap. text ed. 8.75 (ISBN 0-934742-40-5, Inst Study Diplomacy). Geo U Sch For Serv.

Private Diplomacy with the Soviet Union. Ed. by David D. Newsom. LC 86-28926. 166p. (Orig.). 1987. lib. bdg. 22.50 (ISBN 0-8191-5820-8, Pub. by Inst Study Diplomacy); pap. text ed. 8.75 (ISBN 0-8191-5821-6, Pub. by Inst Study Diplomacy). U Pr of Amer.

Private Direct Foreign Investment in Developing Countries. K. Billerbeck & Y. Yasugi. (Working Paper: No. 348). iv, 97p. 1979. 5.00 (ISBN 0-686-36174-1, WP-0348). World Bank.

Private Disgrace: Lizzie Borden by Daylight. Victoria Lincoln. 1986. pap. 5.95 (ISBN 0-930330-35-8). Intl Polygonics.

Private-Do Not Open. Sasha Soldatow. 192p. 1988. pap. 5.95 (ISBN 0-14-008526-2). Penguin.

Private Domain. Paul Taylor. 1987. 22.95 (ISBN 0-394-51683-4). Knopf.

Private Domain: An Autobiography. Paul Taylor. LC 87-82586. 408p. 1988. pap. 12.95 (ISBN 0-86547-322-6). N Point Pr.

Private Education & Public Policy: Studies in Choice & Public Policy. Ed. by Daniel C. Levy. LC 85-15568. 1986. text ed. 38.00x (ISBN 0-19-503710-3). Oxford U Pr.

Private Education in Britain. Clive Griggs. 220p. 1985. 33.00x (ISBN 1-85000-073-5, Falmer Pr); pap. 18.00x (ISBN 1-85000-074-3, Falmer Pr). Taylor & Francis.

Private Elisha Stockwell, Jr. Sees the Civil War. Elisha Stockwell, Jr. Ed. by Byron R. Abernethy. LC 58-6855. (Illus.). 224p. (Orig.). 1985. pap. 6.95 (ISBN 0-8061-1921-7). U of Okla Pr.

Private Employers' Potential Legal Liabilities for Cost Containment Provisions. Norma L. Nielson & W. Alfred Mikatis. Date not set. price not set (ISBN 0-89154-339-2). Intl Found Employ.

Private Enemy, Public Eye: The Work of Bruce Charlesworth. Charles Hagen & Bruce Charlesworth. (Illus.). 96p. 1988. 25.00 (ISBN 0-89381-337-0). Aperture.

Private Enforcement of the Antitrust Laws: An Economic Critique. Warren F. Schwartz. 33p. 1981. pap. 3.25 (ISBN 0-8447-3444-6). Am Enterprise.

Private Enterprise & Public Emulation. Mario Deaglio. (Institute of Economic Affairs, Research Monographs: No. 5). pap. 2.50 technical (ISBN 0-255-69593-4). Transatl Arts.

Private Enterprise & the East African Company. Ed. by Philip A. Thomas. 1969. 35.00x (ISBN 0-678-08021-6). Kelley.

Private Enterprise in Africa: Creating a Better Environment. Keith Marsden & Therese Belot. 1987. 6.50 (ISBN 0-8213-0945-5, DP0017). World Bank.

Private Enterprise in Developing Countries. W. M. Clarke. 1969. pap. 5.50 (ISBN 0-08-012142-X). Pergamon.

Private Enterprise in Eastern Europe: The Non-Agricultural Private Sector in Poland & the GDR, 1945-83. Anders Aslund. LC 84-40388. 320p. 1985. 29.95 (ISBN 0-312-64706-9). St Martin.

Private Exercise of Public Functions. Ed. by Dennis L. Thompson. LC 84-9254. (Policy Studies Organization). 264p. 1985. text ed. 28.00x (ISBN 0-8046-9368-4, 9368). Assoc Faculty Pr.

Private Eye Cartoon Book. Marc Bilgrey. LC 85-71047. (Illus.). 104p. (Orig.). 1985. pap. 7.00 (ISBN 0-933773-10-2). Andrion Bks.

Private Eyes. Julia Winfield. (Sweet Dreams Ser.: No. 113). 160p. (Orig.). (YA) (gr. 7-12). 1986. pap. 2.50 (ISBN 0-553-25814-1). Bantam.

Private Eyes Don't Blink. Robert Kraus. LC 87-40697. (Illus.). 32p. (gr. 2-6). 1988. pap. 2.50 (ISBN 1-55782-059-7). Warner Bks.

Private Eyes: One Hundred & One Knights. Robert Baker & Mike Nietzel. LC 85-70857. 385p. 1985. 29.95 (ISBN 0-87972-329-7); pap. 17.95 (ISBN 0-87972-330-0). Bowling Green Univ.

Private File. Jerry Hurter. (Illus.). 221p. (Orig.). 1986. pap. 12.95 (ISBN 0-9615054-0-0). J Hurter.

Private File Creation-Data Base Construction: A Proceeding with Five Case Studies. Ed. by Marjorie M. Hlava. 120p. 1984. pap. 15.00 (ISBN 0-87111-312-0). SLA.

Private Fire Brigades. National Fire Protection Association Staff. 1986. 10.50 (ISBN 0-317-63486-0, 600-86). Natl Fire Prot.

Private Fire Brigades. (Tenty Ser). 1967. pap. 2.00 (ISBN 0-685-58115-2, 27). Natl Fire Prot.

Private Fire Protection & Detection Systems. International Fire Service Training Association Committee. Ed. by Gene P. Carlson. LC 79-55670. (Illus.). 184p. (Orig.). 1979. pap. 11.00 (ISBN 0-87939-036-0). Fire Protect Pubns.

Private Fleet Management Guide. Ed. by J. J. Keller & Associates, Inc. LC 82-84709. (24M). 350p. 1987. loose-leaf 65.00 (ISBN 0-934674-47-7). J J Keller.

Private Foreign Aid: U. S. Philanthropy in Relief & Development. Landrum R. Bolling & Craig Smith. LC 82-1867. (Illus.). 330p. 1982. pap. 38.50x (ISBN 0-86531-393-8). Westview.

Private Foreign Investment & Economic Development. R. Vedavalli. LC 75-16868. 1976. 39.50 (ISBN 0-521-21019-4). Cambridge U Pr.

Private Foreign Investment in Developing Countries: A Quantitative Study on the Evaluation of Its Macro-Economic Impact. H. C. Bos et al. LC 73-91763. (International Studies in Economics & Econometrics: No. 7). 300p. 1974. lib. bdg. 53.00 (ISBN 90-277-0410-4, Pub. by Reidel Holland); pap. text ed. 28.00 (ISBN 90-277-0439-2, Pub. by Reidel Holland). Kluwer Academic.

Private Foreign Investment: Legal & Economic Realities. Seymour J. Rubin. LC 56-7594. pap. 30.00 (ISBN 0-317-28469-X, 2020751). Bks Demand UMI.

Private Foundations - Self-Dealing (Section 4941) Charles E. Muller, II & Charles D. Rubin. (Tax Management Portfolio Ser.: No. 89). 1987. looselef 50.00. BNA.

Private Foundations: A/Key to Tax Benefits for Charitable Giving. Ernst & Whinney. 4p. 1986. write for info. Am Inst CPA.

Private Franklin: The Man & His Family. Claude-Anne Lopez & Eugenia W. Herbert. (Illus.). 400p. 1985. pap. 7.95 (ISBN 0-393-30227-X). Norton.

Private Freight Cars & American Railways. Louis D. Weld. LC 70-76679. (Columbia University. Studies in the Social Sciences: No. 81). Repr. of 1908 ed. 17.50 (ISBN 0-404-51081-7). AMS Pr.

Private Function. Alan Bennett. LC 84-28734. 110p. (Orig.). 1985. pap. 8.95 (ISBN 0-571-13571-4). Faber & Faber.

Private Gardens of England. Penelope Hobhouse. (Illus.). 224p. 1987. 40.00 (ISBN 0-517-56267-7, Harmony). Crown.

Private Gardens of Germany. M. Sayn-Wittgenstein & Ursula Dohna. (Illus.). 224p. 1987. 60.00 (ISBN 0-517-56512-9, Harmony). Crown.

Private Gardens of Scotland. James Truscott. (Illus.). 160p. 1988. 50.00 (ISBN 0-517-56974-4, Harmony). Crown.

Private Government of Public Money: Community & Policy in British Political Administration. Hugh Heclo & Aaron Wildavsky. LC 73-79474. 1974. 42.50x (ISBN 0-520-02497-4). U of Cal Pr.

Private Grazing & Public Lands. Wesley Calef. Ed. by Stuart Bruchey. LC 78-56701. (Management of Public Land Law in the U. S. Ser.). 1979. Repr. of 1960 ed. lib. bdg. 25.50x (ISBN 0-405-11321-8). Ayer Co Pubs.

Private High. Thomas Martin. 25p. (Orig.). (YA) (gr. 7 up). 1986. pap. 3.00 playscript (ISBN 0-87602-267-0). Anchorage.

Private House of Prayer. Leslie D. Weatherhead. (Festival Bks). 1979. pap. 2.95 (ISBN 0-687-34220-1). Abingdon.

Private Household Consumption in China: A Study of People's Livelihood. Jacques Van der Gaag. (Working Paper: No. 701). 106p. 1985. 5.00 (ISBN 0-8213-0465-8, WP 0701). World Bank.

Private "I". Imogene Forte. LC 84-62933. (Tabletop Learning Ser.). (Illus.). 80p. (gr. k-6). 1985. wkbk 3.95 (ISBN 0-86530-096-8, IP 91-0). Incentive Pubns.

Private Independent Schools: The Bunting & Lyon Blue Book, 1987. 40th ed. LC 72-122324. (Illus.). 1987. 55.00x (ISBN 0-913094-40-4). Bunting.

Private Innovations in Public Transit. Ed. by John C. Weicher. LC 87-33667. (AEI Studies: No. 468). (Illus.). 148p. 1988. lib. bdg. 17.50 (ISBN 0-8447-3647-3). Am Enterprise.

Private Intelligence Secrets. James L. Drake. (Illus.). 140p. (Orig.). 1988. pap. 19.95 (ISBN 0-939427-28-1, 10030). Alpha Pubns OH.

Private Interest & Public Gain: The Dartmouth College Case, 1819. Francis N. Stites. LC 72-77574. 192p. 1972. 17.50x (ISBN 0-87023-112-X); pap. 9.95x (ISBN 0-87023-113-8). U of Mass Pr.

Private Interest Government Beyond Market & State. Ed. by Wolfgang Streek & Phillipe C. Schmitter. (Studies in Neo-Corporatism). 288p. (Orig.). 1986. text ed. 49.95 (ISBN 0-8039-9722-1); pap. text ed. 18.95 (ISBN 0-8039-9723-X). Sage.

Private Interests, Public Policy, & American Agriculture. William P. Browne. LC 87-23131. (Studies in Government & Public Policy). x, 342p. 1988. 29.95x (ISBN 0-7006-0334-4); pap. 12.95x (ISBN 0-7006-0335-2). U Pr of KS.

Private International Investment: An Exercise in Theory & Policy. rev. ed. Robert R. Miller & John Kilpatrick. (CISE Learning Packages on International Studies). 56p. pap. text ed. 3.00x (ISBN 0-317-34810-8). LRIS.

Private International Law. Joseph A. Thomas. LC 74-31362. 174p. 1975. Repr. of 1955 ed. lib. bdg. 35.00x (ISBN 0-8371-7929-7, THPI). Greenwood.

Private International Law: A Comparative Treatise on American International Conflicts Law, Vols. 2 & 3. Albert A. Ehrenzweig. LC 67-28516. 176p. 1973. 75.00 set (ISBN 0-379-00353-8); 37.50 ea. Oceana.

Private International Law in the Netherlands. R. Van Rooij & Maurice V. Polak. LC 87-2601. 1987. 73.00 (ISBN 9-06-544286-3). Kluwer Academic.

Private Investigations: The Novels of Dashiell Hammett. Sinda Gregory. 221p. 1984. text ed. 19.95x (ISBN 0-8093-1165-8). S Ill U Pr.

Private Investigator. Jack Rudman. (Career Examination Ser.: C-2462). (Cloth bdg. avail. on request). pap. 14.00 (ISBN 0-8373-2462-9). Natl Learning.

Private Investigator's Basic Manual. Richard H. Akin. 208p. 1979. 21.75x (ISBN 0-398-03520-2). C C Thomas.

Private Investment: The Key to International Industrial Development: a Report of the San Francisco Conference. Ed. by James Daniel & Stuart Bruchley. LC 80-606. (Multinational Corporations Ser.). 1980. Repr. of 1958 ed. lib. bdg. 30.50x (ISBN 0-405-13355-3). Ayer Co Pubs.

Private Investors Abroad. Southwestern Legal Foundation. 1967. New proceedings annually. 75.00 (662); 99.00. Bender.

Private Journal of Aaron Burr, 2 vols. Aaron Burr. LC 75-31113. (Reprinted from orig. MS). Repr. of 1903 ed. 86.50 set (ISBN 0-404-13710-5). AMS Pr.

Private Journal of Louis McLane, U. S. N. 1844-1848. Louis McLane. Ed. by Jay Monaghan. 1972. 10.00 (ISBN 0-87093-155-5). Dawsons.

Private Journal of Margaret Morris, Kept During a Portion of the Revolutionary War. Margaret Morris. Ed. by Peter Decker. LC 71-77107. (Eyewitness Accounts of the American Revolution Ser., No. 2). 1969. Repr. of 1836 ed. 13.50 (ISBN 0-405-01168-7). Ayer Co Pubs.

Private Journals of the Long Parliament. Vernon Snow & Anne S. Young. LC 81-3323. 560p. 1987. text ed. 75.00 (ISBN 0-300-03604-3). Yale U Pr.

Private Journals of the Long Parliament: January 3 to March 5, 1642. Ed. by Willson H. Coates et al. LC 81-3323. 630p. 1982. text ed. 80.00t (ISBN 0-300-02545-9). Yale U Pr.

Private Jurisdiction in England. Warren O. Ault. LC 80-1998. Repr. of 1923 ed. 41.00 (ISBN 0-404-18550-9). AMS Pr.

Private Jurisdiction in England. Warren O. Ault. Ed. by R. H. Helmholz & Bernard D. Reams, Jr. LC 80-84955. (Historical Writings in Law & Jurisprudence Ser.: No. 25, Bk. 39). 370p. 1981. Repr. of 1923 ed. lib. bdg. 40.00 (ISBN 0-89941-091-X). W S Hein.

Private Justice: Towards Integrative Theorising in the Sociology of Law. Stuart Henry. LC 83-10926. 245p. (Orig.). 1984. pap. 14.95x (ISBN 0-7100-9703-4). Routledge Chapman & Hall.

Private Keepers of the Public Interest. Paul T. Heyne. 144p. 1983. pap. text ed. 9.25 (ISBN 0-8191-2166-5). U Pr of Amer.

Private Lands & Public Recreation. 34p. 1979. 1.00 (ISBN 0-318-23131-X). Wildlife Mgmt.

Private Law Librarians 1986: Commercial Law and Practice Course Handbook, Vol 396. 677p. 1986. 45.00 (A4-4163). PLI.

Private Law Sources & Analogies of International Law, with Special Reference to International Arbitration. Hersh Lauterpacht. LC 71-95030. xxiv, 326p. 1970. Repr. of 1927 ed. 32.50 (ISBN 0-208-00814-4, Archon). Shoe String.

Private Letter-Books of Sir Walter Scott. Wilfred Partington. 1930. Repr. 35.00 (ISBN 0-8274-3204-6). R West.

Private Letter Rulings. (Information Services Ser.). Date not set. price not set ring bound loose leaf. P-H.

Private Letters from an American in England to His Friends in America, 1769. (Novel in England, 1700-1775 Ser.) 1974. lib. bdg. 61.00 (ISBN 0-8240-1186-4). Garland Pub.

Private Letters of Edward Gibbon, 2 Vols. Edward Gibbon. Ed. by Rowland E. Prothero. LC 71-151596. Repr. of 1896 ed. Set. 75.00 (ISBN 0-404-02751-2). AMS Pr.

Private Letters of Princess Lieven to Prince Metternich: 1820-1826. Princess Lieven. 1948. 39.50x (ISBN 0-317-27535-6). Elliots Bks.

Private Letters of the Marquess of Dalhousie. J. G. Baird. (Illus.). 448p. 1984. Repr. of 1910 ed. text ed. 75.00x (ISBN 0-86590-374-3, Pub. by B R Pub Corp Delhi). Apt Bks.

Private Letters of the Marquis of Dalhousie. Ed. by J. G. Baird. (Illus.). 461p. 1972. Repr. of 1910 ed. 37.50x (ISBN 0-7165-2053-2, BBA 03051, Pub. by Irish Academic Pr). Biblio Dist.

Private Liberal Arts Colleges in Minnesota: Their History & Contributions. Merrill E. Jarchow. LC 73-14591. (Illus.). 345p. 1973. 17.00 (ISBN 0-87351-081-X). Minn Hist.

Private Life. Cynthia P. Seton. 192p. 1984. pap. 4.95 (ISBN 0-393-30187-7). Norton.

Private Life see Altar of the Dead.

Private Life of Axie Reed. John Knowles. LC 85-20598. 1986. 15.95 (ISBN 0-525-24403-4, Pub. by W Abrahams Bk). Dutton.

Private Life of H. P. Lovecraft. Sonia H. Davis. Frwd. by S. T. Joshi. 38p. (Orig.). 1985. pap. 4.95 (ISBN 0-318-04718-7). Necronomicon.

Private Life of Henry Maitland. Morley Roberts. 1912. 40.00 (ISBN 0-8274-3205-4). R West.

Private Life of Henry VIII. Lajos Biro & Arthur Wimperis. Ed. by Bruce S. Kupelnick. LC 76-52090. (Classics of Film Literature Ser.). 1978. lib. bdg. 22.00 (ISBN 0-8240-2866-X). Garland Pub.

Private Life of Sherlock Holmes. V. Starrett. LC 78-130268. (English Literature Ser., No. 33). 1970. Repr. of 1934 ed. lib. bdg. 75.00x (ISBN 0-8383-1175-X). Haskell.

Private Property & the Public Interest: The Brandywine Experience. Ann L. Strong. LC 74-24390. (Illus.). 232p. 1975. 27.50x (ISBN 0-8018-1662-9). Johns Hopkins.

Private Property: The History of an Idea. Richard B. Schlatter. LC 72-85007. 284p. 1973. Repr. of 1951 ed. 22.00x (ISBN 0-8462-1697-3). Russell.

Private Prosecution. Eileen Dewhurst. LC 86-32867. (Crime Club Ser.). 192p. 1987. 12.95 (ISBN 0-385-24146-1). Doubleday.

Private Provision of Public Services in Developing Countries. Gabriel Roth. (World Bank Publication). 320p. 1987. 27.00 (ISBN 0-19-520544-8). Oxford U Pr.

Private Provision of Public Welfare: Market, State & Family. Elim Papadakis & Peter Taylor-Gooby. LC 87-9425. 240p. 1987. 35.00 (ISBN 0-312-00950-X). St Martin.

Private Real Estate Syndications. Michael Constas & Richard D. Harroch. LC 83-9417. 1983. looseleaf 75.00 (00581). NY Law Pub.

Private Real Property Syndications After the 1986 Tax Reform. 346p. 1986. pap. 32.00 (RE-49036). Cal Cont Ed Bar.

Private Redevelopment of the Central City: Spatial Processes of Structural Change in the City of Toronto. Larry S. Bourne. LC 66-30638. (Research Papers Ser.: No. 112). 199p. 1967. pap. 12.00 (ISBN 0-89065-020-9). U Chicago Comm Geo.

Private Religious Foundations in the Byzantine Empire. John Philip Thomas. LC 87-8870. (Dumbarton Oaks Studies Ser.: Vol. 24). 322p. 1988. 22.50X (ISBN 0-88402-164-5). Dumbarton Oaks.

Private Rented Housing in the United States & Europe. Michael Harloe. LC 84-17770. 400p. 1985. 32.50 (ISBN 0-312-64718-2). St Martin.

Private Rights & Public Lands. Ed. by Phillip N. Truluck. 95p. 1983. pap. 4.00 (ISBN 0-89195-033-8, 82-8433). Heritage Found.

Private Rights, Public Wrongs: The Computer & Personal Privacy. Michael R. Rubin. Ed. by Brenda Dervin. (Communication & Information Science Ser.). 176p. 1988. text ed. 29.50 (ISBN 0-89391-518-1). Ablex Pub.

Private Road. Forrest Reid. LC 75-41225. Repr. of 1940 ed. 18.50 (ISBN 0-404-14587-6). AMS Pr.

Private Rules in Career Decision Making. John D. Krumboltz. 33p. 1983. 5.75 (ISBN 0-318-22179-9, SN38). Natl Ctr Res Voc Ed.

Private Saving & Public Debt. Ed. by Michael J. Boskin et al. 256p. 1987. text ed. 55.00 (ISBN 0-631-15142-7). Basil Blackwell.

Private School Education in the U. S. An Annotated Bibliography, 1950-1980. Alice H. Songe. LC 81-20884. 89p. (Orig.). 1982. pap. text ed. 15.95x (ISBN 0-89950-045-5). McFarland & Co.

Private School Law in America. Data Research, Inc. Staff. Ed. by Craig W. Andresen. LC 87-5271. 200p. 1987. 45.00 (ISBN 0-939675-06-4); pap. 45.00 (ISBN 0-939675-05-6). Data Res MN.

Private School Management. William J. McMillan. 1977. 7.95 (ISBN 0-918214-00-9, 76-51885). F E Peters.

Private School Management. 2nd ed. William J. McMillan. LC 79-50904. 1979. 14.95 (ISBN 0-918214-03-3). F E Peters.

Private Schools & Private School Teachers: Final Report of the 1985-86 Private School Study. Michael J. Brick & Jeffrey W. Williams. (SC Ser.: 87-346c). (Illus.). 153p. 1987. pap. 8.00 (ISBN 0-318-22745-2, S/N 065-000-00287-6). USGPO.

Private Schools & Public Issues. I. Fox. 220p. 1984. text ed. 38.50 (ISBN 0-333-36328-0, Pub. by Macmillan UK). Humanities.

Private Schools & State Schools: Two Systems or One? Daphne Johnson. 192p. 1987. 65.00x (ISBN 0-335-15998-2, Open Univ Pr); pap. 21.00x (ISBN 0-335-15997-4, Open Univ Pr). Taylor & Francis.

Private Schools: Boards & Heads. new ed. William J. McMillan. LC 80-81654. 88p. (Orig.). 1980. pap. 5.95 (ISBN 0-918214-06-8). F E Peters.

Private Schools: From the Puritans to the Present. Otto F. Kraushaar. LC 75-28648. (Fastback Ser.: No. 73). 53p. (Orig.). 1976. pap. 0.90 (ISBN 0-87367-078-7). Phi Delta Kappa.

Private Schools of Colonial Boston. Robert F. Seybolt. LC 77-89232. (American Education: Its Men, Institutions & Ideas, Ser. 1). 1969. Repr. of 1935 ed. 9.00 (ISBN 0-405-01468-6). Ayer Co Pubs.

Private Schools of Colonial Boston. Robert F. Seybolt. 1935. 7.50x (ISBN 0-686-51291-X). Elliots Bks.

Private Schools of the Future. William J. McMillan. LC 81-66535. 117p. 1981. pap. 12.95 spiral binding (ISBN 0-918214-07-6). F E Peters.

Private Schools of the United States: Council for American Private Education Schools, 1985-86 Edition. Curriculum Information Center Staff. 959p. 1985. pap. 75.00 (ISBN 0-89770-339-1). Market Data Ret.

Private Scores. Anne T. Wallach. 384p. 1986. 16.50 (ISBN 0-453-00512-8). NAL.

Private Scores. Anne T. Wallach. 1987. pap. 4.50 (ISBN 0-451-14952-1, Sig). NAL.

Private Screening. Richard N. Patterson. LC 85-40185. 1986. 16.45 (ISBN 0-394-54275-4, Pub. by Villard Bks). Random.

Private Screening. Richard N. Patterson. 448p. 1986. pap. 3.95 (ISBN 0-345-31139-6). Ballantine.

Private Secretary (Female)--Gold Coast. Erica Powell. LC 83-40285. 240p. 1984. 19.95 (ISBN 0-312-64719-0). St Martin.

Private Secretary's Encyclopedic Dictionary. 3rd ed. Mary A. DeVries. LC 83-11004. 556p. 1983. 24.95 (ISBN 0-13-711093-6, Busn). P-H.

Private Sector. J. Wilson Newman. (Credibility of Institutions, Policies & Leadership Ser.: Vol. 6). 140p. (Orig.). 1985. lib. bdg. 21.50 (ISBN 0-8191-4765-6, Co-Pub. by White Burkett Miller Center of Public Affairs, Univeristy of Virginia, Charlottesville); pap. 8.25 (ISBN 0-8191-4766-4). U Pr of Amer.

Private Sector Alternatives for Preventing Reading Failure: A Directory. Patrick Groff. (Illus.). 91p. (Orig.). 1987. pap. 3.50 (S/N 065-000-00311-2). USGPO.

Private Sector & Public Transit: The Role of the States. Gordon Meeks. (State Legislative Reports: Vol. 13, No. 9). 1988. pap. 5.00 (ISBN 1-55516-194-4). Natl Conf State Legis.

Private Sector Funding Available to Foreign Scholars & Students in the U. S. 54p. (Orig.). 1984. pap. 2.95 (ISBN 0-912207-09-4). NAFSA Washington.

Private Sector in Soviet Agriculture. 2nd enl. & rev ed. Karl-Eugen Wadekin. Ed. by George Karcz. Tr. by Keith Bush from Ger. LC 76-95322. (Russian & East European Studies). Orig. Title: Privatproduzenten in der Sowjetischen Landwirtschaft. 350p. 1973. 44.50x (ISBN 0-520-01558-4). U of Cal Pr.

Private Sector in State Correctional Industries: The Control Data Program in Minnesota. (Innovations Reports). 12p. 1985. 4.00 (ISBN 0-317-45837-X, RM-756). Coun State Govts.

Private Sector in the Public School. Ed. by Marsha Levine. 1985. pap. 7.00 (ISBN 0-8447-2251-0). Am Enterprise.

Private Sector Involvement with the Vocational Community: An Analysis of Policy Options. Clyde F. Maurice. 106p. 1984. 8.75 (ISBN 0-318-22180-2, IN281). Natl Ctr Res Voc Ed.

Private Sector Role in Rural Outdoor Recreation in the United States: An Annotated Bibliography. H. Ken Cordell & Barbara Stanley-Saunders. (Bibliographic Ser.: No. 8). 118p. 1984. pap. 20.00 (ISBN 0-88329-135-5). IAAO.

Private Sector Role in Rural Outdoor Recreation in the United States: An Annotated Bibliography. Ken Cordell & Barbara Stanley-Saunders. (CPL Bibliographies Ser.: No. 106). 118p. 1983. 15.00 (ISBN 0-86602-106-X). Coun Plan Librarians.

Private Sector Task Force on Juvenile Justice. 7.00 (ISBN 0-318-20315-4). Natl Coun Crime.

Private Sector Task Force on Juvenile Justice: Final Report. 1987. 8.65 (ISBN 0-318-23565-X). Natl Coun Crime.

Private Sectors in Higher Education: Structures, Function, & Change in Eight Countries. Roger L. Geiger. 288p. 1986. text ed. 25.00 (ISBN 0-472-09368-1); pap. text ed. 16.95 (ISBN 0-472-06368-5). U of Mich Pr.

Private Security & Private Justice: The Challenge of the 80s. Clifford D. Shearing & Philip C. Stenning. 70p. (Orig.). 1984. pap. text ed. 6.00x (ISBN 0-88645-000-4, Pub. by Inst Res Pub Canada). Brookfield Pub Co.

Private Security & the Law. Charles P. Nemeth. (Illus.). 250p. 1988. pap. text ed. write for info. (ISBN 0-87084-625-6). Anderson Pub Co.

Private Self: Theory & Practice of Women's Autobiographical Writings. Shari Benstock. LC 88-1282. vii, 319p. 1988. 34.95x (ISBN 0-8078-1791-0); pap. 10.95x (ISBN 0-8078-4218-4). U of NC Pr.

Private Side of American History: Readings in Everyday Life. 4th ed. Nash. 1986. Vol. 1, 548 pgs. pap. text ed. 11.50 (ISBN 0-15-571960-2); Vol. 2, 548 pgs. pap. text ed. 13.95 (ISBN 0-15-571961-0). HarBraceJ.

Private Signal: Poems New & Selected. Barbara Howes. LC 77-74559. 192p. 1977. 17.00x (ISBN 0-8195-5013-2); pap. 8.95 (ISBN 0-8195-6051-0). Wesleyan U Pr.

Private Soldier under Washington. Charles K. Bolton. (Illus.). 258p. 1976. Repr. of 1902 ed. 20.00 (ISBN 0-87928-072-7). Corner Hse.

Private Stock. Raymond Oliver. (First Pamphlet Ser.). 16p. (Orig.). 1983. pap. 4.00 (ISBN 0-941150-05-4). Barth.

Private-Stock Cookbook. United Airlines Friendship Guild. 410p. (Orig.). 1982. pap. 11.95 (ISBN 0-89716-109-2). Peanut Butter.

Private Supply of Public Services: Evaluation of Real Estate Exactions, Linkage, & Alternate Land Policies. Ed. by Rachelle Alterman. 256p. 1987. 40.00x (ISBN 0-8147-0589-8). NYU Pr.

Private Swimming Pools. Michigan Municipal League. (Technical Topics Ser.: No. 26). 1987. write for info. MI Municipal.

Private T. Pigeon's Tale. Jaimy Gordon. (Treacle Story Ser.: No. 5). (Illus.). 36p. 1979. signed 8.00 (ISBN 0-914232-19-3). McPherson & Co.

Private Telecommunication Networks - Equipment & Services Markets. Int'l Resource Development Inc. 195p. 1987. 1850.00x (ISBN 0-88694-740-5). Intl Res Dev.

Private Telecommunications Networks: Equipment & Services Markets. 195p. 1987. 1850.00 (740). Intl Res Dev.

Private Television Communications: The New Directions. Judith M. Brush & Douglas P. Brush. (Brush Report Ser.: No. 4). 188p. (Orig.). 1986. pap. 39.95 (ISBN 0-9615988-0-8). HI Pr.

Private Testimony & Public Policy. Phillips Ruopp. 1959. pap. 2.50x (ISBN 0-87574-105-3, 105). Pendle Hill.

Private Thoughts. Matanah, pseud. Ed. by Delores F. Ridge. 32p. (Orig.). 1988. pap. text ed. 3.95 (ISBN 0-9600978-0-5). Knees Pbk.

Private Universe. facsimile ed. Andre Maurois. Tr. by Hamish Miles. LC 70-177963. (Essay Index Reprint Ser). Repr. of 1932 ed. 19.50 (ISBN 0-8369-2564-5). Ayer Co Pubs.

Private Vices, Public Benefits: Bernard Mandeville's Social & Political Thought. M. M. Goldsmith. (Ideas in Context Ser.). 220p. 1985. 37.50 (ISBN 0-521-30036-3). Cambridge U Pr.

Private View. Irene M. Selznick. LC 82-49192. 385p. 1983. 16.95 (ISBN 0-394-40192-1). Knopf.

Private View: Essays on Literature. Walter J. De La Mare. LC 78-14114. 1985. Repr. of 1953 ed. 25.00 (ISBN 0-88355-786-X). Hyperion Conn.

Private Viewdata in the U. K. Penelope A. Yates-Mercer. 206p. 1985. pap. 59.95 (ISBN 0-566-02521-3, Pub. by Gower Pub England). Gower Pub Co.

Private Violence & Public Policy: The Needs of Battered Women & the Response of the Public. Ed. by Jan Pahl. 208p. (Orig.). 1985. pap. 12.95x (ISBN 0-7100-9992-4). Routledge Chapman & Hall.

Private Voluntary Organizations As Agents of Development. Ed. by Robert F. Gorman. 160p. 1984. 29.50x (ISBN 0-86531-997-9). Westview.

Private Wants & Public Needs. rev. ed. Ed. by Edmund S. Phelps. (Problems of Modern Economy Ser.). (Orig.). 1965. pap. 4.95x (ISBN 0-393-09496-0, NortonC). Norton.

Private Wants, Public Means: An Economic Analysis of the Desirable Scope of Government. Gordon Tullock. (Illus.). 272p. 1987. pap. text ed. 12.75 (ISBN 0-8191-6370-8, Pub. by Ctr Study Public Choice). U Pr of Amer.

Private War: Letters & Diaries of Madge Preston, 1862-1867. Virginia Beauchamp. (Douglass Series on Women's Lives & the Meaning of Gender). 365p. 1987. 29.95 (ISBN 0-8135-1206-9). Rutgers U Pr.

Private War: Surviving in Poland on False Papers, 1941-1945. Bruno Shatyn. LC 84-21905. (Illus.). 330p. 1985. 25.00x (ISBN 0-8143-1775-8). Wayne St U Pr.

Private Water Systems Handbook. 4th ed. Midwest Plan Service Personnel. LC 79-19040. (Illus.). 72p. 1979. pap. 6.00 (ISBN 0-89373-045-9, MWPS-14). Midwest Plan Serv.

Private Woman, Public Stage: Literary Domesticity in Nineteenth Century America. Mary Kelley. 432p. 1984. 32.95 (ISBN 0-19-503351-5); pap. 9.95 (ISBN 0-19-503581-X). Oxford U Pr.

Private Woodsrors. Sandrs C. Moore. 288p. 1988. 18.95 (ISBN 0-15-174710-5). HarBraceJ.

Private World of Congress. Rochelle Jones & Peter Woll. LC 79-7371. 1979. 14.95 (ISBN 0-02-916680-2). Free Pr.

Private World of Jean Giono. Walter D. Redfern. LC 67-20396. Repr. of 1967 ed. 54.30 (ISBN 0-8357-9115-7, 2017924). Bks Demand UMI.

Private World of the Last Tsar in the Photographs & Notes of General Count Alexander Grabbe. P. Grabbe & B. Grabbe. 199p. 1985. 85.00x (ISBN 0-317-40708-2, Pub. by Collets UK). State Mutual Bk.

Private World: Selected Works of Miguel de Unamuno, Vol. 2. Miguel de Unamuno. Tr. by Martin Nozick et al from Span. LC 83-43054. (Bollingen Ser.: LXXXV: 2). (Illus.). 356p. 1984. 36.50x (ISBN 0-691-09927-8). Princeton U Pr.

Private Worlds of Dying Children. Myra Bluebond-Langner. LC 77-85529. 298p. 1980. 32.00x (ISBN 0-691-09374-1); pap. 9.95x (ISBN 0-691-02820-6). Princeton U Pr.

Private Worlds of Julia Redfern. Eleanor Cameron. LC 87-30695. 224p. (gr. 6 up). 1988. 13.95 (ISBN 0-525-44394-0, 01354-410). Dutton.

Private Yankee Doodle. Joseph P. Martin. LC 67-29036. (Eyewitness Accounts of the American Revolution Ser., No. 1). 1968. Repr. of 1962 ed. 25.50 (ISBN 0-405-01137-7). Ayer Co Pubs.

Private Zone. Frances S. Dayee. 32p. (Orig.). 1988. pap. text ed. 3.50 (ISBN 0-446-38053-9). Warner Bks.

Private Zone: A Book Teaching Children Sexual Assault Prevention Tools. Frances S. Dayee. Ed. by Linda D. Meyer. (Illus.). 30p. (Orig.). (ps-3). 1982. PLB 9.00 (ISBN 0-9603516-5-5). Franklin Pr WA.

Privateer. Josephine Tey. (Portway Ser.). 424p. 1987. lib. bdg. 17.50 (ISBN 0-7451-7085-4, Pub. by Chivers Pr UK). G K Hall.

Privateering & Colonisation in the Reign of Elizabeth I. Ed. by Joyce Youings. (Exeter Studies in History: Vol. 10). 128p. 1986. pap. text ed. 12.50 (ISBN 0-85989-252-2, Pub. by U of Exeter UK). Humanities.

Privateers. Ben Bova. 432p. (Orig.). 1985. 15.95 (ISBN 0-312-93604-4, Dist. by St. Martin's Press). Tor Bks.

Privateers. Ben Bova. 432p. (Orig.). 1986. pap. 3.50 (ISBN 0-8125-3223-6, Dist. by Warner Pub Services & St. Martin's Press). Tor Bks.

Privately Printed Papers of A. A. Girault. Gordh & Gordon. (Memoir Ser.: No.28). 400p. 1979. 30.00 (ISBN 0-686-40426-2). Am Entom Inst.

Privates. Gene Horowitz. 256p. 1986. 15.95 (ISBN 0-312-64716-6). St Martin.

Privates. Gene Horowitz. (Gay Bks.). 256p. 1988. pap. 7.95x (ISBN 0-312-01496-1). St Martin.

Privates on Parade. Peter Nichols. 112p. 1977. pap. 5.95 (ISBN 0-571-11142-4). Faber & Faber.

Privatisation? Sue Hastings & Hugo Levie. 205p. 75.00x (ISBN 0-85124-359-2, Pub. by Bertrand Russell Hse); pap. 21.25x (ISBN 0-85124-360-6). State Mutual Bk.

Privatisation. Ed. by Richard Parry. (Research Highlights in Social Work Ser.: No. 18). 144p. 1988. price not set (ISBN 1-85302-015-X, Pub. by J Kingsley Pubs UK). UNIPUB.

Privatisation & Planning in Declining Areas. Stephen Young. 240p. 1987. 34.50 (ISBN 0-7099-2906-4, Pub. by Croom Helm UK). Routledge Chapman & Hall.

Privatisation & Planning in Declining Areas. Stephen Young. 240p. 1987. lib. bdg. 42.00x (ISBN 0-317-64368-1, Pub. by Croom Helm UK). Routledge Chapman & Hall.

Privatisation & the National Health Service: The Scope for Collaboration. Ed. by Jeffrey Chandra & Andrew Kakabadse. LC 85-16857. 120p. 1985. text ed. 29.95 (ISBN 0-566-00813-0). Gower Pub Co.

Privatisation & the Welfare State. Ed. by Julian Le Grand & Ray Robinson. 256p. 1984. text ed. 37.95x (ISBN 0-04-336079-3); pap. text ed. 14.95x (ISBN 0-04-336080-7). Unwin Hyman.

Privatisation in the UK. V. V. Ramanadham. 256p. 1988. lib. bdg. 62.50 (ISBN 0-415-00150-1). Routledge Chapman & Hall.

Privatised World. Arthur Brittan. (International Library of Sociology Ser.). 1978. 22.95x (ISBN 0-7100-8769-1). Routledge Chapman & Hall.

Privatization. Ed. by John C. Goodman. 1985. pap. 10.00 (ISBN 0-943802-13-X). Natl Ctr Pol.

Privatization. Hamline University, Advanced Legal Education Staff. 1986. 3-ring binder 47.70 (ISBN 0-317-42509-9). Hamline Law.

Privatization: A Selective Bibliography. Alva W. Stewart. (Public Administration Ser.: P 1936). 11p. 1986. 3.75 (ISBN 0-89028-856-9). Vance Biblios.

Privatization: A Strategy for Taming the Federal Budget. Ed. by Stephen Moore & Stuart M. Butler. 109p. 1987. pap. 8.00. Heritage Found.

Privatization & Development. Steve Hanke. 237p. 1987. 29.95 (ISBN 0-917616-86-3); pap. 12.95 (ISBN 0-917616-85-5). ICS Pr.

Privatization & Provincial Social Services in Canada: Policy, Administration & Delivery. Ed. by Jacqueline S. Ismael & Yves Baillancourt. 225p. 1988. 24.95x (ISBN 0-88864-132-X, Pub. by Univ of Alta Pr Canada); pap. 16.95x (ISBN 0-88864-133-8, Pub. by Univ of Alta Pr Canada). U of Nebr Pr.

Privatization & Public Enterprises. Richard Henning & Ali M. Mansoor. (Occasional Papers: No. 56). vi, 22p. 1988. pap. 7.50 (ISBN 1-55775-005-X). Intl Monetary.

Privatization & Regulation: The U. K. Experience. D. Thompson & J. A. Kay. 288p. 1987. 44.00x (ISBN 0-19-877254-8). Oxford U Pr.

Privatization in Less Developed Countries. Ed. by Paul Cook & Colin Kirkpatrick. LC 87-36937. 256p. 1988. 49.95 (ISBN 0-312-01955-6). St Martin.

Privatization Policy - An International Perspective, 1985-1986. Dale E. Casper. (Public Administration Ser.: P 2185). 8p. 1987. 3.00 (ISBN 1-55590-365-7). Vance Biblios.

Privatization: The Key to Better Government. E. S. Savas. LC 87-23821. (Chatham House Series on Change in American Politics). 320p. 1987. 25.00 (ISBN 0-934540-59-4); pap. 14.95x (ISBN 0-934540-58-6). Chatham Hse Pubs.

Privatization: Toward More Effective Government--Report of the President's Commission on Privatization. Ed. by David F. Linowes. 1988. pap. 9.95 (ISBN 0-252-06058-X). U of Ill Pr.

Privatization: Toward More Effective Government, Report, March 1988. 300p. (Orig.). 1988. pap. 9.00 (S/N 040-000-00526-9). USGPO.

Privatizing Federal Spending: A Strategy to Eliminate the Deficit. Stuart M. Butler. LC 84-8805. 176p. 1985. 15.00 (ISBN 0-87663-454-4). Universe.

Privatizing Public Charities. John C. Goodman. 1986. 10.00 (ISBN 0-943802-15-6). Natl Ctr Pol.

Privatizing the Public Sector: How to Shrink Government. E. S. Savas. LC 82-4207. (Chatham House Series on Change in American Politics). 192p. 1982. 15.00 (ISBN 0-934540-15-2); pap. text ed. 11.95x (ISBN 0-934540-14-4). Chatham Hse Pubs.

Privatproduzenten in der Sowjetischen Landwirtschaft see Private Sector in Soviet Agriculture.

Priviledged Generation: Children in the Soviet Union. N. Vishneva-Sarafanova. 214p. 1984. pap. 10.00x (ISBN 0-317-53869-1, Pub. by Collets (UK)). State Mutual Bk.

Privileges & Practice of Parliaments in England. LC 74-80218. (English Experience Ser.: No. 654). 1974. Repr. of 1628 ed. 5.00 (ISBN 90-221-0654-3). Walter J Johnson.

Privilege. Leona Blair. LC 85-48227. 480p. 1986. 17.95 (ISBN 0-553-05132-6). Bantam.

Privilege. Leona Blair. 480p. (Orig.). 1988. pap. 4.95 (ISBN 0-553-26513-X). Bantam.

Privilege & Creative Destruction: The Charles River Bridge Case. Stanley I. Kutler. 1978. pap. 4.95x (ISBN 0-393-00885-1, Norton Lib). Norton.

Privilege & Democracy in America. facsimile ed. Frederic C. Howe. Ed. by Dan C. McCurry & Richard E. Rubenstein. LC 74-30634. (American Farmers & the Rise of Agribusiness Ser.). 1975. Repr. of 1910 ed. 29.00x (ISBN 0-405-06803-4). Ayer Co Pubs.

Privilege & Profit: A Family of Naval Contractors in 18th-Century France. P. W. Bamford. (Illus.). 448p. 1988. text ed. 45.95x (ISBN 0-8122-8135-7). U of Pa Pr.

Privilege in the Soviet Union. Mervyn Matthews. (Illus.). 1978. pap. text ed. 8.95x (ISBN 0-04-323021-0). Unwin Hyman.

Privilege of All Believers. John Waldron. 1987. pap. 5.95 (ISBN 0-86544-040-9). Salv Army Suppl South.

Privilege of Being a Physicist. Victor F. Weisskopf. 1988. 17.95 (ISBN 0-7167-1982-7). W H Freeman.

Privilege of Darkness. Bert Underwood. LC 85-72808. (Illus.). 395p. 1986. 13.95 (ISBN 0-935763-00-7); pap. 5.95 (ISBN 0-935763-01-5). Chester Hse Pubs.

Privilege, Persecution & Prophecy: The Catholic Church in Spain, 1875-1975. Frances Lannon. (Illus.). 350p. 1987. 55.00 (ISBN 0-19-821923-7). Oxford U Pr.

Privilege: The Enigma of Sasha Bruce. Joan Mellen. 1983. pap. 3.50 (ISBN 0-451-12469-3, Sig). NAL.

Privileged Characters. Morris R. Werner. LC 73-19184. (Politics & People Ser.). 518p. 1974. Repr. 35.50x (ISBN 0-405-05905-1). Ayer Co Pubs.

Privileged Children. Frances Vernon. 1987. 15.95 (ISBN 0-396-09007-9). Dodd.

Privileged Class: Senior Year at Beverly Hills High School. Michael Leahy. 320p. 1988. 17.95 (ISBN 0-316-51815-8). Little.

Privileged Communications As a Branch of Legal Evidence. John F. Hageman. xxix, 328p. 1983. Repr. of 1889 ed. lib. bdg. 32.50x (ISBN 0-8377-0708-0). Rothman.

Privileged Communications in the Mental Health Professions. Samuel J. Knapp & Leon D. VandeCreek. LC 86-24764. 208p. 1987. 27.95 (ISBN 0-442-24055-4). Van Nos Reinhold.

Privileged Eye: Essays on Photography. Max Kozloff. LC 86-16062. (Illus.). 320p. 1987. text ed. 29.95x (ISBN 0-8263-0891-0); pap. text ed. 15.95 (ISBN 0-8263-0892-9). U of NM Pr.

Privileged Generation: Children in the Soviet Union. N. Vishneva-Sarafanova. Tr. by Galina Glasgoleva. 214p. 1984. pap. 3.95 (ISBN 0-8285-2832-2, Pub. by Progress Pubs USSR). Imported Pubns.

Privileged Gifts: Marriage & Motherhood. Anne Dearing. 96p. 1987. pap. 3.95 (ISBN 0-310-55332-6, 19035P). Zondervan.

Privileged Information. Tom Alibrandi & Frank H. Armani. 256p. 1984. 15.95. Dodd.

Privileged Information. 1984. 15.95 (ISBN 0-396-08363-3). North Country.

Privileged Lives. Edward Stewart. 512p. 1988. pap. 18.95 (ISBN 0-385-29652-5). Delacorte.

Privileged Lives. Edward Stewart. (YA) (gr. 9-12). 1989. pap. 4.95 (ISBN 0-440-20230-2). Dell.

Privileged Mortals: The French Heroic Novel, 1630-1660. Mark Bannister. (Modern Languages & Literature Monographs). 1983. 34.00x (ISBN 0-19-815539-5). Oxford U Pr.

Privileged Partnership: Franco-German Relations in the European Community 1969-1984. Haig Simonian. 1985. 34.50x (ISBN 0-19-821959-8). Oxford U Pr.

Privileged Playgoers of Shakespeare's London, 1576-1642. Ann J. Cook. LC 80-8542. (Illus.). 280p. 1981. 30.50x (ISBN 0-691-06454-7). Princeton U Pr.

Privileges & Immunities of Citizens of the United States. Arnold J. Lien. LC 68-56667. (Columbia University. Studies in the Social Sciences: No. 132). Repr. of 1913 ed. 16.50 (ISBN 0-404-51132-5). AMS Pr.

Privileges & Immunities of State Citizenship, No. 3. Roger Howell. LC 78-63966. (Johns Hopkins University. Studies in the Social Sciences, 1918: 36). Repr. of 1918 ed. 16.00 (ISBN 0-404-61212-1). AMS Pr.

Privileges des Clercs Au Moyen-Age. Rene Poncet. 230p. (Fr.). Repr. of 1901 ed. lib. bdg. 42.50x. Coronet Bks.

Privileges for Trial & Business Lawyers. 331p. 1986. pap. 32.00 (CP-49024). Cal Cont Ed Bar.

Privileges of the University of Cambridge, 2 Vols. George Dyer. Repr. of 1824 ed. Set. 105.00 (ISBN 0-404-07306-9). AMS Pr.

Privitization Policy - An International Perspective, 1985-1986. Dale E. Casper. 1987. pap. 3.00 (ISBN 1-55590-365-7). Vance Biblios.

Privy Council. Albert V. Dicey. LC 79-1625. 1981. Repr. of 1887 ed. 17.50 (ISBN 0-88355-930-7). Hyperion Conn.

Privy Piping: A Most Curious Collection of Tunes Arranged for the Highland Bagpipe. 56p. 1985. pap. 6.50 (ISBN 0-912951-39-7). ScotPr.

Privy: The Classic Outhouse Book. rev. ed. Janet A. Strombeck & Richard H. Strombeck. Ed. by Ann Tomasic. (Illus.). 92p. 1984. pap. 7.95 (ISBN 0-912355-03-4). Sun Designs.

Prix et Leur Formation see Cahiers de l'Institut de Science Economique Appliquee.

Prix Nobel en. Nobel Foundation. Incl. 1966. 42.00 (ISBN 0-444-99977-9); 1967. 42.00 (ISBN 0-444-99921-3); 1968. 89.50 (ISBN 0-444-99935-3); 1969. 89.50 (ISBN 0-444-40931-9); 1970. 89.50 (ISBN 0-444-99909-4); 1971. 68.00 (ISBN 0-686-95242-1); 12/1972. 89.50 (ISBN 0-444-99882-9); 1973. 84.25 (ISBN 0-444-99859-4); 1974. 84.25 (ISBN 0-444-99834-9); 1975. 84.25 (ISBN 0-444-99815-2). 1968-77. Elsevier.

Prix Nobel 1984: Nobel Prizes, Presentations, Biographies, & Lectures. (Illus.). 288p. 1985. lib. bdg. 44.50x (ISBN 91-85848-08-5). Coronet Bks.

Priyadarsika, a Sanskrit Drama. Harshadeva. Tr. by G. K. Nariman et al. LC 76-180683. (Columbia University. Indo-Iranian Ser.: No. 10). Repr. of 1923 ed. 20.00 (ISBN 0-404-50480-9). AMS Pr.

Priyadarsika of Sri Harsa-Deva. Tr. by M. R. Kale. 1977. pap. 4.50 (ISBN 0-89684-299-1). Orient Bk Dist.

Prize. Irving Wallace. 704p. pap. 4.95 (ISBN 0-451-13759-0, Sig). NAL.

Prize: A Collection of Stories. Flavia M. Weedn. (Illus.). 128p. (Orig.). 1983. pap. 5.95 (ISBN 0-913289-00-0). Roserich Ltd.

Prize Cases Decided in the United States Supreme Court, 1789-1918, 3 vols. U. S. Supreme Court. LC 74-19623. Repr. of 1923 ed. Set. 167.50 (ISBN 0-404-12467-4). AMS Pr.

Prize for Percival. Allan Langoulant. Ed. by Rhoda Sherwood. LC 88-42912. (Illus.). 32p. (ps-1). 1988. PLB 11.25 (ISBN 1-55532-931-4). Stevens Inc.

Prize Homes. Hiawatha T. Estes. (Illus.). 1988. 2.95x. Hiawatha Homes.

Prize Meets Murder. R. T. Edwards & Otto Penzler. (Whodunit Mystery Ser.: No. 1). 176p. (Orig.). 1984. pap. 2.95 (ISBN 0-671-50988-8). PB.

Prize of Fear. Anne Nash. (Orig.). 1980. pap. 1.75 (ISBN 0-8439-8006-0, Tiara Bks). Leisure NY.

Prize Pig Surprise. Lisa C. Ernst. LC 83-26760. (Illus.). 32p. (ps-2). 1984. 10.25 (ISBN 0-688-03797-6); lib. bdg. 9.55 (ISBN 0-688-03798-4). Lothrop.

Prize Pulitzer. Roxanne Pulitzer & Kathy Maxa. LC 87-40191. 320p. 1988. 17.95 (ISBN 0-394-55761-1, Pub. by Villard Bks). Random.

Prize Pulitzer: The Scandal That Rocked Palm Beach - The Real Story. Roxanne Pulitzer & Kathleen Maxa. 1988. 19.95 (ISBN 0-317-66206-6, Pub. by Villard Bks). Random.

Prize Recipes from Great Restaurants: The Southern States & the Tropics. Ed. by James Stroman. LC 78-27415. (Prize Recipes Ser.). 128p. 1983. pap. 8.95 (ISBN 0-88289-293-2). Pelican.

Prize Recipes from Great Restaurants: The Western States. James Stroman. LC 78-27415. 128p. 1979. pap. 8.95 (ISBN 0-88289-068-9). Pelican.

Prize Stories of the Seventies: From the O. Henry Awards. Ed. by William Abrahams. 512p. 1981. pap. 4.95 (ISBN 0-671-41866-1). WSP.

Prize Stories of the Texas Institute of Letters. Ed. & intro. by Marshall Terry. LC 85-27953. 224p. 1986. 18.95 (ISBN 0-933841-04-3). Still Point Tx.

Prize Stories 1987: The O. Henry Awards. William Abrahams. LC 87-9372. 336p. 1987. 17.95 (ISBN 0-385-23594-1). Doubleday.

Prize Stories 1987: The O. Henry Awards. Ed. by William Abrahams, 336p. 1987. pap. 9.95 (ISBN 0-385-23595-X, Anchor Pr). Doubleday.

Prize Stories 1988: The O. Henry Awards. Ed. by William Abrahams. 312p. 1988. 18.95 (ISBN 0-385-24183-6). Doubleday.

Prize Stories 1988: The O. Henry Awards. Intro. by William Abrahams. 1988. pap. 9.95 (ISBN 0-385-24184-4, Anchor Pr). Doubleday.

Prize Stories 1989: The O. Henry Awards. Ed. by William Abrahams. 1989. 18.95 (ISBN 0-385-24633-1); pap. 9.95 (ISBN 0-385-24634-X, Achor Pr). Doubleday.

Prize Tomatoes Mystery. Thomas F. Pursell. LC 77-74010. (Carolrhoda Mini-Mysteries Ser.). (Illus.). (gr. k-4). 1977. PLB 5.95 (ISBN 0-87614-089-4). Carolrhoda Bks.

Prize Winners: Recipes & Menu Ideas from Award Winning Foodservice Personalities. Raymond B. Peddersen. 340p. 1983. 26.95 (ISBN 0-8436-2253-9). Van Nos Reinhold.

Prize-Winning Ads Used by Night Clubs, Cafes, Drive-Ins, & Hotels-Motels. rev. ed. Compiled by Arnold Fochs. 1982. pap. 29.95 (ISBN 0-685-58280-9). A J Pub.

Prize-Winning Recipes. Selma Glasser. 128p. 1984. 9.95 (ISBN 0-531-09829-X). Watts.

Prize-Winning Stories from China, 1980-1981. Ke Yunlu et al. Tr. by W. C. Chau et al from Chinese. (Illus.). 437p. (Orig.). 1985. pap. 9.95 (ISBN 0-8351-1313-2). China Bks.

Prizewinning Books for Children: Themes & Stereotypes in U. S. Prizewinning Prose Fiction for Children. Jacqueline S. Weiss. LC 82-48624. (Libraries & Librarianship Special Ser.). 480p. 1983. 22.00x (ISBN 0-669-06352-5). Lexington Bks.

Prizzi's Family. Richard Condon. 1987. pap. price not set. Berkley Pub.

Prizzi's Family. Richard Condon. 1986. 17.95 (ISBN 0-399-13210-4, Perigee). Putnam Pub Group.

Prizzi's Family. Richard Condon. 320p. 1987. pap. 4.50 (ISBN 0-515-09106-5). Jove Pubns.

Prizzi's Glory. Richard Condon. 1988. 17.95 (ISBN 0-525-24689-4). Dutton.

Prizzi's Honor. Richard Condon. 320p. 1983. pap. 3.95 (ISBN 0-425-09507-X). Berkley Pub.

Prnciples & Applications of Millimeter-Wave Radar. Charles E. Brown & Nicholas C. Currie. 600p. 1987. text ed. 79.00 (ISBN 0-89006-202-1). Artech Hse.

Pro. Gordon R. Dickson. 192p. 1986. pap. 2.95 (ISBN 0-8125-3575-8, Dist. by Warner Publisher Services & St. Martin's Press). Tor Bks.

Pro. Bob Packard. 1979. pap. 2.25 (ISBN 0-8439-0647-2, Leisure Bks). Leisure NY.

Pro-Allied Putsch in Croatia in 1944 & the Massacre of Croatians by Tito Communists in 1945. Ivo Omrcanin. 128p. 1975. pap. 2.95 (ISBN 0-8059-2128-1). Dorrance.

Pro Am Guide to U. S. Books About Music: Annotated Subject Guide to Current & Backlist Titles. Thomas P. Lewis. (Pro-Am General Music Ser.: Gms-6). 211p. (Orig.). 1987. pap. 35.00x (ISBN 0-912483-03-2, Pub. by Kahn & Averill UK). Pro-Am Music.

Pro-Am Murders. Patrick Cake. LC 78-70580. (Illus.). 1979. 8.95 (ISBN 0-932864-00-7). Proteus Calif.

Pro & College Football's Fifty Greatest Games. George Allen & Ben Olan. LC 83-3800. 272p. 1983. 14.95 (ISBN 0-672-52778-2). Bobbs.

Pro Archia. Cicero. Bd. with Post Redifum in Senatu; Post Redifum Ad Quirites; De Domo Sua; De Haruspicum Responsis; Pro Cn. Plancio. (Loeb Classical Library: No. 158). (Lat. & Eng.). 13.95x (ISBN 0-674-99174-5). Harvard U Pr.

Pro Balbo see Pro Caelio.

Pro-Boers: The Anatomy of an Anti-War Movement. Stephen Koss. (Studies in Imperialism). 1973. text ed. 25.00x (ISBN 0-226-45134-8). U of Chicago Pr.

Pro Caelio. Cicero. Bd. with De Provinciis Consularibus; Pro Balbo. (Loeb Classical Library: No. 447). 13.95x (ISBN 0-674-99492-2). Harvard U Pr.

Pro-Drugs as Novel Drug Delivery Systems. Ed. by T. Higuchi & V. Stella. LC 75-11721. (ACS Symposium Ser.: No. 14). 1975. 29.95 (ISBN 0-8412-0291-5). Am Chemical.

Pro Earth: Readings on Current Land & Water Issues in the Global Environment. 1985. 6.95 (ISBN 0-377-00154-6). Friendship Pr.

Pro Football Hall of Fame Presents Their Deeds & Dogged Faith. Mike Rathet & Don R. Smith. LC 84-11188. (Illus.). 1984. 24.95 (ISBN 0-917439-02-3). Balsam Pr.

Pro Football: NFL Facts & Statistics. Herman E. Burke. 1986. 15.00 (ISBN 0-533-06758-8). Vantage.

Pro Football Scorebook. 2nd ed. Kenneth N. Carlson. (Illus.). 488p. 1986. pap. 12.50 (ISBN 0-938428-07-1). Rain Belt.

Pro Football Strategy: What the Sunday Fan Should Know to be a Monday Quarterback. James E. Hopkinson. LC 81-83104. 265p. (Orig.). 1982. pap. 8.95 (ISBN 0-940950-00-6). Knowledge Builders.

Pro Football's Greatest Upsets. George Sullivan. LC 74-163175. (Garrard Sports Library). (Illus.). 96p. (gr. 3-6). 1972. PLB 7.12 (ISBN 0-8116-6662-X). Garrard.

Pro Game. Megan Terry. (Illus.). 12p. (Orig.). 1984. pap. 1.50 (ISBN 0-88680-217-2); royalty 25.00 (ISBN 0-317-11926-5). I E Clark.

Pro Game see Two by Terry Plus One: An Anthology of Plays by Women.

Pro Golf Teaching Manual. Robert Bernier. pap. 2.95x (ISBN 0-89741-008-4). Roadrunner Tech.

Pro-Lawn Service Accounting Application. 4th ed. David H. Weaver et al. 168p. 1982. text ed. 9.04 (ISBN 0-07-069334-X). McGraw.

Pro Lege Manilia. Cicero. Bd. with Pro Caecina; Pro Cluentio; Pro Rabirio Perduellionis Reo. (Loeb Classical Library: No. 198). (Lat. & Eng.). 13.95x (ISBN 0-674-99218-0). Harvard U Pr.

Pro-Life Catechism. 3.25 (ISBN 0-8198-5818-8); 2.00 (ISBN 0-8198-5819-6). Dghtrs St Paul.

Pro-Life Feminism: Different Voices. Ed. by Gail Grenier-Sweet. 256p. (Orig.). 1985. pap. 9.95 (ISBN 0-919225-22-5). Life Cycle Bks.

Pro-Life Manifesto. Thomas Klasen. LC 87-71890. 160p. (Orig.). 1988. pap. 6.95 (ISBN 0-89107-469-4, Crossway Bks). Good News.

Pro-Life Media Handbook. Judie Brown. Date not set. price not set (ISBN 0-913631-01-9). Anastasia VA.

Pro-Life, Pro-Peace: Life Affirming Alternatives to Abortion, War, Mercy Killing, & the Death Penalty. Lowell O. Erdahl. LC 86-3552. 160p. (Orig.). 1986. pap. 9.95 (ISBN 0-8066-2209-1, 10-5240). Augsburg.

Pro M. Caelio Oratio. 3rd ed. Cicero. Ed. by R. G. Austin. 1960. 12.95x (ISBN 0-19-814401-6). Oxford U Pr.

Pro M. Caelio Oratio. 3rd ed. Cicero. Ed. by R. G. Austin. 212p. 1988. pap. 17.95 (ISBN 0-19-814062-2). Oxford U Pr.

Pro Milone. Cicero. Bd. with In Prisonen; Pro Sauro; Pro Fonteio; Pro Rabirio Postumo; Pro Marcello; Pro Ligario; Pro Rege Deiotaro. (Loeb Classical Library: No. 252). 13.95x (ISBN 0-674-99278-4). Harvard U Pr.

Pro Musica Antiqua: Poems. O. B Hardison, Jr. LC 77-3932. vii, 55p. 1977. 13.95x (ISBN 0-8071-0295-4); pap. 6.95 (ISBN 0-8071-0296-2). La State U Pr.

Pro Quinctio. Cicero. Bd. with Pro Roscio Amerino; Pro Roscio Comoedo; Three Speeches on the Agrarian Law Against Rullus. (Loeb Classical Library: No. 240). (Lat. & Eng.). 13.95x (ISBN 0-674-99265-2). Harvard U Pr.

Pro Sestio. Cicero. Bd. with In Vatinium. (Loeb Classical Library: No. 309). 13.95x (ISBN 0-674-99341-1). Harvard U Pr.

Pro-Slavery Overthrown & the True Principles of Abolitionism Declared. Thomas Lounsbury. 13.00 (ISBN 0-8369-9169-9, 9044). Ayer Co Pubs.

Pro-Slavery Thought in the Old South. William Jenkins. 1959. 11.75 (ISBN 0-8446-1247-2). Peter Smith.

Pro Sports' Greatest Rivalries. Nathan Aaseng. (Sports Talk Ser.). (Illus.). 80p. (gr. 4 up). 1987. PLB 8.95 (ISBN 0-8225-1530-X). Lerner Pubns.

Pro-Style Bodybuilding. Tom Platz & Bill Reynolds. LC 84-23950. (Illus.). 1985. pap. 9.95 (ISBN 0-8069-7910-0). Sterling.

Pro Techniques of Beauty & Glamour Photography. Gary Bernstein. LC 85-60457. 160p. 1985. 14.95 (ISBN 0-89586-364-2). Price Stern.

Pro Techniques of Creative Photography. Ian Bradshaw. LC 85-81329. 192p. pap. 14.95 (ISBN 0-89586-380-4). Price Stern.

Pro Techniques of Landscape Photography. Josef Muench. LC 85-80585. 144p. pap. 14.95 (ISBN 0-89586-418-5). Price Stern.

Pro Techniques of Making Home Video Movies. Thomas I. Ford. LC 85-80600. 160p. 1986. 12.95 (ISBN 0-89586-300-6). Price Stern.

Pro Techniques of People Photography. Gary Bernstein. LC 84-80199. (Illus.). 160p. 1984. pap. 14.95 (ISBN 0-89586-269-7). Price Stern.

Pro Techniques of Photographing Children. Erika Stone. LC 86-80359. 128p. 1986. 9.95 (ISBN 0-89586-390-1). Price Stern.

Pro Techniques of Studio Photography. Jerry Fruchtman. LC 86-81084. (Illus.). 144p. 1986. pap. 14.95 (ISBN 0-89586-384-7). Price Stern.

Pro Vita Monastica: An Essay in Defence of the Contemplative Virtues. Henry D. Sedgwick. 164p. 1986. Repr. of 1923 ed. lib. bdg. 25.00 (ISBN 0-89987-843-1). Darby Bks.

Pro-Wrestling Finishing Holds. Judo G. LeBell. LC 85-61959. (Illus.). 160p. (Orig.). 1985. pap. 10.95 (ISBN 0-9615126-0-1). Pro Action Pub.

Pro 3-4: Winning Football with a Multipurpose Defense. Mike McDaniels. 264p. 1986. 19.95 (ISBN 0-13-711433-8). P-H.

Proact. David K. Kauf. (Illus.). 103p. 1980. 49.50 (ISBN 0-936804-00-9, Pub. by Proact Pubs). Kauf Pubs.

Proactive Approach to Discipline. Kevin J. Swick. 32p. 1985. 4.95 (ISBN 0-8106-1530-4). NEA.

Proactive Manager: The Complete Book of Problem-Solving & Decision-Making. Lorne C. Plunkett & Guy A. Hale. LC 81-11382. 221p. 1982. 25.95x (ISBN 0-471-08509-X, Pub. by Wiley-Interscience). Wiley.

Proactive Manager: The Complete Book of Problem Solving & Decision Making. Lorne C. Plunkett & Guy A. Hale. 221p. 1984. pap. 14.95 (ISBN 0-471-81522-5). Wiley.

Proactive Police Management. Edward A. Thibault et al. LC 84-13364. 1985. text ed. 35.00 (ISBN 0-13-711441-9). P-H.

Proactive Procurement: The Key to Increased Profits, Productivity, & Quality. David N. Burt. (Illus.). 288p. 1984. 40.00 (ISBN 0-13-711465-6). P-H.

Probabalistic Revolution, 2 vols. Ed. by Lorenz Kruger et al. (Illus.). 1987. Set. 60.00x (ISBN 0-262-11125-X). MIT Pr.

Probabilidad E Inferencia Estadistica. rev. ed. (Serie De Matematica: No. 11). (Span.). 1975. pap. 3.50 (ISBN 0-8270-6275-3). OAS.

Probabilistic Algorithms. Andrew Yao. (Progress in Computer Science Ser.: No. 8). 280p. 1988. 35.00 (ISBN 0-8176-3374-X). Birkhauser.

Probabilistic Analysis & Design of Nuclear Power Plant Structures: PVP-PB-030. Ed. by C. Sundararajan. 1978. 18.00 (ISBN 0-685-66810-X, H00135). ASME.

Probabilistic Analysis & Related Topics, Vol. 2. Ed. by A. T. Bharucha-Reid. 1979. 53.50 (ISBN 0-12-095602-0). Acad Pr.

Probabilistic Analysis & Related Topics, Vol. 3. Ed. by A. T. Bharucha-Reid. LC 78-106053. 166p. 1983. 55.50 (ISBN 0-12-095603-9). Acad Pr.

Probabilistic Analysis in Applied Mathematics, 4 vols. Ed. by Albert T. Bharucha-Reid. Vol. 1 1968. 81.50 (ISBN 0-12-095701-9); Vol. 3 1973. 91.50 (ISBN 0-12-095703-5). Acad Pr.

Probabilistic Analysis of Algorithms. M. Hofri. (Texts & Monographs in Computer Science). (Illus.). 255p. 1987. 45.00 (ISBN 0-387-96578-5). Springer Verlag.

Probabilistic Analysis of Redundant Systems. S. K. Srinivasan & R. Subramanian. (Lecture Notes in Economics & Mathematical Systems Ser.: Vol. 175). (Illus.). 356p. 1980. pap. 33.00 (ISBN 3-540-09736-8). Springer-Verlag.

Probabilistic Approach to Mechanisms. B. Z. Sandler. (Studies in Applied Mechanics: Vol. 8). 1984. 94.75 (ISBN 0-444-42306-0, I-098-84). Elsevier.

Probabilistic Basis for Design Criteria in Reinforced Concrete. (Reinforced Concrete Research Council Bulletin Ser.: vol. 22). 134p. 1985. 16.00x (ISBN 0-87262-487-0). Am Soc Civil Eng.

Probabilistic Characterization of Soil Properties: Bridge Between Theory & Practice. Ed. by David S. Bowels & Hon Yim Ko. 189p. 1984. 22.00x (ISBN 0-87262-398-X). Am Soc Civil Eng.

Probabilistic Choice Models & Information, Vol. 24. Ronald W. Hilton. LC 85-72948. (Studies in Accounting Research). 194p. 1985. 15.00 (ISBN 0-86539-083-5). Am Accounting.

Probabilistic Engineering Design. Siddall. (Mechanical Engineering Ser.). 632p. 1983. 79.75 (ISBN 0-8247-7022-6). Dekker.

Probabilistic Fracture Mechanics & Reliability. Ed. by James W. Provan. 1986. lib. bdg. 135.00 (ISBN 90-247-3334-0, Pub. by Martinus Nijhoff Netherlands). Kluwer Academic.

Probabilistic Fracture Mechanics & Fatigue Methods: Applications for Structural Design & Maintenance - STP 798. Ed. by J. M. Bloom & J. C. Ekvall. LC 82-83518. 215p. 1983. text ed. 36.00 (ISBN 0-8031-0242-9, 04-798000-30). ASTM.

Probabilistic Mechanical Design. Edward B. Haugen. LC 80-13428. 650p. 1980. 59.95x (ISBN 0-471-05847-5, Pub. by Wiley Interscience). Krieger.

Probabilistic Mechanics & Structural Reliability: Proceedings of a Conference Sponsored by the Engineering Mechanics, Geotechnical, & Structural Division. Ed. by Y. K. Wen. 458p. 1984. 38.00x (ISBN 0-87262-390-4). Am Soc Civil Eng.

Probabilistic Metaphysics. Patrick Suppes. 250p. 1984. 29.95x (ISBN 0-631-13332-1). Basil Blackwell.

Probabilistic Metaphysics. Patrick Suppes. 264p. 1986. pap. text ed. 15.95x (ISBN 0-631-15049-8). Basil Blackwell.

Probabilistic Methods Applied to Electric Power Systems: Proceedings of the International Symposium on Probabilistic Methods Applied to Electric Power Systems, June 11-13, 1986, Toronto, Ontario. Ed. by S. Krishnasamy. (Illus.). 678p. 1987. 145.00 (ISBN 0-08-031874-6, PBI). Pergamon.

Probabilistic Methods in Civil Engineering. Ed. by P. D. Spanos. (Conference Proceedings Ser.). 528p. 1988. 39.00 (ISBN 0-87262-659-8). Am Soc Civil Eng.

Probabilistic Methods in Differential Equations: Proceedings. Probabilistic Conference, the University of Victoria, August 1974. (Lecture Notes in Mathematics Ser.: Vol. 451). 190p. (Orig.). 1975. pap. 14.00 (ISBN 0-387-07153-9). Springer-Verlag.

Probabilistic Methods in Mathematical Physics. Ed. by Kiyoshi Ito & Nobuyuki Ikeda. 449p. 1989. 59.50 (ISBN 0-12-375660-X). Acad Pr.

Probabilistic Methods in Structural Engineering. G. Augusti & A. Barath. (Illus.). 636p. 1984. 90.00 (ISBN 0-412-22230-2, NO. 6823, Pub. by Chapman & Hall). Routledge Chapman & Hall.

Probabilistic Methods in Structural Engineering. Ed. by M. Shinozuka & James T. Yao. LC 81-69228. 415p. 1981. pap. 30.00x (ISBN 0-87262-286-X). Am Soc Civil Eng.

Probabilistic Methods in the Mechanics of Solids & Structures. Ed. by S. Eggwertz & N. C. Lind. (International Union of Theoretical & Applied Mechanics Ser.). (Illus.). xxiv, 610p. 1985. 58.00 (ISBN 0-387-15087-0). Springer-Verlag.

Probabilistic Methods in the Theory of Numbers. Jonas Kubilius. LC 63-21549. (Translations of Mathematical Monographs: Vol. 11). 182p. 1978. pap. 33.00 (ISBN 0-8218-1561-X, MMONO-11). Am Math.

Probabilistic Methods in the Theory of Structures. Isaac Elishakoff. LC 82-13470. 489p. 1983. 52.95x (ISBN 0-471-87572-4, Pub. by Wiley Interscience). Wiley.

Probabilistic Methods of Signal & System Analysis. George R. Cooper & Clare D. McGillem. LC 73-136170. 1971. text ed. 41.95 (ISBN 0-03-084291-3). HR&W.

Probabilistic Metric Spaces. B. Schweizer & A. Sklar. (Probability & Applied Mathematics Ser.: Vol. 5). 276p. 1982. 61.75 (ISBN 0-444-00666-4, North-Holland). Elsevier.

Probabilistic Models in Engineering Sciences, 2 vols. Harold J. Larson & Bruno O. Shubert. Incl. Vol. 1. Pobabilistic Models in Engineering Sciences: Random Variables & Stochastic Processes. Harold J. Larson & Bruno O. Shubert. LC 79-755. 544p. 1979; Vol. 2. Probabilistic Models in Engineering Sciences: Random Noise Signals & Dynamic Systems. Harold J. Larson & Bruno O. Shubert. 737p. 1979. text ed. 54.90 (ISBN 0-471-05179-9). LC 79-755. 544p. 1979. Wiley.

Probabilistic Models in Engineering Sciences: Random Noise Signals & Dynamic Systems see Probabilistic Models in Engineering Sciences.

Probabilistic Models of Cumulative Damage. John L. Bogdanoff & Frank Kozin. LC 84-11799. 341p. 1985. text ed. 57.50 (ISBN 0-471-88180-5). Wiley.

Probabilistic Number Theory One: Mean-Value Theorems. P. D. Elliot. (Grundlehren der Mathematischen Wissenschaften: Vol. 239). 1979. 59.00 (ISBN 0-387-90437-9). Springer-Verlag.

Probabilistic Number Theory Two: Central Limit Theorems. P. D. Eliott. (Grundlehren der Mathematischen Wissenschaften: Vol. 240). 1980. 56.00 (ISBN 0-387-90438-7). Springer-Verlag.

Probabilistic Performance Models of Language. Raoul N. Smith. 1973. pap. text ed. 9.60x (ISBN 90-2792-414-7). Mouton.

Probabilistic Problems of Discrete Mathematics. (STEKLO Ser.: No. 177). 224p. Date not set. price not set. Am Math.

Probabilistic Programming. S. Vajda. (Probability & Mathematical Statistics Ser.). 1972. 39.50 (ISBN 0-12-710150-0). Acad Pr.

Probabilistic Properties of Deterministic Systems. Andrzej Lasota & Michael C. Mackey. 400p. 1985. 57.50 (ISBN 0-521-30248-X). Cambridge U Pr.

Probabilistic Reliability: An Engineering Approach. rev. ed. Martin L. Shooman. LC 85-14727. 1988. lib. bdg. price not set (ISBN 0-89874-883-6). Krieger.

Probabilistic Revolution, Vol. 1: Ideas in History. Ed. by Lorenz Kruger et al. (Illus.). 456p. 1987. text ed. 32.50x (ISBN 0-262-11118-7). MIT Pr.

Probabilistic Revolution, Vol. 2: Ideas in the Sciences. Ed. by Lorenz Kruger et al. (Illus.). 440p. 1987. text ed. 32.50x (ISBN 0-262-11119-5). MIT Pr.

Probabilistic Risk Assessment in the Nuclear Power Industry: Fundamentals & Applications. Ralph R. Fullwood & Robert E. Hall. (Illus.). 275p. 1988. text ed. 65.00 (ISBN 0-08-036362-8). Pergamon.

Probabilistic System Analysis: An Introduction to Probabilistic Models, Decisions & Applications of Random Processes. Arthur M. Breipohl. LC 77-94920. 352p. 1970. write for info. (ISBN 0-471-10181-8). Wiley.

Probabilistic Theory of Structural Dynamics. Y. K. Lin. LC 75-42154. 380p. 1976. Repr. of 1967 ed. 28.50 (ISBN 0-88275-377-0). Krieger.

Probabilities & Potential. C. Dellacherie & P. A. Meyer. (North Holland Mathematical Studies: No. 29). 190p. 1979. 66.00 (ISBN 0-7204-0701-X, North-Holland). Elsevier.

Probabilities in Everyday Life. John D. McGervey. LC 86-2406. 269p. 1986. 23.95 (ISBN 0-8304-1045-7). Nelson-Hall.

Probabilities of the Quantum World. D. Danin. Tr. by oles Glebov & Vitaly Kisin. 270p. 1983. 6.95 (ISBN 0-8285-2739-3, Pub. by Mir Pubs USSR). Imported Pubns.

Probabilities, Random Variables & Random Processes. 1987. pap. write for info. (ISBN 0-471-61141-7). Wiley.

Probability. Lieberman. (Probability & Mathematical Statistics Ser.). 1988. price not set (ISBN 0-471-87875-8). Wiley.

Probability. Seymour Lipschutz. (Schaum's Outline Ser). 1968. pap. text ed. 7.95 (ISBN 0-07-037982-3). McGraw.

Probability. (Tops Cards Ser.: No. 8). 1978. pap. 10.50 (ISBN 0-941008-08-8). Tops Learning.

Probability. Rubinstein. (Probability & Mathematical Statistics Ser.). 1988. price not set (ISBN 0-471-81928-X). Wiley.

Probability: A Noncalculus Introduction. John T. Baskin. 224p. 1986. pap. 9.95 (ISBN 0-8226-0397-7, Helix Bks). Rowman.

Probability: An Introduction. Samuel Goldberg. xiv, 322p. 1987. pap. text ed. 7.95 (ISBN 0-486-65252-1). Dover.

Probability: An Introduction. G. Grimmett. 1986. 19.95 (ISBN 0-317-58316-6). Oxford U Pr.

Probability: An Introduction. Geoffrey Grimmett. (Illus.). 210p. 1986. 39.95 (ISBN 0-19-853272-5); pap. 19.95 (ISBN 0-19-853264-4). Oxford U Pr.

Probability & Analysis. Ed. by G. Letta & M. Pratelli. (Lectures Notes in Mathematics Ser.: Vol. 1206). viii, 283p. 1986. pap. 23.40 (ISBN 0-387-16787-0). Springer-Verlag.

Probability & Banach Spaces. Ed. by J. Bastero & M. San Miguel. (Lecture Notes in Mathematics Ser.: Vol. 1221). ix, 222p. 1986. pap. 19.40 (ISBN 0-387-17186-X). Springer-Verlag.

Probability & Bayesian Statistics. Ed. by R. Viertl. LC 87-15298. (Illus.). 522p. 1987. 89.50x (ISBN 0-306-42570-X, Plenum Pr). Plenum Pub.

Probability & Causality. Ed. by James H. Fetzer. 1988. lib. bdg. 79.00 (ISBN 90-277-2607-8, Pub. by Reidel Holland); pap. 27.50 (ISBN 1-55608-052-2, Pub. by Reidel Holland). Kluwer Academic.

Probability & Chi Square. 2nd ed. Thomas R. Mertens & Sandra F. Cooper. LC 77-79901. (Programed Biology Ser.). 1974. pap. text ed. 6.95 (ISBN 0-88462-024-7, 3304-21, Ed Methods). Longman Finan.

Probability & Errors: For the Physical Sciences. S. K. Muthu. 568p. 1982. text ed. 35.00x (ISBN 0-86131-137-X, Pub. by Orient Longman Ltd India). Apt Bks.

Probability & Evidence. Paul Horwich. LC 81-18144. (Cambridge Studies in Philosophy). 160p. 1982. 34.50 (ISBN 0-521-23758-0). Cambridge U Pr.

Probability & Information. A. M. Yaglom & I. M. Yaglom. 1983. lib. bdg. 69.00 (ISBN 0-318-00432-1, Pub. by Reidel Holland). Kluwer Academic.

Probability & Information Theory: With Applications to Radar. Philip M. Woodward. LC 80-70175. (Illus.). 138p. pap. 35.90 (2030133). Bks Demand UMI.

Probability & Information Theory 2. Ed. by M. Behara et al. LC 75-406171. (Lecture Notes in Mathematics: Vol. 296). v, 223p. 1973. pap. 19.00 (ISBN 0-387-06211-4). Springer-Verlag.

Probability & Its Applications. Port. (Probability & Mathematical Statistics Ser.). 1988. price not set (ISBN 0-471-63216-3). Wiley.

Probability & Literary Form: Philosophic Theory & Literary Practice in the Augustan Age. Douglas L. Patey. LC 83-7819. 464p. 1984. 49.50 (ISBN 0-521-25456-6). Cambridge U Pr.

Probability & Mathematical Statistics: An Introduction. Eugene Lukacs. 1972. 35.00 (ISBN 0-12-459850-1). Acad Pr.

Probability & Measure. Patrick Billingsley. LC 78-25632. (Probability & Mathematical Statistics Ser.). 515p. 1979. 41.95x (ISBN 0-471-03173-9, Pub. by Wiley-Interscience). Wiley.

Probability & Measure. 2nd ed. Patrick Billingsley. LC 85-6526. (Probability & Mathematical Statistics Ser.). 622p. 1986. 46.95 (ISBN 0-471-80478-9). Wiley.

Probability & Physical Problems. D. I. Blohincev et al. (Translations Ser.: No. 1, Vol. 11). 1968. Repr. of 1962 ed. 27.00 (ISBN 0-8218-1611-X, TRANS 1-11). Am Math.

Probability & Random Processes. Geoffrey Grimmett & David Stirzaker. (Illus.). 1982. pap. 24.95x (ISBN 0-19-853185-0). Oxford U Pr.

Probability & Random Processes: A First Course with Applications. 2nd ed. A. Bruce Clarke & Ralph L. Disney. LC 84-15312. (Probability & Mathematical Statistics Ser.). 324p. 1985. write for info. (ISBN 0-471-08535-9). Wiley.

Probability & Random Processes: An Introduction for Applied Scientists & Engineers. W. B. Davenport. 1970. text ed. 56.95 (ISBN 0-07-015440-6). McGraw.

Probability & Random Processes for Electrical Engineering. Alberto Leon-Garcia. (Electrical & Computer Engineering Ser.). (Illus.). 488p. 1988. text ed. price not set (ISBN 0-201-12906-X). Addison-Wesley.

Probability & Random Variables. G. P. Beaumont. LC 86-4728. (Mathematics & Its Applications Ser.). 345p. 1987. pap. 34.95 (ISBN 0-470-20907-0). Halsted Pr.

Probability & Related Topics in Physical Sciences. Mark Kac. LC 59-10443. (Lectures in Applied Mathematics Ser.: Vol. 1A). 266p. 1984. pap. 35.00 (ISBN 0-8218-0047-7, LAM-1.1). Am Math.

Probability & Statistical Decision Theory. Ed. by F. Konecny et al. 1985. lib. bdg. 56.00 (ISBN 90-277-2089-4, Pub. by Reidel Holland). Kluwer Academic.

Probability & Statistical Inference. Ed. by W. Grossman & G. Pflug. 1982. lib. bdg. 49.50 (ISBN 90-277-1427-4, Pub. by Reidel Holland). Kluwer Academic.

Probability & Statistical Inference. 3rd ed. Robert V. Hogg & Elliot A. Tanis. 1988. text ed. write for info. (ISBN 0-02-355810-5). Macmillan.

Probability & Statistical Inference. R. G. Krutchkoff. 306p. 1970. 82.00 (ISBN 0-677-02530-0). Gordon & Breach.

Probability & Statistical Inference in Ancient & Medieval Jewish Literature. Nachum L. Rabinovitch. LC 79-187394. pap. 54.80 (ISBN 0-317-08544-1, 2014349). Bks Demand UMI.

Probability & Statistical Inference, Vol. 1: Probability. 2nd ed. J. G. Kalbfleisch. (Texts in Statistics Ser.). (Illus.). xiii, 343p. 1985. Repr. of 1979 ed. 33.00 (ISBN 0-387-96144-5). Springer-Verlag.

Probability & Statistical Inference, Vol. 2: Statistical Inference. 2nd ed. J. G. Kalbfleisch. (Texts in Statistics Ser.). (Illus.). xiii, 360p. 1985. Repr. of 1979 ed. 33.00 (ISBN 0-387-96183-6). Springer-Verlag.

Probability & Statistics. 2nd ed. Carnegie-Mellon University Staff & Morris H. DeGroot. LC 84-6269. 678p. 1985. text ed. 41.95 (ISBN 0-201-11366-X); pap. write for info. instr's. manual. Addison-Wesley.

Probability & Statistics. Morris Degroot. LC 74-19691. (Behavioral Science Quantitative Methods Ser). (Illus.). 624p. 1975. text ed. write for info. (ISBN 0-201-01503-X); sol. manual o.p. 7.95 (ISBN 0-201-01509-9). Addison-Wesley.

Probability & Statistics. Murray R. Spiegel. 304p. (Orig.). 1975. pap. text ed. 10.95 (ISBN 0-07-060220-4). McGraw.

Probability & Statistics Cumulative Index, 1940-1984: Sections 60 & 62, 2 vols. (STAPIN Ser.: No. 40-84). 1000p. 1986. pap. 115.00 (ISBN 0-8218-0108-2). Am Math.

Probability & Statistics Exam File. Ed. by Thomas L. Ward. LC 84-24707. (Exam File Ser.). 346p. (Orig.). 1985. pap. 9.95 (ISBN 0-910554-45-5). Engineering.

Probability & Statistics for Decision-Making. Ya-Lun Chou. 1982. Repr. of 1972 ed. text ed. cancelled (ISBN 0-8290-0599-4). Irvington.

Probability & Statistics for Engineers & Scientists. 3rd ed. Ronald E. Walpole & Raymond H. Myers. 650p. 1985. text ed. write for info. (ISBN 0-02-424170-9). Macmillan.

Probability & Statistics for Engineers & Scientists. 4th ed. Ronald E. Walpole & Raymond H. Myers. 838p. 1989. write for info. (ISBN 0-02-424210-1). Macmillan.

Probability & Statistics for Engineering & the Sciences. 2nd ed. Jay L. Devore. LC 86-20731. (Statistics Ser.). 675p. 1986. text ed. 32.50 pub. net (ISBN 0-534-06828-6). Brooks-Cole.

Probability & Statistics for Engineers. R. E. Little. (Illus.). 552p. 1978. 32.95 (ISBN 0-916460-04-5, Matrix Pubs Inc). Weber Systems.

Probability & Statistics for Engineers. 3rd ed. Irwin Miller & John E. Freund. (Illus.). 544p. 1985. text ed. write for info. (ISBN 0-13-711938-0). P-H.

Probability & Statistics I. D. Dacunha-Castelle & M. Duflo. Tr. by D. McHale from Fr. (Illus.). vi, 362p. 1986. 36.00 (ISBN 0-387-96067-8). Springer-Verlag.

Probability & Statistics II. D. Dacunha-Castelle & M. Duflo. Tr. by D. McHale from Fr. (Illus.). 400p. 1986. 32.50 (ISBN 0-387-96213-1). Springer-Verlag.

Probability & Statistics in Civil Engineering. Geoffrey N. Smith. (Illus.). 256p. 1986. 42.50 (ISBN 0-89397-251-7). Nichols Pub.

Probability & Statistics in Engineering & Management Science. 2nd ed. William W. Hines & Douglas C. Montgomery. LC 79-26257. 634p. 1980. text ed. write for info. (ISBN 0-471-04759-7). Wiley.

Probability & Statistics in Geodesy & Geophysics. L. Kubachkova. 1987. 139.50 (ISBN 0-444-98945-5). Elsevier.

Probability & Statistics in Hydrology. Vujica Yevjevich. LC 74-168494. 1972. 25.00 (ISBN 0-918334-00-4). WRP.

Probability & Statistics in Psychological Research & Theory. Donald W. Stilson. LC 66-11141. (Holden-Day Series in Psychology). 1966. pap. 129.80 (ISBN 0-317-08078-4, 2016295). Bks Demand UMI.

Probability & Statistics in the Engineering & Computing Sciences. J. Susan Milton & J. C. Arnold. 672p. 1985. text ed. 43.95 (ISBN 0-07-042351-2). McGraw.

Probability & Statistics with Reliability, Queuing & Computer Science Applications. Kishar S. Trivedi. (Illus.). 672p. 1982. text ed. 48.00 (ISBN 0-13-711564-4). P-H.

Probability & Stochastic Processes. Frederick Solomon. (Illus.). 400p. 1987. text ed. write for info. (ISBN 0-13-711961-5). P-H.

Probability & Stochastic Processes for Engineers. Carl W. Helstrom. (Illus.). 368p. 1984. text ed. write for info. (ISBN 0-02-353560-1). Macmillan.

Probability & Stochastic Processes: With a View Toward Applications. 2nd ed. Leo Breiman. 324p. 1986. Repr. of 1969 ed. text ed. 40.00 (ISBN 0-89426-076-6). Scientific Pr.

Probability & the Logic of Rational Belief. Henry Ely Kyburg. LC 61-11615. pap. 89.00 (ISBN 0-317-08261-2, 2005437). Bks Demand UMI.

Probability Based on Radon Measures. Tue Tjur. LC 80-40503. (Wiley Series in Probability & Mathematical Statistics). pap. 63.50 (2030751). Bks Demand UMI.

Probability Broach. L. Neil Smith. pap. 1.95 (ISBN 0-345-28593-X, Del Rey). Ballantine.

Probability Concepts in Engineering, Planning & Design, Vol. I. 2nd ed. Ang. 1988. write for info. (ISBN 0-471-82181-0). Wiley.

Probability Concepts in Engineering Planning & Design, Vol. I. Alfredo H. Ang & Wilson H. Tang. LC 75-5892. 409p. 1975. text ed. write for info. (ISBN 0-471-03200-X). Wiley.

Probability Concepts in Engineering Planning & Design, Vol. II. Alfredo H. Ang & Wilson H. Tang. LC 75-5892. 562p. 1984. text ed. write for info. (ISBN 0-471-03201-8). Wiley.

Probability Distributions. V. Rothschild & N. Logothetis. LC 85-20308. 80p. 1986. pap. 7.95 (ISBN 0-471-83814-4). Wiley.

Probability Distributions in Quantum Statistical Mechanics. M. A. Kon. (Lecture Notes in Mathematics Ser.: Vol. 1148). v, 120p. 1985. pap. 11.00 (ISBN 0-387-15690-9). Springer-Verlag.

Probability Distributions on Banach Spaces. N. N. Vakhania et al. 1987. lib. bdg. 99.00 (ISBN 90-277-2496-2, Pub. by Reidel Holland). Kluwer Academic.

Probation & Parole: Legal & Social Dimensions. Louis P. Carney. (Illus.). 1976. text ed. 43.95 (ISBN 0-07-010126-4). McGraw.

Probation & Parole: Theory & Practice. 3rd ed. Howard Abadinsky. (Illus.). 464p. 1987. text ed. write for info. (ISBN 0-13-715996-X). P-H.

Probation & the Community: A Practice & Policy Reader. Ed. by John Harding. 240p. 1987. text ed. 39.95 (ISBN 0-422-79590-9, 1134, Pub. by Tavistock England). Routledge Chapman & Hall.

Probation As an Alternative to Custody: A Case Study. Peter Raynor. 214p. 1988. text ed. 44.40 (ISBN 0-566-05588-0, Pub. by Gower Pub England). Gower Pub Co.

Probation Assistant. Jack Rudman. (Career Examination Ser.: C-2577). (Cloth bdg. avail. on request). pap. 14.00 (ISBN 0-8373-2577-3). Natl Learning.

Probation Casework: The Convergence of Theory with Practice. Joan Luxenburg. (Illus.). 174p. (Orig.). 1983. lib. bdg. 26.25 (ISBN 0-8191-3270-5); pap. text ed. 12.00 (ISBN 0-8191-3271-3). U Pr of Amer.

Probation Consultant. Jack Rudman. (Career Examination Ser.: C-980). (Cloth bdg. avail. on request). pap. 16.00 (ISBN 0-8373-0980-8). Natl Learning.

Probation Counselor. Jack Rudman. (Career Examination Ser.: C-1981). (Cloth bdg. avail. on request). pap. 16.00 (ISBN 0-8373-1981-1). Natl Learning.

Probation Director. Jack Rudman. (Career Examination Ser.: C-2266). (Cloth bdg. avail. on request). 1988. pap. 18.00 (ISBN 0-8373-2266-9). Natl Learning.

Probation Employment Officer. Jack Rudman. (Career Examination Ser.: C-1428). (Cloth bdg. avail. on request). pap. 16.00 (ISBN 0-8373-1428-3). Natl Learning.

Probation Investigator. Jack Rudman. (Career Examination Ser.: C-981). (Cloth bdg. avail. on request). pap. 14.00 (ISBN 0-8373-0981-6). Natl Learning.

Probation Officer. Jack Rudman. (Career Examination Ser.: C-619). (Cloth bdg. avail. on request). pap. 12.00 (ISBN 0-8373-0619-1). Natl Learning.

Probation Officer & Parole Officer. 4th ed. Ed. by Hy Hammer. LC 82-18416. 192p. (Orig.). 1984. pap. 8.00 (ISBN 0-668-05619-3). Arco.

Probation Officer Trainee. Jack Rudman. (Career Examination Ser.: C-1429). (Cloth bdg. avail. on request). pap. 12.00 (ISBN 0-8373-1429-1). Natl Learning.

Probation, Parole & Community Corrections: A Reader. Ed. by Lawrence F. Travis. 199p. (Orig.). 1985. pap. text ed. 10.95 (ISBN 0-88133-097-3). Waveland Pr.

Probation, Parole & Community Corrections. 3rd ed. Ed. by Robert Carter. LC 83-23283. 432p. 1984. 29.95 (ISBN 0-471-87461-2). Wiley.

Probation Practice. Nigel Fielding. LC 84-1543. 174p. 1984. text ed. 42.95x (ISBN 0-566-00730-4). Gower Pub Co.

Probation Supervisor. Jack Rudman. (Career Examination Ser.: C-2262). (Cloth bdg. avail. on request). 1988. pap. 14.00 (ISBN 0-8373-2262-6). Natl Learning.

Probation Supervisor I. Jack Rudman. (Career Examination Ser.: C-1828). (Cloth bdg. avail. on request). pap. 14.00 (ISBN 0-8373-1828-9). Natl Learning.

Probation Supervisor II. Jack Rudman. (Career Examination Ser.: C-1829). (Cloth bdg. avail. on request). pap. 14.00 (ISBN 0-8373-1829-7). Natl Learning.

Probation Training Director. (Career Examination Ser.: C-3283). Date not set. pap. 18.00 (ISBN 0-8373-3283-4). Natl Learning.

Probe. Carole N. Douglas. 320p. (Orig.). 1985. pap. 6.95 (ISBN 0-8125-3585-5, Dist. by Warner Pub Services & St. Martin's Press). Tor Bks.

Probe. Carole N. Douglas. 384p. 1986. pap. 3.50 (ISBN 0-8125-3587-1, Dist. by Warner Publisher Services & St. Martin's Press). Tor Bks.

Probe: A Handbook of Classroom Ideas to Motivate the Teaching of Primary Science. (Spice Ser). 1976. 8.95 (ISBN 0-89273-102-8). Educ Serv.

Probe: College Developmental Reading. 3rd ed. Marvin Glock et al. (Communication Skills Ser.: No. 174). 384p. 1984. pap. text ed. 19.95 (ISBN 0-675-20146-2). Merrill.

Probe: College Developmental Reading. 2nd ed. Marvin D. Glock & David S. Bender. 1980. text ed. 14.95 (ISBN 0-675-08144-0). Additional supplements may be obtained from publisher. Merrill.

Probe Duplicating Masters: Primary Science, 2 vols. (Spice Ser.). 1977. 8.95 ea. Vol. 1, Grades K-2 (ISBN 0-89273-546-5). Vol. 2, Grades 2-4 (ISBN 0-89273-547-3). Educ Serv.

Probe into the History of Ashura. Ibrahim Ayati. 234p. 1985. pap. 9.00 (ISBN 0-941724-41-7). Islamic Seminary.

Probe Probe. Jane D. Mook. (Illus., Orig.). (gr. 3-10). 1970. pap. 1.75 (ISBN 0-377-62051-3). Friendship Pr.

Probe Two: A Short Course in College Reading. Marvin D. Glock & David Bender. 1978. pap. text ed. 16.95x (ISBN 0-675-08373-7); 1 set o.p. 80.00 (ISBN 0-675-08372-9). Merrill.

Proben Deutscher Prosa. Robert Kauf & Daniel C. McCluney. 1970. text ed. 6.95x. (ISBN 0-393-09911-3, NortonC); free tchrs. ed. (ISBN 0-393-09985-7); tapes 85.00 (ISBN 0-393-99117-2). Norton.

PROBES: A Prospectus on Processes & Resources of the Bering Sea Shelf Nineteen Seventy-Five to Nineteen Eighty-Five. write for info. (ISBN 0-914500-05-8). U of AK Inst Marine.

Probetes et Prophetes. Antonin Artaud & Louis de Gonzague-Frick. 1976. 9.95 (ISBN 0-686-53836-6). French & Eur.

Probing America's Past: A Critical Examination of Major Myths & Misconceptions, 2 vols. Thoms A. Bailey. 1973. pap. text ed. 13.00 ea.; Vol. 1. (ISBN 0-669-84350-4); Vol. 2. (ISBN 0-669-84368-7). Heath.

Probing Lance. L. Martin. (Illus.). 64p. pap. 9.95 (ISBN 0-317-65041-6). Pleasure Trove.

Probing Our Problems. R. O. Covey. 176p. (Orig.). 1986. pap. 5.95 (ISBN 0-934942-59-5, 3950). White Wing Pub.

Probing the Earth: Contemporary Land Projects. John Beardsley. LC 77-12419. (Illus.). 112p. 1978. 24.95 (ISBN 0-87474-232-3, BEPE). Smithsonian.

Probit Analysis. 3rd ed. D. J. Finney. LC 78-134618. (Illus.). 1971. 80.00 (ISBN 0-521-08041-X). Cambridge U Pr.

Probity Chorus. Richard Lemon. LC 85-18880. 1986. 15.95 (ISBN 0-393-02265-X). Norton.

Problem & Failed Institutions in the Commercial Banking Industry. Joseph F. Sinkey, Jr. Ed. by Edward I. Altman & Ingo Walter. LC 76-5760. (Contemporary Studies in Economic & Financial Analysis: Vol. 4). 1979. lib. bdg. 52.50 (ISBN 0-89232-005-2). Jai Pr.

Problem-Based Learning: An Approach to Medical Education. Howard S. Barrows & Robin M. Tamblyn. (Medical Education Ser.: Vol. 1). 224p. 1980. text ed. 23.95 (ISBN 0-8261-2840-8). Springer Pub.

Problem Behavior & Psychological Development. R. Jessor. 1977. 34.00 (ISBN 0-12-384750-8). Acad Pr.

Problem Behavior in People with Severe Learning Disabilities: A Practical Guide to a Constructional Approach. Ewa Zarkowska & John Clements. 180p. 1988. pap. text ed. 20.00 (ISBN 0-7099-3014-3). P H Brookes.

Problem Behavior Management: Educator's Resource Service. Robert Algozzine. LC 82-1663. 350p. 1982. text ed. 105.00 looseleaf updated semi-annually (ISBN 0-89443-678-3). Aspen Pub.

Problem Behaviour in the Secondary School: A Systems Approach. Ed. by Bill Gillham. 195p. 1981. 26.00 (ISBN 0-7099-0129-1, Pub. by Croom Helm Ltd); pap. 9.75 (ISBN 0-7099-1102-5). Routledge Chapman & Hall.

Problem Book for First Year Calculus. G. W. Bluman. (Problem Books in Mathematics Ser.). (Illus.). 350p. 1984. 47.50 (ISBN 0-387-90920-6). Springer-Verlag.

Problem Book in Mathematical Analysis. G. N. Berman. 483p. 1988. 13.95 (ISBN 0-8285-1958-7, Pub. by Mir Pubs USSR). Imported Pubns.

Problem Book in Phonology: A Workbook for Introductory Courses in Linguistics & in Modern Phonology. Morris Halle & George N. Clements. 96p. (Orig.). 1982. pap. text ed. 9.95x (ISBN 0-262-58059-4). MIT Pr.

Problem Book in Relativity & Gravitation. Alan P. Lightman et al. 500p. 1975. 57.00x (ISBN 0-691-08160-3); pap. 19.95 (ISBN 0-691-08162-X). Princeton U Pr.

Problem Book in the Theory of Functions, 2 vols. Konrad Knopp. Incl. Vol. 1. Problems in the Elementary Theory of Functions. Tr. by Lipman Bers. pap. 4.50 (ISBN 0-486-60158-7); Vol. 2. Problems in the Advanced Theory of Functions. pap. 3.95 (ISBN 0-486-60159-5). 1968. pap. Dover.

Problem Bosses: Who They Are & How to Deal with Them. Marcey Grothe & Peter Wylie. 384p. 1987. pap. 4.95 (ISBN 0-449-21486-9, Crest). Fawcett.

Problem Bosses: Who They Are & How to Deal With Them. Mardy Grothe & Peter Wylie. 320p. 1987. 19.95 (ISBN 0-8160-1264-4). Facts on File.

Problem Called Chavie. Eva Vogiel. (Illus.). 152p. (gr. 4-7). 1985. 9.95 (ISBN 0-87306-386-4); pap. 6.95 (ISBN 0-87306-389-9). Feldheim.

Problem Child in School. Mary B. Sayles. LC 72-2576. (Select Bibliographies Reprint Series). 1972. Repr. of 1925 ed. 18.00 (ISBN 0-8369-6863-8). Ayer Co Pubs.

Problem Complexity & Method Efficiency in Optimization. A. S. Nemirovsky & D. B. Yudin. LC 82-11065. 388p. 1983. 84.95 (ISBN 0-471-10345-4). Wiley.

Problem de L'acte de Foi: Donnees Traditionnelles et Resultants des Controverses Recentes. Roger Aubert. 1978. Repr. of 1958 ed. lib. bdg. 85.00 (ISBN 0-8492-0092-X). R West.

Problem Definition in Policy Analysis. David Dery. LC 84-8662. (Studies in Government & Public Policy). xiv, 146p. 1984. 19.95x (ISBN 0-7006-0261-5). U Pr of KS.

Problem der Parusieverzoegerung in den Synoptischen Evangelien und in der Apostelgeschichte. 3rd ed. Erich Graesser. (Beihefte zur Zeitschrift fuer die Alttestamentliche Wissenschaft 22). 1977. 36.40x (ISBN 3-11-007512-1). De Gruyter.

Problem Des Ich in der Phan. Husserls. Marbach. (Phaenomenologica Ser.). 1974. lib. bdg. 47.50 (ISBN 90-247-1587-3, Pub. by Martinus Nijhoff Netherlands). Kluwer Academic.

Problem Des Todes in der Deutschen Lyrik Des 17 Jahrhunderts. Friedrich W. Wentzlaff-Eggebert. (Ger). pap. 22.00. Johnson Repr.

Problem Drinkers: A National Survey. Don Cahalan. LC 73-133617. (Jossey-Bass Behavioral Science Ser.). (Illus.). pap. 55.00 (ISBN 0-317-42371-1, 2052163). Bks Demand UMI.

Problem Drinkers Seeking Treatment. Eileen M. Corrigan. LC 73-620006. (Rutgers Center of Alcohol Studies: Monograph No. 8). 1974. 5.00 (ISBN 0-911290-39-7). Rutgers Ctr Alcohol.

Problem Drinking among American Men. Don Cahalan & Robin Room. 1974. 18.95x (ISBN 0-8084-0380-X). New Coll U Pr.

Problem Drinking Among American Men. Don Cahalan & Robin Room. LC 72-619570. (Rutgers Center of Alcohol Studies: Monograph No. 7). 1974. 8.25 (ISBN 0-911290-38-9). Rutgers Ctr Alcohol.

Problem Drinking: Experiments in Detoxification. 177p. 1985. pap. 11.95x (ISBN 0-7199-1115-X, Pub. by Bedford England). Brookfield Pub Co.

Problem Employees: How to Improve Their Performance. Peter Wylie & Mardy Grothe. LC 81-82032. 1981. pap. 17.95 (ISBN 0-8224-9373-X). D S Lake Pubs.

Problem Exercises for General Chemistry. 3rd ed. G. Gilbert Long & Forrest C. Hentz. LC 86-13347. 464p. 1986. pap. 12.95 (ISBN 0-471-82840-8). Wiley.

Problem Exercises for General Chemistry. 2nd ed. Gilbert G. Long & Forrest C. Hentz. LC 81-19686. 351p. 1982. pap. text ed. 16.50 (ISBN 0-471-08251-1). Wiley.

Problem Finding & Problem Solving. Alfred W. Schoennauer. LC 81-9591. 208p. 1981. text ed. 20.95x (ISBN 0-88229-590-X); pap. text ed. 10.95x (ISBN 0-88229-792-9). Nelson-Hall.

Problem-Finding Approach to Effective Corporate Planning. Robert J. Thierauf. LC 87-5971. 232p. 1987. lib. bdg. 37.95 (ISBN 0-89930-262-9, TPF/, Quorum Bks). Greenwood.

Problem-Finding in Educational Administration: Trends in Research & Theory. Ed. by Glenn L. Immegart & William L. Boyd. LC 78-19912. 320p. 1979. 29.00x (ISBN 0-669-02438-4). Lexington Bks.

Problem for Mother Christmas. Ted Willis. (Illus.). 160p. (gr. 3-5). 13.95 (ISBN 0-575-03884-5, Pub. by Gollancz England). David & Charles.

Problem Horse. R. S. Summerhays. (Illus.). pap. write for info. (ISBN 0-85131-225-X, NL51, Pub. by J A Allen U K). S R Smith Sporting Bks.

Problem Horses - Tested Guide for Curing Most Common & Serious Horse Behavior Habits. Reginald S. Summerhays. pap. 4.00 (ISBN 0-87980-200-6). Wilshire.

Problem Housing Estate: An Account of Omega & Its People. Frances Reynolds. 200p. 1985. text ed. 38.95 (ISBN 0-566-05008-0). Gower Pub Co.

Problem in Greek Ethics. John A. Symonds. LC 71-163126. (Studies in Philosophy, No. 40). 1971. lib. bdg. 31.95x (ISBN 0-8383-1253-5). Haskell.

Problem in Modern Ethics. John A. Symonds. LC 73-173185. Repr. of 1896 ed. 10.75 (ISBN 0-405-09019-6, Pub. by Blom). Ayer Co Pubs.

Problem Is God: The Selection & Care of Your Personal God. C. Alan Anderson. LC 84-50108. (Illus.). 304p. (Orig.). 1985. pap. 9.95 (ISBN 0-913299-02-2, Dist by NAL). Stillpoint.

Problem Isn't Age: Work & Older Americans. Ed. by Steven H. Sandell. LC 86-30642. 278p. 1987. lib. bdg. 35.95 (ISBN 0-275-92371-1, C2371). Praeger.

Problem Knee: Diagnosis & Management in the Younger Patient. M. F. Macnicol. (Illus.). 220p. 1986. 38.00 (ISBN 0-87189-306-1). Aspen Pub.

Problem Loan Strategies. John E. McKinley, III et al. LC 84-27222. (Illus.). 168p. (Orig.). 1985. pap. text ed. 31.00 (ISBN 0-936742-20-8). Robt Morris Assocs.

Problem Loans: A Special Collection from the Journal of Commercial Bank Lending. Ed. by Charlotte Weisman. LC 85-25874. (Illus.). 100p. 1985. pap. 28.00 (ISBN 0-936742-27-5). Robt Morris Assocs.

Problem Loans & Creditor Options in State: An In-Depth Guide to the Legal & Practical Aspects of Foreclosure, Repossession, Commercial Loan Workouts, & other Creditor Remedies. National Business Institute Staff. LC 85-212902. (Illus.). cancelled. Natl Busn Inst.

Problem Loans in State: Bankruptcy & Foreclosure Practice for the Secured Lender & Its Counsel. National Business Institute Staff. LC 85-241593. (Illus.). 1987. 30.00. Natl Busn Inst.

Problem of Abortion. 2nd ed. Ed. by Joel Feinberg. 201p. 1984. pap. text ed. write for info. (ISBN 0-534-02890-X). Wadsworth Pub.

Problem of Age, Growth, & Death. Charles S. Minot. Ed. by Robert Kastenbaum. LC 78-22211. (Aging & Old Age Ser.). (Illus.). 1979. Repr. of 1908 ed. lib. bdg. 23.00x (ISBN 0-405-11824-4). Ayer Co Pubs.

Problem of Alcoholism: Past, Present & Future. Maurice B. Gordon. 1968. pap. 4.95 (ISBN 0-911566-01-5). Ventnor.

Problem of Altruism: Freudian & Darwinian Solutions. Christopher R. Badcock. 234p. 1986. 24.95 (ISBN 0-631-13814-5). Basil Blackwell.

Problem of Americanization in the Catholic Schools of Puerto Rico. Charles J. Beirne. 144p. (Orig.). 1976. pap. 5.00 (ISBN 0-8477-2725-4). U of PR Pr.

Problem of Arnold Bennett. Geoffrey West. LC 74-31098. 1932. lib. bdg. 17.00 (ISBN 0-8414-9583-1). Folcroft.

Problem of Asia. Alfred T. Mahan. LC 70-115204. 1971. Repr. of 1900 ed. 22.50x (ISBN 0-8046-1097-5, Pub. by Kennikat). Assoc Faculty Pr.

Problem of Assistance to the Indigent Accused. Monrad G. Paulsen. 103p. 1961. pap. 2.00 (ISBN 0-317-30872-6, B169). Am Law Inst.

Problem of Authority in America. Ed. by John P. Diggins & Mark E. Kann. 255p. 1981. 34.95 (ISBN 0-87722-220-7). Temple U Pr.

Problem of Authority in the Early Development of the Individual. Kenneth Lambert. 1985. 10.00x (ISBN 0-317-62257-9, Guild of Pastoral Psych). State Mutual Bk.

Problem of Change: A Study of North-East India. B. P. Singh. 236p. 1988. 15.95 (ISBN 0-19-562052-6). Oxford U Pr.

Problem of Chemical & Biological Warfare: A Study of the Historical, Technical, Military, Legal & Political Aspects of CBW, & Possible Disarmament Measures, Vol. 6, Technical Aspects of Early Warning & Verification 1975. Stockholm International Peace Research Institute. 1975. text ed. 24.00x (ISBN 0-391-00205-8). Humanities.

Problem of Christianity. Josiah Royce. LC 68-16716. 1968. 25.00x (ISBN 0-226-73058-1). U of Chicago Pr.

Problem of Contact with the Animus. Barbara Hannah. 1985. 10.00x (ISBN 0-317-62261-7, Guild of Pastoral Psych). State Mutual Bk.

Problem of Dark Cutting in Beef: Current Topics in Veterinary Medicine & Animal Science, No. 10. Ed. by D. E. Hood & P. V. Tarrant. xii, 504p. 1981. 43.00 (ISBN 90-247-2522-4, Pub. by Martinus Nijhoff Netherlands). Kluwer Academic.

Problem of Democracy in Latin America. Martin C. Needler. (Illus.). 192p. 1987. 28.00x (ISBN 0-669-15333-8). Lexington Bks.

Problem of Discovery in Criminal Cases. Monrad G. Paulsen. 61p. 1961. pap. 1.00 (ISBN 0-317-30874-2, B170). Am Law Inst.

Problem of Education. M. K. Gandhi. Ed. by J. D. Desai. 327p. (Orig.). 1983. pap. 7.00 (ISBN 0-934676-62-3). Greenlf Bks.

Problem of 'Edwin Drood' W. Robertson Nicoll. LC 72-1330. (Studies in Dickens, No. 52). 1972. Repr. of 1912 ed. lib. bdg. 39.95x (ISBN 0-8383-1442-2). Haskell.

Problem of Embodiment. Zaner. (Phaenomenologica Ser.: No. 17). 1964. lib. bdg. 24.00 (ISBN 90-247-5093-8, Pub. by Martinus Nijhoff Netherlands). Kluwer Academic.

Problem of Error from Plato to Kant. Leo W. Keeler. 1977. lib. bdg. 59.95 (ISBN 0-8490-2482-X). Gordon Pr.

Problem of Eschatology. Ed. by Edward Schillebeeckx & Boniface Willems. LC 79-76195. (Concilium Ser.: Vol. 41). 175p. 1969. 7.95 (ISBN 0-8091-0117-3). Paulist Pr.

Problem of Essence & Form in Christianity. Philip Metman. 1985. 10.00x (ISBN 0-317-62268-4, Guild of Pastoral Psych). State Mutual Bk.

Problem of Etiological Narrative in the Old Testament. Burke O. Long. (Beiheft 108 zur Zeitschrift fuer die alttestamentliche Wissenschaft). 1968. 15.50x (ISBN 3-11-005590-2). De Gruyter.

Problem of Evil. Cornelius Hagerty. LC 77-3022. 1978. 9.95 (ISBN 0-8158-0352-4). Chris Mass.

Problem of Evil. Errol E. Harris & D. Litt. LC 77-72325. (Aquinas Lecture Ser.). 1977. 7.95 (ISBN 0-87462-142-9). Marquette.

Problem of Evil & the Judgments of God. A. E. Knoch. 351p. 1976. pap. text ed. 5.00 (ISBN 0-910424-59-4). Concordant.

Problem of Freedom. George H. Palmer. LC 75-173487. Repr. of 1911 ed. 18.50 (ISBN 0-404-04868-4). AMS Pr.

Problem of Freedom & Determinism. Edward D'Angelo. LC 68-63295. 1968. 13.00x (ISBN 0-8262-7713-6). U of Mo Pr.

Problem of Freedom in Marxist Thought: An Analysis of the Treatment of Human Freedom by Marx, Engels, Lenin & Contemporary Soviet Philosophy. J. J. O'Rourke. LC 73-86095. (Sovietica Ser: No. 32). 240p. 1974. lib. bdg. 39.50 (ISBN 90-277-0383-3, Pub. by Reidel Holland). Kluwer Academic.

Problem of God. Edgar S. Brightman. LC 75-3085. (Philosophy in America Ser.). Repr. of 1930 ed. 27.50 (ISBN 0-404-59084-5). AMS Pr.

Problem of God: A Short Introduction. rev. ed. Peter A. Angeles. LC 73-85469. 156p. 1981. pap. text ed. 12.95 (ISBN 0-87975-216-5). Prometheus Bks.

Problem of God & the Emotional Equilibrium of Man. Bonaventura, Sr. (Illus.). 78p. 1984. pap. 97.75 (ISBN 0-89266-490-8). Am Classical Coll Pr.

Problem of God in Philosophy of Religion: A Critical Examination of the Category of the Absolute & the Scheme of Transcendence. Henry Dumery. Tr. by Charles Courtney. (Studies in Phenomenology & Existential Philosophy). 135p. 1964. 22.95x (ISBN 0-8101-0083-5); pap. 11.95 (ISBN 0-8101-0606-X). Northwestern U Pr.

Problem of God: Yesterday & Today. John C. Murray. (St. Thomas More Lectures Ser.: No. 1). (Orig.). 1964. pap. 7.95x (ISBN 0-300-00171-1, Y138). Yale U Pr.

Problem of Grace. Mark Craver. LC 85-81601. (Lost Roads Ser.: No. 29). 64p. (Orig.). 1986. pap. 6.95 (ISBN 0-918786-33-9). Lost Roads.

Problem of Group Responsibility to Society. John H. Randall, Jr. LC 72-89760. (American Labor, from Conspiracy to Collective Bargaining Ser., No. 1). 296p. 1969. Repr. of 1922 ed. 17.00 (ISBN 0-405-02145-3). Ayer Co Pubs.

Problem of Hamlet. Andrew S. Caircross. 1978. Repr. of 1936 ed. lib. bdg. 35.50 (ISBN 0-8495-0765-0). Arden Lib.

Problem of "Hamlet". J. M. Robertson. LC 72-195242. 1973. lib. bdg. 29.50 (ISBN 0-8414-7456-7). Folcroft.

Problem of Hamlet: A Solution. Andrew S. Cairncross. 1936. lib. bdg. 17.00 (ISBN 0-8414-1599-4). Folcroft.

Problem of Heredity & the Phenomena of Development in Man, 2 vols. E. G. Conklin. (Illus.). 278p. 1988. Set. 187.75 (ISBN 0-89920-177-6). Am Inst Psych.

Problem of Hexateuch. Von Rad. Date not set. pap. 19.50 (Pub. by SCM Pr England). Fortress.

Problem of Historical Knowledge: An Answer to Relativism. facsimile ed. Maurice H. Mandelbaum. LC 74-152993. (Select Bibliographies Reprint Ser). Repr. of 1938 ed. 22.00 (ISBN 0-8369-5745-8). Ayer Co Pubs.

Problem of Immigration. Ed. by Steven Anzovin. LC 84-29941. (Reference Shelf Ser.: Vol. 57, No. 1). 156p. 1985. pap. text ed. 10.00. Wilson.

Problem of Induction & Its Solution. Jerrold J. Katz. LC 62-18116. pap. 34.80 (ISBN 0-317-08127-6, 2015758). Bks Demand UMI.

Problem of Inflation. Ed. by Karl Brunner & A. H. Meltzer. (Carnegie-Rochester Conference Series on Public Policy: Vol. 8). 372p. 1978. pap. 39.50 (ISBN 0-444-85147-X, North-Holland). Elsevier.

Problem of International Confrontations see Trilateral Commission Task Force Reports.

Problem of International Consultations. Egidio Ortano et al. 1976. 15.00 (ISBN 0-318-02788-7); pap. 4.95 (ISBN 0-318-02789-5). Trilateral Comm.

Problem of International Debt. Christopher A. Kojm. (Reference Shelf Ser.: Vol. 56, No. 1). 203p. 1984. 8.00 (ISBN 0-8242-0696-7). Wilson.

Problem of Japanese Trade Expansion in the Post-War Situation. Miriam S. Farley. LC 75-30106. (Institute of Pacific Relations Ser.). Repr. of 1940 ed. 11.50 (ISBN 0-404-59523-5). AMS Pr.

Problem of Knowledge. Alfred J. Ayer. (Orig.). 1957. pap. 6.95 (ISBN 0-14-020377-X, Pelican). Penguin.

Problem of Knowledge: Philosophy, Science, & History Since Hegel. Ernst Cassirer. Tr. by William H. Woglom & Charles W. Hendel. 1950. pap. 12.95x (ISBN 0-300-01098-2, Y211). Yale U Pr.

Problem of Lefthandedness. Gerda Hueck. Tr. by R. Finser. 1986. pap. 4.95 (ISBN 0-916786-83-8). St George Bk Serv.

Problem of Liberalism in the Thought of John Stuart Mill. Neil Thornton. Ed. by Maurice Cranston. (Political Theory & Political Philosophy Ser.). 350p. 1987. lib. bdg. 50.00 (ISBN 0-8240-0831-6). Garland Pub.

Problem of Loss & Mourning: New Psychoanalytic Perspectives. Ed. by David R. Dietrich & Peter Shabad. 1988. text ed. price not set (ISBN 0-8236-4349-2, BN 04349). Intl Univs Pr.

Problem of Man's Antiquity. Kenneth P. Oakley. (Illus.). 1964. 15.00 (ISBN 0-384-42700-6); pap. 10.00 (ISBN 0-384-42701-4). Johnson Repr.

Problem of Mental Disorder. National Research Council Committee on Psychiatric Investigations. Ed. by Gerald N. Grob. LC 78-22580. (Historical Issues in Mental Health Ser.). 1979. Repr. of 1934 ed. lib. bdg. 27.50x (ISBN 0-405-11932-1). Ayer Co Pubs.

Problem of Metaphysics. D. M. MacKinnon. LC 73-79309. 180p. 1974. 29.95 (ISBN 0-521-20275-2). Cambridge U Pr.

Problem of Metaphysics & the Meaning of Metaphysical Explanation. Hartley B. Alexander. LC 72-38480. Repr. of 1902 ed. 14.00 (ISBN 0-404-00322-2). AMS Pr.

Problem of Method; Symbols from Jewish Cult see Jewish Symbols in the Greco-Roman Period.

Problem of Military Readiness. Melvin R. Laird & Lawrence J. Korb. 1980. pap. 6.00 (ISBN 0-8447-1087-3). Am Enterprise.

Problem of Moments. J. A. Shohat & J. D. Tamarkin. LC 51-96. (Mathematical Surveys Ser.: No. 1). 144p. 1983. Repr. of 1950 ed. 33.00 (ISBN 0-8218-1501-6, SURV-1). Am Math.

Problem of National Security, Some Economic & Administrative Aspects: A Statement on National Policy by the Research & Policy Committee of the Committee for Economic Development. Committee for Economic Development. LC 58-13649. pap. 21.50 (ISBN 0-317-08288-4, 2007033). Bks Demand UMI.

Problem of Organic Form. Edmund G. Sinnott. 1963. 42.50x (ISBN 0-685-69864-5). Elliots Bks.

Problem of Pain. C. S. Lewis. 1978. pap. 4.50 (ISBN 0-02-086850-2, Collier). Macmillan.

Problem of Participation: A Radical Critique of Contemporary Democratic Theory. Lee A. Osbun. LC 85-5308. 146p. (Orig.). 1985. lib. bdg. 23.25 (ISBN 0-8191-4640-4); pap. text ed. 9.25 (ISBN 0-8191-4641-2). U Pr of Amer.

Problem of Party Government. Richard Rose. LC 74-30329. (Illus.). 1975. 20.95 (ISBN 0-02-926780-3). Free Pr.

Problem of "Poetry & Belief" in Contemporary Criticism. William J. Rooney. LC 50-2632. pap. 43.80 (2029494). Bks Demand UMI.

Problem of Political Obligation. Noel O'Sullivan. Ed. by Maurice Cranston. (Political Theory & Political Philosophy Ser.). 300p. 1987. lib. bdg. 40.00 (ISBN 0-8240-0828-6). Garland Pub.

Problem of Political Obligation: A Critical Analysis of Liberal Theory. Carole Pateman. LC 78-18460. 205p. 1979. 48.95 (ISBN 0-471-99699-8, Pub. by Wiley-Interscience). Wiley.

Problem of Political Obligation: A Critical Analysis of Liberal Theory. Carole Pateman. LC 85-8719. 1985. 11.95x (ISBN 0-520-05650-7). U of Cal Pr.

Problem of Political Obligation: A Critical Analysis of Liberal Theory. Carole Pateman. LC 78-18460. 217p. pap. 56.50 (2030536). Bks Demand UMI.

Problem of Preaching. Donald MacLeod. LC 86-46417. (Resources for Preaching Ser.). 251p. (Orig.). Date not set. pap. 4.95 (ISBN 0-8006-1145-4). Fortress.

Problem of Presentative Sentences in Modern Dutch. R. S. Kirsner. (Linguistic Ser.: Vol. 43). 215p. 1979. 60.75 (ISBN 0-444-85404-5, North Holland). Elsevier.

Problem of Progress. Sander Griffioen. (Lecture Ser.). 56p. (Orig.). 1987. pap. 1.75 (ISBN 0-932914-14-4). Dordt Coll Pr.

Problem of Proof: Especially As Exemplified in Disputed Documents Trials. Albert S. Osborn. LC 75-20212. 564p. 1975. Repr. of 1926 ed. 44.95x (ISBN 0-88229-300-1). Nelson-Hall.

Problem of Rebirth. Sri Aurobindo. 186p. 1983. 7.50 (ISBN 0-89071-305-7, Pub. by Sri Aurobindo Ashram India); pap. 5.50 (ISBN 0-89071-304-9, Pub. by Sri Aurobindo Ashram India). Aurobindo Assn.

Problem of Rebirth. Sri Aurobindo. 1979. pap. 15.00 (ISBN 0-89744-913-4). Auromere.

Problem of Religious Knowledge. Margaret L. Furse et al. (Rice University Studies: Vol. 60, No. 1). 129p. 1974. pap. 10.00x (ISBN 0-89263-219-4). Rice Univ.

Problem of Seam Strength & Thread Durability. 15p. 1953. 7.00 (ISBN 0-318-19653-0). Clothing Mfrs.

Problem of Self-Love in Saint Augustine. Oliver O'Donovan. LC 80-5397. 208p. 1980. text ed. 25.00t (ISBN 0-300-02468-1). Yale U Pr.

Problem of Sentencing. Monrad G. Paulsen. 123p. 1962. pap. 1.00 (ISBN 0-317-30876-9, B173). Am Law Inst.

Problem of Shape in the Prelude: The Conflict of Private & Public Speech. Jonathan Grandine. LC 68-54018. (LeBaron Russell Briggs Prize Honors Essays in English Ser.: 1968). (Orig.). 1968. pap. 3.50x (ISBN 0-674-70800-8). Harvard U Pr.

Problem of Slavery in the Age of Revolution, 1770-1823. David B. Davis. LC 74-9214. (Paperback Ser.). 576p. 1975. 42.50x (ISBN 0-8014-0888-1); pap. 12.95x (ISBN 0-8014-9156-8). Cornell U Pr.

Problem of Slavery in Western Culture. David B. Davis. 528p. 1988. pap. 12.95 (ISBN 0-19-505639-6). Oxford U Pr.

Problem of Social Change. Newell L. Sims. 1939. 20.00 (ISBN 0-686-17708-8). Quality Lib.

Problem of Sociology: An Introduction to the Discipline. Howard Newby & David Lee. 379p. 1984. pap. 12.95 (ISBN 0-09-151511-4, Pub. by Hutchinson Educ). Longwood Pub Group.

Problem of Sovereignty in the Later Middle Ages: The Papal Monarchy with Augustinus Triumphus & the Publicists. Michael Wilks. (Cambridge Studies in Medieval Life & Thought New: Vol. 9). pap. 158.30 (ISBN 0-317-09407-6, 2013890). Bks Demand UMI.

Problem of Space in Jewish Medieval Philosophy. Israel I. Efros. LC 77-164765. (Columbia University. Oriental Studies: No. 11). Repr. of 1917 ed. 14.75 (ISBN 0-404-50501-5). AMS Pr.

Problem of Space in Jewish Medieval Philosophy. facsimile ed. Israel I. Efros. lib. bdg. 37.50x (ISBN 0-697-00037-0); pap. 7.95 (ISBN 0-89197-904-2). Irvington.

Problem of Stagflation. Gottfried Haberler. 1985. pap. 7.00 (ISBN 0-8447-3578-7). Am Enterprise.

Problem of Stuttering: Theory & Therapy. Ed. by Robert W. Rieber. LC 77-4910. 212p. 1977. 25.25 (ISBN 0-444-00222-7, Biomedical Pr). Elsevier.

Problem of Style. Ed. by J. V. Cunningham. 300p. Date not set. pap. cancelled (ISBN 0-941324-03-6). Van Vactor & Goodheart.

Problem of Style. John M. Murry. LC 80-21463. x, 133p. 1980. Repr. of 1960 ed. lib. bdg. 35.00x (ISBN 0-313-22523-0, MUPR). Greenwood.

Problem of Substance: Lectures. University Of California Philosophical Union - 1926-1927. (Publications in Philosophy Ser: Vol. 9). 1927. 20.00 (ISBN 0-384-07110-4). Johnson Repr.

Problem of Teaching High School Pupils How to Study. Joseph S. Butterweck. LC 75-176620. (Columbia University. Teachers College. Contributions to Education: No. 237). Repr. of 1926 ed. 22.50 (ISBN 0-404-55237-4). AMS Pr.

Problem of the Beginning of Dogma in Recent Theology: Theology. Paul Schrodt. (European University Studies: Ser. 23, Vol. 103). xxvi, 339p. 1978. pap. 40.40 (ISBN 3-261-02464-X). P Lang Pubs.

Problem of the Criterion (Nineteen Seventy-Three Aquinas Lecture) Roderick M. Chisholm. gold stamped titles 7.95 (ISBN 0-87462-138-0). Marquette.

Problem of the Day. Shrii Prabhat Rainjain Sarkar. 64p. 1968. pap. 1.00 (ISBN 0-686-95454-8). Ananda Marga.

Problem of the Distressed Areas. Wal Hannington. (English Workers & the Coming of the Welfare State Ser., 1918-1945). 286p. 1985. lib. bdg. 39.00 (ISBN 0-8240-7613-3). Garland Pub.

Problem of the Green Capsule. John D. Carr. (Library of Crime Classics). 1986. pap. 4.95 (ISBN 0-317-52726-6). Intl Polygonics.

Problem of the Individual: Lectures. University Of California Philosophical Union - 1936. (Publications in Philosophy Ser: Vol. 20). 1936. 20.00 (ISBN 0-384-07120-1). Johnson Repr.

Problem of the Irrational in History. Benedetto Croce. 180p. 1985. 147.75 (ISBN 0-89920-082-6). Am Inst Psych.

Problem of the Judgment: Eleven Approaches to Kafka's Story. Angel Flores. LC 76-48958. 1977. 30.00x (ISBN 0-87752-210-3). Gordian.

Problem of the Lord's Supper. Albert Schweitzer & Mattill A. J. LC 81-22590. xiv, 144p. 1982. 10.95 (ISBN 0-86554-025-X, MUP-H25). Mercer Univ Pr.

Problem of the Merry Wives of Windsor. John M. Robertson. 1917. Repr. lib. bdg. 35.00 (ISBN 0-8414-7466-4). Folcroft.

Problem of the Minimum of a Quadratic Functional. Solomon G. Minkhlin. Tr. by A. Feinstein. LC 64-24626. (Holden-Day Series in Mathematical Physics). pap. 41.00 (ISBN 0-317-09170-0, 2016292). Bks Demand UMI.

Problem of the Northmen. E. N. Horsford. 1977. lib. bdg. 59.95 (ISBN 0-8490-2483-8). Gordon Pr.

Problem of the Ohio Mounds. Cyrus Thomas. Repr. of 1889 ed. 19.00x. Scholarly.

Problem of the Ohio Mounds. Cyrus Thomas. 1988. Repr. of 1889 ed. lib. bdg. 49.00x. Am Biog Serv.

Problem of the Pacific in the Twentieth Century. Nikolai N. Golovin & A. D. Bubnov. LC 79-111758. (American Imperialism: Viewpoints of United States Foreign Policy, 1898-1941). 1970. Repr. of 1922 ed. 17.00 (ISBN 0-405-02023-6). Ayer Co Pubs.

Problem of the Phytolyma Gall Bug in the Establishment of Chlorophora. M. G. White. 1966. 30.00x (ISBN 0-686-45545-2, Pub. by For Lib Comm England). State Mutual Bk.

Problem of the Reign of King Edward the Third: A Statistical Approach. Eliot Slater. (New Cambridge Shakespeare Studies & Supplementary Texts). (Illus.). 250p. Date not set. price not set (ISBN 0-521-34353-4). Cambridge U Pr.

Problem of the Self. Henry W. Johnstone, Jr. LC 71-84666. 1970. 19.95 (ISBN 0-271-00102-X). Pa St U Pr.

Problem of the Shakespeare Plays. George C. Bompas. 1902. lib. bdg. 20.00 (ISBN 0-8414-3282-1). Folcroft.

Problem of the Third Generation Immigrant. Marcus L. Hansen. LC 86-64029. (Occasional Paper: No. 16). 27p. 1987. pap. write for info. Augustana Coll.

Problem of the Transformation of Man. Karl Mannheim. (Illus.). 161p. 1986. 117.45 (ISBN 0-89266-540-8). Am Classical Coll Pr.

Problem of the Two Prologues to Chaucer's Legend of Good Women. John C. French. LC 79-168140. Repr. of 1905 ed. 5.00 (ISBN 0-404-02576-5). AMS Pr.

Problem of the Two Prologues to Chaucer's Legend of Good Women. John C. French. LC 72-195907. 1905. lib. bdg. 17.00 (ISBN 0-8414-4283-5). Folcroft.

Problem of the Two Prologues to Chaucer's Legend of Good Women. John C. French. 1976. lib. bdg. 59.95 (ISBN 0-8490-2484-6). Gordon Pr.

Problem of the Unity of the Sciences: Bacon to Kant. Robert McRae. LC 62-2304. pap. 40.00 (ISBN 0-317-08188-8, 2014318). Bks Demand UMI.

Problem of the Wire Cage. John D. Carr. 224p. 1982. 20.00x (ISBN 0-7278-0249-6, Pub. by Severn Hse). State Mutual Bk.

Problem of Time in Nietzsche. Joan Stambaugh. Tr. by John Humphrey. LC 86-47767. 224p. 1987. 29.50x (ISBN 0-8387-5113-X). Bucknell U Pr.

Problem of Time: Lectures. University Of California Philosophical Union - 1934. (Publications in Philosophy Ser: Vol. 18). 1935. 20.00 (ISBN 0-384-07130-9). Johnson Repr.

Problem of Timon of Athens. Parrott. Repr. of 1923 ed. lib. bdg. 10.00 (ISBN 0-8495-4325-8). Arden Lib.

Problem of Truth: Lectures. University Of California Philosophical Union - 1927-1928. (Publications in Philosophy Ser: Vol. 10). 1928. 20.00 (ISBN 0-384-07140-6). Johnson Repr.

Problem of Unbelief in the Sixteenth Century: The Religion of Rabelais. Lucien Febvre. Tr. by Beatrice Gottlieb from Fr. (Illus.). 528p. 1982. text ed. 42.00x (ISBN 0-674-70825-3). Harvard U Pr.

Problem of Unbelief in the Sixteenth Century: The Religion of Rabelais. Lucien Febvre. Tr. by Beatrice Gottlieb. 552p. 1985. pap. 11.95x (ISBN 0-674-70826-1). Harvard U Pr.

Problem of Unemployment. Paul H. Douglas & Aaron Director. LC 75-17217. (Social Problems & Social Policy Ser.). (Illus.). 1976. Repr. of 1931 ed. 38.50x (ISBN 0-405-07488-3). Ayer Co Pubs.

Problem of Universals in Indian Philosophy. R. R. Dravid. 1972. 9.95 (ISBN 0-89684-486-2). Orient Bk Dist.

Problem of Values in Educational Thought. Philip L. Smith. 92p. 1982. pap. text ed. 7.50x (ISBN 0-8138-1853-2). Iowa St U Pr.

Problem of Verse Language. Yury Tynyanov. Tr. by Michael Sosa & Brent Harvey. 1981. 25.00 (ISBN 0-88233-464-6); pap. 6.50x (ISBN 0-88233-465-4). Ardis Pubs.

Problem of Volcanism. Joseph P. Iddings. 1914. 85.00x (ISBN 0-686-50031-8). Elliots Bks.

Problem of Wales & Other Essays. Frederick Rees. 146p. 1963. text ed. 12.50x (ISBN 0-7083-0069-3, Pub. by U of Wales). Humanities.

Problem of War in the Old Testament. Peter C. Craigie. LC 78-17698. 1979. pap. 5.95 (ISBN 0-8028-1742-4). Eerdmans.

Problem of Wastelands in India. Abha L. Singh. (Illus.). xii, 140p. 1985. text ed. 30.00x (ISBN 0-86590-597-5, Pub. by B R Pub Corp Delhi). Apt Bks.

Problem of Weak Railroads. James M. Herring. Ed. by Stuart Bruchey. LC 80-1316. (Railroads Ser.). 1981. Repr. of 1929 ed. lib. bdg. 15.00x (ISBN 0-405-13788-5). Ayer Co Pubs.

Problem of Wineland. Halldor Hermannsson. LC 36-18884. (Islandica Ser.: Vol. 25). 1936. pap. 16.00 (ISBN 0-527-00355-7). Kraus Repr.

Problem of Wineskins: Church Renewal in Technological Age. Howard A. Snyder. LC 74-31842. (Illus.). 216p. 1975. pap. text ed. 7.95 (ISBN 0-87784-769-X). Inter-Varsity.

Problem of World-History & the Destiny of Mankind, 2 vols. Oswald Spengler. (Illus.). 257p. 1987. Set. 189.75 (ISBN 0-86722-159-3). Inst Econ Pol.

Problem-Oriented Approach to Physical Therapy Care. Jane Ratcliff Hill. 1977. pap. 3.50 (ISBN 0-912452-17-X). Am Phys Therapy Assn.

Problem-Oriented Medical Diagnosis. 4th ed. Ed. by H. Harold Friedman. (SPIRAL Manual Ser.). 1987. spiralbound 21.00 (ISBN 0-316-29378-4). Little.

Problem-Oriented Medical Record for High-Risk Obstetrics. Ed. by Curtis L. Cetrulo et al. LC 83-17712. 510p. 1984. 69.50x (ISBN 0-306-41325-6, Plenum Pr). Plenum Pub.

Problem-Oriented Medical Records in Correctional Health Care. 51p. Date not set. 4.00. NCCHC.

Problem-Oriented Nursing Assessment. Patricia Larkin & Barbara Backer. 1977. pap. 17.95 (ISBN 0-07-036450-8). McGraw.

Problem-Oriented Programming Languages. Hans J. Schneider. Tr. by Valerie H. Cottrell. LC 83-16688. 151p. 1984. 39.95x (ISBN 0-471-90111-3, Pub. by Wiley-Interscience). Wiley.

Problem-Oriented Record in Psychiatry & Mental Health Care. 2nd ed. Ralph S. Ryback et al. Ed. by Richard Longabaugh & Robert D. Fowler. 270p. 1981. pap. 49.50 (ISBN 0-8089-1308-5, 793701). Grune.

Problem-Play. R. Balmforth. LC 76-52915. (Studies in Drama, No. 39). 1977. lib. bdg. 41.95x (ISBN 0-8383-2129-1). Haskell.

Problem Play in British Drama: 1890-1914. Elliott M. Simon. Ed. by James Hogg. (Poetic Drama & Poetic Theory Ser.). 340p. (Orig.). 1978. pap. 15.00 (ISBN 3-7052-0873-X, Pub. by Salzburg Studies). Longwood Pub Group.

Problem Pregnancy Centers. (How-to Manual for Community Programs Ser.). 40p. (Orig.). 1986. pap. 5.00 (ISBN 0-936597-00-3). Project Share.

Problem-Projects in Acting. Katharine Kester. 1937. 5.50 (ISBN 0-573-69020-0). French.

Problem Recognition in Public Policy & Business Management. Ed. by V. Subramaniam. 1986. 27.50 (ISBN 81-7024-037-9, Pub. by Ashish India). South Asia Bks.

Problem Seeking, CRSS. 212p. 1987. pap. 19.95x (ISBN 0-913962-87-2). Am Inst Arch.

Problem Seminar. D. J. Newman. (Problem Books in Mathematics). 113p. 1982. 21.00 (ISBN 0-387-90765-3). Springer-Verlag.

Problem Shared... A History of the Institute of London Underwriters 1884-1984. C Hewer. 152p. 1984. 135.00 (ISBN 0-317-61274-3, Pub. by Witherby & Co England). State Mutual Bk.

Problem Situations in Teaching. Gordon E. Greenwood & Thomas L. Good. LC 83-5784. 174p. 1983. pap. text ed. 10.25 (ISBN 0-8191-3089-3). U Pr of Amer.

Problem Solver. Patti Waldo. (Educational Game Activity Ser.). (Orig.). 1986. 29.00X (ISBN 0-930599-05-5). Thinking Pubns.

Problem Solver in Business, Management & Finance. rev. ed. Research & Education Association Staff. LC 78-64582. (Illus.). 864p. 1986. pap. text ed. 19.85 (ISBN 0-87891-516-8). Res & Educ.

Problem Solver in Strength of Materials & Mechanics of Solids. rev. ed. Research & Education Association Staff. LC 80-83305. (Illus.). 1152p. (Orig.). 1986. pap. text ed. 23.85 (ISBN 0-87891-522-2). Res & Educ.

Problem Solvers. Nate Aaseng. (Inside Business). (Illus.). 80p. (gr. 5 up). 1988. lib. bdg. 9.95 (ISBN 0-8225-0675-0). Lerner Pubns.

Problem Solvers: A History of Arthur D. Little, Inc. E. J. Kahn, Jr. 1986. 19.95 (ISBN 0-316-48212-9). Little.

Problem Solver's Guide to Logic. William J. Edgar. LC 82-20285. 106p. (Orig.). 1983. pap. text ed. 8.00 (ISBN 0-8191-2876-7). U Pr of Amer.

Problem Solver's Universal Checklist. Leon Segal. 17p. (Orig.). 1983. pap. text ed. 5.00 (ISBN 0-9607160-0-9). Ed Acad.

Problem Solving. F. H. George. 194p. 1980. 19.50 (ISBN 0-7156-1004-X, Pub. by Duckworth London); pap. 11.95 (ISBN 0-7156-1662-5). Longwood Pub Group.

Problem Solving. Ed. by J. T. Sears et al. LC 83-15515. (AIChE Symposium: Vol. 79). 63p. 1983. pap. 24.00 (ISBN 0-8169-0255-0, S-228). Am Inst Chem Eng.

Problem Solving, Vol. 1-5. Ed. by Julia S. Hough & Donald Woods. (Problem Solving Ser.). 375p. 1984. pap. text ed. 24.95 (ISBN 0-89859-743-9). L Erlbaum Assocs.

Problem Solving: A Cognitive Approach. Hank Kahney. LC 85-21651. (Open Guides to Psychology Ser.). 192p. 1986. pap. 21.00x (ISBN 0-335-15327-5, Open Univ Pr). Taylor & Francis.

Problem-Solving: A Handbook for Elementary School Teachers. Krulik & Rudnick. 1987. pap. text ed. 33.95x (ISBN 0-205-11132-7, Pub. by Longwood Div). Allyn.

Problem Solving: A Handbook for Teachers. 2nd ed. Krulik & Rudnick. 1987. 35.95 (ISBN 0-205-10289-1, Pub. by Longwood Div). Allyn.

Problem-Solving: A Logical & Creative Approach. Harvey J. Brightman. LC 80-25078. 1980. 24.95 (ISBN 0-88406-131-0). Ga St U Busn Pub.

Problem Solving: A Structural-Process with Instructional Implications. Joseph M. Scandura et al. 1977. 39.95 (ISBN 0-12-620650-3). Acad Pr.

Problem Solving: A Systems Approach. Joseph E. Robertshaw & Stephen J. Mecca. (Illus.). 1979. text ed. 25.00 (ISBN 0-89433-075-6). Petrocelli.

Problem Solving Activities for Teaching Daily Living Skills: A Curriculum Handbook. Virginia H. Lucas et al. LC 81-71180. 220p. 1982. pap. text ed. 19.00 (ISBN 0-936326-01-8). Cedars Pr.

Problem Solving & BASIC. 2nd ed. Frances G. Gustavson & Marian V. Sackson. 352p. 1986. pap. text ed. write for info. (ISBN 0-574-21950-1, 13-4950); write for info. instr's guide (ISBN 0-574-21951-X, 13-4951). Sci Res Assoc Coll.

Problem Solving & Comprehension. 4th, rev. ed. Arthur Whimbey & Jack Lochhead. (Illus.). 352p. (gr. 11-12). 1986. pap. 12.50 (ISBN 0-89859-785-4); problem cards 19.50 (ISBN 0-89859-752-8). L Erlbaum Assocs.

Problem Solving & Computer Programming In. P. Grogono & S. H. Nelson. 1982. pap. text ed. write for info. Addison-Wesley.

Problem Solving & Education: Issues in Teaching & Research. Ed. by David T. Tuma & F. Reif. LC 79-22461. 224p. 1980. text ed. 24.95 (ISBN 0-89859-008-6). L Erlbaum Assocs.

Problem Solving & Intelligence. Helga A. Rowe. 416p. 1985. text ed. 45.00 (ISBN 0-89859-347-6). L Erlbaum Assocs.

Problem-Solving & Learning Disabilities: An Information Processing Approach. Melinda Parrill-Burnstein. (Illus.). 212p. 1981. 26.50 (ISBN 0-8089-1340-9, 793247). Grune.

Problem Solving & Mathematics for Physics. 2nd ed. Thomas Nykl. 268p. 1988. pap. text ed. 28.95 (ISBN 0-8403-4706-5). Kendall-Hunt.

Problem Solving & Programming Concepts. Maureen Sprankle. 320p. 1989. case bound 21.95 (ISBN 0-675-20867-X); supplements avail. Merrill.

Problem Solving & Structured Programming in BASIC. Elliot B. Koffman & Frank L. Friedman. LC 78-65355. 1979. pap. text ed. write for info. (ISBN 0-201-03888-9). Addison-Wesley.

Problem Solving & Structured Programming in FORTRAN. 2nd ed. Frank L. Friedman & E. B. Koffman. 1981. write for info. wkbk. (ISBN 0-201-02465-9). Addison-Wesley.

Problem Solving & Structured Programming in FORTRAN. 3rd ed. E. B. Koffman & F. L. Friedman. LC 86-8055. 544p. 1986. pap. text ed. write for info. (ISBN 0-201-11561-1). Addison-Wesley.

Problem Solving & Structured Programming in Modula-2. Elliot B. Koffman. (Illus.). 681p. 1988. pap. text ed. 29.25x (ISBN 0-201-07828-7). Addison-Wesley.

Problem Solving & Structured Programming in Pascal. 2nd ed. Elliot B. Koffman. LC 84-16811. 1985. text ed. write for info. (ISBN 0-201-11736-3); write for info. instr's. manual (ISBN 0-201-11737-1); transparency masters avail. (ISBN 0-201-11738-X). Addison-Wesley.

Problem Solving & Structured Programming in WATFIV. Frank Friedman & Elliot Koffman. LC 81-20598. (Illus.). 480p. 1982. pap. text ed. write for info. (ISBN 0-201-10482-2). Addison-Wesley.

Problem Solving & Structured Programming with FORTRAN 77. Martin O. Holoien & Ali Behforooz. LC 82-24436. 560p. 1983. pap. text ed. 22.00 pub net (ISBN 0-534-01275-2). Brooks-Cole.

Problem Solving & Structured Programming with PASCAL. Ali Behforooz & Martin O. Holoien. LC 85-28008. (Computer Science Ser.). 480p. 1986. pap. text ed. 22.00 (ISBN 0-534-05736-5). Brooks-Cole.

Problem Solving & the Computer: A Structured Concept with PL 1 (PLC) 2nd ed. Joseph Shortt & Thomas C. Wilson. 1979. pap. text ed. write for info. (ISBN 0-201-06916-4). Addison-Wesley.

Problem-Solving Approach to Adjustment. George Spivack et al. (Jossey-Bass Behaviorial Science Ser.). pap. 84.00 (ISBN 0-317-20850-0, 2023881). Bks Demand UMI.

Problem-Solving Approach to Introductory Algebra. 2nd ed. Mervin L. Keedy & Marvin L. Bittinger. LC 85-18592. 1986. text ed. write for info. (ISBN 0-201-12968-X); write for info. instr's. manual (ISBN 0-201-12969-8); write for info. student's guide (ISBN 0-201-12970-1); test bank avail. (ISBN 0-201-12971-X); write for info. instructional software (ISBN 0-201-14896-X); placement test avail. Addison-Wesley.

Problem Solving Approach to Mathematics for Elementary School Teachers. 3rd ed. Billstein et al. 1987. 33.95 (ISBN 0-8053-0865-2); instr's guide 15.95 (ISBN 0-8053-0868-7); lab manual 9.95 (ISBN 0-8053-0867-9). Benjamin Cummings.

Problem Solving Arts: Part One Syllabus. Norman H. Crowhurst. 1976. pap. text ed. 9.95 (ISBN 0-89420-085-2, 256040); cassette recordings 227.10 (ISBN 0-89420-175-1, 256000). Natl Book.

Problem Solving Arts: Part Three Syllabus. Norman E. Crowhurst. 1978. pap. text ed. 10.45 (ISBN 0-89420-040-2, 256130); cassette recordings 196.20 (ISBN 0-89420-177-8, 256090). Natl Book.

Problem Solving Arts: Part Two Syllabus. Norman H. Crowhurst. 1977. pap. text ed. 10.25 (ISBN 0-89420-029-1); cassette recordings 195.80 (ISBN 0-89420-176-X, 256050). Natl Book.

Problem Solving Assessment. Avish Dworkin & Nancy Dworkin. Ed. by Betty L. Kratoville. 219p. (Orig.). 1988. pap. text ed. 16.50 (ISBN 0-87879-593-6). Acad Therapy.

Problem-Solving at Work. Bruce Burgess. 147p. 1987. 169.00x (ISBN 1-85008-000-3, Pub. by Framework UK). State Mutual Bk.

Problem-Solving at Work - Update. Bruce Burgess. 103p. 1987. 160.00x (ISBN 1-85008-055-0, Pub. by Framework UK). State Mutual Bk.

Problem Solving: Concepts & Methods for Community Organizations. Ralph Brody. LC 81-7221. 240p. 1982. 34.95x (ISBN 0-89885-078-9); pap. 16.95x (ISBN 0-89885-079-7). Human Sci Pr.

Problem Solving Environments for Scientific Computing: Proceedings of the IFIP TC2 WG2.5 Working Conf. on Problem Solving Environments for Scientific Computing, Sophia, Antipolis, France, 17-21 June, 1985. Ed. by B. Ford & F. Chatelin. 416p. 1987. 78.00 (ISBN 0-444-70254-7, North Holland). Elsevier.

Problem-Solving Excerises for Basic Nutrition. Betty Clamp et al. (Illus.). 171p. 1986. pap. text ed. 13.00x (ISBN 0-89787-119-7). Gorsuch Scarisbrick.

Problem Solving for Chemistry. 2nd ed. Edward I. Peters. LC 75-12493. (Illus.). 300p. 1976. pap. text ed. 19.50 (ISBN 0-7216-7206-X, CBS C). SCP.

Problem Solving for Managers. William F. Roth, Jr. LC 84-18280. 224p. 1985. 37.95 (ISBN 0-275-91756-8, C1756). Praeger.

Problem Solving for Oil Painters. Gregg Kreutz. (Illus.). 144p. 1986. 24.95 (ISBN 0-8230-4408-4). Watson-Guptill.

Problem Solving for Understanding - Decimals. Allan D. Suter. (Programmed Math Ser.). (Illus.). 30p. (Orig.). (gr. 3-12). 1987. pap. text ed. 3.95 (ISBN 0-945915-11-X). Programmed Lrn.

Problem Solving for Understanding - Fractions. Allan D. Suter. (Programmed Math Ser.). (Illus.). 30p. (Orig.). (gr. 3-12). 1987. pap. text ed. 3.95 (ISBN 0-945915-19-5). Programmed Lrn.

Problem Solving for Understanding - Whole Numbers. Allan D. Suter. (Programmed Math Ser.). (Illus.). 38p. (Orig.). (gr. 3-12). 1987. pap. text ed. 3.95 (ISBN 0-945915-06-3). Programmed Lrn.

Problem Solving Guide: Electronic Circuits. Kosow. (Electronic Technology Ser.). 1988. pap. write for info. (ISBN 0-471-01663-2). Wiley.

Problem Solving in a Project Environment: A Consulting Process. L. Thomas King. LC 80-20063. 204p. 1981. 32.50x (ISBN 0-471-08115-9, Pub. by Wiley-Interscience). Wiley.

Problem Solving in a Project Environment: A Consulting Process. L. Thomas King. LC 80-20063. 216p. 1981. 32.50 (JW). Krieger.

Problem Solving in Apple PASCAL. Lowell A. Carmony et al. (Computers & Math Ser.). 213p. (gr. 10-12). 1984. 28.95 (ISBN 0-88175-006-9, Computer Sci Pr); tchr's. guide 15.00 (ISBN 0-88175-021-2); student diskette 20.00 (ISBN 0-88175-022-0); tchr's. diskette 20.00 (ISBN 0-88175-023-9). W H Freeman.

Problem Solving in Arithmetic. Leon N. Neulen. LC 70-177116. (Columbia University. Teachers College. Contributions to Education: No. 483). Repr. of 1931 ed. 22.50 (ISBN 0-404-55483-0). AMS Pr.

Problem Solving in Biochemistry: A Practical Approach. Jane Magill. 323p. 1988. text ed. price not set (ISBN 0-02-432100-1). Macmillan.

Problem Solving in Biology. 3rd ed. Eugene H. Kaplan. 448p. 1983. pap. text ed. write for info. (ISBN 0-02-362050-1). Macmillan.

Problem Solving in Clinical Medicine: From Data to Diagnosis. 2nd ed. Paul Cutler. 400p. 1985. pap. text ed. 29.00 (ISBN 0-683-02252-0). Williams & Wilkins.

Problem Solving in General Chemistry. Ronald De Lorenzo. 496p. 1981. pap. text ed. 17.00 (ISBN 0-669-02924-6). Heath.

Problem Solving in General Chemistry. 2nd ed. Kenneth W. Whitten & Kenneth D. Gailey. 1984. pap. text ed. 19.50. SCP.

Problem Solving in Immuniohematology. 3rd ed. Ed. by Herbert Silver et al. LC 87-17456. (Illus.). 123p. 1988. text ed. 22.00 (ISBN 0-89189-263-X). Am Soc Clinical.

Problem Solving in Immunohematology. 3rd ed. Ed. by Herbert Silver et al. (Illus.). 148p. 1988. 22.00 (ISBN 0-317-62396-6). Am Soc Clinical.

Problem Solving in Mathematics. Butts. 1988. pap. write for info. (ISBN 0-471-09673-3). Wiley.

Problem Solving in Mathematics: Level A. Contemporary Perspectives, Inc. Staff. (Problem Solving in Mathematics Ser.). 96p. (gr. 1). 1982. text ed. write for info. (ISBN 0-8136-3001-0); tchr's. guide avail. (ISBN 0-8136-3013-4). Modern Curr.

Problem Solving in Mathematics: Level B. Contemporary Perspectives, Inc. Staff. (Problem Solving in Mathematics Ser.). 96p. (gr. 2). 1982. text ed. write for info. (ISBN 0-8136-3002-9); tchr's. guide avail. (ISBN 0-8136-3014-2). Modern Curr.

Problem Solving in Mathematics: Level C. Contemporary Perspectives, Inc. Staff. (Problem Solving in Mathematics Ser.). 96p. (gr. 3). 1982. text ed. write for info.; tchr's. guide avail. (ISBN 0-8136-3003-7). Modern Curr.

Problem Solving in Mathematics: Level D. Contemporary Perspectives, Inc. Staff. (Problem Solving in Mathematics Ser.). 96p. (gr. 4). 1982. text ed. write for info. (ISBN 0-8136-3004-5); tchr's. guide avail. (ISBN 0-8136-3016-9). Modern Curr.

Problem Solving in Mathematics: Level E. Contemporary Perspectives, Inc. Staff. (Problem Solving in Mathematics Ser.). 96p. (gr. 5). 1982. text ed. write for info. (ISBN 0-8136-3005-3); tchr's. guide avail. (ISBN 0-8136-3017-7). Modern Curr.

Problem Solving in Mathematics: Level F. Contemporary Perspectives, Inc. Staff. (Problem Solving in Mathematics Ser.). 96p. (gr. 6). 1982. text ed. write for info. (ISBN 0-8136-3006-1); tchr's. guide avail. (ISBN 0-8136-3018-5). Modern Curr.

Problem Solving in Physical Chemistry. Roland Roskos. LC 74-24649. 189p. 1974. pap. text ed. 22.25 (ISBN 0-8299-0028-4). West Pub.

Problem Solving in Recreation & Parks. 2nd ed. Joseph J. Bannon. 400p. 1981. P-H.

Problem Solving in School Mathematics, 1980 Yearbook. National Council of Teachers of Mathematics. LC 79-27145. (Illus.). 256p. 1980. 18.00 (ISBN 0-87353-162-0). NCTM.

Problem Solving in Structured BASIC-Plus & Vax-II BASIC. Elliot B. Koffman & Frank L. Friedman. LC 83-2566. (Illus.). 448p. 1984. pap. write for info. (ISBN 0-201-10344-3); write for info. instr's. manual (ISBN 0-201-10347-8). Addison-Wesley.

Problem Solving in the Mathematics Curriculum: A Report, Recommendations & An Annotated Bibliography. 140p. 1983. pap. 6.75 (ISBN 0-88385-051-6, NTE-01). Math Assn.

Problem-Solving Methods in Artificial Intelligence. Nils J. Nilsson. 1971. text ed. 56.95 (ISBN 0-07-046573-8). McGraw.

Problem-Solving Methods with Examples in Ada. Nico Lomuto. (Illus.). 176p. 1987. pap. text ed. 23.00 (ISBN 0-13-721325-5). P-H.

Problem Solving Pascal. Francis L. Schneider. Ed. by Pamela S. Cooper & Byron Riggan. (Computer Science Ser.). (Illus.). 471p. 1987. pap. text ed. write for info. (ISBN 0-574-21985-4, 13-4985). SRA.

Problem-Solving Principles: Programming with PASCAL. Ronald E. Prather. (Illus.). 352p. 1982. pap. text ed. write for info. (ISBN 0-13-721308-5). P-H.

Problem-Solving Process: A Planner's Handbook for Program Improvement. Carol P. Kowle et al. 119p. 1982. 8.75 (ISBN 0-318-22181-0, LT63). Natl Ctr Res Voc Ed.

Problem Solving: Research, Method & Theory. Ed. by Benjamin Kleinmuntz. LC 74-14881. (Carnegie-Mellon University Cognition Ser.). 416p. 1975. Repr. of 1966 ed. 29.50 (ISBN 0-88275-219-7). Krieger.

Problem-Solving Skills see Productive Supervisor: A Program of Practical Managerial Skills.

Problem Solving Software to Accompany Engler, Managerial Accounting (Apple) 20.50 (ISBN 0-317-59842-2). Irwin.

Problem Solving Software, to Accompany Engler, Managerial Accounting (IBM) 20.50 (ISBN 0-256-05845-8). Irwin.

Problem Solving Software, to Accompany Rayburn Principles of Cost Accounting (Apple) 18.95x (ISBN 0-256-05580-7). Irwin.

Problem Solving Software to Accompany Rayburn, Principles of Cost Accounting (IBM) Date not set. 18.95 (ISBN 0-256-05581-5). Irwin.

Problem-Solving Strategies for Writing. 2nd ed. Linda Flower. 256p. 1985. pap. text ed. 14.00 net (ISBN 0-15-571976-9, HC); instr's. manual avail. (ISBN 0-15-571977-7). HarBraceJ.

Problem-Solving Techniques Helpful in Math & Science. Charles A. Reeves. LC 87-12219. (Illus.). 35p. 1987. pap. 4.50 (ISBN 0-87353-246-5). NCTM.

Problem Solving Techniques Pascal. Peter Grogono. (Business & Computer Science Ser.). 320p. 1982. pap. text ed. write for info. Addison-Wesley.

Problem-Solving Therapy. 2nd ed. Jay Haley. LC 87-45413. (Social & Behavioral Science Ser.). 1987. text ed. 22.95x (ISBN 1-55542-058-3). Jossey-Bass.

Problem-Solving Therapy: A Social Competence Approach to Clinical Intervention. Thomas J. D'Zurilla. (Behavior Therapy & Behavioral Medicine Ser.). 256p. 1986. text ed. 26.95 (ISBN 0-8261-5680-0). Springer Pub.

Problem Solving Therapy for Depression: Theory Research & Clinical Guidelines. Nezu. (Personality Processes Ser.). 1988. price not set (ISBN 0-471-62885-9). Wiley.

Problem Solving Therapy: New Strategies for Effective Family Therapy. Jay Haley. 275p. 1984. pap. 8.95x (ISBN 0-06-090583-2, TB1991, Torch). Har-Row.

Problem-Solving Therapy with Socially Anxious Children. J. J. Meijers. 290p. 1978. pap. text ed. 26.50 (ISBN 90-265-0282-6, Pub. by Swets & Zeitlinger Netherlands). Hogrefe Intl.

Problem Solving: Tips for Teachers. Ed. by Phares G. O'Daffer. (Illus.). 80p. 1988. pap. 7.00 (ISBN 0-87353-264-3). NCTM.

Problem Solving Using IBM PC PASCAL. Keith Harrow & Jacqueline A. Jones. (Illus.). 592p. 1986. pap. text ed. 28.00 (ISBN 0-13-721358-1). P-H.

Problem Solving Using PASCAL: Algorithm Developmental & Programming Concepts. R. Skvarcius. 640p. 1984. pap. text ed. 25.00 (ISBN 0-87150-440-5, 8080). PWS Kent Pub.

Problem Solving Using PL-1 & PL-C. Keith Harrow. (Illus.). 464p. 1984. pap. text ed. write for info. (ISBN 0-13-711796-5). P-H.

Problem Solving Using Turbo PASCAL. Jacqueline A. Jones & Keith Harrow. (Illus.). 560p. 1986. pap. text ed. 28.00 (ISBN 0-13-721366-2). P-H.

Problem Solving Using UCSD Pascal. 2nd ed. K. L. Bowles et al. (Illus.). 350p. 1984. pap. 22.00 (ISBN 0-387-90822-6). Springer Verlag.

Problem Solving with ANSI Structured BASIC. Rina Yarmish & Joshua Yarmish. 528p. 1988. pap. text ed. write for info. (ISBN 0-574-18680-8, 13-1680); write for info. instr's. guide (ISBN 0-574-18681-6, 13-1681); write for info. test bank bklet. (ISBN 0-574-18683-2, 13-1683); write for info. test generator (ISBN 0-574-21842-4, 13-4842); write for info interpretive pkg. 512k (ISBN 0-574-21894-7, 13-4894). SRA.

Problem Solving with BASIC. Jeff Feeman & Maryellen Feeman. (Stick-Out-Your-Neck Ser.). (Illus.). 32p. (gr. 5 up). 1984. pap. 1.98 (ISBN 0-88724-105-0, CD-9048). Carson-Dellos.

Problem Solving with BASIC. Donald D. Spencer. LC 82-17875. 160p. (YA) (gr. 8 up). 1983. pap. 4.95x (ISBN 0-89218-075-7, NO. 1135). Camelot Pub.

Problem Solving with Borlands Eureka. Tront. 104p. 1988. pap. write for info. (ISBN 0-471-60706-1). Wiley.

Problem Solving with FORTRAN. Donald D. Spencer. LC 76-26040. (Illus.). 1977. pap. text ed. write for info. (ISBN 0-13-720094-3). P-H.

Problem Solving with FORTRAN 77. Richard W. Dillman. 354p. 1985. pap. text ed. 23.95 (ISBN 0-03-063734-1). HR&W.

Problem Solving with FORTRAN 77. Larry Nyhoff & Sanford Leestma. 368p. 1983. pap. text ed. write for info. (ISBN 0-02-388720-6). Macmillan.

Problem Solving with Microbeam Analysis. K. Kiss. (Studies in Analytical Chemistry: Vol. 7). 1987. 119.50 (ISBN 0-444-98949-8). Elsevier.

Problem Solving with Pascal. Kolman W. Brand. 402p. 1986. pap. text ed. 21.50 (ISBN 0-534-06210-5). PWS Kent Pub.

Problem Solving with Pascal. Hugo T. D'Alarcao & Robert F. Sutherland. 973p. 1988. text ed. write for info. (ISBN 0-02-327030-6). Macmillan.

Problem Solving with Pascal. James F. Peters. 832p. 1986. pap. text ed. 26.95 (ISBN 0-03-069848-0, HoltC). HR&W.

Problem Solving with People: The Cycle Process. Thomas J. Gallagher. LC 87-21583. 130p. (Orig.). 1988. lib. bdg. 21.75 (ISBN 0-8191-6643-X); pap. text ed. 7.95 (ISBN 0-8191-6644-8). U Pr of Amer.

Problem Solving with Structured FORTRAN 77. D. M. Etter. 1984. 28.95 (ISBN 0-8053-2522-0); instr's. manual 5.95 (ISBN 0-8053-2523-9); software supplement with tape 50.00 (ISBN 0-8053-2524-7); supplemext 10.00 (ISBN 0-8053-2526-3). Benjamin-Cummings.

Problem Solving with the Calculator. 2nd ed. Russell F. Jacobs. (Illus.). 160p. 1982. pap. text ed. 5.00 (ISBN 0-918272-08-4); ans. key & tchr's guide 1.50 (ISBN 0-918272-09-2). Jacobs.

Problem Solving with the Computer. Edwin R. Sage. (Illus.). 244p. (Orig.). 1969. pap. 16.95 (ISBN 0-87567-030-X). Entelek.

Problem with Management: Is It a Science or a Lot of Nonsense Taken Seriously? Anselm Z. Villeneuve. (Illus.). 131p. 1988. 55.85 (ISBN 0-86654-259-0). Inst Econ Finan.

Problem with Public Education Is Administrative. James M. Carroll. 70p. 1984. pap. 3.95 (ISBN 0-89826-012-4). Natl Paperback.

Problem with Pulcifer. Florence P. Heide. LC 81-48606. (Illus.). 64p. (gr. 3-6). 1982. 10.70i (ISBN 0-397-32001-9, Lipp Jr Bks); PLB 12.89g (ISBN 0-397-32002-7). HarpJ.

Problem Wounds: The Role of Oxygen. J. C. Davis & T. K. Hunt. 1987. 63.00 (ISBN 0-444-01235-4). Elsevier.

Problem Wounds: The Role of Oxygen. Ed. by J. C. Davis & T. K. Hunt. 340p. 1988. 59.50 (ISBN 0-317-67240-1). Elsevier.

Problema Campesino en Francia y en Alemania. Friedrich Engels. 29p. (Span.). 1979. pap. 1.95 (ISBN 0-8285-1673-1, Pub. by Progress Pubs USSR). Imported Pubns.

Problema de la "Americanizacion" en las Escuelas Catolicas de Puerto Rico. Charles J. Beirne. Tr. by Maria E. Estades De Camara. LC 76-10347. 228p. (Span.). 1976. pap. 5.00 (ISBN 0-8477-2726-2). U of PR Pr.

Problema de la Tierra y la Lucha por la Libertad. V. I. Lenin. 151p. (Span.). 1979. pap. 1.95 (ISBN 0-8285-1399-6, Pub. by Progress Pubs USSR). Imported Pubns.

Problema de Liberalismo. 2nd ed. Francisco Ayala. pap. 4.35 (ISBN 0-8477-2402-6). U of PR Pr.

Problema del Dolor. C. S. Lewis. Tr. by Ernesto S. Vilela from Eng. LC 77-16715. 156p. (Span.). 1977. pap. 3.95 (ISBN 0-89922-097-5). Edit Caribe.

Problema en America: The American Problem, Spanish Text. Jose C. Cuchi. LC 74-14227. (Puerto Rican Experience Ser.). (Illus.). 246p. 1975. Repr. 18.00x (ISBN 0-405-06217-6). Ayer Co Pubs.

Problema Pola. Tigorin. 54p. (Rus.). Repr. of 1908 ed. 9.75 (ISBN 0-935005-90-0). Ibis Pub VA.

Problemas Administrativos del Poder Judicial en Puerto Rico. Nelida M. Amato. pap. 3.75 (ISBN 0-8477-2210-4). U of PR Pr.

Problemas De Actualidad. Foy Valentine. Tr. by Ana M. Swenson. 38p. 1983. Repr. of 1981 ed. 1.50 (ISBN 0-311-46039-9). Casa Bautista.

Problemas de la Cultura en Puerto Rico (Foro Auspiciado por el Ateneo Puertorriqueno En 1940) Ateneo Puertorriqueno. LC 76-10701. 444p. (Orig., Span.). 1976. 10.00 (ISBN 0-8477-2430-1). U of PR Pr.

Problemas de la Filosofia: Textos Filosoficos y Contemporaneos. Ed. by Luis O. Gomez & Roberto Torretti. Tr. by Ramon Castilla et al. 1979. pap. 11.25 (ISBN 0-8477-2812-9). U of PR Pr.

Problemas de la Traduccion: Problems in Translation. LC 77-12171. 1978. pap. 7.00 (ISBN 0-8477-3187-1). U of PR Pr.

Problemas Elementales de Maximo y Minimo y Suma de Cantidades Infintamente Pequenas. I. P. Natanson. 107p. (Span.). 1977. pap. 1.95 (ISBN 0-8285-1690-1, Pub. by Mir Pubs USSR). Imported Pubns.

Problemas Filosoficos de la Ciencia. Alfred Stern. LC 76-22489. (Coleccion Mente y Palabra). (Span.). 1976. 6.25 (ISBN 0-8477-2813-7); pap. 5.00 (ISBN 0-8477-2814-5). U of PR Pr.

Problemas y Experimentos Recreativos. Ya Perelman. 423p. (Span.). 1975. 8.95 (ISBN 0-8285-1698-7, Pub. by Mir Pubs USSR). Imported Pubns.

Problematic Characters. Friedrich Spielhagen. Tr. by S. DeVere from Ger. LC 76-28509. viii, 507p. 1977. Repr. of 1888 ed. 35.00x (ISBN 0-86527-296-4). Fertig.

Problematic Fictions of Poe, James, & Hawthorne. Judith Sutherland. LC 83-16817. 192p. 1984. text ed. 19.00x (ISBN 0-8262-0434-1). U of MO Pr.

Problematic Fossil Taxa. Ed. by Matthew N. Nitecki. Antoni Hoffman. (Illus.). 277p. 1986. 69.00 (ISBN 0-19-503992-0). Oxford U Pr.

Problematic Musculoskeletal Injuries in Children (BIMR Orthopedics, Vol. 1) Gregory R. Houghton & George H. Thompson. 234p. 1983. text ed. 55.00 (ISBN 0-407-02346-1). Butterworth.

Problematic Rebel: Melville, Dostoievsky, Kafka, Camus. rev. ed. Maurice Friedman. LC 72-101360. 1970. pap. 3.95x (ISBN 0-226-26396-7, P358, Phoen). U of Chicago Pr.

Problematic Rebel: Melville, Dostoievsky, Kafka, Camus. rev. ed. Maurice Friedman. LC 72-101360. 1970. 18.00x (ISBN 0-226-26395-9). U of Chicago Pr.

Problematic Science. Ed. by William R. Woodward. LC 81-21080. 410p. 1982. 46.95 (ISBN 0-275-90926-3, C0926). Praeger.

Problematic Self: Approaches to Identity in Stendhal, D.H. Lawrence, & Malraux. Elizabeth B. Tenenbaum. 1978. 15.00x (ISBN 0-674-70769-9). Harvard U Pr.

Problematica Sicologica de los Solteros. Jorge Leon. 144p. (Orig., Span.). 1981. pap. 4.95 (ISBN 0-89922-219-6). Edit Caribe.

Problematique de la Psychologie. Thines. (Phaenomenologica Ser.: No. 29). 1968. lib. bdg. 18.50 (ISBN 90-247-0265-8, Pub. by Martinus Nijhoff Netherlands); pap. 16.00 (ISBN 90-247-0264-X, Pub. by Martinus Nijhoff Netherlands). Kluwer Academic.

Probleme Aus der Physik. H. Vogel. LC 75-15907. (Illus.). 224p. 1975. pap. text ed. 11.70 (ISBN 0-387-07119-9). Springer-Verlag.

Probleme de Dieu dans la Pensee de Karl Barth. Sebastian A. Matczak. (Philosophical Questions Ser.: No. 1). 1968. pap. 19.50 (ISBN 0-912116-00-5). Learned Pubns.

Probleme de la Methode Critique chez Jean le Clerc. Maria C. Pitassi. (Kerkhistorische Bijdragen Ser.: No. 14). 401p. 1987. 32.75 (ISBN 90-04-08091-0, Pub. by E J Brill). Heinman.

Probleme de la Sexualite Chez les Champignons: Recherches sur le Genre Coprinus. A. Quintanilha. (Illus.). 1968. pap. 24.00x (ISBN 3-7682-0556-8). Lubrecht & Cramer.

Probleme de la Valeur-Travail see Cahiers de l'Institut de Science Economique Appliquee.

Probleme der Interventionspolitik am Devisenmarkt unter Besonderer Beruecksichtigung des Europaischen Wahrungssystems. Ursula Sommer-Herberich. (European University Studies: No. 5, Vol. 442). 490p. (Ger.). 1983. 43.15 (ISBN 3-8204-7728-4). P Lang Pubs.

Probleme der Kontrazeption Bei der Jugendlichen. Ed. by A. Huber. 276p. 1981. 58.00 (ISBN 90-219-9450-X, Excerpta Medica). Elsevier.

Probleme der Krebsnachsorge. Ed. by A. Pfleiderer. (Beitraege zur Onkologie: Band 4). (Illus.). 112p. 1980. pap. 22.00 (ISBN 3-8055-1378-X). S Karger.

Probleme des adnominalen Attributs in der deutschen Sprache der Gegenwart. Peter Schaeublin. LC 70-174176. (Studia Linguistica Germanica). 1972. 25.60x (ISBN 3-1100-3346-1). De Gruyter.

Probleme des Subsistances a l'epoque Louis XIV. I: La Production des Cereales dans la France du XVIIe et du XVIIIe Siecle Texte-Notes, 2 pts. Jean Meuvret. (Civilisations et Societes Ser.: No. 50). 1977. pap. 21.60x set (ISBN 0-686-26041-4). Mouton.

Probleme du style. Remy de Gourmont. LC 78-64031. (Des Imagistes: Literature of the Imagist Movement). Repr. of 1907 ed. 27.00 (ISBN 0-404-17109-5). AMS Pr.

Probleme General de la Stabilite du Mouvement. M. A. Liapounoff. (Annals of Math Studies). 1947. 23.00 (ISBN 0-527-02733-2). Kraus Repr.

Probleme National Catalan. Jaume Rossinyol. (Illus.). 1974. pap. 30.40x (ISBN 90-2797-258-3). Mouton.

Probleme Unserer Zeit. Ed. by Edmund P. Kurz & Karl H. Ruhleder. LC 72-130785. (Orig., Ger.). 1971. pap. text ed. 6.95x (ISBN 0-89197-359-1). Irvington.

Problemes aux Limites de la Physique Mathematique. H. G. Garnir. (Mathematische Reihe Ser.: No. 23). (Illus.). 234p. (Fr.). 1958. 36.95x (ISBN 0-8176-0134-1). Birkhauser.

Problemes de Civilisation: Avec: Traite de Depart, Fables de ma Vie, La Medicine au 20e Siecle. Georges Duhamel. 232p. 1961. 9.95 (ISBN 0-686-55191-5). French & Eur.

Problemes de la Guerre a Rome. Jean P. Brisson. (Civilisations et Societes: No. 12). 1969. pap. 14.00x (ISBN 0-686-20921-4). Mouton.

Problemes de la Personne: Colloque du Centre de Recherche de Psychologie Comparative. Ed. by Ignace Meyerson. (Congres de Colloques: No. 13). 1973. pap. 27.60x (ISBN 90-2797-243-5). Mouton.

Problemes de L'Admission du Royaume-Uni au Marche Commun. (Economies et Societes Series R: No. 6). 1962. pap. 19.00 (ISBN 0-8115-0786-6). Kraus Repr.

Problemes de L'Agriculture dans la Croissance Economique see Cahiers de l'Institut de Science Economique Applique.

Problemes de L'Investissement dans les Pays d'Outre-Mer: Algerie, Tunisie, Maroc, Afrique Occidentale et Equatoriale, Sud-Vietnam et Cambodge. (Economies et Societes Series F: No. 16). 1961. pap. 26.00 (ISBN 0-8115-0687-8). Kraus Repr.

Problemes de Socio-Economie Polynesienne see Cahiers de l'Institut de Science Economique Appliquee.

Problemes Economiques de l'Europe Orientale. (Economies et Societes Series G: No. 22). 1965. pap. 34.00 (ISBN 0-8115-0713-0). Kraus Repr.

Problemes Fonciers Chez les Kongo Nord-Quest see Cahiers de l'Institut de Science Economique Appliquee.

Problemes Sociaux de la Population Agricole Francaise see Cahiers de l'Institut de Science Economique Appliquee.

Problemoids: Math Challenge, Grades 5 & 6. Bill McCandliss & Albert Watson. Grade 5. tchr's. manual & solution cards 25.00 (ISBN 0-89824-044-1); student's wkbk. 4.95 (ISBN 0-89824-033-6); student computer suppl. 1.00 (ISBN 0-89824-069-7); tchr's. manual 10.00 (ISBN 0-89824-070-0); Grade 6. tchr's. manual & solution cards 25.00 (ISBN 0-89824-039-5); student's wkbk 4.95 (ISBN 0-89824-071-9); student computer suppl. 1.00; tchr's. manual 10.00 (ISBN 0-89824-072-7). Trillium Pr.

Problems, Bks. 1-21. Aristotle. (Loeb Classical Library: No. 316). 13.95x (ISBN 0-674-99349-7). Harvard U Pr.

Problems & Answers in Navigation & Piloting. 2nd ed. Elbert S. Maloney. 96p. 1985. pap. 4.95 (ISBN 0-87021-150-1). Naval Inst Pr.

Problems & Cases for Decisions in Management. Saul Gellerman. Ed. by Paul S. Donnelly. (Random House Business Division Ser.). 1984. pap. text ed. write for info (ISBN 0-394-33559-7, RanC); write for info. tchr's. ed. (ISBN 0-394-33786-7). Random.

Problems & Cases in Trial Advocacy: Cases, Vol. II. 4th ed. (Continuing Legal Education Edition Ser.). 571p. 1986. cancelled (ISBN 0-318-20424-X). Natl Inst Trial Ad.

Problems & Cases in Trial Advocacy: CLE Ed, 2 vols. 4th ed. (Continuing Legal Education Edition). 1986. 45.00 set (ISBN 1-55681-004-0). Teacher's manual $17.50. Natl Inst Trial Ad.

Problems & Cases in Trial Advocacy: Law School, 2 vols. (Law School Edition Ser.). Set. 34.95 (ISBN 1-55681-050-4). Teacher's manual $15.00. Natl Inst Trial Ad.

Problems & Cases in Trial Advocacy: Volume II (Cases) 4th ed. (Continuing Legal Education Edition). 571p. 1986. 25.00 (ISBN 1-55681-006-7). Natl Inst Trial Ad.

Problems & Cases in Trial Advocacy: Volume I (Problems) 4th ed. (Continuing Legal Education Edition). 1986. 20.00 (ISBN 1-55681-005-9). Natl Inst Trial Ad.

Problems & Concerns of Indian Women. Ed. by B. K. Pal. 243p. 1988. text ed. 27.50x (ISBN 0-89891-024-2). Advent NY.

Problems & Concerns of Indian Women. Ed. by B. K. Pal. 260p. text ed. 27.50x (Pub. by ABC Pub Hse). Advent NY.

Problems & Controversies in Gastroenterology. Ed. by G. Dobrilla et al. 304p. 1986. text ed. 47.00 (ISBN 8-88503-775-5). Raven.

Problems & Controversies in Television & Radio: Basic Readings. Ed. by Harry J. Skornia & Jack W. Kitson. LC 67-20825. 1968. 19.95x (ISBN 0-87015-167-3). Pacific Bks.

Problems & Emotional Difficulties of Negro Children As Studied in Selected Communities & Attributed by Parents - Children to the Fact That They Are Negro. Regina M. Goff. LC 76-476808. (Columbia University. Teachers College. Contributions to Education: No. 960). Repr. of 1949 ed. 22.50 (ISBN 0-404-55960-3). AMS Pr.

Problems & Exercises in Organic Chemistry. A. Agronomov et al. Tr. by MIR Publishers. 400p. 1975. 22.50 (ISBN 0-8464-0756-6). Beekman Pubs.

Problems & Exercises in Organic Chemistry. T. K. Ueselorskaya. 311p. 1979. 8.95 (ISBN 0-8285-1530-1, Pub. by Mir Pubs USSR). Imported Pubns.

Problems & Exercises in Physical Chemistry. E. V. Kiselyova et al. 511p. 1987. 14.95 (ISBN 0-8285-3764-X, Pub. by Mir Pubs USSR). Imported Pubns.

Problems & Instruments of Business Cycle Analysis: A Selection of Papers Presented at the 13th CIRET Conference Proceedings, Munich, Sept 1977. Ed. by W. H. Striegel. (Lecture Notes in Economics & Mathematical System Ser.: Vol. 154). 1978. pap. 25.00 (ISBN 0-387-08664-1). Springer-Verlag.

Problems & Issues in Current Econometric Practice. Econometrics Conferences, Ohio State U., 1967 & 1968. Ed. by Karl Brunner. 1973. 11.00 (ISBN 0-87776-306-2, AA6). Ohio St U Admin Sci.

Problems & Issues in Microeconomics: A Study Guide for the Applied Theory of Price. 2nd ed. Joel D. Scheraga. 294p. 1985. pap. write for info. (ISBN 0-02-378500-4). Macmillan.

Problems & Issues in Social Casework. Scott Briar & Henry Miller. LC 79-170924. 274p. 1971. 27.50x (ISBN 0-231-02771-0). Columbia U Pr.

Problems & Laboratory Experiments in Inorganic Chemistry. N. Akhmetov. 256p. 1982. 8.95 (ISBN 0-8285-2443-2, Pub. by Mir Pubs USSR). Imported Pubns.

Problems & Materials in Business Planning, 1987 Supplement. 2nd ed. William H. Painter. (American Casebook Ser.). 180p. 1987. pap. text ed. 8.95 (ISBN 0-314-35452-2). West Pub.

Problems & Materials in Federal Income Taxation. Sanford M. Guerin & Philip F. Postlewaite. 1056p. 1986. case bk. 33.00 (ISBN 0-316-33081-7). Little.

Problems & Materials in Federal Income Taxation. 2nd ed. Sanford M. Guerin & Philip E. Postlewaite. 1056p. 1988. text ed. 37.00 (ISBN 0-316-33083-3). Little.

Problems & Materials on Commercial Law. Douglas J. Whaley. 1008p. 1986. case bk. 36.00 (ISBN 0-316-93213-2). Little.

Problems & Materials on Commercial Paper. Robert J. Nordstrom & Albert L. Clovis. 458p. 1972. write for info. West Pub.

Problems & Materials on Decedent's Estates & Trusts. 4th ed. Eugene F. Scoles & Edward C. Halbach. 850p. 1987. text ed. 36.00 (ISBN 0-316-77633-5). Little.

Problems and Materials on Future Interests. Edward C. Halbach & Eugene F. Scoles. 1977. pap. text ed. 19.50 (ISBN 0-316-33840-0). Little.

Problems & Materials on Negotiable Instruments. 2nd ed. Douglas J. Whaley. 1988. case bk. 29.00 (ISBN 0-316-93219-1). Little.

Problems & Materials on Professional Responsibility. 3rd ed. Thomas D. Morgan & Ronald D. Rotunda. LC 84-7982. (University Casebook Ser.). 482p. 1984. text ed. 21.50 (ISBN 0-88277-180-9); write for info. tchr's. manual, 279 pp (ISBN 0-88277-209-0). Foundation Pr.

Problems & Materials on Sales. Douglas J. Whaley & Rhonda Rivera. 384p. 1983. 26.00 (ISBN 0-316-93221-3). Little.

Problems & Materials on Secured Transactions. Douglas J. Whaley. LC 81-86024. 1982. text ed. 27.00 (ISBN 0-316-93216-7). Little.

Problems & Methodolgies in Mathematical Software Production, Sorrento, Italy 1980: Proceedings. Ed. by P. C. Messina & A. Murli. (Lecture Notes in Computer Sciences: Vol. 142). 271p. 1982. pap. 15.50 (ISBN 0-387-11603-6). Springer-Verlag.

Problems & Methods for Lithospheric Exploration. Ed. by R. Cassinis. (Ettore Majorana International Science Series, Physical Sciences: Vol. 19). 230p. 1984. 52.50x (ISBN 0-306-41721-9, Plenum Pr). Plenum Pub.

Problems & Methods in Orthopedic Shoe Repairing. Clyde Edwards. (Illus.). 1981. pap. text ed. 4.50 (ISBN 0-931424-07-0). Shoe Serv Inst.

Problems & Methods in the History of Medicine. Roy Porter & Andrew Wear. (Welcome Institute Series in the History of Medicine). 256p. 1987. 52.00 (ISBN 0-7099-3687-7, Pub. by Croom Helm UK). Routledge Chapman & Hall.

Problems & Methods of Literary History. Andre Morize. LC 66-13475. 1922. 15.00 (ISBN 0-8196-0168-3). Biblo.

Problems & Methods of Optimal Structural Design. N. V. Banichuk. LC 83-8103. (Mathematical Concepts & Methods in Science & Engineering Ser.: Vol. 26). (Illus.). 336p. 1983. 49.50x (ISBN 0-306-41284-5, Plenum Pr). Plenum Pub.

Problems & Models in Operations Management. 2nd ed. Richard J. Tersine et al. LC 79-21810. (Management Ser.). 292p. 1984. pap. text ed. 23.50 (ISBN 0-471-84207-9, Pub. by Grid). Wiley.

Problems & Opportunies in Solid Waste Management: A Data Base for New Jersey Decision-Makers. Ed. by Brenda Platt & Neil Seldman. LC 87-3297. 150p. (Orig.). 1987. pap. 50.00 (ISBN 0-917582-43-8). Inst Local Self Re.

Problems & Opportunities in Economic Development. Alan H. Leader. (Illus.). 1977. pap. text ed. 2.95 (ISBN 0-932826-11-3). New Issues MI.

Problems & Opportunities in U. S.-Quebec Relations. Ed. by Alfred O. Hero, Jr. & Marcel Daneau. 250p. 1984. 34.00x (ISBN 0-86531-634-1). Westview.

Problems & Other Stories. John Updike. 288p. 1985. pap. 3.50 (ISBN 0-449-21103-7, Crest). Fawcett.

Problems & Other Stories. John Updike. LC 79-1480. (Illus.). 1979. 14.45 (ISBN 0-394-50705-3); signed ed. o.p. 27.50 (ISBN 0-394-50709-6). Knopf.

Problems & Persons. facs. ed. Wilfrid P. Ward. LC 68-29254. (Essay Index Reprint Ser.). 1903. 19.00 (ISBN 0-8369-0097-9). Ayer Co Pubs.

Problems & Perspectives: A Collection of Essays on German Baroque Literature. Blake L. Spahr. (European University Studies: Series 1, German Language & Literature: Vol. 423). 286p. 1981. pap. 37.55 (ISBN 3-8204-7084-0). P Lang Pubs.

Problems & Perspectives of Fundamental Theology. Ed. by Rene Latourelle & Gerald O'Collins. 416p. 1982. pap. 12.95 (ISBN 0-8091-2466-1). Paulist Pr.

Problems & Perspectives of Watering the Crops. B. L. Sharma. 1987. 21.00 (ISBN 81-7022-191-9, Pub. by Concept India). South Asia Bks.

Problems & Planning in Third World Cities. Ed. by Michael Pacione. 1981. 30.00 (ISBN 0-312-64737-9). St Martin.

Problems & Policies in Small Economies. Bimal Jalan. LC 81-21291. 1982. 30.00 (ISBN 0-312-64741-7). St Martin.

Problems & Policies of Malesherbes As Directeur de la Librarie in France, 1750-1763. Edward P. Shaw. LC 66-63787. 164p. 1966. 49.50x (ISBN 0-87395-018-6). State U NY Pr.

Problems & Possibilities for Religious Education. Edwin Cox. (Studies in Teaching & Learning). 152p. (Orig.). 1983. pap. text ed. 16.95 (ISBN 0-340-28433-1). Princeton Bk Co.

Problems & Potential of Branched Chain Amino Acids in Physiology & Medicine. R. Odessey. 356p. 1986. 152.00 (ISBN 0-444-80775-6). Elsevier.

Problems & Practices in Advertising Research: Readings & Workbook. Alan D. Fletcher & Donald W. Jugenheimer. (Advertising & Journalism Ser.). 210p. 1982. pap. text ed. 16.95 (ISBN 0-88244-237-6, Pub. by Grid). Wiley.

Problems & Programmes Related to Alcohol & Drug Dependence in 33 Countries. J. Moser. (Offset Pub.: No. 6). (Also avail. in French). 1974. pap. 8.00 (ISBN 92-4-170006-8). World Health.

Problems & Projects. Nelson Goodman. LC 73-165221. 478p. 1973. 19.50 (ISBN 0-915144-37-9); pap. text ed. 9.95 (ISBN 0-915144-36-0). Hackett Pub.

Problems & Propositions in Analysis. Klambauer. (Lecture Notes in Pure & Applied Mathematics Ser.: Vol. 49). 1979. 45.00 (ISBN 0-8247-6887-6). Dekker.

Problems & Prospects for U. S. Agriculture in World Markets. Timothy Josling. LC 81-83300. (Committee on Changing International Realities Ser.). 68p. 1981. 6.00 (ISBN 0-89068-057-4). Natl Planning.

Problems & Prospects in Continuing Professional Education. Ed. by Ronald M. Cervero & Craig L. Scanlan. LC 85-60828. (Continuing Education Ser.: No. 27). (Orig.). 1985. pap. text ed. 12.95x (ISBN 0-87589-745-2). Jossey-Bass.

Problems & Prospects in Long & Medium Range Weather Forecasting. Ed. by D. M. Burridge & E. Kallen. (Topics in Atmospheric & Oceanographic Sciences Ser.). (Illus.). 290p. 1984. pap. 24.80 (ISBN 0-387-12827-1). Springer-Verlag.

Problems & Prospects in the Study of Learning Disabilities see Review of Child Development Research.

Problems & Prospects of Economic Integration in West Africa. Nicholas G. Plessz. (Keith Callard Lectures Ser.). 1968. 19.95c (ISBN 0-7735-0045-6). McGill-Queens U Pr.

Problems & Prospects of Presidential Leadership in the Nineteen-Eighties, Vol. I. Ed. by James S. Young. LC 82-19981. (Problems & Prospects of the Presidency). (Illus.). 136p. (Orig.). 1982. lib. bdg. 23.00 (ISBN 0-8191-2837-6); pap. text ed. 7.75 (ISBN 0-8191-2838-4). U Pr of Amer.

Problems & Prospects of Presidential Leadership in the Nineteen Eighties, Vol. II. Ed. by James S. Young. (Problems & Prospects of the Presidency Ser.). 92p. (Orig.). 1983. lib. bdg. 22.00 (ISBN 0-8191-2907-0, Pub. by White Miller Center); pap. text ed. 7.25 (ISBN 0-8191-2908-9). U Pr of Amer.

Problems & Prospects of Presidential Leadership in the Nineteen Eighties, Vol. III. Ed. by James S. Young. LC 82-19981. (Problems & Prospects of the Presidency Ser.). 114p. (Orig.). 1984. lib. bdg. 20.50 (ISBN 0-8191-2909-7, Co-pub. by White Burkett Miller Center); pap. text ed. 7.25 (ISBN 0-8191-2910-0). U Pr of Amer.

Problems & Prospects of the Organization of American States: Perceptions of the Member States' Leaders. Henry H. Han. (American University Studies X: Political Science: Vol. 10). 548p. 1987. text ed. 63.50 (ISBN 0-8204-0508-6). P Lang Pubs.

Problems & Prospects: Papers on Presidential Transitions in Foreign Policy, Vol. II. Ed. by Kenneth W. Thompson. 156p. (Orig.). 1986. lib. bdg. 23.75 (ISBN 0-8191-4863-6, Co-Pub. by White Miller Center); pap. text ed. 11.50 (ISBN 0-8191-4864-4, Co-Pub. by White Miller Center). U Pr of Amer.

Problems & Recommendations in Disciplinary Enforcement: "The Clark Report". Center for Professional Responsibility Staff. 193p. 1970. 14.95. Amer Bar Assn.

Problems & Roles of the American Artist As Portrayed by the American Novelist. T. Tanner. (Sarah Tryphena Phillips Lectures in American Literature & History). 1971. pap. 5.50 (ISBN 0-902732-09-9, Pub. by British Acad). Longwood Pub Group.

Problems & Solutions for Proprietors & Partnerships Business. rev. & abr. ed. Luanna C. Blagrove. (AMERCE Business Ser.). (Illus.). 250p. 1988. 24.95 (ISBN 0-939776-12-X). Blagrove Pubns.

Problems & Solutions in Advanced Accountancy, Vol. 1. S. N. Maheshwari. 1988. text ed. 50.00x (ISBN 0-7069-3420-2, Pub. by Vikas Pub Hse India). Advent NY.

Problems & Solutions in Economic Theory. K. A. Lawler & H. A. Seddighi. 1986. 90.00x (ISBN 0-317-61989-6, Peter Andrew Pubs). State Mutual Bk.

Problems & Solutions in Electromagnetic Theory. C. M. Lerner. LC 83-6548. 800p. 1985. pap. 34.95X (ISBN 0-471-88678-5, Pub. by Wiley-Interscience). Wiley.

Problems & Solutions in Introductory Accounting. Sanford R. Kahn & Joseph A. Burnett. 224p. 1978. pap. text ed. 17.95 shrink wrap (ISBN 0-8403-3266-1, 40326602). Kendall-Hunt.

Problems & Solutions in Logic Design. 2nd ed. D. Zissos. (Illus.). 1979. 38.95x (ISBN 0-19-859362-7). Oxford U Pr.

Problems & Solutions in Quantum Chemistry & Physics. Charles S. Johnson, Jr. & Lee G. Pedersen. xviii, 430p. 1986. pap. text ed. 10.95 (ISBN 0-486-65236-X). Dover.

Problems & Solutions in Theoretical Statistics. D. R. Cox. 1978. pap. 18.95 (ISBN 0-412-15370-X, NO. 6066, Pub. by Chapman & Hall). Routledge Chapman & Hall.

Problems & Solutions to Accompany Quellette's Introduction to General, Organic, & Biological Chemistry. Wendy W. Sonntag & Claire Rothenbuhler. 304p. 1984. pap. write for info. (ISBN 0-02-413780-4). Macmillan.

Problems & Teaching Strategies in ESL Composition. Ann Raimes. (Language in Education Ser.: No. 14). 24p. 1979. pap. 3.67x (ISBN 0-13-711987-9, Dist. by P-H). Ctr Appl Ling.

Problems & Their Solutions in Organic Chemistry. Ivor L. Finar. LC 73-166074. pap. 92.30 (ISBN 0-317-09079-8, 2010050). Bks Demand UMI.

Problems & Theorems in Analysis I: Series, Integral Calculus, Theory of Functions. G. Polya & G. Szego. (Illus.). 1970. pap. 26.00 (ISBN 0-387-90224-4). Springer-Verlag.

Problems & Theorems in Analysis I: Series, Integral Calculus, Theory of Functions. G. Polya & G. Szegoe. (Grundlehren der Mathematischen Wissenschaften: Vol. 193). 1978. 70.00 (ISBN 0-387-05672-6). Springer-Verlag.

Problems & Theorems in Analysis II: Theory of Functions, Zeros, Polynomials, Determinants, Number Theory, Geometry. G. Polya & G. Szego. Tr. by C. E. Billigheimer. (Illus.). 1977. pap. text ed. 29.50 (ISBN 0-387-90291-0). Springer-Verlag.

Problems & Theories of Philosophy. K. Ajdukiewicz. Tr. by A. Quinton & H. Skolimowski. LC 72-97878. 160p. 1973. pap. 7.95 (ISBN 0-521-09993-5). Cambridge U Pr.

Problems Are for Solving. Carroll V. Newsom. LC 83-90791. 416p. 1983. 15.95 (ISBN 0-8059-2877-4). Dorrance.

Problems Are the Doors Through Which We Walk to Peace. Stephen R. Schwartz. 117p. 1987. 12.00 (ISBN 0-936415-04-5). Riverrun Piermont.

Problems Associated with Export of Nuclear Power Plants. (Proceedings Ser.). (Illus.). 484p. 1979. pap. 51.25 (ISBN 92-0-020178-4, ISP488, IAEA). UNIPUB.

Problems, Bks 22-38. Aristotle. Bd. with Rhetorica ad Alexandrum. (Loeb Classical Library: No. 317). 13.95x (ISBN 0-674-99350-0). Harvard U Pr.

Problems Book: Engineering Drawing & Graphic Technology. 13th ed. Hartley Rogers. (Illus.). 256p. 1986. pap. text ed. 16.95 (ISBN 0-07-053491-8). McGraw.

Problems, Cases & Materials on Evidence. Eric D. Green & Charles R. Nessen. 1983. text ed. 35.00 (ISBN 0-316-32646-1). Little.

Problems Concerning the Origin & Early Development of the Etruscan Orientalizing Style, 2 vols. (Odense Classical Studies: No. 2). 404p. (Orig.). 1971. Set. pap. 44.50x (ISBN 87-7492-033-2, Pub. by Odense Universitets Forlag (Odense Denmark)). Coronet Bks.

Problems Confronting the Investigator of Gullah see Oil Refinery Terms in Oklahoma.

Problems Faced by Da'wah & Da'iyah. F. Yakal. 1988. 7.95. Kazi Pubns.

Problems for General Chemistry & Qualitative Analysis. 4th ed. C. J. Nyman et al. LC 79-24489. 342p. 1980. pap. text ed. write for info. (ISBN 0-471-05299-X). Wiley.

Problems for Inorganic Chemistry. 3rd ed. Bodie E. Douglas et al. 298p. 1983. pap. 15.95 (ISBN 0-471-89505-9). Wiley.

Problems for Molecular Biology: With Answers & Solutions. David Freifelder. 299p. 1983. pap. text ed. 12.50 (ISBN 0-86720-013-8). Jones & Bartlett.

Problems for Musical Acoustics. William R. Savage. 1977. pap. text ed. 7.95x (ISBN 0-19-502251-3). Oxford U Pr.

Problems for Physics Students: With Hints & Answers. K. F. Riley. LC 82-4575. 100p. 1982. 29.95 (ISBN 0-521-24921-X); pap. 17.95 (ISBN 0-521-27073-1). Cambridge U Pr.

Problems from Locke. J. L. Mackie. (Illus.). 1976. text ed. 32.00x (ISBN 0-19-824555-6); pap. text ed. 14.95x (ISBN 0-19-875036-6). Oxford U Pr.

Problems, Functions & Semantic Roles: A Pragmatists' Analysis of Montague's Theory of Sentence Meaning. E. M. Barth & R. T. Wiche. (Foundations of Communication Ser.). xviii, 198p. 1986. lib. bdg. 57.25 (ISBN 3-11-009861-X). De Gruyter.

Problems in a New Medium: Autobiographies by Three Artists. Catherine C. Fraser. LC 84-47906. (American University Studies I (Germanic Languages & Literature): Vol. 33). 150p. 1984. text ed. 19.00 (ISBN 0-8204-0160-9). P Lang Pubs.

Problems in Administrative Reform. Ed. by Robert D. Miewald & Michael Steinman. LC 83-15399. (Illus.). 280p. 1984. 27.95x (ISBN 0-88229-747-3). Nelson-Hall.

Problems in Advanced Organic Chemistry. J. March. LC 70-176119. Repr. of 1971 ed. 81.90 (ISBN 0-8357-9093-2, 2055049). Bks Demand UMI.

Problems in Advanced Organic Chemistry. Jerry March. LC 70-176119. pap. 112.10 (2030860). Bks Demand UMI.

Problems in Aesthetic Surgery: Biological Causes & Clinical Solutions. Rudolph. 1986. 80.00 (ISBN 0-8016-4245-0). Mosby.

Problems in American Social Policy Research. Ed. by Clark C. Abt. LC 79-55772. (Illus.). 1980. text ed. 29.50 (ISBN 0-89011-540-0). Abt Bks.

Problems in American Social Policy Research. Ed. by Clark C. Abt. 300p. 1984. Repr. of 1980 ed. lib. bdg. 31.00 (ISBN 0-8191-4108-9). U Pr of Amer.

Problems in Analysis. B. R. Gelbaum. (Problem Books in Mathematics). (Illus.). 224p. 1982. 39.00 (ISBN 0-387-90692-4). Springer-Verlag.

Problems in Analysis: A Symposium in Honor of Salomon Bochner. R. C. Gunning. (Mathematical Series, No. 31). 1970. 46.00 (ISBN 0-691-08076-3). Princeton U Pr.

Problems in Analytic Geometry. D. Kletenik. Tr. by MIR Publishers. (Illus.). 298p. 1975. text ed. 19.95 (ISBN 0-8464-0757-4). Beekman Pubs.

Problems in Ancient History, Vol.1. 2nd ed. D. Kagan. 1975. pap. write for info. (ISBN 0-02-361820-5). Macmillan.

Problems in Ancient History, Vol. 2. 2nd ed. Donald Kagan. (Illus.). 464p. 1975. pap. text ed. write for info. (ISBN 0-02-361830-2). Macmillan.

Problems in Anesthesia. Ed. by Robert R. Kirby & David L. Brown. 1988. 55.00 (Lippincott Medical). Lippincott.

Problems in Anesthesia: A Case Study Approach. Mark B. Ravin. 1981. pap. text ed. 17.50 (ISBN 0-316-73461-6). Little.

Problems in Applied Educational Sociolinguistics: Readings on Language & Culture Problems of United States Ethnic Groups. Ed. by Glenn G. Gilbert & Jacob Ornstein. (Janua Linguarum, Series Minor: No. 162). 1978. pap. text ed. 13.40x (ISBN 90-279-7726-7). Mouton.

Problems in Applied Hydrology. E. F. Schulz. 1974. 25.00. WRP.

Problems in Applied Thermodynamics. Colin Bodsworth & A. S. Appleton. LC 66-78638. pap. 55.80 (ISBN 0-317-08450-X, 2003636). Bks Demand UMI.

Problems in Argument Analysis & Evaluation. T. Govier. vii, 303p. 1987. pap. write for info. (ISBN 90-6765-341-1). Foris Pubns.

Problems in Biochemistry. Michael E. Friedman & Paul Melius. 220p. (Orig.). 1984. pap. text ed. 16.95x (ISBN 0-89892-056-6). Contemp Pub Co of Raleigh.

Problems in Biology. Carol Knox & Katheryn Rowsey. (Illus.). 90p. (Orig.). (gr. 10-11). 1980. lab manual 4.95x (ISBN 0-88334-132-8). Ind Sch Pr.

Problems in Breast Pathology. John G. Azzopardi. (Major Problems in Pathology Ser.: Vol. 11). (Illus.). 466p. 1979. 70.00 (ISBN 0-7216-1463-9). Saunders.

Problems in Calculus & Related Topics. Colin R. Jones. LC 66-3023. pap. 50.00 (ISBN 0-317-09413-0, 2019396). Bks Demand UMI.

Problems in Chemical Kinetics. Ed. by N. Emanual. 223p. 1981. pap. 7.00 (ISBN 0-8285-2076-3, Pub. by Mir Pubs USSR). Imported Pubns.

Problems in Chemistry. 2nd ed. Daley & O'Malley. 504p. 1988. 39.50 (ISBN 0-8247-7826-X). Dekker.

Problems in Class Analysis. Guglielmo Carchedi. 300p. (Orig.). 1983. pap. 14.95x (ISBN 0-7100-9426-4). Routledge Chapman & Hall.

Problems in Combinatorics & Graph Theory. I. Tomescu & R. A. Melter. LC 84-21701. (Discrete Mathematics Ser.). 335p. 1985. 36.95 (ISBN 0-471-80155-0). Wiley.

Problems in Community Wastes Management. H. M. Ellis et al. (Public Health Papers Ser: No. 38). 89p. 1969. pap. 2.80 (ISBN 92-4-130038-8, 1352). World Health.

Problems in Conducting. rev. ed. Daniel Moe. 1968. pap. 4.50 (ISBN 0-8066-0834-X, 11-9369). Augsburg.

Problems in Constitutional Law: A Symposium. K. E. Vanlandingham et al. LC 70-152835. (Symposia on Law & Society Ser). 1971. Repr. of 1968 ed. lib. bdg. 25.00 (ISBN 0-306-70148-0). Da Capo.

Problems in Continuing Education. Jerold W. Apps. 1979. text ed. 25.95 (ISBN 0-07-002159-7). McGraw.

Problems in Contract Law: Cases & Materials. 2nd ed. Charles L. Knapp & Nathan M. Crystal. 1232p. 1987. text ed. 37.00 (ISBN 0-316-49926-9). Little.

Problems in Criminal Procedure. 2nd ed. Joseph D. Grano. LC 81-7577. (American Casebook Ser.). 176p. 1981. pap. text ed. 10.95 (ISBN 0-314-59979-7); pap. text ed. tchr's. manual avail. (ISBN 0-314-79133-7). West Pub.

Problems in Crystal Physics with Solutions. N. V. Perelomova & M. M. Tagieva. 336p. 1983. 42.00x (ISBN 0-317-46691-7, Pub. by Collets (UK)). State Mutual Bk.

Problems in Crystal Physics with Solutions. N. V. Perelomova & M. M. Tagieva. 336p. 1983. 8.95 (ISBN 0-8285-2613-3, Pub. by Mir Pubs USSR). Imported Pubns.

Problems in Descriptive Geometry, Bk. 2. Joseph A. Bennett. pap. 20.00 (ISBN 0-317-08629-4, 2007319). Bks Demand UMI.

Problems in Developing Academic Library Collections. Jasper G. Schad & Norman E. Tanis. LC 72-1944. (Bowker Series in Problem-Centered Approaches to Librarianship). pap. 51.80 (ISBN 0-317-19841-6, 2023053). Bks Demand UMI.

Problems in Diagnosis & Management of Polycystic Kidney Disease: Proceedings of the First International Workshop on PKD. Ed. by Jared J. Grantham & Kenneth D. Gardner, Jr. (Illus.). 216p. 1985. 14.95 (ISBN 0-9614567-0-1). PKR Foundation.

Problems in Differential Geometry & Topology. A. S. Mischenko et al. 207p. 1985. 6.95 (ISBN 0-317-47666-1, Pub. by Mir Pubs USSR). Imported Pubns.

Problems in Diplomatic History, Vol. II. Daniel M. Smith. LC 63-22521. 677p. 1964. pap. text ed. 10.00 (ISBN 0-669-23077-4). Heath.

Problems in Distributions & Partial Differnetial Equations. C. Zuily. (Mathematical Studies: No. 143). 248p. 1988. 79.00 (ISBN 0-444-70248-2, North Holland). Elsevier.

Problems in Early Irish & Welsh Literature. Kuno Meyer. 1988. pap. 10.00 (ISBN 0-89979-048-8). British Am Bks.

Problems in Electrodynamics. 2nd ed. V. V. Batygin & I. N. Toptygin. 1978. 61.00 (ISBN 0-12-082160-5). Acad Pr.

Problems in Electronics. J. Auvray & M. Fourrier. LC 73-7617. 444p. 1974. pap. text ed. 23.00 (ISBN 0-08-017871-5). Pergamon.

Problems in Electronics with Solutions. 5th ed. F. A. Benson. 1976. pap. 14.95x (ISBN 0-412-14770-X, NO. 6036, Pub. by Chapman & Hall). Routledge Chapman & Hall.

Problems in Engineering. T. C. Hartley & D. C. O'Bryant. (Graphics Ser.: No. 31). 1975. pap. 8.80x (ISBN 0-87563-109-6). Stipes.

Problems in Engineering Drawing & Geometry, Series 12, 13, 15, 16, 21. J. S. Dobrovolny et al. 1964. pap. 7.80x ea. Stipes.

Problems in Engineering Drawing, Series A, B, C, D, & E. Randolph P. Hoelscher et al. pap. 8.80x ea. Stipes.

Problems in Engineering Drawing Workbook with an Introduction to Interactive Computer. 9th ed. Warren J. Luzadder & Kenneth E. Botkin. (Graphics for Design & Production Ser.: Vol. 1). (Illus.). xvi, 160p. 1986. pap. text ed. write for info. (ISBN 0-13-716366-5). P-H.

Problems in Engineering Geometry, Nos. 1 & 2. Randolph P. Hoelscher et al. pap. 8.80x ea. Stipes.

Problems in Engineering Graphics. Carl A. Arnbal & Joe V. Crawford. 208p. 1982. pap. text ed. 16.95 (ISBN 0-8403-2646-7). Kendall-Hunt.

Problems in Engineering Graphics. D. C. O'Bryant et al. (Engineering Graphics Ser.: Vol. 87). 90p. 1987. wkbk. 11.80 (ISBN 0-87563-292-0). Stipes.

Problems in Engineering Graphics & Design. Andre M. Skaff. 208p. 1983. pap. 15.50 (ISBN 0-8403-3748-5). Kendall-Hunt.

Problems in Engineering Graphics Fundamentals. James A. Leach. (Ser. A). (Illus.). 50p. 1984. pap. text ed. 9.95x (ISBN 0-89892-055-8). Contemp Pub Co of Raleigh.

Problems in Engineering Graphics Fundamentals: Series B. James A. Leach. (Illus.). 46p. 1985. pap. text ed. 9.95x (ISBN 0-89892-058-2). Contemp Pub Co of Raleigh.

Problems in Engineering Soils. 3rd ed. P. L. Capper et al. 1980. 14.95x (ISBN 0-419-11840-3, NO. 2966, Pub. by E & FN Spon). Routledge Chapman & Hall.

Problems in Eugenics: Papers Communicated to the First International Congress. First International Congress of Eugenics & Charles Rosenberg. LC 83-48620. (History of Hereditarian Thought Ser.). 679p. 1985. lib. bdg. 80.00 (ISBN 0-8240-5806-2). Garland Pub.

Problems in Evidence. 3rd ed. Kenneth S. Broun et al. (American Casebook Ser.). 420p. 1988. pap. text ed. write for info. (ISBN 0-314-42363-X); tchr's. manual avail. (ISBN 0-314-46936-2). West Pub.

Problems in Form & Function. Ann Borkin. Ed. by John R. Ross & George Lakoff. LC 82-11417. (Language & Being Ser.). 192p. 1984. 35.00 (ISBN 0-89391-116-X). Ablex Pub.

Problems in Gaba Research from Brain to Bacteria. Ed. by Okada. (International Congress Ser.: Vol. 565). 444p. 1982. 173.25 (ISBN 0-444-90236-8, Excerpta Medica). Elsevier.

Problems in General Chemistry. N. Glinka. 256p. 1973. 22.00 (ISBN 0-8464-1121-0). Beekman Pubs.

Problems in General Linguistics. Emile Benveniste. (Miami Linguistic Ser.: No. 8). 317p. 1973. 17.95 (ISBN 0-87024-310-1). U of Miami Pr.

Problems in General Physics. V. S. Wolkenstein. Tr. by MIR Publishers. (Illus.). 360p. 1975. text ed. 22.00 (ISBN 0-8464-0759-0). Beekman Pubs.

Problems in General Physics. V. S. Wolkenstein. 349p. 1975. 9.45 (ISBN 0-8285-1957-9, Pub. by Mir Pubs USSR). Imported Pubns.

Problems In General Surgery. Ed. by Jack Pickleman. LC 81-22702. (Reviewing Surgical Topics Ser.). 382p. 1982. 55.00x (ISBN 0-306-40765-5, Plenum Med Bk). Plenum Pub.

TITLE INDEX PROBLEMS, ISSUES & CONCEPTS

Problems in Geometry. M. Berger et al. (Problem Books in Mathematics). (Illus.). 184p. 1984. 36.00 (ISBN 0-387-90971-0). Springer-Verlag.
Problems in Geometry for Architects, 2 pts. W. L. Schick et al. pap. 7.80x ea. Stipes.
Problems in German Literary History of the Fifteenth & Sixteenth Centuries. Archer Taylor. (MLA GS). 1939. 21.00 (ISBN 0-527-89056-1). Kraus Repr.
Problems in Greek History. J. P. Mahaffy. 240p. Repr. of 1892 ed. lib. bdg. 75.00 (ISBN 0-89984-759-5). Century Bookbindery.
Problems in Group Theory. John D. Dixon. LC 72-76597. 1973. pap. 4.95 (ISBN 0-486-61574-X). Dover.
Problems in Gynaecology. E. P. Tatford. (Problems in Practice Ser.). 1986. lib. bdg. 70.25 (ISBN 0-85200-278-5, Pub. by MTP Pr England). Kluwer Academic.
Problems in Head & Neck Surgery. O. H. Shaheen. (Illus.). 210p. 1984. 52.00 (ISBN 0-7216-0966-X, Bailliere-Tindall). Saunders.
Problems in Historical Epistemology. Jerzy Kmita. 1988. lib. bdg. 69.00 (ISBN 90-277-2199-8, Pub. by Reidel Holland). Kluwer Academic.
Problems in Hospital Law. 5th ed. Robert D. Miller. LC 86-1160. 366p. 1986. 34.95 (ISBN 0-87189-353-3). Aspen Pub.
Problems in Human Assessment. Douglas H. Jackson & Samuel Messick. LC 77-8209. (Illus.). 890p. 1978. Repr. of 1967 ed. 48.50 (ISBN 0-88275-567-6). Krieger.
Problems in Human Biology: A Study of Brazilian Populations. Francisco M. Salzano & Newton Freire-Maia. LC 76-83524. 203p. 1970. text ed. 22.50x (ISBN 0-8143-1397-3). Wayne St U Pr.
Problems in Implementing Statutory Requirements for Title One ESEA Parent Advisory Councils. Linda Brown. (IRE Reports: No. 2). 1981. pap. 2.50 (ISBN 0-317-00495-6). Inst Responsive.
Problems in Inorganic & Structural Chemistry. T. C. Mak et al. 284p. 1982. pap. text ed. 27.50x (ISBN 962-201-253-1, Pub. by Chinese U HK). Coronet Bks.
Problems in Inorganic Chemistry. B. J. Aylett & B. C. Smith. LC 66-18189. pap. 40.00 (ISBN 0-317-09068-2, 2007643). Bks Demand UMI.
Problems in Intellectual Freedom & Censorship. Arthur J. Anderson. LC 74-4107. (Bowker Series in Problem-Centered Approaches to Librarianship). pap. 54.80 (ISBN 0-317-19839-4, 2023054). Bks Demand UMI.
Problems in Interdisciplinary Studies. Ed. by Ray Jurkovich & Jean H. Paelinck. LC 84-13833. (Issues in Interdisciplinary Studies: No. 2). 196p. 1984. text ed. 39.00x (ISBN 0-566-00689-8). Gower Pub Co.
Problems in International Comparative Research in the Social Sciences. Jan Berting et al. 186p. 1979. 44.00 (ISBN 0-08-025247-8). Pergamon.
Problems in Intrahepatic Cholestasis. International Symposium on Intrahepatic Cholestasis, 2nd, Florence, October 13-14, 1978. Ed. by P. Gentilini et al. (Illus.). 1979. 77.50 (ISBN 3-8055-3009-9). S Karger.
Problems in Introductory Accounting. Sanford R. Kahn et al. 224p. 1978. 15.95 (ISBN 0-8403-1957-6). Kendall-Hunt.
Problems in Labor Relations. Herman Feldman. LC 78-89732. (American Labor, from Conspiracy to Collective Bargaining Ser., no. 1). 353p. 1969. Repr. of 1937 ed. 20.00 (ISBN 0-405-02120-8). Ayer Co Pubs.
Problems in Legal Ethics. 2nd ed. Mortimer D. Schwartz & Richard C. Wydick. (American Casebook Ser.). 330p. 1988. text ed. 18.95 (ISBN 0-314-65743-6); write for info. tchr's manual (ISBN 0-314-42957-3). West Pub.
Problems in Library Management. K. Umapathy Setty. 1976. 10.50 (ISBN 0-7069-0439-7). Intl Bk Dist.
Problems in Library Management. 2nd, rev. ed. K. S. Umapathy. 140p. 1983. text ed. 15.95x (ISBN 0-7069-2490-8, Pub. by Vikas India); (Pub. by Vikas India). Advent NY.
Problems in Library Supervision. Ellen Altman & Kenneth Plate. (Libraries & Information Sciences Ser.). Date not set. price not set (ISBN 0-89391-111-9). Ablex Pub.
Problems in Linear Algebra. A. Proskuryakov. 384p. 1978. 8.95 (ISBN 0-8285-0740-6, Pub. by Mir Pubs USSR). Imported Pubns.
Problems in Linear & Non-Linear Programming. S. Vajda. (Charles Griffin Bk.). 259p. 29.95 (ISBN 0-19-520590-1). Oxford U Pr.
Problems in Linear & Non-Linear Programming. Steven Vajda. LC 74-2565. 1974. 18.50x (ISBN 0-02-854070-0). Hafner.
Problems in Literary Research: A Guide to Selected Reference Works. 2nd rev. & enl. ed. Dorothea Kehler. LC 81-8825. 196p. 1981. 16.50 (ISBN 0-8108-1452-8); instr's. index avail. (ISBN 0-8108-1453-6). Scarecrow.
Problems in Literary Research: A Guide to Select Reference Works. 3rd ed. Dorthea Kehler. LC 86-31626. 237p. 1987. 20.00 (ISBN 0-8108-1978-3). Scarecrow.
Problems in Literary Research: Instructor's Index & Solutions to the Research Problems. 3rd ed. Dorothea Kehler. LC 86-31626. 62p. 1987. pap. text ed. write for info (ISBN 0-8108-1979-1). Scarecrow.
Problems in Management of Locally Abundant Wild Mammals. Ed. by Peter A. Jewell. 1982. 39.50 (ISBN 0-12-385280-3). Acad Pr.
Problems in Marketing. 6th ed. Corey E. Raymond et al. (Marketing Ser.). (Illus.). 832p. 1981. text ed. 41.95 (ISBN 0-07-013141-4). McGraw.
Problems in Marketing Management. Jack Z. Sissors. (Illus.). 64p. 1984. write for info. wkbk. (ISBN 0-13-717611-2). P-H.
Problems in Material Science. Harish D. Merchant. 486p. 1972. 167.00 (ISBN 0-677-13450-9). Gordon & Breach.
Problems in Mathematical Analysis. Ed. by B. Demidovich. (Russian Monographs). 496p. 1969. 135.00 (ISBN 0-677-20840-5). Gordon & Breach.
Problems in Mathematical Analysis. Ed. by Boris Demidovich. Tr. by MIR Publishers. 496p. 1975. text ed. 24.95 (ISBN 0-8464-0761-2). Beekman Pubs.
Problems in Measuring Change: Proceedings of a Conference Sponsored by the Committee on Personality Development in Youth of the Social Science Research Council, 1962. Ed. by Chester W. Harris. LC 63-19211. pap. 67.30 (ISBN 0-317-10541-8, 2004972). Bks Demand UMI.
Problems in Mechanical Drawing. 6th ed. A. S. Levens & S. J. Cooper. (Illus.). 224p. 1985. write for info. (ISBN 0-07-022334-3). McGraw.
Problems in Mechanical Drawing. 4th ed. A. S. Levens & A. E. Edstrom. 1974. text ed. 23.16 (ISBN 0-07-037349-3). McGraw.
Problems in Metallurgical Thermodynamics & Kinetics. G S Upadhyaya & R. K. Dube. LC 77-7376. 1977. pap. text ed. 27.00 (ISBN 0-08-020864-9). Pergamon.
Problems in Microeconomics. Marcia L. Stigum. 1975. pap. 19.95 (ISBN 0-256-01734-4). Irwin.
Problems in Modern Physics. W. Smith. 190p. 1970. 55.00 (ISBN 0-677-02850-4). Gordon & Breach.
Problems in Molecular Structure. Ed. by G. J. Bullen & D. J. Greenslade. (Illus.). 466p. 1983. 32.00 (ISBN 0-85086-083-0, NO. 8007, Pub. by Pion). Routledge Chapman & Hall.
Problems in National Literary Identity & the Writer As Social Critic: Selected Papers of the Fourth Annual NDEA Seminar on Foreign Area Studies, Columbia University, February 28-29, 1980. Ed. by Anne Paolucci. 72p. pap. 6.95 (ISBN 0-918680-11-5). Griffon Hse.
Problems in Neolithic Archaeology. Alasdair Whittle. (Illus.). 235p. Date not set. price not set (ISBN 0-521-35121-9). Cambridge U Pr.
Problems in Nutrition Research Today. H. Aebi et al. LC 81-66375. 1981. 51.00 (ISBN 0-12-044420-8). Acad Pr.
Problems in Optics. M. Rousseau & Jean P. Mathieu. 376p. 1973. text ed. 50.00 (ISBN 0-08-016980-5). Pergamon.
Problems in Organic Chemistry: A Lead-Oriented Approach. David E. Horn & Michael J. Strauss. LC 85-12476. 208p. 1986. pap. text ed. write for info. (ISBN 0-471-81649-3). Wiley.
Problems in Organic Reaction Mechanisms. Fredric M. Menger. LC 68-28060. (Appleton-Century-Crofts Series in Chemistry). pap. 32.00 (ISBN 0-317-26294-7, 2055691). Bks Demand UMI.
Problems in Organotransition Metal Chemistry. Susan Kegley & Alan R. Pinhas. (Illus.). 323p. (Orig.). 1986. pap. text ed. 20.00x (ISBN 0-935702-23-7). Univ Sci Bks.
Problems in Otolaryngology. P. Ratnesar. (Problems in Practice Ser.). 1984. lib. bdg. 13.25 (ISBN 0-85200-320-X, Pub. by MTP Pr England). Kluwer Academic.
Problems in Packaging: The Environmental Issue. Ed. by I. Boustead & K. Lidgren. LC 83-3743. (Series in Energy & Fuel Science: 1-624). 174p. 1984. text ed. 47.95x (ISBN 0-470-20068-5). Halsted Pr.
Problems in Pain: Proceedings. Australia-New Zealand Conference on Pain, Melbourne, Dec. 1978. Ed. by Connie Peck & Meredith Wallace. (Illus.). 304p. 1980. pap. 28.00 (ISBN 0-08-024792-X). Pergamon.
Problems in Pediatric Drug Therapy. 2nd ed. Ed. by Louis A. Pagliaro et al. LC 87-5254. 313p. 1987. text ed. 38.50 (ISBN 0-914768-45-X). Drug Intell Pubns.
Problems in Pediatric Endocrinology. C. La Cuaza & A. W. Root. LC 80-49991. (Serono Symposia: No. 32). 1980. 92.00 (ISBN 0-12-432450-9). Acad Pr.
Problems in Perturbation. Nayfeh. LC 85-3173. 1985. 41.95 (ISBN 0-471-82292-2). Wiley.
Problems in Philosophical Inquiry. Julius R. Weinberg & Keith Yandell. LC 73-148058. 1971. 49.50x (ISBN 0-03-083380-9); pap. text ed. 19.95x (ISBN 0-89197-905-0). Irvington.
Problems in Philosophy: West & East. Ed. by A. L. Herman & R. T. Blackwood. 544p. 1975. P-H.
Problems in Physical Chemistry. Sneh Kumar Dogra & Sulekha Dogra. LC 83-12819. 674p. 1984. 31.95x (ISBN 0-470-27491-3). Halsted Pr.
Problems in Physical Electronics. Ed. by R. L. Ferrari & A. K. Jonscher. 1973. 32.00x (ISBN 0-85086-038-5, NO. 2956, Pub. by Pion England). Routledge Chapman & Hall.
Problems in Physical Organic Chemistry. Anthony R. Bulter. LC 72-617. pap. 28.80 (ISBN 0-317-09092-5, 2016972). Bks Demand UMI.
Problems in Physiochemical Analysis. L. Lyalikov. Tr. by MIR Publishers. 268p. 1975. 20.00 (ISBN 0-8464-0762-0). Beekman Pubs.
Problems in Play: First Book of Bridge Problems. Denis Priest. LC 81-19815. 167p. (Orig.). 1982. 9.95 (ISBN 0-7022-1675-5). U of Queensland Pr.
Problems in Play: Second Book of Bridge Problems. Denis Priest. LC 83-14740. 197p. (Orig.). 1984. pap. 9.95 (ISBN 0-7022-1964-9). U of Queensland Pr.
Problems in Political Economy: An Urban Perspective. 2nd ed. David M. Gordon. 1977. pap. text ed. 16.50 (ISBN 0-669-92841-0). Heath.
Problems in Pre-Columbian Textile Classification. Ina VanStan. LC 59-9294. (Florida State University Studies: 29). (Illus.). pap. 31.80 (ISBN 0-317-10829-8, 2012104). Bks Demand UMI.
Problems in Prehistory: North Africa & the Levant. Ed. by Fred Wendorf & Anthony E. Marks. LC 74-14722. (Southern Methodist University Contributions in Anthropology: No. 13). pap. 117.00 (ISBN 0-317-41765-7, 2023246). Bks Demand UMI.
Problems in Prejudice. Eugene Hartley. LC 70-96197. 1970. Repr. of 1946 ed. lib. bdg. 15.00x (ISBN 0-374-93705-2, Octagon). Hippocrene Bks.
Problems in Price Theory. David De Meza & Michael Osborne. LC 80-16597. (Illus.). xiv, 302p. 1980. pap. 13.00x (ISBN 0-226-14294-9). U of Chicago Pr.
Problems in Primary Education. R. F. Dearden. (Students Library of Education Ser.). 1976. 18.95x (ISBN 0-7100-8363-7); pap. 8.95x (ISBN 0-7100-8364-5). Routledge Chapman & Hall.
Problems in Probability Theory, Mathematical Statistics & Theory of Random Functions. A. A. Sveshnikov. Tr. by Richard A. Silverman from Rus. 1979. pap. text ed. 8.95 (ISBN 0-486-63717-4). Dover.
Problems in Professional Responsibility. 2nd ed. Andrew Kaufman. LC 83-82906. 883p. 1984. text ed. 31.00 (ISBN 0-316-48338-9). Little.
Problems in Public Expenditure Analysis: Papers Presented at a Conference of Experts: Sept. 15-16 1966. Ed. by Samuel B. Chase, Jr. LC 67-30589. (Brookings Institution Studies of Government Finance). pap. 70.80 (ISBN 0-317-20786-5, 2025369). Bks Demand UMI.
Problems in Pulmonary Medicine for the Primary Physician. Ed. by Robert H. Poe & Robert H. Israel. LC 82-8972. (Illus.). 410p. 1982. text ed. 32.50 (ISBN 0-8121-0829-9). Lea & Febiger.
Problems in Quantum Mechanics. F. Constantinescu & E. Magyari. 1971. pap. write for info.; pap. text ed. 32.00 (ISBN 0-08-019008-1). Pergamon.
Problems in Quantum Mechanics. Ed. by D. Ter Haar. 1975. 32.00x (ISBN 0-85086-050-4, NO. 2927, Pub. by Pion England). Routledge Chapman & Hall.
Problems in Quantum Physics (Recent & Future Experiments & Interpretations) Proceedings on the Summer Research Workshop. Ed. by L. Kostro. 500p. 1988. 75.00 (ISBN 9971-50-449-9). World Scientific Pub.
Problems in Remedies. Dan B. Dobbs. 137p. 1974. pap. 7.95 (ISBN 0-314-28158-4). West Pub.
Problems in Retail Merchandising. 6th ed. John W. Wingate et al. (Illus.). 336p. 1973. pap. text ed. write for info. (ISBN 0-13-720680-1). P-H.
Problems in Rock Mechanics. N. G. Cook. (Illus.). 1985. 19.95x (ISBN 0-412-24110-2, NO. 6750, Pub. by Chapman & Hall). Routledge Chapman & Hall.
Problems in Service Life Prediction of Building & Construction Materials. Ed. by Larry W. Masters. 1985. lib. bdg. 49.50 (ISBN 90-247-3181-X, Pub. by Martinus). Kluwer Academic.
Problems in Shakespeare's Penmanship. Samuel A. Tannenbaum. (MLA Rev. Fund Ser.: No. 2). 1927. 24.00 (ISBN 0-527-88750-1). Kraus Repr.
Problems in Soil Engineering. Shamsher Prakash & G. Ranjan. LC 83-166963. 268p. (Orig.). 1976. pap. 11.95 (ISBN 0-9605004-7-2, Pub. by Sarita Prakashan India). Eng Pubns.
Problems in Solid Geometry. I. F. Sharygin. 247p. 1986. pap. 4.95 (ISBN 0-8285-3299-0, Pub. by Mir Pubs USSR). Imported Pubns.
Problems in Solid State Physics. Ed. by H. J. Goldsmid. 1968. 32.00x (ISBN 0-85086-000-8, NO. 2940, Pub. by Pion England). Routledge Chapman & Hall.
Problems in Solid-State Physics. A. M. Prokhorov & A. S. Prokhorov. 365p. 1984. 11.95 (ISBN 0-8285-2897-7, Pub by Mir Pubs USSR). Imported Pubns.
Problems in Solid-State Physics. A. M. Prokhorov & A. S. Prokhorov. 366p. 1984. 42.00x (ISBN 0-317-46693-3, Pub. by Collets (UK)). State Mutual Bk.
Problems in Stellar Atmospheres & Envelopes. Ed. by B. Baschek et al. LC 74-32493. (Illus.). 390p. 1975. 34.00 (ISBN 0-387-07092-3). Springer-Verlag.
Problems in Survival Analysis. Lachenbruch. (Probability & Mathematical Statistics Ser.). 1987. write for info. (ISBN 0-471-83625-7). Wiley.
Problems in Syntax. Ed. by Liliane Tasmowski & Dominique Willems. 414p. 1984. 55.00x (ISBN 0-306-41564-X, Plenum Pr). Plenum Pub.
Problems in Teaching Secondary School Mathematics. Ernest R. Breslich. 348p. 1981. Repr. of 1940 ed. lib. bdg. 40.00 (ISBN 0-89987-078-3). Darby Bks.
Problems in the Classification of Antagonistic Actinomycetes. G. F. Gauze. Tr. by F. Danga. 1959. 5.00 (ISBN 0-934454-69-8). Lubrecht & Cramer.
Problems in the Construction of a Theory of Natural Language. Philip Tartaglia. (Janua Linguarum, Ser. Minor: No. 124). 252p. (Orig.). 1972. pap. text ed. 24.00x (ISBN 90-2792-186-5). Mouton.
Problems in the Constructive Trend in Mathematics: Part VI. Ed. by V. P. Orevkov & N. A. Sanin. LC 75-11951. (Proceedings of the Steklov Institute of Mathematics: No. 129). 1976. 111.00 (ISBN 0-8218-3029-5, STEKLO 129). Am Math.
Problems in the Constructive Trend in Mathematics: Pt. V Proceedings. Steklov Institute of Mathematics, Academy of Sciences, U. S. S. R. Ed. by V. P. Orevkov & N. A. Sanin. (Proceedings of the Steklov Institute of Mathematics: No. 113). 292p. 1972. 53.00 (ISBN 0-8218-3013-9, STEKLO-113). Am Math.
Problems in the Control of Hospital Infection. Ed. by S. W. Newsom & A. D. Caldwell. (International Congress & Symposium Ser.: No. 23). 108p. 1980. pap. 15.00 (ISBN 1-85315-011-8, Pub. by Royal Society of Medicine Services Ltd). Longwood Pub Group.
Problems in the Description of Modal Verbs: An Investigation of Latin. A. M. Bolkestein. (Studies in Greek & Latin Linguistics: No. 1). 180p. 1980. pap. text ed. 18.00 (ISBN 90-232-1764-0, Pub. by Van Gorcum Holland). Longwood Pub Group.
Problems in the Fundamentals of Federal Income Taxation. 2nd ed. Norton L. Steuben & William J. Turnier. 1985. pap. write for info. Foundation Pr.
Problems in the History of Philosophy. T. Oizerman. 463p. 1973. 7.95 (ISBN 0-8285-0206-4, Pub. by Progress Pubs USSR). Imported Pubns.
Problems in the History of Philosophy. Theodor Oizerman. 463p. 1975. 15.00x (ISBN 0-8464-0763-9). Beekman Pubs.
Problems in the Law of Mass Communications: Programmed Instruction. 1982 ed. David Gordon. 183p. 1982. pap. text ed. 4.75 (ISBN 0-88277-104-3). Foundation Pr.
Problems in the Literary Biography of Mikhail Sholokhov. Roi Medvedev. Tr. by A. D. Briggs. LC 76-14032. pap. 58.80 (ISBN 0-317-20597-8, 2024491). Bks Demand UMI.
Problems in the Origins & Development of the English Language. 3rd ed. John Algeo. 288p. 1982. pap. 10.50 net (ISBN 0-15-567609-1, HC); instr's key (ISBN 0-15-567610-5). HarBraceJ.
Problems in the Psychology of Reading. J. Q. Quantz. Bd. with Fluctuation of Attention. John P. Hylan. Repr. of 1896 ed; Mental Imagery. Wilfrid Lay. Repr. of 1898 ed; Animal Intelligence. Edward L. Thorndike. Repr. of 1898 ed; Emotion of Joy. George van N. Dearborn. Repr. of 1899 ed; Conduct & the Weather. Edwin G. Dexter. Repr. of 1899 ed. (Psychology Monographs General & Applied: Vol. 2). pap. 29.00 (ISBN 0-8115-1401-3). Kraus Repr.
Problems in the Sense of Riemann & Klein: Interscience Tracts in Pure & Applied Math. J. Plemji. (Vol. 16). 175p. (Orig.). 1964. lib. bdg. 15.00 (ISBN 0-470-69125-5, JW). Krieger.
Problems in the Theory of Point Explosion in Gases: Proceedings. Steklov Institute of Mathematics, Academy of Sciences, U. S. S. R. Ed. by V. P. Korobeinikov. (Proceedings of the Steklov Institute of Mathematics: No. 119). 311p. 1976. 74.00 (ISBN 0-8218-3019-8, STEKLO-119). Am Math.
Problems in the Theory of Probability. B. Sevastyanov. 235p. 1985. 7.95 (ISBN 0-8285-3044-0, Pub. by Mir Pubs USSR). Imported Pubns.
Problems in the Training of Certain Special-Class Teachers. Louis M. Schleier. LC 70-177809. (Columbia University. Teachers College. Contributions to Education: No. 475). Repr. of 1931 ed. 22.50 (ISBN 0-404-55475-X). AMS Pr.
Problems in Thermodynamics & Statistical Physics. Ed. by P. T. Landsberg. 1971. 34.95x (ISBN 0-85086-023-7, NO. 2938, Pub. by Pion England). Routledge Chapman & Hall.
Problems in Undergraduate Physics. Ed. by D. Ter Haar. Incl. Vol. 1. S. P. Strelkov & I. A. Yakovlev. 1965; Vol. 2. S. P. Strelkov & I. A. El'Tsin. 1965; Vol. 3. V. L. Ginzburg et al. 1965; Vol. 4. V. L. Ginzburg et al. 1965. Pergamon.
Problems in Unification & Supergravity: Conference Proceedings, La Jolla Institute, 1983. Ed. by Glennys Farrar & Frank Henyey. LC 84-71246. (AIP Conference Proceedings Ser.: No. 116). 185p. 1984. lib. bdg. 35.50 (ISBN 0-88318-315-3). Am Inst Physics.
Problems in Vertebrate Evolution. Ed. by S. Mahala Andrews et al. (Linnean Society Symposium Ser.). 1977. 96.00 (ISBN 0-12-059950-3). Acad Pr.
Problems, Issues & Concepts in Therapeutic Recreation. Ronald P. Reynolds & Gerald S. O'Morrow. 304p. 1985. text ed. 30.00 (ISBN 0-13-717430-6). P-H.

Problems of a Changing Population: Report of the Committee on Population Problems to the National Resources Committee. U. S. National Resources Committee, May 1938. LC 75-38145. (Demography Ser.). (Illus.). 1976. Repr. of 1938 ed. 23.50x (ISBN 0-405-07998-2). Ayer Co Pubs.
Problems of a Great City. Arnold White. Ed. by Lynn H. Lees & Andrew Lees. LC 84-48285. (Rise of Urban Britain Ser.). 1985. Repr. of 1886 ed. lib. bdg. 35.00 (ISBN 0-8240-6287-6). Garland Pub.
Problems of a Sociology of Knowledge. Max Scheler. Ed. by Kenneth Strikkers. Tr. by Manfred S. Frings from Ger. (International Library of Sociology). 1980. 25.00x (ISBN 0-7100-0302-1). Routledge Chapman & Hall.
Problems of a World Monetary Order. 2nd ed. Gerald M. Meier. (Illus.). 1982. pap. text ed. 12.95x (ISBN 0-19-503010-9). Oxford U Pr.
Problems of Absenteeism in the Men's & Boys' Clothing Industry. 11p. 1964. 7.00 (ISBN 0-318-19669-7). Clothing Mfrs.
Problems of Accountancy. J. N. Dey. 1985. 69.00x (ISBN 0-317-38792-8, Pub. by Current Dist). State Mutual Bk.
Problems of Adolescence in the Secondary School. Ed. by Geoff Lindsay. (Illus.). 240p. 1984. 31.00 (ISBN 0-7099-1621-3, Pub. by Croom Helm Ltd); pap. 15.95 (ISBN 0-7099-1643-4). Routledge Chapman & Hall.
Problems of Adrenergic Mechanisms in Blood Vessel. Ed. by W. Osswald. (Journal Blood Vessel: Vol. 21, No. 3, 1984). (Illus.). 44p. 1984. pap. 26.75 (ISBN 3-8055-3927-4). S Karger.
Problems of Advanced Economics. Ed. by N. Miyawaki. (Studies in Contemporary Economics: Vol. 10). vi, 319p. 1984. pap. 29.50 (ISBN 0-387-13740-8). Springer-Verlag.
Problems of Africa. Ed. by Janelle Rohr. LC 86-19600. (Opposing Viewpoints Ser.). (Illus.). 175p. 1986. lib. bdg. 13.95 (ISBN 0-89908-390-0); pap. text ed. 6.95 (ISBN 0-89908-365-X). Greenhaven.
Problems of Africa Today. P. Manchkha. 286p. 1983. 7.95 (ISBN 0-8285-2731-8, Pub. by Progress Pubs USSR). Imported Pubns.
Problems of Aging: Biological & Medical Aspects. Ed. by E. V. Cowdry & Robert Kastenbaum. LC 78-22196. (Aging & Old Age Ser.). (Illus.). 1979. Repr. of 1939 ed. lib. bdg. 53.50x (ISBN 0-405-11813-9). Ayer Co Pubs.
Problems of Agricultural Trade. OECD Staff. 178p. 1982. pap. 18.00x (ISBN 92-64-12368-7). OECD.
Problems of America's Aging Population. Ed. by T. Lynn Smith. (Center for Gerontological Studies & Programs: No. 1). (Illus.). 1951. pap. 8.00x (ISBN 0-8130-0213-3). U Presses Fla.
Problems of an Empirical Sociology of Knowledge. Bjorn Eriksson. 171p. 1975. pap. 17.50x (ISBN 0-317-46426-4, Pub. by Almqvist & Wiksell). Coronet Bks.
Problems of an Industrial Society. 2nd ed. William A. Faunce. Ed. by Eric M. Munson. 256p. 1981. pap. 21.95 (ISBN 0-07-020105-6). McGraw.
Problems of Analysis: Philosophical Essays. Max Black. LC 74-139124. 1971. Repr. of 1954 ed. lib. bdg. 35.00x (ISBN 0-8371-5740-4, BLPA). Greenwood.
Problems of Antibiotic Therapy. Ed. by H. C. Neu & A. D. Caldwell. (International Congress & Symposium Ser.: No. 13). 82p. 1979. pap. 15.00 (ISBN 1-85315-060-6, Pub. by Royal Society of Medicine Services Ltd). Longwood Pub Group.
Problems of Antiviral Therapy. Ed. by Charles Stuart-Harris & John Oxford. (Beecham Colloquia Ser.). 360p. 1984. 42.00 (ISBN 0-12-674760-1). Acad Pr.
Problems of Aphasia. Ed. by Yvan Lebrun & Richard Hoops. (Neurolinguistics Ser.: Vol. 9). 198p. 1979. text ed. 42.75 (ISBN 90-265-0309-1, Pub. by Swets & Zeitlinger Netherlands). Hogrefe Intl.
Problems of Applied Analysis. Ed. by Bruno Brosowski & Erich Martensen. (Methoden und Verfahren der Mathematischen Physik: Vol. 33). 176p. 1987. 25.65 (ISBN 3-8204-9838-9). P Lang Pubs.
Problems of Arab Economic Development & Integration. Ed. by Adda Guecioueur. (Special Studies on the Middle East). 275p. 1984. 31.50x (ISBN 0-86531-595-7). Westview.
Problems of Art. Susanne Langer. 184p. 1977. pap. text ed. write for info. (ISBN 0-02-367510-1, Pub. by Scribner). Macmillan.
Problems of Articulation Between the Units of Secondary Education. James W. Richardson. LC 76-177190. (Columbia University. Teachers College. Contributions to Education: No. 804). Repr. of 1940 ed. 22.50 (ISBN 0-404-55804-6). AMS Pr.
Problems of Asia & Its Effect upon the International-Political Balance of Power in the World, 2 vols. Alfred T. Mahan. (Illus.). 255p. 1985. Set. 187.50x. Inst Econ Pol.
Problems of Autistic Behavior: Experimental Analysis of Autism, Vol. 1. O. Ivar Lovaas et al. 300p. Date not set. text ed. price not set (ISBN 0-8290-0740-7). Irvington.
Problems of Balance of Payment & Trade. Ed. by Nasrollah S. Fatemi. LC 74-4971. 261p. 1975. 18.50 (ISBN 0-8386-1587-2). Fairleigh Dickinson.
Problems of Belief. Ferdinand C. Schiller. LC 75-3349. 1976. Repr. of 1924 ed. 22.00 (ISBN 0-404-59348-8). AMS Pr.
Problems of Biblical Theology in the 20th Century. Henning G. Reventlow. LC 86-4722. 1986. pap. 14.95 (ISBN 0-8006-1935-8, 1-1935). Fortress.
Problems of Biological Physics. L. A. Blumenfeld. (Series in Synergetics: Vol. 7). (Illus.). 300p. 1981. 39.00 (ISBN 0-387-10401-1). Springer-Verlag.
Problems of Biology. John M. Smith. (Illus.). 160p. 1986. 21.95x (ISBN 0-19-219213-2); pap. 7.95 (ISBN 0-19-289198-7). Oxford U Pr.
Problems of British Economic Policy, 1870-1945. Jim Tomlinson. 1981. 22.00x (ISBN 0-416-30430-3, NO. 3442); pap. 9.95x (ISBN 0-416-30440-0, NO. 3441). Routledge Chapman & Hall.
Problems of Calibration of Absolute Magnitudes & Temperature of Stars: Proceedings. International Astronomical Union Symposium, No. 54. Ed. by B. Hauck & B. Westerlund. LC 73-83562. 1973. lib. bdg. 47.50 (ISBN 90-277-0365-5, Pub. by Reidel Holland); pap. text ed. 36.00 (ISBN 90-277-0372-8, Pub. by Reidel Holland). Kluwer Academic.
Problems of Capital Formation: Concepts, Measurement, & Controlling Factors. Conference on Research in Income & Wealth. LC 75-19707. (National Bureau of Economic Research Ser.). (Illus.). 1975. Repr. of 1957 ed. 45.50x (ISBN 0-405-07587-1). Ayer Co Pubs.
Problems of Cartesianism: Studies in the History of Ideas. Ed. by Thomas M. Lennon et al. 272p. 1982. 29.75x (ISBN 0-7735-1000-1). McGill Queens U Pr.
Problems of Change in Urban Government. Ed. by M. O. Dickerson et al. 249p. 1980. pap. text ed. 12.50x (ISBN 0-88920-089-0, Pub. by Wilfrid Laurier Canada). Humanities.
Problems of Chemistry. Richards W. Graham. (Opus Ser). 112p. 1986. 24.95x (ISBN 0-19-219191-8); pap. 8.95x (ISBN 0-19-289172-3). Oxford U Pr.
Problems of Collapse & Numerical Relativity. Ed. by Daniel Bancel & Monique Signore. 1984. lib. bdg. 59.00 (ISBN 90-277-1816-4, Pub. by Reidel Holland). Kluwer Academic.
Problems of Computational Mathematics & Mathematical Modelling. G. I. Marchuk & V. P. Dymnikov. 270p. 1985. pap. 8.95 (ISBN 0-8285-3374-1, Pub. by Mir Pubs USSR). Imported Pubns.
Problems of Contemporary Aesthetics: A Collection of Articles. Compiled by A. Zis et al. 334p. 1984. 21.25x (ISBN 0-317-53776-8, Pub. by Collets (UK)). State Mutual Bk.
Problems of Contemporary French Politics. Dorothy Pickles. LC 81-18804. 190p. 1982. 22.00x (ISBN 0-416-73230-5, NO. 3612); pap. 9.95x (ISBN 0-416-73240-2, NO. 3613). Routledge Chapman & Hall.
Problems of Contemporary Militarism. Ed. by Asbjorn Eide & Marek Thee. LC 79-3379. 1980. 35.00x (ISBN 0-312-64744-1). St Martin.
Problems of Continuum Mechanics. Ed. by J. R. M. Radok. xx, 601p. 1961. text ed. 50.00 (ISBN 0-89871-040-5). Soc Indus-Appl Math.
Problems of Cooperation for Development. Gerald M. Meier. 1974. pap. text ed. 6.95x (ISBN 0-19-501867-2). Oxford U Pr.
Problems of Cooperative Development in India, with Special Reference to West Bengal. Pranab J. Chakrabarti. 1983. text ed. 22.00x. Coronet Bks.
Problems of Cytology & Prostitology. 376p. 1964. text ed. 77.00x (ISBN 0-7065-0183-7, Pub. by Keter Pub Jerusalem). Coronet Bks.
Problems of Democracy in Latin America. Lasso G. Plaza. LC 81-36. (Weil Lectures on American Citizenship Ser.). vi, 88p. 1981. Repr. of 1955 ed. lib. bdg. 35.00x (ISBN 0-313-22877-9, PLPD). Greenwood.
Problems of Development in Beautiful Countries: Perspectives on the Caribbean. Ransford W. Palmer. LC 83-83126. (Illus.). vii, 91p. 1984. pap. text ed. 12.50 (ISBN 0-913897-02-7). NS Pub Co Inc.
Problems of Developmental Biology. N. Krushchov. 207p. 1981. pap. 6.95 (ISBN 0-8285-2444-0, Pub. by Mir Pubs USSR). Imported Pubns.
Problems of Diglossia in Arabic: A Comparative Study of Classical & Iraqi Arabic. Salih J. Altoma. LC 69-11663. (Middle Eastern Monographs Ser: No. 21). 1969. pap. text ed. 4.50x (ISBN 0-674-70775-3). Harvard U Pr.
Problems of Dostoevsky's Poetics. Mikhail Bakhtin. Ed. by Caryl Emerson. Tr. by Carl Emerson from Rus. LC 83-12348. (Theory & History of Literature Ser.: No. 8). 352p. 1984. 35.00x (ISBN 0-8166-1227-7); pap. 14.95 (ISBN 0-8166-1228-5). U of Minn Pr.
Problems of Early Childhood: An Annotated Bibliography & Guide. Elisabeth Hirsch. LC 82-49031. 225p. 1983. lib. bdg. 30.00 (ISBN 0-8240-9216-3). Garland Pub.
Problems of Economic Growth in Latin America. Bela Kadar. Tr. by Pal Felix from Hungarian. LC 79-17824. 1980. Repr. of 1977 ed. 35.00x (ISBN 0-312-64758-1). St Martin.
Problems of Economic Planning. Evan F. Durbin. LC 68-29483. 1968. Repr. of 1949 ed. 27.50x (ISBN 0-678-06514-4). Kelley.
Problems of Elastic Stability & Vibrations. Ed. by Vadim Komkov. LC 81-12833. (Contemporary Mathematics Ser.: Vol. 4). 137p. 1981. pap. 12.00 (ISBN 0-8218-5005-9, CONM-4). Am Math.
Problems of Electronic Eavesdropping. 136p. 1977. 2.50 (B175). Am Law Inst.
Problems of Elite Cohesion: Perspective from a Minority Community. Ismail Kassim. 160p. 1974. pap. 6.00x (ISBN 0-8214-0473-3, Pub. by Singapore U Pr). Ohio U Pr.
Problems of Empire. 2nd ed. Thomas A. Brassey. LC 75-118478. 1971. Repr. of 1913 ed. 23.00x (ISBN 0-8046-1227-7, Pub. by Kennikat). Assoc Faculty Pr.
Problems of Empiricism: Philosophical Papers, Vol. 2. P. K. Feyerabend. LC 80-41931. 260p. 1981. 49.50 (ISBN 0-521-23964-8). Cambridge U Pr.
Problems of Estimating Changes in Frequency of Mental Disorders, Vol. 4. GAP Committee on Preventive Psychiatry. (Report No. 50). 1961. pap. 5.00 (ISBN 0-87318-067-4, Pub. by GAP). Brunner-Mazel.
Problems of Ethics & of Aesthetics & the Philosophy of History. Benedetto Croce. (Illus.). 159p. 1986. 137.50 (ISBN 0-89901-254-X). Found Class Reprints.
Problems of Ethnomusicology. Constantin Brailoiu. Ed. by A. L. Lloyd. LC 83-15224. (Illus.). 400p. 1984. 57.50 (ISBN 0-521-24528-1). Cambridge U Pr.
Problems of Everyday Life: And Other Writings on Culture & Science. Leon Trotsky. Tr. by G. R. Fidler et al. LC 79-186693. 352p. 1973. 25.00 (ISBN 0-913460-14-1, Dist. by Path Pr NY); pap. 10.95 (ISBN 0-913460-15-X, Dist. by Path Pr NY). Anchor Found.
Problems of Evolution. Mark Ridley. LC 84-27300. (Illus.). 160p. 1985. 24.95x (ISBN 0-19-219194-2); pap. 9.95x (ISBN 0-19-289175-8). Oxford U Pr.
Problems of Evolution of Physiological Functions. 168p. 1960. text ed. 35.00x (ISBN 0-7065-0115-2). Coronet Bks.
Problems of Family Life. Ed. by Maxwell S. Stewart. LC 70-132094. (Essay & General Literature Index Reprint Ser). 1971. Repr. of 1956 ed. 23.00x (ISBN 0-8046-1422-9, Pub. by Kennikat). Assoc Faculty Pr.
Problems of Fish Culture Economics with Special Reference to Carp Culture in Eastern Europe. Marian Leopold. (European Inland Fisheries Advisory Commission (EIFAC): Technical Papers: No. 40). 107p. 1981. pap. 7.50 (ISBN 92-5-101152-4, F2284, FAO). UNIPUB.
Problems of Flight by Jet Propulsion: Interplanetary Flights. F. A. Tsander. 400p. 1964. text ed. 80.00 (ISBN 0-7065-0282-5, Pub. by Keter Pub Jerusalem). Coronet Bks.
Problems of Futurology. V. Narayan Reddy. viii, 176p. 1985. text ed. 22.50x (ISBN 0-86590-728-5, Pub. by Sterling Pubs India). APT Bks.
Problems of Genetics. Bateson. LC 79-15467. 1979. text ed. 35.00t (ISBN 0-300-02435-5); pap. 11.95x (ISBN 0-300-02436-3, Y-350). Yale U Pr.
Problems of Greek History. John P. Mahaffy. Repr. of 1892 ed. 35.00 (ISBN 0-8274-3925-3). R West.
Problems of Hamlet. G. F. Bradby. (Studies in Shakespeare Ser.: No. 24). 1970. pap. 39.95x (ISBN 0-8383-0006-5). Haskell.
Problems of Hemispheric Defense. California University Committee on International Relations. LC 77-167322. (Essay Index Reprint Ser.). Repr. of 1942 ed. 14.50 (ISBN 0-8369-2759-1). Ayer Co Pubs.
Problems of Heuristics. V. N. Pushkin. 208p. 1972. text ed. 42.00x (ISBN 0-7065-1279-0, Pub. by Keter Pub Jerusalem). Coronet Bks.
Problems of Higher Education in India. K. L. Joshi. 312p. 1977. 8.95. Asia Bk Corp.
Problems of Higher Education in India. C. M. Ramachandron. 1987. 27.50x (ISBN 0-8364-2218-X, Pub. by Mittal). South Asia Bks.
Problems of Higher Education in India: An Annotated Bibliography of Source Material. D. Kamalavijayan. 1979. 12.50x (ISBN 0-8364-0505-6). South Asia Bks.
Problems of Historical Psychology. Zevedei Barbu. LC 75-28659. 1976. Repr. of 1960 ed. lib. bdg. 35.00x (ISBN 0-8371-8476-2, BAHP). Greenwood.
Problems of Human Pleasure & Behavior. Michael Balint. 1973. pap. 3.95 (ISBN 0-87140-279-3). Liveright.
Problems of Humanity. Alice A. Bailey. 1983. pap. 7.00 (ISBN 0-85330-113-1). Lucis.
Problems of Hydrodynamics & Continuum Mechanics. Ed. by M. A. Lavrent'ev. xi, 815p. 1969. text ed. 58.00 (ISBN 0-89871-039-1). Soc Indus-Appl Math.
Problems of Immigration. Ed. by Steven Anzovin. (Reference Shelf Ser: Vol. 57, No. 1). 156p. 1985. pap. text ed. 10.00 (ISBN 0-8242-0710-6). Wilson.
Problems of Implementing Multiple Categorical Education Programs. Jackie Kimbrough & Paul T. Hill. LC 83-15929. 1983. 4.00 (ISBN 0-8330-0515-4, R-2957-ED). Rand Corp.
Problems of Indenture Trustees & Bondholders, 1988: Defaulted Bonds & Bankruptcy. (Real Estate Law & Practice Ser.). 585p. 1988. 45.00 (N4-4483). PLI.
Problems of Indian Economic Development: National & Regional Dimensions. K. N. Prasad. 1983. 45.00x (ISBN 0-86590-116-3, Pub. by Sterling India). Apt Bks.
Problems of Information Processing & Perceptual Organization. Ed. by Collet's Holdings, Ltd. Staff. 94p. 1978. pap. 42.00x (ISBN 0-569-08454-7, Pub. by Collets (UK)). State Mutual Bk.
Problems of Information Processing & Perceptual Organization. Ed. by L. Kardos. 1978. cancelled (ISBN 963-05-1417-6, Pub. by Kiado Hungary). IPS.
Problems of International Finance. Ed. by John Black & Graeme S. Dorrance. LC 83-24747. 188p. 1984. 29.95 (ISBN 0-312-64767-0). St Martin.
Problems of International Justice. Steven Luper-Foy. LC 87-13570. 336p. 1988. text ed. 39.50 (ISBN 0-8133-0392-3); pap. 18.95 (ISBN 0-8133-0393-1). Westview.
Problems of International Money, 1972-85. Ed. by Michael Posner. 200p. 1986. pap. 8.50 (ISBN 0-939934-58-2). Intl Monetary.
Problems of Juvenile Courts & the Rights of Children. Monrad G. Paulsen. 174p. 1975. pap. 2.50 (ISBN 0-317-30878-5, B174). Am Law Inst.
Problems of Knowledge & Freedom: The Russell Lectures. Noam Chomsky. 1972. pap. 2.95 (ISBN 0-394-71815-1, V815, Vin). Random.
Problems of Knowledge: Essays at Unriddling Some Perplexing Nexus of Knowledge Problems. Herman Tennessen. (Methodology & Science Ser.). 86p. 1980. pap. text ed. 8.00 (ISBN 90-232-1762-4, Pub. by Van Gorcum Holland). Longwood Pub Group.
Problems of Knowledge in Legal Scholarship. Philip Shuchman. LC 79-80252. 136p. 1979. pap. text ed. 11.00 (ISBN 0-939328-00-3). U Ct Law Sch Found.
Problems of Labour & Inflation. Hilde Behrend. LC 84-14263. 256p. 1984. 29.00 (ISBN 0-7099-3222-7, Pub. by Croom Helm Ltd). Routledge Chapman & Hall.
Problems of Land Reform Implementation in Rural Ethiopia. Mengistu Woube. (Illus.). 174p. (Orig.). 1986. pap. text ed. 39.50x (ISBN 91-506-0482-1, Pub. by Almqvist & Wiksell). Coronet Bks.
Problems of Lasting Peace. Herbert C. Hoover & H. Gibson. 1943. 18.50x (ISBN 0-686-51292-8). Elliots Bks.
Problems of Lasting Peace. Herbert C. Hoover & H. Gibson. LC 42-16570. 1969. Repr. of 1942 ed. 20.00 (ISBN 0-527-42420-X). Kraus Repr.
Problems of Lasting Peace Revisted. 185p. 1986. 10.00 (ISBN 0-938469-00-2). Hoover Lib.
Problems of Law: Its Past, Present, & Future. John H. Wigmore. 136p. 1988. Repr. of 1920 ed. lib. bdg. 22.50 (ISBN 0-8377-2742-1). Rothman.
Problems of Liberty & Justice. J. P. Day. 240p. write for info. (Pub. by Croom Helm UK). Routledge Chapman & Hall.
Problems of Life. Lev D. Trotsky. Tr. by Z. Vengerova from Rus. LC 73-857. (Russian Studies: Perspectives on the Revolution Ser). 114p. 1980. Repr. of 1924 ed. 15.00 (ISBN 0-88355-054-7). Hyperion Conn.
Problems of Life & Death. Lucius Annaeus Seneca. 154p. 1985. 117.75 (ISBN 0-89266-517-3). Am Classical Coll Pr.
Problems of Life & Mind, 5 vols. George H. Lewes. Incl. Foundations of a Creed, 2 vols. LC 78-72806. 75.00 (ISBN 0-404-60871-X); Physical Basis of Mind. LC 78-72807. 42.50 (ISBN 0-404-60874-4); Study of Psychology & Mind As a Function of the Organism, 2 vols. LC 78-72809. 62.50 (ISBN 0-404-60875-2). LC 78-72805. Set. 180.00 (ISBN 0-404-60870-1). AMS Pr.
Problems of Linear Electron Transport Theory in Semiconductors. M. I. Klinger. LC 78-40821. 1979. 240.00 (ISBN 0-08-018224-0). Pergamon.
Problems of Literary Evaluation. Ed. by Joseph P. Strelka. LC 68-56136. (Yearbook of Comparative Criticism, Vol. 2). 1969. 25.00x (ISBN 0-271-00085-6). Pa St U Pr.
Problems of Lithography in Microelectronics. Ed. by T. M. Makhviladze. (Proceedings of the Institute of General Physics of the Academy of Sciences of the U. S. S. R.: Vol. 8). 207p. 1988. text ed. 62.00 (ISBN 0-941743-30-6). Nova Sci Pubs.
Problems of Long-Term Imprisonment. Anthony E. Bottoms & Roy Light. (Cambridge Criminology Ser.: No. 58). 250p. 1987. text ed. 45.00x (ISBN 0-566-05427-2, Pub. by Gower Pub England). Gower Pub Co.
Problems of Management in a Developing Environment: The Case of Tanzania (State Enterprises Between 1967 & 1975) M. S. El-Namaki. 270p. 1979. 73.75 (ISBN 0-444-85303-0, North Holland). Elsevier.
Problems of Mathematics. Ian Stewart. (Illus.). 224p. 1987. 32.50 (ISBN 0-19-219201-9); pap. 9.95 (ISBN 0-19-289182-0). Oxford U Pr.
Problems of Medieval Popular Culture. Aron I. Gurevich. Tr. by Janos M. Bak & Paul A. Hollomgsworth. (Cambridge Studies in Oral & Literature Culture). 312p. 1988. 44.50 (ISBN 0-521-30369-9). Cambridge U Pr.
Problems of Men. John Dewey. LC 68-19266. 1968. Repr. of 1946 ed. lib. bdg. 35.00x (ISBN 0-8371-0382-7, DEPM). Greenwood.
Problems of Metal Fatigue. V. I. Belyaev. 84p. 1963. pap. text ed. 20.00x (ISBN 0-7065-0520-4, Pub. by Keter Pub Jerusalem). Coronet Bks.

Problems of Typological & Genetic Linguistics Viewed in a Generative Framework. Henrik Birnbaum. LC 70-123298. (Janua Linguarum, Ser. Minor: No. 106). (Orig.). 1970. pap. text ed. 11.20x (ISBN 90-2791-541-5). Mouton.
Problems of Urban Transport in India: Proceedings of the International Seminar Held on April 20-22, 1985. D. Panduranga Rao. (Illus.). xxiii, 376p. 1986. text ed. 50.00x (ISBN 81-210-0066-1, Pub. by Inter India Pubns N Delhi). Apt Bks.
"Problems" of Verbal Inspiration. Alva J. McClain. 1968. pap. 0.50 (ISBN 0-88469-116-0). BMH Bks.
Problems of Verification. R. Timberbayve. 96p. 1984. 13.00x (ISBN 0-317-46696-8, Pub. by Collets (UK)). State Mutual Bk.
Problems of War & Peace in the Society of Nations. facs. ed. California University Committee on International Relations. LC 67-23188. (Essay Index Reprint Ser). 1937. 17.00 (ISBN 0-8369-0270-X). Ayer Co Pubs.
Problems of Women's Liberation: A Marxist Approach. new & rev. ed. Evelyn Reed. LC 78-143808. (Orig.). 1971. 12.00 (ISBN 0-87348-166-6); pap. 3.95 (ISBN 0-87348-167-4). Path Pr NY.
Problems of Women's Plots in the Evil Vineyard. Barbara Hannah. 1985. 10.00x (ISBN 0-317-62271-4, Guild of Pastoral Psych). State Mutual Bk.
Problems of Work. L. Ron Hubbard. 20.00 (ISBN 0-686-30789-5). Church Scient NY.
Problems of Work: How to Solve them & Succeed. L. Ron Hubbard. (Illus.). 179p. 1983. 6.95 (ISBN 0-88404-132-8). Bridge Pubns Inc.
Problems of Work: Scientology Applied to the Work-a-Day World. L. Ron Hubbard. 106p. 1956. 21.44 (ISBN 0-88404-007-0). Bridge Pubns Inc.
Problems of Your Child's Vital Years. Audrey Bilski. (Illus.). 1977. 10.95 (ISBN 0-285-62188-2, Pub. by Souvenir Pr). Intl Spec Bk.
Problems on Quantitative Genetics. D. S. Falconer. LC 82-4965. 128p. 1983. pap. 7.95x (ISBN 0-582-44679-1). Wiley.
Problems on the Design of Machine Elements. 4th ed. Virgil M. Faires & Roy M. Wingren. 1965. text ed. write for info. (ISBN 0-02-335960-9, 33596). Macmillan.
Problems on the Equations of Mathematical Physics. M. M. Smirnov. 102p. 1968. 42.00 (ISBN 0-677-61310-5). Gordon & Breach.
Problems on the Job: A Supervisor's Guide to Coping. The U. S. Office of Personnel Management. 16p. 1.50 (ISBN 0-89486-085-2). Hazelden.
Problems on Thermodynamics. 6th ed. Virgil M. Faires & Clifford M. Simmang. 1978. pap. write for info. (ISBN 0-02-335230-2, 33523). Macmillan.
Problems, Readings & Materials on the Lawyer as a Negotiator. Harry T. Edwards & James J. White. 484p. 1977. 25.95 (ISBN 0-314-31913-1). West Pub.
Problems Supplement for Technical Mathematics. Thomas Stark & Lawrence Pucke. 1984. pap. 16.95 (ISBN 0-8053-9537-7). Benjamin-Cummings.
Problems, Tasks & Outcomes. Matilda E. Goldberg et al. 1985. 106.25x (ISBN 0-317-40636-1, Pub. by Natl Inst Social Work). State Mutual Bk.
Problems, Tasks & Outcomes: The Evaluation of Task-Centered Casework in Three Settings. E. Matilda Goldberg et al. (National Institute Social Services Library: No. 47). 320p. 1985. text ed. 39.95x (ISBN 0-04-361053-6). Unwin Hyman.
Problems to Keep in Mind When It Comes to Tax Reform. William Fellner. LC 77-81191. 1977. pap. 5.00 (ISBN 0-8447-3266-4). Am Enterprise.
Problems with Eating: Interventions for Children & Adults with Developmental Disabilities. 140p. 1987. pap. 23.50 (ISBN 0-910317-42-9). Am Occup Therapy.
Problems with Meat As Human Food. John A. Scharffenberg. LC 79-13056. (Illus., Orig.). 1979. pap. 5.95 (ISBN 0-912800-65-8). Woodbridge Pr.
Problems with Solutions see HMO Model & Its Application.
Problems with Temperature Regulation During Exercise. Ed. by Ethan R. Nadel & John B. Pierce. 1977. 32.50 (ISBN 0-12-513550-5). Acad Pr.
Probo's Amazing Trunk. (Beginning to Read Ser.). (gr. 2 up). PLB 5.95 (ISBN 0-8136-5184-0); pap. 2.95 (ISBN 0-8136-5684-2). Modern Curr.
Probots & People: The Age of the Personal Robot. Timothy O. Knight. (Illus.). 144p. 1984. pap. text ed. 9.95 (ISBN 0-07-035106-6). McGraw.
Probrabilities & Potential: Potential Theory for Discrete & Continuous Semigroups. C. Dellacherie & P. A. Meyer. (Mathematics Studies: Vol. 151). 416p. 1988. 92.00 (ISBN 0-444-70386-1, North Holland). Elsevier.
Procane Chronicle. Oliver Bleeck, pseud. LC 82-48808. 228p. 1987. pap. 3.50 (ISBN 0-06-080854-3, P 854, PL). Har-Row.
Procatechesis, Catacheses One - Twelve. St. Cyril Of Jerusalem. LC 68-55980. (Fathers of the Church Ser.: Vol. 61). 279p. 1969. 15.95x (ISBN 0-8132-0061-X). Cath U Pr.
Procedes d'art en Photographie. Robert Demacy & C. Puyo Demachy. Ed. by Robert A. Sobieszek & Peter C. Bunnell. LC 76-24673. (Sources of Modern Photography Ser.). (Illus., Fr.). 1979. Repr. of 1906 ed. lib. bdg. 17.00x (ISBN 0-405-09649-6). Ayer Co Pubs.
Procedural Elements for Computer Graphics. David F. Rogers. 1985. text ed. 28.95 (ISBN 0-07-053534-5). McGraw.
Procedural Guide to Automating an Art Library. Ed. by Patricia J. Barnett & Amy E. Lucker. (Occasionaal Papers: No. 7). (Illus.). 48p. 1987. pap. 15.00 (ISBN 0-942740-06-8). Art Libs Soc.
Procedural History of the 1940 Census of Population & Housing. Ed. by Robert M. Jenkins. LC 85-40368. 160p. 1986. text ed. 40.00x (ISBN 0-299-10120-7). U of Wis Pr.
Procedural Justice: A Psychological Analysis. John Thibaut & Laurens Walker. LC 75-15944. 150p. 1975. pap. 7.50 (ISBN 0-470-85868-0, Pub. by Wiley). Krieger.
Procedural Law Affecting Qualified Plans. (Series G). 1978. Three Folios. pap. 4.00 (ISBN 0-317-31243-X). Am Law Inst.
Procedural Manual for Archaeological Field Research Projects of the Museum of New Mexico. Alfred E. Dittert & Fred Wendorf. (Arizona Archaeologist Ser.: No. 10). (Illus., Orig.). 1977. pap. 5.00 (ISBN 0-939071-06-1). AZ Archaeol.
Procedural Manual for Entry Establishment in the Dictionary of the Old Spanish Language. 2nd ed. Victoria Burrus. Tr. by Angel Gomez Moreno from Eng. 104p. (Span.). 1983. 25.00x (ISBN 0-942260-37-6). Hispanic Seminary.
Procedural Structure: Success & Influence in Congress. Terry Sullivan. 224p. 1984. 35.00 (ISBN 0-275-91279-5, C1279). Praeger.
Procedure. Owen M. Fisk & Judith Resnik. (University Casebook Ser.). 1500p. 1988. text ed. write for info. (ISBN 0-88277-626-6). Foundation Pr.
Procedure. L. Griffiths & K. Broadbent. (Criminal Law Library). 544p. 1988. 39.01 (ISBN 0-08-039247-4, Pub. by WAT). Pergamon.
Procedure Amiable, Procedure et Pratique: Mutual Agreement, Procedure & Practice. International Tax Congress et al. LC 81-182272. 414p. 1981. 45.00 (ISBN 9-06-544006-2, Pub. by Kluwer Law Netherlands). Kluwer Academic.
Procedure & Evidence in the Juvenile Court: A Guidebook for Judges. 84p. 1962. 4.00 (ISBN 0-318-15371-8). Natl Coun Crime.
Procedure & Metaphysics: A Study in the Philosophy of Mathematical-Physical Science in the 16-17 Century. Edward W. Strong. 301p. 1977. Repr. of 1936 ed. lib. bdg. 19.50x (ISBN 0-915172-28-3). Richwood Pub.
Procedure Before the Internal Revenue Service. 6th ed. James W. Quiggle & Lipman Redman. LC 84-72251. (Illus.). 269p. 1984. 66.00 (ISBN 0-8318-0449-1, B449); 1985 supplement incl. AM Law Inst.
Procedure Before the IRS 1987. James W. Quiggle & Lipman Redman. 15p. 1987. pap. text ed. 10.00 (ISBN 0-8318-0533-1, B533). Am Law Inst.
Procedure, Extent & Limits of Human Understanding, 1728. Peter Browne. Ed. by Rene Wellek. LC 75-11201. (British Philosophers & Theologians of the 17th & 18th Centuriy Ser.: Vol. 8). 487p. 1976. Repr. of 1728 ed. lib. bdg. 51.00 (ISBN 0-8240-1757-9). Garland Pub.
Procedure for the Determination of Fibrinogen in Biological Samples: Proposed Guideline, Vol. 2. National Committee for Clinical Laboratory Standards. 1982. 20.00 (ISBN 0-318-19451-1, H30-P). Natl Comm Clin Lab Stds.
Procedure for the Estimation of Markov Transition Probabilities. Allen J. Scott. (Discussion Ser.: No. 8). 1965. pap. 6.50 (ISBN 0-686-32177-4). Regional Sci Res Inst.
Procedure for Writing Assessment & Holistic Scoring. Miles Myers. 71p. 1980. 5.95 (ISBN 0-8141-3726-1). NCTE.
Procedure Guides for Evaluation of Speech & Language Disorders in Children. 4th ed. Lois J. Sanders. LC 78-71498. 1979. pap. 6.95x (ISBN 0-8134-2074-1, 2074). Inter Print Pubs.
Procedure Handbook: Surface Preparation & Painting of Tanks & Closed Areas. James A. Giese. (Illus.). 150p. 1981. pap. text ed. 30.00 (ISBN 0-938477-20-X). SSPC.
Procedure in International Court: A Commentary on the 1978 Rules of the International Court of Justice. Shabtai Rosenne. 1983. lib. bdg. 56.50 (ISBN 90-247-3045-7, Pub. by Martinus Nijhoff Netherlands). Kluwer Academic.
Procedure Manual for Clinical Bacteriology: Annotated. Dorothy Branson. (Illus.). 368p. 1982. spiral 43.75x (ISBN 0-398-04660-3). C C Thomas.
Procedure Manual in Speech Pathology with Damaged Children. Joseph S. Keenan. viii, 152p. 1975. pap. text ed. 6.95x (ISBN 0-8134-1677-9, 1677). Inter Print Pubs.
Procedure of the House of Commons, 3 Vols. Joseph Redlich. Tr. by A. Ernest Steinthal. LC 77-77895. Repr. of 1908 ed. Set. 62.50 (ISBN 0-404-05280-0). AMS Pr.
Procedure of the U. N. Security Council. Sydney D. Bailey. (Illus.). 1975. 55.00x (ISBN 0-19-827199-9). Oxford U Pr.
Procedure of the U. N. Security Council. 2nd ed. Sydney D. Bailey. (Illus.). 500p. 1988. 78.00 (ISBN 0-19-827566-8). Oxford U Pr.
Procedure Orale et Procedure Ecrite: Oral & Written Procedure in Civil Litigation. M. Cappelletti. (Studi di Diritto Comparato: No. 4). 113p. 1971. 12.00 (ISBN 0-379-00032-6). Oceana.
Procedure Supplement. Owen M. Fiss & Judith Resnik. 797p. 1988. pap. text ed. write for info. (ISBN 0-88277-672-X). Foundation Pr.
Procedures. Ed. by Helen Hamilton & Minnie B. Rose. LC 82-15643. (Nurse's Reference Library). (Illus.). 845p. 1983. text ed. 27.95 (ISBN 0-916730-40-9). Springhouse Pub.
Procedures & Conservation Standards for Museum Collections in Transit & on Exhibition: Protection of the Cultural Heritage. (Promotion of the Cultural Heritages: Technical Handbooks for Museums & Monuments: No. 3). (Illus.). 56p. 1981. pap. 5.00 (ISBN 92-3-101913-9, U1127, UNESCO). UNIPUB.
Procedures & Functions in BBC Basic. D. Gregory. 128p. 1984. 39.00x (ISBN 0-201-14694-0, Pub. by Addison-Wesley Pubs Ltd). State Mutual Bk.
Procedures & Guidelines for Disaster Preparedness Planning. W. Nick Carter. viii, 195p. 1985. pap. 12.25 (ISBN 0-86638-063-9). EW Ctr HI.
Procedures & Practices in Activated Sludge Process Control. Robert M. Arthur. 42.95 (ISBN 0-250-40630-6). Butterworth.
Procedures & Recommendations for the Ultrasonic Testing of Butt Welds. 42p. 1972. member 38.50 (ISBN 0-318-21483-0, 327); non-member 43.50. Am Soc Nondestructive.
Procedures & Standards for a Multipurpose Cadastre. National Research Council. 1983. pap. text ed. 8.50x (ISBN 0-309-03343-8). Natl Acad Pr.
Procedures for Collecting & Analyzing Mortality Data in LSMS. Susan H. Cochrane et al. (LSMS Working Paper: No. 16). 160p. 1982. 8.00 (ISBN 0-317-59150-9, BK 0043). World Bank.
Procedures for Denying Section 8 Existing Housing Assistance (Certificate or Voucher) to Applicants. 14p. 1985. 2.00 (40,735). NCLS Inc.
Procedures for Improving the Measurement of Local Fire Protection Effectiveness. Urban Institute, NFPA. Ed. by A. E. Dean. LC 77-82347. 1977. pap. text ed. 3.75 (ISBN 0-87765-107-8). Natl Fire Prot.
Procedures for Instructional Systems Development. Ed. by Harold F. O'Neil. LC 79-12002. (Educational Technology Ser.). 1979. 19.95 (ISBN 0-12-526660-X). Acad Pr.
Procedures for Library Media Technical Assistants. Barbara E. Chernik. LC 83-7070. 296p. 1983. 25.00x (ISBN 0-8389-0384-3). ALA.
Procedures for Nursing the Burned Patient. Claudella A. Jones & Irving Feller. LC 75-15372. (Illus.). 1975. plastic 3-ring binder 30.00 (ISBN 0-917478-25-8). Natl Inst Burn.
Procedures for Qualification of Plans. Philip N. Rotgin & Arnold M. Jacobs. (Procedural Law Affecting Qualified Plans Ser.). 42p. 1978. pap. 2.00 (ISBN 0-317-31254-5, B374). Am Law Inst.
Procedures for School District Reorganization. Harold D. Alford. LC 75-176509. (Columbia University. Teachers College. Contributions to Education: No. 852). Repr. of 1942 ed. 22.50 (ISBN 0-404-55852-6). AMS Pr.
Procedures for Structuring & Scheduling Sports Tournaments: Elimination, Consolation, Placement, & Round Robin Design. Francis M. Rokosz. (Illus.). 170p. 1981. spiral bdg. 21.75 (ISBN 0-398-04458-9). C C Thomas.
Procedures for Terminating a Participant from Section 8 Existing Housing Program or Denying a Transfer Certificate or Voucher. 22p. 1985. 2.75 (40,730). NCLS Inc.
Procedures for the Coagulation Laboratory. Douglas A. Triplett & Cathy S. Harms. LC 81-10909. (Illus.). 179p. 1981. lab manual 19.00 (ISBN 0-89189-074-2, 45-5-008-00). Am Soc Clinical.
Procedures for the Control of Ships & Discharges. 22p. 1978. 7.00 (ISBN 0-686-70792-3, IMCO33, Pub. by Intl Mariritme Orgn). UNIPUB.
Procedures for the Detection & Identification of Certain Fish Pathogens. 3rd ed. Ed. by K. H. Amos. LC 85-52206. 114p. 1985. pap. 15.00 (ISBN 0-913235-38-5). Am Fisheries Soc.
Procedures for the Electronic Office. Rita C. Kutie & Joan L. Rhodes. 245p. 1988. pap. 13.00 (ISBN 0-471-61250-2). Wiley.
Procedures for the Electronic Office. Dorothy A. Neal et al. 464p. 1988. text ed. 22.56 (ISBN 0-07-046146-5). McGraw.
Procedures for the Handling & Processing of Blood Specimens: Tentative Standard, Vol. 4. National Committee for Clinical Laboratory Standards. 1984. 20.00 (ISBN 0-318-19444-9, H18-T). Natl Comm Clin Lab Stds.
Procedures for the Handling & Transport of Domestic Diagnostic Specimens & Etiological Agents: Approved Standard, Vol. 5. 2nd ed. National Committee for Clinical Laboratory Standards. 1985. 20.00 (ISBN 0-318-19429-5, H5-A2). Natl Comm Clin Lab Stds.
Procedures for the Modern Office: An Applications Approach. Judith C. Simon & Lilliana H. Chaney. 1988. pap. 24.95 (ISBN 0-471-62438-1). Wiley.
Procedures for the Professional Secretary. Patsy J. Fulton & Joanna D. Hanks. 608p. 1985. text ed. write for info. (ISBN 0-538-11950-0, K95). SW Pub.
Procedures for the Testing of International Food Additives to Establish Their Safety for Use. (Nutrition Meetings Reports: No. 17). 19p. (2nd Printing 1974). 1958. pap. 5.75 (ISBN 92-5-101822-7, F336, FAO). UNIPUB.
Procedures Handbook for Special Needs Work-Study Coordinators. Linda H. Parrish & Marilyn R. Kok. LC 84-29996. 167p. 1985. 39.00 (ISBN 0-87189-092-5). Aspen Pub.
Procedures in Ambulatory Care. R. D. Gillette. (Illus.). 400p. 1987. pap. 17.95 (ISBN 0-07-023265-2). McGraw.
Procedures in Applied Optics. Strong. (Optical Engineering Ser.). 416p. 1988. 79.75 (ISBN 0-8247-7987-8). Dekker.
Procedures in Practice. British Medical Association Staff. 74p. 1981. pap. 13.00x (ISBN 0-7279-0075-7, Pub. by British Med Assoc UK). Taylor & Francis.
Procedures in Skeletal Radiology. Ed. by Amy B. Goldman. 720p. 1984. 99.50 (ISBN 0-8089-1655-6, 7916-41). Grune.
Procedures in the Justice System. 3rd ed. Gilbert B. Stuckey. 368p. 1986. text ed. 30.95 (ISBN 0-675-20360-0). Merrill.
Procedures in Vascular Surgery. 2nd ed. Chilton Crane & Richard Warren. LC 75-22597. 1976. text ed. 47.00 (ISBN 0-316-16014-8). Little.
Procedures of Empirical Science. Victor F. Lenzen. LC 71-131570. (Foundations of the Unity of Science Ser: Vol. 1, No. 5). 1938. pap. 1.95x (ISBN 0-226-57580-2, P404, Phoen). U of Chicago Pr.
Procedures of Industrial Water Treatment. J. N. Tanis. 400p. 1987. 48.00 (ISBN 0-942105-44-3). Ltan Inc.
Procedures Supplement for Fundementals of Nursing. B. Kozier & G. L. Erb. 1984. pap. text ed. write for info. (Hlth-Sci). Addison-Wesley.
Procedures to Investigate Arthropod-Borne & Rodent Borne Illness. 93p. 3.00 (ISBN 0-318-17809-5); bulk rates avail. Intl Assn Milk.
Proceedigs: Symposuim on Incremental Motion Control Systems & Devices. 14th ed. Ed. by B. C. Kuo. (Illus.). 432p. 1985. 55.00x (ISBN 0-931538-07-6). Incremental Motion.
Proceeding of the First Soviet-American Library Seminar. Ed. by Jean E. Lowrie. LC 83-18769. xi, 212p. 1983. pap. 27.50x (ISBN 0-8389-3290-8). ALA.
Proceeding of the Noise & Vibration Conference, 1987. 1987. 60.00 (ISBN 0-89883-456-2, P195). Soc Auto Engineers.
Proceeding of the Third Workshop on Hadronic Mechanics: Held at the University of Patras (Greece), August 25-30, 1986, 2 vols. 90.00 (ISBN 0-911767-47-9). Hadronic Pr Inc.
Proceedings. Academy of Management, Annual Meeting, 39th, 1979. Ed. by Richard C. Huseman. LC 40-2886. (Illus.). 1979. pap. text ed. 11.00 (ISBN 0-915350-18-1). Acad of Mgmt.
Proceedings. Ambulatory ECG Monitoring, First National Conference. Ed. by Nancy Jacobsen & Stephen Yarnall. (Illus.). 150p. 1976. 16.50 (ISBN 0-917054-08-3). Med Communications.
Proceedings. Asiatic Exclusion League, 1907-1913. Ed. by Gerald Grob. LC 76-6064. (Anti-Movements in America Ser). 1977. Repr. of 1907 ed. lib. bdg. 59.50x (ISBN 0-405-09939-8). Ayer Co Pubs.
Proceedings. Association of American Geologists & Naturalists at Philadelphia, 1840 & 1841. Ed. by Claude C. Albritton. LC 77-6507. (History of Geology Ser.). Repr. of 1843 ed. lib. bdg. 46.50x (ISBN 0-405-10430-8). Ayer Co Pubs.
Proceedings. Association of Orthodox Jewish Scientists. (ISBN 0-87306-072-5); Vol. 1. 6.95 (ISBN 0-686-67018-3); Vol. 2. 8.95 (ISBN 0-87306-073-3). Feldheim.
Proceedings, 5 vols. Canadian Cancer Conference Staff. Ed. by R. W. Begg. Incl. Vol. 1. 1st Conference, 1954. 1955 (ISBN 0-12-149001-7); Vol. 2. 2nd Conference, 1956. 1957 (ISBN 0-12-149002-5); Vol. 3. 3rd Conference, 1958. 1959 (ISBN 0-12-149003-3); Vol. 4. 4th Conference, 1960. 1961 (ISBN 0-12-149004-1); Vol. 5. 5th Conference, 1962. 1963 (ISBN 0-12-149005-X). 75.00 ea. Acad Pr.
Proceedings. Colloquium on the Law of Outer Space 13th, Constance, Germany, Oct 4-10 1970. Ed. by Mortimer D. Schwartz. iii, 381p. (Orig.). 1971. pap. text ed. 27.50x. U of Cal Sch Law.
Proceedings. Colloquium on the Law of Outer Space, 15th, Vienna, Oct 1972. Ed. by Mortimer D. Schwartz. iv, 284p. (Orig.). 1973. pap. text ed. 27.50x. U of Cal Sch Law.
Proceedings. Conference in Mathematical Logic, London, 1970. Ed. by W. Hodges. (Lecture Notes in Mathematics: Vol. 255). 351p. 1972. pap. 18.00 (ISBN 0-387-05744-7). Springer-Verlag.
Proceedings. Conference in Orders, Group Rings & Related Topics. Ed. by J. S. Hsia et al. (Lecture Notes in Mathematics: Vol. 353). 224p. 1973. pap. 21.00 (ISBN 0-387-06518-0). Springer-Verlag.
Proceedings, 5 vols. Conference Internationale d'Histoire Economique, 3rd, Munich, 1965. (Congres et Colioques Ser.: No. 10). (Illus.). 504p. (Fr.). 1974. text ed. 123.00x set (ISBN 0-686-22580-5). Mouton.

Proceedings. International Symposium on Smallpox Vaccine, 37th, Bilthoven, October 1972. Ed. by R. H. Regamey et al. (Symposia Series in Immunobiological Standardization: Vol. 19). 365p. 1973. 25.50 (ISBN 3-8055-1773-4). S Karger.

Proceedings. International Symposium on Standardization & Use of Vaccines in the Developing Countries, Guadeloupe, 1978. Ed. by R. H. Regamey. (Developments in Biological Standardization: Vol. 41). (Illus., Fr.). 1978. 74.00 (ISBN 3-8055-2811-6). S Karger.

Proceedings. International Symposium on Stereoencephalotomy Research, 6th, Tokyo, October 1973. Ed. by P. L Gildenberg & H. Narabayashi. (Advances in Stereoencephalotomy: Vol. 7). 350p. 1975. pap. 124.00 (ISBN 3-8055-2186-3). S Karger.

Proceedings. International Symposium On Stress Waves In Anelastic Solids - Providence - 1963. Ed. by H. Kolsky & W. Prager. (Illus.). 1964. 69.70 (ISBN 0-387-03221-5). Springer-Verlag.

Proceedings. International Symposium on the Aerodynamics & Ventilation of Vehicle Tunnels, 1st. 1973. text ed. 47.00x (ISBN 0-900983-28-0, Dist. by Air Science Co.). BHRA Fluid.

Proceedings. International Symposium on the Benefits & Risks of Vaccination, Brussels, November 1978. Ed. by R. H. Regamey. (Developments in Biological Standardization: Vol. 43). (Illus., Fr.). 1978. 66.75 (ISBN 3-8055-2816-7). S Karger.

Proceedings. International Symposium on the Design & Operation of Siphons & Siphon Spillways. 1976. text ed. 47.00x (ISBN 0-900983-44-2, Dist. by Air Science Co.). BHRA Fluid.

Proceedings. International Symposium on the Glomerular Basement Membrane, 1st, Vienna, Sept. 1980. Ed. by G. Lubec. (Renal Physiology Journal: Vol. 4, No. 2-3). (Illus.). 100p. 1981. pap. 20.75 (ISBN 3-8055-3491-4). S Karger.

Proceedings. International Symposium on the Judicial Settlement of International Disputes. Ed. by R. Bernhardt & H. Mosler. LC 74-5923. (Beitrage Zum Auslandischen Oeffentlichen Rechtund Voelkerecht: Vol. 62). 550p. 1974. 46.10 (ISBN 0-387-06756-6). Springer-Verlag.

Proceedings. International Symposium on Theoretical Programming. Ed. by A. Ershov. (Lectures Notes in Computer Science: Vol. 5). vi, 407p. 1974. pap. 21.00 (ISBN 0-387-06720-5). Springer-Verlag.

Proceedings. International Symposium on Unsteady Flow in Open Channels. 1977. text ed. 60.00x (ISBN 0-900983-54-X, Dist. by Air Science Co.). BHRA Fluid.

Proceedings. International Vibramycin Symposium, Paris, June 1974 & H. Swarz. (Chemotherapy: Vol. 21, Supplement 1). (Illus.). vii, 149p. 1975. 20.00 (ISBN 3-8055-2142-1). S Karger.

Proceedings. International Workshop on Ergot Alkaloids, Rome, Dec. 6-7, 1976. Ed. by B. B. Brodie et al. (Pharmacology: Vol. 16, Suppl. 1). (Illus.). 1977. 36.00 (ISBN 3-8055-2769-1). S Karger.

Proceedings. Japan - United States Seminar on Ordinary Differential & Functional Equations, Kyoto, 1971. Ed. by M. Urabe. (Lecture Notes in Mathematics: Vol. 243). viii, 332p. 1971. pap. 18.00 (ISBN 0-387-05708-0). Springer-Verlag.

Proceedings. Japan-USSR Symposium on Probablity Theory, 3rd. Ed. by G. Maruyama & J. V. Prokhorov. (Lecture Notes in Mathematics: Vol. 550). 1976. soft cover 34.00 (ISBN 0-387-07995-5). Springer-Verlag.

Proceedings. Jet Pumps & Ejectors & Gas Lift Techniques, 2nd Symposium. 1975. pap. 54.00x (ISBN 0-900983-43-4, Dist. by Air Science Co.). BHRA Fluid.

Proceedings. Joint FAO-WHO Expert Committee on Brucellosis, 5th, Geneva, 1970. (Technical Report Ser: No. 464). 76p. 1971. pap. 2.00 (ISBN 92-4-120464-8, 198). World Health.

Proceedings. Joint FAO-WHO Expert Committee on Brucellosis, 4th, Geneva, 1963. (Technical Report Ser: No. 289). 65p. 1964. pap. 2.00 (ISBN 92-4-120289-0). World Health.

Proceedings. Ed. by James E. Kruger & Donald E. LaBerge. 320p. 1983. lib. bdg. 26.50 (ISBN 0-86531-535-3). Westview.

Proceedings, 3 vols. Lunar & Planetary Science Conference, 9th, Houston, 1978. Compiled by Lunar & Planetary Institute, Houston, Texas. (Geochimica et Cosmochimicha Acta: Suppl. 10). 1979. Set. 325.00 (ISBN 0-08-022966-2). Pergamon.

Proceedings. Lunar & Planetary Science Conference, 12th, Houston, Mar. 16-20, 1981. Ed. by Lunar & Planetary Institute. (Geochimica et Cosmochimica Acta Ser.: No. 16). (Illus.). 2000p. 1982. 235.00 (ISBN 0-08-028074-9). Pergamon.

Proceedings, 3 vols. Lunar & Planetary Science Conference, 10th, Houston, Texas, March 19-23, 1979. LC 79-22554. (Illus.). 3200p. 1980. 290.00 (ISBN 0-08-025128-5). Pergamon.

Proceedings. Ed. by W. J. McGee & Governors in the White House, Conference, Washington D.C., May 13-15, 1908. LC 72-2855. (Use & Abuse). 1909. 32.00 (ISBN 0-405-04519-0). Ayer Co Pubs.

Proceedings. Machine Tool & Design Research International Conference, 14th & F. Koenigsberger. Ed. by S. A. Tobias. 841p. 1975. 149.95 (ISBN 0-470-49746-7). Halsted Pr.

Proceedings. Meeting on Critical Evaluation of Cardiac Rehabilitation, Tel-Aviv, Nov-Dec, 1975. Ed. by J. J. Kellerman. (Bibliotheca Cardiologica: No. 36). (Illus.). 1977. 41.50 (ISBN 3-8055-2373-4). S Karger.

Proceedings. Meeting on Polarization Nuclear Physics, Ebermannstadt, Germany, 1973. Ed. by D. Fick. (Lecture Notes in Physics Ser.: Vol. 30). (Illus.). ix, 292p. 1974. pap. 17.00 (ISBN 0-387-06978-X). Springer-Verlag.

Proceedings. Membrane Processes for Industry, Symposium, May 19-20,1966. Ed. by Charles E. Feazel & Robert E. Lacey. LC 66-30620. (Illus.). 268p. 1966. pap. 5.00 (ISBN 0-940824-00-0). S Res Inst.

Proceedings. Mixing, Second European Conference. Ed. by H. S. Stephens & J. A. Clarke. 1978. pap. 60.00x (ISBN 0-900983-69-8, Dist. by Air Science Co.). BHRA Fluid.

Proceedings. Ed. by G. P. Moretti. (Series Entomologica: No. 20). 471p. 1981. 89.00 (ISBN 90-6193-130-4, Pub. by Junk Pubs Netherlands). Kluwer Academic.

Proceedings. MUMPS Users' Group Meeting. Ed. by Judith R. Faulkner. 1979. 15.00 (ISBN 0-918118-06-9). MUMPS.

Proceedings. MUMPS Users' Group Meeting, 1973. Ed. by Joan Zimmerman. 9.00 (ISBN 0-918118-00-X). MUMPS.

Proceedings. MUMPS Users' Group Meeting, 1974. Ed. by Joan Zimmerman. 9.00 (ISBN 0-918118-01-8). MUMPS.

Proceedings. MUMPS Users' Group Meeting, 1975. Ed. by Joan Zimmerman. 15.00 (ISBN 0-918118-02-6). MUMPS.

Proceedings. Mumps Users' Group Meeting, 1978. Ed. by Pat Zimmerman. 1978. pap. 15.00 (ISBN 0-918118-05-0). MUMPS.

Proceedings. Myopia International Conference, 3rd, Copenhagen, 1980. Ed. by H. C. Fledelius et al. (Documenta Ophthalmologica Ser.: No. 28). 266p. 1982. 69.00 (ISBN 90-6193-725-6, Pub. by Junk Pubs Netherlands). Kluwer Academic.

Proceedings. Luigi G. Napolitano & International Astronautical Congress, 27th, Anaheim, Ca., Oct. 1976. 1978. 85.00 (ISBN 0-08-021732-X). Pergamon.

Proceedings. NASAGA Conference, 14th Annual. Ed. by Richard T. McGinty & Jolene Elliott. 1976. pap. 20.00 (ISBN 0-88474-034-X). U of S Cal Pr.

Proceedings. National Academy Of Arbitrators, 18th Meeting, 1965. Ed. by Dallas L. Jones. LC 55-57413. (Library of Labor Arbitration Ser.). 278p. 1965. 35.00 (ISBN 0-87179-066-1, 0066). BNA.

Proceedings. National Negro Conference, 1909. LC 69-18544. (American Negro: His History & Literature Ser., No. 2). 1969. Repr. of 1909 ed. 10.50 (ISBN 0-405-01890-8). Ayer Co Pubs.

Proceedings. National Passive Solar Conference, 3rd, San Jose, 1979. Ed. by Harry Miller et al. 1979. pap. text ed. 80.00x (ISBN 0-89553-015-5). Am Solar Energy.

Proceedings. National Passive Solar Conference, 4th, Kansas City, 1979. Ed. by Gregory E. Franta. pap. text ed. 80.00x (ISBN 0-89553-018-X). Am Solar Energy.

Proceedings, 2 vols. National Passive Solar Conference, 5th, Amherst, 1980. Ed. by John Hayes & Rachel Snyder. (Illus.). 1980. Set. pap. text ed. 150.00x (ISBN 0-89553-025-2). Am Solar Energy.

Proceedings. North American Symposium on Carbenoxolone, Montreal, 1975. Ed. by I. Beck. (International Congress Ser.: No. 379). 1976. pap. 48.50 (ISBN 0-444-15212-1, Excerpta Medica). Elsevier.

Proceedings. Nova Scotia Conference on Early Identification of Hearing Loss, Halifax, Nova Scotia, September 9-11, 1974. Ed. by Georges T. Mencher. 1976. 32.75 (ISBN 3-8055-2296-7). S Karger.

Proceedings. Order-Disorder Transformations in Alloys International Symposium, Tubinger, Germany, Sep. 1973. Ed. by H. Warlimont. (Reine Uno Angewandte Metallkunde in Einzel-Darstellungen Ser.: Vol. 24). (Illus.). viii, 556p. 1974. 69.70 (ISBN 0-387-06766-3). Springer-Verlag.

Proceedings. Pharmaceutical Technology Conference, New York, 1982. (Illus.). 700p. 1982. pap. text ed. 75.00 (ISBN 0-943330-01-7). Aster Pub Corp.

Proceedings. Pneumatic Transport of Solids in Pipes, 4th International Conference. Ed. by H. S. Stephens & C. A. Stapleton. (Illus.). 1979. pap. text ed. 62.00x (ISBN 0-900983-86-8, Dist by Air Science Co.). BHRA Fluid.

Proceedings. Pressure Surges, 2nd International Conference. 1977. text ed. 58.00x (ISBN 0-900983-65-5, Dist. by Air Science Co.). BHRA Fluid.

Proceedings. 450p. 1978. pap. 83.00 (ISBN 0-08-022678-7). Pergamon.

Proceedings. 84p. 15.00 (ISBN 0-318-12676-1, M70775). Am Gas Assn.

Proceedings. 105p. softcover 10.00 (ISBN 0-318-12677-X, M70774). Am Gas Assn.

Proceedings. 95p. pap. 10.00 (ISBN 0-318-12679-6, X12371). Am Gas Assn.

Proceedings. 648p. 50.00 (ISBN 0-318-12680-X, L51177). Am Gas Assn.

Proceedings. 559p. 50.00 (ISBN 0-318-12681-8, L51176). Am Gas Assn.

Proceedings. 444p. 50.00 (ISBN 0-318-12682-6, L51175). Am Gas Assn.

Proceedings. 432p. 40.00 (ISBN 0-318-12683-4, L51174). Am Gas Assn.

Proceedings. 556p. 40.00 (ISBN 0-318-12684-2, L51173). Am Gas Assn.

Proceedings. 291p. 20.00 (ISBN 0-318-12685-0, L11173). Am Gas Assn.

Proceedings, 2 vols. 1250p. 1963. 10.00 (ISBN 0-318-12922-1). Am Ornithologists.

Proceedings. 320p. pap. 10.00 (20141). Am Water Wks Assn.

Proceedings. (Proces-Verbeaux of General Assemblies Ser.). 220p. 1974. 8.00 (ISBN 0-318-14526-X). Intl Assoc Phys Sci Ocean.

Proceedings. 133p. softcover 10.00 (ISBN 0-318-12678-8, M11173). Am Gas Assn.

Proceedings. (Proces-Verbeaux of General Assemblies Ser.). 156p. 1972. 7.00 (ISBN 0-318-14527-8). Intl Assoc Phys Sci Ocean.

Proceedings. Protein-Ligand Interactions Symposium, Univ. of Konstanz, Germany, Sep, 1974. Ed. by Gideon Blauer & Horst Sund. 1975. 95.00x (ISBN 3-11-004881-7). De Gruyter.

Proceedings. Ed. by Polly M. Quick. (Conference on Reburial Issues). 175p. 1986. 12.50 (ISBN 0-932839-09-6). Soc Am Arch.

Proceedings. Recent & Fossil Marine Diatoms, 3rd Symposium, 1975. Ed. by R. Simonsen. 1975. 150.00x (ISBN 3-7682-5453-4). Lubrecht & Cramer.

Proceedings. Scandinavian Congress, 15th, Oslo, 1986. Ed. by K. E. Aubert & W. Ljunggren. LC 70-112305. (Lecture Notes in Mathematics: Vol. 118). 1970. pap. 10.70 (ISBN 0-387-04907-X). Springer-Verlag.

Proceedings. Seals in Fluid Power Symposium. 1973. pap. 27.00x (ISBN 0-900983-31-0, Dist. by Air Science Co.). BHRA Fluid.

Proceedings. Seminaire De Probabilites, 9th, Universite De Strasbourg. Ed. by P. A. Meyer. (Lecture Notes in Mathematics: Vol. 465). 598p. 1975. pap. 26.00 (ISBN 0-387-07178-4). Springer-Verlag.

Proceedings. Seminaire Pierre Lelong (Analyse) Annee 1973-4. (Lecture Notes in Mathematics: Vol. 474). 182p. 1975. pap. 10.70 (ISBN 0-387-07189-X). Springer-Verlag.

Proceedings. Seminar on Complex Multiplication, Institute for Advanced Study, Princeton & A. Borel. (Lecture Notes in Mathematics: Vol. 21). 1966. pap. 10.70 (ISBN 0-387-03604-0). Springer-Verlag.

Proceedings. Seminar on Differential Equations & Dynamical Systems, University of Maryland, 1968. Ed. by G. S. Jones. (Lecture Notes in Mathematics: Vol. 60). 1968. pap. 10.70 (ISBN 0-387-04230-X). Springer-Verlag.

Proceedings. Seminar on Fiber Spaces, 1964-65 & E. Thomas. (Lecture Notes in Mathematics: Vol. 13). 1966. pap. 10.70 (ISBN 0-387-03596-6). Springer-Verlag.

Proceedings. Seminar on Functional Operators & Equations, Zurich, 1965-66 & G. I. Targonski. (Lecture Notes in Mathematics: Vol. 33). 1967. pap. 10.70 (ISBN 0-387-03904-X). Springer-Verlag.

Proceedings. Seminar on Periodic Maps. (Lecture Notes in Mathematics: Vol. 46). 1967. pap. 10.70 (ISBN 0-387-03917-1). Springer-Verlag.

Proceedings. Seminar on Potential Theory, 2nd. Ed. by H. Bauer. (Lecture Notes in Mathematics: Vol. 226). iv, 170p. 1971. pap. 11.00 (ISBN 0-387-05638-6). Springer-Verlag.

Proceedings. Seminar on Triples & Categorical Homology. Ed. by B. Eckmann. LC 68-59303. (Lecture Notes in Mathematics: Vol. 80). 1969. pap. 18.30 (ISBN 0-387-04601-1). Springer-Verlag.

Proceedings. Seventh International Conference on Fluid Sealing. 1976. text ed. 56.00x (ISBN 0-900983-48-5, Dist. by Air Science Co.). BHRA Fluid.

Proceedings. Shambaugh International Workshop on Middle Ear Microsurgery & Fluctuant Hearing Loss. Ed. by George E. Shambaugh & John J. Shea. LC 80-54309. 1981. 49.95 (ISBN 0-87397-183-3). Strode.

Proceedings. Society for Technical Communication, Symposium on the State of the Art in Communication, Point Mugu, Calif., Oct., 1975. 1975. 15.00 (ISBN 0-87703-123-1). Univelt Inc.

Proceedings. Specialist Symposium on Geophysical Fluid Dynamics, European Geophysical Society, Fourth Meeting, Munich September, 1977. Ed. by P. A. Davies & P. H. Roberts. 156p. 1978. 33.00 (ISBN 0-677-40115-9). Gordon & Breach.

Proceedings. Summer School on Topological Vector Spaces. Ed. by L. Waelbroeck. LC 73-83244. (Lecture Notes in Mathematics: Vol. 331). vi, 226p. (2 contributions in French). 1973. pap. 21.00 (ISBN 0-387-06367-6). Springer-Verlag.

Proceedings. Symposium on Air Cushion Handling. 1974. pap. 32.00x (ISBN 0-900983-34-5, Dist. by Air Science Co.). BHRA Fluid.

Proceedings. Symposium on Applied Continuum Mechanics, Vienna, 1974. Ed. by J. L. Zeman & F. Ziegler. LC 74-12227. (Illus.). vii, 221p. 1974. 29.00 (ISBN 0-387-81260-1). Springer-Verlag.

Proceedings. Symposium on Artificial Ventilation, Paris, 1969. Ed. by A. Minkowski et al. (Biology of the Neonate: Vol. 16, No. 1-3). 1970. pap. 40.00 (ISBN 3-8055-0755-0). S Karger.

Proceedings. Symposium on Asthma & Chronic Bronchitis in Children & Their Prognosis into Adult Life, 3rd, Davos, 1969. Ed. by F. Suter & R. E. Altounyan. 1970. pap. 56.00 (ISBN 3-8055-0754-2). S Karger.

Proceedings. Symposium on Automatic Demonstration, Versailles, 1968. Ed. by M. Laudet et al. LC 79-117526. (Lecture Notes in Mathematics: Vol. 125). (Illus.). 1970. pap. 18.30 (ISBN 0-387-04914-2). Springer-Verlag.

Proceedings. Symposium on Brain Edema, Vienna, 1965. Ed. by I. Klatzo & F. Seitelberger. (Illus.). 1967. 65.00 (ISBN 0-387-80802-7). Springer-Verlag.

Proceedings. Symposium on Congenital Heart Disease with Cyanosis, Amsterdam, 1968. Ed. by A. C. Klinkhammer. (Radiologia Clinica et Biologica: Vol. 39, No. 2). 1970. pap. 21.50 (ISBN 3-8055-0802-6). S Karger.

Proceedings. Symposium on Cranial Computerized Tomography, Munich, June 1976. Ed. by W. Lanksch & E. Kazner. 1976. softcover 45.00 (ISBN 0-387-07938-6). Springer-Verlag.

Proceedings. Symposium on Differential Equations & Dynamical Systems, Warwickshire, 1968. Ed. by D. Chillingworth. LC 79-164961. (Lecture Notes in Mathematics: Vol. 206). 1971. pap. 11.00 (ISBN 0-387-05495-2). Springer-Verlag.

Proceedings. Symposium on Formalist Criticism. Ed. by William J. Handy. LC 67-63594. (Quarterly Ser). 1965. 10.00 (ISBN 0-87959-071-8). U of Tex H Ransom Ctr.

Proceedings. Symposium on General Topology & Its Relations to Modern Analysis & Algebra - 2nd - Prague - 1967. Ed. by J. Novak. 1967. 76.00 (ISBN 0-12-522556-3). Acad Pr.

Proceedings. Symposium on Incremental Motion & Control Systems & Devices, 7th Annual, Hyatt-Regency Hotel, O'hare, Ill., May 24-27, 1978. Ed. by B. C. Kuo. LC 78-53485. (Illus.). 1978. 40.00x (ISBN 0-931538-00-9). Incremental Motion.

Proceedings. Symposium on Incremental Motion & Control Systems & Devices, 8th, Annual. LC 73-647018. (Illus.). 1979. 40.00x (ISBN 0-931538-01-7). Incremental Motion.

Proceedings. Symposium on Information Processing in the Nervous System - Buffalo - 1968. Ed. by K. N. Leibovic. 1970. 70.40 (ISBN 0-387-04885-5). Springer-Verlag.

Proceedings. Symposium on Jet Pumps & Ejectors, 1st. 1972. 39.00x (ISBN 0-686-71056-8). BHRA Fluid.

Proceedings. Symposium on Meson-, Photo-, & Electroproduction at Low & Intermediate Energies, Bonn, 1970. LC 25-9130. (Springer Tracts in Modern Physics: Vol. 59). 1971. 56.70 (ISBN 0-387-05494-4). Springer-Verlag.

Proceedings. Symposium on Non-Well-Posed Problems & Logarithmic Convexity, Edinburgh, 1972. Ed. by R. J. Knops. LC 72-98023. (Lecture Notes in Mathematics: Vol. 316). v, 176p. 1973. pap. 18.00 (ISBN 0-387-06159-2). Springer-Verlag.

Proceedings. Symposium on Optimization, Nice, 1969. Ed. by A. V. Balakrishna et al. LC 70-120380. (Lecture Notes in Mathematics: Vol. 132). (Illus.). 1970. pap. 18.30 (ISBN 0-387-04921-5). Springer-Verlag.

Proceedings. Symposium on Ordinary Differential Equations, Minneapolis, May, 1972. Ed. by W. A. Harris, Jr. & Y. Sibuya. LC 72-97022. (Lecture Notes in Mathematics: Vol. 312). (Illus.). 204p. 1973. pap. 19.00 (ISBN 0-387-06146-0). Springer-Verlag.

Proceedings. Symposium on Psychophysiological Aspects of Space Flight, Brooks Air Force Base, Texas, 1960. Ed. by Bernard E. Flaherty. LC 60-15809. 1961. 49.00x (ISBN 0-231-02456-8). Columbia U Pr.

Proceedings. Symposium on Recent & Fossil Marine Diatoms, First, 1972. Ed. by R. Simonsen. 1972. 90.00x (ISBN 3-7682-5439-9). Lubrecht & Cramer.

Proceedings. Symposium on Recent & Fossil Marine Diatoms, Second, 1974. Ed. by R. Simonsen. 1974. 150.00x (ISBN 3-7682-5445-3). Lubrecht & Cramer.

Proceedings. Symposium on Semantics of Algorithmic Languages. Ed. by E. Engeler. LC 78-151406. (Lecture Notes in Mathematics: Vol. 188). (Illus.). 1971. pap. 18.00 (ISBN 0-387-05377-8). Springer-Verlag.

Proceedings. Symposium on Semiconducting Ferroeletrics, Rostov-on-Don, U. S. S. R., 1976 et al. Ed. by I. Lefkowitz. 200p. 1978. 176.00 (ISBN 0-677-16205-7). Gordon & Breach.

Proceedings. Symposium on Stereoencephalotomy, 5th International, 1970. Ed. by F. Mundinger et al. (Advances in Stereoencephalotomy: Vol. 6). 1972. pap. 54.00 (ISBN 3-8055-1358-5). S Karger.

Proceedings. Symposium on the Comparative Study of Communist Foreign Policy. Ed. by Peter Berton & Charles Gati. 1976. pap. text ed. 2.75 (ISBN 0-88474-029-3). U of S Cal Pr.

Proceedings. Symposium on the Theory of Numerical Analysis. Ed. by J. L. Morris. LC 70-155916. (Lecture Notes in Mathematics: Vol. 193). 1971. pap. 11.00 (ISBN 0-387-05422-7). Springer-Verlag.

Proceedings. Symposium on Wind Energy, 1st. 1977. 58.00x (ISBN 0-686-71055-X). BHRA Fluid.

Proceedings. Symposium on Wind Energy, 3rd. 1980. pap. 87.00x. BHRA Fluid.

Proceedings. Telecommunications Policy Research Conference, Annual 10th. Ed. by Oscar Gandy et al. LC 83-6408. 256p. 1983. text ed. 24.95 pers. ed. (ISBN 0-89391-195-X); text ed. 49.50 inst. ed. Ablex Pub.

Proceedings. Ed. by Sigmund Timberg & Earle W. Zaidins. Incl. Symposium on Twenty Years of Robinson-Putman, the Record & the Issues; Symposium on the House Counsel; Attorney General's Committee Report. 210p. 1956. 10.00 (ISBN 0-87956-003-7). Fed Legal Pubn.

Proceedings. Topology Symposium, Seigen, 1979. Ed. by W. B. Neumann & Koschorke. (Lecture Notes in Mathematics: Vol. 788). 495p. 1980. pap. 34.00 (ISBN 0-387-09968-9). Springer-Verlag.

Proceedings. Touche Ross Foundation Symposium on Graduate Tax Education, 1982. Ed. by William L. Raby. 1981. 25.00 (ISBN 0-88262-667-1). Warren Gorham & Lamont.

Proceedings. Tulane Tidelands Institute. Ed. by R. Slovenko. 1963. Vols. 1-6. 25.00x set; Vol. 7. 7.50x. Claitors.

Proceedings. U. S. S. R. Symposium on Probability Theory, 2nd, Japan, Aug. 2-9, 1972. Ed. by G. Maruyama & Y. V. Prokhorov. (Lecture Notes in Mathematics: Vol. 330). (Illus.). vi, 550p. 1973. pap. 31.00 (ISBN 0-387-06358-7). Springer-Verlag.

Proceedings. United Nations Conference on the Law of the Sea, 3rd, Geneva, 1975. Ed. by Renate Platzoder. xiv, 322p. 1975. pap. text ed. 17.95x (ISBN 3-7875-2127-5). Rothman.

Proceedings. Victoria Symposium on Nonstandard Analysis. Ed. by A. Hurd & P. Loeb. LC 73-22552. (Lecture Notes in Mathematics: Vol. 369). xviii, 339p. 1974. pap. 21.00 (ISBN 0-387-06656-X). Springer-Verlag.

Proceedings, 2 vols. in 1. Virginia Company of London, 1619-1624. Ed. by Conway Robinson & R. A. Brock. LC 73-589. Repr. of 1889 ed. 37.50 (ISBN 0-404-57657-5). AMS Pr.

Proceedings. Virginia Historical Society Annual Meeting, Dec 21-22, 1891. Ed. by R. A. Brock. LC 73-592. (Virginia Historical Society. Collections, New Ser.: No. 11). Repr. of 1892 ed. 27.50 (ISBN 0-404-57661-3). AMS Pr.

Proceedings, 2 vols. Wave & Tidal Energy International Symposium, 1st. Ed. by H. S. Stephens. (Illus.). 1979. Set. pap. 69.00x (ISBN 0-906085-00-4, Dist. by Air Science Co.). BHRA Fluid.

Proceedings, 2 vols. Wind Energy Systems, 2nd International Symposium. Ed. by H. S. Stephens & I. Fantom. (Illus.). 1979. Set. pap. text ed. 69.00x (ISBN 0-906085-03-9, Dist. by Air Science Co.). BHRA Fluid.

Proceedings. Woman's Rights Convention, Seneca Falls And Rochester, Jul-Aug, 1848. LC 76-79180. (Women's Rights & Liberation Ser.). 1969. Repr. of 1848 ed. 11.00 (ISBN 0-405-00117-7). Ayer Co Pubs.

Proceedings. Workshop on Advances in Experimental Pharmacology of Hydergine Basel, December 1976. Ed. by W. Meier-Ruge. (Gerontology: Vol. 24, Suppl. 1). (Illus.). 1977. 32.75 (ISBN 3-8055-2687-3). S Karger.

Proceedings. Workshop on Cariostatic Mechanism of Fluorides, Naples, Florida, April 1976. Ed. by K. G. Koenig. (Caries Research: Vol. 11, Suppl. 1). 1976. 51.50 (ISBN 3-8055-2430-7). S Karger.

Proceedings, 9 Vols. World Petroleum Congress, 7th. Incl. Vol. 1. Review of the Latest Developments Within the Oil Industry; Vol. 2. Origin of Oil Geology & Geophysics; Vol. 3. Drilling & Production. 804p. 138.75 (ISBN 0-444-20016-9); Vol. 4. Refining. 413p. 74.00 (ISBN 0-444-20017-7); Vol. 5. Petrochemsitry. 465p. 74.00 (ISBN 0-444-20018-5); Vol. 6. Engineering Transport & Operations Research. 596p. 100.00 (ISBN 0-444-20019-3); Vols. 7 & 8. Applications & New Uses, 2 Pts. Pt. 1. 44.50 (ISBN 0-444-20020-7); Pt. 2. 64.75 (ISBN 0-686-44100-1); Vol. 9. Petroleum Industry: General Problems. 358p. 61.00 (ISBN 0-444-20022-3). 1967 (Pub. by Elsevier Applied Sci England). Elsevier.

Proceedings, 6 Vols. World Petroleum Congress, 8th. Incl. Vol. 1. General Review of Congress. 1971. Set. 430.50 (ISBN 0-686-44099-4). Elsevier.

Proceedings. World Society for Stereotactic & Functional Neurosurgery, 8th Meeting, Zurich, July 1981 & European Society for Stereotactic & Functional Neurosurgery, 5th Meeting, Zurich, July, 1981. Ed. by P. L. Gildenberg et al. (Advances in Stereoencephalotomy: Vol. 9). (Illus.). viii, 548p. 1982. pap. 103.50 (ISBN 3-8055-3501-5). S Karger.

Proceedings, Pt. 1. Conference on Compact Transformation Groups, 2nd. LC 72-95314. (Lecture Notes in Mathematics: Vol. 298). xii, 453p. 1972. pap. 23.00 (ISBN 0-387-06077-4). Springer-Verlag.

Proceedings, Vol. 1. National Child Labor Committee, 1905. Ed. by Robert H. Bremner. LC 74-1699. (Children & Youth Ser.). 1974. 33.00x (ISBN 0-405-05976-0). Ayer Co Pubs.

Proceedings, Pt. 2. Conference on Compact Transformation Groups, 2nd. LC 72-95314. (Lecture Notes in Mathematics: Vol. 299). xi, 327p. 1972. pap. 21.00 (ISBN 0-387-06078-2). Springer-Verlag.

Proceedings, Pt. 2. Conference on Optimization Techniques, 5th. Ed. by A. Ruberti. (Lecture Notes in Computer Science: Vol. 4). (Illus.). 389p. 1973. pap. 21.00 (ISBN 0-387-06600-4). Springer-Verlag.

Proceedings, Suppl. To Vol. 3. International Society for Artificial Organs, 2nd, New York, April 18-19, 1979 et al. Ed. by Eli A. Friedman & Monica M. Beyer. LC 81-13627. (Illus.). 512p. 1980. text ed. 80.00 (ISBN 0-936022-02-7); pap. text ed. 65.00x (ISBN 0-936022-01-9). Intl Soc Artifical Organs.

Proceedings, Vol. 5. Association of Orthodox Jewish Scientists. Ed. by Fred Rosner. 1978. pap. 10.95 (ISBN 0-87306-150-0). Feldheim.

Proceedings, Vol. 7, Nos. 1-2. Ed. by African Bibliographic Center Staff. Incl. No. 1; No. 2; Vol. 8, No. 1. lib. bdg. 25.00 (ISBN 0-8371-6261-0, SBH&). (Special Bibliographic Ser.). Repr. Set. lib. bdg. 25.00 (ISBN 0-8371-9916-6, SBK&). Greenwood.

Proceedings - Durability of Glass Fiber Reinforced Concrete Symposium. Date not set. 45.00 (GFRC-2). Prestressed Concrete.

Proceedings - Fifth International Carnahan Conference on Security Technology: Electronic Crime Countermeasures. Ed. by R. William DeVore et al. (Illus.). 255p. (Orig.). 1986. pap. 33.50 (ISBN 0-89779-066-9, UKY BU141). OES Pubns.

Proceedings A Symposium of the Bell Museum, Univ. of Minn. Med. School see Death & Attitudes Towards Death.

Proceedings: ABCA Nineteen Eighty-Two International Convention. Ed. by Sam Bruno. 1983. pap. 8.60 (ISBN 0-931874-13-0). Assn Busn Comm.

Proceedings & Addresses at the Freethinkers' Convention Held at Watkins, N. Y., 1878. LC 73-119051. (Civil Liberties in American History Ser). 1970. Repr. of 1878 ed. lib. bdg. 49.50 (ISBN 0-306-71937-1). Da Capo.

Proceedings & Debates of the British Parliaments Respecting North America, 5 vols. Great Britain, Parliament Staff. Ed. by Leo F. Stock. LC 24-7105. 1976. Set. 320.00 (ISBN 0-527-35720-0). Kraus Repr.

Proceedings & Debates of the Virginia State Convention of 1829-1830, 2 vols. in 1. LC 71-139729. (Law, Politics, & History Ser). 1971. Repr. of 1830 ed. lib. bdg. 95.00 (ISBN 0-306-70077-8). Da Capo.

Proceedings & Final Acts see Official Records of the World Health Organization: International Health Conference.

Proceedings & Interim Report. facsimile ed. National Conference on Bail & Criminal Justice, May 27-29, 1964, & May, 1964-Apr 1965. Ed. by Robert M. Fogelson. LC 74-3839. (Criminal Justice in America Ser.). 1974. Repr. 30.00x (ISBN 0-405-06156-0). Ayer Co Pubs.

Proceedings & Papers of the Georgia Association of Historians, 1984. Ed. by Ann W. Ellis. 145p. (Orig.). 1985. pap. 5.00 (ISBN 0-939346-04-4). GA Assn Hist.

Proceedings & Papers of the Georgia Association of Historians, 1985. Ed. by Ann W. Ellis. 125p. (Orig.). 1985. pap. 5.00 (ISBN 0-939346-05-2). GA Assn Hist.

Proceedings & Papers of the Georgia Association of Historians, 1981. Ed. by Ann W. Ellis et al. 138p. (Orig.). 1982. pap. 5.00 (ISBN 0-939346-01-X). GA Assn Hist.

Proceedings & Papers of the Georgia Association of Historians: 1982. Ed. by Ann W. Ellis et al. 141p. (Orig.). 1983. pap. 5.00 (ISBN 0-939346-02-8). GA Assn Hist.

Proceedings & Papers of the Georgia Association of Historians, 1983. Ed. by Ann W. Ellis et al. 130p. (Orig.). 1984. pap. 5.00 (ISBN 0-939346-03-6). GA Assn Hist.

Proceedings & Papers of the Georgia Association of Historians, 1980. Ed. by Ann W. Ellis et al. 84p. (Orig.). 1981. pap. 5.00 (ISBN 0-939346-00-1). GA Assn Hist.

Proceedings & Technical Papers, Vol. 7. General Fisheries Council for the Mediterranean. 503p. 1964. pap. 26.25 (ISBN 0-685-36297-3, F204, FAO). UNIPUB.

Proceedings & Technical Papers, Vol. 8. General Fisheries Council for the Mediterranean. 1967. pap. 47.00 (ISBN 0-685-36298-1, F205, FAO). UNIPUB.

Proceedings: Assembly of European Seismological Commission, 17th, Budapest, 24-29 Aug. 1980. Ed. by E. Bisztricsany & G. Szeidovitz. (Developments in Solid Earth Geophysics: Vol. 15). 690p. 1983. 152.75 (ISBN 0-444-99662-1). Elsevier.

Proceedings: Bulletin of WHO. International Conference on Hong Kong Influenza, Atlanta, Ga. 1969. (Vol. 41, Nos. 3-5). 414p. 1969. pap. 14.40 (ISBN 0-686-09014-4, 797). World Health.

Proceedings: C. S. Peirce Bicentennial International Congress. Ed. by Kenneth Ketner. (Graduate Studies, Texas Tech Univ.: No. 23). 400p. (Orig.). 1981. 75.00 (ISBN 0-89672-075-6); pap. 50.00 (ISBN 0-89672-074-8). Tex Tech Univ Pr.

Proceedings China USSM Polymer Chemistry, Vol. 1 & 2. Science Press staff. 99.95 (ISBN 0-317-64253-7). Van Nos Reinhold.

Proceedings Consensus Conference: The Relative Roles of Vestibuloplasty & Ridge Augmentation in the Management of the Atrophic Mandible. P. J. W. Stoelinga. (Illus.). 1984. pap. text ed. 40.00 (ISBN 0-86715-155-2). Quint Pub CO.

Proceedings: Eastern Oil Shale Symposium. Ed. by Rhonda Pettit. (Illus.). 135p. 1982. pap. text ed. 25.00x (ISBN 0-86607-007-9). KY Energy Cabnt Lab.

Proceedings: Eastern Oil Shale Symposium, 1985. Ed. by Rhonda Pettit. LC 85-147. (Oil Shale Symposium Ser.). (Illus.). 400p. 1986. pap. text ed. 25.00 (ISBN 0-86607-028-1). KY Energy Cabnt Lab.

Proceedings: Eleventh Lunar & Planetary Science Conference, Houston, Texas, March 17-21, 1980, 3 vols. Compiled by Lunar & Planetary Institute. (Geochimica & Cosmochimica Acta: Suppl. 14). 3000p. 1981. Set. 265.00 (ISBN 0-08-026314-3). Pergamon.

Proceedings: FEBS Meeting, 11th, 9 vols. Ed. by Per Schambye. (Illus.). 1978. Set. 455.00 (ISBN 0-08-021527-0). Pergamon.

Proceedings: Fifth International Bat Research Conference. Ed. by D. E. Wilson & A. L. Gardner. 434p. (Orig.). 1980. pap. 16.00 (ISBN 0-89672-083-7). Tex Tech Univ Pr.

Proceedings: Fifth Kentucky Coal Refuse Disposal & Utilization Seminar & Stability Analysis of Refuse Dams Workshop. Ed. by Jerry G. Rose. 75p. 1980. pap. text ed. 10.00 (ISBN 0-686-94732-0). KY Energy Cabnt Lab.

Proceedings: First International Steel Foundry Congress. 1985. 75.00 (ISBN 0-317-47615-7). Steel Founders.

Proceedings for International Congress on Welding Research, July Thirteenth to Fourteenth, 1984, in Boston Massachussets. 25.00 (ISBN 0-318-18645-4). Welding Res Coun.

Proceedings: Fourteenth International Congress of the Historical Sciences. International Congress of Historical Sciences San Francisco 1975. 12.00 (ISBN 0-405-19039-5, 19487). Ayer Co Pubs.

Proceedings: Fourth International Congress on Metallic Corrosion. LC 64-9547. (Illus.). 822p. 1972. 65.00 (ISBN 0-915567-80-6). Natl Corrosion Eng.

Proceedings from the International Rubber Conference, Goteborg Sweden 1986, 3 Vols. (Illus.). 808p. 1986. Set. pap. 127.50x (ISBN 91-86430-59-9). Coronet Bks.

Proceedings from the International Symposium on Kinetic Modelling in Artificial Organs, Rostock-Warenemunde, 1982. Ed. by H. Klinkmann et al. 30.00 (ISBN 0-936022-10-8). Intl Soc Artifical Organs.

Proceedings from the Second International Conference on Expert Database Systems. Ed. by Larry Kerschberg. (Illus.). 900p. 1988. text ed. 41.95 (ISBN 0-8053-0311-1). Benjamin-Cummings.

Proceedings from the Third Nordic Conference for English Studies, 2 vols. Ed. by Ishrat Lindblad & Magnus Ljung. (Stokholm Studies in English: LXXIII). 806p. (Orig.). 1987. Set. pap. text ed. 87.50x (ISBN 91-22-00870-5, Pub. by Almqvist & Wiksell). Coronet Bks.

Proceedings: Great Lakes Solar Greenhouse Conference IV. Kalamazoo, Michigan, Nov. 6-7, 1981. Ed. by H. Lewis Batts, Jr. & Monica A. Evans. 177p. 1982. pap. 10.00 (ISBN 0-939294-05-2, SB-416-G7-1981). Beech Leaf.

Proceedings: Great Lakes Solar Greenhouse Conference II Kalamazoo, Michigan, June, 8-9, 1979. Ed. by H. Lewis Batts, Jr. & Michael Tenenbaum. (Illus.). xiiii, 137p. (Orig.). 1980. pap. 10.00 (ISBN 0-939294-02-8, SB-416-G7-1979). Beech Leaf.

Proceedings: Image Understanding Workshop. (Illus.). 1000p. (Orig.). 1987. pap. text ed. 40.00 (ISBN 0-934613-36-2). Morgan Kaufmann.

Proceedings in Atmospheric Electricity. Ed. by Lothar H. Ruhnke & John Latham. LC 83-10096. (Illus.). 440p. 1983. 35.00 (ISBN 0-937194-04-2). A Deepak Pub.

Proceedings in Parga & the Ionian Islands. C. P. DeBosset. (Illus.). 1976. 15.00 (ISBN 0-916710-27-0). Obol Intl.

Proceedings in Parliament, 4 vols. Ed. by Robert C. Johnson & Keeler. Incl. Introduction & Reference Materials,Vol.1. 30.00x (ISBN 0-300-02033-3); Vol. II. 17 March-19 April 1628. 60.00t (ISBN 0-300-01946-7); Vol. III. 21 April-27 May 1628. 65.00x (ISBN 0-300-02048-1); Vol. IV. May 28 - June 26, 1628. (Illus.). 1978. 65.00t (ISBN 0-300-02050-3). LC 75-43321. 1977. Set. 155.00t (ISBN 0-300-02161-5). Yale U Pr.

Proceedings in Parliament Sixteen Ten, 2 vols. Ed. by Elizabeth R. Foster. Incl. Vol. 1. The House of Lords. (Illus.). lxix, 366p; Vol. 2. The House of Commons. (Illus.). xxi, 422p. (Historical Publications, Manuscripts & Edited Texts Ser.: No. 22 & 23). 1966. Yale U Pr.

Proceedings in Parliament Sixteen Twenty-Eight. Ed. by Mary F. Keeler & Maija J. Cole. LC 75-43321. (Proceedings in Parliament 1628 Ser.). 700p. 1983. Vol. V: Lords Proceedings Sixteen Twenty-Eight. text ed. 92.00x (ISBN 0-300-02051-1); Vol. VI: Appendixes & Indexes. text ed. 65.00x (ISBN 0-300-02467-3). Yale U Pr.

Proceedings in Parliament 1614 (House of Commons) Maija Jansson. LC 86-71781. (Memoirs Ser.: Vol. 172). (Illus.). 500p. 1988. 40.00 (ISBN 0-87169-172-8). Am Philos.

Proceedings in Parliament 1625. Maija Jansson & William B. Bidwell. LC 86-50026. 832p. 1987. text ed. 95.00 (ISBN 0-300-03544-6). Yale U Pr.

Proceedings in the Court of Vice-Admiralty of Virginia: 1698-1775. Ed. by George Reese. xiii, 121p. 1983. 10.00 (ISBN 0-88490-113-0). Va State Lib.

Proceedings in the Parliaments of Elizabeth I: Part I. Ed. by T. E. Hartley. LC 81-80390. 572p. 1981. 87.00 (ISBN 0-89453-225-1). M Glazier.

Proceedings, International Course on Land Drainage: Twenty-Five Years of Drainage Experience, Symposium 25th. Ed. by J. Vos. (ILRI Publication Ser.: No. 42). (Illus.). 353p. 1987. 42.50 (PDC401, Pub. by PUDOC). UNIPUB.

Proceedings: International Ornithological Congress, 13th, 2 vols. Ed. by Charles G. Sibley & American Ornithologists' Union. 1250p. 1963. 10.00 (ISBN 0-943610-00-1). Am Ornithologists.

Proceedings: International Symposium on Bifonazole, Kopenhagen, June 1984. Ed. by Hamburg Rieth. (Journal: Dermatologica: Vol. 169, Suppl. 1). iv, 148p. 1985. pap. 30.75 (ISBN 3-8055-4021-3). S Karger.

Proceedings: MDS Nineteen Eighty-Six. Ed. by Ray Canada. 611p. 1986. pap. text ed. 50.00 (ISBN 0-933957-03-3). Marine Tech Soc.

Proceedings: MUMPS Users' Group Meeting. Ed. by Jeffrey Rothmeier. 1976. 15.00 (ISBN 0-918118-03-4). MUMPS.

Proceedings: MUMPS Users' Group Meeting. Ed. by Richard E. Zapolin. 1977. 15.00 (ISBN 0-918118-04-2). MUMPS.

Proceedings: National Conference on Bilingual Education. Dissemination Center For Bilingual Bicultural Education. Ed. by Francesco Cordasco. LC 77-90556. (Bilingual-Bicultural Education in the U. S. Ser.). 1978. Repr. of 1975 ed. lib. bdg. 31.00x (ISBN 0-405-11094-4). Ayer Co Pubs.

Proceedings: Ninth National Passive Solar Conference, Columbus. Ed. by John Hayes & Alex Wilson. 1984. 120.00x (ISBN 0-89553-200-X). Am Solar Energy.

Proceedings of a Conference on Multispecies Grazing. Ed. by Frank H. Baker & R. Katherine Jones. 235p. 1985. 10.00 (ISBN 0-933595-02-6). Winrock Intl.

Proceedings of a Symposium on Large Scale Digital Calculating Machinery 1948. Harvard Computation Laboratory Staff. (Charles Babbage Institute Reprint Ser.: No. 8). 340p. 1985. Repr. of 1948 ed. text ed. 37.50x (ISBN 0-262-08152-0). MIT Pr.

Proceedings of a Workshop on Agricultural Potentiality Directed by Nutritional Needs. Ed. by Rajki. 1979. cancelled 24.50 (ISBN 963-05-1991-7, Pub. by Akademiai Kaido Hungary). IPS.

Proceedings of a Workshop on Agricultural Potentiality Directed by Nutritional Needs June 5th-9th, 1978 Martonvaar. Sandor Rajki. 238p. 1979. 93.00x (ISBN 0-569-08563-2, Pub. by Collets (UK)). State Mutual Bk.

Proceedings of a Workshop on the Development & Evaluation of Habitat Suitability Criteria: A Compilation of Papers & Discussions Presented at Colorado State University, Fort Collins, Colo. (Illus.). 418p. (Orig.). 1988. pap. 19.00 (S/N 024-010-00681-1). USGPO.

Proceedings of an Institute on the Roles of Psychology & Psychologists in Rehabilitation Held at Princeton, New Jersey, February 3-7, 1958. Beatrice A. Wright. Ed. by Janet Rosenberg. LC 79-6929. (Physically Handicapped in Society Ser.). 1980. Repr. of 1959 ed. lib. bdg. 16.00x (ISBN 0-405-13136-4). Ayer Co Pubs.

Proceedings of Coastal & Port Engineering in Developing Countries 1987, 2 vols. Ed. by Nanjing Hydraulic Research Institute. 2250p. 1988. pap. price not set (ISBN 7-5027-0052-8, Pub. by A A Balkema). Brookfield Pub Co.

Proceedings of Drag Reduction, 2nd International Conference Staff. Drag Reduction Staff. pap. 54.00x (ISBN 0-900983-71-X, Dist. by Air Science Co.). BHRA Fluid.

Proceedings of Eighth World Petroleum Congress: Geological & Exploration, Vol. 2. World Petroleum Congress. 362p. 1971. 89.00 (ISBN 0-85334-517-1, Pub. by Elsevier Applied Sci England). Elsevier.

Proceedings of Eighth World Petroleum Congress: Geographical Exploration, Vol. 3. World Petroleum Congress. 427p. 1971. 105.50 (ISBN 0-85334-518-X, Pub. by Elsevier Applied Sci England). Elsevier.

Proceedings of Fifth Conference on Dimensioning & Strength Calculations & the Sixth Congress on Materials Testing. Ed. by Collet's Holdings, Ltd. Staff. 800p. 1974. 127.25 (ISBN 0-317-46705-0, Pub. by Collets (UK)). State Mutual Bk.

Proceedings of Fifth International Conference on Zeolites. Ed. by L. Rees. 902p. 1980. 152.95 (ISBN 0-471-25989-6, Wiley Heyden). Wiley.

Proceedings of First International Conference in Simulation in Manufacturing. 1985. 93.00x (ISBN 0-903608-84-7, Pub. by IFS Pubns UK). Air Sci Co.

Proceedings of Fourth Conference on Dimensioning & Strength Calculations. Ed. by Collet's Holdings, Ltd. Staff. 439p. 1973. 93.00x (ISBN 0-569-08002-9, Pub. by Collets (UK)). State Mutual Bk.

Proceedings of Fourth International Conference on Applied Numerical Modeling. Ed. by Han-Min Hsia et al. (Science & Technology Ser.: Vol. 63). (Illus.). 800p. 1986. lib. bdg. 70.00x (ISBN 0-87703-242-4, Pub. by Am Astro Soc). Univelt Inc.

Proceedings of G. I. N. I.'s Third International Polio & Independent Living Conference, May 10-12, 1985, St. Louis, Missouri. Ed. by G. Laurie & J. Raymond. 68p. (Orig.). 1986. pap. 15.00 (ISBN 0-931301-02-5). Gazette Intl.

Proceedings of General Assembly & Technical Meeting, Vol. 1. (IUCN Programme Ser.: No. 4, 1986). (Illus.). 118p. (Orig., Eng. & Fr.). 1986. pap. 12.00 (ISBN 2-88032-093-3, IUCN161, IUCN). UNIPUB.

Proceedings of Groups-St. Andrews, 1985. Ed. by E. F. Robertson & C. M. Campbell. (London Mathematical Society Lecture Note: Series 121). (Illus.). 368p. 1987. pap. 39.50 (ISBN 0-521-33854-9). Cambridge U Pr.

Proceedings of HAZMACON 85: Compilation of Technical Papers Presented April 23-25, at the HAzardous Materials Management Conference in Oakland. 390p. 1985. 20.00 (ISBN 0-318-22712-6). Assn Bay Area.

Proceedings of HAZMACON 86: Compilation of Technical Papers Presented April 29-May 1, at the Hazardous Materials Management Conference in Anaheim. 598p. 1986. 50.00 (ISBN 0-318-22713-4). Assn Bay Area.

Proceedings of Holiness Conferences Held at Cincinnati, November 26th, 1877 & at New York, December 17th, 1877. (Higher Christian Life Ser.). 255p. 1985. lib. bdg. 30.00 (ISBN 0-8240-6438-0). Garland Pub.

Proceedings of Infinite Holomorphy. T. L. Hayden & T. J. Suffridge. (Lecture Notes in Mathematics Ser.: Vol. 364). vii, 212p. 1974. pap. 19.00 (ISBN 0-387-06619-5). Springer-Verlag.

Proceedings of Interface, 1982: G-136. (Illus.). 162p. 1983. pap. 6.50 (ISBN 0-87985-338-7). Eastman Kodak.

Proceedings of International Ciprofloxacin Workshop, 1st, Leverkusen, Germany, November 6-8, 1985. International Ciprofloxacin Workshop Staff. Ed. by H. C. Neu & H. Weuta. (Current Clinical Practice Ser.: No. 34). 466p. 1986. 120.00 (ISBN 0-317-54804-2). Elsevier.

Proceedings of International Conference on Colloid & Surface Science. International Conference on Colloid & Surface Science. Ed. by Wolfram. 1976. cancelled 11.50 (ISBN 963-05-0845-1, Pub. by Akademiai Kaido Hungary). IPS.

Proceedings of International Symposium on Composite Materials & Structures. Loo & Sun. 1986. 150.00 (ISBN 0-318-23254-5). T C Pubns Ca.

Proceedings of International Symposium on Environmental Pollution & Toxicology. Ed. by S. P. Raychaudhuri & D. S. Gupta. (Progress in Ecology Ser.: Vols. V-VII). 333p. 1980. 39.00 (ISBN 0-88065-181-4, Pub. by Messers Today & Tomorrows Printers & Publishers India). Scholarly Pubns.

Proceedings of International Symposium on Housing & Urban Development after Natural Disasters. 1986. write for info. Amer Bar Assn.

Proceedings of MAS'86: Advanced Manufacturing Systems Expositions & Conference. 850p. 141.90 (ISBN 0-948507-34-9, Pub. by IFS Pubns UK). Air Sci Co.

Proceedings of National Conference on Future of Prepaid Legal Services, December 1973. 200p. 1974. pap. 6.00 (ISBN 0-317-63643-X, 716-0008-01). Amer Bar Assn.

Proceedings of National Conference on Prepaid Legal Services, April 1972. 439p. 1972. pap. 6.00 (ISBN 0-317-63644-8, 716-0007-01). Amer Bar Assn.

Proceedings of National Conference on Prepaid Legal Services & Beyond, May 1974. 235p. 1974. pap. 6.00 (ISBN 0-317-63645-6, 716-0009-01). Amer Bar Assn.

Proceedings of National Mediocolegal Symposium. National Conference of Representatives of the American Bar Association & American Medical Association Staff. 106p. 1981. pap. 15.00 (ISBN 0-317-63780-0, 571-0006-01). Amer Bar Assn.

Proceedings of National Mediocolegal Symposium. 106p. 1981. pap. 15.00 (ISBN 0-317-31178-6). Amer Bar Assn.

Proceedings of NECC 1981. Ed. by Diana Harris & Laurie Nelson-Heern. (Illus., Orig.). 1981. pap. 15.00 (ISBN 0-937114-01-4). Weeg Comp.

Proceedings of NECC-2. Ed. by Diana Harris & Beth Collison. (Illus., Orig.). 1980. pap. 15.00 (ISBN 0-937114-00-6). Weeg Comp.

Proceedings of NSDA Legal Briefing Conference: September 23-25, 1985, Four Seasons Hotel, Washington, D.C. National Soft Drink Association Staff. LC 86-203294. 287p. Date not set. price not set. Natl Soft Drink.

Proceedings of Rehabilitation Gazette's Second International Post-Polio Conference & Symposium on Living Independently with Severe Disability. Ed. by G. Laurie & J. Raymond. 74p. (Orig.). 1984. pap. 15.00 (ISBN 0-931301-01-7). Gazette Intl.

Proceedings of Second Hellenic School on Elementary Particle Physics: Corfu, Greece: September 1-20, 1985. Ed. by E. Argyres & G. Zoupanos. 600p. 1986. 75.00 (ISBN 9971-50-206-2). World Scientific Pub.

Proceedings of Second International Conference on Pervaporation Processes in the Chemical Industry. R. Bakish. (Illus.). 210p. 1987. pap. 100.00 (ISBN 0-939997-01-0). Bakish Mat.

Proceedings of Second International Conference on Simulation in Manufacturing. Ed. by John Lenz. 260p. 1986. 108.90 (ISBN 0-948507-14-4, Pub. by IFS Pubns UK). Air Sci Co.

Proceedings of Seventh National Conference on Prepaid Legal Services: October 1978. 184p. 1979. pap. 10.00 (ISBN 0-317-31047-X). Amer Bar Assn.

Proceedings of Sixth International Conference on Robot Vision & Sensory Control. Ed. by Maurice Briot. 260p. 1986. 136.40x (ISBN 0-948507-12-8, Pub. by IFS Pubns UK). Air Sci Co.

Proceedings of Summer Institute on Representative of Finite Groups & Related Topics, Pt. I. Ed. by Fong. (Proceedings of Symposia in Pure Mathematics Ser.: Vol. 47/1). 504p. 1988. 61.00 (ISBN 0-8218-1477-X). Am Math.

Proceedings of Summer Institute on Representative of Finite Groups & Related Topics. Ed. by Fong. (PSPUM Ser.: Vol. 47/2). 560p. 1988. 67.00 (ISBN 0-8218-1478-8). Am Math.

Proceedings of the Academy of Management, 40th Annual Meeting, 1980. Academy of Management Staff. Ed. by Richard C. Huseman. LC 40-2886. 436p. (Orig.). 1980. pap. text ed. 11.00 (ISBN 0-915350-19-X). Acad of Mgmt.

Proceedings of the Advanced Medicine Symposia, 11th, 1975. Advanced Medical Symposia Staff & Royal College of Physicians Staff. Ed. by A. F. Lant. (Illus.). 1975. pap. text ed. 40.00x (ISBN 0-685-83067-5). State Mutual Bk.

Proceedings of the Advanced Medicine Symposia, 10th, 1974. Advanced Medicine Symposia Staff & Royal College of Physicians Staff. Ed. by J. G. Ledingham. (Illus.). 1974. pap. text ed. 50.00x (ISBN 0-685-83066-7). State Mutual Bk.

Proceedings of the Advanced Medicine Symposia, 7th, 1971. Advanced Medicine Symposia Staff. Ed. by I. A. Boucher. 1971. pap. text ed. 30.00x (ISBN 0-685-83065-9). State Mutual Bk.

Proceedings of the Advisory Council of the State of Virginia, April 21-June 19, 1861. Ed. by James I. Robertson, Jr. LC 76-27470. (Illus.). 1977. 12.00 (ISBN 0-88490-007-X). VA State Lib.

Proceedings of the Aerodynamics & Ventilation of Vehicle Tunnels, 2nd International Symposium. Aerodynamics & Ventilation of Vehicle Tunnels Symposium Staff. 1977. text ed. 60.00x (ISBN 0-900983-51-5, Dist. by Air Science Co.). BHRA Fluid.

Proceedings of the AFIPS Conference: National Computer Conference 1986, Vol. 55. Ed. by Addie Mattox. LC 55-44701. (Illus.). xiv, 566p. 1986. 80.00 (ISBN 0-88283-049-X). AFIPS Pr.

Proceedings of the AIDS Conference, 1986 Newcastle upon Tyne, U. K. Ed. & intro. by Peter Jones. (Illus.). 208p. 1986. pap. text ed. 20.00x (ISBN 0-946707-06-5). Scholium Intl.

Proceedings of the All-Union Conference on Radiation Chemistry. 816p. 1964. text ed. 155.00x (ISBN 0-7065-0291-4, Pub. by Keter Pub Jerusalem). Coronet Bks.

Proceedings of the American Anti-Slavery Society at Its Third Decade. American Anti-Slavery Society. Incl. Vol. 1. lib. bdg. 155.00 (ISBN 0-8371-5242-9, AAT/); Vol. 2. lib. bdg. 155.00 (ISBN 0-8371-5243-7, AAU/); Vol. 3. lib. bdg. 155.00 (ISBN 0-8371-5244-5, AAV/); Vol. 4. lib. bdg. 155.00 (ISBN 0-8371-5245-3, AAW/); Vol. 5. lib. bdg. 155.00 (ISBN 0-8371-5246-1, AAX/); Vol. 6. lib. bdg. 155.00 (ISBN 0-8371-5247-X, AAY/); Vol. 7. lib. bdg. 155.00 (ISBN 0-8371-5248-8, AAZ/); Vol. 8. lib. bdg. 155.00 (ISBN 0-8371-5249-6, AAA/); Vol. 9. lib. bdg. 155.00 (ISBN 0-8371-5250-X, AAB/); Vol. 10. lib. bdg. 155.00 (ISBN 0-8371-5251-8, AAC/); Vol. 11. lib. bdg. 155.00 (ISBN 0-8371-5252-6, AAD/); Vol. 12. lib. bdg. 155.00 (ISBN 0-8371-5253-4, AAE/); Vol. 13. lib. bdg. 155.00 (ISBN 0-8371-5254-2, AAF/); Vol. 14. lib. bdg. 155.00 (ISBN 0-8371-5255-0, AAG/); Vol. 15. lib. bdg. 155.00 (ISBN 0-8371-5256-9, AAH/); Vol. 16. lib. bdg. 155.00 (ISBN 0-8371-5257-7, AAI/); Vol. 17. lib. bdg. 155.00 (ISBN 0-8371-5258-5, AAJ/); Vol. 18. lib. bdg. 155.00 (ISBN 0-8371-5259-3, AAK/); Vol. 19. lib. bdg. 155.00 (ISBN 0-8371-5260-7, AAL/); Vol. 20. lib. bdg. 155.00 (ISBN 0-8371-5261-5, AAM/). LC 77-97417. Greenwood.

Proceedings of the American Anti-Slavery Society at Its Third Decade. American Anti-Slavery Society Staff. LC 79-82166. (Anti-Slavery Crusade in America Ser). 1969. Repr. of 1864 ed. 9.00 (ISBN 0-405-00606-3). Ayer Co Pubs.

Proceedings of the American Association for the Study & Cure of Inebriates: 1870 to 1875. American Association for the Study & Cure of Inebriates Staff. Ed. by Gerald N. Grob. LC 80-1271. (Addiction in America Ser.). 1981. lib. bdg. 45.00x (ISBN 0-405-13565-3). Ayer Co Pubs.

Proceedings of the American Association of University Instructors in Accounting, 3 vols. American Association of University Instructors in Accounting Staff. Ed. by Richard P. Brief. LC 80-1468. (Dimensions of Accounting Theory & Practice Ser.). 1981. lib. bdg. 114.50 (ISBN 0-405-13498-3). Ayer Co Pubs.

Proceedings of the American Institute of Aeronautics & Astronautics Structures, Structural Dynamics, & Materials Conference, 27th, with ASME-ASCE-AHS, San Antonio, Texas, 19-21 May, 1986, 2 Vols. American Institute of Aeronautics & Astronautics Structures Staff. pap. 150.00 (ISBN 0-317-55298-8). AIAA.

Proceedings of the American Institute of Aeronautics & Astronautics Space Systems Technology Conference, San Diego, California, 9-12 June, 1986. American Institute of Aeronautics & Astronautics Staff. 1986. pap. 80.00 (ISBN 0-317-55307-0). AIAA.

Proceedings of the American Law Institute-Annual Meetings: Volumes 4,5,6,7,8,9, & 10. each vol. 20.00 (ISBN 0-317-30861-0). Am Law Inst.

Proceedings of the Analysis Conference, Singapore, 1986. S. T. Choy et al. (North Holland Mathematics Studies: Vol. 150). 1987. 85.50 (ISBN 0-444-70341-1). Elsevier.

Proceedings of the Anasazi Symposium. Speakers at Symposium. Ed. by Jack Smith. LC 83-63307. 200p. 1983. pap. write for info. (ISBN 0-937062-07-3). Mesa Verde Museum.

Proceedings of the Annual Congress of Correction, 117th. Ed. by Elizabeth Watts. 160p. 1988. pap. 18.75 (ISBN 0-942974-95-6). Am Correctional.

Proceedings of the Annual Congress of the National Prison Association of the United States. National Prison Association. LC 77-154586. (Police in America Ser). 1971. Repr. of 1874 ed. 13.00 (ISBN 0-405-03377-X). Ayer Co Pubs.

Proceedings of the Annual Conventions of the International Association of Chiefs of Police, 1893-1930, 5 Vols. International Association of Chiefs of Police Staff. LC 75-154599. 1971. Repr. of 1893 ed. Set. 250.00 (ISBN 0-405-03398-2). Ayer Co Pubs.

Proceedings of the Annual Meeting of the International Continence Society, 6th, Antwerp, Sept. 1976. Annual Meeting of the International Continence Society Staff. Ed. by B. Coolsaet. (Urologia Internationalis: Vol. 33, No. 1-3). 1978. pap. 49.50 (ISBN 3-8055-2898-1). S Karger.

Proceedings of the Anti-Sabbath Convention, Melodeon, Boston. Anti-Sabbath Convention Staff. Ed. by Henry M. Parkhurst. LC 79-122662. 1971. Repr. of 1848 ed. 16.50x (ISBN 0-8046-1311-7, Pub. by Kennikat). Assoc Faculty Pr.

Proceedings of the APICS Annual Conference, 25th. APICS Staff. LC 79-640341. 590p. 1982. 20.00 (ISBN 0-935406-20-4). Am Prod & Inventory.

Proceedings of the Arbeitsgemeinschaft Magnetismus Conference, 1974. Ed. by A. J. Freeman. 503p. 1975. 73.75 (ISBN 0-444-10900-5, North-Holland). Elsevier.

Proceedings of the Arbeitsgemeinschaft Magnetismus Conference, 1975. Ed. by E. Freeman. 76. Repr. 84.25 (ISBN 0-7204-0441-X, North Holland). Elsevier.

Proceedings of the Art Symposium, October 30-November 1, 1980. Ed. by John Riordan. 106p. (Orig.). 1982. pap. 5.00 spiral bound (ISBN 0-942746-01-5). SUNYP R Gibson.

Proceedings of the Arthur Purdy Stout Society Symposium, "Current Problems in the Surgical Pathology of Infectious Disease" & the Gastrointestinal Pathology Club Symposium, "Gastrointestinal Endocrine Pathology. Ed. by Stephen S. Sternberg. (Illus.). 104p. 1987. pap. text ed. 26.50 (ISBN 0-88167-320-X). Raven.

Proceedings of the Assembly of the Lower Counties on the Delaware 1770-1776, the Constitutional Convention of 1776 & of the House of Assembly of the Delaware State 1776-1781. Claudia L. Bushman & Harold Bell Hancock. LC 86-30791. (Illus.). 1024p. 1988. 75.00x (ISBN 0-87413-309-2). U Delaware Pr.

Proceedings of the Assembly of the Lower Counties on the Delaware 1770-1776: The Constitutional Convention of 1776, & of the House of Assembly of the Delaware State, 1776-1781. Ed. by Claudia L. Bushman et al. LC 85-40510. 616p. 1986. 49.50x (ISBN 0-87413-284-3). U Delaware Pr.

Proceedings of the Association of Orthodox Jewish Scientists, Vol. 6. 1982. pap. 11.95 (ISBN 0-87306-225-6). Feldheim.

Proceedings of the Association of Orthodox Jewish Scientists Vol. 7: Mental Health. Ed. by Paul Kahn. 240p. 1984. pap. 9.95 (ISBN 0-87203-113-6). Hermon.

Proceedings of the Associations of the Association of Orthodox Jewish Scientists, Vols. 8-9. Ed. by Charles S. Naiman. (Illus.). 304p. (Orig.). 1987. pap. 14.95 (ISBN 0-87203-125-X). Hermon.

Proceedings of the Atoms for Peace Awards, 1957-1969: A Memorial to Henry Ford & Edsel Ford. Ed. by James R. Killian, Jr. 1978. text ed. 32.50x (ISBN 0-262-11068-7). MIT Pr.

Proceedings of the Automotive Corrosion & Prevention Conference. 1986. 50.00 (ISBN 0-89883-450-3, P188). Soc Auto Engineers.

Proceedings of the Berkeley Conference in Honor of Jerzy Neyman & Jack Keifer, 2 vols. Ed. by Lucien M. Le Cam & Richard A. Olshen. 1000p. 1985. Vol. 1, 500p. write for info. (ISBN 0-534-03312-1, Pub. by Wadsworth & Brooks-Cole Advanced Books & Software); Vol. 1, 500p. write for info. (ISBN 0-534-03357-1). Brooks-Cole.

Proceedings of the Biotelemetry International Symposium, 2nd, Davos, May 1974. Biotelemetry International Symposium Staff. Ed. by P. A. Neukomm et al. 1975. 42.75 (ISBN 3-8055-2103-0). S Karger.

Proceedings of the Black National & State Conventions, 1865-1900, Vol. 1. Ed. by Philip S. Foner & George E. Walker. 400p. 1986. text ed. 39.95 (ISBN 0-87722-324-6). Temple U Pr.

Proceedings of the Black State Conventions, Eighteen Forty to Eighteen Sixty-Five, 2 vols. Ed. by Philip S. Foner & George E. Walker. 39.95 ea.; Vol. 1, 1979, 387p. (ISBN 0-87722-145-6); Vol. 2, 1980, 336p. (ISBN 0-87722-149-9). Temple U Pr.

Proceedings of the Boston Area Colloquium in Ancient Philosophy, Vol. 3. Ed. by John J. Cleary. LC 85-26323. (Illus.). 424p. (Orig.). 1988. lib. bdg. 34.50 (ISBN 0-8191-6809-2, Pub. by Boston Area Colloquim in Ancient Philosophy); pap. text ed. 19.75 (ISBN 0-8191-6810-6, Pub. by Boston Area Colloquim in Ancient Philosophy). U Pr of Amer.

Proceedings of the British Academy, Vol. LXX. 655p. 1986. 89.00x (ISBN 0-19-726037-3). Oxford U Pr.

Proceedings of the British Academy, Vol. LXIII, 1977. (Illus.). 1979. 89.00x (ISBN 0-19-725983-9). Oxford U Pr.

Proceedings of the British Academy, Vol. LXV, 1979. (Illus.). 1981. 175.00x (ISBN 0-19-725998-7). Oxford U Pr.

Proceedings of the British Academy Index, Vols. 1 - 63. Ed. by Michael Hope. 1980. 74.00x (ISBN 0-19-725999-5). Oxford U Pr.

Proceedings of the British Academy, Vol. LXXII, 1986. British Academy Staff. (British Academy Ser.). (Illus.). 550p. 1988. 135.00 (ISBN 0-19-726064-0). Oxford U Pr.

Proceedings of the British Academy: 1978, Vol. LXIV. (BA Ser.). (Illus.). 1980. 165.00x (ISBN 0-19-725989-8). Oxford U Pr.

Proceedings of the British Academy, 1980, Vol. LXVI. (Illus.). 1982. 110.00x (ISBN 0-19-726013-6). Oxford U Pr.

Proceedings of the British Academy, 1981, Vol. LXVII. (Illus.). 1982. 125.00x (ISBN 0-19-726015-2). Oxford U Pr.

Proceedings of the British Academy: 1982, Vol. LXVIII. (BA Ser.). (Illus.). 1983. 155.00x (ISBN 0-19-726025-X). Oxford U Pr.

Proceedings of the British Academy, 1983, Vol. LXIX. 1985. 105.00 (ISBN 0-19-726031-4). Oxford U Pr.

Proceedings of the British Academy (1985, Vol. LXXI. (Illus.). 590p. 1987. 145.00 (ISBN 0-19-726049-7). Oxford U Pr.

Proceedings of the Canadian Mathematical Society Annual Seminar, 1986: Oscillation, Bifurcation & Chaos. Ed. by Atkinson et al. (Conference Proceedings of the Canadian Mathematical Society Ser.: Vol. 8). 740p. 1987. pap. text ed. 75.00 (ISBN 0-8218-6013-5). Am Math.

Proceedings of the Canadian Mathematical Society on Number Theory, 1985. Kisilevsky & Labute. (Conference Proceedings of the Canadian Mathematical Society Ser.: Vol. 7). 472p. 1987. pap. text ed. 54.00 (ISBN 0-8218-6012-7). Am Math.

Proceedings of the CAP-NSERC Summer Institute in Theoretical Physics, Edmonton, Alberta 4-10 July 1987, 2 vols. Ed. by H. Umezawa et al. 936p. 1987. Set. 110.00 (ISBN 9971-50-433-2, ZA0479P-P). Vol. 1: Quantum Field Theory As an Interdisciplinary Basis. Vol. 2: Field Theory in Two Dimensions. World Scientific Pub.

Proceedings of the Carnahan Conference on Security Technology, 1987. Carnahan Conference on Security Technology Staff. Ed. by R. William De Vore & John S. Jackson. LC 82-646157. (Illus.). 147p. 1987. pap. 22.50 (ISBN 0-89779-068-5, UKY BU143). OES Pubns.

Proceedings of the Catholic University of America, Washington, D. C., Plasma Space Science Symposium, June 11-14, 1963. Catholic University of America, Washington, D.C. Staff. Ed. by C. C. Chang & S. S. Huang. (Astrophysics & Space Science Library: No.3). 377p. 1965. lib. bdg. 60.50 (ISBN 90-277-0112-1, Pub. by Reidel Holland). Kluwer Academic.

Proceedings of the Cedar Bog Symposium, Urbana College, Nov. 3, 1973. Cedar Bog Symposium Staff. Ed. by Charles C. King & Clara M. Frederick. 1974. 3.00 (ISBN 0-686-86536-7). Ohio Bio Survey.

TITLE INDEX PROCEEDINGS OF THE FIRST

Proceedings of the Chest Imaging Conference '87. Ed. by Walter W. Peppler & Albert A. Alter. (Illus.). 350p. (Orig.). 1988. pap. text ed. 25.00 (ISBN 0-944838-03-0). Med Physics Pub.

Proceedings of the Christmas Foundation Meeting of the General Anthroposophical Society. Rudolf Steiner. Ed. by Sabine Seiler. Tr. by Frances Dawson from Ger. 250p. 1988. 30.00 (ISBN 0-88010-193-8); pap. 20.00 (ISBN 0-88010-194-6). Anthroposophic.

Proceedings of the Clean Energy Research Institute, 1st, Miami Beach, 1976. Ed. by T. Nejat Veziroglu. 1977. pap. 355.00 (ISBN 0-08-021561-0). Pergamon.

Proceedings of the Cleveland Symposium on Macromolecules, 1st, Case Western Reserve Univ., Oct. 1976. Cleveland Symposium on Macromolecules Staff. Ed. by A. G. Walton. 310p. 1977. 89.50 (ISBN 0-444-41561-0). Elsevier.

Proceedings of the colloquium of the Law of Outer Space, 18th, 1975. International Institue of the Space Law of the International Astronauctical Federation Staff. Ed. by Mortimer D. Schwartz. v, 201p. 1976. pap. text ed. 27.50x (ISBN 0-8377-0413-8). Rothman.

Proceedings of the Colloquium on Methods of Optimization, Novosibirsk, U. S. S. R., 1966. Colloquium on Methods of Optimization Staff. Ed. by N. N. Moiseev. LC 77-106194. (Lecture Notes in Mathematics: Vol. 112). (Eng. & Fr.). 1970. pap. 14.70 (ISBN 0-387-04901-0). Springer-Verlag.

Proceedings of the Colloquium on the Law of Outer Space, 12th, 1969. International Institute of Space Law of the International Astronautical Federation Staff. Ed. by Mortimer D. Schwartz. iii, 336p. (Orig.). 1970. pap. text ed. 27.50x (ISBN 0-8377-0407-3). Rothman.

Proceedings of the Colloquium on the Law of Outer Space, 9th, 1966. International Institute of Space Law of the International Astronautical Federation Staff. Ed. by Mortimer D. Schwartz. 221p. 1967. pap. text ed. 27.50x (ISBN 0-8377-0403-0). Rothman.

Proceedings of the Colloquium on the Law of Outer Space, 10th, 1967. International Institute of Space Law of the International Astronautical Federation Staff. Ed. by Mortimer D. Schwartz. 279p. 1968. pap. text ed. 27.50x (ISBN 0-8377-0405-7). Rothman.

Proceedings of the Colloquium on the Law of Outer Space, 11th, 1968. International Institute of Space Law of the International Astronautical Federation Staff. Ed. by Mortimer D. Schwartz. iii, 394p. (Orig.). 1969. pap. text ed. 27.50x (ISBN 0-8377-0406-5). Rothman.

Proceedings of the Colloquium on the Law of Outer Space, 13th, 1970. International Institute of Space Law of the International Astronautical Federation Staff. Ed. by Mortimer D. Schwartz. iii, 381p. 1971. pap. text ed. 27.50x (ISBN 0-8377-0408-1). Rothman.

Proceedings of the Colloquium on the Law of Outer Space, 14th, 1971. International Institute of Space Law of the International Astronautical Federation Staff. Ed. by Mortimer D. Schwartz. iv, 298p. 1972. pap. text ed. 27.50x (ISBN 0-8377-0409-X). Rothman.

Proceedings of the Colloquium on the Law of Outer Space, 15th, 1972. International Institute of Space Law of the International Astronautical Federation Staff. Ed. by Mortimer Schwartz. iv, 284p. 1973. pap. text ed. 27.50x (ISBN 0-8377-0410-3). Rothman.

Proceedings of the Colloquium on the Law of Outer Space, 16th, 1973. International Institute of Space Law of the International Astronautical Federatoin Staff. Ed. by Mortimer Schwartz. vi, 408p. 1974. pap. text ed. 27.50x (ISBN 0-8377-0411-1). Rothman.

Proceedings of the Colloquium on the Law of Outer Space, 20th, 1977. International Institute of Space Law of the International Astronautical Federation Staff. Ed. by Mortimer D. Schwartz. v, 524p. 1978. pap. text ed. 32.50x (ISBN 0-8377-0439-1). Rothman.

Proceedings of the Colloquium on the Law of Outer Space, 21st, 1978. International Institute of Space Law of the International Astronautical Federation Staff. Ed. by Mortimer D. Schwartz. v, 291p. 1979. pap. text ed. 32.50x (ISBN 0-8377-0440-5). Rothman.

Proceedings of the Colloquium on the Law of Outer Space, 19th, 1976. International Institute of Space Law of the International Astronautical Federation Staff. Ed. by Mortimer D. Schwartz. 419p. 1977. pap. text ed. 27.50x (ISBN 0-8377-0414-6). Rothman.

Proceedings of the Colloquium on the Law of Outer Space, 17th, 1974. International Institute of Space Law of the International Astronautical Federation Staff. Ed. by Mortimer D. Schwartz. vi, 401p. 1975. pap. text ed. 27.50x (ISBN 0-8377-0412-X). Rothman.

Proceedings of the Colloquium on the Use of Embryonic Cell Transplantation for Correction of CNS Disorders. Ed. by V. H. Mark et al. (Journal, Applied Neurophysiology: Vol 47, No. 1-2). (Illus.). 96p. 1984. pap. 23.50 (ISBN 3-8055-3952-5). S Karger.

Proceedings of the Commissioners of Indian Affairs. Franklin B. Hough. 1981. Repr. lib. bdg. 59.00 (ISBN 0-403-00389-X). Scholarly.

Proceedings of the Conference Oberwolfach: December 4-10, 1977. Ed. by Bruno Brosowski & Erich Martensen. (Methoden und Verfahren der Mathematischen Physik Ser.: Vol. 17). 172p. 1978. pap. write for info. P Lang Pubs.

Proceedings of the Conference on Biblical Inerrancy, 1987. (Orig.). 1987. pap. 12.95 (ISBN 0-8054-6004-7). Broadman.

Proceedings of the Conference on Biblical Interpretation, 1988. (Orig.). 1988. pap. 9.95 (ISBN 0-8054-6005-5). Broadman.

Proceedings of the Conference on Changes in the Biota of Lakes Erie & Ontario, March 10-11, 1980. Ed. by Roberta K. Cap & V. Ray Frederick, Jr. (Bulletin of the Buffalo Society of Natural Sciences Ser.: Vol. 25, No. 4). (Illus.). 120p. (Orig.). 1981. pap. 4.75 (ISBN 0-944032-32-X). Buffalo SNS.

Proceedings of the Conference on Changes in the Physical Aspects of Lakes Erie & Ontario, November 1-2, 1973. Ed. by Robert A. Sweeney. (Bulletin of the Buffalo Society of Natural Sciences Ser.: Vol. 25, No. 3). (Illus.). 93p. (Orig.). 1975. pap. 4.00 (ISBN 0-944032-31-1). Buffalo SNS.

Proceedings of the Conference on Graduate Education, Vol. 42, No. 12. Ed. by Leonard Bickman. (Special Issue, American Psychologist). 1987. pap. 16.00 (ISBN 1-55798-028-4, 4014212); members 12.00. Am Psychol.

Proceedings of the Conference on Groups & Geometry, 2 vols. Ed. by W. Crowe et al. 350p. 1986. Set. 60.00 (ISBN 0-911767-44-4). Hadronic Pr Inc.

Proceedings of the Conference on Language & Language Behavior. Ed. by Eric M. Zale. LC 68-28144. 1968. 39.50x (ISBN 0-89197-906-9). Irvington.

Proceedings of the Conference on Multi-Ring Basins. Ed. by Lunar & Planetary Institute, Houston, Texas, U. S. A. 300p. 1981. 47.00 (ISBN 0-08-028045-5). Pergamon.

Proceedings of the Conference on Singularities. Randell. (CONM Ser.). Date not set. price not set. Am Math.

Proceedings of the Conference on the Care of Dependent Children. Conference on The Care Of Dependent Children. LC 79-137182. (Poverty U. S. A. Historical Record Ser). 1971. Repr. of 1909 ed. 20.00 (ISBN 0-405-03120-3). Ayer Co Pubs.

Proceedings of the Conference on the Lunar Highlands Crust: Houston, Texas, U. S. A., 14-16 November 1979. Lunar & Planetary Institute. 550p. 1980. 69.00 (ISBN 0-08-026304-6). Pergamon.

Proceedings of the Constitutional Convention of South Carolina. Constitutional Convention of South Carolina Staff. LC 68-29018. (American Negro: His History & Literature Ser., No. 1). 1968. Repr. of 1868 ed. 35.50 (ISBN 0-405-01837-1). Ayer Co Pubs.

Proceedings of the Cosma de Koros Memorial Symposium. Louis Ligeti. 586p. 1978. 142.50x (ISBN 0-569-08468-7, Pub. by Collets (UK)). State Mutual Bk.

Proceedings of the Cranfield Fluidics Conference, 1st. Cranfield Fluidics Conference Staff. 1965. 29.00x (ISBN 0-686-71058-4). BHRA Fluid.

Proceedings of the Cranfield Fluidics Conference, 2nd. Cranfield Fluidics Conference Staff. 1967. text ed. 36.00x (ISBN 0-685-85166-4, Dist. by Air Science Co.). BHRA Fluid.

Proceedings of the Cranfield Fluidics Conference, 3rd. Cranfield Fluidics Conference Staff. 1968. text ed. 47.00x (ISBN 0-900983-01-9, Dist. by Air Science Co.). BHRA Fluid.

Proceedings of the Cranfield Fluidics Conference, 4th. Cranfield Fluidics Conference Staff. 1970. text ed. 54.00x (ISBN 0-900983-08-6, Dist. by Air Science Co.). BHRA Fluid.

Proceedings of the Cranfield Fluidics Conference, 5th. Cranfield Fluidics Conference Staff. 1972. text ed. 54.00x (ISBN 0-900983-24-8, Dist. by Air Science Co.). BHRA Fluid.

Proceedings of the Cranfield Fluidics Conference, 6th. Cranfield Fluidics Conference Staff. 1974. 40.00x (ISBN 0-686-71057-6). BHRA Fluid.

Proceedings of the Cranfield Fluidics Conference, 7th. Cranfield Fluidics Conference Staff. 1977. 51.00x (ISBN 0-900983-50-7). BHRA Fluid.

Proceedings of the Eastern Theoretical Physics Conference. Ed. by M. E. Rose. 472p. 1963. 78.00 (ISBN 0-677-12710-3). Gordon & Breach.

Proceedings of the Econometric Society European Meeting, 1979: Papers in Memory of Stefan Valavanis. Ed. by E. G. Charatsis. (Contributions to Economic Analysis Ser.: Vol. 138). 444p. 1982. 150.00 (ISBN 0-444-86184-X, North-Holland). Elsevier.

Proceedings of the Eighteenth Annual Conference. APLIC International Staff. Ed. by Jane Vanderlin & William Barrow. LC 76-643241. 129p. (Orig.). 1986. pap. 15.00 (ISBN 0-933438-11-7). Aplic Intl.

Proceedings of the Eighteenth Lunar & Planetary Science Conference. Lunar & Planetary Institute. (Illus.). 500p. 1988. 65.00 (ISBN 0-521-35090-5). Cambridge U Pr.

Proceedings of the Eighth Annual International Bilingual Bicultural Education Conference. National Association for Bilingual Education. LC 81-149951. 223p. (Orig.). 1981. pap. 4.50 (ISBN 0-89763-054-8). Natl Clearinghse Bilingual Ed.

Proceedings of the Eighth Annual International Conference on Veterinary Acupuncture. annual Ed. by David H. Jaggar. 312p. (Orig.). 1982. pap. text ed. 40.00 (ISBN 0-318-19685-9). Intl Vet Acup.

Proceedings of the Eighth Annual Meeting of the French Colonial Historical Society, 1982. Ed. by E. P. Fitzgerald. (Illus.). 246p. (Orig.). 1985. lib. bdg. 29.00 (ISBN 0-8191-4408-8, French Colonial Hist Soc); pap. text ed. 13.25 (ISBN 0-8191-4409-6). U Pr of Amer.

Proceedings of the Eighth Colloquium on Microwave Communication, Budapest, Hungary, August 25-29, 1986. Ed. by T. Berceli. (Studies in Electrical & Electronic Engineering: No. 27). 524p. 1987. 205.25 (ISBN 0-444-98989-7). Elsevier.

Proceedings of the Eighth Conference on Roofing Technology. (Illus.). 102p. 1987. 18.00 (ISBN 0-934809-03-8). Natl Roofing Cont.

Proceedings of the Eighth Hawaii Topical Conference in Particle Physics, 1979. Ed. by V. S. Peterson & S. Pakvasa. (Particle Physics Conference Proceedings). 644p. 1980. pap. text ed. 20.00x (ISBN 0-8248-0716-2). UH Pr.

Proceedings of the Eighth International Congress for the Study of the Pre-Columbian Cultures of the Lesser Antilles. Ed. by S. Lewenstein. (No. 22). (Illus.). xiv, 624p. 1980. 27.50. AZ Univ ARP.

Proceedings of the Eighth International Congress of Onomastic Sciences, Amsterdam, 1963. Ed. by D. P. Blok. (Janua Linguarum Series Major: No. 17). 1966. 92.00x (ISBN 90-2790-609-2). Mouton.

Proceedings of the Eighth North American Prairie Conference. Ed. by Richard Brewer. 200p. 1983. pap. text ed. 25.00 (ISBN 0-912244-16-X). Western Michigan.

Proceedings of the Eighth Northeast Conference. Ed. by Igor Paul. LC 80-81642. 552p. 1980. pap. 125.00 flexi-cover (ISBN 0-08-026000-4). Pergamon.

Proceedings of the Eighth World Conference on Earthquake Engineering: Held in San Francisco, CA. July 21-28, 1984, 7 Vols. 6995p. 1984. 210.00. Earthquake Eng.

Proceedings of the Eighth World Petroleum Congress: Index, Vol. 7. World Petroleum Congress. 94p. 1971. 35.25 (ISBN 0-85334-522-8, Pub. by Elsevier Applied Sci England). Elsevier.

Proceedings of the Eighth World Petroleum Congress: Manufacturing, Vol. 4. World Petroleum Congress. (Illus.). 433p. 1971. 105.50 (ISBN 0-85334-519-8, Pub. by Elsevier Applied Sci England). Elsevier.

Proceedings of the Eighth World Petroleum Congress: Products, Vol. 5. World Petroleum Congress. (Illus.). 215p. 1971. 68.50 (ISBN 0-85334-520-1, Pub. by Elsevier Applied Sci England). Elsevier.

Proceedings of the Eighth World Petroleum Congress: Transportation, Conservation & Ground Topics, Vol. 6. World Petroleum Congress. 377p. 1971. 89.00 (ISBN 0-85334-521-X, Pub. by Elsevier Applied Sci England). Elsevier.

Proceedings of the Electoral Commission & of the Two Houses of Congress in Joint Meeting Relative to the Count of Electoral Votes Cast December 6, 1876, for the Presidential Term Commencing March 4, 1877. LC 69-11322. (Law, Politics & History Ser.). 1970. Repr. of 1877 ed. lib. bdg. 115.00 (ISBN 0-306-71185-0). Da Capo.

Proceedings of the Electron Microscopy Society. Electron Microscopy Society Staff. Ed. by Claude Arcenaux. (Annual). 1967-71 eds. 12.50x,; 1971-74 eds. 15.00x ea. Claitors.

Proceedings of the Eleventh International Cryogenic Engineering Conference. Ed. by Gustav Klipping & Ingrid Klipping. 842p. 1986. text ed. 149.95 (ISBN 0-408-01258-7). Butterworth.

Proceedings of the Eleventh International Symposium on Cerebral Blood Flow & Metabolism. Ed. by Andre Bes et al. 704p. 1983. text ed. 99.00 (ISBN 0-89004-748-0). Raven.

Proceedings of the Eleventh International Symposium on Quantum Biology & Quantum Pharmacology. P. O. Lowdin. 1985. pap. 68.95 (ISBN 0-471-81331-1). Wiley.

Proceedings of the Eleventh International Seaweed Symposium. Ed. by Carolyn J. Bird & Mark A. Ragan. (Developments in Hydrobiology Ser.). 1985. lib. bdg. 128.50 (ISBN 90-6193-773-6, Pub. by Junk Pubs Netherlands). Kluwer Academic.

Proceedings of the Eleventh Meeting of the French Colonial Historical Society, Quebec, May, 1985. Ed. by Philip Boucher. (Illus.). 338p. (Orig.). 1987. lib. bdg. 30.00 (ISBN 0-8191-5658-2, Pub. by French Colonial Hist Soc); pap. text ed. 17.50 (ISBN 0-8191-5659-0). U Pr of Amer.

Proceedings of the Eleventh Oil Shale Symposium. Ed. by James H. Gary. (Illus.). 389p. 1978. pap. 5.00 (ISBN 0-918062-03-9). Colo Sch Mines.

Proceedings of the Eleventh World Petroleum Congress: General & Indexes, Vol. 1. 250p. 1983. 240.00 (ISBN 0-471-90247-0). Wiley.

Proceedings of the Ergonomics Society's Conference, 1983. Ed. by K. Coombes. 214p. 1983. pap. 36.00x (ISBN 0-85066-252-4). Taylor & Francis.

Proceedings of the ESCAP-FAO-UNEP Expert Group on Fuelwood & Charcoal. (Energy Resources Development Ser.: No. 24). 120p. 11.00 (ISBN 92-1-119178-5, E.82.II.F.10). UN.

Proceedings of the European Conferences & Centrifugal Separation, 1st. European Conference on Mixing & Centrifugal Separation Staff. 1975. text ed. 49.00x (ISBN 0-900983-39-6, Dist. by Air Science Co.). BHRA Fluid.

Proceedings of the European Conference on Mixing & Centrifugal Separation, 3rd, 2 vols. Eurpoean Conference on Mixing & Centrifugal Separation Staff. Ed. by H. S. Stephens & C. A. Stapleton. (European Conferences on Mixing Ser.). 500p. 1979. Set. PLB 65.00x (ISBN 0-906085-31-4, Dist. by Air Science Co.). BHRA Fluid.

Proceedings of the European Seminar on Computerized Axial Tomography in Clinical Practice, 1st. Computerized Axial Tomography in Clinical Practice Staff. Ed. by I. F. Moseley & G. H. DuBoulay. LC 77-1618. 1977. pap. 49.00 (ISBN 0-387-08116-X). Springer-Verlag.

Proceedings of the European Society for Neurochemistry, Vol. 1. V. Neuhoff. (Illus.). 658p. 1978. 51.80x (ISBN 0-89573-018-9). VCH Pubs.

Proceedings of the FAO Expect Consultation on the Substitution of Imported Concentrate Feeds in Animal Production Systems in Developing Countries. R. Samspicy et al. 242p. 1987. pap. text ed. 15.00 (ISBN 92-5-102541-X, F3086, FAO). UNIPUB.

Proceedings of the FAO Expert Consultation on Fish Technology in Africa: Lusaka, Zambia, 21-25 January. (FAO Fisheries Report: Supplement No. 329). (Illus.). 474p. (Orig., Eng. & Span.). 1986. pap. text ed. 36.25 (ISBN 92-5-002429-0, F2942, FAO). UNIPUB.

Proceedings of the FAO-WHO Expert Committee on Nutrition, 8th. FAO-WHO Joint Committee Expert Committee on Nutrition. (Technical Report Ser: No. 477). 80p. 1971. pap. 2.00 (ISBN 92-4-120477-X, 413). World Health.

Proceedings of the Fifteenth Annual Conference. Ed. by Ann Leonard. LC 76-643241. iii, 79p. (Orig.). 1983. pap. 10.00 (ISBN 0-933438-07-9). APLIC Intl.

Proceedings of the Fifteenth Oil Shale Symposium. Ed. by James H. Gary. LC 82-4294. (Illus.). 597p. 1982. pap. 20.00 (ISBN 0-918062-50-0). Colo Sch Mines.

Proceedings of the Fifth Agriculture Sector Symposium. Ed. by Ted J. Davis. 238p. 1985. 10.00 (ISBN 0-317-59151-7, BK 0593). World Bank.

Proceedings of the Fifth Annual Control Engineering Conference. Ed. & intro. by Byron K. Ledgerwood. (Control Engineering Conference Ser.). 478p. 1986. 87.50 (ISBN 0-914331-55-8). Control Eng.

Proceedings of the Fifth British National Conference on Databases. E. A. Oxborrow. 1986. 44.50 (ISBN 0-521-33260-5). Cambridge U Pr.

Proceedings of the Fifth Budapest Conference on SIL Mechanics & Foundation Engineering. Ed. by A. Kezdi & I Lazanyi. 1976. cancelled 40.00 (ISBN 963-05-1138-X, Pub. by Akademiai Kaido Hungary). IPS.

Proceedings of the Fifth Conference on Dimensioning & Strength Calculation & the Congress on Materials Testing, 6th, 2 vols. Collet's Holdings Ltd. Staff. 1974. Set, Vol. 1, 484p., Vol. 2, 498p. 178.00x (Pub. by Collets (UK)). State Mutual Bk.

Proceedings of the Fifth Conference on Fluid Machinery, 2 Vols. Ed. by Collet's Holdings, Ltd. Staff. 1261p. 1975. 293.00x (ISBN 0-569-08239-0, Pub. by Collets (UK)). State Mutual Bk.

Proceedings of the Fifth Hawaii Topical Conference in Particle Physics (1973) Ed. by P. N. Dobson & V. Z. Peterson. LC 73-92867. 719p. (Orig.). 1974. pap. text ed. 20.00x (ISBN 0-8248-0327-2). UH Pr.

Proceedings of the Fifth International Congress of Aesthetics. Ed. by Jan Aler. 1968. pap. 140.00x (ISBN 90-2791-059-6). Mouton.

Proceedings of the Fifth International Conference on Basement Tectonics. Ed. by S. Riad & D. L. Baars. (Illus.). 350p. 1986. 37.50 (ISBN 0-317-43039-4). Intl Basement.

Proceedings of the Fifth International Congress on Mathematical Education. Ed. by Marjorie Carss. 412p. 1986. 77.00 (ISBN 0-8176-3330-8). Birkhauser.

Proceedings of the Fifth Nordic Ornithological Congress, 1985. Ed. by Mats O. Eriksson. (Acta Regiae Zoologica Ser.: No. 14). (Illus.). 228p. (Orig.). 1987. pap. 52.50x (ISBN 91-85252-40-9, Pub. by Vetenkaps Gothenburg). Coronet Bks.

Proceedings of the Fifth Quadrennial Symposium of the International Association on the Genesis of Ore Deposits: Snowbird, Utah, 1978. Ed. by John D. Ridge. (Illus.). 807p. 1980. text ed. 110.00x (ISBN 3-510-65094-8, Pub. by E Schweizerbartsche). Coronet Bks.

Proceedings of the Fifth Tihany Symposium on Radiation Chemistry. Janos Dobo. 1142p. 1983. 385.00x (ISBN 0-569-08759-7, Pub. by Collets (UK)). State Mutual Bk.

Proceedings of the First British-Soviet Geographical Seminar. Ed. by F. E. Hamilton. (Illus.). 152p. 1981. 47.00 (ISBN 0-08-025795-X). Pergamon.

Proceedings of the First Convention of the Industrial Workers of the World: Officially Approved, Stenographically Reported see Founding Convention of the IWW: Proceedings.

Proceedings of the First Florida AI Research Symposium. First Florida AI Research Symposium Staff. Ed. by Mark B. Fishman. (Illus.). 250p. (Orig.). 1988. pap. text ed. 20.00 (ISBN 0-9620173-0-2). FL AI Research.

Proceedings of the First International Conference on Advances in Communication & Control Systems. Ed. by N. DeClaris. 450p. 1988. pap. text ed. 80.00 (ISBN 0-911575-47-2). Optimization Soft.

Proceedings of the First International Congress on Cataract Surgery, Florence, 1978. International Congress on Cataract Surgery, 1st Florence, 1978. Ed. by J. Francois & E. Maumenee. (Documenta Opthalmologica Proceedings Ser.: No. 21). (Illus.). 1980. lib. bdg. 121.00 (ISBN 90-6193-162-2, Dr W Junk Pub). Kluwer Academic.

Proceedings of the First International Congress on Programming & Control. Ed. by L. W. Neustadt. (Proceedings Ser.). iv, 261p. 1966. 25.00 (ISBN 0-89871-155-X). Soc Indus-Appl Math.

Proceedings of the First International Conference on Vehicle Mechanics, Detroit, 16-18 July, 1968. Ed. by H. K. Sachs. 735p. 1969. text ed. 92.50 (ISBN 90-265-0101-3, Pub. by Swets Pub Serv Holland). Swets North Am.

Proceedings of the First International Conference on Word & Image: Word & Image Special Issue, Vol. 4, No. 1. John D. Hunt et al. 1988. pap. 45.00 (ISBN 0-85066-894-8). Taylor & Francis.

Proceedings of the First International ISA Food Instrumentation Division Symposium, Montreal, 1972. Food & Beverage Instrumentation Symposium Staff. Ed. by E. Nobrega. LC 72-90018. (Instrumentation in the Food & Beverage Industry Ser.: Vol. 1). pap. 23.50 (ISBN 0-317-42087-9, 20251119). Bks Demand UMI.

Proceedings of the First International Symposium on Peizoelectricity in Biomaterials & Biomedical Devices. P. M. Galletti et al. 318p. 1984. text ed. 85.00 (ISBN 0-677-40485-9). Gordon & Breach.

Proceedings of the First International Symposium on Reproduction. Ed. by Gaetano Frajese. (Serono Symposia Publications). Date not set. text ed. cancelled. Raven.

Proceedings of the First Italian International Congress on Spinoza. Ed. by Emilia Giancotti. (Illus.). 556p. 1985. 70.00x (ISBN 88-7088-121-0, Pub. by Bibliopolis Italy). Humanities.

Proceedings of the First Latin American School on Biophysics. Ed. by R. Fayad et al. 256p. 1987. 48.00 (ISBN 9971-50-321-2, Z0411L-P). World Scientific Pub.

Proceedings of the First National Biophysics Conference, Columbus, Ohio, March 4-6th 1957: Proceedings. Ed. by H. Quastler & H. Morowitz. 1959. 135.00x (ISBN 0-686-83712-6). Elliots Bks.

Proceedings of the First San Salvador Conference Columbus & His World. Ed. by Donald T. Gerace. LC 87-70948. 368p. 1987. pap. text ed. 18.00 (ISBN 0-935909-23-0). CCFL Bahamian.

Proceedings of the First Symposium on Space Nuclear Power System, 2 vols. Ed. by Mohamed S. EL-Genk & Mark D. Hoover. LC 84-16634. 610p. (Orig.). 1985. Vol. 1-2. 110.00. Orbit Bk Co.

Proceedings of the First Symposium on the Botany of the Bahamas. Robert R. Smith. 165p. 1986. pap. text ed. 10.00 (ISBN 0-935909-18-4). CCFL Bahamian.

Proceedings of the First Turbomachinery Maintenance Congress. (Illus.). 360p. (Orig.). 1985. pap. 52.50 (ISBN 0-9615256-0-6). Turbomachinery.

Proceedings of the First U. S. National Conference on Earthquake Engineering: Held in Ann Arbor, MI, June 18-20,1975. 1975 ed. 660p. 20.00. Earthquake Eng.

Proceedings of the Fluid Logic Conference, 1st, Milwaukee, 1969. Fluid Logic Conference Staff. 1970. Fluidics Quarterly, Vol. 2, Issue 3 26.00 (ISBN 0-88232-009-2). Delbridge Pub Co.

Proceedings of the Fluid Power Symposium, 5th, 2 vols. Fluid Power Symposium Staff. Ed. by H. S. Stephens & C. A. Stapleton. (Illus.). 1979. Set. lib. bdg. 69.00x (ISBN 0-900983-96-5, Dist by Air Science Co.). BHRA Fluid.

Proceedings of the Fluid Power Symposium, 1st. Fluid Power Symposium Staff. 1969. text ed. 27.00x (ISBN 0-900983-03-5, Dist. by Air Science Co.). BHRA Fluid.

Proceedings of the Fluid Power Symposium, 4th. Fluid Power Symposium Staff. 1975. text ed. 50.00x (ISBN 0-900983-45-0, Dist. by Air Science Co.). BHRA Fluid.

Proceedings of the Fluid Power Symposium, 2nd. Fluid Power Symposium Staff. 1971. text ed. 43.00x (ISBN 0-900983-11-6, Dist. by Air Science Co.). BHRA Fluid.

Proceedings of the Fluid Power Symposium, 3rd. Fluid Power Symposium Staff. 1973. text ed. 47.00x (ISBN 0-900983-30-2, Dist. by Air Science Co.). BHRA Fluid.

Proceedings of the Forty-Sixth Annual Convention. Canon Law Society of America Staff. 308p. (Orig.). 1985. pap. 8.00 (ISBN 0-943616-29-8). Canon Law Soc.

Proceedings of the Forum on Malpractice Issues in Childbirth: 1985. Ed. by Diony Young. 68p. 1985. saddle stitched 6.00 (ISBN 0-934024-09-X). Intl Childbirth.

Proceedings of the Fourteenth Annual Conference: APLIC International. Ed. by Carann G. Turner. LC 76-643241. 159p. (Orig.). 1982. pap. text ed. 14.00 (ISBN 0-933438-06-0). APLIC Intl.

Proceedings of the Fourteenth Oil Shale Symposium. Ed. by James H. Gary. LC 81-10238. (Illus.). 433p. 1981. pap. text ed. 15.00 (ISBN 0-918062-46-2). Colo Sch Mines.

Proceedings of the Fourth Agricultural Symposium. Ed. by Ted J. Davis. 374p. 1984. 20.00 (ISBN 0-8213-0417-8, BK 0417). World Bank.

Proceedings of the Fourth American Water Resources Conference Held November 18-22, 1968, Commodore Hotel, New York, New York. American Water Resources Association Staff. Ed. by Philip Cohen & Martha N. Francisco. (American Water Resources Association Proceedings Ser.: No. 6). pap. 160.00 (ISBN 0-317-28825-3, 2017811). Bks Demand UMI.

Proceedings of the Fourth Annual Conference & Exposition of the National Computer Graphics Association, Inc. Herbert K. Quigley, Jr. (Illus.). 750p. (Orig.). 1983. pap. 20.00 (ISBN 0-941514-02-1). Natl Comp Graphics.

Proceedings of the Fourth Annual Control Engineering Conference. Ed. by Byron K. Ledgerwood. 528p. 1985. 87.50 (ISBN 0-914331-54-X). Control Eng.

Proceedings of the Fourth Annual LS Space Development Conference. Ed. by Frank Hecker. (Science & Technology Ser.: Vol. 68). (Illus.). 268p. 1987. lib. bdg. 50.00 (ISBN 0-317-65288-5, Pub for Am Astro Soc); pap. text ed. 35.00 (ISBN 0-87703-273-4). Univelt Inc.

Proceedings of the Fourth British National Conference on Database. Ed. by A. F. Grundy. (British Computer Society Workshop Ser.). 229p. 1985. 49.50 (ISBN 0-521-32020-8). Cambridge U Pr.

Proceedings of the Fourth Budapest Conference on Soil Mechanics & Foundation Engineering. A. Kezdi. 861p. 1971. 143.00x (ISBN 0-569-06764-2, Pub. by Collets (UK)). State Mutual Bk.

Proceedings of the Fourth European Congress on Biotechnology, 1987, 4 vols. Ed. by O. M. Neijssel et al. 2600p. 1987. Set. 634.50 (ISBN 0-444-42831-3). Elsevier.

Proceedings of the Fourth International Conference on Automated Guided Vehicle Systems. Ed. by Gary Hammond. 330p. 1986. 95.00x (ISBN 0-948507-13-6, Pub. by IFS Pubns UK). Air Sci Co.

Proceedings of the Fourth International Conference on Coccidioidomycosis. Ed. by Einstein & Catanzaro. LC 85-60255. 532p. 1985. 30.00 (ISBN 0-9614520-0-5). NFID.

Proceedings of the Fourth International Colloquium of Developmental Pharmacology, Paris, May 1983. Ed. by G. Olive et al. (Journal: Developmental Pharmacology & Therapeutics: Vol. 7, Suppl. 1). (Illus.). viii, 224p. 1984. pap. 46.75 (ISBN 3-8055-3997-5). S Karger.

Proceedings of the Fourth International Conference on Injection Metallurgy, Lulea Sweden, June 11-13, 1986, 2 vols. Scaninject IV-MEFOS Editors. 1086p. (Orig.). 1986. Set. pap. text ed. 125.00x (ISBN 0-317-62885-2, Pub. by Almqvist & Wiksell). Coronet Bks.

Proceedings of the Fourth International Hamito-Semitic Congress. Hermann Jungraithmayr & Walter W. Mueller. LC 86-17566. (Current Issues in Linguistics Theory Ser.: Vol. 44). xiv, 609p. 1987. 80.00x (ISBN 90-272-3538-4). Benjamins North Am.

Proceedings of the Fourth Meeting of the French Colonial Historical Society. Ed. by Alf A. Heggoy & James J. Cooke. LC 79-63751. 1979. pap. text ed. 13.25 (ISBN 0-8191-0738-7). U Pr of Amer.

Proceedings of the Fourth Meeting of the World Federation for Ultrasound in Medicine & Biology. Ed. by Australian Society of Ultrasound in Medicine Staff. 500p. 1986. pap. 125.00 (ISBN 0-08-032792-3, Pub. by PPA). Pergamon.

Proceedings of the Fourth Topical Conference in Particle Physics (1971) Ed. by David Yount & Peter N. Dobson. 550p. 1972. pap. text ed. 25.00x (ISBN 0-8248-0210-1). UH Pr.

Proceedings of the Fourth Working Group Meeting, 1982: Stratigraphic Correlation Between Sedimentary Basins of the Escap Region, Vol. IX. (Mineral Resources Development Ser.: No. 51). 82p. 1986. pap. text ed. 11.50 (ISBN 92-1-119244-7, E.85.II.F.8). UN.

Proceedings of the Fourth World Congress on Pain, Seattle. Ed. by Howard L. Fields et al. (Advances in Pain Research & Therapy Ser.: Vol. 9). (Illus.). 952p. 1985. text ed. 152.50 (ISBN 0-88167-121-5). Raven.

Proceedings of the French Colonial Historical Society Annual Meetings, Sixth & Seventh, 1980-1981. French Colonial Historical Society Staff. Ed. by James J. Cooke. LC 76-644752. 160p. (Orig.). 1982. lib. bdg. 29.75 (ISBN 0-8191-2333-1); pap. text ed. 12.50 (ISBN 0-8191-2334-X). U Pr of Amer.

Proceedings of the General Anti-Slavery Convention, London, 1843. General Anti-Slavery Convention. Ed. by John F. Johnson. LC 71-83957. Repr. of 1843 ed. 27.50 (ISBN 0-8369-8525-7). Ayer Co Pubs.

Proceedings of the General Assembly of I.A.U., 16th, Grenoble, 1976. International Astronomical Union Staff. Ed. by Arnost Jappel & Edith A. Muller. (Transactions of the International Astronomical Union: Vol. XVIB). 1977. lib. bdg. 66.00 (ISBN 90-277-0836-3, Pub. by Reidel Holland). Kluwer Academic.

Proceedings of the Governor's Conference on Crime, the Criminal & Society, New York, Sept. 30-Oct. 3, 1935. facsimile ed. Governor's Conference on Crime Staff. Ed. by Robert M. Fogeleson. LC 74-3848. (Criminal Justice in America Ser.). 1974. Repr. 92.50x (ISBN 0-405-06161-7). Ayer Co Pubs.

Proceedings of the Great Peace Commission. (American Indian Treaty Ser.: No. 10). 10.00 (ISBN 0-317-57385-3). Inst Dev Indian Law.

Proceedings of the Grisons in the Year 1618. LC 78-171760. (English Experience Ser.: No. 383). 94p. Repr. of 1619 ed. 14.00 (ISBN 90-221-0383-8). Walter J Johnson.

Proceedings of the Group Health Institute, 1982. Group Health Institute of America Staff. Ed. by Marion P. Broderick. 343p. 1982. pap. text ed. 15.00 (ISBN 0-936164-30-1, 312). Group Health Assoc of Amer.

Proceedings of the Harvard Celtic Colloquium, Vol. IV. Ed. by Paul Jefferiss & William J. Mahon. (Harvard Celtic Colloquium Ser.). 256p. (Orig.). 1986. pap. text ed. 16.00x (ISBN 0-934665-05-2). Quinlin C Pubs.

Proceedings of the HazPro '85 Professional Certification Symposium. Ed. by Richard A. Young. (Illus.). 625p. 1985. 65.00. Pudvan Pub.

Proceedings of the HazPro '86 Professional Certification Symposium. Ed. by Richard A. Young. (Illus.). 659p. 1986. 65.00 (ISBN 0-317-46855-3). Pudvan Pub.

Proceedings of the Helen Keller Seminar, 1983: "Blindness-Visual Impairment: A Family Affair". 52p. 1984. pap. 6.00 (ISBN 0-89128-126-6, P1P126). Am Foun Blind.

Proceedings of the Helen Keller Seminar, 1985: "Ethical Issues in the Field of Blindness". 58p. 1986. pap. 5.00 (ISBN 0-89128-146-0, PIP146). Am Foun Blind.

Proceedings of the Helen Keller Seminar, 1982: Standards & Models for Excellence, 27-29 October 1982. 39p. 1983. pap. 5.50 (ISBN 0-89128-120-7, PIP120). Am Foun Blind.

Proceedings of the Helen Keller Seminar, 1984: "Serving the Multiply-Handicapped: More than Just the Blind". 73p. 1985. pap. 6.00 (ISBN 0-89128-140-1, P1P140). Am Foun Blind.

Proceedings of the Herbrand Symposium. Ed. by J. Stern. 384p. 1982. 79.00 (ISBN 0-444-86417-2, North-Holland). Elsevier.

Proceedings of the Hypergraph Seminar, Ohio State University, 1972. Hypergraph Seminar Staff. Ed. by C. Berge & D. Ray-Chaudhuri. (Lecture Notes in Mathematics: Vol. 411). x, 287p. 1974. pap. 24.00 (ISBN 0-387-06846-5). Springer-Verlag.

Proceedings of the IFAC Sixth World Congress, Boston-CAmbridge, Massachusetts, U. S. A., August 24-30, 1975, Part 4. International Federation of Automatic Control (6th: 1975: Boston-Cambridge, MA) LC 62-121. pap. 160.00 (ISBN 0-317-26301-3, 2052149). Bks Demand UMI.

Proceedings of the Institute for Twenty-First Century Studies. Ed. by Theodore Cogswell. Date not set. price not set (ISBN 0-911682-30-9). Advent.

Proceedings of the International Chemistry Symposium, No. 19: International Journal of Quantum Chemistry. Ed. by Per O. Lowdin. 744p. 1986. pap. 118.95 (ISBN 0-471-84879-4). Wiley.

Proceedings of the International Colloquium on the Law of Outer Space XXIX. 350p. 1987. 59.50 (ISBN 0-930403-27-4). AIAA.

Proceedings of the International Conference held at Schwerin, September 10-14, 1984. Ed. by Collet's Holdings, Ltd. Staff. 1985. 85.00x (ISBN 0-317-46697-6, Pub. by Collets (UK)). State Mutual Bk.

Proceedings of the International Conference on Energy Storage, 2 vols. Ed. by H. S. Stephens & B. Jarvis. 700p. 1981. pap. 98.00x (ISBN 0-906085-50-0). BHRA Fluid.

Proceedings of the International Conference on Geomembranes: Held June 1984, 2 vols. (Illus.). 1984. Set. 49.00 (ISBN 0-318-18274-2, 22005); 30.00 ea. Indus Fabrics.

Proceedings of the International Congress of Mathematicians, 2 vols, Vols. 1 & 2. Olech. 1730p. 1985. Set. 95.00 (ISBN 0-444-86661-2); Vol. 1. write for info. (ISBN 0-444-86659-0); Vol. 2. write for info. (ISBN 0-444-86660-4). Elsevier.

Proceedings of the International Congress of Mathematicians, Berkley, CA, Aug. 3-11, 1986, 2 pts. (PICM Ser.: No. 86). 1824p. 1988. pap. text ed. 195.00 (ISBN 0-8218-0110-4). Am Math.

Proceedings of the International Conference on Nuclidic Masses, McMaster University, Hamilton, September 12-16, 1960. International Conference on Nuclidic Masses. Ed. by H. E. Duckworth. LC 61-4023. pap. 138.00 (ISBN 0-317-08945-5, 2014191). Bks Demand UMI.

Proceedings of the International Conference on Nuclear Structure, Kingston, Canada, August 29-September 3, 1960. International Conference on Nuclear Structure. Ed. by D. A. Bromley & E. W. Vogt. pap. 160.00 (ISBN 0-317-08933-1, 2014144). Bks Demand UMI.

Proceedings of the International Congress of Nephrology, 8th, Athens, June 1981. W. Zurukzoglu et al. Ed. by M. Pyroasopoulos & M. Sion. (Illus.). xxiv, 1240p. 1981. 216.75 (ISBN 3-8055-2532-X). S Karger.

Proceedings of the International Conference on Plasma Science & Technology: China. (Illus.). 630p. 1988. lib. bdg. 95.00 (ISBN 0-89573-590-3). VCH Pubs.

Proceedings of the International Conference on Quantitative Genetics: August 16-21, 1976. Ed. by Edward Pollak et al. 1977. text ed. 24.95x (ISBN 0-8138-1895-8). Iowa St U Pr.

Proceedings of the International Conference on Raman Spectroscopy, 10th. Ed. by B. Hudson & W. L. Peticolas. 850p. 1986. 45.00x (ISBN 0-87114-176-0). U of Oreg Bks.

Proceedings of the International Conference of Soil Mechanics & Foundation Engineering San Francisco, 11th, 12-16 August 1985, 5 vols. 3700p. 1987. Set. text ed. 380.00 (ISBN 90-6191-560-0, Pub. by A A Balkema). Brookfield Pub Co.

Proceedings of the International Conference on Tropical Oceanography: November 17-24, 1965, Miami Beach, Florida. LC 67-29907. (Studies in Tropical Oceanography Ser: No. 5). 1967. 25.00x (ISBN 0-87024-086-2). U Miami Marine.

Proceedings of the International Conference of the Planning Forum. 1986. 39.95 (ISBN 0-912841-23-0). Planning Forum.

Proceedings of the International Conference "Temporary Work in Modern Society" Held in Geneva, May 1978. 286p. write for info. (ISBN 90-312-0088-3). Kluwer Academic.

Proceedings of the International Forensic Symposium on Latent Prints. LC 87-619890. (Illus.). 212p. 1988. pap. 10.00 (ISBN 0-932115-08-X, S/N 027-001-00045-9). USGPO.

Proceedings of the International Gemological Symposium, 1982. International Gemological Symposium. Ed. by Dianne Eash. 1982. 10.00 (ISBN 0-87311-011-0). Gemological.

Proceedings of the International Instrumentation Symposium, 31st: (Aerospace & Test Measurement Proceedings), 2 pts. 1985. pap. text ed. 44.95x (85AERO). Instru Soc.

Proceedings of the International Instrumentation Symposium, 32nd: (Aerospace & Test Measurement Proceedings, 2 pts. 1986. pap. text ed. 44.95x (86AERO). Instru Soc.

Proceedings of the International Instrumentation Symposium, 33rd: (Aerospace & Test Measurement Proceedings) 808p. 1987. pap. text ed. 95.00x (ISBN 1-55617-022-X, A022-X). Instru Soc.

Proceedings of the International Instrumentation Symposium, 34th: (Aerospace & Test Measurement Proceedings) 762p. 1988. pap. text ed. 95.00x (ISBN 1-55617-106-4, A106-4). Instru Soc.

Proceedings of the International Joint Conference on Artificial Intelligence, 10th, Milan, Italy: Proceedings, 2 vols. (Illus.). 1228p. (Orig.). 1987. pap. text ed. 55.00 (ISBN 0-934613-43-5). Morgan Kaufmann.

Proceedings of the International Mathematics Conference, Singapore, 1981. Ed. by L. H. Y. Chen et al. (Mathematics Studies: Vol. 74). 202p. 1983. 68.50 (ISBN 0-444-86510-1, North-Holland). Elsevier.

Proceedings of the International Neutrino Conference, Aachen 1976. Ed. by Helmut Faissner et al. 1977. 96.00 (ISBN 3-528-08378-6, Pub. by Vieweg & Sohn Germany). IPS.

Proceedings of the International Numismatic Symposium. I. Gedai & K. Biro-Sey. 220p. 1980. 63.00x (ISBN 0-569-08642-6, Pub. by Collets (UK)). State Mutual Bk.

Proceedings of the International Oxygen Steelmaking Congress. 624p. 1987. pap. 100.00 (ISBN 0-932897-26-6). Iron & Steel.

Proceedings of the International Symposium Dorsal Root Entry Zone (DREZ) Lesions, Durham, N. C., 2nd, April 1987. Ed. by B. S. Nashold, Jr. et al. (Journal: Applied Neurophysiology Ser.: Vol. 51, Nos. 2-5, 1988). (Illus.). 204p. 1988. pap. 120.00 (ISBN 3-8055-4747-1). S Karger.

Proceedings of the International Symposium on Engineering Sciences & Mechanics. Ed. by Han-Min Hsia et al. LC 57-43769. (Advances in the Astronautical Sciences Ser.: Vol. 50, Pts. I & II). (Illus.). 1574p. 1983. lib. bdg. 120.00x (ISBN 0-87703-166-5, Pub. by Am Astronaut). Pt. II (ISBN 0-87703-167-3). fiche suppl. 6.00x (ISBN 0-87703-215-7). Univelt Inc.

Proceedings of the International Symposium on Forensic Hair Comparisons. (Illus.). 234p. 1987. pap. 11.00 (S/N 027-001-00044-1). USGPO.

Proceedings of the Seventh Annual Control Engineering Conference: Held as Part of the Control Engineering Conference & Exposition Center, Rosemont, IL June 7-9, 1988. Intro. by Byron K. Ledgerwood. (Illus., Orig.). 1988. pap. 100.00 (ISBN 0-914331-57-4). Control Eng.

Proceedings of the Seventh Annual Conference on Computers & Industrial Engineering. Ed. by Gary Whitehouse & Hamed Eldin. 1985. 91.00 (ISBN 0-08-033140-8, Pub. by PPI). Pergamon.

Proceedings of the Seventh Conference on Fluid Machinery, 2 vols. L. Kisbocskoi & A. Szabo. 969p. 1983. 401.00x (ISBN 0-569-08766-X, Pub. by Collets (UK)). State Mutual Bk.

Proceedings of the Seventh Hawaii Topical Conference in Particle Physics, 1977. Ed. by R. J. Cence et al. LC 77-27006. (Particle Physics Conference Proceedings Ser). 488p. 1978. pap. text ed. 20.00x (ISBN 0-8248-0619-0). UH Pr.

Proceedings of the Seventh International Conference on Input-Output Techniques. 472p. 1958. 33.00 (ISBN 92-1-106194-6, E.84.II.B.9). UN.

Proceedings of the Seventh International Congress of Logic, Methodology & Philosophy of Science. P. Weingartner et al. (Studies in Logic & the Foundations of Mathematics: Vol. 114). 1986. 132.50 (ISBN 0-444-87656-1). Elsevier.

Proceedings of the Seventh International Conference on Low Temperature Physics, University of Toronto, Canada, 29th August-3rd September, 1960. International Conference on Low Temperature Physics (7th: 1960: University of Toronto) Ed. by G. M. Graham & Hollis A. Hallett. pap. 160.00 (ISBN 0-317-27638-7, 2014223). Bks Demand UMI.

Proceedings of the Seventh International Congress of the Phonetic Sciences, Montreal, 22-28 August 1971-Actes Du Septieme Congres International Des Sciences Phonetiques. Ed. by Andre Rigault & Rene Charbonneau. (Janua Linguarum, Series Maior: No. 57). (Illus.). 1972. 180.00x (ISBN 90-2792-311-6). Mouton.

Proceedings of the Seventh Lunar Science Conference. R. B. Merrill. 1977. 370.00 (ISBN 0-08-021771-0). Pergamon.

Proceedings of the Seventh World Petroleum Congress, Mexico 1967. 537.00 (Pub. by Elsevier Applied Sci England). Elsevier.

Proceedings of the Seventy-Fifth Convention: International Association of Fish & Wildlife Agencies, 1985. Ed. by Kenneth J. Sabol. 325p. 1988. lib. bdg. write for info. (ISBN 0-932108-12-1). IAFWA.

Proceedings of the Seventy-First Annual Meeting: Challenges of Professionalism. 414p. pap. 21.00 (ISBN 0-317-59283-1). Assn Phys Plant Admin.

Proceedings of the Seventy-Fourth Annual Meeting: Patterns for Progress. 300p. pap. 21.00 (ISBN 0-317-59292-0). Assn Phys Plant Admin.

Proceedings of the Seventy-Fourth Annual Meeting: Patterns for Progress. 368p. 1987. pap. 21.00 (ISBN 0-913359-39-4). Assn Phys Plant Admin.

Proceedings of the Seventy-Fourth Convention: International Association of Fish & Wildlife Agencies 1984. Ed. by Ken Sabol. 300p. 1986. lib. bdg. 20.00 (ISBN 0-932108-11-3). IAFWA.

Proceedings of the Seventy-Third Annual Meeting: Improving Management Through New Technologies. 304p. pap. 21.00 (ISBN 0-317-59290-4). Assn Phys Plant Admin.

Proceedings of the Shambaugh Fifth International Workshop on Middle Ear Microsurgery & Fluctant Hearing Loss. George Shambaugh & John J. Shea. LC 77-79552. 1977. 35.00 (ISBN 0-87397-125-6). Strode.

Proceedings of the Short Parliament of 1640. Ed. by Esther S. Cope & Willson H. Coates. (RHS Camden Fourth Ser.: Vol. 19). 340p. 1977. 27.00 (ISBN 0-901050-37-7, Pub. by Boydell & Brewer). Longwood Pub Group.

Proceedings of the Sixteenth International Congress of Papyrology. Roger S. Bagnall et al. LC 81-9025. (American Studies in Papyrology). 1981. text ed. 67.50 (ISBN 0-89130-516-5, 31-00-23). Scholars Pr GA.

Proceedings of the Sixteenth International Symposium on Industrial Robots & the 8th International Conference on Industrial Robot Technology, 1 vols. Ed. by H. Van Brussel. 1200p. 1986. lib. bdg. 145.00x (ISBN 0-948507-15-2, Pub. by IFS Pubns UK). Air Sci Co.

Proceedings of the Sixteenth International Symposium on Quantum Chemistry: Theory of Condensed Matter & Progagator Mehtods in the Quantum Theory of Matter. Per Olov Lowdin & Yngve Ohrn. 674p. 1982. pap. 103.95 (ISBN 0-471-89124-X). Wiley.

Proceedings of the Sixth Annual Control Engineering Conference-1987. Ed. & intro. by Byron K. Ledgerwood. (Control Engineering Conference Ser.). 703p. 1987. pap. 100.00 (ISBN 0-914331-56-6). Control Eng.

Proceedings of the Sixth Canadian Conference on Artificial Intelligence. (Illus.). 265p. (Orig.). 1986. pap. text ed. 30.00 (ISBN 2-7605-0409-3). Morgan Kaufmann.

Proceedings of the Sixth GAMM-Conference on Numerical Methods in Fluid Mechanics. Ed. by D. Rues & W. Kordulla. (Notes on Numerical Fluid Mechanics Ser.: Vol. 13). 407p. 1986. pap. 39.00 (ISBN 3-528-08087-6, Pub. by Vieweg & Sohn). IPS.

Proceedings of the Sixth Hawaii Topical Conference in Particle Physics (1975) Ed. by P. N. Dobson, Jr. et al. 1976. pap. text ed. 20.00x (ISBN 0-8248-0464-3). UH Pr.

Proceedings of the Sixth International Conference on Soil Mechanics & Foundation Engineering, 1965: Montreal, 3 vols. International Conference on Soil Mechanics & Foundation Engineering. Vol. 1. pap. 108.50 (2026392); Vol. 2. pap. 150.50; Vol. 3. pap. 154.80. Bks Demand UMI.

Proceedings of the Sixth International Zeolite Conference. Ed. by A. Bisio & D. H. Olson. 1000p. 1984. text ed. 110.00 (ISBN 0-408-22158-5). Butterworth.

Proceedings of the Sixth Plains Archeological Conference, 1948. Jesse D. Jennings. (Utah Anthropological Papers: No. 11). Repr. of 1959 ed. 32.00 (ISBN 0-404-60611-3). AMS Pr.

Proceedings of the Sixth Quadrennial Symposium of the International Association on the Genesis of Ore Deposits, Tbilisi, U. S. S. R., 1982. Ed. by T. V. Janelidze & A. G. Tvalchrelidze. (Illus.). 552p. 1984. text ed. 110.00x (ISBN 3-510-65095-6, Pub. by E Schweizerbartsche). Coronet Bks.

Proceedings of the Special Committee & 4th World Health Assembly on WHO Regulations No. 2 see Official Records of the World Health Organization: International Health (Sanitary) Regulations.

Proceedings of the Summer 1986 Intensive Workshop in Chinese & Russian. Ed. by Albert Leong. Date not set. price not set. U Oreg Russian Dept.

Proceedings of the Symposium of the International Society for Corneal Research. Ed. by J. Francois et al. (Documenta Ophthalmologica Proceedings Ser.: No. 20). 1979. pap. text ed. 47.50 (ISBN 90-6193-157-6, Pub. by Junk Pubs Netherlands). Kluwer Academic.

Proceedings of the Symposium on Advanced Manufacturing, 1987. Symposium on Advanced Manufacturing Staff. Ed. by R. William De Vore & R. G. Edwards. (Illus.). 142p. (Orig.). 1987. pap. 33.50 (ISBN 0-89779-069-3, UKY BU144). OES Pubns.

Proceedings of the Symposium on Degassing. 1978. pap. 47.00x (ISBN 0-900983-89-2, Dist. by Air Science Co.). BHRA Fluid.

Proceedings of the Symposium on Mining, Hydrology, Sedimentology & Reclamation, 1987. Symposium on Mining, Hydrology, Sedimentology & Reclamation Staff. Ed. by R. William De Vore & Donald H. Graves. LC 83-60966. (Illus.). 438p. (Orig.). 1987. pap. 45.00 (ISBN 0-89779-070-7, UKY BU145). OES Pubns.

Proceedings of the Symposium on "Molecules in Motion", University of Kentucky, Lexington, May 20-21, 1984: Transactions of the American Crystallographic Association, 1984, Vol. 20. Ed. by John J. Stezowski. 166p. 1985. pap. 25.00x (ISBN 0-937140-28-7). Polycrystal Bk Serv.

Proceedings of the Symposium on "Structure Determination With Synchrotron Radiation" at Stanford University, Stanford, CA August 19-20, 1985. Ed. by Benno P. Schoenborn. (Transactions of the American Crystallographic Association Ser.: Vol. 21, 1985). v, 55p. (Orig.). 1986. pap. 25.00x (ISBN 0-937140-29-5). Polycrystal Bk Serv.

Proceedings of the Symposium on Terrestrial & Aquatic Ecological Studies of the Northwest. Ed. by Rollins D. Andrews, III et al. 397p. (Orig.). 1977. pap. 10.00x (ISBN 0-910055-04-1). East Wash Univ.

Proceedings of the Symposium on the Small-Angle Scattering: University of Missouri, Columbia, March, 1983. Ed. by Paul W. Schmidt. (Transactions of the American Crystallographic Association Ser.: Vol. 19). 92p. 1984. pap. 25.00x (ISBN 0-937140-27-9). Polycrystal Bk Serv.

Proceedings of the Tenth Annual Congress on Veterinary Acupuncture. Ed. by David H. Jaggar. 213p. (Orig.). 1984. pap. text ed. 35.00 (ISBN 0-318-19690-5). Intl Vet Acup.

Proceedings of the Tenth Congress of the International Comparative Literature Association: Comparative Poetics. Ed. by Claudio Guillen. LC 84-48469. 600p. 1985. lib. bdg. 100.00. Garland Pub.

Proceedings of the Tenth Hawaii Conference in High Energy Physics 1985. F. A. Harris et al. LC 86-7016. (High Energy Physics Conference Proceedings (Used to Be Particle Physics Conference Proceedings)). 784p. 1986. pap. text ed. 50.00x (ISBN 0-8248-1084-8). UH Pr.

Proceedings of the Tenth International Congress, International Society of Labor Law & Social Security, 3 Vols. Don Farwell & Ben Aaron. 1984. text ed. 38.00 ea. Vol. 1 (ISBN 0-87179-427-6, 0427). Vol. 2 (ISBN 0-87179-428-4, 0428). Vol. 3 (0429). BNA.

Proceedings of the Tenth International Conference on Raman Spectroscopy. Ed. by W. L. Peticolas & B. Hudson. 850p. 1986. 45.00x (ISBN 0-317-58442-1). U of Oreg Bks.

Proceedings of the Tenth International Symposium on Quantum Biology & Quantum Pharmacology, Palm Coast, Florida, March 4-6, 1982. P. O. Lowdin. 416p. 1984. pap. 68.95 (ISBN 0-471-88168-6). Wiley.

Proceedings of the Tenth Meeting of the French Colonial Historical Society, April 12-14, 1984. Ed. by Philip P. Boucher. LC 76-644752. (Illus.). 290p. (Orig.). 1986. lib. bdg. 33.25 (ISBN 0-8191-4916-0); pap. text ed. 15.25 (ISBN 0-8191-4917-9). U Pr of Amer.

Proceedings of the Tenth MSIS National Users Group Conference - Issues in Patient Tracking. Ed. by Linda J. Kline & Carl Cappello. (Orig.). 1987. pap. 20.00 (ISBN 0-936934-06-9). N S Kline Inst.

Proceedings of the Tenth Oil Shale Symposium. Ed. by John Ruebens & J. H. Gary. LC 75-17946. (Illus.). 256p. 1977. pap. 3.50 (ISBN 0-918062-01-2). Colo Sch Mines.

Proceedings of the Tenth Session of the Committee on Natural Resources. (Water Resources Ser.: No. 59). 316p. 1986. 30.00 (E.85.II.F.14). UN.

Proceedings of the Tenth World Petroleum Congress, 6 vols. Ed. by World Petroleum Congress. Incl. Vol. 1. General. 112p. 1980. 114.95 (ISBN 0-471-26090-8); Vol. 2. Exploration: Supply & Demand. 444p. 1980; Vol. 3. 424p. 1980; Vol. 4. Storage, Transportation & Processing & Training. 486p. 1980; Vol. 5. Conservation, Environment, Safety & Training. 372p. 1980; Vol. 6. Index. 1980. (Wiley Heyden). Wiley.

Proceedings of the Third Caltech Conference on VLSI. (Digital Systems Design Ser.). 430p. 1983. 39.95 (ISBN 0-914894-86-2, Computer Sci Pr). W H Freeman.

Proceedings of the Third International Analog Computation Meetings, Opatija, Yugoslavia, Sept. 5-8, 1961. International Assn. for Analog Computation. 712p. 1962. pap. 235.00 (ISBN 0-677-10195-3). Gordon & Breach.

Proceedings of the Third International Biodegradation Symposium. Ed. by J. Miles Sharpley & Arthur M. Kaplan. (Illus.). xiv, 1138p. 1976. 197.00 (ISBN 0-85334-679-8, Pub. by Elsevier Applied Sci England). Elsevier.

Proceedings of the Third International Conference on Automated Materials Handling. Ed. by R. H. Hollier. (Illus.). vii, 417p. 1986. 130.60 (ISBN 0-387-16324-7). Springer-Verlag.

Proceedings of the Third International Conference on Boiotian Antiquities. Ed. by John M. Fossey & Hubert Giroux. (McGill University Monographs in Classical Archaeology & History: No. 2). (Illus.). viii, 198p. 1985. 46.00x (ISBN 90-70265-66-4, Pub. by Gieben Amsterdam). Benjamins North Am.

Proceedings of the Third International Conference on Cyclic Nucleotides. International Conference on Cyclic Nucleotide, 3rd, New Orleans, la., July 1977. Ed. by William J. George & Louis Ignarro. LC 77-84555. (Advances in Cyclic Nucleotide Research: Vol.9). 831p. 1978. 117.00 (ISBN 0-89004-240-3). Raven.

Proceedings of the Third International Colloquium of Developmental Pharmacology, Nancy, June 1981, Journal: Developmental Pharmacology & Therapeutics, Vol. 4, Suppl. 1, 1982. Ed. by P. Vert & J. V. Aranda. 232p. 1982. pap. 48.00 (ISBN 3-8055-3476-0). S Karger.

Proceedings of the Third International Conference on Light Scattering in Solids. Ed. by M. L. Balkanski et al. LC 76-122. 988p. 1975. 58.50 (ISBN 0-470-15034-3, Pub. by Wiley). Krieger.

Proceedings of the Third International Congress on Marine Corrosion & Fouling. Ed. by Robert F. Acker et al. 1974. 36.00x (ISBN 0-8101-0445-8). Northwestern U Pr.

Proceedings of the Third International Conference on Vehicle System Dynamics, Blacksburg, VA, 12-15 August, 1974. Ed. by H. K. Sachs. 324p. 1975. text ed. 63.50 (ISBN 90-265-0197-8, Pub. by Swets Pub Serv Holland). Swets North Am.

Proceedings of the Third International Iron & Steel Congress, 16-20 April 1978, Chicago, Illinois - Sponsored by the American Society for Metals & the Iron & Steel Society of AIME. International Iron & Steel Congress, 3rd, 1978, Chicago. LC 79-4097. pap. 160.00 (2027049). Bks Demand UMI.

Proceedings of the Third International Meeting on Spinal Cord Stimulation. Ed. by Ph. L. Gildenberg. (Illus.). 176p. 1981. pap. 70.00 (ISBN 3-8055-3462-0). S Karger.

Proceedings of the Third International Symposium: Recent Advances in Otitis Media with Effusion. Lim et al. 1984. 44.00 (ISBN 0-8016-3008-8). Mosby.

Proceedings of the Third Symposium of Optical Spectro-Scopy Held in Reinhardsbrunn, September 26-28, 1984. Collet's Holdings, Ltd. Staff. 1986. 112.00 (ISBN 0-317-52957-9, Pub. by Collets (UK)). State Mutual Bk.

Proceedings of the Third Symposium on Technical Diagnostics, Moscow, October 3-5, 1983. Ed. by Collet's Holdings, Ltd. Staff. 512p. pap. 410.00x (ISBN 0-317-46701-8, Pub. by Collets (U.K.)). State Mutual Bk.

Proceedings of the Third Symposium on the Geology of the Bahamas. Ed. by H. Allen Curran. 250p. 1987. pap. text ed. 18.00 (ISBN 0-935909-24-9). CCFL Bahamian.

Proceedings of the Third Symposium on Theoretical Metrology. Ed. by T. Kemeny & K. Havrilla. 230p. (Orig.). 1987. pap. text ed. 57.00 (ISBN 0-941743-32-2). Nova Sci Pubs.

Proceedings of the Third Symposium on the Psychology of Religion in Europe: Current Issues in the Psychology of Religion. Ed. by J. A. Van Belzen & J. M. Van Der Lans. (Amsterdam Studies in Theology Ser.). 292p. 1986. pap. text ed. 65.00 (ISBN 90-6203-758-5, Pub. by Rodopi Holland). Humanities.

Proceedings of the Third World Congress on Pain, Edinburdh. Ed. by John J. Bonica et al. (Advances in Pain Research & Therapy Ser.: Vol. 5). 990p. 1983. text ed. 128.50 (ISBN 0-89004-800-2). Raven.

Proceedings of the Thirteenth Annual Conference. APLIC International Staff. Ed. by Adele B. Burns. LC 76-643241. 157p. 1980. pap. 13.00 (ISBN 0-933438-05-2). APLIC Intl.

Proceedings of the Thirteenth Oil Shale Symposium. Ed. by James H. Gary. LC 80-18711. (Oil Shale Ser.). (Illus.). 391p. (Orig.). 1980. pap. 12.00 (ISBN 0-918062-39-X). Colo Sch Mines.

Proceedings of the Twelfth Oil Shale Symposium. Ed. by J. H. Gary. 395p. 1979. 11.00 (ISBN 0-918062-08-X). Colo Sch Mines.

Proceedings of the Twenty-First FISITA Conference. 1986. 120.00 (ISBN 0-317-52524-7, P187). Soc Auto Engineers.

Proceedings of the Twenty-Fourth Automotive Technology Development Contractors' Coordination Meeting. 1987. 48.00 (ISBN 0-317-62911-5, P197). Soc Auto Engineers.

Proceedings of the Twenty-Sixth International Mineral Processing Congress: Stockholm, Sweden, 5-10 June 1988, 2 vols. Ed. by E. Forrsberg. (Developments in Mineral Processing: No. 10). 1996p. 1988. 365.75 (ISBN 0-444-42975-1). Elsevier.

Proceedings of the URSI International Symposium on Electromagnetic Theory, Budapest, Hungary, August 25-29, 1986, 2 vols. Ed. by T. Berceli. (Studies in Electrical & Electronic Engineering: No. 28). 850p. 1987. Set. 326.50 (ISBN 0-444-98986-2). Elsevier.

Proceedings of the VIIth Congress of the International Federation of Societies of Clasical Studies, Vols. 1 & 2. J. Harmatta. 1077p. 1984. Set. text ed. 90.00x (ISBN 963-05-2928-9, Pub. by Akademiai Kiado Hungary). Vol. 1 (ISBN 963-05-2929-7). Vol. 2 (ISBN 963-05-2930-0). Humanities.

Proceedings of the Virgin Islands' Seminar on Unification Theology. Ed. by Darrol Bryant. LC 80-52594. (Conference Ser.: No. 6). (Illus.). xv, 323p. (Orig.). 1980. pap. text ed. 9.95 (ISBN 0-932894-06-2). Unif Theol Sem.

Proceedings of the West Coast Conference on Formal Linguistics, Vol. 6. Ed. by Megan Crowhurst. 339p. (Orig.). pap. 12.00 (ISBN 0-937073-31-8). Ctr Study Language.

Proceedings of the Workshop on Measurement of Microbial Activities in the Carbon Cycle of Freshwaters. Ed. by Jurgen Overbeck. (Limnology Report: No. 12). (Illus.). 174p. (Orig.). 1979. pap. text ed. 54.50x (ISBN 3-510-47010-9, Pub. by E Schweizerbartsche). Coronet Bks.

Proceedings of the Workshop on Needs & Resources for Occupational Mortality Data, January 21-22, 1987. National Center for Health Statistics Staff. Ed. by Klaudia Cox. LC 88-1463. (Series 4: No. 26). 164p. pap. text ed. 3.60 (ISBN 0-8406-0393-2). Natl Ctr Health Stats.

Proceedings of the Workshop on Urea Deep-Placement Technology. Ed. by Paul J. Stangel & E. N. Roth. LC 86-2805. (Special Publication: SP-61). 143p. (Orig.). 1986. pap. 15.00 (ISBN 0-88090-057-1). Intl Fertilizer.

Proceedings of the World Congress on Fertility & Sterility, 6th. Ed. by Zondek & Zondek. 412p. 1970. 138.00 (ISBN 0-677-62100-0). Gordon & Breach.

Proceedings of the World Food Conference of 1976. World Food Conference, Ames, Iowa June, 1976. Ed. by Frank Schaller. 1977. text ed. 10.50x (ISBN 0-8138-1825-7). Iowa St U Pr.

Proceedings of the XVIth International Congress of Dermatology. Ed. by Atsushi Kukita & Makoto Seiji. 832p. 1983. 125.00 (ISBN 0-86008-329-2, Pub. by U of Tokyo Japan). Columbia U Pr.

Proceedings, 1987 Eastern Oil Shale Symposium. Ed. by Pettit Rhonda. (Illus.). 300p. 1988. pap. text ed. 25.00 (ISBN 0-86607-030-3, KECL87-17S). KY Energy Cabnt Lab.
Proceedings: 28th Annual International Conference. LC 79-640341. 760p. 1985. 35.00 (ISBN 0-935406-72-7). Am Prod & Inventory.
Proceedings of the Ninth World Petroleum Congress: Processing & Storage, Vol. 5. World Petroleum Congress. 130p. 1975. 111.00 (ISBN 0-85334-667-4, Pub. by Elsevier Applied Sci England). Elsevier.
Procelain & the Dutch China Trade. C. J. Jorg. 372p. 1982. 175.00x (ISBN 0-317-44158-2, Pub. by Han-Shan Tang Ltd). State Mutual Bk.
Proces De Condamnation et De Rehabilitation De Jeanne D'Arc, 5 Vols. Saint Jeanne D'Arc. Ed. by Jules Quicherat. 1841-1849. Set. pap. 200.00 (ISBN 0-384-27071-9). Johnson Repr.
Proces De Corruption Sous la Terreur: L'affaire De la Compagnie Des Indes. Albert Mathiez. (Illus.). 1971. Repr. of 1920 ed. lib. bdg. 26.50 (ISBN 0-8337-2299-9). B Franklin.
Proces D'imipiete Intentes Aux Philosophes a Athenes Au Vme & Au Ivme Siecles. facsimile ed. Eudore Derenne. LC 75-13260. (History of Ideas in Ancient Greece Ser.). (Fr.). 1976. Repr. of 1930 ed. 17.00x (ISBN 0-405-07302-X). Ayer Co Pubs.
Procesion de los Ardientes. Pedro G. Valderrama. 127p. (Span.). 1981. pap. 4.00 (ISBN 84-85859-10-3, 2007). Ediciones Norte.
Proceso del las Ideas Politicas en Cuba. Humberto Pinera et al. 132p. (Orig., Span.). 1988. pap. 15.00 (ISBN 0-89729-489-0, Pub. by Laurenty Pub Inc Cuba). Ediciones.
Process. Brion Gysin. LC 86-43064. 360p. 1987. 18.95 (ISBN 0-87951-277-6). Overlook Pr.
Process Analysis & Design for Chemical Engineers. W. Resnick. 1980. text ed. 45.95 (ISBN 0-07-051887-4). McGraw.
Process Analytical Instruction. (Market Research Reports). 1986. write for info. (ISBN 0-86621-820-3, A1641). Frost & Sullivan.
Process Analytical Instrumentation Market. 218p. 1984. 1575.00 (ISBN 0-86621-263-9, A1335). Frost & Sullivan.
Process Analyzer Technology. Kenneth J. Clevett. LC 85-26302. 952p. 1986. 112.00 (ISBN 0-471-88316-6). Wiley.
Process & Action in Work with Groups: The Preconditions for Treatment & Growth. Ken Heap. 1979. 46.00 (ISBN 0-08-023023-7); pap. 15.25 (ISBN 0-08-023022-9). Pergamon.
Process & Conscience: Toward a Theology of Human Emergence. Linda L. Stinson. 202p. (Orig.). 1986. lib. bdg. 23.75 (ISBN 0-8191-5206-4); pap. text ed. 12.25 (ISBN 0-8191-5207-2). U Pr of Amer.
Process & Device Modeling: Advances in CAD for VLSI, Vol. 1. Ed. by W. L. Engl. 462p. 1986. 63.50 (ISBN 0-444-87891-2, North Holland). Elsevier.
Process & Device Simulation for MOS-VLSI Circuits. Ed. by Paolo Antognetti. 1983. lib. bdg. 78.50 (ISBN 90-2472-824-X, Pub. by Martinus Nijhoff Netherlands). Kluwer Academic.
Process & Fundamental Considerations of Selected Hydrometallurgical Systems. Ed. by Martin C. Kuhn. LC 79-57685. (Orig.). 1981. pap. text ed. 5.00x (ISBN 0-89520-282-4). Soc Mining Eng.
Process & Industrial Pipe Estimating. Lloyd K. Burkholder, Sr. LC 82-2448. 240p. (Orig.). 1982. pap. 18.25 (ISBN 0-910460-94-9). Craftsman.
Process & Metaphors in the Evolutionary Paradigm. Ed. by Mae-Wan Ho & Sidney Fox. LC 87-25445. 350p. 1988. 84.95 (ISBN 0-471-91801-6). Wiley.
Process & Organization of Government Planning. John David Millett. LC 76-38753. (FDR & the Era of the New Deal Ser). 188p. 1972. Repr. of 1947 ed. lib. bdg. 29.50 (ISBN 0-306-70444-7). Da Capo.
Process & Outcome in Peer Relationships. Edited Treatise ed. Ed. by Edward C. Mueller & Catherine R. Cooper. (Developmental Psychology Ser.). 1985. 54.00 (ISBN 0-12-509560-0); pap. 29.95 (ISBN 0-12-509561-9). Acad Pr.
Process & Pattern: Controlled Composition Practice for ESL Students. Charles M. Cobb. 354p. 1985. pap. text ed. write for info. (ISBN 0-534-03705-4). Wadsworth Pub.
Process & Pattern in Physical Geography. K. D. Hilton. 1979. 20.00x (ISBN 0-7231-0773-4, Pub. by Univ Tutorial Pr Ltd). State Mutual Bk.
Process & Practice: A Guide to Basic Writing. Philip Eggers. 1986. pap. write for info. (ISBN 0-673-15908-6). Scott F.
Process & Practice in Family Therapy. 2nd ed. Gerald H. Zuk. 202p. 1986. text ed. 26.95 (ISBN 0-89885-276-5, Dist. by Independent Publishers Group). Human Sci Pr.
Process & Reality: An Essay in Cosmology. Corrected Ed. ed. Alfred N. Whitehead. LC 77-90011. 1978. 16.95 (ISBN 0-02-934580-4). Free Pr.
Process & Reality: An Essay in Cosmology. Corrected ed. Alfred N. Whitehead. 416p. pap. 14.95 (ISBN 0-02-934570-7). Free Pr.
Process & Reality: An Essay in Cosmology. Alfred North Whitehead. 509p. 1983. Repr. of 1929 ed. lib. bdg. 45.00 (ISBN 0-89987-884-9). Darby Bks.
Process & Reality: Corrected Edition. Alfred N. Whitehead. LC 77-90011. 1979. pap. text ed. 9.95. Free Pr.
Process & Relation in Discourse & Language Learning. Winifred Crombie. 150p. 1986. pap. 10.95x (ISBN 0-19-437083-6). Oxford U Pr.
Process & Structure in Composition. Barbara Clouse. 448p. 1986. text ed. write for info. (ISBN 0-02-322960-8). Macmillan.
Process & Thought in Composition with Handbook. 3rd ed. Frank D'Angelo. 1985. text ed. write for info. (ISBN 0-673-39203-1). Scott F.
Process Archetype: Self & Divine in Jung, Hillman & Whitehead. Ed. by David Griffin. 350p. 1988. 42.95 (ISBN 0-8101-0815-1); pap. 15.95 (ISBN 0-8101-0816-X). Northwestern U Pr.
Process Camera Comparison Charts: 1987 Edition. Harold Durbin. 1987. pap. 25.00. Durbin Assoc.
Process Chemistry for Water & Wastewater Treatment. Joseph F. Judkins & Larry D. Benefield. (Illus.). 528p. 1982. 54.00 (ISBN 0-13-722975-5). P-H.
Process Concepts. (Instrumentation & Process Control Self-Study Ser.). 100p. 1987. pap. text ed. 22.50x (ISBN 1-55617-066-1, A066-1). Instru Soc.
Process Consultation: Its Role in Organization Development. Edgar H. Schein. LC 76-91149. (Organization Development Ser.). (Orig.). 1969. pap. text ed. 16.25 (ISBN 0-201-06733-1). Addison-Wesley.
Process Consultation: Lessons for Managers & Consultants, Vol. II. Edgar H. Schein. LC 76-91149. (A-W Organization Development Ser.). (Illus.). 208p. 1987. pap. text ed. 16.25 (ISBN 0-201-06744-7). Addison-Wesley.
Process Consultation, Vol. I: Its Role in Organization Development. 2nd ed. Edgar H. Schein. (Organization Developments Ser.). (Illus.). 192p. 1988. pap. text ed. price not set. Addison-Wesley.
Process Control. Peter Harriott. LC 81-18558. 392p. 1983. Repr. of 1964 ed. text ed. 31.50 (ISBN 0-89874-399-0). Krieger.
Process Control: A Primer for the Nonspecialist & the Newcomer. George Platt. 120p. 1988. pap. 29.95 (ISBN 1-55617-096-3, A096-3). Instru Soc.
Process Control & Applied Mathematics. 167p. 1965. pap. 24.00 (ISBN 0-8169-0056-6, S-55). Am Inst Chem Eng.
Process Control & Optimization Handbook for the Hydrocarbon Processing Industries. Ed. by Les A. Kane. LC 80-15243. 248p. (Orig.). 1980. pap. 25.00x (ISBN 0-87201-144-5). Gulf Pub.
Process Control: Automatic Control, Vol. 3. (Bibliographic Ser.: No. 240). 87p. 1969. 9.00 (ISBN 0-317-34419-6). Inst Paper Chem.
Process Control Computer Systems: Guide for Managers. Ed. by Tom G. Stire. LC 82-70705. (Illus.). 296p. 1983. 42.95 (ISBN 0-250-40488-5). Butterworth.
Process Control: Computers, Vol. 1. (Bibliographic Ser.: No. 238). 51p. 1969. 8.00 (ISBN 0-317-34420-X); Supplement 1, 1975. 20.00 (ISBN 0-317-34421-8). Inst Paper Chem.
Process Control Conference, 1987: Proceedings of TAPPI, Opryland Hotel, Nashville, TN, March 22-25. Technical Association of the Pulp & Paper Industry Staff. (Illus.). 167p. pap. 43.50 (2029984). Bks Demand UMI.
Process Control: Control Systems, Vol. 4. (Bibliographic Ser.: No. 241). 101p. 1969. 9.00 (ISBN 0-317-34422-6). Inst Paper Chem.
Process Control for Pulp & Paper Mills. Miller Freeman Publications Inc., Staff. Ed. by Kenneth E. Smith. LC 83-60588. (Illus.). 208p. 1983. pap. 39.50 (ISBN 0-87930-149-X). Miller Freeman.
Process Control Fundamentals, 3 vols. J. P. Jerald & D. W. Powers. (Illus.). 1981. Set. 195.00x (ISBN 0-87683-005-X); Vol. 1; 157p. looseleaf 79.50x (ISBN 0-87683-006-8); Vol. 2; 306p. looseleaf 79.50x (ISBN 0-87683-007-6); Vol. 3, 313p. 79.50x (ISBN 0-87683-008-4); lesson plans 595.00x (ISBN 0-87683-009-2). GP Pub.
Process Control in the Construction Industry. (Transportation Research Record Ser.). 63p. 1978. 3.60 (ISBN 0-309-02837-X). Transport Res Bd.
Process Control: Instrumentation, Vol. 2. (Bibliographic Ser.: No. 239). 105p. 1969. 10.00 (ISBN 0-317-34423-4); 1977 Supplement 1 45.00 (ISBN 0-317-34424-2). Inst Paper Chem.
Process Control Instrumentation Markets in S. Asia & the Far East. 273p. 1985. 1850.00 (ISBN 0-86621-656-1, W728). Frost & Sullivan.
Process Control Instrumentation Technology. 3rd ed. Curtis D. Johnson. LC 87-27995. 573p. 1988. write for info. (ISBN 0-471-85340-2). Wiley.
Process Control Markets. Market Intelligence Research Company Staff. Ed. by Wilmoth Hammersley. 230p. (Orig.). pap. text ed. 995.00x. Market Res Co.
Process Control Markets & Fiber Optics. Market Intelligence Research Company Staff. 135p. (Orig.). 1984. pap. text ed. 495.00x (ISBN 0-916483-02-9). Market Res Co.
Process Control: Sensors & Transducers. 214p. 1985. 985.00x (ISBN 0-88694-646-8). Intl Res Dev.
Process Control Symposium, 1985: Notes of TAPPI. Technical Association of the Pulp & Paper Industry. pap. 32.80 (ISBN 0-317-26841-4, 2025283). Bks Demand UMI.
Process Control Systems. 2nd ed. F. Gregg Shinskey. 1979. text ed. 49.00 (ISBN 0-07-056891-X). McGraw.
Process Control Systems: Application, Design & Tuning. 3rd, rev. ed. F. Greg Shinskey. 544p. 1988. text ed. 49.50 (ISBN 0-07-056903-7). McGraw.
Process Control Systems: Hardware, Software, & Operation. Fran Jovic. LC 85-82050. (Illus.). 600p. 1986. 49.00x (ISBN 0-87201-743-5). Gulf Pub.
Process Design for Reliable Operations. Norman P. Leiberman. LC 83-1630. 208p. 1983. 35.00x (ISBN 0-87201-747-8). Gulf Pub.
Process Design in Water Quality Engineering: New Concepts & Development. Ed. by Edward L. Thackston & W. W. Eckenfelder. (Illus.). 15.00 (ISBN 0-8363-0079-3). Jenkins.
Process Development in Antibiotic Fermentations. C. T. Calam. (Cambridge Studies in Biotechnology: No. 4). (Illus.). 209p. 1987. 54.50 (ISBN 0-521-30490-3). Cambridge U Pr.
Process Dynamics & Control. 172p. 1961. pap. 24.00 (ISBN 0-8169-0302-6, S-36). Am Inst Chem Eng.
Process Dynamics: Automatic Control of Steam Generation Plant. R. Dolezal & L. Varcop. (Illus.). 460p. 1970. 55.00 (ISBN 0-444-20042-8, Pub. by Elsevier Applied Sci England). Elsevier.
Process Dynamics Estimation & Control. A. Johnson. (Control Engineering Ser.: No. 27). 188p. 1985. casebound 54.00 (ISBN 0-86341-032-4, CE027). Inst Elect Eng.
Process Education: The New Direction for Elementary-Secondary Schools. Henry P. Cole. LC 79-178843. 288p. 1972. 33.95 (ISBN 0-87778-030-7). Educ Tech Pubns.
Process Energy Conservation Manual. Fairmont Press Staff. 154p. 1984. text ed. 37.00 (ISBN 0-915586-73-8). Fairmont Pr.
Process Engineering Analysis in Semiconductor Fabrication. Stanley Middleman & Arthur K. Hochberg. (Illus.). 672p. 1988. 49.95 (ISBN 0-07-041853-5). McGraw.
Process Engineering Aspects of Immobilised Cell Systems. Ed. by Webb. (Illus.). 240p. 1986. 41.00 (ISBN 0-08-032646-3, Pub. by PPL). Pergamon.
Process Engineering Calculations: Material & Energy Balances. Mack Tyner. LC 60-7613. pap. 103.50 (ISBN 0-317-10496-9, 2012460). Bks Demand UMI.
Process Engineering Control. Mack Tyner & Frank P. May. LC 67-21681. (Illus.). Repr. of 1968 ed. 90.90 (ISBN 0-8357-9962-X, 2012441). Bks Demand UMI.
Process Engineering Development: Proceedings of the Multi-Stream 85 Subject Group Symposium Held in London U. K., April 16-18 1985. Ed. by Institution of Chemical Engineers Staff. (Institution of Chemical Engineers Symposium Ser.). (Illus.). 300p. 1985. 30.00 (ISBN 0-08-031445-7, Pub. by PPL). Pergamon.
Process Engineering: For Manufacturing. Donald F. Eary & G. E. Johnson. (Illus.). 1962. text ed. 46.00 (ISBN 0-13-723122-9). P-H.
Process Engineering of Pyrometallurgy. Ed. by M. J. Jones. 105p. (Orig.). 1974. pap. text ed. 28.75x (ISBN 0-900488-23-9). IMM North Am.
Process Engineering of Size Reduction: Ball Milling. L. G. Austin et al. LC 83-73512. (Illus.). 561p. 1984. text ed. 15.00x (ISBN 0-89520-421-5). Soc Mining Eng.
Process Engineer's Absorption Pocket Handbook. R. N. Maddox. LC 85-852. (Illus.). 96p. 1985. 19.00x (ISBN 0-87201-016-3). Gulf Pub.
Process Engineer's Pocket Handbook, Vol. 1. Carl R. Branan. LC 76-1680. 136p. (Orig.). 1976. pap. 12.00x (ISBN 0-87201-712-5). Gulf Pub.
Process Equipment Design: Vessel Design. Lloyd E. Brownell & Edwin H. Young. LC 59-5882. 408p. 1959. 85.00 (ISBN 0-471-11319-0, Pub by Wiley-Interscience). Wiley.
Process Ethics. James R. Gray. LC 83-6564. 110p. 1983. lib. bdg. 24.75 (ISBN 0-8191-3237-3); pap. text ed. 9.25 (ISBN 0-8191-3238-1). U Pr of Amer.
Process Ethics: A Constructive System. Kenneth Cauthen. LC 84-16662. (Toronto Studies in Theology: Vol. 18). 365p. 1985. lib. bdg. 59.95x (ISBN 0-88946-764-1). E Mellen.
Process Evaluation & Economic Analysis. Carl Branan & John Mills. LC 76-1680. (Process Engineer's Pocket Handbook Ser.: Vol. 3). 200p. (Orig.). 1984. pap. 15.00x (ISBN 0-87201-715-X). Gulf Pub.
Process Flowsheeting. A. W. Westerberg et al. LC 78-51682. (Illus.). 1979. 44.50 (ISBN 0-521-22043-2). Cambridge U Pr.
Process Fluid Mechanics. M. Denn. 1980. 54.00 (ISBN 0-13-723163-6). P-H.
Process Geomorphology. 2nd ed. Dale F. Ritter. 592p. 1986. text ed. write for info. (ISBN 0-697-05047-5). Wm C Brown.
Process Guide for School Improvement. Herbert J. Klausmeier. LC 85-20193. (Illus.). 258p. (Orig.). 1985. lib. bdg. 29.50 (ISBN 0-8191-4941-1, Wisconsin Ctr Education Res); pap. text ed. 13.50 (ISBN 0-8191-4942-X). U Pr of Amer.
Process Heat Exchange. Chemical Engineering Magazine Editors. (Chemical Engineering Book Ser.). (Illus.). 624p. 1980. text ed. 49.50 (ISBN 0-07-010742-4). McGraw.
Process Heat Transfer. Donald Q. Kern. 1950. text ed. 50.95 (ISBN 0-07-034190-7). McGraw.
Process in Architecture: A Documentation in Six Examples. Lance Laver et al. LC 79-88539. (Illus.). 144p. (Orig.). 1979. pap. 4.00 (ISBN 0-938437-00-3). MIT List Visual Arts.
Process in Continental Lithospheric Deformation. Ed. by Sydney P. Clark, Jr. (Special Paper Ser.: No. 218). (Illus.). 1988. 25.00 (ISBN 0-8137-2218-7). Geol Soc.
Process in Geomorphology. Ed. by Clifford Embleton & John Thornes. LC 79-18747. 436p. 1979. pap. 34.95x (ISBN 0-470-26808-5). Halsted Pr.
Process Industries Corrosion. LC 75-28636. (Illus.). 383p. 1975. 35.00 (ISBN 0-915567-50-4). Natl Corrosion Eng.
Process Industries Seminar Proceedings. Ed. by American Production & Inventory Control Society Staff. LC 83-71959. 66p. 1983. pap. 7.00 (ISBN 0-935406-29-8). Am Prod & Inventory.
Process Industry Reprints. Ed. by S. G. Taylor et al. LC 83-71088. 216p. 1984. pap. 16.00 (ISBN 0-935406-41-7, 40641). Am Prod & Inventory.
Process Instrumentation & Control Fundamentals. R. J. Howarth & D. W. Powers, Jr. (Illus.). 380p. 1976. looseleaf 95.00x (ISBN 0-87683-323-7); Lesson Plans 395.00x (ISBN 0-87683-324-5). GP Pub.
Process Instrumentation & Control Systems. Ed. by Water Pollution Control Federation. LC 84-51934. (Manual of Practice Ser.: No. OM-6). (Illus.). 161p. (Orig.). 1984. pap. text ed. 32.00 (ISBN 0-943244-57-9, MOPOM6). Water Pollution.
Process Instrumentation Primer. Norman Whitaker. 117p. 1980. 39.95 (ISBN 0-87814-128-6, P-4236). Pennwell Bks.
Process Instruments & Controls Handbook. 3rd ed. Ed. by Douglas M. Considine. (Illus.). 1593p. 1985. text ed. 99.50 (ISBN 0-07-012436-1). McGraw.
Process Is the Punishment: Handling Cases in a Lower Criminal Court. Malcolm M. Feeley. LC 79-7349. (Illus.). 330p. 1979. 27.50x (ISBN 0-87154-253-6). Russell Sage.
Process Level Instrumentation & Control. Cheremisinoff. (Engineering Measurement & Instrumentation Ser.: Vol. 2). 256p. 1981. 55.00 (ISBN 0-8247-1212-9). Dekker.
Process Measurement & Instrumentation. Michelini. 1987. write for info. (ISBN 0-471-09586-9). Wiley.
Process Measurement Fundamentals, 3 vols. E. M. Eacho et al. (Illus.). 1981. Set. 195.00x (ISBN 0-87683-000-9); Vol. 1; 177p. looseleaf 79.50x (ISBN 0-87683-001-7); Vol. 2; 29p. looseleaf 79.50x (ISBN 0-87683-002-5); Vol. 3; 175p. looseleaf lab manuals 79.50x (ISBN 0-87683-003-3); looseleaf lesson plans 595.00x (ISBN 0-87683-004-1). GP Pub.
Process Metaphysics & Hua-Yen Buddhism: A Critical Study of Cumulative Penetration vs. Interpretation. Steve Odin. LC 81-9388. 242p. 1983. 49.50 (ISBN 0-87395-568-4); pap. 16.95x (ISBN 0-87395-569-2). State U NY Pr.
Process Mineralogy III. Intro. by William Petruk. LC 84-71244. (Symposia on Process Mineralogy Ser.). (Illus.). 322p. 1984. pap. 10.00 (ISBN 0-89520-426-6, 426-6). Soc Mining Eng.
Process Mineralogy of Ceramic Materials. Ed. by W. Baumgart et al. 229p. 1984. pap. 35.25 (ISBN 0-444-00963-9). Elsevier.
Process Mineralogy: Proceedings of the AIME Annual Meeting, New Orleans, 1979. AIME 110th Annual Meeting Staff. Ed. by Donald M. Hausen & Won C. Park. LC 81-82942. 713p. 15.00 (ISBN 0-89520-379-0). Metal Soc.
Process Mineralogy VI: Applications to Precious Metals Deposits, Etc. Ed. by R. D. Hagni. LC 86-23576. (Illus.). 625p. 1987. text ed. 98.00 (ISBN 0-87339-054-7). Metal Soc.
Process Mineralogy VII: Applications to Mineral Beneficiation Technology & Mineral Exploration, with Special Emphasis on Disseminated Carbonaceous Gold Ores. Ed. by A. H. Vassiliou et al. LC 87-42880. (Illus.). 798p. 1988. 169.00 (ISBN 0-87339-073-3). Metal Soc.
Process Modeling. M. M. Denn. 304p. 1986. 36.95 (ISBN 0-470-20668-3, Co-Pub. with Longman). Wiley.
Process Modeling - Fundamentals & Applications to Metals: Proceedings of American Society for Metals Process Modelling Sessions. American Society for Metals. LC 80-12489. (Material-Metalworking Technology Ser.). Repr. of 1980 ed. 114.00 (2026985). Bks Demand UMI.
Process Modeling, Simulation, & Control for Chemical Engineers. W. L. Luyben. (Civil Engineering Ser.). (Illus.). 500p. 1972. text ed. 49.95 (ISBN 0-07-039157-2). McGraw.
Process Modeling Tools: Proceedings of American Society for Metals Process Modeling Sessions Processes Congress 1980. Materials & Processes Congress. LC 81-52303. (Materials-Metalworking Technology Ser.). pap. 56.00 (2027035). Bks Demand UMI.
Process Modelling for Metal Forming & Thermomechanical Treatment. C. R. Boer et al. (Materials Research & Engineering Ser.). (Illus.). xv, 410p. 1986. 75.00 (ISBN 0-387-16401-4). Springer-Verlag.

Process Modification for Industrial Pollutants Source Reduction. Ed. by James W. Patterson. LC 84-21257. (Industrial Waste Management Ser.). (Illus.). 160p. 1985. 24.95 (ISBN 0-87371-003-7). Lewis Pubs Inc.

Process of Argument. Michael Boylan. (Illus.). 128p. 1988. pap. text ed. price not set (ISBN 0-13-723040-0). P-H.

Process of Awakening: An Overview, Vol. 1. Diane K. Pike. LC 85-8083. (Illus.). 75p. (Orig.). 1985. pap. 5.95 (ISBN 0-916192-29-6). L P Pubns.

Process of Becoming. Henry Dalton. 1977. 5.00 (ISBN 0-8233-0258-X). Golden Quill.

Process of Cable Television Franchising: A New York City Case Study. Rena Friedlander & Michael Botein. 100p. 1980. pap. 40.00 (ISBN 0-941888-08-8). Comm Media.

Process of Change. Peggy Papp. LC 83-12814. (Guilford Family Therapy Ser.). 248p. 1983. text ed. 25.00 (ISBN 0-89862-052-X, 2052). Guilford Pr.

Process of Change: From a Closed to an Open System in a Mental Hospital. Maxwell Jones. (Therapeutic Communities Section, International Library of Group Psychotherapy & Group Processes). 220p. 1982. 26.95x (ISBN 0-7100-9255-5). Routledge Chapman & Hall.

Process of Change in Early Modern Europe: Essays in Honor of Miriam Usher Chrisman. Ed. by Phillip N. Bebb & Sherrin Marshall. (Illus.). 250p. 1988. lib. bdg. 32.95x (ISBN 0-8214-0900-X). Ohio U Pr.

Process of Child Development. Ed. by Peter Neubauer. 384p. 1983. 30.00x (ISBN 0-87668-674-9). Aronson.

Process of Clinical Supervision. Gordon M. Hart, Jr. LC 81-16211. (Illus.). 288p. 1982. text ed. 24.00x (ISBN 0-8391-1700-0, 1179). Pro Ed.

Process of Communication: An Introduction to Theory & Practice. David K. Berlo. 1960. pap. text ed. 15.95 (ISBN 0-03-055686-4). HR&W.

Process of Composition. Joy M. Reid. (Illus.). 224p. 1982. pap. text ed. write for info. (ISBN 0-13-723015-X). P-H.

Process of Composition. 2nd ed. Joy M. Reid. (Illus.). 240p. 1988. pap. text ed. price not set (ISBN 0-13-723065-6). P-H.

Process of Constitutional Revision in New Jersey: 1940-1947. Richard J Connors. 219p. 1970. 1.00 (ISBN 0-318-15813-2). Citizens Forum Gov.

Process of Counseling & Therapy. Janet Moursund. (Illus.). 240p. 1985. pap. text ed. 23.00 (ISBN 0-13-722992-5). P-H.

Process of Divorce: How Professionals & Couples Negotiate Settlements. Kenneth Kressel. LC 84-45346. 1985. 23.95 (ISBN 0-465-06389-6). Basic.

Process of Economic Development in Costa Rica, 1948-1970: Some Political Factors. Helen L. Jacobstein. Ed. by Stuart Bruchey. (South American & Latin American Economic History Ser.). 341p. 1987. lib. bdg. 50.00 (ISBN 0-8240-1363-8). Garland Pub.

Process of Economic Growth. rev. ed. W. W. Rostow. 1962. pap. 2.25x (ISBN 0-393-00176-8, Norton Lib). Norton.

Process of Education. Jerome S. Bruner. LC 60-15235. 1960. pap. 4.95x (ISBN 0-674-71001-0). Harvard U Pr.

Process of Excelling: The Practical How-To Guide for Managers & Supervisors. Roger E. Herman. (Illus.). 174p. 1988. 14.95 (ISBN 0-9619590-1-0); pap. 12.95 (ISBN 0-9619590-0-2). Oakhill Pr.

Process of Fiction: Contemporary Stories & Criticism. 2nd ed. Ed. by Barbara McKenzie. 611p. 1974. pap. text ed. 13.00 net (ISBN 0-15-571986-6, HC). HarBraceJ.

Process of Fine Grinding. B. Beke. 1981. 29.50 (ISBN 90-247-2462-7, Pub. by Martinus Nijhoff Netherlands). Kluwer Academic.

Process of Generalizing Abstraction & Its Product: The General Concept see Mental Measurements of the Blind.

Process of Government Under Jefferson. Noble E. Cunningham, Jr. LC 77-85535. (Illus.). 1978. 44.00x (ISBN 0-691-04651-4). Princeton U Pr.

Process of Grant Proposal Development. Gerald V. Teague & Betty S. Heathington. LC 79-93120. (Fastback Ser.: No. 143). (Orig.). 1980. pap. 0.90 (ISBN 0-87367-143-0). Phi Delta Kappa.

Process of Group Communication. 2nd ed. Ronald Applbaum et al. LC 78-18501. 352p. 1979. text ed. write for info. (ISBN 0-574-22710-5, 13-5710); instr's. guide avail. (ISBN 0-574-22711-3, 13-5711). SRA.

Process of Hazard Control. Robert J. Firenze. (Illus.). 1978. text ed. 30.95 (ISBN 0-8403-8002-X). Kendall-Hunt.

Process of Human Development: A Holistic Approach. 2nd ed. Ed. by Clara S. Schuster & Shirley S. Ashburn. 1986. pap. text ed. write for info. (ISBN 0-673-39404-2). Scott F.

Process of Human Evolution. Grover S. Krantz. LC 81-2745. 493p. 1981. pap. text ed. 15.95 (ISBN 0-87073-348-6). Schenkman Bks Inc.

Process of Industrial Development & Alternative Development Strategies. Bela Balassa. LC 81-1033. (Essays in International Finance Ser.: No. 141). 1980. pap. text ed. 4.50x (ISBN 0-88165-048-X). Princeton U Int Finan Econ.

Process of Industrialization: 1750-1870 see Documents of European Economic History.

Process of Innovation in Education see Educational Technology Reviews Ser.

Process of International Arbitration. Kenneth S. Carlston. LC 74-152591. 318p. 1972. Repr. of 1946 ed. lib. bdg. 35.00x (ISBN 0-8371-6024-3, CAIA). Greenwood.

Process of Intuition. 2nd ed. Virginia B. Tower. LC 87-40128. 109p. 1987. pap. 5.75 (ISBN 0-8356-0622-8, Quest). Theos Pub Hse.

Process of Investigation: Concepts & Strategies for the Security Professional. Charles A. Sennewald. 255p. 1981. text ed. 24.95 (ISBN 0-409-95018-1). Butterworth.

Process of Islamic Revolution. A. A. Maududi. pap. 1.50 (ISBN 0-686-18546-3). Kazi Pubns.

Process of Kafka's Trial. Adrian Jaffe. vii, 160p. 1967. 4.50 (ISBN 0-87013-112-5). Mich St U Pr.

Process of Language Understanding. Ed. by G. B. Flores d'Arcais & R. J. Jarvella. LC 82-23754. 340p. 1983. 89.95x (ISBN 0-471-90129-6). Wiley.

Process of Legal Research. Christina Kunz et al. 384p. 1986. pap. text ed. 15.95 (ISBN 0-316-50728-8). Little.

Process of Literature. Agnes M. Mackenzie. 1929. Repr. 35.00 (ISBN 0-8274-3208-9). R West.

Process of Management. T. S. McAlpine. 1973. 20.00 (ISBN 0-8464-0765-5). Beekman Pubs.

Process of Management: Strategy, Action, Results. 6th ed. (Illus.). 704p. 1987. text ed. 39.00 (ISBN 0-13-723602-6). P-H.

Process of Management: Strategy, Action, Results (CPCU Edition) 5th ed. William H. Newman & E. Kirby Warren. LC 81-11985. 578p. 1982. Repr. of 1982 ed. text ed. 26.00 (ISBN 0-89463-036-9). Am Inst Property.

Process of Model-Building in the Behavioral Sciences. Ed. by Ralph M. Stogdill. 192p. 1972. pap. 2.95x (ISBN 0-393-00641-7, Norton Lib). Norton.

Process of Moral Choice. Benito F. Reyes. (Ethics 101 Ser.). 142p. 1970. pap. 5.50 (ISBN 0-939375-28-1). World Univ Amer.

Process of Neurologic Care in Medical Practice. Thomas H. Glick. (Illus.). 392p. 1984. text ed. 27.00x (ISBN 0-674-71080-0). Harvard U Pr.

Process of Occupational Sex-Typing: The Feminization of Clerical Labor in Great Britain. Samuel Cohn. LC 85-14864. (Women in the Political Economy Ser.). 288p. 1985. 34.95 (ISBN 0-87722-402-1). Temple U Pr.

Process of Opposition in India: Two Case Studies of How Policy Shapes Politics. Robert W. Stern. LC 78-116029. 1970. 16.00x (ISBN 0-226-77314-0). U of Chicago Pr.

Process of Paragraph Writing. Joy M. Reid & M. Lindstrom. (Illus.). 200p. 1985. pap. text ed. write for info. (ISBN 0-13-723529-1). P-H.

Process of Parenting. 2nd ed. Jane Brooks. 496p. 1987. pap. text ed. 21.95 (ISBN 0-87484-753-2). Mayfield Pub.

Process of Patient Education. 6th ed. Redman. (Illus.). 352p. 1988. pap. text ed. 22.95 (ISBN 0-8016-4085-7). Mosby.

Process of Political Domination in Ecuador. Agustin Cueva. Tr. by Danielle Salti. LC 79-809. 109p. 1981. 26.95 (ISBN 0-87855-338-X). Transaction Bks.

Process of Political Succession. Ed. by Peter Calvert. 272p. 1987. 37.50 (ISBN 0-312-00771-X). St Martin.

Process of Presentational Speaking. 2nd ed. William S. Howell & Ernest G. Bormann. 223p. 1987. pap. text ed. 19.95 (ISBN 0-06-042929-1, HarpC). Harper Row.

Process of Program Evaluation. 672p. write for info. (NIDSP). Am Soc Train & Devel.

Process of Psychoanalytic Therapy: Models & Strategies, Vol. 1. Emanuel Peterfreund. 1982. text ed. 29.95 (ISBN 0-88163-003-9). Analytic Pr.

Process of Psychotherapy: An Integration of Clinical Experiences & Empirical Research. John R. Thompson. 424p. (Orig.). 1987. lib. bdg. 32.75 (ISBN 0-8191-6602-2); pap. text ed. 17.50 (ISBN 0-8191-6603-0). U Pr of Amer.

Process of Reading: A Cognitive Analyses of Fluent Reading & Learning to Read. D. C. Mitchell. LC 81-21912. 244p. 1982. 64.95x (ISBN 0-471-10199-0, Pub. by Wiley-Interscience). Wiley.

Process of Religion: Essays in Honor of Dean Shailer Mathews. facsimile ed. Ed. by Miles H. Krumbine. LC 71-38776. (Essay Index Reprint Ser). Repr. of 1933 ed. 18.00 (ISBN 0-8369-2667-6). Ayer Co Pubs.

Process of Response: An Empirically Derived Approach for Managing in Turbulence. R. Jeffrey Ellis. 288p. 1987. cancelled (ISBN 0-03-063936-0). Praeger.

Process of Revolution. George S. Pettee. LC 76-80581. 1971. Repr. 18.50x (ISBN 0-86527-159-3). Fertig.

Process of Rural Transformation: Eastern Europe, Latin America & Australia. Ed. by Ivan Volgyes & Richard E. Lonsdale. LC 79-10190. (Pergamon Policy Studies). 1980. 64.00 (ISBN 0-08-023110-1). Pergamon.

Process of Sculpture. Anthony Padovano. 352p. 1986. 15.95 (ISBN 0-306-80273-2). Da Capo.

Process of Social Degeneration. Laurance Labadie. (Men & Movements in the History & Philosophy of Anarchism Ser.). 1979. lib. bdg. 59.95 (ISBN 0-685-96409-4). Revisionist Pr.

Process of Speech: Puritan Religious Writing & Paradise Lost. Boyd M. Berry. LC 75-36933. pap. 80.00 (ISBN 0-317-41618-9, 2025830). Bks Demand UMI.

Process of Spermatogenesis in Animals. Edward C. Roosen-Runge. LC 76-9169. (Developmental & Cell Biology Ser.: 5). pap. 55.50 (2027239). Bks Demand UMI.

Process of Struggle: The Campaign for Corby Steelmaking in 1979. Allen R. Maunders. 1986. text ed. 44.50 (ISBN 0-566-05227-X, Pub. by Gower Pub England). Gower Pub Co.

Process of Technological Change: New Technological & Social Choice in the Workplace. John Clark et al. (Cambridge Studies in Management: No. 11). (Illus.). 300p. 1988. 49.50 (ISBN 0-521-32303-7). Cambridge U Pr.

Process of Water Resources Project Planning: A Systems Approach. Ed. by Y. Y. Haimes et al. 196p. (Orig.). 1987. pap. text ed. 19.00 (ISBN 92-3-102476-0, U1607, UNESCO). UNIPUB.

Process of Work Establishment. Marcia Freedman. LC 71-76248. (Illus.). 135p. 1969. 21.50x (ISBN 0-231-03225-0). Columbia U Pr.

Process of Writing: Discovery & Control. 2nd ed. A. D. Van Nostrand et al. LC 81-83449. 1982. 21.16 (ISBN 0-395-31755-X); Instr's. manual 1.16 (ISBN 0-395-31756-8). HM.

Process One: A Multi-Media College Writing Program. George R. Bramer. 1976. pap. text ed. 17.95 (ISBN 0-675-08682-5). Merrill.

Process Operations: Design of Equipment. Ed. by James Beckman. (Modular Instruction Ser.: Vol. 3). 70p. 1987. pap. 30.00 (ISBN 0-8169-0416-2, J-36). Am Inst Chem Eng.

Process Philosophy & Social Thought. Ed. by John B. Cobb, Jr. & W. Widick Schroeder. LC 80-70781. (Studies in Religion & Society). 263p. 1981. 26.95x (ISBN 0-913348-18-X); pap. 15.95x (ISBN 0-913348-19-8). Ctr Sci Study.

Process Pipe Drafting. Terence M. Shumaker. 1985. 10.00 (ISBN 0-87006-512-2). Goodheart.

Process Piping Blueprint Reading. Terrence M. Shumaker. (Illus.). 176p. 1982. 24.00 (ISBN 0-13-723502-X). P-H.

Process Piping Design, 2 vols. Rip B. Weaver. LC 72-94062. (Illus.). 1973. 24.00x ea. Vol. 1, LC 72-84332. 210p (ISBN 0-87201-759-1). Vol. 2, LC 72-94062. 166p (ISBN 0-87201-760-5). Gulf Pub.

Process Piping Drafting. 3rd ed. Rip Weaver. LC 84-9009. 275p. 1986. 28.00 (ISBN 0-87201-764-8); text ed. wkbk. 16.00 (ISBN 0-87201-763-X). Gulf Pub.

Process Piping Systems. Chemical Engineering Magazine Editors. Ed. by David J. Deutsch. LC 80-13774. (Chemical Engineering Ser.). 484p. 1980. text ed. 54.50 (ISBN 0-07-010706-8). McGraw.

Process Planning Technology. Mark A. Curtis. LC 87-34605. 253p. 1988. write for info. (ISBN 0-471-83254-5). Wiley.

Process Plant Design. J. R. Backhurst & J. H. Harker. LC 72-12561. 411p. 1973. 46.95 (ISBN 0-444-19566-1). Elsevier.

Process Plant Designer's Pocket Handbook of Codes & Standards. Ray Burklin. LC 79-17599. 172p. (Orig.). 1979. pap. 15.00x (ISBN 0-87201-115-1). Gulf Pub.

Process Plant Layout. J. C. Mecklenburgh. (Illus.). 576p. 1985. cancelled (ISBN 0-87201-421-5). Gulf Pub.

Process Plant Layout. J. C. Mecklenburgh. LC 85-13179. 625p. 1985. 89.95 (ISBN 0-470-20238-6). Halsted Pr.

Process Politics: A Guide for Group Leaders. Eileen Guthrie & Warren S. Miller. LC 81-51484. Orig. Title: Making Change. (Illus.). 183p. 1981. pap. 12.95 (ISBN 0-88390-167-6). Univ Assocs.

Process Quality Control. Ellis R. Ott. (Illus.). 416p. 1975. text ed. 42.95 (ISBN 0-07-047923-2). McGraw.

Process Quality Control: Trouble Shooting & Interpretation of Data. 372p. Members 35.95 (ISBN 0-318-13226-5, P177); LP 39.95. Am Soc QC.

Process Reactor Design. Ning H. Chen. 512p. 1983. 54.00 (ISBN 0-205-07903-2, 327903). Allyn.

Process Reader. Richard Ray et al. 480p. 1986. pap. text ed. write for info. (ISBN 0-13-723586-0). P-H.

Process Server. Jack Rudman. (Career Examination Ser.: C-620). (Cloth bdg. avail. on request). pap. 10.00 (ISBN 0-8373-0620-5). Natl Learning.

Process Simulation & Control in Iron & Steelmaking. Ed. by J. M. Uys & H. L. Bishop. LC 65-27847. (Metallurgical Society Conferences Ser.: Vol. 32). pap. 87.50 (ISBN 0-317-10476-4, 2001520). Bks Demand UMI.

Process Synthesis. Dale F. Rudd et al. LC 73-3331. (International Series in Physical & Chemical Engineering). (Illus.). 320p. 1973. ref. ed. o.p. 45.67 (ISBN 0-13-723353-1). P-H.

Process Systems Analysis & Control. Donald R. Coughanowr & L. B. Koppel. (Chemical Engineering Ser.). (Illus.). 1965. text ed. 52.95 (ISBN 0-07-013210-0). McGraw.

Process Systems Development. Carl Brannan. LC 76-1680. (Process Engineer's Pocket Handbook Ser.: Vol. 2). 102p. (Orig.). 1983. pap. 15.00x (ISBN 0-87201-713-3). Gulf Pub.

Process Systems Engineering: Keynote Papers of the Meeting held in Kyoto, Japan, August 1982. Ed. by T. Takamatsu. 366p. 1983. cancelled 47.51 (ISBN 0-08-030272-6). Pergamon.

Process Technologies for Water Treatment. Ed. by S. Stucki. (Illus.). 240p. 1988. 62.50x (ISBN 0-306-43002-9, Plenum Pr). Plenum Pub.

Process Technology: A Compilation of Recent Engineering Conference Papers on Process Control & Simulation. Technical Association of the Pulp & Paper Industry. pap. 48.00 (ISBN 0-317-28031-7, 2025565). Bks Demand UMI.

Process Technology & Flowsheets. Chemical Engineering Magazine Editors. LC 79-12117. (Chemical Engineering Bks). 384p. 1980. text ed. 36.50 (ISBN 0-07-010741-6). McGraw.

Process Technology & Flowsheets, Vol. 2. Chemical Engineering Magazine Editors. LC 83-12117. 360p. 1983. text ed. 38.50 (ISBN 0-07-024388-3). McGraw.

Process Technology Conference, 1st: Proceedings, Washington, D. C. Meeting, March 25-26, 1980, Vol. 1. Iron & Steel Society of AIME. LC 80-138368. pap. 48.50 (ISBN 0-317-30072-5, 2019237). Bks Demand UMI.

Process Technology Conference, 2nd: Proceedings, Chicago Meeting, Feburary 23-25, 1981 Sponsered by the Process Technology Division, Iron & Steel Society of AIME. Iron & Steel Society of AIME. Vol. 2: Continuous Casting of Steel. pap. 80.80 (ISBN 0-317-41762-2, 2024187). Bks Demand UMI.

Process Technology Division (PTD) Conference Proceedings, Vol. 5: Measurement & Control Instrumentation in the Steel & Iron Industry. 254p. 1985. 60.00 (ISBN 0-932897-05-3). Iron & Steel.

Process Technology (PTD) Conference Proceedings, Vol. 4: Topic Mixed Gas Blowing. 202p. 1984. 60.00 (ISBN 0-89520-162-3). Iron & Steel.

Process Theology. Ed. by Ronald H. Nash. 1987. 17.95 (ISBN 0-8010-6748-0). Baker Bk.

Process Theology: An Introductory Exposition. John B. Cobb, Jr. & David R. Griffin. LC 76-10352. 192p. 1976. pap. 8.95 (ISBN 0-664-24743-1). Westminster John Knox.

Process Theology & Secularization. Edwin C. Garvey. 21p. 1972. pap. 0.75 (ISBN 0-912414-14-6). Lumen Christi.

Process Theology & the Christian Tradition. Illtyd Trethowan. LC 84-26240. (Studies in Historical Theology). 122p. 1985. 11.95 (ISBN 0-932506-36-4). St Bedes Pubns.

Process Theology As Political Theology. John B. Cobb, Jr. LC 82-1845. 174p. (Orig.). 1982. pap. 8.95 (ISBN 0-664-24417-3). Westminster John Knox.

Process Theory of Medicine: Problems in Contemporary Philosophy. Ed. by Marcus P. Ford. LC 87-7865. (Problems in Contemporary Philosophy Ser.: Vol. 5). 240p. 1987. lib. bdg. 49.95x (ISBN 0-88946-328-X). E Mellen.

Process Thought on the Eve of the Twenty-First Century. Ewert H. Cousins. 50p. (Orig.). 1985. pap. 3.95x (ISBN 0-932269-25-7). Wyndham Hall.

Process Vacuum Systems Design & Operation. J. Ryans & D. Roper. 384p. 1986. text ed. 45.00 (ISBN 0-07-054355-0). McGraw.

Processed Apple Products. Ed. by Donald L. Downing. (Illus.). 336p. 1988. 59.95 (ISBN 0-442-22117-7). Van Nos Reinhold.

Processed Foods & the Consumer: Additives, Labeling, Standards & Nutrition. Vernal S. Packard, Jr. LC 75-32670. 370p. 1976. pap. text ed. 8.95x (ISBN 0-8166-0784-2). U of Minn Pr.

Processed Foods Packaging. Ed. by Peter Allen. 200p. 1986. pap. 985.00. FIND SVP.

Processed Fruits & Vegetables. 1985. 650.00 (ISBN 0-318-00496-8). Busn Trend.

Processed Meat Industry. 1988. pap. 795.00 (ISBN 0-318-00494-1). Busn Trend.

Processed Meats. 2nd ed. A. M. Pearson & F. Warren Tauber. (Illus.). 1984. 62.95 (ISBN 0-87055-461-1). AVI.

Processed Protein. Business Communications Staff. 105p. 1985. pap. 1250.00 (ISBN 0-89336-447-9, GA-043R). BCC.

Processes Affecting Subsurface Transport of Leaking Underground Tank Fluids. Scott W. Tyler et al. (Illus.). 64p. (Orig.). 1987. pap. 3.25 (S/N 055-000-00269-0). USGPO.

Processes & Control of Plant Senescence: Developments in Crop Science Ser. Ed. by Y. Y. Leshem et al. (Vol. 8). 1986. 92.00 (ISBN 0-444-42521-7). Elsevier.

Processes & Environments of Glacial Margins. American Quaternary Association. 173p. 5.00 (ISBN 0-318-22004-0). Am Quaternary Assn.

Processes & Materials of Manufacture. 3rd ed. Roy A. Lindberg. 1983. text ed. 57.00 (ISBN 0-205-07888-5, 327888). Allyn.

Processes & Phenomena of Social Change. Ed. by Gerald Zaltman et al. LC 78-8950. 478p. 1978. Repr. of 1973 ed. lib. bdg. 27.50 (ISBN 0-88275-725-3). Krieger.

Processes, Beliefs & Questions: Essays on Formal Semantics of Natural Language & Natural Language Processing. Ed. by Stanley Peters & Esa Saarinen. 232p. 34.95 (ISBN 90-277-1314-6, Pub. by Reidel Holland). Kluwer Academic.

Processes for Major Addition-Type Plastics & Their Monomers. 2nd ed. Lyle F. Albright. LC 80-12568. 300p. 1985. lib. bdg. 32.50 (ISBN 0-89874-074-6). Krieger.

Processes in Cutaneous Epidermal Differentiation. Ed. by I. A. Bernstein. 400p. 1987. lib. bdg. 65.00 (ISBN 0-275-92406-8, C2406). Praeger.

Processes in Karst Systems Physics, Chemistry, & Geology. W. Dreybrodt. (Physical Environment Ser.: Vol. 4). (Illus.). 325p. 1988. 133.00 (ISBN 0-387-18839-8). Springer-Verlag.

Processes in Marine Remote Sensing. Ed. by F John Vernberg & Ferdinand P. Diemer. LC 81-16214. (Belle W.Baruch Library in Marine Science: No. 12). (Illus.). 560p. 1981. lib. bdg. 42.95x (ISBN 0-87249-411-X). U of SC Pr.

Processes in Physical Geography. R. D. Thompson et al. 516p. 1986. pap. 31.95 (ISBN 0-470-20661-6, Co-Pub. with Longman). Wiley.

Processes in Physical Geography. R. D. Thompson et al. (Illus.). 516p. 1986. pap. text ed. 19.95 (ISBN 0-582-30136-X). Wiley.

Processes in Technical Writing. David A. McMurrey. 1303p. 1988. pap. text ed. write for info. (ISBN 0-02-379700-2). Macmillan.

Processes of Acquisition in Individuals with High & Low Baseball Knowledge: The First Inning. Harry L. Chiesi et al. 63p. 1977. 1.50 (ISBN 0-318-14727-0). Learn Res Dev.

Processes of Adult Education. Ed. by Coolie Verner & Thurman White. 57p. 1965. 3.50 (ISBN 0-88379-028-9). A A A C E.

Processes of Adult Education. Ed. by Coolie Verner & Thurman White. 57p. Date not set. 2.45 (AEA-6). A A A C E.

Processes of Animal Memory. Douglas L. Medin et al. LC 76-22197. 267p. 1976. 19.50 (ISBN 0-470-15189-7, Pub. by Wiley). Krieger.

Processes of Cognitive Growth: Infancy. Jerome S. Bruner. LC 68-27831. (Heinz Werner Lec. Ser.: No. 3). 1968. 9.00 (ISBN 0-8271-6810-1). Clark U Pr.

Processes of Constitutional Decision Making. 2nd ed. Paul Brest & Sanford Levinson. LC 81-86686. 1983. text ed. 38.00 (ISBN 0-316-10794-8). Little.

Processes of Constitutional Decision Making: 1986 Supplement. Paul Brest & Sanford Levinson. 250p. 1986. pap. text ed. 12.00 (ISBN 0-316-10789-1). Little.

Processes of Criminal Justice: Adjudication. 2nd ed. H. Richard Uviller. (American Casebook Ser.). 768p. 1979. pap. text ed. 14.95 (ISBN 0-8299-2064-1). West Pub.

Processes of Criminal Justice: Investigation & Adjudication. 2nd ed. H. Richard Uviller. LC 79-16743. (American Casebook Ser.). 1384p. 1979. text ed. 35.95 (ISBN 0-8299-2057-9). West Pub.

Processes of Heredity. Bert W. Winterton. 352p. (Orig.). 1983. pap. 18.95 (ISBN 0-8403-2835-4). Kendall-Hunt.

Processes of Industrial Development & Alternative Development Strategies. Bela Balassa. (Working Paper: No. 438). 127p. 1982. pap. 3.50 (ISBN 0-686-39754-1, WP-0438). World Bank.

Processes of Manufacturing. R. Thomas Wright. LC 86-29563. (Illus.). 464p. 1987. text ed. 22.00 (ISBN 0-87006-633-1). Goodheart.

Processes of Organic Evolution. 3rd ed. G. Ledyard Stebbins. (Illus.). 1977. pap. text ed. write for info. (ISBN 0-13-723452-X). P-H.

Processes of Recovery from Neural Trauma. Ed. by G. Gilad et al. (Experimental Brain Research Ser.: Supplementum 13). (Illus.). 384p. 1986. 69.00 (ISBN 0-387-15781-6). Springer-Verlag.

Processes of Stratification in Science. Paul D. Allison. Ed. by Harriet Zuckerman & Robert K. Merton. LC 80-13567. (Dissertations on Sociology Ser.). 1980. lib. bdg. 23.00x (ISBN 0-405-12946-7). Ayer Co Pubs.

Processes of the Earth's Surface. Susan Vuke. 96p. 1980. pap. 5.00 (ISBN 0-87842-125-4). Mountain Pr.

Processes of the World-System. Ed. by Terence K. Hopkins & Immanuel Wallerstein. LC 79-27385. (Political Economy of the World-System Annuals: Vol. 3). (Illus.). 320p. 1980. 29.95 (ISBN 0-8039-1378-8). Sage.

Processes of Tribal Unification & Integration: Case Study of the Bhils. S. L. Doshi. 1978. 11.00x (ISBN 0-8364-0291-X). South Asia Bks.

Processes of Urbanism: A Multidisciplinary Approach. Ed. by Joyce Aschenbrenner & Lloyd R. Collins. (World Anthropology Ser.). xiv, 424p. 1978. 49.25 (ISBN 90-279-7620-1). Mouton.

Processing & Finishing of Aluminum. National Fire Protection Association. 1987. 10.50 (ISBN 0-317-63212-4, 65-87). Natl Fire Prot.

Processing & Finishing of Aluminum. (Sixty Ser). 1973. pap. 2.00 (ISBN 0-685-58074-1, 65). Natl Fire Prot.

Processing & Marketing of Bauxite, Alumina, Aluminium: Areas for International Co-operation. (Studies in the Processing, Marketing & Distribution of Commodities). 89p. 11.00 (ISBN 92-1-112170-1, E.84.II.D.15). UN.

Processing & Marketing of Manganese: Areas for International Co-operation. (Studies in the Processing, Marketing & Distribution of Commodities Ser.). 57p. 8.00 (ISBN 92-1-112173-6, E.84.II.D.18.). UN.

Processing & Marketing of Phosphates: Areas for International Co-operation. (Studies in the Processing, Marketing & Distribution of Commodities). 72p. 9.50 (ISBN 92-1-112178-7, E.84.II.D.13). UN.

Processing & Presentation Antigens. Ed. by Benvenuto Pernis et al. 324p. 1988. 75.00 (ISBN 0-12-551855-2). Acad Pr.

Processing & Properties of Low Carbon Steel. Ed. by J. M. Gray. LC 73-172124. pap. 106.30 (ISBN 0-317-08694-4, 2012653). Bks Demand UMI.

Processing & Properties of Powder Metallurgy Composites. Ed. by P. Kumar et al. LC 87-43115. (Illus.). 170p. 1988. 64.00 (ISBN 0-87339-034-2). Metal Soc.

Processing & Property Enhancement Utilizing Modifiers & Additives in Polymers: First International Conference - Sponsored by Polymer Modifiers & Additives Division, the Marriot Hotel, Newark Airport, Newark, NJ, Nov. 6-7, 1985. Society of Plastics Engineers Staff. pap. 56.50 (2027695). Bks Demand UMI.

Processing & Storage of Foodgrains by Rural Families. Elizabeth O'Kelly & R. H. Forster. (Agricultural Services Bulletins: No. 53). 129p. (Eng. & Fr.). 1983. pap. text ed. 10.00 (ISBN 92-5-101276-8, F2447, FAO). UNIPUB.

Processing & Synthesis of Hydrogeological Data. A. Gheorghe. 390p. 1978. 38.00 (ISBN 0-85626-107-6). Abacus Pr.

Processing & Testing of Reaction Injection Molding Urethanes - STP 788. Ed. by Ashe & Dunleavy. 95p. 1982. pap. 13.95 (ISBN 0-8031-0779-X, 04-788000-20). ASTM.

Processing & Use of Organic Sludge & Liquid Agricultural Wastes. P. L'Hermite. 1986. lib. bdg. 96.00 (ISBN 90-277-2338-9, Pub. by Reidel Holland). Kluwer Academic.

Processing & Use of Sewage Sludge. Ed. by P. L'Hermite & H. Ott. 600p. 1984. lib. bdg. 79.50 (ISBN 90-277-1727-3, Pub. by Reidel Holland). Kluwer Academic.

Processing & Uses of Carbon Fiber Reinforced Plastics. Ed. by VDI. 282p. 1981. 65.00 (ISBN 3-18-404075-5, Pub. by VDI W Germany). IPS.

Processing & Utilization of High Sulfur Coals II: Proceedings of the Second International Conference, Carbondale, IL, 28 September. Y. P. Chugh. 1987. 127.25 (ISBN 0-444-01292-3). Elsevier.

Processing & Utilization of High Sulfur Coals: Proceedings of the First International Conference, Columbus, OH, Oct. 13-17, 1985. Ed. by Y. A. Attia. (Coal Science & Technology Ser.: No. 9). 788p. 1985. 202.75 (ISBN 0-444-42545-4). Elsevier.

Processing Aquatic Food Products. Frederick Wheaton & Thomas B. Lawson. LC 84-20995. 517p. 1985. 78.50 (ISBN 0-471-09736-5). Wiley.

Processing Before the Export of Cocoa: Areas for International Co-operation. (Studies in the Processing, Marketing & Distribution of Commodities Ser.). 81p. 9.50 (ISBN 92-1-112172-8, E.84.II.D.16). UN.

Processing Composites. (Monograph Ser.). Date not set. price not set. Soc Adv Material.

Processing for Improved Productivity. Ed. by K. M. Nair. (Advances in Ceramics Ser.: Vol. 11). 245p. 1984. 40.00 (ISBN 0-916094-63-4). Am Ceramic.

Processing Juvenile Traffic Cases in Ventura County, California. National Center for State Courts Staff. 96p. 1975. manuscript 5.76 (WRO-014). Natl Ctr St Courts.

Processing, Microstructure & Properties of HSLA Steels. Ed. by A. J. DeArdo. (Illus.). 1988. 92.00 (ISBN 0-317-69865-6). Metal Soc.

Processing Mortage-Backed Securities. Louis J. Karcher. (Illus.). 300p. 1988. 39.50 (ISBN 0-13-723685-9, Busn). P-H.

Processing of Ceramics Glasses & Composites Ultrastructure. John D. Mackenzie. LC 87-28574. 1988. 70.00 (ISBN 0-471-62416-0). Wiley.

Processing of Crystalline Ceramics. Ed. by R. F. Davis et al. LC 78-18441. (Materials Science Research Ser.: Vol. 11). 696p. 1978. 105.00x (ISBN 0-306-40035-9, Plenum Pr). Plenum Pub.

Processing of Electronic Materials. Ed. by Clarence G. Law, Jr. & Richard Pollard. LC 87-81560. 488p. 1987. 60.00 (ISBN 0-8169-0427-8, P-50). Am Inst Chem Eng.

Processing of Energy & Metallic Minerals. Ed. by H. Y. Sohn & S. D. Hill. LC 82-11466. (AIChE Symposium Ser.: Vol. 78, No. 216). 1982. pap. 36.00 (ISBN 0-8169-0228-3, S-216). Am Inst Chem Eng.

Processing of Environmental Information in Vertebrates. Ed. by M. H. Stetson. (Illus.). 330p. 1987. 79.00 (ISBN 0-387-96558-0). Springer-Verlag.

Processing of Guided Wave Optoelectronic Materials, No. I. Ed. by R. L. Holman & D. M. Smyth. 149p. 1984. 43.00 (ISBN 0-89252-495-2, 460). SPIE.

Processing of Information & Structure. Wendall R. Garner. LC 73-22174. 208p. 1974. text ed. 29.95 (ISBN 0-89859-119-8). L Erlbaum Assocs.

Processing of Low-Grade Uranium Ores. (Panel Proceedings Ser.). (Illus.). 247p. 1967. pap. 16.25 (ISBN 92-0-041067-7, ISP146, IAEA). UNIPUB.

Processing of Memories: Forgetting & Retention. N. E. Spear. 554p. 1978. 49.95 (ISBN 0-89859-492-8). L Erlbaum Assocs.

Processing of Memories: Forgetting & Retention. Norman E. Spear. LC 77-19113. (Experimental Psychology Ser.). 553p. 1978. 31.95x (ISBN 0-470-26290-7). Halsted Pr.

Processing of Metal & Ceramic Powders: Proceedings of a Symposium, Sponsored by the Powder Metallurgical Society of AIME & Basic Science Division of the American Ceramic Society...Louisville,KY, October 12-14, 1981. The Metallurgical Society of AIME. Ed. by R. M. German & K. W. Lay. LC 82-61009. pap. 86.30 (2056147). Bks Demand UMI.

Processing of Natural Rubber. pap. 12.25 (ISBN 92-5-100742-X, F711, FAO). UNIPUB.

Processing of Polyester Fibres. Ed. by O. Pajgrt et al. (Textile Science & Technology Ser.: Vol. 2). 550p. 1980. 147.50 (ISBN 0-444-99860-8). Elsevier.

Processing of Polymer Composite Materials. A. E. Gibson. Date not set. cancelled (ISBN 0-08-027617-2); pap. cancelled (ISBN 0-08-027616-4). Pergamon.

Processing of Visible Language. Ed. by P. A. Kolers et al. LC 79-13530. 554p. 1979. 70.00x (ISBN 0-306-40186-X, Plenum Pr). Plenum Pub.

Processing of Visible Language. Ed. by Paul A. Kolers et al. LC 80-22602. 634p. 1980. 90.00x (ISBN 0-306-40576-8, Plenum Pr). Plenum Pub.

Processing Opinion Requests in Attorneys General's Offices. (Management Manual: No. 8). 60p. 1979. 3.00 (ISBN 0-318-15222-3). Natl Attys General.

Processing, Structure & Properties of Block Co-Polymers. Ed. by M. J. Folkes. (Illus.). 224p. 1985. 61.25 (ISBN 0-85334-323-3, Pub. by Elsevier Applied Sci England). Elsevier.

Processing Structures for Perception & Action. Ed. by H. Marko et al. 300p. 1988. lib. bdg. 69.50 (ISBN 0-89573-682-9, Pub. by Deutsche Forschungsgemeinschaft). VCH Pubs.

Processing the News. 2nd ed. Doris A. Graber. 224p. Date not set. pap. text ed. 16.95 (ISBN 0-8013-0047-9). Longman.

Processing the News: How People Tame the Information Tide. Doris A. Graber. LC 83-19537. (Political Communication & Policy Ser.). (Illus.). 256p. 1984. pap. 16.95x (ISBN 0-582-28510-0). Longman.

Processing Unemployment Insurance Claims. Cornelia Spanier. (Orig.). 1986. pap. 39.95 (ISBN 0-938545-01-9). Busn Media Res.

Processing Water-Treatment-Plant Sludge. (AWWA Handbooks - General). (Illus.). 160p. 1974. pap. text ed. 10.80 (ISBN 0-89867-016-0). Am Water Wks Assn.

Processing Words: The Information Manager & Word Processing. Stephen Flood. 1987. pap. write for info. (ISBN 0-85142-216-0). Learned Info.

Processing Words: Writing & Revising on a Microcomputer. Bruce L. Edwards, Jr. (Illus.). 400p. 1987. pap. text ed. write for info. (ISBN 0-13-723636-0). P-H.

Procession. Kahlil Gibran. 1972. pap. 3.95 (ISBN 0-8065-0274-6, Pub. by Citadel Pr). Lyle Stuart.

Procession. Kahlil Gibran. 1958. 5.00 (ISBN 0-8022-0580-1). Philos Lib.

Procession of Friends. Daisy Newman. 484p. 1980. pap. 11.95 (ISBN 0-913408-59-X). Friends United.

Procession of Masks. Herbert S. Gorman. LC 77-99698. (Essay Index Reprint Ser.). 1923. 19.00 (ISBN 0-8369-1352-3). Ayer Co Pubs.

Procession of Saints. James Brodrick. LC 72-5436. (Biography Index Reprint Ser). 1972. Repr. of 1949 ed. 20.50 (ISBN 0-8369-8134-0). Ayer Co Pubs.

Processionale ad Usum Insignis ac Praeclarae Ecclesiae Sarum. W. G. Henderson. 200p. Repr. of 1882 ed. text ed. 62.10x (ISBN 0-576-99143-0, Pub. by Gregg Intl Pubs England). Gregg Intl.

Processive World View for Pragmatic Christians. Joseph T. Culliton. LC 75-3781. 302p. 1975. 13.95 (ISBN 0-8022-2170-X). Philos Lib.

Processo De Cartas De Amores. Juan de Segura. Tr. by Edwin B. Place. LC 70-134270. (Northwestern Humanities Ser.: No. 23). 1970. Repr. of 1950 ed. 22.00 (ISBN 0-404-50723-9). AMS Pr.

Processor Arrays: Architecture & Applications. Terry Fountain. (Microelectronics & Signal Processing Ser.). 1987. 39.00 (ISBN 0-12-262945-0). Acad Pr.

Processor Organization & Microprogramming: A Case Study. Daniel J. Nesin. 288p. (Orig.). 1985. pap. text ed. write for info. (ISBN 0-574-21770-3, 13-4770); instr's. guide avail. (13-4771). SRA.

Processus Phonologiques, Processus Morphologiques et Lapsus Dans un Corpus Aphasique. Marianne Kilani-Schoch. (European University Studies: No. 21, Vol. 17). xvii, 568p. (Fr.). 1982. 55.25 (ISBN 3-261-05029-2). P Lang Pubs.

Proclaim Her Name. Philip Bebie. 58p. 1982. pap. 1.98 (ISBN 0-911988-46-7). AMI Pr.

Proclaim His Marvelous Deeds: How to Give a Personal Testimony. Patti G. Mansfield. 96p. (Orig.). 1987. pap. 3.75 (ISBN 0-940535-06-8, UP107). Franciscan U Pr.

Proclaim His Word: Homiletic Themes for Sundays & Holy Days - Cycle C, Vol. 1. new ed. Joseph Fichtner. LC 73-5726. 238p. (Orig.). 1973. pap. 3.95 (ISBN 0-8189-0274-4). Alba.

Proclaim His Word: Homiletic Themes for Sundays & Holy Days-Cycle A, Vol. 2. new ed. Joseph Fichtner. LC 73-5726. 239p. (Orig.). 1974. pap. 4.95 (ISBN 0-8189-0292-2). Alba.

Proclaim the Good News: Essays in Honor of Gordon G. Johnson. Carl Lundquist et al. Ed. by Norris Magnuson. LC 86-80862. 244p. (Orig.). 1986. pap. 4.95 (ISBN 0-935797-24-6). Harvest IL.

Proclaim the Word! Eugene E. Hall & James L. Heflin. LC 84-17458. 1985. 10.95 (ISBN 0-8054-2102-5). Broadman.

Proclaim Your God. Herbert L. Beierle. 1.00 (ISBN 0-940480-09-3). U of Healing.

Proclaiming Grace & Freedom: The Story of United Methodism in America. John G. McEllhenney. (Orig.). 1982. pap. 7.95 (ISBN 0-687-34323-2). Abingdon.

Proclaiming Harmony. Tr. by William O. Hennessey from Chinese. LC 81-18143. (Michigan Monographs in Chinese Studies: No. 41). 200p. (Orig.). 1981. pap. 7.00 (ISBN 0-89264-041-3). U of Mich Ctr Chinese.

Proclaiming Justice & Peace: Documents from John XXIII to John Paul II. Ed. by Michael Walsh & Brian Davies. LC 85-50138. 370p. 1985. 16.95 (ISBN 0-89622-239-X); pap. 12.95 (ISBN 0-89622-236-5). Twenty Third.

Proclaiming the Good News: Homilies for the A Cycle. John J. Hughes. LC 82-62554. 156p. 1983. pap. 14.95 (ISBN 0-87973-722-0, 722). Our Sunday Visitor.

Proclaiming the Good News: Homilies for the "B" Cycle. John J. Hughes. LC 84-60750. 156p. 1984. 14.95 (ISBN 0-87973-723-9, 723). Our Sunday Visitor.

Proclaiming the Truth. Donald E. Demaray. 1980. pap. 6.95 (ISBN 0-8010-2898-1). Baker Bk.

Proclaiming the Word. 2nd ed. G. B. Harrison & John McCabe. 1976. pap. 4.95 (ISBN 0-916134-00-8). Pueblo Pub Co.

Proclaiming the Word: The Concept of Preaching in the Thought of Ellen G. White. R. Edward Turner. (Andrews University Monographs, Studies in Religion: Vol. XII). x, 183p. 1980. pap. 3.95 (ISBN 0-943872-12-X). Andrews Univ Pr.

Proclamation & Presence: Old Testament Essays in Honor of Gwynne Henton Davies. Ed. by John I. Durham & J. R. Porter. LC 83-17445. xx, 315p. 1983. 17.95 (ISBN 0-86554-101-9, MUP/H93). Mercer Univ Pr.

Proclamation of Baha'u'llah. Baha'u'llah. LC 72-237435. 1967. 8.95 (ISBN 0-87743-064-0, 103-012); pap. 4.95 (ISBN 0-87743-065-9, 103-013). Baha'i.

Proclamation of the Gospel in a Pluralistic World: Essays on Christianity & Culture. George W. Forell. LC 73-79354. pap. 36.00 (2026865). Bks Demand UMI.

Proclamation of the Irish Republic: Easter 1916. Provisional Government of Ireland. Ed. by Malachi McCormick. 8p. 1984. pap. text ed. 3.95 (ISBN 0-943984-04-1). Stone St Pr.

Proclamations II, Chronological Series, 2 vols. Incl. No. 368. Proclamadion for the Marchauntes Adventurers. LC 74-171743. Repr. of 1559 ed (ISBN 90-221-0368-4); No. 369. By the Queene, Forbidding Unlicensed Plays. LC 78-171744. Repr. of 1559 ed (ISBN 90-221-0369-2); No. 370. A Proclamation Agaynst Breaking Monumentes of Antiquitie. LC 71-171745. Repr. of 1560 ed (ISBN 90-221-0370-6); No. 371. By the Queene, Forbidding Export of Armour to Russia. LC 75-171746. Repr. of 1561 ed (ISBN 90-221-0371-4); No. 372. This Is the Ordinance for the Quenes Swannes. LC 79-171747. Repr. of 1564 ed (ISBN 90-221-0371-4); No. 373. By the Queene, Against Ill-Treatment of "Informers". LC 72-171748. Repr. of 1566 ed (ISBN 90-221-0372-2); No. 374. By the Queene, Against the Earl of Northumberland. LC 76-171749. Repr. of 1569 ed (ISBN 90-221-0373-0); No. 375. By the Queene, a Proclamation Concerning Hattes & Cappes. LC 70-171750 (ISBN 90-221-0374-9); No. 376. By the Queene, for Discovering Authors of Libels. LC 74-171751. Repr. of 1576 ed (ISBN 90-221-0375-7); By the Queene, for Sowing Lands with Flax. LC 78-171752. (No. 377). Repr. of 1597 ed (ISBN 90-221-0376-5); No. 243. The King's Maiesties Declaration Concerning Lawfull Sports. LC 77-26398. Repr. of 1618 ed (ISBN 90-221-0377-3). (English Experience Ser.: Nos. 243, 368-377). 1970-71. Set. 21.00 (ISBN 90-221-0368-4). Walter J Johnson.

Proclamations of the Arcane Order. 53p. (J). semiannual 35.00 (ISBN 0-318-13348-2, 1790900894). Arcane Order.

Proclamations of the Tudor Kings. Rudolph W. Heinze. LC 75-22983. pap. 82.30 (ISBN 0-317-55468-9, 2029220). Bks Demand UMI.

Proclamations of the Tudor Queens. Frederic A. Youngs. LC 75-30442. pap. 72.80 (ISBN 0-317-55488-3, 2029225). Bks Demand UMI.

Proclus' Commentary on Plato's "Parmenides". Glenn R. Morrow & John M. Dillion. LC 85-43302. 712p. 1986. text ed. 80.00x (ISBN 0-691-07305-8). Princeton U Pr.

Product Costing Manual. 1981. 100.00x (ISBN 0-317-43692-9, Pub. by F I R A). State Mutual Bk.
Product Counterfeiting: Remedies. (Patents, Copyrights, Trademarks & Literary Property Course Handbook: Vol. 180). 332p. 1984. 15.00 (ISBN 0-317-11486-7, G4-3744). PLI.
Product Data Interfaces in CAD-CAM Applications. Ed. by J. Encarnacao et al. (Symbolic Computation Ser.). (Illus.). 270p. 1986. 68.00 (ISBN 0-387-15118-4). Springer-Verlag.
Product Defects & Hazards: Litigation & Regulatory Strategies. James T. O'Reilly. LC 87-15992. 1987. 95.00 (ISBN 0-471-84786-0). Wiley.
Product Defects & Recalls: What Government Wanted & What Industry Did, Vol. 1. Judy Haberek. Ed. by Robert Varela. 45p. pap. 55.00 1-5 copies (ISBN 0-914176-27-7); pap. 50.00 6-15 copies. Wash Busn Info.
Product Design. Ed. by Industrial Design Magazine Staff & Akiko Busch. LC 84-5915. (Illus.). 256p. 1984. 49.95 (ISBN 0-86636-002-6). PBC Intl Inc.
Product Design & Process Engineering. B. W. Niebel & A. B. Draper. 1974. text ed. 52.95 (ISBN 0-07-046535-5). McGraw.
Product Design & Technological Innovation. Ed. by Robin Roy & David Wield. 320p. 1986. 65.00x (ISBN 0-335-15110-8, Open Univ Pr); pap. 24.00x (ISBN 0-335-15109-4, Open Univ Pr). Taylor & Francis.
Product Design Liability. Richard F. Schaden & Victoria C. Heldman. 393p. 1982. text ed. 15.00 (ISBN 0-686-79682-9, H1-2964). PLI.
Product Design Management: An Annotated Bibliography. Patrick Noon & Timothy Warner. 220p. 1988. text ed. 50.00 (ISBN 0-566-05466-3, Pub. by Gower Pub England). Gower Pub Co.
Product Design Two. Industrial Design Magazine Editors & Sandra Edwards. LC 86-9395. (Library of Applied Design). (Illus.). 256p. 1986. 49.95 (ISBN 0-86636-008-5). PBC Intl Inc.
Product Design with Plastics: A Practical Manual. Joseph B. Dym. LC 82-3091. (Illus.). 288p. 1983. 32.95x (ISBN 0-8311-1141-0). Indus Pr.
Product Design 3. (Illus.). 256p. 1988. 55.00 (ISBN 0-86636-066-2). PBC Intl Inc.
Product Development Directory. 500p. 1988. 132.00 (ISBN 0-942036-22-0). Med Device Reg.
Product Differentiation & Non-Price Competition. Norman J. Ireland. 216p. 1987. text ed. 49.95 (ISBN 0-631-13846-3). Basil Blackwell.
Product Differentiation: The Legal Situation. Jules Stuyck. 134p. 1983. 21.00 (ISBN 90-654-4084-4, Pub. by Kluwer Law Netherlands). Kluwer Academic.
Product Durability & Product Life Extension: Their Contribution to Solid Waste Management. OECD Staff. 129p. (Orig.). 1982. pap. 10.00x (ISBN 92-64-12293-1). OECD.
Product Engineering Design Manual. Ed. by Douglas C. Greenwood. LC 80-23595. (Illus.). 342p. 1982. Repr. of 1959 ed. text ed. 29.50 (ISBN 0-89874-273-0). Krieger.
Product Esthetics: An Interpretation for Designers. Zdzislaw M. Lewalski. (Illus.). 240p. (Orig.). 1988. pap. price not set (ISBN 0-944327-04-4). Design & Dev Engineering Pr.
Product Export Riches Opportunities. 220p. 1987. 35.00 (ISBN 0-317-55713-0). B Klein Pubns.
Product Formula for Surgery Obstructions. J. W. Morgan. LC 78-4581. (Memoirs Ser.: No. 201). 90p. 1978. pap. 14.00 (ISBN 0-8218-2201-2, MEMO 201). Am Math.
Product Formulas, Nonlinear Semigroups & Addition of Unbounded Operators. Paul R. Chernoff. LC 73-22235. (Memoirs: No. 140). 121p. 1974. pap. 13.00 (ISBN 0-8218-1840-6, MEMO-140). Am Math.
Product Improvement Through Environmental Science: Proceedings of the Annual Meeting of the Institute of Environmental Sciences, 8th, 1962. Annual Meeting of the Institute of Environmental Sciences Staff. LC 62-38584. (Illus.). 1962. pap. text ed. 8.00 (ISBN 0-915414-02-3). Inst Environ Sci.
Product Innovation & Development. A. E. Berridge. 236p. 1977. text ed. 29.50x (ISBN 0-220-66325-4, Pub. by Busn Bks England). Brookfield Pub Co.
Product Innovation & Directions of International Trade. Louis T. Wells, Jr. Ed. by Stuart Bruchey. LC 80-602. (Multinational Corporations Ser.). (Illus.). 1980. lib. bdg. 22.00x (ISBN 0-405-13392-8). Ayer Co Pubs.
Product Innovation & Management. 2nd ed. Knut Holt. 192p. 1983. text ed. 37.95 (ISBN 0-408-01441-5). Butterworth.
Product Labeling & Health Risks. Ed. by Louis Morris et al. LC 80-22728. (Banbury Report Ser.: Report 6). 328p. 1980. 52.00x (ISBN 0-87969-205-7). Cold Spring Harbor.
Product Liability. John S. Allee. 550p. 1984. looseleaf 70.00 (ISBN 0-318-20280-8, 00587). NY Law Pub.
Product Liability. Hamline University School of Law Advanced Legal Education Staff. LC 85-160087. 274p. 1985. 42.40. Hamline Law.
Product Liability: A Loss Prevention Manual for Wholesaler-Distributors. Robert Larsen. 100p. 30.00 (ISBN 0-318-15146-4); NAW commodity line association members 25.00 (ISBN 0-318-15147-2); NAW members 22.00 (ISBN 0-318-15148-0). Natl Assn Wholesale Dists.
Product Liability & Quality. LC 84-51730. (Illus.). 40p. 1984. 27.00 (ISBN 0-89883-807-X, SP586). Soc Auto Engineers.
Product Liability Casebook. Ed. by J. Stuart Ashworth. 1984. 60.00 (ISBN 1-85044-015-8). Lloyds London Pr.
Product Liability: Cases & Trends. Victor E. Schwartz. LC 87-401017. Date not set. price not set. P-H.
Product Liability for Corporate Counsels, Controllers & Product Safety Executives. Warren Freedman. 1984. 46.95 (ISBN 0-442-22493-1). Van Nos Reinhold.
Product Liability in Europe. Ed. by Paul Strom. Association Europeene D'etudes Juridiques et Fiscales. 160p. 1975. pap. 21.00 (ISBN 90-268-0815-1, Pub.by Kluwer Law Netherlands). Kluwer Academic.
Product Liability Law: A Guide for Managers. Michael Whincup. LC 84-13713. 304p. 1985. text ed. 38.50 (ISBN 0-566-02494-2). Gower Pub Co.
Product Liability Law in Texas. James B. Sales. LC 85-18150. xv, 700p. 1985. 39.50 (ISBN 0-913797-09-X). Houston Law Review.
Product Liability Mess: How Business Can Be Rescued from State Court Politics. Richard Neely. 325p. 1988. 24.95 (ISBN 0-02-922680-5). Free Pr.
Product Liability of Manufacturers 1986: Prevention & Defense, Vol 310. (Litigation & Administrative Practice Ser.). 453p. 1986. 45.00 (H4-5001). PLI.
Product Liability: The Corporate Response. Nathan Weber. (Report Ser.: No. 893). (Illus.). vi, 21p. (Orig.). 1987. pap. text ed. 60.00 (ISBN 0-8237-0335-5). Conference Bd.
Product Liability: The New Law under the Consumer Protection Act 1987. Rodney Nelson-Jones & Peter Stewart. 208p. 1987. 128.00x (ISBN 1-85190-034-9, Pub. by Fourmat England). State Mutual Bk.
Product Liability: Warnings, Instructions, & Recalls 1984. Richard J. Phelan & Kenneth Ross. 300p. 1984. pap. 15.00 (ISBN 0-317-27552-6, H4-4950). PLI.
Product Life Cycle & International Trade. Ed. by Louis T. Wells, Jr. LC 78-184791. (Illus.). 259p. 1972. pap. 4.95x (ISBN 0-87584-095-7, Dist. by Harper & Row Pubs., Inc.). Harvard Busn.
Product-Line Strategies. Earl L. Bailey. (Report Ser.: 816). (Illus.). vii, 76p. (Orig.). 1982. pap. 50.00 (ISBN 0-8237-0253-7). Conference Bd.
Product Management: A Reader. Patrick M. Dunne & Susan Obenhouse. LC 80-22355. pap. 45.50 (ISBN 0-317-26622-5, 2025427). Bks Demand UMI.
Product Management for Hospitals. James C. Folger. LC 87-318895. 132p. (Orig.). 1988. pap. 29.50 (ISBN 1-55648-012-1, 136102). AHPI.
Product Management Handbook. Richard Handscombe. (Illus.). 256p. 1989. 24.95. McGraw.
Product Management Handbook: A Practical Guide for Bank Product Managers. 84p. 1983. 54.00 (ISBN 0-318-03430-1, 711). Bank Admin Inst.
Product Management in Healthcare Marketing. Edward A. Kelley. 480p. 1989. 65.00 (ISBN 0-915601-04-4). Swansea Pr.
Product Management: Strategy & Organization. 2nd ed. Edgar A. Pessemier. LC 85-23976. 688p. 1986. Repr. of 1982 ed. text ed. 47.50 (ISBN 0-89874-922-0). Krieger.
Product of Web Impregnation of Saturation. (Bibliographic Ser.: No. S40.). 166p. 1971. 24.00 (ISBN 0-317-34425-0). Inst Paper Chem.
Product Planning: An Integrated Approach. Merlin Stone. LC 76-26335. 1976. 29.95x (ISBN 0-470-98915-7). Halsted Pr.
Product Planning: The Relationship Between Product Characteristics & Environmental Impact. Environmental Resources, Ltd. Staff. 312p. 1978. 35.00 (ISBN 0-86010-126-6). Graham & Trotman.
Product Policy: Cases & Concepts. Richard N. Cardozo. LC 78-67939. 1979. text ed. write for info. (ISBN 0-201-00888-2). Addison-Wesley.
Product Policy: Concepts, Methods & Strategies. Yoram J. Wind. 1982. text ed. write for info. (ISBN 0-201-08343-4). Addison-Wesley.
Product Rendering with Markers. Mark Arends. (Illus.). 180p. 1985. 36.95x (ISBN 0-442-20952-5). Van Nos Reinhold.
Product Reports Index: First Quarter 1985. Ed. by Theodore E. Wade, Jr. (Product Reports Index Ser.). 96p. (Orig.). pap. cancelled (ISBN 0-930192-21-4). Gazelle Pubns.
Product Risk Reduction in the Chemical Industry. Miller et al. 1985. pap. 125.00 (ISBN 0-88057-294-9). Exec Ent Pubns.
Product S. O. S. 2000p. 360.00 (ISBN 0-942036-21-2). Med Device Reg.
Product S. O. S. - Historical: Nineteen Eighty-Five. Ed. by P. E. Whelan. 1500p. 1985. 495.00 (ISBN 0-942036-06-9). Med Device Reg.
Product Safety & Liability: A Desk Reference. John Kolb & Steven S. Ross. (Illus.). 1979. text ed. 53.00 (ISBN 0-07-035380-8). McGraw.
Product Safety & Liability Reporter. BNA's Environment & Safety Services Staff. 574.00. BNA.
Product Safety. Developing & Implementing Measures. OECD. 64p. 1987. pap. 10.00x (ISBN 92-64-12924-3). OECD.
Product Safety Engineering for Managers. R. Matthiew Seiden. LC 84-9756. 438p. 1984. 39.95 (ISBN 0-13-724097-X, Busn). P-H.
Product Safety Evaluation. Ed. by Alan M. Goldberg. (Alternative Methods in Toxicology Ser.). 376p. 1983. text ed. 75.00 (ISBN 0-913113-00-X). M Liebert.
Product Safety Evaluation Handbook. Gad. (Drug & Chemical Toxicology Ser.). 664p. 1988. 145.00 (ISBN 0-8247-7829-4). Dekker.
Product-Safety Function: Organization & Operations. E. Patrick McGuire. LC 79-63433. (Report Ser.: No. 754). (Illus.). 118p. 1979. pap. 30.00 (ISBN 0-8237-0190-5). Conference Bd.
Product Safety in America: Final Report of the 1984 Chief Justice Earl Warren Conference on Advocacy in the United States. Roscoe Pound-American Trial Lawyers Foundation Staff. LC 85-60392. 128p. (Orig.). 1985. pap. 10.00 (ISBN 0-933067-00-3). Roscoe Pound Found.
Product Safety: Measures to Protect Children. OECD Staff. 86p. (Orig.). 1984. pap. 9.00x (ISBN 92-64-12588-4). OECD.
Product Safety, Risk Management & Cost-Benefit Analysis. OECD Staff. 106p. 1983. pap. 10.00 (ISBN 92-64-12510-8). OECD.
Product Standard Index. 2nd ed. V. L. Roberts. 1978. 65.00 (ISBN 0-08-022123-8). Pergamon.
Product Standardization & Competitive Strategy. Ed. by H. L. Gabel. (Advanced Series in Management: No. 11). 316p. 1987. 131.75 (ISBN 0-444-70232-6, North Holland). Elsevier.
Product Standardization & Evaluation. Charles E. Housley. 250p. 1985. 36.50 (ISBN 0-87189-267-7). Aspen Pub.
Product Standards Index. Roberts & Thomas. 429p. 1986. 59.95 (ISBN 0-938830-03-1). Inst Product.
Product Support: Buy Words for the 80's. Associated Equipment Distributors Staff. 48p. 1985. Repr. 10.00 (ISBN 0-318-19179-2). Assn Equip Distrs.
Product Survival: Lessons of the Tylenol Terrorism. David Swit & Richard Hadley. LC 82-62917. 250p. 1982. pap. 59.00 (ISBN 0-914176-18-8); pap. 53.00ea. 6-15 copies. Wash Busn Info.
Production. Ed. by Terence A. Oliva. (Core Business Program Ser.). (Illus.). 128p. 1985. pap. 7.95x flexicover (ISBN 0-87196-806-1). Facts on File.
Production Activity Control: A Practical Guide. Steven A. Melnyk & Phillip L. Carter. (APICS Series in Production Management). 200p. 1987. 35.00 (ISBN 0-87094-970-5). Dow Jones-Irwin.
Production Activity Control Reprints. Ed. by American Production & Inventory Control Society, PAC Curricula & Certification Council Subcommittee. 200p. 1986. pap. 15.00 (ISBN 0-317-54384-9). Am Prod & Inventory.
Production, Analysis & Upgrading of Oils from Biomass. American Chemical Society, Division of Fuel Chemistry Staff. (Preprints of Papers: Vol. 32, No. 2). (Illus.). 334p. pap. 86.90 (2029988). Bks Demand UMI.
Production & Application of Fluorescent Brightening Agents. Milos Zahradnik. LC 81-16355. 147p. 1982. 48.95 (ISBN 0-471-10125-7, Pub. by Wiley-Interscience). Wiley.
Production & Application of New Industrial Technology. Edwin Mansfield et al. 1977. 15.95x (ISBN 0-393-09168-6). Norton.
Production & Assessment of Numerical Software. M. A. Hennell & L. M. Delves. LC 80-40073. 1980. 76.00 (ISBN 0-12-340940-3). Acad Pr.
Production & Autonomy: Anthropological Studies & Critiques of Development. Ed. by John W. Bennett & John R. Bowen. LC 88-10779. (Monographs in Economic Anthropology: No. 5). (Illus.). 448p. (Orig.). 1988. lib. bdg. 39.75 (ISBN 0-8191-6984-6, Pub. by Soc Economic Anthropology); pap. text ed. 24.50 (ISBN 0-8191-6985-4, Pub. by Soc Economic Anthropology). U Pr of Amer.
Production & Cost Models of a Multi-Product Firm: A Mathematical Programming Approach. Niels Knudsen. (Odense Studies in History & Social Sciences: No. 13). 300p. (Orig.). 1973. pap. 30.00x (ISBN 87-7492-085-5, Pub. by Odense Universitets Forlag (Odense Denmark)). Coronet Bks.
Production & Creativity in Advertising. Robin B. Evans. (Illus.). 224p. (Orig.). 1988. pap. 29.50x (ISBN 0-273-02728-X, Pub. by Pitman Pub Ltd London). Trans-Atl Phila.
Production & Decay of Inner-Shell Vacancies see Atomic Inner-Shell Processes.
Production & Decay of Light Mesons: Proceedings of the Workshop Organized by the Laboratoire National Satume. Ed. by P. Fleury. 300p. 1988. 46.00 (ISBN 9971-50-677-7). World Scientific Pub.
Production & Decision Theory under Uncertainty. Karl Aiginger. (Uncertainty & Expectations in Economics Ser.). 256p. Date not set. text ed. 49.95 (ISBN 0-631-14792-6). Basil Blackwell.
Production & Distribution of Knowledge in the United States. Fritz Machlup et al. 415p. 1962. pap. 9.50x (ISBN 0-691-00356-4). Princeton U Pr.
Production & Exchange of Stone Age Tools: Prehistoric Obsidian in the Aegean. Robin Torrence. (New Studies in Archaeology). (Illus.). 200p. 1986. 47.50 (ISBN 0-521-25266-0). Cambridge U Pr.
Production & Factory Management: An Information Sourcebook. Christine Zembicki. LC 88-15415. (Sourcebook Series in Business & Management: Vol. 18). 448p. 1988. 45.00 (ISBN 0-89774-340-7). Oryx Pr.
Production & Feeding of Single-Cell Protein: Proceedings of the COST Workshop, Zurich, Switzerland, April 13-15, 1983. Ed. by M. P. Ferranti & A. Fiechter. (Illus.). xi, 205p. 1983. 54.00 (ISBN 0-85334-243-1, I-337-83, Pub. by Elsevier Applied Sci England). Elsevier.
Production & Industrial Systems: Proceedings of the 4th International Conference on Production Research, Tokyo, 1977. Ed. by R. Muramatsu & N. A. Dudley. 1340p. 1978. 187.00x (ISBN 0-85066-138-2). Taylor & Francis.
Production & Inventory Control. Lawrence S. Aft. 308p. 1987. text ed. 26.00 (ISBN 0-15-571993-9); instr's. manual 2.00 (ISBN 0-15-571994-7). HarBraceJ.
Production & Inventory Control: Applications. George W. Plossl. LC 83-81732. (Illus.). 320p. 1983. 42.67 (ISBN 0-926219-04-9). G P Ed Serv.
Production & Inventory Control Handbook. J. H. Greene. 1970. text ed. 76.50 (ISBN 0-07-024332-8). McGraw.
Production & Inventory Control Handbook. 2nd ed. J. H. Greene. 992p. 1986. text ed. 79.95 (ISBN 0-07-024321-2). McGraw.
Production & Inventory Control: Principles & Techniques. 2nd ed. George W. Plossl & Oliver W. Wright. (Illus.). 448p. 1985. 46.00 (ISBN 0-13-725144-0). P-H.
Production & Inventory Management. Donald W. Fogarty & Thomas R. Hoffmann. 1983. text ed. write for info. (ISBN 0-538-07040-4, G04). SW Pub.
Production & Inventory Management. Arnoldo C. Hax & Dan Candea. (Illus.). 512p. 1984. 43.00 (ISBN 0-13-724880-6). P-H.
Production & Inventory Management in the Computer Age. Oliver W. Wight. LC 74-7127. 300p. 1983. 29.95 (ISBN 0-442-29367-4). Van Nos Reinhold.
Production & Inventory Management in the Computer Age. Oliver W. Wight. LC 83-21645. 284p. 1988. Repr. of 1974 ed. 39.95 (ISBN 0-939246-06-6). Oliver Wight.
Production & Marketing of Milkfish in Taiwan: An Economic Analysis. Chaur-Shyan Lee. (ICLARM Technical Reports Ser.: No. 6). (Illus.). 41p. (Orig.). 1983. pap. text ed. 9.50x (ISBN 0-89955-390-7, Pub. by ICLARM Philippines). Intl Spec Bk.
Production & Neutralization of Negative Ion & Beams. Ed. by James G. Alessi. LC 85-71695. (Conference Proceedings Ser.: No. 158). 784p. 1987. lib. bdg. 72.00 (ISBN 0-88318-358-7). Am Inst Physics.
Production & Neutralization of Negative Ions & Beams: International Symposium, Brookhaven, 1983. 3rd ed. Ed. by Krsto Prelec. LC 84-70379. (AIP Conference Proceedings Ser.: No. 111). 778p. 1984. lib. bdg. 53.75 (ISBN 0-88318-310-2). Am Inst Physics.
Production & Observations from Japan: A Study Mission Report. Burnham. LC 85-47688. 28p. 1985. 12.00 (ISBN 0-935406-65-4). Am Prod & Inventory.
Production & Operations Analysis. Nahmias. 1988. 42.95 (ISBN 0-256-05550-5). Irwin.
Production & Operations Management. 5th ed. Chase & Aquilano. 1989. 42.95 (ISBN 0-256-06920-4). Irwin.
Production & Operations Management. Heizer & Render. Ed. by R. Carle. (Illus.). 850p. 1988. pap. text ed. 33.00 (ISBN 0-205-11245-5). Allyn.
Production & Operations Management. 4th ed. Richard A. Hopeman. 608p. 1980. text ed. 39.95 (ISBN 0-675-08140-8). Merrill.
Production & Operations Management. 3rd ed. A. C. Laufer. 1984. text ed. write for info. (ISBN 0-538-07090-0, G09). SW Pub.
Production & Operations Management. 5th ed. Keith Lockyear et al. 608p. 1988. pap. 47.50x (ISBN 0-273-02873-1, Pub. by Pitman Pub Ltd London). Trans-Atl Phila.
Production & Operations Management. 5th ed. Keith Lockyer et al. (Illus.). 592p. 1988. pap. 34.95 (ISBN 0-89397-308-4). Nichols Pub.
Production & Operations Management. 4th ed. Raymond E. Mayer. (Illus.). 688p. 1981. text ed. 40.95x (ISBN 0-07-041025-9). McGraw.
Production & Operations Management. William J. Sawaya, Jr. & William C. Giauque. 736p. 1986. text ed. 31.00 net (ISBN 0-15-571968-8, Pub. by HC); net study guide 9.00 (ISBN 0-15-571969-6); test book with transparencies 17.00. HarBraceJ.
Production & Operations Management: A Life Cycle Approach. 4th ed. Richard B. Chase & Nicholas J. Aquilano. 1985. 40.95x (ISBN 0-256-03226-2); study guide 11.50 (ISBN 0-256-03227-0). Irwin.
Production & Operations Management: A Problem-Solving & Decision-Making Approach. 2nd ed. Norman Gaither. 784p. 1984. text ed. 36.95x (ISBN 0-03-062568-8); instr.'s solutions manual 19.95 (ISBN 0-03-062571-8); instr.'s resource manual w/transparency masters 19.95 (ISBN 0-03-062569-6). Dryden Pr.

Production & Operations Management: A Self Correcting Approach. 2nd ed. Ralph M. Stair, Jr. & Barry Render. 1984. pap. text ed. 22.00 (ISBN 0-205-08137-1, 088137); write for info instrs' manual (ISBN 0-205-08138-X, 088138). Allyn.

Production & Operations Management: Concepts, Models & Behavior. 3rd ed. Everett E. Adam, Jr. & Ronald J. Ebert. (Illus.). 800p. 1986. text ed. 42.00 (ISBN 0-13-724857-1). P-H.

Production & Operations Management: Manufacturing & Nonmanufacturing. 3rd ed. James B. Dilworth. 1986. text ed. 28.00 (ISBN 0-394-35111-8, RanB); pap. 11.00 (ISBN 0-394-35361-7). Random.

Production & Operations Management: Manufacturing & Nonmanufacturing. 4th ed. James B. Dilworth. 800p. 1989. text ed. price not set (ISBN 0-394-38322-2); price not set wkbk. Random.

Production & Operations Management: Models, Information & Decisions. Abdel M. El-Shaieb. 500p. 1986. pap. text ed. 35.95 (ISBN 0-8403-3955-0). Kendall Hunt.

Production & Planning Applied to Building. 2nd ed. R. J. Hollins. 1971. 29.95x (ISBN 0-7121-4606-7). Trans-Atl Phila.

Production & Pricing of Energy Resources. Ed. by Robert S. Pindyke. (Advances in the Economics of Energy & Resources: Vol. 2). 250p. 1979. 54.50 (ISBN 0-89232-079-6). Jai Pr.

Production & Productivity in the Service Industries. Ed. by Victor R. Fuchs. (Studies in Income & Wealth Ser.: No. 34). 404p. 1969. 24.00x (ISBN 0-87014-489-8, Dist. by Columbia U Pr). Natl Bur Econ Res.

Production & Properties of Knitted Fabrics. J. D. Turner. 159p. 1971. 70.00x (ISBN 0-686-63782-8). State Mutual Bk.

Production & Properties of Knitted & Woven Fabrics. M. S. Burnip & J. H. Thomas. 139p. 1969. 70.00x (ISBN 0-686-63783-6). State Mutual Bk.

Production & Properties of Narrow Fabrics. J. P. Turner. 114p. 1976. 70.00x (ISBN 0-686-63784-4). State Mutual Bk.

Production & Properties of Non-Woven Fabrics. A. Newton & J. E. Ford. 93p. 1973. 70.00x (ISBN 0-686-63785-2). State Mutual Bk.

Production & Properties of Staple-Fibre Yarns Made by Recently Developed Techniques. L. Hunter. 168p. 1978. 70.00x (ISBN 0-686-27733-3). State Mutual Bk.

Production & Properties of Warp-Knitted Fabrics. N. Gottlieb. 100p. 1975. 70.00x (ISBN 0-686-63786-0). State Mutual Bk.

Production & Properties of Weft-Knitted Fabrics. J. A. Smirfitt. 113p. 1973. 70.00x (ISBN 0-686-63787-9). State Mutual Bk.

Production & Properties of Wool & Other Animal Fibres. M. L. Ryder. 63p. 1975. 70.00x (ISBN 0-686-63788-7). State Mutual Bk.

Production & Reproduction. Ed. by Jack Goody. LC 76-4238. (Cambridge Studies in Social Anthropology: No.17). (Illus.). 1977. o. p. 34.50 (ISBN 0-521-21294-4); pap. 12.95 (ISBN 0-521-29088-0). Cambridge U Pr.

Production & Separation of U-233: Collected Papers. Ed. by Leonard I. Katzin. AEC Technical Information Center. (National Nuclear Energy Ser.: Div. IV, Vol. 17b). 743p. 1952. pap. 54.95 (ISBN 0-87079-383-7, TID-5223); microfilm 18.75 (ISBN 0-87079-341-1, TID-5223). DOE.

Production & Separation of U-233: Survey. Ed. by Glenn Seaborg & Leonard I. Katzin. AEC Technical Information Center. (National Nuclear Energy Ser.: Division IV, Vol. 17A). 236p. 1951. pap. 24.95 (ISBN 0-87079-384-5, TID-5222); microfilm 10.00 (ISBN 0-87079-342-X, TID-5222). DOE.

Production & Stage Management at the Blackfriars Theatre. J. Isaacs. LC 73-14939. Repr. of 1933 ed. lib. bdg. 16.00 (ISBN 0-8414-5052-8). Folcroft.

Production & Storage of Dried Fish: Proceedings of the Workshop on the Production & Storage of Dried Fish, Serdang, Malaysia, Nov. 1982. (Fisheries Reports: No. 279 supp.). 271p. 1983. pap. text ed. 20.75 (ISBN 92-5-101343-8, F2450, FAO). UNIPUB.

Production & Technical Service, Pack 2. Alan Stoker & Bruce Burgess. 154p. 1987. 150.00x (ISBN 1-85008-001-1, Pub. by Framework UK). State Mutual Bk.

Production & Trade in Services: Policies & Their Underlying Factors Bearing Upon International Service Transactions. United Nations Conference on Trade & Development. 64p. 1985. pap. 9.50 (ISBN 92-1-112196-5, E.84.11.D.2). UN.

Production & Transport of Oil. 2nd; rev. ed. A. P. Szilas. (Gas Developments in Petroleum Science Ser.: Vol. 1). 476p. 1985. 118.50 (ISBN 0-444-99598-6). Elsevier.

Production & Transport of Oil & Gas. A. Szilas. (Developments in Petroleum Science Ser.: Vol. 3). 632p. 1975. 110.75 (ISBN 0-444-99869-1). Elsevier.

Production & Transport of Oil & Gas: Gathering & Transportation, Pt. B. 2nd, rev. ed. A. P. Szilas. (Developments in Petroleum Science Ser.: No. 18B). 354p. 1986. 102.75 (ISBN 0-444-99565-X). Elsevier.

Production & Use of Double Skinned Hardboard Panels for Furniture. 1974. 39.00x (ISBN 0-317-43779-8, Pub. by F I R A). State Mutual Bk.

Production & Use of Economic Forecasts. Giles Keating. 288p. 1985. text ed. 39.95 (ISBN 0-416-35790-3, 9615); pap. text ed. 18.95 (ISBN 0-416-35800-4, 9616). Routledge Chapman & Hall.

Production & Use of Interferon for the Treatment & Prevention of Human Virus Infections. Ed. by Charity Waymouth. (In Vitro Monographs Ser.: No. 3). 74p. 1974. 15.00 (ISBN 0-317-36064-7). Tissue Culture Assn.

Production & Use of Microalgae. Ed. by E. W. Becker. (Advances in Limnology Ser.: No. 20). (Illus.). 195p. 1985. pap. text ed. 62.40x (ISBN 3-510-47018-4). Lubrecht & Cramer.

Production & Use of Microalgae. Ed. by W. Becker. (Limnology Report: No. 20). (Illus.). 200p. (Orig.). 1985. pap. text ed. 72.50x (ISBN 3-510-47018-4, Pub. by E Schweizerbartsche). Coronet Bks.

Production & Use of Newcastle Disease Vaccines. (Illus.). 115p. 1975. pap. 10.25 (ISBN 0-685-54193-2, F1074, FAO). UNIPUB.

Production & Use of Short Lived Radioisotopes From Reactors, 2 Vols. (Proceedings Ser.). (Illus.). 706p. (Vol. 1). Vol. 1. pap. 21.50 (ISBN 92-0-060063-8, ISP64-1, IAEA); Vol. 2. pap. 18.00 (ISBN 92-0-060163-4, ISP64-2). UNIPUB.

Production & Utilisation of Protein in Oilseed Crops. Ed. by E. S. Bunting. 390p. 1981. 52.00 (ISBN 90-247-2532-1, Pub. by Martinus Nijhoff Netherlands). Kluwer Academic.

Production & Utilisation of Synthetic Fuels: An Energy Economics Study. F. R. Benn et al. (Illus.). xv, 250p. 1981. 52.00 (ISBN 0-85334-940-1, Pub. by Elsevier Applied Sci England). Elsevier.

Production & Utilization of Products from Commercial Seaweeds. Ed. by D. J. McHugh. (Fisheries Technical Paper: No. 288). 189p. (Orig.). 1987. pap. text ed. 18.00 (ISBN 92-5-102612-2, F3139, FAO). UNIPUB.

Production & Utilization of Radiation Vaccines Against Helminthic Diseases. (Technical Reports Ser.: No. 30). (Illus.). 84p. 1964. pap. 10.50 (ISBN 92-0-115164-0, IDC30, IAEA). UNIPUB.

Production & Water Use of Several Food & Fodder Crops Under Irrigation in the Desert Area of Southwestern Peru. Th. Alberda. (Agricultural Research Reports: No. 928). (Illus.). 50p. 1985. pap. 8.50 (ISBN 90-220-0869-X, PDC291, Pudoc). UNIPUB.

Production Aspects of Single Point Machined Optics. Ed. by D. P. Brehm. 147p. 1984. 36.00 (ISBN 0-89252-543-6, 508). SPIE.

Production Assistant in TV & Video. Avril Rowlands. (Illus.). 224p. 1987. pap. 19.95 (ISBN 0-240-51255-3). Focal Pr.

Production Automation & Numerical Control. William C. Leone. LC 67-21679. (Illus.). pap. 46.60 (ISBN 0-317-11119-1, 2012419). Bks Demand UMI.

Production Conditions in Indian Agriculture: A Study Based on Farm Management Surveys. Krishna Bharadwaj. LC 78-176251. (University of Cambridge, Dept. of Applied Economics, Occasional Paper: 33). pap. 34.50 (ISBN 0-317-26076-6, 2024413). Bks Demand UMI.

Production Control & Information Systems for Component Manufacturing Shops. J. W. Bertrand & J. C. Wortmann. (Studies in Production & Engineering Economics: Vol. 1). 104p. 1981. 102.75 (ISBN 0-444-41964-0). Elsevier.

Production Control in Engineering. 2nd ed. D. K. Corke. (Illus.). 1977. 42.50x (ISBN 0-7131-3380-5). Trans-Atl Phila.

Production Control Systems & Records. 2nd ed. Desmond Tooley. 168p. 1981. text ed. 45.00x (ISBN 0-566-02253-2). Gower Pub Co.

Production Control Systems & Records. Desmond F. Tooley. 1973. 20.00 (ISBN 0-8464-0766-3). Beekman Pubs.

Production Costs Here & Abroad: A Comparative Study of the Experience of American Manufacturers. Theodore R. Gates & Fabian Linden. Ed. by Stuart Bruchey & Eleanor Bruchey. LC 76-5012. (American Business Abroad Ser.). (Illus.). 1976. 17.00x (ISBN 0-405-09280-6). Ayer Co Pubs.

Production. Distribution, & Growth in Transitional Economies. M. Katherine Perkins. 176p. 1988. 39.95 (ISBN 0-275-92104-2, C2104). Praeger.

Production E l'interet Romanesque: Un Etat Du Texte (1870-1880), un Essai De Constitution De Sa Theorie. Charles Grivel. (Approaches to Semiotics: No. 34). 1973. 46.00x (ISBN 90-2792-413-9). Mouton.

Production Ecology of Ants & Termites. Ed. by M. V. Brian. LC 76-54061. (International Biological Programme Ser.: No. 13). (Illus.). 1977. 95.00 (ISBN 0-521-21519-6). Cambridge U Pr.

Production Ecology of Some British Moors & Montane Grasslands. Ed. by O. W. Heal & D. F. Perkins. (Ecological Studies: Vol. 27). (Illus.). 1978. 62.00 (ISBN 0-387-08457-6). Springer-Verlag.

Production Economics: Mathematical Development & Applications. (Illus.). 330p. 1984. 36.95 (ISBN 0-88738-016-6). Transaction Bks.

Production Economics: Theory with Applications. 2nd ed. John P. Doll & Frank Orazem. LC 83-21575. 470p. 1984. 37.95 (ISBN 0-471-87470-1). Wiley.

Production Economics Trends & Issues: Proceedings of the Third International Working Seminar on Production Economics, Igls, Austria Feb. 20-24 1985. Ed. by R. W. Grubbstrom & H. H. Hunterhuber. (Studies in Production & Engineering Economics: No. 4). 328p. 1985. Repr. 118.50 (ISBN 0-444-42500-4). Elsevier.

Production Engineering. Benjamin W. Niebel & Maurice S. Gjesdahl. LC 72-190969. (Illus.). 148p. 1971. 14.75 (ISBN 92-833-1003-9, APO57, APO). UNIPUB.

Production, Equality & Participation in Rural China. M. Stiefel & W. F. Wertheim. (Illus.). 178p. 1983. pap. 9.25 (ISBN 0-86232-123-9, Pub. by Zed Pr England). Humanities.

Production Factors in Cost Accounting & Works Management. Alexander H. Church. LC 75-18461. (History of Accounting Ser.). (Illus.). 1976. Repr. of 1910 ed. 16.00x (ISBN 0-405-07545-6). Ayer Co Pubs.

Production Figure Book for U. S. Cars. Jerry Heasley. LC 77-4149. 1978. pap. 7.95 (ISBN 0-87938-042-X). Motorbooks Intl.

Production for the Graphic Designer. James Craig. (Illus.). 208p. 1974. 27.50 (ISBN 0-8230-4415-7). Watson-Guptill.

Production Function, Demand Function & Location Theory of the Firm. Noboru Sakashita. (Discussion Paper Ser.: No. 15). 1967. pap. 6.50 (ISBN 0-686-32184-7). Regional Sci Res Inst.

Production Functions. L. Johansen. (Vol. 75). 274p. 1972. 73.75 (ISBN 0-444-11116-6, North-Holland). Elsevier.

Production Functions & Aggregation. K. Sato. LC 74-18773. (Contributions to Economic Analysis: Vol. 90). 314p. 1975. 92.00 (ISBN 0-444-10799-1, North-Holland). Elsevier.

Production Gas Carburizing. G. Parrish & G. S. Harper. (Materials Engineering Practice Ser.). (Illus.). 250p. 1985. text ed. 55.00 (ISBN 0-08-027312-2); pap. text ed. 21.00 (ISBN 0-08-027319-X). Pergamon.

Production Handbook. 3rd ed. Ed. by Harold A. Bolz. Hewitt H. Young et al. (Illus.). 1450p. 1972. 85.50 (ISBN 0-471-06651-6, 12602, Pub. by Ronald Pr). Wiley.

Production Handbook. 4th ed. John A. White. 1100p. 1986. 78.50 (ISBN 0-471-86347-5). Wiley.

Production Improvement in a Rehabilitation Workshop. James W. Caddick. (Illus.). 106p. (Orig.). 1980. pap. 6.00x (ISBN 0-916671-24-0). Material Dev.

Production in Format Radio Handbook. Michael C. Keith. 218p. (Orig.). 1984. lib. bdg. 25.00 (ISBN 0-8191-3886-X); pap. text ed. 13.00 (ISBN 0-8191-3887-8). U Pr of Amer.

Production, Income & Welfare: The Search for an Optimal Social Order. Jan Tinbergen. LC 84-28042. xiv, 210p. 1985. 21.95x (ISBN 0-8032-4412-6). U of Nebr Pr.

Production Innovation Management. 3rd ed. Knut Holt. (Illus.). 352p. 1988. pap. text ed. 59.95 (ISBN 0-408-00536-X). Butterworth.

Production Management. 2nd rev. ed. Lallan Prasad & A. M. Bannerjee. (Illus.). 286p. 1986. text ed. 27.95x (ISBN 0-86590-772-2, Pub. by Sterling Pubs India). Apt Bks.

Production Management: Concepts & Analysis for Operation & Control. Irving Abramowitz. LC 66-16835. (Illus.). pap. 93.00 (ISBN 0-317-10856-5, 2012444). Bks Demand UMI.

Production Management Handbook. 2nd ed. Brian Walley. 500p. 1985. text ed. 65.95x (ISBN 0-566-02532-9). Gower Pub Co.

Production Management: Methods & Studies. Ed. by B. Lev. (Studies in Management Science & Systems: Vol. 13). 250p. 1986. 53.00 (ISBN 0-444-87986-2). Elsevier.

Production Management Systems: Proceedings of the IFIP TC 5 International Workshop on Automation of Production Planning & Control, Trondheim, Norway, Sept. 1980. Ed. by P. Falster & A. Rolstadas. viii, 222p. 1981. 47.50 (ISBN 0-444-86176-9, North-Holland). Elsevier.

Production Management Systems-Strategies & Tools for Design: Proceedings of the IFIP WG 5.7 Work Conference on Strategies for Design & Economic Analysis of Computer Supported Production Management Systems, Vienna, Austria, 28-30 Sept 1984. Ed. by H. Hubner & I. Paterson. 180p. 1984. 55.25 (ISBN 0-444-87543-3, North Holland). Elsevier.

Production, Manufacture & Application of Perfumes see Perfumes, Cosmetics & Soaps.

Production Measurement: Your Key to Higher Performance. 29.95 (ISBN 0-318-02616-3). Print Indus Am.

Production Multi-Sectoral Growth & Planning: Essays in Memory of Leif Johansen, Vol. 154. Ed. by F. R. Forsund et al. (Contributions to Economic Analysis Ser.). 338p. 1985. 73.75 (ISBN 0-444-87838-6, North Holland). Elsevier.

Production of Aluminium & Alumina. A. R. Burkin. LC 86-28964. (Critical Reports on Applied Chemistry). 250p. 1987. 69.95 (ISBN 0-471-91424-X). Wiley.

Production of Amorphous Silicon Spectrally Selective Surfaces for Copper Based Solar Thermal Energy Convertors. 98p. 1983. write for info. (331A). Intl Copper.

Production of Commodities by Means of Commodities. P. Sraffa. (Illus.). 99p. 1975. pap. 16.95 (ISBN 0-521-09969-2). Cambridge U Pr.

Production of Complex Fertilizers. F. G. Margolis & T. P. Unanyants. 146p. 1971. text ed. 58.00x (ISBN 0-7065-1024-0, Pub. by Keter Pub Jerusalem). Coronet Bks.

Production of Culture in the Music Industry: The ASCAP-BMI Controversy. John Ryan. (Illus.). 170p. (Orig.). 1985. lib. bdg. 26.00 (ISBN 0-8191-4742-7); pap. text ed. 12.00 (ISBN 0-8191-4743-5). U Pr of Amer.

Production of Desire: The Integration of Psychoanalysis into Marxist Theory. Richard Lichtman. 320p. 1982. text ed. 27.95 (ISBN 0-02-919010-X, 919010). Free Pr.

Production of Desire: The Integration of Psychoanalysis into Marxist Theory. Richard Lichtman. 317p. 1986. pap. 12.95 (ISBN 0-02-919080-0). Free Pr.

Production of Dried Fish. J. J. Waterman. (Fisheries Technical Papers: No. 160). 57p. (Eng., Fr. & Span., 2nd Printing 1978). 1976. pap. 7.50 (ISBN 92-5-100103-0, F892, FAO). UNIPUB.

Production of Fish Meal & Oil. rev. ed. (FAO Fisheries Technical Paper: No. 142). (Illus.). 63p. 1987. pap. text ed. 7.50 (ISBN 92-5-102464-2, F3012, FAO). UNIPUB.

Production of Grapes & Wine in Cool Climates. David Jackson & Danny Schuster. (Illus.). 210p. 1987. text ed. 39.95 (ISBN 0-409-78784-1). Butterworth.

Production of High Strength Concrete. M. B. Peterman & R. L. Carrasquillo. LC 85-25924. (Illus.). 278p. 1986. 36.00 (ISBN 0-8155-1057-8). Noyes.

Production of Houses. Christopher Alexander & Howard Davis. LC 82-14097. (Center for Environmental Structure Ser.: Vol. 4). (Illus.). 1985. 42.50 (ISBN 0-19-503223-3). Oxford U Pr.

Production of Human Capital: A Study of Minority Achievement. Donald R. Winkler. Ed. by Stuart Bruchey. LC 76-45125. (Nineteen Seventy-Seven Dissertations Ser.). (Illus.). 1977. lib. bdg. 31.00x (ISBN 0-405-09936-3). Ayer Co Pubs.

Production of Inequality: Gender & Exchange among Kewa. L. Josephides. 288p. (Orig.). 1985. 35.00 (ISBN 0-422-79720-0, 9608, Pub. by Tavistock England). Routledge Chapman & Hall.

Production of Isotopes: A Portion of the Proceedings of the All-Union Scientific & Technical Conference on Applications of Radioactive Isotopes. Consultants Bureau Staff. LC 59-14487. pap. 34.80 (ISBN 0-317-09120-4, 2020655). Bks Demand UMI.

Production of Landscape Plants. Carl E. Whitcomb. (Illus.). 487p. 1987. 28.00 (ISBN 0-9613109-3-6). Lacebark Pubns.

Production of Later Nineteenth Century American Drama: A Basis for Teaching. Garrett H. Leverton. LC 74-176991. (Columbia University. Teachers College. Contributions to Education: No. 677). Repr. of 1936 ed. 22.50 (ISBN 0-404-55677-9). AMS Pr.

Production of Man-Made Fibres. A. J. Hughes et al. 177p. 1976. 70.00x (ISBN 0-686-63789-5). State Mutual Bk.

Production of Manpower Specialists: A Volume of Selected Papers. Ed. by John R. Niland. 248p. 1971. pap. 7.50 special hard bdg. (ISBN 0-87546-279-0); pap. 3.50 (ISBN 0-87546-045-3). ILR Pr.

Production of Marketing Plan. David Bennett. 72p. 1988. softcover 12.95 (ISBN 0-317-69286-0). Bennett Comns.

Production of Medieval Church Music-Drama. Fletcher Collins, Jr. LC 78-168610. (Illus.). xiii, 356p. 1972. 25.00x (ISBN 0-8139-0373-4). U Pr of Va.

Production of Micro-Forms. Reginald Hawkins. Ed. & pref. by Ralph Shaw. LC 75-17838. (State of the Library Art Ser.: Vol. 5, Pt. 1). 208p. 1975. Repr. of 1960 ed. lib. bdg. 35.00x (ISBN 0-8371-8235-2, HAPM). Greenwood.

Production of New Potato Varieties: Technological Advances. D. E. Richardson. Ed. by G. J. Jellis. 300p. 1987. 49.50 (ISBN 0-521-32458-0). Cambridge U Pr.

Production of Pipeline Gas by Hydrogasification of Coal: 1954-1964, Vol. 1. E. J. Pyrcioch et al. (Research Bulletin Ser.: No. 39). iv, 225p. 1972. 20.00 (ISBN 0-317-56891-4). Inst Gas Tech.

Production of Pipeline Gas by Hydrogasification of Oil Shale. H F. Feldman & W G. Bair. (Research Bulletin No. 36). iv, 109p. 1966. 5.00. Inst Gas Tech.

Production of Pipeline Gas from Crude Oil Feedstocks. Institute of Gas Technology. 63p. pap. 5.00 (ISBN 0-318-12686-9, F40100). Am Gas Assn.

Production of Quality Woollen Yarn. Ed. by Wira Staff. 30.00x (ISBN 0-317-43584-1, Pub. by Wira Tech Group). State Mutual Bk.

Production of Society: A Marxian Foundation for Social Theory. Michael E. Brown. 176p. 1986. 28.50x (ISBN 0-8476-7472-X); pap. 12.50 (ISBN 0-8476-7473-8). Rowman.

Production of Speech. Ed. by P. F. MacNeilage. (Illus.). 302p. 1983. 41.00 (ISBN 0-387-90735-1). Springer-Verlag.

Production of Synthetic-Polymer Fibres. E. M. Hicks, Jr. et al. 127p. 1971. 70.00x (ISBN 0-686-63790-9). State Mutual Bk.

Production of Textile Yarns by the False-Twist Technique. D. K. Wilson. 66p. 1978. 70.00x (ISBN 0-686-63791-7). State Mutual Bk.

Production of Textured Yarns by Methods Other That the False-Twist Technique. D. K. Wilson. 55p. 1977. 70.00x (ISBN 0-686-63792-5). State Mutual Bk.

Production of Two by Two Inch Slides. rev. ed. Joe Coltharp & Nisim Benjiuja. Ed. by Jane Hazelton. (Bridges for Ideas Handbook Ser.). 1983. pap. text ed. 6.00x (ISBN 0-913648-05-1). U Tex Austin Film Lib.

Production of Woven Fabrics. D. C. Snowden. 94p. 1972. 70.00x (ISBN 0-686-63794-1). State Mutual Bk.

Production of Yellow Cake & Uranium Fluorides. (Panel Proceedings Ser.). (Illus.). 355p. 1981. pap. 55.00 (ISBN 92-0-041080-4, ISP553, IAEA). UNIPUB.

Production Operations, 2 vols. 2nd ed. T. O. Allen & Alan P. Roberts. 1982. Set. 90.00 (ISBN 0-317-13016-1); Vol. 1, 290p. 47.50 (ISBN 0-930972-05-8); Vol. 2, 250p. 47.50 (ISBN 0-930972-04-X). Oil & Gas.

Production-Operations Management. 9th ed. Thomas Hendrick & Franklin G. Moore. 1985. 40.95x (ISBN 0-256-03032-4). Irwin.

Production Operations Management. 2nd ed. R. Tersine. 1984. 36.00 (ISBN 0-444-00923-X); instr's. manual avail. (ISBN 0-444-00954-X); instr's. master manual avail. (ISBN 0-444-00955-8). Elsevier.

Production Operations Management: Concepts & Situations. 3rd ed. Roger Schmenner. Ed. by Robert Horan & Molly Gardiner. (Illus.). 742p. 1987. text ed. write for info. (ISBN 0-574-19570-X, 13-2570). SRA.

Production-Operations Management for Small Business. Robert Murdick. 150p. (Orig.). 1982. pap. text ed. 12.00x (ISBN 0-942280-00-8). Pub Horizons.

Production Operations: Well Completions, Workover, & Stimulation, 2 Vols. Thomas O. Allen & Alan P. Roberts. (Illus.). 530p. 1982. 89.95 set (ISBN 0-930972-00-7); 49.95 ea. Pennwell Bks.

Production Planning & Control: An Integrated Approach. S. Bhattacharya. 332p. 1986. text ed. 35.00x (ISBN 0-7069-3042-8, Pub. by Vikas India). Advent NY.

Production Planning & Control Procedures for Cellular Manufacturing: Concepts & Practices. Urban Wemmerlov. LC 88-81540. (Illus.). Date not set. pap. price not set (ISBN 1-55822-004-6). Am Prod & Inventory.

Production Planning & Inventory Control. Dennis W. McLeavey & Seetharama L. Narasimhan. 1985. 45.00 (ISBN 0-205-08147-9, 088147). Allyn.

Production Planning & Scheduling for Long Line Prestress Products. 64p. 8.00 (ISBN 0-318-16191-5, JR184). Prestressed Concrete.

Production Planning & Scheduling: Mathematical Programming Applications. Ed. by Kenneth D. Lawrence & Stelios H. Zanakis. 1984. pap. text ed. 34.95. Inst Indus Eng.

Production Planning, Scheduling Inventory Control: Concepts, Techniques, & Systems. 3rd ed. Ed. by F. Robert Jacobs & Vincent Mabert. 1986. 39.95 (ISBN 0-317-61608-0). Inst Indus Eng.

Production, Pollution, Protection. Ed. by J. S. Weiner et al. (Wykeham Science Ser.: No. 19). 368p. 1977. pap. 18.00x (ISBN 0-85109-250-0). Taylor & Francis.

Production, Pollution, Protection. W. B. Yapp & M. I. Smith. (Wykeham Science Ser.: No. 19). 196p. 1972. 18.00x (ISBN 0-8448-1121-1, Pub. by Crane Russak & Co). Taylor & Francis.

Production Problems in the Men's Clothing Manufacturing Industry. 16p. 1953. 10.00 (ISBN 0-318-19654-9). Clothing Mfrs.

Production Processes: The Productivity Handbook. 5th ed. Roger W. Bolz. LC 81-6494. 1089p. 1981. 48.00x (ISBN 0-8311-1088-0). Indus Pr.

Production, Processing, Handling, & Storage of Titanium. National Fire Protection Association Staff. 1987. 10.50 (ISBN 0-317-63447-X, 481-87). Natl Fire Prot.

Production, Processing, Handling, & Storage of Zirconium. National Fire Protection Association Staff. 1987. 12.00 (ISBN 0-317-63448-8, 482-87). Natl Fire Prot.

Production, Purpose & Structure. Jeremy Bray. LC 82-42603. 1982. 19.95x (ISBN 0-312-64778-6). St Martin.

Production, Purpose & Structure: Towards a Socialist Theory of Production. Jeremy Bray. 187p. 1983. pap. 8.50 (ISBN 0-86187-264-9, Pub. by Frances Pinter). Longwood Pub Group.

Production Quality Assurance & Diagnostic Testing. Ed. by Network Staff. 1982. 49.00x (ISBN 0-904999-19-X, Pub. by Network Events Ltd). State Mutual Bk.

Production Rig Equipment. (Well Servicing & Workover Ser.: Lesson 6). (Illus.). 39p. (Orig.). 1971. pap. text ed. 5.95 (ISBN 0-88698-062-3, 3.70610). PETEX.

Production Sets. Ed. by Murray Kemp. (Economic Theory, Econometrics & Mathematical Economics Ser.). 158p. 1982. 42.50 (ISBN 0-12-404140-X). Acad Pr.

Production Standards for Profit Planning. Spencer A. Tucker & Thomas H. Lennon. 224p. 1981. 43.95 (ISBN 0-442-88016-2). Van Nos Reinhold.

Production, Storage & Handling of Liquefied Natural Gas (LNG) National Fire Protection Association Staff. 34p. 1985. 12.00 (ISBN 0-317-63206-X, 59A-85). Natl Fire Prot.

Production System: An Efficient Integration of Resources. Ed. by R. Hollier & J. M. Moore. 768p. 1977. 100.00 (ISBN 0-85066-103-X). Taylor & Francis.

Production System Models of Learning & Development. Ed. by David Klahr et al. (Computational Models of Cognition & Perception Ser.). (Illus.). 384p. 1987. text ed. 35.00x (ISBN 0-262-11114-4). MIT Pr.

Production System Version of the Hearsay-Two Speech Understanding System. Donald L. McCracken. LC 81-7459. (Computer Science: Artificial Intelligence Ser.: No. 2). pap. 39.30 (2070044). Bks Demand UMI.

Production Systems & Hierarchies of Centres. J. Gunnarsson. (Studies in Applied Regional Science). 1977. pap. 16.00 (ISBN 90-207-0688-8, Pub. by Martinus Nijhoff Netherlands). Kluwer Academic.

Production Systems Design. David J. Bennett. (Illus.). 256p. 1986. text ed. 65.00 (ISBN 0-408-01546-2). Butterworth.

Production Systems Planning Analysis & Control. 4th ed. Riggs. (Management Ser.). 656p. 1987. write for info. (ISBN 0-471-84793-3). Wiley.

Production Technology & Properties of Heat-Resisting Cast Iron. N. N. Aleksandrov. 152p. 1965. text ed. 33.00x (ISBN 0-7065-0582-4, Pub. by Keter Pub Jerusalem). Coronet Bks.

Production Testing & Testing of PCBs & Components. Ed. by Network Staff. 1980. 95.00x (ISBN 0-904999-78-5, Pub. by Network Events Ltd). State Mutual Bk.

Production Theory & Indivisible Commodities. Charles R. Frank, Jr. LC 68-29383. (Studies in Mathematical Economics Ser.: No. 3). 1968. 28.00x (ISBN 0-691-04192-X). Princeton U Pr.

Production Theory & Its Applications: Proceedings of a Workshop. Ed. by H. Albach & G. Bergendahl. (Lecture Notes in Economics & Mathematical Systems Ser.: Vol. 139). 1977. pap. 13.00 (ISBN 0-387-08062-7). Springer-Verlag.

Production to Near Net Shape: Source Book. Ed. by B. Avitzur & C. J. Van Tyne. 1983. 55.00 (ISBN 0-87170-152-9). ASM.

Production Trends in the United States Since 1870. Arthur F. Burns. Repr. of 1934 ed. 39.50x (ISBN 0-678-00024-7). Kelley.

Production Typing Projects. D. Sue Rigby & Robert N. Hanson. 1980. text ed. 9.88 (ISBN 0-07-052836-5). McGraw.

Production, Work, Territory. Allen Scott & Michael Storper. 352p. 1986. text ed. 40.00x (ISBN 0-04-338126-X); pap. text ed. 18.95x (ISBN 0-04-338127-8). Unwin Hyman.

Productions-Operations Management. 2nd ed. William J. Stevenson. 1986. 40.95x (ISBN 0-256-03379-X); study guide 11.95 (ISBN 0-256-03380-3). Irwin.

Productive Aging: Enhancing Vitality in Later Life. Robert N. Butler & Herbert P. Gleason. 176p. 1985. text ed. 25.95 (ISBN 0-8261-4810-7). Springer Pub.

Productive Agriculture & a Quality Environment. National Research Council. pap. 83.80 (ISBN 0-317-28677-3, 2055290). Bks Demand UMI.

Productive Applications of Mechanical Vibrations. Ed. by H. C. Merchant & T. L. Geers. (AMD Ser.: Vol. 52). 1982. 30.00 (H00238). ASME.

Productive Capacity of Locality As a Function of Soil & Climate with Particular Reference to Forest Land. M. S. Czarnowski. LC 64-16087. (Louisiana State University Studies, Biological Science Ser.: No. 5). pap. 48.00 (ISBN 0-317-29879-8, 2051878). Bks Demand UMI.

Productive Christians in An Age of Guilt Manipulators. 3rd ed. David Chilton. 439p. 1985. pap. 12.50 (ISBN 0-930464-04-4). Inst Christian.

Productive Interaction with Students, Children, & Clients... Things Are Not So Good in a Lot of Homes, Classrooms, & Treatment Facilities... Martin A. Kozloff. 226p. 1988. text ed. 29.75x (ISBN 0-398-05510-6). C C Thomas.

Productive Labour & Effective Demand, Including a Critique of Keynesian Economics. Sydney H. Coontz. LC 66-15567. (Illus.). 1966. 27.50x (ISBN 0-678-06511-X). Kelley.

Productive Morphologique et Emprunt: Etude des Derives Deverbaux Savants en Francais Moderne. Wiecher Zwanenburg. Ed. by Jean C. Chevalier et al. (LingvisTicae Investigationes Supplementa: No. 10). x, 199p. (Fr.). 1983. 36.00x (ISBN 90-272-3120-6). Benjamins North Am.

Productive Parenting Skills. Robert R. Carkhuff. 175p. 1985. pap. 15.00x (ISBN 0-87425-018-8). Human Res Dev Pr.

Productive Performance. Charles Lachenmeyer. (Analysis). 51p. (Orig.). 1980. pap. text ed. 18.00 (ISBN 0-938526-01-4). Inst Analysis.

Productive Problem Solving. Robert Carkhuff. 150p. 1985. pap. text ed. 15.00x (ISBN 0-87425-019-6). Human Res Dev Pr.

Productive Program Development. Robert Carkhuff. 150p. 1985. 15.00x (ISBN 0-87425-020-X). Human Res Dev Pr.

Productive Prolog Programming. Peter Schnupp & Lawrence Bernhard. 320p. 1987. pap. text ed. 27.00 (ISBN 0-13-725110-6). P-H.

Productive Retirement Years of Former Managers. Walter S. Wikstrom. LC 78-58881. (Report Ser.: No. 747). (Illus.). 45p. 1978. pap. 15.00 (ISBN 0-8237-0180-8). Conference Bd.

Productive Roles in an Older Society. Institute of Medicine & National Research Council. (America's Aging Ser.). 168p. 1986. pap. text ed. 16.95x (ISBN 0-309-03637-2). Natl Acad Pr.

Productive School: A Systems Analysis Approach to Educational Administration. J. Alan Thomas. LC 80-12531. 144p. 1981. Repr. of 1971 ed. lib. bdg. 12.50 (ISBN 0-89874-164-5). Krieger.

Productive School Systems for a Nonrational World. Jerry L. Patterson et al. LC 86-71233. 125p. (Orig.). 1986. pap. text ed. 7.50 (ISBN 0-87120-136-4, 611-86022). Assn Supervision.

Productive Software Test Management. Michael W. Evans. LC 84-3585. 218p. 1984. 36.95x (ISBN 0-471-88311-5, Pub. by Wiley-Interscience). Wiley.

Productive Speaking for Business & the Professions. James N. Holm. 466p. 1983. pap. text ed. 12.95x (ISBN 0-89641-024-2). American Pr.

Productive Speech Communication for Business & the Professions. rev. ed. James N. Holm & James N. Holm, Jr. (Illus.). 495p. 1985. pap. text ed. 18.95x (ISBN 0-89641-149-4). American Pr.

Productive Supervision. James L. Riggs. (Illus.). 432p. 1985. pap. text ed. write for info. (ISBN 0-13-725151-3). P-H.

Productive Supervisor. James L. Riggs. (Illus.). 432p. 1985. 30.95 (ISBN 0-13-725367-2). P-H.

Productive Supervisor: A Program of Practical Managerial Skills. Charles Macdonald & Richard Pierce. Incl. Planning Skills (ISBN 0-914234-30-7) (ISBN 0-87425-000-5); Controlling Skills (ISBN 0-87425-001-3); Problem-Solving Skills (ISBN 0-914234-32-3) (ISBN 0-87425-002-1); Feedback Skills (ISBN 0-87425-003-X); Coaching Skills (ISBN 0-914234-34-X) (ISBN 0-87425-004-8); Performance Appraisal Skills (ISBN 0-914234-35-8) (ISBN 0-87425-005-6); Career Counseling Skills (ISBN 0-914234-36-6) (ISBN 0-87425-006-4); Motivative Skills (ISBN 0-914234-37-4) (ISBN 0-87425-007-2); Person-to-Person Communication Skills (ISBN 0-914234-38-2) (ISBN 0-87425-008-0); Group Communication Skills (ISBN 0-914234-39-0) (ISBN 0-87425-009-9); Written Communication Skills (ISBN 0-87425-010-2); Public Relations Skills (ISBN 0-914234-60-9) (ISBN 0-87425-011-0); Priority Setting Skills (ISBN 0-914234-92-7) (ISBN 0-87425-012-9); Delegating Skills (ISBN 0-914234-93-5) (ISBN 0-87425-013-7); Time Management Skills (ISBN 0-914234-94-3) (ISBN 0-87425-014-5); Self-Development Skills (ISBN 0-914234-95-1) (ISBN 0-87425-015-3); Managing by Standards Skills (ISBN 0-914234-96-X) (ISBN 0-87425-016-1). ea participant's manual 5.00; pap. 75.00 ea. trainer's guide. Human Res Dev Pr.

Productive Teacher II: An Introduction to Instruction. Robert R. Carkhuff. 232p. 1984. pap. text ed. 15.00 (ISBN 0-914234-78-1). Human Res Dev Pr.

Productive Tension of Hawthorne's Art. Claudia D. Johnson. LC 80-15634. 176p. 1981. text ed. 15.00x (ISBN 0-8173-0050-3); pap. text ed. 5.95x o. p. (ISBN 0-8173-0051-1). U of Ala Pr.

Productive Thinking. Annette Geistfeld & Joyce Juntune. 45p. (Orig.). 1983. pap. 5.00 (ISBN 0-912773-01-4). One Hund Twenty Creat.

Productive Thinking. enl. ed. Max Wertheimer. LC 82-10913. (Phoenix Ser.). 328p. 1982. pap. 8.95X (ISBN 0-226-89376-6). U of Chicago Pr.

Productive Thinking Activities. Faye Day & Annette Geistfeld. 56p. (Orig.). 1985. pap. 6.25 (ISBN 0-912773-11-1). One Hund Twenty Creat.

Productive Work in Industry & Schools: Becoming Persons Again. Arthur G. Wirth. LC 83-14632. 294p. (Orig.). 1983. lib. bdg. 29.00 (ISBN 0-8191-3435-X); pap. text ed. 12.50 (ISBN 0-8191-3436-8). U Pr of Amer.

Productive Workplaces: Organizing & Managing for Dignity, Meaning, & Community. Marvin R. Weisbord. LC 87-45425. (Management Ser.). 1987. text ed. 28.95x (ISBN 1-55542-054-0). Jossey-Bass.

Productivite des Paturages Saheliens: Une Etude des Sols, des Vegetations et de l'Exploitation de Cette Resource Naturelle. Ed. by F. W. Penning de Vries & M. A. Djiteye. (Agricultural Research Reports: No. 918). 548p. (English summary). 1982. 41.50 (ISBN 90-220-0806-1, PDC246, PUDOC). UNIPUB.

Productivity - Improving Performance. Didactic Systems Staff. (Simulation Game Ser.). 1975. pap. 24.90 (ISBN 0-89401-081-6); pap. 21.50 two or more (ISBN 0-685-78135-6). Didactic Syst.

Productivity: A National Priority. Ed. by James R. Wilburn. 79p. (Orig.). 1982. pap. 7.95 (ISBN 0-932612-13-X). Pepperdine U Pr.

Productivity: A Practical Program for Improving Efficiency. Clair F. Vough & Bernard Asbell. xii, 223p. 1986. Repr. 30.00 (ISBN 0-9616778-0-5). Productivity Rsch.

Productivity Analysis: A Range of Perspectives. A. Dogramaci. (Studies in Productivity Analysis: Vol. 1). 208p. 1980. lib. bdg. 19.95 (ISBN 0-89838-039-1, Pub. by Martinus Nijhoff Netherlands). Kluwer Academic.

Productivity Analysis at the Organizational Level. Ed. by Nabil R. Adam & Ali Dogramaci. (Productivity Analysis Studies). 192p. 1981. lib. bdg. 21.00 (ISBN 0-89838-038-3, Pub. by Martinus Nijhoff). Kluwer Academic.

Productivity & Economic Development. B. N. Bhattasali & Gouri Bhattasali. LC 76-186285. 121p. 1972. 15.25 (ISBN 92-833-1015-2, APO60, APO). UNIPUB.

Productivity & Economic Growth. Zoltan Roman. 276p. 1982. 47.50x (Pub. by Collets (UK)). State Mutual BK.

Productivity & Efficiency in Distribution: Research Perspectives from Marketing, Economics & Operations Research. Ed. by D. A. Gautschi. (Sage Series). 233p. 1983. 68.75 (ISBN 0-444-00735-0, North-Holland). Elsevier.

Productivity & Industrial Structure. S. J. Prais. LC 81-3889. (National Institute of Economic & Social Studies: No. 33). (Illus.). 416p. 1982. 44.50 (ISBN 0-521-24189-8). Cambridge U Pr.

Productivity & Motivation: A Review of State & Local Government Initiatives. John Greiner & Harry Hatry. LC 80-53981. 1981. 22.50x (ISBN 0-87766-283-5, 29600); pap. 10.95x (ISBN 0-87766-295-9, 31900). Urban Inst.

Productivity & Policy Decisions. Richard A. Beaumont. 59p. 1959. 2.75 (ISBN 0-317-34268-1). Indus Rel.

Productivity & Prices: The Consequence of Industrial Concentration. Steven Lustgarten. 1983. pap. 7.00 (ISBN 0-8447-3536-1). Am Enterprise.

Productivity & Public Policy. Mare Holzer & Stuart S. Nagol. LC 84-4862. 296p. 1984. 35.00 (ISBN 0-8039-2129-2); pap. 16.95 (ISBN 0-8039-2130-6). Sage.

Productivity & Quality Improvement: How to Implement Statistical Process Control. J. L. Hradesky. 320p. 1988. text ed. 39.95 (ISBN 0-07-030499-8). McGraw.

Productivity & Quality Improvement in Electronics Assembly. Ed. by Johnson A. Edosomwan & Arvind Ballakur. (Illus.). 650p. 1988. 49.95 (ISBN 0-07-019026-7). McGraw.

Productivity & Quality Through People: Practices of Well-Managed Companies. Ed. by Y. K. Shetty & Vernon M. Buehler. LC 84-24930. (Illus.). xvi, 251p. 1985. lib. bdg. 46.95 (ISBN 0-89930-115-0, BPY/, Quorum). Greenwood.

Productivity & Quality Through Science & Technology. Y. K. Shetty & Vernon M. Buehler. LC 87-32595. 480p. 1988. lib. bdg. 39.95 (ISBN 0-89930-344-7, SYQ/, Quorum Bks). Greenwood.

Productivity & Records Automation. Robert J. Kalthoff & Leonard S. Lee. (Illus.). 400p. 1981. text ed. 40.33 (ISBN 0-13-725234-X). P-H.

Productivity & Role of Top Management. 94p. 1986. pap. 10.50 (ISBN 0-317-59553-9, U-APO203, Pub. by APO). UNIPUB-Kraus Intl.

Productivity & Social Organization: The Ahmedabad Experiment. A. K. Rice. Ed. by Arthur P. Brief. (Continuity in Administrative Science & Ancestral Books in the Management of Organizations). 298p. 1987. lib. bdg. 45.00 (ISBN 0-8240-8216-8). Garland Pub.

Productivity & Technical Change: With an Addendum by W. B. Reddaway. W. E. Salter. (Cambridge University, Department of Applied Economics, Monograph: No. 6). pap. 58.50 (ISBN 0-317-20834-9, 2024543). Bks Demand UMI.

Productivity & Technological Progress in Japanese Agriculture. Ed. by Keizo Tsuchiya. 261p. 1976. 35.00 (ISBN 0-86008-167-2, Pub. by U of Tokyo Japan). Columbia U Pr.

Productivity & the Economy: A Chartbook. (Labor Statistics Bureau Bulletin Ser.: No. 2298). (Illus.). 98p. (Orig.). 1988. pap. 4.75 (S/N 029-001-02967-5). USGPO.

Productivity & the Quality of Work Life in Hospitals. Addison C. Bennett. LC 83-25718. (Illus.). 100p. 1983. pap. 30.00 (ISBN 0-939450-01-1, 088220). AHPI.

Productivity & the R & D Production Interface. S. A. Bergen. 122p. 1983. text ed. 33.00x (ISBN 0-566-00648-0). Gower Pub Co.

Productivity & the Social System-The U. S. S. R. & the West. Abram Bergson. LC 77-15493. 1978. 20.00x (ISBN 0-674-71165-3). Harvard U Pr.

Productivity & the Technological Change in Electric Power Generating Plants. Paul H. Nowill. Ed. by Stuart Bruchey. LC 78-22703. (Energy in the American Economy Ser.). (Illus.). 1979. lib. bdg. 17.00x (ISBN 0-405-12005-2). Ayer Co Pubs.

Productivity & U. S. Economic Growth. Dale Jorgenson et al. LC 87-12098. (Harvard Economic Studies: No. 159). (Illus.). 504p. text ed. 32.00x (ISBN 0-674-71175-0). Harvard U Pr.

Productivity & Value: The Political Economy of Measuring Progress. Folke Dovring. LC 87-2347. 201p. 1987. lib. bdg. 35.00 (ISBN 0-275-92668-0, C2668). Praeger.

Products Liability & the Reasonably Safe Product: A Guide for Management, Design & Marketing. Alvin S. Weinstein et al. LC 78-8749. 323p. 1978. 39.95x (ISBN 0-471-03904-7, Pub. by Wiley-Interscience). Wiley.

Products Liability & the Unreasonably Dangerous Requirement. James E. Beasley. 846p. 1981. 25.00 (ISBN 0-686-32426-9, B189). Am Law Inst.

Products Liability: Are You Vulnerable? Charles O. Smith. (Illus.). 368p. 1981. P-H.

Products Liability, Cases & Materials. David A. Fischer & William C. Powers, Jr. (American Casebook Ser.). 694p. 1988. text ed. write for info. (ISBN 0-314-36441-2); write for info. tchr's. manual (ISBN 0-314-46969-9). West Pub.

Products Liability Cases & Materials. 2nd ed. Dix W. Noel & Jerry J. Phillips. LC 81-21868. (American Casebook Ser.). 821p. 1982. 30.95 (ISBN 0-314-64023-1). West Pub.

Products Liability: Cases & Materials. 3rd ed. Harvey Sklaw. 323p. 1983. looseleaf bdg. 35.00. NJ Inst CLE.

Products Liability, Cases & Materials on. Marshall S. Shapo. LC 80-11639. (University Casebook Ser.). 869p. 1980. text ed. 22.50 (ISBN 0-88277-001-2). Foundation Pr.

Products Liability for the Business Executive. Freedman. 44.95 (ISBN 0-317-64254-5). Van Nos Reinhold.

Products Liability in a Nutshell. 2nd ed. Dix W. Noel & Jerry J. Phillips. LC 80-39726. (Nutshell Ser.). 341p. 1981. pap. text ed. 9.95 (ISBN 0-8299-2121-4). West Pub.

Products Liability in a Nutshell. 3rd ed. Jerry J. Phillips. (Nutshell Ser.). 338p. 1988. pap. text ed. write for info. (ISBN 0-314-37315-2). West Pub.

Products Liability in Florida. 2nd ed. Florida Bar Staff. LC 88-81565. 165p. 1988. casebound 45.00 (ISBN 0-910373-95-7, 260). FL Bar Legal Ed.

Products Liability Law in New Jersey: A Practitioner's Guide (1983) William A. Dreier & Hannah G. Goldman. LC 84-179016. 621p. 1985. looseleaf 45.00. NJ Inst CLE.

Products Liability Law: The 1984 National Conference. 381p. 1988. manual 95.00 (ISBN 0-318-23996-5, 1019B). Natl Prac Inst.

Products Liability Law: The 1985 National Conference. 218p. 1988. manual 95.00 (ISBN 0-318-23997-3, 5322B). Natl Prac Inst.

Products Liability Law: The 1986 National Conference. 198p. 1988. manual 95.00 (ISBN 0-318-23998-1, 6321B). Natl Prac Inst.

Products Liability Law: The 1987 National Conference. 291p. 1988. 95.00 (ISBN 0-318-23999-X, 7328B). Natl Prac Inst.

Products Liability: Problems & Process. James A. Henderson, Jr. & Aaron D. Twerski. 912p. 1987. text ed. 35.00 (ISBN 0-316-35612-3). Little.

Products Liability: Recreation & Sports Equipment. Jeffrey D. Wittenberg. 380p. 1985. looseleaf 70.00 (ISBN 0-318-20293-X, 00591). NY Law Pub.

Products Liability: The First 25 Years, 2 vols. Ed. by Jeffrey R. White. LC 83-70668. 1279p. 1983. Set. 45.00 (ISBN 0-941916-06-5). Vol. 1 (ISBN 0-941916-07-3). Vol. 2 (ISBN 0-941916-08-1). Assn Trial Ed.

Products Liability: What Next? 1978. 15.00 (ISBN 0-686-27828-3). M & A Products.

Products Liability, 1984. Ed. by Anne R. Grant. (Trial Annuals Ser.). (Illus., Orig.). 1985. pap. 18.00 (ISBN 0-941916-20-0). Assn Trial Ed.

Products Liability: 1985 Pocket Part. Stuart M. Madden. (Handbook Ser.). 130p. 1985. pap. text ed. write for info. West Pub.

Products of America. Fred Justus. (Social Studies). 24p. (gr. 3-6). 1979. wkbk. 5.00 (ISBN 0-8209-0267-5, POA-1). ESP.

Products of Automata. F. Gecseg. (EATCS Monographs on Theoretical Computer Science: Vol. 7). (Illus.). 180p. 1986. 35.00 (ISBN 0-387-13719-X). Springer-Verlag.

Products of Binns Road. Peter Randall. (Hornby Companion Ser. II: No. II). (Illus.). 225p. 1984. 35.00 (ISBN 0-904568-06-7, Pub. by New Cavendish England). Schiffer.

Products of Conjugacy Classes in Groups. Ed. by Z. Arad & M. Herzog. (Lecture Notes in Mathematics: Vol. 1112). v, 244p. 1985. pap. 16.00 (ISBN 0-387-13916-8). Springer-Verlag.

Products of Metabolism. Ed. by A. H. Rose. 1978. 99.00 (ISBN 0-12-596552-4). Acad Pr.

Products of Random Matrices with Applications to Schrodinger Operat0rs. Philippe Bougerol & Jean Lacroix. (Progress in Probability & Statistics Ser.: Vol. 8). 1986. 39.95 (ISBN 0-8176-3324-3). Birkhauser.

Products of Reflections in U (P.Q) D. Z. Djokovic & Jerry G. Malzan. LC 81-20544. (Memoirs Ser.: No. 259). 86p. 1982. pap. 11.00 (ISBN 0-8218-2259-4, MEMO-259). Am Math.

Products of the Perfected Civilization: Selected Writings of Chamfort. Chamfort. Tr. by W. S. Merwin from Fr. LC 83-63123. 288p. 1984. pap. 12.50 (ISBN 0-86547-145-2). N Point Pr.

Produit de la France de 1700 a 1958: La Croissance. J. C. Toutain. (Economies et Societes Serie AF: No. 2). 1961. pap. 26.00 (ISBN 0-8115-0626-6). Kraus Repr.

Produit de l'Agriculture Francaise de 1700 a 1958: Estimation du Produit au XVIII Siecle see Histoire Quantitative: Buts et Methodes.

Produit Net Des Physiocrates et la Plus-Value De Karl Marx. Pierre Moride. LC 78-156820. (Research & Source Works Ser.: No. 708). (Selected Essays in History, Economics & Social Science Ser., No. 252). 1971. Repr. of 1908 ed. lib. bdg. 20.50 (ISBN 0-8337-2466-5). B Franklin.

Produit Physique de l'Economie Francaise de 1789 a 1913: (Comparaison avec la Grande-Bretagne) J. Marczewski. Bd. with Industrie Francaise de 1789 a 1964: Sources at Methodes. T. J. Markovitch. (Economies et Societes Serie AF: No. 4). 1965. pap. 26.00 (ISBN 0-8115-0628-2). Kraus Repr.

Produits Tensoriels Topologiques et Espaces Nucleaires. Alexander Grothendieck. LC 52-42839. (Memoirs: No. 16). 336p. 1979. pap. 20.00 (ISBN 0-8218-1216-5, MEMO-16). Am Math.

Produktionsbezogene Kooperationen Zwischen dem Hersteller und dem Verwender Individuell Gefertigter Maschinen. Horst Fischer. (European University Studies: No. 5, Vol. 428). 370p. (Ger.). 1983. 40.00 (ISBN 3-8204-7683-0). P Lang Pubs.

Produzentenhaftpflicht in den U. S. A. und in Deutschland: Product Liability in Germany & the U. S. A. Carl W. Schwarz et al. 184p. 1985. pap. 25.00 (ISBN 0-86640-019-2). German Am Chamber.

Proem see Art of Organ Building.

Proensa: An Anthology of Troubadour Poetry. Tr. by Paul Blackburn. LC 75-7466. 1978. 35.00x (ISBN 0-520-02985-2). U of Cal Pr.

Proensa: An Anthology of Troubadour Peotry. Ed. by George Economou. Tr. by Paul Blackburn. LC 86-18657. 325p. 1986. pap. 8.95 (ISBN 0-913729-51-5). Paragon Hse.

Profane Art: Essays & Reviews. Joyce Carol Oates. 256p. 1983. 13.95 (ISBN 0-525-24166-3). Dutton.

Profane Art: Essays & Reviews. Joyce Carol Oates. 212p. pap. 9.95 (ISBN 0-89255-095-3). Persea Bks.

Profane Book of Irish Comedy. David Krause. 352p. 1982. 32.50x (ISBN 0-8014-1469-5). Cornell U Pr.

Profane Mythology: The Savage Mind of the Cinema. Yvette Biro. Tr. by Imre Goldstein. LC 82-48384. (Midland Bks Ser: No. 293). 160p. 1982. 22.50X (ISBN 0-253-18010-4); pap. 7.95x (ISBN 0-253-20293-0). Ind U Pr.

Profane Virtues: Four Studies of the Eighteenth Century. Peter Quennell. LC 78-11551. (Illus.). 1979. Repr. of 1945 ed. lib. bdg. cancelled (ISBN 0-313-21039-X, QUPV). Greenwood.

Profecia Simbolica de la Gran Piramide. 4th ed. H. Spencer Lewis. Tr. by AMORC Staff. (Illus.). 167p. (Orig., Span.). 1982. pap. 7.00 (ISBN 0-912057-70-X, GS-514). AMORC.

Profecia y Carisma, Que de las Lenguas? Jose Flores. Orig. Title: Prophecy & Charisma. 68p. (Span.). 1974. pap. 2.25 (ISBN 0-8254-1238-2). Kregel.

Profesional Accounting Practice Management. Joseph T. Kastantin. LC 87-32261. 232p. 1988. lib. bdg. 45.00 (ISBN 0-89930-290-4, KPL/, Quorum Bks). Greenwood.

Profess or Perish: Proceedings. Pacific Northwest Conference On Higher Education, 1968. Ed. by Oakley Gordon. LC 48-10303. (Orig.). 1968. pap. 5.00x (ISBN 0-87071-268-3). Oreg St U Pr.

Professing Literature: An Institutional History. Gerald Graff. LC 86-16023. 324p. 1987. lib. bdg. 24.95x (ISBN 0-226-30603-8). U of Chicago Pr.

Professing Poetry. John Wain. 1978. pap. 3.95 (ISBN 0-14-004933-9). Penguin.

Professing Sociology: Studies in the Life Cycle of Social Science. abr. ed. Irving L. Horowitz. LC 75-15534. (Arcturus Books Paperbacks). 238p. 1976. pap. 6.95x (ISBN 0-8093-0741-3). S Ill U Pr.

Profession & Monopoly: A Study of Medicine in the United States & Great Britain. Jeffrey L. Berlant. LC 74-76381. 1975. 40.00x (ISBN 0-520-02734-5). U of Cal Pr.

Profession & Practice of Consultation: A Handbook for Consultants, Trainers of Consultants, & Consumers of Consultation Services. June Gallessich. LC 82-8948. (Social & Behavioral Science Ser.). 1982. text ed. 29.95x (ISBN 0-87589-527-1). Jossey-Bass.

Profession & Practice of Program Evaluation. Scarvia B. Anderson & Samuel Ball. LC 78-1154. (Social & Behavioral Science & Higher Education Ser). (Illus.). 1978. text ed. 25.95x (ISBN 0-87589-375-9). Jossey-Bass.

Profession at Risk. Terry Dozier. 6p. 1986. 1.50 (TR-86-5). Ed Comm States.

Profession at Risk: Eight Schools Face the Faculty Compensation Issue. 1988. pap. 20.00 (ISBN 0-934338-68-X). NAIS.

Profession de Foi du Vicaire Savoyard. Jean-Jacques Rousseau. Ed. by Andre Robinet. 1978. 22.50 (ISBN 0-686-55354-3). French & Eur.

Profession Eighty Seven. Ed. by Phyllis Franklin. 68p. (Orig.). 1987. pap. 7.50x (ISBN 0-87352-322-9, W380). Modern Lang.

Profession Journalist: A Study of the Working Conditions of Journalists. G. Bohere. Orig. Title: Fr. ix, 117p. 1984. pap. 17.50 (ISBN 92-2-103531-X). Intl Labour Office.

Profession: Minister. James D. Glasse. LC 68-17447. Repr. of 1968 ed. 33.50 (ISBN 0-8357-9021-5, 2011670). Bks Demand UMI.

Profession of a Chartered Accountant & Other Lectures: Delivered to the Institute of Chartered Accountants in England & Wales. Francis W. Pixley. Ed. by Richard P. Brief. LC 77-87285. (Development of Contemporary Accounting Thought Ser). 1978. Repr. of 1897 ed. lib. bdg. 24.50x (ISBN 0-405-10913-X). Ayer Co Pubs.

Profession of Government: The Public Service in Europe. Brian Chapman. LC 80-17162. 352p. 1980. Repr. of 1959 ed. lib. bdg. 32.50x (ISBN 0-313-22588-5, CHPG); key 1.25 (ISBN 0-88323-174-3). Greenwood.

Profession of King in 17th Century French Drama. 1973. Repr. of 1941 ed. 14.00 (ISBN 0-384-03556-6). Johnson Repr.

Profession of Labor Arbitration: Proceedings. National Academy of Arbitrators, Staff Meetings 1-7. Ed. by Jean T. McKelvey. LC 55-57413. (Library of Labor Arbitration Ser). 192p. 1957. 35.00 (ISBN 0-87179-065-3, 0065). BNA.

Profession of Letters: A Study of the Relation of Author to Patron Publisher, & Public 1780-1832. A. S. Collins. LC 77-134832. 1973. Repr. of 1928 ed. lib. bdg. 35.00x (ISBN 0-678-00789-6). Kelley.

Profession of Medicine: A Study of the Sociology of Applied Knowledge. Eliot Freidson. xx, 420p. 1988. pap. 14.95 (ISBN 0-226-26228-6). U of Chicago Pr.

Profession of Player in Shakespeare's Time: 1590-1642. Gerald E. Bentley. LC 83-43059. 264p. 1984. 29.50x (ISBN 0-691-06596-9). Princeton U Pr.

Profession of Poetry. H. W. Garrod. 1978. Repr. of 1924 ed. lib. bdg. 15.00 (ISBN 0-8495-1925-X). Arden Lib.

Profession of Poetry. Heathcote W. Garrod. LC 74-16316. 1974. Repr. of 1924 ed. lib. bdg. 15.00 (ISBN 0-8414-4556-7). Folcroft.

Profession of Poetry, & Other Lectures. facs. ed. Heathcote W. Garrod. LC 67-302142. (Essay Index Reprint Ser). 1929. 18.00 (ISBN 0-8369-0469-9). Ayer Co Pubs.

Profession of the Religious & the Falsely-Believed & Forged Donation of Constantine. Lorenzo Valla. Ed. by Olga Z. Pugliese. 82p. 1987. pap. text ed. 12.50 (ISBN 0-7727-2004-5, Pub. by Dovehouse Editions Canada). Humanities.

Profession, Vocation & Culture in Later Medieval England. Ed. by C. Clough. 274p. 1982. text ed. 35.00x (ISBN 0-85323-324-1, Pub. by Liverpool U Pr). Humanities.

Profession '78. Ed. by Richard I. Brod & Jasper P. Neel. 60p. 1978. pap. 7.50x (ISBN 0-87352-313-X). Modern Lang.

Profession '79. Ed. by Richard I. Brod & Jasper P. Neel. 60p. 1979. pap. 7.50x (ISBN 0-87352-314-8). Modern Lang.

Profession '80. Ed. by Richard I. Brod & Dexter Fisher. 60p. (Orig.). 1980. pap. 7.50x (ISBN 0-87352-315-6). Modern Lang.

Profession '81. Ed. by Richard I. Brod & Dexter Fisher. 60p. (Orig.). 1981. pap. 7.50x (ISBN 0-87352-316-4). Modern Lang.

Profession '82. Ed. by Richard I. Brod & Phyllis Franklin. (Illus.). 60p. 1982. pap. 7.50x (ISBN 0-87352-317-2). Modern Lang.

Profession '83. Richard I. Brod & Phyllis Franklin. 60p. (Orig.). 1983. pap. 7.50x (ISBN 0-87352-318-0). Modern Lang.

Profession '84. Ed. by Richard I. Brod & Phyllis Franklin. 60p. 1984. 7.50x (ISBN 0-87352-319-9). Modern Lang.

Profession '85. Richard I. Brod & Phyllis Franklin. 60p. (Orig.). 1985. pap. text ed. 7.50 (ISBN 0-87352-320-2). Modern Lang.

Professional Accident Investigation: Executive Investigator Training. Raymond L. Kuhlman. LC 78-56971. (Illus.). 170p. 1978. Incl. transparency masters. 3-ring binder 79.50 (ISBN 0-88061-014-X). Institute Pr.

Professional Accident Investigation: Investigator's Field Workbook. Raymond L. Kuhlman. LC 77-77275. (Illus.). 120p. 1977. 3-ring binder 39.50 (ISBN 0-88061-013-1). Institute Pr.

Professional Accident Investigation: Methods & Techniques. Raymond Kuhlman. LC 77-77275. (Illus.). 262p. 1977. 3-ring binder 57.00 (ISBN 0-88061-012-3). Institute Pr.

Professional Accident Investigation Series, 4 bks. Raymond L. Kuhlman. Set. 3-ring binders 235.50 (ISBN 0-88061-016-6). Institute Pr.

Professional Accident Investigation: Supervisory Investigator Training. Raymond L. Kuhlman. LC 78-57051. (Illus.). 95p. 1978. Incl. transparency masters & slides. 3-ring binder 59.50 (ISBN 0-88061-015-8). Institute Pr.

Professional Accountability for Social Work Practice. Ed. by Rehr et al. 1979. lib. bdg. 16.95 (ISBN 0-88202-127-3). Watson Pub Intl.

Professional Accountants: An Historical Sketch. Beresford Worthington. Ed. by Richard P. Brief. LC 77-87293. (Contemporary Accounting Thought Ser.). 1978. Repr. of 1895 ed. lib. bdg. 17.00x (ISBN 0-405-10920-2). Ayer Co Pubs.

Professional Accountant's Law, Tax & Accounting Deskbook. David Minars & Howard Davidoff. 450p. 1988. 79.50 (ISBN 0-8240-7309-6). Garland Pub.

Professional Admissions-Recruiter Manual. Richard C. Ireland. 1974. 3 ring bdg. 29.95 (ISBN 0-89103-013-1). Ireland Educ.

Professional Advancement Kit - What to Do Until the Mentor Arrives: Administrative Procedures - A Practice Manual. Kathryn M. Moore & Jo Anne J. Trow. (Orig.). 1982. 13.50 (ISBN 0-686-82337-0). Natl Assn Women.

Professional Altruist: The Emergence of Social Work As a Career, 1880-1930. Roy Lubove. LC 65-12786. 1969. pap. text ed. 5.95x (ISBN 0-689-70130-6, 142). Atheneum.

Professional Amateur: The Biography of Charles Franklin Kettering. Thomas A. Boyd. LC 72-5036. (Technology & Society Ser.). (Illus.). 242p. 1972. Repr. of 1957 ed. 18.00 (ISBN 0-405-04689-8). Ayer Co Pubs.

Professional & Administrative Career Examination. Gary Gruber. (Exam Prep Ser.). 1975. pap. 6.95 (ISBN 0-671-18090-8). Monarch Pr.

Professional & Administrative Career Examination (PACE) Gary R. Gruber. (Exam Preparation). 300p. 1976. pap. 6.95. S&S.

Professional & Administrative Career Examination (PACE) Jack Rudman. (Career Examination Ser.: CS-28). (Cloth bdg. avail. on request). pap. 13.95 (ISBN 0-8373-3728-3). Natl Learning.

Professional & Administrative Career Examination (PACE) Jack Rudman. (Admission Test Ser.: ATS-26). (Cloth bdg. avail. on request). pap. 17.95 (ISBN 0-8373-5026-3). Natl Learning.

Professional & Credentialing Issues: Bibliography. 7.50 (ISBN 0-317-59912-7, 72504C). Am Assn Coun Dev.

Professional & Legal Analysis of the Uniform Guidelines on Employee Selection Procedures. Ad Hoc Group on Uniform Selection Guidelines Staff et al. Ed. by Frank Erwin & Alan Koral. 226p. 1981. 42.00x (ISBN 0-939900-02-5). Am Soc Personnel.

Professional & Popular Medicine in France, 1770-1830: The Social World of Medical Practice. Matthew Ramsey. (Cambridge History of Medicine Ser.). (Illus.). 368p. 1988. 49.50 (ISBN 0-521-30517-9). Cambridge U Pr.

Professional & Quasi-Union Organization & Bargaining Behavior: A Bibliography. Archie Kleingartner. 74p. 1972. 3.00 (ISBN 0-89215-055-6). U Cal LA Indus Rel.

Professional & Scientific Literature on Patient Education: A Guide to Information Sources. Ed. by Lawrence Green & Connie Kansler. (Health Affairs Information Guide Ser.: Vol. 5). 352p. 1980. 68.00x (ISBN 0-8103-1422-3). Gale.

Professional & Technical Writing Strategies. Judith S. Van Alstyne. (Illus.). 320p. 1985. pap. text ed. write for info. (ISBN 0-13-725813-5). P-H.

Professional & Trade Association Job Finder: A Directory of Employment Resources Offered by Associations & Other Organizations. Norman Feingold & Avis Nicholson. LC 83-80691. (Illus.). 195p. (Orig.). 1983. 12.95 (ISBN 0-912048-33-6). Garrett Pk.

Professional Apartmenteering. C. D. Ellington. 348p. 1979. pap. 13.00 (ISBN 0-86718-086-2). Nat Assn H Build.

Professional Approach to Radiology Administration. Royce R. Osborn. (Illus.). 228p. 1980. 34.00 (ISBN 0-398-04097-4). C C Thomas.

Professional Approaches with Parents of Handicapped Children. Elizabeth J. Webster. 292p. 1976. 34.00 (ISBN 0-398-03521-0). C C Thomas.

Professional Army Officer in a Changing Society. Sam C. Sarkesian. LC 74-10917. 264p. 1974. 23.95x (ISBN 0-911012-62-1). Nelson-Hall.

Professional Arranger Composer, Bk. 1. Russ Garcia. 1954. 14.95 (ISBN 0-910468-05-2). Criterion Mus.

Professional Arranger Composer, Bk. 2. Russ Garcia. LC 78-83425. 1978. 14.95 (ISBN 0-910468-06-0). Criterion Mus.

Professional Articles for Elementary Counselors. Ed. by Paul Downes. 160p. 1987. 3-ring looseleaf bndr. 43.00 (ISBN 1-55631-012-9). Chron Guide.

Professional Associations & Municipal Innovation. Richard Bingham et al. 200p. 1981. 27.50x (ISBN 0-299-08330-6). U of Wis Pr.

Professional Baking. Wayne Gisslen. LC 84-26988. 346p. 1985. write for info. (ISBN 0-471-88668-8); Trade Ed. 28.95 (ISBN 0-471-81444-X). Wiley.

Professional Barber Styling State Board Exam Review. 1983. 7.85 (ISBN 0-87350-185-3). Milady Pub.

Professional Bartender's Educator. Jerry R. Elliott. (Illus.). 93p. (Orig.). 1982. pap. 5.95. J R Elliott.

Professional Bartending Basics see Mr. Austin's Commercial Bartending Basics.

Professional Baseball Trainer's Fitness Book. Major League Baseball Trainers Staff. Date not set. pap. 12.95 (ISBN 0-446-38751-7). Warner Bks.

Professional Baseball Trainers' Fitness Book. The Trainers of Major League Baseball Staff & Lee Lowenfish. (Orig.). 1988. pap. 12.95 (ISBN 0-446-38752-5). Warner Bks.

Professional Blackjack. Stanford Wong. LC 81-9523. 240p. 1981. 19.95 (ISBN 0-688-00818-6). Morrow.

Professional Bowlers Association Guide to Better Bowling: 25th Anniversary Edition. rev. ed. Chuck Pezzano. (Illus.). 240p. pap. 8.95 (ISBN 0-671-47244-5, Fireside). S&S.

Professional French Pastry Series, Vol. 4: Decorations, Borders & Letters, Marzipan, & Modern Desserts. Ronald Bilheux & Alain Escoffier. Tr. by Rhona P. Lauvand & James Peterson. (Illus.). 252p. 1988. text ed. 59.95 (ISBN 0-442-20569-4). Van Nos Reinhold.

Professional Guide for Activity Coordinators. Richelle N. Cunninghis. (Illus.). 55p. 1984. pap. text ed. 9.95x (ISBN 0-937663-02-6). Geriatric Educ.

Professional Guide for Young Engineers. William E. Eickenden. 52p. 1967. 2.00 (ISBN 0-318-12197-2, EC43). Accred Bd Eng & Tech.

Professional Guide to Alcoholic Beverages. Kathy Lipinski & Robert Lipinski. (Illus.). 480p. 1988. text ed. 32.95 (ISBN 0-442-25837-2); write for info. tchr's. manual (ISBN 0-442-31913-4). Van Nos Reinhold.

Professional Guide to Diseases. 2nd ed. Helen Hamilton & Barbara McVan. LC 86-14395. 1311p. 1987. 24.95 (ISBN 0-87434-035-7). Springhouse Pub.

Professional Handbook of Architectural Detailing. 2nd ed. Osamu A. Wakita & Richard M. Linde. LC 86-26780. 430p. 1987. 49.95 (ISBN 0-471-84813-1). Wiley.

Professional Handbook of Architectural Working Drawings. Osamu A. Wakita & Richard M. Linde. LC 83-23291. 530p. 1984. 49.95 (ISBN 0-471-88575-4); study guide avail. (ISBN 0-471-89131-2); drawings 154.95 (ISBN 0-471-80203-4). Wiley.

Professional Handbook of Building Construction. Edward Allen. LC 85-12205. 743p. 1985. 49.95 (ISBN 0-471-82524-7); Exercises. pap. write for info. (ISBN 0-471-84578-7). Wiley.

Professional Handicappers Handbook. Baron Von Hoelscher. (Orig.). 1980. pap. 5.95 (ISBN 0-934064-00-8). Publishers Media.

Professional Host. CBI Foodservice Editors. LC 80-15609. (Illus.). 496p. 1983. 24.95 (ISBN 0-8436-2154-0). Van Nos Reinhold.

Professional Housekeeper. 2nd ed. Georgina Tucker & Madelin Schneider. 1983. 34.95 (ISBN 0-8436-2252-0). Van Nos Reinhold.

Professional Houseparent. Eva E. Burmeister. LC 60-6548. 244p. 1960. 34.00x (ISBN 0-231-02370-7). Columbia U Pr.

Professional Hungarian Artists Outside Hungary. English ed. Leslie Konnyu. Ed. by E. Gy Kasas. LC 77-94982. (Illus.). 1978. pap. 8.50 (ISBN 0-685-87437-0). Hungarian Rev.

Professional Hypnotism Manual. rev. ed. John G. Kappas. (Illus.). 276p. 1987. pap. 17.95 (ISBN 0-937671-53-3). Panorama Van Nuys.

Professional Hypnotism Manual: Introducing Physical & Emotional Suggestibility & Sexuality. rev. ed. John Kappas. 1978. pap. 17.95 (ISBN 0-87505-250-9). Borden.

Professional Ideals. Ed. by Albert Flores. 211p. 1988. pap. text ed. write for info. (ISBN 0-534-08688-8). Wadsworth Pub.

Professional Ideals of the Lawyer: A Study of Legal Ethics. Henry W. Jessup. xlii, 292p. 1986. Repr. of 1925 ed. lib. bdg. 37.50x (ISBN 0-8377-2301-9). Rothman.

Professional Identity of the Educational Planner. Adam Curle. (Fundamentals of Educational Planning: No. 11). 49p. (Orig.). 1969. pap. 5.00 (ISBN 92-803-1030-5, U494, UNESCO). UNIPUB.

Professional Image. Susan Bixler. (Illus.). 288p. 1985. pap. 9.95 (ISBN 0-399-51115-6, Perigee). Putnam Pub Group.

Professional Imperialism: Social Work in the Third World. James Midgley. 1981. text ed. 31.50x o. p. (ISBN 0-435-82588-7); pap. text ed. 11.50x (ISBN 0-435-82586-0). Gower Pub Co.

Professional Income of Engineers 1986. R. A. Ellis & Engineering Manpower Commission. 110p. (Orig.). 1987. pap. 77.50 (ISBN 0-87615-138-1). AAES.

Professional Income of Engineers, 1987. R. A. Ellis & Engineering Manpower Commission Staff. 1988. pap. 77.50 (ISBN 0-87615-139-X). AAES.

Professional Inspection of Construction: Proceedings of a Symposium Sponsored by the Construction Division. 62p. 1984. 14.00x (ISBN 0-87262-421-8). Am Soc Civil Eng.

Professional Integration: A Guide for Students from the Developing World. Mary Ann Hood & Kevin Schieffer. 143p. (Orig.). 1984. pap. text ed. write for info. (ISBN 0-912207-02-7); pap. text ed. 1.00 ea. additional copy. NAFSA Washington.

Professional Interviewing. Cal W. Downs et al. (Illus.). 432p. 1980. (HarpC); pap. text ed. 17.95 scp (ISBN 0-06-041736-6). Har-Row.

Professional Issues for Social Workers in Schools: Proceedings from Second NASW Natl Conference on Social Work. 1982. 10.95x (ISBN 0-87101-095-X). Natl Assn Soc Wkrs.

Professional Issues in Nursing. Marvin Levine. LC 80-113444. pap. 9.95x. T Horton & Dghts.

Professional Issues in the Delivery of Mental Health Services: A Syllabus. Harold H. Mosak & Edward J. Laude. 1976. pap. 3.00x (ISBN 0-918560-05-5). A Adler Inst.

Professional Job Search Program: How to Market Yourself. Burton E. Lipman. 1985. pap. 9.95 (ISBN 0-471-82058-X). Wiley.

Professional Journalism. M. V. Kamath. 278p. 1986. text ed. 25.00x (ISBN 0-7069-1488-0, Pub. by Vikas India). Advent NY.

Professional Judgment: A Reader in Clinical Decision Making. Ed. by J. Dowie & Arthur S. Elstein. (Illus.). 500p. 1988. 59.50 (ISBN 0-521-34628-2); 19.95 (ISBN 0-521-34696-7). Cambridge U Pr.

Professional Legacy: The Eleanor Clarke Slagle Lectures in Occupational Therapy, 1955-1984. 486p. 1985. text ed. 32.50 (ISBN 0-910317-11-9). Am Occup Therapy.

Professional Liability Insurance for Attorneys, Accountants & Insurance Brokers, 1986. David W. Ichel & Practising Law Institute Staff. LC 86-60576. (Litigation & Adminstrative Practise Ser.). 604p. 1986. 15.00 (H44992). PLI.

Professional Liability of Architects & Engineers. Harrison Streeter. LC 87-22934. (Engineering Management Ser.). 273p. 1988. 39.95 (ISBN 0-471-84483-7). Wiley.

Professional Liability of Trial Lawyers: The Malpractice Question. 163p. 1979. pap. 15.00 (ISBN 0-686-48198-4). Amer Bar Assn.

Professional Liability Pitfalls for Financial Planners. Cheryl Toman-Cubbage. (Illus.). 208p. 1988. text ed. 35.00 (ISBN 0-13-725565-9). P-H.

Professional Library Examination. Jack Rudman. (Career Examination Ser.: C-623). (Cloth bdg. avail. on request). pap. 14.00 (ISBN 0-8373-0623-X). Natl Learning.

Professional Life of Mr. Dibdin, Written by Himself, 4 vols. in 2. Charles Dibdin. LC 80-2272. Repr. of 1803 ed. Set. 150.00 (ISBN 0-404-18835-4). Vol. 1 (ISBN 0-404-18836-2). Vol. 2 (ISBN 0-404-18837-0). AMS Pr.

Professional Lighting Handbook. Verne Carlson & Sylvia Carlson. (Illus.). 242p. 1985. 26.95 (ISBN 0-240-51721-0). Focal Pr.

Professional Lives in America: Structure & Aspiration, 1750-1850. Daniel H. Calhoun. LC 65-22042. (Center for the Study of the History of Liberty in America Ser). (Illus.). Repr. of 1965 ed. 61.80 (ISBN 0-8357-9174-2, 2017745). Bks Demand UMI.

Professional Magic for Amateurs. Walter B. Gibson. (Illus.). 225p. 1974. pap. 4.95 (ISBN 0-486-23012-0). Dover.

Professional Mail Surveys. Rev. ed. Paul L. Erdos. LC 82-10024. 296p. 1983. lib. bdg. 29.50 (ISBN 0-89874-530-6). Krieger.

Professional Management. Louis A. Allen. 256p. 1973. text ed. 39.95 (ISBN 0-07-001110-9). McGraw.

Professional Management: An Evoluntionary Perspective. Yg Osigweh. 272p. 1985. pap. text ed. 19.95 (ISBN 0-8403-3565-2). Kendall-Hunt.

Professional Management for the Cooperatives. A. K. Shah. 350p. 1984. text ed. 45.00x (ISBN 0-7069-2506-8, Pub. by Vikas India). Advent NY.

Professional Management of Housekeeping Operations. Robert J. Martin. LC 85-6431. 514p. 1986. write for info. (ISBN 0-471-84226-5). Wiley.

Professional Manicure Bible. Betty Morgan. (Illus.). 300p. 1986. text ed. write for info; pap. text ed. 45.00 (ISBN 0-936789-01-8). Ramif Julian.

Professional Mascot Handbook. Karen Ahearn & Art Ballant. LC 81-85624. (Illus.). 224p. (Orig.). 1982. pap. text ed. 6.95 (ISBN 0-940056-01-1). Chapter & Cask.

Professional Mediation of Civil Disputes. Robert Coulson. LC 84-72418. 62p. pap. 7.50 (ISBN 0-943001-18-8); pap. 6.50 members. Am Arbitration.

Professional Medical Secretary. 1983. 18.80 (ISBN 0-87350-333-3); tchr's. manual 26.50 (ISBN 0-87350-336-8). Milady Pub.

Professional Microcomputer Handbook. Ivan Flores. (Illus.). 752p. 1985. 52.95 (ISBN 0-442-22497-4). Van Nos Reinhold.

Professional Multihousing Management. Frank Basile. (Illus.). 250p. 1984. 39.00 (ISBN 0-86718-221-0). Nat Assn H Build.

Professional Musician's Business Kit. Lois R. Duna. 180p. 1984. 3-ring binder 29.95 (ISBN 0-942928-03-2). Duna Studios.

Professional Needs of Teachers of English. Willis B. Coale. LC 75-176655. (Columbia University. Teachers College. Contributions to Education: No. 334). Repr. of 1928 ed. 22.50 (ISBN 0-404-55334-6). AMS Pr.

Professional Negligence. Ed. by Thomas G. Roady, Jr. & William R. Andersen. LC 60-8216. 1960. 17.50x (ISBN 0-8265-1055-8). Vanderbilt U Pr.

Professional Negligence. Ashley Underwood & Stephen Holt. 1981. 60.00x (ISBN 0-686-91584-4, Pub. by Fourmat England). State Mutual Bk.

Professional Negligence: Law of Malpractice in New Jersey. 2nd ed. Albert Cohn & Barry Knopf. 500p. 1985. 75.00. NJ Inst CLE.

Professional Negotiations for Media-Library Professionals: District & School. Rolland G. Billings & Errol Goldman. LC 80-67724. 70p. 1980. pap. 8.50 (ISBN 0-89240-037-4). Assn Ed Comm Tech.

Professional Newswriting. Hiley H. Ward. 615p. 1985. pap. text ed. 18.00 net (ISBN 0-15-572010-4, HC). HarBraceJ.

Professional Nurse. Jack Rudman. (Career Examination Ser.: C-624). (Cloth bdg. avail. on request). pap. 14.00 (ISBN 0-8373-0624-8). Natl Learning.

Professional PAIR, Vol. VIII. Ed. by Dale Yoder & Herbert G. Heneman, Jr. (ASPA Handbook of Personnel & Industrial Relations). 268p. 1979. pap. 12.00 (ISBN 0-87179-207-9, 0207). BNA.

Professional Parents: Parent Participation in Four Western Countries. Nicholas Beattie. 278p. 1985. 36.00x (ISBN 1-85000-077-8, Falmer Pr); pap. 20.00x (ISBN 1-85000-078-6, Falmer Pr). Taylor & Francis.

Professional PASCAL: Essays on the Practice of Programming. Henry Legard. LC 83-30788. 192p. 1986. pap. text ed. write for info. (ISBN 0-201-11776-2). Addison-Wesley.

Professional Pastry Chef. Bo Friberg. LC 84-2214. (Illus.). 320p. 1984. 38.95 (ISBN 0-442-22635-7). Van Nos Reinhold.

Professional Pattern Grading. Jack Handford. LC 79-91230. (Illus.). 1980. 18.95 (ISBN 0-916434-34-6). Plycon Pr.

Professional Pattern Making for Designer's of Women's Wear & Men's Casual Wear. Jack Handford. LC 74-78635. (Illus.). 1984. spiral bdg. 18.95x (ISBN 0-916434-20-6). Plycon Pr.

Professional Performing Arts: Attendence Patterns, Preferences & Motives. 135p. 1984. 40.00 (ISBN 0-318-17636-X). Assn Coll Arts Admin.

Professional Philiosophy. Thomas D. Perry. 1986. lib. bdg. 39.50 (ISBN 90-277-2071-1, Pub. by Reidel Holland); pap. 19.50 (ISBN 90-277-2072-X). Kluwer Academic.

Professional Photographer. Ed. by Alfred DeBat. (Illus.). 80p. (J). subscr. incl. membership 22.10ann., monthly (ISBN 0-318-16209-1). Prof Photog.

Professional Photographer's Business Guide. Frederic W. Rosen. (Illus.). 208p. 1985. 24.95 (ISBN 0-8174-5550-7, Amphoto); pap. 12.95 (ISBN 0-8174-5551-5). Watson-Guptill.

Professional Photographer's Handbook: First Edition. 1st ed. Larry L. Logan. LC 80-80056. (Illus.). 128p. (Orig.). 1980. pap. 11.95 (ISBN 0-9603856-0-6). Logan Design.

Professional Photographer's Handbook-Nikon School Edition. Larry L. Logan. LC 81-90008. (Illus.). 116p. (Orig.). 1981. pap. 11.95 (ISBN 0-9603856-1-4). Logan Design.

Professional Photographer's Survival Guide: The Insider's View of Professionalism. Charles E. Rotkin. 320p. 1982. 19.95 (ISBN 0-8174-5409-8, Amphoto); pap. 12.95 (ISBN 0-8174-5410-1). Watson-Guptill.

Professional Photographic Illustration Techniques. LC 77-99272. (Illus.). 136p. 1978. pap. 7.50 (ISBN 0-87985-190-2, 0-16). Eastman Kodak.

Professional Pilot. John Lowery. (Illus.). 156p. 1983. 23.50 (ISBN 0-8138-1411-1). Iowa St U Pr.

Professional Plumbing Techniques--Illustrated & Simplified. Arthur J. Smith. (Illus.). 294p. pap. 10.95 (ISBN 0-8306-1763-9, 1763). TAB Bks.

Professional Police-Human Relations Training. Arthur I. Siegel et al. (Illus.). 192p. 1970. 21.75 (ISBN 0-398-01753-0). C C Thomas.

Professional Portrait Techniques. LC 72-95689. (Illus.). 116p. 1980. pap. 16.95 (ISBN 0-87985-247-X, 0-4). Eastman Kodak.

Professional Potpourri: Seeds Are Sown. Margaret A. Golton. (Illus., Orig.). 1984. pap. 9.95. Frank Pubns.

Professional Power & Social Welfare. Paul Wilding. 192p. (Orig.). 1982. pap. 10.95x (ISBN 0-7100-0885-6). Routledge Chapman & Hall.

Professional Powers: A Study of the Institutionalization of Formal Knowledge. Eliot Freidson. LC 85-20789. xviii, 242p. 1986. lib. bdg. 22.50 (ISBN 0-226-26224-3). U of Chicago Pr.

Professional Powers: A Study of the Institutionalization of Formal Knowledge. Eliot Freidson. xviii, 242p. 1988. pap. 12.95 (ISBN 0-226-26225-1). U of Chicago Pr.

Professional Practice: A South African Nursing Perspective. Charlotte Searle. 364p. 1987. pap. text ed. 34.95 (ISBN 0-409-10906-1). Butterworth.

Professional Practice Builders Kit. Alan Weisman. (Illus.). 101p. (Orig.). 1987. pap. 100.00 (ISBN 0-934311-46-3). Intl Wealth.

Professional Practice for Interior Designers. Christine M. Piotrowski. (Illus.). 328p. 1988. 34.95 (ISBN 0-442-27519-6). Van Nos Reinhold.

Professional Practice in Architecture. Frank Orr. 144p. 1982. pap. 14.95 (ISBN 0-442-26391-0). Van Nos Reinhold.

Professional Practice in Health Care Marketing: Proceedings of American College of Healthcare Marketing. Ed. by William J. Winston. LC 85-22036. (Health Marketing Quarterly Ser.: Vol. 3). 224p. 1986. 39.95 (ISBN 0-86656-549-3). Haworth Pr.

Professional Practice of Architectural Detailing. 2nd ed. Wakita. 416p. 1987. write for info. (ISBN 0-471-86582-6). Wiley.

Professional Practice of Architectural Working Drawings. Osamu A. Wakita & Richard M. Linde. LC 83-21838. 561p. 1984. text ed. write for info. (ISBN 0-471-05636-7). Wiley.

Professional Practice of Nursing Administration. Lillian M. Simms et al. LC 84-2209. 379p. 1985. 19.95 (ISBN 0-471-08247-3, Pub. by Wiley Medical). Wiley.

Professional Practice of Psychology. Georgiana S. Tryon. Ed. by Glenn R. Caddy. LC 85-13433. (Developments in Clinical Psychology Ser.). 320p. 1986. text ed. 42.50 (ISBN 0-89391-163-1). Ablex Pub.

Professional Practice Standards. 78p. 1985. 20.00 (ISBN 0-318-17645-9). Am Med Record Assn.

Professional Preparation in Athletic Training. Ed. by Gerald W. Bell. LC 82-81094. 184p. 1982. text ed. 16.00x (ISBN 0-931250-32-3, BBEL0032). Human Kinetics.

Professional Printing Estimating. 2nd ed. Gerald A. Silver. LC 83-6533. (Illus.). 224p. 1983. pap. 18.95 (ISBN 0-442-28043-2). Van Nos Reinhold.

Professional Produce Manager's Manual. 130p. 1987. 20.00. Produce Mktg Assn.

Professional Project Management. M. Dean Martin & John Adams. 154p. 1957. 28.00 (ISBN 0-317-54778-X). Univ Tech.

Professional Psychologist Today: New Developments in Law, Health Insurance, & Health Practice. Herbert Dorken et al. LC 75-24011. (Jossey-Bass Behavioral Science Ser.). pap. 108.20 (2030813). Bks Demand UMI.

Professional Psychologist's Handbook. Ed. by Bruce D. Sales. 780p. 1983. 75.00x (ISBN 0-306-40934-8, Plenum Pr). Plenum Pub.

Professional Psychology in Transition: Meeting Today's Challenges. Herbert Dorken et al. LC 85-45900. (Social & Behavioral Science Ser.). 1986. text ed. 35.00 (ISBN 0-87589-678-2). Jossey-Bass.

Professional Public Relations & Political Power. Stanley Kelley. LC 56-8492. pap. 65.80 (ISBN 0-317-19863-7, 2023111). Bks Demand UMI.

Professional Qualifications for Fire Inspector, Fire Investigator & Fire Prevention Education Officer. National Fire Protection Association Staff. 23p. 1982. 12.00 (ISBN 0-317-63526-3, 1031-82). Natl Fire Prot.

Professional Raccoon Trapping. 3rd, rev. ed. David A. Avant, III. LC 78-57404. (Illus.). 61p. pap. 4.95 (ISBN 0-317-03287-9). L'Avant Studios.

Professional Radio Selling. Mark R. Lange. 176p. 1987. pap. text ed. 22.95 (ISBN 0-943987-02-4). Origin Co.

Professional Real Estate Investing: How to Evaluate Complex Investment Alternatives. Fred E. Case. 326p. 1983. pap. 12.95 (ISBN 0-13-725853-4). P-H.

Professional Resource Development. Joe Kranz & Janice Frauen. (Illus.). 352p. 1986. text ed. write for info. (ISBN 0-13-725771-6). P-H.

Professional Responsibilities in Protecting Children: A Public Health Approach to Child Sexual Abuse. Ed. by Ann Maney & Susan Wells. 237p. 1988. lib. bdg. 39.95 (ISBN 0-275-92966-3, C2966). Praeger.

Professional Responsibility. 2nd ed. Monica E. Baly. 154p. 1984. pap. 13.00 (ISBN 0-471-26284-6, Pub. by Wiley Med). Wiley.

Professional Responsibility. 2nd ed. Michael Josephson. (Primer Ser.). 1987. 11.95. Herbert Legal Ser.

Professional Responsibility. (Essential Principles Ser.). 1985. write for info. (ISBN 0-940366-36-3). Herbert Legal Ser.

Professional Responsibility. 2nd ed. (Essential Principles Ser.). 1987. write for info. (ISBN 0-940366-39-8). Herbert Legal Ser.

Professional Responsibility. Ronald D. Rotunda. LC 84-15262. (Black Letter Ser.). 429p. 1984. pap. text ed. 14.95 (ISBN 0-314-83764-7). West Pub.

Professional Responsibility. 2nd ed. Ronald D. Rotunda. (Black Letter Ser.). 414p. 1988. pap. text ed. 16.95 (ISBN 0-314-73052-4). West Pub.

Professional Responsibility: A Problem Approach. 2nd ed. Norman Redlich. 1983. 12.95 (ISBN 0-316-73657-0). Little.

Professional Responsibility & the Lawyer: Avoiding Unintentional Grievances. 16p. 1975. pap. 1.00 (ISBN 0-317-31074-7). Amer Bar Assn.

Professional Responsibility, Cases & Materials. Maynard Pirsig & Kenneth Kirwin. (American Casebook Ser.). 107p. 1986. write for info. tchr's manual (ISBN 0-314-98583-2). West Pub.

Professional Responsibility, Cases & Materials. 4th ed. Maynard E. Pirsig & Kenneth F. Kirwin. LC 84-7566. (American Casebook Ser.). 603p. 1984. text ed. 27.95 (ISBN 0-314-83001-4). West Pub.

Professional Responsibility for Harmful Actions. Illinois Institute of Technology. 32p. 1984. saddle stitch 5.45 (ISBN 0-8403-3335-8). Kendall-Hunt.

Professional Responsibility in a Nutshell. Robert H. Aronson & Donald T. Weckstein. LC 80-15007. (Nutshell Ser.). 399p. 1980. pap. text ed. 9.95 (ISBN 0-8299-2095-1). West Pub.

Professional Responsibility in Selected National Standard Supplement. Thomas D. Morgan & Ronald D. Rotunda. 431p. 1986. pap. 11.75. Foundation Pr.

Professional Responsibility of the Criminal Lawyer. John W. Hall, Jr. LC 87-83036. 1988. 74.50. Lawyers Co-Op.

Professional Responsibility of The Lawyer. Association of The Bar of The City of New York. 815p. 1977. 38.00. Oceana.

Professionals' Guide to Fund Raising, Corporate Giving, & Philanthropy: People Give to People. Lynda L. Adams-Chau. LC 87-32263. 192p. 1988. lib. bdg. 35.95 (ISBN 0-89930-251-3, ACP/, Quorum Bks). Greenwood.

Professional's Guide to Older Adult's Life Review: Releasing the Peace Within. James J. Magee. 112p. 1988. 25.00x (ISBN 0-669-19413-1). Lexington Bks.

Professional's Guide to Public Relations Services. 5th ed. Richard Weiner. LC 84-6284. 534p. 1985. 90.00 (ISBN 0-913046-15-9). Public Relations.

Professional's Guide to Public Relations Services. 6th ed. Richard Weiner. 516p. 1988. text ed. 95.00 (ISBN 0-8144-5932-3). AMACOM.

Professional's Guide to Public Relations Services, 1985. 5th ed. 530p. 1985. 95.00 (ISBN 0-317-55716-5). B Klein Pubns.

Professional's Guide to Publicity. 3rd, rev. ed. Richard Weiner. LC 78-52626. 176p. 1982. 9.50 (ISBN 0-913046-07-8). Public Relations.

Professional's Guide to Purchasing Word Processors & Microcomputers. cancelled (ISBN 0-918528-19-4). Edgepress.

Professional's Guide to Systems Analysis. Martin E. Modell. 256p. 1988. text ed. 34.95 (ISBN 0-07-042632-5). McGraw.

Professional's Guide to the U.S. Government Securities Markets: Treasuries, Angencies, Mortgage-Backed Instruments. George H. Bollenbacher & Samuel P. Peluso. (Illus.). 400p. 1989. 39.50 (ISBN 0-13-725532-2, Busn). P-H.

Professional's Guide to Working Smarter. Lauchland A. Henry. LC 87-23868. (People & the Organization Ser.). (Illus.). 208p. 1988. 25.00 (ISBN 0-935310-03-7). Burrill-Ellsworth.

Professional's Handbook on Geriatric Alcoholism. Deborah L. Sherouse. (Illus.). 236p. 1983. 30.25 (ISBN 0-398-04828-2). C C Thomas.

Professionals in Distress: Issues, Syndromes, & Solutions in Psychology. Ed. by Richard R. Kilburg et al. LC 85-18487. 299p. 1986. 30.00 (ISBN 0-912704-43-8, 4600040); members 24.00. Am Psychol.

Professionals in Organizations: Debunking a Myth. Mary E. Guy. LC 85-509. 208p. 1985. 36.95 (ISBN 0-275-90111-4, C0111). Praeger.

Professionals in Search of Work: Coping with the Stress of Job Loss & Unemployment. H. G. Kaufman. LC 82-2061. 320p. 1982. 37.95x (ISBN 0-471-46069-9, Pub. by Wiley-Interscience). Wiley.

Professional's Investment Guide: How to Multiply the Profits from Your Practice. rev. ed. Martin Bud Schulman. LC 76-8269. 1976. 28.50 (ISBN 0-87491-024-2). Acropolis.

Professional's Library. Elizabeth Sparrow. 60p. 1986. pap. 8.00 (ISBN 0-7123-0121-6, Pub. by British Lib). Longwood Pub Group.

Professionals out of Work. Paula G. Leventman. LC 80-1645. (Illus.). 1981. 24.95 (ISBN 0-02-918800-8). Free Pr.

Professional's Tax Desk Manual. Executive Reports Corporation Editorial Staff. 1971. 89.50 (ISBN 0-13-725432-6). Exec Reports.

Professional's Tax Desk Manual. LC 86-30611. Date not set. price not set (ISBN 0-13-725391-5). P-H.

Professions & Power. Terence J. Johnson. (Studies in Sociology). 1972. pap. text ed. 7.95x (ISBN 0-333-13430-3). Humanities.

Professions & Professional Ideologies in America. Ed. by Gerald L. Geison. LC 83-5853. x, 147p. 1983. 19.00x (ISBN 0-8078-1568-3). U of NC Pr.

Professions & Professionalization. Ed. by John A. Jackson. LC 75-123346. (Sociological Studies: No. 3). 1970. 39.50 (ISBN 0-521-07982-9). Cambridge U Pr.

Professions & Services in the European Economic Community. Dominik Lasok. LC 86-15274. 54p. 1986. 91.00 (ISBN 9-06-544253-7, Pub. by Kluwer Law Netherlands). Kluwer Academic.

Professions & Social Change in England 1680-1730. G. S. Holmes. (Raleigh Lectures on History). 1979. pap. 5.50 (ISBN 0-85672-203-0, Pub. by British Acad). Longwood Pub Group.

Professions & the French State: 1700-1900. Ed. by Gerald Geison. LC 83-14700. 352p. 1984. 42.95x (ISBN 0-8122-7912-3). U of Pa Pr.

Professions & the State: The Mexican Case. Peter S. Cleaves. LC 87-5911. (PROFMEX Ser.). 147p. 1987. monograph 19.95x (ISBN 0-8165-1016-4). U of Ariz Pr.

Professions in American History. Ed. by Nathan O. Hatch. LC 87-40351. 248p. 1987. text ed. 21.95x (ISBN 0-268-01568-6). U of Notre Dame Pr.

Professions of Dramatist & Player in Shakespeare's Time, 1590-1642. Gerald E. Bentley. LC 85-43372. 680p. 1986. pap. 14.50x (ISBN 0-691-01426-4). Princeton U Pr.

Professions: Roles & Rules. Wilbert E. Moore. LC 78-104184. 316p. 1970. 27.50x (ISBN 0-87154-604-3). Russell Sage.

Professions, Work & Careers. Anselm L. Strauss. 313p. 1975. 24.95 (ISBN 0-87855-128-X). Transaction Bks.

Professor, 2 vols. Charlotte Bronte. 688p. 1988. Repr. of 1857 ed. 327.45 (ISBN 0-89901-340-6). Found Class Reprints.

Professor. Charlotte Bronte. Ed. by Margaret Smith & Herbert Rosengarten. (Clarendon Edition of the Novels of the Brontes Ser.). (Illus.). 390p. 1987. 79.00 (ISBN 0-19-812694-8). Oxford U Pr.

Professor. Jack Lynn. LC 84-62280. 278p. 1985. 16.95 (ISBN 0-88186-329-7). Parkwest Pubns.

Professor. Richard Patterson. 36p. (Orig.). 1979. pap. text ed. 2.75 (ISBN 0-936004-00-2). R Patterson.

Professor & Emma. Charlotte Bronte. (Fragment Ser.). 1975. Repr. of 1972 ed. 13.95x (ISBN 0-460-00417-4, Evman). Biblio Dist.

Professor & Emma. Charlotte Bronte. 1985. pap. 5.50 (ISBN 0-460-02508-2, Evman). Biblio Dist.

Professor & the Coed. Edward LeComte. LC 79-63192. 1979. 14.95 (ISBN 0-87949-141-8). Ashley Bks.

Professor & the Commissions. Bernard Schwartz. LC 78-2240. 1978. Repr. of 1959 ed. lib. bdg. 35.00x (ISBN 0-313-20358-X, SCPR). Greenwood.

Professor & the Prostitute: And Other True Tales of Murder & Madness. Linda Wolfe. 1986. 16.95 (ISBN 0-395-40049-X). HM.

Professor & the Prostitute: And Other True Tales of Murder & Madness. Linda Wolfe. 304p. 1987. pap. 3.95 (ISBN 0-345-34367-0). Ballantine.

Professor & the Public: The Role of the Scholar in the Modern World. Goldwin A. Smith. LC 72-2088. (Franklin Memorial Lectures: Vol. 20). Repr. of 1972 ed. 31.00 (2027608). Bks Demand UMI.

Professor at Bay. Burges Johnson. LC 73-107718. (Essay Index Reprint Ser.). 1937. 18.00 (ISBN 0-8369-1520-8). Ayer Co Pubs.

Professor at Large. Stephen P. Duggan. LC 72-4507. (Essay Index Reprint Ser.). Repr. of 1943 ed. 27.50 (ISBN 0-8369-2942-X). Ayer Co Pubs.

Professor at the Breakfast-Table. Oliver W. Holmes. 1977. Repr. lib. bdg. 45.00 (ISBN 0-8495-2219-6). Arden Lib.

Professor at the Breakfast-Table. Oliver W. Holmes. 1986. Repr. lib. bdg. 24.95x (ISBN 0-89966-547-0). Buccaneer Bks.

Professor at the Breakfast Table: With the Story of the Iris. Oliver Wendell Holmes. x, 332p. 1968. Repr. of 1899 ed. deluxe ed. 18.00x (ISBN 0-403-00068-8). Scholarly.

Professor Bernhardi. Arthur Schnitzler. Tr. by Hetty Landstone. LC 77-175444. Repr. of 1928 ed. 15.00 (ISBN 0-404-05616-4). AMS Pr.

Professor Bubbles' Official Bubble Handbook. Richard Farity & John Jama. (Illus., Orig.). Date not set. pap. 8.95. Grnleaf Pubs.

Professor Bubbles' Official Bubble Handbook. Richard Favery & John Javna. (Illus.). 96p. (Orig.). 1988. pap. 5.95 (ISBN 0-913319-05-8). Sunstone Pubns.

Professor Diggins' Dragons. Felice Holman. LC 66-16103. (Illus.). 144p. (gr. 4-6). 1974. pap. 0.95 (ISBN 0-02-043680-7, Collier). Macmillan.

Professor Dowell's Head. G. V. Alekseeva. 88p. 1985. pap. 1.95 (ISBN 0-8285-2872-1, Pub. by Rus Lang Pubs USSR). Imported Pubns.

Professor E. McSquared's Original, Fantastic, & Highly Edifying Calculus Primer. 214p. 1987. pap. 12.50 (ISBN 0-913232-47-5, GK110). Janson Pubns.

Professor Fred & the Fid Fuddlephone. D. L. Pape. LC 68-56825. (Oddo Sound Ser.). (Illus.). 48p. (gr. 2-5). 1968. PLB 10.95 (ISBN 0-87783-032-0). Oddo.

Professor Grover's Cute Furry Little Pennywhistle Book. Peter Pickow & Tony Geiss. 32p. (ps-k). 1982. pap. 3.95 (ISBN 0-8256-9538-4, Putnam). Putnam Pub Group.

Professor in Peril. Anthony Lejune. (Crime Club Ser.). 1989. 12.95 (ISBN 0-385-24603-X). Doubleday.

Professor Longfellow of Harvard. Carl L. Johnson. LC 44-42422. 1943. pap. 1.00 (ISBN 0-87114-003-9). U of Oreg Bks.

Professor MMAA's Lecture. Stefan Themerson. LC 74-21585. (Tusk Bks.). 226p. 1984. 22.50 (ISBN 0-87951-029-3); pap. 8.95 (ISBN 0-87951-966-5). Overlook Pr.

Professor Noah's Spaceship. Brian Wildsmith. (Illus.). (ps-3). 1980. 12.95 (ISBN 0-19-279741-7). Oxford U Pr.

Professor of Democracy: The Life of Charles Henry Pearson, 1830-1894. J. Tregenza. 1968. 15.50x (ISBN 0-522-83894-4, Pub. by Melbourne U Pr). Intl Spec Bk.

Professor of Desire. Philip Roth. 263p. 1977. 8.95 (ISBN 0-374-23756-5). FS&G.

Professor of Desire. Philip Roth. (Fiction Ser.). 272p. 1985. pap. 6.95 (ISBN 0-14-007677-8). Penguin.

Professor of Education: An Assessment of Conditions. Ed. by Ayers Bagley. (SPE Monographs). 125p. 1975. 8.00 (ISBN 0-933669-15-1). Soc Profs Ed.

Professor Oscar J. Goldrick & His Denver. Nolie Mumey. LC 59-11065. 1959. pap. 1.25 (ISBN 0-8040-0080-8, Pub. by Swallow). Ohio U Pr.

Professor Percival Pinkerton's Most Perplexing Puzzles. Percival Pinkerton. 1989. 4.95 (ISBN 0-671-67742-X). Meadowbrook.

Professor Pishposh & the Robots. Adelaide Altman. (Illus.). 48p. (ps-2). 1988. 12.95 (ISBN 0-933905-05-X); pap. 9.95 (ISBN 0-933905-16-5). Claycomb Pr.

Professor Possum's Great Adventure. Michael Pellowski. LC 88-1281. (Fiddlesticks Ser.). (Illus.). 48p. (Orig.). (gr. 1-3). 1988. PLB 9.49 (ISBN 0-8167-1341-3); pap. text ed. 1.95 (ISBN 0-8167-1342-1). Troll Assocs.

Professor Q's Mysterious Machine. Donna F. Crow. (Making Choices Ser.: No. 3). (gr. 3-8). 1983. pap. 2.95 (ISBN 0-89191-562-1). Cook.

Professor Royce's Libel. Francis E. Abbot. Bd. with Public Remonstrance Addressed to the Board of Overseers of Harvard University. LC 75-3011. Repr. of 1892 ed. 11.50 (ISBN 0-404-59003-9). AMS Pr.

Professor Skinner, Alias Montagu Norman. J. Hargrave. 69.95 (ISBN 0-8490-0895-6). Gordon Pr.

Professor, the Institute, & DNA. Rene Dubos. LC 76-26812. (Illus.). 262p. 1976. 15.00x (ISBN 0-87470-022-1). Rockefeller.

Professor Ting Yen Yung Works. K. W. Chen. (Illus.). 160p. 1986. 196.00x (ISBN 0-317-69158-9, Pub. by Han-Shan Tang Ltd). State Mutual Bk.

Professor Zuccini's Traveling Tales. Sylvia Ashby. 44p. 1983. pap. 2.75 (ISBN 0-88680-208-3). I E Clark.

Professors & Gods. Roy Fuller. LC 74-75010. 176p. 1974. 20.00 (ISBN 0-312-64785-9). St Martin.

Professors As Teachers. Kenneth E. Eble. LC 78-186579. (Higher Education Ser.). 1972. 24.95x (ISBN 0-87589-118-7). Jossey-Bass.

Professor's Attitude & Performance. Rafael Colon Cora. LC 78-12813. 1979. pap. 6.25 (ISBN 0-8477-2450-6). U of PR Pr.

Professor's Book of First Names. Thomas V. Busse. LC 83-80773. (Illus.). 120p. (Orig.). 1984. pap. 5.95 (ISBN 0-9610950-1-6). Green Ball Pr.

Professor's House. Willa Cather. LC 72-10470. 288p. 1973. pap. 4.95 (ISBN 0-394-71913-1, Vin). Random.

Professors Like Vodka: A Novel. Harold Loeb. LC 73-16121. (Lost American Fiction Ser.). 267p. 1974. Repr. of 1927 ed. 7.95 (ISBN 0-8093-0664-6). S Ill U Pr.

Professor's Love-Story, etc. see Works of J. M. Barrie.

Professors of Education & Education Librarians. Ed. by Ayers Bagley. (SPE Monograph Ser.). 1985. 5.00 (ISBN 0-933669-34-8). Soc Profs Ed.

Professors of Teaching: An Inquiry. Ed. by Richard Wisniewski & Edward Ducharme. (Teacher Preparation & Development Ser.). 224p. 1988. text ed. 39.50x (ISBN 0-88706-901-0); pap. 14.95x (ISBN 0-88706-902-9). State U NY Pr.

Professors on Guard: The First AAUP Investigations. Ed. by Walter P. Metzger. LC 76-55213. (Academic Profession Ser.). 1977. lib. bdg. 26.50x (ISBN 0-405-10040-X). Ayer Co Pubs.

Professors, Presidents, & Politicians: Civil Rights & the University of Oklahoma, 1890-1968. George L. Cross. LC 81-40288. (Illus.). 325p. 1981. 19.95 (ISBN 0-8061-1781-8). U of Okla Pr.

Profeta da Esperanca. F. B. Meyer. Orig. Title: Prophet of Hope. (Port.). 1986. write for info. (ISBN 0-8297-1607-6). Life Pubs Intl.

Profetas Del Antiguo Testamento. K. M. Yates. Tr. by Simon Corona from Eng. Orig. Title: Preaching from the Prophets. 336p. (Span.). 1985. pap. 4.95 (ISBN 0-311-04026-8). Casa Bautista.

Proffered Crown: Saint-Simonianism & the Doctrine of Hope. Robert B. Carlisle. LC 87-45481. (Studies in Historical & Political Science, One Hundredth Fifth Ser.: No. 3). 288p. 1988. text ed. 37.50x (ISBN 0-8018-3512-7). Johns Hopkins.

Proficiency in Counterpoint: A College Worktext. Paul Fontaine. LC 67-13407. (Illus., Orig.). 1967. pap. text ed. 19.95x (ISBN 0-89197-360-5). Irvington.

Proficiency Plus. Michael McCarthy et al. 256p. 1985. pap. 12.95x (ISBN 0-631-90320-8); cassette 14.95x (ISBN 0-631-90016-0). Basil Blackwell.

Proficient C: The Microsoft Guide to Intermediate & Advanced C Programming. Augie Hansen. 512p. 1987. pap. 22.95 (ISBN 1-55615-007-5). Microsoft.

Proficient Pilot. rev. & enl. ed. Barry Schiff. 320p. 1985. 18.95 (ISBN 0-02-607150-9). Macmillan.

Proficient Pilot II. Barry Schiff. (Illus.). 320p. 1988. 19.95 (ISBN 0-02-607151-7). Macmillan.

Proficient Reader. Ira Epstein. LC 84-87971. 384p. 1985. pap. text ed. 22.36 (ISBN 0-395-35020-4); instr's manual 2.36 (ISBN 0-395-35021-2); support package 23.56 (ISBN 0-395-37710-2). HM.

Profil Perdu. Francoise Sagan. 224p. 1974. 18.50 (ISBN 0-686-55393-4); pap. 3.95 (ISBN 0-686-55394-2). French & Eur.

Profile Analysis: Auditory Intensity Discrimination. David M. Green. (Oxford Psychology Ser.: No. 13). (Illus.). 144p. 1987. 35.00 (ISBN 0-19-504948-9). Oxford U Pr.

Profile for Profitability: Using Cost Control & Profitability Analysis. Thomas S. Dudick. LC 72-4353. (Wiley Systems & Controls for Financial Management Ser.). Repr. of 1972 ed. 67.80 (ISBN 0-8357-9963-8, 2015619). Bks Demand UMI.

Profile: Guatemala. CIIR Staff. 8p. 1984. 15.00x (ISBN 0-946848-02-5, Pub. by CIIR). State Mutual Bk.

Profile: Namibia. CIIR Staff. 50p. 1985. 15.00x (ISBN 0-904393-76-3, Pub. by CIIR). State Mutual Bk.

Profile of a Citizen Soldier. John J. Maginnis. (Illus.). 254p. 1981. 9.95 (ISBN 0-89962-046-9). Todd & Honeywell.

Profile of a Collector: The Collection of Muriel Bultman Francis. Edward P. Caraco. LC 85-43432. (Illus.). 132p. 1985. pap. 18.95 (ISBN 0-89494-024-4). New Orleans Mus Art.

Profile of a Museum Registrar. Marjorie Hoachlander. 120p. (Orig.). 1980. pap. 3.00 (ISBN 0-89492-038-3). Acad Educ Dev.

Profile of a Top-Ranked School of Nursing. University of Texas at Austin, School of Nursing Staff et al. (Illus.). 160p. (Orig.). 1985. pap. 18.95 (ISBN 0-88737-203-1, 41-1990). Natl League Nurse.

Profile of Alabama Black Voting Strength & Political Representation. Richard A. Hudlin & Brimah K. Farouk. 1982. pap. 1.00 (ISBN 0-318-00963-3). Voter Ed Proj.

Profile of Black Museums: African American Museums Association. (Illus.). 1988. pap. write for info. (ISBN 0-910050-94-5). AASLH Pr.

Profile of Brigadier General Alfred N. A. Duffie. Thomas S. Reed. 53p. 1982. 11.00 (ISBN 0-89126-109-5). MA AH Pub.

Profile of Canada's Older Population. L. O. Stone & Susan Fletcher. 119p. 1980. pap. text ed. 7.95x (ISBN 0-920380-31-X, Pub. by Inst Res Pub Canada). Brookfield Pub Co.

Profile of Chronic Illness in Nursing Homes: United States, August 1973-April 1974, Ser. 13, No. 29. Ed. by Audrey Shipp. 1977. pap. 1.95 (ISBN 0-8406-0968-X). Natl Ctr Health Stats.

Profile of Dutch Economic Geography. Ed. by Marc De Smidt & Egbert Wever. (Man & Environment Ser.: No. 16). 201p. 1984. pap. 17.50 (ISBN 90-232-2100-1, Pub. by Van Gorcum Holland). Longwood Pub Group.

Profile of Economic Plants. Ed. by John C. Roecklein & PingSun Leung. 608p. 1987. 89.95 (ISBN 0-88738-167-7). Transaction Bks.

Profile of Education Doctorates: 1976 to 1986. Susan T. Hill. (Education Department Publication Ser.: No. 87-385). (Illus.). 36p. (Orig.). 1987. pap. 2.00 (S/N 065-000-00322-8). USGPO.

Profile of Employee Benefits. Mitchell Meyer & Harland Fox. (Report Ser.: No. 645). (Illus.). 103p. 1974. pap. 15.00 (ISBN 0-8237-0064-X). Conference Bd.

Profile of Employee Benefits: 1981. Ed. by Mitchell Meyer. (Report Ser.: No. 813). (Illus.). vi, 58p. (Orig.). 1981. pap. 50.00 (ISBN 0-8237-0249-9). Conference Bd.

Profile of Employment, Manpower Needs & Business Potential in the Boulder County Area. Gerald L. Allen & J. Richard Montanari. 155p. 1976. 25.00 (ISBN 0-686-64178-7). U CO Busn Res Div.

Profile of General Meade & the Four Military Installations Named for the Victor at Gettysburg. B. C. Corrigan. (Historic Marker Ahead Ser.). (Illus., Orig.). 1985. pap. 1.95 (ISBN 0-9612956-1-9). ADS Pr.

Profile of Georgia's Black Voting Strength & Political Representation. Richard A. Hudlin. 1982. 1.00 (ISBN 0-686-38027-4). Voter Ed Proj.

Profile of Glindy. Esther H. Elias. (Illus.). 128p. 1976. 8.95 (ISBN 0-8158-0337-0). Chris Mass.

Profile of Hawaii's Elderly Population. Eleanor C. Nordyke et al. (Papers of the East-West Population Institute: No. 91). vii, 40p. 1984. pap. text ed. 3.00 (ISBN 0-86638-059-0). EW Ctr HI.

Profile of Horace. D. R. Shackleton Bailey. 152p. 1982. text ed. 22.50x (ISBN 0-674-71325-7). Harvard U Pr.

Profile of Indian Culture. K. Chaitanya. 1975. 15.95. Asia Bk Corp.

Profile of Indian Culture. K. K. Nair, pseud. (India Library Ser., Vol. 1). 202p. 1975. 8.95 (ISBN 0-88253-774-1). Ind-US Inc.

Profile of Legal Malpractice: A Statistical Study of Determinative Characteristics of Claims Asserted Against Attorneys. LC 86-210693. 81p. Date not set. price not set (ISBN 0-89707-254-5). Amer Bar Assn.

Profile of Love. Ferdinand Campbell. LC 78-62758. 96p. Repr. of 1978 ed. 6.95 (ISBN 0-912444-16-9). Gaus.

Profile of Man & Culture in Mexico. Samuel Ramos. Tr. by Peter G. Earle from Span. LC 62-9792. (Texas Pan American Ser.). 220p. 1962. 12.50x (ISBN 0-292-73340-2); pap. 5.95x (ISBN 0-292-70072-5). U of Tex Pr.

Profile of Michigan. Stephen P. Sobotka. LC 63-8423. 1963. 7.50 (ISBN 0-02-929830-X). Free Pr.

Profile of Mississippi's Black Voting Strength & Political Representation. Richard A. Hudlin & Brimah K. Farouk. (1981, 1982). 1.00 ea. (ISBN 0-686-38016-9). Voter Ed Proj.

Profile of Modern Greece: In Search of Identity. Yorgos A. Kourvetaris & Betty A. Dobratz. (Illus.). 240p. 1988. 48.00 (ISBN 0-19-827551-X). Oxford U Pr.

Profile of Pacific Schools. 121p. 1987. 9.95 (ISBN 0-317-66079-9). Northwest Regional.

Profile of Small or Rural Hospitals 1980-1984. 48p. (Orig.). 1986. pap. 15.00 (ISBN 0-87258-446-1, 184200). Am Hospital.

Profit Measurement & Price Changes. Kenneth Lacey. LC 82-48370. (Accountancy in Transition Ser.). 148p. 1982. lib. bdg. 22.00 (ISBN 0-8240-5323-0). Garland Pub.

Profit Minded Florist: A Financial Manual for Retail Florists. Floral Finance, Inc. (Illus.). 192p. 1987. pap. 69.95 (ISBN 0-317-61828-8). Financial Control.

Profit on the Dotted Line: Coupons & Rebates. LC 84-71637. (Illus.). 200p. 1984. 24.95 (ISBN 0-913247-00-6). Commerce Comns.

Profit Opportunities in Real Estate Investments. Calvin L. Greenberg. cancelled 12.95 (ISBN 0-13-726042-3, Parker). P-H.

Profit or People? The New Social Role of Money. James Robertson. (Ideas in Progress Ser.). 96p. 1978. 9.95 (ISBN 0-7145-0848-9, Dist. by Scribner); pap. 4.95 (ISBN 0-7145-0773-3). M Boyars Pubs.

Profit Planning & Budgeting for Law Firms. LC 80-66287. 84p. 1980. pap. 25.00. Amer Bar Assn.

Profit Planning & Budgeting for Law Firms. James F. Rabenhorst. 76p. pap. 25.00. Chicago Review.

Profit Planning & Control. T. S. McAlpine. (Illus.). 164p. 1969. 19.95 (ISBN 0-8464-1122-9). Beekman Pubs.

Profit Planning Decisions with the Break-Even System. Tucker. 32.95 (ISBN 0-317-64255-3). Van Nos Reinhold.

Profit Planning for Small Business. Robert N. Hogsett. 256p. 1981. 26.95 (ISBN 0-442-24907-1). Van Nos Reinhold.

Profit Planning Handbook. B. H. Walley. 325p. 1978. text ed. 36.75x (ISBN 0-220-66342-4, Pub. by Busn Bks England). Brookfield Pub Co.

Profit Plus. James B. Pettijohn. (Illus.). 256p. 1988. pap. price not set (ISBN 0-03-013558-3). Dryden Pr.

Profit Secrets for Small Business. Mark Stevens. 1983. 32.00 (ISBN 0-8359-5647-4, Reston); pap. 23.95 (ISBN 0-8359-5646-6). P-H.

Profit-Sharing & Industrial Co-Partnership in British Industry, 1880-1920: Class Conflict or Class Collaboration. Jihang Park. Ed. by William H. McNeill & Peter Stansky. (Modern European History Ser.). 500p. 1987. lib. bdg. 75.00 (ISBN 0-8240-7827-6). Garland Pub.

Profit Sharing as a Motivator. Bert L. Metzger. 24p. 1984. pap. text ed. 4.50 (ISBN 0-911192-36-0). Profit Sharing.

Profit Sharing Between Employer & Employee: A Study in the Evolution of the Wages System. facsimile ed. Nicholas P. Gilman. LC 78-165635. (Select Bibliographies Reprint Ser). Repr. of 1889 ed. 26.50 (ISBN 0-8369-5944-2). Ayer Co Pubs.

Profit Sharing in Thirty-Eight Large Companies: Piece of the Action for 1,000,000 Participants, 2 vols. Bert L. Metzger. Incl. Vol. 1. 256p. 1976. pap. text ed. 14.00 (ISBN 0-911192-26-3); Vol. 2. 470p. 1978. pap. text ed. 34.00 (ISBN 0-911192-27-1). LC 75-39379. 1978. Set. pap. 39.50 (ISBN 0-911192-25-5). Profit Sharing.

Profit Strategies for Business. Robert Rachlin. LC 79-88674. 127p. 1980. 14.95 (ISBN 0-938712-01-2). Marr Pubns.

Profit System. Miloslav Springer. LC 86-90427. 70p. (Orig.). 1986. pap. 8.00 (ISBN 0-9616955-0-1). M Springer.

Profit System: The Economics of Capitalism. Francis Green & Bob Sutcliffe. 400p. 1987. pap. 7.95 (ISBN 0-14-022716-4, Pelican Bks). Penguin.

Profit Target Program. write for info. Print Indus Am.

Profit Theory & Capitalism. Mark Obrinsky. LC 82-40482. (Illus.). 176p. 1983. 24.95x (ISBN 0-8122-7863-1); pap. 11.95x (ISBN 0-8122-1147-2). U of Pa Pr.

Profit with Delight: The Literary Genre of the Acts of the Apostles. Richard I. Pervo. LC 86-45220. 224p. 1987. 16.95 (ISBN 0-8006-0782-1). Fortress.

PROFITAB: Farm Record System. 144p. 1983. pap. 15.95 (ISBN 0-932250-20-3). Doane Info Servs.

Profitability Accounting & Bidding Strategy for Engineering & Construction Management. Hans J. Lang & Michael DeCoursey. 224p. 1983. 35.95 (ISBN 0-442-26005-9). Van Nos Reinhold.

Profitability Analysis for Managerial & Engineering Decisions. 215p. 1980. pap. 24.00 (APO105, APO). UNIPUB.

Profitability & Economic Choice. Paul H. Jeynes. LC 67-28033. (Illus.). 632p. pap. 160.00 (2029823). Bks Demand UMI.

Profitability & Industrial Robots. G. Martins & M Svensson. (Illus.). 170p. 1988. 50.00 (ISBN 0-387-18685-9). Springer-Verlag.

Profitability & Mobility in Rural America: Successful Approaches to Tackling Rural Transportation Problems. William R. Gillis. LC 87-43187. 224p. 1988. lib. bdg. 24.95x (ISBN 0-271-00632-3). Pa St U Pr.

Profitability & Unemployment. E. Malinvaud. LC 79-21472. 1980. 18.95 (ISBN 0-521-22999-5). Cambridge U Pr.

Profitability in Swedish Manufacturing: Trends & Explanations. Lennart Erixon. (Swedish Institute for Social Research: No. 4). 267p. (Orig.). 1987. pap. text ed. 36.00x (ISBN 91-76-04027-5, Pub by Almqvist & Wiksell). Coronet Bks.

Profitability of Major Oil Companies: Normal Returns or Windfall Profits? Gerald D. Keim et al. 16p. 1980. 1.00s (ISBN 0-86599-003-4). Ctr Educ Res.

Profitable Acquistions: Guidelines for Buying & Selling Companies for Businessmen & Financiers. Thomas H. Hopkins. LC 83-61892. (Illus.). 138p. 1984. Repr. of 1983 ed. 24.95 (ISBN 0-9611864-0-2); leather 92.50 (ISBN 0-9611864-1-0). McTaggart.

Profitable Advertising Manual: A Handbook for Small Business. 2nd, rev. ed. Bruce E. David. LC 82-99849. (Illus.). 130p. 1986. pap. 12.95 (ISBN 0-9609734-1-9); wkbk. 9.95 (ISBN 0-317-13026-9); spiral bd. 8.95 (ISBN 0-317-13027-7). Worthprinting.

Profitable & Necessarie Booke of Observations. William Clowes. LC 73-171740. (English Experience Ser.: No. 366). 1971. Repr. of 1596 ed. 33.50 (ISBN 90-221-0366-8). Walter J Johnson.

Profitable Beef Production. 3rd ed. Ed. by M. McG. Cooper & M. B. Willis. (Illus.). 160p. 1979. 19.95 (ISBN 0-85236-093-2, Pub. by Farming Pr UK). Diamond Farm Bk.

Profitable Book Publishing for the Consultant. Hubert Bermont. 48p. (Orig.). 1987. pap. 19.00 (ISBN 0-930686-29-2, Pub. by Consultants Lib). Bermont Bks.

Profitable Calendar Photography. Date not set. 3.95 (ISBN 0-89816-113-4). Embee Pr.

Profitable Careers in Nonprofit. William Lewis & Carol Milano. 1987. pap. 10.95 (ISBN 0-471-83699-0). Wiley.

Profitable Color Postcard Photography. 3.95 (ISBN 0-89816-049-9). Embee Pr.

Profitable Color Poster Photography. Date not set. 3.95 (ISBN 0-89816-100-2). Embee Pr.

Profitable Company in Literature & Science. John M. McBryde. 1934. 15.00 (ISBN 0-8274-3209-7). R West.

Profitable Company: Milestones & Monuments of the Signers of the Declaration of Independence. Archibald Laird. 1984. 19.50 (ISBN 0-8158-0425-3). Chris Mass.

Profitable Consulting: Helping American Managers Face the Future. Robert O. Metzger. 144p. 1988. 16.95 (ISBN 0-201-09539-4). Addison-Wesley.

Profitable Consumer Lending: A Guide to Lending, Collection & Compliance. Robert D. Hall, Jr. & F. Blake Cloonen. LC 84-319. (Bankers Lending Ser.). 192p. 1984. text ed. 44.00 (ISBN 0-87267-047-3). Bank Admin Inst.

Profitable Corporate Report Photography. Date not set. 3.95 (ISBN 0-89816-103-7). Embee Pr.

Profitable Crafts Marketing: A Complete Guide to Successful Selling. Brian Jefferson. (Illus.). 250p. 1985. 19.95 (ISBN 0-88192-013-4). Timber.

Profitable Crafts Marketing: A Complete Guide to Successful Selling. Brian T. Jefferson. (Madrona Crafts Business Bks.). (Illus.). 256p. pap. 10.95 (ISBN 0-88089-013-4). Madrona Pubs.

Profitable Dance Studio Photography. 3.95 (ISBN 0-89816-033-2). Embee Pr.

Profitable Direct Mail for Travel Agencies. Douglas Thompson & Douglas Haylock. 150p. 1988. binder & software 195.00 (ISBN 0-936831-06-5). Dendrobium Bks.

Profitable Direct Marketing. Jim Kobs. LC 79-53509. 1979. 27.95 (ISBN 0-8442-3037-5, Crain Bks). Natl Textbk.

Profitable Distribution of Low-Cost CAD-CAE Hardware, Software & Systems: Vendor Strategies, Third-Party Channels, Retail Outlets. Summit Strategies Staff. (Illus.). 199p. 1986. 1231.00 (ISBN 0-914849-06-9). TBC Inc.

Profitable Earthworm Farming. Charlie Morgan. 1975. pap. 3.00 (ISBN 0-914116-06-1). Shields.

Profitable Equipment Leasing: A Practical Guide for Bankers. Terry Winders & Bill Williams. LC 86-26601. 277p. 1987. text ed. 58.00 (ISBN 0-87267-101-1). Bank Admin Inst.

Profitable Export Marketing: A Strategy for U. S. Business. Marta Ortiz-Buonafina. (Illus.). 256p. 1984. 21.95 (ISBN 0-13-727991-4); pap. 9.95 (ISBN 0-13-727983-3). P-H.

Profitable Exporting: Complete Guide to Marketing Your Products Abroad. John S. Gordon & J. R. Arnold. LC 88-10815. 1988. 32.95 (ISBN 0-471-61334-7). Wiley.

Profitable Farm Mechanization. 3rd ed. Claude Culpin. (Illus.). 336p. 1975. text ed. 24.95x (ISBN 0-8464-0037-5). Beekman Pubs.

Profitable Farming Now. New Farm Magazine Editors. (Illus.). 100p. 1984. pap. 17.95 (ISBN 0-913107-01-8). Rodale Pr Inc.

Profitable Financial Management for Foodservice Operators thru Profit Planning. William P. Fisher. 26p. 1973. pap. 3.00 (ISBN 0-317-57850-2, MG650). Natl Restaurant Assn.

Profitable Food & Beverage Management: Planning. Eric F. Green et al. 352p. 1987. 25.95 (ISBN 0-930745-02-7). Williams Bk Co.

Profitable Food & Beverage Management: Operations. Eric F. Green et al. 448p. 1987. text ed. 29.95 (ISBN 0-930745-03-5). Williams Bk Co.

Profitable Footwear Retailing. William Rossi. 335p. 1988. lib. bdg. 20.00 (ISBN 0-87005-630-1). Fairchild.

Profitable Garden Center Management. 2nd ed. Louis M. Berninger. (Illus.). 1981. 32.00 (ISBN 0-8359-5633-4, Reston); instrs's. manual o.p. avail. (ISBN 0-8359-5634-2). P-H.

Profitable Grain Trading. Ralph M. Ainsworth. LC 80-53316. 256p. 1980. Repr. of 1933 ed. text ed. 25.00 (ISBN 0-934380-04-X). Traders Pr.

Profitable Hotel Reception. D. Taylor & R. Thomason. (International Series in Hospitality Management). (Illus.). 236p. 1982. text ed. 40.00 (ISBN 0-08-026769-6); pap. 20.00 (ISBN 0-08-026768-8). Pergamon.

Profitable Investing: Fundamentals of the Science of Investing. facsimile ed. John Moody. LC 75-2651. (Wall Street & the Security Market Ser.). 1975. Repr. of 1925 ed. 25.50x (ISBN 0-405-06976-6). Ayer Co Pubs.

Profitable Knowledge: Synposis for Success. Christopher Scott. 100p. Date not set. price not set. Meridith & Winthrop Pubs.

Profitable Logistics Management. rev. ed. Don Firth. 400p. 1988. price not set (ISBN 0-07-549603-8). McGraw.

Profitable Management for the Subcontractors. Robert L. Teets. LC 84-967. 332p. 1984. Repr. of 1976 ed. lib. bdg. 24.50 (ISBN 0-89874-715-5). Krieger.

Profitable Marching Band Photography. 3.95 (ISBN 0-89816-048-0). Embee Pr.

Profitable Methods for Small Business Advertising. Ernest A. Gray. LC 83-19884. (Small Business Management Ser.: 1-471). 285p. 1984. 24.95 (ISBN 0-471-86962-7). Wiley.

Profitable New Commodity Trading Methods. Robert Barnes. 1986. cancelled (ISBN 0-442-21273-9). Van Nos Reinhold.

Profitable Office Management for the Growing Business. Edward N. Rausch. LC 83-45210. 208p. 1984. 17.95 (ISBN 0-317-05554-2). AMACOM.

Profitable Part-Time, Home Based, Businesses. rev. ed. Gary Null. LC 74-13075. 48p. 1978. pap. 2.50 (ISBN 0-87576-030-9). Pilot Bks.

Profitable Pasture Management. Roy A. Chessmore. LC 78-70056. 1979. 25.25 (ISBN 0-8134-2056-3, 2056); text ed. 18.95x. Inter Print Pubs.

Profitable People Planning: A Guide to Effective Human Resource Management. Jon D. Council. (Illus.). 159p. 1978. 12.50 (ISBN 0-682-49104-7). Exposition-Phoenix.

Profitable Pet Photography. Date not set. 3.95 (ISBN 0-89816-110-X). Embee Pr.

Profitable Pricing Strategies. S. L. Montgomery. 192p. 1988. text ed. 24.95 (ISBN 0-07-042860-3). McGraw.

Profitable Product Management. John Ward. (Illus.). 304p. 1984. pap. 35.95 (ISBN 0-434-92215-3, Pub. by W Heinemann Ltd). David & Charles.

Profitable Professional Practice. Donald L. Henry. LC 85-9595. 286p. 1985. 59.95 (ISBN 0-13-728619-8, Busn). P-H.

Profitable Prospecting for the Combination Agent. 88p. 2.50 (ISBN 0-318-14765-3). Life Ins Mktg Res.

Profitable Purchasing. 76p. 1982. pap. 11.00 (MG571). Natl Restaurant Assn.

Profitable Purchasing Management: A Guide for Small Business Owners-Managers. William Messner. (Illus.). 272p. 1982. 21.95 (ISBN 0-8144-5542-5). AMACOM.

Profitable Purchasing Management: A Guide for Small Business Owners-Managers. William A. Messner. LC 81-69367. pap. 79.30 (ISBN 0-317-27186-5, 2023922). Bks Demand UMI.

Profitable Restaurant Management. 2nd ed. K. Solomon. 26.95 (ISBN 0-317-64256-1). Van Nos Reinhold.

Profitable Restaurant Management. 2nd ed. Kenneth L. Solomon & Norman Katz. LC 80-25007. 298p. 1981. 60.00x (ISBN 0-13-728816-6, Busn). P-H.

Profitable Retail Television Advertising. Ed. by NRMA Staff. 1977. pap. 15.00 (ISBN 0-87102-058-0, 60-7661). Natl Ret Merch.

Profitable Risk Control: The Winning Edge. William W. Allison. 1986. 35.00 (ISBN 0-939874-71-7). ASSE.

Profitable Sales Management & Marketing for Growing Businesses. Robert J. Calvin. 1984. 33.95 (ISBN 0-442-21502-9). Van Nos Reinhold.

Profitable Selling. John Lidstone. 240p. 1986. pap. text ed. 14.95x (ISBN 0-7045-0524-X, Pub. by Gower England). Gower Pub Co.

Profitable Service Marketing. Eberhard E. Scheuing et al. 1986. 30.00 (ISBN 0-87094-613-7). Dow Jones-Irwin.

Profitable Sheep Farming. 5th ed. M. McG. Cooper & R. J. Thomas. (Illus.). 192p. 1982. 21.95 (ISBN 0-85236-117-3, Pub. by Farming Pr UK). Diamond Farm Bk.

Profitable Small Product Photography. Date not set. 3.95 (ISBN 0-89816-105-3). Embee Pr.

Profitable Soil Management. 2nd ed. Leo L. Knuti et al. 1970. text ed. 31.52 (ISBN 0-13-729400-X). P-H.

Profitable Thesis Typing. E. Pokress. 5.50 (ISBN 0-685-22757-X). Aurea.

Profitable Trucking. American Trucking Association, National Accounting & Finance Council. 107p. 1981. pap. text ed. 8.95 (ISBN 0-686-46974-7). Am Trucking Assns.

Profitable Way: Carbon Plate Steel Specifying & Purchasing Handbook. John S. Blair. (Illus.). 194p. 1978. 39.95x (ISBN 0-931690-08-0). Genium Pub.

Profitable Way: Carbon Sheet Steel Specifying & Purchasing Handbook. John S. Blair. (Illus.). 158p. 1978. 39.95x (ISBN 0-931690-04-8). Genium Pub.

Profitable Way: Carbon Strip Steel Specifying & Purchasing Handbook. John S. Blair. (Illus.). 194p. 1978. 39.95x (ISBN 0-931690-05-6). Genium Pub.

Profitable Worke to This Whole Kingdome Concerning the Mending of All Highways, As Also for Waters & Iron Workes. Thomas Procter. LC 77-7425. (English Experience Ser.: No. 885). 1977. Repr. of 1610 ed. lib. bdg. 15.00 (ISBN 90-221-0885-6). Walter J Johnson.

Profiting from the Word. A. W. Pink. 1977. pap. 3.95 (ISBN 0-85151-032-9). Banner of Truth.

Profiting with Futures Options. David L. Caplan. 48p. (Orig.). 1986. pap. 4.95 (ISBN 0-915513-16-1). Ctr Futures Ed.

Profits. J. N. Williamson. 304p. 1984. pap. 3.25 (ISBN 0-8439-2176-5, Leisure Bks). Leisure NY.

Profits see Houngan.

Profits & Penny Stocks: An Investor's Guide to Low-Cost Stocks & Company Start-Ups. Robert Irwin. 192p. 1987. pap. 3.95 (ISBN 0-425-10344-7). Berkley Pub.

Profits & Prejudice: Illinois Corporations Investments in South Africa. Norman Watkins. LC 84-72411. 65p. (Orig.). 1985. pap. 2.50 (ISBN 0-931879-00-0). Clergy & Laity.

Profits & Professions: Essays in Business & Professional Ethics. Ed. by Wade L. Robison et al. LC 82-23399. (Contemporary Biomedicine, Ethics, & Society Ser.). 336p. 1983. 39.50 (ISBN 0-89603-039-3). Humana.

Profits & Stability of Monopoly. M. A. Utton. (National Institute of Economic & Social Research Occasional Papers: No. XXXVIII). (Illus.). 142p. 1986. 24.95 (ISBN 0-521-32550-1). Cambridge U Pr.

Profits, Dividends & the Law: Profits Available for Dividends from Standpoint of Law & Best Accounting Practice. Prosper Reiter, Jr. LC 75-18481. (History of Accounting Ser.). (Illus.). 1976. Repr. 20.00x (ISBN 0-405-07563-4). Ayer Co Pubs.

Profits from Power: Readings in Protection Rent & Violence-Controlling Enterprises. Frederic C. Lane. LC 79-13860. 128p. 1979. 39.50x (ISBN 0-87395-403-3); pap. 14.95x (ISBN 0-87395-420-3). State U NY Pr.

Profits from Preempts. C. C. Wei & Ron Andersen. 162p. 1977. pap. 4.95 (ISBN 0-87643-035-3). Barclay Bridge.

Profits from Preempts, No. 3. (Bidding Precisely). 162p. (Orig.). 1977. pap. 4.95 (ISBN 0-686-36625-5). M Lisa Precision.

Profits from Real Estate Publicity. Roger Karvel. 225p. 1980. 21.95 (ISBN 0-88462-385-8, 1973-01, Real Estate Ed). Longman Finan.

Profits from Small Town Properties. James H. Koch. 1984. 23.95 (ISBN 0-442-25330-3). Van Nos Reinhold.

Profits in Economic Theory. Michael Howard. LC 83-3108. 250p. (gr. 10 up). 1983. 27.50x (ISBN 0-312-64794-8). St Martin.

Profits in the British Economy, 1909-1938. George D. Worswick & D. G. Tipping. LC 67-5122. 1967. 27.50x (ISBN 0-678-06264-1). Kelley.

Profits in the Long Run. Dennis C. Mueller. (Illus.). 352p. 1986. 47.50 (ISBN 0-521-30693-0). Cambridge U Pr.

Profits in the Modern Economy: Selected Papers. Conference on Understanding Profits (1964: Macalester College & University of Minnesota) Ed. by Harold W. Stevenson & J. Russell Nelson. LC 67-13120. pap. 53.50 (ISBN 0-317-29470-9, 2055919). Bks Demand UMI.

Profits in the Stock Market. H. M. Gartley. 40p. 1935. 90.00 (ISBN 0-939093-07-3). Lambert Gann Pub.

Profits, Interest & Investment. Friedrich A. Hayek. LC 76-76355. 1969. Repr. of 1939 ed. 35.00x (ISBN 0-678-06501-2). Kelley.

Profits of Religion. Upton B. Sinclair. LC 73-120566. 1970. Repr. of 1918 ed. 22.50 (ISBN 0-404-06093-5). AMS Pr.

Profits of the National Banks. Keith Powlison. Ed. by Stuart Bruchey. LC 80-1166. (Rise of Commercial Banking Ser.). (Illus.). 1981. Repr. of 1931 ed. lib. bdg. 12.00x (ISBN 0-405-13676-5). Ayer Co Pubs.

Profits of Time: How to Invest Yourself in the Gregorian Calendar & Get More Out of Everything in Life. Cairo C. Clingon. LC 87-91122. 178p. (Orig.). 1987. pap. 5.00 (ISBN 0-9618463-0-5). Clingon Pub Hse.

Profits, Politics & Drugs. Duncan W. Reekie & Michael H. Weber. LC 78-24496. 185p. 1979. 49.50x (ISBN 0-8419-0461-8). Holmes & Meier.

Profits, Power, & Prohibition: American Alcohol Reform & the Industrializing of America, 1800-1930. John J. Rumbarger. 301p. 1988. 49.50x (ISBN 0-88706-782-4); pap. 16.95x (ISBN 0-88706-783-2). State U NY Pr.

Profits, Profitability, & the Oil Industry. Edward R. Lehman. Ed. by Stuart Bruchey. LC 78-22694. (Energy in the American Economy Ser.). (Illus.). 1979. lib. bdg. 23.00x (ISBN 0-405-11997-6). Ayer Co Pubs.

Program Housing Standards in the Experimental Housing Allowance Program: Analyzing Differences in the Demand & Supply Experiments. Joseph J. Valenza. write for info. Urban Inst.
Program HYDCYL: A Database for Calculation of Hydrodynamic Loading of Circular Cylinders. Michael M. Bernitsas & S. Guha-Thakurta. (University of Michigan, Dept. of Naval Architecture & Marine Engineering, Report: No. 267). pap. 20.00 (ISBN 0-317-27134-2, 2024682). Bks Demand UMI.
Program Implementation: The Organizational Context. Mary A. Scheirer. LC 81-689. (Contemporary Evaluation Research Ser.: Vol. 5). (Illus.). 232p. 1981. 28.00 (ISBN 0-8039-1540-3). Sage.
Program Issues in Developmental Disabilities: A Resource Manual for Surveyors & Reviewers. Ed. by James F. Gardner et al. LC 80-12555. (Illus.). 176p. (Orig.). 1980. pap. text ed. 19.50 (ISBN 0-933716-05-2, 052). P H Brookes.
Program It Right: Structured Methods in BASIC. Stan Benton & Len Weekes. LC 85-51590. 230p. (Orig.). 1985. pap. text ed. 19.95 (ISBN 0-917072-43-X, Yourdon). P-H.
Program Management Handbook. 99p. 1983. pap. 5.00. Lit Vol Am.
Program Manager. Jack Rudman. (Career Examination Ser.: C-985). (Cloth bdg. avail. on request). pap. 16.00 (ISBN 0-8373-0985-9). Natl Learning.
Program Materials for Family Law for the General Practitioner: August 22, 1986, Savannah, Georgia-August 29, 1986, Atlanta, Georgia. Institute of Continuing Legal Education in Georgia. LC 86-623177. Date not set. price not set. ICLE Georgia.
Program Materials for Fourth Annual Corporate & Banking Law Institute: October 24-26, 1985, Sea Island. LC 86-620858. Date not set. price not set. ICLE Georgia.
Program Materials for Insurance Law Institute: September 25-27, 1986, St. Simons Island, Georgia. Insurance Law Institute & Institute of Continuing Legal Education in Georgia. LC 86-623179. Date not set. price not set. ICLE Georgia.
Program Materials for Real Property Law Institute: May 8-10, 1986, St. Simons, May 22-23, 1986, Atlanta. Real Property Law Institute & Institute of Continuing Legal Education, Georgia. LC 86-623182. Date not set. price not set. ICLE Georgia.
Program Materials for Seminar on Construction Litigation, April 4, 1986, Atlanta, Georgia. LC 86-621892. Date not set. price not set. ICLE Georgia.
Program Materials for Seminar on Employee Benefit Plans, April 11, 1986, Atlanta, Georgia. LC 86-621897. Date not set. price not set. ICLE Georgia.
Program Materials for Seminar on Ethics & Malpractice, December 19, 1985, Atlanta, Georgia. LC 86-621678. Date not set. price not set. ICLE Georgia.
Program Materials for Seminar on Federal Practice & Procedure: March 7, 1986, Savannah, March 14, 1986, Atlanta, GA. Institute of Continuing Legal Education in Georgia. LC 86-621894. Date not set. price not set. ICLE Georgia.
Program Materials for Seminar on Forensic Evidence for the Civil & Criminal Practitioner: March 21, 1986, Atlanta, Georgia. LC 86-622083. Date not set. price not set. ICLE Georgia.
Program Materials for Seminar on Georgia Law School: March 21, 1986, Atlanta, Georgia. Georgia Council of School Board Attorneys & Georgia Institute of Continuing Legal Education Staff. LC 86-194719. Date not set. price not set. ICLE Georgia.
Program Materials for Seminar on How to Market Legal Services: Client Development Techniques for Growth & Profits, February 24, 1984, Atlanta, Georgia. Institute of Continuing Legal Education in Georgia & Seminar on How to Market Legal Services. LC 84-175544. cancelled. ICLE Georgia.
Program Materials for Seminar on Motion Practice, September 20, 1985, Savannah & September 27, 1985, Atlanta. LC 86-620855. Date not set. price not set. ICLE Georgia.
Program Materials for Seminar on Real Property Law: April 21, 22,23, 1983, St. Simons Island, Georgia. Seminar on Real Property & Saint Simons Island, Georgia. Ed. by Institute of Continuing Legal Education in Georgia. LC 83-623096. (Illus.). 16.00. ICLE Georgia.
Program Materials for Seminar on Recent Developments in Georgia Law: November 8, 1985, Amelia Island & November 15, 1985, Atlanta. LC 86-621681. Date not set. price not set. ICLE Georgia.
Program Materials for Seminar on Secured Lending Under the UCC: December 5, 1985, Atlanta, Georgia. LC 86-621679. Date not set. price not set. ICLE Georgia.
Program Materials for Seminar on Special Real Estate Issues: Multi-Owners Development, February 21, 1986, Atlanta, Georgia. Institute of Continuing Legal Education in Georgia, Real Property Law Section. LC 86-621680. Date not set. price not set. ICLE Georgia.
Program Materials for Seminar on Will Drafting & Estate Planning, April 18, 1986, Savannah, April 25, 1986, Atlanta. Institute of Continuing Legal Education in Georgia. LC 86-623186. Date not set. price not set. ICLE Georgia.
Program Materials for Seminar on Workers' Compensation for the General Practitioner: Proceedings of the Seminar, Savannah, April 11, 1986 & Atlanta, April 18, 1986. LC 86-622082. Date not set. price not set. ICLE Georgia.
Program Modification. Jean-Dominique Warnier. 152p. 1978. 21.50 (ISBN 90-207-0777-9, Pub. by Martinus Nijhoff Netherlands). Kluwer Academic.
Program Notes for the Singer's Repertoire. Berton Coffin & Werner Singer. LC 60-7265. 230p. 1962. 18.50 (ISBN 0-8108-0169-8). Scarecrow.
Program of Financial Research: Inventory of Current Research on Financial Problems, Vol. 2. (Financial Research Program Ser.: No. 1). 261p. 1937. 10.00 (ISBN 0-87014-459-6). Natl Bur Econ Res.
Program of Priestly Formation, NCCB. 3rd ed. 174p. 1982. pap. 14.95 (ISBN 1-55586-837-1). US Catholic.
Program of the Communist Party of the Soviet Union. Kommunisticheskaia Partiia & Sovetskogo Soiuza. LC 74-10423. 143p. 1974. Repr. of 1963 ed. lib. bdg. 35.00x (ISBN 0-8371-7685-9, KHCP). Greenwood.
Program of the Good. Edward T. Lyons. 33p. 1986. 6.95 (ISBN 0-533-06363-9). Vantage.
Program of the History of the New World: Vol. II; The Colonial Period in the History of the New World. Silvio Zavala. Tr. by Max Savelle from Span. LC 83-1685. (Illus.). xxviii, 359p. 1983. Repr. of 1962 ed. lib. bdg. 48.50 (ISBN 0-313-23889-8, ZAPR). Greenwood.
Program Optimization. (Infotech Computer State of the Art Reports). 448p. 1976. 61.00 (ISBN 0-08-028508-2). Pergamon.
Program Organization in Western Australia's District High Schools. John Davis. Ed. by Patricia M. Simpson. (Research Ser.: No. 1). (Illus.). xix, 162p. (Orig.). 1983. pap. 21.00x (ISBN 0-909751-74-9, Pub. by U of W Austral Pr). Intl Spec Bk.
Program Outreach Specialist. (Career Examination Ser.: C-3405). Date not set. pap. 14.00 (ISBN 0-8373-3405-5). Natl Learning.
Program Papers: Proceedings. National Workshop, Cape Cod, Mass. 1980. 18.00 (ISBN 0-686-36557-7). Assn Interp Naturalist.
Program Papers: Proceedings. National Workshop Estes Park, CO 1981. 10.00 (ISBN 0-686-36558-5). Assn Interp Naturalist.
Program Papers: Proceedings of the National Workshop Callaway Gardens, 1984. 10.00 (ISBN 0-318-01592-7). Assn Interp Naturalist.
Program Papers: Proceedings of the National Workshop, Purdue University. 1983. 10.00 (ISBN 0-318-00375-9). Assn Interp Naturalist.
Program Planning Aids for Day Care Centers. (Illus.). 72p. pap. 3.50 (ISBN 0-686-15583-1, A50). Day Care Coun.
Program Planning & Evaluation for the Public Manager. Ronald D. Sylvia et al. LC 85-5703. (Public Administration Ser.). 140p. 1985. pap. text ed. 12.25 pub net (ISBN 0-534-04710-6); instr's. manual avail. (ISBN 0-534-04711-4). Brooks-Cole.
Program Planning for Blind & Visually Impaired Children: A Framework for Educational Excellence. Date not set. price not set (ISBN 0-89128-155-X, PEL155). Am Foun Blind.
Program Planning for Health Education & Health Promotion. Mark B. Dignan & Patricia A. Carr. LC 87-3937. (Illus.). 160p. 1987. pap. text ed. 19.50 (ISBN 0-8121-1091-9). Lea & Febiger.
Program Planning for Youth Ministry. John E. Forliti. LC 75-143. 60p. 1975. pap. 4.50 (ISBN 0-88489-061-9). St Marys.
Program Research Analyst. Jack Rudman. (Career Examination Ser.: C-1704). (Cloth bdg. avail. on request). pap. 16.00 (ISBN 0-8373-1704-5). Natl Learning.
Program Research Specialist. Jack Rudman. (Career Examination Ser.: C-3200). 1988. pap. 16.00 (ISBN 0-8373-3200-1). Natl Learning.
Program Specialist. Jack Rudman. (Career Examination Ser.: C-2861). (Cloth bdg. avail. on request). 1988. pap. 16.00 (ISBN 0-8373-2861-6). Natl Learning.
Program Specialist: Aging Services. Jack Rudman. (Career Examination Ser.: C-2820). (Cloth bdg. avail. on request). 1988. pap. 16.00 (ISBN 0-8373-2820-9). Natl Learning.
Program Specialist (Correction) Jack Rudman. (Career Examination Ser.: C-1997). (Cloth bdg. avail. on request). pap. 16.00 (ISBN 0-8373-1997-8). Natl Learning.
Program Specification, Aarhus, Denmark, 1981: Proceedings. Ed. by J. Staunstrup. (Lecture Notes in Computer Science Ser.: Vol. 134). 426p. 1982. pap. 24.00 (ISBN 0-387-11490-4). Springer-Verlag.
Program Specification & Transformation: Proceedings of the IFIP TC2-WG.1 Working Conference, Bad-Tolz, FRG, 15-17 April, 1986. Ed. by L. G. Meertens. 536p. 1987. 105.25 (ISBN 0-444-70223-7, North Holland). Elsevier.
Program STARI-3D: A Program for Static Risers, 3-Dimensional Analysis. A. Imron & M. M. Bernitsas. (University of Michigan, Dept. of Naval Architecture & Marine Engineering, Report: No. 280). pap. 20.00 (ISBN 0-317-27124-5, 2024684). Bks Demand UMI.
Program Strategies for Preventing Fetal Alcohol Syndrome & Alcohol-Related Birth Defects. (DHS Publication ADM Ser.: No. 87-1482). 83p. 1987. pap. 4.00 (ISBN 0-318-22935-8, S/N 017-024-01319-6). USGPO.
Program Style, Design, Efficiency, Debugging & Testing. 2nd, reference ed. Dennis Van Tassel. (Illus.). 1978. ref. ed. 43.00 (ISBN 0-13-729947-8). P-H.
Program Trading: The New Age of Investing: The Role of the Individual Investor in Today's Changing Stock Market. Jeffrey D. Miller & Peter J. Brennan. (Illus.). 356p. 1989. pap. 19.95 (ISBN 0-13-730318-1). P-H.
Program Transformation & Programming Environments. Ed. by P. Pepper. (NATO ASI Ser. Series F Computer & Systems Sciences: No. 8). 400p. 1984. 52.00 (ISBN 0-387-12932-4). Springer-Verlag.
Program Translation Fundamentals: Methods & Issues. Peter Calingaert. 1988. 36.95 (ISBN 0-88175-096-4, Computer Sci Pr). W H Freeman.
Program Verification Using Ada. Andrew D. McGettrick. LC 81-12276. (Cambridge Computer Science Texts: No. 13). (Illus.). 350p. 1982. pap. 24.95 (ISBN 0-521-28531-3). Cambridge U Pr.
Program Verifier. James C. King. LC 76-127837. 262p. 1969. 19.00 (ISBN 0-403-04510-X). Scholarly.
Program Your Heart for Health. Frank Murray. 368p. (Orig.). 1978. pap. 2.95 (ISBN 0-915962-20-9). Comm Channels.
Program Your IBM PC to Program Itself! David D. Bush. (Illus.). 160p. 1986. 18.95 (ISBN 0-8306-0898-2, 1898); pap. 12.95 (ISBN 0-8306-1898-8). Tab Bks.
Program Your Microcomputer in BASIC. Peter Gosling. 110p. 1981. pap. 1.95 (ISBN 0-918398-52-5). Weber Systems.
Program Your Own Life. Michael H. Greene. 230p. 1982. 10.00 (ISBN 0-9610136-0-5). Behavorial Sys Inc.
Program Yourself for Success. Herschel L. Scott, Jr. 12p. 1982. pap. 2.50 (ISBN 0-88083-007-7). Poverty Hill Pr.
Programa de Mayordomia para la Iglesia Local. 48p. (Span.). 1987. pap. 2.25 (ISBN 0-311-27024-7). Casa Bautista.
Programa del Espiritu Santo. George A. Hilgeman. 174p. 1982. pap. 5.95 (ISBN 0-89922-216-1). Edit Caribe.
Programa Para Todo El Pueblo. Felix Ojeda. (Span.). 1966. pap. 0.25 (ISBN 0-87898-013-X). New Outlook.
Programacion financiera aplicada: El caso de Colombia. Instituto del FMI. xvii, 311p. 1984. 20.00 (ISBN 0-939934-35-3); pap. 12.50 (ISBN 0-939934-39-6). Intl Monetary.
Programas Del Dia De la Madre y Poesias. 62p. (Span.). 1986. pap. 1.75 (ISBN 0-311-07303-4). Casa Bautista.
Programas Para Dias Especiales Tomo I. A. Lopez Munoz. 107p. 1986. pap. 2.75 (ISBN 0-311-07005-1). Casa Bautista.
Programas Para Dias Especiales Tomo II. A. Lopez Munoz. 64p. 1984. pap. 2.75 (ISBN 0-311-07006-X). Casa Bautista.
Programas para Reuniones Sociales y Banquetes. Ed. by Viola Campbell. (Illus.). 64p. 1985. pap. 1.95 (ISBN 0-311-11011-8). Casa Bautista.
Programas y Actividades para Muchachos y Jovencitos. (No. 1). 96p. (Span.). 1984. pap. 2.95 (ISBN 0-311-12019-9). Casa Bautista.
Programas y Actividades para Muchachos y Jovencitos, Tomo 3. 94p. (Orig., Span.). 1987. pap. 2.75 (ISBN 0-311-12030-X). Casa Bautista.
Programas y Actividades para Muchachos y Jovencitos, No. 4. 96p. (Span.). (gr. 4-10). 1987. pap. text ed. 2.75 (ISBN 0-311-12036-9). Casa Bautista.
Programas y Actividades para Ninas y Jovencitas. (No. 1). 96p. (Span.). 1984. pap. 2.95 (ISBN 0-311-12018-0). Casa Bautista.
Programas y Actividades para Ninas y Jovencitas, No. 4. 96p. (gr. 4-10). 1987. pap. text ed. 2.75 (ISBN 0-311-12035-0). Casa Bautista.
Programas y Actividades para Senoritas. (No.1). 96p. (Span.). 1984. pap. 2.95 (ISBN 0-311-12020-2). Casa Bautista.
Programas y Actividades para Senoritas, Tomo 3. 96p. (Orig., Span.). 1986. pap. 2.75 (ISBN 0-311-12031-8). Casa Bautista.
Programas y Actividades para Senoritas, No. 4. 96p. (Span.). 1987. pap. text ed. 2.75 (ISBN 0-311-12037-7). Casa Bautista.
Programas y Actividades para Varones. (No. 1). 96p. (Span.). 1984. pap. 2.95 (ISBN 0-311-12021-0). Casa Bautista.
Programas y Actividades para Varones, Tomo 3. 64p. (Span.). 1987. pap. 2.75 (ISBN 0-311-12032-6). Casa Bautista.
Programas y Actividades para Varones, No. 4. 64p. (Span.). 1987. pap. text ed. 2.75 (ISBN 0-311-12038-5). Casa Bautista.
Programed Spelling & Vocabulary. George W. Feinstein. 272p. 1983. pap. text ed. write for info. (ISBN 0-13-729855-2). P-H.
Programm des Thukydides see Melier-Dialog.
Programmable Assembly. Ed. by W. Heginbotham. (International Trends in Manufacturing Technology Ser.). (Illus.). 349p. 1984. 58.00 (ISBN 0-387-13479-4). Springer-Verlag.
Programmable Calculators: Business Applications. Julius S. Aronofsky et al. (Illus.). 1978. pap. text ed. 11.95 (ISBN 0-07-002317-4). McGraw.
Programmable Controller - Theory & Implementation. Luis A. Bryan & Eric A. Bryan. Ed. by Lisa DuPree. (PLCs Ser.). (Illus.). 530p. (Orig.). 1988. pap. text ed. 42.95 (ISBN 0-944107-30-3). Indust Text.
Programmable Controllers for Factory Automation. Johnson. (Manufacturing Engineering Material Processeing). 280p. 1987. 59.75 (ISBN 0-8247-7674-7). Dekker.
Programmable Controllers: Hardware, Software & Applications. George J. Batten, Jr. (Illus.). 300p. 1988. 32.95 (ISBN 0-8306-3147-X, 3147). TAB Bks.
Programmable Controllers: Principles & Applications. John W. Webb. 336p. 1988. case bound 29.95 (ISBN 0-675-20452-6); supplements avail. Merrill.
Programmable Controllers Selected Applications, Vol. 1. Luis A. Bryan & Eric A. Bryan. Ed. by Lisa Dupree. (Selected Application Ser.). (Illus.). 440p. (Orig.). pap. text ed. 49.00 (ISBN 0-944107-25-7). Indust Text.
Programmable Controllers Workbook: PLCs. Luis A. Bryan et al. 260p. pap. text ed. 12.95 (ISBN 0-944107-31-1). Indust Text.
Programmable Controllers 85. (PPL Conference Publication: No. 25). 188p. 1985. pap. 56.00 (ISBN 0-86341-045-6, PC025). Inst Elect Eng.
Programmable Electronic Systems in Safety Related Applications, 2 pts. 1987. pap. text ed. 6.50 ea. (ISBN 0-11-883906-3, HMSO). An Introductory Guide, 17 pgs (ISBN 0-11-883913-6, HM48). General Technical Guidelines, 167 pgs (HM49). UNIPUB.
Programmable Hand Calculator: A Teacher's Tool for Mathematics Classroom Lectures. Bernard Seckler. 207p. (Orig.). 1982. handbk. 15.00 (ISBN 0-686-36869-X). Sigma Pr NY.
Programmable Logic Controllers: Controllers Operation, Interfacing & Programming. J. Den Otter. (Illus.). 304p. 1988. text ed. 36.00 (ISBN 0-13-729575-8). P-H.
Programmable Logic Handbook. Intel Staff. 352p. 1987. pap. 18.00 (ISBN 1-55512-068-7, 296083-002). Intel Corp.
Programmable Logic Handbook, 1988. Intel Staff. 448p. (Orig.). 1988. pap. 18.00 (ISBN 1-55512-028-8). Intel Corp.
Programmatic Elements in the Works of Schoenberg. Walter B. Bailey. Ed. by George Buelow. LC 83-18310. (Studies in Musicology: No. 74). 200p. 1984. 42.95 (ISBN 0-8357-1480-2). UMI Res Pr.
Programmatic German, 2 vols. Foreign Service Institute Staff. (Ger.). 1978. Vol. 1, 647p. 10 audio cassettes incl. 145.00x (ISBN 0-88432-017-0, G141); Vol. 2, 179p. 8 audio cassettes incl. 130.00x (ISBN 0-88432-018-9, G151). J Norton Pubs.
Programmatic Portuguese, Vol. 1. Foreign Service Institute Staff. 783p. (Port.). 1982. plus 16 audio cassettes incl. 185.00x (ISBN 0-88432-019-7, P151). J Norton Pubs.
Programmatic Spanish, 2 vols. Foreign Service Institute Staff. (Span.). 1978. Vol. I, 464p. plus 12 audio cassettes 145.00x (ISBN 0-88432-015-4, S101); Vol. II, 614p. 8 audio cassettes incl. 130.00x (ISBN 0-88432-016-2, S121). J Norton Pubs.
Programme for the Third World War. C. H. Douglas. 59.95 (ISBN 0-8490-0896-4). Gordon Pr.
Programme for the 1960 World Census of Agriculture. 78p. 1957. pap. 5.00 (ISBN 92-5-101723-9, F348, FAO). UNIPUB.
Programme for the 1970 World Census of Agriculture. pap. 15.00 (F1037, FAO). UNIPUB.
Programme for the 1990 World Census of Agriculture. (FAO Statistical Development Ser.: No. 2). (Illus.). 120p. (Orig.). 1986. pap. text ed. 9.50 (ISBN 92-5-102373-5, F2960, FAO). UNIPUB.
Programme: Lowell Musicale & Musical Portrait of the Spindle City. Susanne M. Robertson. (Illus.). 131p. (Orig.). 1986. pap. 8.95 (ISBN 0-9616315-0-3). Euterpe Pr.
Programme-Maker's Handbook or Goodbye Totter TV. Harris Watts. (Illus.). 230p. (Orig.). 1982. pap. 7.50x (ISBN 0-9507582-0-5). Kumarian Pr.
Programme Music in the Last Four Centuries. Frederick Niecks. LC 68-25299. (Studies in Music, No. 42). 1969. Repr. of 1907 ed. lib. bdg. 56.95x (ISBN 0-8383-0311-0). Haskell.
Programme of Industrial Activities Advisory Committee of Salaried Employees & Professional Workers, 8th Session, Geneva, 1981: The Effects of Technological & Structural Changes on the Employment & Working Conditions of Non-Manual Workers, Report II. iv, 117p. (Orig.). 1980. pap. 10.50 (ISBN 92-2-102557-8). Intl Labour Office.

Programme of Industrial Activities: Proceedings. Second Tripartite Technical Meeting for the Clothing Industry, Geneva, September-October 1980. iii, 79p. (Orig.). 1981. pap. 10.50 (ISBN 92-2-102552-7). Intl Labour Office.

Programme of the Communist Party of the Soviet Union. CPSU Central Committee. 88p. 1986. pap. 1.95 (ISBN 0-8285-3161-7, Pub. by Novosti Pr USSR). Imported Pubns.

Programme of the German Green Party. 56p. 1985. 3.50 (ISBN 0-942986-03-2). LongRiver Bks.

Programme on Education & Training. 17p. 1979. pap. 5.00 (ISBN 92-808-0012-4, TUNU016, UNU). UNIPUB.

Programmed Algebra. Bryan Sperry. 358p. 1981. pap. text ed. 18.95 (ISBN 0-8403-2516-9). Kendall-Hunt.

Programmed Approach to Good Spelling! Richard C. Baggett. 160p. 1981. pap. text ed. write for info. (ISBN 0-13-729764-5). P-H.

Programmed Approach to Human Genetics. Allen Vegotsky & Cynthia A. White. LC 73-22395. Repr. of 1974 ed. 41.50 (ISBN 0-8357-9964-6, 2011878). Bks Demand UMI.

Programmed Approach to the Circulatory System. George I. Sackheim. (Illus.). pap. 5.00x (ISBN 0-87563-014-6). Stipes.

Programmed Arabic-Islamic Reader. Raji Rammuny. 1987. manual 10.95x (ISBN 0-86685-413-4); 5.95x (ISBN 0-317-66014-4). Intl Bk Ctr.

Programmed Arabic-Islamic Reader, Bk. 2. Raji M. Rammuny. (Arabic & Islam.). Date not set. 14.95 (ISBN 0-86685-431-2); tchr's. manual 5.95. Intl Bk Ctr.

Programmed Arithmetic. 2nd ed. Robert D. Hackworth & Joseph W. Howland. (Illus.). 410p. (Orig.). 1983. pap. text ed. 18.95x (ISBN 0-943202-08-6). H & H Pub.

Programmed Articulation Therapy: Time to Modify. Cynthia D. Psaltis & Sonja L. Spallato. 248p. 1973. spiral bdg. 28.50 (ISBN 0-398-02745-5). C C Thomas.

Programmed Astronomy: The Solar System. Sullivan & Sullivan. 1972. pap. text ed. 16.00 (ISBN 0-8449-0500-3); tchrs' manual 4.00; test 3.00; Kit Including Text, Test and Teachers Manual. 23.00. Learning Line.

Programmed Blueprint Reading. 3rd ed. Shriver L. Coover. 1975. text ed. 22.92 (ISBN 0-07-013063-9). McGraw.

Programmed Business Mathematics, Bk. 1. 4th ed. Harry Huffman. 1980. pap. 20.20 (ISBN 0-07-030901-9). McGraw.

Programmed Business Mathematics, Bks. 1-3. 5th ed. Harry Huffman. 208p. 1986. Bk. 1, 200p. text ed. 16.25 (ISBN 0-07-030917-5); Bk. 2, 244p. text ed. 17.60 (ISBN 0-07-030918-3); Bk. 3, 200p. text ed. 17.60 (ISBN 0-07-030919-1). McGraw.

Programmed Business Mathematics, Bk. 2. 4th ed. Harry Huffman. (Illus.). 256p. 1980. pap. 20.20 (ISBN 0-07-030902-7). McGraw.

Programmed Business Mathematics, Bk. 3. 4th rev. ed. Harry Huffman. (Illus.). 192p. 1981. pap. 20.20 (ISBN 0-07-030903-5). McGraw.

Programmed Capitalism: A Computer-Mediated Global Society. Maurice Estabrooks. 200p. 1988. text ed. 24.95 (ISBN 0-87332-480-3). M E Sharpe.

Programmed Cleaning Guide. rev. ed. Ed. by Edwin B. Feldman. (Illus.). 1984. pap. text ed. 3.00 (ISBN 0-9601394-2-7). Soap & Detergent.

Programmed College Algebra. Robert D. Hackworth & Joseph W. Howland. (Programmed Algebra Ser.). (Illus.). 535p. 1985. pap. text ed. 23.95x (ISBN 0-943202-11-6). H & H Pub.

Programmed College Vocabulary 3600. 3rd ed. George W. Feinstein. 336p. 1986. pap. text ed. write for info. (ISBN 0-13-729427-1). P-H.

Programmed Course in Modern Literary Arabic Phonology & Script. Ernest McCarus & Raji Rammuny. 1974. 8.00x (ISBN 0-86685-384-7). Intl Bk Ctr.

Programmed Course in Modern Literary Arabic Phonology & Script. rev. ed. Ernest N. McCarus & Raji Rammuny. vi, 175p. 1974. 8.00x (ISBN 0-916798-02-X, Dist. by Intl. Book Ctr.); tapes avail. (Dist. by University of Michigan Media Resources Center). UM Dept NES.

Programmed Ear Training. Leo Horacek & Gerald Lefkoff. Incl. Vol. 1. Intervals. 146p. pap. text ed. 11.00 net (ISBN 0-15-572015-5, HC); 18 tapes 100.00 (ISBN 0-15-572019-8, HC); Vol. 2. Melody & Rhythm. 392p. pap. text ed. 13.00 net (ISBN 0-15-572016-3, HC); 25 tapes 120.00 (ISBN 0-15-572020-1, HC); Vol. 3. Chords, Part 1. 276p. pap. text ed. 11.00 net (ISBN 0-15-572017-1, HC); 14 tapes 75.00 (ISBN 0-15-572021-X, HC); Vol. 4. Chords, Part 2. 392p. pap. text ed. 13.00 net (ISBN 0-15-572018-X, HC); 18 tapes 100.00 (ISBN 0-15-572022-8, HC). (Prog. Bk.). 1970. instr's. manual avail. (ISBN 0-15-572023-6, HC); tests avail. (ISBN 0-15-572024-4, HC); pap. HarBraceJ.

Programmed French Readers, 4 bks. Hugh D. Campbell & Camille Bauer. Incl. Bk. 1. Contes pour Debutants. 1965. pap. text ed. 13.96 (ISBN 0-395-04258-5); Bk. 2. Arsene Lupin. 1965. pap. text ed. 13.96 (ISBN 0-395-04259-3); Bk. 3. Robe et le Couteau. 1966. pap. text ed. 13.96 (ISBN 0-395-04264-X); Bk. 4. Dynamite. 1970. pap. text ed. 13.96 (ISBN 0-395-04265-8). pap. HM.

Programmed French Reading & Writing I. Eliane Burroughs. 1971. pap. text ed. 22.00 (ISBN 0-8449-1700-1); tchrs' manual 2.00; test 1.50; Kit Includes Text, Test and Teachers Manual. 25.50. Learning Line.

Programmed French Reading & Writing II. Eliane Burroughs. 1964. pap. text ed. 18.00 (ISBN 0-8449-1704-4); tchrs' manual 2.00; test 1.50; Kit Includes Text, Test and Teachers Manual. 25.00. Learning Line.

Programmed French Reading & Writing III. Eliane Burroughs. 1972. pap. text ed. 22.00 (ISBN 0-8449-1708-7); tchrs' manual 2.00; test 1.50; Kit includes Text, Test and Teachers Manual. 25.50. Learning Line.

Programmed Functional Anatomy. Glynn A. Leyshon. (Illus.). 1984. pap. text ed. 11.80x (ISBN 0-87563-249-1). Stipes.

Programmed Gregg Shorthand. Russell J. Hosler et al. (Diamond Jubilee Ser.). (Experimental Ed). 1969. text ed. 34.75 (ISBN 0-07-030440-8). McGraw.

Programmed Guide T-A 6FAT. Dobyns. 1986. pap. text ed. 12.00 (ISBN 0-87150-984-9, 33L2985, Prindle). PWS Kent Pub.

Programmed Guide T-A 6FCA. Dobyns. 1986. pap. text ed. 10.50 (ISBN 0-87150-920-2, 33L3015, Prindle). PWS Kent Pub.

Programmed Guide to Increasing Church Attendance. Jimmie Gentle & Dwight Peter Richard. 1980. 10.75 (ISBN 0-89536-446-8, 1641). CSS of Ohio.

Programmed Guide to Tax Research. 3rd ed. James E. Parker & Don C. Marshall. LC 86-7311. 335p. 1986. 15.75 (ISBN 0-534-06042-0). PWS Kent Pub.

Programmed Guide to Tax Research. 2nd ed. James E. Parker & Michael J. Tucker. LC 83-4334. 352p. 1984. pap. text ed. 14.25 (ISBN 0-534-01400-3). PWS Kent Pub.

Programmed Hebrew Series, 2 vols. David Bridger. Incl. Vol. 1. 1971. pap. text ed. 3.50x (ISBN 0-87441-079-7); Vol. 2. 1971. pap. text ed. 3.50x (ISBN 0-87441-080-0). (Reshit Tefillah V'lashon). 62p. (Prog. Bk.). pap. Behrman.

Programmed Instruction. Donald H. Bullock. Ed. by Danny G. Langdon. LC 77-25108. (Instructional Design Library). (Illus.). 112p. 1978. 23.95 (ISBN 0-87778-118-4). Educ Tech Pubns.

Programmed Instruction: Bold New Venture. Ed. by Allen D. Calvin. LC 69-15993. pap. 65.00 (ISBN 0-317-07895-X, 2050121). Bks Demand UMI.

Programmed Instruction in West Africa & the Arab States: A Report on Two Training Workshops (UNESCO) P. Kenneth Komoski & Edward J. Green. (Education Studies & Documents: No. 52). pap. 15.00 (ISBN 0-8115-1376-9). Kraus Repr.

Programmed Instruction Manual of the Human Muscle System. Engerbretson. 176p. 1985. pap. text ed. 14.95 (ISBN 0-8403-3535-0). Kendall-Hunt.

Programmed Introduction to Bowling. Les Palmer. 96p. 1975. pap. 7.95 (ISBN 0-8403-1103-6). Kendall-Hunt.

Programmed Introduction to Dynamics, 2 vols. 2nd ed. Clyde E. Work. LC 75-37492. (Illus.). 1976. pap. text ed. 21.50 (ISBN 0-916572-00-5). Aylsworth.

Programmed Introduction to Gas-Liquid Chromatography. 2nd ed. James B. Pattison. (Illus.). 320p. pap. 83.20 (2030427). Bks Demand UMI.

Programmed Introduction to General & Physical Chemistry. Derrick E. Hoare. LC 67-27670. (Illus.). Repr. of 1967 ed. 28.40 (ISBN 0-8357-9965-4, 2013982). Bks Demand UMI.

Programmed Introduction to Infrared Spectroscopy. B. W. Cook & K. Jones. 207p. 1972. 59.95 (ISBN 0-471-25644-7, Pub. by Wiley Hayden). Wiley.

Programmed Introduction to PERT: Program Evaluation & Review Technique. Federal Electric Corporation Staff. 145p. 1963. pap. 39.95x (ISBN 0-471-25680-3, Pub. by Wiley-Interscience). Wiley.

Programmed Introduction to Probability. John R. Dixon. LC 78-25984. 420p. 1979. pap. text ed. 18.50 (ISBN 0-88275-825-X). Krieger.

Programmed Introduction to Statics, 2 vols. 3rd ed. Clyde E. Work. LC 75-37493. (Illus.). 1978. pap. text ed. 20.50 (ISBN 0-916572-01-3). Aylsworth.

Programmed Introduction to Statics, 2 vols. 4th ed. Clyde E. Work. LC 84-70236. (Illus.). 1984. pap. text ed. 20.50 (ISBN 0-916572-02-1). Aylsworth.

Programmed Introduction to Statistics. 2nd ed. Freeman F. Elzey. LC 79-161489. 385p. (Orig.). 1971. pap. text ed. 15.75 pub net (ISBN 0-8185-0018-2). instr's manual avail. (ISBN 0-685-23471-1). Brooks-Cole.

Programmed Introduction to the Game of Chess. M. W. Sullivan. 1972. text ed. 7.00 (ISBN 0-8449-1800-8). Learning Line.

Programmed Introduction to the Study of Law, Pt. 1. Case Skills. Charles D. Kelso. 700p. 1965. 23.00x (ISBN 0-672-81012-3, Bobbs-Merrill Law). Michie Co.

Programmed Introduction to Upper Gastrointestinal Radiology. Stephen L. Gammill. 1977. pap. text ed. 22.00 (ISBN 0-316-30294-5). Little.

Programmed Journalism Editing. new ed. James P. Alexander. (Illus.). (gr. 10-12). 1979. pap. text ed. 9.50x (ISBN 0-8138-1040-X). Iowa St U Pr.

Programmed Journalism Writing. James P. Alexander. 1979. pap. text ed. 12.95x (ISBN 0-8138-1020-5). Iowa St U Pr.

Programmed Language & Speech Correction Through Perceptual Activities. Bernice E. Heasley & Jacqueline R. Grosklos. (Illus.). 136p. 1980. spiral (lexotone) 18.50 (ISBN 0-398-03956-9). C C Thomas.

Programmed Learning: A Bibliography of Programs & Presentation Devices. 4th ed. Carl H. Hendershot. LC 67-16988. (Incl. suppl. 1-6). 1971. 45.00 (ISBN 0-911832-04-1). Hendershot.

Programmed Learning: A Bibliography of Programs & Presentation Devices. 2nd ed. Compiled by Carl H. Hendershot. 1963. 15.00 (ISBN 0-911832-12-2). Hendershot.

Programmed Learning: A Bibliography of Programs & Presentation Devices. 3rd ed. Compiled by Carl H. Hendershot. LC 64-11824. (Illus.). 1965. 30.00 (ISBN 0-911832-11-4). Hendershot.

Programmed Learning Aid for United States History to 1877. James Shenton & Alan M. Meckler. Ed. by Roger M. Hermanson. (Irwin Programmed Learning Aid Ser.). pap. 61.80 (ISBN 0-317-26327-7, 2024234). Bks Demand UMI.

Programmed Learning & Individually Paced Instruction Bibliography: Inc. Suppl. 1-6, 2 vols. 5th ed. Carl H. Hendershot. 1985. Set. 105.50 (ISBN 0-911832-16-5); supplement 6 35.50 (ISBN 0-911832-15-7). Hendershot.

Programmed Material on Legal Research & Citation: Legal Research & Citation Student Library Exercises. 2nd ed. Larry L. Teply. (American Casebook Ser.). 99p. 1986. 5.95 (ISBN 0-314-26685-2). West Pub.

Programmed Materials on Legal Research & Citation. 2nd ed. Larry L. Teply. (American Casebook Ser.). 358p. 1986. pap. text ed. 13.95 (ISBN 0-314-25477-3). West Pub.

Programmed Math: Grade 1. Fred Justus. (Math Ser.). 24p. 1976. wkbk. 5.00 (ISBN 0-8209-0127-X, PM-1). ESP.

Programmed Math: Grade 2. Fred Justus. (Math Ser.). 24p. 1976. wkbk. 5.00 (ISBN 0-8209-0128-8, PM-2). ESP.

Programmed Math: Grade 3. Fred Justus. (Math Ser.). 24p. 1980. wkbk. 5.00 (ISBN 0-8209-0129-6, PM-3). ESP.

Programmed Math: Grade 4. Fred Justus. (Math Ser.). 24p. wkbk. 5.00 (ISBN 0-8209-0130-X, PM-4). ESP.

Programmed Math: Grade 5. Fred Justus. (Math Ser.). 24p. 1977. wkbk. 5.00 (ISBN 0-8209-0131-8, PM-5). ESP.

Programmed Math: Grade 6. Fred Justus. (Math Ser.). 24p. 1979. wkbk. 5.00 (ISBN 0-8209-0132-6, PM-6). ESP.

Programmed Math: Grade 7. Fred Justus. (Math Ser.). 24p. 1977. 5.00 (ISBN 0-8209-0133-4, PM-7). ESP.

Programmed Math: Grade 8. Fred Justus. (Math Ser.). 24p. 1977. wkbk. 5.00 (ISBN 0-8209-0134-2, PM-8). ESP.

Programmed Math: Kindergarten. Fred Justus. (Math Ser.). 24p. 1977. wkbk. 5.00 (ISBN 0-8209-0126-1, PM-R). ESP.

Programmed Mathematics of Drugs & Solutions. rev. ed. Mabel E. Weaver et al. 128p. 1984. pap. text ed. 10.95 (ISBN 0-397-54475-8, 64-04164, Lippincott Nursing). Lippincott.

Programmed Mathematics Series, Bks. 9-15. 2nd ed. Sullivan Associates Staff. 1975. 6.64 ea. McGraw.

Programmed News Style. Blanche G. Prejean & Wayne A. Danielson. (Basic Skills in Journalism Ser.). 1978. pap. text ed. write for info (ISBN 0-13-730655-5). P-H.

Programmed News Style. Blanche G. Prejean & Wayne A. Danielson. 144p. 1988. pap. text ed. price not set (ISBN 0-13-729070-5). P-H.

Programmed Newswriting. John L. Griffith & Edward G. Weston. (Basic Skills in Journalism Ser.). (Illus.). 1978. pap. text ed. write for info (ISBN 0-13-730630-X). P-H.

Programmed Power Phonics: A Simplified Method of Word Identification. Gary Anderson & Nancy Watson. 192p. 1978. pap. 14.95 (ISBN 0-8403-1882-0). Kendall-Hunt.

Programmed Problem Solving for First Year Chemistry. Arnold B. Loebel. LC 82-83359. 512p. 1983. 23.56 (ISBN 0-395-32626-5). HM.

Programmed Proofreading. 2nd ed. Thadys J. Dewar & H. Frances Daniels. 208p. 1987. write for info. (ISBN 0-538-23020-7, WO2). SW Pub.

Programmed Review for Electrical Engineers. 2nd ed. James Bentley & Karen A. Hess. 1984. 33.95 (ISBN 0-442-21628-9). Van Nos Reinhold.

Programmed Review of Engineering Fundamentals. Allen J. Baldwin & Karen M. Hess. 287p. 1982. pap. 23.95 (ISBN 0-442-21389-1). Van Nos Reinhold.

Programmed Rudiments of Music. Robert W. Ottman & Frank D. Mainous. 1979. pap. write for info. (ISBN 0-13-729962-1). P-H.

Programmed Spelling. Judith M. Smith et al. Ed. by Donald E. Smith. (Michigan Learning Modules Ser.: No. 4). 1978. pap. 4.95x (ISBN 0-914004-07-7). Ulrich.

Programmed Spelling Demons. 2nd ed. George W. Feinstein. 240p. 1985. pap. text ed. write for info (ISBN 0-13-729211-2). P-H.

Programmed Text in Statistics, 4 bks. J. Hine & G. B. Wetherill. 1975. pap. 10.95x ea. (NO. 6152, Pub. by Chapman & Hall England); Bk. 1, Summarizing Data. (ISBN 0-412-13590-6, NO. 6152); Bk. 2, Basic Theory. (ISBN 0-412-13730-5, NO. 6431); Bk. 3, The T-text & X-squared Goodness Of Fit. (ISBN 0-412-13740-2, NO. 6153); Bk. 4, Tests On Variance & Regression. (ISBN 0-412-13750-X, NO. 6154). Routledge Chapman & Hall.

Programmed Therapy for Stuttering in Children & Adults. Bruce P. Ryan. (Illus.). 200p. 1980. spiral bdg. 23.00x (ISBN 0-398-03104-5). C C Thomas.

Programmed to Learn: An Essay on the Evolution of Culture. H. Ronald Pulliam & Christopher Dunford. LC 79-17941. (Illus.). 1980. 21.00x (ISBN 0-231-04838-6). Columbia U Pr.

Programmed Topics in General Chemistry. Armine Paul. 1981. 9.25 (ISBN 0-88252-095-4). Paladin Hse.

Programmed Topics in Organic & Biochemistry. Armine D. Paul. 1981. coil bdg. 6.75 (ISBN 0-88252-060-1). Paladin Hse.

Programmed Vocabulary. 3rd ed. James I. Brown. (The CPD Approach). 1980. pap. text ed. write for info (ISBN 0-13-729707-6). P-H.

Programmed Word Attack for Teachers. Robert M. Wilson & Maryanne Hall. 1984. pap. text ed. 17.95 (ISBN 0-675-20122-5). Merrill.

Programmed Workbook see Spanish: A Modular Approach.

Programmed Writing Skills. George W. Feinstein. 1976. pap. write for info (ISBN 0-13-730523-0); free instr's. manual of tests 0.00 (ISBN 0-13-730515-X). P-H.

Programmer. Bruce Jackson. 224p. 1981. pap. 2.25 (ISBN 0-345-29079-8). Ballantine.

Programmer. Jack Rudman. (Career Examination Ser.: C-1430). (Cloth bdg. avail. on request). pap. 16.00 (ISBN 0-8373-1430-5). Natl Learning.

Programmer - Programmer Analyst. Jack Rudman. (Career Examination Ser.: C-1439). 1988. pap. 16.00 (ISBN 0-8373-1439-9). Natl Learning.

Programmer Aptitude Test (PAT) Jack Rudman. (Career Examination Ser.: C-643). (Cloth bdg. avail. on request). pap. 15.00 (ISBN 0-8373-0643-4). Natl Learning.

Programmer Library. Jeffrey Cooper. (DBASE C Tools Ser.). (Orig.). 1985. pap. 89.95 (ISBN 0-912677-79-1). Ashton-Tate Pub.

Programmer Productivity. Girish Parikh. 1984. text ed. 36.33 (ISBN 0-8359-5650-4, Reston). P-H.

Programmer Productivity: Myths, Methods & Murphy's Law. Lowell J. Arthur. 288p. 1984. pap. 18.95 (ISBN 0-471-81493-8, Pub. by Wiley-Interscience). Wiley.

Programmer Trainee. Jack Rudman. (Career Examination Ser.: C-1431). (Cloth bdg. avail. on request). pap. 14.00 (ISBN 0-8373-1431-3). Natl Learning.

Programmers & Managers: The Routinization of Computer Programming in the United States. Philip Kraft. LC 77-1667. (Illus.). 1977. pap. 16.00 (ISBN 0-387-90248-1). Springer-Verlag.

Programmer's ANSI COBOL Reference Manual. 2nd ed. Donald A. Sordillo. (Illus.). 416p. 1988. text ed. 40.00 (ISBN 0-13-729633-9). P-H.

Programmer's Apple, Mac Sourcebook. Thom Hogan. 1989. softcover 22.95 (ISBN 1-55615-168-3). Microsoft.

Programmers at Work. Ed. by Susan Lammers. (At Work Ser.). 392p. 1986. 19.95 (ISBN 1-55615-014-8); pap. 14.95 (ISBN 0-914845-71-3). Microsoft.

Programmer's Book of Rules. Ledin & Ledin. pap. 19.95 (ISBN 0-317-64257-X). Van Nos Reinhold.

Programmer's Book of Rules. George Ledin, Jr. & Victor Ledin. LC 79-13746. 248p. 1979. pap. 12.95 (ISBN 0-534-97993-9, Lifetime Learn). Van Nos Reinhold.

Programmer's CP-M Handbook. Andy Johnson-Laird. 750p. (Orig.). 1983. pap. text ed. 22.95 (ISBN 0-07-881103-1). Osborne-McGraw.

Programmer's Desk Reference for Your Commodore 64. Mona Reinhardt. write for info. P-H.

Programmer's Essential OS-2 Handbook. David E. Cortesi. (Illus.). 720p. (Orig.). 1988. pap. 24.95 (ISBN 0-934375-82-8); Book & disk. 39.95 (ISBN 0-934375-89-5). M & T Pub Inc.

Programmer's Geometry. Adrian Bowyer & John Woodwark. (Illus.). 160p. 1983. text ed. 42.95 (ISBN 0-408-01303-6); pap. text ed. 24.95 (ISBN 0-408-01242-0). Butterworth.

Programmer's Guide to C. John Lees & Stephanie Rosenhaum. write for info. P-H.

Programmer's Guide to Cobol. Harrison. 26.95 (ISBN 0-317-64258-8). Van Nos Reinhold.

Programmer's Guide to Common LISP. Deborah G. Tatar. (Illus.). 352p. 1987. pap. text ed. 23.00x (ISBN 0-932376-87-8, EY-6706E-OP). Digital Pr.

Programmers Guide to FORTRAN: A Second Choice. Micheal H. Pressman. 400p. 1988. pap. text ed. write for info. (ISBN 0-697-07835-3); Solution Manual. instr's. manual avail. (ISBN 0-697-07836-1). Wm C Brown.

Programmer's Guide to GEM. Phillip Balma & William Fitler. 504p. (Orig.). 1986. pap. 19.95 (ISBN 0-89588-297-3). Sybex.

Programmer's Guide to LISP. Ken Tracton. (Illus.). 1979. 13.95 (ISBN 0-8306-9761-6, 1045). TAB Bks.

Programmer's Guide to MS-DOS. rev. ed. Dennis N. Jump. 1987. pap. 21.95 (ISBN 0-13-729096-9). P-H.

Programmer's Guide to Object-Oriented Programming in Common LISP. Sonya E. Keene. (Illus.). 256p. 1988. pap. text ed. 26.95x (ISBN 0-201-17589-4). Addison-Wesley.

Programmer's Guide to OS-2. Michael J. Young. 525p. (Orig.). 1988. pap. 24.95 (ISBN 0-89588-464-X). Sybex.

Programmer's Guide to PC & PS-2 Video Systems: Maximum Video Performance from the EGA, VGA, HGC, & MCGA. Richard Wilton. 544p. 1987. pap. 24.95 (ISBN 1-55615-103-9). Microsoft.

Programmer's Guide to the Amiga. Robert A. Peck. 310p. (Orig.). 1987. pap. 24.95 (ISBN 0-89588-310-4). SYBEX.

Programmer's Guide to the EGA & VGA Cards. Richard F. Ferraro. 1988. pap. 29.95 (ISBN 0-201-12692-3). Addison-Wesley.

Programmer's Guide to the EGA-VGA. George Sutty & Steve Blair. (Illus.). 300p. 1988. pap. 39.95 with disk (ISBN 0-13-729039-X). Brady Comp Bks.

Programmer's Guide to the Hercules Graphics Cards. David B. Doty. 1988. pap. 24.95 (ISBN 0-201-11885-8). Addison-Wesley.

Programmer's Guide to the UNIX System. Rebecca Thomas & Jean Yates. 496p. 1983. cancelled (ISBN 0-201-08849-5). Addison-Wesley.

Programmer's Guide to the Z80 Chip. Phillip R. Robinson. (Illus.). 364p. (Orig.). 1984. pap. 13.50 (ISBN 0-8306-1656-X, 1656). TAB Bks.

Programmer's Guide to Turbo C. Donna Mosich & Ben Elizer. 1988. pap. 21.95 (ISBN 0-471-63742-4). Wiley.

Programmer's Guide to Video Display Terminals. David Stephens. 335p. (Orig.). 1985. pap. 30.00 (ISBN 0-936158-01-8). Atlan Pub Corp.

Programmer's Guide to Windows. 2nd ed. Durant et al. 750p. 1988. pap. 24.95 (ISBN 0-89588-496-8). Sybex.

Programmers' Handbook of Computer Printer Commands: For Printer Models Through 1984. Ed. by Mary Lou East & Fred B. East. 1985. pap. 37.95 (ISBN 0-932065-00-7). Cardinal Pt.

Programmers' Handbook of Computer Printer Commands-11: For Printer Models As New As 1985, Vol. 2. Ed. by Mary Lou East & Fred B. East. 196p. (Orig.). 1986. pap. 26.95 (ISBN 0-932065-25-2). Cardinal Pt.

Programmer's Introduction to SNOBOL. W. D. Maurer. LC 75-26837. (Elsevier Computer Science Library Ser.: No. 3). 142p. 1976. (North Holland); pap. 26.00 (ISBN 0-444-00172-7). Elsevier.

Programmer's Introduction to SNOBOL. Ward D. Maurer. LC 75-26837. (Programming Languages Ser. (Elsevier Computer Sciences Library)). pap. 37.80 (2026270). Bks Demand UMI.

Programmer's Introduction to the Apple IIGS. Apple Computer Incorporated Staff. (Apple Technical Library). 1988. 32.95 (ISBN 0-201-17745-5). Addison-Wesley.

Programmer's Introduction to the Macintosh Family. Apple Computer, Incorporated Staff. (Illus.). 256p. 1987. 24.95 (ISBN 0-201-19254-3). Addison-Wesley.

Programmer's Notebook. James Keogh. 356p. 1984. pap. 10.95 (ISBN 0-671-47066-3, Pub. by Computer Bks). S&S.

Programmer's Notebook: Utilities for the CP-M-80. David Cortesi. 1983. pap. 19.95 (ISBN 0-8359-5641-5, Reston); incl. disk 35.95. P-H.

Programmer's PC Sourcebook: Reference Tables for the IBM PCs & Compatibles, PS-2 Machines & DOS. Thom Hogan. 560p. 1988. cancelled (ISBN 1-55615-106-3); pap. 24.95 (ISBN 1-55615-118-7). Microsoft.

Programmer's Problem Solver for the IBM PC, XT & AT. Robert L. Jourdain. (Illus.). 320p. 1985. pap. 22.95 (ISBN 0-89303-787-7). Brady Comp Bks.

Programmers Reference Guide For the Atari 400-800 Computers. David Heiserman. LC 83-51616. 21.95 (ISBN 0-672-22277-9). Sams.

Programmer's Reference Guide for the Commodore Plus-4. Cyndie Merten & Sarah Meyer. (Illus.). 464p. 1986. pap. 21.95 (ISBN 0-673-18249-5). Scott F.

Programmer's Reference Guide to Expert Systems. David Hu. 350p. 1987. pap. 19.95 (ISBN 0-672-22566-2). Sams.

Programmer's Reference Guide to the Color Computer. C. Regena. 176p. (Orig.). 1984. pap. 12.95 (ISBN 0-942386-19-1). Compute Pubns.

Programmers Reference Manual - 80286 & 80287. rev. ed. Intel Staff. Orig. Title: APX 286 Programmers Reference Manual. 576p. 1987. pap. 22.00 (ISBN 1-55512-055-5, 210498). Intel Corp.

Programmer's Reference Manual for IBM Personal Computers. Steven Armbrust & Ted Forgeron. 250p. 1987. 30.00 (ISBN 0-87094-765-6). Dow Jones-Irwin.

Programmer's Survival Guide: Career Strategies for Computer Professionals. Janet L. Ruhl. 280p. 1988. pap. 16.95 (ISBN 0-13-730375-0). P-H.

Programmer's Toolbox. Jack Emmerichs. LC 84-3196. 418p. 1984. pap. 19.95 (ISBN 0-88056-303-6). Weber Systems.

Programmer's Toolbox. Jack Emmerichs. 300p. pap. 19.95 (ISBN 0-517-56383-5). Crown.

Programmer's View of the Intel 432 System. E. I. Organick. 432p. 1983. text ed. 35.95 (ISBN 0-07-047719-1). McGraw.

Programmes for Animation Fifty-Seven: Handbook for Animation Technicians. B. Salt. 1978. text ed. 230.00 (ISBN 0-08-023153-5). Pergamon.

Programmes of Analysis of Mortality Trends & Levels: Report. UN-WHO Meeting. Geneva, 1968. (Technical Report Ser.: No. 440). (Also avail. in French, Russian & Spanish). 1970. pap. 2.00 (ISBN 92-4-120440-0). World Health.

Programmes to Promote Breastfeeding. Ed. by Derrick B. Jelliffe & E. Patrice Jelliffe. (Illus.). 500p. 1988. pap. 31.50 (ISBN 0-19-261457-6). Oxford U Pr.

Programmgesteuerte Digitale Rechengerate. H. Rutishauser et al. (MIM Ser.: No. 2). (Illus.). 102p. (Ger.). 1958. pap. 13.95x (ISBN 0-8176-0321-2). Birkhauser.

Programmimg Languages. 2nd ed. Allen B. Tucker. (Computer Science Ser.). 915p. 1985. text ed. 43.95 (ISBN 0-07-065416-6). McGraw.

Programmimg Using VAX Basic. Wayne Muller. 320p. 1985. pap. text ed. 18.95 (ISBN 0-317-38895-9). P-H.

Programming: An Introduction to Computer Techniques. rev. 2nd ed. Ward D. Maurer. LC 70-188126. (Illus.). 1972. text ed. 32.95x (ISBN 0-8162-5453-2). Holden Day.

Programming & Design Handbook-80386. Penn Brumm & Don Brumm. (Illus.). 448p. 1987. 29.95 (ISBN 0-8306-0937-7, 2937, TAB-TPR); pap. 19.95 (ISBN 0-8306-2937-8). TAB Bks.

Programming & Distribution in the New Video Marketplace. LC 86-224329. Date not set. price not set. Amer Bar Assn.

Programming & Interfacing the Sixty-Five Two, with Experiments. Marvin De Jong. LC 79-67130. 416p. 1980. pap. 17.95 (ISBN 0-672-21651-5, 21651). Sams.

Programming & Interregional Input-Output Analysis: An Application to the Problem of Industrial Location in India. A. Ghosh. LC 72-76092. (University of Cambridge, Dept. of Applied Economics, Monograph: 22). pap. 28.00 (ISBN 0-317-26405-2, 2024461). Bks Demand UMI.

Programming & Metaprograming in the Human Biocomputer. John C. Lilly. 192p. 1987. pap. 9.95 (Julian Pr). Crown.

Programming & Problem Solving: A Second Course with Pascal. Lawrence H. Miller. 624p. 1986. text ed. write for info. (ISBN 0-201-05531-7); instr's. manual avail. (ISBN 0-201-05579-1). Addison-Wesley.

Programming & Problem-Solving in Modula-2. Sanford Leestma & Larry Nyhoff. 873p. 1989. write for info. (ISBN 0-02-369691-5). Macmillan.

Programming Apple BASIC. John DiElsi et al. 1984. 19.95 (ISBN 0-03-063733-3). HR&W.

Programming Approach to Computability. A. J. Kfoury et al. (Texts & Monographs in Computer Science). (Illus.). 208p. 1982. 32.00 (ISBN 0-387-90743-2). Springer-Verlag.

Programming Assembler Language. 2nd ed. Peter Abel. 1984. text ed. 34.00 (ISBN 0-8359-5661-X, Reston). P-H.

Programming Business Applications in FORTRAN IV. Phillip T. May. LC 72-7634. 1973. pap. text ed. 25.95 (ISBN 0-395-14047-1); solutions manual 1.75 (ISBN 0-395-17159-8). HM.

Programming Business Systems with BASIC. David R. Adams & William E. Leigh. 1984. text ed. write for info. (ISBN 0-538-10980-7, J98). SW Pub.

Programming by Design: A First Course in Structured Programming. special ed. Philip L. Miller & Lee W. Miller. 567p. 1987. pap. text ed. write for info. (ISBN 0-534-08244-0). Wadsworth Pub.

Programming Byte by Byte: Structured FORTRAN 77. 2nd; rev. ed. Bijan Mashaw. 540p. (Orig.). 1987. pap. 27.95 (ISBN 0-934433-02-X). Am Comp Pr.

Programming C on the Macintosh. Terry A. Ward. (Illus.). 384p. 1986. pap. 21.95 (ISBN 0-673-18274-6). Scott F.

Programming Commodore Graphics with Your 64 or 128. John M. Lane. (Illus.). 224p. 1985. pap. 14.95 (ISBN 0-673-18084-0). Scott F.

Programming Concepts. K. LaBudde. 384p. 1987. pap. text ed. 23.95 (ISBN 0-07-035778-1). McGraw.

Programming Concepts: A Second Course. William B. Jones. (Illus.). 336p. 1982. text ed. write for info (ISBN 0-13-729970-2). P-H.

Programming Concepts & Problem Solving: An Introduction to Computer Science Using Pascal. Peter Linz. 1983. 34.95 (ISBN 0-8053-5710-6); Instr's guide with transparency masters. 4.95 (ISBN 0-8053-5711-4). Benjamin-Cummings.

Programming Concepts with the Ada Reference Manual. Roy S. Freedman. (Illus.). 128p. 1982. pap. text ed. 12.95 (ISBN 0-89433-190-6). Petrocelli.

Programming Customs Applications with Symphony's Command Language. Lawrence M. Honig. 288p. 1986. pap. write for info. (ISBN 0-394-74119-6, RanC). Random.

Programming Dedicated Microprocessors. Colin Walls. (Computer Science Ser.). (Illus.). 198p. (Orig.). 1987. pap. text ed. 22.50x (ISBN 0-333-40952-3). Scholium Intl.

Programming Development Language. Wesley James. 34p. (Orig.). 1985. pap. 5.00 (ISBN 0-935393-04-8). Write Protect.

Programming Digital's Personal Computer: BASIC. Howard Bomze. 1986. text ed. 17.75 (ISBN 0-03-063729-5). HR&W.

Programming Effective Human Services: Strategies for Institutional Change & Client Transition. Ed. by Walter P. Christian et al. 538p. 1984. 49.50x (ISBN 0-306-41526-7, Plenum Pr). Plenum Pub.

Programming Electronic Switching Systems, No. 3. M. T. Hills & S. Kano. (IEE Telecommunications Series). 215p. 1975. casebound 56.00 (ISBN 0-901223-80-8, TE003). Inst Elect Eng.

Programming Embedded Microprocessors: A High-Level Language Solution. R. J. Foulger. 240p. 1982. pap. 27.35 (ISBN 0-471-89421-4). Wiley.

Programming Expert Systems in MODULA-2. Brian Sawyer & Dennis Foster. LC 86-1671. 186p. 1986. pap. 19.95 (ISBN 0-471-84267-2). Wiley.

Programming Expert Systems in Modula 2. Brian Sawyer & Dennis Foster. LC 86-18898. 201p. 1986. pap. 24.95 (ISBN 0-471-85036-5). Wiley.

Programming Expert Systems in OPS5: An Introduction to Rule-Based Programming. Lee Browston et al. (Artificial Intellegence Ser.). 1985. text ed. write for info. (ISBN 0-201-10647-7). Addison-Wesley.

Programming for Agricultural Development. (Agricultural Planning Studies: No. 1). 57p. (Eng., Fr. & Span., 5th Printing 1976). 1963. pap. 7.50 (ISBN 92-5-100814-0, F2058, FAO). UNIPUB.

Programming for Digital Computers. J. F. Davison. (Illus.). 186p. 1962. 66.00 (ISBN 0-677-00210-6). Gordon & Breach.

Programming for Microcomputers: Apple II BASIC. June G. Shane. LC 83-8163. 432p. 1983. pap. text ed. 25.56 (ISBN 0-395-35206-1); Grid sheet bklt. 5.96 (ISBN 0-395-35207-X). HM.

Programming for Non-Programmers. Donald A. Sordillo. (Illus.). 190p. 1987. 29.95 (ISBN 0-89433-287-2, NO. 8226); pap. 21.95 (ISBN 0-89433-299-6). Petrocelli.

Programming for Numerical Control Machines. 2nd ed. Arthur Roberts & Richard Prentice. (Illus.). 1978. text ed. 39.95x (ISBN 0-07-053156-0). McGraw.

Programming for Radio & Television. rev. ed. V. Jackson Smith. LC 82-21887. (Illus.). 180p. 1983. lib. bdg. 25.25 (ISBN 0-8191-2887-2); pap. text ed. 10.00 (ISBN 0-8191-2888-0). U Pr of Amer.

Programming for School-Age Child Care: A Children's Literature Based Guide. Melba Hawkins. 225p. 1987. lib. bdg. 23.50 (ISBN 0-87287-555-5). Libs Unl.

Programming for Software Sharing. D. T. Muxworthy. 1983. lib. bdg. 39.50 (ISBN 90-2771-547-5, Pub. by Reidel Holland). Kluwer Academic.

Programming for the Liberal Arts: An Introduction to PL-C. Cynthia Spencer. LC 85-11775. 120p. pap. 9.95 (ISBN 0-8226-0391-8, Helix). Rowman.

Programming for the Social Sciences: Algorithms & FORTRAN 77 Coding. Ed. by Richard S. Lehman. 588p. 1986. text ed. 59.95 (ISBN 0-89859-588-6). L Erlbaum Assocs.

Programming FORTRAN 77. J. N. Hume & R. C. Holt. (Illus.). 1979. pap. text ed. write for info. (ISBN 0-8359-5671-7, Reston). P-H.

Programming from First Principles. Richard Bornat. (Illus.). 480p. 1987. pap. text ed. 31.00 (ISBN 0-13-729104-3). P-H.

Programming Halo Graphics in C. Robert J. Traister. (Illus.). 128p. 1985. pap. text ed. 21.95 (ISBN 0-13-729310-0). P-H.

Programming IBM Assembly Language. Paul Massie. (Illus.). 500p. 1985. pap. text ed. write for info. (ISBN 0-8087-6405-5). Burgess MN Intl.

Programming Ideas for Target Populations. 106p. 1984. 15.00 (ISBN 0-317-36935-0, C-070800). Am Hospital.

Programming in Ada. 2nd ed. Barnes. 300p. (Orig.). 1983. pap. 25.95 (ISBN 0-201-13799-2). Addison-Wesley.

Programming in Ada. Richard Wiener & Richard Sincovec. 345p. 1983. 34.95 (ISBN 0-471-87089-7). Wiley.

Programming in Ada: A First Course. Robert G. Clark. 350p. 1985. 42.50 (ISBN 0-521-25728-X); pap. 18.95 (ISBN 0-521-27675-6). Cambridge U Pr.

Programming in ANSI C. Stephen Kochan. 400p. 1988. pap. 24.95 (ISBN 0-672-48408-0). Sams.

Programming in Assembly Language. Heath Company Staff. (Illus.). 1979. 49.95 (ISBN 0-87119-085-0, EC-1108). Heathkit-Zenith Ed.

Programming in Assembly Language: Macro-11. Edward F. Sowell. LC 83-3774. (Computer Science Ser.). (Illus.). 512p. 1984. write for info. (ISBN 0-201-07788-4). Addison-Wesley.

Programming in Assembly Language: VAX 11. Edward F. Sowell. LC 86-26577. 1987. text ed. 35.50 (ISBN 0-201-10886-0). Addison-Wesley.

Programming in BASIC. Jerry Cummins et al. 1983. 15.40 (ISBN 0-675-05650-0). Merrill.

Programming in BASIC. M. K. Goel. 204p. 1987. text ed. 20.00x (ISBN 81-207-0650-1, Pub. by Sterling Pubs India). Apt Bks.

Programming in BASIC. Christopher Lampton. LC 83-6483. (Computer Awareness First Bks.). (Illus.). 96p. (gr. 5 up). 1983. PLB 10.40 (ISBN 0-531-04644-3). Watts.

Programming in BASIC. Margaret McRitchie. 1982. pap. text ed. 26.95 (ISBN 0-03-061376-0). HR&W.

Programming in BASIC: A Structured Approach. Matthew H. Stern & Mark Cashman. (Pick: the Easy Way Ser.). (Illus.). 350p. (Orig.). 1988. pap. 27.95 (ISBN 0-936477-03-2). Comp Info Sci.

Programming in BASIC: Communicating with Computers. Jeffrey E. Frates. (Illus.). 304p. 1985. pap. text ed. 27.00 (ISBN 0-13-729369-0). P-H.

Programming in BASIC for Business. 3rd ed. Bruce Bosworth & Harry L. Nagel. (Illus.). 404p. (Orig.). pap. text ed. write for info. (ISBN 0-574-21745-2, 13-4745); instr's. guide avail. (ISBN 0-574-21746-0, 13-4746). SRA.

Programming in Basic for Engineers. Kamal B. Rojiani. 1988. text ed. 28.50 (ISBN 0-534-91899-9). PWS Kent Pub.

Programming in BASIC for the IBM PC. David L. Heiserman. (Illus.). 416p. 1984. text ed. 30.00 (ISBN 0-13-729450-6); pap. text ed. 22.95 (ISBN 0-13-729443-3). P-H.

Programming in BASIC-PLUS: VAX-11 BASIC Compatible. 2nd ed. Jasper J. Sawatzky & Shu-Jen Chen. LC 84-27027. 452p. 1985. pap. write for info. (ISBN 0-471-88655-6). Wiley.

Programming in BASIC: Problem Solving with Structure & Style. Stewart Venit. (Illus.). 441p. (Orig.). 1987. pap. text ed. 32.25 (ISBN 0-314-29521-6); lab manual 9.00 (ISBN 0-314-35431-X). West Pub.

Programming in BASIC: Structured Programming, Cases, Applications & Modules. 3rd ed. Ralph M. Stair, Jr. Ed. by Robert B. Fetter & Claude McMillan. LC 84-81735. (Irwin Series in Information & Decision Sciences). (Illus.). 454p. 1985. pap. 24.95x (ISBN 0-256-03213-0). Irwin.

Programming in BASIC with the TI Home Computer. Herbert D. Peckham. 1979. pap. text ed. 26.95 (ISBN 0-07-049156-9, BYTE Bks). McGraw.

Programming in C. Kris A. Jamsa. 1986. pap. 25.95x (ISBN 0-256-03313-7). Irwin.

Programming in C. 2nd ed. Stephen Kochan. (UNIX Library). (Illus.). 300p. 1988. pap. 24.95 (ISBN 0-672-48420-X). Sams.

Programming in C: For the Microcomputer. Robert J. Traister, Sr. (Illus.). 176p. 1984. pap. 19.95 (ISBN 0-13-729641-X). P-H.

Programming in C for UNIX. C. Schirmer. (Computers & Their Applications Ser.). 250p. 1987. 29.95 (ISBN 0-470-20768-X). Halsted Pr.

Programming in C with a Bit of UNIX. F. Richard Moore. (Illus.). 208p. 1985. pap. text ed. 25.95 (ISBN 0-13-730094-8). P-H.

Programming in C with Let's C. Richard Vile. 1988. pap. 21.95 (ISBN 0-673-18813-2). Scott F.

Programming in Clipper. Stephen J. Straley. 752p. 1988. pap. 29.95 (ISBN 0-201-14583-9). Addison-Wesley.

Programming in Clipper. Margaret Zinky et al. 1988. pap. 21.95 (ISBN 0-673-38361-X). Scott F.

Programming in Clipper: The Definitive Guide to the Clipper dBASE Compiler. Stephen J. Straley. (Apple Technical Library). 1988. pap. 29.95 (ISBN 0-201-11993-5). Addison-Wesley.

Programming in Common LISP. Rodney A. Brooks. LC 85-9587. 303p. 1985. pap. 22.95 (ISBN 0-471-81888-7). Wiley.

Programming in Decision Tables. Peter M. Bell. (Illus.). 176p. (Orig.). 1984. pap. 24.50 (ISBN 0-930953-01-0). Albion PA.

Programming in FORTRAN. Heath Company Staff. (Illus.). 616p. 1981. looseleaf with 6 audiocassettes 99.95 (ISBN 0-87119-084-2, EC-1101). Heathkit-Zenith Ed.

Programming in FORTRAN. Vladimir Zwass. 224p. 1980. pap. 7.95 (ISBN 0-06-460194-3, CO 194, B&N Bks). Har-Row.

Programming in FORTRAN IV. William F. Schallert & Carol R. Clark. LC 78-74039. 1979. pap. text ed. write for info. (ISBN 0-201-06716-1). Addison-Wesley.

Programming in Fortran 77. Jean-Paul Tremblay. 448p. 1988. pap. text ed. 19.95 (ISBN 0-07-065179-5). McGraw.

Programming in IBM PC DOS Pascal. David M. Chess. (Illus.). 240p. 1985. pap. text ed. 23.95 (ISBN 0-13-730292-4). P-H.

Programming in LISP: Tools, Techniques, & Principles. Rajeev Sangal. (Illus.). 384p. 1989. 29.95 (ISBN 0-07-054666-5). McGraw.

Programming in Macintosh BASIC. James Heid. 1985. pap. 24.95 (ISBN 0-912677-48-1). Ashton-Tate Pub.

Programming in Micro-Prolog. Hugh De Saram. LC 85-5610. (Computers & Their Applications Ser.). 166p. 1985. pap. 15.95 (ISBN 0-470-20218-1). Halsted Pr.

Programming in Microsoft BASIC. Heath Company Staff. (Illus.). 920p. 1981. looseleaf with 3 audiocassetes 99.95 (ISBN 0-87119-086-9, EC-1110). Heathkit-Zenith Ed.

Programming in Modula-2. 3rd corrected ed. N. Wirth. (Texts & Monographs in Computer Science). iv, 192p. 1985. 20.50 (ISBN 0-387-15078-1). Springer-Verlag.

Programming with FORTRAN 77. J. Ashcroft et al. 304p. 1981. pap. 22.50x (ISBN 0-246-11573-4, Pub. by Granada England). Sheridan.

Programming with Macintosh Programmer's Workshop. Joel W. West. (Macintosh Performance Library). 512p. 1987. pap. 29.95 (ISBN 0-553-34436-6). Bantam.

Programming with MacIntosh Turbo Pascal. Tom Swam. (Illus.). 416p. 1987. pap. 22.95 (ISBN 0-471-62417-9). Wiley.

Programming with Microsoft BASIC. W. Zage. 152p. 1986. pap. text ed. 9.95 (ISBN 0-07-072734-1). McGraw.

Programming with MS DOS & PC DOS Interrupts in Assembly Language. Thom Hogan & Roger Chapman. Date not set. write for info. S&S.

Programming with MS DOS & PC DOS Interrupts in Assembly Language. Thom Hogan & Roger Chapman. 1986. pap. 23.95 (ISBN 0-89303-788-5). P-H.

Programming with Pascal. Byron S. Gottfried. (Schaum's Outline Ser.). 320p. 1985. pap. text ed. 9.95 (ISBN 0-07-023849-9). McGraw.

Programming with Pascal. J. Konvalina. 640p. 1987. pap. text ed. 28.95 (ISBN 0-07-035224-0). McGraw.

Programming with Pascal. Dean L. Smith. (Illus.). 266p. (Orig.). 1985. wkbk. 30.00x (ISBN 0-918699-07-X). D L Smith.

Programming with PL-1. Henry Ruston. (Illus.). 1978. text ed. 37.95 (ISBN 0-07-054350-X). McGraw.

Programming with R: Base 5000. Cary N. Prague & James E. Hammitt. (Illus.). 304p. 1986. 28.95 (ISBN 0-8306-0366-2, 2666); pap. 19.95 (ISBN 0-8306-0466-9, 2666P). TAB Bks.

Programming with RT-11, Vol. 1: Program Development Facilities. Simon Clinch & Stephen Peters. (DEC Books). (Illus.). 200p. 1984. pap. 28.00 (ISBN 0-932376-32-0, EY-00022-DP). Digital Pr.

Programming with RT-11, Vol. 2: Callable System Facilities. Stephen Peters et al. (DEC Books). (Illus.). 255p. 1984. pap. 32.00 (ISBN 0-932376-33-9, EY-00023-DP). Digital Pr.

Programming with Sets: An Introduction to SETL. Ed. by J. T. Schwartz et al. (Texts & Monographs in Computer Science). (Illus.). 465p. 1986. 45.00 (ISBN 0-387-96399-5). Springer-Verlag.

Programming with Structured Flowcharts. Krishna K. Agarwal. 142p. 1984. pap. 13.50 (ISBN 0-89433-226-0). Petrocelli.

Programming with System 370 Assembler Language. 2nd ed. Robert G. Lavery. 532p. 1984. pap. text ed. 28.50 (ISBN 0-8403-3469-9). Kendall-Hunt.

Programming with the Common Lisp Object System. Daniel Bobrow & Gregor Kiczales. (Illus.). 90p. 1988. pap. text ed. 5.00x (ISBN 0-929280-25-3). Amer Artificial.

Programming with Turbo C. S. Scott Zimmerman & Beverly B. Zimmerman. 1988. pap. 24.95 (ISBN 0-673-38092-0). Scott F.

Programming with Turbo Pascal. David W. Carroll. Date not set. 34.95 (ISBN 0-07-852909-3); disk incl. McGraw.

Programming with Windows. Tim Farrell. 600p. 1987. pap. 22.95 (ISBN 0-88022-299-9, 99). Que Corp.

Programming Your Adam Computer with Ready-to-Run Programs. Susan E. Sutphin. 176p. 1985. pap. 21.95 (ISBN 0-13-729377-1). P-H.

Programming Your ATARI Computer. Mark Thompson. (Illus.). 280p. (Orig.). 1983. 16.95 (ISBN 0-8306-0453-7, 1453H). TAB Bks.

Programming Your Own Adventure Games in Pascal. Richard C. Vile, Jr. (Illus.). 320p. (Orig.). 1984. 19.95 (ISBN 0-8306-0768-4, 1768HB). TAB Bks.

Programming Your Texas Instruments Computer in TI BASIC. F. D'Ignazio. 256p. 1984. pap. 9.95 (ISBN 0-07-016897-0, BYTE Bks). McGraw.

Programs see Reaching for the Stars: A Minicourse for Education of Gifted Students.

Programs & Celebrations. Judy G. Smith. Ed. by Arthur L. Zapel. (Illus.). 112p. (Orig.). 1987. pap. 7.95 (ISBN 0-916260-44-5, B122). Meriwether Pub.

Programs & Data Structures in C. Leendert Ammeraal. LC 87-22184. 206p. 1988. 24.95 (ISBN 0-471-91751-6). Wiley.

Programs & Manifestoes on 20th-Century Architecture. Ed. by Ulrich Conrads. 1971. pap. 6.95 (ISBN 0-262-53030-9). MIT Pr.

Programs & Parties for Christmas. Helen Eisenberg & Larry Eisenberg. 160p. 1980. pap. 4.95 (ISBN 0-8010-3359-4). Baker Bk.

Programs & Promises: Reflections on the Beatitudes. Wallace H. Kirby. 1980. 3.50 (ISBN 0-89536-414-X, 1640). CSS of Ohio.

Programs & Resources for Intermediate City Federations. CJF Community Services Department Staff. 1986. write for info. Coun Jewish Feds.

Programs & Systems: An Evaluation Perspective. Gary Borich & Ron Jemelka. LC 81-17539. (Educational Technology Ser.). 1981. 41.50 (ISBN 0-12-118620-2). Acad Pr.

Programs As Data Objects. Ed. by H. Ganzinger & N. D. Jones. (Lecture Notes in Computer Science Ser.: Vol. 217). ix, 324p. 1986. pap. 20.50 (ISBN 0-387-16446-4). Springer-Verlag.

Programs for Advent & Christmas. Ed. by Vincie Alessi. 1978. pap. 5.95 (ISBN 0-8170-0808-X). Judson.

Programs for Advent & Christmas, Vol. 2. Ed. by Vincie Alessi. 64p. 1981. pap. 4.95 (ISBN 0-8170-0930-2). Judson.

Programs for Digital Signal Processing. Ed. by Digital Signal Processing Committee. LC 79-89028. 592p. 1979. 54.40 (ISBN 0-87942-127-4, PC01180); tape version 88.10 (ISBN 0-686-96748-8). Inst Electrical.

Programs for Electronics Circuit Design. David Leithauser. Tr. by Tech Art Associates. (Illus.). 100p. 1984. 14.95 (ISBN 0-88006-068-9, BK7400, DS740011). Weber Systems.

Programs for Improving the Image of the Judiciary. National Center for State Courts Staff. 94p. 1984. manuscript 6.00 (ICM-001). Natl Ctr St Courts.

Programs for Lent & Easter. Ed. by Vincie Alessi. 1979. pap. 5.95 (ISBN 0-8170-0861-6). Judson.

Programs for Lent & Easter, Vol. 2. Vincie Alessi. 64p. 1983. pap. 4.95 (ISBN 0-8170-1016-5). Judson.

Programs for Older Adults. Ed. by Morris A. Okun. LC 81-48475. (Continuing Education Ser.: No. 14). 1982. pap. text ed. 12.95 (ISBN 0-87589-888-2). Jossey-Bass.

Programs for Older Americans: Evaluations by Academic Gerontologists. Ed. by Gordon F. Streib. LC 81-11645. (Research Ser., Center for Gerontological Studies: Vol. 1). (Illus.). xi, 268p. (Orig.). 1981. pap. 13.00x (ISBN 0-8130-0705-4). U Presses Fla.

Programs for Productivity & Quality of Work Life. Richard A. Guzzo. (Studies in Productivity: No. 32). 38p. 1984. pap. 39.00 (ISBN 0-08-030964-X). Work in Amer.

Programs for Profit: How to Really Make Money with a Personal Computer. R. Zboray & D. Sachs. LC 83-17542. (VTX Ser.). (Illus.). 256p. 1984. pap. text ed. 9.95 (ISBN 0-07-072785-6, Byte Bks). McGraw.

Programs for Spouses of Foreign Students. Rosalie Berg et al. 1986. 5.00 (ISBN 0-912207-28-0). NAFSA Washington.

Programs in Aid of the Poor. 5th ed. Sar A. Levitan. LC 84-28890. 168p. 1985. text ed. 17.50x (ISBN 0-8018-2749-3); pap. text ed. 6.95x (ISBN 0-8018-2760-4). Johns Hopkins.

Programs in Aid of the Poor for the 1980's, No. 1. 4th ed. Sar A. Levitan. LC 80-8093. (Policy Studies in Employment & Welfare: No. 1). pap. 42.30 (ISBN 0-317-42065-8, 2025885). Bks Demand UMI.

Programs in BASIC, a Lecture Notebook. 2nd ed. Bruce Bosworth. 80p. 1982. pap. text ed. 7.95 (ISBN 0-8403-1210-5). Kendall-Hunt.

Programs, Leaders, Consultants & Other Resources in Gifted & Talented Education. Frances A. Karnes & Herschel Q. Peddicord, Jr. 360p. 1980. 32.75x (ISBN 0-398-04099-0). C C Thomas.

Programs of Early Education: The Constructivist View. Rheta DeVries & Lawrence Kohlberg. 423p. 1987. 36.95 (ISBN 0-582-28301-9). Longman.

Programs of Medieval Illumination. Robert G. Calkins. LC 84-51249. (Franklin D. Murphy Lectures V). (Illus.). 158p. 1984. 12.00 (ISBN 0-913689-12-2). Spencer Muse Art.

Programs of the Brain. John Z. Young. (Illus.). 1978. 29.95x (ISBN 0-19-857545-9). Oxford U Pr.

Programs of the Brain. John Z. Young. (Illus.). 1978. pap. 9.95 (ISBN 0-19-286019-4). Oxford U Pr.

Progres Economique et Signification see Cahiers de L'Institut de Science Economique Appliquee.

Progres Technique et la Productivite Sociale du Travail see Cahiers de l'Institut de Science Economique Appliquee.

Progreso. Charles Harbutt. Ed. by Joan Liftin. LC 86-72588. (Illus.). 96p. (Orig.). 1987. 45.00 (ISBN 0-9617575-0-7); pap. 27.50 (ISBN 0-9617575-1-5). Archive Pictures.

Progreso del Peregrino. Juan Bunyan & L. P. Leavell. Tr. by Hiram F. Duffer, Jr. from Eng. (Span.). 1987. pap. 3.25 (ISBN 0-311-37006-3). Casa Bautista.

Progreso del Peregrino Ilustrado. John Bunyan. Orig. Title: Pilgrim's Progress Illustrated. 256p. (Span.). pap. 4.75 (ISBN 0-8254-1096-7). Kregel.

Progress. Barrett Watten. LC 85-61016. 120p. (Orig.). 1985. pap. text ed. 7.50 (ISBN 0-937804-16-9). Segue NYC.

Progress Against Growth: Daniel B. Luten on the American Landscape. Ed. by Thomas R. Vale. LC 86-14296. 366p. 1986. lib. bdg. 35.00 (ISBN 0-89862-665-X). Guilford Pr.

Progress & Archaeology. Vera G. Childe. LC 70-114499. 1971. Repr. of 1944 ed. lib. bdg. 25.00x (ISBN 0-8371-4779-4, CHPA). Greenwood.

Progress & Chaos. Alexander J. Groth. LC 83-17549. 242p. (Eng.). 1984. pap. text ed. 10.50 (ISBN 0-89874-677-9). Krieger.

Progress & Controversies in Oncological Urology. Karl H. Kurth et al. LC 84-5658. (Progress in Clinical & Biological Research Ser.: Vol. 153). 626p. 1984. 95.00 (ISBN 0-8451-5003-0). A R Liss.

Progress & Decline in the History of Church Renewal. Ed. by Roger Aubert. LC 67-30136. (Concilium Ser.: Vol. 27). 191p. 1967. 7.95 (ISBN 0-8091-0119-X). Paulist Pr.

Progress & Democracy: William Godwin's Contribution to Political Philosophy. Frederick Rosen. Ed. by Maurice Cranston. (Political Theory & Political Philosophy Ser.). 350p. 1987. lib. bdg. 50.00 (ISBN 0-8240-0829-4). Garland Pub.

Progress & Eternal Recurrence in the Work of Gabriel Naude. D. Curtis. (Occasional Papers in Modern Languages: No. 4). 53p. 1967. pap. text ed. 6.95x (ISBN 0-317-13264-4, Pub. by U of Hull UK). Humanities.

Progress & Hard Feelings. Doug Lucie. 96p. (Orig.). 1985. pap. 6.95 (ISBN 0-413-57760-0, 9335). Heinemann Ed.

Progress & History: Essays. facs. ed. Ed. by Francis S. Marvin. LC 78-84326. (Essay Index Reprint Ser.). 1916. 17.75 (ISBN 0-8369-1096-6). Ayer Co Pubs.

Progress & Human Value. Ed. by Peter M. Schuller. (Orig.). 1979. 15.65x (ISBN 0-89894-007-9). Advocate Pub Group.

Progress & Intelligence of Americans: Collateral Proof of Slavery, from the First to the Eleventh Chapter of Genesis, As Founded on Organic Law. facs. ed. M. T. Wheat. LC 77-83882. (Black Heritage Library Collection Ser.). 1862. 21.75 (ISBN 0-8369-8684-9). Ayer Co Pubs.

Progress & Its Discontents. Ed. by Gabriel A. Almond et al. LC 81-11643. 550p. 1982. 33.00x (ISBN 0-520-04478-9); pap. 11.95x (ISBN 0-520-05447-4). U of Cal Pr.

Progress & Its Problems: Towards a Theory of Scientific Growth. Larry Laudan. LC 76-24586. 1977. 30.00x (ISBN 0-520-03330-2); pap. 10.95x (ISBN 0-520-03721-9). U of Cal Pr.

Progress & Nostalgia: Silvester-Klausen in Urnasch, Switzerland. Regina Bendix. LC 84-28128. (UC Publications in Folklore & Mythology: Vol. 33). 1985. pap. 23.00x (ISBN 0-520-09959-1). U of Cal Pr.

Progress & Performance. Edwin T. Cornelius, Jr. (New Technology English Ser.: Vol. 3). (Illus.). 125p. 1984. text ed. 8.95 (ISBN 0-89209-164-9); pap. text ed. 6.25 (ISBN 0-89209-402-8); audiocassettes (Set of 4) 17.00 (ISBN 0-89209-165-7). Pace Intl Res.

Progress & Perspectives in the Treatment of Gastrointestinal Tumors. Ed. by A. Gerard. (European Journal of Cancer Ser.: No. 2). (Illus.). 128p. 1981. 40.00 (ISBN 0-08-027979-1). Pergamon.

Progress & Pessimism: Religion, Politics & History in Late Nineteenth Century Britain. Jeffrey P. Von Arx. (Harvard Historical Studies: No. 104). 256p. 1985. text ed. 25.00x (ISBN 0-674-71375-3). Harvard U Pr.

Progress & Planning in Industry: Proceedings of International Conference on Industrial Economics, April, 1970. Collets Staff. 417p. 1972. 45.00x (ISBN 0-317-53867-5, Pub. by Collets (UK)). State Mutual Bk.

Progress & Poverty. Henry George. LC 79-12191. 1979. 10.00 (ISBN 0-914016-60-1). Phoenix Pub.

Progress & Poverty. Henry George. LC 79-12191. 599p. (Avail. in Danish, Dutch, Fr., Ger., Heb., It., Korean, Portugese Span., & Swedish). 1879. Repr. of 1987 ed. centennial ed. 10.00x (ISBN 0-911312-79-X). Schalkenbach.

Progress & Poverty. Henry George. LC 79-12191. 599p. 1984. pap. 5.00 (ISBN 0-911312-58-7). Schalkenbach.

Progress & Poverty. Henry George. LC 85-43339. 220p. 1985. pap. 3.00 abridged (ISBN 0-911312-10-2). Schalkenbach.

Progress & Power. Carl L. Becker. LC 83-45701. Repr. of 1949 ed. 21.50 (ISBN 0-404-20023-0). AMS Pr.

Progress & Pragmatism: James, Dewey, Beard & the American Idea of Progress. David W. Marcell. LC 72-818. (Contributions in American Studies: No. 9). 402p. 1974. lib. bdg. 35.00 (ISBN 0-8371-6387-0, MPR/). Greenwood.

Progress & Problems in Lichenology in the Eighties: Proceedings of an International Symposium at the University of Muenster 1986. Ed. by Elizabeth Peveling. (Bibliotheca Lichenologica Ser.: Vol. 25). (Illus.). 497p. 1987. pap. 93.50x softbound (ISBN 3-443-58004-1). Lubrecht & Cramer.

Progress & Problems in Medical & Dental Education: Federal Support Versus Federal Control. Carnegie Council on Policy Studies in Higher Education Staff. LC 76-11964. (Carnegie Council Ser.). pap. 48.00 (ISBN 0-317-26053-7, 2023780). Bks Demand UMI.

Progress & Problems of Genetic Improvement of Tropical Forest Trees, 2 Vols. D. G. Nikles et al. 1978. 165.00x (ISBN 0-85074-020-7, Pub. by For Lib Comm England). State Mutual Bk.

Progress & Problems of Regional Development & Planning in the Countries of the ECAFE Region. (Working Papers Ser.: No. 75-2). 56p. 1973. pap. 6.00 (ISBN 0-686-75490-5, CRD060, UNCRD). UNIPUB.

Progress & Prospects of Pottery Industry in India: A Case Study of U. P. K. C. Gupta. 250p. 1988. 36.50x (ISBN 81-7099-051-3, Pub. by Mittal). South Asia Bks.

Progress & Rationality of Philosophy As a Cognitive Enterprise. Joseph W. Smith. (Avebury Series in Philosophy). 1987. text ed. 50.00x (ISBN 0-566-05305-5, Pub. by Gower Pub England). Gower Pub Co.

Progress & Regress: J. B. Van Helmont to Claude Bernard see Divided Legacy: A History of the Schism in Medical Thought.

Progress & Religion, an Historical Enquiry. Christopher H. Dawson. LC 79-104266. 1970. Repr. of 1929 ed. lib. bdg. 35.00x (ISBN 0-8371-3917-1, DAPR). Greenwood.

Progress & Science. Robert Shafer. 1922. 49.50x (ISBN 0-686-83714-2). Elliots Bks.

Progress & Supercomputing in Computational Fluid Dynamics: Proceedings of U. S. - Israel Workshop, 1984. Ed. by Earll M. Murman & Saul S. Abarbanel. (Progress in Scientific Computing Ser.: Vol. 6). 1985. 49.50x (ISBN 0-8176-3321-9). Birkhauser.

Progress & Survival: An Essay on the the Future of Mankind. Emile Benoit. Ed. by Jack B. Gohn. 144p. 1980. 35.00 (ISBN 0-275-90452-0, C0452). Praeger.

Progress & the Crisis of Man. Frank Yartz et al. LC 76-44451. 160p. 1976. 19.95x (ISBN 0-88229-165-3). Nelson-Hall.

Progress & Trends in Pheology, Vol. II. Ed. by H. Giesekus & M. F. Hibberd. (Rheologica Acta Ser.: Vol. 27). 456p. 1988. 170.00 (ISBN 0-387-91329-7). Springer-Verlag.

Progress & Uniformity in Child-Labor Legislation. William F. Ogburn. LC 68-56678. (Columbia University. Studies in the Social Sciences: No. 121). Repr. of 1912 ed. 18.50 (ISBN 0-404-51121-X). AMS Pr.

Progress & Welfare in Southeast Asia: A Comparison of Colonial Policy & Practice. John S. Furnivall. LC 75-30055. (Institute of Pacific Relations). Repr. of 1941 ed. 20.00 (ISBN 0-404-59525-1). AMS Pr.

Progress, Dancing. Ann Hayes. 20p. 1986. pap. 4.00 (ISBN 0-941150-49-6). Barth.

Progress Experimental Personality Research: Psychopathology, Vol. 12: Psychopathology. Brendan A. Maher & Winifred B. Maher. (Serial Publication Ser.). 1983. 75.00 (ISBN 0-12-541412-9). Acad Pr.

Progress for a Small Planet. Barbara Ward. 1979. 14.95 (ISBN 0-393-01277-8). Norton.

Progress for Food or Food for Progress? The Political Economy of Agricultural Growth and Development. Folke Dovring. 330p. 1988. lib. bdg. 49.95 (ISBN 0-275-92904-3, C2904). Praeger.

Progress in Adjusting Differences of Amount of Educational Opportunity Offered Under the County Unit Systems of Maryland & Utah. Leonard J. Nuttall. LC 72-177122. (Columbia University. Teachers College. Contributions to Education: No. 43). Repr. of 1931 ed. 22.50 (ISBN 0-404-55431-8). AMS Pr.

Progress in Advanced Materials & Processes Durability, Reliability & Quality Control: Proceedings of the Sixth International European Chapter Conference of the Society for the Advancement of Material & Process Engineering, Scheveningen, The Netherlands May 28-30, 1985. Ed. by G. Bartelds & R. J. Schliekelmann. (Materials Science Monographs: No. 29). 310p. 1985. 87.00 (ISBN 0-444-42499-7). Elsevier.

Progress in Aerospace Sciences (Incorporating Progress in Astronautical Sciences, Vols. 7-8, 10-16. Ed. by D. Kuchemann. Incl. Vol. 7. 1966. 1966; Vol. 8. 1967. write for info.; Vol. 10. 1970. 1970; Vol. 11. 1970. 1970; Vol. 12. 1972. 1972; Vol. 13. 1973. 1972; Vol. 14. 1973. 1973; Vol. 15. 1974. 1974; Vol. 16. 1975-76. 1976. LC 74-618347. Pergamon.

Progress in Agricultural Geography. Ed. by Michael Pacione. (Progress in Geography Ser.). 288p. 1986. 48.25 (ISBN 0-7099-2095-4, Pub. by Croom Helm Ltd). Routledge Chapman & Hall.

Progress in Alcohol Research, Vol. 1: Alcohol Nutrition & the Nervous System. Ed. by S. Parvez et al. 340p. 1985. lib. bdg. 125.00x (ISBN 90-6764-050-6). Coronet Bks.

Progress in Allergy, Vol. 13. Ed. by P. Kallos et al. (Illus.). 300p. 1969. 72.00 (ISBN 3-8055-0378-4). S Karger.

Progress in Allergy, Vol. 14. Ed. by P. Kallos & B. H. Waksman. 1970. 56.75 (ISBN 3-8055-0379-2). S Karger.

Progress in Allergy, Vol. 15. Ed. by P. Kallos & B. H. Waksman. 1971. 73.50 (ISBN 3-8055-1238-4). S Karger.

Progress in Allergy, Vol. 16. Ed. by P. Kallos et al. (Illus.). 1972. 85.50 (ISBN 3-8055-1335-6). S Karger.

Progress in Allergy, Vol. 17. Ed. by P. Kallos et al. (Illus.). 300p. 1973. 64.75 (ISBN 3-8055-1539-1). S Karger.

Progress in Allergy, Vol. 18. Ed. by P. Kallos & B. H. Waksman. 300p. 1975. 124.75 (ISBN 3-8055-1660-6). S Karger.

Progress in Allergy, Vol. 19. Ed. by P. Kallos. (Illus.). 300p. 1975. 85.50 (ISBN 3-8055-2033-6). S Karger.

Progress in Allergy, Vol. 20. Ed. by P. Kallos & B. H. Waksman. (Illus.). 1975. 85.50 (ISBN 3-8055-2189-8). S Karger.

Progress in Allergy, Vol. 21. Ed. by P. Kallos et al. (Illus.). 1976. 102.00 (ISBN 3-8055-2342-4). S Karger.

Progress in Allergy, Vol. 22. Ed. by P. Kallos et al. 1977. 63.50 (ISBN 3-8055-2419-6). S Karger.

Progress in Allergy, Vol. 23. Ed. by P. Kallos et al. (Illus.). 1977. 98.75 (ISBN 3-8055-2665-2). S Karger.

Progress in Allergy, Vol. 24. Ed. by P. Kallos et al. (Illus.). 1977. 99.50 (ISBN 3-8055-2781-0). S Karger.

Progress in Allergy, Vol. 25. Ed. by P. Kallos et al. (Illus.). 1978. 66.00 (ISBN 3-8055-2849-3). S Karger.

Progress in Allergy, Vols. 26 & 27. Ed. by P. Kallos et al. (Illus.). 1979. Vol. 26. 66.00 (ISBN 3-8055-2934-1); Vol. 27. 76.75 (ISBN 3-8055-3053-6). S Karger.

Progress in Analytical Atomic Spectroscopy, 2 vols. C. L. Chakrabarti. (Illus.). 282p. 1981. Set. 100.00 (ISBN 0-08-027126-X). Pergamon.

Progress in Anatomy, Vol. 1. Ed. by R. J. Harrison & R. L. Holmes. (Illus.). 250p. 1981. 77.50 (ISBN 0-521-23603-7). Cambridge U Pr.

Progress in Anatomy, 2 vols, Vols. 2 & 3. Ed. by Richard J. Harrison et al. Vol. 2. pap. 59.30; Vol. 3. pap. 71.00. Bks Demand UMI.

Progress in Anatomy, Vol. 3. V. Navaratnam & R. J. Harrison. 350p. 1984. 74.50 (ISBN 0-521-24953-8). Cambridge U Pr.

Progress in Animal Biometeorology: The Effects of Weather & Climate on Animals; Vol 1 Period 1963-1973, 2 pts. H. D. Johnson. Incl. Pt. 1. Effects of Temperature on Animals: Including Effects of Humidity, Radiation & Wind. 624p. 1976. text ed. 115.00 (ISBN 90-265-0196-X); Effect of Light, High Actitude, Noise, Electric, Magnetic & Electro-Magnetic Fields, Ionization, Gravity & Air Pollutions on Animals. 322p. 1976. text ed. 57.00 (ISBN 90-265-0235-4). (Progress in Biometeorology Ser.). 1976 (Pub. by Swets Pub Serv Holland). Swets North Am.

Progress in Anterior Eye Segment: Research & Practice. Ed. by O. Hockwin & W. B. Rathbun. (Documenta Ophthalmologica Proceedings Ser.: No. 18). (Illus.). 1979. lib. bdg. 79.00 (ISBN 90-6193-158-4, Pub. by Junk Pubs Netherlands). Kluwer Academic.

Progress in Aphasiology. Ed. by F. Clifford Rose. (Advances in Neurology Ser.: Vol. 42). 382p. 1984. text ed. 76.00 (ISBN 0-88167-023-5). Raven.

Progress in Applied Materials Research. Ed. by Edwin G. Stanford et al. 1963-65. Vol. 4, 256p. 92.00x (ISBN 0-677-00920-8); Vol. 5, 248p. 92.00 (ISBN 0-677-00930-5); Vol. 6, 320p. 105.00x (ISBN 0-677-00940-2). Gordon & Breach.

Progress in Applied Mechanics: The Chien Wei-Zang Anniversary Volume. Ed. by Yeh Kai-Yuan. 1986. lib. bdg. 135.50 (ISBN 90-247-3249-2, Pub. by Martinus Nijhoff Netherlands). Kluwer Academic.

Progress in Applied Social Psychology, Vol. 1. Ed. by G. M. Stephenson & James H. Davis. LC 80-41694. (Progress in Applied Social Psychology Ser.). 400p. 1981. 76.95 (ISBN 0-471-27954-4, Pub. by Wiley-Interscience). Wiley.

Progress in Applied Social Psychology, Vol. 2. Ed. by G. M. Stephenson & James H. Davis. LC 83-641069. (Progress in Applied Social Psychology Ser.: 1-536). 325p. 1984. 75.00x (ISBN 0-471-90361-2, Pub. by Wiley-Interscience). Wiley.

Progress in Arms Control? Readings from Scientific American. Bruce M. Russett. LC 78-31864. (Illus.). 238p. 1979. pap. text ed. 11.95x (ISBN 0-7167-1061-7). W H Freeman.

Progress in Artificial Intelligence. Ed. by Luc Steels & J. A. Campbell. LC 84-28956. (Artificial Intelligence Ser.). 1985. 57.95 (ISBN 0-470-20171-1). Halsted Pr.

Progress in Artificial Organs: Proceedings, Fourth International Society for Artificial Organs, Kyoto, 1983. Ed. by K Atsumi et al. 110.00 (ISBN 0-936022-17-5); pap. 100.00 (ISBN 0-936022-16-7). Intl Soc Artifical Organs.

Progress in Artificial Organs-1985: Proceedings from the Fifth International Society for Artificial Organs Congress, Chicago. Ed. by Y. Nose et al. 110.00 (ISBN 0-936022-26-4); pap. 100.00 (ISBN 0-936022-25-6). Intl Soc Artifical Organs.

Progress in Assertiveness, Nineteen Seventy-Three to Nineteen Eighty-Three: An Analytical Bibliography. Douglas H. Ruben. LC 85-1853. 336p. 1985. 25.00 (ISBN 0-8108-1793-4). Scarecrow.

Progress in Atomic Spectroscopy, 4 vols. Ed. by W. Hanle & H. Kleinpoppen. LC 78-18230. (Physics of Atoms & Molecules Ser.). Pt. A, 1978, 756p. 95.00x (ISBN 0-306-31115-1, Plenum Pr); Pt. B, 1978, 820p. 95.00x (ISBN 0-306-31116-X); Pt. C, 1984, 626p. 95.00x (ISBN 0-306-41300-0); Pt. D, 1987, 538p. 110.00x (ISBN 0-306-42528-9, Plenum Pr). Plenum Pub.

Progress in Basic Principles of Imaging Systems. Ed. by F. Granzer & E. Moisar. 850p. 1987. pap. 110.00 (ISBN 3-528-08984-9, Pub. by Vieweg & Sohn). IPS.

Progress in Behavior Modification, Vols. 4-5 & 7. Ed. by Michel Hersen. Incl. Vol. 4. 1977. 52.00 (ISBN 0-12-535604-8); Vol. 5. 1977. 52.00 (ISBN 0-12-535605-6); Vol. 7. 1979. 46.00 (ISBN 0-12-535607-2). LC 74-5697. 1977-79. Acad Pr.

Progress in Behavior Modification, Vol. 8. Ed. by Michel Hersen et al. LC 74-5697. 1979. 62.00 (ISBN 0-12-535608-0). Acad Pr.

Progress in Behavior Modification, Vol. 9. Ed. by Michel Hersen et al. (Serial Publication Ser.). 1980. 62.00 (ISBN 0-12-535609-9). Acad Pr.

Progress in Behavior Modification, Vol. 10. Ed. by Michel Hersen et al. 1980. 62.00 (ISBN 0-12-535610-2). Acad Pr.

Progress in Behavior Modification, Vol. 11. Ed. by Michel Hersen et al. 1981. 62.00 (ISBN 0-12-535611-0). Acad Pr.

Progress in Behavior Modification, Vol. 12. Ed. by Michael Hersen et al. 1981. 62.00 (ISBN 0-12-535612-9). Acad Pr.

Progress in Behavior Modification, Vol. 13. Ed. by Michel Hersen et al. (Serial Publication Ser.). 1982. 62.00 (ISBN 0-12-535613-7). Acad Pr.

Progress in Behavior Modification, Vol. 14. Ed. by Michel Hersen et al. (Serial Publication Ser.). 1983. 62.00 (ISBN 0-12-535614-5). Acad Pr.

Progress in Behavior Modification, Vol. 15. Ed. by Michel Hersen et al. (Serial Publication Ser.). 1983. 62.00 (ISBN 0-12-535615-3). Acad Pr.

Progress in Behavior Modification, Vol. 16. Michel Hersen et al. (Serial Publication Ser.). 1984. 62.00 (ISBN 0-12-535616-1). Acad Pr.

Progress in Behavior Modification, Vol. 17. Michel Hersen et al. (Serial Publication Ser.). 1984. 62.00 (ISBN 0-12-535617-X). Acad Pr.

Progress in Behavior Modification, Vol. 18. Ed. by Michel Hersen et al. LC 74-5697. 1984. 62.00 (ISBN 0-12-535618-8). Acad Pr.

Progress in Behavior Modification, Vol. 19. Ed. by Michel Hersen et al. 394p. 1985. 68.50 (ISBN 0-12-535619-6). Acad Pr.

Progress in Behavior Modification, Vol. 20. Ed. by Michael Hersen et al. (Serial Publication Ser.). 1986. 55.00 (ISBN 0-12-535620-X). Acad Pr.

Progress in Behavior Modification, Vol. 21. Michel Hersen et al. 320p. 1986. text ed. 45.00 (ISBN 0-8039-2851-3). Sage.

Progress in Behavioral Social Work. Ed. by Bruce A. Thyer & Walter W. Hudson. LC 87-19819. (Journal of Social Service Research Ser.). 200p. 1987. text ed. 24.95 (ISBN 0-86656-656-2). Haworth Pr.

Progress in Bio-Organic Chemistry & Molecular Biology. Ed. by Yu Ovchinnikov. (ICSU Press Symposium Ser.: No. 4). 1984. 196.00 (ISBN 0-444-80643-1). ICSU Pr.

Progress in Biomass Conversion, Vol. I. Ed. by Kyosti V. Sarkanen & David Tillman. (Serial Publication). 1979. 60.00 (ISBN 0-12-535901-2). Acad Pr.

Progress in Biomass Conversion, Vol. 3. Ed. by Kyosti V. Sarkanen & David A. Tillman. (Serial Publication). 304p. 1982. 60.00 (ISBN 0-12-535903-9). Acad Pr.

Progress in Biomass Conversion, Vol. 4. David A. Tillman & Edwin C. Jahn. (Serial Publication Ser.). 1983. 60.00 (ISBN 0-12-535904-7). Acad Pr.

Progress in Biomass Conversion, Vol. 5. Ed. by David A. Tillman & Edwin C. Jahn. (Serial Publications). 1984. 60.00 (ISBN 0-12-535905-5). Acad Pr.

Progress in Biophysics & Molecular Biology, Vols. 5-11, & 13-30. Ed. by J. A. Butler & D. Noble. Incl. Vol. 5. 1960. Vol. 10. 87.00 (ISBN 0-08-009293-4); Vol. 6. 1956. write for info.; Vol. 7. 1957. write for info.; Vol. 8. 1958. write for info.; Vol. 9. 1959. write for info.; Vol. 10. 1960. write for info.; Vol. 11. 1961. write for info.; Vol. 13. 1964; Vol. 14. 1964; Vol. 15. 1965; Vol. 16. 1966; Vol. 17. 1967. 84.00 (ISBN 0-08-012046-6); Vol. 18. 1968. 87.00 (ISBN 0-08-012753-3); Vol. 19, Pt. 1. 1969; Vol. 19, Pt. 2. 1969; Vol. 19, Complete. 1969; Vol. 20. 1970. 84.00 (ISBN 0-08-006627-5); Vol. 21. 1970. 84.00 (ISBN 0-08-015696-7); Vol. 22. 1971. 84.00 (ISBN 0-08-016348-3); Vol. 23. 1971. 84.00 (ISBN 0-08-016740-3); Vol. 24. 1972; Vol. 25. 1972. 84.00 (ISBN 0-08-016935-X); Vol. 26. 1973. 84.00 (ISBN 0-08-017048-X); Vol. 27. 1973. 84.00 (ISBN 0-08-017142-7); Vol. 28. 1974. 84.00 (ISBN 0-08-018005-1); Vol. 29. 1976. Vol. 29, Complete, 1976. 84.00 (ISBN 0-08-020201-2). Pergamon.

Progress in Biophysics & Molecular Biology, Vols. 31-33. Ed. by J. A. Butler & D. Noble. Incl. Vol. 31. 1977; Vol. 32, Pt. 1. 1978; Vol. 33. 1978. Pergamon.

Progress in Bone Marrow Transplantation. Ed. by Robert P. Gale & Richard Champlin. LC 87-3965. (UCLA Symposia on Molecular & Cellular Biology Ser.: Vol. 53). 1048p. 1987. 160.00 (ISBN 0-8451-2652-0, 2652). A R Liss.

Progress in Botany. Ed. by H. D. Behnke et al. (Progress in Botany Ser.: Vol. 49). (Illus.). 460p. 1987. 156.40 (ISBN 0-387-18413-9). Springer-Verlag.

Progress in Botany, Vol. 47. (Illus.). 420p. 1985. 69.00 (ISBN 0-387-15924-X). Springer-Verlag.

Progress in Botany, Vol. 48. (Illus.). 480p. 1987. 156.10 (ISBN 0-387-17233-5). Springer-Verlag.

Progress in Bulk Semiconductors Crystal Growth. Wernick. Date not set. price not set (ISBN 0-444-00896-9). Elsevier.

Progress in Cancer Control. Ed. by Curtis Mettlin & Gerald P. Murphy. LC 81-4369. (Progress in Clinical & Biological Research Ser.: Vol. 57). 250p. 1981. 36.00 (ISBN 0-8451-0057-2). A R Liss.

Progress in Cancer Control III: A Regional Approach. Curtis Mettlin & Gerald P. Murphy. LC 83-5374. (Progress in Clinical & Biological Research Ser.: Vol. 121). 342p. 1983. 49.00 (ISBN 0-8451-0121-8). A R Liss.

Progress in Cancer Control: Vol. IV: Research in the Cancer Center. Curtis Mettlin & Gerald P. Murphy. LC 83-48142. (Progress in Clinical & Biological Research Ser.: Vol. 130). 542p. 1983. 73.00 (ISBN 0-8451-0130-7). A R Liss.

Progress in Cardiology, Vol. 1-2. Ed. by Douglas P. Zipes & Derek J. Rowlands. LC 77-157474. (Illus.). 300p. 1988. pap. text ed. 29.50 (ISBN 0-8121-1154-0). Lea & Febiger.

Progress in Cardiology, Vol. 1-1. Ed. by Douglas P. Zipes & Derek J. Rowlands. LC 77-157474. (Illus.). 332p. 1988. pap. 29.50 (ISBN 0-8121-1153-2). Lea & Febiger.

Progress in Cardiology, No. 13. Ed. by Paul N. Yu & John F. Goodwin. LC 77-157474. (Illus.). 204p. 1985. text ed. 30.00 (ISBN 0-8121-0973-2). Lea & Febiger.

Progress in Cardiology, No. 14. Ed. by Paul N. Yu & John F. Goodwin. LC 77-157474. (Illus.). 336p. 1986. text ed. 48.50 (ISBN 0-8121-1018-8). Lea & Febiger.

Progress in Cardiology, No. 15. Ed. by Paul N. Yu & John F. Goodwin. LC 77-157474. (Illus.). 183p. 1987. text ed. 35.00 (ISBN 0-8121-1044-7). Lea & Febiger.

Progress in Cardiology, Vol. 16. Ed. by Paul N. Yu & John F. Goodwin. LC 77-157474. (Illus.). 163p. 1988. text ed. 28.50 (ISBN 0-8121-1144-3). Lea & Febiger.

Progress in Caries Prevention: European Organization for Caries Research (ORCA) - 25th Anniversary. Ed. by Y. Ericsson. (Caries Research: Vol. 12, Suppl. 1). (Illus.). 1978. pap. 20.75 (ISBN 3-8055-2920-1). S Karger.

Progress in Catalyst Deactivation. J. L. Figueiredo. 1982. lib. bdg. 49.50 (ISBN 90-247-2690-5, Pub. by Martinus Nijhoff Netherlands). Kluwer Academic.

Progress in Cereal Chemistry & Technology: Proceedings of the VII World Cereal & Bread Congress, Prague, Czechoslovakia, June 28-July 2, 1982, 2 vols. Ed. by J. Holas & J. Kratochvil. (Developments in Food Science Ser.: No. 5). 1300p. 1983. Set. 208.00 (ISBN 0-444-99649-4). Elsevier.

Progress in Chemical Fibrinolysis & Thrombolysis, Vol. 3. Ed. by John F. Davidson et al. LC 75-14335. 631p. 1978. 100.50 (ISBN 0-89004-137-7). Raven.

Progress in Chemical Toxicology. Ed. by A. Stolman. LC 63-22331. Vols. 1-4. 104.00 ea. Vol. 1, 1963 (ISBN 0-12-536501-2). Vol. 2, 1965 (ISBN 0-12-536502-0). Vol. 3, 1967 (ISBN 0-12-536503-9). Vol. 4, 1969 (ISBN 0-12-536504-7). Acad Pr.

Progress in Child Health, Vol. 3. Ed. by J. A. Macfarlene. (Illus.). 237p. (Orig.). 1987. pap. text ed. 48.00 (ISBN 0-443-03404-4). Churchill.

Progress in Cholinergic Biology: Model Cholinergic Synapses. Ed. by Israel Hanin & Alan M. Goldberg. 382p. 1982. text ed. 104.50 (ISBN 0-89004-758-8). Raven.

Progress in Clinical Biochemistry & Medicine, Vol. 3. (Illus.). 195p. 1986. 49.50 (ISBN 0-387-16249-6). Springer-Verlag.

Progress in Clinical Biochemistry & Medicine, Vol. 4. (Illus.). 160p. 1987. 59.30 (ISBN 0-387-16955-5). Springer-Verlag.

Progress in Clinical Biochemistry & Medicine, Vol. 5. (Illus.). 144p. 1987. 77.60 (ISBN 0-387-18187-3). Springer-Verlag.

Progress in Clinical Biochemistry & Medicine, Vol. 7. (Illus.). 150p. 1988. 77.50 (ISBN 0-387-19002-3). Springer-Verlag.

Progress in Clinical Immunology. Ed. by M. Ricci & G. Marone. (Monographs in Allergy: Vol. 18). (Illus.). x, 314p. 1983. 109.50 (ISBN 3-8055-3697-6). S Karger.

Progress in Clinical Immunology, Vol. IV. Ed. by Robert S. Schwartz. 288p. 1980. 36.50 (ISBN 0-8089-1239-9, 793934). Grune.

Progress in Clinical Kidney Disease & Hypertension, Vol. 2. Franklin D. McDonald. (Illus.). 176p. 1985. text ed. 39.00 (ISBN 0-86577-149-9). Thieme Med Pubs.

Progress in Clinical Pathology, Vols. 2-4. Ed. by Mario Stefanini. Incl. Vol. II. (Illus.). 392p. 1969. 99.50 (ISBN 0-8089-0476-0, 794312); Vol. III. (Illus.). 424p. 1969. 99.50 (ISBN 0-8089-0477-9, 794313); Vol. IV. 352p. 1972. 99.50 (ISBN 0-8089-0766-2, 794314). LC 66-11412. (Review of Significant Advances in the Field of Clinical Pathology Ser.). (Vol. 1 o.p.). Grune.

Progress in Clinical Pathology, Vol. 8. Ed. by Mario Stefanini & Ellis Benson. (Illus.). 352p. 1981. 69.50 (ISBN 0-8089-1310-7, 794318). Grune.

Progress in Clinical Pathology, Vol. 9. Ed. by Mario Stefanini et al. 288p. 1983. 74.50 (ISBN 0-8089-1614-9, 794319). Grune.

Progress in Clinical Pharmacy IV: Proceedings of the European Symposium, Tenth, Stresa, Italy, October 14-17, 1981. Ed. by G. Ostino & N. Martini. (Progress in Clinical Pharmacy: No. IV). 274p. 1982. 85.25 (ISBN 0-444-80437-4, Biomedical Pr). Elsevier.

Progress in Clinical Rheumatology, Vol. I. Ed. by Alan S. Cohen. 224p. 1984. 39.50 (ISBN 0-8089-1646-7, 790881). Grune.

Progress in Combinatorial Optimization. Ed. by William R. Pulleybank. 1984. 55.50 (ISBN 0-12-566780-9). Acad Pr.

Progress in Communication Sciences, Vol. 1. Ed. by Melvin J. Voigt & Gerhard J. Hanneman. (Communication & Information Science Ser.). 1979. isnt. ed. 47.50x (ISBN 0-89391-010-4); pers. ed. 29.50. Ablex Pub.

Progress in Communication Sciences, Vol. 2. Ed. by Melvin J. Voigt & Brenda Dervin. (Communication & Information Science Ser.). 400p. 1980. text ed. 47.50 inst. ed. (ISBN 0-89391-060-0); pers. ed. 29.50. Ablex Pub.

Progress in Communication Sciences, Vol. 3. Brenda Dervin. Ed. by Melvin J. Voigt. (Communication & Information Sciences Ser.). 350p. 1982. text ed. 47.50x inst. ed (ISBN 0-89391-081-3); pers. ed. 29.50. Ablex Pub.

Progress in Communication Sciences, Vol. 4. Ed. by Brenda Dervin & Melvin J. Voigt. (Communication & Information Science Ser.). 304p. 1983. text ed. 47.50 inst. ed. (ISBN 0-89391-102-X); pers. ed. 29.50. Ablex Pub.

Progress in Communication Sciences, Vol. 5. Ed. by Melvin Voigt & Brenda Dervin. (Communication & Information Sciences Ser.). 320p. 1984. text ed. 47.50 inst. ed. (ISBN 0-89391-141-0); pers. ed. 29.50. Ablex Pub.

Progress in Communication Sciences, Vol. 6. Brenda Dervin & Melvin J. Voigt. (Progress in Communication Sciences Ser.). 332p. 1985. text ed. 47.50 inst. ed. (ISBN 0-89391-306-5); text ed. 29.50 pers. ed. Ablex Pub.

Progress in Communication Sciences, Vol. 7. Ed. by Brenda Dervin & Melvin J. Voigt. 304p. 1986. text ed. 29.50 pers. ed. (ISBN 0-89391-325-1); inst. ed. 47.50. Ablex Pub.

Progress in Communication Sciences, Vol. 8. Ed. by Brenda Dervin & Melvin J. Voigt. 320p. 1986. text ed. 45.00 inst. ed. (ISBN 0-89391-392-8); text ed. 29.50 pers. ed. (ISBN 0-317-46095-1). Ablex Pub.

Progress in Community Mental Health, Vol. 1. Ed. by Leopold Bellak & Harvey H. Barten. LC 69-15739. 280p. 1969. 56.50 (ISBN 0-8089-0047-1, 790501). Grune.

Progress in Comparative Placentology. Ed. by K. S. Ludwig & H. Hartels. (Illus.). 1973. 26.75 (ISBN 3-8055-1365-8). S Karger.

Progress in Construction Science & Technology, 2 vols. Ed. by Roger A. Burgess et al. Vol. 1. pap. 82.50 (ISBN 0-317-10675-9, 2015502); Vol. 2. pap. 62.80 (ISBN 0-317-10676-7). Bks Demand UMI.

Progress in Coordination Chemistry. Ed. by Michael Cais. 1969. 73.75 (ISBN 0-444-40746-4). Elsevier.

Progress in Cosmology. Ed. by A. W. Wolfendale. 1982. 54.50 (ISBN 90-277-1441-X, Pub. by Reidel Holland). Kluwer Academic.

Progress in Cybernetics & Systems Research: Cybernetics of Cognition & Learning, Structure & Dynamics of Socio-economic Systems, Health Care Systems, Engineering Systems Methodology see Progress in Cybernetics & Systems Research.

Progress in Cybernetics & Systems Research, 5 vols. Ed. by Robert Trappl et al. Incl. Vol. 1. General Systems, Engineering Systems, Biocybernetics & Neural Systems; Vol. 2. Socio-Economic Systems, Cognition & Learning, Systems Education, Organization & Management; Vol. 3. General Systems Methodology, Fuzzy Mathematics & Fuzzy Systems, Biocybernetics & Theoretical Neurobiology; Vol. 4. Progress in Cybernetics & Systems Research: Cybernetics of Cognition & Learning, Structure & Dynamics of Socio-economic Systems, Health Care Systems, Engineering Systems Methodology. Robert Trappl & Gordon Pask. LC 75-6641. (Progress in Cybernetics & Systems Research Ser.). 547p. 1978. 40.00x (ISBN 0-470-99380-4); Vol. 5. Organization & Management, Organic Problem-Solving in Management System Approach in Urban & Regional Planning, Computer Performance, Control & Evaluation of Computer Linguistics. Ed. by Robert Trappl & F. De P. Hanika. LC 75-6641. (Programs in Cybernetics & Systems Research Ser.). 683p. 1979. 54.95x (ISBN 0-470-26553-1). LC 75-6641. 1975-79. Halsted Pr.

Progress in Cybernetics & Systems Research, Vol. 8. Ed. by Robert Trappl. 1982. text ed. 110.00 (ISBN 0-07-065068-3). McGraw.

Progress in Cybernetics & Systems Research, Vol. 8. Ed. by Robert Trappl et al. LC 75-6641. (Progress in Cybernetics & Systems Research Ser.). (Illus.). 529p. 1982. text ed. 125.00 (ISBN 0-89116-237-2). Hemisphere Pub.

Progress in Cybernetics & Systems Research, Vol. 9. Ed. by Robert Trappl. 1982. text ed. 110.00 (ISBN 0-07-065069-1). McGraw.

Progress in Cybernetics & Systems Research, Vol. 10. Ed. by Robert Trappl. 1982. text ed. 110.00 (ISBN 0-07-065070-5). McGraw.

Progress in Cybernetics & Systems Research: Proceedings of the European Meeting on Cybernetics & Systems Research, 5th, Vienna, Austria, April, 1980, Vol. 9. Cybernetics & Systems Research Staff. Ed. by Robert Trappl et al. LC 75-6641. (Illus.). 532p. 1982. text ed. 125.00 (ISBN 0-89116-238-0). Hemisphere Pub.

Progress in Cybernetics & Systems Research: Proceedings of the Eurpoean Meeting on Cybernetics & Systems Research, 5th, Vienna, Austria, April, 1980, Vol. 11. Cybernetics & Systems Research Staff. Ed. by Robert Trappl et al. LC 75-6641. (Illus.). 601p. 1982. text ed. 125.00 (ISBN 0-89116-240-2). Hemisphere Pub.

Progress in Cybernetics & Systems Research: Symposia of the European Meeting on Cybernetics & Systems Research, Linz, Austria, March 1978, Vol. 6. Cybernetics & Systems Research Staff. Ed. by Franz R. Pichler & Robert Trappl. LC 75-6641. (Progress in Cybernetics & Systems Research: Vol. 6). (Illus.). 398p. 1982. text ed. 110.00 (ISBN 0-89116-194-5). Hemisphere Pub.

Progress in Dermatoglyphic Research. Christos S. Bartsocas. LC 82-215. (Progress in Clinical & Biological Research Ser.: Vol. 84). 474p. 1982. 53.00 (ISBN 0-8451-0084-X). A R Liss.

Progress in Desert Research. Ed. by Louis Berkofsky & Morton G. Wurtele. 350p. 1987. 54.50x (ISBN 0-8476-7480-0). Rowman.

Progress in Developmental Biology, Pts. A & B. Ed. by Harold C. Slavkin. (Progress in Clinical & Biological Research Ser.: Vols. 217A). 1986. Pt. A, 476 pgs. LC 86-7483. 65.00 (ISBN 0-8451-0192-7, 0192); Pt. B, 490 pgs. LC 86-7485. 65.00 (ISBN 0-8451-0193-5, 0193). A R Liss.

Progress in Diet & Nutrition. Ed. by C. Horwitz & P. Rozen. (Frontiers of Gastrointestinal Research Ser.: Vol. 14). (Illus.). x, 226p. 1988. 129.50 (ISBN 3-8055-4608-4). S Karger.

Progress in Digital Angiocardiography. Ed. by P. H. Heintzen & J. H. Bursch. (Developments in Cardiovascular Medicine Ser.). 1988. lib. bdg. 145.00 (ISBN 0-89838-965-8, Pub. by Martinus Nijhoof Netherlands). Kluwer Academic.

Progress in Diseases of the Skin, Vol. I. Ed. by Raul Fleischmajer. 288p. 1981. 49.50 (ISBN 0-8089-1412-X, 791272). Grune.

Progress in Diseases of the Skin, Vol. II. Ed. by Raul Fleischmajer. 288p. 1984. 52.50 (ISBN 0-8089-1623-8, 791273). Grune.

Progress in Drug Meatbolism see Progress in Drug Metabolism.

Progress in Drug Metabolism, Vols. 1-4. Ed. by J. W. Bridges & L. F. Chasseaud. Incl. Vol. 1. Progress in Drug Metabolism. J. W. Bridges & L. F. Chasseaud. LC 75-19446. (Progress in Drug Metabolism Ser.). 286p. 1976. 87.95x (ISBN 0-471-10370-5); Vol. 2. 350p. 1977; Vol. 3. Progress in Drug Meatbolism. J. W. Bridges & L. F. Chasseaud. LC 75-19446. (Progress in Drug Metabolism Ser.). 372p. 1979. 110.00x (ISBN 0-471-99711-0); Vol. 4. LC 79-42723. 335p. 1980. Pub. by Wiley-Interscience). Wiley.

Progress in Drug Metabolism, Vols. 1-6. Ed. by James W. Bridges & L. F. Chasseaud. LC 75-19446. (Illus.). Vol. 1. pap. 78.00 (2030485); Vol. 2. pap. 93.60 (2030485); Vol. 3. pap. 100.10 (2030485); Vol. 4. pap. 90.30 (2030485); Vol. 5. pap. 96.80 (2030485); Vol. 6. pap. 86.10 (2030485). Bks Demand UMI.

Progress in Drug Metabolism, Vol. 6. J. W. Bridges & L. F. Chasseaud. LC 80-42314. (Progress in Drug Metabolism Ser.). 320p. 1981. 112.00x (ISBN 0-471-28023-2, Pub. by Wiley Interscience). Wiley.

Progress in Drug Metabolism, Vol. 7. J. W. Bridges & L. F. Chasseaud. (Drug Metabolism Ser.). 446p. 1983. 135.00 (ISBN 0-471-10487-6). Wiley.

Progress in Drug Metabolism, Vol. 8. Ed. by J. W. Bridges & L. F. Chasseaud. 407p. 1984. 77.00x (ISBN 0-85066-269-9). Taylor & Francis.

Progress in Drug Metabolism, Vol. 9. J. W. Bridges & L. F. Chasseaud. 256p. 1986. 77.00x (ISBN 0-85066-328-8). Taylor & Francis.

Progress in Drug Metabolism, Vol. 10. Ed. by J. W. Bridges et al. 340p. 1988. 88.00x (ISBN 0-85066-372-5). Taylor & Francis.

Progress in Drug Metabolism, Vol. 11. G. G. Gibson. 300p. 1988. 77.00x (ISBN 0-85066-419-5). Taylor & Francis.

Progress in Drug Metabolism see Progress in Drug Metabolism.

Progress in Drug Protein Binding. Ed. by N. Rietbrock & B. G. Woodcock. 1981. 16.50 (ISBN 3-528-07906-1, Pub. by Vieweg & Sohn Germany). IPS.

Progress in Drug Research. Ed. by Ernest Jucker. (Progress in Drug Research Ser.: Vol. 27). 400p. 1983. text ed. 155.95 (ISBN 3-7643-1365-X). Birkhauser.

Progress in Drug Research, Vol. 23. E. Jucker. 320p. 1979. 118.95x (ISBN 0-8176-1070-7). Birkhauser.

Progress in Drug Research, Vol. 24. Ed. by Ernst Jucker. 300p. 1980. text ed. 155.95 (ISBN 0-8176-1148-7). Birkhauser.

Progress in Drug Research, Vol. 25. Ed. by E. Jucker. 500p. 1981. text ed. 181.95x (ISBN 0-8176-1179-7). Birkhauser.

Progress in Drug Research, Vol. 26. Ed. by Ernst Jucker. 412p. 1982. text ed. 155.95 (ISBN 0-8176-1261-0). Birkhauser.

Progress in Drug Research, Vol. 28. Ernst Jucker. 1984. text ed. 138.95 (ISBN 3-76431-556-3). Birkhauser.

Progress in Ecology, Vol. I: Progress of Plant Ecology in India. Ed. by R. Mishra et al. (Illus.). 162p. 1973. 20.00 (ISBN 0-88065-160-1, Pub. by Messers Today & Tomorrows Printers & Publishers India). Scholarly Pubns.

Progress in Ecology, Vol. VIII: Ecological & Anatomical Marvels of the Himalayan Orchids. Purushotam Kaushik. 124p. 1983. 65.00 (ISBN 1-55528-028-5, Pub. by Messers Today & Tomorrow Printers & Publishers). Scholarly Pubns.

Progress in Electrochemistry. Ed. by D. Rand et al. (Studies in Physical & Theoretical Chemistry). 470p. 1981. Repr. 144.75 (ISBN 0-444-41955-1). Elsevier.

Progress in Energy & Combustion Science, Vols. 1-2. Ed. by Norman A. Chigier. Incl. Vol. 1, Pt. 1. 1976; Vol. 1, Pts. 2-3. 1976; Vol. 1, Pt. 4. 1976; Vol. 1, Complete. Pollution Formation & Destruction in Flames. 1976; Vol. 2, Pt. 1. 1976; Vol. 2, Pt. 2. 1976; Vol. 2, Pt. 3. 1977; Vol. 2, Pt. 4. 1978. LC 75-24822. 1976-78. pap. write for info. Pergamon.

Progress in Environmental Mutagenesis & Carcinogenesis. Ed. by A. Kappas. (Progress in Mutation Research Ser.: Vol. 2). 206p. 1981. 123.25 (ISBN 0-444-80334-3, Biomedical Pr). Elsevier.

Progress in Environmental Mutagenesis. Ed. by M. Alacevic. (Developments in Toxicology & Environmental Science Ser.: Vol. 7). 1980. 72.00 (ISBN 0-444-80241-X). Elsevier.

Progress in Ergometry: Quality Control & Test Criteria, Fifth International Seminar on Ergometry. Ed. by H. Loellgen & H. Mellerowicz. (Illus.). 260p. 1984. pap. 29.00 (ISBN 0-387-13570-7). Springer-Verlag.

Progress in Essential Oil Research: Proceedings of the International Symposium on Essential Oils, Holzminden-Neuhaus, Federal Republic of Germany, September 18-21, 1985. Ed. by Ernst-Joachim Brunke. (Illus.). xvi, 668p. 1986. 178.00 (ISBN 0-89925-101-3). De Gruyter.

Progress in Experimental Personality Research, Vols. 1-7. Ed. by B. Maher. Incl. Vol. 1. 1964. 57.50 (ISBN 0-12-541401-3); Vol. 2. 1965. 57.50 (ISBN 0-12-541402-1); Vol. 3. 1966. 57.50 (ISBN 0-12-541403-X); Vol. 4. 1968. 57.50 (ISBN 0-12-541404-8); Vol. 5. 1970. 57.50 (ISBN 0-12-541405-6); Vol. 6. 1972. 57.50 (ISBN 0-12-541406-4); Vol. 7. 1974. 57.50 (ISBN 0-12-541407-2). Acad Pr.

Progress in Experimental Personality Research, Vol. 9. Ed. by Brendan A. Maher. 1979. 75.00 (ISBN 0-12-541409-9). Acad Pr.

Progress in Experimental Personality Research, Vol. 10. Ed. by Brendan A. Maher. (Serial Publication Ser.). 1981. 75.00 (ISBN 0-12-541410-2). Acad Pr.

Progress in Experimental Personality Research, Vol. 11. Ed. by Brendan Maher & W. Maher. (Serial Publication Ser.). 1982. 75.00 (ISBN 0-12-541411-0). Acad Pr.

Progress in Experimental Personality Research, Vol. 14. Ed. by Brendan Maher & Winifred Maher. (Serial Publication). 1986. 55.00 (ISBN 0-12-541414-5). Acad Pr.

Progress in Experimental Tumor Research, Vols. 27-28. (Illus.). xxxii, 500p. 1984. 156.75 (ISBN 3-8055-3857-X). S Karger.

Progress in Extractive Metallurgy Series, Vol. 1. F. Habashi. 248p. 1973. 82.00 (ISBN 0-677-12220-9). Gordon & Breach.

Progress in Extractive Metallurgy Series, Vol. 2. F. Habashi. Date not set. 95.00 (ISBN 0-677-15730-4). Gordon & Breach.

Progress in Family Law. John S. Bradway. Ed. by Richard D. Lambert. LC 71-81088. (Annals Ser.: No. 383). 1969. 15.00 (ISBN 0-87761-116-5); pap. 7.95 (ISBN 0-87761-115-7). Am Acad Pol Soc Sci.

Progress in Fast Neutron Physics. International Conference on Fast Neutron Physics 1963: Houston, TX. Ed. by G. C. Phillips & J. B. Marion. LC 63-18849. (Rice University Semicentennial Publications Ser.). pap. 102.80 (ISBN 0-317-08835-1, 2020204). Bks Demand UMI.

Progress in Filtration & Separation, Vol. 1. Ed. by R. J. Wakeman. 346p. 1979. 94.75 (ISBN 0-444-41819-9). Elsevier.

Progress in Filtration & Separation, Vol. 2. Ed. by R. J. Wakeman. 306p. 1981. 94.75 (ISBN 0-444-42006-1). Elsevier.

Progress in Filtration & Separation, Vol. 3. Ed. by R. J. Wakeman. 270p. 1983. 94.75 (ISBN 0-444-42168-8). Elsevier.

Progress in Filtration & Separation, Vol. 4. Ed. by R. L. Wakeman. 422p. 1986. 155.25 (ISBN 0-444-42581-0). Elsevier.

Progress in Fire Safety: Regulations, Polymers, Chemicals, Markets - Fire Retardant Chemicals Association Conference, March 1982-Oct. 1982. 242p. 1983. 35.00 (ISBN 0-317-17385-5). Technomic.

Progress in Flavour Research. Ed. by D. G. Land & H. E. Nursten. (Illus.). 371p. 1979. 83.00 (ISBN 0-85334-818-9, Pub. by Elsevier Applied Sci England). Elsevier.

Progress in Flavour Research, 1984: Proceedings of the 4th Weurman Flavour Research Symposium, Dourdan, France, 9-11 May, 1984. J. Adda. (Developments in Food Science: Vol. 10). 1985. 179.00 (ISBN 0-444-42432-6). Elsevier.

Progress in Flaw Growth & Fracture Toughness Testing: Proceedings of the 1972 National Symposium on Fracture Mechanics, Philadelphia, PA, 28-30, 1972. American Society for Testing & Materials Staff. LC 73-76198. (American Society for Testing & Materials Special Technical Publication: No. 536). pap. 125.30 (ISBN 0-317-10700-3, 2022546). Bks Demand UMI.

Progress in Flying Machines. Octave Chanute. 12.50 (ISBN 0-916494-00-4, Pub. by Lorenz & Herwig). Aviation.

Progress in Food & Nutrition Science, Vol. 1, Pts. 1-10 & Vol. 2, Pts. 1-9. Ed. by H. M. Sinclair. Incl. Vol. 1, Pt. 1. 1975; Vol. 1, Pt. 2. 1975; Vol. 1, Pt. 3. 1975; Vol. 1, Pt. 4. 1975; Vol. 1, Pt. 5. 1975; Vol. 1, Pt. 6. 1975; Vol. 1, Pts. 7-8. 1975; Vol. 1, Pt. 9. 1975; Vol. 1, Pt. 10. 1975; Vol. 2, Pt. 1. 1976; Vol. 2, Pts. 2-3. 1976; Vol. 2, Pt. 4. 1977; Vol. 2, Pt. 5. 1977; Vol. 2, Pt. 6. 1977; Vol. 2, Pt. 7. 1977; Vol. 2, Pt. 8. 1977; Vol. 2, Pt. 9. 1977. LC 75-7734. 1975-77. pap. write for info. Pergamon.

Progress in Fracture Mechanics: Fracture Mechanics Research & Technological Activities of Nations Around the World. Ed. by G. C. Sih & D. Francois. (International Series on Strength & Fracture of Materials). (Illus.). 96p. 1983. 47.00 (ISBN 0-08-028691-7). Pergamon.

Progress in Fracture Research, 1985. Ed. by P. R. Rama et al. (International Series on the Strength & Fracture of Materials & Structures). (Illus.). 114p. 1987. 35.00 (ISBN 0-08-035903-5). Pergamon.

Progress in Functional Psychoses. Ed. by Robert Cancro et al. LC 78-31828. (Illus.). 250p. 1979. 40.00 (ISBN 0-88331-185-2). Luce.

Progress in Gastroenterology, Vols. I-II. Ed. by George B. Glass. LC 68-11924. (Illus.). 1968. Vol. 1, 1968 528pps. 132.50 (ISBN 0-8089-0149-4, 791561). Grune.

Progress in Gastroenterology, Vol. III. Ed. by George B. Glass. 1072p. 1977. 149.00 (ISBN 0-8089-1025-6, 791563). Grune.

Progress in Gastroenterology. Ed. by George B. Glass & Paul Sherlock. (Vol. 4). 624p. 1983. 106.00 (ISBN 0-8089-1555-X, 791564). Grune.

Progress in Gauge Field Theory. Ed. by G. T'Hooft et al. (NATO ASI Series B, Physics: Vol. 115). 618p. 1984. 97.50x (ISBN 0-306-41829-0, Plenum Press). Plenum Pub.

Progress in Geomorphology: Papers in Honour of David L. Linton. Ed. by E. H. Brown & R. S. Waters. (Special Publication of the Institute of British Geographers: No. 7). 1980. 28.50 (ISBN 0-12-137780-6). Acad Pr.

Progress in Glomerulonephritis. Priscilla Kincaid-Smith et al. LC 79-14186. (Perspectives in Nephrology & Hypertension Ser.). 458p. 1979. 90.00 (ISBN 0-471-04424-5, Pub. by Wiley Med). Wiley.

Progress in Gynecology, Vol. 7. Melvin L. Taymor & James H. Nelson. 480p. 1983. 59.50 (ISBN 0-8089-1587-8, 794547). Grune.

Progress in Health Monitoring (AMHTS) Ed. by T. Yasaka. (International Congress Ser.: No. 539). 546p. 1982. 141.00 (ISBN 0-444-90198-1, Excerpta Medica). Elsevier.

Progress in Heat Transfer: Part I: Laminar Boundary Layer Flow in Transparent: & Gray Media. Part II: Equipment for the Preparation of Semiconductor Materials. Ed. by P. K. Konakov. Tr. by James S. Wood from Rus. LC 65-26629. pap. 41.80 (ISBN 0-317-08027-X, 2020672). Bks Demand UMI.

Progress in Hematology, Vol. 11. Ed. by Elmer B. Brown. 335p. 1979. 59.50 (ISBN 0-8089-1223-2, 790701). Grune.

Progress in Hematology, Vol. 12. Ed. by Elmer B. Brown. 1981. 49.50 (ISBN 0-8089-1410-3, 790702). Grune.

Progress in Hematology, Vol. 13. Elmer B. Brown. 368p. 1983. 55.50 (ISBN 0-8089-1615-7, 790703). Grune.

Progress in Hematology, Vol. 14. Ed. by Elmer B. Brown. LC 79-704. 352p. 1986. 57.50 (ISBN 0-8089-1769-2, 790704). Grune.

Progress in Hematology, Vol. 15. Elmer B. Brown. 352p. 1987. 49.50 (ISBN 0-8089-1861-3, 790705). Grune.

Progress in Hemostasis & Thrombosis, Vol. 1. Ed. by Theodore H. Spaet. LC 72-2917. (Illus.). 250p. 1972. 78.50 (ISBN 0-8089-0760-3, 794191). Grune.

Progress in Hemostasis & Thrombosis, Vol. 5. Ed. by Theodore H. Spaet. (Illus.). 320p. 1980. 59.50 (ISBN 0-8089-1220-8, 794195). Grune.

Progress in Hemostasis & Thrombosis, Vol. 6. Ed. by Theodore Spaet. 368p. 1982. 59.50 (ISBN 0-8089-1493-6, 794196). Grune.

Progress in Hemostasis & Thrombosis, Vol. 7. Ed. by Theodore H. Spaet. 400p. 1984. 59.50 (ISBN 0-8089-1688-2, 794197). Grune.

Progress in Hemostasis & Thrombosis, Vol. 8. Barry S. Coller. 240p. 1987. 49.50 (ISBN 0-8089-1836-2, 790883). Grune.

Progress in High Temperature Physics & Chemistry, 5 vols. Ed. by C. A. Rouse. 1973. Vols. 1 & 5. write for info; Vol. 2-4. 58.00 ea.. Pergamon.

Progress in High Temperature Superconductivity: Proceedings of the Adriatic Research Conference on High Temperature Superconductors, Vol. I. Ed. by S. Lundqvist et al. 532p. 1987. 83.00 (ISBN 9971-50-399-9); pap. 39.00 (ISBN 9971-50-400-6). World Scientific Pub.

Progress in High Temperature Superconductivity: Proceedings of the Beijing International Workshop, Vol. II. Ed. by Z. Z. Gran & G. J. Cui. 596p. 1987. 78.00 (ISBN 9971-50-401-4); pap. 39.00 (ISBN 9971-50-402-2). World Scientific Pub.

Progress in Holographic Applications. Ed. by Ebbeni. 223p. 1985. 43.00 (ISBN 0-89252-635-1, 600). SPIE.

Progress in Holography. Ed. by Ebbeni. 169p. 1987. 43.00 (ISBN 0-89252-847-8, 812). SPIE.

Progress in HPLC, Vol. 1: Gel Permeation & Ion-Exchange Chromatography of Proteins & Peptides. Ed. by H. Parvez et al. 231p. 1985. lib. bdg. 107.00x (ISBN 90-6764-048-4). Coronet Bks.

Progress in HPLC, Vol. 2: Electromechanical Detection in Medicine & Chemistry. Ed. by H. Parvez et al. 480p. 1987. lib. bdg. 175.00x (ISBN 90-6764-062-X). Coronet Bks.

Progress in Human Biometeorology: The Effect of Weather & Climate on Man & His Living Environment, Period 1963 to 1970-75, Vol. 1. Solco W. Tromp. Incl. Pt. 1. Micro & Macroenvironments in the Atmosphere & Their Effects on Basic Physiological Mechanisms of Man. 726p. 1974. pap. text ed. 144.00 (ISBN 90-265-0167-6); Pt. 2. Pathological Biometeorology. 444p. 1977. pap. text ed. 86.50 (ISBN 90-265-0245-1); Pt. 3. Biometeorological Aspects of Plants, Trees & Animals in Human Life. 158p. 1972. pap. text ed. 31.50 (ISBN 90-265-0156-0). (Progress in Biometeorology Ser.). pap. (Pub. by Swets Pub Serv Holland). Swets North Am.

Progress in Hydrogen Energy. Ed. by R. P. Dahiya. 1987. lib. bdg. 59.00 (ISBN 90-277-2440-7, Pub. by Reidel Holland). Kluwer Academic.

Progress in Hypertension, Vol. 1: Neurotransmitters As Modulators of Blood Pressure. Ed. by H. Saito et al. 380p. 1987. lib. bdg. 135.00x (ISBN 90-6764-100-6). Coronet Bks.

Progress in Immunodefeciency Research & Therapy: Proceedings, 2nd Meeting of the European Group for Immunodeficiencies (EGID), Congress Centre Roldue, Kerkrade, the Netherlands, June 11-14, 1986, Vol. II. Ed. by J. Vossen & C. Griscelli. (International Congress Ser.: No. 715). 476p. 1986. 149.50 (ISBN 0-444-80841-8, Excerpta Medica). Elsevier.

Progress in Immunodeficiency Research & Therapy, Vol. 1. C. Griscelli & J. Vossen. (International Congress Ser.: Vol. 645). 1984. 154.25 (ISBN 0-444-80602-4). Elsevier.

Progress in Immunohematology. Ed. by S. Breanndan Moore. 1988. text ed. price not set (ISBN 0-915355-60-4). Am Assn Blood.

Progress in Immunology: Fifth International Congress of Immunology (Symposium, Vol. V. Y. Yamamura & T. Tada. 1984. 130.50 (ISBN 0-12-768240-6). Acad Pr.

Progress in Immunology II, 5 Vols. Ed. by L. Brent & J. Holbrow. 1975. Set. 134.25 (ISBN 0-7204-7033-1, North Holland); Vol. 1. 26.00 (ISBN 0-444-10753-3); Vol. 2. 33.75 (ISBN 0-444-10754-1); Vol. 3. 29.50 (ISBN 0-444-10755-X); Vol. 4. 33.75 (ISBN 0-444-10756-8); Vol. 5. 31.75 (ISBN 0-444-10757-6). Elsevier.

Progress in Immunology VI: International Congress in Immunology. Ed. by B. Cinader & Richard G. Miller. 1115p. 1987. 195.00 (ISBN 0-12-174685-2); pap. 77.00 (ISBN 0-317-54362-8). Acad Pr.

Progress in Industrial Gas Chromatography: Proceedings of the Gas Chromatography Institute, 3rd Annual, Buffalo, N. Y., April 4-6, 1961, Vol. 1. Gas Chromatography Institute Staff. LC 61-15520. pap. 59.80 (ISBN 0-317-10634-1, 2020700). Bks Demand UMI.

Progress in Industrial Geography. Ed. by Michael Pacione. LC 85-14938. (Progress in Geography Ser.). 287p. 1985. 43.00 (ISBN 0-7099-2072-5, Pub. by Croom Helm Ltd). Routledge Chapman & Hall.

Progress in Industrial Microbiology, Vols. 4 & 5. D. J. Hockenhull. Incl. Vol. 4. 214p. 70.00 (ISBN 0-677-10150-3); Vol. 5. 328p. 105.00x (ISBN 0-677-10160-0). 1969. Gordon & Breach.

Progress in Industrial Microbiology, Vol. 14. Ed. by M. J. Bull. 294p. 1978. 63.00 (ISBN 0-444-41665-X). Elsevier.

Progress in Industrial Microbiology, Vol. 16. Ed. by M. J. Bull. 350p. 1982. 108.00 (ISBN 0-444-42037-1). Elsevier.

Progress in Industrial Microbiology, Vol. 17: Industrial Microbiology, Spectroscopy & Pharmaceuticals. Ed. by M. E. Bushell. 232p. 1983. 89.50 (ISBN 0-444-42128-9). Elsevier.

Progress in Industrial Microbiology, Vol. 18: Microbial Polysaccharides. M. E. Bushell. 258p. 1983. 94.75 (ISBN 0-444-42246-3). Elsevier.

Progress in Infertility. 3rd, rev. ed. S. J. Behrman et al. 880p. 1987. text ed. 89.00 (ISBN 0-316-08775-0, Little Med Div). Little.

Progress in Nitrogen Ceramics. Ed. by F. L. Riley. 1983. lib. bdg. 100.00 (ISBN 90-247-2828-2, Pub. by Martinus Nijhoff Netherlands). Kluwer Academic.

Progress in Non-Histone Protein Research. Ed. by Isaac Bekhor. 1985. Vol. I, 224p. 95.00 (ISBN 0-8493-5528-1); Vol. II, 240p. 99.00 (ISBN 0-8493-5529-X). CRC Pr.

Progress in Nonmammalian Brain Research, 2 Vols. Ed. by Giuseppe Nistico & Liana Bolis. 1983. Vol. I, 208p. 77.00 (ISBN 0-8493-6350-0); Vol. II, 240p. 79.00 (ISBN 0-8493-6351-9). CRC Pr.

Progress in Nuclear Energy, Vol. 14. Ed. by M. M. Williams & N. J. McCormick. (Illus.). 260p. 1985. 150.00 (ISBN 0-08-032323-5, Pub. by PPL). Pergamon.

Progress in Nuclear Energy, Series 9. Ed. by H. A. Elion & D. C. Stewart. Incl. Vol. 4, Pt. 3. 1965; Vol. 6. 1966. 105.00 (ISBN 0-08-011583-7); Vol. 7. 1966; Vol. 9. 1969; Vol. 10. 1970. 105.00 (ISBN 0-08-013394-0); Vol. 11. 1972; Vol. 12, Pt. 1. 1975. LC 59-8283. write for info. Pergamon.

Progress in Nuclear Magnetic Resonance Spectroscopy, Vols. 1-10. Ed. by J. W. Emsley & L. H. Sutcliffe. Incl. Vol. 1. 1965; Vol. 2. 1967; Vol. 3. 1967; Vol. 4. 1969; Vol. 5. 1970; Vol. 6. 1971; Vol. 7. 1971; Vol. 8, 3 pts. 1972. Pts. 1-3. pap. 15.50 ea.; Vol. 9, 3 pts. 1975. Vol. 9, Complete. 130.00 (ISBN 0-08-017704-2); Pts. 1-3. pap. 13.75 ea.; Vol. 10. 1976. write for info. Pergamon.

Progress in Nuclear Physics. Ed. by D. M. Brink & J. Mulvey. Incl. Vol. 10. 1969; Vol. 11. 1970; Vol. 12, Pt. 1. 1970; Vol. 12, Pt. 2. 1970. write for info. Pergamon.

Progress in Nuclear Physics. Ed. by O. R. Frisch. 1963. Vol. 6. 1957. 110.00 (ISBN 0-08-009066-4); Vol. 8. 1960. 89.00. Pergamon.

Progress in Nucleic Acid Research, Vol. 28. (Serial Publication). 1983. 39.50 (ISBN 0-12-540028-4). Acad Pr.

Progress in Nucleic Acid Research, Vol. 31. Ed. by J. N. Davidson & W. E. Cohn. 1984. 62.50 (ISBN 0-12-540031-4). Acad Pr.

Progress in Nucleic Acid Research & Molecular Biology, Vol. 23. Ed. by Waldo E. Cohn. LC 63-15847. 1980. 85.00 (ISBN 0-12-540023-3). Acad Pr.

Progress in Nucleic Acid Research & Molecular Biology, Vol. 24. Ed. by Waldo E. Cohn. 1980. 85.00 (ISBN 0-12-540024-1). Acad Pr.

Progress in Nucleic Acid Research & Molecular Biology, Vol. 25. Ed. by Waldo E. Cohn. (Serial Publication). 1981. 85.00 (ISBN 0-12-540025-X). Acad Pr.

Progress in Nucleic Acid Research & Molecular Biology, Vol. 27. Ed. by Waldo Cohn. (Serial Publication). 320p. 1982. 85.00 (ISBN 0-12-540027-6). Acad Pr.

Progress in Nucleic Acid Research & Molecular Biology, Vol. 30. Ed. by Waldo E. Cohn & Kivie Moldave. (Serial Publication Ser.). 1983. 85.00 (ISBN 0-12-540030-6); lib. bdg. 47.00 o.p (ISBN 0-12-540104-3). Acad Pr.

Progress in Nucleic Acid Research & Molecular Biology, Vol. 32. (Serial Publication). 1985. 49.50 (ISBN 0-12-540032-2). Acad Pr.

Progress in Nucleic Acid Research & Molecular Biology, Vol. 33. Ed. by Waldo E. Cohn & Moldave Kivic. 296p. 1986. 59.00 (ISBN 0-12-540033-0). Acad Pr.

Progress in Nucleic Acid Research & Molecular Biology, Vol. 35. Ed. by Waldo E. Cohn & Kivie Moldave. 294p. 1988. 65.00 (ISBN 0-12-540035-7). Acad Pr.

Progress in Nucleic Acid Research & Molecular Biology: An International Series. Ed. by J. N. Davidson et al. Incl. Vol. 3. 1964. 71.50 (ISBN 0-12-540003-9); Vol. 4. 1965. 71.50 (ISBN 0-12-540004-7); Vol. 5. 1966. 71.50 (ISBN 0-12-540005-5); Vol. 6. 1967. 71.50 (ISBN 0-12-540006-3); Vol. 7. 1967. 71.50 (ISBN 0-12-540007-1); Vol. 8. 1968. 71.50 (ISBN 0-12-540008-X); Vol. 9. 1969. 71.50 (ISBN 0-12-540009-8); Vol. 10. 1970. 71.50 (ISBN 0-12-540010-1); Vol. 11. 1971. 75.00 (ISBN 0-12-540011-X); Vol. 12. 1972. 55.00 (ISBN 0-12-540012-8); Vol. 13. 1973. 65.00 (ISBN 0-12-540013-6); Vol. 20. 1977. 59.50 (ISBN 0-12-540020-9); Vol. 21. 1978. 55.00 (ISBN 0-12-540021-7); Vol. 22. 1979. 59.50 (ISBN 0-12-540022-5). Acad Pr.

Progress in Nucleic Acid Research & Molecular Biology: DNA: Multiprotein Interactions, Vol. 26. Ed. by Waldo E. Cohn. (Serial Publication Ser.). 1981. 85.00 (ISBN 0-12-540026-8). Acad Pr.

Progress in Numerical Fluid Dynamics. Short Course Held at the Von Karman Institute for Fluid Dynamics, Rhode-St.-Genese, Belgium, Feb. 11-15, 1974. Ed. by H. J. Wirz. (Lecture Notes in Physics: Vol. 41). 480p. 1975. pap. 26.00 (ISBN 0-387-07408-2). Springer-Verlag.

Progress in Obsterics & Gynaecology, Vol. 6. Ed. by John Studd. LC 81-21699. (Illus.). 442p. (Orig.). 1987. pap. text ed. 36.95 (ISBN 0-443-03572-5). Churchill.

Progress in Oceanography, Vols. 1 & 4-6. Ed. by M. Sears & Bruce Warren. LC 63-15353. 1974. text ed. write for info. Pergamon.

Progress in Oceanography, Vol. 7. Ed. by Mary Swallow. Incl. Pt. 1. Midwater Fishes in the Eastern North Atlantic. 1976; Pt. 2. The Mixing & Spreading of Medoc. 1976; Pt. 3. 1977; Pt. 4. Observations of Rossby Waves Near Site D. 1977; Pts. 5 & 6. 1979; Vol. 7 Complete. 1980. LC 63-15353. pap. write for info. Pergamon.

Progress in Oculomotor Research. Ed. by A. F. Fuchs & W. Becker. (Developments in Neuroscience Ser.: Vol. 12). 686p. 1981. 155.00 (ISBN 0-444-00589-7, Biomedical Pr). Elsevier.

Progress in Operations Research, 2 Vols. Ed. by A. Prekopa. (Colloquia Mathematica Societatis Janos Bolyai: No. 12). 968p. 1976. Set. 118.50 (ISBN 0-7204-2836-X, North-Holland). Elsevier.

Progress in Operations Research, Vol. 1. R. L. Ackoff. LC 61-10415. (Operations Research Ser.: No. 5). Repr. of 1961 ed. 98.30 (ISBN 0-8357-9966-2, 2051575). Bks Demand UMI.

Progress in Optical Communication, Vol. 2. P. J. Clarricoats. (IEE Reprint Ser.: No. 4). 344p. 1982. pap. 68.00 (ISBN 0-906048-84-2, RE004). Inst Elect Eng.

Progress in Optical Communication, 1978-79. Ed. by P. J. Clarricoats. (IEE Reprint Ser: No. 3). 272p. 1980. pap. 57.00 (ISBN 0-906048-32-X, RE003). Inst Elect Eng.

Progress in Optics, Vol. XXIII. Ed. by E. Wolf. 320p. 1986. 84.25 (ISBN 0-444-86982-4, North-Holland). Elsevier.

Progress in Optics, Vol. XXIV. Ed. by E. Wolf. 530p. 1987. 109.75 (ISBN 0-444-87050-4, North Holland). Elsevier.

Progress in Optics, Vol. XXV. Ed. by E. Wolf. 448p. 1988. 97.25 (ISBN 0-444-87076-8, North Holland). Elsevier.

Progress in Optics, Vol. XXVI. Ed. by E. Wolf. 420p. 1988. 108.00 (ISBN 0-444-87096-2, North Holland). Elsevier.

Progress in Optics, Vols. 9-17. Ed. by E. Wolf. (North-Holland); Vol. 11, 1973. 89.50 (ISBN 0-444-10497-6); Vol. 12, 1975. 89.50 (ISBN 0-7204-1512-8); Vol. 13, 1976. 76.50 (ISBN 0-444-10806-8); Vol. 14, 1977. 102.75 (ISBN 0-444-10914-5); Vol. 15, 1978. 68.00 (ISBN 0-7204-1515-2); Vol. 16, 1979. 81.00 (ISBN 0-444-85087-2); Vol. 17, 1980. 94.75 (ISBN 0-444-85309-X). Elsevier.

Progress in Optics, Vol. 18. Ed. by E. Wolf. 364p. 1980. 94.75 (ISBN 0-444-85445-2, North-Holland). Elsevier.

Progress in Optics, Vol. 19. Ed. by E. Wolf. 394p. 1981. 76.50 (ISBN 0-444-85444-4, North Holland). Elsevier.

Progress in Optics, Vol. 20. Ed. by E. Wolf. 400p. 1984. 89.50 (ISBN 0-444-86736-8). Elsevier.

Progress in Optics, Vol. 21. E. Wolf. 1984. 100.00 (ISBN 0-444-86761-9). Elsevier.

Progress in Optics, Vol. 22. Ed. by E. Wolf. 424p. 1985. 92.00 (ISBN 0-444-86923-9, North-Holland). Elsevier.

Progress in Palynology: Cumulation of Journal of Palynology, 2 vols. in 4 pts, Vols. 1-20. P. K. Nair. 3500p. 1986. 300.00 (ISBN 1-55528-077-3, Pub. by Messers Today & Tomorrow Printers & Publishers). Scholarly Pubns.

Progress in Parapsychology. Ed. by J. B. Rhine. LC 76-140922. (Illus.). 313p. 1971. pap. 2.50x (ISBN 0-911106-03-0). Parapsych Pr.

Progress in Parasitology. P. C. Garnham. (Heath Clark Lectures, 1968). (Illus.). 224p. 1971. 45.00 (ISBN 0-485-26321-1, Pub. by Athlone Pr UK). Humanities.

Progress in Passive Solar Energy Systems: Vol. 7, The World Turns to Solar. Ed. by John Hayes. 1985. pap. text ed. 150.00x (ISBN 0-89553-035-X). Am Solar Energy.

Progress in Pattern Recognition, Vol. 1. Ed. by L. N. Kanal & A. Rosenfeld. 392p. 1982. 84.25 (ISBN 0-444-86325-7, North-Holland). Elsevier.

Progress in Pattern Recognition Two. Ed. by L. N. Kanal & A. Rosenfeld. (Machine Intelligence & Pattern Recognition Ser.: Vol. 1). 402p. 1985. 55.00 (ISBN 0-444-87723-1, North-Holland). Elsevier.

Progress in Penal Reform. Ed. by Louis Blom-Cooper. 1974. 52.00x (ISBN 0-19-825325-7). Oxford U Pr.

Progress in Peptic Ulcer. Ed. by Mozsik. 1977. text ed. 52.00 cancelled (ISBN 963-05-1210-6, Pub. by Akademiai Kaido Hungary). IPS.

Progress in Peptic Ulcer. G. Mozsik & T. Javor. 774p. 1976. 254.00x (ISBN 0-569-08386-9, Pub. by Collets (UK)). State Mutual Bk.

Progress in Peptide Research, Vol. 2. Ed. by Saul Lande. LC 76-153298. 404p. 1972. 138.00 (ISBN 0-677-13610-2). Gordon & Breach.

Progress in Perinatal Medicine: Biochemical & Biophysical Diagnostic Procedures. Ed. by A. Albertini & P. G. Crosignani. (International Congress Ser.: Vol. 614). 308p. 1984. 100.00 (ISBN 0-444-90370-4, I-456-83, Excerpta Medica). Elsevier.

Progress in Perinatology. Harold Kaminetzky & Leslie Iffy. LC 77-838000005. (Illus.). 384p. 1977. text ed. 17.50 (ISBN 0-89313-006-0). G F Stickley Co.

Progress in Pesticide Biochemistry, Vol. 1. Ed. by D. H. Hutson & T. R. Roberts. LC 80-41419. (Progress in Pesticide Biochemistry Ser.). 346p. 1981. 104.00 (ISBN 0-471-27920-X, Pub. by Wiley-Interscience). Wiley.

Progress in Pesticide Biochemistry, Vol. 2. Ed. by D. H. Hutson & T. R. Roberts. 226p. 1982. text ed. 85.00 (ISBN 0-471-10118-4, Pub. by Wiley-Interscience). Wiley.

Progress in Pesticide Biochemistry, Vol. 3. D. H. Hutson & T. R. Roberts. 449p. 1983. 152.95 (ISBN 0-471-90053-2, Pub. by Wiley Interscience). Wiley.

Progress in Pesticide Biochemistry, Vol. 4. Ed. by D. H. Hutson & T. R. Roberts. 368p. 1985. 106.00 (ISBN 0-471-90460-0, Pub. by Wiley-Interscience). Wiley.

Progress in Pesticide Biochemistry & Toxicology, Herbicides & Plant Growth Regulations, Vol. 6. Ed. by D. H. Hutson & T. R. Roberts. LC 83-647760. (Progress in Pesticide Biochemistry & Toxicology Ser.). 1988. 102.00 (ISBN 0-471-91619-6). Wiley.

Progress in Petroleum Technology: A Collection of the Papers. Symposium on Twenty-five Years of Progress in Petroleum Technology, New York, 1951. LC 51-6844. (Advances in Chemistry Ser.: No. 5). (Illus.). pap. 98.00 (ISBN 0-317-10874-3, 2050182). Bks Demand UMI.

Progress in Photosynthesis Research, 4 vols. Ed. by J. Biggins. 1987. Set. lib. bdg. 662.00 (ISBN 90-247-3449-5, Pub. by Martinus Nijhoff Netherlands). Kluwer Academic.

Progress in Phycological Research, Vol. 2. F. E. Round & D. J. Chapman. 1983. 181.00 (ISBN 0-444-80502-8, I-355-83). Elsevier.

Progress in Physical Organic Chemistry, Vol. 12. Ed. by Robert W. Taft. LC 63-19364. 382p. 1976. 47.50 (ISBN 0-471-01738-8, JW). Krieger.

Progress in Physical Organic Chemistry, Vol. 13. Robert W. Taft. LC 63-19364. 650p. 1981. 97.00 (ISBN 0-471-06253-7, Pub. by Wiley-Interscience). Krieger.

Progress in Physical Organic Chemistry, Vol. 15. Ed. by Robert W. Taft. 362p. 1985. 70.00 (ISBN 0-471-81474-1). Wiley.

Progress in Physiological Psychology, 5 vols. Ed. by Eliot Stellar & James M. Sprague. Vol. 1., 1967. 75.00 (ISBN 0-12-542101-X); Vol. 2., 1968. 75.00 (ISBN 0-12-542102-8); Vol. 3., 1970. 75.00 (ISBN 0-12-542103-6); Vol. 4, 1971. 75.00 (ISBN 0-12-542104-4); Vol. 5, 1973. 75.00 (ISBN 0-12-542105-2). Acad Pr.

Progress in Phytochemistry, Vols. 1 & 2. Ed. by L. Reinhold & Y. Liwschitz. LC 68-24347. Vol. 1. pap. 160.00 (ISBN 0-317-29865-8, 2016177); Vol. 2. pap. 130.80 (ISBN 0-317-29866-6). Bks Demand UMI.

Progress in Planning, Vols. 1-8. Ed. by Donald R. Diamond & J. B. McLoughlin. Incl. Vol. 1, Pt. 1. Education for Planning: The Development of Knowledge & Capability for Urban Governance. C. C. Cockburn. 1973; Vol. 1, Pt. 2. Office Linkages & Location. J. B. Goddard. 1973; Vol. 1, Pt. 3. Planning & the Innovative Process. R. Jefferson. 1973; Vol. 1, Pt. 4. Transportation Planning & Public Policy. D. Starkie. 1973; Vol. 1 (complete) 1973; Vol. 2, Pt. 1. Urban Planning Law in East Africa. G. W. Kanyeihamba. 1973; Vol. 2, Pt. 2. Towards Measures of Spatial Opportunity. Michael Breheny. 1974; Vol. 2, Pt. 3. Planning & Change. P. Healey. 1974; Vol. 2, Pt. 4. Labor Market Areas. M. W. Smart. 1974; Vol. 2 (complete) 1974; Vol. 3, Pt. 1. City Centre Redevelopment. Ian C. Alexander. 1974; Vol. 3, Pt. 2. Local Authorities & the Attraction of Industry. M. M. Camina. 1974; Vol. 3, Pt. 3. Journey to Work. P. H. O'Farrell. 1979; Vol. 4, Pt. 1. Urban Networks: The Structure of Activity Patterns. I. Cullen & V. Godson. 1975; Vol. 4, Pt. 2. Underdevelopment & Spatial Inequality: Approaches to the Problems of Regional Planning in the Third World. D. Slater. 1975; Vol. 4, Pt. 3. Impact of Regional Policy: A Case Study of Manufactturing Employment in the Northern Region. M. E. Frost. 1979; Vol. 5, Pt. 1. Exploratory Study in Strategic Monitoring. F. Wedgwood-Oppenheim. 1976; Vol. 5, Pt. 2. Participation & the Community. A. R. Long. 1976; Vol. 5 Pt. 3. Road Traffic Noise. 1979; Vol. 6, Pt. 1. Communications Factor in Office Decentralization. 1976; Vol. 6, Pt. 2. New Building & Housing Need. 1977; Vol. 6, Pt. 3. Critique of Urban Modelling. 1979; Vol. 7, Pt. 1. Theoretical Perspectives on Planning Participation. 1977; Vol. 7, Pt. 2. Input-Output Methods in Urban & Regional Planning: A Practical Guide. 1977; Vol. 7, Pt. 3. Transport Modelling: Sensitivity Analysis & Policy Testing. 1979; Vol. 8, Pt. 1. Migration Dynamics & Labour Market Turnover. 1977. pap. write for info. Pergamon.

Progress in Planning: Recent Researh in Urban & Regional Planning, 3 pts, Vol. 10. Ed. by D. R. Diamond & J. B. McLoughlin. Incl. Pt. 1. Internal Migration & the Australian Urban System. J. McKay & J. S. Whitelaw. 1979; Pt. 2. Employment Decentralisation: Policy Instruments for Large Cities in Less Developed Countries. P. M. Townroe. 1979; Pt. 3. The Geography of Industrial Reorganisation. Doreen Massey & Richard A. Meegan. 1979. pap. 17.25 (ISBN 0-08-023706-1). (Illus.). 1979. write for info. Pergamon.

Progress in Plant Biometeorology: The Effect of Weather & Climate on Plants, 1963-1974, Vol. 1. Ed. by L. P. Smith. (Progress in Biometeorology Ser.). 490p. 1975. pap. text ed. 88.00 (ISBN 90-265-0183-8, Pub. by Pub Serv Holland). Swets North Am.

Progress in Plant Breeding, Vol. 1. Ed. by G. E. Russell. (Illus.). 288p. 1985. text ed. 89.95 (ISBN 0-407-00780-6). Butterworth.

Progress in Plant Research: Applied Morphology & Allied Subjects, Vol. 1. Ed. by T. N. Khoshoo & P. K. Nair. 320p. 1979. 50.00 (ISBN 0-88065-145-8, Pub. by Messers Today & Tomorrows Printers & Publishers India). Scholarly Pubns.

Progress in Plant Research: Plant Improvement & Horticulture, Vol. 2. Ed. by T. N. Khoshoo & P. K. Nair. 248p. 1979. 50.00 (ISBN 0-88065-146-6, Pub. by Messers Today & Tomorrows India Printers & Publishers India). Scholarly Pubns.

Progress in Plant Research: Silver Jubilee Publication of NBRI, 2 vols. Ed. by T. N. Khoshoo & P. K. Nair. 1979. Set. 90.00 (ISBN 0-88065-144-X, Pub. by Messers Today & Tomorrows Printers & Publishers India). Scholarly Pubns.

Progress in Plant Research, Vol. 3: Cumulation of New Botanist. Ed. by T. N. Khoshoo & P. K. Nair. (Illus.). 1800p. 1986. 120.00 (ISBN 1-55528-078-1, Pub. by Messers Today & Tomorrow Printers & Publichers). Scholarly Pubns.

Progress in Political Geography. Ed. by Michael Pacione. (Progress in Geography Ser.). 275p. 1985. 33.75 (ISBN 0-7099-2087-3, Pub. by Croom Helm Ltd). Routledge Chapman & Hall.

Progress in Polymer Science, Japan, 6 vols. M. Imoto et al. 1974. Set. 141.95x (ISBN 0-470-42692-6). Halsted Pr.

Progress in Polymer Spectroscopy. Collet's Holdings, Ltd. Staff. 1986. 119.00x (ISBN 0-317-52955-2, Pub. by Collets (UK)). State Mutual Bk.

Progress in Powder Metallurgy see Progress in Powder Metallurgy, 1977: Proceedings.

Progress in Powder Metallurgy: Annual Conference Proceedings, 1983 see Progress in Powder Metallurgy, 1977: Proceedings.

Progress in Powder Metallurgy: Proceedings, National Powder Metallurgy Conference, Los Angeles & Cincinatti, 1978 & 1979 see Progress in Powder Metallurgy, 1977: Proceedings.

Progress in Powder Metallurgy, 1977: Proceedings, Vol. 33. Ed. by S. Mocarski & T. Pietrocini. Incl. Progress in Powder Metallurgy: Proceedings, National Powder Metallurgy Conference, Los Angeles & Cincinatti, 1978 & 1979. Ed. by W. et al. Cebulak. (Vols. 34 & 35). (Illus., Orig.). 1980. pap. 56.00 (ISBN 0-918404-49-5); Progress in Powder Metallurgy: Annual Conference Proceedings, 1983. Ed. by H. et al. Nayar. (Vol. 39). 696p. 1984. pap. 75.00 (ISBN 0-918404-61-4); Progress in Powder Metallurgy. Ed. by Joseph Capus & Donald L. Dyke. (Vol. 37). 417p. (Orig.). 1982. pap. 60.00 (ISBN 0-918404-56-8). 1977. 42.00x (ISBN 0-918404-43-6). Metal Powder.

Progress in Powder Metallurgy 1985, Vol. 41. Ed. by Howard I. Sanderow et al. 869p. pap. 120.00 (ISBN 0-918404-69-X). Metal Powder.

Progress in Proficiency. L. Jones. 1986. student's bk. 9.95 (ISBN 0-521-31342-2); tchr's. bk. 9.95 (ISBN 0-521-31343-0); cassette 24.95 (ISBN 0-521-30850-X). Cambridge U Pr.

Progress in Protein-Lipid Interactions, Vol. 1. Ed. by A. Watts & J. J. DePont. 292p. 1985. 113.75 (ISBN 0-444-80630-X). Elsevier.

Progress in Protein-Lipid Interactions, Vol. 2. Ed. by A. Watts & J. J. DePont. 344p. 1986. 146.50 (ISBN 0-444-80707-1). Elsevier.

Progress in Psychobiology & Physiological Psychology, Vol. 8. Ed. by James Sprague & Alan Epstein. LC 66-29640. 1979. 75.00 (ISBN 0-12-542108-7). Acad Pr.

Progress in Psychobiology & Physiological Psychology, Vol. 9. Ed. by James M. Sprague & Alan N. Epstein. 1980. 75.00 (ISBN 0-12-542109-5). Acad Pr.

Progress in Psychobiology & Physiological Psychology, Vol. 12. Ed. by A. N. Epstein & A. Morrison. 1987. 65.00 (ISBN 0-12-542112-5). Acad Pr.

Progress in Psychobiology & Physiological Psychology, Vol. 13. Ed. by Alan N. Epstein & Adrian Morrison. 440p. 1988. price not set (ISBN 0-12-542113-3). Acad Pr.

Progress in Psychological Research, Vol. 1. Ed. by F. E. Round & D. J. Chapman. 384p. 1982. 169.00 (ISBN 0-444-80396-3, Biomedical Pr). Elsevier.

Progress in Pudsey. Joseph Lawson. 154p. 1978. 16.50 (ISBN 0-904573-07-9, Pub. by Caliban Bks); pap. 8.50 (ISBN 0-904573-46-X). Longwood Pub Group.

Progress in Quantum Electronics, Vols. 1-4. Ed. by J. H. Sanders & S. Stenholm. Incl. Vol. 1, Pt. 1. Parametric Processes. 1969; Vol. 1, Pt. 2. Light Propagation & Light Shifts in Optical Pumping Experiments. 1970; Vol. 1, Pt. 3. Non-Resonant Feedback in Lasers. 1970; Vol. 1, Pt. 4. Semiclassical Theory of the Gas Laser. 1971; Vol. 1, Pt. 5. Laser Lines in Atomic Species. 1971; Vol. 1 (complete) 1971; Vol. 2, Pt. 1. Photon Counting & Photon Statistics. 1972; Vol. 2, Pt. 2. Nonlinear Spectroscopy of Molecules. 1972; Vol. 2, Pt. 3. Collision Broadening of Spectral Lines by Neutral Atoms. 1972; Vol. 2, Pt. 4. Quantum Theory of Josephson Radiation. 1973; Vol. 2 (complete) 1974; Vol. 3, Pt. 1. Three-Level Gas System & Their Interaction with Radiation. 1975; Vol. 3, Pt. 2. Mode-Locking of Lasers. 1974; Vol. 3, Pt. 3. Quantum Theory of the Laser. 1974; Vol. 3 (complete) 1975. text ed. 76.00; Vol. 4, Pt. 1. Self-Focusing: Experimental & Theory. 1975; Vol. 4, Pt. 2. Nonlinear Narrow Optical Resonance by Laser Radiation. 1975; Vol. 4, Pt. 3. Far Infrared Generation by Optical Mixing. 1976; Vol. 4 (complete) 1977. pap. write for info. Pergamon.

Progress in Quantum Electronics, Vol. 8. Ed. by T. S. Moss et al. (Illus.). 278p. 1985. 140.00 (ISBN 0-08-031718-9, Pub. by PPL). Pergamon.

Progress in Quantum Field Theory. Ed. by H. Ezawa & S. Kamefuchi. 675p. 1986. 131.75 (ISBN 0-444-86990-5, North-Holland). Elsevier.

Progress in Radio-Oncology II. Ed. by K. H. Karcher et al. 510p. 1982. text ed. 92.50 (ISBN 0-89004-783-9). Raven.

Progress in Radiopharmacology, 1985. Ed. by P. H. Cox et al. LC 85-13774. (Devolopments in Nuclear Medicine). 1985. lib. bdg. 54.00 (ISBN 0-89838-745-0, Pub. by Martinus Nijhoff Netherlands). Kluwer Academic.

Progress in Radiopharmacology 3. P. H. Cox. 1983. 44.00 (ISBN 90-247-2768-5, Pub. by Martinus Nijhoff Netherlands). Kluwer Academic.

Progress in Radiopharmacy. Ed. by P. H. Cox et al. (Developments in Nuclear Medicine Ser.). 1986. lib. bdg. 155.00 (ISBN 0-89838-823-6, Pub. by Martinus Nijhoff Netherlands). Kluwer Academic.

Progress in Rainfed Lowland Rice. 446p. (Orig.). 1986. pap. 13.70x (ISBN 971-104-167-7, Pub. by Intl Rice Res Philippines). Agribookstore.

Progress in Reaction Kinetics, Vol. 6-7. Ed. by K. R. Jennings & R. B. Cundall. Incl. Vol. 6, Pt. 1. 1971; Vol. 6, Pt. 2. Chemi-Ionization Reactions in the Gas Phase. 1971; Vol. 6, Pt. 3. Salt & Medium Effects on Reaction Rates in Concentrated Solutions of Acids & Bases. 1971; Vol. 6, Pt. 4. Chemical Applications of Metasable Rare Gas Atoms. 1971; Vol. 6, Pt. 5. Primary Salt-Effect in Aqueous Solutions. 1971; Vol. 6, Complete. 1972; Vol. 7, Pts. 1 & 2. 1973; Vol. 7, Complete. 1973. LC 61-1784. pap. write for info. Pergamon.

Progress in Rehabilitation: A Review of Three Studies. M. L. Bowden et al. Ed. by C. Jones. LC 80-83417. (Illus.). 1983. cancelled (ISBN 0-917478-35-5). Natl Inst Burn.

Progress in Resource Management & Environmental Planning. Timothy O'Riordan & R. Kerry Turner. LC 79-41729. (Progress in Resource Management & Environment Planning). 326p. Vol. 1, 1979, 326p. 95.00 (ISBN 0-471-99746-3, Pub. by Wiley-Interscience); Vol. 2, 1980, 246p. 89.95 (ISBN 0-471-27747-9). Wiley.

Progress in Resource Management & Environmental Planning, Vol. 3. Ed. by Timothy O'Riordan & R. Kerry Turner. LC 80-42020. (Progress in Resource Management & Environmental Planning Ser.). 324p. 1981. 110.00 (ISBN 0-471-27968-4, Pub. by Wiley-Interscience). Wiley.

Progress in Reversal Theory. Ed. by M. J. Apter et al. (Advances in Psychology Ser.: Vol. 51). 394p. 1988. 100.00 (ISBN 0-444-70391-8, North Holland). Elsevier.

Progress in Rheumatology. Israel Machtey. (Illus.). 236p. 1982. 32.00 (ISBN 0-7236-7007-2). PSG Pub Co.

Progress in Rubber Technology, Vol. 44. Ed. by S. H. Morrell. 139p. 1981. 46.25 (ISBN 0-85334-984-3, Pub. by Elsevier Applied Sci England). Elsevier.

Progress in Rural Geography. Ed. by Michael Pacione. LC 82-22756. (Illus.). 268p. 1983. text ed. 26.95x (ISBN 0-389-20358-0). B&N Imports.

Progress in Science & Its Social Conditions: Proceedings of a Nobel Symposium. Ed. by T. Ganelius. 335p. 1986. 61.00 (ISBN 0-08-031281-0, Pub. by PPL). Pergamon.

Progress in Self Psychology, Vol. 1. Ed. by Arnold I. Goldberg. (Guilford Self Psychology Ser.). 269p. 1985. text ed. 35.00 (ISBN 0-89862-300-6). Guilford Pr.

Progress in Self Psychology, Vol. 2. Ed. by Arnold I. Goldberg. (Guilford Self Psychology Ser.). 313p. 1986. lib. bdg. 35.00 (ISBN 0-89862-301-4). Guilford Pr.

Progress in Semiconductor Laser Diodes. Ed. by Eichen. 123p. 1986. 43.00 (ISBN 0-89252-758-7, 723). SPIE.

Progress in Sensory Physiology, Vol. 1. Ed. by D. Ottoson et al. (Illus.). 160p. 1981. 39.00 (ISBN 0-387-08413-4). Springer-Verlag.

Progress in Sensory Physiology, Vol. 2. H. Autrum et al. (Illus.). 190p. 1981. 39.00 (ISBN 0-387-10923-4). Springer Verlag.

Progress in Sensory Physiology, Vol. 4. N. Mei et al. (Illus.). 136p. 1983. 34.50 (ISBN 0-387-12498-5). Springer-Verlag.

Progress in Sensory Physiology, Vol. 5. (Illus.). 175p. 1985. 49.00 (ISBN 0-387-15339-X). Springer-Verlag.

Progress in Sensory Physiology, Vol. 6. (Illus.). 220p. 1985. 49.00 (ISBN 0-387-15340-3). Springer-Verlag.

Progress in Sensory Physiology, Vol. 8. W. Skrandies et al. 215p. 1987. 100.70 (ISBN 0-387-16300-X). Springer-Verlag.

Progress In Sexology. Ed. by Robert Gemme & C. C. Wheeler. LC 77-13011. (Perspectives In Sexuality Ser.). 634p. 1978. 60.00x (ISBN 0-306-31104-6, Plenum Pr). Plenum Pub.

Progress in Simulation, 2 vols. Ed. by D. K. Caldwell & Gohring. 1972. Vol. 1,382. 128.00 (ISBN 0-677-14890-9); Vol. 2, 380. 140.00 (ISBN 0-677-12490-2). Gordon & Breach.

Progress in Social Psychology, Vol. 1. Ed. by Martin Fishbein. LC 79-67453. (Illus.). 240p. 1980. text ed. 29.95x (ISBN 0-89859-005-1). L Erlbaum Assocs.

Progress in Solar Energy: Proceedings of the American Section of the International Solar Energy Society, Vol. 6. Ed. by G. E. Franta. 1500p. 1984. pap. 135.00x Preprints (ISBN 0-89553-126-7). Am Solar Energy.

Progress in Solar Energy: Vol. 5, The Renewable Challenge. Ed. by Gregory E. Franta & Keith W. Haggard. 1985. pap. text ed. 185.00x (ISBN 0-89553-034-1). Am Solar Energy.

Progress in Solar Engineering. Yogi Goswami. 378p. 1986. 65.00 (ISBN 0-89116-560-6). Hemisphere Pub.

Progress in Solar Physics. Ed. by C. De Jager & Z. Svestka. 1986. lib. bdg. 99.50 (ISBN 90-277-2180-7, Pub. by Reidel Holland). Kluwer-Academic.

Progress in Solar-Terrestrial Physics. Roederer. 1983. lib. bdg. 91.50 (ISBN 90-277-1559-9, Pub. by Reidel Holland). Kluwer Academic.

Progress in Solid State Chemistry. Ed. by H. Reiss et al. 1972. Vol. 1, 1964. 110.00 (ISBN 0-08-010246-8); Vol. 3, 1967. 110.00 (ISBN 0-08-011886-0). Pergamon.

Progress in Solid State Chemistry, Vols. 8-10. Ed. by J. O. McCaldin & G. Somorjai. Incl. Vol. 8. 1973; Vol. 9. 1975; Vol. 10, Pt. 1. 1975; Vol. 10, Pt. 2. Heterogeneous Catalysis by Metals. Sinfelt. 1975; Vol. 10, Pt. 3. 1975; Vol. 10, Pt. 4. 1976; Vol. 10 (complete) 1976. LC 63-11362. pap. text ed. write for info. Pergamon.

Progress in Spanish. 2nd ed. John Crispin & Ruth Crispin. LC 77-18684. 1978. text ed. write for info (ISBN 0-394-33399-3, RanC); write for info (ISBN 0-394-33400-0). Random.

Progress in Statistics, 2 vols. Ed. by J. Gani et al. (Colloquia Mathematica Societatis Janos Bolyai: No. 9). 912p. 1975. Set. 94.75 (ISBN 0-444-10702-9, North-Holland). Elsevier.

Progress in Stellar Spectral Line Formation Theory. Ed. by John E. Beckman & Lucio Crivellari. 1985. lib. bdg. 59.00 (ISBN 90-277-2007-X, Pub. by Reidel Netherlands). Kluwer Academic.

Progress in Stroke Research, Vol. 1. Roger M. Greenhalgh & F. Clifford Rose. (Illus.). 1980. 61.00 (ISBN 0-8151-3937-3). Year Bk Med.

Progress in Surface & Membrane Science, Vol. 12. Ed. by D. A. Cadenhead & James F. Danielli. 1979. 85.00 (ISBN 0-12-571812-8). Acad Pr.

Progress in Surface & Membrane Science, Vol. 13. Ed. by D. A. Cadenhead. (Serial Publication). 1979. 83.00 (ISBN 0-12-571813-6). Acad Pr.

Progress in Surface & Membrane Science, Vol. 14. Ed. by D. A. Cadenhead & J. F. Danielli. (Serial Publication Ser.). 1981. 83.00 (ISBN 0-12-571814-4). Acad Pr.

Progress in Surface & Membrane Science see Recent Progress in Surface & Membrane Science.

Progress in Surface Science, Vols. 1-7 & 9. Ed. by S. G. Davison. Incl. Vol. 1, 4 pts. 1972. Pts 1-4. pap. 15.50 ea.; Vol. 2, 4 pts. 1972. Pts. 1-4. pap. 15.50 ea.; Vol. 3, 4 pts. 1973. Pts. 1-4. pap. 15.50 ea.; Vol. 4, 3 pts. 1974. Pts. 1-3. pap. 15.50 ea.; Pt. 1-1973. pap.; Vol. 5, 4 pts. 1975. Pts. 1-4. pap. 15.50 ea.; Vol. 6, 3 pts. 1978; Vol. 7, 3 pts. 1976; Vol. 9 Complete. 273p. 1981. pap. write for info. Pergamon.

Progress in Surgery, 2 vols. Ed. by M. Allgoewer et al. (Illus.). 1973. Vol. 11. 44.00 (ISBN 3-8055-1379-8); Vol. 12. 65.50 (ISBN 3-8055-1617-7). S Karger.

Progress in Surgery, Vol. 2. Ed. by I. Taylor. (Illus.). 245p. (Orig.). 1987. pap. text ed. 36.00 (ISBN 0-443-03515-6). Churchill.

Progress in Surgery, Vol. 8. Ed. by M. Allgoewer et al. 1970. 44.00 (ISBN 3-8055-0430-6). S Karger.

Progress in Surgery, Vol. 10. Ed. by M. Allgoewer et al. (Illus.). x, 132p. 1972. 36.75 (ISBN 3-8055-1285-6). S Karger.

Progress in Surgery, Vol. 13. Ed. by M. Allgoewer et al. 300p. 1974. 92.75 (ISBN 3-8055-1741-6). S Karger.

Progress in Surgery, Vol. 15. Ed. by U. F. Gruber et al. 1977. 46.00 (ISBN 3-8055-2365-3). S Karger.

Progress in Surgery of the Liver, Pancreas & Biliary System. Ed. by S. Bengmark. (Developments in Surgery Ser.). 1988. lib. bdg. 119.00 (ISBN 0-89838-956-9, Pub. by Martinus Nijhoff Netherlands). Kluwer Academic.

Progress in Surgery, Vol. 14. Ed. by M. Allgoewer et al. x, 192p. 1975. 61.50 (ISBN 3-8055-2181-2). S Karger.

Progress in Surgical Pathology. Cecilia M. Fenoglio-Preiser. (Vol.VIII). 275p. 1988. 67.50 (ISBN 0-02-336900-0). Macmillan.

Progress in Surgical Pathology, Vol. 6. Cecilia M. Fenoglio-Preiser et al. 400p. 1988. text ed. 70.00 (ISBN 0-938607-00-6). Macmillan.

Progress in the Chemistry of Fats & Other Lipids, Vols. 5-14. Ed. by Ralph T. Holman et al. Incl. Vol. 5. Advances in Technology. 1958; Vol. 6. 1963. 92.00 (ISBN 0-08-009863-0); Vol. 7. 1964; Vol. 9, Pt. 1. Polyunsaturated Acids. 1966; Vol. 9, Pts. 2-5. 1971. pap. 20.00 ea.; 1970. Vol. 10, 1-4. pap. 15.50 ea.; 1972. Vol. 11, Pts. 1-3. pap. 15.50 ea.; Vol. 12. 1972; 1973. Vol. 13, Pts. 1-4. pap. 15.50 ea.; Vol. 14, Pt. 1. 1973; Vol. 14, Pt. 2. Lipids of Fungi. 1974; Vol. 14, Pt. 3. Infrared Absorption Spectroscopy of Normal & Substituted Long-Chain Fatty Acids & Esters in Solid State. Fischmeister. 1975; Vol. 14, Pt. 4. Lipid Metabolism Membrane Functions of the Mammary Gland. S. Patton & R. G. Jensen. 1975; Vol. 14, Complete. 1975. 92.00 (ISBN 0-08-017808-1). LC 53-22998. pap. write for info. Pergamon.

Progress in the Chemistry of Organic Natural Products. Ed. by W. Herz et al. (Vol. 40). (Illus.). 300p. 1981. 79.00 (ISBN 0-387-81624-0). Springer-Verlag.

Progress in the Chemistry of Organic Natural Products. Ed. by W. Herz et al. LC 39-1015. (Vol. 37). (Illus.). 1979. 105.10 (ISBN 0-387-81528-7). Springer-Verlag.

Progress in the Chemistry of Organic Natural Products, Vols. 5-12, 15-20. Ed. by W. Herz et al. Incl. Vol. 5. 1948. 72.00 (ISBN 0-387-80047-6); Vol. 6. 1950. 67.30 (ISBN 0-387-80140-5); Vol. 7. 1950. 57.90 (ISBN 0-387-80141-3); Vol. 8. 1951. 67.30 (ISBN 0-387-80204-5); Vol. 9. 1952. 91.50 (ISBN 0-387-80253-3); Vol. 10. 1953. 91.50 (ISBN 0-387-80300-9); Vol. 11. 1954. 79.10 (ISBN 0-387-80336-X); Vol. 12. 1955. 94.40 (ISBN 0-387-80371-8); Vol. 15. 1958. 40.20 (ISBN 0-387-80474-9); Vol. 16. 1958. 40.20 (ISBN 0-387-80475-7); Vol. 17. 1959. 87.40 (ISBN 0-387-80510-9); Vol. 18. 1960. 103.30 (ISBN 0-387-80540-0); Vol. 19. 1961. 73.20 (ISBN 0-387-80577-X); Vol. 20. 1962. 87.40 (ISBN 0-387-80605-9); Cumulative Index, Vols. 1-20. 1964. 63.80 (ISBN 0-387-80677-6). (Eng., Fr. & Ger.). Springer-Verlag.

Progress in the Chemistry of Organic Natural Products, Vols. 21-31. Ed. by W. Herz et al. Incl. Vol. 21. 1963. 64.90 (ISBN 0-387-80638-5); Vol. 22. 1964. 77.90 (ISBN 0-387-80678-4); Vol. 23. 1965. 81.50 (ISBN 0-387-80716-0); Vol. 24. 1966. 95.60 (ISBN 0-387-80757-8); Vol. 25. 1967. 67.30 (ISBN 0-387-80811-6); Vol. 26. 1968. 107.40 (ISBN 0-387-80864-7); Vol. 27. 1970. 95.60 (ISBN 0-387-80909-0); Vol. 28. 1971. 105.10 (ISBN 0-387-80975-9); Vol. 29. 1972. 122.80 (ISBN 0-387-81024-2); Vol. 30. 1973. 146.40 (ISBN 0-387-81062-5); Vol. 31. 1974. 149.90 (ISBN 0-387-81172-9). Springer-Verlag.

Progress in the Chemistry of Organic Natural Products, Vol. 35. Ed. by W. Herz et al. LC 39-1015. 1978. 152.30 (ISBN 0-387-81460-4). Springer-Verlag.

Progress in the Chemistry of Organic Natural Products, Vol. 36. Ed. by W. Herz et al. (Illus.). 1979. 115.70 (ISBN 0-387-81472-8). Springer-Verlag.

Progress in the Chemistry of Organic Natural Products, Vol. 38. Ed. by W. Herz et al. (Illus.). 450p. 1979. 115.10 (ISBN 0-387-81529-5). Springer-Verlag.

Progress in the Chemistry of Organic Natural Products, Vol. 39. Ed. by W. Herz et al. (Illus.). 330p. 1980. 93.30 (ISBN 0-387-81530-9). Springer-Verlag.

Progress in the Chemistry of Organic Natural Products, Vol. 41. Ed. by W. Herz et al. (Illus.). 373p. 1982. 98.00 (ISBN 0-387-81690-9). Springer-Verlag.

Progress in the Chemistry of Organic Natural Products, Vol. 42. Ed. by W. Herz et al. 330p. 1982. 71.00 (ISBN 0-387-81706-9). Springer-Verlag.

Progress in the Chemistry of Organic Natural Products, Vol. 43. Ed. by W. Herz et al. (Illus.). 383p. 1983. 104.00 (ISBN 0-387-81741-7). Springer-Verlag.

Progress in the Chemistry of Organic Natural Products, Vol. 46. (Illus.). 280p. 1984. 75.00 (ISBN 0-387-81804-9). Springer-Verlag.

Progress in the Development & Use of Antiviral Drugs & Interferon. (Technical Report: No. 754). 25p. pap. 3.00 (ISBN 92-4-120754-X). World Health.

Progress in the Development of Cost-Effective Treatment for Drug Abusers. 1986. lib. bdg. 79.95 (ISBN 0-8490-3517-1). Gordon Pr.

Progress in the Education of the Handicapped & Analysis of P.L. 98-199: The Education of the Handicapped Act Amendments of 1983. Frederick J. Weintraub & Bruce A. Ramirez. LC 85-143730. 73p. 6.00 (ISBN 0-86586-156-0). ERIC Clear.

Progress in the Fundamental Principles of Liquid Chromatography: 1984-1985. Barth et al. 1987. write for info. (ISBN 0-471-01189-4). Wiley.

Progress in the Psychology of Language, 2 Vols. Andrew W. Ellis. 248p. 1985. Vol. I. text ed. 29.95 (ISBN 0-86377-027-4); Vol. II, 272 pgs. text ed. 29.95 (ISBN 0-86377-028-2). L Erlbaum Assocs.

Progress in the Psychology of Language, Vol. 3. Ed. by Andrew W. Ellis. 416p. 1987. text ed. 39.95 (ISBN 0-86377-044-4). L Erlbaum Assocs.

Progress in the Science & Technology of the Rare Earths. L. Eyring. write for info. Pergamon.

Progress in the Study of Point Defects. Ed. by Masa Doyama & Sho Yoshida. 440p. 1977. 87.50 (ISBN 0-86008-185-0, Pub. by U of Tokyo Japan). Columbia U Pr.

Progress in the Treatment of Fluency Disorders. Ed. by Lena Rustin et al. 330p. 1987. 66.00x (ISBN 0-85066-664-3); pap. 33.00x (ISBN 0-85066-683-X). Taylor & Francis.

Progress in the Treatment of Gastrointestinal Motility Disorders: The Role of Cisapride. Ed. by A. G. Johnson & G. Lux. (Clinical Practice Ser.: Vol. 48). 204p. 1988. 79.00 (ISBN 0-444-90500-6, Excerpta Medica). Elsevier.

Progress in Toxicology, Vol. 1. G. Zbinden. LC 73-12957. 1973. pap. 23.00 (ISBN 0-387-06495-8). Springer-Verlag.

Progress in Transfusion Medicine, Vol. 1. Ed. by John D. Cash. (Illus.). 190p. 1986. text ed. 55.50 (ISBN 0-443-03261-0). Churchill.

Progress in Transfusion Medicine, Vol. 2. Ed. by John D. Cash. (Illus.). 188p. 1987. text ed. 70.00 (ISBN 0-443-03715-9). Churchill.

Progress in Transplantation, Vol. 2. Peter J. Morris & Nicholas L. Tilney. (Illus.). 248p. 1986. text ed. 90.00 (ISBN 0-443-03449-4). Churchill.

Progress in Transplantation, Vol. 3. Peter J. Morris & Nicholas L. Tilney. (Illus.). 1987. text ed. 30.00 (ISBN 0-443-03662-4). Churchill.

Progress in Tryptophan & Serotonin Research: Proceedings - Fifth Meeting of the International Study Group for Tryptophan Research (ISTRY) Ed. by D. A. Bender et al. 430p. 1987. text ed. 180.00x (ISBN 3-11-011164-0). De Gruyter.

Progress in Tryptophan & Serotonin Research: Proceedings-Fourth Meeting of the International Study Group for Tryptophan Research (ISTRY) Ed. by H. G. Schlossberger et al. LC 84-1719. xix, 889p. 1984. 155.00 (ISBN 3-11-009760-5). De Gruyter.

Progress in Underwater Acoustics. Ed. by Harold Merklinger. 816p. 1987. 125.00x (ISBN 0-306-42552-1, Plenum Pr). Plenum Pub.

Progress in Upland Rice. 578p. (Orig.). 1986. pap. text ed. 25.00 (ISBN 971-104-150-2, Pub. by Intl Rice Res Philippines). Agribookstore.

Progress in Urban Geography. Ed. by Michael Pacione. LC 82-22757. (Illus.). 296p. 1983. text ed. 26.95x (ISBN 0-389-20357-2). B&N Imports.

Progress in Utility & Risk Theory. Ole Hagen & Fred Wenstop. (Theory & Decision Library). 288p. 1984. 46.00 (ISBN 90-277-1731-1, Pub. by Reidel Holland). Kluwer Academic.

Progress in Vacuum Microbalance Techniques, Vol. 1. T. Gast & E. Robens. 105.00 (ISBN 0-471-25714-1, Wiley Heyden). Wiley.

Progress in Vacuum Microbalance Techniques: Proceedings of the Ninth Conference on Vacuum Microbalance Techniques, Technical University, Berlin, Germany, June, 1970, Vol. 1. Conference on Vacuum Microbalance Techniques (9th: 1970: Berlin, Germany) Ed. by Th. Gast & E. Robens. LC 72-82129. pap. 104.80 (ISBN 0-317-29331-1, 2024022). Bks Demand UMI.

Progress in Vacuum Microbalance Techniques: Proceedings of the 10th Conference on Vacuum Microbalance Techniques, Brunal University, Uxbridge, England, June 1972, Vol. 2. Conference on Vacuum Microbalance Techniques (10th: 1972: Uxbridge, England) Ed. by S. C. Bevan & S. J. Gregg. LC 72-82129. pap. 66.50 (ISBN 0-317-29333-8, 2024023). Bks Demand UMI.

Progress in Vacuum Microbalance Techniques: Proceedings of the 12th Conference on Vacuum Microbalance Techniques, Lyon University, Lyon, France, September 1974, Vol. 3. Conference on Vacuum Microbalance Techniques (12th: 1974: Lyon, France) Ed. by C. Eyraud & M. Escoubes. LC 72-82189. pap. 115.30 (ISBN 0-317-29334-6, 2024024). Bks Demand UMI.

Progress in Vascular Surgery. Najarian. 1988. 69.95 (ISBN 0-8151-6341-X). Year Bk Med.

Progress in Very High Pressure Research: Proceedings of an International Conference. Conference on Very High Pressure. Ed. by F. P. Bundy et al. LC 61-13156. pap. 83.30 (2056178). Bks Demand UMI.

Progress in Water Technology, Vols. 1-7. Ed. by S. H. Jenkins. Incl. Vol. 1. Application of New Concepts of Physical-Chemical Waste Water Treatment. Eckenfelder & Cecil. 1973. 55.00 (ISBN 0-08-017243-1); Vol. 2. Phosphorus in Fresh Water & the Marine Environment. 1973; Vol. 3. Water Quality: Management & Pollution Control Problems. 1973; Vol. 4. Marine, Municipal & Industrial Waste Water Disposal: Proceedings, Sorrento, Italy. 1979; Vol. 5. Design-Operation Interaction at Large Treatment Plants. 1978. pap. 55.00 flexi-cover (ISBN 0-08-018293-3); Vol. 6. Instrumentation, Control & Automation for Waste Water Treatment Systems. 1974. 55.00 (ISBN 0-08-017976-2); Vol. 7. Atlanta Conference Proceedings. 1976. Pts. 2-4, 1976. 110.00 (ISBN 0-08-019839-2); Pts. 2-6, 2 Vols. 215.00 (ISBN 0-08-020225-X); Pts. 5-6, 1976. pap. text ed. 110.00 (ISBN 0-08-019841-4). LC 73-1162. write for info. Pergamon.

Progress Notes on a State of Mind. Patricia Fillingham. 55p. 1980. pap. 2.00 (ISBN 0-942292-07-3). Warthog Pr.

Progress of a Biographer. Hugh Kingsmill. 1973. lib. bdg. 30.00 (ISBN 0-8414-5588-0). Folcroft.

Progress of a Fire. Robert Abel. 1985. 18.95 (ISBN 0-671-50931-4). S&S.

Progress of a Race. J. L. Nichols & William H. Crogman. LC 69-18552. (American Negro: His History & Literature Ser., No. 2). 1969. Repr. of 1920 ed. 21.00 (ISBN 0-405-01883-5). Ayer Co Pubs.

Progress of a Race: Or, Remarkable Advancement of the American Negro. facs. ed. J. W. Gibson & W. H. Crogman. LC 79-81118. (Black Heritage Library Collection Ser.). 1902. 31.25 (ISBN 0-8369-8578-8). Ayer Co Pubs.

Progress of a Race, Or, the Remarkable Advancement of the American Negro. Henry F. Kletzing & William H. Crogman. LC 12-4245. (American Studies). 1970. Repr. of 1898 ed. 45.00 (ISBN 0-384-29805-2). Johnson Repr.

Progress of Afro-American Women: A Selected Bibliography & Resource Guide. Compiled by Janet L. Sims. LC 79-8948. 400p. 1980. lib. bdg. 36.95x (ISBN 0-313-22083-2; SAF/). Greenwood.

Progress of Animal Magnetism. Charles Poyen. (Hypnosis & Altered States of Consciousness Ser.). 1982. Repr. of 1837 ed. lib. bdg. 25.00 (ISBN 0-306-76163-7). Da Capo.

Progress of Another Pilgrim. Frances J. Roberts. 1970. 8.95 (ISBN 0-932814-10-7); pap. 5.95 (ISBN 0-932814-11-5). Kings Farspan.

Progress of Continental Law in the Nineteenth Century. A. Alvarez et al. Tr. by L. B. Register. (Continental Legal History Ser.: Vol. 11). (Illus.). xlix, 558p. 1969. Repr. of 1918 ed. 37.50x (ISBN 0-8377-1900-3). Rothman.

Progress of Cybernetics, 3 vols. J. Rose. 1420p. 1970. Set. 355.00 (ISBN 0-677-14190-4). Gordon & Breach.

Progress of Economics: A History of Economic Thought. Warren B. Catlin. LC 61-15681. 788p. 1962. text ed. 64.50x (ISBN 0-8290-0200-6). Irvington.

Progress of God's People. M. J. Evans. (Discovering the Bible Ser.). (gr. 8-10). pap. 8.95 (ISBN 0-7175-1161-8). Dufour.

Progress of Greek Epigraphy 1937-1953. M. N. Tod. 1979. 30.00 (ISBN 0-89005-292-1). Ares.

Progress of International Government. David Mitrany. 1933. 42.50x (ISBN 0-686-51293-6). Elliots Bks.

Progress of Japan, 1853-1871. John H. Gubbins. LC 79-137237. Repr. of 1911 ed. 24.50 (ISBN 0-404-02939-6). AMS Pr.

Progress of Love. Alice Munro. 1986. 16.45 (ISBN 0-394-55272-5). Knopf.

Progress of Love. Alice Munro. 320p. 1987. pap. 6.95 (ISBN 0-14-009879-8). Penguin.

Progress of Management: Process & Behavior in a Changing Environment. 3rd ed. Jerome E. Schnee et al. (Illus.). 1977. pap. text ed. write for info (ISBN 0-13-730622-9). P-H.

Progress of Medicine. O. V. Jones. 317p. 1985. 63.00x (ISBN 0-86383-131-1, Pub. by Gomer Pr). State Mutual Bk.

Progress of Music. George Dyson. LC 79-93334. (Essay Index Reprint Ser). 1932. 18.00 (ISBN 0-8369-1287-X). Ayer Co Pubs.

Progress of Nucleic Acid Research & Molecular Biology, Vol. 34. Ed. by Waldo E. Cohn & Kivie Moldave. 266p. 1987. 59.00 (ISBN 0-12-540034-9). Acad Pr.

Progress of Physics During 33 Years, 1875-1908. Arthur Schuster. LC 74-26289. (History, Philosophy & Sociology of Science Ser.). 1975. Repr. 14.00x (ISBN 0-405-06615-5). Ayer Co Pubs.

Progress of Piety. John Norden. Repr. of 1847 ed. 21.00 (ISBN 0-384-41910-0). Johnson Repr.

Progress of Plant Ecology in India, Vol. 4. Ed. by V. P. Agarwal & V. K. Sharma. 167p. 1980. 10.00 (ISBN 0-686-82969-7, Pub. by Messers Today & Tomorrows Printers & Publishers India). Scholarly Pubns.

Progress of Poesy. John W. Mackail. LC 74-20680. 1974. Repr. of 1906 ed. lib. bdg. 18.50 (ISBN 0-8414-5940-1). Folcroft.

Progress of Public Health in Western Australia. Dudley Snow. 185p. 1982. 27.00x (ISBN 0-7244-8477-9, Pub. by U of W Austral Pr); pap. 19.00x (ISBN 0-7244-8478-7). Intl Spec Bk.

Progress of Redemption: The Story of Salvation from Creation to the New Jerusalem. Willem A. Van Gemeren. 432p. 1988. 19.95 (ISBN 0-310-23130-2, 10868). Zondervan.

Progress of Romance: The Politics of Popular Fiction. Ed. by Jean Radford. 224p. 1987. 29.95 (ISBN 0-317-54011-4, 07174, Pub. by Routledge UK); pap. 11.95 (ISBN 0-317-54012-2, 09630, Pub. by Routledge UK). Routledge Chapman & Hall.

Progress of Slavery in the United States. facs. ed. George M. Weston. LC 73-83952. (Black Heritage Library Collection Ser.). 1857. 16.50 (ISBN 0-8369-8683-0). Ayer Co Pubs.

Progress of Slavery in the United States. George M. Weston. LC 78-92448. 1857. 11.00 (ISBN 0-403-00175-7). Scholarly.

Progress of Society. Robert Hamilton. LC 68-55729. 1969. Repr. of 1830 ed. 45.00x (ISBN 0-678-00451-X). Kelley.

Progress of Society in Europe: A Historical Outline from the Subversion of the Roman Empire to the Beginning of the 16th Century. William Robertson. Ed. by Felix Gilbert & Leonard Krieger. LC 75-190283. (Classic European Historians Ser.). 224p. 1972. 14.00x (ISBN 0-226-72133-7). U of Chicago Pr.

Progress of Society in Europe: A Historical Outline from the Subversion of the Roman Empire to the Beginning of the 16th Century. William Robertson. Ed. by Felix Gilbert & Leonard Krieger. LC 75-190283. (Classic European Historians Ser.). xxviii, 186p. 1975. pap. 2.45X (ISBN 0-226-72134-5, P466, Phoen). U of Chicago Pr.

Progress of Stories. facsimile ed. Laura Riding. LC 70-167469. (Short Story Index Reprint Ser.). Repr. of 1935 ed. 20.00 (ISBN 0-8369-3995-6). Ayer Co Pubs.

Progress of the Breed: A History of U. S. Holsteins. Richard H. Mansfield. Ed. by Robert H. Hastings. LC 85-60730. 350p. 1985. 34.95 (ISBN 0-9614711-0-7). Holstein-Friesian.

Progress of the Nation. new ed. George R. Porter. Ed. by F. W. Hirst. LC 77-85189. 1970. Repr. of 1912 ed. 50.00x (ISBN 0-678-00538-9). Kelley.

Progress of the United States in Population & Wealth. George Tucker. LC 63-23040. 1964. Repr. of 1855 ed. 37.50x (ISBN 0-678-00033-6). Kelley.

Progress of the United States in Population & Wealth in Fifty Years, As Exhibited by the Decennial Census. George Tucker. LC 79-129036. (Research & Source Works Ser.: No. 532). 1970. Repr. of 1843 ed. lib. bdg. 19.00 (ISBN 0-8337-3572-1). B Franklin.

Progress of the Working Class Eighteen Thirty-Two to Eighteen Sixty-Seven. J. M. Ludlow & Lloyd Jones. LC 83-48490. (World of Labour - English Workers 1850-1890 Ser.). 304p. 1984. lib. bdg. 35.00 (ISBN 0-8240-5717-1). Garland Pub.

Progress of the Working Classes, 1832-1867. John M. Ludlow & Lloyd Jones. LC 72-77050. 1973. Repr. of 1867 ed. 37.50x (ISBN 0-678-00909-0). Kelley.

Progress of the World: In Arts, Agriculture, Commerce, Manufactures, Instruction, Railways & Public Wealth since the Beginnng of the Nineteenth Century. Michael G. Mulhall. (Development of Industrial Society Ser.). 528p. 1971. Repr. of 1880 ed. 55.00x (ISBN 0-7165-1584-9, BBA 03547, Pub. by Irish Academic Pr). Biblio Dist.

Progress of Underdeveloped Areas. Ed. by Bert F. Hoselitz. LC 52-14480. 1952. 20.00x (ISBN 0-226-35406-7). U of Chicago Pr.

Progress on Biomechanics. N. Akkas. (NATO Advaned Study Institute Ser.). 395p. 1979. 37.50x (ISBN 90-286-0479-0, Pub. by Sijthoff & Noordhoff). Kluwer Academic.

Progress on Hemostasis & Thrombosis, Vol. 4. Ed. by Theodore H. Spaet. 432p. 1978. text ed. 81.50 (ISBN 0-8089-1096-5, 794194). Grune.

Progress or Catastrophe: The Nature of Biological Science & Its Impact on Human Society. Bentley Glass. Ed. by Ruth N. Anshen. 160p. 1985. 35.00 (ISBN 0-275-90107-6, C0107); pap. 9.95 (ISBN 0-275-91806-8, B1806). Praeger.

Progress Report to the Advisory Committee on the Implementation of Amendment V to the Vermont Constitution Relating to the Organization of the Judicial System. National Center for State Courts Staff. 31p. (On loan through the NCSC Library). 1974. write for info. (NERO-125). Natl Ctr St Courts.

Progress Shorthand Passages, 4 bks. Marie Quint. LC 80-42139. (Longman Secretarial Studies Ser.). Bk. 1, Speed Development, 0-80 wpm. pap. 20.00 (ISBN 0-317-27729-4, 2025226); Bk. 2, Speed Development, 0-80 wpm. pap. 20.00 (ISBN 0-317-27730-8); Bk. 3, Speed Development, 80-120 wpm. pap. 20.00 (ISBN 0-317-27731-6); Bk. 4, Speed Development, 120-150 wpm. pap. 20.00 (ISBN 0-317-27732-4). Bks Demand UMI.

Progress Tests for the Developmentally Disabled: An Evaluation. John Doucette & Ruth Freedman. 319p. 1980. 27.50 (ISBN 0-89011-539-7). Brookline Bks.

Progress Through Pioneer Evangelism. Dan Beller. pap. 2.00 (ISBN 0-911866-80-9). Advocate.

Progress Through the Grades of City Schools: A Study of Acceleration & Arrest. Charles H. Keyes. LC 70-176963. (Columbia University. Teachers College. Contributions to Education: No. 42). Repr. of 1911 ed. 22.50 (ISBN 0-404-55042-8). AMS Pr.

Progress to Improved Movement: For Handicapped Children & Adults with Poor Posture. K. Hollis. 36p. 1985. 10.00x (ISBN 0-906054-17-6, Pub. by British Inst Mental). State Mutual Bk.

Progress to Standing: For Children with Severe Physical Handicap. K. Hollis. 24p. 1985. 10.00x (ISBN 0-906054-16-8, Pub. by British Inst Mental). State Mutual Bk.

Progress Toward Better Vaccines: Proceedings at a Meeting Organized by the WHO as Part of a Program for Vaccine Developement Held in Bellagio Italy by Courtesy of the Rockefeller Foundation 16-18 April 1985. Ed. by Rosemary Bell & G. Torrigiani. (Illus.). 220p. 1987. 49.95 (ISBN 0-19-261567-X). Oxford U Pr.

Progress Towards a Male Contraceptive. Ed. by S. L. Jeffcoate & M. Sandler. LC 82-2789. (Current Topics in Reproductive Endocrinology Ser.: No. 2). pap. 69.20 (2031939). Bks Demand UMI.

Progress: Vol. I of the International Encyclopedia of Psychiatry, Psychology, Psychoanalysis & Neurology. Ed. by Benjamin B. Wolman. 1983. 89.00 (ISBN 0-918228-28-X). Aesculapius Pubs.

Progress, War & Reaction: 1900-1933. Ed. by David R. Ross et al. LC 78-101951. (Structure of American History Ser: Vol. 5). 1970. pap. 6.95x (ISBN 0-88295-759-7). Harlan Davidson.

Progress with Domperidone, a Gastrokinetic & Anti-Emetic Agent. Ed. by G. Towse. (International Congress & Symposium Ser.: No. 36). 110p. 1981. pap. 18.00 (ISBN 1-85315-076-2, Pub. by Royal Society of Medicine Services Ltd). Longwood Pub Group.

Progress Without Punishment: Effective Approaches for Learners with Behavior Problems. Anne M. Donnellan et al. (Special Education Ser.). 192p. 1988. pap. text ed. 15.95x (ISBN 0-8077-2911-6). Tchrs Coll.

Progressed Horoscope. (Astrologer's Library). 328p. 1981. pap. 7.95 (ISBN 0-89281-180-3). Inner Tradit.

Progressed Horoscope Simplified. Leigh H. Milburn. 180p. 1936. 6.00 (ISBN 0-86690-131-0, 1339-01). Am Fed Astrologers.

Progresses & Public Processions of Queen Elizabeth, 3 Vols. John Nichols. LC 3-17051. Repr. of 1823 ed. 90.00 (ISBN 0-404-04770-X). AMS Pr.

Progresses & Public Processions of Queen Elizabeth, 3 Vols. John Nichols. (Illus.). 1966. Repr. of 1823 ed. Set. 115.00 (ISBN 0-8337-2532-7). B Franklin.

Progresses & Public Processions of Queen Elizabeth, 3 Vols. John Nichols. LC 3-17051. (Illus.). 1968. Repr. of 1823 ed. Set. 90.00 (ISBN 0-527-67160-6). Kraus Repr.

Progresses of Aging: Social & Psychological Perspectives, 2 Vols. Ed. by Richard H. Williams et al. LC 79-8692. (Growing Old Ser.). 1980. Repr. of 1963 ed. lib. bdg. 103.00x (ISBN 0-405-12811-8). Ayer Co Pubs.

Progresses, Processions & Magnificent Festivities of King James First, His Royal Consort, Family & Court, 4 Vols. John Nichols. LC 3-29463. Repr. of 1828 ed. Set. 108.00 (ISBN 0-404-04780-7). AMS Pr.

Progresses, Processions & Magnificent Festivities of King James the First, His Royal Consort, Family & Court, 4 Vols. John Nichols. (Illus.). 1967. Repr. of 1828 ed. Set. 140.00 (ISBN 0-8337-2537-8). B Franklin.

Progresses, Processions & Magnificent Festivities of King James First, His Royal Consort, Family & Court, 4 Vols. John Nichols. LC 3-29463. (Illus.). 1968. Repr. of 1828 ed. Set. 108.00 (ISBN 0-527-67170-3). Kraus Repr.

Progression. Vera Blaine & Scott Clark. (Educational Dance Score Registry Ser.: No. 3). (Illus.). 194p. 1981. dance score 10.00 (ISBN 0-932582-36-2). Dance Notation.

Progression Handbook. Elliott Jaques. LC 68-13863. (Glacier Project Ser.). (Illus.). 72p. 1968. 7.50x (ISBN 0-8093-0301-9). S Ill U Pr.

Progression of Consciousness. William C. Fry. 208p. 1986. 10.95 (ISBN 0-8062-2887-3). Carlton.

Progressions & Other Poems. Albert S. Cook. LC 63-11976. pap. 32.00 (ISBN 0-317-28649-8, 2055348). Bks Demand UMI.

Progressions in Action. Doris C. Doane. LC 77-10370. 256p. 1977. Repr. 10.00 (ISBN 0-86690-074-8, 1869-01). Am Fed Astrologers.

Progressive Audio-Lingual Drills in English. Francine Stieglitz. (gr. 9-12). 1970. pap. 7.00 (ISBN 0-13-730607-5, 17754); cassettes 200.00 (ISBN 0-13-730615-6, 58097). Prentice ESL.

Progressive Basketball Drills: A Coach's Guide. Don Edmonston & Jack Lehane. 260p. 1984. text ed. write for info. (ISBN 0-205-08064-2, Pub. by Longwood Div). Wm C Brown.

Progressive Capitalism & the Imperative Need to Improve the Qualitative Essence of Life. John A. Hobson. 159p. 1985. 147.75 (ISBN 0-86654-146-2). Inst Econ Finan.

Progressive Church in Latin America. Ed. by Scott Mainwaring & Alexander Wilde. 1988. text ed. 32.95x (ISBN 0-268-01573-2). U of Notre Dame Pr.

Progressive Cities: The Commission Government Movement in America, 1901-1920. Bradley R. Rice. 180p. 1977. 12.50x (ISBN 0-292-76441-3). U of Tex Pr.

Progressive City: Planning & Participation, 1969-1984. Pierre Clavel. 300p. 1986. text ed. 30.00 (ISBN 0-8135-1119-4); pap. text ed. 10.00 (ISBN 0-8135-1120-8). Rutgers U Pr.

Progressive Class Piano. 2nd ed. Elmer Heerema. 300p. 1984. pap. 15.95 (ISBN 0-317-02467-1). Alfred Pub.

Progressive Contact Metamorphism of the Biwabik Iron-Formation, Mesabi Range, Minnesota. Bevan M. French. LC 68-66592. (Bulletin: No. 45). (Illus.). 1968. 4.50x (ISBN 0-8166-0478-9). Minn Geol Survey.

Progressive Development & Affordability in the Design of Urban Shelter Projects. Douglas H. Keare & Emmanuel Jimenez. (Working Paper: No. 560). 63p. 1983. 5.00 (ISBN 0-8213-0166-7, WP 0560). World Bank.

Progressive Dictation with Previews. Charles E. Zoubek. 1956. text ed. 29.10 (ISBN 0-07-073032-6). McGraw.

Progressive Dressage. Andre Jousseaume. Tr. by Jeanette Vigneron from Fr. pap. 5.95 (ISBN 0-85131-231-4, BL2328, Pub. by J A Allen U K). S R Smith Sporting Bks.

Progressive Education: A Marxist Interpretation. Gilbert G. Gonzalez. LC 81-5787. (Studies in Marxism: Vol. 8). 197p. 1982. 19.95x (ISBN 0-930656-15-6); pap. 9.95 (ISBN 0-930656-16-4). MEP Pubns.

Progressive Education at the Crossroads. Boyd H. Bode. LC 71-165707. (American Education Ser, No. 2). 1971. Repr. of 1938 ed. 14.00 (ISBN 0-405-03696-5). Ayer Co Pubs.

Progressive Education: Lessons from Three Schools. William B. Lauderdale. LC 81-82472. (Fastback Ser.: No. 166). 50p. 1981. pap. 0.90 (ISBN 0-87367-166-X). Phi Delta Kappa.

Progressive Education Movement: An Annotated Bibliography. Mariann P. Winick. LC 76-24764. (Reference Library of Social Science Ser.: Vol. 29). 1976. lib. bdg. 23.00 (ISBN 0-8240-9913-3). Garland Pub.

Progressive Era. Ed. by Lewis L. Gould. LC 73-20783. (Illus.). 270p. 1974. text ed. 11.95x (ISBN 0-8156-2163-9); pap. text ed. 4.95x (ISBN 0-8156-2164-7). Syracuse U Pr.

Progressive Era & the Great War: 1896-1920. 2nd ed. Compiled by William M. Leary, Jr. & Arthur S. Link. LC 78-70030. (Goldentree Bibliographies in American History). 1978. text ed. 24.95x (ISBN 0-88295-574-8); pap. text ed. 14.95x (ISBN 0-88295-575-6). Harlan Davidson.

Progressive Era in Minnesota, 1899-1918. Carl H. Chrislock. LC 79-178677. (Public Affairs Center Publication Ser.). (Illus.). 242p. 1971. 8.95 (ISBN 0-87351-067-4). Minn Hist.

Progressive Era, 1900-20: The Reform Persuasion. George E. Mowry. LC 72-79737. (AHA Pamphlets: No. 212). 1972. pap. text ed. 1.50 (ISBN 0-87229-005-0). Am Hist Assn.

Progressive Exercise Therapy in Rehabilitation & Physical Education. 4th ed. John H. Colson & Frank Collison. (Illus.). 249p. 1983. pap. text ed. 22.00 (ISBN 0-7236-0665-X). PSG Pub Co.

Progressive Exercises in Chinese Pronunciation. Charles F. Hockett. 1.95 (ISBN 0-88710-058-9). Yale Far Eastern Pubns.

Progressive Filing. 9th ed. Jeffrey R. Stewart et al. Ed. by Ella Pezzuti. LC 79-26178. (Illus.). 160p. (gr. 9-12). 1980. text ed. 18.32 (ISBN 0-07-061445-8). McGraw.

Progressive Gymnastics: The National YMCA Progressive Gymnastics Program for Youth. LC 86-32593. (Illus.). 112p. (Orig.). 1987. pap. text ed. 9.00x (ISBN 0-87322-099-4, Pub. by YMCA USA). Human Kinetics.

Progressive Historians: Turner, Beard, Parrington. Richard Hofstadter. LC 79-12591. 1979. pap. 7.95x (ISBN 0-226-34818-0, P841, Phoen). U of Chicago Pr.

Progressive in English. I. Scheffer. (Linguistics Ser.: Vol. 15). 397p. 1975. pap. 51.00 (ISBN 0-444-10770-3, North-Holland). Elsevier.

Progressive Masks: Letters of Oliver Wendell Holmes, Jr., & Franklin Ford. Ed. by David H. Burton. LC 80-54787. 144p. 1982. 19.50 (ISBN 0-87413-188-X). U Delaware Pr.

Progressive Men, Women & Movements of the Past Twenty-Five Years. Benjamin O. Flower. LC 75-313. (Radical Tradition in America Ser.). 316p. 1975. Repr. of 1914 ed. 25.85 (ISBN 0-88355-217-5). Hyperion Conn.

Progressive Movement, Its Principles & Its Programme. S. J. Duncan-Clark. LC 72-164808. Repr. of 1913 ed. 24.00 (ISBN 0-404-02217-0). AMS Pr.

Progressive Movement, Nineteen Hundred to Nineteen Fifteen. Ed. by Richard Hofstadter. (Orig.). 1964. pap. 4.95 (ISBN 0-13-730721-7, Spec). P-H.

Project Management: A Mangerial Approach. Jack R. Meredith & Samuel J. Mantel. LC 84-21946. (Production-Operations Management Ser.). 494p. 1985. write for info. (ISBN 0-471-80964-0). Wiley.

Project Management: A Short Course for Professionals. 2nd ed. Melvin Silverman. (Professional Development Programs Ser.). 1988. pap. 39.95 (ISBN 0-471-61507-2). Wiley.

Project Management: A Systems Approach to Planning, Scheduling & Controlling. 2nd ed. Harold Kerzner. 672p. 1984. 40.95 (ISBN 0-442-24879-2). Van Nos Reinhold.

Project Management: An Annotated Bibliography. Lee Dyer & Gary D. Paulson. LC 76-2085. (ILR Bibliography Ser.: No. 13). 48p. 1976. pap. 2.75 (ISBN 0-87546-059-3). ILR Pr.

Project Management: An Introduction to Issues in Industrial Research & Development. S. A. Bergen. 208p. 1986. text ed. 45.00 (ISBN 0-631-14705-5); pap. text ed. 15.95 (ISBN 0-631-14706-3). Basil Blackwell.

Project Management: Combining Technical & Behavioral Approaches for Effective Implementation. Robert J. Graham. (Illus.). 256p. 1985. 34.95 (ISBN 0-442-23018-4). Van Nos Reinhold.

Project Management: Course & Reference Manual. Sydney F. Love. (Illus.). 123p. 1984. 125.00 (ISBN 0-920176-07-0). Adv Prof Dev.

Project Management Dictionary of Terms. David I. Cleland & Harold Kerzner. 304p. 1985. 33.95 (ISBN 0-442-21690-4). Van Nos Reinhold.

Project Management for Bankers. Harold Kerzner. 224p. 1980. 33.95 (ISBN 0-442-26091-1). Van Nos Reinhold.

Project Management for Data Processing Application Development. McCarthy. (Computers & Information Processing Systems for Business Ser.). 1987. write for info. (ISBN 0-471-80848-2). Wiley.

Project Management for Engineering & Construction. Albert Thumann. LC 86-46140. 300p. 1987. text ed. 58.00 (ISBN 0-88173-040-8). Fairmont Pr.

Project Management for Engineers. Milton D. Rosenau, Jr. (Illus.). 328p. 1984. 38.95 (ISBN 0-534-03383-0). Van Nos Reinhold.

Project Management for Executives. Harold Kerzner. 400p. 1981. 36.95 (ISBN 0-442-25920-4). Van Nos Reinhold.

Project Management for the Design Professional. Frank Stasiowski & David Burstein. (Illus.). 160p. 1982. 24.95 (ISBN 0-8230-7434-X, Whitney Lib). Watson-Guptill.

Project Management Forms. (Photocopier Bks.). (Orig.). 1984. pap. 14.95 (ISBN 0-87280-018-0). Asher-Gallant.

Project Management Handbook. Ed. by Dennis Lock. 400p. 1987. text ed. 69.95 (ISBN 0-291-39741-7, Gower Pub UK). Gower Pub Co.

Project Management: How to Make It Work. Charles C. Martin. LC 75-37884. (Illus.). 312p. 1976. 16.95 (ISBN 0-8144-5408-9). AMACOM.

Project Management in Construction. Anthony Walker. 224p. 1984. 35.00x (ISBN 0-246-12199-8, Pub. by Granada England). Sheridan.

Project Management in Manufacturing & High Technology Operations. Adedji B. Badiru. LC 88-2516. (Engineering Management Ser.). 320p. 1988. 44.95 (ISBN 0-471-62892-1). Wiley.

Project Management in Progress: Tools & Strategies for the Nineties. Ed. by W. Vriethoff & C. Visser. 330p. 1986. 79.00 (ISBN 0-444-87763-0, North Holland). Elsevier.

Project Management of Data Processing Application Development. M. Dianne McCarthy. (Professional Development Programs Ser.). 1984. 55.95x (ISBN 0-471-80712-5, Pub. by Wiley). Wiley.

Project Management Operating Guidelines. Harold Kerzner & Hans J. Thamhain. 528p. 1986. 49.95 (ISBN 0-442-24824-5). Van Nos Reinhold.

Project Management Problem-Solver: How to Bring Small & Medium Sized Projects in on Time, Within Budget, with the Right Results. Sydney F. Love. 1988. price not set (ISBN 0-471-63522-7). Wiley.

Project Management: Scheduling & Monitoring by PERT-CPM. B. M. Naik. (Illus.). 320p. 1984. pap. text ed. 12.95x (ISBN 0-7069-2631-5, Pub. by Vikas India). Advent NY.

Project Management Software Directory. Jack Gido. LC 85-2879. 120p. 1985. pap. 21.95x (ISBN 0-8311-1163-1). Indus Pr.

Project Management Techniques. Alfred O. Awani. (Illus.). 192p. 24.95 (ISBN 0-89433-197-3). Petrocelli.

Project Management: Techniques, Applications & Managerial Issues. 2nd ed. Ed. by Edward W. Davis. 1983. pap. text ed. 34.95 (ISBN 0-89806-043-5). Inst Indus Eng.

Project Management: Techniques in Planning & Controlling Construction Projects. H. N. Ahuja. (Construction Management & Engineering Ser.). 470p. 1984. 54.95 (ISBN 0-471-87399-3). Wiley.

Project Management Using Microcomputers. Harvey A. Levine. (Illus.). 350p. (Orig.). 1986. pap. text ed. 21.95 (ISBN 0-07-881221-6). Osborne-McGraw.

Project Management with CPM, PERT & PRECEDENCE Diagramming. 3rd ed. J. Moder et al. 464p. 1983. 31.95 (ISBN 0-442-25415-6). Van Nos Reinhold.

Project Manager. Jack Rudman. (Career Examination Ser.: C-1433). (Cloth bdg. avail. on request). pap. 16.00 (ISBN 0-8373-1433-X). Natl Learning.

Project Manager: IBM Critical Path. Software Projections. (Wiley Professional Software Ser.). 1984. incl. disk 125.00 (ISBN 0-471-88196-1, Pub. by Wiley Press). Wiley.

Project Manpower Management Decision Making Processes in Construction Practice. Woodhead. 509p. 1986. 79.95 (ISBN 0-471-86189-8). Wiley.

Project Manual. Bruce Roberts. Date not set. 31.50 (ISBN 0-317-59581-4). Constr Ind Pr.

Project Master Mariner. Cedric Best. 1986. 38.00x (ISBN 0-317-58043-4, Pub. by Book Guild Ltd). State Mutual Bk.

Project Matrix Management Policy & Strategy. Kerzner. 1984. 50.95 (ISBN 0-442-24719-2). Van Nos Reinhold.

Project: Millennium. Curtis H. Hoffman. 208p. 1987. pap. 2.95 (ISBN 0-441-68312-6, Pub. by Ace Science Fiction). Ace Bks.

Project Monitoring & Evaluation in Agriculture. Dennis J. Casley & Krishna Kumar. LC 87-22632. 176p. 1988. text ed. 20.00x (ISBN 0-8018-3615-8); pap. text ed. 12.95x (ISBN 0-8018-3616-6). Johns Hopkins.

Project Named Desire. John W. Corrington & Joyce H. Corrington. 224p. 1987. 14.95 (ISBN 0-670-81192-0). Viking.

Project Named Desire. John W. Corrington & Joyce H. Corrington. 208p. 1988. pap. 3.50 (ISBN 0-449-21368-4, Crest). Fawcett.

Project Numbers Eleven Hundred One to Fifteen Hundred: A Catalogue of Ethiopian Manuscripts Microfilmed for the Ethiopian Manuscript Microfilm Library & for the Hill Monastic Manuscript Library, Collegeville, Vol. 4. Getatchew Haile. (Illus.). xv, 760p. (Orig.). 1979. pap. 38.50 (ISBN 0-8357-0457-2). Hill Monastic.

Project Numbers Fifteen Hundred One to Two Thousand: A Catalogue of Ethiopian Manuscripts Microfilmed for the Ethiopian Manuscript Microfilm Library & the Hill Monastic Manuscript Library, Collegeville, Vol. 5. Getatchew Haile & William F. Macomber. (Illus.). xvii, 623p. (Orig.). 1981. pap. 36.25 (ISBN 0-8357-0581-1). Hill Monastic.

Project Numbers Four Thousand to Forty-Five Hundred: A Catalogue of Ethiopian Manuscripts Microfilmed for the Ethiopian Manuscript Microfilm Library & the Hill Monastic Manuscript Library, Collegeville, Vol. 9. xi, 393p. 1987. 50.00. Hill Monastic.

Project Numbers One to Three Hundred: A Catalogue of Ethiopian Manuscripts Microfilmed for the Ethiopian Manuscript Microfilm Library, Addis Ababa, & the Hill Monastic Manuscript Library, Collegeville, Vol. 1. William F. Macomber. (Illus.). ix, 355p. (Orig.). 1975. pap. 15.00 (ISBN 0-940250-51-9). Hill Monastic.

Project Numbers Seven Hundred One to Eleven Hundred: A Catalogue of Ethiopian Manuscripts Microfilmed for the Ethiopian Manuscript Microfilm Library, Addis Ababa, & the Hill Monastic Manuscript Library, Collegeville, Vol. 3. William F. Macomber. ix, 524p. (Orig.). 1978. pap. 30.50 (ISBN 0-8357-0303-7). Hill Monastic.

Project Numbers Three Hundred One to Seven Hundred: A Catalogue of Ethiopian Manuscripts Microfilmed for the Ethiopian Manuscript Microfilm Library, Addis Ababa, & the Hill Monastic Manuscript Library, Collegeville, Vol. 2. William F. Macomber. v, 524p. (Orig.). 1976. pap. 25.00 (ISBN 0-940250-52-7). Hill Monastic.

Project Numbers Three Thousand to Thirty-Five Hundred: A Catalogue of Ethiopian Manuscript Microfilm Library, Addis Ababa, & the Hill Monastic Manuscript Library, Collegeville, Vol. 8. Getatchew Haile. (Illus., Orig.). 1985. pap. 45.00 (ISBN 0-940250-55-1). Hill Monastic.

Project Numbers Twenty-Five Hundred One to Three Thousand: A Catalogue of Ethiopian Manuscripts Microfilmed for the Ethiopian Manuscript Microfilm Library & the Hill Monastic Manuscript Library, Collegeville, Vol. 7. Getatchew Haile & William F. Macomber. (Illus.). xi, 414p. (Orig.). 1983. pap. 40.00 (ISBN 0-940250-54-3). Hill Monastic.

Project Numbers Two Thousand One to Twenty-Five Hundred: A Catalogue of Ethiopian Manuscripts, Vol. 6. Getatchew Haile & William F. Macomber. (Illus.). xvi, 650p. (Orig.). 1982. pap. 45.00 (ISBN 0-940250-53-5). Hill Monastic.

Project of Universal & Perpetual Peace. Pierre-Andre Gargaz. LC 79-147424. (Library of War & Peace; Proposals for Peace: a History). lib. bdg. 46.00 (ISBN 0-8240-0216-4). Garland Pub.

Project Overview: The Subject of Thinking. Sydney B. Tyler. 74p. (Orig.). (gr. k-6). 1982. pap. text ed. 10.00 report cover (ISBN 0-912781-09-2). Thomas Geale.

Project Panda Watch. Miriam Schlein. LC 84-2914. (Illus.). 96p. (gr. 3 up). 1984. 11.95 (ISBN 0-689-31071-4, Atheneum Childrens Bks). Macmillan.

Project Pendulum. Robert Silverberg. (YA) (gr. 8 up). 1987. 15.95 (ISBN 0-8027-6712-5). Walker & Co.

Project Performance Results for 1986. (World Bank Operations Evaluation Study Ser.). 196p. 1988. 12.00 (ISBN 0-8213-1084-4, BK1084). World Bank.

Project Phoenix: A Concept for Future Existence. Martin A. Moe, Jr. 96p. (Orig.). 1981. pap. 4.50 (ISBN 0-939960-00-1). Green Turtle Pubns.

Project Planning & Control. Albert Lester. (Illus.). 195p. 1982. text ed. 37.95 (ISBN 0-408-01164-5). Butterworth.

Project Planning & Control. M. Mohsin. 373p. 1983. text ed. 35.00x (ISBN 0-7069-2315-4, Pub. by Vikas India). Advent NY.

Project Planning & Control for Construction. David R. Pierce, Jr. Ed. by William Mahoney. (Illus.). 275p. 1988. text ed. 44.95 (ISBN 0-87629-099-3, 67247). R S Means.

Project Planning & Income Distribution. F. Leslie & C. H. Helmers. (Studies in Development & Planning: Vol. 9). 1979. lib. bdg. 22.95 (ISBN 0-89838-010-3, Pub. by Martinus Nijhoff Netherlands). Kluwer Academic.

Project Planning & Management: An Integrated System for Improving Productivity. Louis J. Goodman. (Illus.). 320p. 1987. 41.95 (ISBN 0-442-22762-0). Van Nos Reinhold.

Project Planning for Developing Economies. W. W. Shaner. LC 79-13225. (Praeger Special Studies Ser.). 256p. 1979. 44.95 (ISBN 0-275-90422-9, C0422). Praeger.

Project Plans for All Around the House from the Pages of Better Homes & Gardens. Ed. by Jean E. Attebury. LC 84-80185. (Illus.). 128p. (Orig.). 1984. pap. 3.95 (ISBN 0-938708-09-0). L F Garlinghouse Co.

Project Plans for Outdoor Living from the Pages of Better Homes & Gardens. Ed. by Jean E. Attebury. LC 84-80186. (Illus.). 128p. (Orig.). 1984. pap. 3.95 (ISBN 0-938708-08-2). L F Garlinghouse Co.

Project Plans to Build for Children from the Pages of Better Homes & Gardens. Ed. by Jean E. Attebury. LC 84-80184. (Illus.). 128p. (Orig.). 1984. pap. 3.95 (ISBN 0-938708-07-4). L F Garlinghouse Co.

Project Pope. Clifford D. Simak. 320p. 1982. pap. 2.75 (ISBN 0-345-29139-5, Del Rey). Ballantine.

Project Preparation & Appraisal: Material & Techniques for Agricultural Co-Operative Management Training. 130p. 1983. 24.50 (ISBN 92-2-102446-6). Intl Labour Office.

Project-Readiness: A Guide to Family Emergency Preparedness. Louise E. Nelson. LC 75-307239. (Illus.). 270p. 1975. 13.95 (ISBN 0-88290-036-6). Horizon Utah.

Project Remember: A National Index of Grave Sites of Notable Americans. Arthur S. Koykka. Ed. by Keith Irvine. LC 83-42530. 598p. 1986. 59.95 (ISBN 0-917256-22-0). Ref Pubns.

Project Renewal in Israel: Urban Revitalization Through Partnership. Paul King et al. 194p. (Orig.). 1987. lib. bdg. 24.50 (ISBN 0-8191-5346-X, Co-Pub. by Ctr Jewish Comm Studies); pap. text ed. 13.75 (ISBN 0-8191-5347-8). U Pr of Amer.

Project SEARCH: The Struggle for Control of Criminal Information in America. Gordon K. Zenk. LC 78-67654. (Contributions in Political Science: No. 23). (Illus.). 1979. lib. bdg. 46.95 (ISBN 0-313-20639-2, ZEP/). Greenwood.

Project Self-Esteem. Peggy Bielen & Sandy McDaniel. LC 85-51127. (Creative Teaching Ser.). 280p. (Orig.). (gr. 2-6). 1985. pap. text ed. 24.95 (ISBN 0-935266-16-X). Jalmar Pr.

Project Services Specialist. Jack Rudman. (Career Examination Ser.: C-1660). (Cloth bdg. avail. on request). pap. 14.00 (ISBN 0-8373-1660-X). Natl Learning.

Project Set Strategies. Frans G. Derkinderen & Roy L. Crum. (Nijenrode Studies in Business: Vol. 4). 1979. lib. bdg. 20.75 (ISBN 0-89838-014-6, Pub. by Martinus Nijhoff Netherlands). Kluwer Academic.

Project Space Station. Brian O'Leary. (Illus.). 160p. 1983. 12.95 (ISBN 0-8117-1701-1). Stackpole.

Project Still Images in Training. Ed. by Roy Thorpe. (Illus.). 150p. 1987. 45.00 (ISBN 0-940813-39-4). Parthenon NJ.

Project Studies in Fugue. Hugo Norden. 1977. pap. 6.95 (ISBN 0-8008-6553-7, Crescendo). Taplinger.

Project Sunlight. June Strong. LC 80-13011. (Orion Ser.). 1980. pap. 2.25 (ISBN 0-8127-0289-1). Review & Herald.

Project Surveying: General Adjustment & Optimization Techniques with Applications to Engineering Surveying. Peter Richardus. 1984. pap. text ed. 43.50 (ISBN 90-6191-526-0, Pub. by A A Balkema). Brookfield Pub Co.

Project Surveying: General Adjustment & Optimization Techniques with Applications to Engineering Surveying. Ed. by Peter Richardus. 640p. 1984. text ed. 75.00 (ISBN 90-6191-519-8, Pub. by A A Balkema). Brookfield Pub Co.

Project TALENT Data Bank Handbook. rev. ed. Lauress L. Wise et al. 1979. pap. 14.50 (ISBN 0-89785-606-6). Am Inst Res.

Project Text for Public Speaking. 5th ed. Clark S. Carlile & Arlie V. Daniel. 340p. 1986. pap. text ed. 15.95 scp (ISBN 0-06-041175-9, HarpC). Har-Row.

Project Turn-Around. Lawrence Dixon. LC 84-61674. 61p. 1985. Three ring notebook. 49.95 (ISBN 0-914607-20-0). Master Tchr.

Project Viability in Inflationary Conditions. V. P. Chitale. 144p. 1980. text ed. 17.95x (ISBN 0-7069-1132-6, Pub. by Vikas India). Advent NY.

Project Whirlwind: The History of a Pioneer Computer. Kent C. Redmond & Thomas M. Smith. (Illus.). 280p. 1980. pap. 25.00 (ISBN 0-932376-09-6, EY-AX009-DP). Digital Pr.

Project Work. Diana L. Fried-Booth. 89p. 1986. 7.95x (ISBN 0-19-437092-5). Oxford U Pr.

Project Work in the Geography Curriculum: An Advanced Level Primer. John R. Beaumont & Stephen W. Williams. 332p. 1983. pap. 25.00 (ISBN 0-7099-3211-1, Pub. by Croom Helm Ltd). Routledge Chapman & Hall.

Project Write: Block One, Student Materials Packet. El-Hi Educational Service, District No. 112 Staff. 112p. 1985. pap. text ed. 9.20 (ISBN 0-8403-3780-9). Kendall-Hunt.

Project Write: Block Three, Student Materials Packet. El-Hi Educational Service, District No. 112 Staff. 160p. 1985. pap. text ed. 4.30 (ISBN 0-8403-3782-5). Kendall-Hunt.

Project Write: Block Two, Student Materials Packet. El-Hi Educational Service, Dictrict No. 112 Staff. 224p. 1985. pap. text ed. 5.50 (ISBN 0-8403-3781-7). Kendall-Hunt.

Project X: The Search for the Secrets of Immortality. Gene Savoy. LC 76-44670. (Illus.). 279p. 1977. text ed. 35.00 (ISBN 0-672-52181-4). Intl Comm Christ.

Project Y: The Los Alamos Story. David Hawkins et al. (History of Modern Physics 1800-1950 Ser.: Vol. 2). 1983. 46.00x (ISBN 0-938228-08-0). Tomash Pubs.

Project You. Paris & Casey. 1984. pap. 6.00 (ISBN 0-87980-408-4). Wilshire.

Projected Nineteen Eighty-Six Median Household Income in Virginia's Counties, Cities, MSAs, & Planning Districts. 1986. write for info. U Va Ctr Pub Serv.

Projected Pulp & Paper Mills in the World 1984-1994. 112p. 1985. pap. 8.75 (ISBN 92-5-102258-5, F2782, FAO). UNIPUB.

Projected Pulp & Paper Mills in the World 1985-1995. 114p. (Orig.). 1986. pap. text ed. 9.50 (ISBN 92-5-102463-4, F2961, FAO). UNIPUB.

Projected Pulp & Paper Mills in the World 1986-1996. 111p. (Orig.). 1987. pap. text ed. 11.25 (ISBN 92-5-102581-9, F3113, FAO). UNIPUB.

Projecting a Picture of Home Economics: Public Relations in Secondary Programs. E. P. Anderson & C. J. Ley. 1982. 4.00 (ISBN 0-911365-20-6, A261-08454). Home Econ Educ.

Projecting a Positive Image Through Public Relations. Cosette Kies. (School Media Centers: Focus on Trends & Issues: No. 2). 88p. 1978. pap. 6.00x (ISBN 0-8389-3219-3, 78-21250). ALA.

Projection & Re-Collection in Jungian Psychology: Reflections of the Soul. Marie-Louise Von Franz. Tr. by William H. Kennedy from Ger. (Reality of the Psyche Ser.). Orig. Title: Spiegelungen der Seele: Projektion und Innere Sammlung. 264p. 1985. pap. 11.95 (ISBN 0-87548-417-4). Open Court.

Projection Drawing. Thomas C. Wang. LC 83-25930. (Illus.). 112p. 1984. 31.95 (ISBN 0-442-29232-5); pap. 18.95 (ISBN 0-442-29231-7). Van Nos Reinhold.

Projection, Identification, Projective Identification. Joseph Sandler. 1987. lib. bdg. 27.50x (ISBN 0-8236-4370-0). Intl Univs Pr.

Projection-Iterative Methods for Solution of Operator Equations. N. S. Kurpel. Ed. by R. G. Douglas. Tr. by Israel Program for Scientific Translations. LC 76-17114. (Translations of Mathematical Monographs: No. 46). 1976. 48.00 (ISBN 0-8218-1596-2, MMONO-46). Am Math.

Projection Methods in Constrained Optimization & Applications to Optimal Policy Decisions. B. Rustem. (Lecture Notes in Control & Information Sciences Ser.: Vol. 31). 315p. 1981. pap. 19.50 (ISBN 0-387-10646-4). Springer-Verlag.

Projection of Britain: British Overseas Publicity & Propaganda, 1919-1939. Philip M. Taylor. LC 80-42274. pap. 98.60 (2031733). Bks Demand UMI.

Projection of Power: Perspectives, Perceptions, & Problems. Ed. by Uri Ra'anan et al. LC 82-6697. 351p. 1982. 32.50 (ISBN 0-208-01954-5, Archon). Shoe String.

Projection of the Astral Body. Sylvan Muldoon & Hereward Carrington. (Illus.). 1970. pap. 9.95 (ISBN 0-87728-069-X). Weiser.

Projection Operator Techniques in Nonequilibrium Statistical Mechanics. H. Grabert. (Springer Tratcs in Modern physics Ser.: Vol. 95). (Illus.). 220p. 1982. 38.00 (ISBN 0-387-11635-4). Springer-Verlag.

Projection Principle. George Weinberg & Dianne Rowe. 256p. 1988. 16.95 (ISBN 0-312-00057-X). St Martin.

Projectionists' Programmed Primer. (Illus.). 1982. 6.25 (ISBN 0-9601006-0-1). G T Yeamans.

Projections Model for Small Area Economies. Roger L. Burford. LC 67-64023. (Research Monograph: No. 35). 1966. spiral bdg. 10.00 (ISBN 0-88406-049-7). Ga St U Busn Pub.

Projections of United States Agricultural Production & Demand: An Original Anthology. LC 75-29757. (World Food Supply Ser). (Illus.). 1976. 25.00x (ISBN 0-405-07782-3). Ayer Co Pubs.

Proletarianisation in the Third World: Studies in the Creation of a Labour Force under Dependent Capitalism. Ed. by Barry Munslow & Henry Finch. LC 84-12739. 320p. 1984. 29.00 (ISBN 0-7099-1764-3, Pub. by Croom Helm Ltd). Routledge Chapman & Hall.

Proletarianization & Class Struggle in Africa. Ed. by Bernard Magubane & Nzongola-Ntalaja. (Contemporary Marxism Ser.). (Illus.). 180p. (Orig.). 1983. pap. 8.95 (ISBN 0-89935-019-4, 83-444). Synthesis Pubns.

Proletarianization & Family History. Ed. by David A. Levine. (Studies in Social Discontinuity). 1984. 29.95 (ISBN 0-12-444980-8). Acad Pr.

Proletarians & African Capitalism: The Kenyan Case, 1960-1972. Richard Sandbrook. LC 73-91818. (Perspectives on Development Ser.: Vol. 4). pap. 58.00 (ISBN 0-317-20835-7, 2024545). Bks Demand UMI.

Proletarians & Parties: Five Essays in Social Class. Leslie Benson. 1978. pap. 10.50x (ISBN 0-422-76580-5, NO. 2829, Pub. by Tavistock England). Routledge Chapman & Hall.

Proletarians & Protest: The Roots of Class Formation in an Industrializing World. Ed. by Michael Hanagan & Charles Stephenson. LC 85-5596. (Contributions in Labor Studies: No. 17). (Illus.). 263p. 1986. lib. bdg. 46.95 (ISBN 0-313-23217-2, STI/). Greenwood.

Proletariat: A Challange to Western Civilization. Goetz A. Briefs. LC 74-25742. (European Sociology Ser.). 320p. 1975. Repr. 24.50x (ISBN 0-405-06498-5). Ayer Co Pubs.

Proletariato E la Borghesia Nel Movimento Socialista Italiano: Saggio Di Scienza Sociografico-Politica: Proletariat & Bourgeoisie Within the Socialist Movement: a Sociographic Political Essay. Roberto Michels. LC 74-25769. (European Sociology Ser.). 1975. Repr. 34.00x (ISBN 0-405-06523-X). Ayer Co Pubs.

Proliferation of Different Cell Types in the Brain. H. Korr. (Advances in Anatomy, Embryology & Cell Biology Ser.: Vol. 61). (Illus.). 80p. 1980. pap. 32.00 (ISBN 0-387-09899-2). Springer-Verlag.

Proliferation of Prophets: Essays on German Writers from Nietzsche to Brecht. Michael Hamburger. LC 83-40513. 320p. 1984. 22.50 (ISBN 0-312-65117-1). St Martin.

Proliferation, Plutonium & Policy: Institutional & Technological Impediments to Nuclear Weapons Propogation. Alexander De Volpi. (Pergamon Policy Studies). (Illus.). 1979. 64.00 (ISBN 0-08-023872-6). Pergamon.

Proliferation, Politics, & the IAEA: The Issue of Nuclear Safguards. Ed. by Aspen Institute. 42p. (Orig.). 1985. pap. text ed. 5.00 (ISBN 0-8191-5849-6, Pub. by Aspen Inst for Humanistic Studies). U Pr of Amer.

Proliferation, Politics, & the IAEA: The Issue of Nuclear Safguards Part Two Berlin. Ed. by Aspen Institute. 26p. (Orig.). 1985. pap. text ed. 5.00 (ISBN 0-317-61098-8, Pub. by Aspen Inst for Humanistic Studies). U Pr of Amer.

Proliferative Vitreoretinopathy-Epidemiology of Glaucoma. Ed. by W. Straub. (Developments in Ophthalmology Ser.: Vol. 16). (Illus.). viii, 132p. 1989. 80.00 (ISBN 3-8055-4853-2). S Karger.

Prolific Pencil. Percy F. Rex. Ed. by Fredrika A. Burrows & Stephen W. Sullwold. LC 80-51482. (Illus.). 312p. 1980. 15.00 (ISBN 0-88492-037-2). W S Sullwold.

Prolific Tropical Sheep. I. L. Mason. (Animal Production & Health Papers: No. 17). 130p. (Eng., Fr. & Span.). 1980. pap. 9.50 (ISBN 92-5-100845-0, F2107, FAO). UNIPUB.

Prolog. Francis Giannesini. (ICSS Ser.). 320p. 1986. pap. text ed. write for info. (ISBN 0-201-12911-6). Addison-Wesley.

Prolog. Tom Hankins & Thom Luce. 224p. 1989. pap. text ed. price not set (ISBN 0-394-39296-5). Knopf.

Prolog & Its Applications. John Malpas. (Illus.). 336p. 1987. text ed. 29.00 (ISBN 0-13-730805-1). P-H.

Prolog & Natural Language Analysis. Fernando C. Pereira & Stuart M. Shieber. LC 87-71131. (Center for the Study of Language & Information, Lecture Notes: No. 10). 280p. (Orig.). 1987. 28.95 (ISBN 0-937073-17-2); pap. 13.95 (ISBN 0-937073-18-0). Ctr Study Language.

Prolog & the Tutorial. Logicware Staff & Richard Young. (Illus.). 450p. 1988. text ed. 32.95 (ISBN 0-442-25934-4). Van Nos Reinhold.

Prolog Buducnosti. Milos Acin-Kosta. 195p. (Serbo-Croatian.). 1963. pap. 3.00 (ISBN 0-317-61881-4). Ravnogorski.

Prolog By Example. H. Coelho & J. C. Cotta. (Symbolic Computation Artificial Intelligence Ser.). 305p. 1988. 35.00 (ISBN 0-387-18313-2). Springer-Verlag.

PROLOG Database System. Deyi Li. LC 83-26896. 207p. 1984. 64.95x (ISBN 0-471-90429-5). Wiley.

Prolog for Programmers. Dahl. 1985. pap. write for info. (ISBN 0-471-82495-X). Wiley.

Prolog for Programmers. Feliks Kluzniak & Stanislaw Szpakowicz. 1985. 61.00 (ISBN 0-12-416520-6). Acad Pr.

Prolog for Programmers. Ed. by Feliks Kluzniak & Stanislaw Szpakowicz. (APIC Ser.: No. 24). 320p. 1987. pap. 29.95 (ISBN 0-12-416521-4). Acad Pr.

Prolog Multiprocessors. Michael Wise. (Illus.). 160p. 1987. text ed. 28.00 (ISBN 0-13-730755-1). P-H.

Prolog Primer. Jean B. Rogers. LC 85-22846. 214p. 1986. pap. text ed. 21.50 (ISBN 0-201-06467-7). Addison-Wesley.

Prolog Programming & Applications. W. D. Burnham & A. R. Hall. 1985. pap. 16.95 (ISBN 0-470-20263-7). Halsted Pr.

Prolog Programming: Applications for Database Systems, Expert Systems & Parsers. Arity Corporation Staff & Claudia Marcus. LC 86-17287. 304p. 1986. pap. 22.95 (ISBN 0-201-14647-9). Addison-Wesley.

Prolog Programming for Artificial Intelligence. Ivan Bratko. 272p. 1986. pap. text ed. 29.25 (ISBN 0-201-14224-4). Addison-Wesley.

Prolog: Programming for Tomorrow. Jim Doores et al. 156p. 1987. 21.95 (ISBN 0-905104-52-8, Pub. by Sigma Pr UK). Bk Clearing Hse.

Prolog Programming in Depth. Michael Covington et al. 1987. pap. 24.95 (ISBN 0-673-18659-8). Scott F.

PROLOG: Programming Techniques & Applications. Susan B. Garavaglia. 1987. write for info. (ISBN 0-471-60329-5). Wiley.

Prolog: Sophisticated Applications in Artificial Intelligence. Ramachandran Bharath. (Illus.). 220p. 1988. pap. 17.95 (ISBN 0-8306-9392-0, 3092). TAB Bks.

Prolog to Expert Systems. William Leigh. 288p. (Orig.). 1987. pap. text ed. 32.00 (ISBN 0-394-39065-2). Mitchell Pub.

Prolog Wizard: A Wiley Programmer's Reference. Dennis L. Foster. 1987. pap. 24.95 (ISBN 0-471-85348-8). Wiley.

Prologomena to an Anthropological Physiology. F. J. Buytendijk. LC 72-90636. (Psychological Ser.: No. 6). 1974. text ed. 15.00x (ISBN 0-391-00332-1). Duquesne.

Prologue: A Drama of John Hus. Bob Jones. (Illus.). 85p. 1968. pap. 4.20 (ISBN 0-89084-195-0). Bob Jones Univ Pr.

Prologue & Epilogues of William Caxton. William Caxton. Ed. by W. J. Crotch. (EETS, OS Ser.: No. 176). Repr. of 1927 ed. 36.00 (ISBN 0-527-00173-2). Kraus Repr.

Prologue in the Old French & Provencal Mystery. David H. Carnahan. LC 68-55160. (Studies in French Literature, No. 45). 1969. Repr. of 1905 ed. lib. bdg. 46.95x (ISBN 0-8383-0519-9). Haskell.

Prologue of St. John's Gospel. C. K. Barrett. (Ethel M. Wood Lectures). 28p. 1971. pap. 12.95 (ISBN 0-485-14315-1, Pub. by Athlone Pr UK). Humanities.

Prologue of the Gospel of St. John: Esoteric Studies. E. C. Marion-Wild. Tr. by Helga Roboz & Steven Roboz. 19p. 1984. pap. 3.75 (ISBN 0-919924-22-0). Anthroposophic.

Prologue: The Eurocentric State of the Discipline: Project on Goals, Processes & Indicators of Development. 64p. 1982. pap. 5.00 (ISBN 92-808-0385-9, TUNU204, UNU). UNIPUB.

Prologue, the Knight's Tale, & the Nun's Priest's Tale from Chaucer's Canterbury Tales. Ed. & intro. by Frank J. Mather. 143p. Repr. of 1809 ed. lib. bdg. 20.00 (ISBN 0-8492-1688-5). R West.

Prologue: The Novels of Black American Women, 1891-1965. Carole M. Watson. LC 84-21265. (Contributions in American Studies: No. 79). (Illus.). xviii, 168p. 1985. lib. bdg. 35.00 (ISBN 0-313-23630-5, WPG/). Greenwood.

Prologue to English Literature. W. W. Robson. LC 76-7848. 224p. 1986. 19.95x (ISBN 0-389-20630-X). B&N Imports.

Prologue to Gdansk: A Report on Human Rights by the Polish Helsinki Watch Committee. Helsinki Watch Staff. 144p. 1981. 6.00 (ISBN 0-938579-93-2). Fund Free Expression.

Prologue to Independence: The Trials of James Alexander 1715-1756. Henry N. MacCracken. 1965. 2.50 (ISBN 0-685-11978-5). Heineman.

Prologue to National Development Planning. Jamshid Gharajedaghi. LC 86-9921. (Contributions in Economics & Economic History Ser.: No. 70). 223p. 1986. 36.95 (ISBN 0-313-25285-8, GPG/). Greenwood.

Prologue to New England. Henry F. Howe. LC 68-26231. (Illus.). 1968. Repr. of 1943 ed. 27.00x (ISBN 0-8046-0218-2, Pub. by Kennikat). Assoc Faculty Pr.

Prologue to Nuremberg: The Politics & Diplomacy of Punishing War Criminals of the First World War. James F. Willis. LC 81-1055. (Contributions in Legal Studies Ser.: No. 20). (Illus.). xiii, 292p. 1982. lib. bdg. 35.00 (ISBN 0-313-21454-9, WNU/). Greenwood.

Prologue to Peron: Argentina in Depression & War, 1930-1943. Ed. by Mark Falcoff & Ronald Dolkart. LC 74-22961. 250p. 1976. 35.00x (ISBN 0-520-02874-0). U of Cal Pr.

Prologue to Professionalism. M. Louise Fitzpatrick. LC 83-2526. 288p. 1983. pap. text ed. 18.95 (ISBN 0-89303-773-7). Appleton & Lange.

Prologue to Revolution: Sources & Documents on the Stamp Act Crisis, 1764-1766. Ed. by Edmund S. Morgan. (Documentary Problems in Early American History Ser.). 164p. 1972. pap. text ed. 3.95x (ISBN 0-393-09424-3). Norton.

Prologue to Swedenborg's Animal Kingdom. Emanuel Swedenborg. 14p. pap. 0.50 (ISBN 0-915221-08-X). Swedenborg Sci Assn.

Prologue to the Canterbury Tales of Chaucer. E. F. Willoughby. 59.95 (ISBN 0-8490-0898-0). Gordon Pr.

Prologue to the Chinese Revolution: The Transformation of Ideas & Institutions in Hunan Province, 1891-1907. Charlton M. Lewis. (East Asian Monographs: No. 70). 1976. 21.00x (ISBN 0-674-71441-5). Harvard U Pr.

Prologue to the Present: A Narrative World History, Vol. I to 1415. Elizabeth Pool. (Illus.). 448p. (Orig.). (gr. 9-12). 1984. pap. 10.95x (ISBN 0-88334-142-5). Ind Sch Pr.

Prologue to the Protest Movement: The Missouri Sharecropper Roadside Demonstrations of 1939. Louis Cantor. LC 70-86480. xii, 204p. 1969. 20.50 (ISBN 0-8223-0215-2). Duke.

Prologue to War: England & the United States, 1805-1812. Bradford Perkins. 1961. pap. 11.95x (ISBN 0-520-00996-7). U of Cal Pr.

Prologues & Epilogues of John Dryden. William B. Gardner. 383p. Repr. of 1951 ed. 12.00x (ISBN 0-911858-14-8). Appel.

Prologues & Epilogues of William Caxton. William Caxton. Ed. by Walter J. Crotch. LC 70-170185. (Research & Source Works Ser.: No. 829). 1971. Repr. of 1928 ed. lib. bdg. 22.50 (ISBN 0-8337-0738-8). B Franklin.

Prologues Written by Samuel Johnson & Spoken by David Garrick at a Benefit Performance of Comus. Samuel Johnson. LC 77-13301. Repr. of 1925 ed. 18.00 (ISBN 0-8414-5401-9). Folcroft.

Prolongation of Human Life, 2 vols. Elie Metchnikoff. (Illus.). 327p. 1986. Repr. of 1908 ed. Set. 187.75 (ISBN 0-89901-248-5). Am Classical Coll Pr.

Prolongation of Life: Optimistic Studies. Elie Metchnikoff. Ed. by Robert Kastenaum. Tr. by P. Chalmers Mitchell. LC 76-19583. (Death & Dying Ser.). (Illus.). 1977. Repr. of 1908 ed. lib. bdg. 31.00x (ISBN 0-405-09579-1). Ayer Co Pubs.

Prolonged Connections: Demographic Change & the Rise of the Extended Family. Steven Ruggles. LC 86-40451. (Social Demography Ser.). 288p. 1987. text ed. 37.50x (ISBN 0-299-11030-3); pap. text ed. 15.75x (ISBN 0-299-11034-6). U of Wis Pr.

Prolonged Psychological Effects of a Disaster: A Study of Buffalo Creek. Goldine C. Gleser et al. (Personality & Psychopathology Ser.). 1981. 22.00 (ISBN 0-12-286260-0). Acad Pr.

Prolongevity. Albert Rosenfeld. 1983. pap. 2.50 (ISBN 0-380-01786-5, 35303, Discus). Avon.

Prolongevity II: An Updated Report on the Scientific Prospects for Adding Good Years to Life. Albert Rosenfeld. Ed. by Charles Elliott. LC 84-48662. 335p. 1985. 18.45 (ISBN 0-394-53475-1). Knopf.

Prolongevity II: An Updated Report on the Scientifc Prospects for Adding Good Years to Life. Albert Rosenfeld. 1987. pap. 9.95 (ISBN 0-8050-0164-6). H Holt & Co.

Prom Date. M. E. Cooper. (Couples Ser.: No. 31). 192p. (YA) (gr. 12 up). 1988. pap. 2.50 (ISBN 0-590-41266-3). Scholastic Inc.

Promenade & Other Plays. Maria I. Fornes. 1987. pap. 8.95 (ISBN 1-55554-014-7). Paj Pubns.

Promenade et Poesie: L'experience De la Marche et Du Mouvement Dans L'oeuvre De Rimbaud. Jacques Plessen. (Publications De L'institut D'etudes Francaises et Occitanes De L'universite D'utrecht: No. 1). 1967. pap. 28.80x (ISBN 90-2790-092-2). Mouton.

Promenade Home: Macrobiotics & Women's Health. Gale Jack & Alex Jack. 240p. 1988. 15.95 (ISBN 0-87040-697-3). Japan Pubns USA.

Promenades. Michael Chamberlin. 1976. signed ed. 6.00 (ISBN 0-685-79237-4, Pub. by Grosseteste); pap. 2.00 (ISBN 0-685-79238-2). Small Pr Dist.

Promenades a Cambridge. Frank A. Reeve. (Cambridge Town, Gown & County Ser.: Vol. 26). (Illus., Fr.). 1978. pap. 4.00 (ISBN 0-900891-43-2). Oleander Pr.

Promenades dans Rome, 3 tomes. Stendhal, pseud. Set. 47.90 (ISBN 0-685-35015-0). French & Eur.

Promenades dans Rome, 3 vols. facsimile ed. Stendhal. 150.00 (ISBN 0-686-55078-1). French & Eur.

Promenades dans Rome, 3 vols. Stendhal. Ed. by Ernest Abravanel & Victor Del Litto. (Illus.). 9.95 ea. French & Eur.

Promenades et Souvenirs see Oeuvres.

Promenades of an Impressionist. James G. Huneker. LC 73-134097. (Essay Index Reprint Ser). 1910. 24.50 (ISBN 0-8369-1959-9). Ayer Co Pubs.

Promenades Romaines. Rene de Chateaubriand. 20p. 1963. 99.50 (ISBN 0-686-54373-4). French & Eur.

Promesas de Jesus. David Wilkerson. 95p. (Span.). 1974. pap. 2.95 (ISBN 0-89922-027-4). Edit Caribe.

Promesas Personales de la Biblia. 128p. (Span.). 1982. pap. 2.50 (ISBN 0-87788-692-X). Shaw Pubs.

Promesse De L'Aube. Romain Gary. (Folio Ser.: No. 373). 1966. 7.95 (ISBN 0-685-11515-1). Schoenhof.

Prometean Ethics: Living with Death, Competition, & Triage. Garrett Hardin. LC 79-56592. (Jesse & John Danz Lecture Ser.). 92p. 1980. 10.00x (ISBN 0-295-95717-4). U of Wash Pr.

Promethean Fire: Reflections on the Origin of Mind. Charles J. Lumsden & Edward O. Wilson. (Illus.). 256p. 1983. 18.50x (ISBN 0-674-71445-8). Harvard U Pr.

Promethean Fire: Reflections on the Origin of Mind. Charles J. Lumsden & Edward O. Wilson. 224p. 1984. pap. 8.95 (ISBN 0-674-71446-6). Harvard U Pr.

Prometheans. Ben Bova. 288p. (Orig.). 1986. pap. 2.95 (ISBN 0-8125-3219-8, Dist. by Warner Publisher Services & St. Martin's Press). Tor Bks.

Prometheans: Ancient & Moderns. Burton Rascoe. LC 70-156707. (Essay Index Reprint Ser.). Repr. of 1933 ed. 18.00 (ISBN 0-8369-2855-5). Ayer Co Pubs.

Promethee Mal Enchaine: Nouvelles. Andre Gide. pap. 8.95 (ISBN 0-685-34154-2). French & Eur.

Promethee ou la vie de Balzac. Andre Maurois. 27.50 (ISBN 0-685-36955-2). French & Eur.

Prometheus & the Story of Fire. I. M. Richardson. LC 82-15979. (Illus.). 32p. (gr. 4-8). 1983. PLB 10.79 (ISBN 0-89375-859-0); pap. text ed. 2.50 (ISBN 0-89375-860-4). Troll Assocs.

Prometheus: Archetypal Image of Human Existence. C. Kerenyi. 1963. 50.00 (ISBN 0-8274-3210-0). R West.

Prometheus: Archetypal Image of Human Existence see Archetypal Images in Greek Religion.

Prometheus Bound. Aeschylus. Ed. by W. R. Connor. LC 78-18612. (Greek Texts & Commentaries Ser.). (Illus.). 1979. Repr. of 1932 ed. lib. bdg. 17.00x (ISBN 0-405-11451-6). Ayer Co Pubs.

Prometheus Bound. Aeschylus. Tr. by Warren D. Anderson. (Orig.). 1963. pap. 4.24 scp (ISBN 0-672-60357-8, LLA143). Bobbs.

Prometheus Bound. Aeschylus. Ed. by William Arrowsmith. Tr. by James Scully & C. John Herington. (Greek Tragedy in New Translations Ser.). 1975. 19.95x (ISBN 0-19-501934-2). Oxford U Pr.

Prometheus Bound. Aeschylus. Ed. by Mark Griffith. LC 82-1301. (Cambridge Greek & Latin Classics Ser.). 270p. 1983. 49.50 (ISBN 0-521-24843-4); pap. 18.95 (ISBN 0-521-27011-1). Cambridge U Pr.

Prometheus Bound. Robert Lowell. 67p. 1969. 5.95 (ISBN 0-374-23780-8). FS&G.

Prometheus Bound (Aeschylus) Warren D. Anderson. 1963. pap. text ed. write for info. (ISBN 0-02-303130-1). Macmillan.

Prometheus Bound & Other Plays. Aeschylus. Tr. by Philip Vellacott. Incl. Suppliants; Seven Against Thebes; Persians. (Classics Ser.). (Orig.). 1961. pap. 4.95 (ISBN 0-14-044112-3). Penguin.

Prometheus Bound & the Fragments of Prometheus Loosed. Aeschylus. Ed. by N. Wecklein. Tr. by F. D. Allen. (College Classical Ser.). iv, 178p. (Orig., Gr. & Ger.). 1981. lib. bdg. 25.00x (ISBN 0-89241-358-1); pap. text ed. 12.50x (ISBN 0-89241-126-0). Caratzas.

Prometheus Bound: The Mythic Structure of Karl Marx's Scientific Thinking. Leonard P. Wessell, Jr. LC 84-5740. 312p. 1984. text ed. 35.00 (ISBN 0-8071-1142-2). La State U Pr.

Prometheus Design. Sondra Marshak & Myrna Culbreath. (Gregg Press Science Fiction - Star Trek Ser.). 192p. 1986. lib. bdg. 11.95x (ISBN 0-8398-2936-1, Gregg). G K Hall.

Prometheus Operation. Mark Elder. LC 80-14577. 312p. 1980. text ed. 11.95 (ISBN 0-07-019191-3). McGraw.

Prometheus Reborn. Michael J. Johnson. LC 76-52144. 1977. 7.95 (ISBN 0-87212-073-2). Libra.

Prometheus Rising. Robert A. Wilson. LC 83-81665. 280p. 1983. pap. 9.95 (ISBN 0-941404-19-6). Falcon Pr Az.

Prometheus Syndrome. Bettina L. Knapp. LC 78-69803. 280p. 1979. 15.00x (ISBN 0-87875-147-5). Whitston Pub.

Prometheus the Firebringer. Stephen Sweigart. (Parpaglion Poetry Ser.: No. 7). 1985. 35.00 (ISBN 0-9604252-2-5). Parpaglion.

Prometheus: The Life of Balzac. Andre Maurois. 600p. 1983. pap. 11.95 (ISBN 0-88184-023-8). Carroll & Graf.

Prometheus Trilogy. Ruth F. Birnbaum & Harold F. Birnbaum. 7.50x (ISBN 0-87291-125-X). Coronado Pr.

Prometheus Unbound: An Interpretation. Carl H. Grabo. LC 68-19149. 214p. 1968. Repr. of 1935 ed. 25.00x (ISBN 0-87752-045-3). Gordian.

Prometheus Unbound & Hellas: An Approach to Shelley's Lyrical Dramas. John S. Flagg. Ed. by James Hogg. (Romantic Reassessment Ser.). 278p. (Orig.). 1972. pap. 15.00 (ISBN 0-317-40085-1, Pub. by Salzburg Studies). Longwood Pub Group.

Promethium Technology. James Wheelwright. (ANS Monographs). 416p. 1973. 26.00 (ISBN 0-89448-002-2, 300006). Am Nuclear Soc.

Prometheus Design, No. 5. Sondra Marshak & Myrna Culbreath. pap. 3.50 (ISBN 0-671-62745-7). PB.

Prominent Indians of Victorian Age: A Biographical Dictionary. T. Lethbride. 600p. 1986. 120.00x (ISBN 0-317-61975-6, Pub. by Archives Pubs). State Mutual Bk.

Prominent Men & Women of Provo, Utah. Ed. by Larry L. Richman. 188p. 1983. 10.95 (ISBN 0-941846-00-8). Richman Pub.

Promised Land, the Life & Times of Henry Dodge, First Territorial Governor of Wisconsin: A Historical Drama. Edna Meudt. Ed. by John E. Westburg. LC 80-54737. 56p. 1980. pap. 10.00 (ISBN 0-87423-026-8). Westburg.

Promised Land: The South since Nineteen Forty-Five. David R. Goldfield. Ed. by John H. Franklin & Abraham Eisenstadt. LC 86-16243. (American History Ser.). 280p. 1987. text ed. 19.95 (ISBN 0-88295-850-X); pap. text ed. 9.95 (ISBN 0-88295-843-7). Harlan Davidson.

Promised Lands Revisited: An Update of 1976 Findings on Practices. Richard Morgan et al. 1989. pap. price not set (ISBN 0-918780-44-6). INFORM.

Promised Lands 1: Subdivisions in Deserts & Mountains, Vol. 1. Leslie Allan et al. LC 76-46735. (Promised Lands Ser.). (Illus.). 560p. 1976. pap. 20.00x (ISBN 0-918780-04-7). INFORM.

Promised Lands 3: Subdivisions & the Law, Vol. 3. Patricia A. Simko et al. LC 77-90919. (Promised Lands Ser.). (Illus.). 535p. 1978. pap. 10.00x (ISBN 0-918780-06-3). INFORM.

Promised Messiah. Bruce R. McConkie. LC 78-3478. 636p. 1978. 17.95 (ISBN 0-87747-702-7). Deseret Bk.

Promised One. Louis W. Coscia, pseud. 192p. 1983. 10.95. Todd & Honeywell.

Promised Ones Are Alive & Well on Planet Earth. 1986. write for info. Port Love Intl.

Promised Splendor. Connie Mason. 448p. (Orig.). 1988. pap. 3.95 (ISBN 0-8439-2626-0, Pub. by Leisure Bks CT). Leisure NY.

Promised Woman. Mother M. Angelica. 62p. (Orig.). 1977. pap. text ed. 2.00 (ISBN 1-55794-015-0, B41). Eternal Wrd TV.

Promisekeeper: A Tephramancy. Charles Newman. LC 76-139651. 1971. 20.00 (ISBN 0-671-20822-5). Ultramarine Pub.

Promiseland: A Century of Life in a Negro Community. Elizabeth R. Bethel. 318p. 1981. 29.95 (ISBN 0-87722-211-8). Temple U Pr.

Promiseland: A Century of Life in a Negro Community. Elizabeth R. Bethel. 329p. 1982. pap. 9.95 (ISBN 0-87722-275-4). Temple U Pr.

Promises. Charlotte V. Allen. 464p. (Orig.). 1986. pap. 4.50 (ISBN 0-425-10193-2). Berkley Pub.

Promises. Judith Arnold. (American Romance Ser.: No. 201). 245p. Date not set. pap. 2.50 (ISBN 0-317-63688-X). Harlequin Bks.

Promises. Francine Pascal. (Sweet Valley High Ser.: No. 15). 160p. (Orig.). (YA) (gr. 7-12). 1985. pap. 2.75 (ISBN 0-553-26765-5). Bantam.

Promises, 3 bks. Anita L. Wheatcroft. (Illus.). 80p. (Orig.). (gr. 3-4). 1973. Set. pap. 2.95 (ISBN 0-8192-4043-5); tchrs'. guide 4.75x (ISBN 0-8192-4044-3). Morehouse.

Promises: A Daily Guide to Supernatural Living. Bill Bright. LC 82-72302. 365p. 1983. 9.95 (ISBN 0-317-00638-X). Campus Crusade.

Promises & Performance: Presidential Campaigns As Policy Predictors. Michael G. Krukones. LC 84-13208. 158p. (Orig.). 1984. lib. bdg. 26.75 (ISBN 0-8191-4213-1); pap. text ed. 12.50 (ISBN 0-8191-4214-X). U Pr of Amer.

Promises & Prayers for Healing: Hope for the Future. Carl G. Carlozzi. (Pocketpac Books). 128p. (Orig.). 1985. pap. 2.50 (ISBN 0-87788-336-X). Shaw Pubs.

Promises & Turtle Shells: And Forty-Nine Other Object Lessons for Children. Dorothy B. Francis. 112p. (Orig.). 1984. pap. 7.50 (ISBN 0-687-34337-2). Abingdon.

Promises Broken. Created by Francine Pascal. (Caitlin: The Promise Trilogy Ser.: Bk. 2). 176p. (YA) (gr. 7-12). 1986. pap. 2.95 (ISBN 0-553-26156-8). Bantam.

Promises by the Dozen. Tom Carter. LC 87-71393. 160p. (Orig.). 1988. pap. 6.95 (ISBN 0-88270-635-7). Bridge Pub.

Promises for Kids from the Book. 240p. (gr. 1 up). 1988. 8.95 (ISBN 0-8423-5053-5). Tyndale.

Promises for the Golden Years. Pocketpac Bks. 96p. 1983. pap. 2.50 (ISBN 0-87788-320-3). Shaw Pubs.

Promises for the Graduate. Larry Richards. 128p. 1988. pap. 6.95 (ISBN 0-310-39430-9, 18304). Zondervan.

Promises from God. Marilyn Kunz & Catherine Schell. 64p. 1988. pap. 2.95 (ISBN 0-8423-4981-2). Tyndale.

Promises from Proverbs. David Carder. 1986. pap. 1.95 (ISBN 0-310-36782-4, 12732P). Zondervan.

Promises in the Attic. Elisabeth H. Friermood. LC 60-12790. (gr. 5-9). 1975. pap. 4.95 (ISBN 0-913428-14-0). Landfall Pr.

Promises Kept. Raymond Cook. 50p. (Orig.). 1988. pap. text ed. 6.00 (ISBN 0-9620170-0-0). Stone Mtn Pr.

Promises, Morals, & Law. P. S. Atiyah. 1981. 39.95x (ISBN 0-19-825377-X); pap. 17.95x (ISBN 0-19-825479-2). Oxford U Pr.

Promises of Jesus from the Gospels: Puzzle Book. Ruby Maschke. (Illus.). 48p. (gr. 7 up). 1983. pap. 2.50 (ISBN 0-87239-591-X, 2789). Standard Pub.

Promises of the Good Life: Social Consequences of Private Marketing Decisions. S. Prakash Sethi. LC 78-70945. (Irwin Series in Marketing). pap. 103.50 (ISBN 0-317-27541-0, 2055812). Bks Demand UMI.

Promises of the Messiah. Abram K. Abraham. (Inspirational Library). 341p. 1987. leather case 10.95 (ISBN 1-55748-019-2); pap. 4.95 (ISBN 1-55748-020-6). Barbour & Co.

Promises, Promises. Neil Simon et al. 1969. 6.95 (ISBN 0-394-40685-0). Random.

Promises, Promises, Promises. Joel Nederhood. LC 79-18889. (Orig.). 1979. pap. text ed. 4.95 (ISBN 0-933140-09-6). CRC Pubns.

Promises to Keep. George Bernau. LC 88-40080. 656p. 1988. 19.95 (ISBN 0-446-51453-5). Warner Bks.

Promises to Keep. Sharron Cohen. (Private Library Collection). 1986. 6.95 (ISBN 0-938422-38-3). SOS Pubns CA.

Promises to Keep. Jocelyn Stirling. Ed. by Jim Connor. 320p. 1987. pap. 3.95 (ISBN 0-7701-0645-5). Paperjacks US.

Promises to Keep. Wendy Susans. 400p. (Orig.). 1987. pap. 3.95 (ISBN 0-8439-2503-5, Leisure Bks). Leisure NY.

Promises to Keep: A Handbook for Parents of Learning Disabled, Handicapped, & Brain-Injured Children. David Melton. 256p. 1984. 16.95 (ISBN 0-531-09762-5). Watts.

Promises to Keep: A Workbook of Experiences for Covenant Living. Dennis C. Benson & Marilyn J. Benson. (Orig.). 1978. pap. 3.95 (ISBN 0-377-00077-9). Friendship Pr.

Promises to Keep: The Amway Phenomenon & How It Works. Charles P. Conn. 320p. 1985. 16.95 (ISBN 0-399-13059-4). Putnam Pub Group.

Promises to Keep: The Amway Phenomenon & How it Works. Charles P. Conn. 176p. 1986. pap. 3.50 (ISBN 0-425-09856-7). Berkley Pub.

Promises to Live by. David Wilkerson. LC 72-86208. 96p. (Orig.). 1972. pap. 2.95 (ISBN 0-8307-0197-4, 5007305). Regal.

Promises to the Fathers: Studies on the Patriarchal Narratives. Claus Westermann. LC 79-7395. pap. 51.80 (2027191). Bks Demand UMI.

Promising Education for Community Development. Ed. by Ji-Woong Cheong. 312p. 1987. text ed. 18.00x (ISBN 0-8248-1160-7, Pub. by Seoul U Pr). UH Pr.

Promising, Intending, & Moral Autonomy. Michael H. Robins. (Studies in Philosophy). 160p. 1984. 37.50 (ISBN 0-521-26076-0). Cambridge U Pr.

Promising Practices: A Teacher Resource (Grades K-3) Compiled by Johanna Z. Provenzano. LC 85-61129. 104p. 1985. pap. 6.00 (ISBN 0-89763-108-0). Natl Clearinghse Bilingual Ed.

Promising Practices: Teaching the Disadvantaged Gifted. (Brief Ser.: No. 2). 57p. 4.75 (ISBN 0-318-02116-1). NSLTIGT.

Promising Programs & Practices in Worklife Education: Lessons from the Regional Dialogues. 90p. 1980. 8.00 (ISBN 0-318-15750-0). Natl Inst Work.

Promising Replacements for Conventional Aggregates for Highway Use. (National Cooperative Highway Research Program Report). 53p. 1972. 3.60 (ISBN 0-317-36100-7). Transport Res Bd.

Promissory Note. American Bankers Association Staff. (Loan & Discount Ser.: Book 1). 98p. 1979. 12.50 (ISBN 0-317-32405-5, 167000); members 10.00 (ISBN 0-317-32406-3). Am Bankers.

Promontorium Somnii: Edition Critique. Victor Hugo. 1961. 12.50 (ISBN 0-686-54036-0). French & Eur.

Promotable Woman: Becoming a Successful Manager. rev. ed. Norma Carr-Ruffino. 522p. 1985. pap. text ed. write for info. (ISBN 0-534-05052-2). Wadsworth Pub.

Promoted to Glory: The Apotheosis of George Washington. Patricia A. Anderson. (Illus.). 68p. (Orig.). 1980. pap. 8.75 (ISBN 0-87391-017-6). Smith Coll Mus Art.

Promoter: His Life & Times. P. M. O'Brien. (Illus.). 118p. (YA) (gr. 10-12). 1988. pap. 5.65 (ISBN 0-9620540-0-3). P M O'Brien.

Promoters & Agitators in the Age of Gladstone & Disraeli: A Bibliographical Dictonary of the Leaders of British Pressure Groups Founded Between 1865 & 1886. Howard L. Malchow. LC 82-49263. 300p. 1983. lib. bdg. 65.00 (ISBN 0-8240-9130-2). Garland Pub.

Promoter's Gold. Ed. by Robert H. Morrison. 370p. 1981. 19.95 (ISBN 0-936062-04-5). Morrison Peterson Pub.

Promoters: Structure & Function. Raymond L. Rodriguez. Ed. by Michael J. Chamberlin. LC 81-22740. 540p. 1982. 62.95 (ISBN 0-275-90885-2, C0885). Praeger.

Promoteurs Immobiliers: Contribution a L'analyse de la Production Capitaliste du Logement en France. Christian Topalov. (Recherche Urbaine: No. 4). (Illus.). 1974. pap. 16.40x (ISBN 90-2797-283-4). Mouton.

Promoting Adolescent Health: A Dialog in Research & Practice. Thomas J. Coates. 444p. 1982. 56.50 (ISBN 0-12-177380-9). Acad Pr.

Promoting & Selling Your Art. Carole Katchen. 192p. 1978. 19.95 (ISBN 0-8230-4422-X). Watson-Guptill.

Promoting Business Education. 106p. 1983. 8.00 (ISBN 0-318-18610-1). Natl Busn Ed ASSOC.

Promoting Community Health through Innovative Hospital-Based Programs. Mary E. Longe & Anne Wolf. LC 84-16747. 128p. (Orig.). 1984. pap. 30.00 (ISBN 0-939450-59-3, 070125). AHPI.

Promoting Competence in Clients: A New-Old Approach to Social Work Intervention. Ed. by Anthony N. Maluccio. LC 80-1056. (Illus.). 1981. 24.95 (ISBN 0-02-919830-5). Free Pr.

Promoting Competence in Clients: A New-Old Approach to Social Work Practice. Ed. by Anthony N. Maluccio. 370p. 1986. pap. 13.95 (ISBN 0-02-919860-7). Free Pr.

Promoting Competition in Regulated Markets. Ed. by Almarin Phillips. LC 74-277. (Studies in the Regulation of Economic Activity Ser.). pap. 102.80 (2027741). Bks Demand UMI.

Promoting Continuing Education Programs. Gayle A. Hendrickson. 61p. 1980. 14.50 (ISBN 0-89964-169-5). Coun Adv & Supp Ed.

Promoting Democracy: Opportunities & Issues. Ed. by Ralph M. Goldman & William A. Douglas. LC 87-21482. 304p. 1988. lib. bdg. 39.95 (ISBN 0-275-92814-4, C2814). Praeger.

Promoting Economic Self-Sufficiency Among Youth: Findings of a Survey of OHDS Discretionary Funded Projects. Roy Leavitt et al. 54p. 1985. 10.00 (ISBN 0-86671-077-9). Comm Coun Great NY.

Promoting Effective Discipline in School & Classroom: A Practitioner's Perspective. Donald Grossnickle & Frank Sesko. 80p. (Orig.). 1985. pap. text ed. 7.00 (ISBN 0-88210-170-6). Natl Assn Principals.

Promoting Effective Student Motivation in School & Classroom: A Practitioner's Perspective. Donald Grossnickle & William Thiel. 80p. (Orig.). 1987. pap. 6.00 (ISBN 0-88210-200-1). Natl Assn Principals.

Promoting Effectively for Downtown Business: Dynamic New Case Studies. Ed. by Laurence A. Alexander. LC 83-71250. (Illus.). 64p. (Orig.). 1983. pap. 27.50 (ISBN 0-915910-20-9). Downtown Res.

Promoting Employee Health: A Guide for Worksite Wellness. Rebecca Anderson. 1986. 20.00 (ISBN 0-939874-74-1). ASSE.

Promoting Energy Conservation: An Analysis of Psychological Research. Richard D. Katzev & Theodore R. Johnson. (Special Studies in National Resources & Energy Management). 150p. 1987. pap. 27.50 (ISBN 0-8133-7337-9). Westview.

Promoting Equity, Excellence & Efficiency in Higher Education: Implications for Policy, Planning & Management. 88p. (Orig.). 1987. pap. text ed. 12.50 (UB231, UB). UNIPUB.

Promoting Fund Raising. Roy Evanson. (Clipping Art Ser.). (Illus.). 1975. 3.95 (ISBN 0-916068-01-3). Groupwork Today.

Promoting Hazardous Waste Reduction: Six Steps States Can Take. Warren Muir & Joanna Underwood. 24p. 1987. pap. 3.50 (ISBN 0-918780-45-4). INFORM.

Promoting Health: A Practical Guide to Health Education. Linda Ewles & Ina Simnett. LC 84-29095. 201p. 1985. pap. 12.95 (ISBN 0-471-90514-3). Wiley.

Promoting Health: Consumer Education & National Policy. Ed. by Anne Somers. LC 76-21444. 240p. 1977. 34.50 (ISBN 0-912862-25-4). Aspen Pub.

Promoting Health Education in Schools: Problems & Solutions. Patricia Pine. Ed. by Ben Brodinsky. 96p. (Orig.). 1985. pap. 13.95 (ISBN 0-87652-100-6, 021-00152). Am Assn Sch Admin.

Promoting Health in the Human Environment: Technical Discussions Review. World Health Assembly, 1974, 27th. Ed. by E. E. Meyer & P. Sainsbury. 1975. pap. 4.80 (ISBN 92-4-156046-0). World Health.

Promoting Health Through Public Policy. Nancy Milio. LC 80-25275. 350p. 1981. text ed. 33.00x (ISBN 0-8036-6177-0). Davis Co.

Promoting Health Through Risk Reduction. Marilyn M. Faber & Adina M. Reinhardt. 1982. text ed. write for info. (ISBN 0-02-334850-X). Macmillan.

Promoting Health Through the Schools: A Challenge for the Eighties. Ed. by Donald C. Iverson. LC 80-81022. (A Special Issue of HEQ Ser.: Vol. 8, No. 1). 120p. 1981. pap. 14.95 (ISBN 0-89885-104-1). Human Sci Pr.

Promoting High Standards of Professional Excellence. Francis Horn. 1964. 2.50 (ISBN 0-87060-018-4, OCP 9). Syracuse U Cont Ed.

Promoting High Technology Industry: Initiatives & Policies for State Governments. Ed. by Jurgen Schmandt & Robert Wilson. (Special Studies in Science, Technology, & Public Policy). 283p. 1987. pap. 38.00 (ISBN 0-8133-7427-8). Westview.

Promoting Internatioal Tourism-GH. Katz. Date not set. price not set (ISBN 0-935047-03-4). Americas Group.

Promoting Issues & Ideas: A Guide to Public Relations for Nonprofit Organizations. LC 87-7600. 183p. 1987. 19.95 (ISBN 0-87954-192-X). Foundation Ctr.

Promoting Moral Growth: From Piaget to Kohlberg. Joseph Reimer & Richard Hersh. LC 82-20898. 288p. 1983. pap. text ed. 15.95 (ISBN 0-582-28386-8). Longman.

Promoting Nature in Cities & Towns. Malcolm J. Emery. (Illus.). 320p. 1986. 34.50 (ISBN 0-7099-0966-7, Pub. by Croom Helm Ltd); pap. 17.00 (ISBN 0-7099-0970-5, Pub. by Croom Helm Ltd). Routledge Chapman & Hall.

Promoting Parent Response. 1978. 2.00 (ISBN 0-939418-32-0). Ferguson-Florissant.

Promoting Population Stabilization: Incentives for Small Families. Judith Jacobsen. (Worldwatch Papers Ser.). 1983. pap. text ed. 4.00 (ISBN 0-916468-53-4). Worldwatch Inst.

Promoting Portraits. Paul Castle. 64p. (Orig.). 1988. pap. 15.00 (ISBN 0-317-69898-2). Studio Pr Twain Harte.

Promoting Poverty: The Shift of Resources away from Low-Income New York City School Districts. Susan Breslin & Eleanor Stier. 110p. 1987. pap. text ed. 8.50 (ISBN 0-88156-062-6). Comm Serv Soc NY.

Promoting Pre-School Curriculum & Teaching. Henry E. Hankerson. LC 87-50867. 350p. 1987. text ed. 38.95x (ISBN 1-55605-017-8); pap. text ed. 28.95x (ISBN 1-55605-016-X). Wyndham Hall.

Promoting Productive Thinking. Thelma M. Epley. 1988. 17.75 (ISBN 0-318-23169-7). NSLTIGT.

Promoting Productivity in the Public Sector: Problems, Strategies & Prospects. Ed. by Rita M. Kelly. (Policy Studies Organization). 256p. 1987. 35.00 (ISBN 0-312-00746-9). St Martin.

Promoting Prosperity: Two Eighteenth Century Tracts. LC 75-38470. (Evolution of Capitalism Ser.). 236p. 1972. Repr. of 1972 ed. 21.00 (ISBN 0-405-04133-0). Ayer Co Pubs.

Promoting Psychological Comfort. 3rd ed. Gloria M. Francis & Barbara A. Munjas. (Foundations of Nursing Ser.). 120p. 1979. pap. text ed. write for info. (ISBN 0-697-05544-2). Wm C Brown.

Promoting Racial Harmony. Michael Banton. 146p. 1985. 32.50 (ISBN 0-521-30082-7). Cambridge U Pr.

Promoting Reading Comprehension. Ed. by James Flood. 320p. 1984. 18.00 (ISBN 0-87207-737-3). Intl Reading.

Promoting Reflective Teaching. Gunnar Handal & Per Lauvas. 172p. 1988. 65.00x (ISBN 0-335-15547-2, Open Univ Pr); pap. 26.00x (ISBN 0-335-15546-4, Open Univ Pr). Taylor & Francis.

Promoting Rock Concerts: A Practical Guide. Howard Stein & Ronald Zalkind. LC 79-63032. 1979. 12.95 (ISBN 0-02-872490-9); pap. 6.95 (ISBN 0-02-872470-4). Schirmer Bks.

Promoting Sales: A Systematic Approach to Benefit Selling. Owen Dibbs & Patricia Periera. ix, 248p. (An ILO Programmed Book). 1976. pap. 8.55 (ISBN 92-2-101393-6, ILO30, ILO). UNIPUB.

Promoting Sales: A Systematic Approach to Benefit Selling; an ILO Programmed Book. Owen Dibbs & Patricia Pereira. 1976. 10.50 (ISBN 92-2-101393-6). Intl Labour Office.

Promoting School Art: A Practical Approach. Phillip Dunn. 1987. 12.00 (ISBN 0-317-64398-3). Natl Art Ed.

Promoting School Music: A Practical Guide. 48p. 1984. pap. 5.00 (ISBN 0-317-38597-6, 1038). Music Ed Natl.

Promoting Science Among Elementary School Principals. Kenneth R. Mechling & Donna L. Oliver. 1983. pap. 15.25 (ISBN 0-317-65981-2). Natl Sci Tchrs.

Promoting Sexual Responsibility & Preventing Sexual Problems. Ed. by George W. Albee et al. LC 82-40474. (Primary Prevention of Psychopathology Ser.: No. 7). (Illus.). 462p. 1983. 45.00x (ISBN 0-87451-248-4). U Pr of New Eng.

Promoting Small Power Production: Implementing Section 210 of PURPA, Center for Renewable Resources, Solar Lobby & Others. 49p. 1981. 3.00 (ISBN 0-937446-04-1, 200). Fund Renew Energy.

Promoting Social & Moral Development in Young Children: Creative Approaches for the Classroom. Carolyn P. Edwards. (Early Childhood Education Ser.). 192p. 1986. text ed. 25.95x (ISBN 0-8077-2831-4); pap. text ed. 13.95x (ISBN 0-8077-2820-9). Tchrs Coll.

Promoting Student Development Through Intentionally Structured Groups: Principles, Techniques, & Applications. Roger B. Winston, Jr. et al. LC 88-42803. 1988. 29.95x (ISBN 1-55542-113-X). Jossey-Bass.

Promoting the Education of the Gifted-Talented: Strategies for Advocacy. Ed. by James J. Gallagher et al. 93p. 15.25 (ISBN 0-318-02194-3). NSLTIGT.

Promoting the Necessity to Read. Jennifer Welch. 1980. write for info. (ISBN 0-89992-504-9); pap. 2.86 (ISBN 0-89992-505-7). Coun India Ed.

Promoting the Professional Development of Teachers & Principals. Glen D. Fielding & H. Del Schalock. LC 85-70936. (Illus.). 110p. (Orig.). 1985. pap. 5.95 (ISBN 0-86552-088-7). U of Oreg ERIC.

Promoting the Reading Habit. Richard Bamberger. (Reports & Papers on Mass Communication: No. 72). 52p. 1975. pap. 5.00 (ISBN 92-3-101218-5, U497, UNESCO). UNIPUB.

Promoting the Social Development of Young Children. Charles A. Smith. LC 81-83085. 261p. 1981. pap. 13.95 (ISBN 0-87484-528-9); instr's. guide avail. Mayfield Pub.

Promoting the Well-Being of the Elderly: A Community Diagnosis. Thomas T. Wan et al. LC 82-9209. 227p. 1982. text ed. 34.95 (ISBN 0-917724-38-0, B38); pap. text ed. 14.95 (ISBN 0-917724-39-9, B39). Haworth Pr.

Proofguides for Gregg Typing for Colleges: Lessons 1-75. Alan C. Lloyd et al. (Gregg College Typing: Ser. 4). 48p. 1978. pap. text ed. 6.50 (ISBN 0-07-038260-3). McGraw.

Proofguides for Gregg Typing for Colleges: Lessons 76-150. 4th ed. (Gregg College Typing: Ser. 4). 1978. pap. text ed. 6.50 (ISBN 0-07-038261-1, G). McGraw.

Proofing Is in the Pudding. Julia Alarie & Elizabeth Conlon. Ed. by Ellen Sussman. (Illus.). 44p. (Orig.). (gr. 3-6). 1983. pap. text ed. 5.95 (ISBN 0-933606-22-2, MS620). Monkey Sisters.

Proofreading for Information Processing. Patricia E. Seraydarian. Ed. by Mary C. Konstant & Ann L. Meyer. (Illus.). 210p. 1987. pap. text ed. write for info. (ISBN 0-574-20075-4, 13-3075). SRA.

Proofreading for Word Processing. JoAnn Lee. 47p. 1987. instr's. manual 1.50 (ISBN 0-15-572261-1, HC). HarBraceJ.

Proofreading for Wordprocessing. Jo Ann Lee. 184p. 1988. pap. text ed. 8.00 (ISBN 0-15-572260-3, HC). HarBraceJ.

Proofreading in the Sixteenth, Seventeenth & Eighteenth Centuries. Percy Simpson. LC 74-32124. 1935. lib. bdg. 39.00 (ISBN 0-8414-7535-0). Folcroft.

Proofreading in the Word Processing Age. Jack Friedberg. 128p. 14.95 (ISBN 0-8290-1506-X); pap. 7.95 (ISBN 0-8290-1507-8). J Friedberg.

Proofreading Skills for Business. Visual Education Corporation Staff. LC 85-29608. 194p. 1986. pap. write for info. (ISBN 0-471-82841-6). Wiley.

Proofs & Refutations. E. Lakatos. Ed. by J. Worrall. LC 75-32478. 160p. 1976. 39.50 (ISBN 0-521-21078-X); pap. 11.95 (ISBN 0-521-29038-4). Cambridge U Pr.

Proofs for Eternity, Creation, & the Existence of God in Medieval Islamic & Jewish Philosophy. Herbert Davidson. (Studies in Northeast Culture & Society: Vol. 7). 500p. 1985. write for info. (ISBN 0-89003-180-0); pap. 62.00x (ISBN 0-89003-181-9). Undena Pubns.

Proofs for Eternity, Creation, & the Existence of God in Medieval Islamic & Jewish Philosophy. Herbert Davidson. 448p. 1987. 39.95 (ISBN 0-19-504953-5). Oxford U Pr.

Proofs of a Conspiracy. John Robison. 1979. lib. bdg. 59.95 (ISBN 0-8490-2987-2). Gordon Pr.

Proofs of a Conspiracy. John Robison. 1967. pap. 4.95 (ISBN 0-88279-121-4). Western Islands.

Proofs of Christianity. W. Charles Harris. LC 77-77215. (Radiant Life Ser.). 128p. 1977. pap. 2.50 (ISBN 0-88243-911-1, 02-0911); teacher's guide 3.95 (ISBN 0-88243-181-1, 32-0181). Gospel Pub.

Proofs of the Corruption of Gen. James Wilkinson & of His Connexion with Aaron Burr, with a Full Refutation of His Slanderous Allegations in Relation to the Character of the Principal Witness Against Him. Daniel Clark. LC 70-146383. (First American Frontier Ser.). 1971. Repr. of 1809 ed. 23.50 (ISBN 0-405-02834-2). Ayer Co Pubs.

Proofs of the Corruption of General James Wilkinson, & of His Connexion with Aaron Burr. facs. ed. Daniel Clark. LC 70-117868. (Select Bibliographies Reprint Ser). 1809. 24.50 (ISBN 0-8369-5321-5). Ayer Co Pubs.

ProofWriter, Bk. 1. Michelle Waters & Marybeth Mehlmann. Ed. by Joan Ostacher. (Illus.). 120p. (Orig.). 1987. 17.95 (ISBN 0-913935-40-9). ERA-CCR.

ProofWriter, Bk. 2. Michelle Waters & Marybeth A. Mehlmann. Ed. by Joan Ostacher. (Illus.). 120p. 1987. 17.95 (ISBN 0-913935-41-7). ERA-CCR.

Proomien der Alten Judischen Homilie: Beitrag zur Geschichte der Judischen Schriftauslegung und Homiletik. Wilhelm Bacher. 130p. (Ger.). Repr. of 1913 ed. text ed. 41.40x (ISBN 0-576-80159-3, Pub. by Gregg Intl Pubs England). Gregg Intl.

Prop. Relations & Applications. M. Yalpani. (Progress in Biotechnology Ser.: Vol. 3). 142.00 (ISBN 0-444-42906-9). Elsevier.

Propaganda. Michael Hulse. 72p. 1985. 14.95 (ISBN 0-436-20966-7, Pub. by Secker & Warburg UK). David & Charles.

Propaganda Analysis, 5 vols. Institute for Propaganda Analysis. 1977. Set. lib. bdg. 750.00 (ISBN 0-8490-2486-2). Gordon Pr.

Propaganda & Aesthetics: The Literary Politics of Afro-American Magazines in the Twentieth Century. Abby A. Johnson & Ronald M. Johnson. LC 78-19692. 1979. 17.50x (ISBN 0-87023-269-X). U of Mass Pr.

Propaganda & Aryanization, 1938-1944. John Mendelsohn. LC 81-80312. (Holocaust Ser.). 255p. 1982. lib. bdg. 61.00 (ISBN 0-8240-4878-4). Garland Pub.

Propaganda & Communication in World History, Vol. 3. Ed. by Harold D. Lasswell et al. LC 79-21108. pap. 144.00 (2029588). Bks Demand UMI.

Propaganda & Communication in World History: The Symbolic Instrument in Early Times, Vol. 1. Ed. by Harold Lasswell et al. LC 78-23964. (Propaganda & Communication in World History Ser.). 1979. text ed. 27.50x (ISBN 0-8248-0496-1, Eastwest Ctr). UH Pr.

Propaganda & Dictatorship: A Collection of Papers. Ed. by Harwood L. Childs. LC 72-4659. (International Propaganda & Communications Ser.). 153p. 1972. Repr. of 1936 ed. 11.00 (ISBN 0-405-04742-8). Ayer Co Pubs.

Propaganda & Education. William W. Biddle. LC 73-176562. (Columbia University. Teachers College. Contributions to Education: No. 531). Repr. of 1932 ed. 22.50 (ISBN 0-404-55531-4). AMS Pr.

Propaganda & Empire: The Manipulation of British Public Opinion, 1880-1960. John M. MacKenzie. LC 83-25325. (Illus.). 320p. 1984. (Pub. by Manchester Univ Pr); pap. 15.00 (ISBN 0-7190-1869-2). St Martin.

Propaganda & Myth in Time of War. Charles H. Hamlin. Bd. with War Myth in U. S. History; Educators Present Arms: The Use of the Schools & Colleges As Agents of War Propaganda, 1914-1918. LC 77-147725. (Library of War & Peace; the Character & Causes of War). lib. bdg. 46.00 (ISBN 0-8240-0261-X). Garland Pub.

Propaganda & National Power: The Organization of Public Opinion for National Politics. Eugen Hadamovsky. Tr. by Alice Mavrogordato & Ilse De Witt. LC 72-4667. (International Propaganda & Communications Ser.). 204p. 1972. Repr. of 1954 ed. 13.00 (ISBN 0-405-04748-7). Ayer Co Pubs.

Propaganda & Nationalism in Wartime Russia: The Jewish Anti-Fascist Committee in the U. S. S. R., 1941-1948. Shimon Redlich. (East European Monographs: No. 108). 236p. 1982. 24.00x (ISBN 0-88033-001-5). East Eur Quarterly.

Propaganda & Persuasion. Garth Jowett & Victoria O'Donnell. LC 85-30441. (People & Communication Ser.: Vol. 18). 160p. 1986. 28.00 (ISBN 0-8039-2398-8); pap. 14.00 (ISBN 0-8039-2399-6). Sage.

Propaganda & Promotional Activities: An Annotated Bibliography. Ed. by Harold D. Lasswell et al. LC 75-77979. pap. 118.50 (ISBN 0-317-10305-9, 2020100). Bks Demand UMI.

Propaganda & the American Revolution, 1763-1789. Philip G. Davidson. LC 41-3098. xvi, 460p. 1941. 35.00x (ISBN 0-8078-0343-X). U of NC Pr.

Propaganda & the Cold War: A Princeton University Symposium. Ed. by John B. Whitton. LC 83-22551. iv, 119p. 1984. Repr. of 1963 ed. lib. bdg. 35.00x (ISBN 0-313-24304-2, WHPR). Greenwood.

Propaganda & the German Cinema, 1933-1945. David Welch. (Illus.). 1983. pap. 19.95x (ISBN 0-19-821974-1). Oxford U Pr.

Propaganda & the News: Or, What Makes You Think So. William H. Irwin. Repr. of 1936 ed. lib. bdg. 35.00x (ISBN 0-8371-2818-8, IRPN). Greenwood.

Propaganda & the News: Or, What Makes You Think So. William H. Irwin. (American Studies). 1969. Repr. of 1936 ed. 24.00 (ISBN 0-384-25970-7). Johnson Repr.

Propaganda by Short Wave. Ed. by Harwood L. Childs & John B. Whitton. Bd. with War on the Short Waves. Charles A. Rigby. Repr. of 1944 ed. LC 72-4660. (International Propaganda & Communications Ser.). (Illus.). 365p. 1972. Repr. of 1942 ed. 24.00 (ISBN 0-405-04743-6). Ayer Co Pubs.

Propaganda from China & Japan: A Case Study in Propaganda Analysis. Bruno Lasker & Agnes Roman. LC 75-30126. (Institute of Pacific Relations). Repr. of 1938 ed. 22.00 (ISBN 0-404-59537-5). AMS Pr.

Propaganda Game. Lorne Greene & Robert Allen. 12.00 (ISBN 0-911624-39-2). Wffn Proof.

Propaganda Gap. Walter Joyce. LC 74-20076. 144p. 1975. Repr. of 1963 ed. lib. bdg. 35.00x (ISBN 0-8371-7843-6, JOPG). Greenwood.

Propaganda in an Open Society: The Roosevelt Administration & the Media, 1933-1941. Richard W. Steele. LC 84-27931. (Contributions in American History Ser.: No. 111). x, 231p. 1985. lib. bdg. 36.95 (ISBN 0-313-24830-3, SNS/). Greenwood.

Propaganda in the English Reformation: Heroic & Villainous Images of King John. Carole Levin. LC 87-31949. (Studies in British History: Vol. 11). 306p. 1988. lib. bdg. 59.95x (ISBN 0-88946-463-4). E Mellen.

Propaganda in the Next War. Sidney Rogerson. LC 72-4678. (International Propaganda & Communications Ser.). 188p. 1972. Repr. of 1938 ed. 14.00 (ISBN 0-405-04762-2). Ayer Co Pubs.

Propaganda in War & Crisis. Ed. by Daniel Lerner. LC 72-4669. (International Propaganda & Communications Ser.). 516p. 1972. Repr. of 1951 ed. 27.50 (ISBN 0-405-04754-1). Ayer Co Pubs.

Propaganda Novel. M. Waldman. 59.95 (ISBN 0-8490-0900-6). Gordon Pr.

Propaganda, Polls & Public Opinion: Are the People Manipulated? Malcolm G. Mitchell. (gr. 10-12). pap. 13.24 (ISBN 0-13-731109-5). P-H.

Propaganda: The Art of Persuasion, World War II, 2 Vols. Anthony Rhodes. Ed. by Victor Margolin. LC 75-17545. (Illus.). 320p. 1984. Repr. of 1976 ed. Set. 60.00 (ISBN 0-87754-067-5). Chelsea Hse.

Propaganda: The Formation of Men's Attitudes. Jacques Ellul. 352p. 1973. pap. 5.95 (ISBN 0-394-71874-7, Vin). Random.

Propaganda Towards Disarmament in the War of Words. John B. Whitton & Arthur Larson. LC 63-19593. 305p. 1964. 15.00 (ISBN 0-379-00110-1). Oceana.

Propaganda y Atague. Manuel Gonzalez Prada. 232p. 0.65 (ISBN 0-318-14302-X). Hispanic Inst.

Propagandist's Lament. A. Grosshans. 32p. 1980. pap. 5.00 (ISBN 0-941104-01-X). Real Comet.

Propagate Your Own Plants. Wilma R. James. LC 78-18248. (Illus.). 149p. 1978. 12.95 (ISBN 0-87961-073-5); pap. 6.95 (ISBN 0-87961-072-7). Naturegraph.

Propagation. 3.95 (ISBN 0-686-21126-X). Bklyn Botanic.

Propagation & Instabilities in Plasmas. 7th ed. Lockheed Symposium on Magnetohydrodynamics, Palo Alto, 1962. LC 63-19236. pap. 38.80 (ISBN 0-317-12970-8, 2000318). Bks Demand UMI.

Propagation de l'Innovation dans le Domaine du Caoutchouc en France see Cahiers de l'Institut de Science Economique Appliquee.

Propagation of Alpines. Lawrence D. Hills. (Illus.). 1976. Repr. of 1959 ed. write for info (ISBN 0-913728-11-X). Theophrastus.

Propagation of Electromagnetic Waves in Plasma. V. L. Ginzburg. (Russian Monographs & Texts on the Physical Science Ser.). 846p. 1962. 180.00 (ISBN 0-677-20080-3). Gordon & Breach.

Propagation of Electromagnetic Waves Through, along & over a Three-Dimensional Conduction Half Space: EM Waves over a Conducting Earth. D. S. Gilliam & J. R. Schulenberger. (Methoden und Verfahren der Mathematischen Physik Ser.: Vol. 30). 209p. 1986. pap. 24.00 (ISBN 3-8204-8905-3). P Lang Pubs.

Propagation of Horticultural Plants. 2nd ed. Guy W. Adriance & Fred R. Brison. LC 79-9753. 308p. 1979. Repr. of 1955 ed. lib. bdg. 23.50 (ISBN 0-88275-965-5). Krieger.

Propagation of Mammalian Cells in Culture, Vol. I. J. D. Roth et al. 1976. text ed. 39.50x (ISBN 0-8422-7290-9). Irvington.

Propagation of Radio Waves: The Theory of Radio Waves of Low Power in the Ionosphere & Magnetosphere. K. G. Budden. (Illus.). 660p. 1985. 100.00 (ISBN 0-521-25461-2). Cambridge U Pr.

Propagation of Radio Waves: The Theory of Radio Waves of Low Power in the Ionosphere & Magnetosphere. K. G. Budden. (Illus.). 669p. Date not set. pap. 37.50 (ISBN 0-521-36952-5). Cambridge U Pr.

Propagation of Science Into Wider Culture. Philip C. Ritterbush. 140p. 1980. pap. 24.00 (ISBN 0-942776-02-X, Pub by I.C.P.). Pub Ctr Cult Res.

Propagation of Shock Waves in Solids: Presented at the Applied Mechanics Conference, Salt Lake City, Utah, June 14-17, 1976. Applied Mechanics Conference Staff. LC 76-12662. (American Soceity of Mechanical Engineers, Applied Mechanics Division: Vol. 17). pap. 30.50 (ISBN 0-317-26673-X, 2024185). Bks Demand UMI.

Propagation of Sincularities for Fuchsian Operators. A. Bove et al. (Lecture Notes in Mathematics: Vol. 984). 161p. 1983. pap. 13.00 (ISBN 0-387-12285-0). Springer-Verlag.

Propagation of Transient Elastic Waves in Stratified Anisotropic Media. J. H. Van der Hijden. (Applied Mathematics & Mechanics Ser.: No. 32). 288p. 1987. 78.00 (ISBN 0-444-70294-6, North Holland). Elsevier.

Propagation of Tropical & Subtropical Horticultural Crops. T. K. Bose & S. K. Mitra. 580p. 1986. 82.50x (ISBN 81-85109-40-0, Pub. by Naya Prokash India). South Asia Bks.

Propagation of Visible & Infrared Radiation in the Atmosphere. V. E. Zuev. 420p. 1974. text ed. 83.00 (ISBN 0-7065-1312-6, Pub. by Keter Pub Jerusalem). Coronet Bks.

Propagators for Many-Particle Systems. R. L. Mills. 140p. 1969. 60.00 (ISBN 0-677-02040-6). Gordon & Breach.

Propago Sacri Ordinis Cartusienses per Germaniam Pars 2, 2 Vols. Georgius Schwengel. Ed. by James Hogg. (Analecta Cartusiana Ser.: No. 90/4). 378p. 1982. pap. 50.00 (ISBN 3-7052-0151-4, Pub. by Salzburg Studies). Longwood Pub Group.

Propago Sacri Ordinis Cartusiensis-Apparatus ad Annales Carytusiae Paradisi B.M.V, 2 Vols. (Analecta Cartusiana Ser.: No. 90/10). 454p. 1982. pap. 50.00 (ISBN 3-7052-0157-3, Pub. by Salzburg Studies). Longwood Pub Group.

Propago Sacri Ordinis Cartusiensis-Appartus Annales Sacri Ordinis Cartusiensis, 3 Vols. Georgius Schwengel. Ed. by James Hogg. (Analecta Cartusiana Ser.: No. 90/9). 534p. (Orig.). 1983. pap. 85.00 (ISBN 3-7052-0156-5, Pub. by Salzburg Studies). Longwood Pub Group.

Propago Sacri Ordinis Cartusiensis: Appendix ad Tom I, 2 Vols. Georgius Schwengel. Ed. by James Hogg. (Analecta Cartusiana Ser.: No. 90/5). 440p. (Orig.). 1983. pap. 50.00 (ISBN 3-7052-0152-2, Pub. by Salzburg Studies). Longwood Pub Group.

Propago Sacri Ordinis Cartusiensis: Appendix ad Tom II, 2 Vols. Georgius Schwengel. Ed. by James Hogg. (Analecta Cartusiana: No. 90/6). 397p. (Orig.). 1983. pap. 50.00 (ISBN 0-317-42583-8, Pub. by Salzburg Studies). Longwood Pub Group.

Propago Sacri Ordinis Cartusiensis: Appendix ad Tom III, 2 vols. Georgius Schwengel. Ed. by James Hogg. (Analecta Cartusiana Ser.: No. 90/7). 357p. (Orig.). 1983. pap. 50.00 (ISBN 3-7052-0154-9, Pub. by Salzburg Studies). Longwood Pub Group.

Propago Sacri Ordinis Cartusiensis: Appendix ad Tom IV, 2 Vols. Georgius Schwengel. Ed. by James Hogg. (Analecta Cartusiana: No. 90/8). 412p. (Orig.). 1983. pap. 50.00 (ISBN 3-7052-0155-7, Pub. by Salzburg Studies). Longwood Pub Group.

Propago Sacri Ordinis Cartusiensis de Provinciis Burgundiae, Franciae, Picardiae, Teutoniae et Angliae. Georgius Schwengel. Ed. by James Hogg. (Analecta Cartusiana Ser.: No. 90/2). 276p. (Orig.). 1981. pap. 25.00 (ISBN 3-7052-0149-2, Pub. by Salzburg Studies). Longwood Pub Group.

Propago Sacri Ordinis Cartusiensis-Diplomata Poloniae et Prussiae, 2 Vols. Georgius Schwengel. Ed. by James Hogg. (Analecta Cartusiana Ser.: No. 90/11). 256p. (Orig.). 1982. pap. 50.00 (ISBN 3-7052-0158-1, Pub. by Salzburg Studies). Longwood Pub Group.

Propago Sacri Ordinis Cartusiensis per Franciam, 2 Vols. Georgius Schwengel. Ed. by James Hogg. (Analecta Cartusiana Ser.: No. 90/1). 300p. (Orig.). 1984. pap. 50.00 (ISBN 3-7052-0148-4, Pub. by Salzburg Studies). Longwood Pub Group.

Propago Sacri Ordinis Cartusiensis per Germaniam. Georgius Schwengel. Ed. by James Hogg. (Analecta Cartusiana Ser.: No. 90/3). 480p. (Orig.). 1981. pap. 25.00 (ISBN 3-7052-0150-6, Pub. by Salzburg Studies). Longwood Pub Group.

Propane, Butane & 2-Methylpropane. Ed. by W. Hayduk. (IUPAC Solubility Data Ser.: Vol. 24). 447p. 1986. 110.00 (ISBN 0-08-029202-X, Pub. by PPL). Pergamon.

Propane Conversion of Cars, Trucks & RVs. Larry W. Carley. (Illus.). 224p. 1982. 14.95 (ISBN 0-8306-3103-8); pap. 9.95 (ISBN 0-8306-2103-2, 2103). TAB Bks.

Propedeutics of Children's Diseases. V. Molchanov et al. Tr. by MIR Publishers. (Illus.). 392p. 1975. text ed. 20.00x (ISBN 0-8464-0768-X). Beekman Pubs.

Propellanes: Structure & Reactions. David Ginsburg. (Monographs in Modern Chemistry: Vol. 7). 272p. 1975. 88.00 (ISBN 3-527-25602-4). VCH Pubs.

Propellant Profiles. Ed. by Dave Wolfe. (Illus.). 158p. 1982. pap. text ed. 12.95 (ISBN 0-935632-10-7). Wolfe Pub Co.

Propellants Manufacture, Hazards, & Testing: A Symposium. Carl Boyars. LC 75-87208. (Advances in Chemistry Ser.: No. 88). pap. 105.30 (2052251). Bks Demand UMI.

Proper Attitudes Toward Leadership. Robyn Gool. 144p. 1987. pap. 4.50 (ISBN 0-88144-073-6). Christian Pub.

Proper Balance. Joseph M. Champlin. LC 81-68000. 144p. (Orig.). 1981. pap. 3.95 (ISBN 0-87793-233-6). Ave Maria.

Proper Balance Movement: A Diary of Lameness. Tony Gonzales. LC 86-60039. (Illus.). x, 215p. 1986. text ed. 30.00 (ISBN 0-9612862-2-9). R E F Typesetting Pub.

Proper BASIC. Brian C. Walsh. 384p. 1983. 45.95 (ISBN 0-471-90081-8, Pub. by Wiley-Interscience). Wiley.

Proper Blessing. A. C. Jacobs. 1976. pap. 2.50 (ISBN 0-685-83013-6, Pub. by Menard Pr). Small Pr Dist.

Proper Bostonian or Sex & Birth Control. H. R. Storer. Incl. Why Not? a Book for Every Woman, Boston, 1868; Is It I? a Book for Every Man, Boston, 1867. LC 73-20653. (Sex, Marriage & Society Ser.). 258p. 1974. Repr. 24.50x (ISBN 0-405-05813-6). Ayer Co Pubs.

Proper Bostonians. Cleveland Amory. 384p. 1984. pap. 9.95 (ISBN 0-940160-25-0). Parnassus Imprints.

Proper Definition of AFDC Incapacity in Kentucky. Carl Melcher. 15p. 1985. 2.00 (40,701). NCLS Inc.

Proper Degree of Terror: The Expulsion of the Xhosa from the Suurveld in 1812. Ben Maclennan. LC 82-95933. 224p. 1985. pap. text ed. 17.95x (ISBN 0-86975-235-9, Pub. by Ravan Pr). Ohio U Pr.

Proper Distinction Between Law & Gospel. Carl F. Walther. Tr. by W. H. Dau. 1929. 16.95 (ISBN 0-570-03248-2, 15-1601). Concordia.

Proper Distribution of Expense Burden. A. Hamilton Church. Ed. by Alfred D. Chandler. LC 79-7538. (History of Management Thought & Practice Ser.). 1980. Repr. of 1908 ed. lib. bdg. 12.00x (ISBN 0-405-12323-X). Ayer Co Pubs.

Proper Doctoring. D. Mendel. 1984. pap. 9.50 (ISBN 0-387-13686-X). Springer-Verlag.

Proper Food Combining Cookbook. rev. ed. Lee DuBelle. 220p. 1987. pap. 15.00 (ISBN 0-9618703-0-3). Du-Two Pub.

Proper Food Combining Cookbook. rev. ed. Lee DuBelle. 220p. 1988. pap. 15.00 (ISBN 0-9618703-4-6). Du-Two Pub.

Proper Food Combining Works - Living Testimony. rev. ed. Lee Dubelle. 115p. 1987. pap. 9.00 (ISBN 0-9618703-1-1). Du Two Pub.

Proper Food Combining Works - Living Testimony. Lee DuBelle. 115p. (Span.). 1988. pap. 9.00 (ISBN 0-9618703-3-8). Du Two Pub.

Proper Grammarian: Proper Etiquette for the Eighties. Christine A. Robinson & Richard A. Alden. 188p. 1988. pap. text ed. 17.50 (ISBN 0-943437-38-5). CAT Pub.

Proper Lady & the Woman Writer: Ideology As Style in the Writings of Mary Wollstonecraft, Mary Shelley, & Jane Austen. Mary Poovey. LC 83-3664. 287p. 1984. lib. bdg. 20.00X (ISBN 0-226-67527-0). U of Chicago Pr.

Proper Lady & the Woman Writer: Ideology As Style in the Works of Mary Wollstonecraft, Mary Shelley, & Jane Austen. Mary Poovey. LC 84-3664. xxii, 290p. 1985. pap. 9.95x (ISBN 0-226-67528-9). U of Chicago Pr.

Proper Manners & Health Habits: Grade 2 Health. 2.75 (ISBN 0-686-32328-9); tchr's manual 2.50 (ISBN 0-686-32329-7). Rod & Staff.

Proper Marriage: A Complete Novel from Doris Lessing's Masterwork, Children of Violence. Doris Lessing. 1970. pap. 7.95 (ISBN 0-452-25789-1, Z5093, Plume). NAL.

Proper Name Speller. Jean Emerich. Ed. by Diana Gregory. 320p. (Orig.). 1989. pap. price not set (ISBN 0-944494-11-0). Shining Knight Pr.

Proper Proposal. Dawn Lindsey. (Regency Romances Ser.). 224p. 1988. pap. 2.75 (ISBN 0-451-15286-7, Sig). NAL.

Proper Role of Government. Ezra T. Benson. 32p. 1975. pap. 2.50 (ISBN 0-89036-122-3). Hawkes Pub Inc.

Proper Role of the Lawyer in Residential Real Estate Transactions. 27p. 1978. pap. 1.00 (ISBN 0-317-31139-5). Amer Bar Assn.

Proper Study. Royal Institute of Philosophy. 1971. 25.00 (ISBN 0-312-65135-X). St Martin.

Proper Tea: An English Collection of Recipes. Joanna Isles. (Illus.). 95p. 1987. 13.95 (ISBN 0-312-65142-2). St Martin.

Proper Use of Standardized Tests. James W. Deuink. (Illus.). 64p. (Orig.). 1986. pap. 4.00 (ISBN 0-89084-355-4). Bob Jones Univ Pr.

Proper Woman. Lillian Beckwith. 192p. 1987. 13.95 (ISBN 0-312-00672-1, Pub. by Thomas Dunne Bks). St Martin.

Proper Words in Proper Places. rev. ed. Irving T. Richards & Paul I. Richards. 1965. pap. 6.95 (ISBN 0-8158-0175-0). Chris Mass.

Propertiana. D. R. Shackleton-Bailey. 339p. 1956. Repr. lib. bdg. 47.50x (Pub. by A M Hakkert). Coronet Bks.

Properties & Applications of Glass. H. Rawson. (Glass Science & Technology Ser.: Vol. 3). 318p. 1980. 84.25 (ISBN 0-444-41922-5). Elsevier.

Properties & Applications of Glass. H. Rawson. (Glass Science & Technology Ser.: Vol. 3). 1984. 29.00 (ISBN 0-444-42321-4, I-144-84). Elsevier.

Properties & Interactions of Interplanetary Dust. Ed. by R. H. Giese & P. Lamy. 1985. lib. bdg. 64.00 (ISBN 90-277-2115-7, Pub. by Reidel Holland). Kluwer Academic.

Properties & Management of Forest Soils. 2nd ed. William L. Pritchett & Richard F. Fisher. LC 86-22421. 494p. 1987. write for info. (ISBN 0-471-89572-5). Wiley.

Properties & Management of Soils in the Tropics. Pedro A. Sanchez. LC 76-22761. 618p. 1976. 57.00x (ISBN 0-471-75200-2, Pub. by Wiley-Interscience). Wiley.

Properties & Microstructure see Treatise on Materials Science.

Properties & Performance of Materials in the Coal Gasification Environment: Proceedings of a Conference Held 8-10 September 1980, Pittsburgh, PA - Sponsored by the Gas Research Institute... et al. American Society for Metals Staff. Ed. by V. L. Hill & Herbert L. Black. LC 81-67327. (Materials-Metalworking Technology Ser.). pap. 160.00 (2027041). Bks Demand UMI.

Properties & Processing of Polymers for Engineers. Donald E. Kline. (Illus.). 240p. 1984. 48.00 (ISBN 0-13-731125-7). P-H.

Properties & Production Spectra of Elementary Particles see Landolt-Boernstein Numerical Data & Functional Relationships in Science & Technology, New Series, Group 1: Nuclear Particle & Physics.

Properties & Reactions of Bonds in Organic Molecules. K. F. Reid. LC 79-365421. pap. 142.50 (ISBN 0-317-09882-9, 2004551). Bks Demand Umi.

Properties & Selection of Tool Materials. American Society for Metals Staff & Victor A. Kortesoja. LC 75-26829. pap. 80.00 (ISBN 0-317-27717-0, 2019483). Bks Demand UMI.

Properties & Uses of Ferrous & Nonferrous Metals. rev. ed. H. C. Kazanas. LC 78-70035. (Illus.). 1979. pap. 4.75x (ISBN 0-911168-39-7); instrs'. guide & answer bk. 1.95x (ISBN 0-911168-40-0). Prakken.

Properties, Evaluation & Control of Engineering Materials. William A. Cordon. 1979. text ed. 52.95 (ISBN 0-07-013123-6). McGraw.

Properties of Amorphous Silicon. Ed. by N. Parkman et al. (EMIS Datareviews Ser.: No. 1). 262p. 1985. casebound 195.00 (DA001). Inst Elect Eng.

Properties of Asphalt Cements. V. P. Puzinauskas. 72p. 10.00 (ISBN 0-318-13396-2, RR-80-2). Asphalt Inst.

Properties of Atomic Defects in Metals: Proceedings of the International Conference on the Properties of Atomic Defects in Metals, Argonne, Illinois. Ed. by N. L. Peterson & R. W. Siegel. 1978. 185.50 (ISBN 0-444-85146-1, North-Holland). Elsevier.

Properties of Austenitic Stainless Steels & Their Weld Metals: Influence of Slight Chemistry Variations - STP 679. Ed. by C. R. Brinkman & H. W. Garvin. 153p. 1979. pap. 13.50x (ISBN 0-8031-0537-1, 04-679000-02). ASTM.

Properties of Biomaterials in the Physiological Environment. Stephen D. Bruck. 160p. 1980. 75.00 (ISBN 0-8493-5685-7). CRC Pr.

Properties of Building Materials. H. J. Eldridge. (Illus.). pap. 30.30 (ISBN 0-317-08291-4, 2019627). Bks Demand UMI.

Properties of Ceramic Raw Materials: In SI Units. 2nd ed. W. Ryan. 1978. text ed. 23.00 (ISBN 0-08-022113-0); pap. text ed. 7.75 (ISBN 0-08-022114-9). Pergamon.

Properties of Chlorine in SI Units. Chlorine Institute Staff. LC 81-67483. (Illus.). 87p. 1986. pap. text ed. 27.00 (ISBN 0-940230-02-X). Chlorine Inst.

Properties of Concrete. 3rd ed. A. M. Nevill. 792p. 1981. pap. 44.95 (ISBN 0-470-20552-0, Co-Pub. with Longman). Wiley.

Properties of Diamond. Ed. by J. E. Field. 1979. 136.50 (ISBN 0-12-255350-0). Acad Pr.

Properties of Double Stars: A Survey of Parallaxes & Orbits. Leendert Binnendijk. LC 58-8011. pap. 67.90 (ISBN 0-317-08370-8, 2055279). Bks Demand UMI.

Properties of Electrodeposits, Their Measurement & Significance. Ed. by Richard Sard et al. LC 74-84702. (Illus.). pap. 109.00 (ISBN 0-317-11085-3, 2051243). Bks Demand UMI.

Properties of Elemental & Compound Semiconductors: Proceedings. Ed. by Harry C. Gatos. LC 60-10585. (Metallurgical Society Conference Ser.: Vol. 5). pap. 88.30 (ISBN 0-317-08021-0, 2000668). Bks Demand UMI.

Properties of Engineering Materials. R. A. Higgins. (Illus.). 559p. (Orig.). Date not set. pap. text ed. 14.95 (ISBN 0-340-17909-0, Pub. by E Arnold UK). Routledge Chapman & Hall.

Properties of Engineering Materials. rev. ed. Raymond A. Higgins. LC 77-22284. 448p. 1980. pap. 18.50 (ISBN 0-89874-250-1). Krieger.

Properties of Estimators for the Gamma Distribution. Bowman. Ed. by Shenton. (STM series). 288p. 1987. 65.00 (ISBN 0-8247-7556-2). Dekker.

Properties of Flexible Pavement Materials - STP 807. Ed. by John J. Emery. LC 82-83521. 178p. 1983. text ed. 25.00 (ISBN 0-8031-0257-7, 04-807000-08). ASTM.

Properties of Gallium Arsenide. Ed. by N. Parkman et al. (EMIS Datareviews Ser.: No. 2). 346p. 1986. casebound 195.00 (ISBN 0-85296-323-8, DA002). Inst Elect Eng.

Properties of Gases & Liquids. 4th ed. Robert C. Reid et al. (Illus.). 741p. 1987. text ed. 49.50 (ISBN 0-07-051799-1). McGraw.

Properties of Groundwater. Georg Matthess. Tr. by John C. Harvey. LC 81-7481. 406p. 1982. 61.95x (ISBN 0-471-08513-8, Pub. by Wiley-Interscience). Wiley.

Properties of Hydrocarbons of High Molecular Weight Synthesized by Research Project 42 of the American Petroleum Institute, the Pennsylvania State University College of Science, University Park, Penn., 1940-1961. American Petroleum Institute, Research Project 42 Staff. LC 72-8620. pap. 20.00 (ISBN 0-317-10723-2, 2004349). Bks Demand UMI.

Properties of Incramute I Castings. Ampco Metal Division Staff. 85p. 1974. 12.75 (ISBN 0-317-34541-9, 209). Intl Copper.

Properties of Inorganic & Organic Fluids. P. E. Liley et al. (Cindas Data Series on Material Properties). 300p. 1988. 80.00 (ISBN 0-89116-802-8, 66-57076). Hemisphere Pub.

Properties of Liquid & Solid Helium. John Wilks. (International Series of Monographs on Physics). 1967. 79.00x (ISBN 0-19-851245-7). Oxford U Pr.

Properties of Liquid & Solid Hydrogen. B. N. Esel'son et al. 265p. 1971. text ed. 28.50x (ISBN 0-7065-1134-4, Pub. by Keter Pub Jerusalem). Coronet Bks.

Properties of Liquid Metals. Ed. by Takeuchi Sakae. 670p. 1973. cancelled (ISBN 0-85066-065-3). Taylor & Francis.

Properties of Liquids & Solutions. J. N. Murrell & E. A. Boucher. LC 81-21921. 288p. 1982. 77.95 (ISBN 0-471-10201-6, Pub. by Wiley-Interscience); pap. text ed. 39.95 (ISBN 0-471-10202-4, Pub. by Wiley-Interscience). Wiley.

Properties of Magnetic Electron Lenses. P. W. Hawkes. (Topics in Current Physics Ser.: Vol. 18). (Illus.). 470p. 1982. 49.00 (ISBN 0-387-10296-5). Springer-Verlag.

Properties of Materials for Liquified Natural Gas Tankage - STP 579. 424p. 1975. 39.75 (ISBN 0-8031-0538-X, 04-579000-30). ASTM.

Properties of Matter. B. H. Flower. 318p. 1971. pap. 26.60 (ISBN 0-471-26498-9). Wiley.

Properties of Nuclei. 2nd ed. G. A. Jones. (Physics Ser.). (Illus.). 208p. 1987. 39.95 (ISBN 0-19-851868-4); pap. 19.95 (ISBN 0-19-851869-2). Oxford U Pr.

Properties of Ordinary Water-Substances in All Its Phases: Water-Vapor, Water, & All the Ices. Noah E. Dorsey. LC 68-19563. (American Chemical Society Monograph Ser.: No. 81). pap. 160.00 (ISBN 0-317-09001-1, 2015237). Bks Demand UMI.

Properties of Organic Materials. Center for Occupational Research & Development Staff. (EUTEC Environmental & Chemical Analysis Curriculum Ser.). (Illus.). 304p. 1985. pap. text ed. 31.00 (ISBN 1-55502-204-9). Ctr Res & Dev.

Properties of Petroleum Fluids. William D. McCain, Jr. LC 73-78008. 325p. 1974. 54.95 (ISBN 0-87814-021-2, P-4025). Pennwell Bks.

Properties of Petroleum Reservoir Fluids. Emil J. Burcik. LC 57-5906. (Illus.). 190p. 1979. Repr. of 1957 ed. text ed. 29.00 (ISBN 0-934634-00-9). Intl Human Res.

Properties of Planar Graphs with Uniform Vertex & Face Structure. Joseph Malkevitch. LC 52-42839. (Memoirs: No. 99). 116p. 1970. pap. 11.00 (ISBN 0-8218-1299-8, MEMO-99). Am Math.

Properties of Polymers. R. Jenkins et al. (Advances in Polymer Sciences: Vol. 36). (Illus.). 150p. 1980. 45.00 (ISBN 0-387-10204-3). Springer-Verlag.

Properties of Polymers: Their Estimation & Correlation with Chemical Structure. 2nd ed. D. W. Van Krevelen. 620p. 1976. 208.00 (ISBN 0-444-41467-3). Elsevier.

Properties of Pure Liquids. Ed. by B. M. Goodwin. LC 80-25560. (AIChEMI Modular Instruction D Ser.: Vol. 2: Thermodynamics). 70p. 1981. pap. 30.00 (ISBN 0-8169-0179-1, J-10). Am Inst Chem Eng.

Properties of Purified Cholinergic & Adrenergic Receptors. Ed. by M. Wollemann. (Proceedings). 1975. 17.00 (ISBN 0-444-10937-4). Elsevier.

Properties of Reactor Structural Alloys after Neutron or Particle Irradiation - STP 570. 631p. 1976. 59.50 (ISBN 0-8031-0539-8, 04-570000-35). ASTM.

Properties of Refractory Metals. Walter D. Wilkinson. LC 72-75349. 355p. 1969. 32.00 (ISBN 0-685-58275-2, 450010). Am Nuclear Soc.

Properties of Reservoir Rocks: Core Analysis. R. Monicard. LC 79-56347. 168p. 1980. 27.00x (ISBN 0-87201-765-6). Gulf Pub.

Properties of Roofing Asphalts. 102p. 15.00 (ISBN 0-318-17745-5, RR-82-1). Asphalt Inst.

Properties of Selected Ferrous Alloying Elements, Vol. III. Y. S. Touloukian & C. Y. Ho. (M-H-CINDAS Data Series on Material Properties). 288p. 1981. text ed. 59.95 (ISBN 0-07-065034-9). McGraw.

Properties of Solid Polymeric Materials: Part A see Treatise on Materials Science.

Properties of Solid Polymeric Materials: Part B see Treatise on Materials Science.

Properties of Steam. Ed. by V. V. Sytchev & A. A. Aleksandrov. 872p. 1987. 145.00x (ISBN 0-306-42159-3, Plenum Pr). Plenum Pub.

Properties of Water & Steam in SI-Units. 3rd, rev. ed. Ed. by H. Grigull. (Illus.). 194p. 1982. 39.00 (ISBN 0-387-09601-9). Springer-Verlag.

Properties of Water in Foods in Relation to Quality & Stability. Ed. by D. Simatos & J. L. Multon. 1985. lib. bdg. 79.50 (ISBN 90-247-3153-4, Pub. by Martinus Nijhoff Netherlands). Kluwer Academic.

Properties Related to Fracture Toughness - STP 605. Ed. by W. R. Warke et al. 150p. 1976. pap. 15.00 (ISBN 0-8031-0540-1, 04-605000-30). ASTM.

Propertius. Margaret Hubbard. (Classical Life & Letters Ser.). 182p. 1974. 34.00 (ISBN 0-7156-0666-2, Pub. by Duckworth London); pap. 13.50 (ISBN 0-7156-1581-5). Longwood Pub Group.

Propertius. Ed. by E. H. Warmington. (Loeb Classical Library: No. 18). (Lat. & Eng.). 13.95x (ISBN 0-674-99021-8). Harvard U Pr.

Propertius: A Hellenistic Poet on Love & Death. Theodore D. Papanghelis. 260p. 1987. 49.50 (ISBN 0-521-32314-2). Cambridge U Pr.

Propertius Elegies: Book IV. Propertius. Ed. by W. R. Connor & W. A. Camps. LC 78-67126. (Latin Texts & Commentaries Ser.). (Lat. & Eng.). 1979. Repr. of 1965 ed. lib. bdg. 14.00x (ISBN 0-405-11597-0). Ayer Co Pubs.

Propertius: Elegies Book Three. W. A. Camps. 188p. 1986. Repr. of 1966 ed. 17.50 (ISBN 0-86292-116-3, Pub. by Bristol Classical UK). Focus Info Gr.

Propertius: Elegies Book Two. W. A. Camps. 254p. 1986. Repr. of 1966 ed. 17.50 (ISBN 0-86292-148-1, Pub. by Bristol Classical UK). Focus Info Gr.

Propertius: Love & War, Individual & State Under Augustus. Hans-Peter Stahl. LC 84-16324. 1985. 40.00x (ISBN 0-520-05166-1). U of Cal Pr.

Propertius: Modernist Poet of Antiquity. D. Thomas Benediktson. LC 88-10115. 176p. 1988. text ed. 24.95x (ISBN 0-8093-1453-3). S Ill U Pr.

Property. Roger Bernhardt. LC 83-10320. (Black Letter Ser.). 318p. 1983. pap. text ed. 13.95 (ISBN 0-314-73213-6). West Pub.

Property. Tom Clark. (Tadbooks). (Illus.). 16p. pap. 10.00 (ISBN 0-89807-117-8); 20.00 (ISBN 0-89807-122-4). Illuminati.

Property. 2nd ed. Jesse Dukeminier & James Krier. 1385p. 1988. text ed. 38.00 (ISBN 0-316-19517-0). Little.

Property. Ed. by J. Roland Pennock & John W. Chapman. LC 79-55007. (Nomos XXII). 1980. 32.50x (ISBN 0-8147-6576-9). NYU Pr.

Property. Andrew Reeve. LC 86-7187. (Issues in Political Theory Ser.). 220p. 1986. 35.00 (ISBN 0-391-03438-3); pap. 9.95 (ISBN 0-391-03437-5). Humanities.

Property. Allan Ryan. LC 87-25538. (Concepts in Social Thought Ser.). 100p. (Orig.). 1988. 25.00x (ISBN 0-8166-1669-8); pap. 10.95 (ISBN 0-8166-1670-1). U of Minn Pr.

Property: A Study in Social Psychology. Ernest Beaglehole. LC 73-14147. (Perspectives in Social Inquiry Ser.). 332p. 1974. Repr. of 1932 ed. 50.50x (ISBN 0-405-05493-9). Ayer Co Pubs.

Property: Adaptable to Courses Utilizing Browder, Cunningham & Smith's Casebook on Basic Property Law. Casenotes Publishing Co., Inc. Staff. Ed. by Norman S. Goldenberg et al. (Legal Briefs Ser.). 1984. pap. write for info. (ISBN 0-87457-114-6, 1033). Casenotes Pub.

Property: Adaptable to Courses Utilizing Cribbet & Johnson's Casebook on Property. Casenotes Publishing Co., Inc. Staff. Ed. by Norman S. Goldenberg et al. (Legal Briefs Ser.). 1985. pap. write for info. (ISBN 0-87457-116-2, 1031). Casenotes Pub.

Property: Adaptable to Courses Utilizing Casner & Leach's Casebook on Property. Casenotes Publishing Co., Inc. Staff. Ed. by Norman S. Goldenberg et al. (Legal Briefs Ser.). 1985. pap. write for info. (ISBN 0-87457-115-4, 1030). Casenotes Pub.

Property: Adaptable to Courses Utilizing Dukeminier & Krier's Casebook on Property. Casenotes Publishing Co., Inc. Staff. Ed. by Norman S. Goldenberg et al. (Legal Briefs Ser.). 1984. pap. write for info. (ISBN 0-87457-117-0, 1035). Casenotes Pub.

Property: Adaptable to Courses Utilizing Haar & Liebman's Casebook on Property & Law. Casenotes Publishing Co., Inc. Staff. Ed. by Norman S. Goldenberg et al. (Casenote Legal Briefs). 1985. pap. write for info (ISBN 0-87457-118-9, 1034). Casenotes Pub.

Property: Adaptable to Courses Utilizing Materials by Browder. 2nd. ed. Olin L. Browder. LC 87-130233. (Legalines Ser.). 355p. Date not set. 13.50. HarBraceJ.

Property: Adaptable to Courses Utilizing Rabin's Casebook on Real Property Law. Casenotes Publishing Co., Inc. Staff. Ed. by Norman S. Goldenberg et al. (Legal Briefs Ser.). 1982. pap. write for info. (ISBN 0-87457-119-7, 1032). Casenotes Pub.

Property: An Introduction to the Concept & Institution Cases & Materials. 2nd ed. Charles Donahue, Jr. et al. LC 83-6529. (American Casebook Ser.). 1362p. 1983. 36.95 (ISBN 0-314-72904-6); pap. text ed. tchr's. manual avail. (ISBN 0-314-79129-9). West Pub.

Property & Casualty Insurance. Philip L. Gordis. 750p. 1983. lib. bdg. 34.00 (ISBN 0-942326-09-1, 26520). Rough Notes.

Property & Casualty Insurance: Study Guide. Franklin L. Moore. 1983. 26.00 (ISBN 0-942326-25-3, 26629). Rough Notes.

Property & Compensation Reports: 1950-1985, 50 vols. Bound set. 1625.00x (ISBN 0-686-90020-0). Rothman.

Property & Industrial Development. Stephen Fothergill et al. (Built Environment Ser.). (Illus., Orig.). 1987. pap. 19.95 (ISBN 0-09-170741-2, Pub. by Hutchinson Educ). Longwood Pub Group.

Property & Kinship: Inheritance in Early Connecticut, 1750-1820. Toby L. Ditz. 272p. 1986. text ed. 32.50x (ISBN 0-691-04735-9). Princeton U Pr.

Property & Landscape: A Social History of Land Ownership & the English Countryside. Tom Williamson & Liz Bellamy. 240p. 1987. 34.95 (ISBN 0-540-01125-8, Pub. by G. Phillip UK). Sheridan.

Property & Law. 2nd ed. Charles M. Haar & Lance Liebman. LC 84-81025. 1985. text ed. 37.00 (ISBN 0-316-33682-3). Little.

Property & Liability Insurance. 3rd, reference ed. S. S. Huebner et al. (Illus.). 608p. 1982. write for info. (ISBN 0-13-730978-3). P-H.

Property & Liability Insurance Management Model. W. Ray Bagwell. 1972. 15.95 (ISBN 0-88406-118-3). Ga St U Busn Pub.

Property & Liability Insurance Principles. Barry D. Smith et al. LC 87-80750. 280p. 1987. text ed. 25.00 (ISBN 0-89462-035-5). IIA.

Property & Liability Reinsurance Management: A Recognized Text on P. & L. Reinsurance. Robert C. Reinarz. LC 68-59174. 1969. 15.95 (ISBN 0-916910-01-6); 4 or more copies 12.95 ea. Mission Pub.

Property & Participation: Employee Ownership & Workplace Democracy in Three New England Firms. David Toscano. 202p. 1983. text ed. 29.00x (ISBN 0-8290-0553-6). Irvington.

Property & Political Theory. Alan Ryan. 240p. 1984. 34.95x (ISBN 0-631-13691-6). Basil Blackwell.

Property & Political Theory. Alan Ryan. 208p. 1986. pap. text ed. 14.95x (ISBN 0-631-15062-5). Basil Blackwell.

Property & Politics, Eighteen-Seventy to Nineteen-Fourteen: Landownership, Law, Ideology & Urban Development in England. Avner Offer. LC 80-41010. (Illus.). 480p. 1981. 69.50 (ISBN 0-521-22414-4). Cambridge U Pr.

Property & Politics: Essays in Later Medieval English History. A. J. Pollard. LC 84-40371. 192p. 1985. 25.00 (ISBN 0-312-65173-2). St Martin.
Property & Power. Leszek Nowak. 1983. lib. bdg. 57.00 (ISBN 90-277-1351-0, Pub. by Reidel Holland); pap. 24.60 (ISBN 90-277-1595-5). Kluwer Academic.
Property & Prophets: The Evolution of Economic Institutions & Ideologies. 5th ed. E. K. Hunt. 256p. 1985. pap. text ed. 17.95 scp (ISBN 0-06-043037-0, HarpC). Har-Row.
Property & Riches in the Early Church: Aspects of a Social History of Early Christianity. Martin Hengel. Tr. by John Bowden from Ger. LC 75-305658. pap. 26.00 (2026856). Bks Demand UMI.
Property & Social Relations. Ed. & intro. by Peter G. Hollowell. 202p. 1982. pap. text ed. 15.50x (ISBN 0-435-82435-X). Gower Pub Co.
Property & Virtue in Moral Philosophy. Adam Smith. 131p. 1988. 127.50 (ISBN 0-86654-258-2). Inst Econ Finan.
Property Assessment Valuation. LC 77-8155. 1977. 19.50 (ISBN 0-88329-009-X). IAAO.
Property, Cases & Materials on. 5th ed. John E. Cribbet & Corwin W. Johnson. LC 84-4137. (University Casebook Ser.). 1626p. 1984. text ed. 32.00 (ISBN 0-88277-171-X). Foundation Pr.
Property: Cases, Concepts, Critiques. Lawrence Becker & Kenneth Kipnis. 352p. 1984. pap. text ed. write for info. (ISBN 0-13-730912-0). P-H.
Property, Cases on. 5th ed. Cribbet & Johnson. (University Casebook Ser.). 32.00. Foundation Pr.
Property Clerk. (Career Examination Ser.: C-3465). Date not set. pap. 12.00 (ISBN 0-8373-3465-9). Natl Learning.
Property Companies & the Construction Industry in Britain. Hedley Smyth. (Human Geography Ser.). (Illus.). 256p. 1985. 44.50 (ISBN 0-521-26512-6). Cambridge U Pr.
Property Concepts of the Navaho Indians. Berard Haile. LC 76-43726. Repr. of 1954 ed. 12.50 (ISBN 0-404-15566-9). AMS Pr.
Property Conservation Workbook. 169p. 30.00 (ISBN 0-318-14059-4, P7917). Factory Mutual.
Property Control & Social Strategies: Settlers on a Middle Eastern Plain. Barbara C. Aswad. (Anthropological Papers: No. 44). 1971. pap. 4.00x (ISBN 0-932206-42-5). U Mich Mus Anthro.
Property Crime in Canada: An Econometric Study. K. L. Avio & C. Scott Clark. LC 76-925. (Ontario Economic Council Ser.). 1975. pap. 3.95x (ISBN 0-8020-3334-2). U of Toronto Pr.
Property Development. 2nd ed. John McMahan. 1988. 49.95 (ISBN 0-07-045451-5). McGraw.
Property Development: Effective Decision Making in Uncertain Times. John W. McMahan. 1976. text ed. 44.95 (ISBN 0-07-045450-7). McGraw.
Property Division at Marriage Dissolution Cases. Joan M. Krauskopf. LC 83-23464. (American Casebook Ser.). 250p. 1983. pap. text ed. 7.95 (ISBN 0-314-80327-0). West Pub.
Property in the Eighteenth Century. P. Larkin. LC 68-9655. 1969. Repr. of 1930 ed. 15.75x (ISBN 0-86527-160-7). Fertig.
Property in the Eighteenth Century. Paschal Larkin. LC 75-86034. Repr. of 1930 ed. 23.00x (ISBN 0-8046-0622-6, Pub. by Kennikat). Assoc Faculty Pr.
Property Inspection Workbook. Thomas Roe. 106p. (Orig.). 1985. pap. text ed. 19.95 (ISBN 0-930187-01-6). Impact Pub.
Property Insurance Annotations: Fire & Extended Coverages. LC 77-83224. 415p. 1977. looseleaf with binder 35.00 (ISBN 0-686-47984-X). Amer Bar Assn.
Property Insurance Annotations, Fire & Extended Coverages: First Supplement. LC 83-72659. (Tort & Insurance Practice Section Ser.). 157p. 1983. 55.00 (ISBN 0-89707-120-4). Amer Bar Assn.
Property Insurance (for INS 22) 2nd, rev. ed. R. Robert Rackley. (INS Ser.). 1984. 100.00 (ISBN 0-88171-092-X). Insurance Achiev.
Property Interests in North Carolina City Streets. David M. Lawrence. LC 86-621832. 59p. 1986. 5.00. U of NC Inst Gov.
Property, Kin & Community on Truk. 2nd. ed. Ward H. Goodenough. LC 78-16193. 260p. 1978. 27.50 (ISBN 0-208-01696-1, Archon). Shoe String.
Property: Landlord & Tenant, 2 vols. 2nd ed. (Restatement of the Law-Library Edition: No. 1). 64.00 (ISBN 0-686-90457-5). Am Law Inst.
Property Law in the Arab World. F. Ziadeh. 112p. 1979. 55.00 (ISBN 0-86010-112-6). Graham & Trotman.
Property-Liability Insurance Accounting & Finance. 2nd ed. Terrie E. Troxel & Cormick L. Breslin. LC 83-82389. 349p. 1983. text ed. 20.00 (ISBN 0-89463-040-7). Am Inst Property.
Property-Liability Insurance Accounting. 3rd ed. Ed. by Robert W. Strain. LC 84-70333. 502p. 1986. looseleaf 56.45 (ISBN 0-939727-26-9). R W Strain.
Property Liability Insurance Accounting. 4th ed. Ed. by Robert W. Strain. LC 84-70333. 1988. 79.50 (ISBN 0-939727-27-7). R W Strain.
Property: Mainstream & Critical Positions. Ed. by C. B. Macpherson. LC 78-2311. (Controversy Ser). 1978. 11.95c (ISBN 0-8020-2305-3); pap. 10.95c (ISBN 0-8020-6336-5). U of Toronto Pr.
Property Maintenance Logbook. William Chargar & Morris A. Nunes. LC 84-17818. 612p. 1985. 39.95 (ISBN 0-13-731134-6, Busn). P-H.
Property Management. 2nd ed. Robert C. Kyle. LC 84-3325. 440p. (Orig.). 1984. pap. text ed. 31.95 (ISBN 0-88462-498-6, 1551-10, Real Estate Ed). Longman Finan.
Property Management. 3rd ed. Robert C. Kyle. Ed. by Floyd M. Baird. (Illus.). 429p. 1987. pap. 31.95 (ISBN 0-88462-669-5, Real Estate Ed); pap. text ed. 23.95 (Real Estate Ed). Longman Finan.
Property Management. D. Scarrett. (Illus.). 1983. 29.95 (ISBN 0-419-12380-6, NO. 6828, Pub. by E & FN Spon); pap. 14.95 (ISBN 0-419-12390-3, NO. 6829). Routledge Chapman & Hall.
Property Management Handbook: A Practical Guide to Real Estate Management. Ed. by Robert F. Cushman & Neal I. Rodin. LC 84-10427. (Real Estate for Professional Practitioners Ser.: 1-242). 480p. 1985. 65.00x (ISBN 0-471-87503-1). Wiley.
Property Management in California. 2nd ed. Joseph W. DeCario. (Illus., Orig.). 1987. pap. 22.95 (ISBN 0-317-61553-X). JD Pub & Seminars.
Property Management in California. Joseph W. DeCarlo. (Illus., Orig.). 1986. pap. 22.95 (ISBN 0-937841-01-3). JD Pub & Seminars.
Property Management Reinvented: How to Convert Maintenance & Energy Expenses to Profit. Mel A. Shear. (Illus.). 272p. 1988. text ed. 37.33 (ISBN 0-13-731191-5). P-H.
Property Manager's Relationship with Developers & Lenders. (Journal Reprint Ser.). 8.75 (ISBN 0-686-46433-8, 891). Inst Real Estate.
Property Markets & the State in Adam Smith's System. Robert B. Lamb. Ed. by Maurice Cranston. (Political Theory & Political Philosophy Ser.). 450p. 1987. lib. bdg. 65.00 (ISBN 0-8240-0823-5). Garland Pub.
Property Of. Alice Hoffman. 1988. pap. 3.50 (ISBN 0-449-44546-1, Crest). Fawcett.
Property of a Lady. Anthony Oliver. 272p. 1985. pap. 2.95 (ISBN 0-449-20595-9, Crest). Fawcett.
Property Owing Democracy. John Doling et al. 238p. 1988. text ed. 41.00 (ISBN 0-566-05544-9, Pub. by Gower Pub England). Gower Pub Co.
Property, Paternalism, & Power: A Study of East Anglian Farmers. Howard Newby et al. LC 78-2030. (Illus.). 432p. 1978. Repr. 32.50x (ISBN 0-299-07870-1). U of Wis Pr.
Property, Power, & Public Choice: An Inquiry Into Law & Economics. 2nd ed. A. Allan Schmid. 352p. 1987. lib. bdg. 49.95 (ISBN 0-275-92797-0, C2797); pap. 23.95 (ISBN 0-275-92828-4, B2828). Praeger.
Property Qualifications of Members of Parliament. Helen E. Witmer. LC 68-58644. (Columbia University. Studies in Social Sciences: No. 498). Repr. of 1943 ed. 20.00 (ISBN 0-404-51498-7). AMS Pr.
Property Rights & Eminent Domain. Ellen F. Paul. 277p. 1986. 26.95 (ISBN 0-88738-094-8). Transaction Bks.
Property Rights & Sovereign Rights: The Case of North Sea Oil. Peter D. Cameron. (Law State & Society Ser.). 1984. 50.50 (ISBN 0-12-157060-6). Acad Pr.
Property Rights in the Eighth-Century Prophets: The Conflict & Its Background. John A. Dearman. LC 87-28511. (SBL-Dissertation Ser.). 181p. 1988. 16.95 (ISBN 1-55540-192-9, 06-21-06); pap. 10.95 (ISBN 1-55540-195-3). Scholars Pr GA.
Property Rights in Transition. Ed. by Don A. Derr & Leslie Small. 243p. 1977. text ed. 29.50x (ISBN 0-8422-5252-5); pap. text ed. 8.95x (ISBN 0-8422-0554-3). Irvington.
Property Rights: Philosophic Foundations. Lawrence C. Becker. 148p. 1980. pap. 7.95x (ISBN 0-7100-0606-3). Routledge Chapman & Hall.
Property Rights: Philosophic Foundations. Lawrence C. Becker. 1977. 21.95x (ISBN 0-7100-8679-2). Routledge Chapman & Hall.
Property, Social Structure, & Law in the Modern Middle East. Ed. by Ann E. Mayer. LC 85-2786. (SUNY Series in Near Eastern Studies). 274p. 1985. 59.50 (ISBN 0-87395-988-4); pap. 19.95x (ISBN 0-87395-987-6). State U NY Pr.
Property System Approach to the Electromagnetic Spectrum: A Legal-Economic-Engineering Study. Arthur S. De Vany et al. (Cato Paper Ser.: No. 10). 87p. 1980. pap. 4.00x (ISBN 0-932790-11-9). Cato Inst.
Property Tax: A Revision of P 795. Mary Vance. (Public Administration Ser.: P 1932). 41p. 1986. 11.25 (ISBN 0-89028-852-6). Vance Biblios.
Property Tax After Proposition 13: An Update. 103p. 1987. pap. 22.00 (RE-49093). Cal Cont Ed Bar.
Property Tax & Inflation: Compilation of Papers Presented at the 1980 Property Tax Forum in Washington, D. C. Ed. by Joe Ziemba & Sherry Guariglia. 83p. 1981. pap. 14.00 (ISBN 0-88329-018-9). IAAO.
Property Tax & Its Administration: Proceedings of the Committee on Taxation, Resources & Economic Development Symposium, 1967. Taxation, Resources & Economic Development Committee. Ed. by Arthur D. Lynn, Jr. (Committee on Taxation, Resources & Economic Development Ser., No. 3). 260p. 1969. 25.00x (ISBN 0-299-05210-9); pap. 9.95x (ISBN 0-299-05214-1). U of Wis Pr.
Property Tax & Local Finance. Ed. by C. Lowell Harriss. LC 82-74494. (Academy of Political Science). 242p. 1983. pap. 8.00 (ISBN 0-317-03917-2). Schalkenbach.
Property Tax & Local Finance, Vol. 35, No. 1. LC 83-74494. 1983. 9.95 (ISBN 0-318-01790-3). Acad Poli Sci.
Property Tax & National Income in the U. S., 1929 to 1980. Robert M. Clatanoff. (Research & Information Ser.). 85p. 1982. pap. 14.50 (ISBN 0-88329-042-1). IAAO.
Property Tax Assessment: Processes, Records, & Land Values. Ed. by T. Alexander Majchrowicz & Richard R. Almy. LC 86-7334. 113p. 1986. pap. 15.00 (ISBN 0-88329-055-3). IAAO.
Property Tax Collection in North Carolina. rev. 1988 ed. William Campbell. write for info. U of NC Inst Gov.
Property Tax Collection in North Carolina. 2nd. Rev. ed. William A. Campbell. 334p. 1974. 5.00 (ISBN 0-686-39435-6). U of NC Inst Gov.
Property Tax Exemptions & in Lieu Payments. (Bibliographic Ser.). 30p. 1980. 9.00 (ISBN 0-88329-111-8). IAAO.
Property Tax in North Carolina: An Introduction. 3rd ed. Henry W. Lewis. 1978. pap. 2.75 (ISBN 0-686-17569-7). U of NC Inst Gov.
Property Tax Incentives for Alternative Energy Devices. Patricia Carmean. (Research & Information Ser.). 108p. 1980. pap. 17.00 (ISBN 0-88329-041-3). IAAO.
Property Tax Incentives for Preservation: Use-Value Assessment & the Preservation of Farmland, Open Space & Historic Sites. LC 75-40131. (Studies in Property Taxation). 144p. 1976. pap. 13.00 (ISBN 0-88329-052-9). IAAO.
Property Tax Incidence: An Annotated Bibliography. Robert C. Denne. (Bibliographic Ser.). 23p. 1977. pap. 8.50 (ISBN 0-88329-110-X). IAAO.
Property Tax Legislation in the United States, 1984. Gary Langhoff. LC 85-10838. (Research & Information Ser.: No. I-IX). 79p. 1985. pap. 16.00 (ISBN 0-88329-140-1). IAAO.
Property Tax Legislation in the United States, 1985. Gary M. Langhoff. LC 86-10525. (Research & Information Ser.: No. I-X). 63p. 1986. pap. 14.50 (ISBN 0-88329-057-X). IAAO.
Property Tax Legislation in the United States, 1986. Gary M. Langhoff. (Research & Information Ser.: No. 1). 55p. 1987. pap. 13.50 (ISBN 0-88329-150-9). IAAO.
Property Tax Legislation in the United States, 1978. Stuart Miller. (Research & Information Ser.: No. I-III). 78p. 1979. pap. 14.00 (ISBN 0-88329-039-1). IAAO.
Property Tax Legislation in the United States, 1980. Stuart Miller. (Research & Information Ser.: No. I-IV). 92p. 1981. pap. 15.50 (ISBN 0-88329-034-0). IAAO.
Property Tax Legislation in the United States, 1976, 2 pts. Stuart Miller. (Research & Information Ser.: No. 1). 1977. Pt. 1. 8.00 (ISBN 0-88329-032-4); Pt. 2. pap. 8.00 (ISBN 0-88329-031-6). IAAO.
Property Tax Legislation in the United States, 1983. Stuart Miller. (Research & Information Ser.: No. I-VIII). 83p. 1984. pap. 18.00 (ISBN 0-88329-132-0). IAAO.
Property Tax Legislation in the United States, 1982. Stuart W. Miller. (Research & Information Ser.: No. I-VII). 68p. 1983. pap. 13.00 (ISBN 0-88329-019-7). IAAO.
Property Tax Legislation in the United States, 1977. Stuart W. Miller. (Research & Information Ser.: No. I-II). 83p. 1978. pap. 14.50 (ISBN 0-88329-040-5). IAAO.
Property Tax Legislation in the United States, 1981. (Research & Information Ser.: No. I-VI). 87p. 1982. pap. 15.00 (ISBN 0-88329-033-2). IAAO.
Property Tax Legislation in the United States, 1979. (Research & Information Ser.: No. I-IV). 127p. 1980. pap. 19.00 (ISBN 0-88329-035-9). IAAO.
Property Tax Lien Foreclosure Forms. 3rd. ed. William A. Campbell. 112p. 1985. 10.50 (ISBN 0-686-39436-4). U of NC Inst Gov.
Property Tax Limits. Robert J. Gloudemans. (Research & Information Ser.). 55p. 1978. pap. 11.50 (ISBN 0-88329-030-8). IAAO.
Property Tax Preferences for Agricultural Land. Ed. by Neal A. Roberts & H. James Brown. LC 79-52473. (Illus.). 140p. 1980. text ed. 19.50x (ISBN 0-916672-32-8, Pub. by Allanheld). Rowman.
Property Tax: Problems & Potentials. Alfred G. Buehler. (T.A. Monographs). 1976. Repr. of 1967 ed. 24.00 (ISBN 0-527-89014-6). Kraus Repr.
Property Tax Reform. Ed. by George Peterson. 188p. 1973. pap. 10.50 (ISBN 0-87766-099-9, 49000). Urban Inst.
Property Tax Revolt: The Case of Proposition 13. Ed. by George Kaufman & Kenneth T. Rosen. LC 81-1338. (Real Estate & Urban Economics Ser.). 256p. 1981. prof ref 24.50x (ISBN 0-88410-693-4). Ballinger Pub.
Property Taxation & the Finance of Education. Ed. by Richard W. Lindholm. LC 73-2046. (TRED Ser.). (Illus.). 346p. 1974. 32.50x (ISBN 0-299-06440-9). U of Wis Pr.
Property Taxation & the Preservation of Historic Properties. (Research & Information Ser.). 19p. 1977. pap. 8.00 (ISBN 0-88329-125-8). IAAO.
Property Taxation in the U. S. An Annotated Bibliography, Pt. 1, Alabama-Maine. Robert Denne. (Bibliographic Ser.: No. 3A). 80p. 1978. pap. 14.00 (ISBN 0-88329-024-3). IAAO.
Property Taxation in the U. S. An Annotated Bibliography: Pt. II Maryland - North Carolina. Robert Denne. (Bibliographic Ser.: No. 3B). 82p. 1978. pap. 14.50 (ISBN 0-88329-023-5). IAAO.
Property Taxation in the U. S. An Annotated Bibliography: Pt. III, North Dakota - Wyoming & All States. (Bibliographic Ser.: No. 3C). 99p. 1978. pap. 16.00 (ISBN 0-88329-022-7). IAAO.
Property Taxation in the U. S. An Annotated Bibliography, Supplement No. 1. Stuart W. Miller. (Research & Information Ser.: No. 3-I). 82p. 1979. 14.50 (ISBN 0-88329-021-9). IAAO.
Property Taxation, Land Use & Public Policy. Taxation, Resources & Economic Development Committee. Ed. by Arthur D. Lynn, Jr. 268p. 1976. 29.50x (ISBN 0-299-06920-6). U of Wis Pr.
Property Taxation-U. S. A. University of Wisconsin Press. Ed. by Richard W. Lindholm. LC 67-20762. 268p. 1967. pap. 8.00x. Schalkenbach.
Property Taxation, U. S. A. Proceedings. Ed. by Richard W. Lindholm. (Committee on Taxation, Resources & Economic Development Ser.: No. 2). (Illus.). 332p. 1967. pap. 12.50x (ISBN 0-299-04544-7). U of Wis Pr.
Property Taxes, 11 vols. (Information Services Ser.). 1987. loose leaf 1062.00; 948.00; write for info., weekly updates. P-H.
Property Taxes & House Values. Ed. by John Yinger. (Studies in Urban Economics). 250p. 1988. price not set (ISBN 0-12-771060-4). Acad Pr.
Property Taxes & the Birth & Intraregional Location of New Firms. Marie Howland. (Working Paper Ser.: No. 1). 24p. 1984. 3.00 (ISBN 0-913749-07-9). U MD Inst.
Property: The Law of 1987. Roger A. Cunningham et al. (Hornbook Ser.). 148p. 1986. Pocket Part. pap. 8.95 (ISBN 0-314-33872-1). West Pub.
Property Valuation by Isotropic Patterns. Glenn H. Petry. 1974. 2.50 (ISBN 0-686-64199-X). U CO Busn Res Div.
Property Values & Open Space in Northwest Philadelphia: An Empirical Analysis. Robert E. Coughlin & Tatsuhiko Kawashima. (Discussion Paper Ser.: No. 64). 1973. pap. 6.50 (ISBN 0-686-32230-4). Regional Sci Res Inst.
Property, Wealth, Land: Allocation, Planning & Development. 2nd ed. Myers S. McDougal & Luther L. McDougal. 922p. 1981. 28.00x (ISBN 0-672-84349-8). Michie Co.
Prophecies & Revelations about the Jesuits. Tr. by James S. Terrien. 143p. pap. 3.98 (ISBN 0-913452-27-0). Jesuit Bks.
Prophecies & Transformations. Kosrof Chantikian. LC 75-35012. (Modern Poets Ser.). 88p. (Orig.). 1978. pap. 5.95 (ISBN 0-916426-01-7). KOSMOS.
Prophecies de Merlin, 2 Vols. Ed. by Lucy A. Paton. (MLA MS). 1926-1927. Set. 77.00 (ISBN 0-527-70100-9). Kraus Repr.
Prophecies Fulfilled. Charles Dollen. LC 87-62881. 180p. 1988. 5.95 (ISBN 0-87973-495-7, 495). Our Sunday Visitor.
Prophecies of Daniel. Gordon Lindsay. (Daniel Ser.). 4.00 (ISBN 0-89985-052-9). Christ Nations.
Prophecies of Daniel see Daniel: Prophecies.
Prophecies of Joseph Smith. Duane S. Crowther. LC 83-80664. 413p. 1873. 10.95 (ISBN 0-88290-221-0). Horizon-Utah.
Prophecies of Mother Shipton. 1983. pap. 2.95 (ISBN 0-916411-22-2, Pub. by Sure Fire). Holmes Pub.
Prophecies of Nostradamus. Ed. by Erika Cheetham. 1975. pap. 7.95 (ISBN 0-399-50345-5, Perigee). Putnam Pub Group.
Prophecies of Nostradamus: The Man Who Saw Tomorrow. Ed. & tr. by Erika Cheetham. 448p. 1986. pap. 4.95 (ISBN 0-425-08757-3). Berkley Pub.
Prophecies of St. Malachy. Peter Bander. LC 74-125419. (Illus.). 1973. pap. 3.50 (ISBN 0-89555-038-5). TAN Bks Pubs.
Prophecies of the Holy Quran. Hingora. pap. 4.50 (ISBN 0-686-18509-9). Kazi Pubns.
Prophecies on World Events by Nostradamus. 4th ed. Nostradamus. Tr. by Stewart Robb. (Illus., Orig.). 1970. pap. 4.95 (ISBN 0-87140-220-3). Liveright.
Prophecy. Peter Danielson. (Children of the Lion Ser.: No. 7). 432p. (Orig.). 1987. pap. 4.50 (ISBN 0-553-26325-0). Bantam.
Prophecy. Bruce Yocum. (Orig.). 1976. pap. 5.95 (ISBN 0-89283-029-8). Servant.
Prophecy & Canon: A Contribution to the Study of Jewish Origins. Joseph Blenkinsopp. LC 76-22411. 206p. 1986. pap. 9.95 (ISBN 0-268-01559-7). U of Notre Dame Pr.
Prophecy & Charisma see Profecia y Carisma, Que de las Lenguas?.
Prophecy & Gnosis: Apocalypticism in the Wake of the Lutheran Reformation. Robin B. Barnes. LC 87-24138. 368p. 1988. text ed. 39.50x (ISBN 0-8047-1405-3). Stanford U Pr.
Prophecy & Hermeneutics in Early Christianity: New Testament Essays. E. Earle Ellis. 306p. 1978. lib. bdg. 62.50x. Coronet Bks.
Prophecy & History in Luke-Acts. David L. Tiede. LC 79-8897. pap. 44.00 (ISBN 0-317-55547-2, 2029616). Bks Demand UMI.

Prophetic Words of Hosea: A Morphological Study. Martin J. Buss. (Beiheft 111 Zur Zeitschrift Fuer Die alttestamentliche Wissenschaft). 1969. 30.00- (ISBN 3-11-002579-5). De Gruyter.
Prophetic Works for the Agnostic in Word Imagery. Yann Humphery-Smith. 1987. 5.95 (ISBN 0-533-06910-6). Vantage.
Prophetic Worlds: Indians & Whites on the Columbia Plateau. Christopher L. Miller. 180p. 1985. text ed. 29.00 (ISBN 0-8135-1084-8). Rutgers U Pr.
Prophetical, Educational & Playing Cards. Mrs. John K. Van Rensselaer. LC 77-78249. (Illus.). 392p. 1971. Repr. of 1912 ed. 43.00x (ISBN 0-8103-3867-X). Gale.
Prophetical Walk Through the Holy Land. Hal Lindsey. LC 83-80121. 200p. 1983. text ed. 29.95 (ISBN 0-89081-381-7). Harvest Hse.
Prophets, 2 vols. Abraham J. Heschel. Vol. 1, 1969. pap. 7.95x (ISBN 0-06-131421-8, TB1421, Torch); Vol. 2, 1971. pap. 7.95x (ISBN 0-06-131557-5, TB1557, Torch). Har-Row.
Prophets. Abraham J. Heschel. 520p. 12.95 (ISBN 0-318-14657-6, 182). JPS Phila.
Prophets. James M. Ward. LC 81-20575. (Interpreting Biblical Texts). 160p. (Orig.). 1982. pap. 8.95 (ISBN 0-687-34370-4). Abingdon.
Prophets see Oxford Illustrated Old Testament: With Drawings by Contemporary Artists.
Prophets--Nevi'im: A New Translation of the Holy Scriptures According to the Traditional Hebrew Text. LC 77-87245. 930p. 1978. 10.95 (ISBN 0-8276-0096-8, 55). JPS Phila.
Prophets & Kings. Ellen G. White. 752p. deluxe ed. 10.95 (ISBN 0-8163-0040-2, 16642-1); pap. 5.95 (ISBN 0-8163-0041-0, 16643-9). Pacific Pr Pub Assn.
Prophets & Lovers: In Search of the Holy Spirit. Brennan Manning. 1985. 4.95 (ISBN 0-87193-013-7). Dimension Bks.
Prophets & Markets. Morris Silver. 1982. lib. bdg. 35.00 (ISBN 0-89838-112-6, Pub. by Kluwer-Nijhoff (Netherlands)). Kluwer Academic.
Prophets & Our Times. R. Gerald Culleton. 1974. pap. 8.50 (ISBN 0-89555-050-4). TAN Bks Pubs.
Prophets & Patrons: The French University & the Emergence of the Social Sciences. Terry N. Clark. LC 72-93947. (Illus.). 311p. 1973. 19.50x (ISBN 0-674-71580-2). Harvard U Pr.
Prophets & People: Studies in Nineteenth Century Nationalism. Hans Kohn. LC 75-4697. v, 213p. 1975. Repr. of 1946 ed. lib. bdg. 18.50x (ISBN 0-88254-842-5, Octagon). Hippocrene Bks.
Prophets & Personal Prophecy: God's Prophetic Voice Today. Bill Hamon. 218p. (Orig.). 1987. pap. 7.95 (ISBN 0-939868-03-2). Destiny Image.
Prophets & Prophecies of the Old Testament. 2nd ed. Duane S. Crowther. LC 66-25508. (Comprehensive Bible Ser.). (Illus.). 644p. 1973. Repr. of 1967 ed. 12.95 (ISBN 0-88290-022-6). Horizon Utah.
Prophets & Prophecy: Seven Key Messengers. Frank H. Seilhamer. LC 76-62603. pap. 23.80 (2027878). Bks Demand UMI.
Prophets & the Law. Victor Bergren. 15.00x (ISBN 0-87820-403-2, Pub. by Hebrew Union College Press). Ktav.
Prophets & the Powerless. James Limburg. LC 76-12397. 1976. pap. 6.95 (ISBN 0-8042-0156-0, John Knox). Westminster John Knox.
Prophets & the Rise of Judaism. Adolphe Lods. Tr. by S. H. Hooke. LC 77-109772. (Illus.). 1971. Repr. of 1937 ed. lib. bdg. 35.00x (ISBN 0-8371-4262-8, LOPR). Greenwood.
Prophets & Their Times. rev ed. John M. Smith. Ed. by William A. Irwin. LC 25-6864. 1941. 20.00x (ISBN 0-226-76356-0). U of Chicago Pr.
Prophets & Wise Men. McKane. Date not set. 9.50 (Pub. by SCM Pr England). Fortress.
Prophet's Army: Trotskyists in America 1928-1941. Constance A. Myers. LC 76-15330. (Contributions in American History Ser.: No. 56). 1976. lib. bdg. 46.95 (ISBN 0-8371-9030-4, MPA/). Greenwood.
Prophet's Biography Series for Children: Nos. 8, 9, 10. Abdulhamid Jodah Al Sahhar. Ed. by Mary Shahnaz & Hamid Quinlan. Tr. by Outaiba Elhuwaib from Arabic. LC 82-70350. Orig. Title: Kasas Alsyrah. (Illus.). 16p. 1982. pap. 1.50 (ISBN 0-89259-025-4). Am Trust Pubns.
Prophets Denied Honor: An Anthology on the Hispanic Church in the U. S. Ed. by Antonio Stevens-Arroyo. LC 79-26847. 397p. (Orig.). 1982. pap. 12.95 (ISBN 0-88344-395-3). Orbis Bks.
Prophets for a Day of Judgment. facsimile ed. Albert E. Baker. LC 72-90605. (Essay Index Reprint Ser). 1944. 17.00 (ISBN 0-8369-1390-6). Ayer Co Pubs.
Prophet's Heart. Charles Brown. 95p. (Orig.). 1980. pap. 3.95 (ISBN 0-914903-01-2). Destiny Image.
Prophets in Combat: The Nicaraguan Journal of Bishop Pedro Casaldaliga. Pedro Casaldaliga. Tr. by Phillip Berryman from Span. 128p. (Orig.). 1987. pap. 8.95 (ISBN 0-940989-02-6). Meyer Stone Bks.
Prophets in the Church. Roger Aubert. LC 68-57877. (Concilium Ser.: Vol. 37). 160p. 1964. 7.95 (ISBN 0-8091-0120-3). Paulist Pr.
Prophets, Kings, Commoners & Outcasts: Studies in Western Civilization. James Wright. 208p. (Orig.). 1984. pap. 9.95 (ISBN 0-911541-04-7). Gregory Pub.
Prophet's Mantle in the Nation's Capital. George W. Buchanan. LC 78-59167. 1978. pap. text ed. 8.25 (ISBN 0-8191-0545-7). U Pr of Amer.
Prophets Now. Leslie F. Brandt. 1979. 8.95 (ISBN 0-570-03278-4, 15-2722). Concordia.
Prophets-Now see Popular Devotionals.
Prophets of Deceit. J. L. Davidson. 1960. 5.25 (ISBN 0-88027-016-0). Firm Foun Pub.
Prophets of Deceit: A Study of the Techniques of the American Agitator. 2nd ed. Leo Lowenthal & Norbert Guterman. LC 68-31291. (Pacific Books Paperbounds, PB-8). (Illus.). 1970. pap. 1.95 (ISBN 0-87015-182-7). Pacific Bks.
Prophets of Dissent: Essays on Maeterlinck, Strindberg, Nietzsche & Tolstoy. Otto Heller. LC 68-26246. 1968. Repr. of 1918 ed. 21.50x (ISBN 0-8046-0200-X, Pub. by KennikaT). Assoc Faculty Pr.
Prophets of Doom in an Age of Optimism. V. Kerry Inman. (Orig.). 1981. pap. 4.95 (ISBN 0-934688-02-8). Great Comm Pubns.
Prophets of Doom: Literature As a Socio-Political Phenomenon in Modern Iran. M. R. Ghanoonparvar. LC 84-17304. 242p. 1985. lib. bdg. 27.50 (ISBN 0-8191-4292-1); pap. text ed. 13.00 (ISBN 0-8191-4293-X). U Pr of Amer.
Prophets of Extremity: Nietzsche, Heidegger, Foucault, Derrida. Allan Megill. 1985. 35.00x (ISBN 0-520-05239-0); pap. 11.95x. U of Cal Pr.
Prophets of Extremity: Nietzsche, Heideeger, Foucault, Derrida. Allan Megill. xxiii, 399p. 1987. pap. 11.95 (ISBN 0-520-06028-8). U of Cal Pr.
Prophets of Heaven & Hell. Charles R. Buxton. LC 78-100796. 1970. Repr. of 1945 ed. 39.95x (ISBN 0-8383-0086-3). Haskell.
Prophets of Israel. Leon J. Wood. LC 79-50172. 1979. 18.95 (ISBN 0-8010-9607-3). Baker Bk.
Prophets of Israel & Their Place in History to the Close of the Eighth Century B. C. W. Robertson Smith. 1979. Repr. of 1895 ed. lib. bdg. 50.00 (ISBN 0-8495-4905-1). Arden Lib.
Prophets of Israel: And Their Place in History to the Close of the Eighth Century, B.C. William R. Smith. LC 77-87666. 504p. Repr. of 1907 ed. 47.50 (ISBN 0-404-16403-X). AMS Pr.
Prophets of Order. Donald Stabile. LC 84-50939. 350p. (Orig.). 1984. 25.00 (ISBN 0-89608-230-X); pap. 10.50 (ISBN 0-89608-229-6). South End Pr.
Prophets of Past Time: Seven British Autobiographers, 1880-1914. Carl Dawson. LC 87-30025. 280p. 1988. text ed. 29.50x (ISBN 0-8018-3587-9). Johns Hopkins.
Prophets of Peace. D. Douglas Schneider. Ed. by Henry Mayday. 75p. (Orig.). Date not set. pap. 5.95 (ISBN 0-939169-04-5). World Peace Univ.
Prophets of Rebellion: Millenarian Protest Movements Against the European Colonial Order. Michael Adas. LC 78-26775. xxix, 243p. 1979. 25.00x (ISBN 0-8078-1353-2). U of NC Pr.
Prophets of Rebellion: Millenarian Protest Movements Against the European Colonial Order. Michael Adas. (Studies in Comparative World History). (Illus.). 240p. 1987. pap. 9.95 (ISBN 0-521-33568-X). Cambridge U Pr.
Prophets of Regulation. Thomas K. McCraw. (Illus.). 416p. 1986. pap. 8.95 (ISBN 0-674-71608-6, Belknap Pr). Harvard U Pr.
Prophets of Regulation: Charles Francis Adams, Louis D. Brandeis, James M. Landis, Alfred E. Kahn. Thomas K. McCraw. LC 84-296. 408p. 1984. 22.95 (ISBN 0-674-71607-8, Belknap Pr). Harvard U Pr.
Prophets of the Century: Shelley, Wordsworth, Carlyle, Emerson, Tennyson, Browning, George Eliot, Ruskin, Whitman, William Morris, Tolstoy, Ibsen. Arthur C. Rickett. 1898. Repr. 25.00 (ISBN 0-8274-3212-7). R West.
Prophets of the Century: Wordsworth, Shelley, Carlyle, Emerson, Tennyson, Eliot, Ruskin, Whitman, Morris, Tolstoy, Ibsen. Arthur Rickett. 1977. Repr. of 1898 ed. lib. bdg. 25.00 (ISBN 0-8495-4507-2). Arden Lib.
Prophets of the Left: American Socialist Thought in the Twentieth Century. Robert Hyfler. LC 83-18327. (Contributions in Political Science Ser.: No. 109). x, 187p. 1984. lib. bdg. 35.00 (ISBN 0-313-23390-X, HYP/). Greenwood.
Prophets of the Nineteenth Century: Carlyle, Ruskin, Tolstoi. May A. Ward. LC 76-7949. 1978. Repr. of 1900 ed. lib. bdg. 33.00 (ISBN 0-8414-9437-1). Folcroft.
Prophets of the Resoration: Portraits of Latter-Day Saint Presidents in Counted Cross Stitch. Jean D. Crowther. 24p. (Orig.). 1987. pap. 5.95 (ISBN 0-88290-321-7). Horizon Utah.
Prophets of the Soul. facsimile ed. Joseph M. Gray. LC 71-156655. (Essay Index Reprint Ser). Repr. of 1936 ed. 18.00 (ISBN 0-8369-2277-8). Ayer Co Pubs.
Prophets of Yesterday & Their Message for Today. facs. ed. John Kelman. LC 74-152181. (Essay Index Reprint Ser). 1924. 17.00 (ISBN 0-8369-2193-3). Ayer Co Pubs.
Prophets on the Right. Ronald Radosh. 351p. Date not set. pap. 8.00 (ISBN 0-317-53206-5). Noontide.
Prophets One. Ann Macpherson et al. Ed. by Laurence Bright. LC 71-173033. (Scripture Discussion Commentary Ser.: Pt. 2). 214p. 1971. pap. text ed. 4.95 (ISBN 0-87946-001-6). ACTA Pubns.
Prophets: Preachers for God. Tom McMinn. (BibLearn Ser.). (Illus.). (gr. 1-6). 1979. 5.95 (ISBN 0-8054-4250-2, 4242-50). Broadman.
Prophets' Report on Religion in North America. rev. ed. Peter J. Ediger. LC 78-150650. 1978. pap. 2.00 (ISBN 0-87303-686-7). Faith & Life.
Prophet's Return from Exile. Ruth W. Schuler. (Illus.). 84p. (Orig.). 1984. pap. 4.00 (ISBN 0-910083-17-7). Heritage Trails.
Prophet's Song & Other Poems. Michele Gallatin. LC 87-32666. 54p. 1987. pap. 3.75 (ISBN 0-943851-09-2, ProForma Bks). QED Pr Ann Arbor.
Prophets Speak to Our Time. George Drew. 62p. (Orig.). 1981. pap. 6.95 (ISBN 0-940754-09-6). Ed Ministries.
Prophet's Speech at Tabuk. abr. ed. Abdullah. 16p. (Orig.). 1984. pap. 1.00 (ISBN 0-916157-02-4). African Islam Miss Pubns.
Prophet's Stories. Abul H. Ali-Nadawi. Ed. by Hamid Quinlan. Tr. by Kamal El-Helbawy from Arabic. LC 82-70453. (Illus.). 200p. (Orig.). Date not set. pap. 5.00 (ISBN 0-89259-038-6). Am Trust Pubns.
Prophets-Their Times & Social Ideas: A Marxist Interpretation of Old Testament Radicalism. Shmuel Eisenstadt. Tr. by Max Rosenfeld from Yiddish. 1971. Repr. of 1926 ed. 17.95 (ISBN 0-88286-103-4). C H Kerr.
Prophets True & False. Oswald G. Villard. LC 75-93384. (Essay Index Reprint Ser). 1928. 27.50 (ISBN 0-8369-1386-8). Ayer Co Pubs.
Prophets Two. Francis McDonagh et al. LC 71-173033. (Scripture Discussion Commentary Ser.: Pt. 4). 184p. 1972. pap. text ed. 4.95 (ISBN 0-87946-003-2). ACTA Pubns.
Prophets, Volume One. Klaus Koch. Tr. by Margaret Kohl from Ger. LC 79-8894. 224p. 1982. pap. 10.95 (ISBN 0-8006-1648-0, 1-1648). Vol. 1, The Assyrian Age. Fortress.
Prophets, Volume Two: The Babylonian & Persian Period. Klaus Koch. LC 79-8894. 224p. 1984. pap. 10.95 (ISBN 0-8006-1756-8, 1-1756). Fortress.
Prophets with Honour: A Documentary History of Lekhotla la Bafo. Bob Edgar. 304p. 1987. pap. text ed. 19.95x (ISBN 0-86975-312-6, Pub. by Ravan Pr.). Ohio U Pr.
Propheysing the Visitation of Destruction in Our Nation. Alex Riley & Diane Riley. Date not set. 12.00. Alexian Pr.
Prophylactic Approach to Hypertensive Disease. Ed. by Yukio Yamori et al. (Perspectives in Cardiovascular Research Ser.: Vol. 4). 624p. 1979. 104.50 (ISBN 0-89004-339-6). Raven.
Prophylaxis of Infectious & Other Diseases by Means of Vaccination & the Use of Immunoglobulins. Ed. by T. M. Inderbitzin. (Monographs in Allergy: Vol. 9). (Illus.). 300p. 1975. 50.75 (ISBN 3-8055-1779-3). S Karger.
Prophyry the Philosopher to Marcella. Kathleen O. Wicker. LC 87-23077. (SBL: Texts & Translations Ser.). 205p. 1987. 22.95 (ISBN 1-55540-138-4, 06-02-28); pap. 14.95 (ISBN 1-55540-139-2). Scholars Pr GA.
Propisnaia Ili Strochnaia? D. E. Rozental' 328p. (Rus.). 1985. 39.00x (ISBN 0-317-42777-6, Pib by Collets (UK)). State Mutual Bk.
Propitious Speech from the Beginning, Middle & End. Patrul Rinpoche. Tr. by Thinley Norbu from Tibetan. 46p. (Orig.). 1984. pap. 8.00 (ISBN 0-9607000-6-4). Jewel Pub Hse.
Propjet 1988. Harry Adams & R. W. Simpson. (Illus.). 148p. 1988. pap. 9.95 (ISBN 0-317-57095-1, Pub. by AvCom Intl). Aviation.
Propjet 1988. Harry B. Adams. (Illus.). 170p. 1988. pap. 9.95 (ISBN 0-941024-08-3). Avcom Intl.
Propolis, the Eternal Natural Healer. 1981. 5.95 (ISBN 0-9600356-4-8). F Murat.
Proponents of Limited Monarchy in Sixteenth Century France. Beatrice Reynolds. LC 68-58616. (Columbia University. Studies in the Social Sciences: No. 334). Repr. of 1931 ed. 18.50 (ISBN 0-404-51334-4). AMS Pr.
Proportion. Allan D. Suter. (Programmed Math Ser.). (Illus.). 30p. (Orig.). (gr. 3-12). 1986. pap. text ed. 3.95 (ISBN 0-945915-21-7). Programmed Lrn.
Proportional Grade Workshop Manual. 95p. 5.00 (ISBN 0-318-17523-1); members free. Footwear Indus.
Proportional Misrepresentation. Peter Hain. (Wildwood House Ser.). 140p. 1986. pap. text ed. 8.95 (ISBN 0-7045-0526-6, Pub. by Gower Pub England). Gower Pub Co.
Proportional Representation. 2nd ed. John R. Commons. LC 66-21662. 1967. Repr. of 1907 ed. 37.50x (ISBN 0-678-00222-3). Kelley.
Proportional Representation. Clarence G. Hoag & George A. Hallett. (Political Science Ser). 1969. Repr. of 1926 ed. 36.00 (ISBN 0-384-23670-7). Johnson Repr.
Proportional Representation in Presidential Nominating Politics. Paul T. David & James W. Ceasar. LC 79-4387. xv, 298p. 1980. 20.00x (ISBN 0-8139-0787-X). U Pr of Va.
Proportional Representation: The Key to Democracy. George H. Hallett. LC 79-1629. 1980. Repr. of 1940 ed. 19.25 (ISBN 0-88355-933-1). Hyperion Conn.
Proportional Spacing on WordStar. 4th ed. Writing Consultants Staff et al. 98p. 1984. pap. text ed. 22.50 (ISBN 0-931295-00-9). Microlytics.
Proportionalism: The American Debate & Its European Roots. Bernard Hoose. (Orig.). 1987. 22.95 (ISBN 0-87840-454-6); pap. 10.95 (ISBN 0-87840-455-4). Georgetown U Pr.
Proportioning Concrete Mixes. 240p. 1974. 38.75 (ISBN 0-317-32085-8, SP-46). ACI.
Proportions of the Aesthetic Face. Nelson Powell & Brian Humphreys. (American Academy of Facial Plastic & Reconstructive Surgery Monograph Ser.). (Illus.). 96p. 1983. 39.95 (ISBN 0-86577-117-0). Thieme Med Pubs.
Propos me Concernant: Avec: Berne-Joffe-Roy, Presence de Valery. Paul Valery. 236p. 1944. 12.50 (ISBN 0-686-55113-3). French & Eur.
Proposal. Laurence Craig-Green. (Illus.). 32p. 1983. pap. 4.50 (ISBN 0-916922-05-7). Poet Tree Pr.
Proposal & Analysis of a Unitary System for Review of Criminal Justice. National Center for State Courts Staff. 30p. (On loan through the NCSC Library). 1974. write for info. (MAB-088). Natl Ctr St Courts.
Proposal & Bid Preparation for Construction. Stewart. 1988. price not set (ISBN 0-471-63424-7). Wiley.
Proposal Development: A Winning Approach. Bud Porter-Roth. (Successful Business Library)). 200p. 1986. 3-ring binder 33.95 (ISBN 0-916378-67-5, Oasis). PSI Res.
Proposal for Correcting the English Tongue, Polite Conversations, etc. Jonathan Swift. Ed. by Herbert Davis & L. Landa. (Prose Writings of Jonathan Swift Ser.). 350p. 1986. text ed. 60.00x (ISBN 0-631-00210-3). Basil Blackwell.
Proposal for Deaf Education in Nepal. Krishna R. Khatri. 85p. 1984. 8.50 (ISBN 0-318-04167-7). Am-Nepal Ed.
Proposal for Limiting the Duty of the Trial Judge to Instruct the Jury Sua Sponte. National Center for State Courts Staff. 29p. 1974. manuscript 1.74 (MAB-090). Natl Ctr St Courts.
Proposal for Putting Reform to the Vote Throughout the Kingdom. Percy Bysshe Shelley. LC 74-30280. (Shelley Society, Extra Ser.: No. 5). Repr. of 1887 ed. 20.00 (ISBN 0-404-11523-3). AMS Pr.
Proposal for the Design of a Caseflow Management System, Superior Court. National Center for State Courts Staff. 53p. 1975. manuscript 3.18 (MAB-089). Natl Ctr St Courts.
Proposal for the Establishment of Neighborhood Centers for Music Instruction. Herbert Zipper. 1969. 10.00 (ISBN 0-318-21717-1). NGCSA.
Proposal: Key to an Effective Foreign Policy. Max F. Millikan & W. W. Rostow. LC 76-39842. 1977. Repr. of 1957 ed. lib. bdg. 35.00x (ISBN 0-8371-9346-X, MIAPR). Greenwood.
Proposal Management Using the Modular Technique. Rugh & Manning. LC 84-60601. 136p. 1982. 23.95 (ISBN 0-932146-07-4). Peninsula CA.
Proposal Preparation. Rodney D. Stewart & Ann L. Stewart. LC 83-19827. 319p. 1984. 41.95x (ISBN 0-471-87288-1). Wiley.
Proposal Preparation Process: The Systems Approach. William C. Wall, Jr. LC 86-8557. 117p. 1986. pap. 14.95 spiral bdg. (ISBN 0-938745-00-X). McMallec Pub.
Proposal Writer's Swipe File. Ed. by Susan Ezell-Kalish et al. LC 81-50258. 162p. 1981. pap. 16.95 (ISBN 0-914756-45-1). Taft Group.
Proposal Writing for the Data Processing Consultant. William H. Roetzheim. (Illus.). 224p. 1986. text ed. 29.00 (ISBN 0-13-731381-0). P-H.
Proposal Writing Guide. Norman T. Bell et al. 1984. 9.95. Radio Shack.
Proposal Writing: The Art of Friendly Persuasion. William S. Pfeiffer. 224p. 1988. pap. 14.95 (ISBN 0-675-20988-9). Merrill.
Proposals Affecting Corporate Takeovers: 1985, 99th Congress, 1st Session. American Enterprise Institute for Public Policy Research Staff. LC 86-104191. 74p. 1985. 6.00 (ISBN 0-8447-0270-6). Am Enterprise.
Proposals & Contracts for Library Automation: Guidelines for Preparing RFPs. Edwin M. Cortez. 225p. 1987. pap. 29.00 (ISBN 0-913203-17-3). Pacific Info.
Proposals & Contracts for Library Automation: Guidelines for Preparing RFPs. Edwin M. Cortez. 135p. 1987. pap. text ed. 29.00x (ISBN 0-8389-2043-8). ALA.
Proposals & Their Preparation. Ed. by Gerald A. Mann. (Anthology Ser., No. 1). 1973. 25.00x (ISBN 0-914548-06-9). Soc Tech Comm.
Proposals for Carrying on Certain Public Works in the City of Edinburgh. Gilbert Elliot. LC 78-72778. (Scottish Enlightenment Ser.). Repr. of 1752 ed. 18.50 (ISBN 0-404-17629-1). AMS Pr.
Proposals for Establishing a Public Place of Reception for Penitent Prostitutes. Robert Dingley. LC 83-48597. (Marriage, Sex & the Family in England Ser.). 454p. 1984. lib. bdg. 55.00. Garland Pub.

TITLE INDEX PROSE OF FULKE GREVILLE

Proposals for Line-Item Veto Authority: Legislative Analysis. 30p. 1984. 6.00 (ISBN 0-8447-0256-0). Am Enterprise.

Proposals for Reform of Deposit Insurance System: 1985. Les Analysis. 51p. 1985. 6.00 (ISBN 0-8447-0271-4). Am Enterprise.

Proposals for Reform of Export Controls for Advanced Technology: Legislative Analysis. 32p. 1979. 6.00 (ISBN 0-8447-0220-X). Am Enterprise.

Proposals for the Publisher Seventeen Hundred & Forty-Four. Samuel Johnson. Repr. of 1930 ed. 17.50 (ISBN 0-8414-5389-6). Folcroft.

Proposals on Corporate Acquisitions & Dispositions & Reporter's Study On Corporate Distributions: Subchapter J, Tentative Draft, No. 9. (Federal Income Tax Project SEr.). 160p. 1982. 15.00 (ISBN 0-686-91075-3). Am Law Inst.

Proposals That Work: A Guide for Planning Dissertations & Grant Proposals. 2nd ed. Lawrence F. Locke et al. 264p. 1987. text ed. 29.95 (ISBN 0-8039-2986-2); pap. text ed. 12.95 (ISBN 0-8039-2987-0). Sage.

Proposals to Deregulate Depository Institutions: Legislative Analysis. 66p. 1984. 6.00 (ISBN 0-8447-0255-2). Am Enterprise.

Proposals to Establish a Department of Trade: Legislative Analysis. 49p. 1984. 6.00 (ISBN 0-8447-0258-7). Am Enterprise.

Proposals to Reform Drug Regulation Laws. 50p. 1979. pap. 6.00 (ISBN 0-8447-0223-4). Am Enterprise.

Proposals to Revise the Lobbying Law: Legislative Analysis. 52p. 1980. 6.00 (ISBN 0-8447-0226-9). Am Enterprise.

Proposed Act to Regulate Legal Expense Insurance. American Bar Foundation Staff. 46p. 1981. pap. 2.00 (ISBN 0-317-63647-2, 765-0030-01). Amer Bar Assn.

Proposed Administrative & Accounting System of a Catering Industry & a Study of Past Three Years Operation & Five Years Strategy. Ejaz A. Khan. 120p. 1985. 5.30 (ISBN 0-89697-268-2). Intl Univ Pr.

Proposed Amendments to the Constitution: A Monograph on the Resolutions Introduced in Congress Proposing Amendments to the Constitution of the United States of America. Michael A. Musmanno. LC 75-35374. (U. S. Government Documents Program Ser.). 253p. 1976. Repr. of 1929 ed. lib. bdg. 35.00x (ISBN 0-8371-8610-2, MUPAC). Greenwood.

Proposed Amendments to the Constitution of the U. S., During the First Century of Its History. Herman V. Ames. LC 73-135173. 1970. Repr. of 1896 ed. lib. bdg. 26.00 (ISBN 0-8337-0060-X). B Franklin.

Proposed Amendments to the Constitution of the United States: During the First Century of Its History. Herman V. Ames. 1896. 26.00. Ayer Co Pubs.

Proposed Amendments to the Federal Rules of Evidence. Litigation Section. 155p. 1985. 25.00. Amer Bar Assn.

Proposed Case Processing Time Standards for California's Superior Courts. 193p. 1987. 12.00 (WRO-088). Natl Ctr St Courts.

Proposed Constitutional Amendments & Referred Laws, 1968. Ronald Schmidt. 1968. 1.00 (ISBN 1-55614-097-5). U. of SD Gov Res Bur.

Proposed Debarment & Suspension Reform Act. 155p. 1982. spiral 15.00 (ISBN 0-686-48255-7). Amer Bar Assn.

Proposed Estate Plan for Mr. & Mrs. Richard Harry Black III. rev. ed. A. James Casner. 1983. pap. 18.00 looseleaf (ISBN 0-316-13162-8). Little.

Proposed Federal Securities Code: Proceedings of the Federal Bar Association, Conference, October 1980. Federal Bar Association, Conference Staff. 431p. 45.00 (ISBN 0-318-14074-8, FI-80-2). Federal Bar.

Proposed Funds Statements for Managers & Investors. Harold E. Arnett. 137p. pap. 15.95 (ISBN 0-86641-019-8, 79114). Natl Assn Accts.

Proposed Judicial Article for the Constitution of the State of Washington. National Center for State Courts Staff. 107p. 1976. manuscript 6.42 (MAB-091). Natl Ctr St Courts.

Proposed Model for Visual Information Processing in the Human Brain. Matthew Kabrisky. LC 66-10343. pap. 28.50 (2014937). Bks Demand UMI.

Proposed One-Trial-One-Day Jury System for the Courts Serving Maricopa County, Arizona: Final Report. National Center for State Courts Staff. 77p. 1985. manuscript 5.00 (CJS-008). Natl Ctr St Courts.

Proposed One-Trial-One-Day Jury System for the Courts Serving Maricopa County, Arizona: Data Appendix. National Center for State Courts Staff. 71p. 1985. manuscript 5.00 (CJS-009). Natl Ctr St Courts.

Proposed Pennsylvanian System Stratotype. West Virginia & Virginia. Kenneth J. Englund et al. LC 78-74893. 1979. pap. 20.00 (ISBN 0-913312-08-8). Am Geol.

Proposed Procedures for a Limited Constitutional Convention: 1984, 98th Congress, 2d Session. American Enterprise Institute for Public Policy Research Staff. LC 84-244484. 40p. 1984. 3.95 (ISBN 0-8447-0262-5). Am Enterprise.

Proposed Records Retention Schedule for the First Circuit Court of Hawaii. 26p. 1986. 2.00 (ISBN 0-317-59191-6, WRO-070). Natl Ctr St Courts.

Proposed Revision of Rules of Supreme Court & Appellate Session of Superior Court: To Implement Centralized Processing of Appeals in Connecticut. National Center for State Courts Staff. 80p. 1977. manuscript 4.80 (NERO-037). Natl Ctr St Courts.

Proposed Rules of Judicial Administration for Alabama Trial Courts. National Center for State Courts Staff. 68p. 1976. manuscript 4.08 (MAB-092). Natl Ctr St Courts.

Proposed Rules of Professional Conduct: Recommended to the District of Columbia Court of Appeals Nov. 19, 1986. Long Version. 11.50 (ISBN 0-317-62716-3); Short Version. 9.50 (ISBN 0-317-62717-1). DC Bar Assn.

Proposed Standard for Acoustic Emission Examinations During Application of Pressure. 1975. pap. text ed. 2.50 (ISBN 0-685-62574-5, E00096). ASME.

Proposed Standards for Appellate Court Statistics: Report of the Appellate Statistics Committee, ABA Appellate Judges' Conference. National Center for State Courts Staff. 72p. (On loan through the NCSC Library). 1973. write for info. (MAB-093). Natl Ctr St Courts.

Proposed State of Sequoyah see Constitution of the State of Sequoyah.

Proposed System for Food Safety Assessment: A Comprehensive Report on the Issues of Food Ingredient Testing. new ed. Ed. by Food Safety Council, Columbia, U. S. A. Staff. LC 78-40901. (Illus.). 1979. pap. 34.00 (ISBN 0-08-023752-5). Pergamon.

Proposed Yosemite National Park: Treasures & Features. John Muir. Ed. by William R. Jones. (Illus.). 64p. 1976. pap. text ed. 2.95 (ISBN 0-89646-077-0). Outbooks.

Proposition Fourteen: A Secessionist Remedy. Richard Cummings. LC 80-8917. 128p. (Orig.). 1981. pap. 3.95 (ISBN 0-394-17890-4, E776, BC). Grove.

Proposition Fourteen: A Secessionist Remedy. Richard Cummings. LC 80-80357. 128p. 1980. 11.95 (ISBN 0-932966-09-8); pap. 7.50 (ISBN 0-932966-16-0). Permanent Pr.

Proposition Thirteen: A First Anniversary Assessment. (Lincoln Institute Monograph: No. 80-5). (Illus.). 1980. pap. text ed. 5.00 (ISBN 0-686-29506-4). Lincoln Inst Land.

Proposition Thirteen & Its Consequences for Public Management. Council for Applied Social Research Staff. Ed. by Selma J. Mushkin. LC 79-65017. 1979. 20.00 (ISBN 0-89011-536-2). Abt Bks.

Proposition Thirteen & Its Consequences for Public Management. Ed. by Selma J. Mushkin. 186p. 1984. Repr. of 1979 ed. lib. bdg. 20.00 (ISBN 0-8191-4116-X). U Pr of Amer.

Proposition Thirteen in the Nineteen Seventy-Eight California Primary: A Pre-Election Bibliography. Ed. by Terry J. Dean & Ronald J. Heckart. LC 79-12651. (Occasional Bibliographies Ser.: No. 1). (Orig.). 1979. pap. 6.00x (ISBN 0-87772-267-6). UCB IGS.

Proposition Thirteen in the Nineteen Seventy-Eight California Primary: A Post-Election Bibliography. Compiled by Ronald J. Heckart & Terry J. Dean. LC 80-27111. (Occasional Bibliographies Ser.: No. 2). 168p. 1982. pap. 13.00x (ISBN 0-87772-278-1). UCB IGS.

Proposition Two & One Half: Its Impact on Massachusetts. Lawrence J. Suskind. LC 83-6298. 528p. 1983. 30.00 (ISBN 0-89946-174-3); pap. 17.50 (ISBN 0-89946-175-1). Oelgeschlager.

Propositional Logic of Avicenne. Ed. by N. Shehaby. LC 73-75642. (Synthese Historical Library: No. 7). 1973. lib. bdg. 45.00 (ISBN 90-277-0360-4, Pub. by Reidel Holland). Kluwer Academic.

Propositional Logical Thinking & Comprehension of Language Connectives: A Developmental Analysis. Scott G. Paris. LC 74-75824. (Janua Linguarum, Series Minor: No. 216). (Illus.). 101p. 1975. pap. text ed. 12.00x (ISBN 90-2793-197-6). Mouton.

Propositional Structure & Illocutionary Force: A Study of the Contribution of Sentence Meaning to Speech Acts. Jerrold J. Katz. (Language & Thought Ser). (Illus.). 264p. 1980. pap. 9.95x (ISBN 0-674-71615-9). Harvard U Pr.

Propositions & Attitudes. Ed. by Nathan Salmon & Scott Soames. (Readings in Philosophy Ser.). 296p. 1988. 39.95 (ISBN 0-19-875092-7); pap. text ed. 16.95 (ISBN 0-19-875091-9). Oxford U Pr.

Propositions Concerning Protection & Free Trade. Willard Phillips. LC 67-29515. 1968. Repr. of 1850 ed. 29.50x (ISBN 0-678-00369-6). Kelley.

Propositions on the Dignity & Rights of the Human Person. Tr. by Miceal Ledwith from Lat. (International Theological Commission Ser.). 28p. (Orig.). 1986. pap. 1.95 (ISBN 1-55586-997-1). US Catholic.

Propped & Cantilevered Rigid Walls. 104p. 1986. 33.00 (ISBN 0-7277-0271-8, Pub. by T Telford UK). Am Soc Civil Eng.

Propranolol & Schizophrenia: Proceedings. Conference on Propranolol & Schizophrenia, Santa Ynez, Calif., Dec. 5-8, 1976 et al. Ed. by Eugene Roberts & Peter Amacher. LC 78-1781. (Kroc Foundation Ser.: Vol. 10). 162p. 1978. 27.00 (ISBN 0-8451-0300-8). A R Liss.

Proprietary Capitalism: The Textile Manufacture at Philadelphia, 1800-1885. Philip Scranton. 444p. 1987. pap. 12.95 (ISBN 0-87722-461-7). Temple U Pr.

Proprietary Capitalism: The Textile Manufacture at Philadelphia, 1800-1885. Philip B. Scranton. LC 83-10155. (Illus.). 480p. 1984. 39.50 (ISBN 0-521-25245-8). Cambridge U Pr.

Proprietary Network Architectures. K. C. Gee. 250p. 1981. pap. 109.25 (ISBN 0-471-89423-0). Wiley.

Proprietary Protective Signaling Systems. (Seventy Ser.). 56p. 1974. pap. 3.00 (ISBN 0-685-44175-X, 72D). Natl Fire Prot.

Propriete Fonciere en Grece Jusqua a Conquete Romaine. Paul Guiraud. Ed. by Gregory Vlastos. LC 78-19357. (Morals & Law in Ancient Greece Ser.). 1979. Repr. of 1893 ed. lib. bdg. 46.00x (ISBN 0-405-11549-0). Ayer Co Pubs.

Proprieties & Vagaries: A Philosophical Thesis from Science, Horse Racing, Sexual Customs, Religion, & Politics. Albert L. Hammod. LC 61-13245. pap. 70.50 (ISBN 0-317-08939-0, 2003867). Bks Demand UMi.

Proprietor, Proprietary. abr. ed. Luanna C. Blagrove. (Illus.). 250p. 1988. 24.95 (ISBN 0-939776-19-7). Blagrove Pubns.

Proprietor's Daughter. Lewis Orde. 1988. 18.95 (ISBN 0-316-67340-4). Little.

Proprietors of Carolina. William S. Powell. (Illus.). vi, 70p. 1968. pap. 2.00 (ISBN 0-86526-101-6). NC Archives.

Proprietors, Patronage, & Paper Money: Legislative Politics in New Jersey, 1703-1776. Thomas L. Purvis. LC 85-27895. 360p. 1986. lib. bdg. 38.00 (ISBN 0-8135-1161-5). Rutgers U Pr.

Proprietorship of Maryland: A Documented Account. Vera F. Rollo. LC 87-43200. 550p. 1988. 49.75 (ISBN 0-917882-26-1). MD Hist Pr.

Propriety & Position: A Study of Victorian Manners. Michael Curtin. Ed. by William H. McNeill & Peter Stansky. (Modern European History Ser.). 350p. 1987. lib. bdg. 55.00 (ISBN 0-8240-7803-9). Garland Pub.

Proprioceptive Neuromuscular Facilitation. 3rd ed. Voss. LC 84-25958. 1985. 37.50 (ISBN 0-06-142595-8, Lippincott Medical). Lippincott.

Proprioceptive Neuromuscular Facilitation. 3rd ed. Voss. LC 14-25958. Date not set. 37.50. Lippincott.

Propulsion. Ed. by Flanagan. 1988. 36.00 (ISBN 0-89252-907-5, 872). SPIE.

Propylaia to the Athenian Akropolis Vol. 1: The Predecessors. William B. Dinsmoor, Jr. LC 79-9232. (Illus.). 1980. 12.50x (ISBN 0-87661-940-5). Am Sch Athens.

Propylene Oxide. (Environmental Health Criteria Ser.: No. 56). 53p. 1986. pap. 4.80 (ISBN 92-4-154196-2). World Health.

Proryv. Grigory Svirsky. LC 83-8928. 560p. (Rus.). 1983. pap. 18.00 (ISBN 0-938920-44-8). Hermitage.

Pros & Cons. Bethany Campbell. (Intrigue Ser.: No. 65). Date not set. pap. 2.25 (ISBN 0-317-63672-3). Harlequin Bks.

Pros & Cons in Financial Management for Professionals. Victor I. Eber. LC 71-166924. (Illus.). 12.95 (ISBN 0-686-20664-9). Financial Pr.

Pros & Cons of Ability Grouping. Warren Findley & Miriam Bryan. LC 75-19963. (Fastback Ser.: No. 66). 1975. pap. 0.90 (ISBN 0-87367-066-3). Phi Delta Kappa.

Pros & Cons of Merit Pay. Susan M. Johnson. LC 83-83085. (Fastback Ser.: No. 203). 50p. 1984. pap. 0.90 (ISBN 0-87367-203-8). Phi Delta Kappa.

Pros & Cons of Third World Multinationals: A Case Study of India. Jamuna P. Agarwal. 115p. 1985. lib. bdg. 42.50x (ISBN 3-16-344994-8, Pub. by J C B Mohr BRD). Coronet Bks.

Prosa de la Espana Moderna. Marvin Wasserman & Carol Wasserman. (gr. 11). 1972. pap. text ed. 9.08 (ISBN 0-87720-517-5). AMSCO Sch.

Prosa de Luis Lloren Torres: Estudio y Antologia. Daisy Caraballo. LC 83-27416. xiv, 286p. 1985. pap. 10.50 (ISBN 0-8477-3802-7). U of PR Pr.

Prosa der Gegenwart. Gudrum Isaak & Susan Ray. pap. 10.95. Langenscheidt.

Prosa Hispanoamericana: Evolucion y Antologia. Ed. by Jose Promis & Jorge Roman-Lagunas. LC 88-18742. 502p. (Orig.). 1988. lib. bdg. 37.75 (ISBN 0-8191-7098-4); pap. text ed. 25.50 (ISBN 0-8191-7099-2). U Pr of Amer.

Prosareden des Jeremiabuches. Helga Weippert. LC 72-76045. (Beiheft 132 zur Zeitschrift fuer die alttestamentliche Wissenschaft). (Ger.). 1973. 55.00x (ISBN 3-11-003867-6). De Gruyter.

Prosatori del Novecento. Michele Cantarella. (For 4th-5th semesters). (gr. 10-12). 1967. text ed. 16.95 (ISBN 0-03-055190-0, HoltE). HR&W.

Prose. Paul Claudel. Ed. by Petit & Galperine. (Bibliotheque De la Pleiade). 1965. 80.95 (ISBN 0-685-11455-4). French & Eur.

Prose. Edward R. Sill. LC 70-117844. (Essay Index Reprint Ser.). 1900. 21.50 (ISBN 0-8369-1683-2). Ayer Co Pubs.

Prose & Cons. Felix Pollak. (Juniper Bks.: No. 44). 1983. pap. 5.00 (ISBN 1-55780-043-X). Juniper Pr WI.

Prose & Cons: The Do's & Don'ts of Technical & Business Writing. Carol M. Barnum. 156p. 1986. pap. text ed. 9.95x (ISBN 0-935920-29-3). Natl Pub Black Hills.

Prose & Passion. Gary Gabriel. (Illus.). 166p. (gr. 9-12). 1981. pap. text ed. 7.25 (ISBN 0-13-731159-1, 18838); tchr's. ed. 8.75 (ISBN 0-13-731167-2, 18839); cassettes 12.00 (ISBN 0-13-731175-3, 58840). Prentice ESL.

Prose & Poetic Expression of a Black Woman. Marie D. Ransom. Ed. by Mosezelle N. White. LC 80-54319. 40p. (gr. 7 up). 1984. pap. 5.95x (ISBN 0-936026-13-8). R&M Pub Co.

Prose & Poetry. Stephen Crane. Ed. by J. C. Levenson. Incl. Maggie: A Girl of the Streets; Red Badge of Courage; George's Mother; Third Violet. LC 83-19908. 1379p. 1985. 27.50 (ISBN 0-940450-17-8). Library of America.

Prose & Poetry. Alice C. Meynell. LC 76-117824. (Essay Index Reprint Ser.). 1947. 18.00 (ISBN 0-8369-1983-1). Ayer Co Pubs.

Prose & Poetry, Vol. 4, No. 1. Ed. by Ann L. Dunnington. 1978. pap. 2.50 (ISBN 0-916912-33-7). Hellcoal Pr.

Prose & Poetry of Elinor Wylie. William R. Benet. 1978. Repr. of 1934 ed. lib. bdg. 22.50 (ISBN 0-8495-0356-6). Arden Lib.

Prose & Poetry of Elinor Wylie. William R. Benet. LC 73-1300. 1973. lib. bdg. 15.00 (ISBN 0-8414-1799-7). Folcroft.

Prose & Poetry of Modern Sweden: An Intermediate Swedish Reader. Gosta Franzen. LC 70-78815. x, 155p. 1969. 14.95x (ISBN 0-8032-0047-1). U of Nebr Pr.

Prose & Poetry of the Revolution. Frederick C. Prescott & John H. Nelson. 1973. Repr. of 1925 ed. 12.00 (ISBN 0-8274-1635-0). R West.

Prose & Poetry of the Revolution. Ed. by Frederick C. Prescott & John H. Nelson. LC 68-26293. Repr. of 1925 ed. 23.00x (ISBN 0-8046-0371-5, Pub. by Kennikat). Assoc Faculty Pr.

Prose Characters of Richard Flecknoe: A Critical Edition. Fred Mayer. Ed. by Stephen Orgel. (Satire & Sense Ser.). 628p. 1987. lib. bdg. 95.00 (ISBN 0-8240-6019-9). Garland Pub.

Prose Comprehension Beyond the Word. A. C. Graesser. (Illus.). 310p. 1981. 41.00 (ISBN 0-387-90544-8). Springer-Verlag.

Prose Edda of Snorri Sturluson: Tales from Norse Mythology. Snorri Sturluson. Tr. by Jean I. Young. 1964. pap. 7.95x (ISBN 0-520-01232-1). U of Cal Pr.

Prose, Essays, Poems. Gottfried Benn. Ed. by Richard Becker & Wolkmar Sander. (German Library: Vol. 73). 320p. 1987. 27.50x (ISBN 0-8264-0310-7); pap. 10.95x (ISBN 0-8264-0311-5). Continuum.

Prose Fiction of the Cuban Revolution. Seymour Menton. LC 75-5993. (Latin American Monographs: No. 37). 362p. 1975. 20.00x (ISBN 0-292-76421-9). U of Tex Pr.

Prose Fiction of Veniamin A. Kaverin. Hongor Oulanoff. v, 203p. 1976. pap. 12.95 (ISBN 0-89357-032-X). Slavica.

Prose from the Book That Was Not Published in 1968. Lev Navrozov. 112p. (Orig.). 1984. pap. 9.50 (ISBN 0-914265-00-8). New Eng Pub Ma.

Prose Life of Alexander from the Thorton Ms. (EETS, OS Ser.: No. 143). Repr. of 1911 ed. 25.00 (ISBN 0-527-00139-2). Kraus Repr.

Prose Lives of Women Saints of Our Contrie of England. Ed. by C. Horstmann. (EETS, OS Ser.: No.86). Repr. of 1886 ed. 38.00. Kraus Repr.

Prose Masterpieces from Modern Essayists, 3 Vols. LC 79-121500. (Essay Index Reprint Ser). 1915. 42.50 (ISBN 0-8369-1773-1). Ayer Co Pubs.

Prose Miscellanies. Thomas E. Watson. (Studies in Populism). 1980. lib. bdg. 69.95 (ISBN 0-87700-321-1). Revisionist Pr.

Prose Miscellany. Keith Douglas. 159p. 1985. 20.00 (ISBN 0-85635-526-7). Carcanet.

Prose Models. 7th ed. Gerald Levin. 578p. 1987. pap. text ed. 13.95 (ISBN 0-15-572284-0). HarBraceJ.

Prose Observations. Samuel Butler. Ed. by Hugh De Quehen. (Oxford English Texts Ser.). (Illus.). 1979. text ed. 95.00x (ISBN 0-19-812728-6). Oxford U Pr.

Prose Ocean. Gus Blaisdell. (Illus.). 1975. perfect bound in wrappers 3.00 (ISBN 0-685-78877-6, Pub. by Bear Hug). Small Pr Dist.

Prose of Edward Rowland Sill: With an Introduction Comprising Some Familiar Letters. Edward R. Sill. 1900. Repr. 20.00 (ISBN 0-8274-3213-5). R West.

Prose of Edward Thomas. Compiled by Roland Gant. 228p. 1981. Repr. of 1948 ed. lib. bdg. 25.00 (ISBN 0-89984-455-3). Century Bookbindery.

Prose of Emerson. Andre Caliered. 1978. Repr. of 1936 ed. lib. bdg. 15.00 (ISBN 0-8495-0740-5). Arden Lib.

Prose of Fact. Michael Davidson. 1981. 5.00 (ISBN 0-935724-07-9). Figures.

Prose of Fulke Greville, Lord Brooke. Ed. by Stephen Orgel. (Renaissance Imagination Ser.). 334p. 1987. lib. bdg. 50.00 (ISBN 0-8240-8405-5). Garland Pub.

Prose of John Clare. J. W. Tibble & Anne Tibble. 1973. Repr. of 1951 ed. 20.00 (ISBN 0-8274-0508-1). R West.

Prose of Jorge Luis Borges: Existentialism & the Dynamics of Surprise. Ion T. Agheana. LC 84-47694. (American University Studies II (Romance Languages & Literature): Vol. 13). 336p. (Orig.). 1984. pap. text ed. 31.85 (ISBN 0-8204-0130-7). P Lang Pubs.

Prose of Milton. Richard Garnett. 1894. Repr. 20.00 (ISBN 0-8274-3214-3). R West.

Prose of Royall Tyler. Royall Tyler. Ed. by Marius B. Peladeau. LC 70-152113. 1971. 15.00 (ISBN 0-8048-0970-4). C E Tuttle.

Prose of Samuel Taylor Coleridge. L. M. Grow. Ed. by James Hogg. (Romantic Reassessment Ser.). 161p. (Orig.). 1976. pap. write for info. (ISBN 3-7052-0509-9, Pub. by Salzburg Studies). Longwood Pub Group.

Prose of the English Renaissance. Ed. by J. William Hebel et al. 1952. 56.00x (ISBN 0-89197-362-1). Irvington.

Prose of the Minor Connecticut Wits, 3 vols. Ed. by Benjamin Franklin. LC 74-11124. 1500p. 1974. Repr. 200.00x set (ISBN 0-8201-1132-5). Schol Facsimiles.

Prose of the Romantic Period. Ed. by Carl R. Woodring. LC 61-16304. (YA) (gr. 9 up). 1961. pap. 6.95 (ISBN 0-395-05154-1, RivEd). HM.

Prose of the Victorian Period. Ed. by William E. Buckler. (YA) (gr. 9 up). 1958. pap. 6.95 (ISBN 0-395-05128-2, RivEd). HM.

Prose of the World. Maurice Merleau-Ponty. Ed. by Claude Lefort. Tr. by John O'Neill from Fr. LC 72-96699. (Studies in Phenomenology & Existential Philosophy). 180p. 1973. text ed. 19.95 (ISBN 0-8101-0412-1); pap. 10.95 (ISBN 0-8101-0615-9). Northwestern U Pr.

Prose Pieces. Witter Bynner. Ed. by James Kraft. LC 78-11441. 430p. 1979. 25.00 (ISBN 0-374-23833-2). FS&G.

Prose Pieces. John Riley. 1974. signed 4.00 (ISBN 0-685-78926-8, Pub. by Grosseteste); sewn in wrappers 2.00 (ISBN 0-685-78927-6). Small Pr Dist.

Prose Poem As a Genre in Nineteenth-Century European Literature. John Simon. Ed. by James J. Wilhelm & Richard Saez. (Harvard Dissertations in Comparative Literature Ser.). 730p. 1987. lib. bdg. 110.00 (ISBN 0-8240-8435-7). Garland Pub.

Prose Poem in France: Theory & Practice. Ed. by Mary A. Caws & Hermine Riffaterre. LC 82-20691. 256p. 1983. 36.00x (ISBN 0-231-05434-3); pap. 17.00x (ISBN 0-231-05435-1). Columbia U Pr.

Prose Poems. Kahlil Gibran. (Illus.). 1947. 9.95 (ISBN 0-394-40434-3). Knopf.

Prose, Poems & Parodies. Percy French. Ed. by De Burgh Daly. 204p. (Orig.). 1980. pap. 6.95 (ISBN 0-86167-091-4, Pub. by Educ Co of Ireland). Longwood Pub Group.

Prose Poems from Les Illuminations of Arthur Rimbaud. Jean N. Rimbaud. Tr. by Helen Rootham. LC 77-11478. Repr. of 1932 ed. 13.50 (ISBN 0-404-16339-4). AMS Pr.

Prose Poetry. Sydna Brooks. 14p. 1983. 2.00x (ISBN 0-86516-025-2). Bolchazy-Carducci.

Prose, Poetry & Drama for Oral Interpretation, First Ser. facs. ed. Ed. by William J. Farma. LC 73-139759. (Granger Index Reprint Ser). 1930. 27.00 (ISBN 0-8369-6213-3). Ayer Co Pubs.

Prose, Poetry & Drama for Oral Interpretation. William J. Farma. 1930. Repr. 25.00 (ISBN 0-8274-3215-1). R West.

Prose, Poetry & Drama for Oral Interpretation, Second Ser. facsimile ed. Ed. by William J. Farma. LC 73-139759. (Granger Index Reprint Ser). 1936. 27.00 (ISBN 0-8369-6223-0). Ayer Co Pubs.

Prose, Poetry, & Flows. James J. Carter. (Illus., Orig.). 1979. pap. 4.95 (ISBN 0-937004-01-4). Unicorn NJ.

Prose Poetry of Thomas De Quincey. Lane Cooper. LC 74-6177. 1902. lib. bdg. 15.00 (ISBN 0-8414-3595-2). Folcroft.

Prose Quotations from Socrates to Macaulay. Samuel Allibone. 59.95 (ISBN 0-8490-0902-2). Gordon Pr.

Prose Quotations from Socrates to Macauley. Samuel A. Allibone. LC 68-30642. 764p. 1973. Repr. of 1876 ed. 37.00x (ISBN 0-8103-3181-0). Gale.

Prose Reader: Essays for College Writers. Kim Flachmann & Michael Flachmann. (Illus.). 576p. 1987. pap. text ed. write for info. (ISBN 0-13-731209-1). P-H.

Prose Rhythm in English. Albert C. Clark. LC 74-7411. 1913. lib. bdg. 15.00 (ISBN 0-8414-3589-8). Folcroft.

Prose-Rhythm of Demosthenes. rev. ed. Donald F. McCabe. Ed. by W. R. Connor. LC 80-2658. (Monographs in Classical Studies). 1981. lib. bdg. 25.00 (ISBN 0-405-14044-4). Ayer Co Pubs.

Prose Rhythm of Sallust & Livy. Hans Aili. (Studia Latina Stockholmiensia: No. 24). 151p. (Orig.). 1979. pap. text ed. 16.50x (ISBN 91-22-00280-4, Pub. by Almqvist & Wiksell). Coronet Bks.

Prose Salernitan Questions. Ed. by Brian Lawn. (Auctores Britannici Medii Aevi: Vol. V). 440p. 1980. 56.00 (ISBN 0-85672-630-3, Pub. by British Acad). Longwood Pub Group.

Prose Salernitan Questions: An Anonymous Collection Dealing with Science & Medicine Written by an Englishman Circa 1200, with an Appendix of Ten Related Collections. Ed. by Brian Lawn. (British Academy: Auctores Britannici Medii Aevi: Vol. V). 1979. 89.00x (ISBN 0-19-725978-2). Oxford U Pr.

Prose Sermons of the Book of Jeremiah: A Redescription of the Correspondence with Deuteronomistic Literature in Light of Recent Text-Critical Research. Louis Stulman. LC 86-1935. (Society of Biblical Literature Dissertation Ser.). 166p. 1987. 17.25 (ISBN 0-89130-960-8, 06-01-83); pap. 13.25 (ISBN 0-89130-961-6). Scholars Pr GA.

Prose Sketches & Poems: Written in the Western Country. Albert Pike. Ed. by David J. Weber. LC 86-29994. (Southwest Landmark: No. 6). (Illus.). 336p. 1987. lib. bdg. 27.50x (ISBN 0-317-60717-0); pap. 14.95 (ISBN 0-89096-323-1). Tex A&M Univ Pr.

Prose Solomon & Saturn; & Adrian & Ritheus. Ed. by James E. Cross & Thomas D. Hill. (McMaster Old English & Texts Ser.). 1982. 35.00x (ISBN 0-8020-5472-2); pap. 13.95c (ISBN 0-8020-6509-0). U of Toronto Pr.

Prose Studies in Newman. Gilbert J. Garraghan. 1915. Repr. 25.00 (ISBN 0-8274-3216-X). R West.

Prose Style: A Handbook for Writers. 4th ed. Wilfred Stone & Jess G. Bell. (Illus.). 368p. 1983. pap. 19.95 (ISBN 0-07-061734-1). McGraw.

Prose Style for the Modern Writer. Robert Miles & Marc F. Bertonasco. 1977. pap. text ed. write for info (ISBN 0-13-731521-X). P-H.

Prose Style of Emerson. Andre Celieres. 1936. lib. bdg. 25.00 (ISBN 0-8414-3624-X). Folcroft.

Prose Style of Emerson. Andre Celieres. 59.95 (ISBN 0-8490-0903-0). Gordon Pr.

Prose Style of John Jewel. David K. Weiser. Ed. by James Hogg. (Elizabethan & Renaissance Studies). 194p. (Orig.). 1973. pap. 15.00 (ISBN 3-7052-0658-3, Pub. by Salzburg Studies). Longwood Pub Group.

Prose Style of Samuel Johnson. William K. Wimsatt, Jr. LC 78-179568. (Yale Studies in English Ser.: No. 94). xvi, 166p. 1972. Repr. of 1941 ed. 21.00 (ISBN 0-208-01141-2, Archon). Shoe String.

Prose Tales. facsimile ed. Aleksandr Pushkin. Tr. by T. Keane from Rus. LC 78-150484. (Short Story Index Reprint Ser.). Repr. of 1914 ed. 22.00 (ISBN 0-8369-3825-9). Ayer Co Pubs.

Prose Tales of Longfellow & Whittier. 400p. 1983. Repr. of 1982 ed. lib. bdg. 50.00 (ISBN 0-8495-0232-2). Arden Lib.

Prose Tattoo: Selected Performance Scores. Four Horsemen Staff & B. P. Nichol. 72p. (Orig.). 1983. pap. 6.00. Membrane Pr.

Prose That Works. Suzanne S. Webb. 277p. 1982. net 12.00 (ISBN 0-15-597882-9, HC); instr's manual avail. (ISBN 0-15-597883-7). HarBraceJ.

Prose Works. Mary Baker Eddy. new type ed. 32.50 (ISBN 0-87952-074-4); brown new type ed. o.p. 70.00 (ISBN 0-87952-076-0); standard ed. 25.00 (ISBN 0-87952-070-1); new type bonded lea. ed. o.p. 47.00 (ISBN 0-87952-075-2). First Church.

Prose Works. Mary Baker Eddy. New type edition burgundy. 72.25 (ISBN 0-317-65663-5). First Church.

Prose Works Eighteen Ninety-Two, 2 vols. Walt Whitman. Ed. by Floyd Stovall. Incl. Vol. 1. Specimen Days. 358p. 1963; Vol. 2. Collect & Other Prose. 445p. 1964. 75.00x (ISBN 0-8147-0443-3). LC 60-15980. (Illus.). 75.00 set. NYU Pr.

Prose Works. Letters, Axiochus, A View of the Present State of Ireland, A Brief Note of I see Works of Edmund Spenser: A Variorum Edition.

Prose Works of Alexander Pope, Vol. II: The Major Works, 1725-1744. Ed. by Rosemary Cowler. LC 86-3625. xv, 529p. 1986. 49.50 (ISBN 0-208-02059-4, Archon Bks). Shoe String.

Prose Works of Fulke Greville, Lord Brooke. Fulke Greville. Ed. by John Gouws. 360p. 1986. 76.00x (ISBN 0-19-812746-4). Oxford U Pr.

Prose Works of Jonathan Swift, 12 vols. Jonathan Swift. Ed. by Temple Scott. LC 79-179300. (Repr. of 1898-1909 ed.). Set. 495.00 (ISBN 0-404-10050-3). AMS Pr.

Prose Works of Richard Wagner, 8 vols. Richard Wagner. 1987. Repr. Set. lib. bdg. 800.00 (ISBN 0-317-59637-3). Am Biog Serv.

Prose Works of Robert Burns. Robert Burns. LC 79-144501. Repr. of 1839 ed. 21.50 (ISBN 0-404-08509-1). AMS Pr.

Prose Works of William Byrd of Westover. William Byrd. 29.50x (ISBN 0-674-71650-7). Harvard U Pr.

Prose Works of William Wordsworth, 3 Vols. William Wordsworth. Ed. by Alexander B. Grosart. LC 29-24298. Repr. of 1876 ed. Set. 130.00 (ISBN 0-404-07050-7). Vol. 1 (ISBN 0-404-07051-5). Vol. 2 (ISBN 0-404-07052-3). AMS Pr.

Prose works other than Science & Health. Mary Baker Eddy. Newtype ed. 77.50 (ISBN 0-87952-078-7); Century ed. 65.00 (ISBN 0-87952-073-6); Century ed., green. 27.00 (ISBN 0-87952-072-8); Standard ed. 25.00 (ISBN 0-87952-071-X). First Church.

Prose Worlds. Mary Baker Eddy. New type edition Black Indexed. 83.75 (ISBN 0-87952-080-9). First Church.

Prose Writers of America. Rufus Griswold. 1977. Repr. of 1851 ed. 50.00 (ISBN 0-89984-190-2). Century Bookbindery.

Prose Writers of America. Rufus W. Griswold. 1857. 30.00 (ISBN 0-8274-3217-8). R West.

Prose Writers of America. Rufus W. Griswold. 1986. pap. text ed. 7.95x (ISBN 0-8290-1870-0). Irvington.

Prose Writers of America. Ed. by Rufus W. Griswold. 1972. Repr. of 1857 ed. lib. bdg. 22.00 (ISBN 0-8422-8064-2). Irvington.

Prose Writers of America: A Collection of Eloquent & Interesting Extracts from the Writings of American Authors. George B. Cheever. 1979. Repr. of 1853 ed. lib. bdg. 40.00 (ISBN 0-8495-0939-4). Arden Lib.

Prose Writers of America: A Collection of Eloquent & Interesting Extracts from the Writings of American Authors. George B. Cheever. 468p. 1982. Repr. of 1853 ed. lib. bdg. 75.00 (ISBN 0-89987-132-1). Darby Bks.

Prose Writers of Germany. F. H. Hedge. 580p. Repr. of 1847 ed. lib. bdg. 150.00 (ISBN 0-918377-92-7). Russell Pr.

Prose Writers of Germany. Frederic H. Hedge. 580p. Repr. of 1847 ed. lib. bdg. 85.00 (ISBN 0-89984-713-7). Century Bookbindery.

Prose Writings. Thomas O. Davis. text ed. 14.75 (ISBN 0-8369-8153-7, 8293). Ayer Co Pubs.

Prose Writings. Nathaniel P. Willis. Ed. by Henry A. Beers. LC 70-128984. Repr. of 1885 ed. 16.00 (ISBN 0-404-06990-8). AMS Pr.

Prose Writings of Donald Lamont, 1874-1958. Ed. by Thomas M. Murchison. 1958. 15.00x (ISBN 0-7073-0038-X, Pub. by Scot Acad Pr). Longwood Pub Group.

Prose Writings of Dylan Thomas. Linden Peach. LC 87-1006. 176p. 1987. 25.00 (ISBN 0-389-20733-0). B&N Imports.

Prose Writings of Heinrich Heine. Heinrich Heine. Ed. by Havelock Ellis. LC 73-2205. (Jewish People; History, Religion, Literature Ser.). Repr. of 1887 ed. 26.50 (ISBN 0-405-05270-7). Ayer Co Pubs.

Prose Writings of James Clarence Mangan. James C. Mangan. Ed. by D. J. O'Donoghue. LC 75-28826. Repr. of 1904 ed. 31.25 (ISBN 0-404-13818-7). AMS Pr.

Prose Writings of Milton. John Milton. Ed. by Kathleen Burton. 1970. 12.95x (ISBN 0-460-00795-5, Evman); pap. 2.95x (ISBN 0-460-01795-0, Evman). Biblio Dist.

Prose Writings of Robert Louis Stevenson: A Guide. Roger G. Swearingen. LC 79-26612. xxiii, 217p. 1980. 29.50 (ISBN 0-208-01826-3, Archon). Shoe String.

Prose Writings of Swift. Jonathan Swift. Ed. by Walter Lewin. 1977. Repr. of 1886 ed. lib. bdg. 35.00 (ISBN 0-8414-7868-6). Folcroft.

Prosecuting Construction Claims Against Public Owners. 70p. 1982. 10.00 (ISBN 0-686-47817-7). Amer Bar Assn.

Prosecuting Crime in the Renaissance: England, Germany, France. John H. Langbein. LC 73-81670. (Studies in Legal History). 336p. 1974. text ed. 17.50x (ISBN 0-674-71675-2). Harvard U Pr.

Prosecuting the Shoplifter: A Loss Prevention Strategy. James Cleary, Jr. LC 85-11342. 1986. text ed. 24.95 (ISBN 0-409-95116-1). Butterworth.

Prosecution Alternative to Court Trial (PACT) Program: An Innovative Response to the Problem of DWI Adjudication in Phoenix, Arizona. National Center for State Courts Staff. (Paul Reardon Ser.). 21p. 1981. manuscript 1.26 (PRS-023). Natl Ctr St Courts.

Prosecution & Defense of Criminal Conspiracy Cases. Paul Marcus. 1978. looseleaf 90.00 (365); Updates 1985 70.00; 1986 75.00. Bender.

Prosecution & Defense of Forfeiture Cases. David B. Smith. 1985. looseleaf 90.00 (099); Updates 1986 40.00. Bender.

Prosecution & Defense of RICO & Mail Fraud Cases. 193p. 1980. pap. 14.00 (ISBN 0-686-47917-3, 509-0010). Amer Bar Assn.

Prosecution & Defense of Sex Crimes. B. Anthony Morosco. 1976. looseleaf 90.00 (562); Updates 1985 49.50; 1986 56.50. Bender.

Prosecution & the Public Interest. T. Hetherington. 192p. 1989. 33.51 (ISBN 0-08-033110-6, Pub. by Waterlow). Pergamon.

Prosecution of Economic Crimes in the U. S. S. R. Fridrikh Neznansky. Ed. by Andrew Michta. (Orig.). Date not set. pap. text ed. 35.00 (ISBN 1-55831-031-2). Delphic Associates.

Prosecution of John Wyclyf. Joseph H. Dahmus. xi, 167p. 1970. Repr. of 1952 ed. 22.50 (ISBN 0-208-00953-1, Archon). Shoe String.

Prosecution of the Mentally Disturbed: Dilemmas of Identification & Discretion. D. Chiswick et al. 192p. 1984. text ed. 26.00 (ISBN 0-08-028481-7). Pergamon.

Prosecutor. Ed. by William F. McDonald. LC 79-14388. (Sage Criminal Justice System Annuals Ser.: Vol. 11). (Illus.). 279p. 1979. 29.95 (ISBN 0-8039-0815-6); pap. 14.95 (ISBN 0-8039-0816-4). Sage.

Prosecutor. James Mills. 1988. pap. 4.95 (ISBN 0-440-20092-X). Dell.

Prosecutor. Magdalen Nabb & Paolo Vagheggi. 256p. 1988. 16.95x (ISBN 0-312-01497-X). St Martin.

Prosecutor: An Inquiry into the Exercise of Discretion. Brian A. Grosman. LC 76-461526. 1969. pap. 7.50 (ISBN 0-8020-6341-1). U of Toronto Pr.

Prosecutor Disclosure & Judicial Reform: The Omnibus Hearing in Two Courts. Raymond T. Nimmer. vii, 117p. 1975. 10.00 (ISBN 0-910058-72-5); pap. 5.00 (ISBN 0-910058-71-7). Amer Bar Assn.

Prosecutor in America see Roles & Functions of the Prosecutor.

Prosecutorial Discretion: Revised Edition. James I. Knapp & Ephraim Margolin. 135p. 1983. 35.00 (CR-31860); February '82 supp. 20.00; December '83 supp. 20.00. Cal Cont Ed Bar.

Prosecutorial Misconduct. Bennett L. Gershman. LC 84-12399. 1984. 75.00 (ISBN 0-87632-443-X). Clark Boardman.

Prosecutorial Misconduct: Law, Procedure, Forms. Joseph F. Lawless, Jr. LC 85-9815. (Kluwer Criminal Law Library). 812p. 1985. text ed. 80.00 (ISBN 0-930273-06-0). Kluwer Law Bk.

Prosecutorial Relationships in Criminal Justice see Roles & Functions of the Prosecutor.

Prosecutors. James B. Stewart. 448p. 1987. 19.95 (ISBN 0-671-49747-2). S&S.

Prosecutors: Inside the Offices of the Government's Most Powerful Lawyers. James B. Stewart. 384p. 1988. pap. 7.95 (ISBN 0-671-66835-8, Touchstone Bks). S&S.

Prosencephalies. F. P. Probst. LC 79-11643. (Illus.). 1979. 75.00 (ISBN 0-387-09318-4). Springer-Verlag.

Proserpine. Jean-Baptiste Lully. Ed. by Theodore De Lajarte. (Chefs-d'oeuvre classiques de l'opera francais Ser.: Vol. 24). (Illus.). 376p. (Fr.). 1972. pap. 30.00x (ISBN 0-8450-1124-3). Broude.

Proserpine & Midas. Mary Wollstonecraft Shelley. LC 73-15668. 1974. Repr. of 1922 ed. lib. bdg. 27.50. Folcroft.

Proshchanie s Rossiei. Grigorii Svirskii. (Illus.). 144p. (Rus.). 1986. pap. 8.50 (ISBN 0-938920-80-4). Hermitage.

Prosim: A Production Management Simulation. P. S. Greenlaw & M. P. Hottenstein. 1969. pap. text ed. 20.50 scp (ISBN 0-7002-2224-3, HarpC). scp 700-7000 computer deck 27.50 (ISBN 0-352-07310-1). Har-Row.

Proskauer, His Life & Times. Louis M. Hacker & Mark D. Hirsch. LC 77-1697. 240p. 1978. 18.00 (ISBN 0-8173-9361-7). U of Ala Pr.

Proslavery: A History of the Defense of Slavery in America, 1701-1840. Larry E. Tise. LC 86-14671. (Illus.). 568p. 1988. 40.00x (ISBN 0-8203-0927-3). U of Ga Pr.

Prosodic Cues for Segments. Ed. by K. J. Kohler. (Journal-Phonetica, 1986: Vol. 43, No. 1-3). (Illus.). 154p. 1986. pap. 81.50 (ISBN 3-8055-4474-X). S Karger.

Prosodic Phonology. M. Nespor & G. Vogel. (Studies in Generative Grammar). xiv, 328p. 1986. pap. write for info. (ISBN 90-6765-242-3). Foris Pubns.

Prosodic Systems & Intonation in English. D. Crystal. LC 69-13792. (Cambridge Studies in Linguistics: No. 1). (Illus.). 1969. 57.50 (ISBN 0-521-07387-1); pap. 21.95 (ISBN 0-521-29058-9). Cambridge U Pr.

Prosody: Models & Measurement. Ed. by A. Cutler & D. R. Ladd. (Springer Series in Language & Communication: Vol. 14). (Illus.). 180p. 1983. 31.50 (ISBN 0-387-12428-4). Springer-Verlag.

Prosody of Chaucer & His Followers: Supplementary Chapters to "Verses of Cadence". James G. Southworth. LC 77-16835. 1978. Repr. of 1962 ed. lib. bdg. 35.00x (ISBN 0-313-20008-4, SOPC). Greenwood.

Prosody of the Persians, According to Saifi, Jami & Other Writers. Henry F. Blochmann. 1976. lib. bdg. 59.95 (ISBN 0-8490-2487-0). Gordon Pr.

Prosody of the Tudor Interlude. Jules E. Bernard, Jr. LC 69-15677. (Yale Studies in English Ser.: No. 90). ix, 225p. 1969. Repr. of 1939 ed. 24.50 (ISBN 0-208-00782-2, Archon). Shoe String.

Prosopis Tamarugo: Fodder Tree for Arid Zones. Mario Habit et al. (Plant Production & Protection Papers: No. 25). 119p. (Eng., Fr. & Span.). 1981. pap. 8.25 (ISBN 92-5-101055-2, F2229, FAO). UNIPUB.

Prosopographia Attica, 2 vols. Ed. by J. Kirchner. 1340p. 1981. Repr. of 1901 ed. Set. 125.00 (ISBN 0-89005-387-1). Ares.

Prosopographia Attica: Supplement. J. Sundwall. 177p. 1981. 20.00 (ISBN 0-89005-383-9). Ares.

Prosopographia Cartuaiana Belgica: 1314-1796. Jan De Grauwe. Ed. by James Hogg. (Analecta Cartusiana Ser.: No. 28). 360p. (Orig., Flemish & Fr.). 1976. pap. 25.00 (ISBN 3-7052-0029-1, Pub by Salzburg Studies). Longwood Pub Group.

Prosopographia Imperii Romani, Pt. 5, Fascicle 2. 121p. (Lat.). 43.20 (ISBN 3-11-008902-5). De Gruyter.

Prosopographia Lacaedaemoniorum. P. Poralla. 1985. Repr. of 1913 ed. 20.00 (ISBN 0-89005-521-1). Ares.

Prosopographia Macedonica. D. Kanatzoulis. 183p. 1979. 30.00 (ISBN 0-89005-316-2). Ares.

Prosopography of the Later Roman Empire, Vol. 1. A. D. 260-395. Ed. by A. H. Jones et al. LC 77-118859. (Illus.). 1971. o. p. 160.00 (ISBN 0-521-07233-6). Cambridge U Pr.

Prosopography of the Later Roman Empire, Vol. 2, A.D. 395-527. Ed. by J. R. Martindale. LC 77-118859. (Illus.). 1980. 182.50 (ISBN 0-521-20159-4). Cambridge U Pr.

Prospect & Retrospect: Selected Essays of James Britton. James Britton. Ed. by Gordon M. Pradl. LC 82-14608. 224p. 1982. pap. text ed. 13.50x (ISBN 0-86709-043-X). Boynton Cook Pubs.

Prospect for Gold. Timothy Green. 1987. 29.95 (ISBN 0-8027-1002-6). Walker & Co.

Prospect for Metaphysics: Essays of Metaphysical Exploration. Ed. by Ian T. Ramsey. Repr. of 1961 ed. lib. bdg. 35.00x (ISBN 0-8371-2557-X, RAME). Greenwood.

Prospect of Detachment. Lindsley Cameron. 160p. 1988. 14.95 (ISBN 0-312-02269-7). St Martin.

Prospect of Flowers. Andrew Young. 144p. 1985. 12.95 (ISBN 0-670-80345-6). Viking.

Prospect of Flowers: A Book about Wild Flowers. Andrew Young. 224p. 1986. pap. 5.95 (ISBN 0-14-059010-2). Penguin.

Prospect of Liberal Democracy. Ed. by William S. Livingston. LC 79-63171. 239p. 1979. text ed. 17.50x (ISBN 0-292-76454-5); pap. text ed. 8.95x (ISBN 0-292-76455-3). U of Tex Pr.

Prospect of War: Studies in British Defence Policy 1847-1942. John Gooch. 174p. 1981. 24.00x (ISBN 0-7146-3128-0, F Cass Co). Biblio Dist.

Prospect Research: A How-to Guide. Bobbie J. Strand & Susan Hunt. 150p. (Orig.). 1986. pap. 18.50 (ISBN 0-89964-244-6). Coun Adv & Supp Ed.

Prospecting & Exploration of Mineral Deposits. 2nd, rev. ed. M. Kuzvart & M. Bohmer. 506p. 1986. 139.50 (ISBN 0-444-99515-3). Elsevier.

Prospecting & Operating Small Gold Placers. 2nd ed. William F. Boericke. 144p. 1936. 29.95 (ISBN 0-471-08514-6). Wiley.

Prospecting for Gemstones & Minerals. rev. ed. John Sinkankas. 398p. 1970. pap. 12.95 (ISBN 0-442-27620-6). Van Nos Reinhold.

Prospecting for Gold: From Dogtown to Virginia City, 1852-1864. Granville Stuart. Ed. by Paul C. Phillips. LC 77-7244. (Illus.). 272p. 1977. 22.00x (ISBN 0-8032-0932-0); pap. 8.95 (ISBN 0-8032-5869-0, BB 647, Bison). U of Nebr Pr.

Prospecting for Old Furniture: Your Guide to Buying & Restoring Affordable Antiques for Your Home. Don Marotta. LC 85-7937. (Illus.). 192p. (Orig.). 1985. pap. 12.95 (ISBN 0-8117-2178-7). Stackpole.

Prospecting for Recruits. 58p. 2.00 (ISBN 0-318-14766-1). Life Ins Mktg Res.

Prospecting in Alaska. facs. ed. R. Steinart. (Shorey Prospecting Ser.). 28p. pap. 3.95 (ISBN 0-8466-0038-2, S38). Shorey.

Prospecting in Areas of Glacial Terrain. Ed. by M. J. Jones. 138p. (Orig.). 1973. pap. text ed. 40.25x (ISBN 0-900488-19-0). IMM North Am.

Prospecting in Areas of Glaciated Terrain 1975. Ed. by M. J. Jones. 154p. (Orig.). 1975. pap. text ed. 46.00x (ISBN 0-900488-29-8). IMM North Am.

Prospecting in Areas of Glaciated Terrain 1977. 140p. 1977. pap. text ed. 54.75x (ISBN 0-900488-38-7). IMM North Am.

Prospecting in Areas of Glaciated Terrain 1979. 110p. 1979. pap. text ed. 57.50x (ISBN 0-900488-46-8). IMM North Am.

Prospecting in Areas of Glaciated Terrain 1984, No. 6. (Prospecting in Areas of Glaciated Terrain Ser.). 232p. (Orig.). 1984. pap. text ed. 43.25x (ISBN 0-900488-74-3). IMM North Am.

Prospecting Our Past: Gold, Silver & Tungsten Mills of Boulder County. Harrison Cobb. Ed. by Silvia Pettem. (Illus.). 160p. (Orig.). 1988. pap. 15.95 (ISBN 0-9617799-3-4). Book Lode.

Prospecting: Searching Out the Philanthropic Dollar. 2nd ed. James K. Hickey & Elizabeth Koochoo. LC 84-8846. 101p. 1984. pap. 21.95 (ISBN 0-914756-31-1). Taft Group.

Prospecting to Riches in Real Estate. Albert L. Friedman. 224p. 1986. 10.95 (ISBN 0-8062-2803-2). Carlton.

Prospecting with Old E-Logs. R. W. Frank. (Illus.). 161p. Date not set. text ed. 27.50 (ISBN 0-929119-02-9, 7013). Schlumberger Educ.

Prospecting Your Way to Sales Success: How to Find New Business by Phone. Bill Good. 224p. 1986. 19.95 (ISBN 0-684-18620-9). Scribner.

Prospective Charts. rev. ed. Lawson. 18.95 (ISBN 0-317-64235-9). Van Nos Reinhold.

Prospective City: Economic, Population, Energy, & Environmental Developments Shaping Our Cities & Suburbs. Ed. by Arthur P. Solomon. (MIT-Harvard Joint Center for Urban Studies). 1979. text ed. 40.00x (ISBN 0-262-19182-2); pap. 13.50x (ISBN 0-262-69071-3). MIT Pr.

Prospective Financial Statements Documentation Manual. Larry L. Perry. 432p. 1988. 3-ring binder 69.95 (ISBN 0-13-731373-X, Busn). P-H.

Prospective Issues in Infancy Research. Ed. by Kathleen Bloom. LC 80-17479. 208p. 1981. text ed. 29.95 (ISBN 0-89859-059-0). L Erlbaum Assocs.

Prospective Longitudinal Research in Europe: An Empirical Basis for the Primary Prevention of Psychosocial Disorders. Ed. by Sarnoff A. Mednick & Andre E. Baert. (Illus.). 1981. text ed. 130.00x (ISBN 0-19-261184-4). Oxford U Pr.

Prospective Payment: Implications for Psychiartic Patient Care. Donald J. Scherl et al. 250p. 1988. text ed. 26.50x (ISBN 0-89042-106-4). Am Psychiatric.

Prospective Payment: Laws, Regulations, Guidelines & Decisions. National Health Publishing Editorial Staff. 550p. 1984. looseleaf 125.00 (ISBN 0-932500-27-7). Natl Hlth Pub.

Prospective Payment: Managing for Operational Effectiveness. Howard L. Smith & Myron D. Fottler. 280p. 1985. 45.95 (ISBN 0-87189-097-6). Aspen Pub.

Prospective Payment Systems. Carolyn Baum & Aimee Luebben. LC 85-61727. 100p. 1986. pap. text ed. 19.95 (ISBN 0-943432-52-9). Slack Inc.

Prospective Payment: The Definitive Guide to Reimbursement. Paul L. Grimaldi & Julie A. Micheletti. LC 84-62516. (Illus.). 400p. (Orig.). 1985. 37.95 (ISBN 0-931028-63-9); pap. 32.95 (ISBN 0-931028-61-2). Pluribus Pr.

Prospective Payments: Health Care Revolution. Ed. by Barbara Dreyfuss. 565p. (Orig.). 1984. pap. text ed. 72.00 (ISBN 0-914176-25-0). Wash Busn Info.

Prospective Rate Setting. William L. Dowling. LC 77-18700. 157p. 1977. text ed. 49.50 (ISBN 0-89443-028-9). Aspen Pub.

Prospective Studies of Crime and Deliquency. Katherine Teilmann Van Dusen & Sarnoff A. Mednick. LC 83-178. (Longitudinal Research in the Behavioral, Social, and Medical Sciences). 1983. 57.00 (ISBN 0-89838-131-2, Pub. by Kluwer-Nijhoff (Netherlands)). Kluwer Academic.

Prospective Studies on Children with Sex Chromosome Aneuploidy. Ed. by S. G. Ratcliffe & Natalie Paul. LC 86-21486. (Birth Defects: Original Article Ser.: Vol. 22, No. 3). 344p. 1986. 89.00 (ISBN 0-8451-1062-4, 1062). A R Liss.

Prospector's Chemical Cookbook. W. S. Pardy. (Illus.). 112p. 1977. pap. 10.95 (ISBN 0-318-22523-9). Pardy's Tree Farm.

Prospector's Field Book & Guide. Osborn. 1987. pap. 9.95 (ISBN 0-317-62629-9). Lindsay Pubns.

Prospector's Guide. Steven Taylor & Mary Taylor. LC 79-89343. 48p. (Orig.). 1979. 2.95 (ISBN 0-936528-01-X). Poverty Bay.

Prospectors' Manual. Arthur J. Burdick. (Shorey Prospecting Ser.). (Illus.). 160p. pap. 8.95 (ISBN 0-8466-6018-0, U18). Shorey.

Prospects. Steve Richmond. 40p. 1983. pap. 3.00 (ISBN 0-935390-08-1). Wormwood Rev.

Prospects: An Annual of American Cultural Studies, Vol. 1. Ed. by Jack Salzman. 1975. 24.95 (ISBN 0-89102-061-6). B Franklin.

Prospects: An Annual of American Cultural Studies, Vol. 2. Ed. by Jack Salzman. 1976. 24.95 (ISBN 0-89102-069-1). B Franklin.

Prospects: An Annual of American Cultural Studies, Vol. 3. Ed. by Jack Salzman. 1977. 25.00 (ISBN 0-89102-078-0, Artemis); pap. 11.95 (ISBN 0-89102-099-3). B Franklin.

Prospects for Adjustment in Argentina, Brazil, & Mexico: Responding to the Debt Crisis. Ed. by John Williamson. LC 83-81496. pap. 20.00 (ISBN 0-317-20806-3, 2024791). Bks Demand UMI.

Prospects for Adult Education & Development in Asia & the Pacific: Report of a Regional Seminar, Bangkok, November 24-December 4, 1980. UNESCO Regional Office for Education in Asia & the Pacific. 69p. 1981. pap. 5.00 (ISBN 0-686-81856-3, UB98, UB). UNIPUB.

Prospects for Agricultural Development in Indonesia with Special Reference to Java. (Agricultural Research Reports: No. 705). 1968. pap. 26.25 (ISBN 90-220-0166-0, PDC170, PUDOC). UNIPUB.

Prospects for Agricultural Production & Trade in Eastern Europe: Vol 1, Poland, German Democratic Republic, Hungary. 248p. (Orig.). 1981. pap. 21.00x (ISBN 92-64-12262-1). OECD.

Prospects for Agricultural Production & Trade in Eastern Europe: Bulgaria, Czechoslavakia, Romania, Vol. 2. OECD Staff. 216p. (Orig.). 1982. pap. 26.00x (ISBN 92-64-12369-5). OECD.

Prospects for Change in Socialist Systems: Challenges & Responses. Ed. by Charles J. Bukowski & Mark A. Cichock. LC 86-30614. 157p. 1987. lib. bdg. 34.95 (ISBN 0-275-92434-3, C2434). Praeger.

Prospects for Constitutional Democracy: Essays in Honor of R. Taylor Cole. Ed. by John H. Hallowell. LC 76-4220. pap. 55.50 (ISBN 0-317-26762-0, 2023395). Bks Demand UMI.

Prospects for Conventional Arms Control in Europe. Joachim Krause. (East-West Occasional Papers: No. 8). 52p. 1988. pap. 5.95 (ISBN 0-8133-0657-4). Westview.

Prospects for Democracy in India. K. L. Shrimali. LC 78-112393. 156p. 1970. 6.95x (ISBN 0-8093-0441-4). S Ill U Pr.

Prospects for Food Production & Consumption in Developing Countries. Malcolm D. Bale & Ronald C. Duncan. (Working Paper: No. 596). 40p. 1983. 5.00 (ISBN 0-8213-0194-2, WP 0596). World Bank.

Prospects for Fusion Power. Ed. by Stephen O. Dean. (Illus.). 112p. 1981. 29.00 (ISBN 0-08-028046-3). Pergamon.

Prospects for Growth: Changing Expectations for the Future. 334p. 1977. 12.50 (ISBN 0-317-34108-1, 017759). Edison Electric.

Prospects for Growth: Changing Expectations for the Future. Ed. by Kenneth D. Wilson. LC 77-14567. (Praeger Special Studies). 366p. 1977. 42.95 (ISBN 0-275-90278-1, C0278); pap. 19.95 (ISBN 0-03-041441-5). Praeger.

Prospects for Industrial Electrochemistry. Ed. by G. B. Feilden et al. (Illus.). 165p. 1981. lib. bdg. 54.00x (ISBN 0-85403-174-X, Pub. by Royal Soc London). Scholium Intl.

Prospects for Information Service: Essays in Honour of Daphne Clark. Ed. by Colin Harris & Peter J. Taylor. 128p. 1986. pap. 25.00 (ISBN 0-85142-194-6). Learned Info.

Prospects for Metropolitan Water Management. 240p. 1970. pap. 6.00x (ISBN 0-87262-026-3). Am Soc Civil Eng.

Prospects for Partnership: Industrialization & Trade Policies in the 1970's. Helen Hughes. LC 72-12369. (International Bank for Reconstruction & Development Ser). 309p. 1974. 30.00x (ISBN 0-8018-1498-7); pap. 10.95x (ISBN 0-8018-1500-2). Johns Hopkins.

Prospects for Peace. Frank Barnaby. (Illus.). 105p. 1980. 29.00 (ISBN 0-08-027399-8); pap. 15.50 (ISBN 0-08-027398-X). Pergamon.

Prospects for Peace & Cooperation in the Asian-Pacific Region. Ed. by John W. Lewis. (Special Report of the Center for International Security & Arms Control, Stanford University). 138p. (Orig.). 1986. pap. 12.00 (ISBN 0-935371-14-1). ISIS.

Prospects for Peacemaking: A Citizen's Guide to Safer Nuclear Strategy. Ed. by Harlan Cleveland & Lincoln P. Bloomfield. LC 87-2622. 176p. 1987. 15.00 (ISBN 0-262-03131-0). MIT Pr.

Prospects for Plural Societies, 1982. Ed. by David Maybury-Lewis. (Proceedings of the American Ethnological Society Ser.). 1984. 16.00 (ISBN 0-942976-04-5). Am Anthro Assn.

Prospects for Pragmatism. Ed. by David H. Mellor. 270p. 1981. 34.50 (ISBN 0-521-22548-5). Cambridge U Pr.

Prospects for Privatization, Vol. 36, No. 3. LC 87-70470. 1987. 9.95 (ISBN 0-318-23652-4). Acad Poli Sci.

Prospects for Recovery in the British Economy. Ed. by F. V. Meyer. LC 84-29366. 237p. 1985. 34.50 (ISBN 0-7099-1772-4, Pub. by Croom Helm Ltd). Routledge Chapman & Hall.

Prospects for Research & Development in Education. new ed. Ralph W. Tyler. LC 75-36111. 190p. 1978. 21.00x (ISBN 0-8211-1906-0); text ed. 19.00x. McCutchan.

Prospects for Sexing Mammalian Sperm. Ed. by Rupert Amann. LC 82-70138. 1982. pap. text ed. 37.50 (ISBN 0-87081-134-7). Colo Assoc.

Prospects for Soviet Agriculture & Trade with Special Reference to Meat & Grain. OECD Staff. 117p. (Orig.). 1983. pap. text ed. 12.00 (ISBN 92-64-12471-3). OECD.

Prospects for Soviet Agriculture in the 1980s. D. Gale Johnson & Karen M. Brooks. LC 82-48625. (CSIS Publication Series on the Soviet Union in the 1980's: Midland Bks: No. 300). (Illus.). 224p. 1983. 17.50x (ISBN 0-253-34619-3, MB 300); pap. 8.95x (ISBN 0-253-20300-7). Ind U Pr.

Prospects for Synthetic Fuels in the United States. John M. Deutch. 1982. 2.50x (ISBN 0-317-06611-0). Colo Assoc.

Prospects for the Spanish American Culture of New Mexico. Thomas R. Lopez, Jr. LC 73-82391. 1974. 14.95 (ISBN 0-88247-243-7). R & E Pubs.

Prospects for the World Jute Industry. M. Elton Thigpen & Takamasa Akiyama. (Commodity Working Paper: No. 14). 88p. 1986. 5.00 (ISBN 0-8213-0701-0, BK 0701). World Bank.

Prospects for the World Oil Industry. Ed. by Tim Niblock & Richard Lawless. LC 85-4186. 131p. 1985. 29.00 (ISBN 0-7099-4104-8, Pub. by Croom Helm Ltd). Routledge Chapman & Hall.

Prospects for Traditional & Non-Conventional Energy Sources in Developing Countries. David P. Hughart. (Working Paper: No. 346). ii, 132p. 1979. 8.00 (ISBN 0-686-36159-8, WP-0346). World Bank.

Prospects in Areas of Desert Terrain, 1985. 283p. 1985. pap. text ed. 50.00x (ISBN 0-900488-81-6). Imm North Am.

Prospects in Modern Acoustics: Education & Development. Ed. by G. Budzynski & A. Sliwinski. 472p. 1987. 78.00 (ISBN 9971-50-379-4). World Scientific Pub.

Prospects in Systematics. Ed. by D. L. Hawksworth. (Systematics Association Special Volume Ser.: No. 36). (Illus.). 426p. 1988. 98.00 (ISBN 0-19-857707-9). Oxford U Pr.

Prospects of American Industrial Recovery. John E. Ullmann. LC 84-15923. (Illus.). xi, 244p. 1985. lib. bdg. 36.95 (ISBN 0-89930-063-4, UED/, Quorum). Greenwood.

Prospects of Democracy & Other Essays. facs. ed. Alfred E. Zimmern. LC 68-8506. (Essay Index Reprint Ser). 1929. 19.00 (ISBN 0-8369-1017-6). Ayer Co Pubs.

Prospects of Economic Growth. S. K. Kuipers & G. J. Lanjouw. 288p. 1980. 79.00 (ISBN 0-444-85355-3, North-Holland). Elsevier.

Prospects of Heart Surgery. A. Radley. (Contributions to Psychology & Medicine Ser.). (Illus.). 250p. 1988. 59.00 (ISBN 0-387-96721-4). Springer-Verlag.

Prospects of Humanism. Lawrence Hyde. LC 77-94273. (Select Bibliographies Reprint Ser). 1931. 22.00 (ISBN 0-8369-5047-X). Ayer Co Pubs.

Prospects of Humanism. Lawrence Hyde. LC 71-102574. 1970. Repr. of 1931 ed. 23.00x (ISBN 0-8046-0734-6, Pub. by Kennikat). Assoc Faculty Pr.

Prospects of Humanism. Lawrence Hyde. 1931. Repr. 25.00 (ISBN 0-8274-3218-6). R West.

Prospects of Literature. Logan P. Smith. 1927. lib. bdg. 17.00 (ISBN 0-8414-7857-0). Folcroft.

Prospects of Mathematical Science. Ed. by L. Nagasaka et al. 284p. 1988. 53.00 (ISBN 9971-50-454-5); pap. 28.00 (ISBN 9971-50-465-0). World Scientific Pub.

Prospects of Nuclear Power in Pakistan. (Technical Reports Ser.: No. 7). 1962. pap. 9.00 (ISBN 92-0-165062-0, IDC7, IAEA). UNIPUB.

Prospects of Soviet Power in the Nineteen Eighties. Ed. by Christoph Bertram. LC 80-17058. 126p. 1980. 19.50 (ISBN 0-208-01884-0, Archon). Shoe String.

Prospects of the Industrial Areas of Great Britain. M. P. Fogarty. (English Workers Ser.). 492p. 1985. lib. bdg. 66.00 (ISBN 0-8240-7611-7). Garland Pub.

Prospects of World Urbanization: Revised As of 1984-85. rev. ed. (Population Studies: No. 101). 269p. 1987. pap. 34.00 (ISBN 92-1-151163-1, E.87.XIII.3). UN.

Prospects: The Annual of American Cultural Studies, Vol. 4. Ed. by Jack Salzman. (Illus.). 1978. lib. bdg. 21.95 (ISBN 0-89102-151-5). B Franklin.

Prospectus. Bruce Braunstein. 1986. bk. & cassette 89.95 (ISBN 0-317-52217-5). Tetragrammaton.

Prospectus for the Triumph of Realism. Thomas A. Russman. LC 86-28646. 208p. 1987. 24.95 (ISBN 0-86554-232-5, MUP-H205). Mercer Univ Pr.

Prosper Merimee. Maxwell A. Smith. LC 72-1485. (Twayne's World Authors Ser.). 200p. 1972. lib. bdg. 17.95 (ISBN 0-8290-1747-X). Irvington.

Prosper Merimee: A Mask & a Face. G. Johnston. 59.95 (ISBN 0-8490-0904-9). Gordon Pr.

Prosper Merimees: Letters to an Incognita with Recollections by Lamartine & George Sand. Richard H. Stoddard. Repr. of 1893 ed. 20.00 (ISBN 0-686-19857-3). Ridgeway Bks.

Prosperine Papers. Jan Clausen. 200p. (Orig.). 1988. lib. bdg. 23.95 (ISBN 0-89594-274-7); pap. 8.95 (ISBN 0-89594-273-9). Crossing Pr.

Prospering in Private Practice: A Handbook for Speech-Language Pathology & Audiology. Katharine G. Butler. 320p. 1986. 38.00 (ISBN 0-87189-368-1). Aspen Pub.

Prospering Power of Love. rev. ed. Catherine Ponder. LC 66-25849. 126p. 1984. pap. 4.00 (ISBN 0-87516-525-7). DeVorss.

Prospering Power of Prayer. Catherine Ponder. 80p. 1983. pap. 3.50 (ISBN 0-87516-516-8). DeVorss.

Prospering Woman. Ruth Ross. 224p. 1982. pap. 8.95 (ISBN 0-931432-09-X). New Wrld Lib.

Prospering Woman: A Complete Guide to Achieving the Full, Abundant life. Ruth Ross. 224p. 1985. pap. 4.50 (ISBN 0-553-26429-X). Bantam.

Prosperites du Vice. Donatien Alphonse Francois de Sade. 320p. 1969. 5.95 (ISBN 0-686-55373-X). French & Eur.

Prosperity. Charles Fillmore. 1936. 5.95 (ISBN 0-87159-130-8). Unity School.

Prosperity & Depression: A Theoretical Analysis of Cyclical Movements. 4th ed. Gottfried Haberler. LC 59-6133. (Economic Studies: No. 105). (Illus.). 1964. 32.50x (ISBN 0-674-71750-3). Harvard U Pr.

Prosperity & Misery in Modern Bengal: The Famine of 1943-1944. Paul R. Greenough. (Illus.). 1982. 39.95x (ISBN 0-19-503082-6). Oxford U Pr.

Prosperity & Public Spending: Transformation Growth & the Role of Government. Edward Nell. (Studies in International Political Economy). 224p. 1988. text ed. 34.95 (ISBN 0-04-339044-7). Unwin Hyman.

Prosperity & the Healing Power of Prayer. F. Bernadette Turner. LC 83-21276. (Illus.). 166p. 1984. pap. 6.95 (ISBN 0-13-731324-1). P-H.

Prosperity & Upheaval: The World Economy, 1945-1980. Herman Van der Wee. (History of the World Economy in the Twentieth Century: Vol. 6). 576p. 1986. 37.50x (ISBN 0-520-05709-0). U of Cal Pr.

Prosperity, Great Depression & New Deal. Yoshihiko Hirata. (FDR & the Era of the New Deal Ser.). 1973. Repr. of 1972 ed. 48.50 (ISBN 0-306-71195-8). Da Capo.

Prosperity Handbook: A Guide to Personal & Financial Success. Michael Fries & C. Holland Taylor. Ed. by Diane Frank. LC 83-72180. (Illus.). 512p. 1984. 16.95 (ISBN 0-9611910-0-7); pap. 9.95 (ISBN 0-9611910-4-X). Comm Res.

Prosperity in the End Time. Roger F. Campbell. 1983. pap. 2.95 (ISBN 0-87508-055-3). Chr Lit.

Prosperity Is God's Idea. Margaret M. Stevens. (Illus.). 1978. pap. 5.95 (ISBN 0-87516-264-9). DeVorss.

Prosperity Now! Norvel Hayes. (Orig.). 1986. pap. 5.95 (ISBN 0-89274-416-2). Harrison Hse.

Prosperity References. Compiled by Bibliotheca Press Research Division Staff. 35p. 1983. pap. 1.25 (ISBN 0-939476-62-2, Pub. by Biblio Pr GA). Prosperity & Profits.

Prosperity Restored by the State Rate Tax Plan. Edward A. Ellison. LC 85-10104. write for info. (ISBN 0-934005-00-1). Free State Constitution.

Prosperity Road: The New Deal, Tobacco & North Carolina. Anthony J. Badger. LC 79-310. (Fred Morrison Series in Southern Studies). (Illus.). xviii, 295p. 1980. 27.50x (ISBN 0-8078-1367-2). U of NC Pr.

Prosperity Secrets of the Ages. rev. ed. Catherine Ponder. LC 64-16436. 344p. 1986. pap. 8.95 (ISBN 0-87516-567-2). DeVorss.

Prosperity with Purpose. Marc Carr. Ed. by Florence K. Biros. (Mini Teaching Series). 96p. (Orig.). 1987. pap. 3.95 (ISBN 0-936369-13-2). Son-Rise Pubns.

Prosperity Without Progress: Manila Hemp & Material Life in the Colonial Philippines. Norman G. Owen. (Illus.). 335p. 1984. lib. bdg. 37.50x (ISBN 0-520-04470-3). U of Cal Pr.

Prosperity Without Progress: Manila Hemp & Material Life in the Colonial Philippines. Norman G. Owen. (Illus.). 333p. 1984. pap. 16.50x (ISBN 971-113-029-7, Pub. by Ateneo de Manila U Pr Philippines). Cellar.

Prospero Drill. Carl A. Posey. 192p. 1985. 12.95 (ISBN 0-312-65198-8). St Martin.

Prospero Drill. Carl A. Posey. 288p. 1988. 3.95 (ISBN 0-373-97052-8, Pub. by Worldwide). Harlequin Bks.

Prospero's Magic: Some Thoughts on Class & Race. Philip Mason. LC 75-3739. 151p. 1975. Repr. of 1962 ed. lib. bdg. 35.00x (ISBN 0-8371-8054-6, MAPMA). Greenwood.

Prospero's Staff: Acting & Directing in the Contemporary Theatre. Charles Marowitz. LC 85-45887. (Indiana Studies in Theatre & Drama). (Illus.). 360p. 1986. 22.50x (ISBN 0-253-34622-3). Ind U Pr.

Prosperous People: The Growth of the American Economy. Edwin J. Perkins & Gary M. Walton. LC 84-23719. (Illus.). 256p. 1985. pap. text ed. write for info. (ISBN 0-13-731399-3). P-H.

Prosperous Years: The Economic History of Ontario 1939-1975. Kenneth J. Rea. (Ontario Historical Studies). 304p. 1985. pap. 12.50 (ISBN 0-8020-6592-9). U of Toronto Pr.

Prosser & Keeton on Torts. 5th, student Ed. ed. Ed. by Page Keeton et al. W Prosser. LC 83-19830. (Hornbook Ser.). 1286p. 1984. text ed. 29.95 (ISBN 0-314-74880-6). West Pub.

Prosser & Keeton on Torts: Lawyers Edition. 5th. Ed. ed. William L. Prosser & Page Keeton. LC 83-19714. (Hornbook Ser.). 1456p. 1984. text ed. 42.95 (ISBN 0-314-74442-8). West Pub.

Prosser Nineteen Ten to Nineteen Twenty: Looking Back. Paul Fridlund. 172p. 1985. 19.95 (ISBN 0-87770-367-1). Ye Galleon.

Prostacyclin. Ed. by John R. Vane & Sune Bergstrom. LC 78-601200. 466p. 1979. text ed. 83.50 (ISBN 0-89004-330-2). Raven.

Prostacyclin & Its Stable Analogue Iloprost. Ed. by R. J. Gryglewski & G. Stock. (Illus.). 320p. 1986. 53.90 (ISBN 0-387-16954-7). Springer-Verlag.

Prostacyclin: Clinical Trials. Ed. by Richard J. Gryglewski et al. 160p. 1985. text ed. 49.00 (ISBN 0-88167-051-0). Raven.

Prostacyclin in Pregnancy. Ed. by Peter J. Lewis et al. (Illus.). 246p. 1983. text ed. 52.00 (ISBN 0-89004-889-4). Raven.

Prostaglandin & Fertility Regulation. Ed. by M. Toppozada et al. (Advances in Reproductive Health Care Ser.). 1984. lib. bdg. 72.00 (ISBN 0-85200-804-X, Pub. by MTP Pr England). Kluwer Academic.

Prostaglandin & Lipid Metabolism in Radiation Injury. Ed. by T. L. Walden, Jr. & H. N. Hughes. LC 87-32663. (Illus.). 434p. 1988. 72.50x (ISBN 0-306-42793-1, Plenum Pr). Plenum Pub.

Prostaglandin Research. Ed. by Pierre Crabbe. (Organic Chemistry Ser.). 1977. 85.00 (ISBN 0-12-194660-6). Acad Pr.

Prostaglandin Synthesis. Jasjit S. Bindra. 1977. 66.00 (ISBN 0-12-099460-7). Acad Pr.

Prostaglandin Synthetase Inhibitors. H. Robinson. Ed. by J. E. Vane. 1974. 38.50 (ISBN 0-7204-7529-5, North Holland). Elsevier.

Prostaglandin Synthetase Inhibitors: New Clinical Applications Proceedings. Ed. by Peter Ramwell. LC 80-36705. (Prostaglandins & Related Lipids Ser.: Vol. 1). 438p. 1980. 50.00x (ISBN 0-8451-2100-6). A R Liss.

Prostaglandins. Greenberg et al. (Modern Pharmacology-Toxicology Ser.: Vol. 21). 440p. 1982. 79.75 (ISBN 0-8247-1682-5). Dekker.

Prostaglandins. E. W. Horton. (Monographs on Endocrinology: Vol. 7). (Illus.). 235p. 1972. 36.00 (ISBN 0-387-05571-1). Springer-Verlag.

Prostaglandins & Blood Cell Function. Gerrard. (Hematology Ser.). 280p. 1985. 75.00 (ISBN 0-8247-7259-8). Dekker.

Prostaglandins & Cancer: Proceedings. First International Conference on Prostaglandins & Cancer, Washington, DC, August 30-September 2, 1981. Ed. by Trevor J. Powles et al. LC 82-86. (Prostaglandins & Related Lipids: Vol. 2). 876p. 1982. 93.00 (ISBN 0-8451-2101-4). A R Liss.

Prostaglandins & Cardiovascular Disease. Ed. by Ruth J. Hegyeli. (Atherosclerosis Reviews Ser.: Vol. 8). 218p. 1981. text ed. 45.50 (ISBN 0-89004-516-X). Raven.

Prostaglandins & Immunity. Ed. by James S. Goodwin. LC 85-4989. (Prostaglandins, Leukotrienes, & Cancer Ser.: No. 4). 1985. lib. bdg. 42.50 (ISBN 0-89838-723-X, Pub. by Martinus Nijhoff Netherlands). Kluwer Academic.

Prostaglandins & Inflammation. Ed. by A Ford-Hutchinson & K. Rainsford. (Agents & Actions Supplements: No. 6). (Illus.). 242p. 1979. pap. 34.95x (ISBN 0-8176-1132-0). Birkhauser.

Prostaglandins & Leukotrienes in Gastrointestinal Disease. Ed. by W. Domschke et al. (Illus.). 300p. 1988. pap. 59.40 (ISBN 0-387-18744-8). Springer-Verlag.

Prostaglandins & Membrane Ion Transport. Ed. by P. Braquet et al. (Advances in Ion Transport Regulation Ser.). (Illus.). 430p. 1985. text ed. 75.00 (ISBN 0-88167-052-9). Raven.

Prostaglandins & Other Eicosanoids in the Cardiovascular System. Ed. by K. Schroer. (Illus.). xiv, 570p. 1985. pap. 110.00 (ISBN 3-8055-4007-8). S Karger.

Prostaglandins & Perinatal Medicine. Ed. by Flavio Coceani & Peter M. Olley. LC 77-17758. (Advances in Prostaglandin & Thromboxane Research Ser.: Vol. 4). 428p. 1978. 79.50 (ISBN 0-89004-216-0). Raven.

Prostaglandins & Related Compounds: Sixth International Conference, Florence, Italy, 2 vols. Ed. by Bengt Samuelsson et al. (Advances in Prostaglandin, Thromboxane, & Leukotriene Research Ser.: Vols. 17A-17B). (Illus.). 1244p. 1987. Set. text ed. 149.00 (ISBN 0-88167-280-7). Raven.

Prostaglandins & Related Substances: A Practical Approach. Ed. by C. Benedetto et al. Tr. by T. F. Slater. 330p. 1987. 52.00 (ISBN 1-85221-032-X); pap. 32.00 (ISBN 1-85221-031-1). IRL Pr US.

Prostaglandins & Related Substances. Ed. by C. Pace-Asciak & E. Granstrom. (New Comprehensive Biochemistry Ser.: Vol. 5). 255p. 1983. 78.00 (ISBN 0-444-80517-6, I-380-83, Biomedical Pr). Elsevier.

Prostaglandins & the Cardiovascular System. Ed. by John A. Oates. (Advances in Prostaglandin, Thromboxane, & Leukotriene Research Ser.: Vol. 10). 400p. 1982. 81.00 (ISBN 0-89004-580-1). Raven.

Prostaglandins & the Kidney. Ed. by R. Horton & M. J. Dunn. (Journal: Mineral & Electrolyte Metabolism: Vol. 6, No. 1-2). (Illus.). 104p. 1981. pap. 46.75 (ISBN 3-8055-3406-X). S Karger.

Prostaglandins & the Kidney: Biochemistry, Physiology, Pharmacology, & Clinical Applications. Ed. by Michael J. Dunn. LC 82-18117. 438p. 1982. 69.50x (ISBN 0-306-41054-0, Plenum Med Bk). Plenum Pub.

Prostaglandins & Their Inhibitors in Clinical Obstetrics & Gynaecology. M. Bygdeman et al. 1986. lib. bdg. 157.75 (ISBN 0-85200-874-0, Pub. by MTP Pr England). Kluwer Academic.

Prostaglandins & Thromboxins: Proceedings of the Third International Symposium on Prostaglandins & Thromboxanes in the Cardiovascular System, Hale-Salle, GDR, 5-7 May 1980. Werner Forster et al. LC 80-41802. (Illus.). 500p. 1981. 97.00 (ISBN 0-08-027369-6). Pergamon.

Prostaglandins: Basic & Clinical Aspects. Ed. by J. B. Lee. (Current Endocrinology Ser.: Vol. 4). 378p. 1982. 75.25 (ISBN 0-444-00645-1, Biomedical Pr). Elsevier.

Prostaglandins from Plexaura homomalla: Ecology, Utilization & Conservation of a Major Medical Marine Resource, a Symposium. Ed. by Frederick M. Bayer & Alfred J. Weinheimer. LC 74-3562. (Studies in Tropical Oceanography Ser: No. 12). 1974. 15.00x (ISBN 0-87024-275-X). U Miami Marine.

Prostaglandins in Animal Reproduction, Vol II. Lars-Eric Edqvist & Hans Kindahl. (Developments in Animal & Veterinary Sciences Ser.: Vol. 13). 1984. 97.50 (ISBN 0-444-42294-3, I-049-84). Elsevier.

Prostaglandins in Bone Resorption. Ed. by Wilson Harvey & Alan Bennett. 144p. 1987. 95.00 (ISBN 0-8493-5591-5). CRC PR.

Prostaglandins in Cancer Research: Proceedings. Ed. by E. Garaci et al. (Life Sciences Ser.). (Illus.). 300p. 1987. 81.00 (ISBN 0-387-17548-2). Springer-Verlag.

Prostaglandins in Cardiovascular & Renal Function. Ed. by Alexander Scriabine et al. (Monographs of the Physiology. Soc. of Phila.: Vol. 6). (Illus.). 481p. 1980. text ed. 75.00 (ISBN 0-88331-186-0). Luce.

Prostaglandins in Clinical Research. Ed. by Helmut Sinzinger & Karsten Schror. LC 87-3750. (Progress in Clinical & Biolgical Research: Vol. 242). 526p. 1987. 86.00 (ISBN 0-8451-5092-8, 5092). A R Liss.

Prostaglandins in Reproduction. Norman L. Poyser. (Prostaglandins Research Studies). 260p. 1981. 86.00 (ISBN 0-471-09986-4, Pub. by Res Stud Pr). Wiley.

Prostaglandins, Leukotrienes, & Lipoxins. Ed. by J. Martyn Bailey. LC 85-16941. (GWUMC Department of Biochemistry Annual Spring Symposia Ser.). 722p. 1985. 95.00x (ISBN 0-306-41980-7, Plenum Pr.). Plenum Pub.

Prostaglandins, Leukotrienes, & the Immune Response. John L. Ninneman. (Illus.). 295p. Date not set. price not set (ISBN 0-521-33483-7). Cambridge U Pr.

Prostaglandins, Lipids: New Developments in Arteriosclerosis. H. L. Conn et al. 152p. 1981. 44.00 (ISBN 0-444-00566-8, Biomedical Pr). Elsevier.

Prostaglandins, Prostacyclin, Thromboxanes Measurement. Ed. by J. M. Boeynaems & A. G. Herman. (Developments in Pharmacology Ser.: No. 1.). (Illus.). 209p. 1981. PLB 34.00 (ISBN 90-247-2417-1, Pub. by Martinus Nijhoff Netherlands). Kluwer Academic.

Prostanoids: Pharmacological, Physiological & Clinical Relevance. P. K. Moore. (Illus.). 276p. 1985. 57.50 (ISBN 0-521-26081-7); pap. 20.95 (ISBN 0-521-27827-9). Cambridge U Pr.

Prostanoids: Proceedings of the Third Congress of the Hungarian Pharmacological Society, Budapest, 1979. Ed. by Valeria Kecskemeti & J. Knoll. LC 80-41281. (Advances in Pharmacological Research & Practice Ser.: Vol. VI). 175p. 1981. 46.00 (ISBN 0-08-026391-7). Pergamon.

Prostate. J. P. Blandy & Bernard Lytton. (BIMR Urology Ser.: Vol. 3). 320p. 1986. text ed. 95.00 (ISBN 0-407-02359-3). Butterworth.

Prostate Accessory Male Sex Gland. S. Battaglia. (Journal: Applied Pathology: Vol. 3, No. 4). (Illus.). iv, 72p. 1986. pap. 40.00 (ISBN 3-8055-4464-2). S Karger.

Prostate Book: Sound Advice on Symptoms & Treatment. Stephen Rous. 1988. 18.95 (ISBN 0-393-02592-6). Norton.

Prostate Cancer. William J. Catalona. 224p. 1984. 46.50 (ISBN 0-8089-1648-3, 790819). Grune.

Prostate Cancer & Hormone Receptors: Proceedings. National Prostatic Cancer Project with Fred Hutchinson Cancer Research Center, Seattle, March 4-6, 1979. Ed. by Gerald P. Murphy & Avery A. Sandberg. LC 79-2778. (Progress in Clinical & Biological Research Ser.: Vol. 33). 242p. 1979. 41.00x (ISBN 0-8451-0033-5). A R Liss.

Prostate Cancer, Part A: Research, Endocrine Treatment, & Histopathology. Ed. by Gerald P. Murphy et al. LC 87-3637. (Progress in Clinical & Biological Research Ser.: Vol. 243A). 626p. 1987. 98.00 (ISBN 0-8451-0198-6, 0198). A R Liss.

Prostate Cancer, Part B: Imaging Techinques, Radiotherapy, Chemotherapy, & Management Issues. Ed. by Gerald P. Murphy et al. LC 87-3637. (Progress in Clinical & Biological Research: Vol. 243B). 574p. 1987. 98.00 (ISBN 0-8451-0199-4, 0199). A R Liss.

Prostate Gland & Seminal Vesicle. G. Aumueller. (Handbuch der Mikroskopischen Anatomie Des Menschen: Vol. 7, Pt. 6). (Illus.). 1979. 176.00 (ISBN 0-387-09191-2). Springer-Verlag.

Prostate Troubles. Leon Chaitow. (New Self-Help Ser.). (Illus.). 96p. (Orig.). 1988. pap. 2.99 (ISBN 0-7225-1561-8, Pub. by Thorsons (England)). Sterling.

Prostatic Acid Phosphatase Measurement: Detection & Management of Prostatic Cancer. Intro. by Leslie M. Shaw et al. (Annals of The New York Academy of Science Ser.: Vol. 390). 145p. 1982. lib. bdg. 30.00x (ISBN 0-89766-170-2); pap. 30.00x (ISBN 0-89766-171-0). NY Acad Sci.

Prostatic Cancer. Ablin. (Science Practice of Surgery Ser.: Vol. 1). 288p. 1981. 69.75 (ISBN 0-8247-1524-1). Dekker.

Prostatic Cancer. Ed. by Gerald Murphy. LC 78-55284. (Illus.). 246p. 1979. 36.00 (ISBN 0-88416-190-0). PSG Pub Co.

Prostatic Carcinoma: Biology & Diagnosis. Ed. by E. S. Hafez & E. Spring-Mills. (Clinics in Andrology: No. 6). (Illus.). 200p. 1981. PLB 68.50 (ISBN 9-0247-2379-5, Pub. by Martinus Nijhoff Netherlands). Kluwer Academic.

Prostatic Cell: Structure & Function. Part A: Morphologic, Secretory, & Biochemical Aspects. Gerald P. Murphy et al. LC 81-17146. (Progress in Clinical & Biological Research Ser.: Vol. 75A). 550p. 1981. 88.00 (ISBN 0-8451-0161-7). A R Liss.

Prostatic Cell: Structure & Function. Part B: Prolactin, Carcinogenesis, & Clinical Aspects. Gerald P. Murphy et al. LC 81-17146. (Progress in Clinical & Biological Research Ser.: Vol. 75B). 380p. 1981. 73.00 (ISBN 0-8451-0162-5). A R Liss.

Prostatic Disease: Proceedings of the American - European Symposium, sponsored by Physicians Associated for continuing Education, John Hopkins University, University of Vienna & University of Innsbruck, Vienna, Nov 3-5, 1975. American-European Symposium Staff. Ed. by H. Marberger et al. LC 75-42905. (Progress in Clinical & Biological Research Ser.: Vol. 6). 432p. 1976. 47.00x (ISBN 0-8451-0006-8). A R Liss.

Prostglandins & Cardiovascular Disease. Ed. by T. Ozawa et al. 220p. 1986. 77.00x (ISBN 0-85066-357-1). Taylor & Francis.

Prostheses & Contact Lenses. James R. Critser, Jr. (Ser. 10PC-80). 1981. 80.00 (ISBN 0-914428-85-3). Lexington Data.

Prostheses & Contact Lenses. James R. Critser, Jr. (Ser. 10PC-79). 1981. refer. 70.00 (ISBN 0-914428-67-5). Lexington Data.

Prostheses & Contact Lenses. James R. Critser, Jr. (Ser. 10PC-81). 126p. 1982. 80.00 (ISBN 0-914428-96-9). Lexington Data.

Prostheses & Contact Lenses. James R. Critser, Jr. (Ser. 10PC-83). 101p. 1984. 80.00 (ISBN 0-88178-020-0). Lexington Data.

Prostheses & Contact Lenses. James R. Critser, Jr. (Ser. 10PC-82). 106p. 1983. 80.00 (ISBN 0-88178-008-1). Lexington Data.

Prostheses & Contact Lenses. James R. Critser, Jr. (Ser. 10 PC-84). 126p. 1985. 80.00 (ISBN 0-88178-057-X). Lexington Data.

Prostheses for Reconstructure Surgery. D. F. Williams. (Illus.). 300p. 1987. cancelled (ISBN 0-03-060333-1). Praeger.

Prostheses for Sensory & Internal Organs. International Resource Development Staff. 174p. 1986. 1285.00x (ISBN 0-88694-693-X). Intl Res Dev.

Prosthetic & Orthotic Visual Educational Aids. American Academy of Orthopaedic Surgeons Committee on Prosthetics & Orthotics Staff. 52p. (Orig.). 1987. pap. 10.00 (ISBN 0-89203-021-6). Amer Acad Ortho Surg.

Prosthetic Knee Ligament Reconstruction. Friedman & Ferkel. 1987. write for info. (ISBN 0-8089-1885-0). Grune.

Prosthetic Ligament Reconstruction. Friedman & Ferkel. 240p. 1988. write for info. (ISBN 0-7216-2559-2). Saunders.

Prosthetics: Methods of Producing Facial & Body Restorations. Carl D. Clarke. (Illus.). 336p. 1965. 30.00 (ISBN 0-685-25471-2). Standard Arts.

Prostho Plus. Piers Anthony. 224p. 1986. pap. 2.95 (ISBN 0-8125-3116-7, Dist. by Warner Pub Services & St. Martin's Press). Tor Bks.

Prosthodontic Techniques. John B. Sowter. (Dental Laboratory Technology Manuals Ser.). viii, 305p. 1968. pap. text ed. 16.00x (ISBN 0-8078-7901-0). U of NC Pr.

Prostitute & Her Clients: Your Pleasure Is Her Business. Lewis Diana. 246p. 1985. 27.25x (ISBN 0-398-05042-2). C C Thomas.

Prostitute & the Social Reformer: Commercial Vice in the Progressive Era. LC 73-20647. (Sex, Marriage & Society Ser.). 394p. 1974. Repr. 20.00x (ISBN 0-405-05814-4). Ayer Co Pubs.

Prostitute Faith. Norvel Hayes. 1988. pap. 0.75 (ISBN 0-317-68141-9). Harrison Hse.

Prostitute in African Literature. F. E. Senkoro. 96p. 1982. pap. 8.50 (ISBN 0-89410-617-1, Pub. by Salaam U Pr Tanzania). Three Continents.

Prostitute Murders. Rod Leith. (Illus.). 256p. 1983. 14.95 (ISBN 0-8184-0345-4). Lyle Stuart.

Prostituted Muse: Images of Women & Women Dramatists, 1642-1737. Jacqueline Pearson. LC 87-9497. 256p. 1988. 49.95 (ISBN 0-312-00960-7). St Martin.

Prostitution - A Bibliographical Synthesis. B. Joardar. 131p. 1984. 29.95. Asia Bk Corp.

Prostitution: A Bibliographical Synthesis. Biswanath Joardar. xii, 135p. 1984. text ed. 25.00x (ISBN 0-86590-326-3, Pub. by Inter-India Pubns N Delhi). Apt Bks.

Prostitution & Its Repression in New York City, 1900-1931. Willoughby C. Waterman. LC 68-54305. (Columbia University. Studies in the Social Sciences: No. 352). Repr. of 1932 ed. 14.00 (ISBN 0-404-51352-2). AMS Pr.

Prostitution & the State in Italy, 1860-1915. Mary Gibson. (Crime, Law, Deviance Ser.). 320p. 1986. text ed. 38.00 (ISBN 0-8135-1172-0). Rutgers U Pr.

Prostitution & Victorian Social Reform: The Campaign Against the Contagious Diseases Acts. Paul McHugh. 1980. 29.00 (ISBN 0-312-65211-9). St Martin.

Prostitution & Victorian Society: Women, Class & the State. Judith Walkowitz. LC 79-21050. 347p. 1982. pap. 11.95 (ISBN 0-521-27064-2). Cambridge U Pr.

Prostitution, Considered in Its Moral, Social & Sanitary Aspects in London & Other Large Cities & Garrison Towns. William Acton. 302p. 1972. Repr. of 1870 ed. 27.50x (ISBN 0-7146-2414-4, BHA 02414, F Cass Co). Biblio Dist.

Prostitution in America: Three Investigations, 1902-1914. New York Committee of Fifteen, 1975 et al. Ed. by Syracuse Moral Survey Committee, 1975. Tr. by Massachusetts Commission for Investigation of White Slave Traffic Report, 1975. (Social Problems & Social Policy Ser.). 1976. 38.00 (ISBN 0-405-07511-1). Ayer Co Pubs.

Prostitution in Elizabethan & Jacobean Comedy. Anne M. Haselkorn. LC 82-50415. 158p. 1983. 15.00x (ISBN 0-87875-247-1). Whitston Pub.

Prostitution in Europe. Abraham Flexner. LC 69-14924. (Criminology, Law Enforcement, & Social Problems Ser.: No. 30). 1969. Repr. of 1914 ed. 18.00x (ISBN 0-87585-030-8). Patterson Smith.

Prostitution in Historical & Modern Perspectives. B Joardar. 87p. 1984. text ed. 50.00x (ISBN 0-86590-383-2, Pub. by Inter Pub N Delhi). Apt Bks.

Prostitution in India. Santosh K. Mukherji. xxiv, 528p. 1986. text ed. 60.00x (ISBN 81-210-0054-8, Pub. by Inter India Pubns N Delhi). Apt Bks.

Prostitution in Medieval Society: The History of an Urban Institution in Languedoc. Leah L. Otis. LC 84-16184. (Women in Culture & Society Ser.). (Illus.). 240p. 1985. lib. bdg. 22.50x (ISBN 0-226-64032-9). U of Chicago Pr.

Prostitution in Medieval Society: The History of an Urban Institution in Languedoc. Leah L. Otis. LC 84-16184. (Women in Culture & Society Ser.). (Illus.). xviii, 240p. 1985. pap. 11.95x (ISBN 0-226-64033-7). U of Chicago Pr.

Prostitution in Paris, Considered Morally, Politically, & Medically: Prepared for Philanthropists & Legislators from Statistical Documents. Alexandre J. Parent-Duchatelet. LC 72-9671. Repr. of 1845 ed. 37.50 (ISBN 0-404-57488-2). AMS Pr.

Prostitution in the United States. Howard B. Woolston. LC 69-14953. (Criminology, Law Enforcement, & Social Problems Ser.: No. 29). (Illus.). 1969. Repr. of 1921 ed. 18.00x (ISBN 0-87585-029-4). Patterson Smith.

Prostitution Reform: Four Documents. Robert Dingley. LC 83-48597. (Marriage See & Family Series). 454p. 1985. lib. bdg. 61.00. Garland Pub.

Prostitution: Regulation & Control. John F. Decker. (New York University Criminal Law Education & Research Center Publication Ser.: Vol. 13). xxvi, 572p. 1979. 65.00x (ISBN 0-8377-0507-X). Rothman.

Prostrannij Khristijanskij Katekhisis. Metropolitan Philaret Drozdov. 170p. pap. text ed. 6.00 (ISBN 0-317-29305-2). Holy Trinity.

Prostranstuo I Uremja V Micromire see Space & Time in the Microworld.

Protagonist in Transition. Gila Ramras-Rauch. (Comparative Literature-European University Studies: No. 18, Vol. 29). 258p. 1982. pap. 23.15 (ISBN 3-261-04946-4). P Lang Pubs.

Protagonist Powers & the Third World. Wayne Wilcox. Ed. by Richard D. Lambert. LC 76-102760. (Annals of the American Academy of Political & Social Science: Vol. 386). 1969. 15.00 (ISBN 0-87761-122-X); pap. 7.95 (ISBN 0-87761-121-1). Am Acad Pol Soc Sci.

Protagoras. Plato. Ed. by Gregory Vlastos. Tr. by Benjamin Jowett & Martin Ostwald. LC 56-14580. 1956. pap. 4.79 scp (ISBN 0-672-60232-6, LLA59). Bobbs.

Protagoras. Plato. (College Classical Ser.). ix, 232p. 1984. pap. text ed. 17.50x (ISBN 0-89241-387-5). Caratzas.

Protagoras & Meno. Plato. Tr. by W. K. Guthrie. Bd. with Meno. (Classics Ser.). 1957. pap. 3.95 (ISBN 0-14-044068-2). Penguin.

Protagoras (Plato) Benjamin Jowett & Martin Oswald. 1956. pap. text ed. write for info. (ISBN 0-02-361090-5). Macmillan.

Protales de Esplendor. Elizabeth Elliot. 272p. 1959. pap. 8.95 (ISBN 0-8254-1200-5). Kregel.

Protean Poetic: The Poetry of Sylvia Plath. Mary L. Broe. LC 79-3334. 240p. 1980. text ed. 26.00x (ISBN 0-8262-0291-8). U of Mo Pr.

Proteas in Hawaii. Kay Kepler & Jacob Mau. 80p. 1988. pap. 7.95 (ISBN 0-935180-66-4). Mutual Pub HI.

Protease Inhibitors of Human Plasma-Biochemistry & Pathophysiology, Vol. II. Genesio Murano. (Reviews of Hematology: Vol. II). 1985. 59.95 (ISBN 0-915340-14-3). PJD Pubns.

Proteases & Biological Control (Cold Spring Harbor Conferences on Cell Proliferation, Vol. 2. Ed. by Edward Reich et al. LC 75-18635. (Illus.). 1022p. 1975. 98.00x (ISBN 0-87969-114-X). Cold Spring Harbor.

Proteases in Biological Control & Biotechnology. Ed. by Dennis D. Cunningham & George L. Long. LC 87-3108. (UCLA Symposia on Molecular & Cellular Biology Ser.: Vol. 57). 352p. 1987. 100.00 (ISBN 0-8451-2656-3, 2656). A R Liss.

Proteases: Potential Role In Health & Disease. Ed. by Walter H. Horl & August Heidland. LC 83-19186. (Advances in Experimental Medicine & Biology Ser.: Vol. 167). 606p. 1984. 95.00x (ISBN 0-306-41488-0, Plenum Pr). Plenum Pub.

Protect the President: Outrageous Editorials from the Ultra-Right Newspaper Publisher William Loeb. Ed. by Andrew Mayer et al. LC 79-87929. (Illus.). 1979. pap. 7.25 (ISBN 0-932400-01-9). Intervale Pub Co.

Protect Your Child from Sexual Abuse: A Parent's Guide. Janie Hart-Rossi. LC 84-60586. 64p. 1984. lib. bdg. 11.95 (ISBN 0-943990-07-6); pap. 5.00 (ISBN 0-943990-06-8). Parenting Pr.

Protect Your Dreams, Your Dollars & Your Sanity: Or, How to Deal with Contractors. Feurmin Industries Staff. (Illus.). 51p. 1985. 8.95 (ISBN 0-910531-08-0). Wolcotts.

Protect Your Home: A Common-Sense Guide to Home Security. Richard H. Geiger. LC 87-45010. (Illus.). 180p. (Orig.). 1987. pap. 8.95 (ISBN 0-88266-501-4, Garden Way Pub). Storey Comm Inc.

Protect Your Legal Rights: A Handbook for Teenagers. Edward F. Dolan, Jr. LC 83-8162. (Teen Survival Library). 128p. (YA) (gr. 7 up). 1983. lib. bdg. 11.29 (ISBN 0-671-46121-4); pap. 4.95 (ISBN 0-671-49566-6). Messner.

Protect Yourself. N. H. Mager & S. K. Mager. LC 77-77045. (Illus.). 1978. pap. 1.95 (ISBN 0-87502-055-0). Benjamin Co.

Protect Yourself. 12p. 1977. pap. 2.00 (ISBN 0-317-31077-1). Amer Bar Assn.

Protect Yourself from Becoming an Unwanted Parent. Sol Gordon. (Illus., Orig.). (gr. 9-12). 1983. pap. 1.95 (ISBN 0-934978-08-5). Ed U Pr.

Protect Yourself from Cancer: A Physician's Comprehensive Plan for Cancer Prevention. Howard R. Bierman. (Illus.). 288p. 1988. cancelled (ISBN 0-396-08758-2). Dodd.

Protected Fishes of the United States & Canada. J. E. Johnson. LC 87-71027. 42p. 1987. pap. 10.00 (ISBN 0-913235-43-1). Am Fisheries Soc.

Protecting Abused & Neglected Children. Michael S. Wald et al. LC 87-10208. 275p. 1988. text ed. 32.50x (ISBN 0-8047-1420-7). Stanford U Pr.

Protecting Against Inflation & Maximizing Yield. John M. Bragg. 174p. 1986. pap. 19.95 (ISBN 0-88406-171-X). Ga St U Busn Pub.

Protecting Against the Expropriation Risk in Investing Abroad, No. 950. Richard C. Allison. (International Business Portfolios). 1988. 85.00 (ISBN 0-317-67050-6). Bender.

Protecting American Workers: An Assessment of Government Programs. Sar Levitan et al. 1986. pap. 25.00 (ISBN 0-87179-521-3, 0521). BNA.

Protecting & Exploiting New Technology & Designs. Keith Hodkinson. 400p. 1987. text ed. 55.00 (ISBN 0-419-13810-2, Pub. by E & FN Spon England). Routledge Chapman & Hall.

Protecting Biotechnology Inventions: A Guide for Scientists. Roman Saliwanchik. (Brock-Springer Series in Contemporary Bioscience). (Illus.). 160p. (Orig.). 1988. pap. 22.00 (ISBN 0-910239-20-7). Sci Tech Pubs.

Protecting Child Victim - Witnesses. National Legal Resources Center for Child Advocacy & Protection Staff. 1986. pap. 7.50 (549-0047-01). Amer Bar Assn.

Protecting Children from Abuse & Neglect: Developing & Maintaining Effective Support Systems for Families. James Garbarino & S. Holly Stocking. LC 79-24239. (Social & Behavioral Science Ser.). 1980. text ed. 28.95x (ISBN 0-87589-442-9). Jossey-Bass.

Protecting Children from Abuse & Neglect: Policy & Practice. Ed. by Douglas J. Besharov. 500p. 1988. text ed. 62.50x (ISBN 0-398-05428-2). C C Thomas.

Protecting Children Through the Legal System. National Legal Resources Center for Child Advocacy & Protection Staff. 972p. 1981. pap. 20.00 (549-0023-01). Amer Bar Assn.

Protecting Clients Intellectual Property. Michael Einschlag & Peter Michaelson. (Illus.). 290p. 1986. 25.00. NJ Inst CLE.

Protecting Computer Systems & Software. Ed. by Frank L. Huband & Duane Shelton. 1985. 50.00 (ISBN 0-317-29415-6, #H43937, Pub. by Law & Business). HarBraceJ.

Protecting Contractual & Proprietary Rights in the Computer & High-Technology Industries. Tobey Marzouk. 212p. 1988. 44.95 (ISBN 0-8186-8754-1, EK754); 44.95 (ISBN 0-8186-4754-X, MICROFICHE). IEEE Comp Soc.

Protecting Directors & Officers in an Era of Uncertain D&O Liability Insurance: ALI-ABA Video Law Review Study Materials. American Law Institute-American Bar Association Committee on Continuing Professional Educatio. LC 86-207095. 121p. 1986. 40.00. Am Law Inst.

Protecting Electronic Equipment from Electrostatic Discharge. Edward A. Lacy. LC 84-8902. (Illus.). 176p. (Orig.). 1984. pap. 11.95 (ISBN 0-8306-1820-1, 1820P). TAB Bks.

Protecting Environmental & Nuclear Whistleblowers: A Litigation Manual. Stephen Kohn. write for info. Nuclear Info Res.

Protecting Farmlands. Frederick R. Steiner & John Theilacker. (Illus.). 1984. 38.95 (ISBN 0-87055-452-2). AVI.

Protecting Historic Architecture & Museum Collections from Natural Disasters. Ed. by Barclay G. Jones. 500p. 1986. text ed. 44.95 (ISBN 0-409-90035-4). Butterworth.

Protecting Historic Properties: A Guide to Research & Preservation. Martha Wolf et al. LC 84-72856. (Illus.). 150p. 1984. pap. 15.00 (ISBN 0-940540-03-7). Brandywine Conserv.

Protecting Industrial-Business Facilities & Personnel from Terrorist Activities. 1977. pap. 5.00 (ISBN 0-918734-22-3). Reymont.

Protecting Information in the Electronic Workplace: A Guide for Managers. James Schweitzer. 1983. text ed. 32.00 (ISBN 0-8359-5702-0, Reston). P-H.

Protecting Information on Local Area Networks. James A. Schweitzer. 144p. 1988. text ed. 24.95. Butterworth.

Protecting Intellectual Property Rights: Issues & Controversies. Robert P. Benko. LC 86-32124. (AEI Studies: No. 453). 62p. (Orig.). 1987. lib. bdg. 15.75 (ISBN 0-8447-3617-1); pap. text ed. 6.75 (ISBN 0-8447-3622-8). Am Enterprise.

Protecting Minnesota's Children: Public Issues. League of Women Voters of Minnesota Education Fund Staff. (Illus.). 29p. 1986. pap. 2.50 (ISBN 0-9613566-2-6). League Wmn Voters MN.

Protecting Our Children: The Fight Against Molestation, a National Symposium, Oct. 1-4, 1984. LC 85-20124. 259p. 1984. pap. 9.00 (ISBN 0-318-21665-5, S/N 027-000-01260-4). USGPO.

Protecting Our Environment: Toward a New Agenda. James G. Speth et al. LC 85-71963. (Alternatives for the 1980s Ser.). 45p. (Orig.). 1985. pap. text ed. 9.75 (ISBN 0-944237-12-6, Ctr National Policy). U Pr of Amer.

Protecting Personnel at Hazardous Waste Sites. Ed. by Steven P. Levine & William F. Martin. 384p. 1984. text ed. 28.95 (ISBN 0-250-40642-X). Butterworth.

Protecting the Best Men: An Interpretive History of the Law of Libel. Norman L. Rosenberg. LC 85-1174. (Studies in Legal History). xii, 370p. 1986. 32.50x (ISBN 0-8078-1665-5). U of NC Pr.

Protecting the Environment: A Free Market Strategy. Ed. by Doug Bandow. 88p. 1986. 7.00 (ISBN 0-89195-040-0). Heritage Found.

Protecting the Family Jewels: How to Inventory Your Home Without Losing Your Mind. Kathleen Gura. 120p. 1987. pap. 12.95 (ISBN 0-939355-00-0). Enterpress.

Protecting the Family Jewels: How to Inventory Your Home Without Losing Your Mind. 2nd ed. Kathleen Gura. 116p. 1987. pap. 12.95 (ISBN 0-939355-11-6). Enterpress.

Protecting the Golden Shore: Lessons from the Calif. Coastal Commissions. R. Healy et al. Ed. by Robert G. Healy. LC 78-65565. 257p. (Orig.). 1978. pap. 7.50 (ISBN 0-89164-052-5). Conservation Found.

Protecting the Human Environment. (United Nations Peaceful Settlement Ser.). 8.00 (ISBN 92-1-157002-6, E.77.XV.PS/9). UN.

Protecting the Innocent: Enhancing the Humanitarian Role of the United Nations in Natural Disasters & Other Disaster Situations. Thomas E. Boudreau. 1983. pap. (ISBN 0-87641-310-6). Carnegie Ethics & Intl Affairs.

Protecting the Medically Dependent. Robert Barry. (ISBN 0-913631-07-8). Anastasia VA.

Protecting the Nations: Groundwater from Contamination. Congress of the United States Office of Technology Assessment Staff. 1986. 75.00x (ISBN 81-85046-53-0, Pub. by Scientific). State Mutual Bk.

Protecting the New Jersey Pinelands: A New Direction in Land-Use Management. Ed. by Beryl R. Collins & Emily W. Russell. (Illus.). 234p. 1988. text ed. 35.00 (ISBN 0-8135-1267-0); pap. 12.00 (ISBN 0-8135-1275-1). Rutgers U Pr.

Protecting the President. Dennis V. McCarthy. 1987. pap. 3.95 (ISBN 0-440-17163-6). Dell.

Protecting the President: The Inside Story of Secret Service Agent. Dennis V. McCarthy & Philip W. Smith. LC 85-13737. (Illus.). 224p. 1985. 15.95 (ISBN 0-688-05422-6). Morrow.

Protecting the Public's Right to a Legal Defense: Trends in Legal Aid Service, 1980-1985. Dale E. Casper. (Public Administration Ser.: P 1847). 8p. 1986. 3.00 (ISBN 0-89028-717-1). Vance Biblios.

Protecting the Real Estate Lender: Workout, Bankruptcy, & Financing Strategies. (Real Estate Law & Practice Ser.). 567p. 1988. 45.00 (N4-4492). PLI.

Protecting the Social Service Client: Legal & Structural Controls on Official Discretion. Joel F. Handler. LC 78-22528. (Institute for Research on Poverty Monographs). 1979. 17.50 (ISBN 0-12-322842-5); pap. 10.00 (ISBN 0-12-322848-4). Acad Pr.

Protecting the Trustee & Executor in the 80's. Real Property, Probate & Trust Law Section. 268p. 1985. pap. 45.00 (ISBN 0-89707-164-6). Amer Bar Assn.

Protecting the Vulnerable: A Re-Analysis of Our Social Responsibilities. Robert E. Goodin. LC 85-1127. xii, 236p. 1986. 25.00x (ISBN 0-226-30298-9); pap. 9.95 (ISBN 0-226-30299-7). U of Chicago Pr.

Protecting the Working Man: The Quest for Safety in Logging & Milling in the State of Oregon. David James. 1987. 24.95x (ISBN 0-87595-122-8). Oregon Hist.

Protecting Trade Secrets 1986. 969p. 1986. pap. 45.00 (ISBN 0-317-27497-X, G4-3790). PLI.

Protecting Water Quality. Ed. by Gary E. McCuen. (Ideas in Conflict Ser.). 180p. 1986. lib. bdg. 11.95 (ISBN 0-86596-056-9). G E McCuen Pubns.

Protecting Workers' Lives: A Safety & Health Guide for Unions. 248p. 1983. pap. 20.65 (ISBN 0-87912-121-1, 062.02). Natl Safety Coun.

Protecting Workplace Secrets: Manager's Guide to Confidentiality & the Right to Know. O'Reilly. 1985. pap. 75.00 (ISBN 0-88057-269-8). Exec Ent Pubns.

Protecting Your Business Against Employee Thefts, Shoplifters & Other Hazards. rev. ed. L. R. Nader. LC 72-98094. 40p. 1977. pap. 2.00 (ISBN 0-87576-032-5). Pilot Bks.

Protecting Your Business from the IRS. Robert S. Schriebman. 330p. 1986. 27.50 (ISBN 0-87094-905-5). Dow Jones-Irwin.

Protecting Your Business Secrets. Michael K. Saunders. LC 84-25392. 250p. 1985. 27.50 (ISBN 0-89397-209-6). Nichols Pub.

Protecting Your Collection: A Handbook, Survey, & Guide for the Security of Rare Books, Manuscripts, Archives & Works of Art. Slade R. Gandert. LC 81-7004. (Library & Archival Security Ser.: Vol. 4, Nos. 1 & 2). 144p. 1982. text ed. 24.95 (ISBN 0-917724-78-X, B78). Haworth Pr.

Protecting Your Franchising Trademarks & Trade Secrets. Donald A. Kaul. 20p. 1983. 10.00 (ISBN 0-317-66124-8). Intl Franchise Assn.

Protecting Your Mental Health Practice: How to Minimize Legal & Financial Risk. Robert H. Woody. LC 88-42804. 1988. 24.95x (ISBN 1-55542-111-3). Jossey-Bass.

Protecting Your Microcomputer System. Harold J. Highland. LC 83-5858. 244p. 1984. pap. 14.95 (ISBN 0-471-89216-5, Pub by Wiley Pr). Wiley.

Protecting Your Sales Commission: Professional Liability in Real Estate. Ronald Friedman & Benjamin Henszey. LC 82-5199. 280p. 1982. 24.95 (ISBN 0-88462-438-2, 1974-01, Real Estate Ed). Longman Finan.

Protection Against Anti-Union Discrimination. Bartolomei De la Cruz. 123p. 1976. 14.00 (ISBN 92-2-101348-0). Intl Labour Office.

Protection Against Atmospheric Corrosion: Theories & Methods. Karel Barton. Tr. by John R. Duncan. LC 75-26570. 204p. pap. 53.10 (2030482). Bks Demand UMI.

Protection Against Bombs & Incendiaries: For Business, Industrial & Educational Institutions. photocopy ed. Earl A. Pike. (Illus.). 92p. 1973. 13.00 (ISBN 0-398-02517-7). C C Thomas.

Protection Against Internally Generated Missiles & Their Secondary Effects in Nuclear Power Plants: A Safety Guide. (Safety Ser.: No. 50-SG-D4). (Illus.). 44p. 1980. pap. 10.75 (ISBN 92-0-123880-0, ISP552, IAEA). UNIPUB.

Protection Against Ionizing Radiations: A Survey of Current World Legislation. (International Digest of Health Legislation Ser: Vol. 22, No. 4). 328p. 1972. pap. 11.20 (ISBN 92-4-169224-3, 1024). World Health.

Protection Against Ionizing Radiation in the Teaching of Science. International Commission on Radiological Protection. Ed. by International Commission on Radiological Protection & F. D. Sowby. (ICRP Publications: No. 36). 14p. 1983. pap. 11.00 (ISBN 0-08-029818-4). Pergamon.

Protection Against Neutron Radiation. LC 73-138550. (NCRP Reports Ser.: No. 38). 1971. 13.00 (ISBN 0-913392-20-0). NCRP Pubns.

Protection Against Radiation from Brachytherapy Sources. LC 67-190610. (NCRP Reports Ser.: No. 40). 1972. 12.00 (ISBN 0-913392-22-7). NCRP Pubns.

Protection Against Trichothecene Mycotoxins. Toxicology & Environmental Health Hazards Board, National Research Council. 1983. pap. text ed. 17.95x (ISBN 0-309-03430-2). Natl Acad Pr.

Protection Agent. Jack Rudman. (Career Examination Ser.: C-2397). (Cloth bdg. avail. on request). pap. 14.00 (ISBN 0-8373-2397-5). Natl Learning.

Protection & Competition in International Trade. Ed. by Henryk Kierzkowski. 256p. Date not set. text ed. 45.00 (ISBN 0-631-15004-8). Basil Blackwell.

Protection & Development in Mexico. Robert B. Tenkate & Robert B. Wallace. 1981. 35.00x (ISBN 0-312-65217-8). St Martin.

Protection & Industrial Policy in Europe. Joan Pearce & John Sutton. 208p. (Orig.). 1986. text ed. 29.95 (ISBN 0-7102-0733-6). Routledge Chapman & Hall.

Protection & Liberalization: A Review of Analytical Issues. W. Max Corden. (Occasional Papers: No. 54). 28p. 1987. pap. 7.50 (ISBN 0-939934-94-9). Intl Monetary.

Protection & Politics in Bahrain, 1869-1915. Talal T. Farah. (Illus.). 256p. 1986. text ed. 25.00x (ISBN 0-8156-6074-X, Am U Beirut). Syracuse U Pr.

Protection by Angles. 1982. 3.50 (ISBN 0-89858-041-2). Fill the Gap.

Protection, Cooperation, Integration & Development: Essays in Honour of Professor Hiroshi Kitamura. Ed. by Ali M. El-Agraa. 300p. 1987. text ed. 55.00x (ISBN 0-333-43747-0, Pub. by Macmillan London). Sheridan.

Protection du Patrimoine Culturel Mobilier II: Recveil de Textes Legislatifs. (Fr.). 1981. pap. 12.00 (ISBN 92-3-201891-8, U1159, UNESCO). UNIPUB.

Protection du Patrimoine Culturel Mobilier I: Recueil de Textes Legislatifs. (Fr.). 1979. pap. 14.50 (ISBN 92-3-201638-9, U990, UNESCO). UNIPUB.

Protection from Exposure Fires. National Fire Protection Association Staff. 1987. 10.50 (ISBN 0-317-63231-0, 80A-87). Natl Fire Prot.

Protection from Exposure Fires. (Eighty-Ninety Ser.). 1970. pap. 2.00 (ISBN 0-685-58146-2, 80A). Natl Fire Prot.

Protection from Power under English Law. Lord MacDermott. (Hamlyn Lectures Legal Reprint Ser.). viii, 196p. 1986. Repr. of 1957 ed. lib. bdg. 25.00x (ISBN 0-8377-2430-9). Rothman.

Protection, Growth & Trade: Essays in International Economics. W. Max Corden. 272p. 1985. 45.00x (ISBN 0-631-14529-X). Basil Blackwell.

Protection in Nuclear Medicine & Ultrasound Diagnostic Procedures in Children. National Council on Radiation Protection & Measurements Staff. LC 83-61834. (Report Ser.: No. 73). 81p. 1983. pap. text ed. 13.00 (ISBN 0-913392-63-4). NCRP Pubns.

Protection Made Easy. Warren J. Lucas. Ed. by C. C. Clinkscales, III. LC 80-69587. (Illus.). 162p. (Orig.). 1981. 7.95; pap. 5.95. C & L Pub Co.

Protection, Marketing, & Distribution of Computer-Communications Technology. Ed. by Wake Forest University of Law--Continuing Legal Education Staff. (Orig.). 1987. pap. 125.00 (ISBN 0-942225-28-7). Wake Forest Law.

Protection Mutual Insurance Company: The First Hundred Years. Carole Presser. LC 87-61723. (Illus.). 72p. (Orig.). 1987. pap. price not set (ISBN 0-916371-07-7). Mobium Pr.

Protection of Abused Victims: State Laws & Decisions. Ed. by Irving J. Sloan. LC 82-14104. 1982. Bdr. 1 looseleaf 50.00 (ISBN 0-379-10237-4); 35.00. Oceana.

Protection of Assets Manual. T. J. Walsh & R. J. Healy. 1988. looseleaf 285.00x (ISBN 0-930868-04-8). Merritt Co.

Protection of Children: State Intervention & Family Life. Robert Dingwall et al. 296p. 1985. pap. 12.95 (ISBN 0-631-13608-8). Basil Blackwell.

Protection of Citizens Abroad by the Armed Forces of the United States. M. Offutt. Repr. of 1928 ed. 21.00 (ISBN 0-527-68200-4). Kraus Repr.

Protection of Citizens Abroad by the Armed Forces of the United States. Milton Offutt. LC 78-64130. (Johns Hopkins University. Studies in the Social Sciences. Forty-Sixth Ser. 1928: 4). Repr. of 1928 ed. 12.50 (ISBN 0-404-61243-1). AMS Pr.

Protection of Coastal Fisheries under International Law. Stefan A. Riesenfeld. (Carnegie Endowment for International Peace Monograph). xii, 296p. Repr. of 1942 ed. 37.00 (ISBN 0-384-50838-3). Johnson Repr.

Protection of Computer Software: Its Technology & Application. Ed. by Derrick Grover. (British Computer Society Monographs in Informatics). (Illus.). 224p. Date not set. price not set (ISBN 0-521-35335-1). Cambridge U Pr.

Protection of Computer Systems & Software. Frank L. Huband & R. D. Shelton. LC 86-10271. Date not set. price not set (ISBN 0-15-004393-7). HarBraceJ.

Protection of Corporate Names: A Country by Country Survey. United States Trademark Association. LC 82-4235. 1982. looseleaf 95.00 (ISBN 0-87632-404-9). Clark Boardman.

Protection of Creditors' Rights in Workouts & Bankruptcy Cases in State. National Business Institute Staff. LC 86-190796. 1987. 30.00. Natl Busn Inst.

Protection of Cultural Property & Archaeological Resources: A Comprehensive Bibliography of Law-Related Materials. Frank G. Houdek. (Collection of Bibliographic & Research Resources). 122p. 1988. looseleaf 300.00; pap. text ed. 50.00 (ISBN 0-379-20911-X). Oceana.

Protection of Cultural Property & Archaeological Resources: A Comprehensive Bibliography of Law-Related Materials. Ed. by Frank G. Houdek. (Collection of Bibliographic & Research Resources Ser.). 122p. (Orig.). 1988. fascicle 300.00; pap. text ed. 50.00. Oceana.

Protection of Electronic Computer - Data Processing Equipment. National Fire Protection Association Staff. 1987. 10.50 (ISBN 0-317-63226-4, 75-87). Natl Fire Prot.

Protection of Ethnic Minorities: Comparative Perspectives. Ed. by Robert G. Wirsing. LC 80-25618. (Pergamon Policy Studies on International Politics). 350p. 1981. 60.00 (ISBN 0-08-025556-6). Pergamon.

Protection of Exothermic Reactors & Pressurised Storage Vessels: Proceedings of the Symposium, Chester, U. K., April 25-27, 1984. Ed. by Institution of Chemical Engineers. (Institution of Chemical Engineers Symposium Ser.: Vol. 85). 378p. 1984. 50.00 (ISBN 0-08-030280-7). Pergamon.

Protection of Foreign Interests, a Study in Diplomatic & Consular Practice. William M. Franklin. Repr. of 1947 ed. lib. bdg. 35.00x (ISBN 0-8371-0426-2, FRFI). Greenwood.

Protection of Foreign Investment: Six Procedural Studies. Richard B. Lillich. (Procedural Aspects of International Law Ser.: Vol. 5). 222p. 1965. 20.00x (ISBN 0-8139-0838-8). U Pr of Va.

Protection of Geographic Denominations of Goods & Services. Ed. by H. Cohen Jehoran. (Monographs in Industrial Property & Copyright Law: Vol. III). 216p. 1980. 37.50 (ISBN 90-286-0090-6, Pub. by Sijthoff & Noordhoff). Kluwer Academic.

Protection of Human Research Subjects: A Practical Guide to Federal Laws & Regulations. Dennis M. Maloney. LC 84-4873. 442p. 1984. 39.50x (ISBN 0-306-41522-4, Plenum Pr). Plenum Pub.

Protection of Human Rights in the Light of Scientific & Technological Progress in Biology & Medicine: 8th CIOMS Round Table Conference. (Also avail. in French). 1974. 12.40 (ISBN 92-4-056007-6). World Health.

Protection of Industrial Power Systems. T. Davies. 1984. text ed. 44.00 (ISBN 0-08-029322-0); pap. text ed. 18.75 (ISBN 0-08-029321-2). Pergamon.

Protection of International Personnel Abroad. Carol M. Crosswell. LC 52-10152. 196p. 1952. 12.50 (ISBN 0-379-00036-9). Oceana.

Protection of Know-How in Thirteen Countries: Reports to the VIIIth International Congress of Comparative Law, Pescara, 1970. Ed. by Carl Jehoram. 174p. 1972. 26.00 (ISBN 90-26-80586-1). Kluwer Academic.

Protection of Laboratory Workers from Infectious Disease Transmitted by Blood & Tissue: Proposed Guideline: National Committee for Clinical Laboratory Standards, Vol. 7. 1987. 15.00 (ISBN 0-318-23663-X). Natl Comm Clin Lab Stds.

Protection of Libraries & Library Collections. National Fire Protection Association Staff. 24p. 1985. 12.00 (ISBN 0-317-63517-4, 910-85). Natl Fire Prot.

Protection of Library Collection. (Eight Hundred & Nine Hundred Ser.). 1970. pap. 2.00 (ISBN 0-685-58217-5, 910). Natl Fire Prot.

Protection of Metals from Corrosion in Storage & Transit. Donovan. 1986. 62.95 (ISBN 0-470-20332-3). Halsted Pr.

Protection of Minority Political Participation Abandoned in Supreme Court's Ruling on Mobile Elections. Michael Langley. 1980. 1.00 (ISBN 0-686-38004-5). Voter Ed Proj.

Protection of Movable Cultural Property: Compendium of Legislative Texts. Hanna Saba. 392p. pap. 13.75 (ISBN 92-3-101638-5, U1336, UNESCO). UNIPUB.

Protection of Museum Collections. (Eighteen - Hundred to Nineteen - Hundred Ser.). 1974. pap. 2.50 (ISBN 0-685-58198-5, 911). Natl Fire Prot.

Protection of Museums & Museum Collections. National Fire Protection Association Staff. 24p. 1985. 12.00 (ISBN 0-317-63518-2, 911-85). Natl Fire Prot.

Protection of Nationals. F. S. Dunn. Repr. of 1932 ed. 26.00 (ISBN 0-527-25760-5). Kraus Repr.

Protection of Officials of Foreign States According to International Law. Franciszek Przetacznik. 1983. lib. bdg. 69.50 (ISBN 90-247-2721-9, Pub. by Martinus Nijhoff Netherlands). Kluwer Academic.

Protection of Personal & Commercial Reputation. Robert M. Kunstadt. (IIC Studies: Vol. 3). 98p. 1980. 39.00 (ISBN 0-89573-028-6). VCH Pubs.

Protection of Property Rights in the Ideas Market. Jennifer Skilbeck. (Thames Essays Ser.: No. 52). 100p. 1988. pap. text ed. 16.00 (ISBN 0-566-05341-1, Pub. by Gower Pub England). Gower Pub Co.

Protection of Public Water Supplies from Ground-Water Contamination. Ed. by Wayne A. Pettyjohn. LC 86-31173. (Pollution Technology Review Ser.: No. 141). (Illus.). 177p. 1987. 36.00 (ISBN 0-8155-1119-1). Noyes.

Protection of Records. National Fire Protection Association Staff. 1986. 10.50 (ISBN 0-317-63352-X, 232-86). Natl Fire Prot.

Protection of Records. (Two Hundred Ser.). 93p. 1970. pap. 2.00 (ISBN 0-685-46035-5, 232). Natl Fire Prot.

Protection of Semiconductor Chip Masks in the United States. Ed. by D. Ladd et al. (IIC Studies). 99p. 1986. pap. 40.00 (ISBN 0-89573-484-2). VCH Pubs.

Protection of Steel in Prestressed Concrete Bridges. (National Cooperative Highway Research Project Report). 86p. 1970. 4.00 (ISBN 0-309-01877-3). Transport Res Bd.

Protection of the Engineering Heritage: Brisbane, Australia, May 1982. 92p. (Orig.). 1982. pap. text ed. 27.00x (ISBN 0-85825-164-7, Pub. by Inst Engineering Australia). Brookfield Pub Co.

Protection of the Ischemic Myocardium: Cardioplegia. David J. Hearse et al. 432p. 1981. text ed. 75.50 (ISBN 0-89004-423-6). Raven.

Protection of the Library & Archive: An International Bibliography. Martin H. Sable. LC 83-17169. (Library & Archival Security: Vol. 5, Nos. 2/3). 183p. 1983. text ed. 29.95 (ISBN 0-86656-246-X, B246). Haworth Pr.

Protection of the Patient in Diagnostic Radiology. International Commission on Radiological Protection. Ed. by International Commission on Radiology Protection et al. (ICRP Publications: No. 34). 88p. 1983. pap. 28.00 (ISBN 0-08-029797-8). Pergamon.

Protection of the Patient in Nuclear Medicine. International Commission on Radiological Protection Staff. (International Commission on Radiological Protection Ser.: No. 52). (Illus.). 46p. 1988. pap. 25.00 (ISBN 0-08-033188-2, PBL). Pergamon.

Protection of the Patient in Radiation Therapy. Ed. by F. D. Sowby. (ICRP Publication Ser.: No. 44). (Illus.). 60p. 1985. pap. 24.00 (ISBN 0-08-032336-7). Pergamon.

Protection of the Patient in Radionuclide Investigations. International Commission on Radiological Protection. (ICRP Publication Ser.: No. 17). 1971. pap. 11.00 (ISBN 0-08-016773-X). Pergamon.

Protection of the Public in the Event of Major Radiation Accidents: Principles for Planning. Ed. by F. D. Sowby. (ICRP Publication Ser.: No. 40). (Illus.). 32p. 1984. pap. 24.00 (ISBN 0-08-032302-2). Pergamon.

Protection of the Public in the Event of Radiation Accidents: Proceedings. Food & Agriculture Organization of the United Nations Staff et al. (Illus.). 370p. (Eng., Fr. & Rus.). 1965. 14.40 (ISBN 92-4-156025-8). World Health.

Protection of the Thyroid Gland in the Event of Releases of Radioiodine. LC 77-82607. (NCRP Reports Ser.: No. 55). 1977. 13.00 (ISBN 0-913392-37-5). NCRP Pubns.

Protection of the Underwater Heritage: Protection of the Cultural Heritage. (Promotion of the Cultural Heritage: Technical Handbooks for Museums & Monuments: No. 4). (Illus.). 200p. 1981. pap. 12.75 (ISBN 92-3-101863-9, U1155, UNESCO). UNIPUB.

Protection of the Weak & Unarmed: The Dispute over Counting Human Rights Violations in El Salvador. LC 86-155263. (Americas Watch Report Ser.). 51p. Date not set. price not set. Fund Free Expression.

Protection of the Weak in the Talmud. Mordecai Katz. LC 26-5707. (Columbia University. Oriental Studies: No. 24). Repr. of 1925 ed. 12.50 (ISBN 0-404-50514-7). AMS Pr.

Protection of Vision in Children. photocopy ed. Arnall Patz & Richard E. Hoover. (Illus.). 184p. 1969. 21.75 (ISBN 0-398-01456-6). C C Thomas.

Protection of War Victims: Protocol One to the Nineteen Forty-Nine Geneva Conventions, 4 vols. Howard S. Levie. LC 79-16960. 1980. Vols. 1-4. 45.00 ea. (ISBN 0-379-00786-X); Set. 180.00; Supplement 1985. 10.00 (ISBN 0-379-00799-1). Oceana.

Protection of Women under Law. A. Yaqin & B. Anwar. 200p. 1982. 18.95. Asia Bk Corp.

Protection of Women under the Law: An Annotated Bibliography. Anwarul Yaqin. 1983. 15.00x (ISBN 0-8364-1063-7, Pub. by Deep). South Asia Bks.

Protection of Workers Against Noise & Vibration in the Working Environment: An ILO Code Practice. 90p. (Orig.). 1984. pap. 12.25 (ISBN 92-2-101709-5). Intl Labour Office.

Protection of Workers Against Noise & Vibration in the Working Environment: An ILO Code of Practice. viii, 74p. (2nd Impression). 1980. pap. 12.25 (ISBN 92-2-101709-5, ILO28, ILO). UNIPUB.

Protection of Workers Against Radio-Frequency & Microwave Radiation: A Technical Review. (Occupational Safety & Health Ser.: No. 57). ix, 72p. (Orig.). 1986. pap. 12.25 (ISBN 92-2-105604-X). Intl Labour Office.

Protection of Workers Against Radio-Frequency & Microwave Radiation: A Technical Review. (Occupational Safety & Health Ser.: No. 57). (Illus.). 72p. (Orig.). 1987. pap. text ed. 12.25 (ISBN 0-317-57960-6, ILO591, ILO). UNIPUB.

Protection or Free Trade. Henry George. LC 80-14436. 352p. 1980. 10.00x. Phoenix Pub.

Protection or Free Trade. Henry George. LC 80-14436. 335p. (Avail. in Fr., Ger., Span.). 1980. Repr. of 1886 ed. 10.00x. Schalkenbach.

Protection Racket. A. Ernest Fitzgerald. 1989. 18.95 (ISBN 0-395-36245-8). HM.

Protection System & Related Features in Nuclear Power Plants: A Safety Guide. (Safety Ser.: No. 50-SG-D3). (Illus.). 55p. 1981. pap. 10.00 (ISBN 9-2062-3280-0, ISP551, IAEA). UNIPUB.

Protection Through the Law. 2nd ed. Parnell J. Callahan. LC 78-808956. (Legal Almanac Ser.: No. 55). 128p. (Orig.). 1978. 6.95 (ISBN 0-379-11116-0). Oceana.

Protectionism. Jagdish N. Bhagwati. (Illus.). 168p. 1988. text ed. 16.95t (ISBN 0-262-02282-6). MIT Pr.

Protectionism -- Can the Tide Be Stemmed? James F. Bere. 25p. 1982. pap. 1.50 (ISBN 0-317-65758-5). Japan Soc.

Protectionism: A Bibliography. The Information Access Group Staff. (Public Administration Ser.: P 1983). 8p. 1986. 3.00 (ISBN 0-89028-963-8). Vance Biblios.

Protectionism Again? D. Greenaway & C. Milner. (Institute of Economic Affairs, Hobart Papers Ser.: No. 84). pap. 5.95 technical (ISBN 0-255-36127-0). Transatl Arts.

Protectionism & Structural Adjustment in the World Economy: Report. United Nations Conference on Trade & Development Secretariat. LC 83-207017. iii, 38p. 5.00 (ISBN 92-1-112139-6, E.82.II.D.14). UN.

Protectionism & the European Community, 1983. Ed. by E. L. Volker. 170p. 1983. pap. 28.00 (ISBN 90-65-44127-1). Kluwer Academic.

Protectionism & the Future of International Shipping: The Nature, Development & Role of Flag Discriminations & Preferences, Cargo Reservations & Sabotage Restrictions, State Intervention & Maritime Subsidies. Ademuni-Odeke. LC 83-25055. 1984. text ed. 89.50 (ISBN 9-02-472918-1, Pub. by Martinus Nijhoff Netherlands). Kluwer Academic.

Protectionism or Industrial Adjustment? Ed. by G. K. Helleiner et al. (Atlantic Papers Ser.: No. 39). 72p. 1980. pap. 6.50x (ISBN 0-916672-79-4, Pub. by Allanheld). Rowman.

Protectionist Case in the 1840's. Derek Walker-Smith. LC 72-111294. 1970. Repr. of 1933 ed. 17.50x (ISBN 0-678-00614-8). Kelley.

Protectionist Republicanism: Republican Tariff Policy in the McKinley Period. Clarence A. Stern. 1971. pap. 1.50 (ISBN 0-9600116-4-1). Stern.

Protective Agents in Cancer. Ed. by David McBrien & Trevor F. Slater. (NFCR Symposium Ser.). 1983. 42.00 (ISBN 0-12-481770-X). Acad Pr.

Protective & Decorative Coatings for Paper. Jack Weiner & Lillian Roth. LC 62-6678. (Bibliographic Series: No. 199, Suppl 2). 1976. pap. 25.00 (ISBN 0-87010-039-4). Inst Paper Chem.

Protective & Decorative Coatings for Paper. Jack Weiner & Lillian Roth. (Bibliographic Ser.: No. 199). 300p. 1962. 21.00 (ISBN 0-317-34426-9). Inst Paper Chem.

Protective & Decorative Coatings for Paper. Jack Weiner & Lillian Roth. (Bibliographic Ser.: No. 199, Supplement 3). 133p. 1968. 13.00 (ISBN 0-317-34427-7). Inst Paper Chem.

Protective Clothing for Structural Fire Fighting. National Fire Protection Association Staff. 1986. 10.50 (ISBN 0-317-63569-7, 1971-86). Natl Fire Prot.

Protective Coatings for Highway Structural Steel. John D. Keane. (National Cooperative Highway Research Program Reports: No. 74). (Illus.). 66p. 1969. pap. text ed. 15.00 (ISBN 0-938477-21-8). SSPC.

Protective Coatings for Highway Structural Steel. (National Cooperative Highway Research Program Report). 64p. 1969. 2.80 (ISBN 0-317-36101-5, 1749). Transport Res Bd.

Protective Coatings for Metals. 3rd ed. Robert M. Burns & William W. Bradley. LC 67-20826. (ACS Monograph: No. 163). 1975. 53.95 (ISBN 0-8412-0285-0). Am Chemical.

Protective Coatings for Weathering Steel Tower Joints. Bernard R. Appleman et al. (Illus.). 61p. 1987. pap. text ed. 40.00 (ISBN 0-938477-32-3, 87-03). SSPC.

Protective Coatings on Metals, Vol. 2. Grigorii V. Samonov. LC 69-12517. pap. 53.00 (2056113). Bks Demand UMI.

Protective Coatings on Metals, Vol. 10. G. V. Samsonov. 1987. 42.50 (ISBN 81-7087-010-0, Pub. by Oxford IBH). South Asia Bks.

Protective Coatings on Metals, Vol. 12. V. I. Arakhov. 1986. 42.50 (ISBN 0-8364-2275-9, Pub. by Oxford IBH). South Asia Bks.

Protective Custody. Taylor Lovering. 1982. 15.00x (ISBN 0-906660-43-2, Pub. by New Playwrights Network). State Mutual Bk.

Protective Custody in Adult Correctional Facilities. (Illus.). 81p. 1983. pap. 10.00 (ISBN 0-942974-46-8). Am Correctional.

Protective Devices for Sports & Work II: Research Subject Analysis with Bibliography. Mary R. Bartone. LC 84-45655. 150p. 1985. 34.50 (ISBN 0-88164-220-7); pap. 26.50 (ISBN 0-88164-221-5). ABBE Pubs Assn.

Protective Effect of BCG in Experimental Tuberculosis. Donald W. Smith. (Advances in Tuberculosis Research Ser.: Vol. 22). (Illus.). viii, 100p. 1985. 59.50 (ISBN 3-8055-4089-2). S Karger.

Protective Finish Collection, 2 vols. Ed. by Jerome H. Lieblich. 764p. Set. loose-leaf 99.95x (ISBN 0-912702-14-1, PFC). Global Eng.

Protective Groups in Organic Chemistry. Ed. by J. F. McOmie. LC 72-91038. 418p. 1973. 65.00x (ISBN 0-306-30717-0, Plenum Pr). Plenum Pub.

Protective Groups in Organic Synthesis. Theodora W. Greene. LC 80-25348. 349p. 1981. 44.50 (ISBN 0-471-05764-9). Wiley.

Protective Interlocks. (Principles of Steam Generation Ser.: Module 17). (Illus.). 60p. 1982. spiral bdg. 17.50x (ISBN 0-87683-267-2). GP Pub.

Protective Labor Legislation, with Special Reference to Women in the State of New York. Elizabeth Baker. LC 76-82239. (Columbia University Studies in the Social Sciences: No. 259). Repr. of 1925 ed. 20.00 (ISBN 0-404-51259-3). AMS Pr.

Protective Reinforced Concrete Shells in Hydrotechnic Constructions. M. P. Sedov. 80p. 1962. text ed. 20.00x (ISBN 0-7065-0189-6, Pub. by Keter Pub Jerusalem). Coronet Bks.

Protective Relaying: Principles & Applications. Blackburn. (Electrical Engineering Ser.). 405p. 1987. 85.00 (ISBN 0-8247-7445-0). Dekker.

Protective Relaying for Power Systems. S. H. Horowitz. LC 80-21776. 592p. 1980. 59.00 (ISBN 0-87942-140-1, PC01362). Inst Electrical.

Protective Relays: Their Theory & Practice, 2 vols. A. R. Warrington. Incl. Vol. 1, 2nd ed. LC 70-385616. 484p. 1968. text ed. 44.95x (ISBN 0-412-09060-0, NO. 6310); Vol. 2, 3rd ed. 434p. 1978. 44.95x (ISBN 0-412-15380-7, NO. 6311). Pub. by Chapman & Hall England). Routledge Chapman & Hall.

Protective Security Law. Fred E. Inbau & Marvin E. Aspen. 301p. 1983. text ed. 26.95 (ISBN 0-409-95068-8). Butterworth.

Proteins of the Seminal Plasma. Scheit et al. 1988. write for info. (ISBN 0-471-84685-6). Wiley.

Proteins-Peptides: Preparations & Applications. James R. Critser, Jr. (Ser. 15-84). 182p. 1985. 60.00 (ISBN 0-88178-024-3). Lexington Data.

Proteins: Structure & Function. J. J. L'Italien. 810p. 1987. 115.00x (ISBN 0-306-42299-9, Plenum Pr). Plenum Pub.

Proteinuria. Ed. by M. M. Avram. LC 85-9305. 248p. 1985. 39.50x (ISBN 0-306-41956-4, Plenum Pr). Plenum Pub.

Proteinuria. Ed. by J. Brod et al. (Contributions to Nephrology: Vol. 1). (Illus.). 250p. 1975. 39.50 (ISBN 3-8055-2183-9). S Karger.

Proteinuria: An Integrated Review. A. Z. Pesce & M. R. First. (Kidney Disease Ser.: Vol. 1). 1979. 65.75 (ISBN 0-8247-6874-4). Dekker.

Proteoglycans - Biological & Chemical Aspects in Human Life. J. F. Kennedy. (Studies in Organic Chemistry: Vol. 2). 494p. 1980. 129.00 (ISBN 0-444-41794-X). Elsevier.

Proterozoic Geology: Selected Papers from an International Proterozoic Symposium. Ed. by L. G. Medaris, Jr. et al. (Memoir Ser.: No. 161). (Illus.). 1983. 49.00 (ISBN 0-8137-1161-4). Geol Soc.

Proterozoic Lithospheric Evolution. A. Kroner. (Geodynamics Ser.: Vol. 17). 288p. 35.00 (ISBN 0-87590-517-X). Am Geophysical.

Protest & Conflict in African Literature. Ed. by Cosmo Pieterse & Donald Munro. LC 77-80856. 127p. 1969. 24.50 (ISBN 0-8419-0004-3, Africana); pap. 12.50 (ISBN 0-8419-0005-1, Africana). Holmes & Meier.

Protest & Crime in China: A Bibliography. Ssu-Yu Teng. (History, Political Science & International Affairs Catalog Ser.). 300p. 1981. lib. bdg. 43.00 (ISBN 0-8240-9354-2). Garland Pub.

Protest & Democracy in West Germany: Extra-Parliamentary Opposition & the Democratic Agenda. Ed. by Rob Burns & Wilfried Van der Will. LC 87-33092. 336p. 1988. 45.00 (ISBN 0-312-01681-6). St Martin.

Protest & Participation. J. R. Low-Beer. LC 77-8084. (American Sociological Association Rose Monograph: No. 4). (Illus.). 1978. 29.95 (ISBN 0-521-21782-2); pap. 11.95x (ISBN 0-521-29277-8). Cambridge U Pr.

Protest & Politics: Christianity & Contemporary Affairs. Ed. by Robert G. Clouse et al. 277p. 1968. 5.95 (ISBN 0-87921-000-1). Attic Pr.

Protest & Prejudice: A Study of Belief in the Black Community. Gary Marx. (Patterns of American Prejudice Ser.). 352p. pap. 1.95 (ISBN 0-686-95012-7). ADL.

Protest & Prejudice: A Study of Belief in the Black Community. Gary T. Marx. LC 78-23898. 1979. Repr. of 1969 ed. lib. bdg. 35.00x (ISBN 0-313-20827-1, MAPT). Greenwood.

Protest & Public Policy: World-Wide Anti-Nuclear Movement, 1982-1986. Dale E. Casper. (Public Administration Ser.: P 2206). 11p. 1987. 3.75 (ISBN 1-55590-406-8). Vance Biblios.

Protest & Punishment: The Story of the Social & Political Protesters Transported to Australia, 1788-1868. George Rude. 1978. 34.50x (ISBN 0-19-822430-3). Oxford U Pr.

Protest & Reform: The British Social Narrative by Women, 1827-1867. Joseph A. Kestner. LC 84-40498. 256p. 1985. text ed. 21.50x (ISBN 0-299-10060-X). U of Wis Pr.

Protest & Response in Mexico. Evelyn P. Stevens. 280p. 1974. 40.00x (ISBN 0-262-19128-8). MIT Pr.

Protest at Selma: Martin Luther King, Jr. & the Voting Rights Act of 1965. David J. Garrow. LC 78-5593. (Illus.). 1978. 35.00 (ISBN 0-300-02247-6); pap. 11.95x (ISBN 0-300-02498-3). Yale U Pr.

Protest, Direct Action, Repression. Dissent in American Society from Colonial Times to the Present. Ed. by Dirk Hoerder. xxvi, 434p. 1977. lib. bdg. 28.00 (ISBN 3-7940-7009-7). K G Saur.

Protest-Form-Tradition: Essays on German Exile Literature. Ed. by Joseph P. Strelka et al. LC 78-18190. 157p. 1979. 12.50 (ISBN 0-8173-8008-6). U of Ala Pr.

Protest in Democratic India: Authority's Response to Challenge. Leslie J. Calman. (WVSS on East Asia Ser.). 250p. 1985. pap. 25.50x (ISBN 0-8133-7060-4). Westview.

Protest in Tokyo: The Treaty Crisis of Nineteen Sixty. George R. Packard. LC 78-17982. 1978. Repr. of 1966 ed. lib. bdg. 32.25x (ISBN 0-313-20532-9, PAPT). Greenwood.

Protest Is Not Enough: The Struggle of Blacks & Hispanics for Equality in Urban Politics. Rufus P. Browning et al. LC 83-15552. (Illus.). x, 311p. 1984. 30.00 (ISBN 0-520-05033-9); pap. 11.95x (ISBN 0-520-05730-9). U of Cal Pr.

Protest Makers: The British Nuclear Disarmament Movement 1958-1965, Twenty Years on. Richard Taylor & Colin Pritchard. (Illus.). 180p. 1982. text ed. 35.00 (ISBN 0-08-025211-7); pap. text ed. 15.25 (ISBN 0-08-027940-6). Pergamon.

Protest Movements in America. Michael Useem. LC 74-34014. (Studies in Sociology Ser.). 68p. 1975. pap. text ed. 3.56 scp (ISBN 0-672-61356-5). Bobbs.

Protest Movements in Colonial East Africa-Aspects of Early African Response to European Rule. Robert Strayer et al. LC 73-85549. (Foreign & Comparative Studies-Eastern African Ser.: No.12). 96p. 1973. pap. 5.50x (ISBN 0-915984-09-1). Syracuse U Foreign Comp.

Protest: Studies of Collective Behavior & Social Movements. John Lofland. 400p. 1985. 34.95 (ISBN 0-88738-031-X). Transaction Bks.

Protest, Violence & Social Change. J. Hanley et al. 1972. pap. 4.65 (ISBN 0-13-731406-X). P-H.

Protest Without Illusions. Vernon Richards. 168p. 1981. pap. 5.00 (ISBN 0-900384-19-0). Left Bank.

Protestanism & the National Church in 16th Century England. Peter Lake. LC 87-1181. 224p. 1987. 28.50 (ISBN 0-317-58953-9). B&N Imports.

Protestant & Catholic. Kenneth W. Underwood. LC 72-9051. (Illus.). 484p. 1973. Repr. of 1957 ed. lib. bdg. 35.00x (ISBN 0-8371-6567-9, UNPC). Greenwood.

Protestant & Catholic Reform. Enzo Bellini et al. Ed. & tr. by John Drury. (Illustrated History of the Church Ser.). (Illus.). 124p. (Orig.). (gr. 6-12). 1981. 12.95 (ISBN 0-03-056831-5, HarpR). Har-Row.

Protestant & Roman Catholic Ethics: Prospects for Rapprochement. James M. Gustafson. LC 77-21421. 1980. pap. 9.00x (ISBN 0-226-31108-2, P868); 15.00x (ISBN 0-226-31107-4). U of Chicago Pr.

Protestant Baroque Poet: Pierre Poupo. Ralph M. Hester. (Studies in French Literature: No. 10). 1970. 23.20x (ISBN 90-2790-537-1). Mouton.

Protestant Bible. Paul Todd. 32p. 1987. 6.95 (ISBN 0-89962-611-4). Todd & Honeywell.

Protestant Biblical Interpretation. Bernard Ramm. 11.95 (ISBN 0-8010-7600-5). Baker Bk.

Protestant Biblical Interpretation. Bernard Ramm. Tr. by Silas Chan from Eng. (Chinese.). 1984. pap. write for info. (ISBN 0-941598-10-1). Living Spring Pubns.

Protestant, Catholic, Jew: An Essay in American Religious Sociology. Will Herberg. LC 83-9120. xvi, 310p. 1983. pap. 11.95x (ISBN 0-226-32734-5). U of Chicago Pr.

Protestant Cemetery of Rome. Revalee R. Stevens & Robert K. Steven. LC 81-84484. (North American Records in Italy). (Illus.). 110p. (Orig.). 1982. pap. 9.00 (ISBN 0-88127-003-2). Oracle Pr LA.

Protestant Challenge to Corporate America: Issues of Social Responsibility. Roy W. Morano. Ed. by Richard Farmer. LC 84-8514. (Research for Business Decisions Ser.: No. 69). 256p. 1984. 44.95 (ISBN 0-8357-1592-2). UMI Res Pr.

Protestant Christian Churches. Marcus Ward. 1985. 13.00x (ISBN 0-7062-3597-5, Pub. by Ward Lock Educ Co Ltd). State Mutual Bk.

Protestant Christianity. John Dillenberger & Claude Welch. 340p. 1976. pap. text ed. write for info. (ISBN 0-02-330470-7, Pub. by Scribner). Macmillan.

Protestant Christianity & People's Movements in Kerala, 1850-1936. J. W. Gladstone. 470p. 1986. 12.50x (ISBN 0-8364-1821-2, Pub. by Somaiya). South Asia Bks.

Protestant Christianity: Interpreted Through Its Development. 2nd ed. John Dillenberger & Claude Welch. 537p. 1988. pap. text ed. write for info. (ISBN 0-02-329601-1). Macmillan.

Protestant Church Music in America. Archibald Davison. 59.95 (ISBN 0-8490-0905-7). Gordon Pr.

Protestant Church-Related Colleges. Daniel W. Wynn. LC 74-84861. 108p. 1975. 6.95 (ISBN 0-8022-2157-2). Philos Lib.

Protestant Clergy & Public Issues, Eighteen Twelve to Eighteen Forty-Eight. John R. Bodo. LC 79-12849. (Perspectives in American History Ser: No. 52). 1980. Repr. of 1954 ed. lib. bdg. 35.000 (ISBN 0-87991-854-3). Porcupine Pr.

Protestant Clergy in the Great Plains & Mountain West, 1865-1915. Ferenc M. Szasz. (Illus.). 244p. 1988. 27.50x (ISBN 0-8263-1093-1). U of NM Pr.

Protestant Concepts of Church & State. Thomas G. Sanders. 19.50 (ISBN 0-8446-6185-6). Peter Smith.

Protestant Credo. Virgiulius Ferm. 1953. 5.95 (ISBN 0-8022-0494-5). Philos Lib.

Protestant Crusade in Ireland, 1800-70: A Study of Protestant-Catholic Relations Between the Act of Union & Disestablishment. Desmond Bowen. 1978. 27.50x (ISBN 0-7735-0295-5). McGill-Queens U Pr.

Protestant Dictionary: Containing Articles on the History, Doctrines, & Practices of the Christian Church. Ed. by Charles Wright & Charles Neil. LC 73-155436. 840p. 1971. Repr. of 1933 ed. 65.00x (ISBN 0-8103-3388-0). Gale.

Protestant Dissent in Ireland Sixteen Eighty-Seven to Seventeen Eighty. James C. Beckett. LC 78-20448. 1986. Repr. of 1948 ed. text ed. 20.00 (ISBN 0-88355-828-9). Hyperion Conn.

Protestant Era. abr ed. Paul Tillich. Tr. by James L. Adams. 1957. pap. 7.00x (ISBN 0-226-80342-2, P19, Phoen). U of Chicago Pr.

Protestant Establishment. E. Digby Baltzell. LC 86-24678. 448p. 1987. text ed. 35.00t (ISBN 0-300-03917-4, Y-653); pap. 12.95 (ISBN 0-300-03818-6). Yale U Pr.

Protestant Ethic & the Spirit of Capitalism. rev. ed. Max Weber. 1977. pap. 8.95 (ISBN 0-684-16489-2, ScribT). Scribner.

Protestant Ethic & the Spirit of Capitalism. Max Weber. 1984. 20.50 (ISBN 0-8446-6118-X). Peter Smith.

Protestant Ethic & the Spirit of Capitalism. Max Weber. Tr. by Talcott Parsons. (Counterpoint Paperbacks Ser.). 292p. pap. 8.95 (ISBN 0-04-331101-6). Unwin Hyman.

Protestant Ethic & the Spirit of Capitalism. Max Weber. 292p. 1977. pap. text ed. write for info. (ISBN 0-02-424860-6, Pub. by Scribner). Macmillan.

Protestant Evangelism among Italians in America. Ed. by Francesco Cordasco. LC 74-17943. (Italian American Experience Ser.). (Illus.). 276p. 1975. Repr. 21.00x (ISBN 0-405-06414-4). Ayer Co Pubs.

Protestant Faith. George W. Forell. LC 74-26341. 320p. 1975. pap. 10.95 (ISBN 0-8006-1095-4, 1-1095). Fortress.

Protestant in Purgatory: Richard Whately, Archbishop of Dublin. Donald H. Akenson. LC 81-3522. (Conference on British Studies (CBS) Biography: Vol. II). xiii, 276p. 1981. 25.00 (ISBN 0-208-01917-0, Archon). Shoe String.

Protestant Leadership Education Schools. Floy Hyde. LC 70-176892. (Columbia University. Teachers College. Contributions to Education: No. 965). Repr. of 1950 ed. 22.50 (ISBN 0-404-55965-4). AMS Pr.

Protestant Mind of the English Reformation, 1570-1640. Charles George & Katherine George. LC 77-130746. pap. 116.00 (ISBN 0-317-08472-0, 2000986). Bks Demand UMI.

Protestant Mission Education in Zambia: Eighteen Eighty to Nineteen Fifty-Four. John P. Ragsdale. LC 85-40505. 192p. 1986. 26.50x (ISBN 0-941664-09-0). Susquehanna U Pr.

Protestant Missionaries in the Philippines, 1898-1916: An Inquiry into the American Colonial Mentality. Kenton J. Clymer. LC 85-1278. (Illus.). 284p. 1986. 28.95 (ISBN 0-252-01210-0). U of Ill Pr.

Protestant Movement in Bolivia. C. Peter Wagner. LC 76-126079. (Illus.). 240p. (Orig.). 1970. pap. 3.95 (ISBN 0-87808-402-9). William Carey Lib.

Protestant Nationalists in Revolutionary Ireland: The Stopford Connection. Leon O'Broin. LC 85-2745. 240p. 1985. 26.50x (ISBN 0-389-20569-9). B&N Imports.

Protestant Parish Minister: A Behavioral Science Interpretation. Samuel Blizzard. LC 85-50402. (SSSR Monography: No. 5). 1985. pap. 8.00 (ISBN 0-932566-04-9). Soc Sci Stud Rel.

Protestant Pioneers in Korea. Everett N. Hunt, Jr. LC 79-27089. 128p. (Orig.). 1980. pap. 7.95 (ISBN 0-88344-396-1). Orbis Bks.

Protestant Pluralism & the New York Experience: A Study of Eighteenth-Century Religious Diversity. Richard W. Pointer. LC 87-45371. 224p. 1988. 25.00x (ISBN 0-253-34643-6). Ind U Pr.

Protestant Poetics & the Seventeenth Century Religious Lyric. Barbara K. Lewalski. LC 78-70305. (Illus.). 536p. 1984. 52.50x (ISBN 0-691-06395-8); pap. 15.95x (ISBN 0-691-01415-9). Princeton U Pr.

Protestant Reformation. Ed. by Hans J. Hillerbrand. (Documentary History of Western Civilization Ser). (Orig.). 1968. pap. 9.95x (ISBN 0-06-131342-4, TB 1342, Torch). Har-Row.

Protestant Reformation. Lewis W. Spitz. (Orig.). 1966. pap. 3.95x (ISBN 0-13-731638-0, Spec). P-H.

Protestant Reformation, Fifteen Seventeen to Fifteen Fifty-Nine: The Rise of Modern Europe. Lewis W. Spitz. (Illus.). 448p. 1986. pap. 9.95x (ISBN 0-06-132069-2, TB2069, Torch). Har-Row.

Protestant Reformation in Ireland, 1590-1641: Second Impression. Alan Ford. (Studies in the Intercultural History of Christianity: Vol. 34). 316p. 1987. pap. 43.35 (ISBN 3-8204-7471-4). P Lang Pubs.

Protestant Reformation 1517-1559. Lewis W. Spitz. LC 83-48805. (Rise of Modern Europe Ser.). (Illus.). 444p. 1984. 22.45i (ISBN 0-06-013958-7, HarpT). Har-Row.

Protestant Reformers in Elizabethan England. C. M. Dent. (Oxford Theological Monographs). 1985. 39.95x (ISBN 0-19-826723-1). Oxford U Pr.

Protestant Romance: Patterns of Reality in the Prose of Sir Giovanni Francesco Biondi. William M. Jones. 131p. 1980. 10.00 (ISBN 0-87291-138-1). Coronado Pr.

Protestant Search for Political Realism, 1919-1941. 2nd, rev. ed. Donald Meyer. xxiv, 482p. 1988. 35.00x (ISBN 0-8195-5203-8); pap. 15.95 (ISBN 0-8195-6210-6). Wesleyan U Pr.

Protestant Spiritual Traditions. Ed. by Frank C. Senn. 288p. (Orig.). 1986. pap. 9.95 (ISBN 0-8091-2761-X). Paulist Pr.

Protestant Succession in International Politics, 1710-1716. Edward Gregg. (Outstanding Theses from the London School of Economics & Political Science Ser.). 475p. 1987. lib. bdg. 75.00 (ISBN 0-8240-1918-0). Garland Pub.

Protestant Temperament: Patterns of Child-Rearing, Religious Experience, & the Self in Early America. Philip Greven. xiv, 432p. 1988. pap. 14.95 (ISBN 0-226-30830-8). U of Chicago Pr.

Protestant Theological Education in America: A Bibliography. Heather F. Day. LC 85-18300. (ATLA Biobliography Ser.: No. 15). 523p. 1985. 42.50 (ISBN 0-8108-1842-6). Scarecrow.

Protestant Thought. facs. ed. Karl Barth. LC 73-142606. (Essay Index Reprint Ser). 1959. 23.50 (ISBN 0-8369-2102-X). Ayer Co Pubs.

Protestant Thought & Natural Science: A Historical Interpretation. John Dillenberger. LC 77-7200. 1977. Repr. of 1960 ed. lib. bdg. 35.00x (ISBN 0-8371-9670-1, DIPT). Greenwood.

Protestant Thought & Natural Science. John Dillenberger. 1988. pap. text ed. 12.95x (ISBN 0-268-01575-9). U of Notre Dame Pr.

Protestant Thought Before Kant. A. C. McGiffert. 11.25 (ISBN 0-8446-0204-3). Peter Smith.

Protestant Thought in the Nineteenth Century, Vol. 1. Claude Welch. LC 72-75211. 335p. 1988. pap. 12.95x (ISBN 0-300-04200-0). Yale U Pr.

Protestant Thought in the Nineteenth Century, Vol. 2. Claude Welch. LC 72-75211. 315p. 1988. pap. 12.95x (ISBN 0-300-04201-9). Yale U Pr.

Protestant Thought in the Nineteenth Century, Vol. 1: 1799 to 1870. Claude Welch. LC 72-75211. Repr. of 1972 ed. 84.00 (ISBN 0-8357-9459-8, 2013200). Bks Demand UMI.

Protestant Thought in the Nineteenth Century: Volume 1, 1799-1870. Claude Welch. LC 72-75211. 335p. 1986. Repr. 30.00x (ISBN 0-300-01535-6). Yale U Pr.

Protestant Thought in the Nineteenth Century: Volume 2, 1870-1914. Claude Welch. LC 72-75211. 328p. 1985. 27.00x (ISBN 0-300-03369-9). Yale U Pr.

Protestant Thought in the Twentieth Century: Whence & Whither? Ed. by Arnold S. Nash. LC 78-5860. 1978. Repr. of 1951 ed. lib. bdg. 35.00x (ISBN 0-313-20484-5, NAPT). Greenwood.

Protestant Vision: William Harrison & the Reformation of Elizabethan England. G. J. Parry. LC 86-17091. (Camnbridge Studies in the History & Theory of Politics). 360p. 1987. 49.50 (ISBN 0-521-32997-3). Cambridge U Pr.

Protestant vs. Catholic in Mid-Victorian England: Mr. Newdegate & the Nuns. Walter L. Arnstein. LC 81-11451. 288p. text ed. 28.00x (ISBN 0-8262-0354-X). U of MO Pr.

Protestant Worship Music: Its History & Practice. Charles L. Etherington. LC 77-15990. (Illus.). 1978. Repr. of 1962 ed. lib. bdg. 38.50x (ISBN 0-313-20024-6, ETPW). Greenwood.

Protestantism. facs. ed. Ed. by William K. Anderson. LC 69-18918. (Essay Index Reprint Ser). 1944. 17.50 (ISBN 0-8369-1018-4). Ayer Co Pubs.

Protestantism. Ed. by J. Leslie Dunstan. LC 61-15497. (Great Religions of Modern Man Ser). 1961. 8.95 (ISBN 0-8076-0161-6). Braziller.

Protestantism. Hugh Kerr. LC 76-16065. (World Religions Ser.). 1979. pap. text ed. 6.95 (ISBN 0-8120-0665-8). Barron.

Protestantism - Its Modern Meaning. David A. Rausch & Carl Hermann Voss. LC 86-46413. 224p. 1987. pap. 12.95 (ISBN 0-8006-2060-7, 1-2060). Fortress.

Protestantism & Capitalism & Social Science: The Webster Thesis Controversy. 2nd ed. Ed. by Robert W. Green. (Problems in American Civilization Ser). 1973. pap. text ed. 7.50 (ISBN 0-669-81737-6). Heath.

Protestantism & Latinos in the United States: An Original Anthology. Ed. by Carlos E. Cortes. LC 79-6266. (Hispanics in the United States Ser.). (Illus.). 1981. lib. bdg. 51.50x (ISBN 0-405-13173-9). Ayer Co Pubs.

Protestantism & Progress: The Significance of Protestantism for the Rise of the Modern World. Ernst Troeltsch. LC 86-45221. (Fortress Texts in Modern Theology Ser.). 112p. 1986. pap. 8.95 (ISBN 0-8006-3200-1). Fortress.

Protestantism & Repression: A Brazilian Case Study. Rubem Alves. Tr. by John Drury from Port. LC 82-3594. 256p. (Orig.). 1985. pap. 11.95 (ISBN 0-88344-098-9). Orbis Bks.

Protestantism & Social Reform in New South Wales 1890-1910. J. D. Bollen. (Illus.). 200p. 1972. 6.00 (ISBN 0-522-84023-X, Pub. by Melbourne U Pr). Intl Spec Bk.

Protestantism & the American University: An Intellectual Biography of William Warren Sweet. James L. Ash, Jr. LC 82-10629. (Illus.). 180p. 1982. 15.95x (ISBN 0-87074-183-7). SMU Press.

Protestantism & the Cult of Sentiment: 1700-1740 see Religious Trends in English Poetry.

Protestantism & the National Church in 16th Century England. Peter Lake & Maria Dowling. 224p. 1987. lib. bdg. 55.00x (ISBN 0-7099-1681-7, Pub. by Croom Helm UK). Routledge Chapman & Hall.

Protestantism & the National Church in 16th Century England. Ed. by Peter Lake. 224p. 1987. 28.50 (ISBN 0-389-20725-X). B&N Imports.

Protestantism & the New South: North Carolina Baptists & Methodists in Political Crisis, 1894-1903. Frederick A. Bode. LC 75-1289. 171p. 1975. 15.00x (ISBN 0-8139-0597-4). U Pr of Va.

Protestantism in America: A Narrative History. rev. ed. Jerald C. Brauer. LC 66-12686. 320p. 1972. pap. 8.95 (ISBN 0-664-24956-6). Westminster John Knox.

Protozoa: Sporozoa. B. L. Bhatia. (Fauna of British India Ser.). (Illus.). xx, 508p. 1979. Repr. 30.00 (ISBN 0-88065-103-2, Pub. by Messers Today & Tomorrows Printers & Publishers India). Scholarly Pubns.

Protozoan Nucleus: Morphology & Evolution. I. B. Raikov. Tr. by N. Bobrov & M. Verkhovsteva. (Cell Biology Monographs: Vol. 9). (Illus.). 450p. 1982. 122.50 (ISBN 0-387-81678-X). Springer-Verlag.

Protozoan Phylum Apicomplexa, 2 vols. Ed. by Norman D. Levine. 1988. Vol. I, 240 pgs. 125.00 (ISBN 0-8493-4653-3, 4653); Vol. II, 176 pgs. 99.00 (ISBN 0-8493-4654-1, 4654). CRC Pr.

Protozoology, 2 vols. 5th, photocopy ed. Richard R. Kudo. (Illus.). 1188p. 1977. 120.00 (ISBN 0-398-01058-7). C C Thomas.

Protracted Game: A Wei-Ch'i Interpretation of Maoist Revolutionary Strategy. Scott A. Boorman. LC 70-83039. 1969. 22.50x (ISBN 0-19-500490-6). Oxford U Pr.

Protracted Game: A Wei-Ch'i Interpretation of Maoist Revolutionary Strategy. Scott A. Boorman. (Illus.). 1969. pap. 7.95 (ISBN 0-19-501493-6). Oxford U Pr.

Protractive Verse. Martin J. Rosenblum. 1976. pap. 0.50 (ISBN 0-89018-001-6). Cats Pajamas.

Proud. Arthur Moore. (River of Fortune Ser.). 400p. (Orig.). 1980. pap. 2.50 (ISBN 0-89083-665-5). Zebra.

Proud & Ashamed. Laura Chester. 1977. 5.00 (ISBN 0-87922-128-3). Christophers Bks.

Proud & Fearless Lion. Anne Cartwright & Reg Cartwright. 32p. (ps-1). 1987. 8.95 (ISBN 0-8120-5800-3). Barron.

Proud & on My Feet: Poems by J. W. Rivers. J. W. Rivers. LC 82-4768. (Contemporary Poetry Ser.). 88p. 1983. 9.95x (ISBN 0-8203-0632-0); pap. 5.95 (ISBN 0-8203-0633-9). U of Ga Pr.

Proud & the Free. Howard Fast. Date not set. pap. price not set. HM.

Proud & the Naked of St. Tropez. 1985. write for info. Lloylds Pub.

Proud Beggars. Albert Cossery. Tr. by Thomas Cushing from Fr. LC 81-1095. 200p. 1981. 14.00 (ISBN 0-87685-451-X); signed ed. 20.00 (ISBN 0-87685-452-8); pap. 6.50 (ISBN 0-87685-450-1). Black Sparrow.

Proud Breed. Celeste De Blasis. 832p. 1985. pap. 4.95 (ISBN 0-553-25379-4). Bantam.

Proud Captive. Dianne Price. 496p. 1986. pap. 3.95 (ISBN 0-8217-1925-4). Zebra.

Proud Decades: America in War & in Peace, 1941-1960. John P. Diggins. (Illus., Orig.). 1988. pap. price not set (ISBN 0-393-95656-3). Norton.

Proud Decades: America in War & Peace, 1941-1960. John P. Diggins. (Illus.). 1988. 19.95 (ISBN 0-393-02548-9). Norton.

Proud Empires. Austin Clarke. 224p. 1988. 18.95 (ISBN 0-575-03900-0, Pub. by Gollancz England). David & Charles.

Proud Flesh. James Purdy. 58p. 1981. limited signed ed. 50.00 (ISBN 0-935716-07-6). Lord John.

Proud Glory. Ann F. Barron. 384p. 1987. pap. 3.95 (ISBN 0-380-89599-4). Avon.

Proud Gun. Gordon D. Shirreffs. 1977. pap. 1.25 (ISBN 0-505-51197-5, Pub. by Tower Bks). Leisure NY.

Proud Heart. Suzanne Stephens. 1985. 9.95 (ISBN 0-8034-8553-0, Avalon). Bouregy.

Proud Helper: A Story About 'Abdu'l-Baha in the Holy Land. Anthony A. Lee. (Stories About 'Abdu'l-Baha Ser.). (Illus.). 24p. (gr. k-5). 1979. pap. 2.50 (ISBN 0-933770-03-0). Kalimat.

Proud Heritage. D. Scott Atkinson et al. Ed. by Terry Neff & Michael Sanden. (Two Centuries of American Art Ser.). (Illus.). 1987. write for info. (ISBN 0-932171-01-X). Terra Mus.

Proud Heritage: Two Centuries of American Art Selections from the Collections of the Pennsylvania Academy of the Fine Arts, Philadelphia, & the Terra Museum of American Art, Chicago. Ed. by D. Scott Atkinson et al. 300p. 1988. 49.50 (ISBN 0-8109-1470-0). Abrams.

Proud Island. Peadar O'Donnell. 128p. 1985. pap. 7.95 (ISBN 0-86278-093-4, Pub. by O'Brien Pr Ireland). Irish Bks Media.

Proud Kentuckian: John C. Breckinridge, 1821-1875. Frank H. Heck. LC 76-9502. (Kentucky Bicentennial Bookshelf Ser.). 184p. 1976. 6.95 (ISBN 0-8131-0217-0). U Pr of Ky.

Proud Love. Barbara Riefe. pap. 3.50 (ISBN 0-515-08417-4). Jove Pubns.

Proud Man. R. E. Harrington. 400p. 1983. pap. 3.50 (ISBN 0-345-30032-7). Ballantine.

Proud Mary. Iris Gower. 1985. 14.95 (ISBN 0-312-65225-9). St Martin.

Proud Mary. Iris Gower. 380p. 1987. pap. 3.95 (ISBN 1-55547-178-1). Critics Choice Paper.

Proud Mexicans. Robert Decker & Esther T. Marquez. (Illus.). 250p. (gr. 7-12). 1976. pap. 5.95 (ISBN 0-88345-254-5, 18450). Prentice ESL.

Proud Moments: Generation to Generation. Howard Rainer. (Illus.). 144p. 1988. 39.95 (ISBN 0-89802-496-X). Beautiful Am.

Proud Monster. Ian MacMillan. LC 86-62828. 160p. 1987. 16.95 (ISBN 0-86547-279-3). N Point Pr.

Proud Ones: Poems by Koryne Ortega. Koryne Ortega. (Illus.). 46p. (Orig.). 1988. pap. price not set (ISBN 0-943557-00-3). Esoterica Pr.

Proud Outcasts: The Gypsies of Spain. Merrill F. McLane. LC 86-70790. (Illus.). 192p. (Orig.). 1987. pap. 10.95 (ISBN 0-938813-03-X). Carderock Pr.

Proud Paladin. facsimile ed. Iris Morley. LC 70-144164. (Short Story Index Reprint Ser.). Repr. of 1936 ed. 18.00 (ISBN 0-8369-3779-1). Ayer Co Pubs.

Proud Passion. Kathalyn Kraus. 480p. 1986. pap. 3.95 (ISBN 0-8439-2379-2, Leisure Bks). Leisure NY.

Proud Patriot: Philip Schuyler & the War of Independence, 1775-1783. Don R. Gerlach. (New York State Studies). (Illus.). 720p. 1987. text ed. 45.00x (ISBN 0-8156-2373-9). Syracuse U Pr.

Proud Peacock & the Mallard. Grania Davis. (Jataka Tales Ser.). (Illus.). 24p. (gr. k-4). 1983. pap. 5.95 (ISBN 0-913546-70-4). Dharma Pub.

Proud, Peculiar New Orleans: The Inside Story. G. J. Stall. 1984. 13.95 (ISBN 0-87511-679-5). Claitors.

Proud Sheriff. Eugene M. Rhodes. (WFL Ser.: Vol. 42). 1977. pap. 5.95 (ISBN 0-8061-1426-6, WFL 42). U of Okla Pr.

Proud Shoes: The Story of an American Family. Pauli Murray. LC 77-11807. (Illus.). 304p. 1987. pap. 7.95 (ISBN 0-06-091398-3, PL 1398, PL). Har-Row.

Proud Surrender. Casey Douglas. (Super Romances Ser.). 384p. 1983. pap. 2.95 (ISBN 0-373-70056-3, Pub. by Worldwide). Harlequin Bks.

Proud Surrender. Diana Haviland. 384p. (Orig.). 1983. pap. 3.50 (ISBN 0-449-12406-1, GM). Fawcett.

Proud Taste for Scarlet & Miniver. E. L. Konigsburg. LC 73-76320. (Illus.). 208p. (gr. 6-9). 1973. 13.95 (ISBN 0-689-30111-1, Atheneum Childrens Bks). Macmillan.

Proud Taste for Scarlet & Miniver. E. L. Konigsburg. 208p. (gr. 5-8). 1985. pap. 2.95 (ISBN 0-440-47201-6, YB). Dell.

Proud to Be a Teacher. Bill Halloran. 1988. 12.95 (ISBN 0-943867-00-2). Reading Inc.

Proud to Be White: A Survey of Pakaha Prejudice in New Zealand. Angela Ballara. 205p. 1986. pap. 14.95 (ISBN 0-86863-292-9, Pub. by Heinemann Pubs New Zealand). Intl Spec Bk.

Proud Tower. Barbara Tuchman. (Illus.). 1983. pap. 5.95 (ISBN 0-553-25602-5). Bantam.

Proud Tower. Barbara W. Tuchman. 1966. 21.95 (ISBN 0-02-620300-6). Macmillan.

Proud Tree. Luane Roche. 64p. (gr. 2-6). pap. 1.95 (ISBN 0-89243-146-6). Liguori Pubns.

Proud Viscount. Laura Matthews. 224p. 1987. pap. 2.50 (ISBN 0-451-14809-6, Sig). NAL.

Proud Way. Shirley Seifert. 1976. Repr. of 1948 ed. lib. bdg. 9.95 (ISBN 0-89190-138-8, Pub. by River City Pr). Amereon Ltd.

Proudhon & His Bank of the People. Charles A. Dana. 59.95 (ISBN 0-8490-0906-5). Gordon Pr.

Proudhon & His Bank of the People. Charles A. Dana. Ed. by Paul Avrich. (Young America Ser.: No. 1). 80p. lib. bdg. 22.95 (ISBN 0-88286-067-4); pap. 4.95 (ISBN 0-88286-066-6). C H Kerr.

Proudhon & Max Stirner. Laurance Labadie. (Men & Movements in the History & Philosophy of Anarchism Ser.). 1979. lib. bdg. 59.95 (ISBN 0-685-96411-6). Revisionist Pr.

Proudhon et Son Systeme Economique. Jules Vrau. LC 74-143665. (Research & Source Works Ser: No. 629). 1971. Repr. of 1853 ed. 20.50 (ISBN 0-8337-3662-0). B Franklin.

Proudhonist Materialism & Revolutionary Doctrine. Stephen Condit. 1984. lib. bdg. 79.95 (ISBN 0-87700-633-4). Revisionist Pr.

Proudhon's Solution of the Social Problem. P. J. Proudhon. Ed. by Henry E. Cohen. (Men & Movements in the History of Philosophy of Anarchism Ser.). 1980. lib. bdg. 69.95 (ISBN 0-87700-044-1). Revisionist Pr.

Proudly We Serve: A Guide for Waiters & Waitresses. Gary J. Caulfield. (Illus.). 48p. (Orig.). 1987. pap. 3.95 (ISBN 0-912661-11-9). Woodsong Graph.

Proumenoir de Monsieur de Montaigne. Marie Le Jars De Gournay. LC 85-19662. 1986. Repr. of 1594 ed. 45.00x (ISBN 0-8201-1408-1). Schol Facsimiles.

Prouncing Musical Art. Dudley Buck. lib. bdg. 19.00 (ISBN 0-685-95460-9). Scholarly.

Proust. Samuel Beckett. 1957. 10.00 (ISBN 0-394-47523-2, GP651). Grove.

Proust. Samuel Beckett. (Orig.). 1956. pap. 7.95 (ISBN 0-394-17414-3, E50, Ever). Grove.

Proust. C. Bell. 59.95 (ISBN 0-8490-0907-3). Gordon Pr.

Proust. Clive Bell. 1978. Repr. of 1928 ed. lib. bdg. 20.50 (ISBN 0-8495-0429-5). Arden Lib.

Proust. Clive Bell. LC 74-13466. 1928. lib. bdg. 15.00 (ISBN 0-8414-3265-1). Folcroft.

Proust. Derwent May. (Past Masters Ser.). 1983. 13.95x (ISBN 0-19-287612-0); pap. 4.95 (ISBN 0-19-287611-2). Oxford U Pr.

Proust. (YFS: No. 3). pap. 16.00 (ISBN 0-527-01736-1). Kraus Repr.

Proust. William Sansom. LC 85-51363. (Literary Lives Ser.). (Illus.). 128p. 1986. pap. 9.95 (ISBN 0-500-26020-6). Thames Hudson.

Proust & Hardy: Incidence or Coincidence in Studies in French Language Literature & History Presented to R. L. Graeme Ritchie. L. A. Bisson. 1949. Repr. 40.00 (ISBN 0-8274-3920-2). R West.

Proust & the Art of Love: The Aesthetics of Sexuality in the Life, Times & Art of Marcel Proust. J. E. Rivers. LC 80-2403. 440p. 1981. 34.00x (ISBN 0-231-05036-4); pap. 15.00x (ISBN 0-231-05037-2). Columbia U Pr.

Proust & the Middle Ages. R. Bales. (Illus.). 166p. 1975. text ed. 44.00x (ISBN 0-317-56032-8, Pub. by Droz Switzerland). Coronet Bks.

Proust: Collected Essays on the Writer & His Art. J. M. Cocking. LC 81-6105. (Cambridge Studies in French: No. 1). (Illus.). 344p. 1982. 54.50 (ISBN 0-521-23790-4); pap. 15.95 (ISBN 0-521-28799-5). Cambridge U Pr.

Proust Dictionary. Maxine A. Vogely. LC 80-53035. 765p. 1981. 50.00x (ISBN 0-87875-205-6). Whitston Pub.

Proust on Art & Literature. Marcel Proust. 250p. 1984. pap. 8.95 (ISBN 0-88184-114-5). Carroll & Graf.

Proust: Portrait of a Genius. Andre Maurois. 336p. 1984. pap. 10.95 (ISBN 0-88184-104-8). Carroll & Graf.

Proust Screenplay. Harold Pinter. 1977. 10.00 (ISBN 0-394-42202-3, GP794). Grove.

Proust Screenplay. Harold Pinter. LC 77-78081. 1977. pap. 3.95 (ISBN 0-394-17018-0, E690, Ever). Grove.

Proust Souvenir. William H. Adams. LC 84-7309. (Illus.). 160p. 1984. 17.95 (ISBN 0-86565-043-8). Vendome.

Proust Souvenir. William H. Adams. (Illus.). 144p. 1985. pap. 12.95 (ISBN 0-86565-042-X). Vendome.

Proustian Comedy. Jack Murray. 170p. 1980. 15.95 (ISBN 0-917786-13-0). Summa Pubns.

Proustian Optics of Clothes: Mirrors, Masks, Mores. Diana Festa-McCormick. (Stanford French & Italian Studies: Vol. 29). 224p. 1984. pap. 29.50 (ISBN 0-915838-08-7). Anma Libri.

Proustian Space. Georges Poulet. Tr. by Elliott Coleman. LC 76-47390. pap. 30.00 (ISBN 0-317-41757-6, 2025864). Bks Demand UMI.

Proustian Vision. Milton Hindus. LC 53-11068. (Arcturus Books Paperbacks). 301p. 1967. pap. 2.45x (ISBN 0-8093-0273-X). S Ill U Pr.

Proust's Additions, 2 vols. Alison Winton. Incl. Vol. 1. (ISBN 0-521-21610-9); Vol. 2. (ISBN 0-521-21611-7). LC 76-58869. 1977. 85.00 set (ISBN 0-521-21612-5). Cambridge U Pr.

Proust's Binoculars: A Study of Memory, Time & Recognition in A La Recherche du Temps Perdu. Roger Shattuck. LC 82-48567. 160p. 1983. pap. 9.50x (ISBN 0-691-01403-5). Princeton U Pr.

Proust's "Recherche" A Psychoanalytic Interpretation. Randolph Splitter. 176p. 1981. 21.95x (ISBN 0-7100-0664-0). Routledge Chapman & Hall.

Prout: The Alternative to Capitalism & Marxism. Ravi Batra. 209p. 1980. pap. 5.00 (ISBN 0-686-95463-7). Ananda Marga.

Provability & Truth. Torkel Franzen. (Stockholm Studies in Philosophy: No. 9). 81p. (Orig.). 1987. pap. 20.00x (ISBN 91-22-01158-7, Pub. by Almqvist & Wiksell). Coronet BKs.

Prove It! Gerald Ames & Rose Wyler. LC 62-21288. (Science I Can Read Bks.). (Illus.). 64p. (gr. k-3). 1963. PLB 10.89 (ISBN 0-06-020051-0). HarpJ.

Prove It All Night! The Bruce Springsteen Trivia Book. Deborah Mayer. LC 86-63303. (Illus.). 96p. (Orig.). 1987. pap. 5.95 (ISBN 0-914457-17-9). Mustang Pub.

Proved by Trial. James Hearst. (WNJ Ser.: No. 6). 1977. pap. 6.00 (ISBN 1-55780-055-3). Juniper Pr WI.

Proven Partners: Business, Labor, & Community Colleges. Dale Parnell & Roger Yarrington. (Pocket Reader Ser.: No. 1). 56p. (Orig.). 1982. pap. 5.00 (ISBN 0-87117-116-3); pap. 25.00 12 copies. Am Assn Comm Jr Coll.

Proven Performances: Recipes from Thoroughbred Racing Leaders. Ed. by Bobbee Ferrer. LC 85-51914. (Illus.). 248p. 1985. 13.50 (ISBN 0-9615869-0-7). Proven Perf.

Proven Profits from Pollution Prevention: Case Studies in Resource Conservation & Waste Reduction. Donald Huisingh et al. LC 85-82638. 316p. 1986. pap. 25.00 (ISBN 0-917582-47-0). Inst Local Self Re.

Proven Skills for Successful Learning. Thomas Sherman. (Series No. 174). 256p. 1984. pap. 19.95 (ISBN 0-675-20153-5). Merrill.

Proven Strategies for Successful Test Taking. Thomas M. Sherman & Terry M. Wildman. 160p. 1982. pap. text ed. 14.95 (ISBN 0-675-09843-2). Merrill.

Proven Techniques for Increasing Database Use. Ed. by Fred S. Rosenau & Leslie Chase. LC 83-80073. 1983. 25.00 (ISBN 0-942774-09-4). Info Indus.

Proven Techniques for Troubleshooting the Microprocessor & Home Computer Systems. James W. Coffron. (Illus.). 256p. 1984. pap. 16.95 (ISBN 0-13-731738-7). P-H.

Provenance & Problematics of "Sublime & Alarming Images in Poetry". E. Morgan. (Warton Lectures on English Poetry). 1977. pap. 5.50 (ISBN 0-85672-161-1, Pub. by British Acad). Longwood Pub Group.

Provenance of Arenites. Ed. by G. G Zuffa. 1985. lib. bdg. 54.00 (ISBN 90-277-1944-6, Pub. by Reidel Holland). Kluwer Academic.

Provencal Literature & Language: Including the Local History of Southern France. Daniel C. Haskell. Repr. of 1925 ed. 45.00 (ISBN 0-404-08349-8). AMS Pr.

Provencal Lyric. Lewis F. Mott. LC 73-16487. 1901. Repr. lib. bdg. 22.50 (ISBN 0-8414-6091-4). Folcroft.

Provencal Regionalism. Alphonse V. Roche. LC 74-128942. (Northwestern University Humanities Ser.: No. 30). Repr. of 1954 ed. 28.00 (ISBN 0-404-50730-1). AMS Pr.

Provence. John Flower. (Illus.). 216p. 1987. 29.95 (ISBN 0-88162-276-1). Salem Hse Pubs.

Provence. Ford Madox Ford. LC 78-16071. (Neglected Books of the 20th Century Ser.). (Illus.). 1979. pap. 8.50 (ISBN 0-912946-63-6). Ecco Pr.

Provence. (Panorama Bks.). (Illus., Fr.). 3.95 (ISBN 0-685-11516-X). French & Eur.

Provence & Pound. Peter Makin. LC 77-76186. 1979. 45.00x (ISBN 0-520-03488-0). U of Cal Pr.

Provence & the Cote D'Azur: Phaidon Cultural Guides. 1986. 14.95 (ISBN 0-13-731761-1). P-H.

Provence Memories. Dennis Stock. (Illus.). 1988. 50.00 (ISBN 0-8212-1715-1). NYGS.

Provence: Regions of France, French Edition. (Michelin Green Guides). pap. 12.95 (ISBN 0-686-56425-1). French & Eur.

Provenzalische Chrestomathie, Mit Abriss der Formenlehre & Glossar. 6th ed. Carl Appel. LC 71-38488. Repr. of 1930 ed. 15.00 (ISBN 0-404-08345-5). AMS Pr.

Provenzalische Lautlehre: Mit Einer Karte. Carl L. Appel. LC 80-2165. (Provenzalische Chrestomathie Ser.). Repr. of 1918 ed. 30.00 (ISBN 0-404-19027-8). AMS Pr.

Proverb in Ibsen: Proverbial Sayings & Citations As Elements in His Style. Ansten Anstensen. LC 74-158264. (Columbia University. Germanic Studies, New Ser.: No. 1). Repr. of 1936 ed. 27.00 (ISBN 0-404-50451-5). AMS Pr.

Proverb in Literature: An International Bibliography - German Language & Literature, Vol. 218. Wolfgang Mieder. (European University Studies: Ser. 1). 154p. 1978. 17.05 (ISBN 3-261-03035-6); pap. 17.05 (ISBN 3-261-03034-8). P Lang Pubs.

Proverb Literature. W. Bonser & T. A. Stephens. 59.95 (ISBN 0-8490-0908-1). Gordon Pr.

Proverb Literature. Wilfred Bonser & T. A. Stephens. LC 74-26578. 1930. 55.00 (ISBN 0-8414-3317-8). Folcroft.

Proverb Literature: A Bibliography of Works Relating to Proverbs. Thomas A. Stephens. Ed. by Wilfred Bonser. (Folk-Lore Society, London, Monographs: Vol. 89). pap. 47.00 (ISBN 0-8115-0535-9). Kraus Repr.

Proverb Lore. F. E. Hulme. 59.95 (ISBN 0-8490-0909-X). Gordon Pr.

Proverb Lore. F. Edward Hulme. 1977. Repr. of 1902 ed. lib. bdg. 46.00 (ISBN 0-8414-4961-9). Folcroft.

Proverb Lore. F. Edward Hulme. LC 67-23913. 280p. 1968. Repr. of 1902 ed. 34.00x (ISBN 0-8103-3202-7). Gale.

Proverbial Bestiary. Warren Chappell & Rick Cusick. (Illus.). 64p. 1983. 10.95 (ISBN 0-931474-12-4). TBW Bks.

Proverbial Comparisons & Related Expressions in Spanish: Recorded in Los Angeles, California. Shirley Arora. LC 75-46053. (University of California Publications, Folklore Studies: No. 29). pap. 132.50 (ISBN 0-317-29033-9, 2021208). Bks Demand UMI.

Proverbial Folk-Lore. Alan B. Cheales. 1978. Repr. of 1875 ed. lib. bdg. 42.50 (ISBN 0-8495-0834-7). Arden Lib.

Proverbial Folk-Lore. Alan B. Cheales. LC 76-56174. 1976. Repr. of 1875 ed. lib. bdg. 29.50 (ISBN 0-8414-3598-7). Folcroft.

Proverbial Language in English Drama Exclusive of Shakespeare, 1495-1616: An Index. R. W. Dent. LC 83-17922. 600p. 1984. text ed. 55.00x (ISBN 0-520-05169-6). U of Cal Pr.

Proverbial Mouse. Moira Miller. LC 86-16737. (Illus.). 32p. (ps-3). 1987. 11.95 (ISBN 0-8037-0195-0, 01160-350). Dial Bks Young.

Proverbial Philosophy: With the Collection of Poems Entitled a Thousand Lines. Martin F. Tupper. 266p. 1983. Repr. of 1850 ed. lib. bdg. 45.00 (ISBN 0-89987-824-5). Darby Bks.

Proverbial Wisdom of Shakespeare. Frank P. Wilson. LC 77-10883. 1977. Repr. lib. bdg. 25.00 (ISBN 0-8414-9621-8). Folcroft.

Proverbios Morales Santob de Carrion. Ed. by T. Anthony Perry. (Spanish Ser.: No. 21). 1986. 17.00x (ISBN 0-942260-63-5). Hispanic Seminary.

Proverbs. Kenneth T. Aitken. LC 86-15660. (Daily Study Bible-Old Testament). 276p. 1986. 15.95 (ISBN 0-664-21837-7); pap. 8.95 (ISBN 0-664-24586-2). Westminster John Knox.

Proverbs. Charles Bridges. (Geneva Commentaries Ser.). 1979. 18.95 (ISBN 0-85151-088-4). Banner of Truth.

Proverbs. A. Cohen. 223p. 1946. 12.95 (ISBN 0-900689-33-1). Soncino Pr.

Proverbs. A. Dellinger & S. Fletcher. 16p. (ps-3). pap. 0.59 (ISBN 0-570-08309-5, 56HH1441). Concordia.

Proverbs. J. Terrence Forestell. (Bible Ser.). 1.00 (ISBN 0-8091-5122-7). Paulist Pr.

Proverbs. Irving L. Jensen. (Bible Self-Study Guide Ser.). (Illus.). 96p. 1976. pap. 3.50 (ISBN 0-8024-1020-0). Moody.

Proverbs. F. Derek Kidner. LC 75-23850. (Tyndale Old Testament Commentary Ser.). 14.95 (ISBN 0-87784-861-0); pap. 8.95 (ISBN 0-87784-266-3). Inter-Varsity.

Proverbs. Bob Yandian. 1985. pap. 6.95 (ISBN 0-89274-386-7). Harrison Hse.

Proverbs: A Commentary on an Ancient Book of Timeless Advice. Robert L. Alden. 1989. price not set. Baker Bk.

Proverbs: A New Approach. William McKane. LC 75-108185. (Old Testament Library). 692p. 1970. Westminster John Knox.

Proverbs & Common Sayings from the Chinese. Arthur H. Smith. 374p. 1983. Repr. of 1902 ed. lib. bdg. 250.00 (ISBN 0-89987-976-4). Darby Bks.

Proverbs & Ecclesiastes. John J. Collins. LC 79-92067. (Knox Preaching Guides Ser.). 117p. (Orig., John Hayes series editor). 1980. pap. 4.95 (ISBN 0-8042-3218-0, John Knox). Westminster John Knox.

Proverbs & Ecclesiastes. Ed. by R. B. Scott. LC 65-13988. (Anchor Bible Ser.: No. 18). 1965. pap. 18.00 (ISBN 0-385-02177-1, Anch). Doubleday.

Proverbs & Epigrams of John Heywood. John Heywood. 223p. 1986. Repr. of 1867 ed. lib. bdg. 100.00 (ISBN 0-8492-5359-4). R West.

Proverbs & Epigrams of John Heywood, A.D. 1562. John Heywood. 1966. Repr. of 1562 ed. 32.00 (ISBN 0-8337-1689-1). B Franklin.

Proverbs & How to Collect Them. Margaret M. Bryant. (Publications of the American Dialect Society: No. 4). 25p. 1945. pap. 2.35 (ISBN 0-8173-0604-8). U of Ala Pr.

Proverbs & Parables: God's Wisdom for Living. Dee Brestin & Steve Brestin. (Fisherman Bible Studyguide Ser.). 75p. 1975. saddle-stitch 2.95 (ISBN 0-87788-694-6). Shaw Pubs.

Proverbs & People: A Midrash on the Hebrew Alphabet. Illus. by Stavroulakis & Gordon M. Freeman. 12.00 (ISBN 0-943376-19-X). Magnes Mus.

Proverbs & Sayings of Ireland. rev. ed. Ed. by Seamus Cashman & Sean Gaffney. (Illus.). 1985. pap. 6.95 (ISBN 0-86327-073-5, Pub. by Wolfhound Pr Ireland). Irish Bks Media.

Proverbs: Critical Exegetical Commentary. Crawford H. Toy. Ed. by Samuel R. Driver et al. (International Critical Commentary Ser.). 592p. 1899. 34.95 (ISBN 0-567-05013-0, Pub. by T & T Clark Ltd UK). Fortress.

Proverbs, Ecclesiastes, & Song of Solomon. Frank Johnson. Ed. by Lynne M. Deming & Margaret Rogers. (Cokesbury Basic Bible Commentary Ser.). (Illus., Orig.). 1988. pap. text ed. 4.95 (ISBN 0-939697-19-X). Graded Pr.

Proverbs, Ecclesiastes, Song of Solomon. J. Coert Rylaarsdam. LC 59-10454. (Layman's Bible Commentary Ser: Vol. 10). 1964. (John Knox); pap. 4.95 (ISBN 0-8042-3070-6). Westminster John Knox.

Proverbs: English, French, German, Italian, Spanish, Russian. J. Gluski. 448p. 1971. 84.25 (ISBN 0-444-40904-1). Elsevier.

Proverbs Exemplified & Illustrated by Pictures from Real Life. John Trusler. LC 24-12970. (Illus.). Repr. 18.00 (ISBN 0-384-61770-0). Johnson Repr.

Proverbs-Ezekiel. Albert Barnes. 10.95 (ISBN 0-8010-0839-5). Baker Bk.

Proverbs for Graduates. Brent D. Earles. 1984. 5.95 (ISBN 0-8010-3415-9). Baker Bk.

Proverbs for Kids from the Book. Compiled by Richard Osborne. (Illus.). 240p. (gr. k). 1987. 8.95 (ISBN 0-8423-4975-8). Tyndale.

Proverbs for Parenting: A Topical Guide for Child Raising from the Book of Proverbs. Barbara O. Decker. LC 87-50633. 283p. 1988. 14.95 (ISBN 0-9618608-1-2). Lynn's Bookshelf.

Proverbs for Pentecost see Word to the Wise.

Proverbs For People. Vern McLellan. LC 82-83841. (Illus.). 1983. pap. 3.95 (ISBN 0-89081-326-4). Harvest Hse.

Proverbs for Programming in PASCAL. Louise E. Moser & Andrew A. Turnbull. LC 85-16870. 304p. 1986. pap. 15.95 (ISBN 0-471-82309-0). Wiley.

Proverbs from the Armenian. Tr. by P. M. Manuelian from Armenian. LC 80-13387. (Illus.). 150p. 1980. 8.95 (ISBN 0-933706-20-0). Ararat Pr.

Proverbs, God's Powerhouse of Wisdom. Chuck Colclasure. 1981. pap. 2.50 (ISBN 0-8423-4928-6). Tyndale.

Proverbs-Important Things to Know. Carol Greene. 1980. pap. 1.29 (ISBN 0-570-06140-7, 59-1303, Arch Bk). Concordia.

Proverbs in the Earlier English Drama. B. J. Whiting. LC 70-86290. 1969. Repr. of 1938 ed. lib. bdg. 34.50x (ISBN 0-374-98513-8, Octagon). Hippocrene Bks.

Proverbs-Isaiah 39. Christopher Wright. (Bible Study Commentary Ser.). 1983. pap. 4.95 (ISBN 0-87508-158-4). Chr Lit.

Proverbs of Alfred. Walter W. Skeat. LC 74-9509. 1976. Repr. of 1907 ed. lib. bdg. 39.00 (ISBN 0-8414-7766-3). Folcroft.

Proverbs of Alfred. Helen P. South. LC 71-133287. (English Literature, No. 33). 1970. Repr. of 1931 ed. lib. bdg. 49.95x (ISBN 0-8383-1186-5). Haskell.

Proverbs of John Heywood. Julian Sharman. LC 72-10636. 1972. Repr. of 1874 ed. lib. bdg. 42.00 (ISBN 0-8414-0729-0). Folcroft.

Proverbs of Scotland. A. Hislop. 59.95 (ISBN 0-8490-0910-3). Gordon Pr.

Proverbs of Scotland. Alexander Hislop. LC 68-21774. 368p. 1968. Repr. of 1868 ed. 43.00x (ISBN 0-8103-3201-9). Gale.

Proverbs of the Meadow & the Mountain. Thomas A. Clark. Ed. by Laurie Clark. (Illus.). 62p. 1986. pap. 6.00 (ISBN 0-87924-059-8). Membrane Pr.

Proverbs or Adages. Desiderius Erasmus. Tr. by Richard Taverner. LC 55-11634. 1977. Repr. of 1569 ed. 35.00x (ISBN 0-8201-1232-1). Schol Facsimiles.

Proverbs: Practical Directions for Living. James T. Draper, Jr. (Living Studies). pap. 4.95 (ISBN 0-8423-4922-7); leader's guide 2.95 (ISBN 0-8423-4923-5). Tyndale.

Proverbs, Promises & Principles. pap. 3.50 (ISBN 0-89081-460-0). Harvest Hse.

Proverbs, Proverbial Expressions & Popular Rhymes of Scotland. A. Cheviot. 59.95 (ISBN 0-8490-0911-1). Gordon Pr.

Proverbs, Proverbial Expressions, & Popular Rhymes of Scotland. Ed. by Andrew Cheviot. LC 68-23144. 448p. 1969. Repr. of 1896 ed. 40.00x (ISBN 0-8103-3198-5). Gale.

Proverbs Puzzle. Fannie L. Houck. 48p. 1986. pap. 2.50 (ISBN 0-87403-048-X, 2692). Standard Pub.

Proverbs, Sentences & Proverbial Phrases from English Writings Before 1500. Bartlett J. Whiting & Helen W. Whiting. LC 67-22874. 1968. text ed. 50.00x (ISBN 0-674-71950-6, Belknap Pr). Harvard U Pr.

Proverbs, Song of Solomon. H. A. Ironside. 12.95 (ISBN 0-87213-395-8). Loizeaux.

Proverbs Thirty-One Lady & Other Impossible Dreams. Marsha Drake. LC 84-6453. 192p. (Orig.). 1984. pap. 5.95 (ISBN 0-87123-595-1, 210595). Bethany Hse.

Proverbs Twisted with Wit & Humor for Laughs or Tumor. Vito C. Vanderbilt. LC 88-47610. 150p. 1988. 21.50 (ISBN 0-88164-872-8); pap. 19.95 (ISBN 0-88164-873-6). ABBE Pubs Assn.

Proverbs Ungame Cards. 1.50 (ISBN 0-317-15783-3). Chr Marriage.

Proverbs: Wisdom for All Ages. Thomas L. Seals. 5.50 (ISBN 0-89137-529-5). Quality Pubns.

Proverbs, with Introduction to Sapiential Books. Dermot Cox. LC 81-85271. (Old Testament Ser.: Vol. 17). 1982. 12.95 (ISBN 0-89453-417-3); pap. 9.95 (ISBN 0-89453-251-0). M Glazier.

Providence. Anita Brookner. 192p. 1984. 13.45 (ISBN 0-394-52945-6). Pantheon.

Providence. Anita Brookner. 1985. pap. 7.95 (ISBN 0-525-48157-5, Obelisk). Dutton.

Providence. Langford. Date not set. 10.95 (Pub. by SCM Pr England). Fortress.

Providence. Stephen Wallin. (Burning Deck Poetry Ser.). 20p. (Orig.). 1981. pap. 10.00 signed ed. (ISBN 0-930900-86-3). Burning Deck.

Providence. Geoffrey Wolff. 215p. 1986. 16.95 (ISBN 0-670-80461-4, E Sifton Bks). Viking.

Providence. Geoffrey Wolff. 256p. 1987. pap. 3.95 (ISBN 0-14-010012-1). Penguin.

Providence see Summa Contra Gentiles.

Providence, A Citywide Survey of Historic Resources. W. McKenzie Woodward et al. (Statewide Historical Preservaton Report P-P-7 Phode Island Historical Preservation Commission Ser.). (Illus.). 288p. (Orig.). 1986. pap. 14.95. RI Hist Preserv.

Providence: A Pictorial History. Patrick Conley & Paul Campbell. LC 80-27671. 208p. 1983. 19.95 (ISBN 0-89865-128-X). Donning Co.

Providence & Evil. P. T. Geach. LC 76-28005. 1977. 24.95 (ISBN 0-521-21477-7). Cambridge U Pr.

Providence & Free Will in Human Actions. Daniel W. Goodenough. 132p. 1986. pap. 5.95 (ISBN 0-915221-63-2). Swedenborg Sci Assn.

Providence & Patriotism in Early America, 1640-1815. John F. Berens. LC 78-5889. 1978. 17.95x (ISBN 0-8139-0779-9). U Pr of Va.

Providence & Predestination: Questions 5 & 6 of "Truth". St. Thomas Aquinas. Tr. by Robert W. Mulligan. 154p. 1961. pap. 5.95 (ISBN 0-89526-937-6). Regnery Gateway.

Providence As "Idee-Maitresse" in the Works of Bossuet. Georgiana Terstegge. LC 73-128931. (Catholic University of America. Studies in Romance Languages & Literature: No. 43). 1970. Repr. of 1948 ed. 29.00 (ISBN 0-404-50334-9). AMS Pr.

Providence Episode in the Irish Literary Renaissance. Horace Reynolds. 1929. 5.00 (ISBN 0-685-67667-6). RI Hist Soc.

Providence in Colonial Times. Gertrude S. Kimball. LC 76-87452. (American Scene Ser.). (Illus.). 391p. 1972. Repr. of 1912 ed. lib. bdg. 65.00 (ISBN 0-306-71524-4). Da Capo.

Providence of God see Studies in Dogmatics: Theology.

Providence of God in Reformed Perspective. Benjamin W. Farley. 264p. 1988. 16.95 (ISBN 0-8010-3540-6). Baker Bk.

Providence of Wit: Aspects of Form in Augustan Literature & the Arts. Martin C. Battestin. x, 331p. 1974. 25.00x (ISBN 0-19-812052-4, Pub. by Oxford Univ Pr UK). U Pr of Va.

Providence of Wit in English Letter Writers. William H. Irving. 1973. lib. bdg. 26.00x (ISBN 0-374-94118-1, Octagon). Hippocrene Bks.

Providence: Reconstruction of Social & Moral Order. Richard Quinney. 120p. 1986. 12.95 (ISBN 0-932930-72-7). Anderson Pub Co.

Provident: A Centennial History. John Longwith. (Illus.). 192p. 1986. 9.95 (ISBN 0-9617768-0-3). Provident Life.

Provident Sea. D. H. Cushing. (Illus.). 336p. Date not set. 65.00 (ISBN 0-521-25727-1). Cambridge U Pr.

Providential Aesthetic in Victorian Fiction. Thomas Vargish. LC 84-29098. 256p. 1985. 20.00x (ISBN 0-8139-1062-5). U Pr of Va.

Providential Order of the World. Alexander B. Bruce. LC 77-27225. (Gifford Lectures: 1897). 1978. Repr. of 1897 ed. 37.50 (ISBN 0-404-60455-2). AMS Pr.

Providers. Steven Irwin. (Illus.). 296p. 1984. pap. text ed. 12.95 (ISBN 0-88839-181-1). Hancock House.

Provider's Guide to Hospital-Based Psychiatric Services. Allen H. Collins & Herbert Krauss. 456p. 1985. 59.50 (ISBN 0-87189-232-4). Aspen Pub.

Providing Access for Adults to Alternative College Programs. Ed. by Ronald H. Miller. LC 81-9395. (Alliance Manual Ser.: No. 1). 132p. 1981. pap. 12.50 (ISBN 0-8108-1468-4). Scarecrow.

Providing for Future Change: Adaptability & Flexibility in School Building. (OECD Programme on Educational Building Ser.). 110p. 1976. 7.00x (ISBN 92-64-11487-4). OECD.

Providing for Individual Differences in Student Learning: A Mastery Learning Approach. Jackson F. Lee, Jr. & W. Wayne Pruitt. (Illus.). 130p. 1984. 21.75x (ISBN 0-398-05028-7). C C Thomas.

Providing for the Older Adult: A Gerontological Handbook. Sandra C. Lewis. LC 82-50202. 232p. 1983. 21.95 (ISBN 0-913590-82-7). Slack Inc.

Providing for the Preschool Child with Problems. rev. ed. 1986. 6.00 (ISBN 0-939418-29-0). Ferguson-Florissant.

Providing Legal Services for Prisoners: A Tool for Correctional Administrators. Rev. ed. American Association of Law Libraries Staff. 104p. 1982. pap. 10.00 (ISBN 0-942974-02-6). Am Correctional.

Providing Legal Services to Indigents in Colorado. National Center for State Courts Staff. 126p. 1982. manuscript 7.56 (WRO-050). Natl Ctr St Courts.

Providing Mental Health Benefits: Alternatives for Employers. Theresea J. Flynn & Sean Sullivan. LC 86-30215. (Health Policy Ser.). 54p. (Orig.). 1987. pap. text ed. 5.75 (ISBN 0-8447-3616-3). Am Enterprise.

Providing Opportunities for the Mathematically Gifted, K-12. Ed. by Peggy A. House. 100p. (Orig.). 1987. pap. 9.00 (ISBN 0-87353-239-2). NCTM.

Providing Programs for the Gifted & Talented: A Handbook. Sandra Kaplan. 264p. 22.50 (ISBN 0-318-16017-X, 5); excerpt for teachers 1.50 (ISBN 0-318-16018-8); excerpt for administrators 1.50 (ISBN 0-318-16019-6). NSLTIGT.

Providing Psychological Services to Children & Adolescents: A Comprehensive Guidebook. Sebastian Striefel & Phyllis Cole. LC 86-29925. (Illus.). 336p. (Orig.). pap. text ed. 24.95 (ISBN 0-933716-68-0, 680). P H Brookes.

Providing Recognition: A Handbook of Ideas. Recognition Systems Staff. 1974. looseleaf bdg. 24.90 (ISBN 0-89401-103-0). Didactic Syst.

Providing Reference Service in Church & Synagogue Libraries. Jennifer Pritchett. LC 87-15776. (Guide Ser.: No. 15). 60p. 1987. pap. 6.95 (ISBN 0-915324-26-1). CSLA.

Providing Vision Care to an Area of Vision Care Shortage. O. D. Killingbeck. 63p. 1980. text ed. 4.15 (ISBN 0-318-15089-1, 154). Natl Assn Comm Health Ctrs.

Providings. Elspeth Davie. (Orig.). pap. 7.95 (ISBN 0-7145-0665-6). Riverrun NY.

Providings. Carl Thayler. (Orig.). 1971. 7.50 (ISBN 0-912090-13-8); pap. 2.45 (ISBN 0-912090-12-X). Sumac Mich.

Province & Function of Law: Law As Logic, Justice & Social Control. A Study in Jurisprudence. 2nd ed. Julius Stone. LC 46-21845. lxi, 918p. 1973. Repr. of 1946 ed. lib. bdg. 42.00 (ISBN 0-930342-75-5). W S Hein.

Province Beyond the River: The Diary of a Protestant at a Trappist Monastery. W. Paul Jones. 160p. (Orig.). 1986. pap. 6.95 (ISBN 0-8358-0546-8). Upper Room.

Province in Rebellion: A Documentary History of the Founding of the Commonwealth of Massachusetts, 1774-1775. Ed. by L. Kinvin Wroth et al. 350p. (Incl. microfiche cards). 1975. paper covers 100.00x (ISBN 0-674-71955-7). Harvard U Pr.

Province into Being. Skip Baldwin. Ed. by Douglas Anderson. (Illus.). 80p. (Orig.). 1984. pap. 6.95 (ISBN 0-912549-04-1). Bread and Butter.

Province of Buenos Aires & Argentine Politics, 1912-1943. Richard J. Walter. (Cambridge Latin American Studies: No. 53). 268p. 1985. 42.50 (ISBN 0-521-30337-0). Cambridge U Pr.

Province of East New Jersey, Sixteen Hundred & Nine to Seventeen Hundred & Two. John E. Pomfret. 1980. Repr. of 1962 ed. lib. bdg. 31.50x (ISBN 0-374-96515-3, Octagon). Hippocrene Bks.

Province of New Jersey, 1664-1738. Edwin P. Tanner. LC 8-33297. (Columbia University. Studies in the Social Sciences: No. 80). Repr. of 1908 ed. 42.50 (ISBN 0-404-51080-9). AMS Pr.

Province of Piety: Moral History in Hawthorne's Early Tales. Michael J. Colacurcio. LC 83-26586. 688p. 1984. text ed. 32.00x (ISBN 0-674-71957-3). Harvard U Pr.

Province of Reason. Sam B. Warner, Jr. 320p. 1984. 20.00x (ISBN 0-674-71956-5, Belknap Pr). Harvard U Pr.

Province of Reason. Sam B. Warner, Jr. LC 84-7653. (Illus.). 320p. 1988. pap. 10.95 (ISBN 0-674-71958-1, Belknap Pr). Harvard U Pr.

Province of Sociology: Selected Profiles. William A. Pearman & Robert A. Rotz. LC 79-17996. 212p. 1981. text ed. 19.95x (ISBN 0-88229-434-2); pap. text ed. 10.95x (ISBN 0-88229-735-X). Nelson-Hall.

Province of West New Jersey, 1609-1702. John E. Pomfret. 1973. lib. bdg. 21.50x (ISBN 0-374-96516-1, Octagon). Hippocrene Bks.

Province sous l'Ancien Regime, 2 vols. Albert A. Babeau. LC 77-161720. Set 65.00 (ISBN 0-404-07506-1). AMS Pr.

Provinces. Richard Grossinger. 5.00 (ISBN 0-913028-31-2). North Atlantic.

Provinces & Provincial Capitals of the World. 2nd ed. Compiled by Morris Fisher. LC 83-22125. 258p. 1985. 19.50 (ISBN 0-8108-1758-6). Scarecrow.

Provinces of Early Mexico: Variants of Spanish American Regional Evolution. Ed. by Ida Altman & James Lockhart. LC 76-620055. (Latin American Studies: Vol. 36). (Illus.). 1976. text ed. 12.00 (ISBN 0-87903-036-4); pap. 11.95 (ISBN 0-87903-110-7). UCLA Lat Am Ctr.

Provinces of the Roman Empire, 2 vols. Theodor Mommsen. 756p. 1974. 50.00 set (ISBN 0-89005-052-X). Ares.

Provinces of the Roman Empire: The European Provinces. Theodor Mommsen. Ed. by T. Robert Broughton. LC 68-16707. (Classic European Historians Ser.). (Illus.). 1968. pap. 4.50x (ISBN 0-226-53395-6, P305, Phoen). U of Chicago Pr.

Provincetown. Edmund G. Gillon. (Illus.). 128p. 1986. pap. 12.95 (ISBN 0-88740-061-2). Schiffer.

Provincetown. Mary Oliver. Ed. by John Wheatcroft. (Bucknell University Fine Editions Ser.). (Illus.). 40p. 1987. 120.00 (ISBN 0-916375-06-4). Press Alley.

Provincetown Arts: Annual 1988. Ed. by Christopher Busa & Raymond S. Elman. (Robert Motherwell Cover Ser.). (Illus.). 160p. (Orig.). 1988. pap. 4.00 (ISBN 0-944854-00-1). Provincetown Arts.

Provincetown Massachusetts Cemetery Inscriptions. Lurana H. Cook et al. 255p. (Orig.). 1980. 25.00 (ISBN 0-917890-18-3). Heritage Bk.

Provincetown Plays: Second Series. LC 76-40392. (One-Act Plays in Reprint Ser.). 1976. Repr. of 1916 ed. 15.00x (ISBN 0-8486-2007-0). Roth Pub Inc.

Provincetown! Questions You Don't Dare Ask (& Answers) Noel W. Beyle. (No. 18). (Illus.). 48p. (Orig., Recipes by Lee Baldwin). 1983. pap. 0.95 (ISBN 0-912609-02-8). First Encounter.

Provincetown Review, 2 vols, Nos. 1-7. Repr. of 1969 ed. 87.50 (ISBN 0-404-19544-X). AMS Pr.

Provincetown Seafood Cookbook. Howard Mitcham. 288p. 1986. pap. 12.50 (ISBN 0-940160-33-1). Parnassus Imprints.

Provincial America, Sixteen Hundred Ninety to Seventeen Hundred Forty. Evarts B. Greene. LC 79-25852. (Field Museum of Natural History: Vol. 6). (Illus.). xxi, 356p. 1980. Repr. of 1905 ed. lib. bdg. 35.00x (ISBN 0-313-22242-8, GRPR). Greenwood.

Provincial American & Other Papers. facs. ed. Meredith Nicholson. LC 79-152205. (Essay Index Reprint Ser). 1912. 18.00 (ISBN 0-8369-2211-5). Ayer Co Pubs.

Provincial & Local Taxation in Canada. Solomon Vineberg. LC 70-76698. (Columbia University. Studies in the Social Sciences: No. 128). Repr. of 1912 ed. 16.50 (ISBN 0-404-51128-7). AMS Pr.

Provincial & State Papers, 18 Vols. New Hampshire State Legislature. Ed. by Nathaniel Bouton & I. W. Hammond. LC 70-173073. Repr. of 1867 ed. Set. 1530.00 (ISBN 0-404-07450-2); 85.00 ea. AMS Pr.

Provincial Atlas of PRC. Date not set. 29.95 (ISBN 0-8351-1031-1). China Bks.

Provincial Book Trade in Eighteenth Century England. John P. Feather. (Cambridge Studies in Publishing & Printing History). 206p. 1985. 42.50 (ISBN 0-521-30334-6). Cambridge U Pr.

Provincial Cemetery of the Pyramid Age, Naga-Ed-Der, Pt. 3. George A. Reisner. (UC Publications in Egyptian Archaeology: Vol. 6). 1932. 110.00x (ISBN 0-520-01060-4). U of Cal Pr.

Provincial Committees of Safety of the American Revolution. Agnes Hunt. LC 68-24986. (American History & Americana Ser., No. 47). 1969. Repr. of 1904 ed. lib. bdg. 44.95x (ISBN 0-8383-0207-6). Haskell.

Provincial Development in Russia: Catherine II & Jakob Sievers. Robert E. Jones. 225p. 1984. text ed. 38.00 (ISBN 0-8135-1026-0). Rutgers U Pr.

Provincial Governments As Employers: A Survey of Public Personnel Administration in Canada's Provinces. J. E. Hodgetts & O. P. Dwivedi. (Canadian Public Administration Ser.). 224p. 1974. pap. 14.95c (ISBN 0-7735-0234-3). McGill-Queens U Pr.

Provincial Lady in America. E. M. Delafield. (Illus.). 245p. 1984. pap. 8.95 (ISBN 0-89733-110-9). Academy Chi Pubs.

Provincial Lady in London. E. M. Delafield. (Illus.). 392p. 1983. pap. 8.95 (ISBN 0-89733-085-4). Academy Chi Pubs.

Provincial Lady in Wartime. E. M. Delafield. 349p. 1986. pap. 8.95 (ISBN 0-89733-210-5). Academy Chi Pubs.

Provincial Leadership in China: The Cultural Revolution & Its Aftermath. Fredrick Teiwes. (East Asia Papers: No. 4). 170p. 1974. 3.00 (ISBN 0-939657-04-X). Cornell East Asia Pgm.

Provincial Leaderships in Syria Fifteen Seventy-Five to Sixteen Fifty. Abdul-Rahim Abu-Husayn. 230p. 1985. text ed. 29.95 (ISBN 0-8156-6072-3, Am U Beirut). Syracuse U Pr.

Provincial Letters. Blaise Pascal. 1982. pap. 5.95 (ISBN 0-14-044196-4). Penguin.

Provincial Magistrates & Revolutionary Politics in France, 1789-1795. Philip Dawson. LC 74-182816. (Historical Monographs Ser: No. 66). (Illus.). 416p. 1972. 27.50x (ISBN 0-674-71960-3). Harvard U Pr.

Provincial Matters. Mary B. Whidden. LC 85-8577. (Illus.). 204p. 1985. 10.95 (ISBN 0-8263-0832-5). U of NM Pr.

Provincial Militarism & the Chinese Republic: The Yunnan Army, Nineteen Hundred & Five to Nineteen Twenty-Five. Donald S. Sutton. (Michigan Studies on China). (Illus.). 424p. 1980. 22.95x (ISBN 0-472-08813-0). U of Mich Pr.

Provincial Names & Folk Lore of British Birds. Charles Swainson. (English Dialect Society Publications Ser.: No. 47). pap. 25.00 (ISBN 0-8115-0471-9). Kraus Repr.

Provincial Party Personnel in Mainland China. Frederick C. Teiwes. (Occasional Papers of the East Asian Institute). 114p. 1967. pap. 4.00 (ISBN 0-317-17104-6). Columbia U E Asian Inst.

Provincial Patriarchs: Land Tenure & the Economics of Power in Colonial Peru. Susan E. Ramirez. LC 85-13934. (Illus.). 481p. 1986. 37.50x (ISBN 0-8263-0818-X). U of NM Pr.

Provincial Public Finance in Ontario: An Empirical Analysis of the Last Twenty-Five Years. D. K. Foot. (Ontario Economic Council Research Studies). 1977. 8.50x (ISBN 0-8020-3350-4). U of Toronto Pr.

Provincial Rebellion: Revolutionary Civil Wars, 1560-1660 see Rebels & Rulers, Fifteen Hundred to Sixteen-Sixty.

Provincial Stock Exchanges. W. A. Thomas. (Illus.). 360p. 1973. 32.50x (ISBN 0-7146-2981-2, F Cass Co). Biblio Dist.

Provincial Types in American Fiction. Horace S. Fiske. LC 67-27596. 1968. Repr. of 1903 ed. 23.00x (ISBN 0-8046-0148-8, Pub. by Kennikat). Assoc Faculty Pr.

Provinciales. Jean Giraudoux. (Coll. Diamant). 12.95 (ISBN 0-685-23908-X). French & Eur.

Provinciales. Jean Giraudoux. 9.95 (ISBN 0-686-54010-7); pap. 3.95 (ISBN 0-686-54011-5). French & Eur.

Provinciales. Blaise Pascal. 1966. 9.95 (ISBN 0-686-54852-3). French & Eur.

Proving. Thomas Szollosi. LC 87-19711. 246p. 1988. 17.95 (ISBN 0-385-24239-5). Doubleday.

Proving Construction Contract Damages: Course Manual. John B. Tieder & Julian F. Hoffar. LC 86-215277. 484p. Date not set. price not set. Fed Pubns Inc.

Proving Ground: An Account of the Radiobiological Studies in the Pacific, 1946-61. Neal O. Hines. LC 62-18853. (Illus.). 480p. 1962. 20.00x (ISBN 0-295-73894-4). U of Wash Pr.

Proving Gun: The Yesterday Rider. Ray Hogan. 1984. pap. 3.50 (ISBN 0-451-12974-1, Sig). NAL.

Proving It. Diane Hoh. (Cheerleaders Ser.: No. 23). 176p. (Orig.). (gr. 7 up). 1986. pap. 2.50 (ISBN 0-590-40371-0). Scholastic Inc.

Proving Medical Diagnosis & Prognosis, 13 vols. Marshall Houts & Leonard Marmor. 1970. looseleaf set 750.00 (564); Updates. 1985 372.00; 1986 550.50. Bender.

Proving New Drugs: A Guide to Clinical Trials. Ben-Zion Taber. LC 69-19150. (Illus.). 182p. 1969. Geron-x.

Proving Operating Systems Correct. Richard A. Karp. Ed. by Harold Stone. LC 82-13378. (Computer Science: System Programming: No. 16). 172p. 1983. 42.95 (ISBN 0-8357-1365-2). UMI Res Pr.

Proving Punitive Damages: The Complete Handbook. Tom Riley. LC 81-2062. 347p. 1981. 37.50 (ISBN 0-13-731778-6, Busn). P-H.

Proving Sex-Based Wage Discrimination under Federal Law. American Nurses Association Staff & Dennis J. Alessi. LC 84-208867. 1983. 12.00. ANA.

Proving Systems. (Manual of Petroleum Measurement Standards: Chap. 4). 49p. 1978. 9.00 (ISBN 0-317-33093-4, 852-30080). Am Petroleum.

Proving Trail. Louis L'Amour. 1985. pap. 2.95 (ISBN 0-553-25304-2). Bantam.

Proving Your Arbitration Case. Boaz Siegel. LC 61-3879. (Illus.). pap. 20.00 (ISBN 0-317-58788-9, 2029669). Bks Demand UMI.

Proving Yourself: A Study of James. Anna M. Orr. (Basic Bible Study Ser.). 64p. pap. 2.95 (ISBN 0-930756-75-4, 521015). Aglow Pubns.

Provision of Radiological Protection Services. (Safety Ser.: No. 13). (Illus.). 82p. 1965. pap. 7.75 (ISBN 92-0-123365-5, ISP94, IAEA). UNIPUB.

Provisional Austrian Regime in Lombardy-Venetia (1814-1815) R. John Rath. LC 69-63009. 426p. 1969. 23.50x (ISBN 0-292-78385-X). U of Tex Pr.

Provisional Constitution & Ordinances for the People of the United States. John Brown. 32p. 1969. 10.00x (ISBN 0-87730-001-1). M&S Pr.

Provisional Government of Maryland: 1774-1777. J. A. Silver. 1973. pap. 9.00 (ISBN 0-384-55380-X). Johnson Repr.

Provisional Government of Maryland (1774-1777) John A. Silver. LC 78-63844. (Johns Hopkins University. Studies in the Social Sciences. Thirteenth Ser. 1895: 10). Repr. of 1895 ed. 11.50 (ISBN 0-404-61101-X). AMS Pr.

Provisional Guidelines on Statistics of International Tourism. pap. 5.00 (E.78.XVII.6). UN.

Provisional Indicative World Plan for Agricultural Development: A Synthesis & Analysis of Factors Relevant to World, Regional & Agricultural Development, 2 Vols. 744p. (Orig.). 1970. Set. pap. 28.75 (ISBN 92-5-101652-6, F349, FAO); Vol. 2. pap. 5.00 (ISBN 92-5-101653-4, F350). UNIPUB.

Provisional Methodology for Soil Degradation Assessment. (Illus.). 84p. 1980. pap. 33.75 (ISBN 92-5-100869-8, F1958, FAO). UNIPUB.

Provisional Rules of Procedure of the Security Council: December 1982. (Rules of Procedure). pap. 2.00 (ISBN 92-1-100087-4, E.83.I.4). UN.

Provisional Substantive & Procedural Guidelines for Involuntary Civil Commitment. National Center for State Courts Staff. 246p. 1982. manuscript 14.76 (NCSC-022). Natl Ctr St Courts.

Provisional World List of Periodicals Dealing with Science & Technology Policies: 1973. (Science Policy Studies & Documents: No. 33). 112p. 1974. pap. 5.00 (ISBN 92-3-101189-8, U500, UNESCO). UNIPUB.

Provisioning Paris: Merchants & Millers in the Grain & Flour Trade During the Eighteenth Century. Steven L. Kaplan. LC 84-7004. (Illus.). 592p. 1984. 44.50x (ISBN 0-8014-1600-0). Cornell U Pr.

Provisions. Anselm Parlatore. 1971. pap. 1.00 (ISBN 0-685-90032-0). Stone-Marrow Pr.

Provisions: A Reader from Nineteenth-Century American Women. Ed. by Judith Fetterley. LC 84-42840. (Everywoman: Studies in History, Literature, & Culture). 480p. 1985. 35.00x (ISBN 0-253-17040-0); pap. 12.95X (ISBN 0-253-20349-X). Ind U Pr.

Provisions for Disqualification & Substitution of Judges. National Center for State Courts Staff. (Research Essay Ser.). 6p. 1978. manuscript 0.36 (E-009). Natl Ctr St Courts.

Provisions for General Theory Courses in the Professional Education of Teachers. Obed J. Williamson. LC 78-177634. (Columbia University. Teachers College. Contributions to Education: No. 684). Repr. of 1936 ed. 34.50 (ISBN 0-404-55684-1). AMS Pr.

Provisions of Federal Law Held Unconstitutional by the Supreme Court of the United States. U. S. Library of Congress Legislative Reference Service. Ed. by Wilfred C. Gilbert. LC 75-35364. (U. S. Government Documents Program Ser.). 148p. 1976. Repr. of 1936 ed. lib. bdg. 22.50x (ISBN 0-8371-8605-6, USPF). Greenwood.

Provisions of State Codes of Professional Responsibility Governing Lawyer Advertising & Solicitation. ABA, Commn. on Advertising. 1987. pap. write for info. Amer Bar Assn.

Provisions of the Internal Revenue Code & Treasury Regulations Pertaining to the Federal Taxation of Gifts, Trusts & Estates: 1983 Edition. Douglas A. Kahn & Lawrence W. Waggoner. 1983. 14.00 (ISBN 0-316-48209-9). Little.

Provisions: One Hundred & Nine Great Places to Shop for Food in the Capital District. Peter Zaas et al. 144p. (Orig.). 1987. pap. write for info. (ISBN 0-9605460-6-5). Wash Park.

Provo, Pioneer Mormon City. Writers Program, Utah. LC 73-3654. (American Guide Ser.). 1942. Repr. 11.50 (ISBN 0-404-57954-X). AMS Pr.

Provocateurs Against the People. Art Shields. 32p. 1972. pap. 0.50 (ISBN 0-87898-079-2). New Outlook.

Provocative Facts for West Coast Interpreters. Ed. by Phyllis Ford. 194p. 1983. 10.00 (ISBN 0-943272-05-X). Inst Recreation Res.

Provocative Perspectives: When We Were 20 & Now That We're 60. John D. Black et al. LC 82-60220. 137p. 1982. pap. 6.95 (ISBN 0-936988-07-X, Dist. by Shoe String Press). Tompson Rutter Inc.

Provocative Therapy. Frank Farrelly & Jeff Brandsma. LC 74-78101. 1974. Repr. 12.95 (ISBN 0-916990-03-6). Meta Pubns.

Provoked Husband. John Vanbrugh & Colley Cibber. Ed. by Peter Dixon. LC 79-128911. (Regents Restoration Drama Ser.). xxviii, 176p. 1973. 17.95x (ISBN 0-8032-0378-0). U of Nebr Pr.

Provoked Wife. John Vanbrugh. Ed. by James L. Smith. (New Mermaids Ser.). pap. 2.95x (ISBN 0-393-90031-2). Norton.

Provoked Wife. John Vanbrugh. Ed. by Curt A. Zimansky. LC 69-12337. (Regents Restoration Drama Ser.). xxii, 145p. 1970. 15.95x (ISBN 0-8032-0374-8); pap. 3.95x (ISBN 0-8032-5373-7, BB 272, Bison). U of Nebr Pr.

Provoked Wife. John Vanbrugh. Ed. by Antony Coleman. (Revels Plays Ser.). 224p. 1983. 50.00 (ISBN 0-7190-1526-X, Pub. by Manchester Univ Pr). St Martin.

Provoker. Earl Paulk. Ed. by Trisha Weeks. 400p. (Orig.). 1986. pap. 9.95 (ISBN 0-917595-09-2). K-Dimension.

Provost. John Galt. Ed. by Ian A. Gordon. (World's Classics Ser.). 1982. pap. 5.95 (ISBN 0-19-281629-2). Oxford U Pr.

Provozvjestnik Karl Bozhijej Russkomy Narodu. Archbishop Averky Taushev. 30p. 1968. pap. 1.00 (ISBN 0-317-29066-5). Holy Trinity.

PROWAY-LAN Industrial Data Highway: ANSI-ISA Standard S72.01. 200p. 1986. pap. text ed. 50.00x (ISBN 0-87664-896-0, I896-0). Instru Soc.

Prowl. Shane Dowlen. 50p. pap. 4.95. Gondwana Bks.

Prowl: A Lioness Stalks in the Wake of the Moon Poems. Shane Wake. 50p. 1981. 4.95 (ISBN 0-931926-14-9). Alta Napa.

Prowler of Mount Hebrew. George H. Attwood. 48p. 1985. 6.95 (ISBN 0-89962-458-8). Todd & Honeywell.

Prowler of Mount Hebron. George H. Atwood. 64p. 1986. 5.95 (ISBN 0-8059-3036-1). Dorrance.

Proxemic Behavior: A Cross-Cultural Study. O. Michael Watson. 1970. text ed. 14.00x (ISBN 0-686-22399-3). Mouton.

Proximal Flows. M. S. Glasner. (Lecture Notes in Mathematics: Vol. 517). 1976. pap. 13.00 (ISBN 0-387-07689-1). Springer-Verlag.

Proximity & Preference: Problems in the Multidimensional Analysis of Large Data Sets. Ed. by Reginald G. Golledge & John N. Rayner. LC 81-14634. (Illus.). xxxix, 304p. 1982. 35.00x (ISBN 0-8166-1042-8). U of Minn Pr.

Proximity, Levinas, Blanchot, Bataille & Communication. J. Libertson. 1982. 55.00 (ISBN 90-247-2506-2, Pub. by Martinus Nijhoff Netherlands). Kluwer Academic.

Proximo Paso. Jack T. Chick. (Illus.). 64p. (Orig., Span.). 1983. pap. 1.95 (ISBN 0-937958-15-8). Chick Pubns.

Proxopera. Benedict Kiely. LC 86-45536. 128p. 1986. 13.95 (ISBN 0-87923-651-5). Godine.

Proxy Bride. Martha J. Powers. (Orig.). 1987. pap. 2.50 (ISBN 0-449-21293-9, Crest). Fawcett.

Proxy Communications & Management Disclosure: SEC Proxy Review Program 1983. 128p. 1983. pap. 8.00 (ISBN 0-317-04292-0, 4857). Commerce.

Proxy Contests. 2nd ed. Graham B. Moody & Constance E. Bagley. LC 83-224920. (Corporate Practice Ser.: No. 20). (Orig.). 1983. 92.00. BNA.

Proxy Statements: Fifth Annual Institute. 35.00 (ISBN 0-317-29520-9, #CO2283, Law & Business). HarBraceJ.

Proyecto de Construccion de Una Nacion. (Ayacucho Library Collection Ser.: Vol. 68). (Span.). 1980. 25.00 (ISBN 0-317-56550-8, Pub. by Biblioteca Ayacucho); pap. 11.50 (ISBN 0-317-56551-6, Pub. by Biblioteca Ayacucho). Humanities.

Proyecto "Red de Sistemas Educativos Para el Centroamerica y Panama". (Experiments & Innovations in Education Ser.: No. 44). 1980. pap. 5.00 (ISBN 92-3-301849-0, U1091, UNESCO). UNIPUB.

Proza. Osip Mandelshtam. (Illus.). 179p. (Rus.). 1983. 22.50 (ISBN 0-88233-850-1). Ardis Pubs.

Proza Pushkina see Pushkin's Prose.

Proza, Vol. 1: Pervaia Kniga Rasskazov. Mikhail A. Kuzmin. Ed. by Vladimir Markov. (Modern Russian Literature & Culture, Studies & Texts: Vol. 14). 329p. (Orig., Rus.). 1984. pap. 16.00 (ISBN 0-933884-41-9). Berkeley Slavic.

Proza, Vol. 2: Vtoraia Kniga Rasskazov. Mikhail A. Kuzmin. Ed. by Vladimir Markov. (Modern Russian Literature & Culture, Studies & Texts: Vol. 15). 391p. (Orig., Rus.). 1984. pap. 16.00 (ISBN 0-933884-42-7). Berkeley Slavic.

Proza, Vol. 3: Tret'ia Kniga Rasskazov. Mikhail A. Kuzmin. Ed. by Vladimir Markov. (Modern Russian Literature & Culture, Studies & Texts: Vol. 16). 437p. (Orig., Rus.). 1984. 16.00 (ISBN 0-933884-43-5). Berkeley Slavic.

Proza, Vol. 4: Pokoinitsa v Dome, Zelenyi Solovei. Mikhail A. Kuzmin. Ed. by Vladimir Markov. (Modern Russian Literature & Culture Studies & Texts: Vol. 17). 370p. (Orig., Rus.). 1985. pap. 16.00 (ISBN 0-933884-44-3). Berkeley Slavic.

Proza, Vol. 5: Plavaiushchie-puteshestvuiushchie; Voennye Rasskazy. Mikhail A. Kuzmin. Ed. by Vladimir Markov. (Modern Russian Literature & Culture, Studies & Texts: Vol. 18). 381p. (Orig., Rus.). 1985. pap. 16.00 (ISBN 0-933884-45-1). Berkeley Slavic.

Proza, Vol. 6: Tikhii Strazh; Babushkina Shkatulka. Mikhail A. Kuzmin. Ed. by Vladimir Markov. (Modern Russian Literature & Culture, Studies & Texts: Vol. 19). 374p. (Orig., Rus.). 1986. pap. 16.00 (ISBN 0-933884-46-X). Berkeley Slavic.

Proza, Vol. 7: Antrakt v Ovrage. Devstvennyi Viktor. Mikhail A. Kuzmin. Ed. by Vladimir Markov. (Modern Russian Literature & Culture Studies & Texts: Vol. 20). 380p. (Rus.). 1987. pap. 16.00 (ISBN 0-933884-47-8). Berkeley Slavic.

Proza, Vol. 8: Nesobrannaia Proza. Mikhail A. Kuzmin. Ed. by Vladimir Markov. (Modern Russian Literature & Culture, Studies & Texts: Vol. 21). 400p. (Orig., Rus.). 1988. pap. 20.00 (ISBN 0-933884-48-6). Berkeley Slavic.

Prozess. Franz Kafka. Ed. by H. F. Brookes & C. E. Gawne-Cain. (Ger.). 1969. pap. text ed. 9.00x (ISBN 0-435-38501-1). Heinemann Ed.

Prudence. Jilly Cooper. 192p. 1981. pap. 1.95 (ISBN 0-449-24361-3, Crest). Fawcett.

Prudence Crandall: A Biography. Marvis O. Welch. LC 83-83334. (Illus.). 234p. (Orig.). 1984. pap. 10.00 (ISBN 0-9613180-0-7). Jason Pub.

Prudence in Victory: The Dynamics of Post-War Settlements. Nissan Oren. 16p. (Orig.). 1977. pap. text ed. 5.00 (ISBN 0-8191-5830-5, Pub. by Aspen Inst for Humanistic Studies). U Pr of Amer.

Prudence, Morality & the Prisoner's Dilemma. D. Parfit. (Philosophical Lectures (Henriette Hertz Trust)). 1978. pap. 5.50 (ISBN 0-85672-211-1, Pub. by British Acad). Longwood Pub Group.

Prudent Heart. Timothy Steele. 39p. (Orig.). 1983. s & l, wrappers 35.00 (ISBN 0-936576-08-1). Symposium Pr.

Prudent Man. Bruce W. Marcus. (Illus.). 1978. 49.95 (ISBN 0-9601610-0-7). ESP Corp.

Prudent Partnership. Barbara Allister. 1989. pap. 3.50 (ISBN 0-451-15758-3, Sig). NAL.

Prudent Peace: Law As Foreign Policy. John A. Perkins. LC 81-1200. 1981. lib. bdg. 28.00x (ISBN 0-226-65873-2). U of Chicago Pr.

Prudent Practices for Disposal of Chemicals from Laboratories. 304p. 1983. 16.50x (ISBN 0-309-03390-X). Natl Acad Pr.

Prudent Practices for Handling Hazardous Chemicals in Laboratories. National Research Council. 291p. 1981. 16.95x (ISBN 0-309-03128-1); pap. text ed. 9.95 o. p. (ISBN 0-309-03234-2). Natl Acad Pr.

Prudent Revolutionaries: Potraits of British Feminists Between the Wars. Brian Harrison. (Illus.). 384p. 1987. 64.00 (ISBN 0-19-820119-2). Oxford U Pr.

Prudential Supervision in Banking. OECD. 298p. (Orig.). 1987. pap. 26.00x (ISBN 92-64-12916-2, ECD148). OECD.

Prudentius 'Psychomachia' A Re-examination. Macklin Smith. LC 75-37192. 1976. 34.00x (ISBN 0-691-06299-4). Princeton U Pr.

Prudhomme Family Cookbook: Old Time Louisiana Recipes. Paul Prudhomme. LC 87-18345. (Cookbook Library). (Illus.). 384p. 1987. 19.95 (ISBN 0-688-07549-5). Morrow.

Prudie Finds Out. Natania Jansz & Litza Jansz. 32p. 1983. pap. 5.95 (ISBN 0-86358-003-3, Pandora Pr). Routledge Chapman & Hall.

Prufung in der Tertigung - Production Testing & Testability. Network Staff. 1983. 95.00x (ISBN 0-907634-17-6, Pub. by Network Events Ltd). State Mutual Bk.

Prufung von elektronischen Bauelementen und mechanischen Teilen: Electronic Component & Non-Electronic Product Testing. Network Staff. 1983. 95.00x (ISBN 0-317-43556-6, Pub. by Network Events Ltd). State Mutual Bk.

Prune. Ramon R. Ross. LC 84-3018. (Illus.). 192p. (gr. 3 up). 1984. 11.95 (ISBN 0-689-31056-0, Atheneum Childrens Bks). Macmillan.

Prune Book: The Toughest Management & Policymaking Jobs in Washington. John H. Trattner. 512p. 1988. 34.95 (ISBN 0-8191-7000-3). Madison Bks UPA.

Prune Country Railroading. Norman W. Holmes. (Illus.). 1985. 34.95 (ISBN 0-930742-11-7). Shade Tree.

Prune Orchard Management. David Ramos. LC 80-71944. (Illus.). 144p. (Orig.). 1981. pap. 10.00x (ISBN 0-931876-45-1, 3269). ANR Pubns CA.

Prunes & Prism: With Other Odds & Ends. facsimile ed. Charles H. Grandgent. LC 70-128251. (Essay Index Reprint Ser). Repr. of 1928 ed. 15.00 (ISBN 0-8369-2227-1). Ayer Co Pubs.

Pruning. Christopher Brickell. 1988. pap. 9.95 (ISBN 0-671-65841-7, Fireside). S&S.

Pruning. 3.95 (ISBN 0-686-21129-4). Bklyn Botanic.

Pruning: A Practical Guide. Rodger Elliot. 128p. 1987. pap. 12.95 (ISBN 0-85091-180-X, Pub. by Lothian). Intl Spec Bk.

Pruning Handbook. Sunset Editors. LC 82-83213. (Illus.). 120p. 1983. pap. 6.95 (ISBN 0-376-03605-2, Sunset Bks.). Sunset-Lane.

Pruning: How to Guide for Gardeners. Michael MacCaskey & Robert L. Stebbins. LC 82-83307. 160p. 1982. pap. 12.95 (ISBN 0-89586-188-7). Price Stern.

Pruning Manual. Liberty H. Bailey. Rev. by E. P. Christopher. 1954. 15.95 (ISBN 0-02-525420-0). Macmillan.

Pruning Shade Trees & Practicing Tree Surgery. facs. ed. (Shorey Lost Arts Ser.). 52p. pap. 2.95 (ISBN 0-8466-6041-5, U41). Shorey.

Pruning Simplified. updated ed. Lewis Hill. LC 85-45605. (Illus.). 200p. 1986. (Garden Way Pub); pap. 12.95 (ISBN 0-88266-417-4, Garden Way Pub). Storey Comm Inc.

TITLE INDEX PSALMS OF THE HEART.

Pruning Word: The Parables of Flannery O'Connor. John R. May. LC 75-19878. pap. 51.00 (ISBN 0-317-29674-4, 2022075). Bks Demand UMI.

Prunings-Accruings. Richard Kostelanetz. 24p. 1978. pap. 25.00 signed & lettered. A-Z (ISBN 0-932360-22-X). RK Edns.

Prussia in Transition: Society & Politics under the Stein Reform Ministry. Marion W. Gray. LC 84-45902. (Transactions Ser.: Vol. 76, Pt. 1). 150p. 1986. 18.00 (ISBN 0-87169-761-0). Am Philos.

Prussia: The History of a Lost State. Rudolf Von Thadden. Tr. by Angi Rutter from Ger. (Illus.). 172p. 1987. 29.95 (ISBN 0-521-30417-2). Cambridge U Pr.

Prussian-American Relations, Seventeen Seventy-Five to Eighteen Seventy-One. Henry M. Adams. LC 79-25884. 135p. 1980. Repr. of 1960 ed. lib. bdg. 35.00x (ISBN 0-313-22270-3, ADPA). Greenwood.

Prussian & Saxon Casualties of the Franco-Prussian War (1870-1871) Maralyn A. Wellauer. 31p. 1987. pap. 7.00 (ISBN 0-932019-08-0). Roots Intl.

Prussian Bureaucracy in Crisis, 1840-1860: Origins of an Administrative Ethos. John R. Gillis. LC 70-130826. 1971. 27.50x (ISBN 0-8047-0756-1). Stanford U Pr.

Prussian Liberal: The Life of Eduard Von Simson. James E. Dow. LC 81-40312. 226p. (Orig.). 1982. lib. bdg. 28.25 (ISBN 0-8191-1984-9); pap. text ed. 12.50 (ISBN 0-8191-1985-7). U Pr of Amer.

Prussian Military Reforms, 1786-1813. William O. Shanahan. LC 73-182584. (Columbia University. Studies in the Social Sciences: No. 520). Repr. of 1945 ed. 32.50 (ISBN 0-404-51520-7). AMS Pr.

Prussian Nights. Alexander Solzhenitsyn. Tr. by Robert Conquest from Rus. 128p. (Bilingual ed.). 1977. 8.95 (ISBN 0-374-23845-6); pap. 2.95 (ISBN 0-374-51391-0). FS&G.

Prussian Officer. D. H. Lawrence. (Creative's Classics Ser.). 64p. (gr. 6 up). 1982. PLB 8.95 (ISBN 0-87191-892-7). Creative Ed.

Prussian Officer & Other Stories. D. H. Lawrence. Ed. by John Worthen. LC 82-17792. (Cambridge Edition of the Works of D. H. Lawrence Ser.). 400p. 1983. 49.50 (ISBN 0-521-24822-1). Cambridge U Pr.

Prussian Officer & Other Stories. D. H. Lawrence. (Cambridge Edition Texts Ser.). 272p. 1985. 18.95 (ISBN 0-670-58053-8). Viking.

Prussian Officer, & Other Stories. facsimile ed. David H. Lawrence. LC 72-160939. (Short Story Index Reprint Ser.). Repr. of 1914 ed. 21.00 (ISBN 0-8369-3918-2). Ayer Co Pubs.

Prussian Poland in the German Empire, 1871-1900. Richard Blanke. (East European Monograph: No. 86). 268p. 1981. 25.00x (ISBN 0-914710-80-X). East Eur Quarterly.

Prussian Schoolteachers: Profession & Office, 1763-1848. Anthony J. La Vopa. LC 79-24873. x, 220p. 1980. 25.00x (ISBN 0-8078-1426-1). U of NC Pr.

Prussian Society & the German Order: An Aristocratic Corporation in Crisis c. 1410-1466. Michael Burleigh. LC 83-18896. (Cambridge Studies in Early Modern History). 232p. 1984. 44.50 (ISBN 0-521-26104-X). Cambridge U Pr.

Prussian Spirit: A Survey of German Literature & Politics, 1914-1940. S. D. Stirk. 59.95 (ISBN 0-8490-0912-X). Gordon Pr.

Prussian Welfare State Before 1740. Reinhold A. Dorwart. LC 77-134954. (Illus.). 1971. 24.50x (ISBN 0-674-71975-1). Harvard U Pr.

Prymer, or Lay Folks Prayer Book, Pts. 1 & 2. Ed. by H. Littlehales. (EETS, OS Ser.: No. 109). Repr. of 1897 ed. Kraus Repr.

Prytaneion: Its Function & Architectural Form. Stephen G. Miller. LC 76-24590. 1978. 38.00x (ISBN 0-520-03316-7). U of Cal Pr.

Przerwany Bieg. Stanislawa Pijanowska. 1000p. (Orig., Pol.). 1988. pap. 18.95 (ISBN 0-930401-16-6). Artex Pr.

Przewalski Horse & Restoration to Its Natural Habitat in Mongolia. FAO Staff. (FAO Animal Production & Health Paper Ser.: No. 61). (Illus.). 181p. (Orig.). 1987. pap. text ed. 14.50 (ISBN 92-5-102441-3, F2984, FAO). UNIPUB.

P'S & Cues for Travellers in Japan. Boye De Mente. (Illus.). 102p. (Orig.). 1974. pap. 6.50 (ISBN 4-07-971838-1, Pub. by Shufunmoto Co Ltd Japan). C E Tuttle.

PS: Caring about You. John Heidtke. 48p. 1988. 6.95 (ISBN 0-89962-754-4). Todd & Honeywell.

P's Three Women. Paulo E. Gomes & Salles Gomes. 144p. 1984. pap. 3.50 (ISBN 0-380-86256-5, 86256-5, Bard). Avon.

P.S. Write Soon. Colby Rodowsky. 160p. (YA) (gr. 5-7). 1980. pap. 1.50 (ISBN 0-440-97119-5, LFL). Dell.

P.S. Your Shrink Is Dead. John Reisan. 1979. pap. 1.95 (ISBN 0-8439-0687-1, Leisure Bks). Leisure NY.

PSA Offical Publication of the Pirandello Society of America. 1985. 15.00; lib. bdg. 30.00. Griffon Hse.

PSA Yield Tables for Gnma MBS. Ed. by Financial Publishing Co. Staff. 384p. Date not set. pap. 42.00 (ISBN 0-87600-664-0). Finan Pub.

PSA 1974: Proceedings. Philosophy of Science Association 1974 Biennial Meeting. Ed. by A. C. Michalos & R. S. Cohen. (Synthese Library Ser.: No. 91). 1976. lib. bdg. 76.00 (ISBN 90-277-0647-6, Pub. by Reidel Holland); pap. 47.50 (ISBN 90-277-0648-4, Pub. by Reidel Holland). Kluwer Academic.

PSA 1976, Vol. 1. Ed. by F. Suppe & P. D. Asquith. LC 72-624169. 312p. 1976. 8.50 (ISBN 0-917586-02-6). Philos Sci Assn.

PSA 1976, Vol. 2. LC 72-624169. 618p. 1977. pap. 6.25 (ISBN 0-917586-03-4). Philos Sci Assn.

PSA 1978, 2 vols, Vol. I. Ed. by Peter D. Asquith & Ian Hacking. LC 72-624169. 314p. 1978. 9.00x (ISBN 0-917586-06-9); pap. 6.00 (ISBN 0-917586-05-0); Vol. II, 478P. 22.50 (ISBN 0-917586-10-7). Philos Sci Assn.

PSA 1980, 2 Vols. Ed. by Peter D. Asquith & Ronald Giere. 370p. 1980. Vol. I. 9.50 (ISBN 0-917586-14-X); Vol. II, 678P. 1981. 23.75 (ISBN 0-917586-16-6). Philos Sci Assn.

PSA 1982, 2 Vols. Ed. by Peter D. Asquith & Thomas Nickles. 414p. 1982. Vol. I. 21.00 (ISBN 0-917586-18-2); pap. 19.00 (ISBN 0-917586-17-4); Vol. II, 730P. 1983. 25.00 (ISBN 0-917586-19-0). Philos Sci Assn.

PSA, 1984, Vol. 1. Ed. by Peter D. Asquith & Philip Kitcher. 223p. 1984. 15.50 (ISBN 0-917586-21-2); pap. 13.50 (ISBN 0-917586-20-4). Philos Sci Assn.

PSA 1984, Vol. 2. Ed. by Peter D. Asquith & Philip Kitcher. 903p. 1985. 30.00 (ISBN 0-917586-24-7). Philos Sci Assn.

PSA 1986, Vol. 1. Ed. by Arthur I. Fine & Peter K. Machamer. 521p. 1986. 20.00 (ISBN 0-917586-23-9); pap. 17.50 (ISBN 0-917586-22-0). Philos Sci Assn.

PSA, 1986, Vol. 2. Ed. by Arthur I. Fine & Peter K. Machamer. LC 72-624169. 383p. 1988. 13.50x (ISBN 0-917586-25-5). Philos Sci Assn.

Psalm for the Frightened & Frustrated Sheep. James D. Bales. 1977. pap. 1.50 (ISBN 0-89315-216-1). Lambert Bk.

Psalm Journal. Joan Chittister & Mary L. Kownacki. LC 85-50308. 104p. (Orig.). 1985. pap. 6.95 (ISBN 0-934134-28-6, Leaven Pr). Sheed & Ward MO.

Psalm Locator. 2nd ed. Ed. by Anthony Lawrence. (Orig.). 1986. pap. 10.95 (ISBN 0-89390-085-0). Resource Pubns.

Psalm of Christ: Forty Poems on the Twenty-Second Psalm. Chad Walsh. LC 82-5566. (Wheaton Literary Ser.). 74p. 1982. pap. 5.95 (ISBN 0-87788-700-4). Shaw Pubs.

Psalm of Saiva-being. T. Isaac Tamby. 506p. 1986. Repr. of 1925 ed. 30.00X (ISBN 0-8364-1682-1, PUb. by Abhinav India). South Asia Bks.

Psalm of Vietnam. Richard A. Hill. 144p. 1987. 9.95 (ISBN 0-8062-3139-4). Carlton.

Psalm One Hundred Four. Dorsey Alexander & Joyce Alexander. 32p. (Calligraphy & Illus.). 1978. pap. 5.00 (ISBN 0-912020-19-9). Turtles Quill.

Psalm One Hundred Nineteen. Charles Bridges. 1977. 19.95 (ISBN 0-85151-176-7). Banner of Truth.

Psalm Sampler. Office of Worship for the Presbyterian Church (U. S. A.) & The Cumberland Presbyterian Church. LC 85-753089. (Illus.). 48p. 1986. pap. 4.95 ea. (ISBN 0-664-24681-8). Westminster John Knox.

Psalm Singer's Amusement. William Billings. LC 73-5100. (Earlier American Music Ser.: Vol. 20). 104p. 1974. Repr. of 1781 ed. lib. bdg. 25.00 (ISBN 0-306-70587-7). Da Capo.

Psalm to Remember. (Americana Books Ser.). (Illus.). 1980. 3.00 (ISBN 0-911410-49-X). Applied Arts.

Psalmbook of the White Butterfly. Jay B. Fowler, Jr. LC 85-2887. 64p. (Orig.). 1985. pap. 5.00 (ISBN 0-914061-03-8). Orchises Pr.

Psalmen Des Koniglichen Propheten Davids. Johann P. Von Schonborn. xl, 872p. Repr. of 1658 ed. 62.00. Johnson Repr.

Psalmen: Stilistische Verfahren und Aufbau mit besonderer Beruecksichtigung von Ps. 1-41. N. H. Ridderbos. Tr. by Karl E. Mittring from Dutch. (Beiheft 117 zur Zeitschrift fuer die alttestamentliche Wissenschaft). 305p. 1972. 41.60x (ISBN 3-11-001834-9). De Gruyter.

Psalmenkommentare aus der Katenenueberlieferung, Vol. 1. Ekkehard Muehlenberg. LC 73-91808. (Patristische Texte und Studien, Band 15). (Ger.). 1974. 58.40x (ISBN 3-11-004182-0). De Gruyter.

Psalmenkommentare aus der Katenenueberlieferung: Untersuchungen zu den Psalmenkatenen, Vol. 3. Ekkehard Muehlenberg. (Patristische Texte und Studien: No. 19). 1978. 41.20x (ISBN 3-11-006959-8). De Gruyter.

Psalmenkommentware aus Katenenveberlieferung, Vol. 2. Ekkehard Muehlenberg. (Patristische Texte und Studien: Vol. 16). 1977. 59.60x (ISBN 3-11-005717-4). De Gruyter.

Psalmes of David, 2 vols. in 1. George Wither. 1967. Repr. of 1632 ed. 89.00 (ISBN 0-8337-3838-0). B Franklin.

Psalmist with a Camera. Gail Rubin. LC 79-5086. (Illus.). 116p. 1979. 29.95 (ISBN 0-89659-076-3); pap. 16.95 (ISBN 0-89659-071-2). Abbeville Pr.

Psalmnary: Gradual Psalms for Cantor & Congregation. James E. Barrett. 196p. 1982. incl. binder 24.00 (ISBN 0-942466-04-7); 21.00 (ISBN 0-942466-03-9). Hymnary Pr.

Psalmody in Seventeenth Century America: Series 1, the Ainsworth Psalter. Ed. by Carleton S. Smith. price on application (ISBN 0-685-18958-9, Dist. by C. F. Peters Corp). NY Pub Lib.

Psalms. Joseph A. Alexander. 570p. 1989. lib. bdg. 22.95 (ISBN 0-8254-2141-1); pap. 16.95 (ISBN 0-8254-2140-3). Kregel.

Psalms. Anthony L. Ash. 1980. 17.95 (ISBN 0-915547-42-2). Abilene Christ U.

Psalms. Albert Barnes. 29.95 (ISBN 0-8010-0838-7). Baker Bk.

Psalms. A. Cohen. 488p. 1945. 12.95 (ISBN 0-900689-32-3). Soncino Pr.

Psalms. Toni Craven. (Message Biblical Spirituality Ser.: Vol. 6). 1988. 12.95 (ISBN 0-89453-556-0); pap. 8.95 (ISBN 0-89453-572-2). M Glazier.

Psalms. David Dickson. (Geneva Commentary Ser.). 1064p. 1985. Repr. of 1653 ed. 26.95 (ISBN 0-85151-481-2). Banner of Truth.

Psalms. Arno C. Gaebelein. 1939. 10.95 (ISBN 0-87213-222-6). Loizeaux.

Psalms. Irving L. Jensen. (Bible Self-Study Guides). 1968. pap. 3.50 (ISBN 0-8024-1019-7). Moody.

Psalms. Peter Levi. Tr. by Nicholas De Lange. (Penguin Classics Ser.). 272p. 1986. pap. 6.95 (ISBN 0-14-044319-3). Penguin.

Psalms. David G. Mobberley. Ed. by Lynne M. Deming & Margaret Rogers. (Cokesbury Basic Bible Commentary Ser.). (Illus.). 159p. (Orig.). 1988. pap. text ed. 4.95 (ISBN 0-939697-18-1). Graded Pr.

Psalms. Robert North. (Bible Ser.). Pt. 3. pap. 1.00 (ISBN 0-8091-5125-1); Pt. 4. pap. 1.00 (ISBN 0-8091-5126-X); Pt. 5. pap. 1.00 (ISBN 0-8091-5127-8); Pt. 6. pap. 1.00 (ISBN 0-8091-5128-6). Paulist Pr.

Psalms. W. S. Plumer. (Geneva Commentaries Ser.). 1978. 33.95 (ISBN 0-85151-209-7). Banner of Truth.

Psalms. Arnold B. Rhodes. LC 59-10454. (Layman's Bible Commentary Ser: Vol. 9). 1960. 5.95 (ISBN 0-8042-3009-9, John Knox); pap. 4.95 (ISBN 0-8042-3069-2). Westminster John Knox.

Psalms. Charles H. Spurgeon. Ed. by David O. Fuller. LC 76-12085. 704p. 1977. pap. 18.95 (ISBN 0-8254-3714-8). Kregel.

Psalms. Carroll Stuhlmueller. (Read & Pray Ser.). 1979. 1.75 (ISBN 0-8199-0631-X). Franciscan Herald.

Psalms. Stafford Wright. (Bible Study Commentaries Ser.). 152p. 1982. pap. 4.95 (ISBN 0-87508-157-6). Chr Lit.

Psalms--Heartbeat of Life & Worship. Benedict Janecko. LC 86-72734. 86p. (Orig.). 1987. pap. 4.95 (ISBN 0-317-58186-4, 20296-0). Abbey.

Psalms: A Commentary. Artur Weiser. LC 62-16760. (Old Testament Library). 842p. 1962. 29.95 (ISBN 0-664-20418-X). Westminster John Knox.

Psalms: A Form-Critical Introduction. Hermann Gunkel. Ed. by John Reumann. Tr. by Thomas M. Horner from Ger. LC 67-22983. (Facet Bks.). 64p. (Orig.). 1967. pap. 3.95 (ISBN 0-8006-3043-2, 1-3043). Fortress.

Psalms: A Guide to Victorious Holy Living. Carl E. Foster. Ed. by Linda L. Foster. LC 87-51577. 275p. 1988. wkbk. 15.00 (ISBN 0-9619962-1-8). Victorious Holy Living.

Psalms: A Matchless Treasury. Richard A. Hufton. LC 84-82058. 106p. (Orig.). 1984. pap. 4.00 (ISBN 0-933643-02-0). Grace World Outreach.

Psalms: A New Translation. Bonaventure Zerr. 8.95 (ISBN 0-8091-2218-9). Paulist Pr.

Psalms: A New Translation for Prayer & Worship. Tr. by Gary Chamberlain. LC 84-50842. 192p. (Orig.). 1984. pap. 6.95 (ISBN 0-8358-0485-2). Upper Room.

Psalms: A New Version. Roy E. Koeblitz. LC 85-63357. 208p. 1986. 12.95 (ISBN 0-936187-11-5). Palm Pub Co.

Psalms: A Singing Version. Joseph Gelineau. 256p. 1968. pap. 3.95 (ISBN 0-8091-1669-3, Deus). Paulist Pr.

Psalms: A Study Guide. Dale J. Cooper. (Revelation Series for Adults). 1979. pap. text ed. 2.75 (ISBN 0-933140-08-8). CRC Pubns.

Psalms & Prayers for Congregational Participation: Series A. B. David Hostetter. 1983. 7.75 (ISBN 0-89536-639-8, 1633). CSS of Ohio.

Psalms & Prayers for Congregational Participation: Series B (Common Consensus Lectionary) B. David Hostetter. 1984. 7.75 (ISBN 0-89536-694-0, 4871). CSS of Ohio.

Psalms & Prayers for Congregational Participation: Series C (Common Consensus Lectionary) B. David Hostetter. 1985. 7.75 (ISBN 0-89536-770-X, 5865). CSS of Ohio.

Psalms & Proverbs. Alice J. Davidson. (Alice in Bibleland Storybooks). (Illus.). 32p. (ps-3). 1984. 4.95 (ISBN 0-8378-5069-X). Gibson.

Psalms & Proverbs, Neighborhood Bible Study. Marilyn Kunz & Catherine Schell. 1971. pap. 2.95 (ISBN 0-8423-4991-X). Tyndale.

Psalms & Wisdom. Leonard Johnston & Michael Smith. Ed. by Laurence Bright. LC 71-173033. (Scripture Discussion Commentary Ser.: Pt. 6). 256p. 1972. pap. text ed. 4.95. ACTA Pubns.

Psalms Anew. Nancy Schreck & Maureen Leach. 200p. (Orig.). 1986. pap. 6.95 (ISBN 0-88489-174-7). St Mary's.

Psalms (CC, Vol. 13. Donald Williams. 448p. 1986. 23.95 (ISBN 0-8499-0419-6). Word Bks.

Psalms: Chronologically Treated with a New Translation. rev. ed. Moses Buttenwieser. (Library of Biblical Studies Ser.). 1969. 59.50x (ISBN 0-87068-044-7). Ktav.

Psalms Come Alive: Capturing the Voice & the Art of Israel's Songs. John H. Eaton. LC 86-20115. (Illus.). 180p. 1986. pap. 7.95 (ISBN 0-87784-387-2). Inter-Varsity.

Psalms: Critical & Exegetical Commentary, Vols. 1 & 2. Charles Briggs & Emile G. Briggs. Ed. by Samuel R. Driver et al. (International Critical Commentary). 34.95 ea. (Pub. by T & T Clark Ltd UK). Vol. 1, 1906, 580 pgs (ISBN 0-567-05011-4). Vol. 2, 1907, 580 pgs (ISBN 0-567-05012-2). Fortress.

Psalms: Faith Songs for the Faith-Filled. Mary Jo Tully. 96p. 1982. pap. 3.75 (ISBN 0-697-01824-5). Wm C Brown.

Psalms for Children: Series B. Eldon Weisheit. LC 84-18562. 128p. (Orig.). 1984. pap. 7.95 (ISBN 0-8066-2096-X, 10-5304). Augsburg.

Psalms for Children: Series C. Eldon Weisheit. LC 85-11154. 128p. (Orig.). (gr. k-4). 1985. pap. 7.95 (ISBN 0-8066-2169-9, 10-5305). Augsburg.

Psalms for Children: Sixty Object Lessons. Eldon Weisheit. LC 83-70510. (Series A). 128p. (Orig.). 1983. pap. 7.95 (ISBN 0-8066-2016-1, 10-5303). Augsburg.

Psalms for God's People. Robert Johnston. LC 82-5344. (Bible Commentary for Laymen Ser.). 160p. 1982. pap. 3.95 (ISBN 0-8307-0820-0, S362105). Regal.

Psalms for Graduates. Brent D. Earles. 5.95 (ISBN 0-8010-3426-4). Baker Bk.

Psalms for Singing: Twenty-Six Psalms with Musical Settings for Congregation & Choir. Tr. by Gary Chamberlain. LC 84-50778. 141p. (Orig.). 1984. pap. 7.50 (ISBN 0-8358-0495-X). Upper Room.

Psalms for Sojourners. James Limburg. LC 86-2621. (Illus.). 112p. (Orig.). 1986. pap. 6.95 (ISBN 0-8066-2206-7, 10-5306). Augsburg.

Psalms from Prison. Benjamin F. Chavis, Jr. 192p. 1983. 10.95 (ISBN 0-8298-0661-X); pap. 7.95 (ISBN 0-8298-0666-0). Pilgrim NY.

Psalms from the Sea. A. Morgan Parker. 1982. pap. 1.95 (ISBN 0-8341-0745-7). Beacon Hill.

Psalms in Scots. (Illus.). 1987. Repr. of 1871 ed. 7.45 (ISBN 0-317-59593-8, AUP). Pergamon.

Psalms in Scots: Reprint of the Psalms - Frae Hebrew intil Scottis. P. Hately Waddell. (Illus.). 128p. 1987. pap. text ed. 8.95 (ISBN 0-08-035075-5, AUP). Pergamon.

Psalms in Song for the White Cavalry. 3rd ed. Frank M. Wakeman. (Illus.). 1979. 5.00 (ISBN 0-910840-19-9). Kingdom.

Psalms, Meditations in the Psalms. Erling C. Olsen. 1050p. 1975. Repr. 19.95 (ISBN 0-87213-680-9). Loizeaux.

Psalms: Nos. 1-72, Vol. 1. George A. Knight. LC 82-20134. (Daily Study Bible Old Testament Ser.). 350p. 1982. 12.95 (ISBN 0-664-21805-9); pap. 7.95 (ISBN 0-664-24572-2). Westminster John Knox.

Psalms: Nos. 73-150, Vol. 2. George A. Knight. LC 82-20134. (Daily Study Bible Old Testament Ser.). 384p. 1983. 15.95 (ISBN 0-664-21808-3); pap. 8.95 (ISBN 0-664-24575-7). Westminster John Knox.

Psalms-Now. Leslie Brandt. LC 73-78108. 1973. 8.95 (ISBN 0-570-03230-X, 15-2125). Concordia.

Psalms-Now see Popular Devotionals.

Psalms of a Laywoman. Edwina Gateley. (Illus.). 116p. (Orig.). 1987. pap. 5.95 (ISBN 0-940147-00-9). Source Bks CA.

Psalms of Comfort. Tr. by Leslie Brandt. (Psalms Now Gift Books). 1977. pap. 1.95 (ISBN 0-570-07452-5, 12-2686). Concordia.

Psalms of David. Contrib. by James S. Freemantle. 1987. 19.95 (ISBN 0-688-01312-0). Morrow.

Psalms of David. (Classics Ser.). 1982. 9.95 (ISBN 0-88088-965-9). Peter Pauper.

Psalms of Joy. Tr. by Leslie Brandt. (Psalms Now Gift Books). 1977. pap. 1.95 (ISBN 0-570-07451-7, 12-2685). Concordia.

Psalms of Joy & Faith. Kyle M. Yates. 216p. 1984. pap. 7.95 (ISBN 0-913029-03-3). Stevens Bk Pr.

Psalms of My Life. Joseph Bayly. 1987. 9.95 (ISBN 1-55513-281-2, Life Journey). Cook.

Psalms of Praise. Tr. by Leslie Brandt. (Psalms Now Gift Books). 1977. pap. 1.95 (ISBN 0-570-07453-3, 12-2687). Concordia.

Psalms of Redemption. Kiarri T-H Cheatwood. LC 82-83855. 50p. 1983. pap. 4.00x perf. bnd. (ISBN 0-916418-41-3). Lotus.

Psalms of Reflection: A Selection of Psalm Verses for Those Who Mourn. Elmwood Publishing Company Staff. 1979. pap. 1.25 (ISBN 0-931396-00-X). Elmwood Pub Co.

Psalms of Strength. Leslie Brandt. (Psalms Now Gift Books). 1977. pap. 1.95 (ISBN 0-570-07450-9, 12-2684). Concordia.

Psalms of the Early Buddhists, 2 vols. Carolina A. Davids. LC 78-72413. Date not set. Repr. of 1909 ed. Set. 67.50 (ISBN 0-404-17590-2). AMS Pr.

Psalms of the Heart. George Sweeting. 132p. 1988. pap. 5.50 (ISBN 0-89693-435-7). SP Pubns.

Psalms of the Rabbi Physician. Eric R. Braverman. (Illus.). 112p. (Orig.). 1986. pap. 9.95 (ISBN 1-55630-003-4). Brentwood Comm.
Psalms of the Still Country. Edward J. Ingebretsen. 1982. pap. 7.95 (ISBN 0-89390-036-2). Resource Pubns.
Psalms One. Carroll Stuhlmueller. LC 82-83727. (Old Testament Message Ser.: Vol. 21). 16.95 (ISBN 0-89453-421-1); pap. 12.95 (ISBN 0-89453-255-3). M Glazier.
Psalms One - Seventy-Two. D. Kidner. LC 75-23852. 1973. 14.95 (ISBN 0-87784-868-8); pap. 8.95 (ISBN 0-87784-264-7). Inter-Varsity.
Psalms One, One - Fifty. Ed. by Mitchell Dahood. (Anchor Bible Ser.: Vol. 16). 1966. pap. 18.00 (ISBN 0-385-02765-6, Anchor Pr). Doubleday.
Psalms: Prayer Power for Your Problems. Carrie Pevarnik & Robert Chaney. LC 78-58146. (Illus.). 1978. pap. 9.95 (ISBN 0-918936-05-5). Astara.
Psalms: Prayers for the Ups, Downs & In-Betweens of Life: A Literary Experiential Approach. John Craghan. LC 84-81245. (Background Bks.: Vol. 2). 1985. pap. 7.95 (ISBN 0-89453-439-4). M Glazier.
Psalms: Prayers of the Heart. Eugene Peterson. (LifeGuide Bible Studies). 64p. (Orig.). 1987. pap. 2.95 (ISBN 0-8308-1034-X). Inter-Varsity.
Psalms: Songs of Discipleship, 3 vols. Robert L. Alden. (Everyman's Bible Commentary Ser.). 1975. pap. 5.95 ea. Vol. 1 (ISBN 0-8024-2018-4). Vol. 2 (ISBN 0-8024-2019-2). Vol. 3 (ISBN 0-8024-2020-6). Moody.
Psalms: Structure, Content, & Message. Claus Westermann. Tr. by Ralph D. Gehrke from Ger. LC 79-54127. 136p. (Orig.). 1980. pap. 8.95 (ISBN 0-8066-1762-4, 10-5300). Augsburg.
Psalms, Studies on Book One. H. A. Ironside. 9.95 (ISBN 0-87213-383-4). Loizeaux.
Psalms: The Divine Journey. Mark S. Smith. 96p. 1987. pap. 4.95 (ISBN 0-8091-2897-7). Paulist Pr.
Psalms: The Poetry of Palestine. Woodrow M. Kroll. 464p. (Orig.). 1987. lib. bdg. 37.50 (ISBN 0-8191-5750-3); pap. text ed. 24.75 (ISBN 0-8191-5751-1). U Pr of Amer.
Psalms: The Prayer Book of the Bible. 2nd ed. Dietrich Bonhoeffer. Tr. by James H. Burtness from Ger. LC 73-101111. 88p. 1970. 4.95 (ISBN 0-8066-1439-0, 10-5321). Augsburg.
Psalms: Their Origin & Meaning. Leopold Sabourin. LC 73-16459. 560p. (Orig.). 1974. pap. 12.95 (ISBN 0-8189-0121-7). Alba.
Psalms Three, One Hundred One - One Hundred Fifty. Ed. by Mitchell Dahood. LC 66-11766. (Anchor Bible Ser.: Vol. 17A). 1970. pap. 22.00 (ISBN 0-385-00607-1, Anchor Pr). Doubleday.
Psalms: Translation & Commentary by Rabbi Samson Raphael Hirsch. Tr. by Gertrude Hirschler from Ger. (Compact Ser.). 1978. 17.95 (ISBN 0-87306-135-7). Feldheim.
Psalms Two. Carroll Stuhlmueller. LC 82-83728. (Old Testament Message Ser.: Vol. 22). 15.95 (ISBN 0-89453-422-X); pap. 12.95 (ISBN 0-89453-257-X). M Glazier.
Psalms Two, Fifty-One to One Hundred. Ed. by Mitchell Dahood. LC 66-11766. (Anchor Bible Ser.: Vol. 17). 1968. pap. 18.00 (ISBN 0-385-03759-7, Anchor Pr). Doubleday.
Psalms: With Introduction to Cultic Poetry, Prt. I. Ed. by Erhard Gerstenberger. (Forms of the Old Testament Literature Ser.: Vol. XIV). 224p. (Orig.). 1988. pap. 24.95 (ISBN 0-8028-0255-9). Eerdmans.
Psalms with Their Spoils. Jon Silkin. (Orig.). 1980. pap. 7.95 (ISBN 0-7100-0497-4). Routledge Chapman & Hall.
Psalms 1-50. Peter C. Craigie. (Word Biblical Commentary Ser.: Vol. 19). 378p. 1983. 22.95 (ISBN 0-8499-0218-5). Word Bks.
Psalms, 1-50. John W. Rogerson. LC 76-27911. (Cambridge Bible Commentary on the New English Bible, Old Testament Ser.). 1977. 37.50 (ISBN 0-521-21463-7); pap. 13.95 (ISBN 0-521-29160-7). Cambridge U Pr.
Psalms 1-59. Tr. by Hilton C. Oswald. LC 87-19552. 560p. 1988. 36.95 (ISBN 0-8066-2284-9, 10-5301). Augsburg.
Psalms 1-72. Richard J. Clifford. (Collegeville Bible Commentary: Old Testament Ser.: Vol. 22). 80p. 1986. pap. 2.95. Liturgical Pr.
Psalms 101-150. Leslie C. Allen. (Word Biblical Commentary Ser.: Vol. 21). 362p. 1983. 22.95 (ISBN 0-8499-0220-7). Word Bks.
Psalms, 101-150. John W. Rogerson. LC 76-27911. (Cambridge Bible Commentary on the New English Bible, Old Testament Ser.). 1977. 37.50 (ISBN 0-521-21465-3); pap. 12.95 (ISBN 0-521-29162-3). Cambridge U Pr.
Psalms, 51-100. John W. Rogerson. LC 76-27911. (Cambridge Bible Commentary on the New English Bible, Old Testament Ser.). 1977. 37.50 (ISBN 0-521-21464-5); pap. 12.95 (ISBN 0-521-29161-5). Cambridge U Pr.
Psalms 73-150. Richard J. Clifford. (Collegeville Bible Commentary: Old Testament Ser.: Vol. 23). 88p. 1986. pap. 2.95 (ISBN 0-8146-1479-5). Liturgical Pr.
Psalm 118. Theophan the Recluse. 496p. 22.00 (ISBN 0-317-28925-X); pap. 17.00 (ISBN 0-317-28926-8). Holy Trinity.
Psalter. Tr. by The Monks of New Skete. 286p. 1984. 39.50x (ISBN 0-9607924-5-7). Monks of New Skete.
Psalter. 3.50 (ISBN 0-8164-0311-2, HarpR). Har-Row.
Psalter & Hours of Yolande of Soissons. Karen Gould. LC 78-55888. 1978. 11.00x (ISBN 0-910956-78-2, SAM4); pap. 5.00x (ISBN 0-910956-64-2). Medieval Acad.
Psalter of Robert de Lisle. Lucy F. Sandler. (Harvey Miller Publication Ser.). (Illus.). 1983. 105.00x (ISBN 0-19-921028-4). Oxford U Pr.
PSAT (Preliminary Scholastic Aptitude Test) Preparation Guide. Jerry Bobrow & William A. Covino. (Cliffs Test Preparation Ser.). (Illus.). (gr. 10-11). 1982. pap. 3.25 (ISBN 0-8220-2002-5). Cliffs.
Psaumes. Paul Claudel. 280p. 1966. 12.95 (ISBN 0-686-54426-9). French & Eur.
Psaumes Choisis. Henry Morris. 192p. (Fr.). 1986. pap. 3.50 (ISBN 0-8297-0697-6). Life Pubs Intl.
Psaumes mesures a l'antique de J.-A. de Baif see Florilege du concert vocal de la Renaissance.
Pseaumes des Meslanges de 1612; Dialoque e a sept parties see Monuments de la musique francaise au temps de la Renaissance.
Pseaumes en vers Mezurez see Maitres Musiciens de la Renaissance Francaise.
Pseaumes en Vers Mezurez, Premier Fascicule see Maitres Musiciens de la Renaissance Francaise.
Pseaumes en vers Mezurez, Troisieme Fascicule see Maitres Musiciens de la Renaissance Francaise.
Pselaphidae of Oceania, with Special Reference to the Fiji Islands. O. Park. (BMB). pap. 10.00 (ISBN 0-527-02315-9). Kraus Repr.
PSES: Purdue Self-Evaluation System for School Media Centers-Elementary Catalog. David V. Loertscher & Janet G. Stroud. 1976. 2.50x (ISBN 0-931510-01-5). Hi Willow.
PSES: Purdue Self-Evaluation System for School Media Centers-Jr. Sr. High Catalog. David V. Loertscher & Janet G. Stroud. 1976. 2.50x (ISBN 0-931510-00-7). Hi Willow.
Pseudepigrapha & Modern Research, with a Supplement. James H. Charlesworth. LC 76-25921. (Society Biblical Literature Septuagint & Cognate Studies). 344p. 1981. pap. 12.75 (ISBN 0-89130-441-X, 06-04-07A). Scholars Pr GA.
Pseudo-Archytas ueber die Kategorien: Texte zur griechischen Aristoteles-Exegese. Ed. & Thomas Slezak. (Peripatoi Bd. 4). 184p. 1972. 35.60x (ISBN 3-11-003676-2). De Gruyter.
Pseudo-Boolean Methods for Bivalent Programming: Proceedings of the European Meeting, Warsaw, 1966. Institute of Management Sciences Staff & Econometric Institute Staff. Ed. by P. L. Ivanescu & S. Rudeanu. (Lecture Notes in Mathematics: Vol. 23). 1966. pap. 10.70 (ISBN 0-387-03606-7). Springer-Verlag.
Pseudo-Boolean Programming & Applications. Colloquium on Mathematics & Cybernetics in the Economy Staff. Ed. by P. L. Ivanescu. (Lecture Notes in Mathematics: Vol. 9). 1965. pap. 10.70 (ISBN 0-387-03352-1). Springer-Verlag.
Pseudo-Cleft Construction in English. F. R. Higgins. Ed. by Jorge Hankamer. LC 78-66547. (Outstanding Dissertations in Linguistics Ser.). 1985. 53.00 (ISBN 0-8240-9683-5). Garland Pub.
Pseudo-Convexite, Convexite Polynomiale et Domaines D'holomorphie En Dimension Infinie. Ph. Noverraz. (Mathematics Studies: Vol. 3). 1975. pap. 21.00 (ISBN 0-444-10692-8, North-Holland). Elsevier.
Pseudo-Differential Operators. Ed. by H. O. Cordes et al. (Lecture Notes in Mathematics Ser.: Vol. 1256). x, 479p. 1987. 41.70 (ISBN 0-387-17856-2). Springer-Verlag.
Pseudo-Differential Operators. Hitoshi Kumano-Go. Tr. by Remi Vaillancourt & Michihiro Nagase. 560p. 1982. 75.00x (ISBN 0-262-11080-6). MIT Pr.
Pseudo-Dionysius Aeropagite: The Divine Names & Mystical Theology. Tr. by John D. Jones. (Mediaeval Philosophical Texts in Translation: No. 21). 320p. 24.95 (ISBN 0-87462-221-2). Marquette.
Pseudo Dionysius: The Complete Works. Ed. by Colm Luibheid. (Classics of Western Spirituality Ser.: Vol. 54). 336p. 1987. 15.95 (ISBN 0-8091-0383-4); pap. 12.95 (ISBN 0-8091-2838-1). Paulist Pr.
Pseudo Discipleship. George Verwer. 1970. pap. 1.50 (ISBN 0-87508-548-2). Chr Lit.
Pseudo-Epiphanius Testimony Book. Robert V. Hotchkiss. LC 74-15203. (Society of Biblical Literature. Texts & Translation-Early Christian Literature Ser.). 1974. pap. 8.95 (060204). Scholars Pr GA.
Pseudo-Ezekiel & the Original Prophecy. Torrey & Spiegel. Date not set. 25.00. Ktav.
Pseudo-Ezekiel & the Original Prophecy. Charles C. Torrey. LC 78-63562. (Yale Oriental Ser. Researches: No. 18). Repr. of 1930 ed. 15.00 (ISBN 0-404-60288-6). AMS Pr.
Pseudo-Gregorian Dialogues, Vols. 1 & 2. F. Clark. (Studies in the History of Christian Thought: No. 37-38). 1987. Set. 125.50 (ISBN 90-04-07773-1, Pub. by E J Brill). Vol. 1, 420pp. Vol. 2, 376pp. Heinman.
Pseudo-Martyr. John Donne. LC 74-16215. 450p. 1974. 60.00x (ISBN 0-8201-1140-6). Schol Facsimiles.
Pseudo-Melesko: A Ukrainian Apocryphal Parliamentary Speech of 1615-1618. Bohdan A. Struminsky. LC 84-80992. (Harvard Ukrainian Research Institute Monograph). 175p. 1984. 21.95x (ISBN 0-916458-11-3). Harvard Ukrainian.
Pseudo-Plato, Axiochus. Jackson P. Hershbell. Tr. by Jackson P. Hershbell. LC 79-20127. (Society of Biblical Literature, Text & Translations: 21). 90p. 1981. pap. 13.50 (ISBN 0-89130-354-5, 06 02 21). Scholars Pr GA.
Pseudo-Platonica: A Dissertation Presented to the Faculty of Arts, Literature & Science of the University of Chicago in Candidacy for the Degree of Doctor of Philosophy, 1896 see Plato's Euthyphro.
Pseudo-Riemannian Symmetric Spaces. Michel Cahen & Monique Parker. LC 79-27541. (Memoirs Ser.: No. 229). 108p. 1980. pap. 12.00 (ISBN 0-8218-2229-2, MEMO-229). Am Math.
Pseudo-science & Society in Nineteenth Century America. Ed. by Arthur Wrobel. LC 87-12464. (Illus.). 256p. 1987. text ed. 24.00 (ISBN 0-8131-1632-5). U Pr of Ky.
Pseudo-Shakespearian Plays, 5 vols. in 1. Ed. by Karl Warnke & Ludwig Proescholdt. LC 74-148325. Repr. of 1883 ed. 31.50 (ISBN 0-404-06845-6). AMS Pr.
Pseudo-Turpin. Ed. by Hamilton M. Smyser. (Medieval Academy of America: Publ., Vol. 30). Repr. of 1937 ed. 20.00 (ISBN 0-527-01698-5). Kraus Repr.
Pseudocarcinoma of the Skin. Boris A. Berenbein. Tr. by V. E. Tatarchenko from Rus. LC 84-24988. 278p. 1985. 59.50x (ISBN 0-306-10981-6, Consultants). Plenum Pub.
Pseudococcidae. Pt. 1 see Atlas of the Scale Insects of North America.
Pseudodifferential Operators. Michael E. Taylor. LC 80-8580. (Princeton Mathematical Ser.: No. 34). 468p. 1981. 52.50 (ISBN 0-691-08282-0). Princeton U Pr.
Pseudodifferential Operators & Applications. Ed. by F. Treves. LC 85-1419. (Proceedings of Symposia in Pure Mathematics: Vol. 43). 301p. 1985. text ed. 48.00 (ISBN 0-8218-1469-9). Am Math.
Pseudodifferential Operators & Spectral Theory. M. A. Shubin. (Soviet Mathematics Ser.). 305p. 1987. 55.00 (ISBN 0-387-13621-5). Springer-Verlag.
Pseudoepigraphy & Ethical Arguments in the Pastoral Epistles. Lewis R. Donelson. 260p. 1986. lib. bdg. 63.50x (ISBN 3-16-145009-4, Pub. by J C B Mohr BRD). Coronet Bks.
Pseudoepilepsy: The Clinical Aspects of False Seizures. Ed. by Meir Gross. LC 82-49081. 288p. 1983. 30.00x (ISBN 0-669-06418-1). Lexington Bks.
Pseudoklassizistisches und Romantisches in Thomson's Seasons. Erna Anwander. 12.00 (ISBN 0-384-01665-0). Johnson Repr.
Pseudolus see Little Carthaginian.
Pseudomagia: A Neo-Latin Drama. William Mewe. Ed. by John C. Coldewey & Brian P. Copenhaver. Tr. by John C. Coldewey & Brian P. Copenhaver. 177p. 1979. text ed. 48.50x (ISBN 0-317-55879-X, Pub. by B De Graaf Netherlands). Coronet Bks.
Pseudomonas Aeruginosa. Ed. by D. P. Speert & R. E. Hancock. (Antibiotics & Chemotherapy: Vol. 36). (Illus.). viii, 176p. 1985. 98.75 (ISBN 3-8055-3966-5). S Karger.
Pseudomonas Aeruginosa: Clinical Manifestations of Infection & Current Therapy. Ed. by R. G. Doggett. 1979. 86.00 (ISBN 0-12-219550-7). Acad Pr.
Pseudomonas Aeruginosa: Ecological Aspects & Patient Colonization. Ed. by Viola M. Young. LC 76-56919. 155p. 1977. 25.50 (ISBN 0-89004-149-0). Raven.
Pseudonymity & Canon: An Investigation into the Relationship of Authorship & Authority in Jewish & Earliest Christian Tradition. David G Meade. 268p. (Orig.). 1987. pap. 35.00 (ISBN 0-8028-3645-3). Eerdmans.
Pseudonymity & Canon: An Investigation into the Relationship of Authorship & Authority in Jewish & Earliest Christian Tradition. David G. Meade. vii, 257p. 1986. lib. bdg. 63.50x (ISBN 3-16-145044-2, Pub. by J C B Mohr BRD). Coronet Bks.
Pseudonyms & Nicknames Dictionary, 2 vols. 3rd ed. Ed. by Jennifer Mossman. 2207p. 1986. Set. 230.00x (ISBN 0-8103-0541-0). Gale.
Pseudonyms of Authors. John E. Haynes. LC 68-30620. 112p. 1969. Repr. of 1882 ed. 38.00x (ISBN 0-8103-3142-X). Gale.
Pseudopotential Theory of Atoms & Molecules. Levente Szasz. 400p. 1985. 61.00 (ISBN 0-471-82417-8). Wiley.
Pseudoscience & Mental Ability: The Origins & Fallacies of the IQ Controversy. Jeffrey Blum. LC 77-81371. 240p. 1979. pap. 5.95 (ISBN 0-85345-496-5). Monthly Rev.
Pseudoscience & the Paranormal: A Critical Examination of the Evidence. Terence Hines. LC 87-43318. 372p. (Orig.). 1988. pap. text ed. 17.95 (ISBN 0-87975-419-2). Prometheus Bks.
PSI & Altered States of Consciousness: Proceedings. International Conference on Hypnosis, Drugs, Dreams, & Psi, France, June 9-12, 1967. Ed. by Roberto Cavanna & Montague Ullman. LC 68-8909. 1968. 16.00 (ISBN 0-912328-11-8). Parapsych Foun.
PSI & Psychoanalysis. Jule Eisenbud. LC 71-75145. 368p. 1970. 62.50 (ISBN 0-8089-0126-5, 791150). Grune.
PSI & States of Awareness. Proceedings of the International Conference, Paris, France, Aug. 24-26, 1977. Ed. by Betty Shapin & Lisette Coly. LC 78-50167. 1978. 17.00 (ISBN 0-912328-30-4). Parapsych Foun.
PSI & the Consciousness Explosion. Stuart Holroyd. 1976. 9.95 (ISBN 0-8008-6556-1). Taplinger.
PSI & the Mind: An Information Processing Approach. H. J. Irwin. LC 79-20587. 181p. 1979. 16.50 (ISBN 0-8108-1258-4). Scarecrow.
PSI Development Systems. Jeffery Mishlue. 432p. 1988. pap. 4.95 (ISBN 0-345-35204-1). Ballantine.
PSI Factors in Creativity. Proceedings of an International Conference, France, June 16-18, 1969. Ed. by Allan Angoff & Betty Shapin. LC 71-140141. 1970. 16.00 (ISBN 0-912328-18-5). Parapsych Foun.
PSI Favorable States of Consciousness: Proceedings of an International Conference on Methodology in Psi Research, France, Sept. 2-6, 1968. Ed. by Roberto Cavanna. LC 75-97821. 1970. 16.00 (ISBN 0-912328-17-7). Parapsych Foun.
PSI Trek. Laile Bartlett. 300p. 1981. text ed. 12.95 (ISBN 0-07-003915-1). McGraw.
Psicologia: Curso Basico. Dario Casado. LC 81-65574. (Coleccion Textos Ser.). 384p. (Orig., Span.). 1984. pap. 12.00 (ISBN 0-89729-285-5). Ediciones.
Psicologia de Jesus y la Salud Mental. Raymond L. Cramer. Tr. by Carlos A. Vargas from Eng. LC 76-16438. 191p. (Span.). 1976. pap. 5.25 (ISBN 0-89922-074-6). Edit Caribe.
Psicologia De la Comunicacion. 8th ed. Ana M. O'Neill. 8.10 (ISBN 0-8477-2901-X). U of PR Pr.
Psicologia de la Comunicacion. Ana Maria O'Neill. 541p. (Span.). 1986. Repr. of 1984 ed. 8.00 (ISBN 0-8477-2907-9). U of PR Pr.
Psicologia De la Vejez. Efrain Sanchez Hidalgo & Lydia Sanchez Hidalgo. pap. 4.80 (ISBN 0-8477-2905-2). U of PR Pr.
Psicologia en Prevencion de Accidentes. 7.50 (ISBN 0-318-18012-X). Inter-Am Safety.
Psicologia Pastoral de la Iglesia. Jorge A. Leon. LC 77-43121. 192p. (Orig., Span.). pap. 6.25 (ISBN 0-89922-113-0). Edit Caribe.
Psicologia Pastoral para Todos los Cristianos. Jorge A. Leon. LC 76-43121. 181p. (Orig., Span.). 1976. pap. 6.25 (ISBN 0-89922-020-7). Edit Caribe.
Psicologia y el Ministerio Cristiano. James E. Giles. 384p. 1982. Repr. of 1978 ed. 3.25 (ISBN 0-311-42059-1). Casa Bautista.
Psicologia y Religion. J. W. Drakeford. 384p. 1980. pap. 8.95 (ISBN 0-311-46035-6, Edit Mundo). Casa Bautista.
Psicologo Perverso. new ed. Juan Castellanos. (Pimienta Collection Ser). 160p. 1974. pap. 1.00 (ISBN 0-88473-194-4). Fiesta Pub.
Psilocybe Mushrooms & Their Allies. Paul Stamets. Ed. by Bob Harris. LC 77-26546. (Illus.). 1982. pap. 12.95 (ISBN 0-930180-03-8). Homestead Bk.
Psion. Joan D. Vinge. LC 82-70323. 256p. (gr. 7 up). 1982. pap. 12.95 (ISBN 0-385-28780-1). Delacorte.
Psion. Joan D. Vinge. 352p. (gr. k-12). 1985. pap. 2.95 (ISBN 0-440-97192-6, LFL). Dell.
Psionic Medicine: The Study & Treatment of the Causative Factors in Illness. J. H. Reyner et al. 160p. 1982. pap. 8.95 (ISBN 0-7100-9088-9). Routledge Chapman & Hall.
Psionics 101. Charles Cosimano. (Psi Tech Ser.). 250p. (Orig.). 1987. pap. 7.95 (ISBN 0-87542-099-0). Llewellyn Pubns.
Psiquis la Hoz. St John Troya. 115p. (Orig.). 1986. pap. 7.95 (ISBN 0-89729-384-3). Ediciones.
Psittacosaurus. F. Swann. (Dinosaur Library). (Illus.). 24p. (gr. 3 up). Date not set. PLB 13.27 (ISBN 0-86592-518-6). Rourke Corp.
Pskov: A Guide. Y. Morozkina. 192p. 1984. 7.95 (ISBN 0-8285-2842-X, Pub. by Raduga Pubs USSR). Imported Pubns.
Pskovian Land. L. Maliakov. 188p. (Rus. & Eng.). 1982. 99.00x (ISBN 0-317-57307-1, Pub. by Collets UK). State Mutual Bk.
Psmith in the City. P. G. Wodehouse. 402p. 1981. Repr. lib. bdg. 14.95 (ISBN 0-89968-222-7). Lightyear.
Psmith: Journalist. P. G. Wodehouse. 187p. 1981. pap. 3.95 (ISBN 0-14-003214-2). Penguin.
Psocoptera of the Oriental Region: A Review. T. R. New. 1977. 30.00 (ISBN 0-318-18591-1). Oriental Insects.
Psoralen DNA Photobiology. Ed. by Francis P. Gasparro. 1988. 95.00 ea. Vol. I, 160 pgs (ISBN 0-8493-4379-8, 4379). Vol. II, 176 pgs (ISBN 0-8493-4380-1, 4380). CRC Pr.
Psoriasis. Roenigk & Maibach. (Dermatology Ser.). 720p. 1985. 115.00 (ISBN 0-8247-7295-4). Dekker.
Psoriasis: Proceedings. International Symposium on Psoriasis-Stanford University, 1971. Ed. by Eugene M. Farber & Alvin J. Cox. (Illus.). 1971. 35.00x (ISBN 0-8047-0801-0). Stanford U Pr.

Psychiatric Justice. Thomas S. Szasz. LC 77-18804. 281p. 1978. Repr. of 1965 ed. lib. bdg. 35.00 (ISBN 0-313-20196-X, SZPJ). Greenwood.

Psychiatric Malpractice: Liability of Mental Health Professionals. Jeffrey D. Robertson. LC 87-28059. 575p. 1988. 95.00 (ISBN 0-471-84098-X). Wiley.

Psychiatric Management for Medical Practitioners. D. S. Kornfeld & J. Finkel. 496p. 1982. 32.50 (ISBN 0-8089-1420-0, 792373). Grune.

Psychiatric Medicine. Ed. by Gene Usdin. LC 77-10139. 1977. 30.00 (ISBN 0-87630-151-0). Brunner-Mazel.

Psychiatric Medicine: A Handbook. James L. Mathis. Ed. by James F. Gardner. (Allied Health Professions Monograph). 212p. 1984. 22.50 (ISBN 0-87527-320-3). Green.

Psychiatric Medicine Update, 1984. T. C. Manschreck. 1984. 52.75 (ISBN 0-444-00804-7). Elsevier.

Psychiatric Mental Health Nursing. 4th ed. P. A. Clunn & D. B. Payne. (Nursing Outline Ser.: Vol. 7). 626p. 1985. pap. 24.00 (ISBN 0-87488-528-0). Med Exam.

Psychiatric Mental Health Nursing. Ellen H. Janosik & Janet L. Davies. 761p. 1986. text ed. 38.75 (ISBN 0-86720-352-8); write for info. instr's manual. Jones & Bartlett.

Psychiatric-Mental Health Nursing. Jack Rudman. (College Proficiency Examination Ser.: CPEP-34). (Cloth bdg. avail. on request). pap. 13.95 (ISBN 0-8373-5434-X). Natl Learning.

Psychiatric-Mental Health Nursing. Jack Rudman. (ACT Proficiency Examination Program: PEP-40). (Cloth bdg. avail. on request). pap. 13.95 (ISBN 0-8373-5540-0). Natl Learning.

Psychiatric-Mental Health Nursing: Adaptation & Growth. Barbara S. Johnson. LC 64-3349. (Illus.). 736p. 1986. text ed. 39.95 (ISBN 0-397-54393-X, Lippincott Nursing). Lippincott.

Psychiatric Mental Health Nursing: Contemporary Readings. 2nd ed. Barbara A. Backer et al. LC 84-29937. (Contemporary Readings Ser.). 300p. 1985. pap. text ed. 20.00 (ISBN 0-534-04644-4). Jones & Bartlett.

Psychiatric Models in Medicine: Guidebook for Research & Reference. Rollie P. Zwigg. LC 88-47602. 150p. 1988. 34.50 (ISBN 0-88164-644-X); pap. 26.50 (ISBN 0-88164-645-8). Abbe Pubs Assn.

Psychiatric Music Therapy: Origins & Development. Florence Tyson. (Illus.). 1982. 19.95 (ISBN 0-9606876-0-2); pap. 9.95 (ISBN 0-9606876-1-0). CARC.

Psychiatric Nurse. Jack Rudman. (Career Examination Ser.: C-986). (Cloth bdg. avail. on request). pap. 16.00 (ISBN 0-8373-0986-7). Natl Learning.

Psychiatric Nursing. Ed. by Annie T. Altschul. LC 84-12661. (Recent Advances in Nursing Ser.: Vol. 12). (Illus.). 220p. 1985. pap. text ed. 23.00 (ISBN 0-443-02985-7). Churchill.

Psychiatric Nursing. Fields. (Nursing Examination Review Ser.: Vol. 5). 1984. 14.50 (ISBN 0-87488-500-0). Med Exam.

Psychiatric Nursing. 2nd ed. Holly S. Wilson & Carol R. Kneisl. 1983. write for info. (ISBN 0-201-11702-9, 11702, Hlth-Sci); write for info. activity bk. (ISBN 0-201-11703-7, Hlth-Sci); write for info. instr's. manual (ISBN 0-201-11704-5). Addison-Wesley.

Psychiatric Nursing: A Basic Text. Patricia C. Pothier. 1980. pap. text ed. 14.00 (ISBN 0-316-71484-4). Little.

Psychiatric Nursing: A Manual of Clinical Practice. Rawlins & Heacock. 528p. 1987. pap. 24.95 (ISBN 0-8016-4096-2). Mosby.

Psychiatric Nursing As a Human Experience. 3rd ed. Lisa Robinson. (Illus.). 1983. text ed. 33.95 (ISBN 0-7216-7622-7). Saunders.

Psychiatric Nursing: Case Studies, Nursing Diagnosis & Care Plans. Luc R. Pelletier. LC 87-7108. 494p. 1987. pap. 19.95 (ISBN 0-87434-090-X). Springhouse Pub.

Psychiatric Nursing Handbook. Lloyd A. Wells. (Allied Health Professions Handbks.). 440p. 1988. 47.50 (ISBN 0-87527-295-9). Green.

Psychiatric Nursing in the Hospital & the Community. 4th ed. Ann W. Burgess. (Illus.). 900p. 1985. pap. text ed. 33.95 (ISBN 0-13-731951-7). P-H.

Psychiatric Nursing: International Subject Analysis with Reference Bibliography. Greta T. Lithmond. LC 85-48185. 150p. 1987. 34.50 (ISBN 0-88164-482-X); pap. 26.50 (ISBN 0-88164-483-8). ABBE Pubs Assn.

Psychiatric Nursing: PreTest Self-Assessment & Review. Nancy Rozendal & Patricia Fallon. LC 78-50596. 193p. 1978. pap. 13.95 (ISBN 0-07-051569-7). McGraw-Pretest.

Psychiatric Nursing Research. Ed. by Julia Brooking. LC 85-20402. 247p. 1986. pap. 14.95 (ISBN 0-471-90907-6, Pub. by Wiley Medical). Wiley.

Psychiatric Nursing Skills: A Patient-Centred Approach. Graham Dexter & Michael Wash. LC 85-13252. 320p. (Orig.). 1985. pap. 19.00 (ISBN 0-7099-3617-6, Pub. by Croom Helm Ltd). Routledge Chapman & Hall.

Psychiatric Nursing: Theory & Application. Lucille A. Joel & Doris L. Collins. (Illus.). 1978. text ed. 32.00 (ISBN 0-07-032537-5). McGraw.

Psychiatric Occupational Therapy in the Army. Ed. by Paul D. Ellsworth & Diane Gibson. LC 83-10859. (Occupational Therapy in Mental Health Ser.: Vol. 3, No. 2). 88p. 1983. text ed. 22.95 (ISBN 0-86656-234-6, B234). Haworth Pr.

Psychiatric Patient Rights & Patient Advocacy: Issues & Evidence. Ed. by Bernard L. Bloom & Shirley J. Asher. LC 81-13165. (Community Psychology Ser.: Vol. VII). 287p. 1982. 34.95 (ISBN 0-89885-056-8). Human Sci Pr.

Psychiatric Peer Review: Prelude & Promise. Ed. by John Hamilton. LC 85-13517. 240p. 1985. text ed. 22.50x (ISBN 0-88048-211-7, 48-211-7). Am Psychiatric.

Psychiatric Polarities: Methodology & Practice. Phillip R. Slavney & Paul R. McHugh. LC 86-21446. (Johns Hopkins Series in Contemporary Medicine & Public Health). 144p. 1987. text ed. 17.50x (ISBN 0-8018-3428-7). Johns Hopkins.

Psychiatric Presentations of Medical Illness: Somatopsychic Disorders. Ed. by Richard C. Hall. (Illus.). 428p. 1980. text ed. 47.50 (ISBN 0-89335-098-2). PMA Pub Corp.

Psychiatric Programming of People: Neo-Behavioral Orthomolecular Psychiatry. H. L. Newbold. 170p. 1972. 27.00 (ISBN 0-08-016791-8). Pergamon.

Psychiatric Record Manual for the Hospital. Dorothy S. Keller. LC 77-117468. (Contemporary Community Health Ser). Repr. of 1970 ed. 62.50 (ISBN 0-8357-9760-0, 2015568). Bks Demand UMI.

Psychiatric Records in Mental Health Care. Carole Siegel & Susan K. Fischer. LC 80-23099. (Illus.). 352p. (Orig.). 1981. pap. 35.00 (ISBN 0-87630-241-X). Brunner Mazel.

Psychiatric Rehabilitation of Chronic Mental Patients. Robert Paul Liberman. LC 87-1492. 312p. Date not set. pap. text ed. 22.00x (ISBN 0-88048-201-X, 48-201-X). Am Psychiatric.

Psychiatric Research in America: Two Studies, Nineteen Thirty-Six to Nineteen Forty-One, 2 vols. in one. Ed. by Gerald N. Grob. LC 78-22583. (Historical Issues in Mental Health Ser.). 1979. Repr. lib. bdg. 28.50x (ISBN 0-405-11935-6). Ayer Co Pubs.

Psychiatric Self-Help. Gordon R. Forrer. LC 72-85870. 1973. 5.00 (ISBN 0-87212-029-5). Libra.

Psychiatric Senior Attendant. Jack Rudman. (Career Examination Ser.: C-1435). (Cloth bdg. avail. on request). pap. 14.00 (ISBN 0-8373-1435-6). Natl Learning.

Psychiatric Sequelae of Child Abuse: Reconnaissance of Child Abuse & Neglect--Evaluation, Prospects, Recommendations. Jamia J. Jacobsen. (Illus.). 230p. 1986. 29.25 (ISBN 0-398-05233-6). C C Thomas.

Psychiatric Services & Architecture. A. Baker et al. (Public Health Papers Ser.: No. 1). (Illus.). 59p. (Eng. & Span.). 1959. pap. 1.20 (ISBN 92-4-130001-9). World Health.

Psychiatric Services for Underserved Rural Populations. Ed. by L. Ralph Jones & Richard R. Parlour. LC 85-7747. 320p. 1985. 45.00 (ISBN 0-87630-390-4). Brunner-Mazel.

Psychiatric Services in the Community: Developments & Innovations. Ed. by John Reed & Gillian Lomas. 256p. 1984. 28.50 (ISBN 0-7099-2264-7, Pub. by Croom Helm Ltd). Routledge Chapman & Hall.

Psychiatric Slavery: The Dilemmas of Involuntary Psychiatry As Exemplified by the Case of Kenneth Donaldson. Thomas S. Szasz. LC 76-27154. 1977. 17.95 (ISBN 0-02-931600-6). Free Pr.

Psychiatric Social Work Assistant. Jack Rudman. (Career Examination Ser.: C-2414). (Cloth bdg. avail. on request). pap. 12.00 (ISBN 0-8373-2414-9). Natl Learning.

Psychiatric Social Work Supervisor. Jack Rudman. (Career Examination Ser.: C-2357). (Cloth bdg. avail. on request). pap. 16.00 (ISBN 0-8373-2357-6). Natl Learning.

Psychiatric Social Worker. Jack Rudman. (Career Examination Ser.: C-987). (Cloth bdg. avail. on request). pap. 16.00 (ISBN 0-8373-0987-5). Natl Learning.

Psychiatric Social Worker Trainee. Jack Rudman. (Career Examination Ser.: C-988). (Cloth bdg. avail. on request). pap. 14.00 (ISBN 0-8373-0988-3). Natl Learning.

Psychiatric Society. Francoise Castel & Robert Castel. Tr. by Arthur Goldhammer from Fr. LC 81-15504. (European Perspectives Ser.). 368p. 1982. 34.00x (ISBN 0-231-05244-8). Columbia U Pr.

Psychiatric Staff Attendant. Jack Rudman. (Career Examination Ser.: C-1436). (Cloth bdg. avail. on request). pap. 12.00 (ISBN 0-8373-1436-4). Natl Learning.

Psychiatric Status Rating Scales in Medicine & Psychology: Guidebook for Reference & Research. Jacob L. Liehaus. LC 83-46108. 150p. 1985. 34.50 (ISBN 0-88164-150-2); pap. 26.50 (ISBN 0-88164-151-0). ABBE Pubs Assn.

Psychiatric Study of Jesus. Albert Schweitzer. 14.75 (ISBN 0-8446-2894-8). Peter Smith.

Psychiatric Study of Myths & Fairy Tales: Their Origins, Meaning & Usefulness. 2nd ed. Julius E. Heuscher. (Illus.). 440p. 1974. 23.75x (ISBN 0-398-02851-6). C C Thomas.

Psychiatric Syndromes & Drug Treatment. Nathan Kline & Jules Angst. LC 79-5193. 320p. 1979. 30.00x (ISBN 0-87668-379-0). Aronson.

Psychiatric Technician's Handbook. Edwin Robbins. (Allied Health Professions Monograph Ser.). 1988. 16.00 (ISBN 0-87527-285-1). Green.

Psychiatric Therapy Aide. Jack Rudman. (Career Examination Ser.: C-2124). (Cloth bdg. avail. on request). 1988. pap. 12.00 (ISBN 0-8373-2124-7). Natl Learning.

Psychiatric Treatment of Adolescents. Ed. by Aaron H. Esman. LC 83-208. xiii, 543p. 1983. text ed. 50.00x (ISBN 0-8236-5595-4). Intl Univs Pr.

Psychiatric Treatment of Alzheimer's Disease. GAP Committee on Aging Staff. (GAP Report Ser.: No. 125). 172p. 1988. 18.95 (ISBN 0-87630-519-2). Brunner-Mazel.

Psychiatric Treatment of the Child. Ed. by John F. McDermott & Saul I. Harrison. LC 76-45569. 839p. 1977. 40.00x (ISBN 0-87668-289-1). Aronson.

Psychiatric Unit in a General Hospital: Its Current & Future Role. Ed. by M. Ralph Kaufman. LC 65-24003. 482p. 1965. text ed. 50.00x (ISBN 0-8236-5600-4). Intl Univs Pr.

Psychiatrie: Ein Lehrbuch Fur Studirende und Aerzte. 5th ed. Emil Kraepelin. LC 75-16713. (Classics in Psychiatry Ser.). (Ger.). 1976. Repr. of 1896 ed. 63.00x (ISBN 0-405-07442-5). Ayer Co Pubs.

Psychiatrie und Psychotherapie. 9th ed. H. Feldmann. (Illus.). viii, 420p. 1984. pap. 19.50 (ISBN 3-8055-3754-9). S Karger.

Psychiatrist. Jack Rudman. (Career Examination Ser.: C-626). (Cloth bdg. avail. on request). pap. 23.95 (ISBN 0-8373-0626-4). Natl Learning.

Psychiatrist & Public Issues, Vol. 7. GAP Committee on International Relations. LC 62-2872. (Report No. 74). 1969. pap. 5.00 (ISBN 0-87318-103-4, Pub. by GAP). Brunner-Mazel.

Psychiatrist & the Dying Patient. Kurt R. Eissler. 1970. pap. text ed. 19.95 (ISBN 0-8236-8265-X, 25720). Intl Univs Pr.

Psychiatrist of America: The Life of Harry Stack Sullivan. Helen S. Perry. LC 81-7066. (Illus.). 458p. 1982. 25.00x (ISBN 0-674-72076-8, Belknap Pr). Harvard U Pr.

Psychiatrist of America: The Life of Harry Stack Sullivan. Helen S. Perry. 496p. 1987. pap. text ed. 12.50x (ISBN 0-674-72077-6, Belknap Pr). Harvard U Pr.

Psychiatrist Recollects: Stories from the Lives of Psychiatric Patients. Malcolm B. Bowers, Jr. 160p. 1989. 19.95 (ISBN 0-89885-433-4). Human Sci Pr.

Psychiatrist Works with Blindness. Louis S. Cholden. 119p. 1958. pap. 7.00 (ISBN 0-89128-032-4, PPP032). Am Foun Blind.

Psychiatrists & Community Mental Health Centers. Jerome V. Vaccaro. 68p. (Orig.). 1987. pap. 9.95x (ISBN 0-89885-381-8). Human Sci Pr.

Psychiatrists As Teachers in Schools of Social Work, Vol. 4. GAP Committee on Psychiatry & Community. (Report No. 53). 1962. pap. 5.00 (ISBN 0-87318-071-2, Pub. by GAP). Brunner-Mazel.

Psychiatrist's Casebook (The DSM Case Book) Robert L. Spitzer & Andrew E. Skodol. 384p. 1986. pap. 12.50 (ISBN 0-446-38371-6). Warner Bks.

Psychiatrist's Guide to Diseases of the Nervous System. Richard Lechtenberg. LC 82-2790. 478p. 1982. 39.95 (ISBN 0-471-08727-0, Pub. by Wiley Medical). Wiley.

Psychiatrists on Psychiatry. Ed. by Michael Shepherd. LC 81-21750. (Illus.). 200p. 1983. 34.50 (ISBN 0-521-24480-3); pap. 15.95 (ISBN 0-521-28863-0). Cambridge U Pr.

Psychiatry, 6 vols. Ed. by Jesse O. Cavenar, Jr. et al. 1986. 300.00 set (ISBN 0-397-50685-6); Vol. I: The Personality Disorders & Neuroses. 60.00 (ISBN 0-397-50810-7); Vol. II: Psychoses, Affective Disorders & Neuroses. 50.00 (ISBN 0-397-50811-5); Vol. III: Consultation-Liaison Psychiatry & Behavioral Medicine. 60.00 (ISBN 0-397-50813-1); Vol. IV: Psychobiological Foundations of Clinical Psychiatry. 50.00 (ISBN 0-397-50815-8); Vol. V: Social, Epidemiologic, & Legal Psychiatry. 60.00 (ISBN 0-317-52307-4); Vol. VI: Child Psychiatry. 60.00 (ISBN 0-397-50812-3). Basic.

Psychiatry. Flaherty. (Clinical Manual Ser.). 1988. pap. text ed. 19.95 spiral wire (ISBN 0-8385-1277-1). Appleton & Lange.

Psychiatry. (National Medical Ser. for Independent Study). 240p. 1985. pap. 21.00 (ISBN 0-471-82345-7, Pub. by Wiley Medical). Wiley.

Psychiatry. 5th ed. W. H. Trethowan & A. C. Sims. 406p. 1983. pap. 17.95 (ISBN 0-7216-0939-2, Bailliere-Tindall). Saunders.

Psychiatry. R. M. Turner & P. Williams. (Management of Common Diseases in Family Practice Ser.). 1986. lib. bdg. 33.25 (ISBN 0-85200-794-9, Pub. by MTP Pr England). Kluwer Academic.

Psychiatry: A Clinical Treatise on Disease of the Fore-Brain Based Upon a Study of Its Structure, Functions and Nutrition. Theodor Meynert. Tr. by H. Sachs. LC 78-72811. Repr. of 1885 ed. 27.50 (ISBN 0-404-60881-7). AMS Pr.

Psychiatry: A Problem-Oriented Approach. H. Steven Moffic et al. (Problem-Oriented Ser.: Vol. 4). 1986. pap. text ed. 33.25 (ISBN 0-444-01007-6). Med Exam.

Psychiatry & Criminal Law. Sol Rubin. LC 64-19354. 240p. 1965. 12.50 (ISBN 0-379-00225-6). Oceana.

Psychiatry & Ethics: Insanity, Rational Autonomy, & Mental Health Care. Ed. by Rem B. Edwards. LC 82-62135. 609p. 1982. 30.95 (ISBN 0-87975-178-9); pap. 19.95 (ISBN 0-87975-179-7). Prometheus Bks.

Psychiatry & General Practice. Ed. by A. W. Clare & M. Lader. 1982. 42.00 (ISBN 0-12-174720-4). Acad Pr.

Psychiatry & Health. Jules H. Masserman. 253p. 1986. 29.95 (ISBN 0-89885-256-0, Dist. by Independent Publishers Group). Human Sci Pr.

Psychiatry & Its History: Methodological Problems in Research. George Mora & Jeanne L. Brand. 304p. 1970. 30.75 (ISBN 0-398-01342-X). C C Thomas.

Psychiatry & Law. Ralph Slovenko. 1973. 38.50 (ISBN 0-316-79868-1). Little.

Psychiatry & Medical Education: Two Studies, 2 vols. in one. Ed. by Gerald N. Grob. LC 78-22582. (Historical Issues in Mental Health Ser.). (Illus.). 1979. Repr. lib. bdg. 48.00x (ISBN 0-405-11934-8). Ayer Co Pubs.

Psychiatry & Medical Practice in a General Hospital. Ed. by Norman E. Zinberg. LC 64-24868. 364p. 1964. text ed. 37.50x (ISBN 0-8236-5540-7). Intl Univs Pr.

Psychiatry & Medicine: Medical Subject Analysis & Research Guidebook with Bibliography. Marissa G. Thatcher. LC 84-45873. 150p. 1987. 34.50 (ISBN 0-88164-274-6); pap. 26.50 (ISBN 0-88164-275-4). ABBE Pubs Assn.

Psychiatry & Modern Life. Arvindrai N. Desai. 304p. 1988. text ed. 40.00x (Pub. by Sterling Pubs India). Apt Bks.

Psychiatry & Mysticism. Stanley R. Dean. LC 75-8771. (Illus.). 446p. 1975. 30.95x (ISBN 0-88229-189-0). Nelson-Hall.

Psychiatry & Pastoral Care. Edgar Draper. LC 65-23861. (Successful Pastoral Counseling Series). pap. 34.50 (2026894). Bks Demand UMI.

Psychiatry & Psychology in the U. S. S. R. Ed. by Samuel A. Corson & Elizabeth O. Corson. LC 76-47482. 310p. 1976. 59.50x (ISBN 0-306-30992-0, Plenum Pr). Plenum Pub.

Psychiatry & Psychology in the Visual Arts & Aesthetics: A Bibliography. Ed. by Norman Kiell. 264p. 1965. 27.50x (ISBN 0-299-03500-X). U of Wis Pr.

Psychiatry & Religion: Overlapping Concerns (Clinical Insights Monograph) Lillian H. Robinson. LC 85-28728. 192p. 1986. pap. text ed. 12.00x (ISBN 0-88048-099-8, 48-099-8). Am Psychiatric.

Psychiatry & the Aged: An Introductory Approach, Vol. 5. GAP Committee on Aging. LC 62-2872. (Report No. 59A). 1965. pap. 5.00 (ISBN 0-87318-111-5, Pub. by GAP). Brunner-Mazel.

Psychiatry & the Biology of the Human Brain: A Symposium Dedicated to Seymour S. Kety. Ed. by S. Mattysse. 310p. 1981. 79.75 (ISBN 0-444-00649-4, Biomedical Pr). Elsevier.

Psychiatry & the Cinema. Krin Gabbard & Glen O. Gabbard. LC 86-25000. (Illus.). xx, 304p. 1987. 24.95 (ISBN 0-226-27790-9). U of Chicago Pr.

Psychiatry & the Criminal: A Guide to Psychiatric Examinations for the Criminal Courts. 3rd ed. John M. Macdonald. 524p. 1976. 64.50 (ISBN 0-398-03480-X). C C Thomas.

Psychiatry & the Criminal Process. Ed. by Ronald D. Mckay & Kenneth V. Russell. (Leicester Polytechnic Law School Monographs). 48p. 1986. pap. 5.00 (ISBN 0-948097-28-1, Pub. by Leicester Poly Law Schl). Pickering Pubns.

Psychiatry & the Cults: An Annotated Bibliography. John A. Saliba. LC 87-19668. (Garland Reference Library: No. 349). 601p. 1987. 60.00 (ISBN 0-8240-8586-8). Garland Pub.

Psychiatry & the Humanities, Vol. 1. Joseph H. Smith. LC 75-32283. 256p. 1976. 40.00x (ISBN 0-300-01982-3). Yale U Pr.

Psychiatry & the Humanities, Vol. 6. Joseph H. Smith & Walter Kerrigan. LC 83-7022. 320p. 1987. pap. 11.95x (ISBN 0-300-03935-2). Yale U Pr.

Psychiatry & the Mental Health Professionals: New Roles for Changing Times. Group for the Advancement of Psychiatry Staff. LC 87-14588. (GAP Report Ser.: No. 122). 192p. 1987. 20.00 (ISBN 0-87630-474-9); pap. 13.95 (ISBN 0-87630-473-0). Brunner-Mazel.

Psychiatry Around the Globe. Leff. (Experimental Clinical Psychiatry Ser.: No. 5). 224p. 1981. 45.00 (ISBN 0-8247-1532-2). Dekker.

Psychiatry As Medicine: Contemporary Psychotherapies. Yehuda Fried & Joseph Agassi. 1983. lib. bdg. 34.95 (ISBN 90-247-2837-1, Pub. by Martinus Nijhoff Netherlands). Kluwer Academic.

Psychiatry Between the Wars, Nineteen Eighteen to Nineteen Forty-Five: A Recollection. Walter Bromberg. LC 82-6153. (Contributions in Medical History Ser.: No. 10). xxix, 184p. 1982. 36.95 (ISBN 0-313-23460-4, BWN/). Greenwood.

Psychic Thread: Paranormal & Transpersonal Aspects of Psychotherapy. Elizabeth Mintz & R. Schmeidler. 232p. 1983. 29.95 (ISBN 0-89885-139-4). Human Sci Pr.

Psychic Vibrations of Crystals, Gems & Stones. Maria D'Andrea. (Illus.). 116p. 1988. pap. 5.00 (ISBN 0-938294-57-1). Global Comm.

Psychic Voyages. Time-Life Books Editors. (Illus.). 144p. 1988. 12.95 (ISBN 0-8094-6316-4); lib. bdg. write for info. (ISBN 0-8094-6317-2). Time-Life.

Psychic Warfare: Fact or Fiction? John White. (Illus.). 224p. (Orig.). 1988. pap. 9.99 (ISBN 0-85030-644-2, Pub. by Aquarian Pr England). Sterling.

Psychic Wholeness & Healing: Using All the Powers of the Human Psyche. Conrad W. Baars & Anna A. Terruwe. LC 81-4964. 245p. (Orig.). 1981. pap. 8.95 (ISBN 0-8189-0410-0). Alba.

Psychic Women. Antionette May. 1984. pap. 6.95 (ISBN 0-915689-03-0). Hickman Systems.

Psychical Phenomena & the Physical World. Charles McCreery. 20.00x (ISBN 0-900076-04-6, Pub. by Inst Psych Res). State Mutual bk.

Psychical Research & Phenomena of Spiritual Intercourse. Gerald P. Hyslop. (Illus.). 399p. 1988. 117.75 (ISBN 0-89920-182-2). Am Inst Psych.

Psychical Research & Spiritualism. Sanford E. Coates. (Illus.). 1980. deluxe ed. 127.75 (ISBN 0-89920-006-0). Am Classical Coll Pr.

Psychical Research: The Science of the Super-Normal. Hans Driesch. Tr. by Theodore Besterman. LC 75-7376. (Perspectives in Psychical Research Ser.). 1975. Repr. of 1933 ed. 20.00x (ISBN 0-405-07026-8). Ayer Co Pubs.

Psychiczne Zrodla Komunizmu. rev. ed. Marian Wasilewski. Ed. & illus. by Malgorzata Barton. (Illus.). 80p. (Pol.). 1983. pap. 4.50 (ISBN 0-9612122-0-9). Polish Am Ethnic.

Psyching. Judd Biasiotto. 80p. (Orig.). 1988. pap. 6.00 (ISBN 0-933079-08-7). World Class Enterprises.

Psyching for Sport: Mental Training for Athletes & Coaches Training Manual to Psyching for Sport, 2 vols. Terry Orlick. 1986. Set. pap. 18.95x (ISBN 0-88011-275-1, PORL0275). Leisure Pr.

Psyching for Sport: Mental Training for Athletes. Terry Orlick. LC 85-23293. 215p. (Orig.). 1986. pap. 11.95 (ISBN 0-88011-273-5, PORL 0273). Leisure Pr.

Psyching It Out: Over 250 Questions & Answers about Your Body, Mind, & Sports. Eric Margenau et al. 1988. 18.95 (ISBN 0-89876-161-1). Gardner Pr.

Psyching Out Vegas. Marvin Karlins. (Illus.). 280p. 1983. 12.00 (ISBN 0-914314-03-3). Lyle Stuart.

Psyching the Ads: The Case Book of Advertising; the Methods & Results of 180 Advertisements. Carroll Rheinstrom. LC 75-39271. (Getting & Spending: the Consumer's Dilemma). (Illus.). 1976. Repr. of 1929 ed. 29.00x (ISBN 0-405-08043-3). Ayer Co Pubs.

Psychischen Storungen Des Kindesalters. Hermann Emminghaus. LC 75-16701. (Classics in Psychiatry Ser.). (Illus., Ger.). 1976. Repr. of 1887 ed. 23.50x (ISBN 0-405-07428-X). Ayer Co Pubs.

Psychism & the Unconscious Mind. Theosophical Research Centre, London. (Orig.). 1968. pap. 2.75 (ISBN 0-8356-0412-8, Quest). Theos Pub Hse.

Psychlone. Greg Bear. 320p. 1988. pap. 3.95 (ISBN 0-8125-3165-5, Dist. by St Martin's Pr & Warner Pub Servs). Tor Bks.

Psycho. Ed. by Richard Anobile. (Film Classics Library). (Illus.). 256p. 1974. pap. 5.45 (ISBN 0-380-00085-7, 21063, Flare). Avon.

Psycho. Robert Bloch. Repr. lib. bdg. 18.95x (ISBN 0-88411-077-X, Pub. by Aeonian Pr). Amereon Ltd.

Psycho-Analysis As History: Negation & Freedom in Freud. Michael S. Roth. LC 86-29192. 208p. 1987. 22.50x (ISBN 0-8014-1957-3). Cornell U Pr.

Psycho-Analysis of Children, Vol. 2. Melanie Klein. (Writings of Melanie Klein Ser.). 352p. 1984. 25.00x (ISBN 0-02-918430-4). Free Pr.

Psycho-Analytical Treatment of Children. Anna Freud. LC 68-18382. 90p. 1965. text ed. 20.00x (ISBN 0-8236-5080-4). Intl Univs Pr.

Psycho & Neuro-Pharmacology. Ed. by M. J. Parnham & J. Bruinvels. (Discoveries in Pharmacology Ser.: Vol. 1). 507p. 1984. 202.75 (ISBN 0-444-80493-5, Biomedical Pr). Elsevier.

Psycho-Birds. Robert J. Lifton. LC 78-13463. (Illus.). 1978. pap. 3.95 (ISBN 0-914378-41-4). Countryman.

Psycho-Cosmic Symbolism of the Buddhist Stupa. Lama A. Govinda. LC 76-797. (Illus.). 144p. 1976. pap. 9.95 (ISBN 0-913546-36-4). Dharma Pub.

Psycho-Cosmic Symbolism of the Buddhist Stupa. Lama A. Govinda. 102p. 1976. 20.00x (ISBN 0-317-39141-0, Pub. by Luzac & Co Ltd). State Mutual Bk.

Psycho-Cybernetics. Maxwell Maltz. 1983. pap. 3.95 (ISBN 0-671-47213-5). PB.

Psycho-Cybernetics. Maxwell Maltz. pap. 5.00 (ISBN 0-87980-127-1). Wilshire.

Psycho-Cybernetics. Maxwell Maltz. Date not set. pap. 4.95 (ISBN 0-671-63258-2). PB.

Psycho-Cybernetics: A New Way to Get More Living out of life. Maltz Maxwell. pap. 7.95 (ISBN 0-671-22150-7, Fireside). S&S.

Psycho-Cybernetics & Self-Fulfillment. Maxwell Maltz. 256p. 1973. pap. 4.50 (ISBN 0-553-26009-X). Bantam.

Psycho-Cybernetics for Creative Living. Maxwell Maltz. Date not set. pap. 4.50 (ISBN 0-671-61737-0). PB.

Psycho-Dynamic Synthesis. Myron S. Allen. LC 66-17160. 248p. 1979. Repr. of 1966 ed. soft cover 11.95 (ISBN 0-918936-07-1). Astara.

Psycho-Ecological Dimensions of Poverty. Ed. by M. G. Husain. 1983. 12.00x (ISBN 0-8364-1072-6, Pub. by Manohar). South Asia Bks.

Psycho-Educational Battery. Lillie Pope. 1976. incl. specimen set 15.95 (ISBN 0-87594-155-9). Book-Lab.

Psycho-Generative Spanish: A Psycho-Linguistics Approach to Learning. Samuel Nodarse. 592p. 1986. pap. text ed. 33.95 (ISBN 0-8403-4043-5). Kendall-Hunt.

Psycho-History: Readings in the Methods of Psychology, Psychoanalysis & History. Geoffrey Cocks & Travis L. Crosby. LC 86-23411. 356p. 1987. text ed. 35.00 (ISBN 0-300-03681-7); pap. 14.95x (ISBN 0-300-03682-5). Yale U Pr.

Psycho II. Robert Bloch. 224p. 1982. 16.00 (ISBN 0-918372-09-7); signed & slipcased 36.00x (ISBN 0-918372-08-9). Whispers.

Psycho II. Robert Bloch. 320p. (Orig.). 1982. pap. 3.50 (ISBN 0-446-90804-5). Warner Bks.

Psycho-Logic. J. Smedslund. 130p. 1988. 35.00 (ISBN 0-387-18518-6). Springer-Verlag.

Psycho-Mathematical Basic Skills Learning Workbooklet. Andre Joseph. 67p. (gr. 6-7). 1980. 8.00 (ISBN 0-936264-00-4); write for info. (ISBN 0-936264-01-2). Andre's & Co.

Psycho-Mathematical Mini-Math Packs. 81p. 1982. pap. text ed. 10.00 (ISBN 0-936264-07-1); 8.00 (ISBN 0-317-12242-8). Andre's & Co.

Psycho-Mathematical PreAlgebra Learning Workbooklet. Andre Joseph. 85p. 1981. tchr's. ed. 8.00 (ISBN 0-936264-03-9); wkbk. 9.00 (ISBN 0-936264-02-0). Andre's & Co.

Psycho-Mathematics: The Key to the Universe, 2 vols. William B. Conner. Incl. Vol. 1-Creativity through Calculator Harmonic Braiding. LC 82-5100. 140p (ISBN 0-9603536-5-8); Vol. 2-Creativity through Keyboard Harmonic Braiding. LC 82-74235. Orig. Title: Math's & Music's Metasonics. 213p. Repr. of 1983 ed. pap. 36.50 (ISBN 0-9603536-6-6). Orig. Title: Math's & Music's Metasonics. (Orig.). 1983. Set. pap. text ed. 36.50 GBC punched (ISBN 0-9603536-7-4). Tesla Bk Co.

Psycho-Motor Norms for Practical Diagnosis see Voluntary Isolation of Control in a Natural Muscle Group.

Psycho-Neurobiology. Ed. by M. Monnier & M. Meulders. (Functions of the Nervous System Ser.: Vol. 4). 716p. 1983. 278.00 (ISBN 0-444-80469-2, I-365-83, Biomedical Pr). Elsevier.

Psycho-Nutrition. Carlton Fredericks. (Health, Nutrition & Well Being Bks). 224p. 1983. pap. 5.95 (ISBN 0-399-50789-2, G&D). Putnam Pub Group.

Psycho-Nutrition. Carlton Fredericks. 1988. pap. 3.95 (ISBN 0-425-11055-9). Berkley Pub.

Psycho-Organic Syndrome: Its Assessment & Treatment. Abraham Elizur. 54p. 1969. pap. 22.00x (ISBN 0-87424-104-9). Western Psych.

Psycho-Physiological Disorders: General & Medical Research Subject Directory with Bibliography. American Health Research Institute Staff. Ed. by John C. Bartone. LC 82-72012. 236p. 1982. 39.95 (ISBN 0-941864-40-5); pap. 29.95 (ISBN 0-941864-41-3). ABBE Pubs Assn.

Psycho-Physiological Disorders II: Medical Subject Analysis & Research Index with Bibliography. Ellen E. Sandison. LC 84-45993. 150p. 1985. 34.50 (ISBN 0-88164-308-4); pap. 26.50 (ISBN 0-88164-309-2). ABBE Pubs Assn.

Psycho-Physiological Effect of the Elements of Speech in Relation to Poetry see On the Function of the Cerebrum.

Psycho-Physiology of Fatigue: Subject Analysis & Reference Guidebook with Bibliography. Martha G. Gorman. LC 84-45990. 150p. 1987. 34.50 (ISBN 0-88164-302-5); pap. 26.50 (ISBN 0-88164-303-3). ABBE Pubs Assn.

Psycho-Pictography: The New Way to Use the Miracle Power of Your Mind. Vernon Howard. 1968. pap. 5.95 (ISBN 0-13-732222-4, Reward). P-H.

Psycho-Political Muse: American Poetry Since the Fifties. Paul Breslin. LC 87-10863. 296p. 1987. 27.50x (ISBN 0-226-07410-2). U of Chicago Pr.

Psycho-Sales-Analysis. Jack Huttig. LC 74-173598. (Illus.). 232p. 1971. 19.95 (ISBN 0-911012-09-5). Nelson-Hall.

Psycho-Sales Analysis: The New Art of Self-Taught Sales Success. Jack Huttig. (Quality Paperback Ser.: No. 263). 232p. 1978. pap. 5.95 (ISBN 0-8226-0263-6). Littlefield.

Psycho-Sexual Problems: Proceedings of the Bradford Congress 1974. Ed. by Hugo Milne & Shirley J. Hardy. 210p. 1976. 17.95x (ISBN 0-8464-1124-5): Beekman Pubs.

Psycho-Sinology: The Universe of Dreams in Chinese Culture. Carolyn Brown. 94p. (Orig.). 1988. lib. bdg. 22.00 (ISBN 0-8191-6728-2, Pub. by Woodrow Wilson Intl Ctr); pap. text ed. 11.50 (ISBN 0-8191-6729-0). U Pr of Amer.

Psycho-Social Aspects of a Severe Burn: A Review of the Literature. Ed. by M. L. Bowden & I. Feller. C. A. Jones. LC 79-89259. 1979. 16.00 (ISBN 0-917478-34-7). Natl Inst Burn.

Psycho-Social Aspects of Stress Following Abortion. Anne Speckhard. LC 86-63589. 144p. (Orig.). 1987. pap. 7.95 (ISBN 1-55612-059-1). Sheed & Ward MO.

Psycho-Social Matrix of Psychiatry. M. Shepherd. LC 83-456. 1983. 27.00 (ISBN 0-422-78350-1, NO. 3808, Pub. by Tavistock). Routledge Chapman & Hall.

Psycho Squad, Bk. 1: Execution Night. Rick Dade. 1988. pap. 2.95 (ISBN 0-425-11146-6). Berkley Pub.

Psycho-Yoga: The Practice of Mind Control. B. Edwin. 1969. pap. 2.95 (ISBN 0-8065-0071-9, Pub. by Citadel Pr). Lyle Stuart.

Psychoacoustics. J. Donald Harris. pap. text ed. 5.95x (ISBN 0-8290-0327-4). Irvington.

Psychoactive Drugs & Sex. Ernest L. Abel. 242p. 1985. 32.50x (ISBN 0-306-41869-X, Plenum Pr). Plenum Pub.

Psychoactive Drugs: Including Combinations. Ed. by F. Wider. (Data Processing in Medicine Ser.: Vol. 3). 260p. 1974. 80.00 (ISBN 3-8055-1740-8). S Karger.

Psychoalchemy. Oscar Ichazo. (Illus.). 54p. 1978. pap. 20.00 (ISBN 0-916554-08-2). Arica Inst Pr.

Psychoanalysis. Ed. by Bernard Fine. Shelley Orgel. LC 79-51910. (Downstate Ser.: Vol. I). 1977. 30.00x (ISBN 0-87668-267-0). Aronson.

Psychoanalysis. Lawrence J. Friedman. LC 68-8037. 192p. 1977. pap. 4.95 (ISBN 0-8397-6901-6). Eriksson.

Psychoanalysis - A Theory in Crisis. Marshall Edelson. (Illus.). 416p. 1988. 39.95x (ISBN 0-226-18437-4). U of Chicago Pr.

Psychoanalysis: A General Psychology. Ed. by Rudolph M. Loewenstein et al. LC 66-26681. 684p. 1966. text ed. 60.00x (ISBN 0-8236-5220-3). Intl Univs Pr.

Psychoanalysis & American Medicine, 1894-1918: Medicine, Science, & Culture. John C. Burnham. LC 67-31293. (Psychological Issues Monograph: No. 20, Vol. 5, No. 4). 249p. (Orig.). 1967. text ed. 25.00x (ISBN 0-8236-5100-2). Intl Univs Pr.

Psychoanalysis & Anthropology. Geza Roheim. 496p. 1968. text ed. 47.50x (ISBN 0-8236-5120-7); pap. text ed. 19.95 (ISBN 0-8236-8234-X, 25120). Intl Univs Pr.

Psychoanalysis & Behavior Therapy: Toward an Integration. Paul L. Wachtel. LC 76-9348. 1977. text ed. 21.95x (ISBN 0-465-06562-7). Basic.

Psychoanalysis & Beyond. Charles Rycroft. 316p. 1986. pap. 12.50 (ISBN 0-226-73289-4). U of Chicago Pr.

Psychoanalysis & Civilization. Paul Rosenfels. LC 62-18668. 1963. 4.95 (ISBN 0-87212-016-3). Libra.

Psychoanalysis & Cognitive Psychology: A Formalization of Freud's Theory. Cornelius Wegman. 1985. 53.00 (ISBN 0-12-741380-4). Acad Pr.

Psychoanalysis & Contemporary Science: An Annual of Integrative & Interdisciplinary Studies, Vol. 1. Robert R. Holt & Emanuel Peterfruend. LC 72-84741. 1972. 14.95 (ISBN 0-02-896130-7). Macmillan.

Psychoanalysis & Contemporary Science, Vol. 2. Ed. by Benjamin B. Rubinstein. LC 72-84741. 1973. 14.95 (ISBN 0-02-896140-4). Macmillan.

Psychoanalysis & Contemporary Thought. facsimile ed. Ed. by John D. Sutherland. LC 75-134139. (Essay Index Reprint Ser). Repr. of 1958 ed. 15.00 (ISBN 0-8369-2373-1). Ayer Co Pubs.

Psychoanalysis & Culture: Essays in Honor of Geza Roheim. Ed. by George B. Wilbur & Warner Muensterberger. (Illus.). 462p. 1965. text ed. 50.00x (ISBN 0-8236-5140-1). Intl Univs Pr.

Psychoanalysis & Current Biological Thought. Ed. by Norman S. Greenfield & William C. Lewis. LC 64-7725. 1965. pap. 97.50 (ISBN 0-317-08160-8, 2021133). Bks Demand UMI.

Psychoanalysis & Daseinsanalysis. Medard Boss. (Psychoanalysis Examined & Re-Examined Ser.). 295p. 1982. Repr. of 1963 ed. lib. bdg. 25.00 (ISBN 0-306-79708-9). Da Capo.

Psychoanalysis & Discourse. Patrick Mahony. Ed. by David Tuckett. (New Library of Psychoanalysis Ser.). 250p. 1987. lib. bdg. 39.95x (ISBN 0-422-61030-5, Pub. by Tavistock England); pap. 12.95x (ISBN 0-422-61720-2, Pub. by Tavistock England). Routledge Chapman & Hall.

Psychoanalysis & Ethics. Lewis S. Feuer. LC 73-1433. 134p. 1973. Repr. of 1955 ed. lib. bdg. 48.50x (ISBN 0-8371-6795-7, FEPE). Greenwood.

Psychoanalysis & Family Therapy. Helm Stierlin. LC 77-2275. 355p. 1987. Repr. of 1977 ed. 25.00x (ISBN 0-87668-257-3, 25734). Aronson.

Psychoanalysis & Female Sexuality. Ed. by Hendrik M. Ruitenbeek. 1966. pap. 9.95x (ISBN 0-8084-0254-4). New Coll U Pr.

Psychoanalysis & Feminism. Juliet Mitchell. LC 74-19067. 1975. pap. 5.95 (ISBN 0-394-71442-3, Vin). Random.

Psychoanalysis & Fiction: An Exploration of Literary & Psychoanalytic Borders. Daniel Gunn. 256p. 1988. 39.50 (ISBN 0-521-35068-9). Cambridge U Pr.

Psychoanalysis & Group Behavior: A Study of Freudian Group Psychology. Saul Scheidlinger. LC 77-141267. 1971. Repr. of 1952 ed. lib. bdg. 66.50x (ISBN 0-8371-5838-9, SCPS). Greenwood.

Psychoanalysis & Infant Research. Joseph Lichtenberg. 280p. 1983. text ed. 29.95 (ISBN 0-88163-002-0). Analytic Pr.

Psychoanalysis & Its Discontents. John E. Gedo. LC 84-4615. 209p. 1984. 25.00 (ISBN 0-89862-639-0). Guilford Pr.

Psychoanalysis & Judaism. Mortimer Ostow. 1982. 14.95x (ISBN 0-87068-713-1). Ktav.

Psychoanalysis & Language: Psychiatry & the Humanities, Vol. 3. Ed. by Joseph H. Smith. LC 78-9156. 1978. 40.00x (ISBN 0-300-02249-2). Yale U Pr.

Psychoanalysis & Literature: An Introduction. Robert N. Mollinger. LC 80-26256. 192p. 1981. 18.95x (ISBN 0-88229-363-X). Nelson-Hall.

Psychoanalysis & Male Sexuality. Ed. by Hendrik M. Ruitenbeek. 1966. 13.95x (ISBN 0-8084-0255-2); pap. 9.95x (ISBN 0-8084-0256-0). New Coll U Pr.

Psychoanalysis & Moral Values. Heinz Hartmann. LC 58-9230. (New York Psychoanalytic Institute Freud Anniversary Lecture Ser.). 121p. 1960. text ed. 22.50x (ISBN 0-8236-5240-8). Intl Univs Pr.

Psychoanalysis & Philosophy. Ed. by Charles Hanly & Morris Lazerowitz. LC 73-138247. 362p. 1971. text ed. 37.50x (ISBN 0-8236-5185-1). Intl Univs Pr.

Psychoanalysis & Politics: A Contribution to the Psychology of Politics & Morals. R. E. Money-Kyrle. LC 72-12143. 182p. 1973. Repr. of 1951 ed. lib. bdg. 48.50 (ISBN 0-8371-6714-0, MOPS). Greenwood.

Psychoanalysis & Psychosis. Ann S. Silver. (Illus.). 1988. lib. bdg. 60.00 (ISBN 0-8236-5183-5). Intl Univs Pr.

Psychoanalysis & Psychotherapy: Selected Papers. Frieda Fromm-Reichmann. Ed. by Dexter M. Bullard. LC 59-10746. 368p. 1974. pap. 12.95 (ISBN 0-226-26597-8, P580, Phoen). U of Chicago Pr.

Psychoanalysis & Psychotherapy: 36 Systems. Robert A. Harper. LC 73-18625. 190p. (Orig.). 1974. 20.00x (ISBN 0-87668-131-3). Aronson.

Psychoanalysis & Religion. Erich Fromm. (Terry Lectures Ser.). 1950. pap. 5.95 (ISBN 0-300-00089-8, Y12). Yale U Pr.

Psychoanalysis & Religion. W. W. Meissner. LC 83-51296. 320p. 1984. 30.00x (ISBN 0-300-03049-5). Yale U Pr.

Psychoanalysis & Religious Experience. W. W. Meissner. LC 83-51296. 272p. 1986. pap. 11.95x (ISBN 0-300-03751-1, Y-599). Yale U Pr.

Psychoanalysis & Religious Mysticism. David C. McMlelland. 1959. pap. 2.50x (ISBN 0-87574-104-5, 104). Pendle Hill.

Psychoanalysis & the Bible: A Study in Depth of Seven Leaders. Dorothy F. Zeligs. LC 73-85071. 1973. 19.95x (ISBN 0-8197-0360-5). Bloch.

Psychoanalysis & the Bible: A Study in Depth of Seven Leaders. Dorothy F. Zeligs. 372p. 1988. Repr. of 1974 ed. 39.95x (ISBN 0-89885-389-3). Human Sci Pr.

Psychoanalysis & the History of the Individual. Hans W. Loewald. LC 77-11992. (Freud Lectures at Yale Ser.). 1978. 19.00x (ISBN 0-300-02172-0). Yale U Pr.

Psychoanalysis & the Nuclear Threat: Clinical & Theoretical Studies. Ed. by Howard B. Levine et al. 304p. 1988. text ed. price not set (ISBN 0-88163-062-4). Analytic Pr.

Psychoanalysis & the Occult. Ed. by George Devereux. 432p. 1970. text ed. 42.50x (ISBN 0-8236-5180-0); pap. text ed. 17.95 (ISBN 0-8236-8240-4, 25180). Intl Univs Pr.

Psychoanalysis & the Question of the Text. Ed. by Geoffrey Hartman. LC 78-7656. 192p. 1985. pap. text ed. 7.95x (ISBN 0-8018-3160-1). Johns Hopkins.

Psychoanalysis & the Social Sciences. Ed. by W. Muensterberger & S. Axelrad. LC 47-12480. Vol. 4. pap. 73.80 (ISBN 0-317-10715-1, 2010452); Vol. 5. pap. 76.80 (ISBN 0-317-10716-X). Bks Demand UMI.

Psychoanalysis & Women: Contemporary Reappraisals. Judith L. Alpert. 336p. 1986. text ed. 36.00 (ISBN 0-88163-039-X). Analytic Pr.

Psychoanalysis Applied to the Law. C. G. Schoenfeld. LC 83-15342. (New Studies on Law & Society). 220p. 1984. 26.50x (ISBN 0-86733-055-4). Assoc Faculty Pr.

Psychoanalysis As Science: The Hixon Lectures on the Scientific Status of Psychoanalysis. Ed. by Eugene Pumpian-Mindlin. 1970. Repr. of 1952 ed. lib. bdg. 35.00x (ISBN 0-8371-3365-3, PUMP). Greenwood.

Psychoanalysis: Creativity & Literature, a French-American Inquiry. Ed. by Alan Roland. LC 77-26613. 368p. 1978. 34.00x (ISBN 0-231-04324-4). Columbia U Pr.

Psychoanalysis: Critical Explorations in Contemporary Theory & Practice. Ed. by Alan M. Jacobson & Dean X. Parmelee. LC 81-17991. 250p. 1982. 30.00 (ISBN 0-87630-269-X). Brunner-Mazel.

Psychoanalytic Theory & Social Work Practice. Herbet S. Strean. Ed. by Francis J. Turner. LC 78-65223. (Treatment Approaches in the Human Services Ser.). 1978. text ed. 24.95 (ISBN 0-02-932220-0). Free Pr.

Psychoanalytic Theory of Art: A Philosophy of Art on Developmental Principles. Richard Kuhns. LC 82-23499. 192p. 1983. 29.00x (ISBN 0-231-05620-6); pap. 14.50x (ISBN 0-231-05621-4). Columbia U Pr.

Psychoanalytic Theory of Male Homosexuality. Kenneth Lewes. 352p. 1988. 19.95 (ISBN 0-671-62391-5). S&S.

Psychoanalytic Theory of Neurosis. Otto Fenichel. 1945. 29.95 (ISBN 0-393-01019-8). Norton.

Psychoanalytic Theory, Therapy & the Self. Harry Guntrip. LC 79-135563. 1973. pap. 10.95x (ISBN 0-465-09511-9, TB-5012). Basic.

Psychoanalytic Therapy & Behavior Therapy: Is Integration Possible? Ed. by Hal Arkowitz & Stanley Messer. 370p. 1984. 39.50x (ISBN 0-306-41578-X, Plenum Pr). Plenum Pub.

Psychoanalytic Therapy: Principles & Application. Franz Alexander et al. LC 79-24893. xiv, 353p. 1980. 30.00x (ISBN 0-8032-1007-8); pap. 7.95x (ISBN 0-8032-5903-4, BB 732, Bison). U of Nebr Pr.

Psychoanalytic Treatment: An Intersubjective Approach. Robert Stolorow et al. (Psychoanalytic Bk.). 1987. text ed. 22.50 (ISBN 0-88163-061-6). Analytic Pr.

Psychoanalytic Treatment of Schizophrenic Borderline & Characterological Disorders. Peter Giovachinni & Bryce L. Boyer. LC 80-66352. 422p. 1980. 35.00x (ISBN 0-87668-408-8). Aronson.

Psychoanalytic Understanding of the Dream. Paul Sloane. LC 79-50290. 288p. 1983. 25.00x (ISBN 0-87668-362-6). Aronson.

Psychoanalytic Vision: A Controversial Reappraisal of the Freudian Revolution. Reuben Fine. LC 80-2154. 608p. 1981. 19.95 (ISBN 0-02-910270-7). Free Pr.

Psychoanalytic Years. Carl G. Jung. Tr. by R. F. Hull. (Bollingen Ser.: Vol. 20). 144p. 1974. pap. 7.95 (ISBN 0-691-01799-9). Princeton U Pr.

Psychoanalytical Approach to Juvenile Delinquency: Theory, Case Studies, Treatment. Kate Friedlander. 296p. 1960. text ed. 35.00x (ISBN 0-8236-4400-6). Intl Univs Pr.

Psychoanalytical Method & the Doctrine of Freud, 2 vols. facsimile ed. Roland Dalbiez. Tr. by T. F. Lindsay from Fr. (Select Bibliographies Reprint Ser). Repr. of 1941 ed. 47.50 (ISBN 0-8369-6715-1). Ayer Co Pubs.

Psychoanalytical Theory of Love in the Variety of Its Manifestations, 2 vols. Andrews S. Terriot. (Illus.). 1985. Set. 255.50 (ISBN 0-89920-091-5). Am Inst Psych.

Psychoanalytische Literaturwissenschaft und Literatursoziologie. Henning Krauss & Reinhold Wolff. 253p. (Ger.). 1982. 24.20 (ISBN 3-8204-6211-2). P Lang Pubs.

Psychoanalyzing Psychoanalysis: Freud & the Hidden Fault of the Father. Marie Balmary. Tr. by Ned Lukacher from Fr. LC 81-18568. 208p. 1982. text ed. 22.50x (ISBN 0-8018-2349-8). Johns Hopkins.

Psychoanalyzing the Twelve Zodiacal Types. Manly P. Hall. pap. 2.95 (ISBN 0-89314-813-X). Philos Res.

Psychoanthropology of American Culture. Howard F. Stein. 150p. 1985. 17.95x (ISBN 0-914434-25-X). Psychohistory Pr.

Psychobattery: A Chronicle of Psychotherapeutic Abuse. Therese Spitzer. LC 79-92083. 272p. 1980. 17.95 (ISBN 0-89603-014-8). Humana.

Psychobiological Approaches to Social Behavior. Ed. by P. Herbert Leiderman & David Shapiro. 1964. 19.50x (ISBN 0-8047-0202-0). Stanford U Pr.

Psychobiological Aspects of Allergic Disorders. Ed. by Stuart H. Young et al. LC 85-19390. 400p. 1985. 42.95 (ISBN 0-275-91301-5, C1301). Praeger.

Psychobiological Aspects of Cognitive Growth. R. Kohen-Raz. 1977. 19.95 (ISBN 0-12-418050-7). Acad Pr.

Psychobiology & Early Development. Ed. by H. Rauh & H. C. Steinhausen. 298p. 1987. 102.75 (ISBN 0-444-70256-3, North Holland). Elsevier.

Psychobiology & Human Disease. H. Weiner. 1977. 78.50 (ISBN 0-444-00212-X, Biomedical Pr). Elsevier.

Psychobiology & Psychopharmacology. Ed. by Frederic F. Flach. (Directions in Psychiatry Monograph: No. 2). 1988. 29.95 (ISBN 0-393-70045-3). Norton.

Psychobiology of Affective Development. Ed. by Nathan A. Fox & Richard J. Davidson. 424p. 1984. text ed. 39.95x (ISBN 0-89859-269-0). L Erlbaum Assocs.

Psychobiology of Affective Disorders. Ed. by J. Mendels. (Illus.). viii, 220p. 1981. pap. 26.00 (ISBN 3-8055-1400-X). S Karger.

Psychobiology of Aggression & Violence. Luigi Valzelli. 262p. 1981. text ed. 47.50 (ISBN 0-89004-403-1). Raven.

Psychobiology of Aging. D. G. Stein. 446p. 1980. 96.25 (ISBN 0-444-00391-6, Biomedical Pr). Elsevier.

Psychobiology of Anorexia Nervosa. Ed. by K. M. Pirke & D. Ploog. (Illus.). 200p. 1984. 45.00 (ISBN 0-387-13196-5). Springer-Verlag.

Psychobiology of Attachment. Ed. by Martin Reite & Tiffany Field. (Behavioral Biology Ser.). 1985. 45.00 (ISBN 0-12-586780-8). Acad Pr.

Psychobiology of Bulimia. James I. Hudson & Harrison Pope. LC 87-14431. (Progress in Psychiatry Ser.). 250p. 1988. pap. text ed. 15.95 (ISBN 0-88048-139-0). Am Psychiatric.

Psychobiology of Bulimia Nervosa. Ed. by K. M. Pirke et al. (Illus.). 120p. 1988. pap. 44.00 (ISBN 0-387-18670-0). Springer-Verlag.

Psychobiology of Cancer: Automatization & Boredom in Health & Disease. Augustin De la Pena. 256p. 1983. 27.95x. Bergin & Garvey.

Psychobiology of Cancer: Automatization & Boredom in Health & Disease. Augustin De la Pena. 240p. 1983. 35.00 (ISBN 0-275-90968-9, C0968). Praeger.

Psychobiology of Childhood. Ed. by Lawrence Greenhill & Baron Shopsin. 288p. 1984. text ed. 40.00 (ISBN 0-88331-189-5). Luce.

Psychobiology of Chronic Headache. Donald A. Bakal. 176p. 1982. text ed. 17.95 (ISBN 0-8261-3890-X). Springer Pub.

Psychobiology of Consciousness. Ed. by Richard J. Davidson & Julian M. Davidson. LC 79-316. 508p. 1980. 55.00x (ISBN 0-306-40138-X, Plenum Pr). Plenum Pub.

Psychobiology of Down Syndrome. Ed. by Lynn Nadel. (Issues in the Biology of Language & Cognition Ser.). 300p. 1988. text ed. 35.00x (ISBN 0-262-14043-8, Pub. by Bradford). MIT Pr.

Psychobiology of Emotions. Jack G. Thompson. LC 88-5937. (Emotions, Personality, & Psychotherapy Ser.). (Illus.). 418p. 1988. 45.00x (ISBN 0-306-42843-1, Plenum Pr). Plenum Pub.

Psychobiology of Language. Ed. by Michael Studdert-Kennedy & David Caplan. (MIT Press Series in Neuropsychology & Neurolinguistics). (Illus.). 144p. 1983. 25.00x (ISBN 0-262-19217-9). MIT Pr.

Psychobiology of Mind. William R. Uttal. LC 78-1443. 785p. 1978. 31.95x (ISBN 0-470-26316-4). Halsted Pr.

Psychobiology of Mind-Body Healing: New Concepts of Therapeutic Hypnosis. Ernest L. Rossi. (Professional Bks.). (Illus.). 1986. text ed. 25.95 (ISBN 0-393-70034-8). Norton.

Psychobiology of Mind-Body Healing: New Concepts of Therapeutic Hypnosis. Ernest L. Rossi. 1988. pap. 9.95 (ISBN 0-393-30554-6). Norton.

Psychobiology of Reproduction. Crews. (Neurobiology Ser.). 1985. write for info. (ISBN 0-471-83095-X). Wiley.

Psychobiology of Reproduction. David Greene. (Illus.). 368p. 1987. pap. text ed. 20.00 (ISBN 0-13-732090-6). P-H.

Psychobiology of Stress: A Study of Coping Men. Ed. by Holger Ursin et al. (Behavioral Biology Ser.). 1978. 24.95 (ISBN 0-12-709250-1). Acad Pr.

Psychobiology of the Human Newborn. Peter Stratton. LC 81-14756. (Developmental Psychology & Its Applications Ser.). 456p. 1982. 97.00 (ISBN 0-471-10093-5, Pub. by Wiley-Interscience). Wiley.

Psychobiology: The Neuron & Behavior. K. Blick Hoyenga & Kermit T. Hoyenga. LC 86-26837. 544p. 1987. 27.00 (ISBN 0-534-06978-9). Brooks-Cole.

Psychocriticism: An Annotated Bibliography. Compiled by Joseph P. Natoli & Frederik L. Rusch. LC 84-4689. (Bibliographies & Indexes in World Literature Ser.: No. 1). xxiii, 268p. 1984. lib. bdg. 36.95 (ISBN 0-313-23641-0, NPL/). Greenwood.

Psychocultural Change & the American Indian: An Ethnohistorical Analysis. Laurence French. LC 86-33567. (Reference Library of Social Science: Vol. 381). 1987. lib. bdg. 34.00 (ISBN 0-8240-9785-8). Garland Pub.

Psychocutaneous Diseases. Ed. by Caroline Koblenzer. 1987. write for info. (ISBN 0-8089-1865-6, 792329). Grune.

Psychocybernetic Model of Art Therapy. Aina O. Nucho. (Illus.). 248p. 1987. 34.50 (ISBN 0-398-05339-1). C C Thomas.

Psychodiagnosis: Selected Papers. Paul E. Meehl. LC 72-95440. (Illus.). 334p. 1973. 22.50x (ISBN 0-8166-0685-4). U of Minn Pr.

Psychodiagnostic Evaluation of Children: A Casebook Approach. Barbara R. Slater & John M. Thomas. 1983. pap. text ed. 25.95x (ISBN 0-8077-2734-2). Tchrs Coll.

Pschodiagnostics & Personality Assessment: A Handbook. 2nd ed. Donald P. Ogdon. LC 66-29866. (Professional Handbook Ser.). 144p. 1967. pap. 18.50x (ISBN 0-87424-095-6). Western Psych.

Psychodrama, 3 vols. J. L. Moreno. Incl. Vol. 1. Collected Papers. o. s. i. 16.00; pap. 20.00 (ISBN 0-685-22530-5); Vol. 2. Foundations of Psychotherapy. 20.00 (ISBN 0-685-22531-3); pap. 19.00; Vol. 3. Action-Therapy & Principles of Practice. 20.00 (ISBN 0-685-22532-1); pap. 19.00 (ISBN 0-685-22533-X). Beacon Hse.

Psychodrama. Adaline Starr. LC 76-49045. 382p. 1977. 26.95x (ISBN 0-88229-224-2); pap. 14.95x (ISBN 0-88229-468-7). Nelson-Hall.

Psychodrama & Audience Attitude Change. Ira A. Greenberg. LC 68-54532. 1968. 10.00 (ISBN 0-911958-00-2); pap. 5.95 (ISBN 0-685-06839-0). Behavioral Studies.

Psychodrama & Sociodrama in American Education. 14.00 (ISBN 0-685-22536-4). Beacon Hse.

Psychodrama: Experience & Process. Goldman-Morrison. 144p. 1984. pap. text ed. 13.95 (ISBN 0-8403-3322-6). Kendall-Hunt.

Psychodrama: Resolving Emotional Problems Through Role-Playing. Lewis Yablonsky. 300p. 1981. pap. text ed. 14.95 (ISBN 0-89876-016-X). Gardner Pr.

Psychodrome. Simon Hawke. 1987. pap. 2.95 (ISBN 0-441-68791-1, Pub. by Ace Science Fiction). Ace Bks.

Psychodrome Two: The Shapechanger Scenario. Simon Hawke. 1988. pap. 2.95 (ISBN 0-317-68254-7). Ace Bks.

Psychodynamic Approach to Adolescent Psychiatry. D. Heacock. (Experimental & Clinical Psychiatry Ser.: Vol. 2). 384p. 1980. 49.75 (ISBN 0-8247-6873-6). Dekker.

Psychodynamic Foundations of Morality. R. M. Henry. (Contributions to Human Development Ser.: Vol. 7). (Illus.). viii, 148p. 1983. pap. 32.75 (ISBN 3-8055-3603-8). S Karger.

Psychodynamic Group Psychotherapy. J. Scott Rutan & Walter N. Stone. LC 82-73289. 256p. 1984. 20.00 (ISBN 0-669-06300-2, Collamore). Heath.

Psychodynamic Perspectives on Religion, Sect & Cult. D. A. Halperin. 416p. 1983. pap. text ed. 49.00 (ISBN 0-7236-7029-3). PSG Pub Co.

Psychodynamic Psychiatry, Theory & Practice, 2 Vols. John Frosch. 1989. 45.00x ea. (BN#05645/05646). Intl Univs Pr.

Psychodynamic Psychotherapy of Children. Henry P. Coppolillo. 1987. 35.00x (ISBN 0-8236-4455-3, BN#04455). Intl Univs Pr.

Psychodynamic Studies on Aging: Creativity, Reminiscing & Dying. Ed. by Sidney Levin & Ralph J. Kahana. LC 67-27427. 345p. 1967. text ed. 42.50x (ISBN 0-8236-5640-3). Intl Univs Pr.

Psychodynamic Understanding of Depression: The Meaning of Despair. rev. & 2nd ed. Wilard Gaylin. LC 84-45120. 436p. 1984. 30.00x (ISBN 0-87668-673-0). Aronson.

Psychodynamics & Cognition. Mardi J. Horowitz. (Illus.). xii, 390p. 1988. 27.50x (ISBN 0-226-35368-0). U of Chicago pr.

Psychodynamics of Alcoholism: A Current Synthesis. William J. Light. (Illus.). 218p. 1986. 31.75x (ISBN 0-398-05244-1). C C Thomas.

Psychodynamics of Family Life: Diagnosis & Treatment of Family Relationships. Nathan W. Ackerman. LC 58-13043. 1972. pap. 12.95x (ISBN 0-465-09503-8, TB5004). Basic.

Psychodynamics of Inconjunctions. Alan Epstein. LC 83-5908. (Illus.). 224p. 1984. pap. 8.95 (ISBN 0-87728-555-1). Weiser.

Psychodynamics of Medical Practice. Howard R. Stein. LC 84-28046. 1985. 20.00x (ISBN 0-520-05480-6). U of Cal Pr.

Psychodynamics of Stuttering. Dominick A. Barbara. 104p. 1982. 15.25x (ISBN 0-398-04714-6). C C Thomas.

Psychodynamics of the Emotionally Uncomfortable. David W. Shave. LC 79-50191. 489p. 1980. 27.75 (ISBN 0-87527-233-9). Green.

Psychodynamics of Yoga. H. L. Sharma. 160p. 1981. 16.95x (ISBN 0-317-12326-2, Pub. by G D K Pubns India). Asia Bk Corp.

Psychodynamics, Psychotherapy & Counseling: Collected Papers. Rudolf Dreikurs. LC 68-2060. pap. 10.00x (ISBN 0-918560-12-8). A Adler Inst.

Psychoeducational Approaches to Family Therapy & Counseling. Ed. by Ronald F. Levant. 336p. 1986. text ed. 28.95 (ISBN 0-8261-4850-6). Springer Pub.

Psychoeducational Assessment: Intergrating Concepts & Techniques. George Helton et al. 364p. 1982. 34.50 (ISBN 0-8089-1482-0, 791963). Grune.

Psychoeducational Assessment of Minority Group Children: A Casebook. Ed. by Reginald L. Jones. LC 87-20861. 429p. (Orig.). 1988. pap. text ed. 24.95x (ISBN 0-943539-00-5). Cobb & Henry Pubs.

Psychoeducational Assessment of Pre-School Children. Ed. by Kathleen Paget & Bruce Brackett. (Illus.). 551p. 1982. 39.50 (ISBN 0-8089-1475-8, 793230). Grune.

Psychoeducational Assessment of Visually Impaired & Blind Students. Sharon Bradley-Johnson. 140p. (Orig.). 1986. pap. text ed. 18.00x (ISBN 0-89079-108-2, 1394). Pro Ed.

Psychoeducational Diagnosis of Exceptional Children. Milton V. Wisland. (Illus.). 408p. 1977. 21.75 (ISBN 0-398-02843-5). C C Thomas.

Psychoeducational Diagnostic Services for Learning Disabled Youths: Research Procedures. National Center for State Courts Staff. 38p. 1977. manuscript 2.28 (LDJD-011). Natl Ctr St Courts.

Psychoeducational Diagnostic Services for Learning Disabled Youths: Validation Analysis. National Center for State Courts Staff. 80p. 1979. manuscript 4.80 (LDJD-015). Natl Ctr St Courts.

Psychoeducational Evaluation of Children & Adolescents with Low Incidence Handicaps. Philip J. Lazarus & Stephen S. Strichart. 336p. 1986. 39.50 (ISBN 0-8089-1779-X, 794415). Grune.

Psychoeducational Evaluation of the Preschool Child: A Manual Utilizing the Haeussermann Approach. Eleonora Jedrysek et al. LC 75-168848. (Illus.). 160p. 1972. pap. 42.50 (ISBN 0-8089-0735-2, 792175); 50 test forms 29.00 (ISBN 0-8089-0769-7, 792177). Grune.

Psychoeducational Interventions in the Schools: Methods & Procedures for Enhancing Student Competence. Ed. by Charles A. Maher. (General Psychology Ser.: No. 150). 240p. 1987. text ed. 27.50 (ISBN 0-08-033632-9, PBI); pap. text ed. 13.95 (ISBN 0-08-033631-0, PBI). Pergamon.

Psychoeducational Profile (PEP, Vol. I. Eric Schopler et al. LC 78-13415. (Individualized Assessment & Treatment for Autistic & Developmentally Disabled Children Ser.). (Illus.). 256p. 1979. spiral 29.00x (1137). Pro Ed.

Psychoeducational Use & Interpretation of the Wechsler Adult Intelligence Scale-Revised. Hazel Z. Sprandel. 230p. 1985. 28.50 (ISBN 0-398-05126-7). C C Thomas.

Psychoendocrine Aspects of Epilepsy. Harold E. Simmons. 1974. pap. 5.00 (ISBN 0-87312-004-3). Psychogenic Disease.

Psychoendocrinology of Human Sexual Behavior. Harold Persky. LC 87-6976. (Sexual Medicine Ser.: Vol. 6). 272p. 1987. lib. bdg. 45.00 (ISBN 0-275-92526-9, C2526). Praeger.

Psychoenergetic Systems: Interaction of Conciousness, Energy & Matter. Stanley Krippner. (Psychic Studies). 288p. 1979. 58.00 (ISBN 0-677-14870-4). Gordon & Breach.

Psychoenergetics: A Breath of Life. Jan Kennedy. LC 82-72904. (Illus.). 176p. (Orig.). 1982. pap. 14.95 (ISBN 0-938954-02-4). Cosmoenergetics Pubns.

Psychoenergetics: A Key to Health. Jan Kennedy. LC 80-54782. (Illus.). 180p. (Orig.). 1981. pap. 9.95 (ISBN 0-938954-00-8); 80 cards 9.95 (ISBN 0-938954-01-6). Cosmoenergetics Pubns.

Psychoenergetics: A Key to Health. rev. ed. Jan Kennedy. Ed. & illus. by Richard Blanchard. (Illus.). 400p. 1988. pap. 14.95 (ISBN 0-938954-06-7). Cosmoenergetics Pubns.

Psychofeedback: Practical Psychocybernetics. Paul G. Thomas. LC 79-18695. (Illus.). 201p. 1979. Repr. 14.95 (ISBN 0-9609762-0-5). Classic CA.

Psychofraud & Ethical Therapy. John D. Garcia. LC 73-92028. 200p. 1974. 6.95 (ISBN 0-87426-032-9). Whitmore.

Psychogalvanic Reactions of Exceptional & Normal School Children. Robin D. Collmann. LC 79-176664. (Columbia University. Teachers College. Contributions to Education: No. 469). Repr. of 1931 ed. 22.50 (ISBN 0-404-55469-5). AMS Pr.

Psychogenese de la Personne D'Apres "L'Initiation Philosophique" D'Amedee Ponceau see Cahiers de l'Institut de Science Economique Appliquee.

Psychogenesis & the History of Science. Jean Piaget & Rolando Garcia. Tr. by Helga Feider from Fr. (Illus.). 336p. 1988. 37.50x (ISBN 0-231-05992-2). Columbia U Pr.

Psychogenesis: The Early Development of Gender Identity. Elizabeth R. Moberly. 120p. 1983. 19.95x (ISBN 0-7100-9271-7). Routledge Chapman & Hall.

Psychogenic Biochemical Aspects of Cancer. Harold E. Simmons. 1979. pap. 15.00 (ISBN 0-87312-010-8). Psychogenic Disease.

Psychogenic Theory of Disease: A New Approach to Cancer Research. Harold E. Simmons. 1966. pap. 10.00 (ISBN 0-87312-000-0). Gen Welfare Pubns.

Psychogeometrics: How to Use Geometric Psychology to Influence People. Susan Dellinger. (Illus.). 225p. 1989. pap. 8.95 (ISBN 0-13-732835-4). P-H.

Psychogeriatrics: A Hopeful Approach. Philip Ernst. 1987. 12.95 (ISBN 0-533-06882-7). Vantage.

Psychogeriatrics: A Report. WHO Scientific Group. (Technical Report Ser: No. 507). 48p. 1972. pap. 1.60 (ISBN 92-4-120507-5, 58). World Health.

Psychogeriatrics: An International Handbook. Manfred Bergener. (Springer Series on Psychiatry). 576p. 1987. text ed. 53.00 (ISBN 0-8261-5070-5). Springer Pub.

Psychographics in Personal Growth. George Burtt. LC 72-95846. 1972. pap. 3.50 (ISBN 0-913596-00-0). Vector Counsel.

PsychoHeresy: The Psychological Seduction of Christianity. Martin Bobgan & Deidre Bobgan. LC 87-80001. 272p. (Orig.). 14.95 (ISBN 0-941717-01-1); pap. 8.95 (ISBN 0-941717-00-3). EastGate Pubs.

Psychohistorian's Handbook. Henry Lawton. 130p. 1988. 21.95x (ISBN 0-914434-27-6). Psychohistory Pr.

Psychohistorical Inquiry: A Comprehensive Bibliography. William J. Cilmore. LC 82-49165. (Reference Library of Social Science). 400p. 1983. lib. bdg. 53.00 (ISBN 0-8240-9167-1). Garland Pub.

Psychohistory & Religion: The Case of Young Man Luther. Roger A. Johnson et al. LC 76-7870. pap. 51.50 (2026895). Bks Demand UMI.

Psychoimmunity & the Healing Process: A Holistic Approach to Immunity & AIDS. Ed. by Jason Serinus. LC 86-11701. 372p. (Orig.). 1986. pap. 10.95 (ISBN 0-89087-461-1). Celestial Arts.

Psychological Development in Health & Disease. George L. Engel. LC 62-13582. Repr. of 1962 ed. 89.20 (ISBN 0-8357-9556-X, 2013069). Bks Demand UMI.

Psychological Development in the Elementary Years. Ed. by Judith Worell. (Educational Psychology Ser.). 504p. 1982. 35.00 (ISBN 0-12-764050-9). Acad Pr.

Psychological Differences: Causes Consequences & Uses in Education & Guidance. James A. Wakefield & Nancy A. Goad. LC 82-71256. 1982. pap. 9.95 (ISBN 0-912736-27-5). EDITS Pubs.

Psychological Dimensions of Near Eastern Studies. Ed. by L. Carl Brown & Norman Itzkowitz. LC 75-43499. 382p. 1977. 9.95x (ISBN 0-87850-028-6). Darwin Pr.

Psychological Disorders & Their Treatments Series, 13 vols. Ed. by Dale C. Garell & Solomon H. Snyder. (Illus.). 1248p. 1988. lib. bdg. 233.35x (ISBN 0-7910-0010-9). Chelsea Hse.

Psychological Disorders in Obstetrics & Gynecology. R. G. Priest. (Illus.). 256p. 1985. text ed. 80.00 (ISBN 0-407-00373-8). Butterworth.

Psychological Disorders of Children: A Behavioral Approach to Theory, Research & Therapy. Alan O. Ross. (Psychology Ser.). (Illus.). 1979. text ed. 42.95 (ISBN 0-07-053883-2). McGraw.

Psychological Disorders of Young Children. S. Dutta Ray. 259p. 1980. 19.95. Asia Bk Corp.

Psychological Distress in Aging: A Family Management Model. Donna R. Eyde & Jay Rich. LC 82-164440. 240p. 1982. 36.00 (ISBN 0-89443-667-8). Aspen Pub.

Psychological Disturbance in Adolescence. Irving B. Weiner. (Personality Processes Ser.). 400p. 1970. 48.50x (ISBN 0-471-92568-3, Pub. by Wiley-Interscience). Wiley.

Psychological Disturbance in Adolescence. 2nd ed. Irving B. Weiner. 1986. write for info. (ISBN 0-471-82596-4). Wiley.

Psychological Dynamics of Sport. Diane L. Gill. LC 86-10440. (Illus.). 304p. 1986. text ed. 23.95x (ISBN 0-87322-070-6, BGIL0070). Human Kinetics.

Psychological Economics. George Katona. LC 75-8272. pap. 112.00 (2026276). Bks Demand UMI.

Psychological Effects of the Crowded Environment. Lynn E. McCutcheon. 1973. pap. 5.50 (ISBN 0-87948-031-9). Beatty.

Psychological Element in the English Sociological Novel of the 19th Century. Sijna De Vooys. LC 68-2022. (Studies in Fiction, No. 34). 1969. Repr. of 1927 ed. lib. bdg. 75.00x (ISBN 0-8383-0539-3). Haskell.

Psychological Evaluation of Children's Human Figure Drawings. Elizabeth M. Koppitz. (Illus.). 352p. 1967. 29.50 (ISBN 0-8089-0240-7, 792355); scoring forms 19.50 (ISBN 0-8089-0241-5, 7923-57). Grune.

Psychological Evaluation of Exceptional Children. Harold D. Love. (Illus.). 132p. 1985. 20.75x (ISBN 0-398-05045-7). C C Thomas.

Psychological Evaluation of Human Figure Drawings by Middle School Students. Elizabeth M. Koppitz. 208p. 1984. 22.50 (ISBN 0-8089-1682-3, 792355). Grune.

Psychological Evaluation of the Developmentally & Physically Disabled. Ed. by V. B. Van Hasselt & M. Hersen. LC 87-15275. (Illus.). 348p. 1987. 45.00x (ISBN 0-306-42514-9, Plenum Pr). Plenum Pub.

Psychological Evaluations & Expert Testimony. D. Shapiro. 1983. 26.95 (ISBN 0-442-28183-8). Van Nos Reinhold.

Psychological Evaluations for the Courts: A Handbook for Mental Health Professionals & Lawyers. Gary B. Melton et al. LC 86-26992. (Guilford Perspectives on Law &Behavior Ser.). 511p. 1987. lib. bdg. 50.00 (ISBN 0-89862-276-X). Guilford Pr.

Psychological Examination: A Guide for Clinicians. Paul W. Pruyser. LC 78-70234. 311p. 1979. text ed. 35.00x (ISBN 0-8236-5605-5). Intl Univs Pr.

Psychological Examination of Political Leaders. Ed. by Margaret G. Hermann & Thomas W. Milburn. LC 75-32366. 1977. 22.95 (ISBN 0-02-914590-2). Free Pr.

Psychological Exercises & Essays. Alfred R. Orage. LC 72-181083. (Orig.). 1974. pap. 5.95 (ISBN 0-87728-265-X). Weiser.

Psychological Experience of Surgery. Richard S. Blacker. LC 86-11124. (General & Clinical Psychology Ser.). 236p. 1987. 31.50 (ISBN 0-471-81831-3). Wiley.

Psychological Experiences Connected with Different Parts of Speech. Ed. by Eleanor H. Rowland. Bd. with Kinaesthethic & Organic Sensations. John B. Watson. Repr. of 1907 ed; Vol. I, No. 2. Yale Psychology Studies N. S. Ed. by Charles H. Judd. Repr. of 1907 ed; Experimental Study of Visual Fixation. Ed. by Raymond Dodge. Repr. of 1908 ed. (Psychology Monographs General & Applied: Vol. 8). pap. 29.00 (ISBN 0-8115-1407-2). Kraus Repr.

Psychological Experiments & Demonstrations. Louis Snellgrove. LC 67-16937. pap. 39.00 (ISBN 0-317-10576-0, 2004417). Bks Demand UMI.

Psychological Factors in Cardiovascular Disorders. Andrew Steptoe. 1981. 69.00 (ISBN 0-12-666450-1). Acad Pr.

Psychological Factors in Marital Happiness. Lewis M. Terman. 474p. 1981. Repr. of 1938 ed. lib. bdg. 45.00 (ISBN 0-89987-818-0). Darby Bks.

Psychological Foundation of Economics. Ronald Allibrant. (Illus.). 127p. 1983. 147.75 (ISBN 0-86654-087-3). Inst Econ Finan.

Psychological Foundation of Managerial Action, 2 vols. Spencer Fleming. (Illus.). 259p. 1985. Set. 227.45 (ISBN 0-86654-182-9). Inst Econ Finan.

Psychological Foundations of Criminal Justice: Contemporary Perpectives on Forensic Psychiartry & Psychology, Vol. 2. Ed. by Harold J. Vetter & Robert W. Rieber. LC 78-18781. (Illus.). 416p. 1980. 20.00x (ISBN 0-89444-025-X). John Jay Pr.

Psychological Foundations of Criminal Justice: Historical Perspectives on Forensic Psychology, Vol. 1. Ed. by Robert W. Rieber & Harold J. Vetter. LC 78-18781. (Illus.). 1978. 15.00x (ISBN 0-89444-009-8). John Jay Pr.

Psychological Foundations of Economic Behavior. Ed. by Paul J. Albanese. LC 87-38476. 192p. 1988. lib. bdg. 39.95 (ISBN 0-275-92742-3, C2742). Praeger.

Psychological Foundations of Education: A Guide to Information Sources. Ed. by Charles A. Baatz & Olga K. Baatz. (Education Information Guide Ser.: Vol. 10). 480p. 1981. 68.00x (ISBN 0-8103-1467-3). Gale.

Psychological Foundations of Education. Stanley J. Gray. 534p. 1981. Repr. of 1935 ed. lib. bdg. 57.50 (ISBN 0-89984-236-4). Century Bookbindery.

Psychological Foundations of Education. Jack Rudman. (National Teachers Examination Ser.: NC-1). (Cloth bdg. avail. on request). pap. 13.95 (ISBN 0-8373-8401-X). Natl Learning.

Psychological Foundations of Education: Readings. Ed. by Miriam Goldbert & Martha Werle. 350p. 1974. text ed. 34.50x (ISBN 0-8422-5187-1). Irvington.

Psychological Foundations of Educational Technology. Ed. by W. Clark Trow & Eugene E. Haddan. LC 75-35605. 410p. 1976. 34.95 (ISBN 0-87778-086-2); pap. 27.95 (ISBN 0-87778-092-7). Educ Tech Pubn.

Psychological Foundations of Management. Ed. by Henry C. Metcalf. LC 73-8505. (Management History Ser.: No. 67). (Illus.). 316p. 1973. Repr. of 1927 ed. 25.00 (ISBN 0-87960-073-X). Hive Pub.

Psychological Foundations of Moral Education & Character Development: An Integrated Theory of Moral Development. Ed. by Richard T. Knowles & George F. McLean. 374p. (Orig.). 1986. lib. bdg. 28.25 (ISBN 0-8191-5406-7, Pub. by The Council for Research in Values & Philosophy); pap. 15.25 (ISBN 0-8191-5407-5, Pub by The Council for Research in Values & Philosophy). U Pr of Amer.

Psychological Foundations of Musical Behavior. Rudolf E. Radocy & J. David Boyle. (Illus.). 360p. 1979. 28.50 (ISBN 0-398-03841-4). C C Thomas.

Psychological Foundations of Organizational Behavior. 2nd ed. Barry Staw. 1983. pap. text ed. write for info. (ISBN 0-673-16005-X). Scott F.

Psychological Foundations of Sport. Ed. by John M. Silva, III & Robert S. Weinberg. LC 83-83239. 552p. 1984. text ed. 27.00x (ISBN 0-931250-59-5, BSIL0059). Human Kinetics.

Psychological Foundations of the Curriculum (UNESCO) (Education Studies & Documents: No. 26). pap. 15.00 (ISBN 0-8115-1350-5). Kraus Repr.

Psychological Frontiers of Society. Abram Kardiner et al. LC 45-3605. 475p. 1945. pap. 16.50x (ISBN 0-231-08548-6). Columbia U Pr.

Psychological Frontiers of Society. Abram Kardiner et al. LC 80-29605. xxiv, 475p. 1981. Repr. of 1959 ed. lib. bdg. 45.00x (ISBN 0-313-22388-2, KAPF). Greenwood.

Psychological Games: A Book of Tests & Puzzles to Teach You More about Yourself & Those Around You. Nicola A. De Carlo. (Illus.). 184p. 22.95 (ISBN 0-87196-188-1); pap. 12.95 (ISBN 0-87196-983-1). Facts on File.

Psychological Healing: A Historical & Clinical Study, 2 vols. Pierre M. Janet. LC 75-16710. (Classics in Psychiatry Ser.). 1976. Repr. of 1925 ed. Set. 92.50x (ISBN 0-405-07437-9); 46.50x ea. Vol. 1 (ISBN 0-405-07438-7). Vol. 2 (ISBN 0-405-07439-5). Ayer Co Pubs.

Psychological Improvements for Corporate Management with High Impact Foreign Words & Phrases. Brenda Reynolds et al. Ed. by J. C. Bartone. 142p. 1982. 26.00 (ISBN 0-941864-38-3); pap. 18.00 (ISBN 0-941864-39-1). ABBE Pubs Assn.

Psychological Influence of Street Gangs on School-Aged Youth: A Case Study in Hartford, Connecticut. Roland G. Axelson. 13p. 1984. 2.00 (ISBN 0-317-17788-5). I N Thut World Educ Ctr.

Psychological Inquiries: A Series of Essays Intended to Illustrate the Mutual Relations of the Physical Organization & the Mental Faculties. Benjamin Brodie. Bd. with On Animal Electricity. E. DuBois-Reymond. (Contributions to the History of Psychology Ser., Vol. VI, Pt. E). 1983. Repr. of 1854 ed. 30.00 (ISBN 0-89093-325-1). U Pubns Amer.

Psychological Interpretations of Society. Michael M. Davis, Jr. LC 71-76682. (Columbia University. Studies in the Social Sciences: No. 87). Repr. of 1909 ed. 20.00 (ISBN 0-404-51087-6). AMS Pr.

Psychological Investigations. Jose Ortega y Gasset. Tr. by Jorge Garcia-Gomez from Span. LC 86-16246. 1987. 19.95 (ISBN 0-393-02401-6). Norton.

Psychological Issues of Human-Computer Interaction in the Work Place. M. Frese et al. 1987. 95.25 (ISBN 0-444-70318-7). Elsevier.

Psychological Life: From Science to Metaphor. Robert D. Romanyshyn. (Illus.). 227p. 1982. text ed. 19.95x (ISBN 0-292-76473-1). U of Tex Pr.

Psychological Linguistics. J. R. Kantor. 1977. 15.00 (ISBN 0-911188-53-3). Principia Pr.

Psychological Maltreatment of Children & Youth. Ed. by Marla R. Brassard et al. (General Psychology Ser.: No. 143). 400p. 1987. 49.50 (ISBN 0-08-032775-3, J115, PBI). Pergamon.

Psychological Man. Harry Levinson. LC 76-2583. 147p. (Orig.). 1976. pap. text ed. 6.95 (ISBN 0-916516-02-4). Levinson Inst.

Psychological Management of Chronic Pain: A Treatment Manual. H. Claire Philips. (Behavior Therapy & Behavior Medicine Ser.). 240p. 1988. 20.95 (ISBN 0-8261-6110-3). Springer Pub.

Psychological Meaning of the Sacred Symbols in Art, 2 vols. E. E. Goldsmith. (Illus.). 311p. 1987. Set. 167.50 (ISBN 0-89920-149-0). Am Inst Psych.

Psychological Measurements in Psychopharmacology. Ed. by P. Pichot & R. Olivier-Martin. (Modern Problems of Pharmacopsychiatry Ser.: Vol. 7). (Illus.). 1974. 65.50 (ISBN 3-8055-1630-4). S Karger.

Psychological Mechanisms of Language. Ed. by H. C. Longuet-Higgins et al. (Illus.). 209p. 1981. lib. bdg. 64.00x (ISBN 0-85403-172-3, Pub. by Royal Soc London). Scholium Intl.

Psychological Mechanisms of Language. Ed. by Royal Society. 209p. 1981. text ed. 65.00x (Pub. by British Academy). Humanities.

Psychological Medicine Insights: Treating Patients' Medical Psychological Problems. Harry Ireton. LC 85-73695. 80p. (Orig.). 1985. pap. text ed. 15.00 (ISBN 0-936787-00-7). Behavior Sci Systs.

Psychological Methods of Child Assessment. Jacquelin Goldman et al. LC 83-20889. 384p. 1984. 30.00 (ISBN 0-87630-348-3). Brunner-Mazel.

Psychological Methods of Testing Intelligence. William L. Stern. Tr. by G. M. Whipple from Ger. Bd. with Selected Essays. Alfred Binet et al. LC 77-72191. (Contributions to the History of Psychology Ser., Vol. IV, Pt. B: Psychometrics & Educational Psychology). 496p. 1978. Repr. of 1914 ed. 30.00 (ISBN 0-89093-164-X). U Pubns Amer.

Psychological Milieu of Lytton Strachey. Martin Kallich. 1961. pap. 7.95x (ISBN 0-8084-0408-3). New Coll U Pr.

Psychological Models & Neural Mechanisms: An Examination of Reductionism in Psychology. Austen Clark. (CLLP Ser.). (Illus.). 1980. text ed. 47.00x (ISBN 0-19-824422-3). Oxford U Pr.

Psychological Needs & Political Behavior: A Theory of Personality & Political Efficacy. Stanley A. Renshon. LC 73-11735. 1974. 17.95 (ISBN 0-02-926320-4). Free Pr.

Psychological Needs of Adults: A Symposium. Gardner Murphy & Raymond G. Kuhlen. (Notes & Essays on Education for Adults Ser.: 12). pap. 20.00 (ISBN 0-317-08265-5, 2000410). Bks Demand UMI.

Psychological, Neuropsychiatric, & Substance Abuse Aspects of AIDS. Ed. by T. Peter Bridge et al. (Advances in Biochemical Psychopharmacology Ser.: Vol. 44). (Illus.). 280p. 1988. text ed. 30.00 (ISBN 0-88167-396-X). Raven.

Psychological Operations in Guerilla Warfare: The CIA's Nicaragua Manual. 128p. pap. 4.95 (ISBN 0-394-74061-0, Vin). Random.

Psychological Operations: The Soviet Challenge. Joseph S. Gordon. (Special Studies in International Security). 216p. 1988. pap. 22.50 (ISBN 0-8133-7395-6). Westview.

Psychological Origin & the Nature of Religion. James H. Leuba. LC 78-1577. 20.00 (ISBN 0-8414-5837-5). Folcroft.

Psychological Patterns of Jesus Christ. Frank Jakubowsky. 342p. (Orig.). 1982. pap. 14.95 (ISBN 0-932588-02-6). Jesus Bks.

Psychological Perspectives in Psychiatry. Ed. by Brendan P. Bradley & Chris Thompson. LC 85-9383. 260p. 1986. 52.95 (ISBN 0-471-90790-1). Wiley.

Psychological Perspectives of Essential Hypertension. W. Linden. (Karger Biobehavioral Medicine Ser.: Vol. 3). (Illus.). x, 130p. 1984. pap. 46.00 (ISBN 3-8055-3662-3). S Karger.

Psychological Perspectives of the Holocaust & of Its Aftermath. Ed. by Randolph L. Braham. (Holocaust Studies Series Social Science Monographs). 320p. 1988. 40.00 (ISBN 0-88033-960-8). East Eur Quarterly.

Psychological Perspectives on Childhood Exceptionality: A Handbook. Ed. by Robert T. Brown & Cecil R. Reynolds. LC 85-17967. (Wiley Ser. on Personality Processes). 675p. 1986. 45.00 (ISBN 0-471-08589-8, Pub. by Wiley Interscience). Wiley.

Psychological Perspectives on Literature: Freudian Dissidents & Non-Freudian, a Casebook. Ed. by Joseph P. Natoli. LC 83-22452. vii, 288p. 1984. 29.50 (ISBN 0-208-01989-8, Archon Bks). Shoe String.

Psychological Perspectives on the Self, Vol. 1. Ed. by Jerry Suls. 272p. 1982. 29.95 (ISBN 0-89859-197-X). L Erlbaum Assocs.

Psychological Perspectives on the Self, Vol. 2. Ed. by Jerry Suls & Anthony G. Greenwald. 408p. 1983. text ed. 29.95x (ISBN 0-89859-276-3). L Erlbaum Assocs.

Psychological Perspectives on the Self, Vol. 3. Jerry Suls & G. Greenwald. 232p. 1986. text ed. 24.95 (ISBN 0-89859-703-X). L Erlbaum Assocs.

Psychological Perspectives: Politics. Carol Barner-Barry & Robert Rosenwein. (Illus.). 352p. 1985. pap. text ed. 26.00 (ISBN 0-13-732298-4). P-H.

Psychological Portraits of Children: An Integrated Developmental Approach to Psychological Test Data. Lillian Schwarts & Carol J. Eagle. LC 85-45076. 288p. 1986. 35.00x (ISBN 0-669-11199-6). Lexington Bks.

Psychological Power & Business Success: Scientific Psychological Formulas for Better Business, 2 vols. W. C. Shaw. 385p. 1987. Set. 198.75 (ISBN 0-89920-168-7). Am Inst Psych.

Psychological Practices with the Physically Disabled. Ed. by James F. Garrett & Edna S. Levine. LC 62-9708. 463p. 1962. 45.00x (ISBN 0-231-02463-0). Columbia U Pr.

Psychological Preparation & Athletic Excellence. Bryant J. Cratty. 200p. 1984. pap. 14.95 (ISBN 0-932392-12-1). Mouvement Pubns.

Psychological Principles of Education. Herman H. Horne. 435p. 1981. Repr. of 1911 ed. lib. bdg. 30.00 (ISBN 0-89987-372-3). Darby Bks.

Psychological Problems Before & after Myocardial Infarction. Ed. by H. Denolin. (Advances in Cardiology: Vol. 29). viii, 156p. 1982. 65.50 (ISBN 3-8055-3424-8). S Karger.

Psychological Problems in the Father-Son Relationship. Harold A. Abramson. LC 71-81849. 1969. 7.50 (ISBN 0-8079-0154-7). October.

Psychological Problems of the Child in the Family. 2nd ed. Ed. by Paul D. Stienhauer & Quentin Rae-Grant. LC 82-72960. 1983. text ed. 39.95 (ISBN 0-465-06676-3). Basic.

Psychological Processes & Advertising Effects: Theory, Research, & Applications. Ed. by Linda F. Alwitt & Andrew A. Mitchell. 320p. 1985. text ed. 29.95 (ISBN 0-89859-515-0). L Erlbaum Assocs.

Psychological Processes in Cognition & Personality. Ed. by Werner Froehlich & Gudmund Smith. LC 82-21230. (Clinical & Community Psychology Ser.). (Illus.). 284p. 1983. text ed. 47.95 (ISBN 0-89116-243-7). Hemisphere Pub.

Psychological Processes in Pattern Recognition. Stephen K. Reed. (Cognition & Perception Ser.). 1973. 29.95 (ISBN 0-12-585350-5). Acad Pr.

Psychological Profiles of Conjoined Twins: Heredity, Environment, & Identity. J. David Smith. LC 88-1592. 176p. 1988. lib. bdg. 39.95 (ISBN 0-275-92965-5, C2965). Praeger.

Psychological Rackets & the Racket Diagram. Franklin H. Ernst, Jr. 1981. pap. 9.50x (ISBN 0-916944-34-4). Addresso'set.

Psychological Reactance: A Theory of Freedom & Control. 2nd ed. Sharon Brehm & Jack Brehm. LC 81-12796. 1981. 49.95 (ISBN 0-12-129840-X). Acad Pr.

Psychological Readings for the Dental Profession. Ed. by Brenda L. Van Zoost. LC 75-15892. 186p. 1975. 21.95x (ISBN 0-88229-244-7). Nelson-Hall.

Psychological Reality. K. P. Hillner. (Advances in Psychology Ser.: Vol. 26). 418p. 1985. 79.00 (ISBN 0-444-87741-X, North-Holland). Elsevier.

Psychological Reality in Phonology. Per Linell. LC 78-67429. (Cambridge Studies in Linguistics: No. 25). (Illus.). 1979. 52.50 (ISBN 0-521-22234-6). Cambridge U Pr.

Psychological Reflections: A New Anthology of His Writings, 1905-1961. Carl G. Jung. Ed. by Jolande Jacobi & R. F. Hull. (Bollingen Ser.: Vol. 31). 332p. 1970. 34.50x (ISBN 0-691-09862-X); pap. 9.50 (ISBN 0-691-01786-7). Princeton U Pr.

Psychological Rehabilitation of the Amputee. Lawrence W. Friedmann. (Illus.). 176p. 1978. photocopy ed. 23.00x (ISBN 0-398-03707-8). C C Thomas.

Psychological Report Writing. 2nd ed. Norman Tallent. (Illus.). 320p. 1983. 40.33 (ISBN 0-13-732511-8). P-H.

Psychological Report Writing. 3rd ed. Norman Tallent. 1988. text ed. 40.00 (ISBN 0-13-732553-3). P-H.

Psychological Report Writing: Theory & Practice. 2nd ed. Joseph Hollis & Patsy Donn. LC 79-64499. 296p. 1979. pap. text ed. 14.95x (ISBN 0-915202-21-2). Accel Devel.

Psychological Reports: A Guide to Report Writing in Professional Psychology. Raymond L. Ownby. 175p. 1987. pap. 18.95 (ISBN 0-88422-019-2). Clinical Psych.

Psychological Research: An Introduction. 4th ed. Arthur J. Bachrach. 205p. 1981. pap. text ed. write for info (ISBN 0-394-32288-6, RanC). Random.

Psychological Research & Human Values. Lucien A. Buck. LC 76-4267. 80p. 1976. 8.95 (ISBN 0-8158-0340-0). Chris Mass.

Psychology, 4 bks. Ed. by Arthur W. Biddle. LC 86-82608. (Writer's Guide Ser.). 192p. 1987. pap. text ed. 6.50 (ISBN 0-669-12004-9). Heath.

Psychology. 2nd ed. Andrew B. Crider et al. 1986. text ed. write for info. (ISBN 0-673-18217-7); instr's. manual avail. Scott F.

Psychology. 3rd ed. Andrew B. Crider et al. 1988. text ed. price not set (ISBN 0-673-38240-0). Scott F.

Psychology. 2nd ed. John M. Darley et al. (Illus.). 672p. 1984. By Gordon J. Hodge. study guide with practice tests 9.95. P-H.

Psychology. 4th ed. John M. Darley et al. (Illus.). 800p. 1988. text ed. price not set (ISBN 0-13-733650-0). P-H.

Psychology. 3rd ed. John M. Darley et al. (Illus.). 736p. 1986. By Gordon G. Hodge. study guide 9.95. P-H.

Psychology. 2nd ed. John P. Dworetzky. (Illus.). 708p. 1985. text ed. 38.50 (ISBN 0-314-85231-X). West Pub.

Psychology. 3rd ed. John P. Dworetzky. 672p. 1988. text ed. 39.75 (ISBN 0-314-62479-1). West Pub.

Psychology. Henry Gleitman. (Illus.). 1981. study guide o.p. 10.95x (ISBN 0-393-95110-3); instr's. manual avail. (ISBN 0-393-95105-7). Norton.

Psychology. 2nd ed. Henry Gleitman. 1986. text ed. 32.95x (ISBN 0-393-95378-5); instr's. manual avail. (ISBN 0-393-95384-X); study guide 12.95x (ISBN 0-393-95381-5); write for info. test item file (ISBN 0-393-95387-4); set transparencies avail. (ISBN 0-393-95592-3). Norton.

Psychology. David Hothersall. 1985. Repr. text ed. write for info. (ISBN 0-673-18666-0). Scott F.

Psychology. Frank J. Landy. 1985. write for info. (ISBN 0-13-733437-0); study guide incl. P-H.

Psychology. 3rd ed. Lester A. Lefton. 1984. text ed. 38.00 (ISBN 0-205-08177-0, 798177); write for info. study guide (ISBN 0-205-08262-9, 798262). Allyn.

Psychology. 2nd ed. Gardner Lindzey et al. LC 77-86622. (Illus.). 712p. 1978. 32.95x; study guide 9.95x (ISBN 0-87901-090-8). Worth.

Psychology. 3rd ed. Gardner Lindzey et al. 1988. text ed. 34.95 (ISBN 0-87901-361-3); study guide 8.95 (ISBN 0-87901-354-0). Worth.

Psychology. 4th ed. Michael Maher. (Stonyhurst Philosophical Ser.). 608p. 1982. pap. text ed. 10.00x (ISBN 0-87343-051-4). Magi Bks.

Psychology. Richard W. Malott & Donald Whaley. LC 82-84677. 680p. 1983. text ed. 26.95 (ISBN 0-918452-43-0). Learning Pubns.

Psychology. David G. Myers. 693p. 1986. text ed. 31.95x (ISBN 0-87901-311-7); study guide 8.95x (ISBN 0-87901-312-5). Worth.

Psychology. Diane E. Papalia. 736p. 1985. text ed. 36.95 (ISBN 0-07-048401-5); study guide 16.95 (ISBN 0-07-048403-1). McGraw.

Psychology. 2nd ed. Diane E. Papalia & Sally W. Olds. 816p. 1988. text ed. 35.95 (ISBN 0-07-048534-8). McGraw.

Psychology. 1985. 2.25 (ISBN 0-471-63991-5). Wiley.

Psychology. (National Teachers Examination Ser.: NT-42). Date not set. pap. 13.95 (ISBN 0-8373-8452-4). Natl Learning.

Psychology. 2nd ed. Spencer A. Rathus. LC 83-10647. 645p. 1984. text ed. 31.95 (ISBN 0-03-063177-7); study guide 11.95 (ISBN 0-03-063179-3). HR&W.

Psychology. 3rd ed. Spencer A. Rathus. 688p. 1987. text ed. write for info. (ISBN 0-03-001608-8). HR&W.

Psychology. 2nd ed. Henry L. Roediger, III et al. 1987. text ed. write for info. (ISBN 0-673-39530-8); tchr's. ed. avail.; write for info. (ISBN 0-673-39531-6). Scott F.

Psychology. Jack Rudman. (Graduate Record Examination Ser.: GRE-17). (Cloth bdg. avail. on request). pap. 13.95 (ISBN 0-8373-5217-7). Natl Learning.

Psychology. Jack Rudman. (Undergraduate Program Field Test Ser.: UPFT-21). (Cloth bdg. avail. on request). pap. 13.95 (ISBN 0-8373-6021-8). Natl Learning.

Psychology. Saccuzzo. 1986. 38.00 (ISBN 0-205-08842-2); instr's manual avail. (ISBN 0-205-08843-0); study guide avail. (ISBN 0-205-08845-7). Allyn.

Psychology. 5th ed. Robert E. Silverman. (Illus.). 624p. 1985. pap. text ed. write for info. (ISBN 0-13-733601-2); By John Baldsare & Rhoda Mandel-304pp. write for info. (ISBN 0-13-733635-7). P-H.

Psychology. Janet Simons et al. (Illus.). 716p. 1987. text ed. 39.00 (ISBN 0-314-26213-X). West Pub.

Psychology. Carole Wade & Carol Tavris. 700p. 1987. text ed. 37.95 scp (ISBN 0-06-044924-1, HarpC). Har-Row.

Psychology. 2nd ed. Camille Wortman & Elizabeth Loftus. 672p. 1984. text ed. 24.00 (ISBN 0-394-33189-3, KnopfC); 8.00 (ISBN 0-394-34341-7). Knopf.

Psychology. 3rd ed. Camille B. Wortman & Elizabeth F. Loftus. 672p. 1988. text ed. 31.50 (ISBN 0-394-36537-2, RanC); wkbk. 8.00 (ISBN 0-394-37616-1). Random.

Psychology see Comprehensive Dissertation Index 1861-1972: Supplement, 1973.

Psychology: A Biosocial Study of Behavior. Edwin T. Prothro & P. T. Teska. LC 79-164472. 546p. 1972. Repr. of 1950 ed. lib. bdg. 35.00x (ISBN 0-8371-6215-7, PRPS). Greenwood.

Psychology: A Concise Introduction. Lyle E. Bourne, Jr. et al. 464p. Date not set. text ed. price not set (ISBN 0-03-012854-4). HR&W.

Psychology: A Concise Introduction. Terry F. Pettijohn. LC 86-72445. (Illus.). 416p. 1987. pap. text ed. 19.95 (ISBN 0-87967-421-0). Dushkin Pub.

Psychology: A First Encounter. Dennis Krebs & Robert Blackman. 900p. 1988. text ed. 29.00 net (ISBN 0-15-572562-9, HC); instr's. resource manual 6.25 (ISBN 0-15-572563-7); study guide 8.00 (ISBN 0-15-572565-3). HarBraceJ.

Psychology: A First Encounter: Test Book. Rex Bierley. 261p. 1988. pap. text ed. 8.00 net (ISBN 0-15-572564-5). HarBraceJ.

Psychology, a Joyous Subject. James Latimer. 112p. 1987. 8.95 (ISBN 0-8059-3045-0). Dorrance.

Psychology: A Science in Conflict. Howard H. Kendler. (Illus.). 1981. text ed. 25.95x (ISBN 0-19-502900-3); pap. text ed. 16.95x (ISBN 0-19-502901-1). Oxford U Pr.

Psychology: A Way to Grow. William R. Sanford & Carl R. Green. (Orig.). (gr. 10-12). 1982. text ed. 23.92 (ISBN 0-87720-637-6); pap. text ed. 17.92 (ISBN 0-87720-636-8). AMSCO Sch.

Psychology: Advanced Test for the G. R. E. James W. Morrison. LC 79-11444. 144p. 1980. pap. 6.95 (ISBN 0-668-04762-3, 4762-3). Arco.

Psychology: An Elementary Text-Book. Hermann Ebbinghaus. Ed. & tr. by Max Meyer. LC 73-2965. (Classics in Psychology Ser.). Repr. of 1908 ed. 17.00 (ISBN 0-405-05138-7). Ayer Co Pubs.

Psychology: An Introduction. Josh R. Gerow. 1986. text ed. write for info. (ISBN 0-673-18622-9). Scott F.

Psychology: An Introduction. 2nd ed. Josh R. Gerow. 1988. text ed. price not set (ISBN 0-673-38002-5). Scott F.

Psychology: An Introduction. 6th ed. Ed. by Jerome Kagan. 704p. 1988. text ed. 27.00 (ISBN 0-15-572639-0, HC). HarBraceJ.

Psychology: An Introduction. 2nd ed. Benjamin B. Lahey. 744p. 1986. text ed. write for info. (ISBN 0-697-00844-4); pap. text ed. write for info. (ISBN 0-697-00617-4); write for info. instr's. manual (ISBN 0-697-00845-2); write for info. student study guide (ISBN 0-697-00819-3); write for info. lecture enrichment kit (ISBN 0-697-00885-1); write for info. transparencies (ISBN 0-697-01062-7); write for info. audio tape (ISBN 0-697-08435-3). Wm C Brown.

Psychology: An Introduction. 5th ed. Charles G. Morris. (Illus.). 624p. 1985. text ed. write for info. (ISBN 0-13-734385-X). P-H.

Psychology: An Introduction. 5th ed. Charles G. Morris. 1986. write for info. (ISBN 0-13-734435-X). P-H.

Psychology: An Introduction. 6th ed. Charles G. Morris. (Illus.). 640p. 1988. text ed. price not set (ISBN 0-13-734450-3). P-H.

Psychology: An Introduction. brief ed. Paul Mussen et al. 1979. text ed. 24.00 (ISBN 0-669-01672-1); instr's. manual 2.00 (ISBN 0-669-01680-2); study guide 7.00 (ISBN 0-669-01681-0). Heath.

Psychology: An Introduction. Rodney Plotnick et al. 704p. 1986. text ed. write for info (ISBN 0-394-35261-0, RanC). Random.

Psychology: An Introduction. Smith. 1988. write for info. (ISBN 0-471-89366-8). Wiley.

Psychology: An Introduction. 5th ed. Jay G. Watkins. (Illus.). 320p. 1985. write for info. (ISBN 0-13-734427-9). P-H.

Psychology: An Introduction. Arno F. Wittig. 288p. 1984. pap. text ed. 14.95 study guide (ISBN 0-07-071204-2). McGraw.

Psychology: An Introduction: Instructor's Manual. 6th ed. Henry O. Patterson. 1988. pap. text ed. 4.50 net, 147p. (ISBN 0-15-572641-2); net study guide, 195p. 9.00 (ISBN 0-15-572640-4); net test bk., 208p. 6.25 (ISBN 0-15-572643-9). HarBraceJ.

Psychology: An Introduction Study Guide. Rodney Plotnik & Sandra Mollenauer. 160p. 1986. write for info (ISBN 0-394-35262-9, RanC). Random.

Psychology: An Introductory Study of the Structure & Function of Human Consciousness. 4th ed. James R. Angell. LC 73-2957. (Classics in Psychology Ser.). Repr. of 1908 ed. 25.00 (ISBN 0-405-05131-X). Ayer Co Pubs.

Psychology: An Introductory Workbook. Aubry Bissett. 224p. 1987. pap. text ed. 9.95 (ISBN 0-8403-4550-X). Kendall-Hunt.

Psychology: An Orthodox Christian Perspective. Apostolos Makrakis. Ed. by Orthodox Christian Educational Society. Tr. by Denver Cummings from Hellenic. (Logos & Holy Spirit in the Unity of Christian Thought Ser.: Vol. 2). 151p. 1977. pap. 4.25x (ISBN 0-938366-05-X). Orthodox Chr.

Psychology, Ancient & Modern. George Brett. LC 63-10293. (Our Debt to Greece & Rome Ser). Repr. of 1930 ed. 18.50x (ISBN 0-8154-0031-4). Cooper Sq.

Psychology & Adult Learning. Mark Tennant. 224p. 1988. lib. bdg. 42.50 (ISBN 0-415-00560-4). Routledge Chapman & Hall.

Psychology & Aging. Diana Woodruff-Pak. (Illus.). 500p. 1988. text ed. price not set (ISBN 0-13-733064-2). P-H.

Psychology & A.I.D.S. Index of Modern Information. Roth Polinski. LC 88-47613. 150p. 1988. 34.50 (ISBN 0-88164-828-0); pap. 26.50 (ISBN 0-88164-829-9). ABBE Pubs Assn.

Psychology & American Law. Curt R. Bartol. 373p. 1983. text ed. write for info. (ISBN 0-534-01217-5). Wadsworth Pub.

Psychology & Anthropology: A Psychological Perspective. G. Jahoda. 1982. 42.00 (ISBN 0-12-379820-5). Acad Pr.

Psychology & Arthur Miller. Richard I. Evans. 156p. 1981. 35.00 (ISBN 0-275-90620-5, C0620). Praeger.

Psychology & Behavior of Animals in Zoos & Circuses. H. Hediger. Tr. by Geoffrey Sircom. LC 68-55533. 1969. pap. text ed. 4.00 (ISBN 0-486-62218-5). Dover.

Psychology & Behavior of Animals in Zoos & Circuses. H. Hediger. 1983. 13.00 (ISBN 0-8446-2230-3). Peter Smith.

Psychology & Biology of Language & Thought: Essays in Honor of Eric Lenneberg. Ed. by George A. Miller & Elizabeth Lenneberg. 1978. 24.95 (ISBN 0-12-497750-2). Acad Pr.

Psychology & Child Custody Determinations: Knowledge, Roles, & Expertise. Lois A. Weithorn. LC 86-25071. (Children & the Law Ser.). xii, 213p. 1987. 21.95x (ISBN 0-8032-4732-X). U of Nebr Pr.

Psychology & Children: Current Research & Practice. Ed. by Sandra Scarr. (Special Issues American Psychologist, Oct., 1979). 16.00 (ISBN 0-912704-59-4, 4013410); members 12.00. Am Psychol.

Psychology & Christianity. David Cox. 1985. 10.00x (ISBN 0-317-62290-0, Guild of Pastoral Psych). State Mutual Bk.

Psychology & Christianity: An Introduction to Controversial Issues. Ronald P. Philipchalk. 234p. (Orig.). 1987. lib. bdg. 26.25 (ISBN 0-8191-6537-9); pap. text ed. 12.75 (ISBN 0-8191-6538-7). U Pr of Amer.

Psychology & Christianity: Integrative Readings. Ed. by J. Roland Fleck & John D. Carter. LC 81-7911. 400p. (Orig.). 1981. pap. 15.95 (ISBN 0-687-34740-8). Abingdon.

Psychology & Communication in Deaf Children. R. D. Savage et al. 304p. 1981. 44.50 (ISBN 0-8089-1339-5, 793798). Grune.

Psychology & Community Change: Challanges of the Future. 2nd rev., ed. Kenneth Heller et al. 436p. 1984. 33.00x (ISBN 0-256-02860-5). Dorsey.

Psychology & Deterrence. Robert Jervis et al. LC 85-8060. (Perspectives in Security Ser.). 288p. 1985. text ed. 28.50x (ISBN 0-8018-3277-2). Johns Hopkins.

Psychology & Diabetes: Psychosocial Factors in Management & Control. R. W. Shillitoe. (Psychology & Medicine Ser.). 288p. 1988. text ed. 55.00x (ISBN 0-412-33300-7, Pub. by Chapman & Hall UK). Sheridan Med Bks.

Psychology & Education. Robert M. Ogden. 350p. 1982. Repr. of 1932 ed. lib. bdg. 40.00 (ISBN 0-89984-364-6). Century Bookbindery.

Psychology & Education. Hirsch L. Silverman. LC 60-15961. 1961. 5.95 (ISBN 0-8022-1570-X). Philos Lib.

Psychology & Education of Exceptional Children & Adolescents: United States & International Perspectives. Ivan Z. Holowinsky. LC 82-61527. 352p. 1983. text ed. 26.95 (ISBN 0-916622-26-6). Princeton Bk Co.

Psychology & Education of the Gifted. 3rd ed. Ed. by Walter B. Barbe & Joseph S. Renzulli. LC 80-11174. 544p. 1981. pap. text ed. 19.95x (ISBN 0-8290-0234-0). Irvington.

Psychology & Education: The State of the Union. Ed. by Frank Farley & Neal J. Gordon. LC 80-82902. (National Society for the Study of Education Series on Contemporary Educational Issues). 400p. 1981. 28.00x (ISBN 0-8211-0506-X); text ed. 25.25x 10 or more copies. McCutchan.

Psychology & Educational Policy. Ed. by Jeri A. Sechzer & Sheila M. Pfafflin. (Annals of the New York Academy of Sciences: Vol. 517). 153p. 1987. 38.00 (ISBN 0-89766-429-9). NY Acad Sci.

Psychology & Environment. Claude Levy-Leboyer. Tr. by David Canter & Ian Griffiths. 200p. 1982. 29.95 (ISBN 0-8039-1789-9); pap. 14.95 (ISBN 0-8039-1790-2). Sage.

Psychology & FolkLore. Robert R. Marett. LC 74-10825. 286p. Repr. of 1920 ed. 34.00x (ISBN 0-8103-4045-3). Gale.

Psychology & Freudian Theory. Paul Kline. 200p. 1985. 26.00 (ISBN 0-416-36650-3, NO. 4076); pap. 9.95 (ISBN 0-416-36660-0, NO. 4077). Routledge Chapman & Hall.

Psychology & Gynaecological Problems. Annabel Broome & Louise Wallace. 320p. (Orig.). 1985. pap. 35.00x (ISBN 0-422-79460-0, 9250, Pub. by Tavistock England); pap. 13.95x (ISBN 0-422-78590-3, 9251). Routledge Chapman & Hall.

Psychology & Health. Myles Genest & Sharon Genest. LC 86-63680. (Health Psychology Ser.). 254p. (Orig.). 1986. pap. text ed. 16.95 (ISBN 0-87822-280-4). Res Press.

Psychology & Health. Ed. by Barbara L. Hammonds & C. James Scheirer. LC 84-71435. (Master Lecture Ser.: Vol. 3). 194p. (Orig.). 1984. pap. 24.00 (ISBN 0-912704-90-X, 4410030); members 18.00. Am Psychol.

Psychology & Health: Index of Modern Information. Manfred J. Robineault. LC 88-47616. 150p. 1988. 34.50 (ISBN 0-88164-858-2); pap. 26.50 (ISBN 0-88164-859-0). ABBE Pubs Assn.

Psychology & Historical Interpretation. Ed. by William M. Runyan. (Illus.). 320p. 1988. 24.95 (ISBN 0-19-505327-3); pap. text ed. 12.95 (ISBN 0-19-505328-1). Oxford U Pr.

Psychology & History. Harry E. Barnes. 59.95 (ISBN 0-87700-034-4). Revisionist Pr.

Psychology & Industrial Efficiency. Hugo Munsterberg. LC 73-2979. (Classics in Psychology Ser.). Repr. of 1913 ed. 20.00 (ISBN 0-405-05151-4). Ayer Co Pubs.

Psychology & Industrial Efficiency. Hugo Munsterberg. LC 72-9517. (Management History Ser.: No. 19). 329p. 1973. Repr. of 1913 ed. 25.00 (ISBN 0-87960-022-5). Hive Pub.

Psychology & Industry Today: An Introduction to Industrial & Organizational Psychology. 4th ed. Duane Schultz & Sydney E. Schultz. 735p. 1986. text ed. write for info. (ISBN 0-02-407610-4); instr's. manual avail. Macmillan.

Psychology & Instruction: A Practical Approach to Educational Psychology. Benjamin B. Lahey & Martha S. Johnson. 1978. pap. write for info. (ISBN 0-673-15040-2). Scott F.

Psychology & Its Allied Disciplines: Psychology & the Natural Sciences, Vol. III. Ed. by Marc H. Bornstein. 336p. 1984. pap. 24.95 (ISBN 0-89859-322-0). L Erlbaum Assocs.

Psychology & Its Allied Disciplines. Ed. by Marc H. Bornstein. (Cross Currents in Contemporary Psychology Bornstein Ser.). 992p. 1984. lib. bdg. 74.95 (ISBN 0-89859-318-2). L Erlbaum Assocs.

Psychology & Its Allied Disciplines, Vol. I: Psychology & the Humanities. Ed. by Marc H. Bornstein. 352p. 1984. 24.95 (ISBN 0-89859-320-4). L Erlbaum Assocs.

Psychology & Its Allied Disciplines, Vol. II: The Social Sciences. Ed. by Marc H. Bornstein. 304p. 1984. 24.95 (ISBN 0-89859-321-2). L Erlbaum Assocs.

Psychology & Its Practice: Index of Modern Information. Althea Y. Peltier. LC 88-47854. 150p. 1988. 34.50 (ISBN 0-88164-948-1); pap. text ed. 26.50 (ISBN 0-88164-949-X). ABBE Pubs Assn.

Psychology & Language: An Introduction to Psycholinguistics. Herbert H. Clark & Eve V. Clark. (Illus.). 608p. 1977. text ed. 28.00 (ISBN 0-15-572815-6, HC). HarBraceJ.

Psychology & Law: Can Justice Survive the Social Sciences? Daniel N. Robinson. 1980. pap. text ed. 9.95x (ISBN 0-19-502726-4). Oxford U Pr.

Psychology & Law: Topics from an International Conference. Ed. by Dave J. Muller et al. LC 83-21684. 496p. 1984. 76.00x (ISBN 0-471-90336-1). Wiley.

Psychology & Learning. Ed. by Barbara L. Hammonds. LC 84-73343. (Master Lecture Ser.: Vol. 4). 252p. (Orig.). 1985. pap. 24.00 (ISBN 0-912704-93-4, 4410040); members 18.00. Am Psychol.

Psychology & Life. 11th ed. Philip G. Zimbardo. 1985. text ed. write for info. (ISBN 0-673-15418-1). Scott F.

Psychology & Life. 12th ed. Philip G. Zimbardo. 1987. text ed. write for info. (ISBN 0-673-18938-4). Scott F.

Psychology & Literature in the Eighteenth Century. Ed. by Christopher Fox. LC 86-48001. (Studies in the Eighteenth Century: No. 8). 1987. 42.50 (ISBN 0-404-61474-4). AMS Pr.

Psychology & Logic, 2 Vols. J. R. Kantor. 1945-50. Set. 25.00 (ISBN 0-911188-36-3). Principia Pr.

Psychology & Marketing. 1986. write for info. Wiley.

Psychology & Mathematics: An Essay on Theory. Clyde H. Coombs. 104p. 1983. text ed. 13.95x (ISBN 0-472-10034-3). U of Mich Pr.

Psychology & Medical Care. 2nd ed. G. Kent & M. Dalgleish. (Illus.). 1100p. 1986. write for info. (ISBN 0-7020-1166-5, Bailliere-Tindall). Saunders.

Psychology & Medicine of Appetite Disorders: Research Subject Analysis with Reference Bibliography. Barbara C. Poole. LC 85-48101. 150p. 1987. 34.50 (ISBN 0-88164-474-9); pap. 26.50 (ISBN 0-88164-475-7). ABBE Pubs Assn.

Psychology & Medicine: Psychobiological Dimensions of Health & Illness. Donald A. Bakal. 288p. 1979. text ed. 27.95 (ISBN 0-8261-2580-8); pap. text ed. 19.95 (ISBN 0-8261-2581-6). Springer Pub.

Psychology & Mental Health of Afro-American Women: A Selected Bibliography. Ed. by Glenell S. Young & Janet Sims-Wood. LC 83-51604. (Resources on Afro-American Women Ser.: No. 1). 102p. 1984. pap. 6.95 (ISBN 0-915549-00-X). Afro Res Inc.

Psychology & Mental Retardation. Seymour B. Sarason. LC 85-603. 310p. 1985. pap. 21.00x (ISBN 0-936104-46-5, 1292). Pro Ed.

Psychology & Methods of Survival. Bernd W. Weiss & Frank Puskas. LC 84-82061. (Illus., Orig.). 1985. pap. text ed. 8.00 (ISBN 0-931373-01-8). Hiles & Hardin Pubs.

Psychology & Military Proficiency. Charles W. Bray. LC 69-13837. 1969. Repr. of 1948 ed. lib. bdg. 35.50x (ISBN 0-8371-1444-6, BRMI). Greenwood.

Psychology in Foreign Language Teaching. 2nd ed. Steven H. McDonough. (Illus.). 192p. 1987. pap. text ed. 13.95 (ISBN 0-04-418006-3). Unwin Hyman.

Psychology in India: The State-of-the-Art, Vol. 1: Personality & Mental Process. Ed. by Janak Pandey. 336p. 1988. text ed. 35.00 (ISBN 0-8039-9552-0). Sage.

Psychology in India: The State-of-the-Art, Vol. 2: Basic & Applied Social Psychology. Ed. by Janak Pandey. 356p. 1988. text ed. 35.00. Sage.

Psychology in India: The State-of-the-Art, Vol. 3: Organizational Behavior & Mental Health. Ed. by Janak Pandey. 342p. 1988. text ed. 35.00. Sage.

Psychology in Industrial Organizations. 5th ed. Norman R. Maier & Trudy G. Verser. LC 81-81702. (Illus.). 672p. 1982. text ed. 39.16 (ISBN 0-395-31740-1); instr's. Manual 1.56 (ISBN 0-395-31741-X). HM.

Psychology in Perspective. James Hassett. 640p. 1984. text ed. 39.50 scp (ISBN 0-06-042688-8, HarpC). Har-Row.

Psychology in Perspective. 2nd ed. James Hassett & Kathleen M. White. 750p. 1988. text ed. 36.95t (ISBN 0-06-042696-9, HarpC). Har-Row.

Psychology in Product Liability & Personal Injury Litigation. Martin I. Kurke & Robt. G. Meyer. 240p. 1986. 44.50 (ISBN 0-89116-467-7). Hemisphere Pub.

Psychology in Progress: An Interim Report, Vol. 270. Kurt Salzinger. (Annals of the New York Academy of Sciences). 1976. 9.50x (ISBN 0-89072-024-X). NY Acad Sci.

Psychology in Search of a Soul. John W. Drakeford. LC 64-15096. 1964. 13.95 (ISBN 0-8054-6701-7). Broadman.

Psychology in Teaching, Learning & Growth. 3rd ed. Don E. Hamachek. 1984. pap. text ed. 33.33 (ISBN 0-205-08248-3, 248248). Allyn.

Psychology in Teaching Reading. 2nd ed. Emarld V. Dechant. 1977. text ed. write for info. (ISBN 0-13-736686-8). P-H.

Psychology in the Common Cause. B. R. Bugelski. 1989. 39.85 (ISBN 0-275-93034-3, C3034). Praeger.

Psychology in the Dental Office. Ann Ehrlich. (Illus.). 1983. 5.50 (ISBN 0-940012-15-4). Colwell Syst.

Psychology in the Nineteen Nineties. Ed. by K. M. Lagerspetz & P. Niemi. (Advances in Psychology Ser.: Vol. 18). 534p. 1984. 92.00 (ISBN 0-444-86881-X). Elsevier.

Psychology in the Nursery School. Nelly Wolffheim. Tr. by Charles L. Hannam. LC 77-162630. 143p. 1972. Repr. of 1953 ed. lib. bdg. 35.00 (ISBN 0-8371-6197-5, WONS). Greenwood.

Psychology in the Schools in International Perspective, 3 Vols. Ed. by Calvin D. Catterall. 1976. Vol. I, pap. text ed. 7.50 (ISBN 0-917668-02-2); Vol. II, 1977. pap. text ed. 7.50 (ISBN 0-917668-01-4); Vol. III, 253P. 1979. pap. 7.50 (ISBN 0-917668-00-6). Intl Schl Psych.

Psychology in the U. S. S. R. An Historical Perspective. Ed. by Josef Brozek & Dan I. Slobin. LC 72-112930. 1972. Repr. 78.00 (ISBN 0-317-08146-2, 2021853). Bks Demand UMI.

Psychology in Twentieth Century Thought & Society. Ed. by Mitchell G. Ash & William R. Woodward. (Illus.). 304p. 1988. 42.50 (ISBN 0-521-32523-4). Cambridge U Pr.

Psychology in Use: Applications to Everyday Life. Duane P. Schultz. 1979. text ed. write for info. (ISBN 0-02-408060-8). Macmillan.

Psychology in Utopia: Toward a Social History of Soviet Psychology. Alex Kozulin. 180p. 1984. 22.00x (ISBN 0-262-11087-3). MIT Pr.

Psychology Is About People. H. J. Eysenck. LC 73-39003. 385p. 1972. 23.95 (ISBN 0-912050-19-5, Library Pr). Open Court.

Psychology Is Social: Readings & Conversations in Social Psychology. 2nd ed. Edward Krupat. 1982. pap. text ed. write for info. (ISBN 0-673-15382-7). Scott F.

Psychology-Judaism Reader. Reuven P. Bulka & Moshe H. Spero. (Illus.). 338p. 1982. pap. 27.00x (ISBN 0-398-04582-8). C C Thomas.

Psychology Made Simple. Abraham P. Sperling. (Made Simple Ser.). 1957. pap. 6.95 (ISBN 0-385-01248-7). Doubleday.

Psychology, Medicine & Christian Healing: A Revised & Expanded Edition of Healing & Christianity. Morton T. Kelsey. LC 87-46213. 448p. 1988. 24.95 (ISBN 0-317-67212-6, RD-742, HarpR); pap. 14.95 (ISBN 0-06-064383-8). Har-Row.

Psychology Misdirected. Seymour B. Sarason. LC 80-69283. 1981. 22.95 (ISBN 0-02-928100-8). Free Pr.

Psychology Moving East: The Status of Western Psychology in Asia. Geoffrey H. Blowers & Alison M. Turtle. (A WVSS Ser.). 300p. 1986. pap. 28.50 (ISBN 0-8133-7331-X). Westview.

Psychology of a Broken Heart: An Essay on Romantic Love. Gary Streit. (Orig.). 1987. pap. 9.95 (ISBN 0-9618180-0-X). Golden Blossom Pub.

Psychology of a Fairy Tale. David Hart. Ed. by Harriett Crosby. LC 76-56563. (Orig.). 1976. pap. 2.50x (ISBN 0-87574-210-6). Pendle-Hill.

Psychology of a Musical Prodigy. facs. ed. Geza Revesz. LC 70-114890. (Select Bibliographies Reprint Ser.). 1925. 17.00 (ISBN 0-8369-5294-4). Ayer Co Pubs.

Psychology of a Musical Prodigy. Geza Revesz. LC 77-173178. (Illus.). Repr. of 1925 ed. 18.00 (ISBN 0-405-08879-5). Ayer Co Pubs.

Psychology of a Musical Prodigy. Geza Revesz. 180p. 1980. Repr. of 1925 ed. lib. bdg. 45.00 (ISBN 0-89987-715-X). Darby Bks.

Psychology of a Musical Prodigy. Geza Revesz. 1970. Repr. of 1925 ed. lib. bdg. 35.00x (ISBN 0-8371-4004-8, REMP). Greenwood.

Psychology of a Musical Prodigy. Geza Revesz. (Psychology Ser.). 1970. Repr. of 1925 ed. 18.00 (ISBN 0-384-50360-8). Johnson Repr.

Psychology of a Primitive People: Study of the Australian Aborigine. facsimile ed. Stanley D. Porteus. LC 71-37910. (Select Bibliographies Reprint Ser.). Repr. of 1931 ed. 38.00 (ISBN 0-8369-6748-8). Ayer Co Pubs.

Psychology of Abnormal Behavior. Harold J. Vetter. LC 70-188883. pap. 156.00 (ISBN 0-317-07904-2, 2012422). Bks Demand UMI.

Psychology of Abnormal Behavior: A Dynamic Approach. Louis P. Thorpe & Barney Katz. LC 61-9428. (Illus.). pap. 160.00 (ISBN 0-317-10452-7, 2012531). Bks Demand UMI.

Psychology of Abuse. Michael C. Macpherson. LC 83-62297. 125p. (Orig.). 1985. pap. text ed. 11.95 (ISBN 0-88247-722-6). R & E Pubs.

Psychology of Adjustment. Houston. 1988. write for info. (ISBN 0-471-84808-5). Wiley.

Psychology of Adjustment. Kaplan & Stein. 446p. write for info. (ISBN 0-534-03245-1); write for info. study guide 125p. Watts.

Psychology of Adjustment. Paul S. Kaplan & Jean Stein. 446p. 1984. text ed. write for info. (ISBN 0-534-01031-8). Wadsworth Pub.

Psychology of Adjustment. Jack Rudman. (DANTES Ser.: No. 34). 1988. 25.95 (ISBN 0-8373-6684-4); pap. 13.95 (ISBN 0-8373-6634-8). Natl Learning.

Psychology of Adjustment & Human Relationships. 2nd ed. James F. Calhoun & Joan Acocella. LC 82-18078. 1983. text ed. write for info (ISBN 0-394-32906-6, RanC); study guide 8.00 (ISBN 0-394-33116-8). Random.

Psychology of Adjustment & Human Relationships. 3rd ed. James F. Calhoun & Joan R. Acocella. 608p. 1989. text ed. price not set (ISBN 0-394-38176-9); price not set study guide (ISBN 0-394-38737-6). Random.

Psychology of Adjustment & Well-Being. Stan Brodsky. 480p. 1988. pap. text ed. write for info. HR&W.

Psychology of Adjustment: Personal Experience & Development. Richard W. Coan. LC 82-13413. 558p. 1983. write for info tchr's. ed. (ISBN 0-471-87196-6). Wiley.

Psychology of Adjustment: Personal Growth in a Changing World. 3rd ed. Eastwood Atwater. (Illus.). 448p. Date not set. write for info. (ISBN 0-13-734864-9). P-H.

Psychology of Adolescence: Essential Readings. Ed. by Aaron H. Esman. LC 74-21177. 425p. (Orig.). 1975. text ed. 50.00x (ISBN 0-8236-5565-2). Intl Univs Pr.

Psychology of Advertising. Walter D. Scott. Ed. by Henry Assael. LC 78-305. (Century of Marketing Ser.). 1978. Repr. of 1913 ed. lib. bdg. 23.50x (ISBN 0-405-11171-1). Ayer Co Pubs.

Psychology of Affiliation: Experimental Studies of the Sources of Gregariousness. Stanley Schachter. 1959. 10.00x (ISBN 0-8047-0566-6). Stanford U Pr.

Psychology of Aging: Theory, Research & Practice. Janet K. Belsky. LC 83-20923. (Psychology Ser.). 550p. 1984. text ed. 21.50 pub net (ISBN 0-534-02868-3). Brooks-Cole.

Psychology of Alcoholism. George B. Cutten. Ed. by Gerald N. Grob. LC 80-1223. (Addiction in America Ser.). 1981. Repr. of 1907 ed. lib. bdg. 32.00x (ISBN 0-405-13579-3). Ayer Co Pubs.

Psychology of Alcoholism: Medical & Scientific Guide for Reference & Research. Kathleen U. Langston. LC 83-46097. 150p. 1985. 34.50 (ISBN 0-88164-126-X); pap. 26.50 (ISBN 0-88164-127-8). ABBE Pubs Assn.

Psychology of Animal Learning. N. J. Mackintosh. 1974. 60.00 (ISBN 0-12-464650-6). Acad Pr.

Psychology of Anomalous Experience. rev. ed. Graham Reed. 210p. 1988. pap. 15.95 (ISBN 0-87975-435-4). Prometheus Bks.

Psychology of Anxiety. 2nd ed. Eugene E. Levitt. LC 80-107. 188p. 1980. text ed. 19.50 (ISBN 0-89859-040-X). L Erlbaum Assocs.

Psychology of Apartheid. Peter Lambley. LC 80-53595. 318p. 1981. 25.00x (ISBN 0-8203-0548-0). U of Ga Pr.

Psychology of Architectural Design. Akin Omer. (Architecture & Design Ser.). 205p. 1986. 29.95 (ISBN 0-85086-120-9, 9982, Pub. by Pion England). Routledge Chapman & Hall.

Psychology of Aristotle: In Particular His Doctrine of the Active Intellect with an Appendix Concerning the Activity of Aristotle's God. Franz Brentano. Tr. by Rolf George. LC 75-17303. 1977. 30.00x (ISBN 0-520-03081-8). U of Cal Pr.

Psychology of Attachment & Bonding: Index of Modern Information. Lottie F. Lydeen. LC 88-47600. 150p. 1988. 34.50 (ISBN 0-88164-790-X); pap. 26.50 (ISBN 0-88164-791-8). ABBE Pubs Assn.

Psychology of Attempted Suicide: A Medical Subject Analysis with Reference Bibliography. Harold P. Drummond. LC 85-48081. 150p. (Orig.). 1986. 34.50 (ISBN 0-88164-434-X); pap. 26.50 (ISBN 0-88164-435-8). ABBE Pubs Assn.

Psychology of Beauty. Ethel D. Puffer. 286p. 1979. Repr. of 1905 ed. lib. bdg. 40.00 (ISBN 0-8495-4378-9). R West.

Psychology of Behavior in Organization. Elizabeth Chell. 252p. 1987. 53.00x (ISBN 0-333-39676-6, Pub. by Macmillan Pr Ltd). Intl Spec Bk.

Psychology of Birth. Leslie Feher. 224p. 1985. Repr. of 1980 ed. text ed. 15.00 (ISBN 0-9612182-1-5). Assn Birth Psych.

Psychology of Blacks: An Afro-American Perspective. Joseph L. White. 180p. 1984. pap. 16.00 (ISBN 0-13-735134-8). P-H.

Psychology of Blindness. Donald D. Kirtley. LC 74-17155. 376p. 1974. 25.95x (ISBN 0-88229-178-5). Nelson-Hall.

Psychology of C. G. Jung. Jolande Jacobi. Tr. by Ralph Manheim. (Illus.). 1973. pap. 10.95 (ISBN 0-300-01674-3, Y75). Yale U Pr.

Psychology of C. G. Jung. C. A. Meier. Tr. by Eugene Rolfe. LC 85-13996. (Unconscious in Its Empirical Manifestations Ser.: Vol. I). (Illus.). 236p. 1985. 25.50 (ISBN 0-938434-10-1). Sigo Pr.

Psychology of C. G. Jung: The Meaning & Significance of Dreams, Vol. II. C. A. Meier. 1987. 25.50 (ISBN 0-938434-11-X). Sigo Pr.

Psychology of Call-Reluctance: How to Overcome the Fear of Self-Promotion. George W. Dudley. LC 85-73334. 208p. (Orig.). 1986. 26.95 (ISBN 0-935907-00-9); pap. 18.95 (ISBN 0-935907-01-7). Behavioral Sci.

Psychology of Cancer: Prevention & Survival. Peter Lambley. 240p. 1987. 26.50x (ISBN 0-356-10513-X, Pub. by MacD & Co). Trans-Atl Phila.

Psychology of Character: With a Survey of Temperament. Abraham A. Roback. LC 73-2988. (Classics in Psychology Ser.). Repr. of 1927 ed. 34.00 (ISBN 0-405-05160-3). Ayer Co Pubs.

Psychology of Chess. W. R. Hartston & P. C. Wason. (Illus.). 144p. 15.95 (ISBN 0-87196-226-8). Facts on File.

Psychology of Chess Skill. Dennis H. Holding. 228p. 1985. text ed. 34.50 (ISBN 0-89859-575-4). L Erlbaum Assocs.

Psychology of Child Development. S. Bhattacharya. 1986. text ed. 25.00x (ISBN 81-207-0041-4, Pub. by Sterling Pubs India). Apt Bks.

Psychology of Child Firesetting: Detection & Intervention. Jessica Gaynor & Chris Hatcher. LC 88-21642. 180p. 1986. 27.50 (ISBN 0-87630-445-5). Brunner-Mazel.

Psychology of Child Firesetting: Detection & Intervention. Jessica Gaynor & Chris Hatcher. 1986. 25.00 (ISBN 0-318-23305-3). Phoenix Soc.

Psychology of Childbirth. Aidan Macfarlane. (Developing Child Ser.). 1977. pap. 3.95 (ISBN 0-674-72106-3). Harvard U Pr.

Psychology of Childbirth: An Introduction for Mothers & Midwives. 2nd ed. Joyce Prince & Margret E. Adams. LC 86-26359. (Illus.). 219p. (Orig.). 1987. pap. text ed. 14.50 (ISBN 0-443-03388-9). Churchill.

Psychology of Childhood Illness. C. Eiser. (Contributions to Psychology & Medicine). (Illus.). 210p. 1985. 30.00 (ISBN 0-387-96096-1). Springer-Verlag.

Psychology of Choice & the Assumptions of Economics. Richard Thaler. (Working Papers on Risk & Rationality). Date not set. 2.50 (RR3). IPPP.

Psychology of Christian Personality. Ernest M. Ligon. LC 35-22951. 1975. 7.00 (ISBN 0-915744-00-7); pap. 4.00 (ISBN 0-915744-01-5). Character Res.

Psychology of Closing Sales. Forrest H. Patton. 192p. 1984. pap. 7.95 (ISBN 0-13-735663-3). P-H.

Psychology of Clothes. J. C. Flugel. (Illus.). 1969. text ed. 30.00x (ISBN 0-8236-5580-6); pap. 9.95x (ISBN 0-8236-8260-9). Intl Univs Pr.

Psychology of Clothes. John C. Flugel. LC 75-41097. Repr. of 1930 ed. 32.50 (ISBN 0-404-14721-6). AMS Pr.

Psychology of Clothing. George Van Ness Dearborn. Bd. with Some Imaginal Factors Influencing Verbal Expression. E. E. Shaw. Repr. of 1918 ed; Learning Curve Equation. L. L. Thurstone. Repr. of 1919 ed; Effect of Alcohol on the Intelligent Behavior of the White Rat & Its Progeny. A. H. Arlitt. Repr. of 1919 ed; Form of the Learning Curves for Memory. C. L. Kjerstad. Repr. of 1919 ed; Introspective Analysis of the Process of Comparing. S. W. Fernberger. Repr. of 1919 ed. (Psychological Monographs, General & Applied: Vol. 26). pap. 36.00 (ISBN 0-8115-1425-0). Kraus Repr.

Psychology of Cognition. 2nd ed. Gillian Cohen. 1983. 36.00 (ISBN 0-12-178760-5); pap. 17.50 (ISBN 0-12-178762-1). Acad Pr.

Psychology of College Success: A Dynamic Approach. Henry C. Lindgren. LC 79-25614. 158p. 1980. Repr. of 1969 ed. lib. bdg. 9.50 (ISBN 0-89874-035-5). Krieger.

Psychology of Color & Design. Deborah T. Sharpe. (Quality Paperback: No. 313). 170p. 1975. pap. 7.95 (ISBN 0-8226-0313-6). Littlefield.

Psychology of Color & Design. Deborah T. Sharpe. LC 73-91308. 184p. 1974. 16.95x (ISBN 0-88229-107-6). Nelson-Hall.

Psychology of Commitment: Experiments Linking Behavior to Belief. Charles A. Kiesler. (Social Psychology Ser.). 1971. 19.95 (ISBN 0-12-406450-7). Acad Pr.

Psychology of Computer Programming. Gerald M. Weinberg. 228p. 1988. pap. text ed. 25.95 (ISBN 0-442-20764-6). Van Nos Reinhold.

Psychology of Computer Use. Ed. by Thomas Green et al. (Computers & People Ser.). 1983. 30.00 (ISBN 0-12-297420-4). Acad Pr.

Psychology of Conflict & Combat. Ben Shalit. LC 87-23729. 224p. 1988. lib. bdg. 39.95 (ISBN 0-275-92753-9, C2753). Praeger.

Psychology of Consciousness. Ruth Norman. (Illus.). 725p. (Orig.). 1985. spiral bdg. 55.00 (ISBN 0-932642-97-7). Unarius Pubns.

Psychology of Consciousness. 2nd ed. Robert E. Ornstein. (Illus.). 255p. (Orig.). 1977. pap. text ed. 15.00 net (ISBN 0-15-573082-7, HC). HarBraceJ.

Psychology of Consciousness. Robert E. Ornstein. 1975. pap. 5.95 (ISBN 0-14-021679-0, Pelican). Penguin.

Psychology of Control. Ellen J. Langer. 312p. 1983. pap. 12.95 (ISBN 0-8039-1963-8). Sage.

Psychology of Control & Aging. Ed. by Margaret M. Baltes & Paul B. Baltes. 456p. 1986. text ed. 49.95 (ISBN 0-89859-701-3). L Erlbaum Assocs.

Psychology of Conviction: A Study of Beliefs & Attitudes. Joseph Jastrow. 1979. Repr. of 1918 ed. lib. bdg. 40.00 (ISBN 0-8495-2744-9). Arden Lib.

Psychology of Coronary & CV (Cardiovascular) Diseases: A Subject Analysis & Bibliography. Rosetta R. Hardine. LC 85-48079. 150p. (Orig.). 1987. 34.50 (ISBN 0-88164-430-7); pap. 26.50 (ISBN 0-88164-431-5). ABBE Pubs Assn.

Psychology of Cosmetic Treatments. Jean A. Graham & A. M. Klingman. 1985. 29.95 (ISBN 0-318-23307-X). Phoenix Soc.

Psychology of Cosmetic Treatments. Ed. by Jean Ann Graham & Albert M. Kligman. LC 84-26657. 272p. 1985. 40.95 (ISBN 0-275-91315-5, C1315). Praeger.

Psychology of Counseling. Clyde M. Narramore. 14.95 (ISBN 0-310-29930-6, 10409). Zondervan.

Psychology of Creative Dating. Jack DeFilippis & Richard Kraus. LC 85-72774. 198p. 1986. pap. 15.95 (ISBN 0-915202-55-7). Accel Devel.

Psychology of Creativity. Margaret Gilchrist. (Second Century in Australian Education Ser.: Vol. 4). 102p. 1972. pap. 7.50x (ISBN 0-522-84024-8, Pub. by Melbourne U Pr). Intl Spec Bk.

Psychology of Creativity & Discovery: Scientists & Their Work. Richard S. Mansfield & Thomas V. Busse. LC 80-29219. 164p. 1981. 19.95x (ISBN 0-88229-653-1). Nelson-Hall.

Psychology of Crime. David Abrahamsen. LC 59-13606. 1960. 27.50x (ISBN 0-231-02274-3). Columbia U Pr.

Psychology of Crime. David Abrahamsen. LC 59-13606. pap. 93.00 (ISBN 0-317-26424-9, 2024976). Bks Demand UMI.

Psychology of Crime & Criminal Justice. Ed. by Hans Toch. 497p. 1986. pap. text ed. 17.95x (ISBN 0-88133-228-3). Waveland Pr.

Psychology of Deafness: Senory Deprivation, Learning & Adjustment. 2nd ed. Helmer R. Myklebust. (Illus.). 436p. 1964. 44.50 (ISBN 0-8089-0339-X, 793027). Grune.

Psychology of Death. Robert Kastenbaum & Ruth Aisenberg. LC 75-28203. 460p. 1976. pap. text ed. 22.95 (ISBN 0-8261-1920-4). Springer Pub.

Psychology of Deductive Reasoning. Jonathan S. Evans. (International Library of Psychology). 190p. 1982. 29.95x (ISBN 0-7100-0923-2). Routledge Chapman & Hall.

Psychology of Dementia Praecox. Carl G. Jung. (Nervous & Mental Disease Monographs: No. 3). 1909. 19.00 (ISBN 0-384-28229-6). Johnson Repr.

Psychology of Dental Care. G. Kent. (Dental Practitional Handbk.: No. 34). (Illus.). 168p. 1984. pap. 22.00 (ISBN 0-7236-0757-5). PSG Pub Co.

Psychology of Development & History. Klaus F. Riegel. LC 76-26547. (Illus.). 272p. 1976. 45.00x (ISBN 0-306-30930-0, Plenum Pr). Plenum Pub.

Psychology of Dictatorship: Based on an Examination of the Leaders of Nazi Germany. G. M. Gilbert. LC 79-15335. (Illus.). 1979. Repr. of 1950 ed. lib. bdg. 35.00x (ISBN 0-313-21975-3, GIPD). Greenwood.

Psychology of Disability. Carolyn L. Vash. (Springer Series on Rehabilitation: Vol. 1). 288p. 1981. text ed. 24.95; adoption orders 16.95 (ISBN 0-8261-3340-1). Springer Pub.

Psychology of Discipleship. Douglas Baker. 1987. 110.00x (ISBN 0-906006-05-8, Pub. by Claregate Coll UK). State Mutual Bk.

Psychology of Discipline: Six Approaches to Discipline. Darwin Dorr et al. LC 81-20775. xi, 253p. 1981. text ed. 30.00X (ISBN 0-8236-5581-4). Intl Univs Pr.

Psychology of Dreams. Paul R. Robbins. LC 87-29889. 183p. 1988. lib. bdg. 19.95x (ISBN 0-89950-270-9). McFarland & Co.

Psychology of Dreams & of Mental Conflicts. C. D. Valentine. (Illus.). 116p. 1987. 127.75 (ISBN 0-89920-178-4). Am Inst Psych.

Psychology of Medicine. T. W. Mitchell. 1922. 30.00 (ISBN 0-8274-4240-8). R West.

Psychology of Meditation. Ed. by Michael A. West. (Illus.). 272p. 1987. 65.00 (ISBN 0-19-852169-3). Oxford U Pr.

Psychology of Men. Reuben Fine. 250p. cancelled. Aronson.

Psychology of Men: New Psychoanalytic Perspectives. Ed. by Gerald J. Fogel et al. LC 85-48022. 320p. 1986. text ed. 27.95x (ISBN 0-465-06718-2). Basic.

Psychology of Mental Disorders: Medical Guidebook for Reference & Research. Althea Y. Peltier. LC 84-45216. 150p. 1985. 34.50 (ISBN 0-88164-184-7); pap. 26.50 (ISBN 0-88164-185-5). ABBE Pubs Assn.

Psychology of Mental Retardation. I. Biler & M. Sternlicht. LC 77-4137. 800p. 1977. 39.95x (ISBN 0-88437-013-5). Psych Dimensions.

Psychology of Misconduct, Vice & Crime. Bernard Hollander. (Historical Foundations of Forensic Psychiatry & Psychology Ser.). 220p. 1980. Repr. of 1922 ed. lib. bdg. 27.50 (ISBN 0-306-76063-0). Da Capo.

Psychology of Money Making & How to Master It. F. W. Taussig. (Library of Scientific Psychology). (Illus.). 121p. 1983. 117.75 (ISBN 0-89266-381-2). Am Classical Coll Pr.

Psychology of Moral Development. Lawerence Kohlberg. LC 83-47726. (Essays on Moral Development Ser.: Vol. 2). 496p. 1983. 35.95 (ISBN 0-06-064761-2, HarpR). Har-Row.

Psychology of Motor Behavior. Ed. by Leonard Zaichkowsky & C. Zvi Fuchs. (Illus.). 300p. 1986. pap. 29.95 (ISBN 0-932392-24-5). Mouvement Pubns.

Psychology of Motor Behavior & Sport, 1976, 2 vols. North American Society for the Psychology of Sport & Physical Activity Staff. Ed. by Robert W. Christina & Daniel M. Landers. LC 78-641529. Vol. 1. pap. 74.00 (ISBN 0-317-55475-1, 2029528); Vol. 2. pap. 70.80 (ISBN 0-317-55476-X). Bks Demand UMI.

Psychology of Motor Behavior & Sport, 1979. North American Society for the Psychology of Sport & Physical Activity Staff. Ed. by Claude H. Nadeau. LC 78-641529. pap. 160.00 (ISBN 0-317-55485-9, 2029530). Bks Demand UMI.

Psychology of Motor Behavior & Sport, 1978. North American Society for the Psychology of Sport & Physical Activity Staff. Ed. by Glyn C. Roberts & Karl M. Newell. LC 78-641529. pap. 77.30 (ISBN 0-317-55489-1, 2029531). Bks Demand UMI.

Psychology of Motor Behavior & Sport, 1980. North American Society for the Psychology of Sport & Physical Staff. Ed. by Glyn C. Roberts & Daniel M. Landers. LC 78-641529. pap. 55.00 (ISBN 0-317-55496-4, 2029533). Bks Demand UMI.

Psychology of Motor Learning. Joseph B. Oxendine. (Illus.). 352p. 1984. write for info. (ISBN 0-13-736603-5). P-H.

Psychology of Murder: A Study in Criminal Psychology. Andreas Bjerre. Tr. by E. Classen from Swedish. (Historical Foundations of Forensic Psychiatry & Psychology Ser.). 164p. 1980. Repr. lib. bdg. 22.50 (ISBN 0-306-76067-3). Da Capo.

Psychology of Music. John B. Davies. LC 77-92339. (Illus.). 240p. 1978. 22.50x (ISBN 0-8047-0980-7); pap. 7.95 (ISBN 0-8047-1057-0, SP-158). Stanford U Pr.

Psychology of Music. Diana Deutsch. 1984. pap. 32.95 (ISBN 0-12-213562-8). Acad Pr.

Psychology of Music. Ed. by Diana Deutsch. LC 82-1646. (AO Series in Cognition & Perception). 1982. 56.50 (ISBN 0-12-213560-1). Acad Pr.

Psychology of Music. James Mursell. 1988. Repr. lib. bdg. 25.00x. Am Biog Serv.

Psychology of Music. James L. Mursell. LC 77-110274. (Illus.). 389p. 1971. Repr. of 1937 ed. lib. bdg. 41.50x (ISBN 0-8371-4500-7, MUPM). Greenwood.

Psychology of Music. James L. Mursell. LC 37-28429. (Music - Practice & Theory Ser). 1970. Repr. of 1937 ed. 26.00 (ISBN 0-384-40680-7). Johnson Repr.

Psychology of Music. James L. Mursell. lib. bdg. 25.00x (ISBN 0-403-01750-5). Scholarly.

Psychology of Music. H. P. Rao. (Illus.). 80p. 1986. Repr. 15.00X (ISBN 0-8364-1765-8, Pub. by Abhinav India). South Asia Bks.

Psychology of Music. Carl E. Seashore. pap. 6.95 (ISBN 0-486-21851-1). Dover.

Psychology of Music. Carl E. Seashore. (Illus.). 14.25 (ISBN 0-8446-2898-0). Peter Smith.

Psychology of Music: A Survey for Teacher & Musician. Max Schoen. LC 73-181248. 258p. 1940. Repr. 39.00x (ISBN 0-403-01673-8). Scholarly.

Psychology of Music: A Survey for Teacher & Musician. Max Schoen. 1988. Repr. of 1940 ed. lib. bdg. 49.00x. Am Biog Serv.

Psychology of Music Teaching. Edwin Gordon. (Contemporary Perspectives in Music Education Ser.). (Illus.). 1971. ref. ed. o.p. 14.95 (ISBN 0-13-736215-3). P-H.

Psychology of Musical Ability. 2nd ed. Rosamund Shuter-Dyson & Clive Gabriel. 1982. 25.00x (ISBN 0-416-71300-9, NO. 3498). Routledge Chapman & Hall.

Psychology of Mysticism, 2 Vols. Max Nordau. 271p. 1985. Set. 249.50 (ISBN 0-89920-099-0). Am Inst Psych.

Psychology of Myth, Folklore & Religion. Leo Schneiderman. LC 81-9471. 232p. 1981. text ed. 21.95x (ISBN 0-88229-659-0); pap. text ed. 10.95x (ISBN 0-88229-783-X). Nelson-Hall.

Psychology of Occupations. Anne Roe. Ed. by Leon Stein. LC 77-70529. (Work Ser.). (Illus.). 1977. Repr. of 1956 ed. lib. bdg. 32.00x (ISBN 0-405-10197-X). Ayer Co Pubs.

Psychology of Ordinary Explanations of Social Behavior. Ed. by Charles Antaki. (European Monographs in Social Psychology: No. 23). 352p. 1981. 66.00 (ISBN 0-12-058960-5). Acad Pr.

Psychology of Pain. 2nd ed. Ed. by Richard A. Sternbach. 256p. 1986. text ed. 36.00 (ISBN 0-88167-248-3). Raven.

Psychology of Pain in Health & Disease: Medical Analysis Index with Research Bibliography. Cristina Valencia. LC 85-47859. 150p. 1988. 34.50 (ISBN 0-88164-394-7); pap. 26.50 (ISBN 0-88164-395-5). ABBE Pubs Assn.

Psychology of Peoples. Gustave Le Bon. LC 73-14164. (Perspectives in Social Inquiry Ser.). 252p. 1974. Repr. 17.00x (ISBN 0-405-05509-9). Ayer Co Pubs.

Psychology of Perception: A Philosophical Examination of Gestalt Theory & Derivative Theories of Perception. D. W. Hamlyn. (Studies in Philosophical Psychology). 1961. pap. text ed. 7.95x (ISBN 0-391-01104-9). Humanities.

Psychology of Performing Arts. Glenn Wilson. LC 85-12533. 180p. 1985. 27.50 (ISBN 0-312-65316-6). St Martin.

Psychology of Person Identification. Brian Clifford & Ray Bull. 1978. 29.95x (ISBN 0-7100-8867-1). Routledge Chapman & Hall.

Psychology of Personality. English Bagby. Repr. of 1928 ed. 25.00. Darby Bks.

Psychology of Personality. English Bagby. 236p. 1980. Repr. of 1928 ed. lib. bdg. 35.00 (ISBN 0-8492-3590-1). R West.

Psychology of Personality. Carducci. 1988. write for info. (ISBN 0-471-81146-7). Wiley.

Psychology of Personality. Bernard Notcutt. 1953. 6.95 (ISBN 0-8022-1228-X). Philos Lib.

Psychology of Personality. P. F. Valentine. 1936. 30.00 (ISBN 0-8495-6259-7). Arden Lib.

Psychology of Personality: An Epistemological Inquiry. James T. Lamiell. (Critical Assessments of Contemporary Psychology). (Illus.). 256p. 1987. text ed. 30.00 (ISBN 0-231-06020-3). Columbia U Pr.

Psychology of Perspective & Renaissance Art. Michael Kubovy. 200p. 1986. 39.50 (ISBN 0-521-25376-4). Cambridge U Pr.

Psychology of Perspective & Renaissance Art. Michael Kubovy. (Illus.). 208p. Date not set. pap. 15.95 (ISBN 0-521-36849-9). Cambridge U Pr.

Psychology of Pessimism & Optimism & Its Effects upon Literature, Science, Morality & the History of Mankind. Elie Metchnikoff. (Illus.). 137p. 1987. 137.75 (ISBN 0-89920-167-9). Am Inst Psych.

Psychology of Phantasy. I. Roset. 247p. 1984. 7.95 (ISBN 0-8285-2977-9, Pub. by Progress Pubs USSR). Imported Pubns.

Psychology of Physical Symptoms. James W. Pennebaker. (Illus.). 192p. 1982. 32.00 (ISBN 0-387-90730-0). Springer-Verlag.

Psychology of Picture Perception. John Kennedy. (Jossey-Bass Behavioral Science Ser.). pap. 47.50 (ISBN 0-317-20844-6, 2023880). Bks Demand UMI.

Psychology of Place. David Canter. LC 77-73621. (Illus.). 1977. write for info. (ISBN 0-312-65322-0). St Martin.

Psychology of Play. Susanna Millar. LC 74-4394. 288p. 1974. 20.00x (ISBN 0-87668-140-2). Aronson.

Psychology of Play. Brian Sutton-Smith. LC 75-35082. (Studies in Play & Games). (Illus.). 1976. Repr. 32.00x (ISBN 0-405-07930-3). Ayer Co Pubs.

Psychology of Play Activities. Harvey C. Lehman & Paul A. Witty. LC 75-35074. (Studies in Play & Games). (Illus.). 1976. Repr. 20.00x (ISBN 0-405-07924-9). Ayer Co Pubs.

Psychology of Political Control. Ann E. Freedman & P. E. Freedman. LC 75-10556. 224p. 1975. pap. text ed. 11.50 (ISBN 0-312-65310-7). St Martin.

Psychology of Political Science: With Special Consideration for the Political Acumen of Destutt de Tracy. John M. Dorsey. 262p. 1973. 24.95x (ISBN 0-8143-1641-7). Wayne St U Pr.

Psychology of Political Violence. Emma Goldman. 59.95 (ISBN 0-87968-160-8). Gordon Pr.

Psychology of Politics. 2nd ed. W. F. Stone & P. E. Shaffner. (Illus.). 330p. 1988. 34.00 (ISBN 0-387-96674-9). Springer-Verlag.

Psychology of Politics. William F. Stone. LC 73-17647. (Illus.). 1974. 17.00 (ISBN 0-02-931690-1); pap. text ed. 8.95 (ISBN 0-02-931680-4). Free Pr.

Psychology of Preschool Children. A. V. Zaporozhets & D. B. Elkonin. Tr. by J. Shybut & S. Simon. 1971. pap. 6.95x (ISBN 0-262-74011-7). MIT Pr.

Psychology of Psinging. Al Berkman. 1977. 12.95 (ISBN 0-934972-08-7). Melrose Bk Co.

Psychology of Questions. Ed. by Arthur C. Graesser & John B. Black. 392p. 1985. text ed. 39.95 (ISBN 0-89859-444-8). L Erlbaum Assocs.

Psychology of Radio. Hadley Cantril & Gordon W. Allport. LC 72-161159. (History of Broadcasting: Radio to Television Ser). 1971. Repr. of 1935 ed. 23.50 (ISBN 0-405-03574-8). Ayer Co Pubs.

Psychology of Re-education. Paul Diel. Tr. by Raymond Rosenthal from Fr. LC 86-29687. 250p. 1987. 27.50 (ISBN 0-87773-367-8). Shambhala Pubns.

Psychology of Reading. Robert G. Crowder. (Illus.). 1982. pap. text ed. 12.95x (ISBN 0-19-503139-3). Oxford U Pr.

Psychology of Reading. Eleanor J. Gibson & Harry Levin. 1975. pap. 13.95x (ISBN 0-262-57052-1). MIT Pr.

Psychology of Reading. Alan Kennedy. 180p. 1984. pap. 9.95 (ISBN 0-416-35940-X, NO. 3931); 22.00 (ISBN 0-416-38220-7, 3930). Routledge Chapman & Hall.

Psychology of Reading. Insup Taylor & Martin Taylor. 1983. 33.00 (ISBN 0-12-684080-6). Acad Pr.

Psychology of Reading & Language Comprehension. Just & Carpenter. 1986. 37.33 (ISBN 0-205-08760-4). Allyn.

Psychology of Reading & Spelling. A. I. Gates. LC 73-176798. (Columbia University. Teachers College. Contributions to Education: No. 129). Repr. of 1922 ed. 22.50 (ISBN 0-404-55129-7). AMS Pr.

Psychology of Reading & Spelling Disabilities. A. F. Jorm. (International Library of Psychology). 150p. 1983. pap. 12.95x (ISBN 0-7100-9344-6). Routledge Chapman & Hall.

Psychology of Reasoning. Eugenio Rignano. Tr. by Winifred A. Holl. 1978. Repr. of 1923 ed. 40.00 (ISBN 0-8492-2373-3). R West.

Psychology of Reasoning: Structure & Content. P. C. Wason & P. N. Johnson-Laird. LC 78-189160. 1972. 16.00x (ISBN 0-674-72126-8); pap. 8.95x (ISBN 0-674-72127-6). Harvard U Pr.

Psychology of Redemption. Oswald Chambers. 1955. pap. 3.95 (ISBN 0-87508-124-X). Chr Lit.

Psychology of Relaxation. George T. Patrick. Repr. of 1916 ed. 25.00. Darby Bks.

Psychology of Religion. Joseph F. Byrnes. LC 84-47854. 320p. 1984. 27.95x (ISBN 0-02-903580-5). Free Pr.

Psychology of Religion. George A. Coe. LC 75-3113. Repr. of 1916 ed. 40.00 (ISBN 0-404-59109-4). AMS Pr.

Psychology of Religion. George A. Coe. Repr. of 1916 ed. 25.00. Darby Bks.

Psychology of Religion. Heije Faber. LC 75-43721. 348p. 1976. 13.95 (ISBN 0-664-20748-0). Westminster John Knox.

Psychology of Religion: A Guide to Information Sources. Ed. by Donald Capps et al. LC 73-17530. (Philosophy & Religion Information Guide Ser.: Vol. 1). vii, 364p. 1976. 68.00x (ISBN 0-8103-1356-1). Gale.

Psychology of Religion: An Empirical Approach. Bernard Spilka et al. (Illus.). 400p. 1985. text ed. write for info. (ISBN 0-13-736398-2). P-H.

Psychology of Religion: Religion in Individual Lives. Mary J. Meadow & Richard D. Kahoe. 488p. 1984. text ed. 27.50 scp (ISBN 0-06-044411-8, HarpC). Har-Row.

Psychology of Religious Belief. L. B. Brown. 1987. 48.00 (ISBN 0-12-136355-4); pap. 24.00 (ISBN 0-12-136356-2). Acad Pr.

Psychology of Religious Belief. James B. Pratt. LC 75-3326. (Philosophy of America Ser.). Repr. of 1907 ed. 34.00 (ISBN 0-404-59321-6). AMS Pr.

Psychology of Religious Experiences. Erwin R. Goodenough. (Brown Classics in Judaica Ser.). 214p. 1986. pap. text ed. 11.50 (ISBN 0-8191-4489-4). U Pr of Amer.

Psychology of Religious Knowing. Fraser Watts & Mark Williams. (Illus.). 180p. 1988. 34.50 (ISBN 0-521-32610-9). Cambridge U Pr.

Psychology of Religious Ritual. Manly P. Hall. pap. 2.50 (ISBN 0-89314-347-2). Philos Res.

Psychology of Religious Sects. Henry C. McComas. LC 70-172763. Repr. of 1912 ed. 20.00 (ISBN 0-404-04107-8). AMS Pr.

Psychology of Religious Vocations: Problems of the Religious Life. Andre Godin. Ed. by LeRoy A. Wauck. LC 82-24708. 136p. (Orig.). 1983. lib. bdg. 25.25 (ISBN 0-8191-3007-9); pap. text ed. 10.00 (ISBN 0-8191-3008-7). U Pr of Amer.

Psychology of Revolution. Gustave Le Bon. LC 68-29699. 1968. Repr. of 1913 ed. flexible cover 12.00 (ISBN 0-87034-026-3). Fraser Pub Co.

Psychology of Rigorous Humanism. Joseph F. Rychlak. LC 76-54838. (Illus.). 1977. pap. 140.30 (ISBN 0-317-07998-0, 2019889). Bks Demand UMI.

Psychology of Rigorous Humanism. 2nd ed. Joseph F. Rychlak. 560p. 1988. 32.00x (ISBN 0-8147-7402-4). NYU Pr.

Psychology of Rollo May: A Study in Existential Theory & Psychotherapy. Clement Reeves. LC 76-50708. (Social & Behavioral Science Ser.). 1977. text ed. 35.95x (ISBN 0-87589-303-1). Jossey-Bass.

Psychology of Romantic Love. Nathaniel Branden. 288p. 1981. pap. 4.50 (ISBN 0-553-25309-3). Bantam.

Psychology of Rumor. Gordon W. Allport & Leo Postman. LC 65-18784. (Illus.). 1965. Repr. of 1947 ed. 20.00x (ISBN 0-8462-0564-5). Russell.

Psychology of Schizophrenia. John Cutting. LC 84-15578. (Illus.). 457p. 1985. text ed. 72.00 (ISBN 0-443-02663-7). Churchill.

Psychology of Science: A Reconnaissance. Abraham H. Maslow. LC 66-11479. 190p. 1966. pap. 3.95 (ISBN 0-89526-972-4). Regnery Gateway.

Psychology of Science & Morality in the Internal Evolution of Man. Elie Metchnikoff. (Illus.). 127p. 1988. 127.45 (ISBN 0-89920-175-X). Am Inst Psych.

Psychology of Scientific Thinking. Ernst Friedlander. LC 65-11636. 1965. 5.95 (ISBN 0-8022-0548-8). Philos Lib.

Psychology of Second Language Learning: Papers from the Second International Congress of Applied Linguistics, Cambridge, 8-12 Sept., 1969. International Congress of Applied Linguistics (2nd: 1969: Cambridge, Enlgand) Ed. by Paul Pimsleur & Terence Quinn. LC 75-173811. pap. 51.50 (ISBN 0-317-27583-6, 2024517). Bks Demand UMI.

Psychology of Self & Other. Elizabeth Moberly. 112p. 1985. 17.95 (ISBN 0-422-79740-5, 9417, Pub. by Tavistock England). Routledge Chapman & Hall.

Psychology of Self-Determination. Edward L. Deci. LC 80-8373. 1980. 26.00x (ISBN 0-669-04045-2); pap. 14.00x (ISBN 0-669-09813-2). Lexington Bks.

Psychology of Self-Esteem. Nathaniel Branden. 1971. pap. 4.95 (ISBN 0-553-25990-3). Bantam.

Psychology of Separation & Loss: Perspectives on Development, Life Transitions, & Clinical Practice. Jonathan Bloom-Feshbach et al. LC 87-3786. (Social & Behavioral Science Ser.). 1987. text ed. 39.95x (ISBN 1-55542-040-0). Jossey-Bass.

Psychology of Set. Dmitri N. Uznadze. LC 65-21186. (International Behavioral Sciences Ser.). pap. 67.00 (ISBN 0-317-28005-8, 2055803). Bks Demand UMI.

Psychology of Sex Differences. Hilary M. Lips & Nina L. Colwill. (Illus.). 1978. 13.95 (ISBN 0-13-736561-6, Spec). P-H.

Psychology of Sex Differences, 2 vols. in 1. Eleanor E. Maccoby & Carol N. Jacklin. LC 73-94488. 1974. Vol. I: text. pap. 11.95x (ISBN 0-8047-0974-2); Vol. II: Annotated Bibliography. pap. 7.95x (ISBN 0-8047-0975-0). Stanford U Pr.

Psychology of Sex Offenders. Albert Ellis & Ralph Brancale. 148p. 1956. 17.25x (ISBN 0-398-04252-7). C C Thomas.

Psychology of Sex Relations. Theodor Reik. LC 74-28525. 243p. 1975. Repr. of 1945 ed. lib. bdg. 35.00x (ISBN 0-8371-7916-5, RESR). Greenwood.

Psychology of Sex Roles. Ed. by David J. Hargreaves & Ann M. Colley. 323p. 1987. 35.00 (ISBN 0-89116-776-5). Hemisphere Pub.

Psychology of Sexual Diversity. Ed. by Kevin Howells. 300p. 1984. 29.95x (ISBN 0-631-13669-X). Basil Blackwell.

Psychology of Sexual Diversity. Ed. by Kevin Howells. 276p. 1985. pap. text ed. 14.95 (ISBN 0-631-15017-X). Basil Blackwell.

Psychology of Sexual Emotion: The Basis of Selective Attraction. Vernon W. Grant. LC 75-36356. 1979. Repr. of 1957 ed. lib. bdg. 35.00x (ISBN 0-8371-8631-5, GRPS). Greenwood.

Psychology of Shakespeare. John C. Bucknill. LC 72-131514. Repr. of 1859 ed. 21.00 (ISBN 0-404-01147-0). AMS Pr.

Psychology of Skill: Three Studies. William F. Book & William L. Bryan. LC 73-3029. (Classics in Psychology Ser.). 1973. Repr. of 1973 ed. 16.00 (ISBN 0-405-05157-3). Ayer Co Pubs.

Psychology of Social Change. Leo Schneiderman. 240p. 1988. 34.95 (ISBN 0-89885-372-9); pap. 16.95 (ISBN 0-89885-379-6). Human Sci Pr.

Psychology of Social Classes: A Study of Class Consciousness. Richard Centers. LC 61-13778. (Illus.). 1961. Repr. of 1949 ed. 11.00x (ISBN 0-8462-0148-8). Russell.

Psychology of Social Influence: Constraint, Conviction & Persuasion. Genevieve Paicheler. Tr. by Angela S. Emler & Nichales Emler. (Illus.). 225p. 1988. 39.50 (ISBN 0-521-30940-9). Cambridge U Pr.

Psychology of Social Institutions. Charles H. Judd. LC 73-14160. (Perspectives in Social Inquiry Ser.). 360p. 1974. Repr. 21.00x (ISBN 0-405-05506-4). Ayer Co Pubs.

Psychology of Social Movements. Pryns Hopkins. 59.95 (ISBN 0-8490-0913-8). Gordon Pr.

Psychology of Social Situations: Selected Readings. Ed. by A. Furnham & M. Argyle. LC 80-41189. 350p. 1981. text ed. 69.00 (ISBN 0-08-024319-3); pap. text ed. 25.00 (ISBN 0-08-023719-3). Pergamon.

Psychology of Socialism. Henry Deman. LC 73-14152. (Perspectives in Social Inquiry Ser.). 514p. 1974. Repr. 30.00x (ISBN 0-405-05498-X). Ayer Co Pubs.

Psychology of Socialism. Gustave LeBon. LC 64-25423. 1965. Repr. of 1899 ed. flexible cover 15.00 (ISBN 0-87034-025-5). Fraser Pub Co.

Psychology of Socialism. Gustave LeBon. LC 81-1973. 415p. 1982. 39.95 (ISBN 0-87855-321-5); pap. 21.95 (ISBN 0-87855-703-2). Transaction Bks.

TITLE INDEX PSYCHOLOGY: UNDERSTANDING BEHAVIOR.

Psychology of Society: An Anthology of Classic Writings on the Basic Issues, Developmental Concepts & Leading Theories of Social Psychology. Richard Sennett. 1977. pap. 4.95 (ISBN 0-394-72234-5, Vin). Random.
Psychology of Special Disability in Spelling. Leta Hollingworth. LC 79-176873. (Columbia University. Teachers College. Contributions to Education: No. 88). Repr. of 1918 ed. 22.50 (ISBN 0-404-55088-6). AMS Pr.
Psychology of Speculation. Henry H. Harper. LC 66-26207. 1966. Repr. of 1926 ed. flexible cover 6.00 (ISBN 0-87034-015-8). Fraser Pub Co.
Psychology of Spiritual Growth. Mary E. Carreiro. (Gentle Wind Bks.: Vol.I). 160p. 1987. 24.95 (ISBN 0-89789-123-6); pap. 8.95 (ISBN 0-89789-124-4). Bergin & Garvey.
Psychology of Sport. Dorcas S. Butt. LC 82-12661. 208p. 1982. Repr. of 1976 ed. lib. bdg. 14.95 (ISBN 0-89874-535-7). Krieger.
Psychology of Sport. 2nd ed. Dorcas S. Butt. (Illus.). 336p. 1987. pap. 21.95 (ISBN 0-442-21437-5). Van Nos Reinhold.
Psychology of Sport. Robert W. Grant. LC 87-43197. 186p. 1988. lib. bdg. 15.95x (ISBN 0-89950-271-7). McFarland & Co.
Psychology of Sport. Seppo E. Iso-Ahola & Brad A. Hatfield. 384p. 1986. pap. text ed. write for info. (ISBN 0-697-00062-1). Wm C Brown.
Psychology of Status. Herbert H. Hyman. Ed. by Harriet Zuckerman & Robert K. Merton. LC 79-9005. (Dissertations on Sociology Ser.). 1980. lib. bdg. 12.00x (ISBN 0-405-12974-2). Ayer Co Pubs.
Psychology of Strange Killers. James M. Reinhardt. 212p. 1962. 23.00x (ISBN 0-398-01566-X). C C Thomas.
Psychology of Subnormal Children. Leta S. Hollingworth. 1979. Repr. of 1926 ed. lib. bdg. 25.00 (ISBN 0-8495-2264-1). Arden Lib.
Psychology of Subnormal Children. Leta S. Hollingworth. 1928. 30.00 (ISBN 0-932062-83-0). Sharon Hill.
Psychology of Success. Emery Stoops. 140p. 1982. pap. 7.50 (ISBN 0-87881-104-4). Mojave Bks.
Psychology of Successful Living: An Advanced Guide to All Achievement Based on the Laws & Psychology of Right Human Relationship with Oneself, Mankind, & God. Gene H. Lawrence. 1985. pap. 4.95 (ISBN 0-682-40252-4). Exposition-Phoenix.
Psychology of Successful Selling. Kenneth Schock. 320p. 1987. pap. text ed. 26.95 (ISBN 0-8403-4208-X). Kendall-Hunt.
Psychology of Successful Weight Control. Mary C. Tyson & Robert Tyson. LC 73-84207. 192p. 1974. 17.95 (ISBN 0-88229-103-3). Nelson-Hall.
Psychology of Suggestion: A Research into the Subconscious Nature of Man & Society. Boris Sidis. LC 73-2415. (Mental Illness & Social Policy; the American Experience Ser.). Repr. of 1899 ed. 23.00 (ISBN 0-405-05225-1). Ayer Co Pubs.
Psychology of Suicide. Edwin S. Shneidman et al. LC 84-2818. 744p. 1983. 45.00x (ISBN 0-87668-668-4). Aronson.
Psychology of Taxation. Alan Lewis. LC 82-10656. 224p. 1982. 28.50 (ISBN 0-312-65330-1). St Martin.
Psychology of Teaching. rev. ed. Asahel D. Woodruff. LC 73-136091. (Illus.). 617p. 1974. Repr. of 1951 ed. lib. bdg. 35.00 (ISBN 0-8371-5241-0, WOPT). Greenwood.
Psychology of the Adolescent. Leta S. Hollingworth. 256p. 1980. Repr. lib. bdg. 37.50 (ISBN 0-89984-294-1). Century Bookbindery.
Psychology of the Afro-American: A Humanistic Approach. Adelbert H. Jenkins. (Pergamon General Psychology Ser.: No. 103). (Illus.). 270p. 1982. pap. text ed. 18.50 (ISBN 0-08-027205-3). Pergamon.
Psychology of the Americas: Mestizo Perspectives on Personality & Mental Health. Manuel Ramirez, III. (Pergamon General Psychology Ser.: No. 126). (Illus.). 200p. 1983. text ed. 35.00 (ISBN 0-08-026311-9). Pergamon.
Psychology of the Artist. Sheldon Cholst. LC 91-7319. 1978. pap. 9.95 (ISBN 0-931174-00-7). Beau Rivage.
Psychology of the Arts. Hans Kreitler & Shulamith Kreitler. LC 70-185566. (Illus.). 1972. 38.50 (ISBN 0-8223-0269-1); pap. 15.75 (ISBN 0-8223-0437-6). Duke.
Psychology of the Catholic Intellectual. Ed. by A. Von Raum. (Synthesis Ser.). 1967. pap. 0.75 (ISBN 0-8199-0241-1, L38669). Franciscan Herald.
Psychology of the Child. Jean Piaget & Barbel Inhelder. Tr. by Helen Weaver. LC 73-78449. 1969. 14.95x (ISBN 0-465-06735-2); pap. 8.95x (ISBN 0-465-09500-3, TB5001). Basic.
Psychology of the Child in the Middle Class. Allison Davis. LC 60-15158. (Horace Mann Lecture, 1960 Ser.). pap. 15.20 (ISBN 0-317-08019-9, 2017875). Bks Demand UMI.
Psychology of the Chinese People. Ed. by Michael H. Bond. 368p. 1987. 29.95 (ISBN 0-317-66367-4). Oxford U Pr.
Psychology of the Chinese People. Ed. by Michael H. Bond. 368p. 1988. pap. 18.95 (ISBN 0-19-584279-0). Oxford U Pr.
Psychology of the Courtroom. Norbert Kerr & Robert Bray. LC 81-14884. 1981. 29.95 (ISBN 0-12-404920-6). Acad Pr.
Psychology of the Criminal. M. Hamblin Smith. (Historical Foundations of Forensic Psychiatry & Psychology Ser.). viii, 182p. 1983. Repr. of 1922 ed. lib. bdg. 22.50 (ISBN 0-306-76176-9). Da Capo.
Psychology of the Crminal Act & Punishment. Gregory Zilboorg. LC 68-54445. (Illus.). 1968. Repr. of 1954 ed. lib. bdg. 35.00 (ISBN 0-8371-0773-3, ZIPC). Greenwood.
Psychology of the Dentist-Patient Relationship. S. Bochner. (Contributions to Psychology & Medicine Ser.). (Illus.). 200p. 1988. 50.00 (ISBN 0-387-96642-0). Springer-Verlag.
Psychology of the Human Memory. Arthur Wingfield & Dennis L. Byrnes. 429p. 1981. Acad Pr.
Psychology of the Master Counterfeiters, 2 vols. (Illus.). 237p. 1986. Set. 189.50 (ISBN 0-89920-135-0). Am Inst Psych.
Psychology of the Mexican: Culture & Personality. R. Diaz-Guerrero. LC 74-23309. (Texas Pan American Ser.). 193p. 1975. 16.95x (ISBN 0-292-77512-1); pap. 7.95x (ISBN 0-292-76430-8). U of Tex Pr.
Psychology of the Negro: An Experimental Study. George O. Ferguson. LC 74-107481. 1970. Repr. of 1916 ed. 35.00x (ISBN 0-8371-3783-7, FEP&). Greenwood.
Psychology of the Observer. Richard Rose. 1979. pap. 6.00 (ISBN 0-686-27738-4). Pyramid WV.
Psychology of the Physically Handicapped. Rudolf Pitner & Jon Eisenson. Ed. by William R. Phillips & Janet Rosenberg. LC 79-6922. (Physically Handicapped in Society Ser.). 1980. Repr. of 1941 ed. lib. bdg. 34.50x (ISBN 0-405-13130-5). Ayer Co Pubs.
Psychology of the Physically Ill Patient: A Clinician's Guide. M. E. Backman. (Illus.). 290p. Date not set. price not set (ISBN 0-306-43051-7, Plenum Pr). Plenum Pub.
Psychology of the Planets. Francoise Gauquelin. 128p. (Orig.). 1982. pap. 8.95 (ISBN 0-917086-32-5). A C S Pubns Inc.
Psychology of the Planned Community: The New Town Experience. Ed. by Donald Klein & Daniel Adelson. LC 77-15502. (Community Psychology Ser.: Vol. IV). 182p. 1978. 26.95 (ISBN 0-87705-317-0). Human Sci Pr.
Psychology of the Poet Shelley. Edward Carpenter & George Barnefield. LC 72-1334. (English Literature Ser., No. 33). 1972. Repr. of 1925 ed. lib. bdg. 75.00x (ISBN 0-8383-1431-7). Haskell.
Psychology of the Poet Shelley. Edward Carpenter & George Barnfield. 1925. lib. bdg. 27.00 (ISBN 0-8414-3590-1). Folcroft.
Psychology of the Psychic. David Marks & Richard Kammann. LC 80-7458. (Science & the Paranormal Ser.). 232p. 1980. 18.95 (ISBN 0-87975-121-5); pap. 14.95 (ISBN 0-87975-122-3). Prometheus Bks.
Psychology of the Self: A Casebook. Ed. by Arnold I. Goldberg & H. Kohut. LC 77-92188. 460p. 1978. text ed. 47.50x (ISBN 0-8236-5582-2). Intl Univs Pr.
Psychology of the Self & the Treatment of Narcissism. Richard Chessick. LC 85-15621. 366p. 1985. 35.00x (ISBN 0-87668-745-1). Aronson.
Psychology of the Soul, 2 vols. Otto Rank. (Illus.). 201p. 1986. Set. 257.75 (ISBN 0-89920-127-X). Am Inst Psych.
Psychology of the Spirit. C. G. Jung. 1985. 10.00x (ISBN 0-317-62298-6, Guild of Pastoral Psych). State Mutual Bk.
Psychology of the Stock Market. G. C. Selden. LC 65-20560. 1965. Repr. of 1912 ed. flexible cover 5.00 (ISBN 0-87034-016-6). Fraser Pub Co.
Psychology of the Transference. C. G. Jung. (Bollingen Ser.: Vol. 20). pap. 8.95 (ISBN 0-691-01752-2, 158). Princeton U Pr.
Psychology of the Vow. Niel Micklem. 1985. 10.00x (ISBN 0-317-62297-8, Guild of Pastoral Psych). State Mutual Bk.
Psychology of the Youthful Offender. 2nd ed. Robert N. Walker. 164p. 1973. 21.75 (ISBN 0-398-02859-1). C C Thomas.
Psychology of Today's Woman: New Psychoanalytic Vision. Ed. by Toni Bernay & Dorothy W. Cantor. 400p. 1986. text ed. 39.95 (ISBN 0-88163-036-5). Analytic Pr.
Psychology of Touch: A Special Issue of Journal of Nonverbal Behavior. Ed. by Stephen Thayer. LC 80-649435. 80p. 1986. pap. 9.95 (ISBN 0-89885-321-4). Human Sci Pr.
Psychology of Twinship. Ricardo C. Ainslie. LC 84-19591. xvi, 204p. 1985. 19.95x (ISBN 0-8032-1017-5). U of Nebr Pr.
Psychology of Underachievement: Differential Diagnosis & Differential Treatment. Harvey P. Mandel & Sander I. Marcus. LC 87-37127. (Personality Processes Ser.). 397p. 1988. 42.50 (ISBN 0-471-84855-7). Wiley.
Psychology of Vigilance. D. R. Davies & R. Parasuraman. LC 81-67890. (Organizational & Occupational Psychology Ser.). 1982. 53.00 (ISBN 0-12-206180-2). Acad Pr.
Psychology of Vision. Royal Society Discussion, March 7 & 8, 1979. Ed. by H. C. Longuet-Higgins & N. S. Sutherland. (Illus.). 218p. 1980. text ed. 61.00x (ISBN 0-85403-141-3, Pub. by Royal Soc London). Scholium Intl.
Psychology of Western Culture. John C. Myer. LC 72-82791. (Illus.). 160p. 1973. 9.95 (ISBN 0-8022-2096-7). Philos Lib.
Psychology of Winning. Denis Waitley. 160p. 1984. pap. 3.50 (ISBN 0-425-09999-7). Berkley Pub.
Psychology of Winning. Denis Waitley. 1988. 8.95 (ISBN 1-55525-227-3). Nightingale-Conant.
Psychology of Women, 2 vols. Helene Deutsch. Incl. Vol. I. Girlhood. 413p. 1944. 64.50 (ISBN 0-8089-0115-X, 791031); Vol. II. Motherhood. 505p. 1945. 54.50 (ISBN 0-8089-0116-8, 791032). LC 44-5287. Grune.
Psychology of Women. Margaret W. Matlin. 608p. 1987. text ed. write for info. (ISBN 0-03-063409-1). HR&W.
Psychology of Women. Mary R. Walsh. LC 87-6167. 480p. 1987. text ed. 40.00 (ISBN 0-300-03965-4); pap. 12.95x (ISBN 0-300-03966-2). Yale U Pr.
Psychology of Women: A Partially Annotated Bibliography. Joyce J. Walstedt. 76p. 1973. pap. 2.50 (ISBN 0-912786-23-X). Know Inc.
Psychology of Women: Behavior in a Biosocial Context. 3rd ed. Juanita H. Williams. 470p. 1987. pap. text ed. 16.95x (ISBN 0-393-95567-2). Norton.
Psychology of Women: Future Directions in Research. J. A. Sherman & F. L. Denmark. LC 78-31824. 800p. 1979. 59.95x (ISBN 0-88437-009-7). Psych Dimensions.
Psychology of Women: Selected Readings. 2nd ed. Ed. by Juanita H. Williams. 1985. pap. text ed. 14.95x (ISBN 0-393-95379-3). Norton.
Psychology of Work & Human Performance. Robert Smither. 482p. 1988. text ed. 37.95 (ISBN 0-06-046339-2, HarpC). Har-Row.
Psychology of Work & Organization: Current Trends & Issues. Ed. by G. Debus & H. W. Schroiff. 416p. 1986. 102.75 (ISBN 0-444-70029-3, North-Holland). Elsevier.
Psychology of Work & Unemployment. Gordon E. O'Brien. LC 85-29604. (Psychology & Productivity at Work Ser.). 315p. 1986. 54.95 (ISBN 0-471-10533-3). Wiley.
Psychology of Work Behavior. 3rd. ed. Frank J. Landy. 1985. 39.00x (ISBN 0-256-03046-4); study guide 10.00 (ISBN 0-256-03305-6). Dorsey.
Psychology of Written Composition. Ed. by C. Bereiter & M. Scardamalia. 408p. 1987. text ed. 49.95 (ISBN 0-89859-647-5); pap. text ed. 24.95 (ISBN 0-8058-0038-7). L Erlbaum Assocs.
Psychology of Written Language: Developmental & Educational Perspectives. Ed. by Margaret Martlew. LC 82-21933. (Developmental Psychology & Its Applications Ser.). 428p. 1983. 84.95x (ISBN 0-471-10291-1). Wiley.
Psychology; or, a View of the Human Soul, Including Anthropology. Friedrich Rauch. LC 74-22335. (History of Psychology Ser.). 1975. 60.00x (ISBN 0-8201-1142-2). Schol Facsimiles.
Psychology: Perspectives on Behavior. Peter D. Spear et al. LC 87-25340. 825p. 1988. write for info. (ISBN 0-471-82425-9); study guide avail. (ISBN 0-471-63449-2). Wiley.
Psychology: Principles & Applications. Stephen R. Schmidt et al. 256p. 1983. write for info. (ISBN 0-13-732354-9); pap. text ed. practice tests incl. P-H.
Psychology: Principles & Applications. 2nd ed. Stephen Worche & Wayne Shebilske. (Illus.). 672p. 1986. text ed. write for info. (ISBN 0-13-732694-7). P-H.
Psychology: Principles & Applications. Stephen Worchel. (Illus.). 672p. 1983. text ed. write for info (ISBN 0-13-732453-7). P-H.
Psychology: Principles & Applications: Study Guide with Practice Tests. 2nd ed. John M. Tucker. 400p. 1986. pap. text ed. write for info. (ISBN 0-13-732710-2). P-H.
Psychology: Principles & Meanings. 5th ed. Lyle E. Bourne & Bruce R. Ekstrand. 624p. 1985. 28.95 (ISBN 0-03-069816-2, HoltC). Holt Inc.
Psychology Problem Solver. rev. ed. Research & Education Association Staff. LC 80-53174. (Illus.). 1056p. (Orig.). 1986. pap. text ed. 19.85 (ISBN 0-87891-523-0). Res & Educ.
Psychology, Psychiatry & the Law: A Clinical & Forensic Handbook. Ed. by Charles P. Ewing. LC 85-60449. 576p. 1985. text ed. 39.95 (ISBN 0-943158-11-7). Pro Resource.
Psychology Readings Catalogue of the North East London Polytechnic, London, England, 2 vols. North East London Polytechnic London, England. 1976. Set. lib. bdg. 155.00 (ISBN 0-8161-1179-0, Hall Library). G K Hall.
Psychology, Religion, & Ethics in Galdos' Novels: The Quest for Authenticity. Arnold M. Penuel. LC 87-8303. 208p. (Orig.). 1987. lib. bdg. 23.00 (ISBN 0-8191-6333-3); pap. text ed. 12.75 (ISBN 0-8191-6334-1). U Pr of Amer.
Psychology Research & Public Policy. R. Kasschau. 1985. 40.95 (ISBN 0-275-90126-2, C0126). Praeger.
Psychology: Science & Application. Mark G. McGee & David W. Wilson. (Illus.). 666p. 1984. text ed. 37.75 (ISBN 0-314-77927-2). West Pub.
Psychology: Science & Application. Mark G. McGee & David W. Wilson. 666p. 1984. instr's. manual 37.75 (ISBN 0-314-79143-4); study guide 11.00 (ISBN 0-314-79144-2). West Pub.
Psychology: Science, Behavior & Life. Robert L. Crooks & Jean Stein. 800p. 1988. text ed. write for info. (ISBN 0-03-006758-8). HR&W.
Psychology: Strategies for Success. David P. Cantrell. LC 83-70800. (Illus.). 174p. (Orig.). 1983. pap. 5.95 (ISBN 0-913011-01-0). Ambleside.
Psychology: Studying the Behavior of People. 2nd ed. A. Christine Parham. 608p. 1988. text ed. write for info. (ISBN 0-538-16110-8, P11). SW Pub.
Psychology Survey Six. Ed. by Halla Beloff & Andrew Colman. 200p. 1987. 32.50x (ISBN 0-262-02261-3). MIT Pr.
Psychology Teacher's Resource Book: First Course. 3rd ed. Ed. by Margo Johnson & Michael Wertheimer. 209p. (Orig.). 1979. pap. 14.50 (ISBN 0-912704-10-1, 4280040); members 12.00. Am Psychol.
Psychology: The Basic Principles. John F. Hahn & Sanford Lopater. (Quality Paperback Ser.: No. 324). 220p. 1977. pap. 5.95 (ISBN 0-8226-0324-1). Littlefield.
Psychology: The Briefer Course. William James. Ed. by Gordon Allport. LC 84-40821. 360p. 1985. pap. text ed. 8.95 (ISBN 0-268-01557-0). U of Notre Dame Pr.
Psychology: The Cognitive Powers. James McCosh. LC 75-3263. Repr. of 1886 ed. 17.00 (ISBN 0-404-59249-X). AMS Pr.
Psychology: The Frontiers of Behavior. 3rd ed. Ronald E. Smith et al. 656p. 1986. pap. text ed. 39.50 (ISBN 0-06-045728-7, HarpC). Har-Row.
Psychology: The Hybrid Science. 2nd ed. Frank B. McMahon & Judith W. McMahon. 1986. 15.00x (ISBN 0-256-03246-7). Dorsey.
Psychology: The Leading Edge. Ed. by Florence L. Denmark. (Annals of the New York Academy of Sciences: Vol. 340). 114p. 1980. 22.00x (ISBN 0-89766-068-4); pap. 22.00x (ISBN 0-89766-069-2). NY Acad Sci.
Psychology: The Motive Powers-Emotions, Conscience, Will. James McCosh. LC 75-3264. Repr. of 1887 ed. 18.00 (ISBN 0-404-59250-3). AMS Pr.
Psychology: The Personal Science. John Ruch. 674p. write for info. (ISBN 0-534-02671-0); write for info. study guide. Watts.
Psychology: The Personal Science. John C. Ruch. 674p. 1984. text ed. write for info. (ISBN 0-534-02672-9). Wadsworth Pub.
Psychology: The Science of Behavior. 2nd ed. Carlson. 750p. 1986. 39.00 (ISBN 0-205-10272-7). Allyn.
Psychology: The Science of Mind & Behavior. John W. Santrock. 712p. 1986. text ed. write for info. (ISBN 0-697-00310-8); pap. text ed. write for info. (ISBN 0-697-00576-3); write for info. student study guide (ISBN 0-697-00577-1); write for info. instr's. manual (ISBN 0-697-00578-X); write for info. transparencies (ISBN 0-697-01029-5); write for info. test item file (ISBN 0-697-00579-8). Wm C Brown.
Psychology: The Science of Mind & Behavior. 2nd ed. John W. Santrock. 736p. 1988. Instr's manual. text ed. write for info. (ISBN 0-697-06725-4); Student study guide. write for info. instr's. manual; Test item file. student study guide avail.; Transparencies. test item file avail.; transparencies avail. (ISBN 0-697-06728-9). Wm C Brown.
Psychology: The Science of People. 2nd ed. Frank J. Landy. (Illus.). 672p. 1987. text ed. write for info. (ISBN 0-13-732405-7); Study guide with practice tests & software activity. pap. text ed. write for info. P-H.
Psychology: The State of the Art. Ed. by Kurt Salzinger & Florence L. Denmark. (Annals of the New York Academy of Sciences: Vol. 309). 1978. pap. 12.00x (ISBN 0-89072-065-7). NY Acad Sci.
Psychology: The Study of Human Experience. 2nd ed. Robert Ornstein. 766p. 1988. text ed. 27.00 (ISBN 0-15-572680-3, HC); pap. text ed. 1.75 (ISBN 0-15-572681-1); study guide 9.50 (ISBN 0-15-572683-8). HarBraceJ.
Psychology: The Study of Human Experience: Test Book. 2nd ed. Douglas K. Smith. 246p. 1988. pap. text ed. 6.50 net (ISBN 0-15-572682-X). HarBraceJ.
Psychology: Theoretical-Historical Perspectives. Ed. by Robert W. Rieber & Kurt Salzinger. LC 79-6790. 1980. 41.00 (ISBN 0-12-588265-3). Acad Pr.
Psychology: Through the Eyes of Faith. David Myers & Malcolm Jeeves. 176p. 1987. pap. 9.95 (ISBN 0-06-065557-7, HarpR). Har-Row.
Psychology Today. 5th ed. Bootzin et al. LC 82-20450. 1982. text ed. write for info (ISBN 0-394-32581-8, RanC). Random.
Psychology Today: An Introduction. 6th ed. Richard Bootzin et al. 736p. 1986. text ed. write for info. (ISBN 0-394-34359-X, RanC); write for info. (ISBN 0-394-35496-6, RanC). Random.
Psychology: Understanding Behavior. 2nd ed. Robert Baron et al. LC 79-22453. 848p. 1980. text ed. 30.95 (ISBN 0-03-054241-3, HoltC); instr's. manual 25.00 (ISBN 0-03-057044-1); study guide 11.95 (ISBN 0-03-055106-4). HR&W.

Psychology Versus Metapsychology: Psychoanalytic Essays in Memory of George S. Klein. Ed. by Merton M. Gill & Philip S. Holzman. LC 75-23354. (Psychological Issues Monograph: No. 36, Vol. 9, No. 4). 376p. 1975. text ed. 37.50x (ISBN 0-8236-5586-5). Intl Univs Pr.

Psychology Words. Gilda Berger. LC 85-8889. (Illus.). 96p. (gr. 7 up). 1986. PLB 9.59 (ISBN 0-671-54291-5). Messner.

Psychology's Compositional Problem. (Advances in Psychology Ser.: No. 41). 424p. 1987. 100.00 (ISBN 0-444-70115-X, North Holland). Elsevier.

Psychology's Crisis of Disunity: Philosophy & Method for a Unified Science. Arthur W. Staats. 400p. 1983. 46.95 (ISBN 0-275-91082-2, C1082). Praeger.

Psychology's Occult Doubles: Psychology & the Problem of Pseudoscience. Thomas H. Leahey & Grace E. Leahey. LC 82-24635. 296p. 1983. lib. bdg. 25.95x (ISBN 0-88229-717-1). Nelson-Hall.

Psychology's Sanction for Selfishness: The Error of Egoism in Theory & Therapy. Michael A. Wallach & Lise Wallach. LC 82-18391. 307p. 1983. pap. text ed. 14.95 (ISBN 0-7167-1466-3). W H Freeman.

Psychology's Second Century: Enduring Issues, Vol 2. Richard A. Kasschau & Charles N. Cofer. LC 81-11882. 320p. 1981. 42.95 (ISBN 0-275-90659-0, C06592). Praeger.

Psychomancy & Crystal Gazing. William W. Atkinson. pap. 2.00 (ISBN 0-911662-41-3). Yoga.

Psychomental Complex of the Tungus. Sergei M. Shirokogorov. LC 76-44788. 488p. Repr. of 1935 ed. 120.00 (ISBN 0-404-15879-X). AMS Pr.

Psychometabolic Blues: Practical Solutions for Anxiety, Depression, Fatigue, Hypoglycemia & Related Stressful Problems. Jerome Marmorstein & Nanette Marmorstein. LC 79-4271. 1979. 9.95 (ISBN 0-912800-58-5); pap. 4.95 (ISBN 0-912800-59-3). Woodbridge Pr.

Psychometric Analysis. Max F. Long. 1959. pap. 5.95 (ISBN 0-87516-045-X). DeVorss.

Psychometric Tables & Charts. O. T. Zimmerman. 1964. 35.00. Indus Res Serv.

Psychometric Theory. 2nd ed. Jim C. Nunnally. (McGraw-Hill Psychology Ser.). 1978. text ed. 54.95 (ISBN 0-07-047465-6). McGraw.

Psychometrician. Jack Rudman. (Career Examination Ser.: C-1830). (Cloth bdg. avail. on request). pap. 18.00 (ISBN 0-8373-1830-0). Natl Learning.

Psychometrics & Psychology. P. Kline. 1979. 82.50 (ISBN 0-12-415150-7). Acad Pr.

Psychometrics for Educational Debates. International Symposium on Educational Testing (3d: 1977: Leyden) Staff. Ed. by Leo J. Van der Kamp et al. LC 79-4308. 347p. pap. 90.30 (2030442). Bks Demand UMI.

Psychometrics for Educational Debates. Ed. by Leo J. VanDerKamp et al. LC 79-4308. 337p. 1980. 97.95x (ISBN 0-471-27596-4, Pub. by Wiley-Interscience). Wiley.

Psychometrics of Fatigue. Vladimir Zinchenko et al. (Illus.). 80p. 1985. 20.00x (ISBN 0-85066-258-3). Taylor & Francis.

Psychometrics of Similarity. Robert Gregson. 1975. 44.00 (ISBN 0-12-301550-2). Acad Pr.

Psychometry: The Science of Touch. Beverly C. Jaegers. (Illus.). 125p. 1985. pap. text ed. 5.00 (ISBN 0-317-20489-0). Aries Prod.

Psychomotor Domain & the Seriously Handicapped. 2nd ed. Ed. by Paul Jansma. LC 84-2278. (Illus.). 636p. 1984. lib. bdg. 36.50 (ISBN 0-8191-3847-9). U Pr of Amer.

Psychomotor Domain: Movement Behaviors. Ed. by Robert N. Singer. LC 72-79355. (Illus.). pap. 107.30 (ISBN 0-8357-9417-2, 2014582). Bks Demand UMI.

Psychomotor Learning. Robert Kerr. 350p. 1982. text ed. write for info. (ISBN 0-697-06143-4). Wm C Brown.

Psychomotor Performances: Medical & Psychological Subject Index with Bibliography. Katie L. Holt. LC 88-47606. 150p. 1988. 34.50 (ISBN 0-88164-740-3); pap. 26.50 (ISBN 0-88164-741-1). ABBE Pubs Assn.

Psychomotor Skills Teaching Manual. 90p. 1979. pap. 10.00 (ISBN 0-317-33275-9, 4000014). Amer Acad Ortho Surg.

Psychonephrology, Vol. 1: Psychological Factors in Hemodialysis & Transplantation. Ed. by Norman B. Levy. LC 80-20681. 306p. 1981. 49.50x (ISBN 0-306-40586-5, Plenum Pr). Plenum Pub.

Psychonephrology, Vol. 2: Psychological Problems in Kidney Failure & Their Treatment. Ed. by Norman B. Levy. LC 83-8015. 312p. 1983. 49.50x (ISBN 0-306-41154-7, Plenum Pr). Plenum Pub.

Psychoneuroendocrine Dysfunction. Ed. by Nandkumar S. Shah & Alexander G. Donald. LC 83-19202. 660p. 1984. 89.50x (ISBN 0-306-41320-5, Plenum Pr). Plenum Pub.

Psychoneuroendocrinology & Abnormal Behavior. Ed. by J. Mendlewicz. (Advances in Biological Psychiatry: Vol. 5). (Illus.). vi, 130p. 1980. pap. 38.75 (ISBN 3-8055-0599-X). S Karger.

Psychoneuroendocrinology: Proceedings. Conference of the International Society for Psychoneuroendocrinology, Mieken, Sept., 1973. Ed. by N. Hatotani. (Illus.). 450p. 1974. 89.50 (ISBN 3-8055-1711-4). S Karger.

Psychoneuroimmunology. Ed. by Robert Ader. LC 80-265. (Behavioral Medicine Ser.). 1981. 55.00 (ISBN 0-12-043780-5). Acad Pr.

Psychoneuroses & Their Treatment by Psychotherapy. Joseph J. Dejerine & E. Gauckler. Tr. by Smith E. Jelliffe. LC 75-16697. (Classics in Psychiatry Ser.). 1976. Repr. of 1913 ed. 31.00x (ISBN 0-405-07425-5). Ayer Co Pubs.

Psychoneurosis, Organic Brain Disease, Psychopharmacology see Teaching Program in Psychiatry.

Psychopath: A Comprehensive Study of Antisocial Disorders & Behaviors. Ed. by William H. Reid. LC 78-8629. 1978. 30.00 (ISBN 0-87630-172-3). Brunner-Mazel.

Psychopath in Society. Ed. by Robert J. Smith. (Personality & Psychopathology Ser.). 1978. 15.95 (ISBN 0-12-652550-1). Acad Pr.

Psychopath Plague. Steven Spruill. 256p. (Orig.). 1986. pap. 2.95 (ISBN 0-8125-5490-6, Dist. by Warner Pub Services & St. Martin's Press). Tor Bks.

Psychopathic Behaviour: Approaches to Research. Ed. by Robert D. Hare & D. Schalling. LC 77-22873. 406p. pap. 116.00 (2030505). Bks Demand UMI.

Psychopathic God: Adolf Hitler. Robert G. Waite. 1983. pap. 4.95 (ISBN 0-451-62155-7, Ment). NAL.

Psychopathic Mind: Origins, Dynamics, & Treatment. J. Reid Meloy. LC 88-3454. 470p. 1988. 40.00x (ISBN 0-87668-922-5). Aronson.

Psychopathic Racial Personality: And Other Essays. Bobby E. Wright. (Orig.). 1985. pap. 5.95 (ISBN 0-88378-071-2). Third World.

Psychopathological & Neurological Dysfunctions Following Open-Heart Surgery, Milwaukee 1980: Proceedings. Ed. by R. Becker et al. (Illus.). 384p. 1982. 64.00 (ISBN 0-387-11621-4). Springer-Verlag.

Psychopathological Disorders in Childhood: Theoretical Considerations & a Proposed Classification. Group for the Advancement of Psychiatry Staff. LC 73-17784. 175p. 1974. 17.50x (ISBN 0-87668-130-5). Aronson.

Psychopathological Disorders in Childhood: Theoretical Considerations & a Proposed Classification, Vol. 6. GAP Committee on Child Psychiatry. LC 62-2872. (Report No. 62). 1983. pap. 14.95 (ISBN 0-87630-352-1, Pub. by GAP). Brunner-Mazel.

Psychopathological Disorders of Childhood. 3rd ed. Ed. by Herbert C. Quay & John S. Werry. LC 86-11105. 690p. 1986. write for info. (ISBN 0-471-88974-1). Wiley.

Psychopathological Researches. Boris Sidis. 329p. 1980. Repr. of 1902 ed. lib. bdg. 75.00 (ISBN 0-89984-411-1). Century Bookbindery.

Psychopathologie de l'Expression: Tome IV. (Ser. 19-22, & 25). (Illus.). 1978. dans une cassette 80.00 (ISBN 3-8055-2930-9). S Karger.

Psychopathology. Edward J. Kempf. LC 75-16711. (Classics in Psychiatry Ser.). (Illus.). 1976. Repr. of 1920 ed. 59.50x (ISBN 0-405-07440-9). Ayer Co Pubs.

Psychopathology: A Case Book. Robert L. Spitzer. (Illus.). 320p. 1983. pap. 24.95 (ISBN 0-07-060350-2). McGraw.

Psychopathology: A Source Book. Ed. by Charles F. Reed et al. LC 58-10405. (Illus.). 1958. 65.00x (ISBN 0-674-72200-0). Harvard U Pr.

Psychopathology among Mentally Retarded Children & Adolescents. Johnny L. Matson & Cynthia L. Frame. Ed. by Alan E. Kazdin. (Developmental Clinical Psychology Psychiatry Ser.: Vol. 6). 200p. (Orig.). 1985. text ed. 19.95 (ISBN 0-8039-2533-6); pap. text ed. 12.95 (ISBN 0-8039-2534-4). Sage.

Psychopathology: An Interactional Perspective. Ed. by David Magnusson & Arne Ohman. (Personality, Psychopathology & Psychotherapy Ser.). 394p. 1987. 49.50 (ISBN 0-12-465485-1). Acad Pr.

Psychopathology & Adaptation in Infancy & Early Childhood. Stanley I. Greenspan. LC 81-19282. (Clinical Infant Reports Ser.: No. 1). 263p. 1983. 30.00x (ISBN 0-8236-5660-8). Intl Univs Pr.

Psychopathology & Addictive Disorders. Ed. by Roger E. Meyer. LC 85-30547. 384p. 1986. lib. bdg. 37.50 (ISBN 0-89862-680-3). Guilford Pr.

Psychopathology & Brain Dysfunction. Ed. by Charles Shagass et al. LC 76-55487. (American Psychopathological Association Ser.). 399p. 1977. 51.00 (ISBN 0-89004-120-2). Raven.

Psychopathology & Differential Diagnosis: A Primer. Henry Kellerman & Anthony Burry. (History of Psychopathology, Personality, Psychopathology, & Psychotherapy: Theoretical & Clinical Perspectives Ser.: Vol. I). 296p. 1988. 30.00 (ISBN 0-231-06702-X). Columbia U Pr.

Psychopathology & Education of the Brain-Injured Child. Alfred A. Straus & L. E. Lehtinen. Incl. Vol. I. Fundamentals & Treatment. Lehtinen Straus. (Illus.). 206p. 1947. 37.50 (ISBN 0-8089-0487-6, 794391); Vol. II. Progress in Theory & Clinic. Kephart Straus. (Illus.). 277p. 1955. 37.50 (ISBN 0-8089-0488-4, 794392). 1953. Grune.

Psychopathology & Milieu Therapy: A Longitudinal Study. William J. McCord. 296p. 1982. 39.00 (ISBN 0-12-482180-4). Acad Pr.

Psychopathology & Nosology. Ed. by E. Gabriel & H. G. Zapotoczky. (Journal: Psychopathology: Vol. 8, No. 2-3, 1985). 124p. 1985. pap. 50.00 (ISBN 3-8055-4218-6). S Karger.

Psychopathology & Pictorial Expression, Vol. IV. Ed. by Sandoz. (Series 19-22, & 25). (Illus.). 1978. in box 80.00 (ISBN 3-8055-2929-5). S Karger.

Psychopathology & Pictorial Expression, Vol. III. Ed. by Sandoz Ltd. Staff. (Series 13-18). 1973. 96.00 (ISBN 3-8055-1627-4). S Karger.

Psychopathology & Political Leadership, Vol. 16. R. S. Robins et al. LC 77-85747. 1977. pap. text ed. 11.00 (ISBN 0-930598-16-4). Tulane Stud Pol.

Psychopathology & Politics. Harold D. Lasswell. xxvi, 340p. 1986. pap. 18.00x (ISBN 0-226-46919-0). U of Chicago Pr.

Psychopathology & Psychopharmacology: Proceedings of the Sixty-Second Annual Meeting. American Psychopathological Association Staff. Ed. by Jonathan O. Cole et al. LC 72-12347. pap. 78.00 (ISBN 0-317-41752-5, 2023091). Bks Demand UMI.

Psychopathology & Psychotherapy in Homosexuality. Ed. by Michael Ross. LC 87-30826. (Journal of Homosexuality Ser.). 230p. 1988. text ed. 29.95 (ISBN 0-86656-499-3). Haworth Pr.

Psychopathology & Society. 2nd ed. Peter E. Nathan & Sandra L. Harris. LC 79-15683. (Illus.). 1980. text ed. 42.95 (ISBN 0-07-046053-1). McGraw.

Psychopathology: Experimental Models. Ed. by Jack D. Maser & Martin E. Seligman. LC 77-5032. (Psychology Ser.). (Illus.). 474p. 1977. pap. text ed. 18.95x (ISBN 0-7167-0367-X). W H Freeman.

Psychopathology in Childhood. Ed. by Juliana R. Lachenmeyer & Margaret S. Gibbs. 1982. text ed. 39.95 (ISBN 0-89876-014-3). Gardner Pr.

Psychopathology in Childhood: Social, Diagnostic, & Therapeutic Aspects. Mary Engel. 183p. 1972. pap. text ed. 10.00 net (ISBN 0-15-573028-2, HC). HarBraceJ.

Psychopathology in Epilepsy: Social Factors. Ed. by Steven Whiteman & Bruce P. Herman. (Illus.). 327p. 1987. 39.95 (ISBN 0-19-503656-5). Oxford U Pr.

Psychopathology in the Aged. Ed. by Jonathan O. Cole & James E. Barrett. (American Psychopathological Association Ser.). 322p. 1980. text ed. 58.00 (ISBN 0-89004-406-6). Raven.

Psychopathology in the Mentally Retarded. Ed. by Johnny L. Matson & Rowland P. Barrett. 1982. 37.50 (ISBN 0-8089-1511-8, 792808). Grune.

Psychopathology: Its Causes & Symptoms. rev. ed. Frederick K. Taylor. LC 78-31648. pap. 93.00 (2026704). Bks Demand UMI.

Psychopathology of Adolescence: Proceedings, Vol. 26. American Psychopathological Association Publications Staff. Ed. by Joseph Zubin & Alfred Freedman. 354p. 1970. 79.50 (ISBN 0-8089-0558-9, 794986). Grune.

Psychopathology of Aging. Ed. by Oscar J. Kaplan. LC 79-21829. 1979. 29.95 (ISBN 0-12-396950-6). Acad Pr.

Psychopathology of Childhood. Jane W. Kessler. (Illus.). 1966. text ed. 38.00 (ISBN 0-13-736751-1). P-H.

Psychopathology of Childhood. 2nd ed. Jane W. Kessler. 416p. 1988. text ed. price not set (ISBN 0-13-736778-3). P-H.

Psychopathology of Childhood: A Clinical-Experimental Approach. 2nd ed. Steven Schwartz & James H. Johnson. (General Psychology Ser.: No. 95). 464p. 1985. text ed. 24.50 (ISBN 0-08-030935-6). Pergamon.

Psychopathology of Denial. Daniel A. Anderson. 48p. 1981. 4.95 (ISBN 0-89486-143-3). Hazelden.

Psychopathology of Everyday Life. Sigmund Freud. Ed. by James Strachey. Tr. by Alan Tyson. 1971. pap. 6.95 (ISBN 0-393-00611-5). Norton.

Psychopathology of Everyday Racism & Sexism. Ed. by Lenora Fulani. LC 88-6159. (Women & Therapy Ser.: Vol. 6, No. 4). 130p. 1988. text ed. write for info. (ISBN 0-918393-51-5). Harrington Pk.

Psychopathology of Homicide. Eugene Revitch & Louis B. Schlesinger. (Illus.). 272p. 1981. 30.25x (ISBN 0-398-04178-4). C C Thomas.

Psychopathology of the Psychoses. Thomas Freeman. LC 72-86647. 1969. text ed. 30.00x (ISBN 0-8236-5670-5). Intl Univs Pr.

Psychopathology Today. 3rd, rev. ed. Ed. by William S. Sahakian et al. LC 84-61421. 581p. 1986. pap. text ed. 21.95 (ISBN 0-87581-306-2). Peacock Pubs.

Psychopathy: A History of the Concepts. Henry Werlinder. 218p. 1978. pap. text ed. 22.00x (ISBN 91-554-0782-X, Pub. by Almqvist & Wiksell). Coronet Bks.

Psychopedagogy: Psychological Theory & the Practice of Teaching. E. Stones. 490p. 1979. pap. 13.95x (ISBN 0-416-71340-8, NO. 6420). Routledge Chapman & Hall.

Psychopharmachology of Childhood. Ed. by D. Siva Sankar. LC 74-27253. 1976. 37.50 (ISBN 0-915340-00-3). PJD Pubns.

Psychopharmacologic Agents for the Terminally Ill & Bereaved. Ed. by Ivan K. Goldberg et al. LC 72-9895. (Foundation of Thanatology Ser.). 339p. 1973. 37.50x (ISBN 0-88238-700-6). Columbia U Pr.

Psychopharmacologic Drugs: A Pocket Reference. R. G. Sample et al. LC 78-56085. (Illus.). 140p. 1978. pap. text ed. 7.95 (ISBN 0-89313-010-9). G F Stickley Co.

Psychopharmacological Agents, 3 vols. Ed. by Maxwell Gordon. Incl. Vol. 1. 1964. 90.00 (ISBN 0-12-290550-4); Vol. 2. 1967. 80.00 (ISBN 0-12-290556-3); Vol. 3. 1974. 80.00 (ISBN 0-12-290558-X). (Medicinal Chemistry Ser.). Acad Pr.

Psychopharmacological Treatment: Theory & Practice. Ed. by Herman C. Denber. (Modern Pharmacology-Toxicology Ser: Vol. 2). 320p. 1975. 65.00 (ISBN 0-8247-6229-0). Dekker.

Psychopharmacology, Vol. 1. Ed. by D. G. Grahame-Smith & H. Hippius. 935p. 1983. Part 1: Basic Preclinical Neuropharmacology. 126.50 (ISBN 0-444-90240-6, Excerpta Medica); Part 2: Clinical Psychopharmacology. 126.50 (ISBN 0-444-90282-1); 166.00 set (ISBN 0-444-90294-5). Elsevier.

Psychopharmacology & Drug Treatment of Schizophrenia. Ed. by P. Bradley & S. R. Hirsch. (British Association for Psychopharmacology Mongraphs). (Illus.). 475p. 1986. 69.00 (ISBN 0-19-261260-3). Oxford U Pr.

Psychopharmacology & Food. Ed. by Merton Sandler & Trevor Silverstone. 200p. 1986. 52.50 (ISBN 0-19-261458-4). Oxford U Pr.

Psychopharmacology & Psychotherapy. Ed. by Maurice H. Greenhill & Alexander Gralnick. 1982. text ed. 29.95 (ISBN 0-02-912780-7). Free Pr.

Psychopharmacology & Psychotherapy: Synthesis or Antithesis? Norman Rosenzweig & Hilda Griscom. LC 78-4088. 1978. text ed. 29.95 (ISBN 0-87705-354-5). Human Sci Pr.

Psychopharmacology & Reaction Time. Ed. by Bernd Aufdembrinke et al. LC 87-29469. 194p. 1988. 59.95 (ISBN 0-471-91818-0). Wiley.

Psychopharmacology & Sexual Disorders. David Wheatley. (Illus.). 1983. 39.00x (ISBN 0-19-261415-0). Oxford U Pr.

Psychopharmacology, Behavior Modification, Dynamic Psychotherapy: Towards an Integrated Approach. Ed. by G. A. Fava & H. Freyberger. (Journal: Psychotherapy & Psychosomatics: Vol. 46, No. 1-2, 1986). (Illus.). 104p. 1987. pap. 50.75 (ISBN 3-8055-4574-6). S Karger.

Psychopharmacology Case Studies. David S. Janowsky et al. LC 86-27049. 259p. 1987. lib. bdg. 35.00 (ISBN 0-89862-687-0); pap. 18.95 (ISBN 0-89862-921-7). Guilford Pr.

Psychopharmacology Consultation. Ed. by David C. Jimerson & John P. Docherty. LC 86-14136. (Clinical Insights Monograph). (Illus.). 144p. 1986. pap. text ed. 12.00 (ISBN 0-88048-141-2, 48-141-2). Am Psychiatric.

Psychopharmacology: Current Trends. Ed. by D. E. Casey & A. V. Christensen. (Psychopharmacology Ser.: Vol. 5). (Illus.). 250p. 1988. 77.50 (ISBN 0-387-18693-X). Springer-Verlag.

Psychopharmacology for Everyday Practice. T. A. Ban & M. H. Hollender. x, 198p. 1981. pap. 25.00 (ISBN 3-8055-2241-X). S Karger.

Psychopharmacology for Non-Physician. Charles R. Bowden. (Dorsey Professional Bks.). cancelled (ISBN 0-256-03489-3). Dow Jones-Irwin.

Psychopharmacology for Primary Care Physicians. Charles L. Bowden & Martin B. Griffen. LC 77-27297. 92p. (Orig.). 1978. pap. 8.95 (ISBN 0-683-01005-0, WW). Krieger.

Psychopharmacology for the Aged. Ed. by T. H. Ban. xii, 216p. 1980. softcover 26.00 (ISBN 3-8055-1204-X). S Karger.

Psychopharmacology: From Theory to Practice. Ed. by Jack D. Barchas et al. (Illus.). 1977. pap. text ed. 23.95x (ISBN 0-19-502215-7). Oxford U Pr.

Psychopharmacology: Impact on Clinical Psychiatry. Morgan et al. 1985. 27.50 (ISBN 0-912791-06-3). Ishiyaku Euro.

Psychopharmacology in Psychiatric Nursing. Ed. by Richard I. Shader & Judith Kerble. Date not set. price not set (ISBN 0-89004-428-7, 486). Raven.

Psychopharmacology of Addiction. Ed. by Malcolm Lader. (British Association for Psychopharmacology Monographs: No. 10). (Illus.). 194p. 1988. 55.00 (ISBN 0-19-261626-9). Oxford U Pr.

Psychopharmacology of Affective Disorders. Ed. by E. S. Paykel & A. Coppen. (British Association for Psychopharmacology Ser.). (Illus.). 1979. pap. text ed. 19.95x (ISBN 0-19-261278-6). Oxford U Pr.

Psychopharmacology of Aggression. Ed. by Merton Sandler. 247p. 1979. 45.00 (ISBN 0-89004-392-2). Raven.

Psychopharmacology of Aggression. Ed. by L. Valtelli et al. (Modern Problems of Pharmacopsychiatry: Vol. 13). (Illus.). 1978. 52.00 (ISBN 3-8055-2751-9). S Karger.

Psychopharmacology of Aging. Ed. by C. Eisdorfer & W. E. Fann. (Illus.). 327p. 1980. text ed. 55.00 (ISBN 0-88331-190-9). Luce.

Psychopharmacology of Alcohol. Ed. by Merton Sandler. 294p. 1980. text ed. 58.00 (ISBN 0-89004-506-2). Raven.

Psychopharmacology of Anticonvulsants. Ed. by Merton Sandler. (British Association for Psychopharmacology Ser.). (Illus.). 1982. text ed. 37.50x (ISBN 0-19-261341-3). Oxford U Pr.

TITLE INDEX PSYCHOSOMATIC DIAGNOSIS.

Psychopharmacology of Aversively Motivated Behavior. Ed. by H. Anisman & G. Bignami. LC 77-17998. (Illus.). 576p. 1978. 79.50x (ISBN 0-306-31055-4, Plenum Pr). Plenum Pub.
Psychopharmacology of Clonidine. Harbans Lal & Stuart Fielding. LC 81-14275. (Progress in Clinical & Biological Research Ser.: Vol. 71). 334p. 1981. 63.00 (ISBN 0-8451-0071-8). A R Liss.
Psychopharmacology of Depression. Thomas A. Ban. (Illus.). vi, 130p. 1981. pap. 21.50 (ISBN 3-8055-1154-X). S Karger.
Psychopharmacology of Hallucinogens. Ed. by R. C. Stillman & R. E. Willette. LC 78-14019. 1979. 66.00 (ISBN 0-08-021938-1). Pergamon.
Psychopharmacology of Old Age. Ed. by David Wheatley. (British Association for Psychopharmacology Monographs). (Illus.). 1982. pap. 19.95x (ISBN 0-19-261456-8). Oxford U Pr.
Psychopharmacology of Sleep. Ed. by David Wheatley. 256p. 1981. text ed. 52.50 (ISBN 0-89004-593-3). Raven.
Psychopharmacology of Smoking. G. L. Mangan & J. F. Golding. LC 83-15275. (Illus.). 200p. 1984. 52.50 (ISBN 0-521-25806-5). Cambridge U Pr.
Psychopharmacology of the Developmental Disabilities. Ed. by M. G. Aman & N. N. Singh. (Disorders of Human Learning, Behavior, & Communication Ser.). (Illus.). 235p. 1988. 49.00 (ISBN 0-387-96679-X). Springer-Verlag.
Psychopharmacology of the Limbic System. Ed. by Michael R. Trimble & E. Zarifian. (Illus.). 1984. 35.00x (ISBN 0-19-261425-8); pap. 18.95x (ISBN 0-19-261575-0). Oxford U Pr.
Psychopharmacology: Recent Advances & Future Prospects. Ed. by Susan D. Iversen. (British Association for Psychopharmacology Monographs). (Illus.). 300p. 1985. 42.50x (ISBN 0-19-261478-9); pap. 24.95 (ISBN 0-19-261627-7). Oxford U Pr.
Psychopharmacology: The Third Generation of Progress. Ed. by Herbert Y. Meltzer. (Illus.). 1824p. 1987. text ed. 150.00 (ISBN 0-88167-273-4). Raven.
Psychopharmacology Update. Ed. by Jonathan O. Cole. LC 79-48064. 195p. 1980. 16.95 (ISBN 0-669-03695-1, Collomore Pr). Heath.
Psychopharmaka, Gehirntaetigkeit & Schlaf: Neurophysiologische Aspekte der Psychopharmakologie & Pharmakopsychiatrie. B. Saletu. (Biblioteca Psychiatrica: No. 155). (Illus.). 1976. 65.50 (ISBN 3-8055-2352-1). S Karger.
Psychophysical Elements in Parapsychological Traditions. A. Tanagras. LC 67-19168. (Parapsychological Monograph: No. 7). 1967. pap. 6.00 (ISBN 0-912328-10-X). Parapsych Foun.
Psychophysical Judgement & the Process of Perception. H. G. Geissler et al. 288p. 1983. 97.50 (ISBN 0-444-86353-2, North-Holland). Elsevier.
Psychophysical Physiological & Behavioral Studies in Hearing: Proceedings. International Symposium on Hearing, Fifth, Noordwijkerhout, the Netherlands, April 8-12, 1980. Ed. by G. Van den Brink & F. A. Bilsen. 480p. 1980. 42.50x (ISBN 90-286-0780-3, Pub. by Sijthoff & Noordhoff). Kluwer Academic.
Psychophysics & Physiology of Hearing. Ed. by E. F. Evans & J. P. Wilson. 1978. 101.00 (ISBN 0-12-244050-1). Acad Pr.
Psychophysics: Introduction to Its Perceptual, Neural, & Social Prospects. S. S. Stevens. 335p. 1986. pap. text ed. 16.95x (ISBN 0-88738-643-1). Transaction Bks.
Psychophysics: Introduction to Its Perceptual, Neural, & Social Prospects. Stanley S. Stevens. Ed. by Geraldine Stevens. LC 74-13473. pap. 84.00 (ISBN 0-317-28122-4, 2022493). Bks Demand UMI.
Psychophysics: Method, Theory, & Application. 2nd ed. George A. Gescheider. 304p. 1984. text ed. 24.95 (ISBN 0-89859-375-1). L Erlbaum Assocs.
Psychophysiological Aspects of Reading. Victor Rentel et al. (Monographs in Psychobiology). 390p. 1985. text ed. 66.00 (ISBN 2-88124-000-3); pap. 26.00 (ISBN 2-88124-025-9). Gordon & Breach.
Psychophysiological Aspects of Sleep. Ed. by Ismet Karacan. LC 81-38367. (Illus.). 225p. 1981. 32.00 (ISBN 0-8155-0858-1). Noyes.
Psychophysiological Gastrointestinal Disorders. William E. Whitehead & Marvin M. Schuster. (Behavioral Medicine Ser.). 1985. 46.50 (ISBN 0-12-747030-1). Acad Pr.
Psychophysiological Management of Chronic Pain: A Biofeedback Workbook. Barbara J. Headley. (Illus.). 210p. (Orig.). 1988. write for info. wkbk. Pain Resc Ltd.
Psychophysiological Recording. Robert M. Stern et al. (Illus.). 1980. text ed. 23.50x o.p (ISBN 0-19-502695-0); pap. text ed. 15.95x (ISBN 0-19-502696-9). Oxford U Pr.
Psychophysiology & the Electronic Workplace. Ed. by Anthony Gale & Bruce Christie. LC 87-2148. 350p. 1987. 74.95 (ISBN 0-471-91272-7). Wiley.
Psychophysiology: Guidebook for Medicine, Reference & Research. Denise J. Randall. LC 83-46104. 150p. 1985. 34.50 (ISBN 0-88164-142-1); pap. 26.50 (ISBN 0-88164-143-X). ABBE Pubs Assn.
Psychophysiology: Human Behavior & Physiological Response. John L. Andreassi. 1980. pap. 15.95x (ISBN 0-19-502581-4). Oxford U Pr.
Psychophysiology Measurement of Covert Behavior: A Guide for the Laboratory. F. J. McGuigan. (Century Psychology Ser.). 144p. 1979. text ed. 19.95 (ISBN 0-89859-479-0). L Erlbaum Assocs.
Psychophysiology of Cardiovascular Control: Models, Methods, & Data. Ed. by J. F. Orlebeke et al. LC 85-9469. (NATO Conference Series III, Human Factors: Vol. 26). 972p. 1985. 135.00x (ISBN 0-306-42007-4, Plenum Pr). Plenum Pub.
Psychophysiology of the Gastrointestinal Tract: Experimental & Clinical Applications. Ed. by Rupert Holzl & William E. Whitehead. 390p. 1983. 55.00x (ISBN 0-306-41089-3, Plenum Pr). Plenum Pub.
Psychophysiology: Some Simple Concepts & Models. Walter W. Surwillo. (Illus.). 214p. 1986. 28.75 (ISBN 0-398-05254-9). C C Thomas.
Psychophysiology: Systems, Processes, & Applications. Ed. by Michael G. Coles. Emanuel Donchin & Stephen W. Porges. LC 85-17621. 761p. 1986. text ed. 100.00 (ISBN 0-89862-640-4). Guilford Pr.
Psychophysiology Today & Tomorrow. N. P. Bechtereva. 1981. 83.00 (ISBN 0-08-025930-8). Pergamon.
Psychophysiology, 1980: Memory, Motivation & Event-Related Potentials in Mental Operations. Ed. by R. Sinz & M. R. Rosenzweig. 572p. 1983. 136.00 (ISBN 0-444-80370-X). Elsevier.
Psychopolitics. Milton Greenblatt. 352p. 1978. 44.50 (ISBN 0-8089-1062-0, 791729). Grune.
Psychorheumatologie. A. Weintraub. (Illus.). viii, 92p. 1983. 12.75 (ISBN 3-8055-3628-3). S Karger.
Psychos: Eighty Years of Mad Movies, Maniacs, & Murderous Deeds. John McCarty. (Illus.). 224p. 1986. pap. 12.95 (ISBN 0-312-65341-7). St Martin.
Psychosemantics: The Problem of Meaning in the Philosophy of Mind. Jerry A. Fodor. LC 86-33173. 224p. 1987. 19.95x (ISBN 0-262-06106-6). MIT Pr.
Psychoses of Power: African Personal Dictatorships. Samuel Decalo. 232p. 1988. 29.95 (ISBN 0-8133-7617-3). Westview.
Psychoses of Uncertain Aetiology. Ed. by J. K. Wing & Lorna Wing. LC 81-17092. (Handbook of Psychiatry Ser.: Vol. 3). (Illus.). 1982. 57.50 (ISBN 0-521-24101-4); pap. 21.95 (ISBN 0-521-28438-4). Cambridge U Pr.
Psychosexual Imperatives: Their Role in Identity Formation, Vol. II. Ed. by Marie C. Nelson & Jean Ikenberry. LC 78-17739. (Self-in-Process Ser.). 397p. 1979. 39.95 (ISBN 0-87705-302-2). Human Sci Pr.
Psychosis & Civilization. Herbert Goldhamer & Andrew W. Marshall. Ed. by Gerald N. Grob. LC 78-22560. (Historical Issues in Mental Health Ser.). (Illus.). 1979. Repr. of 1953 ed. lib. bdg. 14,00x (ISBN 0-405-11914-3). Ayer Co Pubs.
Psychosis & Sexual Identity: Toward a Post-Analytic View of the Schreber Case. Ed. by David Allison et al. LC 87-10077. (Intersections: Philosophy & Critical Theory Ser.). (Illus.). 368p. 1988. 44.50 (ISBN 0-88706-616-X); pap. 14.95 (ISBN 0-88706-617-8). State U NY Pr.
Psychosocial Adaptation in Pregnancy: Assessment of Seven Dimensions of Maternal Development. Regina P. Lederman. 240p. 1984. 31.95 (ISBN 0-13-736760-0). Appleton & Lange.
Psychosocial Aspects of Cancer. Ed. by Jerome Cohen et al. Orig. Title: Research Issues in Psychological Dimensions of Cancer. 336p. 1982. text ed. 60.00 (ISBN 0-89004-494-5). Raven.
Psychosocial Aspects of Cardiovascular Disease. Ed. by James Reiffel et al. 365p. 1980. 12.50 (ISBN 0-930194-32-2). Ctr Thanatology.
Psychosocial Aspects of Cardiovascular Disease: The Life-Threatened Patient, the Family & the Staff. Ed. by James Reiffel et al. Austin H. Kutscher. LC 79-27765. (Foundation of Thanatology Ser.). (Illus.). 1980. 40.00x (ISBN 0-231-04354-6). Columbia U Pr.
Psychosocial Aspects of Chemotherapy in Cancer Care: The Patient, Family, & Staff. Ed. by Robert DeBellis et al. LC 86-33623. (Loss, Grief & Care Ser.: Vol. 1, No. 3-4). 152p. 1987. text ed. 24.95 (ISBN 0-86656-627-9). Haworth Pr.
Psychosocial Aspects of Clinical Practice. Ed. by Otto D. Payton. (Clinics in Physical Therapy Ser.: Vol. 8). (Illus.). 161p. 1985. text ed. 30.00 (ISBN 0-443-08396-7). Churchill.
Psychosocial Aspects of Cystic Fibrosis: A Model for Chronic Lung Disease. P. R. Patterson et al. LC 72-9893. 1973. 29.00x (ISBN 0-88238-702-2). Columbia U Pr.
Psychosocial Aspects of Cystic Fibrosis: A Model for Chronic Lung Disease. Ed. by Paul Patterson et al. 234p. 1973. 6.25 (ISBN 0-930194-33-0). Ctr Thanatology.
Psychosocial Aspects of Depression: No Way Out? Lars Freden. 240p. 1982. 54.95x (ISBN 0-471-10023-4, Pub. by Wiley-Interscience). Wiley.
Psychosocial Aspects of Disability. George Henderson & Willie V. Bryan. 334p. 1984. 35.75x (ISBN 0-398-05006-6). C C Thomas.
Psychosocial Aspects of Disaster. Gist. (Personality Processes Ser.). 1988. write for info. (ISBN 0-471-84894-8). Wiley.
Psychosocial Aspects of Muscular Dystrophy & Allied Diseases: Commitment to Life, Health & Function. Leon I. Charash et al. (Illus.). 332p. 1983. 32.75x (ISBN 0-398-04811-8). C C Thomas.
Psychosocial Aspects of Nonresponse to Antidepressant Drugs. Ed. by Uriel Halbreich & S. Shalom Feinberg. LC 86-10859. (Clinical Insights Monograph). 128p. 1986. pap. text ed. 12.00x (ISBN 0-88048-129-3, 48-129-3). Am Psychiatric.
Psychosocial Aspects of Nuclear Developments, Task Force Report, No. 20. American Psychiatric Association Staff. LC 82-71902. (Monographs). 104p. 1982. 12.00x (ISBN 0-89042-220-6, 42-220-6). Am Psychiatric.
Psychosocial Aspects of Nursing Home Care. 1978. 3.50 (ISBN 0-938846-08-6). Ebenezer Ctr.
Psychosocial Aspects of Pediatric Care. Ed. by Elizabeth Gellert. 288p. 1978. 42.50 (ISBN 0-8089-1091-4, 791535). Grune.
Psychosocial Aspects of Terminal Care. Ed. by Bernard Schoenberg et al. 388p. 1972. 12.50 (ISBN 0-930194-34-9). Ctr Thanatology.
Psychosocial Aspects of Terminal Care. Ed. by Bernard Schoenberg et al. LC 73-184747. 385p. 1972. 37.00x (ISBN 0-231-03614-0). Columbia U Pr.
Psychosocial Aspects of the "Cleft Palate Problem", 2 vols. D. C. Spriestersbach. LC 73-620015. 560p. 1973. text ed. 35.00s (ISBN 0-87745-044-7). U of Iowa Pr.
Psychosocial Aspects of the Family: The New Pediatrics. Morris Green. LC 84-48800. (Johnson & Johnson Round Table Ser.). (Illus.). 304p. 1985. 40.00x (ISBN 0-669-09768-3). Lexington Bks.
Psychosocial Assessment in Terminal Care. David M. Dush & Barrie R. Cassileth. LC 86-22801. (Hospice Journal Ser.). 144p. 1986. text ed. 22.95 (ISBN 0-86656-461-6). Haworth Pr.
Psychosocial Assessment Tools for Health Evaluation. Lois Long et al. 1987. 19.95 (ISBN 0-8385-8030-0). Appleton & Lange.
Psychosocial Care of the Physically Ill: What Every Nurse Should Know. 2nd ed. Vickie A. Lambert & Clinton E. Lambert, Jr. (Illus.). 384p. 1985. pap. text ed. 21.95 (ISBN 0-13-736869-0). Appleton & Lange.
Psychosocial Caring Throughout the Life Span. Irene M. Burnside & Priscilla Ebersole. (Illus.). 1979. text ed. 32.50 (ISBN 0-07-009213-3). McGraw.
Psychosocial Components of Occupational Therapy. Anne C. Mosey. 624p. 1986. text ed. 41.50 (ISBN 0-89004-334-5). Raven.
Psychosocial Consequence of Natural & Alienated Labor. Michael L. Schwalbe. LC 86-5771. (Sociology of Work Ser.). 233p. (Orig.). 1986. 52.50 (ISBN 0-88706-188-5); pap. 17.95 (ISBN 0-88706-187-7). State U NY Pr.
Psychosocial Constructs of Alcoholism & Substance Abuse. Ed. by Barry Stimmel. LC 83-12615. (Advances in Alcohol & Substances Abuse Ser.: Vol. 2, No. 4). 110p. 1983. text ed. 29.95 (ISBN 0-86656-244-3, B244). Haworth Pr.
Psychosocial Costs of Police Corruption. Charles Bahn. (Criminal Justice Center Monographs). 1979. pap. text ed. 1.00x. John Jay Pr.
Psychosocial Development of Children. 2nd ed. Irene M. Josselyn. LC 78-3112. 1977. pap. 10.95 (ISBN 0-87304-154-2). Family Serv.
Psychosocial Development of Children. Irene M. Josselyn. LC 78-3112. 192p. 20.00x. Aronson.
Psychosocial Development of Minority Group Children. Ed. by Gloria J. Powell. LC 82-22677. 600p. 1983. 70.00 (ISBN 0-87630-277-0). Brunner-Mazel.
Psychosocial Dimensions of Cancer. Richard T. Goldberg & Robert M. Tull. LC 83-48069. 1983. 24.95x (ISBN 0-02-911980-4). Free Pr.
Psychosocial Dimensions of the Pregnant Family. Laurie Sherwen. 256p. 1987. text ed. 25.95 (ISBN 0-8261-4830-1); student ed. 19.95. Springer Pub.
Psychosocial Disorders in General Practice. P. Williams & A. Clare. 356p. 1980. 39.50 (ISBN 0-8089-1252-6, 794853). Grune.
Psychosocial Factors Affecting Health. Lipkin. LC 82-11249. 396p. 1982. 48.95 (ISBN 0-275-91371-6, C1371). Praeger.
Psychosocial Factors at Work & Their Relation to Health. Ed. by R. Kalimo et al. C. L. Cooper. 254p. 1987. pap. 23.40 (ISBN 92-4-156102-5). World Health.
Psychosocial Family Interventions In Chronic Pediatric Illness. Ed. by Adolph E. Christ & Kalman Flomenhaft. LC 82-5309. (Downstate Series of Research In Psychiatry & Psychology: Vol. 4). 224p. 1982. 49.50x (ISBN 0-306-41013-3, Plenum Pr). Plenum Pub.
Psychosocial Interior of the Family. 3rd ed. Ed. by Gerald Handel. LC 84-18398. 520p. 1985. lib. bdg. 49.95x (ISBN 0-202-30317-9); pap. text ed. 23.95x (ISBN 0-202-30318-7). Aldine de Gruyter.
Psychosocial Interventions in Schizophrenia: An International View. Ed. by H. Stierlin et al. (Illus.). 270p. 1983. pap. 34.00 (ISBN 0-387-12195-1). Springer-Verlag.
Psychosocial Interventions with Sensorially Disabled Persons. Ed. by Bruce W. Heller et al. (Mind & Medicine Ser.: No. III). 288p. 1987. 47.50 (ISBN 0-8089-1826-5, 791962). Grune.
Psychosocial Issues in Malignant Disease: Proceedings of the First Annual Conference of the British Psychosocial Oncology Group, London, 7-8 November, 1984. Ed. by M. Watson & S. Greer. 100p. 1986. 25.00 (ISBN 0-08-032010-4, Pub. by PPL). Pergamon.
Psychosocial Issues in the Treatment of Alcoholism. Ed. by David Cook et al. LC 84-28966. (Alcoholism Treatment Quarterly: Vol. 2, No. 1). 134p. 1985. text ed. 27.95 (ISBN 0-86656-363-6); pap. text ed. 19.95 (ISBN 0-86656-401-2). Haworth Pr.
Psychosocial Needs of the Aged: A Health Care Perspective. rev. ed. Ed. by Eugene Seymour. LC 78-60818. 1978. pap. 8.00x (ISBN 0-88474-048-X, 05750-9). Lexington Bks.
Psychosocial Nursing. 3rd ed. Frances M. Carter. 1981. text ed. write for info. (ISBN 0-02-319660-2). Macmillan.
Psychosocial Nursing Assessment & Intervention. Patricia D. Barry. 400p. 1984. pap. text ed. 18.95 (ISBN 0-397-54392-1, 64-03331, Lippincott Nursing). Lippincott.
Psychosocial Occupational Therapy: Practice in a Pluralistic Arena. R. Barris & G. Kielhofner. LC 83-62206. (Illus.). 352p. 1983. pap. text ed. 22.50 (ISBN 0-943596-03-3, RAMSCO 00600). Ramsco Pub.
Psychosocial Oncology: Proceedings of the 2nd & 3rd Meetings of the British Psychosocial Oncology Group, London & Leicester, 1985 & 1986. Ed. by M. Watson et al. (BPOG Ser.: No. 2). (Illus.). 216p. 1988. 57.95 (ISBN 0-08-035745-8). Pergamon.
Psychosocial Origins of Mental Retardation. Harold E. Simmons. 1980. pap. 10.00 (ISBN 0-87312-011-6). Psychogenic Disease.
Psychosocial Problems of College Men. Yale University Division of Student Mental Hygiene Staff. Ed. by Bryant M. Wedge. LC 72-85303. 304p. 1973. Repr. of 1958 ed. 29.50x (ISBN 0-8046-1710-4, Pub. by Kennikat). Assoc Faculty Pr.
Psychosocial Problems of College Men. Yale University Division of Student Mental Hygiene Staff. Ed. by Bryant M. Wedge. 1958. 27.50x (ISBN 0-686-83715-0). Elliots Bks.
Psychosocial Rehabilitative Programs for Older Adults. Sue V. Saxon & Mary J. Etten. (Illus.). 164p. 1984. 21.75 (ISBN 0-398-04966-1). C C Thomas.
Psychosocial Research on American Indian & Alaska Native Youth: An Indexed Guide to Recent Dissertations. Ed. by Spero M. Manson et al. LC 84-6583. (Bibliographies & Indexes in Psychology Ser.: No. 1). (Illus.). viii, 228p. 1984. lib. bdg. 36.95 (ISBN 0-313-23991-6, MPY/). Greenwood.
Psychosocial Research on Pediatric Hospitalization & Health Care: A Review of the Literature. Richard H. Thompson. (Illus.). 364p. 1985. 38.25 (ISBN 0-398-05070-8). C C Thomas.
Psychosocial Stress. A. Vingerhoets. 160p. 1985. pap. text ed. 14.50 (ISBN 90-265-0629-5, Pub. by Swets Zeitlinger Netherlands). Hogrefe Intl.
Psychosocial Stress & Cancer. Ed. by Carey L. Cooper. LC 84-5264. 263p. 1985. 34.95 (ISBN 0-471-90477-5). Wiley.
Psychosocial Stress: Trends in Theory & Research. Howard B. Kaplan. 1983. 42.50 (ISBN 0-12-397560-3). Acad Pr.
Psychosocial Studies. Ed. by Phyllis Caroff & Mary Gottesfeld. 185p. 1987. text ed. 24.95 (ISBN 0-89876-100-X). Gardner Pr.
Psychosocial Theories of the Self. Benjamin Lee. (Path in Psychology Ser.). 230p. 1982. 39.50x (ISBN 0-306-41117-2, Plenum Pr). Plenum Pub.
Psychosocial Therapy: A Social Work Perspective. Ed. by Francis J. Turner. LC 77-90456. (Treatment Approaches in the Human Servics Ser.). 1978. text ed. 19.95 (ISBN 0-02-932720-2). Free Pr.
Psychosocial Treatment of Schizophrenia: Multidimentional Concepts, Psychological, Family & Self-Help Perspectives. Ed. by J. S. Strauss et al. 260p. 1987. text ed. 39.00 (ISBN 0-920887-10-4, H Huber Canada). Hogrefe Intl.
Psychosoical Scenarios for Pediatrics. P. V. Trad. 265p. 1987. pap. 44.00 (ISBN 0-387-96586-6). Springer-Verlag.
Psychosomatic Approach to Illness. Ed. by R. L. Gallon. 320p. 1982. 60.50 (ISBN 0-444-00656-7, Biomedical Pr). Elsevier.
Psychosomatic Aspects of Allergy. C. Frazier. 1977. 31.95 (ISBN 0-442-21685-8). Van Nos Reinhold.
Psychosomatic Aspects of Gynecological Disorders: Seven Psychoanalytic Case Studies. Alfred O. Ludwig et al. LC 69-18039. (Commonwealth Fund Publications Ser). 1969. text ed. 11.00x (ISBN 0-674-72215-9). Harvard U Pr.
Psychosomatic Classics: Selected Papers from Psychosomatic Medicine, 1939-1958. Psychosomatic Medicine, Editorial Committee. 1972. pap. 23.75 (ISBN 3-8055-1232-5). S Karger.
Psychosomatic Concepts. Roy R. Grinker. LC 84-451254. 228p. 1983. 20.00x (ISBN 0-87668-698-6). Aronson.
Psychosomatic Diagnosis. Helen F. Dunbar. (Psychology Ser). 1968. Repr. of 1948 ed. 48.00 (ISBN 0-384-13285-5). Johnson Repr.

Psychosomatic Disorders. B. B. Wolman. (Illus.). 302p. 1988. 39.50x (ISBN 0-306-42945-4, Plenum Med Bk). Plenum Pub.
Psychosomatic Disorders in Childhood. Melitta Sperling. LC 76-22870. 1978. 35.00x (ISBN 0-87668-274-3). Aronson.
Psychosomatic Families: Anorexia Nervosa in Context. Salvador Minuchin et al. 1978. 20.00x (ISBN 0-674-72220-5). Harvard U Pr.
Psychosomatic Medicine: A Core Approach to Clinical Medicine. Ed. by Y. Ikemi & H. Ishikawa. (Illus.). 1979. pap. 86.75 (ISBN 3-8055-3022-6). S Karger.
Psychosomatic Medicine & Contemporary Psychoanalysis. Graeme J. Taylor. LC 86-27698. (Stress & Health Ser.: No. 3). 1987. 35.00x (ISBN 0-8236-5723-X, BN#05723). Intl Univs Pr.
Psychosomatic Medicine & Liaison Psychiatry: Selected Papers. Z. J. Lipowski. LC 85-12474. 470p. 1985. 49.50x (ISBN 0-306-42038-4, Plenum Med.). Plenum Pub.
Psychosomatic Medicine & Logotherapy. Hiroshi Takashima. (Illus.). 91p. (Orig.). 1977. pap. 6.95 (ISBN 0-917867-03-3). Inst Logo.
Psychosomatic Medicine as an Integrated Approach to Life, Education & Doctor-Patient Cooperation: Fourteenth European Conference on Psychosomatic Research, Noordwijkerhout, September 1982. Ed. by H. E. Pelser. (Journal-Psychotherapy & Psychosomatics: Vol. 40, No. 1-4). (Illus.). 272p. 1983. pap. 93.50 (ISBN 3-8055-3785-9). S Karger.
Psychosomatic Medicine: Current Trends & Clinical Applications. Ed. by Z. J. Lipowski et al. (Illus.). 1977. text ed. 37.50x (ISBN 0-19-502169-X). Oxford U Pr.
Psychosomatic Medicine in a Changing World: Theoretical, Clinical & Transcultural Aspects. Ed. by A. J. Krakowski & C. P. Kimball. (Journal: Psychotherapy & Psychosomatics: Vol. 38, No. 1-4). (Illus.). 310p. 1982. pap. 88.00 (ISBN 3-8055-3544-9). S Karger.
Psychosomatic Medicine in Obstetrics & Gynecology: Proceedings. International Congress of Psychosomatic Medicine in Obstetrics & Gynecology, 3rd, London, 1971. Ed. by Norman Morris. (Illus.). 1972. 100.00 (ISBN 3-8055-1314-3). S Karger.
Psychosomatic Medicine: Its Principles & Applications. Franz Alexander. 1987. 29.95 (ISBN 0-393-70036-4). Norton.
Psychosomatic Medicine: New Facts & Old Controversies: Proceedings of the World Congress of the International College of Psychosomatic Medicine Held in Sydney-Australia, 9th, August-September, 1987, Pt. II. Ed. by G. A. Fava et al. (Journal: Psychotherapy & Psychosomatics: Vol. 48, No. 1-3, 1987). (Illus.). 196p. 1988. pap. 95.50 (ISBN 3-8055-4847-8). S Karger.
Psychosomatic Medicine: New Facts & Old Controversies: Proceedings of the World Congress of the International College of Psychosomatic Medicine Held in Sydney-Australia, 9th, August-September, 1987, Pt. 1. Ed. by G. A. Fava et al. (Journal: Psychotherapy & Psychosomatics: Vol. 47, No. 3-4, 1987). (Illus.). iv, 108p. 1988. pap. 76.00 (ISBN 3-8055-4845-1). S Karger.
Psychosomatic Medicine: Past & Future. Ed. by G. N. Christodoulou. LC 87-29075. (Illus.). 396p. 1988. 65.00x (ISBN 0-306-42780-X, Plenum Pr). Plenum Pub.
Psychosomatic Medicine: Theoretical, Clinical & Transcultural Aspects. Ed. by Adam J. Krakowski & Chase P. Kimbell. LC 83-3977. 846p. 1983. 125.00x (ISBN 0-306-41279-9, Plenum Pr). Plenum Pub.
Psychosomatic Medicine: Theory, Physiology, & Practice. Ed. by Stanley Cheren. (Stress & Health Ser.: No. 1-2). 1000p. 1988. Set. text ed. 40.00x (ISBN 0-8236-5725-6, BN#05725); text ed. 40.00x ea. (ISBN 0-8236-5726-4, BN#05726). Intl Univs Pr.
Psychosomatic Obstetrics & Gynecology. Ed. by Miriam B. Rosenthal & D. H. Smith. (Advances in Psychosomatic Medicine: Vol. 12). (Illus.). vi, 190p. 1985. 54.75 (ISBN 3-8055-3967-3). S Karger.
Psychosomatic Practice & Research: International College of Psychosomatic Medicine, 7th. World Congress, Hamburg, July 1983. Ed. by A. J. Krakowski & C. P. Kimball. (Psychotherapy & Psychosomatics: Vol. 42, Nos. 1-4, 1984). (Illus.). 224p. 1984. pap. 86.75 (ISBN 3-8055-3975-4). S Karger.
Psychosomatic Research & Practice. Ed. by Adam J. Krakowski & Chase P. Kimball. 248p. 1985. pap. 78.00x. Transaction Bks.
Psychosomatic Research: Proceedings of the European Conference on Psychosomatic Research, 12th, Bodo, July 1978. European Conference on Psychosomatic Research Staff. Ed. by H. Freyberger. (Psychotherapy & Psychosomatics: Vol. 32, No. 1-4). (Illus.). 86.75 (ISBN 3-8055-3044-7). S Karger.
Psychosomatic Symptoms: Psychodynamic Treatment of Their Underlying Personality Disorder. C. Philip Wilson & Ira L. Mintz. 400p. 1989. 40.00x (ISBN 0-87668-877-6). Aronson.
Psychosomatic Yoga. J. Mumford. (Paths to Inner Power Ser.). 96p. 1974. 1.25 (ISBN 0-85030-208-0, Pub. by Thorsons UK). Weiser.
Psychosomatics & Biofeedback. Ed. by W. H. Wolters & G. Sinnema. 1979. pap. 13.00 (ISBN 90-313-0348-8, Pub. by Martinus Nijhoff Netherlands). Kluwer Academic.
Psychosomatics in Essential Hypertension. Ed. by M. Koster et al. (Bibliotheca Psychiatrica: No. 144). 1970. pap. 39.50 (ISBN 3-8055-0332-6). S Karger.
Psychosomatische Medizin: Grundlagen und Anwendungsgebiete. 4th, rev. ed. Franz Alexander. (Illus.). xvi, 244p. (Ger.). 1985. pap. text ed. 19.20x (ISBN 3-11-010192-0). De Gruyter.
PsychoSpiritual Power. A. Lee Henderson. (Illus.). 225p. (Orig.). 1988. pap. 7.95 (ISBN 0-929386-01-9); wkbk 5.95. AMEC Sunday Schl Union.
Psychosurgery: A Scientific Analysis. Ed. by A. J. O'Callaghan & D. Carroll. 1983. lib. bdg. 48.00 (ISBN 0-85200-458-3, Pub. by MTP Pr England). Kluwer Academic.
Psychosurgery & Society: A Symposium Organised by the Neuropsychiatric Institute, Sydney, Australia. Ed. by J. Sydney Smith & L. G. Kiloh. 1977. 55.00 (ISBN 0-08-021836-9). Pergamon.
Psychosurgery & the Medical Control of Violence: Autonomy & Deviance. Samuel I. Shuman. LC 77-23374. 360p. 1977. 27.50x (ISBN 0-8143-1579-8). Wayne St U Pr.
Psychosynthesis. Roberto Assagioli. 1971. pap. 6.95 (ISBN 0-14-004263-6). Penguin.
Psychosynthesis in Education: A Guide to the Joy of Learning. Diana Whitmore. 244p. (Orig.). 1986. pap. 9.95 (ISBN 0-89281-120-X). Inner Tradit.
Psychotechnic League. Poul Anderson. 1985. pap. 2.95 (ISBN 0-8125-3059-4, Dist. by Warner Pub Services & Saint Martin's Press). Tor Bks.
Psychotechniques: Act Right Feel Right. Salvatore V. Didato. 304p. 1986. pap. 3.95 (ISBN 0-425-08790-5). Berkley Pub.
Psychotherapeutic Action of the Physician: Proceedings, Vol. 21, Nos. 1-6. International Congress of Psychosomatic Medicine, 4th, Paris, Sept. 1970. Ed. by L. Chertok & M. Sapir. (Illus.). 1973. Repr. 57.50 (ISBN 3-8055-1482-4). S Karger.
Psychotherapeutic Approaches to Specific DSM-III-R Categories: A Resource Book for Treatment Planning. Kenneth U. Gutsch. 276p. 1988. text ed. 36.50x (ISBN 0-398-05398-7). C C Thomas.
Psychotherapeutic Approaches to the Resistant Child. Richard A. Gardner. LC 75-5591. 408p. 1975. 35.00x (ISBN 0-87668-203-4). Aronson.
Psychotherapeutic Attraction. Arnold P. Goldstein. LC 79-119598. 260p. 1971. 25.00 (ISBN 0-08-016398-X). Pergamon.
Psychotherapeutic Change: An Alternative Approach to Meaning & Measurment. Alvin R. Mahrer. LC 85-588. 1985. 22.95 (ISBN 0-393-70007-0). Norton.
Psychotherapeutic Conspiracy. Robert Langs. LC 81-20601. 352p. 1982. 30.00x (ISBN 0-87668-488-6). Aronson.
Psychotherapeutic Drug Market. Frost & Sullivan, Inc. Staff. 340p. 1986. 1800.00 (ISBN 0-86621-489-5, A1562). Frost & Sullivan.
Psychotherapeutic Impasse. Myron F. Weiner. 1982. text ed. 19.95x (ISBN 0-02-934620-7). Free Pr.
Psychotherapeutic Instrument. Stanley L. Olinick. LC 80-620. 216p. 1980. 25.00x (ISBN 0-87668-403-7). Aronson.
Psychotherapeutic Intervention in Hysterical Disorders. William J. Mueller & Albert S. Aniskiewicz. LC 85-15000075. 300p. 1986. 30.00x (ISBN 0-87668-913-6). Aronson.
Psychotherapeutic Intervention in Schizophrenia. Lewis B. Hill. LC 55-5128. 1955. 8.00x (ISBN 0-226-33649-2). U of Chicago Pr.
Psychotherapeutic Interventions in Life-Threatening Illness. Ed. by H. Freyberger. (Advances in Psychosomatic Medicine: Vol. 10). (Illus.). xviii, 206p. 1980. 63.50 (ISBN 3-8055-3066-8). S Karger.
Psychotherapeutic Management in the Day Program: Practices in Day Hospital Psychiatry. Jerzy E. Henisz. (Illus.). 194p. 1984. 32.50x (ISBN 0-398-04874-6). C C Thomas.
Psychotherapeutic Process. International Congress of Psychotherapy, 10th, Paris, July 1976. Ed. by J. C. Benoit et al. (Psychotherapy & Psychosomatics: Vol. 29, Nos. 1-4). 1978. 94.75 (ISBN 3-8055-2762-4). S Karger.
Psychotherapeutic Process: A Research Handbook. Ed. by Leslie S. Greenberg & William M. Pinsof. LC 85-30596. 734p. 1986. text ed. 65.00 (ISBN 0-89862-651-X). Guilford Pr.
Psychotherapeutic Strategies in Late Latency Through Early Adolescence. Charles Sarnoff. LC 87-19474. 275p. 1987. 30.00x (ISBN 0-87668-937-3). Aronson.
Psychotherapeutic Strategies in the Latency Years. Charles Sarnoff. LC 87-24194. 550p. 1987. 37.50x (ISBN 0-87668-936-5). Aronson.
Psychotherapeutic Techniques of Richard A. Gardner. Richard A. Gardner. LC 86-11531. 950p. 1986. 35.00 (ISBN 0-933812-14-0). Creative Therapeutics.
Psychotherapeutic Treatment of Cancer Patients. Ed. by Jane C. Goldberg. LC 81-66326. 344p. 1981. 34.95 (ISBN 0-02-911960-X). Free Pr.
Psychotherapeutics: A Symposium. Morton Prince et al. LC 75-16728. (Classics in Psychiatry Ser.). 1976. Repr. of 1910 ed. 15.00x (ISBN 0-405-07451-4). Ayer Co Pubs.
Psychotherapeutics in Primary Care. Steven L. Dubovsky. 240p. 1981. 34.50 (ISBN 0-8089-1337-9, 791090). Grune.
Psychotheraphy & Culture Conflict in Community Mental Health. Georgene H. Seward. LC 74-190213. pap. 59.50 (ISBN 0-317-07901-8, 2012537). Bks Demand UMI.
Psychotheraphy & Multiple Personality: Selected Essays. Morton Prince. Ed. by Nathan G. Hale, Jr. LC 74-82574. 336p. 1975. text ed. 24.50x (ISBN 0-674-72225-6). Harvard U Pr.
Psychotheraphy of Everyday Life. N. Peseschkian. (Illus.). 265p. 1985. pap. 14.00 (ISBN 0-387-15767-0). Springer-Verlag.
Psychotheraphy Today. Ed. by Ved Varma. LC 74-180779. pap. 87.80 (ISBN 0-317-28430-4, 2051266). Bks Demand UMI.
Psychotherapist-Patient Privilege: A Critical Examination. Daniel W. Shuman & Myron F. Weiner. 168p. 1987. 29.75x (ISBN 0-398-05338-3). C C Thomas.
Psychotherapist's Casebook: Theory & Technique in the Practice of Modern Therapies. Ed. by Irwin L. Kutash & Alexander Wolf. LC 85-45907. (Social & Behavioral Science Ser.). 1986. text ed. 39.95x (ISBN 0-87589-685-5). Jossey-Bass.
Psychotherapists in Action. H. H. Strupp. LC 60-6020. (Illus.). 352p. 1960. 55.50 (ISBN 0-8089-0490-6, 794430). Grune.
Psychotherapists in Clinical Practice: Cognitive & Behavioral Perspectives. Ed. by Neil S. Jacobson. LC 84-18474. 451p. 1987. lib. bdg. 35.00 (ISBN 0-89862-690-0). Guilford Pr.
Psychotherapy. 2nd ed. Paul A. Dewald. LC 72-145664. 1971. text ed. 19.95x (ISBN 0-465-06766-2). Basic.
Psychotherapy: A Basic Text. Robert Langs. LC 81-17663. 800p. 1982. 45.00x (ISBN 0-87668-466-5). Aronson.
Psychotherapy: A Cognitive Integration of Theory & Practice. Anthony Ryle. 196p. 1982. 31.50 (ISBN 0-8089-1488-X, 793710). Grune.
Psychotherapy: An Eclectic Approach. Sol. L. Garfield. LC 79-17724. (Personality Processes Ser.). 1980. 38.50x (ISBN 0-471-04490-3, Pub. by Wiley-Interscience). Wiley.
Psychotherapy & Behavior Change: Social, Cultural & Methodological Perspectives. H. N. Higginbotham et al. (General Psychology Ser.: No. 152). 416p. 1988. text ed. 47.50 (ISBN 0-08-028089-7); pap. text ed. 19.50 (ISBN 0-08-028088-9). Pergamon.
Psychotherapy & Culture. rev. ed. Theodora M. Abel et al. LC 86-19191. 256p. 1987. 29.95x (ISBN 0-8263-0893-7); pap. 15.95 (ISBN 0-8263-0894-5). U of NM Pr.
Psychotherapy & Existentialism. Victor E. Frankl. 1968. pap. 9.95 (ISBN 0-671-20056-9, Touchstone Bks). S&S.
Psychotherapy & Existentialism. Viktor E. Frankl. 1985. pap. 3.95 (ISBN 0-671-54729-1). WSP.
Psychotherapy & Existentialism. Date not set. pap. 3.95 (ISBN 0-317-56688-1). PB.
Psychotherapy & Human Science see Proceedings.
Psychotherapy & Human Science: Proceedings, Pt.1. International Congress of Psychotherapy, 8th, Milan, Aug. 1970. Ed. by H. K. Fierz & T. Spoerri. 1972. Repr. 24.00 (ISBN 3-8055-1475-1). S Karger.
Psychotherapy & Patient Relationships. Ed. by Michael J. Lambert. LC 82-71876. (Dorsey Professional Bks.). 324p. 1983. 33.00 (ISBN 0-256-24900-8). Dorsey.
Psychotherapy & Process: The Fundamentals of an Existential-Humanistic Approach. James F. Bugental. 163p. 1978. pap. text ed. write for info (ISBN 0-394-34758-7, RanC). Random.
Psychotherapy & Psychoanalysis: Theory, Practice, Research. Robert Wallerstein. LC 73-16854. 400p. 1975. text ed. 50.00x (ISBN 0-8236-5410-9). Intl Univs Pr.
Psychotherapy & Religion. Josef Rudin. Tr. by Paul C. Bailey & Elisabeth Reinecke. LC 68-12291. 1968. pap. 8.95x (ISBN 0-268-00226-6). U of Notre Dame Pr.
Psychotherapy & Society. W. G. Eliasberg. 236p. 1959. 6.95 (ISBN 0-8022-0446-5). Philos Lib.
Psychotherapy & the Abrasive Patient. Ed. by E. Mark Stern. LC 84-6644. (Psychotherapy Patient: Vol. 1, No. 1). 140p. 1984. text ed. 19.95 (ISBN 0-86656-325-3, B325). Haworth Pr.
Psychotherapy & the Behavioral Sciences. Lewis R. Wolberg. LC 66-78287. 206p. 1966. 52.50 (ISBN 0-8089-0535-X, 794869). Grune.
Psychotherapy & the Bored Patient. Ed. by E. Mark Stern. LC 87-31085. (Psychotherapy Patient Ser.). (Illus.). 160p. 1988. text ed. 19.95 (ISBN 0-86656-641-4). Haworth Pr.
Psychotherapy & the Confrontation Problem-Solving Technique. Harry H. Garner. LC 74-110426. 362p. 1971. 18.50 (ISBN 0-87527-011-5). Green.
Psychotherapy & the Creative Patient. Ed. by E. Mark Stern. LC 88-2694. (Psychotherapy Patient Ser.: Vol. 4, No. 1). (Illus.). 180p. 1988. pap. text ed. 14.95 (ISBN 0-86656-831-X). Haworth Pr.
Psychotherapy & the Creative Patient. Ed. by E. Mark Stern. LC 88-2694. (Psychotherapy Patient Ser.: Vol. 4, No. 1). (Illus.). 180p. 1988. text ed. 24.95 (ISBN 0-86656-642-2). Haworth Pr.
Psychotherapy & the Dual Research Tradition, Vol. 7. GAP Committee on Therapy. LC 62-2872. (Report No. 73). 1969. pap. 5.00 (ISBN 0-87318-102-6, Pub. by GAP). Brunner-Mazel.
Psychotherapy & the Grieving Patient. Ed. by E. Mark Stern. LC 85-17619. 138p. 1986. pap. text ed. 8.95 (ISBN 0-918393-24-8). Harrington Pk.
Psychotherapy & the Grieving Patient. Ed. by E. Mark Stern. LC 85-17618. (Psychotherapy Patient Ser.: Vol. 2, No. 1). 138p. 1986. text ed. 19.95 (ISBN 0-86656-514-0, B514). Haworth Pr.
Psychotherapy & the Law. Ed. by Louis Everstine & Diana Sullivan-Everstine. 288p. 1986. 34.50 (ISBN 0-8089-1780-3, 791172). Grune.
Psychotherapy & the Lonely Patient. Ed. by Samuel M. Natale. LC 86-12101. 152p. 1986. pap. 9.95 (ISBN 0-918393-26-4). Harrington PK.
Psychotherapy & the Lonely Patient. Ed. by Samuel M. Natale. LC 86-12108. (Psychotherapy Patient Ser.). 152p. 1986. text ed. 19.95 (ISBN 0-86656-517-5). Haworth Pr.
Psychotherapy & the Memorable Patient. William Kir-Stimon. LC 86-22852. 160p. 1986. pap. 9.95 (ISBN 0-918393-25-6). Harrington PK.
Psychotherapy & the Memorable Patient. Ed. by William Kir-Stimon & Mark Stern. LC 86-25648. (Psychotherapy Patient Ser.). 160p. 1986. text ed. 19.95 (ISBN 0-86656-516-7). Haworth Pr.
Psychotherapy & the Paranoid Process. William W. Meissner. LC 85-15614. 385p. 1986. 40.00x (ISBN 0-87668-752-4). Aronson.
Psychotherapy & the Religiously Committed Patient. Ed. by E. Mark Stern. LC 84-25276. (Psychotherapy Patient Ser.: Vol. 1, No. 3). 158p. 1985. text ed. 19.95 (ISBN 0-86656-394-6); pap. text ed. 14.95 (ISBN 0-86656-396-2). Haworth Pr.
Psychotherapy & the Role of the Environment. Harold M. Voth & Marjorie H. Orth. LC 72-13818. 354p. 1973. text ed. 39.95 (ISBN 0-87705-102-X). Human Sci Pr.
Psychotherapy & the Selfless Patient. Ed. by Jerome A. Travers. LC 85-24817. (Psychotherapy Patient Ser.: Vol. 2, No. 2). 109p. 1986. text ed. 19.95 (ISBN 0-86656-515-9, B515). Haworth Pr.
Psychotherapy & the Somatizing Patient. Ed. by E. Mark Stern & Virginia F. Stern. (Psychotherapy Patient: Vol. 4, No. 2). 208p. 1988. text ed. 19.95 (ISBN 0-86656-753-4). Haworth Pr.
Psychotherapy & the Spiritual Quest. David G. Benner. 176p. 1988. 13.95 (ISBN 0-8010-0948-0). Baker Bk.
Psychotherapy & the Terrorized Patient. Ed. by E. Mark Stern. LC 85-8468. (Psychotherapy Patient Ser.: Vol. 1, No. 4). 116p. 1985. text ed. 19.95 (ISBN 0-86656-442-X). Haworth Pr.
Psychotherapy & the Uncommitted Patient. Ed. by Jerome A. Travers & E. Mark Stern. LC 84-19754. (Psychotherapy Patient Ser.: Vol. 1, No. 2). 105p. 1985. text ed. 19.95 (ISBN 0-86656-371-7). Haworth Pr.
Psychotherapy & Training in Clinical Social Work. Ed. by Judith Mishne. LC 78-57616. (Clinical Social Work Ser.). 288p. 1978. 22.95x (ISBN 0-470-26387-3). Halsted Pr.
Psychotherapy Based on Human Longing. Robert Murphy, Jr. LC 60-14173. (Orig.). 1960. pap. 2.50x (ISBN 0-87574-111-8, 111). Pendle Hill.
Psychotherapy by Reciprocal Inhibition. Joseph Wolpe. 1958. 22.50x (ISBN 0-8047-0509-7). Stanford U Pr.
Psychotherapy by Structured Learning Theory. Raymond B. Cattell. (Illus.). 192p. 1987. text ed. 29.95 (ISBN 0-8261-5080-2). Springer Pub.
Psychotherapy: Clinical, Research & Theoretical Issues. Hans Strupp. LC 72-96537. 816p. 1973. 45.00x (ISBN 0-87668-059-7). Aronson.
Psychotherapy East & West. Alan W. Watts. 1975. pap. 3.95 (ISBN 0-394-71609-4, Vin). Random.
Psychotherapy East & West: A Unifying Paradigm. Swami Ajaya. 340p. (Orig.). pap. 9.95 (ISBN 0-89389-087-1). Himalayan Pubs.
Psychotherapy for Better or Worse: The Problem of Negative Effects. Hans Strupp et al. LC 77-2439. 1977. 22.50x (ISBN 0-87668-306-5). Aronson.
Psychotherapy for Men: Transcending the Masculine Mystique. Robert A. Silverberg. 332p. 1986. 32.75 (ISBN 0-398-05183-6). C C Thomas.
Psychotherapy for Women: Treatment Toward Equality. Edna I. Rawlings & Dianne K. Carter. (Illus.). 500p. 1977. 39.50 (ISBN 0-398-03584-9). C C Thomas.
Psychotherapy Handbook. Ed. by Richie Herink. (Orig.). 1980. pap. 14.95 (ISBN 0-452-00832-8, Mer). NAL.
Psychotherapy: Impact on Psychoanalytic Training. Ed. by Edward D. Joseph & Robert S. Wallerstein. LC 82-12719. (Influence of the Practice & Theory of Psychotherapy on Education in Psychoanalysis International Psycho-Analytical Association Monograph: No. 1). xvi, 174p. 1983. 27.50x (ISBN 0-8236-5405-2). Intl Univs Pr.
Psychotherapy in a New Key: A Guide to Time-Limited Dynamic Psychotherapy. Hans H. Strupp & Jeffrey L. Binder. LC 83-46075. 320p. 1985. 26.95x (ISBN 0-465-06747-6). Basic.

Psychotherapy in a Religious Framework. Rebecca L. Propst. LC 86-27582. 209p. 1988. text ed. 29.95 (ISBN 0-89885-350-8). Human Sci Pr.

Psychotherapy in Child Guidance. Gordon Hamilton. LC 47-2486. 340p. 1947. 29.00 (ISBN 0-231-01637-9). Columbia U Pr.

Psychotherapy in Christian Perspective. Ed. by David G. Benner. 300p. 1987. pap. 14.95 (ISBN 0-8010-0942-1). Baker Bk.

Psychotherapy in Chronic Ulcerative Colitis. Aeron Karush et al. LC 76-28939. pap. 39.50 (ISBN 0-317-07787-2, 2016668). Bks Demand UMI.

Psychotherapy in the Community. Eric Lager & Isreal Zwerling. Ed. by Alvjn F. Gardner. (Allied Health Professions Monograph Ser.). 200p. 1983. 22.50 (ISBN 0-87527-315-7). Green.

Psychotherapy in the Third Reich: The Goring Institute. Geoffrey Cocks. (Illus.). 1985. 29.95 (ISBN 0-19-503461-9). Oxford U Pr.

Psychotherapy in the Third Reich: The Goring Institute. Geoffrey Cocks. 416p. 1986. pap. 9.95 (ISBN 0-19-504227-1). Oxford U Pr.

Psychotherapy Insight & Style: The Existential Moment. Len Bergantino. LC 86-71119. 288p. 1986. 25.00x (ISBN 0-87668-906-3). Aronson.

Psychotherapy Maze: A Consumer's Guide to Getting In & Out of Therapy. rev. ed. Otto Ehrenberg & Miriam Ehrenberg. 1986. pap. text ed. 6.95 (ISBN 0-671-62287-0, Fireside). S&S.

Psychotherapy Maze: A Consumer's Guide to Getting in & Out of Therapy. rev. ed. Otto Ehrenberg & Miriam Ehrenberg. LC 86-28748. 240p. 1986. 17.95x (ISBN 0-87668-959-4). Aronson.

Psychotherapy, Medical & Psychological Research Subject Index with Bibliography. John C. Bartone. LC 82-72022. 120p. 1983. 34.50 (ISBN 0-941864-60-X); pap. 26.50 (ISBN 0-941864-61-8). ABBE Pubs Assn.

Psychotherapy of People with Physical Symptoms: Brief Strategic Approaches. Steven Goldsmith. LC 86-11037. (Illus.). 196p. (Orig.). 1986. lib. bdg. 19.75 (ISBN 0-8191-5411-3); pap. text ed. 12.50 (ISBN 0-8191-5412-1). U Pr of Amer.

Psychotherapy of Preoedipal Conditions. Hyman Spotnitz. LC 75-37489. 448p. 1987. 35.00x (ISBN 0-87668-242-5). Aronson.

Psychotherapy of Schizophrenia. Gaetano Benedetti. 1987. 42.50x (ISBN 0-317-60230-6). NYU Pr.

Psychotherapy of Schizophrenia. Ed. by John G. Gunderson & Loren Mosher. LC 75-6844. 448p. 1975. 35.00x (ISBN 0-87668-208-5). Aronson.

Psychotherapy of Schizophrenia. Ed. by John S. Strauss et al. LC 80-16524. 320p. 1980. 49.50x (ISBN 0-306-40497-4, Plenum Med. Bk.). Plenum Pub.

Psychotherapy of Schizophrenia: The Treatment of Choice. Bertram P. Karon & Gary R. VandenBos. LC 81-65785. 528p. 1981. 35.00x (ISBN 0-87668-444-4). Aronson.

Psychotherapy of the Adolescent: At Different Levels of Psychiatric Practice with Special Emphasis on the Role of the School. Ed. by Benjamin H. Balser. LC 57-9326. 270p. (Orig.). 1959. text ed. 32.50x (ISBN 0-8236-5400-1); pap. text ed. 17.95 (ISBN 0-8236-8249-8, 225400). Intl Univs Pr.

Psychotherapy of the Borderline Adult. James F. Masterson. LC 76-16564. 1976. 30.00 (ISBN 0-87630-127-8). Brunner-Mazel.

Psychotherapy of the Combat Veteran. Ed. by Harvey J. Schwartz. LC 83-23022. 315p. text ed. 29.95 (ISBN 0-88331-191-7). Luce.

Psychotherapy of the Disorders of the Self: The Masterson Approach. Ed. by James F. Masterson & Ralph Klein. 475p. 1988. 45.00 (ISBN 0-87630-533-8). Brunner-Mazel.

Psychotherapy of the Psychoses: Perspectives on Current Techiques of Treatment. Ed. by Arthur Burton. LC 76-13507. 396p. 1976. Repr. of 1961 ed. 26.50 (ISBN 0-88275-413-0). Krieger.

Psychotherapy of the Religious Patient. Ed. by Moshe H. Spero. 250p. 1985. 32.75 (ISBN 0-398-05058-9). C C Thomas.

Psychotherapy of the Self. Hyman L. Muslin & Eduardo R. Val. LC 87-6356. 240p. 1987. 25.00 (ISBN 0-87630-464-1). Brunner-Mazel.

Psychotherapy: Portraits in Fiction. Jesse Geller & Paul Spector. LC 87-17528. 302p. 1987. 25.00 (ISBN 0-87668-935-7). Aronson.

Psychotherapy: Practice, Research, Policy. Ed. by Gary VandenBos. LC 80-23098. (Sage Studies in Community Mental Health: Vol. 1). (Illus.). 1980. 29.95 (ISBN 0-8039-1536-5); pap. 16.95 (ISBN 0-8039-1537-3). Sage.

Psychotherapy Process: Current Issues & Future Directions. Ed. by M. J. Mahoney. LC 79-9134. (Illus.). 420p. 1980. 39.50x (ISBN 0-306-40244-0, Plenum Pr). Plenum Pub.

Psychotherapy Research. Ed. by Alan E. Kazdin. (Special Issue, Journal of Consulting & Clinical Psychology: Vol. 54, No. 1). 118p. 1986. pap. 16.00 (ISBN 0-912704-64-0, 2065401); members 12.00. Am Psychol.

Psychotherapy Research. Gary R. VandenBos. (Special Issue, American Psychologist: Vol. 41, No. 2). 1986. pap. 16.00 (ISBN 0-912704-65-9, 4014102); members 12.00. Am Psychol.

Psychotherapy Research & Behavior Change. Ed. by John H. Harvey & Marjorie M. Parks. LC 82-1668. (Master Lecture Ser.: Vol. 1). 193p. (Orig.). 1982. 24.00 (ISBN 0-912704-61-6, 4410010); members 18.00. Am Psychol.

Psychotherapy Research: Methodological & Efficacy Issues. APA Commission on Psychiatric Therapies. LC 82-8763. (Illus.). 280p. 1982. pap. 15.00x Report (ISBN 0-89042-101-3, 42-101-3). Am Psychiatric.

Psychotherapy Research: Where Are We & Where Should We Go? Ed. by Janet B. Williams & Robert L. Spitzer. LC 83-26660. (Annual Proceedings for APPA Ser.). 424p. 1984. 50.00 (ISBN 0-89862-635-8). Guilford Pr.

Psychotherapy Revised: New Frontiers in Research & Practice. E. Lakin Phillips. 264p. 1985. text ed. 29.95 (ISBN 0-89859-571-1). L Erlbaum Assocs.

Psychotherapy: The Art of Wooing Nature. Sheldon Roth. LC 86-28763. 294p. 1987. 30.00x (ISBN 0-87668-945-4). Aronson.

Psychotherapy: The Listening Voice. Richard Leva & Rogers. 275p. 1987. 21.95 (ISBN 0-915202-68-9). Accel Devel.

Psychotherapy: The Mystery Solved. Charles W. Patterson. LC 84-61941. 118p. (Orig.). 1984. pap. 8.00 (ISBN 0-9614334-1-8). Passages.

Psychotherapy: The Private & Very Personal Viewpoints of Doctor & Patient. Harold E. McNeely & Norma Obele. LC 72-88581. 304p. 1973. 20.95x (ISBN 0-911012-35-4). Nelson-Hall.

Psychotherapy: the Promised Land. Michael Dinoff et al. LC 77-324. 142p. 1977. 11.00 (ISBN 0-8173-2730-4). U of Ala Pr.

Psychotherapy: The Purchase of Friendship. William Schofield. 212p. 1986. pap. 19.95 (ISBN 0-88738-659-8). Transaction Bks.

Psychotherapy Through Clinical Role Playing. David A. Kipper. LC 86-14744. 408p. 1986. 40.00 (ISBN 0-87630-433-1). Brunner-Mazel.

Psychotherapy Through Imagery. 2nd ed. Joseph E. Shorr. (Illus.). 476p. 1983. 24.50 (ISBN 0-86577-083-2). Thieme Med Pubs.

Psychotherapy Through the Group Process. Dorothy S. Whitaker & Morton A. Lieberman. LC 64-10206. 1964. 28.95x (ISBN 0-202-26056-9). Aldine de Gruyter.

Psychotherapy Tradecraft: The Technique & Style of Doing Therapy. Theodore H. Blau. LC 87-21786. 328p. 1988. 27.50 (ISBN 0-87630-479-X). Brunner-Mazel.

Psychotherapy Versus Iatrogeny: A Confrontation for Physicians. Nikola Schipkowensky. LC 76-49515. 508p. 1977. text ed. 35.00x (ISBN 0-8143-1555-0). Wayne St U Pr.

Psychotherapy with Adolescent Girls. Doris Lamb. LC 78-62560. (Social & Behavioral Science Ser.). 1978. text ed. 26.95x (ISBN 0-87589-382-1). Jossey-Bass.

Psychotherapy with Adolescent Girls. 2nd ed. Doris Lamb. LC 86-12211. 278p. 1986. 29.50x (ISBN 0-306-42242-5, Plenum Pr). Plenum Pub.

Psychotherapy with Adolescents. Richard A. Gardner. 750p. 1988. 35.00 (ISBN 0-933812-18-3). Creative Therapeutics.

Psychotherapy with Children. Frederick H. Allen. LC 79-52647. vi, 311p. 1979. 26.95x (ISBN 0-8032-1002-7); pap. 5.95x (ISBN 0-8032-5900-X, BB 707, Bison). U of Nebr Pr.

Psychotherapy with Children of Divorce. Richard A. Gardner. LC 75-42543. 552p. 1976. 35.00x (ISBN 0-87668-240-9). Aronson.

Psychotherapy with Families: An Analytic Approach. Ed. by Sally Box et al. 160p. (Orig.). 1981. pap. 13.95x (ISBN 0-7100-0854-6). Routledge Chapman & Hall.

Psychotherapy with Older Adults. Bob Knight. 240p. 1985. text ed. 27.50 (ISBN 0-8039-2633-2). Sage.

Psychotherapy with Psychotherapists. Florence W. Kaslow. LC 83-18655. 202p. 1984. text ed. 24.95 (ISBN 0-86656-207-9). Haworth Pr.

Psychotherapy with Schizophrenics. Ed. by Eugene B. Brody & Fredrick C. Redlich. (Monograph Series on Schizophrenia: No. 3). 246p. (Orig.). 1964. text ed. 30.00x (ISBN 0-8236-5420-6). Intl Univs Pr.

Psychotherapy with Severely Deprived Children. Ed. by Mary Boston & Rolene Szur. 176p. (Orig.). 1983. pap. 10.95X (ISBN 0-7100-9536-8). Routledge Chapman & Hall.

Psychotherapys. Ed. by Frederic Flach. (Directions in Psychiatry Ser.: No. 5). 1989. 29.95 (ISBN 0-393-70063-1). Norton.

Psychotic Children Grown Up: A Prospective Follow-Up Study in Adolescence & Adulthood. William Goldfarb et al. LC 77-93594. (Special Issue of Issues in Child Mental Health). 96p. 1979. pap. 16.95 (ISBN 0-87705-331-6). Human Sci Pr.

Psychotic Conflict & Reality. Edith Jacobson. LC 67-29736. (New York Psychoanalytic Institute Freud Anniversary Lecture Ser.). 80p. 1967. text ed. 22.50x (ISBN 0-8236-5680-2). Intl Univs Pr.

Psychotic Core. Michael Eigen. LC 85-3956. 387p. 1986. 30.00x (ISBN 0-87668-895-4). Aronson.

Psychotic Patient: Medication & Psychotherapy. David Greenfeld. 192p. 1984. 25.95x (ISBN 0-02-912830-7). Free Pr.

Psychotic Personality. Leon J. Saul & Silas L. Warner. 320p. 1982. 27.95 (ISBN 0-442-27764-4). Van Nos Reinhold.

Psychotic Process. John Frosch. LC 82-21392. xiii, 521p. 1983. text ed. 52.50x (ISBN 0-8236-5690-X). Intl Univs Pr.

Psychotic Reactions & Carburetor Dung: An Anthology. Lester Bangs. Ed. by Greil Marcus. LC 87-45122. 416p. 1987. 19.95 (ISBN 0-394-53896-X). Knopf.

Psychotic Reactions & Carburetor Dung. Lester Bangs. 1988. 9.95 (ISBN 0-679-72045-6, Vin). Random.

Psychotic States: A Psychoanalytic Approach. Herbert A. Rosenfeld. 264p. 1966. text ed. 30.00x (ISBN 0-8236-5700-0). Intl Univs Pr.

Psychotomimetic Drugs. Ed. by D. Efron. 1970. 33.25 (ISBN 0-7204-4063-7, North Holland). Elsevier.

Psychotron Plot see Complot del Psicotron.

Psychotronic Encyclopedia of Film. Michael Weldon. 832p. 1983. pap. 17.95 (ISBN 0-345-34345-X). Ballantine.

Psychotronics: A Primer on Instruments Using Variable Capacity Tuning. rev. ed. Ed. by Peter J. Kelly. 106p. 1986. pap. text ed. 11.00 (ISBN 0-943975-01-8). Interdimens Sci.

Psychotropic Agents, Anxiolytics, Gerontopsychopharmacological Agents, & Psychomotor Stimulants. Ed. by F. Hoffmeister & G. Stille. (Handbook of Experimental Pharmacology Ser.: Pt. II). (Illus.). 830p. 1981. 202.00 (ISBN 0-387-10300-7). Springer-Verlag.

Psychotropic Agents: Part I, Antipsychotics & Antidepressants. Ed. by G. Stille & Hoffmeister. (Handbook of Experimental Pharmacology: Vol. 55, Pt. 1). (Illus.). 800p. 1980. 174.00 (ISBN 0-387-09858-5). Springer-Verlag.

Psychotropic Agents: Pt. III, Alcohol & Psychotomimetics, Psychotropic & Effects of Central Acting Drugs. Ed. by F. Hoffmeister & G. Stille. (Handbook of Experimental Pharmacology Ser.: Vol. 55). (Illus.). 585p. 1982. 145.00 (ISBN 0-387-10301-5). Springer-Verlag.

Psychotropic & Neurotropic Drugs & Neurotransmitter Receptors: Proceedings of the 3rd Workshop on Neurotransmitters & Diseases, Tokyo, Japan, June 21, 1986. Ed. by R. Takahashi. 96p. 1987. 94.75 (ISBN 0-444-80867-1, Excerpta Medica). Elsevier.

Psychotropic Drug Handbook. 5th ed. Paul J. Perry et al. LC 81-51776. (Illus.). vi, 346p. 1988. pap. text ed. 15.00 (ISBN 0-9606488-5-2). H W Bks.

Psychotropic Drug Side Effects: Clinical & Theoretical Perspectives. Richard Shader & Alberto Dimascio. LC 76-40021. 302p. 1977. Repr. of 1970 ed. 21.50 (ISBN 0-88275-464-5). Krieger.

Psychotropic Drugs: A Guide for the Practitioner. H. M. Van Praag. 488p. 1978. text ed. 62.50x (ISBN 0-317-62929-8, Pub. by Van Gorcum Holland). Coronet Bks.

Psychotropic Drugs & Nursing Intervention. Patricia Irons. (Illus.). 1978. pap. 20.95 (ISBN 0-07-032052-7). McGraw.

Psychotropic Drugs & Related Compounds. 2nd ed. Earl Usdin & Daniel H. Efron. LC 79-42886. 780p. 1979. 63.00 (ISBN 0-08-025510-8). Pergamon.

Psychotropic Drugs & the Human EEG. Ed. by M. Itil Turan et al. (Modern Problems of Pharmacopsychiatry: Vol. 8). (Illus.). 300p. 1974. 100.00 (ISBN 3-8055-1419-0). S Karger.

Psychotropic Drugs in Psychiatry. Michael Shepherd. LC 77-17731. 288p. 1979. 30.00x (ISBN 0-87668-273-5). Aronson.

Psychotropic Drugs in the Year 2000: Use by Normal Humans. Ed. by Wayne O. Evans & Nathan S. Kline. 192p. 1971. 21.50x (ISBN 0-398-02191-0). C C Thomas.

Psychotropic Drugs: Plasma Concentration & Clinical Response. Ed. by Graham D. Burrows & Trevor R. Norman. (Experimental & Clinical Psychiatry Ser.: Vol. 4). (Illus.). 544p. 1981. 85.00 (ISBN 0-8247-1009-6). Dekker.

Psychovenereology: Personality & Lifestyle Factors in Sexually Transmitted Diseases in Homosexual Men, Vol. 3. Michael W. Ross. LC 85-25683. (Series in Sexual Medicine). 258p. 1986. lib. bdg. 38.95 (ISBN 0-275-92122-0, C2122). Praeger.

Psychrotrophic Microorganisms in Spoilage & Pathogenicity. Ed. by T. A. Roberts et al. LC 81-67902. 552p. 1982. 72.00 (ISBN 0-12-589720-0). Acad Pr.

Psychware Sourcebook. 2nd ed. Ed. by Samuel E. Krug. LC 87-10176. 472p. 1987. pap. 39.00 (ISBN 0-933701-07-1, Test Corp America). Westport Pubs.

Psychware Sourcebook. 3rd ed. Ed. by Samuel E. Krug. 1988. text ed. 85.00 (ISBN 0-933701-27-6, Test Corp America); pap. 39.00 (ISBN 0-933701-26-8, Test Corp America). Westport Pubs.

PsycINFO Retrospective: Learning & Communication Disorders, 1971-1980. 1982. pap. 31.50 (ISBN 0-912704-71-3, 3120010). Am Psychol.

PsycINFO Retrospective: Mental Retardation 1971-1980. 1982. pap. 31.50 (ISBN 0-912704-73-X, 3130010); members 25.00. Am Psychol.

PsycINFO User Manual. Ed. by PsycINFO, APA Staff. LC 86-32244. 1987. looseleaf binder 60.00 (ISBN 0-912704-75-6, 3910020); to all foreign addresses 75.00. Am Psychol.

Psycological Dynamics of Religious Experience. Andre Godin. Tr. by Mary Turton from Fr. Orig. Title: Psychologie des Experiences Religieuses. 279p. 1985. pap. 13.95 (ISBN 0-89135-039-X). Religious Educ.

Psycological Emergencies & Crisis Intervention. Brent Hafen. 380p. 1985. text ed. 16.95x (ISBN 0-89582-139-7). Morton Pub.

Pt. B: Applications, Systems Design & Economics see Solar Energy Technology Handbook, Pt. A: Engineering Fundamentals.

Pt 1 The Hellenistic World see Cambridge Ancient History Series.

PTA with a Purpose. 2.00 (ISBN 0-914131-49-4, L01). Torah Umesorah.

Ptarmigan Valley. Ann F. Chandonnet. LC 79-84634. (Lightning Tree Contemporary Poets Ser.: No. 5). 1980. 12.95 (ISBN 0-89016-054-6); pap. 4.95 (ISBN 0-89016-053-8). Lightning Tree.

PTC 19.5-1972 Application, Part Two of Fluid Meters: Interim Supplement on Instruments & Apparatus. 1972. pap. text ed. 14.00 (ISBN 0-685-30666-6, G00018). ASME.

PTC 20.1-1977: Speed & Load Governing Systems for Steam Turbine-Generator Units. 1977. pap. text ed. 12.00 (ISBN 0-685-81975-2, C00019). ASME.

PTC 31-1973. 1974: Ion Exchange Equipment. 1979. pap. text ed. 8.00 (ISBN 0-685-41933-9, C00016). ASME.

PTC '84 Proceedings. Pacific Telecommunications Council. Ed. by Dan J. Wedemeyer & L. S. Harms. 236p. 1984. pap. text ed. 12.50x (ISBN 0-8248-0958-0). Pac Telecom.

PTC '85 Proceedings. Ed. by Dan J. Wedemeyer. 425p. 1985. pap. text ed. 22.50x (ISBN 0-8248-1009-0). Pac Telecom.

PTCA: Percutaneous Transluminal Coronary Angioplasty. Ronald E. Vlietstra & David R. Holmes, Jr. LC 86-11557. (Illus.). 268p. 1986. text ed. 54.00 (ISBN 0-8036-8962-4). Davis Co.

Ptentsy Gnedzda Petrova. N. J. Pavlenko. 334p. (Rus.). 1984. 39.00x (ISBN 0-317-40826-7, Pub. by Collets (UK)). State Mutual Bk.

Pteranodon: The Flying Reptile. Elizabeth Sandell. Ed. by Marjorie Oelerich & Howard Schroeder. LC 88-953. (Dinosaur Discovery Era Ser.). (Illus.). 32p. (gr. k-5). 1988. PLB 9.95 (ISBN 0-944280-05-6); pap. 4.95 (ISBN 0-944280-11-0). BSP Pub Inc.

Pteridophyte Flora of Fiji. G. Brownlie. (Beihefte Zur Nova Hedwigia 55). 1977. lib. bdg. 110.00x (ISBN 3-7682-5455-0). Lubrecht & Cramer.

Pteridophyte Flora of Oaxaca, Mexico. J. Mickel & J. Beitel. (Memoirs of the New York Botanical Garden Ser.: Vol. 46). 1988. text ed. 90.00x (ISBN 0-89327-323-6). NY Botanical.

Pteridophytes. Allan R. Smith. Ed. by Dennis E. Breedlove. (Flora of Chiapas Ser.: Pt. 2). (Illus.). 370p. (Orig.). 1981. pap. 30.00 (ISBN 0-940228-01-7). Calif Acad Sci.

Pteridophytes of Kansas, Nebraska, South Dakota & North Dakota, U. S. A. Nova Hedwigia Beiheft, No. 61. A. J. Petrik-Ott. 1979. lib. bdg. 47.50x (ISBN 3-7682-5461-5). Lubrecht & Cramer.

Pteridophytes of the Society Islands. E. B. Copeland. (BMB Ser.). Repr. of 1932 ed. 13.00 (ISBN 0-527-02199-7). Kraus Repr.

Pteridophytes: Some Aspects of Their Structure & Morphology. S. S. Bir. (Aspects of Plant Sciences Ser.: Vol. III). 170p. 1980. 15.00 (ISBN 0-88065-064-8, Pub. by Messers Today & Tomorrows Printers & Publishers India). Scholarly Pubns.

Pteridophytes: Their Morphology, Cytology, Taxonomy & Phytogeny. S. S. Bir. (Aspects of Plant Sciences Ser.: Vol. 6). vii, 253p. 1983. 19.00 (ISBN 1-55528-012-9, Pub. by Messers Today & Tomorrow Printers & Publishers). Scholarly Pubns.

Pterocarpus (Leguminosae-Papilionaceae) Revised for the World. J. P. Rojo. 1971. 36.00x (ISBN 3-7682-0726-9). Lubrecht & Cramer.

Pterodactyl in the Wilderness. Chuck Oliveros. 56p. (Orig.). 1983. pap. 3.00 (ISBN 0-911757-00-7). Dead Angel.

Pterosauria. P. Wellnhofer. (Handbook of Paleoherpatology: Pt. 19). (Illus.). 82p. 1978. pap. text ed. 60.00x (ISBN 3-437-30269-8). Lubrecht & Cramer.

Pterosaurs: The Flying Reptiles. Illus. by Richard Courtney. (Prehistoric Animals Pop-Up Bks.). (Illus.). 12p. (ps-3). 1988. 5.95 (ISBN 0-448-19301-9, G&D). Putnam Pub Group.

Pterosaurs: The Flying Reptiles. Helen R. Sattler. LC 84-4428. (Illus.). 48p. (gr. 1-4). 1985. 13.00 (ISBN 0-688-03995-2); PLB 12.88 (ISBN 0-688-03996-0). Lothrop.

PTFE Seals in Reciprocating Compressors: Manual of Material Selection, Design & Operating Practices. American Society of Mechanical Engineers Staff. LC 74-32657. pap. 22.50 (ISBN 0-317-11225-2, 2016824). Bks Demand UMI.

Ptici i Slavuji; Hawks & Nightingales: Burgenland Croatian & English. Ed. by Peter Tyran. Tr. by Herbert Kuhner. 171p. 1983. 11.95 (ISBN 3-7003-0504-4). Slavica.

P'tit Bonhomme. Jules Verne. 1978. 8.95 (ISBN 0-686-55942-8). French & Eur.

Ptolemaic Alexandria, 3 vols. P. M. Fraser. 1984. Repr. of 1972 ed. Set. 175.00x (ISBN 0-19-814278-1). Oxford U Pr.

Ptolemaic Oinochoai & Portraits in Faience: Aspects of the Ruler-Cult. Dorothy B. Thompson. (Oxford Monographs on Classical Archeology). (Illus.). 1973. 75.00x (ISBN 0-19-813211-5). Oxford U Pr.

Ptolemaios und Porphyrios Uber Die Musik. Ingemar During. LC 78-20290. (Ancient Philosophy Ser.). 293p. 1980. lib. bdg. 34.00 (ISBN 0-8240-9599-5). Garland Pub.

Ptolemais: City of the Libyan Pentapolis. Carl H. Kraeling. LC 62-9742. 1963. 40.00x (ISBN 0-226-62193-6, OIP90). U of Chicago Pr.

Ptolemais Cyrenaica. The Oriental Institute, Chicago & David Nasgowitz. LC 80-26769. (Illus.). 75p. 1981. text-fiche 50.00 (ISBN 0-226-69474-7). U of Chicago Pr.

Ptolemy's Almagest. G. J. Toomer. (Illus.). 693p. 1984. 77.50 (ISBN 0-387-91220-7). Springer-Verlag.

Ptolia, Bk. 1. Fred Baker. LC 82-81453. 175p. (Orig.). 1982. pap. 4.95 (ISBN 0-914766-83-X, 0197). Illum Way Pub.

PTRE Workbook Supplement. Sherman Keene. 1986. 14.50 (ISBN 0-942080-06-8). SKE Pub.

Pub & the People: Mass Observation. (Cresset Library). (Illus.). 350p. 1987. pap. 13.95 (ISBN 0-09-170421-9, Pub. by Century Hutchinson). David & Charles.

Pub Crawler. Maurice Procter. Ed. by J. Barzun & W. H. Taylor. LC 81-47386. (Crime Fiction 1950-1975 Ser.). 180p. 1982. lib. bdg. 18.00 (ISBN 0-8240-4997-7). Garland Pub.

Pub Games of England. Patrick T. Finn. (Oleander Games & Pastimes Ser.: Vol. 5). (Illus.). 156p. 1981. 18.95 (ISBN 0-900891-66-1); pap. 13.50 (ISBN 0-900891-67-X). Oleander Pr.

Pub Guide to Oxford & Area. A. Cree. 1985. 15.00x (ISBN 0-317-54313-X, Pub. by J Richardson UK). State Mutual Bk.

Puberty. S. R. Berenberg. 1975. lib. bdg. 45.00 (ISBN 90-207-0539-3, Pub. by Martinuus Nijhoff Netherlands). Kluwer Academic.

Puberty & Adolescence. Jean C. Lipke. LC 70-104888. (Being Together Bks.). (Illus.). (gr. 5-11). 1971. PLB 5.95 (ISBN 0-8225-0591-6). Lerner Pubns.

Puberty to Manhood in Italy & America. Harben B. Young & Lucy R. Ferguson. (Development Psychology Ser.). 294p. 1981. 19.95 (ISBN 0-12-773150-4). Acad Pr.

Pubis Angelical. Manuel Puig. LC 86-40172. 256p. 1986. pap. 6.95 (ISBN 0-394-74664-3, Vin). Random.

Public Acceptance of New Technologies. Stephen Mills & Roger Williams. 368p. 1986. 47.50 (ISBN 0-7099-4319-9, Pub. by Croom Helm Ltd). Routledge Chapman & Hall.

Public Accepts: Stories Behind Famous Trade-Marks, Names, & Slogans. Isaac E. Lambert. LC 75-39256. (Getting & Spending: the Consumer's Dilemma). (Illus.). 1976. Repr. of 1941 ed. 18.00x (ISBN 0-405-08029-8). Ayer Co Pubs.

Public Access: Citizens & Collective Bargaining in the Public Schools. Ed. by Robert E. Doherty. LC 79-13189. 112p. 1979. pap. 7.95 (ISBN 0-87546-073-9). ILR Pr.

Public Access Microcomputers in Academic Libraries: The Mann Library Model at Cornell University. Ed. by Howard Curtis. LC 86-22315. 1987. pap. text ed. 14.95x (ISBN 0-8389-0464-5). ALA.

Public Access-Public Interest. 1975. 2.00, institutions 5.00 (ISBN 0-686-09559-6). Network Project.

Public Access Terminals: Determining Quantity Requirements. John E. Tolle. LC 84-164540. (OCLC Library, Information, & Computer Science Ser.: No. 3). (Illus.). 182p. (Orig.). 1983. pap. 14.50 (ISBN 0-933418-51-5). OCLC Online Comp.

Public Access to Government Information. rev. ed. Peter Hernon & Charles R. McClure. (Information Management, Policies & Services Ser.). 336p. 1988. text ed. 45.00 (ISBN 0-89391-522-X); pap. text ed. 29.50 (ISBN 0-89391-523-8). Ablex Pub.

Public Access to Government Publications. Peter Hernon & Charles R. McClure. LC 83-25797. (Libraries & Information Science Ser.). 472p. 1984. text ed. 59.50 (ISBN 0-89391-100-3); pap. text ed. 29.50. Ablex Pub.

Public Access to Information. Ed. by Andrew C. Gordon & John P. Heinz. LC 78-63009. 400p. 1979. Repr. 29.95 (ISBN 0-87855-278-2). Transaction Bks.

Public Access to Online Catalogs. 2nd ed. Joseph R. Matthews. LC 84-20706. (Library Automation Planning Guides Ser.). 497p. 1985. pap. text ed. 37.50 (ISBN 0-918212-89-8). Neal Schuman.

Public Accommodations Law of 1964: Arguments, Issues & Attitudes in a Legal Debate. L. Carothers. LC 67-21036. (Edwin H. Land Prize Essays). 1968. 2.00 (ISBN 0-87391-003-6). Smith Coll.

Public Accounting Firm Practices & CPA Attitudes in Ohio. James C. Yocum. 1973. pap. 6.00 (ISBN 0-87776-403-4, S3). Ohio St U Admin Sci.

Public Address Handbook. Vivian Capel. 224p. 1981. 40.00x (ISBN 0-907266-02-9, Pub. by Dickson England). State Mutual Bk.

Public Administration. 2nd ed. Gerald E. Caiden. LC 82-82054. 1982. pap. 10.95x (ISBN 0-913530-29-8). Palisades Pub.

Public Administration. 5th ed. Marshall E. Dimock et al. 1983. pap. text ed. 29.95 (ISBN 0-03-056212-0). HR&W.

Public Administration. Robert Lorch. 314p. 1977. pap. text ed. 21.25 (ISBN 0-8299-0144-2). West Pub.

Public Administration. David H. Rosenbloom & Deborah Goldman. 1986. text ed. 22.00 (ISBN 0-394-33121-4). Random.

Public Administration. Jeffrey D. Straussman. 424p. 1985. text ed. 26.95x (ISBN 0-03-059544-4). HR&W.

Public Administration. William Thornhill. LC 85-5339. 141p. 1985. 28.95 (ISBN 0-902197-23-1, Pub. by Woodhead-Faulkner); pap. 18.25 (ISBN 0-902197-24-X, Pub. by Woodhead-Faulkner). Longwood Pub Group.

Public Administration: A Bibliographic Guide to the Literature. Howard E. McCurdy. (Public Administration-Public Policy a Comprehensive Publication Ser.). 328p. 1986. 29.75 (ISBN 0-8247-7518-X). Dekker.

Public Administration: A Comparative Perspective. 3rd ed. Ferrel Heady. LC 83-26231. (Public Administration & Public Policy Ser.). 1984. 34.75 (ISBN 0-8247-7205-9). Dekker.

Public Administration: A Management Approach. Donald Klingner. 432p. 1983. text ed. 25.96 (ISBN 0-395-32796-2); instr's. manual 2.36 (ISBN 0-395-32797-0). HM.

Public Administration & Development. 1987. write for info. Wiley.

Public Administration & Legislatures: Examination & Exploration. John A. Worthley. LC 75-23150. 310p. 1976. 24.95x (ISBN 0-88229-233-1). Nelson-Hall.

Public Administration & Management: Problems of Adaptation in Different Socio-Cultural Contexts. (Illus.). 170p. (Co-published with Abhinav Publications, India). 1982. text ed. 10.50 (ISBN 92-3-102024-2, U1282, UNESCO). UNIPUB.

Public Administration & Nation-Building in Nepal. Madhab Poudyal. 1984. 11.00x (ISBN 0-8364-1140-4, Pub. by NB Pubns). South Asia Bks.

Public Administration & Policy Analysis. R. A. Rhodes. 128p. 1979. text ed. 28.50x (ISBN 0-566-00239-6). Gower Pub Co.

Public Administration & Public Affairs. 2nd ed. N. Henry. LC 79-15414. 1980. write for info. (ISBN 0-13-737296-5). P-H.

Public Administration & Public Affairs. 3rd ed. Nicholas L. Henry. LC 85-12414. (Illus.). 400p. 1986. text ed. write for info. (ISBN 0-13-737305-8). P-H.

Public Administration & Public Opinion in Bengal (1854-1885) Anuradha Chanda. 187p. 1986. 17.50x (ISBN 0-8364-2002-0, Pub. by KP Bagchi India). South Asia Bks.

Public Administration & the Department of Agriculture. John M. Gaus & Leon O. Wolcott. LC 75-8788. (FDR & the Era of the New Deal Ser.). 1975. Repr. of 1940 ed. lib. bdg. 65.00 (ISBN 0-306-70704-7). Da Capo.

Public Administration & Tourism Development: A Bibliography. Linda K. Richter. (Public Administration Ser.: P 1946). 21p. 1986. 6.25 (ISBN 0-89028-886-0). Vance Biblios.

Public Administration As a Developing Discipline: Perspectives on Past & Present, Pt. 1. Robert T. Golembiewski. (Public Administration & Public Policy Ser.: Vol. 1). 1977. 32.75 (ISBN 0-8247-6565-6). Dekker.

Public Administration: Balancing Power & Accountability. Jerome B. McKinney & Lawrence C. Howard. LC 79-12796. (Orig.). 1979. pap. 14.00 (ISBN 0-935610-06-5). Moore Pub IL.

Public Administration: Concepts & Cases. 3rd ed. Richard J. Stillman. LC 83-80895. 512p. 1984. pap. text ed. 19.95 (ISBN 0-395-34371-2); instr's. manual 2.00 (ISBN 0-395-34372-0). HM.

Public Administration: Concepts & Cases. 4th. ed. Richard J. Stillman, II. LC 87-80690. 544p. 1988. pap. text ed. 23.56 (ISBN 0-395-35969-4); instr's manual 2.36 (ISBN 0-395-44728-3). HM.

Public Administration: Concepts & Theories. Rumki Basu. 298p. 1987. text ed. 32.50x (ISBN 81-207-0580-7, Pub. by Sterling Pubs India). Apt Bks.

Public Administration Debated. Herbert M. Levine. 336p. 1987. pap. text ed. write for info. (ISBN 0-13-737313-9). P-H.

Public Administration: Design & Problem Solving. John S. Jun. 384p. 1986. write for info. (ISBN 0-02-360700-9); write for info. tchr's. manual (ISBN 0-02-360710-6). Macmillan.

Public Administration Dictionary. 2nd ed. Ralph C. Chandler & Jack C. Plano. (Clio Dictionaries in Political Science Ser.). 430p. 1988. lib. bdg. 39.50 (ISBN 0-87436-498-1); pap. 18.00 (ISBN 0-87436-499-X). ABC-Clio.

Public Administration: History & Theory in Contemporary Perspective. Uveges. LC 81-19428. (Annual Public Administration Ser.: Vol. 1). 144p. 1982. 29.75 (ISBN 0-8247-1557-8). Dekker.

Public Administration in a Secrecy Setting: A Selected Bibliography. Anthony G. White. (Public Administration Ser.: P 1964). 11p. 1986. 3.75 (ISBN 0-89028-924-7). Vance Biblios.

Public Administration in America. 3rd ed. George J. Gordon. LC 85-61286. 625p. 1986. text ed. 22.00 (ISBN 0-312-65391-3); instr's. manual avail. (ISBN 0-312-65390-5). St Martin.

Public Administration in American Society: A Guide to Information Sources. Ed. by John E. Rouse, Jr. (American Government & History Information Guide Ser.: Vol. 11). 576p. 1980. 68.00x (ISBN 0-8103-1424-X). Gale.

Public Administration in an Era of Growing Complexity: The Role of Technical Information & the Holding of Policy-Relevant Information. Dennis L. Soden. (Public Administration Ser.: P 1839). 10p. 1986. 3.00 (ISBN 0-89028-709-0). Vance Biblios.

Public Administration in Ancient India. Pramathanath Banerjea. 316p. 1973. Repr. 18.75x (ISBN 0-89684-445-5). Orient Bk Dist.

Public Administration in Britain. (Illus.). Date not set. pap. text ed. 14.95x (ISBN 0-04-352110-X). Unwin Hyman.

Public Administration in Developed Democracies: A Comparative Study. Rowat. (Public Administration-Public Policy, a Comprehensive Publicat Program Ser.). 512p. 1987. 75.00 (ISBN 0-8247-7807-3). Dekker.

Public Administration in Hong Kong. Charles H. Collins. LC 70-179180. Repr. of 1952 ed. 23.50 (ISBN 0-404-54810-5). AMS Pr.

Public Administration in Japan. Ed. by Kiyoaki Tsuji. 271p. 1983. 22.50x (ISBN 0-86008-330-6, Pub. by U of Tokyo Pr). Columbia U Pr.

Public Administration in Latin America: A Bibliography. Ed. by Jorge Grossman. 1976. lib. bdg. 59.95 (ISBN 0-8490-2488-9). Gordon Pr.

Public Administration in Massachusetts: The Relation of Central to Local Activity. Robert H. Whitten. LC 73-82249. (Columbia University. Studies in the Social Sciences: No. 22). Repr. of 1898 ed. 16.50 (ISBN 0-404-51022-1). AMS Pr.

Public Administration in Modern Society. John J. Corson & Joseph P. Harris. LC 81-7262. (Foundations of American Government & Political Science Ser.). 155p. 1981. Repr. of 1963 ed. lib. bdg. 35.00x (ISBN 0-313-22668-7, COPU/). Greenwood.

Public Administration in Nigeria. R. O. Ola. 220p. 1984. write for info. (ISBN 0-7103-0043-3, Kegan Paul); pap. 20.00x (ISBN 0-7103-0044-1). Routledge Chapman & Hall.

Public Administration in Rural Areas & Small Jurisdictions: A Guide to the Literature. Beth W. Honadle. LC 82-49176. (Public Affairs & Administration Ser.). 177p. 1983. lib. bdg. 32.00 (ISBN 0-8240-9179-5). Garland Pub.

Public Administration in Siam. W. D. Reeve. LC 74-179236. Repr. of 1951 ed. 19.00 (ISBN 0-404-54863-6). AMS Pr.

Public Administration in the Federal Republic of Germany. Ed. by K. Konig et al. 350p. 1983. pap. 20.00 (ISBN 90-65-4412-63). Kluwer Academic.

Public Administration in the FRG. N. J. Von Oertzen et al. (Orig.). 1983. pap. text ed. 19.60 (ISBN 90-654-4141-7, Pub. by Kluwer Law & Taxation). Kluwer Academic.

Public Administration Intern. Jack Rudman. (Career Examination Ser.: C-628). (Cloth bdg. avail. on request). pap. 14.00 (ISBN 0-8373-0628-0). Natl Learning.

Public Administration, Politics, & the People: Selected Readings for Managers, Employees, & Citizens. Dean L. Yarwood. LC 86-10381. (Illus.). 421p. (Orig.). 1986. pap. text ed. 19.95 (ISBN 0-582-29024-4). Longman.

Public Administration: Politics, Policy & the Political System. 2nd ed. William L. Morrow. 387p. 1980. pap. text ed. write for info (ISBN 0-394-32426-9, RanC). Random.

Public Administration Professional - The Court Administrator: A Selected Bibliography. Mark A. Zaffarano. (Public Administration Ser.: P 2311). 7p. 1987. 3.00 (ISBN 1-55590-611-7). Vance Biblios.

Public Administration Professional -- The Court Administrator: A Selected Biliography. Mark A. Zaffarano. 7p. 1987. pap. 3.00 (ISBN 1-55590-611-7). Vance Biblios.

Public Administration Review Cumulative Index, 1940-1979. Ed. by Louis C. Gawthrop & Virginia L. Gawthrop. 160p. 1980. 34.50 (ISBN 0-936678-02-X). Am Soc Pub Admin.

Public Administration: Social Change & Adaptive Management. N. Joseph Cayer & Louis F. Weschler. LC 87-60564. 224p. 1988. pap. text ed. write for info. (ISBN 0-312-00330-7). St Martin.

Public Administration: The Work of Government. Charles R. Barton & William L. Chappell. 1985. text ed. write for info. (ISBN 0-673-15646-X). Scott F.

Public Administration: Theory & Practice. James Fesler. (Illus.). 1980. P-H.

Public Administration: Understanding Management, Politics, & Law in the Public Sector. 2nd ed. David H. Rosenbloom & Deborah D. Goldman. (Illus.). 576p. 1989. text ed. price not set. Random.

Public Administration Workbook. Mark W. Huddleston. (Illus.). 241p. 1987. pap. text ed. 13.95 (ISBN 0-582-29028-7). Longman.

Public Administrator. Jack Rudman. (Career Examination Ser.: C-1440). (Cloth bdg. avail. on request). pap. 16.00 (ISBN 0-8373-1440-2). Natl Learning.

Public Administrator & the Courts. John C. Pine & Patricia A. Hollander. 122p. (Orig.). 1985. pap. 28.50 (ISBN 0-318-12122-0). Res Pubns NC.

Public Adminsitration in the United States. David F. Schuman & Dick W. Olufs. 464p. 1988. pap. text ed. 24.50 (ISBN 0-669-11267-4); Instr. Guide 2.00 (ISBN 0-669-16539-5). Heath.

Public Adminstration & Law. Rosenbloom. (Public Adminstration Public Policy Ser.). 280p. 1983. 32.50 (ISBN 0-8247-1791-0). Dekker.

Public Affairs for the Judiciary: The Means By Which Public Confidence Can Be Fostered to Provide Effective & Efficient Judicial Service. National Center for State Courts. (Paul Reardon Ser.). 13p. 1981. manuscript 0.78 (PRS-019). Natl Ctr St Courts.

Public Affairs Handbook. Ed. by Joseph S. Nagelschmidt. LC 82-6710. pap. 79.80 (ISBN 0-317-26318-8, 2055750). Bks Demand UMI.

Public Affairs in Financial Services. Kathryn L. Troy. (Report Ser.: No. 899). (Illus.). vi, 41p. (Orig.). 1987. pap. text ed. 60.00 (ISBN 0-8237-0342-8). Conference Bd.

Public Affairs Information Service: Cumulative Author Index 1965-1969. Ed. by C. Edward Wall. LC 70-143248. (Cumulative Author Index Ser.: No. 3). 1973. 110.00 (ISBN 0-87650-014-9). Pierian.

Public Affairs Internships: Theory & Practice. Ed. by Joseph C. Honan & Alan P. Balutis. 297p. 1984. 18.95 (ISBN 0-87073-727-9); pap. 11.95 (ISBN 0-87073-728-7). Schenkman Bks Inc.

Public Agency Communication: Theory & Practice. Hindy L. Schachter. LC 82-14144. (Illus.). 256p. 1983. 23.95 (ISBN 0-88229-742-2). Nelson-Hall.

Public Agenda. Brewster. 1987. write for info. (ISBN 0-312-01146-6). St Martin.

Public & Academic History. Phyllis K. Leffler. 1989. pap. price not set (ISBN 0-89464-298-7). Krieger.

Public & Atlantic Defense. Ed. by Gregory Flynn & Hans Rattinger. LC 84-15894. (Atlantic Institute Research Ser.). (Illus.). 416p. 1985. 45.00x (ISBN 0-8476-7365-0, Rowman & Allanheld). Rowman.

Public & Business Planning in the United States: A Bibliography. Ed. by Martha B. Lightwood. LC 79-165488. (Management Information Guide Ser.: No. 26). 314p. 1972. 68.00x (ISBN 0-8103-0826-6). Gale.

Public & Community Health. W. S. Parker & A. M. Nelson. (Illus.). 176p. 1971. pap. text ed. 17.95 (ISBN 0-8464-1269-1). Beekman Pubs.

Public & Health Aspects of Periodontal Disease. Ed. by Frandsen. (Illus.). 220p. 1984. pap. text ed. 36.00 (ISBN 0-86715-153-6). Quint Pub Co.

Public & Its Problems. John Dewey. LC 76-178242. 236p. 1954. pap. 5.95x (ISBN 0-8040-0254-1, Pub. by Swallow). Ohio U Pr.

Public & Nonprofit Marketing: Cases & Readings. Christopher H. Lovelock & Charles B. Weinberg. 400p. 1984. pap. text ed. write for info. (ISBN 0-471-88578-9). Wiley.

Public & Play Without a Title: Two Posthumous Plays. Federico Garcia Lorca. Tr. by Carlos Bauer from Span. LC 83-12117. 96p. (Orig.). 1983. 12.50 (ISBN 0-8112-0880-X); pap. 5.25 (ISBN 0-8112-0881-8, NDP561). New Directions.

Public & Private Economy, 3 vols. in 1. Theodore Sedgwick. LC 68-27855. 1974. Repr. of 1936 ed. 57.50x (ISBN 0-678-01258-X). Kelley.

Public & Private Economy, Pt. 1. Theodore Sedgwick. LC 77-137187. (Poverty U. S. A. Historical Record Ser). 1971. Repr. of 1836 ed. 24.50 (ISBN 0-405-03125-4). Ayer Co Pubs.

Public & Private Education: The Australian Dimension. Don Anderson. 298p. 1986. 39.00 (ISBN 0-949614-26-2, Pub. by Croom Helm UK); pap. 19.00 (ISBN 0-949614-27-0, Pub. by Croom Helm UK). Routledge Chapman & Hall.

Public & Private Enterprise. John Jewkes. LC 66-12709. (Lindsay Memorial Lectures: 1964). pap. 25.00 (ISBN 0-317-20706-7, 2024118). Bks Demand UMI.

Public & Private Enterprise & the Energy Future. Ed. by Gregory Daneke. 192p. (Orig.). 1985. pap. 8.00 (ISBN 0-918592-78-X). Policy Studies.

Public & Private Enterprise in Mixed Economies. Ed. by Wolfgang Friedmann. LC 73-12406. 410p. 1974. 50.00x (ISBN 0-231-03776-7). Columbia U Pr.

Public & Private Faces of Welfare: Social Policy in Transition. Ed. by Wintersberger et al. 1986. text ed. 28.50 (ISBN 0-435-82334-5, Pub. by Gower Pub England). Gower Pub Co.

Public & Private Health Services. Ed. by A. J. Culyer & Bengt Jonsson. 256p. 1987. text ed. 45.00 (ISBN 0-631-15088-9, 12-3081). Basil Blackwell.

Public & Private Hearth. Patricia Wilcox. 1978. 12.95. Bellevue Pr.

Public & Private High Schools: The Impact of Communities. James S. Coleman & Thomas Hoffer. LC 85-43105. (Illus.). 256p. 1987. 21.95 (ISBN 0-465-06767-0). Basic.

Public & Private in Social Life. Ed. by S. I. Benn & Gerlad F. Gaus. LC 83-9539. 430p. 1983. 35.00 (ISBN 0-312-65357-3). St Martin.

Public & Private in Vergil's Aeneid. Susan F. Wiltshire. 184p. 1989. lib. bdg. 22.50x (ISBN 0-87023-650-4). U of Mass Pr.

Public Education in America: A New Interpretation of Purpose & Practice. Ed. by George Z. Bereday & Luigi Volpicelli. LC 77-23510. 1977. Repr. of 1958 ed. lib. bdg. 35.00x (ISBN 0-8371-9702-3, BEPU). Greenwood.

Public Education in California: Its Origin & Development with Personal Reminiscences of Half a Century. John Swett. LC 74-89242. (American Education: Its Men, Institutions & Ideas, Ser. 1). 1969. Repr. of 1911 ed. 13.00 (ISBN 0-405-01479-1). Ayer Co Pubs.

Public Education in Detroit. Arthur B. Moehlman. LC 73-11930. (Metropolitan America Ser.). (Illus.). 268p. 1974. Repr. 20.00x (ISBN 0-405-05404-1). Ayer Co Pubs.

Public Education in Hungary. Jozsef Bencedy. 44p. 1982. 7.50x (ISBN 0-317-53866-7, Pub. by Collets (UK)). State Mutual Bk.

Public Education in Soviet Azerbaijan: Appraisal of an Achievement. Ed. by K. Aliev. 239p. 1985. 12.75 (ISBN 92-803-1110-7, U1383, UNESCO). UNIPUB.

Public Education in Upper Canada. Herbert T. Coleman. LC 78-176661. (Columbia University. Teachers College. Contributions to Education: No. 15). Repr. of 1907 ed. 22.50 (ISBN 0-404-55015-0). AMS Pr.

Public Education Religion Studies: An Overview. N. Piediscalzi et al. Ed. by B. Swyhart. LC 76-26670. (American Academy of Religion. Section Papers). 1976. pap. 12.00 (ISBN 0-89130-082-1, 01-09-18). Scholars Pr GA.

Public Education Religion Studies: An Overview. Paul J. Will et al. LC 80-12237. (Aids for the Study of Religion Ser.). 1981. pap. 12.00 (ISBN 0-89130-402-9, 01-03-07). Scholars Pr GA.

Public Education under Criticism. Ed. by Cecil W. Scott & Clyde M. Hill. LC 72-167416. (Essay Index Reprint Ser.). Repr. of 1954 ed. 26.50 (ISBN 0-8369-2520-3). Ayer Co Pubs.

Public Education under Scrutiny. Richard M. Brandt. LC 80-6080. 197p. 1981. lib. bdg. 26.75 (ISBN 0-8191-1566-5); pap. text ed. 11.75 (ISBN 0-8191-1567-3). U Pr of Amer.

Public Educational Work in Baltimore. Herbert B. Adams. LC 78-63872. (Johns Hopkins University. Studies in the Social Sciences. Seventeenth Ser. 1899: 12). Repr. of 1899 ed. 11.50 (ISBN 0-404-61128-1). AMS Pr.

Public Educational Work in Baltimore. Herbert B. Adams. pap. 9.00 (ISBN 0-384-00324-9). Johnson Repr.

Public Employee Benefit Plans - 1986. Ed. by Mary E. Brennan. 95p. (Orig.). 1986. pap. text ed. 16.00 (ISBN 0-89154-319-8). Intl Found Employ.

Public Employee Benefit Plans - 1987. Ed. by June M. Lehman. (Illus.). 141p. (Orig.). 1987. pap. write for info. (ISBN 0-89154-345-7). Intl Found Employ.

Public Employee Benefit Plans-1985. Ed. by June M. Lehman. 96p. (Orig.). 1986. pap. 14.00 (ISBN 0-89154-300-7). Intl Found Employ.

Public Employee Compensation: A Twelve City Comparison. 2nd ed. Elizabeth Dickson & George Peterson. LC 81-53060. 213p. 1981. pap. text ed. 12.00x (ISBN 0-87766-310-6, URI 32800). Urban Inst.

Public Employee Labor Relations in Japan: Three Aspects. Alice H. Cook et al. LC 71-634401. (Comparative Studies in Public Employment Labor Relations Ser.). 1971. 10.00x (ISBN 0-87736-019-7); pap. 5.00x (ISBN 0-87736-020-0). U of Mich Inst Labor.

Public Employee Organizing & the Law. Michael T. Leibig & Wendy L. Kahn. 258p. 1987. pap. 25.00 (ISBN 0-87179-499-3, 0499). BNA.

Public Employee Pension Funds: A Twentieth-Century Fund Report. Robert Tilove. LC 75-33733. 384p. 1976. 52.00x (ISBN 0-231-04015-6). Columbia U Pr.

Public Employee Pension Funds: New Strategies for Investment. Ed. by Lee Webb. William Schweke. 180p. 1979. 9.95 (ISBN 0-318-13769-0); institutions 19.95 (ISBN 0-318-13770-4). NCPA Washington.

Public Employee Relations in West Germany. William H. McPherson. LC 77-634396. (Comparative Studies in Public Employment Labor Relations Ser.). 1971. 10.95x (ISBN 0-87736-009-X); pap. 5.95x (ISBN 0-87736-010-3). U of Mich Inst Labor.

Public Employee Relations Library, Nos. 41-46. Incl. No. 41. Resolving Internal Management Conflicts for Labor Negotiations. Thomas A. Kochan (ISBN 0-87373-141-7). 1973. pap. 6.00 ea. Intl Personnel Mgmt.

Public Employee Reporter for California. Labor Relation Press Staff. text ed. 325.00 (ISBN 0-934753-01-6). LRP Pubns.

Public Employee Reporter for California, Vol. 10. Ed. by LRP Publications Staff. 1987. text ed. 350.00 (ISBN 0-934753-18-0). LRP Pubns.

Public Employee Retirement Administration. MFOA Committee on Public Employee Retirement Administration. 134p. 1977. 15.00 (ISBN 0-686-84367-3). Municipal.

Public Employee Retirement Plans in South Dakota. W. H. Cape. 1956. 5.00 (ISBN 1-55614-099-1). U of SD Gov Res Bur.

Public Employee Retirement Systems: The Structure & Politics of Teacher Pensions. Suzanne S. Taylor. LC 86-2993. 200p. (Orig.). 1986. 26.00 (ISBN 0-87546-123-9); pap. 14.95 (ISBN 0-87546-124-7). ILR Pr.

Public Employee Trade Unionism in the United Kingdom: The Legal Framework. B. A. Hepple & Paul O'Higgins. LC 70-634397. (Comparative Studies in Public Employment Labor Relations Ser.). 1971. 10.00x (ISBN 0-87736-011-1); pap. 5.00x (ISBN 0-87736-012-X). U of Mich Inst Labor.

Public Employee Turnover in State Government: Costs & Beneifits. Kenneth Meyer et al. 1978. 1.00 (ISBN 1-55614-100-9). U of SD Gov Res Bur.

Public Employee Unionism in Belgium. Roger Blanpain. LC 76-634393. (Comparative Studies in Public Employment Labor Relations Ser.). 1971. 10.00x (ISBN 0-87736-003-0); pap. 5.00x (ISBN 0-87736-004-9). U of Mich Inst Labor.

Public Employee Unionism in Israel. Jerome Lefkowitz. LC 78-634400. (Comparative Studies in Public Employment Labor Relations Ser.). 1971. 6.00x (ISBN 0-87736-017-0); pap. 3.00x (ISBN 0-87736-018-9). U of Mich Inst Labor.

Public Employee Unionism: Structure, Growth, Policy. Jack Stieber. LC 73-1591. (Studies of Unionism in Government). 256p. 1973. 26.95 (ISBN 0-8157-8160-1); pap. 9.95 (ISBN 0-8157-8159-8). Brookings.

Public Employees & Collective Bargaining: A Selective Bibliography. Tim J. Watts. (Public Administration Ser.: P 2216). 29p. 1987. 7.50 (ISBN 1-55590-416-5). Vance Biblios.

Public Employees & Policymaking. Alan Saltzstein. LC 79-87843. 1979. pap. text ed. 7.50 (ISBN 0-913530-15-8). Palisades Pub.

Public Employees, Unions, & the Erosion of Civic Trust: A Study of San Francisco in the 1970s. Randolph H. Boehm & Dan C. Heldman. LC 82-51293. 265p. 1982. lib. bdg. 25.00 (ISBN 0-89093-473-8, Aletheia Bks); pap. 9.00 (ISBN 0-89093-499-1, Aletheia Bks). U Pubns Amer.

Public Employment & Compensation in Canada: Myths & Realities. David K. Foot. 188p. 1978. pap. text ed. 10.95x (ISBN 0-409-88600-9, Pub. by Inst Res Pub Canada). Brookfield Pub Co.

Public Employment Bibliography, Vol. 1. Richard Pegnetter. 60p. 1971. pap. 2.00 (ISBN 0-87546-036-4). ILR Pr.

Public Employment Bibliography, Vol. 2. Robert V. Pezdek. LC 73-620038. (ILR Bibliography Ser.: No. 11). 196p. 1973. pap. 3.00 (ISBN 0-87546-051-8); special hard bdg. 7.00 (ISBN 0-87546-282-0). ILR Pr.

Public Employment Compulsory Arbitration in Australia. Gerald E. Caiden. LC 79-634392. (Comparative Studies in Public Employment Labor Relations Ser.). 1971. 10.00x (ISBN 0-87736-001-4); pap. 5.00x (ISBN 0-87736-002-2). U of Mich Inst Labor.

Public Employment in Canada. David K. Foot. (Statistical Ser.). 217p. 1979. pap. text ed. 15.00x (ISBN 0-409-88603-3, Pub. by Inst Res Pub Canada). Brookfield Pub Co.

Public Employment in Western Nations. Richard Rose et al. 256p. 1985. 44.50 (ISBN 0-521-25411-6). Cambridge U Pr.

Public Employment Labor Relations: An Overview of Eleven Nations. Ed. by Charles M. Rehmus. LC 74-22858. (Comparative Studies in Public Employment Labor Relations Ser.). 1974. 10.00x (ISBN 0-87736-025-1); pap. 5.00x (ISBN 0-87736-026-X). U of Mich Inst Labor.

Public Employment Service in a Changing Labour Market. OECD Staff. 54p. 1984. pap. 8.00 (ISBN 92-64-12557-4). OECD.

Public Employment Service in the United States. Raymond C. Atkinson et al. LC 72-69. (Select Bibliographies Reprint Ser). 1972. Repr. of 1938 ed. 22.50 (ISBN 0-8369-9950-9). Ayer Co Pubs.

Public Employment Service in Transition, 1933-1968: Evolution of a Placement Service into a Manpower Agency. Leonard P. Adams. LC 68-66941. (Cornell Studies in Industrial & Labor Relations: No. 16). 264p. 1969. pap. 3.50 (ISBN 0-87546-037-2); pap. 7.50 special hard bdg. (ISBN 0-87546-274-X). ILR Pr.

Public Employment Service: Organization in Change. Frank H. Cassell. LC 68-27448. (Orig.). 1968. pap. 5.00x (ISBN 0-87736-310-2). U of Mich Inst Labor.

Public Encounter: Where State & Citizen Meet. Ed. by Charles T. Goodsell. LC 81-47007. (Illus.). 280p. 1981. 25.00x (ISBN 0-253-15363-8). Ind U Pr.

Public Enemy. Ed. by Henry Cohen. LC 80-52292. (Wisconsin-Warner Bros. Screenplay Ser.). (Illus.). 190p. (Orig.). 1981. 18.95x (ISBN 0-299-08460-4); pap. 8.95 (ISBN 0-299-08464-7). U of Wis Pr.

Public Enquiry. Picton Publishing Staff. 1987. 11.00x (Pub. by Picton UK). State Mutual Bk.

Public Enterprise: A Modern Approach. Peter J. Curwen. LC 85-26234. 1986. 29.95 (ISBN 0-312-65435-9). St Martin.

Public Enterprise: An International Bibliography, a Supplement. Compiled by Alfred H. Saulniers. LC 86-15290. (Special Publications Ser.). xxiii, 208p. 1986. 22.50x (ISBN 0-86728-017-4); pap. 14.95x (ISBN 0-86728-018-2). U TX Inst Lat Am Stud.

Public Enterprise: An International Bibliography. Compiled by Alfred H. Saulniers. LC 85-14601. (Special Publications Ser.). xxv, 469p. (Orig.). 1985. 37.50x (ISBN 0-86728-014-X); pap. 24.95x (ISBN 0-86728-013-1). U Tx Inst Lat Am Stud.

Public Enterprise & Economic Development: The Korea Case. Leroy P. Jones. 300p. 1975. text ed. 14.00x (ISBN 0-8248-0538-0). UH Pr.

Public Enterprise & the Developing World. Ed. by V. V. Ramanadham. 234p. 1984. 28.00 (ISBN 0-7099-2275-2, Pub. By Croom Helm Ltd). Routledge Chapman & Hall.

Public Enterprise: Developments in Social Ownership & Control in Great Britain. Ed. by William A. Robson. (English Workers & the Coming of the Welfare State Ser., 1918-1945). 416p. 1985. lib. bdg. 55.00 (ISBN 0-8240-7626-5). Garland Pub.

Public Enterprise Economics. 2nd ed. Ray Rees. LC 84-40334. 238p. 1984. 27.50 (ISBN 0-312-65439-1). St Martin.

Public Enterprise Economics: Theory & Applications. D. Bos. (Advanced Textbooks in Economics: Vol. 23). 472p. 1986. 32.50 (ISBN 0-444-87899-8, North-Holland). Elsevier.

Public Enterprise in Europe. Henry Parris. 256p. 1986. 43.00 (ISBN 0-7099-0548-3, Pub. by Croom Helm UK). Routledge Chapman & Hall.

Public Enterprise in India. A. Khan & R. K. Arora. 1975. 12.00 (ISBN 0-686-20293-7). Intl Bk Dist.

Public Enterprise in Mixed Economies: Some Macroeconomic Aspects. Robert H. Floyd et al. pap. 53.50 (ISBN 0-317-26168-1, 2024270). Bks Demand UMI.

Public Enterprise in Mixed Economies: Some Macroeconomic Aspects. Robert H. Floyd et al. xiv, 196p. 1984. pap. 12.00 (ISBN 0-939934-30-2). Intl Monetary.

Public Enterprise in South Asia. Muzaffer Ahmad. (ICPE Monograph). 57p. 1982. pap. 10.00x (ISBN 92-9038-902-8, Pub. by Intl Ctr Pub Yugoslavia). Kumarian Pr.

Public Enterprise: Studies in Organisational Structure. Ed. by V. V. Ramanadham. 275p. 1986. 32.50x (ISBN 0-7146-3248-1, F Cass Co). Biblio Dist.

Public Enterprises: A State Level Perspective. Y. Saraswathy Rao. (Illus.). xix, 287p. 1987. text ed. 37.50x (ISBN 81-7018-370-7, Pub. by B R Pub Corp Delhi). Apt Bks.

Public Enterprises & Development in the Arab Countries: Legal & Managerial Aspects. 236p. 1978. pap. 10.00 (ISBN 0-686-35907-0). Intl Ctr Law.

Public Enterprises & Employment in Developing Countries. Ed. by W. D. Lakshman. (ICPE Bks.). 182p. 1984. pap. 20.00x (ISBN 92-9038-031-4). Kumarian Pr.

Public Enterprises & Privatization in Africa. African Association of Public Administration & Management Staff. 1987. text ed. 50.00x (ISBN 0-7069-3341-9, Pub. by Vikas India). Advent NY.

Public Enterprises in Developing Countries: Legal Status. S. A. Sosna. 128p. 1983. 7.50x (ISBN 0-317-53865-9, Pub. by Collets (UK)). State Mutual Bk.

Public Enterprises in Perspective. B. P. Mathur & R. P. Misra. 1973. 9.50 (ISBN 0-89684-533-8). Orient Bk Dist.

Public Enterprises in Peru: Public Sector Growth & Reform. Alfred H. Saulniers. (Special Studies on Latin America & the Caribbean). 250p. 1988. pap. 29.95 (ISBN 0-8133-7565-7). Westview.

Public Enterprises in Sub-Saharan Africa. John Nellis. 1986. 6.50 (ISBN 0-8213-0845-9, DP0001). World Bank.

Public Entrepreneurship: Toward a Theory of Bureaucratic Political Power. Eugene Lewis. LC 79-2451. (Midland Bks: No. 322). 288p. 1980. 22.50x (ISBN 0-253-17384-1); pap. 9.50X (ISBN 0-253-20322-8). Ind U Pr.

Public Environments. Ed. by Joan Harvey & Don Henning. 1987. 36.00 (ISBN 0-939922-10-X). EDRA.

Public Environments: An International Forum on Environmental Design Research. Ed. by Joan Harvey & Don Henning. 1987. 38.00 (ISBN 0-317-58653-X). EDRA.

Public Evaluation of Government Spending. G. Bruce Doern & Allan M. Maslove. 192p. 1979. pap. text ed. 10.95x (ISBN 0-920380-19-0, Pub. by Inst Res Pub Canada). Brookfield Pub Co.

Public Examinations: A Critique. H. S. Singha. 144p. 1984. text ed. 18.95x (ISBN 0-7069-2590-4, Pub. by Vikas India). Advent NY.

Public Expenditure: Allocation Between Competing Ends. Ed. by Michael Posner. LC 76-53522. pap. 72.30 (2031712). Bks Demand UMI.

Public Expenditure & Economic Development. Sibani Dutta. 395p. 1986. 42.00x (ISBN 81-7024-020-4, Pub. by Ashish India). South Asia Bks.

Public Expenditure & Income Distribution in India. Mohammad Zahir. 1972. 12.00 (ISBN 0-686-20294-5). Intl Bk Dist.

Public Expenditure & Indian Development Policy, 1960-1970. F. J. Toye. LC 80-41011. 284p. 1981. 44.50 (ISBN 0-521-23081-0). Cambridge U Pr.

Public Expenditure & Policy Analysis. 3rd ed. Robert Haveman & Julius Margolis. LC 82-81354. 608p. pap. text ed. 33.56 (ISBN 0-395-32576-5). HM.

Public Expenditure & Select Committees of the Commons. Wilma Flegmann. 160p. 1986. text ed. 19.95 (ISBN 0-566-05013-7). Gower Pub Co.

Public Expenditure & Social Policy: An Examination of Social Spending & Social Priorities. Ed. by Alan Walker. xii, 212p. 1982. text ed. 27.50x (ISBN 0-435-82905-X). Gower Pub Co.

Public Expenditure & Taxation in the U. K. Regions. John Short. 120p. 1981. text ed. 38.50x (ISBN 0-566-00403-8). Gower Pub Co.

Public Expenditure Decisions: Behavior, Institutions Procedures & Performance. Ed. by E. R. Brubaker. (Political Economy & Public Policy Ser.: Vol. 5). 1988. 56.50 (ISBN 0-89232-835-5). Jai Pr.

Public Expenditure in Latin America: Effects on Poverty. Guy P. Pfeffermann. (Discussion Paper: No. 5). 38p. 1987. 5.00 (ISBN 0-8213-0906-4, DP0005). World Bank.

Public Expenditure in Malaysia: Who Benefits & Why. Jacob P. Meerman. (World Bank Research Publications Ser.). (Illus.). 1979. pap. 16.95x (ISBN 0-19-520097-7). Oxford U Pr.

Public Expenditure in Malaysia: Who Benefits & Why. Jacob P. Meerman. (World Bank Research Publication Ser.). (Illus.). 404p. 1979. 35.00; pap. 16.95. Oxford U Pr.

Public Expenditure in Nepal: Growth, Pattern & Impact. Dilli R. Khanal. 208p. 1988. text ed. 35.00x (ISBN 81-207-0861-X, Pub. by Sterling Pubs India). Apt Bks.

Public Expenditure in the Urban Community: Papers Presented at a Conference May 14-15, 1962, under the Sponsorship of the Committee on Urban Economics of Resources for the Future Inc. Ed. by Howard G. Scheller. LC 63-22774. pap. 52.00 (ISBN 0-317-09627-3, 2020951). Bks Demand UMI.

Public Expenditure, Inflation & Growth: A Macro-Econometric Analysis for India. B. B. Bhattacharya. 1985. 21.00x (ISBN 0-19-561713-4). Oxford U Pr.

Public Expenditure: Its Defense & Reform. David Heald. 368p. 1984. pap. 14.95 (ISBN 0-85520-419-2). Basil Blackwell.

Public Expenditure Policy, Nineteen Eighty-Four to Nineteen Eighty-Five. Ed. by Paul Cockle. LC 85-22215. 256p. 1985. 27.50 (ISBN 0-312-65459-6). St Martin.

Public Expenditure Policy, 1985-86. Ed. by Paul Cockle. LC 85-22215. 276p. 1986. 32.50 (ISBN 0-312-65460-X). St Martin.

Public Expenditures on Education & Income Distribution in Colombia. Jean-Pierre Jallade. LC 74-4216. (World Bank Staff Occasional Paper Ser: No. 18). 90p. 1974. pap. 5.00x (ISBN 0-8018-1628-9). Johns Hopkins.

Public Expenditures, Taxes & the Distribution of Income: The U. S. 1950, 1961, 1970. Ed. by M. Reynolds & E. Smolensky. 1977. 20.00 (ISBN 0-12-586550-3). Acad Pr.

Public Eye: Television & the Politics of Canadian Broadcasting, 1952-68. Frank W. Peers. 1979. 27.50 (ISBN 0-8020-5436-6). U of Toronto Pr.

Public Face of Architecture: Civic Culture & Public Spaces. Ed. by Nathan Glazer & Mark Lilla. 448p. 1987. 35.00 (ISBN 0-02-911811-5). Free Pr.

Public Finance. R. Aronson. 576p. 1985. text ed. 42.95 (ISBN 0-07-002362-X). McGraw.

Public Finance. Ed. by H. L. Bhatia. 688p. 1987. text ed. 40.00x (ISBN 0-7069-3352-4, Pub. by Vikas India). Advent NY.

Public Finance. J. Ronnie Davis & Charles W. Meyer. (Illus.). 448p. 1983. write for info (ISBN 0-13-709881-2). P-H.

Public Finance. 4th ed. Otto Eckstein. (Foundations of Modern Economics Ser.). (Illus.). 1979. pap. text ed. write for info. (ISBN 0-13-737445-3). P-H.

Public Finance. 2nd ed. Harvey S. Rosen. (Economics Ser.). 1987. text ed. 37.95 (ISBN 0-256-05808-3). Irwin.

Public Finance. Carl S. Shoup. LC 69-11227. 652p. 1969. text ed. 39.50x (ISBN 0-932400-02-7). Intervale Pub Co.

Public Finance. Michael Veseth. 1984. text ed. write for info. (ISBN 0-8359-5749-7, Reston); instr's. manual avail. (ISBN 0-8359-5750-0). P-H.

Public Finance: A Contemporary Application of Theory to Policy. David N. Hyman. 689p. 1983. 31.95x (ISBN 0-03-059349-2). Dryden Pr.

Public Finance: A Contemporary Application of Theory to Policy. 2nd ed. David N. Hyman. 1987. 36.95 (ISBN 0-03-007498-3). Dryden Pr.

Public Finance: An Information Sourcebook. Compiled by Marion B. Marshall & Paul Wasserman. (Oryx Sourcebook Series in Business and Management: No. 6). 296p. 1987. 45.00 (ISBN 0-89774-276-1). Oryx Pr.

Public Finance & Development Strategy. Dirk J. Wolfson. LC 78-23240. 288p. 1979. 29.50x (ISBN 0-8018-2164-9). Johns Hopkins.

Public Finance & Economic Development of Natal, 1893-1910. Zbigniew A. Konczacki. LC 67-23301. pap. 60.50 (ISBN 0-317-55486-7, 2052210). Bks Demand UMI.

TITLE INDEX PUBLIC IMAGE OF COURTS.

Public Finance & Economic Development: Spotlight on Jamaica. Hugh N. Dawes. LC 81-40176. (Illus.). 162p. (Orig.). 1982. lib. bdg. 28.25 (ISBN 0-8191-2091-X); pap. text ed. 12.25 (ISBN 0-8191-2092-8). U Pr of Amer.

Public Finance & Economic Growth: Proceedings of the 37th Congress of the International Institute of Public Finance, Tokyo 1981. Ed. by Dieter Biehl et al. LC 83-12477. 448p. 1983. 45.00x (ISBN 0-8143-1750-2). Wayne St U Pr.

Public Finance & Public Debt: Proceedings of the 40th Congress of the International Institute of Public Finance, Innsbruck, 1984. Ed. by Bernard P. Herber. LC 86-7747. 383p. 1986. 40.00X (ISBN 0-8143-1810-X). Wayne St U Pr.

Public Finance & Public Employment: Proceedings of the 36th Congress of the International Institute of Public Finance, Jerusalem 1980. Ed. by Robert H. Haveman. LC 82-1844. 358p. 1982. 40.00x (ISBN 0-8143-1712-X). Wayne St U Pr.

Public Finance & Social Policy: Proceedings of the 39th Congress of the International Institute of Public Finance, Budapest, 1983. Ed. by Guy Terny & A. J. Culyer. LC 85-8907. 391p. 1985. 40.00x (ISBN 0-8143-1791-X). Wayne St U Pr.

Public Finance & Stabilization Policy. Ed. by W. L. Smith & J. M. Culbertson. 368p. 1974. 73.75 (ISBN 0-444-10682-0, North-Holland). Elsevier.

Public Finance & the Political Process. Randall G. Holcombe. LC 82-10803. (Political & Social Economy Ser.). 224p. 1983. 19.50x (ISBN 0-8093-1082-1). S Ill U Pr.

Public Finance & the Price Systems. 3rd ed. Edgar K. Browning & Jacqueline Browning. (Illus.). 592p. 1987. text ed. write for info. (ISBN 0-02-315720-8). Macmillan.

Public Finance & the Quest for Efficiency: Proceedings of the 38th Congress of the International Institute of Public Finance, Copenhagen, 1982. Ed. by Horst Hanusch. LC 84-7561. 378p. 1984. 40.00x (ISBN 0-8143-1776-6). Wayne St U Pr.

Public Finance & Welfare: Essays in Honor of C. Ward Macy. Ed. by Paul L. Kleinsorge. LC 66-4750. 1966. 7.50 (ISBN 0-87114-013-6). U of Oreg Bks.

Public Finance During the Korean Modernization Process. Roy Bahl et al. (Harvard East Asian Monographs: No. 107). 1985. text ed. 15.00x (ISBN 0-674-72233-7, Pub. by Coun East Asian Stud). Harvard U Pr.

Public Finance Exams, Puzzles & Problems, Vol. 12. Compiled by Edward Tower. 190p. 1985. 14.00 (ISBN 0-88024-212-4). Eno River Pr.

Public Finance in Democratic Process: Fiscal Institutions & Individual Choice. James M. Buchanan. LC 66-25359. xiv, 307p. 1987. pap. 14.95x (ISBN 0-8078-4190-0). U of NC Pr.

Public Finance in Developing Countries. 3rd ed. A. R. Prest. LC 85-1955. 256p. 1985. 29.95x (ISBN 0-312-65462-6). St Martin.

Public Finance in Egypt: Its Structure & Trends. Sadiq Ahmed. (World Bank Staff Working Papers: No. 639). 112p. 1985. 5.00 (ISBN 0-8213-0359-7, WP0639). World Bank.

Public Finance in Islam. S. A. Siddiqui. 12.50 (ISBN 0-686-18375-4). Kazi Pubns.

Public Finance in Japan. Ed. by Tokue Shibata. 250p. 1986. pap. 19.50 (ISBN 0-86008-387-X, Pub. by U of Tokyo Japan). Columbia U Pr.

Public Finance in Theory & Practice. 3rd ed. Richard A. Musgrave & Peggy B. Musgrave. (Illus.). 1980. text ed. 38.50 (ISBN 0-07-044122-7). McGraw.

Public Finance in Theory & Practice. 4th ed. Richard A. Musgrave & Peggy B. Musgrave. 1984. text ed. 44.95 (ISBN 0-07-044126-X). McGraw.

Public Finance in Theory & Practice. 5th ed. Richard A. Musgrave & Peggy B. Musgrave. (Illus.). 736p. 1989. 39.95 (ISBN 0-07-044127-8). McGraw.

Public Finance: In Theory & Practice. 6th ed. A. R. Prest & N. A. Barr. (Illus.). 568p. 1979. 37.50x (ISBN 0-297-77648-7, GWN 03699, Pub. by Weidenfeld & Nicolson England). Biblio Dist.

Public Finance: In Theory & Practice. 7th ed. A. R. Prest & N. A. Barr. 576p. 1986. 28.95x (ISBN 0-297-78752-7, Pub. by Weidenfeld & Nicolson England). Biblio Dist.

Public Finance in Underdeveloped Countries. R. N. Tripathy. 335p. 1985. text ed. 37.50x (ISBN 0-86590-539-8, Pub. by Sterling Pubs India). Apt Bks.

Public Finance Information Sources. Ed. by Vera H. Knox. LC 64-16503. (Management Information Guide Ser.: No. 3). 150p. 1964. 68.00x (ISBN 0-8103-0803-7). Gale.

Public Finance, Planning & Economic Development: Essays in Honor of Ursula Hicks. Ed. by Wilfred L. David. LC 73-77734. (Illus.). 349p. 1973. 39.50x (ISBN 0-8290-0201-4). Irvington.

Public Finance, Public Choice & Public Policy. Ed. by David Greenaway & G. K. Shaw. 272p. 1985. 45.00x (ISBN 0-631-14313-0). Basil Blackwell.

Public Finance Reading Lists, Vol. 11. Compiled by Edward Tower. 200p. 1985. 14.00 (ISBN 0-88024-211-6). Eno River Pr.

Public Finances. 6th ed. Buchanan & Flowers. 1987. 35.95 (ISBN 0-256-03340-4). Irwin.

Public Financial Institutions & Their Role in Development. Ed. by Ari E. Mir. 261p. 1984. pap. 20.00x (Pub. by Intl Ctr Pub Yugoslavia). Kumarian Pr.

Public Financial Institutions in India. J. S. Uppal. 1985. 11.50x (ISBN 0-8364-1323-7, Pub. by Macmillan India). South Asia Bks.

Public Financing in a Democratic Society: Fiscal Doctrine, Growth & Institutions, Vol. II. Richard A. Musgrave. LC 85-32053. 416p. 1986. 65.00x (ISBN 0-8147-5429-5). NYU Pr.

Public Financing in a Democratic Society: Social Goods, Taxation & Fiscal Policy, Vol. I. Richard A. Musgrave. LC 85-32053. 416p. 1986. 65.00x (ISBN 0-8147-5428-7). NYU Pr.

Public Fire Education. International Fire Service Training Association Staff. Ed. by Connie Osterhout et al. LC 79-89165. (Illus.). 180p. (Orig.). 1979. pap. 11.00 (ISBN 0-87939-034-4). Fire Protect Pubns.

Public Fire Prevention Criteria. National Fire Protection Association Staff. 1984. 10.50 (ISBN 0-317-63541-7, 1301-84). Natl Fire Prot.

Public Fire Safety Organization: A Systems Approach. Harry E. Hickey. LC 73-90984. 224p. 1973. 12.50 (ISBN 0-685-40229-0, SPP-21). Natl Fire Prot.

Public Fire Service Communications. (Seventy Ser.). 68p. 1973. pap. 2.00 (ISBN 0-685-44176-8, 73). Natl Fire Prot.

Public Firesafety Symbols. National Fire Protection Association Staff. 1986. 10.50 (ISBN 0-317-63323-6, 171-86). Natl Fire Prot.

Public Forestry Administration in Latin America. J. Prats-Llaurado & G. Speidel. (Forestry Papers: No. 25). 185p. 1981. pap. 13.75 (ISBN 92-5-101051-X, F2179, FAO). UNIPUB.

Public General Acts - All. 1988. Table of Derivations & Table of Destinations. 11.50 (ISBN 0-11-840282-X, HM3132, Pub. by Her Maj Station Ofc); Income & Corporation Taxes Act 1988, 1037 pgs. 79.00 (ISBN 0-10-540188-9, HM3133, Pub. by Her Maj Station Ofc). UNIPUB.

Public Good & Political Authority: A Pragmatic Proposal. William J. Meyer. (National University Publications Series in American Studies). 1975. 21.95x (ISBN 0-8046-9112-6, Pub. by Kennikat). Assoc Faculty Pr.

Public Goods & Public Policy. Ed. by William Loehr & Todd Sandler. LC 77-17865. (Comparative Political Economy & Public Policy Ser.: Vol. 3). pap. 60.00 (ISBN 0-317-09000-3, 2021923). Bks Demand UMI.

Public Goods & Public Welfare. John G. Head. LC 73-81736. xii, 291p. 1975. 27.95 (ISBN 0-8223-0312-4). Duke.

Public Grazing Lands: Use & Misuse by Industry & Government. William Voigt, Jr. LC 75-42250. (Illus.). 365p. 1976. 37.00x (ISBN 0-8135-0819-3). Rutgers U Pr.

Public Health. Ed. by Dale C. Garell & Solomon H. Snyder. (Encyclopedia of Health Ser.). (Illus.). (YA) (gr. 7-12). 1989. 17.95 (ISBN 0-7910-0091-5). Chelsea Hse.

Public Health. (Illus.). 56p. (gr. 6-12). 1985. pap. 1.25x (ISBN 0-8395-3251-2, 3251). BSA.

Public Health Action in Emergencies Caused by Epidemics: A Practical Guide. P. Bres. 299p. 1986. pap. 29.40 (ISBN 92-4-154207-1). World Health.

Public Health Administration. S. L. Goel. xiii, 472p. 1984. text ed. 50.00x (ISBN 0-86590-527-4, Pub. by Sterling Pubs India). Apt Bks.

Public Health Administration: An Instrument for Evaluation. Ray Biggerstaff. 123p. 1983. pap. text ed. 10.95 (ISBN 0-89917-382-9). Tichenor Pub.

Public Health: Administration & Practice. 8th ed. John J. Hanlon & George E. Pickett. LC 83-24981. (Illus.). 637p. 1983. text ed. 39.95 (ISBN 0-8016-2061-9). Mosby.

Public Health Administration Practice. 9th ed. Hanlon & Pickett. (Illus.). 600p. 1989. 39.95 (ISBN 0-8016-2501-7). Mosby.

Public Health Administrator. Jack Rudman. (Career Examination Ser.: C-2082). (Cloth bdg. avail. on request). 1988. pap. 16.00 (ISBN 0-8373-2082-8). Natl Learning.

Public Health Adviser. Jack Rudman. (Career Examination Ser.: C-3093). 1988. pap. 14.00 (ISBN 0-8373-3093-9). Natl Learning.

Public Health Aide. Jack Rudman. (Career Examination Ser.: C-1441). (Cloth bdg. avail. on request). pap. 14.00 (ISBN 0-8373-1441-0). Natl Learning.

Public Health Aide I. Jack Rudman. (Career Examination Ser.: C-2334). (Cloth bdg. avail. on request). pap. 14.00 (ISBN 0-8373-2334-7). Natl Learning.

Public Health Aide II. Jack Rudman. (Career Examination Ser.: C-1812). (Cloth bdg. avail. on request). pap. 14.00 (ISBN 0-8373-1812-2). Natl Learning.

Public Health & Community Optometry. Robert D. Newcomb & Jerry L. Jolley. (Illus.). 534p. 1980. 60.00x (ISBN 0-398-03918-6). C C Thomas.

Public Health & Development. Ed. by Ismail Sirageldin. (Research in Human Capital & Development Ser.: Vol. 5). 1988. price not set. Jai Pr.

Public Health & Development. Ed. by Ismall Sirageldin & Gary S. Fields. (Research in Human Capital & Development Ser.: Vol. 6). 1988. price not set (ISBN 0-89232-508-9). Jai Pr.

Public Health & Human Ecology. John M. Last. 1987. pap. 29.95 (ISBN 0-8385-8045-9). Appleton & Lange.

Public Health & Insurance. Arthur Newsholme. LC 78-19270. 25.50 (ISBN 0-405-10617-3). Ayer Co Pubs.

Public Health & Podiatric Medicine. Arthur Helfand. 288p. 1987. 31.95 (ISBN 0-683-03952-0). Williams & Wilkins.

Public Health & Preventative Medicine Review. 2nd. ed. Rafael A. Penalver. LC 78-31347. 1983. pap. 14.95. Appleton & Lange.

Public Health & Preventive Medicine Review. 2nd ed. Rafael A. Penalver. 120p. 1984. pap. text ed. 17.95 (ISBN 0-317-60691-3, E5936-9). Appleton & Lange.

Public Health & the Environment: The United States Experience. Ed. by Michael R. Greenberg. LC 86-18373. 395p. 1987. lib. bdg. 35.00 (ISBN 0-89862-778-8). Guilford Pr.

Public Health & the Law: Issues & Trends. Lynn Hogue. LC 80-15041. 427p. 1980. text ed. 71.50 (ISBN 0-89443-289-3). Aspen Pub.

Public Health & the Medical Profession in the Renaissance. Carlo M. Cipolla. LC 75-22984. pap. 37.50 (2031631). Bks Demand UMI.

Public Health & the State: Changing Views in Massachusetts, 1842-1936. Barbara G. Rosenkrantz. LC 70-172321. (Illus.). 1972. 18.50x (ISBN 0-674-72235-3); pap. text ed. 7.95x (ISBN 0-674-72236-1). Harvard U Pr.

Public Health Assistant. Jack Rudman. (Career Examination Ser.: C-629). (Cloth bdg. avail. on request). pap. 14.00 (ISBN 0-8373-0629-9). Natl Learning.

Public Health Consultant. Jack Rudman. (Career Examination Ser.: C-989). 1988. pap. 16.00. Natl Learning.

Public Health Director. Jack Rudman. (Career Examination Ser.: C-2240). (Cloth bdg. avail. on request). pap. 18.00 (ISBN 0-8373-2240-5). Natl Learning.

Public Health Education Trainee. Jack Rudman. (Career Examination Ser.: C-983). (Cloth bdg. avail. on request). pap. 12.00 (ISBN 0-8373-0983-2). Natl Learning.

Public Health Educator. Jack Rudman. (Career Examination Ser.: C-630). (Cloth bdg. avail. on request). pap. 16.00 (ISBN 0-8373-0630-2). Natl Learning.

Public Health Educator 1. Jack Rudman. (Career Examination Ser.: C-2354). (Cloth bdg. avail. on request). pap. 16.00 (ISBN 0-8373-2354-1). Natl Learning.

Public Health Engineer. Jack Rudman. (Career Examination Ser.: C-1979). (Cloth bdg. avail. on request). pap. 14.00 (ISBN 0-8373-1979-X). Natl Learning.

Public Health Engineer Trainee. Jack Rudman. (Career Examination Ser.: C-1881). (Cloth bdg. avail. on request). pap. 12.00 (ISBN 0-8373-1881-5). Natl Learning.

Public Health Engineering-Sewarage. 2nd ed. R. E. Bartlett. 196p. 1979. 54.00 (ISBN 0-85334-796-4, Pub. by Elsevier Applied Sci England). Elsevier.

Public Health Epidemiologist. Jack Rudman. (Career Examination Ser.: C-2246). (Cloth bdg. avail. on request). pap. 14.00 (ISBN 0-8373-2246-4). Natl Learning.

Public Health Implications of Radioactive Waste Releases. C. W. Straub. 61p. 1970. pap. 3.60 (ISBN 92-4-156006-1, 597). World Health.

Public Health in a Retrenchment Era: An Alternative to Managerialism. Helen J. Muller & Curtis Ventriss. LC 84-16432. (SUNY Series in Public Administration). 162p. 1985. 52.50 (ISBN 0-87395-985-X); pap. 17.95 (ISBN 0-87395-986-8). State U NY Pr.

Public Health in America, 46 bks. Ed. by Barbara G. Rosenkrantz. (Public Health in America Ser.). 1977. Repr. lib. bdg. 1242.50x set (ISBN 0-405-09804-9). Ayer Co Pubs.

Public Health in the Town of Boston, 1630-1822. John B. Blake. LC 59-10314. (Historical Studies: No. 72). (Illus.). 288p. 1959. 18.50x (ISBN 0-674-72250-7). Harvard U Pr.

Public Health Inspector. Jack Rudman. (Career Examination Ser.: C-1753). (Cloth bdg. avail. on request). pap. 14.00. Natl Learning.

Public Health: Its Promise for the Future. Wilson G. Smillie. LC 75-22841. (America in Two Centuries Ser.). (Illus.). 1976. Repr. of 1955 ed. 37.50x (ISBN 0-405-07712-2). Ayer Co Pubs.

Public Health: Myth, Mysticism & Reality. U. Ko Ko. (SEARO Regional Health Papers: No. 14). 72p. 1987. pap. 7.20 (ISBN 92-9022-183-6). World Health.

Public Health Nurse. Jack Rudman. (Career Examination Ser.: C-631). (Cloth bdg. avail. on request). pap. 14.00 (ISBN 0-8373-0631-0). Natl Learning.

Public Health Nursing. Mary S. Gardner. Ed. by Barbara G. Rosenkrantz. LC 76-25664. (Public Health in America Ser.). 1977. Repr. lib. bdg. 24.50x (ISBN 0-405-09819-7). Ayer Co Pubs.

Public Health Nutritionist. Jack Rudman. (Career Examination Ser.: C-632). (Cloth bdg. avail. on request). pap. 14.00 (ISBN 0-8373-0632-9). Natl Learning.

Public Health Policy: A World View, 1981-1987. Dale E. Casper. (Public Administration Ser.: P 2291). 11p. 1987. 3.75 (ISBN 1-55590-571-4). Vance Biblios.

Public Health Policy & Planning: A World View, 1982-1987. Dale E. Casper. (Public Administration Ser.: P 2292). 13p. 1987. 3.75 (ISBN 1-55590-572-2). Vance Biblios.

Public Health Representative. Jack Rudman. (Career Examination Ser.: C-2369). (Cloth bdg. avail. on request). pap. 14.00 (ISBN 0-8373-2369-X). Natl Learning.

Public Health Representative I. Jack Rudman. (Career Examination Ser.: C-2972). 1988. pap. 14.00 (ISBN 0-8373-2972-8). Natl Learning.

Public Health Representative II. Jack Rudman. (Career Examination Ser.: C-2973). 1988. pap. 14.00 (ISBN 0-8373-2973-6). Natl Learning.

Public Health Sanitarian. Jack Rudman. (Career Examination Ser.: C-633). (Cloth bdg. avail. on request). pap. 14.00 (ISBN 0-8373-0633-7). Natl Learning.

Public Health Sanitarian Trainee. Jack Rudman. (Career Examination Ser.: C-984). (Cloth bdg. avail. on request). pap. 12.00 (ISBN 0-8373-0984-0). Natl Learning.

Public Health Scientist. Jack Rudman. (Career Examination Ser.: C-634). (Cloth bdg. avail. on request). pap. 16.00 (ISBN 0-8373-0634-5). Natl Learning.

Public Health Service. Ed. by Arthur M. Schlesinger, Jr. (Know Your Government Ser.). (Illus.). (gr. 5 up). 1989. 14.95 (ISBN 0-87754-830-7). Chelsea Hse.

Public Health Service Grants Policy Statement. rev. ed. (DHHS Publication OASH 82-50,000 Ser.). 1987. pap. 4.50 (ISBN 0-318-22596-4, S/N 017-020-00092-7). USGPO.

Public Health Service: Its History, Activities & Organization. Laurence F. Schmeckebier. LC 72-3023. (Brookings Institution. Institute for Government Research. Service Monographs of the U. S. Government: No. 10). Repr. of 1923 ed. 32.00 (ISBN 0-404-57110-7). AMS Pr.

Public Health Social Work Assistant. Jack Rudman. (Career Examination Ser.: C-1442). (Cloth bdg. avail. on request). pap. 14.00 (ISBN 0-8373-1442-9). Natl Learning.

Public Health Technician. Jack Rudman. (Career Examination Ser.: C-2226). (Cloth bdg. avail. on request). pap. 14.00 (ISBN 0-8373-2226-X). Natl Learning.

Public History: An Introduction. Ed. by Barbara J. Howe & Emory L. Kemp. LC 85-23665. 516p. 1986. text ed. 39.95 (ISBN 0-89874-881-X); pap. 27.50. Krieger.

Public History in North Carolina 1903-1978. Ed. by Jeffrey J. Crow. (Illus.). x, 110p. 1979. pap. 4.00 (ISBN 0-86526-098-2). NC Archives.

Public Hospitals under Private Management: The California Experience. William Shonick & Ruth Roemer. LC 82-25854. 127p. pap. 7.75x (ISBN 0-87772-290-0). UCB IGS.

Public Houses & Beerhouses in Nineteenth Century Portsmouth. R. C. Riley & Philip Elly. 1983. 42.00x (ISBN 0-317-43796-8, Pub. by City of Portsmouth). State Mutual Bk.

Public Housing. Ed. by M. A. Muttalib & Akbar A. Mohd. 345p. 1986. text ed. 40.00x (ISBN 0-86590-799-4, Pub. by Sterling Pubs India). Apt Bks.

Public Housing: A Review of Recent Trends. Dale E. Casper. (Public Administration Ser.: P 2335). 35p. 1988. 3.00 (ISBN 1-55590-645-1). Vance Biblios.

Public Housing Advocacy. 3.00 (37,357PH). NCLS Inc.

Public Housing & Private Property. Stephanie Cooper. 200p. 1985. text ed. 38.95 (ISBN 0-566-05004-8). Gower Pub Co.

Public Housing & Selected Housing Issues. Texas Legal Services Center. 275p. 1985. 18.00 (39,401). NCLS Inc.

Public Housing Energy Efficiency Through Private Financing. 57p. 1982. 10.00 (ISBN 0-318-17333-6, DG82-302). Pub Tech Inc.

Public Housing, Race & Renewal: Urban Planning in Philadelphia 1920-1974. John F. Bauman. LC 86-5907. (Illus.). 288p. 1987. 34.95 (ISBN 0-87722-444-7). Temple U Pr.

Public Hug: Poems. Robert Hershon. LC 79-9446. 92p. 1980. 13.95x (ISBN 0-8071-0597-X); pap. 6.95 (ISBN 0-8071-0598-8). La State U Pr.

Public Hygiene in America. Henry I. Bowditch. LC 70-180557. (Medicine & Society in America Ser). (Illus.). 415p. 1972. Repr. of 1877 ed. 27.00 (ISBN 0-405-03937-9). Ayer Co Pubs.

Public Image of Big Business in America, 1880-1940: A Quantitative Study in Social Change. Louis P. Galambos & Barbara Barrow Spence. LC 75-11347. (Illus.). 336p. 1975. 37.50x (ISBN 0-8018-1635-1). Johns Hopkins.

Public Image of Courts. National Center for State Courts Staff. 104p. 1978. manuscript 6.24 (SC-001). Natl Ctr St Courts.

Public Image of Courts, 1977: General Public Data. US Department of Justice, Bureau of Justice Statistics. LC 79-91248. 260p. 1980. write for info., codebk. ICPSR.

Public Image of Courts, 1977: Special Publics Data. U. S. Department of Justice, Bureau of Justice Statistics. LC 79-91248. 260p. 1980. write for info. ICPSR.

Public Image of Henry Ford: An American Folk Hero & His Company. David Lewis. LC 76-807. (Illus.). 600p. 1976. pap. 35.00x (ISBN 0-8143-1553-4). Wayne St U Pr.

Public Image of Henry Ford: An American Folk Hero & His Company. David L. Lewis. (Illus.). 600p. 1987. pap. 17.50x (ISBN 0-8143-1892-4). Wayne St U Pr.

Public Images of Western Security. Gregory Flynn et al. (Atlantic Paper Ser.: 54-55). 92p. 1985. pap. 14.00x (ISBN 0-8476-7491-6, Rowman & Allanheld). Rowman.

Public Industrial Enterprises: Determinants of Performance. Mahmood A. Ayub & Sven O. Hegstad. (Industry & Finance Paper: 17). 90p. 1986. pap. 5.00 (BK0815). World Bank.

Public Information Assistant. Jack Rudman. (Career Examination Ser.: C-2956). (Cloth bdg. avail. on request). pap. 14.00 (ISBN 0-8373-2956-6). Natl Learning.

Public Information Contact Directory 1988-89. Compiled by AAAS Office of Communications Staff. 94p. 1988. pap. 10.00 (ISBN 0-87168-334-2). AAAS.

Public Information Manual for Human Services. Janis A. Martineau. (Serving the Elderly Ser.: Pt. 3). 1978. pap. 5.00 (ISBN 0-89634-004-X, 045). Systems Planning.

Public Information Officer. Jack Rudman. (Career Examination Ser.: C-2950). (Cloth bdg. avail. on request). pap. 14.00 (ISBN 0-8373-2950-7). Natl Learning.

Public Information Programs for Attorneys General's Offices. (Management Manual: No. 4). 59p. 1976. 3.00 (ISBN 0-318-15223-1). Natl Attys General.

Public Information Specialist. Jack Rudman. (Career Examination Ser.: C-2111). (Cloth bdg. avail. on request). pap. 14.00 (ISBN 0-8373-2111-5). Natl Learning.

Public Infrastructure Planning & Management. Ed. by Jay M. Stein. (Urban Affairs Annual Reviews Ser.: Vol. 33). 270p. 1988. text ed. 35.00 (ISBN 0-8039-2690-1); pap. text ed. 16.95 (ISBN 0-8039-2691-X). Sage.

Public Interest: A Critique of the Theory of a Political Concept. Glendon A. Schubert. LC 82-15509. x, 244p. 1982. Repr. of 1960 ed. lib. bdg. 35.00x (ISBN 0-313-22364-5, SCPU). Greenwood.

Public Interest & the Business of Broadcasting: The Broadcast Industry Looks at Itself. Ed. by Jon T. Powell & Wally Gair. LC 88-3098. 208p. 1988. lib. bdg. 39.95 (ISBN 0-89930-198-3, PLI/, Quorum Bks). Greenwood.

Public Interest Handbook: A Guide to Legal Careers in Public Interest Organizations. Geoffrey Kaiser & Barbara Mule. LC 86-33815. 484p. (Orig.). 1987. pap. text ed. 29.95 (ISBN 0-933951-08-6). Locust Hill Pr.

Public Interest in National Labor Policy. 158p. 1961. 2.00 (ISBN 0-317-33996-6, 306). Comm Econ Dev.

Public Interest Law. Ed. by Jeremy Cooper & Rajeev Dhavan. 320p. 1986. 45.00x (ISBN 0-631-14299-1). Basil Blackwell.

Public Interest Law: An Economic & Institutional Analysis. Burton A. Weisbrod et al. 1978. 54.00x (ISBN 0-520-03355-8); pap. 11.95 (ISBN 0-520-03568-2). U of Cal Pr.

Public Interest Law: Where Law Meets Social Action. Robert A. Baum. Ed. by Irving J. Sloan. LC 86-28551. (Legal Almanac Ser.: No. 86). 141p. 1987. lib. bdg. 8.50 (ISBN 0-379-11162-4). Oceana.

Public Interest Liberalism, & the Crisis of Affluence. Robert D. Holsworth. 320p. 1981. pap. text ed. 10.95x (ISBN 0-87073-061-4). Schenkman Bks Inc.

Public Interest Lobbies: Decision Making on Energy. Andrew S. McFarland. LC 76-51340. 1976. pap. 8.50 (ISBN 0-8447-3229-X). Am Enterprise.

Public-Interest Media Reform Movement: A Look at the Mandate & a New Agenda. Theodore J. Schneyer & Frank LLoyd. 44p. (Orig.). 1977. pap. text ed. 5.00 (ISBN 0-8191-5827-5, Pub. by Aspen Inst for Humanistic Studies). U Pr of Amer.

Public Interest on Crime & Punishment. Nathan Glazer. LC 83-25861. 1984. 31.00 (ISBN 0-89011-589-3); pap. 12.25. Abt Bks.

Public Interest on Crime & Punishment. Ed. by Nathan Glazer. 294p. 1984. lib. bdg. 32.75 (ISBN 0-8191-4138-0); pap. text ed. 13.00 (ISBN 0-8191-4139-9). U Pr of Amer.

Public Interest on Education. Ed. by Nathan Glazer. 1984. 31.00 (ISBN 0-89011-590-7); pap. 12.00. Abt Bks.

Public Interest on Education. Ed. by Nathan Glazer. (Illus.). 280p. 1984. lib. bdg. 32.75 (ISBN 0-8191-4140-2); pap. text ed. 12.75 (ISBN 0-8191-4141-0). U Pr of Amer.

Public Interest Report, No. Two: Fluoride Industry's Phantom Air Pollutant Poisoning Animals, Farm & Forest. pap. 1.50 (ISBN 0-318-03956-7). Top Ecol Pr.

Public Interest Report, No. 1: Fluoride Fallout from Factories Making Man the Endangered Species. pap. 1.50 (ISBN 0-318-03955-9). Top Ecol Pr.

Public International Air Transport Law in a New Era: Economic Regulation of International Air Carrier Operations. H. A. Wassenbergh. 176p. 1976. 29.00 (ISBN 90-268-0860-7, Pub. by Kluwer Law Netherlands). Kluwer Academic.

Public International Air Transportation Law in a New Era: Economic Regulation of International Air Carrier Operations. H. A. Wassenbergh. ix, 165p. 1976. text ed. 25.75x (ISBN 90-268-0860-7). Rothman.

Public International Law. Branimir M. Jankovic. LC 83-9155. 450p. 1983. lib. bdg. 55.00 (ISBN 0-941320-16-2); pap. text ed. 26.50 (ISBN 0-941320-19-7). Transnatl Pubs.

Public International Law & International Organizations. Simone-Marie Kleckner. LC 83-61734. (Collection of Bibliographic & Research Resources Ser.). 99p. 1984. including other bibliographies in looseleaf 300.00 (ISBN 0-379-20891-1); pap. 35.00. Oceana.

Public International Law & the Future World Order: Liber Amicorum in Honor of A. J. Thomas, Jr. Ed. by Joseph J. Norton. LC 87-4688. (Illus.). xxxii, 583p. 1987. text ed. 47.50x (ISBN 0-8377-2510-0). Rothman.

Public International Law in a Nutshell. Thomas Buergenthal & Harold G. Maier. LC 85-17836. (Nutshell Ser.). 250p. 1985. pap. text ed. 8.95 (ISBN 0-314-93816-8). West Pub.

Public Intervention & Industrial Restructuring in China, India & the Republic of Korea. 162p. (Orig.). 1987. pap. text ed. 8.00 (ISBN 92-2-105774-7, ILO1469, ILO). UNIPUB.

Public Investment & Full Employment. (I.L.O. Studies & Reports New Ser.: No. 3). Repr. of 1946 ed. 51.00 (ISBN 0-8115-3329-8). Kraus Repr.

Public Investment Planning in Civilian Nuclear Power. John M. Vernon. LC 78-132029. pap. 45.30 (ISBN 0-317-26882-1, 2023464). Bks Demand UMI.

Public Investment, the Rate of Return, & Optimal Fiscal Policy. Kenneth J. Arrow & Mordecai Kurz. LC 73-108380. pap. 62.00 (2025627). Bks Demand UMI.

Public Investor's Guide to Money Market Instruments. Girard Miller. LC 82-80937. (Illus.). 111p. 1982. pap. 13.00 Nonmember (ISBN 0-686-84370-3); pap. 11.00 Member (ISBN 0-686-84371-1). Municipal.

Public Involvement & Social Impact Assessment. Ed. by Gregory A. Daneke & Margot W. Garcia. (Social Impact Assessment Ser.: No. 9). 300p. 1983. lib. bdg. 38.50x (ISBN 0-86531-624-4). Westview.

Public Involvement in Energy Facility Planning: The Electric Utility Experience. Ed. by Dennis W. Ducsik. (Special Studies in Natural Resources & Energy Management). 451p. 1986. pap. 40.50 (ISBN 0-8133-7212-7). Westview.

Public Involvement in Environmental Decisionmaking: An Annotated Bibliography. B. Jaffray. (CPL Bibliographies Ser.: No. 61). 57p. 1981. 11.00 (ISBN 0-86602-061-6). Coun Plan Librarians.

Public Involvement in the Introduction of Power Plants. Myhra. 1988. write for info. (ISBN 0-471-04856-9). Wiley.

Public Involvement Manual. James L. Creighton. LC 81-66306. (Illus.). 344p. 1981. text ed. 40.50x (ISBN 0-89011-557-5). Abt Bks.

Public Involvement Manual. James L. Creighton. 344p. 1984. Repr. of 1981 ed. lib. bdg. 42.75 (ISBN 0-8191-4097-X). U Pr of Amer.

Public Is Invited to Dance: Representation, the Body & Dialogue in Gertrude Stein. Harriet S. Chessman. 288p. 1989. 29.50x (ISBN 0-8047-1484-3). Stanford U Pr.

Public Issues Handbook: A Guide for the Concerned Citizen. Robert A. Rosenbaum. LC 82-15812. (Illus.). vii, 409p. 1983. lib. bdg. 36.95 (ISBN 0-313-23504-X, RPI/). Greenwood.

Public Ivys: A Guide to America's Best Public Undergraduate Colleges & Universities. Richard Moll. LC 83-40659. 320p. 1985. 18.95 (ISBN 0-670-58205-0). Viking.

Public Ivys: A Guide to America's Best State Colleges & Universities. Richard Moll. 304p. 1986. pap. 7.95 (ISBN 0-14-009384-2). Penguin.

Public Knowledge & Christian Education. Theodore Plantinga. LC 87-3555000002. (Studies in Religious Education: Vol. 1). 136p. 1988. 39.95 (ISBN 0-88946-477-4). E Mellen.

Public Knowledge & Environmental Politics in Japan & the United States. John C. Pierce et al. (Special Studies in Public Policy & Public Systems Management). 256p. 1988. pap. 24.00. Westview.

Public Knowledge, Private Ignorance: Toward a Library & Information Policy. Patrick Wilson. LC 76-52327. (Contributions in Librarianship & Information Science Ser.: No. 10). ix, 156p. 1977. lib. bdg. 35.00 (ISBN 0-8371-9485-7, WPN/). Greenwood.

Public Land & Mining Law. 3rd ed. Loren Mall. LC 81-68524. 464p. 1982. 40.00 (ISBN 0-409-23017-0); pap. 29.50 (ISBN 0-409-23018-9). Butterworth WA.

Public Land & the U. S. Economy: Balancing Conservation & Development. Ed. by George M. Johnston & Peter M. Emerson. 290p. 1983. pap. 36.50x (ISBN 0-86531-819-0). Westview.

Public Land Laws. Henry N. Copp. Ed. by Stuart Bruchey. LC 78-53559. (Development of Public Land Law in the U. S. Ser.). 1979. Repr. of 1875 ed. lib. bdg. 63.00x (ISBN 0-405-11372-2). Ayer Co Pubs.

Public Land Policies: An Original Anthology. Ed. by Paul W. Gates & Stuart Bruchey. LC 78-56714. (Management of Public Lands in the U. S. Ser.). 1979. lib. bdg. 40.00x (ISBN 0-405-11360-9). Ayer Co Pubs.

Public Land Surveys. Lowell O. Stewart. Ed. by Stuart Bruchey. LC 78-53567. (Development of Public Lands Law in the U. S. Ser.). 1979. Repr. of 1935 ed. lib. bdg. 17.00x (ISBN 0-405-11386-2). Ayer Co Pubs.

Public Land System of Texas, Eighteen Twenty-Three to Nineteen Ten. Reuben McKitrick. Ed. by Stuart Bruchey. LC 78-56659. (Management of Public Lands in the U. S. Ser.). (Illus.). 1979. Repr. of 1918 ed. lib. bdg. 14.00x (ISBN 0-405-11342-0). Ayer Co Pubs.

Public Lands & Agrarian Laws of the Roman Republic. Andrew Stephenson. LC 78-63804. (Johns Hopkins University. Studies in the Social Sciences. Ninth Ser. 1891: 7-8). Repr. of 1891 ed. 11.50 (ISBN 0-404-61067-6). AMS Pr.

Public Lands & Pioneer Farmers, Gage County, Nebraska, 1850-1900. Yasue Okada. Ed. by Stuart Bruchey. LC 78-56687. (Management of Public Lands in the U. S. Ser.). (Illus.). 1979. Repr. of 1971 ed. lib. bdg. 16.00x (ISBN 0-405-11348-X). Ayer Co Pubs.

Public Lands Conflict & Resolution: Managing National Forest Disputes. Julia M. Wondolleck. LC 88-13991. (Environment, Development, & Public Policy Series: Environmental Policy & Planning). (Illus.). 280p. 1988. 39.50x (ISBN 0-306-42861-X, Plenum Pr). Plenum Pub.

Public Lands in Jacksonian Politics. Daniel Feller. LC 84-40149. 288p. 1984. text ed. 29.50x (ISBN 0-299-09850-8). U of Wis Pr.

Public Lands of Texas, 1519-1970. Thomas L. Miller. LC 75-160500. (Illus.). 1972. 24.95 (ISBN 0-8061-0972-6); pap. 12.95 (ISBN 0-8061-1302-2). U of Okla Pr.

Public Lands Politics: Interest Group Influence on the Forest Service & the Bureau of Land Management. Paul J. Culhane. 398p. 1981. 32.50 (ISBN 0-8018-2598-9); pap. 14.95 (ISBN 0-8018-2599-7). Resources Future.

Public Lands: Studies in the History of the Public Domain. Ed. by Vernon Carstensen. 548p. 1963. pap. 13.95x (ISBN 0-299-02754-6). U of Wis Pr.

Public Landscape of the New Deal. Phoebe Cutler. LC 85-2437. 200p. 1986. 27.50x (ISBN 0-300-03256-0). Yale U Pr.

Public Law & Public Administration. 2nd ed. Phillip J. Cooper. (Illus.). 512p. 1988. text ed. price not set (ISBN 0-13-737594-8). P-H.

Public Law Ninety-Four To One Forty-Two: A Guide for the Education for All Handicapped Children Act. Clarence J. Jones & Ted F. Rabold. 1979. pap. 3.75x (ISBN 0-931992-32-X). Penns Valley.

Public Law Two-Eighty. Carole E. Goldberg. (American Indian Treaties Publications Ser.). 60p. 1975. pap. 5.00 (ISBN 0-935626-19-0). U Cal AISC.

Public Law: 1956-1985, 30 vols. Bound set. 1125.00x (ISBN 0-686-90026-X). Rothman.

Public Law 94-142: Special Education in Transition. Don R. Barbacovi & Richard W. Clelland. 1978. pap. 4.95 (ISBN 0-686-02453-2, 02100323). Am Assn Sch Admin.

Public Law 99-661: Increased Contract Goal for Minorities. rev. ed. Barry L. McVay & Vivina H. McVay. 24p. (Orig.). 1988. pap. 15.00 (ISBN 0-912481-06-4). Panoptic Ent.

Public Law 99-661: Increased Contract Goal for Minorities. rev. ed. Barry L. McVay & Vivina H. McVay. 24p. (Orig.). 1988. pap. 15.00 (ISBN 0-912481-07-2). Panoptic Ent.

Public Legal Services in the 1980's. Jim Buchanan. (Public Administration Ser.: P 2247). 32p. 1987. 8.75 (ISBN 1-55590-487-4). Vance Biblios.

Public Lending Right. H. Cohen Jehoram. 1983. pap. text ed. 30.00 (ISBN 90-654-4134-4, Pub. by Kluwer Law & Taxation). Kluwer Academic.

Public Letters. 2nd ed. John Bright. Ed. by H. J. Leech. 1969. Repr. of 1895 ed. 21.00 (ISBN 0-527-10910-X). Kraus Repr.

Public Librarian. Jack Rudman. (Career Examination Ser.: C-989). (Cloth bdg. avail. on request). pap. 14.00 (ISBN 0-8373-0989-1). Natl Learning.

Public Librarian As Adult Learners' Advisor: An Innovation in Human Services. Jane A. Reilly. (Contributions in Librarianship & Information Science Ser.: No. 38). (Illus.). 184p. lib. bdg. 35.00 (ISBN 0-313-22134-0, REP/). Greenwood.

Public Libraries: An Economic View. Malcolm Getz. LC 80-10651. 208p. 1980. text ed. 27.50x (ISBN 0-8018-2395-1). Johns Hopkins.

Public Libraries & the Challenges of the Next Two Decades. Alphonse F. Trezza. LC 85-24205. 266p. 1985. lib. bdg. 35.00 (ISBN 0-87287-427-3). Libs Unl.

Public Libraries & Nontraditional Clienteles: The Politics of Special Services. Marcia J. Nauratil. LC 84-19342. (New Directions in Librarianship Ser.: No. 8). xi, 180p. 1985. lib. bdg. 35.00 (ISBN 0-313-23818-9, NAP/). Greenwood.

Public Libraries & Organizations Serving the Unemployed. John Barugh & Roger G. Woodhouse. (British Library Research Paper: No. 13). 1987. pap. text ed. 7.50 (ISBN 0-7123-3104-2, Pub. By British Lib). Longwood Pub Group.

Public Libraries: Legislation, Administration, & Finance. B. J. Phillips et al. 40p. 1977. pap. text ed. 10.50x (ISBN 0-85365-750-5, Pub. by Library Assn Pub London). ALA.

Public Libraries of the Pacific Northwest. Ed. by Morton Kroll. LC 60-9873. (PNLA Library Development Project Reports, Ser.: Vol. 1). 461p. 1960. 16.50x (ISBN 0-295-73897-9). U of Wash Pr.

Public Libraries since Nineteen Forty-Five: The Impact of the McColvin Report. Philip Whiteman. 219p. 1987. 39.50 (ISBN 0-85157-371-1, Pub. by Bingley England). ALA.

Public Libraries: Smart Practices in Personnel. Peggy Sullivan & William Ptacek. LC 81-15638. 95p. 1982. lib. bdg. 13.50 (ISBN 0-87287-278-5). Libs Unl.

Public Libraries Today. K. C. Harrison. 1963. 6.95 (ISBN 0-8022-0686-7). Philos Lib.

Public Library: A Guide Book for North Carolina Library Trustees. Robert E. Phay. 74p. 1984. 5.00 (ISBN 0-686-39481-X). U of NC Inst Gov.

Public Library Administration. Royston Brown. (Outline of Modern Librarianship Ser.). 1979. 12.00 (ISBN 0-85157-276-6, Pub. by Bingley England). ALA.

Public Library Administration. George Jefferson. 75p. 1966. 6.95 (ISBN 0-8022-0796-0). Philos Lib.

Public Library Administrator's Planning Guide to Automation. Donald J. Sager. (OCLC Library, Information, & Computer Science Ser.: No. 2). 144p. (Orig.). 1983. pap. 12.50 (ISBN 0-933418-43-4). OCLC Online Comp.

Public Library & Blind People. Peter Craddock. (LIR Report Ser.: No. 36). 122p. 1985. pap. 22.50 (ISBN 0-7123-3051-8, Pub. by British Lib). Longwood Pub Group.

Public Library & Federal Policy. Ed. by J. B. Wellisch et al. LC 73-20302. 1974. lib. bdg. 46.95 (ISBN 0-8371-7334-5, PLF/). Greenwood.

Public Library Catalog. 8th ed. LC 84-3508. 1442p. 1984. 140.00 (ISBN 0-8242-0702-5). Wilson.

Public Library: Circumstances & Prospects: Proceedings of the Thirty-Ninth Conference of the Graduate Library School, April 10-11, 1978. Chicago University, Graduate Library School Staff. Ed. by W. Boyd Rayward. LC 78-19604. pap. 42.00 (2026739). Bks Demand UMI.

Public Library Decision-Making: Process, Participants & Power. Roberta H. Gellert. Date not set. text ed. cancelled (ISBN 0-208-02052-7, Lib Prof Pubns); pap. text ed. cancelled (ISBN 0-208-02053-5, Lib Prof Pubns). Shoe String.

Public Library Development Program: Manual for Trainers. Peggy O'Donnell. 154p. 1988. 3-ring binder 20.00x (ISBN 0-8389-3347-5). ALA.

Public Library Finance. Ann E. Prentice. LC 77-9096. 156p. 1977. pap. 8.00x (ISBN 0-8389-0240-5). ALA.

Public Library in Non-Traditional Education. Jean S. Brooks & David L. Reich. LC 73-21903. (Illus.). 256p. 1974. 19.95 (ISBN 0-88280-008-6). ETC Pubns.

Public Library in the Bibliographic Network. Ed. by Betty J. Turock. LC 86-14915. (Resource Sharing & Information Networks Ser.). 104p. 1986. text ed. 24.95 (ISBN 0-86656-595-7). Haworth Pr.

Public Library in the Nineteen Eighties: The Problems of Choice. Lawrence J. White. LC 82-48604. (Lexington Books Special Series in Libraries & Librarianship). 244p. 1983. 26.00x (ISBN 0-669-06342-8). Lexington Bks.

Public Library in the Urban Setting. Ed. by Leon Carnovsky. LC 68-55802. (Studies in Library Science Ser). 1968. 8.00x (ISBN 0-226-09411-1). U of Chicago Pr.

Public Library Information & Referral Service. Ed. by Clara S. Jones. 265p. 1981. pap. 18.50x (ISBN 0-915794-06-3, Lib Prof Pubns). Shoe String.

Public Library Movement in the United States. Samuel S. Greene. 59.95 (ISBN 0-8490-0914-6). Gordon Pr.

Public Library Networking & Inter-Library Co-Operation. Ed. by Debra Shaw & Ann E. Prentice. (Public Library Quarterly: Vol. 2, Nos. 3-4). 113p. 1982. pap. text ed. 20.00 (ISBN 0-86656-116-1, B116). Haworth Pr.

Public Library of the City of St. Louis: A Facsimile Reproduction, Original Edition Nineteen Twelve. 1979. 1.00 (ISBN 0-937322-05-9). St Louis Pub Lib.

TITLE INDEX PUBLIC PARKS & THE

Public Library Policy. Ed. by K. C. Harrison. (IFLA Publication Ser.: No. 19). 152p. 1981. lib. bdg. 15.00 (ISBN 3-598-20380-2). K G Saur.

Public Library Research: A Study of the Development & Current State of Public Library Research in Great Britain. N. Moore. (R&D Report 5419). 44p. (Orig.). 1978. pap. 8.25 (ISBN 0-905984-15-3, Pub. by British Lib). Longwood Pub Group.

Public Library Service for Ethnic Minorities in Great Britain. Ed. by Eric Clough & Jacqueline Quarmby. LC 78-13622. (Illus.). 1978. lib. bdg. 56.95 (ISBN 0-313-21201-5, CPL). Greenwood.

Public Library Service to Children. Elizabeth H. Gross. LC 67-24347. 152p. 1967. 9.00 (ISBN 0-379-00309-0). Oceana.

Public Library Services for Children. Lionel R. McColvin. (Manuals for Libraries: No. 9). 103p. (3rd Printing 1968). 1957. pap. 5.00 (ISBN 92-3-100426-3, U503, UNESCO). UNIPUB.

Public Library Services for Children. Barbara Rollock. 250p. 1988. 27.50 (ISBN 0-208-02016-0, Lib Prof Pubns). Shoe String.

Public Library User Fees: The Use & Finance of Public Libraries. Nancy A. Van House. LC 82-11741. (Contributions in Librarianship & Information Science Ser.: No. 43). (Illus.). ix, 140p. 1983. lib. bdg. 35.00 (ISBN 0-313-22753-5, DPU/). Greenwood.

Public Library Users & Uses: A Market Research Handbook. Choong H. Kim & Robert D. Little. LC 87-13126. 384p. 1987. 29.50 (ISBN 0-8108-2021-8). Scarecrow.

Public Library User's Consultative Councils. W. J. Murison. (R&D Report 5499). 84p. (Orig.). 1979. pap. 12.00 (ISBN 0-905984-42-0, Pub. by British Lib). Longwood Pub Group.

Public Life & Late Capitalism: Toward a Socialist Theory of Democracy. John Keane. LC 83-10584. 554p. 1984. 47.50 (ISBN 0-521-25543-0). Cambridge U Pr.

Public Life in England. Philippe Daryl. Tr. by Henry Frith. 1978. Repr. lib. bdg. 25.00 (ISBN 0-8495-1038-4). Arden Lib.

Public Life in Renaissance Florence. Richard C. Trexler. LC 80-979. (Studies in Discontinuity). 1980. 24.95 (ISBN 0-12-699550-8). Acad Pr.

Public Life in Urban Places. Suzanne H. Crowhurst-Lennard & Henry L. Lennard. LC 83-83342. 80p. (Orig.). 1984. pap. 8.95 (ISBN 0-935824-03-0). Gondolier.

Public Life of Captain John Brown. facs. ed. James Redpath. LC 79-126251. (Select Bibliographies Reprint Ser). 1860. 21.00 (ISBN 0-8369-5478-5). Ayer Co Pubs.

Public Life of Eugene Semple: Promoter & Politician of the Pacific Northwest. Alan Hynding. LC 73-9903. 220p. 1973. 20.00x (ISBN 0-295-95288-1). U of Wash Pr.

Public Life of Henry Dearborn. Richard A. Erney. Ed. by Richard H. Kohn. LC 78-22419. (American Military of Experience Ser.). 1979. lib. bdg. 27.50x (ISBN 0-405-11893-7). Ayer Co Pubs.

Public Life of Our Lord Jesus Christ, 2 vols. A. Goodier. 1978. Set. 15.95 (ISBN 0-8198-0551-3); Set. pap. 13.95 (ISBN 0-8198-0552-1). Dghtrs St Paul.

Public Life of Thomas Cooper, 1783-1839. Dumas Malone. LC 75-3122. Repr. of 1926 ed. 46.00 (ISBN 0-404-59117-5). AMS Pr.

Public Loans to Private Business. John D. Glover. Ed. by Stuart Bruchey & Vincent P. Carosso. LC 78-18961. (Small Business Enterprise in America Ser.). (Illus.). 1979. lib. bdg. 37.00x (ISBN 0-405-11465-6). Ayer Co Pubs.

Public Man, Private Woman: Women in Social & Political Thought. Jean B. Elshtain. LC 81-47122. 376p. 1981. 38.50x (ISBN 0-691-07632-4); pap. 10.95x (ISBN 0-691-02206-2). Princeton U Pr.

Public Management & Policy Analysis. Barry Bozeman. LC 78-65247. 1979. pap. write for info. (ISBN 0-312-65471-5). St Martin.

Public Management Education - U. S. Military Commissioned Officers: A Selected Bibliography. Anthony G. White. (Public Administration Ser.: P 2009). 15p. 1986. 3.75 (ISBN 1-55590-009-7). Vance Biblios.

Public Management Education - U. S. Military Noncommissioned Officers: A Selected Bibliography. Anthony G. White. (Public Administration Ser.: P 2010). 6p. 1986. 3.00 (ISBN 1-55590-010-0). Vance Biblios.

Public Management Research: A Guide to Research Capability Development. Donald B. Tweedy. (Illus.). 124p. 1981. 24.00 (ISBN 0-398-04481-3). C C Thomas.

Public Management Research in the U. S. G. David Garson & E. Samuel Overman. LC 83-2400. 204p. 1983. 35.00 (ISBN 0-275-90984-0, C0984). Praeger.

Public Manager's Guide to Union Representation. Marvin J. Levine. (Public Employee Relations Library: No. 51). 1975. pap. 14.00 non-members (ISBN 0-686-81165-8); pap. 12.00 members. Intl Personnel Mgmt.

Public Men & Events, 2 vols. Nathan Sargent. LC 79-106496. (American Public Figures Ser). 1970. Repr. of 1875 ed. lib. bdg. 75.00 (ISBN 0-306-71873-1). Da Capo.

Public Men in & out of Office. John Thomas Salter. LC 76-39131. (FDR & the Era of the New Deal Ser). (Illus.). 514p. 1972. Repr. of 1946 ed. lib. bdg. 55.00 (ISBN 0-306-70457-9). Da Capo.

Public Microcomputing: Facilities & Usage in Public Libraries. Steven D. Robertson. (Consulting Report Ser.). 100p. 1986. pap. 24.50 (ISBN 0-913203-16-5). Pacific Info.

Public Money & Parochial Education: Bishop Hughes, Governor Seward & the New York School Controversy. Vincent Lannie. 294p. (Pub. by Press of Case Western University). 1968. 19.95 (ISBN 0-268-00565-6). U of Notre Dame Pr.

Public Money Managers Handbook. Peter Rousmaniere. LC 81-67754. (Illus.). 320p. 1982. 39.95 (ISBN 0-8442-3065-0, Crain Bks). Natl Textbk.

Public Monument & Its Audience. Marianne Doezema & June Hargrove. LC 77-25428. (Themes in Art Ser.). (Illus.). 76p. 1977. pap. 4.95x (ISBN 0-910386-38-2, Pub. by Cleveland Mus Art). Ind U Pr.

Public, Municipal & Community Buildings. Architectural Record Magazine Editors. 1980. text ed. 44.95 (ISBN 0-07-002351-4). McGraw.

Public Murders. Bill Granger. Date not set. pap. 3.95 (ISBN 0-446-34406-0). Warner Bks.

Public of Herondas. G. Mastromarco. (London Studies of Classical Philology: Vol. 11). 122p. 1984. text ed. 28.50x (ISBN 90-70265-94-X, Pub. by Gieben Holland). Humanities.

Public of Herondas. Giuseppe Mastromarco. (London Studies in Classical Philology: Vol. II). xiii, 122p. 1984. 41.00x (ISBN 90-70265-94-X, Pub. by Gieben Amsterdam). Benjamins North Am.

Public of the Music Theatre--Louis Riel: A Case Study. R. Murray Schafer. 1972. pap. 10.00 (ISBN 0-685-93739-9, UE26702). Eur-Am Music.

Public Office Index: U. S. Presidents, Vice-Presidents, Cabinet Members, Supreme Court Justices, Vol. 1. Keith L. Justice. LC 84-43216. 191p. 1985. lib. bdg. 19.95x (ISBN 0-89950-137-0). McFarland & Co.

Public Officials, Elected & Appointed. H. Y. Bernard. LC 68-54014. (Legal Almanac Ser.: No. 26). 119p. 1969. 6.95 (ISBN 0-379-11026-1). Oceana.

Public Opinion. 5th ed. Bernard Hennessy. LC 84-20073. (Political Science Ser.). 325p. 1985. pap. text ed. 14.25 pub net (ISBN 0-534-04920-6). Brooks-Cole.

Public Opinion. 2nd ed. Harry Holloway & John George. LC 83-61602. 286p. 1986. pap. text ed. write for info. (ISBN 0-312-65484-7); instr's. manual avail. (ISBN 0-312-65486-3). St Martin.

Public Opinion. Walter Lippmann. 1965. pap. 12.95x (ISBN 0-02-919130-0). Free Pr.

Public Opinion & Collective Action: The Boston School Desegregation Conflict. D. Garth Taylor. LC 86-4359. 320p. 1986. lib. bdg. 29.00x (ISBN 0-226-79155-6). U of Chicago Pr.

Public Opinion & Congressional Elections. Ed. by William N. McPhee & William A. Glaser. LC 80-29534. (Illus.). x, 326p. 1981. Repr. of 1962 ed. lib. bdg. 35.00x (ISBN 0-313-22779-9, MCOP). Greenwood.

Public Opinion & Constitution Making in Pakistan 1958-1962. Edgar A. Schuler & Katherine R. Schuler. v, 274p. 1966. 6.00 (ISBN 0-87013-103-6). Mich St U Pr.

Public Opinion & Foreign Policy. Lester Markel et al. LC 78-167404. (Essay Index Reprint Ser). 1972. Repr. of 1949 ed. 19.00 (ISBN 0-8369-7242-2). Ayer Co Pubs.

Public Opinion & Foreign Policy: America's China Policy, 1949-1979. Leonard A. Kusnitz. LC 83-26508. (Contributions in Political Science Ser.: No. 114). (Illus.). xii, 191p. 1984. lib. bdg. 35.00 (ISBN 0-313-24264-X, KPO/). Greenwood.

Public Opinion & Political Change in Poland, 1980-1982. David S. Mason. (Soviet & East European Studies). (Illus.). 289p. 1985. 42.50 (ISBN 0-521-30798-8). Cambridge U Pr.

Public Opinion & Political Development in Pakistan, 1947-1958. Inamur Rehman. (Orig.). 1982. pap. text ed. 26.00x (ISBN 0-19-577268-7). Oxford U Pr.

Public Opinion & Politics in Eighteenth-Century England to the Fall of Walpole. William T. Laprade. 1973. lib. bdg. 29.00x (ISBN 0-374-94784-8, Octagon). Hippocrene Bks.

Public Opinion & Propaganda. 2nd ed. Leonard W. Doob. LC 66-16084. x, 612p. 1966. 45.00 (ISBN 0-208-00513-7, Archon). Shoe String.

Public Opinion & Public Policy. 3rd ed. Ed. by Norman R. Luttbeg. LC 80-52446. 467p. 1981. pap. text ed. 21.95 (ISBN 0-87581-259-7). Peacock Pubs.

Public Opinion & Public Policy in Canada. Richard Johnston. (Collected Research Studies of the Royal Commission on the Economic Union & Development Prospects for Canada: Vol. 35). 262p. 1986. 20.95c (ISBN 0-8020-7279-8). U of Toronto PR.

Public Opinion & the Immigrant: Mass Media Coverage, 1880 to 1980. Rita J. Simon. LC 81-48146. (Illus.). 256p. 1984. 27.00x (ISBN 0-669-05291-4). Lexington Bks.

Public Opinion & the Palestine Question. Ed. by Elia Zureik & Moughrabi Fouad. 256p. 1987. 32.50 (ISBN 0-312-00738-8). St Martin.

Public Opinion & the Steel Strike. Interchurch World Movement, Commission of Inquiry. LC 77-119052. (Civil Liberties in American History Ser.). 1970. Repr. of 1921 ed. lib. bdg. 47.50 (ISBN 0-306-71938-X). Da Capo.

Public Opinion & the Teaching of History in the United States. Bessie L. Pierce. LC 71-107416. (Civil Liberties in American History Ser.). 1970. Repr. of 1926 ed. lib. bdg. 45.00 (ISBN 0-306-71883-9). Da Capo.

Public Opinion & the War in Vietnam Study, 1966. Sidney Verba et al. 1975. Repr. of 1971 ed. codebk. write for info. (ISBN 0-89138-053-1). ICPSR.

Public Opinion & World-Politics. Ed. by Quincy Wright. LC 72-4687. (International Propaganda & Communications Ser.). 251p. 1972. Repr. of 1933 ed. 15.00 (ISBN 0-405-04771-1). Ayer Co Pubs.

Public Opinion as the Shaper of Public Policy, 1982-1987. Dale E. Casper. (Public Administration Ser.: P 2304). 9p. 1987. 3.00 (ISBN 1-55590-604-4). Vance Biblios.

Public Opinion During the Reagan Administration. John L. Goodman. (Changing Domestic Priorities Ser.). 1983. pap. text ed. 5.95x nfo. (ISBN 0-87766-330-0). Urban Inst.

Public Opinion: Ideology & State Welfare. Peter Taylor-Gooby. (Radical Social Policy Ser.). 192p. (Orig.). 1985. pap. 14.95x (ISBN 0-7100-9968-1). Routledge Chapman & Hall.

Public Opinion in American Politics. W. Lance Bennett. 420p. 1980. pap. text ed. 10.00 net (ISBN 0-15-573810-0, HC). HarBraceJ.

Public Opinion in Occupied Germany: The OMGUS Surveys, 1945. Ed. by Anna J. Merritt & Richard L. Merritt. LC 74-943397. (Illus.). pap. 87.50 (ISBN 0-317-08637-5, 2020223). Bks Demand UMI.

Public Opinion in Semisovereign Germany: The HICOG Surveys, 1949-1955. Ed. by Anna J. Merritt & Richard L. Merritt. LC 78-20995. 303p. 1980. 24.95 (ISBN 0-252-00731-X). U of Ill Pr.

Public Opinion in Soviet Russia: A Study in Mass Persuasion. 2nd ed. Alex Inkeles. LC 58-4768. (Russian Research Center Studies: No. 1). 1950. 22.50x (ISBN 0-674-72350-3). Harvard U Pr.

Public Opinion in War & Peace. Abbott L. Lowell. LC 73-14167. (Perspectives in Social Inquiry Ser.). 320p. 1974. Repr. 19.00x (ISBN 0-405-05512-9). Ayer Co Pubs.

Public Opinion, Nineteen Thirty-Five to Nineteen Forty-Six. Ed. by Hadley Cantril. LC 78-12745. 1978. Repr. of 1951 ed. lib. bdg. 98.50x (ISBN 0-313-21165-5, CAUE). Greenwood.

Public Opinion Polling: A Handbook for Public Interest & Citizen Advocacy Groups. Celinda Lake & Pat Harper. 192p. (Orig.). 1987. pap. 19.95x (ISBN 0-933280-32-7). Island CA.

Public Opinion Polling in Czechoslovakia, 1968-1969: Results & Analysis of Surveys Conducted During the Dubcek Era. Jaroslaw Piekalkiewicz & Barry Bede. LC 70-176398. (Special Studies in International Politics & Government). 1972. 29.50x (ISBN 0-275-28631-2). Irvington.

Public Opinion, Propaganda, & Politics in Eighteenth Century England: A Study of the Jew Bill of 1753. Thomas W. Perry. LC 62-17222. (Historical Monographs Ser: No. 51). 1962. 15.00x (ISBN 0-674-72400-3). Harvard U Pr.

Public Opinion: The Visible Politics. 2nd ed. Jerry L. Yeric & John R. Todd. LC 82-81415. 243p. 1987. pap. text ed. 11.95 (ISBN 0-87581-281-3). Peacock Pubs.

Public Opinion: Tracking & Targeting. H. L. Nieburg. LC 83-24499. 302p. 1984. 35.00 (ISBN 0-275-91234-5, C1234); pap. 14.95 (ISBN 0-275-91621-9, B1621). Praeger.

Public Opinions & Private Conversations You Should Know About. Cliff E. Delaney. (Illus.). 150p. 1988. 34.50 (ISBN 0-88164-908-2); pap. 26.50 (ISBN 0-88164-909-0). ABBE Pubs Assn.

Public Order: A Guide to the 1986 Public Order Act. John Marston. 189p. 1987. 88.00x (ISBN 1-85190-024-1, Pub. by Fourmat England). State Mutual Bk.

Public Order Campaign Badges: Protest: While You Still Can in Red & Black. NCCL Staff. 20.00x (ISBN 0-317-54913-8, Pub. by NCCL UK). State Mutual Bk.

Public Order Criminal Behavior & Criminal Laws: The Question of Legal Decriminalization. Kenneth A. Johnson. LC 76-56560. 1977. soft bdg. 10.95 (ISBN 0-88247-441-3). R & E Pubs.

Public Order in the Age of the Chartists. Frederick C. Mather. LC 84-12768. ix, 260p. 1984. Repr. of 1959 ed. lib. bdg. 38.50x (ISBN 0-313-24527-4, MAPU). Greenwood.

Public Order of Ocean Resources: A Critique of the Contemporary Law of the Sea. P. Sreenivasa Rao. LC 75-12741. 336p. 1975. text ed. 42.50x (ISBN 0-262-18072-3). MIT Pr.

Public Order of the Oceans: A Contemporary International Law of the Sea. Myres S. McDougal & William T. Burke. LC 86-14171. (New Haven Studies in International Law & World Public Order: No. 5). 1987. 179.50 (ISBN 0-89838-901-1, Pub. by Kluwer-Nijhoff (Netherlands)). Kluwer Academic.

Public Organization Behavior & Development. William B. Eddy. 1981. text ed. write for info.; pap. text ed. 13.00 (ISBN 0-673-39434-4). Scott F.

Public Organization in Ancient Greece. Nicholas F. Jones. LC 86-72885. (Memoirs Ser.: Vol. 176). (Illus.). 1987. 35.00 (ISBN 0-87169-176-0). Am Philos.

Public Organizations & Policy. David A. Bresnick. 1982. pap. text ed. write for info. (ISBN 0-673-16054-8). Scott F.

Public Ownership of Government. Edward P. Costigan. LC 68-15821. 1968. Repr. of 1940 ed. 28.50x (ISBN 0-8046-0090-2, Pub. by Kennikat). Assoc Faculty Pr.

Public Papers. Louis Sullivan. Ed. by Robert Twombly. (Illus.). xxii, 258p. 1988. 29.95x (ISBN 0-226-77996-3). U of Chicago Pr.

Public Papers & Addresses of Benjamin Harrison, 1889-1893. Benjamin Harrison. LC 12-20445. 1893. 29.00 (ISBN 0-527-38350-3). Kraus Repr.

Public Papers of George Clinton, 10 Vols. George Clinton. Ed. by Hugh Hastings & J. A. Holden. LC 72-968. Repr. of 1914 ed. Set. 700.00 (ISBN 0-404-01620-0); 70.00 ea. AMS Pr.

Public Papers of Governor Bert T. Combs, 1959-1963. Bert T. Combs. Ed. by George W. Robinson. LC 78-58103. (Public Papers of the Governors of Kentucky). 568p. 1980. 30.00x (ISBN 0-8131-0604-4). U Pr of Ky.

Public Papers of Governor Edward T. Breathitt, 1963-1967. Edward T. Breathitt. LC 83-25968. (Public Papers of the Governors of Kentucky). 632p. 1984. 30.00x (ISBN 0-8131-0603-6). U Pr of KY.

Public Papers of Governor Keen Johnson, Nineteen Thirty-Nine to Nineteen Forty-Three. Keen Johnson. Ed. by Frederic D. Ogden. LC 79-57562. (Public Papers of the Governors of Kentucky). 618p. 1982. 30.00x (ISBN 0-8131-0605-2). U Pr of Ky.

Public Papers of Governor Lawrence W. Wetherby, 1950-1955. Lawrence W. Wetherby. Ed. by John E. Kleber. LC 82-40182. (Public Papers of the Governors of Kentucky Ser.). 344p. 1983. 30.00 (ISBN 0-8131-0606-0). U Pr of Ky.

Public Papers of Governor Louie B. Nunn, 1967-1971. Louie B. Nunn. Ed. by Robert F. Sexton. LC 74-18938. (Public Papers of the Governors of Kentucky). 640p. 1975. 30.00 (ISBN 0-8131-0601-X). U Pr of Ky.

Public Papers of Governor Simeon Willis, 1943-1947. Ed. by James C. Klotter. LC 87-24085. (Illus.). 424p. 1988. text ed. 30.00x (ISBN 0-8131-0607-9). U Pr of Ky.

Public Papers of Governor Wendell H. Ford: 1971-1974. Wendell H. Ford. Ed. by W. Landis Jones. (Public Papers of the Governors of Kentucky). 722p. 1978. 30.00x (ISBN 0-8131-0602-8). U Pr of Ky.

Public Papers of the Presidents of the United States, 1983, Bk. 2: Ronald Reagan. 863p. 1985. text ed. 32.00 (S/N 022-003-01120-0). USGPO.

Public Papers of the Secretaries-General of the United Nations, Vol. 8: U Thant 1968-1971. Ed. by Andrew Cordier. LC 68-8873. 1977. 60.00x. Columbia U Pr.

Public Papers of the Secretaries-General of the United Nations, Vol 1: Trygve Lie, 1946-1953. Ed. by Andrew W. Cordier & Wilder Foote. LC 68-8873. 535p. 1969. 45.00x (ISBN 0-231-03137-8). Columbia U Pr.

Public Papers of the Secretaries-General of the United Nations, Vol. 2: Dag Hammarskjold, 1953-1956. Ed. by Andrew W. Cordier & Wilder Foote. LC 68-8873. 115p. 1972. 40.00x (ISBN 0-231-03633-7). Columbia U Pr.

Public Papers of the Secretaries General of the United Nations, Vol. 3: Dag Hammarskjold, 1956-1957. Ed. by Andrew W. Cordier & Wilder Foote. LC 68-88873. 729p. 1973. 45.00x (ISBN 0-231-03735-X). Columbia U Pr.

Public Papers of the Secretaries-General of the United Nations, Vol. 5: Dag Hammarskjold, 1960-1961. Ed. by Andrew W. Cordier & Wilder Foote. LC 68-8873. 592p. 1975. 45.00x (ISBN 0-231-03897-6). Columbia U Pr.

Public Papers of the Secretaries-General of the United Nations, Vol. 6: U Thant, 1961-1964. Ed. by Andrew W. Cordier & Max Harrelson. LC 68-8873. 708p. 1976. 45.00x (ISBN 0-231-03966-2). Columbia U Pr.

Public Papers of the Secretaries General of the United Nations, Vol. 7: U Thant, 1965-1967. Ed. by Andrew W. Cordier & Max Harrelson. LC 68-8873. 633p. 1976. 45.00 (ISBN 0-231-04098-9). Columbia U Pr.

Public Papers of the Secretaries General of the United Nations, Vol 4: Dag Hammarskjold, 1958-1960, Vol. 4. Ed. by Andrew W. Cordier & Wilder Foote. LC 68-8873. 659p. 1974. 45.00x (ISBN 0-231-03810-0). Columbia U Pr.

Public Parks & Recreation Administration: Behavior & Dynamics. Linn Rockwood. LC 82-1294. (Brighton Recreation & Leisure Ser.). 397p. 1986. 30.00x (ISBN 0-89832-021-6); text ed. 25.00. Pub Horizons.

Public Parks & the Enlargement of Towns. Frederick L. Olmsted. LC 76-112564. (Rise of Urban America). 1970. Repr. of 1870 ed. 12.00 (ISBN 0-405-02469-X). Ayer Co Pubs.

Public Participation in Development & Health Programs: Lessons from Rural Bangladesh. Wasim A. Zaman. 312p. (Orig.). 1984. lib. bdg. 29.00 (ISBN 0-8191-3874-6); pap. text ed. 15.25 (ISBN 0-8191-3875-4). U Pr of Amer.
Public Participation in Development Planning & Management: Cases from Africa & Asia. Ed. by Jean-Claude Garcia-Zamor. (Westview Replica Ser.). 240p. 1985. pap. 29.95x (ISBN 0-86531-874-3). Westview.
Public Participation in Planning. Ed. by W. Derrick Sewell & J. T. Coppock. LC 76-56800. pap. 57.80 (ISBN 0-317-30323-6, 2024804). Bks Demand UMI.
Public Participation in Quasi-Judicial Administrative Hearings: A Training Manual. Nancy E. Stroud. 53p. 1985. 10.00. FLA Atlantic.
Public Parts. Ed. by Maxim Jukubowski. 1982. 7.95 (ISBN 0-688-01405-4). Morrow.
Public Pension Administration. Archibald L. Patterson. 116p. (Orig.). 1982. pap. 9.50 (ISBN 0-89854-082-8). U of GA Inst Govt.
Public Pension Fiduciary Responsibility & Liability. Hamline University School of Law Staff & Advanced Legal Education Staff. 238p. 1986. 36.80 (ISBN 0-317-55355-0). Hamline Law.
Public Pension Plans: The State Regulatory Framework. Sarah C. Reilly. LC 85-62686. 115p. Date not set. price not set. Natl Coun Teach.
Public Pensions: A Legislator's Guide. 47p. 1985. 10.00 (ISBN 1-55516-537-0). Natl Conf State Legis.
Public Perceptions of Biotechnology. Ed. by Waldemar Klassen & Lekh Batra. LC 87-72504. 271p. (Orig.). 1987. pap. text ed. write for info. (ISBN 0-944919-00-6). Agri Research Inst.
Public Perceptions of the Police in Texas. Raymond H. Teske. 28p. 1982. 2.00 (ISBN 0-318-02512-4). S Houston Employ.
Public Personnel Administration. Robert H. Elliott. LC 84-24892. 1985. pap. text ed. write for info. (ISBN 0-8359-5998-8, Reston); instr's. manual avail. (ISBN 0-8359-5999-6). P-H.
Public Personnel Administration. 1986. pap. text ed. 45.00x (ISBN 0-86590-764-1). Apt Bks.
Public Personnel Administration. Jay Shafritz & Sarah Bowman. Ed. by John Bowman. LC 82-49150. (Public Affairs & Administration Ser.). 320p. 1986. lib. bdg. 42.00 (ISBN 0-8240-9151-5). Garland Pub.
Public Personnel Administration: Concepts & Practices. Gilbert B. Siegel & Robert C. Myrtle. LC 84-82246. 480p. 1985. text ed. 35.16 (ISBN 0-395-35966-X). HM.
Public Personnel Administration in the U. S. 2nd ed. N. Joseph Cayer. LC 85-61242. 175p. 1986. pap. text ed. write for info. (ISBN 0-312-65521-5). St Martin.
Public Personnel Administration-Labor-Management Relations. (Information Services Ser.). Date not set. price not set ring bound looseleaf. P-H.
Public Personnel Administration: Policies & Practices for Personnel. (Information Services Ser.). Date not set. price not set ring bound looseleaf. P-H.
Public Personnel Administration: Problems & Prospects. Steven W. Hays & Richard C. Kearney. (Illus.). 384p. 1983. pap. write for info. (ISBN 0-13-737973-0). P-H.
Public Personnel Management: A Contingency Approach. Perry Moore. LC 83-49502. 352p. 1985. text ed. 27.95x (ISBN 0-669-08202-3). Lexington Bks.
Public Personnel Management & Public Policy. Dennis L. Dresang. 1984. text ed. 29.75 (ISBN 0-673-39433-6). Scott F.
Public Personnel Management: Contexts & Strategies. 2nd ed. Donald E. Klingner & John Nalbandian. LC 84-8287. (Illus.). 496p. 1985. text ed. 35.00 (ISBN 0-13-737990-0). P-H.
Public Personnel Management: Readings, Cases & Contingency Plans. Ed. by Marvin J. Levine. 424p. 1980. 26.95x (ISBN 0-89832-006-2); pap. text ed. 24.95. Pub Horizons.
Public Personnel Management: Readings in Contexts & Strategies. Ed. by Donald E. Klingner. LC 80-84019. (Illus.). 422p. 1981. 13.95 (ISBN 0-87484-517-3). Intl Personnel Mgmt.
Public Personnel Management: Readings in Contexts & Strategies. Ed. by Donald E. Klingner. 422p. 1981. pap. text ed. 15.95 (ISBN 0-317-54240-0). Mayfield Pub.
Public Personnel Management: Structure, Process & Practice. Marvin J. Levine. 1983. 22.95x (ISBN 0-913878-27-8). T Horton & Dghts.
Public Personnel Policy in a Political Environment: A Symposium. Ed. by David Rosenbloom. (Orig.). 1982. pap. 8.00 (ISBN 0-918592-59-3). Policy Studies.
Public Personnel Policy: The Politics of Civil Service. Ed. by David H. Rosenbloom. LC 83-15795. (Policy Studies Organization). 244p. 1985. text ed. 28.00x (Pub. by Natl U). Assoc Faculty Pr.
Public Personnel Update. Cohen & Glombiewski. (Public Administration & Public Policy Ser.). 352p. 1984. 39.75 (ISBN 0-8247-7237-7). Dekker.
Public Persons. Walter Lippmann. Ed. by Gilbert A. Harrison. 1976. 7.95 (ISBN 0-87140-620-9). Liveright.
Public Philosopher: Selected Letters of Walter Lippman. Ed. by John M. Blum. 544p. 1985. 29.95 (ISBN 0-89919-260-2). Ticknor & Fields.
Public Places & Private Spaces: The Psychology of Work, Play, & Living Environments. Albert Mehrabian. LC 76-9341. 354p. 1980. pap. 11.95x (ISBN 0-465-06770-0, TB-5070). Basic.
Public Places: Exploring Their History. Gerald A. Danzer. Ed. by Myron A. Marty. (Nearby History Ser.: Vol. 3). (Illus.). 132p. 1987. 11.95 (ISBN 0-910050-88-0). AASLH Pr.
Public Planning & Control of Urban & Land Development Cases & Materials. 2nd ed. Donald G. Hagman. LC 80-36684. (American Casebook Ser.). 1301p. 1980. text ed. 35.95 (ISBN 0-8299-2100-1). West Pub.
Public Planning & Control of Urban & Land Development-Cases & Materials: 1982 Supplement to Teacher's Manual. 2nd ed. Donald G. Hagman. (American Casebook Ser.). 51p. 1982. pap. text ed. write for info. (ISBN 0-314-66383-5). West Pub.
Public Planning in the Netherlands. Ed. by Ashok K. Dutt & Frank J. Costa. (Illus.). 1984. 38.00x (ISBN 0-19-823248-9). Oxford U Pr.
Public Policies Affecting Lignite Development in Texas, No. 20. (Policy Research Project Reports Ser.). 240p. 1977. 3.00 (ISBN 0-89940-613-0). LBJ Sch Pub Aff.
Public Policies & Industrial Economy of India since Independence. Kalipada Deb. 380p. 1988. text ed. 40.00x (ISBN 81-207-0705-2, Pub. by Sterling Pubs India). Apt Bks.
Public Policies & Political Development in Canada. Ronald Manzer. 256p. 1985. 15.95c (ISBN 0-8020-2564-1); pap. 14.95 (ISBN 0-8020-6559-7). U of Toronto Pr.
Public Policies & Private Actions: A Multinational Study of Local Energy Conservation Schemes. George Gaskell & Bernward Joerges. 324p. 1987. text ed. 39.50x (ISBN 0-566-05436-1, Gower Pub England). Gower Pub Co.
Public Policies & Their Politics. Randall Ripley. 1967. 4.50x (ISBN 0-393-05337-7); pap. 3.95x (ISBN 0-393-09689-0, NortonC). Norton.
Public Policies for an Aging Population. Ed. by Elizabeth Markson & Gretchen Batra. LC 79-3249. (Boston University Series in Gerontology). 1980. 25.00x (ISBN 0-669-03398-7). Lexington Bks.
Public Policies for Communities in Economic Crisis. F. Stevens Redburn & Terry Buss. 1981. pap. 8.00 (ISBN 0-918592-54-2). Policy Studies.
Public Policies Toward Adoption. Barbara Joe. 84p. 1979. pap. text ed. 11.75x (ISBN 0-87766-253-3). Urban Inst.
Public Policies Toward Business. 7th ed. William G. Shepherd. 1985. 35.95x (ISBN 0-256-02815-X). Irwin.
Public Policies Toward Business: Readings & Cases. rev ed. Ed. by William G. Shepherd. 1979. pap. 20.95x (ISBN 0-256-02236-4). Irwin.
Public Policy. Peter Woll. LC 81-40886. 272p. 1982. lib. bdg. 30.50 (ISBN 0-8191-2097-9); pap. text ed. 13.75 (ISBN 0-8191-2098-7). U Pr of Amer.
Public Policy: A Guide to Information Sources. Ed. by William J. Murin et al. LC 80-25872. (American Government & History Information Guide Ser.: Vol. 13). 296p. 1981. 68.00x (ISBN 0-8103-1490-8). Gale.
Public Policy Across States & Cities. Ed. by Denis Judd. (Public Policy Studies: Vol. 7). 1985. 57.50 (ISBN 0-89232-513-5). Jai Pr.
Public Policy Agenda of the Nation council on the Aging: Perspective on Aging, Vol. XV, March-April, 1986. 1986. 3.50 (4178). Natl Coun Aging.
Public Policy Analysis. John S. Robey. LC 82-49149. 550p. 1983. lib. bdg. 43.00 (ISBN 0-8240-9150-7). Garland Pub.
Public Policy Analysis: An Introduction. W. Dunn. 1981. pap. write for info. (ISBN 0-13-737957-9). P-H.
Public Policy Analysis of Bilingual Education in California. David J. Alexander & Alfonso Nava. LC 75-41665. 1976. pap. 10.95 perfect bdg. (ISBN 0-88247-371-9). R & E Pubs.
Public Policy & Administration. Ed. by M. Kistaiah. 257p. 1986. text ed. 32.50x (ISBN 81-207-0154-2, Pub. by Sterling Pubs India). Apt Bks.
Public Policy & Administration. Ed. by M. Kistaiah. 257p. 1986. 29.95. Asia Bk Corp.
Public Policy & Administration in Australia. R. N. Spann & G. R. Curnow. 586p. 1988. pap. 28.95 (ISBN 0-471-81466-0). Wiley.
Public Policy & Administrative Reform. Ed. by Gerald Caiden. (Orig.). 1981. pap. 8.00 (ISBN 0-918592-47-X). Policy Studies.
Public Policy & Agricultural Development in Africa. O. A. Akoto. 1988. text ed. 37.00x (ISBN 0-566-05404-3, Pub. by Gower Pub England). Gower Pub Co.
Public Policy & Agricultural Technology: Adversity Despite Achievement. Ed. by Don F. Hadwiger & William P. Browne. LC 87-4323. (Policy Studies Organization). 300p. 1987. 37.50 (ISBN 0-312-00748-5). St Martin.
Public Policy & Agriculture Economics: A Checklist of Journal Articles, 1983-1985. Dale E. Casper. (Public Administration Ser.: P 2027). 18p. 1986. 5.00 (ISBN 1-55590-047-X). Vance Biblios.
Public Policy & Collective Bargaining. Ed. by Joseph Shister et al. LC 81-20181. (Industrial Relations Research Association Publication Ser.: No. 27). vii, 248p. 1982. Repr. of 1962 ed. lib. bdg. 35.00x (ISBN 0-313-23455-8, SHPA). Greenwood.
Public Policy & College Management: Title III of the Higher Education Act. Edward P. St. John. LC 81-5204. 300p. 1981. 40.95 (ISBN 0-275-90723-6, C0723). Praeger.
Public Policy & Development Politics: The Politics of Technical Expertise in Africa. Mekki Mtewa. LC 79-48041. 364p. 1980. pap. text ed. 16.25 (ISBN 0-8191-1004-3). U Pr of Amer.
Public Policy & Educating Handicapped Persons. Ed. by Maynard Reynolds & John Brandl. 1983. pap. 8.00 (ISBN 0-918592-61-5). Policy Studies.
Public Policy & Federalism: Issues in State & Local Politics. Jeffrey R. Henig. LC 84-51680. 400p. 1985. pap. text ed. write for info. (ISBN 0-312-65560-6). St Martin.
Public Policy & Federalism: Issues in State & Local Politics. Jeffrey R. Henig. LC 84-51680. 400p. 1985. 32.50 (ISBN 0-312-65557-6). St Martin.
Public Policy & Industrial Development: The Case of Mexican Auto Parts Industry. Mark Bennet. LC 83-23456. (Replica Edition Ser.). 115p. 1984. pap. 18.50x (ISBN 0-86531-821-2). Westview.
Public Policy & International Lending: A World Perspective. Dale E. Casper. (Public Administration Ser.: P 2106). 12p. 1987. 3.75 (ISBN 1-55590-206-5). Vance Biblios.
Public Policy & Mental Illness: Four Investigations, 1915-1939, an Original Anthology. Ed. by Gerald N. Grob. LC 78-22585. (Historical Issues in Mental Health Ser.). (Illus.). 1979. lib. bdg. 50.50x (ISBN 0-405-11936-4). Ayer Co Pubs.
Public Policy & Natural Environment, Vol. 4. Ed. by Kenneth Godwin & Helen Ingram. 1985. 57.50 (ISBN 0-89232-452-X). Jai Pr.
Public Policy & Police Discretion. David E. Aaronson et al. LC 83-11882. 1984. 25.00 (ISBN 0-87632-347-6). Clark Boardman.
Public Policy & Political Institutions: Defense & Foreign Policy. Duncan L. Clark. LC 85-12705. (Public Policy Studies: A Multi-Volume Treatise: Vol. 5). 1985. 57.50 (ISBN 0-89232-374-4). Jai Pr.
Public Policy & Politics in America. 2nd ed. James E. Anderson et al. LC 83-21066. (Political Science Ser.). 450p. 1984. text ed. 17.00 pub net (ISBN 0-534-03094-7). Brooks-Cole.
Public Policy & Population Change in Singapore. Ed. by Peter S. Chen & James T. Fawcett. LC 79-21096. 275p. (Orig.). 1979. pap. text ed. 6.95 (ISBN 0-87834-034-3). Population Coun.
Public Policy & Private Education in Japan. Estelle James & Gail R. Benjamin. LC 87-35606. 200p. 1988. 39.95 (ISBN 0-312-01337-X). St Martin.
Public Policy & Private Higher Education. Ed. by David W. Breneman & Chester E. Finn. LC 77-91798. (Studies in Higher Education Policy). 468p. 1978. 29.95 (ISBN 0-8157-1066-6); pap. 11.95 (ISBN 0-8157-1065-8). Brookings.
Public Policy & Public Analysis in India. Ed. by R. S. Ganapathy et al. 280p. 1986. text ed. 25.00 (ISBN 0-8039-9496-6). Sage.
Public Policy & the Aging. William Lammers. LC 82-22138. 265p. 1983. pap. 9.50 (ISBN 0-87187-246-3). Congr Quarterly.
Public Policy & the Corporation. M. A. King. (Cambridge Studies in Applied Econometrics). 1977. 36.00x (ISBN 0-412-15330-0, NO. 6171, Pub. by Chapman & Hall). Routledge Chapman & Hall.
Public Policy & the Diffusion of Technology. John H. DeYoung, Jr. & John E. Tilton. LC 78-50067. (Penn State Studies: No. 43). (Illus.). 1978. pap. text ed. 5.50x (ISBN 0-271-00547-5). Pa St U Pr.
Public Policy & the Economy of Metropolitan Areas: Recent Journal Articles. Dale E. Casper. (Public Administration Ser.: P 2090). 13p. 1987. 3.75 (ISBN 1-55590-170-0). Vance Biblios.
Public Policy & the Law: A Bibliography. Information Access Group, Washington, D.C. LC 87-400423. (Public Administration Bibliography Ser. P2062). 1986. 3.00 (ISBN 1-55590-122-0). Vance Biblios.
Public Policy & the Misuse of Forest Resources. Ed. by Robert Repetto & Malcolm Gillis. 200p. Date not set. price not set (ISBN 0-521-34022-5); pap. price not set (ISBN 0-521-33574-4). Cambridge U Pr.
Public Policy & the Practice & the Problems of Accounting. Ahmed Belkaoui. LC 85-3568. (Illus.). xiv, 204p. 1985. lib. bdg. 38.95 (ISBN 0-89930-105-3, BIF/, Quorum Bks.). Greenwood.
Public Policy & the Problem of Addiction: Four Studies, 1914 to 1924, an Original Anthology. Ed. by Gerald N. Grob. LC 70-1208. (Addiction in America Ser.). 1981. lib. bdg. 15.00x (ISBN 0-405-13564-5). Ayer Co Pubs.
Public Policy & the Regulation of Monopolies & Competition: Recent Journal Articles. Dale E. Casper. 1986. pap. 3.75 (ISBN 0-89028-854-2). Vance Biblios.
Public Policy & the Special Education Task of the 1980's. 1983. 10.00 (ISBN 0-317-17624-2). AACTE.
Public Policy & the Supply of Coal to London, 1700-1770. William J. Hausman. Ed. by Stuart Bruchey. LC 80-2809. (Dissertations in European Economic History II). (Illus.). 1981. lib. bdg. 31.00x (ISBN 0-405-13993-4). Ayer Co Pubs.
Public Policy & World Food Sufficiency. Ed. by Don Hadwiger & William Browne. (Orig.). 1984. pap. 8.00 (ISBN 0-918592-73-9). Policy Studies.
Public Policy, Canada, & the United States. Ed. by Martin Lubin. 164p. (Orig.). 1986. pap. 8.00 (ISBN 0-918592-89-5). Policy Studies.
Public Policy Dictionary. Earl R. Kruschke & Byron M. Jackson. (Dictionaries Political Science Ser.: No. 15). 256p. 1987. lib. bdg. 35.00 (ISBN 0-87436-443-4); pap. text ed. 15.00 (ISBN 0-87436-460-4). ABC-Clio.
Public Policy Evaluation: Approaches & Methods. David Nachimas. 1978. text ed. write for info. (ISBN 0-312-65561-4); pap. text ed. 13.00 (ISBN 0-312-65562-2). St Martin.
Public Policy for Chemicals: National & International Issues. Sam Gusman et al. LC 80-68965. 152p. (Orig.). 1980. pap. 8.50 (ISBN 0-89164-062-2). Conservation Foun.
Public Policy for Developing Market Economies. Manuel Velez Montes. pap. 3.10 (ISBN 0-8477-2425-5). U of PR Pr.
Public Policy for Local Government. J. A. Chandler. 224p. 1986. 39.00 (ISBN 0-7099-3455-6, Pub. by Croom Helm UK). Routledge Chapman & Hall.
Public Policy for Local Government. J. A. Chandler. 192p. 1988. lib. bdg. 49.95x (ISBN 0-317-64369-X, Pub. by Croom Helm UK). Routledge Chapman & Hall.
Public Policy for the Humanities in Texas. (Policy Research Project Reports: No. 74). 185p. 1986. 10.00 (ISBN 0-89940-676-9). LBJ Sch Pub Aff.
Public Policy for the Use of the Seas. rev. ed. Norman J. Padelford. 1970. pap. 14.00x (ISBN 0-262-66001-6). MIT Pr.
Public Policy Formation. R. Eyestone. (Public Policy Studies: A Multi-Volume Treatise: Vol. 2). 1985. 55.00 (ISBN 0-89232-372-8). Jai Pr.
Public Policy: Goals, Means & Methods. Stuart S. Nagel. LC 83-61613. 546p. 1984. write for info. (ISBN 0-312-65558-4); instr's. manual avail. St Martin.
Public Policy Implementation. G. C. Edwards. (Public Policy Studies: A Multi Volume-Treatise: Vol. 3). 1985. 55.00 (ISBN 0-89232-453-8). Jai Pr.
Public Policy in a No-Party State: Spanish Planning & Budgeting in the Twilight of the Franquist Era. Richard Gunther. LC 78-62839. 1980. 32.50x (ISBN 0-520-03752-9). U of Cal Pr.
Public Policy in America: Government in Action. Dennis J. Palumbo. 385p. 1988. text ed. 21.00 (ISBN 0-15-573811-9). HarBraceJ.
Public Policy in Britain. Martin Burch & Bruce Wood. 256p. 1983. 45.00x (ISBN 0-85520-586-5). Basil Blackwell.
Public Policy in Industrial Growth: The Case of the Early Ruhr Mining Region, 1766-1865. Manfred Jankowski. Ed. by Stuart Bruchey. LC 77-77175. (Dissertations in European Economic History Ser.). (Illus.). 1977. lib. bdg. 36.50x (ISBN 0-405-10788-9). Ayer Co Pubs.
Public Policy in Latin America: A Comparative Survey. John W. Sloan. LC 84-40093. (Pitt Latin American Ser.). (Illus.). 296p. 1984. 30.95x (ISBN 0-8229-3810-3); pap. text ed. 13.95x (ISBN 0-8229-4800-1). U of Pittsburgh Pr.
Public Policy in Temporal Perspective. William Michelson. 1978. pap. text ed. 11.20x (ISBN 90-279-7824-7). Mouton.
Public Policy in Texas. 2nd ed. Wendell M. Bedichek & Neal Tannahill. 1986. pap. text ed. write for info. (ISBN 0-673-18001-8). Scott F.
Public Policy Issues & Latin American Library Resources. Ed. by Pamela Howard. (Papers of the Seminar on the Acquisition of Latin American Library Materials: No. 27). 234p. 1984. pap. 45.00 (ISBN 0-917617-01-0). SALALM.
Public Policy Issues for Management. Rogene A. Buchholz. (Illus.). 400p. 1988. pap. text ed. price not set (ISBN 0-13-738840-3). P-H.
Public Policy Issues in Marketing. Ed. by Cynthia J. Frey et al. Thomas C. Kinnear & Bonnie B. Reece. LC 79-24126. (Illus.). 160p. (Orig.). 1980. pap. 6.00 (ISBN 0-87712-202-4). UMI Div Res GSBA.
Public Policy-Making. 3rd ed. James E. Anderson. 1984. pap. text ed. 16.95 (ISBN 0-03-062394-4). HR&W.
Public Policy Making in a Federal System. Ed. by Robert D. Jones. (Policy Studies Organization Ser.). 288p. 1976. pap. 7.50 (ISBN 0-317-35634-8). Policy Studies.
Public Policy Opinion & the Elderly, 1952-1978: A Kaleidoscope of Culture. John E. Tropman. LC 86-27150. (Contributions to the Study of Aging: No. 6). (Illus.). 265p. 1987. lib. bdg. 35.00 (ISBN 0-313-25432-X, TPO/). Greenwood.
Public Policy, Science, & Environmental Risk. Ed. by Sandra Panem. LC 83-73029. 65p. 1983. pap. 10.95 (ISBN 0-8157-6901-6). Brookings.
Public Policy Studies: A Multi-Volume Treatise. Harrell Rogers. (Public Policy & Social Institutions Ser.: Vol. 1). 1984. 55.00 (ISBN 0-317-13509-0). Jai Pr.

Public Relations: Strategies & Tactics. Dennis L. Wilcox et al. 640p. 1985. text ed. 36.50 scp (ISBN 0-06-040176-1, HarpC). Har-Row.

Public Relations: Strategies & Tactics. 2nd ed. Dennis L. Wilcox et al. 624p. 1988. text ed. 36.50t (ISBN 0-06-047106-9, HarpC). Har-Row.

Public Relations: The Necessary Art. David A. Haberman & Harry A. Dolphin. 436p. 1988. text ed. 28.95x (ISBN 0-8138-1457-X). Iowa St U Pr.

Public Relations: The Profession & the Practice. 2nd ed. Otis W. Baskin & Craig Aronoff. 512p. 1988. text ed. write for info. (ISBN 0-697-01485-1); write for info. (ISBN 0-697-01486-X). Wm C Brown.

Public Relations: What Research Tells Us. John V. Pavlik. (Commtext Ser.: Vol. 16). 1987. text ed. 19.95 (ISBN 0-8039-2950-1); pap. text ed. 9.95 (ISBN 0-8039-2951-X). Sage.

Public Relations Writer in a Computer Age: Worktext. Frank E. Walsh. 216p. 1986. write for info. wkbk. (ISBN 0-13-738766-0). P-H.

Public Relations Writer in Computer Age. Frank E. Walsh. (Illus.). 320p. 1985. pap. text ed. write for info. (ISBN 0-13-738733-4). P-H.

Public Relations Writing: Form & Style. 2nd ed. Doug Newsom & Bob Carrell. 442p. 1986. pap. text ed. write for info. (ISBN 0-534-06096-X). Wadsworth Pub.

Public Relief & Private Charity. Josephine S. Lowell. LC 76-137176. (Poverty U. S. A. Historical Record Ser.). 1971. Repr. of 1884 ed. 13.00 (ISBN 0-405-03115-7). Ayer Co Pubs.

Public Religion in American Culture. John F. Wilson. 240p. 1981. pap. 9.95 (ISBN 0-87722-226-6). Temple U Pr.

Public Religion in American Culture. John F. Wilson. 240p. 1979. lib. bdg. 24.95 (ISBN 0-87722-159-6). Temple U Pr.

Public Remonstrance Addressed to the Board of Overseers of Harvard University see Professor Royce's Libel.

Public Reporting Standards & Auditing. 2nd ed. Grant W. Newton. (Certificate in Management Accounting Review Ser.). 287p. 1983. 19.95 (ISBN 0-918937-02-7); cassette tapes 120.00 (ISBN 0-918937-09-4). Malibu Pub.

Public Revenue & Economic Policy in African Countries: An Overview of Issues & Policy Options. Dennis Anderson. (Discussion Paper Ser.: No. 19). 56p. 1987. 6.50 (ISBN 0-8213-0981-1, BK0981). World Bank.

Public Review Draft of the Proposed ABA Model Procurement Ordinance for Local Governments. 24p. 1981. pap. 2.00 (ISBN 0-317-31122-0). Amer Bar Assn.

Public Rights in Shoreline Recreation Areas: A Selectively Annotated Bibliography, No. 894. David W. Owens. 1975. 5.00 (ISBN 0-686-20369-0). CPL Biblios.

Public Role in the Dairy Economy: Why & How Governments Intervene in the Milk Business. Alden C. Manchester. (Special Studies in Agriculture-Aquaculture Science & Policy). 304p. 1983. 39.00x (ISBN 0-86531-590-6). Westview.

Public Safety & the Justice System in Alaskan Native Villages. John E. Angell. 88p. 1981. pap. 6.95 (ISBN 0-932930-35-2). Pilgrimage Inc.

Public Safety & Underground Nuclear Detonations. AEC Technical Information Center Staff & Samuel Glasstone. 276p. 1971. 23.50 (ISBN 0-87079-315-2, TID-25708). DOE.

Public Safety Dispatcher I. Jack Rudman. (Career Examination Ser.: C-116). (Cloth bdg. avail. on request). pap. 12.00 (ISBN 0-8373-0116-5). Natl Learning.

Public Safety Dispatcher II. Jack Rudman. (Career Examination Ser.: C-117). (Cloth bdg. avail. on request). pap. 14.00 (ISBN 0-8373-0117-3). Natl Learning.

Public Safety Officer I. Jack Rudman. (Career Examination Ser.: C-2895). (Cloth bdg. avail. on request). pap. 12.00 (ISBN 0-8373-2895-0). Natl Learning.

Public Safety Officer II. Jack Rudman. (Career Examination Ser.: C-2896). (Cloth bdg. avail. on request). pap. 12.00 (ISBN 0-8373-2896-9). Natl Learning.

Public Safety Officer III. Jack Rudman. (Career Examination Ser.: C-2897). (Cloth bdg. avail. on request). pap. 14.00 (ISBN 0-8373-2897-7). Natl Learning.

Public Safety Officer IV. Jack Rudman. (Career Examination Ser.: C-3053). 1988. pap. 14.00 (ISBN 0-8373-3053-X). Natl Learning.

Public Sale of Securities in the United States: A Guide for Foreign Bankers. Peat Marwick, Mitchell, & Company. LC 81-187002. iv, 133p. Date not set. price not set. Peat Marwick.

Public Scandal, Odium & Contempt: An Investigation of Recent Libel Cases. David Hooper. 256p. 1984. 30.95 (ISBN 0-436-20093-7, Pub. by Secker & Warburg UK). David & Charles.

Public School Administration. 3rd ed. Calvin Grieder et al. LC 76-75638. (Illus.). pap. 160.00 (ISBN 0-8357-9971-9, 2012544). Bks Demand UMI.

Public, School & Academic Media Centers: A Guide to Information Sources. Ed. by Esther Dyer & Pam Berger. LC 74-11554. (Books, Publishing & Libraries Information Guide Ser.: Vol. 3). 256p. 1980. 68.00x (ISBN 0-8103-1286-7). Gale.

Public School & Finances. Mary F. Williams. LC 80-20771. (Education of the Public & the Public School Ser.). 64p. 1980. pap. 3.95 (ISBN 0-8298-0414-5). Pilgrim NY.

Public School & Moral Education. Henry C. Johnson, Jr. LC 80-20768. (Education of the Public & the Public School Ser.). 96p. (Orig.). 1981. pap. 5.95 (ISBN 0-8298-0420-X). Pilgrim NY.

Public School & Public Policy. Stanley. 1980. pap. 1.95 (ISBN 0-8298-0419-6). Pilgrim NY.

Public School & the Challenge of Ethnic Pluralism. Carl A. Grant et al. LC 80-21315. 1981. pap. 2.95 (ISBN 0-8298-0421-8). Pilgrim NY.

Public School & the Family. Leichter. 1980. pap. 1.95 (ISBN 0-8298-0416-1). Pilgrim NY.

Public School & the Whole Person. Mary Richards. 1980. pap. 2.95 (ISBN 0-8298-0417-X). Pilgrim NY.

Public School Desegregation in the United States, 1968-1980. Gary Orfield. (Illus.). 66p. (Orig.). 1983. pap. 4.95 (ISBN 0-941410-29-3). Jt Ctr Pol Studies.

Public School Education of Second-Generation Japanese in California. Reginald Bell. Ed. by Roger Daniels. LC 78-54808. (Asian Experience in North America Ser.). 1979. Repr. of 1935 ed. lib. bdg. 12.00x (ISBN 0-405-11264-5). Ayer Co Pubs.

Public School Finance: A Bibliography. Mary Vance. (Public Administration Ser.: P 2111). 35p. 1987. 8.75 (ISBN 1-55590-211-1). Vance Biblios.

Public School Health Programs in Thirty-Five U. S. Cities: No Standards, No Systems. Mona Geller. (Municipal Performance Report Ser.: No. 7). 1979. pap. text ed. 5.00x (ISBN 0-916450-26-0). Nat Civic League.

Public School in the New Society: The Social Foundations of Education. Grace Graham. pap. 104.00 (ISBN 0-8357-9149-1, 2013229). Bks Demand UMI.

Public School Law. 2nd ed. McCarthy & Cambron. 1987. 34.95x (ISBN 0-205-10489-4, Pub. by Longwood Div). Allyn.

Public School Monopoly: A Critical Analysis of Education & the State in American Society. Ed. by Robert B. Everhart. LC 81-20635. (Illus.). 583p. 1982. 34.95 (ISBN 0-88410-383-8); pap. 14.95 (ISBN 0-88410-388-9). PRIPP.

Public School Plumbing Equipment. Minor W. Thomas. LC 75-177715. (Columbia University. Teachers College. Contributions to Education: No. 282). Repr. of 1928 ed. 22.50 (ISBN 0-404-55282-X). AMS Pr.

Public School System: A Voice to Revitalize. Rishel L. Whitham. LC 82-81315. 176p. (Orig.). 1982. pap. 7.95 (ISBN 0-88100-008-6). Natl Writ Pr.

Public School System of the United States. J. M. Rice. LC 77-89224. (American Education: Its Men, Institutions & Ideas, Ser. 1). 1969. Repr. of 1893 ed. 24.00 (ISBN 0-405-01461-9). Ayer Co Pubs.

Public School Tax Management in Texas. Eugene G. Wilkins. LC 78-177642. (Columbia University. Teachers College. Contributions to Education: No. 703). Repr. of 1937 ed. 22.50 (ISBN 0-404-55703-1). AMS Pr.

Public School Word-Book. John S. Farmer. LC 68-17988. 256p. 1968. Repr. of 1900 ed. 35.00x (ISBN 0-8103-3280-9). Gale.

Public School Word-Book. John S. Farmer. 1900. 30.00 (ISBN 0-8274-3224-0). R West.

Public Schooling & the Education of Democratic Citizens. Richard M. Battistoni. LC 85-9133. 1985. 20.00x (ISBN 0-87805-280-1). U Pr of Miss.

Public Schools: A Law Treatise on the Rights, Powers, Duties & Liabilities of School Boards, Officers & Teachers. Irwin Taylor. 411p. 1980. Repr. of 1893 ed. lib. bdg. 30.00x (ISBN 0-8377-1204-1). Rothman.

Public Schools: An Evangelical Appraisal. Frank C. Nelsen. (Crucial Questions Ser.). 224p. 14.95 (ISBN 0-8007-1525-X). Revell.

Public Schools & British Opinion since 1860. Edward C. Mack. LC 73-13947. xii, 511p. 1973. Repr. lib. bdg. 34.50x (ISBN 0-374-95243-4, Octagon). Hippocrene Bks.

Public Schools & British Opinion Since 1860: The Relationship Between Contemporary Ideas & the Evolution of an English Institution. Edward C. Mack. 1971. Repr. of 1941 ed. lib. bdg. 35.00x (ISBN 0-8371-4267-9, MAPS). Greenwood.

Public Schools in Hard Times: The Great Depression & Recent Years. David Tyack et al. LC 83-22679. (Illus.). 328p. 1984. 20.00x (ISBN 0-674-73800-4). Harvard U Pr.

Public Schools in Hard Times: The Great Depression & Recent Years. David Tyack et al. 228p. 1987. pap. text ed. 8.95x (ISBN 0-674-73801-2). Harvard U Pr.

Public Schools in Renaissance France. George Huppert. LC 83-1333. 184p. 1984. 19.95 (ISBN 0-252-01053-1). U of Ill Pr.

Public Schools: Issues in Budgeting & Financial Management. Ed. by John Augenblick. 204p. (Orig.). 1985. pap. text ed. 17.95x (ISBN 0-88738-626-1). Transaction Bks.

Public Schools of Colonial Boston. Robert F. Seybolt. LC 73-89231. (American Education: Its Men, Institutions & Ideas, Ser. 1). 1969. Repr. of 1935 ed. 12.00 (ISBN 0-405-01469-4). Ayer Co Pubs.

Public Schools U. S. A. A Comparative Guide to School Districts. Charles Harrison. Ed. by Susan Williamson. 268p. (Orig.). 1988. pap. 17.95 (ISBN 0-913589-36-5). Williamson Pub Co.

Public Schools vs. American Political Liberty: Restoring Freedom of Education in a Nation Imperiled by Public Schools. George L. Bate. LC 87-82986. 91p. (Orig.). 1987. pap. 4.95 (ISBN 0-944776-00-0). Freesponse Pr.

Public Science-Private View. D. W. Budworth. (Illus.). 199p. 1981. 40.00x (ISBN 0-85274-449-8, Pub. by A Hilger UK); pap. 19.00x (ISBN 0-85274-452-8, Pub. by A Hilger UK). Taylor & Francis.

Public Scrutiny of Protection. Olivier Long. 114p. 1988. text ed. write for info. (ISBN 0-566-05780-8, Pub. by Gower Pub England). Gower Pub Co.

Public Sculptor: Lorado Taft & the Beautification of Chicago. Timothy J. Garvey. LC 87-24481. (Illus.). 240p. 1988. 19.95 (ISBN 0-252-01501-0). U of Ill Pr.

Public Secondary Education for Negroes in North Carolina. Hollis M. Long. LC 71-177008. (Columbia University. Teachers College. Contributions to Education: No. 529). Repr. of 1932 ed. 22.50 (ISBN 0-404-55529-2). AMS Pr.

Public Secondary Education in Canada. Walter F. Dyde. LC 72-176736. (Columbia University. Teachers College. Contributions to Education: No. 345). Repr. of 1929 ed. 22.50 (ISBN 0-404-55345-1). AMS Pr.

Public Secrets: A Study in the Development of Government Secrecy. K. G. Robertson. LC 81-5666. 288p. 1982. 25.00 (ISBN 0-312-65566-5). St Martin.

Public Secrets: EastEnders & Its Audience. David Buckingham. 1988. pap. 15.50 (ISBN 0-85170-210-4, Pub. by British Film England). U of Ill Pr.

Public Sector Accountability: A Selected Bibliography with Emphasis on Canada. Ontario Ministry of Treasury & Economics, Library Services Staff. (Public Administration Ser.: P 1669). 16p. 1985. 2.25 (ISBN 0-89028-379-6). Vance Biblios.

Public Sector Accounting. 2nd ed. Henley. 1987. pap. 31.95 (ISBN 0-442-31751-4). Van Nos Reinhold.

Public Sector Bargaining. Ed. by Benjamin Aaron et al. 341p. 1988. text ed. 27.00 (ISBN 0-87179-565-5, 0565). BNA.

Public-Sector Bargaining. 2nd ed. Ed. by Benjamin Aaron et al. LC 87-32025. 334p. 1988. write for info. (207). BNA.

Public Sector Bargaining in the 1980's. John Sheldrake & Rene Saran. 104p. 1988. text ed. 33.50 (ISBN 0-566-05597-X, Pub. by Gower Pub England). Gower Pub Co.

Public Sector Contemporary Series, 3 vols. Ed. by Harry Kershen. Incl. Vol. 1. Impasse & Grievance Resolution; Vol. 2. Labor-Management Relations among Government Employees; Vol. 3. Collective Bargaining by Government Workers: The Public Employee. Set. pap. 34.50x (ISBN 0-89503-030-6). Baywood Pub.

Public Sector Decision Making: Legal Fringe Benefits & Union Parameters. Ed. by Paul A. Weinstein. LC 78-70342. (Public Sector Labor Relations Conference Board Ser.: No. 3). 1978. pap. 7.50 (ISBN 0-913400-02-5). Pub Sect Lab Rel.

Public Sector Deficits in OECD Countries: Causes, Consequences & Remedies. Ed. by Henry Cavanna. LC 87-11876. 256p. 1988. 49.95 (ISBN 0-312-00533-4). St Martin.

Public Sector Designs. Clint Page & Penelope Cuff. LC 83-82147. (Illus.). 64p. (Orig.). 1984. pap. 12.00 (ISBN 0-941182-12-6). Partners Livable.

Public Sector Economics. 2nd ed. Robin W. Boadway et al. 1984. 30.95 (ISBN 0-673-39116-7). Little.

Public Sector Economics. British Association for the Advancement of Science, Section F, Economics Staff. Ed. by A. R. Prest. LC 68-6526. 1968. 27.50x (ISBN 0-678-06765-1). Kelley.

Public Sector Economics. 3rd ed. C. V. Brown & Peter M. Jackson. LC 86-6119. 512p. 1986. pap. text ed. 24.95x (ISBN 0-631-14588-5). Basil Blackwell.

Public Sector Economics. Ed. by Jorg Finsinger. LC 82-42576. 352p. 1983. 27.50 (ISBN 0-312-65567-3). St Martin.

Public Sector Economics. Randall G. Holcombe. 414p. 1988. text ed. write for info. (ISBN 0-534-08190-8). Wadsworth Pub.

Public Sector Financial Control & Accounting. John Glynn. 280p. Date not set. text ed. 45.00 (ISBN 0-631-14686-5). Basil Blackwell.

Public Sector in Developing Countries: Role & Efficiency. I. Shhilin & S. Cheema. 157p. 1987. pap. 4.95 (ISBN 0-8285-3769-0, Pub. by Progress Pubs USSR). Imported Pubns.

Public Sector in Latin America. Ed. by Alfred H. Saulniers. LC 83-3646. (Special Publications Ser.). x, 235p. (Orig.). 1984. pap. 19.95x (ISBN 0-86728-009-3). U TX Inst Lat Am Stud.

Public Sector Investment Planning for Developing Countries. E. V. FitzGerald. 200p. 1978. 28.50x (ISBN 0-8419-5027-X). Holmes & Meier.

Public Sector Labor & Employment Law. Jerome Lefkowitz. 1100p. 1987. text ed. 70.00 (ISBN 0-942954-18-1). NYS Bar.

Public Sector Labor Markets. Ed. by P. Mieszkowski & G. Peterson. 216p. 1981. pap. 12.00x (ISBN 0-87766-285-1, 29100). Urban Inst.

Public Sector Labor Relations. David Lewin et al. LC 82-64038. 672p. 1988. 45.00x (ISBN 0-669-17125-5); pap. 21.95x (ISBN 0-669-12893-7). Lexington Bks.

Public Sector Labor Relations: Analysis & Readings. 2nd. ed. David Lewin et al. LC 82-3021. 1981. pap. 18.95x (ISBN 0-913878-23-5); pap. 18.95x. T Horton & Dghts.

Public Sector Labor Relations in Maryland: Issues & Prospects. Ed. by Donald W. O'Connell. LC 72-92069. (PSLRCB Publication Ser.: No. 1). (Illus., Orig.). 1972. pap. 7.50 (ISBN 0-913400-00-9). Pub Sect Lab Rel.

Public Sector Labor Relations in South Carolina. Thomas L. Stephenson. Ed. & intro. by William E. Tomes. 60p. (Orig.). 1987. pap. text ed. 5.00 (ISBN 0-917069-05-6). Bur Univ Gov SC.

Public Sector Labor Relations Law in New York State. Wade J. Newhouse. LC 78-50698. 1300p. 1978. lib. bdg. 35.00 (ISBN 0-930342-57-7). W S Hein.

Public Sector Management in Botswana: Lessons in Pragmatism. Nimrod Raphaeli et al. (Working Paper: No. 709). 104p. 1985. 5.00 (ISBN 0-8213-0452-6, WP 0709). World Bank.

Public Sector Management, Systems, & Ethics. Louis C. Gawthrop. LC 83-48176. (Illus.). 184p. 1984. 25.00x (ISBN 0-253-34675-4). Ind U Pr.

Public-Sector Marketing: A Guide for Practitioners. Larry Coffman. (Business Strategy Ser.). 160p. 1986. 22.95 (ISBN 0-471-01161-4). Wiley.

Public Sector Mediation. Arnold M. Zack. 216p. 1985. pap. text ed. 23.00 (ISBN 0-87179-477-2, 0477). BNA.

Public Sector Payrolls. Ed. by David A. Wise. LC 86-24962. (NBER Project Report Ser.). x, 328p. 1987. text ed. 40.00x (ISBN 0-226-90291-9). U of Chicago Pr.

Public Sector Performance: A Turning Point. Trudi C. Miller. LC 83-23895. 288p. 1984. 32.00x (ISBN 0-8018-3146-6); pap. 12.95x (ISBN 0-8018-3147-4). Johns Hopkins.

Public Sector Productivity Programs: Background & Analysis with Special Reference to State Governments, No. 19. (Policy Research Project Reports Ser.). 44p. 1977. 3.00 (ISBN 0-89940-612-2). LBJ Sch Pub Aff.

Public Self & Private Self. Ed. by R. F. Baumeister. (Springer Series in Social Psychology). (Illus.). 270p. 1986. 34.00 (ISBN 0-387-96303-0). Springer-Verlag.

Public Servant, Private Woman. Alix Meynell. (Illus.). 288p. 1988. 39.95 (ISBN 0-575-04086-6, Pub. by Gollancz England). David & Charles.

Public Service, Vol. 3. Ed. by James E. Rush. LC 83-9584. (Library Systems Evaluation Guides Ser.). (Illus.). 267p. 1983. velo bound 59.50 (ISBN 0-912803-03-7). Rush Assoc.

Public Service Alliance of Canada: A Look at a Union in the Public Sector. Maurice Lemelin. (Monograph & Research Ser.: No. 21). 1978. 6.50 (ISBN 0-89215-085-8). U Cal LA Indus Rel.

Public Service Employment: A Field Evaluation. Richard P. Nathan et al. LC 81-4596. 121p. 1981. pap. 9.95 (ISBN 0-8157-5987-8). Brookings.

Public Service Employment: An Analysis of Its History, Problems & Prospects. Ed. by Alan Gartner et al. LC 72-93186. (Special Studies in U. S. Economics, Social, & Political Issues). 1973. 59.50x (ISBN 0-275-06630-4). Irvington.

Public Service Employment in the Rural South. Vernon M. Briggs, Jr. Ed. by Brian Rungeling & Lewis H. Smith. LC 83-51266. (Policy Ser.: No. 1). 144p. (Orig.). 1984. pap. 8.00 (ISBN 0-87755-285-1). Bureau Busn UT.

Public Service in Higher Education: Practices & Priorities. Patricia H. Crosson. Ed. & frwd. by Jonathan D. Fife. LC 84-166237. (ASHE-ERIC Higher Education Report Ser.: No. 7, 1983). 138p. (Orig.). 1983. pap. 7.50x (ISBN 0-913317-06-3). Assn Study Higher Ed.

Public Service in the New States: A Study in Some Trained Manpower Problems. Kenneth G. Younger. LC 87-8684. 128p. 1987. Repr. of 1960 ed. lib. bdg. 35.00x (ISBN 0-313-25959-3, YOPS). Greenwood.

Public Service Labour Relations: Recent Trends & Future Prospects. Tiziano Treu et al. v, 287p. (Orig.). 1987. pap. 22.75 (ISBN 92-2-106049-7). Intl Labour Office.

Public Service Provision & Urban Politics. Ed. by Andrew Kirby et al. LC 83-40485. 420p. 1984. 35.00 (ISBN 0-312-65568-1). St Martin.

Public Service Responsibility of Broadcast Licensees. Federal Communications Commission. LC 74-5225. (Telecommunications Ser). 64p. 1974. Repr. of 1946 ed. 18.00x (ISBN 0-405-06064-5). Ayer Co Pubs.

Public Service: The Quiet Crisis. Paul A. Volcker. (Francis Boyer Lectures on Public Policy). 32p. (Orig.). 1988. pap. text ed. 4.95 (ISBN 0-8447-1385-6). Am Enterprise.

Public Service Unions & the European Community. Ed. by Emil J. Kirchner. 176p. 1983. pap. text ed. 35.00x (ISBN 0-566-00492-5). Gower Pub Co.

Public Services Goals & Objectives. (SPEC Kit & Flyer Ser.: No. 84). 108p. 1982. (10.00 for ARL members 20.00 (ISBN 0-318-03470-0). OMS.

Public Works Wage Rate & Some of Its Economic Effects. Viola Wyckoff. LC 72-76650. (Columbia University. Studies in the Social Sciences: No. 521). Repr. of 1946 ed. 22.50 (ISBN 0-404-51521-5). AMS Pr.

Public Worship of God: A Source Book. Henry S. Coffin. 16.00 (ISBN 0-8369-7272-4, 8071). Ayer Co Pubs.

Publica Carmina: Ovid's Books from Exile. Harry B. Evans. LC 82-10899. xii, 202p. 1983. 23.50x (ISBN 0-8032-1806-0). U of Nebr Pr.

Publication Design. 4th ed. Roy P. Nelson. 344p. 1987. pap. write for info. (ISBN 0-697-00493-7). WM C Brown.

Publication Manual of the American Psychological Association. 3rd ed. LC 83-2521. 208p. 1983. pap. 16.50 (ISBN 0-912704-57-8, 4200030); members 12.50. Am Psychol.

Publication of Guiana's Plantation. LC 72-7836. (English Experience Ser.: No. 525). 24p. 1972. Repr. of 1632 ed. 6.00 (ISBN 90-221-0726-4). Walter J Johnson.

Publication of the Monk. Andre Parreaux. 1960. Repr. 40.00 (ISBN 0-8274-3225-9). R West.

Publication Opportunities for Tax Researchers. J. Burns et al. 206p. 1981. 10.00. Am Accounting.

Publication Style Manual for Author & Editor. 1977. 12.50 (ISBN 0-89982-066-2, 420300); write for info. Am Bankers.

Publication Style Manual for Author & Editor. 27.00 (ISBN 0-686-95658-3, 240100); write for info. (ISBN 0-686-99561-9). Am Bankers.

Publications, 18 vols. Nos. 1-108. Augustan Reprint Society Staff. 1974. (ISBN 0-527-03250-6); Set. pap. 684.00; Kraus Repr.

Publications. Shelley Society, London. LC 74-2680. (4 series in 23 nos.). Repr. of 1892 ed. Set. 518.00 (ISBN 0-404-11500-4). AMS Pr.

Publications, Nos. 1-14 In 33 Vols. Shakespeare Society of New York. Repr. Set. 845.50 (ISBN 0-404-54200-X). AMS Pr.

Publications Based on Project TALENT: An Annotated Bibliography. Emily A. Campbell. 1979. pap. 10.00 (ISBN 0-89785-628-7). Am Inst Res.

Publications by the Fellows: Winterthur Program in Early American Culture, 1954 to 1979. 1981. pap. 5.00 (ISBN 0-912724-11-0). Winterthur.

Publications by Women on American Domestic Architecture. Lamia Doumato. (Architecture Ser.: A 1491). 12p. 1985. 2.00 (ISBN 0-89028-621-3). Vance Biblios.

Publications Cost Management. Ed. by Helen G. Caird. (Anthology Ser., No. 3). 1975. pap. 25.00x (ISBN 0-914548-14-X). Soc Tech Comm.

Publications, Documentation & Means for Their Dissemination in the Commission of the European Communities. M. Hopkins. LC 81-180937. (R&D Report 5618). 40p. (Orig.). 1981. pap. 8.25 (ISBN 0-905984-69-2, Pub. by British Lib). Longwood Pub Group.

Publications Editor. Jack Rudman. (Career Examination Ser.: C-3146). 1988. pap. 14.00 (ISBN 0-8373-3146-3). Natl Learning.

Publications in Continuing Education. Alexander N. Charters. (MS Ser.: No. 12). 1980. 4.50 (ISBN 0-686-64687-8, MSS 12). Syracuse U Cont Ed.

Publications in Continuing Education. Ed. by Alexander N. Charters. 1983. 8.00 (ISBN 0-87060-038-9, MSS 26). Syracuse U Cont Ed.

Publications in Economics, Vols. 1-15. University of California. 1908-50. pap. 360.00 (ISBN 0-384-07034-5). Johnson Repr.

Publications in Education, Vols. 1-11. University of California. Set. 440.00 (ISBN 0-384-07035-3); Set. pap. 375.00 (ISBN 0-685-23264-6). Johnson Repr.

Publications in Geography, Vols. 1-10. University of California. Set. 400.00 (ISBN 0-384-07036-1); Set. pap. 340.00 (ISBN 0-685-23262-X). Johnson Repr.

Publications in International Relations, 5 Vols. University of California. 1923-57. 155.00 (ISBN 0-384-07037-X); pap. 125.00 (ISBN 0-685-13625-6). Johnson Repr.

Publications in Mathematical & Physical Sciences, Vol. 1-3. University of California. (Partly in the original edition). pap. 55.00 (ISBN 0-384-07038-8). Johnson Repr.

Publications in Philosophy, Vols. 1-25. University of California. Set. 640.00 (ISBN 0-384-07039-6); Set. pap. 500.00 (ISBN 0-685-13568-3). Johnson Repr.

Publications in Southern California Art 1, 2, & 3. Nancy D. Moure. (Illus.). 297p. 80.00 (ISBN 0-317-54894-8). Apollo.

Publications in Southern California Art 1, 2, 3, 3 vols. in 1. rev. ed. Ed. by Nancy D. Moure. Incl. Vol. 1. Index to the California Watercolor Society Exhibitions 1921-1954; Vol. 2. Index to Artists Clubs & Exhibitions in Los Angeles Before 1930; Vol. 3. Dictionary of Art & Artists in Southern California Before 1930. 525p. 1984. 80.00 (ISBN 0-9614622-0-5). Dustin Pubns.

Publications of Resources for the Future, Inc, 12 vols. Resources for the Future, Inc. Repr. Set. write for info (ISBN 0-404-60325-4). AMS Pr.

Publications of the Alabama Historical Society, 5 vols. Ed. by Thomas M. Owen. 1989. Repr. of 1898 ed. Set. lib. bdg. 150.00x (ISBN 0-942301-07-2). Vol. I, 450pgs. Vol. II, 204pgs. Vol. III, 251pgs. Vol. IV, 639pgs. Vol. V, 282pgs. Birm Pub Lib.

Publications of the American Association for Netherlandic Studies: Papers from the Third Interdisciplinary Conference on Netherlandic Studies. Ed. by Ton J. Broos. 342p. 1988. lib. bdg. 28.50 (ISBN 0-8191-7056-9, Pub. by Amer Assn Netherlandic Studies). U Pr of Amer.

Publications of the American Ethnological Society, Vols. 1-22. American Ethnological Society Staff. (Reprint of 1907-1952). 820.00 (ISBN 0-404-58150-1). AMS Pr.

Publications of the Ballad Society, 14 vols, Nos. 1-38. Ballad Society. (Ballad Society Ser.: Nos. 1-38). Repr. of 1899 ed. Set. 815.00 (ISBN 0-404-50820-0). AMS Pr.

Publications of the Bannatyne Club, Nos. 1-120 & 8 Extra Vols. Bannatyne Club Staff. Repr. of 1875 ed. Set. write for info. (ISBN 0-404-52700-0). AMS Pr.

Publications of the Caxton Society, 16 Vols. Caxton Society Staff. 1966. Repr. of 1854 ed. Set. 320.00 (ISBN 0-8337-0507-5). B Franklin.

Publications of the International Agricultural Research & Development Centers: 1986 Supplement. 167p. (Orig.). 1986. pap. 9.70x (ISBN 971-104-145-6, Pub. by Intl Rice Res Philippines). Agribookstore.

Publications of the IRS, 3 vols. (Information Services Ser.). 1987. 252.00; 225.00; write for info. P-H.

Publications of the Maitland Club, Numbers 1-75. Maitland Club. Repr. of 1859 ed. write for info. (ISBN 0-404-52920-8). AMS Pr.

Publications of the Nebraska State Historical Society, Vol. XX. Ed. by Albert Watkins. 400p. 1922. write for info. Nebraska Hist.

Publications of the Venice Biennale 1895-1977 on Microfiche: Bibliography & Subject Index. (Illus.). 60p. (Orig.). 1986. pap. text ed. 4000.00 incl. 1105 microfiche (ISBN 0-85964-162-7). Chadwyck-Healey.

Publications of the World Health Organization, 1958-1962: A Bibliography. 125p. (Eng. & Fr.). 1964. 5.60 (ISBN 92-4-152001-9). World Health.

Publications of the World Health Organization, 1963-1967: A Bibliography. 152p. (Eng. & Fr.). 1969. 8.00 (ISBN 92-4-152002-7). World Health.

Publications of the World Health Organization, 1968-1972: A Bibliography. (Also avail. in French). 1974. pap. 8.00 (ISBN 92-4-152004-3). World Health.

Publications of William Pain, 1730 to 1790: Architect & Carpenter. Carole Cable. (Architecture Ser.: Bibliography A 1338). 1985. pap. 2.00 (ISBN 0-89028-308-7). Vance Biblios.

Publications Proscribed by the Government of India: A Catalogue. Ed. by Mary Lloyd & Graham Shaw. (Illus.). 224p. 1985. 37.50 (ISBN 0-7123-0029-5, Pub. by British Lib). Longwood Pub Group.

Publichnye Chteniia O Petre Velikom. S. M. Solov'ev. 232p. (Rus.). 1984. 39.00x (ISBN 0-317-40868-2, Pub. by Collets (UK)). State Mutual Bk.

Publicidad en Puerto Rico: Como Fue, Como es, Como se Hace. Rafael H. Benitez. LC 85-1017. (Illus., Span.). 1985. 9.00 (ISBN 0-8477-2908-7). U of PR pr.

Publicistes Modernes. Henri Baudrillart. Ed. by J. P. Mayer. LC 78-67330. (European Political Thought Ser.). 1979. Repr. of 1863 ed. lib. bdg. 39.00x (ISBN 0-405-11676-4). Ayer Co Pubs.

Publicity Advice & How-to Handbook. Rolf Gompertz. LC 88-50026. (Illus.). 132p. (Orig.). 1988. pap. 15.95 (ISBN 0-918248-07-8). Word Doctor.

Publicity & Customer Relations in Transport Management. David W. Wragg. 160p. 1982. text ed. 33.00x (ISBN 0-566-00442-9). Gower Pub Co.

Publicity & Diplomacy with Special Reference to England & Germany (1890-1914) O. J. Hale. 11.75 (ISBN 0-8446-1215-4). Peter Smith.

Publicity & Promotion Handbook: A Complete Guide for Small Business. Linda Carlson. 272p. 1982. 24.95 (ISBN 0-8436-0865-X). Van Nos Reinhold.

Publicity & Public Relations Guide for Business. Bruce A. Brough. (Successful Business Library). 125p. 1986. 3-ring binder 33.95 (ISBN 0-916378-41-1, Oasis). PSI Res.

Publicity & Public Relations in Libraries: A Selected Bibliography. Dittakavi N. Rao. (Public Administration Ser.: Bibliography P 1636). 1985. pap. 2.25 (ISBN 0-89028-306-0). Vance Biblios.

Publicity & Public Relations Worktext. 5th ed. Raymond Simon. LC 82-9305. (Advertising & Journalism Ser.). 340p. 1983. write for info. (ISBN 0-02-411090-6, Pub. by Grid). Macmillan.

Publicity, Budget & Finance Management. Khan Lynch. 1986. lib. bdg. 28.00 (ISBN 0-8240-9005-5). Garland Pub.

Publicity for Authors. Date not set. price not set (ISBN 0-937571-05-9). Trudco Pub.

Publicity for Books & Authors: A Do-It-Yourself Handbook for Small Publishing Firms & Enterprising Authors. Peggy Glenn. LC 84-28288. (Illus.). 180p. 1985. 16.95 (ISBN 0-936930-92-6); pap. 12.95 (ISBN 0-936930-91-8). Aames-Allen.

Publicity for Volunteers: A Handbook. Virginia Bortin. LC 81-50233. 128p. 1981. 10.95 (ISBN 0-8027-0685-1); pap. 6.95 (ISBN 0-8027-7176-9). Walker & Co.

Publicity for Volunteers: A Handbook. Virginia Bortin. 159p. 1981. pap. 7.50 (ISBN 0-318-17151-1, C81). VTNC Arlington.

Publicity Guide for Nutrition Education. 21p. 1985. pap. 8.00 (ISBN 0-910869-22-7). Soc Nutrition Ed.

Publicity Handbook for Churches & Christian Organizations. Jim A. Vitti. 160p. (Orig.). 1987. pap. 6.95 (ISBN 0-310-37601-7, 12089P). Zondervan.

Publicity, How To. Martin Pollack & Jeffrey Pollack. 96p. (Orig.). 1988. pap. 14.95 (ISBN 0-936836-13-X). Alliance Pubs.

Publicity Manual. Kate Kelly. LC 79-55946. 184p. 1980. 29.95 (ISBN 0-9603740-1-9). Visibility Ent.

Publicity Process. 3rd, rev. ed. Ed. by Christine F. Goff. (Illus.). 256p. 1988. pap. text ed. 18.95xt (ISBN 0-8138-1316-6). Iowa St U Pr.

Publicizing & Promoting Programs. Helen Farlow. 1979. text ed. 28.95x (ISBN 0-07-019947-7). McGraw.

Publick Employment & the Active Life Prefer'd to Solitude. John Evelyn. Ed. by Brian Vickers. LC 86-137650. (Public & Private Life in the Seventeenth Century Ser.). 1986. 50.00x. Schol Facsimiles.

Public's Business: The Politics & Practices of Government Corporations. Annmarie Hauck Walsh. LC 77-15595. (A Twentieth Century Fund Study). 456p. 1978. pap. 13.95x (ISBN 0-262-73055-3). MIT Pr.

Public's First Right to Federally Generated Power: An Analysis of the Preference Clause. American Public Power Association Staff et al. LC 85-243014. 38p. 1985. 10.00. APPA.

Public's Impact on Foreign Policy. Bernard C. Cohen. LC 83-6550. 236p. 1983. pap. text ed. 12.00 (ISBN 0-8191-3244-6). U Pr of Amer.

Public's Right to Know: The Supreme Court & the First Amendment. David M. O'Brien. LC 81-988. 218p. 1981. 35.00 (ISBN 0-275-90694-9, C0694). Praeger.

Public's Use of Television: Who Watches & Why. Ronald E. Frank & Marshall G. Greenberg. LC 79-27067. (People & Communication: Vol. 9). (Illus.). 368p. 1980. 35.00 (ISBN 0-8039-1389-3). Sage.

Public's View of the Outdoor Environment As Interpreted by Magazine Ad-Makers. Robert E. Coughlin & Karen A. Goldstein. (Discussion Paper Ser.: No. 25). 1968. pap. 6.50 (ISBN 0-686-32194-4). Regional Sci Res Inst.

Publikation Aelterer Praktischer und Theoretischer Musikwerke, 29 vols. in 27. Ed. by Robert Eitner. Incl. Vols. 1-3. Johann Ott's Mehrstimmiges Deutsches Liederbuch Von 1544. Set. 95.00x; Vol. 4. Einleitung, Biographieen, Melodieen, und Gedichte Zu Johann Ott's Uedersammlung Von 1544. 35.00x; Vol. 5. Musikalische Spicilegien ueber das Liturgische Drama, Orgelbau und Orgelspiel, das Ausserliturgische Lied und die Instrumentalmusik desmittelalters von P. Anselm Schubiger. 30.00x; Vol. 6. Josquin Depris - eine Sammlung Ausgewaehlter Kompositionen Zu 4, 5 und 6 Stimmen. 45.00x (ISBN 0-8450-1706-3); Vol. 7. Johann Walther - Wittembergische Geistliche Gesangbuch Von 1524 Zu 3, 4 und 5 Stimmen. 45.00x; Vol. 8. Heinrich Finck - eine Sammlung Ausgewaehlter Kompositionen Zu Vier und Fuenf Stimmen: Hermann Finck-Sechs Tonsaetzen. 45.00x (ISBN 0-8450-1708-X); Vol. 19. Erhart Oeglin's Liederbuch Von 1512. 45.00x; Vol. 10. Die Oper Von Ihren Ersten Anfaengen Bis Zur Mitte des 18; Jahrunderts Pt. 1. 53.00x (ISBN 0-8450-1710-1); Vol. 11. Sebastian Virdung: Musica Getutscht 1511. 30.00x; Vol. 12. Die Oper Von Ihren Ersten Anfaengen Bis Zur Mitte des 18, Jahrhunderts Pt. 2. 53.00x (ISBN 0-8450-1712-8); Vol. 13. Michael Praetorius - Syntagma Musicum: Tomus Secundus Se Organographia. 30.00x; Vol. 14. Die Oper Von Ihren Ersten Anfaengen Bis Zur Mitte des 18, Jahrhunderts Pt. 3. 53.00x; Vol. 15. Lustgarten - eine Sammlung Deutsche Lieder Zu Vier, Fuenf, Sechs und Acht Stimmen Von Hans Leo Hassler 1601. 45.00x; Vol. 17. Die Oper Von Ihren Ersten Anfaengen Bis Zur Mitte des 18, Jahrhunderts Pt. 4. 53.00x; Vol. 18. Die Oper Von Ihren Ersten Anfaengen Bis Zur Mitte des 18, Jahrhunderts Pt. 5. 53.00x; Vol. 19. Jakob Regnart's Deutsche Dreistimmige Lieder. 45.00x; Vol. 20. Martin Agricola - Musica Instrumentalis Deutsch, Erste und Vierte Ausgabe, 1528 und 1545. 30.00x; Vol. 21. Johann Eccard - Neue Geistliche und Weltliche Lieder Zu Fuenf und Vier Stimmen 1589. 45.00x; Vol. 22. Joachim Von Burck - Zwanzig Deutsch Geistliche Vierstimmige Lieder, 1575; Passionem 1567 und 1574. 45.00x; Vol. 23. 60 Chansons Zu Vier Stimmer Aus der Ersten Haelfte Des 16. 45.00x; Vol. 24. Gallus Dressler - 17 Motetten Zu Vier und Fuenf Stimmen. 45.00x; Vol. 25. Gregor Langus -eine Ausgewaehlte Sammlung Motetten Zu 4, 5, 6 und 8 Stimmen. 45.00x; Vol. 26. Orazio Vecchi: L'Amfiparnaso. 45.00x; Vol. 27. Jean -Marie Leclair, 12 Sonaten Fuer Violine und Generalbass. 45.00x; Vol. 28. Martin Zeuner, 82 Geistliche Kirchenlieder Zu Fuenf Stimmen; Nuernberg 1616. 45.00x; Vol. 29. Georg Forster: der Zweite Teil der Kurtzweiligen Guten Frischen Teutschen Liedlein. 45.00x. 5176p. 1967. Repr. of 1873 ed. Set. 1000.00x (ISBN 0-8450-1700-4). Broude.

Publikationen, Vols 1-4. Osterreichisches Historisches Institut In Rom. Repr. of 1910 ed. Set. 55.00 (ISBN 0-384-43010-4). Johnson Repr.

Publish & Be Free: A Catalogue of Clandestine Books Printed in the Netherlands, 1940-1945 in the British Library. Ed. by Anna E. Simoni. (Illus.). 289p. (Orig.). pap. 18.00 (ISBN 90-247-1764-7, Pub. by British Lib). Longwood Pub Group.

Publish & Be Killed. Anne Morice. 192p. 1987. 12.95 (ISBN 0-312-00178-9). St Martin.

Publish & Be Killed. Anne Morice. (Nightingale Ser.). 294p. 1988. pap. 12.95x (ISBN 0-8161-4394-3, Large Print Bks). G K Hall.

Publish & Perish: The Organizational Ecology of Newspaper Industries. Samuel B. Bacharach & Glenn R. Carroll. (Monographs in Organizational Behavior & Industrial Relations: Vol. 8). 1987. 56.50 (ISBN 0-89232-440-6). Jai Pr.

Publish Good News: A Resource Guide for Self-Publishing Church Groups. Gerald L. Hastings. (Illus.). 80p. (Orig.). 1986. pap. 6.50 (ISBN 0-937641-01-4). Stone Canyon Pr.

Publish It Not: The Middle East Cover-Up. Michael Adams & Christopher Mayhew. LC 76-363688. pap. 51.00 (ISBN 0-317-11305-4, 2016300). Bks Demand UMI.

Publish It Yourself. Charles Chickadel. 208p. 1984. write for info. Meridian Learn Systs.

Publish It Yourself: A Manual. Netti Schreiner-Yantis. 200p. Date not set. pap. price not set (ISBN 0-89157-018-7); price not set. GBIP.

Publish-It-Yourself Handbook: Literary Tradition & How-to. 3rd, rev. ed. Ed. by Bill Henderson. 1987. pap. 11.95 (ISBN 0-916366-44-8). Pushcart Pr.

Publish Your Own Book: A Resource Book for Young Authors. Mary Bold. (Children's Resources Ser.). (Illus.). 36p. (Orig.). (gr. 5 up). 1986. pap. 9.95 (ISBN 0-938267-02-7). Bold Prodns.

Publish Your Own Book (& Pocket the Profits!) Jacquelyn Peake. (Illus.). 96p. (Orig.). 1985. pap. 4.95 (ISBN 0-9613830-1-1). J Peake Assocs.

Publish Your Own Handbound Books. Betty Doty. LC 80-67947. (Illus.). 127p. 1980. 8.95 (ISBN 0-930822-02-1); lib. bdg. 7.95 (ISBN 0-930822-03-X). Bookery.

Publish Yourself Without Killing Yourself. L. A. Tattan. LC 81-80473. 191p. (Orig.). 1981. pap. 9.95 (ISBN 0-937362-01-8). InPrint.

Published in Paris: A Literary Chronicle of Paris in the 1920's & 1930's. Hugh Ford. 1988. pap. 14.95 (ISBN 0-02-032550-9, Collier). Macmillan.

Published Music for the Viola Dagamba & Other Viols. Robin De Smet. LC 75-151302. (Detroit Studies in Music Bibliography Ser.: No. 18). 1971. pap. 6.00 (ISBN 0-911772-40-5). Harmonie Pk Pr.

Published Offical Sources of Financial Statistics. OECD. (Illus.). 132p. (Orig.). 1980. pap. 11.00x (ISBN 92-64-02095-0). OECD.

Published Radio, Television & Film Scripts: A Bibliography. G. Howard Poteet. LC 74-18201. iii, 245p. 1975. 15.00x (ISBN 0-87875-063-0). Whitston Pub.

Published Screenplays: A Checklist. Clifford McCarty. LC 73-138656. (Serif Ser.: No. 18). 137p. 1971. 12.00x (ISBN 0-87338-112-2). Kent St U Pr.

Publisher & His Friends, 2 Vols. Samuel Smiles. LC 77-148304. Repr. of 1891 ed. Set. 85.00 (ISBN 0-404-07492-8). AMS Pr.

Publisher Gene Pulliam: Last of the Newspaper Titans. Russell Pulliam. LC 85-149654. 250p. 1984. 16.95 (ISBN 0-915463-02-4, Pub. by Jameson Bks, Dist. by Kampmann). Green Hill.

Publisher (John Murray) & His Friends, 2 vols. S. Smiles. 1891. Repr. 75.00 (ISBN 0-8274-3226-7). R West.

Publishers & Distributors of Paperback Books for Young People. John T. Gillespie. LC 86-32260. 188p. 1987. pap. text ed. 15.00x (ISBN 0-8389-0471-8). ALA.

Publishers & Librarians: A Foundation for Dialogue: Proceedings of the 42nd Annual Conference of the Graduate Library School. Ed. by Mary Biggs. LC 83-18124. (Library Science Ser.). 120p. 1984. pap. 5.95 (ISBN 0-226-04847-0). U of Chicago Pr.

Publishers Association, 1896-1946: With an Epilogue. Reginald J. Kingsford. LC 74-101445. pap. 59.50 (ISBN 0-317-20604-4, 2024483). Bks Demand UMI.

Publisher's Business System: 4.8 Version. Eugene D. Wheeler et al. 66p. 1987. 995.00 (ISBN 0-934793-10-7); software manual diskettes incl. Pathfinder CA.

Publishers Business System: 5.0 Version. Eugene D. Wheeler et al. 100p. 1988. 14.95 (ISBN 0-934793-13-1); software manual diskettes incl. Pathfinder CA.

Publishers' Catalogs Annual: 1986-1987. 1985. pap. text ed. 235.00 with microfiche (ISBN 0-317-46491-4). Chadwyck-Healey.

Publisher's Direct Mail Handbook. Nat G. Bodian. 283p. 1987. 37.95 (ISBN 0-89495-079-7). ISI Pr.

Publishers Directory, 2 vols. 8th ed. Ed. by Linda S. Hubbard. 2206p. 1987. Set. 275.00x (ISBN 0-8103-2513-6). Gale.

Publishers Directory, 1988: Supplement. 8th ed. Ed. by Linda S. Hubbard. 250p. 1987. 155.00x (ISBN 0-8103-2516-0). Gale.

Publishers Directory: 1989, 2 vols. 9th ed. Ed. by Linda S. Hubbard. 1988. 195.00 (ISBN 0-8103-2592-6). Gale.

Publishers, Distributors & Wholesalers of the United States, 1988-1989. Ed. by Bowker, R. R., Staff. 1988. 95.00 (ISBN 0-8352-2475-9). Bowker.

Publisher's Guide to Printing in Hong Kong, 1984. Sally A. Taylor et al. (Illus.). 32p. 1983. pap. 5.00 (ISBN 0-9604904-6-9). S Taylor & Friends.

Publisher's Guide to Successful Multinational Mailings. Alfred M. Goodloe. (Illus.). 117p. 1986. write for info. (ISBN 0-9616409-0-1). Direct Intl.

Publisher's International Directory with ISBN Index, 1988, 2 vols. 15th ed. Ed. by Helmut Opitz & Karl H. Strasser. 3444p. 1988. 275.00 (ISBN 3-598-20537-6). K G Saur.

Publishers Office Manual: How to Do Your Paperwork in the Music Publishing Industry. Walter E. Hurst & William S. Hale. LC 66-19600. (Entertainment Industry Ser., Vol. 3). 1966. 25.00 (ISBN 0-911370-58-7); pap. 10.00 (ISBN 0-911370-57-9). Seven Arts.

Publisher's Practical Dictionary in 20 Languages. Ed. by Imre Mora. 418p. 1984. lib. bdg. 65.00 (ISBN 3-598-10449-9). K G Saur.

Publisher's Trade List Annual Index, 1903-1963. Ed. by Anthony Abbott. 150p. 1980. lib. bdg. 49.50x (ISBN 0-930466-25-X). Meckler Corp.

Publishers' Trade List Annual Index, 1964-1980. Ed. by Anthony Abbott. 175p. 1984. lib. bdg. 75.00x (ISBN 0-88736-015-7). Meckler Corp.

Publishers' Trade List Annual 1988, 4 vols. Ed. by Bowker, R. R., Staff. 1988. 179.95 (ISBN 0-8352-2479-1). Bowker.

Publishers' Trade List Annual 1989, 4 vols. Ed. by Bowker, R. R., Staff. Date not set. Set. price not set (ISBN 0-8352-2633-6). Vol. I (ISBN 0-8352-2634-4). Vol. II (ISBN 0-8352-2635-2). Vol. III (ISBN 0-8352-2636-0). Vol. IV (ISBN 0-8352-2637-9). Bowker.

Publishing: A Complete Guide for Schools, Small Presses, & Entrepreneurs. Robert L. Holt. LC 82-83565. (Calif. Financial Publications Ser.). 1982. pap. 19.95 (ISBN 0-930926-09-9). Calif Health.

Publishing a Professional Journal: An Editor's Guide. 15.00 (ISBN 0-934510-21-0, K022). Am Dental.

Publishing & Review of Reference Sources. Ed. by Bill Katz & Robin Kinder. LC 86-22910. (Reference Librarian Ser.). 336p. 1987. text ed. 34.95 (ISBN 0-86656-571-X). Haworth Pr.

Publishing Child-Oriented Articles in Psychology: A Compendium of Publication Outlets. Ed. by Michael C. Roberts & Robert D. Lyman. LC 82-45067. 178p. (Orig.). 1982. lib. bdg. 29.25 (ISBN 0-8191-2660-8); pap. text ed. 12.25 (ISBN 0-8191-2661-6). U Pr of Amer.

Publishing Children's Books in America: An Annotated Bibliography, 1919-1976. Robin Gottlieb. 208p. pap. 10.00. Child Bk Coun.

Publishing Contracts: Sample Agreements for Book Publishers on Disk. Dan Poynter & Charles Kent. LC 87-6872. (Orig.). 1987. 29.95 (ISBN 0-915516-46-2). Para Pub.

Publishing for Professional Development. Fred Dorn. 202p. 1985. 13.95 (ISBN 0-915202-46-8). Accel Devel.

Publishing for Schools: Textbooks & the Less Developed Countries. Peter H. Neumann. (Working Paper: No. 398). ii, 79p. 1980. 5.00 (ISBN 0-686-36042-7, WP-0398). World Bank.

Publishing for the People: The Firm Posrednik, 1885-1905. Robert C. Otto. Ed. by William H. McNeill & Barbara Jelavich. 260p. 1987. lib. bdg. 40.00 (ISBN 0-8240-8060-2). Garland Pub.

Publishing Forms: A Collection of Applications & Information for the Beginning Publisher. 3rd, rev. ed. Dan Poynter. (Orig.). 1986. pap. 14.95 (ISBN 0-915516-38-1). Para Pub.

Publishing from a Full Text Data Base. 1986. lib. bdg. 79.95 (ISBN 0-8490-3541-4). Gordon Pr.

Publishing from the Desktop. John Seybold & Fritz Dressler. 1987. pap. 19.95 (ISBN 0-553-34401-3). Bantam.

Publishing in English Education. Ed. by Stephen N. Tchudi. LC 81-15525. 208p. (Orig.). 1981. pap. 13.50x (ISBN 0-86709-011-1). Boynton Cook Pubs.

Publishing in the Organizational Sciences. L. L. Cummings & Peter Frost. 1985. 11.00x (ISBN 0-317-19954-4). Irwin.

Publishing in the Pacific Islands. Ed. by Jim Richstad & Miles M. Jackson. 146p. 1984. pap. text ed. 11.00 (ISBN 0-8248-1022-8, Pub. by Graduate Schl of Lib Studies Univ of Hawaii Manoa). UH Pr.

Publishing in the Third World: Knowledge & Development. Ed. by Philip G. Altbach et al. LC 84-27920. 240p. 1985. text ed. 35.00x (ISBN 0-435-08006-7). Heinemann Ed.

Publishing in the Third World: Trend Report & Bibliography. Philip G. Altbach & Eva-Maria Rathgeber. LC 80-20146. 200p. 1980. 40.95 (ISBN 0-275-90446-6, C0446). Praeger.

Publishing in the U. S. S. R, Vol. 19. LC 59-63390. (Indiana University, Indiana University Publications, Russian & East European Ser.). pap. 79.80 (ISBN 0-317-10385-7, 2055225). Bks Demand UMI.

Publishing in the West: Alan Swallow. Ed. by William F. Claire. LC 73-89794. 1974. 10.00 (ISBN 0-89016-003-1). Lightning Tree.

Publishing Newsletters. rev. ed. Howard P. Hudson. 224p. 1988. pap. 12.95 (ISBN 0-684-18954-2). Scribner.

Publishing Opportunities for Energy Research: A Descriptive Guide to Selective Serials in the Social & Technical Sciences. Compiled by Roberta A. Scull. LC 86-14975. (Bibliographies & Indexes in Science & Technology Ser.: No. 1). 416p. 1986. 50.95 (ISBN 0-313-25160-6, SPG/). Greenwood.

Publishing Power with Ventura. Martha Lubow & Jesse Berst. LC 88-60084. (Illus.). 576p. 1988. pap. 24.95 (ISBN 0-934035-19-9); Publishing Power Disk 14.95 (ISBN 0-934035-35-0). New Riders Pub.

Publishing, Printing, & the Origins of Intellectual Life in Russia, 1700-1800. Gary Marker. LC 84-42893. 312p. 1985. text ed. 33.50x (ISBN 0-691-05441-X). Princeton U Pr.

Publishing, Promoting & Selling Your Book for Self-Publishers & Impatient Writers. John C. Bartone. LC 88-47598. (Illus.). 150p. 1988. 24.50 (ISBN 0-88164-624-5); pap. 19.50 (ISBN 0-88164-643-1). ABBE Pubs Assn.

Publishing Short-Run Books: How to Paste up & Reproduce Books Instantly Using Your Quick Print Shop. 5th, rev. ed. Dan Poynter. LC 80-13614. (Illus.). 144p. 1988. pap. 5.95 (ISBN 0-915516-44-6). Para Pub.

Publishing Short-Run Books: How to Paste up & Reproduce Books Instantly Using Your Quick Print Shop. 5th, rev. ed. Ed. by Dan Poynter. (Illus.). 144p. 1988. pap. 5.95. Para Pub.

Publishing Tactics. D. W. Skrabanek. (S & S How-to Ser.: No. 2). (Orig.). 1981. pap. 2.00 (ISBN 0-934646-03-1). TX S & S Pr.

Publishing: The Creative Business. Harald Bohne & Harry Van Ierssel. LC 72-96455. pap. 25.00 (ISBN 0-317-10315-6, 2020456). Bks Demand UMI.

Publishing with a Purpose: A Guide to Association Publishing. American Society of Association Executives, Communication Section Staff. Ed. by Marshall Jorpeland. 72p. (Orig.). 1982. pap. text ed. 20.00 (ISBN 0-88034-002-9). Am Soc Assn Execs.

Publishing with CD-ROM. Patti Myers. 1987. pap. text ed. 22.95 (ISBN 0-88736-181-1). Meckler Corp.

Publit. Ferdinand Kriwet. (Illus.). 96p. (Orig.). 1971. pap. 4.50 (ISBN 0-89366-018-3). Ultramarine Pub.

Publius: Annual Review of American Federalism: 1981. Ed. by Stephen L. Schechter. LC 83-5960. 228p. (Orig.). 1983. lib. bdg. 27.50 (ISBN 0-8191-3170-9); pap. text ed. 12.50 (ISBN 0-8191-3171-7). U Pr of Amer.

Publizist Helmut von Gerlach, 1866-1935: Welt und Werk eines Demokraten und Pazifisten. Franz G. Schulte. 388p. (Ger.). 1988. pap. text ed. 40.00 (ISBN 3-598-20549-X). K G Saur.

Publizistikwissenschaftlicher Referatedienst. (Vol. 17, 1982). 602p. 1985. lib. bdg. 62.00 (ISBN 3-598-20477-9). K G Saur.

Publizistikwissenschaftlicher Referatedienst (prd, Vol. 18 1983. Ed. by Institut fur Dokumentationswissenschaft der Freien Universitat Berlin. 200p. (Ger.). 1989. lib. bdg. 80.00 (ISBN 3-598-20478-7). K G Saur.

Publizistikwissenschaftlicher Referatedienst (prd, Vol. 19: 1984. Ed. by Institut fur Dokumentationswissenschaft der Freien Universitat Berlin. 200p. (Ger.). 1989. lib. bdg. 80.00 (ISBN 3-598-20479-5). K G Saur.

Pubs of Portsmouth. Ron Brown. (Down Memory Lane, Old Hampshire Ser.). (Illus.). 80p. (Orig.). 1987. pap. 4.95 (ISBN 0-903852-64-0, Pub. by Milestone Pubns UK). Seven Hills Bks.

Puccini. (Portraits of Greatness Ser.: No. II). 1987. 15.00 (ISBN 0-918367-06-9); pap. 12.50 (ISBN 0-317-57564-3). Elite.

Puccini. Giuseppe Tarozzi. Ed. by John W. Freeman. Tr. by Susan Sawry from Eng. (Portraits of Greatness Ser.). (Illus.). 94p. (Span.). 1987. 12.50 (ISBN 0-918367-24-7). Elite.

Puccini. Giuseppe Tarozzi. Ed. by John W. Freeman. Tr. by Richard Martet from Eng. (Portraits of Greatness Ser.). (Illus.). 94p. (Fr.). 1987. 12.50 (ISBN 0-918367-48-4). Elite.

Puccini: A Critical Biography. 2nd ed. Mosco Carner. LC 76-30456. (Illus.). 519p. 1977. 55.00x (ISBN 0-8419-0302-6). Holmes & Meier.

Puccini the Thinker: The Composer's Intellectual & Dramatic Development. John L. DiGaetani. 176p. 1987. text ed. 33.00 (ISBN 0-8204-0370-9). P Lang Pubs.

Pucciniosireae: Uredinales, Pucciniaceae. P. Buritica & J. F. Hennen. LC 79-27151. (Flora Neotropica Monograph: No. 24). (Illus.). 50p. 1980. pap. 7.75x (ISBN 0-89327-219-1). NY Botanical.

Puccini's La Boheme. Giacomo Puccini. (Music (General) Ser.). 75p. 1984. pap. 2.95 (ISBN 0-486-24607-8). Dover.

Puccini's Madama Butterfly. Giacomo Puccini. (Opera Libretto Ser.). 64p. (Orig.). 1983. pap. 2.95 (ISBN 0-486-24465-2). Dover.

Puck of Pook's Hill. Rudyard Kipling. Ed. by Sarah H. Wintle. LC 87-50328. 224p. (gr. 5 up). 1987. pap. 3.95 (ISBN 0-14-043284-1). Penguin.

Puck of Pook's Hill. Rudyard Kipling. 272p. 1988. pap. 3.50 (ISBN 0-451-52168-4, Sig Classics). NAL.

Puck of the Droms: The Lives & Literatures of the Irish Tinkers. Artelia Court. 1985. 30.00x (ISBN 0-520-03711-1). U of Cal Pr.

Puck'em All: We've Got the Magick. Rachel L. Manning & Al G. Manning. 150p. (Orig.). 1985. pap. 5.95 (ISBN 0-941698-10-6). Pan Ishtar.

Pudding Is Nice. Dorothy Kunhardt. LC 75-19948. (Illus.). 64p. (gr. 1 up). 1975. 10.00 (ISBN 0-912846-18-6); pap. 5.00 (ISBN 0-912846-12-7). Bookstore Pr.

Pudding Magazine. Ed. by Jennifer G. Welch & Doug Swisher. Incl. Pudding One: Client-Theraputic Section. 50p. 1980. pap. 25.00 (ISBN 0-318-17414-6, 2001); Pudding Two. 71p. 1980. pap. 15.00 (ISBN 0-318-17415-4, 2002); Pudding Three. 68p. 1980. pap. 5.00 (ISBN 0-318-17416-2, 2003); Pudding Four: "The Manner in Which We Say Goodbye". 60p. 1981. pap. 5.00 (ISBN 0-318-17417-0, 2004); Pudding Five: "Learning Disabilities". 54p. 1981. pap. 3.50 (ISBN 0-318-17418-9, 2005); Pudding Six: "Somewhere the Child". 106p. 1982. pap. 5.00 (ISBN 0-318-17419-7, 2006); Pudding Seven: "Addictions". 80p. 1982. pap. 15.00 (ISBN 0-318-17420-0, 2007); Pudding Eight: "Creating the Solution: Turning Problems into Projects Through the Creative Process". 78p. 1983. pap. 3.50 (ISBN 0-318-17421-9, 2008); Pudding Nine: "Working". 96p. 1983. pap. 3.50 (ISBN 0-318-17422-7, 2009); Pudding Ten: 1982 Looking Glass Competition Winners. 108p. 1983. pap. 3.50 (ISBN 0-318-17423-5, 2010); Pudding Eleven: "Disasters". 1984. pap. 5.30 (ISBN 0-318-17424-3, 2011). Pudding Hse Pubns.

Puddles & Wings & Grapevine Swings. Imogene Forte & Marge Frank. LC 81-85014. (Illus.). 304p. (ps-6). 1982. pap. text ed. 14.95 (ISBN 0-86530-004-6, IP-046). Incentive Pubns.

Puddles of Knowing. Marlene Halpin. pap. 6.95 (ISBN 0-697-02003-7). Wm C Brown.

Puddling Against Dry Plowing for Lowland Rice Culture in Surinam: Effect on Soil & Plant, & Interaction with Irrigation & Nitrogen Dressing. W. Scheltema. (Agricultural Research Reports: No. 828). (Illus.). viii, 241p. (Dutch & Eng.). 1975. pap. 28.00 (ISBN 90-220-0538-0, PDC76, PUDOC). UNIPUB.

Pudd'nhead Wilson. Samuel L. Clemens. (Works of Mark Twain). 1988. Repr. of 1899 ed. lib. bdg. 59.00x. Am Biog Serv.

Pudd'nhead Wilson. Mark Twain. (Airmont Classics Ser.). (Illus.). (gr. 8 up). pap. 1.75 (ISBN 0-8049-0124-4, CL-124). Airmont.

Pudd'nhead Wilson. Mark Twain. (Bantam Classics Ser.). 1984. pap. 1.95 (ISBN 0-553-21158-7). Bantam.

Pudd'nhead Wilson. Mark Twain. pap. 1.95 (ISBN 0-451-51925-6, Sig Classics). NAL.

Pudd'nhead Wilson. Mark Twain. Ed. by Malcolm Bradbury. (English Library Ser). (Orig.). 1969. pap. 2.50 (ISBN 0-14-043040-7). Penguin.

Pudd'nhead Wilson. Mark Twain. 15.95 (ISBN 0-89190-348-8, Pub. by Am Repr). Amereon Ltd.

Pudd'nhead Wilson see Mississippi Writings.

Pudd'nhead Wilson see Writings of Mark Twain.

Pudd'nhead Wilson & Those Extraordinary Twins. Samuel L. Clemens. Ed. by Sidney E. Berger. (Norton Critical Edition Ser.). (Illus.). 1981. 22.50 (ISBN 0-393-01337-5); pap. text ed. 7.95x (ISBN 0-393-95027-1). Norton.

Pudgy Book of Babies. Illus. by Kathy Wilburn. (Pudgy Bks.). (Illus.). 16p. (gr. k). 1984. pap. 2.95 (ISBN 0-448-10207-2, G&D). Putnam Pub Group.

Pudgy Book of Farm Animals. Illus. by Julie Durrell. (Pudgy Bks.). (Illus.). 16p. (gr. k). 1984. 2.95 (ISBN 0-448-10211-0, G&D). Putnam Pub Group.

Pudgy Book of Here We Go. Illus. by Beth L. Weiner. (Pudgy Bks.). (Illus.). 16p. (gr. k). 1984. pap. 2.95 (ISBN 0-448-10208-0, G&D). Putnam Pub Group.

Pudgy Book of Make-Believe. Illus. by Andreas Brooks. (Pudgy Bks.). (Illus.). 16p. (gr. k). 1984. 2.95 (ISBN 0-448-10209-9, G&D). Putnam Pub Group.

Pudgy Book of Mother Goose. Illus. by Richard Walz. (Pudgy Bks.). (Illus.). 16p. (gr. k). 1984. 2.95 (ISBN 0-448-10212-9, G&D). Putnam Pub Group.

Pudgy Book of Toys. Illus. by Julie Durrell. (Pudgy Board Bks.). (Illus.). 16p. (ps-3). 1983. pap. 2.95 (ISBN 0-448-10201-3, G&D). Putnam Pub Group.

Pudgy Bunny Book. Illus. by Ruth Sanderson. (Pudgy Bks.). (Illus.). 16p. (gr. k). 1984. 2.95 (ISBN 0-448-10210-2, G&D). Putnam Pub Group.

Pudgy Fingers Counting Book. Illus. by Doug Cushman. (Pudgy Board Bks.). (Illus.). 16p. (ps-3). 1983. pap. 2.95 (ISBN 0-448-10202-1, G&D). Putnam Pub Group.

Pudgy I Love You Book. Deborah Shine. (Pudgy Board Bks.). (Illus.). 18p. (ps). 1988. bds. 2.95 (ISBN 0-448-19056-7, G&D). Putnam Pub Group.

Pudgy Noisy Book. Deborah Shine. (Pudgy Board Bks.). (Illus.). 18p. (ps). 1988. bds. 2.95 (ISBN 0-448-19055-9, G&D). Putnam Pub Group.

Pudgy Pals. Illus. by Kathy Wilburn. (Pudgy Board Bks.). (Illus.). 16p. (ps). 1983. pap. 2.95 (ISBN 0-448-10203-X, G&D). Putnam Pub Group.

Pudgy Pat-a-Cake. Illus. by Terri Super. (Pudgy Board Bks.). (Illus.). 16p. (ps). 1983. pap. 2.95 (ISBN 0-448-10204-8, G&D). Putnam Pub Group.

Pudgy Peek-a-Boo Book. Illus. by Amye Rosenberg. (Pudgy Board Bks.). (Illus.). 16p. (ps). 1983. pap. 2.95 (ISBN 0-448-10205-6, G&D). Putnam Pub Group.

Pudgy Rock-a-Bye Book. Illus. by Kathy Wilburn. (Pudgy Board Bks.). (Illus.). 16p. (ps). 1983. pap. 2.95 (ISBN 0-448-10206-4, G&D). Putnam Pub Group.

Pudovkin's Films & Film Theory. Peter Dart. LC 74-986. (Dissertations on Film Ser.). 1974. 15.00 (ISBN 0-405-04874-2). Ayer Co Pubs.

Pud's in Practice. Colleen G. Moore. LC 85-51488. 96p. 1985. pap. 32.00 (ISBN 0-87420-644-8, P36). Urban Land.

Puebla: A Pilgrimage of Faith. Pope John Paul II. 1979. pap. 2.00 (ISBN 0-8198-0629-3). Dghtrs St Paul.

Puebla & Beyond. Ed. by John Eagleson & Philip J. Scharper. LC 79-24098. 370p. (Orig.). 1979. pap. 9.95 (ISBN 0-88344-399-6). Orbis Bks.

Puebla Document. Bonaventure Kloppenburg. cancelled. Franciscan Herald.

Pueblo. David Yue & Charlotte Yue. (Illus.). (gr. 8-11). 1986. 12.95 (ISBN 0-395-38350-1). HM.

Pueblo Birds & Myths. Hamilton A. Tyler. LC 78-58069. (Civilization of the American Indian Ser: No. 147). (Illus.). 1979. 19.95 (ISBN 0-8061-1483-5). U of Okla Pr.

Pueblo Blues. Tony Moffeit. 96p. (Orig.). 1986. pap. 5.00x (ISBN 0-916156-71-0). Cherry Valley.

Pueblo Children of the Earth Mother, 2 vols. Thomas E. Mails. LC 74-1772. (Illus.). 1156p. 1988. Vol. I, 544p. pap. 50.00 (ISBN 0-385-03645-0); Vol. II, 528p. pap. 50.00 (ISBN 0-385-18754-8); Vol. I, ltd. ed. pap. write for info. (ISBN 0-385-18117-5); Vol. II, ltd. ed. pap. write for info. (ISBN 0-385-18755-6). Doubleday.

Pueblo Crafts. Ruth M. Underhill. Ed. by Willard W. Beatty. LC 76-43880. (U. S. Office of Indian Affairs Indian Handcrafts: 7). Repr. of 1945 ed. 32.50 (ISBN 0-404-15737-8). AMS Pr.

Pueblo Crafts. Ruth M. Underhill. (Wild & Woolly West Ser.: No. 36). (Illus.). 1979. 11.00 (ISBN 0-910584-87-7); pap. 8.00 (ISBN 0-910584-51-6). Filter.

Pueblo Crafts. Ruth M. Underhill. (Illus.). 147p. 1984. pap. 7.95 (ISBN 0-936984-07-4). Schneider Pubs.

Pueblo Cultures. B. Wright. (Iconography of Religions X Ser.: No. 4). (Illus.). xii, 29p. 1986. pap. 29.00 (ISBN 90-04-07106-7, Pub. by E J Brill). Heinman.

Pueblo Designs: One Hundred Seventy-Six Illustrations of the Rain Bird. H. Mera. 1970. pap. 5.95 (ISBN 0-486-22073-7). Dover.

Pueblo Designs: One Hundred Seventy-Six Illustrations of the Rain Bird. H. Mera. (Illus.). 14.25 (ISBN 0-8446-0206-X). Peter Smith.

Pueblo en la Cruz see Tragedy of Bolivia: A People Crucified.

Pueblo God & Myths. Hamilton A. Tyler. LC 64-11317. (Civilization of the American Indians Ser.: Vol. 71). (Illus.). 336p. 1984. pap. 8.95 (ISBN 0-8061-1112-7). U of Okla Pr.

Pueblo Indian. Joe Sando. 1976. pap. 12.25 (ISBN 0-685-65151-7). Indian Hist Pr.

Pueblo Indian Cookbook. rev. ed. Phyllis Hughes. LC 77-76238. (Illus.). 1977. pap. 7.95 (ISBN 0-89013-094-9). Museum NM Pr.

Pueblo Indian Embroidery. H. Mera. LC 74-31607. (Illus.). 80p. 1975. lib. bdg. 15.00x (ISBN 0-88307-512-1); pap. 7.95 (ISBN 0-88307-513-X). Gannon.

Pueblo Indian Journal. Elsie C. Parsons. LC 65-104022. (American Anthro. Association Memoirs). 1925. 20.00 (ISBN 0-527-00531-2). Kraus Repr.

Pueblo Indian Land Grants of the "Rio Abajo", New Mexico. Herbert O. Brayer. Ed. by Stuart Bruchey. LC 78-56700. (Management of Public Lands in the U. S. Ser.). 1979. Repr. of 1938 ed. lib. bdg. 12.00x (ISBN 0-405-11320-X). Ayer Co Pubs.

Pueblo Indian Revolt of Sixteen Ninety-Six & the Franciscan Missions in New Mexico: Letters of the Missionaries & Related Documents. Intro. by & tr. by J. Manuel Espinosa. LC 88-10022. (Illus.). 336p. 1988. 27.95 (ISBN 0-8061-2139-4). U of Okla Pr.

Pueblo Indian Textiles: A Living Tradition. Kate P. Kent. LC 83-3346. (Studies in American Indian Art). (Illus.). 136p. 1983. 30.00 (ISBN 0-933452-07-1); pap. 14.95 (ISBN 0-933452-08-X). Schol Am Res.

Pueblo Indian Textiles: A Living Tradition. Kate P. Kent. LC 83-3345. (Illus.). 136p. (Orig.). 1983. 30.00x (ISBN 0-295-96056-6); pap. 14.95 (ISBN 0-295-96057-4). U of Wash Pr.

Pueblo Indian Water Rights: Struggle for a Precious Resource. Ed. by Charles T. DuMars et al. LC 84-2490. 183p. 1984. 22.50x (ISBN 0-8165-0832-1). U of Ariz Pr.

Pueblo Indian World. Edgar L. Hewett & Bertha P. Dutton. Ed. by John P. Harrington. LC 76-43737. Repr. of 1945 ed. 37.50 (ISBN 0-404-15578-2). AMS Pr.

Pueblo Indians of New Mexico: Their Land, Economy & Civil Organization. S. B. De Aberle. LC 49-2640. (American Anthropological Association Memoirs). Repr. of 1948 ed. 12.00 (ISBN 0-527-00569-X). Kraus Repr.

Pueblo Indians of North America. Edward P. Dozier. (Illus.). 224p. 1983. pap. text ed. 9.50x (ISBN 0-88133-059-0). Waveland Pr.

Pueblo Indians of San Ildefonso. William Whitman. LC 73-82352. (Columbia Univ. Contributions to Anthropology Ser.: Vol. 34). Repr. of 1947 ed. 22.00 (ISBN 0-404-50584-8). AMS Pr.

Pueblo Indians, Vol. Two: Archaeologic & Ethnologic Data: Acoma-Laguna Land Claims. Florence H. Ellis. (American Indian Ethnohistory Ser: Indians of the Southwest). (Illus.). lib. bdg. 51.00 (ISBN 0-8240-0726-3). Garland Pub.

Pueblo of Jemez. Elsie W. Parsons. LC 76-43805. (Phillips Academy. Papers of the Southwest Expedition: No. 3). Repr. of 1925 ed. 47.50 (ISBN 0-404-15661-4). AMS Pr.

Pueblo of San Felipe. Leslie A. White. LC 32-30651. (American Anthro. Association Memoirs). 1932. 34.00 (ISBN 0-527-00537-1). Kraus Repr.

Pueblo of Santa Ana, New Mexico. Leslie A. White. LC 43-10004. (American Anthro. Association Memoirs). 1942. 31.00 (ISBN 0-527-00559-2). Kraus Repr.

Pueblo of Santo Domingo, New Mexico. Leslie A. White. LC 35-17202. (American Anthro. Association Memoirs). 1935. 23.00 (ISBN 0-527-00542-8). Kraus Repr.

Pueblo: Plays, Players, Playhouses in the Gilded Age, 1865-1900. Alice Eikenberry. (Illus.). 52p. (Orig.). 1985. pap. 3.75 (ISBN 0-915617-08-0). Pueblo Co Hist Soc.

Pueblo Population & Society: The Arroyo Hondo Skeletal & Mortuary Remains. Ann M. Palkovich. LC 80-51310. (Arroyo Hondo Archaeological Ser.: Vol. 3). (Illus.). 222p. 1981. pap. 12.00 (ISBN 0-933452-03-9). Schol Am Res.

Pueblo Potter: A Study of Creative Imagination in Primitive Art. Ruth L. Bunzel. LC 73-82257. (Columbia Univ. Contributions to Anthropology Ser.: Vol. 8). (Illus.). Repr. of 1929 ed. 55.00 (ISBN 0-404-50558-9). AMS Pr.

Pueblo Potter: A Study of Creative Imagination in Primitive Art. Ruth L. Bunzel. (Illus.). 160p. 1973. pap. 5.95 (ISBN 0-486-22875-4). Dover.

Pueblo Potter: A Study of Creative Imagination in Primitive Art. Ruth L. Bunzel. (Illus.). 14.00 (ISBN 0-8446-4622-9). Peter Smith.

Pueblo Pottery Making: A Study of the Village of San Ildefonso. Carl E. Guthe. LC 76-43718. Repr. of 1925 ed. 30.00 (ISBN 0-404-15554-5). AMS Pr.

Pueblo Pottery of the New Mexico Indians. Betty Toulouse. LC 77-71898. (Guidebooks Ser.). (Illus.). 1977. pap. 8.95 (ISBN 0-89013-091-4). Museum NM Pr.

Pueblo: Southwest. Ed. by Frank W. Porter. (Indians of North America Ser.). (Illus.). (gr. 5 up). 1989. 16.95 (ISBN 1-55546-727-X). Chelsea Hse.

Pueblo Stories. Edward W. Dolch & M. P. Dolch. (Basic Vocabulary Ser.). 176p. (gr. 1-6). 1956. PLB 6.57 (ISBN 0-8116-2503-6). Garrard.

Pueblo Stories & Storytellers. Mark Bathi. 48p. (Orig.). 1988. pap. 9.95 (ISBN 0-918080-16-9). Treasure Chest.

Pueblo Storyteller: Development of a Figurative Ceramic Tradition. Barbara Babcock et al. LC 86-4279. (Illus.). 201p. 1986. 40.00 (ISBN 0-8165-0870-4). U of Ariz Pr.

Pueblo Village. Illus. by Hilda Aragon. (Illus.). 8p. (Orig.). (ps-7). 1982. pap. 4.00 (ISBN 0-915347-17-2). Pueblo Acoma Pr.

Puedo Ser Conductor de Camion. June Behrens. Tr. by Lada Kratky. LC 85-31402. (Spanish Edition--I Can Be Bks.). (Illus.). 32p. (Span.). (gr. k-3). 1986. PLB 11.93 (ISBN 0-516-31848-9); pap. 2.95 (ISBN 0-516-51848-8). Childrens.

Puedo ser jugador de beisbol. Carol Greene. Tr. by Lada Kratky. LC 86-996. (Spanish edition--I Can Be Bks.). (Illus.). 32p. (Span.). (gr. k-3). 1986. PLB 11.93 (ISBN 0-516-31845-4); pap. 2.95 (ISBN 0-516-51845-3). Childrens.

Puedo ser un Astronauta. June Behrens. Tr. by Lada Kratky from Eng. LC 84-7601. (Spanish--I Can Be Bks.). (Illus.). 32p. (Span.). (gr. k-3). 1984. lib. bdg. 11.93 (ISBN 0-516-31837-3); pap. 2.95 (ISBN 0-516-51837-2). Childrens.

Puedo Ser un Policia. Catherine Matthias. LC 84-12106. (Spanish - I Can Be Bks.). (Illus.). 32p. (Span.). (gr. k-3). 1987. PLB 11.93 (ISBN 0-516-31840-3); pap. 2.95 (ISBN 0-516-51840-2). Childrens.

Puer Aeternus. 2nd ed. Marie-Louise Von Franz. LC 80-28090. (Illus.). 292p. 1981. 17.95 (ISBN 0-938434-03-9); pap. 10.95 (ISBN 0-938434-01-2). Sigo Pr.

Puer Papers. Ed. by James Hillman. LC 86-31566. 246p. (Orig.). 1979. 17.00 (ISBN 0-88214-310-7). Spring Pubns.

Puericultura: Manual. pap. 8.75 (F1292, FAO). UNIPUB.

Puertas a la Lengua Espanola. 2nd ed. John G. Copeland & Ralph Kite. 357p. (appendix). 1986. text ed. write for info (ISBN 0-394-34247-X, RanC); Puertas al mundo reader. pap. text ed. write for info (ISBN 0-394-34246-1); Puertas a la communication activity manual. pap. text ed. write for info (ISBN 0-394-34245-3); write for info (ISBN 0-394-34244-5); write for info (ISBN 0-394-34243-7). Random.

Puertas a la Lengua Espanola. Ralph Kite et al. 300p. 1982. write for info (ISBN 0-394-32879-5, RanC); Puertas Al Mundo Hispanico Cultural Reader, 224p. pap. text ed. 8.00 O.P; Puertas A La Communication Activity Manual, 224p. pap. text ed. write for info (ISBN 0-394-32881-7); write for info (ISBN 0-394-33012-9); lab manual 8.00 (ISBN 0-394-32880-9). Random.

Puertas de Madera Solida. (Productos Latinoamericanos Incluidos En el Sistema Generalizado De Preferencias De los Estados Unidos Ser.). 21p. 1977. pap. text ed. 3.00 (ISBN 0-8270-3465-2). OAS.

Puerto Rican Americans: The Meaning of Migration to the Mainland. reference ed. Joseph P. Fitzpatrick. 1971. pap. 17.00 (ISBN 0-13-740100-0). P-H.

Puerto Rican Americans: The Meaning of Migration to the Mainland. 2nd ed. Joseph P. Fitzpatrick. (Illus.). 224p. 1987. pap. text ed. write for info. (ISBN 0-13-740135-3). P-H.

Puerto Rican & Caribbean Cookbook. Ed. by Raoul Gordon. (Puerto Rico Ser.). 1982. lib. bdg. 72.95 (ISBN 0-8490-3228-8). Gordon Pr.

Puerto Rican Chicago. Felix M. Padilla. LC 86-40244. 256p. 1987. 26.95x (ISBN 0-268-01564-3). U of Notre Dame Pr.

Puerto Rican Chicago. Felix M. Padilla. 1988. pap. text ed. 11.95x (ISBN 0-268-01565-1). U of Notre Dame Pr.

Puerto Rican Community & Its Children on the Mainland: A Source Book for Teachers, Social Workers & Other Professionals. rev., 3rd ed. Francesco Cordasco & Eugene Bucchioni. LC 81-21250. 469p. 1982. 25.00 (ISBN 0-8108-1506-0). Scarecrow.

Puerto Rican Community Development Project. Puerto Rican Forum. LC 74-14243. (Puerto Rican Experience Ser.). (Illus.). 162p. 1975. Repr. 11.00x (ISBN 0-405-06230-3). Ayer Co Pubs.

Puerto Rican Cookery. 8th ed. Carmen A. Valldejuli. LC 83-2149. (Illus.). 389p. 1983. Repr. of 1977 ed. 14.95 (ISBN 0-88289-411-0). Pelican.

Puerto Rican Creole Cuisine: Barbecue al Fresco. Ed. by Jesus Velez de las Marias. (Illus.). 160p. (Orig., Span.). 1988. 12.95 (ISBN 0-318-24012-2); pap. 9.95 (ISBN 0-318-24013-0). Pubs j Velez Marias.

Puerto Rican Culture. Ed. by Raoul Gordon. 1976. lib. bdg. 59.95 (ISBN 0-8490-0915-4). Gordon Pr.

Puerto Rican Culture: An Introduction. Ed. by Raoul Gordon. (Puerto Rico Ser.). 1982. lib. bdg. 59.95 (ISBN 0-8490-3226-1). Gordon Pr.

Puerto Rican Curriculum Development Workshop. Date not set. 3.85. Coun Soc Wk Ed.

Puerto Rican Danza, with an Essay on la Borinquena. Ernesto J. Fonfrias. (Puerto Rico Ser.). 1979. lib. bdg. 59.95 (ISBN 0-8490-2988-0). Gordon Pr.

Puerto Rican Dilemma. Sakari Sariola. (National Univ. Pubns. Ser.). 1979. 23.50x (ISBN 0-8046-9217-3, Pub. by Kennikat). Assoc Faculty Pr.

Puerto Rican Dishes. 3rd ed. Berta Cabanillas. 1971. 15.00x. Adlers Foreign Bks.

Puerto Rican Dishes. 4th ed. Berta Cabanillas & Carmen Ginorio. 5.60. U of PR Pr.

Puerto Rican Drama. Ed. by Raoul Gordon. 1976. lib. bdg. 59.95 (ISBN 0-8490-0916-2). Gordon Pr.

Puerto Rican Experience. Ed. by Francesco Cordasco. (Illus.). 10610p. 1975. 827.50 set (ISBN 0-405-06210-9). Ayer Co Pubs.

Puerto Rican Experience: A Sociological Sourcebook. Francesco Cordasco et al. (Quality Paperback: No. 259). 370p. (Orig.). 1975. pap. 5.95 (ISBN 0-8226-0259-8). Littlefield.

Puerto Rican Families in New York City: Intergenerational Processes. Lloyd H. Rogler & Rosemary S. Cooney. 216p. 1985. lib. bdg. 18.95 (ISBN 0-943862-24-8); pap. 9.95 (ISBN 0-943862-25-6). Waterfront NJ.

Puerto Rican Folk-Tales. Ed. by Raoul Gordon. (Puerto Rico Ser.). 1982. lib. bdg. 59.95 (ISBN 0-8490-3229-6). Gordon Pr.

Puerto Rican Folklore. J. Alden Mason. Ed. by Aurelio M. Espinosa. (Puerto Rico Ser.). 1979. lib. bdg. 59.95 (ISBN 0-8490-2989-9). Gordon Pr.

Puerto Rican Historiography. Ed. by Raoul Gordon. 1976. lib. bdg. 59.95 (ISBN 0-8490-0917-0). Gordon Pr.

Puerto Rican Historiography. Allen L. Woll. (Studies in Puerto Rican History, Literature & Culture). 1979. lib. bdg. 69.95 (ISBN 0-8490-1393-3). Gordon Pr.

Puerto Rican Houses in Sociohistorical Perspective. Carol F. Jopling. LC 87-6025. (Illus.). 320p. 1988. text ed. 34.95x alk. paper (ISBN 0-87049-543-7). U of Tenn Pr.

Puerto Rican in New York & Other Sketches. Jesus Colon. LC 74-14229. (Puerto Rican Experience Ser). 206p. 1975. Repr. 18.00x (ISBN 0-405-06218-4). Ayer Co Pubs.

Puerto Rican in New York & Other Sketches. Jesus Colon. LC 82-6100. (Illus.). 204p. (Orig.). 1982. pap. 3.75 (ISBN 0-7178-0589-1). Intl Pubs Co.

Puerto Rican Literature: A Bibliography of Secondary Sources. David W. Foster. LC 82-6198. xxiii, 232p. 1982. lib. bdg. 40.95 (ISBN 0-313-23419-1, FPR/). Greenwood.

Puerto Rican Migrants of New York City. Manual Alers-Montalvo. LC 83-45349. (Immigrant Communities & Ethnic Minorities in the United States & Canada Ser.: No. 8). 1985. 37.50 (ISBN 0-404-19400-1). AMS Pr.

Puerto Rican Music. Ed. by Raoul Gordon. 1976. lib. bdg. 59.95 (ISBN 0-8490-0918-9). Gordon Pr.

Puerto Rican Music Following the Spanish American War: 1898, the Aftermath of the Spanish American War & Its Influence on the Musical Culture of Puerto Rico. Catherine Dower. LC 83-10290. (Illus.). 212p. (Orig.). 1983. lib. bdg. 30.00 (ISBN 0-8191-3333-7); pap. text ed. 12.50 (ISBN 0-8191-3334-5). U Pr of Amer.

Puerto Rican Neighbor. Roy Schuckman. 1954. pap. 2.50x (ISBN 0-87574-075-8, 075). Pendle Hill.

Puerto Rican Novel & Short Story. Ed. by Raoul Gordon. 1976. lib. bdg. 59.95 (ISBN 0-8490-0919-7). Gordon Pr.

Puerto Rican Obituary. Pedro Pietri. LC 73-8058. 128p. 1974. pap. 6.50 (ISBN 0-85345-330-6, PB3306). Monthly Rev.

Puerto Rican People. Date not set. 3.30. Coun Soc Wk Ed.

Puerto Rican Perspectives. Ed. by Edward Mapp. LC 73-20175. 179p. 1974. 16.50 (ISBN 0-8108-0691-6). Scarecrow.

Puerto Rican Politics & the New Deal. Thomas Mathews. LC 76-1934. 345p. 1976. Repr. of 1960 ed. lib. bdg. 39.50 (ISBN 0-306-70752-7). Da Capo.

Puerto Rican Politics in Urban America. Ed. by James Jennings & Monte Rivera. LC 83-10739. (Contributions in Political Science Ser.: No. 107). (Illus.). xiii, 166p. 1984. lib. bdg. 35.00 (ISBN 0-313-23801-4, JER/). Greenwood.

Puerto Rican Population: A Study of Human Biology. Frederick P. Thieme. (Anthropological Papers Ser.: No. 13). (Illus.). 1959. pap. 2.50x (ISBN 0-932206-19-0). U Mich Mus Anthro.

Puerto Rican Population of New York City. Ed. by Jaffe Abram. LC 74-14328. (Puerto Rican Experience Ser.). 65p. 1975. Repr. of 1954 ed. 11.00x (ISBN 0-405-06226-5). Ayer Co Pubs.

Puerto Rican Poverty & Migration: We Just Had to Try Elsewhere. Julio Morales, Jr. 271p. 1986. 33.95 (ISBN 0-275-92020-8, C2020). Praeger.

Puerto Rican Presence in the History of Cuba. Joaquin Freire. (Puerto Rico Ser.). 1979. lib. bdg. 59.95 (ISBN 0-8490-2990-2). Gordon Pr.

Puerto Rican Press Reaction to the United States, 1888-1898. Paul N. Chiles. LC 74-14225. (Puerto Rican Experience Ser.). 124p. 1975. Repr. 11.00x (ISBN 0-405-06215-X). Ayer Co Pubs.

Puerto Rican Public Papers of R. G. Tugwell, Governor. Rexford G. Tugwell. LC 74-14251. (Puerto Rican Experience Ser.). 1975. Repr. 29.00x (ISBN 0-405-06237-0). Ayer Co Pubs.

Puerto Rican Question. Jorge Heine & Juan M. Garcia-Passalacqua. LC 84-80499. (Headline Ser.: 266). 1983. pap. 4.00 (ISBN 0-87124-088-2, HS 266). Foreign Policy.

Puerto Rican Struggle: Essays on Survival in the U. S. 2nd ed. Ed. by Clara E. Rodriguez et al. 151p. 1984. 16.50 (ISBN 0-943862-20-5); pap. 7.50 (ISBN 0-943862-19-1). Waterfront NJ.

Puerto Rican Study, 1953-1957. J. Cayce Morrison. Ed. by Carlos E. Cortes. LC 79-6217. (Hispanics in the United States Ser.). (Illus.). 1981. Repr. of 1958 ed. lib. bdg. 28.50x (ISBN 0-405-13165-8). Ayer Co Pubs.

Puerto Rican Task Force Report. Date not set. 1.10. Coun Soc Wk Ed.

Puerto Rican Tourist Industry. Ed. by Raoul Gordon. 1976. lib. bdg. 69.95 (ISBN 0-8490-0920-0). Gordon Pr.

Puerto Rican Woman. Edna Acosta-Belen & Eli H. Christensen. LC 79-17638. 186p. 1979. 31.95 (ISBN 0-275-90325-7, C0325). Praeger.

Puerto Rican Woman: Perspectives on Culture, History & Society. 2nd ed. Ed. by Edna Acosta-Belen. 224p. 1986. lib. bdg. 36.95 (ISBN 0-275-92133-6, C2133); pap. 13.95 (ISBN 0-275-92134-4, B2134). Praeger.

Puerto Rican Workers & the Socialist Party, 1932-1940 see Trabajadores Puertoriquenos y el Partido Socialista, 1932 a 1940.

Puerto Rican Youth Employment. Jose Hernandez. 155p. (Orig.). 1984. pap. text ed. 7.50x (ISBN 0-943862-08-6). Waterfront NJ.

Puerto Ricans: A Brief Look at Their History. (Illus.). 96p. pap. 1.95 (ISBN 0-686-74907-3). ADL.

Puerto Ricans: A Resource Unit for Teachers. 64p. pap. 1.25 (ISBN 0-686-74908-1). ADL.

Puerto Ricans & Educational Opportunity: An Orginal Anthology. Francesco Cordasco. LC 74-14246. (Puerto Rican Experience Ser). (Illus.). 1975. Repr. 20.00x (ISBN 0-405-06231-1). Ayer Co Pubs.

Puerto Ricans & Other Minority Groups in the Continental United States: An Annotated Bibliography. Ed. by Diane Herrera. 1979. Repr. of 1973 ed. 30.00 (ISBN 0-87917-067-0). Ethridge.

Puerto Ricans: Culture Change & Language Deviance. Ruby R. Leavitt. LC 73-90914. (Viking Fund Publications in Anthropology: No. 51). 268p. 1974. pap. 4.95x (ISBN 0-8165-0457-1). U of Ariz Pr.

Puerto Ricans, Fourteen Ninety-Three to Nineteen Seventy-Three: A Chronology & Fact Book. Francesco Cordasco. LC 73-5840. (Ethnic Chronology Ser.: No. 11). 137p. 1973. lib. bdg. 8.50 (ISBN 0-379-00509-3). Oceana.

Puerto Ricans in America. Ronald J. Larsen. LC 72-3590. (In America Bks.). (Illus.). 96p. (gr. 5-11). 1973. PLB 8.95 (ISBN 0-8225-0225-9); pap. 3.95 (ISBN 0-8225-1020-0). Lerner Pubns.

Puerto Ricans in New York City. Welfare Council, New York City. LC 74-14230. (Puerto Rican Experience Ser). (Illus.). 64p. 1975. Repr. 9.00x (ISBN 0-405-06219-2). Ayer Co Pubs.

Puerto Ricans in Philadelphia. Arthur Siegel et al. LC 74-14250. (Puerto Rican Experience Ser). (Illus.). 150p. 1975. Repr. 10.00x (ISBN 0-405-06236-2). Ayer Co Pubs.

Puerto Ricans in the U. S. Ed. by Catarino Garza. LC 77-81291. 1977. 12.00 (ISBN 0-87348-552-1). Path Pr NY.

Puerto Ricans: Migration & General Bibliography. Francesco Cordasco. LC 74-14245. (Puerto Rican Experience Ser). (Illus.). 1975. Repr. 35.50x (ISBN 0-405-06232-X). Ayer Co Pubs.

Puerto Ricans: On the Island, on the Mainland, In Connecticut see Peoples of Connecticut Multinational Ethnic Heritage Studies.

Puerto Ricans: Their History, Culture & Society. Ed. by Adalberto Lopez. 490p. 1981. pap. text ed. 16.95 (ISBN 0-87073-845-3). Schenkman Bks Inc.

Puerto Rico. Elena E. Cevallos. (World Bibliographical Ser.: No. 52). 193p. 1985. lib. bdg. 40.00 (ISBN 0-903450-89-5). ABC-Clio.

Puerto Rico. Pamela Falk. (Westview Special Study on Latin America & the Caribbean). Date not set. 28.00x (ISBN 0-86531-629-5). Westview.

Puerto Rico. Turner Program Services, Inc. Staff & James I. Clark. (Portrait of America Library). 48p. (gr. 4 up). 1985. PLB 15.33 (ISBN 0-86514-443-5); pap. text ed. 9.27 (ISBN 0-86514-518-0); tchr's guide 13.27 (ISBN 0-86514-293-9); student activity bk. 6.60 (ISBN 0-86514-368-4); 3/4" video 136.00 (ISBN 0-86514-218-1); beta video 113.33 (ISBN 0-86514-068-5); VHS video 113.33 (ISBN 0-86514-143-6); index 13.27. Raintree Pubs.

Puerto Rico. Zachery Winslow. (Let's Visit Ser.). (Illus.). 96p. 1986. lib. bdg. 12.95x (ISBN 1-55546-154-9). Chelsea Hse.

Puerto Rico: A Colonial Experiment. Raymond Carr. (Twentieth Century Fund Studies). 477p. 1984. 25.00x (ISBN 0-8147-1389-0). NYU Pr.

Puerto Rico: A Colonial Experiment. Raymond Carr. (Twentieth Century Fund Study). 477p. 1984. pap. 12.95 (ISBN 0-394-72431-3, Vin). Random.

Puerto Rico: A Guide to the Island of Boriquen. Ed. by Gordon Raoul. 1976. lib. bdg. 75.00 (ISBN 0-8490-1375-5). Gordon Pr.

Puerto Rico: A Guide to the Island of Boriquen. Writers Program, Puerto Rico. LC 73-3650. (American Guide Ser.). 1940. Repr. 23.50 (ISBN 0-404-57950-7). AMS Pr.

Puerto Rico: A Political & Cultural History. Arturo M. Carrion. (Illus.). 400p. 1984. pap. text ed. 10.95x (ISBN 0-393-30193-1). Norton.

Puerto Rico: A Political & Cultural Odyssey. Arturo M. Carrion et al. (Illus.). 1983. 19.50 (ISBN 0-393-01740-0). Norton.

Puerto Rico: A Socio-Historic Interpretation. Manuel Maldonado-Denis. 1972. (Vin). Random.

Puerto Rico: A Survey of Historical, Economic, & Political Affairs. United States Congress House Committee on Interior & Insular Affairs. Ed. by Robert J. Hunter. LC 78-10360. 1979. Repr. of 1959 ed. lib. bdg. 35.00x (ISBN 0-313-20692-9, HUPU). Greenwood.

Puerto Rico: An Introduction. Ed. by Raoul Gordon. (Pureto Rico Ser.). 1982. lib. bdg. 69.95 (ISBN 0-8490-3227-X). Gordon Pr.

Puerto Rico & Its People. Trumbull White. LC 74-14258. (Puerto Rican Experience Ser). (Illus.). 434p. 1975. 32.00x (ISBN 0-405-06243-5). Ayer Co Pubs.

Puerto Rico & Its Problems. Victor S. Clark et al. LC 74-14226. (Puerto Rican Experience Ser). (Illus.). 748p. 1975. Repr. 56.50x (ISBN 0-405-06216-8). Ayer Co Pubs.

Puerto Rico & the Caribbean. Ed. by Raoul Gordon. 1976. lib. bdg. 59.95 (ISBN 0-8490-0921-9). Gordon Pr.

Puerto Rico & the Non-Hispanic Caribbean: A Study in the Decline of Spanish Exclusivism. Arturo M. Carrion. pap. 3.10 (ISBN 0-8477-0835-7). U of PR Pr.

Puerto Rico & the Puerto Ricans. Clifford A. Hauberg. LC 74-15755. 211p. 1984. pap. 3.95 (ISBN 0-88254-308-3). Hippocrene Bks.

Puerto Rico & the Sea. Ed. by William S. Beller. Tr. by Irma Balzac. (Illus.). 1974. pap. 6.25 (ISBN 0-8477-2301-1). U of PR Pr.

Puerto Rico & the United States in the Revolutionary Period of Europe & America. Arturo F. Santana. (Puerto Rico Ser.). 1979. lib. bdg. 69.95 (ISBN 0-8490-2991-0). Gordon Pr.

Puerto Rico & the United States, 1917-1933. Truman R. Clark. LC 74-26019. (Pitt Latin American Ser.). pap. 63.50 (ISBN 0-317-26631-4, 2025433). Bks Demand UMI.

Pulmonary & Respiratory Physiology. Ed. by Julius H. Comroe. LC 75-33085. (Benchmark Papers in Human Physiology: Vol. 5, Pt. 1). 400p. 1976. 87.00 (ISBN 0-12-786251-X). Acad Pr.

Pulmonary & Respiratory Physiology. Ed. by Julius H. Comroe. LC 75-33063. (Benchmark Papers in Human Physiology: Vol. 6, Pt. 2). 400p. 1976. 87.00 (ISBN 0-12-786252-8). Acad Pr.

Pulmonary Aspects of Neurological Diseases. Ed. by Stephan L. Kamholz. (Neurologic Illness: Diagnosis & Treatment Ser.). 1987. text ed. 50.00 (ISBN 0-89335-239-X). PMA Pub Corp.

Pulmonary Assessment: A Clinical Guide. Witkowski. LC 65-7925. 1984. 15.75 (ISBN 0-397-50627-9, Lippincott Medical). Lippincott.

Pulmonary Blood Volume in Health & Disease. Paul N. Yu. LC 68-18860. pap. 82.00 (ISBN 0-317-29257-9, 2055450). Bks Demand UMI.

Pulmonary Circulation. Symposium on Pulmonary Circulation, Prague, 1969. Ed. by J. Widimsky et al. (Progress in Respiration Research: Vol. 5). 1970. 96.00 (ISBN 3-8055-1152-3). S Karger.

Pulmonary Circulation & Acute Lung Injury. Ed. by Sami I. Said & John Vane. (Illus.). 650p. 1985. monograph 65.00 (ISBN 0-87993-249-X). Futura Pub.

Pulmonary Circulation in Chronic Lung Diseases. Ed. by J. Widimsky et al. (Progress in Respiration Research: Vol. 20). (Illus.). viii, 192p. 1985. 92.00 (ISBN 3-8055-3961-4). S Karger.

Pulmonary Circulation in Health & Disease. Ed. by James A. Will et al. 592p. 1987. 59.00 (ISBN 0-12-752085-6). Acad Pr.

Pulmonary Development: Transition from Intrauterine to Extrauterine Life. Nelson. (Lung Biology Ser.). 544p. 1985. 85.00 (ISBN 0-8247-7316-0). Dekker.

Pulmonary Disease. Paul A Selecky. LC 82-1903. 358p. 1982. 42.95 (ISBN 0-471-09554-0, JW). Krieger.

Pulmonary Disease Review. William J. Hall. LC 77-11665. (Medical Review Ser.). 1977. pap. 14.95 (ISBN 0-668-04008-4). Appleton & Lange.

Pulmonary Disease Reviews. Roger C. Bone. (Pulmonary Disease Ser.: Vol. 2). 642p. 1981. 60.00x (ISBN 0-471-09047-6, Pub. by Wiley Med). Wiley.

Pulmonary Disease Reviews, 2 Vols. Ed. by Roger C. Bone. LC 80-648256. Vol. 1. pap. 145.30 (ISBN 0-317-28954-3, 2055984); Vol. 2. pap. 160.00 (ISBN 0-317-28955-1). Bks Demand UMI.

Pulmonary Disease Reviews, Vol. 1. Roger C. Bone. (Pulmonary Disease Review Ser.). 581p. 1980. 60.00 (ISBN 0-471-05736-3, Pub. by Wiley Med). Wiley.

Pulmonary Diseases & Disorders, 2 vols. Alfred P. Fishman. (Illus.). 1696p. 1980. Set. text ed. 225.00 (ISBN 0-07-021116-7). McGraw.

Pulmonary Diseases & Disorders, 3 vols. 2nd ed. Alfred P. Fishman. 1680p. 1988. Set. text ed. 295.00 (ISBN 0-07-079982-2). McGraw.

Pulmonary Diseases & Disorders: Update 1. Ed. by Alfred P. Fishman. (Illus.). 496p. 1982. text ed. 60.00 (ISBN 0-07-021119-1). McGraw.

Pulmonary Diseases: Clinicopathological Correlations. Ed. by K. M. Mueller. (Current Topics in Pathology Ser.: Vol. 73). (Illus.). 310p. 1983. 74.00 (ISBN 0-387-12453-5). Springer-Verlag.

Pulmonary Diseases: Mechanisms of Altered Structure & Function. Adam Wanner & Marvin A. Sackner. (Physiopathology Ser.). 282p. 1983. pap. text ed. 21.00 (ISBN 0-316-92150-5). Little.

Pulmonary Edema in Man & Animals. Aldo A. Luisada. LC 71-96988. (Illus.). 168p. 1970. 15.00 (ISBN 0-87527-050-6). Green.

Pulmonary Embolism. Frank D. Gray. LC 66-19290. pap. 58.50 (ISBN 0-317-07818-6, 2055298). Bks Demand UMI.

Pulmonary Embolism. Ed. by J. Widimsky. (Progress in Respiration Research: Vol. 13). (Illus.). viii, 192p. 1980. 96.75 (ISBN 3-8055-0487-X). S Karger.

Pulmonary Embolism & Deep Venous Thrombosis. Contrib. by Samuel Z. Goldhaber. (Illus.). 295p. 1985. 63.00 (ISBN 0-7216-4151-2). Saunders.

Pulmonary Emergencies. Ed. by Steven A. Sahn. (Illus.). 1982. 45.00 (ISBN 0-443-08169-7). Churchill.

Pulmonary Emphysema & Proteolysis, 1986. Ed. by Joseph C. Taylor & Charles Mittman. 568p. 1987. 55.00 (ISBN 0-12-684570-0). Acad Pr.

Pulmonary Emphysema: Proceedings. International Symposium on Pathophysiology & Diagnostic Methods in Incipient Pulmonary Emphysema. Ed. by G. L. Scarpa. (Progress in Respiration Research: Vol. 10). 1976. 65.50 (ISBN 3-8055-2273-8). S Karger.

Pulmonary Endothelium in Health & Disease. Ryan. (Lung Biology in Health & Disease Ser.). 528p. 1987. 125.00 (ISBN 0-8247-7758-1). Dekker.

Pulmonary Eosinophilia. F. E. Udwadia. Ed. by H. Herzog. (Progress in Respiration Research: Vol. 7). (Illus.). xi, 286p. 1975. 93.50 (ISBN 3-8055-1739-4). S Karger.

Pulmonary Function Indices in Critical Care Patients. J. Brunner & G. Wolff. 180p. 1987. pap. 49.00 (ISBN 0-387-18432-5). Springer-Verlag.

Pulmonary Function Technology: The Basics. Mark Esenwein. (Illus.). 900p. 1985. pap. text ed. 155.00 (ISBN 0-933195-09-5). CA College Health Sci.

Pulmonary Function Testing. Reuben M. Cherniack. LC 77-75533. (Illus.). 1977. pap. text ed. 22.95 (ISBN 0-7216-2528-2). Saunders.

Pulmonary Function Testing. Ed. by Jack L. Clausen & Irwin Zimet. LC 82-3968. (Continuing Medical Education Ser.). 1982. 56.50 (ISBN 0-12-788125-5). Acad Pr.

Pulmonary Function Testing: Indications & Interpertations: A Project of the California Thoracic Society. Ed. by Archie Wilson. 384p. 1985. 44.50 (ISBN 0-8089-1692-0, 794854). Grune.

Pulmonary Function Testing: Principles & Practice. Ed. by Stephen A. Conrad et al. (Illus.). 378p. 1984. text ed. 33.50 (ISBN 0-443-08182-4). Churchill.

Pulmonary Function Tests: A Guide for the Student & House Officer. Ed. by Albert Miller. 304p. 1987. 29.50 (ISBN 0-8089-1764-1, 792923). Grune.

Pulmonary Function Tests in Clinical & Occupational Lung Disease. Ed. by Albert Miller. 512p. 1986. 69.50 (ISBN 0-8089-1749-8, 792929). Grune.

Pulmonary Gas Exchange. Ed. by M. Meyer & J. Piiper. (Progress in Respiration Research Ser.: Vol. 21). (Illus.). xiv, 274p. 1986. 166.00 (ISBN 3-8055-4330-1). S Karger.

Pulmonary Heart Disease. Ed. by Lewis J. Rubin. 1984. lib. bdg. 75.00 (ISBN 0-89838-632-2, Pub. by Martinus Nijhoff Netherlands). Kluwer Academic.

Pulmonary Hypertension. Ed. by E. Kenneth Weir & John T. Reeves. (Illus.). 496p. 1984. 55.00 (ISBN 0-87993-206-6). Futura Pub.

Pulmonary Hypertension: Proceedings. International Symposium on Pulmonary Circulation 2, Prague, June 1974. Ed. by J. Widimsky. (Progress in Respiration Research: Vol. 9). (Illus.). 320p. 1975. 118.75 (ISBN 3-8055-2171-5). S Karger.

Pulmonary Lesions Induced by Bleomycin. Gebbers & A. Burkhardt. (LITS 13 Lectures in Taxicology Ser.). (Illus.). 12p. 73.00 (ISBN 0-317-66864-1). Pergamon.

Pulmonary Macrophage & Epithelial Cells: Proceedings. Ed. by Charles L. Sanders & Richard P. Schneider. LC 77-12024. (ERDA Symposium Ser.). 628p. 1977. pap. 23.75 (ISBN 0-87079-204-0, CONF-760927); microfiche 6.50 (ISBN 0-87079-316-0, CONF-760927). DOE.

Pulmonary Manifestations of Hypersensitivity & Immunodeficiency. Stephen B. Sulavik & Herbert Y. Reynolds. Date not set. price not set (ISBN 0-89004-431-7, 489). Raven.

Pulmonary Manifestations of Systemic Disease. U. B. Prakash. 1988. 39.00 (ISBN 0-8151-6830-6). Year Bk Med.

Pulmonary Medicine. 2nd ed. Ed. by Clarence A. Guenter & Martin H. Welch. (Illus.). 896p. 1982. text ed. 89.50 (ISBN 0-397-50444-6, 65-05895, Lippincott Medical). Lippincott.

Pulmonary Medicine Case Studies. Daniel J. Stone. (Case Study Ser.: Vol. 34). 1982. pap. text ed. 22.25 (ISBN 0-87488-051-3). Med Exam.

Pulmonary Nuclear Medicine. Harold L. Atkins. (Lung Biology in Health & Diseases Ser.). 344p. 1984. 75.00 (ISBN 0-8247-7233-4). Dekker.

Pulmonary Nuclear Medicine. Merle K. Loken. (Current Practice in Nuclear Medicine Ser.). 1987. 89.95 (ISBN 0-8385-8070-X). Appleton & Lange.

Pulmonary Nuclear Medicine. Ed. by Merle K. Loken. 1986. text ed. 89.95 (ISBN 0-317-60694-8). Appleton & Lange.

Pulmonary Pathology. Ed. by D. H. Dail & S. P. Hammar. (Illus.). 1190p. 1987. 200.00 (ISBN 0-387-96491-6). Springer Verlag.

Pulmonary Pathology: Proceedings of the Annual Anatomic Pathology Slide Seminar, 46th. Merle A. Legg & Lynne M. Reid. LC 86-7992. 156p. 1986. pap. text ed. 28.00 (ISBN 0-89189-178-1); 25 glass slides 60.00 (ISBN 0-317-58156-2). Am Soc Clinical.

Pulmonary Pathophysiology: The Essentials. 3rd ed. John West. 250p. 1987. pap. text ed. 17.95 (ISBN 0-683-08941-2). Williams & Wilkins.

Pulmonary Pathophysiology: The Essentials. 2nd ed. John B. West. 232p. 1981. pap. 18.50 (ISBN 0-683-08935-8). Williams & Wilkins.

Pulmonary Physiology. 2nd ed. M. G. Levitzky. 288p. 1986. pap. text ed. 18.95 (ISBN 0-07-037468-6). McGraw.

Pulmonary Physiology in Clinical Medicine. 2nd ed. Gennaro M. Tisi. (Illus.). 296p. 1983. lib. bdg. 42.95 (ISBN 0-683-08271-X). Williams & Wilkins.

Pulmonary Physiology in Clinical Practice: The Essentials for Patient Care & Evaluation. Martin. 1986. 22.95 (ISBN 0-8016-3192-0). Mosby.

Pulmonary Physiology of the Fetus, Newborn & Child. Ed. by Emile M. Scarpelli & Peter A. Auld. LC 75-26531. pap. 95.80 (ISBN 0-317-55511-1, 2056326). Bks Demand UMI.

Pulmonary Rehabilitation. J. A. O'Ryan. 1984. 36.50 (ISBN 0-8151-6550-1). Year Bk Med.

Pulmonary Rehabilitation: Guidelines to Success. Ed. by John E. Hodgkin et al. 1984. text ed. 44.95 (ISBN 0-409-95061-0). Butterworth.

Pulmonary Restriction & Obstruction: A Programmed Text. Patricia R. Hercules et al. (Illus.). 1979. 33.50 (ISBN 0-8151-4361-3). Year Bk Med.

Pulmonary Surfactant. B. Robertson et al. 1984. 211.00 (ISBN 0-444-80553-2). Elsevier.

Pulmonary Surfactant System. Ed. by E. V. Cosmi & E. M. Scarpelli. (Symposia of the Giovanni Lorenzini Foundation: Vol. 16). 404p. 1984. 125.25 (ISBN 0-444-80514-1, Biomedical Pr). Elsevier.

Pulmonary System: Practical Approaches to Pulmonary Diagnosis. Ed. by Stanley S. Siegelman et al. (Multiple Imaging Procedure Ser.: Vol. 1). (Illus.). 384p. 1979. 59.50 (ISBN 0-8089-1143-0, 794052). Grune.

Pulmonary Toxicology of Respirable Particles: Proceedings. Ed. by Charles L. Sanders et al. (DOE Symposium Ser.). 688p. 1980. pap. 25.25 (ISBN 0-87079-121-4, CONF-791002); microfiche 6.50 (ISBN 0-87079-404-3, CONF-791002). DOE.

Pulmonary Tuberculosis: A Journey down the Centuries. Robert Y. Keers. 1979. text ed. write for info. (ISBN 0-7216-0741-1, Bailliere-Tindall). Saunders.

Pulmonary Vascular Diseases. K. M. Moser. (Lung Biology in Health & Disease Ser.: Vol. 14). 1979. 110.00 (ISBN 0-8247-6609-1). Dekker.

Pulmonary Vascular Physiology & Pathophysiology. Weir & Reeves. (Lung Biology in Health & Disease Ser.). 744p. 1988. 125.00 (ISBN 0-8247-7972-X). Dekker.

Pulmonates: Functional Anatomy & Physiology, Vol. 1. Ed. by V. Fretter & J. Peake. 1975. 95.00 (ISBN 0-12-267501-0). Acad Pr.

Pulmonates: Vol. 2A, Systematics, Evolution & Ecology. Ed. by Vera Fretter & J. Peake. 1979. 106.00 (ISBN 0-12-267502-9). Acad Pr.

Pulmonates: Vol. 2b, Economic Malacology with Particular Reference to Achatina Fulica. Ed. by Vera Fretter & J. Peake. 1979. 67.50 (ISBN 0-12-267541-X). Acad Pr.

Pulp & Paper. Boy Scouts of America. (Illus.). 40p. (gr. 6-12). 1974. pap. 1.25x (ISBN 0-8395-3343-8, 3343). BSA.

Pulp & Paper Capacities Survey 1984-1989. 178p. (Eng., Fr. & Span.). 1985. pap. 18.75 (ISBN 92-5-002254-9, F2761, FAO). UNIPUB.

Pulp & Paper Capacities Survey, 1985-1990. FAO Staff. (Illus.). 200p. (Orig., Eng., Fr. & Span.). 1987. pap. text ed. 18.75 (ISBN 92-5-002452-5, F2988, FAO). UNIPUB.

Pulp & Paper Capacities Survey 1986-1991. (Pulp & Paper Capacities Ser.). 200p. (Orig., Eng., Fr., & Span.). 1987. pap. text ed. 22.50 (ISBN 92-5-002571-8, F3069, FAO). UNIPUB.

Pulp & Paper Chemical Market. 336p. 1985. 1800.00 (ISBN 0-86621-686-3, E758). Frost & Sullivan.

Pulp & Paper Chemicals (U. S.) 1985. write for info. (ISBN 0-86621-346-5, A1430). Frost & Sullivan.

Pulp & Paper: Chemistry & Chemical Technology, 3 vols. 3rd ed. Ed. by James P. Casey. LC 79-13435. 1980. Vol. 1, 820 p. 110.00 (ISBN 0-471-03175-5); Vol. 2, 625 p. 110.00 (ISBN 0-471-03176-3); Vol. 3. 84.00 (ISBN 0-471-03177-1). Wiley.

Pulp & Paper: Chemistry & Chemical Technology. 3rd ed. Ed. by James P. Casey. LC 79-13435. 596p. 1983. 95.00 (ISBN 0-471-03178-X). Wiley.

Pulp & Paper: Chemistry & Chemical Technology, 4 vols. 3rd ed. Ed. by James P. Casey. 1983. Set. 340.00 (ISBN 0-471-88186-4). Wiley.

Pulp & Paper Development in Africa & the Near East, Vol. 1. pap. 8.75 (F351, FAO). UNIPUB.

Pulp & Paper Dictionary. John R. Lavigne. Ed. by Kenneth L. Patrick. 370p. 1986. 47.50 (ISBN 0-87930-168-6, 530). Miller Freeman.

Pulp & Paper Industry Corrosion Problems: Vol. 2. LC 77-76737. (Illus.). 154p. 1977. 40.00 (ISBN 0-915567-79-2). Natl Corrosion Eng.

Pulp & Paper Industry Corrosion Problems, Vol. 3. LC 82-60909. (Illus.). 360p. 1982. 50.00 (ISBN 0-915567-78-4). Natl Corrosion Eng.

Pulp & Paper Industry Division Index to Technical Papers, 1960-1983. 80p. 1984. pap. text ed. 16.00x (ISBN 0-87664-804-9). Instru Soc.

Pulp & Paper Industry, 1982. OECD. 102p. (Orig.). 1984. pap. 12.00x (ISBN 92-64-02617-7). OECD.

Pulp & Paper Industry 1983. OECD. 100p. (Orig.). 1986. pap. 15.00x (ISBN 92-64-02870-6). OECD.

Pulp & Paper Manufacture, Vol. 1: Pulping of Wood. 2nd ed. Pulp & Paper Manufacture Staff. 1968. text ed. 59.95 (ISBN 0-07-050924-7). McGraw.

Pulp & Paper Manufacture, Vol. 2: Control, Secondary Fiber, Structural Board, Coating. 2nd ed. Pulp & Paper Manufacture Staff. 1969. text ed. 79.95 (ISBN 0-07-050925-5). McGraw.

Pulp & Paper Pricebook Two. Miller Freman Staff. 150p. 1987. 3-ring binder 297.00 (ISBN 0-87930-170-8). Miller Freeman.

Pulp & Paper Primer. David Saltman. 1983. pap. 8.45 (ISBN 0-89852-410-5); pap. 5.66 members. TAPPI.

Pulp & Paper Primer. David Saltman. LC 83-50324. pap. 20.00 (ISBN 0-317-20540-4, 2022830). Bks Demand UMI.

Pulp & Wood Densitometric Properties of Pinus Caribaea from Fiji. J. Burley & E. R. Palmer. 1979. 30.00x (ISBN 0-85074-046-0, Pub. by For Lib Comm England). State Mutual Bk.

Pulp Cutter' Nativity. David Budbill. LC 81-12506. 64p. 1981. 11.95 (ISBN 0-914378-79-1); pap. 6.95 (ISBN 0-914378-80-5). Countryman.

Pulp-itations: The Graphic Art of Spicy Dectective Stories. (Odd Books for Odd Moments: No. 14). (Illus.). iv, 100p. (Orig.). 1986. pap. 4.95 (ISBN 0-930937-44-9). Winds World Pr.

Pulp Man's Odyssey. Audrey Parente. (Starmont Popular Culture Ser.: No. 6). 146p. 1988. lib. bdg. 19.95x (ISBN 0-8095-5302-3). Borgo Pr.

Pulp Man's Odyssey. Audrey Parente. (Popular Culture Studies: Vol. 6). 1988. 19.95x (ISBN 1-55742-041-6); pap. 9.95x (ISBN 1-55742-038-6). Starmont Hse.

Pulp, Paper, & Board: Proceedings of a Seminar Organized by the Commssion of the European Communities, Directorate-General for Science, Research, & Development (Directorate G) under the Patronage of Dr. Karl-Heinz Narjes. Ed. by I. F. Hendry & W. J. Hanssens. 198p. 1988. 38.00 (ISBN 1-85166-173-5). Elsevier.

Pulp Technology & Treatment for Paper. 2nd ed. James d'A. Clark. LC 85-62603. (Illus.). 880p. 1985. 97.00 (ISBN 0-87930-164-3). Miller Freeman.

Pulp Voices or Science Fiction Voices, No. 6: Interviews with Pulp Magazine Writers & Editors. Jeffrey M. Elliot. LC 81-21632. (Milford Ser.: Popular Writers of Today: Vol. 37). (Illus.). 63p. 1983. lib. bdg. 16.95x (ISBN 0-89370-157-2); pap. text ed. 7.95x (ISBN 0-89370-257-9). Borgo Pr.

Pulp Western: A Popular History of the Western Fiction Magazine in America. John A. Dinan. LC 81-21697. (I. O. Evans Studies in the Philosophy & Criticism of Literature: Vol. 2). (Illus.). 128p. 1983. lib. bdg. 19.95x (ISBN 0-89370-161-0); pap. text ed. 9.95x (ISBN 0-89370-261-7). Borgo Pr.

Pulping & Paper-Making Properties of Fast Growing Plantation Wood Species, 2 Vols. (Forestry Papers: Nos. 19-1 & 19-2). 886p. 1980. pap. 47.00 set (ISBN 0-686-68193-2, F1969, FAO). Vol. 1, 486p (ISBN 92-5-100865-5). Vol. 2, 400p (ISBN 92-5-100866-3). UNIPUB.

Pulping & Papermaking Properties of Fast-Growing Plantation Wood Species. 1976. pap. 26.25 (ISBN 0-685-71579-5, F1177, FAO). UNIPUB.

Pulping Conference: 1984, Proceedings of the Technical Association of the Pulp & Paper Industry, Hyatt Regency, San Francisco, Ca., November 12-14. Technical Association of the Pulp & Paper Industry. Bk. 1. pap. 43.30 (ISBN 0-317-20767-9, 2024786); Bk. 2. pap. 75.00 (ISBN 0-317-20768-7); Bk. 3. pap. 45.00 (ISBN 0-317-20769-5). Bks Demand UMI.

Pulping Conference, 1986: Sheraton Center, Toronto, Ontario, October 26-30. Technical Association of the Pulp & Paper Industry. (TAPPI Proceedings Ser.). (Illus.). Bk. 1. pap. 58.00 (ISBN 0-317-58145-7, 2029690); Bk. 2. pap. 74.70 (ISBN 0-317-58146-5); Bk. 3. pap. 55.90 (ISBN 0-317-58147-3). Bks Demand UMI.

Pulping of Bagasse & Other Papermaking Fibers. Louise Louden. LC 76-29080. (Bibliographic Ser.: No. 270). 1976. pap. 20.00 (ISBN 0-87010-045-9). Inst Paper Chem.

Pulping of Bagasse & Other Papermaking Fibers. (Bibliographic Ser.: No. S41). 483p. 1970. 45.00 (ISBN 0-317-34428-5). Inst Paper Chem.

Pulping Processes. Sven A. Rydholm. LC 85-4324. 1280p. 1985. Repr. of 1965 ed. lib. bdg. 130.00 (ISBN 0-89874-856-9). Krieger.

Pulping Processes: Mill Operations, Techology, & Practices. Miller Freeman Publications, Inc., Staff. Ed. by Kenneth E. Smith. LC 81-81386. (Pulp & Paper Focus Bk). (Illus.). 216p. 1981. pap. 35.00 (ISBN 0-87930-126-0). Miller Freeman.

Pulping Processes: Semichemical Process, Vol. 4. 2nd ed. (Bibliographic Ser.: No. 175-2). 329p. 1955. 15.00 (ISBN 0-317-34432-3); Supplement 1, 1963. 9.00 (ISBN 0-317-34433-1); Supplement 2, 1970. 8.00 (ISBN 0-317-34434-X). Inst Paper Chem.

Pulping Processes V: Mechanical Processes. Louise Louden. LC 78-385. (Bibliographic Ser.: No. 283). pap. 45.00 (ISBN 0-87010-034-3). Inst Paper Chem.

Pulpit & Press. Mary Baker Eddy. pap. 4.50 (ISBN 0-87952-046-9). First Church.

Pulpit & Press. 90p. (Orig.). pap. 7.50 (ISBN 0-317-65705-4). First Church.

Pulpit & the Pew. Charles H. Parkhurst. 1913. 39.50x (ISBN 0-686-83717-7). Elliots Bks.

Pulpit Commentary, 23 vols. H. D. Spence & T. S. Exell. Incl. Old Testament only, 14 Vols. 320.00 (ISBN 0-8028-8056-8, 2209); New Testament only, 8 Vols. 200.00 (ISBN 0-8028-8057-6, 2210). 1959. Repr. Set. 520.00 (ISBN 0-8028-8055-X). Eerdmans.

Pulpit Commentary, 23 vols. Ed. by H. D. Spence & Joseph S. Exell. 26612p. Date not set. Set. 520.00 (ISBN 0-917006-32-1). Hendrickson MA.

Pulpit in the American Revolution. Ed. by John W. Thornton. LC 77-114833. (Research & Source Works Ser: No. 440). 1970. Repr. of 1860 ed. 26.50 (ISBN 0-8337-3534-9). B Franklin.

Pulpit of the American Revolution: Political Sermons of the Period of 1776. Ed. by John W. Thornton. LC 71-109611. (Era of the American Revolution Ser). 1970. Repr. of 1860 ed. lib. bdg. 49.50 (ISBN 0-306-71907-X). Da Capo.

Pulpit Preparation. Paul Hamsher. (Orig.). 1981. pap. 5.25 (ISBN 0-937172-29-4). JLJ Pubs.

Pulpit under the Sky: A Life of Hans Nielson Hauge. Joseph M. Shaw. LC 78-12391. 1979. Repr. of 1955 ed. lib. bdg. 35.00x (ISBN 0-313-21123-X, SHPU). Greenwood.

Punctuation & Capitalization. Doris Rikkers. Ed. by Joan Hoffman. (I Know It! Bks.). (Illus.). 32p. (gr. 5 up). 1979. wkbk. 1.95 (ISBN 0-938256-24-6). Sch Zone Pub Co.

Punctuation & Mechanics. Mary Lewick-Wallace. 240p. 1982. text ed. 18.95 (ISBN 0-07-067903-7). McGraw.

Punctuation Drills & Exercises. 2nd ed. LeRoy A. Brendel & Doris Near. (gr. 9-12). 1978. pap. 12.88 (ISBN 0-07-007479-8). McGraw.

Punctuation for Shorthand Reporters. Nathaniel Weiss. 72p. 15.50 (ISBN 0-318-15865-5). Natl Shorthand Rptr.

Punctuation Partners. Rita Lerin. (Language Arts Ser.). 48p. (gr. 2-4). 1983. 5.95 (ISBN 0-88160-098-9, LW 121). Learning Wks.

Punctuation Passport. Beverly Armstrong. (Language Arts Ser.). 38p. (gr. 4-7). 1979. 4.95 (ISBN 0-88160-029-6, LW 214). Learning Wks.

Punctuation Pockets: A Student Folder. Patrick Sebranek & Verne Meyer. (Illus.). (YA) (gr. 7-12). 1984. pap. text ed. 0.95x (ISBN 0-9605312-8-9). Write Source.

Punctuation, Proofreading & Printing: How to Prepare a Manuscript for Publication. rev. ed. Alan C. Wares & Iris M. Wares. 1975. microfiche 2.00 (ISBN 0-88312-491-2). Summer Inst Ling.

Punctuation: Syllabus. 2nd ed. Theodore Yerian & Carl W. Salser. 1972. pap. text ed. 6.35 (ISBN 0-89420-020-8, 357498); cassette recordings 56.20 (ISBN 0-89420-178-6, 357500). Natl Book.

Punctuation the Easy Way. Robert Brittain. 225p. (gr. 10-12). Date not set. pap. text ed. cancelled (ISBN 0-8120-2426-5). Barron.

Puncture Prevention Techniques for Low Cost Vehicles. Michael Ayre & Alan Smith. (Illus.). 46p. (Orig.). 1987. pap. 7.50x (ISBN 0-946688-14-1, Pub. by Intermed Tech England). Intermediate Tech.

Pundemonium: Puns Are Everywhere! Harvey C. Gordon. LC 83-61419. (Illus.). 108p. (Orig.). 1983. pap. 3.95 (ISBN 0-9601402-2-0); prepack 47.40. Punster's Pr.

Pundits: British Exploration of Tibet & Central Asia. Derek Waller. (Illus.). 264p. 1989. 25.00 (ISBN 0-8131-1666-X). U Pr of Ky.

Pundles. Bruce Nash & Greg Nash. 96p. 1980. pap. 2.95 (ISBN 0-399-50963-1, G&D). Putnam Pub Group.

Puniana: Or Thoughts Wise & Other Wise. Hugh Rowley. Repr. of 1902 ed. 25.00 (ISBN 0-8274-4175-4). R West.

Punic Coins of Ancient Spain. E. S. Robinson. 29p. 1978. pap. 4.00 (ISBN 0-89005-125-9). Ares.

Punica, 2 Vols. Silius Italicus. (Loeb Classical Library: No. 277-278). 13.95x ea. Vol. 1 (ISBN 0-674-99305-5). Vol. 2 (ISBN 0-674-99306-3). Harvard U Pr.

Puniddles. Bruce McMillan & Brett McMillan. (Illus.). (gr. 2 up). PLB 7.95 (ISBN 0-395-32082-8); pap. 2.95 (ISBN 0-395-32076-3). HM.

Punish Me with Kisses. William Bayer. 1981. pap. 3.50 (ISBN 0-671-60697-2). PB.

Punish the Sinners. John Saul. 416p. 1986. pap. 4.50 (ISBN 0-440-17084-2). Dell.

Punished Land. Dennis Silk. (Poets Ser.). 1980. pap. 7.95 (ISBN 0-14-042276-5). Penguin.

Punished Land. Dennis Silk. 1980. 12.95 (ISBN 0-670-58226-3). Viking.

Punished Peoples. Aleksandr Nekrich. 1978. 10.95 (ISBN 0-393-05646-5). Norton.

Punishing Criminals: Concerning Very Old & Painful Question. Ernest Van den Haag. LC 75-3758. 1975. pap. 10.95x (ISBN 0-465-09729-4, TB-5080). Basic.

Punishing International Terrorists: The Legal Framework for Policy Initiatives. John F. Murphy. LC 85-15845. 152p. 1985. 24.95x (ISBN 0-8476-7449-5, Rowman & Allanheld). Rowman.

Punishing the Perpetrators of the Holocaust: The Brandt, Pohl & Ohlendorf Cases. John Mendelsohn. LC 81-80325. 269p. 1982. lib. bdg. 61.00 (ISBN 0-8240-4891-1). Garland Pub.

Punishing the Perpetrators of the Holocaust: The Ohlendorf & Von Weizsaecker Cases. John Mendelsohn. LC 81-80326. (Holocaust Ser.). 310p. 1982. lib. bdg. 61.00 (ISBN 0-8240-4892-X). Garland Pub.

Punishment: A Philosophical & Criminological Inquiry. Philip Bean. 224p. 1982. pap. 12.95x (ISBN 0-85520-478-8). Basil Blackwell.

Punishment & - or Treatment for Driving under the Influence of Alcohol & Other Drugs: Current Concepts, Experiences, & Prospective. (Illus.). 272p. (Orig.). 1985. pap. text ed. 68.50x (Pub. by Almqvist & Wiksell). Coronet Bks.

Punishment & Aversive Stimulation in Special Education: Legal, Theoretical, & Practical Issues in Their Use with Emotionally Disturbed Children & Youth. Ed. by Frank H. Wood & K. Charlie Lakin. 130p. 1982. pap. 8.50 (ISBN 0-86586-131-5). Coun Exc Child.

Punishment & Deterrence. Johannes Andenaes. LC 73-90883. 1974. text ed. 12.50x (ISBN 0-472-08013-X). U of Mich Pr.

Punishment & Human Rights. Milton Goldinger. 1974. 11.25 (ISBN 0-87073-527-6). Schenkman Bks Inc.

Punishment & Its Alternatives: A New Perspective for Behavior Modification. Johnny L. Matson & Thomas M. DiLorenzo. (Springer Series on Behavior Therapy & Behavioral Medicine: Vol. 13). 288p. 1983. text ed. 22.95 (ISBN 0-8261-4560-4). Springer Pub.

Punishment & Penal Discipline: Essays on the Prison & the Prisoner's Movement. 2nd ed. Ed. by Tony Platt & Paul Takagi. LC 79-90275. (Illus., Orig.). 1982. pap. 10.95 (ISBN 0-935206-00-0). Crime & Soc Justice.

Punishment & Prevention of Crime. Edmund Du Cane. LC 83-49247. (Crime & Punishment in England, 1850-1922 Ser.). 231p. 1984. lib. bdg. 30.00 (ISBN 0-8240-6212-4). Garland Pub.

Punishment & Privilege. Ed. by W. Byron Groves. Graeme Newman. (Illus.). 180p. 1987. text ed. 32.00 (ISBN 0-911577-09-2); pap. text ed. 17.50 (ISBN 0-911577-10-6). Harrow & Heston.

Punishment & Reformation. Frederick H. Wines. (Historical Foundations of Forensic Psychiatry & Psychology Ser.). xi, 481p. 1983. Repr. of 1919 ed. lib. bdg. 45.00 (ISBN 0-306-76184-X). Da Capo.

Punishment & Reformation: A Study of the Penitentiary System. new rev. enl. ed. Frederick H. Wines. LC 73-38676. (Foundations of Criminal Justice Ser.). Repr. of 1919 ed. 30.00 (ISBN 0-404-09192-X). AMS Pr.

Punishment & Rehabilitation. 2nd ed. Ed. by Jeffrie G. Murphy. 233p. 1985. pap. text ed. write for info. (ISBN 0-534-04614-2). Wadsworth Pub.

Punishment & Responsibility: Essays in the Philosophy of Law. Herbert L. Hart. (Orig.). 1968. pap. 10.95x (ISBN 0-19-825181-5). Oxford U Pr.

Punishment & Restitution: A Restitutionary Approach to Crime & the Criminal. Charles F. Abel & Frank H. Marsh. LC 83-22837. (Contributions in Criminology & Penology Ser.: No. 5). (Illus.). 214p. 1984. lib. bdg. 32.95 (ISBN 0-313-23717-4, ABP/). Greenwood.

Punishment & Social Structure. Georg Rusche & Otto Kirchheimer. Tr. by M. I. Finkelstein & Otto Kirchheimer. LC 68-15157. (Illus.). 1968. Repr. of 1939 ed. 23.00x (ISBN 0-8462-1176-9). Russell.

Punishment & Welfare: A History of Penal Strategies. David Garland. 291p. 1985. text ed. 41.95 (ISBN 0-566-00855-6). Gower Pub Co.

Punishment & Welfare: A History of Penal Strategies. David Garland. 297p. 1987. pap. text ed. 17.95x (ISBN 0-566-05431-0, Pub. by Gower Pub England). Gower Pub Co.

Punishment by Death: Its Authority & Expediency. George B. Cheever. (Capital Punishment Ser.). Date not set. Repr. of 1842 ed. 37.50 (ISBN 0-404-62409-X). AMS Pr.

Punishment Chart for Motor Vehicle Offenses in North Carolina. Ben F. Loeb & James C. Drennan. 1987. pap. 4.00. U of NC Inst Gov.

Punishment, Danger & Stigma: The Morality of Criminal Justice. Nigel Walker. LC 81-112572. 206p. 1980. 27.50x (ISBN 0-389-20129-4, 06905). B&N Imports.

Punishment in Islamic Law. M. S. El Awa. 162p. 1985. pap. 6.00 (ISBN 0-89259-015-7). Am Trust Pubns.

Punishment: Issues & Experiments. Ed. by Erling E. Boe & Russell M. Church. LC 68-23894. (Century Psychology Ser.). (Illus., Orig.). 1968. pap. text ed. 10.95x (ISBN 0-89197-367-2). Irvington.

Punishment: Its Origin, Purpose, & Psychology. Hans Von Hentig. LC 74-172566. (Criminology, Law Enforcement, & Social Problems Ser.: No. 147). 270p. (With new intro. & index). 1973. Repr. of 1937 ed. 16.00x (ISBN 0-87585-147-9). Patterson Smith.

Punishment of Apostasy in Islam. S. A. Rahman. pap. 9.00 (ISBN 0-686-18551-X). Kazi Pubns.

Punishment of the Stingy & Other Indian Stories. George B. Grinnell. LC 81-21922. (Illus.). xx, 265p. 1982. 22.95x (ISBN 0-8032-2113-4); pap. 5.95 (ISBN 0-8032-7008-9, BB 783, Bison). U of Nebr Pr.

Punishment Response. 2nd ed. Graeme Newman. LC 85-80304. 340p. 1985. pap. text ed. 17.50 (ISBN 0-911577-02-5). Harrow & Heston.

Punishment Short of Death: A History of the Penal Settlement at Norfolk Island. Margaret Hazzard. 304p. 1987. 25.00 (ISBN 0-908090-64-1, Pub. by Hyland Australia). Intl Spec Bk.

Punishment Without Walls: Community Service Sentences in New York City. Douglas C. McDonald. (Crime, Law & Deviance Ser.). 224p. 1986. text ed. 30.00 (ISBN 0-8135-1147-X). Rutgers U Pr.

Punishments Imposed on Federal Offenders, 2 vols. A. Partridge & P. Lombard. LC 86-81506. v, 1336p. 1986. Repr. Set. lib. bdg. 145.00 (ISBN 0-89941-469-9). W S Hein.

Punishments of Former Days. Ernest W. Pettifer. (Illus.). 1976. Repr. 15.00x (ISBN 0-7158-1021-9). Charles River Bks.

Punitive Damage. Chester Oksner. Ed. by Thomas Congdon. LC 87-7883. 288p. 1987. 17.45 (ISBN 0-688-07220-8). Morrow.

Punitive Damage. Chester Oksner. 1988. pap. 4.95 (ISBN 0-944276-21-0). Tudor Pub NYC.

Punitive Damages. Kenneth R. Redden. 1009p. 1980. with 1987 suppl. 75.00x (ISBN 0-87215-303-7); 1987 suppl. only 37.50x (ISBN 0-87215-696-6). Michie Co.

Punitive Damages: A Constructive Examination. American Bar Association, Special Committee on Punitive Damages. LC 87-400150. 104p. Date not set. price not set. Amer Bar Assn.

Punitive Damages in Bad Faith Cases. 3rd ed. John C. McCarthy. LC 83-81290. 436p. 1983. 65.00 (ISBN 0-915544-11-3). Lawpress Ca.

Punitive Damages in Bad Faith Cases. John C. McCarthy. LC 87-81538. 718p. 1987. 80.00 (ISBN 0-915544-18-0). Lawpress CA.

Punitive Damages in Wrongful Discharge Cases. John C. McCarthy. LC 85-50568. 543p. 1985. 75.00 (ISBN 0-915544-16-4). Lawpress Ca.

Punitive Damages: 1981-1983, 2 vols. James Ghiardi & John Kircher. LC 81-10088. 145.00; Suppl., 1982. 20.00; Suppl., 1983. 25.00. Callaghan.

Punitive Expedition: Pershing's Pursuit of Villa, 1916-1917. Ed. by Donald Smythe. 1985. 31.95 (ISBN 0-8488-0022-2, Pub. by J M C & Co). Amereon Ltd.

Punitive Medicine. Alexander Podrabinek. Tr. by Alexander Lehrman from Rus. (Illus.). 236p. 1980. 8.95 (ISBN 0-89720-022-5). Karoma.

Punjab: A Cultural Profile Illustrated. V. N. Tewari. (Illus.). 90p. 1984. 30.00x (ISBN 0-7069-2568-8, Pub. by Vikas India). Advent NY.

Punjab Accord & Elections Retrospect & Prospect. A. S. Narang. 1986. pap. 8.50x (ISBN 0-8364-1796-8, Pub. by Minerva India). South Asia Bks.

Punjab & the Raj Eighteen Forty-Nine to Nineteen Forty-Seven. Ian Talbot. LC 87-61957. 1988. 34.00 (ISBN 0-913215-28-7). Riverdale Co.

Punjab Campaign: Casualty Roll, 1849-9. Picton Publishing Staff. 76p. 1987. 105.00x (Pub. by Picton UK). State Mutual Bk.

Punjab Crisis. A. C. Kapur. 316p. 1986. 34.95. Asia Bk Corp.

Punjab Crisis: Challenge & Response. Ed. by Abida Samiuddin. xxviii, 714p. 1985. 44.00 (ISBN 0-318-18470-2, Pub. by Mittal Pubs Dist India). Nataraj Bks.

Punjab Crisis: Context & Trends. Ed. by Pramod Kumar. 1985. 21.00x (ISBN 0-8364-1464-0, Pub. by Ctr Res Chandigarh). South Asia Bks.

Punjab: Imperial Gazetteer of India, 1908. 1985. Repr. of 1908 ed. 75.00x (ISBN 0-8364-1318-0, Pub. by Usha). South Asia Bks.

Punjab in Indian Politics: Issues & Trends. Ed. by Amrik Singh. 1986. 37.50x (ISBN 0-317-44237-6, Pub. by Ajanta). South Asia Bks.

Punjab in Indian Politics: Issues & Trends. Ed. by Amrik Singh. xvi, 479p. 1985. 25.00 (ISBN 0-318-23242-1, Pub. by Ajanta Pubns). Nataraj Bks.

Punjab in Peace & War. S. S. Thorburn. LC 73-137301. Repr. of 1904 ed. 26.50 (ISBN 0-404-06424-8). AMS Pr.

Punjab in Peace & War. S. S. Thorburn. 1987. 36.00x (ISBN 0-8364-2021-7, Pub. by Usha). South Asia Bks.

Punjab Mail Murder. 2nd, enl. ed. Roger Perkins. 108p. 1987. 84.00x (ISBN 0-948251-09-3, Pub. by Picton UK). State Mutual Bk.

Punjab Peasant in Prosperity & Debt. rev. ed. Malcolm L. Darling. Ed. by Clive Dewey. 1978. 14.00x (ISBN 0-8364-0070-4). South Asia Bks.

Punjab Plants: Compromising Botanical & Vernacular Names, & Uses of Most of the Trees, Shrubs, & Herbs of Economical Value, Growing Within the Province Intended As a Hand-Book for Officers & Residents in the Punjab. J. L. Stewart. 1978. Repr. of 1869 ed. 37.50x (ISBN 0-89955-301-X, Pub. by Intl Bk Dist). Intl Spec Bk.

Punjab Politics: Socio-Politico Orientations of the Sikh Gurus. Gurdev Singh. xxvi, 122p. 1986. text ed. 22.50x (ISBN 81-7018-318-9, Pub. by B R Pub Corp Delhi). Apt Bks.

Punjab Politics: The Role of Sir Chhotu Ram. Prem Chowdhury. 336p. 1984. text ed. 40.00x (ISBN 0-7069-2473-8, Pub. by Vikas India). Advent NY.

Punjab Problem: The Muslim Connection. Balraj Madhok. 1985. 14.00x (ISBN 0-8364-1519-1, Pub. by Vision). South Asia Bks.

Punjab Since Partition. Satya M. Rai. 1986. 45.00 (ISBN 0-8364-1944-8, Pub. by Deep). South Asia Bks.

Punjab Story. Ed. by A. Kaur et al. 199p. 1984. 19.95. Asia Bk Corp.

Punjab: The Fatal Miscalculation. Ed. by Patwant Singh & Harji Malik. 252p. 1985. 12.00 (ISBN 0-318-23241-3, Pub. by Patwant Singh). Nataraj Bks.

Punjab Today. Ed. by Gopal Singh. 1987. 48.50x (ISBN 81-7076-006-2, Pub. by Macmillan India). South Asia Bks.

Punjab under Imperialism, 1885-1947. Imran Ali. (Illus.). 270p. 1988. 49.50 (ISBN 0-691-05527-0). Princeton U Pr.

Punjabi Century, 1857-1947. Prakash Tandon. 1968. pap. 7.95x (ISBN 0-520-01253-4). U of Cal Pr.

Punjabi Manual & Grammar. 1986. Repr. 22.50 (ISBN 0-8364-1688-0, Pub. by Chanakya India). South Asia Bks.

Punjabi Short Stories: An Anthology. Ed. by G. S. Khosla. (Vikas Library of Modern Moian Writing Ser.: No. 17). 140p. 1981. text ed. 15.95x (ISBN 0-7069-1311-6, Pub. by Vikas India). Advent NY.

Punjabis in New Zealand. W. H. McLeod. 198p. 1986. 16.00x (ISBN 0-8364-1907-3, Pub. by Nanak Dev Univ India). South Asia Bks.

Punjabis, War & Women: The Short Stories of Gulzar Singh Sandhu. Marcus Franda. 1983. 17.00x (ISBN 0-8364-0936-1, Pub. by Heritage India). South Asia Bks.

Punk Petro: The Music of the "No-Future" Generation. Debora Hill. 1987. 39.00x (ISBN 0-317-68327-6, Pub. by Harrap Ltd England). State Mutual Bk.

Punkin Center Stories. Cal Stewart. (Illus.). 192p. 1986. pap. 25.00 limited special ed. (ISBN 0-940152-04-5). McNutt Pubns.

Punky Brewster at Camp Chipmunk. Ann Matthews. (Punky Brewster Ser.). (Illus.). (gr. 2-5). 1987. pap. 2.50 (ISBN 0-671-62729-5, Minstrel Bks). S&S.

Puns. W. D. Redfern. 256p. 1985. 24.95 (ISBN 0-631-13793-9). Basil Blackwell.

Puns. Walter Redfern. (Language Library). 256p. 1986. pap. 8.95 (ISBN 0-631-14909-0). Basil Blackwell.

Punta Gorda. D. C. Kip. (Illus.). 111p. (Orig.). 1984. pap. 5.00 (ISBN 0-9614549-0-3). Maedon.

Punta Rassa. Ann O. Rust. 320p. (Orig.). Date not set. pap. price not set. Amaro Bks.

Punti Controversi di Sintassi Latina. Gaetano Dall'Olio. (Studi Pubblicati Dall'Istituto di Filologia Classica (Universita di Bologna): No. VI). 112p. (Ital.). 1959. pap. text ed. 6.75 (ISBN 0-905205-42-1, Pub. by F Cairns). Longwood Pub Group.

Punto de Partida: An Invitation to Spanish. 2nd ed. Marty Knorre et al. 1985. text ed. write for info (ISBN 0-394-33655-0, RanC); write for info (ISBN 0-394-33657-7); write for info (ISBN 0-394-33658-5). Random.

Punto Tagliato Lace. Nenia Lovesey. (Illus.). 1986. 19.95 (ISBN 0-85219-632-6). Branford.

Puntos de Vista: Voces de Espana e Hispanoamerica. 2nd ed. Solomon Tilles. 236p. 1986. pap. text ed. 11.75 (ISBN 0-8191-5383-4). U Pr of Amer.

Pup Pup & Murray Find a New Home. Jean C. Stoneback. (Illus.). 45p. (Orig.). (ps). 1984. pap. 4.00 (ISBN 0-931440-09-2). Stoneback Pub.

Pup Went Up. Mary Blocksma. LC 82-19862. (Just One More Ser.). (Illus.). 24p. (ps-2). 1983. PLB 10.60 (ISBN 0-516-01583-4); pap. 2.95 (ISBN 0-516-41583-2). Childrens.

Pupa Digging. Joseph Greene. 1984. 25.00x (ISBN 0-317-07171-8, Pub. by FW Classey UK). State Mutual Bk.

Pupi, the Rag Doll. Dan Feller. 25p. 1988. 5.95 (ISBN 0-533-07751-6). Vantage.

Pupil. E. Alexandridis. Tr. by T. Telger from Ger. (Illus.). 115p. 1985. 35.95 (ISBN 0-387-96109-7). Springer-Verlag.

Pupil. Keith M. Zinn. (Illus.). 152p. 1972. 21.75 (ISBN 0-398-02320-4). C C Thomas.

Pupil see What Maisie Knew.

Pupil: A Memory of Love. Monk Gibbon. 128p. 1981. 10.95 (ISBN 0-905473-68-X, Pub. by Wolfhound Pr Ireland). Irish Bks Media.

Pupil As Scientist? Ed. by Rosalind Driver. 128p. 1983. pap. 21.00x (ISBN 0-335-10178-X, Pub. by Open Univ Pr). Taylor & Francis.

Pupil Assistant in the School Library. Mary P. Douglas. LC 57-9534. 68p. 1957. pap. 4.00x (ISBN 0-8389-0050-X). ALA.

Pupil Evaluation in Science. 30p. 1986. pap. text ed. 5.00 (ISBN 0-317-43831-X, UB185, UB). UNIPUB.

Pupil Evaluation in the Classroom: An All Level Guide to Practice. Douglas M. Brooks & David W. Van Cleaf. LC 82-13650. (Illus.). 170p. 1983. lib. bdg. 29.25 (ISBN 0-8191-2736-1); pap. text ed. 12.25 (ISBN 0-8191-2737-X). U Pr of Amer.

Pupil Experience. John F. Schostak & Tom Logan. 258p. 1984. (Pub. by Croom Helm Ltd); pap. 14.50 (ISBN 0-7099-3332-0). Routledge Chapman & Hall.

Pupil, Parent & School: A Hong Kong Study. Robert E. Mitchell. (Asian Folklore & Social Life Monograph: No. 26). 1972. 18.00x (ISBN 0-89986-027-3). Oriental Bk Store.

Pupil Power: Deviance & Gender in School. Lynn Davies. 190p. 1984. 33.00x (ISBN 1-85000-007-7, Falmer Pr); pap. 19.00x (ISBN 1-85000-006-9, Falmer Pr). Taylor & Francis.

Pupil Profiles. Roger C. Reeds. (Sunday School Workers Training Course Ser.: No. 3). 1973. pap. 3.95 (ISBN 0-89265-010-9). Randall Hse.

Pupil Profiles: Teacher's Guide. Larry D. Hampton. 1978. pap. 1.50 (ISBN 0-89265-057-5). Randall Hse.

Pupil Progress Policies & Practices. Garth H. Akridge. LC 70-176505. (Columbia University. Teachers College. Contributions to Education: No. 691). Repr. of 1937 ed. 22.50 (ISBN 0-404-55691-4). AMS Pr.

Pupil Rating of Secondary School Teachers. Roy C. Bryan. LC 73-176609. (Columbia University. Teachers College. Contributions to Education: No. 708). Repr. of 1937 ed. 22.50 (ISBN 0-404-55708-2). AMS Pr.

Pupil Rating Scale Revised: Screening for Learning Disabilities. rev. ed. Helmer R. Myklebust. 84p. 1980. 23.00 (ISBN 0-8089-1358-1, 793067); specimen set & manual 15.50 (ISBN 0-8089-1329-8, 793066); fifty record forms 14.50 (ISBN 0-8089-1364-6, 793068). Grune.

Purchase & Sale of Assets in Bankruptcy: 1988 Cumulative Supplement. Richard N. Tilton. (Business Practice Library). 1988. pap. price not set (ISBN 0-471-61154-9). Wiley.

Purchase & Sale of Real Property. Ed. by Karl B. Holtzschue. (Real Estate Transaction Ser.). 1987. write for info. (NO. 658). Bender.

Purchase & Sale of Small Businesses: Tax & Legal Aspects. Marc J. Lane. LC 84-19693. (Business Practice Library: 1-692). 737p. 1985. 85.00x (ISBN 0-471-89070-7). Wiley.

Purchase & Sale of Small Businesses: Tax & Legal Aspects, 1988 Cumulative Supplement. Marc J. Lane. (Business Practice Library). 1988. write for info. (ISBN 0-471-60906-4). Wiley.

Purchase Inspector. Jack Rudman. (Career Examination Ser.: C-637). (Cloth bdg. avail. on request). pap. 14.00 (ISBN 0-8373-0637-X). Natl Learning.

Purchase Inspector (Shop Steel) Jack Rudman. (Career Examination Ser.: C-2258). (Cloth bdg. avail. on request). 1988. pap. 16.00 (ISBN 0-8373-2258-8). Natl Learning.

Purchase of Alaska. Victor J. Farrar. 1971. Repr. of 1935 ed. 39.00x (ISBN 0-403-00590-6). Scholarly.

Purchase of Alaska. Archie W. Shiels. 208p. 1967. 6.50 (ISBN 0-912006-14-5); pap. 2.95 (ISBN 0-912006-15-3). U of Alaska Pr.

Purchase of Medical Care Through Fixed Periodic Payment. Pierce Williams. LC 75-17251. (National Bureau of Economic Research Ser.). 1975. Repr. 26.00x (ISBN 0-405-07525-1). Ayer Co Pubs.

Purchase of Order. Gail G. Adams. LC 88-4724. 176p. 1988. 4.95 (ISBN 0-8203-1040-9). U of GA Pr.

Purchase of Service Contracting. Peter M. Kettner & Lawrence L. Martin. (Sage Human Services Guides Ser.: Vol. 44). 174p. (Orig.). 1987. pap. 12.95 (ISBN 0-8039-2630-8). Sage.

Purchase of the Danish West Indies. Charles C. Tansill. LC 68-23332. 1968. Repr. of 1932 ed. lib. bdg. 29.75x (ISBN 0-8371-0245-6, TADI). Greenwood.

Purchase of the North Pole. Jules Verne. 4.95 (ISBN 0-685-06592-8). Assoc Bk.

Purchase Specifications Assistant. Jack Rudman. (Career Examination Ser.: C-2542). (Cloth bdg. avail. on request). pap. 14.00 (ISBN 0-8373-2542-0). Natl Learning.

Purchaser's Formbook of Contracts and Agreements. first year 32.50 renewal 65.00. Busn Laws Inc.

Purchaser's Guide to the Uniform Commercial Code. 124.95. Busn Laws Inc.

Purchases & Sales - Corporate Bonds. (Transaction Reports). 1988. 135.00 (ISBN 0-317-53424-6). A M Best.

Purchases & Sales - Municipal Bonds. (Transaction Reports). 1988. 170.00 (ISBN 0-317-53430-0). A M Best.

Purchasing. C. K. Lysons. 211p. 1982. pap. text ed. 18.50x (ISBN 0-7121-1752-0). Trans-Atl Phila.

Purchasing. C. L. Murphy. 188p. 1987. cancelled. Carlton.

Purchasing. Coursebook ed. 1988. write for info. (ISBN 0-471-61350-9). Wiley.

Purchasing Agent. Jack Rudman. (Career Examination Ser.: C-638). (Cloth bdg. avail. on request). pap. 14.00 (ISBN 0-8373-0638-8). Natl Learning.

Purchasing Agent: Food. Jack Rudman. (Career Examination Ser.: C-2731). (Cloth bdg. avail. on request). 1988. pap. 16.00 (ISBN 0-8373-2731-8). Natl Learning.

Purchasing Agent: Lumber. Jack Rudman. (Career Examination Ser.: C-2732). (Cloth bdg. avail. on request). 1988. pap. 16.00 (ISBN 0-8373-2732-6). Natl Learning.

Purchasing Agent: Medical. Jack Rudman. (Career Examination Ser.: C-2733). (Cloth bdg. avail. on request). 1988. pap. 16.00 (ISBN 0-8373-2733-4). Natl Learning.

Purchasing Agent: Printing. Jack Rudman. (Career Examination Ser.: C-2734). (Cloth bdg. avail. on request). 1988. pap. 16.00 (ISBN 0-8373-2734-2). Natl Learning.

Purchasing Agent's Guide to the Naked Salesman. Barry J. Hersker & Thomas F. Stroh. LC 75-17522. 1975. 16.95 (ISBN 0-8436-1308-4). Van Nos Reinhold.

Purchasing an Encyclopedia: 12 Points to Consider. 2nd ed. Reference Books Bulletin Editorial Board Staff. LC 88-2178. 40p. 1988. pap. text ed. 4.95x (ISBN 0-8389-3351-3). ALA.

Purchasing & Materials Management. 3rd ed. Lamar Lee, Jr. & Donald W. Dobler. 1976. text ed. 40.95 (ISBN 0-07-037027-3). McGraw.

Purchasing & Materials Management. 9th ed. Leenders et al. 1989. 41.95 (ISBN 0-256-06984-0). Irwin.

Purchasing & Materials Management. 8th ed. Michael R. Leenders et al. 1985. 40.95x (ISBN 0-256-03029-4). Irwin.

Purchasing & Materials Management for Health-Care Institutions. 2nd ed. Dean S. Ammer. LC 83-47985. 288p. 1983. 29.00x (ISBN 0-669-04908-5). Lexington Bks.

Purchasing & Materials Management: Integrative Strategies. Joseph L. Cavinato. (Illus.). 475p. 1984. text ed. 39.75 (ISBN 0-314-77869-1); instr's. manual avail. (ISBN 0-314-77870-5). West Pub.

Purchasing & Materials Management: Texts & Cases. 4th ed. Dean D. Dobler & Lamar Lee. (Management & Marketing Ser.). (Illus.). 736p. 1984. text ed. 45.95 (ISBN 0-07-037042-7). McGraw.

Purchasing & Supply Management. P. J. Baily. 1978. pap. 18.50x (ISBN 0-412-15690-3, NO. 6021, Pub. by Chapman & Hall England). Routledge Chapman & Hall.

Purchasing & Supply Management. 5th ed. P. J. Baily. 304p. 1987. pap. text ed. 27.50 (ISBN 0-412-28940-7, Pub. by Chapman & Hall). Routledge Chapman & Hall.

Purchasing & the Management of Materials. 6th ed. Gary J. Zenz. LC 86-32589. 576p. 1987. write for info. (ISBN 0-471-81802-X). Wiley.

Purchasing Computer Software Products. Cliff Dilloway. 170p. 1985. text ed. 39.00 (ISBN 0-566-02520-5). Gower Pub Co.

Purchasing Computers. Edward R. Sambridge. 172p. 1979. text ed. 45.00 (ISBN 0-566-02193-5, Pub. by Gower Pub England). Gower Pub Co.

Purchasing Factomatic. R. Jerry Baker et al. 1976. 54.95 (ISBN 0-13-742031-5, Busn). P-H.

Purchasing for Food Service Managers. rev. ed. M. C. Warfel & Marion Cremer. LC 84-61509. (Illus.). 464p. 1985. 32.00x (ISBN 0-8211-2264-9); text ed. 29.00. McCutchan.

Purchasing for Food Service: Self-Instruction. Lynne N. Ross. (Illus.). 162p. 1985. pap. text ed. 15.95x (ISBN 0-8138-1461-8). Iowa St U Pr.

Purchasing for Hospitality Operations. William B. Virts. Ed. by Kent F. Premo. LC 86-29196. (Illus.). 282p. 1987. 36.95 (ISBN 0-86612-033-5). Educ Inst Am Hotel.

Purchasing from Small and Minority Businesses. 300p. first year 30.50 renewal (supplemented annually) 66.50. Busn Laws Inc.

Purchasing Guide for Banks. 68p. 1978. 24.00 (ISBN 0-317-33808-0, 652). Bank Admin Inst.

Purchasing Handbook. 3rd ed. George W. Aljian. 1152p. 1973. 59.95 (ISBN 0-07-001068-4). McGraw.

Purchasing Influence of OR Nurses in Hospital Settings & Freestanding Ambulatory Surgical Centers. 33p. 1985. 12.00 (ISBN 0-939583-16-X). Assn Oper Rm Nurses.

Purchasing Information Sources. Ed. by Douglas C. Basil et al. LC 76-7037. (Management Information Guide Ser.: No. 30). 256p. 1977. 68.00x (ISBN 0-8103-0830-4). Gale.

Purchasing International Freight Services. G. J. Davies. Ed. by R. Gray. 200p. 1985. text ed. 41.95x (ISBN 0-566-02497-7). Gower Pub Co.

Purchasing Management Handbook. David Farmer. LC 84-18659. 712p. 1985. text ed. 64.95 (ISBN 0-566-02471-3). Gower Pub Co.

Purchasing Manager's Desk Book of Purchasing Law. James J. Ritterskamp. 470p. 1987. 59.95 (ISBN 0-13-742115-X, Busn). P-H.

Purchasing Negotiations. C. W. Barlow & Glen P. Eisen. 200p. 1983. 23.95 (ISBN 0-8436-0881-1). Van Nos Reinhold.

Purchasing Performance: Measurement & Control. Robert M. Monczka & Phillip L. Carter. LC 78-620032. 1979. pap. 17.00x (ISBN 0-87744-155-3). Mich St U Pr.

Purchasing Power of Money. 2nd ed. Irving Fisher. LC 85-152. (Illus.). 1985. Repr. of 1922 ed. 45.00x (ISBN 0-678-00011-5). Kelley.

Purchasing Power of the Consumer: A Statistical Index. William A. Berridge et al. LC 75-39232. (Getting & Spending: the Consumer's Dilemma). (Illus.). 1976. Repr. of 1925 ed. 26.50x (ISBN 0-405-08009-3). Ayer Co Pubs.

Purchasing Power Parities & Real Expenditures in the OECD. OECD Staff & Michael Ward. 95p. (Orig.). 1985. pap. 12.00x (ISBN 0-318-19009-5). OECD.

Purchasing Power Parities & Real Expenditures, 1985. OECD. (Orig., Eng. & Fr.). 1988. pap. 15.50x (ISBN 92-64-03018-2). OECD.

Purchasing Power Parity & Exchange Rates: Theory, Evidence, & Relevance. Lawrence H. Officer. LC 81-81650. (Contemporary Studies in Economic & Financial Analysis Ser.: Vol. 35). 361p. 1982. 52.50 (ISBN 0-89232-229-2). Jai Pr.

Purchasing Power Parity & the International Transmission of Price Disturbances under Alternative Exchange Regimes: The Swiss Experience. Georg Junge. 251p. 1984. pap. 19.95x (ISBN 3-87895-263-5, Pub. by HWWA Inst Econc Res). Transaction Bks.

Purchasing: Principles & Applications. 6th ed. Stuart F. Heinritz & Paul V. Farrell. (Illus.). 448p. 1981. text ed. write for info. (ISBN 0-13-742163-X). P-H.

Purchasing: Principles & Applications. 7th ed. Stuart F. Heinritz et al. (Illus.). 512p. 1986. text ed. 41.00 (ISBN 0-13-742180-X). P-H.

Purchasing Principles & Management. 5th ed. Peter Baily & David Farmer. 336p. (Orig.). 1986. pap. 26.50x (ISBN 0-273-02242-3). Trans Atl Phila.

Purchasing, Receiving & Storage: A Systems Manual for Restaurants, Hotels & Clubs. Jack D. Ninemeier. 360p. 1983. 3 ring binder 66.95 (ISBN 0-8436-2261-X). Van Nos Reinhold.

Purchasing Role: A View from the Top. Charles F. Carpenter. LC 77-6349. (AMA Management Briefing Ser.). pap. 20.00 (ISBN 0-317-29943-3, 2051698). Bks Demand UMI.

Purchasing: Selection & Procurement for the Hospitality Industry. John M. Stefanelli. LC 80-20604. (Service Management Ser.). 502p. 1981. 28.95 (ISBN 0-471-04538-1); supplementary materials avail. (ISBN 0-471-05953-6). Wiley.

Purchasing: Selection & Procurement for the Hospitality Industry. 2nd ed. John M. Stefanelli. LC 84-7544. (Management Ser.). 543p. 1985. write for info. (ISBN 0-471-87430-2). Wiley.

Purchasing Supervisor. Jack Rudman. (Career Examination Ser.: C-2720). (Cloth bdg. avail. on request). 1988. pap. 16.00 (ISBN 0-8373-2720-2). Natl Learning.

Purchasing Systems & Records. 2nd ed. Peter Baily. 127p. 1983. text ed. 45.00x (ISBN 0-566-02337-7). Gower Pub Co.

Purchasing Technician. Jack Rudman. (Career Examination Ser.: C-913). (Cloth bdg. avail. on request). pap. 14.00 (ISBN 0-8373-0913-1). Natl Learning.

Purdah & the Status of Women in Islam. A. A. Maududi. pap. 12.00 (ISBN 0-686-18464-5). Kazi Pubns.

Purdah: The Status of Indian Women. S. Das. 287p. 1979. 19.95. Asia Bk Corp.

Purdah to Profession (A Case Study of Working Women in M.P.) Indira Chauhan. (Illus.). viii, 295p. 1987. text ed. 35.00x (ISBN 81-7018-375-8, Pub. by B R Pub Corp Delhi). Apt Bks.

Purdey's: The Guns & the Family 1815-1984. Richard Beaumont. (Illus.). 256p. 1984. 34.95 (ISBN 0-7153-8624-7). David & Charles.

Purdue Grain Elevator Management Game. Emerson M. Babb. 1979. Repr. of 1973 ed. 6.25x (ISBN 0-933836-06-6). Simtek.

Purdue Industrial Waste Conference Proceedings, 42nd. Purdue Industrial Waste Staff & Bell. 900p. 1988. write for info. (ISBN 0-471-60942-0). Wiley.

Purdue Industrial Waste Conference, 41st: Proceedings. Ed. by John Bell. LC 86-640717. (Illus.). 785p. 1987. 89.95 (ISBN 0-87371-094-0). Lewis Pubs Inc.

Purdue Pharmacy: The First Century. Robert B. Eckles. LC 78-58099. (Illus.). 114p. 1979. 10.00 (ISBN 0-931682-01-0). Purdue U Pubns.

Purdue Supermarket Chain Management Game. rev. ed. Emerson M. Babb. 1979. student's manual 6.25x (ISBN 0-933836-07-4). Simtek.

Purdue Thirty-Eighth Industrial Waste Conference: Proceedings. Ed. by John M. Bell. 1000p. 1984. text ed. 90.00 (ISBN 0-250-40639-X). Butterworth.

Purdue Thirty-Ninth Industrial Waste Conference. Ed. by John B. Bell. 1008p. 1985. text ed. 90.00 (ISBN 0-250-40640-3). Butterworth.

Purdy's Eagle Lake. Tim I. Purdy. (Illus.). 160p. Date not set. pap. 11.95 (ISBN 0-938373-04-8). Lahontan Images.

Pure & Applied Science Books, 1876-1982, 6 vols. 7784p. 1982. Set. 345.00 (ISBN 0-8352-1437-0). Bowker.

Pure & Simple Natural Weight Control. Norman W. Walker. LC 81-11080. 1981. pap. 4.95 (ISBN 0-89019-078-X). Norwalk Pr.

Pure & the Impure. Colette. Tr. by Herma Briffault from Fr. 175p. 1975. 7.95 (ISBN 0-374-23920-7); pap. 6.25 (ISBN 0-374-50692-2). FS&G.

Pure & Wholesome. LC 81-70989. 181p. 1982. pap. 18.00x (ISBN 0-87262-290-8). Am Soc Civil Eng.

Pure Bred Arabian Horse. Carlo Guarmani. 112p. 1984. 120.00x (ISBN 0-907151-26-4, Pub. by IMMEL UK). State Mutual Bk.

Pure Breed Poultry Raising. Rick Kemp. 80p. (Orig.). 1985. pap. 10.95 (ISBN 0-86417-058-0, Pub. by Kangaroo Pr). Intl Spec Bk.

Pure Chemistry. Naomi Horton. (Silhouette Desire Ser.). pap. 2.50 (ISBN 0-373-05386-X). Harlequin Bks.

Pure Clear Word: Essays on the Poetry of James Wright. Ed. by Dave Smith. LC 81-2976. 288p. 1982. 22.95 (ISBN 0-252-00876-6). U of Ill Pr.

Pure Concept of Diplomacy. Jose Calvet De Magalhaes. Tr. by Bernardo F. Pereira. (Contributions in Political Science Ser.: No. 212). 1988. price not set (ISBN 0-313-26259-4, CPT/). Greenwood.

Pure Drop: A Book of Irish Drinking. John Killen. (Illus.). 196p. 1987. pap. 15.95 (ISBN 0-85640-385-7, Pub. by Blackstaff Ireland). Irish Bks Media.

Pure Economics. Maffeo Pantaleoni. 1957. Repr. of 1898 ed. 37.50x (ISBN 0-678-00674-1). Kelley.

Pure English of the Soil see Fate of French-E in English: The Plural of Nouns Ending in-th.

Pure Fabrication: Fabric Ideas for the Home. Maggie Colvin. LC 84-71909. 192p. (Orig.). 1985. pap. 15.95 (ISBN 0-8019-7603-0). Chilton.

Pure Gold. Bud Allen & Diana Bosta. 87p. 1981. vinyl 8.95 (ISBN 0-9605226-7-0). Rae John.

Pure Gold. Ole E. Rolvaag. Tr. by Sivert Erdahl. LC 73-11846. 346p. 1973. Repr. of 1930 ed. lib. bdg. 35.00x (ISBN 0-8371-7070-2, ROPG). Greenwood.

Pure Grace. Bro. Stanley. 96p. 1984. 6.95 (ISBN 0-89962-414-6). Todd & Honeywell.

Pure Joy: My Spiritual Journey Through India. Sondra Ray. 290p. 1988. pap. 9.95 (ISBN 0-89087-491-3). Celestial Arts.

Pure Land. David Foster. (Fiction Ser.). 240p. 1986. pap. 4.95 (ISBN 0-14-007700-6). Penguin.

Pure Land Buddhist Paintings. Joji Okazaki. Tr. by Elizabeth T. Grotenhuis from Japanese. LC 76-9354. (Japanese Arts Library: Vol. 4). 1977. 27.95 (ISBN 0-87011-287-2). Kodansha.

Pure Lives: The Early Biographers. Reed Whittemore. LC 87-16822. 176p. 1988. text ed. 16.95x (ISBN 0-8018-3548-8). Johns Hopkins.

Pure Logic & Other Minor Works. W. S. Jevons. 1986. lib. bdg. 25.00x (ISBN 0-318-20448-7); pap. text ed. 13.50x (ISBN 0-935005-49-8). Ibis Pub VA.

Pure Logic & Other Minor Works. W. Stanley Jevons. Ed. by R. Adamson & H. A. Jevons. LC 71-160420. (Research & Source Works Ser.: No. 773). 1971. Repr. of 1890 ed. lib. bdg. 22.50 (ISBN 0-8337-1842-8). B Franklin.

Pure Logic of Choice. Richard D. Fuerle. 1986. 13.95 (ISBN 0-533-06401-5). Vantage.

Pure Logistics. George C. Thorpe. LC 85-600393. 1986. pap. 4.25 (ISBN 0-318-20388-X, S/N 008-020-01055-3). USGPO.

Pure Lust: Elemental Feminist Philosophy. Mary Daly. LC 83-71944. 488p. 1984. pap. 11.95 (ISBN 0-8070-1505-9, BP 692). Beacon Pr.

Pure Magic! Henry Gross. LC 77-15069. (Illus.). 1978. 4.95 (ISBN 0-684-15338-6, SL 751, ScribT); (ScribJ). Scribner.

Pure Magic see Werefox.

Pure Mathematics. Godfrey H. Hardy. 1959. text ed. 75.00 (ISBN 0-521-05203-3). Cambridge U Pr.

Pure Mathematics, 2 vols. S. L. Parsonson. LC 70-100026. (Illus.). 1971. Vol. 1. text ed. 16.95x (ISBN 0-521-07683-8). Cambridge U Pr.

Pure Nostalgia: Memories of Early Iowa. Ed. by Carl Hamilton. (Illus.). 1979. pap. 11.95 (ISBN 0-8138-0976-2). Iowa St U Pr.

Pure Nostalgia: Memories of Early Iowa. Ed. by Carl Hamilton. (Iowa Heritage Collection). (Illus.). 212p. 1988. pap. 5.95t (ISBN 0-8138-0977-0). Iowa St U Pr.

Pure Notations. Steve Levine. LC 81-16404. (Illus., Orig.). 1981. signed 35.00 (ISBN 0-915124-51-3, Pub. by Toothpaste); pap. 6.00 (ISBN 0-915124-52-1, Bookslinger). Coffee Hse.

Pure Politics & Impure Science: The Swine Flu Affair. Arthur M. Silverstein. LC 81-47590. (Illus.). 192p. 1981. text ed. 22.50x (ISBN 0-8018-2632-2). Johns Hopkins.

Pure Pragmatics & Possible Worlds: The Early Essays of Wilfrid Sellars. Wilfrid Sellars. Ed. by Jeffrey Sicha. LC 78-65271. (Orig.). 1980. lib. bdg. 27.00 (ISBN 0-917930-26-6); pap. text ed. 10.40 (ISBN 0-917930-06-1). Ridgeview.

Pure Prairie League Songbook. 8.95 (ISBN 0-89524-127-7). Cherry Lane.

Pure Principle: An Introduction to the Philosophy of Shankara. Y. Keshava Menon & Richard F. Allen. xii, 127p. 1960. 3.50 (ISBN 0-87013-048-X). Mich St U Pr.

Pure Red Cell Aplasia. Emmanuel N. Dessypris. LC 87-27378. (Contemporary Medicine & Public Health Ser.). (Illus.). 176p. 1988. text ed. 32.50x (ISBN 0-8018-3572-0). Johns Hopkins.

Pure Silver: The Second Best of Everything. David Reid & Jonathan Jerald. 320p. 1988. pap. 10.95 (ISBN 0-15-679960-X). HarBraceJ.

Pure Sociology. 2nd ed. Lester F. Ward. LC 74-117916. 1970. Repr. of 1909 ed. 45.00x (ISBN 0-678-00653-9). Kelley.

Pure Spring: Craft & Craftsmen of the U. S. S. R. Alexander Milovsky. 255p. 1987. 13.95 (ISBN 0-8285-3590-6, Pub. by Raduga Pubs USSR). Imported Pubns.

Pure Theory of Capital. Friedrich A. Hayek. LC 41-2440. (Midway Reprint Ser.). xxxii, 454p. 1975. pap. 27.00x (ISBN 0-226-32081-2). U of Chicago Pr.

Pure Theory of Foreign Trade & the Pure Theory of Domestic Values. Alfred Marshall. LC 73-22013. (Illus.). Repr. of 1897 ed. lib. bdg. 15.00x (ISBN 0-678-01194-X). Kelley.

Pure Theory of Law. William Ebenstein. xii, 211p. 1970. Repr. of 1945 ed. text ed. 17.50x (ISBN 0-8377-2100-8). Rothman.

Pure Thoughts. Eileen C. Wood. 1985. 5.95 (ISBN 0-533-06662-X). Vantage.

Pure Types Are Rare: Myths & Meanings of Madness. Irwin Silverman. 144p. 1983. 35.00 (ISBN 0-275-91079-2, C1079). Praeger.

Pure Vegetarian Indian Cookery. Pritam Uberoi. 167p. 1983. pap. 12.95 (ISBN 0-940500-61-2, Pub. by Sterling India). Asia Bk Corp.

Pure Vegetarian Indian Cookery. Pritam Uberoi. 1983. 12.95. Asia Bk Corp.

Purely Original Verse. J. Gordon Coogler. (Illus.). 1974. Repr. limited ed. 6.00 (ISBN 0-686-09908-7). C H Neuffer.

Purer Than Diamond see Mas Puro Que el Diamante.

Pureza en el Hogar Cristiano. Paul M. Landis. (Span.). pap. 1.25 (ISBN 0-686-32330-0). Rod & Staff.

Purgatorio. Raul Zurita. Ed. by Yvette E. Miller. Tr. by Jeremy Jacobson. LC 85-8058. 96p. (Span. & Eng.). 1985. pap. 11.95 (ISBN 0-935480-21-8). Lat Am Lit Rev Pr.

Purgatorio see Divine Comedy.

Purgatorio by Dante. Tr. by John Ciardi. 1971. pap. 3.95 (ISBN 0-451-62206-5, ME2206, Ment). NAL.

Puritans & Radicals in North England: Essays on the English Revolution. Roger Howell, Jr. LC 84-10411. 226p. (Orig.). 1984. lib. bdg. 25.50 (ISBN 0-8191-4013-9); pap. text ed. 13.00 (ISBN 0-8191-4014-7). U Pr of Amer.

Puritans & Regicide: Presbiterian-Independent Difference over the Trial & Execution of Charles (I) Stuart. Noel H. Mayfield. 282p. (Orig.). 1988. lib. bdg. 24.50 (ISBN 0-8191-6773-8). U Pr of Amer.

Puritans & Revolutionaries: Essays in Seventeenth-Century History Presented to Christopher Hill. Ed. by Donald Pennington & Keith Thomas. 1982. Repr. of 1978 ed. 24.00x (ISBN 0-19-822686-1). Oxford U Pr.

Puritans & Yankees: Selected Articles on New England Colonial History, 1974-1984. Ed. by Peter C. Hoffer. (Early American History Ser.). 365p. 1987. lib. bdg. 60.00 (ISBN 0-8240-6235-3). Garland Pub.

Puritans in America: A Narrative Anthology. Ed. by Alan Heimert & Nicholas Delbanco. 456p. 1985. text ed. 27.00x (ISBN 0-674-74065-3); pap. text ed. 9.95x (ISBN 0-674-74066-1). Harvard U Pr.

Puritans: Their Origins & Successors. David M. Lloyd-Jones. 436p. 1987. 25.95 (ISBN 0-85151-496-0). Banner-of-Truth.

Purity: A Middle English Poem. Ed. by Robert J. Menner. LC 78-91187. (Yale Studies in English Ser.: No. 61). lxii, 230p. 1970. Repr. of 1920 ed. 26.00 (ISBN 0-208-00914-0, Archon). Shoe String.

Purity & Danger: An Analysis of the Concepts of Pollution & Taboo. Mary Douglas. 196p. 1984. pap. 6.95 (ISBN 0-7448-0011-0, Ark Paperbks). Routledge Chapman & Hall.

Purity & Defilement in Gulliver's Travels. Charles H. Hinnant. LC 87-4624. 128p. 1987. 29.95 (ISBN 0-312-00829-5). St Martin.

Purity & Pollution in Zoroastrianism: Triumph over Evil. Jamesheed K. Choksky. (Illus.). 204p. 1988. text ed. 22.50x (ISBN 0-292-79802-4). U of Tex Pr.

Purity Crusade: Sexual Morality & Social Control, 1868-1900. David J. Pivar. LC 70-179650. (Contributions in American History Ser.: No. 23). 308p. 1973. lib. bdg. 35.00 (ISBN 0-8371-6319-6, PPC/). Greenwood.

Purity Determinations by Thermal Methods - STP 838. Ed. by R. L. Blaine & C. K. Schoff. LC 83-72815. 150p. 1984. text ed. 24.00 (ISBN 0-8031-0222-4, 04-838000-40). ASTM.

Purity in the Christian Home. Paul M. Landis. 1978. 0.95 (ISBN 0-686-25260-8). Rod & Staff.

Purity Makes the Heart Grow Stronger: Sexuality & the Single Christian. Julia Duin. (Illus.). 150p. (Orig.). 1988. pap. 6.95 (ISBN 0-89283-373-4). Servant.

Purity of Childhood. Heini Arnold & Annemarie Arnold. 10p. 1974. pap. 1.25 (ISBN 0-87486-118-7). Plough.

Purity of Heart. Soren Kierkegaard. Tr. by Douglas Steere. pap. 8.95x (ISBN 0-06-130004-7, TB4, Torch). Har-Row.

Purloined Letter. Edgar Allan Poe. LC 86-4156. (Creative's Classic Short Stories Ser.). 48p. (YA) (gr. 9 up). 1986. PLB 8.95 (ISBN 0-88682-061-8). Creative Ed.

Purloined Paperweight. P. G. Wodehouse. LC 86-71036. 188p. 1986. Repr. of 1967 ed. 14.95 (ISBN 0-933756-09-7, Dist. by Charles Tuttle Publishing Co.). Paperweight Pr.

Purloined Poe: Lacan, Derrida, & Psychoanalytic Reading. Ed. by John P. Muller & William J. Richardson. LC 87-2760. 424p. 1988. text ed. 35.00x (ISBN 0-8018-3292-6); pap. text ed. 12.95x (ISBN 0-8018-3293-4). Johns Hopkins.

Puro Mexicano. Ed. by J. Frank Dobie. LC 75-26679. (Texas Folklore Society Publications Ser.: No. 12). 278p. 1980. Repr. of 1935 ed. 12.95 (ISBN 0-87074-041-5). SMU Press.

Puroxylin Plastics in Warehouses, Wholesale & Retail Stores. (Forty Ser). 1967. pap. 2.00 (ISBN 0-685-58099-7, 43). Natl Fire Prot.

Purpaleanie & Other Permutations. Sietze Buning. LC 78-61207. 1978. pap. 5.95 (ISBN 0-931940-00-1). Middleburg Pr.

Purple & Fine Women. Edgar Saltus. LC 79-182714. Repr. of 1925 ed. 17.50 (ISBN 0-404-05549-4). AMS Pr.

Purple & Green: Poems By 33 Women Poets. Ed. by Rivelin Grapheme Press Staff. 228p. 40.00x (ISBN 0-947612-15-7, Pub. by Rivelin Grapheme Pr); pap. 25.00x (ISBN 0-317-43697-X, Pub. by Rivelin Grapheme Pr). State Mutual Bk.

Purple Bear. Nancy Reese. Ed. by Alton Jordan. (Elephant Ser.). (Illus.). (gr. k-3). 1975. PLB 3.95 (ISBN 0-89868-013-1, Read Res); pap. text ed. 1.75 (ISBN 0-89868-046-8). ARO Pub.

Purple Bird. Yu. Kovol. 156p. 1985. pap. 2.99 (ISBN 0-8285-2797-0, Pub. by Raduga Pubs USSR). Imported Pubns.

Purple-Braided People. Shree Devi. 8.00 (ISBN 0-89253-652-7); flexible cloth 4.80 (ISBN 0-89253-653-5). Ind-US Inc.

Purple Climbing Days. Patricia R. Giff. (Kids of the Polk Street School Ser.: No. 9). (Illus.). 80p. (gr. 5 up). 1985. pap. 2.50 (ISBN 0-440-47309-8, YB). Dell.

Purple Climbing Days. Patricia R. Giff. (Kids of the Polk Street School Ser.). (Illus.). (ps-2). 1986. pap. 8.95 (ISBN 0-385-29500-6). Delacorte.

Purple Cloud. M. P. Shiel. lib. bdg. 14.95x (ISBN 0-89966-228-5). Buccaneer Bks.

Purple Cloud. M. P. Shiel. 1985. 29.00x (ISBN 0-900001-18-6, Pub. by Centaur Bks). State Mutual Bk.

Purple Coat. Amy Hest. LC 85-29186. (Illus.). 32p. (gr. k-3). 1986. 12.95 (ISBN 0-02-743640-3, Four Winds). Macmillan.

Purple Connection. Philip H. Warren. (Illus.). 140p. 1987. pap. 10.95 (ISBN 0-915081-01-6). Williams Coll.

Purple Cow--Handset Type. Miniature ed. Gelett Burgess. 1987. pap. 7.95 (ISBN 0-89979-039-9). British Am Bks.

Purple Cow & Its Parodies. Gelett Burgess & Carolyn Wells. 1987. pap. 4.95 (ISBN 0-89979-038-0). British Am Bks.

Purple Cow to the Rescue. Ann Cole & Carolyn Haas. LC 82-47913. (Illus.). 160p. (gr. 1-5). 1982. 14.95 (ISBN 0-316-15104-1); pap. 8.95 (ISBN 0-316-15106-8). Little.

Purple Cows & Potato Chips. MaryAnn Christison & Sharron Bassano. (Illus.). 120p. (gr. 5-12). 1987. pap. text ed. 14.95 (ISBN 0-88084-230-X). Alemany Pr.

Purple Decades: A Reader. Tom Wolfe. (Illus.). 416p. 1987. pap. 4.95 (ISBN 0-425-10345-5). Berkley Pub.

Purple Decades: A Reader. Tom Wolfe. (Illus.). 396p. 1982. 17.50 (ISBN 0-374-23927-4); limited ed. 60.00 (ISBN 0-374-23928-2). FS&G.

Purple Decades: A Reader. Tom Wolfe. 1987. pap. 7.95 (ISBN 0-425-06266-X). Berkley Pub.

Purple Dyeing: Ancient & Modern. (Shorey Historical Ser.). 220p. pap. 3.95 (ISBN 0-8466-4077-5, I77). Shorey.

Purple Ghosts of Damnation Row. Albert Wass. LC 84-72034. 272p. (Orig.). 1984. pap. 7.00 (ISBN 0-87934-030-4). Danubian.

Purple Is Part of the Rainbow. Carolyn Kowalczyk. LC 85-11693. (Rookie Readers Ser.). (Illus.). 32p. (gr. 1-2). 1985. PLB 9.93 (ISBN 0-516-02068-4); pap. 2.50 (ISBN 0-516-42068-2). Childrens.

Purple Island. Phineas Fletcher. LC 72-196. (English Experience Ser.: No. 313). 132p. 1971. Repr. of 1633 ed. 75.00 (ISBN 90-221-0313-7). Walter J Johnson.

Purple Land. William H. Hudson. Repr. of 1922 ed. 35.00 (ISBN 0-404-03391-1). AMS Pr.

Purple Level Student Book. Chicago Board of Education Staff. (Vocabulary Learning Strategies Ser.). (Orig.). (gr. 7). 1984. wkbk. 3.75 (ISBN 0-88106-087-9, 7130). Mastery Ed.

Purple Level Teacher Manual. Chicago Board of Education Staff. (Vocabulary Learning Strategies Ser.). (Orig.). (gr. 7). 1984. tchr's. ed. 12.00 (ISBN 0-88106-088-7, 7230). Mastery Ed.

Purple Martin. R. B. Layton. LC 71-92883. (Illus.). 192p. 1969. pap. 8.95x (ISBN 0-912542-01-2). Nature Bks Pubs.

Purple Power. Dick Dilley. (People Patch Ser.). (Illus.). 48p. (gr. 1-5). 1986. PLB 9.95 (ISBN 0-936535-02-4). People Patch.

Purple Prairie. 1987. pap. 3.95 (ISBN 0-317-64771-7). Herald Pr.

Purple Private. Talbot Mundy. Repr. lib. bdg. 21.95x (ISBN 0-89190-489-1, Pub. by River City Pr). Amereon Ltd.

Purple Pterodactyls: The Adventures of W. Wilson Newbury, Ensorcelled Financier. L. Sprague De Camp. (W. Wilson Newbury Ser.). 1979. 15.00 (ISBN 0-932096-02-6). Phantasia Pr.

Purple Pussycat. Margaret Hillert. (Just-Beginning-to-Read Ser.). (Illus.). 32p. (gr. k-3). 1980. PLB 4.39 (Dist. by Caroline Hse); pap. 1.95 (ISBN 0-8136-5572-2). Modern Curr.

Purple Runner. Paul Christman. 229p. (Orig.). 1983. pap. 8.95. Cedarwinds.

Purple Sage & Other Pleasures. Ed. by Junior League of Tucson. (Illus.). 256p. 18.95 (ISBN 0-9616403-0-8). Jr League Tucson.

Purple Sea Horse & Other Stories. Loretta M. King. LC 79-56712. (Illus., Orig.). (gr. k-3). 1979. pap. 4.95 (ISBN 0-934104-02-6). Woodland.

Purple Sea: More Splashes of Chinese Color. Frank Owen. Ed. by R. Reginald & Douglas Melville. LC 77-84262. (Lost Race & Adult Fantasy Ser.). 1978. Repr. of 1930 ed. lib. bdg. 17.00x (ISBN 0-405-11003-0). Ayer Co Pubs.

Purple Shit! Onspot - On Location in the Street. Philip L. Sherrod. 1986. write for info. Carrousel Pubns.

Purple Tale. John Judson. (Illus.). 1978. saddlestitched 2.00 (ISBN 0-912284-94-3). New Rivers Pr.

Purple Turkey & Other Thanksgiving Riddles. David A. Adler. LC 86-310. (Illus.). 64p. (gr. 1-4). 1986. reinforced bdg. 9.95 (ISBN 0-8234-0613-X). Holiday.

Purple Turtle's Mother Goose. Gilson Henry. Ed. by Ronnie Hansen. LC 87-62125. (Illus.). 24p. (ps-5). 1987. pap. 3.95 (ISBN 0-943925-02-9). Purple Turtle Pub.

Purple Turtles Say No, No, to Drugs. Gilson Henry. Ed. & illus. by Ronnie Hansen. LC 87-62124. (Illus.). 24p. (ps-4). 1987. pap. 3.95 (ISBN 0-943925-00-2). Purple Turtle Pub.

Purpose. Jim Wilson. 80p. pap. 4.50 (ISBN 0-227-67707-2). Attic Pr.

Purpose: A Little Gift in the Adventure of Life. Buddy Sears. 169p. (Orig.). 1986. pap. 6.95 (ISBN 0-87418-023-6, 160). Coleman Pub.

Purpose & Admiration: A Law Study of the Visual Arts. J. E. Barton. 1978. Repr. of 1933 ed. lib. bdg. 30.00 (ISBN 0-8492-3562-6). R West.

Purpose & Necessity in Social Theory. Maurice Mandelbaum. LC 86-46283. 224p. 1987. text ed. 25.00x (ISBN 0-8018-3470-8). Johns Hopkins.

Purpose & Pattern: A Rhetoric Reader. Elizabeth Penfield. 1982. pap. text ed. write for info. (ISBN 0-673-15459-9). Scott F.

Purpose & Process. Jeffrey D. Hoeper & James H. Pickering. 870p. 1989. text ed. price not set (ISBN 0-02-395470-1). Macmillan.

Purpose & Thought: The Meaning of Pragmatism. John E. Smith. LC 83-18136. 236p. 1984. pap. 8.95 (ISBN 0-226-76383-8). U of Chicago Pr.

Purpose, Financing & Governance of Museums: Three Conferences on Present & Future Issues. June B. Arey. 1978. pap. text ed. 2.50 (ISBN 0-932676-01-4). Spring Hill.

Purpose in Prayer. E. M. Bounds. (Direction Bks). 1978. pap. 3.95 (ISBN 0-8010-0738-0). Baker Bk.

Purpose of a Christian School. Ed. by David Cummings. 1979. pap. 4.50 (ISBN 0-87552-157-6). Presby & Reformed.

Purpose of American Politics. Hans J. Morgenthau. LC 82-20057. 382p. 1983. pap. text ed. 14.75 (ISBN 0-8191-2847-3). U Pr of Amer.

Purpose of Authority? Lucius Annese. LC 78-72295. (Orig.). 1978. 50.00 (ISBN 0-933402-12-0). Charisma Pr.

Purpose of Biblical Genealogies: With Special Reference to the Setting of the Genealogies of Jesus. 2nd ed. Marshall D. Johnson. (Society for New Testament Studies Monograph Ser.: No. 8). 340p. Date not set. price not set (ISBN 0-521-35644-X). Cambridge U Pr.

Purpose of Church-Related Colleges. Leslie K. Patton. LC 78-177145. (Columbia University. Studies in the Social Sciences: No. 783). Repr. of 1940 ed. 22.50 (ISBN 0-404-55783-X). AMS Pr.

Purpose of Forests. Jack Westoby. (Illus.). 320p. Date not set. text ed. 60.00 (ISBN 0-631-15657-7). Basil Blackwell.

Purpose of Genesis. Stephen D. Eckstein, Jr. 1976. pap. 2.75 (ISBN 0-88027-037-3). Firm Foun Pub.

Purpose of Higher Education. Johann G. Fichte. Tr. by Jorn K. Bramann. LC 87-63358. 1988. pap. 7.00 (ISBN 0-945073-04-6). Nightsun MD.

Purpose of History. Frederick J. Woodbridge. LC 65-27115. 1916. Repr. 16.50x (ISBN 0-8046-0513-0, Pub. by Kennikat). Assoc Faculty Pr.

Purpose of Islam. M. Yameen Zubairi. LC 84-90999. 100p. (Orig.). 1984. pap. text ed. write for info. (ISBN 0-930895-02-9). Byron Daven Pub.

Purpose of Life. Maximilian Beyer. LC 76-47246. 181p. 1977. 12.50 (ISBN 0-8022-2191-2). Philos Lib.

Purpose of Life. Satguru S. Keshavadas. LC 78-50754. (Illus.). 112p. 1978. 5.95 (ISBN 0-533-03147-8). Vishwa.

Purpose of Luke-Acts. Robert Maddox. Ed. by John Riches. 220p. 1982. 33.95 (ISBN 0-567-09312-3, Pub. by T&T Clark Ltd UK). Fortress.

Purpose of Physical Reality: The Kingdom of Names. John S. Hatcher. Ed. by Betty J. Fisher & Richard A. Hill. 250p. 1987. pap. 12.95 (ISBN 0-87743-208-2). Baha'i.

Purpose of the Church & Its Ministry. H. Richard Niebuhr. LC 76-62925. (Orig.). 1977. pap. 8.95 (ISBN 0-06-066174-7, RD 211, HarpR). Har-Row.

Purpose Perspective. Joanne S. Hayden. 1989. pap. price not set (ISBN 0-9619427-3-8). J S Hayden.

Purposes & Aims of the German American Bund. 1984. lib. bdg. 79.95 (ISBN 0-87700-567-2). Revisionist Pr.

Purposes & Conditions Affecting the Nature & Extent of Participation of Adults in Courses in the Home Study Department of Columbia University, 1925-1932. George B. Smith. LC 78-177772. (Columbia University. Teachers College. Contributions to Education: No. 663). Repr. of 1935 ed. 22.50 (ISBN 0-404-55663-9). AMS Pr.

Purposes & Leadership, Vol. 2. (Current Issues in Catholic Higher Education: No. 1). 50p. 1981. 2.40 (ISBN 0-318-17917-2). Natl Cath Educ.

Purposes of American Power: An Essay on National Security. Robert W. Tucker. LC 81-8675. 200p. 1981. 35.00 (ISBN 0-275-91704-5, C1704); pap. 12.95 (ISBN 0-275-91522-0, B1522). Praeger.

Purposes of Groups & Organizations. Alvin Zander. LC 85-45068. (Management Ser.). 1985. text ed. 24.95x (ISBN 0-87589-651-0). Jossey-Bass.

Purposes of Pentecost. Derek Prince. (Foundation Ser.: Bk. IV). 1965-66. pap. 3.95 (ISBN 0-934920-03-6). Derek Prince.

Purposes of Pleasure. Richard A. Hawley. (gr. 9-12). 1983. pap. text ed. 7.95x (ISBN 0-88334-171-9). Ind Sch Pr.

Purposes of Reference Measurement. 81p. 1978. 4.50 (ISBN 0-317-34819-1). Library Admin.

Purposive Behavior in Animals & Men. Edward C. Tolman. LC 67-20666. (Century Psychology Ser.). (Illus.). 1967. text ed. 49.50x (ISBN 0-89197-544-6). Irvington.

Purposive Behaviour & Teleological Explanations. Ed. by Frank George & Les Johnson. (Studies in Cybernetics: Vol. 8). 334p. 1985. text ed. 64.00 (ISBN 2-88124-110-7). Gordon & Breach.

Purposive Biology. Li Kung Shaw. LC 81-90747. (Illus.). 359p. 1982. text ed. 20.00 (ISBN 0-9607806-0-2); pap. text ed. 15.00 (ISBN 0-9607806-1-0). Li Kung Shaw.

Purposive Brain. Ragnar Granit. 1977. text ed. 27.50x (ISBN 0-262-07069-3); pap. 7.95x (ISBN 0-262-57054-8). MIT Pr.

Purposive Explanation in Psychology. Margaret A. Boden. LC 73-169858. (Illus.). 432p. 1972. 29.50x (ISBN 0-674-73902-7). Harvard U Pr.

Purr Baby, Furr Baby. Jean Fredeking. (Illus.). 40p. 1988. 8.95 (ISBN 0-913211-55-9, Am Liberty Pub). Jackson Assocs.

Purrfect Parenting. Beverly Guhl & Don Fontenelle. 160p. 1987. pap. 7.95 (ISBN 1-55561-004-8). Fisher Bks.

Purse. Kathy Caple. LC 86-2889. (Illus.). 32p. (gr. k-3). 1986. 12.95 (ISBN 0-395-41852-6). HM.

Purse. Nieh Hua-Ling. 95p. 1980. 10.95 (ISBN 0-89955-173-4, Pub. by Mei Ya China). Intl Spec Bk.

Purse-Seining With Small Boats. (FAO Training Ser.: No. 13). 97p. (Orig.). 1987. pap. text ed. 12.00 (ISBN 92-5-102267-4, F3109, FAO). UNIPUB.

Purser's Handbook. William E. Armstrong. LC 65-21748. 287p. 1966. 10.00x (ISBN 0-87033-086-1). Cornell Maritime.

Pursue & Destroy. Leonard C. Carson. (Illus.). 1978. text ed. 19.95 (ISBN 0-913194-05-0). Sentry.

Pursued. rev. ed. J. Vera Schlamm & Bob Friedman. LC 86-600. 189p. 1986. pap. 3.95 (ISBN 0-8307-1146-5, 5018631). Regal.

Pursued by the Crooked Man. Susan Trott. Date not set. 16.95 (ISBN 0-317-67703-9). Har-Row.

Pursuing a Just & Durable Peace: John Foster Dulles & International Organization. Anthony C. Arend. LC 87-37552. (Contributions in Political Science Ser.: No. 212). 256p. 1988. lib. bdg. 39.95 (ISBN 0-313-25637-3, ADJ/). Greenwood.

Pursuing Excellence in a Time of Declining Resources - The Role of Automated Information Systems: Proceedings, Ninth Annual MSIS National Users Group Conference. Ed. by Joan DiBlasi et al. (Orig.). 1986. pap. 20.00 (ISBN 0-936934-05-0). N S Kline Inst.

Pursuing Food Security: Strategies & Obstacles in Africa, Asia, Latin America, & the Middle East. Ed. by W. Ladd Hollist & F. LaMond Tullis. LC 87-4524. (International Political Economy Yearbook: Vol. 3). 390p. 1987. lib. bdg. 40.00x (ISBN 1-55587-032-5); pap. text ed. 16.95x (ISBN 1-55587-033-3). Lynne Rienner.

Pursuing Innocent Pleasures: The Gardening World of Alexander Pope. Peter Martin. LC 84-488. (Illus.). xvii, 309p. 1985. 35.00 (ISBN 0-208-02011-X, Archon Bks). Shoe String.

Pursuing Justice for the Child. Ed. by Margaret K. Rosenheim. LC 75-43238. (Studies in Crime & Justice). (Illus.). 1976. lib. bdg. 22.50x (ISBN 0-226-72789-0). U of Chicago Pr.

Pursuing Justice for the Child. Ed. by Margaret K. Rosenheim. LC 75-43238. (Studies in Crime & Justice). (Illus.). 1978. pap. 6.50X (ISBN 0-226-72788-2, P774, Phoen). U of Chicago Pr.

Pursuing Justice in a Sinful World. Stephen V. Monsma. 100p. (Orig.). 1984. pap. 6.95 (ISBN 0-8028-0023-8). Eerdmans.

Pursuing Life's Adventures. Dorothy M. Schmidt. LC 85-40650. 168p. 1985. pap. 5.95 (ISBN 0-938232-84-3, Dist. by Baker & Taylor Co.). Winston-Derek.

Pursuing Melville: Nineteen Forty to Nineteen Eighty. Merton M. Sealts, Jr. LC 81-70014. 432p. 1982. 32.50x (ISBN 0-299-08870-7). U of Wis Pr.

Pursuing the American Dream. Ed. by Kenneth S. Knodt. 336p. 1976. pap. text ed. write for info. (ISBN 0-13-742742-5). P-H.

Pursuing the Just Cause of Their People: A Study of Contemporary Armenian Terrorism. Michael M. Gunter. LC 85-27295. (Contributions in Political Science Ser.: No. 152). 190p. 1986. lib. bdg. 35.00 (ISBN 0-313-25247-5, GUA/). Greenwood.

Pursuing the Whale: A Quarter Century of Whaling in the Arctic. John A. Cook. 1977. lib. bdg. 59.95 (ISBN 0-8490-2493-5). Gordon Pr.

Pursuit. Michael French. LC 82-70319. 192p. (gr. 7 up). 1982. 9.95 (ISBN 0-385-28781-X). Delacorte.

Pursuit. Michael French. 192p. (YA) (gr. 9 up). 1983. pap. 2.95 (ISBN 0-440-96665-5, LFL). Dell.

Pursuit. James S. Thayer. LC 85-14997. 416p. 1986. 15.95 (ISBN 0-517-55813-0). Crown.

Pursuit. James S. Thayer. 416p. 1987. pap. 3.95 (ISBN 0-446-34479-6). Warner Bks.

Pursuit-Evasion Differential Games: I.S. in Modern Applied Mathematics & Computer Science. Ed. by Y. Yavin & M. Pachter. (International Series in Modern Applied Mathematics & Computer Science: No. 14). 250p. 1987. 89.00 (ISBN 0-08-034862-9, PBL). Pergamon.

Pursuit Games: An Introduction to the Theory & Applications of Differential Games of Pursuit & Evasion. Otomar Hajek. (Mathematics in Science & Engineering Ser.). 1975. 49.50 (ISBN 0-12-317260-8). Acad Pr.

Pursuit of a Dream. Janet S. Hermann. (Illus.). 1981. 21.95x (ISBN 0-19-502887-2). Oxford U Pr.

Pushkin Museum of Fine Arts. 1981. 69.00x (ISBN 0-317-14317-4, Pub. by Collets (UK)). State Mutual Bk.

Pushkin Museum of Fine Arts, Moscow Painting. Irina Antonova. 176p. 1983. 50.00x (ISBN 0-317-57422-1, Pub. by Collets UK). State Mutual Bk.

Pushkin Museum of Fine Arts Painting. 128p. 30.00x (ISBN 0-317-14281-X, Pub. by Collets (UK)). State Mutual Bk.

Pushkin on Literature. Pushkin. Ed. & tr. by Tatiana Wolff. LC 85-51799. 580p. 1986. Repr. of 1971 ed. 39.50x (ISBN 0-8047-1322-7). Stanford U Pr.

Pushkin State Museum of Fine Arts. I. A. Antonova. (Rus. & Fr.). 1981. 116.00x (ISBN 0-317-57423-X, Pub. by Collets UK). State Mutual Bk.

Pushkin's Drawings: Risunki Pushkina. 446p. 1983. 32.00x (ISBN 0-317-57434-5, Pub. by Collets UK). State Mutual Bk.

Pushkin's "Egyptian Nights" The Bibliography of a Work. Leslie O'Bell. 160p. 1984. 21.50 (ISBN 0-88233-925-7). Ardis Pubs.

Pushkin's I. P. Belkin. Andrej Kodjak. 112p. 1979. pap. 9.95 (ISBN 0-89357-057-5). Slavica.

Pushkin's Prose. A. Lezhnev. Tr. by Roberta Reeder. 225p. pap. 45.00x (ISBN 0-317-40744-9, Pub. by Collets UK). State Mutual Bk.

Pushkin's Prose. Abram Lezhnev. Tr. by Roberta Reeder from Rus. Orig. Title: Proza Pushkina. 300p. 1983. 27.95 (ISBN 0-88233-627-4). Ardis Pubs.

Pushkinskill Dom. Andrei Bitov. (Rus.). 1978. pap. 8.95 (ISBN 0-88233-351-8). Ardis Pubs.

Pusillum, 4 vols. Athanasius Bierbaum. Vol. 1. 7.50 (ISBN 0-8199-0089-3, L38675). Vol. 2 (ISBN 0-8199-0090-7). Vol. 3 (ISBN 0-8199-0091-5). Vol. 4 (ISBN 0-8199-0092-3). Set. Franciscan Herald.

Puskin & His Sculptural Myth. Roman Jakobson. Ed. & tr. by John Burbank. (De Proprietatibus Litterarum, Ser Practica: No. 116). (Illus.). 88p. (Orig.). 1975. pap. text ed. 15.75x (ISBN 90-2793-426-6). Mouton.

Puss in Books & Other Stories. Retold by Anne Rockwell. LC 87-14976. 96p. 1988. 15.95. Macmillan.

Puss in Boots. Lorinda B. Cauley. LC 86-7629. (Illus.). 32p. (ps-1). 1986. 13.95 (ISBN 0-15-264227-7, HJ). HarBraceJ.

Puss in Boots. Retold by Lorinda B. Cauley. (Illus.). 32p. (gr. k-4). 1988. 3.95 (VoyB). HarBraceJ.

Puss in Boots. Margaret Davidson & Carson Davidson. (Make Believe It's You Ser.). (Illus.). 80p. (Orig.). (gr. 2-6). 1987. pap. 2.25 (ISBN 0-590-41088-1). Scholastic Inc.

Puss In Boots. Mark Friesen. (Children's Theatre Playscript ser.). 1986. pap. 2.50x (ISBN 0-88020-119-3). Coach Hse.

Puss in Boots. Paul Galdone. LC 75-25505. (Illus.). 32p. (ps-4). 1976. 7.95 (ISBN 0-395-28808-8, Clarion). HM.

Puss in Boots. Paul Galdone. LC 75-25505. 32p. (gr. k-3). 1983. pap. 3.95 (ISBN 0-89919-192-4, Pub. by Clarion). Ticknor & Fields.

Puss in Boots. Ed McBain. LC 86-22887. 1987. 15.95 (ISBN 0-8050-0371-1). H Holt & Co.

Puss in Boots. Ed McBain. 1988. pap. 3.95. Mysterious Pr.

Puss in Boots. Illus. by Morin. (Picture Classics Ser.). (Illus.). 32p. (ps up). 1988. 8.95 (ISBN 0-8120-5901-8). Barron.

Puss in Boots. Sally Netzel. (Illus.). 32p. 1979. pap. 2.50 (ISBN 0-88680-157-5); royalty 25.00 (ISBN 0-317-03611-4). I E Clark.

Puss in Boots. new ed. Charles Perrault. LC 78-18061. (Illus.). 32p. (gr. k-3). 1979. PLB 9.79 (ISBN 0-89375-130-8); pap. 1.95 (ISBN 0-89375-108-1). Troll Assocs.

Puss in Boots. Charles Perrault. LC 84-52784. (Tell Me a Story Ser.). (Illus.). 18p. (ps-1). 1985. 3.75 (ISBN 0-382-09069-1). Silver.

Puss in Boots. Charles Perrault. LC 85-81137. (Golden Storytime Bks.). (Illus.). 24p. (ps-1). 1987. pap. 2.95 (ISBN 0-307-11969-6, Golden Bks). Western Pub.

Puss in Boots. (Illus., Arabic.). (gr. 2-6). 3.50x (ISBN 0-86685-220-4). Intl Bk Ctr.

Puss in Boots. abr. ed. (Pic-a-Story Bks.). (Illus.). 24p. (gr. k-1). 1981. 4.95 (ISBN 0-89531-106-2); pap. 1.95 (ISBN 0-686-79396-X). Sharon Pubns.

Puss in Boots. (Favorite Tale Pop-Up Bks.). (Illus.). (ps-1). 1.79 (ISBN 0-517-46234-6). Outlet Bk Co.

Puss in Boots. (Classic Fairytales Pop-Ups Ser.). (Illus.). (ps-1). 1.98 (ISBN 0-517-39464-2). Outlet Bk Co.

Puss-In-Boots. Sabrina Saponaro. (Once upon a Time Ser.). (Illus.). 30p. (ps-1). 1987. 3.95 (ISBN 0-8120-5810-0). Barron.

Puss in Boots & Other Stories. As told by & illus. by Anne Rockwell. LC 87-14976. (Illus.). 96p. (gr. k-4). 1988. PLB 15.95 (ISBN 0-02-777861-2). Macmillan.

Puss in Boots: Fairy Tales. Perrault. Ed. by Tony Tallarico. (Tuffy Story Bks). (Illus.). 32p. (ps-3). 1987. pap. text ed. 2.95 (ISBN 0-89828-329-9, 83299). Tuffy Bks.

Puss 'N Boots. Paul Galdone. (Book & Cassette Favorites Ser.). (ps-3). 1987. incl. cass. 6.95 (ISBN 0-317-64571-4). HM.

Puss 'n Boots. (Fr.). (gr. k-3). 9.95 (ISBN 0-685-28440-9). French & Eur.

Pussy Cat, Pussy Cat. Ferelith E. Williams. (Nursery Rhyme Board Bks.). (Illus.). 8p. (ps-k). 1985. 4.95 (ISBN 0-437-86009-4, Pub. by Worlds Work). David & Charles.

Pussycat Kite. Sharon Peters. LC 84-8632. (Giant First Start Reader Ser.). (Illus.). 32p. (gr. k-2). 1985. PLB 9.89 (ISBN 0-8167-0358-2); pap. text ed. 2.95 (ISBN 0-8167-0438-4). Troll Assocs.

Pussycat Tales. 128p. 1987. 24.00x (ISBN 0-948397-86-1, Pub. by M O'Mara UK). State Mutual Bk.

Put a Frog in Your Pocket. Mary L. Blansett & Lorraine Schimminger. (Illus.). 112p. (gr. 3-6). 1985. guide 7.95 (ISBN 0-86530-085-2, IP 85-2). Incentive Pubns.

Put a Little Starch in Your Faith. Otis Bernard. 150p. 1980. pap. 4.95 (ISBN 0-89221-095-8). New Leaf.

Put-Down Pro: Getting along With Friends. Jack Canario. (Read on! - Write on! Ser.). (Illus.). 64p. (gr. 6-12). 1980. pap. text ed. 3.95 (ISBN 0-915510-39-1). Janus Bks.

Put It in Writing. David Blot & David Davidson. 150p. 1988. pap. text ed. 8.50 (ISBN 0-06-632137-9). Newbury Hse.

Put It in Writing. E. Ellman. 1984. pap. 23.95 (ISBN 0-442-22171-1). Van Nos Reinhold.

Put it in Writing. 3rd ed. Albert M. Joseph. LC 86-81013. 114p. 1986. write for info. (ISBN 0-911481-02-8). Intl Writing Inst.

Put it in Writing. 2nd ed. Albert M. Joseph. LC 72-90427. 101p. 1979. write for info. Intl Writing Inst.

Put It in Writing. John Whale. 151p. 1987. 12.95 (ISBN 0-460-04582-2, Pub. by J. M. Dent England). Biblio Dist.

Put It in Writing, Bk. 1. Brian Schenk. (Writing Ser.). (Orig.). 1986. pap. text ed. 3.65 (ISBN 0-8428-9717-8); wkbk. 1.95 (ISBN 0-8428-9720-8). Cambridge Bk.

Put It in Writing, Bk. 2. Brian Schenk & Laura Daly. (Put It in Writing Ser.). 128p. 1986. pap. text ed. 3.65 (ISBN 0-8428-9718-6); wkbk. 1.95 (ISBN 0-8428-9721-6). Cambridge Bk.

Put It in Writing, Bk. 3. Ed. by Laura Daly. (Writing Ser.). 1987. pap. text ed. 3.65 (ISBN 0-8428-9719-4); wkbk. 1.95 (ISBN 0-8428-9722-4). Cambridge Bk.

Put It in Writing: A Complete Guide for Preparing Employee Policy Handbooks. Edgar S. Ellman. 160p. 1983. pap. 23.95 comb-bound (ISBN 0-8436-0884-6). Van Nos Reinhold.

Put It in Writing: Writing Activities for Students of ESL. David Blot & David Davidson. (Illus.). 104p. (Orig.). 1981. pap. text ed. 8.50 (ISBN 0-88377-175-6). Newbury Hse.

Put Me in the Zoo. Robert Lopshire. LC 60-13494. (Illus.). 72p. (gr. 1-2). 1960. 5.95 (ISBN 0-394-80017-6); lib. bdg. 6.99 (ISBN 0-394-90017-0). Beginner.

Put More Leadership into Your Style. Elwood N. Chapman. 144p. 1984. pap. text ed. write for info. (ISBN 0-574-20710-4, 13-3710); leader's guide avail. (ISBN 0-574-20711-2, 13-3711). SRA.

Put on My Crown. Betty Levin. 208p. (gr. 7 up). 1985. 12.95 (ISBN 0-525-67163-3, 01258-430). Lodestar Bks.

Put on Your Dancing Shoes. Nancy Telfer. Ed. by Frances Clark & Louise Goss. 12p. 1985. pap. text ed. 2.95 (ISBN 0-913277-16-9). New Schl Mus Study.

Put' Otrecheniya. Mark Altshuller & Elena Dryzhakova. LC 85-24728. 350p. (Rus.). 1985. pap. 16.50 (ISBN 0-938920-53-7). Hermitage.

Put Out. David L. Barre. 53p. (Orig.). 1986. pap. 6.95 (ISBN 0-934553-03-3). Wainwright.

Put out More Flags. Evelyn Waugh. 1977. 15.95 (ISBN 0-316-92615-9); pap. 7.95 (ISBN 0-316-92612-4). Little.

Put out the Light. Sara Woods. 224p. 1985. 13.95 (ISBN 0-312-65702-1). St Martin.

Put Out the Light. Sara Woods. 240p. 1987. pap. 3.50 (ISBN 0-380-70476-5). Avon.

Put That in Writing. Jonathan Price. 224p. 1984. pap. 5.95 (ISBN 0-14-007338-8). Penguin.

Put That in Writing. Jonathan Price. 224p. 1984. 15.95 (ISBN 0-670-79149-0). Viking.

Put the Law on Your Side: Strategies for Winning the Legal Game. Bertram Harnett. LC 84-25196. 384p. 1985. 17.95 (ISBN 0-15-175352-0). HarBraceJ.

Put the Law on Your Side: Strategies for Winning the Legal Game. Bertram Harnett. LC 86-45112. 336p. 1986. pap. 6.95 (ISBN 0-06-097056-1, PL/7056, PL). Har-Row.

Put Your Arms Around the World. Marcus V. Hand. LC 78-66976. 112p. (Orig.). 1978. pap. text ed. 1.25 (ISBN 0-87148-698-9). Pathway Pr.

Put Your Degree to Work: Job-Hunting Success for the New Professional. Marcia R. Fox. 1979. pap. 7.95 (ISBN 0-393-00938-6). Norton.

Put Your Degree to Work: The New Professional's Guide to Career Planning & Job Hunting. 2nd ed. Marcia R. Fox. 1988. 17.95 (ISBN 0-393-02580-2); pap. 8.95 (ISBN 0-393-30550-3). Norton.

Put Your English to Work. David Prince & Julia Gage. (Illus.). 160p. 1986. pap. text ed. 9.95 (ISBN 0-13-744350-1). P-H.

Put Your Foot in Your Mouth & Other Silly Sayings. James A. Cox. LC 80-12877. (Step-up Book: No. 31). (Illus.). 72p. (gr. 2-5). 1980. bds. 3.95 (ISBN 0-394-84503-X). Random.

Put Your Future in Ruins: Essays in Honor of Robert Jehu Bull. Ed. by Henry O. Thompson. LC 85-51754. 160p. (Orig.). 1985. pap. text ed. 14.95x (ISBN 0-932269-65-6). Wyndham Hall.

Put Your Mind at Ease. Joyce S. Hifler. 128p. (Orig.). 1983. pap. 7.75 (ISBN 0-687-34929-X). Abingdon.

Put Your Money Down: Buying on Credit. Marilyn Thypin & Lynne Glasner. LC 78-12666. (Consumer Education Ser.). 1979. pap. text ed. 3.95 (ISBN 0-88436-510-7, 30255). EMC.

Put Your Money Where Your Mouth Is: How to Make a Fortune from Public Speaking. Robert Anthony. 176p. 1985. pap. 3.50 (ISBN 0-425-08030-7). Berkley Pub.

Put Your Mother on the Ceiling. Robert Demille. 1976. pap. 4.95 (ISBN 0-14-004379-9). Penguin.

Put Your Mother on the Ceiling: Children's Imagination Games. Richard De Mille. 192p. 1981. 9.95 (ISBN 0-915520-39-7). Santa Barb Pr.

Put Your Psychic Powers to Work: A Practical Guide to Parapsychology. Evelyn Monahan & Terry Bakken. LC 73-84208. 151p. 1973. 16.95 (ISBN 0-88229-132-7). Nelson-Hall.

Put Yourself on the Fast Track: A Guide for Supervisors & Managers Who Want to Get Promoted. Doug Mealy. LC 84-28648. (Illus.). 104p. 1986. pap. 9.95 (ISBN 0-88280-110-4). ETC Pubns.

Putain Respectueuse. Jean-Paul Sartre. Bd. with Morts Sans Sepulture. (Folio Ser.: No. 868). pap. 6.95 (ISBN 0-685-35916-6). Schoenhof.

Putain Respectueuse. Jean-Paul Sartre. Incl. Morts Sans Sepulture. write for info.. write for info. French & Eur.

Putain Respectueuse see Diable et le Bon Dieu.

Putain Respectueuse see Theatre.

Putera Reports: Problems in Indonesian-Japanese Wartime Co-Operation. Mohammad Hatta. Tr. & intro. by William H. Frederick. 114p. 1971. pap. 4.00 (ISBN 0-87763-009-7). Cornell Mod Indo.

Puteshestvie V Arzrum. Aleksandr Pushkin. (Illus., Rus.). 1978. pap. 4.00 (ISBN 0-88233-454-9). Ardis Pubs.

Puteshestvie V. Drevnost' V. L. Janin. 270p. (Rus.). 1983. 39.00x (ISBN 0-317-40803-8, Pub. by Collets (UK)). State Mutual Bk.

Putevoditel' Po Bibliografii. Aleksandr G. Fomin. Repr. of 1934 ed. 24.00 (ISBN 0-384-16350-5). Johnson Repr.

Puti Izgnaniia. Zinaida Zhemchuzhnaia. LC 87-8905. (Illus.). 302p. (Rus.). 1987. pap. 14.00 (ISBN 0-938920-88-X). Hermitage.

Putian Respectueuse see Diable et le Bon Dieu.

Putman's Digital Electronics: Lac Manual. James W. Nice. (Illus.). 144p. 1986. text ed. 16.00 (ISBN 0-13-212549-8). P-H.

Putnam Anniversary Volume: Anthropological Essays Presented to Frederic Ward Putnam, in Honor of His Seventieth Birthday, April 16, 1909, by His Friends & Associates. Ed. by Stephen Williams. LC 72-5222. (Illus.). Repr. of 1909 ed. 62.50 (ISBN 0-404-10626-9). AMS Pr.

Putnam Division. Daniel Gallo & Frederick Kramer. 1981. pap. 8.95 (ISBN 0-915276-29-1). Quadrant Pr.

Putnam's Geology. 5th, rev. ed. Peter W. Birkeland & Edwin E. Larson. (Illus.). 768p. 1989. text ed. 49.95 (ISBN 0-19-505630-2); pap. text ed. 26.95 (ISBN 0-19-505517-9). Oxford U Pr.

Putnam's Geology. 4th ed. Ed. by Peter W. Birkeland & Edwin E. Larson. (Illus.). 1982. text ed. 31.95x (ISBN 0-19-503002-8); tchr's. manual avail. (ISBN 0-19-503004-4); study guide 11.95x (ISBN 0-19-503003-6). Oxford U Pr.

Putnam's Handbook of Expression. 1915. 15.00 (ISBN 0-8274-3230-5). R West.

Putnam's Minute-a-Day English for Busy People. Compiled by Edwin H. Carr. 316p. 1983. Repr. of 1921 ed. text ed. 40.00. Century Bookbindery.

Putnam's Phrase Book: An Aid to Social Letter Writing & to Ready & Effective Conversation. Compiled by Edwin H. Carr. 327p. 1983. Repr. of 1919 ed. text ed. 40.00. Century Bookbindery.

Putnam's Word Book: A Practical Aid in Expressing Ideas Through the Use of an Exact & Varied Vocabulary. Louis A. Flemming. 709p. 1983. Repr. of 1913 ed. text ed. 40.00. Century Bookbindery.

Putney School. Susan M. Lloyd. LC 86-24638. 294p. 1987. 27.50x (ISBN 0-300-03742-2). Yale U Pr.

Putt Like the Pros: Dave Peltz's Scientific Way to Improving Your Stroke, Reading Greens, & Lowering Your Score. Dave Peltz & Nick Mastroni. LC 86-46095. (Illus.). 192p. 1988. 17.95 (ISBN 0-06-015745-3, HarpT). Har-Row.

Putt Like the Pros: Dave Pelz's Scientific Guide to Improving Your Stroke, Reading Greens & Lowering Your Score. Dave Pelz. 1988. 17.95 (ISBN 0-317-67798-5). Har-Row.

Puttering Around in a Small Land. Philip K. Dick. 291p. 1985. 16.95 (ISBN 0-89733-149-4). Academy Chi Pubs.

Puttin' on the Peachtree. Compiled by Junior League of Dekalb County. 352p. 1979. 8.95 (ISBN 0-918544-69-6). Wimmer Bks.

Putting a Lid on Legal Fees: How to Deal Effectively with Lawyers. Raymond M. Klein. LC 86-82987. (Illus.). 192p. 1987. 27.50 (ISBN 0-9617950-7-7); pap. 17.95 (ISBN 0-9617950-8-5). Interlink Pr.

Putting a Plough to the Ground: Accumulation & Dispossession in Rural South Africa, 1850-1930. Ed. by William Beinart et al. 480p. 1986. pap. 23.95x (ISBN 0-86975-283-9, Pub. by Ravan Pr). Ohio U Pr.

Putting America Back to Work: The Kellogg Leadership Initiative. Ed. by James Mahoney. (Illus.). 58p. (Orig.). 1984. pap. 8.50 (ISBN 0-87117-134-1). Am Assn Comm Jr Coll.

Putting America First: A Conservative Trade Alternative. Anthony H. Harrigan et al. LC 87-50998. (Illus.). 86p. (Orig.). 1987. pap. 6.95 (ISBN 0-944468-00-4). USIC Ed Found.

Putting Artifical Intelligence to Work: Evaluating & Implementing Business Applications. Sy Schoen & Wendell Sykes. LC 87-15940. 264p. 1987. pap. 24.95 (ISBN 0-471-85704-1). Wiley.

Putting Asunder: A History of Divorce in Western Society. Roderick Phillips. (Illus.). 816p. Date not set. 39.50 (ISBN 0-521-32434-3). Cambridge U Pr.

Putting Away Childish Things. David A. Seamands. 144p. 1982. pap. 5.95 (ISBN 0-88207-308-7). Victor Bks.

Putting Children First: A Volume in Honor of Mia Kellmer Pringle. Ed. by Ian Vallender & Ken Fogelman. 200p. 1987. 36.00x (ISBN 1-85000-218-5, Falmer Pr); pap. 19.00x (ISBN 1-85000-219-3, Falmer Pr). Taylor & Francis.

Putting Christ First: A Woman's Workshop on Colossians. Margaret Fromer & Paul Fromer. Ed. by Janet Kobobel. (Woman's Workshop Ser.). 128p. 1986. pap. 5.95 (ISBN 0-310-44801-8, 11313P). Zondervan.

Putting Computer Power in School: A Step-by-Step Approach. Jerry L. Patterson & Janice H. Patterson. 1984. 17.95x (ISBN 0-317-38248-9, Parker); pap. 12.95 (ISBN 0-317-38249-7). P-H.

Putting Computer Power in Schools: A Step-by-Step Approach. Jerry L. Patterson & Janice H. Patterson. LC 83-8017. 227p. 1983. 17.95x (ISBN 0-13-744474-5, Busn); pap. 12.95 (ISBN 0-13-744467-2). P-H.

Putting Dell on the Map: A History of the Dell Paperbacks. William H. Lyles. LC 83-1641. (Contributions to the Study of Popular Culture Ser.: No. 5). xxiv, 178p. 1983. lib. bdg. 35.00 (ISBN 0-313-23667-4, LPD/). Greenwood.

Putting Democracy to Work: A Practical Guide for Starting Worker-Owned Businesses. Frank T. Adams & Gary B. Hansen. LC 87-4246. 360p. 1987. pap. 14.95 (ISBN 0-938493-03-5). Hulogos'i Inc.

Putting Expert Systems into Practice. Robert G. Bowerman & David E. Glover. (Illus.). 384p. 1988. 39.95 (ISBN 0-442-20842-1). Van Nos Reinhold.

Putting Food by. 4th ed. Janet Greene et al. (Illus.). 512p. 1988. 22.95 (ISBN 0-8289-0644-0); pap. 9.95 (ISBN 0-8289-0645-9). Greene.

Putting Food by. 3rd ed. Ruth Hertzberg et al. LC 82-9176. (Illus.). 550p. 1984. 18.95 (ISBN 0-8289-0468-5); pap. 11.95 deluxe ed. (ISBN 0-8289-0469-3); pap. 7.95 (ISBN 0-8289-0538-X). Greene.

Putting Forgiveness into Practice. Doris Donnelly. LC 82-71967. 192p. 1982. 8.95 (ISBN 0-89505-087-0). Tabor Pub.

Putting God First. Jim Burns. (Illus.). 64p. (gr. 7-10). 1983. wkbk. 4.95 (ISBN 0-89081-366-3). Harvest Hse.

Putting God First: The Tithe. Norma Gaskill. (Orig.). 1988. pap. 4.95 (ISBN 0-88177-058-2, DR058B). Discipleship Res.

Putting It All Together: A Guide to Strategic Thinking. William E. Rothschild. LC 76-10535. (Illus.). 272p. 1976. 17.95 (ISBN 0-8144-5405-4). AMACOM.

Putting It All Together: A Guide to Strategic Thinking. William E. Rothschild. LC 76-10535. 272p. 1981. pap. 7.95 (ISBN 0-8144-7555-8). AMACOM.

Putting It All Together in a Puppet Ministry. Fredda Marsh. LC 77-91674. (Illus.). 144p. 1978. pap. 6.95 (ISBN 0-88243-578-7, 02-0578). Gospel Pub.

Putting It Together. Michael T. Meyer & Don Meyer. 160p. 1985. pap. text ed. 17.95 (ISBN 0-8403-3648-9). Kendall-Hunt.

Putting It Together. Nieman & Sokolow. LC 83-72008. 200p. 1984. 13.00 (ISBN 0-86690-257-0, 2402-01). Am Fed Astrologers.

Putting It Together: Teenagers Talk about Family Breakup. Paula McGuire. LC 86-29238. 224p. (YA) (gr. 7 up). 1987. pap. 15.95 (ISBN 0-385-29564-2). Delacorte.

Putting It up with Honey. Susan Geiskopf. LC 78-59871. 224p. 1979. pap. 7.95 (ISBN 0-930356-13-6). Quicksilver Prod.

Putting Junior to Work: A Guide to the IBM PCjr. Donald Trivette. Ed. by Compute Editors. 164p. (Orig.). 1985. pap. 8.95 (ISBN 0-942386-90-6). Compute Pubns.

Putting Knowledge to Use: Facilitating the Diffusion of Knowledge & the Implementation of Planned Change. Edward M. Glaser et al. LC 83-11281. (Social & Behavioral Science Ser.). 1983. text ed. 42.95x (ISBN 0-87589-572-7). Jossey-Bass.

Putting Knowledge to Work. Pauline Atherton. 1973. 6.00 (ISBN 0-7069-0264-5). Intl Bk Dist.

Pygmalion Grows Up. Harris M. Cooper & Thomas L. Good. LC 82-14876. (Research in Writing Ser.). (Illus.). 224p. 1982. 32.95x (ISBN 0-582-28401-5). Longman.

Pygmalion in the Classroom: Teacher Expectation & Pupils' Intellectual Developement. enl. ed. Robert Rosenthal & Lenore Jacobson. 265p. 1988. text ed. 39.50x (ISBN 0-8290-1768-2); pap. text ed. 14.95x (ISBN 0-8290-1265-6). Irvington.

Pygmalion in the Gym. Thomas J. Martinek & Patricia B. Crowe. Ed. by Walker J. Rejeski. LC 81-81634. 160p. (Orig.). 1982. pap. text ed. 13.95x (ISBN 0-918438-75-6, PMAR0075). Leisure Pr.

Pygmalion; les surprises de l'amour see Oeuvres Completes De Jean-Philippe Rameau.

Pygmies & Papuans: The Stone Age To-Day in Dutch New Guinea. Alexander F. Wollaston. LC 75-34889. Repr. of 1912 ed. 36.50 (ISBN 0-404-14451-9). AMS Pr.

Pygmy Chimpanzee: Evolutionary Biology & Behavior. Randall L. Susman. LC 84-13236. 464p. 1984. 69.50x (ISBN 0-306-41595-X, Plenum Pr). Plenum Pub.

Pygmy Forest. Robert E. Sholars. (Illus.). 50p. (Orig.). 1982. pap. 6.95 (ISBN 0-9611178-0-X). Sholars.

Pygmy(Goat) in America. Alice Hall. (Illus.). 100p. (Orig.). 1982. pap. 7.50x (ISBN 0-932218-13-X). Hall Pr.

Pyjama. Pierre Daninos. 1972. 15.95 (ISBN 0-686-55573-2). French & Eur.

Pylgremage of the Sowle. Guillaume de Deguileville. Tr. by J. Lydgate. LC 74-28845. (English Experience Ser.: No. 726). 1975. Repr. of 1483 ed. 24.00 (ISBN 90-221-0740-X). Walter J Johnson.

Pylgrymage of Sir Richard Guylforde to the Holy Land, A. D. 1506. Ed. by Henry Ellis. LC 75-166023. (Camden Society, London. Publications, First Ser.: No. 51). Repr. of 1851 ed. 19.00 (ISBN 0-404-50151-6). AMS Pr.

Pylgrymage of Sir Richard Guylforde to the Holy Land A. D. 1506. 1851. 19.00 (ISBN 0-384-48440-9). Johnson Repr.

Pylon. reissue ed. William Faulkner. 1965. 13.95 (ISBN 0-394-44156-7). Random.

Pylon. William Faulkner. Ed. by Noel Polk. LC 86-40166. (Illus.). 336p. 1987. pap. 4.95 (ISBN 0-394-74741-0, Vin). Random.

Pylon see Novels Nineteen Thirty to Nineteen Thirty-Five.

Pylon (1935) William Faulkner. Ed. by Blotner et al. (William Faulkner Manuscripts Ser.). 1987. lib. bdg. 100.00 (ISBN 0-8240-6816-5). Garland Pub.

Pylos Comes Alive: Industry & Administration in the Mycenaean Palace. 107p. 1984. 10.00 (ISBN 0-318-17842-7). Archaeological Inst.

Pylos Four Hundred Twenty-Five B. C. Thucydides. Ed. by J. Wilson. 49.00 (ISBN 0-86516-111-9); pap. 16.50 (ISBN 0-86516-112-7). Bolchazy Carducci.

Pylos in Elis. John E. Coleman. (Hesperia Supplement: No. 21). (Illus.). 176p. 1986. 25.00x (ISBN 0-87661-521-3). Am Sch Athens.

Pylos 425 B.C. J. Wilson. 147p. 1981. text ed. 37.50x (ISBN 0-85668-145-8); pap. text ed. 16.50x (ISBN 0-85668-179-2, Pub. by Aris & Phillips UK). Humanities.

Pynchon Papers: Selections from the Account Books of John Pynchon, Vol. II. John Pynchon. Ed. by Carl Bridenbaugh & Juliette Tomlinson. xxiv, 513p. 1985. 30.00x (ISBN 0-8139-1074-9, Colonial Soc MA). U Pr of Va.

Pynchon Papers, Vol. 1: Letters of John Pynchon, 1654-1700. John Pynchon. Intro. by Carl Bridenbaugh. LC 81-70057. 338p. 1982. 30.00x (ISBN 0-8139-0978-3, Colonial Soc MA). U Pr of Va.

Pynchon: The Voice of Ambiguity. Thomas H. Schaub. LC 80-11944. 176p. 1981. 15.95 (ISBN 0-252-00816-2). U of Ill Pr.

Pynchon's Fictions: Thomas Pynchon & the Literature of Information. John O. Stark. LC 79-28466. x, 183p. 1980. 18.95x (ISBN 0-8214-0419-9). Ohio U Pr.

Pynchon's Mythography: An Approach to Gravity's Rainbow. Kathryn Hume. (Crosscurrents-Modern Critiques-Third Ser.). 232p. 1987. text ed. 22.50x (ISBN 0-8093-1357-X). S Ill U Pr.

Pyongyang Between Peking & Moscow: North Korea's Involvement in the Sino-Soviet Dispute, 1958-1975. Chin O. Chung. LC 76-44261. 240p. 1978. 17.95 (ISBN 0-8173-4728-3). U of Ala Pr.

Pyongyang Conference: Primary Health Care in Action. (SEARO Regional Health Papers: No. 6). 352p. 1985. pap. 12.00 (ISBN 92-9022-175-5). World Health.

Pyquag Poetry. Lawrence J. Babin. 1971. pap. 1.00x (ISBN 0-912492-02-3). Pyquag.

Pyralidae & Microlepidoptera of the Marquesas Archipelago. John F. Clarke. LC 85-600124. (Smithsonian Contributions to Zoology Ser.: No. 416). pap. 122.30 (ISBN 0-317-55743-2, 2029357). Bks Demand UMI.

Pyraloidea Pyralidae (part) Phycitinae (Acrobasis & Allies) Fascicle 15.2. H. H. Neunzig. Ed. by Ronald W. Hodges et al. LC 85-51913. (Moths of America North of Mexico including Greenland Ser.). (Illus.). xii, 114p. (Orig.). 1986. pap. text ed. 45.00 (ISBN 0-933003-01-3). Wedge Entomological.

Pyramid. William Golding. LC 67-19198. 192p. 1981. pap. 3.95 (ISBN 0-15-674703-0, Harv). HarBraceJ.

Pyramid. David Macaulay. (Illus.). 80p. (gr. 7 up). 1975. 14.95 (ISBN 0-395-21407-6). HM.

Pyramid & the Grail. M. Beckett. 1985. 60.00 (ISBN 0-317-68635-6, Pub. by J Richardson); pap. 40.00 (ISBN 0-317-68636-4). State Mutual Bk.

Pyramid & the Rose. Richard H. Weidig. Ed. by Clair Burch & Mark Weiman. LC 87-70972. (Philosophical Ser.). (Illus.). 194p. (Orig.). 1988. 18.95 (ISBN 0-9618245-2-2); pap. 9.95 (ISBN 0-9618245-3-0). Berkeley West Pub.

Pyramid Builders of Ancient Egypt: A Modern Investigation of Pharoah's Workforce. A. R. David. 258p. 1986. text ed. 34.95 (ISBN 0-7100-9909-6). Routledge Chapman & Hall.

Pyramid Is a Pure Crystal. John Taggart. 1974. 16.00 (ISBN 0-685-40875-2); pap. 8.00 (ISBN 0-685-40876-0). Elizabeth Pr.

Pyramid Lake Indian War Guidebook. Jamison Station Press Staff. (Desert Rat Guidebook Ser.: No. 1). (Illus.). 21p. 1984. 1.95. Jamison Stn.

Pyramid Odyssey. William R. Fix. LC 78-14540. (Illus.). 291p. 1984. pap. 12.95 (ISBN 0-932487-00-9). Mercury Media.

Pyramid of Bone. Thylias Moss. Ed. by Charles H. Rowell. (Callaloo Poetry Ser.). ix, 56p. 1989. pap. 8.95 (ISBN 0-8139-1202-4). U Pr of Va.

Pyramid of Ice. F. Sanders. pap. 1.50 (ISBN 0-937816-30-2). Tech Data.

Pyramid of the Sun - Pyramid of the Moon. Leonard E. Fisher. LC 88-1410. (Illus.). 32p. (gr. 1-5). 1988. 13.95 (ISBN 0-02-735300-1). Macmillan.

Pyramid PA. David Macaulay. (Illus.). (gr. 5 up). 1982. pap. 6.95 (ISBN 0-395-32121-2). HM.

Pyramid Power. Max Toth & Greg Nielson. (Illus.). 207p. 1985. pap. 4.95 (ISBN 0-89281-106-4, Destiny Bks). Inner Tradit.

Pyramid Power: A New Reality. Bill Schul & Ed Pettit. (Illus.). 270p. 1987. pap. 9.95 (ISBN 0-913299-41-3, Dist. by NAL). Stillpoint.

Pyramid Prophecies. Max Toth. (Illus.). 382p. 1988. pap. 6.95 (ISBN 0-89281-203-6, Destiny Bks). Inner Tradit.

Pyramidal Systems for Computer Vision. Ed. by V. Cantoni & S. Levialdi. (NATO ASI Ser.: No. F25). viii, 390p. 1987. 82.50 (ISBN 0-387-17165-7). Springer-Verlag.

Pyramids. Harriette Abels. Ed. by Howard Schroeder. LC 87-15455. (Mystery of...Ser.). (Illus.). 48p. (gr. 5-6). 1987. PLB 10.95 (ISBN 0-89686-345-X). Crestwood Hse.

Pyramids. 2nd ed. Ahmed Fakhry. LC 61-8645. 272p. 1974. pap. 9.95 (ISBN 0-226-23473-8, P571, Phoen). U of Chicago Pr.

Pyramids. Fred Saberhagen. pap. 3.50 (ISBN 0-671-65609-0). PB.

Pyramids. James Tandy. LC 86-42675. (Investigate Ser.). 48p. (gr. 3-7). Date not set. cancelled (ISBN 0-382-09279-1); pap. cancelled (ISBN 0-382-09280-5). Silver.

Pyramids. John Weeks. (Cambridge Introduction to World History Topic Bks.). (Illus.). 48p. (YA) (gr. 7 up). 1971. 4.95 (ISBN 0-521-07240-9). Cambridge U Pr.

Pyramids. John Weeks. LC 76-22457. (Cambridge Topic Bks.). (Illus.). (gr. 5-10). 1977. PLB 8.95 (ISBN 0-8225-1209-2). Lerner Pubns.

Pyramids: An Enigma Solved. Joseph Davidovits & Margie Morris. (Illus.). 224p. 1988. 16.95 (ISBN 0-87052-559-X). Hippocrene Bks.

Pyramids & the Second Reality. Bill Schul & Ed Pettit. 1979. pap. 4.95 (ISBN 0-449-90008-8, Columbine). Fawcett.

Pyramids of Egypt. I. E. Edwards. 1986. pap. 6.95 (ISBN 0-14-022549-8). Penguin.

Pyramids of Egypt. I. E. S. Edwards. 368p. 1987. 25.00 (ISBN 0-670-80153-4). Viking.

Pyramids of Power: The Story of Roosevelt, Insull & the Utility Wars. Marion L. Ramsay. (FDR & the Era of the New Deal Ser.). (Illus.). 342p. 1975. Repr. of 1937 ed. lib. bdg. 37.50 (ISBN 0-306-70707-1). Da Capo.

Pyramids of Sacrifice: Political Ethics & Social Change. Peter L. Berger. 240p. 1976. pap. 3.50 (ISBN 0-385-07101-9, Anch). Doubleday.

Pyramids: Opposing Viewpoints. Barbara Mitchell. LC 87-8392. (Great Mysteries Ser.). (Illus.). 96p. (gr. 3-10). 1987. lib. bdg. 12.95 (ISBN 0-89908-051-0). Greenhaven.

Pyramids: Structurally Based Tasks for E. S. L. Learners. Carolyn G. Madden & Susan M. Reinhart. (English As a 2nd Language Ser.). (Illus.). 1987. pap. text ed. 8.95x, 80p. (ISBN 0-472-08072-5); 144p. 6.95x, (ISBN 0-472-08073-3). U of Mich Pr.

Pyramus & Thisbe. rev. ed. William-Alan Landes. (gr. 3 up). 1984. pap. text ed. 5.00 (ISBN 0-88734-103-9). Players Pr.

Pyrates. George M. Fraser. LC 84-47771. 416p. 1984. 16.45 (ISBN 0-394-53837-4). Knopf.

Pyrates. George M. Fraser. 1985. pap. 8.95 (ISBN 0-452-25764-6, Plume). NAL.

Pyrenean Festivals: Calendar Customs, Music & Magic, Drama & Dance. Violet Alford. LC 77-87730. 1977. Repr. of 1937 ed. 25.00 (ISBN 0-404-16577-X). AMS Pr.

Pyrenean Prehistory: A Paleoeconomic Survey of the French Sites. P. Bahn. 511p. 1984. pap. 60.00x (ISBN 0-85668-260-8, Pub. by Aris & Phillips UK). Humanities.

Pyrenees. (Michelin Travel Guides). (Fr.). pap. 12.95 (ISBN 0-685-36092-X). French & Eur.

Pyrenees, French Edition: Regions of France. (Michelin Green Guides). pap. 12.95 (ISBN 0-686-56426-X). French & Eur.

Pyrenomycetous Fungi. Lewis E. Wehmeyer. (Mycologia Memoir: No. 6). 1975. text ed. 48.00x (ISBN 3-7682-0967-9). Lubrecht & Cramer.

Pyrethrin & Piperonyl Butoxide. (Specifications for Plant Protection Products: No. 7). 1978. pap. 7.50 (F1992, FAO). UNIPUB.

Pyrethroid Insecticides. J. P. Leahey. 450p. 1985. 99.00x (ISBN 0-85066-283-4). Taylor & Francis.

Pyretics & Antipyretics. Ed. by A. S. Milton. (Handbook of Experimental Pharmacology: Vol. 60). 715p. 1982. 245.00 (ISBN 0-387-11511-0). Springer-Verlag.

Pyridazines, Vol. 28. Ed. by Raymond N. Castle. LC 72-13270. (Hetercyclic Compounds Ser.). 905p. 1973. 109.00 (ISBN 0-471-38213-2, JW). Krieger.

Pyridine & Its Derivatives, Vol. 14, Pt. 4. Ed. by E. Klingsberg. 711p. 1964. 255.95x (ISBN 0-470-38016-0, Pub. by Wiley-Interscience). Wiley.

Pyridine & Its Derivatives, Vol. 14, Pt. 5. Ed. by George R. Newkome. LC 59-103038. (Chemistry of Heterocyclic Compounds Ser.: 1-079). 714p. 1984. 194.00 (ISBN 0-471-05072-5, 1-079). Wiley.

Pyridine-Metal Compounds, Vol. 14, Pt. 6. Piotr Tomasik & Zbigniew Ratajewicz. LC 84-26939. (Chemistry of Heterocyclic Compounds, A Ser. of Monographs). 2246p. 1985. 656.00 (ISBN 0-471-05073-3, Pub. by Wiley-Interscience). Wiley.

Pyridine Nucleotide Coenzymes. Ed. by Johannes Everse et al. 416p. 1982. 78.50 (ISBN 0-12-244750-6). Acad Pr.

Pyridine Nucleotide Coenzymes: Chemical, Biological, & Medical Aspects. Ed. by David Dolphin et al. LC 86-7744. (Coenzymes & Cofactors Ser.). 672p. 1986. Vol. 2, Pt. A. write for info. (ISBN 0-471-01125-8); Vol. 2, Pt. B. write for info. (ISBN 0-471-01126-6). Wiley.

Pyridine Nucleotide Coenzymes: Chemical, Biochemical, & Medical Aspects, Vol. 2A-B. Ed. by David Dolphin et al. (Coenzymes & Cofactors Ser.). 1987. 199.90 (ISBN 0-471-01138-X). Wiley.

Pyridine Nucleotide: Dependent Dehydrogenases. Ed. by Horst Sund. 513p. 1977. text ed. 87.00x (ISBN 3-11007-091-X). De Gruyter.

Pyrimidines: Supplement 2. D. J. Brown. (Chemistry of Hetercyclic Compounds Monographs). 1184p. 1985. 215.00 (ISBN 0-471-02745-6). Wiley.

Pyroclastic Geology of Oahu. C. K. Wentworth. (BMB). Repr. of 1926 ed. 20.00 (ISBN 0-527-02133-4). Kraus Repr.

Pyroclastic Rocks. R. V. Fisher & H. U. Schmincke. (Illus.). 350p. 1984. 54.00 (ISBN 0-387-12756-9). Springer-Verlag.

Pyroclastic Volcanism & Deposits of Cenozoic Intermediate to Felsic Volcanic Islands with Implications for Precambrian Greenstone-Belt Volcanoes. Ed. by L. D. Ayres. (Geological Association of Canada. Short Course Notes: Vol. 2). pap. 93.30 (2027847). Bks Demand UMI.

Pyrocysteen der Plankton-Expedition der Humboldt-Stiftung. C. Apstein. 1971. Repr. of 1909 ed. 12.50x (ISBN 3-7682-0807-9). Lubrecht & Cramer.

Pyrogens, Endotoxins, LAL Testing & Depyrogenation. Pearson. 272p. 1985. 59.75 (ISBN 0-8247-7436-1). Dekker.

Pyrolysis Mass Spectrometry of Recent & Fossil Biomaterials. H. L. Meuzelaar & J. Haverkamp. (Techniques & Instrumentation in Analytical Chemistry Ser.: Vol. 3). 294p. 1982. 79.00 (ISBN 0-444-42099-1). Elsevier.

Pyrolysis of Polymers, Vol. 13. Ed. by Carlos J. Hilado. LC 73-82115. (Fire & Flammability Ser.). (Illus.). 210p. 1976. pap. 14.95 (ISBN 0-87762-173-X). Technomic.

Pyrolysis: Theory & Industrial Practice. Lyle Albright et al. 446p. 1983. 85.00 (ISBN 0-12-048880-9). Acad Pr.

Pyrolytic Methods in Organic Chemistry: Applications of Flow & Flash Vacuum Pyrolytic Techniques. Roger F. Brown. LC 79-52787. (Organic Chemistry Ser.). 1980. 65.50 (ISBN 0-12-138050-5). Acad Pr.

Pyrometallurgical Processes in Nonferrous Metallurgy. Ed. by J. N. Anderson & P. E. Queneau. LC 67-26570. (Metallurgical Society Conferences: Vol. 39). pap. 132.30 (ISBN 0-317-10578-7, 2001528). Bks Demand UMI.

Pyrometallurgy 87. (Illus.). 1105p. text ed. 132.00 (ISBN 0-900488-97-2). IMM-North Am.

Pyrotechnics. Joseph H. McLain. (Illus.). 243p. 1980. 29.95 (ISBN 0-89859-732-3). L Erlbaum Assocs.

Pyrotechnics. George W. Weingart. (Illus.). 1968. Repr. of 1947 ed. 18.50 (ISBN 0-8206-0112-8). Chem Pub.

Pyrotechnics in Industry. Richard T. Barbour. LC 80-11152. (Illus.). 190p. 1981. text ed. 38.00 (ISBN 0-07-003653-5). McGraw.

Pyroxenes. Ed. by C. T. Prewitt. (Reviews in Mineralogy: Vol. 7). 525p. 1980. 18.00 (ISBN 0-939950-07-3). Mineralogical Soc.

Pyrrhon et le Scepticisme Grec. Leon Robin. LC 78-66561. (Ancient Philosophy Ser.). 264p. 1980. lib. bdg. 32.00 (ISBN 0-8240-9589-8). Garland Pub.

Pyrrhus, King of Epirus. Petros Garoufalias. (Illus.). 492p. 1979. text ed. 19.95 (ISBN 0-905743-13-X, Pub. by Stacey Intl UK). Humanities.

Pyruvate Carboxylase. John C. Wallace & D. Bruce Keech. 280p. 1985. 155.00 (ISBN 0-8493-6552-X). CRC Pr.

Pythagoras: A Life. Peter Gorman. 1978. 19.95 (ISBN 0-7100-0006-5). Routledge Chapman & Hall.

Pythagoras & Early Pythagoreanism. James A. Philip. LC 66-9226. (Phoenix Series Supplement: Supplementary Vol. 7). pap. 58.00 (ISBN 0-317-08752-5, 2014340). Bks Demand UMi.

Pythagoras: His Life & Teachings. Thomas Stanley. 15.00 (ISBN 0-89314-408-8). Philos Res.

Pythagoras: Lover of Wisdom. Ward Rutherford. 128p. 1984. pap. 13.95 (ISBN 0-85030-379-6, Pub. by Thorsons UK). Weiser.

Pythagorean Plato: Prelude to the Song Itself. Ernest G. McClain. (Illus.). 192p. (Orig.). 1984. pap. 8.95 (ISBN 0-89254-010-9). Nicolas-Hays.

Pythagorean Politics in Southern Italy. Kurt Von Fritz. 1973. Repr. lib. bdg. 16.50x (ISBN 0-374-92939-4, Octagon). Hippocrene Bks.

Pythagorean Precepts. Thomas Taylor. 1983. pap. 6.95 (ISBN 0-916411-00-1, Pub. by Alexandrian Pr). Holmes pub.

Pythagorean Proposition. Elisha S. Loomis. (Classics in Mathematics Education Ser.: Vol. 1). (Illus.). 306p. 1968. 14.00 (ISBN 0-87353-036-5). NCTM.

Pythagorean Sourcebook & Library: An Anthology of Ancient Writings Which Relate to Pythagoras & Pythagorean Philosophy. Iamblichus et al. Ed. by Kenneth S. Guthrie. LC 87-60459. (Illus.). 361p. 1987. 30.00 (ISBN 0-933999-50-X); pap. 17.00 (ISBN 0-933999-51-8). Phanes Pr.

Pythagorean Triangle. George Oliver. LC 75-16015. (Secret Doctrine Reference Ser). 250p. 1975. Repr. of 1875 ed. 13.00 (ISBN 0-913510-17-3). Wizards.

Pythagorean Writings: Hellenistic Texts from the 1st c. B.C. to 3rd c. A.D. Ed. by Robert Navon. Tr. by Kenneth Guthrie & Thomas Taylor. (Great Works of Philosophy Ser.: Vol. 3). 190p. (Orig.). 1986. text ed. 32.00 (ISBN 0-933601-01-8); pap. text ed. 16.50 (ISBN 0-933601-02-6). Selene Bks.

Pythagoreans & Eleatics. J. E. Raven. 196p. 1981. 12.50 (ISBN 0-89005-367-7). Ares.

Pythia's Drunken Song. Jerry A. Dibble. (International Archives of the History of Ideas, Series Minor: No. 19). 1978. pap. 9.00 (ISBN 90-247-2011-7, Pub. by Martinus Nijhoff Netherlands). Kluwer Academic.

Python. Joseph Fontenrose. 1959. 28.00 (ISBN 0-8196-0285-X). Biblo.

Python: A Study of Delphic Myth & Its Origins. Joseph Fontenrose. 637p. 1981. pap. 10.95x (ISBN 0-520-04091-0). U of Cal Pr.

Python Killer: Stories of Nzema Life. Vinigi L. Grottanelli. (Illus.). xii, 224p. 1988. 24.95x (ISBN 0-226-31005-1). U of Chicago Pr.

Pythons. Bargar & Johnson. (Snake Discovery Library Set). (Illus.). 24p. (gr. 1-4). 1987. PLB 69.96 6 bk. set (ISBN 0-317-60581-X); PLB 11.66 (ISBN 0-86592-244-6). Rourke Corp.

Pythons & Constrictors. Lionel Bender. Ed. by Franklin Watts Ltd. (First Sight Ser.). (Illus.). 32p. (gr. k-9). 1988. 10.90 (ISBN 0-531-17076-4, Gloucester Pr). Watts.

PzKpfw IV in Action. (Armor in Action Ser.). (Illus.). 1984. pap. 4.95 (ISBN 0-89747-045-1, 2012). Squad Sig Pubns.

P3M: A Guide to Productivity, Pricing & Profits. David B. Uman. 1986. cancelled (ISBN 0-87094-500-9). Dow Jones-Irwin.

P.38 Pistol, Vol. 2: The Contract Pistols 1940-1945. Warren H. Buxton. LC 78-51018. (Illus.). 256p. 1985. 45.50 (ISBN 0-9614024-0-7). Ucross Bks.

Q & A about the Silva Method. 3.95 (ISBN 0-913343-45-5). Inst Psych Inc.

Q & A: Employee Drug Screening. 12p. (Orig.). 1987. pap. text ed. 2.95 (ISBN 0-9610026-9-7). Perf Resource Pr.

Q

Q-Baltimore & Ohio Railroad Q-Class Mikado Locomotives. Howard N. Barr & W. A. Barringer. LC 78-52708. (Illus.). 1978. 30.00 (ISBN 0-934118-15-9). Barnard Roberts.

Q Clearance. Peter Benchley. LC 85-28092. 336p. 1986. 16.45 (ISBN 0-394-55360-8). Random.

Q Clearance. Peter Benchley. 1987. pap. 4.50 (ISBN 0-441-69400-4, Charter Pub). Berkley Pub.

Q Dramatists of the Present Day, London 1871. Thomas Purnell. Ed. by Fredeman et al. (Victorian Muse Ser.). 146p. 1985. lib. bdg. 25.00 (ISBN 0-8240-8614-7). Garland Pub.

Q Factor. Philip Kirk. (Butler Ser.). 240p. 1984. pap. 2.50 (ISBN 0-8439-2096-3, Leisure Bks). Leisure NY.

Q. Horatius Flaccus: His Art of Poetry: Englished by Ben Johnson, with Other Works of the Author Never Printed Before. Q. Horatius Flaccus. Tr. by Ben Jonson. LC 74-80190. (English Experience Ser.: No. 670). 166p. 1974. Repr. of 1640 ed. 45.00 (ISBN 90-221-0670-5). Walter J Johnson.

Q Hypergeometric Functions & Applications. H. Exton. (Mathematics & its Applications Ser.). 355p. 1983. 57.95x (ISBN 0-470-27453-0). Halsted Pr.

Q Is for Duck. Mary Elting & Michael Folsom. LC 80-13854. (Illus.). 64p. (ps-3). 1980. 11.95 (ISBN 0-395-29437-1, Clarion); pap. 4.95 (ISBN 0-395-30062-2). HM.

Q Methodology. Bruce McKeown & Dan Thomas. (Quantitative Applications in the Social Sciences Ser.: No. 66). 93p. 1988. pap. text ed. 6.50 (ISBN 0-8039-2753-3). Sage.

"Q" Model: Effective Management of Personal Stress. Edward Zerin & Marjory Zerin. 156p. 1986. text ed. 19.95 (ISBN 0-89876-107-7). Gardner Pr.

Q Parallels: Synopis, Critical Notes & Concordance. John S. Kloppenborg. (Foundations & Facets Ser.). (Illus.). 352p. 1988. 29.95 (ISBN 0-944344-00-3); pap. 19.95 (ISBN 0-944344-01-1). Polebridge Pr.

Q-Series: Their Development & Application in Analysis, Number Theory, Combinatorics, Physics & Computer Algebra. G. Andrews. LC 86-14061. (CBMS Ser.: Vol. 66). 110p. 1986. pap. text ed. 17.00 (ISBN 0-8218-0716-1). Am Math.

Q-Ships & Their Story. E. Keble Chatterton. LC 79-6105. (Navies & Men Ser.). (Illus.). 1980. Repr. of 1972 ed. lib. bdg. 28.50x (ISBN 0-405-13034-1). Ayer Co Pubs.

Q-Sort As a Needs Assessment Technique. Sean Tate. (Technical Note Ser.: No. 21). 20p. (Orig.). 1982. pap. 2.00 (ISBN 0-932288-92-8). Ctr Intl Ed U of MA.

Q-Sort Method in Personality Assessment. Jack Block. Ed. by Molly Harrower. LC 61-10370. 161p. 1978. pap. 14.75x (ISBN 0-89106-000-6, 0791). Consulting Psychol.

Q T C: (I Have a Message for You) Ray Redwood. Ed. by Tom Noe. LC 88-90627. (Illus.). 350p. (Orig.). 1988. 15.00 (ISBN 0-945845-00-6); pap. 8.95 (ISBN 0-945845-01-4). Sequoia TX.

Q: The Sayings of Jesus. Ivan Havener. LC 84-81243. (Good News Studies: Vol. 19). (Orig.). 1986. pap. 8.95 (ISBN 0-89453-441-6). M Glazier.

Q-Values & Excitation Functions of Nuclear Reactions, Pt.A: Q-Values see Landolt-Boernstein Numerical Data & Functional Relationships in Science & Technology, New Series, Group 1: Nuclear Particle & Physics.

Q-Values & Excitation Functions of Nuclear Reactions, Pt. B: Excitation Functions for Charged-Particle Induced Nuclear Reactions see Landolt-Boernstein Numerical Data & Functional Relationships in Science & Technology, New Series, Group 1: Nuclear Particle & Physics.

Qabalah. Papus. 1977. pap. 12.95 (ISBN 0-85030-340-0, Pub. by Thorsons UK). Weiser.

Qabalism. Henry B. Pullen-Burry. 167p. 1972. Repr. of 1925 ed. 10.00 (ISBN 0-911662-45-6). Yoga.

Qabalistic Tarot: A Textbook of Mystical Philosophy. Robert Wang. (Illus.). 304p. 1987. pap. 16.95 (ISBN 0-87728-672-8). Weiser.

Qabbalah: The Philosophical Writings of Solomon Ben Yehudah Ibn Gabirol. Isaac Myer. 69.95 (ISBN 0-8490-0922-7). Gordon Pr.

Qaddafi & the Libyan Revolution. David Blundy & Andrew Lycett. 1987. 17.95 (ISBN 0-316-10042-0). Little.

Qaddafi: His Ideology in Theory & Practice. Mohamed El-khawas. (Illus.). 200p. (Orig.). 1986. 18.95 (ISBN 0-915597-24-1); pap. 9.95 (ISBN 0-915597-23-3). Amana Bks.

Qaddafi-His Ideology in Theory & Practice. Mohamed El-Khawas. 1987. lib. bdg. 79.95 (ISBN 0-8490-3940-1). Gordon Pr.

Qaddafi's Green Book: An Unauthorized Edition. Intro. by Henry M. Christman. 140p. 1988. 17.95 (ISBN 0-87975-431-1). Prometheus Bks.

Qadhafi's Libya. Jonathan Bearman. (Illus.). 324p. 1986. 35.00 (ISBN 0-86232-433-5, Pub. by Zed Pr); pap. 12.50 (ISBN 0-86232-434-3, Pub. by Zed Pr). Humanities.

Qadianism: A Critique. A. H. Nadvi. pap. 1.00 (ISBN 0-686-18539-0). Kazi Pubns.

Qaids, Captains, & Colons: French Military Administration in the Colonial Maghrib 1844-1934. Kenneth J. Perkins. LC 80-13114. 278p. 1981. 45.00 (ISBN 0-8419-0564-9, Africana). Holmes & Meier.

Qajar Iran, Eighteen Hundred to Nineteen Twenty-Five: Political, Social & Cultural Change. Ed. by E. Bosworth & Carole Hillenbrand. LC 84-673453. 414p. 1983. 40.00x (ISBN 0-85224-459-2, Pub. by Edinburgh U Pr Scotland). Columbia U Pr.

Qajar Persia: Eleven Studies. Ann K. Lambton. 359p. 1988. 27.50x (ISBN 0-292-76900-8). U of Tex Pr.

Q&A Simplified. David Bolocan. 1987. pap. 18.95 (ISBN 0-8306-2828-2, 2828). Tab Bks.

Qaryat Al-Fau: A Portrait of Pre-Islamic Civilization in Saudi Arabia. Rahman Al-Ansary. LC 81-21329. 1982. 37.50 (ISBN 0-312-65742-0). St Martin.

Qashqa'i of Iran. Lois Beck. LC 85-23404. 368p. 1986. text ed. 30.00t (ISBN 0-300-03212-9). Yale U Pr.

Qasida & Creation. Ed. by Arthur Wormhoudt. (Arab Translation Ser.: No. 99). 150p. 1988. pap. text ed. 6.50 (ISBN 0-940307-01-4). Wormhoudt.

Qasida & Creed. Intro. by Arthur Wormhoudt. (Arab Translation Ser.: No. 104). (Illus.). 175p. 1988. pap. text ed. 6.50 (ISBN 0-940307-06-5). Wormhoudt.

Qasida & Shih. Tr. & intro. by Arthur Wormhoudt. (Arab Translation Ser.: No. 89). 160p. (Orig.). 1986. pap. 6.50x (ISBN 0-916358-41-0). Wormhoudt.

Qasida & Veda. Arthur Wormhoudt. (Arab Translation Ser.: No. 94). 175p. 1987. pap. text ed. 6.50x (ISBN 0-916358-46-1). Wormhoudt.

Qasr Kharana in the Transjordan. Stephen K. Urice. LC 87-14326. 184p. 1987. 28.50 (ISBN 0-89757-207-6, Dist. by Eisenbrauns). Am Sch Orient Res.

Qatar. Ed. by Martin Caiger-Smith. (Illus.). 160p. 1986. 50.00 (ISBN 0-905743-43-1, Pub. by Stacey Intl UK). Humanities.

Qatar. 2nd. ed. Middle East Economic Digest Staff. Ed. by John Whelan. (MEED Practical Guides Ser.). (Illus.). 176p. (Orig.). 1985. pap. 16.95x (ISBN 0-9505211-9-1). Lynne Rienner.

Qatar. (Let's Visit Places & Peoples - - Nations, Dependencies, & Sovereignties of the World Ser.). (Illus.). (gr. 5 up). 1988. 12.95 (ISBN 1-55546-173-5). Chelsea Hse.

Qatar. Ed. by P. T. Unwin. (World Bibliographical Ser.: No. 36). 162p. 1982. 30.00 (ISBN 0-903450-66-6). ABC-Clio.

Qatar: Development of an Oil Economy. Ragaei El Mallakh. LC 78-12167. (Illus.). 1979. 25.00 (ISBN 0-312-65751-X). St Martin.

Qatar: Energy & Development. Ragaei E. Mallakh. LC 84-29317. 184p. 1985. 31.00 (ISBN 0-7099-0955-1, Pub. by Croom Helm Ltd). Routledge Chapman & Hall.

Qatari Women: Past & Present. Abeer Abu Saud. (Illus.). 184p. 1984. text ed. 32.95 (ISBN 0-582-78372-0). Longman.

Qawiaraq Inupiaq Literacy Manual. Lawrence D. Kaplan. iv, 50p. (Orig., Inupiaq Eskimo.). 1987. pap. 5.00 (ISBN 1-55500-028-2). Alaska Native.

QB Seven. Leon Uris. 1972. pap. 4.95 (ISBN 0-553-25957-1). Bantam.

QC Circles: Applications, Tools & Theory. Ed. by Davida M. Amsden & Robert T. Amsden. 174p. 10.00 (ISBN 0-318-13230-3, 104); members 8.50 (ISBN 0-318-13231-1). Am Soc QC.

QC Sources. Charles Bastien. 420p. (Orig.). 1984. 17.95 (ISBN 0-916429-00-8). IAQC Pr.

QCD: Renormalization for the Practitioner. P. Pascual & R. Tarrach. (Lecture Notes in Physics Ser.: Vol. 194). v, 277p. 1984. pap. 14.50 (ISBN 0-387-12908-1). Springer Verlag.

QCD Spectral Sum Rules: Toward a Theory for Hadrons. Stephan Narison. 250p. 1988. 38.00 (ISBN 9971-50-653-X, ZB0647PB). World Scientific Pub.

QCD Vacuum, Hadrons, & Superdense Matter. E. V. Shuryak. 416p. 1987. 78.00 (ISBN 9971-978-32-6); pap. 36.00 (ISBN 9971-978-33-4). World Scientific Pub.

QC's & Unions: Together QC's & Unions. spiralbound 8.95 (ISBN 0-317-69751-X). IAQC Pr.

QE Two. William H. Flayhart, III & Ronald Warwick. (Illus.). 1985. 19.95 (ISBN 0-393-01885-7). Norton.

QED Report on Venture Capital Financial Analysis. James L. Plummer. 217p. 1987. hard cover bndr. 295.00 (ISBN 0-9620093-0-X). QED Research.

QED: The Strange Theory of Light & Matter. Richard P. Feynman. LC 85-42685. (Alix G. Mautner Memorial Lectures). (Illus.). 152p. 1985. 18.50 (ISBN 0-691-08388-6); pap. 8.95 (ISBN 0-691-02417-0). Princeton U Pr.

QED's Guide to U. S. School Districts 1987-88. Quality Education Data Staff. (School Trend Ser.). 400p. 1988. pap. 79.975 (ISBN 0-88747-295-8, 2958Q). Quality Ed Data.

Qemant: A Pagan-Hebraic Peasantry of Ethiopia. Frederick C. Gamst. (Illus.). 128p. 1984. pap. text ed. 7.95x (ISBN 0-88133-047-7). Waveland Pr.

QE8 - Eighth National Quantum Electronics Conference: Special Issue - Journal of Modern Optics, Vol. 35 No. 3. A. Maitland & W. Sibbett. 320p. 1988. pap. 66.00 (ISBN 0-85066-899-9). Taylor & Francis.

QF-Three & QF-One Rings. H. Tachikawa. Ed. by C. M. Ringel. (Lecture Notes in Mathematics: Vol. 351). 172p. 1973. pap. 19.00 (ISBN 0-387-06501-6). Springer-Verlag.

Qhawalali: Water Coming down Place; a History of Gualala, Mendocino County; California. Annette W. Parks. LC 80-82462. (Illus.). 150p. 1981. 24.95 (ISBN 0-9605550-0-5). FreshCut.

Qi Lai: An Introduction to the Chinese Communication System. Robert L Bishop. LC 87-36153. 128p. (Orig.). 1988. pap. 12.95x (ISBN 0-8138-0296-2). Iowa St U Pr.

Qigong for Health. Masaru Takahashi. 1986. pap. 9.95. Japan Pubns USA.

Qin Han Jin Wenlu. Rong Geng. 1931. 700.00x (ISBN 0-317-68557-0, Pub. by Han-Shan Tang Ltd). State Mutual Bk.

Qing Gong Zhenbao Baimei Tu, 4 Vols. 1925. 2100.00 (ISBN 0-317-69034-5, Pub. by Han-Shan Tang Ltd). State Mutual Bk.

Qing Mark & Period Blue & White. S. Marchant & Son. 40p. 1984. 70.00x (ISBN 0-317-44181-7, Pub. by Han-Shan Tang Ltd). State Mutual Bk.

Qing Porcelain. Michel Beurdeley & Raindre Beurdeley. 320p. 1987. 340.00x (ISBN 0-317-68617-8, Pub. by Han-Shan Tang Ltd). State Mutual Bk.

Qing Porcelain: Famille Rose, Famille Verte. Michel Beurdeley & Guy Raindre. LC 86-42701. (Illus.). 300p. 1987. 150.00 (ISBN 0-8478-0737-1). Rizzoli Intl.

Qingdai Taoci Daquan. He Zheng-guang. 516p. 1986. 210.00x (ISBN 0-317-68991-6, Pub. by Han-Shan Tang Ltd). State Mutual Bk.

Qinghai Caitao. 41p. 1980. 85.00x (ISBN 0-317-45186-3, Pub. by Han-Shan Tang Ltd). State Mutual Bk.

Qinghua Ciqi. Fu Yang. 66p. 1957. 110.00x (ISBN 0-317-43775-5, Pub. by Han-Shan Tang Ltd). State Mutual Bk.

Qintsvisi Murals. O. D. Piralishvili. 184p. 1979. 62.00x (ISBN 0-317-14282-8, Pub. by Collets (UK)). State Mutual Bk.

QL Compendium. Martin Gandoff & Robin Kinge. 176p. 1984. 39.00x (ISBN 0-201-15438-2, Pub. by Addison-Wesley Pubs Ltd). State Mutual Bk.

QL Computing. Ian Sinclair. (Illus.). 182p. (Orig.). 1984. pap. 11.95 (ISBN 0-246-12595-0, Pub. by Granada England). Sheridan.

QRB Special Edition - Drug & Antibiotic Review: Effect on Quality & Cost. 90p. 1984. pap. 25.00 (ISBN 0-86688-074-7). Joint Comm Hlthcare.

QRB Special Edition: Data Management in Cost Containment & Quality Review Strategies. 104p. 1983. pap. 20.00. Joint Comm Hlthcare.

QRB Special Edition, Quality Assurance in Mental Health: Theory, Technology, & Practice. 104p. 1983. pap. 20.00 (ISBN 0-86688-063-1). Joint Comm Hlthcare.

QRB Ten-Year Cumulative Index. cancelled (ISBN 0-317-41166-7, QRB-301). Joint Comm Hlthcare.

QRB Tenth Anniversary Publication. 300p. 1984. pap. 25.00 (ISBN 0-86688-087-9, QRB-84-12). Joint Comm Hlthcare.

QRP Notebook. DeMaw. 1986. 5.00 (ISBN 0-87259-500-5). Am Radio.

Q's in Albuquerque. Glenna Luschei. 1988. Handoriented artist bk. 200.00 (ISBN 0-318-22929-3); 7.25 (ISBN 0-318-22930-7). Solo Pr.

Q's Legacy. Helene Hanff. 1986. pap. 6.95 (ISBN 0-14-008936-5). Penguin.

Q's Who in Pay-per-View. Dantia Quirk. 80p. 1988. 24.95 (ISBN 0-910767-17-3). QV Pub.

Q's Who in Television Sports. Dantia Quirk. 130p. 1987. 19.95 (ISBN 0-910767-20-3). QV Pub.

QSAR & Strategies in the Design of Bioactive Compounds. Ed. & intro. by J. K. Seydel. LC 85-2408. (Illus.). 442p. 1985. 73.00 (ISBN 0-89573-433-8). VCH Pubs.

Qsar Es-Seghir: An Archaeological View of Medieval Life. Charles L. Redman. 1985. 70.00 (ISBN 0-12-584630-4); pap. 24.95 (ISBN 0-12-584631-2). Acad Pr.

QSAR in Drug Design & Toxicology: Proceedings of the 6th European Symposium on Quantitative Structure-Activity Relationships, Protoroz, September 22-26, 1986. Ed. by D. Hadzi & B. Jerman-Blazic. (Pharmacochemistry Library: No. 10). 376p. 1987. 116.00 (ISBN 0-444-42767-8). Elsevier.

Qsar in Environmental Toxicology - II. Ed. by Klaus L. Kaiser. 1987. lib. bdg. 99.50 (ISBN 90-277-2555-1, Pub. by Reidel Holland). Kluwer Academic.

Qsar in Toxicology & Xenobiochemistry: Proceedings of a Symposium, Prague Czechoslovakia, Sept. 12-14, 1984. Ed. by M. Tichy. (Pharmacochemistry Library: No. 8). 474p. 1985. 155.25 (ISBN 0-444-42483-0). Elsevier.

QSL Adress Book see KODAK Complete Darkroom DATAGUIDE: Processing & Printing Information for Black-&-White & Color.

Quaaludes: The Quest for Oblivion. Marilyn Carroll & Gary Gallo. (Encyclopedia of Psychoactive Drugs Ser.). (Illus.). 1985. PLB 17.95 (ISBN 0-87754-766-1). Chelsea Hse.

Quabbin: The Story of a Small Town with Outlooks upon Puritan Life. Francis H. Underwood. 400p. 1986. pap. text ed. 10.95x (ISBN 0-930350-88-X). NE U Pr.

Quack Quack. Patricia Casey. LC 87-17301. (Illus.). (ps-1). 1988. 12.95 (ISBN 0-688-07765-X). Lothrop.

Quack-Quack. Frederic Stehr. LC 86-46349. (Illus.). 32p. (ps up). 1987. 10.95 (ISBN 0-374-36161-4). FS&G.

Quack-Quack. Frederic Stehr. (Illus.). 28p. (ps up). 1988. pap. 3.95 (ISBN 0-374-46141-4, Sunburst). FS&G.

Quack! Said the Billy-Goat. Charles Causley. LC 85-27167. (Trophy Picture Bks.). (Illus.). 24p. (ps-2). 1986. pap. 2.50 (ISBN 0-06-443104-5, Trophy). HarpJ.

Quack! Said the Billy-Goat. Charles Causley. LC 85-23856. (Illus.). 24p. (ps-2). 1986. PLB 11.89 (ISBN 0-397-32192-9, Lipp Jr Bks). HarpJ.

Quackers, an Idea Book for Preschool Teachers. Rev. ed. Susan Majors. 288p. 1986. pap. text ed. 20.00 (ISBN 0-317-57809-X). Programs Comm.

Quackery & You. William T. Jarvis. Ed. by Gerald Wheeler. (Better Living Ser.). (Illus., Orig.). 1983. pap. 1.25 (ISBN 0-8280-0148-0). Review & Herald.

Quacks of Old London. C. J. Thompson. LC 75-89296. (Tower Bks). (Illus.). 364p. 1971. Repr. of 1929 ed. 43.00x (ISBN 0-8103-3212-4). Gale.

Quacky & the Crazy Curve Ball. Walter Oleksy. 1981. text ed. 9.95 (ISBN 0-07-047752-3). McGraw.

Quacky & the Haunted Amusement Park. Walter Oleksy. (gr. 6-9). 1982. text ed. 8.95 (ISBN 0-07-047753-1). McGraw.

Quacky & Wacky-Buzz Bee. Ethel Barrett. (ps-1). 1978. pap. 6.95 book & cassette pac (ISBN 0-8307-0418-3, 5602593). Regal.

Quad Cities Guide: 1988. Basil Williams & Blake Lewis. (Guides U. S. A.). (Illus.). 72p. (Orig.). 1987. pap. text ed. 4.95 (ISBN 0-938185-01-2). Wms & Assocs IA.

Quad Cities U. S A. Book. Basil Williams & Blake Lewis. (Illus.). 48p. (Orig.). 1986. pap. text ed. 6.95 (ISBN 0-938185-00-4). Williams & Assocs.

Quaderno Di Esercizi Avanti con L'Italiano. Stefano Morel. 1988. wkbk. 5.42 (ISBN 0-87720-574-4). Amsco Sch.

Quaderno of Illustrations in Full Colors of Spanish & Moslem Architecture & Life. Quentin G. Worthington. 121p. 1987. 167.15 (ISBN 0-86650-236-X). Gloucester Art.

Quaderno of the Most Impressive Paintings by Gerome. Jean L. Gerome. (Illus.). 1980. 147.75 (ISBN 0-930582-53-5). Gloucester Art.

Quaderno of Twenty-Five Illustrations in Full Colors of the City of Paris, France. Gaston E. Warren. 97p. 1988. 157.85 (ISBN 0-86650-235-1). Gloucester Art.

Quadpack: A Subroutine Package for Automatic Integration. R. Piessens et al. (Springer Series in Computational Mathematics: Vol. 1). (Illus.). 301p. 1983. pap. 32.50 (ISBN 0-387-12553-1). Springer-Verlag.

Quadratic & Hermitian Forms. W. Scharlau. (Grundlehren der Mathematischen Wissenschaften Ser.: A Series of Comprehensive Studies in Mathematics Vol. 270). 430p. 1984. 73.00 (ISBN 0-387-13724-6). Springer-Verlag.

Quadratic Differentials. K. Strebel. (Ergebnisse der Mathematik und ihrer Grenzgebiete, 3. Folge A Series of Modern Surveys in Mathematics: Vol. 5). (Illus.). 200p. 1984. 52.00 (ISBN 0-387-13035-7). Springer Verlag.

Quadratic Form Theory & Differential Equations. Ed. by John Gregory. LC 80-520. (Mathematics in Science & Engineering Ser.). 1981. 49.50 (ISBN 0-12-301450-6). Acad Pr.

Quadratic Forms & Hecke Operators. A. N. Andrianov. (Grundlehren der Mathematischen Wissenschaften Ser.: Band 286). (Illus.). 400p. 1987. 102.00 (ISBN 0-387-15294-6). Springer-Verlag.

Quadratic Forms in Infinite Dimensional Vector Spaces. Herbert Gross. (Progress in Mathematics: Vol. 1). 431p. 1979. pap. 34.95x (ISBN 0-8176-1111-8). Birkhauser.

Quadratic Forms over Semilocal Rings. R. Baeza. (Lecture Notes in Mathematics Ser.: Vol. 655). 1978. pap. 16.00 (ISBN 0-387-08845-8). Springer-Verlag.

Quadratic Programming Models Applied to Agricultural Policies. Anton D. Meister et al. (Illus.). 1978. text ed. 9.95x (ISBN 0-8138-1930-X). Iowa St U Pr.

Quadrature Domains. M. Sakai. (Lecture Notes in Mathematics: Vol. 934). 133p. 1982. pap. 11.00 (ISBN 0-387-11562-5). Springer-Verlag.

Quadrature Formulae. A. Ghizzetti & A. Ossicini. (International Series of Numerical Mathematics: No. 13). 192p. 1970. 37.95x (ISBN 0-8176-0530-4). Birkhauser.

Quadrifariam. Frank Samperi. 1973. 15.00 (ISBN 0-685-78988-8, Pub. by Mushinsha Bks). Small Pr Dist.

Quadrilingual Business Dictionary. (Eng., Fr., Ger. & Span.). 1982. 90.00x (ISBN 0-686-75659-2, Pub. by European Schoolbks England). State Mutual Bk.

Quadrilingual Economics Dictionary. Ed. by Frits J. De Jong et al. 1981. lib. bdg. 48.00 (ISBN 90-247-2243-8, Pub. by Martinus Nijhoff Netherlands). Kluwer Academic.

Quadrille. Marion Chesney. 224p. 1987. pap. 2.50 (ISBN 0-449-21410-9, Crest). Fawcett.

Quadrille. Illus. by Cynthia Kintzer. (Illus.). 48p. 1982. Repr. of 1841 ed. 24.00 (ISBN 0-88014-037-2). Mosaic Pr OH.

Quadrille for Tigers. Christine Craig. LC 82-60727. (Illus.). 1984. pap. 5.95 (ISBN 0-942610-02-4). Mina Pr.

Quadrille of Gender: Casanova's Memoirs. Francois Roustang. Tr. by Anne C. Vila from Fr. LC 87-27807. 184p. 1988. text ed. 25.00x (ISBN 0-8047-1456-8). Stanford U Pr.

Quadrillen see Werke fuer Pianoforte.

Quadripartite Structures: Categories, Relations & Homologies in Bush Mekeo Culture. Mark S. Mosko. (Illus.). 304p. 1985. 44.50 (ISBN 0-521-26452-9). Cambridge U Pr.

Quadroon: or, Adventures in the Far West. facsimile ed. Thomas M. Reid. LC 67-29278. (Americans in Fiction Ser.). (Illus.). 447p. lib. bdg. 36.00 (ISBN 0-8398-1751-7); pap. text ed. 6.95x (ISBN 0-89197-912-3). Irvington.

Quadrupeds of North America, 3 vols. John J. Audubon & John Bachman. LC 73-17796. (Natural Sciences of America Ser.). (Illus.). 1406p. 1974. Repr. Set. 99.00x (ISBN 0-405-05706-7); Vol. 1. 33.00x (ISBN 0-405-05707-5); Vol. 2. 33.00x (ISBN 0-405-05708-3); Vol. 3. 33.00x (ISBN 0-405-05709-1). Ayer Co Pubs.

Quadruples in Electron Lens Design see Advances in Electronics & Electron Physics: Supplements.

Quadrupole Mass Spectrometry. March et al. (Chemical Analysis Ser.). 1988. write for info. (ISBN 0-471-85794-7). Wiley.

Quaestio Disputata de Unitate Formae: A Critical Edition. Richard Knapwell. Ed. by Francis E. Kelley. LC 83-789. (Medieval & Renaissance Texts & Studies: Vol. 15). 100p. 1982. 15.00 (ISBN 0-86698-022-9). Medieval & Renaissance NY.

Quaestiones Alberti de Modis Significandi: Psuedo-Albertus Magnus. Tr. by L. G. Kelly. (Studies in the History of Linguistics Ser.: No. 15). xxxvii, 191p. 1977. 36.00x (ISBN 90-272-4510-X). Benjamins North Am.

Quaestiones in Quatuor Libros Sentntiarum et Quodlibetales. John Baconthorpe. 1582p. 1618. text ed. 372.60x (ISBN 0-576-99128-7, Pub. by Gregg Intl Pubs England). Gregg Intl.

Quaestiones Parisiis Disputatae. Joannes Neapolitanus. 448p. 1618. text ed. 74.52x (ISBN 0-576-99494-4, Pub. by Gregg Intl Pubs England). Gregg Intl.

Quaestiones Quodlibetales see John Duns Scotus: God & Creatures; the Quodlibetal Questions.

Quag Keep. Andre Norton. (Science Fiction Ser.). 1987. pap. 2.95 (ISBN 0-88677-250-8). DAW Bks.

Quai Malaquais: A Story of Paris. John Guenther. 200p. 1984. pap. 5.00 (ISBN 0-938266-02-0). Purchase Pr.

Quail Hunting in America: Tactics for Finding & Taking Bobwhite, Valley, GambelMountain, Scaled, & Mearns Quail by Season & Habitat. Tom Huggler. (Illus.). 288p. 1987. 19.95 (ISBN 0-8117-1277-X). Stackpole.

Quail's Egg: A Folk Tale from Sri Lanka. Retold by & illus. by Joanna Troughton. (Folk Tales of the World Ser.). (Illus.). (ps-3). 1988. 12.95. P Bedrick Bks.

Quails, Partridges, & Francolins of the World. Paul A. Johnsgard. (Illus.). 288p. 1988. 75.00 (ISBN 0-19-857193-3). Oxford U Pr.

Quaint Corners of Ancient Empires: Southern India, Burma & Manila. Michael M. Shoemaker. LC 72-4582. (Essay Index Reprint Ser.). Repr. of 1899 ed. 33.00 (ISBN 0-8369-2978-0). Ayer Co Pubs.

Quaint Cuts in the Chap Book Style. Joseph Crawhall. 88p. 1974. Repr. of 1889 ed. 5.95 (ISBN 0-486-23020-1). Dover.

Quaint Cuts in the Chap Book Style. Joseph Crawhall. Ed. by Theodore Menten. (Illus.). 9.00 (ISBN 0-8446-5020-X). Peter Smith.

Quaint Furniture. Ed. by Stephen Gray. (Mission Furniture Catalogues Ser.: No. 1). 80p. 1981. pap. 5.95 (ISBN 0-940326-01-9). Turn of Cent.

Quaint Furniture in Arts & Crafts. Ed. by Stephen Gray. (Mission Furniture Catalogues Ser.: No. 9). 144p. 1988. pap. 15.95 (ISBN 0-940326-11-6). Turn of Cent.

Quaint Furniture: Stickley Bros. (Illus.). 88p. 1985. pap. 5.95 (ISBN 0-87905-412-3). Gibbs Smith Pub.

Quaint Irish Customs & Superstitions. Gregory Wilde. 96p. (Orig.). (YA) (gr. 9 up). 1988. pap. 9.95 (ISBN 0-85342-841-7, Pub. by Mercier Pr Ireland). Irish Bks Media.

Quaisey, a Nantucket Quail. Barbara L. Loucka. 1987. 7.95 (ISBN 0-533-07200-X). Vantage.

Quake. Michael Hardcastle. (YA) (gr. 7 up). 1988. 11.95 (ISBN 0-317-69550-9). Faber & Faber.

Quaker: A Study in Costume. Amelia M. Gummere. LC 68-56494. (Illus.). 1968. Repr. of 1901 ed. 20.00 (ISBN 0-405-08585-0, Blom Pubns). Ayer Co Pubs.

Quaker Adventures: Three Hundred Years in Carolina. Mary E. Hinshaw. (Illus.). 74p. (Orig.). (gr. 5-7). 1971. pap. 1.50x (ISBN 0-942727-01-0). NC Yrly Pubns Bd.

Quaker Anecdotes. Irvin C. Poley & Ruth V. Poley. 1983. pap. 2.50x (ISBN 0-87574-033-2, 033). Pendle Hill.

Quaker Approach to Contemporary Problems. Ed. by John Kavanaugh. Repr. of 1953 ed. lib. bdg. 35.00x (ISBN 0-8371-4432-9, KAGA). Greenwood.

Quaker Cavalier: William Penn. Joyce Reason. 1971. pap. 3.50 (ISBN 0-87508-618-7). Chr Lit.

Quaker Colonies see Chronicles of America.

Quaker Doctrine of Inward Peace. Howard H. Brinton. LC 64-23230. (Orig.). 1948. pap. 2.50x (ISBN 0-87574-044-8). Pendle Hill.

Quaker Education in the Colony & State of New Jersey. Thomas Woody. LC 76-89256. (American Education: Its Men, Institutions & Ideas, Ser. 1). 1969. Repr. of 1923 ed. 32.00 (ISBN 0-405-01494-5). Ayer Co Pubs.

Quaker Education in Theory & Practice. rev. ed. Howard H. Brinton. LC 58-12843. 1949. pap. 7.00x (ISBN 0-87574-009-X). Pendle Hill.

Quaker Experiences in International Conciliation. C. H. Yarrow. LC 78-7415. 1978. 29.00x (ISBN 0-300-02260-3). Yale U Pr.

Quaker Funeral. Rev. ed. 32p. (Orig.). 1986. pap. 1.50x (ISBN 0-942727-12-6). NC Yrly Pubns Bd.

Quaker Genealogies: A Selected List of Books. Willard Heiss & Thomas D. Hamm. LC 85-18909. 73p. (Orig.). 1985. pap. text ed. 4.95 (ISBN 0-88082-013-6). New Eng Hist.

Quaker Heritage in Medicine. Russell J. Elkinton & Robert A. Clark. (Illus.). 1978. pap. 3.95 (ISBN 0-910286-68-X). Boxwood.

Quaker Idyls. Sarah M. Gardner. LC 70-110193. (Short Story Index Reprint Ser.). 1894. 17.00 (ISBN 0-8369-3344-3). Ayer Co Pubs.

Quaker Influence in American Literature. Howard W. Hintz. 1970. Repr. of 1940 ed. lib. bdg. 18.75 (ISBN 0-8371-3945-7, HIGA). Greenwood.

Quaker Influence on America Ideals. Seth B. Hinshaw. (Orig.). 1976. pap. 1.50x (ISBN 0-942727-03-7). NC Yrly Pubns Bd.

Quaker Invasion of Massachusetts. Richard P. Hallowell. 13.50 (ISBN 0-8369-7139-6, 7972). Ayer Co Pubs.

Quaker Invasion of Massachusetts. Richard P. Hallowell. vi, 227p. 1987. pap. 14.50 (ISBN 1-55613-085-6). Heritage Bk.

Quaker Journals: Varieties of Religious Experience among Friends. Howard H. Brinton. LC 78-188399. (Illus., Orig.). 1972. 7.00 (ISBN 0-87574-952-6). Pendle Hill.

Quaker Looks at Yoga. Dorothy Ackerman. LC 76-23909. (Orig.). 1976. pap. 2.50x (ISBN 0-87574-207-6, 207). Pendle Hill.

Quaker Meeting. Howard E. Collier. 1983. pap. 2.50x (ISBN 0-87574-026-X, 026). Pendle Hill.

Quaker Message. Sidney Lucas. 1948. pap. 2.50x (ISBN 0-87574-040-5, 040). Pendle Hill.

Quaker Message: A Personal Affirmation. Hugh L. Doncaster. 1977. pap. 2.50x (ISBN 0-87574-181-9, 181). Pendle Hill.

Quaker Mutation. Gerald Heard. 1983. pap. 2.50x (ISBN 0-87574-007-3, 007). Pendle Hill.

Quaker Poets Past & Present. Mary H. Jones. LC 75-7414. 32p. (Orig.). 1975. pap. 2.50x (ISBN 0-87574-202-5). Pendle Hill.

Quaker Relief During the Siege of Boston. Henry J. Cadbury. 1983. pap. 2.50x (ISBN 0-686-43965-1, 004). Pendle Hill.

Quaker Singer's Recollections. David Bispham. Ed. by Andrew Farkas. LC 76-29927. (Opera Biographies). (Illus.). 1977. Repr. of 1921 ed. lib. bdg. 27.50x (ISBN 0-405-09669-0). Ayer Co Pubs.

Quaker Sloopers: From the Fjords to the Prairies. Wilmer L. Tjossem. LC 84-80195. 80p. 1984. pap. 8.95 (ISBN 0-913408-85-9). Friends United.

Quaker Social History: Sixteen Sixty-Nine to Seventeen Thirty-Eight. Arnold Lloyd. LC 79-4398. 1979. Repr. of 1950 ed. lib. bdg. 35.00x (ISBN 0-313-20943-X, LLQU). Greenwood.

Quaker Spirituality: Selected Writings. Ed. by Douglas V. Steere. (Classics of Western Spirituality Ser.). 384p. 1984. pap. 9.95 (ISBN 0-8091-2510-2). Paulist Pr.

Quaker Strongholds. Caroline Stephen. Ed. by Mary G. Ogilvie. LC 51-4625. 32p. (Orig.). 1951. pap. 2.50x (ISBN 0-87574-059-6, 059). Pendle Hill.

Quaker Struggle for the Rights of Women. pap. 0.75 (ISBN 0-686-95360-6). Am Fr Serv Comm.

Quaker Testimonies & Economic Alternatives. Severyn Broyn. LC 80-80915. 35p. pap. 2.50x (ISBN 0-87574-231-9). Pendle Hill.

Quaker Woman's Cookbook: The Domestic Cookery of Elizabeth Ellicott Lea. Elizabeth E. Lea. Ed. by William W. Weaver. LC 82-60260. 402p. 1982. 23.95 (ISBN 0-8122-7848-8). U of Pa Pr.

Quaker Worship & Techniques of Meditation. Scott Crom. 1974. pap. 2.50x (ISBN 0-87574-195-9, 195). Pendle Hill.

Quakerism: A Study Guide on the Religious Society of Friends. Leonard S. Kenworthy. LC 81-80656. 224p. 1981. pap. 5.00 (ISBN 0-932970-21-4). Prinit Pr.

Quakerism & Christianity. Edwin B. Bronner. LC 67-18689. (Orig.). 1967. pap. 2.50x (ISBN 0-87574-152-5, 152). Pendle Hill.

Quakerism & Other Religions. Howard H. Brinton. 1983. pap. 2.50x (ISBN 0-87574-093-6, 093). Pendle Hill.

Quakerism in India. Horace Alexander. 1945. pap. 2.50x (ISBN 0-87574-031-6, 031). Pendle Hill.

Quakerism of the Future: Mystical, Prophetic & Evangelical. John Yungblut. LC 74-81830. (Orig.). 1974. pap. 2.50x (ISBN 0-87574-194-0). Pendle Hill.

Quakerism on the Eastern Shore. Kenneth Carroll. LC 70-112986. (Illus.). 328p. 1970. 15.00x (ISBN 0-938420-15-1). Md Hist.

Quakers. Hugh Barbour & J. William Frost. (Denominations in America Ser.: No. 3). 1988. price not set (ISBN 0-313-22816-7, BSF/). Greenwood.

Quakers. Hope Hay. 1985. 13.00x (ISBN 0-7062-4025-1, Pub. by Ward Lock Educ Co Ltd). State Mutual Bk.

Quakers & Education. W. A. Stewart. LC 76-115330. 1971. Repr. of 1953 ed. 32.50x (ISBN 0-8046-1121-1, Pub. by Kennikat). Assoc Faculty Pr.

Quakers & Slavery: A Divided Spirit. Jean R. Soderlund. LC 85-42707. (Illus.). 233p. 1985. text ed. 29.00x (ISBN 0-691-04732-4); pap. 14.95 (ISBN 0-691-10243-0). Princeton U Pr.

Quakers & the American Family: British Quakers in the Delaware Valley, 1650-1765. Barry Levy. (Illus.). 352p. 1988. 24.95 (ISBN 0-19-504975-6). Oxford U Pr.

Quakers & the Atlantic Culture. Frederick Tolles. 1980. Repr. of 1960 ed. lib. bdg. 16.00x (ISBN 0-374-97949-9, Octagon). Hippocrene Bks.

Quakers & the English Legal System, 1660-1688. Craig W. Horle. 336p. 1988. text ed. 34.95x (ISBN 0-8122-8101-2). U of Pa Pr.

Quakers & the English Revolution. Barry Reay. LC 84-22355. 200p. 1985. 27.50 (ISBN 0-312-65808-7). St Martin.

Quakers & the Use of Power. Paul Lacey. LC 81-85558. (Pendle Hill Pamphlets Ser.). 32p. (Orig.). 1982. pap. 2.50x (ISBN 0-87574-241-6, 241). Pendle Hill.

Quakers As Pioneers in Social Work. Auguste Jorns. LC 68-8232. 1969. Repr. of 1931 ed. 26.50x (ISBN 0-8046-0244-1, Pub. by Kennikat). Assoc Faculty Pr.

Quakers As Pioneers in Social Work. Auguste Jorns. Tr. by Thomas K. Brown. LC 69-14934. (Criminology, Law Enforcement, & Social Problems Ser.: No. 27). 1969. Repr. of 1931 ed. 8.50x (ISBN 0-87585-027-8). Patterson Smith.

Quakers in Conflict: The Hicksite Reformation. H. Larry Ingle. LC 86-1528. 330p. 1986. text ed. 29.95x (ISBN 0-87049-501-1). U of Tenn Pr.

Quakers in Nazi Germany. Michael Seadle. (Studies in Quakerism: No. 5). 44p. (Orig.). 1978. pap. 2.00 (ISBN 0-89670-006-2). Progresiv Pub.

Quakers in Peace & War. Margaret E. Hirst. LC 70-147671. (Library of War & Peace; Relig. & Ethical Positions on War Ser.). lib. bdg. 46.00 (ISBN 0-8240-0429-9). Garland Pub.

Quakers in Peace & War: An Account of Their Peace Principles & Practice. Margaret E. Hirst. LC 73-137545. (Peace Movement in America Ser). 560p. 1972. Repr. of 1923 ed. lib. bdg. 32.95x (ISBN 0-89198-073-3). Ozer.

Quakers in Pennsylvania. Albert C. Applegarth. LC 78-63813. (Johns Hopkins University. Studies in the Social Sciences. Tenth Ser. 1892: 8-9). Repr. of 1892 ed. 11.50 (ISBN 0-404-61076-5). AMS Pr.

Quakers in Pennsylvania. Albert C. Applegarth. pap. 9.00 (ISBN 0-384-01765-7). Johnson Repr.

Quakers in Puritan England. Hugh Barbour. LC 85-6963. 300p. 1985. pap. 14.95 (ISBN 0-913408-87-5). Friends United.

Quakers in Science & Industry. Arthur Raistrick. LC 68-18641. (Illus.). 1968. Repr. of 1950 ed. 39.50x (ISBN 0-678-05622-6). Kelley.

Quakers in the Colonial Northeast. Arthur J. Worrall. LC 79-63086. 248p. 1980. 25.00x (ISBN 0-87451-174-7). U Pr of New Eng.

Quakers Uniting in Publications Catalog, 1987. Ed. by Barbara Mays. 54p. 1987. 2.00 (ISBN 0-913408-99-9). Friends United.

Quaking Aspen Grove. Phyllis Walsh. (Haiku Ser.: No. 18). 1985. pap. 3.00 (ISBN 1-55780-087-1). Juniper Pr WI.

Qualification of Nuclear Power Plant Personnel: A Guidebook. 290p. 1985. pap. 51.00 (ISBN 92-0-155584-9, IDC242, IAEA). UNIPUB.

Qualifications & Certification of Instrumentation & Control Technicians in Nuclear Power Plants: ANSI/ISA Standard S67.14. 16p. 1983. pap. text ed. 16.00x (ISBN 0-87664-788-3). Instru Soc.

Qualifications & Training of Staff of the Regulatory Body for Nuclear Power Plants: A Safety Guide. (Safety Ser.: No. 50-SG-01). 30p. (Eng., Fr., Rus. & Span.). 1979. pap. 7.75 (ISBN 92-0-123179-2, ISP513, IAEA). UNIPUB.

Qualifications Division Five of the Organization Executive Course see Organization Executive Course: An Encyclopedia of Scientology Policy (1950-1951, 1953-1974,.

Qualifications for a Score. rev. ed. Muriel Topaz. 1988. pap. write for info. (ISBN 0-932582-40-0). Dance Notation.

Qualifications of Foreign Language Teachers see Foreign Language Teachers & Tests.

Qualified Deferred Compensation Plans: Forms, 1 vol. Neil Mancoff & Allen Steinberg. LC 83-23222. 798p. 1984. 80.00 (ISBN 0-317-11358-5). Callaghan.

Qualified Deferred Compensation Plans: Treatise, 1 vol. Gary Boren. LC 83-23912. 1446p. 1983. 95.00 (ISBN 0-317-11357-7). Callaghan.

Qualified Immunity from Liability for Violations of Federal Rights: A Modification. Michael Smith. LC 83-622201. (Local Government Law Bulletin Ser.: No. 23). 1983. 3.00. U of NC Inst Gov.

Qualified Joint & Survivor Annuities. Jack M. Elkin. (Requirements for Qualification of Plans Ser.). 13p. 1983. pap. 2.50 (ISBN 0-317-31165-4, B447). Am Law Inst.

Qualified Products List & Sources, No. 66. Global Engineering Documents Staff. 304p. 1987. perfect binding 59.95 (ISBN 0-912702-33-8). Global Eng.

Qualified Retirement & Other Employee Benefit Plans, 1988. Michael J. Canan. (Handbook Ser.). (Illus.). 870p. 1988. pap. text ed. write for info. (ISBN 0-314-77713-X). West Pub.

Qualified Retirement Plans. Ray R. Benner & Leslie L. Wellman. 500p. 1982. looseleaf 145.00 (ISBN 0-932500-18-8). Natl Hlth Pub.

Qualified Retirement Plans. Michael J. Canan & David R. Baker. (Handbook Ser.). 730p. 1986. write for info. (ISBN 0-314-28486-9). West Pub.

Qualified Student: A History of Selective College Admission in America. Harold S. Wechsler. LC 76-47692. pap. 90.30 (ISBN 0-317-09624-9, 2015845). Bks Demand UMI.

Qualifying Adjective in Spanish. Ernesto Zierer. LC 72-94516. (Janua Linguarum, Ser. Practica: No. 192). 54p. 1974. pap. text ed. 8.80x (ISBN 90-2792-722-7). Mouton.

Qualifying Examination: Management Service. Jack Rudman. (Career Examination Ser.: CS-39). (Cloth bdg. avail. on request). pap. 14.00 (ISBN 0-8373-3739-9). Natl Learning.

Qualifying for Admission to the Service Academies: A Student's Guide. Robert F. Collins. Ed. by Ruth Rosen. (Military Opportunity Ser.). (Illus.). 154p. (YA) (gr. 7 up). 1987. lib. bdg. 14.95 (ISBN 0-8239-0696-5). Rosen Group.

Qualitative Analysis. Ray U. Brumblay. (Illus., Orig). 1964. pap. 5.95 (ISBN 0-06-460116-1, CO 116, B&N Bks). Har-Row.

Qualitative Analysis: An Introduction. W. David Moseley. 128p. 1984. pap. text ed. 9.00 (ISBN 0-8403-3453-2). Kendall-Hunt.

Qualitative Analysis & Econometric Estimation of Continuous Time Dynamic Models. G. Gandolfo. (Contributions to Economic Analysis Ser.: Vol. 136). 254p. 1981. 58.00 (ISBN 0-444-86025-8, North-Holland). Elsevier.

Qualitative Analysis & Ionic Equilibrium. George H. Schenk & Darrell D. Ebbing. LC 84-81935. 256p. 1985. pap. text ed. 11.56 (ISBN 0-395-36517-1). HM.

Qualitative Analysis & the Properties of Ions in Aqueous Solution. Emil Slowinski & William Masterton. LC 75-145567. 1971. 18.00 (ISBN 0-7216-8369-X, CBS C). SCP.

Qualitative Analysis by Gas Chromatography. Seaton T. Preston, Jr. et al. 30p. 1982. write for info. (ISBN 0-913106-18-6). PolyScience.

Qualitative Analysis for Social Scientists. Anselm Strauss. LC 86-21608. (Illus.). 352p. 1987. 49.50 (ISBN 0-521-32845-4); pap. 14.95 (ISBN 0-521-33806-9). Cambridge U Pr.

Qualitative Analysis of Behavior: Foraging, Vol. 6. Ed. by Michael L. Commons & A. Kacelnick Shettleworth. (Roitblat-Bever Olton: Comparative Cognition & Neuroscience Ser.). 328p. 1987. text ed. 45.00 (ISBN 0-89859-550-9). L Erlbaum Assocs.

Qualitative Analysis of Flavor & Fragrance Volatiles by Glass Capillary Gas Chromtography. Walter Jennings & Takayuki Shibamoto. LC 79-26034. 1980. 63.00 (ISBN 0-12-384250-6). Acad Pr.

Qualitative Analysis of Large Scale Dynamical Systems. Anthony N. Michel & Richard K. Miller. 1977. 65.50 (ISBN 0-12-493850-7). Acad Pr.

Qualitative Analysis of Physical Problems. Ed. by M. Gitterman & V. Halpern. LC 80-767. 1981. 32.95 (ISBN 0-12-285150-1). Acad Pr.

Qualitative Analysis of the Anistropic Kepler Problem. Josefina Casasayas & Jaume Llibre. LC 84-18521. (Memoirs of the American Mathematical Society: No. 312). 115p. 1984. pap. 15.00 (ISBN 0-8218-2309-4). Am Math.

Qualitative Analysis of the Periodically Forced Relaxation Oscillations. Mark Levi. LC 81-3642. (Memoirs of the American Mathematical Society: No. 244). 148p. 1981. pap. 12.00 (ISBN 0-8218-2244-6, MEMO-244). Am Math.

Qualitative & Quantitative Analyses of Plankton Diatoms. Matthew H. Hohn. 1969. 6.00 (ISBN 0-86727-057-8). Ohio Bio Survey.

Qualitative & Quantitative Mathematical Economics. J. H. Paelinck. 1982. lib. bdg. 34.50 (ISBN 90-247-2623-9, Pub. by Martinus Nijhoff Netherlands). Kluwer Academic.

Qualitative & Quantitative Social Research: Papers in Honor of Paul F. Lazarsfeld. Ed. by Robert K. Merton et al. LC 78-24752. 1979. 23.95 (ISBN 0-02-920930-7). Free Pr.

Qualitative Approaches to Evaluation in Education: The Silent Scientific Revolution. Ed. by David M. Fetterman. LC 88-2746. (Illus.). 320p. 1988. lib. bdg. 45.00 (ISBN 0-275-92917-5, C2917). Praeger.

Qualitative Aspects of Large Systems. O. I. Franksen et al. (Lecture Notes in Control & Information Science: Vol. 17). 1979. pap. 13.00 (ISBN 0-387-09609-4). Springer-Verlag.

Qualitative Change in Human Geography. Ed. by S. S. Duncan. (Illus.). 127p. 1981. 39.00 (ISBN 0-08-025222-2). Pergamon.

Qualitative Choice Analysis: Theory, Econometrics, & an Application to Automobile Demand. Kenneth Train. (MIT Press Series in Transportation Studies). 224p. 1986. text ed. 30.00x (ISBN 0-262-20055-4). MIT Pr.

Qualitative Credit Control. William E. Dunkman. (Columbia University. Studies in the Social Sciences: No. 395). Repr. of 1933 ed. 24.50 (ISBN 0-404-51395-6). AMS Pr.

Qualitative Data Analysis: A Sourcebook of New Methods. Matthew B. Miles & A. Michael Huberman. 240p. 1984. text ed. 35.00 (ISBN 0-8039-2274-4). Sage.

Quality Assurance: The Route to Efficiency & Competitiveness. Lionel Stebbing. 231p. 1986. 62.95 (ISBN 0-470-20298-X). Halsted Pr.

Quality, Careers & Training in Educational & Social Research. Caroline H. Persell. LC 76-9294. (Illus.). 321p. 1976. lib. bdg. 28.95x (ISBN 0-930390-32-6); pap. text ed. 16.95x (ISBN 0-930390-31-8). Gen Hall.

Quality Circle Handbook. Donald L. Dewar. (Quality Circle Leader Manual & Instructional Guide, Quality Circle Member Manual Ser.). 640p. 1980. pap. 69.00 (ISBN 0-937670-03-0). Quality Circle.

Quality Circle Handbook for Financial Institutions. 3rd ed. Donald L. Dewar. (Illus.). 496p. 1982. pap. 69.00 (ISBN 0-937670-14-6). Quality Circle.

Quality Circle Handbook for Health Care Facilities. 2nd ed. Donald L. Dewar. (Illus.). 496p. (Orig.). 1982. pap. 60.00 (ISBN 0-937670-07-3). Quality Circle.

Quality Circle Leader Manual & Instructional Guide. Donald L. Dewar. (Quality Circle Member Manual: Quality Circle Handbook Ser.). 248p. 1980. pap. 18.50 (ISBN 0-937670-02-2). Quality Circle.

Quality Circle Leader Manual & Instructional Guide for Financial Institutions. 3rd ed. Donald L. Dewar. (Illus.). 235p. (Orig.). 1982. 18.50 (ISBN 0-937670-12-X). Quality Circle.

Quality Circle Leader Manual & Instructional Guide for Health Care Facilities. 2nd ed. (Illus.). 235p. (Orig.). 1982. pap. 18.50 (ISBN 0-937670-06-5). Quality Circle.

Quality Circle Management: The Human Side of Quality. Harry Katzan, Jr. (Illus.). 180p. 1988. 24.95 (ISBN 0-89433-326-7, 8260). Petrocelli.

Quality Circle Member Manual. Donald L. Dewar. (Quality Circle Handbook & Quality Circle Leader Manual & Instructional Guide Ser.). (Illus.). 268p. (Orig.). 1980. pap. 12.75 (ISBN 0-937670-01-4). Quality Circle.

Quality Circle Member Manual for Financial Institutions. 3rd ed. Donald L. Dewar. (Illus.). 268p. 1982. pap. 12.75 (ISBN 0-937670-13-8). Quality Circle.

Quality Circle Member Manual for Health Care Facilities. 2nd ed. Donald L. Dewar. (Illus.). 268p. (Orig.). 1982. pap. 12.75 (ISBN 0-937670-05-7). Quality Circle.

Quality Circle Member's Packet. Roger G. James & Aaron J. Elkins. 34p. 1983. for pkg. of six 26.50 (ISBN 0-88390-182-X). Univ Assocs.

Quality Circle: What You Should Know about It. Donald L. Dewar. (Illus.). 29p. 1980. pap. 1.15 (ISBN 0-937670-04-9). Quality Circle.

Quality Circle: What You Should Know about It - Financial Institutions. 3rd ed. Donald L. Dewar. (Illus.). 29p. 1982. pap. 1.15 (ISBN 0-937670-17-0). Quality Circle.

Quality Circle: What You Should Know about It - Health Care Facilities. 2nd ed. Donald L. Dewar. (Illus.). 29p. (Orig.). 1982. pap. 1.15 (ISBN 0-937670-16-2). Quality Circle.

Quality Circles. B. L. Maheshwari. 1987. 16.00 (ISBN 81-204-0235-9, Pub. by Oxford IBH). South Asia Bks.

Quality Circles. 1982. 61.95 (ISBN 0-85013-136-7). Dartnell Corp.

Quality Circles. Mike Robson. (Practical Guides to Quality Circles Ser.: No. 1). 224p. 1982. text ed. 32.00x (ISBN 0-566-02343-1). Gower Pub Co.

Quality Circles. Philip C. Thompson. 16.95 (ISBN 0-8144-5731-2). AMACOM.

Quality Circles: A Guide to Participation & Productivity. Charmey Crocker & Chiu Crocker. 1986. pap. 4.95 (ISBN 0-451-62464-5, Pub. by Ment). NAL.

Quality Circles: A Guide to Participation & Productivity. Olga Crocker et al. 312p. 1985. 24.95 (ISBN 0-8160-1161-3). Facts on File.

Quality Circles: A Practical Guide. 2nd ed. Mike Robson. 256p. 1988. text ed. 46.80 (ISBN 0-566-02748-8, Pub. by Gower Pub England). Gower Pub Co.

Quality Circles: An Approach to Productivity Improvement. Price Gibson. (Studies in Productivity: Highlights of the Literature Ser.: Vol. 26). 79p. 1982. pap. 39.00 (ISBN 0-08-029507-X). Work in Amer.

Quality Circles: An Introduction for Management. 30.00 (ISBN 0-318-02548-5); members 15.00 (ISBN 0-318-02549-3). Print Indus Am.

Quality Circles: Answers to One Hundred Frequently Asked Questions. rev. ed. Donald L. Dewar. (Illus.). 1980. pap. 4.95 (ISBN 0-937670-00-6). Quality Circle.

Quality Circles: Applications in Vocational Education. Russell F. Lloyd & Virgil R. Rehg. 47p. 1983. 4.95 (ISBN 0-318-22183-7, IN249). Natl Ctr Res Voc Ed.

Quality Circles: Changing Images of People at Work. William L. Mohr & Harriet Mohr. LC 83-5970. (Illus.). 256p. 1983. write for info. (ISBN 0-201-05207-5). Addison-Wesley.

Quality Circles Data Bank. Cathy Kramer. 44.95 (ISBN 0-317-07128-9). IAQC Pr.

Quality Circles: Facilitator's Manual. John E. Baird, Jr. & David J. Rittof. (Illus.). 247p. (Orig.). 1983. 39.95X (ISBN 0-88133-010-8). Waveland Pr.

Quality Circles Handbook. David Hutchins. 256p. 1985. pap. 23.50 (ISBN 0-273-02644-5). Nichols Pub.

Quality Circles: Implications for Training. Carl L. Harshman. 74p. 1982. 6.50 (ISBN 0-318-22184-5, IN243). Natl Ctr Res Voc Ed.

Quality Circles in Action. Mike Robson. LC 84-4095. 176p. 1984. text ed. 32.95x (ISBN 0-566-02433-0). Gower Pub Co.

Quality Circles in Health Care Facilities. Alvin Goldberg & C. Carl Pegels. 192p. 1984. 36.50. Aspen Pub.

Quality Circles: Leader's Manual. John E. Baird, Jr. 256p. 1982. pap. text ed. 14.95 (ISBN 0-917974-88-3). Waveland Pr.

Quality Circles Master Guide: Increasing Productivity with People Power. Sud Ingle. 288p. 1982. 25.95 (ISBN 0-13-745018-4); pap. 14.95 (ISBN 0-13-745000-1). P-H.

Quality Circles: One Approach to Productivity Improvement. Price Gibson. (Work in America Institute Studies in Productivity). 1982. pap. 35.00. Pergamon.

Quality Circles: Participant's Manual. John E. Baird, Jr. (Illus.). 192p. 1982. pap. text ed. 9.95x (ISBN 0-917974-79-4). Waveland Pr.

Quality (Concepts) from Start to Finish: Proceedings. Food Processors Institute Staff. 39p. (Orig.). 1984. pap. 10.00 (ISBN 0-937774-10-3). Food Processors.

Quality Concrete. rev. ed. Thomas A. Hoerner & W. Forrest Bear. (Illus.). 36p. 1971. pap. text ed. 3.15x (ISBN 0-913163-00-7, 164). Hobar Pubns.

Quality Control. 2nd ed. Dale H. Besterfield. (Illus.). 336p. 1986. text ed. 39.00 (ISBN 0-13-745258-6). P-H.

Quality Control. Richard C. Vaughn. (Illus.). 234p. 1974. text ed. 12.95x (ISBN 0-8138-1265-8). Iowa St U Pr.

Quality Control: A Practical Approach. Dale H. Besterfield. (Illus.). 1979. ref. o.p. 35.00 (ISBN 0-13-745232-2). P-H.

Quality Control & Application. Bertrand L. Hansen & Prabbaker M. Ghare. (Illus.). 512p. 1987. text ed. 51.00 (ISBN 0-13-745225-X). P-H.

Quality Control & Data Analysis of Binder-Ligand Assays: Radioimmunoassay, Enzymeimmunoassay, Fluoroimmunoassay & Other Immunoassay Methods: A Programmed Text, Volume II, Statistical Considerations. Richard C. Rodgers. (Illus.). 1981. text ed. 38.50 (ISBN 0-930914-08-2). Sci Newsletters.

Quality Control & Data Analysis of Binder-Ligand Assays: Radiommunoassay, Enzymeimmmunoassay, Fluoroimmunoassay, a Programmed Text, Vol. I. Richard C. Rodgers. (Illus.). 1981. 36.00 (ISBN 0-930914-07-4). Sci Newsletters.

Quality Control & Industrial Statistics. Duncan. 1012p. 27.50 (ISBN 0-318-13233-8, P 48). Am Soc QC.

Quality Control & Industrial Statistics. 5th ed. Acheson J. Duncan. 1986. 44.95x (ISBN 0-256-03535-0). Irwin.

Quality Control & Peer Review: A Practice Manual for CPAs. James W. Pattillo. LC 83-14607. (Modern Accounting Perspectives & Practice Ser.: 1-466). 301p. 1984. 49.50 (ISBN 0-471-86986-4). Wiley.

Quality Control & Performance Appraisal, Vol. 1. Ed. by Journal of Nursing Administration. LC 75-41590. 62p. 1976. pap. text ed. 25.25 (ISBN 0-913654-23-X). Aspen Pub.

Quality Control & Performance Appraisal, Vol. 2. Journal of Nursing Administration. LC 75-41590. 48p. 1976. pap. 25.25 (ISBN 0-913654-34-5). Aspen Pub.

Quality Control & Performance Appraisal, Vol. 3. Ed. by Journal of Nursing Administration. LC 77-85307. 44p. 1977. pap. 25.25 (ISBN 0-913654-37-X). Aspen Pub.

Quality Control & Quality Assurance - the Asian Experience: Papers from APO Symposium, Indonesia. 192p. 1980. pap. 14.75 (ISBN 92-833-1486-7, APO123, APO). UNIPUB.

Quality Control: ASTM Standards on Precision & Bias for Various Applications. 570p. 1985. pap. 24.00. ASTM.

Quality Control Audit: A Management Evalulation Tool. Charles E. Mills. 288p. 1988. 42.50 (ISBN 0-07-042428-4). McGraw.

Quality Control Circle Activities in the Service Sector: A Symposium Report. 170p. 1986. pap. 10.50 (ISBN 0-317-59555-5, U-APO230, Pub. by APO). UNIPUB-Kraus Intl.

Quality Control Circle Approach to Police Community Relations. Ralph Hogges. Ed. by Beryl Davis & Irving J. Klein. LC 88-80358. 78p. 1988. 8.50 (ISBN 0-938993-03-8). Coral Gables Pub.

Quality Control Circles: An Important Tool for Productivity. Cheryl E. Lees-Haley. (Illus.). 1982. pap. text ed. 6.95 (ISBN 0-317-03935-0). Rubicon.

Quality Control for Hot Mix Asphalt Manufacturing Facilities & Paving Operations. (Quality Improvemtn Program Ser.: No. 97). 64p. 1986. 38.00 (ISBN 0-317-58383-2). Natl Asphalt Pavement.

Quality Control for Management. Kenneth Kivenko. LC 83-26928. 324p. 1984. 59.95x (ISBN 0-13-745217-9, Busn). P-H.

Quality Control for Plastics: How to Set up & Run a Quality Program in a Plastics Processing Facility. William J. Tobin et al. 150p. 1986. 55.00 (ISBN 0-938648-26-8). T-C Pubns CA.

Quality Control for Profit. Lester et al. (Quality Control Ser.). 312p. 1985. 69.75 (ISBN 0-8247-7424-8). Dekker.

Quality Control for Rehabilitation Workshops. David A. Hietala. (Illus.). 61p. (Orig.). 1980. pap. 6.25x (ISBN 0-916671-30-5). Material Dev.

Quality Control Handbook. rev. 3rd ed. Joseph M. Juran. 1600p. 1974. text ed. 85.00 (ISBN 0-07-033175-8). McGraw.

Quality Control in Analytical Chemistry. G. Kateman & F. W. Pijpers. LC 80-23146. (Chemical Analysis Ser.: Vol. 60). 276p. 1981. 68.00x (ISBN 0-471-46020-6, Pub. by Wiley-Interscience). Wiley.

Quality Control in Architectural & Engineering Offices: A Selective Bibliography & Sources for Information. David K. Ballast. (Architecture Ser.: A 1865). 8p. 1987. 3.00 (ISBN 1-55590-395-9). Vance Biblios.

Quality Control in Automation. Ken Stout. (Illus.). 224p. 1985. text ed. 32.00 (ISBN 0-13-745159-8). P-H.

Quality Control in Clinical Chemistry. T. P. Whitehead. LC 76-44522. (Quality Control Methods in the Clinical Laboratory Ser.). 144p. 1977. text ed. 42.00 (ISBN 0-471-94075-5, Pub. by Wiley Medical). Krieger.

Quality Control in Foodservice. rev. ed. Marvin E. Thorner & Peter B. Manning. (Illus.). 1983. 34.95 (ISBN 0-87055-431-X). AVI.

Quality Control in Haematology. Ed. by S. M. Lewis & J. Coster. 1976. 51.50 (ISBN 0-12-446850-0). Acad Pr.

Quality Control in Higher Education. Charles P. Hogarth. 154p. (Orig.). 1987. lib. bdg. 24.75 (ISBN 0-8191-6174-8); pap. text ed. 11.50 (ISBN 0-8191-6175-6). U Pr of Amer.

Quality Control in Japan. Ed. by K Noro. (Ergonomics Special Issue Ser.: Vol. 27, No. 7). 102p. 1984. pap. 24.00x (ISBN 0-85066-992-8). Taylor & Francis.

Quality Control in Lumber Manufacturing. Terence D. Brown. LC 82-80244. (Forest Industries Bk.). (Illus.). 288p. 1982. 55.00 (ISBN 0-87930-138-4, 463); pap. 44.50 (ISBN 0-87930-142-2). Miller Freeman.

Quality Control in Remedial Site Investigation: Hazardous & Industrial Solid Waste Testing, Vol. 5. Ed. by Cary L. Perket. LC 86-25873. (Special Technical Publications: No. 925). (Illus.). 227p. 1986. text ed. 29.00 (ISBN 0-8031-0451-0, 04-925000-16). ASTM.

Quality Control in the Food Industry, 4 vols. 2nd ed. S. M. Herschdoerfer. (Food Science & Technology Ser.). 1985. Vol. 1. 65.00 (ISBN 0-12-343001-1); Vol. 2, 1986. 75.00 (ISBN 0-12-343002-X); Vol. 3, 1987. 69.50 (ISBN 0-12-343003-8); Vol. 4: 1988, 512p. 89.00 (ISBN 0-12-343004-6). Acad Pr.

Quality Control in the Hospital Discharge Survey. W. Kenneth Harris & Keith L. Hoffman. Ed. by Taloria Stevenson. LC 75-619242. (Data Evaluation & Methods Research Ser 2: No.68). 1976. pap. text ed. 1.50 (ISBN 0-8406-0050-X). Natl Ctr Health Stats.

Quality Control in the Pharmaceutical Industry, 3 vols. Ed. by Murray S. Cooper. Vol. 1, 1972. 78.50 (ISBN 0-12-187601-2); Vol. 2, 1973. 93.50 (ISBN 0-12-187602-0); Vol. 3, 1979. 65.00 (ISBN 0-12-187603-9). Acad Pr.

Quality Control in the Pulp & Paper Industry, 3 Vols. Jack Weiner & Vera Pollock. (Bibliographic Ser.: No. 189, Supplement 1 & 2). 1973. 10.00 (ISBN 0-87010-007-6); Supp. 2, 81P. 1973. 8.00; 73P. 1959 8.00,. Inst Paper Chem.

Quality Control Inspector (U.S.P.S.) Jack Rudman. (Career Examination Ser.: C-2458). (Cloth bdg. avail. on request). pap. 18.00 (ISBN 0-8373-2458-0). Natl Learning.

Quality Control Investigator. Jack Rudman. (Career Examination Ser.: C-2137). (Cloth bdg. avail. on request). pap. 16.00 (ISBN 0-8373-2137-9). Natl Learning.

Quality Control Manual for Injection Molding. William J. Tobin. 101p. 1985. pap. 36.00 (ISBN 0-938648-13-6, 0909). T-C Pubns CA.

Quality Control of Cloth Dimensions & the Shrinkage of Yarns & Fabrics. Ed. by Wira. 1977. 30.00x (ISBN 0-686-87172-3, Pub. by Wira Tech Group). State Mutual Bk.

Quality Control, Reliability, & Engineering Design. Dhillon. (Industrial Engineering Ser.). 392p. 1985. 59.75 (ISBN 0-8247-7278-4). Dekker.

Quality Control, Robust Design & the Taguchi Method. Ed. by Khosrow Dehnad. 500p. 1988. 39.95 (ISBN 0-534-09048-6). Brooks-Cole.

Quality Control: Source Book. Ed. by A. K. Hingwe. 1982. 55.00 (ISBN 0-87170-147-2). ASM.

Quality Control Specialist. Jack Rudman. (Career Examination Ser.: C-1618). (Cloth bdg. avail. on request). pap. 18.00 (ISBN 0-8373-1618-9). Natl Learning.

Quality Control Systems: Procedures for Planning Quality Programs. 640p. 1988. text ed. 49.50 (ISBN 0-07-063160-3). McGraw.

Quality Control Technician-Inspector Training Manual. 235p. Date not set. 30.00 (TM-101). Prestressed Concrete.

Quality Control Techniques for Phototypesetting Film. 10.00 (ISBN 0-318-02629-5). Print Indus Am.

Quality Costs: Ideas & Applications, Vol. I. 2nd ed. Quality Costs Committee Staff. Ed. by Andrew F. Grimm. (Illus.). 588p. 1988. pap. 35.95 (ISBN 0-87389-046-9, H0565). ASQC Qual Pr.

Quality Criteria & Inspection Standards. 2nd ed. 48p. 1980. 5.00 (ISBN 0-318-22852-1, S323). Am Inst Steel Construct.

Quality Criteria for Water Reuse. National Research Council Board on Toxicology & Environmental Health Hazards. 1982. pap. text ed. 11.25x (ISBN 0-309-03326-8). Natl Acad Pr.

Quality Customer Service. William B. Martin. Ed. by Michael G. Crisp. LC 86-71574. (Fifty-Minute Ser.). (Illus.). 72p. (Orig.). 1986. pap. 6.95 (ISBN 0-931961-17-3). Crisp Pubns.

Quality Customer Service. William B. Martin. (CRISP Publications 50-Minute Ser.). Date not set. 6.95. Human Res Dev Pr.

Quality Data Processing. Claude W. Burrill & Leon W. Ellsworth. LC 79-9623. (Data Processing Handbook Ser.). (Illus.). 208p. 1982. text ed. 25.00 (ISBN 0-935310-01-0). Burrill-Ellsworth.

Quality Day Care: A Handbook of Choices for Parents & Caregivers. Richard Endsley & Marilyn Bradbard. (Illus.). 256p. 1981. (Spectrum); pap. 5.95 (ISBN 0-13-745422-8). P-H.

Quality Detection in Foods. 225p. 1976. 25.00 (ISBN 0-916150-04-6, CO176); pap. 19.00 (ISBN 0-317-33226-0). Am Soc Ag Eng.

Quality Ductile Iron Production Today & Tomorrow: Proceedings of the AFS-DIS Conference, 1975. AFS-DIS Conference Staff. 347p. 40.00 (ISBN 0-317-32662-7, FC7510); members 20.00 (ISBN 0-317-32663-5). Am Foundrymen.

Quality Education for All Americans: An Assessment of Gains of Black Americans with Proposals for Program Development in American Schools & Colleges for the Next Quarter Century. William F. Brazziel. LC 73-88966. 264p. 1974. 10.95 (ISBN 0-88258-007-8). Howard U Pr.

Quality Education for Less Money. Louis R. Meeth. LC 73-18502. (Jossey-Bass Series in Higher Education). pap. 56.00 (ISBN 0-317-41803-3, 2025663). Bks Demand UMI.

Quality Enlarging with Kodak B-W Papers (G-1) Eastman Kodak Company. LC 81-68717. (Illus.). 132p. 1985. pap. 12.00 (ISBN 0-87985-279-8). Eastman Kodak.

Quality Environments: Developmentally Appropriate Experiences for Young Children. Ed. by Mac H. Brown. 109p. (Orig.). 1988. pap. text ed. 6.80 (ISBN 0-87563-321-8). Stipes.

Quality Factor in Radiation Protection. Ed. by International Commission on Radiation Units & measurement Staff. LC 86-181. (ICRU Report Ser.: No. 40). 30p. 1986. 15.00 (ISBN 0-913394-34-3). Intl Comm Rad Meas.

Quality Friendship. Gary Inrig. LC 81-38379. 192p. (Orig.). 1981. pap. 7.95 (ISBN 0-8024-2891-6). Moody.

Quality Health Care: The Role of Continuing Medical Education. Ed. by Richard H. Egdahl & Paul M. Gertman. LC 77-70434. 276p. 1977. 51.95 (ISBN 0-912862-37-8). Aspen Pub.

Quality Higher Education in Times of Financial Stress: Proceedings. Pacific Northwest Conference on Higher Education, 1975. Ed. by Richard Landini & Patricia Douglas. LC 76-6137. 1976. pap. 5.00x (ISBN 0-87071-275-6). Oreg St U Pr.

Quality Hospice Care: Administration, Organization, & Models. Alice McDonnell. LC 85-62898. 307p. 1985. text ed. 25.00 (ISBN 0-932500-36-6). Natl Hlth Pub.

Quality Impact of Home Care for the Elderly. Ed. by Francis G. Caro & Arthur E. Blank. (Home Health Care Services Quarterly Ser.: Vol. 9, Nos. 2 & 3). (Illus.). 207p. 1988. text ed. 24.95 (ISBN 0-86656-820-4). Haworth Pr.

Quality Improvement Using Statistical Process Control. Lawrence S. Aft. 395p. 1988. text ed. 31.00 net (ISBN 0-15-574103-9). HarBraceJ.

Quality in Canadian Public Education: A Critical Assessment. Ed. by Hugh A. Stevenson & J. Donald Wilson. 185p. 1988. 44.00x (ISBN 1-85000-325-4, Falmer Pr); pap. 23.00x (ISBN 1-85000-326-2, Falmer Pr). Taylor & Francis.

Quality in Continuing Education: Principles, Practices & Standards for Colleges & Universities. Leonard Freedman. LC 86-27508. (Higher Education Ser.). 1987. text ed. 22.95x (ISBN 1-55542-041-9). Jossey-Bass.

Quality in Early Childhood Programs: Four Perspectives. Gwen Morgan et al. 70p. (Orig.). 1985. pap. 10.00 (ISBN 0-931114-35-7). High-Scope.

Quality in Liberal Learning: Curricular Innovations in Higher Education. Katherine S. Guroff. 272p. (Orig.). 1981. pap. 7.00 (ISBN 0-911696-09-1). Assn Am Coll.

Quality in Science. Ed. by Marcel Chotkowski La Follette. 250p. 1982. 35.00x (ISBN 0-262-12099-2); pap. 15.00x (ISBN 0-262-62040-5). MIT Pr.

Quality in the Construction Project: Proceedings of a Workshop Sponsored by ASCE. Ed. by Arthur J. Fox, Jr. & Holly A. Cornell. 200p. 1985. 16.00x (ISBN 0-87262-457-9). Am Soc Civil Eng.

Quandary of Life, Science & Religion. Parker L. Johnstone. LC 82-83297. 212p. 1982. cloth 7.95 (ISBN 0-917802-04-7). Theoscience Found.

Quandt'sche Gebuhrentabellen: Fur Rechtsanwaite und Notare, Gerichtsvollzieher und Rechtsbelstande, Ordentliche Gerichte und Arbeitsgerichte, Gerichte der Verwaltungs, Sozial und Finanzgerichtsbarkeit, Freiwillige Gerichtsbarkeit und Strafsachen. Begrundet V. Quant. 72p. (Ger.). 1985. pap. 8.80x (ISBN 3-11-010335-4). De Gruyter.

Quangle Wangle's Hat. Edward Lear. (Illus.). 32p. (ps-3). 1988. 12.95 (ISBN 0-15-264450-4). HarBraceJ.

Quanguo Jiben Jianshe Gongcheng Zhong Chutu Wenwu Zhanlan Tulu. 34p. 1956. 770.00x (ISBN 0-317-69026-4, Pub. by Han-Shan Tang Ltd). State Mutual Bk.

Quant on Make-Up. Mary Quant. (Illus.). 160p. 1987. 19.95 (ISBN 0-7126-1206-8). Salem Hse Pubs.

Quanta: A Handbook of Concepts. P. W. Atkins. (Oxford Chemistry Ser.). (Illus.). 1977. pap. 29.95x (ISBN 0-19-855494-X). Oxford U Pr.

Quanta: Essays in Theorectical Physics Dedicated to Gregory Wentzel. Ed. by Peter G. Freund & C. J. Goebel. LC 70-108268. pap. 107.50 (ISBN 0-317-08085-7, 2019966). Bks Demand UMI.

Quantative Chemical Analysis: A Laboratory Manual. 4th ed. R. A. Chalmers & M. S. Cresser. (Analytical Chemistry Ser.). 420p. 1983. 79.95x (ISBN 0-470-27228-7). Halsted Pr.

Quantative Description & Analysis of the Growth of the Pennsylvania Anthracite Coal Industry, 1820-1865. Donald F. Schaefer. Ed. by Stuart Bruchey. LC 76-45113. (Nineteen Seventy-Seven Dissertations Ser.). (Illus.). 1977. lib. bdg. 24.50x (ISBN 0-405-09924-X). Ayer Co Pubs.

Quantative Methods for Market Oriented Economic Analysis over Space & Time. Ed. by W. C. Labys et al. (Contemporary Studies in Energy Analysis & Policy: Vol. 9). 1988. price not set (ISBN 0-89232-607-7). Jai Pr.

Quantenmechanik, Band Two: Zwei Auflage Ubersetzt aus dem Franzosischen von Joachim Streubel. Albert Messiah. (Illus.). 585p. (Ger.). 1985. 27.60x (ISBN 3-11-010265-X). De Gruyter.

Quantification: A History of the Meaning of Measurement in the Natural & Social Sciences. Ed. by Harry Woolf. 1961. text ed. 39.50x (ISBN 0-672-60844-8). Irvington.

Quantification in Cultural Anthropology: An Introduction to Research Design. Allen W. Johnson. LC 76-54091. 1978. 7.95x (ISBN 0-8047-0941-6); pap. 6.95 (ISBN 0-8047-1058-9, SP-159). Stanford U Pr.

Quantification in the History of Political Thought: Toward a Qualitative Approach. Robert Schware. LC 80-1704. (Contributions in Political Science Ser.: No. 55). ix, 168p. 1981. lib. bdg. 46.95 (ISBN 0-313-22228-2, SPT/). Greenwood.

Quantification of Circulating Proteins. W. T. Hermens. 1983. 44.00 (ISBN 90-247-2755-3, Pub. by Martinus Nijhoff Netherlands). Kluwer Academic.

Quantification of Occupational Cancer. Ed. by Richard Peto & Marvin Schneiderman. LC 81-10218. (Banbury Report Ser.: Vol. 9). 756p. 1981. 99.00x (ISBN 0-87969-208-1). Cold Spring Harbor.

Quantification of Steady State Operant Behavior. Ed. by C. M. Bradshaw et al. 1981. 70.25 (ISBN 0-444-80298-3). Elsevier.

Quantifications & Syntactic Theory. Robin Cooper. 1983. lib. bdg. 47.50 (ISBN 90-277-1484-3, Pub. by Reidel Holland). Kluwer Academic.

Quantifier Meanings. Cushing. (Linguistics Ser.: Vol. 48). 388p. 1982. pap. 73.75 (ISBN 0-444-86445-8, North Holland). Elsevier.

Quantifying Archaelology. Stephen Shennan. 364p. 1988. 34.95 (ISBN 0-12-639860-7). Acad Pr.

Quantifying Archaeology. Stephen Shennan. 300p. 1987. 25.00 (ISBN 0-85224-460-6, Pub. by Edinburgh U Pr Scotland); pap. 15.00 (ISBN 0-85224-473-8). Columbia U Pr.

Quantifying Diversity in Archaeology. Ed. by Robert D. Leonard & George T. Jones. (New Directions in Archaeology Ser.). (Illus.). 170p. Date not set. price not set (ISBN 0-521-35030-1). Cambridge U Pr.

Quantifying Music. H. F. Cohen. 1984. lib. bdg. 54.50 (ISBN 90-277-1637-4, Pub. by Reidel Holland). Kluwer Academic.

Quantifying the Benefits of Separating Pedestrians & Vehicles. (National Cooperative Highway Research Program Report). 127p. 1978. 7.00 (ISBN 0-317-36102-3). Transport Res Bd.

Quantile Processes with Statistical Applications. Miklos Csorgo. LC 83-60222. (CBMS-NSF Regional Conference Ser.: No. 42). xiii, 156p. 1983. pap. text ed. 21.00 (ISBN 0-89871-185-1). Soc Indus-Appl Math.

Quantitative Acid-Base Physiology. Poul Kildeberg. LC 80-81619. (Illus.). 142p. 1981. 27.50 (ISBN 0-89640-048-4). Igaku-Shoin.

Quantitative Aids for Management Decision Making. Colin Palmer. 212p. 1979. text ed. 30.50x (ISBN 0-566-00284-1). Gower Pub Co.

Quantitative Analyses of Behavior: The Effects of Delay & of Intervening Events on Reinforcement Value, Vol. 5. Ed. by Michael L. Commons et al. (Roitblat-Bever-Olton: Comparative Cognition & Neuroscience Ser.). 304p. 1986. text ed. 45.00 (ISBN 0-89859-800-1). L Erlbaum Assocs.

Quantitative Analysis. Vladimir Alexeyev. Tr. by MIR Publishers. (Illus.). 563p. 1975. text ed. 19.95 (ISBN 0-8464-0774-4). Beekman Pubs.

Quantitative Analysis. Vladimir Alexeyev. (Russian Monographs & Texts on the Physical Sciences). 501p. 1969. 89.00 (ISBN 0-677-20860-X). Gordon & Breach.

Quantitative Analysis. 5th ed. R. A. Day & Arthur L. Underwood. (Illus.). 704p. 1986. text ed. write for info. (ISBN 0-13-746728-1). P-H.

Quantitative Analysis. Lawrence W. Potts. text ed. 49.95t scp (ISBN 0-06-045269-2, HarpC). Har-Row.

Quantitative Analysis. Ed. by E. Woolf et al. 500p. (Orig.). 1985. pap. text ed. 38.50x (ISBN 0-7121-0490-9). Trans-Atl Phila.

Quantitative Analysis by Gas Chromatography. 2nd ed. Novak. (Chromatographic Science Ser.). 296p. 1987. 89.75 (ISBN 0-8247-7818-9). Dekker.

Quantitative Analysis for Business. Andrew J. Vazsonyi & Herbert F. Spirer. (Illus.). 1072p. 1984. text ed. write for info. (ISBN 0-13-746578-5). P-H.

Quantitative Analysis for Business Decisions. 7th ed. Harold Bierman, Jr. et al. 1986. 38.95x (ISBN 0-256-03381-1). Irwin.

Quantitative Analysis for Management. 3rd ed. Render & Stair. (Illus.). 800p. 1988. pap. text ed. 31.50 (ISBN 0-205-10566-1). Allyn.

Quantitative Analysis for Public Policy. John K. Gohagan. (Quantitative Methods for Management Ser.). (Illus.). 1980. text ed. 42.95 (ISBN 0-07-023570-8). McGraw.

Quantitative Analysis in Sobolev Imbedding Theorems & Applications to Spectral Theory. M. S. Birman & M. Z. Solomjak. (Translations Ser. 2: Vol. 114). 1980. 38.00 (ISBN 0-8218-3064-3, TRANS2-114). Am Math.

Quantitative Analysis: Laboratory Manual. 5th ed. R. A. Day, Jr. & Arthur L. Underwood. (Illus.). 208p. 1986. pap. text ed. write for info. (ISBN 0-13-746751-6). P-H.

Quantitative Analysis of Catecholamines & Related Compounds. Ante M. Krstulovic. (Analytical Chemistry Ser.). 378p. 1986. 74.95 (ISBN 0-470-20719-1). Wiley.

Quantitative Analysis of Computer Systems. Clement H. Leung. LC 87-2046. (Computing Ser.). 1987. write for info. (ISBN 0-471-91509-2). Wiley.

Quantitative Analysis of Mineral & Energy Resources. Ed. by C. F. Chung et al. 1988. lib. bdg. 139.00 (ISBN 90-277-2635-3, Pub. by Reidel Holland). Kluwer Academic.

Quantitative Analysis of Organic Mixtures: General Principles, Pt. 1. Tsu-Sheng Ma. LC 78-23202. pap. 96.00 (ISBN 0-317-08874-2, 2055601). Bks Demand UMI.

Quantitative Analysis of Plant Growth. G. Clifford Evans. LC 77-183156. (Studies in Ecology: Vol. 1). 1973. 45.00x (ISBN 0-520-02204-1). U of Cal Pr.

Quantitative Analysis of Steroids. S. Gorog. (Studies in Analytical Chemistry: No. 5). 440p. 1983. 123.75 (ISBN 0-444-99698-2). Elsevier.

Quantitative Analysis of the Growth & Diffusion of Steam Power in Manufacturing in the U. S., 1919-1938. Allen H. Fenichel. Ed. by Stuart Bruchey. LC 78-22679. (Energy in the American Economy Ser.). (Illus.). 1979. lib. bdg. 19.00x (ISBN 0-405-11982-8). Ayer Co Pubs.

Quantitative Analysis of Voting Behavior in the General Assembly: Who Voted with Whom Within the United Nations: Pacific Nations Case Study. (Policy & Efficacy Studies: No. 2). 79p. 1981. pap. 5.00 (ISBN 0-686-97561-8, UN81/15PE2, UNITAR). UNIPUB.

Quantitative Analysis of Voting Behavior in the General Assembly: Who Voted with Whom Within the United Nations. Vladislav Tikhomirov. (Unitar Policy & Efficacy Studies). 79p. 1981. 5.00 (ISBN 92-1-157034-4, E.81.XV.PE/2). UN.

Quantitative Analysis: Solutions to Problems. 5th ed. R. A. Day, Jr. & Arthur L. Underwood, Jr. 180p. 1986. pap. text ed. 12.95 (ISBN 0-317-40029-0). P-H.

Quantitative Analysis Using Chromatographic Techniques. Ed. by Elena Katz. LC 86-26715. (Separation Science Ser.). 400p. 1987. 69.95 (ISBN 0-471-91406-1). Wiley.

Quantitative Analysis, Vol. II: TV Coverage of the Oil Crises: How Well Was the Public Served? The Media Institute. Ed. by Leonard J. Theberge. LC 81-86030. (Illus.). 81p. (Orig.). 1982. pap. 5.00 (ISBN 0-937790-06-0). Media Inst.

Quantitative Analyst. Jack Rudman. (Career Examination Ser.: C-1714). (Cloth bdg. avail. on request). pap. 16.00 (ISBN 0-8373-1714-2). Natl Learning.

Quantitative Analytic Studies in Epilepsy. Ed. by Peter Kellaway & Ingemar S. Petersen. LC 76-22912. 588p. 1976. 87.50 (ISBN 0-89004-133-4). Raven.

Quantitative Analytical Chemistry. 5th ed. Fritz & Schenk. 1987. 50.00 (ISBN 0-205-10480-0). Allyn.

Quantitative & Analytical Studies in East-West Economic Relations. Ed. by Josef C. Brada. LC 76-10986. (Studies in East European & Soviet Planning Development & Trade: No. 24). (Illus.). 1976. pap. text ed. 6.00 (ISBN 0-89249-015-2). Intl Development.

Quantitative & Comparative Study of the B-V Alternation in Latin Inscriptions from Britain, the Balkans, Dalmatia, North Africa, Spain & Italy. Joseph Barbarino. LC 78-20445. (Studies in the Romance Languages & Literatures Ser.: No. 203). 184p. 1979. pap. 15.00x (ISBN 0-8078-9203-3). U of NC Pr.

Quantitative & Comparative Study of the Vocalism of the Latin Inscriptions of North American, Britain, Dalmatia, & the Balkans. Stephen Omeltchenko. (Studies in the Romance Languages & Literature Ser: No. 180). 310p. 1977. 25.00x (ISBN 0-8078-9180-0). U of NC Pr.

Quantitative & Numerical Methods in Soil Classification & Survey. R. Webster. (Monographs on Soil Survey). (Illus.). 1977. 46.00x (ISBN 0-19-854512-6). Oxford U Pr.

Quantitative & Qualitative NMR Spectroscopy. David Williams & Norma Chadwick. LC 86-15694. 272p. 1986. pap. 21.95 (ISBN 0-471-91177-1). Wiley.

Quantitative & Statistical Approaches to Geography: A Practical Manual. John A. Matthews. (Pergamon Oxford Geographies). (Illus.). 224p. 1981. pap. text ed. 21.00 (ISBN 0-08-024295-2). Pergamon.

Quantitative Applications in the Social Sciences, 65 vols. (University Papers Ser.). 1983. pap. text ed. 6.50 ea. Sage.

Quantitative Approach in Political Science: An Introduction. Scott Bennett. 376p. 1986. lib. bdg. 59.95x (ISBN 0-88946-205-4). E Mellen.

Quantitative Approaches in Business Studies. C. A. Morris. (Higher Business Education Ser.). 288p. 1983. text ed. 26.50x (ISBN 0-7121-1706-7). Trans-Atl Phila.

Quantitative Approaches to Drug Design: Proceedings of the European Symposium on Chemical Structure Biological Activity, 4th, Bath, U. K., Sept. 6-9, 1982. Ed. by J. C. Dearden. (Pharmacochemistry Library: Vol. 6). 296p. 1983. 97.50 (ISBN 0-444-42200-5). Elsevier.

Quantitative Approaches to Management. 5th ed. Richard I. Levin & Charles A. Kirkpatrick. 798p. 1982. text ed. 38.95x (ISBN 0-07-037436-8). McGraw.

Quantitative Approaches to Management. 7th ed. Richard I. Levin & David Rubin. 832p. 1988. text ed. 39.95 (ISBN 0-07-037478-3). McGraw.

Quantitative Approaches to Metabolism: The Role of Tracers & Models in Clinical Medicine. Ed. by D. G. Cramp. LC 81-21992. 390p. 1982. 104.00 (ISBN 0-471-10172-9, Pub. by Wiley-Interscience). Wiley.

Quantitative Approaches to Metabolism: The Role of Tracers & Models in Clinical Medicine. Ed. by D. G. Cramp. LC 81-21992. pap. 104.60 (2031936). Bks Demand UMI.

Quantitative Approximation. Ed. by R. A. DeVore & K. Scherer. LC 80-17554. 1980. 44.50 (ISBN 0-12-213650-0). Acad Pr.

Quantitative Aquatic Biological Indicators: Their Use to Monitor Trace Metal & Organochlorine Pollution. David J. Phillips. (Pollution Monitoring Ser.: No. 1). (Illus.). 460p. 1980. 90.00 (ISBN 0-85334-884-7, Pub. by Elsevier Applied Sci England). Elsevier.

Quantitative Aspects of Allosteric Mechanisms. A. Levitzki. (Molecular Biology, Biochemistry & Biophysics Ser.: Vol. 28). (Illus.). 1978. 27.00 (ISBN 0-387-08696-X). Springer-Verlag.

Quantitative Aspects of the Ecology of Biological Invasions. Ed. by H. Kornberg & M. H. Williamson. (Royal Society Discussion Volume Ser.). 250p. 1988. 69.50 (ISBN 0-521-35073-5). Cambridge U Pr.

Quantitative Aspects of the Ecology of Biological Invasions. Intro. by Hans Kornberg & M. H. Williamson. (Philosophical Transactions of the Royal Society, Series B: Vol. 314, 1986). (Illus.). 232p. 1987. lib. bdg. 87.00x (ISBN 0-85403-302-5, Pub. by Royal Soc London). Scholium Intl.

Quantitative Aspects of the Evolution of Concepts. Clark L. Hull. Bd. with Experimental Analysis of a Case Trial & Error Learning in the Human Subject. G. S. Snoddy. Repr. of 1920 ed; Work with Knowledge of Results. G. F. Arps. Repr. of 1920 ed; Individual Differences in Finger Reactions. E. L. Gatewood. Repr. of 1920 ed; Lag of Visual Sensation in Its Relation to Wave Lengths & Intensity of Light. M. A. Bills. Repr. of 1920 ed; Some Factors Determining the Degree of Retroactive Inhibition. E. S. Robinson. Repr. of 1920 ed; Higher Mental Process of Learning. J. C. Peterson. Repr. of 1920 ed. (Psychology Monographs General & Applied: Vol. 28). pap. 36.00 (ISBN 0-8115-1427-7). Kraus Repr.

Quantitative Assessment in Arms Control: Mathematical Modeling & Simulation in the Analysis of Arms Control Problems. Ed. by Rudolf Avenhaus & Reiner K. Huber. 488p. 1984. 75.00x (ISBN 0-306-41818-5, Plenum Pr). Plenum Pub.

Quantitative Bases for Developing an Index of Harm: ICRP Publication Number Forty-Five. Ed. by M. C. Thorne. 90p. 1986. pap. 25.00 (ISBN 0-08-033665-5, Pub. by PPL). Pergamon.

Quantitative Bioassay. David Hawcroft et al. (Analytical Chemistry by Open Learning Ser.). 300p. 1988. pap. 26.95 (ISBN 0-471-91401-0). Wiley.

Quantitative Business Analysis. William M. Bassin. LC 80-21090. 256p. (gr. 11-12). 1981. text ed. 21.17 scp (ISBN 0-672-97696-X); scp tchr's. ed. 3.67 (ISBN 0-672-97697-8). Bobbs.

Quantitative Business Analysis. David E. Smith. LC 82-7833. 670p. 1982. Repr. of 1977 ed. lib. bdg. 43.50 (ISBN 0-89874-504-7). Krieger.

Quantitative Cellular Biology: An Approach to the Quantitative Analysis of Life Processes. Ferdinand Heinmets. LC 70-84774. (Quantitative Approach to Life Science Ser.). pap. 85.30 (2027113). Bks Demand UMI.

Quantitative Characterization & Performance of Porous Implants for Hard Tissue Applications. Ed. by Jack E. Lemons. LC 87-33430. (Special Technical Publications: No. 953). 420p. 1988. text ed. 75.00 (ISBN 0-8031-0965-2, 04-053000-54). ASTM.

Quantitative Chemical Analysis. 2nd ed. Daniel Harris. LC 86-25810. (Chemistry Ser.). (Illus.). 640p. 1987. text ed. 48.95 (ISBN 0-7167-1817-0). W H Freeman.

Quantitative Chemical Analysis. Stanley E. Manahan. LC 86-2590. (Chemistry Ser.). 720p. 1986. text ed. 34.50 pub net (ISBN 0-534-05538-9). Brooks-Cole.

Quantitative Chromatography. Walker. 1987. write for info. (ISBN 0-471-09911-2). Wiley.

Quantitative Column Liquid Chromatography: A Survey of Chemometric Methods. S. T. Balke. (Journal of Chromatography Library: Vol. 29). 1984. 92.00 (ISBN 0-444-42393-1). Elsevier.

Quantitative Concepts for Management: Decision-Making Without Algorithms. 2nd ed. Gary D. Eppen & Floyd J. Gould. (Illus.). 768p. 1985. text ed. 38.00 (ISBN 0-13-746637-4). P-H.

Quantitative Concepts for Management: Decision-Making Without Algorithms. 2nd ed. Lawrence W. Robinson. (Illus.). 384p. 1985. write for info. (ISBN 0-13-746652-8). P-H.

Quantitative Criteria for Academic Research Libraries. K. L. Stubbs. 135p. 1984. 19.00 (ISBN 0-8389-6788-4). Assn Coll & Res Libs.

Quantitative Criteria for Academic Research Libraries. K. L. Stubbs. 135p. 1984. 19.00x; members 15.00 (ISBN 0-317-37015-4). ALA.

Quantitative Cryofixation. W. B. Bald. 192p. 1987. 87.00x (ISBN 0-85274-448-X, Pub. by A Hilger UK). Taylor & Francis.

Quantitative Cytochemical Study of Shock Wave Effects on Spiral Ganglion Cells. Gunnar Hammer. 1956. 12.00 (ISBN 0-384-21250-6). Johnson Repr.

Quantitative Data File for Ore Minerals. Ed. by A. J. Criddle & C. J. Stanley. 460p. 1986. 101.50x (ISBN 0-565-00997-4, Pub. by Brit Mus Nat Hist England). Sabbot-Natural Hist Bks.

Quantitative Decision Aiding Techniques for Research & Development Management. Ed. by Marvin J. Cetron et al. LC 70-129677. (Illus.). 214p. 1972. 59.00 (ISBN 0-677-14250-1). Gordon & Breach.

Quantitative Decision Making for Business. 2nd ed. Gilbert Gordon & Israel Pressman. (Illus.). 576p. 1983. text ed. write for info. (ISBN 0-13-746685-4). P-H.

Quantitative Dermatoglyphics: Classification, Genetics, & Pathology. Danuta Z. Loesch. (Oxford Monographs on Medical Genetics). (Illus.). 1983. 63.00x (ISBN 0-19-261305-7). Oxford U Pr.

Quantitative Drug Design. Yvonne C. Martin. LC 77-26709. (Medicinal Research Ser.: Vol. 8). 1978. 95.00 (ISBN 0-8247-7963-0). Dekker.

Quantitative Ecological Theory: An Introduction to Basic Models. Michael R. Rose. LC 86-46274. 200p. 1987. text ed. 25.00x (ISBN 0-8018-3509-7). Johns Hopkins.

Quantitative Economic & Development: Essays in Memory of T. C. Liu. Ed. by L. R. Klein et al. LC 79-8855. (Economic Theory, Econometrics & Mathematical Economic Ser.). 1980. 35.00 (ISBN 0-12-413350-9). Acad Pr.

Quantitative Economic Policies & Interactive Planning: A Reconstruction of the Theory of Economic Policy. Andrew Hughes-Hallett & Hedley Rees. LC 82-4204. 370p. 1983. 52.50 (ISBN 0-521-23718-1). Cambridge U Pr.

Quantitative Electron-Probe Microanalysis. Ed. by V. D. Scott & G. Love. LC 83-18366. 343p. 1984. 51.95x (ISBN 0-470-27510-3). Halsted Pr.

Quantitative Ethology. Ed. by Patrick W. Colgan. LC 78-999. 380p. 1978. 47.50 (ISBN 0-471-02236-5, Pub. by John Wiley). Krieger.

Quantitative Evaluation of Predicted Reserves of Oil & Gas (Authorized Translation from the Russian) N. I. Buialov et al. LC 64-7759. pap. 20.00 (ISBN 0-317-10640-6, 2003359). Bks Demand UMI.

TITLE INDEX QUANTITATIVE TOOLS FOR DECISION

Quantitative Examination of Neurologic Functions, 2 vols. Ed. by Alfred R. Potvin & Wallace W. Tourtellotte. LC 84-3152. 224p. 1985. Vol. I: Scientific Basis & Design of Instrumented Tests, 272p. 99.00 (ISBN 0-8493-5926-0); Vol. II: Methodology for the Test & Patient Assessments & Design of a Computer-Automated System, 224p. 95.00 (ISBN 0-8493-5927-9). CRC Pr.

Quantitative Explorations in Drug Abuse Policy. Ed. by I. Leveson. LC 79-21399. 183p. 1980. 45.00 (ISBN 0-88331-192-5). Luce.

Quantitative Foundations of Counseling Psychology Research. Ed. by Bruce E. Wampold. (Special Issues, Journal of Counseling Psychology). 1987. pap. 16.00 (ISBN 1-55798-007-1, 2113404). Am Psychol.

Quantitative Gas Chromatography for Laboratory Analyses & On-Line Process Control. G. Guichon & C. L. Guillemin. (Journal of Chromatography Library: Vol. 42). 780p. 1988. 165.75 (ISBN 0-444-42857-7). Elsevier.

Quantitative Genetic Variation. Ed. by James N. Thompson & J. M. Thoday. LC 79-9917. 1979. 41.50 (ISBN 0-12-688850-7). Acad Pr.

Quantitative Genetics & Maize Breeding. rev. ed. A. R. Hallauer & J. B. Miranda. (Illus.). 480p. 1988. text ed. 44.95x (ISBN 0-317-69830-3). Iowa St U Pr.

Quantitative Genetics & Maize Breeding. 2nd, rev. ed. A. R. Hallauer & J. B. Miranda. (Illus.). 480p. 1989. text ed. 44.95x (ISBN 0-8138-1522-3). Iowa St U Pr.

Quantitative Genetics & Selection in Plant Breeding. Gunter Wricke & Eberhard Weber. (Illus.). xii, 405p. 1986. 89.95x (ISBN 3-11-007561-X). De Gruyter.

Quantitative Genetics in Maize Breeding. Arnel R. Hallauer & J. B. Miranda, Jr. (Illus.). 468p. 1981. 33.95x (ISBN 0-8138-1520-7); pap. 37.95x (ISBN 0-8138-1519-3). Iowa St U Pr.

Quantitative Genetics, Pt. II: The Selection. Hill. 52.95 (ISBN 0-317-64262-6). Van Nos Reinhold.

Quantitative Genetics, Pt.I & Pt. II, 2 Vol. set. Hill. 94.95 (ISBN 0-317-64261-8). Van Nos Reinhold.

Quantitative Genetics: The Exploration & Analysis of Continuous Variation. Ed. by William Hill. 384p. 1984. Pt. I. 55.95 (ISBN 0-442-23219-5); Pt. II. 55.95 (ISBN 0-442-23218-7); Set. 99.95 (ISBN 0-442-23217-9). Van Nos Reinhold.

Quantitative Geography in Britain: Retrospect & Prospect. Ed. by Neil Wrigley & Robert J. Bennett. 448p. 1981. 65.00x (ISBN 0-7100-0731-0). Routledge Chapman & Hall.

Quantitative History: Selected Readings in the Quantitative Analysis of Historical Data. Don Karl Rowney & James Q. Graham. LC 76-90239. pap. 127.00 (ISBN 0-317-09235-9, 2006453). Bks Demand UMI.

Quantitative Hydrogeology. G. De Marsily. 1986. 66.00 (ISBN 0-12-208915-4); pap. 33.00 (ISBN 0-12-208916-2). Acad Pr.

Quantitative Image Analysis in Cancer Cytology & Histology. Ed. by J. Y. Mary & J. P. Rigaut. 406p. 1986. 116.50 (ISBN 0-444-80805-1). Elsevier.

Quantitative Indicators in World Politics: Timely Assurance & Early Warning. Ed. by David J. Singer. LC 83-17792. 236p. 1984. 35.00 (ISBN 0-275-91269-8, C1269). Praeger.

Quantitative Industrial Hygiene. Harry J. Beaulieu & Roy M. Buchan. 1981. lib. bdg. 19.00 (ISBN 0-8240-7180-8). Garland Pub.

Quantitative Layer-by-Layer Perimetry: An Extended Analysis. Jay M. Enoch et al. (Current Ophthalmology Monographs). (Illus.). 256p. 1980. 44.50 (ISBN 0-8089-1282-8, 791165). Grune.

Quantitative Management: An Introduction. 2nd ed. Michael Q. Anderson & R. J. Lievano. 873p. 1986. text ed. 33.00 (ISBN 0-534-05958-9). PWS Kent Pub.

Quantitative Mass Spectrometry in Life Sciences, Vol. II. Ed. by A. P. De Leenheer & R. R. Roncucci. 502p. 1979. 126.50 (ISBN 0-444-41760-5). Elsevier.

Quantitative Mass Spectrometry in Life Sciences: Proceedings. International Symposium on Quantitative Mass Spectrometry in Life Sciences, 1st, State University of Ghent Belgium June 16-18 1976. Ed. by A. P. DeLeenheer & Romeo R Roncucci. LC 77-3404. 254p. 1977. 89.50 (ISBN 0-444-41557-2). Elsevier.

Quantitative Measurement & Dynamic Library Service. Ed. by Ching-Chih Chen. (Neal-Schuman Professional Bk.). 312p. 1978. lib. bdg. 33.00x (ISBN 0-912700-17-3). Oryx Pr.

Quantitative Measurement of Fetal Hemoglobin by the Alkali Denaturation Method: Proposed Guideline, Vol. 2. National Committee for Clinical Laboratory Standards. 1982. 20.00 (ISBN 0-318-19439-2, H13-P). Natl Comm Clin Lab Stds.

Quantitative Measures of China's Economic Output. Alexander Eckstein & Robert Dernberger. (Illus.). 1979. text ed. 26.50x (ISBN 0-472-08754-1). U of Mich Pr.

Quantitative Method for Deriving Cultural Chronology. James A. Ford. LC 75-24231. (Museum Brief Ser.: No. 9). (Illus.). vi, 62p. 1972. pap. 3.25 (ISBN 0-913134-08-2). Mus Anthro Mo.

Quantitative Methods & Computer Applications in Business, Vol. 9. Compiled by James W. Dean & Richard Schwindt. 222p. 1985. 14.00 (ISBN 0-88024-109-8). Eno River Pr.

Quantitative Methods: Applications to Managerial Decision Making. Robert E. Markland & James R. Sweigart. LC 87-2025. 560p. 1987. 40.25 (ISBN 0-471-87885-5); study guide avail. Wiley.

Quantitative Methods for Business. 3rd ed. David R. Anderson et al. LC 85-20115. (Illus.). 751p. 1986. text ed. 41.00 (ISBN 0-314-93147-3). West Pub.

Quantitative Methods for Business Decisions. C. A. Gallagher & H. J. Watson. 1980. text ed. 42.95 (ISBN 0-07-022751-9). McGraw.

Quantitative Methods for Business Decisions. Christopher K. McKenna. (Quantitative Methods for Management Ser.). (Illus.). 1980. text ed. 42.95 (ISBN 0-07-045351-9). McGraw.

Quantitative Methods for Business Decisions with Cases. 4th ed. Lawrence Lapin. 847p. 1988. text ed. 30.00 (ISBN 0-15-574327-9, HC). HarBraceJ.

Quantitative Methods for Decision Making in Business. Richard E. Trueman. LC 80-65810. 736p. 1981. text ed. 38.95x (ISBN 0-03-051356-1). Dryden Pr.

Quantitative Methods for Economics. Peter Holl. 192p. (Orig.). 1987. pap. text ed. 23.50x (ISBN 0-273-02539-2, Pub. by Pitman Pub Ltd London). Trans-Atl Phila.

Quantitative Methods for Financial Analysis. Stephen J. Brown & Mark P. Kritzman. 229p. 1987. 40.00 (ISBN 0-87094-978-0). Dow Jones-Irwin.

Quantitative Methods for Library & Information Science. 1985. 10.00 (ISBN 0-471-63884-6). Wiley.

Quantitative Methods for Life Safety Analysis: Proceedings of the 1986 Symposium. Harold E. Nelson et al. 1988. 35.30 (ISBN 0-318-24020-3). Society Fire Protect.

Quantitative Methods for Management Decisions. W. P. Cooke. 704p. 1985. text ed. 41.95 (ISBN 0-07-012518-X); study guide 14.95 (ISBN 0-07-012519-8). McGraw.

Quantitative Methods for Management Decision Making. Robert E. Marklund & James R. Sweigart. LC 87-2025. 1987. write for info; pap. write for info study guide. Wiley.

Quantitative Methods for Managers. A. I. Godfrey. 1977. pap. text ed. 22.50x (ISBN 0-7131-3349-X). Trans-Atl Phila.

Quantitative Methods for Planning & Urban Studies. Barry J. Simpson. 176p. 1985. text ed. 38.95 (ISBN 0-566-00843-2). Gower Pub Co.

Quantitative Methods for Public Administration in Developing Countries. Scott C. Iverson. LC 85-638. 167p. 1985. 46.95 (ISBN 0-471-90755-3). Wiley.

Quantitative Methods for Public Administration: Techniques & Applications. 2nd ed. Susan Welch & John Comer. 1987. pap. text ed. 21.00 (ISBN 0-256-03669-1). Dorsey.

Quantitative Methods in Biology. M. A. Williams. (Vol. 6). 1978. pap. 29.50 (ISBN 0-7204-0638-2, North Holland). Elsevier.

Quantitative Methods in Budgeting. Ed. by C. B. Tilanus. 1976. lib. bdg. 23.00 (ISBN 90-207-0649-7, Martinus Nijhoff Pubs). Kluwer Academic.

Quantitative Methods in Business. Curwin & Slater. 1985. pap. 25.95 (ISBN 0-442-30640-7). Van Nos Reinhold.

Quantitative Methods in Epidemiology: Relative Risk Regression. Prentice et al. (Probability & Mathematical Statistics Ser.). 1987. write for info. (ISBN 0-471-88278-X). Wiley.

Quantitative Methods in Geography. Peter J. Taylor. (Illus.). 386p. 1983. Repr. of 1977 ed. text ed. 29.95x (ISBN 0-88133-072-8). Waveland Pr.

Quantitative Methods in Law: Studies in the Application of Mathematical Probability & Statistics to Legal Problems. Michael O. Finkelstein. LC 77-94081. 1978. 22.95 (ISBN 0-02-910260-X). Free Pr.

Quantitative Methods in Librarianship: Standards, Research, & Management. Ed. by Irene B. Hoadley & Alice S. Clark. LC 73-149962. (Contributions in Librarianship & Information Science: No. 4). 256p. 1972. lib. bdg. 35.00 (ISBN 0-8371-6061-8, HOQ/). Greenwood.

Quantitative Methods in Library & Information Science. Inna K. Rao. LC 82-21375. 271p. 1983. 33.95x (ISBN 0-470-27393-3). Halsted Pr.

Quantitative Methods in Management. John Ullmann. (Schaum's Outline Ser). 256p. (Orig.). 1976. pap. text ed. 8.95 (ISBN 0-07-065742-4). McGraw.

Quantitative Methods in Management: Case Studies of Failures & Successes. C. B. Tilanus et al. LC 85-12351. 279p. 1986. 42.95 (ISBN 0-471-90841-X). Wiley.

Quantitative Methods in Management: Text & Cases. Paul A. Vatter et al. 1978. 35.95x (ISBN 0-256-02006-X). Irwin.

Quantitative Microanalysis with High Spatial Resolution. 288p. 1981. text ed. 70.00x (ISBN 0-904357-38-4, Pub. by Inst Metals). Brookfield Pub Co.

Quantitative Modeling of Magnetospheric Processes. Ed. by W. P. Olson. (Geophysical Monograph Ser.: Vol. 21). (Illus.). 655p. 1979. 30.00 (ISBN 0-87590-021-6, GM2100). Am Geophysical.

Quantitative Models for Management. 2nd ed. K. Roscoe Davis & Patrick G. McKeown. LC 83-24813. 768p. 1984. text ed. 33.00 (ISBN 0-534-03122-6). PWS Kent Pub.

Quantitative Models in Accounting: A Procedural Guide for Professionals. Ahmed Belkaoui. LC 86-16993. 368p. 1987. lib. bdg. 55.00 (ISBN 0-89930-186-X, BQU/, Quorum Bks). Greenwood.

Quantitative NDE in the Nuclear Industry: Proceedings of the Fifth International Conference on Nondestructive Evaluation in the Nuclear Industry, San Diego, CA, 10-13 May 1982--Sponsored by the American Society for Metals. Ed. by Roger B. Clough. LC 82-74019. pap. 121.80 (2027043). Bks Demand UMI.

Quantitative Neuroanatomy in Transmitter Research. Ed. by Luigi F. Agnati & Kjell Fuxe. (Wenner-Gren Center International Symposium Ser.: Vol. 42). 432p. 1986. 69.50x (ISBN 0-306-42160-7, Plenum Pr). Plenum Pub.

Quantitative Nuclear Cardiology. Ed. by Richard N. Pierson, Jr. LC 74-20990. (Illus.). pap. 74.80 (ISBN 0-317-07862-3, 2012582). Bks Demand UMI.

Quantitative Organic Analysis Via Functional Groups. 4th ed. Sidney Siggia & Gordan Hanna. 996p. 1988. Repr. of 1979 ed. lib. bdg. 110.00 (ISBN 0-89464-283-9). Krieger.

Quantitative Organic Microanalysis. 2nd ed. Al Steyermark. 1961. 77.00 (ISBN 0-12-670450-3). Acad Pr.

Quantitative Pharmaceutical Chemistry. 7th ed. Adelbert M. Knevel & Frank E. DiGangi. (Illus.). 518p. 1982. Repr. of 1977 ed. text ed. 29.95x (ISBN 0-88133-001-9). Waveland Pr.

Quantitative Planning & Control: In Honor of William W. Cooper. Ed. by Yuji Ijiri & Andrew B. Whinston. LC 78-22529. 1979. 59.00 (ISBN 0-12-370450-2). Acad Pr.

Quantitative Plant Ecology. 3rd ed. Peter Greig-Smith. LC 83-1302. (Studies in Ecology: Vol. 9). 355p. 1983. pap. text ed. 37.50x (ISBN 0-520-05080-0). U of Cal Pr.

Quantitative Population Dynamics. Ed. by D. G. Chapman & V. F. Gallucci. (Statistical Ecology Ser.). 290p. 1981. 30.00 (ISBN 0-89974-010-3). Intl Co-Op.

Quantitative Practice of Anesthesia: Use of Closed Circuit. Harry J. Lowe & Edward A. Ernst. LC 80-21803. (Illus.). pap. 64.80 (ISBN 0-317-58237-2, 2056386). Bks Demand UMI.

Quantitative Problems in Biochemical Sciences. 2nd ed. Rex Montgomery & Charles A. Swenson. LC 75-42234. (Illus.). 370p. 1976. text ed. 17.50 (ISBN 0-7167-0178-2); answer bk. o.p. avail. W H Freeman.

Quantitative Problems in Physical & Chemical Biology. D. Siva Sankar. Date not set. price not set (ISBN 0-685-77285-3). PJD Pubns.

Quantitative Psychology. M. Nowakowska. (Advances in Psychology Ser.: Vol. 15). 1984. 110.75 (ISBN 0-444-86708-2, I-232-83). Elsevier.

Quantitative Receptor Autoradiography. Ed. by Carl Boast et al. LC 85-24036. (NN Ser.: Vol. 19). (Illus.). 280p. 1986. 49.50 (ISBN 0-8451-2721-7, 2721). A R Liss.

Quantitative Research in Archaeology: Progress & Prospects. Ed. by Mark S. Aldenderfer. 360p. 1986. text ed. 35.00 (ISBN 0-8039-2844-0). Sage.

Quantitative Research in Public Administration & Policy Analysis: A Methodologically Annotated Bibliography. T. R. Carr et al. 1977. 4.50 (ISBN 0-686-22970-3). Univ OK Gov Res.

Quantitative Risk Assessment: Biomedical Ethics Reviews, 1986. Ed. by R. Almeder & J. Humber. LC 84-640015. 296p. 1987. 35.00 (ISBN 0-89603-056-3). Humana.

Quantitative Risk Assessment for Environmental & Occupational Health. Bill Hallenbeck. (Illus.). 200p. 1986. 39.95 (ISBN 0-87371-055-X). Lewis Pubs Inc.

Quantitative Risk Assessment in Regulation. Ed. by Lester B. Lave. LC 82-22603. (Studies in the Regulation of Economic Activity). 264p. 1983. 31.95 (ISBN 0-8157-5164-8); pap. 11.95 (ISBN 0-8157-5163-X). Brookings.

Quantitative Risk in Standards Setting: Proceedings of 16th Annual Meeting. 1981. 15.00 (ISBN 0-318-02042-4). NCRP Pubns.

Quantitative Seismology: Theory & Methods, Vol. I. Keiiti Aki & Paul G. Richards. LC 79-17434. (Geology Bks.). (Illus.). 573p. 1980. text ed. 47.95 (ISBN 0-7167-1058-7). W H Freeman.

Quantitative Seismology: Theory & Methods, Vol. II. Keiiti Aki & Paul G. Richards. LC 79-17434. (Geology Bks.). (Illus.). 389p. 1980. text ed. 47.95 (ISBN 0-7167-1059-5). W H Freeman.

Quantitative Slope Models. Ed. by Frank Ahnert. (Annals of Gemorphology Supplement Ser.: No. 25). (Illus.). 176p. (Orig.). 1976. pap. text ed. 67.50x (ISBN 3-443-21025-2, Pub. by Gebruder Borntraeger). Coronet Bks.

Quantitative Social Science Research on Latin America. Ed. by Robert S. Byars & Joseph L. Love. LC 72-95001. (University of Illinois at Urbana-Champaign Center for Latin American & Caribbean Studies Monograph: No. 1). pap. 70.00 (ISBN 0-317-29006-1, 2020245). Bks Demand UMI.

Quantitative Stratigraphic Correlation. Ed. by J. M. Cubitt & R. A. Reyment. LC 81-21926. (International Geological Correlation Programme Ser.). 301p. 1983. 81.95 (ISBN 0-471-10171-0, Pub. by Wiley-Interscience). Wiley.

Quantitative Stratigraphy. F. M. Gradstein et al. LC 85-18331. 1985. lib. bdg. 77.00 (ISBN 0-318-18267-X, Pub. by Reidel Holland). Kluwer Academic.

Quantitative Stratigraphy. F. M. Gradstein et al. (Illus.). 598p. (Orig.). 1986. pap. text ed. 80.00 (ISBN 92-3-102336-5, U1506, Unesco). UNIPUB.

Quantitative, Structural & Institutional Changes in Soviet Agriculture During the Khrushchev Era 1953-1964 see Deux Etudes de V. S. Nemtchinov.

Quantitative Structure-Activity Relations in Environmental Toxicology. Klaus L. Kaiser. 1984. lib. bdg. 54.50 (ISBN 90-277-1776-1, Pub. by Reidel Holland). Kluwer Academic.

Quantitative Structure-Activity Relationships of Drugs. Ed. by John G. Topliss. 1983. 82.00 (ISBN 0-12-695150-0). Acad Pr.

Quantitative Structure: Chromatographic Retention Relationships. Roman Kaliszan. LC 87-14802. (Chemical Analysis Ser.). 303p. 1987. 65.00 (ISBN 0-471-85983-4). Wiley.

Quantitative Studies in the Geological Sciences: A Memoir in Honor of William C. Krumbein. Ed. by E. H. Whitten. LC 74-15932. (Geological Society of America Memoir Ser.: No. 142). pap. 106.00 (ISBN 0-317-29108-4, 2023733). Bks Demand UMI.

Quantitative Studies of International Economic Relations. Ed. by H. Glejser. 282p. 1976. 55.25 (ISBN 0-444-10902-1, North-Holland). Elsevier.

Quantitative Study of Chromatic Adaptation see Effect of Intensity of Light, State Adaptation of the Eye.

Quantitative Study of Rotatoria in Terwilliger's Pond, Put-in Bay, Ohio. Elbert H. Ahlstrom. 1934. 1.00 (ISBN 0-86727-029-2). Ohio Bio Survey.

Quantitative Surface Analysis of Materials - STP 643. 217p. 1978. 21.50 (ISBN 0-8031-0543-6, 04-643000-39). ASTM.

Quantitative System Performance: Computer System Analysis Using Queueing Network Models. Edward D. Lazowska et al. LC 83-13791. (Illus.). 417p. 1984. text ed. 51.00 (ISBN 0-13-746975-6). P-H.

Quantitative Systemic Analysis & Control. Ralph F. Breyer. Ed. by Henry Assael. LC 78-250. (Century of Marketing Ser.). 1978. Repr. of 1949 ed. lib. bdg. 30.00x (ISBN 0-405-11164-9). Ayer Co Pubs.

Quantitative Systems for Business. Yih-Long Chang & Robert S. Sullivan. 192p. 1986. pap. text ed. 19.95 (ISBN 0-13-747007-X); write for info. wkbk. (ISBN 0-13-747015-0); write for info. disk. (ISBN 0-13-747023-1). P-H.

Quantitative Techniques. C. R. Kothari. 1979. text ed. 22.50x (ISBN 0-7069-0642-X, Pub. by Vikas India). Advent NY.

Quantitative Techniques. T. Lucey. 352p. 1979. 37.00x (ISBN 0-905435-09-5, Pub. by DP Pubns). State Mutual Bk.

Quantitative Techniques for Internal Auditing. Donald Ricketts & Horton L. Sorkin. Ed. by Richard Holman. (Research Report Ser.: No. 27). (Illus.). 106p. 1983. pap. text ed. 33.00 (ISBN 0-89413-108-7). Inst Inter Aud.

Quantitative Techniques for Management: A Practical Approach. Thomas Payne. (Illus.). 464p. 1982. (Reston); calculator manual 15.00 (ISBN 0-8359-6118-4); instr's. manual o.p. avail. (ISBN 0-8359-6117-6); sample package avail. (ISBN 0-8359-6119-2). P-H.

Quantitative Techniques for Managerial Decision Making. 1985. 5.50 (ISBN 0-471-63954-0). Wiley.

Quantitative Techniques in Geography. 2nd ed. R. Hammond & P. S. McCullagh. 1978. 28.00x (ISBN 0-19-874066-2); pap. 14.95x (ISBN 0-19-874067-0). Oxford U Pr.

Quantitative Techniques in Management. Israel Brosh. 1983. text ed. write for info. (ISBN 0-8359-6113-3, Reston); instr's. manual avail. (ISBN 0-8359-6114-1). P-H.

Quantitative Texture Analysis. Ed. by H. J. Bunge & C. Esling. (Illus.). 562p. 1982. (Pub. by DGM Metallurgy Germany); pap. text ed. 28.00 (Pub. by DGM Metallurgy Germany). IR Pubns.

Quantitative Texture Analysis. Ed. by H. J. Bunge & C. Esling. 551p. 1981. cancelled 100.00. IPS.

Quantitative Theory of Foliations. H. Blaine Lawson, Jr. LC 76-51339. (Conference Board of the Mathematical Sciences Ser.: No. 27). 65p. 1981. pap. 16.00 (ISBN 0-8218-1677-2, CBMS27). Am Math.

Quantitative Thin-Layer Chromatography. Ed. by Joseph C. Touchstone. LC 72-13689. (Illus.). pap. 86.00 (ISBN 0-317-09311-8, 2055519). Bks Demand UMI.

Quantitative TLC & It's Industrial Applications. Treiber. (Chromatographic Science Ser.). 344p. 1986. 89.75 (ISBN 0-8247-7597-X). Dekker.

Quantitative Tools for Decision Support Using IFPS-Optimum. Donald R. Plane & Roy E. Crummer. LC 84-24368. 400p. 1986. pap. text ed. write for info. (ISBN 0-201-05844-8). Addison-Wesley.

Quantitative Toxicology: Selected Topics. V. A. Filov et al. LC 78-12530. (Environmental Science & Technology Ser.). 462p. 1980. 98.50 (ISBN 0-471-02109-1, Pub. by Wiley-Interscience). Wiley.
Quantitative Toxicology Selected Topics. V. A. Filvo et al. LC 78-12530. 480p. 1979. 98.50. Krieger.
Quantitative Videoangiocardiography. R. P. Wijk Van Brievingh. 220p. (Orig.). 1975. pap. text ed. 37.50x (ISBN 0-317-63130-6, Pub. by Delft Univ Pr). Coronet Bks.
Quantitative X-Ray Spectrometry. Jenkins. 608p. 1981. 95.00 (ISBN 0-8247-1266-8). Dekker.
Quantitative Zooarchaeology: Topics in the Analysis of Archaeological Faunas. Donald K. Grayson. Ed. by G. W. Dimbleby. (Studies in Archaeological Science). 1984. 29.50 (ISBN 0-12-297280-5). Acad Pr.
Quantities & Units - SI: Committee Report, Vol. 3. National Committee for Clinical Laboratory Standards. 1983. 20.00 (ISBN 0-318-19374-4, C11-CR). Natl Comm Clin Lab Stds.
Quantities: Damages. Richard Howard. (Wesleyan Poetry Ser.). 160p. 1984. 17.50x (ISBN 0-8195-5105-8); pap. 9.95 (ISBN 0-8195-6094-4). Wesleyan U Pr.
Quantity & Price Indexes in National Accounts. Richard Stone. 124p. 1956. 6.00x (ISBN 0-686-14788-X). OECD.
Quantity & Quality in Economic Research, Vol. I. Ed. by Roy C. Brown. (Illus.). 438p. (Orig.). 1986. lib. bdg. 40.50 (ISBN 0-8191-5112-2, Intl Soc Statisical Sci Economics); pap. text ed. 23.75 (ISBN 0-8191-5113-0, Intl Soc Statistical Sci Economics). U Pr of Amer.
Quantity & Quality in Economic Research, Vol. 2. Ed. by Roy C. Brown. LC 85-26360. 212p. (Orig.). 1988. lib. bdg. 27.50 (ISBN 0-8191-6701-0); pap. text ed. 14.75 (ISBN 0-8191-6702-9). U Pr of Amer.
Quantity & Quality in Economic Research, Vol. 3. Ed. by Roy Brown & George Johnson. LC 85-26360. (Illus.). 285p. (Orig.). 1988. 50.99 (ISBN 0-942004-19-1); pap. 38.96 (ISBN 0-942004-18-3). Throwkoff Pr.
Quantity & Quiddity: Essays in American Economic History. Ed. by Peter Kilby. x, 440p. 1987. 40.00x (ISBN 0-8195-5154-6). Wesleyan U Pr.
Quantity Baking Recipes: Combined Edition, 2 vols. Nathan Cotton. Incl. Vol. I. Cakes, Icings & Cheesecakes. 292p. 1983. pap. 26.95 (ISBN 0-8436-2265-2); Vol. II. Breads, Pastries, Pies & Cookies. 284p. 1983. 1983. Set. pap. 48.95 (ISBN 0-8436-2273-3). Van Nos Reinhold.
Quantity Cookery. 4th rev. ed. Nola Treat & Lenore Richards. 1967. 24.95 (ISBN 0-316-85251-1). Little.
Quantity Cooking. rev. ed. Thomas Mario. (Illus.). 1978. pap. 29.95 (ISBN 0-87055-497-2). AVI.
Quantity Cooking: Tested Recipes for Twenty or More. Darrell Miles & William Bigley. LC 75-46351. (Cookbook Ser.). Orig. Title: Dare to Excel in Cooking. (Illus.). 64p. 1976. pap. 2.95 (ISBN 0-486-23318-9). Dover.
Quantity Food Preparation. Jack Rudman. (Occupational Competency Examination Ser.: OCE-30). (Cloth bdg. avail. on request). pap. 13.95 (ISBN 0-8373-5730-6). Natl Learning.
Quantity Food Preparation: Standardizing Recipes & Controlling Ingredients. Polly W. Buchanan. (Standardizing Recipes for Institutional Use Ser.). (Illus.). 32p. 1983. pap. text ed. 11.95 (ISBN 0-88091-008-9, 0203). Am Dietetic Assn.
Quantity Food Production. 3rd ed. L. H Kotschevar. (Illus.). x, 662p. 1975. 55.00 (ISBN 0-85334-632-1, Pub. by Elsevier Applied Sci England). Elsevier.
Quantity Food Production, Planning & Management. 2nd ed. John Knight & Lendal Kotschevar. (Illus.). 640p. 1988. text ed. 28.95 (ISBN 0-442-24016-3). Van Nos Reinhold.
Quantity Food Production, Planning & Management. John B. Knight & Lendal H. Kotschevar. LC 79-12094. 589p. (Orig.). 1985. pap. 22.95 (ISBN 0-442-25745-7). Van Nos Reinhold.
Quantity Food Purchasing. 3rd ed. Lendal H. Kotschevar & Charles Levinson. (Illus.). iv, 690p. 1988. text ed. write for info. (ISBN 0-02-366220-4). Macmillan.
Quantity Food Sanitation. 4th ed. Karla Longree & Gertrude Armbruster. 452p. 1987. 39.95 (ISBN 0-471-81902-6). Wiley.
Quantity in Historical Phonology. K. Arnason. LC 79-41363. (Cambridge Studies in Linguistics: No. 30). (Illus.). 256p. 1980. 52.50 (ISBN 0-521-23040-3). Cambridge U Pr.
Quantity Surveying Practice. Ivor Seeley. 220p. 1984. 90.00x (ISBN 0-333-37860-1, Pub. by Macmillan Ed UK). State Mutual Bk.
Quantity Theory of Money. Hugo Hegeland. LC 68-55731. 1969. Repr. of 1951 ed. 29.50x (ISBN 0-678-00500-1). Kelley.
Quantity Tofu Recipes for Institutions & Restaurants: Tested Recipes for 50 or More. Gary Landgrebe. LC 83-81312. 96p. 1983. pap. 10.95 (ISBN 0-9601398-5-0). Fresh Pr.
Quantization. Ed. by Peter F. Swaszek. 352p. 1985. 54.95 (ISBN 0-442-28124-2). Van Nos Reinhold.
Quantization, Gravitation & Group Methods in Physics. Ed. by A. A. Komar. (Proceedings of the Lebedev Physics Institute of the Academy of Sciences of the U. S. S. R. Ser.: Vol. 176 Supplemental Volume). 314p. 1988. text ed. 98.00 (ISBN 0-941743-17-9). Nova Sci Pubs.
Quantocks & Their Library Associates. W. Nichols. Repr. 20.00 (ISBN 0-8274-3231-3). R West.
Quantrell's Raiders. Frank Gruber. Bd. with Town Tamer. 352p. 1984. pap. 3.50 (ISBN 0-451-12777-3, Sig). NAL.
Quantum & Beyond. William M. Honig. (Illus.). 312p. 1986. 25.00 (ISBN 0-8022-2517-9); pap. 17.50 (ISBN 0-8022-2518-7). Philos Lib.
Quantum & Fermion Differential Geometry, Pt. A. Robert Hermann. (Interdisciplinary Mathematics Ser.: No. 16). 196p. 1977. 24.00 (ISBN 0-915692-22-8, 991600339). Math Sci Pr.
Quantum Aspects of Molecular Motions in Solids: Proceedings of an ILL-IFF Workshop, Grenoble, France, September 24-26, 1986. Ed. by A. Heidemann et al. (Proceedings in Physics Ser.: Vol. 17). (Illus.). xii, 221p. 1987. 51.50 (ISBN 0-387-17562-8). Springer-Verlag.
Quantum Aspects of Polypeptides & Polynucleotides: A Symposium Held at Stanford University, California, March 25-29, 1963. Ed. by Mitchel Weissbluth. LC 64-9806. (Biopolymers Symposia: No.1). pap. 143.30 (ISBN 0-317-08769-X, 2007395). Bks Demand UMI.
Quantum Biochemistry & Specific Interactions. Z. Simon. 251p. 1976. 26.00 (ISBN 0-85626-087-8). Abacus Pr.
Quantum Chaos & Statistical Nuclear Physics. Ed. by T. H. Seligman & H. Nishioka. (Lecture Notes in Physics: Vol. 263). ix, 382p. 1986. 36.90 (ISBN 0-387-17171-1). Springer-Verlag.
Quantum Chemistry. Raymond Daudel et al. LC 82-23688. 558p. 1984. 143.00x (ISBN 0-471-90135-0). Wiley.
Quantum Chemistry. Hendrik F. Hameka. LC 81-3430. 340p. 1981. 42.95 (ISBN 0-471-09223-1, Pub. by Wiley-Interscience). Krieger.
Quantum Chemistry. 3rd ed ed. Ira N. Levine. 592p. 1983. text ed. 49.00 (ISBN 0-205-07793-5, 6877931). Allyn.
Quantum Chemistry. Donald A. McQuarrie. LC 82-51234. (Physical Chemistry Ser.). (Illus.). 517p. 1983. text ed. 36.00x (ISBN 0-935702-13-X). Univ Sci Bks.
Quantum Chemistry: An Introduction. Robert L. Flurry, Jr. (Illus.). 480p. 1983. write for info. (ISBN 0-13-747832-1). P-H.
Quantum Chemistry in Biomedical Sciences, Vol. 367. Ed. by Harel Weinstein & Jack P. Green. 552p. 1981. 108.00x (ISBN 0-89766-121-4); pap. 108.00x (ISBN 0-89766-122-2). NY Acad Sci.
Quantum Chemistry Literature Data Base: Bibliography of AB Initio Calculations for 1978-80. K. Ohno & K. Morokuma. (Physical Sciences Data Ser.: Vol. 12). 460p. 1982. 147.50 (ISBN 0-444-42074-6). Elsevier.
Quantum Chemistry of Atoms & Molecules. Philip S. Matthews. (Illus.). 200p. 1987. 44.50 (ISBN 0-521-24854-X); pap. 17.95 (ISBN 0-521-27025-1). Cambridge U Pr.
Quantum Chemistry of Polymers: Solid State Aspects. Ed. by Janos Ladik & Jean-Marie Andre. LC 84-3367. 1984. lib. bdg. 59.00 (ISBN 90-277-1741-9, Pub. by Reidel Holland). Kluwer Academic.
Quantum Chemistry Solutions Manual. Donald A. McQuarrie. (Physical Chemistry Ser.). 241p. 1985. student manual 18.00x (ISBN 0-935702-16-4). Univ Sci Bks.
Quantum Chemistry: Student Edition. John Lowe. 1979. 33.75 (ISBN 0-12-457552-8). Acad Pr.
Quantum Chemistry Symposium: Proceedings from the the International Journal of Quantum Chemistry, No. 17. Ed. by Per-Olov Lowdin et al. 652p. 1984. pap. text ed. 99.95x (ISBN 0-471-88169-4, Pub. by Wiley-Interscience). Wiley.
Quantum Chemistry: The Challenge of Transition Metals & Coordination Chemistry. Ed. by A. Veillard. 1986. lib. bdg. 89.50 (ISBN 90-277-2237-4, Pub. by Reidel Holland). Kluwer Academic.
Quantum Chemistry: The Development of AB Initio Methods in Molecular Electronic Structure Theory. Henry F. Schaefer, III. 144p. 1984. 29.95x (ISBN 0-19-855183-5). Oxford U Pr.
Quantum Chromodynamics. Ed. by William Frazer & Frank Henyey. LC 79-54969. (AIP Conference Ser.; Particles & Fields Sub-Ser.: No. 55; No. 18). (Illus.). 1979. lib. bdg. 20.50 (ISBN 0-88318-154-1). Am Inst Physics.
Quantum Chromodynamics - Theory & Experiment: Proceedings of the Third Lake Louise Winter Institute, Chateau Lake Louis, Canada, March 6-12, 1988. Ed. by B. A. Campbell et al. 600p. 1988. 78.00 (ISBN 9971-50-657-2, ZB0651PP). World Scientific Pub.
Quantum Chromodynamics: An Introduction to the Theory of Quarks & Gluons. F. J. Yndurain. (Texts & Monographs in Physics). (Illus.). 227p. 1983. 39.00 (ISBN 0-387-11752-0). Springer-Verlag.
Quantum Chromodynamics: Proceedings. Ed. by J. L. Alonso & R. Tarrach. (Lecture Notes in Physics: Vol. 113). 306p. 1980. pap. 26.00 (ISBN 0-387-09731-7). Springer-Verlag.
Quantum Collision Theory, Pts. 1 & 2. rev. ed. Ed. by C. J. Joachain. 710p. 1984. pap. 34.50 (ISBN 0-444-86773-2). Elsevier.
Quantum Concepts in Space & Time. Ed. by R. Penrose & C. J. Isham. (Illus.). 320p. 1986. 80.00 (ISBN 0-19-851972-9). Oxford U Pr.
Quantum Cosmology. Ed. by L. Z. Fang & R. Ruffini. (Advanced Series on Astrophysics & Cosmology: Vol. 3). 340p. 1987. 67.00x (ISBN 9971-50-293-3); pap. 32.00 (ISBN 9971-50-312-3). World Scientific Pub.
Quantum Description of High-Resolution NMR in Liquids. Maurice Goldman. (International Series of Monographs on Chemistry: No. 15). (Illus.). 288p. 1988. 75.00 (ISBN 0-19-855639-X). Oxford U Pr.
Quantum Dynamical Semigroups & Applications. R. Alicki & K. Lendi. (Lecture Notes in Physics: Vol. 286). viii, 196p. 1987. 22.30 (ISBN 0-387-18276-4). Springer Verlag.
Quantum Dynamics: Models & Mathematics. (Acta Physica Austriaca Ser.: Supplementum 16). 1976. 39.00 (ISBN 0-387-81414-0). Springer-Verlag.
Quantum Dynamics of Molecules: The New Experimental Challenge to Theorists. Ed. by R. G. Woolley. LC 80-16321. (NATO ASI Series B, Physics: Vol. 57). 572p. 1980. 95.00x (ISBN 0-306-40462-1, Plenum Pr). Plenum Pub.
Quantum Electrochemistry. J. O. M. Bockris & S. U. Khan. LC 78-11167. 538p. 1978. 79.50x (ISBN 0-306-31143-7, Plenum Pr). Plenum Pub.
Quantum Electrodynamics. J. Bialyniccy-Birula. LC 74-4473. 541p. 1975. 69.00 (ISBN 0-08-017188-5). Pergamon.
Quantum Electrodynamics. Richard P. Feynman. LC 61-18179. (Frontiers in Physics Ser.: No. 3). (Illus.). 1961. pap. 30.25 (ISBN 0-8053-2501-8, Adv Bk Prog MSP). Addison-Wesley.
Quantum Electrodynamics. S. N. Gupta. 238p. 1977. 75.00 (ISBN 0-677-04240-X). Gordon & Breach.
Quantum Electrodynamics. 2nd ed. Landau & et al. (Course of Theoretical Physics Ser.: Vol. 4). (Illus.). 550p. 1982. text ed. 100.00 (ISBN 0-08-026503-0); pap. text ed. 37.50 (ISBN 0-08-026504-9). Pergamon.
Quantum Electrodynamics & Quantum Optics. Ed. by A. O. Barut. (NATO ASI Ser. B, Physics: Vol. 110). 482p. 1984. 85.00x (ISBN 0-306-41730-8, Plenum Pr). Plenum Pub.
Quantum Electrodynamics of Particle Beams. Don McAllister. (Illus.). 370p. (Orig.). 1988. 40.00 (ISBN 0-937949-06-X); pap. 20.00 (ISBN 0-937949-07-8). Mind Matters Pub.
Quantum Electrodynamics of Particle Beams. Don McAllister. LC 88-11689. (Illus.). 370p. 1988. pap. 20.00. Quark Pub.
Quantum Electrodynamics of Strong Fields. Ed. by W. Greiner. (NATO ASI Series B, Physics: Vol. 80). 912p. 1982. 135.00x (ISBN 0-306-41010-9, Plenum Pr). Plenum Pub.
Quantum Electrodynamics of Strong Fields. W. Greiner et al. (Texts & Monographs in Physics). (Illus.). 610p. 1985. 43.00 (ISBN 0-387-13404-2). Springer-Verlag.
Quantum Electronic. 3rd ed. Yariv. 608p. 1988. write for info. (ISBN 0-471-60997-8). Wiley.
Quantum Electronics. 2nd ed. Amnon Yariv. LC 75-1392. 570p. 1975. write for info. (ISBN 0-471-97176-6). Wiley.
Quantum Electronics & Electro-Optics: Proceedings of the Fifth National Quantum Electronics Conference. Ed. by P. L. Knight. LC 82-24778. 456p. 1983. 100.00 (ISBN 0-471-10278-4). Wiley.
Quantum Field Theory. C. Itzykson & J. B. Zuber. 1980. text ed. 79.95 (ISBN 0-07-032071-3). McGraw.
Quantum Field Theory. F. Mandi & G. Shaw. LC 84-5229. 354p. 1985. pap. 44.95 (ISBN 0-471-90650-6). Wiley.
Quantum Field Theory. Lewis H. Ryder. (Illus.). 350p. 1985. pap. 85.00 (ISBN 0-521-23764-5). Cambridge U Pr.
Quantum Field Theory. Lewis H. Ryder. (Illus.). 440p. 1986. pap. 24.95 (ISBN 0-521-33859-X). Cambridge U Pr.
Quantum Field Theory & Parastatistics. Y. Ohnuki & S. Kamefuchi. (Illus.). 489p. 1982. 77.00 (ISBN 0-387-11643-5). Springer-Verlag.
Quantum Field Theory & Quantum Statistics: Essays in Honor of the Sixtieth Birtday of E. S. Fradkin, 2 Vols. Ed. by I. A. Batalin et al. 1987. Set. 220.00x (ISBN 0-85274-525-7, Pub. by A Hilger UK); Quantum Statistics & Methods of Field Theory, Vol. 1, 720pgs. 132.00x (ISBN 0-85274-573-7, Pub. by A Hilger UK); Models of Field Theory, Vol. 2, 630pgs. 132.00x (ISBN 0-85274-574-5). Taylor & Francis.
Quantum Field Theory & Statistical Mechanics, 2 vols. Jaffee & Glimm. (Contemporary Physicists Ser.). 951p. 1985. Set. lib. bdg. 139.90 (ISBN 0-8176-3273-5); Vol. 1. 64.95 (ISBN 0-8176-3271-9); Vol. 2. 74.95 (ISBN 0-8176-3272-7). Birkhauser.
Quantum Field Theory & the Many-Body Problem. Theodore D. Schultz. (Many-Body Problem: Current Research & Reviews Ser.). 158p. 1964. 48.00 (ISBN 0-677-01130-X). Gordon & Breach.
Quantum Field Theory in Curved Spacetime: Fundamentals (A Collection of Reprints) B. L. Hu & L. Parker. 500p. 1989. 83.00 (ISBN 9971-50-443-X); pap. 44.00 (ISBN 9971-50-444-8). World Scientific Pub.
Quantum Field Theory of Point Particles & Strings. Brian Hatfield. (Frontiers in Physics Ser.: Vol. 75). 608p. 1989. 48.50 (ISBN 0-201-11982-X). Addison-Wesley.
Quantum Field Theory of Solids. Ed. by H. Haken. 330p. 1983. pap. 42.00 (ISBN 0-444-86737-6, North-Holland). Elsevier.
Quantum Field Theory: Proceedings of the International Symposium in Honour of Hiroomi Umezawa, Positano, Salerno, Italy, 5-7 June, 1985. Ed. by F. Mancini. 696p. 1986. 79.00 (ISBN 0-444-87001-6). Elsevier.
Quantum Fields. M. N. Bogoliubov & D. V. Shirkov. 403p. 1983. text ed. 53.75 (ISBN 0-8053-0983-7, Adv Bk Prog MSP). Addison-Wesley.
Quantum Fields: Algebras, Processes. Ed. by L. Streit. (Illus.). 144p. 1980. 48.00 (ISBN 0-387-81607-0). Springer-Verlag.
Quantum Fields in Curved Space. N. D. Birrell & P. C. Davies. LC 81-3851. (Cambridge Monographs on Mathematical Physics: No. 7). (Illus.). 340p. 1982. 67.50 (ISBN 0-521-23385-2). Cambridge U Pr.
Quantum Fields in Curved Space. N. D. Birrell & P. C. Davies. (Cambridge Monographs in Mathematical Physics). 360p. 1984. pap. 29.95 (ISBN 0-521-27858-9). Cambridge U Pr.
Quantum Fitness: Breakthrough to Excellence. Irving Dardik & Denis Waitley. 1984. 12.70 (ISBN 0-671-50903-9). PB.
Quantum Fitness: Breakthrough to Excellence. Irving Dardik et al. 1986. pap. 3.95 (ISBN 0-671-61825-3). PB.
Quantum Flavordynamics, Quantum Chromodynamics & Unified Theories. Ed. by K. T. Mahanthappa & James Randa. LC 80-12289. (NATO ASI Series B, Physics: Vol. 54). 506p. 1980. 85.00x (ISBN 0-306-40436-2, Plenum Pr). Plenum Pub.
Quantum Fluctuations. Edward Nelson. LC 84-26449. (Princeton Series in Physics). 155p. 1985. 36.00x (ISBN 0-691-08378-9); pap. 14.50 (ISBN 0-691-08379-7). Princeton U Pr.
Quantum Fluids. Ed. by N. Wiser & D. J. Amit. 624p. 1970. 210.00 (ISBN 0-677-13700-1). Gordon & Breach.
Quantum Fluids & Solids, 1983: AIP Conference Proceedings No. 103, Sanibel Island, Florida. Ed. by E. D. Adams & G. G. Ihas. LC 83-72240. 512p. 1983. lib. bdg. 39.75 (ISBN 0-88318-202-5). Am Inst Physics.
Quantum Gravity, 2 vols. Ed. by M. Markov et al. 1000p. 1988. 113.00 (ISBN 9971-50-409-X). World Scientific Pub.
Quantum Gravity. Ed. by M. A. Markov & P. C. West. 536p. 1984. 89.50x (ISBN 0-306-41513-5, Plenum Pr). Plenum Pub.
Quantum Gravity & Cosmology: Proceedings of the 8th Summer Kyoto Institute (KSI'85) Kyoto, Japan, May 1985. Ed. by H. Sato & T. Inami. 420p. 1986. 74.00 (ISBN 9971-50-043-4); pap. 44.00 (ISBN 9971-50-047-7). World Scientific Pub.
Quantum Gravity: Proceedings of the Third Seminar, Moscow, 1984. Ed. by M. A. Markov et al. 716p. 1985. 99.00x (ISBN 9971-978-90-3). World Scientific Pub.
Quantum Gravity Two: A Second Oxford Symposium. Ed. by C. J. Isham et al. (Illus.). 1981. 63.00x (ISBN 0-19-851952-4). Oxford U Pr.
Quantum Hall Effect. Ed. by R. E. Prange & S. M. Girvin. (Graduate Texts in Contemporary Physics). (Illus.). 440p. 1986. 27.50 (ISBN 0-387-96286-7). Springer-Verlag.
Quantum Implications: Essays in Honour of David Bohn. Ed. by Basil Hiley & F. David Peat. 384p. 1987. 49.95 (ISBN 0-7102-0806-5, 08065, Pub. by Routledge UK). Routledge Chapman & Hall.
Quantum Man: Introduction to Uniphysics, the Science of Synthesis. Yaounde Olu. (Illus.). 50p. 1985. pap. 7.00 (ISBN 0-9615454-0-2). Astropoint Res.
Quantum Many-Particle Systems. J. Negele & H. Orland. (Frontiers in Physics Ser.). (Illus.). 500p. 1988. text ed. 46.25 (ISBN 0-201-12593-5, Adv Bk Prog MSP). Addison-Wesley.
Quantum Measurement & Chaos. Ed. by E. R. Pike & S. Sarker. LC 87-18934. (NATO ASI Series B, Physics: Vol. 161). (Illus.). 304p. 1987. 55.00x (ISBN 0-306-42669-2, Plenum Pr). Plenum Pub.
Quantum Mechanical Few-Body Problem. W. Gloeckle. (Texts & Monographs in Physics). (Illus.). 220p. 1983. 41.00 (ISBN 0-387-12587-6). Springer-Verlag.
Quantum Mechanical Three-Body Problem. E. W. Schmid & H. Ziegelmann. 222p. 1974. 63.00 (ISBN 0-08-018240-2). Pergamon.
Quantum Mechanical Tunnelling & Its Applications. D. Roy. 400p. 1986. 53.00 (ISBN 9971-50-024-8, Z0217P-B). World Scientific Pub.
Quantum Mechanical Tunnelling in Biological Systems. 2nd ed. Don DeVault. LC 83-15445. (Illus.). 200p. 1984. 47.50 (ISBN 0-521-24904-X). Cambridge U Pr.
Quantum Mechanics. D. I. Blokhintsev. Tr. by J. B. Sykes & M. J. Kearsley. 535p. 1964. lib. bdg. 39.50 (ISBN 90-277-0104-0, Pub. by Reidel Holland). Kluwer Academic.
Quantum Mechanics. 2nd, enl. ed. A. Bohm. LC 85-4710. (Texts & Monographs in Physics). (Illus.). 550p. 1986. pap. 49.50 (ISBN 0-387-13985-0). Springer-Verlag.

Quantum Theory's Growing Competitor. James S. Hughes. (Illus.). 16p. 1975. 15.00 (ISBN 0-915386-01-1). Arctinurus Co.

Quantum Uncertainties: Recent & Future Experiments & Interpretations. Ed. by W. M. Honig et al. LC 87-20223. (NATO ASI Series B, Physics: Vol. 162). (Illus.). 496p. 1987. 89.50x (ISBN 0-306-42670-6, Plenum Pr). Plenum Pub.

Quantum Universe. A. J. Hey & P. Walters. (Illus.). 192p. 1987. 47.50 (ISBN 0-521-26744-7); pap. 16.95 (ISBN 0-521-31845-9). Cambridge U Pr.

Quantum Velocity of Light h: The Unification of Quantum & Classical Physics. John A. Mayes. LC 83-61674. 1984. text ed. 35.00 (ISBN 0-9611548-0-2). Quantum Pubns.

Quantum Well & Superlattice Physics, No. II. Ed. by Capasso et al. 1988. 50.00 (ISBN 0-89252-978-4, 943). SPIE.

Quantum Well & Superlattice Physics. Ed. by Dohler & Schulman. 326p. 1987. 50.00 (ISBN 0-89252-827-3, 792). SPIE.

Quantum Wells & Superlattices in Optoelectronic Devices & Integrated Optics. Ed. by Adams. 1988. 43.00 (ISBN 0-89252-896-6, 861). SPIE.

Quantum World. J. C. Polkinghorne. LC 83-9411. (Illus.). 112p. 1984. text ed. 14.95 (ISBN 0-582-44682-1). Wiley.

Quantum World. J. C. Polkinghorne. LC 84-42953. 112p. 1985. pap. 7.95x (ISBN 0-691-02388-3). Princeton U Pr.

Quapaw. W. D. Baird. (Indians of North America Ser.). (Illus.). 104p. 1989. lib. bdg. 16.95x (ISBN 1-55546-728-8). Chelsea Hse.

Quapaw: Great Plains. Ed. by Frank W. Porter, III. (Indians of North America Ser.). (Illus.). (gr. 5 up). 1989. 16.95. Chelsea Hse.

Quapaw Indians: A History of the Downstream People. W. David Baird. LC 79-4731. (Civilization of the American Indian Ser.: Vol. 152). (Illus.). 1980. 22.95 (ISBN 0-8061-1542-4). U of Okla Pr.

Quaranic Commentary & Tradition: Studies in Arabic Literary Papyri, Vol. 2. Nabia Abbott. LC 56-5027. (Oriental Inst. Pubns. Ser: No. 76). 1967. 35.00x (ISBN 0-226-62177-4, OIP76). U of Chicago Pr.

Quarante-Cinq. Alexandre Dumas. 12.50 (ISBN 0-686-55830-8). French & Eur.

Quarantine. Josh Webster. 384p. Date not set. pap. 3.95 (ISBN 0-373-97063-3, Pub. by Worldwide). Harlequin Bks.

Quare Fellow see Behan: The Complete Plays.

Quare Geg. John Pepper. (Illus.). 64p. 1979. pap. 4.50 (ISBN 0-85640-193-5, Pub. by Blackstaff Pr). Longwood Pub Group.

Quark. Jana Price. Ed. by Jim Gross. (Illus.). 88p. 1988. 12.95 (ISBN 0-912949-12-0). Uni-Sun.

Quark Confinement & Liberation: Numerical Results & Theory: Proceedings of the Conference held at Berkeley, California, May, 1985. Ed. by M. B. Halpern & F. R. Klinkhamer. 620p. 1985. 63.00 (ISBN 9971-50-000-0). World Scientific Pub.

Quark-Gluon Plasma: Proceedings of the Int'l Conference on Physics & Astro-Physics. Ed. by B. Sinha & S. Raha. 600p. (Orig.). 1988. 75.00 (ISBN 9971-50-553-3); pap. 38.00 (ISBN 9971-50-555-X). World Scientific Pub.

Quark Matter Eighty-Four. Ed. by K. Kajantie. (Lecture Notes in Physics Ser.: Vol. 221). vi, 305p. 1985. pap. 22.50 (ISBN 0-387-15183-4). Springer-Verlag.

Quark Matter Formation & Heavy Ion Collisions: Proceedings of the Bielefeld Workshop, May 10-14, 1982. Ed. by M. Jacob & H. Satz. v, 586p. 1982. 67.00 (ISBN 9971-950-46-4); pap. 29.00 (ISBN 9971-950-47-2, Pub. by World Sci Singpore). World Scientific Pub.

Quark Model & High Energy Collisions. V. V. Anisovich et al. 280p. 1985. 38.00 (ISBN 9971-966-68-9). World Scientific Pub.

Quark Structure of Matter: Proceedings of the Strasbourg-Karlsruhe Conference, September 26-October 1, 1985. Ed. by M. Jacob & K. Winter. 700p. 1986. 82.00 (ISBN 9971-50-075-2); pap. 41.00 (ISBN 9971-50-076-0). World Scientific Pub.

Quark Structure of Matter: Proceedings of the Yukon Advanced Study Institute, Canada, August 1984. Ed. by N. Isgur et al. 350p. 1985. 47.00 (ISBN 9971-978-30-X). World Scientific Pub.

Quarks & Hadronic Structure. Ed. by G. Morpurgo. LC 76-47490. 328p. 1977. 59.50x (ISBN 0-306-38141-9, Plenum Pr). Plenum Pub.

Quarks & Leptons. Ed. by R. H. Dalitz & P. I. Kalmus. (Illus.). 148p. 1986. pap. text ed. 35.00X (ISBN 0-85403-276-2, Pub. by Royal Soc London). Scholium Intl.

Quarks & Leptons. Ed. by C. A. Engelbrecht. (Lecture Notes in Physics Ser.: Vol. 248). x, 417p. 1986. pap. 30.00 (ISBN 0-387-16457-X). Springer-Verlag.

Quarks & Leptons: An Introductory Course in Modern Particle Physics. Francis Halzen & Alan D. Martin. LC 83-14649. 396p. 1984. text ed. write for info. (ISBN 0-471-88741-2). Wiley.

Quarks & Leptons As Fundamental Particles. Ed. by P. Urban. (Acta Physica Austriaca Supplemetum Ser.: No. 21). (Illus.). 720p. 1979. 88.00 (ISBN 0-387-81564-3). Springer-Verlag.

Quarks & Leptons: Cargese 1979. Ed. by Maurice Levy et al. LC 80-25583. (NATO ASI Series B, Physics: Vol. 61). 736p. 1981. 115.00x (ISBN 0-306-40560-1, Plenum Pr). Plenum Pub.

Quarks & Nuclear Forces. Ed. by D. E. Fries & B. Zeitnitz. (Tracts in Modern Physics Ser.: Vol. 100). (Illus.). 223p. 1982. 39.00 (ISBN 0-387-11717-2). Springer-Verlag.

Quarks & Nuclear Structure: Proceedings of the Klaus Erkelenz Symposium, 3rd Held at Bad Honnef June 13-16, 1983. Ed. by k. Bleuler. (Lecture Notes in Physics Ser.: Vol. 197). viii, 414p. 1984. pap. 26.00 (ISBN 0-387-12922-7). Springer Verlag.

Quarks & Nuclei. W. Weise. (International Review of Nuclear Physics Ser.: Vol. 1). 620p. 1985. 67.00 (ISBN 9971-966-61-1); pap. 36.00 (ISBN 9971-966-62-X, Pub. by World Sci Singapore). World Scientific Pub.

Quarks: Frontiers in Elementary Particle Physics. Y. Nambu. 250p. 1985. 36.00 (ISBN 9971-966-65-4); pap. 21.00 (ISBN 9971-966-66-2, Pub. by World Sci Singapore). World Scientific Pub.

Quarks, Gluons & Hadronic Matter: Proceedings of the International Workshop on Quarks, Gluons & Hadronic Matter. Ed. by R. Violler. 484p. 74.00 (ISBN 9971-50-415-4). World Scientific Pub.

Quarks, Gluons & Lattices. Michael Creutz. LC 83-2089. (Cambridge Monographs on Mathematical Physics). 175p. 1984. 39.50 (ISBN 0-521-24405-6). Cambridge U Pr.

Quarks, Gluons & Lattices. Michael Creutz. (Monographs on Mathematical Physics). (Illus.). 175p. 1985. pap. 14.95 (ISBN 0-521-31535-2). Cambridge U Pr.

Quarks, Leptons, & Beyond. Ed. by H. Fritzsch et al. (NATO ASI Series B, Physics: Vol. 122). 564p. 1985. 89.50x (ISBN 0-306-41925-4, Plenum Pr). Plenum Pub.

Quarks, Leptons & Gauge Fields. K. Huang. 292p. 1982. 38.00 (ISBN 9971-950-03-0). World Scientific Pub.

Quarks, Leptons, & Their Constituents. Ed. by A. Zichichi. LC 86-22672. (The Subnuclear Ser.: Vol. 22). (Illus.). 584p. 1988. 95.00x (ISBN 0-306-42401-0, Plenum Pr). Plenum Pub.

Quarks, Mesons & Isobars in Nuclei: Proceedings of the Fifth Topical School Motril, Granada, Spain, Sept. 6-11, 1982. Ed. by R. Guardiola & A. Polls. vi, 328p. 1983. 45.00 (ISBN 9971-950-49-9). World Scientific Pub.

Quarks, Strings, Dark Matter & All the Rest: Proceedings of the Vanderbilt High Energy Physics Conference, 7th, Nashville, Tennessee, May 15-17, 1987. Ed. by R. S. Panvini & T. Weiler. 344p. 60.00 (ISBN 9971-50-272-0); pap. 28.00. World Scientific Pub.

Quarks: The Stuff of Matter. Harald Fritzsch. LC 82-72395. (Illus.). 1983. 19.95 (ISBN 0-465-06781-6). Basic.

Quarks, 1986: Proceedings of the U. S. S. R. Seminar. Ed. by A. N. Tavkhelidze et al. 526p. 1987. lib. bdg. 137.50x (ISBN 90-6764-097-2). Coronet Bks.

Quarles' Emblems. Illus. by Charles Bennett & W. H. Rogers. (Illus.). 321p. 1980. Repr. lib. bdg. 50.00 (ISBN 0-8495-4576-5). Arden Lib.

Quarrel Between Philosophy & Poetry: Studies in Ancient Thought. Stanley Rosen. 256p. 1988. text ed. 29.95. Routledge Chapman & Hall.

Quarrel Between the Earl of Manchester & Oliver Cromwell: An Episode of the English Civil War. Ed. by David Masson. Repr. of 1875 ed. 27.00 (ISBN 0-384-35850-0). Johnson Repr.

Quarrel of Reason with Itself: Essays on Hamann, Nietzsche, Lessing & Michaelis. James C. O'Flaherty. LC 87-70862. (Studies in German Literature, Linguistics, & Culture: Vol. 35). (Illus.). 230p. 1988. 32.00x (ISBN 0-938100-56-4). Camden Hse.

Quarrel of the Six Beasts. LC 87-70711. (Lac-Viet Ser.: No. 4). x, 92p. 1987. pap. 7.00 (ISBN 0-938692-27-5). Yale U SE Asia.

Quarrel with the Moon. J. C. Conaway. 320p. 1988. pap. 3.95 (ISBN 0-8125-1636-2). Tor Bks.

Quarrel with the Rose. James L. Weil. (Illus.). 1978. 24.00 (ISBN 0-686-59674-9). Elizabeth Pr.

Quarrel Within: Art & Morality in Milton's Poetry. Lawrence Hyman. LC 76-189559. 1972. 17.50x (ISBN 0-8046-9018-9, Pub. by Kennikat). Assoc Faculty Pr.

Quarreling Book. Charlotte Zolotow. LC 63-14445. (Illus.). (gr. k-3). 1963. 9.70i (ISBN 0-06-026975-8); PLB 9.89 (ISBN 0-06-026976-6). HarpJ.

Quarreling Book. Charlotte Zolotow. LC 63-14445. (Trophy Picture Bks.). (Illus.). 32p. (gr. k-3). 1982. pap. 2.95 (ISBN 0-06-443034-0, Trophy). HarpJ.

Quarrels of Authors: Or Some Memoirs for Our Literary History, 3 vols. Isaac D'Israeli. 1814. Set. 70.00 (ISBN 0-384-11870-4). Johnson Repr.

Quarrels That Have Shaped the Constitution. rev. & expanded ed. John A. Garraty. LC 86-46066. 320p. 1987. 22.95i (ISBN 0-06-055062-7, HarpT). Har-Row.

Quarrels That Have Shaped the Constitution. rev. & expanded ed. John A. Garraty. 320p. 1987. pap. 10.95 (ISBN 0-06-096166-X, PL6166, PL). Har-Row.

Quarry. C. Terry Cline, Jr. 1987. 17.95 (ISBN 0-453-00514-4). NAL.

Quarry. Max A. Collins. (Quarry Ser.). 224p. 1985. pap. 4.95 (ISBN 0-88150-057-7, Foul Play). Countryman.

Quarry. 2nd ed. Friedrich Durrenmatt. Bd. with Judge & His Hangman. (Double Detective Ser.: No. 2). 256p. 1983. pap. 7.95 (ISBN 0-87923-408-3). Godine.

Quarry. Carole Oles. (Poetry Ser.). 96p. (Orig.). 1983. pap. 7.95 (ISBN 0-87480-217-2). U of Utah Pr.

Quarry. Rochelle Ratner. (Orig.). 1978. pap. 2.75 (ISBN 0-912284-98-6). New Rivers Pr.

Quarry: A Collection in Lieu of Memoirs by Lincoln Kirstein. Lincoln Kirstein. (Illus.). 112p. 1986. 40.00 (ISBN 0-942642-27-9). Twelvetrees Pr.

Quarry: New Poems. Richard Eberhart. 1964. 12.95x (ISBN 0-19-500536-8). Oxford U Pr.

Quarry Wood. Nan Shepard. (Canongate Classics Ser.). 213p. 1988. pap. 8.95 (ISBN 0-86241-141-6, Pub. by Cnngt Pub Ltd). David & Charles.

Quarrying & Rockbreaking: The Operation & Maintenance of Mobile Plants. D. Lester. 117p. 1984. pap. text ed. 15.00x. Brookfield Pub Co.

Quarrying & Rockbreaking: The Operation & Maintenance of Mobile Processing Plants. David Lester. (Illus.). 117p. 1981. 19.50x (ISBN 0-903031-80-9, Pub. by Intermediate Tech England). Intermediate Tech.

Quarrying in Antiquity: Technology, Tradition & Social Change. J. B. Ward-Perkins. (Mortimer Wheeler Archaeological Lectures). 1971. pap. 5.50 (ISBN 0-85672-053-4, Pub. by British Acad). Longwood Pub Group.

Quarrying, Opencast & Alluvial Mining. John Sinclair. (Illus.). 375p. 1969. 75.75 (ISBN 0-444-20040-1, Pub. by Elsevier Applied Sci England). Elsevier.

Quarry's Contact. Robin Hunter. 300p. 1989. 16.95 (ISBN 1-55710-021-7, Arbor Hse). Morrow.

Quarry's Cut. Max A. Collins. (Quarry Ser.). 224p. 1986. pap. 4.95 (ISBN 0-88150-069-0, Foul Play). Countryman.

Quarry's Deal. Max A. Collins. (Quarry Ser.). 192p. 1986. pap. 4.95 (ISBN 0-88150-068-2, Foul Play). Countryman.

Quarry's List. Max A. Collins. 192p. 1985. pap. 4.95 (ISBN 0-88150-058-5). Countryman.

Quart Livre. Francois Rabelais. 607p. 1967. 9.95 (ISBN 0-686-54703-9). French & Eur.

Quart Livre. Ed. by Albert Seay. (Transcriptions Ser.: No. 6). v, 48p. 1981. 4.00 (ISBN 0-933894-09-0). Colo Coll Music.

Quarter-Acre of Heartache. Claude C. Smith. LC 85-28097. (Illus.). 160p. 1985. 12.95 (ISBN 0-936015-01-2); pap. 8.95 (ISBN 0-936015-00-4). Pocahontas Pr.

Quarter Century in Lawrence County, Indiana 1917-1941. James M. Guthrie. LC 84-8009. (Illus.). 432p. 1984. 40.00 (ISBN 0-318-03788-2). J M Guthrie.

Quarter Century of IFIP -- The IFIP Silver Summary: Proceedings of the 25th Anniversary Celebration of IFIP, Munich, FRG, 27 March, 1985. Ed. by H. Zemanek. 500p. 1986. 45.00 (ISBN 0-444-70003-X). Elsevier.

Quarter Century of Learning, 1904-1929. facs. ed. Columbia University Staff. LC 68-58780. (Essay Index Reprint Ser). 1931. 21.50 (ISBN 0-8369-1028-1). Ayer Co Pubs.

Quarter Century of Social Work Education. Ed. by Miriam Dinerman & Ludwig Geisman. LC 84-6951. 258p. 1984. 17.95x (ISBN 0-87101-124-7). Natl Assn Soc Wkrs.

Quarter-Century of Social Work Education. Ed. by Miriam Dinerman & Ludwig L. Geismar. 1984. 5.00. Coun Soc WK Ed.

Quarter Century of Social Work Education. Date not set. 17.95. Coun Soc Wk Ed.

Quarter Horse. Bob Denhardt. LC 82-45893. (Illus.). 280p. 1983. Repr. of 1941 ed. 16.95 (ISBN 0-89096-144-1). Tex A&M Univ Pr.

Quarter Horses. Dorothy H. Patent. LC 85-904. (Illus.). 96p. (gr. 3-7). 1985. reinforced bdg. 12.95 (ISBN 0-8234-0573-7). Holiday.

Quarter Horses: A Story of Two Centuries. Robert M. Denhardt. (Illus.). 1967. 19.95 (ISBN 0-8061-0753-7). U of Okla Pr.

Quarter-Midget Racing Is for Me. Mark Lerner. LC 81-41. (Sports for Me Bks.). (Illus.). (gr. 2-5). 1981. PLB 7.95 (ISBN 0-8225-1125-8). Lerner Pubns.

Quarter Note Cowpoke. James Potter & Gale Potter. (Illus.). 40p. (gr. k-2). 1987. 13.95 (ISBN 0-918825-51-2, Dist. by Kampmann & Co.). Moyer Bell Limited.

Quarter of a Millennium: The Library Company of Philadelphia, 1731-1981. Ed. by Edwin Wolf & Marie E. Korey. LC 81-80392. (Illus.). viii, 355p. 1981. pap. 25.00x (ISBN 0-914076-81-7). Lib Co Phila.

Quarter Race in Kentucky & Other Sketches Illustrative of Scenes, Characters & Incidents Throughout the Universal Yankee Nation. Ed. by William T. Porter. LC 78-174281. Repr. of 1847 ed. 27.50 (ISBN 0-404-05088-3). AMS Pr.

Quarter Running Horse: America's Oldest Breed. Robert M. Denhardt. LC 78-21381. 1979. 29.95 (ISBN 0-8061-1500-9). U of Okla Pr.

Quarter Sessions Records for Family Historians. 1987. 30.00x (Pub. by Birmingham Midland Soc UK). State Mutual Bk.

Quarterback. Terry Shea. (Illus.). 88p. (Orig.). 1980. pap. write for info. (ISBN 0-89279-060-1). Championship Bks.

Quarterback. George Sullivan. LC 81-43889. (Illus.). 64p. (gr. 4 up). 1982. 11.70i (ISBN 0-690-04241-8, Crowell Jr Bks); PLB 11.89g (ISBN 0-690-04242-6). HarpJ.

Quarterback Speaks to His God. Herbert Wilner. 288p. 1987. 17.95 (ISBN 0-933529-04-X); pap. 8.95 (ISBN 0-933529-03-1). Cayuse Pr.

Quarterback Walk-On. Thomas J. Dygard. LC 81-18715. 224p. (gr. 7-9). 1982. 12.95 (ISBN 0-688-01065-2). Morrow.

Quarterbacks. Mickey Herskowitz. 288p. 1988. 18.95 (ISBN 0-688-07387-5). Morrow.

Quarterdeck & Saddlehorn: The Story of Edward F. Beale, 1822-1893. Carl Briggs & Clyde F. Trudell. (Western Frontiersmen Ser.: Vol. xx). (Illus.). 300p. 1983. 29.50 (ISBN 0-87062-148-3). A H Clark.

Quarterdecks & Spanish Grants. Raymond C. Clar. (Illus.). 156p. 1984. pap. 15.00 (ISBN 0-910845-23-9, 909). Landmark Ent.

Quartered in Hell: The Story of the American North Russia Expeditionary Force 1918-1919. Dennis Gordon. LC 81-71127. (Illus.). 320p. (Orig.). 1982. pap. 12.95 (ISBN 0-942258-00-2). Gos Inc.

Quartered Questions & Queries. Monika Varma. 9.00 (ISBN 0-89253-747-7); flexible cloth 4.00 (ISBN 0-89253-748-5). Ind-US Inc.

Quarterly, No. 3. Ed. by Gordon Lish. 288p. 1987. pap. 5.95 (ISBN 0-394-75536-7, Vin). Random.

Quarterly, No. 4. Ed. by Gordon Lish. 256p. 1987. pap. 5.95 (ISBN 0-394-75537-5, Vin). Random.

Quarterly Bulletin of Statistics for Asia & the Pacific. (ST-ESCAP Series 436: Vol. XV, No.4). 75p. 1985. pap. 9.50 (ISBN 92-1-119423-7, E.86.II.F.14). UN.

Quarterly Bulletin of Statistics for Asia & the Pacific: Volume XIV, No. 2: June 1984. UN Economic & Social Commission for Asia & the Pacific. 86p. 1985. pap. 9.50 (ISBN 92-1-119233-1, E.84.II.F21). UN.

Quarterly Bulletin of Statistics for Asia & the Pacific. March 1985, Vol. XV, No. 1. 86p. 1986. 11.50 (ISBN 92-1-119415-6, E.86.II.F.2). UN.

Quarterly Bulletin of Statistics for Asia & the Pacific, Vol. XIV, No. 1. 93p. 1985. 11.00 (ISBN 92-1-119245-5, E.84.II.F11). UN.

Quarterly Bulletin of Statistics for Asia & the Pacific, Vol. XV, No. 2. 87p. 1985. 9.50 (ISBN 92-1-119418-0, E.86.11.F.8). UN.

Quarterly Bulletin of Statistics for Asia & the Pacific, Vol. XIV, No. 3. 85p. 9.50 (ISBN 92-1-119275-7, E.85.11.F.12). UN.

Quarterly Bulletin of Statistics for Asia & the Pacific, Vol. XV, No. 3. 85p. 1985. 9.50 (ISBN 92-1-119421-0, E.86.11.F.11). UN.

Quarterly Bulletin of Statistics for Asia & the Pacific, December 1984, Vol. XIV, No. 4. 75p. 1986. 9.50 (ISBN 92-1-119274-9, E.85.II.F.15). UN.

Quarterly: Fall 1988, No. 7. Ed. by Gordon Lish. (Orig.). 1988. 6.95 (ISBN 0-394-75936-2, Vin). Random.

Quarterly Review of Literature - Retrospective Anthologies: Poetry Volume. Ed. by T. Weiss & R. Weiss. 500p. 25.00 (ISBN 0-686-40289-8); pap. 20.00 (ISBN 0-686-40290-1). Quarterly Rev.

Quarterly Review of Literature Retrospective - Anthology: Criticism Volume. Ed. by T. Weiss & R. Weiss. 350p. 1982. 25.00 (ISBN 0-686-40295-2); pap. 20.00 (ISBN 0-686-40296-0). Quarterly Rev.

Quarterly Review of Literature Retrospective - Anthology: Fiction Volume. Ed. by T. Weiss & R. Weiss. 600p. 25.00 (ISBN 0-686-40291-X); pap. 20.00 (ISBN 0-686-40292-8). Quarterly Rev.

Quarterly Review of Literature Retrospective - Anthology: Special & Translation Volume. Ed. by T. Weiss & R. Weiss. 550p. 1982. 25.00 (ISBN 0-686-40293-6); pap. 20.00 (ISBN 0-686-40294-4). Quarterly Rev.

Quarterly Selections. Danny Licten. Ed. by Joyce Thomas & Irene Souter. LC 83-73466. 1983. 5.00 (ISBN 0-916183-00-9). Cal Poet.

Quarterly, Semiannual & Annual Payment Tables. Financial Publishing Co. Staff. 208p. 1982. pap. 19.95 (ISBN 0-87600-298-X). Finan Pub.

Quarterly: Winter 1988, No. 8. Ed. by Gordon Lish. (Orig.). 1988. 6.95 (ISBN 0-394-75937-0, Vin). Random.

Quartermaine's Terms. Simon Gray. (Modern Plays Ser.). 79p. 1983. pap. 6.95 (ISBN 0-413-52830-8, NO. 3887). Heinemann Ed.

Quarternary Coastlines & Marine Archaeology: Towards the Prehistory of Land Bridges & Continental Shelves. P. M. Masters. Ed. by N. C. Fleming. LC 82-45021. 1983. 58.50 (ISBN 0-12-479250-2). Acad Pr.

Quarternary Geology of Lake Zurich: An Interdisciplinary Investigation by Deep-Lake Drilling. Ed. by K. J. Hsu & K. R. Kelts. (Contributions to Sedimentology Ser.: No. 13). (Illus.). 210p. 1984. pap. text ed. 44.00x (ISBN 3-510-57013-8). Lubrecht & Cramer.

Que Gusto! Robert J. Brett. Ed. by James Funston. 1987. text ed. 19.75 (ISBN 0-8219-0267-9, 70453); tchr's. ed. 20.00 (ISBN 0-8219-0308-X, TE-70820); wkbk. 5.95 (ISBN 0-8219-0307-1, WK-70658); test bklt. 4.25 (ISBN 0-8219-0283-0, TB-70903); tape program 168.00 (ISBN 0-8219-0369-1, 70042); 60.00 (ISBN 0-8219-0370-5, 70951). EMC.
Que hay de nuevo? Jose B. Fernandez & Nasario Garcia. LC 84-81196. 216p. 1985. pap. text ed. 14.50 (ISBN 0-669-05908-0). Heath.
Que Linda es la Creacion: Beautiful Creation. (Games for Children Ser.). 32p. (Span. & Eng.). 1987. pap. 1.25 (ISBN 0-311-26611-8). Casa Bautista.
Que Ma Joie Demeure. Jean Giono. 512p. 1959. 8.95 (ISBN 0-686-53984-2). French & Eur.
Que Ma Joie Demeure see Oeuvres Romanesques.
Que Ma Vie Demeure. Jean Giono. 12.95 (ISBN 0-686-53985-0). French & Eur.
Que Mandan (Those Who Rule) Jose L. de Imaz. Tr. by Carlos A. Astiz from Span. LC 69-12100. 1970. 34.50x (ISBN 0-87395-044-5); pap. 10.95x (ISBN 0-87395-073-9). State U NY Pr.
Que Me Pasa con las Matematicas? Ana H. Quintero. LC 85-24617. (Illus.). 119p. 1986. pap. 11.50 (ISBN 0-8477-2749-1). U of PR Pr.
Que Mi Pueblo Adore. Edward W. Nelson. Tr. by Salomon C. Mussiett from Eng. 184p. (Span.). 1986. pap. 5.25 (ISBN 0-311-17029-3). Casa Bautista.
Que Pasa? Beverly Leetch & Philip Grundlehner. 1984. pap. text ed. 17.95 (ISBN 0-03-060558-X). HR&W.
Que Pasa Despues de la Muerte? 2nd ed. H. Rossier. Ed. by Gordon H. Bennett. Tr. by Sara Bautista from Eng. (Serie Diamante). (Illus.). 36p. (Span.). 1982. pap. 0.85 (ISBN 0-942504-07-0). Overcomer Pr.
Que Paso? An English-Spanish Guide for Medical Personnel. 4th, rev. ed. Martin P. Kantrowitz et al. LC 83-14670. (Illus.). 84p. 1984. pap. 5.95 (ISBN 0-8263-0725-6). U of NM Pr.
Que Paso con Estos Pecados? P. A. Deiros. 144p. 1979. pap. 2.50 (ISBN 0-311-42063-X). Casa Bautista.
Que Queda Enterrado. Carmen M. Gaite. (Unabridged Spanish Readers Ser.). 64p. 1987. pap. text ed. 5.95 (ISBN 0-88436-996-X, 70288). EMC.
Que Sabes Del Reloj? Y. Dlugolenski. 26p. (Span.). 1982. pap. 1.99 (ISBN 0-8285-2497-1, Pub. by Progress Pubs USSR). Imported Pubns.
Que Son las Necesidades Humanas. Vincent W. Kafka. 12p. 1988. pap. 3.95 (ISBN 0-913261-18-1). Effect Learn Sys.
Que Tal? An Introductory Course. 2nd ed. Thalia Dorwick et al. LC 82-21434. 474p. 1987. text ed. write for info. (ISBN 0-394-35314-5, RanC); write for info. wkbk. (ISBN 0-394-35315-3); write for info. lab manual (ISBN 0-394-35316-1). Random.
Que Tiempos Aquellos! Andino Acevedo Gonzales. LC 84-25639. 1988. UPREX: Ensayo, 69. pap. price not set (ISBN 0-8477-0069-0). U of PR Pr.
Que Tiene Sed. Abelardo Castillo. 257p. (Span.). 1985. pap. 9.00 (ISBN 0-317-46764-6). Ediciones Norte.
Que Va-T-Il Arriver? Lowell Lundstrom. Ed. by Annie L. Cosson. Tr. by Valerie Chardenal from Eng. 304p. (Fr.). 1985. pap. text ed. 3.00 (ISBN 0-8297-0435-3). Life Pubs Intl.
Que Veinte Anos No Es Nada. Celedonio Gonzales. LC 87-80170. (Coleccion Caniqui). 126p. (Orig., Span.). 1987. pap. 9.95 (ISBN 0-89729-435-1). Ediciones.
Que Viva Mexico! S. M. Eisenstein. LC 70-169341. (Arno Press Cinema Program). (Illus.). 94p. 1972. Repr. of 1951 ed. 12.00 (ISBN 0-405-03916-6). Ayer Co Pubs.
Quebec. Ed. by Fernand Grenier. (Studies in Canadian Geography). (Illus., Fr.). 1972. pap. 6.00x (ISBN 0-8020-6159-1). U of Toronto Pr.
Quebec Act: A Study in Statesmanship. Reginald Coupland. LC 83-45424. Repr. of 1925 ed. 28.00 (ISBN 0-404-20068-0). AMS Pr.
Quebec & Canada: Past, Present & Future. John Fitzmaurice. LC 85-2086. 240p. 1985. 37.50 (ISBN 0-312-65921-0). St Martin.
Quebec & Radical Social Change. Ed. by Dimitrios I. Roussopoulos. 225p. 1974. 16.95 (ISBN 0-919618-52-9, Dist. by U of Toronto Pr); pap. 5.95 (ISBN 0-919618-51-0, Dist. by the U of Toronto). Black Rose Bks.
Quebec & Related Silver at the Detroit Institute of Arts. Ed. by Ross A. Fox. (Illus.). 176p. 1978. 2.00. Detroit Inst Arts.
Quebec Before Duplessis: The Political Career of Louis-Alexandre Taschereau. Bernard L. Vigod. 328p. 1986. 35.00x (ISBN 0-7735-0588-1). McGill-Queens U Pr.
Quebec City, Seventeen Sixty-Five to Eighteen Thirty-Two. David T. Ruddel. (Mercury Ser.). (Illus.). 293p. 1988. pap. 24.95 (ISBN 0-660-10771-6, Pub. by CN Mus Civilization Canada). U of Chicago Pr.
Quebec Establishment: The Ruling Class & the State. Pierre Fournier. 236p. 1978. 19.95 (ISBN 0-919618-28-6, Dist by U of Toronto Pr); pap. 9.95 (ISBN 0-919618-27-8, Dist. by U of Toronto Pr). Black Rose Bks.
Quebec, I Love You: Je t'Aime. Miyuki Tanobe. (Illus.). 48p. (gr. 5 up). 1971. pap. 2.95 (ISBN 0-88776-156-9). Tundra Bks.
Quebec Inc. Matthew Fraser. 288p. 1987. 24.95 (ISBN 1-55013-043-9, Pub. by Key Porter Canada). U of Toronto Pr.
Quebec Labour. Intro. by Marcel Pepin. 224p. 1972. 18.95 (ISBN 0-919618-14-6, Dist by U of Toronto Pr); pap. 7.95 (ISBN 0-919618-15-4, Dist. by U of Toronto Pr). Black Rose Bks.
Quebec Nationalism in Crisis. Dominique Clift. Orig. Title: Declin du Nationalisme au Quebec. 162p. 1982. 25.00x (ISBN 0-7735-0381-1); pap. 9.95 (ISBN 0-7735-0383-8). McGill Queen's U Pr.
Quebec Sales Tax--with Related Taxes, 1986. 15th ed. 112p. (Orig.). 1986. pap. 9.95 (3910). Commerce.
Quebec Sales Tax-With Related Taxes. 14th ed. 104p. 1984. 9.00 (ISBN 0-317-44630-4, 4040). Commerce.
Quebec: The Challenge of Independence. Anne Griffin. LC 81-72054. 260p. 1983. 27.50 (ISBN 0-8386-3135-5). Fairleigh Dickinson.
Quebec: The Unfinished Revolution. rev. & enl. ed. Leon Dion. 1976. text ed. 29.95x (ISBN 0-7735-0242-4); pap. 14.95c (ISBN 0-7735-0279-3). McGill-Queens U Pr.
Quechua Peoples Poetry. Jesus Lara. Tr. by Maria Proser & James Scully. LC 76-26704. Orig. Title: Poesia Popular Quechua. 1977. pap. 7.50 (ISBN 0-915306-09-3). Curbstone.
Quechua Peoples Poetry. Tr. by Maria A. Proser & James Scully. 1986. pap. 7.50 (ISBN 0-317-52698-7). Curbstone.
Queen. Ann Morrow. (Illus.). 272p. 1986. pap. 8.95 (ISBN 0-586-05860-5). Academy Chi Pubs.
Queen: A Magic Tour. (Illus.). 96p. (Orig.). 1987. pap. 9.95 (ISBN 0-283-99488-6, 00183587, Pub. by Sidgwich & Jackson England). H Leonard Pub Corp.
Queen Alexandra's Christmas Gift Book. Queen Alexandra. Intro. by Georgina Battiscombe. (English Heritage Ser.). (Illus.). 160p. 1987. Repr. of 1908 ed. 34.00 (ISBN 0-948285-01-X). Archival Facsimiles.
Queen & Her Court: A Guide to the British Monarchy Today. Jerrold M. Packard. (Illus.). 256p. 1981. (ScribT); pap. 6.95 (ISBN 0-684-17648-3). Scribner.
Queen & I. Barbara J. Crane. (Crane Reading System-English Ser.). (Illus.). (gr. k-2). 1977. pap. text ed. 3.86 (ISBN 0-89075-093-9). Crane Pub Co.
Queen & Lord M. Jean Plaidy. 268p. Repr. of 1973 ed. lib. bdg. 15.95x (ISBN 0-88411-895-9, Pub. by Aeonian Pr.). Amereon Ltd.
Queen & Mister Gladstone. Queen Victoria. Ed. by Philip Guedella. LC 34-6053. 1969. Repr. of 1934 ed. 36.00 (ISBN 0-527-93152-7). Kraus Repr.
Queen & the Axe. Barry L. Hillman. 1982. 15.00x (ISBN 0-903653-40-0, Pub. by New Playwrights Network). State Mutual Bk.
Queen Anne. Edward Gregg. (Illus.). 1984. 29.95x (ISBN 0-7100-0400-1); pap. 9.95 (ISBN 0-7448-0018-8, Ark Paperbks). Routledge Chapman & Hall.
Queen Anne. Herbert Paul. 1973. Repr. of 1906 ed. 35.00 (ISBN 0-8274-1233-9). R West.
Queen Anne & Georgian Looking Glasses: Old English & Early American. F. Lewis Hinckley. (Illus.). 256p. 1987. 60.00x (ISBN 0-8147-3447-2, Pub. by Washington Mews). NYU Pr.
Queen Anne's American Kings. Richmond P. Bond. 1972. lib. bdg. 18.00x (ISBN 0-374-90783-8, Octagon). Hippocrene Bks.
Queen Anne's Gate Mystery: A Novel, 2 vols. in 1. Richard Arkwright. LC 75-32733. (Literature of Mystery & Detection). 1976. Repr. of 1889 ed. 37.50x (ISBN 0-405-07863-3). Ayer Co Pubs.
Queen Anne's Lace. Genevieve S. Whitford. (Illus.). 64p. 1987. 9.95 (ISBN 0-02-627190-7). Macmillan.
Queen Anne's Lace & Other Poems. Genevieve Smith Whitford. (Illus.). 53p. Repr. of 1982 ed. 9.95 (ISBN 0-9610456-0-4). Harp Pr.
Queen Bee. Jacob Grimm & Wilhelm K. Grimm. (Creative's Collection of Fairy Tales). (Illus.). 32p. (gr. 4 up). 1986. 10.95 (ISBN 0-87191-939-7). Creative Ed.
Queen Bee. Barbara Hazard. 240p. (Orig.). 1988. pap. 2.95 (ISBN 0-451-15474-6, Sig). NAL.
Queen Christina. Pam Gems. 80p. 1983. pap. 4.95 (ISBN 0-9508443-0-6, NO.3938). Routledge Chapman & Hall.
Queen Christina, Charles XII, Gustav III. August Strindberg. Tr. by Walter Johnson. LC 55-7573. (American-Scandinavian Foundation Scandinavian Studies). (Illus.). 293p. 1968. 16.50x (ISBN 0-295-73899-5); pap. 5.95x (ISBN 0-295-78570-5, WP45). U of Wash Pr.
Queen City: A History of Denver. Lyle W. Dorsett. LC 85-30176. (Western Urban History Ser.). (Illus.). 1986. 19.95 (ISBN 0-87108-698-0). Pruett.
Queen City: A History of Denver. Lyle W. Dorsett. LC 85-30176. (Western Urban History Ser.). (Illus.). 350p. 1986. pap. 12.95 (ISBN 0-87108-704-9). Pruett.
Queen Conch. Katherine S. Orr & Carl J. Berg, Jr. (Illus.). 32p. 1987. pap. 2.50 (ISBN 0-89317-038-0). Windward Pub.
Queen Eleanor: Independent Spirit of the Medieval World: a Biography of Eleanor of Aquitaine. Polly S. Brooks. LC 82-48776. (Illus.). 160p. (gr. 6 up). 1983. 11.70i (ISBN 0-397-31994-0, Lipp Jr Bks); PLB 12.89 (ISBN 0-397-31995-9). HarpJ.
Queen Elizabeth. Jacob Abbott. 281p. 1982. Repr. of 1903 ed. lib. bdg. 32.50 (ISBN 0-89987-037-6). Darby Bks.
Queen Elizabeth. Katherine Anthony. 1979. Repr. of 1929 ed. lib. bdg. 29.00 (ISBN 0-8495-0148-2). Arden Lib.
Queen Elizabeth. Edward S. Beesley. 1978. Repr. of 1908 ed. lib. bdg. 22.50 (ISBN 0-8495-0374-4). Arden Lib.
Queen Elizabeth. Edward S. Beesly. LC 74-39408. (Select Bibliographies Reprint Ser.). 1972. Repr. of 1892 ed. 16.25 (ISBN 0-8369-9901-0). Ayer Co Pubs.
Queen Elizabeth: A Life of the Queen Mother. Penelope Mortimer. (Illus.). 304p. 1986. 17.95 (ISBN 0-312-65984-9, J Kahn). St Martin.
Queen Elizabeth & Her Subjects. Alfred Rowse & George Harrison. LC 79-76913. (Essay Index Reprint Ser). 1935. 13.00 (ISBN 0-8369-1895-9). Ayer Co Pubs.
Queen Elizabeth & the Making of Policy, 1572-1588. Wallace T. MacCaffrey. LC 80-8564. 536p. 1981. 58.50x (ISBN 0-691-05324-3); pap. 22.50 (ISBN 0-691-10112-4). Princeton U Pr.
Queen Elizabeth & the Revolt of the Netherlands. 2nd ed. Charles Wilson. (Illus.). 168p. 1980. pap. 19.00 (ISBN 90-247-2273-X, Pub. by Martinus Nijhoff Netherlands). Kluwer Academic.
Queen Elizabeth at War. Chris Konings. (Illus.). 128p. 1985. 17.95 (ISBN 0-85059-725-0, Pub. by PSL P Stephens England). Sterling.
Queen Elizabeth I. Dorothy Turner. (Great Lives Ser.). 32p. (gr. 1-6). 1987. lib. bdg. 11.90 (ISBN 0-531-18132-4, Pub. by Bookwright Pr). Watts.
Queen Elizabeth I. Betka Zamoyska. Ed. by Eleanor Nichols. (Great Leaders Ser.). (Illus.). 69p. 1981. text ed. 7.95 (ISBN 0-07-072721-X). McGraw.
Queen Elizabeth II. Dorothy Turner. LC 84-73574. (Great Lives Ser.). (Illus.). 32p. (gr. 7-9). 1985. s&l 11.90 (ISBN 0-531-18017-4, Pub. by Bookwright Pr). Watts.
Queen Elizabeth in Drama & Related Studies. facs. ed. Frederick S. Boas. LC 78-119954. (Select Bibliographies Reprint Ser). 1950. 19.00 (ISBN 0-8369-5397-5). Ayer Co Pubs.
Queen Elizabeth in Drama & Related Studies. Frederick S. Boas. (Select Bibliographies Reprint Ser.). 212p. 1982. Repr. of 1950 ed. lib. bdg. 11.00 (ISBN 0-8290-0828-4). Irvington.
Queen Elizabeth in Drama & Related Studies. Frederick S. Boas. 212p. 1980. Repr. lib. bdg. 25.00 (ISBN 0-8492-3588-X). R West.
Queen Elizabeth in Drama & Related Studies. Frederick S. Boas. LC 71-158905. 1971. Repr. of 1950 ed. 12.00x (ISBN 0-403-01317-8). Scholarly.
Queen Elizabeth in Drama & Related Studies. Frederick S. Boas. 212p. 1983. Repr. of 1950 ed. lib. bdg. 40.00 (ISBN 0-8495-0635-2). Arden Lib.
Queen Elizabeth, the Queen Mother. Alan Hamilton. (Profiles Ser.). (Illus.). 63p. (gr. 6-9). 1984. 9.95 (ISBN 0-241-11030-0, Pub. by Hamish Hamilton England). David & Charles.
Queen Emma & the Bishop. 2nd ed. Katherine S. Thompson. (Illus.). 1987. Repr. of 1963 ed. text ed. write for info. (ISBN 0-938851-04-7). Daughters of HI.
Queen Ester. rev. ed. Tomie De Paola. (Bible Story Cutout Bks.). (Illus.). 40p. (Orig.). (gr. k-5). 1987. 12.95 (ISBN 0-06-255539-1); lib. bdg. 12.89 (ISBN 0-06-255617-7); pap. 5.95 (ISBN 0-06-255540-5). Har-Row.
Queen Fish. V. Astafiev. 444p. 1982. 12.95 (ISBN 0-8285-2523-4, Pub. by Progress Pubs USSR). Imported Pubns.
Queen Fussy. Mister Tom. (Illus.). 48p. (gr. 2-4). 1973. Cassette. write for info. Oddo.
Queen Has Been Pleased: British Honours System at Work. John Walker. 192p. 1986. 30.95 (ISBN 0-436-56111-5, Pub. by Secker & Warburg UK). David & Charles.
Queen in Waiting. Jean Plaidy. 1987. pap. 3.95 (ISBN 0-449-21096-0, Crest). Fawcett.
Queen Kapiolani. Maili Yardley & Miriam Rogers. 1985. pap. text ed. 7.95 (ISBN 0-914916-73-4). Topgallant.
Queen Lucia. E. F. Benson. (Large Print Bks). 369p. 1987. lib. bdg. 16.95 (ISBN 0-8161-4163-0, Large Print Bks). G K Hall.
Queen Lucia, Pt. 1. E. F. Benson. LC 83-48324. (Make Way for Lucia Ser.). 288p. 1986. pap. 5.95 (ISBN 0-06-091372-X, PL 1372, PL). Har-Row.
Queen Mary: Her Early Years Recalled. C. W. Winter. (Illus.). 1986. 24.95 (ISBN 0-393-02351-6). Norton.
Queen Mary: The Official Pictorial History. Robert O. Maguglin. LC 85-50967. (Illus.). 120p. Date not set. pap. 10.95 (ISBN 0-917859-21-9). Sunrise SBCA.
Queen Mary's Dolls' House. Mary Stewart-Wilson. (Illus.). 192p. Date not set. 35.00 (ISBN 0-89659-876-4). Abbeville Pr.
Queen Mary's Grammar School, Clitheroe, Pt. 1. C. W. Stokes. Repr. of 1934 ed. 24.00 (ISBN 0-384-58360-1). Johnson Repr.
Queen Mother. Robert Lacey. (Illus.). 128p. 1987. 17.95 (ISBN 0-316-51167-6). Little.
Queen Mother. Elizabeth Longford. (Illus.). 185p. 1986. pap. 10.95 (ISBN 0-586-05603-3). Academy Chi Pubs.
Queen Must Die & Other Affairs of Bees & Men. William Longgood. (Illus.). 1985. 12.95 (ISBN 0-393-01896-2). Norton.
Queen Must Die & Other Affairs of Bees & Men. William Longgood. (Illus.). 1988. pap. 7.95 (ISBN 0-393-30528-7). Norton.
Queen Named King: Henrietta of the King Ranch. Mary V. Fox. 96p. (gr. 4-7). 1986. 8.95 (ISBN 0-89015-562-3). Eakin Pr.
Queen of Apostles Prayerbook. James Alberione. 7.50 (ISBN 0-8198-0266-2); plastic bdg. 6.00 (ISBN 0-8198-0267-0). Dghtrs St Paul.
Queen of Atlantis: Romance of the Caribbean Sea. Frank Aubrey. LC 74-15949. (Science Fiction Ser). 394p. 1975. Repr. of 1899 ed. 30.00x (ISBN 0-405-06275-3). Ayer Co Pubs.
Queen of Canada Colouring Book. Charles Pachter. 24p. 1977. pap. 1.00 (ISBN 0-88784-060-4, Pub. by Hse Anansi Pr Canada). U of Toronto Pr.
Queen of Cowtowns: Dodge City. Stanley Vestal. LC 51-11962. (Illus.). xii, 285p. 1972. pap. 7.95 (ISBN 0-8032-5758-9, BB 551, Bison). U of Nebr Pr.
Queen of Death. John Milne. (Heinemann Guided Readers). 1979. pap. text ed. 3.00x (ISBN 0-435-27049-4). Heinemann Ed.
Queen of Eene. Jack Prelutsky. LC 77-17311. (Illus.). 32p. (gr. k-3). 1978. PLB 11.88 (ISBN 0-688-84144-9). Greenwillow.
Queen of Hearts. Jill Briscoe. (Quality Paper). 1986. pap. 6.95 (ISBN 0-8007-5225-2). Revell.
Queen of Hearts. Vera Cleaver & Bill Cleaver. LC 77-18252. 160p. (gr. 6 up). 1987. 12.70i (ISBN 0-397-31771-9, Lipp Jr Bks). HarpJ.
Queen of Hearts. Vera Cleaver & Bill Cleaver. LC 77-18252. (Trophy Bks.). 160p. (gr. 5 up). 1987. pap. 2.95 (ISBN 0-06-440196-0, Trophy). HarpJ.
Queen of Hearts. Wilkie Collins. LC 75-32740. (Literature of Mystery & Detection Ser.). 1976. Repr. of 1859 ed. 35.50x (ISBN 0-405-07868-4). Ayer Co Pubs.
Queen of Hearts. Megan Daniel. 224p. 1986. pap. 2.50 (ISBN 0-451-14437-6, Sig). NAL.
Queen of Hearts. Susan Shreve. 1988. pap. 4.50 (ISBN 0-671-64764-4). PB.
Queen of Hearts. Susan R. Shreve. 352p. 1987. 17.95 (ISBN 0-671-60102-4). S&S.
Queen of Hearts: The Passionate Pilgrimage of Lola Montez. Isaac Goldberg. LC 75-91505. 308p. 1936. 18.00 (ISBN 0-405-08563-X). Ayer Co Pubs.
Queen of Hell. J. N. Williamson. 288p. (Orig.). 1981. pap. 2.50 (ISBN 0-8439-0995-1, Leisure Bks). Leisure NY.
Queen of Letter Writers: Marquise De Sevigne Dame De Bourbilly, 1626-1696. Janet Aldis. 1977. Repr. of 1907 ed. lib. bdg. 27.50 (ISBN 0-8495-0015-X). Arden Lib.
Queen of Letter Writers: Marquise De Sevigne Dame De Bourbilly 1626-1696. Janet Aldis. 1973. Repr. of 1907 ed. 35.00 (ISBN 0-8274-1209-6). R West.
Queen of Letter Writers: Marquise De Sevigne Dame De Bourbilly 1626-1696. Janet Aldis. 1907. 39.00 (ISBN 0-932062-03-2). Sharon Hill.
Queen of Lost Baggage. Barbara Lefcowitz. LC 85-52078. (Series X). 72p. (Orig.). 1986. pap. 5.00 (ISBN 0-931846-29-3). Wash Writers Pub.
Queen of Navarre, Jeanne D'Albret, 1528-1572. Nancy L. Roelker. LC 68-54024. (Illus.). 1968. 34.50x (ISBN 0-674-74150-1, Belknap Pr). Harvard U Pr.
Queen of Paradox: A Stuart Tragedy (Mary Stuart, Queen of Scots) Katherine Bregy. 221p. 1982. Repr. of 1950 ed. lib. bdg. 35.00 (ISBN 0-8495-0612-3). Arden Lib.
Queen of Peace, Echo of the Eternal Word. Tomislav Pervan. (Illus.). 58p. (Orig.). 1986. pap. 3.50 (ISBN 0-940535-05-X). Franciscan U Pr.
Queen of Shaba: The Story of an African Leopard. Joy Adamson. LC 80-7931. (Helen & Kurt Wolff Bk.). (Illus.). 256p. 1980. 14.95 (ISBN 0-15-175651-1). HarBraceJ.
Queen of Sheba's Heirs: Cultural Patterns of Ethiopia. Edith Lord. LC 74-75127. (Illus.). 250p. 1970. 12.50 (ISBN 0-87491-012-9). Acropolis.
Queen of Sorcery. David Eddings. (Belgariad Ser.: Bk. 2). 327p. (Orig.). 1988. pap. 3.95 (ISBN 0-345-33565-1, Del Rey). Ballantine.
Queen of Spades. Harold H. Henderson. LC 82-83127. 208p. 1983. 12.95 (ISBN 0-932966-27-6). Permanent Pr.
Queen of Spades. Harold H. Henderson. 208p. 1985. pap. 9.95 (ISBN 0-932966-58-6). Permanent Pr.
Queen of Spades. Aleksandr Pushkin. Ed. by James Forsyth. (Library of Russian Classics). 128p. pap. text ed. 9.95x (ISBN 0-631-14383-1). Basil Blackwell.
Queen of Spades & Other Stories. Aleksandr Pushkin. Tr. by Rosemary Edmonds from Rus. (Classics Ser.). 1978. pap. 4.95 (ISBN 0-14-044119-0). Penguin.
Queen of Swords. Anne E. Crompton. LC 79-26496. 1980. 8.95 (ISBN 0-416-30611-X, NO. 0165). Routledge Chapman & Hall.
Queen of Swords. Judy Grahn. LC 87-47537. 192p. 1987. 14.95 (ISBN 0-8070-6802-0). Beacon Pr.

Quelques Aspects de l'Evolution de la Population Active Masculine Agricole de 1946 a 1962 see Cahiers de l'Institut de Science Economique Appliquee.

Quelques Documents Inedits Sur Paul Lafargue see Cahiers de l'Institut de Science Economique Appliquee.

Quelques Lettres d'Ivan Tourguenev a Pauline Viardot: Texte Integral d'Apres l'Apres les Originaux de la Collection Maupoil de 29 Lettres de l'Edition Halperine-Kaminski avec en Appendice 8 Lettres Inedites en France d'Ivan Tourguenev a Pauline Viardot. Ed. by Heri Granjard. (Etudes Sur l'Historie l'Economie et la Sociologie des Pays Slaves: No. 16). 1974. 16.40x (ISBN 90-2797-309-1). Mouton.

Quelques Methodes de Prevision a Court Terme: Analyses des Tendances Recentes, Indices Precurseurs & Tests Conjoncturels. J. Meraud. (Economies & Societes Serie AK: No. 1). 1961. pap. 13.00 (ISBN 0-8115-0638-X). Kraus Repr.

Quelques Methodes de Resolutions de Problemes aux Limites de la Physique Mathematiques. Robert Lattes. (Cours & Documents de Mathematiques & de Physique Ser.). 196p. (Orig.). 1967. 76.00 (ISBN 0-677-50060-2). Gordon & Breach.

Quelques Moeurs et Coutumes des Paysans Haitiens. J. B. Romain. LC 75-1057. Repr. of 1958 ed. lib. bdg. 57.00 (ISBN 0-8414-7370-6). Folcroft.

Quelques Notions de Base pour l'Economie. L. Couffignal. Bd. with Connaissance Cybernetique de L'Economie et l'Information Statistique. V. Rouquet-la-Garrigue; Methodes Nouvelles d'Expoitation des Courbes-Reponses. G. Coulmy. (Economies et Societes Ser N: No. 4). 1962. pap. 11.00 (ISBN 0-8115-0768-8). Kraus Repr.

Quelques Observations Sur L'Ethnologie Britannique Actuelle see Cahiers de l'Institut de Science Economique Appliquee.

Quelques Peintures de Lettres, XIV-XX Siecles. Vadime Elisseeff. (Illus.). 58p. 1962. 175.00x (ISBN 0-317-68558-9, Pub. by Han-Shan Tang Ltd). State Mutual Bk.

Quelques Pianos. Simon Cutts. LC 75-37301. 1976. pap. 5.00 (ISBN 0-912330-35-X, Dist. by Inland Bk). Jargon Soc.

Quelques Relexions sur la Methode des Plans pour le Developpement Regional see Cahiers de l'Institut de Science Economique Applique.

Quelques Riens Pour Album, 1 vol. Gioachino Rossini. Ed. by Marvin Tartak. Tr. by Bruno Cagli et al from Ital. (Works of Gioachino Rossini Ser.). xxii, 224p. 1986. text ed. 65.00x (ISBN 0-317-46885-5, 728390, Pub. by Fondazione Rossini). U of Chicago Pr.

Quelqu'un. Robert Pinget. 264p. 1965. 12.95 (ISBN 0-686-54879-5). French & Eur.

Quench Hardening in Metals. H. Kimura & R. Maddin. LC 74-140489. (Defects in Crystalline Solids Ser.: Vol. 3). (Illus.). 133p. 1971. 21.00 (ISBN 0-444-10114-4, North-Holland). Elsevier.

Quench Not the Spirit. rev. ed. Myron S. Augsburger. LC 62-7330. 1975. pap. 2.95 (ISBN 0-8361-1477-9). Herald Pr.

Quench the Moon. Walter Macken. 399p. 1974. pap. 8.50 (ISBN 0-330-23894-9). Bks Britain.

Queneau: Zazie dans le Metro. W. D. Redfern. (Critical Guides to French Texts Ser.). 94p. 1980. pap. 3.50 (ISBN 0-7293-0086-2, Pub. by Grant & Cutler). Longwood Pub Group.

Queneau's Fiction: An Introductory Study. Christopher Shorley. 256p. 1985. 44.50 (ISBN 0-521-30397-4). Cambridge U Pr.

Quenells. Laurence Meynell. 224p. 1985. 24.95x (ISBN 0-7090-2177-1, Pub. by R Hale Ltd UK). State Mutual Bk.

Quentin. Kerry Kenihan. (Nonfiction Ser.). 224p. 1985. pap. 4.95 (ISBN 0-14-007008-7). Penguin.

Quentin: A Spy. David Selves. 1986. 39.00x (ISBN 0-86332-058-9, Pub. by Book Guild Ltd). State Mutual Bk.

Quentin Blake's Nursery Rhyme Book. Quentin Blake. LC 83-48171. (Illus.). 32p. (gr. k-3). 1984. PLB 11.89g (ISBN 0-06-020532-6). HarpJ.

Quentin Corn. Mary Stolz. LC 84-48321. (Illus.). 128p. (gr. 1-7). 1985. pap. 12.95 (ISBN 0-87923-553-5). Godine.

Quentin Corn. Mary Stolz. 1988. pap. 2.75 (ISBN 0-440-40043-0, YB). Dell.

Quentin Durward. Walter Scott. (Airmont Classics Ser.). (gr. 9 up). pap. 2.50 (ISBN 0-8049-0132-5, CL-132). Airmont.

Querelle. Jean Genet. Tr. by Anselm Hollo from Fr. LC 74-24898. 1975. pap. 4.95 (ISBN 0-394-17838-6, B382, BC). Grove.

Querelle. Jean Genet. Tr. by Anselm Hollo. 1987. 7.95 (ISBN 0-394-62368-1). Grove.

Querelle de Brest see Oeuvres Completes.

Querelle de la Rose: Letters & Documents. J. L. Baird & John R. Kane. (Studies in the Romance Languages & Literatures: No. 199). 172p. 1978. pap. 12.50x (ISBN 0-8078-9199-1). U of NC Pr.

Querelle des Images Huitieme-Neuvieme Siecle. Louis Brehier. 1969. 14.00 (ISBN 0-8337-0362-5). B Franklin.

Querelle: The Film Book. Rainer Werner Fassbinder. LC 83-80816. (Illus.). 180p. 1983. pap. 16.95 (ISBN 0-394-62477-7, E861, Ever). Grove.

Querelles de Famille. Georges Duhamel. 224p. 1959. 9.95 (ISBN 0-686-55192-3). French & Eur.

Querencia. Daniel J. Langton. 64p. 1976. 7.00. Cheltenham Pr.

Querencia: Poems. Daniel J. Langton. LC 76-740443. (Devins Award Breakthrough Ser). 64p. 1976. 6.95 (ISBN 0-8262-0192-X). U of Mo Pr.

Queries & Theories: Game of Science & Language. Layman Allen et al. 15.00 (ISBN 0-911624-42-2). Wffn Proof.

Querist, Containing Several Queries Proposed to the Consideration of the Public. George Berkley. Repr. of 1737 ed. 16.00 (ISBN 0-384-04010-1). Johnson Repr.

Querschnitt. Ed. by Ian C. Loram & Leland R. Phelps. (Orig., Ger.). 1962. pap. 6.95x (ISBN 0-393-09575-4, NortonC). Norton.

Query Letters-Cover Letters: How They Sell Your Writing. Gordon Burgett. LC 85-51216. 204p. 1986. 12.95 (ISBN 0-9605078-8-4); pap. 9.95 (ISBN 0-9605078-7-6). Write to Sell.

Query Optimization by Semantic Reasoning. Jonathan J. King. Ed. by Harold Stone. LC 84-37. (Computer Science: Artificial Intelligence: No. 15). 136p. 1984. 37.95 (ISBN 0-8357-1541-8). UMI Res Pr.

Query Processing in Database Systems. Ed. by W. Kim et al. (Topics in Information Systems Ser.). (Illus.). 352p. 1985. 32.50 (ISBN 0-387-13831-5). Springer-Verlag.

Quesnay's Tableau Economique. 3rd ed. Francois Quesnay. Tr. by Marguerite Kuczynski & Ronald L. Meek. LC 78-157694. 160p. (Fr.). 1971. lib. bdg. 27.50x (ISBN 0-678-07007-5). Kelley.

Quest. Stephen Carman & Robert Owen. 160p. (Orig.). 1986. pap. 5.95 (ISBN 0-8423-5112-4). Tyndale.

Quest. Derek Gill. 1982. pap. 3.95 (ISBN 0-345-30094-7). Ballantine.

Quest. Thanos Mellos. (Illus.). 144p. 1984. 6.95 (ISBN 0-89962-352-2). Todd & Honeywell.

Quest. Richard B. Sapir. 384p. 1987. 18.95 (ISBN 0-525-24548-0). Dutton.

Quest. Richard B. Sapir. 1988. pap. 4.50 (ISBN 0-451-40076-3, Onyx). NAL.

Quest. Eleanor C. Slater. LC 75-144728. (Yale Series of Younger Poets: No. 21). Repr. of 1926 ed. 18.00 (ISBN 0-404-53821-5). AMS Pr.

Quest. J. Marvin Spiegelman. LC 84-80966. 192p. 1984. pap. 8.95 (ISBN 0-941404-30-7). Falcon Pr Az.

Quest: A Search for Self. 2nd ed. Sarah Cirese. 448p. 1985. text ed. 26.95 (ISBN 0-03-063191-2, HoltC). HR&W.

Quest: Academic Skills Program. Ruth Cohen et al. 293p. 1973. pap. text ed. 10.00 net (ISBN 0-15-574610-3, HC); instr's. manual avail. (ISBN 0-15-574611-1). HarBraceJ.

Quest: An Autobiography. Leopold Infeld. LC 79-55510. viii, 361p. 1980. 17.95 (ISBN 0-8284-0309-0). Chelsea Pub.

Quest & Occupation of Tahiti, by Emissaries of Spain During the Years 1772-1776, 3 vols. B. Glanville Corney. (Hakluyt Society Works Ser.: No. 2, Vols. 32, 36 & 43). (Illus.). Repr. of 1913 ed. Set. 200.00 (ISBN 0-8115-0348-8). Kraus Repr.

Quest & Response: Minority Rights & the Truman Administration. Donald R. McCoy & Richard T. Ruetten. LC 72-87820. xii, 428p. 1973. 35.00x (ISBN 0-7006-0099-X). U Pr of KS.

Quest & Vision. William J. Dawson. 286p. 1980. Repr. of 1892 ed. lib. bdg. 38.00 (ISBN 0-8495-1058-9). Arden Lib.

Quest & Vision: Essays in Life & Literature (Shelley, Meredith, Wordsworth, Longfellow, Eliot) W. J. Dawson. LC 76-15282. 1973. lib. bdg. 27.00 (ISBN 0-8414-3720-3). Folcroft.

Quest Anthology. Ed. by James Webb. LC 75-36916. (Occult Ser.). 1976. Repr. of 1976 ed. 46.50x (ISBN 0-405-07971-0). Ayer Co Pubs.

Qu'est-ce Que la Litterature? Jean-Paul Sartre. (Folio Essay Ser.: No. 19). pap. 8.95 (ISBN 0-685-36564-6). Schoenhof.

Qu'est-ce Que le Medecin? Etude Psychologique de la Relation Medecin-Malade. Peirre Guicheney. (Interaction-l'Homme et Son Environnement Sociales Ser.: No. 1). 225p. (Fr.). 1974. pap. text ed. 12.80x (ISBN 90-2797-324-5). Mouton.

Qu'est-ce Que le Tiers Etat? & Sieyes, 2 vols. in 1. Emmanuel Sieyes & Charles A. Sainte Beuve. Ed. by J. P. Mayer. LC 78-67389. (European Political Thought Ser.). (Fr.). 1979. Repr. of 1885 ed. lib. bdg. 12.00x (ISBN 0-405-11740-X). Ayer Co Pubs.

Quest Crosstime. Andre Norton. 256p. 1981. pap. 2.50 (ISBN 0-441-69685-6, Pub. by Ace Science Fiction). Ace Bks.

Quest for a Black Theology. Ed. by James J. Gardiner & J. Deotis Roberts. LC 76-151250. 128p. 1971. 6.95 (ISBN 0-8298-0196-0). Pilgrim NY.

Quest for a Classic Winner: Pedigree Patterns of the Racehorse. Ken McLean. (Illus.). 280p. 1987. 60.00 (ISBN 0-9619432-0-3). K A & C J McLean.

Quest for a Constitution: A Man Who Wouldn't Quit-A Political Biography of Samuel Witwer of Illinois. Elmer Gertz et al. LC 84-13226. 1984. 21.50 (ISBN 0-8191-4208-5); pap. text ed. 12.50 (ISBN 0-8191-4209-3). U Pr of Amer.

Quest for a Cure: The Public Hospital in Williamsburg, Virginia, 1773-1885. Shomer S. Zwelling. LC 84-28567. (Illus.). 72p. (Orig.). 1985. pap. 4.95 (ISBN 0-87935-110-1). Williamsburg.

Quest for a Golden Key. Geoffrey Thornber. 1982. 15.00x (ISBN 0-903653-33-8, Pub. by New Playwrights Network). State Mutual Bk.

Quest for a Just World Order. Samuel S. Kim. LC 83-10327. (Special Studies in International Relations). (Illus.). 440p. 1983. pap. 21.00 (ISBN 0-86531-433-0). Westview.

Quest for a Kelpie. Frances Hendry. LC 87-19666. 160p. (gr. 4-7). 1988. 12.95 (ISBN 0-8234-0680-6). Holiday.

Quest for a Philosophical Jesus: Christianity & Philosophy in Rousseau, Kant, Hegel, & Schelling. Vincent A. McCarthy. LC 86-2521. xv, 240p. 1986. 28.95 (ISBN 0-86554-210-4, MUP-H190). Mercer Univ Pr.

Quest for a Public: French Popular Theatre Since 1945. Vera Lee. 200p. 1976. text ed. 8.95 (ISBN 0-87073-180-7). Schenkman Bks Inc.

Quest for a Theology of Judaism: The Divine, the Human & the Ethical Dimensions in the Structure-of-Faith of Judaism. Manfred H. Vogel. (Studies in Judaism). 328p. (Orig.). 1987. lib. bdg. 28.50 (ISBN 0-8191-6593-X, Pub. by Studies in Judaism); pap. text ed. 15.75 (ISBN 0-8191-6594-8, Pub. by Studies in Judaism). U Pr of Amer.

Quest for a United Germany. Ferenc A. Vali. LC 67-16914. pap. 82.80 (ISBN 0-317-42363-0, 2025879). Bks Demand UMI.

Quest for Absolute Zero. K. Mendelssohn. 280p. 1977. pap. 27.00x (ISBN 0-85066-119-6). Taylor & Francis.

Quest for Adventure. Chris Bonington. (Illus.). 448p. 1982. 30.00 (ISBN 0-517-54696-5). Crown.

Quest for an African Eldorado: Sofala, Southern Zambezia & the Portuguese, 1500-1865. T. H. Elkiss. 120p. 1981. 12.00 (ISBN 0-918456-41-X). African Studies Assn.

Quest for an American Sociology: Robert E. Park & the Chicago School. Fred Matthews. 1977. lib. bdg. 29.95x (ISBN 0-7735-0243-2). McGill-Queens U Pr.

Quest for an Image of Brain: Computerized Tomography in the Perpective of Past & Future Imaging Methods. William H. Oldendorf. 167p. 1980. text ed. 38.50 (ISBN 0-89004-429-5). Raven.

Quest for an International Order in the Indian Ocean. K. P. Misra. 159p. 1977. 14.95. Asia Bk Corp.

Quest for An Island. Vassily Aksyonov. 250p. 1987. 17.95 (ISBN 1-55554-020-1). PAJ Pubns.

Quest for Arthur's Britain. Geoffrey Ashe. (Illus.). 320p. 1980. pap. 8.95 (ISBN 0-89733-287-3). Academy Chi Pubs.

Quest for Arthur's Britain. Ed. by Geoffrey Ashe. 1987. pap. 8.95. Academy Chi Pubs.

Quest for Artificial Intelligence. Dorothy Hinshaw Patent. LC 85-27042. (Illus.). 224p. (gr. 7-8). 1986. 13.95 (ISBN 0-15-264550-0, HJ). Harbracej.

Quest for Better Preaching: Resources for Renewal in the Pulpit. Edward F. Markquart. LC 85-13500. 240p. (Orig.). 1985. pap. 12.95 (ISBN 0-8066-2170-2, 10-5349). Augsburg.

Quest for Bowie's Blade. J. T. Edson. 1987. pap. 2.50 (ISBN 0-425-09113-9). Berkley Pub.

Quest for Bruton Vault. Marie B. Hall. Date not set. pap. 21.50 (ISBN 0-938760-08-4). Veritat Found.

Quest for Cathay. Percy Sykes. 280p. 1936. 210.00x (ISBN 0-317-68569-4, Pub. by Han-Shan Tang Ltd). State Mutual Bk.

Quest for Certainty: Vol. 4: 1929. abr. ed. John Dewey. Ed. by Jo Ann Boydston. LC 80-2789. (Later Works of John Dewey, 1925-1953 Ser.). 288p. 1988. pap. text ed. 9.95x (ISBN 0-8093-1493-2). S Ill U Pr.

Quest for Certitude in E. M. Forster's Fiction. David Shusterman. LC 72-6784. (Studies in Fiction, No. 34). 1972. Repr. of 1965 ed. lib. bdg. 49.95x (ISBN 0-8383-1662-X). Haskell.

Quest for Character. Charles R. Swindoll. Ed. by Larry R. Libby. 1987. 13.95. Multnomah.

Quest for Christa T. Christa Wolf. Tr. by Christopher Middleton from Ger. 185p. 1970. pap. 8.95 (ISBN 0-374-51534-4). FS&G.

Quest for Church Unity: From John Calvin to Isaac d'Huisseau. Richard Stauffer. (Pittsburgh Theological Monographs: No. 19). (Orig.). 1986. pap. 15.00 (ISBN 0-915138-63-8). Pickwick.

Quest for Clues. Ed. & illus. by Shay Addams. 192p. (Orig.). 1988. pap. 24.99 (ISBN 0-929373-00-6). Origin Syst.

Quest for Common Learning: The Aims of General Education. Ernest L. Boyer & Arthur Levine. LC 81-66307. 68p. 1981. pap. 6.95 (ISBN 0-931050-18-9). Carnegie Found.

Quest for Community. O. H. Mowrer. LC 65-167. (Augustana College Library Occasional Papers: No. 8). 15p. 1962. pap. 0.50 (ISBN 0-910182-38-8). Augustana Coll.

Quest for Community: Tomorrow's Parish Today. Dennis J. Geaney. LC 87-71612. 144p. (Orig.). 1987. pap. 3.95 (ISBN 0-87793-368-5). Ave Maria.

Quest for Control: A Critique of the Rational-Central-Rule Approach in Public Affairs. Herman R. Van Gunsteren. LC 75-19228. 194p. pap. 42.50 (ISBN 0-317-09430-0, 2020431). Bks Demand UMI.

Quest for Courage. Stormy Rodolph. (Indian Culture Ser.). (Illus.). 102p. (Orig.). (gr. 5-12). 1984. lib. bdg. 12.95 (ISBN 0-89992-392-5); pap. 6.95 (ISBN 0-89992-092-6). Coun India Ed.

Quest for Discipleship. Claude Buchanan. 1987. pap. 4.95 (ISBN 0-940543-03-6). Magnificat Pr.

Quest for Eastern Christians: Travels & Rumor in the Age of Discovery. Francis M. Rogers. LC 62-18138. pap. 58.30 (ISBN 0-317-41750-9, 2055901). Bks Demand UMI.

Quest for Economic Stability: Roosevelt to Reagan. Hugh S. Norton. 352p. 1985. 22.95 (ISBN 0-87249-456-X). U of SC Pr.

Quest for Economic Stabilization. Tony Killick. 1984. text ed. 23.50x (ISBN 0-566-05040-4, Pub. by Gower Pub England). Gower Pub Co.

Quest for Eden. Elena M. Marsella. LC 66-16172. 275p. 1966. 8.95 (ISBN 0-8022-1063-5). Philos Lib.

Quest for Empire: The Saga for Russian America. Kyra P. Wayne. 415p. 1986. 27.95 (ISBN 0-88839-193-5); pap. 14.95 (ISBN 0-88839-191-9). Hancock House.

Quest for Equality in Freedom. Francis M. Wilhoit. LC 78-55940. 350p. 1979. 28.95 (ISBN 0-87855-240-5). Transaction Bks.

Quest for Equality: The Constitution, Congress & the Supreme Court. Robert J. Harris. LC 77-1851. 172p. 1977. Repr. of 1960 ed. lib. bdg. 41.50x (ISBN 0-8371-9524-1, HAQE). Greenwood.

Quest for Equilibrium: America & the Balance of Power on Land & Sea. George Liska. LC 77-4780. 280p. 1977. text ed. 32.50x (ISBN 0-8018-1968-7). Johns Hopkins.

Quest for Equivalence: On Translating Villon. Margaret J. Draskau. 370p. (Orig.). 1987. pap. 47.50x. Coronet Bks.

Quest for Eros: Browning & Fifine. Samuel B. Southwell. LC 79-4945. 288p. 1980. 25.00 (ISBN 0-8131-1399-7). U Pr of Ky.

Quest for Eternity. Susan Caroselli. (Illus.). 161p. 1987. pap. 112.00x (ISBN 0-317-69164-3, Pub. by Han-Shan Tang Ltd). State Mutual Bk.

Quest for Eternity: An Outline of the Philosophy of Religion. J. C. Gaskin. (Pelican Ser.). 192p. 1984. pap. 5.95 (ISBN 0-14-022538-2). Penguin.

Quest for Eternity: Chinese Ceramic Sculptures from the People's Republic of China. George Kuwayama. LC 86-27528. (Illus.). 162p. 1987. pap. 19.95 (ISBN 0-87701-428-0). Chronicle Bks.

Quest for Eternity: Manners & Morals in the Age of Chivalry. Charles T. Wood. LC 82-40476. (Illus.). 172p. 1983. pap. 9.00x (ISBN 0-87451-259-X). U Pr of New Eng.

Quest for Ethics. James R. Simmons. LC 62-15036. 1962. 5.95 (ISBN 0-8022-1573-4). Philos Lib.

Quest for Evil. Katrina Smith. LC 85-90151. 72p. 1988. 8.95 (ISBN 0-533-06651-4). Vantage.

Quest for Excellence, Final Report: Appendix. (Illus.). 384p. (Orig.). 1986. pap. 19.00 (ISBN 0-318-21306-0, S/N 040-000-00499-8). USGPO.

Quest for Excellence in Medical Education: A Personal Survey of Medical Education. George Pickering. 1978. 14.95x (ISBN 0-19-721399-5). Oxford U Pr.

Quest for Excellence: The Story of the Olympic Games. Knowledge Unlimited Staff. (Illus.). 20p. (gr. 4-12). 1983. tchr's. guide & color filmstrips 13.00 (ISBN 0-915291-03-7, 5029). Know Unltd.

Quest for Excitement: Sport & Leisure in the Civilizing Process. Norbert Elias & Eric Dunning. 288p. 1986. 24.95 (ISBN 0-631-14654-7). Basil Blackwell.

Quest for Extraterrestrial Life: A Book of Readings. Donald Goldsmith. LC 79-57423. (Illus.). 308p. 1980. 24.00x (ISBN 0-935702-08-3); pap. text ed. 19.00x (ISBN 0-935702-02-4). Univ Sci Bks.

Quest for Failure: A Study of William Faulkner. Walter J. Slatoff. LC 72-4084. 275p. 1973. Repr. of 1960 ed. lib. bdg. 35.00x (ISBN 0-8371-6432-X, SLQF). Greenwood.

Quest for Faith. C. Stephens Evans. LC 86-7436. 144p. (Orig.). 1986. pap. 5.95 (ISBN 0-87784-511-5). Inter-Varsity.

Quest for Faith, Quest for Freedom: Aspects of Pennsylvania's Religious Experience. Ed. by Otto Reimherr. LC 86-61790. (Illus.). 208p. 1987. 28.50x (ISBN 0-941664-26-0). Susquehanna U Pr.

Quest for Federal Manpower Partnership. Sar A. Levitan & Joyce K. Zickler. LC 74-16541. 144p. 1974. text ed. 11.00x (ISBN 0-674-74125-0). Harvard U Pr.

Quest for Fire. J. H. Rosny. 128p. 1982. pap. 2.50 (ISBN 0-345-30067-X). Ballantine.

Quest For Freedom. Velma B. Clark. LC 86-91155. 1986. 15.00 (ISBN 0-682-40298-2). Exposition-Phoenix.

Quest for God: A Journey into Prayer & Symbolism. Abraham J. Heschel. (Crossroad Paperback Ser.). 176p. 1982. pap. 7.95 (ISBN 0-8245-0436-4). Crossroad NY.

Quest for Gold: The Encyclopedia of American Olympians. Bill Mallon & Ian Buchanan. (PMAL0217). (Illus.). 496p. 1984. text ed. 29.95 cancelled (ISBN 0-88011-243-3); pap. 21.95 (ISBN 0-88011-217-4). Leisure Pr.

Quest for Harmony: The Dialectics of Communication in the Poetry of Eugenio Florit. Mirella D. Servodidio. LC 78-66111. 1979. pap. 12.00 (ISBN 0-89295-008-0). Society Sp & Sp-Am.

Quest for Holiness & Unity. John W. Smith. 1980. 16.95 (ISBN 0-87162-231-9, D6250). Warner Pr.

Quest for Identity. Allen Wheelis. 1966. pap. 7.95 (ISBN 0-393-00745-6). Norton.

Quest of Enlightenment: A Selection of the Buddhist Scriptures. Tr. by E. J. Thomas from Sanskrit. LC 78-70130. Repr. of 1950 ed. 17.50 (ISBN 0-404-17389-6). AMS Pr.

Quest of Excalibur. Leonard Wibberley. LC 79-192. (Illus.). 190p. 1979. lib. bdg. 17.95x (ISBN 0-89370-131-9); pap. 7.95x (ISBN 0-89370-231-5). Borgo Pr.

Quest of Inquirie: Some Contexts of Tudor Literature. Howard C. Cole. LC 73-91621. 1973. 39.50 (ISBN 0-672-53583-1). Irvington.

Quest of Justice. Harold Potter. (Legal Reprint Ser.). ix, 88p. 1986. Repr. of 1951 ed. lib. bdg. 17.50x (ISBN 0-421-35510-7). Rothman.

Quest of Prince Ferdinand. Jessie Hale. 1985. 4.95 (ISBN 0-533-06182-2). Vantage.

Quest of Self in the Collected Poems of Wallace Stevens. Michael Sexson. LC 81-16942. (Studies in Art & Religious Interpretation: Vol. 1). 216p. 1982. lib. bdg. 49.95x (ISBN 0-88946-957-1). E Mellen.

Quest of the Ballad. W. Roy MacKenzie. LC 68-815. (Studies in Poetry, No. 38). 1969. Repr. of 1919 ed. lib. bdg. 75.00x (ISBN 0-8383-0591-1). Haskell.

Quest of the Colonial. Robert Shackleton & Elizabeth Shackleton. LC 72-99075. (Illus.). 440p. 1970. Repr. of 1907 ed. 43.00x (ISBN 0-8103-3574-3). Gale.

Quest of the Dawnstar. Gordon McBain. 144p. (Orig.). (gr. 7 up). 1984. pap. 2.25 (ISBN 0-380-86520-3, 86520, Flare). Avon.

Quest of the Faes. Catharine Geenen. (Illus.). 144p. 1985. pap. 7.95 (ISBN 0-9606240-6-6). Pearl-Win.

Quest of the Fish-Dog Skin. James W. Schultz. LC 83-73495. (James Willard Schultz Reprint Ser.). (Illus.). 144p. (gr. 3 up). 1986. 15.95 (ISBN 0-8253-0326-5); pap. 7.95 (ISBN 0-8253-0321-4). Beaufort Bks NY.

Quest of the Fish-Dog Skin. James W. Schultz. (J. W. Schultz Reprint Ser.). 15.95 (ISBN 0-317-65106-4); pap. 7.95 (ISBN 0-317-65107-2). Confluence Pr.

Quest of the Four: A Story of the Comanches & Buena Vista. Joseph A. Altsheler. 386p. Repr. of 1911 ed. lib. bdg. 18.95x (ISBN 0-88411-939-4, Pub. by Aeonian Pr). Amereon Ltd.

Quest of the Golden Boy: The Life & Letters of Richard Le Gallienne. Richard Whittington-Egan & Geoffrey Smerdon. LC 79-8087. Repr. of 1962 ed. 49.50 (ISBN 0-404-18395-6). AMS Pr.

Quest of the Golden Stairs: A Mystery of Kinghood in Faerie. Arthur E. Waite. LC 80-19659. 176p. 1980. Repr. of 1974 ed. lib. bdg. 22.95x (ISBN 0-89370-628-0). Borgo Pr.

Quest of the Holy Grail. Tr. by P. M. Matarasso. (Classics Ser.). 304p. 1969. pap. 4.95 (ISBN 0-14-044220-0). Penguin.

Quest of the Holy Grail. Jessie L. Weston. 59.95 (ISBN 0-87968-094-6). Gordon Pr.

Quest of the Holy Grail. Jessie L. Weston. LC 72-10823. (Arthurian Legend & Literature Ser., No. 1). 1973. Repr. of 1913 ed. lib. bdg. 75.00x (ISBN 0-8383-0642-X). Haskell.

Quest of the Missing Map. Carolyn Keene. LC 70-86692. (Nancy Drew Ser.: Vol. 19). (Illus.). (gr. 4-7). 1942. 4.50 (ISBN 0-448-09519-X, G&D); PLB 3.29 (ISBN 0-448-19519-4). Putnam Pub Group.

Quest of the One Best Way. Lillian M. Gilbreth. LC 73-1170. (Management History Ser.: No. 21). (Illus.). 65p. 1973. Repr. of 1928 ed. 15.00 (ISBN 0-87960-032-2). Hive Pub.

Quest of the Overself. rev. 1984 ed. Paul Brunton. LC 83-159508. 240p. (Orig.). 1970. pap. 7.95 (ISBN 0-87728-594-2). Weiser.

Quest of the Riddlemaster, 4 vols. Patricia McKillip. (YA) (gr. 7-12). 1982. Boxed Set. pap. 6.75 (ISBN 0-345-29089-5, Del Rey). Ballantine.

Quest of the Silver Fleece. W. E. B. Dubois. LC 73-144599. Repr. of 1911 ed. 12.50 (ISBN 0-404-00154-8). AMS Pr.

Quest of the Silver Fleece. W. E. B. Dubois. LC 73-86658. (American Negro: His History & Literature, Series No. 3). 1970. Repr. of 1911 ed. 21.00 (ISBN 0-405-01922-X). Ayer Co Pubs.

Quest of the Silver Fleece. facs. ed. W. E. B. Dubois. LC 71-83922. (Black Heritage Library Collection Ser). (Illus.). 1911. 21.00 (ISBN 0-8369-8553-2). Ayer Co Pubs.

Quest of the Silver Fleece. W. E. B. Dubois. LC 74-7364. 451p. 1975. Repr. of 1911 ed. lib. bdg. 26.00 (ISBN 0-527-25325-1). Kraus Intl.

Quest of the Silver Fleece: A Novel. W. E. B. Dubois. LC 70-92742. 1970. Repr. of 1911 ed. 35.00x (ISBN 0-8371-2066-7, DSF&). Greenwood.

Quest of the Three Worlds. Cordwainer Smith. 224p. 1986. pap. 2.95 (ISBN 0-345-32931-7, Del Rey Bks). Ballantine.

Quest One: Active Living, a Guide to Fitness, Conditioning & Health. 3rd ed. James J. Burd & Leonard T. Serfustini. 272p. 1982. pap. 14.95 (ISBN 0-8403-2520-7). Kendall Hunt.

Quest: Research & Inquiry in Arts Education. Richard Courtney. LC 86-24693. 148p. 1987. lib. bdg. 23.50 (ISBN 0-8191-5744-9); pap. text ed. 9.75 (ISBN 0-8191-5745-7). U Pr of Amer.

Quest: The Search for the Grail of Immortality. Rhuddlwm Gawr. LC 78-61716. (Illus., Orig.). (YA) 1985. 14.95 (ISBN 0-931760-02-X, CP10101); pap. text ed. 12.95 (ISBN 0-931760-01-1). Camelot GA.

Quest: The Search for the Grail of Immortality. Rhuddlwm Gawr. LC 78-61716. (Illus.). 186p. 1987. 15.95 (ISBN 0-318-23765-2); pap. 12.95 (ISBN 0-318-23766-0). Camelot GA.

Quest There Is. Elizabeth G. Vining. 1982. pap. 2.50x (ISBN 0-87574-246-7, 246). Pendle Hill.

Questers: Dare to Change Your Job, & Your Life. Carole J. Kanchier. LC 87-60351. 220p. (Orig.). 1987. pap. 9.95 (ISBN 0-88247-767-6). R & E Pubs.

Quester's Endgame: A Novel of the Diadem. Jo Clayton. 384p. 1986. pap. 3.50 (ISBN 0-88677-138-2). DAW Bks.

Questing Fictions: Latin America's Family Romance. Djelal Kadir. LC 86-16019. (Theory & History of Literature Ser.: Vol. 32). 186p. 1986. 29.50x (ISBN 0-8166-1516-0); pap. 12.95 (ISBN 0-8166-1517-9). U of Minn Pr.

Questing Heart. Nelma Haynes. (Orig.). 1980. pap. 1.75 (ISBN 0-8439-8011-7, Tiara Bks). Leisure NY.

Questing Heart. Deborah Joyce. (Super Romances Ser.). 384p. 1983. pap. 2.95 (ISBN 0-373-70061-X, Pub. by Worldwide). Harlequin Bks.

Questing of Kedrigern. John Morressy. 208p. 1987. pap. 2.95 (ISBN 0-441-69721-6, Pub. by Ace Science Fiction). Ace Bks.

Question & Answer Book of Nature. (Illus.). (gr. k-4). 1962. Random.

Question & Answer Catholic Catechism. John A. Hardon. LC 80-2961. 408p. 1981. (Im); pap. 10.95 (ISBN 0-385-13664-1). Doubleday.

Question & Answer: Graded Oral Comprehension. new ed. L. G. Alexander. (English As a Second Language Bk.). 1977. pap. text ed. 4.95 (ISBN 0-582-55206-0). Longman.

Question & Answer Guide to Successful Franchising. rev. ed. LC 79-103723. 31p. 1988. pap. 3.50 (ISBN 0-87576-005-8). Pilot Bks.

Question & Answers for FHA, VA & Conventional Loans. rev., 2nd ed. Albert Santi. LC 85-63137. (Illus.). 260p. (Orig.). 1986. 15.95 (ISBN 0-9615886-2-4); pap. 8.95 (ISBN 0-9615886-1-6). Mortgage Tech.

Question Arabe et le Congo, 1883-1892. P. Ceulemans. (Academie Royale des Sciences d'Outre-Mer, Memoires Ser: Vol. 22, No. 1, N.S.). (Fr). 1969. Repr. of 1959 ed. 33.00 (ISBN 0-384-28459-0). Johnson Repr.

Question As a Measure of Efficiency in Instruction. Romiett Stevens. LC 70-177825. (Columbia University. Teachers College. Contributions to Education: No. 48). Repr. of 1912 ed. 22.50 (ISBN 0-404-55048-7). AMS Pr.

Question Concerning Technology & Other Essays. Martin Heidegger. Tr. by William Lovitt from Ger. LC 77-87181. 1978. lib. bdg. 24.00x (ISBN 0-8240-2427-3). Garland Pub.

Question Concerning Technology & Other Essays. Martin Heidegger. Tr. by William Lovitt. (Orig.). 1977. pap. 8.95x (ISBN 0-06-131969-4, TB 1969, Torch). Har-Row.

Question Framing & Response Consistency. Ed. by Robin M. Hogarth. LC 81-48486. (Methodology of Social & Behavioral Science Ser.: No. 11). 1982. 16.95x (ISBN 0-87589-911-0). Jossey-Bass.

Question in Baptist History: Whether the Anabaptists in England Practiced Immersion Before the Year 1641? William H. Whitsitt. Ed. by Edwin S. Gaustad. LC 79-52611. (Baptist Tradition Ser.). 1980. Repr. of 1896 ed. lib. bdg. 14.00x (ISBN 0-405-12476-7). Ayer Co Pubs.

Question in Search of an Answer: Understanding Learning Disability in Jewish Education. Roberta M. Greene & Elaine Heavenrich. LC 8-18059. (Illus.). 262p. 1981. pap. 5.00 (ISBN 0-8074-0029-7). UAHC.

Question Is the Answer. Siegmund Frost. cancelled (ISBN 0-87306-075-X). Feldheim.

Question of a Reference to International Law in the United Nations Code of Conduct of Transnational Corporations. (Working Paper Ser.: No. 1). 4.00 (ISBN 92-1-104178-3, E.86.II.A.5). UN.

Question of a Reference to International Law in the United Nations Code of Conduct on Transnational Corporations. (UNCTC Current Studies: Vol. A, No I). 22p. 1986. pap. 4.00 (ISBN 92-1-104178-3, E.86.II.A.5). UN.

Question of a Reference to International Obligations in the United Nations Code of Conduct on Transnational Corporations: A Different View. (UNCTC Current Studies: Vol. A, No. 2). 17p. 1986. pap. 4.00 (ISBN 92-1-104186-4, E.86.II.A.11). UN.

Question of Aborigines in the Law & Practice of Nations. Alpheus H. Snow. LC 79-99409. 218p. 1972. Repr. of 1919 ed. lib. bdg. 14.50 (ISBN 0-8411-0082-9). Metro Bks.

Question of Age: The Dorm & I. Kathryn Martin. LC 80-27057. 245p. (Orig.). 1981. 14.95 (ISBN 0-936988-01-0, Dist. by Shoe String Press). Tompson Rutter Inc.

Question of AIDS. Ed. by Richard Liebmann-Smith. 89p. 1985. pap. text ed. 6.00x (ISBN 0-89766-302-0). NY Acad Sci.

Question of Animal Awareness: Evolutionary Continuity of Mental Experience. rev. ed. Donald R. Griffin. LC 81-51221. 224p. 1981. 13.95x (ISBN 0-87470-035-3). Rockefeller.

Question of Animal Awareness: Evolutionary Continuity of Mental Experience. 2nd ed. Donald R. Griffin. LC 81-51221. (Illus.). 221p. pap. 9.95 (ISBN 0-86576-002-0). W Kaufmann.

Question of Arbitrability: Challenges to the Arbitrator's Jurisdiction & Authority. Mark M. Grossman. LC 84-6568. (Practitioner Guides Ser.). 128p. (Orig.). 1984. pap. 9.95 (ISBN 0-87546-106-9). ILR Pr.

Question of Artificial Intelligence: Philosophical & Sociological Perspectives. Ed. by Brian P. Bloomfield. 256p. 1988. lib. bdg. 49.95x (ISBN 0-7099-3957-4, Pub. by Croom Helm UK). Routledge Chapman & Hall.

Question of Being. Martin Heidegger. 1958. pap. 5.95x (ISBN 0-8084-0258-7). New Coll U Pr.

Question of Being: East-West Perspectives. Ed. by Mervyn Sprung. 1978. text ed. 19.50x (ISBN 0-271-01242-0). Pa St U Pr.

Question of Being in Husserl's Logical Investigations. James R. Mensch. 1981. 39.00 (ISBN 90-247-2413-9, Pub. by Martinus Nijhoff Netherlands). Kluwer Academic.

Question of Choice: An Australian Aboriginal Dilemma. Ed. by Ronald M. Berndt. LC 72-188167. 123p. 1971. pap. 11.95 (ISBN 0-85564-054-5, Pub. by U of W Austral Pr). Intl Spec Bk.

Question of Class. Marion Devon. 1988. pap. 2.50 (ISBN 0-449-21340-4, Crest). Fawcett.

Question of Class: Capital, the State & Uneven Development in Malaya. Jomo K. Sundara. (East Asian Social Science Monographs). (Illus.). 1986. 56.00x (ISBN 0-19-582552-7). Oxford U Pr.

Question of Class: Capital, the State, & Uneven Development in Malaya. Jomo K. Sundaram. 400p. (Orig.). 1988. pap. 12.00 (ISBN 0-85345-750-6). Monthly Rev.

Question of Class Struggle: The Social Foundation of Popular Radicalism During the Industrial Revolution. Craig Calhoun. LC 81-2018. xiv, 322p. 1982. pap. 11.00x (ISBN 0-226-09091-4). U of Chicago Pr.

Question of Destiny. Pamela Service. LC 85-21466. 160p. (gr. 6-9). 1986. 12.95 (ISBN 0-689-31181-8, Atheneum Childrens Bks). Macmillan.

Question of Destiny. Pamela F. Service. 168p. (gr. 7 up). 1988. pap. 2.95 (ISBN 0-02-044981-X, Collier). Macmillan.

Question of Eclecticism: Studies in Later Greek Philosophy. Ed. by J. M. Dillon & A. A. Long. (Culture & Society Ser.: Vol. 3). 1988. 32.50x (ISBN 0-520-06008-3). U of Cal Pr.

Question of Economics: The Impact of Phased Increases in Canadian Oil & Gas Prices. Irving Leveson et al. 96p. 1981. 50.00 (ISBN 0-318-14353-4, HI3291RR); Summary. 25.00 (ISBN 0-318-14354-2). Hudson Inst.

Question of Elites: An Essay on the Cultural Elitism of Nietzche, George & Hesse. Stanley J. Antosik. (New York University Ottendorfer Series, Neue Folge: Vol. 11). 204p. 1978. 22.75 (ISBN 3-261-03102-6). P Lang Pubs.

Question of Empire: Leopold I & the War of Spanish Succession, 1701-1705. Linda Frey & Marsha Frey. LC 83-80628. (Studies on Society in Change: No. 28). 1983. write for info (ISBN 0-88033-038-4). Brooklyn Coll Pr.

Question of Eros: Irony in Sterne, Kierkegaard, & Barthes. John V. Smyth. LC 85-17786. (Kierkegaard & Postmodernism Ser.). 512p. (Orig.). 1986. pap. 29.95x (ISBN 0-8130-0834-4). U Presses Fla.

Question of Ethics. Ed. by Marilyn C. Rivkin. 58p. 1985. pap. text ed. 10.00 (ISBN 0-936164-36-0, 422). Group Health Assoc of Amer.

Question of Expatriation in America Prior to 1907. I-Mien Tsiang. LC 78-64187. (Johns Hopkins University. Studies in the Social Sciences. Sixtieth Ser. 1942: 3). Repr. of 1942 ed. 16.50 (ISBN 0-404-61294-6). AMS Pr.

Question of Freedom. Basil Sacavanos. 1986. 34.00x (ISBN 0-86332-061-9, Pub. by Book Guild Ltd). State Mutual Bk.

Question of Geography. John Berger & Nella Bielski. (Orig.). Date not set. pap. 6.95 (ISBN 0-86316-125-1). Writers & Readers.

Question of Greek Independence: A Study of British Policy in the Near East, 1821-1833. C. W. Crawley. LC 74-144130. 272p. 1973. Repr. of 1930 ed. 27.50x (ISBN 0-86527-161-5). Fertig.

Question of Hamlet. Harry Levin. LC 59-5784. 1970. pap. 5.95 (ISBN 0-19-500808-1). Oxford U Pr.

Question of Happiness. Janine Boissard. 224p. 1985. pap. 2.50 (ISBN 0-449-70133-6, Juniper). Fawcett.

Question of Height Revisited: Assaults on Police. Cheryl Swanson & Charles D. Hale. (Criminal Justice Policy & Administration Research Ser: No. 7). 12p. 1974. pap. 1.00 (ISBN 0-686-20791-2). Univ OK Gov Res.

Question of Honor. Jacqueline Ashley. (American Romance Ser.: No. 208). 245p. Date not set. pap. 2.50 (ISBN 0-317-63696-0). Harlequin Bks.

Question of Honor. Ana Leigh. (Kirkland Chronicles Ser.: Vol. II). 432p. (Orig.). 1986. pap. 3.95 (ISBN 0-8439-2377-6, Leisure Bks). Leisure NY.

Question of Hu. Jonathan D. Spence. LC 88-45271. 192p. 1988. 18.95 (ISBN 0-394-57190-8). Knopf.

Question of Identitiy. Michael Braude. 12.95x (ISBN 0-317-07057-6). Lieber-Atherton.

Question of Identity. Michael Braude. LC 76-4203. 1976. 6.95 (ISBN 0-88311-900-5). Horizon.

Question of Imperialism: The Political Economy of Dominance & Dependence. Benjamin J. Cohen. LC 73-81036. (Illus.). 245p. 1973. text ed. 17.95x (ISBN 0-465-06780-8). Basic.

Question of Law. Montague Jon. LC 81-21444. 196p. 1982. 9.95 (ISBN 0-312-66031-6). St Martin.

Question of Lay Analysis. Sigmund Freud. Ed. & tr. by James Strachey. (Standard ed.). 1969. pap. 3.95 (ISBN 0-393-00503-8). Norton.

Question of Life: The Warnock Report on Human Fertilization a Embryology. Mary Warnock. 128p. 1985. pap. 12.95x (ISBN 0-631-14257-6). Basil Blackwell.

Question of Loyalty. Paul M. Sniderman. LC 80-22932. 224p. 1981. 30.00x (ISBN 0-520-04196-8); pap. 9.95 (ISBN 0-520-04413-4). U of Cal Pr.

Question of Madness. Zhores A. Medvedev & Roy A. Medvedev. Tr. by Ellen De Kadt from Rus. 1979. pap. 5.95 (ISBN 0-393-00921-1). Norton.

Question of Mary Rose see Pregunta de Maria Rosa.

Question of Max. Amanda Cross. pap. 3.50 (ISBN 0-345-35489-3). Ballantine.

Question of Murder. Eric Wright. 208p. 1988. 15.95 (ISBN 0-684-19000-1). Scribner.

Question of Offshore Oil. Ed. by Edward J. Mitchell. LC 76-16665. pap. 42.80 (ISBN 0-317-29838-0, 2017492). Bks Demand UMI.

Question of Our Speech: Lesson on Balzac. Henry James. LC 74-28338. 1905. lib. bdg. 27.00 (ISBN 0-8414-5335-7). Folcroft.

Question of Palestine. Edward Said. 1980. write for info. (ISBN 0-8129-0832-5). Times Bks.

Question of Palestine. Edward W. Said. LC 80-12146. 288p. 1980. pap. 6.95 (ISBN 0-394-74527-2, Vin). Random.

Question of Place. 2nd ed. Eric Fischer et al. 1969. 39.50 (ISBN 0-87948-004-1). Beatty.

Question of Play. Drew A. Hyland. LC 84-8460. 190p. (Orig.). 1984. lib. bdg. 25.50 (ISBN 0-8191-4005-8); pap. text ed. 12.25 (ISBN 0-8191-4006-6). U Pr of Amer.

Question of Polish: The Antique Market in Australia. Terry Ingram. (Illus.). 192p. 24.95 (ISBN 0-00-216412-4, Pub. by W Collins Australia). Intl Spec Bk.

Question of Pornography: Research Findings & Policy Implications. Edward Donnerstein et al. 288p. 1987. 22.95 (ISBN 0-02-907521-1). Free Pr.

Question of Power. Bessie Head. (African Writers Ser.). 1974. pap. text ed. 7.00 (ISBN 0-435-90720-4). Heinemann Ed.

Question of Principle. Jeffrey Ashford. 192p. 1987. 13.95 (ISBN 0-312-01078-8). St Martin.

Question of Quality. Filler. 1976. 13.95 (ISBN 0-87972-077-8); pap. 7.95 (ISBN 0-87972-078-6). Bowling Green Univ.

Question of Sedition: The Federal Government's Investigation of the Black Press During World War II. Patrick S. Washburn. LC 85-21683. 272p. 1986. 24.95 (ISBN 0-19-503984-X). Oxford U Pr.

Question of Separatism: Quebec & the Struggle over Sovereignty. Jane Jacobs. LC 80-5268. (Illus.). 160p. 1980. 8.95 (ISBN 0-394-50981-1). Random.

Question of Separatism: Quebec & the Struggle over Sovereignty. Jane Jacobs. LC 81-40076. 144p. 1981. pap. 3.95 (ISBN 0-394-74748-8, Vin). Random.

Question of Speech-The Lesson of Balzac: Two Lectures. Henry James. LC 72-334. (Studies of Henry James, No. 17). 1972. Repr. of 1905 ed. lib. bdg. 39.95x (ISBN 0-8383-1411-2). Haskell.

Question of Survival. Julian F. Thompson. 320p. (gr. 8 up). 1984. pap. 2.95 (ISBN 0-380-87775-9, 87775-9, Flare). Avon.

Question of Survival: Quakers in Australia in the Nineteenth Century. William N. Oats. LC 84-2351. (Illus.). 409p. 1985. text ed. 35.00x (ISBN 0-7022-1708-5). U of Queensland Pr.

Question of Syllables: Essays in Nineteenth Century French Verse. Clive Scott. (Cambridge Studies in French). 288p. 1986. 44.50 (ISBN 0-521-32584-6). Cambridge U Pr.

Question of Textuality: Strategies of Reading in Contemporary American Criticism. Ed. by William V. Spanos et al. LC 81-47566. 384p. 1982. 20.00x (ISBN 0-253-34750-5). Ind U Pr.

Question of the Atom: From the Karlsruhe Congress to the First Solvay Conference, 1860-1911. Ed. by Mary J. Nye. (History of Modern Physics 1800-1950 Ser.: Vol. 4). (Illus.). 1984. 48.00x (ISBN 0-938228-07-2). Tomash Pubs.

Question of the Commons: The Culture & Ecology of Communal Resources. Ed. by Bonnie J. McCay & James M. Acheson. LC 87-19833. (Arizona Studies in Human Ecology). 439p. 1987. 35.00x (ISBN 0-8165-0972-7). U of Ariz Pr.

Question of Time. Dina Anastasio. (Illus.). 96p. (gr. 4-6). 1983. pap. 1.95 (ISBN 0-590-62028-2, Apple Paperbacks). Scholastic Inc.

Question of Trust: The Memoirs of Loy Henderson. George W. Baer. 579p. 1987. text ed. 44.95x (ISBN 0-8179-8331-7). Hoover Inst Pr.

Question of Upbringing. Anthony Powell. 224p. 1985. pap. 3.95 (ISBN 0-445-20010-3, Pub. by Popular Lib). Warner Bks.

Question of Values. Paul L. Errington. 196p. 1987. 18.95 (ISBN 0-8138-1444-8). Iowa St U Pr.

Questions of Special Urgency: The Church in the Modern World Two Decades after Vatican II. Ed. by Judith A. Dwyer. 256p. (Orig.). 1986. 17.95 (ISBN 0-87840-434-1); pap. 9.95 (ISBN 0-87840-425-2). Georgetown U Pr.

Questions of the Day. facs. ed. John A. Ryan. LC 67-26779. (Essay Index Reprint Ser). 1931. 20.00 (ISBN 0-8369-0846-5). Ayer Co Pubs.

Questions of the Day & of the Fray. Galton, Francis, Laboratory for National Eugenics Staff & Karl Pearson. Ed. by Charles Rosenberg. LC 83-48539. (History of Hereditarian Thought Ser.). 350p. 1985. Repr. lib. bdg. 45.00 (ISBN 0-8240-5813-5). Garland Pub.

Questions of the Heart. Edward Chinn. (Orig.). 1987. pap. 6.25 (ISBN 0-89536-877-3, 7863). CSS of Ohio.

Questions of the Soul. Isaac T. Hecker. 24.50 (ISBN 0-405-10834-6, 11840). Ayer Co Pubs.

Questions of Uniqueness & Resolution in Reconstruction of 2-D & 3-D Objects from Their Projections. M. B. Katz. (Lecture Notes in Biomathematics: Vol. 26). 1978. pap. 19.00 (ISBN 0-387-09087-8). Springer-Verlag.

Questions of Uniqueness, Stability, & Transient Behaviour see Mathematical Theory of Diffusion & Reaction in Permeable Catalysts.

Questions on Banking Practice. 11th ed. Ed. by Institute of Bankers Staff. 1978. 55.00x (ISBN 0-85297-045-5, Pub. by Inst of Bankers). State Mutual Bk.

Questions on Economics & Planning of Scientific Research (Collection of Articles) L. S. Blyakhman et al. LC 77-136731. 287p. 1969. 34.50. Scholarly.

Questions on Geologic Principles. Edward Reyer. Tr. by Allen Keller et al. LC 79-89374. (Microform Publication: No. 9). (Illus.). 1979. 3.20 (ISBN 0-8137-6009-7). Geol Soc.

Questions on International Law-Hungarian Perspectives. Ed. by Hanna Bokor-Szego. 1986. lib. bdg. 59.00 (ISBN 90-247-3293-X, Pub. by Martinus Nijhoff Netherlands). Kluwer Academic.

Questions on Occultism. Ernest Wood. Ed. by Kwaku Adzei. LC 78-8791. (Orig.). 1978. pap. 3.75 (ISBN 0-8356-0517-5, Quest). Theos Pub Hse.

Questions on Shakespeare, 2 vols. Albert H. Tolman. 354p. 1984. Repr. of 1910 ed. lib. bdg. 100.00 set (ISBN 0-918377-26-9). Russell Pr.

Questions on Social Explanation: Piagetian Themes Reconsidered. Ed. by Luigia Camaioni & Claudia De Lemos. LC 85-26727. (Pragmatics & Beyond Ser.: VI-4). viii, 141p. (Orig.). 1986. pap. 33.00x (ISBN 0-915027-66-6). Benjamins North Am.

Questions on the Way. Beverley D. Tucker. 128p. (Orig.). 1987. pap. 2.80 (ISBN 0-88028-056-5). Forward Movement.

Questions on Wittgenstein. Rudolf Haller. LC 87-4718. 208p. 1988. 24.95x; pap. 9.95x (ISBN 0-8032-7240-5). U of Nebr Pr.

Questions Parents Ask: Straight Answers from Louise Bates Ames, Ph.D., Associate Director of the Gesell Institute of Child Development. Louise B. Ames. LC 87-29078. (Illus.). 288p. 1988. 18.95 (ISBN 0-517-56797-0, C N Potter Bks). Crown.

Questions Pentecostals Ask. David F. Gray. Ed. by David Bernard. LC 86-26784. 304p. (Orig.). 1986. pap. 8.50 (ISBN 0-932581-07-2). Word Aflame.

Questions People Ask Ministers Most. Harold Hazelip. 1986. pap. 3.95 (ISBN 0-8010-4302-6). Baker Bk.

Questions Quakers Are Asking. Seth B. Hinshaw. 59p. (Orig.). 1982. pap. 1.50x (ISBN 0-942727-09-6). NC Yrly Pubns Bd.

Questions, Questions! Not Another Question! Dave Eaton. LC 86-80703. (Questions, Questions Ser.). 32p. (ps-3). 1986. 2.95 (ISBN 0-89081-548-8). Harvest Hse.

Questions Smart Kids Ask. 1987. 7.95 (ISBN 0-88047-076-3). DOK Pubs.

Questions sur la Vie. Vercors. 224p. 1973. 12.95 (ISBN 0-686-55134-6). French & Eur.

Questions Teenagers Ask. Caroline Goforth. 160p. (Orig.). 1987. pap. text ed. 6.95 (ISBN 0-939697-42-4). Graded Pr.

Questions Teenagers Ask about Dating & Sex. Barry Wood. 160p. (Orig.). 1981. pap. 5.95 (ISBN 0-8007-5058-6, Power Bks). Revell.

Questions Teens Are Asking. Theodore W. Schroeder & Dean Nadasdy. 1987. pap. 5.95 (ISBN 0-570-04454-5, 12-3062). Concordia.

Questions That Count: British Literature to 1750. J. David Williams. LC 82-15893. 98p. (Orig.). 1983. lib. bdg. 24.75 (ISBN 0-8191-2742-6); pap. text ed. 5.00 (ISBN 0-8191-2743-4). U Pr of Amer.

Questions: The Perfect Companion to Your Trivia Games. Fred L. Worth. Date not set. pap. 3.95 (ISBN 0-446-32500-7). Warner Bks.

Questions Through Pictures. Harris Winitz. (Language Through Pictures Ser.). (Illus.). 100p. (gr. 2-12). 1982. pap. 4.95 (ISBN 0-939990-33-4). Intl Linguistics.

Questions to a Zen Master. Taisen Deshimaru. 160p. 1985. pap. 8.95 (ISBN 0-525-48141-9). Dutton.

Questions to the Universe: Ten Lectures on the Foundations of Physics & Cosmology. Michael Heller. LC 86-61669. (Astronomy & Astrophysics Ser.: Vol 14). (Illus.). 152p. 1987. pap. 38.00 (ISBN 0-88126-008-8). Pachart Pub Hse.

Questions You Always Wanted to Ask about English but Were Afraid to Raise Your Hand. Maxwell Nurnberg. 272p. 1972. pap. 2.95 (ISBN 0-671-47419-7). WSP.

Questions You Have Always Wanted to Ask about Tongues, but... William Banks. (Illus.). 1979. pap. 2.75 (ISBN 0-89957-526-9). AMG Pubs.

Questor Tapes. D. C. Fontana. 1976. Repr. of 1974 ed. lib. bdg. 15.95x (ISBN 0-88411-091-5, Pub. by Aeonian Pr). Amereon Ltd.

Quests Beyond the Mirror: A Trio of Tales. Elbert Rynberg. 64p. 1981. 5.00 (ISBN 0-682-49735-5). Exposition-Phoenix.

Quests for a Promised Land: The Works of Martin Andersen Nexo. Faith Ingwersen & Niels Ingwersen. LC 84-8916. (Contributions to the Study of World Literature Ser.: No. 8). xvi, 156p. 1984. lib. bdg. 35.00 (ISBN 0-313-24469-3, IAT/). Greenwood.

Quests for Spices & New Worlds. Bertha S. Dodge. LC 87-24192. 232p. 1988. 25.00 (ISBN 0-208-02170-1, Archon Bks). Shoe String.

Quests of Difference: Reading Pope's Poems. G. Douglas Atkins. LC 85-20228. 208p. 1986. 19.00x (ISBN 0-8131-1565-5). U Pr of Ky.

Quests of Simon Ark. Edward D. Hoch. LC 84-60556. 1984. 14.95 (ISBN 0-89296-113-9). Mysterious Pr.

Quete de Paul Gadenne: Une Morale pour Notre Epoque. James B. Davis. 96p. (Fr.). 1979. 9.95 (ISBN 0-917786-18-1). Summa Pubns.

Quetelet, Statisticien et Sociologue. Joseph Lottin. (Research & Source Works Ser.: No. 270). 1969. Repr. of 1912 ed. 32.00 (ISBN 0-8337-2150-X). B Franklin.

Quetico Wolf. R. Oetting. LC 71-190274. (Illus.). 48p. (gr. 4 up). 1972. PLB 9.95 (ISBN 0-87783-059-2); pap. 3.94 deluxe ed. (ISBN 0-87783-103-3). Oddo.

Quetzal. Amilcar Lobos & Leland Mellot. Ed. by Rolando Castellon & Carlos Perez. LC 73-74385. 112p. (Orig., Eng. & Span.). 1973. pap. 3.50 (ISBN 0-912078-29-4). Volcano Pr.

Quetzalcoatl & Guadalupe: The Formation of Mexican National Consciousness 1531-1813. Jacques Lafaye. Tr. by Benjamin Keen. LC 75-20889. xxx, 336p. 1987. pap. 14.95 (ISBN 0-226-46788-0). U of Chicago Pr.

Quetzalcoatl & the Irony of Empire: Myth & Prophecies in the Aztec Tradition. David Carrasco. LC 82-13356. (Illus.). xii, 234p. 1984. lib. bdg. 25.00x (ISBN 0-226-09487-1); pap. 10.00x (ISBN 0-226-09489-8). U of Chicago Pr.

Quetzalcotl & Company. Ed. by Peter M. Briscoe & R. Reginald. (Studies in Literary Criticism: No. 19). Date not set. 19.95; pap. 9.95. Starmont Hse.

Queue. Vladimir Sorokin. Tr. by Sally Laird. (Rus.). 1988. 16.95 (ISBN 0-930523-44-X); pap. 8.95 (ISBN 0-930523-45-8). Readers Intl.

Queue de la Poire de la Boule de Monseigneur. Gustave Flaubert. (Illus.). 53p. 1958. 13.50 (ISBN 0-686-55988-6). French & Eur.

Queueing: Basic Theory & Application. Walter C. Giffen. LC 76-44996. (Grid Industrial Engineering Ser.). Repr. of 1978 ed. 92.50 (ISBN 0-8357-9144-0, 2015244). Bks Demand UMI.

Queueing Systems, 2 vols. Leonard Kleinrock. Incl. Vol. 1. Theory. Leonard Kleinrock. 417p. 1975. 42.50x (ISBN 0-471-49110-1); Vol. 2. Computer Applications. 549p. 49.50x (ISBN 0-471-49111-X). LC 44-9846. 417p. 1975-76 (Pub. by Wiley-Interscience). Wiley.

Queueing Tables & Graphs. F. S. Hillier et al. (Publications in Operations Research Ser.: Vol. 3). 232p. 1981. 54.50 (ISBN 0-444-00582-X, North-Holland). Elsevier.

Queueing Theory: A Solving Approach. Len Gorney. (Illus.). 300p. 1981. 24.95 (ISBN 0-89433-128-0). Petrocelli.

Queues & Point Processes. Peter Franken et al. (Probability & Mathematical Statistics Ser.). 208p. 1983. 41.95x (ISBN 0-471-10074-9, Pub. by Wiley-Interscience). Wiley.

Queues: Receptors & Recognition Series B. D. R. Cox & W. L. Smith. Incl. Vol. 13. Receptor Regulation. 59.95 (2245); Vol. 12. Purinergic Receptors. 63.00 (2142); Vol. 11. Membrane Receptors. 49.95 (2156); Vol. 10. Neurotransmitter Receptors, Part 2: Biogenic Amines. 49.95 (49.95); Vol. 9. Neurotransmitter Receptors, Part 1: Amino Acids, Peptides & Benzodiazepines. 49.95 (NO.6456); Vol. 8. Virus Receptors, Part 2: Animal Viruses. 43.00 (NO.6413); Vol. 7. Virus Receptors, Part 1: Bacterial Viruses. 43.00 (NO.6416); Vol. 6. Bacterial Adherence. 69.95 (6453); Vol. 5. Taxis & Behavior. 63.00 (NO.6452); Vol. 4. Specificity of Embryological Interactions. 49.95 (NO.6118); Vol. 3. Microbial Interactions. 49.95 (NO.6236); Vol. 2. Intercellular Junctions & Synapses. 53.00 (NO.6107); Vol. 1. Specificity & Action of Animal, Bacterial & Plant Toxins. 63.00 (NO. 6078). Pub. by Chapman & Hall England). Routledge Chapman & Hall.

Queues: Will This Wait Never End! Clifford Sloyer et al. (Contemporary Applied Mathematics Ser.). (Illus.). 47p. (Orig.). 1987. pap. text ed. 7.95 (ISBN 0-939765-08-X, G105). Janson Pubns.

Queuing & Waiting: Studies in the Social Organization of Access & Delay. Barry Schwartz. LC 75-11607. (Illus.). vi, 217p. 1975. lib. bdg. 12.00x (ISBN 0-226-74210-5). U of Chicago Pr.

Quevedo. Donald W. Bleznick. 192p. Repr. of 1972 ed. text ed. 22.50x cancelled (ISBN 0-8290-0730-X). Irvington.

Quevedo & the Grotesque. James Iffland. (Serie A: Monagrafias, LXIX). 174p. 1978. 24.00 (ISBN 0-7293-0061-7, Pub. by Tamesis Bks Ltd). Longwood Pub Group.

Quevedo & the Grotesque, Vol. II. (Serie A: Monagrafias, XCII). 283p. 1982. 36.00 (ISBN 0-7293-0140-0, Pub. by Tamesis Bks Ltd). Longwood Pub Group.

Quevedo, Hombre y Escritor en Conflicto con su Epoca. Ela R. Gomez-Quintero. LC 77-88534. 1978. pap. 10.00 (ISBN 0-89729-181-6). Ediciones.

Quevedo: Los Suenos. R. M. Price. (Critical Guides to Spanish Texts Ser.: No. 39). 87p. (Orig.). 1983. pap. 4.95 (ISBN 0-7293-0168-0, Pub. by Grant & Cutler). Longwood Pub Group.

Qufu Luguo Gucheng. 1982. 175.00x (ISBN 0-317-69023-X, Pub. by Han-Shan Tang Ltd). State Mutual Bk.

Qui a Obstrue la Cascade? Analyse Semantique du Rituel de la Circoncision chez les Komo au Zaire. Wauthier de Mahieu. (Atelier d'Anthropologie Sociale). 464p. 1986. 49.50 (ISBN 0-521-30043-6). Cambridge U Pr.

Qui Ne Souffre Pas... Reflexions sur le Probleme Social. Paul Claudel. 160p. 1958. 8.95 (ISBN 0-686-54427-7). French & Eur.

Quia Absurdum: Sur la Terre Comme au Ciel. Pierre Boulle. 224p. 1970. 9.95 (ISBN 0-686-54113-8). French & Eur.

Quiche & Pate. Peter Kump. Ed. by Gladys Topkis. LC 81-70444. (Great American Cooking Schools Ser.). (Illus.). 84p. 1982. pap. 5.95 (ISBN 0-941034-10-0). I Chalmers.

Quiche & Souffle. Paul Mayer. LC 77-670105. (Illus.). 192p. (Orig.). 1972. pap. 6.95 (ISBN 0-911954-72-4). Bristol Pub Ent CA.

Quiche-English Dictionary. Munro S. Edmonson. 168p. 1976. Repr. of 1965 ed. 17.50. Tulane MARI.

Quiche Mayas of Utatlan: The Evolution of a Highland Guatemala Kingdom. Robert M. Carmack. LC 80-5241. (Civilization of the American Indian Ser.: No. 155). (Illus.). 400p. 1981. 29.50x (ISBN 0-8061-1546-7). U of Okla Pr.

Quichean Civilization: The Ethnohistoric, Ethnographic & Archaeological Sources. Robert M. Carmack. LC 70-149948. (Illus.). 1973. 45.00x (ISBN 0-520-01963-6). U of Cal Pr.

Quick Algebra Review. Peter H. Selby. LC 82-21966. (Self Teaching Guide Ser.). 231p. 1983. pap. 9.95 (ISBN 0-471-86471-4). Wiley.

Quick Analysis, Vol. 1. Joseph Zmuda. (Illus.). 48p. (Orig.). 1986. pap. 22.00 (ISBN 0-941572-04-8). Z Graphic Pubns.

Quick Analysis, Vol. 2. Joseph Zmuda. (Illus.). 48p. 1986. pap. 22.00 (ISBN 0-941572-05-6). Z Graphic Pubns.

Quick Analysis for Busy Decision Makers. Robert D. Behn & James W. Vaupel. LC 81-68402. 1982. 18.95 (ISBN 0-465-06787-5). Basic.

Quick Analysis for Busy Decision Makers. Robert D. Behn & James W. Vaupel. LC 81-68402. 415p. 1984. pap. 12.95x (ISBN 0-465-06789-1, TB-5118). Basic.

Quick & Dirty Guide to War: Briefings on Present & Potential Wars. James F. Dunnigan & Austin Bay. LC 84-22797. (Illus.). 384p. 1985. 17.95 (ISBN 0-688-04199-X). Morrow.

Quick & Dirty Guide to War: Briefings on Present & Potential Wars. James F. Dunnigan & Austin Bay. (Illus.). 416p. 1986. pap. 9.95 (ISBN 0-688-06256-3, Quill). Morrow.

Quick & Easy. Ed. by Shelly Melvin. (Chosen Ser.). (Illus.). 260p. (Orig.). 1984. pap. 8.95 (ISBN 0-937404-55-1); printed plastic comb 11.95 (ISBN 0-937404-56-X). Triad Pub FL.

Quick & Easy Armour Cookbook. Armour & Company Kitchens Staff. LC 80-66316. (Orig.). 5.95 (ISBN 0-87502-082-8). Benjamin Co.

Quick & Easy Cassette Pack: Japanese. incl. 2 cassettes 13.95 (ISBN 0-88729-906-7). Langenscheidt.

Quick-&-Easy Cholesterol & Calorie Counter. Compiled by Lynn Sonberg. 112p. (Orig.). 1988. pap. 3.95 (ISBN 0-380-75573-4). Avon.

Quick & Easy Cookbook. Lee Cannon. LC 79-88365. (Illus.). 256p. 1979. 17.95 (ISBN 0-8487-0509-2). Oxmoor Hse.

Quick & Easy Cookbook. Robyn Supraner. LC 80-24021. (Illus.). 48p. (gr. 1-5). 1981. PLB 9.49 (ISBN 0-89375-438-2); pap. 1.95 (ISBN 0-89375-439-0). Troll Assocs.

Quick & Easy Cooking. Cheryl T. Caviness. 128p. (Orig.). 1988. pap. write for info. (ISBN 0-8280-0445-5). Review & Herald.

Quick & Easy Cooking. Pamela Westland. LC 85-60086. (Creative Cuisine Ser.). 80p. 1985. pap. 4.95 (ISBN 0-89586-342-1). Price Stern.

Quick & Easy Cooking: The Art of Living Litely. Ed. by A. Grimm-Richardson. (Orig.). 1988. pap. price not set (ISBN 0-937953-07-5). Tiptoe Pub.

Quick & Easy Creative Art Lessons. Anne Martin. LC 80-17558. 254p. 1981. 18.95 (ISBN 0-13-749663-X, Parker). P-H.

Quick & Easy dBASE II. Joseph Reymann. (Handy Guide Ser.). 64p. (Orig.). 1984. pap. 3.50 (ISBN 0-88284-291-9). Manusoft.

Quick & Easy Exercises for Figure Beauty. Judy Smithdeal. pap. 2.00 (ISBN 0-87980-381-9). Wilshire.

Quick & Easy Gas Grill Cookbook. Structo. LC 84-72095. 1984. 11.95 (ISBN 0-87502-132-8). Benjamin Co.

Quick & Easy Giant Dahlia Quilt on the Sewing Machine: Step-By-Step Instructions & Full Size Templates for Three Quilt Sizes. Susan A. Murwin & Suzzy C. Payne. (Illus.). 80p. (Orig.). 1983. pap. 3.95 (ISBN 0-486-24501-2). Dover.

Quick & Easy Guide to Database Management on the IBM PC. Amy Woodis & Evan Lim. 128p. 1984. pap. 4.95 (ISBN 0-912003-23-5). Bk Co.

Quick & Easy Guide to Educational Software on the Apple. Robert P. Wells. 128p. pap. 4.95 (ISBN 0-912003-27-8). Bk Co.

Quick & Easy Guide to Spreadsheets on the Apple. Tom Simondi. 128p. 1984. pap. 4.95 (ISBN 0-912003-28-6). Bk Co.

Quick & Easy Guide to Word Processing on the Apple. Steve Adams. 128p. 1984. 4.95 (ISBN 0-912003-29-4). Bk Co.

Quick & Easy Guide to Wordprocessing with the IBM PC. David Lansing. 128p. 1984. pap. 4.95 (ISBN 0-912003-25-1). Bk Co.

Quick-&-Easy Heart Motif Quilts: Instructions & Full-Size Templates for Applique Projects. Karen O'Dowd. 48p. (Orig.). 1986. pap. 3.50 (ISBN 0-486-25136-5). Dover.

Quick & Easy Home Repair. Graham Blackburn. 160p. (Orig.). 1986. pap. 6.95 (ISBN 0-345-33035-8). Ballantine.

Quick & Easy Knit & Crochet. Leslie Linsley. (Illus.). 160p. 1983. 18.95 (ISBN 0-312-66047-2, Pub. by Marek). St Martin.

Quick-&-Easy "Little Folk" Charted Designs. Georgia L. Gorham. 32p. (Orig.). 1987. pap. 2.50 (ISBN 0-486-25342-2). Dover.

Quick & Easy Math. Isaac Asimov. (gr. 7 up). 1964. 10.95 (ISBN 0-395-06573-9). HM.

Quick & Easy Microwaving Chicken. Microwave Cooking Institute Staff. LC 86-16611. (Illus.). 96p. 1986. pap. 5.95 (ISBN 0-86573-528-X); 8.95 (ISBN 0-86573-526-3). Cy De Cosse.

Quick & Easy Microwaving Chicken. Microwave Cooking Institute Staff. (Quick & Easy Microwaving Ser.). 1987. 8.95 (ISBN 0-317-56567-2). Prentice Hall Pr.

Quick & Easy Microwaving Chicken. The Microwave Cooking Institute Staff. (Quick & Easy Microwaving Ser.: Vol. II). (Illus.). 1987. pap. 8.95 (ISBN 0-13-749433-5). P-H.

Quick & Easy Microwaving Ground Beef. Microwave Cooking Institute Staff. LC 86-32771. 96p. 1987. 8.95 (ISBN 0-86573-531-X); pap. 5.95 (ISBN 0-86573-532-8). Cy De Cosse.

Quick & Easy Microwaving Ground Beef. Microwave Cooking Institute Staff. (Quick & Easy Microwaving Ser.). 1987. 8.95 (ISBN 0-13-749425-4). Prentice Hall Pr.

Quick & Easy Microwaving Seafood. Microwave Cooking Institute Staff. LC 87-622. (Illus.). 96p. Date not set. 8.95 (ISBN 0-86573-535-2); pap. 5.95 (ISBN 0-86573-536-0). Cy De Cosse.

Quick & Easy Microwaving Secrets. Microwave Cooking Institute Staff. LC 86-16612. (Illus.). 96p. 1986. 8.95 (ISBN 0-86573-525-5); pap. 5.95 (ISBN 0-86573-527-1). Cy De Cosse.

Quick & Easy Microwaving Secrets. Microwave Cooking Institute Staff. (Quick & Easy Microwaving Ser.). 1987. 8.95 (ISBN 0-317-56566-4). Prentice Hall Pr.

Quick & Easy Microwaving Secrets. The Microwave Cooking Institute Staff. (Quick & Easy Microwaving Ser.: Vol. I). (Illus.). 96p. 1987. pap. 8.95 (ISBN 0-13-749672-9). P-H.

Quick & Easy Microwaving Snacks & Appetizers. Microwave Cooking Institute Staff. LC 86-32788. (Illus.). 96p. 1987. 8.95 (ISBN 0-86573-529-8); pap. 5.95 (ISBN 0-86573-530-1). Cy De Cosse.

Quick & Easy Microwaving Snacks & Appetizers. Microwave Cooking Institute Staff. (Quick & Easy Microwaving Ser.). 1987. 8.95 (ISBN 0-317-56568-0). Prentice Hall Pr.

Quick & Easy Microwaving Snacks & Appetizers. The Microwave Cooking Institute Staff. (Quick & Easy Microwaving Ser.: Vol. III). (Illus.). 96p. 1987. pap. 8.95 (ISBN 0-13-749391-6). P-H.

Quick & Easy Microwaving Vegetables. Microwave Cooking Institute Staff. LC 87-626. (Illus.). 96p. Date not set. 8.95 (ISBN 0-86573-533-6); pap. 5.95 (ISBN 0-86573-534-4). Cy De Cosse.

Quick & Easy Miniature Samplers for Cross-Stitch. Barbara Christopher. 32p. 1986. pap. 2.75 (ISBN 0-486-25209-4). Dover.

Quick & Easy Monarch Notes on Salinger's Catcher in the Rye. (Orig.). pap. 2.25 (ISBN 0-671-52870-X). Monarch Pr.

Quick & Easy Multiplan. Richard O. Jones. 1984. pap. 3.50 (ISBN 0-88284-326-5). Manusoft.

Quick & Easy Origami. Toshie Takahama. 62p. 1988. pap. 13.95 (ISBN 0-87040-771-6). Japan Pubns USA.

Quick & Easy Paper Toys. E. Richard Churchill. LC 87-33531. (Illus.). 128p. 1988. 12.95 (ISBN 0-8069-6748-X); lib. bdg. 15.69 (ISBN 0-8069-6749-8). Sterling.

Quick & Easy Pasta Recipes. Bob Simmons & Coleen Simmons. (Illus.). 216p. 1983. 7.95 (ISBN 0-911954-79-1). Bristol Pub Ent CA.

Quick & Easy Patchwork on the Sewing Machine: Instructions & Full-Size Templates for 12 Quilts. Susan A. Murwin & Suzzy C. Payne. LC 78-74751. (Illus.). 1979. pap. 3.95 (ISBN 0-486-23770-2). Dover.

Quick & Easy PC-DOS & MS-DOS. Henry Sollarzano. 1984. pap. 3.50 (ISBN 0-88284-327-3). Manusoft.

Quick & Easy Plastic Canvas Projects. Illus. by Marie Thiesen. (Embroidery, Needlepoint, Charted Designs Ser.). (Illus.). 48p. 1984. pap. 2.95 (ISBN 0-486-24655-8). Dover.

Quick & Easy SuperCalc. Carlton Shrum. 1984. pap. 3.50 (ISBN 0-88284-325-7). Manusoft.

Quick & Easy Taxes. The J. K. Lasser Tax Institute Staff. 80p. 1987. pap. 3.95 (ISBN 0-13-509639-1). P-H.

Quick & Easy Vegetarian Cookbook. Ruth A. Manners & William Mannners. LC 78-2259. 288p. 1978. 12.50 (ISBN 0-87131-260-3); pap. 7.95 (ISBN 0-87131-303-0). M Evans.

Quick & Easy VisiCalc. Carlton Shrum. 1984. cancelled; pap. cancelled (ISBN 0-88284-324-9). Manusoft.

Quick & Easy Ways to Effective Speaking. Dale Carnegie. (gr. 10 up). 1983. pap. 3.95 (ISBN 0-671-60197-0). PB.

Quick & Easy Wood Crafts. Better Homes & Gardens Editors. 1987. pap. 7.95 (ISBN 0-696-01611-7). BH&G.

Quick & Easy Wooden Toys. Alan Pinder. (Illus.). 128p. 1986. 19.95 (ISBN 0-85532-561-5). Pathway Bk Serv.

Quick & Easy Word Processing with Your TI Professional Computer. Shirley R. Radl et al. LC 84-91755. 256p. (Orig.). 1986. pap. 19.95 (ISBN 0-911061-07-X). S Davis Pub.

Quick & Easy WordStar. William Urschel. (Handy Guide Ser.). 64p. (Orig.). 1984. pap. 3.50 (ISBN 0-88284-275-7). Manusoft.

Quick & Easy Wordstar 2000. Janet Crider. LC 85-80116. 192p. pap. 14.95 (ISBN 0-89586-408-8). Price Stern.

Quick & the Dead. Gamaliel Bradford. LC 70-85991. (Essay & General Literature Index Reprint Ser). 1969. Repr. of 1931 ed. 24.50x (ISBN 0-8046-0544-0, Pub By Kennikat). Assoc Faculty Pr.

Quick & the Dead. Louis L'Amour. (gr. 8-12). 1982. pap. 2.95 (ISBN 0-553-25478-2). Bantam.

Quick & the Dead. Z. Vance Wilson. 408p. 1987. pap. 3.95 (ISBN 0-345-34634-3). Ballantine.

Quick, Annie, Give Me a Catchy Line! Robert Quackenbush. (Illus.). 32p. (gr. 3-7). 1983. 10.95 (ISBN 0-13-749762-8). P-H.

Quick Arithmetic: A Self-Teaching Guide. 2nd ed. Robert A. Carman & Marilyn J. Carman. LC 83-3531. 286p. 1984. pap. 8.95 (ISBN 0-471-88966-0, 1-581). Wiley.

Quick As a Cricket. Audrey Wood. (Illus.). 32p. (ps-2). 1982. 10.00 (ISBN 0-85953-151-1, Pub. by Child's Play England). Playspaces.

Quick As a Dodo. Ralph McInerny. LC 77-93301. (Illus.). 1978. 14.95 (ISBN 0-8149-0806-3). Vanguard.

Quick Badge. Martin Ryerson. 1981. pap. 1.95 (ISBN 0-8439-0863-7, Leisure Bks). Leisure NY.

Quick Basic 4.0 Programming for the IBM. Carl Townsend. 1988. pap. cancelled (ISBN 0-672-22633-2). Sams.

Quick C Complete! Strawberry Software. Ed. by Bonnie Derman. 1988. pap. 22.95 (ISBN 0-673-38102-1). Scott F.

Quick C Programmer's Guide. Lance Leventhal. 1988. pap. 22.95 (ISBN 0-553-34674-1). Bantam.

Quick Calculus: A Self-Teaching Guide. 2nd ed. Daniel Kleppner & Norman Ramsey. LC 85-12349. 262p. 1985. pap. 10.95 (ISBN 0-471-82722-3). Wiley.

Quick Change Displays. Paula Corbett & Leslee Huntsman. (Teacher Aid Ser.). 43p. 1985. saddle-stitch 6.95 (ISBN 0-513-01772-0). Denison.

Quick Check for Children's Learning Styles Handbook: Infancy-First Grade. Lauren C. Bradway. (Illus.). 14p. 1987. tchr's ed. 19.95 (ISBN 0-944697-03-8). Beeby Champ.

Quick COBOL. 2nd ed. L. Coddington. (Computer Monograph Ser.: Vol. 16). 308p. 1978. 31.25 (ISBN 0-444-19460-6). Elsevier.

Quick Cost Estimating Manual. Ken Laviana. Ed. by E. D. Cormier. 120p. (Orig.). 1985. pap. 35.00 (ISBN 0-912227-03-6). C E Pub.

Quick Crowdbreakers & Games for Youth Groups. Ed. by Lane Eskew. (Illus., Orig.). 1988. pap. write for info. (ISBN 0-931529-46-8). Group Bks.

Quick Cuisine. Elizabeth Fraser. LC 83-82661. 144p. 1984. pap. 6.95 (ISBN 0-89709-130-2). Liberty Pub.

Quick Cuisine. Sunset Books & Sunset Magazine Editors. 96p. (Orig.). 1987. pap. text ed. 6.95 (ISBN 0-376-02563-8). Sunset-Lane.

Quick Cuisine International: Easy French Country Classics. (Illus.). 128p. 1984. 10.00 (ISBN 0-89535-146-3). Knapp Pr.

Quick Cuisine International: New Recipes for Italian Favorites. LC 84-14402. (Illus.). 128p. 1984. 10.00 (ISBN 0-89535-147-1). Knapp Pr.

Quick Delicious Low-Fat, Low-Salt Cookbook. Jacqueline B. Williams & Goldie Silverman. 192p. 1986. pap. 8.95 (ISBN 0-399-51225-X, Perigee). Putnam Pub Group.

Quick Dos Utilities. Alonso. 1988. pap. 19.95 (ISBN 0-471-60905-6). Wiley.

Quick Fire Hombre. Nelson Nye. 1977. pap. 1.25 (ISBN 0-505-51177-0, Pub. by Tower Bks). Leisure NY.

Quick Fix Decorating Ideas. Karen Fisher. LC 83-23775. (Illus.). 176p. 1984. pap. 8.95 (ISBN 0-452-25519-8, Plume). NAL.

Quick-Fix Home Repair. rev. ed. Richard D'Arezzo. Ed. by Christie Alexander. (Quick-Fix Ser.). (Illus.). 160p. 1987. pap. 6.95 (ISBN 0-939353-08-3). Alexander & Alexander.

Quick Fixes & Small Comforts: How Every Woman Can Resist Those Irresistible Urges. Georgia Witkin. LC 87-40572. 256p. 1988. 17.95 (ISBN 0-394-56040-X, Pub. by Villard Bks). Random.

Quick Gourmet Meals. Julian. (Easy Cooking Ser.). 1984. 5.95 (ISBN 0-8120-5558-6). Barron.

Quick Guide to Football Terms. Frances Seese. Date not set. cancelled. Betterway Pubns.

Quick Guide to Loans & Emergency Funds. rev. ed. (Memoranda Ser.). 9p. 1982. 2.00. Ctr for Arts Info.

Quick Kitchen Cabinets. rev. ed. John Ward. (Illus.). 92p. (Orig.). 1986. pap. cancelled (ISBN 0-941936-04-X). Linden Pub Fresno.

Quick Knife: Unnecessary Surgery U. S. A. Duane F. Stroman. (National University Publications Ser.). 1979. 22.50x (ISBN 0-8046-9226-2, PUB by Kennikat). Assoc Faculty Pr.

Quick Knits. Debbie Bliss & Mary Norden. (Illus.). 128p. (Orig.). 1987. pap. 15.95 (ISBN 0-7135-2664-5). Salem Hse Pubs.

Quick Legal Terminology. Randolph Z. Volkell. LC 79-13647. (Self-Teaching Guides Ser.). 161p. 1979. pap. text ed. 8.95 (ISBN 0-471-03786-9). Wiley.

Quick, Let's Get out of Here. Michael Rosen. (Illus.). 96p. (gr. k-5). 1984. 10.95 (ISBN 0-233-97559-4). Andre Deutsch.

Quick-Line Stories for Young Children. Judith B. Kaiser. 1975. spiral bdg. 3.95 (ISBN 0-916406-12-1). Accent Bks.

Quick Marches. John Moon. LC 75-19259. (Music of the Fifes & Drums Ser: Vol. 1). 24p. 1976. pap. 5.95 (ISBN 0-87935-031-8). Williamsburg.

Quick Meals. Cecilia J. Au-Yeung. (Chopsticks Recipes Ser.). (Illus.). 128p. (Orig., Eng. & Chinese.). 1985. pap. 4.95 (ISBN 9-627-01804-X). Parkwest Pubns.

Quick Meals Cookbook. Lorene Froehling. (Illus.). 64p. (Orig.). 1985. pap. 3.95 (ISBN 0-8249-3056-8). Ideals.

Quick Meals with Fresh Foods. Sunset Editors. LC 83-81000. (Illus.). 96p. 1983. pap. 5.95 (ISBN 0-376-02552-2, Sunset Bks). Sunset-Lane.

Quick Medical Terminology: A Self-Teaching Guide. 2nd ed. Genevieve L. Smith et al. LC 83-21612. 241p. 1984. pap. 10.95 (ISBN 0-471-88451-0, 1581); cassette 8.95 (ISBN 0-471-80771-0). Wiley.

Quick-Mini Stress-Management Strategies for You: A Person with a Disability. David G. Danskin & Dorothy V. Danskin. LC 87-72520. 1988. 12.50 (ISBN 0-9619661-0-6); Braille ed. 12.50 (ISBN 0-9619661-2-2); cass. 12.50 (ISBN 0-9619661-1-4). Guild Hall Pubns.

Quick 'n' Easy Calendar Learning. Ina Tabibian. (gr. 1-4). 1986. pap. 4.95 (ISBN 0-8224-5654-0). D S Lake Pubs.

Quick-N-Easy Electronics Projects. Bob Greene. 7.95 (ISBN 0-86668-049-7). ARCsoft.

Quick 'n' Easy Learning Tasks. Charlene H. Lutz. (gr. 1-4). 1986. pap. 10.95 (ISBN 0-8224-5653-2). D S Lake Pubs.

Quick 'n Fun Games for the IBM Personal Computer. Michael Fox. 96p. 1984. 8.95 (ISBN 0-86668-044-6). ARCsoft.

Quick Neurological Screening Test. Harold Sterling et al. 1978. pap. 35.00 incl. manual, 25 recording forms, 25 geometric reproduction sheets, administration & scoring flip cards in vinyl folder (ISBN 0-87879-185-X). Acad Therapy.

Quick Pascal. David L. Matuszek. LC 82-8354. 179p. 1982. pap. text ed. 17.95x (ISBN 0-471-86644-X). Wiley.

Quick Print Shop-How to Set up a Successful Quick Print Operation of Your Own. 1987. lib. bdg. 79.95 (ISBN 0-8490-3946-0). Gordon Pr.

Quick Printing Encyclopedia. 7th ed. William Friday. (Illus.). 523p. 1988. 49.50. Prudential Pub Co.

Quick Proposal Workbook. Daniel L. Conrad. LC 80-84209. 119p. 1980. 19.00x (ISBN 0-916664-38-4). Public Management.

Quick Quackers. Bernard Wiseman. LC 79-14216. (Easy Venture Ser.). (Illus.). (gr. k-2). 1979. PLB 7.47 (ISBN 0-8116-6077-X). Garrard.

Quick Ready Reference. Biokinesiology Institute Staff & John Barton. (Illus.). 250p. (Orig.). 1981. pap. text ed. 25.00 (ISBN 0-937216-06-2). Biokinesiology.

Quick Reference Chinese. Date not set. 7.95 (ISBN 0-8351-2036-8). China Bks.

Quick Reference Data for Mechanical Drafters-Designers. rev. 2nd ed. William E. Rybolt. Ed. by Arthur Schultz. LC 87-61108. (Illus.). 52p. 1987. pap. 7.95 (ISBN 0-941801-13-6). Rybolt Pubns.

Quick Reference Guide to Bayonets from Janzen's Notebook. Jerry L. Janzen. (Illus.). 64p. 1989. pap. price not set. J L Janzen.

Quick Reference Guide to dBASE III PLUS: A Handy, Alphabetic Guide to dBASE III PLUS Commands & Functions. (Quick Reference Ser.). 72p. (Orig.). 1987. pap. 5.95 (ISBN 1-55615-040-7). Microsoft.

Quick Reference Guide to Hard-Disk Management. Van Wolverton. (Programmer's Quick Reference Ser.). (Orig.). 1988. pap. 5.95 (ISBN 1-55615-105-5). Microsoft.

Quick Reference Guide to Microsoft C: A Complete Reference to Microsoft & ANSI Standard Libraries. 72p. Date not set. pap. 5.95 (ISBN 1-55615-109-8). Microsoft.

Quick Reference Guide to Microsoft Word for the IBM PC. Peter Rinearson. (Programmer's Quick Reference Ser.). 128p. (Orig.). 1988. pap. 5.95 (ISBN 1-55615-154-3). Microsoft.

Quick Reference Guide to MS-DOS Commands. Van Wolverton. (Quick Reference Ser.). 48p. (Orig.). 1987. pap. text ed. 4.95 (ISBN 1-55615-025-3). Microsoft.

Quick Reference Guide to MS-DOS Commands. rev. ed. Van Wolverton. (Programmer's Quick Reference Ser.). 96p. (Orig.). 1988. pap. 5.95 (ISBN 1-55615-182-9). Microsoft.

Quick Reference Guide to Polygraph Admissibility, Licensing Laws & Limiting Laws. 10th ed. Norman Ansley. LC 85-108798. 1985. write for info. Am Polygraph.

Quick Reference Guide to Polygraphy Admissibility, Licensing Laws & Limiting Laws. 11th ed. Norman Ansley. 1987. 4.95. Am Polygraph.

Quick Reference Guide to Tax Reform Act of 1986. 44p. 1987. 3.50 (ISBN 0-88462-593-1, 5606-10, Pub. by Longman Fin Serv Pub). Longman Finan.

Quick Reference Guide to the Norton Utilities: A Great Reference to All the Features & Commands of This Popular Utility. (Quick Reference Ser.). 1988. softcover 5.95 (ISBN 1-55615-180-2). Microsoft.

Quick Reference Guide to the Tax Reform Act of 1986. H. David Megaw. LC 86-21438. Date not set. cancelled (ISBN 0-88462-578-8). Longman Finan.

Quick Reference Guide to the Tax Reform Act, 1988. Ernst & Whinney. 44p. 1987. pap. 27.00 (ISBN 0-88462-720-9). Longman Finan.

Quick Reference Guide to Using Early Recollections in Treating Personality Disorders. Michael Meier. LC 87-92202. (Orig.). 1988. pap. text ed. write for info. (ISBN 0-945628-00-5). NPCI.

Quick Reference Guide to WordStar. T. M. Nash & C. Robert Nash. 82p. 1985. lab manual 19.95 (ISBN 0-934569-99-1). Nash Group.

Quick Reference Guide to XENIX Mail: Communicating on the XENIX-UNIX Multiuser Operating System. 48p. 1987. pap. 4.95 (ISBN 1-55615-038-5). Microsoft.

Quick Reference Manual for Silicon Integrated Circuit Technology. Ed. by W. E. Beadle et al. LC 84-25667. 736p. 1985. 71.95 (ISBN 0-471-81588-8). Wiley.

Quick Reference Scripture Handbook. Dick Mills. 50p. (Orig.). 1984. pap. 1.95 (ISBN 0-89274-323-9). Harrison Hse.

Quick Reference to Allergic Skin Diseases in Dogs & Cats. Reedy & Miller. 256p. 1988. price not set (ISBN 0-7216-2432-4). Saunders.

Quick Reference to Cardiovascular Disease. 3rd ed. Edward Chung. 456p. 1987. 39.50 (ISBN 0-683-01566-4). Williams & Wilkins.

Quick Reference to Clinical Cardiology. Emmanuel Goldberger. LC 65-10432. (Illus.). 500p. 1989. price not set (ISBN 0-397-50878-6, Lippincott Medical). Lippincott.

Quick Reference to Clinical Nutrition. 2nd ed. Seymour L. Halpern. LC 65-8410. (Illus.). 496p. 1987. pap. 29.95 (ISBN 0-397-50675-9, Lippincott Medical). Lippincott.

Quick Reference to Critical Care Nursing. Fletcher. LC 64-3091. 1988. 15.75 (Lippincott & Nursing). Lippincott.

Quick Reference to Emergency Nursing. Belinda B. Hammond & Gennell Lee. (Illus.). 426p. 1984. pap. text ed. 14.75 (ISBN 0-397-54430-8, 64-03711, Lippincott Nursing). Lippincott.

Quick Reference to Fluid Balance. Norma M. Metheny. (Quick Reference for Nurses Ser.). (Illus.). 368p. 1984. pap. text ed. 15.75 (ISBN 0-397-54448-0, 64-03893, Lippincott Nursing). Lippincott.

Quick Reference to Intravenous Drugs. Diane P. Sager & Suzanne K. Bomar. (Quick References for Nurses Ser.). 375p. 1982. pap. text ed. 15.95 (ISBN 0-397-54411-1, 00712897, Lippincott Nursing). Lippincott.

GYN Procedures. 3rd ed. Hugh R. Barber et al. LC 65-5580. (Illus.). 352p. 1989. price not set (Lippincott Medical). Lippincott.

Quick Reference to Pediatric Emergencies. 3rd ed. Delmer J. Pascoe & Moses Grossman. (Illus.). 618p. 1984. text ed. 34.50 (ISBN 0-397-50650-3, 65-08147, Lippincott Medical). Lippincott.

Quick Reference to Surgical Emergencies. 2nd ed. Bernard Gardner & Gerald W. Shaftan. LC 65-8667. (Illus.). 736p. 1986. 39.50 (ISBN 0-397-50702-X, Lippincott Medical). Lippincott.

Quick Reference to the Diagnostic Criteria from DSM-III-R. American Psychiatric Association Staff. 288p. 1987. pap. text ed. 15.00x (ISBN 0-89042-020-3, 0-89042-020-3). Am Psychiatric.

Quick Reference to Therapeutic Nutrition. Barbara G. Morrissey. (Quick Reference for Nurses Ser.). (Illus.). 400p. 1984. pap. text ed. 15.75 (ISBN 0-397-54416-2, 64-03570, Lippincott Nursing). Lippincott.

Quick Reference to Veterinary Medicine. William R. Fenner. (Illus.). 448p. 1982. pap. text ed. 34.50 (ISBN 0-397-50448-9, 65-05937, Lippincott Medical). Lippincott.

Quick Response Therapy: A Time Limited Treatment Approach. Judith Goldring. LC 80-11362. 142p. 1980. 26.95 (ISBN 0-87705-499-1). Human Sci Pr.

Quick-Response Urban Travel Estimation Techniques & Transferable Parameters: A User's Guide. (National Cooperative Highway Research Program Report). 229p. 1978. 10.20 (ISBN 0-309-02775-6). Transport Res Bd.

Quick Return. K. T. Giddins. 1982. 15.00x (ISBN 0-903653-90-7, Pub. by New Playwrights Network). State Mutual Bk.

Quick Science: Science Experiments You Can Do in a Minute. Herman Schneider & Nina Schneider. 64p. (Orig.). (gr. 4-6). 1987. pap. 2.95 activity bk. (ISBN 0-590-41354-6). Scholastic Inc.

Quick Scientific Terminology: A Self-Teaching Guide. Kenneth J. Rose. LC 88-725. 352p. 1988. pap. 12.95 (ISBN 0-471-85763-7). Wiley.

Quick Scripture Reference for Counseling. John G. Kruis. 80p. 1988. pap. 5.95 (ISBN 0-8010-5488-5). Baker Bk.

Quick Service. P. G. Wodehouse. 1981. pap. 3.95 (ISBN 0-14-000994-9). Penguin.

Quick Silver. Clark Howard. 544p. 1988. 19.95 (ISBN 0-525-24603-7). Dutton.

Quick-Sketch: A New Technique in Interior Design Graphics. Richard W. Henton. 144p. 1980. pap. text ed. 12.95 (ISBN 0-8403-2233-X). Kendall-Hunt.

Quick Solutions: 500 People Problems Managers Face & How to Solve Them. Thomas L. Quick. 377p. 1987. 22.95 (ISBN 0-471-85229-5); pap. 14.95. Wiley.

Quick Springs of Sense: Studies in the Eighteenth Century. Ed. by Larry S. Champion. LC 72-86783. pap. 68.20 (2031065). Bks Demand UMI.

Quick! Start Writing: Original Ideas to Motivate Writing. Elsie Lang & Park Lang. (gr. 4-8). 1985. pap. 8.95 (ISBN 0-673-18063-8). Scott F.

Quick Survey Course in Forms Typing. E. G. Blendon & B. H. Nalepa. 1967. text ed. 8.52 standard ed. (ISBN 0-07-005892-X); pap. text ed. 8.52 facsimile ed. (ISBN 0-07-005891-1). McGraw.

Quick Tempo Foxtrot. (Ballroom Dance Ser.). 1985. lib. bdg. 70.00 (ISBN 0-87700-704-7). Revisionist Pr.

Quick Test for Understanding Alcoholism. rev. ed. Jon R. Weinberg. 20p. 1983. pap. 0.85 (ISBN 0-89486-218-9). Hazelden.

Quick, Thrifty Cooking. Reader's Digest Editors. LC 84-3465. 256p. 1985. 21.99 (ISBN 0-89577-181-0). RD Assn.

Quick Tips from the CBS Tennis Spot. Shep Campbell. LC 80-84952. (Illus.). 188p. 1981. pap. 6.95 (ISBN 0-914178-45-8, A Tennis Mag. Bk). Golf Digest.

Quick to Fix Desserts. Eulalia C. Blair. LC 80-13124. (Foodservice Menu Planning Ser.). 309p. 1983. 20.95 (ISBN 0-8436-2183-4). Van Nos Reinhold.

Quick to Fix Western States Cookbook. Ed. by Joice Hansell & Vange Hendrix. JoAnn Blanchard & Kathleen Hendrix. LC 86-29684. (Illus.). 128p. (Orig.). 1987. pap. 8.95 (ISBN 0-9610156-2-4). Rainbow Clackamas.

Quick Trigger Country. Nelson Nye. 192p. 1985. pap. 2.25 (ISBN 0-8439-2214-1, Leisure Bks). Leisure NY.

Quick Tunes & Good Times. Newton F. Tolman. (YA) (gr. 7 up). 1972. 7.50 (ISBN 0-87233-018-4). Bauhan.

Quick Typing: A Self-Teaching Guide. Jeremy Grossman. LC 79-26243. (Self-Teaching Guides Ser.). 157p. 1980. pap. text ed. 8.95 (ISBN 0-471-05287-6). Wiley.

Quick Workouts. Time-Life Books Editors. (Fitness, Health & Nutrition Ser.). 144p. 1987. 17.27 (ISBN 0-8094-6179-X); lib. bdg. 21.27 (ISBN 0-8094-6180-3). Time-Life.

QuickBASIC. Fred Scott. 1988. pap. text ed. write for info. (ISBN 0-673-38082-3). Scott F.

QuickBASIC Made Easy. Bob Albrecht et al. 350p. 1988. 19.95 (ISBN 0-07-881421-9). Osborne-McGraw.

QuickBASIC: Programming Techniques & Library Development. Namir C. Shammas. 1988. 19.95 (ISBN 1-55851-003-6). M & T Pub Inc.

QuickBASIC: The Complete Reference. Steven Nameroff. 700p. 1988. cancelled (ISBN 0-07-881363-8); pap. text ed. 24.95 (ISBN 0-07-881362-X). Osborne-McGraw.

QuickBook: Genetic Engineering of Plants. Steven C. Witt. (Illus.). 53p. (Orig.). 1983. pap. 11.50 (ISBN 0-912005-02-5). Ctr Sci Info.

QuickC: Memory-Resident Utilities, Screen I-O & Programming Techniques. Al Stevens. 336p. (Orig.). 1988. pap. 24.95 (ISBN 0-943518-80-6); with disk 49.95 (ISBN 0-317-69869-9). MIS Press.

QuickC Programming. Carl Townsend. (Orig.). 1988. pap. 22.95 (ISBN 0-672-22622-7). Sams.
Quickened Seed. Clarence L. Weaver. (Echo XII). 101p. (Orig.). 1981. pap. text ed. 3.50x (ISBN 0-915020-20-3). Bardic.
Quickening Flame: A Scriptural Study of Revival. Winifred Ascroft. (Basic Bible Study). 64p. 1985. pap. 2.95 (ISBN 0-932305-20-2, 521020). Aglow Pubns.
Quickening Seed: Death in the Sermons of John. Bettie A. Doebler. (Elizabethan & Renaissance Studies). 297p. (Orig.). 1974. pap. 15.00 (ISBN 3-7052-0678-8, Pub. by Salzburg Studies). Longwood Pub Group.
Quickening Universe: Cosmic Evolution & Human Destiny. Eugene F. Mallove. 288p. 1987. 18.95 (ISBN 0-312-00062-6, Pub. by Thomas Dunne Bks). St Martin.
Quicker Quilts. Linda J. Rimel. (Illus.). 144p. 1984. 16.95 (ISBN 0-668-06119-7, 6119). Arco.
Quickest Way to Draw Well. Frederic Taubes. (Handbook Ser.). (Illus.). 96p. 1977. pap. 6.95 (ISBN 0-14-046275-9). Penguin.
Quickest Way to Get a Raise & Promotion. Barile Ebeh. LC 85-51789. 96p. 1986. pap. 12.00 (ISBN 0-933245-01-7). Zest Pub.
Quickhand. Jeremy Grossman. 128p. 1976. pap. text ed. 8.95 (ISBN 0-471-32887-1). Wiley.
Quickie Quizzes from the Bible. Charles Vander Meer. (Quiz & Puzzle Bks.: No. 1). 48p. (gr. 7 up). 1976. pap. 2.50 (ISBN 0-8010-9252-3). Baker Bk.
Quickie Quizzes No. 2. Charles Vander Meer. (Quiz & Puzzle Bks.). pap. 2.50 (ISBN 0-8010-9266-3). Baker Bk.
Quickies for Singles. Fellowship Church, Baton Rouge, La, Members. Ed. by Gwen McKee. (Cookbook Ser.: No. 4). (Illus.). 80p. 1980. pap. 5.95 (ISBN 0-937552-03-8). Quail Ridge.
Quickies That Can Be Taught in Less Than Ten Minutes: Cha Cha, Paso Doble, Merengue, Rumba & Foxtrot. (Ballroom Dance Ser.). 1985. lib. bdg. 49.95 (ISBN 0-87700-781-0). Revisionist Pr.
Quickies That Can Be Taught in Less Than Ten Minutes: Cha Cha, Paso Doble, Merengue, Ruma & Foxtrot. (Ballroom Dance Ser.). 1986. lib. bdg. 59.95 (ISBN 0-8490-3289-X). Gordon Pr.
Quicksand. Nella Larsen. LC 74-75553. 1970. Repr. of 1928 ed. 35.00 (ISBN 0-8371-1127-7, LAQ&). Greenwood.
Quicksand & Cactus: A Memoir of the Southern Mormon Frontier. Juanita Brooks. LC 82-11698. (Illus.). 400p. 1982. pap. 12.50 (ISBN 0-935704-39-6). Howe Brothers.
Quicksand & Passing. Nella Larson. Ed. by Deborah McDowell. (American Women Writers Ser.). 300p. 1986. text ed. 30.00 (ISBN 0-8135-1169-0); pap. text ed. 9.95 (ISBN 0-8135-1170-4). Rutgers U Pr.
Quicksand Book. Tomie De Paola. LC 76-28762. (Illus.). 32p. (gr. k-3). 1977. reinforcd bdg. 12.95 (ISBN 0-8234-0291-6). Holiday.
Quicksand Book. Tomie DePaola. LC 76-28762. (Illus.). (gr. k-3). 1984. pap. 5.95 (ISBN 0-8234-0532-X). Holiday.
Quicksand Through the Hourglass. Dave Morice. LC 79-25714. (Illus.). 56p. (Orig.). 1979. signed 20.00 (ISBN 0-915124-28-9, Pub. by Toothpaste); pap. 4.50 (ISBN 0-915124-27-0). Coffee Hse.
Quicksilver. James Farnsworth. (Gunsmoke Western Ser.). 176p. 1988. text ed. 12.95x (ISBN 0-85997-853-2, Pub. by Firecrest Pub Ltd). Prescott Pr NH.
Quicksilver. Bill Pronzini. Ed. by Nancy Parent. (Nameless Detective Ser.). 160p. 1987. pap. 3.50 (ISBN 0-7701-0704-4). Paperjacks US.
Quicksilver Lady, No. 148. Barbara Whitehead. 224p. 1981. pap. 1.50 (ISBN 0-449-50220-1, Coventry). Fawcett.
Quicksilver Love. Rose Flynn. (YA) (gr. 7 up). 1980. 9.95 (ISBN 0-686-73941-8, Avalon). Bouregy.
Quicksilver Pool. Phyllis A. Whitney. 304p. (Orig.). 1981. pap. 3.50 (ISBN 0-449-23983-7, Crest). Fawcett.
Quicksilver: Terlingua & the Chisos Mining Company. Kenneth B. Ragsdale. LC 75-4081. 368p. 1976. pap. 11.95 (ISBN 0-89096-188-3). Tex A&M Univ Pr.
Quicksilver Years: The Hopes & Fears of Early Adolescence. Peter L. Benson et al. 264p. (Orig.). 1986. 14.95 (ISBN 0-86683-535-0, HarpR); pap. 13.95. Har-Row.
Quickstep. Earl Atkinson. (Ballroom Dance Ser.). 1986. lib. bdg. 79.95 (ISBN 0-8490-3644-5). Gordon Pr.
Quickstep Variations. (Ballroom Dance Ser.). 1985. lib. bdg. 69.00 (ISBN 0-87700-772-1). Revisionist Pr.
Quickstep Variations. (Ballroom Dance Ser.). 1986. lib. bdg. 79.95 (ISBN 0-8490-3419-1). Gordon Pr.
QuickWrite: Commodore Sixty-Four. Robert Hime. 128p. 1984. pap. cancelled (ISBN 0-88056-220-X). Dilithium Pr.
QuickWrite: IBMPC & PCjr. Robert Hime. 128p. 1984. cancelled (ISBN 0-88056-219-6). Dilithium Pr.
Quid Nunc: A Contemplative Perspective of the American Dream Turned Nightmare. Iris Kern & William E. Needham. LC 81-69060. 196p. 1981. text ed. 19.95 (ISBN 0-939296-01-2). Bond Pub Co.
Quid Pro Quo: Equity & Claims of Money. Michael Kirchberger. 1981. 3.00 (ISBN 0-682-49779-7). Exposition-Phoenix.
Quiddities: An Intermittently Philosophical Dictionary. W. V. Quine. LC 87-11974. 288p. 1987. 20.00 (ISBN 0-674-74351-2). Harvard U Pr.
Quien Era Ella? Santa I Roman. (Romance Real Ser.). 192p. (Span.). 1981. pap. 1.50 (ISBN 0-88025-005-4). Roca Pub.
Quien es Jesuscristo? William Hendricks. Tr. by Jose L. Martinez from Eng. (Biblioteca de Doctrina Cristiana Ser.). 164p. (Span.). 1986. pap. 5.95 (ISBN 0-311-09112-1). Casa Bautista.
Quien Es Quien en las Lettras Espanolas (S-37344) 495p. (Span.). 1979. 29.95 (ISBN 84-85635-05-1). French & Eur.
Quien Jala los Hilos? Irene Sendin. Ed. by Rosa M. Icaza. (Illus.). 135p. (Span.). 1985. pap. 4.95 (ISBN 0-932545-01-7). Mex Am Cult.
Quien Me Robo a Mi Hija? M. K. Callie. Tr. by Jacinto De Torres from Eng. (Compadre Collection Ser). Orig. Title: Where Have All the Little Girls Gone. 160p. (Span.). 1974. pap. 0.85 (ISBN 0-88473-707-1). Fiesta Pub.
Quien Movio la Piedra? Frank Morison. Tr. by Rhode Ward from Eng. LC 77-11752. 206p. (Span.). 1977. pap. 6.25 (ISBN 0-89922-100-9). Edit Caribe.
Quien Sabe? A Preliminary List of Chicano Reference Materials. Francisco Garcia-Ayvens. (Bibliography & Reference Ser.: No. 11). 116p. (Orig.). 1981. pap. text ed. 6.00 (ISBN 0-89551-000-6). UCLA Chicano Stud.
Quiet American. Graham Greene. 1977. pap. 3.95 (ISBN 0-14-001792-5). Penguin.
Quiet American. Graham Greene. 228p. 1956. 16.95 (ISBN 0-670-58552-1). Viking.
Quiet American. Graham Greene. 17.95 (ISBN 0-88411-657-3, Pub. by Aeonian Pr). Amereon Ltd.
Quiet & Peaceable Life. rev. ed. John L. Ruth. LC 85-70284. (People's Place Booklet: No. 2). (Illus.). 96p. (Orig.). 1985. pap. 4.50 (ISBN 0-934672-25-3). Good Bks PA.
Quiet Answer. Hugh Prather. LC 80-2979. 176p. 1982. pap. 6.95 (ISBN 0-385-17605-8, Dolp). Doubleday.
Quiet Approach. (United Nations Peaceful Settlement Ser.). 4.00 (ISBN 92-1-157003-4, E.75.XV.PS/6). UN.
Quiet As a Nun. Antonia Fraser. 1982. pap. 3.95 (ISBN 0-393-30120-6). Norton.
Quiet Assassin. Thomas Kirkwood. LC 84-73451. 288p. 1985. 16.95 (ISBN 0-917657-14-4). D I Fine.
Quiet Athenian. L. B. Carter. 224p. 1986. 49.95 (ISBN 0-19-814870-4). Oxford U Pr.
Quiet Beauty of China. Pat Fok. LC 87-45447. (Illus.). 136p. 1987. 40.00 (ISBN 0-8478-0859-9). Rizzoli Intl.
Quiet Because. Vera Groomer. (Come Unto Me Ser.). (ps). 1979. pap. 1.95 (ISBN 0-8127-0253-0). Review & Herald.
Quiet Broker? A Way Out of the Irish Conflict. William V. Shannon. 52p. (Orig.). 1985. pap. 8.00x (ISBN 0-87078-163-4). Priority Pr Pubns.
Quiet Comfort of Quilts: Stitches of Love from Lahoma. Lahoma Rackley. Ed. by Molly L. Griffis. LC 87-83113. (Land we Belong to is Grand Ser.: Bk. 4). (Illus.). 65p. 1988. pap. 5.00 (ISBN 0-9618634-3-9). Levite Apache.
Quiet Companion: Peter Favre S. J., 1506-1546. Mary Purcell. vi, 198p. 1981. 8.95 (ISBN 0-8294-0377-9). Loyola.
Quiet Company: A Modern History of Northwestern Mutual Life. John Gurda. LC 83-238714. (Illus.). 334p. 1983. 14.95 (ISBN 0-9612010-0-2). NW Mutual Life.
Quiet Corner in a Library. facs. ed. William H. Hudson. LC 68-16940. (Essay Index Reprint Ser). 1915. 17.00 (ISBN 0-8369-0550-4). Ayer Co Pubs.
Quiet Days in Clichy. Henry Miller. 160p. 1987. pap. 6.95 (ISBN 0-8021-3016-X, Ever). Grove.
Quiet Days in Clichy & The World of Sex. Henry Miller. LC 77-91353. 1978. pap. 2.95 (ISBN 0-394-17037-7, B409, BC). Grove.
Quiet Desperation. Bill Weiner. 1980. 10.95 (ISBN 0-686-65059-X). Lyle Stuart.
Quiet Desperation: The Truth about Successful Men. Jan Halper. LC 87-31585. 320p. 1988. 18.95 (ISBN 0-446-51359-8). Warner Bks.
Quiet Dogs. John Gardner. 1988. pap. 3.95 (ISBN 1-55773-053-9, Charter Pub). Berkley Pub.
Quiet Ear: Deafness in Literature. Ed. by Brian Grant. 244p. 1988. 14.95 (ISBN 0-571-12976-5). Faber & Faber.
Quiet Enemy. Cecil Dawkins. 224p. 1986. pap. 5.95 (ISBN 0-14-008011-2). Penguin.
Quiet Eye. Sylvia S. Judson. (Illus.). 74p. 1982. 8.95 (ISBN 0-89526-638-5). Regnery Gateway.
Quiet Eye. Sylvia S. Judson. 1988. 9.95. Regnery Gateway.
Quiet Fire: Memoirs of Older Gay Men. Keith Vacha. LC 85-5699. (Gay Ser.). 160p. (Orig.). 1985. 21.95 (ISBN 0-89594-158-9); pap. 8.95 (ISBN 0-89594-157-0). Crossing Pr.
Quiet Furies: Man & Disorder. Elton B. McNeil. 1967. pap. text ed. 19.00 (ISBN 0-13-749770-9). P-H.
Quiet Gathering. David Scott. 1986. pap. 13.95 (ISBN 0-906427-68-1, Pub. by Bloodaxe Bks). Dufour.
Quiet Gentleman. Georgette Heyer. 288p. 1987. pap. 3.50 (ISBN 0-425-10527-X). Berkley Pub.
Quiet Healing Zone. Herbert L. Beierle. 1980. 10.00 (ISBN 0-940480-10-7). U of Healing.
Quiet Heart, a Quiet Mind. Georgia Hainline. 28p. 1987. 5.95 (ISBN 0-533-07037-6). Vantage.
Quiet Heart: Daily Devotionals for Women. June M. Bacher. LC 87-82261. 368p. (Orig.). 1988. pap. 8.95 (ISBN 0-89081-624-7). Harvest Hse.
Quiet Hour. facsimile ed. Ed. by Fitzroy Carrington. LC 71-160901. (Granger Index Reprint Ser). Repr. of 1915 ed. 17.00 (ISBN 0-8369-6264-8). Ayer Co Pubs.
Quiet Hour. Ed. by FitzRoy Carrington. LC 78-74813. (Granger Poetry Library). (Illus.). 1979. Repr. of 1915 ed. 17.00x (ISBN 0-89609-131-7). Roth Pub Inc.
Quiet Hours in Poets' Corner. Stephen Coleridge. 131p. 1980. Repr. lib. bdg. 27.00. Darby Bks.
Quiet Imperative: Meditations on Justice & Peace Based on Readings from the New Testament. John Carmody. 176p. (Orig.). 1986. pap. 6.95 (ISBN 0-8358-0518-2). Upper Room.
Quiet in the Grave & Other Poems. Gerald Garbarini. 1976. pap. 2.00 (ISBN 0-918466-02-4). Quintessence.
Quiet Is Too Loud. Alexis Satchell. (Illus., Orig.). 1986. pap. 6.95 (ISBN 0-931841-04-6). Satchells Pub.
Quiet Killers, Vol. 1. J. David Truby. (Illus.). 80p. 1972. pap. 8.00 (ISBN 0-87364-014-4). Paladin Pr.
Quiet Killers II: Silencer Update. J. David Truby. (Illus.). 92p. (Orig.). 1979. pap. 8.00 (ISBN 0-87364-163-9). Paladin Pr.
Quiet Land. James A. Warner. (Illus.). 176p. 1988. 24.95 (ISBN 0-912608-58-7); pap. 14.95 (ISBN 0-912608-64-1). Mid Atlantic.
Quiet Light. John Sexton. (Illus.). 128p. 1988. 75.00 (ISBN 0-912383-80-1). Van Der Marck.
Quiet Lives. David Cope. LC 83-172. (Vox Humana Ser.). 1983. 12.95 (ISBN 0-89603-048-2); pap. 4.95 (ISBN 0-89603-049-0). Humana.
Quiet Mind. White Eagle. 1972. 4.50 (ISBN 0-85487-009-1). DeVorss.
Quiet Mind. White Eagle. 96p. 1983. Repr. of 1972 ed. large print 5.95 (ISBN 0-85487-060-1). DeVorss.
Quiet Moment: Devotions for the Golden Years. Jeanette Lockerbie. LC 82-7344. (Illus.). 96p. (Orig.). 1982. pap. 4.95 (ISBN 0-87239-606-1, 3009). Standard Pub.
Quiet Moments for a New Mother. Jennifer B. Owen. (Illus.). 80p. (Orig.). 1987. pap. 3.95 (ISBN 0-936625-12-0). Womans Mission Union.
Quiet Moments for Women: A Daily Devotional. June M. Bacher. LC 79-84722. 1979. pap. 8.95 (ISBN 0-89081-187-3). Harvest Hse.
Quiet Moments Kid's Relaxation: A Guide to the Tape Series for Parents & Teachers. Gary K. Mills. 27p. (Orig.). 1986. pap. 6.00x (ISBN 0-938669-07-9); Set. 20.00xcassettes (ISBN 0-938669-12-5). MediaHlth Pubns.
Quiet Moments Preschoolers. Louise B. Wyly. Ed. by Shirley Wigginton. (Illus.). 128p. (Orig.). (ps-k). 1988. pap. 3.95 (ISBN 0-87403-471-X). Standard Pub.
Quiet Moments Relaxation: A Guide to Deep Relaxation for Adults. Gary K. Mills. LC 86-16464. (Illus.). 72p. (Orig.). 1986. pap. 10.00 (ISBN 0-938669-00-1); cassettes 60.00xincl. (ISBN 0-938669-11-7). MediaHlth Pubns.
Quiet Moments with God. Joseph Murphy. pap. 3.50 (ISBN 0-87516-276-2). DeVorss.
Quiet Moments with Older Children. Jane B. Sorenson. Ed. by Shirley Wigginton. (Illus.). 128p. (Orig.). Date not set. pap. 3.95 (ISBN 0-87403-473-6, 2810). Standard Pub.
Quiet Moments with Young Children. Jane B. Sorenson. Ed. by Shirley Wigginton. Tr. by Diane Johnson. 128p. (Orig.). (gr. 1-3). 1988. pap. 3.95 (ISBN 0-87403-472-8). Standard Pub.
Quiet Neighborhood. George MacDonald. 240p. 1985. pap. 5.95 (ISBN 0-89693-328-8). Victor Bks.
Quiet Neighbors: Prosecuting Nazi War Criminals in America. Allan A. Ryan. LC 84-6540. 400p. 1984. 15.95 (ISBN 0-15-175823-9). HarBraceJ.
Quiet Night. Ann Morris. (Little Read-A-Long Library). (Illus.). 32p. (ps-k). 1987. 3.95 (ISBN 0-671-63367-8, Little Simon). S&S.
Quiet Night: A Play for Christmas. Thomas J. Hatton. 24p. (Orig.). 1980. pap. text ed. 5.25 (ISBN 0-89536-438-7, 1703). CSS of Ohio.
Quiet on Account of Dinosaur. Jane Thayer. (Illus.). (ps-3). 1964. PLB 11.88 (ISBN 0-688-31632-8). Morrow.
Quiet on Account of Dinosaur. Jane Thayer. (Illus.). Date not set. pap. 3.95 (ISBN 0-688-08292-0). Morrow.
Quiet on the Set: Motion Picture History at the Iverson Movie Location Ranch. Robert G. Sherman. Ed. by Dean Davis. LC 83-60720. (Illus.). 150p. (Orig.). 1984. pap. 14.95 (ISBN 0-912641-00-2). Sherway Pub.
Quiet Passages: The Exchange of Civilians Between the United States & Japan During World War II. P. Scott Corbett. LC 87-2069. 242p. 1987. 22.00x (ISBN 0-87338-343-5). Kent St U Pr.
Quiet Past & Stormy Present? War Powers in American History. Harold M. Hyman. LC 87-73602. 67p. 5.00 (ISBN 0-87229-035-2). Am Hist Assn.
Quiet People of the Land: A Story of the North Carolina Moravians in Revolutionary Times. Hunter James. LC 75-44042. (Old Salem Ser). (Illus.). xiv, 156p. 1976. 8.95 (ISBN 0-8078-1282-X). U of NC Pr.
Quiet Places. Sam Bate. 1982. 15.00x (ISBN 0-903653-56-7, Pub. by New Playwrights Network). State Mutual Bk.
Quiet Places, Warm Thoughts. Janette Oke. 112p. 1983. pap. 4.95 (ISBN 0-934998-15-9). Bethel Pub.
Quiet Places with Jesus. Isaias Powers. LC 78-64452. 128p. 1978. pap. 4.95 (ISBN 0-89622-086-9). Twenty-Third.
Quiet Places with Mary. Isaias Powers. LC 86-50123. 160p. (Orig.). 1986. pap. 4.95 (ISBN 0-89622-297-7). Twenty-THird.
Quiet Please. Phil Baron. (Teddy Ruxpin Adventure Ser.). (Illus.). 34p. (ps). 1987. incl. cassettes 9.95 (ISBN 0-934323-40-2). Alchemy Comms.
Quiet, Please. James B. Cabell. 1952. 6.00x (ISBN 0-8130-0040-8). U Presses Fla.
Quiet Please. Richard Flint. 1986. pap. text ed. write for info. (ISBN 0-937851-21-3). Pendelton Lane.
Quiet Please, It's Andy Capp! Reginald Smythe. (Orig.). 1980. pap. 1.50 (ISBN 0-449-14322-8, GM). Fawcett.
Quiet Poems. Gene Fowler. 70p. (Orig.). 1982. pap. 5.00 (ISBN 0-932112-13-7). Carolina Wren.
Quiet Power: Words of Faith, Hope, & Love. Helen L. Marshall. 64p. 1985. pap. 3.95 (ISBN 0-8010-6197-0). Baker Bk.
Quiet Presence. Dyke Hendrickson. pap. 6.95 (ISBN 0-930096-06-1). G Gannett.
Quiet Rage: Bernie Goetz in a Time of Madness. Lillian Rubin. (Orig.). 1988. pap. price not set. U of Cal Pr.
Quiet Rage: Bernie Goetz in a Time of Madness. Lillian B. Rubin. 256p. 1986. 16.95 (ISBN 0-374-24063-9). FS&G.
Quiet Rebel: How to Survive As a Woman & Businessperson. Glynis M. Breakwell. 224p. 1987. Repr. of 1985 ed. 15.95 (ISBN 0-394-55560-0). Grove.
Quiet Rebellion: The Fictional Heroines of Eliza Fowler Haywood. Mary A. Schofield. LC 81-40664. 148p. (Orig.). 1982. pap. text ed. 10.00 (ISBN 0-8191-2151-7). U Pr of Amer.
Quiet Rebels: The Story of the Quakers in America. Margaret H. Bacon. 260p. 1985. lib. bdg. 24.95 (ISBN 0-86571-058-9); pap. 10.95 (ISBN 0-86571-057-0). New Soc Pubs.
Quiet Revolution. Peter Ambrose. 1974. 15.00x (ISBN 0-85621-034-X, Pub. by Scot Acad Pr). Longwood Pub Group.
Quiet Revolution. Sara Harris & Robert F. Allen. LC 77-17645. (Story of a Small Miracle in America Life Ser.). 283p. 2.95 (ISBN 0-451-08367-9). Human Res Inst.
Quiet Revolution: British Sculpture Since 1965. Charles Harrison et al. LC 86-16325. (Illus.). 1987. 35.00 (ISBN 0-500-23480-9). Thames Hudson.
Quiet Revolution: Political Development in the Republic of China. John F. Copper. LC 87-32930. 76p. (Orig.). 1988. lib. bdg. 19.75 (ISBN 0-89633-127-X); pap. text ed. 7.95 (ISBN 0-89633-128-8). Ethics & Public Policy.
Quiet Revolution: Power, Planning, & Profits in New York State. Michael K. Heiman. 337p. 1988. 49.95 (ISBN 0-275-92476-9, C2476). Praeger.
Quiet Revolution: The Electrification of Rural Ireland 1946-1976. Michael Shiel. (Illus.). 320p. 1984. 26.95 (ISBN 0-86278-056-X, Pub. by O'Brien Pr Ireland). Irish Bks Media.
Quiet Revolution: The Struggle for the Democratic Party & the Shaping of Post-Reform Politics. Bryon E. Shafer. LC 83-71445. 628p. 1983. 37.50x (ISBN 0-87154-765-1). Russell Sage.
Quiet Revolution: The United Nations Convention on the Law of the Sea. 61p. (Orig.). 1984. pap. 5.00 (E.83.V.7, +003). UN.
Quiet Revolution: Women in Transition in Rural Bangladesh. Marth A. Chen. 256p. 1983. 24.95 (ISBN 0-87073-452-0); pap. 15.95 (ISBN 0-87073-453-9). Schenkman Bks Inc.
Quiet Riot. (Metal Mania Ser.). (Illus.). 48p. (gr. 4-12). 1984. 6.95 (ISBN 0-88188-298-4, Robus Books). H Leonard Pub Corp.
Quiet Riot (Official) 48p. 1985. 4.95 (ISBN 0-89524-279-6). Cherry Lane.
Quiet Riots: Race & Poverty in the United States. Ed. by Fred Harris & Roger Wilkins. LC 88-42770. 1988. 18.95 (ISBN 0-394-57473-7); 7.95 (ISBN 0-679-72100-2). Pantheon.
Quiet Road to Death. Sheila Radley. (Crime Monthly Ser.). 192p. 1985. pap. 3.95 (ISBN 0-14-007746-4). Penguin.
Quiet Rumors: An Anarcha-Feminist Anthology. Lynne Farrow et al. 72p. (Orig.). Date not set. pap. 4.95 (ISBN 0-939306-46-8). Left Bank.
Quiet Rumors: An Anarcho-Feminist Anthology. P. Kornegger et al. 1984. lib. bdg. 79.95 (ISBN 0-87700-640-7). Revisionist Pr.
Quiet Storm. Helene Storm. LC 81-70299. 210p. 1981. pap. 7.95 (ISBN 0-9607412-0-8). Celebrity Pr.

Quinolines & Its Derivativers, 2 pts, Vol. 32. rev. ed. Gurnos Jones. (Chemistry of Heterocyclic Compounds Monographs Ser.). (Orig.). 1978. (Pub. by Wiley-Interscience); Pt. 2, 685p. 245.00 (ISBN 0-471-28055-0). Wiley.

Quinolones. Ed. by Vincent T. Andriole. 300p. 1988. price not set (ISBN 0-12-059515-X). Acad Pr.

Quinolones - Their Future in Clinical Practice. Ed. by Alan Percival. (International Congress & Symposium Ser.: No. 104). 72p. 1986. pap. 12.00 (ISBN 0-905958-33-0, Pub. by Royal Society of Medicine Services Ltd). Longwood Pub Group.

Quinonediazides. V. V. Ershov & G. A. Nikiforov. (Studies in Organic Chemistry: Vol. 7). 302p. 1981. 108.00 (ISBN 0-444-42008-8). Elsevier.

Quinquennales: An Historical Study. Ralph V. Magoffin. LC 78-63946. (Johns Hopkins University. Studies in the Social Sciences. Thirty-First Ser. 1913: 4). Repr. of 1913 ed. 11.50 (ISBN 0-404-61195-8). AMS Pr.

Quinquennial Cumulative Personal Author Index, 1961-65 see Cumulative Personal Author Indexes for the Monthly Catalog of U. S. Government Publications, 1941-1975.

Quinquennial Cumulative Personal Author Index, 1966-70 see Cumulative Personal Author Indexes for the Monthly Catalog of U. S. Government Publications, 1941-1975.

Quinquennnial Cumulative Personal Author Index, 1971-75 see Cumulative Personal Author Indexes for the Monthly Catalog of U. S. Government Publications, 1941-1975.

Quin's Shanghai Circus. Edward Wittemore. 304p. 1982. pap. 3.50 (ISBN 0-380-61200-3, 61200-3, Bard). Avon.

Quinsai. A. C. Moule. 92p. 1957. pap. 180.00x (ISBN 0-317-69443-X, Pub. by Han-Shan Tang Ltd). State Mutual Bk.

Quint Etudes. Shinichi Suzuki. (Suzuki Violin School Ser.). 48p. (Japanese.). (gr. k-12). 1976. pap. text ed. 7.95 (ISBN 0-87487-095-X, Suzuki Method). Birch Tree Gr.

Quintana & Friends. John G. Dunne. 304p. 1988. pap. 4.50 (ISBN 0-671-66025-X). WSP.

Quintesse. Kevin Kiely. 176p. 1985. 11.95 (ISBN 0-312-66114-2, Pub. by Marek). St Martin.

Quintessence of Bernard Shaw. Henry C. Duffin. LC 75-34135. 1975. Repr. of 1920 ed. lib. bdg. 25.00 (ISBN 0-8414-3748-3). Folcroft.

Quintessence of Capitalism. Werner Sombart. 1967. 45.00x (ISBN 0-86527-162-3). Fertig.

Quintessence of G. B. S. Stephen Winsten. 1949. 30.00 (ISBN 0-8274-3233-X). R West.

Quintessence of Islamic History & Culture. S. P. Gulati. 225p. 1986. 23.00X (ISBN 81-85061-44-0, Pub. by Manohar India). South Asia Bks.

Quintessence of the Animate & Inanimate: A Discourse on the Holy Dharma. Venerable Larma Lodo. Ed. by Nancy Clark & Caroline Parke. LC 85-2290. (Illus.). 238p. 1985. pap. 11.95 (ISBN 0-910165-01-7). KDK Pubns.

Quintessence: The Quality of Having It & How to Know It When You See It. Owen Edwards et al. (Illus.). 1983. pap. 12.95 (ISBN 0-517-55090-3). Crown.

Quintessential Dictionary. I. Moyer Hunsburger. 448p. 1984. pap. 3.95 (ISBN 0-446-32443-4). Warner Bks.

Quintet. Robert Killoren et al. LC 81-670230. 1979. 4.95 (ISBN 0-933532-04-0). BKMK.

Quintet for Piano & Strings in A Minor,(Opus 38) Arthur Foote. LC 82-17251. (Earlier American Music Ser.: No. 26). 108p. 1983. Repr. of 1898 ed. lib. bdg. 27.50. Da Capo.

Quintet for Piano & Strings in F-Sharp Minor, Op. 67. Amy Beach. LC 79-18593. (Women Composers Ser.: No. 1). 1979. Repr. of 1909 ed. lib. bdg. 27.50 (ISBN 0-306-79550-7). Da Capo.

Quintet in a Flat. Basil Ashmore. 1982. 15.00x (ISBN 0-903653-10-9, Pub. by New Playwrights Network). State Mutual Bk.

Quintets for Orchestra: Study Score. Lukas Foss. 60p. (Orig.). 1980. pap. 20.00 (ISBN 0-8258-0065-X, PCB115). Fischer Inc NY.

Quintilian. Ed. by W. Peterson. (Institutionis Oratiae Liber: No. X). 130p. Date not set. pap. 11.00 (ISBN 0-86516-009-0). Bolchazy-Carducci.

Quintilian on the Teaching of Speaking & Writing: Translations from Books One, Two, & Ten of the Institutio Oratoria. Ed. by James J. Murphy. (Landmarks in Rhetoric & Public Address Ser.). 200p. 1987. text ed. 16.95x (ISBN 0-8093-1377-4); pap. text ed. 9.95x (ISBN 0-8093-1378-2). S Ill U Pr.

Quintilian: The Preface to Book VIII & Comparable Passages in the Institutio Oratoria. Frans Ahlheid. 204p. (Orig.). 1983. pap. 32.00x (ISBN 90-6032-240-1, Pub. by B R Gruener Netherlands). Benjamins North Am.

Quint's World. Samuel Fuller. 256p. Date not set. pap. 3.95 (ISBN 0-373-97061-7, Pub. by Worldwide). Harlequin Bks.

Quintuples. Luis R. Sanchez. 100p. (Span.). 1985. pap. 8.00 (ISBN 0-910061-28-9, 1310). Ediciones Norte.

Quintus Sertorius & the Legacy of Sulla. Philip O. Spann. LC 85-28921. 280p. 1987. 22.00 (ISBN 0-938626-64-7). U of Ark Pr.

Quinx, or the Ripper's Tale. Lawrence Durrell. 224p. 1985. 15.95 (ISBN 0-670-80658-7). Viking.

Quinx: Or the Ripper's Tale. Lawrence Durrell. 1986. pap. 5.95 (ISBN 0-14-008059-7). Penguin.

Quinzaine for This Yule. Ezra Pound. 59.95 (ISBN 0-87968-087-3). Gordon Pr.

Quinzaine for This Yule. facsimile ed. Ezra Pound. 32p. 1984. 10.00x (ISBN 0-8139-1045-5). U Pr of Va.

Quinzaine in Return for a Portrait of Mary Sun. Barry Gifford. 1977. pap. 2.50 (ISBN 0-935388-04-4). Workingmans Pr.

Quinze Aventures dans la Jungle. Jules Verne & Rudyard Kipling. 224p. 1976. 7.95 (ISBN 0-686-55943-6). French & Eur.

Quinze Aventures de Mousquetaires. Alexandre Dumas et al. 256p. 1976. 9.95 (ISBN 0-686-55831-6). French & Eur.

Quinze Chasses au Tresor. Alexandre Dumas et al. (Illus.). 224p. 1974. 9.95 (ISBN 0-686-55832-4). French & Eur.

Quinze Contes. Guy De Maupassant. Ed. by F. C. Green. (Fr). 1943. text ed. 8.95 (ISBN 0-521-05693-4). Cambridge U Pr.

Quinze Histoires de Provence. Alphonse Daudet et al. (Illus.). 220p. 1977. 8.95 (ISBN 0-686-55595-3). French & Eur.

Quinze Recits de Noel. Victor Hugo et al. 224p. 1975. 8.95 (ISBN 0-686-54037-9). French & Eur.

Quiotepec Chinantec Grammar. Frank E. Robbins. 150p. 1968. pap. 1.00 (ISBN 0-88312-799-7); microfiche (2) 4.00 (ISBN 0-88312-492-0). Summer Inst Ling.

Quips & Quotes. William E. Darton. 64p. 1986. 6.95 (ISBN 0-8062-2934-9). Carlton.

Quips & Quotes about Fashion. Eleanor Lambert. LC 77-18242. 48p. 1978. pap. 2.95 (ISBN 0-87576-065-1). Pilot Bks.

Quips & Quotes for Church Bulletins. E. C. McKenzie. (Direction Bks). 1978. pap. 3.95 (ISBN 0-8010-6221-7). Baker Bk.

Quips, Quotes & Quests. Vernon K. McLellan. LC 81-85544. 176p. (Orig.). 1982. pap. 3.50 (ISBN 0-89081-310-8). Harvest Hse.

Quips, Quotes & Quiddities. Jacob W. Spatz. 120p. (Orig.). 1987. pap. 6.00 (ISBN 0-938033-09-3). Alert Pubs.

Quirigua: A Classic Maya Center & Its Sculptures. Robert J. Sharer. LC 86-71809. (Centers of Civilization Ser.). (Illus.). 144p. 1988. lib. bdg. 29.75 (ISBN 0-89089-260-1). Carolina Acad Pr.

Quirigua Reports, Vol. I, Papers 1-5. Wendy Ashmore et al. Ed. by Robert J. Sharer & Wendy Ashmore. (University Museum Monographs: No. 37). (Illus.). ix, 73p. (Orig.). 1979. pap. 20.00x (ISBN 0-934718-26-1). Univ Mus of U PA.

Quirigua Reports: Unfolded Drawings of Monument 23 (Altar D) and Monument 24 (Altar P, Vol. II, Papers 6-15. 1983. unbound 10.00 (ISBN 0-318-04192-8). Univ Mus of U PA.

Quirigua Reports: Vol. II, Papers 6-15. Ed. by Edward Schortman & Patricia Urban. (University Museum Monographs: No. 49). (Illus.). 152p. 1983. text ed. 40.00 (ISBN 0-934718-48-2). Univ Mus of U Pa.

Quiroga, a Mexican Municipio. Donald D. Brand. LC 76-44693. Repr. of 1951 ed. 22.50 (ISBN 0-404-15853-6). AMS Pr.

Quiroga: A Mexican Municipio. Donald D. Brand. 1976. lib. bdg. 59.95 (ISBN 0-8490-2494-3). Gordon Pr.

Quiroga: Cuentos de Amor, de Locura y de Muerte. Peter R. Beardsell. (Critical Guides to Spanish Texts Ser.: No. 44). 105p. (Orig.). 1986. pap. 5.50 (ISBN 0-7293-0247-4, Pub. by Grant & Cutler). Longwood Pub Group.

Quislings or Realists: A Documentary Study of "Coloured" Politics in South Africa. Pierre Hugo. 744p. 1978. text ed. 26.95x (ISBN 0-86975-067-4, Pub. by Ravan Pr). Ohio U Pr.

Quisqueya: Panoramic Anthology of Dominican Verse. Ed. by Francis E. Townsend. 1976. lib. bdg. 34.95 (ISBN 0-8490-2495-1). Gordon Pr.

Quit. rev. ed. Charles F. Wetherall. (Illus.). 208p. 1987. pap. 2.95. Running Pr.

Quit & Win: The War of Cigarette Withdrawal Once & for All. Peggy Keigley. 112p. (Orig.). 1987. pap. 7.95 (ISBN 0-942285-00-X). PBK Pubns.

Quit for Life: The Sensational New Program for Smokers. Robert S. Sobel. LC 88-90751. 125p. (Orig.). 1988. pap. write for info. MDTA Pr.

Quit India: American Response to the 1942 Struggle. M. S. Venkataramani. 350p. 1979. 20.95. Asia Bk Corp.

Quit Pulling My Leg! A Story of Davy Crockett. Robert Quackenbush. (Illus.). (gr. 2-6). 1987. 11.95 (ISBN 0-13-749755-5). P-H.

Quit: Read This Book & Stop Smoking. rev. ed. Charles F. Wetherall. 208p. 1988. pap. 2.95 (ISBN 0-89471-672-7). Running Pr.

Quit-Rent System in the American Colonies. Beverley W. Bond. 1919. 11.75 (ISBN 0-8446-1082-8). Peter Smith.

Quit Rents of Virginia, 1704. Annie L. Smith. LC 75-7833. 114p. 1980. pap. 6.50 (ISBN 0-8063-0674-2). Genealog Pub.

Quit Rents of Virginia, 1704. Compiled by Annie L. Smith. 114p. 1987. Repr. of 1957 ed. 7.50 (5440). Genealog Pub.

Quit Smart Leader Manual: Scientific Foundations & Implementation Guidelines. Robert H. Shipley. (Illus.). 140p. 1988. 3-ring notebook 75.00 (ISBN 0-9614881-5-8). J B Pr.

Quit-Smoking Painlessly. George B. Kish. 84p. (Orig.). 1988. lib. bdg. 17.50 (ISBN 0-8191-7064-X); pap. text ed. 7.50 (ISBN 0-8191-7065-8). U Pr of Amer.

Quit Your Job! Jay C. Levinson. 240p. 1987. 16.95 (ISBN 0-396-08882-1, Gamut Bk); pap. 8.95 (ISBN 0-396-09197-0, Gamut Bk). Dodd.

Quite Early One Morning. Dylan Thomas. LC 54-12907. pap. 5.95 (ISBN 0-8112-0208-9, NDP90). New Directions.

Quite the Other Way. Kaylie Jones. 1988. 17.95 (ISBN 0-385-24119-4). Doubleday.

Quito see Monumental Cities.

QuitSmart: A Guide to Freedom from Cigarettes. rev. ed. Robert H. Shipley. LC 86-80034. (Illus.). 96p. 1986. pap. 5.95 (ISBN 0-9614881-3-1); bk. & self-hypnosis cassette 12.95 (ISBN 0-9614881-4-X). J B Pr.

Quitte pour la Peur see Chatterton.

Quitting Smoking: A Psychological Experiment Using Community Research. Richard J. Coelho. LC 84-47787. (American University Studies VIII (Psychology): Vol. 5). 309p. 1985. text ed. 33.50 (ISBN 0-8204-0139-0). P Lang Pubs.

Quiver Full of Arrows. Jeffery Archer. 1987. pap. 3.95 (ISBN 0-671-60408-2). PB.

Quiver of Quizzes for Quidnuncs. Nan Carpenter. 1985. pap. 6.95 (ISBN 0-8158-0420-2). Chris Mass.

Quivira Society Publications, 13 vols. 1967. Repr. Set. 202.00 (ISBN 0-405-00071-5). Ayer Co Pubs.

Quixotes. R. C. Hutchinson. Ed. by Robert Green. 237p. 1984. 14.95 (ISBN 0-85635-515-1). Carcanet.

Quixotic Scriptures: Essays on the Texuality of Hispanic Literature. Elias L. Rivers. LC 82-49300. 176p. 1984. 17.50x (ISBN 0-253-34761-0). Ind U Pr.

Quixotic Vision of Sinclair Lewis. Martin Light. LC 74-82792. 176p. 1975. 6.50 (ISBN 0-911198-40-7). Purdue U Pr.

Quiz Book on Black America. Clarence N. Blake & Donald F. Martin. (Illus.). 224p. (gr. 7 up). 1976. 6.95 (ISBN 0-395-24389-0). HM.

Quiz Book on Black America. Clarence N. Blake & Donald F. Martin. (gr. 7 up). 1976. pap. 3.95 o.s. (ISBN 0-395-24974-0, Sandpiper). HM.

Quiz Bowl Crash Course. Carole Marsh. (gr. 5 up). Date not set. pap. 14.95. Gallopade Pub Group.

Quiz Bowl I. Richard Lahey. (Illus.). 56p. (Orig.). (gr. 4-12). 1982. tchr's manual 5.95 (ISBN 0-88047-012-7, 8216). DOK Pubs.

Quiz Bowl II. Richard Lahey. (Illus.). 56p. (Orig.). (gr. 4-12). 1984. 5.95 (ISBN 0-88047-037-2, 8408). DOK Pubs.

Quiz for Christian Wives. Mae Erickson. 32p. 1976. pap. 0.95 (ISBN 0-930756-20-7, 541003). Aglow Pubns.

Quizzes for Two Hundred & Twenty Great Children's Books. Polly J. Wickstrom. 443p. 1988. 24.50 (ISBN 0-87287-603-9). Libs Unl.

Quizzes for Whizzes: The Ultimate Challenge Quiz Book. Minnie Hickman & Norman Hickman. 1983. pap. 6.45 (ISBN 0-688-02194-8, Quill NY). Morrow.

Quizzes, Tricks, Stunts, Puzzles & Brain Teasers from Tell Me Why. Arkady Leokum. (Illus.). 80p. (gr. 1-7). 1973. 4.95 (ISBN 0-448-11536-0, G&D). Putnam Pub Group.

Quizzical Administration: Employee Benefits Trivia. Irving Baldinger. Ed. by Mary E. Brennan. (Illus.). 38p. (Orig.). 1987. pap. 7.95 (ISBN 0-89154-336-8). Intl Found Employ.

Quizzical Look at the Rock Era. Rick Roeder. Ed. by Diane McLean. (Illus.). 136p. (Orig.). pap. 7.95 (ISBN 0-9619648-0-4). Big Bop Bks.

Quizzical Pursuits: Test Yourself & Discover the Real You. Sherry S. Cohen. 128p. (Orig.). 1985. pap. 4.95 (ISBN 0-671-53070-4, Pub. by Fireside). S&S.

Quizzism & Its Key. Albert P. Southwick. LC 68-22051. 238p. 1970. Repr. of 1884 ed. 35.00x (ISBN 0-8103-3094-6). Gale.

Quliaqtuat Mumiaksrat Ilisaqtuanun Savaaksriat. Edna A. Maclean. (Illus.). iv, 35p. (Orig., Inupiaq Eskimo.). 1986. pap. 4.00 (ISBN 1-55500-027-4). Alaska Native.

Qumran & Corinth. Martin H. Scharlemann. 1962. pap. 5.95x (ISBN 0-8084-0358-3). New Coll U Pr.

Qumran & Corinth. Martin H. Scharlemann. 78p. 1962. write for info. Concordia Schl Grad Studies.

Qumran & the History of the Biblical Text. Ed. by Frank M. Cross & Shemaryahu Talmon. LC 75-12529. 415p. 1975. pap. text ed. 10.95x (ISBN 0-674-74362-8). Harvard U Pr.

Qumran Community. Ed. by Michael A. Knibb. LC 86-24450. (Cambridge Commentaries on Writings of the Jewish & Christian World 200 B.C. to A.D. 200). 260p. 1987. 49.50 (ISBN 0-521-24247-9); pap. 16.95 (ISBN 0-521-28552-6). Cambridge U Pr.

Qumran Community: Its History & Scrolls. Charles T. Fritsch. 1973. Repr. of 1956 ed. 20.00 (ISBN 0-8196-0279-5). Biblo.

Qumran Grotte Four, No. III. Ed. by Maurice Baillet. (Discoveries in the Judean Desert Ser.: Vol. 7). (Illus.). 1982. 140.00x (ISBN 0-19-826321-X). Oxford U Pr.

Qumran Origins of the Christian Church. B. E. Thiering. (Austrailian & New Zealand Studies in Theology & Religion). (Illus.). 314p. 1983. 29.95 (ISBN 0-85821-308-7, Pub. by Theol Explor); pap. 16.95 (ISBN 0-318-23173-5, Pub. by Theol Explor). ANZ Religious Pubns.

Qumran Text of Samuel & Josephus. Eugene C. Ulrich, Jr. LC 78-15254. (Harvard Semitic Museum. Harvard Semitic Monographs: No. 19). 1983. 15.00 (ISBN 0-89130-256-5, 040019). Scholars Pr GA.

Quo, Musa, Tendis? Robert Dunn. (Illus.). 64p. (Orig.). 1983. pap. 4.95 (ISBN 0-914339-02-8). P E Randall Pub.

Quo Vadimus? or, the Case for the Bicycle. facsimile ed. Elwyn B. White. LC 74-167438. (Essay Index Reprint Ser). Repr. of 1939 ed. 17.00 (ISBN 0-8369-2678-1). Ayer Co Pubs.

Quo Vadis. Hendryk Sienkiewicz. Repr. lib. bdg. 28.95 (ISBN 0-89190-484-0, Pub. by River City Pr). Amereon Ltd.

Quo Vadis. Henryk Sienkiewicz. (Airmont Classics Ser.). (gr. 10 up). 1968. pap. 2.50 (ISBN 0-8049-0188-0, CL-188). Airmont.

Quo Vadis? A Just Censure of Travell As It Is Commonly Undertaken by the Gentlemen of Our Nation. Joseph Hall. LC 74-28860. (English Experience Ser.: No. 740). 1975. Repr. of 1617 ed. 25.00 (ISBN 90-221-0165-7). Walter J Johnson.

Quo Vadis, Africa? Letters from Ghana Prison, 1972. Kwame Safo-Adu. 1985. 7.95 (ISBN 0-533-05941-0). Vantage.

Quo Vadis, America? Phil E. Gafford. LC 76-57068. 112p. 1977. 6.95 (ISBN 0-918354-01-3). Huntleigh.

Quoat-Quoat. Jacques Audiberti. 9.95 (ISBN 0-686-54501-X). French & Eur.

Quodlibet. John P. Kennedy. LC 75-104502. 350p. Repr. of 1840 ed. lib. bdg. 29.00 (ISBN 0-8398-1052-0). Irvington.

Quodlibet. John P. Kennedy. 350p. 1986. pap. text ed. 6.95x (ISBN 0-8290-1919-7). Irvington.

Quodlibeta. Hadrianus. 180p. text ed. 49.68x (ISBN 0-576-99427-8, Pub. by Gregg Intl Pubs England). Gregg Intl.

Quonset Huts on the River Styx: The Bomb Shelter Design Book. Architects, Designers, & Planners for Social Responsibility (ADPSR) (Illus.). 72p. 1987. 30.00 (ISBN 1-55643-028-0); pap. 12.95 (ISBN 1-55643-027-2). North Atlantic.

Quoof. Paul Muldoon. LC 83-50028. 64p. 1983. pap. 4.95 (ISBN 0-916390-19-5). Wake Forest.

Quota ou les Plethoriens. Vercors. 300p. 1966. 8.95 (ISBN 0-686-55135-4). French & Eur.

Quotable Bresee. Compiled by Harold I. Smith. 224p. (Orig.). 1983. pap. 5.95 (ISBN 0-8341-0835-6). Beacon Hill.

Quotable Chesterton. Ed. by G. Marlin et al. LC 86-80788. 391p. 1986. 24.95 (ISBN 0-89870-102-3); pap. 16.95 (ISBN 0-89870-122-8). Ignatius Pr.

Quotable Chesterton: A Topical Compilation of the Wit, Wisdom & Satire of G. K. Chesterton. George J. Martin et al. LC 87-8878. 409p. 1987. pap. 9.95 (ISBN 0-385-23925-4, Im). Doubleday.

Quotable Lawyer. Ed. by David S. Shrager & Elizabeth Frost. LC 85-10380. 384p. 1986. 27.95x (ISBN 0-8160-1184-2). Facts On File.

Quotable Mario Cuomo. Bill Adler, Jr. 1988. 15.95 (ISBN 0-688-08190-8). Morrow.

Quotable Poems: An Anthology of Modern Verse. Thomas C. Clark & Esther A. Gillespie. 1979. Repr. of 1928 ed. lib. bdg. 20.00 (ISBN 0-8495-0781-2). Arden Lib.

Quotable Quotations. Compiled by Lloyd Cory. 400p. 1985. pap. 12.95 (ISBN 0-88207-823-2). Victor Bks.

Quotable Quotes of Benjamin E. Mays. Benjamin E. Mays. LC 82-91028. 20p. 1983. 10.00 (ISBN 0-533-05685-3). Vantage.

Quotable Shakespeare: A Topical Dictionary. Charles DeLoach. LC 87-46384. 568p. 1988. lib. bdg. 39.95x (ISBN 0-89950-303-9). McFarland & Co.

Quotable Teddy Bear. (Illus.). 96p. (gr. 1-12). 1988. 6.98 (ISBN 0-89471-609-3, Pub. by Courage Bks.). Running Pr.

Quotable Woman: Eve to 1799. Elaine Partnow. LC 82-15511. 550p. 1986. 29.95 (ISBN 0-87196-307-8); pap. 14.95 (ISBN 0-8160-1385-3). Facts on File.

Quotable Woman: 1800-1981. Elaine Partnow. LC 82-2350. 608p. 1983. 29.95x (ISBN 0-87196-580-1). Facts on File.

Quotas & Affirmative Action. Ed. by Lester A. Sobel et al. LC 79-26722. pap. 49.80 (ISBN 0-317-26064-2, 2025160). Bks Demand UMI.

Quotation Marks & Underlining. Sheldon Tilkin. (Horizons II Ser.). (Illus.). 24p. (gr. 3-4). 1980. 2.50 (ISBN 0-89403-594-0). EDC.

Quotations & References in Charles Dickens. James S. Stevens. LC 73-17241. 1973. lib. bdg. 17.00 (ISBN 0-8414-7705-1). Folcroft.

Quotations for All Occasions. Katherine B. Wood. 1973. Repr. of 1896 ed. 30.00 (ISBN 0-8274-0554-5). R West.

R. H. Hutton, Critic & Theologian: The Writings of R. H. Hutton on Newman, Arnold, Tennyson, Wordsworth & George Eliot. Ed. by Malcom Woodfield. 240p. 48.00x (ISBN 0-19-818564-2). Oxford U Pr.

R. H. Jahns Memorial Issue: The Mineralogy, Petrology & Geochemistry of Granitic Pegmatites & Related Granitic Rocks. Ed. by G. E. Brown, Jr. & R. C. Ewing. 424p. 1986. 20.00. Mineralogical Soc.

R. H. Stetson's Phonetics: A Retrospective Edition. J. A. Kelso & K. G. Munhall. (Illus.). 248p. 1988. text ed. 35.00 (ISBN 0-316-48702-3, 487023). College-Hill.

R. H. Tawney. Anthony Wright. (Lives of the Left Ser.). 192p. 1988. 29.00 (ISBN 0-7190-1998-2, Pub. by Manchester Univ Pr); pap. 8.75 (ISBN 0-7190-1999-0). St Martin.

R. H. Tawney & His Times: Socialism As Fellowship. Ross Terrill. LC 72-188350. 1973. 18.50x (ISBN 0-674-74376-8); pap. 8.95x (ISBN 0-674-74377-6). Harvard U Pr.

R. Holmes & Co. Being the Remarkable Adventure of Raffles Holmes. John K. Bangs. LC 78-91073. (American Humorists Ser.). Repr. of 1906 ed. lib. bdg. 44.50 (ISBN 0-8398-0151-3). Irvington.

R. I. M., the Rebel Robot. Nora Logan. (Pick A Path Bks.: No. 14). (Illus.). 64p. (gr. 3-6). 1984. pap. 1.95 (ISBN 0-590-33289-9). Scholastic Inc.

R. I., the Most Pleasant History of Tom A. Lincolne. Richard Johnson. Ed. by Richard S. Hirsch. (Renaissance English Text Society Ser.: Vol. 7-8). 121p. 1978. 7.50 (ISBN 0-911028-21-8). Newberry.

R Is for Rocket. Ray Bradbury. (gr. 9-12). 1969. pap. 3.50 (ISBN 0-553-25040-X). Bantam.

R. J. Reynolds Tobacco Company. Nannie M. Tilley. LC 84-20811. (Illus.). xxi, 706p. 1985. 37.50x (ISBN 0-8078-1642-6). U of NC Pr.

R K F D V: German Resettlement & Population Policy, 1939-1945: A History of the Reich Commission for the Strengthening of Germandom. Robert Koehl. LC 57-8625. (Historical Monographs Ser: No. 31). 1957. 17.50x (ISBN 0-674-77326-8). Harvard U Pr.

R. K. Narayan. P. S. Sundaram. (Indian Writers Ser.). 1973. 8.50 (ISBN 0-89253-510-5). Ind-US Inc.

R. K. Narayan: A Critical Appreciation. William Walsh. LC 82-40320. (Illus.). 192p. 1983. lib. bdg. 12.50x (ISBN 0-226-87213-0). U of Chicago Pr.

R. L. S. Francis Watt. 1973. Repr. of 1913 ed. 20.00 (ISBN 0-8274-0437-9). R West.

R. L. S. Francis Watt. 311p. 1983. lib. bdg. 40.00 (ISBN 0-89987-886-5). Darby Bks.

R. L. S. & His Sina Qua Non. Adelaide A. Boodle. 1926. Repr. 25.00 (ISBN 0-8274-3286-0). R West.

R. L. Stevenson. Janet A. Smith. 1937. lib. bdg. 17.00 (ISBN 0-8414-7856-2). Folcroft.

R. L. Stevenson & the Bridge of Alan. J. A. Macculloch. 1973. Repr. of 1927 ed. 20.00 (ISBN 0-8274-1026-3). R West.

R. L. Stevenson: Poet in Paradise. Maxine Mrantz. LC 87-123117. (Hawaiiana Ser.). (Illus.). 30p. (Orig.). 1977. pap. 2.25 (ISBN 0-941351-07-6). Aloha Pub.

R-Linear Endomorphisms of R(n) Preserving Invariants. Bernard R. McDonald. LC 83-15648. (Memoirs Ser.: No. 287). 68p. 1983. pap. 12.00 (ISBN 0-8218-2287-X). Am Math.

R. M. Fischer. Nina Felshin. (Illus.). 1981. 4.00. Contemp Arts.

R. M. Fischer. Elisabeth Kirsch & Susan Feagin. Ed. by Craig Subler. (Illus.). 13p. (Orig.). 1984. pap. 5.00 (ISBN 0-914489-02-X). Univ Miss KS Art.

R. M. Rilke: Aspects of His Mind & Poetry. William Rose et al. Ed. by G. C. Houston. LC 72-6484. (Studies in German Literature, No. 13). (Illus.). 190p. 1972. Repr. of 1938 ed. lib. bdg. 39.95x (ISBN 0-8383-1617-4). Haskell.

R. M. S. Titanic. Anthony Cronin. (Raven Long Poems Ser.). 1981. 8.95 (ISBN 0-906897-31-9). Dufour.

R. M. Schindler: Architect Eighteen Eighty-Seven to Nineteen Fifty-Three. August Sarnitz. LC 88-42693. (Illus.). 216p. 1988. 35.00 (ISBN 0-8478-0921-8). Rizzoli Intl.

R. Madison Mitchell: His Life & Decoys. Charles L. Robbins. (Illus.). 1988. 24.95 (ISBN 0-9620028-0-1). C L Robbins.

R. Murray Schafer. Stephen Adams. (Canadian Composers Ser.: No. 4). 256p. 1983. 30.00x (ISBN 0-8020-5571-0). U of Toronto Pr.

R. N. Sharon Webb. (Orig.). 1982. pap. 2.95 (ISBN 0-89083-915-8). Zebra.

R. P. Blackmur, Poet-Critic: Toward a View of Poetic Objects. Robert Boyers. LC 80-15414. (Literary Frontiers Editions). 96p. 1980. pap. text ed. 7.95x (ISBN 0-8262-0315-9). U of Mo Pr.

R. P. Vondel & Milton. Jehangir Mody. LC 76-29704. 1942. lib. bdg. 39.50 (ISBN 0-8414-6127-9). Folcroft.

R Reinforcement Contracts. Marilyn J. Click & Jerrie K. Ueberle. 1981. text ed. 6.95x (ISBN 0-8134-2198-5). Inter Print Pubs.

R. S. Crane: An Annotated Bibliography. John C. Sherwood. LC 82-48277. 100p. 1983. lib. bdg. 43.00 (ISBN 0-8240-9250-3). Garland Pub.

R. S. S. Myth & Reality. Dina N. Mishra. 240p. 1980. text ed. 17.50x (ISBN 0-7069-1020-6, Pub. by Vikas India). Advent NY.

R. S. Thomas: Poet of the Hidden God. D. Z. Phillips. LC 85-31998. (Princeton Theologographical Monograph Ser.: No. 2). 192p. (Orig.). 1986. pap. 18.00 (ISBN 0-915138-83-2). Pickwick.

R. S. Thomas: Selected Prose. R. S. Thomas. Ed. by Sandra Anstey. LC 84-71579. 187p. 1984. (Pub. by Poetry Wales Pr UK); pap. 18.95. Dufour.

R. S. V. P. Junior League of Orange County, California, Incorporated. 1982. 14.95 (ISBN 0-9608306-0-X). Jun League NH.

R. Tait McKenzie: The Sculptor of Athletes. Andrew J. Kozar. LC 74-34421. (Illus.). 140p. 1975. 16.50x (ISBN 0-87049-168-7). U of Tenn Pr.

R-Ticulation. Mary Zellmer. (Illus.). 1986. 12.00 (ISBN 0-930599-23-3). Thinking Pubns.

R. U. R. Josef Capek & Karel Capek. Bd. with Insect Play. 1961. pap. 6.95x (ISBN 0-19-281010-3). Oxford U Pr.

R. V. H. Manual on Palliative-Hospice Care: A Resource Book. Ed. by Ina Ajemian & Balfour M. Mount. pap. 34.00 (ISBN 0-405-13934-9). Ayer Co Pubs.

R-V Pillsbury Deep-Sea Biological Expedition to the Gulf of Guinea, 1964-1965. Incl. Part 1. 1966. 5.50x (ISBN 0-87024-085-4); Part 2. 1970. 7.95x (ISBN 0-87024-190-7). (Studies in Tropical Oceanography Ser: No. 4). U Miami Marine.

R. V. W. A Biography of Ralph Vaughan Williams. Ursula Vaughan Williams. (Illus.). 1964. 37.50x (ISBN 0-19-315411-0). Oxford U Pr.

R. V. W. A Biography of Ralph Vaughan Williams. Ursula V. Williams. (Illus.). 480p. 1988. pap. 15.95 (ISBN 0-19-282082-6). Oxford U Pr.

R. W. Emerson, Tourist. Lois Rather. (Illus.). 1979. ltd ed. 25.00 (ISBN 0-686-26147-X). Rather Pr.

R. W. Seton-Watson & the Yugoslavs: Correspondence 1906-1941, 2 vols. G. H. Seton-Watson et al. 468p. 1979. 90.00x. State Mutual Bk.

R. W. Seton-Watson & the Yugoslavs, Correspondence 1906-1941, 2 vols. R. W. Seton-Watson. 1976. Set. 40.00 (Pub. by British Acad). Vol. I, 474 pgs. Vol. II, 468 pgs. Longwood Pub Group.

RA Material: An Ancient Astronaut Speaks. Don Elkins et al. Ed. by Hank Stine. LC 82-12967. (Illus.). 234p. (Orig.). 1984. pap. 6.95 (ISBN 0-89865-260-X). Donning Co.

Rab & Dab. Elizabeth A. Pringle. LC 84-24887. (South Caroliniana Ser.: No. 9). 112p. 1985. Repr. of 1984 ed. 17.50 (ISBN 0-87152-405-8). Reprint.

Rab & Dab. Elizabeth A. Pringle. Ed. & intro. by Anne Blythe. 1985. ltd. ed. 27.50. Seajay Society.

Rab & His Friends. John Brown. LC 72-5910. (Short Story Index Reprint Ser.). 1972. Repr. of 1906 ed. 19.00 (ISBN 0-8369-4193-4). Ayer Co Pubs.

Rab & His Friends & Other Papers. John Brown. 1970. 14.95x (ISBN 0-460-00116-7, Evman); pap. 2.95x (ISBN 0-460-01116-2, Evman). Biblio Dist.

Rab Saadia Gaon: Studies in His Honor. Ed. by Louis Finkelstein & Steven Katz. LC 79-7169. (Jewish Philosophy, Mysticism & History of Ideas Ser.). 1980. Repr. of 1944 ed. lib. bdg. 19.00x (ISBN 0-405-12250-0). Ayer Co Pubs.

Rabad of Posquieres: A Twelfth-Century Talmudist. Isadore Twersky. LC 62-7192. (Semitic Ser: No. 18). 1962. 22.50x (ISBN 0-674-74550-7). Harvard U Pr.

Rabat: Urban Apartheid in Morocco. Janet L. Abu-Lughod. LC 80-7508. (Princeton Studies on the Near East). (Illus.). 400p. 1981. 50.00x (ISBN 0-691-05315-4); pap. 18.50x (ISBN 0-691-10098-5). Princeton U Pr.

Rabban Gamaliel II: The Legal Traditions. Shamai Kanter. LC 80-12229. (Brown Judaic Studies: No. 8). 1980. 15.00x (ISBN 0-89130-403-7, 14 00 08); pap. 10.50x (ISBN 0-89130-404-5). Scholars Pr GA.

Rabbi. Noah Gordon. 408p. 1987. pap. 4.95 (ISBN 0-449-21454-0, Crest). Fawcett.

Rabbi & Minister: The Friendship of Stephen S. Wise & John Haynes Holmes. Carl H. Voss. LC 80-7453. (Library of Liberal Religion). 384p. 1980. pap. 13.95 (ISBN 0-87975-130-4). Prometheus Bks.

Rabbi & the Priest. Y. B. Arrarat. 224p. 1988. 12.95 (ISBN 0-944070-02-7). Targum Pr.

Rabbi & the Priest. Y. B. Arrarat. 1988. 12.95. Feldheim.

Rabbi Eizik: Hasidic Stories about the Zaddik of Kallo. Ed. & tr. by Andrew Handler. LC 75-5245. 195p. 1976. 16.50 (ISBN 0-8386-1739-5). Fairleigh Dickinson.

Rabbi Emil G. Hirsch: The Reform Advocate. David E. Hirsch. LC 68-24717. 1968. pap. 3.00x (ISBN 0-87655-502-4). Collage Inc.

Rabbi from Burbank. Isidor Zwirn & Bob Owen. 128p. pap. 4.95 (ISBN 0-8423-5120-5). Tyndale.

Rabbi Is a Lady. Alex J. Goldman. 288p. 1987. 14.95 (ISBN 0-87052-306-6). Hippocrene Bks.

Rabbi Isaac Jacob Reines: His Life & Thought. Joseph Wanefsky. LC 79-118314. 181p. 1970. 6.95 (ISBN 0-8022-2349-4). Philos Lib.

Rabbi Jonah of Gerona. cancelled (ISBN 0-686-76524-9). Feldheim.

Rabbi Joseph H. Lookstein Memorial Volume. Leo Landman. 1979. 35.00x (ISBN 0-87068-705-0). Ktav.

Rabbi Letters, No. 1. Lillian M. Rossini. (Illus.). 32p. 1986. 5.95 (ISBN 0-89962-506-1). Todd & Honeywell.

Rabbi Levine Challenges Father Treacy: Examine Your Jewish Roots. Levine & William Treacy. Ed. by Martha Ireland. 168p. (Orig.). 1987. pap. 11.95 (ISBN 0-910303-09-6). Writers Pub Serv.

Rabbi Moses Nahmanides: Explorations in His Religious & Literary Virtuosity. Ed. by Isadore Twersky. (Center for Jewish Studies Ser.). 110p. (Orig.). 1983. pap. text ed. 9.50x (ISBN 0-674-74560-4). Harvard U Pr.

Rabbi Must Be Married. Harry T. Zankel. 1986. 11.95 (ISBN 0-533-06865-7). Vantage.

Rabbi Nachman De Breslov. Rabbi Nachman of Breslov & Rabbi Nathan of Breslov. Ed. by Alon Dimermanas. (Illus.). 442p. 1986. pap. 15.00 (ISBN 0-930213-20-3). Breslov Res Inst.

Rabbi Nachman's Stories. Nachman of Breslov. Tr. by Aryeh Kaplan from Hebrew. LC 83-70201. 552p. 1983. 15.00 (ISBN 0-930213-02-5). Breslov Res Inst.

Rabbi Nachman's Stories: Skazocnniji Histori Rabbi Nechman iz Bratzlav. Nachman of Breslov. Tr. by Baruch Avni from Hebrew & Rus. (Illus.). 332p. (Orig.). 1987. pap. 10.00 (ISBN 0-930213-29-7). Breslov Res Inst.

Rabbi Nachman's Tikkun: The Comprehensive Remedy. Nachman of Breslov. Tr. by Avraham Greenbaum from Hebrew. 240p. 1984. 10.00 (ISBN 0-930213-06-8). Breslov Res Inst.

Rabbi Nachman's Wisdom. Nachman of Breslov. Ed. by Zvi A. Rosenfeld. Tr. by Aryeh Kaplan from Hebrew. (Illus.). 510p. 1984. 14.00 (ISBN 0-930213-00-9); pap. 11.00 (ISBN 0-930213-01-7). Breslov Res Inst.

Rabbi of Casino Boulevard. Allan Appel. 320p. 1986. 16.95 (ISBN 0-312-66127-4). St Martin.

Rabbi of Lud. Stanley Elkin. 222p. 1987. 17.95 (ISBN 0-684-18902-X). Scribner.

Rabbi of Lud. Stanley Elkin. 256p. 1988. pap. 8.95 (ISBN 0-684-19013-3). Scribner.

Rabbi Tarfon: The Tradition, the Man & Early Rabbinic Judaism. Joel Gereboff. LC 78-15220. (Brown Judaic Studies: No. 7). 1979. 16.50 (ISBN 0-89130-257-3, 140007); pap. 12.00 (ISBN 0-89130-258-1). Scholars Pr GA.

Rabbi Yisroel Baal Shem Tov. Moshe Prager. (Illus., Hebrew.). 1.75 (ISBN 0-914131-51-6, D50). Torah Umesorah.

Rabbinic Anthology. Ed. by C. G. Montefiore & H. Loewe. LC 73-91340. 1970. pap. 16.95 (ISBN 0-8052-0442-3). Schocken.

Rabbinic Authority. Elliot Stevens. 1982. 15.00x (ISBN 0-916694-88-7). Ktav.

Rabbinic Authority. Ed. by Elliot L. Stevens. 184p. 1982. 15.00 (ISBN 0-317-01466-8). Central Conf.

Rabbinic Commentary on the New Testament: The Gospels of Matthew, Mark & Luke. Samuel T. Lachs. 600p. 1987. 39.50 (ISBN 0-88125-089-9); pap. 19.95 (ISBN 0-88125-115-1). Ktav.

Rabbinic Essays. Jacob Z. Lauterbach. LC 52-18170. pap. 146.50 (ISBN 0-317-42031-3, 2025693). Bks Demand UMI.

Rabbinic Mind. 3rd ed. Max Kadushin. LC 75-189016. 1972. 15.00 (ISBN 0-8197-0007-X). Bloch.

Rabbinic Psychology. W. Hirsch. LC 73-2208. (Jewish People; History, Religion, Literature Ser.). Repr. of 1947 ed. 24.50 (ISBN 0-405-05272-3). Ayer Co Pubs.

Rabbinic Responsa of the Holocaust Era. Ed. by Robert S. Kirschner. LC 84-23509. 204p. 1985. 17.95 (ISBN 0-8052-3978-2). Schocken.

Rabbinical Assembly Mahzor. 12.00 (ISBN 0-686-96025-4). United Syn Bk.

Rabbinical Mathematics & Astronomy. rev. ed. W. M. Feldman. LC 78-60816. (Judaic Studies Library: No. SHP4). 1978. pap. text ed. 10.95 (ISBN 0-87203-026-1). Hermon.

Rabbinical Seminary of Budapest, 1877-1977: A Centennial Volume. Ed. by Moshe Carmilly-Weinberger. (Illus.). 420p. 1986. 35.00 (ISBN 0-87203-148-9). Hermon.

Rabbinischen Gleichnisse und der Gleichniserzaehler Jesus. David Flusser. (Judaica et Christiana: Vol. 4). 322p. (Ger.). 1981. 31.60 (ISBN 3-261-04778-X). P Lang Pubs.

Rabbis & Wives. Chaim Grade. LC 82-14. 1982. 15.45 (ISBN 0-394-50979-X). Knopf.

Rabbis & Wives. Chaim Grade. LC 83-5855. 320p. 1983. pap. 5.95 (ISBN 0-394-71647-7, Vin). Random.

Rabbis & Wives. Chaim Grade. Tr. by Harold Rabinowitz & Inna H. Grade. LC 87-9745. 320p. (Orig.). 1987. pap. 8.95 (ISBN 0-8052-0840-2). Schocken.

Rabbis' Bible, Vol. 1: Torah. Solomon Simon & Morrison D. Bial. (gr. 5-6). 6.95 (ISBN 0-317-70149-5); tchr's guide 12.50 (ISBN 0-317-70150-9); tchr's resource bk. 14.95 (ISBN 0-317-70151-7); student activity bk. 2.95 (ISBN 0-317-70152-5). Behrman.

Rabbis' Bible, Vol. 2: Early Prophets. Solomon Simon & Morrison D. Bial. (gr. 6-7). 6.95 (ISBN 0-317-70153-3); tchr's guide 12.50 (ISBN 0-317-70154-1); tchr's resource bk. 14.95 (ISBN 0-317-70155-X). Behrman.

Rabbis' Bible, Vol. 3: Later Prophets. Solomon Simon & Abraham Rothberg. (YA) (gr. 7-8). 6.95 (ISBN 0-317-70159-2); tchr's guide 12.50 (ISBN 0-317-70160-6); tchr's resource bk. 14.95 (ISBN 0-317-70161-4). Behrman.

Rabbi's Blessing. 1982. 7.50 (ISBN 0-686-76249-5). Feldheim.

Rabbi's Girls. Johanna Hurwitz. LC 82-2102. (Illus.). 192p. (gr. 4-6). 1982. 10.95 (ISBN 0-688-01089-X). Morrow.

Rabbi's Rovings. Israel Mowshowitz. 385p. 1985. 20.00 (ISBN 0-88125-069-4). Ktav.

Rabbit. John Burningham. LC 75-4566. (Illus.). (ps-1). 1975. (Crowell Jr Bks); PLB 11.89 (ISBN 0-690-00907-0). HarpJ.

Rabbit. Nadine Saunier. (Animal Companions Ser.). (Illus.). 20p. (ps). 1988. 5.95 (ISBN 0-8120-5932-8). Barron.

Rabbit: A Model for the Principles of Mammalian Physiology & Surgery. Harold M. Kaplan & Edward H. Timmons. LC 78-67878. 1979. 35.00 (ISBN 0-12-397450-X). Acad Pr.

Rabbit & Skunk & the Scary Rock. Carla Stevens. (Illus.). (gr. k-3). 1970. pap. 1.50 (ISBN 0-590-00111-6). Scholastic Inc.

Rabbit & the Turnip. Addison-Wesley Staff. (ESL Ser.). (Illus.). 16p. (gr. k-2). 1988. pap. text ed. 31.75 (ISBN 0-201-19326-4). Addison-Wesley.

Rabbit Christmas. Thomas J. Hatton. (Orig.). 1982. pap. 3.95 (ISBN 0-937172-40-5). JLJ Pubs.

Rabbit Dissection Manual. Bruce D. Wingerd. LC 84-15761. 80p. 1985. 9.95x (ISBN 0-8018-2470-2). Johns Hopkins.

Rabbit Ears. Robert Montgomery. 160p. 1985. pap. 2.50 (ISBN 0-451-13631-4, Sig Vista). NAL.

Rabbit Ears. Alfred Slote. LC 81-47760. (Trophy Bks.). 128p. (gr. 4-7). 1983. pap. 3.50 (ISBN 0-06-440134-0, Trophy). HarpJ.

Rabbit Express. Michel Gay. LC 84-29608. (Illus.). 40p. (ps-3). 1985. 11.75 (ISBN 0-688-04647-9, Morrow Junior Books); lib. bdg. 11.88 (ISBN 0-688-04648-7). Morrow.

Rabbit Feeding & Nutrition. Peter R. Cheeke. (Animal Feeding & Nutrition Ser.). 376p. 1987. 45.00 (ISBN 0-12-170605-2). Acad Pr.

Rabbit Finds a Way. Judy Delton. (Illus.). 32p. (ps-3). 1986. pap. 2.95 (ISBN 0-517-55948-X). Crown.

Rabbit Goes to Night School. Judy Delton. Ed. by Kathleen Tucker. LC 86-15998. (Illus.). 32p. (gr. k-2). 1986. PLB 10.50 (ISBN 0-8075-6725-6). A Whitman.

Rabbit Hill. Robert Lawson. (Illus.). (gr. 1-3). 1977. pap. 3.95 (ISBN 0-14-031010-X, Puffin). Penguin.

Rabbit Hill. Robert Lawson. (Illus.). (gr. 4-6). 1944. lib. bdg. 12.95 (ISBN 0-670-58675-7). Viking.

Rabbit Hunting. Charles Fergus et al. LC 85-72451. 1985. pap. 7.95 (ISBN 0-910042-50-0). Allegheny.

Rabbit: Husbandry, Health & Production. F. Lebas et al. (Animal Health & Production Ser.: No. 21). (Illus.). 235p. (Orig.). 1987. pap. text ed. 33.75 (ISBN 92-5-101253-9, F3017, FAO). UNIPUB.

Rabbit in Contemporary Immunological Research. Ed. by Stanislaw Dubiski. (Monographs & Surveys in the Biosciences). 206p. 1988. 89.95 (ISBN 0-470-20948-8). Wiley.

Rabbit in Eye Research. photocopy ed. Jack H. Prince. (Illus.). 672p. 1964. 73.50 (ISBN 0-398-01525-2). C C Thomas.

Rabbit in the Fields. Jennifer Coldrey. LC 85-30298. (Animal Habitats Ser.). (Illus.). 32p. (gr. 4-6). 1987. 9.95 (ISBN 1-55532-061-9). Stevens Inc.

Rabbit in the Moon: Haiku. Raymond Roesliep. LC 83-6445. (Illus.). 128p. 1983. 12.00 (ISBN 0-934184-15-1); pap. 6.00 (ISBN 0-934184-16-X). Alembic Pr.

Rabbit Is Rich. John Updike. 448p. 1982. pap. 3.95 (ISBN 0-449-24548-9, Crest). Fawcett.

Rabbit Is Rich. John Updike. LC 81-1287. 480p. 1981. ltd. ed. o.p. 40.00 (ISBN 0-394-52047-5); 14.45 (ISBN 0-394-52087-4). Knopf.

Rabbit Island. Jorg Steiner. Tr. by Ann C. Lammers. (Illus.). 30p. (ps-3). 9.95 (ISBN 0-930267-00-1). Bergh Pub.

Rabbit Keeping. Gay Nightingale. (Illus.). 95p. 1984. pap. 3.95 (ISBN 0-7028-1099-1). Avian Pubns.

Rabbit Pie. Gerald Rose. 32p. (ps-5). 1986. pap. 4.95 (ISBN 0-571-13930-2). Faber & Faber.

Rabbit Production. Cheeke et al. 472p. 1987. 19.95 (ISBN 0-8134-2580-8); text ed. 14.95x (ISBN 0-317-61482-7). Inter Print Pubs.

Rabbit Raising. (Illus.). 32p. (gr. 6-12). 1974. pap. 1.25x (ISBN 0-8395-3375-6, 3375). BSA.

Rabbit Raising. Paul Sawin. (Illus.). 83p. pap. 2.00 (ISBN 0-936622-18-0). A R Harding Pub.

Rabbit Redux. John Updike. 352p. 1985. pap. 3.95 (ISBN 0-449-20934-2, Crest). Fawcett.

Rabbit Redux. John Updike. 1971. 14.95 (ISBN 0-394-47273-X). Knopf.

Rabbit Run. John Updike. 1983. pap. 3.95 (ISBN 0-449-20506-1, Crest). Fawcett.

Rabbit Run. John Updike. 1960. 15.45 (ISBN 0-394-44206-7). Knopf.

Rabbit Seeds. Bijou Le Tord. LC 84-28736. (Illus.). (gr. 4-5). 1984. 10.95 (ISBN 0-02-756420-7, Four Winds). Macmillan.

Rabbit Spring. Tilde Michaels. LC 87-18107. (Illus.). 96p. (gr. 7-11). 1988. 10.95 (ISBN 0-15-200568-4, Gulliver Bks). HarBraceJ.

Race & Ethnicity in Modern America. Richard Meister. (Problems in American History Ser.). 1975. pap. 7.50 (ISBN 0-669-91124-0). Heath.

Race & Family in the Colonial South. Ed. by Winthrop D. Jordan & Sheila L. Skemp. LC 87-23157. (Chancellor's Symposium Ser.). 1987. 27.50x (ISBN 0-87805-333-6); pap. 9.95x (ISBN 0-87805-334-4). U Pr of Miss.

Race & Gender: Equal Opportunities Policies in Education. Ed. by M. Arnot. 154p. 1985. text ed. 18.25 (ISBN 0-08-032675-7, M110, M115, M125, Pub. by PPL); pap. text ed. 9.00 (ISBN 0-08-032674-9). Pergamon.

Race & Health Policy. Allan McNaught. 160p. 1988. lib. bdg. 35.00x (ISBN 0-7099-4673-2, Pub. by Croom Helm UK). Routledge Chapman & Hall.

Race & Inequality: A Study in American Values. Paul M. Sniderman & Michael G. Hagen. LC 85-24247. (Chatham House Series on Change in American Politics). (Illus.). 176p. 1985. pap. text ed. 11.95x (ISBN 0-934540-24-1). Chatham Hse Pubs.

Race & Intelligence. Ed. by Melvin M. Tumin. write for info. ADL.

Race & Kinship in a Midwestern Town: The Black Experience in Monroe Michigan, 1900-1915. James E. DeVries. LC 83-6508. (Blacks in the New World Ser.). (Illus.). 206p. 1984. 19.95 (ISBN 0-252-01084-1). U of Ill Pr.

Race & Labour in Twentieth-Century Britain. Ed. by Kenneth Lunn. 192p. 1986. 29.50x (ISBN 0-7146-3238-4, F Cass Co); pap. 14.95x (F Cass Co). Biblio Dist.

Race & Law in Great Britain. Anthony Lester & Geoffrey Bindman. LC 73-189159. 1972. 29.50x (ISBN 0-674-74570-1). Harvard U Pr.

Race & Manifest Destiny: The Origins of American Racial Anglo-Saxonism. Reginald Horsman. LC 81-4293. 352p. 1981. text ed. 27.00x (ISBN 0-674-74572-8). Harvard U Pr.

Race & Manifest Destiny: The Origins of American Racial Anglo-Saxonism. Reginald Horsman. 384p. 1986. pap. text ed. 10.95. Harvard U Pr.

Race & Modern Science. Robert E. Kuttner. 1986. 11.00 (ISBN 0-317-53271-5). Noontide.

Race & Nationalism in Trinidad & Tobago: A Study of Decolonization in Multiracial Society. Selwyn D. Ryan. LC 70-185735. pap. 131.30 (ISBN 0-317-55731-9, 2029348). Bks Demand UMI.

Race & Nationalism: The Struggle for Power in Rhodesia-Nyasaland. Thomas M. Franck. LC 73-11853. 369p. 1973. Repr. of 1960 ed. lib. bdg. 35.00x (ISBN 0-8371-7074-5, FRRN). Greenwood.

Race & Nationalism: The Struggle for Power in Rhodesia-Nyasaland. Thomas M. Franck. 1960. 10.00 (ISBN 0-685-99549-6). Univ Place.

Race & Party Competition in Britain. Anthony M. Messina. (Illus.). 192p. 1989. 44.00 (ISBN 0-19-827534-X). Oxford U Pr.

Race & Place: A Legal History of the Neighborhood School. Meyer Weinberg. 1968. pap. 3.60 (ISBN 0-912008-06-7). Equity & Excel.

Race & Political Strategy. Ed. by Thomas E. Cavanagh. LC 83-22189. 60p. (Orig.). 1983. pap. 4.95 (ISBN 0-941410-33-1). Jt Ctr Pol Studies.

Race & Politics. Muhammad Anwar. 256p. 1986. 29.95 (ISBN 0-422-79840-1, 9913, Pub. by Tavistock England). Routledge Chapman & Hall.

Race & Politics. Ed. by Elizabeth Burgoyne. (Reference Shelf Ser.: Vol. 56, No. 6). 174p. pap. text ed. 10.00 (ISBN 0-8242-0700-9). Wilson.

Race & Politics: "Bleeding Kansas" & the Coming of the Civil War. James A. Rawley. LC 79-14856. (Illus.). xvi, 304p. 1979. 25.95x (ISBN 0-8032-3854-1); pap. 6.95x (ISBN 0-8032-8901-4, BB 714, Bison). U of Nebr Pr.

Race & Politics in Fiji. Robert Norton. LC 77-78122. (Illus.). 1978. 26.00x (ISBN 0-312-66138-X). St Martin.

Race & Politics in North Carolina, 1872-1901: The Black Second. Eric Anderson. LC 80-16342. xiii, 379p. 1981. 40.00x (ISBN 0-8071-0685-2); pap. 15.95x (ISBN 0-8071-0784-0). La State U Pr.

Race & Politics in South Africa. Ed. by Ian Robertson & Phillip Whitten. LC 76-50334. 274p. 1978. text ed. 24.95 (ISBN 0-87855-137-9). Transaction Bks.

Race & Politics in the Bahamas. Colin A. Hughes. 1981. 26.00x (ISBN 0-312-66136-3). St Martin.

Race & Politics in Urban Malaya. Alvin Rabushka. LC 72-91040. (Studies: No. 35). 150p. 1973. 7.95x (ISBN 0-8179-3351-4). Hoover Inst Pr.

Race & Race Relations. Jessica Kuper. (Today's World Ser.). (Illus.). 72p. (gr. 7-12). 1984. 17.95 (ISBN 0-7134-1985-7, Pub. by Batsford England). David & Charles.

Race & Racism: Essays in Social Geography. Ed. by Peter Jackson. 320p. 1987. text ed. 45.00x (ISBN 0-04-305002-6). Unwin Hyman.

Race & Rally Car Sourcebook. rev ed. Allan Staniforth. LC 86-80433. (Illus.). 204p. 1987. 24.95 (ISBN 0-85429-572-0, F572, Pub. by G T Foulis Ltd). Haynes Pubns.

Race & Rapprochement. Stuart Anderson. LC 79-24185. 240p. 1981. 23.50 (ISBN 0-8386-3001-4). Fairleigh Dickinson.

Race & Reality. Carleton Putnam. LC 67-19407. 192p. 1980. pap. 5.00 (ISBN 0-914576-14-3). Howard Allen.

Race & Reason. Carleton Putnam. LC 61-8447. 125p. 1977. pap. 5.00 (ISBN 0-914576-08-9). Howard Allen.

Race & Region. Ed. by E. T. Thompson & Alma M. Thompson. Repr. of 1949 ed. 23.00 (ISBN 0-527-89750-7). Kraus Repr.

Race & Residence: An Analysis of Property Values in Transitional Areas, Atlanta, Georgia, 1960-1971. Howard Openshaw. LC 74-620726. (Research Monograph: No. 53). 1973. spiral bdg. 15.95 (ISBN 0-88406-019-5). Ga St U Busn Pub.

Race & Residence in American Cities. Ed. by Wade C. Roof & Ralph B. Ginsberg. LC 78-72993. (Annals: No. 441). 1979. 15.00 (ISBN 0-87761-236-6). Am Acad Pol Soc Sci.

Race & Schooling in the City. Adam Yarmolinsky et al. LC 80-20424. 304p. 1981. text ed. 20.00x (ISBN 0-674-74577-9). Harvard U Pr.

Race & Sex Effects in the Conformity Behavior of Children. Gordon N. Cantor. (Augustana College Library Occasional Paper Ser.: No. 14). 16p. 1978. pap. 1.00x (ISBN 0-910182-37-X). Augustana Coll.

Race & Slavery in the Western Hemisphere. Stanley L. Engerman & Eugene D. Genovese. LC 74-2965. (Quantitative Studies in History Ser). 472p. 1974. 54.00x (ISBN 0-691-04625-5); 19.50x (ISBN 0-691-10024-1). Princeton U Pr.

Race & State in Capitalist Development: Studies on South Africa, Alabama, Northern Ireland, & Israel. Stanley B. Greenberg. LC 79-22324. (Illus.). 416p. 1980. text ed. 70.00x (ISBN 0-300-02444-4); pap. 16.95x (ISBN 0-300-02527-0). Yale U Pr.

Race & the South: Two Studies, 1914-1922, 2 bks. Lily H. Hammond. Incl. In Black & White; In the Vanguard of a Race. LC 72-38448. (Religion in America, Ser. 2). 486p. 1972. Repr. of 1972 ed. 32.00 (ISBN 0-405-04067-9). Ayer Co Pubs.

Race & You. Alain Corcos. 1986. spiral bdg. 7.00 (ISBN 0-88252-131-4). Paladin Hse.

Race Around the World. David Gantz. (My Modern World of Words Ser.). 48p. (ps-2). 1987. 8.95 (ISBN 0-516-08308-2). Childrens.

Race as News. 174p. (Orig.). 1976. pap. 5.00 (ISBN 92-3-101191-X, U508, UNESCO). UNIPUB.

Race Car Engineering & Mechanics. 2nd ed. Paul Van Valkenburgh. (Illus.). 176p. 1986. pap. 18.95 (ISBN 0-9617425-0-X). Van Valkenburgh.

Race Car Woman. Laurie Simons. 1977. pap. 1.50 (ISBN 0-8439-0445-3, LB445, Leisure Bks). Leisure NY.

Race Cars. Norman Barrett. (Picture Library). (Illus.). 32p. (gr. k-3). 1987. PLB 9.90 (ISBN 0-531-10275-0). Watts.

Race Cars. Illus. by Tony Roberts. (Fast Rolling Race Cars Ser.). (Illus.). (ps-2). 1987. 3.95 (ISBN 0-448-09887-3, G&D). Putnam Pub Group.

Race: Challenge to Religion. National Conference on Religion & Race. Ed. by Mathew Ahmann. LC 78-24276. 1979. Repr. of 1963 ed. lib. bdg. 35.00x (ISBN 0-313-20796-8, NCRA). Greenwood.

Race, Change & Urban Society. Ed. by Peter Orleans & William R. Ellis, Jr. LC 70-127992. (Urban Affairs Annual Reviews Ser.: Vol. 5). pap. 160.00 (ISBN 0-317-08723-1, 2021939). Bks Demand UMI.

Race, Class & Conservatism. Thomas D. Boston. 1988. 34.95 (ISBN 0-04-330368-4); pap. 11.95 (ISBN 0-04-330369-2). Unwin Hyman.

Race, Class & Education. Ed. by Len Barton & Stephen Walker. 235p. 1983. pap. 13.95 (ISBN 0-7099-0684-6, Pub. by Croom Helm Ltd). Routledge Chapman & Hall.

Race, Class, & Party: A History of Negro Suffrage & White Politics in the South. Paul Lewinson. LC 63-15168. (Illus.). 1963. Repr. of 1932 ed. 21.00x (ISBN 0-8462-0366-9). Russell.

Race, Class & Political Activism. D. G. Pearson. 216p. 1980. text ed. 34.25x (ISBN 0-566-00353-8). Gower Pub Co.

Race, Class & Political Consciousness. John Leggett. 243p. 1972. text ed. 18.95x (ISBN 0-87073-256-0). Schenkman Bks Inc.

Race, Class & Political Symbols: Rastafari & Reggae in Jamaican Politics. Anita M. Waters. 224p. 1985. 34.95 (ISBN 0-88738-024-7). Transaction Bks.

Race, Class, & Politics: Essays on American Colonial & Revolutionary Society. Gary B. Nash. 400p. 1986. pap. 15.95 (ISBN 0-252-01313-1). U of Ill Pr.

Race, Class, & Power in Brazil. Ed. by Pierre-Michel Fontaine. LC 85-19543. (CAAS Special Publication Ser.: Vol. 7). (Illus.). xi, 160p. (Orig.). 1986. text ed. 19.95 (ISBN 0-934934-22-3); pap. text ed. 11.95 (ISBN 0-934934-23-1). UCLA CAAS.

Race, Class & State Housing: Inequality & the Allocation of Public Housing in Britain. Valerie Karn & Jeff Henderson. (Centre for Urban & Regional Studies: Vol. 3). 354p. 1987. text ed. 39.95 (ISBN 0-566-00785-1, Gower Pub UK). Gower Pub Co.

Race, Class & the Apartheid State. H. Wolpe. (Apartheid & Society Ser.). 118p. 1988. pap. 13.00 (ISBN 92-3-102510-4, U1653, UNESCO). UNIPUB.

Race, Class, & the World System: The Sociology of Oliver C. Cox. Ed. by Herbert H. Hunter & Sameer Abraham. 384p. 1986. 28.00 (ISBN 0-85345-683-6); pap. 12.00 (ISBN 0-85345-684-4). Monthly Rev.

Race, Color, & the Young Child. John E. Williams & J. Kenneth Morland. LC 76-812. xiv, 360p. 1976. 30.00x (ISBN 0-8078-1261-7). U of NC Pr.

Race, Conflict & the International Order: From Empire to United Nations. Hugh Tinker. LC 77-79017. (Making of the 20th Century Ser.). (Illus.). 1977. 22.50x (ISBN 0-312-66130-4). St Martin.

Race Conflict in New Zealand, 1814-1865. Harold G. Miller. LC 81-20183. (Illus.). xxvii, 328p. 1982. Repr. of 1966 ed. lib. bdg. 35.00x (ISBN 0-313-23443-4, MIRC). Greenwood.

Race Crossing in Jamaica. Charles B. Davenport. LC 77-106833. 1970. Repr. of 1929 ed. 35.00x (ISBN 0-8371-3455-2, DRC&). Greenwood.

Race, Culture, & Evolution: Essays in the History of Anthropology. George W. Stocking, Jr. LC 81-23154. (Phoenix Ser.). xviii, 380p. 1982. pap. 12.00x (ISBN 0-226-77494-5). U of Chicago Pr.

Race, Culture, & Mental Disorder. Philip Rack. 300p. 1982. 33.00 (ISBN 0-422-78160-6, NO. 3801, Tavistock). Routledge Chapman & Hall.

Race, Culture & Portuguese Colonialism in Cabo Verde. Deirdre Meintel. (Foreign & Comparative Studies Program African Ser.: No. 41). (Orig.). 1984. pap. text ed. 12.50x (ISBN 0-915984-66-0). Syracuse U Foreign Comp.

Race Culture: Or Race Suicide? A Plea for the Unborn. Robert R. Rentoul. Ed. by Charles Rosenberg. LC 83-48556. (History of Hereditarian Thought Ser.). 182p. 1985. lib. bdg. 25.00 (ISBN 0-8240-5826-7). Garland Pub.

Race Decadence: An Examination of the Causes of Racial Degeneration in the United States. William S. Sadler. 75.00 (ISBN 0-87968-343-0). Gordon Pr.

Race des Hommes: Avec: L'Empire et la Trappe. Jacques Audiberti. 224p. 1968. 9.95 (ISBN 0-686-54502-8). French & Eur.

Race Differences. Otto Klineberg. LC 74-5777. 367p. 1974. Repr. of 1935 ed. lib. bdg. 35.00x (ISBN 0-8371-7519-4, KLRD). Greenwood.

Race: Discipleship for the Long Run. John White. LC 84-6695. 216p. 1984. pap. 6.95 (ISBN 0-87784-976-5). Inter-Varsity.

Race Distinctions in American Law. G. T. Stephenson. 1977. lib. bdg. 69.95 (ISBN 0-8490-2496-X). Gordon Pr.

Race Distinctions in American Law. Gilbert T. Stephenson. LC 70-99889. Repr. of 1910 ed. 16.00 (ISBN 0-404-00215-3). AMS Pr.

Race Distinctions in American Law. facs. ed. Gilbert T. Stephenson. LC 71-89445. (Black Heritage Library Collection Ser). 1910. 14.75 (ISBN 0-8369-8656-3). Ayer Co Pubs.

Race Distinctions in American Law. Gilbert T. Stephenson. LC 10-21327. (Basic Afro-American Reprint Library). 20.00 (ISBN 0-384-58030-0). Johnson Repr.

Race Down the Mountain. As told by Mary C. Olsen. (Step Ahead Beginning Readers Ser.). (Illus.). 32p. (gr. 4-8). 1987. pap. write for info. (ISBN 0-307-03675-8, Pub. by Golden Bks). Western Pub.

Race Drivers' Wives: Twenty-Four Women Talk about Their Lives. Jean S. Berry & John R. Berry. LC 82-70755. (Illus.). 181p. (Orig.). 1982. pap. 4.95 (ISBN 0-942556-00-3). Berry Pub.

Race, Economics, & Corporate America. John W. Work. LC 84-1233. 324p. 1984. lib. bdg. 35.00 (ISBN 0-8420-2217-1). Scholarly Res Inc.

Race Elements in the White Population of North Carolina. R. D. Connor. Ed. by W. C. Jackson. LC 73-149343. 115p. 1971. Repr. of 1920 ed. 15.00 (ISBN 0-87152-062-1). Reprint.

Race, Ethnicity, & Class in American Social Thought, 1865-1919. Glenn C. Altschuler. LC 81-173970. (American History Ser.). 168p. (Orig.). 1982. pap. text ed. 7.95x (ISBN 0-88295-808-9). Harlan Davidson.

Race, Ethnicity, & Minority Housing in the United States. Ed. by Jamshid A. Momeni. LC 86-9971. (Contributions in Ethnic Studies: No. 16). (Illus.). 249p. 1986. lib. bdg. 36.95 (ISBN 0-313-24848-6, MRY/). Greenwood.

Race, Ethnicity & Power: A Comparative Study. Ed. by Donald G. Baker. 224p. 1983. 24.95x (ISBN 0-7100-9467-1). Routledge Chapman & Hall.

Race, Ethnicity & Socioeconomic Status: A Theoretical Analysis of Their Interrelationship. Charles V. Willie. LC 83-80157. 279p. (Orig.). 1983. lib. bdg. 26.95X (ISBN 0-930390-48-2); pap. text ed. 11.95x (ISBN 0-930390-47-4). Gen Hall.

Race First: The Ideological & Organizational Struggles of Marcus Garvey & the Universal Negro Improvement Association. Tony Martin. (New Marcus Garvey Library: No. 8). (Illus.). x, 421p. (Orig.). 1986. text ed. 29.95 (ISBN 0-912469-22-6); pap. text ed. 10.95 (ISBN 0-912469-23-4). Majority Pr.

Race, Folk, Individuality & Mankind. Albert Steffen. Tr. by Arvia MacKaye. 30p. 1982. pap. 3.50 (ISBN 0-932776-04-3). Adonis Pr.

Race for Life: The Joel Sonnenberg Story. Janet Sonnenberg. 1983. 9.95x (ISBN 0-310-25930-4). Phoenix Soc.

Race for Modernization: Britain & Germany Since the Industrial Revolution. Ed. by Adolf Birke & Lothar Kettenacker. (Prince Albert Studies: Vol. 6). 1988. 42.00 (ISBN 3-598-21406-5). K G Saur.

Race for Resources: Continuing Struggles over Minerals & Fuels. Michael Tanzer. LC 80-18027. 285p. 1981. pap. 6.50 (ISBN 0-85345-541-4). Monthly Rev.

Race for Revenge. Lynsey Stevens. (Harlequin Romances Ser.). 192p. 1982. pap. 1.50 (ISBN 0-373-02495-9). Harlequin Bks.

Race for Security: Arms & Arms Control in the Reagan Years. Ed. by Robert T. Scott. LC 84-48507. 320p. 1986. 39.00x (ISBN 0-669-09552-4); pap. text ed. 16.95x (ISBN 0-669-09553-2). Lexington Bks.

Race for the Eighth: The Making of a Congressional Campaign: Joe Kennedy's Successful Pursuit of a Political Legacy. Gerald Sullivan & Michael Kenney. LC 87-45079. 288p. 1987. 19.95 (ISBN 0-06-015816-6, HarpT). Har-Row.

Race for the Moon. Robin Kerrod. LC 79-2347. (Lerner Question & Answer Bks.). (Illus.). (gr. 3-6). 1980. PLB 8.95 (ISBN 0-8225-1183-5). Lerner Pubns.

Race for the Presidency: The Media & the Nominating Process. Ed. by James D. Barber. LC 78-111878. (Guides). (Illus.). 1978. 11.95 (ISBN 0-13-750141-2); pap. 4.95 (ISBN 0-13-750133-1). Am Assembly.

Race for the Presidency: Winning the 1988 Nomination. Rhodes Cook. 121p. 1987. pap. 12.95 (ISBN 0-87187-444-X). Congr Quarterly.

Race for the Rhine. Alexander McKee. (World at War Ser.: No. 12). 1979. pap. 2.50 (ISBN 0-89083-460-1). Zebra.

Race for the Twenty-First Century. Tim LaHaye. LC 86-19339. 256p. 1986. pap. 7.95 (ISBN 0-8407-7757-4). Nelson.

Race for Your Life, Charlie Brown. Charles M. Schulz. LC 77-15208. (Illus.). 1978. 12.95 (ISBN 0-03-042646-4). H Holt & Co.

Race Forever. Montgomery. (Choose Your Own Adventure Ser.: No. 17). (ps-7). 1987. pap. 2.25 (ISBN 0-553-25988-1). Bantam.

Race Forever. Raymond A. Montgomery. (Choose Your Own Adventure Ser.). 116p. (gr. 2-7). 1987. Repr. of 1983 ed. 8.95 (ISBN 0-942545-12-5); lib. bdg. 9.95 (ISBN 0-942545-17-6). Grey Castle.

Race, Government & Politics in Britain. Ed. by Zig Layton-Henry & Paul B. Rich. 224p. 1986. text ed. 39.50x (ISBN 0-333-39349-X, Pub. by Macmillan London); pap. text ed. 19.50x (ISBN 0-333-39350-3). Sheridan.

Race Horse. Bob Buess. 1978. pap. 2.50 (ISBN 0-934244-08-1). Sweeter Than Honey.

Race Hygiene & National Efficiency: The Eugenics of Wilhelm Schallmayer. Sheila F. Weiss. LC 86-24895. (Illus.). 244p. 1987. 37.50x (ISBN 0-520-05823-2). U of Cal Pr.

Race, I. Q. & Jensen. James R. Flynn. 320p. 1980. 29.95x (ISBN 0-7100-0651-9). Routledge Chapman & Hall.

Race in Britain: Continuity & Change. Ed. by Charles Husband. (Illus.). 320p. 1984. pap. 11.95 (ISBN 0-09-146911-2, Pub. by Hutchinson Educ). Longwood Pub Group.

Race into the Past. Megan Stine & H. William Stine. (Twistaplot Ser.). (Illus.). 96p. (Orig.). (gr. 7 up). 1984. pap. 1.95 (ISBN 0-590-32868-9). Scholastic Inc.

Race, Language, & Culture. Franz Boas. xx, 648p. 1988. pap. 23.95x (ISBN 0-226-06242-2, Midway Reprint). U of Chicago Pr.

Race Life of the Aryan Peoples, 2 vols. Joseph P. Widney. Repr. of 1907 ed. lib. bdg. 65.00 set. (ISBN 0-8495-5908-1). Arden Lib.

Race, Migration & Schooling. J. Tierney et al. 202p. 1982. pap. 13.00x (ISBN 0-03-910362-5, Pub. by Cassell UK). Taylor & Francis.

Race Mixing in Public Schools. Charles V. Willie & Jerome Beker. LC 73-10947. (Special Studies in U. S. Economic, Social & Political Issues). 1973. 29.50x (ISBN 0-275-28812-9). Irvington.

Race Mixture. Harry L. Shapiro. (Race Question in Modern Science). 58p. (Orig., 3rd Printing 1965). 1953. pap. 5.00 (ISBN 92-3-100416-6, U509, UNESCO). UNIPUB.

Race Mixture: Studies in Intermarriage & Miscegenation. Edward B. Reuter. (Basic Afro-American Reprint Library Ser). 1970. Repr. of 1931 ed. 14.00 (ISBN 0-384-50340-3). Johnson Repr.

Race, Nation, Person: Total Aspects of the Race Problem. facs. ed. LC 70-128291. (Essay Index Reprint Ser). 1944. 25.50 (ISBN 0-8369-2019-8). Ayer Co Pubs.

Race Navigation. S. Quarrie. 1982. 15.00 (ISBN 0-540-07408-X). Heinman.

Race of Flitty Hummingbird & Flappy Crane. Margaret Z. Searcy. (Illus.). (gr. 2-4). 1980. 7.50 (ISBN 0-916620-21-2). Portals Pr.

Race of the Radical. Fanny Howe. LC 86-30274. 144p. (gr. 3-7). 1987. pap. 3.95 (ISBN 0-14-031870-4, Puffin Bks). Penguin.

Race of the Radicals. Fanny Howe. LC 85-40445. (Viking Kestrel Novels). 150p. (gr. 5-8). 1985. 11.95 (ISBN 0-670-80557-2, Viking Kestrel). Viking.

Race on the Edge of Time: How Radar Helped Win World War II. D. E. Fisher. 400p. 1988. text ed. 19.95 (ISBN 0-07-021088-8). McGraw.

Race or Mongrel. Alfred P. Schultz. 1977. lib. bdg. 69.95 (ISBN 0-8490-2497-8). Gordon Pr.

Race or Mongrel: History of the Rise & Fall of the Ancient Races of Earth. Alfred P. Schultz. Ed. by Gerald Grob. LC 76-46103. (Anti-Movements in America). 1977. Repr. of 1908 ed. lib. bdg. 29.00x (ISBN 0-405-09974-6). Ayer Co Pubs.

Race or Nation: Conflict of Divided Loyalties. Gino Speranza. LC 74-17955. (Italian American Experience Ser). 284p. 1975. Repr. 21.00x (ISBN 0-405-06424-1). Ayer Co Pubs.

Race Orthodoxy in the South & Other Aspects of the Negro Question. Thomas P. Bailey. Repr. of 1914 ed. 15.00 (ISBN 0-404-00136-X). AMS Pr.

Race, Peace, Law & Southern Africa. Howard J. Taubenfeld & Rita Taubenfeld. Ed. by J. Carey. LC 67-25906. (Hammarskjold Forum Ser.: No. 10). 211p. 1968. Repr. 12.50 (ISBN 0-379-11810-6). Oceana.

Race, Politics & Culture: Critical Essays on the Radicalism of the 1960s. Ed. by Adolph Reed, Jr. LC 85-27162. (Contributions in Afro-American & African Studies: No. 95). 304p. 1985. 36.95 (ISBN 0-313-24480-4, RRA/). Greenwood.

Race, Poverty & the Cities: Hyperinnovation in Complex Policy Systems. Madeline Landau. LC 88-1298. 73p. (Orig.). 1988. pap. 6.95 (ISBN 0-87772-316-8). UCB IGS.

Race, Power & Resistance. Chris Mullard. 256p. 1985. 39.95x (ISBN 0-7100-9774-3). Routledge Chapman & Hall.

Race, Power, & Social Segmentation in Colonial Society: Plantation Guyana After Slavery 1838-1891. Brian L. Moore. (Carribbean Studies: Vol. 4). 315p. 1987. text ed. 38.00 (ISBN 0-677-21980-6). Gordon & Breach.

Race Prejudice. facs. ed. Jean Finot. Tr. by Florence Wade-Evans. LC 72-89413. (Black Heritage Library Collection Ser). 1906. 16.00 (ISBN 0-8369-8570-2). Ayer Co Pubs.

Race, Prejudice & the Origins of Slavery in America. Ed. by Raymond Starr & Robert Detweiler. 165p. 1975. pap. text ed. 9.95 (ISBN 0-87073-665-5). Schenkman Bks Inc.

Race Prejudice: How It Began, When Will It End. George Breitman. pap. 0.35 (ISBN 0-87348-256-5). Path Pr NY.

Race Problem in the South. facs. ed. Joseph Le Conte. LC 78-81123. (Black Heritage Library Collection Ser). 1892. 9.00 (ISBN 0-8369-8619-9). Ayer Co Pubs.

Race Questions, Provincialism, & Other American Problems. facs. ed. Josiah Royce. LC 67-23266. (Essay Index Reprint Ser). 1908. 18.00 (ISBN 0-8369-0842-2). Ayer Co Pubs.

Race, Racism, & American Law. 2nd ed. Derrick A. Bell, Jr. 1980. text ed. 31.00 (ISBN 0-316-08821-8). Little.

Race, Radicalism, & Reform: Selected Papers of Abram L. Harris. Abram L. Harris. 500p. 1988. 49.95 (ISBN 0-88738-210-X). Transaction Bks.

Race, Reform & Rebellion: The Second Reconstruction in Black America, 1945-1982. Manning Marable. LC 84-7436. 256p. 1984. pap. 9.95 (ISBN 0-87805-225-9). U Pr of Miss.

Race Relations. 3rd ed. Harry H. Kitano. LC 84-11598. (Illus.). 320p. 1985. text ed. write for info. (ISBN 0-13-750167-6). P-H.

Race Relations. Ed. by J. Masuoka & P. Valien. (New Reprints in Essay & General Literature Index Ser.). 1975. Repr. of 1961 ed. 22.75 (ISBN 0-518-10205-X, 10205). Ayer Co Pubs.

Race Relations & American Law. Jack Greenberg. LC 59-11179. 481p. 1959. 40.00x (ISBN 0-231-02313-8). Columbia U Pr.

Race Relations & American Law. Jack Greenberg. LC 59-11179. pap. 123.30 (ISBN 0-317-26579-2, 2023967). Bks Demand UMI.

Race Relations & Cultural Differences. Ed. by Gajendra K. Verma. LC 83-43000. 290p. 1984. 27.50 (ISBN 0-312-66140-1). St Martin.

Race Relations & the Law in American History. Ed. by Kermit L. Hall. (United States Constitutional & Legal History Ser.). 662p. 1987. lib. bdg. 75.00 (ISBN 0-8240-0136-2). Garland Pub.

Race Relations at the Cape of Good Hope, 1652-1795: A Select Bibliography. P. L. Scholtz. 1981. lib. bdg. 34.50 (ISBN 0-8161-8500-X, Hall Reference). G K Hall.

Race Relations: Elements & Social Dynamics. Oliver C. Cox. LC 75-38572. pap. 88.50 (ISBN 0-317-30024-5, 2025022). Bks Demand UMI.

Race Relations in British North America, 1607-1783. Bruce Glasrud & Alan Smith. LC 81-18824. 368p. 1982. 24.95x (ISBN 0-88229-388-5). Nelson-Hall.

Race Relations in Colonial Queensland: A History of Exclusion, Exploitation & Extermination. Raymond Evans et al. (Illus.). 460p. (Orig.). 1988. pap. text ed. 19.95x (ISBN 0-7022-2099-X). U of Queensland Pr.

Race Relations in Colonial Trinidad 1870-1900. Bridget Brereton. LC 78-72081. (Illus.). 1980. 52.50 (ISBN 0-521-22428-4). Cambridge U Pr.

Race Relations in Malaysia. Wan Hashim. xvii, 127p. 1983. pap. text ed. 8.50x (ISBN 967-925-003-2, 00158). Heinemann Ed.

Race Relations in Sociological Theory. John Rex. 180p. (Orig.). 1983. pap. 11.95x (ISBN 0-7100-9299-7). Routledge Chapman & Hall.

Race Relations in South Africa, Nineteen Twenty-Nine to Nineteen Seventy-Nine. Ed. by Ellen Hellmann & Henry Lever. LC 80-7473. 278p. 1980. 27.50 (ISBN 0-312-66142-8). St Martin.

Race Relations in the Portuguese Colonial Empire 1415-1825. Charles R. Boxer. LC 85-740. vii, 136p. 1985. Repr. of 1963 ed. lib. bdg. 38.50x (ISBN 0-313-24733-1, BORR). Greenwood.

Race Relations in the United States: Material Published 1980-1984. Mary Vance. (Public Administration Ser.: P 1702). 27p. 1985. 3.75 (ISBN 0-89028-452-0). Vance Biblios.

Race Relations in the Urban South, 1865-1890. Howard N. Rabinowitz. LC 79-28674. (Blacks in the New World Ser.). 461p. 1980. pap. 10.95 (ISBN 0-252-00811-1). U of Ill Pr.

Race Relations in Virginia & Miscegenation in the South: 1776-1860. James H. Johnston. LC 78-87833. 376p. 1970. 25.00x (ISBN 0-87023-050-6). U of Mass Pr.

Race Relations in Wartime Detroit: The Soujourner Truth Housing Controversy, 1937-1942. Dominic J. Capeci, Jr. 328p. 1984. lib. bdg. 37.95 (ISBN 0-87722-339-4). Temple U Pr.

Race Relations Magazine: A Monthly Summary & Events & Trends, 5 vols. 1970. Repr. of 1948 ed. Vol. 1. 28.00 (ISBN 0-8371-1254-0, RA1&); Vol. 2. 28.00 (ISBN 0-8371-1255-9, RA2&); Vol. 3. 28.00 (ISBN 0-8371-1256-7, RA3&); Vol. 4. 28.00 (ISBN 0-8371-1257-5, RA4&); Vol. 5. 28.00 (ISBN 0-8371-1258-3, RA5&). Greenwood.

Race Relations Rights. Paul Gordon et al. 1982. 20.00x (ISBN 0-946088-02-0, Pub. by NCCL UK). State Mutual Bk.

Race, Religion, & the Continuing American Dilemma. C. Eric Lincoln. 304p. 1984. 17.95 (ISBN 0-8090-8016-8). Hill & Wang.

Race, Religion, & the Continuing American Dilemma. C. Eric Lincoln. (American Century Ser.). 304p. 1985. pap. 7.95 (ISBN 0-8090-0163-2); 17.95. Hill & Wang.

Race, Religion, & the Promotion of the American Executive. Reed M. Powell. 1970. 9.50 (ISBN 0-87776-303-8, AA3). Ohio St U Admin Sci.

Race, Research, & Reason: Social Work Perspectives: Report. Institute on Research Toward Improving Race Relations (1967: Warrenton, VA) Ed. by Roger R. Miller. LC 68-59483. pap. 47.50 (ISBN 0-317-55746-7, 2029277). Bks Demand UMI.

Race Riot: A First Hand Observation of the 1943 Detroit Riots. Alfred M. Lee & Norman D. Humphrey. 1967. lib. bdg. 19.00x (ISBN 0-374-94883-6, Octagon). Hippocrene Bks.

Race Riot at East St. Louis July 2, 1917. Elliott M. Rudwick. LC 82-1940. (Black in the New World Ser.). 320p. 1982. pap. 9.95 (ISBN 0-252-00951-7). U of Ill Pr.

Race Riot: Chicago in the Red Summer of 1919. William M. Tuttle, Jr. LC 71-130983. (Illus.). 1970. 8.95 (ISBN 0-689-10372-7); pap. text ed. 6.95x (ISBN 0-689-70287-6, NL30). Atheneum.

Race Rock. Peter Matthiessen. LC 87-40096. 320p. 1988. pap. 8.95 (ISBN 0-394-74538-8, Vin). Random.

Race, Rock & Religion: Profiles from a Southern Journalist. Frye Gaillard. LC 82-11325. (Illus.). 192p. 1982. 12.95 (ISBN 0-914788-59-0). Globe Pequot.

Race: Science & Politics. Ruth Benedict. 206p. 1982. Repr. of 1950 ed. lib. bdg. 35.00 (ISBN 0-313-23597-X, BENR). Greenwood.

Race, Science & Society. 364p. (Co-published with George Allen & Unwin Ltd., London and; Columbia University Press, New York). 1975. pap. 20.50 (ISBN 92-3-101155-3, UM18, UNESCO). UNIPUB.

Race, Sex & National Origin: Public Attitudes of Desegregation see Readings on Equal Education, Vol. 9: Education Policy in an Era of Conservative Reform.

Race: The History of an Idea in America. rev. ed. Thomas F. Gossett. LC 63-21187. (Sourcebooks in Negro History). (YA) (gr. 7 up). 1965. pap. 9.50 (ISBN 0-8052-0106-8). Schocken.

Race: The History of an Idea in America. Thomas F. Gossett. LC 63-21187. 228p. 1975. Repr. of 1963 ed. 17.95x (ISBN 0-87074-065-2). SMU Press.

Race to Fashoda: European Colonialism & African Resistance in the Scramble for Africa. David L. Lewis. LC 86-28256. (Illus.). 352p. 1987. 24.95 (ISBN 1-55584-058-2). Weidenfeld.

Race to Fashoda: European Colonialism & African Resistance in the Scramble for Africa. David L. Lewis. (Illus.). 1989. pap. 11.95 (ISBN 1-55584-278-X). Weidenfeld.

Race to Grace. George Harper. (H. B. Bible Adventures Ser.). 216p. (Orig.). 1986. pap. 5.95 (ISBN 0-934318-74-3). Falcon Pr MT.

Race to Mars: The Harper & Row Mars Flight Atlas. Frank Miles & Nicholas Booth. LC 88-3514. (Illus.). 192p. 1988. 19.95 (ISBN 0-06-016005-5, HarpT). Har-Row.

Race to Pearl Harbor: The Failure of the Second London Naval Conference & the Onset of World War II. Stephen E. Pelz. LC 73-89711. (Studies in American-East Asian Relations: No. 5). 416p. 1974. text ed. 24.50x (ISBN 0-674-74575-2). Harvard U Pr.

Race to the Swift: Thoughts on Twenty-First Century Warfare. R. Simpkin. (Illus.). 376p. 1985. 36.00 (ISBN 0-08-031170-9). Pergamon.

Race, Training & Employment. Ed. by Gajendra K. Verma & D. S. Darby. 150p. 1987. 33.00x (ISBN 1-85000-243-6, Falmer Pr); pap. 18.00x (ISBN 1-85000-244-4, Falmer Pr). Taylor & Francis.

Race Traits & Tendencies of the American Negro. Frederick L. Hoffman. LC 70-169474. Repr. of 1896 ed. 24.50 (ISBN 0-404-00065-7). AMS Pr.

Race Versus Robe: The Dilemma of Black Judges. Michael D. Smith. 205p. 1983. 21.50 (ISBN 0-8046-9320-X, 5320). Assoc Faculty Pr.

Race, Writing, & Difference. Ed. by Henry L. Gates, Jr. LC 86-6921. (Illus.). 424p. 1986. text ed. 30.00x (ISBN 0-226-28434-4); pap. text ed. 15.00 (ISBN 0-226-28435-2). U of Chicago Pr.

Racehoss: Big Emma's Boy. Albert R. Sample. 272p. 1984. 14.95 (ISBN 0-89015-442-2). Eakin Pr.

Racehoss: Big Emma's Boy. Albert R. Sample. 160p. 1988. pap. 3.95 (ISBN 0-345-00696-8). Ballantine.

Racehoss: Big Emma's Boy. Albert R. Sample. 1988. pap. 3.95 (ISBN 0-345-32807-8, Pub. by Ballantine Epiphany). Ballantine.

Races: A Study of the Problems of Race Formation in Man. Carleton S. Coon et al. LC 80-24479. (American Lecture Ser.: No. 77). (Illus.). xiv, 153p. 1981. Repr. of 1950 ed. lib. bdg. 35.00x (ISBN 0-313-22878-7, CORA). Greenwood.

Races & Ethnic Groups in American Life. T. J. Woofter. Repr. of 1933 ed. 26.00 (ISBN 0-527-97980-5). Kraus Repr.

Races & Immigrants in America. 2nd ed. John R. Commons. LC 67-27834. 1967. Repr. of 1920 ed. 29.50x (ISBN 0-678-00321-1). Kelley.

Races & Peoples of Europe. B. J. Lundman. 1984. lib. bdg. 79.95 (ISBN 0-87700-622-9). Revisionist Pr.

Races of Britain. John Beddoe. 300p. 1983. Repr. 50.00 (ISBN 0-941694-13-5). Cliveden Pr.

Races of Burma. 2nd ed. Collin M. Enriquez. LC 77-87013. (Illus.). 152p. Repr. of 1933 ed. 29.50 (ISBN 0-404-16816-7). AMS Pr.

Races of Central Europe: A Footnote to History. Geoffrey M. Morant. LC 77-87532. Repr. of 1939 ed. 16.50 (ISBN 0-404-16598-2). AMS Pr.

Races of Europe. Carleton S. Coon. LC 76-184840. (Illus.). 739p. 1972. Repr. of 1939 ed. lib. bdg. 52.50x (ISBN 0-8371-6328-5, CORE). Greenwood.

Races of Europe: A Sociological Study. William Z. Ripley. (Illus.). Repr. of 1899 ed. 46.00 (ISBN 0-384-50930-4). Johnson Repr.

Races of Maize in Peru: Their Origins, Evolution & Classification. Alexander Grobman & Ricardo Sevilla. LC 61-60080. (National Research Council, Publication: 915). pap. 96.00 (ISBN 0-317-28682-X, 2055288). Bks Demand UMI.

Races of Man & Their Distribution. A. C. Haddon. 75.00 (ISBN 0-87968-288-4). Gordon Pr.

Races of Man: Outline of Anthropology & Ethnography. facsimile ed. Joseph Deniker. (Select Bibliographies Reprint Ser). Repr. of 1900 ed. 45.00 (ISBN 0-8369-5932-9). Ayer Co Pubs.

Races of Mankind. H. J. Fleure. 1979. Repr. of 1927 ed. lib. bdg. 15.50 (ISBN 0-8495-1649-8). Arden Lib.

Races of Men. facs. ed. Robert Knox. LC 78-89401. (Black Heritage Library Collection Ser). 1850. 16.50 (ISBN 0-8369-8617-2). Ayer Co Pubs.

Racetrack Betting: The Professors' Guide to Strategies. Richard Quandt & Peter Asch. 250p. 1986. 24.95 (ISBN 0-86569-147-9). Auburn Hse.

Racewalking. Marion Weinstein & William Finley. (Illus.). 128p. 1985. pap. 9.95 (ISBN 0-8289-0534-7). Greene.

Racewalking for Fun & Fitness. John Gray. 176p. 1985. 15.95 (ISBN 0-13-944711-3); pap. 7.95 (ISBN 0-13-944703-2). P-H.

Raceway. rev. ed. Sue Dickson. (Illus.). 96p. (gr. k-3). 1984. pap. 4.97 (ISBN 1-55574-002-2, WB-140). CBN Publishing.

Raceways: Having Fun with Balls & Tracks. Bernard Zubrowski. LC 84-20600. (Illus.). 96p. (gr. 3-7). 1985. PLB 10.25 (ISBN 0-688-04159-0, Morrow Junior Books); pap. 5.95 (ISBN 0-688-04160-4, Morrow Junior Books). Morrow.

Rachel. James Agate. LC 72-84504. 1928. 16.00 (ISBN 0-405-08192-8, Pub. by Blom). Ayer Co Pubs.

Rachel. James Agate. 94p. Repr. of 1924 ed. text ed. 7.00x cancelled (ISBN 0-8290-1453-5). Irvington.

Rachel. Leila P. Golding. (Heartsong Ser.). 176p. (Orig.). (YA) (gr. 10-12). 1988. pap. 3.50 mass market (ISBN 0-87123-963-9). Bethany Hse.

Rachel. Nina H. Kennard. 1975. Repr. of 1886 ed. 20.00 (ISBN 0-8274-4128-2). R West.

Rachel. Ivan Southall. LC 86-45509. 147p. (gr. 5 up). 1986. 11.95 (ISBN 0-374-36163-0). FS&G.

Rachel, No. 21. Vivian Schurfranz. 224p. (Orig.). (gr. 7 up). 1986. pap. 2.50 (ISBN 0-590-40394-X, Sunfire). Scholastic Inc.

Rachel & Her Children: Homeless Families in America. Jonathan Kozol. 320p. 1988. 17.95 (ISBN 0-517-56730-X). Crown.

Rachel & Mischa. Steven Bayar & Ilene Bayar. LC 88-9450. (Illus.). 32p. (ps-3). 1988. pap. 4.95 (ISBN 0-930494-77-6). Kar Ben.

Rachel & Obadiah. Brinton Turkle. LC 77-15661. (Illus.). (gr. k-3). 1978. 11.95 (ISBN 0-525-38020-5). Dutton.

Rachel & Obadiah. Brinton Turkle. (Unicorn Paperbacks Ser.). (gr. 1-3). 1987. pap. 3.95 (ISBN 0-525-44303-7). Dutton.

Rachel & the Angel & Other Stories. Robert Westall. LC 86-33523. (Illus.). 192p. (YA) (gr. 7 up). 1987. 10.25 (ISBN 0-688-07370-0). Greenwillow.

Rachel Carson. Carol B. Gartner. LC 82-40285. (Literature & Life Ser.). 175p. 1983. 16.95x (ISBN 0-8044-5425-6). Ungar.

Rachel Carson. Marty Jezer. (American Women of Achievement Ser.). (Illus.). 112p. (gr. 5 up). 1988. lib. bdg. 16.95x (ISBN 1-55546-646-X). Chelsea Hse.

Rachel Carson: Pioneer of Ecology. Kathleen V. Kudlinski. (Illus.). 64p. (gr. 2-7). 1988. 10.95 (ISBN 0-670-81488-1). Viking.

Rachel Carson: Who Loved the Sea. Jean L. Latham. LC 72-11475. (Garrard Discovery Ser.). (Illus.). 80p. (gr. 2-5). 1973. PLB 6.69 (ISBN 0-8116-6312-4). Garrard.

Rachel Dyer. John Neal. LC 64-10667. 1979. Repr. of 1828 ed. 45.00x (ISBN 0-8201-1263-1). Schol Facsimiles.

Rachel Dyer, a North American Story. John Neal. 1988. Repr. of 1828 ed. lib. bdg. 49.00x. Am Biog Serv.

Rachel Giese: The Donegal Pictures. Rachel Giese. LC 87-50534. (Illus.). 100p. 1987. 29.95 (ISBN 0-317-66482-4). Wake Forest.

Rachel Has a Secret. Elizabeth Van Steenwyk. (Impressions Ser.). 128p. (Orig.). (gr. 5-8). 1987. pap. 2.50 (ISBN 0-87406-249-7). Willowisp Pr.

Rachel: Her Stage Life & Her Real Life. Francis Gribble. LC 70-93163. (Illus.). 1972. Repr. of 1911 ed. lib. bdg. 22.00 (ISBN 0-405-08582-6, Blom Pubns). Ayer Co Pubs.

Rachel McMasters Miller Hunt Botanical Library. (Illus.). viii, 35p. 1961. 5.00 (ISBN 0-913196-37-1). Hunt Inst Botanical.

Rachel Marie. Illus. by Pat Sustendal. (Cabbage Patch Kids Ser.). (Illus.). (ps-3). cancelled (ISBN 0-910313-69-5). Parker Bros.

Rachel of Old Louisiana. Avery O. Craven. LC 74-15921. (Illus.). xiv, 122p. 1975. 16.95 (ISBN 0-8071-0095-1). La State U Pr.

Rachel on the Run. Maggie Prince. 96p. (gr. 5-7). 1988. 15.95 (ISBN 0-340-33806-7, Pub. by Hodder & Stoughton UK). David & Charles.

Rachel Papers. Martin Amis. 224p. 1988. pap. 8.95 (ISBN 0-517-56777-6, Harmony). Crown.

Rachel Ray, 2 vols. Anthony Trollope. Ed. by N. John Hall. LC 80-1881. (Selected Works of Anthony Trollope Ser.). 1981. Repr. of 1863 ed. lib. bdg. 65.00 (ISBN 0-405-14140-8). Ayer Co Pubs.

Rachel Ray. Anthony Trollope. 1980. pap. 6.95 (ISBN 0-486-23930-6). Dover.

Rachel Ray. Anthony Trollope. Ed. by Rose D'Agostino. (Harding Grange Library). (Illus.). 557p. 1986. 25.00 (ISBN 0-932282-50-4); pap. cancelled (ISBN 0-932282-51-2). Caledonia Pr.

Rachel Ray. Anthony Trollope. Intro. by P. D. Edwards. (World's Classics Ser.). 464p. 1989. pap. 8.95 (ISBN 0-19-281809-0). Oxford U Pr.

Rachel the Immortal. Bernard Falk. LC 70-91900. 1935. 22.00 (ISBN 0-405-08495-1, Blom Pubns). Ayer Co Pubs.

Rachel Victoria. Robert S. Macdonald. 350p. 1984. 15.95 (ISBN 0-89433-224-4). Petrocelli.

Rachel Weeping for Her Children, Uncomforted. Hazel Lin. LC 75-2434. 1975. 10.00 (ISBN 0-8283-1616-3). Branden Pub Co.

Rachel Weeping: The Case Against Abortion. James T. Burtchaell. LC 83-48986. 400p. 1984. pap. 10.95 (ISBN 0-06-061251-7, RD 517, HarpR). Har-Row.

Rachel's Rainbow. Sharon Morphew. (Happy Day Bks.). (Illus.). 32p. (gr. k-2). 1987. 1.59 (ISBN 0-87403-279-2, 3779). Standard Pub.

Rachel's Walk. Jonathan Berman. LC 84-90285. 83p. 1985. 8.95 (ISBN 0-533-06325-6). Vantage.

Rachmaninoff. Watson Lyle. LC 74-24140. 1976. Repr. of 1939 ed. 19.00 (ISBN 0-404-13003-8). AMS Pr.

Rachmaninoff. Victor I. Seroff. (Biography Index Reprint Ser). Repr. of 1950 ed. 21.00 (ISBN 0-8369-8034-4). Ayer Co Pubs.

Rachmaninoff: His Life & Times. expanded ed. Robert Walker. (Illus.). 152p. 1981. Repr. of 1980 ed. 12.95 (ISBN 0-87666-582-2, Z-51). Paganiniana Pubns.

Rachmaninoff's Recollections Told to Oskar Von Riesemann. Sergei Rachmaninoff. LC 74-111100. (Select Bibliographies Reprint Ser). 1934. 29.00 (ISBN 0-8369-5232-4). Ayer Co Pubs.

Rachmaninov. N. Bazhanov. 343p. 1983. 11.95 (ISBN 0-8285-2624-9, Pub. by Raduga Pubs USSR). Imported Pubns.

Rachz: The True Story of a Fox. Sue Chambers. (Illus.). 160p. Date not set. 16.00 (ISBN 0-85362-217-5, Oriel). Routledge Chapman & Hall.

Racial Adaptations. Carleton S. Coon. LC 82-8010. (Illus.). 1982. text ed. 24.95 (ISBN 0-8304-1012-0); pap. text ed. 12.95 (ISBN 0-88229-806-2). Nelson-Hall.

Racial & Cultural Minorities: An Analysis of Prejudice & Discrimination. 5th ed. George E. Simpson & Milton Yinger. (Environment, Development, & Public Policy Ser.). 506p. 29.50x (ISBN 0-306-41777-4, Plenum Pr). Plenum Pub.

Racial & Ethnic Competition. Michael Banton. LC 82-23558. (Comparative Ethnic & Race Relations Ser.). (Illus.). 500p. 1983. o. p. 54.50 (ISBN 0-521-25463-9); pap. 17.95 (ISBN 0-521-27475-3). Cambridge U Pr.

Racial & Ethnic Groups. 2nd ed. Richard T. Schaefer. 1984. text ed. write for info. (ISBN 0-673-39595-2). Scott F.

Racial & Ethnic Groups. 3rd ed. Richard T. Schaefer. 1988. text ed. write for info. (ISBN 0-673-39747-5). Scott F.

Racial & Ethnic Relations. 2nd ed. Joe R. Feagin. (Illus.). 400p. 1984. text ed. write for info. (ISBN 0-13-750125-0). P-H.

Racial & Ethnic Relations in America. 2nd ed. S. Dale McLemore. (Illus.). 1983. text ed. 36.00 (ISBN 0-205-07969-5, 8179697); test items avail. Allyn.

Racial Aspects of the Far Eastern War of 1941-45. C. Thorne. (Raleigh Lectures on History). 1980. pap. 5.50 (ISBN 0-85672-243-X, Pub. by British Acad). Longwood Pub Group.

Racial Attitudes in America: Trends & Interpretations. Howard Schuman et al. (Social Trends in the United States Ser.). (Illus.). 288p. 1985. text ed. 25.00x (ISBN 0-674-74574-4). Harvard U Pr.

Racial Attitudes in America: Trends & Interpretations. Howard Schuman et al. (Social Trends in the United States Ser.). 276p. 1988. pap. text ed. 10.95. Harvard U Pr.

Racial Attitudes in English-Canadian Fiction, 1905-1980. Terrence Craig. 224p. 1987. text ed. 29.95 (ISBN 0-88920-952-9, Pub. by Wilfrid Laurier U Pr). Humanities.

Racial Biology of the Jews. Otmar Von Verschuer. (Illus.). 1984. lib. bdg. 79.95 (ISBN 0-87700-560-5). Revisionist Pr.

Racial Biology of the Jews. Otmar Von Verschuer. 1987. lib. bdg. 75.00 (ISBN 0-8490-3945-2). Gordon Pr.

Racial Change & Community Crisis: St. Augustine, Florida, 1877-1980. David R. Colburn. 320p. 1985. 33.50s (ISBN 0-231-06046-7). Columbia U Pr.

Racial Chaos & Criminal Anarchy: The Prelude to Black Revolution. W. J. Davis. 1982. lib. bdg. 59.95 (ISBN 0-87700-412-9). Revisionist Pr.

Racial Characteristics of Syrians & Armenians. Carl C. Seltzer. (HU PMP). 1936. 12.00 (ISBN 0-527-01230-0). Kraus Repr.

Racial Conflict & Economic Development. W. Arthur Lewis. (W. E. B. Du Bois Lectures). (Illus.). 128p. 1985. text ed. 13.50x (ISBN 0-674-74579-5). Harvard U Pr.

Racial Conflict & Negotiations: Perspectives & First Case Studies. Ed. by W. E. Chalmers & G. W. Cormick. LC 72-634167. (Orig.). 1971. 12.00x (ISBN 0-87736-313-7); pap. 5.95x (ISBN 0-87736-314-5). U of Mich Inst Labor.

Racial Conflict, Discrimination, & Power: Historical & Contemporary Studies. Ed. by William Barclay et al. LC 75-11964. (Studies in Modern Society: Political & Social Issues: No. 9). 1976. lib. bdg. 32.50 (ISBN 0-404-13140-9); pap. 11.95 (ISBN 0-404-13144-1). AMS Pr.

Racial Conflict in Contemporary Society. John Stone. 192p. 1986. text ed. 19.50x (ISBN 0-674-74565-5); pap. text ed. 7.95x (ISBN 0-674-74566-3). Harvard U Pr.

Racial Consciousness. Michael Banton. (Illus.). 176p. (Orig.). 1988. text ed. 28.95 (ISBN 0-582-02385-8); pap. text ed. 12.95 (ISBN 0-582-02384-X). Longman.

Racial Decay: A Compilation of Evidence from World Sources. O. C. Beale. 1976. lib. bdg. 59.95 (ISBN 0-8490-2498-6). Gordon Pr.

Racial Discrimination. pap. 6.00 (E.71.XIV.2). UN.

Racial Discrimination Against Neither-White-nor-Black American Minorities. Ed. by Kananur V. Chandras. LC 77-91409. 1978. soft cover 12.95 (ISBN 0-88247-497-9). R & E Pubs.

Racial Discrimination in Canada: Asian Minorities. Kananur V. Chandra. LC 73-76006. lib. bdg. 10.95 (ISBN 0-88247-208-9). R & E Pubs.

Racial Disparities in the Criminal Justice System. Joan Petersilia. LC 83-9777. 128p. 1983. 10.00 (ISBN 0-8330-0506-5, R-2947-NIC). Rand Corp.

Racial Elements of European History. Hans F. Gunther. 59.95 (ISBN 0-8490-0926-X). Gordon Pr.

Racial Elements of Europeon History. Hans F. Gunther. Tr. by G. C. Wheeler. LC 77-110905. 1970. Repr. of 1927 ed. 23.50x (ISBN 0-8046-0888-1, Pub by Kennikat). Assoc Faculty Pr.

Racial Equality. L. McDonald. Ed. by Franklyn S. Haiman. (To Protect These Rights Ser.). 168p. 1983. pap. 12.95 (ISBN 0-8442-6004-5, Passport Bks.). Natl Textbk.

Racial Equality in America. John H. Franklin. LC 76-26168. 1976. 7.95x (ISBN 0-226-26073-9). U of Chicago Pr.

Racial Equation: Pontius Pilate Plus Judus Iscariot Equals Crucification. Arthur T. Davidson. 1986. write for info. (ISBN 0-933389-00-0). Northeastern Pub.

Racial, Ethnic & Sexual Composition of Library Staff in Academic & Public Libraries. 52p. 1981. 5.00x (ISBN 0-8389-6515-6). ALA.

Racial-Ethnic Minorities & Women in School Administration: A Selected Bibliography. 40p. (Orig.). 1983. pap. 6.50 (ISBN 0-87652-080-8, 021-00121). Am Assn Sch Admin.

Racial Exclusionism & the City: The Urban Support of the National Front. Christopher T. Husbands. 240p. 1983. text ed. 39.95x (ISBN 0-04-329045-0). Unwin Hyman.

Racial Factors in Psychiatric Intervention. Benjamin D. Singer. LC 76-56468. 1977. soft cover 11.95 (ISBN 0-88247-452-9). R & E Pubs.

Racial Forces & the Tranformation of the American Culture. Frederick V. D'Armand. 137p. 1988. 97.75 (ISBN 0-86722-188-7). Inst Econ Finan.

Racial Formation in the United States from the 1960's to the 1980's. Michael Omi & Howard Winant. 224p. 1986. 24.95 (ISBN 0-7102-0566-X, 0566X); pap. 10.95 (ISBN 0-7102-0970-3, 09703). Routledge Chapman & Hall.

Racial Foundation of the History of Mankind, 3 vols. Charles L. Brace. (Illus.). 445p. 1985. 178.75 (ISBN 0-86722-097-X). Inst Econ Pol.

Racial History of Man, 2 vols. Roland Dixon. Set. 250.00 (ISBN 0-87968-273-6). Gordon Pr.

Racial Hybridity. Philip T. Jones. (Illus.). 241p. (Orig.). 1979. pap. 5.50x (ISBN 0-911038-77-9, Uriel Pubns). Noontide.

Racial Hygiene: Medicine Under the Nazis. Robert Proctor. LC 87-31116. 496p. 1988. text ed. 34.95 (ISBN 0-674-74580-9). Harvard U Pr.

Racial Inequality: A Political-Economic Analysis. Michael Reich. LC 80-8573. 345p. 1981. 34.00x (ISBN 0-691-04227-6); pap. 9.95x (ISBN 0-691-00365-3). Princeton U Pr.

Racial Integration in American Neighborhoods: A Comparative Study. Norman M Bradburn et al. (Report Ser: No. IIIB). 6.50x (ISBN 0-932132-08-1). NORC.

Racial Integrity & Other Features of the Negro Problem. facsimile ed. Alexander H. Shannon. LC 70-38024. (Black Heritage Library Collection). Repr. of 1907 ed. 19.25 (ISBN 0-8369-8990-2). Ayer Co Pubs.

Racial Minorities & Public Housing. David Smith & Anne Whalley. 119p. 1975. 18.00x (ISBN 0-686-87321-1, Pub. by Policy Studies). State Mutual Bk.

Racial Minorities in Banking: New Workers in the Banking Industry. R. D. Corwin. 1971. pap. 9.95x (ISBN 0-8084-0042-8). New Coll U Pr.

Racial Myth in English History: Trojans, Teutons, & Anglo-Saxons. Hugh A. MacDougall. LC 81-69941. 160p. 1982. 15.00x (ISBN 0-87451-228-X); pap. 7.95x (ISBN 0-87451-229-8). U Pr of New Eng.

Racial Myths. Juan Comas. LC 76-5909. (Race Question in Modern Science Ser.). 51p. 1976. Repr. of 1965 ed. lib. bdg. 25.00x (ISBN 0-8371-8801-6, CORM). Greenwood.

Racial Negotiations: Potentials & Limitations. W. Ellison Chalmers. LC 74-78509. 1974. 15.00 (ISBN 0-87736-321-8). U of Mich Inst Labor.

Racial Origin & Earliest Racial History of the Hebrews. Eugen Fischer. 1987. lib. bdg. 75.00 (ISBN 0-8490-3931-2). Gordon Pr.

Racial Origins of English Character. R. N. Bradley. LC 72-118461. 1971. Repr. of 1926 ed. 21.00x (ISBN 0-8046-1210-2, Pub by Kennikat). Assoc Faculty Pr.

Racial Policies & Practices of Real Estate Brokers. Rose Helper. LC 73-81398. pap. 100.80 (ISBN 0-317-41746-0, 2055874). Bks Demand UMI.

Racial Politics in Little Rock, 1954-1964. Irving J. Spitzberg, Jr. Ed. by Harold Hyman & Stuart Bruchey. LC 86-27030. (American Legal & Constitutional History Ser.). 200p. 1987. lib. bdg. 30.00 (ISBN 0-8240-8296-6). Garland Pub.

Racial Prehistory in the Southwest & the Hawikuh Zunis. Carl C. Seltzer. (HU PMP). 1944. pap. 16.00 (ISBN 0-527-01256-4). Kraus Repr.

Racial Prejudice. Elaine Pascoe. LC 85-8816. (Issues in American History Ser.). (Illus.). 128p. (gr. 7 up). 1985. PLB 12.90 (ISBN 0-531-10057-X). Watts.

Racial Pride & Prejudice. Eric J. Dingwall. LC 78-32177. 1979. Repr. of 1946 ed. lib. bdg. 35.00x (ISBN 0-8371-5940-7, DIR&). Greenwood.

Racial Problems in Hungary. R. W. Seton-Watson. 540p. 1973. Repr. of 1908 ed. 45.00x (ISBN 0-86527-163-1). Fertig.

Racial Segregation: Two Policy Views. Gary Orfield & William Taylor. LC 79-3166. (Illus.). 68p. 1979. pap. text ed. 4.50 (ISBN 0-916584-13-5). Ford Found.

Racial Study of the West Nakanai. Daris R. Swindler. (University Museum Monographs: No. 24). (Illus.). viii, 39p. 1962. pap. 15.00 (ISBN 0-934718-16-4). Univ Mus of U PA.

Racial Tensions & National Identity. Ed. by Ernest Q. Campbell. LC 70-185873. (Illus.). 232p. 1972. 14.95x (ISBN 0-8265-1179-1). Vanderbilt U Pr.

Racial Theories. Michael Banton. LC 86-32734. 250p. 1987. 44.50 (ISBN 0-521-33456-X); pap. 12.95 (ISBN 0-521-33675-9). Cambridge U Pr.

Racial Variations in Man: Proceedings of a Symposium Held at the Royal Geographical Society, London, 1974. Ed. by F. J. Ebling & W. V. Ewens. LC 75-12803. (Symposia of the Institute of Biology Ser.). 245p. 1976. 57.95x (ISBN 0-470-22955-1). Halsted Pr.

Racine. Jean Giraudoux. LC 77-24244. 1938. lib. bdg. 16.00 (ISBN 0-8414-4604-0). Folcroft.

Racine. Jean Giraudoux. 1980. Repr. of 1938 ed. lib. bdg. 15.00 (ISBN 0-8492-4948-1). R West.

Racine. Lucien Goldmann. Tr. by Alastair Hamilton from Fr. (Orig.). 1981. pap. 4.95 (ISBN 0-906495-77-6). Writers & Readers.

Racine. P. J. Yarrow. (Plays & Playwrights Ser.). 197p. 1978. 18.50x (ISBN 0-87471-830-9). Rowman.

Racine & Seneca. Ronald W. Tobin. (Studies in the Romance Languages & Literatures: No. 96). 156p. 1971. pap. 8.50x (ISBN 0-8078-9096-0). U of NC Pr.

Racine & the Art Poetique of Boileau. Marie Haley. 1973. lib. bdg. 18.50 (ISBN 0-374-93379-0, Octagon). Hippocrene Bks.

Racine Berenice. James J. Supple. Ed. by Roger Little & Wolfgang Van Emden. (Critical Guides to French Texts: No. 57). 89p. 1986. pap. 4.95 (ISBN 0-7293-0230-X, Pub. by Grant & Cutler). Longwood Pub Group.

Racine et Shakespeare. facsimile ed. Stendhal. 1928. 50.00 (ISBN 0-686-55079-X). French & Eur.

Racine et Shakespeare: Etudes sur le Romantisme. Stendhal. (Coll GF). pap. 3.95 (ISBN 0-685-35016-9). French & Eur.

Racine in England. F. Y. Eccles. LC 74-7036. 1922. lib. bdg. 15.50 (ISBN 0-8414-3936-2). Folcroft.

Racine: Phedre. J. P. Short. (Critical Guides to French Texts Ser.: No. 20). 84p. 1983. pap. 3.95 (ISBN 0-7293-0149-4, Pub. by Grant & Cutler). Longwood Pub Group.

Racines du Ciel. Romain Gary. (Folio Ser.: No. 242). 1956. 8.95 (ISBN 0-685-11521-6). Schoenhof.

Racine's Iphigenie: Literary Rehearsal & Tragic Recognition. R. Pfohl. 240p. 1974. text ed. 43.50x (ISBN 0-317-56034-4, Pub. by Droz Switzerland). Coronet Bks.

Racine's La Thebaide: Political, Moral, & Aesthetic Dimensions. Robert L. Myers. LC 81-51476. (Rice University Studies: Vol. 67, No. 2). 51p. (Orig.). 1981. pap. 5.50x (ISBN 0-89263-249-6). Rice Univ.

Racine's Theatre: The Politics of Love. William J. Cloonan. LC 77-8683. (Romance Monographs, Inc: No. 28). 1978. 18.00x (ISBN 84-399-7422-1). Romance.

Racinet's Full-Color Pictorial History of Western Costume: With 92 Plates Showing Over 950 Authentic Costumes from the Middle Ages to 1800. Auguste Racinet. (Dover Fine Arts Ser.). (Illus.). iv, 92p. (Orig.). 1987. pap. 10.95 (ISBN 0-486-25464-X). Dover.

Racinet's Historic Ornament in Full Color. Auguste Racinet. 112p. 1988. pap. 14.95 (ISBN 0-486-25787-8). Dover.

Racing Alone: Houses Made with Earth & Fire. Nader Khalili. LC 82-48419. 224p. 1983. 14.45 (ISBN 0-06-250445-2, HarpR). Har-Row.

Racing & Sports Car Chassis Design. Michael Costin & David Phipps. LC 68-4344. (Illus.). 148p. 1965. lib. bdg. 16.95 (ISBN 0-8376-0296-3). Bentley.

Racing & Wagering Assistant. Jack Rudman. (Career Examination Ser.: C-2714). (Cloth bdg. avail. on request). 1988. pap. 14.00 (ISBN 0-8373-2714-8). Natl Learning.

Racing Breed. Helen Ueltzen. LC 83-20706. (Illus.). 233p. 1984. 34.95 (ISBN 0-915309-00-9). GFI Assocs.

Racing Breed. Helen Ueltzen. (Illus.). 234p. 1986. 34.95 (ISBN 0-8119-0694-9). Fell.

Racing Car Design & Development. Len Terry & Alan Baker. LC 73-85159. 272p. 1973. 14.95 (ISBN 0-8376-0080-4). Bentley.

Racing Cars. N. S. Barrett. LC 84-50018. (Picture Library). (Illus.). 32p. (gr. k-3). 1985. PLB 10.90 (ISBN 0-531-03784-3). Watts.

Racing Cars. P. Harmer. (Great Bks.). (Illus.). 48p. (gr. 3-8). Date not set. PLB 17.27 (ISBN 0-86592-455-4). Rourke Corp.

Racing Cars. A. D. Lefage. LC 86-42676. (Investigate Ser.). 48p. (gr. 3-7). Date not set. cancelled (ISBN 0-382-09265-1); pap. cancelled (ISBN 0-382-09273-2). Silver.

Racing Cars. Kate Petty. (First Library). 32p. (gr. 1-3). 1986. PLB 10.90 (ISBN 0-531-10203-3). Watts.

Racing Cart see Three Little Friends Series.

Racing Certainty. Martin Coutts. 160p. 1984. 12.95 (ISBN 0-89962-339-5). Todd & Honeywell.

Racing-Cruiser. 2nd ed. Richard Henderson. LC 82-84658. (Illus.). 240p. 1983. 6.95 (ISBN 0-87742-169-2, R586). Intl Marine.

Racing Days. Brendan Boyd. LC 87-40062. (Illus.). 192p. 1987. 30.00 (ISBN 0-670-81873-9). Viking.

Racing Dragsters. Angelo G. Resciniti. (Illus.). 32p. (gr. 3-8). 1986. 2.95 (ISBN 0-87406-039-7). Willowisp Pr.

Racing Driver: The Theory & Practice of Fast Driving. Denis Jenkinson. LC 59-3790. (Illus.). 1959. 8.95 (ISBN 0-8376-0200-9). Bentley.

Racing Driver's Diary. Y. Klemanov. 150p. 1982. pap. 2.95 (ISBN 0-8285-2513-7, Pub. by Progress Pubs USSR). Imported Pubns.

Racing Edge. Ted Turner & Gary Jobson. (Illus.). 192p. pap. 7.95 (ISBN 0-671-49819-3, Wallaby). S&S.

Racing for Gold: Or, Incidents in the Life of a Turf Commissioner with Examples of the Most Successful Systems of Speculating on the Turf & in Games of Chance. James Peddie. 1979. Repr. of 1891 ed. lib. bdg. 50.00 (ISBN 0-8495-4333-9). Arden Lib.

Racing for the Stars. Maggie Dana. LC 87-16246. (Best Friends Ser.). (Illus.). 128p. (gr. 4-8). 1987. PLB 9.49 (ISBN 0-8167-1195-X); pap. text ed. 2.95 (ISBN 0-8167-1196-8). Troll Assocs.

Racing Game (Odds Against) Dick Francis. 1984. pap. 3.50 (ISBN 0-671-53086-0). PB.

Racing Hearts. Ruth Burnett. (YA) (gr. 7 up). 1984. 9.95 (ISBN 0-8034-8452-6, Avalon). Bouregy.

Racing Hearts. Francine Pascal. (Sweet Valley High Ser.: No. 9). (gr. 7 up). 1984. pap. 2.75 (ISBN 0-553-26626-8). Bantam.

Racing Hearts. Eileen Witton. 208p. 1988. pap. 3.50 (ISBN 0-446-35160-1). Warner Bks.

Racing in Her Blood. Millys N. Altman. LC 79-3018. (YA) (gr. 7 up). 1980. (Lipp Jr Bks); PLB 9.89 (ISBN 0-397-31895-2). HarpJ.

Racing into Tomorrow: ASPRS-ACSM Fall Convention Technical Papers. American Congress on Surveying & Mapping. 996p. 1985. 20.00 (ISBN 0-317-59915-1, T665). Am Congrs Survey.

Racing Kinsers. Carl Hungness. 1988. lib. bdg. 24.95 (ISBN 0-915088-48-7). C Hungness.

Racing Men of TV. new ed. Miles Napier. 1978. pap. 3.95 (ISBN 0-85131-301-9, NL51, Pub. by J A Allen U K). S R Smith Sporting Bks.

Racing Minicycles. Ray Paprocki. (Winning Streak Ser.). (Illus.). 32p. (Orig.). (gr. 3-8). 1987. 2.50 (ISBN 0-87406-217-9). Willowisp Pr.

Racing Planes & Pilots. Joe Christy. (Illus.). 208p. 1982. pap. 8.95 (ISBN 0-8306-2322-1, 2322). TAB Bks.

Racing Porsches R to RSR. John Starkey. LC 87-81697. (Illus.). 128p. 1988. 24.95 (ISBN 0-85429-604-2, Pub. by G T Foulis Ltd). Haynes Pubns.

Racing Sled Dogs: An Original North American Sport. Michael Cooper. LC 87-25007. (Illus.). 96p. (gr. 4-7). 1988. 13.95 (ISBN 0-89919-499-0, Pub. by Clarion). Ticknor & Fields.

Racing the Sun. Paul Pitts. 160p. 1988. pap. 2.50 (ISBN 0-380-75496-7, Camelot). Avon.

Racing Through Paradise: A Pacific Passage. Willam F. Buckley, Jr. 1988. pap. 10.95 (ISBN 0-316-11448-0). Little.

Racing Through Paradise: A Pacific Passage. William F. Buckley, Jr. LC 86-26209. (Illus.). 384p. 1987. 25.00 (ISBN 0-394-55781-6); deluxe ed. 150.00 ltd. (ISBN 0-394-56128-7). Random.

Racing to Love. Caroline Cooney. (Follow Your Heart Romance Ser.: No. 7). (Orig.). (gr. 5 up). 1985. pap. 2.25. Archway.

Racing to Win: The Salt Flats. new ed. Stephen Gregory. LC 75-21845. (Illus.). (gr. 5-10). 1976. PLB 9.79 (ISBN 0-89375-010-7); pap. 2.50 (ISBN 0-89375-026-3). Troll Assocs.

Racing Without Tears. Caroline Ramsden. (Illus.). pap. 2.95 (ISBN 0-85131-004-4, NL51, Pub. by J A Allen U K). S R Smith Sporting Bks.

Racing Without Tears: Horses. Caroline Ramsden. (Illus.). 5.00x (ISBN 0-87556-247-7). Saifer.

Racing Yesterday's Cars. Richard L. Knudson. (Superwheels & Thrill Sports Bks.). (Illus.). 48p. (gr. 4-9). 1986. PLB 8.95 (ISBN 0-8225-0512-6). Lerner Pubns.

Racism & Apartheid in Southern Africa: South Africa & Namibia. 156p. (Orig.). 1974. pap. 5.00 (ISBN 92-3-101199-5, U512, UNESCO). UNIPUB.

Racism & Colonialism. Robert J. Ross. 1982. 39.50 (ISBN 90-247-2634-4, Pub. by Martinus Nijhoff Netherlands). Kluwer Academic.

Racism & Equal Opportunity Policies in the 1980's. Ed. by Richard Jenkins & John Solomos. (Comparative Ethnic & Race Relations Ser.). (Illus.). 250p. 1987. 42.50 (ISBN 0-521-33013-0). Cambridge U Pr.

Racism & Its Elimination. 144p. 1981. pap. 15.00 (ISBN 0-686-78457-X, UN81 15ST18, Unitar). UNIPUB.

Racism & Mental Health: Essays. Ed. by Charles V. Willie et al. LC 72-78933. (Contemporary Community Health Ser.). 1974. pap. 19.95x (ISBN 0-8229-5233-5). U of Pittsburgh Pr.

Racism & Migrant Labour: A Critical Text. Robert Miles. 206p. (Orig.). 1983. pap. 10.95x (ISBN 0-7100-9212-1). Routledge Chapman & Hall.

Racism & Psychiatry. Alexander Thomas & Samuel Sillen. 180p. 1974. pap. 4.95 (ISBN 0-8065-0409-9, Pub. by Citadel Pr). Lyle Stuart.

Racism & Recruitment: Managers, Organisations & Equal Opportunities in the Labour Market. Richard Jenkins. (Comparative Ethnic & Race Relations Ser.). (Illus.). 220p. 1986. 52.50 (ISBN 0-521-32028-3). Cambridge U Pr.

Racism & Sexism: An Integrated Study. Paula S. Rothenberg. LC 87-60522. 464p. 1987. pap. text ed. write for info. (ISBN 0-312-00312-9). St Martin.

Racism & Sexism: An Integrated Study. Paula S. Rothenberg. 464p. 1987. 39.95 (ISBN 0-312-01217-9). St Martin.

Racism & Sexism in Children's Books. Council on Interracial Books for Children, Inc. Staff. (Interracial Digest Ser.: No. 1). (Illus.). 48p. (Orig.). (gr. 11-12). 1976. pap. 3.95x (ISBN 0-930040-28-7). CIBC.

Racism & Sexism in Children's Books. Council on Interracial Books for Children, Inc. Staff. (Interracial Digest Ser.: No. 2). (Illus.). 48p. (Orig.). (gr. 11-12). 1978. pap. 4.95 (ISBN 0-930040-29-5). CIBC.

Radial Keratotomy. Waring. (Illus.). 400p. 1989. 65.00 (ISBN 0-8016-5349-5). Mosby.

Radial Tire Wear Conditions & Causes: A Guide to Wear Pattern Analysis. American Trucking Association Maintenance Council. 1984. updated loose-leaf 40.00 (ISBN 0-88711-095-9). Am Trucking Assns.

Radiance & Reflections: Medieval Art from the Raymond Pitcairn Collection. Jane Hayward et al. (Illus.). 261p. 1982. 25.00 (ISBN 0-87099-298-8). Metro Mus Art.

Radiance & Virtue: The R. Norris Shreve Collection of Chinese Jade & Other Oriental Works of Art. Katherine R. Tsiang. LC 82-84074. (Illus.). 88p. 1983. 15.00x (ISBN 0-936260-15-7); pap. 7.00x. Ind Mus Art.

Radiance from the Waters: Ideals of Feminine Beauty in Mende Art. Sylvia A. Boone. LC 85-19077. 304p. 1986. text ed. 35.00x (ISBN 0-300-03576-4). Yale U Pr.

Radiance in the Gulag. Nijole Sadunaite. 148p. (Orig.). 1987. 9.95 (ISBN 0-937495-08-5); pap. 5.95 (ISBN 0-317-65641-4). Trinity Comns.

Radiance Like Wind or Water. Richard Ronan. LC 83-72376. 73p. 1984. 14.00 (ISBN 0-937872-14-8); pap. 6.00 (ISBN 0-937872-15-6). Dragon Gate.

Radiance of Shabbos. Simcha Cohen-Bunim. (ArtScroll Mesorah Ser.). (Illus.). 200p. 1986. 11.95 (ISBN 0-89906-212-1); pap. 8.95 (ISBN 0-89906-213-X). Mesorah Pubns.

Radiance of the Inner Splendor. Lloyd J. Ogilvie. LC 80-51524. 144p. 1980. pap. text ed. 4.95x (ISBN 0-8358-0405-4). Upper Room.

Radiance Technique on the Job. Fred W. Wright, Jr. 76p. 1987. pap. text ed. 7.50 (ISBN 0-933267-01-0). Radiance Assocs.

Radiant Child. Thomas Armstrong. LC 85-40409. 220p. (Orig.). 1985. pap. 6.75 (ISBN 0-8356-0600-7, Quest). Theos Pub Hse.

Radiant Daughters: Fictional American Women. Thelma J. Shinn. LC 85-27196. (Contributions in Women's Studies Ser.: No. 66). 230p. 1986. lib. bdg. 35.00 (ISBN 0-313-25197-5, SRD/). Greenwood.

Radiant Energy & the Eye. Ed. by Sidney Lerman. (Illus.). 1980. text ed. write for info. (ISBN 0-02-369970-1). Macmillan.

Radiant Energy Cure Systems. Business Communications Staff. 111p. 1988. 1750.00 (ISBN 0-89336-645-5, C-026R). BCC.

Radiant Energy in Relation to Forests. William E. Reifsynder & Howard W. Lull. LC 77-10239. (U. S. Department of Agriculture. Technical Bulletin: 1344). Repr. of 1965 ed. 21.50 (ISBN 0-404-16217-7). AMS Pr.

Radiant Faith. Rudolph F. Norden. Ed. by Oscar E. Feucht. 1966. pap. 1.60 study guide (ISBN 0-570-03527-9, 14-1330); pap. 1.95 leader's manual (ISBN 0-570-03528-7, 14-1331). Concordia.

Radiant Heart. Linda Sabbath. 1986. Repr. of 1985 ed. 4.95 (ISBN 0-87193-003-X). Dimension Bks.

Radiant Properties of Materials. A. Sala. (Physical Science Data Ser.: Vol. 21). 1986. 171.00 (ISBN 0-444-99599-4). Elsevier.

Radiant Science, Dark Politics: A Memoir of the Nuclear Age. Martin D. Kamen. LC 83-13510. 350p. 1985. 25.00 (ISBN 0-520-04929-2); pap. 8.95. U of Cal Pr.

Radiant Tree. Sylvia Spencer. 1988. 9.95. Folder Edns.

Radiant Tree, & Other Stories. facs. ed. Temple Bailey. LC 73-116932. (Short Story Index Reprint Ser). 1934. 19.00 (ISBN 0-8369-3434-2). Ayer Co Pubs.

Radiant Way. Margaret Drabble. LC 87-45126. 432p. 1987. 18.95 (ISBN 0-394-56143-0). Knopf.

Radiating Atmosphere: Proceeding. Summer Advanced Study Institute, Queen's University, Kingston, Ontario, August 3-14, 1970. Ed. by B. M. Mc Cormac. LC 70-154742. (Astrophysics & Space Science Library: No.24). 455p. 1971. lib. bdg. 58.00 (ISBN 90-277-0184-9, Pub. by Reidel Holland). Kluwer Academic.

Radiation. Dennis Fradin. (New True Bks.). (Illus.). (gr. k-4). pap. 3.95 (ISBN 0-516-41238-8). Childrens.

Radiation. Sandra McPherson. LC 73-81356. (American Poetry Ser.: Vol. 1). 80p. 1973. 12.95 (ISBN 0-912946-04-0); pap. 6.95 (ISBN 0-912946-05-9). Ecco Pr.

Radiation. Mark Pettigrew. (Science Today Ser.). (Illus.). 32p. (gr. 4). Date not set. PLB 10.90 (ISBN 0-531-17023-3, Pub. by Gloucester). Watts.

Radiation. Price, Stern & Sloan Staff. (How & Why Wonder Bks.). (Illus.). 32p. (gr. 7-12). 1987. pap. 1.95 (ISBN 0-8431-4291-X). Price Stern.

Radiation Accident Preparedness: Medical & Managerial Aspects. Eugene L. Saenger et al. 89p. (Orig.). 1981. Boxed Set. 205.00 (ISBN 0-918473-04-7); cassettes, text & self-assessment exam incl. Sci-Thru-Media.

Radiation Alarms & Access Control Systems. LC 86-28486. (NCRP Report Ser.: No. 88). 81p. 1986. pap. text ed. 16.00 (ISBN 0-913392-84-7). NCRP Pubns.

Radiation: All You Need to Know to Stop Worrying...or Start. Martin D. Eckert & Norton J. Bramesco. LC 80-6137. (Illus.). 256p. (Orig.). 1981. pap. 4.95 (ISBN 0-394-74650-3, V-650, Vin). Random.

Radiation & Aging. Ed. by Patricia J. Lindop & G. A. Sacher. 1966. 32.50x (ISBN 0-89563-020-6). Trans-Atl Phila.

Radiation & Cellular Response. Ed. by George P. Scott & Heinz W. Wahner. (Illus.). 246p. 1983. pap. text ed. 12.95x (ISBN 0-8138-1496-0). Iowa St U Pr.

Radiation & Combined Heat Transfer in Channels. M. Tamonis. Ed. by A. Zukauskas. (Experimental & Applied Heat Transfer Equipment: A Series of Guide Books). 239p. 1987. 74.95 (ISBN 0-89116-570-3). Hemisphere Pub.

Radiation & Health. Audery S. Bomberger & Betty A. Dannenfelser. 272p. 1984. 56.95 (ISBN 0-89443-586-8). Aspen Pub.

Radiation & Health: The Biological Effects of Low Level Exposure to Ionising Radiation. Ed. by Robin R. Jones & Richard Southwood. LC 87-18972. 292p. 1987. 41.95 (ISBN 0-471-91674-9). Wiley.

Radiation & Human Health. J. T. Mensah. 1986. 29.00x (ISBN 0-86332-013-9, Pub. by Book Guild Ltd). State Mutual Bk.

Radiation & Human Health: A Comprehensive Investigation of the Evidence Relating Low-Level Radiation to Cancer & Other Diseases. John W. Gofman. LC 80-26484. (Illus.). 928p. 1981. 29.95 (ISBN 0-87156-275-8). Sierra.

Radiation & Life. 2nd ed. Eric J. Hall. 1984. 27.50 (ISBN 0-08-028819-7). Pergamon.

Radiation & Noise in Quantum Electronics. William H. Louisell. LC 76-56801. 318p. 1977. Repr. of 1964 ed. lib. bdg. 21.50 (ISBN 0-88275-503-X). Krieger.

Radiation & Propagation of Electromagnetic Waves. G. Tyras. (Electrical Science Ser). 1969. 95.00 (ISBN 0-12-705650-5). Acad Pr.

Radiation & Radioisotopes Applied to Insects of Agricultural Importance. (Proceedings Ser.). (Illus.). 508p. 1963. 25.25 (ISBN 92-0-010263-8, ISP74, IAEA). UNIPUB.

Radiation & Radioisotopes for Industrial Microorganisms. 1971. pap. 27.00 (ISBN 92-0-010371-5, ISP287, IAEA). UNIPUB.

Radiation & Skin. C. S. Potten. 226p. 1985. 47.00x (ISBN 0-85066-257-5). Taylor & Francis.

Radiation & the Control of Immune Response. (Panel Proceedings Ser.). (Illus.). 126p. 1968. pap. 9.25 (ISBN 92-0-011168-8, ISP175, IAEA). UNIPUB.

Radiation & the Lymphatic System: Proceedings. Ed. by John E. Ballou. LC 75-38685. (ERDA Symposium Ser.). 264p. 1976. pap. 14.50 (ISBN 0-87079-030-7, CONF-740930); microfiche 6.50 (ISBN 0-87079-317-9, CONF-740930). DOE.

Radiation & Waves in Plasmas. Lockheed Symposium on Magnetohydrodynamics, (5th: 1960: Palo Alto) Ed. by Morton Mitchner. LC 61-14651. pap. 41.80 (ISBN 0-317-07864-X, 2000319). Bks Demand UMI.

Radiation Biochemistry, 2 vols. Kurt I. Altman. Incl. Vol. 1. Cells. Shigefumi Okada (ISBN 0-12-054501-2); Vol. 2. Tissues & Body Fluids. Kurt I. Altman & Georg B. Gerber (ISBN 0-12-054502-0). 1970. Vol. 1. o.p. 75.00 ea.; Vol. 2. 98.00. Acad Pr.

Radiation Biochemistry. A. M. Kuzin. 288p. 1964. text ed. 57.00x (ISBN 0-7065-0534-4, Pub. by Keter Pub Jerusalem). Coronet Bks.

Radiation Biology. Alison P. Casarett. (Illus.). 1968. 43.00 (ISBN 0-13-750356-3). P-H.

Radiation Biology. Ed. by Donald J. Pizzarello. 312p. 1982. 99.00 (ISBN 0-8493-6011-0). CRC Pr.

Radiation Biology. (Advanced Health Physics Training Ser.). (Illus.). 255p. 1983. looseleaf 75.00x (ISBN 0-87683-203-6). GP Pub.

Radiation Biology, 2 Pts. Ed. by A. Zuppinger. (Handbook of Medical Radiology: Vol. 2, Pts. 1 & 2). (Illus.). 1966. Pt. 1. 224.20 (ISBN 0-387-03544-3); Pt. 2. 224.20 (ISBN 0-387-03545-1). Springer-Verlag.

Radiation Biology & Chemistry: Research Developments: Proceedings. Association for Radiation Research, Winter Meeting Jan. 3-5, 1979. Ed. by H. E. Edwards et al. LC 79-15532. (Studies in Physical & Theoretical Chemistry Ser.: Vol. 6). 505p. 1979. 131.75 (ISBN 0-444-41821-0). Elsevier.

Radiation Biology in Cancer Research. Ed. by Raymond Meyn & H. Rodney Withers. (Thirty-Second M. D. Anderson Symposium on Fundamental Cancer Research). 681p. 1980. text ed. 103.50 (ISBN 0-89004-402-3). Raven.

Radiation Biology of the Fetal & Juvenile Mammal: Proceedings. Ed. by Melvin R. Sikov & D. Dennis Mahlum. LC 74-603748. (AEC Symposium Ser.). 1026p. 1969. pap. 33.75 (ISBN 0-87079-318-7, CONF-690501); microfiche 6.50 (ISBN 0-87079-319-5, CONF-690501). DOE.

Radiation Budget at Plateau Station, Antarctica: Paper 5 in Meteorological Studies at Plateau Station, Antarctica. M. Kuhn et al. Ed. by Joost A. Businger. (Antarctic Research Ser.: Vol. 25). (Illus.). 1977. pap. 16.90 (ISBN 0-87590-139-5). Am Geophysical.

Radiation Carcinogenesis. Arthur C. Upton et al. (Current Onocology Ser.: Vol. 2). 600p. 1986. 73.75 (ISBN 0-444-00859-4). Elsevier.

Radiation Carcinogenesis & DNA Alterations. Ed. by F. J. Burns et al. LC 87-2224. (NATO ASI Series A, Life Sciences: Vol. 124). 630p. 1987. 97.50x (ISBN 0-306-42495-9, Plenum Pr). Plenum Pub.

Radiation Carcinogenesis: Epidemiology & Biological Significance. Ed. by John D. Boice, Jr. & Joseph F. Fraumeni, Jr. (Progress in Cancer Research & Therapy Ser.: Vol. 26). 510p. 1984. text ed. 104.50 (ISBN 0-89004-907-6). Raven.

Radiation Chemistry. 1981. 8.40 (ISBN 0-910362-15-7). Chem Educ.

Radiation Chemistry & Its Applications. (Technical Reports Ser.: No. 84). (Illus.). 182p. 1968. pap. 17.50 (ISBN 92-0-045068-7, IDC84, IAEA). UNIPUB.

Radiation Chemistry of Aqueous Solutions: A Portion of Proceedings of the First All-Union Conference on Radiation Chemistry, 1st: 1957: Moscow. All-Union Conference on Radiation Chemistry Staff. pap. 20.00 (ISBN 0-317-27217-9, 2024708). Bks Demand UMI.

Radiation Chemistry of Hydrocarbons. G. Foldiak. (Studies in Physical & Theoretical Chemistry: Vol. 14). 476p. 1982. 118.50 (ISBN 0-444-99746-6). Elsevier.

Radiation Chemistry of Major Food Components. P. S. Elias & A. J. Cohen. 220p. 1977. 50.75 (ISBN 0-444-41587-4, Biomedical Pr). Elsevier.

Radiation Chemistry of Monomers, Polymers & Plastics. Joseph E. Wilson. 640p. 1974. 115.00 (ISBN 0-8247-6095-6). Dekker.

Radiation Chemistry of Water. Ivan G. Draganic & Zorica D. Draganic. (Physical Chemistry Ser.: Vol. 26). 1971. 85.00 (ISBN 0-12-221650-4). Acad Pr.

Radiation Chemistry: Principles & Applications. Farhataziz & M. A. Rodgers. 640p. 1987. lib. bdg. 103.00 (ISBN 0-89573-127-4). VCH Pubs.

Radiation Climate of the Arctic. M. K. Gavrilova. 184p. 1966. text ed. 40.00x (ISBN 0-317-46476-0, Pub. by Keter Pub Jerusalem). Coronet Bks.

Radiation Control. A. A. Keil. 256p. 1960. pap. 4.75 (ISBN 0-685-46052-5, SPP-4). Natl Fire Prot.

Radiation Controversy. 2nd ed. Ralph E. Lapp. LC 78-83841. (Illus.). 1979. pap. 4.95 ea. (ISBN 0-9603716-0-5). Reddy Comm.

Radiation Corrosion. A. V. Byalobzheskii. 186p. 1970. text ed. 39.00x (ISBN 0-7065-1013-5, Pub. by Keter Pub Jerusalem). Coronet Bks.

Radiation-Cured Polymers (U. S.) 236p. 1985. 1875.00 (ISBN 0-86621-331-7, A1414). Frost & Sullivan.

Radiation Curing. Jim Lacey & Allen H. Keough. (Illus.). 96p. 1980. pap. 33.00 (ISBN 0-938648-15-2, 2004). T-C Pubns CA.

Radiation Curing: A Discussion of Advantages, Features & Applications. Jim Lacey & Allen H. Keough. LC 80-52815. pap. 24.30 (ISBN 0-317-10943-X, 2019120). Bks Demand UMI.

Radiation Curing: An Introduction to Coatings, Varnishes, Adhesives, & Inks. Ed. by A. Berejka & J. Rie. 95p. 1986. 20.00 (ISBN 0-87263-248-2). SME.

Radiation Curing: An Introduction to Coatings, Varnishes, Adhesives, & Inks. Society of Manufacturing Engineers. LC 84-51595. pap. 28.80 (2026701). Bks Demand UMI.

Radiation Curing Buyer's Guide, Vol. 5. Technology Marketing Corporation Staff Editors. 40p. 1983. pap. text ed. 22.00 (ISBN 0-318-01981-7). Tech Marketing.

Radiation Curing Buyer's Guide, Vol. 6. Technology Marketing Corporation Staff Editors. 40p. 1984. pap. text ed. 22.00 (ISBN 0-318-01982-5). Tech Marketing.

Radiation Curing Buyer's Guide Nineteen Eighty-Five. Technology Marketing Corporation Editors. 1980. soft cover 22.00 (ISBN 0-686-26255-7). Tech Marketing.

Radiation Curing Buyer's Guide, 1981, Vol. 3. Ed. by Technology Marketing Corporation Staff Editors. 48p. 1981. pap. text ed. 22.00 (ISBN 0-936840-05-6). Tech Marketing.

Radiation Curing Buyer's Guide, 1982, Vol. 4. Technology Marketing Corporation Staff Editors. 50p. 1982. pap. text ed. 22.00 (ISBN 0-936840-06-4). Tech Marketing.

Radiation Curing of Polymers: Proceedings of a Symposium Organized by the North West Region of the Industrial Division of Royal Society of Chemistry, University of Lancaster, September 18-19, 1986. Ed. by D. R. Randall. (Special Publication: No. 64). (Illus.). 210p. 1987. flexbound 63.00x (ISBN 0-85186-696-4, Pub. by Royal Soc Chem). Scholium Intl.

Radiation Curing VI: Conference Proceedings, September 20-23, 1982, Chicago, IL. International Conference on Radiation Curing (6th: 1982: Chicago, IL) Staff. LC 82-60954. pap. 111.30 (2030900). Bks Demand UMI.

Radiation Damage & Defects in Semiconductors: Reading 1972. (Institute of Physics Conference Ser.: No. 16). 1972. cancelled 49.00 (ISBN 0-85498-106-3, Pub. by Inst Physics England). IPS.

Radiation Damage & Sulphydryl Compounds. (Panel Proceedings Ser.). (Illus.). 191p. 1969. pap. 14.50 (ISBN 92-0-011169-6, ISP221, IAEA). UNIPUB.

Radiation Damage in Materials. 2nd ed. Frank L. Bouquet. (Illus.). 100p. 1987. text ed. 80.00x (ISBN 0-937041-28-9); pap. text ed. 55.00x (ISBN 0-937041-29-7). Systems Co.

Radiation Damage in Metals: Papers Presented at a Seminar of the American Society for Metals, Nov. 9-10, 197. Ed. by N. L. Peterson & S. D. Harkness. LC 76-25094. (Illus.). pap. 103.80 (ISBN 0-317-08178-0, 2019485). Bks Demand UMI.

Radiation Damage in Reactor Materials: 1969, 2 vols. (Proceedings Ser.). (Illus.). 1071p. (Vol. 1). 1969. Vol. 1. pap. 34.25 (ISBN 92-0-030069-3, ISP230-1, IAEA). UNIPUB.

Radiation Damage in Solids. Douglas Billington et al. LC 60-16414. pap. 115.50 (ISBN 0-317-07756-2, 2000985). Bks Demand UMI.

Radiation Damage to Skin: British Journal of Radiology Supplement 19. 1986. pap. text ed. 90.00 (ISBN 0-905749-13-8). Butterworth.

Radiation Detection. W. H. Tait. LC 80-40240. 1980. text ed. 75.00 (ISBN 0-408-10645-X). Butterworth.

Radiation Detection & Measurement. G. F. Knoll. 816p. 1979. member 55.00 (ISBN 0-318-21471-7, 228); 73.00. Am Soc Nondestructive.

Radiation Detection & Measurement. Glenn F. Knoll. LC 78-12387. 816p. 1979. write for info. (ISBN 0-471-49545-X). Wiley.

Radiation Dose to Patients from Radiopharmaceuticals. International Commission on Radiological Protection Staff. (ICRP Publication Ser.: No. 53). (Illus.). 386p. 1988. 105.00 (ISBN 0-08-035591-9). Pergamon.

Radiation Doses, Effects, Risks. 64p. 1986. pap. 10.00 (ISBN 92-807-1104-0, E.86.III.D.4). UN.

Radiation Dosimetry, 3 vols. 2nd ed. F. Attix & William Roesch. Incl. Vol. 1. Fundamentals. 1968. 69.50 (ISBN 0-12-066401-1); Vol. 2. Instrumentation. 1967. 69.50 (ISBN 0-12-066402-X); Vol. 3. Sources, Field Measurements & Applications. Ed. by F. Attix & E. Tochilin. 1969. 113.50 (ISBN 0-12-066403-8); Suppl. 1. Topics in Radiation Dosimetry. 1972. 77.00 (ISBN 0-12-066501-8). Acad Pr.

Radiation Dosimetry. Ed. by Gerald J. Hine. 1956. 123.50 (ISBN 0-12-349456-7). Acad Pr.

Radiation Dosimetry: Electron Beams with Energies Between 1 & 50 MeV. International Commission on Radiation Units & Measurement. LC 84-12763. (ICRU Report Ser.: No. 35). 154p. 1984. pap. text ed. 23.00 (ISBN 0-913394-29-7). Intl Comm Rad Meas.

Radiation Dosimetry: Physical & Biological Aspects. Ed. by Colin G. Orton. 340p. 1986. 59.50x (ISBN 0-306-42056-2, Plenum Pr). Plenum Pub.

Radiation Dosimetry: X Rays & Gamma Rays with Maximum Photon Energies Between 0.6 & 50 MeV, No. 14. International Commission on Radiation Units & Measurements. LC 70-97640. 1969. 8.00. Intl Comm Rad Meas.

Radiation Dosimetry: X Rays Generated at Potentials of 5 to 150 kV, No. 17. International Commission on Radiation Units & Measurements. LC 74-126755. 1970. 9.00. Intl Comm Rad Meas.

Radiation Education Notebook. Atomic Industrial Forum Staff. (Public Affairs & Information Program: General). 1983. 15.00 (ISBN 0-318-02249-4). US Coun Energy Awareness.

Radiation Effect & Tolerance, Normal Tissue in the Optimal Treatment of Cancer. Ed. by J. M. Vaeth & J. L. Meyer. (Frontiers of Radiation Therapy & Oncology Ser.: Vol. 23). (Illus.). x, 200p. 1989. 118.75 (ISBN 3-8055-4837-0). S Karger.

Radiation Effects. Ed. by W. F. Sheely. LC 67-26579. (Metallurgical Society Conferences Ser.: Vol. 37). pap. 160.00 (ISBN 0-317-11268-6, 2001526). Bks Demand UMI.

Radiation Effects & After-Effects in the Clear Polymethyl Methacrylate Dosimeter. (Agricultural Research Reports Ser.: 763). Date not set. pap. 12.00 (ISBN 90-220-0361-2, PDC78, PUDOC). UNIPUB.

Radiation Effects Computer Experiments. J. R. Beeler. (Defects in Solids Ser.: Vol. 13). 882p. 1983. 234.25 (ISBN 0-444-86315-X, North Holland). Elsevier.

Radiation Effects in Electronics. American Society for Testing & Materials Staff. LC 65-18216. (American Society for Testing & Materials. Special Technical Publication: No. 384). pap. 60.80 (ISBN 0-317-08042-3, 2000743). Bks Demand UMI.

Radiation Effects in Insulators, Vol. 3: A Special Issue of the Journal "Radiation Effects", 2 vols. Ian H. Wilson & Roger P. Webb. 805p. 1986. Set. text ed. 255.00 (ISBN 0-677-21440-5). Gordon & Breach.

Radiation Effects in MOS Devices & Circuits. Ma. 1987. write for info. (ISBN 0-471-84893-X). Wiley.

Radiation Effects in Semiconductors. J. W. Corbett & G. D. Watkins. 456p. 1971. 145.00 (ISBN 0-677-15080-6). Gordon & Breach.

Radiation Effects in Semiconductors: 1976. (Institute of Physics Conference Ser.: No. 31). 1977. cancelled 59.00 (ISBN 0-85498-121-7, Pub. by Inst Physics England). IPS.

Radiation Effects Information Generated on the ASTM Reference Correlation-Monitor Steels - DS 54. 84p. 1974. pap. 9.75 (ISBN 0-8031-0544-4, 05-054000-35). ASTM.

Radiation Effects on & Dose Enhancement of Electronic Materials. J. R. Srour et al. LC 84-14770. (Illus.). 128p. 1985. 32.00 (ISBN 0-8155-1007-1). Noyes.

Radiation Effects on Electronics. 2nd ed. Frank L. Bouquet. (Illus.). 60p. 1987. text ed. 80.00x (ISBN 0-937041-26-2); pap. text ed. 55.00x (ISBN 0-937041-27-0); lib. bdg. 90.00x (ISBN 0-937041-49-1). Systems Co.

Radiation Effects on Optical Materials: Critical Reviews. Ed. by P. W. Levy. 186p. 1985. 43.00 (ISBN 0-89252-576-2, 541). SPIE.

Radiation Electrochemical Processes: A Portion of Proceedings of the First All-Union Conference on Radiation Chemistry,1st: 1957: Moscow) All-Union Conference on Radiation Chemistry Staff. pap. 20.00 (ISBN 0-317-27216-0, 2024709). Bks Demand UMI.

Radiation Embrittlement & Surveillance of Nuclear Reactor Pressure Vessels: An International Study - STP 819. Ed. by Lendell E. Steele. LC 83-70258. 218p. 1983. text ed. 34.00 (ISBN 0-8031-0263-1, 04-819000-35). ASTM.

Radiation Embrittlement of Nuclear Reactor Pressure Vessel Steels: An International Review, Vol. 2. Lendell E. Steele. LC 86-10811. (Special Technical Publications: No. 909). (Illus.). viii, 201p. 1986. text ed. 59.00 (ISBN 0-8031-0473-1, 04-909000-35). ASTM.

Radiation Energy Conversion in Space, PAAS61. Ed. by Kenneth W. Billman. LC 78-8566. (Illus.). 670p. 1978. 69.50 (ISBN 0-915928-26-4). AIAA.

Radiation Engineering in the Academic Curriculum: Study Group Meeting, Haifa, Aug. 27-Sept. 4, 1973. (Panel Proceedings Ser.). (Illus.). 362p. 1975. pap. 40.00 (ISBN 92-0-161075-0, ISP372, IAEA). UNIPUB.

Radiation Exposure from Consumer Products & Miscellaneous Sources. LC 77-85462. (NCRP Reports Ser.: No. 56). 1977. 12.00 (ISBN 0-913392-38-3). NCRP Pubns.

Radiation Exposure from Consumer Products & Miscellaneous Sources. (NCRP Report: No. 95). 100p. (Orig.). 1987. pap. text ed. 14.00 (ISBN 0-913392-94-4). NCRP Pubns.

Radiation for a Clean Environment: Proceedings. (Proceedings Ser.). (Illus.). 672p. 1976. pap. 60.00 (ISBN 92-0-060075-1, ISP402, IAEA). UNIPUB.

Radiation from Apertures in Convex Bodies: Flush-Mounted Antennas. L. N. Zakharyev et al. Tr. by Petr Beckmann from Rus. LC 76-114987. (Electromagnetics Ser.: Vol. 4). 1970. 25.00x (ISBN 0-911762-06-X). Golem.

Radiation from Relativistic Electrons. A. A. Sokolov & I. M. Ternov. Ed. by C. W. Kilmister. Tr. by S. Chomet from Rus. LC 86-26618. (Translation Ser.). (Illus.). 328p. 1986. text ed. 40.00 (ISBN 0-88318-507-5). Am Inst Physics.

Radiation Hazards in Mining: Control, Measurement, & Medical Aspects. Ed. by Manuel Gomez. LC 81-70691. (Illus.). 1105p. 1982. 5.00x (ISBN 0-89520-290-5). Soc Mining Eng.

Radiation Heat Transfer. Sparrow & Cess. 366p. 1978. 51.00 (ISBN 0-89116-508-8). Hemisphere Pub.

Radiation Heat Transfer Notes. Don K. Edwards. LC 81-4539. (Hemisphere Engineering Paperback Ser.). (Illus.). 370p. (Orig.). 1981. pap. text ed. 33.00 (ISBN 0-89116-231-3). Hemisphere Pub.

Radiation Histopathology, 2 vols. George W. Casarett. 1981. Vol. 1, 160p. 69.00 (ISBN 0-8493-5357-2); Vol. 2, 176p. 69.00 (ISBN 0-8493-5358-0). CRC Pr.

Radiation Hydrodynamics in Stars & Compact Objects. Ed. by D. Mihalas & K. H. Winkler. (Lecture Notes in Physics: Vol. 255). vi, 454p. 1986. 38.50 (ISBN 0-387-16764-1). Springer-Verlag.

Radiation in a Cloudy Atmosphere. Ed. by E. M. Feigelson. 1984. lib. bdg. 64.00 (ISBN 90-277-1803-2, Pub. by Reidel Holland). Kluwer Academic.

Radiation in Plasmas: Proceedings of the Topical Conference on Radiation in Plasmas, Trieste, Italy, 1983, 2 vols. Ed. by B. McNamara. 1000p. 1984. Set. 109.00 (ISBN 9971-966-37-9). World Scientific Pub.

Radiation in the Atmosphere. K. Ya Kondratyav. (International Geophysics Ser.: Vol. 12). 1969. 112.00 (ISBN 0-12-419050-2). Acad Pr.

Radiation-Induced Cancer. (Proceedings Ser.). (Illus.). 498p. 1969. pap. 40.00 (ISBN 92-0-010269-7, ISP228, IAEA). UNIPUB.

Radiation Induced Changes in Microstructure: Thirteenth International Symposium, Part I. Ed. by F. A. Garner et al. LC 87-24104. (Special Technical Publications: No. 955). (Illus.). 940p. 1987. text ed. 121.00 (ISBN 0-8031-0962-8, 04-955000-35). ASTM.

Radiation-Induced Decomposition of Inorganic Molecular Ions. Everett R. Johnson. 154p. 1970. 65.00 (ISBN 0-677-02650-1). Gordon & Breach.

Radiation-Induced Voids in Metals: Proceedings. Ed. by James W. Corbett & Louis C. Ianniello. LC 72-600048. (AEC Symposium Ser.). 884p. 1972. pap. 30.00 (ISBN 0-87079-320-9, CONF-710601); microfiche 6.50 (ISBN 0-87079-321-7, CONF-710601). DOE.

Radiation Injury: Effects, Principles, & Perspectives. Arthur C. Upton. LC 69-17672. pap. 34.00 (ISBN 0-317-07735-X, 2019988). Bks Demand UMI.

Radiation Injury of Bone: Bone Injuries Following Radiation Therapy of Tumors. K. Shimanovskaya & Alexander Shiman. Tr. by Basil Haigh. (Illus.). 300p. 1983. 61.00 (ISBN 0-08-028821-9). Pergamon.

Radiation, Isotopes, & Bone. F. C. McLean & A. M. Budy. (Atomic Energy Commission Monographs). 1964. 14.50 (ISBN 0-12-484950-4). Acad Pr.

Radiation Issues for the Nuclear Industry: Set of Papers from AIF Conference on Radiation. Atomic Industrial Forum Staff. (Technical & Economic Reports: Radiation Protection & Environmental Considerations). 1982. 150.00 (ISBN 0-318-02244-3). US Coun Energy Awareness.

Radiation Measurements in Nuclear Power 1966. Institute of Physics. (Institute of Physics Conference Ser.: No. 2). 1967. cancelled 49.00 (ISBN 0-85498-403-8, Pub. by Inst Physics England). IPS.

Radiation Monitoring: A Programmed Instruction Book. AEC Technical Information Center Staff et al. 286p. 1967. write for info. (ISBN 0-87079-322-5, EDM-123). DOE.

Radiation Oncology. Ed. by B. E. Amendola & M. A. Amendola. 350p. 1984. 80.25 (ISBN 0-444-00846-2, Biomedical Pr). Elsevier.

Radiation Oncology. Stewart M. Jackson & Ann Johnson. 264p. 1985. 37.50 (ISBN 0-87527-334-3). Green.

Radiation Oncology, Vol. 2. Ed. by Theodore L. Phillips & William Wara. 184p. 1987. text ed. 75.50 (ISBN 0-89004-957-2). Raven.

Radiation Oncology Annual, 1983. Ed. by Theodore L. Phillips & David A. Pistenmaa. 288p. 1983. text ed. 58.00 (ISBN 0-89004-956-4). Raven.

Radiation Oncology Annual, 1984. Ed. by Theodore L. Phillips & David A. Pistenmaa. text ed. cancelled (ISBN 0-88167-004-9). Raven.

Radiation Oncology: Rationale Technique Results. Moss & Cox. (Illus.). 704p. 1988. 75.00 (ISBN 0-8016-3570-5). Mosby.

Radiation Oncology: Rationale, Technique, Results. 5th ed. William T. Moss et al. LC 79-14367. (Illus.). 660p. 1979. 67.95 (ISBN 0-8016-3556-X). Mosby.

Radiation: One Story of the M. I. T. Radiation Lab. 1940-1945. Ernest C. Pollard. (Illus.). 197p. 1982. pap. 8.00 (ISBN 0-9612798-1-8). Woodburn Pr.

Radiation Physics & Chemistry of Polymers. F. A. Makhlis. 300p. 1974. text ed. 59.00x (Pub. by Keter Pub Jerusalem). Coronet Bks.

Radiation Physics Laboratory Manual. Tortorici. 1985. 14.95 (ISBN 0-8016-5010-0). Mosby.

Radiation Physics Laboratory Manual. Marianne R. Tortorici & Hiram M. Hunt. (Illus.). 194p. (Orig.). 1984. 14.95x (ISBN 0-940122-14-6); instr's. manual 15.95x (ISBN 0-940122-15-4). Mosby Multi-Media.

Radiation Preservation of Food. (Proceedings Ser.). (Illus.). 774p. (Orig.). 1972. pap. 75.00 (ISBN 92-0-010373-1, ISP317, IAEA). UNIPUB.

Radiation Preservation of Foods: A Symposium. Edward S. Josephson. LC 67-25568. (Advances in Chemistry Series: No. 65). (Illus.). 192p. pap. 50.00 (2052229). Bks Demand UMI.

Radiation Processes in Astrophysics. Wallace H. Tucker. LC 75-29236. 311p. 1975. pap. 9.95x (ISBN 0-262-70010-7). MIT Pr.

Radiation Processing: Transactions of the First International Meeting on Radiation Processing, 2 vols. Ed. by Joseph Silverman & A. R. Van Dyken. LC 76-58383. 1977. Set. 235.00 (ISBN 0-08-021640-4). Pergamon.

Radiation Protection. Ronald L. Kathren. Ed. by J. M. Lenihan. (Medical Physics Handbooks Ser.: No. 16). (Illus.). 212p. 1985. 53.00x (ISBN 0-85274-554-0, Pub. by A Hilger UK). Taylor & Francis.

Radiation Protection. rev. ed. (Illus.). 184p. 1981. text ed. 79.50x (ISBN 0-87683-173-0). GP Pub.

Radiation Protection - Recommendations of the ICRP. 2nd ed. International Commission on Radiological Protection. (ICRP Publication Ser.: No. 26). 1977. pap. 17.25 (ISBN 0-08-021511-4). Pergamon.

Radiation Protection: A Guide for Scientists & Physicians. 2nd ed. Jacob Shapiro. LC 80-23096. (Illus.). 480p. 1981. text ed. 32.00x (ISBN 0-674-74584-1). Harvard U Pr.

Radiation Protection: A Systematic Approach to Safety: Proceedings of the 5th Congress of the International Radiation Protection Society, March 1980, Jerusalem, 2 vols. Ed. by Eisenberg. (Illus.). 1055p. 1980. Set. 255.00 (ISBN 0-08-025912-X). Pergamon.

Radiation Protection & Measurements for Low-Voltage Neutron Generators. National Council on Radiation Protection & Measurements Staff. LC 83-62802. (Report Ser.: No. 72). 80p. 1983. pap. text ed. 13.00 (ISBN 0-913392-61-8). NCRP Pubns.

Radiation Protection & Measurements for Low Voltage Neutron Generators. (Report Ser.: No. 72). 1983. 13.00. NCRP Pubns.

Radiation Protection & New Medical Diagnostic Approaches, Proceedings of the Eighteenth Annual Meeting, Held on April 6-7, 1982. (Taylor Lectures: No. 6). 1983. 16.00. NCRP Pubns.

Radiation Protection: Concepts & Trade Offs. Hymer L. Friedell. (Taylor Lecture Ser.: No. 3). 8.00 (ISBN 0-686-30848-4). NCRP Pubns.

Radiation Protection Design Guidelines for 0.1-100 MeV Particle Accelerator Facilities. LC 76-52067. (Report Ser.: No. 51). 1977. 14.00 (ISBN 0-913392-33-2). NCRP Pubns.

Radiation Protection Dose Limit Standards & Regulations. (Advanced Health Physics Training Ser.). (Illus.). 70p. 1983. 39.95x (ISBN 0-87683-353-9). GP Pub.

Radiation Protection During Operation of Nuclear Power Plants: A Safety Guide. (Safety Ser.: No. 50-SG-05). 54p. 1983. pap. text ed. 12.00 (ISBN 92-0-123783-9, ISP654, IAEA). UNIPUB.

Radiation Protection for Dental Radiographers. Edwards. 1985. 17.95 (ISBN 0-8016-1501-1). Mosby.

Radiation Protection for Dental Radiographers. Cris Edwards et al. LC 84-42910. (Illus.). 300p. (Orig.). 1984. pap. text ed. 17.95x (ISBN 0-940122-16-2, MAP-12). Mosby Multi-Media.

Radiation Protection for Medical & Allied Health Personnel. LC 76-19728. (NCRP Reports Ser.: No. 48). 1976. 13.00 (ISBN 0-913392-30-8). NCRP Pubns.

Radiation Protection for Radiologic Technologists. Robert Frankel. (Illus.). 1976. text ed. 36.95 (ISBN 0-07-021875-7). McGraw.

Radiation Protection for Student Radiographers. Statkiewicz. 1985. 18.95 (ISBN 0-8016-4738-X). Mosby.

Radiation Protection for Student Radiographers. Mary A. Statkiewicz & E. Russell Ritenour. LC 83-19480. (Illus.). 277p. (Orig.). 1983. pap. 17.95X (ISBN 0-940122-10-3). Mosby Multi-Media.

Radiation Protection Glossary. 76p. 1976. looseleaf 18.95x (ISBN 0-87683-213-3). GP Pub.

Radiation Protection Glossary. (Safety Ser.: No. 76). 166p. (Orig.). 1986. pap. text ed. 40.00 (ISBN 92-0-023086-5, ISP726, IAEA). UNIPUB.

Radiation Protection in Educational Institutions. LC 66-25710. (NCRP Reports Ser.: No. 32). 1966. 10.00 (ISBN 0-913392-14-6). NCRP Pubns.

Radiation Protection in Hospitals. Richard F. Mould. (Medical Science Ser.). (Illus.). 224p. 1985. 59.00x (ISBN 0-85274-802-7, Pub. by A Hilger UK). Taylor & Francis.

Radiation Protection in Mining & Milling of Uranium & Thorium. iv, 346p. 1976. 24.50 (ISBN 92-2-101504-1). Intl Labour Office.

Radiation Protection in Occupational Health: Manual for Occupational Physicians. (Safety Ser.: No. 83). 200p. (Orig.). 1987. pap. text ed. 44.00 (ISP744, IAEA). UNIPUB.

Radiation Protection in Pediatric Radiology. LC 81-80187. (Report Ser.: No. 68). 1981. 14.00 (ISBN 0-913392-54-5). NCRP Pubns.

Radiation Protection in the Radiologic & Health Sciences. 2nd ed. Marilyn E. Noz & Gerald Q. Maguire, Jr. LC 84-20187. (Illus.). 277p. 1985. pap. 24.50 (ISBN 0-8121-0962-7). Lea & Febiger.

Radiation Protection in Veterinary Medicine. LC 77-121706. (NCRP Reports Ser.: No. 36). 1970. 12.00 (ISBN 0-913392-18-9). NCRP Pubns.

Radiation Protection Instrumentation & Its Application, No. 20. International Commission on Radiation Units and Measurements. LC 70-177297. (Illus.). v, 60p. 1971. 12.00 (ISBN 0-913394-38-6). Intl Comm Rad Meas.

Radiation Protection Monitoring. (Proceedings Ser.). (Illus.). 556p. 1969. pap. 44.00 (ISBN 92-0-020069-9, ISP199, IAEA). UNIPUB.

Radiation Protection of the Patient: A Manual of Good Practice, Vol. 1. Ed. by Walter A. Langmead. 62p. 1984. text ed. 9.95x (ISBN 0-19-261503-3). Oxford U Pr.

Radiation Protection of the Patient in Nuclear Medicine: A Manual of Good Practice. Walter A. Langmead. 1983. pap. 13.95x (ISBN 0-19-261422-3). Oxford U Pr.

Radiation Protection of Workers - Ionising Radiations: An International Labour Office Code of Practice. 71p. (Orig.). 1987. pap. 10.50 (ISBN 92-2-105996-0). Intl Labour Office.

Radiation Protection of Workers in Mining & Milling of Radioactive Ores. (Safety Ser.: No. 26). 108p. 1983. pap. 15.00 (ISBN 92-0-123683-2, ISP637, IAEA). UNIPUB.

Radiation Protection of Workers in Mines. Ed. by M. C. Thorne. (ICRP Publication: No. 47). 1986. pap. 25.00 (ISBN 0-08-034020-2, Pub. by PPL). Pergamon.

Radiation Protection Optimization-Present Experience & Methods: Proceedings of the European Scientific Seminar, Luxembourg, Oct. 1979. Ed. by H. Ebert et al. LC 80-41671. (Illus.). 330p. 1981. 67.00 (ISBN 0-08-027291-6). Pergamon.

Radiation Protection Practice, 3 vols. IRPA 7 Staff. 1739p. 1988. Set. pap. 118.00 (ISBN 0-08-034443-7, Pub. by PPA). Pergamon.

Radiation Protection Practice, Vol. 1. IRPA 7 Staff. 620p. 1988. pap. 57.00 (ISBN 0-08-034440-2, Pub. by PPA). Pergamon.

Radiation Protection Practice, Vol. 2. IRPA 7 Staff. 575p. 1988. pap. 57.00 (ISBN 0-08-034441-0, Pub. by PPA). Pergamon.

Radiation Protection Practice, Vol. 3. IRPA 7 Staff. 544p. 1988. pap. 57.00 (ISBN 0-08-034442-9, Pub. by PPA). Pergamon.

Radiation Protection Principles for the Disposal of Solid Radioactive Waste. Ed. by M. C. Thorne. (ICRP Publication: No. 46). 35p. 1986. pap. 25.00 (ISBN 0-08-033666-3, Pub. by PPL). Pergamon.

Radiation Protection Procedures. P. N. Krishnamoorthy & J. U. Ahmed. (Safety Ser.: No. 38). (Illus.). 198p. (Orig.). 1973. pap. 22.00 (ISBN 92-0-123373-6, ISP257, IAEA). UNIPUB.

Radiation Protection Programmes in the Soviet Union, Poland & Czechoslovakia. (Study Tour Reports). (Illus.). 100p. 1971. pap. 9.25 (ISBN 92-0-127071-2, ISTR2, IAEA). UNIPUB.

Radiation Protection Progress Reports, 1978. (Commission of the European Communities Symposium Ser.). 870p. 1979. 144.00 (ISBN 3-7186-0011-0). Harwood Academic.

Radiation Protection Progress Reports, 1980. (Commission of the European Communities Symposium Ser.). 1358p. 1981. 258.00 (ISBN 3-7186-0062-5). Harwood Academic.

Radiation Protection Progress Reports, 1979. (Commission of the European Communities Symposium Ser.). 924p. 1980. 205.00 (ISBN 3-7186-0047-1). Harwood Academic.

Radiation Protection Quantities for External Exposure. G. Burger et al. (Commission of the European Communities Symposium Ser.). 268p. 1981. 90.00 (ISBN 3-7186-0063-3). Harwood Academic.

Radiation Protection Standards. Lauriston S. Taylor. (Monotopic Reprint Ser.). 112p. 1971. 29.00 (ISBN 0-8493-0111-4). CRC Pr.

Radiation Protection Standards for Radioluminous Timepieces. (Safety Ser.: No. 23). 37p. 1967. pap. 6.25 (ISBN 92-0-123467-8, ISP167, IAEA). UNIPUB.

Radiation Protection Technician Program Planning Guide. Center for Occupational Research & Develpoment Staff. (Nuclear Technology Ser.). 76p. 1980. pap. text ed. 20.00 (ISBN 1-55502-061-5). Ctr Res & Dev.

Radiation Protection Technology: Student Manual, a Self-Study Course. Daniel A. Gollnick. 195p. 1984. wkbk. 175.00 (ISBN 0-916339-02-5). Pacific Rad.

Radiation-Protective Drugs & Their Reaction Mechanisms. J. C. Livesey et al. LC 85-15451. (Illus.). 146p. 1986. 32.00 (ISBN 0-8155-1051-9). Noyes.

Radiation Quantities & Units, No. 33. International Commission on Radiation Units & Measurements. LC 80-812758. 1980. 11.00 (ISBN 0-913394-27-0, SC 33). Intl Comm Rad Meas.

Radiation Regime & Architecture of Plant Stands. Juhan Ross. (Tasks for Vegetation Science Ser.: No. 3). 480p. 1982. 115.00 (ISBN 90-6193-607-1, Pub. by Junk Pubs Netherlands). Kluwer Academic.

Radiation Research: Proceedings of the Eighth International Congress of Radiation Research, Edingburgh, July 1987, 2 vols. Ed. by E. M. Fielden et al. 1988. Vol. 1: 450 pgs. 110.00x (ISBN 0-85066-399-7); Vol. 2: 1000 pgs. 308.00x (ISBN 0-85066-385-7); Two Vol. set. 374.00x (ISBN 0-85066-428-4). Taylor & Francis.

Radiation Risks in Medical Imaging. J. Whalen. 1984. 36.50 (ISBN 0-8151-9254-1). Year Bk Med.

Radiation Risks to the Developing Nervous System. Kriegel et al. 435p. 1986. 63.00 (ISBN 0-89574-225-X, Pub. by Gustav Fischer Verlag). VCH Pubs.

Radiation Safety for Laboratory Technicians. Charles A. Kelsey. Ed. by Alvin F. Gardner. (Allied Health Professions Monographs). 42p. 1983. 5.00 (ISBN 0-87527-319-X). Green.

Radiation Safety Handbook. 69p. Date not set. member 10.00 (ISBN 0-318-21477-6, 227); non-member 13.50. Am Soc Nondestructive.

Radiation Safety in Hot Facilities. (Proceedings Ser.: No. 238). (Illus.). 754p. (Orig.). 1970. pap. 57.25 (ISBN 92-0-020070-2, ISP238, IAEA). UNIPUB.

Radiation Safety Training Criteria for Industrial Radiography. LC 78-61401. (NCRP Reports Ser.: No. 61). 1978. 10.00 (ISBN 0-913392-45-6). NCRP Pubns.

Radiation: Self-Help Guide. National Veterans Law Center Staff. Ed. by Keith D. Snyder. 1982. pap. text ed. 5.00x (ISBN 0-941486-03-6). Vets Ed Proj.

Radiation Sensitivity of Toxins & Animal Poisons. (Panel Proceedings Ser.). (Illus., Orig.). 1970. pap. 9.25 (ISBN 92-0-111270-X, ISP243, IAEA). UNIPUB.

Radiation Technician. Jack Rudman. (Career Examination Ser.: C-681). (Cloth bdg. avail. on request). pap. 16.00 (ISBN 0-8373-0681-7). Natl Learning.

Radiation Techniques for Water-Use Efficiency Studies. (Technical Reports Ser.: No. 168). (Illus.). 127p. 1975. pap. 20.00 (ISBN 92-0-115075-X, IDC168, IAEA). UNIPUB.

Radiation Therapy & Thanatology. Richard J. Torpie et al. 194p. 1984. 24.00 (ISBN 0-398-04885-1). C C Thomas.

Radiation Therapy for Head & Neck Neoplasms. C. C. Wang. 336p. 1983. text ed. 55.00 (ISBN 0-7236-7049-8). PSG Pub Co.

Radiation Therapy Mold Technology: Principles, Design & Applications. B. Watkins. (Illus.). 224p. 1981. 39.00 (ISBN 0-08-025373-3). Pergamon.

Radiation Therapy of Gynecological Cancer. Ed. by Dattatreyudu Nori & Basil S. Hilaris. LC 86-18602. 444p. 1987. 69.50 (ISBN 0-8451-4219-4, 4219). A R Liss.

Radiation Therapy of Tumors & Diseases of the Nervous System. Jean J. Bouchard. LC 66-23233. (Illus.). pap. 46.40 (ISBN 0-317-07855-0, 2014527). Bks Demand UMI.

Radiation Therapy Planning, Vol. 1. Bleehan & Glatstein. (Fundamentals of Cancer Management). 792p. 1983. 99.75 (ISBN 0-8247-1830-5). Dekker.

Radiation Therapy Simulation Workbook. Sue Mizer et al. 192p. 1986. 57.50 (ISBN 0-08-033652-3, PBI). Pergamon.

Radiation Therapy with Heavy Particles & Fast Electrons. Ed. by R. Silverman & J. DiStasio. LC 79-27925. (Radiology Review: No. 2). (Illus.). 560p. 1980. 48.00 (ISBN 0-8155-0790-9). Noyes.

Radiation Transfer & Stellar Atmospheres. Thomas L. Swihart. (Astronomy & Astrophysics Ser.: Vol. 12). 142p. 1981. 38.00 (ISBN 0-912918-18-7, 0018). Pachart Pub Hse.

Radiation Transmission Through Inhomogeneities in Shields. V. G. Zolotukhin. 368p. 1971. text ed. 74.00 (ISBN 0-7065-1206-5). Coronet Bks.

Radiation Transport in Spectral Lines. R. G. Athay. LC 72-188002. (Geophysics & Astrophysics Monographs: No. 1). 266p. 1972. lib. bdg. 39.50 (ISBN 90-277-0228-4, Pub. by Reidel Holland); pap. 21.50 (ISBN 90-277-0241-1, Pub. by Reidel Holland). Kluwer Academic.

Radiation Trapped in the Earth's Magnetic Field. B. M. McCormac. 908p. 1966. 110.00 (ISBN 0-677-01210-1). Gordon & Breach.

Radiation Trapped in the Earth's Magnetic Field: Proceedings of the Advanced Study Institute, Bergen Norway, 1965. Advanced Study Institute, Bergen, Norway, Staff. Ed. by B. M. McCormac. (Astrophysics & Space Library: No. 5). 901p. 1966. lib. bdg. 79.00 (ISBN 90-277-0130-X, Pub. by Reidel Holland). Kluwer Academic.

Radiation: Waves & Particles-Benefits & Risks. Laurence Pringle. LC 82-16721. (Illus.). 64p. (gr. 7-12). 1983. PLB 12.95 (ISBN 0-89490-054-4). Enslow Pubs.

Radiationless Processes. Ed. by Baldassare Di Bartolo. LC 80-21961. (NATO ASI Series B, Physical Sciences: Vol. 62). 566p. 1981. 89.50x (ISBN 0-306-40577-6, Plenum Pr). Plenum Pub.

Radiationless Processes in Molecules & Crystals. Ed. by F. K. Fong. (Topics in Applied Physics: Vol. 15). (Illus.). 1976. 61.00 (ISBN 0-387-07830-4). Springer-Verlag.

Radiationless Transition. Ed. by Sheng H. Lin. LC 79-26781. 1980. 70.50 (ISBN 0-12-450650-X). Acad Pr.

Radiative Corrections in SU (2) O X U (1) Proceedings of the Workshop on Radiative Corrections in SU (2) O X U (1), Miramore, Trieste, Italy, June 6-8. Ed. by B. W. Lynn & J. F. Wheater. 340p. 1984. 38.00 (ISBN 9971-966-26-3); pap. 23.00 (ISBN 9971-966-28-X, Pub. by World Sci Singapore). World Scientific Pub.

Radiative Heat Transfer in High Temperature Gases: A Handbook. Ed. by R. I. Soloukhin. Tr. by Dov Lederman from Rus. 309p. 1987. 95.00 (ISBN 0-89116-569-X). Hemisphere Pub.

Radiative Processes in Astrophysics. George B. Rybicki & Alan P. Lightman. LC 79-15531. 382p. 1979. 56.95 (ISBN 0-471-04815-1); pap. 22.95 (ISBN 0-471-82759-2). Wiley.

Radiative Processes in Discharge Plasmas. Ed. by Joseph M. Proud & Lawrence H. Luessen. (NATO ASI Series B, Physical Sciences: Vol. 149). 592p. 1987. 97.50x (ISBN 0-306-42550-5, Plenum Pr). Plenum Pub.

Radiative Processes in Meteorology & Climatology. G. Paltridge & C. Platt. (Developments in Atmospheric Science: Vol. 5). 318p. 1976. 105.25 (ISBN 0-444-41444-4). Elsevier.

Radiative Properties of Hot Dense Matter III: Proceedings of the Third International Conference, Williamsburgh, Virginia, October 14-18, 1985. Ed. by C. Hooper, Jr. et al. 576p. 1987. 74.00 (ISBN 9971-50-235-6, Z0369P-P). World Scientific Pub.

Radiative Properties of Hot Dense Plasma Matter. Ed. by J. Davis et al. LC 85-10720. 500p. 1985. 71.00 (ISBN 9971-978-37-7). World Scientific Pub.

Radiative Transfer. Subrahmanyan Chandrasekhar. (Illus.). 1960. pap. 7.95 (ISBN 0-486-60590-6). Dover.

Radiative Transfer & Thermal Control, PAAS49. Ed. by Allie M. Smith. LC 76-40978. (Illus.). 551p. 1976. 59.50 (ISBN 0-915928-13-2). AIAA.

Radiative Transfer in Nontransparent, Dispersed Media. H. Reiss. (Tracts in Modern Physics Ser.: Vol. 113). (Illus.). 200p. 1988. 65.50 (ISBN 0-387-18608-5). Springer-Verlag.

Radiative Transfer in Scattering & Absorbing Atmospheres: Standard Computational Procedures. Ed. by Jacqueline Lenoble. LC 85-31116. 315p. 1985. 48.00 (ISBN 0-937194-05-0). A Deepak Pub.

Radiator Service Work. Peter Novellino. (Series 466). (Orig.). 1978. pap. 5.00 wkbk. (ISBN 0-8064-0183-4, 466); audio visual pkg. 79.00 (ISBN 0-8064-0184-2). Bergwall.

Radical, Vol. 1-10. Repr. of 1872 ed. Set. 775.00 (ISBN 0-404-19545-8); 77.50 ea. (ISBN 0-686-47851-7). AMS Pr.

Radical Abolitionism: Anarchy & the Government of God in Anti-Slavery Thought. Lewis Perry. 328p. 1973. 27.50x (ISBN 0-8014-0754-0). Cornell U Pr.

Radical Adult Education: A Political & Philosophical Critique. Brendan Evans. LC 87-13572. (Volume in Radical Forum on Adult Education Ser.). 256p. 1987. 29.00 (ISBN 0-7099-0942-X, Pub. by Croom Helm UK). Routledge Chapman & Hall.

Radical Analysis of Special Education: Focus on Historical Development & Learning Disabilities. Scott B. Sigmon. 136p. 1987. 36.00x (ISBN 1-85000-230-4, Pub. by Falmer Pr); pap. 17.00x (ISBN 1-85000-231-2). Taylor & Francis.

Radical: And Advocate of Equality. Paul Brown. LC 75-307. (Radical Tradition in America Ser). 170p. 1975. Repr. of 1834 ed. 18.70 (ISBN 0-88355-211-6). Hyperion Conn.

Radical Approaches to Adult Education. Tom Lovett. 240p. 1988. lib. bdg. 42.00x (ISBN 0-415-00561-2, Pub. by Croom Helm UK). Routledge Chapman & Hall.

Radical Approaches to Adult Education. Ed. by Tom Lovett. (Radical Forum on Adult Education Ser.). 240p. 1986. 34.50 (ISBN 0-7099-4141-2, Pub. by Croom Helm UK). Routledge Chapman & Hall.

Radical Approaches to Social Skills Training. Ed. by Peter Trower. 384p. 1984. 33.00 (ISBN 0-416-00931-X, NO. 5076). Routledge Chapman & Hall.

Radical Arts. J. A. Dorsten. (Publications of Sir Thomas Browne Institute Ser.: No. 4). 1973. lib. bdg. 24.00 (ISBN 90-6021-001-8, Pub. by Leiden Univ Holland). Kluwer Academic.

Radical Banach Algebras & Automatic Continuity: Long Beach, California, 1981, Proceedings. Ed. by J. M. Bacher et al. (Lecture Notes in Mathematics: Vol. 975). 470p. 1983. pap. 27.50 (ISBN 0-387-11985-X). Springer-Verlag.

Radical Beginnings: Richard Hofstadter & the 1930's. Susan S. Baker. LC 84-27930. (Contributins in American History Ser.: No. 112). xxi, 268p. 1985. lib. bdg. 36.95 (ISBN 0-313-24713-7, BHO/). Greenwood.

Radical Bible. 1972. pap. 1.95 (ISBN 0-377-02141-5). Friendship Pr.

Radical Bibliographies. Leon Kramer. 1979. lib. bdg. 59.95 (ISBN 0-87700-307-6). Revisionist Pr.

Radical Bourgeoisie: The Ligue de l'Enseignement & the Origins of the Third Republic. Katherine Auspitz. LC 81-15462. 320p. 1982. 34.50 (ISBN 0-521-23861-7). Cambridge U Pr.

Radical Brethren. Irvin B. Horst. 216p. 1972. 43.95 (ISBN 0-8361-1193-1). Herald Pr.

Radical by Design: The Life & Style of Elizabeth Hawes. Bettina Berch. (Illus.). 1988. 19.95 (ISBN 0-525-24715-7). Dutton.

Radical Career Change: Life Beyond Work. David L. Krantz. LC 78-50720. 1978. 11.95 (ISBN 0-02-916760-4). Free Pr.

Radical Center. Alan Baron & William Schneider. Date not set. price not set. S&S.

Radical Center: Middle Americans & the Politics of Alienation. Donald I. Warren. LC 75-19880. (Illus.). 276p. 1976. text ed. 22.95 (ISBN 0-268-01594-5); pap. 9.95x (ISBN 0-268-01595-3). U of Notre Dame Pr.

Radical Challenge: The Response of Social Democracy. Alastair Kilmarnock. (Illus.). 228p. 1988. pap. 15.95 (ISBN 0-233-98179-9, Pub. by A Deutsch England). David & Charles.

Radical Change Through Communication in Mao's China. Godwin Chu. LC 77-3874. 350p. 1977. text ed. 17.50x (ISBN 0-8248-0515-1, Eastwest Ctr). UH Pr.

Radical Chic & Mau-Mauing the Flak Catchers. Tom Wolfe. 153p. 1987. 16.95 (ISBN 0-374-24600-9); pap. 5.95 (ISBN 0-374-52072-0). FS&G.

Radical Christian. Arthur Wallis. Ed. by Dick Myhre. 189p. (Orig.). 1987. pap. 5.95 (ISBN 0-939159-05-8). Cityhill Pub.

Radical Christian Living. Richard Booker. LC 84-90103. (Illus.). 124p. (Orig.). 1985. pap. 4.95 (ISBN 0-932081-03-7). Victory Hse.

Radical Christianity. Tim Timmons. 144p. 1986. pap. 4.95 (ISBN 0-89693-531-0). Victor Bks.

Radical Christianity: A Reading of Recovery. Christopher Rowland. 250p. 1988. 27.95 (ISBN 0-88344-370-8, 370-8); pap. 14.95 (ISBN 0-88344-369-4, 369-4). Orbis Bks.

Radical Commitment: Getting Serious about Christian Growth. Vernon Grounds. LC 84-3344. 1984. pap. 5.95 (ISBN 0-88070-051-3). Multnomah.

Radical Constructionism: Rethinking the Dynamics of Development. Melvin Feffer. 240p. 1988. 35.00x (ISBN 0-8147-2590-2). NYU Pr.

Radical Criminology. Michael Lynch & W. Byron Groves. LC 85-81734. (Special Edge Texts Ser.). 115p. (Orig.). 1986. pap. 7.99 (ISBN 0-911577-06-8). Harrow & Heston.

Radical Currents in Contemporary Philosophy. David H. DeGrood. LC 73-110806. 286p. 1971. 15.00 (ISBN 0-87527-029-8). Fireside Bks.

Radical Democracy: Progress Through Disunity. Edward Speyer. 384p. (Orig.). 1984. pap. 9.75 (ISBN 0-9613359-0-4). E Speyer.

Radical Departure. Lia Matera. 224p. (Orig.). 1988. pap. 3.50 (ISBN 0-553-27072-9). Bantam.

Radical Departures: Desparate Detours to Growing Up. Saul V. Levine. LC 83-26491. 216p. 1986. pap. 4.95 (ISBN 0-15-675799-0, Harv). HarBraceJ.

Radical Departures: Desperate Detours to Growing Up. Saul V. Levine. LC 83-26491. 288p. 1984. 15.95 (ISBN 0-15-175840-9). HarBraceJ.

Radical Discontinuities: American Romanticism & Christian Consciousness. Harold P. Simonson. LC 81-72051. 180p. 1983. 24.50 (ISBN 0-8386-3159-2). Fairleigh Dickinson.

Radical Doctor Smollett. Donald Bruce. 240p. 1985. Repr. of 1964 ed. lib. bdg. 45.00 (ISBN 0-89984-136-8). Century Bookbindery.

Radical Earnestness: English Social Theory, 1880-1980. Fred Inglis. 264p. 1982. pap. 9.95x (ISBN 0-85520-401-X). Basil Blackwell.

Radical Economics. Bruce McFarlane. LC 81-21278. 1982. 26.50 (ISBN 0-312-66148-7). St Martin.

Radical Empiricism of William James. John D. Wild. LC 80-17547. xiv, 430p. 1980. Repr. of 1969 ed. lib. bdg. 41.50 (ISBN 0-313-22641-5, WIRW). Greenwood.

Radical Enlightenment: Pantheists, Freemasons & Republicans. Margaret C. Jacob. (Early Modern Europe Today Ser.). (Illus.). 352p. 1981. text ed. 14.95 (ISBN 0-04-901029-8). Unwin Hyman.

Radical Essays. B. P. Beckwith. 1981. 6.00 (ISBN 0-9603262-2-7). Beckwith.

Radical Feminists of Heterodoxy: Greenwich Village, 1912-1940. 2nd, rev. ed. Judith Schwarz. LC 86-62342. (Illus.). 180p. 1986. pap. 8.95 (ISBN 0-934678-08-1). New Victoria Pubs.

Radical Forecasting Power of the Philosophy of History Expressed in Meaningful & Dramatic Charts, 2 vols. Georg W. Hegel. (Illus.). 241p. 1986. Set. 245.75 (ISBN 0-89901-258-2). Found Class Reprints.

Radical Future of Liberal Feminism. Zillah Eisenstein. (Northeastern Series in Feminist Theory). 270p. 1981. pap. text ed. 11.95x (ISBN 0-582-28206-3). NE U Pr.

Radical Heritage: Labor, Socialism, & Reform in Washington & British Columbia, 1885-1917. Carlos A. Schwantes. LC 78-21757. (Emil & Kathleen Sick Lecture-Bk. Ser. in Western History & Biography). 306p. 1979. 22.50x (ISBN 0-295-95653-4). U of Wash Pr.

Radical Hermeneutics: Repetition, Deconstruction & the Hermeneutic Project. John D. Caputo. LC 86-46143. (Studies in Phenomenology & Existential Philosophy). 332p. 1987. 37.50 (ISBN 0-253-34785-8); pap. 17.50 (ISBN 0-253-20442-9). Ind U Pr.

Radical Hospitality. David Rupprecht & Ruth Rupprecht. LC 83-3259. 110p. 1983. pap. 4.95. Presby & Reformed.

Radical Hospitality: Leader's Guide. David Rupprecht & Ruth Rupprecht. 1985. pap. 2.95 (ISBN 0-87552-419-2). Presby & Reformed.

Radical Humanism: Selected Essays. Jean Amery. Ed. by Sidney Rosenfeld & Stella P. Rosenfeld. Tr. by Stella Rosenfeld & Sidney Rosenfeld. LC 83-49525. 160p. 1984. 22.50x (ISBN 0-253-34770-X). Ind U Pr.

Radical Imagination. Kathe Kollwitz & Josef Herman. (Illus.). 150p. (Orig.). 1985. pap. 4.50 (Pub. by Journeyman Pr Canda). Riverrun NY.

Radical Innocence: A Critical Study of the Hollywood Ten. Bernard F. Dick. 304p. 1988. 27.00 (ISBN 0-8131-1660-0). U Pr of Ky.

Radical Islam. Emmanuel Sivan. LC 84-20999. 224p. 1987. pap. 10.95x (ISBN 0-300-03888-7). Yale U Pr.

Radical Islam: Medieval Theology & Modern Politics. Emmanuel Sivan. LC 84-20999. 224p. 1985. 25.00t (ISBN 0-300-03263-3). Yale U Pr.

Radical Issues in Criminology. Ed. by Pat Carlen & Mike Collison. 212p. 1980. 28.50x (ISBN 0-389-20083-2, 06856). B&N Imports.

Radical Kingdom: The Western Experience of Messianic Hope. Rosemary R. Ruether. LC 70-109080. 324p. 1975. pap. 5.95 (ISBN 0-8091-1860-2). Paulist Pr.

Radical Knowledge: A Philosophical Inquiry into the Nature & Limits of Science. Gonzalo Munevar. LC 81-4258. 135p. 1981. 25.00 (ISBN 0-915145-17-0); pap. 12.50 (ISBN 0-915145-16-2). Hackett Pub.

Radical Left & American Foreign Policy. Robert W. Tucker. LC 73-156476. (Washington Center of Foreign Policy Research: Studies in International Affairs: No. 15). pap. 42.00 (ISBN 0-317-55519-7, 2029236). Bks Demand UMI.

Radical Left in Britain Nineteen Thirty-One to Nineteen Forty-One. James Jupp. 270p. 1982. 30.00x (ISBN 0-7146-3123-X, F Cass Co). Biblio Dist.

Radical Left in the Hungarian Revolution of 1848. Lazlo Deme & Laszlo Deme. (East European Monographs: No. 19). 162p. 1976. 20.00x (ISBN 0-914710-12-5). East Eur Quarterly.

Radical Liberation Theology: An Evangelical Response. Raymond C. Hundley. 128p. 1987. 12.95 (ISBN 0-917851-04-8). Forum Script.

Radical Life: The Autobiography of a Woman Radical. Vera B. Weisbord. 330p. 1977. 17.95 (ISBN 0-88286-101-8). C H Kerr.

Radical Literary Education: A Classroom Experiment with Wordsworth's "Ode". Jeffrey C. Robinson. LC 86-23366. 224p. 1987. text ed. 30.00x (ISBN 0-299-11060-5); pap. text ed. 13.95x (ISBN 0-299-11064-8). U of Wis Pr.

Radical Lord Radnor: The Public Life of Viscount Folkestone, Third Earl of Radnor, 1779-1869. Ronald K. Huch. (Minnesota Monographs in the Humanities: Vol. 10). 1977. 18.50x (ISBN 0-8166-0809-1). U of Minn Pr.

Radical Love: Toward a Sexual Spirituality. Dorothy H. Donnelly. 144p. 1984. pap. 6.95 (ISBN 0-86683-817-1, AY8407, HarpR). Har-Row.

Radical Management: Power-Politics & the Pursuit of Trust. Samuel A. Culbert & John J. McDonough. 240p. 17.95 (ISBN 0-02-905940-2). Free Pr.

Radical Media: The Political Experience of Alternative Communication. John Downing. LC 83-61475. 350p. 1984. 20.00 (ISBN 0-89608-192-3); pap. 8.00 (ISBN 0-89608-191-5). South End Pr.

Radical Monotheism in Western Culture. H. Richard Niebuhr. pap. 6.95x (ISBN 0-06-131491-9, TB1491, Torch). Har-Row.

Radical Movement of the Nineteen Sixties. Roger G. Betsworth. LC 80-12534. (ATLA Monograph Ser.: No. 14). viii, 363p. 1980. 22.50 (ISBN 0-8108-1307-6). Scarecrow.

Radical Nationalist in Japan: Kita Ikki, 1883-1937. George W. Wilson. LC 69-12740. (East Asian Ser: No. 37). (Illus.). 1969. 17.50x (ISBN 0-674-74590-6). Harvard U Pr.

Radical Nature of Christianity: Church Growth Eyes Look at the Supernatural Mission of the Christian & the Church. Waldo J. Werning. LC 76-8359. 220p. 1976. pap. 5.85 (ISBN 0-87808-730-3, Pub. by Mandate Pr). William Carey Lib.

Radical New Road to Wealth: How to Raise Venture Capital for a New Business. 3rd, rev. ed. A. David Silver. 1987. pap. 15.00 (ISBN 0-934311-15-3). Intl Wealth.

Radical Papers. Ed. by Dimitrios I. Roussopoulos. 168p. 1987. 29.95 (ISBN 0-920057-87-X, Dist. by U of Toronto Press); pap. 12.95 (ISBN 0-920057-86-1, Dist. by U of Toronto Pr). Black Rose Bks.

Radical Papers, No. 2. Ed. by Dimitrios I. Roussopoulos. 168p. 1987. 22.95 (ISBN 0-921689-13-6, Dist. by U of Toronto Pr); pap. 12.95 (ISBN 0-921689-12-8, Dist. by U of Toronto Pr). Black Rose Bks.

Radical Paradoxes: Dilemmas of the American Left, 1945-1970. Peter Clecak. LC 73-4072. 1973. 29.50x (ISBN 0-06-010819-3). Irvington.

Radical People's Theatre. Eugene Van Erven. LC 87-46368. 256p. 1988. 27.50 (ISBN 0-253-34788-2). Ind U Pr.

Radical Periodicals in America, 1890-1950: A Bibliography with Brief Notes. Walter Goldwater. 1977. 17.50 (ISBN 0-685-77028-1). Univ Place.

Radical Perspectives in Psychology. Nick Heather. (Essential Psychology Ser.). 1976. pap. 4.50x (ISBN 0-416-81860-9, NO. 2745). Routledge Chapman & Hall.

Radical Perspectives on Social Problems: Readings in Critical Sociology. 3rd ed. Ed. by Frank Lindenfeld. 414p. (Orig.). 1987. lib. bdg. 29.95x (ISBN 0-930390-74-1); pap. text ed. 16.95x (ISBN 0-930390-73-3). Gen Hall.

Radical Perspectives on the Rise of Fascism in Germany, 1919 to 1945. Ed. by Michael N. Dobkowski & Isidor Wallimann. 320p. 1988. 28.00 (ISBN 0-85345-757-3); pap. 12.00 (ISBN 0-85345-758-1). Monthly Rev.

Radical Persuasion, 1890-1917: Aspects of the Intellectual History & the Historiography of Three American Radical Organizations. Aileen S. Kraditor. LC 80-18996. 372p. 1981. 40.00 (ISBN 0-8071-0767-0); pap. 12.95x o. p. (ISBN 0-8071-0864-2). La State U Pr.

Radical Philosophy. Agnes Heller. 256p. 1984. 34.95x (ISBN 0-631-12567-1). Basil Blackwell.

Radical Philosophy. Agnes Heller. 224p. 1986. pap. text ed. 12.95 (ISBN 0-631-15022-6). Basil Blackwell.

Radical Pietists. Delburn Carpenter. LC 72-13586. (Illus.). 30.00 (ISBN 0-404-11008-8). AMS Pr.

Radical Political Economy: An Introduction to the Alternative Economics. Brian Burkitt. 208p. 1984. 30.00x (ISBN 0-8147-1057-3); pap. 15.00x (ISBN 0-8147-1058-1). NYU Pr.

Radical Political Economy since the Sixties: A Sociology of Knowledge Analysis. Paul A. Attewell. LC 83-24650. 1984. text ed. 32.00 (ISBN 0-8135-1053-8). Rutgers U Pr.

Radical Politics in South Asia. Ed. by Paul R. Brass & Marcus F. Franda. (Studies in Communism, Revisionism, & Revolution: No.19). 475p. 1973. 32.50x (ISBN 0-262-02099-8). MIT Pr.

Radical Politics in West Bengal. Marcus F. Franda. (Studies in Communism, Revisionism, & Revolution). 1971. 30.00x (ISBN 0-262-06040-X). MIT Pr.

Radical Politics of Thomas Jefferson. Richard K. Matthews. LC 84-5240. xii, 172p. 1984. pap. 7.95x (ISBN 0-7006-0293-3). U Pr of KS.

Radical Pragmatics. Ed. by Peter Cole. 1981. 29.95 (ISBN 0-12-179660-4). Acad Pr.

Radio Comedy. Arthur F. Wertheim. LC 78-10679. (Illus.). 1979. 29.95x (ISBN 0-19-502481-8) Oxford U Pr.
Radio Common Carriers. 62p. 1976. loose-leaf ed. 3.50 (ISBN 0-318-15019-0). NARUC.
Radio Communication Requirements for Oceanography. (Intergovernmental Oceanographic Commission (IOC) Technical Ser.: No. 3). 1967. pap. 5.00 (ISBN 92-3-100665-7, U515, UNESCO). UNIPUB.
Radio Communications & Navigational Aids see IMAS Seventy-Three: Proceedings.
Radio Contacts Directory, 1988. Ed. by Bob Del Pazzo. 1988. 239.00 (ISBN 0-935224-33-5). Larimi Comm.
Radio Continua During Solar Flares: Selected Contributions to the Workshop Held at Duino, Italy, May 1985. Ed. by Arnold O. Benz. 1986. lib. bdg. 79.00 (ISBN 90-277-2291-9, Pub. by Reidel Holland). Kluwer Academic.
Radio Contrast Agents, 2 Vols. P. R. Knoefel. 1971. Set. 250.00 (ISBN 0-08-016144-8). Pergamon.
Radio Control Model Aircraft. A. M. Vale. 192p. 1984. 27.00x (ISBN 0-905418-04-2, Pub. by Gresham England). State Mutual Bk.
Radio Control Model Helicopter Handbook. Don Lodge. (Illus.). 192p. (Orig.). 1983. pap. 10.95 (ISBN 0-8306-1509-1, 1509). TAB Bks.
Radio Controlled Gliding. Dave Jones. (Illus.). 192p. 1987. pap. 24.95 (ISBN 0-85242-884-7, Argus Bks). Motorbooks Intl.
Radio-Controlled Models: Design & Construction. Graham Goodchild. (Illus.). 120p. 1986. 24.95 (ISBN 0-7134-4532-7, Pub. by Batsford England). David & Charles.
Radio Correspondence Education Planning in Thailand. Boonlert Supadhiloke. (Institute of Culture & Communication Case Studies: No. 9). 122p. (Orig.). 1983. pap. text ed. 5.00 (ISBN 0-86638-040-X). EW Ctr HI.
Radio-Diagnosis of Pleuro-Pulmonary Affections. J. Barjon. 1918. 75.00x (ISBN 0-685-89775-3). Elliots Bks.
Radio Dial. Alicia S. O'Drago. LC 88-70857. 133p. (Orig.). 1988. pap. 9.95 (ISBN 0-929273-00-1). AMP Publishing.
Radio Direction Finding. P. J. Gething. Ed. by J. R. Wait et al. (Electromagnetic Waves Ser.). 253p. 1986. pap. 39.00 (ISBN 0-86341-055-3, EWR04). Inst Elect Eng.
Radio Director's Manual. Edgar E. Willis. 1961. pap. 9.62 (ISBN 0-87506-033-1). Campus.
Radio Dispatcher. Jack Rudman. (Career Examination Ser.: C-540). (Cloth bdg. avail. on request). pap. 14.00 (ISBN 0-8373-0540-3). Natl Learning.
Radio Documentary Handbook: Creating, Producing & Selling for Broadcast. Jurgen Hesse. (Illus.). 152p. (Orig.). 1987. pap. 8.95 (ISBN 0-88908-653-2, 9555P). ISC Pr.
Radio Electronic Measurements. G. Mirsky. 503p. 1978. 10.20 (ISBN 0-8285-0692-2, Pub. by Mir Pubs USSR). Imported Pubns.
Radio-Electronics: From "Drawing Board" to Finished Project. Editors of Radio-Electronics Staff. (Illus.). 160p. 1988. 13.95 (ISBN 0-8306-9133-2, 3133); pap. 10.95 (ISBN 0-8306-3133-X, 3133). TAB Bks.
Radio-Electronics' Guide to Computer Circuits. Radio-Electronics Editors. (Illus.). 170p. 1988. 14.95 (ISBN 0-8306-0333-6); pap. 9.95 (ISBN 0-8306-9333-5, 3033P). TAB Bks.
Radio Electronics State of Solid State. Radio Electronics Editors. LC 87-10190. 168p. 1987. 14.95 (ISBN 0-8306-7733-X, 2733); pap. 9.95 (ISBN 0-8306-2733-2). TAB Bks.
Radio Emission of the Sun & Planets. V. V. Zheleznyakov. LC 75-76797. 1970. 180.00 (ISBN 0-08-013061-5). Pergamon.
Radio Format Conundrum. Edd Routt et al. LC 78-9068. (Illus.). 1978. 13.00x (ISBN 0-8038-6355-1). Hastings.
Radio Free Albemulh. Philip K. Dick. 224p. 1987. pap. 3.50 (ISBN 0-380-70288-6). Avon.
Radio Free Albemuth. Philip K. Dick. 207p. 1986. 14.95 (ISBN 0-87795-762-2). Morrow.
Radio Free Europe. Robert T. Holt. LC 58-7621. pap. 65.80 (ISBN 0-317-41747-9, 2055879). Bks Demand UMI.
Radio Frequency Bridges. Ed. by A. C. Lynch & A. E. Bailey. (Electrical Measurement Ser.). 1988. write for info. Inst Elect Eng.
Radio Frequency Interference. American Radio Play League Staff. 1987. 4.00 (ISBN 0-317-57034-X). Am Radio.
Radio Frequency, Radiation & Plasma Processing. Ed. by Paul N. Cheremisinoff et al. LC 84-52116. 213p. 1984. 45.00 (ISBN 0-87762-382-1). Technomic.
Radio: From Marconi to the Space Age. Alden R. Carter. (First Bks.). (Illus.). 96p. (gr. 4-9). 1987. PLB 9.90 (ISBN 0-531-10310-2). Watts.
Radio Hacker's Code Book. George Sassoon. (Home Computing Ser.). (Illus.). 239p. (Orig.). 1986. pap. 10.50 (ISBN 0-7156-2068-1, Pub. by Duckworth London). Longwood Pub Group.
Radio Handbook. 23rd ed. William I. Orr. 672p. 1986. 29.95 (ISBN 0-672-22424-0). Sams.
Radio in the Television Age. Peter Fornatale. LC 79-67675. 240p. 1983. 22.50 (ISBN 0-87951-106-0); pap. 9.95 (ISBN 0-87951-172-9). Overlook Pr.
Radio Industry: The Story of Its Development. Ed. by Christopher H. Sterling. LC 74-4687. (Telecommunications Ser). (Illus.). 344p. 1974. Repr. of 1928 ed. 23.00x (ISBN 0-405-06055-6). Ayer Co Pubs.
Radio Is My Bomb: A Do-it-Yourself Manual for Pirates. Frear Waves & Joanna Soap. (Illus.). 72p. (Orig.). Date not set. pap. 6.95 (ISBN 1-86980-203-9). Left Bank.
Radio Listening in America: The People Look at Radio-Again. Paul F. Lazarsfeld & Patricia L. Kendall. Ed. by Lewis A. Coser & Walter W. Powell. LC 79-7002. (Perennial Works in Sociology Ser.). (Illus.). 1979. Repr. of 1948 ed. lib. bdg. 15.00x (ISBN 0-405-12100-8). Ayer Co Pubs.
Radio Man: Miles Cabot on Venus. Farley. 5.00 (ISBN 0-686-00476-0); pap. 2.00 (ISBN 0-686-00477-9). Fantasy Pub Co.
Radio Manufacturers of the 1920's, Vol. I: A-C Dayton to J. B. Ferguson, Inc. Alan S. Douglas. LC 87-31088. (Illus.). 256p. 1988. 29.95 (ISBN 0-911572-67-8, K-17); pap. 19.95 (ISBN 0-911572-68-6, K-18). Vestal.
Radio Mechanic. Jack Rudman. (Career Examination Ser.: C-660). (Cloth bdg. avail. on request). pap. 14.00 (ISBN 0-8373-0660-4). Natl Learning.
Radio, Motion Picture & Reading Interests: A Study of High School Pupils. Alice P. Sterner. LC 77-177824. (Columbia University. Teachers College. Contributions to Education: No. 932). Repr. of 1947 ed. 22.50 (ISBN 0-404-55932-8). AMS Pr.
Radio Navigation Engineering. Raab. 1987. write for info. (ISBN 0-471-09781-0). Wiley.
Radio Networks & the Federal Government. Thomas P. Robinson. Ed. by Christopher H. Sterling. LC 78-21735. (Dissertations in Broadcasting Ser.). 1979. Repr. of 1943 ed. lib. bdg. 21.00x (ISBN 0-405-11772-8). Ayer Co Pubs.
Radio Noise Spectrum. Ed. by Donald H. Menzel. LC 60-7997. (Illus.). 1960. 15.00x (ISBN 0-674-74675-9). Harvard U Pr.
Radio Operator. Jack Rudman. (Career Examination Ser.: C-683). (Cloth bdg. avail. on request). pap. 14.00 (ISBN 0-8373-0683-3). Natl Learning.
Radio Paging Market. 295p. 1984. 1550.00 (ISBN 0-86621-279-5, A1355). Frost & Sullivan.
Radio Papers: From KRAB to KCHU-Essays on the Art & Practice of Radio Transmission. Lorenzo W. Milam. (Twenty-Five Years of Community Broadcasting Ser.). (Illus.). 224p. 1986. o.s. 14.95 (ISBN 0-917320-18-2); pap. 9.95 (ISBN 0-917320-19-0). MHO & MHO.
Radio Physics of the Sun: Proceedings. IUA Symposium, College Park, Md., Aug. 7-10, 1979. Ed. by T. E. Gergely & M. R. Kundu. (International Astronomical Union Symposium Ser.: No. 86). 472p. 1980. lib. bdg. 60.50 (ISBN 90-277-1120-8, Pub. by Reidel Holland); pap. 29.00 (ISBN 90-277-1121-6, Pub. by Reidel Holland). Kluwer Academic.
Radio Programming: Consultancy & Formatics. Michael C. Keith. (Illus.). 224p. 1987. pap. 21.95x (ISBN 0-240-51792-X). Focal Pr.
Radio Programs Source Book. 2nd ed. Broadcast Information Bureau, Inc. Staff. Ed. by Avra Fliegelman & Liz Doris. 240p. 1983. pap. write for info. (ISBN 0-943174-02-3). Broadcast Info.
Radio Programs Source Book. Broadcast Information Bureau, Inc. Staff. Ed. by Liz Doris. (Illus., Orig.). 1982. pap. 62.95 (ISBN 0-943174-00-7). Broadcast Info.
Radio Programs Source Book. 3rd, Rev. Suppl. ed. Broadcast Information Bureau, Inc. Staff. Ed. by Liz Doris. LC 82-654122. 300p. (Orig.). 1984. pap. 64.95 (ISBN 0-943174-04-X). Broadcast Info.
Radio Programs Source Book. 3rd ed. Broadcast Information Bureau, Inc. Staff. Ed. by Liz Doris. 150p. (Orig.). 1984. pap. 64.95 (ISBN 0-943174-05-8). Broadcast Info.
Radio Programs Source Book Supplement. Broadcast Information Bureau, Inc. Staff. Ed. by Liz Doris. 100p. (Orig.). 1982. pap. 62.95 (ISBN 0-943174-01-5). Broadcast Info.
Radio Receiver--Chance or Choice. Rainer Lichte. Ed. by Jeanne C. Ferrell. LC 85-80383. 224p. (Orig.). 1985. pap. 18.50 (ISBN 0-914542-16-8). Gilfer.
Radio Receiver: LF-UHF. Ed. by W. Gosling. 456p. 1986. 86.00 (ISBN 0-86341-056-1, TE015). Inst Elect Eng.
Radio Recombination Lines: Proceedings of a Workshop Held in Ottawa, Canada, August 22-24, 1979. Ed. by Peter A. Shaver. (Astrophysics & Space Science Library: No. 80). 294p. 1980. lib. bdg. 37.00 (ISBN 90-277-1103-8, Pub. by Reidel Holland). Kluwer Academic.
Radio Refractivity & Meteorological Data Plots from Radiosonde Launches Trade Winds: March 1969. L. G. Rowlandson & J. S. Schwarz. LC 77-135079. 242p. 1970. 29.00 (ISBN 0-403-04534-7). Scholarly.
Radio Regulations First Series, 25 vols. 1948-1963. Pike & Fischer. LC 48-2103. 1980. Repr. of 1963 ed. lib. bdg. 1150.00 set (ISBN 0-89941-207-6); lib. bdg. 50.00 ea. W S Hein.
Radio Regulations Second Series, 59 vols. 1963-1986. Pike & Fischer. LC 70-24229. 1978. Repr. of 1963 ed. Set. lib. bdg. 3470.00 (ISBN 0-89941-208-4); lib. bdg. 60.00 ea. Vols. 1-49; lib. bdg. 75.00 Vol. 50. W S Hein.
Radio Replies, 3 vols. Leslie Rumble & Charles M. Carty. LC 79-51938. 1979. Set. pap. 33.00 (ISBN 0-89555-159-4). Vol. 1 (ISBN 0-89555-089-X). Vol. 2 (ISBN 0-89555-090-3). Vol. 3 (ISBN 0-89555-091-1). TAN Bks Pubs.
Radio Rescue. Charlotte B. Chorpenning. (Children's Theatre Playscript Ser.). (gr. k-12). 1970. pap. 2.00x (ISBN 0-88020-046-4). Coach Hse.
Radio Research, Nineteen Hundred Forty-Two to Nineteen Hundred Forty-Three. Ed. by Paul F. Lazarsfeld et al. LC 79-7004. (Perennial Works in Sociology Ser.). (Illus.). 1979. Repr. of 1944 ed. lib. bdg. 45.00x (ISBN 0-405-12102-4). Ayer Co Pubs.
Radio Research, Nineteen Hundred Forty-One. Ed. by Paul F. Lazarsfeld et al. LC 79-7003. (Perennial Works in Sociology Ser.). (Illus.). 1979. Repr. of 1941 ed. lib. bdg. 26.50x (ISBN 0-405-12101-6). Ayer Co Pubs.
Radio: Selected AAPSS Surveys, 1929-1941: Radio: the Fifth Estate. American Academy of Political & Social Science, Philadelphia Staff & Irvin Stewart. 1972. cancelled 34.00 (ISBN 0-405-03556-X, 11244). Ayer Co Pubs.
Radio Servicing. Jack Rudman. (DANTES Ser.: No. 35). 1988. 25.95 (ISBN 0-8373-6685-2); pap. 13.95 (ISBN 0-8373-6635-6). Natl Learning.
Radio Shack TRS-80 Educational Software Sourcebook. 6.95 (ISBN 0-317-11010-1). Radio Shack.
Radio Soundtracks: A Reference Guide. 2nd ed. Michael R. Pitts. LC 85-30409. 349p. 1986. 27.50 (ISBN 0-8108-1875-2). Scarecrow.
Radio Speeches of Charles A. Lindbergh: 1939-1940. Charles A. Lindbergh. 1982. lib. bdg. 69.95 (ISBN 0-87700-455-2). Revisionist Pr.
Radio Stars. Ed. by Robert M. Hjellming & David M. Gibson. 1985. lib. bdg. 59.00 (ISBN 90-277-2063-0, Pub. by Reidel Netherlands). Kluwer Academic.
Radio Station. Michael C. Keith & Joseph M. Krause. (Illus.). 320p. (Orig.). 1986. pap. text ed. 22.95x (ISBN 0-240-51747-4). Focal Pr.
Radio Station K-E-R-M. Sindy McKay & Larry Swerdlove. (Muppet Magic Ser.). (Illus.). 26p. (ps up). 1987. 12.95 (ISBN 1-55578-607-3). Worlds Wonder.
Radio Station Manager. Jack Rudman. (Career Examination Ser.: C-2935). (Cloth bdg. avail. on request). pap. 18.00 (ISBN 0-8373-2935-3). Natl Learning.
Radio Station Operations: Management & Employee Perspectives. Lewis B. O'Donnell et al. Date not set. pap. text ed. write for info. (ISBN 0-534-09540-2). Wadsworth Pub.
Radio Station Treasury (Nineteen Hundred to Nineteen Forty-Six) Tom Kneitel. (Illus.). 176p. (Orig.). 1986. pap. 12.95 (ISBN 0-939780-04-6). CRB Res.
Radio Stations Operations. Mark R. Lange. 118p. 1985. pap. text ed. 16.95 (ISBN 0-943987-04-0). Origin Co.
Radio System Design for Telecommunications (1-100 GHz) Roger L. Freeman. 560p. 1987. 44.95 (ISBN 0-471-81236-6). Wiley.
Radio Tech Talk. Ed Radlauer. LC 84-7805. (Tech Talk Bks.). (Illus.). 64p. (gr. 4 up). 1984. 14.60 (ISBN 0-516-08255-8). Childrens.
Radio Technologist. Jack Rudman. (Career Examination Ser.: C-1957). (Cloth bdg. avail. on request). pap. 14.00 (ISBN 0-8373-1957-9). Natl Learning.
Radio Telephone Operator. Jack Rudman. (Career Examination Ser.: C-2883). (Cloth bdg. avail. on request). pap. 14.00 (ISBN 0-8373-2883-7). Natl Learning.
Radio, Television & Sound System Repair: An Introduction. Joel Goldberg. (Illus.). 1978. ref. 37.33 (ISBN 0-13-752238-X). P-H.
Radio-Television-Cable: A Telecommunications Approach. Marvin Smith. 386p. 1985. text ed. 26.95 (ISBN 0-03-060567-9, HoltC). HR&W.
Radio: The Psychology of an Art of Sound. Rudolf Arnheim. LC 73-164504. (Cinema Ser). 1972. Repr. of 1936 ed. lib. bdg. 39.50 (ISBN 0-306-70291-6). Da Capo.
Radio Today: The Present State of Broadcasting. Arno Huth. LC 77-161179. (History of Broadcasting: Radio to Television Ser). 1971. Repr. of 1942 ed. 14.00 (ISBN 0-405-03585-3). Ayer Co Pubs.
Radio Transcript, Dr. Kurt Oster Interview, Tiny Markle Show. 20p. pap. 1.00 (ISBN 0-318-00545-X). Park City Pr.
Radio Universe. 3rd ed. J. S. Hey. LC 82-18982. (Illus.). 260p. 1983. text ed. 40.00 (ISBN 0-08-029152-X); pap. text ed. 17.25 (ISBN 0-08-029151-1). Pergamon.
Radio Universe: An Introduction to Radio Astronomy & Outer Space. Stephen Weston. 20.00 (ISBN 0-900707-42-9, Pub. by Kahn & Averill). State Mutual Bk.
Radio Wave Propagation & the Ionosphere. I. L. Al'pert. LC 61-17727. pap. 101.00 (ISBN 0-317-09200-6, 2020656). Bks Demand UMI.
Radio Waves in the Ionosphere: The Mathematical Theory of the Reflection of Radio Waves from Stratified Ionized Layers. K. G. Budden. pap. 141.50 (ISBN 0-317-27909-2, 2055781). Bks Demand UMI.
Radioactive Contamination of Soil & Plants. R. M. Aleksakhin. 112p. 1965. text ed. 26.00x (ISBN 0-7065-0400-3, Pub. by Keter Pub Jerusalem). Coronet Bks.
Radioactive Contamination of the Marine Environment. (Proceedings Ser.). (Illus.). 786p. (Orig.). 1973. pap. 73.75 (ISBN 92-0-020073-7, ISP313, IAEA). UNIPUB.
Radioactive Contamination of the Sea. Ed. by V. I. Baranov & L. M. Khitrov. 200p. 1966. text ed. 41.00x (ISBN 0-7065-0425-9, Pub. by Keter Pub Jerusalem). Coronet Bks.
Radioactive Decay Data Tables. David C. Kocher & DOE Technical Information Center Staff. LC 81-607800. 227p. 1981. pap. 13.75 (ISBN 0-87079-124-9, DOE/TIC-11026); microfiche 6.50 (ISBN 0-87079-496-5, DOE/TIC-11026). DOE.
Radioactive Fallout from Nuclear Weapons Tests: Proceedings. Ed. by Alfred W. Klement, Jr. LC 65-62945. (AEC Symposium Ser.). 965p. 1965. pap. 32.25 (ISBN 0-87079-323-3, CONF-765); microfiche 6.50 (ISBN 0-87079-324-1, CONF-765). DOE.
Radioactive Isotopes & Global Transport in the Atmosphere. I. L. Karol. 337p. 1974. text ed. 70.00 (ISBN 0-7065-1489-0, Pub. by Keter Pub Jerusalem). Coronet Bks.
Radioactive Isotopes in the Atmosphere & Their Use in Meteorology. I. L. Karol' et al. 376p. 1967. text ed. 75.00x (ISBN 0-7065-0452-6, Pub. by Keter Pub Jerusalem). Coronet Bks.
Radioactive Nuclides in Medicine & Biology. 3rd ed. Edith H. Quimby. LC 68-18868. pap. 100.50 (ISBN 0-317-26277-7, 2055701). Bks Demand UMI.
Radioactive Pharmaceuticals: Proceedings. Ed. by Gould A. Andrews et al. LC 66-60068. (AEC Symposium Ser.). 702p. 1966. pap. 25.50 (ISBN 0-87079-325-X, CONF-651111); microfiche 6.50 (ISBN 0-87079-326-8, CONF-651111). DOE.
Radioactive Phosphorus in the Diagnosis of Gastrointestinal Cancer. R. S. Nelson. (Recent Results in Cancer Research: Vol. 10). (Illus.). 1967. 15.00 (ISBN 0-387-03958-9). Springer-Verlag.
Radioactive Substances. Marie Curie. (Philosophical Paperbook Serie). 94p. 1983. pap. 4.95 (ISBN 0-8022-2433-4). Philos Lib.
Radioactive Tracers in Microbial Immunology. (Illus.). 130p. (Orig.). 1973. pap. 12.00 (ISBN 92-0-111172-X, ISP330, IAEA). UNIPUB.
Radioactive Waste: Advanced Management Methods for Medium-Active Liquid Waste. Ed. by K. W. Carley-Macauly. (Radioactive Waste Management Ser.). 352p. 1981. 102.00 (ISBN 3-7186-0060-9). Harwood Academic.
Radioactive Waste Disposal: A Bibliography. Mary Vance. (Public Administration Ser.: P-1676). 102p. 1985. pap. 15.00 (ISBN 0-89028-386-9). Vance Biblios.
Radioactive Waste Disposal & Geology. Konrad B. Krauskopf. (Topics in the Earth Sciences Ser.). 120p. 1988. text ed. 29.95 (ISBN 0-412-28630-0, Pub. by Chapman & Hall England). Routledge Chapman & Hall.
Radioactive Waste Disposal in Situ Experiments in Granite. OECD. (Nuclear Energy Agency Ser.). 266p. (Orig.). 1985. pap. 34.00x (ISBN 92-64-02728-9). OECD.
Radioactive Waste Disposal in the Ocean: A Bibliography of Politics & Law. Frederick Frankena & Joann K. Frankena. (Public Administration Ser.: P 2007). 20p. 1986. 5.00 (ISBN 1-55590-007-0). Vance Biblios.
Radioactive Waste Disposal in the Ocean. (NCRP Reports Ser.: No. 16). 1954. 8.00 (ISBN 0-913392-05-7). NCRP Pubns.
Radioactive Waste Disposal into a Plastic Clay Formation: A Site-Specific Exercise of Probabilistic Assessment of Geological Containment. M. D'Allessandro & A. Bonne. (Radioactive Waste Management Ser.). 150p. 1981. 35.00 (ISBN 3-7186-0084-6). Harwood Academic.
Radioactive Waste Disposal into the Ground. (Safety Ser.: No. 15). (Illus.). 111p. 1965. pap. 9.50 (ISBN 92-0-123565-8, ISP103, IAEA). UNIPUB.
Radioactive Waste Disposal: The Waste Package, Vol. 1. Roy. (Radioactive Waste Disposal Ser.: No. 1). (Illus.). 256p. 1982. 41.00 (ISBN 0-08-027541-9, A145). Pergamon.
Radioactive Waste from Nuclear Power Plants. Thomas B. Johansson & Peter Steen. LC 80-6052. (Illus.). 1981. 22.50x (ISBN 0-520-04199-2). U of Cal Pr.
Radioactive Waste in Geologic Storage. Ed. by Sherman Fried. LC 79-9754. (ACS Symposium Ser.: No. 100). 1979. 39.95 (ISBN 0-8412-0498-5). Am Chemical.
Radioactive Waste Management. Berlin. 1988. write for info. (ISBN 0-471-85792-0). Wiley.
Radioactive Waste Management: Airborne Radioactive Effluents: Releases & Processing: A Bibliography. DOE Technical Information Center Staff. 244p. 1982. pap. 16.00 (ISBN 0-87079-479-5, DOE/TIC-3397); microfiche 6.50 (ISBN 0-87079-480-9, DOE/TIC-3397). DOE.
Radioactive Waste Management & Disposal. R. Simon. 734p. 1986. 97.50 (ISBN 0-521-32580-3). Cambridge U Pr.

Radiography of Infants & Children: A Problem Oriented Manual of Radiographic & Fluoroscopic Procedures. 3rd ed. Donald B. Darling. (Illus.). 584p. 1979. 84.25x (ISBN 0-398-03740-X). C C Thomas.

Radiography Question & Answer Book A. 1979. 22.25 (2026). Am Soc Nondestructive.

Radiography Workbook. Robert DeAngelis. (Illus.). 167p. Date not set. wkbk. 18.95 (ISBN 0-943589-00-2). Health & Allied.

Radiography Workbook Two. Robert DeAngelis & Michelle Edgar. (Illus.). 178p. Date not set. pap. text ed. 24.95 (ISBN 0-943589-01-0). Health & Allied.

Radioimmunoassay. Ed. by Leonard M. Freeman & M. Donald Blaufox. (Seminars in Nuclear Medicine Reprint Ser.). 176p. 1975. 57.50 (ISBN 0-8089-0933-9, 791374). Grune.

Radioimmunoassay. Ed. by Rosalyn S. Yalow. LC 83-8594. (Benchmark Papers in Microbiology: Vol. 20). 416p. 1983. 55.95 (ISBN 0-87933-109-7). Van Nos Reinhold.

Radioimmunoassay & Related Procedures in Medicine. (Illus.). 471p. (Orig.). 1974. pap. 39.50 ea. (ISP350-1, IAEA); Vol. 1. pap. (ISBN 92-0-010274-3); Vol. 2. pap. (ISBN 92-0-010374-X, ISP350-2). UNIPUB.

Radioimmunoassay & Related Procedures in Medicine: 1977, 2 vols. 1979. Vol. 1. pap. 69.00 (ISBN 92-0-010078-3, ISP469-1, IAEA); Vol. 2. pap. 64.50 (ISBN 92-0-010178-X, ISP469-2). UNIPUB.

Radioimmunoassay & Related Procedures in Medicine 1982. (Illus.). 825p. 1983. pap. 104.00 (ISBN 92-0-010482-7, ISP625, IAEA). UNIPUB.

Radioimmunoassay in Basic & Clinical Pharmacology. Ed. by C. Patrono & B. A. Peskar. (Handbook of Experimental Pharmacology Ser.: Vol. 82). (Illus.). 615p. 1987. 295.00 (ISBN 0-387-17413-3). Springer-Verlag.

Radioimmunoassay in Clinical Biochemistry. Ed. by Charles A. Pasternak. LC 76-675546. pap. 79.30 (ISBN 0-317-29335-4, 2024025). Bks Demand UMI.

Radioimmunoassay of Antibody & Its Clinical Applications. David Parratt. LC 81-12939. pap. 45.30 (2031940). Bks Demand UMI.

Radioimmunoassay of Antibody & It's Clinical Applications. David Parratt et al. LC 81-12939. 234p. 1982. 54.95x (ISBN 0-471-10061-7, Pub. by Wiley-Interscience). Wiley.

Radioimmunoassay of Drugs & Hormones in Cardiovascular Medicine. Ed. by A. Albertini et al. (Symposia Giovanni Lorenzini Foundation: Vol. 3). 364p. 1979. 80.75 (ISBN 0-444-80176-6, North Holland). Elsevier.

Radioimmunoassay of Gut Regulatory Peptides. Stephen R. Bloom & R. G. Long. 256p. 1982. 46.95 (ISBN 0-275-91360-0, C1360). Praeger.

Radioimmunoassay of Hormones for Clinical Trials of Fertility Regulating Agents in Developing Countries: Report. (Technical Report Ser.: No. 578). (Also avail. in French & Spanish). 1975. pap. 2.00 (ISBN 92-4-120578-4). World Health.

Radioimmunoassay of Hormones, Proteins & Enzymes. Ed. by Albertini. (International Congress Ser.: Vol. 528). 1981. 75.25 (ISBN 0-444-90173-6). Elsevier.

Radioimmunoassay of Steroid Hormones. 2nd ed. Derek Gupta. (Illus.). 265p. 1980. 48.80x (ISBN 3-527-25863-9). VCH Pubs.

Radioimmunoassays for Insulin, C-peptide & Proinsulin. L. G. Heding. 1988. lib. bdg. 35.00 (ISBN 0-7462-0085-4, Pub. by MTP Pr England). Kluwer Academic.

Radioimmunoimaging & Radioimmunotherapy. Ed. by S. W. Burchiel & B. A. Rhodes. 416p. 1983. 120.25 (ISBN 0-444-00806-3, Biomedical Pr). Elsevier.

Radioiodine Removal in Nuclear Facilities: Methods & Techniques for Normal & Emergency Situations. (Technical Reports Ser.: No. 201). (Illus.). 98p. 1981. pap. 20.00 (ISBN 92-0-125280-3, IDC201, IAEA). UNIPUB.

Radioisotope Engineering. Ed. by Geoffrey G. Eichholz. LC 77-142891. (Illus.). pap. 106.80 (ISBN 0-317-07974-3, 2055012). Bks Demand UMI.

Radioisotope in Geburtshilfe und Gynekologie. H. Janisch et al. Ed. by E. Gitsch. 1977. 98.00x (ISBN 3-11-004532-X). De Gruyter.

Radioisotope Laboratory Techniques. 4th ed. R. A. Faires & G. G. Boswell. LC 80-41045. 272p. 1980. text ed. 54.95 (ISBN 0-408-70940-5). Butterworth.

Radioisotope Production & Quality Control. (Technical Reports Ser.: No. 128). (Illus.). 969p. (Orig.). 1971. pap. 69.00 (ISBN 92-0-145171-7, IDC128, IAEA). UNIPUB.

Radioisotope Sample Measurement Techniques in Medicine & Biology. (Proceedings Ser.). 724p. 1965. pap. 38.50 (ISBN 92-0-010165-8, ISP106, IAEA). UNIPUB.

Radioisotope Studies in Cardiology. Ed. by H. J. Biersack & P. H. Cox. (Developments in Nuclear Medicine Ser.). 1985. lib. bdg. 59.50 (ISBN 0-318-04531-1, Martinus Nijhoff Netherlands). Kluwer Academic.

Radioisotope Study of Salivary Glands. Ed. by Giuseppe De Rossi. 198p. 1987. 124.95 (ISBN 0-8493-6072-2). CRC Pr.

Radioisotope Techniques for Problem-Solving in Industrial Process Plants. Ed. by J. S. Charlton. LC 85-82076. (Illus.). 320p. 1986. 69.00x (ISBN 0-87201-778-8). Gulf Pub.

Radioisotope Techniques in the Study of Protein Metabolism. (Technical Reports Ser.: No. 45). 1965. pap. 20.00 (ISBN 92-0-115165-9, IDC45, IAEA). UNIPUB.

Radioisotope Tracers in Industry & Geophysics. (Proceedings Ser.). (Illus.). 710p. 1967. pap. 40.00 (ISBN 92-0-060067-0, ISP142, IAEA). UNIPUB.

Radioisotope X-Ray Fluorescence Spectrometry. (Technical Reports Ser.: No. 115). (Illus.). 102p. (Orig.). 1970. pap. 13.00 (ISBN 92-0-165170-8, IDC115, IAEA). UNIPUB.

Radioisotopes & Ionizing Radiations in Entomology: 1961-1963. (Bibliographical Ser.: No. 15). 565p. 1965. pap. 29.00 (ISBN 92-0-014065-3, ISP21/15, IAEA). UNIPUB.

Radioisotopes & Ionizing Radiations in Entomology: 1964-1965. (Bibliographical Ser.: No. 24). 454p. 1976. pap. 34.00 (ISBN 92-0-014067-X, ISP21 24, IAEA). UNIPUB.

Radioisotopes & Ionizing Radiations in Entomology: 1966-1967. (Bibliographical Ser.: No. 36). 818p. 1969. pap. 65.00 (ISBN 92-0-014069-6, ISP21/36, IAEA). UNIPUB.

Radioisotopes & Radiation: Recent Advances in Medicine, Agriculture, & Industry. J. H. Lawrence et al. (Illus.). 12.00 (ISBN 0-8446-0765-7). Peter Smith.

Radioisotopes in Animal Nutrition & Physiology. (Proceedings Ser.). (Illus.). 884p. 1965. pap. 24.00 (ISBN 92-0-010065-1, ISP90, IAEA). UNIPUB.

Radioisotopes in Biology & Medicine: Introductory Principles & Techniques. Audrey V. Wegst et al. 1964. pap. 8.65 (ISBN 0-87506-031-5, 87506-031-5). Campus.

Radioisotopes in Cardiology. Ed. by Marco Salvatore & Ernesto Porta. LC 82-24690. 342p. 1983. 65.00x (ISBN 0-306-41267-5, Plenum Pr). Plenum Pub.

Radioisotopes in Hydrology. (Proceedings Ser.). (Illus.). 459p. 1963. 26.00 (ISBN 92-0-040063-9, ISP71, IAEA). UNIPUB.

Radioisotopes in Medicine-In Vitro Studies: Proceedings. Ed. by Raymond L. Hayes et al. LC 68-60071. (AEC Symposium Ser.). 753p. 1968. pap. 26.75 (ISBN 0-87079-327-6, CONF-671111); microfiche 6.50 (ISBN 0-87079-328-4, CONF-671111). DOE.

Radioisotopes in the Detection of Pesticide Residues. (Panel Proceedings Ser.). (Illus.). 116p. 1966. pap. 7.25 (ISBN 92-0-111166-5, ISP123, IAEA). UNIPUB.

Radioisotopes in the Human Body. Frederick W. Spiers. LC 68-16515. (Atomic Energy Commission Monographs). 1968. 32.00 (ISBN 0-12-657750-1). Acad Pr.

Radioisotopes in the Pulp & Paper Industry. (Panel Proceedings Ser.). (Illus.). 117p. 1968. pap. 9.25 (ISBN 92-0-161068-8, ISP202, IAEA). UNIPUB.

Radiolabeled Monoclonal Antibodies for Imaging & Therapy. Ed. by S. C. Srivastava. (NATO ASI Series A, Life Sciences: Vol. 152). (Illus.). 884p. 1988. 129.50x (ISBN 0-306-42982-9, Plenum Pr). Plenum Pub.

Radiolabelled Cellular Blood Elements: Pathophysiology, Techniques, & Scintigraphic Techniques. Ed. by M. L. Thakur. LC 85-3628. (NATO ASI Series A, Life Sciences: Vol. 88). 444p. 1985. 79.50x (ISBN 0-306-41935-1, Plenum Pr). Plenum Pub.

Radiolaria. O. R. Anderson. (Illus.). 350p. 1983. 76.50 (ISBN 0-387-90832-3). Springer-Verlag.

Radiolarian Zonation & Stratigraphy of the Upper Cretaceous Portion of the Great Valley Sequence, California Coast Ranges. E. A. Pessagno, Jr. (Micropaleontology Special Publications Ser.: No. 2). 95p. 1976. 20.00 (ISBN 0-686-84250-2). Am Mus Natl Hist.

Radiologic Anatomy of the Brain. G. Salamon & Y. P. Huang. LC 75-45294. (Illus.). 1976. 199.00 (ISBN 3-540-07528-3). Springer-Verlag.

Radiologic Anatomy of the Jaws. Harrison M. Berry, Jr. LC 82-60263. (Illus.). 144p. (Orig.). 1982. pap. 18.95x (ISBN 0-8122-1130-8). U of Pa Pr.

Radiologic Atlas of Pulmonary Abnormalities in Children. 2nd ed. David B. Singleton et al. (Illus.). 368p. 1988. 75.00 (ISBN 0-7216-2062-0). Saunders.

Radiologic Atlas of the Colon & Rectum. Jakob Altaras. Ed. by George D. Dimitrijevic. Orig. Title: Radiologischer Atlas Kolon und Rectum. (Illus.). 318p. 1983. text ed. 65.00 (ISBN 0-8067-0141-2). Urban & S.

Radiologic Diagnosis of Renal Transplant Complications. Ed. by W. R. Casteneda-Zuniga. LC 85-2542. (Illus.). 305p. 1986. 49.50x (ISBN 0-8166-1232-3). U of Minn Pr.

Radiologic Diagnosis of the Sella Trucica. Henry W. Pribram. (Illus.). 244p. 1988. 16.50 (ISBN 0-87527-228-2). Green.

Radiologic Examination of the Orohypopharynx & Esophagus. C. Zaino & T. C. Beneventano. (Illus.). 1977. 103.00 (ISBN 0-387-90239-2). Springer-Verlag.

Radiologic Management of Musculoskeletal Tumors. H. Pettersson et al. (Illus.). 170p. 1986. 89.00 (ISBN 0-387-16756-0). Springer-Verlag.

Radiologic Management of Pelvic Ring Fractures: Systematic Radiographic Diagnosis. Jeremy W. Young & Andrew R. Burgess. 128p. 1987. 39.50 (ISBN 0-8067-2531-1). Urban & S.

Radiologic-Oncology of the Abdomen & Pelvis. Shirkhoda. 1988. 99.00 (ISBN 0-8151-7652-X). Year Bk Med.

Radiologic Pathologic Correlation of Musculoskeletal Lesions. T. M. Hudson. (Illus.). 670p. 1987. 134.50 (ISBN 0-683-04250-5). Williams & Wilkins.

Radiologic Physics, Equipment, & Quality Control. William R. Hendee et al. LC 77-204. pap. 75.30 (ISBN 0-317-26174-6, 2024265). Bks Demand UMI.

Radiologic Science for Technologists. Bushong. (Illus.). 688p. 1988. 39.95 (ISBN 0-8016-1532-1); pap. 19.95 wkbk. & lab manual (ISBN 0-8016-1539-9); instr's. manual incl. Mosby.

Radiologic Science: Workbook & Laboratory Manual. 3rd ed. Stewart Bushong. (Illus.). 287p. 1984. pap. text ed. 17.95 (ISBN 0-8016-0975-5). Mosby.

Radiologic Technologist. Jack Rudman. (Career Examination Ser.: C-1544). (Cloth bdg. avail. on request). pap. 16.00 (ISBN 0-8373-1544-1). Natl Learning.

Radiologic Technology. 1986. lib. bdg. 155.00 (ISBN 0-8490-3805-7). Gordon Pr.

Radiologic Technology. (Illus.). 569p. (Orig.). 1983. pap. 26.00 (ISBN 0-318-22428-3, S/N 008-070-00581-6). USGPO.

Radiologic Technology Examination Review. 2nd ed. Howard J. Naidech & Lorraine Damon. LC 82-13908. (Illus.). 304p. (Orig.). 1983. pap. 16.95 (ISBN 0-668-05366-6). Appleton & Lange.

Radiological Anatomy. D. Nagy. 1966. 120.00 (ISBN 0-08-010675-7). Pergamon.

Radiological Aspects of Renal Transplantation: Proceedings. Microsymposium, Nijmegen, 1977. Ed. by William Penn. (Radiologia Clinica: Vol. 47, No. 1). (Illus.). 1977. 13.00 (ISBN 3-8055-2844-2). S Karger.

Radiological Assessment: Predicting the Transport, Bioaccumulation, & Uptake by Man of Radionuclides Released to the Environment. National Council on Radiation Protection & Measurements Staff. LC 84-4773. (Report Ser.: No. 76). 300p. 1984. pap. text ed. 22.00 (ISBN 0-913392-66-9). NCRP Pubns.

Radiological Atlas of Bone Tumours, 2 vols. Ed. by Netherlands Committee on Bone Tumours. Incl. Vol. 1. 1966. 132.25x (ISBN 90-2796-403-3); Vol. II. 1972. 136.00x (ISBN 0-686-22177-X). (Illus.). Mouton.

Radiological Atlas of Common Diseases of the Small Bowel. J. L. Sellink. 1976. lib. bdg. 95.00 (ISBN 90-207-0476-1, Pub. by Martinus Nijhoff Netherlands). Kluwer Academic.

Radiological Casebook: Seventy-Five Cases with Clinico-Radiological Discussion. N. M. Perry & A. N. Chauhan. (Illus.). 176p. 1988. pap. 28.00 (ISBN 0-7236-0868-7). PSG Pub Co.

Radiological Diagnosis in Canine & Feline Emergencies: An Atlas of Thoracic & Abdominal Changes. Sten E. Olsson. LC 71-146031. pap. 55.40 (2056522). Bks Demand UMI.

Radiological Diagnosis of Fractures. D. Finlay & M. Allen. (Illus.). 255p. 1984. 34.95 (ISBN 0-7216-0961-9, Bailliere-Tindall). Saunders.

Radiological Effect of Nuclear War: British Journal of Radiology Reprint. 50p. 1983. pap. text ed. 4.95 (ISBN 0-444-40823-1). Butterworth.

Radiological Evaluation of the Spinal Cord, 2 vols. Milosh Perovitch. 1981. Vol. 1, 256p. 87.50 (ISBN 0-8493-5041-7); Vol. 2, 192p. 70.50 (ISBN 0-8493-5043-3). CRC Pr.

Radiological Examination of the Colon. R. E. Miller & J. Skucas. 1983. 128.00 (ISBN 90-247-2666-2, Pub. by Martinus Nijhoff Netherlands). Kluwer Academic.

Radiological Exploration of the Ventricles & Subarachnoid Space. G. Ruggiero et al. LC 73-19548. (Illus.). 200p. 1974. 105.00 (ISBN 0-387-06572-5). Springer-Verlag.

Radiological Factors Affecting Decision-Making in a Nuclear Attack. LC 74-20064. (NCRP Reports Ser.: No. 42). 1974. 12.00 (ISBN 0-913392-24-3). NCRP Pubns.

Radiological Functional Analysis of the Vascular System: Contrast Media Methods-Results. Ed. by F. H. Heuck. (Illus.). 296p. 1983. 57.50 (ISBN 0-387-12185-4). Springer-Verlag.

Radiological Health Specialist. Jack Rudman. (Career Examination Ser.: C-3118). 1988. pap. 16.00 (ISBN 0-8373-3118-8). Natl Learning.

Radiological Imaging: The Theory of Formation & Detection & Processing, Vol. 2. H. H. Barrett & W. Swindell. LC 80-69416. (Biophysics & Bioengineering Ser.). 1981. 55.00 (ISBN 0-12-079602-3). Acad Pr.

Radiological Imaging, Vol. I: The Theory of Image Formation, Detection, & Processing. H. H. Barrett. Ed. by W. Swindell. LC 80-69416. 1981. 55.00 (ISBN 0-12-079601-5). Acad Pr.

Radiological Impact of Radionuclides Dispersed on a Regional & Global Scale: Methods for Assessment & Their Application: Report Based on an Advisory Group Meeting Organized by the International Atomic Energy Agency & Held in Vienna, 1-4 June 1982. (Technical Reports Ser.: No. 250). 81p. 1986. pap. 23.00 (ISBN 92-0-125285-4, IDC250, IAEA). UNIPUB.

Radiological Impact of the Chernobyl Accident in OECD Countries. OECD Staff & NEA. 184p. (Orig.). 1988. pap. 31.00x (ISBN 92-64-13043-8). OECD.

Radiological Methods & Equipment. James R. Critser, Jr. (Ser. 10R-80). 1981. 80.00 (ISBN 0-914428-86-1). Lexington Data.

Radiological Methods & Equipment. James R. Critser, Jr. (Ser. 10R-79). 1980. 70.00 (ISBN 0-914428-68-3). Lexington Data.

Radiological Methods & Equipment. James R. Critser, Jr. (Ser. 10R-81). 115p. 1982. 80.00 (ISBN 0-914428-97-7). Lexington Data.

Radiological Methods & Equipment. James R. Critser, Jr. (Ser. 10R-82). 1983. 80.00 (ISBN 0-88178-007-3). Lexington Data.

Radiological Methods & Equipment. James R. Critser, Jr. (Ser. 10R-83). 88p. 1984. 80.00 (ISBN 0-88178-018-9). Lexington Data.

Radiological Methods & Equipment. James R. Critser, Jr. (Ser. 10R-84). 124p. 1985. 90.00 (ISBN 0-88178-055-3). Lexington Data.

Radiological Methods & Equipment. James R. Critser, Jr. (Ser. 10R-86). 242p. 1987. 93.00x (ISBN 0-88178-049-9). Lexington Data.

Radiological Methods & Equipment. James R. Critser, Jr. (Series 10R-87). 1988. 95.00x (ISBN 0-88178-066-9). Lexington Data.

Radiological Officer. (Career Examination Ser.: C-3406). Date not set. pap. 16.00 (ISBN 0-8373-3406-3). Natl Learning.

Radiological Safety Aspects of the Operation of Electron Linear Accelerators. (Technical Reports Ser.: No. 188). (Illus.). 327p. 1979. pap. 57.00 (ISBN 92-0-125179-3, IDC188, IAEA). UNIPUB.

Radiological Safety Aspects of the Operation of Neutron Generators. R. F. Boggs. (Safety Ser.: No. 42). (Illus.). 42p. 1976. pap. 9.25 (ISBN 92-0-123076-1, ISP427, IAEA). UNIPUB.

Radiological Safety in Uranium & Thorium Mines & Mills. (Safety Ser.: No. 43). 1976. pap. 11.75 (ISBN 92-0-123176-8, ISP449, IAEA). UNIPUB.

Radiological Significance & Management of Tritium, Carbon-14, Krypton-85, Iodine-129, Arising from the Nuclear Fuel Cycle. OECD-Nuclear Energy Agency. (Illus.). 222p. (Orig.). 1980. pap. text ed. 19.00x (ISBN 92-64-12083-1, 66-80-06-1) (ISBN 92-64-12083-1). OECD.

Radiological Surveillance of Airborne Contaminants in the Working Environment. (Safety Ser.: No. 49). (Illus.). 138p. 1980. pap. 20.25 (ISBN 92-0-623279-7, ISP484, IAEA). UNIPUB.

Radiologischer Atlas Kolon und Rectum see Radiologic Atlas of the Colon & Rectum.

Radiologist. Jack Rudman. (Career Examination Ser.: C-1447). (Cloth bdg. avail. on request). pap. 19.95 (ISBN 0-8373-1447-X). Natl Learning.

Radiologists Guide to Detection of Early Breast Cancer by Mammography, Thermography, & Xeroradiography. American College of Radiology Staff. 169p. 10.00 (ISBN 0-318-12467-X); members 7.50 (ISBN 0-318-12468-8). Am Coll Radiology.

Radiology. Robert F. Bury. (Practical Guides for General Practice). (Illus.). 82p. 1988. pap. 10.95 (ISBN 0-19-261681-1). Oxford U Pr.

Radiology & Imaging for Medical Students. 4th ed. David Sutton. 1982. pap. text ed. 22.50 (ISBN 0-443-02669-6). Churchill.

Radiology & the Kidney: Some Present Concepts. Ed. by C. J. Hodson. (Contributions to Nephrology: Vol. 5). (Illus.). 1977. 32.75 (ISBN 3-8055-2385-8). S Karger.

Radiology & the Law. Ed. by Albert L. Bundy. 222p. 1987. 45.00 (ISBN 0-87189-865-9). Aspen Pub.

Radiology Atlas of Rheumatic Diseases. Wolfgang Dihlmann. (Illus.). 386p. 1986. text ed. 110.00 (ISBN 0-86577-237-1). Thieme Med Pubs.

Radiology: Faculty Proceedings of the 6th European Congress of Radiology, Lisbon, Portugal, 31 May to 6 June, 1987. Ed. by M. E. Silvestre et al. (International Congress Ser.: No. 749). 674p. 1987. 200.00 (ISBN 0-444-80947-3, Excerpta Medica). Elsevier.

Radiology for Anesthesia & Critical Care. Murphy & Murphy. 1987. 50.00 (ISBN 0-443-08306-1). Churchill.

Radiology for Dental Auxiliaries. 4th ed. Frommer. (Illus.). 352p. 1987. 25.95 (ISBN 0-8016-1700-6). Mosby.

Radiology for Dental Hygienists & Dental Assistants. Olaf E. Langland et al. (Illus.). 252p. Date not set. text ed. 29.75x (ISBN 0-398-05470-3). C C Thomas.

Radiology in Disorders of the Liver, Biliary Tract & Pancreas. Joe Ariyama et al. LC 81-82117. (Illus.). 208p. 1981. text ed. 41.00 (ISBN 0-89640-059-X). Igaku-Shoin.

Radiology in Emergency Medicine. Ed. by Murray K. Dalinka & Jeremy Kaye. (Clinics in Emergency Medicine Ser.: Vol. 3). (Illus.). 364p. 1984. text ed. 39.00 (ISBN 0-443-08287-1). Churchill.

Raiders of the Lost Ark: A Novelization Adapted from the Screenplay by Lawrence Kasden. Campbell Clark. 192p. 1981. 6.95 (ISBN 0-345-28480-1); pap. 2.95 (ISBN 0-345-35375-7). Ballantine.

Raiders of the Lost Ark Storybook. Les Martin. (Movie Storybooks Ser.). (Illus.). 64p. (gr. 5-9). 1981. lib. bdg. 6.99 (ISBN 0-394-94802-5); pap. 5.95 boards (ISBN 0-394-84802-0). Random.

Raiders on Zeta. John Tully. (Starpol Ser.). (Illus.). 48p. (gr. 3-8). 1987. pap. 4.95 (ISBN 1-55624-905-5, RF9055). Wright Group.

Raider's Sky. Mary Haynes. LC 85-23788. 192p. (gr. 6-9). 1987. 11.75 (ISBN 0-688-06455-8). Lothrop.

Raids: A Guide to Planning, Coordinating, & Executing Searches & Arrests. James M. Davis. 138p. 1982. 26.00x (ISBN 0-398-04649-2). C C Thomas.

Raids & Rallies. Ernie O'Malley. 208p. 1982. 17.95 (ISBN 0-900068-62-0, Pub. by Anvil Bks Ireland). Irish Bks Media.

Raids & Rallies. Ernie O'Malley. 208p. (Orig.). 1985. pap. 6.95 (ISBN 0-900068-63-9, Pub. by Anvil Bks. Ltd Ireland). Irish Bks Media.

Raids on the Unspeakable. Thomas Merton. LC 66-17823. 1970. pap. 6.95 (ISBN 0-8112-0101-5, NDP213). New Directions.

Raigne of King Edward the Third. Fred Lapides. LC 79-54346. (Renaissance Drama Ser.). 265p. 1982. lib. bdg. 36.00 (ISBN 0-8240-4463-0). Garland Pub.

Rail Across India: A Photographic Journey. Geoffrey Moorhouse & Brian Hollingsworth. (Illus.). 244p. 1986. 85.00 (ISBN 0-89659-652-4). Abbeville Pr.

Rail & Motor Carrier Reports. (Special Report). 80p. 1979. 4.40 (ISBN 0-309-02971-6). Transport Res Bd.

Rail & Road in East Africa. Arthur Hazelwood. LC 65-6406. (Illus.). 1964. 29.50x (ISBN 0-678-06271-4). Kelley.

Rail & Sea Transport. D. H. Aldcroft & D. Mort. 280p. 1981. 50.00 (ISBN 0-08-026105-1). Pergamon.

Rail Book Bibliography: A Comprehensive Guide & Index. LC 72-96485. (Illus.). 1972. 7.50 (ISBN 0-913556-01-7); pap. 5.00 (ISBN 0-913556-00-9). Spec Pr NJ.

Rail Car, Locomotive & Trolley Builders: An All-Time Directory. Spencer Crump. cancelled (ISBN 0-87046-032-3, Pub. by Trans-Anglo). Interurban.

Rail Fences & Roosters: Poems & Almost Poems. Hazel B. Girard & Marvin E. Girard. LC 78-4802. 96p. 1978. 6.00 (ISBN 0-8233-0276-8). Golden Quill.

Rail Planning. (Transportation Research Record Ser.). 72p. 1977. 4.80 (ISBN 0-309-02685-7). Transport Res Bd.

Rail Rogues. Glebe Morgan. (Orig.). 1980. pap. 1.75 (ISBN 0-505-51490-7, Pub. by Tower Bks). Leisure NY.

Rail Steels: Developments Processing & Use, STP 644. Ed. by D. H. Stone & G. G. Knupp. 488p. 1978. 45.00 (ISBN 0-8031-0545-2). ASTM.

Rail: The Records. John Marshall. (Illus.). 200p. (Orig.). 1985. cancelled 14.95 (ISBN 0-85112-441-0, Pub. by Guinness Superlatives England); pap. 9.95 (ISBN 0-85112-447-X, Pub. by Guinness Superlatives England). Sterling.

Rail Three Hundred: The World High Speed Train Race. Murray Hughes. (Illus.). 192p. 1988. 24.95 (ISBN 0-7153-8963-7). David & Charles.

Rail Transit Development: Five Reports. (Transportation Research Record Ser.). 57p. 1975. 2.60 (ISBN 0-309-02458-7). Transport Res Bd.

Rail Transit Planning & Rail Sections. (Transportation Research Record Ser.). 53p. 1980. 5.40 (ISBN 0-309-03100-1). Transport Res Bd.

Rail Transport of Solid Wastes. (Special Reports Ser: No. 40). 150p. 1970. 10.00 (ISBN 0-917084-10-1). Am Public Works.

Rail Transport of Spent Fuel & High-Level Waste. Barbara Foster & Julie Jordan. (State Legislative Report: Vol. 11, No. 12). 16p. 1986. pap. 5.00 (ISBN 1-55516-168-5). Natl Conf State Legis.

Rail Transport Research Needs. (Special Report). 77p. 1977. 3.60 (ISBN 0-309-02586-9). Transport Res Bd.

Rail Vehicle Energy Design Considerations. B. C. Houser. 1984. 84.25 (ISBN 0-444-86864-X, I-071-84). Elsevier.

Rail Ventures. 3rd ed. Jack Swanson & Jeff Karsh. (Illus.). 360p. 1988. pap. 12.95 (ISBN 0-9608764-9-9). Wayfinder Pr.

Railbird. Rex Jones. (Illus.). 157p. 1984. pap. 5.95 (ISBN 0-89746-028-6). Gambling Times.

Railfan's Guide to Colorado. Edgar H. Sibert. (Illus.). pap. 7.95 (ISBN 0-87108-556-9). Pruett.

Railfreight Rolling Stock. Brian Handley. (Transport Ser.). (Illus.). 1985. 20.00x (ISBN 0-86025-873-4, Pub. by Ian Henry Pubns England). State Mutual Bk.

Railfreight Rolling Stock. Brian Handley. 1988. 30.00x (Pub. by Ian Henry Pubns England). State Mutual Bk.

Raillery & Rage: A Study of Eighteenth Century Satire. David Nokes. LC 87-9487. 256p. 1987. 35.00 (ISBN 0-312-00958-5). St Martin.

Railroad Accidents in Colorado. Eleanor Fry. (Illus.). 24p. 1982. pap. 2.00 (ISBN 0-915617-02-1). Pueblo Co Hist Soc.

Railroad & the City: A Technological & Urbanistic History of Cincinnati. Carl W. Condit. LC 76-55346. (Illus.). 347p. 1977. 15.00x (ISBN 0-8142-0265-9). Ohio St U Pr.

Railroad Book. E. Boyd Smith. (Illus.). 56p. (gr. 3-5). 1983. PLB 12.95 (ISBN 0-395-34832-3). HM.

Railroad Builders. John Moody. 1919. 8.50x (ISBN 0-686-83721-5). Elliots Bks.

Railroad Builders see No Break Here.

Railroad Caboose. William F. Knapke & Freeman Hubbard. LC 67-28316. (Illus.). (gr. 10 up). 1968. 16.95 (ISBN 0-87095-011-8). Gldn West Bks.

Railroad Capitalization. James C. Bonbright. LC 70-78003. (Columbia University Studies in the Social Sciences: No. 215). Repr. of 1920 ed. 24.50 (ISBN 0-404-51215-1). AMS Pr.

Railroad Car Builders Pictorial Dictionary. Matthias N. Forney. (Illus.). 13.25 (ISBN 0-8446-5187-7). Peter Smith.

Railroad Caretaker. Jack Rudman. (Career Examination Ser.: C-684). (Cloth bdg. avail. on request). pap. 14.00 (ISBN 0-8373-0684-1). Natl Learning.

Railroad Clerk. 3rd ed. Ed. by Hy Hammer. LC 82-18431. 176p. (Orig.). 1984. pap. 8.00 (ISBN 0-668-05643-6). Arco.

Railroad Clerk. Jack Rudman. (Career Examination Ser.: C-661). (Cloth bdg. avail. on request). pap. 12.00 (ISBN 0-8373-0661-2). Natl Learning.

Railroad Collectibles. 3rd, rev. ed. Stanley Baker. 160p. 1985. 17.95 (ISBN 0-89145-280-X, 1543). Collector Bks.

Railroad Competition & the Oil Trade: 1855-1873. Rolland H. Maybee. LC 73-16234. (Perspectives in American History Ser.: No. 16). (Illus.). 451p. 1974. Repr. of 1940 ed. lib. bdg. 45.00x (ISBN 0-87991-341-X). Porcupine Pr.

Railroad Consolidation under the Transportation Act of 1920. William N. Leonard. LC 68-58602. (Columbia University. Studies in the Social Sciences: No. 522). Repr. of 1946 ed. 24.50 (ISBN 0-404-51522-3). AMS Pr.

Railroad Consolidation West of the Mississippi River. Stuart Daggett. Ed. by Stuart Bruchey. LC 80-1302. (Railroads Ser.). (Illus.). 1981. Repr. of 1933 ed. lib. bdg. 12.00x (ISBN 0-405-13771-0). Ayer Co Pubs.

Railroad Development Programs in the Twentieth Century. Roy V. Scott. (Henry A. Wallace Serieson Agricultural History & Rural Studies: Vol. 3). 234p. 1985. text ed. 24.95x (ISBN 0-8138-1506-1). Iowa St U Pr.

Railroad Electrification: The Issues. (Special Report). 85p. 1978. 3.80 (ISBN 0-309-02654-7). Transport Res Bd.

Railroad Engineering. 2nd ed. William W. Hay. LC 81-23117. 758p. 1982. 58.95x (ISBN 0-471-36400-2, Pub. by Wiley-Interscience). Wiley.

Railroad Equipment Inspector. Jack Rudman. (Career Examination Ser.: C-210). (Cloth bdg. avail. on request). pap. 14.00 (ISBN 0-8373-0210-2). Natl Learning.

Railroad Ferries of the Hudson & the Stories of a Deckhand. Raymond J. Baxter. Ed. by Arthur G. Adams. (Illus.). 264p. 29.95 (ISBN 0-317-62578-0). Lind Grap Pubns.

Railroad-Highway Crossings, Visibility & Human Factors. (Transportation Research Record Ser.). 68p. 1976. 3.20 (ISBN 0-309-02587-7). Transport Res Bd.

Railroad History: Essays on Entrepreneurial & Managerial Ability & Performance. Charles J. Kennedy et al. 200p. 1988. 45.50 (ISBN 0-935662-02-2); Set. price not set (ISBN 0-935662-03-0). EBHA Pr.

Railroad History Index, Nineteen Twenty-One to Nineteen Eighty-Four. Ed. by Thomas T. Taber, III. (Illus.). 176p. (Orig.). 1985. pap. 12.50 (ISBN 0-9616102-0-4). Railway Loco Hist.

Railroad in American Art: Representations of Technological Change. Ed. by Susan Danly & Leo Marx. (Illus.). 1988. pap. 35.00. MIT Pr.

Railroad Inspector. Jack Rudman. (Career Examination Ser.: C-685). (Cloth bdg. avail. on request). pap. 14.00 (ISBN 0-8373-0685-X). Natl Learning.

Railroad Labor Board: Its History, Activities & Organization. Joshua Bernhardt. LC 72-3037. (Brookings Institution. Institute for Government Research. Service Monographs of the U. S. Government: No. 19). Repr. of 1923 ed. 21.50 (ISBN 0-404-57119-0). AMS Pr.

Railroad Land Grants. American Bar Association, Natural Resources Law Staff. LC 87-70130. 121p. 1987. pap. 29.95 (ISBN 0-89707-284-7). Amer Bar Assn.

Railroad Law Digest. 2nd ed. R. V. Laverty. Ed. by J. R. Laverty. lib. bdg. 47.00x (ISBN 0-318-04011-5). J R Laverty.

Railroad Line Abandonment: A Bibliography. Mary E. Huls. (Public Administration Ser.: P 2018). 6p. 1986. 3.00 (ISBN 1-55590-038-0). Vance Biblios.

Railroad Maps of North America: The First Hundred Years. Andrew M. Modelski. LC 82-675134. (Illus.). 186p. 1984. 28.00 (ISBN 0-8444-0396-2). Lib Congress.

Railroad Maps of North America: The First Hundred Years. Andrew M. Modelski. LC 82-675134. (Illus.). 207p. 1984. 28.00 (ISBN 0-318-18823-6, S/N 030-004-00021-3). USGPO.

Railroad Maps of North America: The First 100 Years. (Americana Ser.). 1986. lib. bdg. 85.00 (ISBN 0-8490-3798-0). Gordon Pr.

Railroad Maps of the United States: A Selected Annotated Bibliography of Original 19th-century Maps in the Geography & Map Division of the Library of Congress. Ed. by Andrew M. Modelski. LC 75-619007. (Illus.). v, 112p. 1975. pap. 5.50 (ISBN 0-317-59988-7). Lib Congress.

Railroad Mergers & Abandoments. Michael Conant. LC 82-15834. (Publications of the Institute of Business & Economic Research, University of California). xiii, 212p. 1982. Repr. of 1964 ed. lib. bdg. 35.00x (ISBN 0-313-23694-1, CORAM). Greenwood.

Railroad Passenger Car: An Illustrated History of the First Hundred Years, with Accounts by Contemporary Passengers. August Mencken. LC 57-13290. pap. 55.80 (ISBN 0-317-11162-0, 2002915). Bks Demand UMI.

Railroad Porter. 3rd ed. Hy Hammer. LC 82-18430. 128p. (Orig.). 1984. pap. 8.00 (ISBN 0-668-05637-1, 5637-1). Arco.

Railroad Porter. Jack Rudman. (Career Examination Ser.: C-662). (Cloth bdg. avail. on request). pap. 12.00 (ISBN 0-8373-0662-0). Natl Learning.

Railroad Promotion & Capitalization in the United States. Frederick A. Cleveland & Fred W. Powell. Ed. by Stuart Bruchey. LC 80-1698. (Railroads Ser.). 1981. Repr. of 1909 ed. lib. bdg. 35.00x (ISBN 0-405-13770-2). Ayer Co Pubs.

Railroad Question. facs. ed. William Larrabee. LC 76-150190. (Select Bibliographies Reprint Ser). 1893. 25.50 (ISBN 0-8369-5703-2). Ayer Co Pubs.

Railroad Reorganization. Stuart Daggett. 1908. 35.00 (ISBN 0-384-10665-X). Johnson Repr.

Railroad Reorganization. Stuart Daggett. LC 67-18576. 1967. Repr. of 1908 ed. 39.50x (ISBN 0-678-00239-8). Kelley.

Railroad Signal Specialist. Jack Rudman. (Career Examination Ser.: C-663). (Cloth bdg. avail. on request). pap. 14.00 (ISBN 0-8373-0663-9). Natl Learning.

Railroad Sirens. Allan N. Campbell. 1979. 8.95 (ISBN 0-533-03906-1). C I L Inc.

Railroad Spikes: A Collectors Guide. James M. Joyce. LC 85-2805. (Illus.). 64p. (Orig.). 1985. pap. 6.95 (ISBN 0-915010-33-X). Sutter House.

Railroad Station Planbook. Ed. by Harold A. Edmonson. LC 76-52194. (Illus.). 1977. pap. 4.00 (ISBN 0-89024-531-2). Kalmbach.

Railroad Stations in Nebraska: An Era of Use & Reuse. 3rd, rev. ed. James J. Reisdorff & Michael M. Bartels. (Illus.). 100p. 1987. pap. 20.00 (ISBN 0-942035-03-8). South Platte.

Railroad Stock Assistant. Jack Rudman. (Career Examination Ser.: C-1448). (Cloth bdg. avail. on request). pap. 12.00 (ISBN 0-8373-1448-8). Natl Learning.

Railroad Stockman. Jack Rudman. (Career Examination Ser.: C-664). (Cloth bdg. avail. on request). pap. 12.00 (ISBN 0-8373-0664-7). Natl Learning.

Railroad Street. Bruce Hunsberger. 1970. 5.95 (ISBN 0-8184-0116-8). Lyle Stuart.

Railroad That Died at Sea. Pat Parks. 1972. pap. 4.95 (ISBN 0-8289-0151-1). Penguin.

Railroad That Died at Sea: The Florida East Coast's Key West Extension. Pat Parks. LC 68-54448. (Illus.). 48p. 1986. pap. 5.95 (ISBN 0-911607-05-6). Langley Pr.

Railroad That Ran by the Tide. Raymond J. Feagans. (Illus.). 146p. 1981. Repr. of 1972 ed. 19.95 (ISBN 0-8310-7094-3). Howell-North.

Railroad to the Pacific. Edwin Johnson. 186p. 1982. 14.95 (ISBN 0-87770-264-0). Ye Galleon.

Railroad Track & Electrification Studies. (Transportation Research Record Ser.). 72p. 1978. 4.00. Transport Res Bd.

Railroad Track & Facilities. (Transportation Research Record Ser.). 66p. 1980. 5.20 (ISBN 0-309-03052-8). Transport Res Bd.

Railroad Track & Structure Inspector. Jack Rudman. (Career Examination Ser.: C-209). (Cloth bdg. avail. on request). pap. 14.00 (ISBN 0-8373-0209-9). Natl Learning.

Railroad Track Briefs for the Plant Engineer. W. L. Anderson. (Illus.). 1979. 10.00 (ISBN 0-682-49448-8). Exposition-Phoenix.

Railroad Transportation: Its History & Its Laws. Arthur T. Hadley. (History of American Economy Ser). Repr. of 1903 ed. 16.00 (ISBN 0-384-20685-9). Johnson Repr.

Railroaded! The Battle for Woodhead Pass. Simon Bain. (Orig.). 1986. pap. 9.95 (ISBN 0-571-13909-4). Faber & Faber.

Railroaded to Resurrection. Donald De Simone. 204p. 1982. 13.95. ETC Pubns.

Railroader. Fred W. Cottrell. (Russell Sage Foundation Reprint Ser). 1971. lib. bdg. 19.00 (ISBN 0-697-00210-1). Irvington.

Railroaders. L. Matthews. (Wild West in American History Ser.). (Illus.). 32p. (gr. 3-8). Date not set. PLB 15.93 (ISBN 0-86625-366-1). Rourke Corp.

Railroaders. K. Wheeler. LC 73-84316. (Old West Ser). (Illus.). (gr. 7 up). 1973. 19.94 (ISBN 0-8094-1467-8, Pub. by Time-Life). Silver.

Railroaders. Keith Wheeler. (Old West Ser.). (Illus.). 1973. 14.95 (ISBN 0-8094-1466-X). Time-Life.

Railroading. (Illus.). 48p. (gr. 6-12). 1978. pap. 1.25x (ISBN 0-8395-3292-X, 3292). BSA.

Railroading in Southern Oregon & the Founding of Medford. Bert Webber. 256p. 1985. 19.95 (ISBN 0-87770-351-5); pap. 14.95 (ISBN 0-87770-352-3). Ye Galleon.

Railroading in the Carolina Sandhills: "The Hoffman & Troy Railroad" & "Sandhill Shays", Vol. 3. S. David Carriker. (Illus.). 80p. Date not set. 16.00 (ISBN 0-936013-03-6); Set. price not set. Herit Pub NC.

Railroading in the Carolina Sandhills: The 19th Century (1825-1900, Vol. 1. S. David Carriker. (Illus.). 224p. 1986. text ed. 35.00 (ISBN 0-936013-01-X). Herit Pub NC.

Railroading in the Carolina Sandhills: The 20th Century (1900-1985, Vol. 2. S. David Carriker. (Illus.). 272p. 1987. 39.95 (ISBN 0-936013-02-8); Set. (vol. 1 & 2) 74.95. Herit Pub NC.

Railroading on the Washington Line. E. R. Corner, III. 143p. 1987. 25.00. R E F Typesetting Pub.

Railroads. Don Ball, Jr. (Illus.). 1985. 37.50 (ISBN 0-393-02236-6). Norton.

Railroads. Leonard E. Fisher. LC 79-1458. (Nineteenth Century America Ser.). (Illus.). 64p. (gr. 5 up). 1979. reinforced bdg. 9.95 (ISBN 0-8234-0352-1). Holiday.

Railroads. Bill Gunston. Ed. by Janet Caulkins. (Illus.). 32p. (gr. k-6). 1988. 10.40 (ISBN 0-531-18182-0, Pub. by Bookwright Pr). Watts.

Railroads. T. Harvey. LC 79-5062. (Lerner Question & Answer Bks.). (Illus.). (gr. 3-6). 1980. PLB 8.95 (ISBN 0-8225-1184-3). Lerner Pubns.

Railroads see West on Wood: Antique Wood Engravings of the Old West.

Railroads & American Economic Growth: Essays in Econometric History. Robert W. Fogel. LC 64-25069. (Illus.). 311p. 1970. pap. 9.95x (ISBN 0-8018-1148-1). Johns Hopkins.

Railroads & Land Grant Policy: A Study of Government Intervention. Lloyd Mercer. 258p. 1982. 29.95 (ISBN 0-12-491180-3). Acad Pr.

Railroads & Railroad Regulations in New York State, 1900-1913. Bruce W. Dearstyne. Ed. by Harold Hyman & Stuart Bruchey. LC 86-22960. (American Legal & Constitutional History Ser.). 393p. 1987. lib. bdg. 50.00 (ISBN 0-8240-8258-3). Garland Pub.

Railroads & Regulation, Eighteen Seventy-Seven to Nineteen Sixteen. Gabriel Kolko. LC 76-8917. vii, 273p. 1976. Repr. of 1965 ed. lib. bdg. 35.00x (ISBN 0-8371-8885-7, KORR). Greenwood.

Railroads & Revolutions: The Story of L. R. Hoard. J. F. Hulse. LC 86-61738. 128p. 1986. 19.95 (ISBN 0-930208-20-X). Mangan Bks.

Railroads & Rifles: Soldiers, Technology & the Unification of Germany. Dennis E. Showalter. 267p. 1986. pap. 17.50 (ISBN 0-208-02137-X). Shoe String.

Railroads & Rifles: Soldiers, Technology & Unification of Germany. Dennis E. Showalter. LC 75-17710. (Illus.). 267p. 1975. 27.50 (ISBN 0-208-01505-1, Archon). Shoe String.

Railroads & the Character of America: Eighteen Twenty to Eighteen Eighty-Seven. James A. Ward. LC 85-22658. (Illus.). 216p. 1986. 14.95 (ISBN 0-87049-498-8). U of Tenn Pr.

Railroads & the Granger Laws. George H. Miller. LC 75-138059. 308p. 1971. 25.00x (ISBN 0-299-05870-0). U of Wis Pr.

Railroads: Finance & Organization. William Z. Ripley. Ed. by Stuart Bruchey. LC 80-1699. (Railroads Ser.). (Illus.). 1981. Repr. of 1915 ed. lib. bdg. 55.00x (ISBN 0-405-13823-7). Ayer Co Pubs.

Railroads: Finance & Organization. William Z. Ripley. LC 15-4849. 1915. 39.00 (ISBN 0-527-75500-1). Kraus Repr.

Railroads for Rent: The Local Rail Assistance Program. William R. Black. LC 84-48546. 352p. 1985. 35.00x (ISBN 0-253-34774-2). Ind U Pr.

Railroads, Freight, & Public Policy. Theodore E. Keeler. LC 82-45985. (Studies in the Regulation of Economic Activity). 180p. 1983. 26.95 (ISBN 0-8157-4856-6); pap. 9.95 (ISBN 0-8157-4855-8). Brookings.

Railroads in Mexico: An Illustrated History, Vol. I. Francisco G. Franco. Ed. by Ben B. Massie. Tr. by Hector L. Hernandez & Ben B. Massie. (Illus.). 224p. 1985. 39.00x (ISBN 0-913582-39-5). Sundance.

Railroads in Mexico, Vol. 2: An Illustrated History. Francisco F. Garma. Ed. by Ben B. Massie. Tr. by Hector L. Hernandez from Span. (Illus.). 376p. 1988. 39.00 (ISBN 0-913582-01-8). Sundance.

Railroads in Michigan: A Catalog of Company Publications, 1836-1980. Dr. LeRoy Barnett. LC 85-63480. 1986. 16.00 (ISBN 0-918616-14-X); pap. 13.50. Northern Mich.

Railroads in the Nineteenth Century. Robert L. Frey. (Illus.). 352p. 1988. 75.00 (ISBN 0-8160-2012-4). Facts on File.

Railroads in the West. Ed. by Don L. Hofsommer. (Illus.). 118p. 1978. pap. text ed. 9.95x (ISBN 0-89745-002-7). Sunflower U Pr.

Railroads, Lands & Politics: The Taxation of the Railroad Land Grants, 1864-1897. Leslie E. Decker. LC 64-11940. (Illus.). 447p. 1964. 45.00x (ISBN 0-87057-084-6). U Pr of New Eng.

Railroads of Arizona, Vol. 1. David F. Myrick. (Illus.). 480p. 1981. Repr. of 1975 ed. 35.00 (ISBN 0-8310-7111-7). Howell-North.

Railroads of Arizona, Vol. 2. David F. Myrick. LC 75-27787. (Illus.). 480p. 35.00 (ISBN 0-8310-7118-4). Howell-North.

Railroads of Arizona: Vol. III-Clifton, Morenci & Metcalf; Rails & Copper Mines. David F. Myrick. Ed. by Jim Walker. (Trans Anglo Bks.: No. 265). (Illus.). 344p. 1984. 44.95 (ISBN 0-87046-065-X, Pub. by Trans-Anglo). Interurban.

Railroads of Kansas City. Terry Lynch. LC 82-16662. 1984. 14.95 (ISBN 0-87108-637-9). Pruett.

Railroads of Lawrence, Kansas: 1854-1900. I. E. Quastler. (Illus.). pap. 10.00x (ISBN 0-87291-094-6). Coronado Pr.

Railroads of Nevada & Eastern California, 2 Vols. David F. Myrick. LC 62-22034. (Illus.). 34.95 ea. Vol. 1 (ISBN 0-8310-7033-1). Vol. 2 o.s.i (ISBN 0-8310-7039-0). Howell-North.

Railroads of North America. Joseph Gross. (Illus.). 320p. 1986. write for info. (ISBN 0-9616476-0-4). J Gross.

Railroads of the United States. Henry M. Flint. LC 75-22818. (America in Two Centuries Ser). 1976. Repr. of 1868 ed. 34.50x (ISBN 0-405-07690-8). Ayer Co Pubs.

Railroads of the Yosemite Valley. 3rd ed. Hank Johnston. LC 80-51157. (Illus.). 1980. 17.95 (ISBN 0-87046-055-2, Pub. by Trans-Anglo). Interurban.

Railroads One Hundred Years Ago. Abbott & Anon. (Sun Historical Ser.). (Illus.). 1980. 3.50 (ISBN 0-89540-048-0, SB-048). Sun Pub.

Railroads: Pioneers in Modern Management, an Original Anthology. Ed. by Alfred D. Chandler. LC 79-7528. (History of Management Thought & Practice Ser.). 1980. lib. bdg. 28.50x (ISBN 0-405-12312-4). Ayer Co Pubs.

Railroads: Rates & Regulation. William Z. Ripley. LC 73-2532. (Big Business; Economic Power in a Free Society Ser.). Repr. of 1912 ed. 43.00 (ISBN 0-405-05110-7). Ayer Co Pubs.

Railroads, Reconstruction & the Gospel of Prosperity. Mark W. Summers. LC 83-43094. (Illus.). 361p. 1984. 44.00x (ISBN 0-691-04695-6). Princeton U Pr.

Railroads Series, 63 bks. in 65 vols. Ed. by Stuart Bruchey. 1981. Set. lib. bdg. 1781.00x (ISBN 0-405-13750-8). Ayer Co Pubs.

Railroads: The Free Enterprise Alternative. Daniel L. Overbey. LC 82-7503. (Illus.). 296p. 1982. lib. bdg. 29.95 (ISBN 0-89930-031-6, OVR/, Quorum). Greenwood.

Railroads: The Nation's First Big Business Sources & Readings. Ed. by Alfred D. Chandler, Jr. & Stuart Bruchey. LC 80-1298. (Railroads Ser.). 1981. Repr. of 1965 ed. lib. bdg. 20.00x (ISBN 0-405-13768-0). Ayer Co Pubs.

Railroads: Their Origin & Problems. Charles F. Adams, Jr. Ed. by Stuart Bruchey. LC 80-1294. (Railroads Ser.). 1981. Repr. of 1878 ed. lib. bdg. 20.00x (ISBN 0-405-13764-8). Ayer Co Pubs.

Railroads: Their Rise & Fall. Herbert E. Bixler. 115p. (Orig.). 1982. pap. 7.95 (ISBN 0-9610066-0-9). H E Bixler.

Railroads Through the Coeur d'Alenes. John V. Wood. LC 82-4168. (Illus.). 230p. (Orig.). 1983. 19.95 (ISBN 0-87004-297-1); pap. 14.95 (ISBN 0-87004-291-2). Caxton.

Rails. Don Ball, Jr. (Illus.). 1981. 24.95 (ISBN 0-393-01480-0). Norton.

Rails Across the Ranchos. Loren Nicholson. (Illus.). 197p. 1980. 18.95 (ISBN 0-913548-72-3, Valley Calif). Western Tanager.

Rails Across the Tundra: A Historical Album of the Alaska Railroad. Stan B. Cohen. LC 84-60465. (Illus.). 152p. 1984. pap. 9.95 (ISBN 0-933126-43-3). Pictorial Hist.

Rails Along the Hudson. Thomas Crawford & Frederick Kramer. 1976. pap. 8.50 (ISBN 0-915276-25-9). Quadrant Pr.

Rails at the Pass of the North. Edward A. Leonard. (Southwestern Studies: No. 63). 1981. pap. 5.00 (ISBN 0-87404-122-8). Tex Western.

Rails I Tote: A Collection of Short Stories. Christopher Manson. (Illus.). 96p. 1987. pap. 7.95 (ISBN 0-8050-0113-1). H Holt & Co.

Rails in the Isle of Wight. P. C. Allen & A. B. MacLeod. (Illus.). 128p. 1987. 24.95 (ISBN 0-7153-8701-4). David & Charles.

Rails 'Neath the Palms. Robert Mann. (Illus.). 220p. 1984. 29.95 (ISBN 0-933506-08-2). Darwin Pubns.

Rails of the World. S. Dillon Ripley. LC 75-619273. (Illus.). 432p. 1977. 125.00 (ISBN 0-87923-198-X); ltd. ed. 400.00x (ISBN 0-87923-199-8). Godine.

Rails of the World: A Compilation of New Information, 1975-1983 (Aves Hallidae) Sidney Ripley & Bruce M. Beenler. LC 84-600393. (Smithsonian Contribution to Zoology Ser.: No. 417). pap. 20.00 (ISBN 0-317-41853-X, 2026178). Bks Demand UMI.

Rails of the World: A Monograph of the Family Rallidae. Portfolio ed. S. Dillon Ripley. LC 83-81671. (Illus.). 32p. 1984. 39.95x (ISBN 0-87474-804-6, RIRW). Smithsonian.

Rails, Rivalry, & Romance. Don Banwart. (Illus.). 577p. 24.95 (ISBN 0-9601568-7-9); pap. 19.95 (ISBN 0-9601568-8-7). Historic Pres Bourbon.

Rails That Climb: A Narrative History of the Moffat Road. Edward T. Bollinger. Ed. by William C. Jones. LC 79-14634. (Illus.). 1979. 24.95 (ISBN 0-918654-29-7). CO RR Mus.

Rails Through Dixie. John Krause & H. Reid. LC 65-27038. (Illus.). 1965. 21.95 (ISBN 0-87095-020-7). Gldn West Bks.

Railway Adventure. L. T. Rolt. 1977. 15.95 (ISBN 0-7153-7389-7). David & Charles.

Railway Age's Comprehensive Railroad Dictionary. abr. ed. Simmons-Boardman Publishing Corp. LC 83-51791. 162p. 1984. 17.95 (ISBN 0-911382-00-3). Simmons Boardman.

Railway Braking. 326p. 1979. pap. 99.00 (ISBN 0-85298-441-3, MEP-111). Soc Auto Engineers.

Railway Builders: Lives & Works of the Victorian Railway Contractors. R. S. Joby. 1983. 45.00X (ISBN 0-317-52173-X, Pub. by Pinhorns UK). State Mutual Bk.

Railway Children. E. Nesbit. (Puffin Classics Ser.). 240p. (gr. 3-7). 1983. pap. 2.25 (ISBN 0-14-035005-5, Puffin). Penguin.

Railway Children. E. Nesbit. (gr. 5-8). 1988. 13.50 (ISBN 0-8446-6345-X). Peter Smith.

Railway Clearing House in the British Economy 1842-1922. Philip Bagwell. LC 71-355685. (Illus.). 1968. 29.95x (ISBN 0-678-06013-4). Kelley.

Railway Conductors. Edwin C. Robbins. LC 76-127435. (Columbia University. Studies in the Social Sciences: No. 148). Repr. of 1914 ed. 17.50 (ISBN 0-404-51148-1). AMS Pr.

Railway Construction As Viewed from Local Society. 34p. 1980. pap. 5.00 (ISBN 92-808-0097-3, TUNU058, UNU). UNIPUB.

Railway Country. Dudley Witney & Brian Johnson. (Illus.). 200p. Date not set. 29.95 (ISBN 0-919493-64-5, Pub. by Key Porter Canada). U of Toronto Pr.

Railway Country: Across Canada by Train. Dudley Whitney & Brian D. Johnson. (Illus.). 1985. 45.00 (ISBN 0-393-02234-X). Norton.

Railway Directory & Yearbook, 1986. 91st ed. 1986. 90.00 (ISBN 0-617-00443-9). Intl Pubns Serv.

Railway Economy. Dionysius Lardner. LC 67-29509. 1968. Repr. of 1850 ed. 45.00x (ISBN 0-678-00361-0). Kelley.

Railway Engineering Symposium: Upgrading of Australia's Rail Transport Systems. 235p. 1983. pap. text ed. 15.00x (ISBN 0-85825-203-1, Pub. by Inst Engineering Australia). Brookfield Pub Co.

Railway Engineering, 1985: Electrification Railways to the Year 2000. 262p. 1985. pap. text ed. 30.00x (ISBN 0-85825-258-9, Pub. by Inst Engineering Australia). Brookfield Pub Co.

Railway Expenditures: Their Extent, Object & Economy, 2 vols. Marshall M. Kirkman. Ed. by Alfred D. Chandler. LC 79-7547. (History of Management Thought & Practice Ser.). 1980. Repr. of 1880 ed. Set. lib. bdg. 69.00x (ISBN 0-405-12331-0). Ayer Co Pubs.

Railway Ghosts. W. B. Herbert. 128p. 1985. 16.95 (ISBN 0-7153-8647-6). David & Charles.

Railway Guns. John E. Lewis. 1983. 9.95 (ISBN 0-686-84193-X, Avalon). Bouregy.

Railway History in Pictures: Chilterns & Cotswolds. R. Davies & M. D. Grant. 1977. 16.95 (ISBN 0-7153-7299-8). David & Charles.

Railway History in Pictures: North East England. K. Hoole. LC 68-23818. (Illus.). 1969. 17.95x (ISBN 0-678-05603-X). Kelley.

Railway History in Pictures: The Midlands. H. C. Casserly & C. C. Dorman. LC 78-77871. (Illus.). 1969. 19.95x (ISBN 0-678-05557-2). Kelley.

Railway History in Pictures: West Country. R. C. Riley. (Illus.). 160p. 1987. 24.95 (ISBN 0-7153-8641-7). David & Charles.

Railway History Monograph, Vol. 4. LC 73-75503. 1976. lib. bdg. 10.00 (ISBN 0-916170-08-X). J-B Pub.

Railway History Monographs, Vol. 1: The Railroads of Nebraska. 2.50 (ISBN 0-916170-35-7). J-B Pub.

Railway in Town & Country, Eighteen Thirty to Nineteen Fourteen. Jack Simmons. (Illus.). 416p. 1986. 35.95 (ISBN 0-7153-8699-9). David & Charles.

Railway Journey: The Industrialization & Perception of Time & Space. Wolfgang Schivelbusch. 1986. 30.00x (ISBN 0-520-05812-7); pap. 10.95 (ISBN 0-520-05929-8). U of Cal Pr.

Railway Legislation in the United States. Balthasar H. Meyer. LC 73-2523. (Big Business; Economic Power in a Free Society Ser.). Repr. of 1909 ed. 23.50 (ISBN 0-405-05102-6). Ayer Co Pubs.

Railway Mania & Its Aftermath: Eighteen Forty-Five to Eighteen Fifty-Two. Henry G. Lewin. LC 68-26159. (Illus.). xxii, 526p. 1968. Repr. of 1936 ed. lib. bdg. 45.00x (ISBN 0-678-05213-1). Kelley.

Railway Mechanical Engineering: A Century of Progress - Car & Locomotive Design. Ed. by D. Blaine & J. Van Overeen. 446p. 1979. 35.00 (ISBN 0-317-33605-3, H00155); members 25.00 (ISBN 0-317-33606-1). ASME.

Railway Modelling: An Introduction. W. A. Corkill. 1979. 14.95 (ISBN 0-7153-7571-7). David & Charles.

Railway Monopoly & Rate Regulation. Robert J. McFall. LC 79-76704. (Columbia University Studies in the Social Sciences: No. 164). Repr. of 1916 ed. 16.50 (ISBN 0-404-51164-3). AMS Pr.

Railway Murders. Ed. by Jonathan Goodman. 176p. 1985. 13.95 (ISBN 0-8052-8223-8, Pub. by Allison & Busby England). Schocken.

Railway Nationalization in Canada: The Problem of the Canadian National Railways. Leslie T. Fournier. Ed. by Stuart Bruchey. LC 80-1308. (Railroads Ser.). 1981. Repr. of 1935 ed. lib. bdg. 30.00x (ISBN 0-405-13776-1). Ayer Co Pubs.

Railway Painting of Terence Cuneo. Terence Cuneo. (Illus.). 130p. 1984. 27.50 (ISBN 0-904568-43-1, Pub. by New Cavendish, England). Schiffer.

Railway Paintings of Alan Fearnley. Alan Fearnley. 95p. 1988. 65.00 (ISBN 0-7153-9088-0). David & Charles.

Railway Paintings of Don Breckon. Don Breckon. LC 81-67015. (Illus.). 200p. 1982. 40.00 (ISBN 0-7153-8206-3). David & Charles.

Railway Paintings of Don Breckon. Don Breckon. (Illus.). 80p. 1988. 24.95 (ISBN 0-7153-9078-3). David & Charles.

Railway Passenger Lists of Overland Trains to San Francisco & the West, 2 vols. Louis J. Rasmussen. Incl. Vol. 1 o.p. 1966; Vol. 2. November 12, 1871 to April 23, 1873. 1968. 9.75 (ISBN 0-911792-51-1). LC 66-12617. SF Hist Records.

Railway Practice. Samuel C. Brees. (Industrial Antiquites Ser.). (Illus.). 296p. 1987. Repr. of 1837 ed. 145.00 (ISBN 1-85297-013-8). Archival Facsimiles.

Railway Problems in China. Mongton C. Hsu. LC 70-76707. (Columbia University. Studies in the Social Sciences: No. 159). 1969. Repr. of 1915 ed. 17.50 (ISBN 0-404-51159-7). AMS Pr.

Railway Property (Unlawful Possession) Act, 1966. Askari Hasan. 471p. 1983. 180.00x (ISBN 0-317-54690-2, Pub. by Eastern Bk India). State Mutual Bk.

Railway Revenue: A Treatise on the Organization of Railroads & the Collection of Railway Receipts. Marshall M. Kirkman. Ed. by Alfred D. Chandler. LC 79-7548. (History of Management Thought & Practice Ser.). 1980. Repr. of 1879 ed. lib. bdg. 49.50x (ISBN 0-405-12332-9). Ayer Co Pubs.

Railway Revolution in Mexico. Bernard Moses. 1976. lib. bdg. 59.95 (ISBN 0-8490-2499-4). Gordon Pr.

Railway Ribaldry. Heath Robinson. (Illus.). 96p. 1974. text ed. 13.50 (Pub. by Duckworth London). Longwood Pub Group.

Railway Road Vehicles. Leslie Geary. 1988. 30.00x (ISBN 0-86025-411-9, Pub. by Ian Henry Pubns England). State Mutual Bk.

Railway Station: A Social History. Jeffrey Richards & John M. MacKenzie. (Illus.). 480p. 1986. 27.95 (ISBN 0-19-215876-7). Oxford U Pr.

Railway Station Man. Jennifer Johnston. 1985. 15.95 (ISBN 0-670-80593-9). Viking.

Railway Stations of Britain: Just a Glimpse. J. A. Coltas. (Illus.). 1979. 9.00 (ISBN 0-916170-09-8). J-B Pub.

Railway Stations of the North East. Ken Hoole. (Illus.). 216p. 1985. 29.95 (ISBN 0-7153-8527-5). David & Charles.

Railway Traction: The Principles of Mechanical & Electrical Railway Traction. H. I. Andrews. (Studies in Mechanical Engineering: No. 5). 412p. 1986. 144.75 (ISBN 0-444-42489-X). Elsevier.

Railway Walks: Exploring Disused Railways in Britain. Gareth L. Jones. (Illus.). 288p. 1983. 18.95 (ISBN 0-7153-8543-7). David & Charles.

Railwayman Thiel & Other Novellen. Gerhart Hauptmann. 96p. 1988. 21.00 (ISBN 0-946162-27-1, Pub. by Angel Bks); pap. 11.95 (ISBN 0-946162-28-X, Pub. by Angel Bks). Dufour.

Railwaymen & Revolution: Russia 1905. Henry Reichman. 1987. 38.00x (ISBN 0-520-05716-3). U of Cal Pr.

Railways. Arthur N. Evans. (Cambridge Introduction to World History Topic Bks.). (Illus.). 48p. (YA) (gr. 7 up). 1988. pap. 4.95 (ISBN 0-521-26918-0). Cambridge U Pr.

Railways & Energy. Liviu L. Alston. 94p. (Eng. & Fr.). Eng. Ed. 5.00 (ISBN 0-318-02821-2, WP0634); Fr. Ed. avail. World Bank.

Railways & the Economic Development of Western Europe: 1830-1914. Patrick O'Brien. LC 81-23261. 356p. 1983. 32.50x (ISBN 0-312-66277-7). St Martin.

Railways at War. John Westwood. LC 80-25429. 224p. 1981. 17.50 (ISBN 0-8310-7138-9). Howell-North.

Railways Atlas of the World. John E. Mahoney. 116p. 1982. pap. 23.00 (ISBN 0-9615046-0-9). Railways.

Railways for Pleasure: The Complete Guide to Steam & Scenic Lines in Great Britain & Ireland. Kenneth W. Jones. (Illus.). 160p. 1982. pap. 12.95 (ISBN 0-7188-2446-6). Salem Hse Pubs.

Railways in Burton & the Trent Valley Through 145 Years. Trent Valley Publications Staff. (Illus.). 84p. 1988. 39.00x (ISBN 0-948131-00-4, Pub. by Trent Valley UK). State Mutual Bk.

Railways in the Victorian Economy. Compiled by M. C. Reed. LC 69-10863. 1969. 27.50x (ISBN 0-678-05623-4). Kelley.

Railways of Canada. Robert F. Leggett. (Illus.). 255p. (Orig.). 1983. pap. 9.95 (ISBN 0-88894-269-9, Pub. by Douglas McIntyre-Grounwood). Salem Hse Pubs.

Railways of Great Britain & Ireland. Francis Whishaw. LC 68-56390. (Illus.). Repr. of 1842 ed. 49.50x (ISBN 0-678-05629-3). Kelley.

Railways of the Cotswolds. Colin Maggs. (Illus.). 96p. 1987. 32.00x (Pub. by Picton UK). State Mutual Bk.

Railways of the Twentieth Century. Geoffrey F. Allen. (Illus.). 1983. 27.50 (ISBN 0-393-01603-X). Norton.

Railways of Wharfedale. Peter E. Baughan. LC 76-91236. (Illus.). 1969. 22.95x (ISBN 0-678-05650-1). Kelley.

Railways or No Railways. Robert Fairlie. 147p. 1984. 14.95 (ISBN 0-912113-07-3). Railhead Pubns.

Railways Revisited: A Guide to Little-Known Railways of Austria & Germany. Bernard C. Winn. LC 87-83256. (Illus.). 96p. (Orig.). 1988. pap. 8.95 (ISBN 0-9615161-1-9). Incline Pr.

Railways to Cambridge Actual & Proposed. Reginald B. Fellows. (Cambridge Town, Gown & County Ser.: Vol. 2). (Illus.). 32p. 1976. pap. 4.00 (ISBN 0-902675-62-1). Oleander Pr.

Raiment of Light: A Study of the Human Aura. David Tansley. (Illus.). 224p. (Orig.). 1985. pap. 9.95 (ISBN 0-7100-9972-X). Routledge Chapman & Hall.

Rain. Barbara Hill. (Illus.). 20p. (gr. k-3). pap. 2.50 (ISBN 0-590-21581-7). Scholastic Inc.

Rain. Robert Kalan. LC 77-25312. (Illus.). 24p. (gr. k-3). 1978. PLB 11.88 (ISBN 0-688-84139-2). Greenwillow.

Rain. Keith Peterson. 1989. pap. 3.50 (ISBN 0-553-27663-8). Bantam.

Rain. Alana Willoughby. Ed. by Alton Jordan. (I Can Read Underwater Bks.). (Illus.). (gr. k-3). 1974. PLB 3.95 (ISBN 0-89868-003-4, Read Res); pap. text ed. 1.75 (ISBN 0-89868-036-0). ARO Pub.

Rain, No. 1. David Bennett. (Bear Facts Bks.). 32p. (Orig.). 1988. pap. 3.95 (ISBN 0-553-05474-0). Bantam.

Rain & Hail. Franklyn M. Branley. LC 83-45058. (Let's Read-&-Find-Out Science Bks.). (Illus.). 40p. (gr. k-3). 1983. 12.70 (ISBN 0-690-04352-X, Crowell Jr Bks); PLB 12.89 (ISBN 0-690-04353-8). HarpJ.

Rain & Shine. Paul Rogers. LC 88-1453. (Illus.). 128p. (gr. 2-5). 1988. 12.95 (ISBN 0-531-05771-2); PLB 12.99 (ISBN 0-531-08371-3). Orchard Bks Watts.

Rain Dance. John Hewitt. 56p. 1978. pap. 3.75 (ISBN 0-85640-152-8, Pub. by Blackstaff Pr). Longwood Pub Group.

Rain Door. Russell Hoban. LC 86-47719. (Illus.). 32p. (ps-3). 1986. 11.95i (ISBN 0-690-04575-1, Crowell Jr Bks); PLB 11.89 (ISBN 0-690-04577-8). HarpJ.

Rain Drop Splash. Alvin R. Tresselt. (Illus.). 36p. (gr. k-3). 1946. PLB 12.88 (ISBN 0-688-51165-1). Lothrop.

Rain, Fire, & the Will of God. Donald Wetzel. 208p. 1985. 16.95 (ISBN 0-933256-58-2); pap. 11.95 (ISBN 0-933256-59-0). Second Chance.

Rain Following: Poems. Susan J. Lenier. (Oleander Modern Poets Ser.: Vol. 13). 64p. 1984. 15.00 (ISBN 0-906672-19-8); pap. 8.95 (ISBN 0-906672-20-1). Oleander Pr.

Rain Forest. Helen Cowcher. (Illus.). 32p. (ps up). 1988. 13.95 (ISBN 0-374-36167-3). FS&G.

Rain Forests of Golfo Dulce. Paul H. Allen. LC 77-76150. (Illus.). 1956. 35.00x (ISBN 0-8047-0955-6). Stanford U Pr.

Rain Frog. LaRue Selman. Ed. by Alton Jordan. (Buppet Ser.). (Illus.). (gr. k-3). 1981. PLB 5.95 (ISBN 0-89868-091-3, Read Res); pap. text ed. 1.95 (ISBN 0-89868-102-2). ARO Pub.

Rain God: A Desert Tale. Arturo Islas. 180p. (Orig.). 1984. pap. 6.95 (ISBN 0-916485-01-3). Alexandrian Pr.

Rain, Hail, Sleet & Snow. Nancy Larrick. LC 61-5488. (E. G. Junior Science Ser.). (gr. 2-5). 1961. PLB 6.69 (ISBN 0-8116-6157-1). Garrard.

Rain in Her Voice. Lawrence Fitzgerald. 24p. 1978. 10.00 (ISBN 0-913719-05-6); pap. 3.50 (ISBN 0-913719-04-8). High-Coo Pr.

Rain in the Desert Music Book. 5.95 (ISBN 0-8198-0727-3). Dghtrs St Paul.

Rain in the Distance. Suzanne Falkiner. 176p. 1986. pap. 5.95 (ISBN 0-14-008436-3). Penguin.

Rain in the Forest, Light in the Trees: Contemporary Poetry from the Northwest. Ed. by Rich Ives. 448p. (Orig.). 1983. pap. 8.00 (ISBN 0-937669-08-3). Owl Creek Pr.

Rain in the Lyle Hollow. Douglas F. Miller. 192p. 1986. 10.95 (ISBN 0-8062-2916-0). Carlton.

Rain in the Trees. W. S. Merwin. LC 87-46081. 96p. 1988. 16.95 (ISBN 0-394-57039-1); pap. 8.95 (ISBN 0-394-75858-7). Knopf.

Rain Lover. Dave Burkey. 1985. pap. 2.95 (ISBN 0-345-31963-X). Ballantine.

Rain Maiden. Jill M. Phillips. 570p. 1987. 16.95 (ISBN 0-8065-1008-0, Pub. by Citadel Pr). Lyle Stuart.

Rain Maiden. Jill M. Phillips. 1988. pap. 4.95. Tudor Pub NYC.

Rain-Makers: Indians of Arizona & New Mexico. Mary E. Coolidge. LC 76-43681. (Illus.). 376p. Repr. of 1929 ed. 35.00 (ISBN 0-404-15514-6). AMS Pr.

Rain Makes Applesauce. Julian Scheer. (Illus.). 36p. (gr. k-3). 1964. 12.95 (ISBN 0-8234-0091-3). Holiday.

Rain Making & Other Weather Vagaries. William J. Humphreys. LC 77-10228. Repr. of 1926 ed. 21.50 (ISBN 0-404-16208-8). AMS Pr.

Rain of Darts: The Mexica Aztecs. Burr C. Brundage. LC 72-680. (Texas Pan American Ser.). 372p. 1972. 20.00x (ISBN 0-292-77002-2). U of Tex Pr.

Rain of Dollars: U. S. Economic Intervention in Central America. Tom Barry. 1986. write for info. (ISBN 0-911213-08-2). Inter-Hem Educ.

Rain of Doom. (Able Team Ser.: No. 16). Date not set. pap. 2.25 (ISBN 0-317-63979-X, Pub. by Worldwide). Harlequin Bks.

Rain of Fire. Marion D. Bauer. LC 83-2065. 160p. (gr. 4-8). 1983. 10.95 (ISBN 0-89919-190-8, Clarion). HM.

Rain of Fire, Air War. John Morrocco. Ed. by Robert Manning. LC 84-73511. (Vietnam Experience Ser.: Vol. XIV). (Illus.). 192p. 1984. 16.95 (ISBN 0-939526-14-X). Boston Pub Co.

Rain of Terror. W. Murphy & R. Sapir. (Destroyer Ser.: No. 75). 1989. pap. 3.95 (ISBN 0-451-15752-4, Sig). NAL.

Rain of Troubles: The Science & Politics of Acid Rain. Laurence Pringle. LC 87-34950. (Science for Survival Ser.). (Illus.). 128p. (YA) (gr. 7 up). 1988. PLB 13.95 (ISBN 0-02-775370-0). Macmillan.

Rain of Wisdom: The Essence of the Ocean of True Meaning. Ed. by Kendra Crossen. Tr. by Nalanda Translation Committee Staff & Chogyam Trungpa. LC 85-245. 414p. 1989. 35.00 (ISBN 0-87773-196-9). Shambhala Pubns.

Rain on the Just: A Novel. Kathleen M. Morehouse. LC 79-18762. (Lost American Fiction Ser.). 333p. 1980. Repr. of 1936 ed. 13.95 (ISBN 0-8093-0945-9). S Ill U Pr.

Rain One Step Away. Melih C. Anday. Tr. by Talat Halman & Brian Swann. LC 80-68880. 1980. 7.50 (ISBN 0-910350-00-0). Charioteer.

Rain or Shine. Cyra McFadden. 1987. pap. 4.95 (ISBN 0-394-74879-4, Vin). Random.

Rain or Shine: A Family Memoir. Cyra McFadden. (Illus.). 224p. 1986. 16.45 (ISBN 0-394-51937-X). Knopf.

Rain or Shine: A Family Memoir. Cyra McFadden. 297p. 1987. lib. bdg. 17.95x (ISBN 0-8161-4252-1, Large Print Bks). G K Hall.

Rain: Poems. William Carpenter. (Samuel French Morse Poetry Prize Ser.: Vol. 2). 82p. (Orig.). 1985. pap. 7.95x (ISBN 0-930350-80-4). NE U Pr.

Rain Puddle. Adelaide Holl. LC 65-22026. (Illus.). 32p. (gr. k-3). 1965. PLB 12.88 (ISBN 0-688-51096-5). Lothrop.

Rain! Rain! Carol Greene. LC 82-9509. (Rookie Readers Ser.). (Illus.). (ps-2). 1982. PLB 9.93 (ISBN 0-516-02034-X); pap. 2.50 (ISBN 0-516-42034-8). Childrens.

Rain Rain Rivers. Uri Shulevitz. LC 73-85370. (Illus.). 32p. (ps-3). 1969. 11.95 (ISBN 0-374-36171-1). FS&G.

Rain Rain Rivers. Uri Shulevitz. (Michael Di Capua Bks.). (Illus.). 32p. 1988. pap. 3.95 (ISBN 0-374-46195-3, Sunburst). FS&G.

Rain Shadow. James R. Newton. LC 82-45927. (Illus.). 32p. (gr. 2-6). 1983. 11.70i (ISBN 0-690-04344-9, Crowell Jr Bks); PLB 11.89 (ISBN 0-690-04345-7). HarpJ.

Rain Through the Night. Buddladeva Bose. Tr. by Clinton B. Seely from Bengali. (Orient Paperbacks). 139p. 1974. pap. 1.80 (ISBN 0-88253-285-5). Ind-US Inc.

Rainbird's Revenge. Marion Chesney. LC 87-27962. 176p. 1988. 13.95x (ISBN 0-312-01506-2). St Martin.

Rainbow. Pearl S. Buck. 1976. pap. 1.75 (ISBN 0-671-80319-0). PB.

Rainbow. Fitzgerald. (Dear God Kids Ser.). Date not set. 3.95 (ISBN 0-671-50681-1). S&S.

Rainbow. D. H. Lawrence. 1981. pap. 4.95 (ISBN 0-14-000692-3). Penguin.

Rainbow. D. H. Lawrence. Ed. by John Worthen. (English Library). 576p. 1982. pap. 4.95 (ISBN 0-14-043155-1). Penguin.

Rainbow. Nancy Lecourt. (Books I Can Read). 32p. (gr. 2). 1980. pap. 1.95 (ISBN 0-8127-0290-5). Review & Herald.

Rainbow: A History of the Honolulu Japanese Chamber of Commerce. 246p. 10.40 (ISBN 0-318-14327-5). Honolulu Japanese.

Rainbow & the Kings: A History of the Luba Empire to 1891. Thomas O. Reefe. LC 80-17627. 1981. 30.00x (ISBN 0-520-04140-2). U of Cal Pr.

Rainbow at Dusk. Emilie Loring. 1976. Repr. of 1942 ed. lib. bdg. 19.95x (ISBN 0-88411-360-4, Pub. by Aeonian Pr). Amereon Ltd.

Rainbow Bags: Instructions for Making Six Colorful Bags of Soft Toys. Lois Brokering. 48p. (Orig.). 1986. pap. 5.95 (ISBN 0-8066-2256-3, 10-5380). Augsburg.

Rainbow Below. Hugh Atkinson. Ed. by Kent Oswald. 304p. 1987. 17.95 (ISBN 0-531-15037-2). Watts.

Rainbow Book. S. Marshak. 95p. 1974. 2.95 (ISBN 0-8285-1220-5, Pub. by Progress Pubs USSR). Imported Pubns.

Rainbow Book of Adventures. Ed. by Susan Remini. (Illus.). 114p. (Orig.). 1983. pap. 7.95 (ISBN 0-932471-01-3). Falsoft.

Rainbow Book of Poems. Ruth Baker. 1984. 3.95 (ISBN 0-89536-993-1, 7544). CSS of Ohio.

Rainbow Book of Simulations. Ed. by Charles L. Springer. (Illus.). 202p. (Orig.). 1984. pap. 9.95 (ISBN 0-932471-02-1). Falsoft.

Rainbow Bridge. Bhagwan Shree Rajneesh. Ed. by Krishna Prabhu. LC 85-42535. (Initiation Talks Ser.). 368p. (Orig.). 1985. pap. 3.95 (ISBN 0-88050-618-0). Chidvilas Inc.

Rainbow Bridge. Mary W. Cushing. Ed. by Andrew Farkas. LC 76-29932. (Opera Biographies). (Illus.). 1977. Repr. of 1954 ed. lib. bdg. 30.00x (ISBN 0-405-09674-7). Ayer Co Pubs.

Rainbow Bridge. R. Farrer. 383p. 1986. pap. 49.00x (ISBN 0-317-68560-0, Pub. by Han-Shan Tang Ltd). State Mutual Bk.

Rainbow Bridge. Reginald Farrer. LC 76-47496. (Illus.). 1976. Repr. of 1921 ed. 15.00 (ISBN 0-913728-15-2). Theophrastus.

Rainbow Bridge. Reginald Farrer. (Plant Hunter Ser.). 416p. 1987. pap. 9.95 (ISBN 0-946313-48-2). Timber.

Rainbow Bridge II: Link with the Soul Purification. 1981. pap. 8.50. New Age.

Rainbow Bridge to the Inner Worlds. Ruth E. Norman. 400p. 1985. text ed. 14.95 (ISBN 0-932642-87-X). Unarius Pubns.

Rainbow Bridge: Two Disciples. 1981. casebound 10.00 (ISBN 0-87613-069-4); pap. 8.50 (ISBN 0-87613-068-6); pap. text ed. Write for info. New Age.

Rainbow Cafe. David Ossman. (Illus.). 20p. 1982. limited ed. 10.00x (ISBN 0-918824-37-0). Turkey Pr.

Rainbow Candles: A Chanukah Counting Book. Myra Shostak. LC 86-81718. (Illus.). 12p. (ps). 1986. bds. 4.95 (ISBN 0-930494-59-8). Kar Ben.

Rainbow Challenge: The Jackson Campaign & the Future of U. S. Politics. Sheila Collins. 384p. (Orig.). 1986. 27.00 (ISBN 0-85345-690-9); pap. 11.00 (ISBN 0-85345-691-7). Monthly Rev.

Rainbow Chasers. Kay Peterson. (Illus.). 216p. 1982. pap. 6.75 (ISBN 0-910449-01-5). Roving Pr Pub.

Rainbow Collection: Quilt Patterns for Rainbow Colors. Judy Martin. 44p. (Orig.). 1987. pap. 10.95 (ISBN 0-9602970-2-2). Moon Over Mntn.

Rainbow Color Book of Song: Key of "C" Book. Beverly M. Hale. (Illus.). 51p. 1986. 7.95 (ISBN 0-533-06527-5). Vantage.

Rainbow Countries of Central America. Wallace Thompson. 1978. lib. bdg. 59.95 (ISBN 0-8490-2500-1). Gordon Pr.

Rainbow Drive. Roderick Thorp. 320p. 1986. 18.95 (ISBN 0-671-49981-5). Summit Bks.

Rainbow Drive. Roderick Thorp. 1987. pap. 4.95 (ISBN 0-8041-0170-1, Pub. by Ivy). Ballantine.

Rainbow Effect: Interracial Families. Kathlyn Gay. LC 86-26689. (Illus.). 144p. (YA) (gr. 7-12). 1987. lib. bdg. 11.90 (ISBN 0-531-10343-9). Watts.

Rainbow Encyclopedia of Prehistoric Life. Mark Lambert. Ed. by Adrian Sington. LC 82-80987. (Illus.). 144p. (gr. 4 up). 1982. 12.95 (ISBN 0-528-82388-4). Macmillan.

Rainbow Factor. Raboo Rodgers. LC 84-22567. 178p. (gr. 5 up). 1985. 11.95 (ISBN 0-395-35643-1). HM.

Rainbow Flower. V. Katayev. 23p. 1977. pap. 1.49 (ISBN 0-8285-1221-3, Pub. by Progress Pubs USSR). Imported Pubns.

Rainbow for the Christian West. Rene Depestre. Tr. by Joan Dayan. LC 76-45047. 272p. 1977. 20.00x (ISBN 0-87023-229-0). U of Mass Pr.

Rainbow Freeware. Bruce Jackson. 170p. (Orig.). 1986. pap. 20.00x (ISBN 0-939731-00-2). South Moulton Pr.

Rainbow Friends Game Book. 1985. pap. 0.49 (ISBN 0-317-28259-X). Pacific Pr Pub Assn.

Rainbow: From Myth to Mathematics. Carl B. Boyer. (Illus.). 376p. 1987. 40.00 (ISBN 0-691-08457-2); pap. 12.95 (ISBN 0-691-02405-7). Princeton U Pr.

Rainbow Fun: Rainbows to Keep, Share & Give Away. Imogene Forte. LC 86-82873. (Tabletop Learning Ser.). 80p. (gr. k-6). 1987. pap. text ed. 3.95 (ISBN 0-86530-161-1, IP-94-5). Incentive Pubns.

Rainbow Garden. Patricia M. St. John. (gr. 2-5). pap. 4.50 (ISBN 0-8024-0028-0). Moody.

Rainbow Goblins. Ul De Rico. (Illus.). 1978. 24.95 (ISBN 0-500-95005-9). Thames Hudson.

Rainbow Goblins. Ul De Rico. (Illus.). 36p. 1979. pap. 13.95 (ISBN 0-446-38204-3). Warner Bks.

Rainbow Guide to Introductory Statistics. Michael Plog & Norman Stenzel. Ed. by Belinda Kirby. 150p. (Orig.). 1987. 6.95 (ISBN 0-932471-05-6). Falsoft.

Rainbow Hammock. Becky L. Weyrich. 304p. (Orig.). 1983. pap. 3.50 (ISBN 0-449-12445-2, GM). Fawcett.

Rainbow in the Mist. Phyllis A. Whitney. 1989. 17.95 (ISBN 0-385-24954-3). Doubleday.

Rainbow in the Morning. Ed. by J. Frank Dobie. LC 74-32243. (Texas Folklore Society Publications: No. 5). 208p. 1975. Repr. of 1926 ed. 12.95 (ISBN 0-87074-150-0). SMU Press.

Rainbow in the Sky. May S. Hilburn. 54p. 1966. pap. 1.50 (ISBN 0-88053-315-3, S-260). Macoy Pub.

Rainbow in the Sky: Golden Anniversary Edition. Ed. by Louis Untermeyer. LC 84-19306. (Illus.). 528p. (gr. 3-6). 1985. 19.95 (ISBN 0-15-265479-8, HJ). HarBraceJ.

Rainbow in the Spray. Pamela Wynne. (Barbara Cartland's Library of Love: No. 13). 218p. 1980. 12.95 (ISBN 0-7156-1473-8, Pub. by Duckworth London). Longwood Pub Group.

Rainbow in Your Eyes: Yes You Can Find Your Colors & for Others, Too. Bernice Kentner. (Illus.). 146p. 1981. 14.95 (ISBN 0-941522-01-6). Ken Kra Pubs.

Rainbow in Your Hands. Albert R. Davis & Walter C. Rawls, Jr. 1976. 8.00 (ISBN 0-682-48543-8). Exposition-Phoenix.

Rainbow Is Not Enough. Leydel J. Willis. 72p. 1982. pap. 4.95 (ISBN 0-930416-07-4). Clodele.

Rainbow Jordan. Alice Childress. (Illus.). (gr. 7 up). 1981. 9.95 (ISBN 0-698-20531-6, Coward). Putnam Pub Group.

Rainbow Jordan. Alice Childress. 128p. 1982. pap. 2.50 (ISBN 0-380-58974-5, Flare). Avon.

Rainbow Kid. Jeanne Betancourt. 112p. (Orig.). (gr. 3-7). 1988. pap. 2.50 (ISBN 0-380-84665-9, 84665, Camelot). Avon.

Rainbow Man: A Musical Entertainment. Paul Harrington et al. 1984. 35.00x (ISBN 0-906549-40-X, Pub. by J Clare Bks); pap. 22.00x (ISBN 0-317-07188-2, Pub. by J Clare Bks). State Mutual Bk.

Rainbow Night. Marie D. Cameron. (Stories for Young Americans Ser.). (Illus.). 32p. (gr. k up). 1986. 9.95 (ISBN 0-89015-543-7). Eakin Pr.

Rainbow Obsidian. Phillips Kloss. LC 85-2628. 128p. 1985. 10.95 (ISBN 0-86534-070-6). Sunstone Pr.

Rainbow of Hope. Ada R. Dogger. 382p. (Orig.). Date not set. pap. 12.95 (ISBN 1-55523-167-5). Winston-Derek.

Rainbow of My Own. Don Freeman. 32p. (ps-2). 1978. pap. 3.95 (ISBN 0-14-050328-5, Puffin). Penguin.

Rainbow of My Own. Don Freeman. (Illus.). (gr. k-3). 1966. lib. bdg. 12.95 (ISBN 0-670-58928-4). Viking.

Rainbow of My Own. Don Freeman. (Illus.). (gr. k-3). 1982. incl. cass. 19.95 (ISBN 0-941078-20-5); pap. 12.95 incl. cass. (ISBN 0-941078-18-3); user's guide incl. 4 pbs. & cass. 27.95 (ISBN 0-941078-19-1). Live Oak Media.

Rainbow of Readiness: Parental Guide for Better Beginnings. Ruth D. Summerlin. (Illus.). 128p. (Orig.). 1987. pap. 9.95 (ISBN 0-9618841-1-8). Readiness Pubns.

Rainbow of Reflections. Karen Styons. LC 85-61902. 96p. 1985. 6.95 (ISBN 0-938232-80-0). Winston-Derek.

Rainbow Path. Louise Kinoshita & Joyce Sanderson. 1983. pap. 6.95. Conner & Sanderson.

Rainbow Path: Healing Ourselves. Louise Kinoshita & Joyce Sanderson. 78p. 1982. pap. 6.95. Coleman Pub.

Rainbow Quest of Thomas Pynchon. Douglas A. Mackey. LC 80-11219. (Milford Ser.: Popular Writers of Today: Vol. 28). 62p. 1980. lib. bdg. 19.95x (ISBN 0-89370-142-4). Borgo Pr.

Rainbow Rhino. Peter Sis. LC 87-2679. (Illus.). 40p. (ps-1). 1987. 11.95 (ISBN 0-394-89009-4); lib. bdg. 12.99 (ISBN 0-394-99009-9). Knopf.

Rainbow Riddle. Margaret Sutton. (Judy Bolton Mysteries). 1976. Repr. of 1946 ed. lib. bdg. 15.95x (ISBN 0-88411-711-1, Pub. by Aeonian Pr). Amereon Ltd.

Rainbow Rider. Jane Yolen. LC 73-19700. (Illus.). (ps-3). 1974. PLB 12.89 (ISBN 0-690-00311-0, Crowell Jr Bks). HarpJ.

Rainbow, River & Tree. Myron S. Hoyt. LC 85-80095. 104p. (Orig.). 1985. pap. 3.95 (ISBN 0-9614817-0-6). Green Meadow Bks.

Rainbow Roun' Mah Shoulder. Linda B. Bragg. 140p. (Orig.). 1984. pap. 7.00 (ISBN 0-932112-20-X). Carolina Wren.

Rainbow Round Her Shoulder: The Zora Neale Hurston Symposium Papers. Ed. by Ruthe T. Sheffey. LC 82-238000078. (Illus.). 134p. (Orig.). 1982. pap. 8.95 (ISBN 0-9610324-0-5). Morgan State.

Rainbow Round the Sun. Elizabeth Van Buren. 185p. 1984. 29.00x (ISBN 0-7212-0564-X, Pub. by Regency Pr). State Mutual Bk.

Rainbow Route: An Illustrated History of the Silverton Railroad, the Silverton Northern Railroad & the Silverton, Gladstone & Northerly Railroad. Robert E. Sloan & Carl A. Skowronski. Ed. by Jackson C. Thode et al. (Illus.). 416p. 1975. 55.00x (ISBN 0-913582-12-3). Sundance.

Rainbow Ryder. Linda Hampton. (Loveswept Ser.: No. 218). 192p. (Orig.). 1987. pap. 2.50 (ISBN 0-553-21793-3). Bantam.

Rainbow Ryder. Linda Hampton. (Loveswept Ser.: No. 222). 192p. (Orig.). 1987. pap. 2.50 (Loveswept). Bantam.

Rainbow Serpent: A Chromatic Piece. Ed. by Ira R. Buchler & Kenneth Maddock. (World Anthropology Ser.). (Illus.). x, 228p. 1978. 36.25 (ISBN 90-279-7680-5). Mouton.

Rainbow Songs. James E. Haas. 40p. (Orig.). (gr. 1-8). 1975. pap. 3.95 (ISBN 0-8192-1201-6). Morehouse.

Rainbow Sticker Riot. Linda W. Aber & Hal Aber. (Stuck on Stickers Ser.). (Illus.). 24p. (Orig.). (gr. 2-6). 1985. pap. 2.95 (ISBN 0-590-33388-7). Scholastic Inc.

Rainbow Sword. Adrienne Martine-Barnes. 224p. 1988. pap. 3.50 (ISBN 0-380-75455-X). Avon.

Rainbow Trail. Zane Grey. (Zane Grey's West Ser.). 288p. 1985. Repr. lib. bdg. 12.95 (ISBN 0-915643-04-9). Santa Barb Pr.

Rainbow Trail. Zane Grey. 1985. 20.00x (ISBN 0-86025-195-0, Pub. by Ian Henry Pubns England). State Mutual Bk.

Rainbow Valley. L. M. Montgomery. (Anne of Green Gables Ser.: No. 7). 240p. (gr. 6 up). 1985. pap. 2.95 (ISBN 0-553-25213-5). Bantam.

Rainbow Valley. L. M. Montgomery. 1986. 24.75X (ISBN 0-245-52798-2, Pub. by Harrap Ltd England). State Mutual Bk.

Rainbow Walkers. Doris Schwerin. Ed. by Marc Jaffe. LC 84-40483. 1985. 16.45 (ISBN 0-394-53950-8, Pub. by Villard Bks). Random.

Rainbow Walkers. Doris Schwerin. 384p. 1986. pap. 3.95 (ISBN 0-345-30387-3). Ballantine.

Rainbow Warrior: The French Attempt to Sink Greenpeace. The Sunday Times Insight Team. 302p. 1987. 30.95 (ISBN 0-09-164360-0, Pub. by Century Hutchinson). David & Charles.

Rainbow World. N. Sladkov. 99p. 1986. 11.95 (ISBN 0-8285-3455-1, Pub. by Raduga Pubs USSR). Imported Pubns.

Rainbow: Writing the Research Paper. Blomain et al. 64p. 1987. pap. text ed. 11.95 (ISBN 0-8403-4557-7). Kendall-Hunt.

Rainbowfishes of Australia & Papua New Guinea. G. R. Allen & N. J. Cross. (Illus.). 160p. 1982. 19.95 (ISBN 0-87666-547-4, H-1047). TFH Pubns.

Rainbows & Children: Three Monographs. Naomi Hale. 1986. 7.95 (ISBN 0-533-06701-4). Vantage.

Rainbows & Frogs: A Story about Colors. Joy Kim. LC 81-4685. (Illus.). 32p. (gr. k-2). 1981. PLB 9.89 (ISBN 0-89375-505-2); pap. text ed. 2.95 (ISBN 0-89375-506-0). Troll Assocs.

Rainbows & Unicorns: And Other Such Realities. Ann Wilmer-Lasky. (Illus.). 28p. (Orig.). 1988. pap. 4.95 (ISBN 0-945152-02-7). Skye Isle Ent.

Rainbows Are Made: Poems by Carl Sandburg. Lee B. Hopkins. (Illus.). 1984. pap. 7.95 (ISBN 0-15-265481-X, VoyB). HarBraceJ.

Rainbows Are Made: Poems by Carl Sandburg. Ed. by Lee B. Hopkins. LC 82-47934. (Illus.). (gr. k up). 1984. 13.95 (ISBN 0-15-265480-1, HJ). HarBraceJ.

Rainbow's End. Carole Buck. Ed. by Joan Marlowe. (Second Chance At Love Ser.: No. 436). 192p. (Orig.). 1988. pap. 2.50 (ISBN 0-425-10708-6). Berkley Pub.

Rainbow's End. James M. Cain. 240p. (Orig.). 1982. pap. 2.50 (ISBN 0-8439-1054-2, Leisure Bks). Leisure NY.

Rainbow's End. Genaro Gonzalez. 200p. (Orig.). 1988. pap. 8.50 (ISBN 0-934770-81-6). Arte Publico.

Rainbow's End. Luanne Tovey & Louise DeFelice. 175p. 1985. pap. 3.00 (ISBN 0-9613765-1-1). Rainbow Pubns.

Rainbow's End: Irish-American & The Dilemmas of Urban Machine Politics, 1840-1985. Steven P. Erie. Date not set. 27.50 (ISBN 0-520-06119-5). U of Cal Pr.

Rainbows Falling on My Head: The Magic of the Great God Pan. Al G. Manning. LC 82-90133. (Illus.). 1982. 12.95 (ISBN 0-941698-02-5); pap. 5.95 (ISBN 0-941698-03-3). Pan-Ishtar.

Rainbows, Fleas, & Flowers: A Nature Anthology. Geoffrey Grigson. 280p. Date not set. 12.95 (ISBN 0-8149-0754-7). Vanguard.

Rainbows for the Fallen World. C. Seerveld. 1980. pap. 9.95x (ISBN 0-919071-01-5). Radix Bks.

Rainbows, Halos & Glories. Robert Greenler. LC 80-143722. (Illus.). 304p. 1980. 39.50 (ISBN 0-521-23605-3). Cambridge U Pr.

Rainbows, Mirages & Sundogs. Roy A. Gallant. LC 86-23728. (Illus.). 112p. (gr. 3-7). 1987. 12.95 (ISBN 0-02-737010-0). Macmillan.

Rainbows of Promise. Ivy D. Doherty. Ed. by Gerald Wheeler. (Banner Bks.). (Illus.). 92p. (Orig.). (gr. 2 up). 1984. pap. 6.95 (ISBN 0-8280-0213-4). Review & Herald.

Rainbows of Song. Georgiana L. Lahr. 3.95 (ISBN 0-533-01774-2). Vantage.

Rainbows of Your Aura. Lea Sanders. (Illus.). 124p. 1987. pap. write for info. (ISBN 0-936415-07-X). Riverrun Piermont.

Rainbows, Snowflakes & Quarks: Physics & the World Around Us. Hans C. Von Baeyer. (Illus.). 192p. 1984. text ed. 16.95 (ISBN 0-07-067545-7). McGraw.

Rainbows Through Tears. Eva H. Groce. (Illus.). 1979. pap. 2.00x (ISBN 0-9602440-2-6). Jesus-First.

Raindancer. Barbara Hock. 1983. pap. 4.00 (ISBN 0-934834-35-0). White Pine.

Raindrops Keep Falling on My Tent. Joy Mackay. 20p. 1981. pap. 4.00 (ISBN 0-686-79517-2). Am Camping.

Rainer Maria Rilke. Arnold Bauer. Tr. by Ursula Lamm. LC 75-163151. (Literature & Life Ser.). 128p. 1972. 16.95x (ISBN 0-8044-2025-4). Ungar.

Rainer Maria Rilke. Patricia P. Brodsky. (Twayne World Author Ser.: Vol. 796). 192p. 1988. lib. bdg. 24.95x (ISBN 0-8057-8226-5, Twayne). G K Hall.

Rainer Maria Rilke. Eliza M. Butler. 437p. 1973. Repr. of 1941 ed. lib. bdg. 29.00x (ISBN 0-374-91120-7, Octagon). Hippocrene Bks.

Rainer Maria Rilke: A Study of His Later Poetry. Hans E. Holthusen. LC 74-17400. 1974. Repr. of 1952 ed. lib. bdg. 18.00 (ISBN 0-8414-4883-3). Folcroft.

Raising Less Corn & More Hell: Midwestern Farmers Speak Out. Jim Schwab. (Illus.). 320p. 1988. 24.95 (ISBN 0-252-01398-0). U of Ill Pr.

Raising Livestock & Poultry: A Smallholder's Guide. Ed. by Katie Thear & Alistair Fraser. 240p. 1981. 40.00 (ISBN 0-906348-11-0, Pub. by Dunitz). State Mutual Bk.

Raising Milk Goats Successfully. Gail Luttmann. Ed. by Roger Griffith. 192p. (Orig.). 1986. pap. 8.95 (ISBN 0-913589-24-1). Williamson Pub Co.

Raising Milk Goats the Modern Way. Jerry Belanger. LC 75-3493. (Illus.). 160p. 1975. pap. 6.95 (ISBN 0-88266-062-4, Garden Way Pub). Storey Comm Inc.

Raising Money for Women: A Survivors' Guide. Marion Bowman & Michael Norton. 128p. 1986. pap. text ed. 11.90x (ISBN 0-7199-1170-2, Pub. by Bedford England). Brookfield Pub Co.

Raising Money from Grants & Other Sources Success Kit. 3rd ed. Tyler G. Hicks. 496p. 1987. pap. 99.50 (ISBN 0-934311-07-2). Intl Wealth.

Raising Money Through an Institutionally Related Foundation. Ed. by Timothy A. Reilley. 83p. 1985. 16.50 (ISBN 0-89964-225-X). Coun Adv & Supp Ed.

Raising Money Through Gift Clubs: A Survey of Techniques at 42 Institutions. Compiled by Robert D. Sweeney. 71p. 1982. 14.50 (ISBN 0-89964-191-1). Coun Adv & Supp Ed.

Raising of Intelligence: A Selected History of Attempts to Raise Retarded Intelligence. Herman H. Spitz. 288p. 1986. text ed. 29.95 (ISBN 0-89859-836-2). L Erlbaum Assocs.

Raising of Lazarus. John Cornish. 1979. pap. 2.95 (ISBN 0-916786-36-6). St George Bk Serv.

Raising of Money: Thirty-Five Essentials (Accompanied by a Guide for the Professional) James G. Lord. LC 84-50377. 128p. 1984. 34.50 (ISBN 0-939120-02-X). Third Sector.

Raising PG Kids in an X-Rated Society: Leader's Guide. 1988. pap. 1.75 (ISBN 0-687-35281-9). Abingdon.

Raising PG Kids in an X-Rated Society. Tipper Gore. 240p. 1987. 12.95 (ISBN 0-687-35283-5); pap. 8.95 (ISBN 0-687-35282-7). Abingdon.

Raising Pigs Successfully. Kathy & Bob Kellog. (Illus.). 224p. 1985. pap. 8.95 (ISBN 0-913589-15-2). Williamson Pub Co.

Raising Positive Kids in a Negative World. Zig Ziglar. 288p. 1985. 14.95 (ISBN 0-8407-9039-2). Nelson.

Raising Poultry Successfully. Will Graves. (Illus.). 196p. (Orig.). 1985. pap. 8.95 (ISBN 0-913589-09-8). Williamson Pub Co.

Raising Poultry the Modern Way. Leonard S. Mercia. LC 74-75463. (Illus.). 240p. 1975. pap. 8.95 (ISBN 0-88266-058-6, Garden Way Pub). Storey Comm Inc.

Raising Rabbits. Harlan H. D. Attfield. 90p. (Fr.). 1977. perfect bdg. 5.50 (ISBN 0-86619-060-0, 11040-BK); In French. 4.35 (ISBN 0-86619-061-9, 19040-BK). Vols Tech Asst.

Raising Rabbits. Ann Kanable. LC 77-23926. 208p. 1977. pap. 7.95 (ISBN 0-87857-314-3). Rodale Pr Inc.

Raising Rabbits Successfully. Bob Bennett. (Illus.). 192p. (Orig.). 1984. pap. 8.95 (ISBN 0-913589-03-9). Williamson Pub Co.

Raising Rabbits the Modern Way. rev. ed. Bob Bennett. Ed. by Constance Oxley. LC 87-45579. (Illus.). 192p. (Orig.). 1988. pap. 8.95 (ISBN 0-88266-479-4, Garden Way Pub). Storey Comm Inc.

Raising School Quality in Developing Countries: What Investments Boost Learning? Bruce Fuller. (Discussion Paper: No. 2). 90p. 1986. 5.00 (ISBN 0-8213-0846-7, DP 0002). World Bank.

Raising Seed Money for Your Own Business. Brian Smith. LC 84-791. (Illus.). 192p. 1984. 19.95 (ISBN 0-86616-041-8). Greene.

Raising Self-Reliant Children in a Self-Indulgent World: Seven Building Blocks for Developing Capable Young People. rev. ed. H. Stephen Glenn & Jane Nelsen. LC 87-31866. 210p. 1988. 16.95 (ISBN 0-914629-64-6). Prima Pub Comm.

Raising Sheep the Modern Way. Paula Simmons. Ed. by Roger Griffith. LC 76-44530. (Illus.). 240p. 1976. pap. 8.95 (ISBN 0-88266-093-4, Garden Way Pub). Storey Comm Inc.

Raising Sons: Practical Strategies for Single Mothers. Joan E. Rodgers & Michael F. Catalado. 1984. 14.95 (ISBN 0-453-00470-9). NAL.

Raising Standards in Schools: Problems & Solutions. Patricia Pine. Ed. by Shirley B. Neill. 80p. (Orig.). 1985. pap. write for info. (ISBN 0-87652-099-9, 021-00145). Am Assn Sch Admin.

Raising Teenagers Right. James Dobson. 96p. 1988. pap. 2.25. Tyndale.

Raising the Achievement Level of Children in Primary Education. 48p. 1986. pap. text ed. 7.50 (ISBN 0-317-53611-7, UB221, UB). UNIPUB.

Raising the African Nightcrawler. Charlie Morgan. 1978. pap. 3.00 (ISBN 0-9600102-9-7). Shields.

Raising the Dead: A Moses Wine Mystery. Roger L. Simon. LC 87-40578. 224p. 1988. 15.95 (ISBN 0-394-56441-3, Pub. by Villard Bks). Random.

Raising the Home Duck Flock. rev. ed. Dave Holderread. LC 80-10992. (Illus.). 192p. 1980. pap. 7.95 (ISBN 0-88266-169-8, Garden Way Pub). Storey Comm Inc.

Raising the Only Child. Murray Kappelman. 1977. pap. 2.50 (ISBN 0-451-09939-7, E9939, Sig). NAL.

Raising the Stakes, 3 vols. Edward Doyle & Samuel Lipsman. Ed. by Boston Publishing Company Staff & Robert Manning. (Illus.). 1982. write for info. Vol. I: Setting The Stage (pre-1946) 192p (ISBN 0-201-11260-4). Vol. II: Passing The Torch (1946-1960) 208p. write for info. (ISBN 0-201-11261-2); Vol. III: Raising The Stakes (1960-1965) 192p. write for info. (ISBN 0-201-11262-0). Addison-Wesley.

Raising the Stakes, Vol. III. Terrence Maitland & Stephen Weiss. Ed. by Robert Manning. LC 82-71280. (Vietnam Experience Ser.). (Illus.). 192p. 1982. 16.95 (ISBN 0-939526-02-6). Boston Pub Co.

Raising the Torch of Good News: Catholic Authority & Dialogue with the World. Ed. by Bernard P. Prusak. LC 87-31695. (CTS Annual Publication: Vol. 32). 342p. (Orig.). 1988. lib. bdg. 28.75 (ISBN 0-8191-6699-5, Pub. by College Theology Society); pap. text ed. 15.75 (ISBN 0-8191-6700-2, Pub. by College Theology Society). U Pr of Amer.

Raising the Veil, or, Scenes in the Courts. Ball Fenner. LC 77-172580. (Criminology, Law Enforcement, & Social Problems Ser.: No. 168). (Illus.). Date not set. 12.50x (ISBN 0-87585-168-1). Patterson Smith.

Raising the Wind: The Legend of Lapland & Finland Wizards in Literature. Ernest J. Moyne. Ed. by Wayne R. Kime. (Illus.). 224p. 1981. 27.50 (ISBN 0-87413-146-4). U Delaware Pr.

Raising the Young Blind Child: A Guide for Parents & Educators. Shulamith Kastein et al. LC 79-17820. 208p. 1980. text ed. 29.95 (ISBN 0-87705-422-3); pap. 14.95 (ISBN 0-89885-288-9). Human Sci Pr.

Raising Turkeys, Ducks, Geese, Pigeon, & Guineas. Cynthia Haynes. (Illus.). 368p. (Orig.). 1987. 24.95 (ISBN 0-8306-0803-6); pap. 16.95 (ISBN 0-8306-2803-7). TAB Bks.

Raising Venture Capital & Other Musings on Risky Business. Leonard A. Batterson. 400p. 1986. text ed. 34.00 (ISBN 0-13-752684-9). P-H.

Raising Your Adopted Child: A Complete & Loving Guide. Stephanie Seigel. 224p. 1989. 16.45 (ISBN 0-13-815325-6). Prentice Hall Pr.

Raising Your Blessings: How to Bring up Your Kids Without Climbing the Walls! Larry G. Brady. (Illus.). 120p. (Orig.). 1986. pap. text ed. 10.95 (ISBN 0-935489-02-9). Larry G Brady.

Raising Your Child, Not by Force But by Love. Sidney D. Craig. LC 72-10436. 192p. 1982. pap. 7.95 (ISBN 0-664-24413-0). Westminster John Knox.

Raising Your Child, Not Your Voice. Duane Cuthbertson. 168p. 1986. pap. 5.95 (ISBN 0-89693-342-3). Victor Bks.

Raising Your Child to Be Mensch. Neil Kurshan. LC 85-48149. 128p. 1987. 14.95 (ISBN 0-689-11655-1). Atheneum.

Raising Your Family Naturally. Joy Gross. 224p. 1988. Repr. of 1983 ed. 12.95 (ISBN 0-8184-0459-0). Lyle Stuart.

Raising Your Hearing-Impaired Child: Guideline for Parents. Shirley H. McArthur. 256p. 1982. pap. 12.95 (ISBN 0-88200-150-7). Alexander Graham.

Raising Your Jewish-Christian Child: Wise Choices for Interfaith Parents. Lee F. Gruzen. 1987. 16.95 (ISBN 0-396-08551-2). Dodd.

Raising Your Own Livestock. Claudia Weisburd. (Illus.). 1980. 15.95 (ISBN 0-13-752758-6, Spec). P-H.

Raising Your Own Meat for Pennies a Day. Will Graves. Ed. by Fred Stetson. LC 83-1595. (Illus.). 160p. (Orig.). 1983. pap. 6.95 (ISBN 0-88266-330-5, Garden Way Pub). Storey Comm Inc.

Raising Your Own Turkeys. Leonard S. Mercia. LC 81-6353. (Illus.). 160p. (Orig.). 1981. pap. 6.95 (ISBN 0-88266-253-8, Garden Way Pub). Storey Comm Inc.

Raising Your Wellness Grade. American Association of School Administrators Staff. 24p. 1986. pap. write for info. (ISBN 0-87652-104-9, 021-00158). Am Assn Sch Admin.

Raisins in Motion. (California Raisins Storybooks Ser.). (Illus.). 24p. (ps-4). 1988. pap. 1.95 (ISBN 0-02-688828-9, Checkerboard Pr). Macmillan.

Raison et Alterite chez Fadrique Furio Ceriol, Philosphe Pollitique Espagnol du XVIe Siecle. Ed. by Henri Mechoulan. 1973. pap. 14.40x (ISBN 90-2797-194-3). Mouton.

Raison et Deraison dans le Theatre de Pierre Corneille. Carlo Francois. 178p. (Fr.). 1979. 13.95 (ISBN 0-917786-17-3). Summa Pubns.

Raisonnement Modal: Etude Genetique. Gilberte Pieraut-Le Bonniec. (Connaissance et Language Ser.: No. 2). 288p. (Fr.). 1975. pap. text ed. 28.00x (ISBN 90-2797-516-7). Mouton.

Raissa's Journal. Raissa Maritain. LC 72-95648. 1974. 12.95x (ISBN 0-87343-041-7). Magi Bks.

Raj. Donald H. Robinson. pap. 3.95 (ISBN 0-515-08223-6). Jove Pubns.

Raj in Fiction. Udayon Misra. x, 198p. 1987. text ed. 27.50x (ISBN 81-7018-433-9, Pub. by B R Pub Corp Delhi). Apt Bks.

Raj Kapoor's Films: Harmony & Discourses. W. Dissanayake & M. Sahai. 1988. text ed. 35.00 (ISBN 0-7069-4040-7). Advent NY.

Raj Marwar During the British Paramountcy. P. R. Shah. 47p. 1982. 75.00x (ISBN 0-317-62306-0, Pub. by Scientific). State Mutual Bk.

Raj Quartet. Paul Scott. LC 76-13249. 1950p. 27.50 (ISBN 0-688-04212-0). Morrow.

Raj, the Indian Mutiny, & the Kingdom of Oudh, 1801-1859. John Pemble. LC 76-55892. 303p. 1978. 27.50 (ISBN 0-8386-2092-2). Fairleigh Dickinson.

Raja Rammohun Roy. Mini Thakur. 1987. 22.50x (ISBN 0-8364-2020-9, Pub. by Deep). South Asia Bks.

Raja Rammohun Roy & Progressive Movement in India. J. K. Majumdar. 1988. Repr. 72.50 (ISBN 81-7041-071-1, Pub. by Anmol Delhi). South Asia Bks.

Raja Rammohun Roy & the New Learning. Ed. by B. P. Barua. 134p. 1988. text ed. 22.50x (ISBN 0-86131-886-2, Pub. by Orient Longman LTD India). Apt bks.

Raja Rammohun Roy: India's Great Social Reformer. Jamuna Nag. (Illus.). 167p. 1972. 6.00x (ISBN 0-89684-446-3). Orient Bk Dist.

Raja Rammohun Roy: Letters & Documents. Ram P. Chanda & Jatindra K. Majumdar. 1987. Repr. 72.50 (ISBN 81-7041-067-3, Pub. by Anmol Delhi). South Asia Bks.

Raja Rao. C. D. Narasimaiah. (Indian Writers Ser.). 8.50 (ISBN 0-89253-511-3). Ind-US Inc.

Raja Rao & Cultural Tradition. Paul Sharrad. 180p. 1988. text ed. 25.00 (Pub. by Sterling Pubs India). Apt Bks.

Raja Rao, Novelist As Sadhaka. Shiva Niranjan. 154p. 1986. 13.50X (ISBN 0-8364-1664-3, Pub. by Popular Prakashan). South Asia Bks.

Raja-Vidya: The King of Knowledge. Swami A. C. Bhaktivedanta. LC 72-84845. (Illus.). 1973. pap. 1.95 (ISBN 0-912776-40-4). Bhaktivedanta.

Raja Yoga. Yogi Ramacharaka. 8.00 (ISBN 0-911662-03-0). Yoga.

Raja Yoga. Swami Sivananda. Ed. by Swami Venkatesananda. (Life & Works of Swami Sivananda Ser.). 373p. (Orig.). 1986. pap. 11.95 (ISBN 0-949027-07-3). Integral Yoga Pubns.

Raja Yoga. Subramuniya. (Illus.). 193p. 1973. 7.00 (ISBN 0-87516-348-3). DeVorss.

Raja-Yoga. Swami Vivekananda. LC 55-12231. 310p. pocket ed. 7.95 (ISBN 0-911206-06-X); pap. 7.95 large size (ISBN 0-911206-23-X). Ramakrishna.

Raja Yoga: A Simplified & Practical Course. Wallace Slater. LC 71-3051. 1969. pap. 4.50 (ISBN 0-8356-0131-5, Quest). Theos Pub Hse.

Raja Yoga Sutras. Patanjali. Tr. by Swami Jyotir Maya Nanda from Sanskrit. (Illus.). 1978. pap. 2.99 (ISBN 0-934664-38-2). Yoga Res Foun.

Raja Yoga (The Study of the Mind) Swami Jyotir Maya Nanda. (Illus.). 1970. 5.99 (ISBN 0-934664-09-9). Yoga Res Foun.

Raja-Yoga: The Yoga Aphorisms of Patanjali. Tr. by Swami Vivekananda. pap. 3.50 (ISBN 0-87481-160-0). Vedanta Pr.

Rajahs & Rebels: The Ibans of Sarawak under Brooke Rule, 1841-1941. Robert M. Pringle. LC 79-102935. 432p. 1970. 42.50x (ISBN 0-8014-0552-1). Cornell U Pr.

Rajah's Sapphire. M. P. Shiel. (Nautilus Ser.). (Illus.). 163p. 1981. pap. 6.00 (ISBN 0-686-92118-6). Highflyer Pr.

Rajah's Sapphire. M. P. Shiel. 139p. pap. 6.00 (ISBN 0-317-14710-2). Reynolds Morse.

Rajah's Servant. A. B. Ward. 204p. 1966. pap. 2.50 (ISBN 0-87727-061-9, DP 61). Cornell SE Asia.

Rajaji Story: Warrior from the South. Rajmohan Gandhi. 1979. 12.50x (ISBN 0-8364-0562-5, Pub. by Bharathan India). South Asia Bks.

Rajarsi Janakananda: A Great Western Yogi. (Illus.). 95p. 1984. pap. 2.00 (ISBN 0-87612-181-4). Self Realization.

Rajasthan: A Bibliographic Index of Social Science. S. N. Sahai. Ed. by D. V. Kothari. 418p. 1985. 75.00x (ISBN 0-317-62309-5, Pub. by Scientific). State Mutual Bk.

Rajasthan: Land of Kings. Sylvia Matheson. LC 84-7319. (Illus.). 200p. 1984. 50.00 (ISBN 0-86565-046-2). Vendome.

Rajasthan: The Painted Walls of Shekhavati. Francis Wacziarg & Aman Nath. (Illus.). 120p. 1983. 35.00 (ISBN 0-8390-0309-9). Abner Schram Ltd.

Rajesh. Curt Kaufman & Gita Kaufman. LC 85-7510. (Illus.). 32p. (gr. k-3). 1985. 8.95 (ISBN 0-689-31074-9, Atheneum Childrens Bks). Macmillan.

Rajiv Gandhi: Breaking New Grounds. B. K. Ahluwalia & S. Alhuwalia. 202p. 1985. 34.95. Asia Bk Corp.

Rajiv Gandhi: Challenges & Choices. V. K. Murthi & G. Sharma. 1985. 22.95. Asia Bk Corp.

Rajiv Gandhi: Challenges & Choices. V. K. Murthi & Gautam Sharma. viii, 141p. 1986. text ed. 18.95x (ISBN 81-7027-089-8, Pub. by Radiant Pubs India). Advent NY.

Rajiv Gandhi: Future of India. Jagdish C. Tokas. 134p. 1987. 32.95. Asia Bk Corp.

Rajiv Gandhi: The Brave New Leader. P. Sood. 227p. 1986. 28.00x (ISBN 0-8364-1815-8, Pub. by Marwah). South Asia Bks.

Rajneesh & the U. S. Postal Service. Bert Webber. (Orig.). 1988. pap. price not set (ISBN 0-936738-29-4). Webb Research.

Rajneesh Bible, Vol. II. Bhagwan S. Rajneesh. Ed. by Rajneesh Academy Staff. LC 85-42539. 839p. (Orig.). 1985. pap. 9.95x (ISBN 0-88050-201-0, 201-0). Chidvilas Inc.

Rajneesh Bible, Vol. III. Bhagwan S. Rajneesh. Ed. by Rajneesh Academy Staff. LC 85-42539. 1072p. (Orig.). 1985. pap. 9.95 (ISBN 0-88050-202-9). Chidvilas Inc.

Rajneesh Bible, Vol. IV. Bhagwan Shree Rajneesh. LC 85-42539. (Illus.). 800p. (Orig.). 1987. pap. 9.95 (ISBN 3-907757-02-5). Chidvilas Inc.

Rajneesh Bible, Vol. 1. Baghwan S. Rajneesh. Ed. by Rajneesh Academy Staff. LC 85-42539. 800p. (Orig.). 1985. pap. 9.95 (ISBN 0-88050-200-2). Chidvilas Inc.

Rajneesh: The Mystic of Feeling. Ram C. Prasad. 239p. 1978. 16.95. Asia Bk Corp.

Rajneesh: The Mystic of Feeling. 2nrev. ed. Ram Chandra Prasad. 1978. 10.95 (ISBN 0-89684-023-9, Pub. by Motilal Banarsidass India). Orient Bk Dist.

Rajneesh Upanishad. Bhagwan S. Rajneesh. Ed. by Ma Deva Sarito. 1032p. 1986. pap. 9.95 (ISBN 0-88050-301-7). Chidvilas Inc.

Rajneeshpuram: How the U. S. Postal Service Handled Mail for 20,000 Rajneeshes--an Illustrated History. Bert Webber. (Illus., Orig.). Date not set. pap. price not set (ISBN 0-936738-24-3). Webb Research.

Rajneeshpuram: The Unwelcome Society-"Cultures Collide in a Quest for Utopia". Kirk Braun. 256p. 1984. pap. 9.95 (ISBN 0-930219-00-7). Scout Creek Pr.

Rajpur: Last of the Bengal Tigers. Robert M. McClung. LC 82-3478. (Illus.). 96p. (gr. 4-6). 1982. 10.25 (ISBN 0-688-01495-X). Morrow.

Rajput Art & Architecture. Hermann Goetz. Ed. by Jyotindra Jain & Jutta Jain-Neubauer. (Illus.). 250p. (Orig.). 1978. pap. 48.50x (ISBN 3-515-02912-6, Pub by Franz Steiner). Coronet Bks.

Rajput Painting, 2 vols. in 1. Ananda K. Coomaraswamy. LC 72-87768. 1975. Repr. of 1916 ed. lib. bdg. 75.00 (ISBN 0-87817-118-5). Hacker.

Rajput Painting, 2 vols. 2nd ed. Ananda K. Coomaraswamy. (Illus.). 1976. Set. 150.00x (ISBN 0-89684-301-7). Orient Bk Dist.

Rajput Palace Architecture. G. H. Tillotson. LC 86-24544. 245p. 1987. 45.00x (ISBN 0-300-03738-4). Yale U Pr.

Rajput Polity: A Study of Politics & Administration of the State of Marwar, 1638-1749. G. D. Sharma. 1977. 14.00x (ISBN 0-88386-887-3). South Asia Bks.

Rajput Rebellion Against Aurangzeb: A Study of the Mughal Empire in Seventeenth-Century India. Robert C. Hallissey. LC 77-268. (Illus.). 136p. 1977. 13.00x (ISBN 0-8262-0222-5). U of Mo Pr.

Rakehell. Deirdre Stiles. 1978. pap. 1.95 (ISBN 0-8439-0541-7, Leisure Bks). Leisure NY.

Rakehell Dynasty. Michael W. Scott. 544p. (Orig.). 1980. pap. 3.95 (ISBN 0-446-32018-8). Warner Bks.

Rakehell Dynasty, No. 2: China Bride. Michael W. Scott. 512p. (Orig.). 1981. pap. 3.95 (ISBN 0-446-30948-6). Warner Bks.

Rakehell Dynasty, No. 4: Mission to Cathay. Michael W. Scott. 432p. (Orig.). 1984. pap. 3.95 (ISBN 0-446-90239-X). Warner Bks.

Rakehell Dynasty: Orient Affair, No. 3. Michael W. Scott. 1984. pap. 3.95 (ISBN 0-446-30771-8). Warner Bks.

Rakehell's Widow. Sandra Heath. 224p. 1987. pap. 2.50 (ISBN 0-451-15062-7, Sig). NAL.

Rakes & Rogues. Neil King. (Drama Ser.). pap. 11.95 (ISBN 0-7175-1234-7). Dufour.

Rake's Progress. Marion Chesney. 176p. 1987. 12.95 (ISBN 0-312-00674-8). St Martin.

Rake's Ransom. Barbara Metzger. 224p. 1986. 15.95 (ISBN 0-8027-0911-7). Walker & Co.

Rakhmaninov. Geoffrey Norris. (Master Musicians Ser.: M-175). (Illus.). 1978. pap. 7.95 (ISBN 0-8226-0701-8). Littlefield.

Raking the Snow. Elisavietta Ritchie. LC 81-86642. 55p. 1982. pap. 4.00 (ISBN 0-931846-21-8). Wash Writers Pub.

Rakish Stage: Studies in English Drama, 1660-1800. Robert D. Hume. LC 82-16984. 382p. 1983. 27.50x (ISBN 0-8093-1100-3). S Ill U Pr.

Rakkasan! The 187th Regimental Combat Team. Arch E. Roberts. (Airborne Ser.: No. 8). (Illus.). 1978. 20.00 (ISBN 0-89839-008-7). Battery Pr.

Raku & Smoke North America. American Craft Council Staff. 28p. 1984. 7.50 (ISBN 0-88321-056-8). Am Craft.

Rakuyo Kinson Kobo Shuei. Umehara Sueji. 70p. 1939. 1050.00x (ISBN 0-317-68992-4, Pub. by Han-Shan Tang Ltd). State Mutual Bk.

Rakuyo Kinson Kobo Shuei, Zotei (Old Tombs of Jincun at Luoyang) Umehara Sueji. 90p. 1944. 1260.00x (ISBN 0-317-68995-9, Pub. by Han-Shan Tang Ltd). State Mutual Bk.

Ralegh's Country: The South West of England in the Reign of Queen Elizabeth I. Joyce Youings. (America's 400th Anniversary Ser.). (Illus.). xiv, 74p. (Orig.). 1986. pap. 5.00 (ISBN 0-86526-207-1). NC Archives.

Raleigh. Edmund W. Gosse. LC 74-14939. 1974. Repr. of 1888 ed. lib. bdg. 20.00 (ISBN 0-8414-4532-X). Folcroft.

Raman Spectroscopy, Vol. 1. Ed. by Herman A. Szymanski. LC 64-23241. 250p. 1967. 49.50x (ISBN 0-306-37741-1, Plenum Pr). Plenum Pub.

Raman Spectroscopy, Vol. 2. Ed. by Herman A. Szymanski. LC 64-23241. 222p. 1970. 49.50x (ISBN 0-306-37742-X, Plenum Pr). Plenum Pub.

Raman Spectroscopy in Biology: Principles & Applications. Anthony T. Tu. LC 82-6901. 448p. 1982. text ed. 83.00x (ISBN 0-471-07984-7, Pub. by Wiley-Interscience). Wiley.

Raman Spectroscopy: Linear & Nonlinear. International Conference on Raman Spectroscopy 8th, 1982, Bordeaux et al. Ed. by Jean Lascombe & Pham V. Huong. pap. 160.00 (ISBN 0-317-08718-5, 2022542). Bks Demand UMI.

Raman Spectroscopy of Gases & Liquids. Ed. by A. Weber. (Topics in Current Physics Ser.: Vol. 11). (Illus.). 1979. 37.00 (ISBN 0-387-09036-3). Springer-Verlag.

Raman Spectroscopy: Proceedings of the 6th International Conference on Raman Spectroscopy, Bangalore, India, 4-9 September 1978, 2 vols, Vols. 1 & 2. International Conference on Raman Spectroscopy (6th: 1978: Bangalore, India) Ed. by E. D. Schmid & R. S. Krishnan. LC 83-131239. Vol. 1 - Invited Lectures. pap. 112.30 (ISBN 0-317-29336-2, 2024026); Vol. 2 - Contributed Papers. pap. 135.50 (ISBN 0-317-29337-0): Bks Demand UMI.

Ramana Maharshi. K. Swaminathan. (National Biography Ser.). 1979. pap. 3.95 (ISBN 0-89744-197-4). Auromere.

Ramanujan. 3rd ed. Godfrey H. Hardy. LC 59-10268. 1978. 14.95 (ISBN 0-8284-0136-5). Chelsea Pub.

Ramanujan Revisited: Proceedings of the Centenary Conference. Ed. by George E. Andrews et al. 609p. 1988. 49.50 (ISBN 0-12-058560-X). Acad Pr.

Ramanujan's Notebooks, Pt. 1. B. C. Berndt. (Illus.). 430p. 1985. 59.50 (ISBN 0-387-96110-0). Springer-Verlag.

Ramapo Mountain People. David S. Cohen. 285p. 1986. pap. 12.95 (ISBN 0-8135-1195-X). Rutgers U Pr.

Ramaria of Western Washington. C. D. Marr. 1973. 25.00x (ISBN 3-7682-0902-4). Lubrecht & Cramer.

Ramaria, Subgenus Lentoramaria, with Emphasis on North American Taxa. R. H. Petersen. (Bibliotheca Mycologica Ser.: No. 43). 1975. text ed. 30.00x (ISBN 3-7682-0961-X). Lubrecht & Cramer.

Ramayana. William Buck. 1978. pap. 3.50 (ISBN 0-451-62346-0, Ment). NAL.

Ramayana. William Buck. LC 78-153549. (Illus.). 1976. pap. 10.95x (ISBN 0-520-04394-4). U of Cal Pr.

Ramayana. Tr. by Romesh C. Dutt. Bd. with Mahabharata. 1972. 12.95x (ISBN 0-460-00403-4, Evman). Biblio Dist.

Ramayana. Shudha Mazumdar. 542p. 1974. 12.95. Asia Bk Corp.

Ramayana. R. K. Narayan. (Illus.). 1977. pap. 4.95 (ISBN 0-14-004428-0). Penguin.

Ramayana. C. Rajagopalachari. 1979. pap. 5.95 (ISBN 0-89744-930-4). Auromere.

Ramayana. Kamala Subramaniam. 596p. 1983. 29.95. Asia Bk Corp.

Ramayana: As Told by Audrey Menen. Audrey Menen. LC 72-598. 276p. Repr. of 1954 ed. lib. bdg. 35.00x (ISBN 0-8371-6181-9, VARA). Greenwood.

Ramayana at a Glance. Satguru S. Keshavadas. (Illus.). 184p. (Orig.). 1978. pap. 3.50. Vishwa.

Ramayana in Historical Perspective. H. D. Sankalia. 1983. 18.50x (ISBN 0-8364-0997-3, Pub. by Macmillan India). South Asia Bks.

Ramayana of R. K. Narayan: A Shortened Modern Prose Version of the Indian Epic, Suggested by the Tamil Version of Kamban. R. K. Narayan. LC 79-189514. (Illus.). 192p. 1972. 13.95 (ISBN 0-670-58950-0). Viking.

Ramayana of Tulasidasa. 2nd, rev. ed. Ed. by R. C. Prasad. Tr. by F. S. Growse from Hindi. 719p. 1987. 23.00 (ISBN 81-208-0205-5, Pub. by Motilal Banarsidass India); pap. 17.50 (ISBN 81-208-0209-8, Pub. by Motilal Banarsidass India). Orient Bk Dist.

Ramayana of Tulasidasa. Tulasidas. Tr. by F. S. Growse. 1979. 26.00x (ISBN 0-8364-0363-0). South Asia Bks.

Ramayana of Valmiki, 3 vols. 3rd ed. Tr. by H. P. Shastri. 1976. Set. pap. 58.00x (ISBN 0-85424-016-0); Vol. 1. Vol. 2. (ISBN 0-85424-000-4); Vol. 3. (ISBN 0-85424-017-9). Orient Bk Dist.

Ramayana of Valmiki, 3 vols. Shri Valmiki. Tr. by Hari P. Shastri. 1985. pap. 60.00 (ISBN 0-7103-0136-7, Kegan Paul). Routledge Chapman & Hall.

Ramayana of Valmiki: An Epic of Ancient India, Vol II. Ed. by Robert P. Goldman. Tr. by Sheldon I. Pollock from Sanskrit. LC 85-61364. (Princeton Library of Asian Translations). (Illus.). 525p. 1986. text ed. 60.00x (ISBN 0-691-06654-X). Princeton U Pr.

Ramayana of Valmiki Balakanda, Vol. I. Tr. by Robert P. Goldman. LC 82-61364. (Princeton Library of Asian Translations: Vol. 1). 450p. 1984. 55.50x (ISBN 0-691-06561-6). Princeton U Pr.

Ramayana: The Story of Rama. Valmiki. LC 74-77601. (Illus.). 72p. (gr. 5-12). 1975. 8.50 (ISBN 0-88253-292-8); pap. 3.50 (ISBN 0-88253-291-X). Ind-US Inc.

Ramayana Tradition in Asia. Ed. by V. Raghavan. 1982. 18.00x (ISBN 0-8364-0899-3, Pub. by National Sahitya Akademi). South Asia Bks.

Rambam, Readings in the Philosophy of Moses Maimonides. Ed. & tr. by Lenn E. Goodman. LC 75-14476. 460p. 1985. 14.95x (ISBN 0-917232-19-4). Gee Tee Bee.

Ramban: His Life & Teachings. Charles B. Chavel. LC 63-1543. pap. 5.95 (ISBN 0-87306-037-7). Feldheim.

Ramban (Nachmanides) Commentary on the Torah, 5 vols. Charles B. Chavel. 2575p. 1971. 89.75 set (ISBN 0-686-86743-2); Vol. I, Book Of Genesis. 17.95 ea. (ISBN 0-88328-006-X). Vol. II, Book Of Exodus (ISBN 0-88328-007-8). Vol. III, Book Of Leviticus (ISBN 0-88328-008-6). Vol. IV, Book Of Numbers (ISBN 0-88328-009-4). Vol. V, Book Of Deuteronomy (ISBN 0-88328-010-8). Shilo Pub Hse.

Ramban (Nachmanides) Writings & Discourses, 2 vols. Charles B. Chavel. 768p. 1978. Set. slipcase 35.00 (ISBN 0-88328-013-2). Shilo Pub Hse.

Ramble among the Musicians of Germany. 2nd ed. Edward Holmes. LC 68-16239. 1969. Repr. of 1828 ed. lib. bdg. 39.50 (ISBN 0-306-71086-2). Da Capo.

Rambler, 3 Vols. Samuel Johnson. Ed. by W. J. Bate & Albrecht Strauss. (Works of Samuel Johnson Ser.: Nos. 3, 4 & 5). 1969. Set. 100.00t (ISBN 0-300-01157-1). Yale U Pr.

Rambler in North America, 2 Vols. 2nd ed. Charles J. Latrobe. LC 1-26855. (Illus.). 1971. Repr. of 1836 ed. Set. 50.00 (ISBN 0-384-31520-8). Johnson Repr.

Rambler's Guide to the Trails of the East Bay Hills: Central Section Including Redwood, Chabot, Las Trampas, Sibley & Joaquin Miller Parks & Lands of East Bay MUD. Gerald W. Olmsted. (Illus.). 1987. 5.95 (ISBN 0-941969-00-2). Olmsted Bros Map.

Rambles about Portsmouth, 2 vols. Charles Brewster. LC 70-181350. 1972. Repr. 55.00x set; Vol. 1, 1971. 0.00 (ISBN 0-912274-12-3); Vol. 2, 1972. 0.00 (ISBN 0-912274-21-2). NH Pub Co.

Rambles & Studies in Greece. J. P. Mahaffey. 459p. Repr. of 1913 ed. lib. bdg. 52.50 (ISBN 0-89984-762-5). Century Bookbindery.

Rambles Beyond Railways. Wilkie Collins. 196p. 1982. pap. 7.50 (ISBN 0-907746-05-5, Pub. by A Mott Ltd). Longwood Pub Group.

Rambles in Dickens' Land. R. Allbut. LC 76-52947. (Studies in Dickens, No. 52). 1977. lib. bdg. 48.95x (ISBN 0-8383-2139-9). Haskell.

Rambles in Dickens' Land. Robert Allbut. 1899. 17.50 (ISBN 0-8274-3240-2). R West.

Rambles in Germany & Italy in Eighteen Forty, Eighteen Forty-Two, & Eighteen Forty-Three, 2 vols. Mary Wollstonecraft Shelley. LC 75-26765. Repr. of 1844 ed. Set. lib. bdg. 97.50 (ISBN 0-8414-7826-0). Folcroft.

Rambles in Ireland. 2nd rev. ed. Monie Begley. LC 77-78830. (Illus.). 1985. 15.00 (ISBN 0-8159-5214-7). Devin.

Rambles in the Footsteps of Don Quixote. H. D. Inglis. 1973. Repr. of 1837 ed. 25.00 (ISBN 0-8274-0365-8). R West.

Rambles in the Mammoth Cave During the Year 1844 by a Visiter. Alexander C. Bullitt. LC 85-6698. (Illus.). 134p. 1985. pap. 5.00 (ISBN 0-939748-16-9). Cave Bks MO.

Rambles in the West of Ireland. abr. ed. William Bulfin. 90p. 1979. pap. 5.25 (ISBN 0-85342-585-X, Pub. by Mercier Pr Ireland). Irish Bks Media.

Rambles in Vedanta. B. R. Iyer. 1974. Repr. 22.50 (ISBN 0-8426-0601-7). Orient Bk Dist.

Rambles of a Botanist among the Plants & Climates of California. John Muir. Intro. by William F. Kimes. (Illus.). 43p. 1974. 10.00 (ISBN 0-87093-301-9). Dawsons.

Rambles Round Donegal. Patrick Campbell. 128p. (Orig.). 1986. pap. 7.95 (ISBN 0-85342-642-2, Pub. by Mercier Pr Ireland). Irish Bks Media.

Rambles Through an Alaskan Wild: Katmai & the Valley of the Smokes. Dave Bohn. LC 79-14527. (Illus.). 176p. 1979. 20.00 (ISBN 0-88496-125-7, Noel Young Bk). Capra Pr.

Rambling Recollections of Ninety Happy Years. Levi T. Pennington. (Illus.). 8.95 (ISBN 0-8323-0198-1). Binford-Metropolitan.

Rambling Through Baja California with Pen & Brush: Painting & Sketching Baja's Landscape & Missions. Anthony Quartuccio. LC 83-90130. (Illus.). 120p. 1984. 12.00 (ISBN 0-9606934-1-6). A Quartuccio.

Rambling Through British Columbia. Robert S. Wilson. (Illus.). 1978. pap. 4.00 (ISBN 0-934944-11-3). Wilson Bros.

Rambling Through Science. Adolph L. De Leevw. LC 72-315. (Essay Index Reprint Ser.). Repr. of 1932 ed. 21.00 (ISBN 0-8369-2788-5). Ayer Co Pubs.

Ramblings. Carola Lewis. 1974. 6.50 (ISBN 0-87012-161-8). McClain.

Ramblings in the Clover-Absorbing Shock. Eileen M. Greco. (Illus.). 48p. 1982. 5.00 (ISBN 0-682-49885-8). Exposition-Phoenix.

Ramblings in the Elucidation of the Autograph of Milton. S. L. Sotheby. 1974. Repr. of 1861 ed. lib. bdg. 125.00 limited ed. (ISBN 0-8414-8008-7). Folcroft.

Ramblings of an Ascetic. Yuacharya Shri Mahaprajna. xvi, 127p. 1979. 9.00 (ISBN 0-88065-212-8, Pub. by Messers Today & Tomorrows Printers & Publishers India). Scholarly Pubns.

Rambo: First Blood, Pt. II. David Morrell. 1985. pap. 3.50 (ISBN 0-515-08399-2). Jove Pubns.

Rambo III. David Morrell. 1988. pap. 3.50 (ISBN 0-515-09333-5). Jove Pubns.

Rambunctious Lady Royston. Kasey Michaels. 224p. 1988. pap. 2.95 (ISBN 0-380-81448-X, 81448). Avon.

Rameau's Nephew & D'Alembert's Dream. Denis Diderot. (Classics Ser). 1976. pap. 6.95 (ISBN 0-14-044173-5). Penguin.

Rameau's Nephew & Other Works. Denis Diderot. Tr. by Jacques Barzun & Ralph Bowen. LC 55-9755. 1964. pap. write for info. (ISBN 0-02-306550-8, LLA200). Macmillan.

Rameau's Nephew & Other Works. Denis Diderot. Tr. by Jacques Barzun & Ralph H. Brown. LC 55-9755. 1964. 29.50x (ISBN 0-672-51089-8). Irvington.

Ramera Fogosa. Abel Castano. (Pimienta Collection Ser.). 1977. pap. 1.00 (ISBN 0-88473-268-1). Fiesta Pub.

Ramesses II: A Chronological Structure of His Reign. John D. Schmidt. LC 72-6558. (Near Eastern Studies). Repr. of 1973 ed. 56.00 (ISBN 0-8357-9282-X, 2011503). Bks Demand UMI.

Ramesside Administrative Documents. Ed. by Alan Gardiner. 101p. 1968. Repr. of 1948 ed. text ed. 28.50x (ISBN 0-900416-40-8, Pub. by Aris & Phillips UK). Humanities.

Ramessium Papyri. Ed. by Alan Gardiner. (Illus.). 18p. 1955. text ed. 55.00x (ISBN 0-900416-37-8, Pub. by Aris & Phillips England). Humanities.

Ramillies. Barbara Whitehead. 1988. pap. 2.95 (ISBN 0-312-90512-2). St Martin.

Ramism in William Perkins' Theology. Donald K. McKim. (American University Studies, Series VII: Theology & Religion: Vol. 15). 249p. 1987. text ed. 38.90 (ISBN 0-8204-0285-0). P Lang Pubs.

Rammhoun Roy: A Biographical Inquiry into the Making of Modern India, Vol. 1. Iqbal Singh. viii, 342p. 1983. text ed. 40.00x (ISBN 0-210-40644-5, Pub. by Jaisingh Mehta India). Apt Bks.

Rammohum Roy & the Process of Modernization. Ed. by P. C. Joshi. 1975. 12.00 (ISBN 0-7069-0349-8). Intl Bk Dist.

Rammohun Roy: A Biographical Inquiry into the Making of Modern India, Vol. II & III. Iqbal Singh. (Illus.). 634p. 1987. text ed. 50.00x (ISBN 0-210-40645-3, Pub. by Jaisingh Mehta India). Apt Bks.

Ramon Betances: Father of the Poor. Irving Gerber. (American Destiny Ser.: Puerto Rico: Puerto Rico). (gr. 4-12). 1979. 12.95 set (ISBN 0-87594-180-X). Book-Lab.

Ramon de la Cruz. John Moore. LC 70-153997. (Twayne's World Authors Ser.). 181p. 1972. lib. bdg. 17.95 (ISBN 0-8290-1746-1). Irvington.

Ramon de la Sagra: A Chronology. V. Munoz. Tr. by W. Scott Johnson. (Libertarian & Anarchist Chronology Ser.). 1979. lib. bdg. 59.95 (ISBN 0-8490-3042-0). Gordon Pr.

Ramon de Mesonero Romanos. Richard A. Curry. LC 76-25. (Twayne's World Authors Ser.). 1976. lib. bdg. 17.95 (ISBN 0-8057-6226-4). Irvington.

Ramon Del Valle-Inclan. Robert Lima. LC 72-186643. (Columbia Essays on Modern Writers Ser.: No. 59). 1972. pap. 5.00 (ISBN 0-231-03499-7). Columbia U Pr.

Ramon Guthrie's Maximum Security Ward: An American Classic. Sally M. Gall. LC 83-16836. 104p. 1984. 7.95 (ISBN 0-8262-0430-9). U of Mo Pr.

Ramon J. Sender. Charles L. King. LC 73-19612. (Twayne's World Authors Ser.). 196p. 1974. lib. bdg. 17.95 (ISBN 0-8057-2815-5). Irvington.

Ramon J. Sender: An Annotated Bibliography, 1928-1974. Charles L. King. LC 76-9020. 301p. 1976. 25.00 (ISBN 0-8108-0933-8). Scarecrow.

Ramon Lull: A Biography. Edgar A. Peers. LC 77-76019. (Bibliography & Reference Ser.: No. 266). 1969. Repr. of 1929 ed. 29.50 (ISBN 0-8337-2706-0). B Franklin.

Ramon Lull: A Biography. Edgar A. Peers. 1980. lib. bdg. 75.00 (ISBN 0-8490-3186-9). Gordon Pr.

Ramon Perez de Ayala. Marguerite C. Rand. (Twayne's World Authors Ser.). 175p. 1971. lib. bdg. 17.95 (ISBN 0-8290-1734-8). Irvington.

Ramon Perez de Ayala: A Annotated Bibliography of Criticism. Marigold Berst. (Research Bibliographies & Checklists Ser.: No. 33). 81p. (Orig.). 1980. pap. 8.95 (ISBN 0-7293-0102-8, Pub. by Grant & Cutler). Longwood Pub Group.

Ramon y Cajal's Contribution to the Neurosciences. S. Grisolia et al. 1983. 114.25 (ISBN 0-444-80486-2). Elsevier.

Ramona. Helen H. Jackson. 1970. pap. 3.95 (ISBN 0-380-00383-X, 60174-5). Avon.

Ramona. Helen H. Jackson. 1976. lib. bdg. 20.10x (ISBN 0-89968-051-8). Lightyear.

Ramona. Helen H. Jackson. (Illus.). (gr. 6 up). 1939. Repr. of 1884 ed. 17.95 (ISBN 0-316-45467-2). Little.

Ramona. Helen H. Jackson. 384p. 1988. pap. 3.50 (ISBN 0-451-52208-7, Sig Classics). NAL.

Ramona & Her Family see Meet Ramona Quimby.

Ramona & Her Father. Beverly Cleary. LC 77-1614. (Illus.). (gr. 3-7). 1977. 11.95 (ISBN 0-688-22114-9); PLB 11.88 (ISBN 0-688-32114-3). Morrow.

Ramona & Her Father. Beverly Cleary. (Illus.). 196p. (gr. 3-7). 1979. pap. 3.25 (ISBN 0-440-47241-5, YB). Dell.

Ramona & Her Father see Meet Ramona Quimby.

Ramona & Her Friends. Beverly Cleary. pap. 9.00 (ISBN 0-440-47222-9). Dell.

Ramona & Her Mother. Beverly Cleary. 208p. (gr. k-6). 1980. pap. 3.25 (ISBN 0-440-47243-1, YB). Dell.

Ramona & Her Mother. Beverly Cleary. LC 79-10323. (Illus.). (gr. 4-6). 1979. 12.95 (ISBN 0-688-22195-5); PLB 12.88 (ISBN 0-688-32195-X). Morrow.

Ramona & Her Mother see Meet Ramona Quimby.

Ramona: Behind the Scenes of a Television Show. Elaine Scott. LC 87-33313. (Reading Rainbow Review Book). (Illus.). 96p. (YA) (gr. 3-7). 1988. 13.95 (ISBN 0-688-06818-9); PLB 13.88 (ISBN 0-688-06819-7). Morrow.

Ramona, Forever. Beverly Cleary. LC 84-704. (Illus.). 192p. (gr. 3-7). 1984. 11.75 (ISBN 0-688-03785-2, Morrow Junior Books); PLB 11.88 (ISBN 0-688-03786-0). Morrow.

Ramona, Forever. Beverly Cleary. 192p. (gr. k-6). 1985. pap. 3.25 (ISBN 0-440-47210-5, YB). Dell.

Ramona Forever see Meet Ramona Quimby.

Ramona Quimby, Age Eight. Beverly Cleary. LC 80-28425. (Illus.). 192p. (gr. 4-6). 1981. 11.95 (ISBN 0-688-00477-6); PLB 11.88 (ISBN 0-688-00478-4). Morrow.

Ramona Quimby, Age Eight. Beverly Cleary. (Illus.). 192p. (gr. 3-7). 1982. pap. 3.25 (ISBN 0-440-47350-0, YB). Dell.

Ramona Quimby, Age Eight. Beverly Cleary. (Illus.). (gr. k-9). 1988. pap. 2.95. Scholastic Inc.

Ramona Quimby, Age Eight see Meet Ramona Quimby.

Ramona Quimby Age Eight see Meet Ramona Quimby.

Ramona Quimby, Age 8. Beverly Cleary. (Illus.). 142p. (gr. 2-6). 1987. Repr. of 1981 ed. lib. bdg. 13.95 (ISBN 1-55736-000-6). ABC-Clio.

Ramona Quimby Diary. Beverly Cleary. (Illus.). 160p. (gr. 3-7). 1984. pap. 7.95 (ISBN 0-688-03883-2, Morrow Junior Books). Morrow.

Ramona Quimby Diary. Beverly Cleary. 160p. (gr. 2-5). 1988. spiral bdg. 8.95. Morrow.

Ramona Quimby: The Making of a Television Film. Beverly Cleary. 1988. 3.95 (YB). Dell.

Ramona the Brave. Beverly Cleary. LC 74-164968. (Illus.). 192p. (gr. 3-7). 1975. 12.95 (ISBN 0-688-22015-0); PLB 12.88 (ISBN 0-688-32015-5). Morrow.

Ramona the Brave. Beverly Cleary. (Illus.). 192p. (gr. k-6). 1984. pap. 3.25 (ISBN 0-440-47351-9, YB). Dell.

Ramona the Pest. Beverly Cleary. 192p. (gr. 4-7). 1982. pap. 3.25 (ISBN 0-440-47209-1, YB). Dell.

Ramona the Pest. Beverly Cleary. (Illus.). (gr. 3-7). 1968. 11.75 (ISBN 0-688-21721-4); PLB 11.88 (ISBN 0-688-31721-9). Morrow.

Ramona the Pest. Beverly Cleary. Tr. by Argentina Palacios. LC 83-23805. (Illus.). 208p. (Span.). (gr. 3-7). 1984. 12.95 (ISBN 0-688-02783-0). Morrow.

Ramona the Pest see Meet Ramona Quimby.

Ramon's Adventures in the Library. Elizabeth Vreeken. LC 67-31108. (Illus.). 48p. (gr. 1-3). 1967. 3.95 (ISBN 0-379-00243-4). Oceana.

Ramor's Conch. Le Tendre & Loisel. Tr. by T. Nantier from Fr. (Roxanna & the Quest for the Time Bird Ser.). 48p. 1987. pap. 7.95X (ISBN 0-918348-30-7). NBM.

Ramp Creek Rhythms: A Book of Poems. Helena Ashby. LC 85-90773. 54p. 1985. 8.00 (ISBN 0-9614781-0-1); pap. 4.00 (ISBN 0-9614781-1-X). H Ashby Bks.

Rampage. Justin Scott. 432p. 1986. 17.95 (ISBN 0-671-53047-X). S&S.

Rampage. Justin Scott. 416p. 1988. pap. 4.50 (ISBN 0-671-64852-7). PB.

Rampage. William P. Wood. pap. 4.50 (ISBN 0-312-90306-5). St Martin.

Rampage. William P. Wood. 1987. pap. 4.50 (ISBN 0-312-90983-7). St Martin.

Rampaging Frontier. Thomas D. Clark. LC 75-17477. 350p. 1976. Repr. of 1939 ed. lib. bdg. 35.00x (ISBN 0-8371-8313-8, CLRF). Greenwood.

Rampaging Herd: A Bibliography of Books & Pamphlets on Men & Events in the Cattle Industry. Ramon F. Adams. 464p. 38.00x (ISBN 0-939738-05-8). Zubal Inc.

Ramparts We Guard. R. M. MacIver. 1952. 34.50x (ISBN 0-686-51296-0). Elliots Bks.

Rampion. Inka Pucmer. (Illus.). 25p. (gr. 2-4). 1982. 22.95 (ISBN 0-88010-064-8, Pub. by Walter Keller Pr). Anthroposophic.

Ramrod Vengeance. William Hopson. 1978. pap. 1.25 (ISBN 0-8439-0564-6, Leisure Bks). Leisure NY.

Rams: Five Decades of Football. Joseph Hession. LC 86-22902. (Illus.). 200p. (Orig.). 1987. pap. 16.95 (ISBN 0-935701-40-0). Foghorn Pr.

RAMs, ROMs & Robots: The Inside Story of Computers. James Jespersen & Jane Fitz-Randolph. LC 84-3001. (Illus.). 160p. (YA) (gr. 7 up). 1984. 13.95 (ISBN 0-689-31063-3, Atheneum Childrens Bks). Macmillan.

Ramses II, the Pharaoh in His Time: Exhibition Catalog, Jacksonville Art Museum, 17 November 1986 - 15 March 1987. Lisa K. Sabbahy. Ed. by C. Wilfred Griggs. Date not set. price not set (ISBN 0-8425-2257-3). Jacksonville Art.

Ramsey & the Road Warrior. Elizabeth Dear. 200p. (Orig.). 1988. pap. text ed. 8.95 (ISBN 0-934678-17-0). New Victoria Pubs.

Ramsey Campbell. Gary W. Crawford. (Starmont Reader's Guide Ser.: No. 48). 74p. 1988. lib. bdg. 17.95x (ISBN 0-8095-5001-6). Borgo Pr.

Ramsey Campbell. Gary W. Crawford. Ed. by Roger C. Schlobin. (Reader's Guides to Contemporary Science Fiction & Fantasy Authors Ser.: Vol. 48). (Orig.). 1988. 17.95x (ISBN 1-55742-037-8); pap. 8.95x (ISBN 1-55742-036-X). Starmont Hse.

Ramsey County Jury Study for the Second Judicial District: Final Report. National Center for State Courts Staff. 211p. 1979. manuscript 12.66 (NCRO-017). Natl Ctr St Courts.

Ramsey County Municipal Court Administrative Hearing Office. National Center for State Courts Staff. (Paul Reardon Ser.). 7p. 1982. manuscript 0.42 (PRS-038). Natl Ctr St COurts.

Ramsey Theory. Ronald Graham et al. LC 80-14110. (Discrete Mathematics Ser.). 174p. 1980. 39.95x (ISBN 0-471-05997-8). Wiley.

Ramsey's Best: Collector of the Badges. J. L. Foster. 1987. 10.95 (ISBN 0-533-07154-2). Vantage.

Ramtha. Ramtha. Ed. by Steven L. Weinberg. LC 85-61768. 224p. 1986. 19.95 (ISBN 0-932201-11-3). Sovereignty.

Ramtha. Ramtha. Ed. by Steven Weinberg. 224p. 1986. 19.95. Sovereignty.

Ramtha: An Introduction. Ramtha. Ed. by Steve L. Weinberg. 200p. (Orig.). 1987. pap. 9.95 (ISBN 0-932201-76-8). Sovereignty.

Ramtha Intensive: Change, the Days to Come. Ramtha. Ed. by Steven L. Weinberg et al. 144p. (Orig.). 1987. pap. 10.00 (ISBN 0-932201-99-7). Sovereignty.

Ramtha Intensive: Soulmates. Ramtha. Ed. by Steven L. Weinberg et al. 160p. (Orig.). 1987. pap. 10.00 (ISBN 0-932201-58-X). Sovereignty.

Ramtha: The New Kingdom of God. Ronald G. Kaufman. (Illus.). 225p. (Orig.). 1988. pap. 12.95 (ISBN 0-940539-09-8). Heridonius.

Ramu of Lemura Speaks. Ruth Norman. 430p. 1988. 14.95 (ISBN 0-935097-08-2). Unarius Pubns.

Ramus, Method, & the Decay of Dialogue: From the Art of Discourse to the Art of Reason. Walter J. Ong. 432p. 1983. pap. text ed. 10.95x (ISBN 0-674-74802-6). Harvard U Pr.

Ramus (Pierre de la Ramee): Sa Vie, Ses Ecrits et Ses Opinions. Charles Waddington. (Medieval Studies Reprint Ser.). Repr. of 1855 ed. lib. bdg. 44.00 (ISBN 0-697-00020-6). Irvington.

Ran. Akira Kurosawa et al. LC 86-13016. (Illus.). 110p. (Orig.). 1986. pap. 19.95 (ISBN 0-87773-387-2). Shambhala Pubns.

Rana Mozelle: Surrealist Texts. Paul Garon. (Illus.). 16p. 1978. pap. 3.50 (ISBN 0-941194-05-1). Black Swan Pr.

Rana Viajera. V. Garshin. (Illus.). 12p. (Span.). 1975. pap. 1.49 (ISBN 0-8285-1301-5, Pub. by Progress Pubs USSR). Imported Pubns.

Ranade & the Roots of Indian Nationalism. Richard P. Tucker. (Midway Reprint Ser.). pap. 11.00x (ISBN 0-226-81532-3). U of Chicago Pr.

Ranald S. Mackenzie's Official Correspondence Relating to Texas, 1873-1879. Ed. by Ernest Wallace. 241p. 1968. 10.00 (ISBN 0-911618-03-1). West Tex Mus.

Ranald S. Mackenzie's Official Correspondence Relating to Texas, 1871-1873. Ed. by Ernest Wallace. 202p. 1967. 10.00 (ISBN 0-911618-04-X). West Tex Mus.

Rance & the Trappist Legacy. A. J. Krailsheimer. 16.95 (ISBN 0-87907-886-3); pap. 6.95. Cistercian Pubns.

Ranch & Modern Homes. Hiawatha T. Estes. (Illus.). 1988. 3.20. Hiawatha Homes.

Ranch Life & the Hunting Trail. Theodore Roosevelt. LC 76-125761. (American Environmental Studies). 1970. Repr. of 1901 ed. 15.00 (ISBN 0-405-02688-9). Ayer Co Pubs.

Ranch Life & the Hunting-Trail. Theodore Roosevelt. LC 82-20091. (Illus.). x, 210p. 1983. 19.95x (ISBN 0-8032-3865-7); pap. 8.95 (ISBN 0-8032-8913-8, BB 833, Bison). U of Nebr Pr.

Ranch Life & the Hunting Trail. Theodore Roosevelt. (Illus.). 208p. (Orig.). 1985. pap. 8.95 (ISBN 0-87052-212-4). Hippocrene Bks.

Ranch Life & the Hunting-Trail. Theodore Roosevelt. LC 85-18253. (Illus.). 1986. Repr. of 1888 ed. 14.95 (ISBN 0-312-66365-X). St Martin.

Ranch Life in Southern Kansas & the Indian Territory, As Told by a Novice: How a Fortune Was Made in Cattle. facsimile ed. Benjamin S. Miller. LC 75-111. (Mid-American Frontier Ser.). 1975. Repr. of 1896 ed. 17.00x (ISBN 0-405-06878-6). Ayer Co Pubs.

Ranch Life in the Far West. Theodore Roosevelt. (Illus.). 1978. pap. 5.95 (ISBN 0-89646-034-7). Outbooks.

Ranch Papers: A California Memoir. Jane H. Wheelwright. LC 87-80275. (Illus.). 164p. 1987. pap. 19.95 (ISBN 0-932499-19-8). Lapis Pr.

Ranch Rodeos in West Texas. Lawrence R. Clayton. (Illus., Orig.). Date not set. pap. text ed. 10.00 (ISBN 0-910075-08-5). Hardin-Simmons.

Ranch Woman's Manual. Gwen Petersen. (Orig.). 1976. pap. 2.95 (ISBN 0-87970-138-2). North Plains.

Ranchero Revolt: The Mexican Revolution in Guerrero. Ian Jacobs. (Texas Pan American Ser.). (Illus.). 256p. 1983. text ed. 25.00x (ISBN 0-292-77026-X). U of Tex Pr.

Rancheros of Pisaflores: The History of a Peasant Bourgeoisie in Twentieth-Century Mexico. Frans J. Schryer. LC 79-20686. 1979. 27.50X (ISBN 0-8020-5466-8). U of Toronto Pr.

Ranchers. Ogden Tanner. LC 77-85283. (Old West Ser.). (Illus.). (gr. 7 up). 1977. 19.94 (ISBN 0-8094-1510-0, Pub. by Time-Life). Silver.

Ranchers. Ed. by Time-Life Books. (Old West Ser.). (Illus.). 1978. 14.95 (ISBN 0-8094-1508-9). Time-Life.

Ranchers: A Book of Generations. Stan Steiner. LC 84-15201. (Illus.). 256p. (Orig.). 1985. pap. 8.95 (ISBN 0-8061-1923-3). U of Okla Pr.

Ranchers Legacy: Alberta Essays by Lewis G. Thomas. Lewis G. Thomas. Ed. by Patrick A. Dunae. (Western Canada Reprint Ser.). xxv, 217p. 1986. pap. 14.95x (ISBN 0-88864-095-1, Univ of Atla Pr Canada). U of Nebr Pr.

Ranchers, Ramblers & Renegades: True Tales of Territorial New Mexico. Marc Simmons. LC 83-73398. (Illus.). 128p. 1984. pap. text ed. 6.95 (ISBN 0-941270-17-3). Ancient City Pr.

Ranches & Ranching in Spanish Texas. Lyle W. Williams. (Texas History Ser.). (Illus.). 35p. 1982. pap. text ed. 2.95x (ISBN 0-89641-121-4). American Pr.

Ranching, Mining, & the Human Impact of Natural Resources Development. Raymond L. Gold. (Illus.). 200p. 1984. 24.95 (ISBN 0-88738-025-5). Transaction Bks.

Ranching Saga: The Lives of William Electious Halsell & Ewing Halsell, 2 vols. William C. Holden. LC 75-9300. Vol. 1. pap. 75.50 (ISBN 0-317-28178-X, 2022567); Vol. 2. pap. 71.50. Bks Demand UMI.

Ranching with Lords & Commons: Or, Twenty Years on the Range. John R. Craig. LC 79-132387. Repr. of 1903 ed. 19.50 (ISBN 0-404-01798-3). AMS Pr.

Ranchman's Recollections. Frank S. Hastings. LC 85-51948. (Illus.). 266p. 1985. 17.95 (ISBN 0-87611-077-4); pap. 9.95 (ISBN 0-87611-079-0); ltd. ed. 50.00. Tex St Hist Assn.

Rancho Armadillo. Judith Stephens. LC 85-73253. 165p. (Orig.). Date not set. pap. 7.00 (ISBN 0-933529-02-3). Cayuse Pr.

Rancho Gumbo: Five Thousand Days in Montana's Piegan County. Abner M. Wagner. (Illus.). 1983. ltd. ed. 20.00x (ISBN 0-930704-15-0). Sagebrush Pr.

Rancho La Brea: Treasures of the Tar Pits. Ed. by John M. Harris & George Jefferson. (Science Ser.: No. 31). (Illus.). 96p. (Orig.). 1985. pap. 9.95 (ISBN 0-938644-19-X). Nat Hist Mus.

Rancho La Brea: Treasures of the Tar Pits. Ed. by John M. Harris & George Jefferson. (Illus.). 96p. 1985. pap. 9.95. U of Wash Pr.

Rancho los Alamitos. George Salzer. (Illus.). 1975. pap. 2.00 (ISBN 0-916552-04-7). Acoma Bks.

Rancho los Cerritos. Loretta Berner. (Illus.). 1975. pap. 2.00 (ISBN 0-916552-01-2). Acoma Bks.

Rancho Maria. Jerry Oster. LC 85-45218. 232p. 1986. 14.45i (ISBN 0-06-015519-1, HarpT). Har-Row.

Ranchos De Taos: San Francisco De Asis Church. Wolfgang Pogzeba & Joy Overbeck. LC 81-82257. (Illus.). 68p. (Orig.). 1981. pap. 7.95 (ISBN 0-913504-66-1). Lowell Pr.

Ranchos of California: A List of Spanish Concessions 1775-1822, & Mexican Grants 1822-1846. Robert G. Cowan. LC 85-21289. 151p. 1985. Repr. of 1977 ed. lib. bdg. 19.95x (ISBN 0-89370-863-1). Borgo Pr.

Rancidity in Foods. Ed. by J. C. Allen & R. J. Hamilton. 198p. 1984. 57.75 (ISBN 0-85334-219-9, Pub. by Elsevier Applied Sci England). Elsevier.

Rancor Against Time: The Phenomenology of "Ressentiment". Richard I. Sugarman. 162p. 1980. 40.00 (ISBN 3-7873-0456-8). Philosophia Pr.

Rand Corporation: Case Study of a Non-Profit Advisory Corporation. Bruce L. Smith. LC 66-14454. (Harvard Political Studies Ser.). pap. 87.50 (ISBN 0-317-09149-2, 2011025). Bks Demand UMI.

Rand House, Short Stories. Etienne Noir. 1987. 9.95 (ISBN 0-934536-37-6). Merging Media.

Rand McNally Atlas of World History. rev. ed. (Illus.). 192p. (Orig.). 1987. pap. 17.95 (ISBN 0-528-83288-3). Rand McNally.

Rand McNally Book of Favorite Christmas Stories. (Illus.). 112p. (ps-3). 1985. 8.95 (ISBN 0-528-82678-6). Macmillan.

Rand McNally Children's Atlas of the World. Bruce Ogilvie & Douglas Waitley. (Illus.). 96p. (gr. 4 up). 1985. 11.95 (ISBN 0-528-82418-X). Rand McNally.

Rand McNally Classroom Atlas. rev. ed. (Illus.). 96p. (gr. 5-8). 1986. pap. text ed. 2.94 (ISBN 0-528-17720-6). Rand McNally.

Rand McNally Compact Road Atlas. annual ed. (Illus.). 224p. (Orig.). 1987. pap. 4.95 (ISBN 0-528-89716-0). Rand McNally.

Rand McNally Concise World Atlas. (Illus.). 232p. 1987. 24.95 (ISBN 0-528-83285-9). Rand McNally.

Rand McNally Contemporary World Atlas. rev. ed. Jon Leverenz. (Illus.). 224p. 1986. pap. 9.95 (ISBN 0-528-83146-1). Rand McNally.

Rand McNally Contemporary World Atlas. (Illus.). 256p. (Orig.). 1988. pap. 9.95 (ISBN 0-528-83328-6). Rand McNally.

Rand McNally Cosmopolitan World Atlas. rev. ed. (Illus.). 344p. 1987. 55.00 (ISBN 0-528-83284-0). Rand McNally.

Rand McNally Deluxe Motor Carriers Road Atlas. rev. ed. (Illus.). 208p. (Orig.). 1988. pap. 59.95 (ISBN 0-528-89826-4). Rand McNally.

Rand McNally Desk Reference World Atlas. (Illus.). 528p. 1987. 17.95 (ISBN 0-528-83287-5). Rand McNally.

Rand McNally Encyclopedia of War World II. Ed. by John Keegan. 1985. 12.98 (ISBN 0-517-43897-6). Outlet Bk Co.

Rand McNally Fact Books. Incl. Aircraft. Chris Maynard & John Paton (ISBN 0-528-87851-4); Astronomy. John Paton (ISBN 0-528-87852-2); Space Flight. Stewart Cowley. (Fact Bk). 96p. (gr. 4-7). pap. 3.50 (ISBN 0-528-87853-0); Dinosaur World. David Lambert (ISBN 0-528-87854-9). (Illus.). 96p. (gr. 3-7). 1982. 3.50 ea. Macmillan.

Rand McNally Fact Books. Incl. Computer World. Stephen Hoare (ISBN 0-528-87857-3); Ships & Other Sea Craft. Brian Williams. (Fact Bks). 96p. (gr. 4-7). pap. 3.50 (ISBN 0-528-87858-1). 96p. (gr. 4-7). 3.50 ea. Macmillan.

Rand McNally Family World Atlas. (Illus.). 256p. 1988. 16.95 (ISBN 0-528-83145-3). Rand McNally.

Rand McNally Glove Compartment Road Atlas. 1988. pap. 3.95. Rand McNally.

Rand McNally Goode's World Atlas. 17th ed. Ed. by Edward Epenshade, Jr. & Joel L. Morrison. (Illus.). 384p. 1986. text ed. 19.95 (ISBN 0-528-63005-9); pap. text ed. 13.28 (ISBN 0-528-63006-7). Rand McNally.

Rand McNally Goode's World Atlas. Ed. by Edward B. Espenshade, Jr. & Joel L. Morrison. (Illus.). 367p. 1986. 22.95 (ISBN 0-528-83127-5). Rand McNally.

Rand McNally Great National Park Vacations, 1988. annual ed. 224p. (Orig.). 1988. pap. 12.95 (ISBN 0-528-88256-2). S&S.

Rand McNally Green Guide: U. S. Places with over 100 People. (Illus.). 298p. 1983. pap. 17.95 (ISBN 0-528-21066-1). Rand McNally.

Rand McNally Handy Railroad Atlas. (Illus.). 64p. 1988. pap. 14.95 (ISBN 0-528-21001-7). Rand McNally.

Rand McNally Images of the World. LC 83-60038. 160p. 1984. 24.95 (ISBN 0-528-83034-1). Rand McNally.

Rand McNally Interstate Road Atlas: United States, Canada, Mexico. Ed. by John Manning. 1988. pap. 3.95 (ISBN 0-528-89812-4). Rand McNally.

Rand McNally Mathematics Encyclopedia. Leslie Foster. LC 86-70402. (Encyclopedia Ser.). 144p. (gr. 4 up). 1986. 12.95 (ISBN 0-528-82799-5, Checkerboard Pr). Macmillan.

Rand McNally Motor Carriers' Road Atlas, 1988. 1988. pap. 14.95 (ISBN 0-528-89810-8). Rand McNally.

Rand McNally New Century World Atlas. Ed. by Jon Leverenz. 504p. 1986. 39.95 (ISBN 0-528-83213-1). Rand McNally.

Rand McNally Pocket City Atlas. 1988. pap. 1.95. Rand McNally.

Rand McNally Question Books: The Senses. Kathie B. Smith & Victoria E. Crenson. Incl. Seeing (ISBN 0-528-87152-8); Touching (ISBN 0-528-87150-1); Hearing (ISBN 0-528-87151-X); Thinking (ISBN 0-528-87154-4); Tasting (ISBN 0-528-87149-8); Smelling (ISBN 0-528-87153-6). (Illus.). 24p. (Orig.). (gr. k-3). 1986. pap. 1.50 ea. Macmillan.

Rand McNally Quick Reference World Atlas. rev. ed. (Illus.). 64p. (Orig.). 1987. pap. 3.95 (ISBN 0-528-83226-3). Rand McNally.

Rand McNally Road Atlas & City Guide of Europe, 1988. 1988. pap. 12.95 (ISBN 0-528-89817-5). Rand McNally.

Rand McNally Road Atlas & Vacation Guide, 1988. 1988. pap. 13.95 (ISBN 0-528-89808-6). Rand McNally.

Rand McNally Road Atlas of Britain, 1988. 1988. pap. 13.95 (ISBN 0-528-89818-3). Rand McNally.

Rand McNally Road Atlas of Europe, 1988. 1988. pap. 6.95 (ISBN 0-528-89816-7). Rand McNally.

Rand McNally Road Atlas of France. (Illus.). 128p. (Orig.). 1988. pap. 12.95 (ISBN 0-528-89837-X). Rand McNally.

Rand McNally Road Atlas, 1988: United States, Canada, Mexico. 1988. deluxe ed. 9.95 (ISBN 0-528-89805-1); pap. 6.95 (ISBN 0-528-89823-X); gift ed. 8.95 (ISBN 0-528-89803-5). Rand McNally.

Rand McNally RV Park & Campground Directory, 3 vols. rev., annual ed. (Orig.). 1988. National, 934 pgs. pap. 13.95 (ISBN 0-528-88222-8); Western, 472 pgs. pap. 9.95 (ISBN 0-528-88226-0); Eastern, 582 pgs. pap. 9.95 (ISBN 0-528-88224-4). S&S.

Rand McNally Sales & Marketing Atlas. rev. ed. (Illus.). 168p. 1986. pap. 16.95 (ISBN 0-528-22429-8). Rand McNally.

Rand McNally Student's World Atlas. rev. ed. (Illus.). 96p. (Orig.). (YA) (gr. 4-8). 1988. pap. 5.95 (ISBN 0-528-83286-7). Rand McNally.

Rand McNally World Atlas of Nations. (Illus.). 232p. 1988. 34.95 (ISBN 0-528-83315-4). Rand McNally.

Rand McNally World Atlas, 1986. (Illus.). 64p. 1986. pap. cancelled (ISBN 0-528-83225-5). Rand McNally.

Rand McNally World Atlas: 1987. Jon Leverenz. 1986. pap. cancelled (ISBN 0-317-52751-7). Rand McNally.

Rand McNally Zip Code Atlas. rev. ed. (Illus.). 160p. (Orig.). 1986. pap. 17.95. Rand McNally.

Rand McNally Zip Code Finder. 672p. (Orig.). 1988. pap. 6.95 (ISBN 0-528-22448-4). Rand McNally.

Rand McNally's America. (Illus.). 272p. 1987. 69.95 (ISBN 0-528-81143-6). Rand McNally.

Rand McNally's Campground & Trailer Park Guide. 768p. 1988. 13.95. RV Indus Assn.

Randall & the River of Time. C. S. Forester. 21.95 (ISBN 0-89190-610-X, Pub. by Am Repr). Amereon Ltd.

Randall County Story: From Fifteen Forty-One to Nineteen Ten. Ed. by Mrs. Clyde W. Warwick. (Illus.). 376p. 1969. 12.50 (ISBN 0-933512-03-1). Pioneer Bk Tx.

Randall House Bible Commentary: Galatians, Ephesians, Philippians, & Colossians. Thomas Marberry et al. Ed. by H. D. Harrison. (Bible Commentary Ser.). 400p. 1988. 19.95 (ISBN 0-89265-134-2). Randall Hse.

Randall House Bible Commentary: Romans. F. Leroy Forlines. (Bible Commentary Ser.). 381p. 1987. 19.95 (ISBN 0-89265-116-4). Randall Hse.

Randall House Bible Commentary Series, 3 vols. Ed. by Robert E. Picirilli & H D. Harrison. 1988. Set. 19.95 ea. (ISBN 0-89265-115-6). Randall Hse.

Randall House Bible Commentary: 1, 2 Corinthians. Robert E. Picirilli. Ed. by H. D. Harrison. 434p. 1987. 19.95 (ISBN 0-89265-118-0). Randall Hse.

Randall Jarrell. Charles M. Adams. 1978. Repr. of 1958 ed. lib. bdg. 15.00 (ISBN 0-8495-0028-1). Arden Lib.

Randall Jarrell. M. L. Rosenthal. (Pamphlets on American Writers Ser: No. 103). 1972. pap. 1.25x (ISBN 0-8166-0646-3). U of Minn Pr.

Randall Jarrell: A Bibliography. Charles M. Adams. LC 74-8205. Repr. of 1958 ed. lib. bdg. 16.50 (ISBN 0-8414-2977-4). Folcroft.

Randall Jarrell: A Descriptive Bibliography 1929-1983. Stuart Wright. LC 85-3132. (Linton R. Massey Descriptive Bibliography Ser.). (Illus.). xvi, 372p. 1986. 35.00x (ISBN 0-8139-1055-2). U Pr of Va.

Randall Jarrell's Letters: An Autobiographical & Literary Selection. Randall Jarrell. Ed. by Mary Jarrell. 1985. 29.95 (ISBN 0-395-34405-0). HM.

Randall Thompson: A Choral Legacy. Alfred Mann. 1983. pap. 10.00 (ISBN 0-911318-12-7). E C Schirmer.

Randax Education Guide: A Guide to Colleges Seeking Students, 1984 Edition. 13th ed. Stephen E. Marshall. (Illus.). 128p. (Orig.). 1984. pap. 8.95 (ISBN 0-914880-14-4, 14R). Educ Guide.

Randax Education Guide: A Guide to Colleges Seeking Students, 1983 Edition. 12th ed. Ed. by Stephen E. Marshall. (Illus.). 128p. (Orig.). 1983. pap. 8.95 (ISBN 0-914880-13-6). Educ Guide.

Randax Education Guide to Colleges Seeking Students. 15th ed. Stephen E. Marshall. (Illus.). 128p. (Orig.). 1986. pap. 9.95 (ISBN 0-914880-16-0). Educ Guide.

Randax Education Guide to Colleges Seeking Students. 16th ed. Stephen E. Marshall. (New Ser.). (Illus.). 128p. (Orig.). 1987. pap. 9.95 (ISBN 0-914880-17-9). Educ Guide.

Randax Education Guide: To Colleges Seeking Students, 1988. 17th ed. Stephen E. Marshall. (Illus.). 128p. (Orig.). 1988. pap. 10.95 (ISBN 0-914880-18-7). Educ Guide.

Randax Education Guide to Colleges Seeking Students, 1985 Edition. 14th ed. Stephen E. Marshall. (Illus.). 128p. (Orig.). 1985. pap. 8.95 (ISBN 0-914880-15-2). Educ Guide.

Randax Education Guide: 1980. 9th ed. Ed. by Stephen E. Marshall. (Illus., Orig.). 1980. pap. 6.50 (ISBN 0-914880-10-1). Educ Guide.

Randax Education Guide: 1981. 10th ed. 128p. 1981. pap. 7.95 (ISBN 0-914880-11-X). Educ Guide.

Randax Education Guide: 1982. 11th ed. Ed. by Stephen E. Marshall. (Illus.). 128p. (Orig.). 1982. pap. 8.95 (ISBN 0-914880-12-8). Educ Guide.

Randax Graduate School Directory. new ed. Ed. by Robert A. Pastman. LC 75-41652. 303p. 1976. lib. bdg. 21.50 (ISBN 0-914880-06-3). Educ Guide.

R&D Management Systems in Japanese Industry. Ed. by H. Eto & K. Matsui. 332p. 1984. 84.25 (ISBN 0-444-86808-9, North Holland). Elsevier.

R&D Partnerships: Structuring the Transactions. 2nd ed. Lee Petillon & Robert J. Hull. (Securities Law Ser.). 1985. 85.00 (ISBN 0-87632-471-5). Clark Boardman.

Randlords. P. H. Emden. 59.95 (ISBN 0-8490-0927-8). Gordon Pr.

Randlords: South Africa's Robber Barons & the Mines That Forged a Nation. Geoffrey Wheatcroft. 1987. pap. 9.95 (ISBN 0-671-63993-5, Touchstone Bks). S&S.

Randolph: A Study of Churchill's Son. Brian Roberts. (Illus.). 320p. 1986. 30.95 (ISBN 0-241-11109-9, Pub. by Hamish Hamilton England). David & Charles.

Randolph Bourne. Sherman Paul. (Pamphlets on American Writers Ser: No. 60). (Orig.). 1966. pap. 1.25x (ISBN 0-8166-0405-3, MPAW60). U of Minn Pr.

Randolph Bourne: Legend & Reality. John Moreau. 1943. 9.00 (ISBN 0-8183-0203-8). Pub Aff Pr.

Randolph Caldecott. Henry Blackburn. LC 68-21757. 232p. 1969. Repr. of 1886 ed. 35.00x (ISBN 0-8103-3490-9). Gale.

Randolph Caldecott Treasury. Elizabeth T. Billington. LC 76-45308. (Illus.). 1978. 30.00 (ISBN 0-7232-6139-3). Warne.

Randolph County Profile: 1976. Anna D. Kek. 1976. 5.00 (ISBN 0-87012-243-6). McClain.

Randolph Cranstone & the Glass Thimble. Michael Bullock. (Illus.). 118p. 1978. 10.95 (ISBN 0-7145-2506-5, Dist by Scribner). M Boyars Pubs.

Randolph-Macon College: A Southern History, 1825-1967. James E. Scanlon. LC 82-16072. 1983. 15.00x (ISBN 0-8139-0928-7). U Pr of Va.

Randolph Rogers: American Sculptor in Rome. Millard F. Rogers, Jr. LC 75-164439. (Illus.). 256p. 1971. 20.00x (ISBN 0-87023-087-5). U of Mass Pr.

Randolph Scott: The Gentleman from Virginia. Jefferson B Crow, III. (Illus.). 336p. 1987. 29.95 (ISBN 0-940375-00-1). WindRiver Pub.

Randolph Scott: The Gentleman from Virginia. rev. ed. Jefferson B. Crow, III. (Illus.). 336p. 1990. pap. 14.95 (ISBN 0-940375-11-7). WindRiver Pub.

Randolph: The Biography of Winston Churchill's Son. Anita Leslie. 1985. 16.95 (ISBN 0-8253-0284-6). Beaufort Bks NY.

Random Access & Data File Programming with the IBM PC, Vol. I. 1984. write for info. (ISBN 0-910985-15-4); disk avail. (ISBN 0-910985-17-0). D S C Pub.

Random Access & Data File Programming with the IBM PC, Vol. II. 1984. write for info. (ISBN 0-910985-16-2); disk avail. (ISBN 0-910985-18-9). D S C Pub.

Random Access Murder. Linda Grant. 192p. 1988. pap. 2.95 (ISBN 0-380-75534-3). Avon.

Random & Restricted Walks: Theory & Applications. M. N. Barber & B. W. Ninham. (Mathematics & Its Applications Ser.). 190p. 1970. 58.00 (ISBN 0-677-02620-X). Gordon & Breach.

Random Coefficient Autoregressive Models: An Introduction. D. F. Nicholls & B. G. Quinn. (Lecture Notes in Statistics: Vol. 11). (Illus.). 154p. 1982. pap. 17.00 (ISBN 0-387-90766-1). Springer-Verlag.

Random Counts in Scientific Work, 3 vols. G. P. Patil. Incl. Vol. 1. Random Counts in Models & Structures. 276p. 1970 (ISBN 0-271-00114-3); Vol. 2. Random Counts in Biomedical & Social Sciences. 232p. 1970 (ISBN 0-271-00115-1); Vol. 3. Random Counts in Physical Science, Geoscience, & Business. 215p. 1970 (ISBN 0-271-00116-X). LC 73-114351. (Illus.). 25.00x ea. Pa St U Pr.

Random Data: Analysis & Measurement Procedures. Julius S. Bendat & Allan G. Piersol. LC 71-160211. (Illus.). 407p. 1971. 45.50x (ISBN 0-471-06470-X, Pub. by Wiley-Interscience). Wiley.

Random Data: Analysis & Measurement Procedures. 2nd, exp. & rev. ed. Julius S. Bendat & Allan G. Piersol. LC 85-17996. 566p. 1986. 51.95 (ISBN 0-471-04000-2). Wiley.

Random Differential Equations in Science & Engineering. T. T. Soong. (Mathematics in Science & Engineering Ser.). 1973. 79.50 (ISBN 0-12-654850-1). Acad Pr.

Random Differential Inequalities. G. S. Ladde & V. Laksmikantham. LC 80-521. (Mathematics in Science & Engineering Ser.). 1980. 56.50 (ISBN 0-12-432750-8). Acad Pr.

Random Eigenvalue Problems. Collet's Holding Ltd. Staff. 1985. 112.00x (Pub. by Collets (UK)). State Mutual Bk.

Random Eigenvalue Problems. J. Vom Scheidt & W. Purkert. (North-Holland Series in Probability & Applied Mathematics). 176p. 1984. 25.00 (ISBN 0-444-00769-5, North-Holland). Elsevier.

Random Fatigue Life Prediction. Ed. by Y. S. Shin & M. K. Au-Yang. (PVP Ser.: Vol. 72). 148p. 1983. pap. text ed. 30.00 (ISBN 0-317-02643-7, H00258). ASME.

Random Fields, 2 vols. J. Fritz et al. (Colloquia Mathematica Ser.: Vol. 27). 1112p. 1982. Set. 242.00 (ISBN 0-444-85441-X, North-Holland). Elsevier.

Random Fields: Analysis & Synthesis. Erik Vanmarcke. (Illus.). 416p. 1983. 50.00x (ISBN 0-262-22026-1). MIT Pr.

Random Fourier Series with Application to Harmonic Analysis. Michael B. Marcus & Gilles Pisier. LC 81-47145. (Annals of Mathematical Studies: No.101). 192p. 1981. 27.00x (ISBN 0-691-08289-8); pap. 10.50 (ISBN 0-691-08292-8). Princeton U Pr.

Random Functions: A Laplacian Random Function Depending on a Point of Hilbert Space. Paul Levy. LC 56-8639. (University of California Publications in Statistics Ser.: Vol. 2, No. 10). pap. 20.00 (ISBN 0-317-11008-X, 2021182). Bks Demand UMI.

Random Gentleman. Elizabeth Chater. 224p. 1981. pap. 1.50 (ISBN 0-449-50210-4, Crest). Fawcett.

Random Giblets Written. Wayne Cargile. 1973. 1.50 (ISBN 0-87012-162-6). McClain.

Random Graphs. Bela Bollobas. 1985. 69.50 (ISBN 0-12-111755-3); pap. 35.00 (ISBN 0-12-111756-1). Acad Pr.

Random Graphs '83. Ed. by M. Karonski & A. Rucinski. 364p. 1986. 84.25 (ISBN 0-444-87821-1, North-Holland). Elsevier.

Random Harvest. James Hilton. 1982. Repr. lib. bdg. 18.95x (ISBN 0-89966-414-8). Buccaneer Bks.

Random Harvest. James Hilton. 327p. 1985. pap. 4.50 (ISBN 0-88184-125-0). Carroll & Graf.

Random Hearts. Warren Adler. 1985. pap. 3.95 (ISBN 0-451-13395-1, Sig). NAL.

Random House Basic Dictionary: French. Ed. by Francesca L. Langbaum. (Fr. & Eng.). 1986. pap. 2.50 (ISBN 0-345-33712-3). Ballantine.

Random House Basic Dictionary: German. Ed. by Jenni K. Moulton. 1987. pap. 2.25 (ISBN 0-345-34600-9). Ballantine.

Random House Basic Dictionary: Italian. Robert A. Hall, Jr. 1986. pap. 2.25 (ISBN 0-345-34603-3). Ballantine.

Random House Basic Dictionary: Spanish. Ed. by Donald P. Sola. 1986. pap. 2.95 (ISBN 0-345-33711-5). Ballantine.

Random House Basic Dictionary: Synonyms & Antonyms. Ed. by Lawrence Urdang. 1981. pap. 1.50 (ISBN 0-345-29712-1). Ballantine.

Random House Basic Speller-Divider. Jess Stein. 1987. pap. 2.50 (ISBN 0-317-58574-6). Ballantine.

Random House Basic Speller-Divider. Ed. by Jess Stein. 1981. pap. 2.95 (ISBN 0-345-29255-3). Ballantine.

Random House Book of Computer Literacy. Ellen Richman. LC 83-40008. 192p. 1984. 10.95 (ISBN 0-394-72125-X, Vin). Random.

Random House Book of Fairy Tales. Adapted by Amy Ehrlich. LC 83-13833. (Illus.). 224p. (gr. k-4). 1985. bds. 14.95 (ISBN 0-394-85693-7, BYR); lib. bdg. 14.99 (ISBN 0-394-95693-1). Random.

Random House Book of Humor for Children. Compiled by Pamela Pollack. LC 86-31478. (Illus.). 320p. (gr. 2-6). 1988. 14.95 (ISBN 0-394-88049-8); lib. bdg. 14.99 (ISBN 0-394-98049-2). Random.

Random House Book of Mother Goose: A Treasury of 306 Timeless Nursery Rhymes. Selected by & illus. by Arnold Lobel. LC 86-47532. 176p. (gr. 2-6). 1986. 14.95 (ISBN 0-394-86799-8, BYR); lib. bdg. 14.99 (ISBN 0-394-96799-2, BYR). Random.

Random House Book of Poetry for Children. Jack Prelutsky. LC 81-85940. (Illus.). 248p. (gr. 1-5). 1983. 14.95 (ISBN 0-394-85010-6); lib. bdg. 15.99 (ISBN 0-394-95010-0). Random.

Random House Book of Twentieth Century French Poetry. Ed. by Paul Auster. LC 82-17342. 688p. 1984. pap. 11.95 (ISBN 0-394-71748-1, Vin). Random.

Random House College Dictionary. Ed. by Stuart B. Flexner. (Illus.). 1979. 19.93 (ISBN 0-394-05433-4); thumbed index 21.27 (ISBN 0-394-05434-2). Random.

Random House College Dictionary. rev. ed. 1975. regular ed. 16.95 (ISBN 0-394-43500-1); thumb-indexed ed. 16.95 (ISBN 0-394-43600-8); deluxe ed. 16.95 (ISBN 0-394-51192-1). Random.

Random House College Dictionary. rev. ed. 1982. thumb-indexed ed. incl. Pocket Thesaurus 15.95 (ISBN 0-394-52760-7); thumb-indexed ed. incl. Bad Speller's Dictionary 14.95 (ISBN 0-394-52762-3). Random.

Random House College Dictionary & the Random House Thesaurus. 1987. Boxed set. 31.90 (ISBN 0-394-54210-X). Random.

Random House College Dictionary: Leather Edition. (Illus.). 1600p. 1988. leather ed. 50.00 (ISBN 0-394-57350-1). Random.

Random House Concise World Atlas. John Bartholomew. 1985. 9.95 (ISBN 0-394-74007-6). Random.

Random House Crossword Puzzle Dictionary. 1988. 19.95 (ISBN 0-394-53513-8). Random.

Random House Dictionary. 1088p. 1987. Red, with gold stamp. 12.95 (ISBN 0-394-53440-9); Blue, with silver stamp. 12.95 (ISBN 0-394-53441-7); Brown, with gold stamp. 12.45 (ISBN 0-394-53442-5). Random.

Random House Dictionary. Ed. by Jess Stein. (Orig.). 1984. pap. 3.50 (ISBN 0-345-32298-3). Ballantine.

Random House Dictionary: Concise Edition. Random House, Inc. 1980. 2.38 (ISBN 0-394-51200-6). Random.

Random House Dictionary of New Information Technology. Ed. by A. J. Meadows & M. Gordon. LC 82-40026. 200p. 1982. pap. 7.95 (ISBN 0-394-71202-1, Vin). Random.

Random House Dictionary of the English Language. 1966. 59.95 (ISBN 0-394-47176-8). Random.

Random House Dictionary of the English Language. 2nd, unabridged ed. 2500p. 1987. 79.95 (ISBN 0-394-50050-4); deluxe ed. 99.95 (ISBN 0-394-56500-2). Random.

Random House Dictionary: Synonyms & Antonyms. Ed. by Lawrence Urdang. 1987. pap. 1.50 (ISBN 0-317-58573-8). Ballantine.

Random House Encyclopedia. rev. ed. Ed. by James Mitchell. LC 83-9596. (Illus.). 2920p. 1983. 94.95 (ISBN 0-394-52883-2). Random.

Random House Encyclopedia. 1977. 79.95 (ISBN 0-394-40730-X). Random.

Random House Guide to Natural Areas of the Eastern United States. John Perry & Jane G. Perry. LC 79-5552. (Illus.). 1980. pap. 11.95 (ISBN 0-394-73506-4). Random.

Random House Guide to Research Writing. Thomas S. Kane & Leonard J. Peters. 1989. pap. text ed. price not set (ISBN 0-394-35607-1). Random.

Random House Guide to Technical & Scientific Communication. David Clark & Donald Zimmerman. 576p. 1987. text ed. write for info. (ISBN 0-394-33260-1, RanC). Random.

Random House Guide to Writing. 3rd ed. Sandra Schor & Judith Fishman. 464p. 1986. pap. text ed. write for info (ISBN 0-394-33796-4, RanC). Random.

Random House Handbook. 4th ed. Frederick Crews. 1983. text ed. write for info (ISBN 0-394-32395-5, RanC). Random.

Random House Handbook. 5th ed. Frederick Crews. 528p. 1988. text ed. 17.00 (ISBN 0-394-33944-4, RanC). Random.

Random House Handbook of Business Terms. Jay N. Nisber. 352p. 1988. 14.95 (ISBN 0-394-53047-0). Random.

Random House Library of Painting & Sculpture, 4 vols. David Piper. LC 80-28604. (Illus.). 960p. 1981. Boxed Set. boxed set 99.50 (ISBN 0-394-50092-X). Random.

Random House Mini World Atlas. John Bartholomew. 1985. 4.95 (ISBN 0-394-74008-4). Random.

Random House Reader. Frederick Crews. 432p. 1981. pap. text ed. write for info (ISBN 0-394-32268-1, RanC). Random.

Random House School Dictionary. Ed. by Stuart B. Flexner. (Illus.). 966p. 1983. 22.64 (ISBN 0-676-39289-X). Random.

Random House Thesaurus: College Edition. LC 84-4914. 812p. 1984. Thumb indexed 14.95 (ISBN 0-394-52949-9). Random.

Random House Workbook. 4th ed. Ann V. Sant. 1984. pap. text ed. write for info (ISBN 0-394-33249-0, RanC). Random.

Random Integral Equations. A. T. Bharucha-Reid. (Mathematics in Science & Engineering Ser.: Vol. 96). 1972. 83.00 (ISBN 0-12-095750-7). Acad Pr.

Random Lengths Buyers' & Sellers' Guide, 1988: A Directory of the Forest Products Industry. rev. ed. Ed. by David Bartel. 1988. text ed. 130.00 (ISBN 0-9614042-2-1). Random Lgths Pubns.

Random Linear Operators. A. V. Skorohod. 1984. lib. bdg. 43.00 (ISBN 0-318-00431-3, Pub. by Reidel Holland). Kluwer Academic.

Random Mappings. V. F. Kolchin. xiv, 207p. 1986. 80.00 (ISBN 0-387-96154-2). Springer-Verlag.

Random Mappings. V. F. Kolchin. Ed. by A. V. Balakrishnan. LC 86-9316. (Translations Series in Mathematics & Engineering). 224p. 1986. text ed. 72.00 (ISBN 0-911575-16-2). Optimization Soft.

Random Matrices. Madan L. Mehta. 1967. 85.50 (ISBN 0-12-488050-9). Acad Pr.

Random Matrices & Their Applications. Ed. by J. Cohen et al. LC 85-30842. (Contemporary Mathematics Ser.: Vol. 50). 376p. 1986. pap. text ed. 34.00 (ISBN 0-8218-5044-X). Am Math.

Random Measures. O. Kallenberg. 1984. 36.00 (ISBN 0-12-394960-2). Acad Pr.

Random Measures. Olav Kallenberg. 1976. pap. cancelled (ISBN 0-685-74757-3). Adlers Foreign Bks.

Random Media. Ed. by G. Papanicolaou. (IMA Volumes in Mathematics & its Applications Ser.: Vol. 7). (Illus.). 345p. 1987. 34.00 (ISBN 0-387-96524-6). Springer-Verlag.

Random Noise Techniques in Nuclear Reactor Systems. Robert E. Uhrig. LC 71-110558. (Illus.). pap. 95.40 (ISBN 0-317-08879-3, 2012436). Bks Demand UMI.

Random Notes of Early Settlers of Brunswick-Topsham (ME) 24p. 1986. pap. 3.50 (ISBN 0-935207-31-7). DanBury Hse Bks.

Random Notes on Red China, Nineteen Thirty-Six to Nineteen Forty-Five. Edgar Snow. LC 58-146. (East Asian Monographs Ser: No. 5). pap. text ed. 11.00x (ISBN 0-674-74900-6). Harvard U Pr.

Random Packings & Packed Towers: Design & Applications. Ralph F. Strigle. 288p. 1987. 38.00 (ISBN 0-87201-669-2). Gulf Pub.

Random Perturbations of Dynamical Systems. M. I. Freidlin & A. D. Wentzell. (Grundlehren der Mathematischen Wissenschaften Ser.: Bd. 260). (Illus.). 340p. 1983. 70.00 (ISBN 0-387-90858-7). Springer-Verlag.

Random Polynomials. A. T. Bharucha-Reid & M. Sambandham. (Probability & Mathematical Statistics Ser.). 1986. 49.50 (ISBN 0-12-095710-8); pap. 19.95 (ISBN 0-12-095711-6). Acad Pr.

Random Processes. Murray Rosenblatt. LC 74-10956. (Graduate Texts in Mathematics Ser.: Vol. 17). (Illus.). 225p. 1974. 34.00 (ISBN 0-387-90085-3). Springer-Verlag.

Random Processes. 2nd ed. Syski. (Statistics Textbooks & Monographs). 276p. 1988. 49.75 (ISBN 0-8247-8028-0). Dekker.

Random Processes: A First Look. Syski. (Statistics; Textbooks & Monographs Ser.: Vol. 29). 1979. 34.75 (ISBN 0-8247-6893-0). Dekker.

Random Processes: A Mathematical Approach for Engineers. Robert M. Gray & Lee D. Davisson. (Illus.). 272p. 1985. text ed. 42.00 (ISBN 0-13-752882-5). P-H.

Random Processes & the Growth of Firms: A Study of the Pareto Law. J. Steindl. 249p. 1965. text ed. 22.00x (ISBN 0-85264-063-3). Lubrecht & Cramer.

Random Processes: Filtering & Estimation. Ludeman. 1988. price not set (ISBN 0-471-60756-8). Wiley.

Random Processes in Electrical & Mechanical Systems. V. L. Lebedev. 128p. 1961. text ed. 27.00x (ISBN 0-7065-0121-7, Pub. by Keter Pub Jerusalem). Coronet Bks.

Random Processes in Mechanical Sciences. CISM (International Center for Mechanical Sciences) Ed. by H. Parkus. (CISM Pubns. Ser.: No. 9). (Illus.). vi, 169p. 1973. pap. 19.80 (ISBN 0-387-81086-2). Springer-Verlag.

Random Processes in Nuclear Reactors. M. M. Williams. LC 74-4066. 1974. 65.00 (ISBN 0-08-017920-7). Pergamon.

Random Processes: Measurement Analysis & Simulation. J Cacko. (Fundamental Studies in Engineering: Vol. 8). 1987. 94.75 (ISBN 0-444-98942-0). Elsevier.

Random Pulse Trains: Their Measurement & Statistical Properties. C. H. Vincent. (Monographs: No. 13). 278p. 1973. casebound 44.00 (ISBN 0-901223-37-9, MO013). Inst Elect Eng.

Random Ramblings. D. A. Mecca. 1988. 6.95 (ISBN 0-533-07518-1). Vantage.

Random Recollections of an Anachronism. Keyes D. Metcalf. 401p. 1980. 35.00 (ISBN 0-918414-02-4). Readex Bks.

Random Recollections of Early Days in Mississippi. H. S. Fulkerson. 1972. 10.00 (ISBN 0-87511-597-7). Claitors.

Random Reminiscences of Lord Fletcher of Islington. Lord Eric Fletcher. (Illus.). 269p. 1987. 12.95 (ISBN 0-317-64184-0, Pub. by Bishopsgate Pr London). Intl Spec Bk.

Random Reminiscences of Men & Events. John D. Rockefeller. LC 73-2533. (Big Business; Economic Power in a Free Society Ser.). Repr. of 1909 ed. 17.00 (ISBN 0-405-05111-5). Ayer Co Pubs.

Random Reminiscences of Men & Events. John D. Rockefeller. (Illus.). 124p. 1984. 12.95 (ISBN 0-912882-58-1). Sleepy Hollow.

Random Ruminations. Dhe Bradley. LC 87-90078. 113p. 1987. 7.95 (ISBN 0-533-07449-5). Vantage.

Random Search Algorithms: Their Development & Application in the U. S. S. R. George Tarasenko. Ed. by Rebecca Kraft. (Illus., Orig.). Date not set. pap. text ed. 35.00 (ISBN 1-55831-049-5). Delphic Associates.

Random Seas & Design of Maritime Structures. Yoshimi Goda. 320p. 1985. 44.50 (ISBN 0-86008-369-1, Pub. by U of Tokyo Japan). Columbia U Pr.

Random Shots. facsimile ed. Charles H. Clark. LC 70-164557. (American Fiction Reprint Ser). Repr. of 1879 ed. 24.50 (ISBN 0-8369-7033-0). Ayer Co Pubs.

Random Signal Analysis in Engineering Systems. John J. Komo. 302p. 1987. 39.95 (ISBN 0-12-418660-2). Acad Pr.

Random Signals & Systems. Richard E. Mortensen. LC 86-19007. 252p. 1986. 33.95 (ISBN 0-471-84364-4). Wiley.

Random Signals Estimation & Identification: Analysis & Applications. Nirode C. Mohanty. 640p. 1986. 62.95 (ISBN 0-442-26396-1). Van Nos Reinhold.

Random Signals Noise & Filtering. Arthur M. Breipohl & Sam K. Shanmugan. LC 87-37273. 576p. 1988. write for info. (ISBN 0-471-81555-1). Wiley.

Random Signals: Noise & Filtering. Sam K. Shanmugan. 528p. 1988. pap. write for info. (ISBN 0-471-61274-X). Wiley.

Random Talks with the Living Christ. Francis L. L'Estrange. 107p. 1988. 30.00X (ISBN 0-7223-2038-8, Pub. by A H Stockwell England). State Mutual Bk.

Random Thoughts: Aphorisms, Reflections. Karl T. Marx. 1956. 5.00 (ISBN 0-686-31254-6). Freedom Univ-FSP.

Random Thoughts on Dickens. Chester N. Farr. LC 77-21125. 1977. Repr. of 1931 ed. lib. bdg. 15.00 (ISBN 0-8414-4351-3). Folcroft.

Random Variables & Probability Distribution. 3rd ed. Harold Cramer. (Cambridge Tracts in Mathematics & Mathematical Physics). 1970. 29.95 (ISBN 0-521-07685-4). Cambridge U Pr.

Random Vibration -- Status & Recent Developments: The Stephen Harry Crandall Festschrift. Ed. by I. Elishakoff & R. H. Lyon. (Studies in Applied Mechanics: No. 14). 564p. 1986. 260.75 (ISBN 0-444-42665-5). Elsevier.

Random Vibration in Mechanical Systems. Stephen H. Crandall & W. D. Mark. 1963. 43.00 (ISBN 0-12-196750-6). Acad Pr.

Random Vibration in Perspective. Wayne Tustin & Robert Mercado. LC 84-80801. (Illus.). 208p. 1984. text ed. 100.00x (ISBN 0-918247-00-4). Tustin Tech.

Random Vibration of Mechanical Systems. K. Piszczek & J. Niziol. LC 85-16338. (Mechanical Engineering Ser.). 343p. 1986. 118.00 (ISBN 0-470-20247-5). Wiley.

Random Vibration of Structures. C. Y. Yang. 295p. 1986. 49.95 (ISBN 0-471-80262-X, Pub. by Wiley-Interscience). Wiley.

Random Vibrations. CISM (International Center for Mechanical Sciences. Ed. by Robson et al. (CISM Pubns. Ser.: No. 115). (Illus.). 219p. 1974. pap. 20.50 (ISBN 0-387-81223-7). Springer-Verlag.

Random Vibrations & Reliability: Proceedings of the Iutam Symposium, Frankfurt. Collet's Holdings, Ltd. Staff. 1986. 224.00x (ISBN 0-317-52959-5, Pub. by Collets (UK)). State Mutual Bk.

Random Vibrations of Elastic Systems. V. V. Bolotin. (Mechanics of Elastic Stability: No. 8). 480p. 1984. lib. bdg. 86.00 (ISBN 90-247-2981-5, Pub. by Martinus Nijhoff Netherlands). Kluwer Academic.

Random Walk: A Novel for the New Age. Lawrence Block. 352p. 1988. 18.95 (ISBN 0-312-93092-5). Tor Bks.

Random Walk & Beyond: An Inside Guide to the Stock Market. Mark A. Johnson. LC 87-31602. 245p. 1988. 22.95 (ISBN 0-471-63223-6). Wiley.

Random Walk down Wall Street. rev. ed. Burton G. Malkiel. (Illus.). 1973. 13.95 (ISBN 0-393-05500-0). Norton.

Random Walk down Wall Street. 2nd ed. Burton G. Malkiel. 1981. 8.95x (ISBN 0-393-95117-0). Norton.

Random Walk down Wall Street. 4th ed. Burton G. Malkiel. 1985. pap. text ed. 9.95x (ISBN 0-393-95460-9). Norton.

Random Walk in Relativity & Cosmology: Essays in Honor of P. C. Vaidya & A. K. Raychaudhuri. Ed. by N. Dadhich et al. LC 85-9490. 236p. 1985. 38.95 (ISBN 0-470-20198-3). Halsted Pr.

Random Walk in Science: An Anthology. R. L. Weber & E. Mendoza. 1973. 29.00x (ISBN 0-85498-027-X, Pub. by A Hilger UK). Taylor & Francis.

Random Walks. M. Shlesinger. 400p. 1987. write for info. (ISBN 9971-50-247-X). World Scientific Pub.

Random Walks & Electric Networks. Peter G. Boyle & J. Laurie Snell. LC 84-61495. 173p. 1984. 25.00 (ISBN 0-88385-024-9, CAM-22); avail. Math Assn.

Random Walks & Their Applications in the Physical & Biological Sciences: NBS-La Jolla Institute - 1982. Ed. by Michael F. Shlesinger & Bruce J. West. LC 84-7028. (AIP Conference Proceedings Ser.: No. 109). 243p. 1984. lib. bdg. 38.75 (ISBN 0-88318-308-0). Am Inst Physics.

Random Walks in Biology. Howard C. Berg. LC 83-42549. (Illus.). 160p. 1984. 18.50x (ISBN 0-691-08245-6). Princeton U Pr.

Random Wavelets & Cybernetic Systems. 136p. 20.00 (ISBN 0-910835-06-3). Goose Pond Pr.

Random Wavelets & Cybernetic Systems. Enders A. Robinson. (Griffin's Statistical Monographs: No. 9). 125p. 1962. pap. text ed. 17.95x (ISBN 0-85264-075-7). Lubrecht & Cramer.

Random Winds. Belva Plain. 1980. pap. 13.95 (ISBN 0-385-28808-5). Delacorte.

Random Winds. Belva Plain. 1987. pap. 4.95 (ISBN 0-440-17562-3). Dell.

Randomised Controlled Clinical Trials. Christopher J. Bulpitt. 1983. lib. bdg. 52.50 (ISBN 90-247-2749-9, Pub. by Martinus Nijhoff Netherlands). Kluwer Academic.

Randomization & Field Experimentation. Ed. by Robert F. Boruch & Werner Wothke. LC 85-81897. (Program Evaluation Ser.: No. 28). (Orig.). 1985. pap. text ed. 14.95x (ISBN 0-87589-766-5). Jossey-Bass.

Randomization Tests, Vol. 77. 2nd ed. Eugene S. Edgington. (Statistics: Textbooks & Monographs). 396p. 1987. 55.00 (ISBN 0-8247-7656-9). Dekker.

Randomized Clinical Trial & Therapeutic Diseases. Niels Tygstrup et al. (Statistics Ser.). 400p. 1982. 55.00 (ISBN 0-8247-1856-9). Dekker.

Randomized Response. James A. Fox. (Quantitative Applications in the Social Sciences Ser.: Vol. 58). 96p. (Orig.). 1986. pap. text ed. 6.50 (ISBN 0-8039-2309-0). Sage.

Randomized Response: Theory & Techniques. Chaudhuri & Mukerjee. (Statistics Textbook & Monograph Ser.). 192p. 1987. 69.75 (ISBN 0-8247-7785-9). Dekker.

Randomized Trials in Cancer: A Critical Review by Sites. Ed. by Maurice L. Slevin & Maurice J. Staquet. (European Organization for Research on Treatment of Cancer (EORTC) Monograph: Vol. 15). 716p. 1986. text ed. 104.50 (ISBN 0-88167-157-6). Raven.

Randomn Perturbations of Dynamical Systems. Yuri Kifer. (Progress in Probability & Statistics Ser.: No. 16). 304p. 1988. 47.00 (ISBN 0-8176-3384-7). Birkhauser.

Randomness, Statistics & Emergence. Philip McShane. LC 78-122619. 1970. 22.95x (ISBN 0-268-00436-6). U of Notre Dame Pr.

Randonnees aux Environs de Montreal. William G. Scheller. Tr. by Janine Booth from Eng. (Country Walks Bks.). (Illus.). 152p. (Orig., Fr.). 1983. Fr. ed. pap. 7.95 (ISBN 0-910146-46-2). Eng. ed. Appalach Mtn.

Randy. John LaCrosse. 224p. 1980. 10.95 (ISBN 0-932282-47-4). Caledonia Pr.

Randy Roy Persnazznur. David B. Creps. LC 80-51270. (Orig.). 1980. pap. 4.95 (ISBN 0-930830-32-6). Great Basin.

Randy the Rooster. Rose Labrie. LC 83-50688. (Illus.). 32p. (Orig.). (gr. 3-5). 1986. pap. 9.95 over boards (ISBN 0-931474-24-8). TBW Bks.

Randy's Dandy Lions. Bill Peet. (Illus.). (gr. k-3). 1964. PLB 12.95 (ISBN 0-395-18507-6). HM.

Randy's Dandy Lions. Bill Peet. (Illus.). (gr. k-3). 1979. pap. 3.95 (ISBN 0-395-27498-2). HM.

Raney. Clyde Edgerton. 232p. 1985. 12.95 (ISBN 0-912697-17-2). Algonquin Bks.

Raney. Clyde Edgerton. 256p. 1988. pap. 3.95 (ISBN 0-345-32982-1). Ballantine.

Ranganathan's Philosophy: Assessment, Impact & Relevance. T. S. Rajagopalan. 725p. 1986. text ed. 60.00x (ISBN 0-7069-3027-4, Pub. by Vikas India). Advent NY.

Range Camp. W. F. Bragg. 1980. pap. 1.75 (ISBN 0-8439-0852-1, Leisure Bks). Leisure NY.

Range Conservationist. Jack Rudman. (Career Examination Ser.: C-686). (Cloth bdg. avail. on request). pap. 14.00 (ISBN 0-8373-0686-8). Natl Learning.

Range Development & Improvements. 2nd ed. John F. Vallentine. LC 79-26676. (Illus.). 1980. text ed. 18.95x (ISBN 0-8425-1708-1). Brigham.

Range Development & Research in Kenya. Ed. by Richard M. Hansen et al. (Illus.). 474p. 1986. perfect bdg. 13.50 (ISBN 0-933595-06-9). Winrock Intl.

Range Ecology. Robert R. Humphrey. LC 62-20671. pap. 60.00 (2015179). Bks Demand UMI.

Range Economics. John P. Workman. (Biological Resource Management Ser.). (Illus.). 240p. 1986. 34.50x (ISBN 0-02-948810-9). Macmillan.

Range Management. 3rd ed. L. A. Stoddart et al. (Illus.). 480p. 1975. text ed. 48.95 (ISBN 0-07-061596-9). McGraw.

Range of Choice in Water Management: A Study of Dissolved Oxygen in the Potomac Estuary. Robert K. Davis et al. LC 68-27737. (Illus.). pap. 53.50 (ISBN 0-317-10648-1, 2019821). Bks Demand UMI.

Range of Literature see Houghton Books in Literature.

Range Rebel. Gordon D. Shirreffs. 1978. pap. 1.50 (ISBN 0-505-51226-2, Pub. by Tower Bks). Leisure NY.

Range Research: Basic Problems & Techniques. C. Wayne Cook & James Stubbendieck. LC 85-63270. 317p. Date not set. 30.00 (ISBN 0-9603692-3-6). Soc Range Mgmt.

Range Rover - Land Rover. Graham Robson. (Illus.). 208p. 1986. 30.95 (ISBN 0-7153-8786-3). David & Charles.

Range Rover: Super Profile. Treveor Alder. LC 86-81435. (Super Profile Ser.). (Illus.). 56p. 1987. 8.95 (ISBN 0-85429-534-8, Pub. by G T Foulis Ltd). Haynes Pubns.

Range Science: A Guide to Information Sources. Ed. by John F. Vallentine & Phillip L. Sims. (Natural World Information Guide Ser.: Vol. 2). 248p. 1980. 68.00x (ISBN 0-8103-1420-7). Gale.

Range Service (Gas, Electric, Microwave) Ed. by A. Ross Sabin. (Illus.). 254p. (gr. 11). 1980. 20.00 (ISBN 0-938336-06-1). Whirlpool.

Range Site: Archaic Through Late Woodland Occupations. John E. Kelly et al. (American Bottom Archaelogy - Selected FAI-270 Site Reports: Vol. 16). (Illus.). 480p. 1987. pap. 23.95 (ISBN 0-252-01078-7). U of Ill Pr.

Range Site 2: Emergent Mississippian, Dohack, & Range Phase Occupations. John E. Kelly et al. (American Bottom Archaelogy - Selected FAI-270 Site Reports: Vol. 20). (Illus.). 1988. pap. price not set (ISBN 0-252-01082-5). U of Ill Pr.

Range War. Cole Westan. 1987. pap. 3.50 (ISBN 0-8041-0060-8, Pub. by Ivy). Ballantine.

Range Wars: Heated Debates, Sober Reflections, & Other Assessments of Texas Writing. Ed. by Craig Clifford & Tom Pilkington. LC 88-42632. (Southwest Life & Letters Ser.). 224p. 1988. 22.50x (ISBN 0-87074-282-5); pap. 10.95 (ISBN 0-87074-273-6). SMU Press.

Rangeland Avenger. Max Brand. 256p. 1986. pap. 2.95 (ISBN 0-446-34121-5). Warner Bks.

Rangeland Avenger. Max Brand. 340p. 1986. lib. bdg. 14.95x (ISBN 0-8161-3962-8, Large Print Bks). G K Hall.

Rangeland Hydrology. 2nd ed. Branson. 340p. 15.00 (ISBN 0-318-16600-3). Soc Range Mgmt.

Rangeland Plant Physiology. Ed. by R. Sosebee. 290p. 14.50 (ISBN 0-318-16601-1). Soc Range Mgmt.

Rangeland Through Time: A Photographic Study of Vegetation Change in Wyoming. Kendall L. Johnson. (Illus.). 196p. (Orig.). 1987. pap. 18.00 (ISBN 0-941570-05-3). U of Wyoming.

Rangelands. Ed. by Bruce A. Buchanan. (Committee on Desert & Arid Zones Research-Soutwestern & Rocky Mountain Div.). 104p. 1988. 22.50x (ISBN 0-8263-1088-5). U of NM Pr.

Rangelands: A Resource under Siege. Ed. by P. J. Joss & P. W. Lynch. 750p. 1987. 79.50 (ISBN 0-521-30936-0). Cambridge U Pr.

Ranger, Vol. I. 2nd rev. ed. Theodore Enslin. 432p. 1980. 30.00 (ISBN 0-913028-79-7); pap. 12.95 (ISBN 0-913028-78-9). North Atlantic.

Ranger, Vol. 1. Theodore Enslin. (Illus.). 432p. 1978. 30.00 (ISBN 0-913028-58-4); pap. 8.95 (ISBN 0-913028-51-7). North Atlantic.

Ranger & Other Stories. Max Brand. pap. 2.95 (ISBN 0-671-83596-3). PB.

Ranger Escort West of the Pecos. Tom Lea. 1965. 3.00 (ISBN 0-292-77003-0). U of Tex Pr.

Ranger Handbook. U. S. Army Infantry School, Ft. Benning, Ga. (Illus.). 202p. 1972. pap. 8.00 (ISBN 0-87364-044-6). Paladin Pr.

Ranger Mosby. Virgil C. Jones. 368p. 1987. pap. 12.95 (ISBN 0-939009-01-3). EPM Pubns.

Ranger Rick's Dinosaur Book. Ed. by Victor H. Waldrop. LC 84-14680. (Illus.). 96p. (gr. 2-7). 1985. Repr. of 1984 ed. PLB 12.95 (ISBN 0-912186-54-2). Natl Wildlife.

Ranger Rick's Storybook. Ed. by Victor H. Waldrop. LC 83-8060. (Illus.). 96p. (gr. 1-6). 1983. 10.95 (ISBN 0-912186-47-X). Natl Wildlife.

Ranger Training & Operations. Department of the Army. 1982. lib. bdg. 75.00 (ISBN 0-87700-376-9). Revisionist Pr.

Ranger: U. S. Park Service. Jack Rudman. (Career Examination Ser.: C-665). (Cloth bdg. avail. on request). pap. 15.00 (ISBN 0-8373-0665-5). Natl Learning.

Ranger Volume II. Theodore Enslin. 256p. (Orig.). 1980. 30.00 (ISBN 0-913028-75-4); pap. 9.95 (ISBN 0-913028-74-6). North Atlantic.

Rangers & Sovereignty. Dan W. Roberts & D. W. Roberts. Bd. with Woman's Reminiscences of Six Years in Camp with the Texas Rangers. Repr. of 1928 ed. LC 87-42527. (Illus.). 288p. 1987. 19.95 (ISBN 0-938349-16-3); ltd. ed. 50.00 (ISBN 0-938349-14-7); pap. 12.95 (ISBN 0-938349-15-5). State House Pr.

Ranger's Guide to Useful Plants of Eastern Wilds. Deganawidah. (Illus.). 1964. 3.95 (ISBN 0-8158-0086-X). Chris Mass.

Ranger's Impartial List of the Ladies of Pleasure in Edinburgh. (Illus.). 1979. Repr. of 1775 ed. 12.95 (ISBN 0-8464-0783-3). Beekman Pubs.

Rangers of the North. John D. Ruemmler. (Illus.). 56p. (YA) (gr. 10-12). 1985. pap. 12.00 (ISBN 0-915795-22-1). Iron Crown Ent Inc.

Rangers Quiz Book. Compiled by Alex Hosie. 176p. 1987. 25.00x (ISBN 1-85158-091-3, Pub. by Mainstream Scotland). State Mutual Bk.

Rangers: Selected Combat Operations During World War 2. Michael J. King. LC 85-15691. (Leavenworth Papers: No. 11). (Illus.). 95p. (Orig.). 1985. pap. 3.25 (ISBN 0-318-19923-8, S/N 008-020-01057-0). USGPO.

Rangers: The Illustrated History of the Vietnam War. James R. Arnold. LC 87-47800. (Illus.). 160p. 1988. pap. 6.95 (ISBN 0-553-34509-5). Bantam.

Rani of Jhansi: A Study of Female Heroism in India. Joyce Lebra-Chapman. LC 85-20677. (Illus.). 224p. 1986. 25.00x (ISBN 0-8248-0984-X). UH Pr.

Ranibow Cadenza. J. Neil Schulman. 368p. 1986. pap. 3.50 (ISBN 0-380-75123-2). Avon.

Ranitidine. Ed. by A. J. Riley & P. R. Salmon. (Current Clinical Practice Ser.: Vol. 1). 217p. 1983. 80.00 (ISBN 0-444-90319-4, Excerpta Medica). Elsevier.

Ranitidine: Therapeutic Advances. Ed. by J. J. Misiewicz & J. R. Woods. (Current Clinical Practice Ser.: Vol. 15). 220p. 1985. 80.00 (ISBN 0-444-90386-0). Elsevier.

Rank among the Canaanite Gods: El, Baal, & the Raphaim. Conrad E. L'Heureux. LC 79-15582. (Harvard Semitic Monographs: No. 21). 1979. 10.50 (ISBN 0-89130-326-X, 040021). Scholars Pr GA.

Rank & File: Personal Histories by Working-Class Organizers. Ed. by Alice Lynd & Staughton Lynd. 320p. (YA) (gr. 9-12). 1988. pap. 10.00 (ISBN 0-85345-752-2). Monthly Rev.

Rank & Rivalry: The Politics of Inequality in Rural West Bengal. Marvin Davis. LC 82-9747. (Cambridge Studies in Cultural Systems: No. 7). pap. 64.80 (2031638). Bks Demand UMI.

Rank & Warfare among the Plains Indians. Bernard Mishkin. LC 84-45510. (American Ethnological Society Monographs: No. 3). 1988. Repr. of 1940 ed. 20.00 (ISBN 0-404-62903-2). AMS Pr.

Rank Correlation Methods. 4th ed. Maurice Kendall. (Charles Griffin Bk.). (Illus.). 202p. 1987. 35.00 (ISBN 0-19-520572-3). Oxford U Pr.

Rank Correlation Methods. 4th ed. Maurice G. Kendall. 1962. 34.95x (ISBN 0-02-847750-2). Hafner.

Rank-in-Class & Other Factors in College Admissions. NASSP Staff. 60p. 1983. pap. text ed. 6.00 (ISBN 0-88210-146-3). Natl Assn Principals.

Ranke: The Meaning of History. Leonard Krieger. LC 76-25633. 1977. lib. bdg. 31.00x (ISBN 0-226-45349-9). U of Chicago Pr.

Rankin: Enemy of the State. John Osier. LC 85-27651. 160p. 1986. 12.95 (ISBN 0-918518-43-1, St Luke TN). Peachtree Pubs.

Rankin: Enemy of the State. John Osier. 224p. 1987. pap. 3.50 (ISBN 0-14-009818-6). Penguin.

Rankin Family. G. T. Ridlon. LC 79-133881. (Saco Valley Settlements Ser). 1970. pap. 2.00 (ISBN 0-8048-0827-9). C E Tuttle.

Rankine, His Life & Times. Hugh B. Sutherland. 30p. 1973. 6.50 (ISBN 0-901948-75-6, Pub. by T Telford UK). Am Soc Civil Eng.

Ranks of Bronze. David Drake. 320p. 3.50 (ISBN 0-671-65568-X). Baen Bks.

Ranks of Death: A Medical History of the Conquest of America. Percy M. Ashburn. Ed. by Frank D. Ashburn. LC 80-24672. (Perspectives in Latin American History Ser.: No. 2). xix, 298p. 1981. Repr. of 1947 ed. lib. bdg. 37.50x (ISBN 0-87991-599-4). Porcupine Pr.

Ranniaia Proza. Mikhail Bulgakov. Ed. by Ellendea Proffer. (Sobranie Sochinenii Ser.: Vol. 2). 539p. (Rus.). 1985. lib. bdg. 35.00 (ISBN 0-88233-699-1). Ardis Pubs.

Rannoch Line. Picton Publishing Staff. (Illus.). 1987. 14.00x (Pub. by Picton UK). State Mutual Bk.

Rannyaya Proza Fedora Sologuba. Ludmila Kleyman. 192p. (Rus.). 1984. pap. text ed. 14.00 (ISBN 0-938920-41-3). Hermitage.

Ransack. 2nd ed. Michael Henson. 96p. 1987. pap. 5.95 (ISBN 0-931122-44-9). West End.

Ransacked. Nancy Holt. LC 79-92752. 1980. pap. 7.50 (ISBN 0-930378-11-3). Printed Matter.

Ransom. Lois Duncan. 144p. (gr. 7-12). 1984. pap. 2.95 (ISBN 0-440-97292-2, LFL). Dell.

Ransom. Grace L. Hill. Repr. lib. bdg. 19.95 (ISBN 0-89190-045-4, Pub. by River City Pr). Amereon Ltd.

Ransom. Jay McInerney. 280p. 1985. pap. text ed. 5.95 (ISBN 0-394-74118-8, Vin). Random.

Ransom. Jay McInerney. LC 87-45956. 288p. 1987. pap. 4.95 (ISBN 0-394-75803-X, Vin). Random.

Ransom from a Poet. Jerry W. Elkins. LC 81-50913. 116p. 1981. 7.95 (ISBN 0-938232-01-0); pap. 5.95 (ISBN 0-938232-02-9). Winston-Derek.

Ransom Game. Howard Engel. (Crime Monthly Ser.). 224p. 1986. pap. 3.95 (ISBN 0-14-007741-3). Penguin.

Ransom in Jade. Fran Earley. (Intrigue Ser.: No. 69). Date not set. pap. 2.25 (ISBN 0-317-63676-6). Harlequin Bks.

Ransom Kidnapping in America, Eighteen Seventy-Four to Nineteen Seventy-Four: The Creation of a Capital Crime. Ernest K. Alix. LC 78-1985. (Perspectives in Sociology Ser.). 256p. 1978. 22.50x (ISBN 0-8093-0849-5). S Ill U Pr.

Ransom Kidnapping in America, Eighteen Seventy-Four to Nineteen Seventy-Four: The Creation of a Capital Crime. Ernest K. Alix. LC 78-1985. 256p. 1980. pap. 9.95x (ISBN 0-8093-0976-9). S Ill U Pr.

Ransom of Red Chief. Brian Kral. (Orig.). (gr. 3 up). 1980. playscript 3.00 (ISBN 0-87602-227-1). Anchorage.

Ransom of Red Chief. O. Henry. (Creative's Classic Short Stories Ser.). (Illus.). 40p. (gr. 4 up). 1980. PLB 8.95 (ISBN 0-87191-776-9). Creative Ed.

Ransom of Red Chief. O. Henry. Ed. by Walter Pauk & Raymond Harris. (Classics Ser.). (Illus.). 40p. (Orig.). (gr. 6-12). 1979. pap. text ed. 3.00x (ISBN 0-89061-189-0, 405); tchrs. ed. 4.00x (ISBN 0-89061-191-2, 407); cassette 12.00 (406). Jamestown Pubs.

Ransom of Red Chief. O. Henry. 15.95 (ISBN 0-89190-342-9, Pub. by Am Repr). Amereon Ltd.

Ransom of the Golden Bridge. Proctor Jones. LC 83-80825. 176p. 1983. pap. 3.95 (ISBN 0-9608860-2-8). Proctor Jones.

Ransom Trail. Robert E. Trevathan. (YA) (gr. 7 up). 1984. 9.95 (ISBN 0-8034-8415-1, Avalon). Bouregy.

Ransomed Wait. May Miller. LC 82-83856. 72p. 1983. pap. 4.50x perf. bnd (ISBN 0-916418-40-5). Lotus.

Ransoming Captives in Crusader Spain: The Order of Merced on the Christian-Islamic Frontier. James W. Brodman. LC 85-20362. (Middle Ages Ser.). (Illus.). 216p. 1986. text ed. 25.95 (ISBN 0-8122-8001-6). U of PA Pr.

Ransoming the Mind: An Integration of Yoga & Modern Therapy. Charles Bates. LC 86-50084. (Illus.). 329p. (Orig.). 1986. pap. 11.95 (ISBN 0-936663-00-6). Yes Intl.

Ransoming the Time. Jacques Maritain. Tr. by Harry L. Binsse. LC 70-165665. 322p. 1972. Repr. of 1941 ed. 30.00x (ISBN 0-87752-153-0). Gordian.

Ransoms to Time: Selected Poems. Adonis Decavalles. Tr. by Kimon Friar from Gr. LC 82-49314. 144p. 1984. 18.50 (ISBN 0-8386-3180-0). Fairleigh Dickinson.

Ranson's Folly. facsimile ed. Richard H. Davis. LC 79-152938. (Short Story Index Reprint Ser.). (Illus.). Repr. of 1902 ed. 20.00 (ISBN 0-8369-3797-X). Ayer Co Pubs.

Ranson's Folly & Other Stories. Richard H. Davis. (Airmont Classics Ser.). (gr. 9 up). 1968. pap. 1.95 (ISBN 0-8049-0192-9, CL-192). Airmont.

Ranthorpe. George H. Lewes. Ed. by Barbara Smalley. LC 74-82496. lvii, 369p. 1974. 12.00x (ISBN 0-8214-0167-X); pap. 4.25x (ISBN 0-8214-0168-8). Ohio U Pr.

Ranting Dog: The Life of Robert Burns. John Lindsey. 402p. 1981. lib. bdg. 47.50 (ISBN 0-89984-305-0). Century Bookbindery.

Ranulf of Chester: A Relic of the Conquest. James W. Alexander. LC 83-3459. 208p. 1983. 20.00x (ISBN 0-8203-0673-8). U of Ga Pr.

Ranunculaceae. (Flora del Paraguay Ser.). (Span.). Date not set. price not set (ISBN 0-915279-05-3). Miss Botan.

Ranuzzi Manuscripts: An Exhibit. Maria X. Wells. 1980. 9.50 (ISBN 0-87959-094-7). U of Tex H Ransom Ctr.

Ranxerox in New York. 2nd ed. Stefano Tamburini. (Ranxerox Ser.). (Illus.). 60p. 1986. pap. 10.95 (ISBN 0-87416-027-8). Catalan Communs.

Ranxerox, No. Two: Happy Birthday, Lubna. 2nd ed. Stefano Tamburini. Ed. by Bernd Metz. (Illus.). 64p. 1987. pap. 10.95 (ISBN 0-87416-038-3). Catalan Communs.

Raoul Dufy: Catalogue Raisonne des Aquarelles, Gouaches, et Pastels, 2 Vols, Fr. Fanny L. Guilion. 48p. 1981. 385.00x (ISBN 2-86574-002-1). Hacker.

Raoul Hausmann & Berlin Dada. Timothy Benson. Ed. by Stephen Foster. LC 86-28049. (Studies in the Fine Arts: The Avant-Garde: No. 55). 298p. 1987. 44.95 (ISBN 0-8357-1785-2). UMI Res Pr.

Raoul Wallenberg. Michael Nicholson. Ed. by Rhoda Sherwood. LC 88-2078. (People Who Have Helped the World Ser.). (Illus.). 68p. (gr. 5-6). 1989. PLB 12.45 (ISBN 1-55532-820-2). Stevens Inc.

Raoul Wallenberg: Hero of the Holocaust. Thelma I. Pangburn. Ed. by John G. Buchanan. (Outstanding Personalities Ser.: No. 97). (Orig.). (YA) (gr. 7-12). 1987. lib. bdg. 3.75 incl. catalog cards (ISBN 0-87157-597-3); pap. 2.50 vinyl laminated covers (ISBN 0-87157-097-1). SamHar Pr.

Rap. Keith E. Greenberg. (Entertainment World Ser.). (Illus.). (gr. 4-9). 1987. 8.95 (ISBN 0-8225-1617-9). Lerner Pubns.

Rap Attack: African Jive to New York Hip Hop. David Toop. 160p. (Orig.). 1984. 20.00 (ISBN 0-89608-238-5); pap. 8.00 (ISBN 0-89608-239-3). South End Pr.

Rap Master Ronnie. G. B. Trudeau. 60p. 1986. deluxe ed. 50.00 signed (ISBN 0-935716-35-1). Lord John.

Rap Reiplinger's How You Figgah? Rap Reiplinger. (Illus.). 64p. (Orig.). 1984. pap. 1.95 (ISBN 0-935848-26-6). Bess Pr.

Rapala Fishing Guide: Secrets from Pros. LC 76-15852. (Illus.). 1976. pap. 2.95 (ISBN 0-686-17472-0). Normark Corp.

Rapan Lifeways: Society & History on a Polynesian Island. F. Allan Hanson. (Illus.). 227p. 1983. pap. text ed. 8.95x (ISBN 0-88133-029-9). Waveland Pr.

Rapanui: Tradition & Survival on Easter Island. Grant McCall. LC 80-54833. 197p. 1981. text ed. 16.95x (ISBN 0-8248-0746-4). UH Pr.

Rape. Susan Griffin. 1986. pap. 7.95 (ISBN 0-06-250351-0, PL 4132, HarpR). Har-Row.

Rape. Ed. by Roy Porter & Sylvana Tomaselli. LC 86-6148. (Illus.). 304p. 1986. 24.95 (ISBN 0-631-13748-3). Basil Blackwell.

Rape: A Bibliography Nineteen Sixty-Five to Nineteen Seventy-Five. Dorothy L. Barnes. LC 77-89641. 1977. 15.00x (ISBN 0-87875-120-3). Whitston Pub.

Rape-A How to Fight, Prevent, Use Protective Psychology & Later Identify Rapist. Patricia L. Miketta. (Illus.). 150p. 1988. 34.50 (ISBN 0-88164-906-6); pap. 26.50 (ISBN 0-88164-907-4). ABBE Pubs Assn.

Rape & Inequality. Julia R. Schwendinger & Herman Schwendinger. (Sage Library of Social Research: Vol. 148). 240p. 1983. 35.00 (ISBN 0-8039-1967-0); pap. 16.95 (ISBN 0-8039-1968-9). Sage.

Rape & Rape Related Issues: An Annotated Bibliography. Elizabeth J. Kemmer. (Reference Library of Social Science: Vol. 39). (LC 76-052701). 1977. lib. bdg. 26.00 (ISBN 0-8240-9873-0). Garland Pub.

Rape & Sexual Assault: A Research Handbook. Ann W. Burgess. LC 83-48217. (Reference Library of Social Science). 452p. 1985. lib. bdg. 50.00 (ISBN 0-8240-9049-7). Garland Pub.

Rape & Sexual Assault: Management & Intervention. Carmen G. Warner. LC 79-24643. 364p. 1980. text ed. 54.50 (ISBN 0-89443-172-2). Aspen Pub.

Rape & the Limits of Law Reform. Jeanne C. Marsh et al. 171p. 1982. 26.95 (ISBN 0-86569-083-9). Auburn Hse.

Rape & Victims of Rape. Vimala Veeraraghavan. 126p. 1987. 24.95. Asia Bk Corp.

Rape & Woman's Identity. William B. Sanders. LC 80-13346. (Sage Library of Social Research: Vol. 106). (Illus.). 184p. 1980. 24.50 (ISBN 0-8039-1449-0); pap. 12.50 (ISBN 0-8039-1450-4). Sage.

Rape Controversy. Melissa Benn et al. 1986. 20.00x (ISBN 0-946088-23-3, Pub. by NCCL UK). State Mutual Bk.

Rape: Crisis & Recovery. Ann W. Burgess & Lynda L. Holmstrom. LC 79-51507. (Illus.). 350p. 1979. pap. 18.95 (ISBN 0-87619-433-1). P-H.

Rape Crisis Intervention Handbook: A Guide to Victim Care. Ed. by Sharon L. McCombie. LC 80-14191. (Illus.). 250p. 1980. 27.50x (ISBN 0-306-40401-X, Plenum Pr). Plenum Pub.

Rape in Medieval England: An Historical & Sociological Study. John M. Carter. 196p. (Orig.). 1985. lib. bdg. 26.25 (ISBN 0-8191-4503-3); pap. text ed. 12.00 (ISBN 0-8191-4504-1). U Pr of Amer.

Rape in Paradise. Theon Wright. (Orig.). 1981. pap. 2.75 (ISBN 0-505-51716-7, Pub. by Tower Bks). Leisure NY.

Rape: Index of Modern Information with Bibliography. Marie R. Drake. LC 88-47798. 150p. (Orig.). 1988. 34.50 (ISBN 0-88164-880-9); pap. 26.50 (ISBN 0-88164-881-7). ABBE Pubs Assn.

Rape Intervention Resource Manual. Patrick Mills. 300p. 1977. 37.25 (ISBN 0-398-03594-6). C C Thomas.

Rape of a Nation. Jimmy Swaggart. 1985. 12.95 (ISBN 0-935113-00-2). Swaggart Ministries.

Rape of a Noble Ideology. Aslam Munjee. 487p. 1986. write for info. (ISBN 0-9617573-0-2). First Amend Pubs.

Rape of Clarissa: Writing, Sexuality & Class-Struggle in Richardson. Terry Eagleton. 128p. 1982. 25.00x (ISBN 0-8166-1204-8); pap. 11.95 (ISBN 0-8166-1209-9). U of Minn Pr.

Rape of Florida. facs. ed. Albery A. Whitman. LC 75-83895. (Black Heritage Library Collection Ser). 1884. 9.00 (ISBN 0-8369-8689-X). Ayer Co Pubs.

Rape of Florida. facsimile ed. Albery A. Whitman. LC 71-104595. Repr. of 1885 ed. lib. bdg. 8.00 (ISBN 0-8398-2166-2). Irvington.

Rape of Justice: MacArthur & the New Guinea Hangings. Walter A. Luszki. LC 86-21424. (Illus.). 210p. 1987. 25.00 (ISBN 0-89727-075-4). ISHI PA.

Rape of Lucrece. Ed. by J. W. Lever. 1981. pap. 3.75 (ISBN 0-14-070723-9). Penguin.

Rape of Ma Bell: The Criminal. Constantine R. Kraus & Alfred W. Duerig. 386p. 1988. 19.95 (ISBN 0-8184-0468-X). Lyle Stuart.

Rape of Nations: A Study in Societal Economics. C. Pensare. LC 73-88364. 1969. 18.50x (ISBN 0-912010-01-0); 14.50x, spiral bdg. (ISBN 0-912010-00-2). Goss.

Rape of Poland. Stanislaw Mikolajczyk. LC 73-141282. (Illus.). 309p. 1972. Repr. of 1948 ed. lib. bdg. 38.50x (ISBN 0-8371-5879-6, MIRP). Greenwood.

Rape of Shavi. Buchi Emecheta. 178p. 1985. pap. 6.95 (ISBN 0-8076-1118-2). Braziller.

Rape of the Blindfolded Lady. Carole Raft. 1979. pap. 2.25 (ISBN 0-933664-00-1). Motiv Methods.

Rape of the Indian Lands: An Original Anthology. Ed. by Paul W. Gates & Stuart Bruchey. LC 78-56698. (Management of Public Lands in the U. S. Ser.). 1979. lib. bdg. 23.00x (ISBN 0-405-11358-7). Ayer Co Pubs.

Rape of the Lock. Aubrey Beardsley & Alexander Pope. pap. 3.95 (ISBN 0-486-21963-1). Dover.

Rape of the Lock. 3rd ed. Alexander Pope. Ed. by G. Tillotson. 1971. pap. 4.95x (ISBN 0-423-87290-7, NO. 2389). Routledge Chapman & Hall.

Rape of the Lock. Alexander Pope. Ed. by J. S. Cunningham. 1966. pap. 4.95x (ISBN 0-19-911012-3). Oxford U Pr.

Rape of the Lock & Its Illustrations 1714-1896. Robert Halsband. 1980. 39.95x (ISBN 0-19-812098-2). Oxford U Pr.

Rape of the Lock. Flaubert's Mythic Realism. Robert Griffin. LC 87-81916. (French Forum Monographs: No. 70). 352p. (Orig.). 1988. pap. 24.95x (ISBN 0-917058-71-2). French Forum.

Rape of the Locks. Menander. Tr. by Gilbert Murray. 1942. pap. text ed. 3.95x (ISBN 0-04-882046-6). Unwin Hyman.

Rape of the Male. Richard F. Doyle. LC 76-3141. (Illus.). 286p. 1976. pap. 5.95 (ISBN 0-917212-01-0). Poor Richards.

Rape of the Masses: The Psychology of Totalitarian Political Propaganda. Serge Chakotin. LC 77-157553. (Studies in Philosophy, No. 40). 1971. lib. bdg. 49.95x (ISBN 0-8383-1264-0). Haskell.

Rape of the Nicollet Mall Mannequin. Steve Hall. LC 78-64893. 1978. pap. 2.50 (ISBN 0-9602068-0-9). Con Brio.

Rape of the Nile: Tomb Robbers, Tourists, and Archaeologists in Egypt. Brian Fagan. LC 75-11857. (Illus.). 416p. 1975. 14.95 (ISBN 0-684-14235-X, ScribT). Scribner.

Rape of the Powerless. Ed. by William Osborne. 212p. 1971. 66.00 (ISBN 0-677-14720-1); pap. 32.00 (ISBN 0-677-14725-2). Gordon & Breach.

Rape of the Sabine Women. Janemarie Luecke. 1978. 5.95 (ISBN 0-87482-097-9). Wake-Brook.

Rape: Offenders & Their Victims. John M. Macdonald. 352p. 1979. 42.50x (ISBN 0-398-01181-8). C C Thomas.

Rape on Trial. Zsuzsanna Adler. LC 86-15586. 224p. 1987. 35.00 (ISBN 0-7102-0804-9, 08049, Pub. by Routledge UK). Routledge Chapman & Hall.

Rape: Social Facts from England & America. Donna I. Qureshi. 293p. 1979. pap. text ed. 8.60x (ISBN 0-87563-178-9). Stipes.

Rape: The Evidential Examination & Management of the Sexual Assault Survivor. William M. Green. LC 88-45224. 192p. 1988. 30.00xt (ISBN 0-669-19412-3). Lexington Bks.

Rape: The New Attitude for Prevention. R. R. Green. LC 86-82844. (Illus.). 104p. (Orig.). 1986. 6.95; pap. 4.95. Green Prodns.

Rape Victim. Elaine Hilberman. LC 76-5627. 112p. 1976. pap. 12.00x (ISBN 0-89042-142-0, 42-142-0). Am Psychiatric.

Rape Victim. Koss & Harvey. 1987. 19.95 (ISBN 0-8289-0616-5). Greene.

Rape Victimology. LeRoy G. Schultz. 424p. 1975. 46.75 (ISBN 0-398-03183-5). C C Thomas.

Rape Victims, Offenders, Treatment & Jurisprudence: Medical Subject Analysis & Research Guide. American Health Research Institute Staff. Ed. by John C. Bartone. LC 83-45537. 140p. 1984. 34.50 (ISBN 0-88164-122-7); pap. 26.50 (ISBN 0-88164-123-5). ABBE Pubs Assn.

Rape: What Would You Do If...? Dianna D. Booher. LC 81-914. 128p. (gr. 7 up). 1981. PLB 11.29 (ISBN 0-671-42201-4); pap. 4.95 (ISBN 0-671-49485-6). Messner.

Rape Within Marriage: A Moral Analysis Delayed. Edward J. Bayer. LC 85-5289. 160p. (Orig.). 1985. lib. bdg. 26.25 (ISBN 0-8191-4613-7); pap. text ed. 10.25 (ISBN 0-8191-4614-5). U Pr of Amer.

Rapes of Lucretia: A Myth & Its Transformations. Ian Donaldson. (Illus.). 1982. 34.95x (ISBN 0-19-812638-7). Oxford U Pr.

Rapeseed. Ed. by L. A. Appelqvist & R. Ohlson. 391p. 1973. 144.75 (ISBN 0-444-40892-4). Elsevier.

Raphael. James Beck. LC 73-12198. (Library of Great Painters). 1976. 45.00 (ISBN 0-8109-0432-2). Abrams.

Raphael. Leopold D. Ettlinger & Helen S. Ettlinger. (Illus.). 240p. 1987. 75.00 (ISBN 0-7148-2303-1). Salem Hse Pubs.

Raphael. Geoffrey Hinton. 10p. 1982. 6.50x (ISBN 0-317-54589-2, Pub. by Ashmolean Museum). State Mutual Bk.

Raphael. Roger Jones & Nicholas Penny. LC 83-1390. 240p. 1983. 45.00x (ISBN 0-300-03061-4). Yale U Pr.

Raphael. Roger Jones & Nicholas Penny. LC 83-1390. 256p. 1987. pap. 19.95x (ISBN 0-300-04052-0, Y-673). Yale U Pr.

Raphael. R. A. MacAvoy. 240p. 1984. pap. 2.95 (ISBN 0-553-25978-4). Bantam.

Raphael. Bruno Santi. (Illus.). 80p. (Orig.). 1981. pap. 13.95 (ISBN 0-935748-21-0). Scala Books.

Raphael & America. David A. Brown. LC 82-22405. (Illus.). pap. 5.00 (ISBN 0-89468-064-1). Natl Gallery Art.

Raphael Before Rome: A Symposium. Ed. by James Beck. (Studies in the History of Art: No. 17). (Illus.). 260p. (Orig.). 1985. pap. 27.50x (ISBN 0-89468-080-3, Dist. by U Pr New Eng). Natl Gallery Art.

Raphael Drawings in the Ashmolean Museum. pap. 12.50 (ISBN 0-900090-99-5, Pub. by Ashmolean Mus). Longwood Pub Group.

Raphael: His Life & His Art with a Portfolio in Full Color of His Best Known Masterpieces. Edward Mc Curdy. (Illus.). 217p. 1987. 277.75 (ISBN 0-86650-212-2). Gloucester Art.

Raphael, His Life & Works. Joseph A. Crowe. LC 72-2584. (Select Bibliographies Reprint Ser). 1972. Repr. of 1885 ed. 48.00 (ISBN 0-8369-6852-2). Ayer Co Pubs.

Raphael: His Life, His Art, His Fortunes, 2 vols. Vincent Golzio. (Great Masters of the World Ser.). (Illus.). 765p. 1982. Repr. of 1968 ed. 237.45 (ISBN 0-89901-089-X). Found Class Reprints.

Raphael: His Life, Works & Times. Eugene Muntz. Ed. by Walter Armstrong. LC 77-9327. 1977. Repr. of 1888 ed. lib. bdg. 65.00 (ISBN 0-89341-202-3). Longwood Pub Group.

Raphael Sanzio. Ernest Raboff. LC 87-45299. (Trophy Nonfiction Art for Children). (Illus.). 32p. (gr. 1 up). 1988. pap. 5.95 (ISBN 0-06-446075-4, Trophy). HarpJ.

Raphael Sanzio. Ernest Raboff. LC 87-45314. (Art for Children Ser.). (Illus.). 32p. (gr. 1 up). 1988. Repr. of 1971 ed. 11.95i (ISBN 0-397-32227-5, Lipp Jr Bks). HarpJ.

Raphael Semmes, Rear Admiral, Confederate States Navy, Brigadier General, Confederate States Army. Ed. by Caldwell Delaney. (Illus.). 1978. 25.00 (ISBN 0-914334-05-0); pap. 10.00 (ISBN 0-914334-06-9). Museum Mobile.

Raphael Soriano: A Bibliography. Sara S. Richardson. (Architecture Ser.: A 1766). 10p. 1987. 3.00 (ISBN 1-55590-196-4). Vance Biblios.

Raphael Soyer: Fifty Years of Printmaking, 1917-1967. Sylvan Cole, Jr. LC 67-29917. (Graphic Art Ser.). 1967. 39.50 (ISBN 0-306-70986-4). Da Capo.

Raphael Soyer Life Drawings & Portraits: 42 Plates. Raphael Soyer. (Art Library). 48p. (Orig.). 1986. pap. 3.50 (ISBN 0-486-25100-4). Dover.

Raphael: Tables of Houses. Raphael. 4.95x (ISBN 0-685-38474-8). Wehman.

Raphael's Astro Ephemeris (Any Year) Raphael. pap. 4.95x (ISBN 0-685-22085-0). Wehman.

Raphael's Bible: A Study of the Vatican Logge. Bernice F. Davidson. LC 84-43088. (College Art Association Monographs: Vol. 39). (Illus.). 198p. 1985. 30.00 (ISBN 0-271-00388-X). Pa St U Pr.

Raphael's Drawings. Sanzio Raffaele. LC 83-45844. Repr. of 1945 ed. 37.50 (ISBN 0-404-20208-X). AMS Pr.

Raphael's Key to Astrology. Raphael. 118p. Date not set. pap. 7.00 (ISBN 0-89540-142-8, SB-142). Sun Pub.

Rapid Access Guide to Physical Examination. Novey. 1988. 22.50 (ISBN 0-8151-6434-3). Year Bk Med.

Rapid & Reliable Analysis. Reinhold Ebertin. 68p. 1970. 7.00 (ISBN 0-86690-093-4, 1099-01). Am Fed Astrologers.

Rapid Assessement Procedures for Nutrition & Primary Health Care: Anthropological Approaches to Improving Programme Effectiveness, Vol.11. Susan C. Scrimshaw & Elena Hurtado. LC 87-3193. 70p. 1987. pap. 8.95 (ISBN 0-317-65403-9). UCLA Lat Am Ctr.

Rapid Assessment Procedures for Nutrition & Primary Health Care. Susan C. Scrimshaw & Elena Hurtado. LC 87-3193. (Reference Ser.). 69p. (Orig.). 1987. wkbk. 8.95 (ISBN 0-87903-111-5). UCLA Lat Am Ctr.

Rapid Company Growth: How to Plan & Manage Small Company Expansion. A. C. Hazel & A. S. Reid. 166p. 1979. 24.75x (ISBN 0-220-67025-0, Pub. by Busn Bks England). Brookfield Pub Co.

Rapid Construction: A Bibliography. Mary Vance. (Architecture Ser.: Bibliography A 1330). 1985. pap. 2.00 (ISBN 0-89028-280-3). Vance Biblios.

Rapid Deployment Force & U. S. Military Intervention in the Persian Gulf. 2nd ed. Jeffrey Record. LC 83-81086. (Special Report Ser.). 83p. 1983. 7.50 (ISBN 0-89549-053-6). Inst Foreign Policy Anal.

Rapid Deployment Underwater Search & Rescue: Organizing, Training & Equipping an Emergency Service Dive Team. Eric Tackett. Ed. by Ruth A. Hunsinger. (Illus.). 150p. (Orig.). 1987. pap. 16.95 (ISBN 0-318-22568-9); instr's. guide 15.95 (ISBN 0-943155-06-1, 1021). Lasertech.

Rapid Detection & Identification of Infectious Agents. Ed. by David Kingsbury & Stanley Falkow. 1985. 35.00 (ISBN 0-12-408550-4). Acad Pr.

Rapid Diagnosis in Infectious Diseases. Michael J. Rytel. 224p. 1979. 89.00 (ISBN 0-8493-5535-4). CRC Pr.

Rapid Electrical Estimating & Pricing. 4th, rev. ed. C. Kenneth Kolstad & Gerald V. Kohnert. (Illus.). 352p. 1986. text ed. 49.75 (ISBN 0-07-035131-7). McGraw.

Rapid Evaluation of Potential Fields in Particle Systems. Leslie F. Greengard. (ACM Distinguished Dissertation Ser.). 110p. 1988. text ed. 25.00x (ISBN 0-262-07110-X). MIT Pr.

Rapid Excavation & Tunneling Conference Proceedings, 1983, 2 vols. Ed. by Harry Sutcliffe & John W. Wilson. LC 83-70933. (Illus.). 1258p. 1983. Set. 70.00x (ISBN 0-89520-411-8, 411-8). Soc Mining Eng.

Rapid Excavation: Problems & Progress Proceedings. Tunnel & Shaft Conference, Minneapolis, 1968. Ed. by Donald H. Yardley. LC 78-98023. (Illus.). pap. 105.00 (ISBN 0-317-10974-X, 2002907). Bks Demand UMI.

Rapid Guide to Hazardous Chemicals in the Workplace. Sax & Lewis. 1986. pap. 21.95 (ISBN 0-442-28220-6). Van Nos Reinhold.

Rapid Guide to Hazardous Chemicals in the Workplace. N. Irving Sax & Richard J. Lewis. 1986. 19.95. Van Nos Reinhold.

Rapid Healing Foods. Ben Davis. LC 79-22770. 1980. 18.95 (ISBN 0-13-753137-0, Parker). P-H.

Rapid Healing Foods. Ben Davis. 1982. pap. 5.95 (ISBN 0-13-753038-2, Reward). P-H.

Rapid Induction Hypnosis & Self Hypnosis. Arnold Furst. 1982. 15.00 (ISBN 0-87505-326-2). Borden.

Rapid Interpretation of EKG's. 3rd ed. Dale Dubin. 1974. pap. 19.95 (ISBN 0-912912-00-6). Cover Pub.

Rapid Interpretation of EKG's. 4th ed. Dale B. Dubin. (Illus.). 310p. 1988. pap. text ed. 24.50 (ISBN 0-912912-01-4). Cover Pub.

Rapid Interpretation of Heart Sounds & Murmurs. 2nd. ed. Emanuel Stein & Abner J. Delman. (Illus.). 64p. 1985. 18.50 (ISBN 0-8121-0983-X). Lea & Febiger.

Rapid Italian for Students & Tourists. Michael Cagno & Ben D'Arlon. 1979. pap. 5.95x (ISBN 0-913298-05-0). S F Vanni.

Rapid Math Without a Calculator. A. Frederick Collins. Orig. Title: Magic with Figures. 120p. (YA) 1987. pap. 4.95 (ISBN 0-8065-1058-7, Pub. by Citadel Pr). Lyle Stuart.

Rapid Maxillary Expansion. Donald S. Timms. 1981. 46.00 (ISBN 0-931386-49-7). Quint Pub Co.

Rapid Measurement of Concrete Pavement Thickness & Reinforcement Location: Field Evaluation of Nondestructive Systems. (National Cooperative Highway Research Program Report). 63p. 1976. 4.80 (ISBN 0-309-02777-2). Transport Res Bd.

Rapid Methods & Automation in Microbiology & Immunology. Ed. by K. O. Habermehl. (Illus.). 780p. 1985. 95.00 (ISBN 0-387-13695-9). Springer-Verlag.

Rapid Methods for Measuring Radioactivity in the Environment. (Proceedings Ser.). (Illus.). 967p. (Orig.). 1972. pap. 71.50 (ISBN 92-0-020371-X, ISP289, IAEA). UNIPUB.

Rare & Unlisted Toothpick Holders. William Heacock. (Illus.). 96p. (Orig.). 1984. pap. 11.95 (ISBN 0-915410-18-4). Antique Pubns.

Rare & Valuable Antique Arms. Jamese. Serven. 1976. 4.95 (ISBN 0-913150-37-1). Pioneer Pr.

Rare Animals. I. Akimushkin. (Illus.). 16p. 1978. pap. 1.99 (ISBN 0-8285-8817-1, Pub. by Progress Pubs USSR). Imported Pubns.

Rare Art Traditions: A History of Art Collecting & Its Linked Phenomena. Joseph Alsop. LC 81-47218. (Illus.). 464p. 1982. 59.45i (ISBN 0-06-010091-5, HarpT). Har-Row.

Rare Birds of Southern Africa. P. A. Clancey. (Illus.). Date not set. 69.95. Saifer.

Rare Birds of the West Coast of North America. Don Roberson. LC 80-51054. (Illus.). 548p. 1980. 24.95 (ISBN 0-9605352-0-9, Dist. by American Birding Association). Woodcock.

Rare Book & Manuscript Library of Columbia University: Collections & Treasures. Ed. by Kenneth A. Lohf & Rudolph Ellenbogen. 138p. 1985. pap. 25.00 (ISBN 0-9607862-1-X). Columbia U Libs.

Rare Book Collections: Some Theoretical & Practical Suggestions for Use by Librarians & Students. Ed. by Horace R. Archer. LC 81-13311. (ACRL Monograph: No. 27). viii, 128p. 1982. Repr. of 1965 ed. lib. bdg. 35.00x (ISBN 0-313-23226-1, ARRB). Greenwood.

Rare Book Librarianship. 2nd rev. ed. Roderick Cave. 162p. 1982. 20.00 (ISBN 0-85157-328-2, Pub. by Bingley England). ALA.

Rare Books for Law Libraries. Thomas H. Reynolds. (Law Library Information Reports: Vol. 5). 141p. 1983. pap. 100.00 (ISBN 0-87802-080-2). Glanville.

Rare Books of Freemasonry. Lionel Vibert. 1987. pap. 5.95 (ISBN 0-916411-73-7, Sure Fire). Holmes Pub.

Rare Books Slavica from the University of Colorado Libraries. Sonia Jacobs & Eugene Petriwsky. (Illus.). 1988. 40.00x (ISBN 0-911797-39-4). R Rinehart Inc.

Rare Books, 1983-84: Trends, Collections, Sources. Ed. by Alice Schreyer. 581p. 1984. 49.95 (ISBN 0-8352-1756-6). Bowker.

Rare Brass Rubbings from the Ashmolean Collection. Jerome Bertram. (Illus.). 40p. (Orig.). 1977. 2.50 (ISBN 0-900090-34-0, Pub. by Ashmolean Museum). State Mutual Bk.

Rare Brass Rubbings from the Ashmolean Collection. Jerome Bertram. (Illus.). 40p. (Orig.). 1977. pap. 5.50 (ISBN 0-317-58650-5, Pub. by Ashmolean Mus). Longwood Pub Group.

Rare Breed: The Entrepreneur, an American Culture. Wiliam MacPhee. 225p. 1987. 19.95 (ISBN 0-917253-75-2). Probus Pub Co.

Rare Character Dolls. Maree Tarnowska. (Illus.). 144p. 1987. 25.00 (ISBN 0-87588-306-0). Hobby Hse.

Rare Coin Score. Richard Stark. 160p. 1984. 13.95 (ISBN 0-8052-8182-7, Pub. by Allison & Busb y England). Schocken.

Rare Collection: Superb Recipes. Junior League of Galveston County, Inc. & Paula Roberts. LC 84-81639. (Illus.). 320p. 1985. 15.95 (ISBN 0-9613779-0-9). Jr League Galveston.

Rare Early Essays on George Eliot. Carmen J. Dello Buono. 211p. 1980. lib. bdg. 32.50 (ISBN 0-8482-3660-2). R West.

Rare Earth Element Geochemistry. Ed. by P. Henderson. (Developments in Geochemistry: Vol. 2). 510p. 1984. 121.00 (ISBN 0-444-42148-3). Elsevier.

Rare Earth Elements. Moscow. 368p. Repr. of 1963 ed. text ed. 70.00X (ISBN 0-7065-0095-4, Pub. by Keter Pub Jerusalem). Coronet Bks.

Rare Earth Permanent Magnets. E. A. Nesbitt & J. A. Wernick. (Materials Science Ser). 1973. 30.00 (ISBN 0-12-515450-X). Acad Pr.

Rare Earth Permanent Magnets. Parker. 1987. write for info. (ISBN 0-471-82293-0). Wiley.

Rare Earth Research, Vol. 1. Ed. by Joseph F. Nachman & C. E. Lundin. (Rare Earth Research Ser.). 370p. 1962. 140.00 (ISBN 0-677-10490-1). Gordon & Breach.

Rare Earth Research, Vol. 2. Ed. by Karl S. Vorres. (Rare Earth Research Ser.). 638p. 1964. 188.00 (ISBN 0-677-10620-3). Gordon & Breach.

Rare Earth Research, Vol. 3. Ed. by L. Eyring. (Rare Earth Research Ser.). 770p. 1965. 228.00 (ISBN 0-677-10130-9). Gordon & Breach.

Rare Earth Technology & Applications. Ed. by F. Villani. LC 80-42. (Chemical Technology Review: No. 154). (Illus.). 367p. 1980. 48.00 (ISBN 0-8155-0795-X). Noyes.

Rare Earths. C. K. Jorgenson et al. (Structure & Bonding Ser.: Vol. 25). (Illus.). iv, 152p. 1976. 46.00 (ISBN 0-387-07508-9). Springer-Verlag.

Rare Earths. E. Nieboehr et al. LC 67-11280. (Structure & Bonding Ser.: Vol. 22). iv, 1p. 1975. 43.00 (ISBN 0-387-07268-3). Springer-Verlag.

Rare Earths. Ed. by S. P. Sinha et al. LC 67-11280. (Structure & Bonding Ser: Vol. 30). 1976. 42.00 (ISBN 0-387-07887-8). Springer-Verlag.

Rare Earths. Ed. by F. H. Spedding & A. H. Danne. LC 61-15413. 654p. 1971. Repr. of 1961 ed. 42.50 (ISBN 0-88275-052-6). Krieger.

Rare Earths & Actinides Nineteen Seventy-Seven: Durham. (Institute of Physics Conference Ser.: No. 37). 1978. cancelled 49.00 (ISBN 0-85498-128-4, Pub. by Inst Physics England). IPS.

Rare Earths in Modern Science & Technology, Vol. 3. Ed. by Gregory J. McCarthy & Herbert B. Silber. LC 78-5365. 610p. 1982. 85.00x (ISBN 0-306-40919-4, Plenum Pr). Plenum Pub.

Rare Earths Spectroscopy: Proceedings of the International Symposium on Rare Earth Spectroscopy. Ed. by B. Jezowska-Trzebiatowska et al. 500p. 1985. 86.00 (ISBN 9971-978-38-5). World Scientific Pub.

Rare Gas Solids. (Springer Tracts in Modern Physics Ser.: Vol. 103). (Illus.). 115p. 1984. 34.00 (ISBN 0-387-13272-4). Springer-Verlag.

Rare Gas Solids, Vol. 1. Ed. by M. L. Klein & J. A. Venables. 1976. 127.00 (ISBN 0-12-413501-3). Acad Pr.

Rare Gas Solids, Vol. 2. Ed. by M. L. Klein & J. A. Venables. 1977. 112.00 (ISBN 0-12-413502-1). Acad Pr.

Rare Halos, Mirages, Anomalous Rainbows, & Related Electromagnetic Phenomena. William R. Corliss. (Catalog of Geophysical Anomalies Ser.). (Illus.). 244p. 1984. 12.95 (ISBN 0-915554-12-7). Sourcebook.

Rare Integrity: The Biography of L. W. Payne, Jr., A Noble Texan. Hansen Alexander. 50p. 1986. 35.00 (ISBN 0-932119-02-6). Wind River Pr.

Rare Jewel of Christian Contentment. Jeremiah Burroughs. 1979. pap. 5.95 (ISBN 0-85151-091-4). Banner of Truth.

Rare Masterpieces of Arab & Islamic Art. Prisse D'Avenes. 1840. 125.00x (ISBN 0-86685-373-1). Intl Bk Ctr.

Rare Masterpieces of Russian Piano Music. Ed. by Dmitry Feofanov. (Music Scores & Music to Play Ser.). 144p. 1984. pap. 6.95 (ISBN 0-486-24659-0). Dover.

Rare Metals. O. A. Songina. 565p. 1970. text ed. 109.00x (ISBN 0-7065-1029-1, Pub. by Keter Pub Jerusalem). Coronet Bks.

Rare Metals Handbook. 2nd ed. Ed. by Clifford A. Hampel. LC 61-10449. 732p. 1971. Repr. of 1961 ed. 52.50 (ISBN 0-88275-024-0). Krieger.

Rare People & Rare Books. 2nd ed. E. Millicent Sowerby. (Illus.). xxii, 248p. 1987. Repr. of 1967 ed. 22.50 (ISBN 0-916271-04-8). BkPr Ltd.

Rare Plant Conservation: Geographical Data Organization. Ed. by L. E. Morse & M. S. Henifin. 377p. 1981. pap. 25.00x (ISBN 0-89327-223-X). NY Botanical.

Rare Poems of the Sixteenth & Seventeenth Centuries. Repr. of 1883 ed. 25.00 (ISBN 0-686-19856-5). Ridgeway Bks.

Rare Prologues & Epilogues 1642-1700. Ed. by Autrey N. Wiley. LC 79-113350. (Illus.). 1970. Repr. of 1940 ed. 26.00x (ISBN 0-8046-0988-8, Pub. by Kennikat). Assoc Faculty Pr.

Rare Quarto Edition of Lord Byron's "Fugitive Pieces". Herbert C. Roe. LC 72-13685. 1973. lib. bdg. 25.00 (ISBN 0-8414-1262-6). Folcroft.

Rare Sculptures-Selections from Some Indian Museums. Contrib. by Laxmi P. Sihare. (Illus.). 48p. 1984. 15.00. Asia Bk Corp.

Rare Sir William Davenant: Poet Laureate, Playwright, Civil War General, Restoration Theatre Manager. Mary Edmond. LC 86-33913. 1987. 29.95 (ISBN 0-312-00783-3). St Martin.

Rare Triumphs of Love & Fortune. Ed. by W. W. Greg. LC 82-45799. (Malone Society Reprint Ser.: No. 69). Repr. of 1930 ed. 40.00 (ISBN 0-404-63069-3). AMS Pr.

Rare Wild Flowers of North America. rev. 2nd ed. Leonard Wiley. LC 73-80863. 1969. 15.00 (ISBN 0-911742-02-6); limited ed. 15.00 (ISBN 0-911742-00-X). L Wiley.

Rarefied Gas Dynamics. Ed. by O. M. Belotserkovskii et al. 1418p. 1985. 195.00x (ISBN 0-306-41932-7, Plenum Pr). Plenum Pub.

Rarefied Gas Dynamics, 2 vols. Hakuro Oguchi. 1130p. 1985. 125.00 (ISBN 0-86008-383-7, Pub. by U of Tokyo Japan). Columbia U Pr.

Rarefied Gas Dynamics, PAAS51, 2 vols. Ed. by J. Leith Potter. LC 76-57748. (Illus.). 1337p. 1977. 94.50 (ISBN 0-915928-15-9). AIAA.

Rarefied Gas Dynamics, PAAS74, 2 vols. Ed. by Sam S. Fisher. LC 81-7913. (Illus.). 1224p. 1981. 119.50 (ISBN 0-915928-51-5). AIAA.

Rarefied Gas Dynamics: Proceedings see Advances in Applied Mechanics: Supplements.

Rarefied Gas Flows: Theory & Experiment. Ed. by W. Fiszdon. (CISM-International Centre for Mechanical Sciences, Courses & Lectures: Vol. 224). (Illus.). 524p. 1982. pap. 49.00 (ISBN 0-387-81595-3). Springer-Verlag.

Rarefield Gas Dynamics. Ed. by K. Karamcheti. 1974. 84.50 (ISBN 0-12-398150-6). Acad Pr.

Rarest of These Is Hope. Harold C. Warlick, Jr. 1985. 7.50 (ISBN 0-89536-743-2, 5826). CSS of Ohio.

Raring to Retire. Alwyn James & Sheila Mackay. 120p. 1982. 35.00x (ISBN 0-904265-91-9, Pub. by Macdonald Pub UK); pap. 20.00x (ISBN 0-904265-92-7). State Mutual Bk.

Rarities of the Musee Guimet. Jeannine Auboyer. 123p. 1975. pap. 84.00x (Pub. by Han-Shan Tang Ltd). State Mutual Bk.

Rarotonga & the Cook Islands-A Travel Survival Kit. Tony Wheeler. (Illus.). 120p. (Orig.). 1986. pap. 7.95 (ISBN 0-908086-97-0). Lonely Planet.

Ras Shamra & the Bible. Charles F. Pfeiffer. (Baker Studies in Biblical Archaeology). 1976. pap. 2.95 (ISBN 0-8010-7003-1). Baker Bk.

Ras Shamra Mythological Texts. James A. Montgomery & Zellig S. Harris. LC 36-2726. (American Philosophical Society. Philadelphia. Memoirs: Vol. 4). pap. 34.80 (ISBN 0-317-09878-0, 2000354). Bks Demand UMI.

Rasa, or Knowledge of the Self. Rene Daumal. Tr. by Louise L. Levi from Fr. LC 81-22389. 128p. 1982. 12.95 (ISBN 0-8112-0824-9); pap. 5.95 (ISBN 0-8112-0825-7, NDP530). New Directions.

Rasa Tantra: Blood Marriage, The Sacred Initiation, A Marriage of the Faiths of East & West. Tsampa Yeshe Norbu. (Illus.). 36p. 1980. pap. 6.95 (ISBN 0-9609802-2-9). Life Science.

Rasas & Lament of the Sudra. Desmond O'Brien. LC 78-65696. (SCOP III Ser.). 1979. pap. 5.00 (ISBN 0-930526-02-3). SCOP Pubns.

Rasayana Siddhi: Medicine & Alchemy in the Buddhist Tantras. Edward T. Fenner. (Traditional Healing Ser.). 300p. 1984. 39.95 (ISBN 0-932426-28-X). Trado-Medic.

Rascal. Sterling North. (gr. 5 up). 1975. pap. 2.75 (ISBN 0-380-01518-8, Flare). Avon.

Rascal: A Memoir of a Better Era. Sterling North. LC 63-13882. (Illus.). (gr. 4 up). 1984. 12.95 (ISBN 0-525-18839-8). Dutton.

Rascal Says, "I'm Sorry". Paula J. Bussard. Ed. by Shirley Wigginton. (Critter County Ser.). (Illus.). 30p. (gr. k-4). 1987. 1.39 (ISBN 0-87403-253-9, 3453). Standard Pub.

Rascal's Choice. Paula J. Bussard. (Critter County Ser.). (Illus.). 32p. (gr. k-6). 1986. 1.29 (ISBN 0-87403-103-6, 3433). Standard Pub.

Rascal's Close Call. Paula Bussard. (Critter County Ser.). (Illus.). 28p. (gr. k-3). 1985. 1.29 (ISBN 0-87239-962-1, 3382). Standard Pub.

Rascals Heaven. F. Van Wyck Mason. 1976. Repr. of 1964 ed. lib. bdg. 26.95 (ISBN 0-89190-351-8, Pub. by River City Pr). Amereon Ltd.

Rascals in Paradise. James A. Michener. 384p. 1987. pap. 4.95 (ISBN 0-449-21459-1, Crest). Fawcett.

Rascals in Paradise. James A. Michener & A. Grove Day. 1957. 17.95 (ISBN 0-394-44220-2). Random.

Rasco & the Rats of NIMH. Jane L. Conly. LC 85-42634. (Illus.). 288p. (gr. 4-7). 1986. 12.95i (ISBN 0-06-021361-2); PLB 12.89 (ISBN 0-06-021362-0). HarpJ.

Rasco & the Rats of NIMH. Jane L. Conly. LC 85-42634. (Illus.). 288p. (gr. 4-7). 1988. pap. 3.50 (ISBN 0-06-440246-0, Trophy). HarpJ.

Rash Act. Ford Madox Ford. 348p. 1982. Repr. of 1933 ed. lib. bdg. 39.50. Century Bookbindery.

Rash Act. Ford Madox Ford. 348p. 1985. 14.95 (ISBN 0-85635-399-X); pap. 8.50 (ISBN 0-85635-529-1). Carcanet.

Rash, Reckless Love. Valerie Sherwood. 576p. (Orig.). 1983. pap. 4.95 (ISBN 0-446-32756-5). Warner Bks.

Rash Resolve; or, the Untimely Discovery. Eliza Haywood. Bd. with Life & Adventures of the Lady Lucy. Penelope Aubin. LC 74-170561. (Foundations of the Novel Ser.: Vol. 43). lib. bdg. 61.00 (ISBN 0-8240-0555-4). Garland Pub.

Rashad. Ahmad Rashad. 1988. 19.95 (ISBN 0-670-82301-5). Viking.

Rashanyn Dark. William Tedford. (Timequest Ser.: No. 1). 1981. pap. 2.25 (ISBN 0-8439-0869-6, Leisure Bks). Leisure NY.

Rashi. Chaim Pearl. 128p. 1988. 15.95 (ISBN 0-8021-1063-0). Grove.

Rashi: The Man & His World. Esra Shereshevsky. 288p. 1982. 17.50 (ISBN 0-87203-101-2). Hermon.

Rashi Vocalized for Beginners. text ed. 2.50 (ISBN 0-914131-52-4, B01). Torah Umesorah.

Rashid Ali-Al-Gailani: Political & Military Study of the British Campaign in Iraq. W. Hamdi. 290p. 1987. 150.00x (ISBN 1-85077-164-2, Pub. by Darf Pubs Ltd). State Mutual Bk.

Rashie Coat. Joan Hassall. 1985. 20.00x (ISBN 0-85411-040-2, Pub. by Saltire Soc.). State Mutual Bk.

Rashomon. Ed. by Donald Richie. (Films in Print Ser.). 226p. 1987. text ed. 28.00 (ISBN 0-8135-1179-8); pap. text ed. 13.00 (ISBN 0-8135-1180-1). Rutgers U Pr.

Rashomon & Other Stories. new ed. Ryunosuke Akutagawa. Tr. by Kojima Takashi. LC 52-9665. (Illus.). 1970. pap. 5.95 (ISBN 0-87140-214-9). Liveright.

Rashomon & Other Stories. Ryunosuke Akutagawa. Tr. by Kojima Takashi from Japanese. LC 83-50837. (Illus.). 102p. 1952. pap. 4.95 (ISBN 0-8048-1457-0). C E Tuttle.

Rashtriya Swayam Sewak Sangh. D. R. Goyal. 232p. 1979. 14.95. Asia Bk Corp.

Rashtriya Swayamsevak Sangh. Des Raj Goyal. 1979. 10.00x (ISBN 0-8364-0566-8, Pub. by Radha Krishna India). South Asia Bks.

Rasikapriya of Keshavadasa. Tr. by K. P. Bahadur. 1972. 18.50 (ISBN 0-89684-303-3). Orient Bk Dist.

Rasmus & the Vagabond. Astrid Lindgren. LC 86-30248. 192p. (gr. 3-7). 1987. pap. 4.95 (ISBN 0-14-032304-X, Puffin Bks). Penguin.

Rasmus Bjorn Anderson. Lloyd Hustvedt. Ed. by Franklyn D. Scott. LC 78-15189. (Scandinavians in America Ser.). (Illus.). 1979. Repr. of 1966 ed. lib. bdg. 30.50x (ISBN 0-405-11642-X). Ayer Co Pubs.

Rasp. Philip MacDonald. 1979. pap. 4.50 (ISBN 0-486-23864-4). Dover.

Rasp. Philip MacDonald. Date not set. pap. 3.95 (ISBN 0-394-72435-6, Vin). Random.

Rasp. Philip MacDonald. 280p. 1984. pap. 3.50 (ISBN 0-88184-094-7). Carroll & Graf.

Rasp. Philip MacDonald. 18.95 (ISBN 0-89190-094-2, Pub. by Am Repr). Amereon Ltd.

Raspail, Scientist & Reformer. Dora B. Weiner. LC 68-19761. (Illus.). 1968. 39.50x (ISBN 0-231-03059-2). Columbia U Pr.

Raspberries & Blackberries: Their Breeding, Diseases & Growth. D. L. Jennings. (Applied Botany & Crop Science Ser.). 230p. 1988. 39.95 (ISBN 0-12-384240-9). Acad Pr.

Raspberry Kingdom. Renee Hermanson. LC 78-62985. 1978. pap. 4.50 (ISBN 0-8358-0374-0). Upper Room.

Raspberry One. Charles Ferry. LC 82-25476. 224p. (gr. 7 up). 1983. 11.95 (ISBN 0-395-34069-1). HM.

Rasputin the Holy Devil. Rene Fulop-Miller. 1977. Repr. of 1928 ed. lib. bdg. 47.00 (ISBN 0-8414-4308-4). Folcroft.

Rasputin's Revenge. John T. Lescroart. LC 86-82179. 288p. 1987. 17.95 (ISBN 1-55611-011-1). D I Fine.

Rasputin's Revenge. John T. Lescroart. 288p. 1988. pap. 3.50 (ISBN 0-8439-2671-6, Pub. by Leisure Bks CT). Leisure NY.

Rasselas. Samuel Johnson. Ed. by Warren Fleischauer. LC 61-18208. (gr. 9 up). 1977. text ed. 6.95 (ISBN 0-8120-5070-3); pap. text ed. 4.95 (ISBN 0-8120-0153-2). Barron.

Rasselas, Prince of Abissinia. Samuel Johnson. Intro. by J. P. Hardy. (World's Classics Ser.). 216p. 1989. pap. 4.95 (ISBN 0-19-281778-7). Oxford U Pr.

Rassiia Nakanune 'Smutnogo Vremeni. R. G. Skrynnikov. 206p. (Rus.). 1980. 39.00x (ISBN 0-317-40857-7, Pub. by Collets (UK)). State Mutual Bk.

Rasskazy Nazara Il'icha, Gospodina Sinebriukhova. Mikhail Zoshchenko. 89p. (Rus.). 1982. pap. 3.50 (ISBN 0-933884-33-8). Berkeley Slavic.

Rasskazy O Tovarishche Staline i Drugikh Tovarishchakh: Tales about Com Stalin & Other Comrades. Ilia Suslov. LC 81-6312. 140p. (Rus.). 1981. pap. 7.50 (ISBN 0-938920-03-0). Hermitage.

Rasskazy: Stories. Fedor Sologub. Ed. by Evelyn Bristol. LC 79-25535. (Rus.). 1979. 22.50 (ISBN 0-933884-11-7); pap. 12.50 (ISBN 0-933884-10-9). Berkeley Slavic.

Rasta & Resistance: From Marcus Garvey to Walter Rodney. Horace Campbell. LC 85-73332. 240p. (Orig.). 1987. 32.95 (ISBN 0-86543-034-9); pap. 10.95 (ISBN 0-86543-035-7). Africa World.

Rastafarians. Kathy Williams. 1985. 13.00x (ISBN 0-7062-4063-4, Pub. by Ward Lock Educ Co Ltd). State Mutual Bk.

Rastafarians: Sounds of Cultural Dissonance. Leonard E. Barrett. LC 76-48491. (Illus.). 1977. pap. 9.95 (ISBN 0-8070-1115-0, BP559). Beacon Pr.

Rastafarians: Sounds of Cultural Dissonance. rev. ed. Leonard E. Barrett, Sr. LC 88-47662. (Illus.). 257p. 1988. pap. 11.95 (ISBN 0-8070-1027-8, BP 795). Beacon Pr.

Rastaman: The Rastafarian Movement in England. Ernest Cashmore. (Illus.). 272p. 1980. pap. text ed. 12.95 (ISBN 0-04-301116-4). Unwin Hyman.

Rastaman: The Rastafarian Movement in England. Ernest Cashmore. (Counterpoint Ser.). 263p. 1983. pap. 9.95 (ISBN 0-04-301164-0). Unwin Hyman.

Raster Graphics Handbook. 2nd ed. Conrac Corporation Staff. (Illus.). 360p. 1985. 44.95 (ISBN 0-442-21608-4). Van Nos Reinhold.

Raster Scanning, Processing, & Plotting of Cartographic Documents. Donna J. Peuquet & A. Raymond Boyle. 130p. (Orig.). 1984. pap. text ed. 39.95x (ISBN 0-913913-01-4). Spad Sys.

Rastus on Capitol Hill. Samuel Edison. LC 86-21135. 228p. (Orig.). 1986. pap. 8.45 (ISBN 0-89793-045-2). Hunter Hse.

Rastus on Capitol Hill. Samuel Edison. LC 87-32176. 221p. 1987. lib. bdg. 19.95x (ISBN 0-8095-6304-5). Borgo Pr.

Rasutin's Vintage. Kelly Buchanan. 239p. (Orig.). 1988. pap. 10.00 (ISBN 0-945679-00-9). XAXI Pr Pub.

Rat. Gunter Grass. Tr. by Ralph Manheim. LC 86-31817. 1987. 17.95 (ISBN 0-15-175920-0). HarBraceJ.

Rat: A Study in Behavior. 3rd, rev. ed. S. A. Barnett. LC 74-33509. xiv, 318p. 1976. lib. bdg. 22.00x (ISBN 0-226-03740-1); pap. 11.00x (ISBN 0-226-03742-8). U of Chicago Pr.

Rat-a-Tat, Pitter Pat. Alan Benjamin. LC 87-568. (Illus.). 40p. (ps-k). 1987. 11.95i (ISBN 0-690-04609-X, Crowell Jr Bks); PLB 11.89 (ISBN 0-690-04611-1). HarpJ.

Rat-a-Tat, Pitter Pat. Alan Benjamin. (Illus.). (ps-k). 11.95 (ISBN 0-317-62898-4, Crowell Jr Bks). HarpJ.

Rational-Emotive Therapy: Fundamentals & Innovations. Windy Dryden. 192p. 1983. 25.00 (ISBN 0-7099-0848-2, Pub. by Croom Helm Ltd). Routledge Chapman & Hall.

Rational-Emotive Therapy with Children & Adolescents: Theory, Treatment Strategies, Preventative Methods. Michael E. Bernard & Marie R. Joyce. LC 83-23442. (Personality Processes Ser.: 1-341). 489p. 1984. 45.95x (ISBN 0-471-87543-0). Wiley.

Rational Enterprise: Logos in Plato's Theaetetus. Rosemary Desjardins. (Ancient Greek Philosophy Ser.). 288p. 1988. 49.50 (ISBN 0-88706-837-5); pap. 16.95 (ISBN 0-88706-838-3). State U NY Pr.

Rational Expectation in Macroeconomics. C. L. E. Attfield et al. 232p. 1985. 39.95x (ISBN 0-631-13963-X); pap. 17.95x (ISBN 0-631-13964-8). Basil Blackwell.

Rational Expectations. Steven M. Shefrin. LC 82-19747. (Cambridge Surveys of Economic Literature Ser.). 215p. 1983. pap. 12.95 (ISBN 0-521-28595-X). Cambridge U Pr.

Rational Expectations: An Elementary Exposition. G. K. Shaw. LC 83-40180. 200p. 1984. 22.95 (ISBN 0-312-66402-8). St Martin.

Rational Expectations: An Elementary Exposition. G. K. Shaw. LC 83-19252. 131p. 1985. pap. 9.95 (ISBN 0-312-66403-6). St Martin.

Rational Expectations & Econometric Practice, 2 vols. Ed. by Robert E. Lucas, Jr. & Thomas J. Sargent. LC 80-24602. 776p. 1981. Set 2 Vols In 1. 60.00x (ISBN 0-8166-0916-0); Vol. 1. pap. 15.95x (ISBN 0-8166-0917-9); Vol. 2. pap. 15.95x (ISBN 0-8166-1071-1); Paperbound Set. pap. 31.90x (ISBN 0-8166-1098-3). U of Minn Pr.

Rational Expectations & Economic Policy. Ed. by Stanley Fischer. LC 79-22661. x, 294p. 1982. pap. text ed. 11.00x (ISBN 0-226-25134-9). U of Chicago Pr.

Rational Expectations & Inflation. Thomas Sargent. 208p. 1985. pap. text ed. 14.95 scp (ISBN 0-06-045741-4, HarpC). Har-Row.

Rational Expectations & Monetary Policies. J. J. Sijben. LC 79-56565. 144p. 1980. 37.50x (ISBN 0-686-27288-9, Pub. by Sijthoff & Noordhoff). Kluwer Academic.

Rational Expectations & the New Macroeconomics. Patrick Minford & David Peel. 230p. 1984. 34.95x (ISBN 0-85520-713-2); pap. 14.95x (ISBN 0-85520-714-0). Basil Blackwell.

Rational Expectations Approach to Macroeconomics: Testing Policy Ineffectiveness & Efficient-Markets Models. Frederic S. Mishkin. LC 82-20049. (National Bureau of Economic Research-Monograph). 192p. 1983. lib. bdg. 20.00x (ISBN 0-226-53186-4). U of Chicago Pr.

Rational Expectations Approach to Macroeconomics: Testing Policy Ineffectiveness & Efficient-Markets Models. Frederick S. Mishkin. LC 82-20049. (National Bureau of Economic Research Monograph). (Illus.). xii, 172p. 1984. pap. text ed. 9.00x (ISBN 0-226-53187-2). U of Chicago Pr.

Rational Expectations: Macroeconomics for the 1980s? M. Carter & R. Maddock. 165p. 1984. text ed. 35.00x (ISBN 0-333-33143-5, Pub. by Macmillan UK). Humanities.

Rational Expectations, Non-Market Clearing & Investment Theory. Mark Precious. (Illus.). 176p. 1987. 45.00 (ISBN 0-19-877256-4); pap. 19.95 (ISBN 0-19-877255-6). Oxford U Pr.

Rational Expectations Revolution in Macroeconomics: Theories & Evidence. David K. Begg. LC 82-47785. 304p. (Orig.). 1982. pap. 12.95x (ISBN 0-8018-2882-1). Johns Hopkins.

Rational Exultation. Seelye. 1985. 3.50 (ISBN 0-912296-70-4, Dist. by U Pr of Va). Am Antiquarian.

Rational Faith: Essays in Honor of Levi A. Olan. Ed. by J. Bemporad. 15.00x (ISBN 0-87068-448-5). Ktav.

Rational Fault Analysis. Ed. by Richard Saeks & Stanley Liberty. (Electrical Engineering & Electronics Ser.: Vol. 1). 1977. 65.00 (ISBN 0-8247-6541-9). Dekker.

Rational Finite Element Basis. Eugene L. Wachspress. (Mathematics in Science & Engineering Ser.). 1975. 65.50 (ISBN 0-12-728950-X). Acad Pr.

Rational Foundation of Ethics. Timothy Sprigge. 272p. 1988. text ed. 47.50 (ISBN 0-7102-0705-0, Pub. by Kegan Paul). Routledge Chapman & Hall.

Rational Geriatric Drug Therapy: An Interdisciplinary Approach, 2 vols. Ed. by Cyrelle K. Gerson & Eleanor Beavers. 1979. pap. text ed. 25.00 (ISBN 0-917330-43-9). Am Pharm Assn.

Rational Grammar. Jean-Louis Gardies. Tr. by Kevin Mulligan. LC 84-23002. 360p. (Fr.). 1986. 59.95x (ISBN 0-8132-0611-1). Cath U Pr.

Rational Homotopy Theory & Differential Forms. P. A. Griffiths & J. Morgan. (Progress in Mathematics Ser.: Vol. 16). 256p. 1981. text ed. 22.50x (ISBN 0-8176-3041-4). Birkhauser.

Rational Homotopy Type. W Wu. (Lecture Notes in Mathematics Ser.: Vol. 1264). viii, 219p. 1987. pap. 20.00 (ISBN 0-387-13611-8). Springer-Verlag.

Rational Investment Behavior in the Face of Floods. C. B. McGuire. LC 79-135090. 151p. 1969. 29.00 (ISBN 0-403-04517-7). Scholarly.

Rational Irrational Man: Torah Psychology. Avrohom Amsel. 1976. pap. 7.95 (ISBN 0-87306-129-2). Feldheim.

Rational Landscapes & Humanistic Geography. Edward Relph. LC 81-10782. 232p. 1981. 27.50x (ISBN 0-389-20237-1, 07033). B&N Imports.

Rational Legitimacy: A Theory of Political Support. Ronald Rogowski. LC 74-2975. 256p. 1974. 37.00x (ISBN 0-691-07563-8). Princeton U Pr.

Rational Love. Warren Shibles. LC 77-93187. 1978. pap. 7.00 (ISBN 0-912386-13-4). Language Pr.

Rational Man: A Modern Interpretation of Aristotelian Ethics. Henry B. Veatch. LC 62-16161. (Midland Bks.: No. 71). 228p. 1962. pap. 8.95x (ISBN 0-253-20071-7). Ind U Pr.

Rational Man & Irrational Society? An Introduction & Sourcebook. Brian Barry & Russell Hardin. (Illus.). 432p. 1982. 30.00 (ISBN 0-8039-1850-X); pap. 14.95 (ISBN 0-8039-1851-8). Sage.

Rational Management of Children. 2nd rev ed. Paul Hauck. 1972. 7.95 (ISBN 0-87212-018-X). Libra.

Rational Manager. Charles H. Kepner & Benjamin Tregoe. LC 65-21586. 240p. 1976. Repr. of 1965 ed. 17.50 (ISBN 0-686-38777-5). Princet Res Pr.

Rational Mechanics of Materials see Continuum Mechanics.

Rational Methods in Lie Algebras. George Seligman. (Lecture Notes in Pure and Applied Mathematics: Vol. 17). 1976. 65.00 (ISBN 0-8247-6480-3). Dekker.

Rational Millennium: Puritan Utopias of Seventeenth-Century England & America. James Holstun. 354p. 1987. 29.95x (ISBN 0-19-504141-0). Oxford U Pr.

Rational Moral Education. J. Watt. Ed. by R. J. Selleck. (Second Century in Australian Education Ser.). 1976. pap. 7.50x (ISBN 0-522-84102-3, Pub. by Melbourne U Pr). Intl Spec Bk.

Rational Numbers, Algebra & Solving Equations. rev. ed. Mervin Keedy & Marvin Bittinger. (Algebra, a Modern Introduction Ser.). (gr. 7-9). 1981. pap. text ed. write for info. (ISBN 0-201-03983-4). Addison-Wesley.

Rational Numbers Study Aid. Richard C. Davis et al. 1976. pap. 3.00 (ISBN 0-87738-039-2). Youth Ed.

Rational Peasant: The Political Economy of Rural Society in Vietnam. Samuel Popkin. LC 77-83105. 1979. 33.00x (ISBN 0-520-03561-5); pap. 11.95x (ISBN 0-520-03954-8). U of Cal Pr.

Rational Pesticide Use. Ed. by E. J. Brent & E. K. Atkin. (Illus.). 358p. 1987. 49.50 (ISBN 0-521-32068-2). Cambridge U Pr.

Rational Philosophy in History & in System: An Introduction to a Logical & Metaphysical Course. Alexander C. Fraser. LC 73-21803. 1974. Repr. of 1858 ed. lib. bdg. 21.00 (ISBN 0-8337-1235-7). B Franklin.

Rational Points, Vol. 6. G. Faltings & G. Wustholz. (Aspects of Mathematics Ser.). 1984. 23.00 (ISBN 3-528-08593-2, Pub. by Vieweg & Sohn Germany). IPS.

Rational Politics: Decisions, Games & Strategies. C Q Press Staff & Steven J. Brams. LC 85-17117. 233p. 1985. pap. 16.95 (ISBN 0-87187-337-0). Congr Quarterly.

Rational Praise & Natural Lamentation: Johnson, Lycidas, & Principles of Criticism. James L. Battersby. LC 77-89774. 288p. 1979. 22.50 (ISBN 0-8386-2148-1). Fairleigh Dickinson.

Rational Psychology. L. P. Hickok. LC 72-13798. (Hist. of Psych. Ser.). 756p. Repr. of 1849 ed. lib. bdg. 90.00x (ISBN 0-8201-1117-1). Schol Facsimiles.

Rational Psychology. Emanuel Swedenborg. Ed. by Alfred Acton. Tr. by Norbert H. Rogers & Alfred Acton. 343p. 1950. 7.00 (ISBN 0-915221-05-5). Swedenborg Sci Assn.

Rational Quadratic Forms. J. W. Cassels. (London Mathematical Society Monograph). 1979. 82.50 (ISBN 0-12-163260-1). Acad Pr.

Rational Representation of Algebraic Groups. S. Donkin. (Lecture Notes in Mathematics: Vol. 1140). vii, 254p. 1985. pap. 20.00 (ISBN 0-387-15668-2). Springer-Verlag.

Rational Series & Their Languages. J. Berstel & C. Reutenauer. (EATCS Monographs on Theoretical Computer Science: Vol. 12). 150p. 1988. 49.50 (ISBN 0-387-18626-3). Springer-Verlag.

Rational Society: A Critical Reading of Santayana's Social Thought. Beth J. Singer. 1970. 10.00 (ISBN 0-8295-0194-0). UPB.

Rational Society: A Critical Study of Santayana's Social Thought. Beth J. Singer. LC 77-99237. pap. 38.80 (ISBN 0-317-08959-5, 2003261). Bks Demand UMI.

Rational Stories for Children. Virginia Waters. (Illus.). pap. 8.95 (ISBN 0-686-36825-8). Inst Rational-Emotive.

Rational System: Eighteen Thirty-Seven to Eighteen Forty-One. LC 72-2537. (British Labour Struggles Before 1850 Ser). (7 pamphlets). 21.00 (ISBN 0-405-04430-5). Ayer Co Pubs.

Rational Techniques in Policy Analysis. Michael Carley. 1980. text ed. 28.95x (ISBN 0-435-83801-6); pap. text ed. 17.95x (ISBN 0-435-83802-4). Gower Pub Co.

Rational Theology & the Creativity of God. Keith Ward. LC 82-81888. 256p. 1982. 17.95 (ISBN 0-8298-0618-0). Pilgrim NY.

Rational Thermodynamics. 2nd ed. C. Truesdell. 560p. 1984. Repr. of 1969 ed. 83.50 (ISBN 0-387-90874-9). Springer-Verlag.

Rational Thinking: A Study in Basic Logic. John B. Bennett. 1980. 22.95x (ISBN 0-88229-285-4); pap. 10.95x (ISBN 0-88229-739-2). Nelson-Hall.

Rational Use of Drugs: Report of the Conference of Experts, Nirobi (25-29 November 1985) 329p. 1987. pap. 31.20 (ISBN 92-4-156104-1). World Health.

Rational Use of Drugs Report of the Conference of Experts, Nairobi (25-29 November 1985) 329p. 1987. pap. 31.20 (ISBN 9-2415-6104-1). World Health.

Rational Use of Psychotropic Drugs with Special Emphasis in Tranquillizers on Non-Psychiatric Settings: Proceedings of the International Symposium, Moscow, USSR, September 29-October 1, 1986. Ed. by M. E. Vartanian et al. (International Congress Ser.: No. 739). 154p. 1987. 88.00 (ISBN 0-444-80860-4). Elsevier.

Rational Utilization of Natural Resources & the Protection of the Environment: The Practice, Problems & Prospects of Socialism. Ed. by Collets Staff. 328p. 1983. pap. 9.75x (ISBN 0-317-53864-0, Pub. by Collets (UK)). State Mutual Bk.

Rational View. Charles C. Moore. (Illus.). 190p. 1984. pap. 5.00 (ISBN 0-910309-17-5). Am Atheist.

Rational Welding Design. 2nd ed. T. G. Gray & John Spence. 315p. 1982. 44.95 (ISBN 0-408-01200-5). Butterworth.

Rationale. Robert S. Cunningham. (Poetry for Today Ser.: Vol. 1). 80p. 1974. 6.50 (ISBN 0-87881-013-7). Mojave Bks.

Rationale & Design of a Primary Grades Reading System for an Individualized Classroom. Isabel L. Beck & Donna D. Mitroff. 89p. 1972. 1.50 (ISBN 0-318-14729-7, ED 063 100). Learn Res Dev.

Rationale & Design of a Program to Teach Vocabulary to Fourth-Grade Students. Isabel L. Beck et al. 49p. 1980. 1.00 (ISBN 0-318-14730-0). Learn Res Dev.

Rationale & Design of an Adaptive Beginning School Learning Environment: Curriculum Objectives. Margaret C. Wang & Alexander W. Siegel. (Illus.). 59p. 1975. 1.50 (ISBN 0-318-14731-9, ED 116 421). Learn Res Dev.

Rationale & Design of the Self-Schedule System. Margaret C. Wang. 52p. 1974. 1.50 (ISBN 0-318-14732-7, ED 101 861). Learn Res Dev.

Rationale for Child Care: Programs vs. Politics. Ed. by Stevanne Auerbach. LC 74-11877. (Childcare: a Comprehensive Guide Ser.: Vol. I). 215p. 1975. 29.95 (ISBN 0-87705-218-2). Human Sci Pr.

Rationale for Sampling & Interpretation of Ecological Data in the Assessment of Freshwater Ecosystems, STP 894. Ed. by Billy G. Isom. LC 86-3323. (Special Technical Publications). (Illus.). 194p. 1986. text ed. 39.00 (ISBN 0-8031-0455-3, 04-894000-16). ASTM.

Rationale of Beings: Recent Developments in Particle, Nuclear & General Physics Festschrift in Honor of Gyo Takeda, Japan, October 13, 1984. Ed. by K. Ishikawa et al. LC 86-5573. 430p. 1986. 70.00 (ISBN 9971-50-117-1). World Scientific Pub.

Rationale of Biological Response Modifiers in Cancer Treatment: Proceedings of the Sixth Symposium in Rationale of Biological Modifiers in Cancer Treatment, Hakone, Japan. Ed. by E. Tsubura et al. (International Congress Ser.: No. 690). 276p. 1985. 114.75 (ISBN 0-444-80700-4, Excerpta Medica). Elsevier.

Rationale of Crime & Its Appropriate Treatment: Being a Treatise on Criminal Jurisprudence Considered in Relation to Cerebral Organization. 2nd ed. Marmaduke B. Sampson. (Criminology, Law Enforcement, & Social Problems Ser.: No. 174). (Illus., With index & intro. added & notes & ils. by Eliza W. Farnham). 1973. Repr. of 1846 ed. 12.00x (ISBN 0-87585-174-6). Patterson Smith.

Rationale of Operative Fracture Care. J. Schatzker & M. Tile. (Illus.). 545p. 1987. 195.00 (ISBN 0-387-10675-8). Springer-Verlag.

Rationale of Punishment: With Intro. & Index Added. Heinrich Oppenheimer. LC 72-172579. (Criminology, Law Enforcement, & Social Problems Ser.: No. 167). 1975. 22.00x (ISBN 0-87585-167-3). Patterson Smith.

Rationale of the China Question. Gideon Nye. LC 72-79834. (China Library Ser.). 1972. Repr. of 1860 ed. lib. bdg. 14.00. Scholarly Res Inc.

Rationalism & Revolution Sixteen Sixty to Eighteen Fifteen, Vol. II. Ed. by Thomas G. Barnes & Gerald D. Feldman. LC 79-66686. 1979. pap. text ed. 10.50 (ISBN 0-8191-0850-2). U Pr of Amer.

Rationalism, Empiricism, & Idealism. Anthony Kenny. (British Academy Lectures on the History of Philosophy). 192p. 1986. 44.00x (ISBN 0-19-824669-2); pap. 13.50x (ISBN 0-19-824670-6). Oxford U Pr.

Rationalism, Empiricism & Pragmaticism: An Introduction. Bruce A. Aune. 1970. pap. text ed. write for info (ISBN 0-394-30017-3, RanC). Random.

Rationalism in Greek Philosophy. George Boas. LC 61-15638. pap. 97.70 (ISBN 0-317-08864-5, 2013173). Bks Demand UMI.

Rationalism in Politics: And Other Essays. Michael Oakeshott. LC 80-42279. 344p. 1981. pap. 12.50x (ISBN 0-416-69950-2, NO. 3488). Routledge Chapman & Hall.

Rationalist Architecture: A Bibliography of Recent Literature. Mary E. Huls. (Architecture Ser.: A 1892). 6p. 1987. 3.00 (ISBN 1-55590-462-9). Vance Biblios.

Rationalist Encyclopaedia: A Book of Reference on Religion, Philosophy, Ethics, & Science. Joseph McCabe. LC 79-164054. 642p. 1971. Repr. of 1948 ed. 51.00x (ISBN 0-8103-3754-1). Gale.

Rationalist Methodology for the Social Sciences. David Sylvan & Barry Glassner. 200p. 1985. 29.95x (ISBN 0-631-13443-3). Basil Blackwell.

Rationalists. John Cottingham. (History of Western Philosophy Ser.: No. 4). 192p. 1988. 29.95 (ISBN 0-19-219209-4); pap. text ed. 9.95 (ISBN 0-19-289190-1). Oxford U Pr.

Rationalists: Five Basic Works on Rationalism. Rene Descartes et al. Incl. Discourse on Method. Rene Descartes; Meditations. Rene Descartes; Ethics. Benedict Spinoza; Monadology. Gottfried W. Liebniz; Discourse on Metaphysics. Gottfried W. Liebniz. 1960. pap. 6.95 (ISBN 0-385-09540-6, Anch). Doubleday.

Rationalite et Calcul Economiques en U. S. S. R. (Economies et Societes Ser. G: No. 19). 1964. pap. 34.00 (ISBN 0-8115-0710-6). Kraus Repr.

Rationalite et Croissance Economiques Sovietiques. (Economies et Societes Series G: No. 9). 1960. pap. 19.00 (ISBN 0-8115-0700-9). Kraus Repr.

Rationality. Ed. by Bryan R. Wilson. 294p. 1973. pap. 15.95x (ISBN 0-631-09900-X). Basil Blackwell.

Rationality & Collective Belief. Anthony Harris. Ed. by Gerald Platt. LC 85-20152. (Modern Sociology Ser.). 256p. 1986. text ed. 39.50 (ISBN 0-89391-044-9). Ablex Pub.

Rationality & Intelligence. Jonathon Baron. 332p. 1985. 34.50 (ISBN 0-521-26717-X). Cambridge U Pr.

Rationality & Irrationality in Economics. Maurice Godelier. Tr. by Brian Pearce from Fr. LC 72-92033. 336p. (Eng.). 1975. pap. 7.50 (ISBN 0-85345-349-7). Monthly Rev.

Rationality & Mind in Early Buddhism. Frank J. Hoffman. 1986. 20.00 (ISBN 81-208-0211-X, Pub. by Motilal Banarsidass). South Asia Bks.

Rationality & Mind in Early Buddhism. Frank J. Hoffman. 138p. 1987. 19.95. Asia Bk Corp.

Rationality & Relativism. Ed. by Martin Hollis & Steven Lukes. 320p. 1983. 34.00x (ISBN 0-262-08130-X); pap. 13.50x (ISBN 0-262-58061-6). MIT Pr.

Rationality & Relativism: In Search of a Philosophy & History of Anthropology. I. C. Jarvie. (International Library of Sociology). 180p. 1984. 30.00x (ISBN 0-7102-0078-1). Routledge Chapman & Hall.

Rationality & Revolution. Ed. by Michael Taylor. (Studies in Marxism & Social Theory). 275p. 1988. 37.50 (ISBN 0-521-34419-0). Cambridge U Pr.

Rationality & the Social Sciences: Contributions to the Philosophy & Methodology of the Social Sciences. Ed. by S. I. Benn & G. W. Mortimore. 400p. 1976. 36.95x (ISBN 0-7100-8170-7). Routledge Chapman & Hall.

Rationality in Planning: Critical Essays on the Role of Rationality in Urban & Regional Planning. Ed. by M. Breheny & A. Hooper. 252p. 1985. 25.95x (ISBN 0-85086-112-8, 9130, Pub. by Pion England). Routledge Chapman & Hall.

Rationality in Science & Politics. Ed. by Gunnar Andersson. 1983. lib. bdg. write for info (Pub. by D. Reidel Holland). Kluwer Academic.

Rationality in Thought & Action. Ed. by Martin Tamny & K. D. Irani. LC 85-21868. (Contributions in Philosophy Ser.: No. 29). (Illus.). 306p. 1986. lib. bdg. 38.95 (ISBN 0-313-25017-0, TRA/). Greenwood.

Rationality of Emotion. Ronald de Sousa. 448p. 1987. text ed. 25.00x (ISBN 0-262-04092-1, Pub. by Bradford). MIT Pr.

Rationality of Indecisive Choice Functions. Tony E. Smith. (Discussion Paper Ser.: No. 62). 1971. pap. 6.50 (ISBN 0-686-32229-0). Regional Sci Res Inst.

Rationality of Induction. David C. Stove. 250p. 1986. 37.00x (ISBN 0-19-824789-3). Oxford U Pr.

Rationality of Islam. Murtaza Mutahhery. Tr. by M. A. Ansari. 170p. 1983. pap. 6.00 (ISBN 0-941724-17-4). Islamic Seminary.

Rationality of Religious Belief: Essays in Honour of Basil Mitchell. Ed. by William J. Abraham & Steven W. Holtzer. 278p. 1987. 56.00 (ISBN 0-19-826675-8). Oxford U Pr.

Rationality of Science. W. H. Newton-Smith. (International Library of Philosophy). 300p. 1981. pap. 11.95x (ISBN 0-7100-0913-5). Routledge Chapman & Hall.

Rationality: Problems of Philosophy. 224p. 1988. text ed. 29.50 (ISBN 0-415-00181-1, Pub. by Kegan Paul). Routledge Chapman & Hall.

Rationality, Relativism & the Human Sciences. J. Margolis et al. 1986. lib. bdg. 58.90 (ISBN 90-247-3271-9, Pub. by Martinus Nijhoff Netherlands); pap. text ed. 17.50 (ISBN 90-247-3417-7, Pub. by Martinus Nijhoff Netherlands). Kluwer Academic.

Ravishing the Women of Conquered Europe. Austin J. App. 1984. lib. bdg. 79.95 (ISBN 0-87700-522-2). Revisionist Pr.

Ravissement de Lol V. Stein. Marguerite Duras. (Folio Ser.: No. 810). 1976. 5.95 (ISBN 0-686-55850-2). Schoenhof.

Ravitaillement et Alimentation en Provence aux XIVe & XVe Siecles. Louis Stouff. (Civilisations et Societes: No. 20). (Illus.). 1971. pap. 36.00x (ISBN 90-2796-886-1). Mouton.

Raw & the Cooked. Claude Levi-Strauss. (Science of Mythology Ser.). 1979. Repr. of 1970 ed. lib. bdg. 29.00x (ISBN 0-374-94953-0, Octagon). Hippocrene Bks.

Raw & the Cooked: Introduction to a Science of Mythology, Vol. 1. Claude Levi-Strauss. Tr. by John Weightman & Doreen Weightman. LC 82-15895. (Illus.). xiv, 388p. 1969. pap. 14.95x (ISBN 0-226-47487-9). U of Chicago Pr.

Raw Deal. Gary DeVore & Norman Wexler. (Orig.). 1986. pap. 3.95 (ISBN 0-446-30201-5). Warner Bks.

Raw Dog. Eric Priestly. (Orig.). 1985. pap. 3.25 (ISBN 0-87067-809-4, BH809). Holloway.

Raw Energy. Leslie Kenton & Susannah Kenton. 1986. pap. 7.95 (ISBN 0-446-37018-5). Warner Bks.

Raw Fruit & Vegetable Juices & Drinks. William Lee. LC 82-82323. 32p. (Orig.). 1982. pap. 2.95 (ISBN 0-87983-306-8). Keats.

Raw Hands & Bagging. Coco Gordon. (Illus.). 1978. pap. 6.00 (ISBN 0-931956-00-5). Water Mark.

Raw Heaven. Molly Peacock. LC 84-42627. 96p. 1984. pap. 6.95 (ISBN 0-394-72707-X, Vin). Random.

Raw Honey. Marie Harris. LC 75-21787. 72p. 1975. pap. 7.95 (ISBN 0-914086-09-X). Alicejamesbooks.

Raw Juices for Health: How to Use Freshly Pressed Juices for Restoring Vitality. Vivienne Lewis. (Illus.). 96p. 1988. pap. cancelled (ISBN 0-909911-11-8). Sterling.

Raw-Material Problems & Policies. Eugene Staley & K. E. Knorr. LC 82-48324. (World Economy Ser.). 116p. 1982. lib. bdg. 17.00 (ISBN 0-8240-5372-9). Garland Pub.

Raw Materials & Colonies see Report on the Problem of Raw Materials & Foodstuffs.

Raw Materials & Processing of Paper Making. H. F. Rance. (Handbook of Paper Science: Vol. 1). 298p. 1980. 116.00 (ISBN 0-444-41778-8). Elsevier.

Raw Materials for Industrial Polymers. H. Ulrich. (Illus.). 220p. 1988. price not set (ISBN 0-19-520762-9). Oxford U Pr.

Raw Materials for Industrial Polymers. Henri Ulrich. 150p. 1988. 45.00x (ISBN 0-02-949789-2, Pub. by Hanser International). Macmillan.

Raw Materials for the Pulp & Paper Industry. Ed. by Ted Dickson & Peter Harben. 100p. (Orig.). 1984. pap. text ed. 38.50 (ISBN 0-913333-01-8). Metal Bulletin.

Raw Materials in Peace & War. Eugene Staley. Ed. by Stuart Bruchey & Eleanor Bruchey. LC 76-5034. (American Business Abroad Ser.). 1976. Repr. of 1937 ed. 29.00x (ISBN 0-405-09300-4). Ayer Co Pubs.

Raw Materials in the Glass Industry: Minor Ingredients, 2 pts. Ed. by Alexis G. Pincus & David H. Davies. LC 83-70137. (Processing in the Glass Industry). (Illus.). 454p. 1983. Set. text ed. 59.90 (ISBN 0-911993-02-9). Ashlee Pub Co.

Raw Materials in the Glass Industry, Pt. I: Major Ingredients. Ed. by Alexis G. Pincus & David H. Davies. LC 83-70137. (Processing in the Glass Industry Ser.). (Illus.). 254p. 1983. text ed. 29.95 (ISBN 0-911993-00-2). Ashlee Pub Co.

Raw Materials of Industrialism. Hugh B. Killough & Lucy W. Killough. LC 79-137951. (Economic Thought, History & Challenge Ser). 1971. Repr. of 1929 ed. 27.50x (ISBN 0-8046-1453-9, Pub. by Kennikat). Assoc Faculty Pr.

Raw Materials of Perfumery see Perfumes, Cosmetics & Soaps.

Raw Materials Purchasing: An Operational Research Approach. B. G. Kingsman. (Frontiers of Operational Research & Applied Systems Analysis Ser.: Vol. 4). (Illus.). 376p. 1985. text ed. 61.00 (ISBN 0-08-029976-8); pap. text ed. 43.00 (ISBN 0-08-029975-X). Pergamon.

Raw Opals. Lyn. 60p. (Orig.). 1987. pap. 7.95 (ISBN 0-89807-251-4). Illuminati.

Raw Pain Max. C. Dean Andersson. 1988. pap. 3.95 (Pub. by Popular Lib). Warner Bks.

Raw Passion. Charles Martin. 1979. pap. 1.75 (ISBN 0-8439-0695-2, Leisure Bks). Leisure NY.

Raw Pearl. Pearl Bailey. LC 67-11963. (Illus.). 1968. 10.95 (ISBN 0-15-175930-8). HarBraceJ.

Raw-Robed Few & Other Poems. Guy R. Beining. 1979. pap. 4.95 (ISBN 0-930090-11-X). Applezaba.

Raw Sienna see Mike's Place: Every Monday.

Raw: The Graphic Aspirin for War Fever. Ed. by Francoise Mouly & Art Spiegelman. (Illus.). 80p. 1986. pap. 7.95 (ISBN 0-317-60862-2). Raw Bks & Graph.

Raw Youth: A Play. Neal Bell. 53p. 1986. pap. 3.35 (ISBN 0-317-45786-1). Dramatists Play.

Rawhide. Frank Bosworth. (Lythway Ser.). 160p. 1988. lib. bdg. 17.50x (ISBN 0-7451-0661-7, Pub. by Chivers Pr UK). G K HAll.

Rawhide Justice. Max Brand. 1985. pap. 2.50 (ISBN 0-671-41589-1). PB.

Rawhide Justice. Max Brand. (General Ser.). 1984. lib. bdg. 14.95 (ISBN 0-8161-3532-0, Large Print Bks). G K Hall.

Rawhide Justice. Jake Logan. 192p. (Orig.). 1986. pap. 2.50 (ISBN 0-425-09342-5). Berkley Pub.

Rawhide Knot & Other Stories. Conrad Richter. LC 84-20799. xii, 207p. 1985. pap. 6.50 (ISBN 0-8032-8916-2, BB 888, Bison). U of Nebr Pr.

Rawhide Laureate: John G. Neihardt, a Selected Annotated Bibliography. John T. Richards. LC 83-10117. (Scarecrow Author Bibliographies Ser.: No. 65). 189p. 1983. 17.50 (ISBN 0-8108-1640-7). Scarecrow.

Rawhide Legacy. Robert E. Trevathan. (YA) (gr. 7 up). 1983. 9.95 (ISBN 0-317-17585-8, Avalon). Bouregy.

Rawhide Railroad. George Estes. (Shorey Historical Ser.). (Illus.). 56p. pap. 3.95 (ISBN 0-8466-0266-0, S266). Shorey.

Rawhide Redeemer. Jerome Gardner. (Lythway Ser.). 1987. lib. bdg. 16.50x (ISBN 0-7451-0580-7, Pub. by Chivers Pr UK). G K Hall.

Rawhiders. Ray Hogan. 224p. 1986. pap. 2.75 (ISBN 0-451-14392-2, Sig). NAL.

Rawhiders. Ray Hogan. (General Ser.). 255p. 1986. lib. bdg. 14.95x (ISBN 0-8161-4053-7, Large Print Bks). G K Hall.

Rawhider's Woman. Dirk Fletcher. (Spur Ser.: No. 16). 208p. (Orig.). 1986. pap. 2.50 (ISBN 0-8439-2365-2, Leisure Bks). Leisure NY.

Rawls & Rights. Rex Martin. LC 84-27044. xii, 244p. 1985. 25.00x (ISBN 0-7006-0266-6); pap. 14.95x (ISBN 0-7006-0310-7). U Pr of KS.

Ray. Barry Hannah. LC 80-11195. 128p. 1980. 7.95 (ISBN 0-394-50972-2). Knopf.

Ray. Barry Hannah. 128p. 1987. pap. 5.95 (ISBN 0-14-010515-8). Penguin.

Ray Berwick's Complete Guide to Training Your Cat. Ray Berwick & Karen Thure. LC 85-81841. 224p. pap. 6.95 (ISBN 0-89586-423-1). Price Stern.

Ray Bradbury. David Mogen. (Twayne's United States Authors Ser.: No. 504). 184p. 1986. lib. bdg. 17.95x (ISBN 0-8057-7464-5, Twayne). G K Hall.

Ray Bradbury. Ed. by Joseph D. Olander & Martin H. Greenberg. LC 77-76721. (Writers of the 21st Century Ser.). 1980. pap. 5.95 (ISBN 0-8008-6639-8). Taplinger.

Ray Bradbury. William F. Touponce. (Starmont Reader's Guide Ser.: No. 31). 144p. 1988. lib. bdg. 17.95x (ISBN 0-89370-958-1). Borgo Pr.

Ray Bradbury. William F. Touponce. Ed. by Roger C. Schlobin. (Reader's Guides to Contemporary Science Fiction & Fantasy Authors Ser.: Vol. 31). (Orig.). 1988. 17.95x (ISBN 0-930261-23-2); pap. 9.95x (ISBN 0-930261-22-4). Starmont Hse.

Ray Bradbury & the Poetics of Reverie: Fantasy, Science Fiction, & the Reader. William F. Touponce. Ed. by Robert Scholes. LC 84-2553. (Studies in Speculative Fiction: No. 2). 156p. 1984. 37.95 (ISBN 0-8357-1569-8). UMI Res Pr.

Ray Bradbury: Dramatist. Ben P. Indick. (Essays on Fantastic Literature Ser.: No. 3). 40p. 1988. lib. bdg. 15.95x (ISBN 0-89370-540-3). Borgo Pr.

Ray Bradbury Review. Ray Bradbury. Ed. by William F. Nolan. (Illus.). 75p. 1988. Repr. of 1952 ed. 45.00 (ISBN 0-940941-05-8). Blood & Guts Pr.

Ray Buckland's Complete Book of Witchcraft. Raymond Buckland. Ed. by Carl L. Weschcke. LC 85-45280. (Sourcebook Ser.). (Illus.). 320p. (Orig.). 1986. wkbk. 12.95 (ISBN 0-87542-050-8). Llewellyn Pubns.

Ray-Centered Astrology. Ruth Mierswa & Richard Mierswa. LC 84-90404. 16.00 (ISBN 0-87212-185-2). Libra.

Ray Flacke: Solos. Ray Flack. 26p. 1986. pap. 14.95 (ISBN 0-931759-08-0); cassette tape avail. Centerstream Pub.

Ray Johnson's Total Security. Ray Johnson & Carroll Stoianoff. 256p. 1986. pap. 3.95 (ISBN 0-451-14615-8, Sig). NAL.

Ray Johnson's Total Security: How to Protect Yourself from Crime. Ray Johnson & Carroll Stoianoff. (Illus.). 256p. 1985. pap. 6.95 (ISBN 0-452-25601-1, Plume). NAL.

Ray Keene's Good Move Guide. Ray Keene & Andrew Whiteley. (Illus.). 1982. pap. 9.95 (ISBN 0-19-217582-3). Oxford U Pr.

Ray Lindwall. David Frith. 192p. 1986. 65.00x (ISBN 0-946771-15-4, Pub. by Spellmount Ltd Pubs). State Mutual Bk.

Ray Lum: Mule Trader -- an Essay. Bill Ferris. Ed. by Jack Friedman. LC 76-53834. (Illus.). 1977. 2.50 (ISBN 0-89267-003-7); film transcript 2.50 (ISBN 0-89267-001-0); record transcript 2.50 (ISBN 0-89267-002-9). Ctr South Folklore.

Ray Manley's Collecting Southwestern Indian Arts & Crafts. 3rd rev. ed. Clara L. Tanner et al. (Illus.). 1979. pap. 6.00 (ISBN 0-931418-03-8). R Manley.

Ray Manley's Hopi Kachina. Clara L. Tanner. (Illus.). 1980. 6.00 (ISBN 0-931418-06-2). R Manley.

Ray Manley's Indian Lands. Clara L. Tanner. (Illus., Eng., Ger. & Japanese.). 1979. pap. 7.95 (ISBN 0-931418-05-4). R Manley.

Ray Manley's "The Fine Art of Navajo Weaving". Steve Getzwiller. (Illus.). 1984. pap. 9.95 (ISBN 0-931418-08-9); 19.95 (ISBN 0-931418-09-7). R Manley.

Ray Manley's "The Vanishing Indian". Clara L. Tanner. (Illus.). 1983. pap. 6.00 (ISBN 0-931418-07-0). R Manley.

Ray Methods for Waves in Elastic Solids: With Applications to Scattering by Cracks. Achenbach. 272p. 1982. 54.95 (ISBN 0-470-20400-1, Co-Pub. with Longman). Wiley.

Ray Miller's Eyes of Texas Travel Guide: Dallas - East Texas. 2nd ed. (Illus.). 224p. 1988. pap. 10.95 (ISBN 0-88415-232-4). Gulf Pub.

Ray Miller's Galveston. Ray Miller. (Illus.). 280p. 1983. 19.95 (ISBN 0-89123-032-7). Cordovan Pr.

Ray Miller's Houston. Ray Miller. (Illus.). 248p. pap. 19.95 (ISBN 0-89123-039-4). Cordovan Pr.

Ray Miller's Texas Forts: A History & Guide. Ray Miller. 240p. 1985. pap. 13.95 (ISBN 0-89123-036-X). Cordovan Pr.

Ray Miller's Texas Parks: A History & Guide. Ray Miller. (Illus.). 248p. (Orig.). 1984. pap. 13.95 (ISBN 0-89123-046-7). Cordovan Pr.

Ray of Darkness. Margiad Evans. 192p. (Orig.). 1986. pap. 4.95 (ISBN 0-7145-3607-5). Riverrun NY.

Ray Reardon. Ray Reardon & Peter Buxton. (Illus.). 160p. 1982. 19.95 (ISBN 0-7153-8262-4). David & Charles.

Ray Reardon's Fifty Best Trick Shots. Ray Reardon. LC 80-69348. (Illus.). 128p. 1980. 15.95 (ISBN 0-7153-7993-3). David & Charles.

Rayburn: A Biography. D. B. Hardeman & Donald C. Bacon. LC 86-30061. 356p. 1987. 21.95 (ISBN 0-932012-03-5). Texas Month Pr.

Rayleigh Wave Theory & Application. E. A. Ash & E. G. Paige. (Springer Seriess on Wave Phenomena: Vol. 2). (Illus.). x, 360p. 1985. 39.50 (ISBN 0-387-15933-9). Springer-Verlag.

Raymond. Mark Geller. LC 87-45282. (Charlotte Zolotow Bk.). 96p. (gr. 6 up). 1988. 10.95i (ISBN 0-06-022206-9); PLB 10.89 (ISBN 0-06-022207-7). HarpJ.

Raymond A. Bidwell Collection of Chinese Bronzes & Ceramics. M. C. Dailey. 85p. 1965. pap. 70.00x (ISBN 0-317-68561-9, Pub. by Han-Shan Tang Ltd). State Mutual Bk.

Raymond Asquith: Life & Letters. Ed. by John Jolliffe. 312p. 1987. pap. 13.95 (ISBN 0-7126-1491-5, Pub. by Century Hutchinson). David & Charles.

Raymond Berry Years. Skipper Steely. (Illus.). 269p. 1982. 25.00 (ISBN 0-915263-04-1). Wright Pr.

Raymond Berry's Complete Guide to Coaching Pass Receivers. Raymond Berry & C. H. Gilbert, Jr. LC 82-2140. 180p. 1982. 19.95 (ISBN 0-13-753210-5, Parker). P-H.

Raymond Chandler. William Marling. (Twayne's United States Authors Ser.: No. 508). 184p. 1986. lib. bdg. 18.95x (ISBN 0-8057-7472-6, Twayne). G K Hall.

Raymond Chandler. Jerry Speir. LC 80-5347. (Recognitions Ser.). 180p. 1981. 16.95x (ISBN 0-8044-2826-3). Ungar.

Raymond Chandler: A Checklist. Matthew J. Bruccoli. LC 68-16892. (Serif Ser.: No. 2). pap. 15.00 (ISBN 0-8357-9373-7, 2015383). Bks Demand UMI.

Raymond Chandler: A Descriptive Bibliography. Matthew J. Bruccoli. LC 78-4280. (Pittsburgh Series in Bibliography). 1979. 60.00x (ISBN 0-8229-3382-9). U of Pittsburgh Pr.

Raymond Chandler Mystery Map of Los Angeles. Ed. by Molly Maguire. (Literary Maps Ser.). (Orig.). 1986. pap. 4.95 (ISBN 0-937609-00-5). Aaron Blake Pubs.

Raymond Chandler Omnibus. Raymond Chandler. LC 79-92498. 625p. 1980. 13.95 (ISBN 0-394-60492-X). Modern Lib.

Raymond Chandler on Screen: His Novels into Film. Stephen Pendo. LC 76-9855. 255p. 1976. lib. bdg. 20.00 (ISBN 0-8108-0931-1). Scarecrow.

Raymond Chandler Speaking. fascimile ed. Raymond Chandler. Ed. by Dorothy Gardiner & Kathrine Sorley. LC 76-146855. (Select Bibliographies Reprint Ser.). 1972. Repr. of 1962 ed. 20.00 (ISBN 0-8369-5622-2). Ayer Co Pubs.

Raymond Chandler Speaking. Dorothy Gardiner & K. Sorley Walker. 276p. 1984. pap. 5.95 (ISBN 0-8052-8208-4, Pub. by Allison & Busby, England). Schocken.

Raymond Chandler's Los Angeles. Elizabeth Ward & Alain Silver. LC 86-18007. (Illus.). 1987. 25.00 (ISBN 0-87951-266-0). Overlook Pr.

Raymond Chandler's Philip Marlowe: A Centennial Celebration. Ed. by Byron Preiss. LC 88-45344. (Illus.). 352p. 1988. 18.95 (ISBN 0-394-57327-7). Knopf.

Raymond Chandler's Unknown Thriller: The Screenplay of Playback. Raymond Chandler. 192p. 1985. 15.95 (ISBN 0-89296-128-7). Mysterious Pr.

Raymond Chandler's Unknown Thriller: The Screenplay of Playback. Raymond Chandler. 192p. (Orig.). 1987. pap. 9.95 (ISBN 0-89296-904-0). Mysterious Pr.

Raymond D'Aguilers: Historia Francorum Qui Ceperunt Iherusalem. John H. Hill & Laurita L. Hill. LC 68-24358. (Memoirs Ser: Vol. 71). (Illus.). 1968. 12.00 (ISBN 0-87169-071-3). Am Philos.

Raymond Hood, Architect of Ideas. Walter H. Kilham, Jr. (Illus.). 1974. 14.95 (ISBN 0-8038-0218-8). Architectural.

Raymond III of Tripolis & the Fall of Jerusalem: 1140-1187. Marshall W. Baldwin. LC 76-29830. Repr. of 1936 ed. 28.50 (ISBN 0-404-15411-5). AMS Pr.

Raymond McIntyre: A New Zealand Painter. Auckland Art Gallery Staff. (Illus.). 112p. 1984. 21.75 (ISBN 0-86863-051-9, Pub. by Heinemann Pub New Zealand). Intl Spec Bk.

Raymond Poincare & the French Presidency. Gordon Wright. 1967. Repr. lib. bdg. 20.00x (ISBN 0-374-98797-1, Octagon). Hippocrene Bks.

Raymond Queneau. Bergens. 34.50 (ISBN 0-685-37074-7). French & Eur.

Raymond Queneau. Jacques Guicharnaud. LC 65-26340. (Columbia Essays on Modern Writers Ser.: No. 14). (Orig.). 1965. pap. 5.00 (ISBN 0-231-02706-0). Columbia U Pr.

Raymond Queneau. Allen Thiher. (Twayne World Author Ser.). 160p. 1985. lib. bdg. 27.95 (ISBN 0-8057-6613-8, Twayne). G K Hall.

Raymond Rabbit Goes Shopping. Lynne Dennis. LC 87-20210. (Illus.). 32p. (ps). 1988. 11.95 (ISBN 0-525-44362-2, 01160-350). Dutton.

Raymond Rabbit's Early Morning. Lynne Dennis. (ps). 1987. 10.95 (ISBN 0-525-44316-9). Dutton.

Raymond Radiguet. James McNab. (World Authors Ser.: No. 725). 1984. lib. bdg. 23.95 (ISBN 0-8057-6572-7, Twayne). G K Hall.

Raymond Radiguet. Noakes. (Coll. Poetes d'aujourd'hui). pap. 14.95 (ISBN 0-685-37076-3). French & Eur.

Raymond Robins' Own Story. William Hard. LC 72-150950. (Russia Observed Ser). (Illus.). 1971. Repr. of 1920 ed. 17.00 (ISBN 0-405-03080-0). Ayer Co Pubs.

Raymund Lully: Christian Mystic. Arthur E. Waite. 69.95 (ISBN 0-87968-100-4). Gordon Pr.

Raynal et Sa Machine de Guerre. Hans Wolpe. LC 57-5448. (Stanford University. Stanford Studies in Language & Literature: No. 15). Repr. of 1957 ed. 28.00 (ISBN 0-404-51825-7). AMS Pr.

Raynaud Update: Pathophysiology & Treatment. Ed. by E. Davis. (Advances in Microcirculation: Vol. 12). (Illus.). vi, 162p. 1985. 92.00 (ISBN 3-8055-3992-4). S Karger.

Rayon Vert. Jules Verne. 8.95 (ISBN 0-686-55944-4). French & Eur.

Rays: A History of Radiology in the United States & Canada. Edward Brecher & Ruth Brecher. LC 69-19071. 522p. 1977. Repr. of 1969 ed. 36.00 (ISBN 0-88275-926-4). Krieger.

Rays Adventures with New Neighbors. Edith Witmer. (gr. 3 up). 1981. 6.50 (ISBN 0-686-30774-7). Rod & Staff.

Rays First Spaceship Ride. 60p. (gr. 3-4). Date not set. pap. price not set. Rapcom Enter.

Ray's Light, Too. Charles R. Dietz. (Illus.). 168p. (Orig.). pap. 6.95 (ISBN 0-9618284-0-4). Spirited Comns.

Rays of Hope. Denis Hayes. 1977. pap. 4.95 (ISBN 0-393-06422-0). Norton.

Rays of Hope. D. O. Teasley. 95p. pap. 0.75 (ISBN 0-686-29137-9). Faith Pub Hse.

Rays of Light. Mary Light. pap. 1.00 (ISBN 0-910924-59-7). Macalester.

Rays of Light: A Book on Life, Love & Spiritual Growth. Dan Latour. (Illus.). 110p. 1987. pap. 9.50x spiral bound (ISBN 0-318-22770-3). NAFSG.

Rays of the Same Light: Parallel Passages, with Commentary, from the Bible & the Bhagavad Gita, 3 vols. J. Donald Walters. (Illus.). 480p. (Orig.). Set. pap. 26.95 (ISBN 0-916124-50-9); Vol. I, 1987. pap. 9.95 (ISBN 0-916124-38-X, CCP1); Vol. II, 1988. pap. 9.95 (ISBN 0-916124-48-7, CCP12); Vol. III, 1989. pap. 9.95 (ISBN 0-916124-49-5, CCP13). Crystal Clarity.

Rayuela. Julio Cortazar. (Ayacucho Library Collection Ser.: Vol. 77). (Span.). 1980. 45.00 (ISBN 0-317-56594-X, Pub. by Biblioteca Ayacucho); pap. 21.50 (ISBN 0-317-56595-8, Pub. by Biblioteca Ayacucho). Humanities.

Raz-Ma-Taz. Stephen Cosgrove. (Serendipity Bks.). (Illus.). 32p. (gr. 1-6). 1982. pap. 2.50 (ISBN 0-8431-0588-7). Price Stern.

Raza: Forgotten Americans. Ed. by Julian Samora. 1966. pap. 5.95x (ISBN 0-268-00534-3). U of Notre Dame Pr.

Razgovor O Dante. Osip Mandelstam. 80p. (Rus.). 1983. 15.00 (ISBN 0-88233-902-8). Ardis Pubs.

Razmishljenije o Bozhestvennoj Liturgii. Nikolai Gogol. 48p. pap. 2.00 (ISBN 0-317-29135-1). Holy Trinity.

Razmyshleniia Posle Vstrechi. M. N. Liubomudrov. 352p. 1984. 39.00x (Pub. by Collets UK). State Mutual Bk.

Razon de Algunos Refranes. Francisco Del Rosel. Ed. by B. Russell Thompson. (Serie B: Textos, XII). 178p. (Span.). 1975. 22.50 (ISBN 0-7293-0007-2, Pub. by Tamesis Bks Ltd). Longwood Pub Group.

Razor. Barry Sadler. 1988. pap. 3.95 (ISBN 0-317-67474-9). Charter Pr.

Razor Candy. Scott Sonders. LC 83-70241. (Illus.). 91p. (Orig.). 1983. pap. 5.95x (ISBN 0-912159-77-4). Caravan Pr.

Razor Edge Book of Sharpening. John Juranitch. (Orig.). 1985. pap. 12.50 (ISBN 0-446-38002-4). Warner Bks.

Razor Edge of Balance: A Study of Virginia Woolf. Jane Novak. LC 72-85111. 192p. 1973. 8.95x (ISBN 0-87024-247-4). U of Miami Pr.

Razor Eyes. Richard Hough. LC 83-11574. 112p. (gr. 7 up). 1983. 11.95 (ISBN 0-525-66916-7, 01160-350). Lodestar Bks.

Razor's Edge. W. Somerset Maugham. LC 75-25363. (Works of W. Somerset Maugham Ser.). 1977. Repr. of 1943 ed. 5.95 (ISBN 0-405-07821-8). Ayer Co Pubs.

Razor's Edge. W. Somerset Maugham. 1978. pap. 4.95 (ISBN 0-14-001860-3). Penguin.

Razor's Edge: Boundaries & Boundary Disputes in Southeast Asia. Lee Y. Leng. 29p. (Orig.). 1980. pap. text ed. 7.50x (ISBN 9971-902-05-2, Pub. by Inst Southeast Asian Stud). Gower Pub Co.

Razvitie Russkoi Srednevekovoi Politiko-Pravovoi Mysli. N. M. Zolotukhina. 1985. 29.00x (ISBN 0-317-42807-1, Pub by Collets (UK)). State Mutual Bk.

Razzamatazz. Jack Early. 320p. 1985. 16.95 (ISBN 0-531-09796-X). Watts.

Razzle Dazzle! Magic Tricks for You. Larry White & Ray Broekel. Ed. by Ann Fay. (Illus.). 48p. (gr. 3-8). 1987. PLB 10.50 (ISBN 0-8075-6857-0). A Whitman.

Razzle-Dazzle Riddles. Giulio Maestro. LC 85-3785. (Illus.). 64p. (Orig.). (gr. 2-5). 1985. 11.95 (ISBN 0-89919-382-X, Clarion); pap. 4.95 (ISBN 0-89919-405-2). Ticknor & Fields.

Razzmatazz. Christopher Middleton. 1976. 17.50x (ISBN 0-935072-02-0). W T Taylor.

RB Nineteen Eighty. Ed. by Timothy Fry et al. LC 81-1013. 627p. 1981. 24.95 (ISBN 0-8146-1211-3); pap. 17.50 (ISBN 0-8146-1220-2). Liturgical Pr.

RB Nineteen-Eighty: The Rule of St. Benedict in Latin & English with Notes & Thematic Index. abr. ed. Ed. by Timothy Fry et al. LC 81-12434. xii, 198p. 1981. pap. 8.95 (ISBN 0-8146-1243-1). Liturgical Pr.

Rbase System V: Database Fundamentals. Carl Opel. 275p. 1988. pap. 24.95 (ISBN 0-938862-87-1). Weber Systems.

Rbase 5000 for the Programmer. Nelson T. Dinerstein. (Illus.). 320p. 1986. pap. 21.95 (ISBN 0-673-18404-8). Scott F.

RBDC's Telecommunication Equipment Resale. Market Intelligence Research Co. Staff. (Orig.). 1987. pap. 995.00x (ISBN 0-916483-01-0). Market Res Co.

RBP Pattern Resource Book. Ed. by Valerie Wilson. (Illus.). 1975. wire spiral 3.25 (ISBN 0-87227-016-5). Reg Baptist.

RC Buyers Guide. 12th ed. Ed. by George Zombakis. (Illus.). 386p. (Orig.). 1988. pap. 11.95 (ISBN 0-89024-093-0). Kalmbach.

RCA & the VideoDisc: The Business of Research. Margaret B. Graham. (Studies in Economic History & Policy: The United States in the Twentieth Century). (Illus.). 256p. 1986. 21.95 (ISBN 0-521-32282-0). Cambridge U Pr.

RCA Electro-Optics Handbook. RCA Staff. (Illus.). 1974. 4.95 (ISBN 0-913970-11-5, EOH-11). RCA Solid State.

RCIA: A Total Parish Process. William A. Anderson. 1986. pap. 12.95 (ISBN 0-697-02200-5). Wm C Brown.

RCIA Team Manual: How to Implement the Rite of Christian Initiation of Adults in Your Parish. Patricia Barbernitz. 88p. 1986. pap. 7.95 (ISBN 0-8091-2814-4). Paulist Pr.

RCIA: The Rite of Christian Initiation of Adults. Patricia Barbernitz. 48p. 1983. pap. 3.95 (ISBN 0-89243-190-3). Liguori Pubns.

RCIC: Let the Children Come to Me. Thomas L. Long & Emily Filippi. (gr. 1 up). 1988. Program Manual. pap. text ed. 12.95 (ISBN 0-697-02571-3); Primary Student. pap. text ed. 4.25 (ISBN 0-697-02572-1); Intermediate Student. pap. text ed. 4.25 (ISBN 0-697-02573-X); Upper Student. pap. text ed. 5.45 (ISBN 0-697-02574-8). Wm C Brown.

RCR-CERCLA: Practical Report. Ed. by Government Institutes, Inc. Staff. 140p. 1986. text ed. 45.00 (ISBN 0-86587-150-7). Gov Insts.

RCRA-CERCLA Case Management Handbook. U. S. Environmental Protection Agency Staff & U. S. Department of Justice Staff. 109p. 1985. pap. 34.00 (ISBN 0-86587-038-1). Gov Insts.

RCRA Compliance-Enforcement Guidance Manual. U. S. Environmental Protection Agency Staff. (Illus.). 392p. 1985. pap. text ed. 58.00 (ISBN 0-86587-033-0). Gov Insts.

RCRA Ground Water Monitoring Technical Guidance Document. 1987. 18.75 (ISBN 0-318-23014-3). Natl Water Well.

RCRA Ground-Water Monitoring Technical Guidance Document (TEGD) (Illus.). 342p. 1986. pap. 16.00 (ISBN 0-318-21554-3, S/N 055-000-00260-6). USGPO.

RCRA-Hazardous Wastes Handbook. 7th ed. Ridgway M. Hall, Jr. et al. (Hazardous Wastes Handbook Ser.). 548p. 1987. pap. text ed. 95.00 (ISBN 0-86587-705-X). Gov Insts.

RCRA Policy Compendium. U. S. Environmental Protection Agency Staff. 302p. 1985. pap. text ed. 52.00 (ISBN 0-86587-034-9). Gov Insts.

Rct Mathematics Workbook. John Allasio et al. 170p. (gr. 8-12). 1986. pap. 7.45 (ISBN 0-937820-52-0). Westsea Pub.

RCT Reading: A Workbook. Marie Lackner & Cynthia Paterno. 165p. 1982. pap. 6.47 (ISBN 0-937820-25-3); answer key 2.25 (ISBN 0-937820-28-8). Westsea Pub.

RCT Writing: A Workbook. Rosalie Rafter & Cheri Alaia. 200p. (gr. 9-12). 1981. pap. 7.31 (ISBN 0-937820-10-5). Westsea Pub.

RDF Handbook (Robotech) Kevin Siembieda. Ed. by Florence Siembieda. 1987. pap. 6.95 (ISBN 0-916211-23-1, 551). Palladium Bks.

RDF Sourcebook. Frank Frey. (Twilight: 2000 Ser.). (Illus.). 49p. (Orig.). 1986. pap. 7.00 (ISBN 0-943580-14-5). Game Designers.

RDI Evaluates Popular Outdoor Antennas. Ed. by Lawrence Magne. (Radio Database International White Paper). (Illus.). 30p. (Orig.). 1988. pap. 5.95 (ISBN 0-914941-14-3). IBS PA.

RDI Evaluates the Grunding Satellit 650 Reciever. (Radio Database International White Paper). (Illus.). 14p. (Orig.). 1988. pap. 5.95 (ISBN 0-914941-07-0). IBS PA.

RDI Evaluates the ICOM IC-R71 Reciever. Ed. by Lawrence Magne. (Radio Basabase International White Paper). (Illus.). 20p. (Orig.). 1988. pap. 5.95 (ISBN 0-914941-08-9). IBS PA.

RDI Evaluates the Japan Radio NRD-525 Receiver. Ed. by J. Robert Sherwood. (Radio Database International White Paper). 25p. 1988. 5.95 (ISBN 0-914941-04-6). IBS PA.

RDI Evaluates the Japan Radio NRD-93 Reciever. Lawrence Magne. (Radio Database International White Paper). (Illus.). 13p. (Orig.). 1987. pap. 4.00 (ISBN 0-914941-11-9). IBS PA.

RDI Evaluates the Kenwood R-5000 Reciever. J. Robert Sherwood. (Radio Database International White Paper). (Illus.). 30p. (Orig.). 1988. pap. 5.95 (ISBN 0-914941-12-7). IBS PA.

RDI Evaluates the Lowe HF-125 Reciever. J. Robert Sherwood. (Radio Database International White Paper). (Illus.). 25p. (Orig.). 1988. pap. 5.95 (ISBN 0-914941-13-5). IBS PA.

RDI Evaluates the Sony ICF-2010 Reciever. Lawrence Magne. (Radio Database International White Paper). (Illus.). 22p. (Orig.). 1988. pap. 5.95 (ISBN 0-914941-06-2). IBS PA.

RDI Evaluates the Ten-Tec RX325 Reciever. Lawrence Magne. (Radio Database International White Paper). (Illus.). 12p. (Orig.). 1987. pap. 4.00 (ISBN 0-914941-09-7). IBS PA.

RDI Evaluates the Yaesu FRG-8800 Reciever. Lawrence Magne. (Radio Database International White Paper). (Illus.). 10p. (Orig.). 1988. pap. 5.95 (ISBN 0-914941-10-0). IBS PA.

RE AIDS Packet see AIDS Packet.

Re-Animator. Jeff Rovin. 304p. 1987. pap. 3.50 (ISBN 0-671-63723-1). PB.

Re-Appraisals: Some Commonsense Readings in American Literature. Martin Green. 1967. pap. 1.65x (ISBN 0-393-00400-7, Norton Lib). Norton.

Re-Assessment of the Telmatobiine Leptodactylid Frogs of Patagonia. John D. Lynch. (Occasional Papers: No. 72). 57p. 1978. pap. 3.00 (ISBN 0-686-80373-6). U of KS Mus Nat Hist.

Re-Assessmnent of the Theoretical & Therapeutical Meaning of Anal Symbolism. Karl Abenheimer. 1985. 10.00x (ISBN 0-317-62113-0, Guild of Pastoral Psych). State Mutual Bk.

Re-Attribution of Certain Tetradrachms of Alexander the Great. Edward T. Newell. (Alexander the Great Ser.). (Illus.). 160p. 1981. 50.00 (ISBN 0-916710-84-X). Obol Intl.

Re-Biographing & Deviance: Psychotherapeutic Narrativism & the Midrash. Mordechai Rotenberg. LC 87-2451. 256p. 1987. lib. bdg. 39.95 (ISBN 0-275-92391-6, C2391). Praeger.

Re-Careering in Turbulent Times: Skills & Strategies for Success in Today's Job Market. Ronald L. Krannich. LC 82-82720. 295p. (Orig.). 1983. pap. 8.95 (ISBN 0-942710-02-9). Impact Va.

Re: Colonized Planet 5-Shikasta. Doris Lessing. LC 81-40194. 384p. 1981. pap. 6.95 (ISBN 0-394-74977-4, Vin). Random.

Re-Competitive Strategies: How to Regain Growth Profits for Mature Businesses. Mack Hanan. LC 86-47588. 192p. 1986. 15.95 (ISBN 0-8144-5888-2). AMACOM.

Re-Conciliation: The Hidden Hyphen. Mary Morrison. LC 74-24007. 24p. (Orig.). 1974. pap. 2.50x (ISBN 0-87574-198-3). Pendle Hill.

Re-Constructing Archaeology: Theory & Practice. Michael Shanks & Christopher Tilley. (New Studies in Archaeology). (Illus.). 280p. 1987. 44.50 (ISBN 0-521-30141-6). Cambridge U Pr.

Re-Creating Your Self. Christopher Stone. LC 86-31125. 176p. 1988. 17.95 (ISBN 0-943920-29-9). Metamorphous Pr.

Re-Creation of Eve. Rosemary Haughton. 1985. pap. 8.95 (ISBN 0-87243-135-5). Templegate.

Re-Creation of Landscape: A Study of Wordsworth, Coleridge, Constable, & Turner. James A. W. Heffernan. LC 84-40302. (Illus.). 278p. 1985. 28.00x (ISBN 0-87451-312-X). U Pr of New Eng.

Re-Creations. Grace L. Hill. Repr. lib. bdg. 21.95 (ISBN 0-89190-046-2, Pub. by River City Pr). Amereon Ltd.

Re-Dact One. Ed. by Peter Frank. (Illus.). 224p. (Orig.). 1983. pap. 7.95 (ISBN 0-930279-00-X). Willis Locker & Owens.

Re-Discovery of the Old Testament. facs. ed. Harold H. Rowley. LC 75-76912. (Essay Index Reprint Ser). 1946. 19.00 (ISBN 0-8369-1154-7). Ayer Co Pubs.

Re-Echo Club. Carolyn Wells. 1987. pap. 8.95 (ISBN 0-89979-046-1). British Am Bks.

Re-Editing Shakespeare for the Modern Reader. Stanley Wells. (Illus.). 1984. 19.95x (ISBN 0-19-812934-3). Oxford U Pr.

Re-Educating Chinese Anti-Communists. J. A. Fyfield. LC 81-84061. 1982. 24.95 (ISBN 0-312-66733-7). St Martin.

Re-Educating Myself: An Introduction to a New Civilization. Bob Gebelein. LC 85-60221. 288p. (Orig.). 1985. pap. 9.95 (ISBN 0-9614611-0-1). Omdega Pr.

Re-Educating Troubled Youth: Environments for Teaching & Treatment. Larry K. Brendtro & Arlin E. Ness. LC 83-11787. (Modern Application of Social Work Ser.). 1983. lib. bdg. 35.95x (ISBN 0-202-36033-4); pap. text ed. 17.95x (ISBN 0-202-36034-2). Aldine de Gruyter.

Re-Education in a Nursery Group: A Study in Clinical Psychology. Ruth W. Washburn. (SRCD Ser.). 1944. 15.00 (ISBN 0-527-01531-8). Kraus Repr.

Re-Electing the Governor: The Nineteen Eighty-Two Elections. Ed. by Thad L. Beyle. LC 85-31582. (Illus.). 378p. (Orig.). 1986. lib. bdg. 31.50 (ISBN 0-8191-5252-8); pap. text ed. 16.75 (ISBN 0-8191-5253-6). U Pr of Amer.

Re-Emergence of Indira Gandhi. P. Sood. 208p. 1981. 14.95x (ISBN 0-686-81394-4, Pub. by S Chand India). Asia Bk Corp.

Re-emergence of Indira Gandhi. P. Sood. 208p. 1981. 14.95. Asia Bk Corp.

Re-Emergence of Indira Ghandi. P. Sood. 1981. text ed. 22.50x. Coronet Bks.

Re-Emergence of the Chinese Peasantry. Ed. by Ashwani Saith. 288p. 1987. lib. bdg. 59.95x (ISBN 0-7099-4409-8, Pub. by Croom Helm UK). Routledge Chapman & Hall.

Re Encarnacion, los Muertos Estan Vivos. Frank Calderon. 96p. (Orig., Span.). 1987. pap. 2.95 (ISBN 0-939193-15-9). Edit Concepts.

Re-Encounters in China: Notes of a Journey in a Time Capsule. Harold R. Isaacs. LC 84-14064. 192p. 1984. 19.95 (ISBN 0-87332-289-4, East Gate Bks). M E Sharpe.

Re-Enter Laughing. Judith Hanson. (Illus.). 36p. (Orig.). 1977. pap. 4.50 (ISBN 0-940592-00-2). Heyeck Pr.

Re-Entry Aerodynamics. Wilbur Hankey. (Educ Ser.). 1988. 49.50 (ISBN 0-317-61874-1). AIAA.

Re-Entry II. John W. White. 1986. pap. 4.95 (ISBN 0-8010-9680-4). Baker Bk.

Re-Entry into the Single Life. Jim Keelan. 1977. 6.00 (ISBN 0-9606554-1-7). Comm Unltd.

Re-Entry Programs for Female Scientists. Alma E. Lantz et al. LC 79-25364. 220p. 1980. 36.95 (ISBN 0-275-90510-1, C0510). Praeger.

Re-entry Technology & the Soviet Space Program (Some Personal Observations) Victor Yevsikov. Ed. by Barbara Dash. 112p. (Orig.). Date not set. pap. text ed. 35.00 (ISBN 1-55831-001-0). Delphic Associates.

Re-Entry: Turning Military Experience into Civilian Success. Keith O. Nyman. LC 82-5765. (Illus.). 176p. (Orig.). 1982. pap. 10.95 (ISBN 0-8117-2139-6). Stackpole.

Re-Entry Vehicle Dynamics. Frank J. Regan. LC 83-16198. (Education Ser.). (Illus.). 414p. 1984. 49.50 (ISBN 0-915928-78-7). AIAA.

Re-Establishment of the Church of England, 1660-1663. I. M. Green. (Oxford Historical Monographs). 1978. 42.00x (ISBN 0-19-821867-2). Oxford U Pr.

Re-Establishment of the Indians in Their Pueblo Life Through the Revival of Their Traditional Crafts. H. K. Burton. LC 36-35586. Repr. of 1936 ed. 18.00 (ISBN 0-527-03236-0). Kraus Repr.

Re-Establishment of the Indians in Their Pueblo Life Through the Revival of Their Traditional Crafts: A Study in Home Extension Education. Henrietta K. Burton. LC 73-176617. (Columbia University. Teachers College. Contributions to Education: No. 673). Repr. of 1936 ed. 22.50 (ISBN 0-404-55673-6). AMS Pr.

Re-Evaluation Counseling Community. Carol Carrig. 1972. pap. 0.50 (ISBN 0-911214-19-4). Rational Isl.

Re-Evaluation Counseling: Social Implications. Thomas Scheff. 1972. pap. 0.50 (ISBN 0-911214-48-8). Rational Isl.

Re-Evaluation of the Eldership. Dayton Keese. pap. 2.50 (ISBN 0-89137-552-X). Quality Pubns.

Re-Evaluation Therapy: Theoretical Framework. Bernard Somers. 1972. pap. 0.50 (ISBN 0-911214-49-6). Rational Isl.

Re-Examination of the Gibson Paradox. T. Windsor Fields. LC 79-53207. (Outstanding Dissertations in Economics Ser.). 235p. 1984. lib. bdg. 31.00 (ISBN 0-8240-4157-7). Garland Pub.

Re-forming the Narrative: Toward a Mechanics of Modernist Fiction. David Hayman. LC 87-47546. (Illus.). 240p. 1987. 24.95x (ISBN 0-8014-2005-9). Cornell U Pr.

Re: Fractions. Roger Steigmeier. 70p. (Orig.). 1988. pap. 6.95 (ISBN 0-910829-08-X). First East.

Re-Imagining American Catholicism. Eugene Kennedy. 256p. pap. 5.95 (ISBN 0-394-74093-9, Vin). Random.

Re-Interpretations: Seven Studies in Nineteenth-Century German Literature. Joseph P. Stern. LC 80-49684. pap. 98.80 (2031729). Bks Demand UMI.

Re-Inventing the Corporation: Transforming Your Job & Your Company for the New Information Society. John Naisbitt & Patricia Aburdene. LC 85-40007. 297p. 1985. 17.50 (ISBN 0-446-51284-2). Warner Bks.

Re-inventing the Corporation: Transforming Your Job & Your Company for the New Information Society. John Naisbitt & Patricia Aburdene. 384p. 1985. 4.95 (ISBN 0-446-30088-8). Warner Bks.

Re Joyce. Anthony Burgess. 1968. pap. 7.95 (ISBN 0-393-00445-7, Norton Lib). Norton.

Re-Learning. James Humphrey. Ed. by John Silbersack. LC 76-8704. (Illus., Orig.). 1976. pap. 2.50 (ISBN 0-916912-01-9). Hellcoal Pr.

Re-Making It New: Contemporary American Poetry & the Modernist Tradition. Lynn Keller. (Cambridge Studies in American Literature & Culture). 368p. 1988. 29.95 (ISBN 0-521-33283-4). Cambridge U Pr.

Re-Making Love: The Feminization of Sex. Barbara Ehrenreich et al. LC 86-2074. 240p. 1986. pap. 15.95 (ISBN 0-385-18498-0, Anchor Pr). Doubleday.

Re-Making Love: The Feminization of Sex. Barbara Ehrenreich et al. LC 86-2074. 240p. 1987. pap. 8.95 (ISBN 0-385-18499-9, Anchor Pr). Doubleday.

Re-Mating Game: Dating & Relating in Middle Life. Max L. Marshall. LC 88-19375. 176p. (Orig.). 1988. pap. 7.95 (ISBN 1-55870-109-5). Betterway Pubns.

Re Publica Librorum sex quae Manserunt. Cicero. xxxvi, 147p. 1985. Repr. of 1915 ed. 15.00 (ISBN 0-89005-455-X). Ares.

Re-Reading English. Ed. by Peter Widdowson. 246p. 1982. pap. 10.95x (ISBN 0-416-31150-4, NO. 2384). Routledge Chapman & Hall.

Re-Search: Industrial Culture Handbook. Ed. by V. Vale. (Illus.). 140p. 1983. pap. 11.99 (ISBN 0-940642-07-7). Re-Search Pubns.

Re-Search: J. G. Ballard. J. G. Ballard. Ed. by V. Vale. (Re-Search Ser.). (Illus.). 176p. 1984. pap. 11.95 (ISBN 0-940642-08-5). Re-Search Pubns.

Re-Search No. 10: Incredibly Strange Films. Ed. by V. Vale et al. (Illus.). 224p. 1986. pap. 16.95 (ISBN 0-940642-09-3). Re-Search Pubns.

Re-Search, No. 11: Pranks. Ed. by V. Vale & A. Juno. (Illus.). 224p. 1987. pap. 14.99 (ISBN 0-940642-10-7). Re-Search Pubns.

Re-Search, No. 12: Modern Primitives. Ed. by V. Vale & A. Juno. (Illus.). 224p. 1987. pap. 16.99 (ISBN 0-940642-13-1). Re-Search Pubns.

Re-Search: Sex & Control. Ed. by V. Vale. 136p. pap. cancelled (ISBN 0-940642-06-9). Re-Search Pubns.

Re-Search: William S. Burroughs, Brion Gysin, Throbbing Gristle. Ed. by V. Vale. (Illus.). 100p. 1982. pap. 11.89 (ISBN 0-940642-05-0). Re-Search Pubns.

Re-Searching Death: Selected Essays in Death Education & Counseling. Ed. by Richard A. Pacholski. (Illus.). vii, 241p. (Orig.). 1986. pap. 15.00 (ISBN 0-9607394-3-2). Assn Death Educ.

Re-Shaping of the Far East. B. L. Weale. 1905. 280.00x (Pub. by Han-Shan Tang Ltd). State Mutual Bk.

Re-Structuring the Government of New York City: Report of the Scott Commission Task Force on Jurisdiction & Structure. Edward N Costikyan & Maxwell Lehman. LC 72-86838. (Special Studies in U. S. Economic, Social & Political Issues). 1972. 24.50x (ISBN 0-275-06320-8). Irvington.

Re-Tell Stories: From Words to Conversation with Meaning. Laura P. Goepfert. (Illus.). 50p. (ps-3). 1986. 16.95 (ISBN 0-937857-02-5, 1441). Speech Bln.

Re: Thinking. Jeanne Hoffman & Elaine Prizzi. (gr. 5 up). 1989. pap. 9.95 (ISBN 0-8224-5789-X). D S Lake Pubs.

Re-Thinking American Education: A Philosophy of Teaching & Learning. J. Glenn Gray. 304p. 1984. pap. 10.95 (ISBN 0-8195-6106-1). Wesleyan U Pr.

Re-Thinking: How to Succeed by Learning How to Think. Daniel Cohen. LC 82-1472. 216p. 1982. 11.95 (ISBN 0-87131-369-3). M Evans.

Re-Thinking the Sources of International Law. F. Van Hoof. 225p. 1983. 40.00 (ISBN 90-65-44085-2). Kluwer Academic.

Re-Treat Your Family to Lent. Sandra De Gidio. 50p. (Orig.). 1983. pap. text ed. 1.95 (ISBN 0-86716-022-5). St Anthony Mess Pr.

Re-Upholstery Techniques. Derek Balfour. 1986. 9.95 (ISBN 0-316-07932-4). Little.

Re-Use of the Muse Theater: A Study of Consumer Preferences. R. K. Piper. 20p. (Orig.). 1986. pap. 2.00 (ISBN 1-55719-089-5). U NE Ctr Applied Urban Rsch.

Re-Used Blocks from the Pyramid of Amenemhet I at Lisht. Hans Goedicke. LC 75-159406. (Illus.). 162p. 1971. 20.00 (ISBN 0-87099-107-8). Metro Mus Art.

Re Views. Frank M. Re. 80p. 1975. pap. 2.95 (ISBN 0-686-14654-9). F M Re.

Re-Vision: Essays in Feminist Film Criticism. Ed. by Mary A. Doane et al. LC 83-23366. 220p. 1983. 25.00 (ISBN 0-89093-585-8); pap. 10.00. U Pubns Amer.

Re-Visioning Psychology. James Hillman. 1977. pap. 7.95 (ISBN 0-06-090563-8, CN563, PL). Har-Row.

Re-Visioning Secondary Art Education. Frances L. Henry & Phyllis Luckenbach-Sawyers. (Illus.). 209p. 1985. pap. text ed. 19.95x (ISBN 0-89641-152-4). American Pr.

Re-Working the Work Ethic: Work & Society in th Eighties. Michael Rose. LC 84-23555. 160p. 1985. 17.00 (ISBN 0-8052-3933-2). Schocken.

Reach Each You Teach. Donald Treffinger et al. (Illus.). 80p. (Orig.). 1979. pap. text ed. 4.95 (ISBN 0-914634-62-3, 7905). DOK Pubs.

Reach for a Different Sky. Linda Grone. 1984. 5.95 (ISBN 0-8062-2411-8). Carlton.

Reach for Charisma: A Personal Guide for Body Language Use. Sidney Vernon. Ed. by Thomas Salter. (Illus.). 50p. (Orig.). 1983. 11.95 (ISBN 0-943150-08-6); pap. 6.95 (ISBN 0-943150-03-5); plastic comb bdg. 6.95 (ISBN 0-943150-07-8). Rovern Pr.

Reach for Fitness. Richard Simmons. 1986. 17.95 (ISBN 0-317-42912-4). Warner Bks.

Reach for Freedom. John D. Burch. 64p. 1986. cancelled (ISBN 0-8062-1536-4). Carlton.

Reach for Heaven. Susan E. Kirby. (YA) (gr. 7 up). 1983. 9.95 (ISBN 0-8034-8327-9, Avalon). Bouregy.

Reach for It. Ardy Friedberg. (Illus.). 96p. 1983. 7.95 (ISBN 0-671-45997-X, Fireside). S&S.

Reach for It... A Handbook of Exercise & Dance Activities for Older Adults. David E. Corbin & Josie Metal-Corbin. (Illus., Orig.). 1983. pap. text ed. 18.95x (ISBN 0-912855-41-X). E Bowers Pub.

Reach for Reading. rev. ed. Alice D. Lorenz. 128p. (gr. 4 up). 1981. write for info. wkbk. (ISBN 0-8136-0317-X); write for info. manual with ans. key (ISBN 0-8136-0318-8). Modern Curr.

Reach for the Cookies. F. Richardo Jachim. (Aphorisms with Illustrations Ser.). (Illus.). 128p. (Orig.). 1987. pap. 11.95 (ISBN 0-940469-00-6). CES Pub.

Reach for Tomorrow. Arthur C. Clarke. (Science Fiction Ser.). (Orig.). 1975. pap. 3.50 (ISBN 0-345-35376-5). Ballantine.

Reach for Your Spiritual Potential. Doris Black. 1986. pap. 4.95 (ISBN 0-89137-438-8). Quality Pubns.

Reach of Art: A Study in the Prosody of Pope. Jacob H. Adler. LC 64-63900. (University of Florida Humanities Monographs: No. 16). 1964. pap. 6.00x (ISBN 0-8130-0002-5). U Presses Fla.

Reach of Criticism: Method & Perception in Literary Theory. Paul H. Fry. LC 83-3535. 256p. 1983. 27.50x (ISBN 0-300-02924-1). Yale U Pr.

Reach of Solitude: The Paintings of Ann Taylor. Barbara Cortright. (Illus.). 1983. 25.00 (ISBN 0-8397-7073-1). Eriksson.

Reach of Song, Bk. VII. Georgia State Poetry Society. 200p. 1987. pap. 9.95 (ISBN 0-87797-155-2). Cherokee.

Reach of the State: Sketches of the Chinese Body Politic. Vivienne Shue. LC 87-27447. 192p. 1988. text ed. 25.00x (ISBN 0-8047-1458-4). Stanford U Pr.

Reach of Tide, Ring of History: A Coulmbia River Voyage. Sam McKinney. (Illus.). 176p. 1987. 19.95 (ISBN 0-87595-196-1). Oregon Hist.

Reach Out. Paul Foust & Richard Kortals. 1984. pap. 4.50 (ISBN 0-570-03933-9, 12-2868). Concordia.

Reach Out. (Illus.). 1969. pap. 6.95 (ISBN 0-8423-5201-5). Tyndale.

Reach out & Sell Someone: Phone Your Way to Success Through the Goodman System of Telemarketing. Gary S. Goodman. 141p. 1983. pap. 7.95 (ISBN 0-13-753624-0). P-H.

Reach Out: Diana Ross Story. Leonard Pitts, Jr. (Star Bks.). (Illus.). 96p. 1983. pap. 6.95 (ISBN 0-89531-036-8). Sharon Pubns.

Reach Out for New Life. Robert H. Schuller. 1979. pap. 3.50 (ISBN 0-553-25222-4). Bantam.

Reach Out for Your Dreams. Ed. by Susan P. Schutz. LC 80-65752. (Illus.). 64p. (Orig.). 1980. pap. 4.95 (ISBN 0-88396-078-8). Blue Mtn Pr Co.

Reach Out to Singles: A Challenge to Ministry. Raymond K. Brown. LC 79-15495. 192p. 1979. pap. 8.95 (ISBN 0-664-24270-7). Westminster John Knox.

Reach to Eternity. Dobrica Cosic. Tr. by Muriel Heppell. LC 79-2234. 480p. 1980. 14.95 (ISBN 0-15-175961-8). HarBraceJ.

Reach with All Your Heart. Marilyn Donahue. LC 88-14807. (Quick Fox Line Ser.). Orig. Title: To Catch a Golden Ring. (gr. 3-7). 1988. pap. 3.95 (ISBN 1-55513-755-5, Chariot Bks). Cook.

Reach Your Career Dreams: CareerTrack's Handbook for Professional Women. 216p. 1986. 15.95 (ISBN 0-943066-19-0). CareerTrack Pubns.

Reachbook see Handbook & Reachbook.

Reaches of Heaven: A Story of the Baal Shem Tov. Isaac Bashevis Singer. (Illus.). 95p. 1981. 15.00 (ISBN 0-374-24733-1); pap. 8.95 (ISBN 0-374-51648-0). FS&G.

Reaching. Connie Hunt. (Illus.). 96p. 1982. pap. 6.00 (ISBN 0-9609442-0-6). Pulsar Pub.

Reaching Adolescents. Arthea J. Reed. LC 84-12905. 490p. 1985. text ed. 22.95 (ISBN 0-03-069342-X, HoltC). HR&W.

Reaching & Teaching Black Young Adults. Walter A. McCray. LC 86-71996. 120p. 1987. pap. 5.95 (ISBN 0-933176-07-4). Black Light Fellow.

Reaching Beyond: Chapters in the History of Perfectionism. Stanley M. Burgess. 292p. 1986. pap. 12.95 (ISBN 0-913573-19-1). Hendrickson MA.

Reaching Decisions. Howard H. Brinton. 1952. pap. 2.50x (ISBN 0-87574-065-0, 065). Pendle Hill.

Reaching Decisions in Public Administration: Methods & Applications. Richard D. Bingham & Marcus E. Ethridge. LC 81-12427. (Illus.). 416p. 1982. pap. text ed. 23.95x (ISBN 0-582-28248-9). Longman.

Reaching Effective Agreements. Ed. by John A. Lemmon. (Mediation Quarterly Ser.: No. 3). (Orig.). 1984. pap. text ed. 15.00x (ISBN 0-87589-979-X). Jossey-Bass.

Reaching Exercises: The IWWG Workshop Book. D. H. Melhem. LC 81-67876. 1981. Repr. 10.95 (ISBN 0-935468-04-8). Dovetail.

Reaching for a Feeling. Bruce Johnson. 1976. pap. 2.00 (ISBN 0-686-14931-9). Goranson Pr.

Reaching for a Star Through Poetical Imagery. Dorothy K. Hunt. 1987. 8.95 (ISBN 0-533-07199-2). Vantage.

Reaching for Art. facs. ed. Guy Eglinton. (Essay Index Reprint Ser). 1931. 17.00 (ISBN 0-8369-0408-7). Ayer Co Pubs.

Reaching for Dreams: A Ballet from Rehearsal to Opening Night. Susan Kuklin. LC 86-15356. (Illus.). (gr. 4-9). 1987. 11.75 (ISBN 0-688-06316-0). Lothrop.

Reaching for Excellence. Tannis Duncan. 67p. (Orig.). 1982. pap. text ed. 2.50 (ISBN 0-87148-737-3). Pathway Pr.

Reaching for Excellence: An Effective Schools Sourcebook. Ed. by Regina M. Kyle. 255p. 1985. looseleaf 9.50 (ISBN 0-318-22429-1, S/N 065-000-00230-2). USGPO.

Reaching for God's Highest. Clyde T. Bryant. 240p. (Orig.). 1987. pap. write for info. (ISBN 0-9618387-0-1). Clyde T Bryant.

Reaching for Language Creativity. Rosemary R. Gallagher. (gr. 4-6). 1987. pap. 6.95 (ISBN 0-8224-4670-7). D S Lake Pubs.

Reaching for More. Pascal Foresi. Tr. by Hugh J. Moran from Ital. 128p. (Orig.). 1982. pap. 4.95 (ISBN 0-911782-40-0). New City.

Reaching for Rainbows: Resources for Creative Worship. Ann Weems. LC 80-19330. 156p. 1980. pap. 8.95 (ISBN 0-664-24355-X). Westminster John Knox.

Reaching for the High Frontier: The American Pro-Space Movement, 1972-84. Michael A. Michaud. LC 86-91456. 462p. 1986. 40.95 (ISBN 0-275-92151-4, C2151); pap. 17.95 (ISBN 0-275-92150-6, B2150). Praeger.

Reaching for the Other Side. Dawn Hill. (Orig.). 1983. pap. 6.95 (ISBN 0-87877-063-1). Newcastle Pub.

Reaching for the Other Side. Dawn Hill. LC 83-8809. 272p. 1983. Repr. of 1893 ed. lib. bdg. 19.95x (ISBN 0-89370-663-9). Borgo Pr.

Reaching for the Rim. Terry Hill. LC 87-7715. (SportsWitness Ser.). 128p. 1987. pap. 5.95 (ISBN 0-8407-7758-2). Nelson.

Reaching for the Sky. Thomas B. Pittman, 3rd. 1976. pap. 3.95 (ISBN 0-87148-731-4). Pathway Pr.

Reaching for the Stars. Moina Ejaz. 176p. 1987. 10.95 (ISBN 0-8062-3073-8). Carlton.

Reaching for the Stars: A Minicourse for Education of Gifted Students, 10 bks. Jackie Mallis. Incl. Bk. 1. Characteristics. Alison Heinemann. 106p. pap. text ed. 19.95x (ISBN 0-86617-001-4); Bk. 2. Needs. Elizabeth Duke. 70p. pap. text ed. 19.95x (ISBN 0-86617-002-2); Bk. 3. Underachieving Gifted. Alison Heinemann. 50p. pap. text ed. 19.95x (ISBN 0-86617-003-0); Bk. 4. Handicapped Gifted. Nancy Alexander. 62p. pap. text ed. 19.95x (ISBN 0-86617-004-9); Bk. 5. Disadvantaged Gifted. Elizabeth Duke. 56p. pap. text ed. 19.95x (ISBN 0-86617-005-7); Bk. 6. Using Knowledge about Intelligence. 70p. pap. text ed. 19.95x (ISBN 0-86617-006-5); Bk. 7. Using Knowledge about Creativity. Alison Heinemann. 57p. pap. text ed. 19.95x (ISBN 0-86617-007-3); Bk. 8. Enrichment. Sharlene Gilman. 125p. pap. text ed. 19.95x (ISBN 0-86617-008-1); Bk. 9. Programs. Alison Heinemann. 169p. pap. text ed. 19.95x (ISBN 0-86617-009-X); Bk. 10. Counseling for the Gifted. Alison Heinemann. 167p. pap. text ed. 19.95x (ISBN 0-86617-010-3). 1979. Set. pap. text ed. 159.95x (ISBN 0-86617-000-6). Multi Media TX.

Reaching for the Stars: The Story of Astronaut Training & the Lunar Landing. Stanley H. Goldstein. LC 87-6937. 208p. 1987. lib. bdg. 35.95 (ISBN 0-275-92601-X, C2601). Praeger.

Reaching God's Ear. C. Samuel Storms. 320p. 1988. pap. 8.95 (ISBN 0-8423-5268-6). Tyndale.

Reaching High: The Psychology of Spiritual Living. Marvin Gawryn. LC 80-24306. 200p. 1981. 11.95 (ISBN 0-938380-00-1); pap. 7.95 (ISBN 0-938380-01-X). Highreach Colorado.

Reaching in Silence. Kay Closson. (Contemporary Poets Ser.: No. 2). 56p. (Orig.). 1983. pap. 3.95 (ISBN 0-916982-27-0, RL227). CCR Pubns.

Reaching Intimacy. De Haan. 1988. pap. 3.95 (ISBN 0-312-90478-9). St Martin.

Reaching Intimacy: A Male Sex Surrogate's Perspective. Jerry DeHaan. 256p. 1986. 14.95 (ISBN 0-312-66434-6). St Martin.

Reaching Marginal Students: A Primary Concern for School Renewal. Robert L. Sinclair & Ward J. Ghory. LC 86-63773. (NSSE Series on Contemporary Educational Issues). 250p. 1987. text ed. write for info. (ISBN 0-8211-1860-9). McCutchan.

Reaching New Students Through New Technologies. Coastline Community College Staff. 448p. 1983. pap. 27.95 (ISBN 0-8403-2954-7). Kendall-Hunt.

Reaching Ninety - My Way: Good Health & Long Life Can Be Yours Too. Zilpha P. Main. LC 84-90575. (Illus.). 75p. (Orig.). 1984. 7.00 (ISBN 0-9601584-5-6); pap. 5.00 (ISBN 0-9601584-6-4). Z Main.

Reaching Our Generation. Wade T. Coggins & Edwin L. Frizen, Jr. LC 82-9751. (Illus., Orig.). 1982. pap. 5.95 (ISBN 0-87808-188-7). William Carey Lib.

Reaching Our Jewish Friends. Lee Belcher & Carol Belcher. (Truthway Ser.). 79p. (Orig.). 1981. pap. text ed. 1.50 (ISBN 0-87148-735-7). Pathway Pr.

Reaching Out. Sandy Mello. LC 84-90182. 239p. 1986. 8.95 (ISBN 0-533-06245-4). Vantage.

Reaching Out - How to Love & Be Loved. Georgie Moore. 1980. 5.00 (ISBN 0-682-49610-3). Exposition-Phoenix.

Reaching Out: A Guide to EAP Casefinding. 92p. (Orig.). 1983. pap. text ed. 9.95 (ISBN 0-9610026-0-3). Perf Resource Pr.

Reaching Out: A History of the Rotary Club of Marquette, Michigan 1916-1981. Richard F. O'Dell. Ed. by Pryse H. Duerfeldt. LC 82-60037. (Illus.). 254p. 1982. 13.00x (ISBN 0-9609764-0-X). Rotary Club.

Reaching Out a Little Farther. Meta Mereday. 32p. 1988. 5.95 (ISBN 0-89962-638-6). Todd & Honeywell.

Reaching Out: Achieving Community Involvement with Developmentally Disabled Children. M. Kay Blackard & Elizabeth T. Barsh. 72p. 1982. pap. text ed. 9.95 (ISBN 0-911227-00-8). Willoughby Wessington.

Reaching Out: Advocacy for the Gifted & Talented. American Association for Gifted Children Staff. Ed. by Abraham J. Tannenbaum. LC 80-14342. (Perspectives on Gifted & Talented Education Ser.). (Orig.). 1980. pap. text ed. 5.75x (ISBN 0-8077-2591-9). Tchrs Coll.

Reaching Out: Interpersonal Effectiveness & Self-Actualization. 3rd ed. David W. Johnson. (Illus.). 336p. 1986. pap. text ed. 25.00 (ISBN 0-13-753351-9). P-H.

Reaching Out: The Prevention of Drug Abuse Through Increased Human Interaction. Gerald D. Edwards. 217p. 1985. pap. 12.00 (ISBN 0-88268-029-3, Pub. by Pulse Bks). Station Hill Pr.

Reaching Out: The Three Movements of the Spiritual Life. Henri J. Nouwen. LC 86-2901. (Illus.). 168p. 1986. pap. 6.95 (ISBN 0-385-23682-4, Im). Doubleday.

Reaching Out through a Perinatal Outreach Education Program. Ruth E. Redmann & Wendy Dorchester. Ed. by Susan C. Pescar & Christine A. Nelson. (Illus.). 174p. 1985. pap. text ed. 19.95 (ISBN 0-932457-00-2). PNLW.

Reaching Out to Others. (Pocket Power Ser.). 16p. (Orig.). 1985. pap. 0.50 (ISBN 0-89486-311-8). Hazelden.

Reaching Out to Prostitutes. Jean Flores. (Orig.). 1988. pap. text ed. 4.72 (ISBN 0-945227-00-0). Brassica Pub.

Reaching Out to the Alcoholic & the Family. Richard Silver. 24p. 1977. 1.95 (ISBN 0-89486-042-9, 1408B). Hazelden.

Reaching Out to the Baptists with Heart & Mind. William J. Whalen. (Reaching Out to...Ser.). 32p. 1984. pap. 1.50 (ISBN 0-89243-209-8). Liguori Pubns.

Reaching Out to the Episcopalians with Heart & Mind. William J. Whalen. (Reaching Out to...Ser.). 32p. 1984. pap. 1.50 (ISBN 0-89243-210-1). Liguori Pubns.

Reaching Out to the Lutherans with Heart & Mind. William J. Whalen. (Reaching Out to...Ser.). 32p. 1984. pap. 1.50 (ISBN 0-89243-206-3). Liguori Pubns.

Reaching Out to the Methodists with Heart & Mind. William J. Whalen. (Reaching Out to...Ser.). 32p. 1984. pap. 1.50 (ISBN 0-89243-207-1). Liguori Pubns.

Reaching Out to the Presbyterians & the Reformed with Heart & Mind. William J. Whalen. (Reaching Out to...Ser.). 32p. 1984. pap. 1.50 (ISBN 0-89243-208-X). Liguori Pubns.

Reaching Out to Troubled Youth. Dwight Spotts & David Veerman. 204p. 1987. pap. 11.95 (ISBN 0-89693-296-6). Victor Bks.

Reaching Out with Love: Encounters with Troubled Youth. Jean M. Campbell. LC 81-50354. 144p. (Orig.). 1981. pap. 3.95 (ISBN 0-87239-453-0, 3652). Standard Pub.

Reaching People from the Pulpit: A Guide to Effective Sermon Delivery. Dwight E. Stevenson & Charles F. Diehl. (Notable Books on Preaching). 1978. pap. 6.95 (ISBN 0-8010-8133-5). Baker Bk.

Reaching: Poems by George P. Elliott. George P. Elliot. (Santa Susana Press Ser.). 1979. numbered 35.00 (ISBN 0-937048-21-6); lettered 60.00 (ISBN 0-937048-28-3). CSUN.

Reaching Port: A Montana Couple Sails Around the World. Keith Jones. (Illus.). 288p. 1983. 13.95 (ISBN 0-312-66431-1). St Martin.

Reaching Port: A Montana Couple Sails Around the World. Keith Jones. 288p. 1984. pap. 6.95 (ISBN 0-312-66432-X). St Martin.

Reaching Rural Families in East Africa. (Programmes for Better Family Living Reports: No. 1). pap. 7.50 (F1075, FAO). UNIPUB.

Reaching Teenagers: Learning Centers for the Secondary Classroom. Don M. Beach. LC 76-40778. (Illus.). 1977. 14.95 (ISBN 0-673-16416-0); pap. 12.95 (ISBN 0-673-16417-9). Scott F.

Reaching Tender Hearts, Vol. 1. Lynn Groth. Ed. by Richard Grunze. (Devotional Readings Ser.). 157p. (ps-k). 1987. pap. 7.95 (ISBN 0-938272-42-X). WELS Board.

Reaching Tender Hearts, Vol. 2. Lynn Groth. Ed. by Richard Grunze. (Devotional Readings Ser.). (Illus.). 176p. (ps-k). 1988. pap. 8.95 (ISBN 0-938272-43-8). WELS Board.

Reaching That Peak: Seventy-Five Years of the Dartmouth Outing Club. David O. Hooke. LC 86-30468. (Illus.). 512p. 1987. 45.00 (ISBN 0-914659-24-3). Phoenix Pub.

Reaching the Aged: Social Services in Forty-Four Countries. Ed. by Morton I. Teicher et al. LC 79-18525. (Social Service Delivery Systems: Vol. 4). 256p. 1979. 29.95 (ISBN 0-8039-1365-6); pap. 14.95 (ISBN 0-8039-1366-4). Sage.

Reaching the Assetless Poor: Projects & Strategies for Their Self-Reliant Development. Cheryl A. Lassen. (Special Series on Landlessness & Near-Landlessness: No. 6). 68p. (Orig.). 1980. pap. text ed. 6.75 (ISBN 0-86731-073-1). Cornell CIS RDC.

Reaching the Autistic Child: A Parent Training Program. Martin A. Kozloff. LC 83-25228. 245p. 1983. pap. text ed. 14.95 (ISBN 0-914797-02-6). Brookline Bks.

Reaching the Disadvantaged Learner. 6th ed. Work Conference on Urban Education. Ed. by Harry A. Passow. LC 69-11364. pap. 93.50 (ISBN 0-317-41868-8, 2026054). Bks Demand UMI.

Reaching the Hispanic Market Effectively: The Media, the Market, the Methods. Antonio Guernica & Irene Kasperuk. LC 81-20687. (Illus.). 224p. 1982. text ed. 36.95 (ISBN 0-07-025107-X). McGraw.

Reaching the Inactive Member. John H. Krahn. 1982. 5.25 (ISBN 0-89536-570-7, 1815). CSS of Ohio.

Reaching the Morning After. Al Kasha & Joel Hirschhorn. LC 86-805. 224p. 1986. 14.95 (ISBN 0-8407-5509-0). Nelson.

Reaching the Peasant Farmer: Organization Theory & Practice in Kenya. David K. Leonard. LC 77-1823. xxii, 298p. 1985. pap. text ed. 17.00x (ISBN 0-226-47261-2). U of Chicago Pr.

Reaching the Underserved: Mental Health Needs of Neglected Populations. Ed. by Lonnie Snowden. (Sage Annual Review of Community Mental Health: Vol. 3). (Illus.). 1982. pap. 35.00 (ISBN 0-8039-1856-9); pap. 16.95 (ISBN 0-8039-1857-7). Sage.

Reaching the Unreached. Ed. by Harvie M. Conn. LC 84-3347. (Orig.). 1985. pap. 8.95 (ISBN 0-87552-209-2). Presby & Reformed.

Reaching the Unreached: The Old-New Challenge. Ed. by Harvie M. Conn. 192p. 1985. pap. 8.95 (ISBN 0-8010-2508-7). Baker Bk.

Reaching the Urban Poor: Project Implementation in Developing Countries. Ed. by G. Shabbir Cheema. (Special Studies Ser.). 1985. pap. 27.50x (ISBN 0-8133-7129-5). Westview.

Reaching, Touching, Teaching: How to Run Successful Days of Retreat. Randy Cooney. 1986. pap. 15.95 (ISBN 0-697-02199-8). Wm C Brown.

Reaching Toward God. Michael Marsh. LC 81-81683. 27p. 1981. pap. 2.50x (ISBN 0-87574-237-8, 237). Pendle Hill.

Reaching Toward the Heights. Richard Wurmbrand. 1979. pap. 7.95x (ISBN 0-88264-142-5). Living Sacrifice Bks.

Reaching Up, Reaching Out. Leland E. Pulley. LC 85-90071. (Orig.). 1985. pap. 5.95 (ISBN 0-9611282-1-6). Stewardship Enters.

Reaching Women: The Way to Go in Marketing Healthcare Services. Barbara B. Alpern. LC 87-60402. 160p. 1987. 24.95 (ISBN 0-931028-94-9). Pluribus Pr.

Reaching Young People Through Media. Nancy B. Pillon. 279p. 1983. lib. bdg. 23.50 (ISBN 0-87287-369-2). Libs Unl.

Reaching Your Full Potential. Richard Furman. 1984. pap. 6.95 (ISBN 0-89081-443-0). Harvest Hse.

Reaching Your Teenager. Elizabeth Winship. LC 83-143. 1983. 14.95 (ISBN 0-395-32219-7); pap. 7.95 (ISBN 0-395-34033-0). HM.

Reaching Youth Today: Heirs to the Whirlwind. Barbara Hargrove & Stephen D. Jones. 1983. pap. 5.95 (ISBN 0-8170-0977-9). Judson.

React Interact: Situations for Communication. Donald R. Byrd & Isis C. Cabetas. (Illus.). 100p. (gr. 10-12). 1980. pap. text ed. 7.50 (ISBN 0-13-753377-2, 18674). Prentice ESL.

Reacting Flows: Combustion & Chemical Reactors, 2 pts. Ed. by G. Ludford. LC 86-1088. (Lectures in Applied Mathematics: Vol. 24). 1048p. Set. text ed. 87.00 (ISBN 0-8218-1124-X); Pt. I, 512p. text ed. 52.00 (ISBN 0-8218-1127-4); Pt. II, 536p. text ed. 52.00 (ISBN 0-8218-1128-2). Am Math.

Reacting Flows: Combustion & Chemical Reactors. Ed. by G. S. Ludford. 160p. 1986. 42.00 (ISBN 0-444-87014-8, North-Holland). Elsevier.

Reaction Against Tennyson. Andrew C. Bradley. 1978. Repr. of 1917 ed. lib. bdg. 15.00 (ISBN 0-8495-0437-6). Arden Lib.

Reaction Against Tennyson. Andrew C. Bradley. LC 74-1188. 1917. lib. bdg. 10.00 (ISBN 0-8414-3290-2). Folcroft.

Reaction Against Tennyson. Andrew C. Bradley. 59.95 (ISBN 0-87968-139-X). Gordon Pr.

Reaction & Accommodation: The United States Supreme Court & Political Conflict 1809-1835. Dwight Jessup. Ed. by Harold Hyman & Stuart Bruchey. (American Legal & Constitutional History Ser.). 484p. 1987. lib. bdg. 60.00 (ISBN 0-8240-8276-1). Garland Pub.

Reaction & Counterrevolution in the Contemporary Arab World. Edward Said et al. (Information Papers: No. 21). 55p. 1978. pap. 4.50 (ISBN 0-937694-37-1). Assn Arab-Amer U Grads.

Reaction & Reconstruction in English Politics, 1832 to 1852. Norman Gash. LC 81-1813. 227p. 1981. Repr. of 1965 ed. lib. bdg. 35.00x (ISBN 0-313-22927-9, GARR). Greenwood.

Reaction Detection in Liquid Chromatography. Krull. (Chromatographic Science Ser.). 376p. 1986. 89.75 (ISBN 0-8247-7579-1). Dekker.

Reaction-Diffusion Equations & Their Applications to Biology. N. F. Britton. 1986. 65.00 (ISBN 0-12-135140-8). Acad Pr.

Reaction Dynamics, 2 pts. H. Feshbach & F. S. Levin. Incl. Pt. 1. Recent Developments in the Theory of Direct Reactions; Pt. 2. Topics in the Theory of Nuclear Reactions. LC 70-183847. (Documents on Modern Physics Ser.). 224p. 1973. Set. 83.00 (ISBN 0-677-04330-9). Gordon & Breach.

Reaction Engineering. Ed. by A. Fiechter. LC 65-6745. (Advances in Biochemical Engineering Ser.: Vol. 24). (Illus.). 150p. 1982. 49.00 (ISBN 0-387-11699-0). Springer-Verlag.

Reaction Engineering of Step Growth Polymerization. Santosh K. Gupta & Anil Kumar. (Chemical Engineering Ser.). 425p. 1987. 65.00x (ISBN 0-306-42339-1, Plenum Pr). Plenum Pub.

Reaction Guide for the Brief Organic Chemistry Course. Michael J Millam. 180p. 1988. pap. text ed. 8.00 (ISBN 0-669-13247-0). Heath.

Reaction Injection Molding & Fast Polymerization Reactions. Jiri E. Kresta. LC 82-12389. (Polymer Science & Technology Ser.: Vol. 18). 310p. 1982. 59.50x (ISBN 0-306-41120-2, Plenum Pr). Plenum Pub.

Reaction Injection Molding Machinery & Processes. Sweeney. (Plastics Engineering Ser.). 336p. 1987. pap. text ed. 89.75 (ISBN 0-8247-7595-3). Dekker.

Reaction Injection Molding of Polymers. 126p. 1984. pap. 85.00 (ISBN 0-686-48332-4, LS43). T-C Pubns CA.

Reaction Injection Molding: Polymer Chemistry & Engineering. Ed. by Jiri E. Kresta. LC 84-24560. (ACS Symposium Ser.: No. 270). 302p. 1985. lib. bdg. 59.95x (ISBN 0-8412-0888-3). Am Chemical.

Reaction Injection Molding (RIM) Ed. by Walter E. Becker, Jr. (Illus.). 336p. 40.00 (ISBN 0-686-48170-4, 0211). T-C Pubns CA.

Reaction Kinetic & Reactor Design. J. Butt. 1980. 56.00 (ISBN 0-13-753335-7). P-H.

Reaction Kinetics, 2 vols. K. J. Laidler. 1963. Vol. 2. 21.00 (ISBN 0-08-009836-3); Vol. 1. text ed. 25.00 (ISBN 0-08-009834-7); Vol. 2. pap. 8.50 (ISBN 0-08-009835-5); Vol. 1. pap. text ed. 10.50 (ISBN 0-08-009833-9). Pergamon.

Reaction Kinetics in Heterogeneous Chemical Systems: Proceedings. International Meeting of the Societe de Chemie Physique, 25th, July, 1974. Ed. by P. Barret. LC 75-31672. 1975. 94.75 (ISBN 0-444-41351-0). Elsevier.

Reaction Kinetics in the Liquid Phase. S. G. Entelis & K. P. Tiger. 380p. 1975. text ed. 76.00x (ISBN 0-7065-1516-1, Pub. by Keter Pub Jerusalem). Coronet Bks.

Reaction Mechanisms see Pentacoordinated Phosphorus.

Reaction Mechanisms in Organic Chemistry. F. Badea. 701p. 1977. 29.00 (ISBN 0-85626-002-9). Abacus Pr.

Reaction Rate Compilation for the H-O-N System. Ed. by Gilbert S. Bahn. LC 68-20396. 254p. 1968. Repr. of 1967 ed. 95.00 (ISBN 0-677-12750-2). Gordon & Breach.

Reaction Rates of Isotopic Molecules. Lars Melander & William H. Saunders, Jr. LC 79-12363. 331p. 1980. 50.95 (ISBN 0-471-04396-6, Pub. by Wiley-Interscience). Wiley.

Reaction Rates of Isotopic Molecules. Lars Melander & William H. Saunders, Jr. LC 85-23200. 348p. 1987. Repr. of 1980 ed. 49.50 (ISBN 0-89874-940-9). Krieger.

Reaction Thermidorienne. Albert Mathiez. 327p. Repr. of 1929 ed. lib. bdg. 62.50x. Coronet Bks.

Reaction Time & Attention after Closed Head Injury. A. H. Zomeren. 176p. 1981. pap. text ed. 17.75 (ISBN 90-265-0369-5, Pub. by Swets & Zeitlinger Netherlands). Hogrefe Intl.

Reaction Times. A. T. Welford. 1981. 93.00 (ISBN 0-12-742880-1). Acad Pr.

Reaction to Opinion Deviance in Small Groups. John M. Levine. 56p. (Reprint from P.B. Paulus (Ed.), Psychology of Group Influence). 1980. 1.50 (ISBN 0-318-14733-5). Learn Res Dev.

Reaction to the Chinese in the Pacific North West & British Columbia, 1850-1910. Robert E. Wynne. Ed. by Roger Daniels. LC 78-54847. (Asian Experience in North America Ser.). 1979. lib. bdg. 39.00x (ISBN 0-405-11298-X). Ayer Co Pubs.

Reaction to the Kennedy Assassination among Political Leaders. Samuel C. Patterson. 1967. 1.00 (ISBN 1-55614-101-7). U of SD Gov Res Bur.

Reaction Transition States. Ed. by Dubois. 304p. 1972. 114.00 (ISBN 0-677-50730-5). Gordon & Breach.

Reactionary Essays on Poetry & Ideas. facs. ed. Allen Tate. LC 68-24856. (Essay Index Reprint Ser). 1968. Repr. of 1936 ed. 18.00 (ISBN 0-8369-0924-0). Ayer Co Pubs.

Reactionary Modernism: Technology, Culture & Politics in Weimar & the Third Reich. Jeffery Herf. 288p. 1985. 37.50 (ISBN 0-521-26566-5). Cambridge U Pr.

Reactionary Modernism: Technology, Culture & Politics in Weimar & the Third Reich. Jeffrey Herf. 272p. 1986. pap. 11.95 (ISBN 0-521-33833-6). Cambridge U Pr.

Reactions. (Advances in Polymer Science Ser.: Vol. 58). (Illus.). 145p. 1984. 41.00 (ISBN 0-387-12793-3). Springer-Verlag.

Reactions & Processes. Ed. by O. Hutzinger. (Handbook of Environmental Chemistry Ser.: Vol. 2 Pt. B). (Illus.). 232p. 1982. 59.50 (ISBN 0-387-11107-7). Springer-Verlag.

Reactions & Processes. Ed. by O. Hutzinger. (Handbook of Environmental Chemistry Ser.: Vol. 2, Pt. C). 180p. 1984. 52.00 (ISBN 0-387-13819-6). Springer-Verlag.

Reactions & Processes. Ed. by O. Hutzinger. (Handbook of Environmental Chemistry Ser.: Vol. 2D). (Illus.). 210p. 1988. 99.50 (ISBN 0-387-15547-3). Springer-Verlag.

Reactions & Processes. (Handbook of Environmental Chemistry: Vol. 2, Pt. A). (Illus.). 320p. 1980. 78.00 (ISBN 0-387-09689-2). Springer-Verlag.

Reactions & Syntheses in the Organic Laboratory. Lutz Tietze & Theophil Eicher. Tr. by Dagmar Ringe. (Illus.). 592p. (Orig., Ger.). 1988. text ed. 52.00x (ISBN 0-935702-24-5). Univ Sci Bks.

Reactions Between Complex Nuclei: Proceedings, 2 vols. Ed. by R. L. Robinson et al. LC 74-81324. 680p. 1975. Set. 92.75 (ISBN 0-685-57108-4); Vol. 1. 29.00 (ISBN 0-444-10664-2); Vol. 2. 78.00 (ISBN 0-444-10746-0). Elsevier.

Reactions Between Dogma & Philosophy Illustrated from the Works of St. Thomas Aquinas. Philip H. Wicksteed. LC 77-27153. (Hibbert Lectures: 1916). Repr. of 1920 ed. 57.50 (ISBN 0-404-60418-8). AMS Pr.

Reactions in Condensed Phases see Physical Chemistry: An Advanced Treatise in Eleven Volumes.

Reactions Macrochimiques chez les Champignons Suives d'Indications sur la Morphologie des Spores. F. Bataille. 1969. Repr. of 1948 ed. 24.00x (ISBN 3-7682-0654-8). Lubrecht & Cramer.

Reactions of Acids & Bases in Analytical Chemistry. Adam Hulanicki. (Analytical Chemistry Ser.). 352p. 1987. 112.00 (ISBN 0-470-20246-7). Wiley.

Reactions of Aromatic Compounds see Comprehensive Chemical Kinetics.

Reactions of Carbon with Carbon Dioxide & with Steam. C. G. Von Fredersdorff. (Research Bulletin: No. 19). iv, 75p. (B). 1955. 7.50. Inst Gas Tech.

Reactions of Coordinated Ligands, Vol. 1. Ed. by Paul S. Braterman. 1020p. 1987. 135.00x (ISBN 0-306-42201-8, Plenum Pr). Plenum Pub.

Reactions of Coordinated Ligands & Homogeneous Catalysis: A Symposium Sponsored by the American Chemical Society, Washington, D.C., March 22-24, 1962. Daryl H. Busch. LC 63-13314. (American Chemical Society Advances in Chemistry Ser.: No. 37). pap. 65.80 (ISBN 0-317-09028-3, 2051256). Bks Demand UMI.

Reactions of Metallic Salts & Complexes & Organometallic Compounds see Comprehensive Chemical Kinetics.

Reactions of Molecules at Electrodes. Ed. by N. S. Hush. LC 70-149570. pap. 128.00 (ISBN 0-317-29338-9, 2024029). Bks Demand UMI.

Reactions of Non-Metallic Inorganic Compounds see Comprehensive Chemical Kinetics.

Reactions of Small Transient Species, Kinetics & Energetics. Ed. by A. Fontijn & M. A. Clyne. 1984. 102.50 (ISBN 0-12-262040-2). Acad Pr.

Reactions of Solids with Gases. C. H. Bamford & C. F. Tipper. (Comprehensive Chemical Kinetics Ser.: Vol. 21). 1984. 118.50 (ISBN 0-444-42288-9, I-450-84). Elsevier.

Reactions of Sulphur with Organic Compounds. Mikhail G. Voronkov et al. 422p. 1984. 79.50x (ISBN 0-306-10978-6, Consultants). Plenum Pub.

Reactions on Polymers: Proceedings of the NATO Advanced Study Institute, No. C-4, Troy, N. Y., July, 1973. NATO Advanced Study Institute Staff. Ed. by James A. Moore. LC 73-91207. 1973. lib. bdg. 53.00 (ISBN 90-277-0416-3, Pub. by Reidel Holland). Kluwer Academic.

Reactions Patterns in Human Teeth. Ivar A. Mjor. 248p. 1983. 85.00 (ISBN 0-8493-6645-3). CRC Pr.

Reactions to Crime: The Public, The Police, Courts & Prisons. Ed. by David P. Farrington & John Gunn. LC 84-17369. (Current Research in Forensic Psychiatry & Psychology Ser.). 189p. 1985. 51.95 (ISBN 0-471-90497-X). Wiley.

Reactions to Irish Nationalism, 1865-1914. Alan O'Day. 422p. 1987. 40.00 (ISBN 0-907628-85-0). Hambledon Press.

Reactions to Motherhood: The Role of Post-Natal Care. Jean A. Ball. (Illus.). 168p. 1987. 34.50 (ISBN 0-521-30331-1); pap. 9.95 (ISBN 0-521-31629-4). Cambridge U Pr.

Reactions to Non-Native English: Native English-Speakers' Assessements of Errors in the Use of English Made by Non-Native Users of the Language, Pt. 1 Acceptability & Intelligibility. Par Hultfors. 264p. (Orig.). 1986. pap. text ed. 26.50x (ISBN 91-22-00806-3, Pub. by Almqvist & Wiksell). Coronet Bks.

Reactions to Non-Native English, Pt. 2: Foreigner Role & Interpretation. Par Hultfors. (Stockholm Studies in English: Vol. LXXI). 240p. (Orig.). 1987. pap. 26.50x (ISBN 91-22-00871-3, Pub. by Almqvist & Wiksell). Coronet Bks.

Reactions to Psychotropic Medication. F. L. Tornatore et al. LC 87-30056. (Illus.). 184p. 1987. 29.50x (ISBN 0-306-42718-4, Plenum Med Bk). Plenum Pub.

Reactions to the English Civil War, 1642-1649. Ed. by John Morrill. LC 82-25538. 257p. 27.50x (ISBN 0-312-66443-5). St Martin.

Reactions under Plasma Conditions. Ed. by M. Venugopalan. LC 78-132857. Vol. 1. pap. 153.30 (ISBN 0-317-10852-2, 22006313); Vol. 2. pap. 155.50 (ISBN 0-317-10853-0). Bks Demand UMI.

Reactions with Variable-Change Soils. N. J. Barrow. (Developments in Plant & Soil Sciences Ser.). 1988. lib. bdg. 54.50 (ISBN 90-247-3589-0, Pub. by Martinus Nijhoff Netherlands). Kluwer Academic.

Reactivated Man. Curtis Zahn. (Illus.). 48p. 1984. pap. 4.00 (ISBN 0-88145-014-6). Broadway Play.

Reactive Arthritis. Ed. by Auli Toivanen & Paavo Toivanen. 192p. 1988. 99.50 (ISBN 0-8493-6118-4, 6118). CRC Pr.

Reactive Dyes in Protein & Enzyme Technology. Ed. by Y. D. Clonis et al. LC 87-21903. 300p. 1987. 80.00x (ISBN 0-935859-26-8, Stockton Pr). Groves Dict Music.

Reactive Intermediates, Vol. 1. Ed. by R. A. Abramovitch. LC 79-344. (Illus.). 536p. 1980. 79.50x (ISBN 0-306-40220-3, Plenum Pr). Plenum Pub.

Reactive Intermediates, Vol. 2. Ed. by R. A. Abramovitch. LC 79-344. 614p. 1982. 89.50x (ISBN 0-306-40594-6, Plenum Pr). Plenum Pub.

Reactive Intermediates, Vol. 3. Ed. by R. A. Abramovitch. LC 82-15139. 644p. 1983. 89.50x (ISBN 0-306-40970-4, Plenum Pr). Plenum Pub.

Reactive Intermediates: A Serial Publication, 2 vols. Ed. by Maitland Jones, Jr. & Robert A. Moss. (Reactive Intermediates: A Serial Publication). 1981. (Pub. by Wiley-Interscience); Vol. 2, 396p. 63.50 (ISBN 0-471-01875-9). Wiley.

Reactive Intermediates: A Serial Publication. Ed. by Maitland Jones, Jr. & Robert A. Moss. (Vol. 3). 435p. 1985. text ed. 85.00x (ISBN 0-471-01893-7). Wiley.

Reactive Intermediates in Organic Chemistry: Carbonium Ions. Ed. by George A. Olah & Paul Schleyer. (John Wiley); Vol. 2 Methods Of Formation & Major Types 500p., 1970. 38.50; Vol. 3 Major Types 536p.,1972. 46.00 (ISBN 0-471-65334-9); Vol. 4 Major Types, 1973 460p. 46.50 (ISBN 0-471-65337-3). Krieger.

Reactive Intermediates in Organic Chemistry. Neil Isaacs. LC 73-8194. 560p. 1975. (Pub. by Wiley-Interscience); pap. 39.95x (ISBN 0-471-42859-0, Pub. by Wiley-Interscience). Wiley.

Reactive Intermediates in Organic Chemistry. Neil S. Isaacs. LC 73-8194. 564p. pap. 146.70 (2030523). Bks Demand UMI.

Reactive Intermediates in the Gas Phase: Generation & Monitoring. Ed. by D. W. Setser. LC 79-51698. 1979. 49.00 (ISBN 0-12-637450-3). Acad Pr.

Reactive Metals: Proceedings of the 3rd Reactive Metals Conference, Buffalo, 1958. Ed. by W. R. Clough. LC 59-14889. (Metallurgical Society Conference: Vol. 2). pap. 156.30 (ISBN 0-317-10823-9, 2000665). Bks Demand UMI.

Reactive Molecules: Neutral Reactive Intermediates in Organic Chemistry. Curt Wentrup. LC 83-16824. 333p. 1984. 41.50 (ISBN 0-471-87639-9, Pub. by Wiley-Interscience). Wiley.

Reactive Oligomers. Frank W. Harris & Harry J. Spinelli. LC 85-9215. (ACS Symposium Ser.: No. 282). 262p. 1985. lib. bdg. 59.95 (ISBN 0-8412-0922-7). Am Chemical.

Reactive Oxygen Species in Chemistry, Biology, & Medicine. Ed. by A. Quintanilha. LC 87-38498. (Illus.). 240p. 1988. 55.00x (ISBN 0-306-42808-3, Plenum Pr). Plenum Pub.

Reactive Power Control in Electric Systems. Ed. by Timothy J. Miller. LC 82-10838. 381p. 1982. 59.95x (ISBN 0-471-86933-3, Pub. by Wiley-Interscience). Wiley.

Reactive Processing of Polymers: Proceedings of the 2nd International Conference, November 2-4, 1982. Society of Plastics Engineers. Ed. by J. T. Lindt. (Illus.). pap. 111.00 (ISBN 0-317-09322-3, 2021697). Bks Demand UMI.

Reactive Risk & Rational Action: Managing Moral Hazard in Insurance Contracts. Carol A. Heimer. (California Series on Social Choice & Political Economy: Vol. 6). 1985. 33.00x (ISBN 0-520-05202-1). U of Cal Pr.

Reactivity Coefficients in Large Fast Power Reactors. Hummel Okrent. LC 73-119000. (ANS Monographs). 386p. 1970. 21.00 (ISBN 0-89448-006-5, 300002). Am Nuclear Soc.

Reactivity in Organic Chemistry. Gerhard W. Klumpp. LC 81-16437. 502p. 1982. 59.50x (ISBN 0-471-06285-5). Wiley.

Reactivity Indices for Biomolecules. Chen-An Chin & Pill-Soon Song. (Graduate Studies: No. 24). (Illus.). 176p. 1981. 33.00 (ISBN 0-89672-093-4); pap. 20.00 (ISBN 0-89672-092-6). Tex Tech Univ Pr.

Reactivity, Mechanism, & Structure in Polymer Chemistry. Ed. by A. D. Jenkins & A. Ledwith. LC 73-2786. pap. 157.80 (ISBN 0-317-29339-7, 2024030). Bks Demand UMI.

Reactivity of Metal-Metal Bonds. Ed. by Malcolm Chisholm. LC 81-361. (ACS Symposium Ser.: No. 155). 1981. 41.95 (ISBN 0-8412-0624-4). Am Chemical.

Reactivity of Solids: Proceedings of the Tenth International Symposium on Reactivity of Solids, Dijon, France, August 27-31, 1984, 2 vols. Ed. by P. Barret & L. C. Dufour. (Materials Science Monographs: Vols. 28A & 28B). 1148p. 1985. Set. 276.00 (ISBN 0-444-42496-2). Elsevier.

Reactivity of Solids: Proceedings of the 9th International Symposium, Cracow, Sept. 1980, 2 vols. Ed. by K. Dyrek et al. (Materials Science Monographs: No. 10). 1500p. 1983. 255.25 (ISBN 0-444-99707-5). Elsevier.

Reactor Burn-up Physics. (Panel Proceedings Ser.). (Illus.). 296p. (Orig.). 1973. pap. 22.50 (ISBN 92-0-051073-6, ISP336, IAEA). UNIPUB.

Reactor Card Index: Technical Directory. pap. 46.50 (ISBN 92-0-152164-2, ISP85, IAEA). UNIPUB.

Reactor Coolant & Associated Systems in Nuclear Power Plants: A Safety Guide. (Safety Ser.: No. 50-SG-D13). (Illus.). 70p. (Orig.). 1987. pap. text ed. 23.00 (ISBN 0-317-55693-2, ISP731, IAEA). UNIPUB.

Reactor Core Fuel Management. P. Silvennoinen. 250p. 1976. 65.00 (ISBN 0-08-019853-8); pap. 25.00 (ISBN 0-08-019852-X). Pergamon.

Reactor Dosimetry, 2 vols. J. P. Genthon & H. Rottger. 1985. Set. lib. bdg. 118.00 (ISBN 90-277-2013-4, Pub. by Reidel Netherlands); Vol. I. lib. bdg. 59.00 (ISBN 90-277-2011-8); Vol. II. lib. bdg. 59.00 (ISBN 90-277-2012-6). Kluwer Academic.

Reactor Handbook, Vol. 1. 2nd ed. LC 60-11027. pap. 160.00 (ISBN 0-317-09150-6, 2055163). Bks Demand UMI.

Reactor Kinetics & Control: Proceedings. Ed. by Lynn E. Weaver. (AEC Symposium Ser.). 593p. 1964. pap. 22.75 (ISBN 0-87079-333-0, TID-7662); microfiche 6.50 (ISBN 0-87079-334-9, TID-7662). DOE.

Reactor-Noise Analysis in the Time Domain. Nicola Pacilio. LC 79-600321. (AEC Critical Review Ser.). 102p. 1969. pap. 10.50 (ISBN 0-87079-335-7, TID-24512); microfiche 6.50 (ISBN 0-87079-336-5, TID-24512). DOE.

Reactor Operation. J. Shaw. 1969. 38.00 (ISBN 0-08-013325-8); pap. 17.25 (ISBN 0-08-013324-X). Pergamon.

Reactor Physics & Nuclear Spectroscopy Research: Proceedings of the Conference on Reactor Physics for Developing Countries & Nuclear Spectroscopy Research. Ed. by K. Lieb & G. Medrano. 770p. 1986. 78.00 (ISBN 9971-50-203-8, Z0343E-P). World Scientific Pub.

Reactor Physics Constants. 2nd ed. Argonne National Laboratory & AEC Technical Information Center Staff. 876p. 1963. pap. 60.95 (ISBN 0-87079-337-3, ANL-5800); microfiche 6.50 (ISBN 0-87079-497-3, ANL-5800). DOE.

Reactor Physics Studies of H20 - DS0 Moderated U02 Cores: A NORA Project Report. (Technical Reports Ser.: No. 67). (Illus.). 76p. 1966. pap. 10.50 (ISBN 92-0-155166-5, IDC67, IAEA). UNIPUB.

Reactor Plant Materials. (Illus.). 298p. 1982. looseleaf bdg. 79.50x (ISBN 0-87683-293-1); looseleaf instr's. lesson plans 195.00x (ISBN 0-87683-294-X). GP Pub.

Reactor Shielding. (Technical Reports Ser.: No. 34). (Illus.). 164p. 1981. pap. 14.00 (ISBN 0-686-93878-X, IDC34, IAEA). UNIPUB.

Reactor Shielding Design Manual. Ed. by Theodore Rockwell, 3rd. AEC Technical Information Center. 478p. 1956. hardbound 36.95 (ISBN 0-87079-338-1, TID-7004). DOE.

Reactor Shielding for Nuclear Engineers. N. M. Schaeffer & AEC Technical Information Center. LC 73-600001. 801p. 1973. pap. 28.00 (ISBN 0-87079-004-8, TID-25951); microfiche 6.50 (ISBN 0-87079-339-X, TID-25951). DOE.

Reactor Stability: Sensitivity & Mixing Effects. Ed. by B. L. Crynes & H. S. Fogler. LC 80-25535. (AIChEMI Modular Instruction E Ser.: Vol. 4: Kinetics). 98p. 1984. pap. 30.00 (ISBN 0-8169-0239-9). Am Inst Chem Eng.

Reactor Theory Course. (Illus.). 1979. looseleaf lesson notes 79.50x (ISBN 0-87683-248-6); looseleaf instr's. lesson plans 95.00x (ISBN 0-87683-249-4). GP Pub.

Reactors & Rate Data. Ed. by B. L. Crynes & H. S. Fogler. LC 80-24435. (AIChEMI Modular Instruction E Ser.: Vol. 2: Kinetics). 94p. 1981. pap. 30.00 (ISBN 0-8169-0180-5, J-11). Am Inst Chem Eng.

Reactors & Reactions. Ed. by A. Fiechter. (Advances in Biochemical Engineering Ser.: Vol. 19). (Illus.). 250p. 1981. 64.00 (ISBN 0-387-10464-X). Springer-Verlag.

Read-a-Rebus: Tales & Rhymes in Words & Pictures. William H. Hooks et al. LC 83-22282. (Picturebacks Ser.). (Illus.). 32p. (ps-1). 1986. lib. bdg. 5.99 (ISBN 0-394-95833-0); pap. 1.95 (ISBN 0-394-85833-6). Random.

Read about China. Pao-Chen Lee. 6.95 (ISBN 0-88710-061-9); tapes avail. (ISBN 0-88710-062-7). Yale Far Eastern Pubns.

Read about It: Beginning Readers. Imogene Forte. LC 82-81720. (Read About It DM Ser.). (Illus.). 80p. (gr. k-1). 1982. pap. text ed. 6.95 (ISBN 0-86530-005-4, IP 05-4). Incentive Pubns.

Read About It DM Ser. Middle Grades. Imogene Forte. LC 82-80502. (Read about It Ser.). (Illus.). 80p. (gr. 4-6). 1982. pap. text ed. 6.95 (ISBN 0-86530-007-0, IP 070). Incentive Pubns.

Read about It: Primary. Imogene Forte. LC 82-80499. (Read About It DM Ser.). (Illus.). 80p. (gr. 2-4). 1982. pap. text ed. 6.95 (ISBN 0-86530-006-2, IP-062). Incentive Pubns.

Read about Rye: Sixteen Sixty to Nineteen Sixty. Arlene D. Hawkins. LC 85-19679. 1985. pap. 4.95 (ISBN 0-9615327-0-X). Rye Hist Soc.

Read All about It. Sidney Zion. 368p. 1984. pap. 9.95 (ISBN 0-425-07209-6). Berkley Pub.

Read All About It! A Day in the Life of a Metropolitan Newspaper. Jane T. Harrigan. LC 87-17798. (Illus.). 324p. 1987. casebound 17.95 (ISBN 0-87106-760-9). Globe Pequot.

Read-Along with "Atariba & Niguayona". Harriet Rohmer & Jesus G. Rea. 1988. Incl. audiocassette. 15.95 (ISBN 0-89239-039-5). Childrens Book Pr.

Read-Along with "How We to the Fifth World". Harriet Rohmer & Mary Anchondo. Incl. audiocassette. 15.95 (ISBN 0-89239-034-4). Childrens Book Pr.

Read-Along-With-Me Series. Ed. by Deborah Shine. (Illus.). 32p. (ps). 1988. 1.29 (ISBN 0-02-688566-2, Checkerboard Pr). Macmillan.

Read-Along with "Mother Scorpion County". Dorminster Wilson. 1988. 15.95 (ISBN 0-89239-037-9). Childrens Book Pr.

Read-Along with "My Aunt Otilia's Spirits". Richard Garcia. 15.95. Childrens Book Pr.

Read-Along with "The Adventures of Connie & Diego". Maria Garcia. 1988. Incl. audiocassette. 15.95 (ISBN 0-89239-033-6). Childrens Book Pr.

Read-Along with "The Invisible Hunters". Octavio Chow & Morris Vidaure. 1988. Incl. audiocassete. 15.95. Childrens Book Pr.

Read-Along with "The Legend of Food Mountain". Harriet Rohmer. 1988. Incl. Audiocassette. 15.95 (ISBN 0-89239-035-2). Childrens Book Pr.

Read-Aloud Bible Stories, Vol. 1. Ella K. Lindvall. LC 82-2114. 160p. (ps). 1982. 16.95 (ISBN 0-8024-7163-3). Moody.

Read-Aloud Bible Stories, Vol. 2. Ella K. Lindvall. (Illus.). 1985. text ed. 16.95 (ISBN 0-8024-7164-1). Moody.

Read-Aloud Handbook. Jim Trelease. 1984. 15.75 (ISBN 0-8446-6172-4). Peter Smith.

Read-Aloud Handbook. rev. ed. Jim Trelease. (Handbooks Ser.). (Illus.). 272p. 1985. pap. 8.95 (ISBN 0-14-046727-0). Penguin.

Read Aloud Rhymes for the Very Young. Ed. by Jack Prelutsky. LC 86-7147. (Illus.). 112p. (ps-3). 1986. 13.95 (ISBN 0-394-87218-5); lib. bdg. 14.99 (ISBN 0-394-97218-X). Knopf.

Read-Aloud Rhymes for the Very Young. Ed. by Jack Prelutsky. LC 86-7147. (Book & Cassette Classics Ser.). (Illus.). 112p. (ps-3). 1988. bk. & cassette pkg. 19.95 (ISBN 0-394-89833-8). Knopf.

Read Aloud Topsy-Turvy Library, 26 vols. Stephen Cosgrove. (Illus.). (ps-3). 1988. Set. 155.48 (ISBN 0-87475-600-6). Stuttman.

Read-Aloud Treasury: Favorite Nursery Rhymes, Poems, Stories & More for the Very Young. Compiled by Joanna Cole & Stephanie Calmenson. (Illus.). 256p. 1988. pap. 17.95 (ISBN 0-385-18560-X). Doubleday.

Read America First. facs. ed. Robert Littell. LC 68-16947. (Essay Index Reprint Ser). 1968. Repr. of 1926 ed. 20.00 (ISBN 0-8369-0620-9). Ayer Co Pubs.

Read & Comprehend: Following Directions. Gail Aemmer. (Stick-Out-Your-Neck Ser.). (Illus.). 20p. (gr. 3-4). pap. 5.95 (ISBN 0-88724-132-8, CD-0565). Carson-Dellos.

Read & Comprehend: Following Directions. Gail Aemmer. (Stick-Out-Your-Neck Ser.). (Illus.). 20p. (gr. 2-3). pap. 5.95 (ISBN 0-88724-131-X, CD-0564). Carson-Dellos.

Read & Comprehend: Following Directions. Gail Aemmer. (Stick-Out-Your-Neck Ser.). (Illus.). 20p. (gr. 1-2). 1985. pap. 5.95 (ISBN 0-88724-130-1, CD-0563). Carson-Dellos.

Read & Comprehend: Main Ideas. Gail Aemmer. (Stick-Out-Your-Neck Ser.). (Illus.). 20p. (gr. 2-3). 1985. pap. 4.95 (ISBN 0-88724-126-3, CD-0559). Carson-Dellos.

Read & Comprehend: Sequencing. Gail Aemmer. (Stick-Out-Your-Neck Ser.). (Illus.). 20p. (gr. 2-3). 1985. pap. 4.95 (ISBN 0-88724-145-X, CD-0554). Carson-Dellos.

Read & Comprehend: Vocabulary Development. Gail Aemmer. (Stick-Out-Your-Neck Ser.). (Illus.). 20p. (gr. 2-3). 1985. pap. 5.95 (ISBN 0-88724-121-2, CD-0549). Carson-Dellos.

Read & Do: Learning to Follow Written Directions. rev. & enl. ed. Katherine H. O'Connor. (Illus.). 51p. (gr. 1-3). 1973. wkbk 1.50 (ISBN 0-910812-09-8). Johnny Reads.

Read & Draw. J. M. Baggiani & V. M. Tewell. (Illus.). 12p. (gr. 1-3). 1966. pap. 2.00 (ISBN 0-934329-06-0). Baggiani-Tewell.

Read & Respond. Janet Swinton & William Agopsowicz. LC 87-23502. (Illus.). 272p. 1987. pap. text ed. 16.95x (ISBN 0-935732-10-1); instr's. manual avail. Roxbury Pub Co.

Read & Think Storybook Series, 15 bks. Sullivan Associates Staff. 1974. Bks. 1-7. 10.72 ea. (ISBN 0-686-76801-9); Bk. 8-15. 12.28 ea. (ISBN 0-686-76802-7). McGraw.

Read & Understand Chinese: A Guide to the Usage of Chinese Characters. Rita M. Choy. 368p. (Chinese.). 1989. pap. text ed. 14.95 (ISBN 0-941340-10-4). China West.

Read & Write: A Guide to Effective Composition. James F. Dorrill & Charles W. Harwell. 1987. pap. text ed. 12.00 (ISBN 0-15-575510-2); instr's. manual 3.25 (ISBN 0-15-575511-0). HarBraceJ.

Read & Write Chinese: A Simplified Guide to the Chinese Characters. rev. ed. Rita Mei-Wah Choy. 336p. (Chinese.). 1982. pap. text ed. 11.95 (ISBN 0-941340-09-0). China West.

Read Better, Read Faster: A New Approach to Efficient Reading. Manya De Leeuw & Eric De Leeuw. 256p. 1966. pap. 6.95 (ISBN 0-14-020740-6). Penguin.

Read Chinese, Vol. I. H. C. Fenn & M. G. Tewksbury. 236p. 1961. includes 4 cassettes 65.00x (ISBN 0-88432-090-1, M301). J Norton Pubs.

Read Chinese, Vol. II. H. C. Fenn & M. G. Tewksbury. 267p. 1983. includes 3 cassettes 55.00x (ISBN 0-88432-091-X, M310). J Norton Pubs.

Read Chinese, Bk. 1. rev. ed. Fred Wang. 8.95 (ISBN 0-88710-064-3); tapes avail. (ISBN 0-88710-065-1). Yale Far Eastern Pubns.

Read Chinese, Bk. 2. rev. ed. Richard Chang. 9.95 (ISBN 0-88710-066-X); tapes avail. (ISBN 0-88710-067-8). Yale Far Eastern Pubns.

Read Chinese, Bk. 3. Fred Wang & Richard Chang. 6.95 (ISBN 0-88710-068-6); tapes avail. (ISBN 0-88710-069-4). Yale Far Eastern Pubns.

Read English, Bk. 3. Demnitz. (Speak English Ser.). (Illus.). 80p. (Orig.). 1981. pap. text ed. 4.95 (ISBN 0-8325-0512-9). Natl Textbk.

Read English, Bk 1. Sherry Royce & Doris Zook. (Speak English Ser.). (Illus.). 80p. (Orig.). 1980. pap. text ed. 4.95 (ISBN 0-8325-0504-8). Natl Textbk.

Read English, Bk. 2. Joseph Coyle. (Speak English Ser.). (Illus.). 64p. (Orig.). 1981. pap. 4.95 (ISBN 0-8325-0508-0). Natl Textbk.

Read for Understanding, Bk. I. new ed. Selma E. Herr. Ed. by Piequet Press Staff. (Illus.). 225p. (Orig.). (gr. 6-12). 1987. pap. 6.95 (ISBN 0-914275-04-6). Piequet Pr.

Read for Your Life: Two Successful Efforts to Help People Read & an Annotated List of Books That Made Them Want To. Julia R. Palmer. LC 73-14695. 508p. 1974. 25.00 (ISBN 0-8108-0654-1). Scarecrow.

Read It Again!, K-2: A Guide for Teaching Reading Through Literature. Liz Rothlein & Terri Christman. 1988. pap. 9.95 (ISBN 0-673-38199-4). Scott F.

Read It Right, & Remember What You Read. Samuel Smith. (Orig.). 1970. pap. 4.50 (ISBN 0-06-463306-3, EH 306, B&N Bks). Har-Row.

Read Japanese Today. Len Walsh. LC 69-12078. 1969. pap. 5.95 (ISBN 0-8048-0496-6). C E Tuttle.

Read Me: A Course of Study to Improve Your Reading Speed, Comprenhension, Memory, & Concentration. Cliff Mauler. (Illus.). 191p. (gr. 9-12). 1979. spiral bdg. 14.95 (ISBN 0-9602842-0-6). Read Me Pub.

Read 'n Grow Picture Bible. Ed. by Libby Weed. LC 84-51093. (Illus.). 319p. (ps-6). 1984. 14.95 (ISBN 0-8344-0124-X, 124). Worthy TX.

Read-O-Mat: Syllabus. Alyce E. Faber. 1976. pap. text ed. 5.85 (ISBN 0-89420-006-2, 114008); cassette recordings 35.85 (ISBN 0-89420-179-4, 114000). Natl Book.

Read On: A Conference Approach to Reading. David Hornsby et al. LC 87-22938. vii, 186p. (Orig.). 1988. pap. text ed. 15.00x (ISBN 0-435-08459-3). Heinemann Ed.

Read on, Speak Out. Linda A. Ferreira & Marjorie Vai. LC 79-314. 1979. pap. text ed. 10.50 (ISBN 0-88377-133-0). Newbury Hse.

Read Out Read-in. Ed. by Robert McGovern & Richard Snyder. 39p. 1971. pap. 1.95 (ISBN 0-912592-09-5). Ashland Poetry.

Read, Reason, Write. 2nd, rev. ed. Dorothy Seyler. 448p. 1986. pap. text ed. write for info. (ISBN 0-394-36295-0, RanC). Random.

Read, Reflect, Write. Carmen Collins. (Illus.). 192p. 1984. pap. text ed. write for info. (ISBN 0-13-753558-9). P-H.

Read Right: Comprehension Power. J. E. Sparks & Carl E. Johnson. 1971. pap. text ed. write for info. (ISBN 0-02-478390-0, 47839). Macmillan.

Read Test: Reading Evaluation Adult Diagnosis. rev. ed. Ruth J. Colvin & Jane Root. 55p. 1982. pap. 5.50 (ISBN 0-930713-23-0). Lit Vol Am.

Read That Label: How to Tell What's Inside a Wine Bottle from What's on the Outside. Bruce M. Fingerhut & Steve Haskin. (Illus.). 128p. (Orig.). 1983. pap. 4.95 (ISBN 0-89651-652-0). B L Pub.

Read the Label: Reducing Risk by Providing Information. Susan Hadden. 300p. 1985. 30.50x (ISBN 0-8133-0244-7). Westview.

Read This Only to Yourself: The Private Writings of Midwestern Women, 1880-1910. Elizabeth Hampsten. LC 81-47008. (Midland jBks: No. 347). 256p. 1982. 25.00x (ISBN 0-253-34836-6); pap. 9.95x (ISBN 0-253-20347-3). Ind U Pr.

Read Through the Bible in a Year. John R. Kohlenberger, III. (Orig.). 1986. pap. 1.95 (ISBN 0-8024-7168-4). Moody.

Read-to-Me Bible ABC Book. Joy MacKenzie. LC 87-18337. 48p. (ps-2). 1988. 7.95 (ISBN 1-55513-861-6, Chariot Bks). Cook.

Read-to-Me Bible 1-2-3 Book. Joy MacKenzie. LC 87-18334. 48p. (ps-2). 1988. 7.95 (ISBN 1-55513-480-7, Chariot Bks). Cook.

Read-to-Me Storybook Staff. Child Study Association of America. LC 47-31488. (Illus.). (ps-1). 1947. 12.70 (ISBN 0-690-68832-6, Crowell Jr Bks). HarpJ.

Read to Me, Talk with Me. Barbara M. Lockhart. Orig. Title: Home Book Program. 208p. 1987. pap. text ed. 24.95 (ISBN 0-88450-210-4, 7370). Communication Skill.

Read to Succeed. 2nd ed. Jane Bracy et al. (Illus.). 192p. 1980. pap. 22.95x (ISBN 0-07-007035-0). McGraw.

Read to Write. Donald M. Murray. 640p. 1986. pap. text ed. 13.95 (ISBN 0-03-069776-X, HoltC). HR&W.

Read to Write. Halsey P. Taylor & Sheila F. Taylor. 1981. pap. text ed. write for info. (ISBN 0-673-15388-6). Scott F.

Read to Write: Using Children's Literature As a Springboard for Teaching Writing. rev. ed. John W. Stewig. LC 80-19047. (Orig.). 1980. pap. 13.95 (ISBN 0-03-056123-X). HR&W.

Read Vietnamese. Nguyen-Dinh-Hoa. LC 66-18965. 189p. 1980. pap. 9.50 (ISBN 0-8048-0497-4). C E Tuttle.

Read, Write, Revise: A Guide to Academic Writing. Mary J. Schenck. LC 87-60515. 300p. 1988. pap. text ed. write for info. (ISBN 0-312-00293-9); write for info. instr's. manual (ISBN 0-312-00294-7); write for info. instr's. ed. (ISBN 0-312-01285-3). St Martin.

Read Your Way to the Top with the Guide. Rose Saperstein & James Joseph. (Bluechip Business Bk.). (Illus.). 88p. 1987. pap. text ed. 7.95x (ISBN 0-930251-00-8). Bluechip Pubs.

Read Yourself Raw. Art Spiegelman & Francoise Mouly. LC 87-43045. (Illus.). 88p. 1987. 14.95 (ISBN 0-394-75551-0). Pantheon.

Readability. Judith M. Smith & Wayne A. King. (Michigan Learning Modules Ser.: No. 5). 1977. pap. 2.45x (ISBN 0-914004-08-5). Ulrich.

Readability Formula. H. Gilliland. 1980. 00.15 (ISBN 0-89992-508-1). Coun India Ed.

Readability: Its Past, Present, & Future. Ed. by Beverley Zakaluk & S. Jay Samuels. 1988. pap. 9.50 (ISBN 0-87207-795-0). Intl Reading.

Readability Machine: Radio Shack, TRS-80 Model 4 (Software & Documentation) Brian Pasch & Jacqueline K. Polk. 48p. 1986. 84.95 (ISBN 0-13-753609-7). P-H.

Readability Machine: The Readability Machine for Apple II; Apple IIe, Apple IIc, & Apple-Compatible Microcomputers. Brian Pasch & Jacqueline K. Polk. 48p. 1986. 84.95 (ISBN 0-13-753617-8). P-H.

Readability of Certain Type Sizes & Forms in Sight-Saving Classes. Harold J. McNally. LC 71-177040. (Columbia University. Teachers College. Contributions to Education: No. 883). Repr. of 1943 ed. 22.50 (ISBN 0-404-55883-6). AMS Pr.

Readable "Beowulf" The Old English Epic Newly Translated. Tr. by Stanley B. Greenfield. LC 81-16933. (Illus.). 173p. 1982. pap. 14.95x (ISBN 0-8093-1060-0). S Ill U Pr.

Readable People of George Meredith. Judith Wilt. 284p. 1975. 30.50x (ISBN 0-691-06275-7). Princeton U Pr.

Readable Writing: Revising for Style. H. Wendell Smith. 307p. 1985. pap. text ed. write for info. (ISBN 0-534-03278-8). Wadsworth Pub.

Read'em & Weep: The Songs You Forgot to Remember. Sigmund Spaeth. LC 79-11319. (Music Reprint Ser.). 1979. Repr. of 1926 ed. lib. bdg. 35.00 (ISBN 0-306-79564-7). Da Capo.

Reader & Study Guide for That Delicate Balance. George McKenna. 320p. 1984. pap. text ed. write for info (ISBN 0-394-34125-2, RanC). Random.

Reader & the Text Interpretative Strategies for Latin American Literatures. Diana S. Goodrich. LC 85-30697. (Purdue University Monographs in Romance Languages 18). xi, 150p. (Orig.). 1986. pap. 26.00x. Benjamins North Am.

Reader & the Writer: Essays for College Writing. Robert E. Yarber et al. 1982. pap. text ed. write for info. (ISBN 0-673-16042-4). Scott F.

Reader As Detective, Bk. III. Burton Goodman. (YA) (gr. 8-9). 1988. pap. text ed. 7.92 (ISBN 0-87720-777-1). Amsco Sch.

Reader As Detective Book I. Goodman. (gr. 6-7). 1985. pap. text ed. 7.92 (ISBN 0-87720-697-X). AMSCO Sch.

Reader As Detective Book II. Goodman. (gr. 7-8). 1986. pap. text ed. 7.92 (ISBN 0-87720-658-9). AMSCO Sch.

Reader for College Writers. 2nd ed. Ralph E. Loewe. (Illus.). 368p. 1985. pap. text ed. write for info. (ISBN 0-13-753641-0). P-H.

Reader in a Strange Land: The Activity of Reading Literary Utopias. Peter Ruppert. LC 85-16512. 192p. 1986. 19.00x. U of GA Pr.

Reader in American Foreign Policy. James M. McCormick. LC 86-70322. 411p. (Orig.). 1986. pap. text ed. 18.95 (ISBN 0-87581-318-6). Peacock Pubs.

Reader in American Library History. Ed. by Michael H. Harris. LC 71-165293. 242p. 1983. 28.50 (ISBN 0-313-24040-X, ZHR/). Greenwood.

Reader in Argument. Jeanne Fahnestock & Marie Secor. 448p. 1985. pap. text ed. write for info (ISBN 0-394-33155-9, RanC). Random.

Reader in Art Librarianship. Philip Pacey. (IFLA Publication: 34). 199p. 1985. lib. bdg. 20.00 (ISBN 3-598-20398-5). K G Saur.

Reader in Bureaucracy. Ed. by Robert K. Merton et al. 1965. pap. text ed. 17.95 (ISBN 0-02-921070-4). Free Pr.

Reader in Children's Librarianship. Joan Foster. 450p. 1983. 28.50 (ISBN 0-313-24039-6, ZRG/). Greenwood.

Reader in Classification & Descriptive Cataloging. Ed. by Ann F. Painter. LC 72-78204. 320p. 1972. 28.50 (ISBN 0-313-24035-3, ZRC/). Greenwood.

Reader in Comparative Librarianship. Ed. by D. J. Foskett. LC 76-10124. 333p. 1983. 28.50 (ISBN 0-313-24037-X, ZRE/). Greenwood.

Reader in Comparative Religion: An Anthropological Approach. 4th ed. William A. Lessa & Evon Z. Vogt. 1979. pap. text ed. 33.50 scp (ISBN 0-06-043991-2, HarpC). Har-Row.

Reader in Cultural Anthropology. Carleton S. Coon. LC 76-78. 634p. 1977. Repr. of 1948 ed. lib. bdg. 28.50 (ISBN 0-88275-394-0). Krieger.

Reader in Czech Sociolinguistics. Ed. by Jan Chloupek et al. LC 86-17024. (Linguistics & Literary Studies in Eastern Europe: No. 23). 344p. 1987. 58.00 (ISBN 90-272-1528-6). Benjamins North Am.

Reader in Documents of International Organizations. Ed. by Robert D. Stevens & Helen C. Stevens. LC 73-93966. 410p. 1983. 28.50 (ISBN 0-313-24036-1, ZRD/). Greenwood.

Reader in Electronics & Telecomunications, English-Italian. M. G. Calasso & M. L. Mirak. 470p. pap. 29.95 (ISBN 88-00-26311-9, M-9194). French & Eur.

Reader in Law Librarianship. Bernard D. Reams. LC 87-82949. xv, 375p. 1987. Repr. of 1976 ed. lib. bdg. 40.00 (ISBN 0-89941-589-X). W S Hein.

Reader in Library Administration. Ed. by Paul Wasserman & Mary Lee Bundy. LC 68-28324. 403p. 1968. 28.50 (ISBN 0-313-24033-7, ZRA/). Greenwood.

Reader in Library Services & the Computer. Ed. by Louis Kaplan. LC 70-149298. 239p. 1983. 28.50 (ISBN 0-313-24041-8, ZRI/). Greenwood.

Reader in Library Technology. Shirley Gray Adamovich. 236p. 1983. 28.50 (ISBN 0-313-24042-6, ZRJ/). Greenwood.

Reader in Marxist Philosophy. Ed. by Howard Selsam & Harry Martel. LC 63-14262. 384p. (Orig.). 1963. pap. 5.25 (ISBN 0-7178-0167-5). Intl Pubs Co.

Reader in Medical Librarianship. Ed. by Winifred Sewell. LC 72-86634. 340p. 1983. 28.50 (ISBN 0-313-24043-4, ZRK/). Greenwood.

Reader in Modern Literary Arabic. Farhat J. Ziadeh. LC 62-11966. 448p. 1981. Repr. of 1964 ed. 17.50x (ISBN 0-295-95840-5). U of Wash Pr.

Reader in Music Librarianship. Ed. by Carol June Bradley. LC 73-82994. 340p. 1983. 28.50 (ISBN 0-313-24044-2, ZRL/). Greenwood.

Reader in Planning Theory. Ed. by Andreas Faludi. LC 72-11536. 416p. 1973. text ed. 42.00 (ISBN 0-08-017066-8); pap. text ed. 15.00 (ISBN 0-08-017067-6). Pergamon.

Reader in Public Opinion & Mass Communication. 3rd ed. Ed. by Morris Janowitz & Paul Hirsch. LC 80-2444. 448p. 1981. pap. 15.95 (ISBN 0-02-916020-0). Free Pr.

Reader in Research Methods for Librarianship. Ed. by Mary L. Bundy & Paul Wasserman. LC 70-86858. 363p. 1983. 28.50 (ISBN 0-313-24045-0, ZRM/). Greenwood.

Reader in Russian & Soviet Literature, Vol. 3. Ed. by T. D. Tikhomirova et al. 223p. 1987. pap. 5.95 (ISBN 0-8285-3431-4, Pub. by Rus Lang Pubs USSR). Imported Pubns.

Reader in Science Information. Ed. by John Sherrod & Alfred Hodina. LC 72-97713. 403p. 1983. 28.50 (ISBN 0-313-24046-9, ZRN/). Greenwood.

Reader in Social Science Documentation. Ed. by Christopher D. Needham. LC 75-8049. 538p. 1983. 28.50 (ISBN 0-313-24047-7, ZRO/). Greenwood.

Reader in Technical Services. Ed. by Edward L. Applebaum. LC 72-87717. 284p. 1983. 28.50 (ISBN 0-313-24048-5, ZRP/). Greenwood.

Reader in the Academic Library. Ed. by Michael M. Reynolds. LC 71-112300. 378p. 1983. 28.50 (ISBN 0-313-24034-5, ZRB/). Greenwood.

Reader in the Dickens World. Susan R. Horton. LC 80-53031. 115p. 1981. 31.95x (ISBN 0-8229-1140-X). U of Pittsburgh Pr.

Reader in the History of Aphasia: From Franz Gall to Norman Geschwind. Ed. by Paul Eling. (Classics in Psycholinguistics Ser.: No. 4). 420p. 1988. 68.00 (ISBN 90-272-1893-5). Benjamins North Am.

Reader in the History of Books & Printing. Ed. by Paul A. Winckler. LC 78-17260. 406p. 1983. 28.50 (ISBN 0-313-24038-8, ZRF/). Greenwood.

Reader in the History of the Eastern Slavic Languages: Russian, Belorussian & Ukrainian. Ed. by George Y. Shevelov & Fred Holling. LC 58-9238. (Columbia Slavic Studies). pap. 22.30 (ISBN 0-317-09819-5, 2015390). Bks Demand UMI.

Reader in the Language of Shakespearean Drama. Vivian Salmon & Edwina Burgess. LC 86-30991. (Studies in the History of Language Sciences: No. 35). xx, 523p. 1987. 70.00x (ISBN 90-272-4516-9); pap. 21.95x (ISBN 0-915027-99-2). Benjamins North Am.

Reader in the Novels of C. M. Wieland. Richard G. Rogan. (American University Studies I (Germanic Languages & Literature): Vol. 1). 87p. 1981. pap. text ed. 10.25 (ISBN 3-261-04898-0). P Lang Pubs.

Reader in the Picaresque Novel. Helen H. Reed. (Serie A: Monagrafias, CXIV). 120p. 1984. 22.00 (ISBN 0-7293-0204-0, Pub. by Tamesis Bks Ltd). Longwood Pub Group.

Reader in the Text: Essays on Audience & Interpretation. Ed. by Susan Suleiman & Inge Crosman. LC 79-27619. 1980. 52.50x (ISBN 0-691-06436-9); pap. 14.50 (ISBN 0-691-10096-9). Princeton U Pr.

Reader Meets Author - Bridging the Gap: A Psycholinguistic & Sociolinguistic Perspective. Judith A. Langer & M. Trika Smith-Burke. 256p. 1982. pap. text ed. 9.50 (ISBN 0-87207-529-X). Intl Reading.

Reader of Classical Urdu Poetry, 3 vols. Muhammad A. Barker. 1977. 3 vol. set 45.00x (ISBN 0-87950-433-1); vol. 1, 530p. 15.00x (ISBN 0-87950-430-7); vol. 2, 430p. 15.00x (ISBN 0-87950-431-5); vol. 3, 500p. 15.00x (ISBN 0-87950-432-3); Set. 3 vols. & cassettes 120.00x (ISBN 0-87950-435-8); cassettes, 6 dual track 75.00x (ISBN 0-87950-434-X). Spoken Lang Serv.

Reader of Handwritten Japanese. P. G. O'Neill. LC 84-81170. 232p. 1985. 30.00x (ISBN 0-87011-698-3). Kodansha.

Reader of Modern Urdu Poetry. M. A. Barker et al. 334p. 1968. pap. 5.00x (ISBN 0-7735-9066-8). McGill-Queens U Pr.

Reader on Choosing an Automated Library System. Ed. by Joseph R. Matthews. LC 83-11821. ix, 390p. 1983. pap. 35.00x (ISBN 0-8389-0383-5). ALA.

Reader on Islam. Ed. by Arthur Jeffery. LC 79-52557. (Islam Ser.). 1980. Repr. of 1962 ed. lib. bdg. 50.00x (ISBN 0-8369-9264-4). Ayer Co Pubs.

Reader on Language Variety, Vol. 1. Ed. by C. S. Butler & R. Hartmann. (Exeter Linguistic Studies). 138p. 1979. pap. text ed. 6.95x (ISBN 0-85989-051-1, Pub. by U of Exeter UK). Humanities.

Reader on Social Sciences. E. F. Borisov & G. I. Libman. 463p. 1985. 7.95 (ISBN 0-8285-3369-5, Pub. by Progress pubs USSR). Imported Pubns.

Reader on the Library Building. Ed. by Hal B. Schell. LC 73-93967. 1983. 28.50 (ISBN 0-313-24049-3, ZRQ). Greenwood.

Reader on the Sanskrit Grammarians. Ed. by J. F. Staal. 557p. 1985. Repr. of 1972 ed. 38.00X (ISBN 81-208-0029-X, Pub. by Motilal Banarsidass India). Orient Bk Dist.

Reader on the Sociology of the Academic Profession. Ed. by Walter P. Metzger. LC 76-55212. (Academic Profession Ser.). 1977. Repr. lib. bdg. 51.00x (ISBN 0-405-10039-6). Ayer Co Pubs.

Reader Over Your Shoulder: A Handbook for Writers of English Prose. Robert Graves & Alan Hodge. LC 78-21367. 1979. pap. 3.95 (ISBN 0-394-72936-6). Random.

Reader Parts, 2 sets. Jon George. Ed. by Louise Goss. (Frances Clark Library for Piano Students). (Illus.). 32p. (Orig.). (gr. k-12). pap. text ed. 5.95 pts. A & B, 1969 (ISBN 0-87487-186-7). Birch Tree Gr.

Reader-Response Criticism: From Formalism to Post-Structuralism. Ed. by Jane P. Tompkins. LC 80-7966. 320p. 1981. pap. text ed. 9.95x (ISBN 0-8018-2401-X). Johns Hopkins.

Reader Response in the Classroom. Ed. by Charles R. Chew et al. 119p. 1986. pap. text ed. 7.00 (ISBN 0-930348-13-3). NY St Eng Coun.

Reader Services in Libraries: A Day in Honor of Margaret E. Monroe. Ed. by John J. Boll. 64p. 1982. pap. 4.00 (ISBN 0-936442-09-3). U Wis Sch Lib.

Reader Services in Polytechnic Libraries. Ed. by John Fletcher. 200p. 1985. text ed. 53.95 (ISBN 0-566-03528-6). Gower Pub Co.

Reader, the Text, the Poem: The Transactional Theory of the Literary Work. Louise Rosenblatt. 196p. 1978. 19.00 (ISBN 0-8141-3835-7). NCTE.

Reader, the Text, the Poem: The Transactional Theory of the Literary Work. Louise M. Rosenblatt. LC 78-16335. 214p. 1978. 22.50x (ISBN 0-8093-0883-5). S Ill U Pr.

Reader's Adviser, 3 vols. 13th ed. Ed. by Barbara A. Chernow & George A. Vallasi. 2500p. 1986. Set. lib. bdg. 195.00 (ISBN 0-8352-0923-7); lib. bdg. 75.00 ea. Bowker.

Reader's Adviser, 6 vols. 13th ed. 1988. Set. 375.00 (ISBN 0-8352-2428-7). Bowker.

Reader's Adviser, Vol. 4: The Best in the Literature of Philosophy & World Religions. 13th ed. Ed. by William L. Reese. 801p. 1988. 75.00 (ISBN 0-8352-2148-2). Bowker.

Reader's Adviser, Vol. 5: The Best in the Literature of Science, Technology, & Medicine. 13th ed. Ed. by Paul T. Durbin. 725p. 1988. 75.00 (ISBN 0-8352-2149-0). Bowker.

Reader's Adviser, Vol. 6: Indexes. 13th ed. Ed. by Bowker, R. R., Staff. 594p. 1988. 75.00 (ISBN 0-8352-2315-9). Bowker.

Readers Advisory Service: Selected Topical Booklists, Vol. 10. Ed. by Leonard Cohan. 1983. 115.00 (ISBN 0-685-79403-2). Sci Assoc Intl.

Readers & Collectors Guide to the Biographies of the American Presidents. Compiled by Jeffrey R. Speirs. 148p. (Orig.). 1988. pap. 19.95 (ISBN 0-945707-00-2). Amer Political.

Readers & Library Users. Martin L. Ward. 96p. 1977. pap. 9.95 (ISBN 0-85365-479-4, Pub. by Library Assn Pub London). ALA.

Readers & Writers. Alfred R. Orage. LC 72-99714. (Essay Index Reprint Ser.). 1922. 17.00 (ISBN 0-8369-1367-1). Ayer Co Pubs.

Reader's & Writer's Thesaurus. John P. Schumake. 556p. (Orig.). 1986. pap. 12.95 (ISBN 0-9616789-0-9, 1B). Earnest Pubns.

Readers & Writers with a Difference: A Holistic Approach to Teaching Learning Disabled & Remedial Students. Lynn K. Rhodes & Curt Dudley-Marling. LC 87-23819. xii, 329p. (Orig.). 1988. pap. text ed. 18.00X (ISBN 0-435-08453-4). Heinemann Ed.

Reader's Art: Virginia Woolf As Literary Critic. Mark Goldman. (Depropriétatibus Litterarum Ser.: No. 19). 1976. pap. text ed. 17.60x (ISBN 90-2793-275-1). Mouton.

Readers As Writers. Kate Kiefer. 448p. 1986. pap. text ed. 16.95 (ISBN 0-03-070409-X, HoltC). HR&W.

Reader's Bible, A Narrative: Selections from the King James Version. Ed. by Roland M. Frye. LC 77-311. 638p. 1979. pap. 14.95 (ISBN 0-691-01995-9). Princeton U Pr.

Reader's Browning. Walter Graham. 486p. 1980. Repr. lib. bdg. 30.00 (ISBN 0-8492-4984-8). R West.

Reader's Choice. 2nd ed. Margaret E. Baudoin et al. (English As a Second Language Ser.). 350p. 1988. pap. text ed. 9.95 (ISBN 0-472-08077-6). U of Mich Pr.

Readers' Comments on Recommendations for Estimating Prestress Losses. (PCI Journal Reprints Ser.). 20p. pap. 5.00 (ISBN 0-318-19753-7, JR171). Prestressed Concrete.

Readers' Comments on Shear & Torsion of Prestressed & Nonprestressed Concrete Beams. (PCI Journal Reprints Ser.). 24p. pap. 5.00 (ISBN 0-318-19760-X, JR228A). Prestressed Concrete.

Reader's Companion to Dante's Divine Comedy. Angelo A. DeGennaro. LC 85-21413. (Paperback Ser.). 130p. (Orig.). 1986. pap. 8.95. Philos Lib.

Reader's Companion to World Literature. rev. ed. Ed. by Lillian H. Hornstein et al. 1973. pap. 5.95 (ISBN 0-451-62441-6, ME2177, Ment). NAL.

Reader's Delight. Noel Perrin. LC 87-40507. (Illus.). 220p. 1988. 16.95 (ISBN 0-87451-430-4); pap. 9.95 (ISBN 0-87451-432-0). U Pr of New Eng.

Reader's Digest Atlas of the World. (Illus.). 240p. 1987. 34.95 (ISBN 0-528-83283-2). Rand McNally.

Reader's Digest Atlas of the World. Reader's Digest Editors. LC 87-675016. (Illus.). 240p. 1987. 34.95 (ISBN 0-89577-264-7). RD Assn.

Reader's Digest Book of Facts. Reader's Digest Editors. LC 86-29744. (Illus.). 416p. 1987. 24.95 (ISBN 0-89577-256-6, Pub. by RD Assn). Random.

Reader's Digest Book of the Great Barrier Reef. Reader's Digest Editors. (Illus.). 384p. 1985. 32.50 (ISBN 0-949819-41-7, Pub. by RD Assn). Random.

Reader's Digest Children's Songbook. Ed. by Reader's Digest Editors. (Illus.). 252p. (ps up). 1985. Lie-flat spiral bdg. 26.95 (ISBN 0-89577-214-0, Pub. by RD Assn). Random.

Reader's Digest Country & Western Songbook. Ed. by Reader's Digest Editors. (Illus.). 252p. 1983. Lie-flat spiral bdg. 25.95 (ISBN 0-89577-147-0, Pub. by RD Assn). Random.

Reader's Digest Family Safety & First Aid. Reader's Digest Editors. 256p. (Orig.). 1984. pap. 4.95 (ISBN 0-425-06817-X). Berkley Pub.

Reader's Digest Great Biographies, Vol. 1. Ed. by Reader's Digest Editors. LC 86-29816. (Open-Ended Ser.). (Illus.). 608p. 1987. 13.95 (ISBN 0-89577-259-0). RD Assn.

Reader's Digest Great Biographies, Vol. 2. Ed. by Reader's Digest Editors. LC 86-29816. (Open-Ended Ser.). (Illus.). 640p. 1987. 13.95 (ISBN 0-89577-260-4). RD Assn.

Reader's Digest Great Biographies, Vol. 3. Ed. by Reader's Digest Editors. LC 86-29816. (Open-ended Ser.). (Illus.). 576p. 1987. 13.95 (ISBN 0-89577-261-2). RD Assn.

Reader's Digest Guide to Creative Gardening. Reader's Digest Editors. LC 87-128856. (Illus.). 384p. 1986. 25.95 (ISBN 0-276-35223-8, Pub. by RD Assn). Random.

Reader's Digest Household Hints & Handy Tips: The Most Comprehensive, Best Organized, Hardest Working Collection of How-to Facts & Shortcuts. 1988. 25.95. Readers Digest Pr.

Reader's Digest Illustrated Book of Dogs. Reader's Digest Editors. (Illus.). 384p. 1984. 19.95 (ISBN 0-89577-206-X, Pub. by RD Assn). Random.

Reader's Digest Illustrated Encyclopedic Dictionary, 2 vols. Reader's Digest Editors. LC 87-9650. (Illus.). 1920p. 1987. Set. 49.96 (ISBN 0-89577-269-8). RD Assn.

Reader's Digest Legal Question & Answer Book. Reader's Digest Editors. LC 87-25963. 704p. 1988. 28.95 (ISBN 0-89577-291-4, Pub. by RD Assn). Random.

Reader's Digest Merry Christmas Songbook. Ed. by Reader's Digest Editors. LC 81-51285. (Illus.). 252p. 1981. 26.95 (ISBN 0-89577-105-5, Pub. by RD Assn). Random.

Reader's Encyclopedia of American Literature. Max J. Herzberg et al. LC 62-16546. (Illus.). 1962. T Y Crowell.

Reader's Encyclopedia of the American West. Howard R. Lamar. LC 76-17236. (Illus.). 1320p. 1987. 29.50i (ISBN 0-06-015726-7, HarpT). Har-Row.

Reader's Eye: Studies in Didactic Literary Theory from Dante to Tasso. Robert L. Montgomery. LC 78-57313. 1979. 35.00x (ISBN 0-520-03700-6). U of Cal Pr.

Reader's Greek-English Lexicon of the New Testament & a Beginner's Guide for the Translation of New Testament Greek. Sakae Kubo. (Andrews University Monographs, Studies in Religion: Vol. IV). x, 327p. 1975. text ed. 14.95 (ISBN 0-943872-04-9). Andrews Univ Pr.

Reader's Greek-English Lexicon of the New Testament & Beginner's Guide. Sakae Kubo. 1975. text ed. 16.95 (ISBN 0-310-26920-2, 6269). Zondervan.

Reader's Guide: The Development of Baha'i Literature in English. Eunice Braun. 176p. 1986. 17.95 (ISBN 0-85398-228-7); pap. 9.50 (ISBN 0-85398-229-5). G Ronald Pub.

Reader's Guide to A. E. van Vogt. Jeffrey M. Elliot. Ed. by Roger C. Schlobin. (Starmont Reader's Guides to Contemporary Science Fiction & Fantasy Authors Ser.: Vol. 17). (Illus., Orig.). 1989. 17.95x (ISBN 0-916732-46-0); pap. text ed. 9.95x (ISBN 0-916732-45-2). Starmont Hse.

Reader's Guide to African Literature. Hans Zell & Helene Silver. LC 76-83165. 1971. pap. 9.50 (ISBN 0-8419-0018-3, Africana); pap. text ed. 9.50 (ISBN 0-8419-0019-1, Africana). Holmes & Meier.

Reader's Guide to Alfred Bester. Carolyn Wendell. Ed. by Roger C. Schlobin. LC 80-19655. (Starmont Reader's Guides to Contemporary Science Fiction & Fantasy Authors Ser.: Vol. 6). (Illus., Orig.). 1982. 15.95x (ISBN 0-916732-17-7); pap. text ed. 7.95x. Starmont Hse.

Reader's Guide to Arthur C. Clarke. rev. ed. Eric S. Rabkin. Ed. by Roger C. Schlobin. LC 79-84709. (Starmont Reader's Guides to Contemporary Science Fiction & Fantasy Author's Ser.: Vol. 1). (Illus., Orig.). 1980. 15.95x; pap. text ed. 7.95x (ISBN 0-916732-21-5). Starmont Hse.

Reader's Guide to C. S. Lewis. Brian Murphy. Ed. by Roger C. Schlobin. LC 82-7346. (Starmont Reader's Guides to Contemporary Science Fiction & Fantasy Authors Ser.: Vol. 14). (Illus., Orig.). 1983. 15.95x (ISBN 0-916732-38-X); pap. text ed. 7.95x (ISBN 0-916732-37-1). Starmont Hse.

Reader's Guide to Canadian History, No. 1: Beginnings to Confederation. Ed. by D. A. Muise. 256p. 1982. pap. 10.95c (ISBN 0-8020-6442-6). U of Toronto Pr.

Reader's Guide to Canadian History, No. 2: Confederation to the Present. Ed. by J. L. Granatstein & Paul Stevens. 288p. 1982. pap. 11.95c (ISBN 0-8020-6490-6). U of Toronto Pr.

Reader's Guide to Contemporary Literary Criticism & Theory. Elisa K. Sparks. (Reference Books-Literature). 300p. 1988. lib. bdg. 25.00x (ISBN 0-8161-8743-6). G K Hall.

Reader's Guide to Contemporary Literary Theory. Raman Selden. LC 85-5353. 160p. 1985. 17.00 (ISBN 0-8131-1560-4); pap. 7.00 (ISBN 0-8131-0167-0). U Pr of Ky.

Reader's Guide to D. H. Lawrence. Phillip Hobsbaum. 160p. 1981. pap. 9.95 (ISBN 0-500-15017-6). Thames Hudson.

Reader's Guide to David Lindsay. Gary K. Wolfe. Ed. by Roger C. Schlobin. LC 82-5563. (Starmont Reader's Guides to Contemporary Science Fiction & Fantasy Authors Ser.: Vol. 9). (Illus., Orig.). 1982. 15.95x (ISBN 0-916732-29-0); pap. text ed. 7.95x (ISBN 0-916732-26-6). Starmont Hse.

Reader's Guide to Dylan Thomas. William Y. Tindall. 1973. lib. bdg. 22.50x (ISBN 0-374-97948-0, Octagon). Hippocrene Bks.

Reader's Guide to E. E. "Doc" Smith. Joe Sanders. Ed. by Roger C. Schlobin. LC 85-30434. (Starmont Reader's Guides to Contemporary Science Fiction & Fantasy Authors Ser.: Vol. 24). (Illus., Orig.). 1986. 15.95x; pap. text ed. 7.95x. Starmont Hse.

Reader's Guide to Ernest Hemingway. Arthur Waldhorn. 1977. Repr. of 1972 ed. lib. bdg. 20.00x (ISBN 0-88254-885-9, Octagon). Hippocrene Bks.

Reader's Guide to Fifty American Novels. Ian Ousby. LC 79-53437. (Reader's Guide Ser.). 351p. 1979. text ed. 24.50x (ISBN 0-06-495318-1). B&N Imports.

Reader's Guide to Fifty American Poets. Peter Jones. (Reader's Guide Ser.). 386p. 1980. 24.50x (ISBN 0-389-20140-5). B&N Imports.

Reader's Guide to Fifty British Plays: 1660-1900. John C. Thompson. (Reader's Guide Ser.). 448p. 1980. 24.50x (ISBN 0-389-20139-1). B&N Imports.

Reader's Guide to Fifty British Poets: 1300-1900. Michael Schmidt. (Reader's Guide Ser.). 430p. 1980. 24.50x (ISBN 0-389-20137-5). B&N Imports.

Reader's Guide to Fifty European Novels. Martin Seymour-Smith. (Reader's Guide Ser.). 528p. 1980. 24.50x (ISBN 0-389-20138-3). B&N Imports.

Reader's Guide to Fifty Modern British Plays. Benedict Nightingale. LC 82-11448. (Reader's Guide). 480p. 1982. text ed. 24.50x (ISBN 0-389-20239-8). B&N Imports.

Reader's Guide to Fifty Modern European Poets. John Pilling. LC 82-11363. (Reader's Guide). 480p. 1982. text ed. 24.50x (ISBN 0-389-20241-X). B&N Imports.

Reader's Guide to Frank Herbert. David M. Miller. Ed. by Roger C. Schlobin. LC 80-20880. (Starmont Reader's Guides to Contemporary Science Fiction & Fantasy Author Ser.: Vol. 5). (Illus., Orig.). 1980. 19.95x (ISBN 0-916732-16-9). Starmont Hse.

Reader's Guide to Frederik Pohl. Thomas Clareson. Ed. by Roger C. Schlobin. (Starmont Reader's Guides to Contemporary Science Fiction & Fantasy Authors Ser.: Vol. 39). (Illus., Orig.). 1987. 17.95x (ISBN 0-930261-34-8); pap. 9.95x (ISBN 0-930261-33-X). Starmont Hse.

Reader's Guide to Fritz Leiber. Jeff Frane. Ed. by Roger C. Scholbin. LC 80-22107. (Starmont Reader's Guides to Contemporary Science Fiction & Fantasy Authors Ser.: Vol. 8). (Illus., Orig.). 1980. 15.95x (ISBN 0-916732-02-9); pap. text ed. 7.95x (ISBN 0-916732-10-X). Starmont Hse.

Reader's Guide to Gene Wolfe. Joan Gordon. Ed. by Roger C. Schlobin. LC 85-17163. (Starmont Reader's Guides to Contemporary Science Fiction & Fantasy Authors Ser.: Vol. 29). (Illus., Orig.). 1986. 15.95x; pap. text ed. 7.95x. Starmont Hse.

Reader's Guide to Gerard Manley Hopkins. Norman H. Mackenzie. LC 80-69275. (Paperback Ser.). 256p. 1981. 34.50x (ISBN 0-8014-1349-4); pap. 13.95x (ISBN 0-8014-9221-1). Cornell U Pr.

Reader's Guide to Graham Greene. Paul O'Prey. LC 88-50134. 160p. (Orig.). 1988. pap. 10.95 (ISBN 0-500-15019-2). Thames Hudson.

Reader's Guide to Great Twentieth-Century English Novels. Frederick R. Karl & Marvin Magalaner. 1972. lib. bdg. 22.50x (ISBN 0-87052-003-2, Octagon). Hippocrene Bks.

Reader's Guide to H. G. Wells. Robert Crossley. Ed. by Roger C. Schlobin. LC 84-2691. (Starmont Reader's Guides to Contemporary Science Fiction & Fantasy Authors Ser.: Vol. 19). (Illus., Orig.). 1986. 15.95x (ISBN 0-916732-51-7); pap. text ed. 7.95x (ISBN 0-916732-50-9). Starmont Hse.

Reader's Guide to H. P. Lovecraft. S. T. Joshi. Ed. by Roger C. Schlobin. LC 82-10236. (Starmont Reader's Guides to Contemporary Science Fiction & Fantasy Authors Ser.: Vol. 13). (Illus., Orig.). 1982. 15.95x (ISBN 0-916732-36-3); pap. text ed. 7.95x (ISBN 0-916732-35-5). Starmont Hse.

Reader's Guide to Hal Clement. Donald M. Hassler. Ed. by Roger C. Schlobin. LC 82-5577. (Starmont Reader's Guides to Contemporary Science Fiction & Fantasy Authors Ser.: Vol. 11). (Illus., Orig.). 1982. 15.95x (ISBN 0-916732-30-4); pap. text ed. 7.95x (ISBN 0-916732-27-4). Starmont Hse.

Reader's Guide to Isaac Asimov. Donald M. Hassler. Ed. by Roger C. Schlobin. (Starmont Reader's Guides to Contemporary Science Fiction & Fantasy Authors Ser.: Vol. 40). (Illus., Orig.). 1988. 17.95x (ISBN 0-930261-32-1); pap. text ed. 9.95x (ISBN 0-930261-31-3). Starmont Hse.

Reader's Guide to Jack London. Gorman Beauchamp. Ed. by Roger C. Schlobin. LC 82-7345. (Starmont Reader's Guides to Contemporary Science Fiction & Fantasy Authors Ser.: Vol. 15). (Illus., Orig.). 1984. 15.95x (ISBN 0-916732-40-1); pap. text ed. 7.95x (ISBN 0-916732-39-8). Starmont Hse.

Reader's Guide to James Joyce. William Y. Tindall. 304p. 1959. pap. 9.95 (ISBN 0-374-50112-2). FS&G.

Reader's Guide to James Tiptree, Jr. Mark Siegel. Ed. by Roger C. Schlobin. (Starmont Reader's Guide to Contemporary Science Fiction & Fantasy Authors Ser.: Vol. 22). (Illus., Orig.). 1985. 15.95x (ISBN 0-916732-68-1); pap. text ed. 7.95x (ISBN 0-916732-67-3). Starmont Hse.

Reader's Guide to Japanese Literature. J. Thomas Rimer. 208p. 1988. pap. 14.95 (ISBN 0-87011-896-X). Kodansha.

Reader's Guide to Joe Haldeman. Joan Gordon. Ed. by Roger C. Schlobin. LC 80-21388. (Starmont Reader's Guide to Contemporary Science Fiction & Fantasy Author Ser.: Vol. 4). (Illus., Orig.). 1980. 15.95x (ISBN 0-916732-15-0). Starmont Hse.

Reader's Guide to Marion Zimmer Bradley. Rosemarie Arbur. Ed. by Roger C. Schlobin. (Starmont Reader's Guide to Contemporary Science Fiction & Fantasy Authors Ser.: Vol. 27). (Illus., Orig.). 1985. 16.95x (ISBN 0-916732-96-7); pap. text ed. 8.95x (ISBN 0-916732-95-9). Starmont Hse.

Reader's Guide to Olaf Stapledon. John Kinnaird. Ed. by Roger C. Schlobin. LC 84-2656. (Starmont Reader's Guides to Contemporary Science Fiction & Fantasy Authors Ser.: Vol. 21). (Illus., Orig.). 1986. 15.95x (ISBN 0-916732-55-X); pap. text ed. 7.95x (ISBN 0-916732-54-1). Starmont Hse.

Readers' Guide to Periodical Literature, 45 Vols. 1900-87. 120.00 ea. Wilson.

Reader's Guide to Philip Jose Farmer. Mary T. Brizzi. Ed. by Roger C. Schlobin. LC 79-17691. (Starmont Reader's Guides to Contemporary Science Fiction & Fantasy Authors Ser.: Vol. 3). (Illus., Orig.). 1980. 15.95x (ISBN 0-916732-14-2); pap. text ed. 7.95x (ISBN 0-916732-05-3). Starmont Hse.

Reader's Guide to Philip K. Dick. Hazel Pierce. Ed. by Roger C. Schlobin. LC 82-6005. (Starmont Reader's Guides to Contemporary Science Fiction & Fantasy Authors Ser.: Vol. 12). (Illus., Orig.). 1982. 15.95x (ISBN 0-916732-34-7); pap. text ed. 7.95x (ISBN 0-916732-33-9). Starmont Hse.

Reader's Guide to Piers Anthony. Michael R. Collings. Ed. by Roger C. Schlobin. LC 83-2466. (Starmont Reader's Guides to Contemporary Science Fiction & Fantasy Authors Ser.: Vol. 20). (Illus., Orig.). 1983. 15.95x (ISBN 0-916732-53-3); pap. text ed. 7.95x (ISBN 0-916732-52-5). Starmont Hse.

Reader's Guide to Proclamation: For Sundays & Major Feasts in Cycle A. Jerome J. DuCharme. 160p. 1974. pap. 2.95 (ISBN 0-8199-0577-1). Franciscan Herald.

Reader's Guide to Remembrance of Things Past. Terence Kilmartin. LC 83-42862. 193p. 1984. 14.45 (ISBN 0-394-53326-7, Vin); pap. 7.95 (ISBN 0-394-72096-2). Random.

Reader's Guide to Robert Bloch. Randall B. Larson. Ed. by Roger C. Schlobin. LC 86-5751. (Starmont Reader's Guides to Contemporary Science Fiction & Fantasy Authors Ser.: Vol. 37). (Illus., Orig.). 1986. 16.95x (ISBN 0-930261-59-3); pap. text ed. 8.95x (ISBN 0-930261-58-5). Starmont Hse.

Reader's Guide to Robert Lowell. Philip Hobsbaum. LC 88-50133. 176p. (Orig.). 1988. pap. 10.95 (ISBN 0-500-15020-6). Thames Hudson.

Reader's Guide to Robert Silverberg. Thomas D. Clareson. Ed. by Roger C. Schlobin. LC 83-542. (Starmont Reader's Guides to Contemporary Science Fiction & Fantasy Authors Ser.: Vol. 18). (Illus., Orig.). 1983. 15.95x (ISBN 0-916732-48-7); pap. text ed. 7.95x (ISBN 0-916732-47-9). Starmont Hse.

Reader's Guide to Roger Zelazny. Carl B. Yoke. Ed. by Roger C. Schlobin. LC 79-17107. (Starmont Reader's Guides to Contemporary Science Fiction & Fantasy Authors Ser.: Vol. 2). (Illus., Orig.). 1979. 19.95x (ISBN 0-916732-42-8). Starmont Hse.

Reader's Guide to Samuel R. Delany. Jane B. Weedman. Ed. by Roger C. Schlobin. LC 82-5545. (Starmont Reader's Guides to Contemporary Science Fiction & Fantasy Authors Ser.: Vol. 10). (Illus., Orig.). 1982. 15.95x (ISBN 0-916732-28-2); pap. text ed. 7.95x (ISBN 0-916732-25-8). Starmont Hse.

Reader's Guide to Shakespeare & His Contemporaries. Marguerite Alexander. LC 79-53435. (Reader's Guide Ser.). 386p. 1979. text ed. 24.50x (ISBN 0-06-490149-1, 06310). B&N Imports.

Reader's Guide to Suzy McKee Charnas, Octavia Butler & Joan Vinge. Marleen S. Barr et al. Ed. by Roger C. Schlobin. (Starmont Reader's Guides to Contemporary Science Fiction & Fantasy Authors Ser.: Vol. 23). (Illus., Orig.). 1985. 17.95x (ISBN 0-916732-92-4); pap. text ed. 9.95x (ISBN 0-916732-91-6). Starmont Hse.

Reader's Guide to T. S. Eliot. George Williamson. 270p. 1974. Repr. lib. bdg. 20.00x (ISBN 0-88254-887-5, Octagon). Hippocrene Bks.

Reader's Guide to the Alexander Technique: A Selected Annotated Bibliography. Phyllis Sanfilippo. 96p. (Orig.). 1987. pap. 25.00 (ISBN 0-913111-17-1). Centerline.

Reader's Guide to the Appraisal Journal, 1970-1980. 99p. 1981. pap. 9.50 (ISBN 0-911780-55-6). Am Inst Real Estate Appraisers.

Reader's Guide to the Best Evangelical Books. Ed. by Mark L. Branson. LC 82-48205. 208p. (Orig.). 1982. pap. 5.95 (ISBN 0-06-061046-8, RD-388, HarpR). Har-Row.

Reader's Guide to the Classic British Mystery. Susan P. Oleksiw. 300p. 1988. lib. bdg. 29.95x (ISBN 0-8161-8787-8, Hall Reference). G K Hall.

Reader's Guide to the Contemporary English Novel. Frederick R. Karl. 1972. lib. bdg. 25.00x (ISBN 0-374-94523-3, Octagon). Hippocrene Bks.

Reader's Guide to the Eighteenth-Century English Novel: The Adversary Literature. Frederick R. Karl. LC 79-143303. 360p. 1974. pap. 4.95 (ISBN 0-374-51248-5). FS&G.

Reader's Guide to the Everyman's Library. Ed. by Donald A. Ross. 1976. 14.95x (ISBN 0-460-00889-7, Evman); pap. 2.50x (ISBN 0-460-01889-2). Biblio Dist.

Reader's Guide to the Great Religions. 2nd ed. Ed. by Charles J. Adams. LC 76-10496. 1977. 24.95 (ISBN 0-02-900240-0). Free Pr.

Reader's Guide to the Mahatma Letters. George Linton & V. Hanson. 4.95 (ISBN 0-8356-7481-9). Theos Pub Hse.

Reader's Guide to the Nineteenth-Century English Novel. Julia P. Brown. 160p. 1986. pap. 7.95 (ISBN 0-02-079560-2, Collier). Macmillan.

Reader's Guide to the Plays of W. B. Yeats. Richard Taylor. LC 81-21295. 192p. 1984. 29.95 (ISBN 0-312-66456-7). St Martin.

Reader's Guide to the Roman de la Rose. Maxwell Luria. LC 81-22767. xii, 282p. 1982. 35.00 (ISBN 0-208-01838-7, Archon). Shoe String.

Reader's Guide to the Short Stories of Ernest Hemingway. Paul Smith. 1988. 35.00 (ISBN 0-8161-8794-0). G K Hall.

Reader's Guide to the Short Stories of Mark Twain. James D. Wilson. 248p. 1987. lib. bdg. 35.00x (ISBN 0-8161-8721-5, Hall Reference). G K Hall.

Reader's Guide to the Short Stories of Herman Melville. Lea B. V. Newman. (Reference Bks). 344p. 1986. lib. bdg. 40.00x (ISBN 0-8161-8653-7). G K Hall.

Reader's Guide to the Short Stories of Nathaniel Hawthorne. Lea B. Newman. 1979. lib. bdg. 40.50 (ISBN 0-8161-8398-8, Hall Reference). G K Hall.

Reader's Guide to the Social Sciences. rev. ed. Ed. by Bert F. Hoselitz. 1972. pap. 3.95 (ISBN 0-02-914990-8). Free Pr.

Readers' Guide to the Tarlton Law Library. rev. & updated ed. (Illus.). 27p. 1980. 2.00 (ISBN 0-686-75485-9). U of Tex Tarlton Law Lib.

Reader's Guide to Theodore Sturgeon. Lahna Diskin. Ed. by Roger C. Schlobin. LC 80-21423. (Starmont Reader's Guides to Contemporary Science Fiction & Fantasy Author Ser.: Vol. 7). (Illus., Orig.). 1981. 15.95x (ISBN 0-686-86765-3); pap. text ed. 7.95x (ISBN 0-916732-09-6). Starmont Hse.

Reader's Guide to Walt Whitman. Gay Wilson Allen. 1971. Repr. lib. bdg. 19.00x (ISBN 0-88254-971-5, Octagon). Hippocrene Bks.

Reader's Guide to William Butler Yeats. John Unterecker. LC 72-154661. 1971. Repr. of 1959 ed. lib. bdg. 22.50x (Octagon). Hippocrene Bks.

Reader's Guide to William Faulkner. Edmond L. Volpe. 427p. 1975. Repr. of 1964 ed. lib. bdg. 27.50x (ISBN 0-88254-966-9, Octagon). Hippocrene Bks.

Reader's Guide to William Gaddis's "The Recognitions". Steven Moore. LC 81-7572. xii, 337p. 1982. 28.95x (ISBN 0-8032-3072-9). U of Nebr Pr.

Reader's Handbook. Rose Wassman & Anne Paye. 1985. pap. text ed. write for info. (ISBN 0-673-15904-3). Scott F.

Reader's Handbook of Famous Names in Fiction. E. Brewer. 69.95 (ISBN 0-8490-0928-6). Gordon Pr.

Reader's Handbook to Proust. Philip A. Spalding. LC 74-20705. 1974. Repr. of 1959 ed. lib. bdg. 45.00 (ISBN 0-8414-7748-5). Folcroft.

Reader's Hebrew-English Lexicon of the Old Testament, Vol. 4. Ed. by Terry A. Armstrong et al. 224p. 1988. text ed. 16.95 (ISBN 0-310-37000-0, 6296). Zondervan.

Reader's Hebrew-English Lexicon of the Old Testament: Genesis-II Kings. Ed. by Terry Armstrong et al. (Hebrew & Eng.). 1982. 16.95 (ISBN 0-310-37040-X, 6291). Zondervan.

Reader's Hebrew-English Lexicon of the Old Testament: Isaiah-Malachi, Vol. 3. Terry A. Armstrong et al. 208p. 1985. 16.95 (ISBN 0-310-37010-8, 6293). Zondervan.

Reader's History of American Literature. T. W. Higginson & A. Boynton. 1973. Repr. of 1903 ed. 30.00 (ISBN 0-8274-0170-1). R West.

Reader's Johnson: A Representative Selection of His Writings. C. H. Conley. 1977. Repr. of 1940 ed. lib. bdg. 30.00 (ISBN 0-8495-0708-1). Arden Lib.

Readers, Texts, Teachers. Ed. by Bill Corcoran & Emrys Evans. 272p. (Orig.). 1987. pap. text ed. 13.50x (ISBN 0-86709-187-8). Boynton Cook Pubs.

Reader's Theatre. 1987. 9.95 (ISBN 0-88047-132-8). DOK Pubs.

Reader's Theatre Comes to Church. 2nd ed. Gordon C. Bennett. LC 85-61999. 128p. 1985. pap. 7.95 (ISBN 0-916260-33-X, B-191). Meriwether Pub.

Readers Theatre Handbook. 3rd ed. Leslie I. Coger & Melvin R. White. 1982. pap. text ed. write for info. (ISBN 0-673-15270-7). Scott F.

Reader's Theatre: Story Dramatization in the Classroom. Shirlee Sloyer. LC 82-8146. (Illus., Orig.). 1982. pap. 12.25 (ISBN 0-8141-3838-1). NCTE.

Readership Research. Guy Consterdine. 200p. 1987. text ed. write for info. (ISBN 0-566-05071-4). Gower Pub Co.

Readership Research: Proceedings of the International Symposim, 2nd, Montreal, 1983. Ed. by H. Henry. 560p. 1984. 137.00 (ISBN 0-444-87599-9, North-Holland). Elsevier.

Readership Research: Theory & Practice, 1987. H. Henry. 1987. 134.50 (ISBN 0-444-70224-5). Elsevier.

Readiness for Kindergarten. James O. Massey. 16p. 1975. pap. 1.75 (ISBN 0-89106-014-6, 1281). Consulting Psychol.

Readiness for Reconciliation. Lynn Buzzard & Juanita Buzzard. 36p. (Orig.). 1982. wkbk 3.00 (ISBN 0-686-39857-2). Chr Legal.

Readiness for Reconciliation. rev. ed. Lynn R. Buzzard & Juanita Buzzard. Ed. by Laury Eck. 32p. (Orig.). 1987. pap. text ed. 3.00 (ISBN 0-944561-07-1). Chr Legal.

Readiness for Reconciliation. rev. ed. Lynn R. Buzzard et al. 32p. 1988. pap. text ed. 3.00 (ISBN 0-944561-18-7). Chr Legal.

Readiness for Religion. Ronald Goldman. 1970. pap. 4.95 (ISBN 0-8164-2060-2, SP70, HarpR). Har-Row.

Readiness for Religion. Harold Loukes. LC 63-11818. (Orig.). 1963. pap. 2.50x (ISBN 0-87574-126-6). Pendle Hill.

Readiness Games & Activities. Arline Nichols & Susan Coleridge. (ps-3). 1980. 5.95 (ISBN 0-916456-93-5, GA 173). Good Apple.

Readiness Level see Competency Tests for Basic Reading Skills.

Readiness Roundup. Patricia Rex. (ps). 1988. pap. 6.95 (ISBN 0-8224-5775-X). D S Lake Pubs.

Readiness to Remember, 2 pts. Ed. by D. P. Kimble. Incl. Vol. 1. 354p. 103.00 (ISBN 0-677-14420-2); Vol. 2. 410p. 103.00 (ISBN 0-677-14430-X). 764p. 1969. Set. 182.00 (ISBN 0-677-13420-7). Gordon & Breach.

Reading. Richard L. Allington & Kathleen Krull. LC 80-16547. (Beginning to Learn about Ser.). (Illus.). 32p. (ps-2). 1980. PLB 15.33 (ISBN 0-8172-1322-8). Raintree Pubs.

Reading. Richard L. Allington & Kathleen Krull. LC 80-16547. (E. G. Beginning to Learn about... Ser.). (Illus.). 32p. (gr. k-2). 1985. pap. 9.27 (ISBN 0-8172-2485-8). Raintree Pubs.

Reading. James T. Martinoff et al. (Language Rehabilitation Ser.). 230p. 1981. spiral bdg. 69.00x (ISBN 0-88120-128-6, 2368). Pro Ed.

Reading. Jan Ormerod. LC 84-12628. (Illus.). 24p. (ps). 1985. 4.95 (ISBN 0-688-04127-2). Lothrop.

Reading. (Illus.). 32p. (gr. 6-12). 1983. pap. 1.25x (ISBN 0-8395-3393-4, 3393). BSA.

Reading. Hugh Walpole. 93p. 1986. Repr. of 1927 ed. lib. bdg. 15.00 (ISBN 0-8495-5927-8). Arden Lib.

Reading - Learning - Enjoying: A College Reader. Harold Newman. LC 88-19495. 94p. 1988. pap. text ed. 15.00 (ISBN 0-9613577-2-X). Prestige Educ.

Reading - Learning Disability: An Ecological Approach. Jill Bartoli & Morton Botel. 280p. 1988. text ed. 29.95x (ISBN 0-8077-2905-1); pap. text ed. 16.95x (ISBN 0-8077-2904-3). Tchrs Coll.

Reading a Newspaper. Phyllis Larned & Nick Randall. (Survival Guides Ser.). (Illus.). 64p. (gr. 7-12). 1978. pap. text ed. 3.95 (ISBN 0-915510-26-X). Janus Bks.

Reading a Novel. Walter E. Allen. 1978. Repr. of 1956 ed. lib. bdg. 18.50 (ISBN 0-8495-0109-1). Arden Lib.

Reading a Novel. Walter E. Allen. LC 72-194361. 1949. 15.00 (ISBN 1-8141-2924-3). Folcroft.

Reading a Novel Approach. Janice Szabos. (Illus.). 112p. (gr. 4-8). 1984. wkbk 8.95 (ISBN 0-86653-186-6). Good Apple.

Reading: A Research Retrospective, 1881-1941. Ed. by John T. Guthrie. 101p. 1984. 7.00 (ISBN 0-87207-959-7). Intl Reading.

Reading Abbey Cartularies, I. Ed. by B. R. Kemp. (RHS Camden Fourth Ser.). 196p. 1986. 27.00 (ISBN 0-86193-108-4, Pub. by Boydell & Brewer). Longwood Pub Group.

Reading Abbey Cartularies, No. II. Ed. by B. R. Kemp. (Royal Historical Society, Camden: 4th, No. 33). 1988. 36.00 (Pub. by Boydell & Brewer). Longwood Pub Group.

Reading Ability. Charles A. Perfetti. (Illus.). 1985. 37.50x (ISBN 0-19-503501-1). Oxford U Pr.

Reading about Science, Skills & Concepts. John F. Mongillo et al. Ed. by Joanne E. Kane. (Reading about Science, Skills & Concepts Ser.). (Illus.). 128p. (gr. 4-7). 1980. Bk. A. pap. text ed. 8.00 (ISBN 0-07-002421-9); Bk. B. pap. text ed. 8.28 (ISBN 0-07-002422-7); Bk. C. pap. text ed. 8.28 (ISBN 0-07-002423-5); Bk. D. pap. text ed. 8.40 (ISBN 0-07-002424-3); Bk. E. pap. text ed. 7.92 (ISBN 0-07-002425-1); Bk. F. pap. text ed. 8.88 (ISBN 0-07-002426-X); Bk. G. pap. text ed. 8.88 (ISBN 0-07-002427-8). McGraw.

Reading (Absent) Character: Towards a Theory of Characterization in Fiction. Thomas Docherty. LC 83-12197. 1983. 45.00x (ISBN 0-19-812822-3). Oxford U Pr.

Reading Achievement Program for the Moderately & Severely Retarded. Sharon Evans & M. Ray Denney. LC 74-81202. xviii, 30p. 1974. pap. text ed. 2.50 (ISBN 0-8134-1665-5, 1665). Inter Print Pubs.

Reading Activities for Every Month of the School Year. Sue J. Erlenbusch. 288p. 1988. pap. 24.95x (ISBN 0-87628-722-4). Ctr Appl Res.

Reading Activities for Middle & Secondary Schools: A Handbook for Teachers. 2nd ed. Carl B. Smith & Peggy G. Elliott. 264p. 1986. pap. 15.95x (ISBN 0-8077-2826-8). Tchrs Coll.

Reading Activities for Today's Elementary Schools. Paul C. Burns & Betty D. Roe. 1979. pap. 22.36 (ISBN 0-395-30573-X). HM.

Reading Activities Handbook. Wilma H. Miller. LC 80-17117. (Illus.). 476p. (gr. 1-8). 1980. pap. 22.95 (ISBN 0-03-051371-5). HR&W.

Reading Activities in Content Areas: An Ideabook for Middle & Secondary Schools. 2nd ed. Dorothy Piercey. 590p. 1982. pap. 28.95x (ISBN 0-205-07372-7, 2373726, Pub. by Longwood Div). Allyn.

Reading Adrienne Rich: Reviews & Re-Visions, 1951-81. Ed. by Jane R. Cooper. 1984. 20.00 (ISBN 0-472-09350-9); pap. 10.95 (ISBN 0-472-06350-2). U of Mich Pr.

Reading Ads, Legal Documents & Reference Materials. Carolyn M. Starkey & Norgina W. Penn. (Essential Life Skills Ser.). 64p. Date not set. pap. 4.95 (ISBN 0-8442-5315-4, Passport Bks). Natl Textbk.

Reading after Freud: Essays on Goethe, Holderlin, Habermas, Nietzsche, Brecht, Celan, & Freud. Rainer Nagele. LC 86-20730. 216p. 1987. 29.00x (ISBN 0-231-06286-9). Columbia U Pr.

Reading Aids Through the Grades: A Guide to Materials & 501 Activities for Individualizing Reading Instruction. 4th rev. ed. David Russell et al. Ed. by Anne M. Mueser. LC 75-15639. 320p. 1981. pap. text ed. 13.95x (ISBN 0-8077-2609-5). Tchrs Coll.

Reading Aloud to Your Child. Elizabeth L. Fontaine. LC 84-60976. 125p. (Orig.). 1985. pap. text ed. 5.50 (ISBN 0-88247-732-3). R & E Pubs.

Reading Althusser: An Essay on Structural Marxism. Steven B. Smith. LC 83-45943. 240p. 1984. 24.95x (ISBN 0-8014-1672-8). Cornell U Pr.

Reading America: Essays on American Literature. Denis Donoghue. 1987. 22.95 (ISBN 0-394-55939-8). Knopf.

Reading America: Essays on American Literature. Denis Donoghue. 320p. (Orig.). 1988. pap. 10.95 (ISBN 0-520-06424-0). U of Cal Pr.

Reading: An Essay. Hugh Walpole. 1979. Repr. of 1927 ed. lib. bdg. 15.00 (ISBN 0-8495-5706-2). Arden Lib.

Reading Analytically. John F. Gardenhire. 76p. 1987. pap. text ed. 17.50 (ISBN 0-8403-4265-9). Kendall Hunt.

Reading Ancient Greek: A Reasonable Approach, 2 Pt. J. D. Ellsworth. 498p. 1982. 22.50x set (ISBN 0-87291-162-4). Coronado Pr.

Reading & Analyzing Medical Records. 232p. 1983. 15.00 (ISBN 0-318-02486-1). ICLE Georgia.

Reading & Believing. Jacob Neusner. LC 86-30399. (Brown Judaic Studies). 138p. 1986. 25.50 (ISBN 0-89130-976-4, 14-01-13); pap. 20.50 (ISBN 0-89130-977-2). Scholars Pr GA.

Reading & Case in Basic Marketing. 5th ed. E. Jerome McCarthy et al. 1987. 14.95x (ISBN 0-256-05795-8). Irwin.

Reading & Cases in Marketing Management. Alvin C. Burns & David W. Cravens. 1987. 17.95x (ISBN 0-256-03161-4). Irwin.

Reading & Computers: Issues for Theory & Practice. Ed. by David Reinking. (Computers & Education Ser.). 220p. 1987. text ed. 22.95x (ISBN 0-8077-2866-7). Tchrs Coll.

Reading & Dating Roman Imperial Coins. Zander Klawans. (Illus.). 1982. Repr. of 1977 ed. softcover 10.00 (ISBN 0-686-79427-3). S J Durst.

Reading & Deafness. C. M. King & S. P. Quigley. 326p. 1985. write for info. (ISBN 0-85066-585-X, Co-pub. by College Hill Pr). Taylor & Francis.

Reading & Deafness. Cynthia King & Stephen Quigley. LC 85-5694. (Illus.). 350p. 1985. 31.00 (ISBN 0-316-49351-1). COllege-Hill.

Reading & Detailing Assembly Drawings: Dies. A. A. Vezzani & Donald Salmonson. LC 61-9841. 1972. 9.25x (ISBN 0-911168-10-9). Prakken.

Reading & Dialect Differences. Walt Wolfram et al. (Dialects & Educational Equity Ser.: No. 4). 20p. 1979. pap. 3.33x (ISBN 0-13-209842-3, Dist. by P-H). Ctr Appl Ling.

Reading Comprehension: Workbook Lessons & Tests. rev. ed. Samuel F. Zimbal & Wilbert J. Levy. (gr. 7-10). 1969. text ed. 9.75 (ISBN 0-87720-363-6); wkbk. 8.83 (ISBN 0-87720-323-7); tchrs' ed. 8.33 (ISBN 0-87720-324-5). AMSCO Sch.
Reading Comprehesion in the Elementary School. Wilson & Gambrell. 350p. 1988. pap. 28.95x (ISBN 0-205-11161-0, Pub. by Longwood Div). Allyn.
Reading Connection. Salvatore J. Iacone. 288p. 1983. text ed. write for info. (ISBN 0-02-359380-6). Macmillan.
Reading Connection: Proceedings of the 16th Annual Conference of the United Kingdom Reading Association 1979. Ed. by Gwen Bray & Tony Pugh. 160p. 1985. 30.00x (ISBN 0-7062-4069-3, Pub. by Ward Lock Educ Co Ltd). State Mutual Bk.
Reading Construction Drawings. Paul I. Wallach & Donald E. Hepler. (Illus.). 1979. pap. text ed. 28.95 (ISBN 0-07-067935-5). McGraw.
Reading Construction Drawings: Trade Edition. Paul I. Wallach & Donald E. Hepler. (Illus.). 320p. 1980. text ed. 39.95 (ISBN 0-07-067940-1). McGraw.
Reading Consultant - Library Media Specialist Team: Building the Reading Habit. Emma L. Benedict & Darla Shaw. LC 87-3947. xvi, 201p. 1987. lib. bdg. 27.50 (ISBN 0-208-02102-7, Lib Prof Pubns); pap. 19.50x (ISBN 0-208-02103-5, Lib Prof Pubns). Shoe String.
Reading Corinthians: A Literary & Theological Commentary on 1 & 2 Corinthians. Charles H. Talbert. 224p. 1987. 15.95 (ISBN 0-8245-0804-1). Crossroad NY.
Reading Corner: Ideas, Games & Activities for Individualizing Reading. Harry W. Forgan. LC 76-28292. (Illus.). 1977. pap. 12.95 (ISBN 0-673-16419-5). Scott F.
Reading Correction Kit. 2nd ed. Wilma H. Miller. 368p. 1982. comb-bound 22.50x (ISBN 0-87628-703-8). Ctr Appl Res.
Reading Critically, Writing Well: A Reader & Guide. Rise B. Axelrod & Charles R. Cooper. LC 86-60657. 640p. 1987. pap. text ed. write for info. (ISBN 0-312-66459-1); write for info. instr's. manual (ISBN 0-312-66463-X). St Martin.
Reading Curriculum: A Reference Guide to Criterion-Based Skill Development in Grades K-8. William A. Gordon. LC 82-9103. 272p. 1982. 42.95 (ISBN 0-275-90807-0, C0807). Praeger.
Reading Dance: The Birth of Choreology. Rudolf Benesh & Joan Benesh. 139p. 1987. pap. 12.95 (ISBN 0-285-64976-0, Pub. by Souvenir Pr). Intl Spec Bk.
Reading Dancing: Bodies & Subjects in Contemporary Dance. Susan Foster. (Illus.). 224p. 1986. 35.00x (ISBN 0-520-05549-7). U of Cal Pr.
Reading De Man Reading. Ed. by Lindsay Waters & Wlad Godzich. LC 88-4580. (Theory & History of Literature Ser.: Vol. 59). 300p. (Orig.). 1988. text ed. 39.50x (ISBN 0-8166-1660-4); pap. 14.95x (ISBN 0-8166-1661-2). U of Minn Pr.
Reading Deconstruction Deconstructive Reading. G. Douglas Atkins. LC 83-10308. 168p. 1983. 18.00x (ISBN 0-8131-1493-4); pap. 7.00 (ISBN 0-8131-0165-4). U Pr of Ky.
Reading Development & Cohesion. John Chapman. x, 147p. 1983. pap. text ed. 12.50x (ISBN 0-435-10161-7). Heinemann Ed.
Reading Development of Non-native Speakers of English. John G. Barnitz. (Language in Education Ser.). 114p. 1985. pap. 9.33 (ISBN 0-13-754805-2, Dist. by P-H). Ctr Appl Ling.
Reading Diagnosis & Instruction: A C-A-L-M Approach. Susan M. Glazer & Lyndon W. Searfoss. (Illus.). 448p. 1988. text ed. price not set (ISBN 0-13-755810-4). P-H.
Reading Diagnosis & Instruction: Theory into Practice. Robert J. Marzano et al. (Illus.). 448p. 1987. text ed. write for info. (ISBN 0-13-755836-8). P-H.
Reading Diagnosis & Remediation. Don A. Brown. (Illus.). 384p. 1982. write for info. (ISBN 0-13-754952-0). P-H.
Reading Diagnosis & Remediation in Classroom & Clinic. Lois A. Bader. (Illus.). 1980. pap. text ed. write for info. (ISBN 0-02-305100-0). Macmillan.
Reading Diagnosis for Teachers. Rebecca Barr & Marilyn Sadow. LC 84-17193. 256p. (Orig.). 1985. pap. text ed. 17.95 (ISBN 0-582-28527-5). Longman.
Reading Diagnosis Kit. 3rd ed. Wilma Miller. 27.95x (ISBN 0-87628-720-8). Ctr Appl Res.
Reading Diagnosis Kit. 3rd ed. Wilma H. Miller. 376p. 1986. pap. 27.95 (ISBN 0-317-66024-1, Ctr Appl Res). P-H.
Reading Difficulties: Analysis & Treatment. Jerry L. Milligan. 128p. 1981. pap. 9.00x (ISBN 0-87562-068-X). Spec Child.
Reading Difficulties, Assessment & Instruction. Barbara M. Taylor et al. 416p. 1988. text ed. write for info (ISBN 0-394-36298-5, RanC). Random.
Reading Difficulties in Schools. Margaret M. Clark. LC 80-670036. (Orig.). 1980. pap. text ed. 12.50x (ISBN 0-435-80221-6). Heinemann Ed.
Reading Difficulties: Their Diagnosis & Correction. 5th ed. Guy L. Bond et al. (Illus.). 368p. 1984. write for info. (ISBN 0-13-754960-1). P-H.
Reading Disabilities: The Interaction of Reading, Leading & Neuropsychological Deficits. Donald Doehring et al. LC 81-10932. (Perspectives in Neurolinguistics, Neuropsychology & Psycholinguistics Ser.). 1981. 46.00 (ISBN 0-12-219180-3). Acad Pr.
Reading Disability: Developmental Dyslexia. Lloyd J. Thompson. (Illus.). 228p. 1974. spiral bdg. 26.25 (ISBN 0-398-03123-1). C C Thomas.
Reading Disability: Progress & Research Needs in Dyslexia. Ed. by John Money. 208p. 1962. 19.50x (ISBN 0-8018-0466-3). Johns Hopkins.
Reading Disorders. Ed. by Robert Piazza. (Special Education Ser.). (Illus., Orig.). 1978. pap. text ed. 16.00 (ISBN 0-89568-085-8). Spec Learn Corp.
Reading Disorders: Varieties & Treatment. Ed. by R. N. Malatesha & P. G. Aaron. LC 82-4039. (Perspectives in Neurolinguistics, Neuropsychology & Psycholinguistics Ser.). 1982. 39.95 (ISBN 0-12-466320-6). Acad Pr.
Reading Drama. 2nd ed. David Scanlan. 181p. 1988. pap. 9.95 (ISBN 0-87484-735-4). Mayfield Pub.
Reading Drama: A Method of Analysis with Selections for Study. Fred B. Millett. LC 71-111110. (Play Anthology Reprint Ser). Repr. of 1950 ed. 18.25 (ISBN 0-8369-8203-7). Ayer Co Pubs.
Reading Drawings: An Introduction to Looking at Drawings. Susan Lambert. (Illus.). 1984. pap. 12.95 (ISBN 0-394-72479-8). Pantheon.
Reading Drills: Advanced Level. Edward B. Fry. (Illus.). 192p. (gr. 9 up). 1975. pap. text ed. 7.20x (ISBN 0-89061-039-8, 751). Jamestown Pubs.
Reading Drills: Middle Level. Edward B. Fry. (Illus.). 224p. (Orig.). (gr. 4-8). 1982. pap. text ed. 7.20x (ISBN 0-89061-245-5, 750). Jamestown Pubs.
Reading Dutch. W. Z. Shetter & R. B. Bird. 1986. pap. text ed. 12.50 (ISBN 90-6890-021-8, Pub. by Martinus Nijhoff Netherlands). Kluwer Academic.
Reading Dutch: Fifteen Annotated Stories from the Low Countries. W. Z. Shetter & B. R. Bird. (Illus.). 1985. 15.00x. Heinman.
Reading Education: Foundations for a Literate America. Ed. by Jean Osborn et al. LC 84-47505. 352p. 1984. 39.00x (ISBN 0-669-08280-5). Lexington Bks.
Reading Educational Research. Andrea Vierra & Judith Pollock. (Orig.). 1988. pap. text ed. 22.00 (ISBN 0-89787-522-2). Gorsuch Scarisbrick.
Reading EKGs Correctly. 2nd ed. Ed. by Susan Williams & Barbara McVan. LC 83-20269. (New Nursing Skillbook). (Illus.). 190p. 1984. pap. 15.95 (ISBN 0-87434-134-5). Springhouse Pub.
Reading Engineering Drawings Through Conceptual Sketching. Jay Helsel. (Illus.). 1979. pap. 29.95 (ISBN 0-07-028031-2). McGraw.
Reading English. Ed. by Donald R. Gallo. 124p. (Reprinted from Fall 1978 Connecticut English Journal). 7.00 (ISBN 0-317-35303-9, 38667). NCTE.
Reading English Discourse: Business, Economics, Law & Political Science. Lyle F. Bachman. 280p. 1986. pap. text ed. write for info. (ISBN 0-13-755844-9). P-H.
Reading English for Academic Study. Michael Long et al. (Illus.). 184p. (Orig.). 1980. pap. text ed. 10.95 (ISBN 0-88377-108-X). Newbury Hse.
Reading Enhancement & Development. Rhonda Atkinson & Debbie Longman. (Illus.). 479p. 1985. pap. text ed. 19.25 (ISBN 0-314-85215-8). West Pub.
Reading Enhancement & Development. 2nd ed. Rhonda H. Atkinson & Debbie G. Longman. 348p. 1988. pap. 21.95 (ISBN 0-314-65673-1). West Pub.
Reading Everyday Stuff. Elaine Prizzi & Jeanne Hoffman. (gr. 4-6). 1985. pap. 6.95 (ISBN 0-8224-3180-7). D S Lake Pubs.
Reading Expository Material. Ed. by Wayne Otto & Sandra White. LC 82-4054. 1982. 24.95 (ISBN 0-12-531050-1). Acad Pr.
Reading Fast. Philly Murtha. Ed. by Ann Redpath. (You Can Be a Reading Athlete Ser.). 32p. (gr. 4 up). 1985. PLB 8.95 (ISBN 0-87191-996-6). Creative Ed.
Reading Faster & Understanding More, 3 Bks. 2nd ed. Wanda M. Miller & Sharon Steeber. 1985. Bk. I. pap. text ed. write for info. (ISBN 0-673-39284-8); Bk. II. pap. text ed. write for info. (ISBN 0-673-39285-6); Bk. III. pap. text ed. write for info. (ISBN 0-673-39286-4). Scott F.
Reading Faster for Ideas. Elaine L. Cohen & Mary A. Poppino. LC 83-18586. 1984. pap. text ed. 14.95 (ISBN 0-03-061959-9). HR&W.
Reading Faulknerian Tragedy. Warwick Wadlington. LC 86-29166. 272p. 1987. 24.95x (ISBN 0-8014-2011-3). Cornell U Pr.
Reading Fiction. Stephen Minot. 160p. 1985. pap. text ed. write for info. (ISBN 0-13-754995-4). P-H.
Reading First: Building Reading Competence. Suzanne D. Robertshaw & Roberta E. Hamblen. 224p. 1984. pap. text ed. write for info. (ISBN 0-02-402100-8). Macmillan.
Reading for A Purpose: Encore, Bk. 4. (Illus.). 164p. 1987. pap. text ed. 10.00 (ISBN 0-317-61467-3). Heinle & Heinle.
Reading for a Purpose: Encore Book 4. (Illus.). 164p. 1987. pap. text ed. 10.00 (ISBN 0-8384-1496-6). Heinle & Heinle.
Reading for Adults. Richard Lewis. (English As a Second Language Bk.). (Illus.). 1977. Bk. 1: Pre-Intermediate. pap. text ed. 7.95 (ISBN 0-582-79320-3); Bk. 2: Intermediate. pap. text ed. 7.95 (ISBN 0-582-79321-1); Bk. 3: High-Intermediate. pap. text ed. 7.95 (ISBN 0-582-52792-9). Longman.
Reading for Boys & Girls: Illinios: a Subject Index & Annotated Bibliography. Dorothy Hinman & Ruth Zimmerman. LC 75-118853. pap. 33.50 (ISBN 0-317-26830-9, 2024215). Bks Demand UMI.
Reading for College & Life. Delphenia M. Carter & Dorothy B. Booher. 288p. 1986. pap. text ed. 19.95 (ISBN 0-8403-3930-5). Kendall-Hunt.
Reading for College Writers. Leonard J. Rosen & Lawrence Behrens. 1987. pap. text ed. write for info. (ISBN 0-673-39197-3). Scott F.
Reading for Concepts: Bks. A-H. 2nd ed. William Liddle. (Illus.). (gr. 3-9). 1977. Bk. A. pap. text ed. 7.40 (ISBN 0-07-037661-1); Bk. B. pap. text ed. 7.40 (ISBN 0-07-037662-X); Bk. C. pap. text ed. 7.40 (ISBN 0-07-037663-8); Bk. D. pap. text ed. 7.40 (ISBN 0-07-037664-6); Bk. E. pap. text ed. 7.40 (ISBN 0-07-037665-4); Bk. F. pap. text ed. 7.96 (ISBN 0-07-037666-2); Bk. G. pap. text ed. 7.96 (ISBN 0-07-037667-0); Bk. H. pap. text ed. 7.96 (ISBN 0-07-037668-9). McGraw.
Reading for Executives. Donna Litherland. (Illus.). 100p. (Orig.). 1982. pap. text ed. 12.50x (ISBN 0-9607888-0-8). Barney Pr.
Reading for Life: A First Book for Adults & Their Tutors. Virginia F. Allen. 288p. (Orig.). 1987. pap. text ed. 15.00 (ISBN 0-940723-00-X). SIIS.
Reading for Mastery & Enrichment. Evelyn Gins et al. 208p. 1985. pap. text ed. 16.95 (ISBN 0-8403-3525-3). Kendall-Hunt.
Reading for Mathematics. Joyce Friedland & Irene Gross. 96p. 1984. pap. 4.00 (ISBN 0-88323-199-9, 218); tchr's. answer key 1.50 (ISBN 0-88323-142-5, 231). Richards Pub.
Reading for Meaning see Language Learning: The Intermediate Phase.
Reading for Pleasure: Guidelines. Dixie L. Spiegel. (Reading Aids Ser.). 98p. (Orig.). 1981. pap. text ed. 5.50 (ISBN 0-87207-226-6). Intl Reading.
Reading for Professional Purposes: Studies & Practices in Native & Foreign Languages. A. K. Pugh & J. M. Ulijn. vi, 243p. (Orig.). 1984. pap. text ed. 22.50x (ISBN 0-435-10718-6). Heinemann Ed.
Reading for Results. 3rd ed. Laraine M. Flemming. LC 86-81106. 1987. pap. text ed. 22.36; instr's. manual with tests 2.36 (ISBN 0-395-42467-4). HM.
Reading for Rhetoric: Applications to Writing. 4th ed. Caroline Shrodes et al. 1979. pap. write for info. (ISBN 0-02-410240-7); instr's. manual avail. Macmillan.
Reading for Success in College: A Guide to Background Reading & Study Skills. Walter Pauk. 1968. pap. 3.00 (ISBN 0-911880-00-3). Academia.
Reading for Survival. Eileen Corcoran. 80p. 1984. pap. 3.75 (ISBN 0-88323-205-7, 234); tchr's. answer key 1.25 (ISBN 0-88323-151-4, 240). Richards Pub.
Reading for Survival in Today's Society, Vol. 1. Ann Adams et al. LC 77-24017. 1978. 14.95 (ISBN 0-673-16421-7); pap. 12.95 (ISBN 0-673-16420-9). Scott F.
Reading for Survival in Today's Society, Vol. 2. Ann Adams et al. LC 77-24017. 1978. 14.95 (ISBN 0-673-16423-3); pap. 12.95 (ISBN 0-673-16422-5). Scott F.
Reading for the Love of It. Michele Landsberg. (Illus.). 20p. 1987. 17.95 (ISBN 0-13-579822-1). P-H.
Reading for the Plot. Peter Brooks. LC 83-48929. 1984. 17.45 (ISBN 0-394-50597-2). Knopf.
Reading for the Point. William J. Kerrigan. 141p. 1979. pap. text ed. 11.00 net (ISBN 0-15-575640-0, HC). HarBraceJ.
Reading For the Real World. Eileen L. Corcoran. 80p. 1977. pap. text ed. 4.00 (ISBN 0-88323-245-6, 221); tchr's key 1.25 (232). Richards Pub.
Reading for TOEFL. Educational Testing Service Staff. Date not set. pap. 13.00 (ISBN 0-446-38522-0). Warner Bks.
Reading for Working. Thomas G. Sticht. 186p. 1975. pap. text ed. write for info (ISBN 0-686-10657-1). Human Resources.
Reading for Young People: Kentucky, Tennessee, West Virginia see Reading for Young People: The Great Plains.
Reading for Young People: New England. Ed. by Elfrieda McCauley. LC 85-11368. (Reading for Young People Ser.). 208p. 1985. pap. text ed. 17.50x (ISBN 0-8389-0432-7). ALA.
Reading for Young People: The Great Plains. Mildred Laughlin. Incl. Reading for Young People: Kentucky, Tennessee, West Virginia. Ed. by Barbara Mertins. LC 84-24562. (Reading for Young People Ser.). 144p. 1985. pap. text ed. 12.00x (ISBN 0-8389-0426-2); Reading for Young People: The Middle Atlantic. Ed. by Arabelle Pennypacker. LC 80-16021. 164p. 1980. pap. 11.00x (ISBN 0-8389-0295-2); Reading for Young People: The Midwest. Dorothy Hinman & Ruth Zimmerman. LC 78-24479. 250p. 1979. pap. 11.00x (ISBN 0-8389-0271-5); Reading for Young People: The Mississippi Delta. Cora Matheny Dorsett. LC 83-14375. (Reading for Young People Ser.: VII). 150p. 1984. pap. 15.00x (ISBN 0-8389-0395-9); Reading for Young People: The Northwest. Ed. by Mary Meacham. LC 80-24192. 152p. 1981. pap. 11.00x (ISBN 0-8389-0318-5); Reading for Young People: The Rocky Mountains. Ed. by Mildred Laughlin. LC 80-10932. 192p. 1980. pap. 11.00x (ISBN 0-8389-0296-0); Reading for Young People: The Southeast. Ed. by Dorothy Heald. 176p. 1980. pap. text ed. 11.00x (ISBN 0-8389-0300-2); Reading for Young People: The Southwest. Elva Harmon & Anna L. Milligan. LC 82-4002. 256p. 1982. pap. text ed. 15.00x (ISBN 0-8389-0362-2); Reading for Young People: The Upper Midwest. Ed. by Marion F. Archer. LC 81-10771. 142p. 1981. pap. 11.00x (ISBN 0-8389-0339-8). LC 78-27242. 166p. 1979. pap. 11.00x (ISBN 0-8389-0265-0). ALA.
Reading for Young People: The Middle Atlantic see Reading for Young People: The Great Plains.
Reading for Young People: The Midwest see Reading for Young People: The Great Plains.
Reading for Young People: The Mississippi Delta see Reading for Young People: The Great Plains.
Reading for Young People: The Northwest see Reading for Young People: The Great Plains.
Reading for Young People: The Rocky Mountains see Reading for Young People: The Great Plains.
Reading for Young People: The Southeast see Reading for Young People: The Great Plains.
Reading for Young People: The Southwest see Reading for Young People: The Great Plains.
Reading for Young People: The Upper Midwest see Reading for Young People: The Great Plains.
Reading Frames in Modern Fiction. Mary A. Caws. LC 84-16092. 275p. 1985. text ed. 30.50x (ISBN 0-691-06625-6). Princeton U Pr.
Reading French in the Arts & Sciences. 4th ed. E. M. Stack. LC 86-80905. 1987. pap. text ed. 21.96 (ISBN 0-395-35968-6). HM.
Reading Freud: Psychology, Neurosis, & Religion. Volney P. Gay. LC 83-2917. (AAR Studies in Religion). 142p. 1983. pap. 8.25 (ISBN 0-89130-613-7, 01 00 32). Scholars Pr GA.
Reading from Left to Right: One Man's Political History. H. S. Ferns. 384p. 1983. 24.95 (ISBN 0-8020-2518-8); 14.95 (ISBN 0-8020-6655-0). U of Toronto Pr.
Reading from Modern Mexican Authors. Frederick Starr. 1976. lib. bdg. 50.00 (ISBN 0-8490-0929-4). Gordon Pr.
Reading Games: A Tournament for Your Mind, 5 vols. Ronald E. Hostetler. (Illus.). 402p. (gr. 2-6). 1982. pap. text ed. 9.95 ea. Vol. II (ISBN 0-9608722-7-2). Vol. III (ISBN 0-9608722-1-3). Vol. IV (ISBN 0-9608722-6-4). Vol. V (ISBN 0-9608722-0-5). Vol VI (ISBN 0-9608722-5-6). Set. pap. text ed. 49.75 (ISBN 0-9608722-8-0). Kitten Pub.
Reading Games for Middle & Upper Grades. Ed. by Flora C. Fowler. LC 74-8367. 198p. 1975. pap. text ed. 6.95x (ISBN 0-8422-0430-X). Irvington.
Reading Genesis by the Light of a Comet. George F. Butterick. LC 76-43367. 1976. pap. 2.95 (ISBN 0-917488-01-6). Ziesing Bros.
Reading Georges Bataille: Beyond the Gift. Michel H. Richman. LC 81-48179. 192p. 1982. text ed. 22.50x (ISBN 0-8018-2593-8). Johns Hopkins.
Reading: Grade Four, Bk. 1. Schaffer, Frank, Publications Staff. (Schaffer Basic Learning Ser.). (Illus.). 48p. (gr. 4). 1983. wkbk. 3.98 (ISBN 0-86734-038-X, FS-2667). Schaffer Pubns.
Reading: Grade Four, Bk. 2. Schaffer, Frank, Publications Staff. (Schaffer Basic Learning Ser.). (Illus.). 48p. (gr. 4). 1983. wkbk. 3.98 (ISBN 0-86734-039-8, FS-2668). Schaffer Pubns.
Reading: Grade Four, Bk. 3. Schaffer, Frank, Publications Staff. (Shaffer Basic Learning Ser.). (Illus.). 48p. (gr. 4). 1983. wkbk. 3.98 (ISBN 0-86734-040-1, FS-2669). Schaffer Pubns.
Reading: Grade One, Bk. 1. Schaffer, Frank, Publications Staff. (Schaffer Basic Learning Ser.). (Illus.). 48p. (gr. 1). 1983. wkbk. 3.98 (ISBN 0-86734-029-0, FS-2658). Schaffer Pubns.
Reading: Grade One, Bk. 2. Schaffer, Frank, Publications Staff. (Schaffer Basic Learning Ser.). (Illus.). 48p. (gr. 1). 1983. wkbk. 3.98 (ISBN 0-86734-030-4, FS-2659). Schaffer Pubns.
Reading: Grade One, Bk. 3. Schaffer, Frank, Publications Staff. (Schaffer Basic Learning Ser.). (Illus.). 48p. (gr. 1). 1983. wkbk. 3.98 (ISBN 0-86734-031-2, FS-2660). Schaffer Pubns.
Reading: Grade Three, Bk. 1. Schaffer, Frank, Publications Staff. (Schaffer Basic Learning Ser.). (Illus.). 48p. (gr. 3). 1983. wkbk. 3.98 (ISBN 0-86734-035-5, FS-2664). Schaffer Pubns.

TITLE INDEX READING OF DANTE'S INFERNO.

Reading: Grade Three, Bk. 2. Schaffer, Frank, Publications Staff. (Schaffer Basic Learning Ser.). (Illus.). 48p. (gr. 3). 1983. wkbk. 3.98 (ISBN 0-86734-036-3, FS-2665). Schaffer Pubns.
Reading: Grade Three, Bk. 3. Schaffer, Frank, Publications Staff. (Schaffer Basic Learning Ser.). (Illus.). 48p. (gr. 3). 1983. wkbk. 3.98 (ISBN 0-86734-037-1, FS-2666). Schaffer Pubns.
Reading: Grade Two, Bk. 1. Schaffer, Frank, Publications Staff. (Schaffer Basic Learning Ser.). (Illus.). 48p. (gr. 2). wkbk. 3.98 (ISBN 0-86734-032-0, FS-2661). Schaffer Pubns.
Reading: Grade Two, Bk. 2. Schaffer, Frank, Publications Staff. (Schaffer Basic Learning Ser.). (Illus.). 48p. (gr. 2). 1983. wkbk. 3.98 (ISBN 0-86734-033-9, FS-2662). Schaffer Pubns.
Reading: Grade Two, Bk. 3. Schaffer, Frank, Publications Staff. (Schaffer Basic Learning Ser.). (Illus.). 48p. (gr. 2). 1983. wkbk. 3.98 (ISBN 0-86734-034-7, FS-2663). Schaffer Pubns.
Reading: Grade 1, Bk. 2. Catherine Schwaller. Ed. by Joan Hoffman. (I Know It! Bks.). (Illus.). 32p. (gr. 1). 1979. wkbk. 1.95 (ISBN 0-938256-07-6). Sch Zone Pub Co.
Reading: Grade 1, Bk. 1. Catherine Schwaller. Ed. by Joan Hoffman. (I Know It! Bks.). (Illus.). 32p. (gr. 1). 1979. wkbk. 1.95 (ISBN 0-938256-06-8). Sch Zone Pub Co.
Reading: Grade 2, Bk. 1. Shirley Lane. Ed. by Joan Hoffman. (I Know It! Bks.). (Illus.). 32p. (gr. 2). 1979. wkbk. 1.95 (ISBN 0-938256-09-2). Sch Zone Pub Co.
Reading: Grade 2, Bk. 2. Shirley Lane. Ed. by Joan Hoffman. (I Know It! Bks.). (Illus.). 32p. (gr. 2). 1979. wkbk. 1.95 (ISBN 0-938256-10-6). Sch Zone Pub Co.
Reading: Grade 3, Bk. 1. Jean Syswerda. Ed. by Joan Hoffman. (I Know It! Bks.). (Illus.). 32p. (gr. 3). 1980. wkbk. 1.95 (ISBN 0-938256-11-4). Sch Zone Pub Co.
Reading: Grade 4. James Hoffman. Ed. by Joan Hoffman. (I Know It! Bks.). (Illus.). 32p. (gr. 4). 1979. wkbk. 1.95 (ISBN 0-938256-13-0). Sch Zone Pub Co.
Reading: Grade 5. James Hoffman. Ed. by Joan Hoffman. (I Know It! Bks). (Illus.). 32p. (gr. 5). 1979. wkbk. 1.95 (ISBN 0-938256-14-9). Sch Zone Pub Co.
Reading: Grade 6. Leona V. Olin. Ed. by Joan Hoffman. (I Know It! Bks.). (Illus.). 32p. (gr. 6). 1980. wkbk. 1.95 (ISBN 0-938256-15-7). Sch Zone Pub Co.
Reading Greek: Grammar, Vocabulary & Exercises. Joint Association of Classical Teachers. LC 77-91090. 1978. 14.95 (ISBN 0-521-21977-9); pap. 6.95 (ISBN 0-521-22052-1). Cambridge U Pr.
Reading Greek Tragedy. Simon Goldhill. 336p. 1986. 42.50 (ISBN 0-521-30583-7); pap. 13.95 (ISBN 0-521-31579-4). Cambridge U Pr.
Reading Guidance & Bibliotherapy in Public, Hospital & Institution Libraries: A Selection of Papers Presented at a Series of Adult Services Institutes, 1965-1968. Ed. by Margaret E. Monroe. 76p. 1971. pap. 3.00 (ISBN 0-936442-02-6). U Wis Sch Lib.
Reading Guidance in a Media Age. Nancy Polette & Marjorie Hamlin. LC 75-26833. (Illus.). 275p. 1975. 16.00 (ISBN 0-8108-0873-0). Scarecrow.
Reading Guide to the Book of Mormon: A Simplified Program Featuring Brief Outlines & Doctrinal Summaries. Duane S. Crowther. LC 75-5322. 169p. 1975. 7.95 (ISBN 0-88290-045-5). Horizon Utah.
Reading Handbook: With This Book, You Can Teach Someone to Read. Maryjane Cable. (YA) (gr. 7-12). 1986. tchrs. ed., 3-ring binder 30.00 (ISBN 0-9619050-0-X, 2 027-282). M Cable.
Reading Hebrew. Lillian W. Adler & C. Castberg. 1972. pap. 4.95x (ISBN 0-87441-042-8); wkbk. 3.50x (ISBN 0-87441-216-1). Behrman.
Reading Help. (ps-1). 1984. 2.50 (ISBN 0-86653-244-7, GA 591). Good Apple.
Reading Help. (Help for Home & School Ser.). (gr. k-2). 2.50 (ISBN 0-86653-245-5, GA 592). Good Apple.
Reading Help. (Help for Home & School Ser.). (gr. 1-3). 2.50 (ISBN 0-86653-246-3, GA 594). Good Apple.
Reading Help. (Help for Home & School Ser.). (gr. 2-4). 2.50 (ISBN 0-86653-247-1, GA 593, Dist. by Ingram). Good Apple.
Reading Ideas Ready to Use! Barbara Gruber. (Instant Idea Bks.). (Illus.). 64p. 1983. 5.95 (ISBN 0-86734-049-5, FS-8303). Schaffer Pubns.
Reading Ideologies: An Investigation into the Marxist Theory of Ideology & Law. Colin Sumner. (Law, State & Society Ser.). 1979. 52.00 (ISBN 0-12-676650-9); pap. 24.00 (ISBN 0-12-676652-5). Acad Pr.
Reading Improvement: A Complete Course for Increasing Speed and Comprehension. Barbara M. Klaeser. LC 76-49042. 306p. 1977. 22.95x (ISBN 0-88229-232-3). Nelson-Hall.
Reading Improvement: Exercises for Students of English As a Second Language. David P. Harris. (Orig.). 1966. pap. text ed. write for info. (ISBN 0-13-755058-8). P-H.
Reading Improvement for Everyone. Robert Westrom. 71p. (Orig.). 1980. pap. 2.95 (ISBN 0-938230-05-0, TX547-673). Westrom.
Reading in a Foreign Language. Ed. by J. Charles Alderson & A. H. Urquhart. (Applied Linguistics & Language Study). 324p. (Orig.). 1983. pap. text ed. 14.95 (ISBN 0-582-55372-5). Longman.
Reading in a Second Language: Hypotheses, Organization & Practice. Ronald Mackay et al. 224p. 1979. pap. text ed. 13.50 (ISBN 0-88377-134-9). Newbury Hse.
Reading in American Schools: A Guide to Information Sources. Ed. by Maria E. Schantz & Joseph F. Brynner. LC 79-23770. (Education Information Guide Ser.: Vol. 5). 280p. 1980. 68.00x (ISBN 0-8103-1456-8). Gale.
Reading in an Age of Mass Communication: Report of the Committee on Reading at the Secondary School & College Levels. National Council of Teachers of English. Ed. by William S. Gray. LC 70-167390. (Essay Index Reprint Ser.). Repr. of 1949 ed. 11.00 (ISBN 0-8369-2811-3). Ayer Co Pubs.
Reading in Art History, Vol. I: Ancient Egypt Through the Middle Ages. 3rd ed. Ed. by Harold Spencer. LC 76-7404. (Illus.). 502p. 1982. pap. text ed. write for info. (ISBN 0-02-414380-4, Pub. by Scribner). Macmillan.
Reading in Attitude Theory & Measurement. Martin Fishbein. LC 67-22410. (Illus.). 1967. pap. 96.80 (ISBN 0-317-08010-5, 2055145). Bks Demand UMI.
Reading in Community Work. Ed. by Paul Henderson & David Thomas. 1981. 46.25x (ISBN 0-317-54598-1, Pub. by Natl Inst Social Work). State Mutual Bk.
Reading in Detail: Aesthetics & the Feminine. Naomi Schor. 1987. 25.00 (ISBN 0-416-01511-5, 1179); pap. 10.95 (ISBN 0-416-01521-2, 1184). Routledge Chapman & Hall.
Reading in Early Childhood. Ragnhild Soderbergh. LC 76-43032. 136p. 1977. 6.95 (ISBN 0-87840-165-2). Georgetown U Pr.
Reading in Elementary Classrooms: Strategies & Observations. James Cunningham & Partricia Cunningham. LC 82-7814. 512p. 1982. text ed. 23.95 (ISBN 0-582-28390-6). Longman.
Reading in English: For Students of ESL. 2nd ed. Dorothy Danielson et al. (Illus.). 1980. pap. text ed. write for info. (ISBN 0-13-753442-6). P-H.
Reading in Focus: Learning to Get the Message. 2nd ed. Esta De Fossard. 352p. 1985. Module A-gr. 4-7. write for info. (ISBN 0-538-05660-6, E66); Module B-gr. 7-10. wkbk. (ISBN 0-538-05670-3, E67). Module C-gr. 10up (ISBN 0-538-05680-0, E68). SW Pub.
Reading in Group Work Practice. Ed. by Robert D. Vinter. 1967. pap. 5.45 (ISBN 0-87506-030-7). Campus.
Reading in Health, Physical Education, Recreation Classes. Page S. Bristow & Alan E. Farstrup. 72p. 1981. 7.95 (ISBN 0-8106-3206-3). NEA.
Reading in Humanistic Psychology. A. Sutich & M. Vich. LC 74-75206. 1969. pap. text ed. 11.95 (ISBN 0-02-932320-7). Free Pr.
Reading: In Memoriam. Timothy Peltason. (Princeton Essays in Literature Ser.). 200p. 1985. text ed. 28.00x (ISBN 0-691-06650-7). Princeton U Pr.
Reading in Modern Dance, Vol. 2. Compiled by Michele J. Varon. LC 76-359498. (Illus.). v, 86p. (Orig.). 1977. pap. text ed. 21.95 (ISBN 0-932582-23-0). Dance Notation.
Reading in Mythology: An Original Anthology. Ed. by Kees W. Bolle. LC 77-139. (Mythology Ser.). (Ger. & Fr.). 1978. lib. bdg. 14.00x (ISBN 0-405-10573-8). Ayer Co Pubs.
Reading in Portuguese Linguistics. new ed. J. Schmidt-Radefeldt. (North Holland Linguistics Ser.: Vol. 22). 480p. 1976. pap. 71.00 (ISBN 0-444-10910-2, North-Holland). Elsevier.
Reading in Property Protection. Insurance Institute of America. LC 86-82905. 333p. (Orig.). 1986. pap. 14.00 (ISBN 0-89462-034-7). IIA.
Reading in the Age of the Computer. Ed. by Malcolm P. Douglass. (Claremont Reading Conference Yearbook). 255p. 1984. pap. write for info. (ISBN 0-941742-02-4). Claremont Grad.
Reading in the Bilingual Classroom: Literacy and Biliteracy. Kenneth Goodman et al. LC 79-84373. 50p. 1978. pap. 5.25 (ISBN 0-89763-011-4). Natl Clearinghse Bilingual Ed.
Reading in the Content Area: Research for Teachers. Ed. by Mary M. Dupuis. 88p. 1984. pap. 6.00 (ISBN 0-87207-857-4). Intl Reading.
Reading in the Content Areas: Improving Classroom Instruction. 2nd ed. Ernest K. Dishner et al. 384p. 1986. pap. text ed. 22.95 (ISBN 0-8403-3918-6). Kendall-Hunt.
Reading in the Content Areas: Strategies for Classroom Teachers. Delva Daines. 1982. text ed. write for info. (ISBN 0-673-16025-4). Scott F.
Reading in the Content Fields. rev. ed. Compiled by Leo Fay. (Annotated Bibliographies Ser.). 1975. 1.25 (ISBN 0-87207-302-5). Intl Reading.
Reading in the Mathematics Classroom. Cyrus F. Smith & Henry S. Kepner. 64p. 1981. 7.95 (ISBN 0-8106-3203-9). NEA.
Reading in the Middle School. Ed. by Gerald G. Duffy. LC 74-23428. (Perspectives in Reading Ser.: No. 18). Repr. of 1974 ed. 55.00 (ISBN 0-317-55487-5, 2029594). Bks Demand UMI.
Reading in the Mind. Leif Fearn. 41p. (gr. 1-7). 1984. 25.00 (ISBN 0-940444-22-4). Kabyn.
Reading in the Psychology of Exceptional Children: Reference Book. (Special Education Ser.). 1978. text ed. 64.00 (ISBN 0-89568-077-7); pap. text ed. 25.95 (ISBN 0-89568-015-7). Spec Learn Corp.
Reading in the Science Classroom. Judith Bechtel & Bettie Franzblau. 64p. 1980. 7.95 (ISBN 0-8106-3201-2). NEA.
Reading in the Secondary School Classroom. Robert C. Aukerman. (Illus.). 425p. 1972. text ed. 31.95 (ISBN 0-07-002483-9). McGraw.
Reading in the Social Studies Classroom. Terry L. Bullock & Karl D. Hesse. 64p. 1981. 7.95 (ISBN 0-8106-3202-0). NEA.
Reading in the 1980's. 257p. 1983. 24.95 (ISBN 0-8352-1758-2). Bowker.
Reading Instruction: Diagnostic Teaching in the Classroom. 4th ed. Larry A. Harris & Carl B. Smith. ix, 769p. 1986. text ed. write for info. (ISBN 0-02-350580-X). Macmillan.
Reading Instruction for the Adult Illiterate. Edward V. Jones. LC 80-23063. 182p. 1981. 15.00x (ISBN 0-8389-0317-7). ALA.
Reading Instruction for the Gifted. Donald C. Cushenbery. 182p. 1987. 29.50x (ISBN 0-398-05332-4). C C Thomas.
Reading Instruction for Today. Jana Mason & Kathryn Au. 1986. text ed. write for info. (ISBN 0-673-18010-7). Scott F.
Reading Instruction for Today's Children. 2nd ed. H. Robinson & N. Smith. 1980. write for info. (ISBN 0-13-755157-6). P-H.
Reading Instruction in the Elementary School. Jack Rudman. (College Proficiency Examination Ser.: CPEP-25). (Cloth bdg. avail. on request). pap. 13.95 (ISBN 0-8373-5425-0). Natl Learning.
Reading Instruction in the Elementary School. Jack Rudman. (ACT Proficiency Examination Program: PEP-31). (Cloth bdg. avail. on request). pap. 13.95 (ISBN 0-8373-5531-1). Natl Learning.
Reading Instruction in the Middle School: A Whole School Approach. Maryann M. Manning & Gary L. Manning. 96p. 1979. pap. 5.95 (ISBN 0-8106-1707-2). NEA.
Reading Instruction Through Content Teaching. Earl H. Cheek, Jr. & Martha C. Cheek. 1983. text ed. 31.95 (ISBN 0-675-20026-1). Merrill.
Reading Interests, Activities & Opportunities of Bright, Average & Dull Children. May Lazar. LC 71-176977. (Columbia University. Teachers College. Contributions to Education: No. 707). Repr. of 1937 ed. 22.50 (ISBN 0-404-55707-4). AMS Pr.
Reading Interests & Needs of Negro College Freshmen Regarding Social Science Materials. Walter G. Daniel. LC 79-176719. (Columbia University. Teachers College. Contributions to Education: No. 862). Repr. of 1942 ed. 22.50 (ISBN 0-404-55862-3). AMS Pr.
Reading Interests of Young Children. George W. Norvelle. 516p. 1974. 10.00x (ISBN 0-87013-177-X). Mich St U Pr.
Reading Interpretation in Social Studies, Natural Sciences & Literature (G. E. D.) Jack Rudman. (Career Examination Ser.: CS-34). (Cloth bdg. avail. on request). pap. 10.00 (ISBN 0-8373-3734-8). Natl Learning.
Reading into Photography: Selected Essays, 1959-1980. Ed. by Thomas F. Barrow et al. LC 81-52051. 264p. 1987. pap. 13.95 (ISBN 0-8263-0647-0). U of NM Pr.
Reading into Racism: Bias in Children's Literature & Learning Materials. Gillian Klein. (Education Bks.). 192p. (Orig.). 1986. pap. text ed. 12.95 (ISBN 0-7102-0160-5). Routledge Chapman & Hall.
Reading into Writing: A Rhetoric, Reader, & Handbook. Eric Gould. 1983. pap. text ed. 25.96 (ISBN 0-395-32607-9); instr's manual 2.36 (ISBN 0-395-32608-7). HM.
Reading Is for Everyone: A Guide for Parents & Teachers of Exceptional Children. Dorothy Jeffree & Margaret Skeffington. (Illus.). 168p. 1984. pap. 6.95 (ISBN 0-13-755216-5). P-H.
Reading Is Fun with Bobby Bookworm. Ed. by Jean L. Scrocco. (Touch, Feel, Look & Learn Ser.). (Illus.). 16p. (ps). 1988. bds. 5.95 (ISBN 0-88101-074-X). Unicorn Pub.
Reading Is Fundamental: Guide to Encouraging Young Readers. Reading Is Fundamental, Inc. Staff. Ed. by Ruth Graves. LC 86-24055. 336p. 1987. pap. 8.95 (ISBN 0-385-23632-8). Doubleday.
Reading Is Thinking. Jelle Roos. 168p. 1983. pap. text ed. 11.95 (ISBN 0-8403-3039-1). Kendall-Hunt.
Reading Japanese. Eleanor H. Jorden. 607p. 1976. includes 17 cassettes 225.00x (ISBN 0-88432-096-0, J450). J Norton Pubs.
Reading Japanese. Eleanor H. Jorden & Hamako I. Chaplin. LC 75-18176. (Linguistic Ser.). 1976. 57.00t (ISBN 0-300-01912-2); pap. text ed. 22.50x (ISBN 0-300-01913-0). Yale U Pr.
Reading Joyce's "Ulysses". Daniel R. Schwarz. 240p. 1987. 27.50 (ISBN 0-312-66458-3). St Martin.
Reading Joyce's "Ulysses". Daniel R. Schwarz. LC 86-6680. 300p. 1987. pap. 11.95 (ISBN 0-312-00086-3). St Martin.
Reading Jung: Science, Psychology, & Religion. Volney P. Gay. LC 84-1322. (AAR-Studies in Religion). 166p. 1984. pap. 8.25 (ISBN 0-89130-731-1, 01 00 34). Scholars Pr GA.
Reading Keyboard Music, 3 vols. rev. ed. C. W. Reid. Ed. by Martha Miner et al. 1988. Vol. I. 44p. pap. 5.95 (ISBN 0-9620268-0-8); Vol. II. 36p. pap. 5.95 (ISBN 0-9620268-1-6); Vol. III. 40p. pap. 5.95 (ISBN 0-9620268-2-4); Set. 120p. pap. 15.00 (ISBN 0-9620268-3-2). Demibach Society.
Reading Knowledge in German: A Course for Art Historians & Archaeologists (1975) 2nd ed. Mary L. Apelt & H. P. Apelt. pap. 18.00. Heinman.
Reading Knowledge in German for Art Historians & Archaeologists: An English-German Course in Art History & Archaeology. H. P. Apelt. 1975. pap. 22.50x (ISBN 3-503-02228-7). Adlers Foreign Bks.
Reading Lab Kit. Caleb Gattegno. 1973. 35.00 (ISBN 0-87825-009-3). Ed Solutions.
Reading Lacan. Jane Gallop. LC 85-7892. 200p. 1985. 24.95x (ISBN 0-8014-1585-3). Cornell U Pr.
Reading Lacan. Jane Gallop. LC 85-7892. (Paperback Ser.). 200p. 1987. pap. 8.95x (ISBN 0-8014-9443-5). Cornell U Pr.
Reading Ladders for Human Relations. 6th ed. Ed. by Eileen Tway. 1980. pap. 9.95 (ISBN 0-02-933040-8). ACE.
Reading Ladders for Human Relations. Ed. by Eileen Tway. 1981. pap. 13.75 (ISBN 0-8141-3894-2, 38942). NCTE.
Reading Latin. Peter Jones & Keith Sidwell. (Illus.). 1986. Text, 176pgs. pap. 9.45 (ISBN 0-521-28623-9); Grammar, Vocabulary & Exercises, 550pgs. pap. 14.95 (ISBN 0-521-28622-0). Cambridge U Pr.
Reading Latin Poetry. Roger Hornsby. 286p. 1969. Repr. of 1967 ed. 13.95x (ISBN 0-8061-0741-3). U of Okla Pr.
Reading List for Students in Conservation of Historic & Artistic Works on Paper & Photographs. Anne Clapp & Roy Perkinson. 1980. 3.75 (ISBN 0-318-18698-5). Am Inst Conser Hist.
Reading Luke: A Literary & Theological Commentary on the Third Gospel. Charles H. Talbert. 256p. 1984. pap. 10.95 (ISBN 0-8245-0668-5). Crossroad NY.
Reading Made Easy: A First Book for Deaf & Dumb Children. W. R. Scott. 59.95 (ISBN 0-8490-0930-8). Gordon Pr.
Reading Maps. Paul Riffel. LC 79-13628. (Illus.). (gr. 7 up). 1973. pap. 6.95 plastic comb bdg. (ISBN 0-8331-1300-3). Hubbard Sci.
Reading Materials Handbook: A Guide to Materials & Sources for Secondary & College Reading Improvement. Allen Berger & Hugo Hartig. 1969. pap. 3.00 (ISBN 0-911880-01-1). Academia.
Reading Matters: A Practical Philosophy. J. Webster. 208p. 1983. text ed. 11.00 (ISBN 0-07-084134-9). McGraw.
Reading Medieval European Coins. Ralph S. Walker. (Illus.). 1979. 6.50 (ISBN 0-915018-41-1). Attic Bks.
Reading "Middlemarch": Reclaiming the Middles Distance. Jeanie Thomas. Ed. by Walton A. Litz. LC 87-5874. (Nineteenth-Century Studies). 124p. 1987. 39.95 (ISBN 0-8357-1797-6). UMI Res Pr.
Reading Modern Russian. Jules F. Levin et al. (Illus.). vi, 321p. 1979. pap. text ed. 13.95 (ISBN 0-89357-059-1). Slavica.
Reading Motivation Idea Book. Elaine P. LeBlanc & Anthony D. Fredericks. 1986. pap. 7.95 (ISBN 0-673-18312-2). Scott F.
Reading My Bible in Fall. Lou Heath & Beth Taylor. LC 85-30947. (Orig.). (gr. 1-6). 1986. pap. 4.50 (ISBN 0-8054-4322-3). Broadman.
Reading My Bible in Spring. Lou Heath & Beth Taylor. (Orig.). (gr. 3-6). 1987. pap. 4.50 (ISBN 0-8054-4320-7). Broadman.
Reading My Bible in Summer. Lou Heath & Beth Taylor. (Orig.). (gr. 3-6). 1987. pap. 4.50 (ISBN 0-8054-4321-5). Broadman.
Reading My Bible in Winter. Lou Heath & Beth Taylor. LC 85-30940. (Orig.). (gr. 1-6). 1986. pap. 4.50 (ISBN 0-8054-4323-1). Broadman.
Reading Myself & Others. Philip Roth. LC 75-2475. 270p. 1975. 8.95 (ISBN 0-374-24753-6). FS&G.
Reading Myself & Others. Philip Roth. (Nonfiction Ser.). 336p. 1985. pap. 6.95 (ISBN 0-14-007681-6). Penguin.
Reading Nabokov. Douglas Fowler. LC 82-17342. 224p. 1983. pap. text ed. 12.50 (ISBN 0-8191-2721-3). U Pr of Amer.
Reading Narrative: Form, Ethics, Ideology. Ed. by James Phelan. (Illus.). 336p. 1988. text ed. 30.00x (ISBN 0-8142-0458-9). Ohio St U Pr.
Reading Nature's Clues: A Guide to the Wild. Doug Sadler. (Illus.). 248p. Date not set. 14.95 (Pub. by Broadview Pr). Lewiston Busn Servs.
Reading Newspapers, Labels & Directions. Carolyn M. Starkey & Norgina W. Penn. (Essential Life Skills Ser.). 64p. Date not set. pap. 4.95 (ISBN 0-8442-5314-6, Passport Bks). Natl Textbk.
Reading Nietzsche. Robert C. Solomon & Kathleen M. Higgins. 288p. 1988. 32.50 (ISBN 0-19-504858-X). Oxford U Pr.
Reading Norwegian. Einar Haugen. LC 75-24258. 1977. cloth 300pg; pap. 8.00x 208pg. (ISBN 0-87950-172-3). Spoken Lang Serv.
Reading of Books. Holbrook Jackson. 1946. Repr. 29.00 (ISBN 0-8274-3245-3). R West.
Reading of Dante's Inferno. Wallace Fowlie. LC 80-19025. 248p. 1981. lib. bdg. 18.00x (ISBN 0-226-25887-4); pap. 6.50x (ISBN 0-226-25888-2). U of Chicago Pr.

Reading of E. M. Forster. Glen Cavaliero. 187p. 1979. 24.50x (ISBN 0-8476-6191-1). Rowman.
Reading of "Gulliver's Travels". Kathleen M. Swaim. 1972. text ed. 20.80x (ISBN 90-2792-304-3). Mouton.
Reading of Hegel's "Phenomenology of Spirit". rev ed. Quentin Lauer. LC 75-41657. x, 303p. 1987. pap. 15.00 (ISBN 0-8232-1001-4). Fordham.
Reading of Henry Green. A. Kingsley Weatherhead. LC 61-8767. 180p. 1961. 20.00x (ISBN 0-295-73902-9). U of Wash Pr.
Reading of I Samuel. Peter D. Miscall. (Literary Bible Ser.). 256p. 1985. cancelled (ISBN 0-8245-0662-6). Crossroad NY.
Reading of Imagery in the Chinese Poetic Tradition. Pauline Yu. 264p. 1987. text ed. 29.50x (ISBN 0-691-06682-5). Princeton U Pr.
Reading of Jane Austen. Barbara Hardy. LC 75-39852. 200p. 1976. pap. 11.00x cusa (ISBN 0-8147-3397-2). NYU Pr.
Reading of Life. facs. ed. Sidney R. Lysaght. LC 70-142659. (Essay Index Reprint Ser). 1936. 18.00 (ISBN 0-8369-2060-0). Ayer Co Pubs.
Reading of "Mansfield Park" An Essay in Critical Synthesis. Avrom Fleishman. 109p. 1970. pap. 4.95x (ISBN 0-8018-1149-X). Johns Hopkins.
Reading of "Moby Dick". Milton O. Percival. 1967. Repr. lib. bdg. 14.00x (ISBN 0-374-96403-3, Octagon). Hippocrene Bks.
Reading of Modern Art. Dore Ashton. LC 68-19064. (Illus.). pap. 63.80 (ISBN 0-317-10195-1, 2002261). Bks Demand UMI.
Reading of Proust. David R. Ellison. LC 83-48057. 232p. 1983. 25.00x (ISBN 0-8018-3048-6). Johns Hopkins.
Reading of Proust. Wallace Fowlie. 11.00 (ISBN 0-8446-0627-8). Peter Smith.
Reading of Proust. 2nd ed. Wallace Fowlie. LC 75-14766. xii, 324p. 1985. pap. 18.00x (ISBN 0-226-25885-8). U of Chicago Pr.
Reading of the Alamo. John F. Rios. 1987. 20.00 (ISBN 0-533-07123-2). Vantage.
Reading of the "Canterbury Tales". Bernard F. Huppe. LC 64-17577. 245p. 1964. 39.50x; pap. 9.95 (ISBN 0-87395-022-4). State U NY Pr.
Reading of the Canterbury Tales. Bernard F. Huppe. 256p. 10.00 (Pub. by SUNY Pr). Medieval & Renaissance NY.
Reading of the "Canterbury Tales". Trevor Whittock. (Orig.). 1969. pap. 13.95 (ISBN 0-521-09557-3). Cambridge U Pr.
Reading of the Will. (Drama Pak Ser.). 1984. 9.95 (ISBN 0-89273-305-5). Educ Serv.
Reading of Verbal Material in Ninth Grade Algebra. Margaret G. McKim. LC 71-177032. (Columbia University. Teachers College. Contributions to Education Ser.: No. 850). Repr. of 1941 ed. 22.50 (ISBN 0-404-55850-X). AMS Pr.
Reading of Villon's Testament. David A. Fein. LC 84-50322. 112p. 1984. pap. 10.95 (ISBN 0-917786-04-1). Summa Pubns.
Reading Old & New. Daphne Phillips. 96p. 1987. pap. 30.00x (ISBN 0-905392-73-6, Countryside Bks). State Mutual Bk.
Reading on Indian Music. G. Kuppuswamy & M. Hariharan. (Illus.). 239p. 1979. 22.95. Asia Bk Corp.
Reading on Purpose: Cognitive Skills for Intermediate Learners. Fraida Dubin & Elite Olshtain. (Illus.). 1987. pap. text ed. 14.95 (ISBN 0-201-11671-5). Addison-Wesley.
Reading Onetti: Language Narrative & the Subject. Mark Millington. (Liverpool Monographs in Hispanic Studies: No. 5). 345p. 1986. text ed. 32.95 (ISBN 0-905205-26-X, Pub. by F Cairns). Longwood Pub Group.
Reading Opera. Ed. by Arthur Groos & Roger Parker. 381p. 1988. 45.00 (ISBN 0-691-09132-3); pap. 14.95 (ISBN 0-691-02709-9). Princeton U Pr.
Reading Other People's Mail: The Best of "Dear Deborah". Katherine N. Nyberg. 1988. pap. 7.95. Abingdon.
Reading Ourselves to Sleep. Donald Finkel et al. 24p. 1985. pap. 15.00 (ISBN 0-931757-23-1). Pterodactyl Pr.
Reading Philip Roth. Ed. by Asher Z. Milbauer & Donald G. Watson. 225p. 1987. 27.50 (ISBN 0-312-00934-8). St Martin.
Reading Photographs: Understanding the Aesthetics of Photography. The Photographer's Gallery & Jonathan Bayes. LC 77-88761. 1978. pap. 11.95 (ISBN 0-394-73584-6). Pantheon.
Reading Poe Reading Freud: The Romantic Imagination in Crisis. Clive Bloom. LC 87-32223. 144p. 1988. 35.00 (ISBN 0-312-01668-9). St Martin.
Reading Poems. Richard Gunter. 1975. pap. text ed. 4.50 (ISBN 0-917496-06-X). Hornbeam Pr.
Reading Pound Reading: Modernism after Nietzsche. Kathryne V. Lindberg. 288p. 1987. 29.95x (ISBN 0-19-504165-8). Oxford U Pr.
Reading Power. Adult ed. Bea Mikulecky & Linda Jeffries. (Illus.). 1986. pap. text ed. 13.96 (ISBN 0-201-15865-5). Addison-Wesley.
Reading Power & Study Skills for College Work. 2nd ed. Carl A. Lefevre & Helen E. Lefevre. 356p. 1984. pap. text ed. 12.00 net (ISBN 0-15-575759-8, HC). HarBraceJ.
Reading Power: Book 1. Angelica W. Cass. 128p. (Orig.). 1984. pap. 6.95 (ISBN 0-668-05968-0). Arco.
Reading Power: Book 2. Angelcia W. Cass. 176p. (Orig.). 1984. pap. 6.95 (ISBN 0-668-05969-9). Arco.
Reading Power: Book 3. Angelica W. Cass. 160p. (Orig.). 1984. pap. 6.95 (ISBN 0-668-05970-2). Arco.
Reading Power: Book 4. Angelica W. Cass. 192p. (Orig.). 1984. pap. 6.95 (ISBN 0-668-05971-0). Arco.
Reading Power: Getting Started. Rosakis. 128p. 1987. pap. 6.95 (ISBN 0-668-06614-8). Arco.
Reading Power Plus. Nicholas Criscuolo. (gr. 1-6). 1986. pap. 10.95 (ISBN 0-8224-5812-8). D S Lake Pubs.
Reading, Preaching & Celebrating the Word. Ed. by Paul Marcoux & Joseph P. LoCigno. pap. 9.95 (ISBN 0-941850-00-5). Liturgical Pubns.
Reading Prisms. 1987. 7.95 (ISBN 0-88047-124-7). DOK Pubs.
Reading; Problems & Practices: Open University Course Reader. Ed. by Jessie F. Reid & Harry Donaldson. 418p. 1985. 30.00x (ISBN 0-317-42665-6, Pub. by Ward Lock Educ Co Ltd). State Mutual Bk.
Reading Problems: Diagnosis & Remediation. Margaret A. Rickek & Lynne K. List. (Illus.). 400p. 1983. 25.50 (ISBN 0-13-755173-8). P-H.
Reading Problems: Identification & Treatment. Peter Edwards. 1978. pap. text ed. 12.50x (ISBN 0-435-10264-8). Heinemann Ed.
Reading Process & Practice: From Socio-Psycholinguistics to Whole Language. Constance Weaver. LC 87-12114. xxvii, 483p. 1987. text ed. 27.50x (ISBN 0-435-08444-5). Heinemann Ed.
Reading Process: The Teacher & the Learner. 4th ed. Miles V. Zintz & Zelda R. Maggart. 656p. 1984. pap. write for info (ISBN 0-697-08274-1); instr's manual avail. (ISBN 0-697-06214-7). Wm C Brown.
Reading Program: Critical Reading, Bk. G. 2nd ed. Amy Awtrey & Carol Markos. 72p. 1982. pap. 3.75x (ISBN 0-88069-006-2). L A Meyer.
Reading Program: Essay Structure, Bk. F. 2nd ed. Amy Awtrey & Carol Markos. 72p. 1982. pap. 3.75x (ISBN 0-88069-005-4). L A Meyer.
Reading Program: Relationships, Bk. E. 3rd ed. Amy Awtrey & Carol Markos. 58p. 1982. pap. 3.75x (ISBN 0-88069-004-6). L A Meyer.
Reading Program: Sentence Structure, Bk. C. 2nd ed. Amy Awtrey & Carol Markos. 48p. 1982. pap. 3.75x (ISBN 0-88069-002-X). L A Meyer.
Reading Program: Signals, Bk. D. 2nd ed. Amy Awtrey & Carol Markos. 62p. 1982. pap. 3.75x (ISBN 0-88069-003-8). L A Meyer.
Reading Program: Vocabulary, Bk. B. 2nd ed. Amy Awtrey & Carol Markos. 48p. 1982. pap. 3.75x (ISBN 0-88069-001-1). L A Meyer.
Reading Program: Word Patterns, Bk. A. 3rd ed. Amy Awtrey & Carol Markos. 48p. 1982. pap. 3.75x (ISBN 0-88069-000-3). L A Meyer.
Reading Progress Feedback System (RFFS) Ellis Richardson & Harold Freeman, Jr. 86p. (Orig.). 1981. pap. 15.00 (ISBN 0-939632-32-2). ILM.
Reading Race: White American Poets & the Racial Discourse in the Twentieth Century. Aldon L. Nielsen. LC 88-3942. 192p. 1988. 24.00x (ISBN 0-8203-1061-1). U of Ga Pr.
Reading Railroad. Barbara Gregorich. Ed. by Joan Hofman. (Fast Forward Enrichment Ser.). (Illus.). 32p. (ps-1). 1986. wkbk. 1.95 (ISBN 0-88743-130-5, 02506). Sch Zone Pub Co.
Reading Readiness, 4 bks. (gr. k-1). 1980. pap. text ed. 3.25 (ISBN 0-8449-3507-7); tchr's. manual & placement exam avail.; 4 bk. set 13.00. Learning Line.
Reading Readiness. (Questron Electronic Workbook Library Ser.). (Illus.). 32p. (ps). 1985. 3.95 (ISBN 0-394-87700-4). Random.
Reading Readiness, Bk. 1. Joan Hoffman. (I Know It! Bks). (Illus.). 32p. (ps-1). 1980. wkbk. 1.95 (ISBN 0-938256-04-1). Sch Zone Pub Co.
Reading Readiness, Bk. 2. Joan Hoffman. (I Know It! Bks.). (Illus.). 32p. (ps-1). 1980. wkbk. 1.95 (ISBN 0-938256-05-X). Sch Zone Pub Co.
Reading Readiness - Teaching. Ann Zimmer. (Let's Learn Ser.). (Illus.). 32p. (ps-1). 1984. pap. 1.98 (ISBN 0-88724-097-6, CD-7036). Carson-Dellos.
Reading Readiness Book One. (Dell Home Activity Ser.). 1979. pap. 0.99 (ISBN 0-440-07468-1). Dell.
Reading Readiness Program, 2 kits. Sullivan Associates Staff. Incl. Kit No. 1. Letters of the Alphabet. 1972. 328.20 (ISBN 0-07-079581-9); Kit No. 2. Sounds & Letters. 1972. 328.00 (ISBN 0-07-079582-7). McGraw.
Reading Readiness Readers, 6 bks. Sullivan Assoc. pap. text ed. 1.50 ea. (ISBN 0-8449-3700-2); Set. 9.00. Learning Line.
Reading Reading. 3rd ed. Peter L. Spencer. LC 78-128391. 1978. pap. 5.00x (ISBN 0-914522-02-7). Alpha Iota.
Reading Reading: Fiftieth Anniversary Perspectives. Ed. by Malcolm P. Douglass. (Claremont Reading Conference Yearbook Ser.). 241p. 1983. pap. 12.00 (ISBN 0-941742-01-6). Claremont Grad.
Reading Realism in Stendhal. Ann Jefferson. (Cambridge Studies in French). 288p. 1988. 44.50 (ISBN 0-521-26274-7). Cambridge U Pr.
Reading Reform. Satsvarupa Das Goswami. Ed. by Dattatreya dasa. 120p. 1985. pap. text ed. 10.00 (ISBN 0-911233-28-8). Gita Nagari.
Reading Report Card. 72p. 1988. 9.00 (ISBN 0-317-67885-X). Educ Testing Serv.
Reading Research, Vol. 5. T. Gary Waller & G. E. Mackinnon. 1985. 59.50 (ISBN 0-12-572305-9); pap. 27.00 (ISBN 0-12-570501-8). Acad Pr.
Reading Research: Advances in Theory & Practice, Vol. 1. Ed. by T. Gary Waller & G. E. Mackinnon. 1979. 41.50 (ISBN 0-12-572301-6). Acad Pr.
Reading Research: Advances in Theory & Practice, Vol. 2. Ed. by Gary T. Waller & G. E. Mackinnon. (Serial Publication). 1981. 41.50 (ISBN 0-12-572302-4). Acad Pr.
Reading Research: Advances in Theory & Practice, Vol. 3. Ed. by T. Gary Waller & G. E. MacKinnon. (Serial Publication Ser.). 1981. 44.50 (ISBN 0-12-572303-2). Acad Pr.
Reading Research: Advances in Theory & Practice, Vol. 4. Ed. by T. Gary Waller & G. E. MacKinnon. 1985. 53.50 (ISBN 0-12-572304-0). Acad Pr.
Reading Research & Librarianship: A History & Anaylsis. Stephen Karetzky. LC 80-1715. (Contributions in Librarianship & Information Science Ser.: No. 36). (Illus.). xxi, 385p. 1982. lib. bdg. 38.95 (ISBN 0-313-22226-6, KRR/). Greenwood.
Reading Research Revisited. Lance M. Gentile & Michael L. Kamil. 1983. text ed. 28.95 (ISBN 0-675-20028-8). Merrill.
Reading Research, Vol. 6: Advances in Theory & Practice. Ed. by Meredyth Daneman et al. 416p. 1988. price not set (ISBN 0-12-572306-7). Acad Pr.
Reading Resource Book. Mary Jett-Simpson. LC 83-81433. 226p. (Orig.). (ps-2). 1984. pap. 16.95 (ISBN 0-89334-095-2). Humanics Ltd.
Reading Resource Book: Tried & True Reading Activities for Elementary Students. Virginia N. Fulk. LC 83-83317. 224p. (Orig.). 1984. pap. text ed. 19.95 (ISBN 0-918452-68-6). Learning Pubns.
Reading, Responding & Writing: Short Essays & Stories. Ed. by Domenick Caruso & Stephen Weidenborner. LC 86-60658. 256p. 1987. pap. text ed. 10.50 (ISBN 0-312-66460-5); 00.29 (ISBN 0-312-66464-8). St Martin.
Reading Retardation & Multi-Sensory Teaching. Charles Hulme. (International Library of Psychology Ser.). 200p. 1981. 31.95x (ISBN 0-7100-0761-2). Routledge Chapman & Hall.
Reading Riddles. 32p. 1989. pap. 1.95. Tor Bks.
Reading Rights for Boys: Sex Role & Development in Language Experiences. David Austin et al. LC 71-130790. (Orig.). 1971. pap. text ed. 5.95x (ISBN 0-89197-369-9). Irvington.
Reading, Riting & Reconstruction: The Education of Freedmen in the South, 1861-1870. Robert C. Morris. LC 80-25370. (Illus.). 1982. lib. bdg. 28.00x (ISBN 0-226-53928-8). U of Chicago Pr.
Reading Room. P. R. Harris. (Illus.). 36p. (Orig.). 1979. pap. 2.95 (ISBN 0-904654-31-1, Pub. by British Lib). Longwood Pub Group.
Reading Round-Ups: One Hundred Ten Ready-to-Use Literature Enrichment Activities. Barbara F. Bannister. 288p. (gr. 5-8). 1988. pap. 24.95x (ISBN 0-87628-750-X). Ctr Appl Res.
Reading Roundups: Thirteen Ready to Use Literature Enrichment Activities for Grades 5-8. Barbara Bannister. 288p. (gr. 5-8). 1988. pap. 24.95 spiral bdg. Ctr Appl Res.
Reading Rules for Russian: A Systematic Approach to Russian Spelling & Pronunciation with Notes on Dialectal & Stylistic Variation. Bruce L. Derwing & Tom M. Priestly. (Illus.). vi, 247p. (Orig.). 1980. pap. 13.95 (ISBN 0-89357-066-4). Slavica.
Reading Schedules. Winifred H. Roderman. (Survival Guides Ser.). (Illus.). 64p. (gr. 7-12). 1978. pap. text ed. 3.95 (ISBN 0-915510-23-5). Janus Bks.
Reading Scripture As the Word of God. Rev. ed. George Martin. 200p. 1982. pap. 5.95 (ISBN 0-89283-152-9). Servant.
Reading: Seventy-Five Years of Progress. Conference on Reading - University Of Chicago. Ed. by H. Alan Robinson. LC 66-23696. 1966. 7.50x (ISBN 0-226-72178-7, SEM96). U of Chicago Pr.
Reading Signs, Directories, Schedules, Maps, Charts & Utility Bills. Carolyn M. Starkey & Norgina W. Penn. (Essential Life Skills). 64p. Date not set. pap. 4.95 (ISBN 0-8442-5317-0, Passport Bks). Natl Textbk.
Reading Skillbuilder: Comprehension Skills. Harry W. Forgan. 1982. pap. 6.95 (ISBN 0-673-16549-3). Scott F.
Reading Skillbuilder: Prereading Skills. Harry W. Forgan. 1982. pap. 6.95 (ISBN 0-673-16547-7). Scott F.
Reading Skillbuilder: Word Recognition Skills. Harry W. Forgan. 1982. pap. 6.95 (ISBN 0-673-16548-5). Scott F.
Reading Skills. 2nd ed. William D. Baker. LC 73-17161. (Illus.). 176p. 1974. pap. text ed. write for info. (ISBN 0-13-762062-4). P-H.
Reading Skills. Lillian Lieberman. 64p. (gr. k-3). 1985. 6.95 (ISBN 0-912107-36-7). Monday Morning Bks.
Reading Skills for College Students. Ophelia Hancock. 384p. 1986. pap. text ed. write for info. (ISBN 0-13-755257-2). P-H.
Reading Skills for College Study. 2nd ed. James F. Shepherd. LC 83-82433. 368p. 1984. pap. text ed. 18.95 (ISBN 0-395-34120-5); instr's manual 1.50 (ISBN 0-395-34121-3). HM.
Reading Skills for College Study. 3rd ed. James F. Shepherd. LC 87-80618. 384p. 1987. pap. text ed. 21.96 (ISBN 0-395-35961-9); Instr's manual 2.36 (ISBN 0-395-45053-5). HM.
Reading Skills for In-Depth Understanding. Calvin Greatsinger. (Illus.). 56p. 1981. pap. text ed. 4.95 (ISBN 0-914634-87-9). DOK Pubs.
Reading Skills for Law Students. Craig K. Mayfield. 170p. 1980. pap. 12.50x (ISBN 0-87215-313-4). Michie Co.
Reading Skills for Social Studies: Social Studies Concepts, Level C. Dale I. Foreman & Sally Allen. (Skillbooster Ser.). 64p. (gr. 3). 1980. 4.12 (ISBN 0-8136-2153-4). Modern Curr.
Reading Skills for Social Studies: Social Studies Concepts, Level E. Dale I. Foreman & Sally Allen. (Skillbooster Ser.). 64p. (gr. 5). 1981. wkbk. 4.12 (ISBN 0-8136-2154-2). Modern Curr.
Reading Skills for Social Studies: Social Studies Concepts, Level F. Dale I. Foreman & Sally Allen. (Skillbooster Ser.). 64p. (gr. 6). 1981. wkbk. 4.12 (ISBN 0-8136-2156-9). Modern Curr.
Reading Skills for Social Studies: Using Maps, Charts & Graphs, Level C. Dale I. Foreman & Sally Allen. (Skillbooster Ser.). 64p. (gr. 3). 1980. wkbk. 4.12 (ISBN 0-8136-2128-3). Modern Curr.
Reading Skills for Social Studies: Using Maps, Charts & Graphs. Dale I. Foreman & Sally Allen. (Skillbooster Ser.: Level D). 64p. (gr. 4). 1980. wkbk. 4.12. Modern Curr.
Reading Skills for Social Studies: Using Maps, Charts & Graphs, Level E. Dale I. Foreman & Sally Allen. (Skillbooster Ser.). 64p. (gr. 5). 1981. wkbk. 4.12 (ISBN 0-8136-2130-5). Modern Curr.
Reading Skills for Social Studies: Using Maps, Charts & Graphs, Level F. Dale I. Foreman & Sally Allen. (Skillbooster Ser.). 64p. (gr. 6). 1981. wkbk. 4.12 (ISBN 0-8136-2131-3). Modern Curr.
Reading Skills for Successful Living. 3rd ed. Irwin L. Joffe. 360p. 1987. pap. text ed. write for info. (ISBN 0-534-07236-4). Wadsworth Pub.
Reading Skills Handbook. 3rd ed. Harvey S. Wiener & Charles Bazerman. 416p. 1985. pap. text ed. 18.95 (ISBN 0-395-35810-8, 718FD); instr's. manual 2.00 (ISBN 0-395-36265-2); test package 2.00 (ISBN 0-395-36266-0). HM.
Reading Skills Handbook. 4th ed. Harvey S. Wiener & Charles Bazerman. 1988. 21.16 (ISBN 0-395-38013-8); test pkg. 3.16 (ISBN 0-395-45054-3). HM.
Reading Skills Register. Kathleen Smith & Jennifer Woods. Ed. by Ellen Sussman. (Illus.). 68p. (Orig.). (gr. 4-6). 1983. pap. text ed. 7.95 (ISBN 0-933606-24-9, MS-623). Monkey Sisters.
Reading Skills Test. rev. ed. Frank Pintozzi. (GED Ser.). 236p. 1985. pap. 7.65 (ISBN 0-8092-5585-5). Contemp Bks.
Reading Specialist. Jack Rudman. (National Teachers Examination Ser.: NT-30). (Cloth bdg. avail. on request). pap. 13.95 (ISBN 0-8373-8440-0). Natl Learning.
Reading Stanley Elkin. Peter J. Bailey. LC 84-8735. 242p. 1985. 18.95 (ISBN 0-252-01172-4). U of Ill Pr.
Reading Statistics & Research. Schuyler W. Huck et al. 1974. pap. text ed. 21.50 scp (ISBN 0-06-042976-3, HarpC). Har-Row.
Reading Stories. 1982. 0.50 (ISBN 0-939418-43-6). Ferguson-Florissant.
Reading Success for Each Child Every Day. Janet L. Prange & David L. Zufelt. (Illus.). 184p. 1980. pap. text ed. 9.95x (ISBN 0-89641-037-4). American Pr.
Reading Success for School & Home. Lucy C. LeGros. (Illus.). 212p. (Orig.). (gr. k-4). 1979. pap. 10.95 (ISBN 0-937306-01-0). Creat Res NC.
Reading T-1 Locomotives: An Unusual Northern. Rod Dirkes. pap. 12.95 (ISBN 0-944119-00-X). Andover Junction.
Reading Teacher's Book of Lists. Edward B. Fry et al. 195p. 1984. 17.50x (ISBN 0-13-762112-4, Busn). P-H.
Reading Teacher's Complete Diagnosis & Correction Manual. Wilma H. Miller. 256p. (gr. 1-12). 1988. pap. 24.95x (ISBN 0-87628-772-0). Ctr Appl Res.
Reading Teacher's Complete Diagnosis & Correction Manual. Wilma H. Miller. 296p. 1988. pap. 24.95. P-H.
Reading Technical Books. Anne Eisenberg. LC 78-672. (Illus.). 1978. pap. write for info. ref. ed. (ISBN 0-13-762138-8). P-H.
Reading Television. John Fiske & John Hartley. (New Accents Ser.). 1978. pap. 10.95x (ISBN 0-416-85560-1, NO. 2781). Routledge Chapman & Hall.
Reading Tests & Reviews I. Ed. by Oscar K. Buros. xxii, 520p. 1968. 20.00x (ISBN 0-910674-09-4). U of Nebr Pr.
Reading Tests & Reviews II: A Monograph Consisting of the Reading Sections of the Seventh Mental Measurements Yearbook (1972) & Tests in Print II (1974) Ed. by Oscar K. Buros. LC 70-13495. pap. 71.30 (2026563). Bks Demand UMI.
Reading Tests & Teachers: A Practical Guide. Ed. by Robert Schreiner. LC 79-17271. 81p. (Orig.). 1979. pap. text ed. 4.00 (ISBN 0-87207-726-8, 726). Intl Reading.

Readings & Cases in Personnel Management. Lloyd L. Byars et al. 1979. 14.95x (ISBN 0-7216-2252-6). Dryden Pr.

Readings & Conversations: About the United States, Its People, Its History & Its Customs, 2 vols. rev. ed. English Language Services Staff. 1976. text ed. 4.50 ea.; Vol. 1. (ISBN 0-87789-195-8); Vol. 2. (ISBN 0-87789-196-6); Set. cassette tapes 95.00 (ISBN 0-87789-201-6). Cassettes 1. Cassettes 2 (ISBN 0-87789-202-4). ELS Educ Servs.

Readings & Feelings: An Introduction to Subjective Criticism. David Bleich. LC 74-84482. 114p. 1975. pap. 6.95 (ISBN 0-8141-3921-3). NCTE.

Readings & Information Systems: A Managerial Perspective. James Wetherbe et al. 486p. 1988. pap. text ed. 25.75 (ISBN 0-314-65767-3). West Pub.

Readings & Interpreting Diagrams in Air Conditioning & Refrigeration. Edward Mahoney. 1983. text ed. 32.00 (ISBN 0-8359-6483-3, Reston); pap. text ed. 24.00 (ISBN 0-8359-6482-5); instr's. manual avail. (ISBN 0-8359-6484-1). P-H.

Readings & Resources in Youth Ministry. Michael Warren. 254p. (Orig.). 1987. pap. 9.95 (ISBN 0-88489-178-X). St Mary's.

Readings & Writing Termcap Entries. John Strang. Ed. by Dale Dougherty. (Nutshell Handbook). 72p. 1985. pap. 7.50 (ISBN 0-937175-03-X). O'Reilly & Assocs.

Readings, Cases, Materials in Canon Law: A Textbook for Ministerial Students. Jordan F. Hite et al. LC 79-24977. 370p. (Orig.). 1980. pap. text ed. 8.50 (ISBN 0-8146-1081-1). Liturgical Pr.

Readings: Child Psychology. Ed. by George R. Smrtic & Victor P. Garlock. LC 73-4447. 145p. 1973. pap. text ed. 12.00x (ISBN 0-8422-5094-8). Irvington.

Readings for a New Public Health. Ed. by Claudia J. Martin & David V. McQueen. 250p. 1988. 37.50x (ISBN 0-85224-598-X, Pub. by Edinburgh U Pr Scotland). Columbia U Pr.

Readings for Anthropology & Education. Ed. by Charles Harrington. 1971. pap. text ed. 7.95x (ISBN 0-8290-1178-1). Irvington.

Readings for Assembly. R. L. Bowley. 1985. 30.00x (ISBN 0-900000-87-2, Pub. by Centaur Bks). State Mutual Bk.

Readings for Enrichment in Secondary School Mathematics. Ed. by Max A. Sobel. LC 87-34855. (Illus., Orig.). 1988. pap. 11.00 (ISBN 0-87353-252-X). NCTM.

Readings for General Psychology. Ed. by R. A. Lockhart et al. 1967. pap. 10.00 (ISBN 0-384-50021-8). Johnson Repr.

Readings for Introducing Sociology. Ed. by Richhard F. Larson. Ronald J. Knapp. (Illus.). 1982. pap. text ed. 10.95x (ISBN 0-19-503007-9). Oxford U Pr.

Readings for Introductory Sociology. 3rd ed. Dennis H. Wrong & H. L. Gracey. 1977. pap. text ed. write for info. (ISBN 0-02-430700-9). Macmillan.

Readings for Older Women. Date not set. price not set (ISBN 0-940483-04-1). Hot Flash Pr.

Readings for Social Psychology. Ed. by Martin F. Kaplan. LC 72-86188. 146p. 1972. 26.50x (ISBN 0-8422-5043-3); pap. text ed. 12.50x (ISBN 0-8422-0228-5). Irvington.

Readings for Social Work Practice, Vol. 1. Everett Busby et al. LC 72-8103. 174p. 1972. pap. text ed. 14.95x (ISBN 0-686-76955-4). Irvington.

Readings for Speed Development. PAR Staff. 1983. 8.35x (ISBN 0-89702-036-7). PAR Inc.

Readings for Technical Writers. Debra Journet & Julie L. Kling. 1984. pap. text ed. write for info. (ISBN 0-673-15557-9). Scott F.

Readings for the History of the English Language. Ed. by Charles T. Scott & Jon L. Erickson. LC 68-20532. 1968. 64.50x (ISBN 0-89197-370-2). Irvington.

Readings for the Managerial Accounting Specialty. (FLMI Insurance Education Program Ser.). 207p. 1981. pap. text ed. 9.50 (ISBN 0-915322-45-5). LOMA.

Readings for Today's Writers. Steven H. Gale. LC 79-21312. 1980. pap. text ed. write for info. (ISBN 0-673-15672-9). Scott F.

Readings for Town & Country Church Workers: An Annotated Bibliography. David M. Byers & Bernard Quinn. LC 74-77445. 120p. 1974. pap. 2.00x (ISBN 0-914422-00-6). Glenmary Res Ctr.

Readings for Women's Programs. Meg Bowman. 98p. 1987. pap. 5.95 (ISBN 0-940483-00-9). Hot Flash Pr.

Readings for Writers. 5th ed. Jo Ray McCuen & Anthony C. Winkler. 741p. 1986. pap. text ed. 13.00 net (ISBN 0-15-575833-0, Pub. by HC); instr's. manual 2.00 (ISBN 0-15-575834-9). HarBraceJ.

Readings for Writing. Elizabeth Cowan. 1983. pap. text ed. write for info. (ISBN 0-673-15845-4). Scott F.

Readings from AI Magazine: Nineteen Eighty to Nineteen Eighty-Four. Ed. by Robert Engelmore. (Illus.). 700p. 1988. pap. text ed. 75.00x (ISBN 0-929280-01-6). Amer Artificial.

Readings from American Literature: A Textbook for Schools & Colleges. Mary E. Calhoun & Emma L. MacAlarney. 1979. Repr. of 1915 ed. lib. bdg. 40.00 (ISBN 0-8495-0938-6). Arden Lib.

Readings from Chinese Writers: Nineteen Nineteen to Nineteen Forty-Nine, Vol. 1. Beijing Language Institute Staff. 335p. (Chinese.). 1982. pap. text ed. 8.95x (ISBN 0-88727-038-7). Cheng & Tsui.

Readings from Chinese Writers: Nineteen Nineteen to Nineteen Forty-Nine, Vol. 2. Beijing Language Institute Staff. 363p. (Chinese.). 1982. pap. text ed. 8.95x (ISBN 0-88727-039-5). Cheng & Tsui.

Readings From Chinese Writers: Nineteen Nineteen to Nineteen Forty-Nine, Bk. 2. Ed. by Beijing Language Institute Staff. (Readings From Chinese Writers Ser.). 360p. (Orig.). 1982. pap. 8.95 (ISBN 0-8351-1122-9). China Bks.

Readings From Chinese Writers Series: Nineteen Nineteen to Nineteen Forty-Nine, Bk. 1. Ed. by Beijing Language Institute Staff. (Readings From Chinese Writers). 333p. (Orig.). 1982. pap. 8.95 (ISBN 0-8351-1117-2). China Bks.

Readings from Durkheim. Selected by Kenneth Thompson. (Key Texts Ser.). 150p. 1985. pap. 9.95 (ISBN 0-85312-901-0, 9585, Pub. by Tavistock England). Routledge Chapman & Hall.

Readings from Progressive Education, Vol. I: A Movement & Its Professional Journal. Ed. by Stephen I. Brown et al. LC 88-5713. 366p. (Orig.). 1988. lib. bdg. 29.50 (ISBN 0-8191-6916-1); pap. text ed. 16.25 (ISBN 0-8191-6917-X). U Pr of Amer.

Readings from Talcott Parsons. Selected by Peter Hamilton. (Key Texts Ser.). 150p. 1985. pap. 9.95 (ISBN 0-85312-854-5, 9586, Pub. by Tavistock England). Routledge Chapman & Hall.

Readings from the American Mercury. facs. ed. American Mercury Staff. Ed. by G. C. Knight. LC 68-16902. (Essay Index Reprint Ser.). 1926. 18.00 (ISBN 0-8369-0150-9). Ayer Co Pubs.

Readings from the Frankfurt School. Ed. by Tom Bottomore. (Key Text Ser.). 1986. pap. 7.50 (ISBN 0-85312-853-7, 9584, Pub. by Tavistock England). Routledge Chapman & Hall.

Readings from the History of the Episcopal Church. Ed. by Robert W. Prichard. 192p. (Orig.). 1986. pap. 14.95 (ISBN 0-8192-1383-7). Morehouse.

Readings from the Literature of Ancient Rome. Dora Pym. 1975. Repr. of 1922 ed. 25.00 (ISBN 0-8274-4053-7). R West.

Readings from the New Book on Nature: Physics & Metaphysics in the Modern Novel. Robert L. Nadeau. LC 81-2625. 224p. 1981. lib. bdg. 17.50x (ISBN 0-87023-331-9). U of Mass Pr.

Readings from the People's Daily. Vivian Hsu. 1974. 7.95 (ISBN 0-88710-070-8). Yale Far Eastern Pubns.

Readings in Accident Investigation: Examples of the Scope, Depth & Sources. Ed. by Ted S. Ferry. (Illus.). 302p. 1984. 38.25x (ISBN 0-398-04950-5). C C Thomas.

Readings in Accident Prevention. Insurance Institute of America. LC 86-81731. 238p. (Orig.). 1986. pap. 14.00 (ISBN 0-89462-031-2). IIA.

Readings in Administration of Special Education. Peter Swatsburg. (Special Education Ser.). (Illus., Orig.). 1980. pap. text ed. 16.00 (ISBN 0-89568-193-5). Spec Learn Corp.

Readings in Adult Psychology: Contemporary Perspectives. 2nd ed. Ed. by Lawrence R. Allman & Dennis T. Jaffe. 407p. 1982. pap. text ed. 14.95 scp (ISBN 0-06-040234-2, HarpC). Har-Row.

Readings in African Law, 2 vols. Ed. by N. N. Rubin & E. Cotran. 351p. 1970. 75.00x set (ISBN 0-7146-2480-2, F Cass Co). Biblio Dist.

Readings in Agnosia. Richard K. Peach. (Special Education Ser.). 125p. 1986. 24.95 (ISBN 0-582-28630-1); pap. text ed. 16.95 (ISBN 0-582-28615-8). Longman.

Readings in Agnosia. 1984. 16.00 (ISBN 0-89568-426-8). Spec Learn Corp.

Readings in American Art since Nineteen Hundred to Nineteen Seventy-Five. Ed. by Barbara Rose. 308p. 1975. pap. text ed. 19.95 (ISBN 0-275-89120-8). HR&W.

Readings in American Democracy. Paul Peterson. 1979. pap. text ed. 12.95 (ISBN 0-8403-2001-9). Kendall-Hunt.

Readings in American Democracy. 2nd ed. Gerald Stourzh et al. 1966. pap. 7.95x (ISBN 0-19-501071-X). Oxford U Pr.

Readings in American Educational History. Ed. by Edgar W. Knight & Clifton L. Hall. Repr. of 1951 ed. lib. bdg. 35.00x (ISBN 0-8371-2835-8, KNAE). Greenwood.

Readings in American Folklore. Jan H. Brunvand. (Illus.). 1979. pap. text ed. 10.95x (ISBN 0-393-95029-8). Norton.

Readings in American Legal History. Ed. by Mark A. Howe. LC 70-155924. (American Constitutional & Legal History Ser). 1971. Repr. of 1949 ed. lib. bdg. 59.50 (ISBN 0-306-70159-6). Da Capo.

Readings in American Political Issues. Franklin Jones et al. 464p. 1987. pap. text ed. 19.95 (ISBN 0-8403-4321-3). Kendall-Hunt.

Readings in Ancient History: Greece & the East. William S. Davis. 1912. 20.00 (ISBN 0-686-20107-8). Quality Lib.

Readings in Ancient History: Thought & Experience from Gilgamesh to St. Augustine. 3rd ed. Nels M. Bailkey. LC 86-80500. 454p. 1987. pap. text ed. 13.00 (ISBN 0-669-11019-1). Heath.

Readings in Anorexia Nervosa & Eating Disorders. 1984. 16.00 (ISBN 0-89568-410-1). Spec Learn Corp.

Readings in Anthropology: People of the Bering Sea. Ed. by Ted Bank. 1971. pap. text ed. 6.95x (ISBN 0-8422-0137-8). Irvington.

Readings in Aphasia. Ed. by Ruben H. Douglas & Nancy R. Macciomei. (Special Education Ser.). 110p. 1986. 24.95 (ISBN 0-582-28631-X); pap. text ed. 16.95 (ISBN 0-582-28617-4). Longman.

Readings in Aphasia. 1984. 16.00 (ISBN 0-89568-427-6). Spec Learn Corp.

Readings in Applied English Linguistics. Harold B. Allen & Michael D. Linn. LC 81-18663. 1981. pap. text ed. 13.00 net (ISBN 0-394-32750-0, KnopfC). Knopf.

Readings in Arab Middle Eastern Societies & Cultures. Abdulla H. Lutfiyya. Ed. by Charles W. Churchill. LC 69-19116. (Orig.). 1970. pap. text ed. 20.00x (ISBN 90-2791-062-6). Mouton.

Readings in Art History: The Renaissance to the Present, Vol. II. 3rd ed. Harold Spencer. LC 76-7404. 520p. 1982. pap. text ed. write for info. (ISBN 0-02-414390-1, Pub. by Scribner). Macmillan.

Readings in Arthritis. 1984. 16.00 (ISBN 0-89568-401-2). Spec Learn Corp.

Readings in Articulation. 1984. 16.00 (ISBN 0-89568-405-5). Spec Learn Corp.

Readings in Artificial Intelligence. Ed. by Bonnie L. Webber & Nils J. Nilsson. LC 85-24203. (Illus.). 547p. (Orig.). 1981. pap. text ed. 27.95 (ISBN 0-934613-03-6). Morgan Kaufmann.

Readings in Artificial Intelligence & Databases. Ed. by John Mylopoulos & Michael Brodie. 600p. 1988. pap. text ed. 29.95 (ISBN 0-934613-53-2). Morgan Kaufmann.

Readings in Artificial Intelligence & Software Engineering. Ed. by Charles Rich & Richard C. Waters. LC 86-18627. (Illus.). 602p. (Orig.). 1986. pap. text ed. 28.95 (ISBN 0-934613-12-5). Morgan Kaufmann.

Readings in Asian Farm Management. Ed. by Bock T. Tan & Saho-er Ong. 362p. 1979. pap. 10.00x (ISBN 0-8214-0514-4, Pub. by Singapore U Pr). Ohio U Pr.

Readings in Audiology. 1984. 16.00 (ISBN 0-89568-429-2). Spec Learn Corp.

Readings in Australian & Pacific Anthropology. Ed. by I. Hogbin & L. R. Hiatt. 1966. pap. 8.50x (ISBN 0-522-83635-6, Pub. by Melbourne U Pr). Intl Spec Bk.

Readings in Autism. rev. ed. Ed. by Loretta T. Leon. (Special Education Ser.). (Illus.). 224p. 1981. pap. text ed. 16.00 (ISBN 0-686-77779-4). Spec Learn Corp.

Readings in Autism. (Special Education Ser.). 1978. pap. text ed. 16.00 (ISBN 0-89568-008-4). Spec Learn Corp.

Readings in Autism. 1984. 16.00 (ISBN 0-89568-428-4). Spec Learn Corp.

Readings in Barrier Free Design. 1984. 16.00 (ISBN 0-89568-408-X). Spec Learn Corp.

Readings in Behavior. Ed. by William G. Van der Kloot et al. LC 73-15700. (Illus.). 1974. pap. text ed. 19.50x (ISBN 0-03-084077-5). Irvington.

Readings in Behavior Modification. Marilyn T. Erickson et al. LC 73-8528. 1973. 29.75x (ISBN 0-8422-5106-5); pap. 14.95x (ISBN 0-8422-0312-5). Irvington.

Readings in Behavior Modification. (Special Education Ser.). 1978. pap. text ed. 16.00 (ISBN 0-89568-004-1). Spec Learn Corp.

Readings in Behavior Modification Research with Children. Marilyn T. Erickson et al. LC 73-8536. 1973. pap. text ed. 24.95x (ISBN 0-8422-0313-3). Irvington.

Readings in Behavioral Issues in Safety. 1985. 10.00 (ISBN 0-939874-63-6). ASSE.

Readings in Biological Science. 3rd ed. Ed. by Irving W. Knobloch. LC 72-93743. 1973. pap. text ed. 14.95x (ISBN 0-89197-371-0). Irvington.

Readings in Biology. Thomas Scandone. 12.50 (ISBN 0-317-47208-9). Paladin Hse.

Readings in Black Aged. Ed. by Peter Chang. 212p. 1977. 29.50x (ISBN 0-8422-0556-X). Irvington.

Readings in Black American Music. Eileen Southern. 1983. 8.95x (ISBN 0-393-95280-0). Norton.

Readings in Brain Impairments. 1984. 16.00 (ISBN 0-89568-403-9). Spec Learn Corp.

Readings in Business Communication. Ed. by Robert D. Gieselman. 1986. pap. 11.60x (ISBN 0-87563-287-4). Stipes.

Readings in Business Cycle Theory. Compiled by American Economic Association Committee. LC 76-29403. (BCL Ser.). 736p. Repr. of 1944 ed. 33.50 (ISBN 0-686-77531-7). AMS Pr.

Readings in Business Policy & Strategy from "Business Week". 2nd ed. William F. Glueck & Neil Snyder. (Management Ser.). (Illus.). 336p. 1982. text ed. 20.95 (ISBN 0-07-059540-2). McGraw.

Readings in California Catholic History. Francis J. Weber. 10.00 (ISBN 0-87026-000-6). Westernlore.

Readings in California Civilization: Interpretative Issues. Howard A. DeWitt. LC 80-83492. 240p. 1980. pap. text ed. 16.95 (ISBN 0-8403-2311-5). Kendall-Hunt.

Readings in Calvin's Theology. Donald K. McKim. 304p. (Orig.). 1984. pap. 15.95 (ISBN 0-8010-6150-4). Baker Bk.

Readings in Canadian Marketing. Ulrike DeBrentani & Michel Laroche. 200p. 1984. pap. 11.50 (ISBN 0-8403-3143-6). Kendall-Hunt.

Readings in Career & Vocational Education for the Handicapped. (Special Education Ser.). 1978. pap. 15.00 (ISBN 0-89568-083-1). Spec Learn Corp.

Readings in Caribbean History & Economics: An Introduction to the Region. Roberta M. Delson. (Caribbean Studies). 360p. 1981. 75.00 (ISBN 0-677-05280-4). Gordon & Breach.

Readings in Cerebral Palsy. 1984. 16.00 (ISBN 0-89568-412-8). Spec Learn Corp.

Readings in Child Abuse. Ed. by Special Learning Corporation. (Special Education Ser.). (Illus., Orig.). 1979. pap. text ed. 16.00 (ISBN 0-89568-103-X). Spec Learn Corp.

Readings in Childhood Language Disorders. Margaret Lahey. LC 83-19991. 448p. 1984. Repr. of 1978 ed. 31.50 (ISBN 0-89874-704-X). Krieger.

Readings in Chinese Communist Ideology: A Manual for Students of the Chinese Language. Wen-Shun Chi. LC 67-11201. 452p. pap. 117.60 (2029949). Bks Demand UMI.

Readings in Chinese Geography: Vol. 1, Chinese Text, Vol. 2, Vocabulary, Notes & Translations. Jack Williams & Yung Teng Chia-Yee. Set. pap. text ed. 15.00x (ISBN 0-87022-862-5). UH Pr.

Readings in Christian Humanism. Ed. by Joseph M. Shaw et al. LC 82-70963. (Orig.). 1982. pap. 25.95 (ISBN 0-8066-1938-4, 10-5400). Augsburg.

Readings in Christian Theology. Ed. by Peter C. Hodgson & Robert H. King. LC 84-48721. 432p. 1985. pap. 19.95 (ISBN 0-8006-1849-1, 1-1849). Fortress.

Readings in Christian Thought. Ed. by Hugh T. Kerr. LC 66-14992. 1966. 25.95. Abingdon.

Readings in Church History, 3 vols. in 1. Ed. by Colman J. Barry. 1985. pap. 50.00 (ISBN 0-87061-104-6). Chr Classics.

Readings in Classical Rhetoric. Ed. by Thomas W. Benson & Michael H. Prosser. LC 76-80478. Repr. of 1969 ed. 87.50 (ISBN 0-8357-9237-4, 2017610). Bks Demand UMI.

Readings in Classical Rhetoric. Ed. by Thomas W. Benson & Michael H. Prosser. xii, 341p. 1988. pap. text ed. 12.95 (ISBN 0-9611800-3-X). Hermagoras Pr.

Readings in Community Health Nursing. 3rd ed. Barbara W. Spradley. 1986. pap. text ed. write for info. (ISBN 0-673-39407-7). Scott F.

Readings in Community Organizations Practice. 3rd ed. Ralph M. Kramer & Harry Specht. (Illus.). 448p. 1983. pap. text ed. write for info. (ISBN 0-13-755751-5). P-H.

Readings in Community Work. Ed. by Paul Henderson & David Thomas. 1981. 40.00x (ISBN 0-317-05809-6, Pub. by Natl Soc Work). State Mutual Bk.

Readings in Comparative Criminology. Ed. by Louise I. Shelley. LC 80-19533. (Science & International Affairs). (Illus.). 312p. 1981. 25.00x (ISBN 0-8093-0938-6). S Ill U Pr.

Readings in Computer Vision: Issues, Principles, Problems, & Paradigms. Ed. by Martin Fischler & Oscar Firschein. LC 86-27692. (Illus.). 802p. (Orig.). 1987. pap. 32.95 (ISBN 0-934613-33-8). Morgan Kaufmann.

Readings in Computers & Software. Ed. by American Production & Inventory Control Society Staff. LC 84-72234. 64p. 1984. pap. 9.00 (ISBN 0-935406-56-5, 40656). Am Prod & Inventory.

Readings in Contemporary Chinese Literature, 3 vols. Ed. by Tien-Yi Li & Wu-Chi Liu. Incl. Vol. 1. Plays & Poems with Notes. 3rd ed. 6.95 (ISBN 0-88710-071-6); Vol. 2. Stories with Notes. rev. ed. 10.95; Vol. 3. Essays with Notes. rev. ed. 6.95 (ISBN 0-686-09921-4). (ISBN 0-88710-073-2); tapes avail. (ISBN 0-88710-074-0). Yale Far Eastern Pubns.

Readings in Contemporary Culture. A. S. Horning. 1979. text ed. 6.00 (ISBN 0-07-030352-5). McGraw.

Readings in Contemporary Korean. Sung-Un Chang & Samuel E. Martin. 4.95 (ISBN 0-88710-075-9). Yale Far Eastern Pubns.

Readings in Contemporary Labor Issues. Gerald P. Glyde & Donald Kennedy. 336p. 1985. pap. text ed. 22.95 (ISBN 0-8403-3841-4). Kendall-Hunt.

Readings in Contemporary Literature. E. Hanes & M. McCoy. Repr. of 1936 ed. lib. bdg. 15.00 (ISBN 0-8414-4989-9). Folcroft.

Readings in Contrastive Spanish Linguistics, Vol II. Ed. by Rose Nash & Domitila Belaval. LC 73-85939. 265p. 1980. pap. 7.95 (ISBN 0-913480-41-X). Inter Am U Pr.

Readings in Controversial Issues in Education of the Mentally Retarded. Ed. by Frank Warner & Robert Thrapp. 1972. 29.50x (ISBN 0-8422-5007-7). Irvington.

Readings in Cost Accounting. Intro. by Richard L. Clarke. 120p. 1987. 15.00 (ISBN 0-930228-59-6); pap. text ed. write for info. Healthcare Fin Mgmt Assn.

Readings in Cost Accounting, Budgeting, & Control. 7th ed. William E. Thomas. 608p. 1988. text ed. write for info. (ISBN 0-538-01340-0, A34). SW Pub.

Readings in Management. 7th ed. Max D. Richards. 1986. text ed. write for info. (ISBN 0-538-07990-8, G99). SW Pub.

Readings in Management & Organizations. Monique A. Pelletier. 304p. 1987. pap. text ed. 19.95 (ISBN 0-8403-4554-2). Kendall-Hunt.

Readings in Management & Personal Development. Ed. by American Production & Inventory Control Society Staff. LC 84-72232. 84p. 1984. pap. 14.00 (ISBN 0-935406-54-9, 40654). Am Prod & Inventory.

Readings in Management Control in Non-Profit Organizations. Kavasseri V. Ramanathan & L. P. Hegstad. LC 82-2025. 380p. 1982. 36.95x (ISBN 0-471-86974-0); pap. text ed. 26.95 (ISBN 0-471-05883-1). Wiley.

Readings in Management Information Systems: An Interdisciplinary Approach. Anderson. (Computers & Information Processing Systems for Business Ser.). 1988. write for info. (ISBN 0-471-80443-6). Wiley.

Readings in Managerial Accounting: From "The Wall Street Journal". Jonathan B. Schiff. 7.95 (ISBN 0-405-12623-9). Ayer Co Pubs.

Readings in Managerial Psychology. 3rd ed. Harold J. Leavitt & Louis R. Pondy. LC 79-21587. xii, 732p. 1980. pap. text ed. 22.00x (ISBN 0-226-46987-5). U of Chicago Pr.

Readings in Managerial Psychology. 4th ed. Harold J. Leavitt et al. (Illus.). 784p. 1989. 60.00x (ISBN 0-226-46991-3); pap. 19.95x (ISBN 0-226-46992-1). U of Chicago Pr.

Readings in Managing Human Resources. 6th ed. Herbert J. Chruden & Arthur W. Sherman, Jr. 1984. text ed. write for info. (ISBN 0-538-07880-4, G88). SW Pub.

Readings in Managing the Marketing Research Function. Lee Adler & Charles S. Mayer. LC 80-11092. 191p. 1980. pap. 23.00 (ISBN 0-87757-136-8). Am Mktg.

Readings in Marine Ecology. 2nd ed. James Nybakken. 737p. 1985. pap. text ed. 31.50 scp (ISBN 0-06-044837-7, HarpC). Har-Row.

Readings in Market Research for Real Estate. Ed. by James D. Vernor. 324p. 1985. pap. 14.50 (ISBN 0-911780-76-9). Am Inst Real Estate Appraisers.

Readings in Market Segmentation. Donald W. Scotton & Ronald L. Zellocco. LC 80-478. pap. 52.00 (2026672). Bks Demand UMI.

Readings in Market Value. 231p. 1981. pap. 14.50 (ISBN 0-911780-57-2). Am Inst Real Estate Appraisers.

Readings in Marketing Management: A Strategic Perspective. Barry Berman & Joel Evans. LC 83-19881. 478p. 1984. pap. text ed. write for info. (ISBN 0-471-86966-X). Wiley.

Readings in Marketing Strategy. Joseph P. Guiltinan & P. Gordon. (Marketing Ser.). 624p. 1982. text ed. 19.95 (ISBN 0-07-048922-X). McGraw.

Readings in Marketing Strategy. Jean-Claude Larreche & Edward C. Strong. 322p. 1982. pap. text ed. 30.00 (ISBN 0-89426-030-8). Scientific Pr.

Readings in Marketing: The Qualitative & Quantitative Areas. Ed. by Philip R. Cateora & Lee Richardson. LC 67-10928. (Illus., Orig.). 1967. pap. text ed. 9.95x (ISBN 0-89197-373-7). Irvington.

Readings in Marketing Today. John T. Mentzer & Forrest S. Carter. 452p. 1985. pap. text ed. 10.00x net (ISBN 0-15-575814-4, HC). HarBraceJ.

Readings in Marxist Sociology. Ed. by Tom Bottomore & Patrick Goode. 1983. text ed. 39.95x (ISBN 0-19-876108-2); pap. text ed. 13.95x (ISBN 0-19-876109-0). Oxford U Pr.

Readings in Mass Communication: Concepts & Issues in the Mass Media. 6th ed. Michael Emery & Ted C. Smythe. 576p. 1986. pap. write for info. (ISBN 0-697-00488-0). Wm C Brown.

Readings in Material & Capacity Requirements Planning. Ed. by American Production & Inventory Control Society Staff. LC 84-72231. 84p. 1984. pap. 9.00 (ISBN 0-935406-53-0, 40653). Am Prod & Inventory.

Readings in Medical Sociology. Ed. by David Mechanic. LC 79-7578. (Illus.). 1980. pap. text ed. 12.95 (ISBN 0-02-920700-2). Free Pr.

Readings in Medieval Poetry. A. C. Spearing. 288p. 1987. 44.50 (ISBN 0-521-32268-5). Cambridge U Pr.

Readings in Mental Handicaps. rev. ed. Ed. by John Venn. (Special Education Ser.). (Illus.). 224p. 1982. pap. text ed. 16.00 (ISBN 0-89568-195-1). Spec Learn Corp.

Readings in Mental Retardation. (Special Education Ser.). 1978. pap. text ed. 16.00 (ISBN 0-89568-002-5). Spec Learn Corp.

Readings in Microcomputers & Emotional Behavioral Disorders. 1984. 16.00 (ISBN 0-89568-423-3). Spec Learn Corp.

Readings in Microcomputers & Individualized Educational Programs. 1984. 16.00 (ISBN 0-89568-418-7). Spec Learn Corp.

Readings in Microcomputers & Learning Disabilities. 1984. 16.00 (ISBN 0-89568-446-2). Spec Learn Corp.

Readings in Microcomputers & Special Education. 1984. 16.00 (ISBN 0-89568-445-4). Spec Learn Corp.

Readings in Microcomputers & the Gifted Child. 1984. 16.00 (ISBN 0-89568-404-7). Spec Learn Corp.

Readings in Microcomputers & the Mentally Handicapped. 1984. 16.00 (ISBN 0-89568-419-5). Spec Learn Corp.

Readings in Microeconomics. Breit et al. 1985. pap. 16.95 (ISBN 0-8016-0795-7). Mosby.

Readings in Missionary Anthropology II. 2nd rev. enl. ed. Ed. by William A. Smalley. LC 78-6009. (Applied Cultural Anthropology Ser.). 912p. 1978. pap. text ed. 16.95x (ISBN 0-87808-731-1). William Carey.

Readings in Modern Dance, Vol. I. Jane Edelson et al. 82p. pap. 21.95 (ISBN 0-932582-13-3); cassette 15.00 (ISBN 0-317-56653-9). Dance Notation.

Readings in Modern Linguistics: An Anthology. Ed. by Bertil Malmberg. 384p. (Orig.). 1972. pap. text ed. 26.40x (ISBN 90-2792-429-5). Mouton.

Readings in Modern Literature, Vol. 2: Stories, Vol. 2. Ed. by Wu-Chi Liu & Tien-Yi Li. (Mirror Ser.). 368p. 1953. pap. text ed. write for info. Yale Far Eastern Pubns.

Readings in Molecular Biology Selected from Nature. Ed. by W. B. Gratzer. 1971. pap. 6.95x (ISBN 0-262-57025-4). MIT Pr.

Readings in Monetary Theory. Friedrich Lutz & Lloyd W. Mints. LC 82-48205. (Gold, Money, Inflation & Deflation Ser.). 514p. 1982. lib. bdg. 66.00 (ISBN 0-8240-5271-4). Garland Pub.

Readings in Moral Theology: No. 1, Moral Norms & Catholic Tradition. Charles E. Curran & Richard McCormick. LC 79-84237. 1979. pap. 9.95 (ISBN 0-8091-2203-0). Paulist Pr.

Readings in Moral Theology, No. 2: The Distinctiveness of Christian Ethics. Ed. by Charles E. Curran & Richard A. McCormick. LC 79-84237. 360p. 1980. pap. 9.95 (ISBN 0-8091-2303-7). Paulist Pr.

Readings in Moral Theology, No. 3: The Magisterium & Morality. Ed. by Charles E. Curran & Richard A. McCormick. LC 81-82436. (Orig.). 1981. pap. 7.95 (ISBN 0-8091-2407-6). Paulist Pr.

Readings in Moral Theology, No. 4: The Use of Scripture in Moral Theology. Charles E. Curran & Richard A. McCormick. 1984. pap. 9.95 (ISBN 0-8091-2563-3). Paulist Pr.

Readings in Moral Theology, No. 5: Official Catholic Social Teaching. Ed. by Richard A. McCormick & Charles Curran. 400p. (Orig.). 1986. pap. 9.95 (ISBN 0-8091-2738-5). Paulist Pr.

Readings in Moral Theology, No. 6: Dissent in the Church. Richard A. McCormick & Charles E. Curran. 1987. pap. 14.95 (ISBN 0-8091-2930-2). Paulist Pr.

Readings in Motor Learning. Ed. by Robert N. Singer. LC 79-146033. Repr. of 1972 ed. 93.10 (ISBN 0-8357-9418-0, 2014583). Bks Demand UMI.

Readings in Multiline Insurance Law & Operations. Ed. by Charles E. Hughes. (Huebner School Ser.). (Orig.). 1986. pap. text ed. 18.00 (ISBN 0-943590-09-4). Amer College.

Readings in Muscular Dystrophy. 1984. 16.00 (ISBN 0-89568-402-0). Spec Learn Corp.

Readings in Natural Language Processing. Ed. by Barbara Grosz et al. LC 86-18488. (Illus.). 664p. (Orig.). 1986. pap. text ed. 28.95 (ISBN 0-934613-11-7). Morgan Kaufmann.

Readings in Natural Resource Economics. John E. Reynolds. 199p. 1974. text ed. 29.00x (ISBN 0-685-50581-2). Irvington.

Readings in Noise Control & Hearing Conservation. 1985. 10.00 (ISBN 0-939874-65-2). ASSE.

Readings in Nonmonotonic Reasoning. Ed. by Matthew Ginsberg. LC 87-24144. 481p. (Orig.). 1987. pap. text ed. 28.95 (ISBN 0-934613-45-1). Morgan Kaufmann.

Readings in Oncology. Stacey B. Day et al. LC 80-80708. (Foundation Publication Ser.). (Illus.). 227p. (Orig.). 1980. pap. 15.00x (ISBN 0-934314-01-2). Intl Found Biosocial Dev.

Readings in Organizational Behavior. Steven Altman & Richard M. Hodgetts. 1979. pap. text ed. 15.95 (ISBN 0-7216-1140-0). HR&W.

Readings in Organizational Behavior: Concepts and Applications. Jerry Gray & Frederick Starke. 1977. pap. text ed. 19.95 (ISBN 0-675-08522-5). Merrill.

Readings in Organizational Behavior: Dimensions of Management Actions. Richard C. Huseman & Archie B. Carroll. 1979. text ed. 24.00 (ISBN 0-205-06515-5, 086515); instr's. manual avail. (ISBN 0-205-06538-4, 086538). Allyn.

Readings in Organizational Decline: Frameworks, Research, & Prescriptions. Ed. by Kim S. Cameron et al. LC 87-27136. 352p. 1988. 39.95x (ISBN 0-88730-223-8); pap. 22.95x (ISBN 0-88730-270-X). Ballinger Pub.

Readings in Perception & Memory. Ed. by Robert Piazza. (Special Education Ser.). (Illus., Orig.). 1978. pap. text ed. 16.00 (ISBN 0-89568-086-6). Spec Learn Corp.

Readings in Personality Assessment. Ed. by Leonard D. Goodstein & Richard I. Lanyon. LC 77-149770. Repr. of 1971 ed. 120.00 (ISBN 0-8357-9972-7, 2012426). Bks Demand UMI.

Readings in Personnel & Human Resource Management. 3rd ed. Schuler. 600p. 1987. 24.50 (ISBN 0-314-33750-4). West Pub.

Readings in Pharmacology. Ed. by Bo Holmstedt & G. Liljestrand. 410p. 1981. pap. text ed. 36.00 (ISBN 0-89004-662-X). Raven.

Readings in Philosophical Analysis. Ed. by Herbert Feigl & Wilfrid Sellars. x, 593p. 1981. lib. bdg. 33.00 (ISBN 0-917930-29-0); pap. text ed. 17.00 (ISBN 0-917930-09-6). Ridgeview.

Readings in Philosophy. 3rd ed. John H. Randall, Jr. et al. 1972. pap. 8.95 (ISBN 0-06-460059-9, CO 59, B&N Bks). Har-Row.

Readings in Philosophy of Law. John Arthur & William Shaw. 640p. 1984. text ed. write for info. (ISBN 0-13-761628-7). P-H.

Readings in Philosophy of Psychology, Vol. I. Ed. by Ned Block. (Language & Thought Ser.). 320p. 1983. pap. text ed. 10.95x (ISBN 0-674-74876-X). Harvard U Pr.

Readings in Philosophy of Psychology, Vol. 2. Ed. by Ned Block. (Language & Thought Ser.). 376p. 1985. pap. text ed. 12.50x (ISBN 0-674-74878-6). Harvard U Pr.

Readings in Physically Handicapped Education. (Special Education Ser.). 1978. pap. text ed. 16.00 (ISBN 0-89568-012-2). Spec Learn Corp.

Readings in Planning for Business Owners & Professionals. 3rd ed. Ed. by Theodore Kurlowicz. (Huebner School Ser.). (Illus.). 350p. 1986. pap. text ed. 18.00 (ISBN 0-943590-03-5). Amer College.

Readings in Pre-School Education for the Handicapped. (Special Education Ser.). 1978. pap. 16.00 (ISBN 0-89568-082-3). Spec Learn Corp.

Readings in Primary Prevention of Psychopathology: Basic Concepts. Ed. by Justin M. Joffe et al. LC 83-40557. (Illus.). 511p. 1984. 40.00x (ISBN 0-87451-295-6); pap. text ed. 18.00x (ISBN 0-87451-303-0). U Pr of New Eng.

Readings in Primary School Management. Ed. by Geoff Southworth. 260p. 1987. 38.00x (ISBN 1-85000-245-2, Falmer Pr); pap. 18.00x (ISBN 1-85000-246-0, Falmer Pr). Taylor & Francis.

Readings in Principles & Curriculum of Secondary Education. D. Quist et al. 1971. pap. text ed. 4.75x (ISBN 0-8422-0178-5). Irvington.

Readings in Prison Education. Albert R. Roberts. (Illus.). 440p. 1973. 49.00 (ISBN 0-398-02520-7). C C Thomas.

Readings in Product Liability & Civil Liability. 1985. 10.00 (ISBN 0-939874-64-4). ASSE.

Readings in Production & Inventory Control & Planning. Ed. by American Production & Inventory Control Society Staff. LC 84-72230. 213p. 1984. pap. 14.00 (ISBN 0-935406-52-2, 40652). Am Prod & Inventory.

Readings in Production & Inventory Control Interfaces. Ed. by American Production & Inventory Control Society Staff. LC 84-72233. 69p. 1984. pap. 9.00 (ISBN 0-935406-55-7, 40655). Am Prod & Inventory.

Readings in Productivity Improvements. Ed. by American Production & Inventory Control Society Staff. LC 84-72235. 134p. 1984. pap. 11.00 (ISBN 0-935406-57-3, 40657). Am Prod & Inventory.

Readings in Professional Personnel Assessment. International Personnel Management Association. 333p. (Orig.). 1984. pap. text ed. 19.00 (ISBN 0-914945-00-9). Intl Personnel Mgmt.

Readings in Prose. Agnes B. Werner et al. LC 80-17845. pap. 6.25 (ISBN 0-8477-3327-0). U of PR Pr.

Readings in Psychology. Raymond H. Wheeler. 597p. 1979. Repr. of 1930 ed. lib. bdg. 40.00 (ISBN 0-89987-850-4). Darby Bks.

Readings in Psychology of Exceptional Children. (Special Education Ser.). 1978. pap. 16.00 (ISBN 0-89568-003-3). Spec Learn Corp.

Readings in Public Policy. Ed. by Lawrence Chickering. 338p. (Orig.). 1984. pap. 9.95 (ISBN 0-917616-66-9). ICS Pr.

Readings in Rabelais. Walter Besant. 1973. Repr. of 1883 ed. 25.00 (ISBN 0-8274-1436-6). R West.

Readings in Race & Ethnic Relations. Anthony H. Richmond. 350p. 1972. pap. 18.75 (ISBN 0-08-016212-6). Pergamon.

Readings in Real Estate Investment Analysis. 252p. 1977. pap. 14.50 (ISBN 0-911780-42-4). Am Inst Real Estate Appraisers.

Readings in Real Property Valuation Principles, Vol. II. 160p. 1985. 14.50 (ISBN 0-911780-83-1). Am Inst Real Estate Appraisers.

Readings in Real Property Valuation Principles, Vol. 1. 322p. 1977. pap. 14.50 (ISBN 0-911780-41-6). Am Inst Real Estate Appraisers.

Readings in Records Management - from Records Management Quarterly. 175p. 1977-1980. 18.00 (ISBN 0-933887-02-7, 4517). Assn Recs Mgrs & Admin.

Readings in Reference Group Theory & Research. Ed. by Herbert H. Hyman & Eleanor D. Singer. LC 68-10366. 1968. 20.50 (ISBN 0-02-915700-5). Free Pr.

Readings in Rehabilitation Administration. Ed. by T. F. Riggar & J. R. Lorenz. LC 85-2576. 260p. 1985. 59.50 (ISBN 0-88706-097-8); pap. 19.95 (ISBN 0-88706-098-6). State U NY Pr.

Readings in Rehabilitation Counseling. Patterson & Moses. 1971. pap. 8.60x (ISBN 0-87563-034-0). Stipes.

Readings in Romance Linguistics. James M. Anderson & JoAnn Creore. (Illus.). 472p. (Orig.). 1972. pap. text ed. 26.00x (ISBN 90-2792-303-5). Mouton.

Readings in Russian Civilization, 3 vols. rev. ed. Ed. by Thomas Riha. Incl. Vol. 1. Russia Before Peter the Great, 900-1700. pap. 10.00x (ISBN 0-226-71853-0); Vol. 2. Imperial Russia, 1700-1917. pap. 9.50x (ISBN 0-226-71855-7); Vol. 3. Soviet Russia, 1917-Present. pap. 12.00x (ISBN 0-226-71857-3). LC 69-14825. 1969. U of Chicago Pr.

Readings in Russian History: From Alexander II to the Soviet Period, Vol. 2. 4th. ed. Warren B. Walsh. 1963. pap. 6.00x (ISBN 0-8156-2082-9). Syracuse U Pr.

Readings in Russian History: From Ancient Times to Nicholas I, Vol. 1. 4th. ed. Ed. by Warren B. Walsh. 1963. pap. 6.00x (ISBN 0-8156-2081-0). Syracuse U Pr.

Readings in Russian History: From Ancient Times to the Eighteenth Century, Vol. I. Ed. by Warren B. Walsh. 1963. 10.95x (ISBN 0-8156-2048-9). Syracuse U Pr.

Readings in Russian History: From the Reign of Paul to Alexander III, Vol. II. Ed. by Warren B. Walsh. 1963. 10.95x (ISBN 0-8156-2050-0); pap. 5.95x (ISBN 0-8156-2051-9). Syracuse U Pr.

Readings in Russian Philosophical Thought: Logic & Aesthetics. Ed. by Louis J. Shein. LC 73-83931. 337p. 1973. pap. text ed. 19.20x (ISBN 0-686-22554-6). Mouton.

Readings in Russian Philosophical Thought. Ed. by Louis J. Shein. LC 68-15528. 1968. pap. text ed. 12.80x (ISBN 0-686-22454-X). Mouton.

Readings in Russian Poetics. Ed. by Ladislav Matejka & Krystyna Pomorska. (Michigan Slavic Contributions Ser.: No. 8). 1978. pap. 10.00 (ISBN 0-930042-25-5). Mich Slavic Pubns.

Readings in Safety Management. 84p. 1984. 10.00 (ISBN 0-939874-61-X). ASSE.

Readings in St. John's Gospel. William Temple. 391p. 1985. pap. 8.95 (ISBN 0-8192-1360-8). Morehouse.

Readings in Sales Force Management. Ed. by Kenneth R. Davis & Frederick E. Webster, Jr. LC 68-20550. (Illus.). pap. 118.80 (ISBN 0-317-10053-X, 2012394). Bks Demand UMI.

Readings in Sayable Chinese, 3 vols. Yuen Ren Chao. (Spoken Language Ser.). 1985. Vol. 1. 10.00x (ISBN 0-87950-325-4); Vol. 2 cloth 296pg. 10.00x (ISBN 0-87950-326-2); Vol. 3 cloth 370pg. 10.00x (ISBN 0-87950-327-0); Set of 3 vols. 30.00x (ISBN 0-87950-328-9); Cassettes for Vol. 1. 80.00x (ISBN 0-87950-333-5); Cassettes for Vol. 2. 60.00x; Cassettes for Vol. 3. 75.00x (ISBN 0-87950-335-1); Set of Cassettes. 215.00x (ISBN 0-87950-336-X). Spoken Lang Serv.

Readings in Schenker Analysis & Other Approaches. Ed. by Maury Yeston. LC 76-40140. 1977. pap. text ed. 11.95x (ISBN 0-300-02114-3). Yale U Pr.

Readings in Scientific German. Ronald L. Crawford. LC 83-4860. (American University Studies VI: Foreign Language Instruction): Vol. 1). 126p. 1983. pap. text ed. 11.05 (ISBN 0-8204-0031-9). P Lang Pubs.

Readings in Semantics. Ed. by Farhang Zabeeh et al. LC 74-639. pap. 160.00 (ISBN 0-317-08056-3, 2022270). Bks Demand UMI.

Readings in Sexology. Mary A. Watson. 396p. 1984. pap. 22.95 (ISBN 0-8403-3427-3). Kendall-Hunt.

Readings in Small Business. Graham Beaver et al. 300p. 1986. text ed. 42.95 (ISBN 0-566-05174-5, Pub. by Gower Pub England). Gower Pub Co.

Readings in Social & Political Philosophy. Ed. by Robert M. Stewart. 512p. 1986. pap. 16.95x (ISBN 0-19-503747-2). Oxford U Pr.

Readings in Social Psychology. Jonathan L. Freedman et al. (Personality, Clinical & Social Psychology Ser). 1971. pap. text ed. write for info. (ISBN 0-13-761072-6). P-H.

Readings in Social Psychology: Contemporary Perspectives. 2nd ed. Ed. by Dennis Krebs. 361p. 1981. pap. text ed. 16.50 scp (ISBN 0-06-043769-3, HarpC). Har-Row.

Readings in Sociology. Russell L. Curtis. 656p. 1987. pap. text ed. 16.95 (ISBN 0-8403-4579-8). Kendall-Hunt.

Readings in Soviet Semiotics: Russian Texts. Ed. by L. Matejka et al. (Michigan Slavic Materials: No. 15). 1977. pap. 10.00 (ISBN 0-930042-08-5). Mich Slavic Pubns.

Readings in Spanish-English Contrastive Linguistics, Vol. I. Ed. by Rose Nash. LC 73-85939. 249p. 1973. pap. 4.50 (ISBN 0-913480-20-7). Inter Am U Pr.

Readings in Spanish-English Contrastive Linguistics, Vol. III. Ed. by Rose Nash & Domitila Belaval. LC 73-85939. 270p. 1982. pap. text ed. 9.95 (ISBN 0-913480-42-8). Inter Am U Pr.

Readings in Spasticity. 1984. 16.00 (ISBN 0-89568-422-5). Spec Learn Corp.

Readings in Special Education. (Special Education Ser.). 1978. pap. text ed. 16.00 (ISBN 0-89568-000-9). Spec Learn Corp.

Readings in Special Education & Language Development. 1984. 16.00 (ISBN 0-89568-415-2). Spec Learn Corp.

Readings in Special Education & Mathematics. 1984. 16.00 (ISBN 0-89568-414-4). Spec Learn Corp.

Readings in Speech & Hearing. (Special Education Ser.). 1978. pap. text ed. 16.00 (ISBN 0-89568-005-X). Spec Learn Corp.

Readings in Speech Communication. Richard L. Weaver. 240p. 1985. pap. text ed. 16.95 (ISBN 0-8403-3729-9). Kendall-Hunt.

Readings in Speech Pathology. 1984. 16.00 (ISBN 0-89568-421-7). Spec Learn Corp.

Readings in Sports. Murray Bromberg & Melvin Gordon. LC 77-29059. (gr. 9-12). 1978. pap. 5.95 (ISBN 0-8120-0975-4). Barron.

Readings in Strategic Management. 2nd ed. Arthur A. Thompson et al. 1987. pap. 20.95 (ISBN 0-256-03718-3). Business Pubns.

Readings in Strategic Marketing: Analysis, Planning & Implementation. Bart Weitz & Robin Wensley. (Illus.). 656p. 1988. pap. price not set (ISBN 0-03-020864-5). Dryden Pr.

Readings in Strategy & Policy from "Business Week". J. A. Pearce & R. Robinson, Jr. 144p. 1986. text ed. 15.95 (ISBN 0-07-049020-1). McGraw.

Readings in Stress Management. 1985. 10.00 (ISBN 0-939874-69-5). ASSE.

Readings in Student Teaching & Special Education. 1984. 16.00 (ISBN 0-89568-417-9). Spec Learn Corp.

Readings in Stuttering. Ed. by Charles E. Healey. (Special Education Ser.). 155p. 1986. 24.95 (ISBN 0-582-28628-X); pap. text ed. 16.95 (ISBN 0-582-28614-X). Longman.

Readings in Stuttering. 1984. 16.00 (ISBN 0-89568-400-4). Spec Learn Corp.

Readings in Survey Research. Ed. by Robert Ferber. LC 78-14428. pap. 153.50 (2026669). Bks Demand UMI.

Readings in Systemic Linguistics. Ed. by N. A. Halliday & J. R. Martin. 320p. 1981. 29.95 (ISBN 0-7134-3678-6, Pub. by Batsford England). David & Charles.

Readings in Tay-Sachs Disease. 1984. 16.00 (ISBN 0-89568-420-9). Spec Learn Corp.

Readings in Technology. Ed. by Nancy Viggiano. 204p. 1984. 16.50 (ISBN 0-87111-297-3). SLA.

Readings in Texas History. Ed. by Robert J. Rosenbaum. (Illus.). 216p. 1982. pap. text ed. 6.95x (ISBN 0-89641-136-2). American Pr.

Readings in Texas History. Ed. by Cary D. Wintz. (Texas History Ser.). (Illus.). 344p. (Orig.). 1983. pap. text ed. 14.95x (ISBN 0-89641-134-6). American Pr.

Readings in the Analysis of Survey Data. Ed. by Robert Ferber. LC 80-12975. 249p. (Orig.). 1980. pap. text ed. 24.00 (ISBN 0-87757-140-6). Am Mktg.

Readings in the Appraisal of Special Purpose Properties. 285p. 1981. pap. 14.50 (ISBN 0-911780-52-1). Am Inst Real Estate Appraisers.

Readings in the Arts & Sciences. Elaine P. Maimon et al. 1984. write for info. (ISBN 0-673-39226-0). Scott F.

Readings in the Concept & Measurement of Income. 2nd ed. R. H. Parker et al. 380p. 1986. 55.00x (ISBN 0-86003-536-0, Pub. by Philip Allan UK). Humanities.

Readings in the Concept & Measurement of Income. Ed. by Robert H. Parker & G. C. Harcourt. LC 75-87137. pap. 102.50 (ISBN 0-317-27570-4, 2024513). Bks Demand UMI.

Readings in the Constitutional History of India. Char S. Desika. 1983. 59.00x (ISBN 0-19-561264-7). Oxford U Pr.

Readings in the Development of Moral Thought. Francis Seaman & Marvin Henberg. 208p. 1986. pap. text ed. 14.95 (ISBN 0-8403-4081-8). Kendall Hunt.

Readings in the Development of Settlement Work. facs. ed. Ed. by Lorene M. Pacey. LC 79-142688. (Essay Index Reprint Ser). 1950. 21.00 (ISBN 0-8369-2198-4). Ayer Co Pubs.

Readings in the Economic History of American Agriculture. Ed. by Louis B. Schmidt & Earle D. Ross. Repr. of 1925 ed. 45.00 (ISBN 0-384-50010-2). Johnson Repr.

Readings in the Economics of Law & Regulation. A. I. Ogus & C. G. Veljanovski. LC 83-25189. 1984. 36.00x (ISBN 0-19-876142-2); pap. 19.95x (ISBN 0-19-876143-0). Oxford U Pr.

Readings in the History of Christian Theology: From Its Beginnings to the Eve of the Reformation, Vol. 1. William C. Placher. LC 87-29540. 204p. (Orig.). 1988. pap. 15.95 (ISBN 0-664-24057-7). Westminster John Knox.

Readings in the History of Christian Theology: From the Reformation to the Present, Vol. 2. William C. Placher. LC 87-29540. 216p. (Orig.). 1988. pap. 15.95 (ISBN 0-664-24058-5). Westminster John Knox.

Readings in the History of Education: Mediaeval Universities. Arthur O. Norton. LC 78-173801. Repr. of 1909 ed. 15.45 (ISBN 0-404-04797-1). AMS Pr.

Readings in the History of Mathematics Education. Ed. by James K. Bidwell & Robert G. Clason. LC 74-113172. (Illus.). 706p. 1970. 27.00 (ISBN 0-87353-087-X). NCTM.

Readings in the History of the American Indian. Ed. by Melvin W. Roe. 1971. pap. 6.95 (ISBN 0-8422-0134-3). Irvington.

Readings in the History of the American Legal Profession. Ed. by Dennis R. Nolan. 329p. (Orig.). 1980. pap. text ed. 19.00x (ISBN 0-672-84197-5). Michie Co.

Readings in the Income Approach to Real Property Valuation, Vol. 1. 226p. 1977. pap. 14.50 (ISBN 0-911780-43-2). Am Inst Real Estate Appraisers.

Readings in the Income Capitalization Approach to Real Property Valuation, Vol. II. 136p. 1985. 14.50 (ISBN 0-911780-84-X). Am Inst Real Estate Appraisers.

Readings in the Latin American Policy of the United States. Ed. by Thomas L. Karnes. LC 70-182882. pap. 79.00 (ISBN 0-317-41737-1, 2022757). Bks Demand UMI.

Readings in the Management of Innovation. Michael L. Tushman & William L. Moore. LC 81-12149. 672p. 1982. text ed. 22.95x (ISBN 0-88730-160-6). Ballinger Pub.

Readings in the Management of Innovation. 2nd ed. Ed. by Michael L. Tushman & William L. Moore. 656p. 1988. 39.95 (ISBN 0-88730-243-2); pap. text ed. 22.95x (ISBN 0-88730-244-0). Ballinger Pub.

Readings in the Modern Essay. facs. ed. Ed. by Edward S. Noyes. LC 70-121494. (Essay Index Reprint Ser). 1933. 33.00 (ISBN 0-8369-2008-2). Ayer Co Pubs.

Readings in the Modern Theory of Economic Growth. Ed. by Joseph E. Stiglitz & Hirofumi Uzawa. 1969. pap. 16.50x (ISBN 0-262-69018-7). MIT Pr.

Readings in the Philosophical Problems of Parapsychology. Antony Flew. LC 86-25342. 24.95 (ISBN 0-87975-382-X); pap. 16.95 (ISBN 0-87975-385-4). Prometheus Bks.

Readings in the Philosophy of Constitutional Law. 2nd ed. Richard Bronaugh et al. LC 82-83807. 304p. 1985. pap. text ed. 16.50 (ISBN 0-8403-3579-2). Kendall-Hunt.

Readings in the Philosophy of Language. Jay F. Rosenberg & Charles Travis. LC 70-132170. 1971. text ed. write for info. (ISBN 0-13-759332-5). P-H.

Readings in the Philosophy of Man. W. L. Kelly & A. Tallon. 1972. text ed. 25.95 (ISBN 0-07-033882-5). McGraw.

Readings in the Philosophy of Psychology, 2 vols. Ed. by Ned Block. LC 79-25593. (Language & Thought Ser.). 1980. Vol. 1. 21.00x (ISBN 0-674-74875-1); Vol. 2, 1981. 27.00x (ISBN 0-674-74877-8). Harvard U Pr.

Readings in the Philosophy of Religion: An Analytic Approach. Ed. by Baruch Brody. LC 73-20485. 608p. 1974. text ed. write for info. (ISBN 0-13-759340-6). P-H.

Readings in the Political Economy of Aging. Ed. by Meredith Minkler & Carroll L. Estes. (Policy, Politics, Health & Medicine Ser.: Vol. 6). 300p. (Orig.). pap. 22.00 (ISBN 0-89503-042-X). Baywood Pub.

Readings in the Psychology of Parent-Child Relations. Ed. by Gene R. Medinnus. LC 67-12565. Repr. of 1967 ed. 96.00 (ISBN 0-8357-9973-5, 2055146). Bks Demand UMI.

Readings in the Psychology of Perception. Ed. by Thomas L. Bennett. 179p. 1971. pap. text ed. 8.95x (ISBN 0-8422-0160-2). Irvington.

Readings in the Psychology of Perception. 2nd ed. Ed. by Thomas L. Bennett. 1973. pap. text ed. 9.95x (ISBN 0-685-48425-4, 0-8422-0325). Irvington.

Readings in the Severely & Profoundly Handicapped Education. Special Learning Corp. (Special Education Ser). (Illus.). 1978. 16.00 (ISBN 0-89568-079-3). Spec Learn Corp.

Readings in the Social Control of Industry. Ed. by American Economic Association Staff. LC 72-14175. (Essay Index Reprint Ser.). Repr. of 1942 ed. 27.50 (ISBN 0-518-10001-4). Ayer Co Pubs.

Readings in the Sociology of Language. Ed. by Joshua A. Fishman. LC 68-17892. (Orig.). 1978. pap. text ed. 31.00x (ISBN 90-2791-528-8). Mouton.

Readings in the Swedish Class Structure. Ed. by Richard Scase. 1976. 55.00 (ISBN 0-08-016663-6); pap. 23.00 (ISBN 0-08-020633-6). Pergamon.

Readings in the Theory & Practice of Medical Social Work. Ed. by Dora Goldstine. LC 54-8906. (Midway Reprint Ser). 345p. 1974. pap. 12.50x (ISBN 0-226-30162-1). U of Chicago Pr.

Readings in the Theory of Action. Ed. by Norman S. Care et al. LC 68-27339. pap. 111.50 (ISBN 0-317-08105-5, 2050050). Bks Demand UMI.

Readings in the Theory of Growth. Ed. by F. H. Hahn. LC 70-140572. 1971. 25.00 (ISBN 0-312-66465-6). St Martin.

Readings in the Theory of Income Distribution. Compiled by American Economic Association Committee. LC 76-29414. (BCL II Ser.). Repr. of 1946 ed. 45.00 (ISBN 0-404-15332-1). AMS Pr.

Readings in Third World Missions: A Collection of Essential Documents. Ed. by Marlin L. Nelson. LC 76-45803. 294p. 1976. pap. 6.95x (ISBN 0-87808-319-7). William Carey Lib.

Readings in Trade Unionism. Ed. by David Saposs. LC 70-89762. (American Labor, from Conspiracy to Collective Bargaining Ser., No. 1). 415p. 1969. Repr. of 1926 ed. 23.50 (ISBN 0-405-02147-X). Ayer Co Pubs.

Readings in Tribal Culture: A Study of the Ollar of Orissa. Makhan Jha. 175p. 1983. text ed. 22.50x (ISBN 0-86590-141-4). Apt Bks.

Readings in Tumor Virology. Ed. by Harold Varmus & Arnold J. Levine. LC 82-72707. 903p. 1983. 39.50X (ISBN 0-87969-157-3). Cold Spring Harbor.

Readings in Urban Dynamics, Vol. 1. Ed. by Nathaniel J. Mass. LC 73-89545. (Illus.). 1974. 42.50x (ISBN 0-262-13140-4). MIT Pr.

Readings in Urban Dynamics, Vol. 2. Ed. by Walter W. Schroeder, III et al. LC 73-89545. (Illus.). 1975. 55.00x (ISBN 0-262-19170-9). MIT Pr.

Readings in Urban Geography. Ed. by Harold M. Mayer & Clyde F. Kohn. LC 59-11973. (Illus.). 1959. 22.50x (ISBN 0-226-51270-3). U of Chicago Pr.

Readings in Urban Structure. G. Vishwanadham. 210p. 1986. 12.75X (ISBN 81-202-0151-5, Pub. by Ajanta). South Asia Bks.

Readings in Urban Transportation. Ed. by George Smerk. LC 68-14613. pap. 87.00 (2056238). Bks Demand UMI.

Readings in Value Development. Brian Hall et al. 1982. pap. 11.95 (ISBN 0-8091-2448-3). Paulist Pr.

Readings in Values Clarification. Howard Kirschenbaum & Sidney B. Simon. 1973. pap. 9.95 (ISBN 0-03-011936-7, 861, HarpR). Har-Row.

Readings in Vedic Literature. Satsvarupa Das Gosvami. 1985. 7.95 (ISBN 0-912776-88-9). Bhaktivedanta.

Readings in Visually Handicapped Education. (Special Education Ser.). 1978. pap. text ed. 16.00 (ISBN 0-89568-010-6). Spec Learn Corp.

Readings in Vocational Guidance. Ed. by Meyer Bloomfield. 723p. 1982. Repr. of 1915 ed. lib. bdg. 65.00 (ISBN 0-89987-090-2). Darby Bks.

Readings in Vocational Training for the Mentally Retarded. (Special Education Ser.). 1978. pap. 16.00. Spec Learn Corp.

Readings in Wealth Accumulation Planning. 2nd. ed. Robert J. Doyle, Jr. (Huebner School Ser.). 1987. pap. text ed. 20.00 (ISBN 0-943590-10-8). Amer College.

Readings in Western Religious Thought: The Ancient World. Ed. by Patrick Reid. 304p. (Orig.). 1987. pap. 12.95 (ISBN 0-8091-2850-0). Paulist Pr.

Readings in Wildlife Conservation. Ed. by James A. Bailey et al. LC 74-28405. (Illus.). 722p. (Orig.). 1974. pap. 10.00 (ISBN 0-933564-02-3). Wildlife Soc.

Readings in Workers Compensation: Loss Prevention-Loss Control. 1985. 10.00 (ISBN 0-939874-66-0). ASSE.

Readings in World Civilizations, Vol. II: The Development of the Modern World. Kevin Reilly. LC 87-60524. 384p. 1987. pap. text ed. write for info. (ISBN 0-312-00430-3). St Martin.

Readings in World Civilizations, Vol. I: The Great Traditions. Kevin Reilly. LC 87-60524. 368p. 1987. pap. text ed. write for info. (ISBN 0-312-00306-4). St Martin.

Readings in World Politics. Ed. by Thomas O. Schlesinger. 84p. 1969. pap. text ed. 9.95x (ISBN 0-8290-1090-4). Irvington.

Readings in Zero Inventory. Ed. by American Production & Inventory Control Society Staff. LC 84-72229. 175p. 1984. pap. 9.00 (ISBN 0-935406-51-4, 40651). Am Prod & Inventory.

Readings, Issues, & Questions in Public Finance. Eleanor Brown. 1988. 17.95 (ISBN 0-256-06316-8). Irwin.

Readings: "John at Patmos" & "A Book of Hours". Catherine de Vinck. LC 78-55341. 68p. 1978. 5.75 (ISBN 0-911726-32-2); pap. 3.75 (ISBN 0-911726-33-0). Alleluia Pr.

Readings of Biological Concern. Ed. by Robert H. Catlett. LC 72-6695. 84p. 1972. pap. text ed. 4.75x (ISBN 0-8422-0239-0). Irvington.

Readings on Accounting Development: Original Anthology. new ed. Ed. by Paul S. Garner & Marilyn Hughes. LC 77-87313. (Development of Contemporary Accounting Thought Ser). 1978. lib. bdg. 34.50x (ISBN 0-405-10926-1). Ayer Co Pubs.

Readings on Biological Foundations of Behavior. Joel Lubar. 1975. text ed. 5.95 (ISBN 0-88429-004-2). Best Bks Pub.

Readings on Chinese Culture. Institute of Far Eastern Languages Staff. Orig. Title: Talks on Chinese Culture. 5.95 (ISBN 0-88710-076-7); tapes avail. (ISBN 0-88710-077-5). Yale Far Eastern Pubns.

Readings on Cognitive Ergonomics: Mind & Computers. Ed. by G. C. Van Der Veer et al. (Lecture Notes in Computer Science: Vol. 178). vi, 269p. 1984. pap. 18.50 (ISBN 0-387-13394-1). Springer-Verlag.

Readings on Curriculum Implementation. 48p. 1980. 4.00 (611-80200). Assn Supervision.

Readings on Deafness. Ed. by Douglas Watson. pap. 5.50 (ISBN 0-317-62991-3, RS010). Natl Assn Deaf.

Readings on Edmund Husserl's Logical Investigations. Ed. by J. N. Mohanty. 1977. lib. bdg. 28.00 (ISBN 90-247-1928-3, Pub. by Martinus Nijhoff Netherlands). Kluwer Academic.

Readings on English As a Second Language: For Teachers & Teacher Trainees. Kenneth Croft. 1980. write for info. (ISBN 0-673-39249-X). Scott F.

Readings on Equal Education, Vol. 9: Education Policy in an Era of Conservative Reform. Ed. by Marguerite R. Barnett et al. Charles C. Harrington & Philip V. White. Incl. Vol. 1. School Year 1968-1969. Ed. by Allan C. Ornstein. buckram 47.50 (ISBN 0-404-10101-1); Vol. 2. School Year 1969-1970. Ed. by Allan C. Ornstein et al. buckram 47.50 (ISBN 0-404-10102-X); Vol. 3. School Year 1970-1971. Ed. by Russell C. Doll. Maxine Hawkins. LC 70-143794. 47.50 (ISBN 0-404-10103-8); Vol. 4. School Year 1971-72. Ed. by Erwin Flaxman. LC 73-9242. 47.50 (ISBN 0-404-10104-6); Vol. 5. School Year 1972-1973. 47.50 (ISBN 0-404-10105-4); Vol. 6. School Year 1975-76. 47.50 (ISBN 0-404-10106-2); Vol. 7. School Year 1976-1978. Ed. by Marguerite R. Barnett. 47.50; Vol. 8. Race, Sex & National Origin: Public Attitudes of Desegregation. 1985. 47.50 (ISBN 0-404-10108-9). LC 77-83137. Orig. Title: Educating the Disadvantaged. Set. 47.50. AMS Pr.

Readings on Fascism & National Socialism. University of Colorado Department of Philosophy. 112p. (Orig.). 1952. pap. 5.95x (ISBN 0-8040-0259-2, Pub. by Swallow). Ohio U Pr.

Readings on Historical Method. E. Lacy. 1969. pap. text ed. 7.95x (ISBN 0-8290-1180-3). Irvington.

Readings on Human Behavior: The Best of Science '80-'86. Alan Hammond & Philip G. Zimbardo. 1988. pap. text ed. write for info. (ISBN 0-673-18941-4). Scott F.

Readings on Interaction in the Classroom. Sara Delamont. (Contemporary Sociology of the School Ser.). 368p. 1984. pap. text ed. 12.95 (ISBN 0-416-35220-0, 3971). Routledge Chapman & Hall.

Readings on Islam in Southeast Asia. Ahmad Ibrahim et al. 224p. 1987. text ed. 45.95x (ISBN 9971-988-04-6, Pub. by Gower Pub England). Gower Pub Co.

Readings on Language, Schools & Classrooms. Ed. by Michael Stubbs & Hilary Hillier. (Contemporary Sociology of the School Ser.). 140p. 1983. pap. 12.95 (ISBN 0-416-35180-8, NO. 3958). Routledge Chapman & Hall.

Readings on Managing Hotels, Restaurants & Institutions. Dunnovan L. Sapienza et al. 416p. 1987. text ed. 18.95 (ISBN 0-930745-05-1). Williams Bk Co.

Readings on Police Use of Deadly Force. James J. Fyfe. LC 81-86057. 1982. write for info. Police Found.

Readings on Population for Law Students. Ed. by L. T. Lee & P. Saney. (Illus.). 123p. 1977. pap. 5.00 (ISBN 92-3-101364-5, U759, UNESCO). UNIPUB.

Readings on Production Planning & Control. Economic Development Foundation. 178p. 1972. 15.75 (ISBN 92-833-1017-9, APO51, APO). UNIPUB.

Readings on Reading Instruction. 3rd ed. Albert J. Harris & Edward R. Sipey. LC 82-24975. (Illus.). 397p. 1983. pap. text ed. 18.95 (ISBN 0-582-28311-6). Longman.

Readings on Religion: From Inside & Outside. Ed. by Robert S. Ellwood, Jr. 1978. pap. text ed. write for info. (ISBN 0-13-760942-6). P-H.

Readings on Strategic Management. Ed. by Arnoldo C. Hax. LC 81-11103. (Institute Of Management Ser.). 240p. 1984. pap. text ed. 16.95x (ISBN 0-88410-973-9). Ballinger Pub.

Readings on Taxation in Developing Countries. 3rd ed. Ed. by Richard Bird & Oliver Oldman. LC 74-24385. (Illus.). 624p. 1975. 55.00x (ISBN 0-8018-1693-9). Johns Hopkins.

Readings on the Body Politic. Fred R. Harris. 1987. pap. text ed. write for info. (ISBN 0-673-18528-1). Scott F.

Readings on the Criminal Justice System in Chicago & Cook County. Gad J. Bensinger. 210p. 1987. pap. text ed. 8.00 (ISBN 0-942854-12-8). Loyola U Crim.

Readings on the Israeli Political System: Structures & Processes. Ed. by Gregory S. Mahler. LC 81-40031. 450p. (Orig.). 1982. lib. bdg. 36.25 (ISBN 0-8191-2117-7); pap. text ed. 17.75 (ISBN 0-8191-2118-5). U Pr of Amer.

Readings on the Management of Working Capital. 2nd ed. Keith V. Smith. (Illus.). 1980. pap. 27.25 (ISBN 0-8299-0296-1). West Pub.

Readings on the Management of Working Capital. 3rd ed. Keith V. Smith & George W. Gallinger. 717p. 1988. pap. text ed. 28.75 (ISBN 0-314-85300-6). West Pub.

Readings on the Multinational Corporation in Kenya. Ed. by Raphael Kaplinsky. 1978. text ed. 29.95x (ISBN 0-19-572446-1). Oxford U Pr.

Readings on the Paradiso of Dante: Chiefly Based on the Commentary of Benvenuto da Imola; with an Introduction by the Bishop of Ripon, 2 vols. William W. Vernon. LC 74-38372. (Select Bibliographies Reprint Ser.). Repr. of 1900 ed. Set. 62.00 (ISBN 0-8369-6789-5). Ayer Co Pubs.

Readings on the Purgatorio of Dante, 2 vols. William W. Vernon. 1973. Repr. of 1889 ed. 75.00 set (ISBN 0-8274-0492-1). R West.

Readings on the Relation of Government to Property & Industry. Ed. by Samuel P. Orth. LC 73-2527. (Big Business; Economic Power in a Free Society Ser.). Repr. of 1915 ed. 40.00 (ISBN 0-405-05106-9). Ayer Co Pubs.

Readings on Wildfires. Ed. by Michael P. Jones. (Illus.). 96p. (Orig.). 1985. text ed. 12.20 (ISBN 0-89904-118-3); pap. text ed. 9.70 (ISBN 0-89904-119-1). Crumb Elbow Pub.

Readings: RE in the School Curriculum. Rosemary Wilcock. 250p. 1988. 38.00x (ISBN 1-85000-220-7, Falmer Pr.); pap. 21.00x (ISBN 1-85000-221-5). Taylor & Francis.

Readings to Accompany: Basic Marketing - A Situational Orientation, 1988 Edition. D. Wayne Norvell. Ed. by C. Glenn Walters & Sam J. Bruno. 600p. 1988. pap. text ed. 20.00 (ISBN 0-938991-27-2). Colonial Pr AL.

Reading...the Ninety Percent Solution. Allan Sack. 256p. 1985. pap. text ed. 24.95 (ISBN 0-89026-068-0); wkbk. 5.95 (ISBN 0-89026-069-9). College Skills.

Readjuster Movement in Virginia. C. C. Pearson. 11.25 (ISBN 0-8446-1344-4). Peter Smith.

Readjustment of Indian Affairs: Hearings. U. S. Congress. House Committee on Indian Affairs. LC 74-15123. Repr. of 1934 ed. 36.00 (ISBN 0-404-11983-2). AMS Pr.

Read's Florida Evidence. Frank T. Read. LC 86-31035. 1987. 135.00. Callaghan.

Ready About! New Course & New Designs for the Sailing World. Garry Hoyt. (Illus.). 120p. 1986. text ed. 14.95 (ISBN 0-87742-229-X). Intl Marine.

Ready, Aim, Your're Hired: How to Job-Interview Successfully Anytime, Anywhere with Anyone. Paul Hellman. LC 85-26676. 144p. (Orig.). 1986. pap. 6.95 (ISBN 0-8144-7650-3). AMACOM.

Ready All: George Yeoman Pocock & Crew Racing. Gordon Newell. (Illus.). 160p. 1987. 19.95 (ISBN 0-295-96473-1). U of Wash Pr.

Ready Always. Stanley M. Horton. LC 74-76802. (Radiant Life Ser). 128p. 1974. pap. 2.50 (ISBN 0-88243-575-2, 02-0575); tchr's. guide 3.95 (ISBN 0-88243-182-X, 32-0182). Gospel Pub.

Ready & Write. Lillian Lieberman et al. (TAB & LIL Reading Ser.). 64p. (gr. k-2). 1986. 6.95 (ISBN 0-912107-54-5). Monday Morning Bks.

Ready-Art Portfolio - Humor in the Workplace. 1987. 39.95 (ISBN 0-87280-905-6). Asher-Gallant.

Ready-Art Portfolio: Borders for Holidays & Special Occasions. 1987. 39.95 (ISBN 0-87280-904-8). Asher-Gallant.

Ready-Art Portfolio: Motivation & Achievement Headings & Illustrations. 1987. 39.95 (ISBN 0-87280-903-X). Asher-Gallant.

Ready, Fire, Aim: Avoiding Management by Impulse. Harry Levinson. Compiled by Janet E. Robinson. LC 86-10593. 304p. 1986. 25.00 (ISBN 0-916516-06-7); pap. 9.95 (ISBN 0-916516-07-5). Levinson Inst.

Ready for Bed. Susanna Gretz. LC 85-13007. (Illus.). 10p. (ps). 1986. bds. 2.95 (ISBN 0-02-737460-2, Four Winds). Macmillan.

Ready for Reading: Classroom Games for Reading Readiness. Markanne Gantt. 149p. 1980. pap. 14.95 (ISBN 0-87762-285-X). Technomic.

Ready for Reference: Media Skills for Intermediate Students. Barbara B. Zlotnick. (Teaching Library, Media, Research & Information Skills Ser.). 290p. 1984. pap. text ed. 19.50 (ISBN 0-87287-411-7). Libs Unl.

Ready for Romance. Mollie Marshall. (Leisure First Romance Ser.: No. 2). 192p. (Orig.). (gr. 6-12). 1982. pap. 1.95 (ISBN 0-8439-1129-8, Leisure Bks). Leisure NY.

Ready for School. (Golden Step Ahead Workbooks). (Illus.). 32p. (ps). 1985. pap. 1.95 (ISBN 0-307-03585-9, Pub. by Golden Bks). Western Pub.

Ready for School: How Parents Can Prepare Children for School Success. Geraldine Chapey. (Illus.). 164p. (Orig.). 1986. lib. bdg. 23.75 (ISBN 0-8191-5316-8); pap. text ed. 9.25 (ISBN 0-8191-5317-6). U Pr of Amer.

Ready for the Defense. Martin Garbus. 300p. 1987. pap. 4.95 (ISBN 0-88184-373-3). Carroll & Graf.

Ready from Within: Septima Clark & the Civil Rights Movements. Septima Clark. Ed. by Cynthia S. Brown. (Illus.). 134p. (Orig.). 1986. pap. 8.95 (ISBN 0-931125-04-9). Wild Trees Press.

Ready, Get Set, Go! Sharon Peters. (Illus.). 32p. (gr. k-2). 1980. PLB 5.41 (ISBN 0-89375-386-6); pap. 1.50 (ISBN 0-89375-285-1). Troll Assocs.

Ready! Get Set! Grow! Jim Plueddemann. (Bible Discovery Guides for Campers Juniors Ser.). (Illus.). 48p. 1987. Camper Ed. pap. 1.50 (ISBN 0-87788-715-2); Counselor Ed. pap. 3.50 (ISBN 0-87788-716-0). Shaw Pubs.

Ready-Mixed Concrete. 160p. 1985. 595.00 (ISBN 0-318-00504-2). Busn Trend.

Ready or Not: Here Come Fourteen Frightening Stories! Joan Kahn. LC 86-31875. (Illus.). 176p. (YA) (gr. 7 up). 1987. 11.75 (ISBN 0-688-07167-8). Greenwillow.

Ready Reading. Faye Crow. (Illus.). 135p. (Orig.). 1987. pap. 10.95 (ISBN 0-9617529-0-4). Ready Work.

Ready Reference Guide to Shipping & Receiving. Patricia Laux. 220p. 1986. pap. 2.95 (ISBN 0-934674-56-6, 13 ORS). J J Keller.

Ready Reference to Philosophy East & West. Eugene F. Bales. 314p. 1988. lib. bdg. 24.50 (ISBN 0-8191-6640-5). U Pr of Amer.

Ready, Run, Fun: Apple IIe-IIc Edition. Joan Targ & Jeff Levinsky. Date not set. write for info. S&S.

Ready, Set, Love. Judith Enderle. (Caprice Ser.: No. 64). 144p. 1985. pap. 2.25 (ISBN 0-441-70834-X, Pub. by Tempo). Ace Bks.

Ready, Set, Read: Best Books to Prepare Preschoolers. Ellen Mahoney & Leah Wilcox. LC 83-27087. 1985. 19.50 (ISBN 0-8108-1684-9). Scarecrow.

Ready, Set Read Books. (Illus.). 32p. 1988. 3.95 (ISBN 0-02-688518-2, Checkerboard Pr). Macmillan.

Ready... Set... Robot! Lillian Hoban & Phoebe Hoban. LC 81-47731. (Trophy I Can Read Bks.). (Illus.). 64p. (ps-3). 1985. pap. 3.50 (ISBN 0-06-444087-7, Trophy). HarpJ.

Ready to Go. Tom Mandel. LC 81-4904. 69p. (Orig.). 1981. pap. 4.00 (ISBN 0-87886-113-0). Greenfld Rev Pr.

Ready-to-Go-Sales Meetings. Dan Kennedy. Date not set. 39.95 (ISBN 0-87280-134-9). Asher-Gallant.

Ready to Hazard: A Biography of Commodore William Bainbridge, 1774-1833. David F. Long. LC 80-29146. pap. 89.80 (ISBN 0-317-30023-7, 2025021). Bks Demand UMI.

Ready to Minister. William M. Pinson, Jr. LC 84-3052. (Broadman Leadership Ser.). 1984. pap. 4.95 (ISBN 0-8054-3109-8). Broadman.

Ready to Read. Janet Fenholt. 128p. 1988. pap. text ed. write for info. (ISBN 0-538-14650-8, N65); write for info. manual (ISBN 0-538-28555-9, N65M). SW Pub.

Ready to Read. Lillian Lieberman et al. (TAB & LIL Reading Ser.). 64p. (gr. k-2). 1986. 6.95 (ISBN 0-912107-52-9). Monday Morning Bks.

Ready to Restore. Jay E. Adams. (Orig.). 1981. pap. 4.95 (ISBN 0-8010-0171-4). Baker Bk.

Ready to Restore. Jay E. Adams. 1981. pap. 5.95 (ISBN 0-87552-070-7). Presby & Reformed.

Ready to Run Accounting with Lotus 1-2-3 & Symphony. William Urschel. 225p. 1984. incl. disk 44.95 (ISBN 0-88284-330-3). Manusoft.

Ready to Survive. Jacqueline Lapidus. LC 75-9593. 24p. 1975. pap. 4.00 (ISBN 0-914610-04-X). Hanging Loose.

Ready-to-Use Accents & Attention-Getters. Carol B. Grafton. 64p. 1984. pap. 3.95 (ISBN 0-486-24692-2). Dover.

Ready-to-Use Arrows. Ed. by Theodore Menten. (Clip Art Ser.). (Illus.). 1979. pap. 3.95 (ISBN 0-486-23783-4). Dover.

Ready-to-Use Art Deco Borders. Theodore Menten. 64p. (Orig.). 1985. pap. 3.50 (ISBN 0-486-24967-0). Dover.

Ready-to-Use Art Nouveau Alphabets. Dan X. Solo. 1986. pap. 3.95 (ISBN 0-486-25140-3). Dover.

Ready-to-Use Art Nouveau Borders. Theodore Menten. (Illus.). 64p. (Orig.). 1983. pap. 3.50 (ISBN 0-486-24431-8). Dover.

Ready-to-Use Art Nouveau Small Frames & Borders. Theodore Menten. 64p. (Orig.). 1985. pap. 3.95 (ISBN 0-486-24975-1). Dover.

Ready-to-Use Banners. Theodore Menten. (Clip Art Ser.). (Illus.). 1979. pap. 3.50 (ISBN 0-486-23899-7). Dover.

Ready-to-Use Borders. Ed. by Theodore Menten. (Clip Art Ser.). (Illus.). 1979. pap. 3.50 (ISBN 0-486-23782-6). Dover.

Ready-to-Use Borders on Layout Grids. Carol B. Grafton. (Clip Art Ser.). 48p. 1985. pap. 3.95 (ISBN 0-486-24812-7). Dover.

Ready-to-Use Business Forms. Ed. by Self-Counsel Press. 112p. 1985. pap. 9.95 (ISBN 0-88908-609-5, 9537). ISC Pr.

Ready to Use Cartoons for Church Publications. Phil Jackson. 160p. 1987. pap. 4.95 (ISBN 0-8010-5221-1). Baker Bk.

Ready-to-Use Christmas Designs. Ed Sibbett, Jr. (Clip Art Ser.). (Illus.). 1979. pap. 3.50 (ISBN 0-486-23900-4). Dover.

Ready-to-Use Christmas Silhouettes. Bob Censoni. 64p. (Orig.). 1985. pap. 3.50 (ISBN 0-486-24954-9). Dover.

Ready-to-Use Computer Literacy Activities Kit, Level I. Dwight E. Mostoller & Margaret F. Campbell. 176p. (gr. 4-6). 1987. tchr's. manual 24.95 (ISBN 0-13-762022-5). P-H.

Ready-to-Use Computer Literacy Activities Kits, Level I. Dwight E. Mostoller & Margaret F. Campbell. 64p. (gr. 4-6). 1987. student wkbk. 5.95 (ISBN 0-317-66399-2). P-H.

Ready-to-Use Computer Literacy Activities Kits, Level II. Dwight E. Mostoller & Margaret F. Campbell. 160p. (gr. 7-10). 1987. tchr's. manual 24.95 (ISBN 0-13-762048-9). P-H.

Ready-to-Use Computer Literacy Activities Kits Level II. Dwight E. Mostoller & Margaret F. Campbell. 64p. (gr. 7-10). 1987. student wkbk. 5.95 (ISBN 0-317-66401-8). P-H.

Ready-to-Use Dollhouse Wallpaper: Six Full-Color Patterns to Decorate Six Rooms. Katzenbach & Warren, Inc. LC 77-70052. (Illus.). 1978. pap. 2.95 (ISBN 0-486-23495-9). Dover.

Ready-to-Use Floral Designs. Ed Sibbett, Jr. (Illus.). 64p. pap. 3.50 (ISBN 0-486-23976-4). Dover.

Ready-to-Use Food & Drink Spot Illustrations. Susan Gaber. (Clip Art Ser.). 1981. pap. 3.50 (ISBN 0-486-24139-4). Dover.

Ready-to-Use Graphic Attention-Getters. Dan X. Solo. 64p. 1988. pap. 3.95 (ISBN 0-486-25744-4). Dover.

Ready-to-Use Headlines. Ed. by Theodore Menten. (Clip Art Ser.). 1979. pap. 3.50 (ISBN 0-486-23454-1). Dover.

Ready-To-Use Humorous Spot Illustrations. Illus. by Bob Censoni. (Clip Art Ser.). (Illus.). 64p. 1984. pap. 3.50 (ISBN 0-486-24644-2). Dover.

Ready-to-Use Illustrations for Holidays & Special Occasions. Ed. by Ed Sibbett, Jr. (Illus.). 64p. (Orig.). 1983. pap. 3.50 (ISBN 0-486-24440-7). Dover.

Ready-to-Use Illustrations of Children (Clip Art) Tom Tierney. (Pictorial Archive Ser.). (Illus.). 64p. (Orig.). 1983. pap. 3.50 (ISBN 0-486-24405-9). Dover.

Ready-to-Use Illustrations of Hands. Illus. by Tom Tierney. (Clip Art Ser.). (Illus., Orig.). 1983. pap. 3.50 (ISBN 0-486-24570-5). Dover.

Ready-to-Use Illustrations of Men's Heads. Tom Tierney. (Pictorial Archive Ser.). (Illus.). 64p. (Orig.). 1982. pap. 3.50 (ISBN 0-486-24413-X). Dover.

Ready-to-Use Illustrations of Women's Heads (Clip Art) Tom Tierney. (Pictorial Archive Ser.). (Illus.). 64p. (Orig.). 1982. pap. 3.50 (ISBN 0-486-24341-9). Dover.

Ready-to-Use Library Skills Games: Reproducible Activities for Building Location & Literature Skills. Ruth Snoddon. 256p. 1987. pap. 22.95 (ISBN 0-87628-721-6). P-H.

Ready-to-Use Literature Activities: With Techniques & Ideas for Using Video in the Classroom. Patricia Altmann & Lisa Luciano. 288p. (YA) (gr. 7-12). 1988. pap. 24.95x (ISBN 0-87628-779-8). Ctr Appl Res.

Ready-to-Use Marbelized Papers. Judith Saurman & Judith Pierce. 28p. 1979. pap. 4.95 (ISBN 0-486-23901-2). Dover.

Ready-to-Use Music Activities Kit. Audrey J. Adair. LC 83-17480. 291p. 1984. pap. text ed. 24.95x (ISBN 0-13-762295-3, Parker). P-H.

Ready-to-Use News Announcements. Jean Larcher. 1981. pap. 3.50 (ISBN 0-486-24173-4). Dover.

Ready-to-Use Old-Fashioned Sports Illustrations. Carol B. Grafton. 64p. 1988. pap. 3.95 (ISBN 0-486-25776-2). Dover.

Ready-to-Use Outdoor Recreations Spot Illustrations. David Carlson. (Clip Art Ser.). 64p. 1985. pap. 3.50 (ISBN 0-486-24784-8). Dover.

Ready-to-Use Sale Announcements. David Gatti. (Dover Clip Art - Pictorial Archive Ser.). (Illus.). 64p. (Orig.). 1980. pap. 3.50 (ISBN 0-486-24012-6). Dover.

Ready-to-Use Science Activities for the Elementary Classroom. Debra Seabury & Susan Peeples. 256p. 1987. pap. 19.95x (ISBN 0-87628-743-7). Ctr Appl Res.

Ready-to-Use Science Activities for the Elementary Classroom. Debra Seabury & Susan Peeples. 224p. 1987. pap. 17.95 (ISBN 0-317-66406-9). P-H.

Ready to Use Sermon Outlines. Russell E. Spray. 80p. 1987. pap. 3.95 (ISBN 0-8010-8268-4). Baker Bk.

Ready-to-Use Silhouette Spot Illustrations. Bob Censoni. 64p. 1984. pap. 3.50 (ISBN 0-486-24711-2). Dover.

Ready-to-Use Small Frames & Borders (Clip Art) Ed. by Carol B. Grafton. (Pictorial Archive Ser.). (Illus.). 64p. (Orig.). 1982. pap. 3.50 (ISBN 0-486-24375-3). Dover.

Ready-to-Use Sports Illustrations (Clip Art) David Carlson. (Pictorial Archive Ser.). (Illus.). 64p. (Orig.). 1982. pap. 3.50 (ISBN 0-486-24344-3). Dover.

Ready-to-Use Teddy Bear Illustrations. Theodore Menten. 64p. (Orig.). 1985. pap. 3.95 (ISBN 0-486-24943-3). Dover.

Ready-to-Use Thematic Borders. Ed Sibbett, Jr. (Illus.). 64p. 1982. pap. 3.50 (ISBN 0-486-24254-4). Dover.

Ready-To-Use Thinking Skills Activities for Grades 4-8. Fred Chernow & Carol Chernow. LC 85-21732. 227p. 1986. pap. 18.95X (ISBN 0-13-762303-8, Parker). P-H.

Ready-to-Use Victorian Alphabets. Dan X. Solo. 1986. pap. 3.95 (ISBN 0-486-25053-9). Dover.

Ready-to-Use Writing Workshop Activities Kit, 6 bks. Judith Schifferle. Incl. Word Skills. 72p. Kit I (ISBN 0-87628-940-5); Sentence Skills. 48p. Kit II (ISBN 0-87628-745-3); Paragraph Writing Skills. 48p. Kit III (ISBN 0-87628-640-6); Editorial Skills. 72p. Kit IV (ISBN 0-87628-290-7); Letter & Report Writing Skills. 48p. Kit V (ISBN 0-87628-522-1); Notetaking & Outlining Skills. 48p. Kit VI (ISBN 0-87628-613-9). (Orig.). 1984. tchng. aids 8.95x ea. Ctr Appl Res.

Ready to Work? Development of Occupational Skills, Attitudes, & Behaviors with Mentally Retarded Persons. David R. Gingland & Bernice W. Carlson. LC 76-58841. Repr. of 1977 ed. 39.80 (ISBN 0-8357-9023-1, 2016397). Bks Demand UMI.

Ready...Aim...Fire! Small Arms Ammunition in the Battle of Gettysburg. Dean S. Thomas. Intro. by Stephen V. Ash. (Illus.). 76p. (Orig.). 1981. pap. 7.50 (ISBN 0-939631-00-8). Thomas Publications.

ReadySetGo for the Macintosh. Manhattan Graphics Staff & David Kater. (Brady Desktop Publishing Library). 320p. 1988. pap. 21.95 (ISBN 0-13-762188-4). Brady Comp Bks.

Ready...Set...Robot! Lillian Hoban & Phoebe Hoban. LC 81-47731. (Trophy I Can Read Bks.). (Illus.). 64p. (gr. k-3). 1982. 9.70i (ISBN 0-06-022345-6); PLB 10.89 (ISBN 0-06-022346-4). HarpJ.

Reaeration Research. Compiled by American Society of Civil Engineers Staff. 376p. 1979. pap. 26.00x (ISBN 0-87262-142-1). Am Soc Civil Eng.

Reaffirmation of Republicanism: Eisenhower & the Eighty-Third Congress. Gary W. Reichard. LC 75-1017. (Twentieth Century America Ser.). 320p. 1975. 28.95x (ISBN 0-87049-167-9). U of Tenn Pr.

Reaffirming Rehabilitation. Francis T. Cullen & Karen E. Gilbert. 315p. (Orig.). 1982. pap. text ed. 16.95 (ISBN 0-87084-175-0). Anderson Pub Co.

Reagan Administration & Human Rights. Tinsley E. Yarbrough. LC 85-16699. 288p. 1985. 36.95 (ISBN 0-275-90239-0, C0239). Praeger.

Reagan Administration & the Palestinian Question: The First Thousand Days. Juliana Peck. 138p. 1984. pap. 7.00 (ISBN 0-88728-140-0). Inst Palestine.

Reagan Administration's Human Rights Policy: A Mid-Term Review. Americas Watch Committee (U.S.) et al. LC 86-151721. Date not set. price not set. Fund Free Expression.

Reagan Administration's Record on Human Rights in 1985. Americas Watch Staff et al. 154p. 1986. 8.00 (ISBN 0-938579-55-X). Fund Free Expression.

Reagan & Gorbachev. Michael Mandelbaum & Strobe Talbott. LC 86-24568. 188p. (Orig.). pap. 5.95 (ISBN 0-394-74721-6, Vin). Random.

Reagan & the Cities. Ed. by George E. Peterson. (Changing Domestic Priorities Ser.). 360p. 1986. text ed. 27.95x (ISBN 0-87766-384-X); pap. text ed. 14.95x (ISBN 0-87766-385-8). Urban Inst.

Reagan & the Economy: The Successes, Failures & Unfinished Agenda. Michael J. Boskin. 301p. 1987. 22.95 (ISBN 0-917616-80-4). ICS Pr.

Reagan & the Middle East. N. Aruri et al. (Monograph: No. 17). 95p. (Orig.). 1983. pap. text ed. 5.50 (ISBN 0-937694-59-2). Assn Arab-Amer U Grads.

Reagan & the States. Richard P. Nathan & Fred C. Doolittle. LC 87-45529. (Illus.). 344p. 1987. text ed. 42.50 (ISBN 0-691-07748-7); pap. text ed. 12.95 (ISBN 0-691-02273-9). Princeton U Pr.

Reagan & the World: Imperial Policy in the New Cold War. Jeff McMahan. 320p. 1985. 26.00 (ISBN 0-85345-677-1); pap. 10.00 (ISBN 0-85345-678-X). Monthly Rev.

Reagan Block Grants: What We Have Learned?? George E. Peterson. 1986. pap. 15.95 (ISBN 0-87766-400-5). Urban Inst.

Reagan Chronicles: A Cartoon Carnival. Dwane Powell. 146p. 1987. pap. 6.95 (ISBN 0-912697-72-5). Algonquin Bks.

Reagan County Story. Compiled by Reagan County Historical Society & Mike Werst. (Illus.). 288p. 1974. 12.50 (ISBN 0-933512-19-8). Pioneer Bk Tx.

Reagan Defense Program: An Interim Assessment. Ed. by Stephen J. Cimbala. LC 86-962. 248p. 1986. 35.00 (ISBN 0-8420-2243-0); pap. 12.95 (ISBN 0-8420-2262-7). Scholarly Res Inc.

Reagan Detour: Conservative Revolutionary. Richard Reeves. 139p. 1985. 14.95 (ISBN 0-671-60652-2); pap. 7.95 (ISBN 0-671-60702-2). S&S.

Reagan Doctrine & Beyond. Christopher C. DeMuth et al. LC 87-31958. (Forum Ser.: No. 67). 54p. (Orig.). 1988. pap. text ed. 5.95 (ISBN 0-8447-2274-X). Am Enterprise.

Reagan Doctrine & U. S. Foreign Policy. Jeane J. Kirkpatrick. 23p. 1985. pap. 4.00 (ISBN 0-317-47101-5). Heritage Found.

Reagan Electionomics: How Reagan Ambushed the Pollsters, 1976-1984. Donald J. Devine. LC 84-108682. 105p. 1984. 14.95 (ISBN 0-89803-130-3, Dist. by Kampmann). Green Hill.

Reagan Energy Plan: A Major Power Failure. NRDC Staff et al. 49p. 1982. 2.50 (ISBN 0-318-20480-0). Natl Resources Defense Coun.

Reagan Experiment: An Examination of Economic & Social Policies under the Reagan Administration. Ed. by John L. Palmer & Isabel V. Sawhill. 530p. 1982. 29.95 (ISBN 0-87766-315-7); pap. 12.95x (ISBN 0-87766-316-5). Urban Inst.

Reagan Foreign Policy. William G. Hyland. 1987. pap. 9.95 (ISBN 0-452-00889-1, Mer). NAL.

Reagan, God & the Bomb. F. H. Knelman. LC 84-43328. 350p. 1985. 21.95 (ISBN 0-87975-310-2). Prometheus Bks.

Reagan in the Workplace: Unraveling the Health & Safety Net. Philip J. Simon. 103p. 1983. pap. 10.00 (ISBN 0-936758-12-0). Ctr Responsive Law.

Reagan Legacy: A Nation Adrift. Sidney Blumenthal & Thomas Edsall. LC 87-43109. 320p. 1988. 19.95 (ISBN 0-394-56555-X); pap. 9.95 (ISBN 0-394-75970-2). Pantheon.

Reagan Legacy: Promise & Performance. Ed. by Charles O. Jones. LC 88-18137. (Illus.). 324p. 1988. 25.00 (ISBN 0-934540-71-3); pap. text ed. 14.95 (ISBN 0-934540-70-5). Chatham Hse Pubs.

Reagan on Cuba: Selected Statements by the President. Ronald Reagan. 1986. 4.00. Cuban Amer Natl Fndtn.

Reagan Phenomenon & Other Speeches on Foreign Policy. Jeane J. Kirkpatrick. LC 82-16434. 230p. 1983. 16.95 (ISBN 0-8447-1361-9). Am Enterprise.

Reagan Presidency: An Early Assessment. Ed. by Fred I. Greenstein. LC 83-48056. 208p. 1983. pap. 8.95x (ISBN 0-8018-3057-5). Johns Hopkins.

Reagan Presidency & the Governing of America: Conference Volume. Ed. by Lester M. Salamon & Michael S. Lund. LC 84-27065. (Changing Domestic Priorities Ser.). 1984. text ed. 28.95x (ISBN 0-87766-370-X); pap. text ed. 15.95x (ISBN 0-87766-347-5). Urban Inst.

Reagan Psalms. A. D. Winans. LC 84-81138. (Illus.). 96p. (Orig.). 1984. lib. bdg. 12.95 (ISBN 0-930131-00-2); pap. 6.95 (ISBN 0-930131-01-0). Integrity Times.

Reagan Record: An Assessment of America's Changing Domestic Priorities. Ed. by John L. Palmer & Isabel V. Sawhill. LC 84-11001. 440p. 1984. prof. ref. o.p. 29.95 (ISBN 0-88730-000-6); pap. 16.95x (ISBN 0-88730-001-4). Ballinger Pub.

Reagan Reflected in Patriotic Prose. Patricia Taylor. (Illus.). 48p. (Orig.). 1987. pap. 5.95 (ISBN 0-943481-02-3). Pumphouse Pr.

Reagan Regulatory Strategy: An Assessment. Ed. by Eads & Fix. (Changing Domestic Priorities Ser.). 240p. 1984. pap. 12.95x (ISBN 0-87766-346-7). Urban Inst.

Reagan Revolution? B. B. Kymlicka & Jean Matthews. 250p. (Orig.). 1987. 22.00 (ISBN 0-256-06135-1); pap. text ed. 12.00 (ISBN 0-256-06237-4). Dorsey.

Reagan Rogue: The Mob That Could Not Think Straight. Klint Westwood. Ed. by Ralph Dominiqu. (Illus.). 350p. (Orig.). 1987. pap. 34.95 (ISBN 0-9619087-3-4). Westwood Irvine.

Reagan Speaks: The Making of an American Myth. Paul D. Erickson. 192p. 1985. 22.50 (ISBN 0-8147-2167-2). NYU Pr.

Reagan Strategic Defense Initiative: A Technical, Political, & Arms Control Assessment. Sidney D. Drell et al. LC 85-3916. 168p. 1985. pap. 14.95x professional reference (ISBN 0-88730-064-2). Ballinger Pub.

Reagan, Thatcher, & the Politics of Decline. Joel Krieger. (Europe & the International Order Ser.). 247p. 1986. 29.95x (ISBN 0-19-520522-7); pap. 11.95x (ISBN 0-19-520529-4). Oxford U Pr.

Reagan: The Man from Main Street. Vance H. Trimble. (Illus.). 64p. hand bound 24.00 (ISBN 0-88014-025-9). Mosaic Pr OH.

Reagan the Man, the President. Hedrick Smith et al. (Leaders of the World Ser.). (Illus.). 228p. 1981. text ed. 15.25 (ISBN 0-08-027916-3). McGraw.

Reagan: The Next Four Years. Congressional Quarterly Inc. Staff. 168p. 1985. pap. 10.95 (ISBN 0-87187-352-4). Congr Quarterly.

Reagan, Trilateralism & the Neoliberals: U. S. Policy in the 1980s. Holly Sklar. (Institute for New Communications Pamphlet Ser.). (Illus.). 75p. (Orig.). 1986. pap. 4.75 perfect bdg. (ISBN 0-89608-213-X). South End Pr.

Reagan versus the Sandinistas: The Undeclared War on Nicaragua. Ed. by Thomas W. Walker. 337p. 1987. 30.00 (ISBN 0-8133-0371-0); pap. 14.85 (ISBN 0-8133-0372-9). Westview.

Reagan Wit. Bill Adler. LC 81-38509. 120p. 1981. 6.95 (ISBN 0-89803-090-0). Green Hill.

Reagan Years. Hodding Carter. 202p. 1988. 17.50 (ISBN 0-8076-1209-X). Braziller.

Reagan Years: Perspectives & Assessments. Ed. by James J. Horgan & Joseph A. Cernik. (Institute for Policy Studies). 221p. (Orig.). 1988. pap. 10.95 (ISBN 0-945759-00-2). St Leo Col Pr.

Reaganomics. Bruce W. Kimzey. (Illus.). 117p. 1983. pap. text ed. 12.25 (ISBN 0-314-73187-3). West Pub.

Reaganomics: A Midterm Report. Ed. by Wm. Craig Stubblebine & Thomas D. Willett. LC 82-258440. 232p. 1983. 14.95 (ISBN 0-917616-54-5). ICS Pr.

Reaganomics: An Insider's Account. William A. Niskanen. (Illus.). 384p. 1988. 22.95 (ISBN 0-19-505394-X). Oxford U Pr.

Reaganomics & New York City. 1982. 5.00 (ISBN 0-686-40509-9). Comm Coun Great NY.

Reaganomics in the Stagflation Economy. Ed. by Sidney Weintraub & Marvin Goodstein. LC 82-60305. (Post Keynesian Economics Ser.). 200p. (Orig.). 1983. pap. 13.95 (ISBN 0-8122-1133-2). U of Pa Pr.

Reaganomics: Meaning, Means & Ends. John Kenneth Galbraith & Paul W. McCracken. LC 83-48640. (Charles E. Moskowitz Memorial Lecture Ser.: Vol. XXIV). 12.95 (ISBN 0-02-922890-5). Free Pr.

Reaganomics: Reagan's Economic Program. Stephen Goode. (Impact Bks). (Illus.). 96p. 1982. PLB 12.90 (ISBN 0-531-04422-X). Watts.

Reaganomics: Rhetoric vs. Reality. Frank Ackerman. 200p. 1982. 20.00 (ISBN 0-89608-142-7); pap. 7.50 (ISBN 0-89608-141-9). South End Pr.

Reaganomics: Successes & Failures. Khalid R. Mehtabdin. LC 86-21674. 1986. pap. 14.95x (ISBN 0-88946-204-6). E Mellen.

Reaganomics: The New Federalism. Carl Lowe. LC 83-26108. 1984. 10.00 (ISBN 0-8242-0686-X). Wilson.

Reagan's America. Lloyd DeMause. LC 82-73581. 200p. 1984. 21.95 (ISBN 0-940508-02-8). Creative Roots.

Reagan's America: Innocents at Home. Garry Wills. LC 86-16493. (Illus.). 480p. 1987. 19.95 (ISBN 0-385-18286-4). Doubleday.

Reagan's America: With a New Chapter on the Legacy of the Reagan Era. Garry Wills. 1988. pap. 8.95 (ISBN 0-14-010557-3). Penguin.

Reagan's First Four Years: A New Beginning? J. D. Lees et al. 224p. 1988. 39.95 (ISBN 0-7190-2539-7, Pub. by Manchester Univ Pr). St Martin.

Reagan's Leadership & the Atlantic Alliance: Views from Europe & America. Ed. by W. F. Goldstein. (Illus.). 256p. 1986. text ed. 21.95 (ISBN 0-08-033982-4, PDP). Pergamon.

Reagan's Nuclear Terrorism. Udai Narain. 1985. 18.50x (ISBN 0-8364-1312-1, Pub. by Deep). South Asia Bks.

Reagan's Ruling Class: Portraits of the President's Top 100 Officials. Ronald Brownstein. Ed. by Nina Easton. LC 82-60917. (Illus.). 759p. 1983. 24.50 (ISBN 0-936486-03-1). Presidential Acct.

Reagan's Secret Wars. Jay Peterzell. LC 83-226461. 100p. 1984. pap. 3.95 (ISBN 0-86566-033-6). Ctr Natl Security.

Reagan's Squeeze on Small Business: How the Adminstration Plan Will Increase Economic Concentration, Vol. 1. Nina Easton. Ed. by Ronald Brownstein. (Presidential Examiner Ser.: Vol. 1, No. 1). 83p. (Orig.). 1981. pap. text ed. 7.00 (ISBN 0-936486-02-3). Presidential Acct.

Reagent Chemicals. 7th ed. LC 86-20569. (Illus.). xiii, 675p. 1986. 89.95 (ISBN 0-8412-0991-X). Am Chemical.

Reagents for Organic Synthesis. Fieser & Fieser's. 1981. Vol. 9, 596pp. 54.50 (ISBN 0-471-05631-6); Vol. 10, 528pp. 49.50 (ISBN 0-471-86636-9). Wiley.

Reagents for Organic Synthesis, 8 vols. Louis F. Fieser & Mary Fieser. LC 66-27894. (Fieser's Reagents for Organic Synthesis Ser.). 1980. Vol. 1, 1967, 1457p. 80.00 (ISBN 0-471-25875-X); Vol. 2, 1969, 538p. 52.50 (ISBN 0-471-25876-8); Vol. 3, 1972, 401p. 47.50x (ISBN 0-471-25879-2); Vol. 4, 1974, 660p. 54.50 (ISBN 0-471-25881-4); Vol. 5, 1975, 864p. 59.50 (ISBN 0-471-25882-2); Vol. 6, 1977, 765p. 56.50 (ISBN 0-471-25873-3); Vol. 7, 1979, 487p. 49.95 (ISBN 0-471-02918-1); Vol. 8, 1980, 602p. 54.50 (ISBN 0-471-04834-8). Wiley.

Reagents for Organic Synthesis, Vol. 11. Fieser & Fieser's. (Fieser's Reagents for Organic Synthesis Ser.). 669p. 1984. 49.50x (ISBN 0-471-88628-9). Wiley.

Reagents for Organic Synthesis, Vol. 12. Fieser. (Fieser's Reagents for Organic Synthesis Ser.). 643p. 1986. 47.50 (ISBN 0-471-83469-6). Wiley.

Reagents in Mineral Technology. Somasundaran & Moudgil. (Surfactant Science Ser.). 664p. 1987. 150.00 (ISBN 0-8247-7715-8). Dekker.

Real Algebraic Differential Topology: Part One. Richard S. Palais. LC 81-81990. (Mathematics Lecture Ser.: No. 10). v, 192p. 1981. text ed. 18.00 (ISBN 0-914098-19-5). Publish or Perish.

Real America. Elijah Brown. LC 73-13124. (Foreign Travelers in America, 1810-1935 Ser.). 308p. 1974. Repr. 24.50x (ISBN 0-405-05447-5). Ayer Co Pubs.

Real American Cowboy. Jack Weston. LC 84-22227. (Illus.). 288p. 1985. 19.95 (ISBN 0-8052-3983-9). Schocken.

Real American Cowboy. Jack Weston. (Illus.). 267p. 1988. pap. 11.95 (ISBN 0-941533-27-1). New Amsterdam Bks.

Real American Food: From Yankee Red Flannel Hash & the Ultimate Navajo Taco to Beautiful Swimmer Pie & General Store Fudge Pie. Jane Stern & Michael Stern. LC 86-45284. (Illus.). 416p. 1986. 19.95 (ISBN 0-394-53953-2). Knopf.

Real American Politics: Changing Perspectives on American Government. Ralph P. Hummel & Robert A. Isaak. (Illus.). 336p. 1986. text ed. 26.00 (ISBN 0-13-762360-7); pap. text ed. write for info. (ISBN 0-13-762352-6). P-H.

Real American Psychomastery. Jordan Wagner. (Illus.). 124p. (Orig.). 1985. pap. 1200.00 (ISBN 0-9613141-1-7). Big Sur Pubs.

Real Analysis. J. A. Anderson. 356p. 1969. 135.00 (ISBN 0-677-61460-8). Gordon & Breach.

Real Analysis. Nicolas Artemiadis. LC 75-29189. 594p. 1976. 15.00x (ISBN 0-8093-0727-8). S Ill U Pr.

Real Analysis. Serge Lang. 533p. 1983. write for info. (ISBN 0-201-14179-5, Adv Bk Prog MSP). Addison Wesley.

Real Analysis. William Ray. 320p. 1988. text ed. price not set (ISBN 0-13-762386-0). P-H.

Real Analysis. 3rd ed. H. L. Royden. 505p. 1988. text ed. write for info. (ISBN 0-02-404151-3). Macmillan.

Real Analysis & Probability. Robert B. Ash. (Probability & Mathematical Statistics Ser.). 476p. 1972. 39.95 (ISBN 0-12-065201-3). solutions to problems 6.75 (ISBN 0-12-065240-4). Acad Pr.

Real Analysis: Modern Techniques & Their Applications. Gerald B. Folland. LC 84-10435. (Pure & Applied Mathematics Ser.: 1-237). 350p. 1984. text ed. 41.95 (ISBN 0-471-80958-6, Pub. by Wiley-Interscience). Wiley.

Real Analysis with Point-Set Topology. Stancl. (Pure & Applied Mathematics Ser.). 304p. 1987. 45.00 (ISBN 0-8247-7790-5). Dekker.

Real & Complex Analysis. 3rd ed. Walter Rudin. (Higher Mathematics Ser.). 480p. 1987. text ed. 47.95 (ISBN 0-07-054234-1). McGraw.

Real & False Alarms. David A. Evans. LC 84-73284. 64p. 1985. pap. 5.25 (ISBN 0-933532-45-8). BkMk.

Real & Functional Analysis, Part A: Real Analysis. 2nd ed. A. Mukherjea & K. Pothoven. (Mathematical Concepts & Methods in Science & Engineering Ser.: Vol. 27). 352p. 1984. 55.00x (ISBN 0-306-41557-7, Plenum Pr). Plenum Pub.

Real & Functional Analysis, Pt B: Functional Analysis. 2nd ed. A. Mukherjea & K. Pothoven. (Mathematical Concepts & Methods in Science & Engineering Ser.: Vol. 28). 276p. 1985. 39.50x (ISBN 0-306-41558-5, Plenum Pr). Plenum Pub.

Real & Imagined Role of Culture in Development: Case Studies from Indonesia. Ed. by Michael R. Dove. LC 87-35567. (Illus.). 304p. 1988. text ed. 32.00 (ISBN 0-8248-1080-5). UH Pr.

Real & Imagined Worlds: The Novel & Social Science. Morroe Berger. 1977. 22.50x (ISBN 0-674-74941-3). Harvard U Pr.

Real & Stochastic Analysis. Ed. by M. M. Rao. LC 85-31492. (Probability & Mathematical Statistics-Applied Probability & Statistics Section Ser.). (Illus.). 347p. 1986. 41.95 (ISBN 0-471-82969-2, Pub. by Wiley Press). Wiley.

Real & the Imaginary: A New Approach to Physics. Ed. by Jean E. Charon. LC 86-25326. (Illus.). 206p. 1987. 24.95 (ISBN 0-89226-027-0, Pub. by ICUS). Paragon Hse.

Real Animal Heroes: Dramatic Recount of the Heroism Demonstrated by a Variety of Animals in Saving a Human Life. Ed. by Paul D. Stevens. LC 86-62119. (Illus.). 208p. 1988. 18.95 (ISBN 0-918495-25-3). Sharp & Dunn.

Real Barbecue: A Guide to the Best Joints, the Best Sauces, the Best Cookers--& Much More, the Only Barbecue Book You'll Ever Need. Greg Johnson & Vince Staten. LC 87-46149. (Illus.). 224p. (Orig.). 1988. pap. 8.95 (ISBN 0-06-096267-4, PL-6267, PL). Har-Row.

Real Battle: How to Win Daily Victories in Spiritual Warfare. Ray Beeson. 1988. pap. 6.95 (ISBN 0-8423-5273-2, 75-5273-2). Tyndale.

Real Beneficiaries of Federal Dredging: A Legal, Political & Economic Assessment of the Fifty-Foot Channel for the Port of Baltimore. pap. 4.00 (ISBN 0-943676-00-2). MD Sea Grant Col.

Real Benjamin Franklin. Andrew M. Allison et al. LC 82-70110. (American Classic Ser.). (Illus.). xx, 504p. (Orig.). 1982. 16.95 (ISBN 0-88080-000-3); pap. 13.95 (ISBN 0-88080-001-1). Natl Ctr Constitutional.

Real Billy Sunday. E. P. Brown. 1986. pap. 6.95 (ISBN 0-937931-13-6). Global TN.

Real Blake. Edwin J. Ellis. LC 75-117994. (Studies in Blake, No. 3). 1970. Repr. of 1906 ed. lib. bdg. 54.95x (ISBN 0-8383-1049-4). Haskell.

Real Bosses Don't Say Thank You. Ellen Nevins. (Illus.). 138p. (Orig.). 1983. pap. 4.95 (ISBN 0-914359-00-2). Nevins Pub Co.

Real Brains, Artificial Minds. Ed. by John L. Casti & Anders Karlqvist. 245p. 1987. 48.00 (ISBN 0-444-01155-2). Elsevier.

Real Bread. Maggie Baylis & Coralie Castle. LC 80-21929. (Illus.). 240p. (Orig.). 1980. pap. 7.95 (ISBN 0-89286-179-7). One Hund One Prods.

Real Caruja de Jesus Nazareno de Valldemossa. James Hogg. (Analecta Cartusiana Ser.: No. 41-9). (Illus.). 66p. (Orig., Span.). 1983. pap. 25.00 (ISBN 3-7052-0057-7, Pub by Salzburg Studies). Longwood Pub Group.

Real Cats Don't Do Talk Shows. Mort Gerberg. 96p. (Orig.). 1983. pap. 2.95 (ISBN 0-8431-0747-2). Price Stern.

Real Chant of the Rolling Wheels. Marco Fontoura. Ed. by Jennifer Leach & Fred Reyes. LC 85-70974. Orig. Title: Canto real das rodas rolantes. (Illus.). 130p. (Orig.). 1986. 10.95 (ISBN 0-934169-01-2); pap. 5.95 (ISBN 0-934169-00-4); avail.talk bk. (4 90 minute cassettes) 19.95 (ISBN 0-934169-02-0). Rolling Hse.

Real Character's in the Making. Lorraine Peterson. 150p. 1985. pap. 5.95 (ISBN 0-87123-824-1, 210824). Bethany Hse.

Real Charlotte. E. O. Somerville & MArtin Ross. 352p. (Orig.). pap. 9.95 (ISBN 0-7043-3099-7, Pub. by Quartet Bks). Salem Hse Pubs.

Real Charlotte. Edith O. Somerville & Martin Ross. Ed. by Virginia Beards. 350p. 1986. text ed. 25.00x (ISBN 0-8135-1133-X); pap. text ed. 10.00 (ISBN 0-8135-1134-8). Rutgers U Pr.

Real Chief: The Story of Liam Lynch. Meda Ryan. 144p. (Orig.). 1986. pap. 13.95 (ISBN 0-85342-764-X, Pub. by Mercier Pr Ireland). Irish Bks Media.

Real Christianity. Bailey E. Smith. LC 79-50336. 1980. 9.95 (ISBN 0-8054-5168-4). Broadman.

Real Christianity: Contrasted with the Prevailing Religious System. William Wilberforce. Ed. by James M. Houston. LC 82-8061. (Classics of Faith & Devotion Ser.). 1982. casebound 12.95 (ISBN 0-930014-90-1). Multnomah.

Real Christians. Charles Price. Orig. Title: Christ for Real. 1987. pap. 5.95 (ISBN 0-89109-145-9). NavPress.

Real Christians Don't Dance. John Fischer. 224p. (Orig.). 1988. 10.95 (ISBN 1-55661-010-6). Bethany Hse.

Real Christmas Tree. Ardith Dorrough. 48p. (Orig.). 1983. pap. 2.50 (ISBN 0-88144-020-5, CPS/020). Christian Pub.

Real CIA: An Insider's View of the Strengths & Weaknesses of Our Government's Most Important Agency. Lyman B. Kirkpatrick, Jr. (Encore Edition Ser.). 312p. 1987. Repr. of 1968 ed. 38.50 (ISBN 0-8133-7492-8). Westview.

Real Coke, the Real Story. Thomas Oliver. LC 86-10151. 224p. 1986. 16.95 (ISBN 0-394-55273-3). Random.

Real Coke: The Real Story. Thomas Oliver. 256p. 1987. pap. 4.50 (ISBN 0-14-010408-9). Penguin.

Real Colonel House. A. D. Smith. PLB 59.95 (ISBN 0-8490-0931-6). Gordon Pr.

Real Conflict Between China & Japan: An Analysis of Opposing Ideologies. Harley F. MacNair. (Double-Page Reprint Ser.). pap. 29.00 (ISBN 0-317-29846-1, 2020114). Bks Demand UMI.

Real Conversations. William Archer. LC 72-195438. 1904. lib. bdg. 25.00 (ISBN 0-8414-1199-9). Folcroft.

Real Conversations. 1978. Repr. of 1904 ed. lib. bdg. 25.00 (ISBN 0-8495-0046-X). Arden Lib.

Real Cooking, by George. George Jacobs. 176p. 1986. 14.95 (ISBN 0-940160-32-3). Parnassus Imprints.

Real Cool Killers. Chester Himes. 160p. (Orig.). 1985. 13.95 (ISBN 0-8052-8237-8, Pub. by Allison & Busby England); pap. 5.95 (ISBN 0-8052-8238-6, Pub. by Allison & Busby England). Schocken.

Real Cool Killers. Chester Himes. 5.95 (ISBN 0-394-72039-3). Pantheon.

Real Cool Killers. Chester Himes. (Crime Ser.). 1988. 5.95 (ISBN 0-679-72039-1, Vin). Random.

Real Corvette: An Illustrated History of Chevrolet's Sports Car. Ray Miller & Glenn Embree. LC 75-8100. (The Chevy Chase Ser.: Vol. 3). (Illus.). 320p. 1975. 39.95 (ISBN 0-913056-06-5). Evergreen Pr.

Real Dakota! Dale Gorder et al. (Real States Ser.). (Orig.). 1988. pap. 11.95 (ISBN 0-933025-07-6). Blue Bird Pub.

Real del Monte: A British Mining Venture in Mexico. Robert W. Randall. LC 78-37944. (Latin American Monographs: No. 26). 275p. 1972. 15.95x (ISBN 0-292-77000-6). U of Tex Pr.

Real Disaster Is Above Ground: A Mine Fire & Social Conflict. J. Stephen Kroll-Smith & Stephen R. Couch. 256p. 1989. 24.00 (ISBN 0-8131-1667-8). U Pr of Ky.

Real Dogs Don't Eat Leftovers: A Guide to All That Is Truly Canine. Lee Lorenz. (Illus.). 1983. write for info. S&S.

Real Dreams. Trevor Griffiths. 112p. (Orig.). 1987. pap. 6.95 (ISBN 0-571-14677-5). Faber & Faber.

Real Effects of Stabilization & Structural Adjustment Policies: An Extension of the Australian Adjustment Model. Deepak Lal. (World Bank Staff Working Papers: No. 636). 80p. 1985. 5.00 (ISBN 0-8213-0353-8). World Bank.

Real Eichmann Trial. Paul Rassinier. 170p. 1980. pap. 4.00 (ISBN 0-911038-48-5). Inst Hist Rev.

Real Elliptic Curves. N. L. Alling. (North-Holland Mathematics Studies: Vol. 54). 350p. 1981. 79.00 (ISBN 0-444-86233-1, North-Holland). Elsevier.

Real Estate. 2nd ed. William R. Beaton et al. 1982. text ed. write for info. (ISBN 0-673-16003-3). Scott F.

Real Estate. 8th ed. George F. Bloom et al. LC 81-15933. 738p. 1982. 37.95 (ISBN 0-471-09398-X, Pub. by Wiley Press); tchr's. manual 16.00 (ISBN 0-471-86234-7). Wiley.

Real Estate. Rodney Davis. LC 79-155. (Career Competencies in Marketing). (Illus.). (gr. 11-12). 1979. pap. 12.04 (ISBN 0-07-015672-7). McGraw.

Real Estate. Jane DeLynn. LC 87-29299. 1988. 17.95 (ISBN 0-671-54424-1, Poseidon Pr). PB.

Real Estate. Gary W. Eldred. 480p. text ed. 47.50t scp (ISBN 0-06-041893-1, HarpC). Har-Row.

Real Estate. J. B. Kau & C. F. Sirmans. 816p. 1985. text ed. 40.95 (ISBN 0-07-033306-8). McGraw.

Real Estate. Louise Page. (Methuen New Theatrescripts Ser.). 48p. (Orig.). 1985. pap. 4.95 (ISBN 0-413-57950-6, 9382). Heinemann Ed.

Real Estate. (Taxsaver Ser.). 144p. 1987. 5.95 (ISBN 0-376-07029-3). Sunset-Lane.

Real Estate. I. Edward Weich. (Orig.). 1967. pap. 5.95 (ISBN 0-06-460060-2, CO 60, B&N Bks). Har-Row.

Real Estate. Larry E. Wofford. LC 85-26462. 658p. 1986. write for info. (ISBN 0-471-83885-3). Wiley.

Real Estate - Bienes Raices: A Bilingual Dictionary, Spanish-English & English-Spanish - Un Diccionario Bilingue, Espanol-Ingles y Ingles-Espanol. Compiled by Howard P. Goldstone. LC 85-23736. 136p. 1986. pap. 15.95x (ISBN 0-89950-196-6). McFarland & Co.

Real Estate - The Great American Hoax: How to Survive the Foreclosure Trap. Marilyn Ross & Tom Ross. 300p. 1986. cancelled (ISBN 0-918880-09-2). Comm Creat.

Real Estate: A Bibliography of the Monographic Literature. Ed. by Peter D. Haikalis & Jean K. Freeman. LC 82-23071. xii, 317p. 1983. lib. bdg. 50.95 (ISBN 0-313-23680-1, HAK/). Greenwood.

Real Estate: A Hidden Corporate Asset. American Society of Real Estate Counselors Staff. 1986. 15.00. Am Soc Rec.

Real Estate Accounting & Mathematics Handbook. Robert J. Wiley. LC 80-12990. (Real Estate for Professional Practitioners Ser.). 310p. 1980. 44.95 (ISBN 0-471-04812-7, Pub by Ronald Pr). Wiley.
Real Estate Accounting & Mathematics Handbook. 2nd ed. Robert J. Wiley. 380p. 1987. 52.50 (ISBN 0-471-81681-7). Wiley.
Real Estate Accounting & Reporting Manual. Benedetto Bongiorno & Robert R. Garland. 1983. text ed. 84.00 (ISBN 0-88262-965-4). Warren Gorham & Lamont.
Real Estate Accounting & Reporting: A Guide for Developers, Investors & Lenders. 2nd ed. James J. Klink. LC 85-3194. 248p. 1985. 45.00 (ISBN 0-471-82266-3, Pub. by Ronald Press). Wiley.
Real Estate Advertising. Lawrence J. Danks. LC 82-18541. (Illus.). 298p. 1983. 27.95 (ISBN 0-88462-420-X, 1929-01, Real Estate Ed). Longman Finan.
Real Estate Advertising Handbook. Donald R. Brown & Wendell G. Mathews. Ed. by Helene Berlin. LC 81-51380. (Illus.). 96p. 1981. Repr. of 1980 ed. 9.95 (ISBN 0-686-73397-5, 340). Realtors Natl.
Real Estate after Tax Reform: A Guide for Investors. Martin M. Shenkman. LC 87-2196. 320p. 1987. 19.95 (ISBN 0-471-85984-2). Wiley.
Real Estate Agent. Jack Rudman. (Career Examination Ser.: C-2179). (Cloth bdg. avail. on request). pap. 14.00 (ISBN 0-8373-2179-4). Natl Learning.
Real Estate Agents Guide to the 1981 Revised Colorado Real Estate Commission's Mandatory & Approved Forms (1981) Kent J. Levine. Date not set. price not set. Prof Pubns & Educ.
Real Estate Aide. Jack Rudman. (Career Examination Ser.: C-687). (Cloth bdg. avail. on request). pap. 12.00 (ISBN 0-8373-0687-6). Natl Learning.
Real Estate Almanac. Ed. by Robert D. Allen & Thomas E. Wolfe. LC 80-12417. (Real Estate for Professional Practitioners Ser.). pap. 117.00 (ISBN 0-317-10964-2, 2055413). Bks Demand UMI.
Real Estate: An Introduction to the Profession. 4th ed. Bruce M. Harwood. 1985. pap. text ed. 22.00 (ISBN 0-8359-6492-2, Reston); tchr's. manual avail. P-H.
Real Estate & Construction Lending: A Special Collection from the Journal of Commercial Bank Lending. Ed. by Charlotte Weisman. LC 86-8567. (Illus.). 116p. 1986. pap. text ed. 28.00 (ISBN 0-936742-31-3). Robt Morris Assocs.
Real Estate & Leasing Transactions in the Shadow of Tax Reform. Mortimer M. Caplin & Michael I. Sanders. LC 85-205569. Date not set. price not set (Pub. by Law & Business). HarBraceJ.
Real Estate & the Bankruptcy Code, 1986: Workouts & Bankruptcies. Richard A. Gitlin & Practising Law Institute Staff. LC 87-103470. (Real Estate Law & Practice Course Handbook Ser.: No. 287). 452p. 1986. 45.00 (ISBN 0-317-59122-3, N44467). PLI.
Real Estate & the "Dog" Factors. Albert C. Smith, Jr. Ed. by Albert Smith, III. (Illus., Orig.). Date not set. pap. price not set (000632). Cromwell-Smith.
Real Estate & the Law. Robert N. Corley et al. 453p. 1982. text ed. 30.00 (ISBN 0-394-32546-X, RanC). Random.
Real Estate Appraisal. Jack Friedman et al. 1985. text ed. 24.33 (ISBN 0-8359-6508-2, Reston); instr's. manual avail. (ISBN 0-8359-6509-0). P-H.
Real Estate Appraisal. 2nd ed. Halbert C. Smith & Jerry D. Belloit. LC 86-24520. (Illus.). 341p. 1987. pap. 22.00; 18.50x. Century VII Pub Co.
Real Estate Appraisal Bibliography. American Institute of Real Estate Appraisers. 346p. 1940-1972. 7.00 (ISBN 0-318-15191-X, NO. 21-1017). Natl Assoc Realtors.
Real Estate Appraisal Bibliography, 1945-1972. 436p. 1973. pap. 7.00 (ISBN 0-911780-33-5). Am Inst Real Estate Appraisers.
Real Estate Appraisal Bibliography, 1973-1980. 146p. 1981. pap. 12.50 (ISBN 0-911780-53-X). Am Inst Real Estate Appraisers.
Real Estate Appraisal Terminology. rev ed. Ed. by Byrl N. Boyce. LC 80-23713. 384p. 1981. 32.00x (ISBN 0-88410-597-0). Ballinger Pub.
Real Estate Appraiser. Jack Rudman. (Career Examination Ser.: C-1640). (Cloth bdg. avail. on request). 1988. pap. 12.00 (ISBN 0-8373-1640-5). Natl Learning.
Real Estate Appraising (Step-by-Step) 2nd ed. Paul G. Creteau. LC 73-90006. 1974. 18.00 (ISBN 0-9603372-1-0). Castle Pub Co.
Real Estate Assistant. Jack Rudman. (Career Examination Ser.: C-688). (Cloth bdg. avail. on request). pap. 12.00 (ISBN 0-8373-0688-4). Natl Learning.
Real Estate Bankruptcies & Workouts: A Practical Perspective. Anthony B. Kuklin & Paul E. Roberts. LC 83-72413. (Section of Real Property, Probate & Trust Law, American Bar Association Ser.). vii, 428p. 1983. 48.00 (ISBN 0-89707-117-4, 543-0054). Amer Bar Assn.
Real Estate Book. rev. ed. Robert L. Nessen. 1983. pap. 4.50 (ISBN 0-451-14096-6, Sig). NAL.
Real Estate Bookkeeper's Guide to ADP. James A. Young. Date not set. pap. text ed. 14.95 (ISBN 0-935351-05-1). Gross Johnson.
Real Estate Books & Periodicals in Print: A Guide to Real Estate Publications, Their Authors, Prices, Publishers' Addresses & Other Bibliographic Data. John R. Johnsich. 1977. 19.95 (ISBN 0-914256-07-6); pap. 15.95 (ISBN 0-914256-08-4). Real Estate Pub.
Real Estate Books & Periodicals in Print: A Guide to Real Estate Publications, Their Authors, Prices, Publishers' Addresses & Other Bibliographic Data. John. R. Johnsich. (Orig.). 1982. pap. 19.95 (ISBN 0-914256-15-7). Real Estate Pub.
Real Estate Books & Periodicals in Print: A Guide to Real Estate Publications, Their Authors, Prices, Publishers Addresses & Other Bibliographic Data. John R. Johnsich. 168p. 1988. pap. 29.95x (ISBN 0-914256-19-X). Real Estate Pub.
Real Estate Books & Periodicals in Print: 1978-79 Supplement. John R. Johnsich. 1979. pap. 9.95 (ISBN 0-914256-10-6). Real Estate Pub.
Real Estate Books & Periodicals in Print: 1984-85 Supplement. John R. Johnsich. (Orig.). 1984. pap. 9.95 (ISBN 0-914256-16-5). Real Estate Pub.
Real Estate Broker. Jack Rudman. (Career Examination Ser.: C-666). (Cloth bdg. avail. on request). pap. 15.00 (ISBN 0-8373-0666-3). Natl Learning.
Real Estate Broker (REB) Jack Rudman. (Admission Test Ser.: ATS-3). 300p. (Cloth bdg. avail. on request). pap. 15.00 (ISBN 0-8373-5003-4). Natl Learning.
Real Estate Brokerage. Bruce Lindeman. 450p. 1981. text ed. 27.00 (ISBN 0-8359-6517-1, Reston); instr's. manual o.p. avail. (ISBN 0-8359-6518-X). P-H.
Real Estate Brokerage: A Success Guide. John Cyr & Joan Sobeck. 336p. 1982. 29.95 (ISBN 0-88462-359-9, 1965-01, Real Estate Ed). Longman Finan.
Real Estate Brokerage: A Success Guide. 2nd ed. John Cyr & Joan Sobeck. 1987. pap. 31.95 (ISBN 0-88462-674-1, Real Estate Ed); pap. text ed. 22.95 (ISBN 0-317-68001-3). Longman Finan.
Real Estate Brokerage: A Systems Approach. 2nd ed. Fred E. Case. (Illus.). 416p. 1982. 36.33 (ISBN 0-13-762344-5). P-H.
Real Estate Brokerage in the Eighties: Survival among the Giants. Thomas W. Dooley. 1980. 18.95 (ISBN 0-88462-364-5, 1978-01, Real Estate Ed). Longman Finan.
Real Estate Brokerage Law. Arthur R. Gaudio. 400p. 1986. text ed. write for info. (ISBN 0-314-31298-6). West Pub.
Real Estate Brokerage: Law & Practice, 1 vol. Patrick Rohan et al. (Real Estate Transactions Ser.). 1985. Updates avail. looseleaf 85.00 (486). Bender.
Real Estate Broker's Guide to Resort Timesharing. Richard Lynge & Keith W. Trowbridge. LC 83-19239. 256p. 1983. 24.95 (ISBN 0-88462-442-0, 1965-03, Real Estate Ed). Longman Finan.
Real Estate Buying - Selling Guide for Washington. 3rd ed. Charles J. Covello. (Illus.). 96p. 1987. pap. 6.95 (ISBN 0-88908-734-2). ISC Pr.
Real Estate: Buying a House or Condo. 2nd ed. HALT Staff. (Citizens Legal Manual Ser.). 150p. 1986. pap. text ed. write for info. (ISBN 0-910073-09-0). HALT DC.
Real Estate Buying-Selling Guide for Alberta. 4th ed. George C. Stewart. 159p. 1985. 7.95 (ISBN 0-88908-238-3). ISC Pr.
Real Estate Buying-Selling Guide for Ontario. 7th ed. Stanley M. Rose. 224p. 1987. 8.50 (ISBN 0-88908-364-9). ISC Pr.
Real Estate Buying-Selling Guide for Oregon. Fred A. Granata. 111p. 1980. 3.95 (ISBN 0-88908-809-8). ISC Pr.
Real Estate Buying-Selling Guide for British Columbia. 8th ed. E. Syberg-Olsen. 204p. 1986. 7.95 (ISBN 0-88908-199-9). ISC Pr.
Real Estate by Yourself. J. James Hasenau. LC 80-85022. (Illus.). 1985. pap. 12.95 (ISBN 0-913042-12-9). Holland Hse Pr.
Real Estate Closing Procedures (1983) Mark Gruber et al. LC 84-153773. 1985. 25.00. NJ Inst CLE.
Real Estate Closings. 2nd ed. Robert E. Schreiner & Robert E. Schreiner, Jr. LC 83-161974. (Illus.). 344p. 1983. text ed. 35.00x (ISBN 0-9618320-1-0). R E Schreiner.
Real Estate Closings. 2nd ed. Raymond J. Werner. 317p. 1988. text ed. 75.00 (N1-1360). PLI.
Real Estate Contracts. Robert E. Schreiner & Robert E. Schreiner, Jr. LC 87-90696. (Illus.). 200p. (Orig.). 1987. pap. text ed. 14.95 (ISBN 0-9618320-0-2). R E Schreiner.
Real Estate Contracts with 1987 Supplement. Karl B. Holtzschue. 333p. 1987. text ed. 60.00 (ISBN 0-317-52200-0, N6-1542). PLI.
Real Estate Coordinator, 8 vols. ann. sub. 522.00. Res Inst Am.
Real Estate Counseling. American Society of Real Estate Counselors Staff. (Illus.). 352p. 1984. text ed. 27.95 (ISBN 0-686-90138-X). P-H.
Real Estate Counseling. American Society of Real Estate Counselors Staff. 316p. 30.00 (ISBN 0-318-19108-3). Am Soc REC.
Real Estate Data: Your Market & Your Firm. George D. Herman. LC 80-18126. (Illus.). 197p. (Orig.). 1980. pap. 16.95 (ISBN 0-913652-23-7). Realtors Natl.
Real Estate Debt Financing. M. A. Hines. LC 87-6200. (Real Estate for Professional Practitioners Ser.). 405p. 1987. 45.00 (ISBN 0-471-85493-X). Wiley.
Real Estate Decision Making Using VisiCalc. Austin J. Jaffe. 1985. pap. cancelled (ISBN 0-8359-6501-5, Reston). P-H.
Real Estate Development & Construction Financing 1986. 721p. 1986. 45.00 (N4-4452). PLI.
Real Estate Development & Construction Financing, 1988. Charles Zalaznick. 788p. 1988. pap. 45.00 (N4-4485). PLI.
Real Estate Development: Business, Commercial, Industrial, & Major Residential Properties, 4 vols, No. 570. J. E. Resende et al. 1987. 360.00 (ISBN 0-317-67052-2). Bender.
Real Estate Development: Financing, Syndication & Business Aspects. Jarchow. 1988. price not set (ISBN 0-471-83742-3). Wiley.
Real Estate Development Syndication. Joseph T. Howell. LC 83-17764. 254p. 1983. 35.00 (ISBN 0-275-91010-5, C1010). Praeger.
Real Estate Dictionary. 4th ed. John Talamo. 192p. 1979. pap. 7.50 (ISBN 0-87600-510-5). Finan Pub.
Real Estate Dictionary. Michael C. Thomsett. LC 87-43196. 232p. 1988. 29.95x (ISBN 0-89950-321-7). McFarland & Co.
Real Estate Dictionary & Reference Guide. Rev. ed. Samuel V. Abraham. Ed. by S. Michele McFadden & Roberta Wilson-Fulkerson. LC 79-9761. 1987. pap. text ed. 6.95x (ISBN 0-89262-059-5). Career Pub.
Real Estate Dictionary of Terms & Definitions. John R. Johnsich. (Orig.). 1973. 8.95 (ISBN 0-914256-00-9). Real Estate Pub.
Real Estate Education Company Real Estate Exam Manual. 3rd ed. Douglas C. Smith & John T. Gibbons. (Illus.). 216p. 1984. pap. 19.95 (ISBN 0-88462-490-0, 1970-01, Real Estate Ed). Longman Finan.
Real Estate Education Company Real Estate Exam Manual. 4th ed. Douglas C. Smith & John T. Gibbons. 1987. pap. 19.95 (ISBN 0-88462-692-X, Real Estate Ed); pap. text ed. 14.95 (ISBN 0-317-68002-1). Longman Finan.
Real Estate Encyclopedia of Home Design, Construction, & Architecture. Leonard Kleeman. LC 80-17891. 330p. 1981. 29.95 (ISBN 0-13-762542-1, Parker). P-H.
Real Estate Ethics. William Pivar. 1979. pap. 9.25 (ISBN 0-88462-371-8, 1966-01, Real Estate Ed). Longman Finan.
Real Estate Exam Ready Book. 2nd ed. Ed Willer. 200p. 1985. pap. 24.50 (ISBN 0-9614931-1-9). Willer.
Real Estate Exchange & Acquisition Techniques. William T. Tappan. 1982. pap. 14.95 (ISBN 0-13-762567-7, Reward). P-H.
Real Estate Exchange Counseling. Robert L. Simpson. 1983. text ed. 28.67 (ISBN 0-8359-6511-2, Reston). P-H.
Real Estate Exchanges. Mark L. Levine. Ed. by Pat Allen. LC 81-50724. 622p. 1981. 24.95 (ISBN 0-913652-27-X, BK 143); members 19.96. Realtors Natl.
Real Estate Exchanges & Non-Tax Considerations (1981) Mark L. Levine. 1987. write for info. Prof Pubns & Educ.
Real Estate Exchanges, Taxation & Investment; a Systems Approach. Harley J. Smith. (Illus.). 1977. perfect bdg. 29.95x (ISBN 0-685-64690-4). Harley Smith Invest.
Real Estate Farming: Campaign for Success. Pauline J. Thompson. LC 85-14878. (Orig.). 1985. pap. 12.95 (ISBN 0-918785-01-4). Kricket.
Real Estate Finance. 2nd ed. William R. Beaton. (Illus.). 480p. 1982. text ed. write for info. (ISBN 0-13-762716-5). P-H.
Real Estate Finance. 8th ed. William Brueggeman & Leo D. Stone. 1989. 37.95x (ISBN 0-256-03033-2). Irwin.
Real Estate Finance. 2nd ed. Michael R. Buchanan & Ronald D. Johnson. (Illus.). 522p. 1988. text ed. 45.00 (ISBN 0-89982-351-3). Am Bankers.
Real Estate Finance. Jerome Dasso & Gerald W. Kuhn. (Illus.). 464p. 1983. write for info. (ISBN 0-13-762757-2). P-H.
Real Estate Finance. Ross H. Johnson & Thomas P. Henderson. 464p. 1985. text ed. 35.95 (ISBN 0-675-20195-0). Additional supplements may be obtained from publisher. Merrill.
Real Estate Finance. Sherman J. Maisel. (Illus.). 450p. 1987. text ed. write for info. (ISBN 0-15-575847-0); instr's. manual 2.00 (ISBN 0-15-575849-7). HarBraceJ.
Real Estate Finance. Sherman J. Maisel. 570p. 1987. text ed. 29.00 net (ISBN 0-317-59189-4, HC); instr's. manual avail. HarBraceJ.
Real Estate Finance. 1976. 27.00 (ISBN 0-89982-063-8, 057200); members 18.00; instr's. manual 6.50 (257200); members 3.00. Am Bankers.
Real Estate Finance. William M. Shenkel. 1988. 33.95 (ISBN 0-256-02206-2); pap. 15.95. Business Pubns.
Real Estate Finance. C. F. Sirmans. 448p. 1985. text ed. 36.95 (ISBN 0-07-057693-9). McGraw.
Real Estate Finance. 2nd ed. C. F. Sirmans. (Illus.). 480p. 1988. 36.95 (ISBN 0-07-057698-X). McGraw.
Real Estate Finance. 2nd ed. Maurice A. Unger & Ronald W. Melicher. 1984. text ed. write for info. (ISBN 0-538-19630-0, S63). SW Pub.
Real Estate Finance. Arthur Warner et al. 1985. text ed. 25.95 (ISBN 0-8359-6565-1, Reston); instr's. manual avail. (ISBN 0-8359-6566-X). P-H.
Real Estate Finance. 5th ed. John P. Weidemer. (Illus.). 384p. 1987. text ed. 28.00 (ISBN 0-13-762774-2). P-H.
Real Estate Finance: A Practical Approach. Tom Morton. 1983. text ed. write for info. (ISBN 0-673-16580-9). Scott F.
Real Estate Finance & Investment Tables. Jack P. Friedman & Peggy Pearson. 1983. text ed. 32.00 (ISBN 0-8359-6525-2, Reston). P-H.
Real Estate Finance & Syndication Form Book. Samuel K. Freshman. 1980. write for info. S K Freshman.
Real Estate Finance in a Nutshell. 2nd ed. John W. Bruce. (Nutshell Ser.). 300p. 1985. pap. text ed. 8.95 (ISBN 0-314-85866-0). West Pub.
Real Estate Finance in California. 2nd ed. Douglas M. Temple. 1981. text ed. write for info. (ISBN 0-673-16524-8). Scott F.
Real Estate Finance Law. 2nd ed. Grant S. Nelson & Dale A. Whitman. LC 85-13660. (Hornbook Ser.). 941p. 1985. text ed. 24.95 lawyer's ed. (ISBN 0-314-91411-0); text ed. write for info. student ed. (ISBN 0-314-91412-9). West Pub.
Real Estate Financial Feasibility Analysis Handbook & Workbook. James C. Canestano. 280p. 1982. Set. 25.00 (ISBN 0-318-03322-4); wkbk. (ISBN 0-936954-04-3); handbk. (ISBN 0-936954-05-1). Natl Assoc Realtors.
Real Estate Financing. Frederick E. Case & John M. Clapp. LC 77-27938. 417p. 1978. tchr's. manual 8.00 (ISBN 0-471-04411-3). Wiley.
Real Estate Financing. Massachusetts Continuing Legal Education Inc. & American Law Institute-American Bar Association Committee for Continuing Professional Education. LC 87-107439. (ALI-ABA Course of Study Materials Ser.). Date not set. price not set. Am Law Inst.
Real Estate Financing: Business, Tax & Accounting Considerations. Ross. (Wiley Tax & Business Guides for Professionals Ser.). 1988. write for info. (ISBN 0-471-81973-5). Wiley.
Real Estate Financing Forms Manual with Commentary. Koppel Douglas. 1985. 72.00 (ISBN 0-88712-443-7). Warren Gorham & Lamont.
Real Estate Financing Manual: a Guide to Money-Making Strategies: Complete Guide to Real Estate Financing. Jack Cummings. 530p. 1987. 49.95 (ISBN 0-13-763418-8). P-H.
Real Estate Financing Manual: A Guide to Money Making Strategies. Jack Cummings. (Illus.). 458p. 1988. pap. 18.95 (ISBN 0-13-762535-9, Busn). P-H.
Real Estate Financing: Text, Forms, Tax Analysis, 6 vols. Patrick J. Rohan. (Real Estate Transactions Ser.). 1973. Set. looseleaf 420.00 (592); Updates 1985. 262.50; Supplement 1986. 350.00. Bender.
Real Estate Folio. ALI-ABA Committee on Continuing Professional Education. LC 84-73129. (Illus.). 121p. Date not set. price not set. Am Law Inst.
Real Estate for Income & Profit: How You Can Stop Working for a Living & Make Living Work for You. David G. Darby. LC 74-84503. (Illus.). 203p. (Orig.). 1974. pap. 14.95 (ISBN 0-915512-01-7). M-L Pub.
Real Estate Foreclosures. National Business Institute Staff. LC 86-232912. (Illus.). 1987. 30.00. Natl Busn Inst.
Real Estate Forms & How to Master Them. Ed Beckley. 103p. 1985. 29.95 (ISBN 0-933623-03-8). Midwest Finan Pubns.
Real Estate Forms Approved for Colorado. Robert E. Schreiner & Robert E. Schreiner, Jr. LC 86-190261. (Illus.). 344p. 1986. text ed. 27.00x (ISBN 0-9618320-2-9). R E Schreiner.
Real Estate Forms from American Law Institute Course Materials. 650p. 1983. looseleaf 70.00 (ISBN 0-686-40801-2, F301); Looseleaf supplement, 1984. 40.00 (F303); F305, 250p. loose leaf, 1985 60.00; looseleaf, 1987, 158 p. 65.00 (F307). Am Law Inst.
Real Estate Fundamentals. 2nd ed. Wade E. Gaddy, Jr. & Robert E. Hart. 372p. (Orig.). 1984. pap. text ed. 22.50 (ISBN 0-88462-506-0, 1513-01, Real Estate Ed). Longman Finan.
Real Estate Fundamentals. Mark L. Levine. write for info. Prof Pubns & Educ.
Real Estate Fundamentals. Mark L. Levine. LC 76-3508. pap. 110.00 (ISBN 0-317-20531-5, 2022843). Bks Demand UMI.
Real Estate Gamble: Lessons From Fifty Years of Boom & Bust. Alan Rabinowitz. LC 80-65706. pap. 80.00 (ISBN 0-317-26698-5, 2023508). Bks Demand UMI.
Real Estate Game & How to Win It. Jim Randel. LC 85-25277. 224p. 1986. 17.95 (ISBN 0-8160-1693-3); pap. 9.95 (ISBN 0-8160-1791-3). Facts on File.
Real Estate Guide. Prentice-Hall Editorial Staff. 1966. 131.50 (ISBN 0-13-762740-8). P-H.
Real Estate Guide to Microcomputers. Christopher B. Reade. (Guides to Microcomputing Ser.). (Illus.). 300p. Date not set. pap. cancelled (ISBN 0-88462-606-7, 1302-02, Pub. by Longman Fin. Serv. Pub.). Longman Finan.

Real Estate, Securities & Syndication Picture Dictionary. Edward Hooper & Darlene Hooper. LC 84-90432. (Illus.). 350p. (Orig.). 1984. pap. 18.95 (ISBN 0-9613648-0-7). Hooper Pub Co.

Real Estate Securities & Title Insurance Terminology. Intro. By John R. Johnsich. (Orig.). 1980. pap. 3.95 (ISBN 0-914256-12-2). Real Estate Pub.

Real Estate Securities (1985) Mark L. Levine. Date not set. write for info. Prof Pubns & Educ.

Real Estate Selling Magic. rev. ed. Gael Himmah. 234p. 1982. 18.00 (ISBN 0-9600488-2-0). Gael Himmah Pub.

Real Estate Settlement Costs. rev. ed. 48p. 1987. 2.50 (5285). Commerce.

Real Estate Settlement Costs: Effective July 1, 1983. 48p. pap. 2.50 (ISBN 0-317-04294-7, 4896). Commerce.

Real Estate Software Guidelines: Property Management. Institute of Real Estate Management & National Association of Realtors. LC 83-83110. (Real Estate Software Guidelines Ser.). (Illus.). 145p. 1984. looseleaf 36.95 (ISBN 0-912104-75-9). Inst Real Estate.

Real Estate Success Habits: A Five Week Career Guide. Talova L. Jones. LC 84-51045. 210p. 1984. pap. 29.95 (ISBN 0-918365-00-7). T L C.

Real Estate Syndication: A Manual for Practitoners & Participants. Robert Newson & Charles Muse. 208p. 1983. pap. text ed. 20.95 (ISBN 0-8403-2973-3). Kendall-Hunt.

Real Estate Syndication: A Selected Bibliography of Articles, Books & Serials. Nathan A. Rosen. (Public Administration Ser.: P 1796). 20p. 1985. 3.00 (ISBN 0-89028-596-9). Vance Biblios.

Real Estate Syndication Manual. Alvin Arnold. 1984. 86.00 (ISBN 0-88712-176-4). Warren Gorham & Lamont.

Real Estate Syndication: Securitization after Tax Reform. 2nd ed. Stephen P. Jarchow. LC 87-37187. (Tax & Business Guides for Professionals Ser.). 1988. 95.00 (ISBN 0-471-63572-3). Wiley.

Real Estate Syndication under the 1984 Tax Act. 35.00 (ISBN 0-317-29638-8, #CO3190, Law & Business). HarBraceJ.

Real Estate Syndications. Pennsylvania Bar Institute. 438p. 1985. 40.00 (ISBN 0-318-19070-2, 293). PA Bar Inst.

Real Estate Syndications: Law, Practice & Forms, 2 vols. Patrick J. Rohan & B. Harrison Franchel. (Real Estate Transactions Ser.). 1985. Updates avail. looseleaf set 170.00 (587). Bender.

Real Estate Syndications 1986: Current techniques and investments vehicles, 2 vols. Practising Law Institute. 1986. pap. 45.00 (N4-4456). PLI.

Real Estate Syndicator's Handbook. Charles Klotsche. LC 85-8319. 360p. 1985. 39.95 (ISBN 0-13-766452-4). P-H.

Real Estate Tax Appeals: Law, Practice & Forms, 3 vols. Patrick J. Rohan. (Real Estate Transaction Ser.). 1984. Set, updates avail. looseleaf 230.00 (575). Bender.

Real Estate Tax Appeals: Law, Practice & Forms, 3 vols, Vols. 8,8A,8B. Patrick J. Rohan. 1984. write for info. (NO. 575). Bender.

Real Estate Tax Digest. Marvin B. Starr. 1983. Updates avail. 155.00 (ISBN 0-317-37694-2, 581); Annual Renewal. 140.00 (ISBN 0-317-37695-0). Bender.

Real Estate Tax Digest: Federal Income, Estate & Gift Taxes. James A. Douglas et al. LC 83-51782. 1984. 78.00 (ISBN 0-88712-008-3). Warren Gorham & Lamont.

Real Estate Tax Exemption for Continuing Education. A. N. Charters. LC 76-189508. (Occasional Paper Ser.: No. 26). 1972. pap. 2.00 (ISBN 0-87060-049-4, OCP 26). Syracuse U Cont Ed.

Real Estate Tax Law after 1986: Unscrambling the Tax Reform Act of 1986. George M. Yeiter. Ed. by Marie-Louise Crozat. (Illus.). 145p. (Orig.). 1987. pap. 24.95 (ISBN 0-942037-16-2). Win Pubs.

Real Estate Tax Problems II. Gary E. Friedman & Robert H. Lipsey. LC 85-214098. (Illus.). 1985. write for info. Am Inst CPA.

Real Estate Tax Reduction Manual. Irving Lew. 137p. 1961. pap. 15.00 (ISBN 0-686-63209-5). Battery Pk.

Real Estate Tax Shelter Deskbook. Mark L. Levine. 1982. 50.00 (ISBN 0-318-02242-7). Prof Pubns & Educ.

Real Estate Tax Update Outline (1987) Mark L. Levine. write for info. Prof Pubns & Educ.

Real Estate Taxation, Tax Problems & Tax Clauses (1978) Mark L. Levine. 1978. Prof Pubns & Educ.

Real Estate Taxes & Abatements Handbook. Robert L. Marzelli. 301p. 1980. 29.50 (ISBN 0-318-03671-1). Lawyers Weekly.

Real Estate Taxes - The Basics - Planning for Depreciation & Investment Tax Credits. Martin M. Shenkman & International Council of Shopping Centers. LC 83-22780. 64.00 (ISBN 0-913598-34-8, 573); members 32.00. Intl Coun Shop.

Real Estate: The Best Game in Town. Wade B. Cook. 143p. (Orig.). pap. 11.95 (ISBN 0-910019-10-X). Regency Bks.

Real Estate: The Most Successful Real Estate Listing & Selling Techniques. Intro. by John R. Johnsich. 1979. pap. 9.95 (ISBN 0-914256-09-2). Real Estate Pub.

Real Estate: The Ultimate Handbook. Andrew J. McLean. (Illus.). 160p. 1981. pap. 7.95 (ISBN 0-8092-5703-3). Contemp Bks.

Real Estate Timesharing & the Property Tax. Ed. by Stuart M. Bloch. (Monograph: No. 85-4). (Illus.). 103p. 1985. pap. text ed. 15.00 (ISBN 0-318-04692-X). Lincoln Inst Land.

Real Estate Title Matters. 397p. 1984. 17.00 (ISBN 0-318-02434-9). ICLE Georgia.

Real Estate Titles. New York State Bar Association Staff. Ed. by James M. Pedowitz. (Illus.). 877p. 1984. 55.00 (ISBN 0-942954-04-1). NYS Bar.

Real Estate Transactions Answer Book. 1986. 45.00 (ISBN 0-916592-63-4). Panel Pubs.

Real Estate Transactions: Cases & Materials on Land Transfer, Development & Finance; Statute, Form & Problem Supplement. 2nd ed. Paul Goldstein. (University Casebook Ser.). 164p. pap. 6.95 (ISBN 0-88277-264-3). Foundation Pr.

Real Estate Transactions, Cases & Materials on Land Transfer, Development & Finance, 1988. Paul Goldstein. (University Casebook Ser.). 1988. text ed. write for info. (ISBN 0-88277-665-7). Foundation Pr.

Real Estate Transactions: Cases & Materials on the Transfer Development & Finance. 2nd ed. Paul Goldstein. LC 85-10335. (University Casebook Ser.). 937p. 1985. text ed. 32.00 (ISBN 0-88277-248-1); write for info. (ISBN 0-88277-276-7). Foundation Pr.

Real Estate Transactions from Kish. Henry F. Lutz. LC 32-813. (University of California Publications in Semitic Philology: Vol. 10, No. 3). pap. 20.00 (ISBN 0-317-10207-9, 2021474). Bks Demand UMI.

Real Estate Transactions, Statutes, Form & Problem Supplement, 1988 Edition. Paul Goldstein. (University Casebook Ser.). 1988. pap. text ed. write for info. (ISBN 0-88277-683-5). Foundation Pr.

Real Estate Transactions, Tax Planning & Consequences Edition, 1988. Mark L. Levine. (West's Handbook Ser.). 1200p. 1988. pap. text ed. write for info. (ISBN 0-314-43044-X). West Pub.

Real Estate Transactions, Tax Planning & Consequences: 1987 Edition. Mark L. Levine. 1227p. 1987. pap. text ed. write for info. (ISBN 0-314-40359-0). West Pub.

Real Estate Transactions, Tax Planning (1987) Mark L. Levine. 1987. write for info. Prof Pubns & Educ.

Real Estate Transfer Deeds in Novgorod 1609-1616: Text & Commentary. Ingegerd Nordlander. (Stockholm Slavic Studies: No. 18). 171p. (Orig.). 1987. pap. text ed. 24.00 (ISBN 91-22-00857-8, Pub. by Almqvist & Wiksell). Coronet Bks.

Real Estate Transfer, Finance & Development: Cases & Materials. 3rd ed. Grant S. Nelson & Dale A. Whitman. (American Casebook Ser.). 1173p. 1987. text ed. 35.95 (ISBN 0-314-35161-2). West Pub.

Real Estate Turnaround. Craig Hall. 1982. pap. 7.95 (ISBN 0-13-765826-5, Reward). P-H.

Real Estate Turnaround Formulas. Dave Glubetich. Ed. by Barbara Bennett. 1985. pap. 49.00 (ISBN 0-930187-00-8). Impact Pub.

Real Estate Valuation Colloquim, 1984: A Redefinition of Real Estate Appraisal Precepts & Processes. Ed. by William N. Kinnard, Jr. LC 86-1388. (Lincoln Institute of Land Policy-OG & H Ser.). (Illus.). 401p. 1987. text ed. 40.00x (ISBN 0-89946-225-1, 225-1). Oelgeschlager.

Real Estate Valuation in Litigation. James D. Eaton. 489p. 1982. 32.50 (ISBN 0-911780-65-3). Am Inst Real Estate Appraisers.

Real Estate Values & You. Howard F. Jackson, Jr. LC 86-81729. 280p. 1986. pap. 19.95 (ISBN 0-9617001-0-6). Innovative Pub.

Real Estate Valuing, Counseling, Forecasting: Selected Writings of John Robert White. John R. White. 275p. 1984. 17.50 (ISBN 0-911780-72-6). Am Inst Real Estate Appraisers.

Real Estate Wealth Building Opportunities. Bernard H. Porter. 1986. 42.50 (ISBN 0-911156-48-8). Bern Porter.

Real Estate Wealth Building Opportunities. 1987. lib. bdg. 79.95 (ISBN 0-8490-3879-0). Gordon Pr.

Real Estate Wealth Building Opportunities. Russ Von Hoelscher. 357p. 1984. 14.95 (ISBN 0-940398-09-5). Profit Ideas.

Real Evangelism. Bailey E. Smith. LC 77-92283. 1978. 8.95 (ISBN 0-8054-6220-1). Broadman.

Real-Exchange-Rate Variability from 1920-1926 & 1973-1982. Paul De Grauwe et al. (Princeton Studies in International Finance: No. 56). 1985. pap. text ed. 6.50x (ISBN 0-88165-228-8). Princeton U Int Finan Econ.

Real Facts about Ethiopia. J. A. Rogers. (Illus.). 34p. 1982. pap. 3.00 (ISBN 0-933121-07-5). Black Classic.

Real Faith. Kenneth E. Hagin. 1970. pap. 1.00 (ISBN 0-89276-017-6). Hagin Ministries.

Real Faith: One of the Classic Faith-Builders. Charles S. Price. 125p. 1972. pap. 5.95 (ISBN 0-88270-000-6). Bridge Pub.

Real Family Stories. Anne Turyn. (Illus.). 24p. (Orig.). 1982. pap. 3.00 (ISBN 0-917061-13-6). Top Stories.

Real Fiction. Telfer Stokes & Helen Douglas. 144p. 1987. pap. 20.00 (ISBN 0-89822-052-1). Visual Studies.

Real-Financial Linkages among Open Economies. Ed. by Sven W. Arndt & J. David Richardson. 216p. 1987. 27.50x (ISBN 0-262-01096-8). MIT Pr.

Real for Sure Sister. Ann Angel. LC 87-29217. (Illus.). 72p. (gr. 3-6). 1988. 12.95 (ISBN 0-9609504-7-8). Perspect Indiana.

Real Francis Bacon. Brian Bevan. 1983. 50.00x (ISBN 0-900000-67-8, Pub. by Centaur Bks). State Mutual Bk.

Real Friends: Becoming the Friend You'd Like to Have. Barbara B. Varenhorst. LC 82-48412. (Illus.). 160p. (Orig.). 1983. pap. 8.95 (ISBN 0-06-250890-3, CN4048, HarpR). Har-Row.

Real Functions. B. S. Thomson. (Lecture Notes in Mathematics Ser.: Vol. 1170). vii, 229p. 1985. pap. 16.00 (ISBN 0-387-16058-2). Springer-Verlag.

Real George Washington. Andrew M. Allison et al. (American Classic Ser.). (Illus.). 950p. 1988. 17.95 (ISBN 0-88080-013-5); pap. 14.95 (ISBN 0-88080-014-3). Natl Ctr Constitutional.

Real Ghosts. Daniel Cohen. (Illus.). 128p. (gr. 4 up). 1984. pap. 2.50 (ISBN 0-671-62670-1). Archway.

Real Ghosts Don't Wear Sheets. Don W. Farrant. (Illus.). 80p. (Orig.). pap. 7.00 (ISBN 0-935604-02-2). Ivystone.

Real Happily Ever after Book: The Kids' Stuff People. LC 80-80256. (Illus.). (gr. k-3). 1980. pap. 7.95 (ISBN 0-913916-66-8, IP 66-8). Incentive Pubns.

Real Hawaii: Its History & Present Conditions Including the True Story of the Revolution. Lucien Young. LC 77-111760. (American Imperialism: Viewpoints of United States Foreign Policy, 1898-1941). 1970. Repr. of 1899 ed. 23.50 (ISBN 0-405-02054-6). Ayer Co Pubs.

Real History of the Rosicrucians, Vol. 20. Arthur E. Waite. LC 76-53632. (Spiritual Science Library). (Illus.). 456p. 1982. lib. bdg. 25.00 (ISBN 0-89345-018-9); pap. 15.00 (ISBN 0-89345-019-7). Garber Comm.

Real Hole. rev. ed. Beverly Cleary. (Illus.). (ps-1). 1986. PLB 10.88 (ISBN 0-688-05851-5); pap. 10.25 (ISBN 0-688-05850-7). Morrow.

Real Hole. Beverly Cleary. (gr. k-6). 1987. pap. 3.95 (ISBN 0-440-47521-X, YB). Dell.

Real Illusions. Russell Haley. LC 84-14866. 132p. 1985. pap. 7.95 (ISBN 0-8112-0929-6, NDP586). New Directions.

Real in the Ideal: Berkeley's Relation to Kant. Ed. by George Pitcher. (Philosophy of George Berkeley Ser.). 315p. 1988. lib. bdg. 50.00 (ISBN 0-8240-2447-8). Garland Pub.

Real Inspector Hound & after Magritte. Tom Stoppard. 1969. pap. 7.95 (ISBN 0-394-17313-9, E489, Ever). Grove.

Real Ireland. Liam Blake & Brendan Kennelly. LC 84-10625. (Illus.). 1988. pap. 12.95 (ISBN 0-87701-507-4). Chronicle Bks.

Real Is Not the Rational. Joan Stambaugh. LC 85-14673. (Buddhist Studies). 130p. (Orig.). 1986. 49.50 (ISBN 0-88706-166-4); pap. 16.95 (ISBN 0-88706-167-2). State U NY Pr.

Real Issue. William A. White. LC 72-98603. (Short Story Index Reprint Ser.). 1896. 17.00 (ISBN 0-8369-3177-7). Ayer Co Pubs.

Real Italians: A Study of European Psychology. Carlo Sforza. LC 42-14340. Repr. of 1942 ed. 14.50 (ISBN 0-404-05758-6). AMS Pr.

Real Japanese Question. Kiyoshi K. Kawakami. Ed. by Roger Daniels. LC 78-54819. (Asian Experience in North America Ser.). 1979. Repr. of 1921 ed. lib. bdg. 20.00x (ISBN 0-405-11275-0). Ayer Co Pubs.

Real Jazz. Hugues Panassie. LC 73-13328. 284p. 1973. Repr. of 1960 ed. lib. bdg. 35.00 (ISBN 0-8371-7123-7, PARJ). Greenwood.

Real Jewish World: A Rabbi's Second Thoughts. Stuart E. Rosenberg. LC 83-17455. 434p. 1984. 19.95 (ISBN 0-8022-2439-3). Philos Lib.

Real Job for You: An Employment Guide for Teens. Rose P. Lee. LC 85-1233. (Illus.). 128p. (YA) (gr. 9 up). 1985. pap. 7.95 (ISBN 0-932620-45-0). Betterway Pubns.

Real Jobs for Real People. Benjamin Piltch. (Illus.). 64p. (gr. 3). Date not set. pap. text ed. 3.75 (ISBN 0-88323-246-4, 208); tchr's. key 1.25 (263). Richards Pub.

Real Lace: America's Irish Rich. Stephen Birmingham. 288p. 1986. pap. 3.95 (ISBN 0-425-08789-1). Berkley Pub.

Real Lies. Craig Mcgregor. LC 87-10770. 126p. (Orig.). 1987. pap. 8.95 (ISBN 0-7022-2088-4). U of Queensland Pr.

Real Life. Kitty B. Florey. LC 85-10605. 256p. 1986. 15.95 (ISBN 0-688-06081-1). Morrow.

Real Life. Kitty B. Florey. 320p. Date not set. pap. 3.95 (ISBN 0-451-40029-1, Onyx). NAL.

Real Life Christianity. Andrew Knowles. (Manuals Ser.). 128p. (Orig.). Date not set. pap. 6.95 (ISBN 0-85648-565-9). Lion USA.

Real Life Christianity Workbook. Andrew Knowles. (Manuals Ser.). 32p. (Orig.). Date not set. pap. 1.95 (ISBN 0-85648-853-4). Lion USA.

Real Life Guide for the Second Time Bride. Anita T. Williams. (Illus.). 172p. 1988. pap. 11.95 (ISBN 0-945633-00-9). Bounty Pr Inc.

Real Life: Louisville in the Twenties. Michael Lesy. LC 76-9977. 1976. pap. 7.95 (ISBN 0-394-73235-9). Pantheon.

Real Life of Alejandro Mayta. Mario V. LLosa. LC 86-40169. 320p. 1986. pap. 6.95 (ISBN 0-394-74776-3, Vin). Random.

Real Life of Alejandro Mayta. Mario Vargas-Llosa. Tr. by Alfred M. Adam. 310p. 1986. 16.95 (ISBN 0-374-24776-5). FS&G.

Real Life of Domingos Xavier. Luandino Vieira. (African Writers Ser.). 1978. pap. text ed. 6.00 (ISBN 0-435-90202-4). Heinemann Ed.

Real Life of Sebastian Knight. Vladimir Nabokov. LC 59-9489. 1959. 16.00 (ISBN 0-8112-0327-1); pap. 7.95 (ISBN 0-8112-0644-0, NDP432). New Directions.

Real Life, Real Answers: Earning, Saving, Investing, Enjoying - A Realistic Guide to Managing Your Money. John Hancock Financial Services Staff & Dana Shilling. Ed. by Liza Dawson. 336p. 1988. 17.95 (ISBN 1-55710-004-7, Arbor Hse). Morrow.

Real Life, Real Answers: Earning, Saving, Investing, Enjoying - A Realistic Guide to Managing Your Money. Dana Shilling & John Hancock Financial Services Staff. 336p. 1988. 17.95 (ISBN 0-87795-942-0, Arbor Hse). Morrow.

Real-Life Scenic Techniques for Model Railroaders. Carl Caiati. (Illus.). 144p. 1987. pap. 14.95 (ISBN 0-8306-2765-0, NO. 2765). TAB Bks.

Real Linear Algebra. Fekete. (Pure & Applied Mathematics Ser.). 448p. 1985. 39.50 (ISBN 0-8247-7238-5). Dekker.

Real Living: A Small-Group Life Experience with the Gospel of Luke, Pt. 1. Mary Nilsen. (Illus.). 1977. pap. text ed. 5.65 (ISBN 0-03-021856-X, HarpR); tchr's. ed. 7.95 (ISBN 0-03-021861-6). Har-Row.

Real Living: A Small Group Life Experience with the Gospel of Luke, Pt. 2. Mary Y. Nilsen. (Illus.). 1978. pap. text ed. 5.65 (ISBN 0-03-022141-2, HarpR); tchr's. guide 7.95 (ISBN 0-03-022146-3). Har-Row.

Real Living: A Small-Group Life Experience with the Gospel of Luke, Pt. 3. Mary Y. Nilsen. (Illus.). (gr. 6-12). 1978. pap. text ed. 5.65 (ISBN 0-03-045696-7, HarpR); tchr's. guide 7.95 (ISBN 0-03-045701-7). Har-Row.

Real Living: A Small-Group Life Experience with the Gospel of Luke, Pt. 4. Mary Y. Nilsen. Ed. by Winston Press Editorial Staff. (Illus.). 1979. pap. text ed. 5.65 (ISBN 0-03-045706-8, HarpR); tchr's. guide 7.95 (ISBN 0-03-045711-4). Har-Row.

Real Long John Silver & Other Plays. Peter Barnes. (Orig.). 1986. pap. 9.95 (ISBN 0-571-14558-2). Faber & Faber.

Real Lord Byron. John C. Jeaffreson. LC 75-29200. 1975. Repr. of 1884 ed. lib. bdg. 55.00 (ISBN 0-8414-5332-2). Folcroft.

Real Love by Appointment. Marie L. Jordan. LC 84-24207. 1986. 11.95 (ISBN 0-87949-247-3). Ashley Bks.

Real McCoy. (Illus.). Vol. I. 5.95 (ISBN 0-9600678-3-3); Vol. II. 7.95 (ISBN 0-685-77478-3). P Coates.

Real McCoy: The Bi-Centennial Price Guide. (Illus.). 1976. 5.95 (ISBN 0-9600678-6-8). P Coates.

Real Majority: Nineteen Seventy-Six. Richard M. Scammon. 1976. 1.00 (ISBN 1-55614-102-5). U of SD Gov Res Bur.

Real Majority: Nineteen Seventy-Two. Richard M. Scammon. 1972. 1.00 (ISBN 1-55614-103-3). U of SD Gov Res Bur.

Real Man Tells All: Confessions of an Eligible Bachelor. Peter Nelson. 176p. 1988. pap. 6.95 (ISBN 0-14-011075-5). Penguin.

Real Managers. Fred Luthans et al. LC 87-19080. 200p. 1987. 26.00x (ISBN 0-88730-103-7). Ballinger Pub.

Real Marijuana Danger. Malcolm E. Smith. 256p. 1981. 9.95 (ISBN 0-936066-02-4). Suffolk Hse.

Real Me. Patricia Aks. (Orig.). 1986. pap. 2.50 (ISBN 0-449-70106-9, Juniper). Fawcett.

Real Me. Betty Miles. LC 74-160. 144p. (gr. 3 up). 1974. lib. bdg. 7.99 (ISBN 0-394-92838-5). Knopf.

Real Men Do. ken Olson. 224p. 1987. pap. 6.95 (ISBN 0-8007-5243-0). Revell.

Real Men Don't Eat Quiche. Bruce Feirstein. (Illus., Orig.). 1983. pap. 4.95 (ISBN 0-671-49228-4). PB.

Real Men Don't Eat Quiche. Bruce Feirstein. pap. 3.95 (ISBN 0-671-44831-5). PB.

Real Men Enjoy Their Kids: How to Spend Quality Time with the Children in Your Life. Stephen Shechtman & Wenda G. Singer. LC 82-24317. 176p. (Orig.). 1983. pap. 6.95 (ISBN 0-687-35598-2). Abingdon.

Real Men Like Violence: Australian Men, Media & Violence. Glen Lewis. 176p. (Orig.). 1985. pap. 6.95 (ISBN 0-949924-55-5, Pub. by Kangaroo Pr). Intl Spec Bk.

Real Menstrual Cycle. Doreen Asso. 214p. 1983. pap. 23.95x (ISBN 0-471-90175-X). Wiley.

Real Mexico. E. Fyfe. 1976. lib. bdg. 59.95 (ISBN 0-8490-2501-X). Gordon Pr.

Real Money. William J. Joseph. 250p. 18.95 (ISBN 0-317-19420-8). Eaton Pub.

Real Money from Home. Valerie Bohigian. 320p. 1987. pap. 4.50 (ISBN 0-451-15010-4, Sig). NAL.

Real Money from Home: How to Start, Manage, & Profit from a Home-Based Service Business. Valerie Bohigian. Date not set. pap. 8.95 (ISBN 0-452-25661-5, Plume). NAL.

Real Money: The Case for the Gold Standard. Lewis E. Lehrman. 13.00 (ISBN 0-394-51904-3). Random.

Real Mormonism. Robert C. Webb. LC 72-2971. Repr. of 1916 ed. 42.50 (ISBN 0-404-10736-2). AMS Pr.

Real Mother Goose. Blanche F. Wright. LC 16-15134. (Illus.). (ps-1). 1916. 9.95 (ISBN 0-528-82322-1). Macmillan.

Real Mother Goose. Illus. by Blanche F. Wright. (Illus.). 128p. (ps-1). 1987. Repr. 9.95 (ISBN 0-02-689038-0, Checkerboard Pr). Macmillan.

Real Mother Goose. Illus. by Blanche F. Wright. (Illus.). 96p. (ps-2). Date not set. Incl. cassettes. pap. 14.98 (ISBN 1-55886-018-5). Smarty Pants.

Real Mother Goose, Vol. I. Illus. by Blanche F. Wright. (Illus.). 24p. (ps-2). Date not set. Incl. cassettes. pap. 4.98 (ISBN 1-55886-012-6). Smarty Pants.

Real Mother Goose, Vol. II. Illus. by Blanche F. Wright. (Illus.). 24p. (ps-2). Date not set. Incl. cassettes. pap. 4.98 (ISBN 1-55886-013-4). Smarty Pants.

Real Mother Goose, Vol. III. Illus. by Blanche F. Wright. (Illus.). 24p. (ps-2). Date not set. Incl. cassettes. pap. 4.98 (ISBN 1-55886-014-2). Smarty Pants.

Real Mother Goose, Vol. IV. Illus. by Blanche F. Wright. (Illus.). 24p. (ps-2). Date not set. Incl. cassettes. pap. 4.98 (ISBN 1-55886-015-0). Smarty Pants.

Real Mother Goose Cassette Board Book. Illus. by Blanche F. Wright. (Illus.). 22p. (ps-2). 1985. 9.95 (ISBN 0-528-82575-5). Macmillan.

Real Mother Goose Clock Book. Mother Goose. (Illus.). (ps-2). 4.95 (ISBN 0-02-689014-3, Checkerboard Pr). Macmillan.

Real Mother Goose Husky Books, 4 vols. 24p. (gr. 2-6). 3.95 ea. Vol. 1 Blue (ISBN 0-528-82424-4). Vol. 2 Yellow (ISBN 0-528-82425-2). Vol. 3 Green (ISBN 0-528-82435-X). Vol. 4 Red (ISBN 0-528-82436-8). Macmillan.

Real Mother Goose Piano Book. Illus. by Blanche F. Wright. 24p. (ps-3). 1987. pap. 12.95 (ISBN 0-02-899500-7, Checkerboard Pr). Macmillan.

Real Mother Goose Picture Word Rhymes. Illus. by Blanche F. Wright. LC 87-18397. (Real Mother Goose Bks.). (Illus.). 64p. (ps-2). 1987. 8.95 (ISBN 0-02-689039-9, Checkerboard Pr). Macmillan.

Real Mother Goose Picture Word Rhymes. Illus. by Blanche F. Wright. (Checkerboard Word Books). 64p. (ps-2). 1987. 10.95 (ISBN 0-516-09893-4). Childrens.

Real Mother Goose TM Cloth Books. Adapted by Nan Pollard. Incl. Hickory, Dickory, Dock (ISBN 0-528-87197-8); Hush-a-Bye, Baby (ISBN 0-528-87195-1); Little Bo-Peep (ISBN 0-528-87196-X); Humpty Dumpty (ISBN 0-528-87198-6). (Illus.). (ps-4). 1986. 3.50 ea. Macmillan.

Real Munchhausen: Baron of Bodenwerder. Angelita Von Munchhausen. (Illus.). 224p. (gr. 6 up). 1960. 10.00 (ISBN 0-8159-6701-2). Devin.

Real Numbers: Arithmetic. Layman E. Allen. 2.50 (ISBN 0-911624-04-X). Wffn Proof.

Real Objects & Models. J. Steven Soulier. Ed. by James E. Duane. LC 80-21450. (Instructional Media Library: Vol. 12). (Illus.). 96p. 1981. 23.95 (ISBN 0-87778-172-9). Educ Tech Pubns.

Real Old Tory Politics: The Political Diaries of Robert Sanders, Lord Bayford, 1910-1935. Ed. by J. Ramsden. 268p. 1984. text ed. 29.95x (ISBN 0-9508900-0-6, Pub. by Historians Pr). Humanities.

Real Oscar Wilde. Robert H. Sherard. LC 73-11157. 1917. lib. bdg. 59.50 (ISBN 0-8414-7570-9). Folcroft.

Real Peace. Richard M. Nixon. LC 83-62597. 107p. 1984. 16.95 (ISBN 0-316-61149-2). Little.

Real People. rev. ed. Martha Denlinger. LC 74-16966. (Illus.). 96p. 1975. pap. 3.95 (ISBN 0-8361-3430-3). Herald Pr.

Real People. Alison Lurie. 160p. 1970. pap. 3.95 (ISBN 0-380-70069-7). Avon.

Real People: Personal Identity Without Thought Experiments. Kathleen V. Wilkes. (Illus.). 264p. 1988. 49.95 (ISBN 0-19-824955-1). Oxford U Pr.

Real People's Economics. Bijan Moeinian. 149p. 1983. text ed. 11.95 (ISBN 0-9611802-1-8); pap. text ed. 8.95 (ISBN 0-317-01246-0). I E C.

Real Play. Nanao Sakaki. (Illus.). 80p. 1981. pap. 5.00 (ISBN 0-940510-01-4). Tooth of Time.

Real Poland: An Anthology of National Self-Perception. Ed. by Alfred Bloch. LC 82-1559. 224p. 1982. 14.95x (ISBN 0-8264-0060-4). Continuum.

Real Power: The Stages of Personal Power in Organizations. Janet O. Hagberg. 324p. (Orig.). 16.95 (ISBN 0-86683-861-9, AY8445, HarpR); pap. 9.95 (ISBN 0-86683-823-6, AY8480). Har-Row.

Real Preacher. Magdalena. 1986. 20.00x (ISBN 0-946270-23-6, Pub. by Pentland Pr UK). State Mutual Bk.

Real Presence: The Christian Worldview of C. S. Lewis As Incarnational Reality. 2nd ed. Leanne Payne. LC 87-73194. 208p. 1988. pap. 7.95 (ISBN 0-89107-483-X, Crossway Bks). Good News.

Real Presence: The Holy Spirit in the Works of C. S. Lewis. Leanne Payne. LC 78-71945. 183p. 1979. pap. 6.95 (ISBN 0-89107-164-4, Crossway Bks). Good News.

Real Presence: Worship, Sacraments, & Commitment. Regis A. Duffy. LC 81-47877. 192p. 1982. pap. 8.95 (ISBN 0-06-062105-2, RD 383, HarpR). Har-Row.

Real Professional Teacher's Role & the Instructional Crisis Action Team. Don Stewart. (Chance for Instructional Excellence Ser.: Bk. 2). (Illus.). 325p. (Orig.). 1988. 16.95 (ISBN 0-913448-18-4); pap. 12.95 (ISBN 0-913448-19-2). Slate Servs.

Real Projective Plane. 2nd ed. Harold Coxeter & Scott Macdonald. LC 60-3540. pap. 59.50 (ISBN 0-317-09189-1, 2050796). Bks Demand UMI.

Real Property. Sara Davidson. 384p. 1981. pap. 2.95 (ISBN 0-671-41269-8). PB.

Real Property. Paul Goldstein. LC 84-5919. (University Casebook Ser.). 1362p. 1984. text ed. 30.00 (ISBN 0-88277-170-1). Foundation Pr.

Real Property. Julian Jergensmeyer. (Essential Principles Ser.). 1982. 8.95. Herbert Legal Ser.

Real Property. (Essential Principles Ser.). 1982. write for info. (ISBN 0-940366-37-1). Herbert Legal Ser.

Real Property & the 1986 Tax Reform Act: What You & Your Clients Should Know. American Bar Association, Real Property, Probate & Trust Law Staff. LC 87-70124. 37p. 1987. pap. 9.95 (ISBN 0-89707-283-9). Amer Bar Assn.

Real Property Appraisal Technician. Jack Rudman. (Career Examination Ser.: C-2185). (Cloth bdg. avail. on request). pap. 12.00 (ISBN 0-8373-2185-9). Natl Learning.

Real Property Appraiser. Jack Rudman. (Career Examination Ser.: C-841). (Cloth bdg. avail. on request). pap. 12.00 (ISBN 0-8373-0841-0). Natl Learning.

Real Property Appraiser-Arbitrator. (Career Examination Ser.: C-3275). Date not set. pap. 16.00 (ISBN 0-8373-3275-3). Natl Learning.

Real Property Appraiser I. Jack Rudman. (Career Examination Ser.: C-842). (Cloth bdg. avail. on request). pap. 12.00 (ISBN 0-8373-0842-9). Natl Learning.

Real Property Appraiser II. Jack Rudman. (Career Examination Ser.: C-843). (Cloth bdg. avail. on request). pap. 12.00 (ISBN 0-8373-0843-7). Natl Learning.

Real Property Appraiser III. Jack Rudman. (Career Examination Ser.: C-844). (Cloth bdg. avail. on request). pap. 12.00 (ISBN 0-8373-0844-5). Natl Learning.

Real Property Appraiser IV. Jack Rudman. (Career Examination Ser.: C-845). (Cloth bdg. avail. on request). pap. 14.00 (ISBN 0-8373-0845-3). Natl Learning.

Real Property Assessor. Jack Rudman. (Career Examination Ser.: C-2199). (Cloth bdg. avail. on request). pap. 12.00 (ISBN 0-8373-2199-9). Natl Learning.

Real Property Assistant. Jack Rudman. (Career Examination Ser.: C-699). (Cloth bdg. avail. on request). 1988. pap. 12.00 (ISBN 0-8373-0699-X). Natl Learning.

Real Property Basics. Renny J. Avey. 1986. perfect bdg. 6.00 (ISBN 0-88252-132-2). Paladin Hse.

Real Property Commercial Real Estate. 392p. 1981. 6.00 (ISBN 0-318-02422-5). ICLE Georgia.

Real Property Examiner. (Career Examination Ser.: C-3345). Date not set. pap. 14.00 (ISBN 0-8373-3345-8). Natl Learning.

Real Property Exchanges. Richard A. Goodman. LC 81-71805. 233p. 1982. 70.00 (ISBN 0-88124-061-3, RE-34530). Cal Cont Ed Bar.

Real Property Exchanges. Richard A. Goodman. 233p. 1986. 70.00 (RE-34530); March '85 supp. 19.00; June '86 supp. 24.00. Cal Cont Ed Bar.

Real Property in a Nutshell. 2nd ed. Roger H. Bernhardt. LC 81-11662. (Nutshell Ser.). 448p. 1981. pap. text ed. 10.95 (ISBN 0-314-60008-6). West Pub.

Real Property Information System Specialist. Jack Rudman. (Career Examination Ser.: C-3138). 1988. pap. 16.00 (ISBN 0-8373-3138-2). Natl Learning.

Real Property Interrogatories. Bender's Editorial Staff. (Bender's Interrogatories System). 1985. incl. disks cancelled 300.00 (652). Bender.

Real Property Law. 350p. 1982. 6.50 (ISBN 0-318-02428-4). ICLE Georgia.

Real Property Law. 736p. 1984. 27.00 (ISBN 0-318-02431-4). ICLE Georgia.

Real Property Law Commercial Seminar. 353p. 1983. 16.00 (ISBN 0-318-02432-2). ICLE Georgia.

Real Property Manager. Jack Rudman. (Career Examination Ser.: C-698). 1988. pap. 14.00 (ISBN 0-8373-0698-1). Natl Learning.

Real Property: New York. Louis A. Kass. (Orig.). 1964. pap. 2.50x (ISBN 0-87526-054-3). Gould.

Real Property Probate & Trust Journal: 1966-1986, 21 vols. Bound set. 735.00x (ISBN 0-686-90032-4). microfilm avail. Rothman.

Real Property Recorder. Jack Rudman. (Career Examination Ser.: C-3102). 1988. pap. 12.00 (ISBN 0-8373-3102-1). Natl Learning.

Real Property Syndications with Limited Partnerships. 2nd ed. Girard P. Miller. (Tax Management Portfolio Ser.: No. 476). 1987. looseleaf 50.00. BNA.

Real Property Tax Considerations in Florida. Florida Bar Staff. LC 78-54785. 494p. 1979. looseleaf, ringbinder 45.00 (ISBN 0-910373-18-3, 258). FL Bar Legal Ed.

Real Property Tax Delinquency & Urban Land Policy. John J. Lawlor et al. (Lincoln Institute Monograph: No. 78-2). 1978. pap. 3.00 (ISBN 0-686-12252-6). Lincoln Inst Land.

Real Property Tax, Differential Assessment, & the Loss of Farmland on the Rural-Urban Fringe. Thomas Plaut. (Discussion Paper Ser.: No. 97). pap. 5.50 (ISBN 0-686-32263-0). Regional Sci Res Inst.

Real Property Tax Examiner. Jack Rudman. (Career Examination Ser.: C-1835). (Cloth bdg. avail. on request). pap. 12.00 (ISBN 0-8373-1835-1). Natl Learning.

Real Property Tax: Monographs. Mary Vance. (Public Administration Ser.: P1795). 54p. 1985. pap. 8.25 (ISBN 0-89028-595-0). Vance Biblios.

Real Property Tax Specialist. Jack Rudman. (Career Examination Ser.: C-2227). (Cloth bdg. avail. on request). pap. 12.00 (ISBN 0-8373-2227-8). Natl Learning.

Real Property, Teacher's Guide. Paul Goldstein. (University Casebook Ser.). 415p. 1984. write for info (ISBN 0-88277-218-X). Foundation Pr.

Real Property Time Shares: An Appraisal Guide & Bibliography. Robert M. Clatanoff. (Bibliographic Ser.). 9p. 1982. pap. 5.00 (ISBN 0-88329-116-9). IAAO.

Real Property Title Examination & Insurance in Florida. 2nd ed. Florida Bar Staff. LC 79-51281. 544p. 1988. looseleaf 65.00 (ISBN 0-910373-91-4, 219). FL Bar Legal Ed.

Real Property Valuation: A Revision of P 791. Mary Vance. (Public Administration Ser.: P 1906). 33p. 1986. 8.75 (ISBN 0-89028-826-7). Vance Biblios.

Real Property, 1988 Supplement. Paul Goldstein. (University Casebook Ser.). 1988. pap. text ed. write for info. (ISBN 0-88277-681-9). Foundation Pr.

Real Questions. David Field & Peter Toon. (Illus.). 96p. Date not set. pap. 9.95 (ISBN 0-85648-290-0). Lion USA.

Real Questions: Searching the Psalms for Answers. Ron Klug. (Young Fisherman Bible Studyguide Ser.). 64p. (gr. 7-12). 1984. saddle-stitched tchr's. ed. 4.95 (ISBN 0-87788-702-0); saddle-stitched student ed. 2.95 (ISBN 0-87788-701-2). Shaw Pubs.

Real Race. Alfred T. Wilkins, Jr. & Joseph Dunn. LC 80-85152. (Illus.). 272p. 1981. 10.95 (ISBN 0-938694-04-9). JCP Corp VA.

Real Race. Skip Wilkins & Joseph Dunn. 240p. 1987. pap. 6.95 (ISBN 0-8423-5283-X). Tyndale.

Real Rape. Susan Estrich. LC 86-22939. 176p. 1987. 15.95 (ISBN 0-674-74943-X). Harvard U Pr.

Real Rape. Susan Estrich. 176p. 1988. pap. 7.95 (ISBN 0-674-74944-8). Harvard U Pr.

Real Reason for Christmas: Letters to Children for the Twelve Nights of Christmas. 123p. (gr. 1-7). Date not set. pap. price not set (ISBN 0-9618730-0-0). M Taliaferro.

Real Reason Why Christians Are Sick. Gordon Lindsay. (Divine Healing & Health Ser.). 3.50 (ISBN 0-89985-029-4). Christ Nations.

Real Reason Why Johnnie Still Can't Read. Stanley L. Sharp. (Illus.). 240p. 1982. 12.95 (ISBN 0-682-49771-1, University). Exposition-Phoenix.

Real Reductive Groups, I. Ed. by Nolan R. Wallach. (Pure & Applied Mathematics Ser.). 412p. 1988. 59.95 (ISBN 0-12-732960-9). Acad Pr.

Real Revival Preaching. Bailey E. Smith. LC 81-86667. 1982. 8.50 (ISBN 0-8054-6235-X). Broadman.

Real Rhythm in English Poetry. Katharine M. Wilson. LC 72-187205. 1929. lib. bdg. 25.00 (ISBN 0-8414-0545-X). Folcroft.

Real Rhythm in English Poetry. Katharine M. Wilson. 171p. 1980. Repr. of 1929 ed. lib. bdg. 32.50 (ISBN 0-89987-860-1). Darby Bks.

Real Right Thing see Altar of the Dead.

Real Ringmaster. Austin Miles & Grace Davis. LC 80-83458. 1980. 8.95 (ISBN 0-89221-079-6). New Leaf.

Real Ritual Magick: For People Ready to Enjoy Life Now. Al G. Manning. LC 86-63701. 180p. (Orig.). 1987. pap. 6.95 (ISBN 0-941698-15-7). Pan Ishtar.

Real Robert Burns. J. L. Hughes. 1973. Repr. of 1922 ed. 20.00 (ISBN 0-8274-0292-9). R West.

Real Robinson Crusoe: Being the Life & Strange Surprising Adventures of Alexander Selkirk of Largo, Fife, Mariner. R. L. Megroz. 1979. Repr. lib. bdg. 40.00 (ISBN 0-8495-3832-7). Arden Lib.

Real Robinson Crusoe: Being the Life & Strange Surprising Adventures of Alexander Selkirk of Largo, Fife, Mariner. R. L. Megroz. 1973. 35.00 (ISBN 0-8274-1014-X). R West.

Real Robots. Grace Maccarone et al. (Illus.). 32p. (Orig.). (ps-5). 1985. pap. 2.95 (ISBN 0-590-40266-8). Scholastic Inc.

Real Runabouts, Book II. Robert G. Speltz. 230p. 1978. 23.95 (ISBN 0-89279-017-2). Graphic Pub.

Real Runabouts, Book III. Robert G. Speltz. 330p. 1980. 29.95 (ISBN 0-89279-018-0). Graphic Pub.

Real Runabouts, Book IV. Robert G. Speltz. 573p. 1983. 39.95 (ISBN 0-89279-048-2). Graphic Pub.

Real Runabouts, Vol. II. Robert G. Speltz. 230p. 1988. Repr. of 1978 ed. 23.95x (ISBN 0-932299-01-6). R G Speltz.

Real Runabouts, Vol. 6. Robert G. Speltz. 354p. 1987. 59.95 ea. (ISBN 0-932299-06-7). R G Speltz.

Real Runabouts V: History of Inboard-Powered Pleasure Boats, Nomenclature & Descriptions. Robert Speltz. 289p. 1984. 38.95 (ISBN 0-932299-04-0). R G Speltz.

Real Sailor-Songs. Ed. by John Ashton. LC 78-160612. (Illus.). Repr. of 1891 ed. 27.50 (ISBN 0-405-08224-X, Pub. by Blom). Ayer Co Pubs.

Real Salesmen Drive Company Cars. Jim Keil. (Illus.). 50p. (Orig.). 1988. pap. 4.95 (ISBN 0-9619809-0-7). Smilin Ed Pr.

Real Self: A Developmental, Self, & Object Relations Approach. James F. Masterson. LC 85-12824. 192p. 1985. 27.50 (ISBN 0-87630-400-5). Brunner-Mazel.

Real Shelley, 2 vols. J. Jeaffreson. 1973. Repr. of 1885 ed. 100.00 (ISBN 0-8274-0019-5). R West.

Real Shelley: New Views of the Poet's Life, 2 Vols. John C. Jeaffreson. 478p. 1982. Repr. of 1885 ed. lib. bdg. 250.00 set (ISBN 0-8495-2801-1). Arden Lib.

Real Skiers' Dictionary. Morten Lund. 1984. Calender. write for info. (Fireside). S&S.

Real Socialism & Ideological Struggle. B. I. Korolyov. 133p. 1985. pap. 1.95 (ISBN 0-8285-3093-9, Pub. by Progress Pubs USSR). Imported Pubns.

Real Solids & Radiation. A. E. Hughes & D. Pooley. (Wykeham Science Ser.: No. 35). 208p. 1975. pap. 18.00x (ISBN 0-85109-011-7). Taylor & Francis.

Real Solids & Radiation. A. E. Hughes et al. LC 74-32348. (Wykeham Science Ser.: No. 35). 208p. 1975. 18.00x (ISBN 0-8448-1162-9, Pub. by Crane Russak & Co). Taylor & Francis.

Real Soviet Russia. David J. Dallin. 1947. 39.50x (ISBN 0-685-69807-6). Elliots Bks.

Real-Space Renormalization. T. W. Burkhardt & J. M. Leeuwen. (Topics in Current Physics Ser.: Vol. 30). (Illus.). 214p. 1982. 35.00 (ISBN 0-387-11459-9). Springer-Verlag.

Real Spiro Agnew. Ed. by James Calhoun. 127p. 1970. 10.00 (ISBN 0-911116-29-X). Pelican.

Real Stories. Gareth Reeves. 60p. 1984. pap. 9.50 (ISBN 0-85635-520-8). Carcanet.

Real Stories from Baltimore County History. Isobel Davidson. LC 70-9245. (Illus.). x, 312p. Repr. of 1917 ed. 35.00x (ISBN 0-8103-5033-5). Gale.

Real Story of a Real Doll. Violet Higgins. (Illus.). 116p. (gr. 4 up). 1981. Repr. of 1929 ed. lib. bdg. 25.00 (ISBN 0-940070-08-1). Doll Works.

Real Story of the Bonobos Who Wore Spectacles. Adela Turin & Nella Bosnia. (Feminist Fables for Children Ser.). Orig. Title: Vera Storia Dei Bonobo Con Gli Occhiali. (Illus.). 32p. (gr. 3-6). 1980. 4.95 (ISBN 0-904613-18-6). Writers & Readers.

Real Stuff: A History of NASA's Astronaut Recruitment Policy. Joseph D. Atkinson, Jr. & Jay M. Shafritz. LC 85-9460. 192p. 1985. pap. 11.95 (ISBN 0-275-91808-4, B1808); 40.95 (ISBN 0-275-90195-5, C0195). Praeger.

Real Supply-Side Economics. Anthony P. Carnevale. 15p. 1982. 1.90 (ISBN 0-318-22185-3, OC80). Natl Ctr Res Voc Ed.

Real Tax Reform: Replacing the Income Tax. John H. Makin. LC 85-18714. (American Enterprise Institute Studies in Fiscal Policy). x, 42p. 1985. 5.00 (ISBN 0-8447-3586-8). Am Enterprise.

Real Terror Network. Edward Herman. 250p. 1982. 20.00 (ISBN 0-89608-135-4); pap. 9.00 (ISBN 0-89608-134-6). South End Pr.

Real Texans Don't Drink Scotch in Their Dr. Pepper. Bill Walraven. (Illus.). 88p. (Orig.). 1982. pap. 3.95 (ISBN 0-9609870-0-2). Sandcrab.

REAL: The Yearbook of Research in English & American Literature, Vol. 5. Ed. by Herbert Grabes et al. 329p. 1988. lib. bdg. 115.00x (ISBN 3-11-011498-4). De Gruyter.

Real Thief. William Steig. LC 73-77910. (Illus.). 64p. (gr. k up). 1973. 9.95 (ISBN 0-374-36217-3, Sunburst); pap. 2.95 (ISBN 0-374-46208-9). FS&G.

Real Thing. Carole Buck. (Second Chance at Love Ser.: No. 448). 1988. pap. 2.50 (ISBN 0-425-10986-0). Berkley Pub.

Real Thing. Tom Stoppard. 88p. (Orig.). 1984. 14.95 (ISBN 0-571-13200-6); pap. 5.95 (ISBN 0-571-11983-2). Faber & Faber.

Real Thing see Daisy Miller.

Real Thing & Other Tales. facsimile ed. Henry James. LC 70-167453. (Short Story Index Reprint Ser.). Repr. of 1893 ed. 18.00 (ISBN 0-8369-3979-4). Ayer Co Pubs.

Real Thing & Other Tales. Henry James. 1973. lib. bdg. 65.00 (ISBN 0-8414-5362-4). Folcroft.

Real Thing, Man Out of Reach, Gone Before Morning. Lillian Peake. (Harlequin Romances Ser.). 576p. 1982. pap. 3.50 (ISBN 0-373-20064-1). Harlequin Bks.

Real Thing: Reading Readiness for American Universities. Stratton Ray & Patricia Nardiello. 200p. 1985. text ed. write for info. (ISBN 0-02-398610-7). Macmillan.

Real Thomas Jefferson. 2nd ed. Andrew M. Allison et al. LC 83-17404. (American Classic Ser.). (Illus.). 709p. 1983. 16.95 (ISBN 0-88080-005-4); pap. 13.95 (ISBN 0-88080-006-2). Natl Ctr Constitutional.

Real Threat & Mere Shadow. Daniel L. Dreisbach. (Rutherford Institute Reports: Vol. 5). 384p. (Orig.). 1987. pap. 15.00 (ISBN 0-89107-418-X, Crossway Bks). Good News.

Real Time. David H. Mellor. 210p. 1985. pap. 13.95 (ISBN 0-521-28468-6). Cambridge U Pr.

Real-Time Computer Control. Ed. by S. Bennett & D. A. Linkens. (IEE Control Engineering Ser.: No. 24). 272p. 1984. casebound 44.00 (ISBN 0-86341-018-9, CE024). Inst Elect Eng.

Real Time Computing: With Applications to Data Acquisition & Control. Ed. by Duncan A. Mellichamp. 469p. 1982. 49.95 (ISBN 0-442-21372-7). Van Nos Reinhold.

Real Time Control of Large Scale Systems. Ed. by G. Schmidt et al. (Lecture Notes in Control & Information Sciences Ser.: Vol. 67). xi, 650p. 1985. pap. 44.00 (ISBN 0-387-15033-1). Springer-Verlag.

Real-Time Control of Walking. Marc Donner. (Progress in Computer Science Ser.: No. 7). 192p. 1986. 29.00 (ISBN 0-8176-3332-4). Birkhauser.

Real Time Data Handling & Process Control, II. Ed. by E. G. Kingham et al. 386p. 1984. 84.25 (ISBN 0-444-86846-1, North-Holland). Elsevier.

Real-Time Data Handling & Process Control. Ed. by H. Meyer. (First European Symposium, Berlin, Germany, 1979). 786p. 1980. 131.75 (ISBN 0-444-85468-1, North-Holland). Elsevier.

Real Time Digital Control Applications: Proceedings of the IFAC Conference, Guadalafara City, Mexico, Jan., 1983. IFAC Conference Staff. Ed. by A. Alonso-Conchiero. (IFAC Proceedings Ser.). 800p. 1984. 225.00 (ISBN 0-08-029980-6). Pergamon.

Real Time Image Processing: Concepts & Technologies. Ed. by Besson. 1988. 43.00 (ISBN 0-89252-895-8, 860). SPIE.

Real-Time Medical Image Processing. Ed. by Morio Onoe et al. LC 80-23779. 258p. 1980. 49.50x (ISBN 0-306-40551-2, Plenum Pr). Plenum Pub.

Real Time Method of Radar Plotting. Max H. Carpenter & Wayne M. Waldo. (Illus.). 48p. 1975. pap. 10.50x (ISBN 0-87033-204-X). Cornell Maritime.

Real-Time Microcomputer System Design: An Introduction. P. Lawrence & K. Mauch. (Electrical Engineering Ser.). 592p. 1987. text ed. 42.95 (ISBN 0-07-036731-0). McGraw.

Real-Time Microprocessor Systems. Stephen R. Savitzky. (Illus.). 416p. 1985. 49.95 (ISBN 0-442-28048-3). Van Nos Reinhold.

Real-Time Object Measurement & Classification. Ed. by A. K. Jain. (NATO ASI Ser.: No. F42). 407p. 1988. 79.50 (ISBN 0-387-18766-9). Springer-Verlag.

Real Time Ophthalmic Ultrasonography. N. Hassani. LC 78-17197. (Illus.). 1978. 60.00 (ISBN 0-387-90318-6). Springer-Verlag.

Real-Time Parallel Computing: Imaging Analysis. Ed. by Morio Onoe et al. LC 80-28025. 424p. 1981. 69.50x (ISBN 0-306-40639-X, Plenum Pr). Plenum Pub.

Real Time Programming, 1978: Proceedings of the IFAC-IFIP Symposium, Mariehamn-Aland, Finland, 1978. IFAC-IFIP Symposium Staff. Ed. by B. Cronhjort. (IFAC Proceedings). (Illus.). 138p. 1979. 43.00 (ISBN 0-08-024492-0). Pergamon.

Real Time Programming, 1980: Proceedings. LC 80-49720. (IFAC Proceedings Ser.). 150p. 1980. 57.00 (ISBN 0-08-027305-X). Pergamon.

Real Time Programming, 1983: Proceedings of the IFAC-IFIP Workshop, 12th, Hertford, U. K., March 1983. Ed. by G. M. Bull. 100p. 1983. 35.00 (ISBN 0-08-030568-7). Pergamon.

Real Time Programming, 1985: Proceedings of the 13th IFAC-IFIP Worshop, West Lafayette, In, U. S. A., 6-8 October 1985. Ed. by G. M. Bull & T. J. Williams. (IFAC Publication). 154p. 1986. 48.00 (ISBN 0-08-033450-4, Pub. by PPL). Pergamon.

Real-Time Programming 1986: Proceedings of an IFAC Workshop, May 26-28, 1986, Balaton, Hungary. Ed. by J. Szlanko. (IFAC Publications). (Illus.). 136p. 1986. 43.00 (ISBN 0-08-034347-3, PBL). Pergamon.

Real-Time Proven Commodity Spreads. George Angell. 1985. 72.00 (ISBN 0-930233-02-6). Windsor.

Real-Time Radiologic Imaging: Medical & Industrial - STP 716. Ed. by D. A. Garrett & D. A. Bracher. 352p. 1980. 36.50x (ISBN 0-8031-0546-0, 04-716000-22). ASTM.

Real Time Signal Processing, No. X. Ed. by Letellier. 259p. 1987. 50.00 (ISBN 0-89252-862-1, 827). SPIE.

Real Time Signal Processing, No. IX. Ed. by Miceli. 287p. 1986. 50.00 (ISBN 0-89252-733-1, 698). SPIE.

Real Time Signal Processing, No. VIII. Ed. by W. J. Miceli & K. Bromley. 230p. 1985. 43.00 (ISBN 0-89252-599-1, 564). SPIE.

Real-Time Software. Robert L. Glass. (Illus.). 464p. 1984. text ed. 43.00 (ISBN 0-13-767103-2). P-H.

Real Time Software Design: A Guide for Microprocessor Systems. Philip Heller. 116p. 1987. 19.95 (ISBN 0-8176-3201-8). Birkhauser.

Real Time Software for Small Systems. A. W. Leigh. 250p. 1988. pap. 26.95 (ISBN 0-470-20980-1). Wiley.

Real-Time Sonography. Arthur C. Fleischer & A. Everette James. 431p. 1983. 65.00 (ISBN 0-8385-8270-2). Appleton & Lange.

Real-Time Systems Symposium, 1987: Proceedings. 302p. 1987. 60.00 (ISBN 0-8186-0815-3, EZ815). IEEE Comp Soc.

Real Time Ultrasound: A Manual for Physician & Technical Personnel. 2nd ed. Royal J. Bartrum, Jr. & Harte C. Crow. LC 77-72802. (Illus.). 1983. text ed. 38.95 (ISBN 0-7216-1552-X). Saunders.

Real-Time Ultrasound Imaging in the Abdomen. M. Leon Skolnick. (Illus.). xi, 241p. 1981. 49.50 (ISBN 0-387-90570-7). Springer-Verlag.

Real Time Ultrasound in Perinatal Medicine. Ed. by R. Chef. (Contributions to Gynecology & Obstetrics: Vol. 6). (Illus.). 1979. pap. 52.75 (ISBN 3-8055-2976-7). S Karger.

Real to Reel. Samuela Eckstut & Despina Scoulos. 236p. 1986. pap. text ed. 11.50 (ISBN 0-88377-316-3); cassette 13.75. Newbury Hse.

Real Tom Thumb. Helen R. Cross. LC 80-11447. (Illus.). 96p. (gr. 3-7). 1980. 8.95 (ISBN 0-02-724600-0, Four Winds). Macmillan.

Real Truth about Health: The Book That Takes the Work Out of Being Healthy. William J. Nelson. Ed. by Charles W. Musey. LC 85-82587. (Illus.). 287p. (Orig.). 1987. lib. bdg. 13.95 (ISBN 0-936987-01-4). Kaptur Pr.

Real Truth about Women & AIDS. Helen S. Kaplan. 1987. pap. 4.95 (ISBN 0-671-65743-7, Fireside). S&S.

Real Truth Concerning Apostolos Makrakis. Themistocles Livadeas & Minas Charitos. Ed. by Orthodox Christian Educational Society. Tr. by Denver Cummings from Hellenic. 230p. (Orig.). 1952. pap. 4.50x (ISBN 0-938366-30-0). Orthodox Chr.

Real Truth: Profiles of Soviet Jews. S. Zivs. 223p. 1986. 6.95 (ISBN 0-8285-3191-9, Pub. by Raduga Pubs USSR). Imported Pubns.

Real Variable & Integration. John J. Benedetto. (Illus.). 1976. pap. 36.00x (ISBN 3-519-02209-5). Adlers Foreign Bks.

Real Variable Method for the Cauchy Transform, & Analytic Capacity. T. Mural. (Lecture Notes in Mathematics Ser.: Vol. 1307). viii, 133p. Date not set. pap. 13.90 (ISBN 0-387-19091-0). Springer-Verlag.

Real Variable Methods in Fourier Analysis. Miguel De Guzman & Miguel. (Mathematical Studies Ser.: Vol. 46). 392p. 1981. 61.75 (ISBN 0-444-86124-6, North-Holland). Elsevier.

Real-Variable Methods in Harmonic Analysis. Alberto Torchinsky. (Pure & Applied Mathematics Ser.). 1986. 89.00 (ISBN 0-12-695460-7); pap. 45.00 (ISBN 0-12-695461-5). Acad Pr.

Real Variables. Murray R. Spiegel. 1969. pap. text ed. 10.95 (ISBN 0-07-060221-2). McGraw.

Real Variables. Torchinsky. 448p. 1988. 43.25 (ISBN 0-201-15675-X). Addison-Wesley.

Real Variables. Alberto Torchinsky. 1987. 39.95 (ISBN 0-317-66920-6, 15675). Addison-Wesley.

Real Vermonters Address Book. Frank Bryan & Bill Mares. (Illus.). 112p. pap. 6.95 spiral bd. (ISBN 0-933050-24-0). New Eng Pr Vt.

Real Vermonters Don't Milk Goats. Frank Bryan & Bill Mares. LC 83-61500. (Illus.). 96p. (Orig.). 1983. pap. 5.95 (ISBN 0-933050-16-X). New Eng Pr VT.

Real Wages & Employment: Keynes, Monetarism & the Labour Market. Andres Drobny. 240p. 1988. lib. bdg. 57.50 (ISBN 0-415-00386-5). Routledge Chapman & Hall.

Real Wages & Exchange Rates in the Philippines, 1956-78: An Application of the Stolper-Samuelson-Rybczynski Model of Trade. Deepak Lal. (Working Paper: No. 604). 60p. 1983. 5.00 (ISBN 0-8213-0213-2, WP 0604). World Bank.

Real Wages in Manufacturing: 1890-1914. Albert Rees. LC 75-19735. (National Bureau of Economic Research Ser.). (Illus.). 1975. Repr. 18.00x (ISBN 0-405-07612-6). Ayer Co Pubs.

Real Wages in the United States, 1890-1926. Paul H. Douglas. LC 66-21671. (Illus.). 1966. Repr. of 1930 ed. 49.50x (ISBN 0-678-00171-5). Kelley.

Real Wagner. Rudolph Sabor. (Illus.). 305p. 1987. 39.95 (ISBN 0-233-97870-4, Pub. by A Deutsch England). David & Charles.

Real War. Richard M. Nixon. 352p. (Orig.). 1980. 12.50 (ISBN 0-446-51201-X); pap. 4.50 (ISBN 0-446-32280-6). Warner Bks.

Real War, Nineteen Fourteen to Nineteen Eighteen. B. H. Liddell Hart. 1964. pap. 11.95 (ISBN 0-316-52505-7). Little.

Real War of the Theatres: Shakespeare's Fellows in Rivalry with the Admiral's Men. Robert B. Sharpe. (MLA MS). 1935. 23.00 (ISBN 0-527-81800-3). Kraus Repr.

Real War on Inflation Has Not Begun. Robert S. Morrison. LC 82-5057. (Illus.). 1982. 15.00 (ISBN 0-912400-25-0); pap. 9.50 (ISBN 0-912400-26-9). Western Res Pr.

Real War: The Classic Reporting on the Vietnam War. Jonathan Schell. LC 87-43046. 400p. 1987. 7.95 (ISBN 0-394-75550-2). Pantheon.

Real Wealth. Wade Cook. 1985. 16.95 (ISBN 0-910019-12-6). Regency Bks.

Real Wealth. Wade Cook. 1986. pap. 9.95 (ISBN 0-446-37037-1). Warner Bks.

Real Wealth of Nations. S. R. Eyre. LC 77-93019. 1978. 27.50x (ISBN 0-312-66525-3). St Martin.

Real Weather. Kathleen Aguero. 1987. pap. 7.00 (ISBN 0-914610-42-2); Casebound 15.00. Hanging Loose.

Real West Marginal Way: A Poet's Autobiography. Richard Hugo. Ed. by Ripley S. Hugo & James Welch. 1986. 16.95 (ISBN 0-393-02326-5). Norton.

Real Winner. Patricia McKissack & Fredrick McKissack. (Reading Well Ser.). (Illus.). 30p. (Orig.). (gr. 1-3). 1987. text ed. 9.95 (ISBN 0-88335-732-1); pap. text ed. 4.95 (ISBN 0-88335-752-6). Milliken Pub Co.

Real Woman Cookbook. Shirley Smith. LC 83-51077. (Illus.). 96p. 1983. pap. 4.95 (ISBN 0-939114-86-0); pap. 5.95 spiral bndg. (ISBN 0-939114-87-9). Wimmer Bks.

Real Women Don't Pump Gas: A Guide to All That Is Divinely Feminine. Joyce Jillson. (Illus., Orig.). 1982. pap. 3.95 (ISBN 0-671-46309-8). PB.

Real Work: Interviews & Talks. Gary Snyder. Ed. by Scott McLean. LC 79-27319. 224p. 1980. 10.00 (ISBN 0-8112-0760-9); pap. 5.95 (ISBN 0-8112-0761-7, NDP499). New Directions.

Real World. Robert Herrick. (Collected Works of Robert Herrick). 1988. Repr. of 1901 ed. lib. bdg. 59.00x. Am Biog Serv.

Real World. Christopher Knowlton. LC 83-45505. 256p. 1984. 15.95 (ISBN 0-689-11439-7). Atheneum.

Real World. Tim Paulson. 400p. 1988. 18.95 (ISBN 0-525-24639-8). Dutton.

Real World. Harriet Sirof. LC 85-13731. 160p. (gr. 7 up). 1985. PLB 11.90 (ISBN 0-531-10080-4). Watts.

Real World see Collected Works.

Real World & Doubting Mind: A Critical Study of the Poetry of John Clare. Tim Chilcott. 316p. 1985. pap. 25.00x (ISBN 0-85958-446-1, Pub. by U of Hull UK). Humanities.

Real World & Mathematics. Hugh Burkhardt. 188p. 1981. pap. text ed. 13.95x (ISBN 0-216-91084-6). Birkhauser.

Real-World Intelligence: Business Information in a Global Economy. Herbert E. Meyer. LC 87-20787. 112p. 1988. 14.95 (ISBN 1-55584-147-3). Weidenfeld.

Real-World Linguist. Peter C. Bjarkman & Victor Raskin. LC 85-46067. 384p. 1986. inst. ed. 47.50 (ISBN 0-89391-357-X); pers ed. 29.50. Ablex Pub.

Real World Measurement. Robert Rohm & John W. Shaw. LC 79-730249. (Illus.). 1979. pap. text ed. 159.00 (ISBN 0-89290-097-0, A513-SATC). Soc for Visual.

Real World of Alternate ID Acquisition. D. P. Rochelle. 28p. (Orig.). 1987. pap. text ed. 8.00 (ISBN 0-87364-440-9). Paladin Pr.

Real World of Buying & Selling Your Home. Bob Dean. Ed. by William W. Denlinger & R. Annabel Rathman. LC 84-23045. (Real Estate Ser.). 208p. 1985. pap. 6.95 (ISBN 0-87714-119-3). Denlingers.

Real World of Democracy. C. B. Macpherson. 1966. pap. 5.95x (ISBN 0-19-501534-7). Oxford U Pr.

Real World of Fairies. Dora Van Gelder. LC 77-5250. (Illus., Orig.). 1977. pap. 4.50 (ISBN 0-8356-0497-7, Quest). Theos Pub Hse.

Real World of Liberalism. David Spitz. LC 81-16262. (Illus.). 1982. lib. bdg. 22.50x (ISBN 0-226-76973-9). U of Chicago Pr.

Real World of the Small Business Owner. Richard Scase & Robert Goffee. 166p. 1980. 27.50 (ISBN 0-7099-0452-5, Pub. by Croom Helm Ltd); pap. 13.50 (ISBN 0-7099-4471-3, Pub. by Croom Helm Ltd). Routledge Chapman & Hall.

Real World of William C. Casey: Professor of Sociology, Columbia University 1931-1959. William C. Casey. LC 86-5852. 224p. 1987. 17.95 (ISBN 0-8069-6338-7). Sterling.

Real World One Hundred One. James Calano & Jeff Salzman. 256p. 1987. pap. 3.95 (ISBN 0-446-34569-5). Warner Bks.

Real World PostScript: Techniques from PostScript. Ed. by Stephen F. Roth. 400p. 1988. pap. 22.95 (ISBN 0-201-06663-7). Addison-Wesley.

Real World Reading Activities for Teachers & Students. Edward F. DeRoche & Robert L. Infantino. 138p. 1983. spiral bdg. 15.25x (ISBN 0-398-04827-4). C C Thomas.

Real Worship. Warren W. Wiersbe. LC 86-8674. 192p. 1986. 12.95 (ISBN 0-8407-9045-7). Oliver-Nelson.

Real Writing: Argumentation, Reflection, Information, with Stylistic Options: The Sentence & the Paragraph. Walter H. Beale et al. 1982. text ed. write for info. (ISBN 0-673-15585-4); pap. text ed. write for info. (ISBN 0-673-15446-7). Scott F.

Real Writing: Argumentation, Reflection, Information. 2nd ed. Walter H. Beale. 1986. pap. text ed. write for info. (ISBN 0-673-18153-7). Scott F.

Realencyclopaedie der Classischen Altertumswissenschaft, 68 vols & 15 suppl. vols. A. F. Pauly & G. Wissowa. write for info. Adlers Foreign Bks.

Realidad Como Resultado. Enrique T. Galvan. pap. 1.85 (ISBN 0-8477-2802-1). U of PR Pr.

Realidad, Ideologia y Literatura en el "Facundo" de D. F. Sarmiento. Noel Salomon. (BHEA: No.1). 169p. (Span.). 1984. pap. text ed. 22.50x (ISBN 90-6203-565-5, Pub. by Rodopi Holland). Humanities.

Realidad Invisible (Nineteen Seventeen-Nineteen Twenty, Nineteen Twenty-Four) Juan R. Jimenez. Ed. by Antonio S. Romeralo. (Serie B: Textos. XXI). (Illus.). 383p. (Span.). 1983. 52.50 (ISBN 0-7293-0070-6, Pub. by Tamesis Bks Ltd). Longwood Pub Group.

Realidad y Fantasia. Boyd & Nogvez. 1984. wkbk. 7.25 (ISBN 0-87720-525-6). AMSCO Sch.

Realidad y Utopia en el Descubrimiento y Conquista de la America Hispana, 1492-1682. Stelio Cro. (Span.). 1984. 20.50x (ISBN 0-936968-07-9). Intl Bk Ctr.

Realignment in American Politics: Toward a Theory. Ed. by Bruce A. Campbell & Richard J. Trilling. 393p. 1979. text ed. 25.00x (ISBN 0-292-77019-7). U of Tex Pr.

Realignment of World Power. Oton Ambroz. LC 73-149631. 744p. 1972. Vol. 1. 13.95 ea. (ISBN 0-8315-0114-6); Vol. 2. (ISBN 0-8315-0115-4). Speller.

Realisation D'une Etude de Faisabilite: Activites de Formation pour Creer Ou Faire le Bilan D'une Petite Entreprise. Ed. by Suzanne Kindervatter. LC 87-63406. (Formation Commerciale Appropriee pour la Femme du Tiers Monde Ser.). (Illus.). 190p. (Orig., Fr.). 1988. pap. text ed. 15.00 (ISBN 0-912917-16-4). OEF Intl.

Realism. Ed. by Daniel O. Dahlstrom. (ACPA Proceedings: Vol. 59). 250p. 1985. 15.00 (ISBN 0-918090-19-9). Am Cath Philo.

Realism. Damian Grant. (Critical Idiom Ser.). 1970. pap. 5.50x (ISBN 0-416-17820-0, NO. 2216). Routledge Chapman & Hall.

Realism. Linda Nochlin. (Style & Civilization Ser). (Orig.). 1972. pap. 7.95 (ISBN 0-14-021305-8, Pelican). Penguin.

Realism: A Critique of Brentano & Meinong. Gustav Bergmann. 468p. (Orig.). 1967. 25.00x (ISBN 0-299-04330-4); pap. 10.95x (ISBN 0-299-04334-7). U of Wis Pr.

Realism: An Attempt to Trace Its Origin & Development in Its Chief Representatives. Saiyid Zafar al-Hasan. LC 74-173110. Repr. of 1928 ed. 20.00 (ISBN 0-405-09111-7). Ayer Co Pubs.

Realism & Allegory in the Early Fiction of Mao Tun. Yu-shih Chen. LC 84-48486. (Studies in Chinese Literature & Society). 272p. 1986. 24.95x (ISBN 0-253-34950-8). Ind U Pr.

Realism & Antirealism. Peter A. French et al. LC 87-16229. (Midwest Studies in Philosophy: Vol. XII). 490p. (Orig.). 1988. 45.00x (ISBN 0-8166-1620-5); pap. 18.95 (ISBN 0-8166-1621-3). U of Minn Pr.

Realism & Consensus in the English Novel. Elizabeth D. Ermarth. LC 82-61360. 296p. 1986. text ed. 31.00x (ISBN 0-691-06560-8); pap. text ed. 14.50 (ISBN 0-691-10214-7). Princeton U Pr.

Realism & Hope. Ronald H. Stone. 1977. pap. text ed. 12.50 (ISBN 0-8191-0128-1). U Pr of Amer.

Realism & Idealism in the Art Expression, 2 vols. Felix H. Rank. (Illus.). 216p. 1986. Set. 187.65 (ISBN 0-86650-188-6). Gloucester Art.

Realism & Illusionism in Hinduism. Bharatan Kumarappa. xvi, 356p. 1986. Repr. text ed. 40.00x (ISBN 81-7047-012-9, Pub. by Mayur Pubns India). Apt Bks.

Realism & Imagination. Joseph Chiari. LC 74-131248. 218p. 1970. Repr. of 1960 ed. 25.00x (ISBN 0-87752-019-4). Gordian.

Realism & Imagination in Ethics. Sabina Lovibond. 252p. 1983. 29.50x (ISBN 0-8166-1268-4); pap. 14.95 (ISBN 0-8166-1269-2). U of Minn Pr.

Realism & Latin American Painting in the 70s. Lawrence Alloway. (Illus., Span. & Eng.). 1980. pap. 3.50 (ISBN 0-89192-312-8, Pub. by Ctr Inter-Am Relations). Interbk Inc.

Realism & Naturalism see Modern Drama in Theory & Practice.

Realism & Naturalism in Nineteenth-Century American Literature. Donald Pizer. LC 75-29942. 176p. 1976. Repr. of 1966 ed. 20.00x (ISBN 0-8462-1794-5). Russell.

Realism & Naturalism in Nineteenth-Century American Literature. Rev. ed. Donald Pizer. 224p. 1984. 17.95x (ISBN 0-8093-1125-9). S Ill U Pr.

Realism & Naturalism in Puerto Rico. Julia M. Guzman. (Puerto Rico Ser.). 1979. lib. bdg. 59.95 (ISBN 0-8490-2993-7). Gordon Pr.

Realism & Nominalism Revisited. Henry Veatch. (Aquinas Lecture Ser.). 1954. 7.95 (ISBN 0-87462-119-4). Marquette.

Realism & Politics in Victorian Art of the Crimean War. Matthew P. Lalumia. Ed. by Linda Seidel. LC 83-24284. (Studies in the Fine Arts: Iconography: No. 9). 304p. 1984. 42.95 (ISBN 0-8357-1499-3). UMI Res Pr.

Realism & Reality. Walter Silz. LC 78-27815. (North Carolina. University. Studies in the Germanic Languages & Literatures: No. 11). Repr. of 1954 ed. 27.00 (ISBN 0-404-50911-8). AMS Pr.

Realism & Reality: The Novel & Society in India. Meenakshi Mukherjee. 1985. 23.95x (ISBN 0-19-561648-0). Oxford U Pr.

Realism & Relativism: A Perspective on Kenneth Burke. Robert L. Heath. LC 86-12825. 320p. 1986. 36.95 (ISBN 0-86554-231-7, MUP-H204). Mercer Univ Pr.

Realism & Romance & Other Essays. Henry MacArthur. LC 78-105804. 1970. Repr. of 1897 ed. 24.50x (ISBN 0-8046-0960-8, Pub. by Kennikat). Assoc Faculty Pr.

Reality & Value Judgment in Policymaking: A Study of Expert Judgments about Alternative Energy Technologies. Robert J. Dillon. Ed. by Stuart Bruchey. LC 78-22674. (Energy in the American Economy Ser.). (Illus.). 1979. lib. bdg. 16.00x (ISBN 0-405-11977-1). Ayer Co Pubs.

Reality at Risk: A Defence of Realism in Philosophy & the Sciences. Roger Trigg. 216p. 1980. 28.50x (ISBN 0-389-20037-9). B&N Imports.

Reality-Centered People Management: Keys to Improved Productivity. Erwin S. Stanton. 160p. 1982. 14.95 (ISBN 0-8144-5676-6). AMACOM.

Reality Club, No. 1. Ed. by John Brockman. (Illus.). 336p. (Orig.). 1988. pap. 9.95 (ISBN 1-55802-192-2). Lynx Bks.

Reality Embraced. Donald C. Boughton. 132p. 1983. 17.95 (ISBN 0-87975-225-4). Prometheus Bks.

Reality Fictions: The Films of Frederick Wiseman. Thomas W. Benson & Carolyn Anderson. LC 88-17613. 480p. 1989. text ed. 45.00x (ISBN 0-8093-1364-2). S Ill U Pr.

Reality Game: A Guide to Humanistic Counselling & Therapy. John Rowan. 204p. (Orig.). 1984. pap. 9.95x (ISBN 0-7100-9814-6). Routledge Chapman & Hall.

Reality Game & How to Win it: Making the Mysteries of Space & Time Work for You. Brad Steiger. LC 86-17625. 263p. 1986. Repr. lib. bdg. 22.95x (ISBN 0-89370-685-X). Borgo Pr.

Reality: Glimpses of Life. Lilian L. Schalet. 64p. (Orig.). 1983. pap. 5.00 (ISBN 0-682-49940-4). Exposition-Phoenix.

Reality in a Looking Glass: Rationality Through an Analysis of Traditional Folly. Anton Zijderveld. 208p. 1982. 26.95x (ISBN 0-7100-0949-6). Routledge Chapman & Hall.

Reality in Advertising. Rosser Reeves. 1961. 13.45 (ISBN 0-394-44228-8). Knopf.

Reality in Transition. Michael S. Spiegel. Ed. by Ellen A. Edelen. (Illus.). 128p. (Orig.). 1985. pap. 10.00 (ISBN 0-932163-00-9). Separate Real.

Reality in Which We Live: Occult Movements Through the Ages. F. Zeylmans. 1973. lib. bdg. 79.95 (ISBN 0-87968-569-7). Krishna Pr.

Reality Inspector. John Caris. (Illus.). 1982. pap. 5.00 (ISBN 0-9607320-0-4). Westgate Hse.

Reality, Knowledge, & Value: A Basic Introduction to Philosophy. Jerome A. Shaffer. 1971. pap. text ed. write for info (ISBN 0-394-31267-8, RanC). Random.

Reality Living. Thomas M. Billings. 80p. 1988. 7.95 (ISBN 0-8062-3369-9). Carlton.

Reality Matrix. John Dalmas. 1986. 2.95 (ISBN 0-671-65583-3). Baen Bks.

Reality, Myths & Illusions. Peter D. Francuch. LC 83-51193. 513p. 1984. 9.95 (ISBN 0-939386-06-2). TMH Pub.

Reality of Christian Learning: Strategies for Faith-Discipline Integration. Ed. by Harold Heie & David L. Wolfe. 448p. 1987. pap. 19.95 (ISBN 0-8028-0233-8). Eerdmans.

Reality of Consciousness. John G. Elliott. 128p. 1988. 11.95 (ISBN 0-918892-05-8); pap. 8.95 (ISBN 0-918892-06-6). Gibson-Hiller.

Reality of Ethnomethodology. Hugh Mehan & Houston Wood. LC 82-20885. 274p. 1983. Repr. of 1975 ed. lib. bdg. 24.50 (ISBN 0-89874-586-1). Krieger.

Reality of God. Schubert M. Ogden. LC 66-20783. 1977. pap. 8.95 (ISBN 0-06-066351-0, RD 241, HarpR). Har-Row.

Reality of God: Thoughts on the Death of God Controversy. Alexander Purdy. LC 67-23314. (Orig.). 1967. pap. 2.50x (ISBN 0-87574-154-1). Pendle Hill.

Reality of Hell & the Goodness of God. Harold T. Bryson. LC 83-51674. 192p. 1984. pap. 4.95 (ISBN 0-8423-5279-1). Tyndale.

Reality of Jesus. Dermont A. Lane. LC 77-70635. (Exploration Book Ser.). 180p. 1977. pap. 6.95 (ISBN 0-8091-2020-8). Paulist Pr.

Reality of Living Yoga. 212p. 1978. pap. 6.95x (ISBN 0-933740-01-8). Mindbody Inc.

Reality of Music. Rutland Boughton. LC 72-80495. Repr. of 1934 ed. 15.50 (ISBN 0-405-08294-0, Blom Pubns). Ayer Co Pubs.

Reality of National Computer Networking for Higher Education. 200p. 16.00 (ISBN 0-318-14032-2); members 9.00 (ISBN 0-318-14033-0). Educom.

Reality of Numbers: A Physicalist's Philosophy of Mathematics. John Bigelow. (Illus.). 208p. 1988. 34.50 (ISBN 0-19-824957-8). Oxford U Pr.

Reality of Prayer. E. M. Bounds. (Direction Bks). 1978. pap. 3.95 (ISBN 0-8010-0739-9). Baker Bk.

Reality of Retirement: The Inner Experience of Becoming a Retired Person. Jules Z. Willing. LC 80-21919. 1981. 10.95 (ISBN 0-688-00298-6); pap. 6.95 (ISBN 0-688-00394-X). Lively Mind Bks.

Reality of Retirement: The Inner Experience of Becoming a Retired Person. Jules Z. Willing. 1988. pap. 9.95. Lively Mind Bks.

Reality of the Cross of Christ. (Christian Library). 132p. 1988. Repr. 6.95 (ISBN 1-55748-013-3). Barbour & Co.

Reality of the Devil see Anatomy of Evil.

Reality of the Historical Past. Paul Ricoeur. LC 84-60012. (Aquinas Lecture Ser.). 51p. 1984. 7.95 (ISBN 0-87462-152-6). Marquette.

Reality of the Mind: Augustine's Philosophical Arguments for the Human Soul As Spiritual Substance. Ludger Holscher. (Studies in Phenomenological & Classical Realism Ser.). 304p. 1986. 32.50 (ISBN 0-7102-0777-8, 07778, Pub. by Routledge UK). Routledge Chapman & Hall.

Reality of the Paranormal. Arthur J. Ellison. 1988. 60.00x (ISBN 0-245-54474-7, Pub. by Harrap Ltd England). State Mutual Bk.

Reality of the Psyche. Ed. by Joseph B. Wheelwright. LC 68-15614. (Illus.). 1968. 16.00x (ISBN 0-913430-16-1). C G Jung Foun.

Reality of the Spiritual World. Thomas Kelly. LC 76-9644. (Orig.). 1942. pap. 2.50x (ISBN 0-87574-021-9). Pendle Hill.

Reality of Time. Errol E. Harris. (Philosophy Ser.). 200p. 1988. 39.50 (ISBN 0-88706-860-X); pap. 12.95 (ISBN 0-88706-861-8). State U NY Pr.

Reality of Time. Andros Loizou. (Avebury Studies in the History & Philosophy of Science). 200p. 1986. text ed. 39.95 (ISBN 0-566-05128-1). Gower Pub Co.

Reality of Time & the Existence of God: The Project of Proving God's Existence. David Braine. 400p. 1988. 74.00 (ISBN 0-19-824459-2). Oxford U Pr.

Reality of Work & Promotion. Fiona Armstrong et al. (Illus.). 208p. 1980. pap. 12.96 (ISBN 0-07-002519-3). McGraw.

Reality on Reels: How to Make Documentaries for Video-Radio-Film. Mike Wolverton. LC 82-12091. 196p. 1983. 22.00x (ISBN 0-87201-776-1). Gulf Pub.

Reality or Illusion: War & Peace in Central America. Frank McNeil. 288p. 1988. 19.95 (ISBN 0-684-18917-8). Scribner.

Reality Orientation. 2nd ed. Holden & Woods. 1987. write for info. (ISBN 0-443-03460-5). Churchill.

Reality Orientation for the Elderly. 3rd ed. Sylvester Kohut, Jr. et al. 150p. (Orig.). 1987. pap. 21.95 (ISBN 0-87489-436-0). Med Economics.

Reality Recruitment. Michael Dani. LC 85-90141. 38p. 1986. 5.95 (ISBN 0-533-06631-X). Vantage.

Reality Revealed: The Theory of Multidimensional Reality. Douglas Vogt & Gary Sultan. Ed. by Jean-Louis Brindamour. LC 77-88915. (Illus.). 1978. 12.95 (ISBN 0-930808-01-0). Vector Assocs.

Reality Sandwiches: Poems, 1953-1960. Allen Ginsberg. LC 63-12219. (Pocket Poets Ser.: No. 18). (Orig.). 1963. pap. 4.95 (ISBN 0-87286-021-3). City Lights.

Reality Therapy: A New Approach to Psychiatry. William Glasser. 1975. pap. 7.95 (ISBN 0-06-090414-3, CN414, PL). Har-Row.

Reality Therapy: A New Approach to Psychiatry. William Glasser. 1975. pap. 4.95 (ISBN 0-06-080348-7, P348, PL). Har-Row.

Reality vs. Romance in South Central Africa. 2nd rev. ed. James Johnston. (Illus.). 353p. 1969. 32.50x (ISBN 0-7146-1871-3, F Cass Co). Biblio Dist.

Reality's Dark Dream: Dejection in Coleridge. Beverly Fields. LC 67-64939. (Kent Studies in English: No. 5). Repr. of 1967 ed. 39.40 (ISBN 0-8357-9374-5, 2011315). Bks Demand UMI.

Reality's Dark Dream: The Narrative Fiction of Ludwig Tieck. William J. Lillyman. 1979. 25.25x (ISBN 3-11007-710-8). De Gruyter.

Realizability Theory for Continuous Linear Systems. A. H. Zemanian. (Mathematics in Science & Engineering Ser.: Vol. 97). 1972. 69.50 (ISBN 0-12-779550-2). Acad Pr.

Realizable Ideals. Theodore Roosevelt. LC 77-90676. (Essay Index Reprint Ser). 1911. 17.00 (ISBN 0-8369-1233-0). Ayer Co Pubs.

Realization of Anti-Racist Teaching. Godfrey L. Brandt. 220p. 1987. 36.00x (ISBN 1-85000-126-X, Falmer Pr); pap. 19.00x (ISBN 1-85000-127-8). Taylor & Francis.

Realization of Data Protection in Health Information Systems: Proceedings of the IFIP-WG Working Conference, Germany, 1976. IFIP-WG Working Conference, Staff. Ed. by G Griesser. LC 77-1802. 214p. 1977. 52.75 (ISBN 0-7204-0462-2, North-Holland). Elsevier.

Realization of Death: A Guide for the Psychological Autopsy. Avery D. Weisman. LC 74-8343. 228p. 1974. 25.00x (ISBN 0-87668-163-1). Aronson.

Realization of Neter Nu: A Kabalistical Guide to the Realization of Self. R. A. Straughn. 1975. pap. 8.00 (ISBN 0-917650-01-8). Maat Pub.

Realization of Oneness: The Practice of Spiritual Healing. Joel S. Goldsmith. 200p. 1974. pap. 5.95 (ISBN 0-8065-0453-6, Pub. by Citadel Pr). Lyle Stuart.

Realization of the Verbal Composition of Speech by Preschool Children. S. Karpova. (Janua Linguarum, Ser. Major: No. 56). 1977. 33.60x (ISBN 90-279-3186-0). Mouton.

Realization: The Anthropology of Pastoral Care. Josef Goldbrunner. 1966. 18.95 (ISBN 0-268-00227-4). U of Notre Dame Pr.

Realization: The Final Report of the Knapp School Libraries Project. American Association of School Librarians, Knapp School Libraries Project Staff. Ed. by Peggy Sullivan. LC 68-29658. pap. 102.50 (ISBN 0-317-27855-X, 2024216). Bks Demand UMI.

Realization Theory of Continuous-Time Dynamical Systems. T. Matsuo. (Lecture Notes in Control & Information Sciences Ser.: Vol. 32). 329p. 1981. pap. 19.50 (ISBN 0-387-10682-0). Springer-Verlag.

Realizations: Narrative, Pictorial, & Theatrical Arts of the Nineteenth Century. Martin Meisel. LC 82-12292. (Illus.). 471p. 1984. 58.50x (ISBN 0-691-06553-5). Princeton U Pr.

Realizations of Usonia: Frank Lloyd Wright in Weschester. Priscilla Henken & David Henken. (Illus.). 36p. (Orig.). 1985. pap. 5.00 (ISBN 0-943651-12-3). Hudson Riv.

Realizations: Personal Empowerment Through Self-Awareness. William A. Guillory. LC 85-60283. (Illus., Orig.). 1985. pap. 7.95 (ISBN 0-933241-00-3). Innovations Inc.

Realizations: The Art of Walter Anderson. 34p. 1985. 15.00 (ISBN 0-317-67964-3). Anderson Estate.

Realize & Rejoice. Richard C. Hoefler. 1981. 4.00 (ISBN 0-89536-468-9, 1803). CSS of Ohio.

Realize Your Potential. V. Pekelis. 311p. 1987. 5.95 (ISBN 0-8285-3475-6, Pub. by Mir Pubs USSR). Imported Pubns.

Realizing Eternal Selfhood. Ivan G. McDaniel. Ed. by Paul P. Ricchio. 297p. 1981. 12.95 (ISBN 0-932785-41-7). Philos Pub.

Realizing the Potential of Computer-Based Information Systems. Myles E. Walsh. LC 83-26764. 275p. 1984. 26.95x (ISBN 0-02-949810-4). Macmillan.

Realizing What's Available in the World of Work. Fiona Armstrong et al. (Lifeworks Ser.). (Illus.). 1979. pap. 12.96 (ISBN 0-07-002516-9). McGraw.

Reallexikon der aegyptischen Religionsgeschichte. 2nd ed. Hans Bonnet. (Illus., Ger.). 1981. 71.20x (ISBN 3-11-003365-8). De Gruyter.

Reallexikon der deutschen Literaturgeschichte, 3 vols. 2nd ed. Ed. by Werner Kohlschmidt & Werner Mohr. Incl. Vol. 1 A-K. 915p. 1958. 56.00x (ISBN 3-11-000294-9); Vol. 2 L-O. 847p. 1964. 56.00 (ISBN 3-11-000295-7); Vol. 3, Pt. 1. 1977. 71.20x (ISBN 3-110073-99-4). De Gruyter.

Reallexikon der Germanischen Altertumskunde. 2nd, rev., enl. ed. Johannes Hoops. Incl. Vol. 1. Aachen-Bajuwaren. (Illus.). xxxiv, 627p. 128.00 (ISBN 3-11-004489-7); Vol. 2. Bake Billigkeit. 128.00 (ISBN 3-11-006740-4). 1976. De Gruyter.

Reallocation: Strategies for Effective Resource Management. James A. Hyatt et al. Ed. by Lanora Welzenbach. 86p. (Orig.). 1984. pap. text ed. 20.00 (ISBN 0-915164-21-3). NACUBO.

Really Bad News. Glasgow University, Media Group Staff. 14.95 (ISBN 0-86316-051-4); pap. 6.95 (ISBN 0-906495-44-X). Writers & Readers.

Really Christmas. Ann S. Gordon. (Illus.). 14p. (ps-k). 1986. write for info. (ISBN 0-9615244-0-5). Pana Pr.

Really Cute Corpse: A Claire Malloy Mystery. Joan Hess. 192p. 1988. 14.95 (ISBN 0-312-02271-9). St Martin.

Really Living. Daughters of St. Paul. LC 68-59042. (Divine Master Ser.). (gr. 11). pap. 3.00 (ISBN 0-8198-0350-2); rev. tchr's. manual 3.95 (ISBN 0-8198-0351-0). Dghtrs St Paul.

Really Managing: The Work of Effective CEOs in Large Health Organizations. Anthony R. Kovner. LC 88-2673. 200p. 1988. 30.00x (ISBN 0-910701-32-6, 0871). Health Admin Pr.

Really Mrs. Austin Do You Feel You Need a Sub? Helen Long. (Illus.). 67p. (Orig.). 1983. pap. 5.95 (ISBN 0-938403-00-1, BB-10). Baker-BerwicK.

Really, Not Really. Lesley Frost. (Illus.). 64p. (ps-3). 1966. 10.00 (ISBN 0-8159-6702-0). Devin.

Really Now, Why Can't Our Johnnies Read? Illus. by Jon Eisenson. (Illus.). 164p. 1988. 17.95 (ISBN 0-87015-258-0). Pacific Bks.

Really Nurse. Roger Brook. 1977. 2.95 (ISBN 0-285-50091-0, Pub. by Souvenir Pr). Intl Spec Bk.

Really Ridiculous Rabbit Riddles. Jeanne Wallace & Margret Wallace. (Illus.). 64p. (gr. k-3). 1979. pap. 1.75 (ISBN 0-590-05764-2, Schol Pap). Scholastic Inc.

Really Rotten Recipes. Norma Ewalt. LC 84-72432. (Illus.). 48p. 1984. pap. 3.95 (ISBN 0-9609318-1-3). Clear Creek.

Really the Blues. Mezz Mezzrow & Bernard Wolfe. 380p. Date not set. pap. cancelled (ISBN 0-88184-326-1). Carroll & Graf.

Really Trying: A Career Guide for the Health Services Manager. Anthony R. Kovner. LC 83-24327. 272p. 1984. pap. 23.00x (ISBN 0-914904-94-9, 0865). Health Admin Pr.

Realm Beneath. B. W. Clough. 1986. pap. 2.95 (ISBN 0-88677-137-4). DAW Bks.

Realm of a Rain-Queen, A Study of the Pattern of Louedu Society. Eileen Krige. LC 75-41168. Repr. of 1943 ed. 32.50 (ISBN 0-404-14564-7). AMS Pr.

Realm of Algebra. Isaac Asimov. 144p. 1982. pap. 2.50 (ISBN 0-449-24398-2, Crest). Fawcett.

Realm of Art. John M. Anderson. LC 67-16195. 5.50 (ISBN 0-932540-03-1). Dialogue Pr Man World.

Realm of Chaos. J. H. Brennan. (Grailquest Ser.: No. 6). (Orig.). (gr. k-12). 1987. pap. 2.50 (ISBN 0-440-97325-2, LFL). Dell.

Realm of Color: Flowers of Japan. Shinzo Maeda. 96p. 1988. 34.95 (ISBN 4-7661-0488-9, Pub. by Graphic Sha Japan). Bks Nippan.

Realm of Ends: Or, Pluralism & Theism. James Ward. LC 77-27173. (Gifford Lectures: 1907-10). Repr. of 1911 ed. 34.50 (ISBN 0-404-60464-1). AMS Pr.

Realm of Fiction: 74 Short Stories. 3rd ed. James B. Hall & Elizabeth Hall. 1977. pap. 23.95 (ISBN 0-07-025594-6). McGraw.

Realm of Literature. Henry W. Wells. LC 65-27135. Repr. of 1927 ed. 17.50x (ISBN 0-8046-0494-0, Pub. by Kennikat). Assoc Faculty Pr.

Realm of Measure. Isaac Asimov. (Illus.). (gr. 8 up). 1960. 8.95 (ISBN 0-395-06564-X). HM.

Realm of Mind: An Essay in Metaphysics. F. J. Woodbridge. Repr. of 1926 ed. 21.00 (ISBN 0-527-97850-7). Kraus Repr.

Realm of Numbers. Isaac Asimov. 144p. 1982. pap. 2.50 (ISBN 0-449-24399-0, Crest). Fawcett.

Realm of the Extra-Human: Agents & Audiences. Ed. by Agehananda Bharati. (World Anthropology Ser.). (Illus.). xii, 556p. 1976. 49.25 (ISBN 90-279-7749-6). Mouton.

Realm of the Extra-Human: Ideas & Actions. Ed. by Agehananda Bharait. (World Anthropology Ser.). (Illus.). xii, 522p. 1976. 43.50 (ISBN 90-279-7759-3). Mouton.

Realm of the Gods. Catherine Cooke. 1988. pap. 3.50 (ISBN 0-441-70840-4). Ace Bks.

Realm of the Immortals: Daoism in the Arts of China. Stephen L. Little. LC 87-35473. 76p. 1988. 14.95 (ISBN 0-910386-92-7). Ind U Pr.

Realm of the Long Eyes: A Brief History of Kitt Peak National Observatory. James E. Kloeppel. (Illus.). 148p. (Orig.). 1983. pap. 15.00x (ISBN 0-912183-01-2). Univelt Inc.

Realm of the Nebulae. Edwin Hubble. LC 81-16155. (Silliman Milestones in Science Ser.). 226p. 1982. 35.00x (ISBN 0-300-02499-1); pap. 11.95x (ISBN 0-300-02500-9, Y-428). Yale U Pr.

Realm of the Universe. 3rd ed. George Abell. 1984. pap. text ed. 28.95 (CBS C); instr's manual 12.00 (ISBN 0-03-058506-6). SCP.

Realm of Totality. Kevin O'Neil. 49p. (Orig.). 1984. pap. 6.00 (ISBN 0-86627-011-6). Crises Res Pr.

Realms. William James. (Illus.). x, 86p. (Orig.). 1977. 8.50 (ISBN 0-940578-01-8); pap. text ed. 5.95 (ISBN 0-940578-02-6). Galahand Pr.

Realms. Paul Kircher. (Illus.). 80p. (Orig.). 1987. pap. 11.95 (ISBN 0-87416-043-X). Catalan Communs.

Realms of Beauty: The Wilderness Areas of East Texas. Edward C. Fritz. (Illus.). 128p. 1986. 18.95 (ISBN 0-292-76440-5); pap. 9.95 (ISBN 0-292-76504-5). U of Tex Pr.

Realms of Fantasy. Robert Holdstock & Malcolm Edwards. 120p. (Orig.). 1988. pap. 15.95 (ISBN 0-905895-83-5, PTB UK). Avery Pub.

Realms of Healing. Stanley Krippner & Alberto Villoldo. LC 75-7858. 320p. (Orig.). 1986. pap. 9.95 (ISBN 0-89087-474-3). Celestial Arts.

Realms of Meaning: A Perspective Through a Retrospective, Vol. 8. Philip H. Phenix. 1986. 22.50 (ISBN 0-318-18970-4). NSLTIGT.

Realms of Philosophy. 3rd ed. William S. Sahakian & Mabel L. Sahakian. 640p. 1981. pap. text ed. 10.60 (ISBN 0-87073-531-4); 29.95. Schenkman Bks Inc.

Realms of Silver. Compton Mackenzie. Ed. by Mira Wilkins. LC 78-3934. (International Finance Ser.). (Illus.). 1978. Repr. of 1954 ed. lib. bdg. 32.00x (ISBN 0-405-11236-X). Ayer Co Pubs.

Realms of Silver. Compton Mackenzie. 338p. 1954. 175.00x (ISBN 0-317-68996-7, Pub. by Han-Shan Tang Ltd). State Mutual Bk.

Realms of the Self: Variations on a Theme in Modern Drama. Arthur Ganz. (Gotham Library). 256p. 1981. 30.00x (ISBN 0-8147-2979-7). NYU Pr.

Realms of the Unconscious: The Enchanted Frontier. V. V. Nalimov. Ed. by Robert G. Colodny. (Illus.). 320p. 1982. 29.95 (ISBN 0-89495-020-7). ISI Pr.

Realtime Ophthalmic Ultrasonography & Biometry. Richard S. Koplin et al. 134p. 1985. pap. text ed. 24.50 (ISBN 0-316-50169-7). Little.

Realtime Simulation of Random Processes. M. Bily & J. Cacko. 1981. 28.00 (ISBN 3-18-145805-8, 996107436S, Pub. by VDI W Germany). IPS.

Realtors Guide to Practice Equal Opportunity in Housing. 57p. 1.00 (ISBN 0-318-15192-8, 111-831); 11-25 copies 0.75 ea.; 26 or more copies 0.50 ea. Natl Assoc Realtors.

Realtors Liability. Mark L. Levine. LC 79-4133. (Real Estate for Professional Practitioners: a Wiley Ser.). pap. 71.30 (ISBN 0-317-09301-0, 2022419). Bks Demand UMI.

Realtors Liability. Mark L. Levine. 1979. 30.00. Prof Pubns & Educ.

Realty Brokerage Operations by Savings Institutions. 134p. 1986. 50.00 (ISBN 0-929097-25-4, 18507). US League Savi Inst.

Realty Joint Ventures 1986: Structuring, Deal points, & Legal Analysis, 2 vols. Practising Law Institute. 1288p. 1986. pap. 45.00 (ISBN 0-317-27703-0, N4-4462). PLI.

Realty Ventures, 1987: Working In & Working Out, 2 vols. (Real Estate Law & Practice Ser.). 1446p. 1987. Set. 45.00 (N4-4479). PLI.

Realval: Apple II Plus Version. Evaluation Consultants, Inc. Staff. 1984. 250.00 (ISBN 0-07-021110-8). McGraw.

Reamker (Ramakerti) The Cambodian Version of the Ramayana. Judith M. Jacob. (Oriental Translation Fund, New Ser.: No. 45). xxxiv, 320p. 1986. 31.75 (ISBN 0-317-60873-8, Pub. by E J Brill). Heinman.

Reams Family Genealogy, Sixteen Hundred & Fifty to Nineteen Hundred & Eighty-Seven. Mildred R. Kantorowicz. 264p. 1987. pap. write for info. (ISBN 0-918292-13-1). Griggs Print.

Reanalyzing Program Evaluations. Ed. by Robert F. Boruch et al. LC 81-2841. (Jossey-Bass Social & Behavioral Science Ser.). pap. 109.50 (2056559). Bks Demand UMI.
Reanimacion Sin Sensaciones. A. Axelrod. 155p. (Span.). 1977. pap. 2.95 (ISBN 0-8285-1699-5, Pub. by Mir Pubs USSR). Imported Pubns.
Reanimation in Philosophy. Palmer Talbutt, Jr. LC 86-23356. (Illus.). 220p. (Orig.). 1987. lib. bdg. 22.50 (ISBN 0-8191-5647-7); pap. text ed. 11.50 (ISBN 0-8191-5648-5). U Pr of Amer.
Reap Ten. Fred Barlow. (Illus.). 1974. pap. 1.50 (ISBN 0-87227-041-6). Reg Baptist.
Reap the Bitter Wind. Jill DuBois. 432p. 1985. pap. 3.50 (ISBN 0-345-32166-9). Ballantine.
Reap the Bitter Winds. June Shiplett. 1979. pap. 3.95 (ISBN 0-451-11690-9, AE1690, Sig). NAL.
Reap the East Wind. Glen Cook. 224p. (Orig.). 1987. pap. 2.95 (ISBN 0-8125-3376-3, Dist. by St Martin's Pr & Warner Pub Servs). Tor Bks.
Reap the Whirlwind. Bernice M. Chappel. LC 87-50674. 410p. (Orig.). 1987. pap. 10.95 (ISBN 0-9611596-8-5). Wilderness Bks.
Reapers of the Dust: A Prairie Chronicle. Lois P. Hudson. LC 84-14720. (Borealis Books Reprint). 173p. 1984. pap. 5.95 (ISBN 0-87351-177-8). Minn Hist.
Reaping. Bernard Taylor. 240p. 1982. pap. 2.50 (ISBN 0-8439-1035-6, Leisure Bks). Leisure NY.
Reaping the Bloody Harvest: Race Riots in the United States During the Age of Jackson, 1824-1849. John M. Werner. Ed. by Harold Hyman & Stuart Bruchey. (America Legal & Constitutional History Ser.). 340p. 1987. lib. bdg. 40.00 (ISBN 0-8240-8301-6). Garland Pub.
Reaping the Whirlwind: A Christian Interpretation of History. Langdon Gilkey. 1977. (HarpR); pap. 12.95 (ISBN 0-8164-2317-2). Har-Row.
Reaping the Whirlwind: The Civil Rights Movement in Tuskegee. Robert J. Norrell. LC 85-40845. (Illus.). 272p. 1985. 19.95 (ISBN 0-394-53688-6). Knopf.
Reaping the Whirlwind: The Civil Rights Movement in Tuskegee. Robert J. Norrell. LC 86-40151. 269p. 1986. pap. 9.95 (ISBN 0-394-74407-1, Vin). Random.
Reappearance of Christ in the Etheric. rev. ed. Rudolf Steiner. 190p. (Orig.). 1983. 18.00 (ISBN 0-88010-017-6); pap. 10.95 (ISBN 0-88010-016-8). Anthroposophic.
Reappearance of the Christ. Alice A. Bailey. 1978. 18.00 (ISBN 0-85330-014-3); pap. 7.00 1985 (ISBN 0-85330-114-X). Lucis.
Reappearance of the Christ & the Masters of Wisdom. Benjamin Creme. LC 80-50639. 253p. 1980. pap. 6.00 (ISBN 0-936604-00-X). Tara Ctr.
Reappearance of the Dove. Helena E. Ruhnau. LC 75-27625. (Illus.). 1978. 12.95 (ISBN 0-941036-03-0). Colleasius Pr.
Reappearing Characters in Balzac's "Comedie Humaine". Arthur G. Canfield. Ed. by Edward B. Ham. LC 77-14166. (Studies in Romance Languages & Literature: No. 37). 1977. Repr. of 1961 ed. lib. bdg. 35.00x (ISBN 0-8371-9836-4, CARC). Greenwood.
Reapportionment in the 1970s. Ed. by Nelson W. Polsby. LC 73-142046. (Institute of Governmental Studies, UC Berkeley: No. 1). 1971. 43.00x (ISBN 0-520-01885-0). U of Cal Pr.
Reapportionment Information Service State: 1981. 110p. 1981. 25.00 (ISBN 0-317-34041-7, R M696). Coun State Govts.
Reapportionment: Law & Technology. 90p. 1980. 5.00 (ISBN 1-55516-712-8). Natl Conf State Legis.
Reapportionment of the Oklahoma House of Representatives: Politics & Process. Richard D. Bingham. (Legislative Research Ser: No. 2). 33p. 1972. pap. 1.50 (ISBN 0-686-20792-0). Univ OK Gov Res.
Reapportionment Policy. Bernard Grofman et al. (Orig.). 1981. pap. 8.00 (ISBN 0-918592-45-3). Policy Studies.
Reapportionment Puzzle. Bruce E. Cain. LC 83-18077. 1984. 32.00x (ISBN 0-520-05028-2). U of Cal Pr.
Reapportionment: The Law & Politics of Equal Representation. R. B. McKay. (Twentieth Century Fund Ser.). Repr. of 1965 ed. 13.00 (ISBN 0-527-02825-8). Kraus Repr.
Reapportionment Update: A Summary of 1980 Legislative & Congressional Litigation. Janice P. Carpenter. 55p. 1987. pap. 8.00 (ISBN 1-55516-726-8). Natl Conf State Legis.
Reappraisal of Franco-American Relations, Eighteen Thirty to Eighteen Seventy-One. Henry Blumenthal. LC 79-25197. 255p. 1980. Repr. of 1959 ed. lib. bdg. 35.00x (ISBN 0-313-22138-3, BLRA). Greenwood.
Reappraisal of Marxian Economics. Murray Wolfson. LC 66-14790. 1966. 30.00x (ISBN 0-231-02880-6). Columbia U Pr.
Reappraisal of Welfare Economics. S. K. Nath. LC 70-80108. 1969. 27.50x (ISBN 0-678-06507-1). Kelley.
Reappraisals in History: New Views on History & Society in Early Modern Europe. 2nd ed. J. H. Hexter. LC 78-55041. 1979. pap. 13.00x (ISBN 0-226-33233-0, P794). U of Chicago Pr.
Reappraisals in Overseas History: Essays on Post-War Historiography About European Expansion. Ed. by P. C. Emmer & H. L. Wesseling. (Comparative Studies in Overseas History: No. 2). 248p. 1979. lib. bdg. 36.00 (ISBN 90-6021-444-7, Pub. by Leiden Univ Holland); pap. 20.00 (ISBN 90-6021-447-1, Pub. by Leiden Univ Holand). Kluwer Academic.
Reappraisals of Rousseau: Studies in Honour of R. A. Leigh. Ed. by Simon Harvey et al. 312p. 1980. 28.50x (ISBN 0-389-20067-0). B&N Imports.
Reappraising an Empire: New Perspectives on Philippine-American History. Intro. by Peter W. Stanley. (Harvard Studies in American-East Asian Relations: No. 10). 300p. 1984. text ed. 20.00x (ISBN 0-674-74975-8). Harvard U Pr.
Reappraising Defense Organization: An Analysis Based on the Defense Organization Study of 1977-1980. Archie D. Barrett. 326p. (Orig.). 1983. pap. 6.00 (ISBN 0-318-20137-2, S/N 008-020-00928-8). USGPO.
Reappraising Social Security: Toward an Alternative System. Jeffrey D. Dunn. 244p. 1982. pap. 5.95 (ISBN 0-89940-850-8). LBJ Sch Pub Aff.
Rear Admiral John Rodgers: 1812-1882. Robert E. Johnson. LC 79-6110. (Navies & Men Ser.). (Illus.). 1980. Repr. of 1967 ed. lib. bdg. 40.00x (ISBN 0-405-13039-2). Ayer Co Pubs.
Rear Column & Other Plays. Simon Gray. (Methuen Modern Plays Ser.). 192p. (Orig.). 1985. pap. 5.50 (ISBN 0-413-39170-1, 9387). Heinemann Ed.
Rear-View Mirrors. Paul Fleischman. LC 85-45387. (Charlotte Zolotow Bks.). 128p. (YA) (gr. 7 up). 1986. 12.70 (ISBN 0-06-021866-5); PLB 12.89 (ISBN 0-06-021867-3). HarpJ.
Rearing of Marine Fish Larvae in Japan. K. Kuronuma & K. Fukosho. 109p. 1984. pap. 10.00 (ISBN 0-88936-406-0, IDRCTS47, IDRC). UNIPUB.
Rearrangement. Nancy Pelletier. pap. 4.50 (ISBN 0-671-62218-8). PB.
Rearrangements & Convexity of Level Sets in PDE. B. Kawohl. (Lecture Notes in Mathematics: Vol. 1150). v, 136p. 1985. pap. 11.00 (ISBN 0-387-15693-3). Springer-Verlag.
Rearrangements in Ground & Excited States, Vol. 1. Ed. by Paul De Mayo. LC 79-51675. (Organic Chemistry Ser.). 1980. 89.00 (ISBN 0-12-481301-1). Acad Pr.
Rearrangements in Ground & Excited States, Vol. 2. Ed. by Paul De Mayo. LC 79-51675. (Organic Chemistry Ser.). 1980. 82.00 (ISBN 0-12-481302-X). Acad Pr.
Reason Aflame: Unamuno & the Heroic Will. Victor Ouimette. (Romantic Studies, Second Ser.: No. 24). 1974. 32.00x (ISBN 0-300-01666-2). Yale U Pr.
Reason & Action. Bruce Aune. (Studies in Philosophy: No. 9). 1977. lib. bdg. 31.50 (ISBN 90-277-0805-3, Pub. by Reidel Holland); pap. 16.00 (ISBN 90-277-0851-7, Pub. by Reidel Holland). Kluwer Academic.
Reason & Analysis. 2nd ed. Brand Blanshard. LC 62-9576. (Paul Carus Lectures Ser.). 505p. 1964. 11.95 (ISBN 0-87548-104-3). Open Court.
Reason & Being. Boris G. Kuznetsov. 1986. lib. bdg. 89.50 (ISBN 90-277-2181-5, Pub. by Reidel Holland). Kluwer Academic.
Reason & Commitment. R. Trigg. LC 72-89806. 192p. 1973. pap. 10.95 (ISBN 0-521-09784-3). Cambridge U Pr.
Reason & Controversy in the Arts. Mortimer R. Kadish. LC 67-27796. pap. 74.00 (ISBN 0-317-13007-2, 2001794). Bks Demand UMI.
Reason & Decision: Bowling Green Studies in Applied Philosophy, Vol. III. Michael Bradie & Kenneth Sayre. 134p. 1981. text ed. 15.00 (ISBN 0-935756-04-3). BGSU Dept Phil.
Reason & Dignity. Raymond Dennehy. LC 81-40364. 152p. 1982. lib. bdg. 26.25 (ISBN 0-8191-1898-2); pap. text ed. 10.25 (ISBN 0-8191-1899-0). U Pr of Amer.
Reason & Emotion in Psychotherapy. Albert Ellis. 445p. 1984. pap. 7.95 (ISBN 0-8065-0909-0, Pub. by Citadel Pr). Lyle Stuart.
Reason & Emotion in Psychotherapy. Albert Ellis. 1962. 15.00 (ISBN 0-8184-0122-2). Lyle Stuart.
Reason & Emotions in Their Process of Fashioning the Personality of Man, 2 vols. William James. (Illus.). 210p. 1987. Set. 187.75 (ISBN 0-89920-159-8). Am Inst Psych.
Reason & Eros: The Social Theory of Herbert Marcuse. Vincent Geoghegan. 122p. 1981. pap. 6.75 (ISBN 0-86104-335-9, Pub. by Pluto Pr). Longwood Pub Group.
Reason & Evidence in Husserl's Phenomenology. David M. Levin. (Studies in Phenomenology & Existential Philosophy). 1970. 26.95x (ISBN 0-8101-0298-6). Northwestern U Pr.
Reason & Experience: Dialogues in Modern Philosophy. John DeLucca. LC 72-91229. 448p. 1973. text ed. 12.00x (ISBN 0-87735-517-7). Freeman Cooper.
Reason & Experience: The Representation of Natural Order in the Work of Carl von Linne. James L. Larson. LC 70-632164. 1971. 35.00x (ISBN 0-520-01834-6). U of Cal Pr.
Reason & Faith Revisited. Francis H. Parker. (Aquinas Lecture 1971). 7.95 (ISBN 0-87462-136-4). Marquette.
Reason & Freedom in Sociological Thought. Frank Hearn. 220p. 1985. text ed. 34.95x (ISBN 0-04-301194-2); pap. text ed. 13.95x (ISBN 0-04-301195-0). Unwin Hyman.
Reason & God: Encounters of Philosophy with Religion. John E. Smith. LC 77-13887. 1978. Repr. of 1961 ed. lib. bdg. 35.00x (ISBN 0-8371-9867-4, SMRG). Greenwood.
Reason & Human Good in Aristotle. John M. Cooper. LC 74-30852. 224p. 1975. text ed. 20.00x (ISBN 0-674-74952-9). Harvard U Pr.
Reason & Human Good in Aristotle. John M. Cooper. 206p. 1986. pap. text ed. 9.95 (ISBN 0-87220-022-1). Hackett Pub.
Reason & Intuition. A. C. Ewing. 1970. pap. 39.95x (ISBN 0-8383-0115-0). Haskell.
Reason & Intuition & Other Essays. John L. Stocks. Ed. by D. Emmet. LC 77-111866. (Essay Index Reprint Ser). 1939. 19.00 (ISBN 0-8369-1777-4). Ayer Co Pubs.
Reason & Justice. Richard D. Winfield. (SUNY Series in Systematic Philosophy). 368p. 1988. 49.50x (ISBN 0-88706-710-7); pap. 18.95x (ISBN 0-88706-711-5). State U NY Pr.
Reason & Life: The Introduction to Philosophy. Julian Marias Aquilera. Tr. by Kenneth S. Reid & Edward Sarmiento. LC 74-25891. 413p. 1975. Repr. of 1956 ed. lib. bdg. 35.00x (ISBN 0-8371-7866-5, MARLI). Greenwood.
Reason & Morality. Alan Gewirth. LC 77-13911. 1978. pap. text ed. 9.95x (ISBN 0-226-28876-5). U of Chicago Pr.
Reason & Morality. Ed. by Joanna Overing. (ASA Monographs). 240p. 1985. 35.00 (ISBN 0-422-79800-2, 9604, Pub. by Tavistock England); pap. 15.95 (ISBN 0-422-79810-X, 9605, Pub. by Tavistock England). Routledge Chapman & Hall.
Reason & Nature. Morris R. Cohen. 1978. pap. 7.50 (ISBN 0-486-23633-1). Dover.
Reason & Rationality in Natural Science: A Group of Essays. Nicholas Rescher. 228p. (Orig.). 1985. lib. bdg. 27.75 (ISBN 0-8191-4763-X, Co-Pub. by Ctr for Philosophy of Science); pap. 13.25 (ISBN 0-8191-4764-8). U Pr of Amer.
Reason & Religion. Ed. by Stuart Brown. LC 77-3115. 336p. 1977. pap. 12.95x (ISBN 0-8014-9166-5). Cornell U Pr.
Reason & Religion: An Introduction to the Philosophy of Religion. Rem B. Edwards. LC 78-66278. 1979. pap. text ed. 13.25 (ISBN 0-8191-0690-9). U Pr of Amer.
Reason & Religion: Essays in Philosophical Theology. Anthony Kenny. 250p. Date not set. text ed. 24.95 (ISBN 0-631-15268-7). Basil Blackwell.
Reason & Responsibility: Readings in Some Basic Problems of Philosophy. 6th ed. Ed. by Joel Feinberg. 602p. 1985. text ed. write for info. (ISBN 0-534-03873-5). Wadsworth Pub.
Reason & Responsibility: Readings in Some Basic Problems of Philosophy. 7th ed. Ed. by Joel Feinberg. Date not set. text ed. write for info. (ISBN 0-534-09648-4). Wadsworth Pub.
Reason & Revelation: John Duns Scotus on Natural Theology. Cecil B. Currey. LC 77-9614. (Synthesis Ser.). 1977. pap. 0.75 (ISBN 0-8199-0717-0). Franciscan Herald.
Reason & Revolution: Hegel & the Rise of Social Theory. 2nd ed. Herbert Marcuse. 439p. 1983. pap. text ed. 17.50x (ISBN 0-391-02999-1). Humanities.
Reason & Revolution: The Political Thought of the Abbe Sieyes. Murray Forsyth. 264p. 1987. 49.50 (ISBN 0-8419-1143-6). Holmes & Meier.
Reason & Rhetoric: The Intellectual Foundations of Twentieth Century Liberal Educational Policy. Walter Feinberg. LC 74-16009. Repr. of 1975 ed. 57.20 (ISBN 0-8357-9974-3, 2055147). Bks Demand UMI.
Reason & Right. Garth Hallett. LC 83-40595. 192p. 1984. 16.95 (ISBN 0-268-01621-6); pap. 8.95 (ISBN 0-268-01622-4). U of Notre Dame Pr.
Reason & Romanticism. Herbert Read. LC 72-6856. (English Literature Ser., No. 33). 1974. lib. bdg. 49.95x (ISBN 0-8383-1640-9). Haskell.
Reason & Society in the Middle Ages. Alexander Murray. (Illus.). 528p. 1985. 55.00x (ISBN 0-19-822540-7); pap. 19.95x (ISBN 0-19-821985-7). Oxford U Pr.
Reason & Spontaneity. A. C. Graham. LC 84-12358. 320p. 1985. 26.50x (ISBN 0-389-20510-9, BNB 08068). B&N Imports.
Reason & Teaching. Israel Scheffler. LC 72-86641. 214p. 1973. lib. bdg. 22.50 (ISBN 0-672-51854-6); pap. text ed. 5.95 (ISBN 0-672-61253-4). Hackett Pub.
Reason & the Lover. John V. Fleming. LC 83-42557. 244p. 1984. 23.00x (ISBN 0-691-06578-0). Princeton U Pr.
Reason & the Passions in the Comedias of Calderon. David J. Hildner. (Purdue University Monographs in Romance Languages: No. 11). xii, 119p. 1982. 22.00x (ISBN 90-272-1721-1). Benjamins North Am.
Reason & the Radical Crisis of Faith. Shabbir Akhtar. (American University Studies VII: Theology & Religion: Vol. 30). 217p. 1987. text ed. 40.00 (ISBN 0-8204-0451-9). P Lang Pubs.
Reason & the Search for Knowledge. Dudley Shapere. 1983. lib. bdg. 59.50 (ISBN 90-277-1551-3, Pub. by Reidel Holland). Kluwer Academic.
Reason & the Search for Knowledge. Dudley Shapere. (Orig.). 1984. pap. text ed. 19.95 (ISBN 90-277-1641-2, Pub. by Reidel Holland). Kluwer Academic.
Reason & Tradition in Islamic Ethics. G. F. Hourani. 282p. 1985. 44.50 (ISBN 0-521-26712-9). Cambridge U Pr.
Reason & Value. E. J. Bond. LC 82-4564. (Cambridge Studies in Philosophy). 220p. 1983. 32.50 (ISBN 0-521-24571-0); pap. 11.95 (ISBN 0-521-27079-0). Cambridge U Pr.
Reason & Violence. David G. Cooper & R. D. Laing. pap. 5.95 (ISBN 0-394-71582-9, V-43, Vin). Random.
Reason & Violence. Ed. by Sherman M. Stanage. 253p. (Orig.). 1975. 10.00x (ISBN 0-87471-603-9). Rowman.
Reason at Work: Introductory Readings in Philosophy. Steven M. Cahn et al. 727p. 1984. text ed. 19.00 net (ISBN 0-15-575990-6, HC). HarBraceJ.
Reason Awake: Science for Man. Rene J. Dubos. LC 70-111327. 280p. 1970. 29.50x (ISBN 0-231-03181-5). Columbia U Pr.
Reason, Emotion & Habit in the Training of a Torah Personality. Nachman Bulman. (Annual Fryer Memorial Lecture Ser.). 0.75 (ISBN 0-914131-53-2, 134). Torah Umesorah.
Reason Enough: A Case for the Christian Faith. Clark H. Pinnock. 126p. 1986. pap. 5.95 (ISBN 0-85364-296-6, Pub. by Paternoster UK). Attic Pr.
Reason, Experience & the Moral Life. Benjamin S. Llamzon. 256p. 1984. 13.50x (ISBN 0-86516-047-3). Bolchazy Carducci.
Reason for a Flower. Ruth Heller. (Illus.). (ps-2). 1983. 8.95 (ISBN 0-448-14495-6, G&D). Putnam Pub Group.
Reason for Being. Emerson M. Clymer. 116p. 1971. 6.95 (ISBN 0-932785-42-5). Philos Pub.
Reason for Being. S. Bradford Williams, Jr. LC 84-71446. (Illus., Orig.). 1984. pap. 4.00 (ISBN 0-9608522-2-0). Copper Orchid.
Reason for Being: The Syl Harris Story. Sylvester L. Harris. 288p. 1988. 12.95 (ISBN 0-8062-3037-1). Carlton.
Reason for Joy. Thomas P. Thigpen. 300p. (Orig.). 1988. pap. 7.95 (ISBN 0-89109-251-X). NavPress.
Reason for Our Hope: A Introduction to Anthropology. Richard Viladesau. LC 83-82019. 1984. pap. 10.95 (ISBN 0-8091-2574-9). Paulist Pr.
Reason for Science. Donald R. Strombeck. Ed. by Walter Hearn. (Illus.). 246p. 1987. 15.95 (ISBN 0-9619272-0-8). Stonegate Davis.
Reason for the Hope Within: Sermons on the Theory of Religious Belief. John H. Newman. 368p. 1985. pap. 14.95 (ISBN 0-87193-219-9). Dimension Bks.
Reason for Visit Classification for Ambulatory Care. Don Schneider et al. Ed. by Taloria Stevenson. (Ser. 2: No. 78). 40p. 1978. pap. 1.50 (ISBN 0-8406-0145-X). Natl Ctr Health Stats.
Reason, Freedom, & Religion: Closing the Gap Between the Humanistic & Scientific Study of Religion. Lorne L. Dawson. (Toronto Studies in Religion: Vol. 6). 247p. 1988. text ed. 46.95 (ISBN 0-8204-0600-7). P Lang Pubs.
Reason, Ideology, & Politics. Shawn W. Rosenberg. 250p. 1988. 37.50 (ISBN 0-691-07785-1). Princeton U Pr.
Reason in Art. George Santayana. 230p. 1982. pap. 5.95 (ISBN 0-486-24358-3). Dover.
Reason in Common Sense. George Santayana. 1980. pap. text ed. 5.00 (ISBN 0-486-23919-5). Dover.
Reason in Common Sense. George Santayana. (Life of Reason Ser.: Vol. 1). 13.50 (ISBN 0-8446-5806-5). Peter Smith.
Reason in Faith. Ralph T. Flewelling. LC 75-3148. Repr. of 1924 ed. 24.00 (ISBN 0-404-59155-8). AMS Pr.
Reason in History: A General Introduction to the Philosophy of History. Georg W. Hegel. Tr. by Robert S. Hartman. LC 53-4476. 1953. pap. 5.99 scp (ISBN 0-672-60200-8, LLA35). Bobbs.
Reason in History: Hegel. Robert S. Hartman. 1953. pap. text ed. write for info. (ISBN 0-02-351320-9). Macmillan.
Reason in Human Affairs. Herbert A. Simon. LC 82-62448. 125p. 1983. 11.50x (ISBN 0-8047-1179-8). Stanford U Pr.
Reason in Law. 2nd ed. Lief Carter. 1984. 19.25 (ISBN 0-673-39425-5). Scott F.
Reason in Law. 3rd ed. Lief H. Carter. 1988. pap. text ed. write for info. (ISBN 0-673-39712-2). Scott F.
Reason in Madness: Critical Essays. facsimile ed. Allen Tate. LC 68-26479. (Essay Index Reprint Ser.). 1968. Repr. of 1941 ed. 19.00 (ISBN 0-8369-0925-9). Ayer Co Pubs.
Reason in Religion. George Santayana. 288p. 1982. pap. 5.95 (ISBN 0-486-24253-6). Dover.
Reason in Science. George Santayana. 320p. 1983. pap. 6.00 (ISBN 0-486-24439-3). Dover.
Reason in Society. George Santayana. 224p. 1980. pap. 4.50 (ISBN 0-486-24003-7). Dover.
Reason in Society. George Santayana. (Life of Reason Ser.: Vol. 2). 13.25 (ISBN 0-8446-5807-3). Peter Smith.
Reason in the Age of Science. Hans-Georg Gadamer. Tr. by Frederick G. Lawrence from Ger. (Studies in Contemporary German Social Thought). 216p. 1982. pap. text ed. 7.95x (ISBN 0-262-57061-0). MIT Pr.

Reason: Lectures. University Of California Philosophical Union - 1938. (Publications in Philosophy Ser: Vol. 21). 1939. 20.00 (ISBN 0-384-07150-3). Johnson Repr.

Reason Not the Need: Eyewitness Chronicles of Israel's War in Lebanon. Ed. by Franklin Lamb. 936p. 60.00x (ISBN 0-85124-432-7, Pub. by Bertrand Russell Hse); pap. 40.00x (ISBN 0-85124-433-5). State Mutual Bk.

Reason of Rules: Constitutional Political Economy. Geoffrey Brennan & James Buchanan. 176p. 1986. 34.50 (ISBN 0-521-25655-0). Cambridge U Pr.

Reason of State & Statecraft in Spanish Political Thought: 1595-1640. J. A. Fernandez-Santamaria. LC 82-25614. 376p. (Orig.). 1983. text ed. 33.00 (ISBN 0-8191-3046-X); pap. text ed. 16.75 (ISBN 0-8191-3047-8). U Pr of Amer.

Reason over Passion: Harriet Martineau & the Novel. Valerie Sanders. LC 86-3938. 272p. 1986. 32.50 (ISBN 0-312-66533-4). St Martin.

Reason, Relativism & God. Joseph Runzo. LC 85-27893. 308p. 1986. 29.95x (ISBN 0-312-66538-5). St Martin.

Reason, Religion, & Kindness. 3rd, rev. ed. Paul Avallone. LC 77-83952. 1977. pap. 4.75 (ISBN 0-89944-030-4). Don Bosco Multimedia.

Reason, Revelation, & the Foundations of Political Philosophy. James V. Schall. LC 86-27624. 264p. 1987. text ed. 27.50 (ISBN 0-8071-1303-4). La State U Pr.

Reason Revisited: The Philosophy of Karl Jaspers. Sebastian Samay. LC 72-160423. pap. 79.50 (ISBN 0-317-26140-1, 2024371). Bks Demand UMI.

Reason, Ridicule & Religion. John Redwood. 1976. 17.50x (ISBN 0-674-74953-7). Harvard U Pr.

Reason, Rule & Revolt in English Classicism. Francis Gallaway. 1965. lib. bdg. 23.00x (ISBN 0-374-92983-1, Octagon). Hippocrene Bks.

Reason, Science & Paradox. Joseph W. Smith. 320p. 1986. 52.50 (ISBN 0-7099-4430-6, Pub. by Croom Helm UK). Routledge Chapman & Hall.

Reason, Science & Paradox: Against Received Opinion in Science & Philosophy. Joseph W. Smith. 272p. cancelled (ISBN 0-312-66540-7). St Martin.

Reason the Only Oracle of Man. E. Allen. LC 40-36196. Repr. of 1940 ed. 39.00 (ISBN 0-527-01240-8). Kraus Repr.

Reason, the Understanding, & Time. Arthur O. Lovejoy. LC 61-8177. pap. 56.00 (ISBN 0-317-20645-1, 2024135). Bks Demand UMI.

Reason to Believe. R. C. Sproul. 160p. 1982. pap. 6.95 (ISBN 0-310-44911-1, 12370P). Zondervan.

Reason to Hope: A Synthesis of Teilhard de Chardin's Vision & Systems Thinking. R. Wayne Kraft. (Systems Inquiry Ser.). 292p. 1983. pap. 13.95x (ISBN 0-914105-14-0). Intersystems Pubns.

Reason to Live. Amy Hempel. (Contemporary American Fiction Ser.). 144p. 1986. pap. 6.95 (ISBN 0-14-008666-8). Penguin.

Reason to Live, a Reason to Die. rev. ed. John Powell. LC 75-24848. (Illus.). 208p. 1972. pap. 5.95 (ISBN 0-913592-61-7). Tabor Pub.

Reason, Truth & God. Renford Bambrough. (Library Reprints Ser.). 174p. 1979. 45.00x (ISBN 0-416-72530-9, NO. 2823). Routledge Chapman & Hall.

Reason vs. the Sword: A Treatise. John M. Washburn. LC 75-137559. (Peace Movement in America Ser.). 470p. 1972. Repr. of 1873 ed. lib. bdg. 26.95x (ISBN 0-89198-090-3). Ozer.

Reason Why. Ethel M. Dell. 402p. Repr. of 1925 ed. lib. bdg. 22.95x (ISBN 0-88411-293-4, Pub. by Aeonian Pr). Amereon Ltd.

Reason Why. Elinor Glyn. (Barbara Cartland's Library of Love: No. 6). 1977. 12.95 (ISBN 0-7156-1382-0, Pub. by Duckworth London). Longwood Pub Group.

Reason Why. Robert A. Laidlaw. 48p. 1975. pap. 2.50 (ISBN 0-310-27112-6, 18243P). Zondervan.

Reason Why. Cecil Woodham-Smith. 1960. pap. 7.95 (ISBN 0-525-47053-0). Dutton.

Reason Why the Closet-Man Is Never Sad. Russell Edson. LC 76-55942. (Wesleyan Poetry Program: Vol. 84). 1977. 17.00 (ISBN 0-8195-2084-5); pap. 9.95 (ISBN 0-8195-1084-X). Wesleyan U Pr.

Reason Within the Bounds of Religion. 2nd ed. Nicholas Wolterstorff. 168p. 1984. pap. 6.95 (ISBN 0-8028-1604-5). Eerdmans.

Reason Wounded: An Experience of India's Emergency. P. Lewis. 207p. 1978. 16.95. Asia Bk Corp.

Reasonable Accommodations for Deaf Employees in White Collar Jobs. Dorothy J. Steffanic. (Readings in Deafness Ser.: No. 10). (Illus.). 1983. pap. text ed. 3.00 (ISBN 0-914494-11-2). Am Deaf & Rehab.

Reasonable Adventurer. Roy Heath. LC 64-12487. 1964. pap. 8.95x (ISBN 0-8229-5071-5). U of Pittsburgh Pr.

Reasonable Arm of the Law? The Law Enforcement Procedures of Environmental Health Officers. Bridget M. Hutter. (Socio-Legal Studies). 256p. 1988. 55.00 (ISBN 0-19-825594-2). Oxford U Pr.

Reasonable Belief: A Funny of the Christian Faith. Anthony Hanson & Richard Hanson. 1980. pap. 11.95x (ISBN 0-19-213238-5). Oxford U Pr.

Reasonable Defense. William W. Kaufmann. LC 85-73331. (Studies in Defense Policy). 113p. 1986. pap. 8.95 (ISBN 0-8157-4879-5). Brookings.

Reasonable Doubt. Steven Barish. 136p. 1985. pap. 5.95 (ISBN 0-9614345-0-3). Hybar Bks.

Reasonable Doubt. Philip Friedman. Date not set. price not set. D I Fine.

Reasonable Doubt: An Investigation into the Assassination of John F. Kennedy. Henry Hurt. LC 85-7571. 1987. pap. 9.95 (ISBN 0-8050-0360-6). H Holt & Co.

Reasonable Doubts. Joan Lingard. 224p. 1987. 18.95 (ISBN 0-241-11696-1, Pub. by Hamish Hamilton). David & Charles.

Reasonable Efforts: A Manual for Judges. Debra Ratterman. LC 87-1015. 1987. pap. 10.00 (ISBN 0-89707-286-3). Amer Bar Assn.

Reasonable Efforts: A Report on Implementation by Social Service Agencies in Five States. American Bar Association, Young Lawyers Division & National Legal Resource Center for Child Advocacy & Protection. 1987. pap. 10.00 (ISBN 0-89707-287-1). Amer Bar Assn.

Reasonable Efforts to Prevent Foster Home Placements. National Legal Resources Center for Child Advocacy & Protection Staff. 125p. 1985. pap. 10.00 (ISBN 0-317-63387-2, 549-0017-01). Amer Bar Assn.

Reasonable Efforts to Prevent Foster Placement: A Guide to Implementation. 2nd ed. Debra Ratterman et al. LC 87-1094. 1987. pap. 20.00 (ISBN 0-89707-288-X). Amer Bar Assn.

Reasonable Faith. Anthony Campolo. 208p. 1985. 8.95 (ISBN 0-8499-3040-5, 3040-5). Word Bks.

Reasonable Life. Arnold Bennett. LC 74-16364. (Collected Works of Arnold Bennett: Vol. 69). 1976. Repr. of 1907 ed. 16.75 (ISBN 0-518-19150-8). Ayer Co Pubs.

Reasonable Man: Trollope's Legal Fictions. Coral Lansbury. LC 80-8560. 260p. 1981. 24.00x (ISBN 0-691-06457-1). Princeton U Pr.

Reasonable Reason to Wait. Jacob Aranza & Theresa Lamson. 101p. (Orig.). 1984. pap. 4.95 (ISBN 0-910311-21-8). Huntington Hse Inc.

Reasonable Religion: A Commonsense Approach. Robert E. Romig. LC 84-42823. 183p. 1984. 19.95 (ISBN 0-87975-252-1). Prometheus Bks.

Reasonable Romantic: Essays on Alessandro Manzoni. Sante Matteo & Larry H. Peer. 293p. 1987. text ed. 49.50 (ISBN 0-8204-0372-5). P Lang Pubs.

Reasonableness of Christianity & a Discourse of Miracles. John Locke. Ed. by I. T. Ramsey. 1958. pap. 6.95x (ISBN 0-8047-0341-8). Stanford U Pr.

Reasonableness of Scripture-Belief. Charles Wolseley. LC 73-2618. 488p. 1973. Repr. of 1672 ed. lib. bdg. 75.00x (ISBN 0-8201-1113-9). Schol Facsimiles.

Reasoned Argument in Social Science. Eugene J. Meehan. LC 80-1198. (Linking Research to Policy Ser.). (Illus.). xvi, 218p. 1981. lib. bdg. 35.00 (ISBN 0-313-22481-1, MRE/). Greenwood.

Reasoned Look at Asian Religions. David L. Johnson. 150p. 1985. pap. 5.95 (ISBN 0-87123-798-9, 210798). Bethany Hse.

Reasoned Space. Timothy Druckrey & Marnie Gillett. (Illus.). 71p. 1980. pap. 5.00 (ISBN 0-938262-02-5). Ctr Creat Photog.

Reasoning. Michael Scriven. 1977. pap. 24.95 (ISBN 0-07-055882-5). McGraw.

Reasoning: A Textbook of Elementary Logic. Peter A. Carmichael. LC 77-80132. (Illus.). 283p. 1978. 12.95 (ISBN 0-8022-2206-4). Philos Lib.

Reasoning Ability of Children in the Fourth, Fifth, & Sixth School Grades. Frederick G. Bonser. LC 70-176580. (Columbia University. Teachers College. Contributions to Education: No. 37). Repr. of 1910 ed. 22.50 (ISBN 0-404-55037-1). AMS Pr.

Reasoning Ability of Mildly Retarded Learners. Herbert Goldstein & Marjorie T. Goldstein. LC 80-65500. 80p. (Orig.). 1980. pap. 6.00 (ISBN 0-86586-102-1). Coun Exc Child.

Reasoning about Actions & Plans: Proceedings of the 1986 Workshop. Ed. by Michael Georgeff & Amy Lansky. LC 86-27748. (Illus.). 425p. (Orig.). 1987. pap. 24.95 (ISBN 0-934613-30-3). Morgan Kaufmann.

Reasoning about Change: Time & Causation from the Standpoint of Artificial Intelligence. Yoav Shoham. (Artificial Intelligence Ser.). (Illus.). 216p. 1987. text ed. 25.00x (ISBN 0-262-19269-1). MIT Pr.

Reasoning about Discrimination: The Analysis of Professional & Executive Work in Federal Antibias Programs. Richard A. Lester. LC 79-3220. 336p. 1980. 32.00x (ISBN 0-691-04224-1). Princeton U Pr.

Reasoning about Madness. J. K. Wing. 1978. 16.95x (ISBN 0-19-217662-5). Oxford U Pr.

Reasoning & Argument in Psychology. P. B. Bell & P. J. Staines. 228p. (Orig.). 1983. pap. 11.95x (ISBN 0-7100-0712-4). Routledge Chapman & Hall.

Reasoning & Concepts. D. N. Osherson. (Child Psychology Ser.: Vol. 4). 256p. 1976. text ed. 29.95x (ISBN 0-89859-503-7). L Erlbaum Assocs.

Reasoning & Concepts see Logical Abilities in Children.

Reasoning & Discourse Processes. Ed. by Terry Myers et al. (Cognitive Science Ser.). 312p. 1986. 69.00 (ISBN 0-12-512320-5); pap. 29.95 (ISBN 0-12-512321-3). Acad Pr.

Reasoning & Logic. Richard B. Angell. LC 63-16209. (Century Philosophy Ser.). (Illus.). 1964. 39.50x (ISBN 0-89197-375-3). Irvington.

Reasoning Criminal: Rational Choice Perspectives on Offending. D. B. Cornish & R. V. Clarke. LC 86-1275. (Research in Criminology Ser.). 1986. 39.50 (ISBN 0-387-96272-7). Springer-Verlag.

Reasoning Heart: Toward a North American Theology. Ed. by Frank M. Oppenheim. 156p. (Orig.). 1986. pap. 17.95. Georgetown U Pr.

Reasoning in Adolescence: Deductive Inference. D. N. Osherson. (Child Psychology Ser.: Vol. 3). 272p. 1975. text ed. 29.95x (ISBN 0-89859-362-X). L Erlbaum Assocs.

Reasoning in Adolescence-Deductive Inference see Logical Abilities in Children.

Reasoning in Medicine: An Introduction to Clinical Inference. Daniel A. Albert et al. LC 87-3243. (Contemporary Medicine & Public Health Ser.). 288p. 1988. text ed. 30.00x (ISBN 0-8018-3426-0). Johns Hopkins.

Reasoning, Inference, & Judgement in Clinical Psychiatry. Ed. by Dennis C. Turk & Peter Salovey. 352p. 1988. 29.95 (ISBN 0-02-933190-0). Free Pr.

Reasoning, Learning, & Action: Individual & Organizational. Chris Argyris. LC 81-48662. (Management Ser.). 1982. text ed. 32.95x (ISBN 0-87589-524-7). Jossey-Bass.

Reasoning Things Out. John Young. 72p. 1982. pap. 2.50 (ISBN 0-909615-05-5). Stella Maris Bks.

Reasoning with a Computer. Daniel Solow. LC 85-15753. 512p. 1986. pap. text ed. write for info. (ISBN 0-201-12060-7); write for info instr's. manual; write for info. solutions manual (ISBN 0-201-12061-5). Addison-Wesley.

Reasoning with a Computer in Pascal. Carolyn K. Cuff. 44p. 1986. write for info. instr's. manual. Addison-Wesley.

Reasoning with Arbitrary Objects. Kit Fine. 240p. 1985. 29.95 (ISBN 0-631-13844-7). Basil Blackwell.

Reasoning with Democratic Values: Ethical Problems in United States History, 2 vols. Alan L. Lockwood & David E. Harris. (gr. 9-12). 1985. Vol. I: 1607-1876. 8.95x (ISBN 0-8077-6094-3); Vol. II: 1877 to Present. 11.95x (ISBN 0-8077-6095-1); tchr's. manual 11.95x (ISBN 0-8077-6101-X). Tchrs Coll.

Reasoning with Incomplete Information. David W. Etherington. (Research Notes in Artificial Intelligence Ser.). (Illus.). 240p. (Orig.). 1988. pap. text ed. 22.95 (ISBN 0-934613-60-5). Morgan Kaufmann.

Reasoning with Juniors for Christs Sake. Lance Colkmire. 1982. pap. 5.95 (ISBN 0-87148-736-5). Pathway Pr.

Reasoning with Statistics. 2nd ed. Frederick Williams. LC 78-15744. 1979. pap. text ed. 16.95 (ISBN 0-03-019536-5, HoltC). HR&W.

Reasoning with Statistics. 3rd ed. Frederick Williams. 224p. 1986. pap. text ed. 16.95 (ISBN 0-03-071847-3, HoltC). HR&W.

Reasoning with Uncertainty for Rule-Based Expert Systems. Togai. 1988. write for info. (ISBN 0-471-85238-4). Wiley.

Reasons. Josh McDowell & Don Stewart. LC 80-67432. (Answers to Tough Questions Ser.: Vol.II). 160p. (Orig.). 1981. pap. 6.95 (ISBN 0-918956-98-6). Campus Crusade.

Reasons. Josh McDowell & Don Stewart. (Living Bks.). 256p. 1986. 3.95 (ISBN 0-8423-5287-2). Tyndale.

Reasons. Kristine Marie. 1988. 6.95 (ISBN 0-533-07502-5). Vantage.

Reasons & Knowledge. Marshall Swain. LC 80-69825. 243p. 1981. 28.50x (ISBN 0-8014-1378-8). Cornell U Pr.

Reasons & Methods: Poems by Kirk Robertson, with Constellations, Typoglifs by Karl Kempton. Kirk Robertson. (Illus.). 20p. (Orig.). 1981. pap. 2.50 (ISBN 0-916918-15-7). Duck Down.

Reasons & Persons. Derek Parfit. (Illus.). 543p. 1985. 36.00x (ISBN 0-19-824615-3); pap. text ed. 12.95x (ISBN 0-19-824908-X). Oxford U Pr.

Reasons & Realpolitik: U. S. Foreign Policy & World Order. Louis R. Beres. LC 83-49102. 160p. 1984. 22.00x (ISBN 0-669-07756-9); pap. 14.95x (ISBN 0-669-07758-5). Lexington Bks.

Reason's Disciples: Seventeenth-Century English Feminists. Hilda Smith. LC 81-14834. 264p. 1982. 24.95 (ISBN 0-252-00912-6). U of Ill Pr.

Reasons for a New Edition of Shakespeare's Works. J. Payne Collier. LC 79-113586. Repr. of 1842 ed. 11.50 (ISBN 0-404-01616-2). AMS Pr.

Reasons for Anger. facs. ed. Robert Briffault. LC 68-58774. (Essay Index Reprint Ser). 1936. 17.75 (ISBN 0-8369-1024-9). Ayer Co Pubs.

Reasons for Going It on Foot. William P. Root. LC 80-69369. Orig. Title: Wheel Turning on the Hub of the Sun. 80p. 1981. 11.95 (ISBN 0-689-11138-X); pap. 6.95 (ISBN 0-689-11164-9). Atheneum.

Reasons for Hope. rev. ed. W. H. Carroll et al. 254p. 1982. pap. 6.95 (ISBN 0-931888-07-7, Chris. Coll. Pr.). Christendom Coll Pr.

Reasons for Hope: Laity in Catholic Health Care Facilities. Kevin D. O'Rourke. LC 83-7426. 60p. (Orig.). 1983. pap. 7.00 (ISBN 0-87125-084-5). Cath Health.

Reasons for Jewish Customs & Traditions. Abraham I. Sperling. Tr. by Abraham Matts. LC 68-31711. cancelled (ISBN 0-8197-0184-X); pap. 11.95 (ISBN 0-8197-0008-8). Bloch.

Reasons for Living: A Basic Ethics. Burton F. Porter. 747p. 1988. pap. text ed. write for info. (ISBN 0-02-396050-7). Macmillan.

Reasons for Moving. Mark Strand. LC 68-19151. 1968. pap. 3.95 (ISBN 0-689-10263-1). Atheneum.

Reasons for Pardoning the Haymarket Anarchists. John P. Altgeld. LC 86-80035. 80p. lib. bdg. 14.95 (ISBN 0-88286-149-2); pap. 3.95 (ISBN 0-88286-124-7). C H Kerr.

Reasons for Realism: Selected Essays of James J. Gibson. E. Reed & R. Jones. (Resources for Ecological Psychology Ser.). (Illus.). 480p. 1982. text ed. 45.00x (ISBN 0-89859-207-0). L Erlbaum Assocs.

Reasons for Rejoicing: Readings in Christian Hope. Kenneth Zanca. (Orig.). 1976. pap. 2.95 (ISBN 0-914544-12-8). Living Flame Pr.

Reasons for Seasons: The Great Cosmic Megagalactic Trip Without Moving from Your Chair. Linda Allison. (Brown Paper School Bks.). (Illus.). 128p. (gr. 4 up). 1975. 13.45 (ISBN 0-316-03439-8); pap. 7.95 (ISBN 0-316-03440-1). Little.

Reasons for the Sky. Jim Hanson. LC 79-10984. (Orig.). 1979. pap. 3.00 (ISBN 0-915124-26-2, Pub. by Toothpaste). Coffee Hse.

Reasons for Welfare: The Political Theory of the Welfare State. Robert E. Goodin. Ed. by Marshall Cohen. (Studies in Moral, Political, & Legal Philosophy). 392p. 1988. text ed. 45.00 (ISBN 0-691-07766-5); pap. text ed. 14.95 (ISBN 0-691-02279-8). Princeton U Pr.

Reasons Four, Explaining the Reformed Perspective. 120p. (Orig.). 1981. pap. text ed. 4.50 (ISBN 0-933140-29-0); tchr's manual, 60pgs 4.50 (ISBN 0-933140-30-4). CRC Pubns.

Reasons of State. Alejo Carpentier. Tr. by Frances Patridge from Span. 320p. 1981. pap. 4.95 (ISBN 0-904613-52-6). Writers & Readers.

Reasons of State. Shashi Tharoor. 438p. 1981. text ed. 40.00x (ISBN 0-7069-1275-6, Pub by Vikas India). Advent NY.

Reasons of State. Shashi Tharoor. 438p. 1982. 30.95. Asia Bk Corp.

Reasons of State: Oil Politics & the Capacities of American Government. G. John Ikenberry. LC 88-3660. (Studies in Political Economy). 232p. 1988. 32.95x (ISBN 0-8014-2155-1); pap. 10.95x (ISBN 0-8014-9488-5). Cornell U Pr.

Reasons of the Heart. Henry Giniger. 1987. 16.95 (ISBN 0-531-15047-X). Watts.

Reasons of the Heart: A Journey into Solitude & Back Again into the Human Circle. John S. Dunne. 1979. pap. 6.95 (ISBN 0-268-01606-2). U of Notre Dame Pr.

Reasons One, Sects & Cults with Non-Christian Roots. Bill Evenhouse. 120p. (Orig.). 1981. pap. text ed. 4.50 (ISBN 0-933140-23-1); tchr's manual, 61 pgs. 4.50 (ISBN 0-933140-24-X). CRC Pubns.

Reasons Three, Objections to Christianity. Richard J. Mouw. (Orig.). 1981. pap. text ed. 4.50 (ISBN 0-933140-27-4); tchr's manual, 64 pgs. 4.50 (ISBN 0-933140-28-2). CRC Pubns.

Reasons to Be Cheerful. Judith Martin. (Illus.). 80p. (ps-4). 1985. pap. 4.50 (ISBN 0-9606662-1-4). Paper Bag.

Reasons to Believe: New Voices in American Fiction. Michael Schumacher. 224p. 1988. pap. 9.95 (ISBN 0-312-01811-8). St Martin.

Reasons to Live. Amy Hempel. Ed. by Gordon Lish. LC 84-48658. 129p. 1985. 11.45 (ISBN 0-394-53993-1). Knopf.

Reasons to Live. Amy Hempel. 144p. 1986. 6.95 (ISBN 0-14-008688-9). Penguin.

Reasons to Stay. Margaret W. Froehlich. LC 86-10322. 192p. (YA) (gr. 6 up). 1986. 12.95 (ISBN 0-395-41068-1). HM.

Reasons Two, Sects & Cults with Christian Roots. Bill Evenhouse. (Orig.). 1981. pap. text ed. 4.50 (ISBN 0-933140-25-8); tchr's manual, 67 pgs. 4.50 (ISBN 0-933140-26-6). CRC Pubns.

Reasons Why. Frank Dawkins. 144p. 1986. 9.95 (ISBN 0-8062-2072-4). Carlton.

Reasons Why I Am Not Perfect. John Judson. (Sparrow Poetry Pamphlets Ser.: No. 42). 32p. 1982. pap. 2.00x (ISBN 0-935552-07-3). Sparrow Pr.

Reassembling Assembling. new ed. Ed. by R. Kostelanetz et al. lib. bdg. 600.00 (ISBN 0-685-96376-4). Assembling Pr.

Reassessing Arms Control: Studies in Disarmament & Conflicts. Ed. by David Carlton & Carlo Schaerf. LC 84-40339. 232p. 1985. 27.50 (ISBN 0-312-66545-8). St Martin.

Reassessing Community Care. Ed. by Nigel Malin. 1987. 34.50 (ISBN 0-7099-1738-4, Pub. by Croom Helm UK). Routledge Chapman & Hall.

Reassessing Fatherhood. Ed. by Charlie Lewis & Margaret O'Brien. LC 87-60199. 288p. 1987. text ed. 45.00 (ISBN 0-8039-8019-1); pap. text ed. 17.50 (ISBN 0-8039-8020-5). Sage.

Reassessing Nuclear Power: The Fallout from Chernobyl. Christopher Flavin. LC 87-50070. 92p. (Orig.). 1987. pap. 4.00 (ISBN 0-916468-76-3). Worldwatch Inst.

Rebellion Record: A Diary of American Events, 12 vols. Ed. by Frank Moore. (Illus.). 1976. Set. pap. 300.00 (ISBN 0-405-09846-4). Ayer Co Pubs.

Rebellion, Revolution, & Armed Force: A Comparative Study of Fifteen Countries with Special Emphasis on Cuba & South Africa. D. E. Russell. 1974. 19.95 (ISBN 0-12-785745-1). Acad Pr.

Rebellious Angels. Laura Parker. Date not set. pap. write for info. Warner Bks.

Rebellious Century: 1830-1930. Charles Tilly et al. LC 74-16802. 1975. pap. 10.95x (ISBN 0-674-74956-1). Harvard U Pr.

Rebellious Colonel Speaks. Willard F. Rockwell. 1964. text ed. 4.95 (ISBN 0-07-053362-8). McGraw.

Rebellious Fraser's: Nol Yorke's Magazine in the Days of Maginn, Thackeray & Carlyle. Miriam M. Thrall. LC 35-1070. Repr. of 1934 ed. 19.50 (ISBN 0-404-06458-2). AMS Pr.

Rebellious Galilean. John Bonforte. LC 81-82691. 327p. 1982. 10.95 (ISBN 0-8022-2391-5). Philos Lib.

Rebellious Heroine. John K. Bangs. 1973. Repr. of 1896 ed. 12.50 (ISBN 0-8274-1491-9). R West.

Rebellious Love. Maura Seger. 1983. pap. 2.50 (ISBN 0-671-46379-9). PB.

Rebellious River. J. P. Kemper. LC 72-2848. (Use & Abuse of America's Natural Resources Ser). 284p. 1972. Repr. of 1949 ed. 20.00 (ISBN 0-405-04514-X). Ayer Co Pubs.

Rebellious Spirit. Bhagwan S. Rajneesh. Ed. by Ma P. Pankaja et al. LC 87-42814. (Rajneesh University of Mysticism Ser.). 325p. (Orig.). 1987. pap. text ed. 14.95 (ISBN 3-907757-16-5, Pub. by Rajeesh Foundation, Europe). Chidvilas Inc.

Rebellious Structures: Women Writers & the Crisis of the Novel, 1880-1900. Gerd Bjorhovde. (Norwegian University Press Publication Ser.). (Illus.). 252p. 1988. 35.00 (ISBN 82-00-02502-0). Oxford U Pr.

Rebellious Ward. Joan Wolf. (Regency Romance Ser.). 224p. 1988. pap. 2.95 (ISBN 0-451-15401-0, Sig). NAL.

Rebello Transcripts: Governor Phillip's Portugese Prelude. Kenneth G. McIntyre. 257p. 1984. 24.95 (ISBN 0-285-62603-5, Pub. by Souvenir Pr). Intl Spec Bk.

Rebels. Lorayne Ashton. (Park Avenue Ser.: No. 7). 1988. pap. 3.95 (ISBN 0-8041-0173-6, Pub. by Ivy). Ballantine.

Rebels. John Jakes. (Kent Family Chronicle Ser.: No. 2). 544p. 1983. pap. 4.95 (ISBN 0-515-09206-1). Jove Pubns.

Rebels Against War: The American Peace Movement, 1933-1983. Lawrence S. Wittner. 384p. 1984. 34.95 (ISBN 0-87722-346-7); pap. 9.95 (ISBN 0-87722-342-4). Temple U Pr.

Rebels & Bureaucrats: China's December 9ers. John Israel & Donald Klein. LC 74-18757. 1976. 45.00x (ISBN 0-520-02861-9). U of Cal Pr.

Rebels & Colleagues: Advertising & Social Change in French Canada. Frederick Elkin. (Illus.). 240p. 1973. 24.95x (ISBN 0-7735-0135-5). McGill-Queens U Pr.

Rebels & Colleagues: Advertising & Social Change in French-Canada. Frederick Elkin. LC 72-88133. pap. 61.80 (ISBN 0-317-41742-8, 2023847). Bks Demand UMI.

Rebels & Democrats. E. P. Douglass. LC 77-160853. (Era of the American Revolution Ser.). 368p. 1971. Repr. of 1955 ed. 45.00 (ISBN 0-306-70402-1). Da Capo.

Rebels & Gentlemen: Philadelphia in the Age of Franklin. Carl Bridenbaugh & Jessica Bridenbaugh. LC 78-657. (Illus.). 1978. Repr. of 1942 ed. lib. bdg. 35.00x (ISBN 0-313-20300-8, BRRE). Greenwood.

Rebels & Redcoats: The American Revolution Throught the Eyes of Those Who Fought & Lived It. George F. Scheer & Hugh F. Rankin. (Quality Paperbacks Ser.). 574p. 1987. pap. 14.95 (ISBN 0-306-80307-0). Da Capo.

Rebels & Reformers of the Airways. R. E. Davies. LC 86-26243. (Illus.). 320p. 1987. 22.50 (ISBN 0-87474-354-0). Smithsonian.

Rebels & Renegades. facs. ed. Max Nomad. LC 68-20326. (Essay Index Reprint Ser). 1932. 21.50 (ISBN 0-8369-0745-0). Ayer Co Pubs.

Rebels & Revolutionaries in North China, 1845-1945. Elizabeth J. Perry. LC 79-65179. xvi, 324p. 1980. 32.50x (ISBN 0-8047-1055-4); pap. 9.95 (ISBN 0-8047-1175-5, SP-62). Stanford U Pr.

Rebels & Rulers, Fifteen Hundred to Sixteen-Sixty, 2 vols. P. Zagorin. Incl. Vol. 1. Society, States, & Early Modern Revolution: Agrarian & Urban Rebellions (ISBN 0-521-24472-2). pap. (ISBN 0-521-28711-1); Vol. 2. Provincial Rebellion: Revolutionary Civil Wars, 1560-1660 (ISBN 0-521-24473-0). pap. (ISBN 0-521-28712-X). LC 81-17039. 304p. 1982. 47.50 ea.; pap. 12.95 ea. Cambridge U Pr.

Rebels & Their Causes: Essays in Honour of A. L. Morton. Maurice Cornforth. 1957. pap. 19.95x (ISBN 0-85315-426-0). Humanities.

Rebels & Victims: The Fiction of Richard Wright & Bernard Malamud. Evelyn Avery. (National Univ. Pubns. Literary Criticism Ser.). 1979. 16.50x (ISBN 0-8046-9234-3, Pub. by Kennikat). Assoc Faculty Pr.

Rebels & Whips: An Analysis of Dissension, Discipline & Cohesion in British Political Parties. Robert J. Jackson. LC 68-19078. 1969. 25.00 (ISBN 0-312-66570-9). St Martin.

Rebels from West Point. Gerard A. Patterson. LC 87-548. (Illus.). 216p. 1987. pap. 16.95 (ISBN 0-385-24248-4). Doubleday.

Rebels in Bohemia: The Radicals of the Masses, 1911-1917. Leslie Fishbein. LC 81-24105. (Illus.). xv, 270p. 1982. 27.50x (ISBN 0-8078-1519-5). U of NC Pr.

Rebels in Hell. Janet Morris et al. (Heroes in Hell Ser.). 1986. 3.50 (ISBN 0-671-65577-9). Baen Bks.

Rebels in Love. Shana Carrol. 384p. 1985. pap. 3.95 (ISBN 0-515-08249-X). Jove Pubns.

Rebels in the Rif: Abd el Krim & the Rif Rebellion. David S. Woolman. (Illus.). 1968. 25.00x (ISBN 0-8047-0664-6). Stanford U Pr.

Rebels in the Shadows. Robert T. Reilly. LC 78-66069. (gr. 3-7). 1979. pap. 7.95 (ISBN 0-8229-5304-8). U of Pittsburgh Pr.

Rebels of Art: Manet to Matisse. George Slocombe. LC 68-8229. (Illus.). 1969. Repr. of 1939 ed. 23.50x (ISBN 0-8046-0425-8, Pub. by Kennikat). Assoc Faculty Pr.

Rebels of Sabrehill. Raymond Giles. 1981. pap. 2.95 (ISBN 0-449-13695-7, GM). Fawcett.

Rebels of the Heavenly Kingdom. Katherine Paterson. 224p. (YA) (gr. 12 up). 1983. 11.95 (ISBN 0-525-66911-6, 01160-350). Lodestar Bks.

Rebels of the Heavenly Kingdom. Katherine Paterson. 249p. (gr. 7 up). 1984. pap. 2.95 (ISBN 0-380-68304-0, 68304, Flare). Avon.

Rebels of the New South. Walter M. Raymond. LC 72-2027. (Black Herietage Library Collection Ser.). (Illus.). Repr. of 1904 ed. 17.25 (ISBN 0-8369-9055-2). Ayer Co Pubs.

Rebels of the Woods: The I.W.W. in the Pacific Northwest. Robert L. Tyler. LC 68-1776. 1967. pap. 7.50 (ISBN 0-87114-018-7). U of Oreg Bks.

Rebels on the Rio Grande: The Civil War Journals of A. B. Peticolas. Ed. by Don E. Alberts. LC 84-17237. (Illus.). 196p. 1984. 19.95 (ISBN 0-8263-0766-3); pap. 9.95 (ISBN 0-8263-0773-6). U of NM Pr.

Rebels; or Boston Before the Revolution. Lydia M. Child. LC 78-64069. Repr. of 1825 ed. 37.50 (ISBN 0-404-17058-7). AMS Pr.

Rebels or Reformers? Dissenting Priests in American Life. William B. Faherty. 1988. 9.95 (ISBN 0-8294-0587-9). Loyola.

Rebel's Progress. Tom Earley. 82p. 1985. 23.50x (ISBN 0-85088-521-3, Pub. by Gomer Pr). State Mutual Bk.

Rebel's Quest. F. M. Busby. 240p. 1985. pap. 2.95 (ISBN 0-553-25994-6). Bantam.

Rebel's Recollections. George C. Eggleston. LC 58-12205. (Indiana University Civil War Centennial Ser.). 1968. Repr. of 1959 ed. 16.00 (ISBN 0-527-26640-X). Kraus Repr.

Rebels Resurgent. William K. Goolrick. LC 84-23984. (Civil War Ser.). 1985. lib. bdg. 19.94 (ISBN 0-8094-4749-5, Pub. by Time-Life) (ISBN 0-8094-4750-9). Silver.

Rebels' Seed. F. M. Busby. 256p. (Orig.). 1986. pap. 2.95 (ISBN 0-553-26115-0, Spectra). Bantam.

Rebels: The Rebel Hero in Films. Joe Morella & Edward Z. Epstein. (Illus.). 224p. 1973. 9.95 (ISBN 0-685-29241-X, Pub. by Citadel Pr); pap. 7.95 (ISBN 0-8065-0360-2). Lyle Stuart.

Rebels United: The Enduring Reality of James Dean. 2nd ed. Joel Brean. Ed. by Elbert Jones. (Illus.). 140p. 1987. pap. 10.50 (ISBN 0-317-63846-7). Brean-Jones Pub.

Rebels Without a Cause? Middle Class Youth & the Transition from School to Work. Peter Aggleton. 160p. 1987. 33.00x (ISBN 1-85000-224-X, Falmer Pr); pap. 18.00x (ISBN 1-85000-225-8, Falmer Pr). Taylor & Francis.

Rebirth & the Western Buddhist. Martin Willson. (Wisdom East-West Book - Grey Ser.). (Orig.). 1987. pap. 6.95 (ISBN 0-86171-215-3). Wisdom MA.

Rebirth for Christianity. Alvin B. Kuhn. LC 76-104032. 1970. 6.50 (ISBN 0-8356-0015-7). Theos Pub Hse.

Rebirth of a Nation: Origins & Rise of Moroccan Nationalism, 1912-1944. John P. Halstead. LC 67-31566. (Middle Eastern Monographs Ser: No. 18). (Orig.). 1967. pap. 8.95x (ISBN 0-674-75000-4). Harvard U Pr.

Rebirth of a Nation: Wales, 1880-1890. Kenneth O. Morgan. (Oxford History of Wales Ser.: Vol. VI). (Illus.). 480p. 1987. pap. 14.95 (ISBN 0-19-821760-9). Oxford U Pr.

Rebirth of a Nation: Wales 1880-1980. Kenneth O. Morgan. (History of Wales Ser.: Vol. VI). 1981. 35.00x (ISBN 0-19-821736-6). Oxford U Pr.

Rebirth of Anthropological Theory. Stanley R. Barrett. 288p. 1984. 27.50x (ISBN 0-8020-5638-5). U of Toronto Pr.

Rebirth of Britain. J. H. Powell et al. (Institute of Economic Affairs Ser.). pap. 2.50 technical (ISBN 0-686-89193-7). Transatl Arts.

Rebirth of Cosmology. Jacques Merleau-Ponty & Bruno Morando. LC 82-60404. (Illus.). xvi, 302p. 1982. pap. text ed. 9.95x (ISBN 0-8214-0606-X). Ohio U Pr.

Rebirth of Images: The Making of St. John's Apocalypse. Austin Farrar. 13.25 (ISBN 0-8446-0617-0). Peter Smith.

Rebirth of Images: The Making of St. John's Apocalypse. Austin Farrer. LC 85-26219. 347p. (Orig.). 1986. 44.50 (ISBN 0-88706-271-7); pap. 14.95 (ISBN 0-88706-272-5). State U NY Pr.

Rebirth of Israel. Ed. by Israel Cohen. LC 75-6427. (Rise of Jewish Nationalism & the Middle East Ser.). 338p. 1975. Repr. of 1952 ed. 25.85 (ISBN 0-88355-314-7). Hyperion Conn.

Rebirth of Jewish Art: The Unfolding of Jewish Art in the Nineteenth Century. Hyman J. Lewbin. LC 74-76483. (Illus.). 1974. 10.00 (ISBN 0-88400-007-9). Shengold.

Rebirth of Ministry: A Study of the Biblical Character of the Church's Ministry. James D. Smart. LC 60-6189. 192p. 1978. pap. 4.95 (ISBN 0-664-24206-5). Westminster John Knox.

Rebirth of Music. LaMar Boshman. 96p. pap. 3.95 (ISBN 0-938612-04-2). Revival Press.

Rebirth of Music: Training Course. Carolyn Smith. 76p. 1985. pap. 4.95 (ISBN 0-938612-10-7). Revival Press.

Rebirth of Norway's Peasantry: Folk Leader Hans Nielsen Hauge. Magnus Nodtuedt. 305p. 1965. octavo 5.95. Holmes.

Rebirth of Power: Overcoming the Effects of Sexual Abuse Through the Experiences of Others. Ed. by Pamela Portwood et al. LC 87-62737. 210p. 1988. pap. 9.95 (ISBN 0-941300-07-2). Mother Courage.

Rebirth of the Congregation. Richard Bieber. 1973. pap. 1.25 (ISBN 0-87508-012-X). Chr Lit.

Rebirth of the Missouri Pacific, 1956-1983. H. Craig Miner. LC 83-45097. (Illus.). 258p. 1983. 19.50 (ISBN 0-89096-159-X). Tex A&M Univ Pr.

Rebirth of the Paraguayan Republic: The First Colorado Era, 1878-1904. Harris G. Warren. LC 84-19528. (Pitt Latin American Ser.). (Illus.). 352p. 1985. 40.95x (ISBN 0-8229-3507-4). U of Pittsburgh Pr.

Rebirth of the Trade Union Movement: 1838-1847. LC 72-2539. (British Labour Struggles Before 1850 Ser). 1972. 20.00 (ISBN 0-405-04431-3). Ayer Co Pubs.

Rebirth. Poems. Forough Farrokhzaad. Tr. by David C. Martin. (Iran-e NO Literary Collection Ser.). (Illus.). 172p. 1985. pap. 9.95 (ISBN 0-939214-30-X). Mazda Pubs.

Rebirth, Reform, & Resilience: Universities in Transition, 1300-1700. Ed. by James M. Kittelson & Pamela J. Transue. LC 83-25095. (Illus.). 373p. 1984. 25.00x (ISBN 0-8142-0356-6). Ohio St U Pr.

Rebirth: When Everyone Forgot. Thomas C. McClary. (Classics of Science Fiction Ser.). 187p. 1976. 15.00 (ISBN 0-88355-373-2); pap. 10.00 (ISBN 0-88355-459-3). Hyperion Conn.

Rebirthing in the New Age. Leonard Orr. pap. 9.95 (ISBN 0-318-23462-9). L Orr.

Rebirthing in the New Age. Leonard Orr & Sondra Ray. LC 76-53337. 1978. pap. 9.95 (ISBN 0-89087-134-5). Celestial Arts.

Rebirthing Made Easy. Colin P. Sisson. 261p. (Orig.). pap. 9.95 (ISBN 0-937611-27-1). Hay House.

Rebirthing: The Science of Enjoying All of Your Life. Jim Leonard & Phil Laut. LC 83-70721. 300p. (Orig.). 1983. pap. 9.95 (ISBN 0-9610132-0-6). Trinity Pubns.

Rebonding: Preventing & Restoring Damaged Relationships. Donald Joy. 192p. 1986. 11.95 (ISBN 0-8499-0519-2, 0519-2). Word Bks.

Reborn Again in the Kingdom. Jacques Sollov. LC 81-71382. (Temple of Love Ser.). (Illus.). 128p. (Orig.). 1982. pap. 10.95 (ISBN 0-941804-04-6). White Eagle Pub.

Reborn As Meaning: Panegyrical Biography from Isocrates to Walton. Michael P. Rewa. 140p. (Orig.). 1983. lib. bdg. 25.00 (ISBN 0-8191-3013-3); pap. text ed. 10.00 (ISBN 0-8191-3014-1). U Pr of Amer.

Reborn Spirit. Margoe Jane. LC 79-84678. (Illus.). 64p. 1979. 3.00x (ISBN 0-9602330-0-8). Margoe Jane.

Reborn to Multiply. Paul Foust. LC 73-9110. 1973. pap. 2.95 (ISBN 0-570-03170-2, 12-2573). Concordia.

Rebound. David Everson. 1988. pap. 3.50 (ISBN 0-8041-0177-9, Pub. by Ivy). Ballantine.

Rebound - Leaders Manual. Aima. 200p. 1986. pap. write for info. (ISBN 0-8403-4171-7). Kendall-Hunt.

Rebound Caper. Thomas J. Dygard. LC 82-18821. 176p. (gr. 7 up). 1983. 11.95 (ISBN 0-688-01707-X). Morrow.

Rebound System. Robert Appel. LC 9-10240. (Illus.). 144p. 1982. pap. 9.95 (ISBN 0-06-091024-0, CN1024, PL). Har-Row.

Rebound: The Autobiography of K. C. Jones & An Inside Look at the Champion Boston Celtics. K. C. Jones & Jack Warner. LC 86-62397. (Illus.). 190p. 1986. 16.95 (ISBN 0-933341-60-1). Quinlan Pr.

Rebound with Weights. Chuck Pfeiffer. LC 83-70893. (Illus.). 136p. (Orig.). 1983. pap. 6.95 (ISBN 0-9611234-0-0). Beaver Pubns.

Rebours. Joris-Karl Huysmans. (Folio Ser.: No. 898). 7.95 (ISBN 0-686-54172-3). Schoenhof.

Rebozos of Love. Ed. by Gloria A. Flores & Juan F. Herrera. (Illus.). 96p. 1974. pap. 3.00 (ISBN 0-317-61560-2). Tolteca Pubns.

Rebuild. Ed. by R. Derricott & S. S. Chissick. LC 81-21942. (Properties of Materials Safety & Environmental Factors Ser.). (Illus.). 300p. pap. 78.00 (2030519). Bks Demand UMI.

Rebuild Your Life. Dale Galloway. 1981. pap. 4.95 (ISBN 0-8423-5323-2). Tyndale.

Rebuilder's Guide. Bill Gothard. LC 80-80352. (Illus.). 250p. 1982. 15.00 (ISBN 0-916888-06-1). Inst Basic Youth.

Rebuilding America. Roger J. Vaughan & Barbara Dyer. Incl. Vol. 1. Financing Public Works in the 1980's. 14.95 (ISBN 0-934842-21-3); Vol. 2. Planning & Managing Public Works in the 1980's. 182p. 14.95 (ISBN 0-934842-22-1). CSPA.

Rebuilding America - Infrastructure Rehabilitation: Proceedings of a Conference Sponsored by the Metropolitan Association of Urban Designers & Environmental Planners. Ed. by Walter H. Kraft & Mary F. Brown. 277p. 1985. 25.00x (ISBN 0-87262-437-4). Am Soc Civil Eng.

Rebuilding America: A Blueprint for the New Economy. Gar Alperovitz & Jeff Faux. 1984. 19.50 (ISBN 0-394-53200-7); pap. 10.95 (ISBN 0-394-71619-1). Pantheon.

Rebuilding America: The Case for Economic Regulation. Frederick C. Thayer, Jr. LC 83-17789. 190p. 1984. 35.00 (ISBN 0-275-91750-9, C1750). Praeger.

Rebuilding American Education. Ed. by Ralph Scott. LC 79-66920. (Orig.). 1979. pap. 4.95 (ISBN 0-9601600-2-7). Quam Pr.

Rebuilding America's Cities: Roads to Recovery. Ed. by Paul R. Porter & David C. Sweet. 224p. 1984. pap. text ed. 14.95x (ISBN 0-88285-099-7). Ctr Urban Pol Res.

Rebuilding America's Infrastructure: An Agenda for the 1980's. Ed. by Michael Barker. (Duke Press Policy Studies). xxxv, 330p. 1983. 33.50 (ISBN 0-8223-0568-2). Duke.

Rebuilding Central Park: A Management & Restoration Plan. Elizabeth B. Rogers et al. Ed. by John Berendt. (Illus.). 176p. 1987. 27.50 (ISBN 0-262-18127-4). MIT Pr.

Rebuilding Grain Reserves: Toward an International System. Philip H. Trezise. LC 76-8911. pap. 20.00 (ISBN 0-317-26592-X, 2025415). Bks Demand UMI.

Rebuilding of Old Commonwealths. Walter H. Page. LC 79-125175. Repr. of 1902 ed. 16.50 (ISBN 0-404-04859-5). AMS Pr.

Rebuilding of Psychology. Gary Collins. 1976. pap. 7.95 (ISBN 0-8423-5315-1). Tyndale.

Rebuilding the Christian Commonwealth: New England Congregationalists & Foreign Missions, 1800-1830. John A. Andrew, III. LC 75-38214. 240p. 1976. 22.00x (ISBN 0-8131-1333-4). U Pr of Ky.

Rebuilding the Famous Ford Flathead. Ron Bishop. (Illus.). 140p. (Orig.). 1981. 9.95 (ISBN 0-8306-9965-1). TAB Bks.

Rebuilding the Liberal Order. D. H. Barran et al. (Institute of Economic Affairs, Occasional Papers Ser.: No. 27). pap. 2.50 technical (ISBN 0-255-69646-9). Transatl Arts.

Rebuilding the Pulp & Paper Workers' Union, 1933-1941. Robert H. Zieger. LC 83-10227. (Twentieth-Century America Ser.). (Illus.). 256p. 1984. 22.95x (ISBN 0-87049-407-4). U of Tenn Pr.

Rebuilding the Real You. Jack W. Hayford. 195p. (Orig.). 1986. pap. 7.95 (ISBN 0-8307-1156-2, 5418849). Regal.

Rebuilding the World. John B. Robinson. 59.95 (ISBN 0-8490-0934-0). Gordon Pr.

Rebuilding the World Economy. Norman S. Buchanan & F. A. Lutz. LC 82-48296. (World Economy Ser.). 434p. 1982. lib. bdg. 55.00 (ISBN 0-8240-5351-6). Garland Pub.

Rebuilding: When Your Relationship Ends. Bruce Fisher. LC 79-24440. 208p. 1981. pap. 7.95 (ISBN 0-915166-30-5). Impact Pubs Cal.

Rebuilding: When Your Relationship Ends. 1981. pap. 7.95 (ISBN 0-317-60869-X). Family Relations.

Rebuilding Your Broken World. Gordon MacDonald. 1988. 12.95 (ISBN 0-8407-9086-4). Oliver-Nelson.

Rebuilt Man. William Beechcroft. 1987. 15.95 (ISBN 0-396-08833-3). Dodd.

Rebuilt Man. William Beechcroft. Ed. by Damaris Rowland. 240p. 1988. pap. 3.50 (ISBN 0-425-10752-3). Berkley Pub.

Rebuke & Challenge: The Point of Jesus' Parables. Norman Young. Ed. by Richard W. Coffen. 96p. (Orig.). 1985. pap. 6.95 (ISBN 0-8280-0286-X). Review & Herald.

Rebus Treasury. Jean Marzollo. LC 85-16133. (Illus.). 64p. (ps up). 1986. 14.95 (ISBN 0-8037-0254-X, 01451-440); PLB 14.89 (ISBN 0-8037-0255-8). Dial Bks Young.

Recalcitrant Rich: A Comparative Analysis of the Northern Responses to the Demands for a New International Economic Order. Ed. by Helge O. Bergesen et al. LC 81-9127. 1982. 26.50x (ISBN 0-312-66573-3). St Martin.

Recall & Recognition. Ed. by John Brown. LC 75-8770. 1976. 85.00 (ISBN 0-471-11229-1, Pub. by Wiley-Interscience). Wiley.

Recall & Recognition. Ed. by John Brown. 285p. pap. 74.10 (2052240). Bks Demand UMI.

Recent Advances in Connective Tissue Research. Ed. by Peter Ghosh. (Agents & Actions Supplements: Vol. 18). 160p. 1986. 29.50 (ISBN 0-8176-1775-2, Pub. by Birkhauser Vlg). Birkhauser.

Recent Advances in Corporate Finance. Edward Altman & Marti G. Subrahmanyam. 1985. 50.00 (ISBN 0-87094-560-2). Dow Jones-Irwin.

Recent Advances in Corporate Finance. Ed. by Jeremy Edwards et al. 320p. 1986. 37.50 (ISBN 0-521-32964-7). Cambridge U Pr.

Recent Advances in Creep & Fracture of Engineering Materials & Structures. Ed. by B. Wilshire & D. R. Owen. 353p. 1982. text ed. 59.00x (ISBN 0-906674-18-2, Pub. by Inst Metals). Brookfield Pub Co.

Recent Advances in Critical Care Medicine, No. 3. Ed. by Iain M. Ledingham. (Illus.). 1988. pap. text ed. 60.00 (ISBN 0-443-03215-7). Churchill.

Recent Advances in Critical Microcirculatory Research: Proceedings of the European Conference on Microcirculation, 8th le Touguet, 1974. European Conference on Microcirculation Staff. Ed. by D. H. Lewis. (Bibliotheca Anatomica: No. 13). (Illus.). 380p. 1975. 94.00 (ISBN 3-8055-2277-0). S Karger.

Recent Advances in Crohn's Disease: Developments in Gastroenterology One. Ed. by A. S. Pena. 549p. 1981. 69.00 (ISBN 90-247-2475-9, Pub. by Martinus Nijhoff Netherlands). Kluwer Academic.

Recent Advances in Cytochalasans. Ed. by G. S. Pendse. 202p. 1987. text ed. 85.00 (ISBN 0-412-29350-1, Pub. by Chapman & Hall). Routledge Chapman & Hall.

Recent Advances In Depression. C. N. Stefanis. 152p. 1982. 26.00 (ISBN 0-08-027954-6). Pergamon.

Recent Advances in Dermatology. Ed. by R. H. Champion. (Illus.). 270p. 1986. 84.00 (ISBN 0-443-03231-9). Churchill.

Recent Advances in Diabetics, Vol. 2. Ed. by Malcolm Nattrass. (Illus.). 213p. 1986. text ed. 64.75 (ISBN 0-443-03467-2). Churchill.

Recent Advances in Diagnosis & Treatment of Infections: Special Issue of Journal of Medicine. Ed. by Thomas R. Beam, Jr. 1983. 19.95 (ISBN 0-915340-12-7). PJD Pubns.

Recent Advances in Differential Equations. Ed. by Roberto Conti. LC 81-15042. 1981. 59.50 (ISBN 0-12-186280-1). Acad Pr.

Recent Advances in Distributed Data Base Management. C. Mohan. (Tutorials Texts Ser.). 341p. 1984. 36.00 (ISBN 0-8186-0571-5). IEEE Comp Soc.

Recent Advances in Drug Delivery Systems. Ed. by James M. Anderson & Sung W. Kim. LC 84-3387. 404p. 1984. 72.50x (ISBN 0-306-41627-1, Plenum Pr). Plenum Pub.

Recent Advances in Dynamical Astronomy: Proceedings of the NATO Advanced Study Institute in Dynamical Astronomy, Cortina D'ampezzo, August, 1972. NATO Advanced Study Institute Staff. Ed. by B. D. Tapley & V. Szebehely. LC 73-83571. (Astrophysics & Space Science Library: No. 39). 490p. 1973. lib. bdg. 71.00 (ISBN 90-277-0348-5, Pub. by Reidel Holland). Kluwer Academic.

Recent Advances in EEG & EMG Data Processing. Ed. by N. Yamaguchi & K. Fujisawa. 422p. 1981. 102.75 (ISBN 0-444-80356-4, Biomedical Pr). Elsevier.

Recent Advances in Electroorganic Synthesis. S. Toril. (Studies in Organic Chemistry: No. 30). 504p. 1987. 194.75 (ISBN 0-444-98963-3). Elsevier.

Recent Advances in Engineering Mechanics & Their Impact on Civil Engineering Practice, 2 Vols. Ed. by W. F. Chen & A. D. Lewis. 1378p. 1983. pap. 106.00x (ISBN 0-87262-358-0). Am Soc Civil Eng.

Recent Advances in Engineering Science, 5 Vols. Ed. by A. C. Eringen. (Orig.). 1967-69. Vol. 1, 878p. 212.00 (ISBN 0-677-10790-0); Vol. 2, 456p. 155.00 (ISBN 0-677-10800-1); Vol. 3, 568p. 170.00 (ISBN 0-677-11880-5); Vol. 4, 362p. 120.00 (ISBN 0-677-13100-3); Vol. 5, 862p., 2 pt. set. 250.00 (ISBN 0-677-13780-X). Gordon & Breach.

Recent Advances in Environmental Analysis. Ed. by Roland W. Frei. (Current Topics in Environmental & Toxicological Chemistry Ser.: Vol.2). 362p. 1979. 110.00 (ISBN 0-677-15950-1). Gordon & Breach.

Recent Advances in Fertility Research, Pt. A: Developments in Reproductive Endocrinology. Ed. by Thomas G. Muldoon & Virendra B. Mahesh. LC 82-20327. (Progress in Clinical & Biological Research Ser.: Vol. 112A). 362p. 1982. 40.00 (ISBN 0-8451-0172-2). A R Liss.

Recent Advances in Fertility Research: Pt. B: Development in the Management of Reproductive Disorders. Thomas G. Muldoon. LC 82-20820. (Progress in Clinical & Biological Research Ser.: Vol. 112B). 288p. 1982. 33.00 (ISBN 0-8451-0173-0). A R Liss.

Recent Advances in Field Theory & Statistical Mechanics: Les Houches, Vol. 39. J Zuber & R. Stora. 1984. 258.00 (ISBN 0-444-86675-2). Elsevier.

Recent Advances in Fluidization & Fluid-Particle Systems. Ed. by D. V. Punwani. LC 81-3525. (AIChE Symposium: Vol. 77). 198p. 1981. pap. 36.00 (ISBN 0-8169-0201-1, S-205). Am Inst Chem Eng.

Recent Advances in Gas Chromatography. Ed. by I. Domsky & J. Perry. 1971. 89.75 (ISBN 0-8247-1146-7). Dekker.

Recent Advances in Gastroenterology, Vol. 6. Ed. by R. E. Pounder. LC 84-642975. (Illus.). 367p. 1986. text ed. 84.00 (ISBN 0-443-03497-4). Churchill.

Recent Advances in Geomathematics: An International Symposium. Ed. by D. F. Merriam. 1978. 69.00 (ISBN 0-08-022095-9). Pergamon.

Recent Advances in Geometric Inequalities. D. S. Mitrinovic et al. 1988. lib. bdg. 149.00 (ISBN 90-277-2565-9, Pub. by Reidel Holland). Kluwer Academic.

Recent Advances in Geriatric Medicine, No. 3. Ed. by Bernard Isaacs. (Illus.). 283p. 1985. text ed. 73.00 (ISBN 0-443-03022-7). Churchill.

Recent Advances in Glaucoma. Ed. by U. Ticho & R. David. (International Congress Ser.: No. 636). 360p. 1984. 133.25 (ISBN 0-444-80611-3, Excerpta Medica). Elsevier.

Recent Advances in Glaucoma: International Glaucoma Symposium, Prague, 1976. Ed. by S. Rehak & G. Paterson. (Illus.). 1977. 51.00 (ISBN 0-387-07944-0). Springer-Verlag.

Recent Advances in Hamiltonian Systems: Proceedings of the International Conference, L'Aquila, June 10-13, 1986. Ed. by G. F. Dell'Antonio & B. D'Onofrio. 256p. 1987. 39.00 (ISBN 9971-50-246-1). World Scientific Pub.

Recent Advances in Hepatology, Vol. 2. Ed. by Howard C. Thomas & E. Anthony Jones. (Illus.). 193p. 1986. text ed. 90.00 (ISBN 0-443-03200-9). Churchill.

Recent Advances in Histopathology, No. 13. Ed. by Peter P. Anthony & Roderick N. MacSween. LC 80-642705. (Illus.). 287p. (Orig.). 1987. pap. text ed. 51.00 (ISBN 0-443-03488-5). Churchill.

Recent Advances in Homotopy Theory. George W. Whitehead. LC 79-145639. (CBMS Regional Conference Series in Mathematics: No. 5). 82p. 1970. pap. 12.00 (ISBN 0-8218-1654-3, CBMS-5). Am Math.

Recent Advances in Immunology. Ed. by Asuman U. Muftuoglu & Nefise Barlas. LC 83-24494. 252p. 1984. 49.50x (ISBN 0-306-41515-1, Plenum Pr). Plenum Pub.

Recent Advances in Inborn Errors of Metabosism. Ed. by K. Tada et al. (Reprint from Journal Enzyme Ser.: Vol. 38, No. 1-4, 198). (Illus.). 332p. 1988. 65.50 (ISBN 3-8055-4772-2). S Karger.

Recent Advances in Insect Physiology Morphology & Ecology. S. C. Pathak. (Illus.). xiii, 324p. 1986. 39.00 (ISBN 1-55528-079-X, Pub. by Messers Today & Tomorrow Printers & Publishers). Scholarly Pubns.

Recent Advances in Knowledge of the Phytoseiidae. Marjorie Hoy. (Illus.). 100p. (Orig.). 1982. pap. 8.00x (ISBN 0-931876-62-1, 3284). ANR Pubns CA.

Recent Advances in Labour Economics. Ed. by G. Hutchinson & J. G. Treble. LC 83-40628. 256p. 1984. 27.50 (ISBN 0-312-66575-X). St Martin.

Recent Advances in Language, Communication & Social Psychology. Ed. by Howard Giles & R. N. St. Clair. 312p. 1986. text ed. 29.95 (ISBN 0-86377-000-2). L Erlbaum Assocs.

Recent Advances in Liquid Crystalline Polymers: Proceedings of the European Science Foundation Sixth Polymer Workshop, Lyngby, Denmark, 12-14 September 1983. Ed. by L. L. Chapoy. (Illus.). 352p. 1985. 81.00 (ISBN 0-85334-313-6, Pub. by Elsevier Applied Sci England). Elsevier.

Recent Advances in Male Reproduction: Molecular Basis & Clinical Implications. Ed. by R. D'Agata et al. (Serono Symposia Publications from Raven Press Ser.: Vol. 7). (Illus.). 350p. 1983. text ed. 75.50 (ISBN 0-89004-918-1). Raven.

Recent Advances in Materials Research. Ed. by C. M. Srivastava. 379p. 1984. text ed. 46.00 (ISBN 90-6191-411-6, Pub. by A A Balkema). Brookfield Pub Co.

Recent Advances in Matrix Theory. Ed. by Hans Schneider. LC 64-20843. (U. S. Army Mathematics Research Center Publication: No. 12). pap. 38.50 (ISBN 0-317-09153-0, 2015372). Bks Demand UMI.

Recent Advances in Mechanistic & Synthetic Aspects of Polymerization. Ed. by M. Fontanille & A. Guyot. 1987. lib. bdg. 99.50 (ISBN 90-277-2602-7, Pub. by Reidel Holland). Kluwer Academic.

Recent Advances in Medical Thermology. Ed. by Francis J. Ring & Barbara Phillips. LC 84-3366. 723p. 1984. 115.00x (ISBN 0-306-41672-7, Plenum Pr). Plenum Pub.

Recent Advances in Microcirculatory Research. Ed. by P. Gaehtgens. (Bibliotheca Anatomica Ser.: No. 20). (Illus.). xvi, 740p. 1981. 196.75 (ISBN 3-8055-2272-X). S Karger.

Recent Advances in Mucosal Immunity. Ed. by Warren Strober et al. 454p. 1982. text ed. 113.50 (ISBN 0-89004-642-5). Raven.

Recent Advances in Nemertean Biology. Ed. by P. Sundberg et al. (Developments in Hydrobiology Ser.). 1988. lib. bdg. 99.00 (ISBN 90-6193-647-0, Pub. by Junk Pubs Netherlands). Kluwer Academic.

Recent Advances in Nervous System Toxicology. Ed. by Corraldo L. Galli et al. LC 85-25805. (NATO ASI Series A: Life Sciences: Vol. 100). 390p. 1987. 69.50x (ISBN 0-306-42209-3, Plenum Pr). Plenum Pub.

Recent Advances in Neuropathology, Vol. 3. Ed. by J. B. Cavanaugh. LC 78-40946. 167p. 1986. text ed. 72.00 (ISBN 0-443-03226-2). Churchill.

Recent Advances in Neuropsychopharmacology: Selected Papers from the 12th Congress of the Collegium Internationale Neuro-Psychopharmacologicum Goteborg, Sweden, 22-26 June, 1980. Ed. by B. Angrist et al. (Illus.). 422p. 1981. 97.00 (ISBN 0-08-026382-8). Pergamon.

Recent Advances in Nuclear Medicine, Vol. IV. Ed. by John H. Lawrence. LC 65-299263. (Illus.). 256p. 1974. 85.50 (ISBN 0-8089-0837-5, 792464). Grune.

Recent Advances in Nuclear Medicine, Vol. V. Ed. by John H. Lawrence & Thomas Budinger. 160p. 1978. 65.50 (ISBN 0-8089-1068-X, 792465). Grune.

Recent Advances in Nuclear Medicine, Vol. 3. Ed. by John H. Lawrence. LC 65-12654. (Illus.). 256p. 1971. 85.50 (ISBN 0-8089-0697-6, 792463). Grune.

Recent Advances in Nuclear Medicine, Vol. 6. Ed. by John H. Lawrence. H. Saul Winchell. 224p. 1983. 65.50 (ISBN 0-8089-1592-4, 792466). Grune.

Recent Advances in Numerical Analysis. Ed. by Carl De Boor & Gene H. Golub. (Mathematics Research Center Symposia Ser.). 1978. 44.50 (ISBN 0-12-208360-1). Acad Pr.

Recent Advances in Obesity & Diabetes Research. Ed. by N. Melchionda et al. (Serono Symposia Publications from Raven Press Ser.: Vol. 8). (Illus.). 442p. 1984. text ed. 104.50 (ISBN 0-89004-969-6). Raven.

Recent Advances in Obesity Research, Vol. 1. Ed. by Alan Howard. LC 76-11950. (Illus.). 1976. 29.00 (ISBN 0-87762-201-9). Technomic.

Recent Advances in Obesity Research, Vol. 2. George A. Bray. LC 78-64353. 510p. 1978. 29.00 (ISBN 0-87762-259-0). Technomic.

Recent Advances in Obstetrics & Gynaecology, No. 15. Ed. by John Bonnar. LC 81-644212. (Illus.). 282p. 1987. text ed. 48.00 (ISBN 0-443-03413-3). Churchill.

Recent Advances in Occupational Health--3. Ed. by J. M. Harrington. LC 85-644853. (Illus.). 350p. 1987. text ed. 74.00 (ISBN 0-443-03577-6). Churchill.

Recent Advances in Optimization Techniques: Proceedings. Symposium on Recent Advances in Optimization Techniques 1965, Carnegie Institute of Technology. Ed. by Abrahim Lavi et al. LC 66-4421. pap. 160.00 (ISBN 0-317-08576-X, 2006349). Bks Demand UMI.

Recent Advances in Pathophysiological Conditions in Pregnancy. J. G. Schenker et al. (International Congress Ser.: Vol. 631). 1984. 175.25 (ISBN 0-444-80588-5, I-346-84). Elsevier.

Recent Advances in Pediatric Nephrology. Ed. by J. F. Pascual & P. L. Calcagno. (Contributions to Nephrology: Vol. 27). (Illus.). vi, 98p. 1981. pap. 43.50 (ISBN 3-8055-1851-X). S Karger.

Recent Advances in Pediatric Nephrology: Proceedings of the Seventh International Congress, Tokyo, Japan, September 7-12, 1986. Ed. by K. Murakami et al. (International Congress Ser.: No. 733). 676p. 1987. 170.75 (ISBN 0-444-80888-4). Elsevier.

Recent Advances in Pediatric Surgery. 2nd ed. A. W. Wilkinson. (Illus.). 288p. 1969. 57.50 (ISBN 0-8089-0593-7, 794845). Grune.

Recent Advances in Perinatal Pathology & Physiology, Vol. 4. Denis N. White. LC 80-41367. (Ultrasound in Biomedicine Ser.). 245p. 1981. 91.95x (ISBN 0-471-27925-0, Pub. by Res Stud Pr). Wiley.

Recent Advances in Perinatology: Proceedings, 4th Asia-Oceania Congress of Perinatology, Tokyo, Japan, April 8-11, 1986. Ed. by K. Maeda et al. (International Congress Ser.: No. 712). 444p. 1987. 138.50 (ISBN 0-444-80842-6, Excerpta Medica). Elsevier.

Recent Advances in Personal Construct Technology. Ed. by M. L. Shaw. (Computers & People Ser.). 1981. 40.50 (ISBN 0-12-639260-9). Acad Pr.

Recent Advances in Phytochemistry, Vol. 2: Proceedings of the 7th Annual Symposium of the Phytochemical Society of North America. Phytochemical Society of North America. Ed. by Margaret K. Seikel. pap. 46.80 (ISBN 0-317-26217-3, 2055689). Bks Demand UMI.

Recent Advances in Planetary Meterology. Ed. by Garry E. Hunt. 300p. 1985. 49.50 (ISBN 0-521-25886-3). Cambridge U Pr.

Recent Advances in Plant Nutrition, 2 vols. R. M. Samish. LC 78-179403. (Illus.). 1972. Set. 175.00 (ISBN 0-677-14390-7); Vol. 1, 368p. 95.00 (ISBN 0-677-12360-4); Vol. 2, 410p. 105.00 (ISBN 0-677-12370-1). Gordon & Breach.

Recent Advances in Plastic Surgery, No. 3. Ed. by Ian Jackson & Brian C. Sommerlad. (Illus.). 260p. 1985. text ed. 95.00 (ISBN 0-443-02975-X). Churchill.

Recent Advances in Postpartum Psychiatric Disorders. David G. Inwood. LC 85-15619. (Clinical Insights Monograph). 144p. 1985. pap. text ed. 12.00x (ISBN 0-88048-083-1, 48-083-1). Am Psychiatric.

Recent Advances in Prenatal Diagnosis: Proceedings of the First International Symposium on Recent Advances in Prenatal Diagnosis, Bologna, September 15-16, 1980. C. Orlandi et al. 344p. 1981. 89.95x (ISBN 0-471-09987-2, Pub. by Res Stud Pr). Wiley.

Recent Advances in Prenatal Diagnosis: Proceedings of the First International Symposium on Recent Advances in Prenatal Diagnosis, Bologna, September 15th-16th, 1980. Ed. by Camillo Orlandi et al. LC 81-198305. (Illus.). pap. 89.50 (ISBN 0-317-58634-3, 2029638). Bks Demand UMI.

Recent Advances in Primary & Acquired Immunodeficiencies. Ed. by F. Aiuti et al. (Serono Symposia Publications from Raven Press Ser.: Vol. 28). 446p. 1986. text ed. 61.50 (ISBN 0-88167-196-7). Raven.

Recent Advances in Primatology, Vols. 1-4. Ed. by David C. Chivers. Vol. 1, 1978. 110.00 (ISBN 0-12-173301-7); Vol. 2, 1978. 78.00 (ISBN 0-12-173302-5); Vol. 3, 1978. 92.00 (ISBN 0-12-173303-3); Vol. 4, 1978. 64.00 (ISBN 0-12-173304-1). Acad Pr.

Recent Advances in Psychogeriatrics, No. 1. Tom Arie. (Illus.). 235p. 1985. text ed. 77.00 (ISBN 0-443-03080-4). Churchill.

Recent Advances in Radiology & Medical Imaging, No. 8. Ed. by R. E. Steiner & T. Sherwood. (Illus.). 213p. 1986. text ed. 95.00 (ISBN 0-443-03108-8). Churchill.

Recent Advances in Receptor Chemistry: Proceedings of the 6th Camerino-Noordwijkerhout Symposium, Camerino, Italy,6-10 Sept., 1987. Ed. by C. Melchiorre & M. Giannella. (Pharmacochemistry Library: No. 11). 334p. 1988. 123.75 (ISBN 0-444-42965-4). Elsevier.

Recent Advances in Renal Cell Carcinoma. Ed. by C. Bollack & J. Cinqualbre. (Progress in Surgery: Vol. 17). (Illus.). viii, 160p. 1983. bound 86.75 (ISBN 3-8055-3621-6). S Karger.

Recent Advances in Renal Metabolism. Ed. by K. Kurokawa & R. Tanner. (Journal: Mineral Electrolyte Metabolism: Vol. 9: No. 5-6). (Illus.). vi, 148p. 1983. 113.50 (ISBN 3-8055-3652-6). S Karger.

Recent Advances in Renal Physiology. International Symposium on Renal Handling of Sodium, Brestenberg, 1971. Ed. by H. Wirz & F. Spinelli. 300p. 1972. 65.50 (ISBN 3-8055-1405-0). S Karger.

Recent Advances in Renal Research: Contributions from Japan. Ed. by K. Maeda et al. (Contributions to Nephrology: Vol. 9). (Illus.). 1978. 32.75 (ISBN 3-8055-2826-4). S Karger.

Recent Advances in Respiratory Medicine, Vol. 4. David C. Fenley & Thomas L. Petty. (Illus.). 285p. 1986. text ed. 90.00 (ISBN 0-443-03411-7). Churchill.

Recent Advances in Robotics. Susan Hackwood & Gerardo Beni. (Advances in Robotics Ser.). 426p. 1985. 32.50 (ISBN 0-471-88383-2, Pub. by Wiley-Interscience). Wiley.

Recent Advances in School Librarianship. Frances L. Carroll. (Recent Advances in Library & Information Science Ser.). (Illus.). 250p. 1981. text ed. 42.00 (ISBN 0-08-026084-5). Pergamon.

Recent Advances in Sensors, Radiometry, & Data Processing for Remote Sensing. Ed. by Slater. 1988. 57.00 (ISBN 0-89252-959-8, 924). SPIE.

Recent Advances in Separation Techniques--III. Ed. by Norman N. Li. LC 86-26513. (Symposium Ser.: Vol. 82, No. 250). 208p. 1986. pap. 44.00 (ISBN 0-8169-0392-1). Am Inst Chem Eng.

Recent Advances in Separation Techniques II. LC 79-24225. 104p. 1980. pap. 22.00 (ISBN 0-8169-0121-X, S-192). Am Inst Chem Eng.

Recent Advances in Separation Techniques. 149p. 1972. pap. 24.00 (ISBN 0-8169-0073-6, S-120). Am Inst Chem Eng.

Recent Advances in Statistical Physics: Proceedings of the International Base Symposium on Statistical Physics. Ed. by B. Dutta & M. Dutta. 176p. 1987. 44.00 (ISBN 9971-50-369-7). World Scientific Pub.

Recent Advances in Statistics: Papers in Honor of Herman Chernoff on his Sixthieth Birthday. Ed. by G. Gaseeb Rizvi & Jagdish Rustage. 1983. 47.00 (ISBN 0-12-589320-5). Acad Pr.

Recent Advances in Steroid Hormone Action. Ed. by V. K. Moudgil. 552p. 1987. lib. bdg. 116.00x (ISBN 0-89925-313-X). De Gruyter.

Recent Advances in Structural Dynamics. Ed. by Gerald C. Pardoen. (Sessions Proceedings Ser.). 53p. 1986. 11.50x (ISBN 0-87262-530-3). Am Soc Civil Eng.

Recent Developments in Civil Aviation in India. Shri J. Tytler. 1987. 26.00 (ISBN 81-7095-004-X, Pub. by Lancer India). South Asia Bks.

Recent Developments in Civil Litigation. 107p. 1987. pap. 25.00 (CP-49049). Cal Cont Ed Bar.

Recent Developments in Classical Wave Scattering: Focus on the T-Matrix Approach. International Symposium on Recent Developments in Classical Wave Scattering, Ohio State Univ., Columbus, 1979. Ed. by V. V. Varadan & V. K. Varadan. (Illus.). 670p. 1980. 115.00 (ISBN 0-08-025096-3). Pergamon.

Recent Developments in Clinical Immunology. Ed. by G. W. Reeves. (Research Monographs in Immunology: Vol. 6). 216p. 1984. 97.00 (ISBN 0-444-80554-0, 1-273-84). Elsevier.

Recent Developments in Clinical Research. Ed. by C. E. Orfanos. (Current Problems in Dermatology: Vol. 13). (Illus.). viii, 192p. 1984. 109.50 (ISBN 3-8055-3928-2). S Karger.

Recent Developments in Competitive Business Practices Litigation. 154p. 1986. pap. 26.00 (BU-49027). Cal Cont Ed Bar.

Recent Developments in Condensed Matter Physics, Vol. 1: Invited Papers. Ed. by J. T. Devreese et al. LC 80-28067. 874p. 1981. 110.00x (ISBN 0-306-40646-2, Plenum Pr). Plenum Pub.

Recent Developments in Condensed Matter Physics, Vol. 2: Metals, Disordered Systems, Surfaces & Interfaces. Ed. by J. T. Devreese et al. LC 80-28067. 496p. 1981. 85.00x (ISBN 0-306-40647-0, Plenum Pr). Plenum Pub.

Recent Developments in Condensed Matter Physics, Vol. 3: Impurities, Excitons, Polarons, & Polaritons. Ed. by J. T. Devreese et al. LC 80-28067. 436p. 1981. 75.00x (ISBN 0-306-40648-9, Plenum Pr). Plenum Pub.

Recent Developments in Condensed Matter Physics, Vol. 4: Low-Dimensional Systems, Phase Changes, & Experimental Techniques. Ed. by J. T. Devreese et al. LC 80-28067. 464p. 1981. 79.50x (ISBN 0-306-40649-7, Plenum Pr); Set (Vols. 1-4) 275.00. Plenum Pub.

Recent Developments in Control Theory & Its Applications: Proceedings of Bilateral Meeting on Control Systems. Ed. by Chinese Association of Automation Staff. 1006p. 1982. 151.95 (ISBN 0-677-31040-4). Gordon & Breach.

Recent Developments in Criminal Law Practice: 1987. 315p. 1987. pap. 29.00 (CR-49052). Cal Cont Ed Bar.

Recent Developments in Electronic Engine Control & Fuel Injection Management. 1987. 32.00 (ISBN 0-89883-974-2, SP703). Soc Auto Engineers.

Recent Developments in European Thought. Ed. by Francis S. Marvin. LC 71-111851. (Essay Index Reprint Ser.). 1920. 19.00 (ISBN 0-8369-1619-0). Ayer Co Pubs.

Recent Developments in External Debt Restructuring. K. Burke Dillon et al. (Occasional Papers: No. 40). vii, 68p. 1985. pap. 7.50 (ISBN 0-939934-52-3). Intl Monetary.

Recent Developments in Fluvial Sedimentology. Ed. by Frank G. Ethridge et al. (Special Publications Ser.: No. 39). 398p. 1987. 49.00 (ISBN 0-918985-67-6). SEPM.

Recent Developments in Food Analysis: Proceedings Euro Food Chem, I. Euro Food Chem Staff. Ed. by W. Baltes et al. (Illus.). 500p. (Orig.). 1982. 61.30x (ISBN 3-527-25942-2). VCH Pubs.

Recent Developments in Gauge Theories. Ed. by Thooft et al. LC 80-18528. (NATO ASI Series B, Physics: Vol. 59). 446p. 1980. 79.50x (ISBN 0-306-40479-6, Plenum Pr). Plenum Pub.

Recent Developments in Georgia Law. 313p. 1983. 12.00 (ISBN 0-318-02435-7). ICLE Georgia.

Recent Developments in Geotechnical Engineering for Hydro Projects: Embankment Dam Instrumentation Performance, Engineering Geology Aspects, Rock Mechanics Studies. Ed. by Fred Kulhavy. LC 81-66345. 253p. 1981. pap. 17.00x (ISBN 0-87262-269-X). Am Soc Civil Eng.

Recent Developments in Graphic Arts Research see Advances in Printing Science & Technology.

Recent Developments in Ground Improvement Techniques: Proceedings of the International Symposium Held at Asian Institute of Technology, Bangkok, 29 November - 3 December 1982. Ed. by A. S. Balasubramaniam et al. 598p. 1985. text ed. 95.00 (ISBN 90-6191-568-6, Pub. by A A Balkema). Brookfield Pub Co.

Recent Developments in High Energy Physics. Ed. by H. Mitter & C. B. Lang. (Acta Physica Austriaca Ser.: Supp. 25). (Illus.). 547p. 1983. 69.00 (ISBN 0-387-81771-9). Springer-Verlag.

Recent Developments in Historical Phonology. Ed. by Jacek Fisiak. (Trends in Linguistics Ser.). 1978. pap. text ed. 69.00x (ISBN 90-279-7706-2). Mouton.

Recent Developments in Hydrogen Technology. Ed. by Kenneth D. Williamson, Jr. & Fred J. Edeskuty. LC 84-29360. 1986. Vol. I, 168p. 79.00 ea. (ISBN 0-8493-5126-X). Vol. II, 168p (ISBN 0-8493-5127-8). CRC Pr.

Recent Developments in Infrared Components & Subsystems. Ed. by Hall. 1988. price not set (ISBN 0-89252-950-4, 915). SPIE.

Recent Developments in Insurance Practice. Hamline University, Advanced Legal Education Staff. 210p. 1985. 3-ring binder 42.40 (ISBN 0-317-42510-2). Hamline Law.

Recent Developments in International Banking - 1986. Sarkis J. Khoury & Alo Ghosh. (Illus.). 304p. 1986. 40.00x (ISBN 0-669-13211-X). Lexington Bks.

Recent Developments in International Banking & Finance, Vol. 2. Ed. by Saskis J. Khoury & Alo Ghosh. LC 85-46007. 448p. 1988. 59.00 (ISBN 0-669-16197-7). Lexington Bks.

Recent Developments in Ion Exchange: Proceeding of the International Conference, Ion-Ex '87, Held at the North East Wales Institue, Wrexham, Clwyd, U.K., 13-16 April, 1987. P. A. Williams & M. J. Hudson. 356p. 1987. 81.00 (ISBN 1-85166-101-8). Elsevier.

Recent Developments in Japanese Economics. Ryuzo Sato & Takashi Negishi. 400p. 1988. price not set (ISBN 0-12-619845-4). Acad Pr.

Recent Developments in Job Security: Layoffs & Discipline in the Public Sector. June Weisberger. LC 76-379018. (IPE Monograph: No. 6). 60p. 1976. pap. 2.25 (ISBN 0-87546-258-8). ILR Pr.

Recent Developments in Laboratory & Field Tests & Analysis of Geotechnical Problems: Proceedings of International Symposium, Bangkok, 6-9 December 1983. Ed. by A. S. Balasubrmaniam et al. 632p. 1986. text ed. 99.50 (ISBN 90-6191-623-2, Pub. by A A Balkema). Brookfield Pub Co.

Recent Developments in Laboratory Identification Techniques. Ed. by R. Facklam et al. (International Congress Ser.: Vol. 519). 210p. 1980. 54.75 (ISBN 0-444-90152-3, Excerpta Medica). Elsevier.

Recent Developments in Lattice Theory. W. Ludwig. (Springer Tracts in Modern Physics: Vol. 43). (Illus.). 1967. 69.70 (ISBN 0-387-03982-1). Springer-Verlag.

Recent Developments in Licensing. 264p. 1981. pap. 20.00 (ISBN 0-686-47987-4). Amer Bar Assn.

Recent Developments in Markow Decision Process. R. Hartley. (IMA Conference Ser.). 1981. 74.50 (ISBN 0-12-328460-0). Acad Pr.

Recent Developments in Mass Spectrometry in Biochemistry & Medicine, Vol. 6. Ed. by Alberto Frigerio & M. McCamish. (Analytical Chemistry Symposia Ser.: Vol. 4). 554p. 1981. 123.00 (ISBN 0-444-41870-9). Elsevier.

Recent Developments in Mass Spectrometry in Biochemistry, Medicine & Environmental Research: Proc. of the 8th International Symposium, Venice, June 18-19, 1983. Ed. by A. Frigerio. (Analytical Chemistry Symposia Ser.: Vol. 12). 346p. 1983. 116.00 (ISBN 0-444-42055-X). Elsevier.

Recent Developments in Mass Spectrometry in Biochemistry, Medicine & Environmental Research. Ed. by Alberto Frigerio. (Analytical Chemistry Symposia Ser.: Vol. 7). 1981. 116.00 (ISBN 0-444-42029-0). Elsevier.

Recent Developments in Materials & Detectors for the Infrared. Ed. by Morten & Seeley. 146p. 1985. 43.00 (ISBN 0-89252-623-8, 588). SPIE.

Recent Developments in Mathematical Physics. Ed. by H. Mitter & L. Pintter. (Illus.). 335p. 1987. 54.00 (ISBN 0-387-18502-X). Springer-Verlag.

Recent Developments in Mechanical Testing - STP 608. Ed. by A. K. Schmieder. 133p. 1976. pap. 14.50 (ISBN 0-8031-0547-9, 04-608000-23). ASTM.

Recent Developments in Medical & Physiological Imaging. Ed. by Ray Clark & Mervyn Goff. 180p. 1986. pap. text ed. 55.00x (ISBN 0-85066-955-3). Taylor & Francis.

Recent Developments in Mucosal Immunology. Ed. by Jiri Mestecky et al. LC 87-14129. (Illus.). 1866p. 1987. Pt. A. 110.00x (ISBN 0-306-42614-5, Plenum Pr); Pt. B. 135.00x (ISBN 0-306-42775-3); Set. 225.00x. Plenum Pub.

Recent Developments in Nitrogen Fixation. W. Newton. 1978. 99.00 (ISBN 0-12-517350-4). Acad Pr.

Recent Developments in Nonequilibrium Thermodynamics: Fluids & Related Topics. Ed. by J. Casas-Vazquez et al. (Lecture Notes in Physics: Vol 253). x, 392p. 1986. 34.30 (ISBN 0-387-16489-8). Springer-Verlag.

Recent Developments in Nonequilibrium Thermodynamics: Proceedings of the Meeting Held at Bellaterra School of Thermodynamics, Autonomous University of Barcelona, Spain, Sept. 26-30, 1983. Ed. by J. Casas-Vazquez et al. (Lecture Notes in Physics Ser.: Vol. 199). xiii, 485p. 1984. pap. 29.00 (ISBN 0-387-12927-8). Springer-Verlag.

Recent Developments in Numerical Integration. Smith. 1988. write for info. (ISBN 0-471-09019-0). Wiley.

Recent Developments in Orthopaedic Surgery. Ed. by J. Noble & C. S. Galasko. 320p. 1988. 60.00 (ISBN 0-7190-2542-7, Pub. by Manchester Univ Pr). St Martin.

Recent Developments in Pacemaker Technology. Kalman Ausubel & Seymour Furman. LC 87-70653. 24p. (Orig.). 1987. write for info. (ISBN 0-935404-65-1). Biomedical Info.

Recent Developments in Parkinson's Disease. Ed. by Stanley Fahn et al. (Illus.). 400p. 1986. text ed. 94.00 (ISBN 0-88167-132-0). Raven.

Recent Developments in Particle & Field Theory. Ed. by W. Dittrich. 1979. casebound 56.00 (ISBN 3-528-08426-X, Pub. by Vieweg & Sohn Germany). IPS.

Recent Developments in Particle Physics. Ed. by M. J. Moravcsik. (Nuclear Physics Ser.). 272p. (Orig.). 1966. 104.00 (ISBN 0-677-11010-3). Gordon & Breach.

Recent Developments in Patent, Trademark & Copyright Law. Patent, Trademark & Copyright Law Section. 75p. 1984. pap. 15.00. Amer Bar Assn.

Recent Developments in Pesticide Toxicology & Registration. Ed. by M. A. Mehlman et al. (Illus.). 250p. 1988. 58.00 (ISBN 0-911131-34-5). Princeton Sci Pubs.

Recent Developments in Pipeline Welding WI: RPW. 82p. 1979. 50.00 (ISBN 0-686-95595-1). Am Welding.

Recent Developments in Plant Sciences: Prof. S. M. Sircar Memorial Volume. Ed. by S. P. Sen. (Illus.). 395p. 1982. 39.00 (ISBN 0-88065-241-1, Pub. by Messers Today & Tomorrow Printers & Publishers). Scholarly Pubns.

Recent Developments in Polyurethanes & Interpenetrating Polymer Networks. Ed. by Kurt C. Frisch, Jr. LC 87-51683. 260p. 1988. pap. 55.00 (ISBN 0-87762-589-1). Technomic.

Recent Developments in Production Research: Selected Papers from the 9th International Conference on Production Research, August 17-20, 1987, Cincinati, Ohio. Ed. by A. Mital. (Manufacturing Research & Technology Ser.: Vol. 6). 900p. 1988. 197.25 (ISBN 0-444-42929-8). Elsevier.

Recent Developments in Psychoanalysis: A Critical Evaluation. Morris N. Eagle. LC 87-196. 272p. 1987. pap. text ed. 9.95x (ISBN 0-674-75080-2). Harvard U Pr.

Recent Developments in Psychoanalysis. M. N. Eagle. 1984. text ed. 21.95 (ISBN 0-07-018597-2). McGraw.

Recent Developments in Psychogeriatrics: A Symposium. Ed. by David Kay & Alexander Walk. LC 70-502113. (British Journal of Psychiatry. Special Publication: No. 6). pap. 35.10 (2031459). Bks Demand UMI.

Recent Developments in Quantum Field Theory: Proceedings of the Niels Bohr Centennial Conference, Copenhagen, Denmark, May 6-10, 1985. Ed. by J. B. Ambjorn et al. 306p. 1985. Set. 55.25 (North Holland); 39.00 (ISBN 0-444-86978-6) (ISBN 0-317-38668-9). Elsevier.

Recent Developments in Reading. Conference On Reading - University Of Chicago - 1965. Ed. by H. Alan Robinson. LC 66-23696. (Supplementary Educational Monographs Ser: No. 95). 1965. 6.50x (ISBN 0-226-72177-9). U of Chicago Pr.

Recent Developments in Real Property Law Practice. 510p. 1987. pap. 35.00 (RE-49058). Cal Cont Ed Bar.

Recent Developments in Regional Science. R. Funck. (Karlsruhe Papers in Regional Science). 153p. 1974. pap. 10.00x (ISBN 0-85086-034-2, NO. 2912, Pub. by Pion England). Routledge Chapman & Hall.

Recent Developments in Ruminant Nutrition, 2. W. Haresign & D. J. Cole. (Illus.). 352p. 1988. text ed. 54.95 (ISBN 0-407-01164-1). Butterworth.

Recent Developments in Separation Science, Vols. VI & VII. Norman N. Li. 1981. Vol. VI, 208p. 85.00 (ISBN 0-8493-5487-0); Vol. VII, 224p. 89.00 (ISBN 0-8493-5488-9). CRC Pr.

Recent Developments in Separation Science, Vol. IX. Ed. by Norman N. Li & Joseph M. Calo. 352p. 1986. 135.00 (ISBN 0-8493-5490-0). CRC Pr.

Recent Developments in Separation Science, Vol. VIII. Ed. by Norman N. Li & James D. Navratil. 344p. 1986. 135.00 (ISBN 0-8493-5489-7). CRC Pr.

Recent Developments in Shock Tube Research: Proceedings. International Shock Tube Symposium, 9th, Stanford Univ., 1973. Ed. by Daniel Bershader & Wayland Griffith. LC 73-80624. (Illus.). 848p. 1973. 50.00x (ISBN 0-8047-0842-8). Stanford U Pr.

Recent Developments in Space Flight Mechanics. Ed. by P. B. Richards. (Science & Technology Ser.: Vol. 9). 1966. 25.00x (ISBN 0-87703-037-5). Univelt Inc.

Recent Developments in Spatial Data Analysis: Methodology, Measurement, Models. Ed. by Gerhard Bahrenberg et al. 426p. 1984. text ed. 41.95x (ISBN 0-566-00685-5). Gower Pub Co.

Recent Developments in Statistical Inference & Data Analysis. Ed. by K. Matusita. 364p. 1980. 102.75 (ISBN 0-444-86104-1, North-Holland). Elsevier.

Recent Developments in Statistics: European Meeting of Statisticians, Sept. 6-11, 1976, Grenoble, France. Ed. by J. R. Barra et al. 808p. 1977. 131.75 (ISBN 0-7204-0751-6, North-Holland). Elsevier.

Recent Developments in Structural Optimization. Ed. by Franklin Y. Cheng. (Sessions Proceedings Ser.). 108p. 1986. 15.00x (ISBN 0-87262-557-5). Am Soc Civil Eng.

Recent Developments in Structured Continual. Ed. by Daniel DeKee & Purna Kaloni. LC 86-13264. (Pitman Research Notes in Mathematics Ser.). 1987. pap. 52.95 (ISBN 0-470-20364-1, Co-Pub. with Longman). Wiley.

Recent Developments in the Algebraic, Analytical, & Topological Theory of Semigroups. Ed. by K. H. Hoffman et al. (Lecture Notes in Mathematics: Vol. 998). 486p. 1983. pap. 27.50 (ISBN 0-387-12321-0). Springer-Verlag.

Recent Developments in the Chemistry of Natural Carbon Compounds, Vol. 6. Bognar. 1975. cancelled 14.00 (ISBN 963-05-0388-3, Pub. by Akademiai Kaido Hungary). IPS.

Recent Developments in the Chemistry of Natural Carbon Compounds, Vol. 6. Ed. by Collet's Holdings, Ltd. Staff. 198p. 1975. 42.00x (ISBN 0-569-08195-5, Pub. by Collets (UK)). State Mutual Bk.

Recent Developments in the Chemistry of Natural Carbon Compound, Vol. 8. C. Szantay & L. Novac. (Synthesis of Prostaglandins Ser.). 267p. 1978. 89.00x (ISBN 0-569-08421-0, Pub. by Collets (UK)). State Mutual Bk.

Recent Developments in the Chemistry of Natural Carbon Compounds, Vol. 9. Bognar et al. 420p. 1979. cancelled 41.00 (ISBN 963-05-1632-2, Pub. by Akademiai Kaido Hungary). IPS.

Recent Developments in the Chemistry of Natural Carbon Compounds, Vol. 9. Ed. by Collet's Holdings, Ltd. Staff. 420p. 1979. 150.00x (ISBN 0-569-08590-X, Pub. by Collets (UK)). State Mutual Bk.

Recent Developments in the Chemistry of Natural Carbon Compounds, Vol. 10. Bognar & Szantay. 1984. cancelled 21.00 (ISBN 963-05-3255-7, Pub. by Akademiai Kaido Hungary). IPS.

Recent Developments in the Design & Construction of Piles. (Conference Proceedings Ser.). 412p. 1980. 65.00 (ISBN 0-7277-0082-0, Pub. by T Telford UK). Am Soc Civil Eng.

Recent Developments in the Foundations of Utility & Risk Theory. L. Daboni et al. 1986. lib. bdg. 74.00 (ISBN 90-277-2201-3, Pub. by Reidel). Kluwer Academic.

Recent Developments in the Nuclear Many-Body Problem. Collet's Holdings, Ltd. Staff. 1986. 49.00x (ISBN 0-317-52961-7, Pub. by Collets (UK)). State Mutual Bk.

Recent Developments in the Nuclear Many Body Problem 11: Nuclear Reactions & Dynamics. Ed. by Collet's Staff. 1986. 35.00x (ISBN 0-317-52962-5, Pub. by Collets (UK)). State Mutual Bk.

Recent Developments in the Pharmacology of Inflammatory Mediators. Ed. by I. L. Bonta. (Agents & Actions Suplements: No. 2). 178p. 1977. pap. 41.95x (ISBN 0-8176-0914-8). Birkhauser.

Recent Developments in the Study of Economic & Business History: Essays in Memory of Herman E. Krooss. Ed. by Robert E. Gallman. LC 76-13956. (Research in Economic History: Suppl. 1). 450p. 1977. lib. bdg. 56.50 (ISBN 0-89232-035-4). Jai Pr.

Recent Developments in the Textual Criticism of the Greek Bible. F. G. Kenyon. (British Academy of London Ser.). pap. 19.00 (ISBN 0-8115-1274-6). Kraus Repr.

Recent Developments in the Theory of Direct Reactions see Reaction Dynamics.

Recent Developments in the Theory of Function Spaces. Hans Triebel. 286p. 1983. text ed. 73.95 (ISBN 3-7643-1381-1). Birkhauser.

Recent Developments in Theoretical & Experimental Fluid Mechanics: Compressible & Incompressible Flows. Ed. by U. Mueller et al. (Illus.). 1979. 55.00 (ISBN 0-387-09228-5). Springer-Verlag.

Recent Developments in Theoretical Physics: Proceedings of the National Symposium. Ed. by E. C. Sudarshan & K. Strinivasa Rao. 352p. 1988. 55.00 (ISBN 9971-50-457-X). World Scientific Pub.

Recent Developments in Thermomechanics of Solids. Ed. by G. Lebon & P. Perzyna. (CISM-Course & Lectures Ser.: Vol. 262). (Illus.). 415p. 1980. pap. 43.70 (ISBN 0-387-81597-X). Springer-Verlag.

Recent Developments in Thermophysical Properties Research: Presented at the Winter Annual Meeting of the ASME, Washington, D. C., Dec. 1, 1971. Ed. by A. Cezairliyan. LC 76-180675. (American Society of Mechanical Engineers. Heat Transfer Division HTD: Vol. 3). pap. 20.00 (ISBN 0-317-08191-8, 2016902). Bks Demand UMI.

Recent Developments in Torts Practice. 45p. 1987. pap. 20.00 (TO-49050). Cal Cont Ed Bar.

Recent Developments in Trusts & Estate Planning & Administration. 104p. 1986. pap. 40.00 (ES-49041). Cal Cont Ed Bar.

Recent Developments in Uranium Enrichment. Ed. by J. R. Merriman & M. Benedict. LC 82-25312. (AIChE Symposium Ser.: Vol. 78, No. 221). 1982. pap. 25.00 (ISBN 0-8169-0245-3, S-221). Am Inst Chem Eng.

Recent Developments in Urban Gaming. Ed. by Phillip D. Patterson. (SCS Simulation Ser.: Vol. 2, No. 2). 1972. 36.00 (ISBN 0-686-36659-X). Soc Computer Sim.

Recent Research in Developmental Psychopathology. Ed. by J. E. Stevenson. (Illus.). 250p. 1984. 31.00 (ISBN 0-08-030828-7). Pergamon.

Recent Research in Mechanical Fastening of Wood: Part II. 51p. 7.00 (ISBN 0-317-34175-8, 625P7923); members 5.00 (ISBN 0-317-34176-6). Forest Prod.

Recent Research in Psychosomatics. Ed. by R. A. Pierloot. (Psychotherapy & Psychosomatics: Vol. 18, No. 1-6). (Illus.). viii, 376p. 1970. Repr. 76.00 (ISBN 3-8055-1219-8). S Karger.

Recent Research in the Biology of Mitoch. B Fiskum. 46.95 (ISBN 0-317-64265-0). Van Nos Reinhold.

Recent Research on Anglo-Irish Writers: A Supplement to "Anglo-Irish Literature: A Review of Research". Richard J. Finneran et al. LC 82-12575. (Reviews of Research Ser.). 361p. 1983. 30.00 (ISBN 0-87352-259-1). Modern Lang.

Recent Research on Ben Jonson. Ed. by James Hogg. (Jacobean Drama Studies). 136p. (Orig.). 1978. pap. 15.00 (ISBN 3-7052-0367-3, Salzburg Studies). Longwood Pub Group.

Recent Research on Cast Iron. Harish D. Merchant. LC 66-28072. 842p. 1968. 212.00 (ISBN 0-677-11000-6). Gordon & Breach.

Recent Research on European Sign Languages. Ed. by F. Loncke et al. 172p. 1984. pap. text ed. 24.00 (ISBN 90-265-0465-9, Pub. by Swets Zeitlinger Netherlands). Hogrefe Intl.

Recent Research on Mechanical Behavior of Solids. Ed. by Hiroshi Miyamoto. 427p. 1979. 52.50 (ISBN 0-86008-247-4, Pub. by U of Tokyo Japan). Columbia U Pr.

Recent Research on Neurotransmitter Receptors. Ed. by H. Yoshida. 116p. 1986. 99.50 (ISBN 0-444-80773-X, Excerpta Medica). Elsevier.

Recent Researches in Palynology: Hensferdinand Linskens Commemoration Volume. Ed. by C. P. Malik. (Illus.). 295p. 1984. 50.00 (ISBN 1-55528-071-4, Pub. by Messers Today & Tomorrow Printers & Publishers). Scholarly Pubns.

Recent Results in Peptide Hormone & Androgenic Steroid Research 9th Congress of the Hungarian Society of Endocrinology. F. A. Laszlo. 326p. 1979. 103.00x (ISBN 0-569-08624-8, Pub. by Collets (UK)). State Mutual Bk.

Recent Results in Stochastic Programming: Proceedings. Ed. by P. Kall & A. Prekopa. (Lecture Notes in Economics & Mathematical Systems: Vol. 179). (Illus.). 256p. 1980. pap. 23.00 (ISBN 0-387-10013-X). Springer-Verlag.

Recent Revolution in Mathematics. Albert Stwertka. (Impact Ser.). (Illus.). 128p. (YA) (gr. 7-12). 1987. lib. bdg. 11.90 (ISBN 0-531-10418-4). Watts.

Recent Revolution in Organ Building. George L. Miller. (Illus.). 9.95 (ISBN 0-911572-02-3, A-53). Vestal.

Recent Revolutions in Anthropology. Maxine P. Fisher. LC 86-9223. (Science Impact Ser.). (Illus.). 128p. (gr. 7-12). 1986. PLB 12.90 (ISBN 0-531-10240-8). Watts.

Recent Revolutions in Astronomy. Larry Kelsey & Darrel Hoff. LC 86-23340. (Science Impact Ser.). (Illus.). 128p. (YA) (gr. 7-12). 1987. lib. bdg. 12.90 (ISBN 0-531-10340-4). Watts.

Recent Revolutions in Biology. James A. Corrick. (Science Impact Ser.). (Illus.). 128p. 1987. lib. bdg. 12.90 (ISBN 0-531-10341-2). Watts.

Recent Revolutions in Chemistry. James A. Corrick. LC 86-5675. (Science Impact Ser.). (Illus.). 128p. (gr. 7-12). 1986. 12.90 (ISBN 0-531-10241-6). Watts.

Recent Revolutions in Geology. Lisa A. Rossbocher. LC 86-9236. (Science Impact Ser.). (Illus.). 128p. (gr. 7-12). 1986. 12.90 (ISBN 0-531-10242-4). Watts.

Recent Revolutions in Physics. Albert Stwertka. Ed. by M. Kline. (Science Impact Books Ser.). (Illus.). 128p. (gr. 7-12). 1986. lib. bdg. 12.90 (ISBN 0-531-10066-9). Watts.

Recent Sediment of Southeast Texas-a Field Guide to the Brazos Alluvial & Deltaic Plains & the Galveston Barrier Island Complex & Resume of the Quaternary Geology of the Northwestern Gulf of Mexico Province. H. A. Bernard & R. J. LeBlanc, Sr. (Guidebook Ser.: GB 11). 132p. 1984. Repr. of 1970 ed. 7.00 (ISBN 0-686-29319-3). Bur Econ Geology.

Recent Social Trends in the United States, 2 vols. President's Research Committee on Social Trends. Ed. by Lewis A. Coser & Walter W. Powell. LC 79-7010. (Perennial Works in Sociology Ser.). (Illus.). 1979. Repr. of 1933 ed. lib. bdg. 111.00 set (ISBN 0-405-12107-5); lib. bdg. 55.50x ea. Vol. 1 (ISBN 0-405-12108-3). Vol. 2 (ISBN 0-405-12109-1). Ayer Co Pubs.

Recent Soviet Psychology. Ed. by N. O'Connor. 1961. 9.50x (ISBN 0-87140-864-3). Liveright.

Recent Spanish Poetry & the Role of the Reader. Margaret Persin. LC 85-43247. 176p. 1987. 27.50x (ISBN 0-8387-5100-8). Bucknell U Pr.

Recent Strategies for the Study of Invasive & Metastatic Cancer. (Journal: Invasion & Metastasis: Vol. 4, Supplement 1, 1984). (Illus.). iv, 68p. 1985. pap. 18.75 (ISBN 3-8055-4008-6). S Karger.

Recent Student Flows in Higher Education. Ignace Hecquet et al. 189p. (Orig.). 1976. pap. text ed. 2.50 (ISBN 0-89192-313-6). Interbk Inc.

Recent Studies in Atomic & Molecular Processes. Ed. by A. E. Kingston. LC 87-7263. (Physics of Atoms & Molecules Ser.). (Illus.). 230p. 1987. 49.50x (ISBN 0-306-42687-0, Plenum Pr). Plenum Pub.

Recent Studies in Modern Armenian History. Ed. by Robert Thomson. (Illus.). 153p. 1972. 12.95 (ISBN 0-935411-07-0); pap. 7.95 (ISBN 0-935411-04-6). Natl Assn Arm.

Recent Studies in Sanskirt & Indology. Dharmendra K. Gupta. 1982. 28.00x (ISBN 0-8364-0913-2, Pub. by Ajanta). South Asia Bks.

Recent Studies of Hypothalamic Function: Proceedings. Symposium, Calgary, Alberta, May, 1973. Ed. by K. Lederis & K. E. Cooper. (Illus.). 450p. 1974. 38.75 (ISBN 3-8055-1694-0). S Karger.

Recent Studies on the Human Thalamus: Proceedings of the Annual Meeting of the Japanese Society for Sterotactic 8, Functional Neurosurgery, 15th, Maebashi, October 1976. Annual Meeting of the Japanese Society for Stereotactic & Functional Neurosurgery Staff. Ed. by Ph. L. Gildenberg & C. Ohye. (Applied Neurophysiology: Vol. 39, No. 3-4). (Illus.). 1977. 38.75 (ISBN 3-8055-2847-7). S Karger.

Recent Synthetic Developments in Polyquinine Chemistry. L. A. Paquette. (Topics in Current Chemistry Ser.: Vol. 119). 160p. 1984. 34.00 (ISBN 0-387-12766-6). Springer-Verlag.

Recent Synthetic Differential Geometry. H. Busemann. LC 13-120381. (Ergebnisse der Mathematik und Ihrer Grenzgebiete: Vol. 54). 1970. 26.00 (ISBN 0-387-04810-3). Springer-Verlag.

Recent Technologies of the Uses of Peat: Reports of the International Symposium. Ed. by G. W. Luettig. (Illus.). 223p. 1983. pap. text ed. 55.00x (ISBN 3-510-65115-4). Lubrecht & Cramer.

Recent Theoretical (Computational) Developments in Atomic Collisions in Solids: Proceedings of a Conference, Strasbourg, France, July 14-16, 1981. Ed. by Y. H. Ohtsuki. iv, 158p. 1983. 31.00 (ISBN 9971-950-33-2). World Scientific Pub.

Recent Theoretical Developments in Control. Ed. by M. J. Gregson. (Institute of Mathematics & Applications Conference Ser.). 1978. 106.00 (ISBN 0-12-301650-9). Acad Pr.

Recent Theories of Citizenship. Carl Brinkman. 1927. 39.50x (ISBN 0-686-51297-9). Elliots Bks.

Recent Theories of Narrative. Wallace Martin. LC 85-22401. (Paperback Ser.). 248p. 1986. 29.95x (ISBN 0-8014-1771-6); pap. 8.95x (ISBN 0-8014-9355-2). Cornell U Pr.

Recent Topics in Mass Spectrometry. R. I. Reed. 368p. 1971. 130.00 (ISBN 0-677-14800-3). Gordon & Breach.

Recent Topics in Non-Linear Partial Differential Equations. Ed. by M. Mimura & T. Nishida. (Mathematics Studies: Vol. 98). 1985. 73.75 (ISBN 0-444-87544-1, North-Holland). Elsevier.

Recent Topics in Nonlinear PDE II. Ed. by K. Masuda & M. Mimura. (North-Holland Mathematics Studies, No. 128; Lecture Notes in Numerical & Applied Analysis, No. 8). 228p. 1986. pap. 70.00 (ISBN 0-444-87938-2, North Holland). Elsevier.

Recent Topics in Nonlinear PDE III. Ed. by K. Masuda & T. Suzuki. (Mathematics Studies, Vol. 148: Lecture Notes in Numerical Applied Analysis, Vol. 9). 266p. 1988. pap. 10.50 (ISBN 0-444-70317-9, North Holland). Elsevier.

Recent Topics in Semiconductor Physics: In Commemoration of the 60th Birthday of Yasutada Vemura Tokyo University, Japan, March 29, 1982. H. Kamimura & Y. Toyozawa. 1983. 41.00 (ISBN 9971-950-54-5); pap. 23.00 (ISBN 9971-950-55-3, Pub. by World Sci Singapore). World Scientific Pub.

Recent Topics in Theoretical Physics. Ed. by H. Takayama. (Proceedings in Physics Ser.: Vol. 24). (Illus.). 150p. 1988. 49.00 (ISBN 0-387-18604-2). Springer-Verlag.

Recent Transportation Literature for Planning & Engineering Librarians (January 1985) Daniel Krummes & Michael Kleiber. (Public Admininstration Ser.: Bibliography P-1598). 55p. 1985. pap. 8.25 (ISBN 0-89028-248-X). Vance Biblios.

Recent Transportation Literature for Planning & Engineering Librarians (February 1985) Daniel Krummes & Michael Kleiber. (Public Administration Ser.: Bibliography P 1617). 1985. pap. 8.25 (ISBN 0-89028-287-0). Vance Biblios.

Recent Transportation Literature for Planning & Engineering Librarians (March 1985) Daniel Krummes & Michael Kleiber. (Public Administration Ser.: Bibliography P 1637). 1985. pap. 8.25 (ISBN 0-89028-327-3). Vance Biblios.

Recent Transportation Literature for Planning & Engineering Librarians (November 1987) Daniel Krummes & Michael Kleiber. (Public Administration Ser.: P 2277). 56p. 1987. 14.50 (ISBN 1-55590-557-9). Vance Biblios.

Recent Transportation Literature for Planning & Engineering Librarians: A Selection Based upon the Acquisitions of the Institute of Transportation Studies Library, University of California, Berkeley, (November 1986) Daniel Krummes & Michael Kleiber. (Public Administration Ser.: P 2037). 55p. 1986. 13.50 (ISBN 1-55590-077-1). Vance Biblios.

Recent Transportation Literature for Planning & Engineering Librarians: A Selection Based upon the Acquisitions of the Institute of Transportation Studies Library, University of California, Berkeley, (September 1986) Daniel Krummes & Michael Kleiber. (Public Administration Ser.: P 1997). 81p. 1986. 19.50 (ISBN 0-89028-997-2). Vance Biblios.

Recent Transportation Literature for Planning & Engineering Librarians: A Selection Based upon the Acquisitions of the Institute of Transportation Studies Library, University of California, Berkeley, (August 1986) Daniel Krummes & Michael Kleiber. (Public Administration Ser.: P 1977). 57p. 1986. 14.50 (ISBN 0-89028-957-3). Vance Biblios.

Recent Transportation Literature for Planning & Engineering Librarians: A Selection Based upon the Acquisitions of the Institute of Transportation Studies Library, University of California, Berkeley, (July 1986) Daniel Krummes & Michael Kleiber. (Public Administration Ser.: P 1957). 84p. 1986. 19.50 (ISBN 0-89028-917-4). Vance Biblios.

Recent Transportation Literature for Planning & Engineering Librarians: A Selection Based upon the Acquisitions of the Institute of Transportation Studies Library, University of California, Berkeley, (June 1986) Daniel Krummes & Michael Kleiber. (Public Administration Ser.: P 1937). 73p. 1986. 17.50 (ISBN 0-89028-877-1). Vance Biblios.

Recent Transportation Literature for Planning & Engineering Librarians: A Selection Based upon the Acquisitions of the Institute of Transportation Studies Library, University of California, Berkeley, (May 1986) Daniel Krummes & Michael Kleiber. (Public Administration Ser.: P 1917). 53p. 1986. 13.50 (ISBN 0-89028-837-2). Vance Biblios.

Recent Transportation Literature for Planning & Engineering Librarians: A Selection Based upon the Acquisitions of the Institute of Transportation Studies Library, University of California, Berkeley, (April 1986) Daniel Krummes & Michael Kleiber. (Public Administration Ser.: P 1897). 68p. 1986. 16.50 (ISBN 0-89028-817-8). Vance Biblios.

Recent Transportation Literature for Planning & Engineering Librarians (November 1987) Daniel Krummes & Michael Kleiber. (Public Administration Ser.: P 2277). 56p. 1987. 14.50 (ISBN 1-55590-557-9). Vance Biblios.

Recent Transportation Literature for Planning & Engineering Librarians (October 1987) Daniel Krummes & Michael Kleiber. (Public Administration Ser.: P 2257). 53p. 1987. 13.50 (ISBN 1-55590-517-X). Vance Biblios.

Recent Transportation Literature for Planning & Engineering Librarians (September 1987) Daniel Krummes & Michael Kleiber. (Public Administration Ser.: P 2237). 82p. 1987. 19.50 (ISBN 1-55590-477-7). Vance Biblios.

Recent Transportation Literature for Planning & Engineering Librarians (August 1987) Daniel Krummes & Michael Kleiber. (Public Administration Ser.: P 2217). 53p. 1987. 13.50 (ISBN 1-55590-437-8). Vance Biblios.

Recent Transportation Literature for Planning & Engineering Librarians (July 1987) Daniel Krummes & Michael Kleiber. (Public Administration Ser.: P 2198). 76p. 1987. 18.50 (ISBN 1-55590-398-3). Vance Biblios.

Recent Transportation Literature for Planning & Engineering Librarians (June 1987) Daniel Krummes & Michael Kleiber. (Public Administration Ser.: P 2177). 75p. 1987. 17.50 (ISBN 1-55590-357-6). Vance Biblios.

Recent Transportation Literature for Planning & Engineering Librarians (May 1987) Daniel Krummes & Michael Kleiber. (Public Administration Ser.: P 2157). 64p. 1987. 15.50 (ISBN 1-55590-317-7). Vance Biblios.

Recent Transportation Literature for Planning & Engineering Librarians (March 1987) Daniel Krummes & Michael Kleiber. (Public Administration Ser.: P 2117). 60p. 1987. 14.50 (ISBN 1-55590-237-5). Vance Biblios.

Recent Transportation Literature for Planning & Engineering Librarians (February 1987) Daniel Krummes & Michael Kleiber. (Public Administration Ser.: P 2097). 51p. 1987. 13.50 (ISBN 1-55590-197-2). Vance Biblios.

Recent Transportation Literature for Planning & Engineering Librarians (January 1987) Daniel Krummes & Michael Kleiber. (Public Administration Ser.: P 2078). 73p. 1987. 17.50 (ISBN 1-55590-158-1). Vance Biblios.

Recent Transportation Literature for Planning & Engineering Librarians: A Selection Based upon the Acquisitions of the Institute of Transportation Studies Library, University of California, Berkeley, (December 1986) Daniel Krummes & Michael Kleiber. (Public Administration Ser.: P 2057). 71p. 1986. 17.50 (ISBN 1-55590-117-4). Vance Biblios.

Recent Transportation Literature for Planning & Engineering Librarians: A Selection Based upon the Acquisitions of the Institute of Transportation Studies Library, University of California, Berkeley, (December 1985) Daniel Krummes & Michael Kleiber. (Public Administration Ser.: P 1817). 58p. 1985. 9.00 (ISBN 0-89028-667-1). Vance Biblios.

Recent Transportation Literature for Planning & Engineering Librarians: A Selection Based upon the Acquisitions of the Institute of Transportation Studies Library, University of California, Berkeley, (November 1985) Daniel Krummes & Michael Kleiber. (Public Administration Ser.: P 1797). 51p. 1985. 7.50 (ISBN 0-89028-627-2). Vance Biblios.

Recent Transportation Literature for Planning & Engineering Librarians: A Selection Based upon the Acquisitions of the Institute of Transportation Studies Library, University of California, Berkeley, (October 1985) Daniel Krummes & Michael Kleiber. (Public Administration Ser.: P 1777). 63p. 1985. 9.75 (ISBN 0-89028-577-2). Vance Biblios.

Recent Transportation Literature for Planning & Engineering Librarians: A Selection Based upon the Acquisitions of the Institute of Transportation Studies Library, University of California, Berkeley (September 1985) Daniel Krummes & Michael Kleiber. (Public Administration Ser.: P 1757). 59p. 1985. 9.00 (ISBN 0-89028-557-8). Vance Biblios.

Recent Transportation Literature for Planning & Engineering Librarians: A Selection Based upon the Acquisitions of the Institute of Transportation Studies Library, University of California, Berkeley (August 1985) Daniel Krummes & Michael Kleiber. (Public Administration Ser.: P 1737). 82p. 1985. 12.00 (ISBN 0-89028-517-9). Vance Biblios.

Recent Transportation Literature for Planning & Engineering Librarians: A Selection Based upon the Acquisitions of the Institute of Transportation Studies Library, University of California, Berkeley (July 1985) Daniel Krummes & Michael Kleiber. (Public Administration Ser.: P 1718). 67p. 1985. 9.75 (ISBN 0-89028-488-1). Vance Biblios.

Recent Transportation Literature for Planning & Engineering Librarians: A Selection Based upon the Acquisitions of the Institute of Transportation Studies Library, University of California, Berkeley (June 1985) Daniel Krummes & Michael Kleiber. (Public Administration Ser.: P 1697). 56p. 1985. 8.25 (ISBN 0-89028-447-4). Vance Biblios.

Recent Transportation Literature for Planning & Engineering Librarians: A Selection Based upon the Acquisitions of the Institute of Transportation Studies Library, University of California, Berkeley (May 1985) Daniel Krummes & Michael Kleiber. (Public Administration Ser.: P 1677). 63p. 1985. 9.75 (ISBN 0-89028-407-5). Vance Biblios.

Recent Transportation Literature for Planning & Engineering Librarians: A Selection Based upon the Acquisitions of the Institute of Transportation Studies Library, University of California, Berkeley (April 1985) Daniel Krummes & Michael Kleiber. (Public Administration Ser.: P 1657). 57p. 1985. 8.25 (ISBN 0-89028-367-2). Vance Biblios.

Recent Transportation Literature for Planning & Engineering Librarians (January 1988) Daniel Krummes & Michael Kleiber. (Public Administration Ser.: P 2318). 57p. 1988. 14.50 (ISBN 1-55590-628-1). Vance Biblios.

Recent Transportation Literature for Planning & Engineering Librarians (December 1987) Daniel Krummes & Michael Kleiber. (Public Administration Ser.: P 2297). 62p. 1987. 15.50 (ISBN 1-55590-597-8). Vance Biblios.

Recent Transportation Literature for Planning & Engineering Librarians: A Selection Based upon the Acquisitions of the Institute of Transportation Studies Library, University of California, Berkeley (March 1986) Daniel Krummes & Michael Kleiber. (Public Administration Ser.: P 1877). 47p. 1986. 12.50 (ISBN 0-89028-787-2). Vance Biblios.

Recent Transportation Literature for Planning & Engineering Librarians: A Selection Based upon the Acquisitions of the Institute of Transportation Studies Library, University of California, Berkeley, (February 1986) Daniel Krummes & Michael Kleiber. (Public Administration Ser.: P 1857). 45p. 1986. 11.25 (ISBN 0-89028-747-3). Vance Biblios.

Recent Transportation Literature for Planning & Engineering Librarians: A Selection Based upon the Acquisitions of the Institute of Transportation Studies Library, University of California, Berkeley, (January 1986) Daniel Krummes & Michael Kleiber. (Public Administration Ser.: P 1838). 39p. 1986. 10.00 (ISBN 0-89028-708-2). Vance Biblios.

Recent Transportation Literature for Planning & Engineering Librarians (April 1987) Daniel Krummes & Michael Kleiber. (Public Administration Ser.: P 2137). 46p. 1987. 12.50 (ISBN 1-55590-277-4). Vance Biblios.

Recent Transportation Literature for Planning & Engineering Librarians: A Selection Based upon the Acquisitions of the Institute of Transportation Studies Library, University of California, Berkeley. (Public Administration Ser.: P 2017). 55p. 1986. 13.50 (ISBN 1-55590-037-2). Vance Biblios.

Recent Trends & Contacts Between Cytogenetics Embryology & Morphology, 1976. Ed. by V. R. Dnyansagar et al. (Current Trends in Life Sciences Ser.: Vol. 5). xiv, 592p. 1977. 50.00 (ISBN 0-88065-081-8, Pub. by Messers Today & Tomorrows Printers & Publishers India). Scholarly Pubns.

Recent Trends & Developments in Nuclear Physics. Ed. by Z. Wilhelmi et al. (Nuclear Science Research Conference Ser.: Vol. 10). 955p. 1986. flexicover 150.00 (ISBN 3-7186-0351-9). Harwood Academic.

Recent Trends in Aeroelasticity, Structures, & Structural Dynamics. Ed. by Prabhat Hajela. (Illus.). 432p. (Orig.). 1987. pap. 15.00x (ISBN 0-8130-0871-9). U Presses Fla.

Recent Trends in Allergen & Complement Research. Ed. by K. Ishizaka et al. (Progress in Allergy: Vol. 30). (Illus.). xiv, 234p. 1982. 88.75 (ISBN 3-8055-2580-X). S Karger.

Recent Trends in Architectural Education in Great Britain: A Survey of Periodical Literature, 1976-1986. Carole Cable. (Architecture Ser.: A 1969). 7p. 1988. 3.00 (ISBN 1-55590-619-2). Vance Biblios.

Recent Trends in Botanical Research. 334p. 1985. 100.00x (ISBN 81-85046-24-7, Pub. by Scientific). State Mutual Bk.

Recent Trends in Data Type Specification. Ed. by H. J. Kreowski. (Informatik-Fachberichte Ser.: Vol. 116). vii, 253p. 1986. pap. 19.30 (ISBN 0-387-16077-9). Springer-Verlag.

Recent Trends in Diabetes Research. Ed. by H. Bostrom. 308p. (Orig.). 1982. text ed. 42.50x (ISBN 91-22-00566-8, Pub. by Almqvist & Wiksell). Coronet Bks.

Recent Trends in Fertility & Mortality in Indonesia. Panel on Indonesia, Committee on Population & Demography et al. (Papers of the East-West Population Institute: No. 105). (Illus.). xvi, 96p. (Orig.). 1987. pap. text ed. 3.00 (ISBN 0-86638-092-2). EW Ctr HI.

Recent Trends in Flexible Manufacturing. 314p. 1986. 33.00 (ISBN 92-1-016183-1, E.85.II.E.35). UN.

Recent Trends in Hydrogeology. Ed. by T. N. Narasimhan & R. Allan Freeze. (Special Paper: No. 189). 1982. 22.00 (ISBN 0-8137-2189-X). Geol Soc.

Recent Trends in International Direct Investment. OECD Staff. (International Investment & Multinational Enterprises Ser.). 214p. (Orig.). 1987. pap. 21.00x (ISBN 92-64-12971-5). OECD.

Recent Trends in Legislation Concerning Rehabilitation Services for Disabled Persons in Selected Countries. 2.50 (ISBN 92-1-130071-1, E.78.IV.1). UN.

Recent Trends in Management of Diabetes Mellitus: Proceedings of the Second International Symposium on Treatment of Diabetes Mellitus, Ngoya, 13-15 Nov., 1985. N. Sakamoto & K. G. Alberti. (International Congress Ser.: No. 726). 630p. 1987. 195.25 (ISBN 0-444-80878-7, Excerpta Medica). Elsevier.

Recent Trends in Mathematics. Collet's Holdings Ltd. Staff. 1982. 70.00x (Pub. by Collets (UK)). State Mutual Bk.

Recent Trends in Mathematics. Ed. by V. Reinhardsbrunn. 1985. 50.00x (ISBN 0-317-46708-5, Pub. by Collets (UK)). State Mutual Bk.

Recent Trends in Medical Genetics: Proceedings of the Conference on Recent Trends in Medical Genetics, Madras, India, 8-10 December, 1983. Ed. by K. M. Marimuthu & P. M. Gopinath. (Illus.). 350p. 1986. 88.00 (ISBN 0-08-031993-9, PBL). Pergamon.

Recent Trends in Mortality Analysis. Kenneth G. Manton & Eric Stallard. LC 83-11736. (Studies in Population). 1984. 39.95 (ISBN 0-12-470020-9). Acad Pr.

Recent Trends in Occupational Mobility. Natalie Rogoff. Ed. by Lewis A. Coser & Walter W. Powell. LC 79-7016. (Perennial Works in Sociology Ser.). (Illus.). 1979. Repr. of 1953 ed. lib. bdg. 15.00x (ISBN 0-405-12115-6). Ayer Co Pubs.

Recent Trends in Optical Systems Design: Computer Lends Design. Ed. by Londono & Fischer. 307p. 1987. 50.00 (ISBN 0-89252-801-X, 766). SPIE.

Recent Trends in Representation of Women & Minorities in School Administration & Problems in Documentation. American Association of School Administrators Staff. 5.00 (ISBN 0-318-01741-5, 021-00910). Am Assn Sch Admin.

Recent Trends in Robotics: Modeling, Control, & Education: Proceedings of the International Symposium on Robot Manipulators: Modeling, Control, & Education, Albuquerque, New Mexico, November 12-14, 1986. International Symposium on Robot Manipulators Staff. Ed. by M. Jamshid et al. 550p. 1986. 79.50 (ISBN 0-444-01140-4, North Holland). Elsevier.

Recent Trends in Soviet Psycho-Linguistics. James V. Wertsch. LC 77-85715. pap. 58.00 (ISBN 0-317-29618-3, 2021863). Bks Demand UMI.

Recent Trends in the Novel. Ed. by Eldred D. Jones. (African Literature Today Ser.: Vol. 13). 245p. 1983. 35.00 (ISBN 0-8419-0804-4, Africana); pap. 23.50 (ISBN 0-8419-0805-2). Holmes & Meier.

Recent Trends in Theoretical Psychology. Ed. by W. J. Baker et al. (Recent Research in Psychology Ser.). (Illus.). 380p. 1988. pap. 33.00 (ISBN 0-387-96757-5). Springer-Verlag.

Recent United States Policy in the Persian Gulf (1971-82) C. Paul Bradley. LC 82-16049. 148p. (Orig.). 1982. pap. text ed. 10.00 (ISBN 0-936988-08-8, Dist. by Shoe String Press). Tompson Rutter Inc.

Recent Views on British History: Essays on Historical Writings since 1966. Richard Schlatter. 897p. 1984. 55.00x (ISBN 0-8135-0959-9). Rutgers U Pr.

Recent Views on Hypertrophic Cardiomyopathy. Ed. by E. Van der Wall & K. I. Lie. (Developments in Cardiovascular Medicine Ser.). 1985. lib. bdg. 35.00 (ISBN 0-89838-694-2, Pub. by Martinus Netherlands). Kluwer Academic.

Recent Vitamin Research. Ed. by M. H. Briggs. 224p. 1984. 99.00 (ISBN 0-8493-5618-0). CRC Pr.

Recent Work in Philosophy. Ed. by Kenneth Lucey & Tibor Machan. LC 82-3741. (APQ Library of Philosophy). 330p. 1983. text ed. 38.95x (ISBN 0-8476-7103-8, Rowman & Allanheld). Rowman.

Recent Work in Women's History: East & West. Ed. by Esther Katz. LC 85-30223. (Trends in History Ser.). 152p. 1986. 24.95 (ISBN 0-86656-139-0). Haworth Pr.

Recent Work of Jurgen Habermas: Reason, Justice, & Modernity. Stephen K. White. 200p. 1988. 29.95 (ISBN 0-521-34360-7). Cambridge U Pr.

Recently Discovered Systems of Enzyme Regulation by Reversible Posphorylation. Ed. by P. Cohen. (Molecular Aspects of Cell Regulation Ser.: Vol. 1). 274p. 1980. 69.00 (ISBN 0-444-80226-6, Biomedical Pr). Elsevier.

Recents Developments in the Adiabatic Engine. 1988. 51.00 (ISBN 0-89883-665-4, SP738). Soc Auto Engineers.

Reception: An Ecumenical Opportunity. William G. Rusch. LC 87-20710. 1987. pap. 3.25 (ISBN 0-8006-2091-7). Fortress.

Reception of Calvinistic Thought in England. Charles D. Cremeans. LC 83-45578. Date not set. Repr. of 1949 ed. 22.00 (ISBN 0-404-19896-1). AMS Pr.

Reception of Classical German Literature in England, 1760-1860: A Documentary History from Contemporary Periodicals, 10 vols. Ed. & intro. by John Boening. Incl. Vol. 1. General Introduction & Reviews from 1760 to 1813 (ISBN 0-8240-0990-8); Vol. 2. Reviews from 1813 to 1835 (ISBN 0-8240-0991-6); Vol. 3. Reviews from 1835 to 1860 (ISBN 0-8240-0992-4); Vol. 4. Authors from Bodmer to Klopstock (ISBN 0-8240-0993-2); Vol. 5. Authors from Lavater to Novalis (ISBN 0-8240-0994-0); Vol. 6. The Reception of Early German Romantics: Richter, the Brothers Schlegel, Tieck & Hoffmann (ISBN 0-8240-0995-9); Vol. 7. General Critical Articles on Goethe & Reviews Which Discuss Goethe & Schiller Together, Arranged in Order of Appearance (ISBN 0-8240-0996-7); Vol. 8. Reviews of Werther, Goethe's Early Works, His Poems & Faust (ISBN 0-8240-0997-5); Vol. 9. The Works of Goethe's Midcareer, Wilhelm Meister & Such Works As Dichtung und Wahrheit, Etc (ISBN 0-8240-0998-3); Vol. 10. The English Reception of Specific Works of Schiller, from the Early Plays to the Historical Works (ISBN 0-8240-0999-1). 1977. Set. lib. bdg. 120.00 each (ISBN 0-686-77265-2). Garland Pub.

Reception of Copernicus' Heliocentric Theory: Proceedings. Symposium of 'Nicolas Copernicus Committee of International Union of History & Philosophy of Science, Torum, Poland, 1973. Ed. by Jerzy Dobrzycki. LC 72-95980. 368p. 1973. lib. bdg. 39.50 (ISBN 90-277-0311-6, Pub. by Reidel Holland). Kluwer Academic.

Reception of English Literature in Germany. Lawrence M. Price. LC 68-21223. 1968. Repr. of 1932 ed. 33.00 (ISBN 0-405-08863-9). Ayer Co Pubs.

Reception of Georg Kaiser (1915-45) Texts & Analysis, 2 vols. Peter K. Tyson. LC 84-47844. (Canadian Studies in German Language & Literature: Vol. 32). 1042p. (Orig.). 1984. pap. text ed. 51.60 (ISBN 0-8204-0145-5). P Lang Pubs.

Reception of German Literature in Iceland, 1775-1850. W. M. Senner. (Amsterdamer Publikationen Zur Sprache Und Literatur: No. 62). 186p. 1985. pap. text ed. 29.95x (ISBN 90-6203-697-X, Pub. by Rodopi Holland). Humanities.

Reception of Goethe's Faust in England in the First Half of the Nineteenth Century. William F. Hauhart. LC 9-17319. (Columbia University. Germanic Studies, Old Series: No. 11). Repr. of 1909 ed. 11.50 (ISBN 0-404-50411-6). AMS Pr.

Reception of Herman Hesse by the Youth in the United States: A Thematic Analysis. Carlee Marrer-Tising. (European University Studies: No. 1, Vol. 502). 487p. 1982. 51.60 (ISBN 3-261-05006-3). P Lang Pubs.

Reception of Jazz in America: A New View. James L. Collier. LC 88-80503. (Monographs: No. 27). 84p. (Orig.). 1988. pap. 11.00 (ISBN 0-914678-30-2). Inst Am Music.

Reception of Pablo Neruda's Works in the German Democratic Republic. Bonnie A. Beckett. (Germanic Studies in America: Vol. 42). 256p. 1981. 27.85 (ISBN 3-261-04896-4). P Lang Pubs.

Reception of Scott's Poetry by His Correspondents, 1796-1817, 2 vols. J. H. Alexander. Ed. by James Hogg. 520p. (Orig.). 1979. pap. 30.00 (ISBN 3-7052-0548-X, Pub. by Salzburg Studies). Longwood Pub Group.

Reception of Vatican II. Ed. by Giuseppe Alberigo et al. Tr. by Matthew J. O'Connell from Fr. 384p. 1987. 39.95x (ISBN 0-8132-0647-2); pap. 19.95 (ISBN 0-8132-0654-5). Cath U Pr.

Reception Theory: A Critical Introduction. Robert C. Holub. LC 83-13385. 189p. 1984. 25.00 (ISBN 0-416-33580-2, NO. 4040); pap. 10.95 (ISBN 0-416-33590-X, NO. 4041). Routledge Chapman & Hall.

Receptionist. Hazel Atkins. 112p. 1981. pap. 14.95x (ISBN 0-7131-0580-1). Trans-Atl Phila.

Receptionist. Jack Rudman. (Career Examination Ser.: C-1636). (Cloth bdg. avail. on request). 1988. pap. 12.00 (ISBN 0-8373-1636-7). Natl Learning.

Receptionist. J. W. Twing & Georgia Alpharetta. 160p. 1983. pap. 13.16 (ISBN 0-07-065641-X). McGraw.

Receptionist: A Practical Course in Office Reception Techniques. Merle W. Wood & Margaret McKenna. 1966. text ed. 25.85 (ISBN 0-07-071590-4). McGraw.

Receptive Mechanisms of Sound in the Ear. Yasuji Katsuki. LC 81-12241. 135p. 1982. 44.50 (ISBN 0-521-24346-7). Cambridge U Pr.

Receptive Prayer: A Christian Approach to Meditation. Grace A. Brame. Ed. by Herbert Lambert. LC 84-29302. 144p. (Orig.). 1985. pap. 9.95 (ISBN 0-8272-3211-X). CBP.

Receptivity. Francis K. Nemeck. 135p. 1985. 10.00 (ISBN 0-533-06057-5). Vantage.

Receptor Binding Radiotracers, Vol. I. Ed. by W. C. Eckelman. 200p. 1982. 69.00 (ISBN 0-8493-6019-6). CRC Pr.

Receptor Binding Radiotracers, Vol. II. Ed. by W. C. Eckelman. 248p. 1982. 79.00 (ISBN 0-8493-6020-X). CRC Pr.

Receptor Binding Studies in Adrenergic Pharmacology. Lewis T. Williams & Robert J. Lefkowitz. LC 78-3011. 167p. 1978. 36.50 (ISBN 0-89004-164-4). Raven.

Receptor Mediated Antisteroid Action. Ed. by M. K. Agarwal. 523p. 1987. lib. bdg. 193.00 (ISBN 0-89925-374-1). De Gruyter.

Receptor-Mediated Binding & Internalization of Toxins & Hormones. Ed. by John H. Middlebrook & Leonard D. Kohn. 1981. 29.95 (ISBN 0-12-494850-2). Acad Pr.

Receptor-Mediated Targeting of Drugs, Vol. 82. Ed. by G. Gregoriadis et al. LC 84-18183. (NATO ASI Series A, Life Sciences). 502p. 1984. 89.50x (ISBN 0-306-41831-2, Plenum Press). Plenum Pub.

Receptor-Mediated Uptake in the Liver. Ed. by H. Greten et al. (Illus.). 240p. 1986. 39.00 (ISBN 0-387-16181-3). Springer-Verlag.

Receptor Modelling in Environmental Chemistry. Philip K. Hopke. LC 84-19568. (Chemical Analysis Ser.). 336p. 1985. 84.00 (ISBN 0-471-89106-1). Wiley.

Receptor Pharmacology & Function. Williams et al. (Clinical Pharmacology Ser.). 784p. 1988. 125.00 (ISBN 0-8247-7841-3). Dekker.

Receptor Purification Procedures. Ed. by J. Craig Venter & Len C. Harrison. LC 83-17504. (Receptor Biochemistry & Methodology Ser.: Vol. 2). 184p. 1984. 34.00 (ISBN 0-8451-3701-8, 3701). A R Liss.

Receptor-Receptor Interactions: A New Intramembrane Integrative Mechanism. Ed. by K. Fuxe & L. F. Agnati. LC 87-942721. (Wenner-Gren International Symposium Ser.: Vol. 48). (Illus.). 580p. 1987. 85.00x (ISBN 0-306-42719-2, Plenum Pr). Plenum Pub.

Receptor Regulation see Queues: Receptors & Recognition Series B.

Receptors. Ed. by P. Michael Conn. 1985. Vol. 2. 85.00 (ISBN 0-12-185202-4); Vol. 3, 1986. 85.00 (ISBN 0-12-185203-2). Acad Pr.

Receptors, Vol. 1. Ed. by P. Michael Conn. 1984. 100.00 (ISBN 0-12-185201-6). Acad Pr.

Receptors, Vol. 1. Ed. by J. Jacob. LC 78-41027. (Illus.). 295p. 1979. 120.00 (ISBN 0-08-023191-8). Pergamon.

Receptors, Vol. 4. Edited Treatise ed. Ed. by P. Michael Conn. 1986. 85.00 (ISBN 0-12-185204-0). Acad Pr.

Receptors: A Comprehensive Treatise. Ed. by R. D. O'Brien & Palmer Taylor. LC 78-24366. (Vol. 1). (Illus.). 362p. 1979. 59.50x (ISBN 0-306-40100-2, Plenum Pr). Plenum Pub.

Receptors: A Quantitative Approach. Alexander Levitzki. 1984. 25.95 (ISBN 0-8053-6410-2). Benjamin Cummings.

Receptors, Again. Ed. by J. W. Lamble & A. C. Abbott. 322p. 1984. 23.50 (ISBN 0-444-80593-1, I-430-84). Elsevier.

Receptors & Centrally Acting Drugs - Pharmacokinetics & Drug Metabolism: Proceedings of the 4th Congress of the Hungarian Pharmacological Society, Budapest, 1985, Vol. 2. Ed. by E. S. Vizi et al. LC 86-9349. 526p. 1987. 120.00 (ISBN 0-08-034191-8, PBL). Pergamon.

Receptors & Hormone Action, Vol. 1. Ed. by B. W. O'Malley & L. Birnbaumer. 1978. 85.00 (ISBN 0-12-526301-5). Acad Pr.

Receptors & Hormone Action, Vol. 3. Ed. by B. W. O'Malley & Lutz Birnbaumer. 1978. 92.00 (ISBN 0-12-526303-1). Acad Pr.

Receptors & Ion Channels: Proceedings of the Symposium on Receptors & Ion Channels, Tashkent, U. S. S. R., October 2-5, 1986. Y. A. Ovchinnikov & F. Hucho. xi, 351p. (Orig.). 1987. lib. bdg. 130.00 (ISBN 0-89925-375-X). De Gruyter.

Receptors & Ligands in Neurological Disorders. Ed. by Amar K. Sen & Tyrone Lee. (Intercellular & Intracellular Communication Ser.: No. 4). (Illus.). 372p. 1988. 90.00 (ISBN 0-521-30720-1). Cambridge U Pr.

Receptors & Ligands in Psychiatry. Ed. by Amar K. Sen & Tyrone Lee. (Intercellular & Intracellular Communications Ser.: No. 3). (Illus.). 500p. 1988. 120.00 (ISBN 0-521-30719-8). Cambridge U Pr.

Receptors & Mechanism of Action of Steroid Hormones, Pt. 2. Jorge Pasqualini. (Modern Pharmacology & Toxicology Ser.: Vol. 8). 1977. 85.00 (ISBN 0-8247-6440-4). Dekker.

Receptors & Other Targets for Toxic Substances. Ed. by P. L. Chambers et al. (Archives of Toxicology Ser.: Suppl. 8). (Illus.). 536p. 1985. pap. 99.00 (ISBN 0-387-13670-3). Springer-Verlag.

Receptors & Recognition, Series A, 6 vols. Ed. by P. Cuatrecasas & M. F. Greaves. Incl. Vol. 1. (No. 6072). 175p. 1976 (ISBN 0-412-13800-X); Vol. 2. 229p. 1976 (ISBN 0-412-13810-7, NO. 6073); Vol. 3. 166p. 1977 (ISBN 0-412-14310-0, NO. 6074); Vol. 4. 258p. 1977 (ISBN 0-412-14330-5, NO. 6075); Vol. 5. 212p. 1978 (ISBN 0-412-15270-3, NO. 6076); Vol. 6. 199p. 1978 (ISBN 0-412-15290-8, NO. 6077). 85.20 set (ISBN 0-412-15950-3, NO. 6878, Pub. by Chapman & Hall England); 15.95 ea. Routledge Chapman & Hall.

Receptors & Sensory Perception. Ragnar Granit. LC 75-14597. (Mrs. Hepsa Ely Silliman Memorial Lectures). (Illus.). 369p. 1975. Repr. of 1955 ed. lib. bdg. 35.00x (ISBN 0-8371-8213-1, GRRS). Greenwood.

Receptors, Antibodies & Disease: Symposium No. 90. CIBA Foundation Symposium. 320p. 1986. 54.95 (ISBN 0-471-91059-7). Wiley.

Receptors As Surramolecular Entities: Proceedings of the Biannual Capo Bio Conference, Cagliari, Italy, 7-10 June, 1981. Ed. by G. Biggio & E. Costa. (Advances in the Biosciences Ser.: Vol. 44). (Illus.). 480p. 1983. 110.00 (ISBN 0-08-029804-4). Pergamon.

Receptors in Cellular Recognition & Developmental Processes. Reginald M. Gorczynski. (Cell Biology Ser.). 1986. 60.50 (ISBN 0-12-290530-X). Acad Pr.

Receptors in Pharmacology. Ed. by John R. Smythies & Ronald J. Bradley. (Modern Parmacology-Toxicology Ser.: Vol. 11). 1978. 95.00 (ISBN 0-8247-6546-X). Dekker.

Receptors in the Cardiovascular System. Peiter A. Van Zweiten & E. Schonbaum. (Progress in Pharmacology Ser.: Vol. 6/2). 193p. 1987. text ed. 59.00 (ISBN 0-89574-227-6, Pub. by Gustav Fisher Verlag). VCH Pubs.

Receptors in Tumour Biology. Ed. by C. M. Chadwick. (Intercellular & Intracellular Communication Ser.: No. 2). (Illus.). 250p. 1986. 49.50 (ISBN 0-521-32117-4). Cambridge U Pr.

Receptors, Membranes & Transport Mechanisms in Medicine: Proceedings of the Symposium Held in Heidelberg, Australia, 22-23 March, 1984. Ed. by A. E. Doyle & F. A. Mendelsohn. (International Congress Ser.: Vol. 660). 288p. 1984. 106.50 (ISBN 0-444-80631-8). Elsevier.

Recerchari, Motetti, Canzoni, Libro Primo see Monuments of Music & Music Literature in Facsimile: Series One.

Recertification: A Look at the Issues, Vol. 9. GAP Committee on Recertification. (Report: No. 96). 1976. pap. 5.00 (ISBN 0-87318-133-6, Pub. by GAP). Brunner-Mazel.

Recertification for Medical Specialists. Ed. by Donald G. Langsley & John S. Lloyd. LC 87-72510. 276p. 1987. lib. bdg. 39.95 (ISBN 0-934277-10-9). Am Bd Med Spec.

Recess. Terry Thornton & Sandy Thornton. (Illus.). 32p. (gr. 2-5). 1987. pap. 5.95 (ISBN 0-687-35660-1). Abingdon.

Recess, or, a Tale of Other Times, 3 Vols. Sophia Lee. LC 77-131325. (Gothic Novels Ser). 1971. Repr. of 1783 ed. Set. 49.50 (ISBN 0-405-00806-6). Ayer Co Pubs.

Recess: Prayer Meditations for Teachers. Elspeth C. Murphy. (Orig.). 1988. 5.95 (ISBN 0-8010-6244-6). Baker Bk.

Recession. 40.45 (ISBN 0-318-02547-7). Print Indus Am.

Recession As a Policy Instrument: Israel, 1965-1969. Carol S. Greenwald. LC 73-2895. 154p. 1973. 16.50 (ISBN 0-8386-1396-9). Fairleigh Dickinson.

Recession, Crime, & Punishment. Steven Box. LC 87-1825. 240p. 1987. 28.50 (ISBN 0-389-20724-1). B&N Imports.

Recession in Africa. Ed. by Jerker Carlsson. 203p. 1982. 29.50 (ISBN 0-8419-9765-9, Africana). Holmes & Meier.

Recession Stopper & Boom Builder. Arthur O. Dahlberg. (Illus.). 192p. 1988. pap. 9.95 (ISBN 0-930170-04-0). Humane Sci Pubs.

Recession, the Western Economies & the Changing World Order. Lars Anell. LC 81-2647. 1981. 25.00 (ISBN 0-312-66576-8). St Martin.

Recession, the Western Economies & the Changing World Order. Lars Anell. 181p. 1981. pap. 11.00 (ISBN 0-86187-243-6, Pub. by Frances Pinter). Longwood Pub Group.

Recetas Norteamericanas En Ingles Y Espanol. 168p. 1980. 5.95 (ISBN 0-686-27595-0, 0-9607690). Lang Svcs CA.

Receuil Arien de Verone. R. Gryson. 1983. 46.00 (ISBN 90-247-2705-7, Pub. by Martinus Nijhoff Netherlands). Kluwer Academic.

Receuil des Cours 1980. Academie de Droit International Staff. (No. IV). 380p. 1984. 50.00 (ISBN 90-247-2976-9, Pub. by Martinus Nijhoff Netherlands). Kluwer Academic.

Rechargeable Batteries: Advances Since 1977. Ed. by Robert W. Graham. LC 80-13152. (Energy Technology Review Ser. No. 55; Chemical Technology Review Ser. No.160). 452p. 1980. 54.00 (ISBN 0-8155-0802-6). Noyes.

Rechenka's Eggs. Patricia Polacco. (Illus.). 32p. (ps-3). 1988. 13.95 (ISBN 0-399-21501-8, Philomel Bks). Putnam Pub Group.

Recherche de la Base et du Sommet. Rene Char. (Poesie Ser.). 192p. 1977. 6.95 (ISBN 0-686-54168-5). Schoenhof.

Recherche de l'Absolu. Honore De Balzac. Bd. with Messe de l'Athee. (Folio Ser.: No. 739). pap. 7.95 (ISBN 0-685-23884-9, 2163). Schoenhof.

Recherche des Bouches du Mississippi et Voyage a Travers le Continent Depuis les Cotes du Texas jusqu'a Quebec (1669-1698) see Decouvertes et Establissements des francais dans l'ouest et dans le sud de l'Amerique septentrional: 1614-1754.

Recherche-Developpement, Concepts et Problemes de Base Environnement. F. Russo & R. Erbes. (Economies et Societes Series T: No. 1). 1959. pap. 11.00 (ISBN 0-8115-0798-X). Kraus Repr.

Recherche-Developpement en Grande-Bretagne. J. M. Collette. (Economies et Societes Series T: No. 2). 1961. pap. 19.00 (ISBN 0-8115-0799-8). Kraus Repr.

Recherche-Developpement et Progres Economique en U. R. S. S. J. M. Collette. (Economies et Societes Series G: No. 15). 1962. pap. 19.00 (ISBN 0-8115-0706-8). Kraus Repr.

Recherche du Don Perdu: Points de Repere dans le Roman de Marcel Proust. Per Nykrog. LC 85-73551. (Harvard Studies in Romance Languages: No. 42). 100p. (Orig., Fr.). 1986. pap. 10.00 (ISBN 0-940940-42-6). Harvard U Romance Lang & Lit.

Recherche d'une Eglise. Jules Romains. 192p. 1962. 4.95 (ISBN 0-686-55289-X). French & Eur.

Recherche Operationnelle et Agriculture see Cahiers de l'Institut de Science Economique Appliquee.

Recherche Recipes from Sound Food Restaurant & Bakery. Ed. by Melane Lohmann. (Illus.). 51p. (Orig.). 1984. pap. 6.95 (ISBN 0-9615672-0-1). Sound Food Co.

Recherches Bibliographiques sur les Oeuvres Imprimes De J. J. Rousseau, 2 vols. in 1. Theophile A. Dufour. 1925. 35.50 (ISBN 0-8337-0949-6). B Franklin.

Recherches Critiques sur l'Age et l'Origine des Traductions Latines d'Aristote sur des Commentaires Grecs ou Arabes Employes par les Docteurs Scolastiques. Amable L. Jourdain. 1960. Repr. of 1843 ed. 30.50 (ISBN 0-8337-1880-0). B Franklin.

Recherches En Delinquance: Principes De L'analyse Quantitative. Travis Hirschi & Hanan C. Selvin. (L'oeuvre Sociologique: No. 4). (Illus.). 294p. (Fr.). 1976. pap. text ed. 24.00x (ISBN 90-2797-912-X). Mouton.

Recherches Historiques Sur le Systeme De (John) Law. Emile Levasseur. LC 74-133549. 1970. Repr. of 1854 ed. lib. bdg. 29.00 (ISBN 0-8337-2091-0). B Franklin.

Recherches Photographiques. Niepce De Saint-Victor. Ed. by Peter C. Bunnell & Robert A. Sobieszek. LC 76-23058. (Sources of Modern Photography Ser.). (Fr.). 1979. Repr. of 1855 ed. lib. bdg. 17.00x (ISBN 0-405-09622-4). Ayer Co Pubs.

Recherches Recentes sur les Etudes de Marche et l'Analyse de la Demande. (Economies et Societes Series K: No. 5). 1961. pap. 26.00 (ISBN 0-8115-0724-6). Kraus Repr.

Recherches sur la Communaute Juive De Manosque Au Moyen Age (1241-1329) Joseph Shatzmiller. (Etudes Juives: No. 15). 1973. pap. 14.00x (ISBN 90-2797-188-9). Mouton.

Recherches sur la Condition de la Femme Kabyle: La coutume et l'oeuvre francaise. Laure M. Bousquet-Lefevre. LC 77-87660. Repr. of 1939 ed. 18.50 (ISBN 0-404-16404-8). AMS Pr.

Recherches sur la poesie de Dafydd ab Gwilym, barde gallois du XIVe siecle. Theodor M. Chotzen. LC 78-72622. (Celtic Language & Literature: Goidelic & Brythonic). Repr. of 1927 ed. 42.50 (ISBN 0-404-17546-5). AMS Pr.

Recherches sur le Probleme de l'Innovation: Perspectives Historiques dans le Cas Francais see Cahiers de l'Institut de Science Economique Appliquee.

Recherches sur le Symbolisme Funeraire des Romains. facsimile ed. Franz Cumont. LC 75-10632. (Ancient Religion & Mythology Ser.). (Illus., Fr.). 1976. Repr. of 1942 ed. 57.50x (ISBN 0-405-07007-1). Ayer Co Pubs.

Recherches sur le vers francais au quinzieme siecle: rimes, metres et strophes. Henri L. Chatelain. LC 79-149950. (Research & Source Works Ser.: No. 725). 1971. Repr. of 1908 ed. lib. bdg. 26.50 (ISBN 0-8337-0550-4). B Franklin.

Recherches sur le Vocabulaire du General de Gaulle: Analyse Statistique des Allocutions Radiodiffusees (1958-1965) Cotteret & Moreau. 23.75 (ISBN 0-685-33949-1). French & Eur.

Recherches sur les Ceramiaceae de la Mediterranee. Genevieve Feldmann-Mazoyer. 1977. pap. text ed. 107.50x (ISBN 3-87429-120-0). Lubrecht & Cramer.

Recherches Sur les Chrysophycees: Morphologie, Phylogenie, Systematique. P. Bourrelly. (Illus.). 1971. Repr. of 1957 ed. 44.00x (ISBN 3-7682-0703-X). Lubrecht & Cramer.

Recherches Sur les Conditions De la Connaissance Essai D'une Theoretique Pure. Gaston Berger. Ed. by Maurice Natanson. LC 78-66755. (Phenomenology Ser.: Vol. 1). 194p. 1979. lib. bdg. 26.00 (ISBN 0-8240-9569-3). Garland Pub.

Recherches Sur les Cours Laiques Du Xe Au XIIIe Siecle. Yvonne Bongert. LC 80-1996. 1981. Repr. of 1949 ed. 38.50 (ISBN 0-404-18554-1). AMS Pr.

Recherches Sur les Ornementations Sporales Des Discomycetes Opercules. M. Le Gal. 1970. Repr. of 1947 ed. 24.00x (ISBN 3-7682-0694-7). Lubrecht & Cramer.

Recherches Sur les Sources Latines Des Contes et Romans Courtois Du Moyen Age. Edmond Faral. LC 72-178580. Repr. of 1913 ed. 35.00 (ISBN 0-404-56600-6). AMS Pr.

Recherches Sur les Systemes Significants: Symposium De Varsovie, 1968. Ed. by Josette Rey-Debove. (Approaches to Semiotics: No. 18). (Illus.). 1973. 72.80x (ISBN 90-2792-379-5). Mouton.

Recherches Sur L'histoire De la Langue Osmanlie Des XVIe et XV11e Siecles: Les Elements Osmanlis De la Langue Hongroise. Suzanne Kakuk. (Near & Middle East Monographs: No. 17). 1974. 72.80 (ISBN 90-2792-626-3). Mouton.

Recherches sur L'Histoire de L'Astronomie Ancienne. facsimile ed. Paul Tannery. LC 75-13297. (History of Ideas in Ancient Greece Ser.). (Fr.). 1976. Repr. of 1893 ed. 23.50x (ISBN 0-405-07341-0). Ayer Co Pubs.

Recherches sur l'Origine, l'Esprit et la Progres des Arts de Arts de la Grece. Pierre D'Hancarville. Ed. by Burton Feldman & Robert D. Richardson. LC 78-60885. (Myth & Romanticism Ser.). 1984. lib. bdg. 240.00 (ISBN 0-8240-3561-5). Garland Pub.

Recht auf Arbeit in Ethisch-Politischer Perspektive. Jorg Eschenauer. (European University Studies: No. 31, Vol. 48). 326p. (Ger.). 1983. 37.35 (ISBN 3-8204-7853-1). P Lang Pubs.

Recht Zu Leben und Die Pflicht Zu Sterben, Sozialphilosophische Betrachtungen. Josef Popper & E. Schwarz. 1972. Repr. of 1924 ed. 26.00 (ISBN 0-384-47260-5). Johnson Repr.

Rechtfertigung und zukuenftiges Heil. Untersuchungen zu Roemer 5, 1-11. Michael Wolter. (Beihefte zur Zeitschrift fuer die Neutestamentliche Wissenschaft: No. 43). 1978. 29.20x (ISBN 3-11-007579-2). De Gruyter.

Rechts-, Wirtschafts- und Sozialgeschichte der Inneralpinen Salzwerke bis zu Deren Monopolisierung. Rudolf Palme. (Rechtshistorischhe Reihe: Vol. 25). 547p. (Ger.). 1983. 45.80 (ISBN 3-8204-7133-2). P Lang Pubs.

Rechtsentwicklungen in Deutschland. 3rd ed. Adolf Laufs. (De Gruyter Lehrbuch). 1984. 15.20x (ISBN 3-11-009758-3). De Gruyter.

Rechtssaetze in gebundener Sprache und Rechtssatzreihen im israelitischen Recht: Ein Beitrag zur Gattungsforschung. Volker Wagner. (Beiheft 127 zur Zeitschrift fuer die alttestamentliche Wissenschaft). 1972. 16.80x (ISBN 3-11-003945-1). De Gruyter.

Rechtssprache Englisch-Deutsch. R. Renner & J. Tooth. 526p. (Ger.). 1971. 35.00 (ISBN 3-19-006280-3, M-7597, Pub. by M. Hueber). French & Eur.

Rechtswoerterbuch. H. Kniepkamp. 216p. (Ger. & Eng., Dictionary of Legal Terms). 1954. 65.00 (ISBN 3-7678-0013-6, M-7598, Pub. by Colloquium Vlg.). French & Eur.

Rechtsworterbuch Fur Die Gewerbliche Wirtschaft. Ursula Becker. 600p. (Ger., Ger. & Fr., Dictionary of Industrial Economics). 1978. 195.00 (ISBN 3-7819-2015-1, M-7599, Pub. by Fritz Knapp Verlag). French & Eur.

Recidivism. Michael D. Maltz. LC 83-15911. (Quantitative Studies in Social Relations). 1984. 24.95 (ISBN 0-12-468980-9). Acad Pr.

Recidivism in Foster Care. Norman M. Block & Arlene Libowitz. 93p. 1983. pap. 15.95 (ISBN 0-87868-212-0, 2120). Child Welfare.

Recife. Manuel Bandeira. Tr. by Eddie Flintoff. 56p. pap. 20.00x (ISBN 0-947612-04-1, Pub. by Rivelin Grapheme Pr). State Mutual Bk.

Recipe Annual 1988. Sunset Bks & Sunset Magazine Editors. (Illus.). 352p. 1988. 19.95 (ISBN 0-376-02689-8). Sunset-Lane.

Recipe Conversion for Microwave. Barbara Methven. LC 79-120586. (Microwave Cooking Library). (Illus.). 160p. 1979. 15.95 (ISBN 0-86573-502-6). Cy De Cosse.

Recipe Finder. Marian Carey. (Illus.). 103p. (Orig.). Date not set. pap. 14.95 (ISBN 0-9620559-0-5). M J Carey.

Recipe for a Great Affair: How to Cater Your Own Party...or Anybody Else's. Annette Annechild & Russell Bennett. LC 81-11806. 207p. 1981. pap. 9.95 (ISBN 0-671-42411-4, Wallaby). S&S.

Recipe for Happy Days. Patricia O'Grady. (Illus.). 65p. (Orig.). 1982. pap. 4.25 (ISBN 0-9601846-2-7). PM Ent.

Recipe for Holiness. Pope Pius Tenth. 125p. 1971. 4.00 (ISBN 0-912414-04-9). Lumen Christi.

Recipe for Math Program. Nina Traub. 1984. 49.95 set (ISBN 0-87594-250-4); tchr's bk. 19.95 (ISBN 0-87594-245-8); student wkbk. 9.95 (ISBN 0-87594-246-6). Book-Lab.

Recipe for Murder. Jeffrey Ashford. 152p. 1980. Walker & Co.

Recipe for Murder. Jeffrey Ashford. LC 80-51721. (British Mystery Ser.). 175p. 1984. Walker & Co.

Recipe for Murder. Carolyn Keene. (Nancy Drew Files Ser.: No. 21). 160p. (Orig.). (YA) (gr. 7 up). 1988. pap. 2.75 (ISBN 0-671-64227-8). Archway.

Recipe for Romance. Terri Fields. 192p. (Orig.). (gr. 7 up). 1986. pap. 2.25 (ISBN 0-590-33872-2, Wildfire). Scholastic Inc.

Recipe for Spelling. Frances Bloom & Deborah Bloom. Ed. by Kenn Goin & Ina C. Jaeger. 240p. (Orig.). 1985. pap. 16.95 (ISBN 0-8027-8042-3). Walker & Co.

Recipe for Spelling. Frances Bloom & Deborah Bloom. 256p. (gr. 2-6). 1986. 16.95 (ISBN 0-317-70004-9). Walker & Co.

Recipe for Survival: Your Daily Food. Doris Grant. LC 73-93654. 224p. 1974. 6.95 (ISBN 0-87983-069-7); pap. 3.95 (ISBN 0-87983-079-4). Keats.

Recipe Index, Nineteen Seventy-One: The Eater's Guide to Periodical Literature. Ed. by John Forsman. LC 72-884. 774p. 1972. 52.00x (ISBN 0-8103-0526-7). Gale.

Recipe Index, Nineteen Seventy: The Eater's Guide to Periodical Literature. Ed. by John Forsman. LC 72-884. 784p. 1972. 52.00x (ISBN 0-8103-0525-9). Gale.

Recipe Ingredient Replacement As a Method for Food Self-Sufficiency. Center for Self-Sufficiency, Reasearch Division Staff. 20p. 1985. pap. text ed. 2.50 (ISBN 0-910811-19-9, Pub. by Center Self Suff). Prosperity & Profits.

Recipe Ingredient Replacement for Small Business, Caterers, Small Restaurants, Deli Shops, Etc. Center for Self-Sufficiency, Research Division Staff. 20p. 1985. pap. text ed. 6.95 (ISBN 0-318-04301-7, Pub. by Center Self Suff). Prosperity & Profits.

Recipe Ingredient Replacement, Variation & Substitution Cookbooks for Library Loan: A Catalog with Recipes. 10p. 1986. pap. 1.00 (ISBN 0-910811-53-9, Pub. by Center Self-Suff.). Prosperity & Profits.

Recipe Ingredient Substitution As a Continuing Education Alternative. Training Manuals Research Division. 27p. 1984. pap. text ed. 6.95 (ISBN 0-318-04562-1, Pub. by Training Manuals). Prosperity & Profits.

Recipe Ingredient Substitution Cookbook. Alpha Pyramis. 60p. Date not set. pap. text ed. 7.95 (ISBN 0-913597-23-6, Pub. by Alpha Pyramis). Prosperity & Profits.

Recipe Ingredient Substitution or Replacement: Food Bank Edition. Recycling Consortium. 25p. 1985. pap. text ed. 3.00 (ISBN 0-318-04377-7, Pub. by Recycling Consort). Prosperity & Profits.

Recipe Ingredient Substitutions & Variety Concept As an Alternative Cooking School. Alpha Pyramis. 30p. 1985. pap. text ed. 8.95 (ISBN 0-913597-81-3, Pub. by Alpha Pyramis). Prosperity & Profits.

Recipe Jubilee. 344p. 1964. spiral bdg. 11.95 (ISBN 0-9603054-1-6). Mobile Jr League Pubns.

Recipe Reflections. Nineteenth Century Club. (Illus.). 352p. 1979. pap. 11.95 (ISBN 0-939114-05-4). Nineteenth Century.

Recipe Reminder. rev. ed. 124p. 1985. 6.95 (ISBN 0-9602448-2-4). Wimmer Bks.

Recipe Research Correspondence Course. Cookbook Consortium Educational Division Staff. 1984. pap. text ed. 9.95 (ISBN 0-318-04319-X, Pub. by Cookbk Consorts). Prosperity & Profits.

Recipe Research Correspondence Course for Pastries & Deserts. Cookbook Consortium Educational Division Staff. 1984. pap. text ed. 9.95 (ISBN 0-318-04320-3, Pub. by Cookbk Consorts). Prosperity & Profits.

Recipe Yearbook 1987. Bon Appetit Magazine Editors. LC 87-4125. (Cooking with Bon Appetit Ser.). 1987. 12.95 (ISBN 0-89535-182-X). Knapp Pr.

Recipe Yearbook 1988. Bon Appetit Magazine Editors. (Cooking with Bon Appetit Ser.). 1987. 12.95 (ISBN 0-89535-194-3). Knapp Pr.

Recipes & Reminiscences of New Orleans. Illus. by Emery Clark. (Illus.). 237p. (Orig.). 1971. pap. 7.95 (ISBN 0-9604718-0-4). Ursuline.

Recipes & Reminiscences of New Orleans, Vol. II. (Our Cultural Heritage Ser.). (Illus.). 389p. (Orig.). 1981. pap. 11.95 (ISBN 0-9604718-1-2). Ursuline.

Recipes & Rendezvous. Gail R. Parker. (Illus.). 108p. (Orig.). 1984. pap. 5.95 (ISBN 0-910115-02-8). PS Pubns.

Recipes for a Small Planet. Ellen B. Ewald. (Illus., Orig.). 1988. pap. 3.95 (ISBN 0-345-00622-4). Ballantine.

Recipes for a Small Planet. Ellen B. Ewald. 1988. pap. 7.95 (ISBN 0-345-29567-6). Ballantine.

Recipes for an Arabian Night. David Scott. (Illus.). 1984. pap. 8.95 (ISBN 0-394-72292-2). Pantheon.

Recipes for Art & Craft Materials. rev. ed. Helen R. Sattler. LC 86-34271. (Illus.). 128p. (gr. 6 up). 1987. 10.95 (ISBN 0-688-07374-3); PLB 10.88 (ISBN 0-688-07375-1). Lothrop.

Recipes for Better Bones. Victor Ettinger & Judy Fredal. 176p. 1988. pap. 11.95 (ISBN 0-399-51401-5, Perigee Bks). Putnam Pub Group.

Recipes for Diabetics. Billie Little. 304p. 1985. pap. 4.50 (ISBN 0-553-25597-5). Bantam.

Recipes for Diabetics. rev. ed. Billie Little. LC 80-84944. 288p. 1981. pap. 7.95 (ISBN 0-399-50957-7, G&D). Putnam Pub Group.

Recipes for Fitness. Eleanor Brown. Date not set. price not set. Fitness Ojai.

Recipes for Fitness for Very Busy People. rev ed. Eleanor A. Brown. (Illus.). 89p. 1985. pap. 6.95 (ISBN 0-9618805-1-1). Fitness Ojai.

Recipes for Health... & Pleasure. David A. Phillips. LC 83-12424. 191p. 1983. pap. 7.95 (ISBN 0-88007-140-0). Woodbridge Pr.

Recipes for Leftovers. Ed. by Linda Wallner. 64p. 1975. pap. 3.95 (ISBN 0-89821-006-2). Reiman Assocs.

Recipes for Longer Life. Ann Wigmore. 196p. pap. 8.95 (ISBN 0-89529-195-9). Avery Pub.

Recipes for Quantity Service. 1986. lib. bdg. 79.95 (ISBN 0-8490-3791-3). Gordon Pr.

Recipes for Remembrance: A Family Album Featuring Stars of the Lawrence Welk Show. Cinda G. Redman & Jo Berry. LC 85-45365. (Illus.). 176p. 1986. pap. 13.95 (ISBN 0-06-250741-9, HarpR). Har-Row.

Recipes for Self-Sufficient Living. Marlynn Phipps et al. LC 84-3117. (Illus.). 160p. (Orig.). 1984. pap. 9.95 (ISBN 0-87747-640-3, Pub. by Shadow Mountain). Deseret Bk.

Recipes for Starving Actors. Victor Izay. (Illus., Orig.). pap. 3.50. Pacifica.

Recipes for the Heart: A Nutrition Guide for People with High Blood Pressure. Lucy M. Williams. (Illus.). 158p. (Orig.). 1988. pap. 13.50 (ISBN 0-945080-40-9). Sandridge Pub.

Recipes for the Rockies. Sara Clark. LC 85-6503. 337p. (Orig.). 1985. pap. 12.95 (ISBN 0-87108-669-7). Pruett.

Recipes from a Kitchen Garden. Renee Shepherd. LC 87-90646. (Illus.). 92p. (Orig.). 1987. pap. 7.95. Shepherds Garden Pubs.

Recipes from America's Restored Villages. 1987. pap. 4.95 (ISBN 0-345-34708-0). Ballantine.

Recipes from an Old Farmhouse. Alison Uttley. (Illus.). 132p. (Orig.). 1973. pap. 3.95 (ISBN 0-571-10178-X). Faber & Faber.

Recipes from an Old New Orleans Kitchen. Suzanne Ormond. 1988. pap. 4.95 (ISBN 0-88289-699-7). Pelican.

Recipes from Arizona with Love. Liza Golden & Ferol Golden. (Orig.). 1985. pap. 8.95 comb bd. (ISBN 0-913703-10-9). New Boundary Design.

Recipes from Around the World. Jules Bond. (Easy Cooking Ser.). (Illus.). 64p. 1984. pap. 5.95 (ISBN 0-8120-5604-3). Barron.

Recipes from Around the World: For Young People 8-14. Cobblestone Publishing, Inc Staff. (Illus.). 36p. (gr. 4-8). 1987. pap. text ed. 4.95 (ISBN 0-942389-03-4). Cobblestone Pub.

Recipes from Home. Bernell Izard & Ann Izard. 64p. (Orig.). 1983. pap. 4.50 (ISBN 0-913431-01-X). Dominion Pub.

Recipes from Iowa: With Love. Peg Hein & Kathy Cramer. Ed. by Dorothy Yeglin. (Illus.). 194p. 1982. comb bdg. 8.95 (ISBN 0-913703-01-X). New Boundary Design.

Recipes from Loch Lomond. Picton Publishing Staff. 1987. 9.00x (Pub. by Picton UK). State Mutual Bk.

Recipes from Maine with Love. Peter Hodgkin. (Illus.). 200p. (Orig.). 1985. pap. 8.95 comb bd. (ISBN 0-913703-08-7). New Boundary Design.

Recipes from Massachusetts with Love. Liz Anton & Beth Dooley. (Illus.). 250p. (Orig.). 1985. pap. 8.95 comb bd. (ISBN 0-913703-07-9). New Boundary Design.

Reclamation, Treatment, & Utilization of Coal Mining Wastes: Proceedings of Second International Conference on the Reclamation, Treatment, & Utilization of Coal Mining Wastes, Nottingham, UK, Sept. 7-11, 1987. Ed. by A. K. Rainbow. (Advances in Mining Science & Technology Ser.: Vol. 2). 668p. 1987. 139.25 (ISBN 0-444-42876-3). Elsevier.

Reclassification of the Perceval Romances. George Woods. (Studies in Comparative Literature, No. 35). 1970. pap. 22.95x (ISBN 0-8383-0083-9). Haskell.

Reclassification-Rationale & Problems, Vol. 1. Ed. by Jean M. Perreault. 1968. pap. 5.00 (ISBN 0-911808-02-7). U of Md Lib Serv.

Recoding Metaphysics. Ed. by Giovanna Borradori. 350p. 1988. 42.95 (ISBN 0-8101-0799-6); pap. 14.95 (ISBN 0-8101-0800-3). Northwestern U Pr.

Recodings: Art, Spectacle, Cultural Politics. Hal Foster. LC 85-70184. (Illus.). 272p. 1985. 16.95 (ISBN 0-941920-03-8); pap. 9.95 (ISBN 0-941920-04-6). Bay Pr.

Recognition, A Logical & Experimental Study see Horizontal-Vertical Illusion of Brightness.

Recognition & Discrimination see Mental & Physical Measurements of Working Children.

Recognition & Enforcement of Foreign Judgments in the Common Law Units of the British Commonwealth. Horace E. Read. LC 38-18887. (Harvard Studies in the Conflict of Laws: Vol. 2). xiv, 371p. 1978. Repr. of 1938 ed. lib. bdg. 40.00 (ISBN 0-89941-127-4). W S Hein.

Recognition & Evaluation of Uraniferous Areas. (Panel Proceedings Ser.). (Illus.). 295p. 1977. pap. 35.00 (ISBN 92-0-041077-4, ISP450, IAEA). UNIPUB.

Recognition & Regulation in Cell-Mediated Immunity. James D. Watson. Ed. by J. Marbrook. (Receptors & Ligands in Intercellular Communication Ser.). 1985. 85.00 (ISBN 0-8247-7268-7). Dekker.

Recognition in Financial Statements: Underlying Concepts & Practical Conventions. L. Todd Johnson & Reed K. Storey. LC 82-71737. (Financial Accounting Standards Board Research Report). (Illus.). 267p. (Orig.). 1982. pap. 20.00 (ISBN 0-910065-16-0). Finan Acct Found.

Recognition in International Law. Hersh Lauterpacht. LC 76-29419. Repr. of 1947 ed. 31.00 (ISBN 0-404-15338-0). AMS Pr.

Recognition in Microbe-Plant Symbiotic & Pathogenic Interactions. Ed. by B. Lugtenberg. (NATO ASI Series H4). xiv, 449p. 1986. 110.00 (ISBN 0-387-17183-5). Springer-Verlag.

Recognition, Investigation & Prevention of Acute Viral Infections. Donald H. McLean. 444p. 1988. 65.00 (ISBN 0-87527-372-6). Green.

Recognition of Ancient Sedimentary Environments. Ed. by J. Keith Rigby & W. K. Hamblin. LC 72-194231. (Society of Economic Paleontologists & Mineralogists, Special Publication: No. 16). pap. 87.50 (ISBN 0-317-27126-1, 2024741). Bks Demand UMI.

Recognition of Contractual Rights & Obligations: An Exploratory Study of Conceptual Issues. Yuji Ijiri. LC 80-71000. (Financial Accounting Standards Board Research Report). (Illus.). 92p. (Orig.). 1980. pap. 9.25 (ISBN 0-910065-10-1). Finan Acct Found.

Recognition of Depreciation by Not-for-Profit Institutions. Ed. by Yamil Kahn. 159p. 1988. 25.00 (ISBN 0-915164-37-X). NACUBO.

Recognition of Excellence. Stern Family Fund. 1960. pap. 6.75 (ISBN 0-02-931390-2). Free Pr.

Recognition of Facial Expression: An Original Anthology. Ed. by Martha Davis. LC 74-9160. (Body Movement Perspectives in Research Ser). 252p. 1975. Repr. 32.00x (ISBN 0-405-06198-6). Ayer Co Pubs.

Recognition of Fluvial Depositional Systems & Their Resource Potential. Romeo M. Flores et al. (Short Course Notes Ser.: No. 19). 290p. 1985. pap. 23.00 (ISBN 0-918985-53-6). SEPM.

Recognition of Health Hazards in Industry: A Review of Materials & Processes. William A. Burgess. LC 81-2132. 275p. 1981. 48.00 (ISBN 0-471-06339-8). Wiley.

Recognition of Henry David Thoreau: Selected Criticism since 1848. Wendell Glick. LC 69-15845. pap. 100.50 (ISBN 0-317-29154-8, 2055608). Bks Demand UMI.

Recognition of Israel, 1948. Ed. by Michael J. Cohen & Howard M. Sachar. (Rise of Israel Ser.). 280p. 1987. lib. bdg. 65.00 (ISBN 0-8240-4937-3). Garland Pub.

Recognition of M. Leprae Antigens. Tom Ottenhoff & Rene De Vries. (Development in Hematology & Immunology Ser.). 1987. lib. bdg. 54.00 (ISBN 0-317-59613-6, Pub. by Martinus Nijhoff Netherlands). Kluwer Academic.

Recognition of Merit in Superintendents' Reports to the Public. Zenas R. Clark. LC 77-176650. (Columbia University. Teachers College. Contributions to Education: No. 471). Repr. of 1931 ed. 22.50 (ISBN 0-404-55471-7). AMS Pr.

Recognition of Nathaniel Hawthorne: Selected Criticism since 1828. Ed. by B. Bernard Cohen. LC 70-83454. pap. 80.00 (ISBN 0-317-29153-X, 2055609). Bks Demand UMI.

Recognition of Pattern & Form, Austin, Texas 1979: Proceedings. Ed. by D. G. Albrecht. (Lecture Notes in Biomathematics: Vol. 44). 225p. 1982. pap. 17.00 (ISBN 0-387-11206-5). Springer-Verlag.

Recognition of Patterns Using the Frequencies of Occurence of Binary Words. 2nd & rev. ed. P. W. Becker. (Illus.). 1978. pap. 26.00 (ISBN 0-387-81506-6). Springer-Verlag.

Recognition of Reason. Edward Pols. LC 63-14296. (Philosophical Exploration Ser.). 269p. 1963. 9.95x (ISBN 0-8093-0111-3). S Ill U Pr.

Recognition of Speech by Machine - A Bibliography. Ed. by A. S. House. 498p. 1988. 49.00 (ISBN 0-12-356785-8). Acad Pr.

Recognition of Uranium Provinces - Proceedings of a Technical Committee Meeting on Recognition of Uranium Provinces Organized by the International Atomic Energy Agency & Held in London from 18 to 20 September, 1985. 459p. (Orig.). 1988. pap. text ed. 93.00 (ISBN 92-0-141088-3, ISP736, IAEA). UNIPUB.

Recognition Policy of the United States. Julius L. Goebel. LC 68-56657. (Columbia University Studies in the Social Sciences: No. 158). Repr. of 1915 ed. 19.50 (ISBN 0-404-51158-9). AMS Pr.

Recognition Proteins, Receptors, & Probes: Invertebrates. Elias Cohen. LC 84-7878. (Progress in Clinical & Biological Research Ser.: Vol. 157). 228p. 1984. 42.00 (ISBN 0-8451-5007-3). A R Liss.

Recognition: Study in the Philosophy of Artificial Intelligence. Kenneth M. Sayre. 1965. 18.95 (ISBN 0-268-00228-2). U of Notre Dame Pr.

Recognitions. Clare Butterfield. Ed. by Johnston William et al. L. Johnston. (Chapbook Ser.: No. 11). 18p. 1983. pap. 3.00 (ISBN 0-932884-10-5). Red Herring.

Recognitions. William Gaddis. 1984. pap. 5.95 (ISBN 0-380-00030-X, 60921-5, Bard). Avon.

Recognitions. William Gaddis. (Contemporary American Fiction Ser.). 954p. 1985. pap. 12.95 (ISBN 0-14-007768-5). Penguin.

Recognitions: A Study in Poetics. Terence Cave. 544p. 1988. 75.00 (ISBN 0-19-815849-1). Oxford U Pr.

Recognitions, Poems Nineteen Seventy-Five to Nineteen Seventy-Seven. Clinton Williams. LC 77-89954. 1977. pap. 2.50 (ISBN 0-934614-02-4). Talisman Research.

Recognizable Image: William Carlos Williams on Art & Artists. William Carlos Williams. Ed. by Bram Dijkstra. LC 78-16919. (Illus.). 1978. 16.00 (ISBN 0-8112-0704-8). New Directions.

Recognizable Patterns of Human Deformation: Identification & Management of Mechanical Effects of Morphogenesis. David W. Smith. (Major Problems in Clinical Pediatrics Ser.: Vol. 21). (Illus.). 240p. 1981. text ed. 34.95 (ISBN 0-7216-8401-7). Saunders.

Recognizable Patterns of Human Malformation: Genetic, Embryologic & Clinical Aspects. David W. Smith. LC 75-21150. (Major Problems in Clinical Pediatrics Ser.: Vol. 7). (Illus.). Repr. of 1970 ed. 97.00 (ISBN 0-8357-9557-8, 2051194). Bks Demand UMI.

Recognizable Patterns of Human Malformation: Genetic, Embryologic & Clinical Aspects. 3rd ed. David W. Smith. (Major Problems in Clinical Pediatrics Ser.: Vol. 7). (Illus.). 688p. 1982. 60.00 (ISBN 0-7216-8381-9). Saunders.

Recognizing & Helping the Learning Disabled Child in Your Classroom. Mary J. Rolando. 24p. 1978. 2.40 (ISBN 0-686-39949-8). Natl Cath Educ.

Recognizing & Producing Behavioral Objectives. Donald E. Smith. (Michigan Learning Modules Ser.: No. 1). 1977. pap. 2.45x (ISBN 0-914004-04-2). Ulrich.

Recognizing & Treating Insulin Reactions. Helen Bowlin et al. 4p. 1987. pap. 1.00 (ISBN 0-937721-12-3). Diabetes Ctr MN.

Recognizing Biography. William H. Epstein. 256p. 1987. text ed. 31.95x (ISBN 0-8122-8081-4). U of Pa Pr.

Recognizing Cause & Effect. Sheldon L. Tilkin. (Horizons E Ser.). (Illus.). 24p. (gr. 3-4). 1980. 2.50 (ISBN 0-89403-574-6). EDC.

Recognizing Cause & Effect. Sheldon L. Tilkin & Judith Conoway. (Horizons F Ser.). (Illus.). 24p. (gr. 4-5). 1980. wkbk. 2.50 (ISBN 0-89403-584-3). EDC.

Recognizing Foreign Governments: The Practice of the United States. Thomas L. Galloway. 1978. pap. 11.00 (ISBN 0-8447-3280-X). Am Enterprise.

Recognizing Inflation in Accounting. Francis J. Walsh, Jr. (Report Ser.: No. 783). (Illus.). v, 50p. (Orig.). 1980. 15.00 (ISBN 0-8237-0219-7). Conference Bd.

Recognizing Islam: Religion & Society in the Modern Word. Micheal Gilsenan. 1983. pap. 7.96 (ISBN 0-394-71332-X). Pantheon.

Recognizing Job Health Hazards. Center for Occupational Research & Development Staff. (Job Safety & Health Instructional Materials Ser.). (Illus.). 46p. 1981. pap. text ed. 3.50 (ISBN 1-55502-086-0). Ctr Res & Dev.

Recognizing Job Safety Hazards. Center for Occupational Research & Development Staff. (Job Safety & Health Instructional Materials Ser.). (Illus.). 32p. 1981. pap. text ed. 2.50 (ISBN 1-55502-087-9). Ctr Res & Dev.

Recognizing Mood, Character & Plot. Sheldon L. Tilkin & Judith Conoway. (Horizons F Ser.). (Illus.). 24p. (gr. 4-5). 1980. wkbk. 2.50 (ISBN 0-89403-586-X). EDC.

Recognizing Mood, Character & Plot. Sheldon L. Tilkin & Judith Conoway. (Horizons E Ser). (Illus.). 24p. (gr. 3-4). 1980. wkbk. 2.50 (ISBN 0-89403-576-2). EDC.

Recognizing Patterns of Ocular Childhood Diseases. Leonard B. Nelson et al. LC 84-52023. 187p. 1985. 65.00 (ISBN 0-943432-37-5). Slack Inc.

Recognizing Points of View: Whose Mind; Where's He Standing? Walter Pauk. (Skill at a Time Ser). 64p. (gr. 9 up). 1975. pap. text ed. 4.00x (ISBN 0-89061-028-2, ST-8). Jamestown Pubs.

Recognizing the Dangers: An Information Book on Child Sexual Abuse. Linda R. Young. 64p. (Orig.). 1986. pap. 1.25 (ISBN 0-940339-00-5). Lineage Pr.

Recognizing Tone: Advanced Level. James A. Giroux & Glenn R. Williston. Ed. by Edward Spargo. (Comprehension Skills Ser). (Illus.). 64p. (gr. 9 up). 1974. pap. text ed. 4.00x (ISBN 0-89061-017-7, CB-6A). Jamestown Pubs.

Recognizing Tone: Middle Level. Glenn R. Williston. (Comprehension Skill Ser.). (Illus.). 64p. (gr. 6-12). 1976. pap. text ed. 4.00x (ISBN 0-89061-069-X, CB-6M). Jamestown Pubs.

Recognizing Traits of Characters: How Does the Author Build His Characters? Walter Pauk. (Skill at a Time Ser). 64p. (gr. 9 up). 1975. pap. text ed. 4.00x (ISBN 0-89061-027-4, ST-7). Jamestown Pubs.

Recoil. Roy LeBeau. (Buckskin Ser.: No. 12). 208p. (Orig.). 1986. pap. 2.50 (ISBN 0-8439-2355-5, Leisure Bks). Leisure NY.

Recoil. Jim Thompson. LC 84-71663. 192p. 1985. pap. 3.95 (ISBN 0-916870-89-8, Black Lizard Bks). Creative Arts Bk.

Recollected Essays, Nineteen Sixty-Five to Nineteen Eighty. Wendell Berry. LC 80-28812. 352p. 1981. 18.00 (ISBN 0-86547-025-1); pap. 10.95 (ISBN 0-86547-026-X). N Point Pr.

Recollected in Tranquillity. Janet E. Courtney. 1973. Repr. of 1926 ed. 20.00 (ISBN 0-8274-1525-7). R West.

Recollecting the Future: A View of Business, Technology & Innovation in the Next 30 Years. Hugh B. Stewart. 1988. 24.95 (ISBN 1-55623-143-1). Dow Jones-Irwin.

Recollection & Discovery: The Rhetoric of Character in William Faulkner's Novels. Cathy Waegner. (Anglo-Saxon Language & Literature-European University Studies: No. 14, Vol. 120). 225p. 1983. pap. 27.90 (ISBN 3-8204-7811-6). P Lang Pubs.

Recollection & Reconstruction. Ed. by Bernard D. Fine et al. Bd. with Reconstruction in Psychoanalysis. LC 74-147778. (Kris Study Group Monograph: No. 4). 128p. (Orig.). 1971. text ed. 17.50 (ISBN 0-8236-5785-X). Intl Univs Pr.

Recollection of a Happy Childhood by Mary Esther Huger, Daughter of Francis Kinloch Huger of Long House Near Pendleton, South Carolina 1826-1848. Ed. & intro. by Mary Stevenson. LC 76-4386. (Illus.). 1976. 15.00 (ISBN 0-912462-07-8). Foun Hist Rest.

Recollection of a Literary Life: Or, Books, Places & People, 3 vols. Mary R. Mitford. 1973. Repr. of 1852 ed. 50.00 set (ISBN 0-8274-1202-9). R West.

Recollection of Marcella Sembrich. H. Goddard Owen. LC 81-22197. (Music Reprint Ser.). (Illus.). 80p. 1982. Repr. of 1950 ed. lib. bdg. 21.50 (ISBN 0-306-76141-6). Da Capo.

Recollections. Andrew J. Chambers. Bd. with Reminiscences. Margaret W. Chambers. 1975. 8.95 (ISBN 0-87770-156-3). Ye Galleon.

Recollections. George W. Childs. 1890. 25.00 (ISBN 0-932062-31-8). Sharon Hill.

Recollections. Colette. 288p. 1986. pap. 8.95 (ISBN 0-02-013360-X, Collier). Macmillan.

Recollections. Harry Frazier. 100p. 1938. 1.00 (ISBN 0-939487-01-2). Ches & OH Hist.

Recollections, 2 vols. John Morley. LC 75-30034. Repr. of 1917 ed. 65.00 set (ISBN 0-404-14080-7). AMS Pr.

Recollections, 2 vols. John Morley. 1978. Repr. of 1917 ed. lib. bdg. 50.00 (ISBN 0-8495-3727-4). Arden Lib.

Recollections, 2 vols. John V. Morley. 1917. 65.00 set (ISBN 0-8274-3253-4). R West.

Recollections & Impressions of James A. McNeill Whistler. Arthur J. Eddy. LC 71-176163. (Illus.). Repr. of 1904 ed. 27.50 (ISBN 0-405-08484-6, Blom Pubns). Ayer Co Pubs.

Recollections & Opinions of an Old Pioneer. Peter H. Burnett. LC 76-87661. (American Scene Ser.). 1969. Repr. of 1880 ed. lib. bdg. 55.00 (ISBN 0-306-71765-4). Da Capo.

Recollections & Reflections. Douglas Black. (Memoir Club Ser.). 132p. 1988. 32.00x (ISBN 0-7279-0209-1, Pub. by British Med Assoc UK). Taylor & Francis.

Recollections & Reflections. James R. Planche. LC 78-17733. (Music Reprint Ser.). (Illus.). 1978. Repr. of 1901 ed. lib. bdg. 65.00 (ISBN 0-306-79501-9). Da Capo.

Recollections & Reflections. Richard Strauss. Ed. by Willi Schuh. Tr. by L. J. Lawrence. LC 74-72. (Illus.). 173p. 1974. Repr. of 1953 ed. lib. bdg. 38.50x (ISBN 0-8371-7366-3, STRF). Greenwood.

Recollections & Reflections. J. J. Thomson. LC 74-26297. (History, Philosophy & Sociology of Science Ser). (Illus.). 1975. Repr. 36.50x (ISBN 0-405-06622-8). Ayer Co Pubs.

Recollections & Reflections of Pedro Arrupe. Tr. by Yolanda De Mola. LC 85-45548. (Orig.). 1986. pap. 7.95 (ISBN 0-317-59710-8). M Glazier.

Recollections: Carlyle, Dickens, Charles Reade, Wilkie Collins, Rudyard Kipling. 1978. Repr. of 1908 ed. lib. bdg. 35.00 (ISBN 0-8495-3754-1). Arden Lib.

Recollections: Carlyle, Dickens, Kipling, Meredith, Barrie, Stevenson. David C. Murray. 1978. Repr. of 1908 ed. lib. bdg. 35.00 (ISBN 0-8492-6743-9). R West.

Recollections from 1860 to 1865. John H. Lewis. 1983. 12.50 (ISBN 0-89029-074-1); pap. 7.50 (ISBN 0-89029-774-6). Pr of Morningside.

Recollections: Literary & Political. J. H. Browne. 1917. Repr. 20.00 (ISBN 0-8274-3252-6). R West.

Recollections of a Busy Life. facsimile ed. James B. Forgan. LC 75-2632. (Wall Street & the Security Market Ser.). (Illus.). 1975. Repr. of 1924 ed. 29.00x (ISBN 0-405-06957-X). Ayer Co Pubs.

Recollections of a Busy Life. facs. ed. Horace Greeley. LC 74-83912. (Black Heritage Library Collection Ser). 1868. 23.50 (ISBN 0-8369-8582-6). Ayer Co Pubs.

Recollections of a Busy Life. Horace Greeley. LC 74-125695. (American Journalists Ser). 1970. Repr. of 1868 ed. 23.50 (ISBN 0-405-01674-3). Ayer Co Pubs.

Recollections of a Busy Life, 2 Vols. Horace Greeley. LC 71-137913. (American History & Culture in the Nineteenth Century Ser). 1971. Repr. of 1873 ed. Set. 66.50x (ISBN 0-8046-1481-4, Pub. by Kennikat). Assoc Faculty Pr.

Recollections of a Georgia Loyalist. Elizabeth L. Johnston. Ed. by Arthur W. Eaton. LC 76-187388. (Illus.). 224p. 1972. Repr. of 1901 ed. 17.50 (ISBN 0-87152-083-4). Reprint.

Recollections of a Golden Age. Rudolph Schevill. Ed. by Yvette E. Miller. LC 84-29985. 224p. 1985. 25.00 (ISBN 0-935480-19-6); pap. 14.95. Lat Am Lit Rev Pr.

Recollections of a Handcart Pioneer of 1860: A Woman's Life on the Mormon Frontier. Mary A. Hafen. LC 82-23868. (Illus.). 100p. 1983. 10.95x (ISBN 0-8032-2325-0); pap. 4.50 (ISBN 0-8032-7219-7, BB 841, Bison). U of Nebr Pr.

Recollections of a Happy Life. Maurice Egan. 1924. Repr. 20.00 (ISBN 0-8274-3254-2). R West.

Recollections of a Happy Life. Elizabeth C. Hobson. 14.00 (ISBN 0-8369-6978-2, 7857). Ayer Co Pubs.

Recollections of a High School District 1893-1968: An Informal History of the Kern County Union High School & Junior College District. J. S. Wallace. 289p. Date not set. 15.00 (ISBN 0-9619924-0-9). Kern HS Dist.

Recollections of a Humourist. Arthur W. Beckett. Repr. of 1907 ed. 15.00 (ISBN 0-8274-4145-2). R West.

Recollections of a Journey Through Tartary, Thibet, & China During the Years of 1844, 1845, & 1846, 2 vols. M. Huc. 1986. Repr. of 1852 ed. 100.00 (ISBN 0-8495-2409-1). Arden Lib.

Recollections of a Labour Pioneer. Francis W. Soutter. LC 83-48499. (World of Labour - English Workers 1850-1890 Ser.). 223p. 1984. lib. bdg. 25.00 (ISBN 0-8240-5726-0). Garland Pub.

Recollections of a Life. Alger Hiss. LC 87-28482. (Illus.). 256p. 1988. 19.95 (ISBN 0-8050-0612-5). Seaver Bks.

Recollections of a Lifetime, or Men & Things I Have Seen. Samuel G. Goodrich. LC 67-23886. 1110p. 1967. Repr. of 1857 ed. 43.00x (ISBN 0-8103-3041-5). Gale.

Recollections of a Literary Life. Mrs. Desmond Humphrey. 1973. Repr. of 1936 ed. 20.00 (ISBN 0-8274-0353-4). R West.

Recollections of a Literary Life. Mary R. Mitford. LC 74-178342. Repr. of 1852 ed. 49.50 (ISBN 0-404-56789-4). AMS Pr.

Recollections of a Long & Satisfactory Life. William Harden. LC 68-55890. (Illus.). Repr. of 1934 ed. cancelled (ISBN 0-8371-0464-5, HAR&). Greenwood.

Recollections of a Long Life. Jeremiah B. Jeter. Ed. by Edwin S. Gaustad. LC 79-52595. (Baptist Tradition Ser.). 1980. Repr. of 1891 ed. lib. bdg. 24.00x (ISBN 0-405-12462-7). Ayer Co Pubs.

Recollections of a Long Life: With Additional Extracts from His Private Diaries, 6 vols. John C. Broughton. Ed. by Lady Dorchester. LC 9-25987. Repr. of 1911 ed. Set. 240.00 (ISBN 0-404-03320-2); 40.00 ea. AMS Pr.

Recollections of a Longshore Gunner. BB. 216p. 1979. 11.25 (ISBN 0-85115-067-5, Pub. by Boydell & Brewer). Longwood Pub Group.

Recollections of a Maryland Confederate Soldier & Staff Officer under Johnston, Jackson & Lee. McHenry Howard. Ed. by James I. Robertson. 1975. 20.00 (ISBN 0-89029-019-9). Pr of Morningside.

Recollections of a Mint Director. Frank A. Leach. (Illus.). 136p. (Orig.). 1987. pap. 9.95 (ISBN 0-943161-01-0). Bowers & Merena.

Recollections of a Naval Office, 1841-1865. William H. Parker. (Classics of Naval Literature Ser.). 320p. 1985. Repr. of 1883 ed. 21.95 (ISBN 0-87021-533-7). Naval Inst Pr.

Recollections of a New England Educator. William A. Mowry. LC 73-89207. (American Education: Its Men, Institutions & Ideas, Ser. 1). 1969. Repr. of 1908 ed. 19.00 (ISBN 0-405-01446-5). Ayer Co Pubs.

Recollections of a New York Chief of Police with Historic Supplement of the Denver Police. George W. Walling. LC 70-129311. (Criminology, Law Enforcement, & Social Problems Ser.: No. 133). (Illus.). 682p. (With intro. & index added). 1972. Repr. of 1890 ed. 20.00x (ISBN 0-87585-133-9). Patterson Smith.

Recollections of a Newspaperman: A Record of Life & Events in California. Frank A. Leach. (American Newspapermen 1790-1933 Ser.). (Illus.). 416p. 1974. Repr. of 1917 ed. 20.00x (ISBN 0-8464-0016-2). Beekman Pubs.

Recollections of a One-Room Schoolhouse: An Interview with Marian Brooks. 1975. pap. 0.75 (ISBN 0-918374-13-8). City Coll Wk.

Recollections of a Picture Dealer. Ambroise Vollard. Tr. by Violet M. MacDonald from Fr. LC 77-88948. (Illus.). 1978. pap. 7.50 (ISBN 0-486-23582-3). Dover.

Recollections of a Picture Dealer. Ambroise Vollard. LC 77-76778. (Illus.). 1978. Repr. of 1936 ed. lib. bdg. 35.00 (ISBN 0-87817-218-1). Hacker.

Recollections of a Pioneering Sovietologist. expanded ed. John N. Hazard. LC 87-62208. 188p. 1987. lib. bdg. 25.00 (ISBN 0-379-20878-4). Oceana.

Recollections of a Private. Warren L. Goss. LC 84-2679. (Collector's Library of the Civil War Ser.). 1984. Kivar binding 26.60 (ISBN 0-8094-4466-6, Pub. by Time-Life). Silver.

Recollections of a Private Soldier in the Army of the Potomac. Frank Wilkeson. LC 70-39471. (Select Bibliographies Reprint Series). 1972. Repr. of 1886 ed. 15.50 (ISBN 0-8369-9923-1). Ayer Co Pubs.

Recollections of a Regimental Medical Officer. H. D. Steward. (Illus.). 169p. 1983. 29.95x (ISBN 0-522-84263-1, Pub. by Melbourne U Pr Australia); pap. 16.95x (ISBN 0-522-84244-5). Intl Spec Bk.

Recollections of a Revolution: Geography As Spatial Science. Ed. by Mark Billinge et al. LC 83-19191. 256p. 1984. 25.00 (ISBN 0-312-66587-3). St Martin.

Recollections of a Texas Educator. Louis H. Hubbard. 1964. 10.00x (ISBN 0-686-72458-5). A Jones.

Recollections of a Tour Made in Scotland, A. D. 1803. Dorothy Wordsworth. Ed. by J. C. Shairp. LC 70-37730. Repr. of 1874 ed. 37.00 (ISBN 0-404-56857-2). AMS Pr.

Recollections of a Tour Made in Scotland: A. D. 1803. Dorothy Wordsworth. Ed. by J. C. Shairp. 1978. Repr. of 1894 ed. lib. bdg. 35.00 (ISBN 0-8495-5633-3). Arden Lib.

Recollections of Alexander H. Stephens: His Diary Kept When a Prisoner at Fort Warren, Boston Harbor, 1865. Ed. by Myrta L. Avary. LC 76-124914. (American Public Figures Ser). 1971. Repr. of 1910 ed. lib. bdg. 69.50 (ISBN 0-306-71984-3). Da Capo.

Recollections of an Excursion. William Beckford. 1983. 60.00x (ISBN 0-900000-78-3, Pub. by Centaur Bks). State Mutual Bk.

Recollections of an Excursion to the Monasteries of Alcobaca & Baltalha. William Beckford. LC 72-13457. 1974. Repr. of 1835 ed. lib. bdg. 37.00 (ISBN 0-8414-1187-5). Folcroft.

Recollections of an Excursion to the Monasteries of Alcobaca & Batalha. William Beckford. 27.50 (ISBN 0-87556-541-7). Saifer.

Recollections of an Irish Rebel. J. Devoy. 508p. 1979. Repr. of 1929 ed. 30.00x (ISBN 0-7165-0045-0, BBA 02226, Pub. by Irish Academic Pr Ireland). Biblio Dist.

Recollections of an Old Cartman: Old New York Street Life. Isaac Lyon. (Illus.). 114p. 1983. Repr. of 1872 ed. 12.95 (ISBN 0-9608788-4-X). NY Bound.

Recollections of an Old Musician. Thomas Ryan. (Music Reprint Ser.). 290p. 1979. Repr. of 1899 ed. lib. bdg. 37.50 (ISBN 0-306-79521-3). Da Capo.

Recollections of Aubrey De Vere. Aubrey De Vere. 1897. Repr. 35.00 (ISBN 0-8274-3255-0). R West.

Recollections of Baron Gros's Embassy to China & Japan in 1857-1858. De Moges. LC 72-79818. (China Library Ser.). (Illus.). 1972. Repr. of 1860 ed. lib. bdg. 35.00 (ISBN 0-8420-1366-0). Scholarly Res Inc.

Recollections of Baron Gros's Embassy to China & Japan in 1857 to 1858. Marquis De Moges. 376p. 1972. Repr. of 1860 ed. 37.50x (ISBN 0-7165-2039-7, Pub. by Irish Academic Pr). Biblio Dist.

Recollections of Benjamin Franklin Bonney. Fred Lockley. 1971. pap. 2.50 (ISBN 0-87770-060-5). Ye Galleon.

Recollections of British Administration in the Cameroons & Northern Nigeria, 1921-1957: "But Always As Friends". Bryan Sharwood-Smith. LC 69-20048. pap. 120.00 (ISBN 0-317-26089-8, 2023768). Bks Demand UMI.

Recollections of Charles Lamb. George Daniel. LC 74-9598. 1927. lib. bdg. 25.00 (ISBN 0-8414-3745-9). Folcroft.

Recollections of Charley Russell. Frank B. Linderman. Ed. by H. G. Merriam. LC 63-18074. 148p. 1984. 14.95 (ISBN 0-8061-0582-8). U of Okla Pr.

Recollections of Charley Russell. Frank B. Linderman. Intro. by H. G. Merriam. LC 63-18074. (Illus.). 196p. 1988. pap. 10.95 (ISBN 0-8061-2112-2). U of Okla Pr.

Recollections of Commander James Anthony Gardner, 1775-1814. R. Vesey Hamilton & J. K. Laughton. 1985. 69.00x (ISBN 0-317-44222-8, Pub. by Navy Rec Soc). State Mutual Bk.

Recollections of Country Joe. S. E. Lee. LC 75-31650. (Illus.). 104p. 1976. 6.95 (ISBN 0-88289-040-9). Pelican.

Recollections of Dante Gabriel Rossetti & His Circle. Henry T. Dunn. Ed. by Gale Pedrick. LC 73-129379. Repr. of 1904 ed. 12.00 (ISBN 0-404-02222-7). AMS Pr.

Recollections of Dr. John Brown. Alexander Peddie. 1978. Repr. of 1892 ed. lib. bdg. 30.00 (ISBN 0-8495-4347-9). Arden Lib.

Recollections of Early Rogers County. Rogers County Historical Soc. Staff. 120p. 1987. 9.95 (ISBN 0-941195-08-2). Country lane.

Recollections of Early Texas: Memoirs of John Holland Jenkins. Ed. by John H. Jenkins, III. (Personal Narratives of the West Ser.). (Illus.). 347p. 1987. pap. 8.95 (ISBN 0-292-77037-5). U of Tex Pr.

Recollections of Edgar A. Poe by Lambert A. Wilmer see Edgar Allan Poe.

Recollections of Edgar Allan Poe see Merlin Baltimore: Eighteen Twenty-Seven.

Recollections of Eminent Men with Other Papers. Edwin P. Whipple. 397p. 1982. Repr. of 1886 ed. lib. bdg. 45.00 (ISBN 0-8495-5840-9). Arden Lib.

Recollections of Fenians & Fenianism, 2 vols. in 1. John O'Leary. 554p. 1968. Repr. of 1896 ed. 30.00x (ISBN 0-7165-0606-8, BBA 02221, Pub. by Irish Academic Pr Ireland). Biblio Dist.

Recollections of Frontier Life. Elizabeth A. Roe. Ed. by Annette K. Baxter. LC 79-8809. (Signal Lives Ser.). (Illus.). 1980. Repr. of 1885 ed. lib. bdg. 31.50x (ISBN 0-405-12855-X). Ayer Co Pubs.

Recollections of Geoffrey Hamlyn. Henry Kingsley. 1899. lib. bdg. 30.00 (ISBN 0-8414-5585-6). Folcroft.

Recollections of Geoffrey Hamlyn. Henry Kingsley. 1971. Repr. of 1924 ed. 24.00x (ISBN 0-403-01057-8). Scholarly.

Recollections of Geoffry Hamlyn. Henry Kingsley. 468p. 1985. Repr. of 1910 ed. lib. bdg. 40.00 (ISBN 0-8495-3101-2). Arden Lib.

Recollections of Gran Apacheria. Edward Dorn. (New World Writing Ser.). 1975. 12.00 (ISBN 0-913666-17-3); pap. 2.00 (ISBN 0-913666-03-3). Turtle Isl Foun.

Recollections of Grover Cleveland. facsimile ed. George F. Parker. LC 70-165649. (Select Bibliographies Reprint Ser). Repr. of 1909 ed. 33.00 (ISBN 0-8369-5958-2). Ayer Co Pubs.

Recollections of Gustav Mahler. Natalie Bauer-Lechner. Ed. by P. Franklin. Tr. by D. Newlin from Ger. LC 80-834. (Illus.). 241p. 1980. 34.50 (ISBN 0-521-23572-3). Cambridge U Pr.

Recollections of Johnson & Higgins. David H. Winton. LC 87-29173. 148p. 1987. 20.00 (ISBN 0-914659-29-4). Phoenix Pub.

Recollections of Life in Ohio from 1813 to 1840. William C. Howells. LC 63-7082. 1977. Repr. of 1895 ed. 40.00x (ISBN 0-8201-1260-7). Schol Facsimiles.

Recollections of Literary Characters & Celebrated Places, 2 vols. in 1. Katherine Thomson. LC 70-37725. (Women of Letters Ser.). Repr. of 1854 ed. 57.50 (ISBN 0-404-56847-5). AMS Pr.

Recollections of Long Life, 1829-1915. Isaac Stephenson. 15.00 (ISBN 0-8369-6991-X, 7868). Ayer Co Pubs.

Recollections of Louisa May Alcott, John Greenleaf Whittier, & Robt. Browning, Together with Several Memorial Poems. Maria S. Porter. LC 76-13453. 1976. Repr. of 1893 ed. lib. bdg. 15.50 (ISBN 0-8414-6701-3). Folcroft.

Recollections of Louisa May Alcott, John Greenleaf Whittier, & Robert Browning, Together with Several Memorial Poems. Maria S. Porter. 1978. Repr. of 1899 ed. lib. bdg. 27.50 (ISBN 0-8492-2088-2). R West.

Recollections of Mount Athos. Archimandrite C. Karambelas. 202p. 1988. pap. 10.00 (ISBN 0-917651-44-8). Holy Cross Orthodox.

Recollections of My Immigrant Grandmother. Dorothea A. Gross. 64p. 1987. 7.95 (ISBN 0-8062-3071-1). Carlton.

Recollections of Phantom Ranch. Elizabeth Simpson. (Illus.). 28p. pap. 1.50 (ISBN 0-938216-08-2). GCNHA.

Recollections of Poe. John H. Hewitt. LC 77-7606. 1949. Repr. lib. bdg. 16.00 (ISBN 0-8414-4778-0). Folcroft.

Recollections of R. Taylor Cole: Educator, Emmissary, Development Planner. R. T. Cole. LC 82-14758. (Illus.). x, 212p. 1983. 20.00 (ISBN 0-8223-0488-0). Duke.

Recollections of Richard Dewey: Pioneer in American Psychiatry. Richard Dewey. Ed. by Ethel L. Dewey. LC 73-2395. (Mental Illness & Social Policy; the American Experience Ser.). Repr. of 1936 ed. 20.00 (ISBN 0-405-05203-0). Ayer Co Pubs.

Recollections of Rifleman Harris. Ed. by Christopher Hibbert. (Century Lives & Letters Ser.). 114p. 1986. pap. 8.95 (ISBN 0-7126-0346-8, Pub. by Century Hutchinson). David & Charles.

Recollections of Robert Louis Stevenson in the Pacific. Arthur Johnstone. LC 74-23652. 1974. Repr. of 1905 ed. lib. bdg. 27.00 (ISBN 0-8414-5324-1). Folcroft.

Recollections of Rossetti. Hall Caine. 59.95 (ISBN 0-8490-0935-9). Gordon Pr.

Recollections of Rossetti. Hall Caine. LC 72-6285. (English Literature Ser., No. 33). 267p. 1972. Repr. of 1928 ed. lib. bdg. 49.95x (ISBN 0-8383-1634-4). Haskell.

Recollections of Seventy Years. Elizabeth R. Farrar. Ed. by Annette K. Baxter. LC 79-8791. (Signal Lives Ser.). 1980. Repr. of 1866 ed. lib. bdg. 30.00x (ISBN 0-405-12838-X). Ayer Co Pubs.

Recollections of Seventy Years. Daniel A. Payne. LC 68-29015. (American Negro: His History & Literature Ser., No. 1). (Illus.). 1968. Repr. of 1888 ed. 14.00 (ISBN 0-405-01834-7). Ayer Co Pubs.

Recollections of Seventy Years. Franklin B. Sanborn. LC 67-23889. 621p. 1967. Repr. of 1909 ed. 48.00x (ISBN 0-8103-3045-8). Gale.

Recollections of Sir Walter Scott, Bart. Robert P. Gillies. LC 73-8885. Repr. of 1837 ed. lib. bdg. 27.00 (ISBN 0-8414-2040-8). Folcroft.

Recollections of Socrates. Xenophon. Tr. by Anna Benjamin. Bd. with Socrates' Defense Before the Jury. LC 64-66080. 1965. pap. 7.20 scp (ISBN 0-672-60449-3, LLA205). Bobbs.

Recollections of Tartar Steppes & Their Inhabitants. Lucy Atkinson. 351p. 1972. Repr. of 1863 ed. 32.50x (ISBN 0-7146-1531-5, F Cass Co). Biblio Dist.

Recollections of Tartar Steppes & Their Inhabitants. Mrs. Thomas W. Atkinson. LC 71-115503. (Russia Observed, Ser., No. 1). 1970. Repr. of 1863 ed. 25.50 (ISBN 0-405-03003-7). Ayer Co Pubs.

Recollections of the Catawba Valley. J. Alexander Mull & Gordon Boger. LC 82-20721. 1983. 6.50 (ISBN 0-913239-05-4). Appalach Consortium.

Recollections of the Early Settlement of the Wabash Valley. facs. ed. Sandford C. Cox. LC 78-117870. (Select Bibliographies Reprint Ser). 1860. 17.00 (ISBN 0-8369-5323-1). Ayer Co Pubs.

Recollections of the Flathead Mission. Gregory Mengarini. Ed. by Gloria Lothrop. LC 74-27573. (Illus.). 1977. 28.50 (ISBN 0-87062-111-4). A H Clark.

Recollections of the Golden Triangle. Alain Robbe-Grillet. Tr. by J. A. Underwood from Fr. Orig. Title: Sourvenirs due triangle d'or. 160p. 1986. 16.95 (ISBN 0-394-55564-3); pap. 6.95. Grove.

Recollections of the Golden Triangle: A Novel. Alain Robbe-Grillet. Tr. by J. A. Underwood. 160p. (Orig.). Date not set. pap. 6.95 (ISBN 0-394-62275-8). Grove.

Recollections of the Jersey Prison Ship: From the Manuscript of Thomas Dring. Albert Greene. 148p. 1986. pap. 6.95 (ISBN 0-918222-92-3). Applewood.

Recollections of the Lakes & the Lake Poets. Thomas DeQuincy. (Classics Ser.). 416p. 1971. pap. 6.95 (ISBN 0-14-043056-3). Penguin.

Recollections of the Last Days of Shelley & Byron. E. J. Trelawney. 304p. 1975. Repr. of 1858 ed. 20.00 (ISBN 0-87928-060-3). Corner Hse.

Recollections of the Last Days of Shelley & Byron. facsimile ed. Edward J. Trelawny. LC 72-160998. (Select Bibliographies Reprint Ser.). Repr. of 1906 ed. 17.00 (ISBN 0-8369-5866-7). Ayer Co Pubs.

Recollections of the Last Ten Years in the Valley of the Mississippi. 2nd ed. Timothy Flint. LC 68-24891. (American Scene Ser). 1968. Repr. of 1826 ed. lib. bdg. 49.50 (ISBN 0-306-71136-2). Da Capo.

Recollections of the Last Ten Years: Passed in Occasional Residences & Journeyings in the Valley of the Mississippi. Timothy Flint. (American Studies). 1968. Repr. of 1826 ed. 24.00 (ISBN 0-384-16030-1). Johnson Repr.

Recollections of the Life of John O'Keeffe, 2 vols. in 1. John O'Keeffe. LC 70-89711. 1826. 44.00 (ISBN 0-405-08828-0). Ayer Co Pubs.

Recollections of the Life of Lord Byron: From the Year 1808 to the End of 1814. Robert C. Dallas. 344p. 1980. Repr. of 1824 ed. lib. bdg. 65.00 (ISBN 0-8495-1057-0). Arden Lib.

Recollections of the Life of Lord Byron from the Year 1808 to the End of 1814. Robert C. Dallas. LC 75-29173. 1975. Repr. of 1824 ed. lib. bdg. 67.50 (ISBN 0-8414-3728-9). Folcroft.

Recollections of the Lyceum & Chautauqua Circuits Plus Notes on Calligraphy & Scribal Writing. Raymond F. DaBoll & Irene B. DaBoll. LC 66-19773. (Illus.). 188p. 1974. 16.95 (ISBN 0-87027-107-5). Cumberland Pr.

Recollections of the Old Quarter. facsimile ed. William S. Gordon. LC 75-39084. (Black Heritage Library Collection). Repr. of 1902 ed. 17.50 (ISBN 0-8369-9022-6). Ayer Co Pubs.

Recollections of the Powys Brothers. Intro. by Belinda Humfrey. 288p. 1980. 30.00 (ISBN 0-317-65921-9, Pub. by P Owen Ltd). Dufour.

Recollections of the Third Republic. Joseph Paul-Boncour. 9.95 (ISBN 0-8315-0050-6). Speller.

Recollections of the Youkon. Francois Mercier. Ed. by Linda F. Yarborough. (Alaska Historical Commission Studies in History: No. 188). (Illus.). 1986p. (Orig.). 1986. pap. 10.00 (ISBN 0-943712-19-X). Alaska Hist.

Recollections of Things to Come. Elena Garro. Tr. by Ruth L. Simms from Span. (Texas Pan American Ser.). (Illus.). 299p. 1986. pap. 10.95 (ISBN 0-292-77032-4). U of Tex Pr.

Recollections of Thirteen Presidents. facs. ed. John S. Wise. LC 68-55865. (Essay Index Reprint Ser). 1906. 20.00 (ISBN 0-8369-1005-2). Ayer Co Pubs.

Recollections of West Hunan. Congwen Shen. Tr. by Gladys Yang from Chinese. 196p. (Orig.). 1982. pap. 4.95 (ISBN 0-295-96016-7, Pub. by Chinese Lit Beijing). U of Wash Pr.

Recollections of Wittgenstein. Ed. by Rush Rhees. (Galaxy Bks.). (Illus.). 1984. pap. 8.95 (ISBN 0-19-287628-7). Oxford U Pr.

Recollections of Woodrow Wilson. Winthrop M. Daniels. 1944. 29.50x (ISBN 0-685-89776-1). Elliots Bks.

Recollections of Writers. Chas Clarke & Mary Cowden. 24.00x (ISBN 0-87556-542-5). Saifer.

Recollections of Writers. Chas Clarke & Mary Cowden. 1985. 59.00x (ISBN 0-900000-09-0, Pub. by Centaur Bks). State Mutual Bk.

Recollections on the French Revolution of 1848. Alexis De Tocqueville. Ed. & intro. by J. P. Mayer. 360p. 1986. pap. 19.95 (ISBN 0-88738-658-X). Transaction Bks.

Recollections, Personal & Literary. Richard H. Stoddard. LC 76-153874. Repr. of 1903 ed. 19.00 (ISBN 0-404-06280-6). AMS Pr.

Recollections: Shakespeare, Milton. George W. Childs. 1973. Repr. of 1890 ed. 20.00 (ISBN 0-8274-1531-1). R West.

Recollections: The Detroit Years (The Motown Sound by the People Who Made It) Jack Ryan. (Illus.). 154p. 1982. pap. 10.95 (ISBN 0-914303-00-7). Whitlaker.

Recollective Resolve: A Phenomenological Understanding of Time & Myth. Sanford Krolick. LC 87-1581. 160p. 1987. 24.95 (ISBN 0-86554-248-1, MUP H-214). Mercer Univ Pr.

Recombinant DNA. Ed. by K. J. Denniston & L. W. Enquist. LC 80-14100. (Benchmark Papers in Microbiology Ser.: Vol. 15). 391p. 1982. 62.95 (ISBN 0-87933-378-2). Van Nos Reinhold.

Recombinant DNA: A Short Course. James D. Watson & John Tooze. LC 83-9069. (Illus.). 256p. 1983. pap. text ed. 17.95 (ISBN 0-7167-1484-1). W H Freeman.

Recombinant DNA & Bacterial Fermentation, 2 vols. Ed. by Jennifer A. Thomson. 1988. 135.00. Vol. I, 285 pgs (ISBN 0-8493-6022-6, 6022). Vol. II, 364 pgs. cancelled (ISBN 0-8493-6023-4, 6023). CRC Pr.

Recombinant DNA & Cell Proliferation. Gary S. Stein & Janet L. Stein. 1984. 60.50 (ISBN 0-12-665080-2). Acad Pr.

Recombinant DNA & Genetic Experimentation: Proceedings. Conference on Recombinant DNA, Committee on Genetic Experimentation (COGENE) & the Royal Society of London, Wye College, Kent, UK, April, 1979. Ed. by Joan Morgan & W. J. Whelan. LC 79-40962. (Illus.). 334p. 1979. 99.00 (ISBN 0-08-024427-0). Pergamon.

Recombinant DNA & Medical Genetics (Symposium) Ed. by Anne Messer & Ian Porter. (Birth Defects Institute Symposia Ser.: Vol. 13). 1983. 29.95 (ISBN 0-12-492220-1). Acad Pr.

Recombinant DNA Debate. David A. Jackson & Stephen P. Stitch. LC 78-26385. 1979. text ed. write for info. (ISBN 0-13-767442-2). P-H.

Recombinant DNA Experiments: An Introduction. R. L. Rodriguez & R. C. Tait. 1983. pap. text ed. 24.95 (ISBN 0-201-10870-4). Benjamin-Cummings.

Recombinant DNA Lab Manual. Fuchs Hackett & Messing. 1984. pap. text ed. 24.95 (ISBN 0-8053-3672-9). Benjamin-Cummings.

Recombinant DNA Methodology. Earle R. Nestman et al. LC 84-20946. 256p. 1985. 22.50 (ISBN 0-471-89851-1). Wiley.

Recombinant DNA: Proceedings 3rd Cleveland Symposium on Macromolecules, Cleveland, June 1981. Ed. by A. G. Walton. 310p. 1982. 78.75 (ISBN 0-444-42039-8). Elsevier.

Recombinant DNA Products: Insulin, Interferon & Growth Hormone. Arthur P. Bollon. 208p. 1984. 85.00 (ISBN 0-8493-5542-7, 5542DA). CRC Pr.

Recombinant DNA Research & the Human Prospect. Ed. by Earl D. Hanson. (Other Technical Bks.). 129p. 1983. text ed. 19.95 (ISBN 0-8412-0750-X); pap. text ed. 14.95 (ISBN 0-8412-0754-2). Am Chemical.

Recombinant DNA Research & Viruses. Ed. by Yechiel Becker. (Developments in Molecular Virology Ser.). 1984. lib. bdg. 59.95 (ISBN 0-89838-683-7, Pub. by Martinus Nijhoff Netherlands). Kluwer Academic.

Recombinant DNA Safety Considerations. OECD Staff. 70p. (Orig.). 1986. pap. 12.00 (ISBN 92-64-12857-3). OECD.

Recombinant DNA Technology. Alan E. Emery. LC 84-11830. 1984. pap. 21.95 (ISBN 0-471-90363-9). Wiley.

Recombinant Intferons: New Aspects in Research & Therapy. Ed. by S. Eckhardt. (Journal: Oncology: Vol. 42, Suppl. 1, 1985). iv, 46p. 1985. pap. 18.75 (ISBN 3-8055-4238-0). S Karger.

Recombinant Lymphokines & Their Receptors. Gillis. (Immunology Ser.). 376p. 1987. 89.75 (ISBN 0-8247-7753-0). Dekker.

Recombinant Molecules: Impact on Science & Society. Ed. by Roland F. Beers, Jr. & Edward G. Bassett. LC 77-5276. (Miles International Symposium Ser: 10th). 556p. 1977. 89.00 (ISBN 0-89004-131-8). Raven.

Recombination at the DNA Level. LC 34-8174. (Symposia on Quantitative Biology Ser.: Vol. 49). 854p. 1984. 130.00 (ISBN 0-87969-049-6). Cold Spring Harbor.

Recombination-Induced Defect Formation in Crystals. Ed. by F. C. Brown & Noriaki Itoh. (Special Topics Issue of Semiconductors & Insulators Ser.). 484p. 1983. 94.00 (ISBN 0-677-40365-8). Gordon & Breach.

Recombination of Genectic Material. Ed. by K. Brooks Low. 506p. 1988. 65.00 (ISBN 0-12-456270-1). Acad Pr.

Recombinations. Perri Klass. 1985. 17.95 (ISBN 0-399-13090-X). Putnam Pub Group.

Recombinations. Perri Klass. 1986. pap. 3.95 (ISBN 0-451-14555-0, Sig). NAL.

Recomendaciones e Informes del Comite Jurico Interamericano Documetos Oficiales: Vol. 2, 1974-1977. OAS General Secretariat. 675p. 1981. 50.00 (ISBN 0-8270-1284-5). OAS.

Recomendaciones e Informes, 1981, Vol. XIII. OAS General Secretariat of Development & Codification of International Law. (Comite Juridico Interamericano). 125p. 1981. pap. 8.00 (ISBN 0-8270-1441-4). OAS.

Recomendations on Equipment for the Towing of Disabled Tankers. OCIMF Staff. 1981. 135.00x (ISBN 0-317-61454-1, Pub. by Witherby & Co England). State Mutual Bk.

Recommendation for Developing an Integrated Municipal-Superior Court Automated Information System in Ventura County, California. National Center for State Courts Staff. 27p. 1976. manuscript 1.62 (MAB-094). Natl Ctr St Courts.

Recommendation for the Format of Bills of Lading. ICS Staff. 1978. 36.00x (ISBN 0-317-61279-4, Pub. by Witherby & Co England). State Mutual Bk.

Recommendation on Marks of Origin. pap. 5.00 (G49, GATT). UNIPUB.

Recommendations Concerning Reservoirs. 1967. pap. 5.00 (ISBN 92-3-100664-9, U520, UNESCO). UNIPUB.

Recommendations de la Comision Internationale de Protection Radiologique. International Commission on Radiological Protection. Ed. by A. Duchene & H. Jammet. (ICRP Publicaton Ser.: No. 26). 63p. (Fr.). 1980. pap. 19.00 (ISBN 0-08-025529-9). Pergamon.

Recommendations for Arc Welded Joints in Clad Steel Construction: II W: IIW. 66p. 1969. 10.00 (ISBN 0-686-43359-9). Am Welding.

Recommendations for Asbestos Abatement Projects. American Industrial Hygiene Association Technical Committees. 24p. 1986. pap. text ed. 10.00 (ISBN 0-317-55221-X). Am Indus Hygiene.

Recommendations for Child Care Centers. Gary T. Moore et al. (Publications in Architecture & Urban Planning Ser.: R79-2). (Illus.). viii, 450p. 1979. 20.00 (ISBN 0-938744-06-2). U of Wis Ctr Arch-Urban.

Recommendations for Child Play Areas. Uriel Cohen et al. (Publications in Architecture & Urban Planning Ser.: R79-1). (Illus.). vi, 380p. 1979. 18.00 (ISBN 0-938744-07-0). U of Wis Ctr Arch-Urban.

Recommendations for Covering Existing Interior Walls & Ceiling with Gypsum Board. 8p. 0.50 (ISBN 0-318-23483-1, GA-650-86). Gypsum Assn.

Recommendations for Estimating Prestress Losses. (PCI Journal Reprints Ser.). 36p. pap. 5.00 (ISBN 0-318-19842-8, JR162). Prestressed Concrete.

Recommendations for Improving the Ohio Victims of Crime Compensation Program's Newsletter: Final Report (A Technical Assistance Report) 54p. 1986. manuscript 3.00 (ISBN 0-317-59193-2, NERO, T/A-535). Natl Ctr St Courts.

Recommendations for Improving the Use of Restitution As a Dispositional Alternative, As Administered by the Connecticut Adult Probation Division. National Center for State Courts Staff. 34p. 1975. manuscript 2.04 (MAB-095). Natl Ctr St Courts.

Recommendations for Improving Trustee Selection in Public Colleges & Universities. 54p. 1980. 11.00 (ISBN 0-318-17384-0). Assn Gov Bds.

Recommendations for the Design & Construction of Refrigerated Liquefied Gas Storage Tanks. EEMUA Staff. 1986. 150.00x (ISBN 0-85931-113-9, Pub. by EEMUA). State Mutual Bk.

Recommendations for the Design, Calculation, Construction & Monitoring of Ground Anchors. 3rd. rev. ed. Ed. by P. Habib. 150p. 1987. text ed. 25.00 (ISBN 90-6191-737-9, Pub. by A A Balkema); pap. text ed. 14.50 (ISBN 90-6191-736-0, Pub. by A A Balkema). Brookfield Pub Co.

Recommendations for the Practice of Clinical Neurophysiology. Cobb. 1983. 11.25 (ISBN 0-444-80505-2, I-402-83). Elsevier.

Recommendations for the Use of Gypsum Board in Manufactured Housing. 16p. 1.00 (ISBN 0-318-23482-3, GA-228-86). Gypsum Assn.

Recommendations for Tube End Welding: Tubular Heat Transfer Equipment, Pt. 1, Ferrous Materials. 1977. 75.00x (ISBN 0-85931-093-0, Pub. by EEMUA). State Mutual Bk.

Recommendations from the Arusha Conference on the African Refugee Problem. 45p. 1982. pap. 9.50 (ISBN 0-8419-9742-X). Holmes & Meier.

Recommendations on Limits for Exposure to Ionizing Radiation. NCRP Staff. LC 87-14070. (NCRP Reports: No. 91). 50p. 1987. pap. text ed. 12.00 (ISBN 0-913392-89-8). NCRP Pubns.

Recommendations on the Mathematical Preparation of Teachers (CUPM) LC 83-6270. (MAA Notes: No. 2). 76p. 1983. pap. 6.00 (ISBN 0-88385-052-4). Math Assn.

Recommendations on the Transport of Dangerous Goods. 5th, rev. ed. 504p. 1987. pap. 55.00 (ISBN 92-1-139023-0, E.87.VIII.1). UN.

Recommendations on the Transport of Dangerous Goods: Tests & Criteria. 189p. 1986. 18.00 (ISBN 92-1-139021-4, E.85.VIII.2). UN.

Recommendations on the Transport of Dangerous Goods: Tests & Criteria - First Edition, Addendum 1. 118p. 1987. pap. 25.00 (ISBN 92-1-139024-9, E.87.VIII.2). UN.

Recommendations pour l'Adaptation aux Conditions Locales les Questionnaires de l'Etude sur la Mesure des Niveaux de Vie. Martha Ainsworth & Jacques Van der Gaag. (LSMS Working Paper Ser.: No. 34F). Orig. Title: Guidelines for Adapting the LSMS Living Standards Questionnaires to Local Conditions. 202p. (Span.). 1988. 12.00 (ISBN 0-8213-1044-5, BK1044). World Bank.

Recommendations Regarding Records Management & Space Utilization in the Clerk's Office of the New Salem District Court, Salem, Massachusetts. National Center for State Courts Staff. 57p. 1977. manuscript 3.42 (MAB-096). Natl Ctr St Courts.

Recommendations to Improve the Court Registries & Court Management Systems in Twelve Caribbean Islands & States. 253p. 1987. 15.00 (SERO-033). Natl Ctr St Courts.

Recommended Aids for the Partially Sighted. 2nd rev. ed. Louise L. Sloan. 64p. 1971. pap. 2.40 (ISBN 0-89128-086-3, PLP956). Am Foun Blind.

Recommended Arizona Jury Instructions: Civil. Civil Jury Instruction Committee. 1987. write for info. AZ St Bar.

Recommended Country Hotels of Britain, 1988. (Illus.). 150p. (Orig.). 1988. pap. 6.95 (ISBN 0-317-57814-6). Hunter Pub NY.

Recommended Country Inns of Arizona, New Mexico & Texas. 2nd ed. Eleanor Morris. (Recommended Country Inns Ser.). (Illus.). 1989. pap. price not set (ISBN 0-87106-630-0). Globe Pequot.

Recommended Country Inns of New England. 11th ed. Elizabeth Squier. (Recommended Country Inns Ser.). (Illus.). 1989. pap. price not set (ISBN 0-87106-626-2). Globe Pequot.

Recommended Country Inns of the Midwest. 2nd ed. Bob Puhala. (Illus.). 1989. pap. price not set (ISBN 0-87106-628-9). Globe Pequot.

Recommended Country Inns of the Rocky Mountain Region. 2nd ed. DOris Kennedy. (Recommended Country Inns Ser.). (Illus.). 1989. pap. price not set (ISBN 0-87106-632-7). Globe Pequot.

Recommended Country Inns of the South. 2nd ed. Sara Pitzer. (Recommended Country Inns Ser.). (Illus.). 1989. pap. price not set (ISBN 0-87106-631-9). Globe Pequot.

Recommended Country Inns of the West Coast. 2nd ed. Julianne Belote. (Recommended Country Inns Ser.). (Illus.). Date not set. pap. price not set (ISBN 0-87106-629-7). Globe Pequot.

Recommended Data of Selected Compounds & Binary Mixtures: Tables, Diagrams & Calculations. K. Stephan & H. Hildwein. (Chemistry Data Ser.: Vol. 4, pts 1 & 2). (Illus.). 715p. 1987. Set. text ed. 253.00x (ISBN 3-921567-80-7, Pub. by Dechema Germany). Pt. I, Pure Compounds. Pt. II, Binary Mixtures. Scholium Intl.

Recommended Data on Atomic Collision Processes Involving Iron & Its Ions. C. Bottcher et al. 131p. (Orig.). 1987. pap. text ed. 29.00 (ISBN 92-0-139087-4, ISP23 87, IAEA). UNIPUB.

Recommended Diagramming Standards for Analysts & Programmers. James Martin. (Illus.). 432p. 1986. text ed. 48.00 (ISBN 0-13-767377-9). P-H.

Recommended Dietary Allowances: Ninth Edition. Food & Nutrition Board Staff. (Illus.). 185p. 1980. pap. 9.50x (ISBN 0-309-02941-4). Natl Acad Pr.

Recommended English Language Arts Curriculum Guides, K-12. 1985. 4.75 (ISBN 0-8141-3951-5). NCTE.

Recommended Good Practice for Community Dump. (Six Hundred Ser.). 1964. pap. 2.00 (ISBN 0-685-58208-6, 602). Natl Fire Prot.

Recommended Grievance & Appeal Procedures for the District of Columbia Courts. National Center for State Courts Staff. 30p. 1978. manuscript 1.80 (MARO-009). Natl Ctr St Courts.

Recommended Guide for the Prediction of the Dispersion of Airborne Effluents, Bk. No. H00037. 3rd ed. Ed. by M. E. Smith & J. R. Martin. LC 90-75471. 87p. 1979. 10.00 (ISBN 0-686-62958-2). ASME.

Recommended Guidelines for Feed Mills Subject to FDA Inspection. 94p. 1983. 15.00 (ISBN 0-318-01823-3). Am Feed Industry.

Recommended Guidelines for Plants Subject to OSHA Inspection. 81p. 1981. 15.00 (ISBN 0-318-01825-X). Am Feed Industry.

Recommended Health-Based Limits in Occupational Exposure to Selected Mineral Dusts (Silica, Coal) (Technical Report Ser.: No. 734). 82p. 1986. pap. 7.20 (ISBN 92-4-120734-5). World Health.

Recommended Instrumentation for Uranium & Thorium Exploration. (Technical Reports Ser.). 104p. (Orig.). 1974. pap. 15.00 (ISBN 92-0-145074-5, IDC158, IAEA). UNIPUB.

Recommended Law Books. 2nd ed. James A. McDermott. LC 86-71141. 168p. 1986. 24.95 (ISBN 0-89707-239-1). ABA Prof Educ Pubns.

Recommended Law Books. 2nd ed. 168p. 1986. pap. 22.95 (ISBN 0-317-63127-6, 507-0070-01). Amer Bar Assn.

Recommended Maintenance Practices Manual. 1983. pap. text ed. 75.00 (ISBN 0-88711-060-6). Am Trucking Assns.

Recommended Methods for Development-Information Systems: Manual for the Preparation of Records in Development-Information Systems, 2 vols. 1983. Vol. 1, 272p. pap. 15.00 (ISBN 0-88936-354-4, IDRCTS40, IDRC); Vol. 2, 196p. pap. 15.00 (ISBN 0-88936-450-8, IDRCTS52, IDRC). UNIPUB.

Recommended Methods for Purification of Solvents. Ed. by J. F. Coetzee. (International Union of Pure & Applied Chemistry). 1982. pap. 28.00 (ISBN 0-08-022370-2). Pergamon.

Recommended Personnel Administration Standards for the Minnesota Judicial System: Executive Summary. National Center for State Courts Staff. 32p. 1978. manuscript 1.92 (NCRO-009). Natl Ctr St Courts.

Recommended Practice for a Demonstration of Nondestructive Evaluation (NDE) Reliability on Aircraft Production Parts. 11p. 1976. member 5.00 (ISBN 0-318-21523-3, 2021); non-member 7.50. Am Soc Nondestructive.

Recommended Practice for Cleanroom Gloves & Finger Cots. LC 62-38584. 11p. 1987. pap. text ed. 12.00 (ISBN 0-317-59760-4, IES-RP-CC-005-87-T). Inst Environ Sci.

Recommended Practice for Cleanroom Product & Support Equipment. LC 62-38584. 10p. (Orig.). 1987. pap. text ed. 15.00 (ISBN 0-317-59762-0, IES-RP-CC-015-87-T). Inst Environ Sci.

Recommended Practice for Design, Manufacture, & Installation of Prestressed Concrete Piling. (PCI Journal Reprints Ser.). 32p. 1985. pap. 6.00 (ISBN 0-318-19763-4, JR187). Prestressed Concrete.

Recommended Practice for Electric Power Distribution for Industrial Plants: Standard 141-1986. 1987. 33.00 (ISBN 0-471-85687-8). Wiley.

Recommended Practice for Electric Power Systems in Commercial Buildings. rev. ed. Institute of Electrical & Electronics Engineers, Inc. (IEEE) 616p. 1983. 33.00 (ISBN 0-471-89357-9). Wiley.

Recommended Practice for Electric Systems in Health Care Facilities. (IEEE Standards Publications). 424p. 1986. 43.00 (ISBN 0-471-82747-9). Wiley.

Recommended Practice for Electrical Installations in Petroleum Processing Plants. 2nd ed. 64p. 1974. 8.00 (ISBN 0-317-33097-7, 82254000). Am Petroleum.

Recommended Practice for Energy Conservation & Cost Effective Planning in Industrial Facilities: Std. 739-1984. 160p. 1985. 23.00 (ISBN 0-471-82037-7). Wiley.

Recommended Practice for Equipment Calibration or Validation Procedures: IES RP CC. 1986. 10.00 (ISBN 0-317-52597-2, IES-RP-CC-013-86-T); pap. 2.00. Inst Environ Sci.

Recommended Practice for Erection of Precast Concrete. 96p. Date not set. 20.00 (MNL-127-85). Prestressed Concrete.

Recommended Practice for Frozen Food Distribution Centers. 10.00. Am Inst Baking.

Recommended Practice for Glass Fiber Reinforced Concrete Panels. 92p. Date not set. 16.00 (MNL-128-87). Prestressed Concrete.

Recommended Practice for Grounding of Industrial & Commercial Power Systems. Institute of Electrical & Electronics Engineers. LC 82-83209. (Illus.). 136p. 1982. 21.00 (ISBN 0-471-89573-3). Wiley.

Recommended Practice for Grouting of Post-Tensioned Prestressed Concrete. Prestressed Concrete Institute. (PCI Journal Reprints Ser.: No. 119). 8p. pap. 4.00 (ISBN 0-318-19838-X, JR119). Prestressed Concrete.

Recommended Practice for Power Systems Analysis. Institute of Electrical & Electronics Engineers, Inc. 224p. 1981. 28.00x (ISBN 0-471-09262-2). Wiley.

Recommended Practice for Precast Post-Tensioned Segmental Construction. 52p. pap. 8.00 (JR-252). Prestressed Concrete.

Recommended Practice for Precast Prestressed Concrete Circular Storage Tanks. 48p. Date not set. 10.00 (JR-334). Prestressed Concrete.

Recommended Practice for Protection & Coordination of Industrial & Commercial Power Systems - Standards 242-1986. (IEEE Standards Publications). 588p. 1987. 33.00 (ISBN 0-471-85392-5). Wiley.

Recommended Practice for Radio Silence When Conducting Wireline Services Involving the Use of Explosives. Institute of Petroleum. LC 84-22045. 37p. 1985. pap. 37.00 (ISBN 0-471-90653-0). Wiley.

Recommended Practice for the Design of Reliable Industrial & Commercial Power Systems. Institute of Electrical & Electronics Engineers, Inc. LC 80-83819. 224p. 1981. 23.00 (ISBN 0-471-09261-4). Wiley.

Recommended Practice for Use of High Range Water Reducing Admixtures in Precast Prestressed Concrete Operations. (PCI Journal Reprints Ser.). 24p. 1985. pap. 6.00 (ISBN 0-318-19774-X, JR247). Prestressed Concrete.

Recommended Practice No. SNT-TC-1A. Date not set. non-member 36.25 (ISBN 0-318-21515-2, 2035); member 28.75 (ISBN 0-318-21516-0, 2025). Am Soc Nondestructive.

Recommended Practice on Static Electricity. (Seventy Ser.). 64p. 1972. pap. 2.00 (ISBN 0-685-46075-4, 77). Natl Fire Prot.

Recommended Practices for Gas Metal Arc Welding: AWS C5.6. (Illus.). 58p. 1979. pap. text ed. 24.00 (ISBN 0-87171-166-4). Am Welding.

Recommended Practices for Plasma-Arc Welding, C5.1. (Illus.). 68p. 1973. pap. text ed. 10.00 (ISBN 0-87171-107-9). Am Welding.

Recommended Practices for Resistance Welding: C1.1. 115p. 1966. 20.00 (ISBN 0-317-33300-3) (ISBN 0-317-33301-1). Am Welding.

Recommended Practices for Underground Storage of Petroleum. 1985. 12.50 (ISBN 0-318-22998-6). Natl Water Well.

Recommended Practices for Welding Austenitic Chromiium-Nickel Stainless Steel Piping & Tubing (D10.4-86) rev ed. American Welding Society Staff. (Illus.). 1986. pap. write for info (ISBN 0-87171-267-9, D10.4-86). Am Welding.

Recommended Practices for Welding of Chromium-Molydenum Steel Piping & Tumbing. rev ed. American Welding Society Staff. (Illus.). 1986. pap. write for info. (ISBN 0-87171-262-8, 010.8-86). Am Welding.

Recommended Practices for Welding of Chromium-Molybdenum Steel Piping & Tubing. rev ed. American Welding Society Staff. (Illus., Orig.). 1986. pap. text ed. 12.00 (ISBN 0-87171-265-2, A4.3-86). Am Welding.

Recommended Provisions & Commentary for Existing High-Rise Buildings. 3.00 (ISBN 0-318-00064-4). Intl Conf Bldg Off.

Recommended Provisions & Commentary for Existing High-rise Buildings. 3.00 (ISBN 0-318-22313-9). Intl Conf Bldg Off.

Recommended Publications for Legal Research, 1984. Oscar J. Miller & Mortimer D. Schwartz. LC 86-3253. 1986. 37.50x (ISBN 0-8377-2528-3). Rothman.

Recommended Publications for Legal Research, 1980. Oscar J. Miller & Mortimer D. Schwartz. LC 86-17669. 1986. 37.50x (ISBN 0-8377-2529-1). Rothman.

Recommended Publications for Legal Research, 1983. Oscar J. Miller & Mortimer D. Schwartz. LC 87-4837. Date not set. price not set (ISBN 0-8377-2531-3). Rothman.

Recommended Publications for Legal Research, 1986. Oscar J. Miller & Mortimer D. Schwartz. LC 87-12723. Date not set. price not set (ISBN 0-8377-2532-1). Rothman.

Recommended Publications for Legal Research, 1981. Oscar J. Miller & Mortimer D. Schwartz. LC 87-10106. Date not set. price not set (ISBN 0-8377-2533-X). Rothman.

Recommended Publications for Legal Research 1979. Compiled by Oscar J. Miller & Mortimer D. Schwartz. (Orig.). 1985. pap. text ed. 37.50 ea. (ISBN 0-8377-2527-5). Rothman.

Recommended Reference Books for Small & Medium-Sized Libraries & Media Centers, 1988. Bohdan J. Wynar. xviii, 261p. 1988. lib. bdg. 32.50 (ISBN 0-87287-682-9). Libs Unl.

Recommended Reference Books for Small & Medium-Sized Libraries & Media Centers, 1985. Ed. by Bohdan S. Wynar. 271p. 1985. lib. bdg. 30.00 (ISBN 0-87287-494-X). Libs Unl.

Recommended Reference Books for Small & Medium-Sized Libraries & Media Centers 1986. Ed. by Bohdan S. Wynar. 300p. 1986. 30.00 (ISBN 0-87287-540-7). Libs Unl.

Recommended Reference Books for Small & Medium-Sized Libraries & Media Centers, 1987. Ed. by Bohdan S. Wynar. 275p. 1987. lib. bdg. 32.50 (ISBN 0-87287-597-0). Libs Unl.

Reconstruction in Georgia: Economic, Social, Political, 1865-1872. facsimile ed. C. Mildred Thompson. LC 76-169777. (Select Bibliographies Reprint Ser.). Repr. of 1915 ed. 24.50 (ISBN 0-8369-5997-3). Ayer Co Pubs.
Reconstruction in Georgia: Economic, Social, Political 1865-1872. C. Mildred Thompson. 1964. 11.75 (ISBN 0-8446-1447-5). Peter Smith.
Reconstruction in Indian Territory. M. Thomas Bailey. LC 77-189551. 1972. 23.95x (ISBN 0-8046-9022-7, PUb. by Kennikat). Assoc Faculty Pr.
Reconstruction in Mississippi. James W. Garner. LC 12-1798. xxx, 422p. 1968. pap. text ed. 14.95 (ISBN 0-8071-0137-0). La State U Pr.
Reconstruction in Mississippi. James W. Garner. 1964. 13.25 (ISBN 0-8446-1196-4). Peter Smith.
Reconstruction in North Carolina. facsimile ed. Joseph G. Hamilton. LC 73-173607. (Black Heritage Library Collection: Columbia University Studies in History, Economics & Public Law). Repr. of 1914 ed. 36.25 (ISBN 0-8369-8899-X). Ayer Co Pubs.
Reconstruction in North Carolina. Joseph G. Hamilton. 1964. 16.50 (ISBN 0-8446-1219-7). Peter Smith.
Reconstruction in Philosophy. John Dewey. 1957. pap. 11.95x (ISBN 0-8070-1585-7, BP48). Beacon Pr.
Reconstruction in Philosophy, & Essays 1920, Vol. 12. John Dewey & Jo Anne Boydston. (Middle Works of John Dewey Ser.: 1899-1924). 322p. (Orig.). 1988. pap. text ed. 9.95x (ISBN 0-8093-1435-5). S Ill U Pr.
Reconstruction in Psychoanalysis see Recollection & Reconstruction.
Reconstruction in Retrospect: Views from the Turn of the Century. Ed. by Richard N. Current. LC 77-80044. xxii, 166p. 1969. 20.00x (ISBN 0-8071-0850-2); pap. text ed. 6.95x (ISBN 0-8071-0140-0). La State U Pr.
Reconstruction in Texas. Charles W. Ramsdell. 1964. 13.25 (ISBN 0-8446-1373-8). Peter Smith.
Reconstruction in Texas. Charles W. Ramsdell. (Texas History Paperbacks Ser.: No. 6). 324p. 1970. pap. 8.95 (ISBN 0-292-70031-8). U of Tex Pr.
Reconstruction in Texas. Cary D. Wintz. (Texas History Ser.). (Illus.). 70p. (Orig.). 1983. pap. text ed. 2.95x (ISBN 0-89641-142-7). American Pr.
Reconstruction in the South. 2nd ed. Ed. by Edwin C. Rozwenc. (Problems in American Civilization Ser.). 1973. pap. text ed. 7.50 (ISBN 0-669-82735-5). Heath.
Reconstruction: Ninety Years of Black Historical Literature. Ed. by Mothobi Mutloatse. (Staffrider Ser.: No. 8). 320p. 1981. pap. text ed. 8.95x (ISBN 0-86975-207-3, Pub. by Ravan Pr). Ohio U Pr.
Reconstruction of a Spanish Golden Age Playhouse: El Corral del Principe (1583-1744) John J. Allen. LC 83-1241. (Illus.). xii, 129p. 1984. 30.00x (ISBN 0-8130-0755-0). U Presses Fla.
Reconstruction of a Tragedy: The Beverly Hills Supper Club Fire. Richard L. Best. Ed. by Amy E. Dean. LC 77-93009. 1978. pap. 5.75 (ISBN 0-87765-113-2, LS-2). Natl Fire Prot.
Reconstruction of American History. Ed. by John Higham. LC 80-14047. 244p. 1980. Repr. of 1962 ed. lib. bdg. 25.00x (ISBN 0-313-22460-9, HIRH). Greenwood.
Reconstruction of American Political Ideology, 1865-1917. Frank Tariello, Jr. LC 81-14734. 200p. 1982. 20.00x (ISBN 0-8139-0906-6). U Pr of Va.
Reconstruction of Cell Evolution: A Periodic System. W. Schwemmler. 256p. 1984. 85.00 (ISBN 0-8493-5532-X). CRC Pr.
Reconstruction of County Representation. Alan L. Clem. 1968. 1.00 (ISBN 1-55614-104-1). U of SD Gov Res Bur.
Reconstruction of Demographic Profiles from Ossuary Skeletal Samples: A Case Study from the Tidewater Potomac. Douglas H. Ubelaker. LC 73-16117. (Smithsonian Contribution to Anthropology Ser.: No. 18). pap. 22.80 (ISBN 0-317-28477-0, 2020309). Bks Demand UMI.
Reconstruction of Economic Theory. Ed. by Philip Mirowski. 1987. lib. bdg. 42.50 (ISBN 0-89838-211-4, Pub. by Kluwer-Nijhoff (Netherlands)). Kluwer Academic.
Reconstruction of Economics: An Analysis of the Fundamentals of Institutional Economics. Allan G. Gruchy. LC 86-25721. (Contributions in Economics & Economic History Ser.: No. 71). 193p. 1987. lib. bdg. 32.95 (ISBN 0-313-25679-9, GRS/). Greenwood.
Reconstruction of Europe. Louis Aubert. 1925. 39.50x (ISBN 0-686-83724-X). Elliots Bks.
Reconstruction of Gann's Stocks & Commodities Wisdom from His Famous Wall Street Reports, 2 vols. W. D. Gann. (Illus.). 117p. 1983. Set. 185.75x (ISBN 0-86654-077-6). Inst Econ Finan.
Reconstruction of Georgia. Alan Conway. LC 66-18867. pap. 63.50 (2056193). Bks Demand UMI.
Reconstruction of Georgia. Edwin C. Woolley. LC 74-120211. (Columbia University. Studies in the Social Sciences: No. 36). Repr. of 1901 ed. 14.50 (ISBN 0-404-51036-1). AMS Pr.
Reconstruction of Historical Materialism. Jorge Larrain. Ed. by T. Bottomore & M. Mulkay. LC 85-18699. (Controversies in Sociology: No. 19). 120p. 1986. text ed. 27.95x (ISBN 0-04-301207-8); pap. text ed. 11.95x (ISBN 0-04-301208-6). Unwin Hyman.
Reconstruction of International Monetary Arrangements. Ed. by Robert Z. Aliber. LC 86-3758. 320p. 1987. 32.50 (ISBN 0-312-66590-3). St Martin.
Reconstruction of Light. John Minczeski. LC 81-80546. (Minnesota Voices Project Ser.: No. 2). (Illus.). 80p. 1981. pap. 3.00 (ISBN 0-89823-023-3). New Rivers Pr.
Reconstruction of Patriotism: Education for Civic Consciousness. Morris Janowitz. LC 83-14540. 240p. 1984. lib. bdg. 25.00x (ISBN 0-226-39304-6). U of Chicago Pr.
Reconstruction of Patriotism: Education for Civic Consciousness. Morris Janowitz. LC 84-14540. xiv, 222p. 1985. pap. 8.95x (ISBN 0-226-39305-4). U of Chicago Pr.
Reconstruction of Proto-Mnong. Henry F. Blood. 110p. 1968. microfiche (2) 4.00 (ISBN 0-88312-493-9). Summer Inst Ling.
Reconstruction of Religious Thoughts in Islam. M. Iqbal. 29.00 (ISBN 0-686-18482-3). Kazi Pubns.
Reconstruction of Santayana's Philosophy of Beauty. Wayne M. Loveridge. (Illus.). 129p. 1982. 147.50 (ISBN 0-86650-028-6). Gloucester Art.
Reconstruction of Savonarola's Thought on the Art of Governing Men. Ronald Labouisse. (Illus.). 117p. 1984. 127.75 (ISBN 0-89901-135-7). Found Class Reprints.
Reconstruction of Secondary Education: Theory, Myth & Practice Since the War. A. McPherson & J. Gray. (Routledge Education Bks.). 300p. 1983. 34.95x (ISBN 0-7100-9265-2); pap. 18.50x (ISBN 0-7100-9268-7). Routledge Chapman & Hall.
Reconstruction of the Christian Revelation Claim: A Philosophical & Critical Apologetic. Stuart C. Hackett. 560p. 1984. pap. 19.95 (ISBN 0-8010-4283-6). Baker Bk.
Reconstruction of the Church. Ed. by James B. Jordan. LC 86-80570. (Christianity & Civilization Ser.: No. 4). xiv, 338p. (Orig.). 1986. pap. 12.95 (ISBN 0-939404-11-7). Geneva Ministr.
Reconstruction of the Elliott Wave Principle, 2 vols. in one. rev. & enl. ed. R. N. Elliott. (Institute for Economic & Financial Research Ser.). (Illus.). 143p. 1975. Set. 277.75 (ISBN 0-913314-63-3). Am Classical Coll Pr.
Reconstruction of the Elliott's Theory of Cycles. Ed. by Ralph N. Elliott & C. M. Flumiani. (Illus.). 118p. 1982. 257.75 (ISBN 0-86654-033-4). Inst Econ Finan.
Reconstruction of the Hogen-Heiji Monogatari Emaki. Penelope E. Mason. LC 76-23639. (Outstanding Dissertations in the Fine Arts). (Illus.). 1977. Repr. of 1970 ed. lib. bdg. 58.00 (ISBN 0-8240-2709-4). Garland Pub.
Reconstruction of the International Monetary System: The Attempts of 1922 & 1933. Stephen V. Clarke. LC 73-9360. (Princeton Studies in International Finance Ser.: No. 33). pap. 20.00 (ISBN 0-317-28836-9, 2017823). Bks Demand UMI.
Reconstruction of the New York Democracy, 1861-1874. Jerome Mushkat. LC 78-16826. 328p. 1981. 25.00 (ISBN 0-8386-3002-2, 3002). Fairleigh Dickinson.
Reconstruction of the Republic. Harold J. Brown. 1981. pap. 5.95 (ISBN 0-915134-86-1, Baker Hse). Mott Media.
Reconstruction of the Spiritual Ideal. Felix Adler. LC 77-27148. (Hibbert Lectures: 1923). Repr. of 1924 ed. 25.00 (ISBN 0-404-60422-6). AMS Pr.
Reconstruction of Thinking. Robert C. Neville. LC 81-5347. 350p. 1981. 44.50x (ISBN 0-87395-494-7); pap. 14.95x (ISBN 0-87395-495-5). State U NY Pr.
Reconstruction of Tokyo. Tokyo Municipal Office Staff. 419p. 1933. 525.00x (ISBN 0-317-69384-0, Pub. by Han-Shan Tang Ltd). State Mutual Bk.
Reconstruction of Trauma: Monograph II. Ed. by Arnold Rothstein. LC 86-10672. (Workshop Series of the American Psychoanalytic Association). 1986. text ed. 32.50x (ISBN 0-8236-5786-8). Intl Univs Pr.
Reconstruction of Western Europe 1945-51. Alan S. Milward. LC 83-17931. 500p. 1984. text ed. 45.00x (ISBN 0-520-05206-4); pap. 15.95x (ISBN 0-520-06035-0). U of Cal Pr.
Reconstruction of Wyckoff's Thoughts on the Formulas for Determining the Intrinsic Value of Securities. Stapley W. Tyndall. (Illus.). 147p. 1987. 117.75 (ISBN 0-86654-212-4). Inst Econ Finan.
Reconstruction Surgery & Traumatology, Vol. 12. Ed. by G. Chapchal. 1971. 65.50 (ISBN 3-8055-1183-3). S Karger.
Reconstruction Surgery & Traumatology, Vol. 13. Ed. by G. Chapchal. Incl. Scoliosis; Traumatology; Operative Treatment of Cerebral Palsy. (Illus.). 1972. 65.50 (ISBN 3-8055-1385-2). S Karger.
Reconstruction Surgery & Traumatology, Vol. 14. G. Chapchal. (Illus.). 200p. 1974. 65.50 (ISBN 3-8055-1563-4). S Karger.
Reconstruction Surgery & Traumatology, Vol. 15. Ed. by G. Chapchal. 1976. 32.75 (ISBN 3-8055-2250-9). S Karger.
Reconstruction Surgery & Traumatology, Vol. 16. Ed. by G. Chapchal. (Illus.). 1977. 38.75 (ISBN 3-8055-2696-2). S Karger.
Reconstructions: Avant-Garde Art in Japan 1945-1965. Ed. by David Elliott. (Illus.). 96p. 1987. pap. 14.95 (ISBN 0-87663-507-9). Universe.
Reconstructions of Early Christian Documents. Herbert J. Bardsley. 1977. lib. bdg. 59.95 (ISBN 0-8490-2504-4). Gordon Pr.
Reconstructive & Esthetic Mammoplasty. Guthrie & Schwartz. 848p. 1988. price not set (ISBN 0-7216-2806-0). Saunders.
Reconstructive Microvascular Surgery. E. Biemer & W. Duspiva. (Illus.). 151p. 1982. 99.00 (ISBN 0-387-11320-7). Springer-Verlag.
Reconstructive Plastic Surgery: Principles & Procedures in Correction Reconstruction & Transplantation, 7 vols. 2nd ed. Ed. by John M. Converse. LC 74-21010. (Illus.). 1977. Set. text ed. 575.00 (ISBN 0-7216-2691-2); Vol. 1. text ed. 89.00 (ISBN 0-7216-2680-7); Vol. 2. text ed. 89.00 (ISBN 0-7216-2681-5); Vol. 3. text ed. 89.00 (ISBN 0-7216-2682-3); Vol. 4. text ed. 89.00 (ISBN 0-7216-2683-1); Vol. 5. text ed. 89.00 (ISBN 0-7216-2684-X); Vol. 6. text ed. 78.00 (ISBN 0-7216-2685-8); Vol. 7. text ed. 78.00 (ISBN 0-7216-2686-6). Saunders.
Reconstructive Preprosthetic Oral & Maxillofacial Surgery. Raymond J. Fonseca & H. Howard Davis. (Illus.). 526p. 1986. 99.00 (ISBN 0-7216-3797-3). Saunders.
Reconstructive Surgery of the Gastrointestinal Tract. Alfred Cuschieri & David B. Skinner. (BIMR Surgery Ser.: Vol. 5). 320p. 1985. text ed. 95.00 (ISBN 0-407-02321-6). Butterworth.
Reconstructive Surgery of the Long Bones with Autogenous & Homogenous Grafts. O. Verbeek et al. 1973. lib. bdg. 45.00 (ISBN 90-207-0343-9, Pub. by Martinus Nijhoff Netherlands). Kluwer Academic.
Reconstructive Surgery of the Trachea. Rodolphe Meyer & Irene Flemming. (Illus.). 148p. 1982. 29.95 (ISBN 0-86577-061-1). Thieme Med Pubs.
Record & Music Publishing Forms of Agreement in Current Use. Compiled by Irwin O. Spiegel & Jay L. Cooper. LC 72-144789. 859p. 1971. looseleaf 59.00 (ISBN 0-88238-028-1). Law-Arts.
Record & Music Publishing Forms of Agreement in Current Use. Compiled by Irwin O. Spiegel & Jay L. Cooper. 859p. 1971. looseleaf 59.00 (ISBN 0-88238-118-0). Law Arts.
Record & Revelation. Ed. by Henry W. Robinson. LC 76-29395. Repr. of 1938 ed. 35.50 (ISBN 0-404-15354-2). AMS Pr.
Record Apart. Richard Heron. 1974. 12.50x (ISBN 0-7073-0147-5, Pub. by Scot Acad Pr). Longwood Pub Group.
Record Book, International Edition: A Guide to the World of the Phonograph. David Hall. LC 78-5686. 1978. Repr. of 1948 ed. lib. bdg. 55.50x (ISBN 0-313-20425-X, HATR). Greenwood.
Record Book of USGA Championships & International Events: 1895 Through 1980, 2 vols. 7.50 (ISBN 0-686-30840-9); 1981 supplement 1.00; 1982 supplement 1.00; 1984 supplement 1.00; 1983 supplement 1.00; 1985 supplement 1.00; 1986 supplement 1.00. US Golf Assn.
Record Breakers of Pro Sports. Nathan Aaseng. (Sports Talk Ser.). (Illus.). 80p. (gr. 4 up). 1987. PLB 8.95 (ISBN 0-8225-1533-4). Lerner Pubns.
Record Breakers: One Hundred & One Winning Streaks in Sports. Zander Hollander. (Illus.). 128p. (Orig.). (gr. 7 up). 1985. pap. 1.95 (ISBN 0-590-33374-7). Scholastic Inc.
Record Breaking Airplanes. Don Berliner. (Superwheels & Thrill Sports Bks.). (Illus.). 48p. (gr. 4-9). 1985. PLB 8.95 (ISBN 0-8225-0429-4). Lerner Pubns.
Record Collector's Fact Book, Vol. I. Chuck Brigermann. LC 82-73474. (Illus.). 96p. 1983. pap. 7.95 (ISBN 0-89709-037-3). Liberty Pub.
Record Collector's Record Books. Alan Leibowitz. Ed. by Roger Adler & Andrew Adler. 1979. pap. 5.95x (ISBN 0-916844-07-2). Turtle Pr.
Record Company Directory. Robert A. Livingston. 1986. 7.95 (ISBN 0-9607558-7-X). GLGLC Music.
Record Forms for the Uzgiris-Hunt Scales, 5 pts. Ina C. Uzgiris & J. McVicker Hunt. 1982. 15.75 set (ISBN 0-252-00905-3). U of Ill Pr.
Record Guide, 2 vols. Edward Sackville-West & Desmond Shawe-Taylor. LC 78-5028. 1978. Repr. of 1955 ed. Vol. 1. lib. bdg. 49.00 (ISBN 0-313-20405-5, SWRG01); Vol. 2. lib. bdg. 16.75 (ISBN 0-313-20406-3, SWRG02). Greenwood.
Record Guide. John Sarian. LC 79-63060. 1979. pap. 3.00 (ISBN 0-933706-05-7). Ararat Pr.
Record Houses, 1987. Architectural Record Magazine Editors. 227p. 1988. pap. text ed. 11.95 (ISBN 0-07-002451-0). McGraw.
Record Houses, 1988. Architectural Record Staff. 200p. 1988. pap. 12.95 (ISBN 0-07-002454-5). McGraw.
Record in Detail: Architectural Photographs of Jack E. Boucher. Jack E. Boucher. LC 87-5828. 120p. 1988. text ed. 34.95 (ISBN 0-8262-0640-9). U of Mo Pr.
Record Industry Book. 7th ed. Walter E. Hurst. 15.00 (ISBN 0-911370-01-3); pap. 10.00. Borden.
Record Industry Book, No. 1. 7th rev. ed. Walter E. Hurst. (Entertainment Industry Ser.). 1979. text ed. 15.00 (ISBN 0-911370-31-5); pap. 10.00 (ISBN 0-911370-32-3). Seven Arts.
Record Interiors, 1985. Architectural Record Magazine Editors. 300p. 1985. pap. text ed. 9.95 (ISBN 0-07-002432-4). McGraw.
Record Keeper: The Workbook That Helps You Organize Your Life. Crystal K. Meriwether & Curtis L. Sippel. LC 84-23899. 1985. pap. 14.95 (ISBN 0-934878-57-9). Dembner Bks.
Record Keeping & Archives in West Germany. Maralyn A. Wellauer. 54p. 1987. pap. 10.00 (ISBN 0-932019-10-2). Roots Intl.
Record Keeping & Self-Administration for Radio Account Executives. John M. Donohue. (Radio Sales Executive Reports). (Illus.). 35p. Date not set. pap. text ed. cancelled (ISBN 0-943382-10-6). Radio Resource.
Record Keeping for Business: Syllabus. Marvin W. Hempel. 1977. pap. text ed. 9.75 (ISBN 0-89420-018-6, 359090); cassette recordings 139.80 (ISBN 0-89420-180-8, 359000). Natl Book.
Record Keeping for Personal Finance: Syllabus. Marvin W. Hempel. 1976. pap. text ed. 8.95 (ISBN 0-89420-005-4, 358080); cassette recordings 124.25 (ISBN 0-89420-181-6, 358000). Natl Book.
Record Keeping for Small Rural Businesses. Eligia Murcia. (Technical Note Ser.: No. 26). (Illus.). 25p. (Orig.). pap. text ed. 2.00 (ISBN 0-932288-75-8). Ctr Intl Ed U of MA.
Record Label Guide for Domestic LPs. Joe Lindsay. (Illus.). 200p. (Orig.). 1986. pap. 14.95 (ISBN 0-9617347-0-1). BIODISC.
Record Makers & Record Breakers. Nick Iversen. LC 76-10227. 240p. 1977. 9.95 (ISBN 0-8246-0208-0). Jonathan David.
Record of a Friendship: The Correspondence of Wilhelm Reich & A. S. Neill. Wilhelm Reich. Ed. by Beverley Placzek. 1981. 20.00 (ISBN 0-374-24807-9); pap. 11.95 (ISBN 0-374-51770-3). FS&G.
Record of a Quaker Conscience see Civil War Diary of Cyrus Pringle: Record of Quaker Conscience.
Record of a School. Elizabeth P. Peabody. LC 74-89218. (American Education: Its Men, Institutions & Ideas, Ser. 1). 1969. Repr. of 1836 ed. 18.00 (ISBN 0-405-01457-0). Ayer Co Pubs.
Record of Achievement of Dr. Lawrence C. Bryant. Lawrence C. Bryant. 1966. 5.00 (ISBN 0-686-05556-X). L C Bryant.
Record of an Adventurous Life. Henry M. Hyndman. LC 83-48486. (World of Labour - English Workers 1850-1890 Ser.). 460p. 1984. 55.00 (ISBN 0-8240-5713-9). Garland Pub.
Record of an Obscure Man. Mary T. Putnam. LC 70-82213. (Anti-Slavery Crusade in America Ser.). 1969. Repr. of 1861 ed. 11.50 (ISBN 0-405-00652-7). Ayer Co Pubs.
Record of Buddhist Monasteries in Lo-Yang. Hsuan-chih Yang & Wang T. Yi-t'ung. LC 83-42586. (Princeton Library of Asian Translations). (Illus.). 340p. 1984. 38.50x (ISBN 0-691-05403-7). Princeton U Pr.
Record of Commissions of Officers in the Tennessee Militia,1796-1815. Mrs. John T. Moore. LC 76-53147. 273p. 1977. Repr. of 1956 ed. 15.00 (ISBN 0-8063-0756-0). Genealog Pub.
Record of Deaths in Columbia South Carolina & Elsewhere As Recorded by John Glass 1859-1877. Brent.H. Holcomb. 223p. 1986. 20.00 (ISBN 0-913363-05-7). SCMAR.
Record of European Armour & Arms Through Seven Centuries, 5 vols. Guy F. Laking. LC 79-8365. (Illus.). Repr. of 1922 ed. 295.00 set (ISBN 0-404-18344-1). AMS Pr.
Record of Evidence & Statements Before the Penitentiary Investigating Committee: Appointed by the Thirty-Third Legislature of Texas. facsimile ed. Texas, Penitentiary Investigating Committee. LC 74-3847. (Criminal Justice in America Ser.). 1974. Repr. of 1913 ed. 31.00x (ISBN 0-405-06171-4). Ayer Co Pubs.
Record of Experience: FFHC-Action for Development. 1978. pap. 7.50 (ISBN 92-5-100316-5, F1361, FAO). UNIPUB.
Record of Hawksbill Church 1788-1850, Page County, Virginia. Klaus Wust. 1979. pap. 5.50 (ISBN 0-917968-06-9). Shenandoah Hist.
Record of Indentures (1771-1773) Excerpted from the Pennsylvania-German Society Proceedings & Addresses 16. Philadelphia Office of Mayor. LC 72-10671. 364p. 1973. Repr. of 1907 ed. 20.00 (ISBN 0-8063-0540-1). Genealog Pub.
Record of My Life-Work in Entomology. C. R. Osten-Sacken. 1978. 45.00x (ISBN 0-317-07172-6, Pub. by FW Classey UK). State Mutual Bk.
Record of Oral Language & Biks & Gutches. Marie M. Clay et al. (Illus.). 91p. (Orig.). 1983. pap. text ed. 12.50x (00571). Heinemann Ed.
Record of Pennsylvania Marriages Prior to 1810, 2 vols. John B. Linn & William H. Egle. 1987. Repr. of 1880 ed. 75.00 (3400). Vol. I, 790 pp. Vol. II, 601 pp. Genealog Pub.
Record of Proceedings: ILO Seventieth Session, Geneva, 1984. 185p. 1985. pap. 56.00 (ISBN 92-2-103451-8, ILO395, ILO). UNIPUB.

Records of Noble Lives. William O. Adams. 1882. Repr. 30.00 (ISBN 0-8274-3256-9). R West.

Records of Noble Lives: A Book of Notable English Biographies. W. H. Adams. 309p. 1985. Repr. of 1882 ed. lib. bdg. 65.00 (ISBN 0-918377-82-X). Russell Pr.

Records of North American Big Game. 8th ed. Ed. by W. H. Nesbitt & Philip L. Wright. (Records of North American Big Game Ser.). (Illus.). xii, 412p. 1981. 30.00 (ISBN 0-940864-00-2). Boone & Crockett.

Records of North American Big Game. 8th ed. Ed. by W. H. Nesbitt & Philip L. Wright. xii, 412p. 1981. leather, ltd. ed. 195.00x (ISBN 0-940864-01-0). Boone & Crockett.

Records of North American Whitetail Deer. Ed. by W. Nesbitt & Jack Reneau. (Illus.). 246p. 1987. pap. 15.00 (ISBN 0-940864-12-6). Boone & Crockett.

Records of Officers & Men of New Jersey in Wars, 1791-1815. New Jersey Adjutant-General's Office. LC 78-117069. 318p. 1970. Repr. of 1909 ed. 27.50 (ISBN 0-8063-0417-0). Genealog Pub.

Records of Pastoral Acts at Emanual Lutheran Church (Known in the Eighteen Century as the Warwick Congregation, Near Brickerville, Elizabeth Township, Lancaster County) 1743-1799. Tr. by Frederick S. Weiser. (Sources & Documents Ser.: No. 8). 229p. 1983. pap. 15.00 (ISBN 0-911122-47-8). Penn German Soc.

Records of Plymouth Colony: Births, Marriages, Deaths, Burials & Other Records 1633-1689. Nathaniel B. Shurtleff. LC 75-34715. 293p. 1979. Repr. of 1857 ed. 17.50 (ISBN 0-8063-0701-3). Genealog Pub.

Records of Salem Lutheran Church, Brenham, Texas 1850-1940. Jack A. Dabbs & Edward C. Breitenkamp. LC 86-72575. (Illus.). 501p. 1986. 35.00 (ISBN 0-911494-10-3). Dabbs.

Records of Salem Witchcraft, 2 vols. in 1. (Woodward's Historical Ser.: Nos. 1 & 2). 1968. Repr. of 1864 ed. 40.50 (ISBN 0-8337-2916-0). B Franklin.

Records of Salem Witchcraft, Copied from the Original Documents, 2 Vols. LC 78-75274. (Law, Politics & History Ser.). 1969. Repr. of 1864 ed. lib. bdg. 45.00 (ISBN 0-306-71309-8). Da Capo.

Records of Shelley, Byron, & the Author. Edward J. Trelaway. Ed. by David Wright. 328p. 1983. pap. 5.95 (ISBN 0-14-043088-1). Penguin.

Records of Shelley, Byron & the Author, 2 vols. in 1. Edward J. Trelawney. LC 68-20230. 1968. Repr. of 1878 ed. 33.00 (ISBN 0-405-09031-5). Ayer Co Pubs.

Records of Social & Economic History: The Compton Census of 1676: A Critical Edition, Vol. X. Anne Whiteman. (Illus.). 812p. 1986. 89.00x (ISBN 0-19-726041-1). Oxford U Pr.

Records of Social & Economic History: The Early Records of Medieval Coventry, Vol. XI. P. R. Coss. 560p. 1986. 135.00 (ISBN 0-19-726038-1). Oxford U Pr.

Records of Tennyson, Ruskin & Browning. Anne Ritchie. 1896. 10.00 (ISBN 0-8274-3915-6). R West.

Records of Tennyson, Ruskin & Browning. Anne Ritchie. 1977. Repr. lib. bdg. 20.00 (ISBN 0-8492-2352-0). R West.

Records of Tennyson, Ruskin & Browning. Anne T. Ritchie. LC 70-172549. Repr. of 1892 ed. 22.00 (ISBN 0-405-08893-0, Pub. by Blom). Ayer Co Pubs.

Records of Tennyson, Ruskin & Browning. Anne T. Ritchie. LC 68-26220. 1969. Repr. of 1899 ed. 23.00x (ISBN 0-8046-0383-9, Pub. by Kennikat). Assoc Faculty Pr.

Records of the American Women's Hospitals 1917-1982: An Inventory. Nancy A. Hewitt. (Illus.). 55p. (Orig.). 1987. 5.00 (ISBN 0-944542-01-8). Med Coll PA ASCWM.

Records of the British Residency & Agencies in the Persian Gulf. Penelope Tuson. 214p. (Orig.). 1979. pap. 34.50 (ISBN 0-7123-0617-X, Pub. by British Lib). Longwood Pub Group.

Records of the Burgh of Prestwick in the Sheriffdom of Ayr. Ed. by John Fullarton. LC 76-174286. (Maitland Club. Glasgow. Publications: No. 27). Repr. of 1834 ed. 20.00 (ISBN 0-404-52983-6). AMS Pr.

Records of the Cape Colony, 36 vols. Cape of Good Hope, Public Record Office, London Staff. LC 74-8329. (Illus.). Repr. of 1905 ed. AMS Pr.

Records of the Church of Christ, Buxton, (ME) 88p. 1985. pap. 10.00 (ISBN 0-935207-16-3). DanBury Hse Bks.

Records of the Church of Christ in Buxton, Maine. rev. ed. Ed. by Lewis B. Rohrbach. 96p. 1988. lib. bdg. 25.00; pap. 15.00. Picton Pr.

Records of the City of Portsmouth, 1835-1955, 5 vols. City of Portsmouth Publications Staff. (Illus.). 1985. 95.00x (ISBN 0-317-43840-9, Pub. by City of Portsmouth). State Mutual Bk.

Records of the Colony of New Plymouth in New England, 12 Vols in 6. Ed. by Nathaniel B. Shurtleff & David Pulsifer. LC 1-12098. Repr. of 1861 ed. Set. 550.00 (ISBN 0-404-06040-4). AMS Pr.

Records of the Colony of Rhode Island & Providence Plantations in New England, 10 Vols. Ed. by John R. Bartlett. Repr. of 1856 ed. Set. lib. bdg. 550.00 (ISBN 0-404-00680-9); lib. bdg. 55.00 ea. AMS Pr.

Records of the Columbia Historical Society of Washington, D. C, Vol. 52. Ed. by J. Kirkpatrick Flack. (Illus.). 450p. 1989. text ed. price not set (ISBN 0-8139-1183-4). U Pr of VA.

Records of the Columbia Historical Society of Washington D.C. 1957-1974. Ed. by Francis C. Rosenberger. Incl. 1957-1959. (Illus.). 1961. 20.00x (ISBN 0-8139-0493-5); 1960-1962. (Illus.). 1963. 20.00x (ISBN 0-8139-0494-3); 1963-1965. (Illus.). 1966. 20.00x (ISBN 0-8139-0495-1); 1966-1968. (Illus.). 1969. 20.00x (ISBN 0-8139-0496-X); 1969-1970. LC 1-17677. (Illus.). 1971. 20.00x (ISBN 0-8139-0497-8); 1971-1972. 1973. 20.00x (ISBN 0-8139-0501-X); 1973-74. 1976. 20.00x (ISBN 0-8139-0641-5). LC 73-84160. cancelled. U Pr of Va.

Records of the Conference for Revision of the Universal Copyright Convention: UNESCO House, Paris, 5-24 July 1971. 295p. 1973. pap. 10.00 (ISBN 92-3-101047-6, U521, UNESCO). UNIPUB.

Records of the Conference Resolutions 14th Resolution. pap. 11.00 (U523, UNESCO). UNIPUB.

Records of the Court of Assistants of the Colony of the Massachusetts Bay, 1630-1692, 3 Vols. Massachusetts Colony Court Of Assistants. LC 70-172853. Repr. of 1928 ed. Set. 97.50 (ISBN 0-404-07350-6); 32.50 ea. Vol. 1 (ISBN 0-404-07351-4). Vol. 2 (ISBN 0-404-07352-2). Vol. 3 (ISBN 0-404-07353-0). AMS Pr.

Records of the Court of the Stationers' Company 1602 to 1640. Ed. by William A. Jackson. 555p. 1985. Repr. of 1957 ed. lib. bdg. 550.00 (ISBN 0-89987-447-9). Darby Bks.

Records of the Department of State Relating to the Internal Affairs of China, 1910-1929: A Descriptive Guide & Subject Index to Microcopy No. 329. Ed. by Mordechai Rozanski. LC 79-13351. 1979. lib. bdg. 30.00 (ISBN 0-8420-2133-7). Scholarly Res Inc.

Records of the Diplomatic Conference on the International Protection of Performers, Producers of Phonograms & Broadcasting Organizations. 1968. pap. 16.50 (ISBN 0-686-53022-5, WIPO37, WIPO). UNIPUB.

Records of the Dutch Reformed Church in New Amsterdam & New York. Samuel S. Purple. 50.00 (ISBN 0-8490-0936-7). Gordon Pr.

Records of the East India College, Haileybury, & Other Institutions. Anthony Farrington. (Illus.). 175p. 1976. 12.75 (ISBN 0-903359-16-2, Pub. by British Lib). Longwood Pub Group.

Records of the English Province of the Society of Jesus, 7 Vols. in 8. Henry Foley. (Illus.). Repr. of 1883 ed. Set. 690.00 (ISBN 0-384-16310-6). Johnson Repr.

Records of the Federal Convention of 1787, 4 vols. Max Farrand. Incl. Vol. 1. (Illus.). 640p. 45.00x (ISBN 0-300-00447-8); pap. 14.95x (ISBN 0-300-00080-4); Vol. 2. (Illus.). 680p. 45.00x (ISBN 0-300-00448-6); pap. 14.95x (ISBN 0-300-00081-2); Vol. 3. 640p. 45.00x (ISBN 0-300-00449-4); pap. 14.95x (ISBN 0-300-00082-0); Vol. 4. 230p. LC 86-50311. 1986. pap. Yale U Pr.

Records of the First Church in Salem, Massachusetts, 1629-1736. Ed. by Richard D. Pierce. LC 73-93302. 1974. 30.00 (ISBN 0-88389-050-X). Essex Inst.

Records of the First Church of Christ, Biddeford (ME) 54p. 1985. pap. 6.50 (ISBN 0-935207-24-4). DanBury Hse Bks.

Records of the First Church of Wareham, Mass., 1739-1891. Ed. by Leonard H. Smith, Jr. pap. 15.00 (ISBN 0-932022-01-4). L H Smith.

Records of the First Congregational Church in Scarborough (Me)-Baptisms. 64p. 1986. pap. 7.50 (ISBN 0-935207-35-X). DanBury Hse Bks.

Records of the First Congregational Church in Scarborough (Me)-Marriages. 21p. 1986. pap. 3.25 (ISBN 0-935207-43-0). DanBury Hse Bks.

Records of the General Conference, Fourth Extraordinary Session: Paris, 23 Nov. - 3 Dec. 1982, 2 Vols. 1983. Vol. 1: Resolutions, 65pp. pap. text ed. 5.00 (ISBN 92-3-102094-3, U1273, UNESCO); Vol. 2: Reports, Commissions I & II, 71pp. pap. 5.00 (ISBN 92-3-102121-4, U1314). UNIPUB.

Records of the General Conference: Twenty-First Session, Belgrade, Sept. 23-Oct. 28, 1980, 3 Vols. Incl. Vol. 1. Resolutions. 1980. pap. 13.25 (ISBN 92-3-101916-3, U1086, UNESCO). UNIPUB; Vol. 2. Reports. 295p. 1982. pap. 15.00 (ISBN 92-3-101960-0, U1222). UNIPUB; Proceedings. 1982. pap. 46.50 (ISBN 92-3-002010-9, U1235). UNIPUB. pap. write for info. (UNESCO). UNIPUB.

Records of the General Conference, Twenty-Third Session, 1985, Vol. 3: Proceedings. 1604p. (Eng., Fr., Span., Rus., Arabic & Chinese.). 1987. pap. 31.50 (ISBN 92-3-002474-0, U1612, UNESCO). UNIPUB.

Records of the General Conference 15th Session: Resolutions. pap. 13.25 (U527, UNESCO). UNIPUB.

Records of the Governor & Company of Massachusetts Bay in New England, 1628-1686, 5 Vols in 6. Ed. by Nathaniel B. Shurtleff. LC 72-1721. Repr. of 1854 ed. Set. lib. bdg. 390.00 (ISBN 0-404-06020-X). AMS Pr.

Records of the Governor & Council of the State of Vermont, 8 Vols. Vermont. Ed. by Eliakim P. Walton. LC 74-177562. Repr. of 1880 ed. Set. 360.00 (ISBN 0-404-07600-9); 45.00 ea. AMS Pr.

Records of the Grand Historian of China, 2 vols. Chien Ssu-ma. Incl. Vol. 1. Early Years of the Han Dynasty, 209 to 141 B.C. pap. 109.30; Vol. 2. Age of Emperor Wu, 140 to c. 100 B.C. pap. 120.00. LC 60-13348. (Records of Civilization: Sources & Studies: No. 65). (Illus.). pap. (2005779). Bks Demand UMI.

Records of the Historian. Tr. by Burton Watson from Chinese. LC 70-89860. (Translations from the Oriental Classics). Orig. Title: Chapters from the Shih Chi of Ssu-Ma Ch'ien. 1970. pap. 17.50 (ISBN 0-231-03321-4). Columbia U Pr.

Records of the Intellectual Property Conference of Stockholm: 1967, Vols. 1 & 2. 1971. Set. 99.00 (ISBN 0-686-53023-3, WIPO30, WIPO). UNIPUB.

Records of the International Conference of States on the Protection of Phonograms: Geneva, 18-29 Oct. 1971. 224p. 1975. pap. 31.50 (ISBN 92-3-101280-0, U540, UNESCO). UNIPUB.

Records of the International Conference of States on the Distribution of Programme Carrying Signals Transmitted by Satellite: Brussels, 6-21 May 1974. 677p. (Co-published with the World Intellectual Property Organization). 1977. pap. 15.00 (ISBN 92-3-101465-X, U860, UNESCO). UNIPUB.

Records of the Joint Chiefs of Staff, 1946-1953, Pt. 2. Joint Chiefs of Staff. 1980. 4200.00 (ISBN 0-89093-202-6). U Pubns Amer.

Records of the Life of Tripitaka Master Hua, Vol. 1. Biography of Master Hsuan Hua Publication Committee. (Illus.). 90p. (Orig.). 1981. pap. 5.00 (ISBN 0-917512-78-2). Buddhist Text.

Records of the Life of Tripitaka Master Hua, Vol. 2. Biography of Master Hsuan Hua Publication Committee. (Illus.). 229p. (Orig.). 1976. pap. 8.00 (ISBN 0-917512-10-3). Buddhist Text.

Records of the Locarno Conference: 1968, for the Purpose of Setting Up an International Classification for Industrial Designs. 1972. 19.25 (ISBN 0-686-53025-X, WIPO31, WIPO). UNIPUB.

Records of the Moravians in North Carolina, 11 vols. Incl. Vol. 1, 1752-1771. 511p. 1968. Repr. of 1925 ed; Vol. 2, 1752-1775. viii, 460p. 1968. Repr. of 1925 ed; Vol. 3, 1776-1779. viii, 513p. 1968. Repr. of 1926 ed; Vol. 4, 1780-1783. v, 471p. 1968. Repr. of 1930 ed; Vol. 5, 1784-1792. ix, 487p. 1970. Repr. of 1943 ed. 15.00x (ISBN 0-86526-060-5); Vol. 6, 1793-1808. x, 566p. 1970. Repr. of 1943 ed. 15.00x (ISBN 0-86526-061-3); Vol. 7, 1809-1822. x, 593p. 1970. Repr. of 1947 ed. 15.00x (ISBN 0-86526-062-1); Vol. 8, 1823-1837. Ed. by Minnie J. Smith. xi, 756p. 1954. 15.00x (ISBN 0-86526-063-X); Vol. 9, 1838-1847. Ed. by Kenneth G. Hamilton. xiii, 685p. 1964; Vol. 10, 1841-1851. Ed. by Kenneth G. Hamilton. xviii, 626p. 1966; Vol. 11, 1852-1879. Ed. by Kenneth G. Hamilton. xvi, 524p. 1969. 15.00x (ISBN 0-86526-066-4). (Illus.). NC Archives.

Records of the New York Stage from 1750 to 1860, 2 Vols. Joseph N. Ireland. LC 68-56716. (Bibliography & Reference Ser: No. 226). 1968. Repr. of 1866 ed. 43.00 (ISBN 0-8337-1810-X). B Franklin.

Records of the New York Stage: Seventeen Fifty to Eighteen Sixty, 2 vols. Joseph N. Ireland. LC 65-27912. Set. 66.00 (ISBN 0-405-08657-1); 33.00 ea. Vol. 1 (ISBN 0-405-08658-X). Vol. 2 (ISBN 0-405-08659-8). Ayer Co Pubs.

Records of the Paris Conference: 1971. 1974. 27.50 (ISBN 0-686-53026-8, WIPO34, WIPO). UNIPUB.

Records of the Particular Court of Connecticut: 1639 to 1663. LC 29-13342. 1928. 6.00. Conn Hist Soc.

Records of the Particular Court of Connecticut: 1639-1663. Connecticut Historical Society. xii, 302p. 1987. pap. 20.00 (ISBN 1-55613-078-3). Heritage Bk.

Records of the Past: Being English Translations of the Ancient Monuments of Egypt & Western Asia, 6 vols. in 2. Ed. by A. H. Sayce. LC 72-83175. Repr. of 1888 ed. Set. 71.00 (ISBN 0-405-08918-X); 35.75 ea. Vol. 1 (ISBN 0-405-08919-8). Vol. 2 (ISBN 0-405-08922-8). Ayer Co Pubs.

Records of the Presbyterian Church in the United States of America, 1706-1788. Presbyterian Church in The United States of America. LC 75-83434. (Religion in America, Ser. 1). 1969. Repr. of 1904 ed. 30.00 (ISBN 0-405-00259-9). Ayer Co Pubs.

Records of the Presidency: Presidential Papers & Libraries from Washington to the Present. Frank L. Schick. 328p. 1988. 49.50 (ISBN 0-89774-277-X). Oryx Pr.

Records of the Recorder's Office of Highland County, Ohio (1805-1850) David N. McBride & Jane N. McBride. (Vital Records of Highland County, Ohio Ser.). Date not set. Repr. lib. bdg. cancelled (ISBN 0-931000-03-3). S Ohio Genealog.

Records of the Reformed Dutch Church of Albany, New York, 1683-1809. Holland Society of New York. LC 78-54063. 922p. (Repr. of the 1904-1927 eds.). 1978. 38.50 (ISBN 0-8063-0808-7). Genealog Pub.

Records of the Reformed Dutch Church of New Paltz, New York. Tr. by Dingman Versteeg. LC 77-77266. 269p. 1977. Repr. of 1896 ed. 15.00 (ISBN 0-8063-0772-2). Genealog Pub.

Records of the Second General Assembly. Nepal National Commission for UNESCO Staff. 136p. 1966. 12.50 (ISBN 0-318-17087-6, 68). Am-Nepal Ed.

Records of the Strasbourg Diplomatic Conference on the International Patent Classification: 1971. 1973. 27.50 (ISBN 0-686-53027-6, WIPO33, WIPO). UNIPUB.

Records of the Templars in England in the Twelfth Century: The Inquest of 1185 with Illustrative Charters & Documents. (British Academy, London, Records of the Social & Economic History Of England & Wales Ser.: Vol. 9). pap. 70.00 (ISBN 0-8115-1249-5). Kraus Repr.

Records of the Town of Cambridge Massachusetts 1630-1703. Ed. by J. Brandon. 397p. 1985. Repr. of 1901 ed. 30.00 (ISBN 0-917890-50-7). Heritage Bk.

Records of the Town of Newark, New Jersey, from its Settlement in 1666 to its Incorporation as a City in 1836, Vol. 6. Ed. by Samuel H. Congar. 308p. 1966. pap. 8.50 (ISBN 0-686-81799-0). NJ Hist Soc.

Records of the Trial of Walter Langeton, 1307-12. Ed. by Royal Historical Society Staff. (Camden Fourth Ser.: No. 6). 1970. 27.00 (ISBN 0-901050-02-4, Pub. by Boydell & Brewer). Longwood Pub Group.

Records of the Tuesday Club of Annapolis, 1745-56. Ed. by Elaine G. Breslaw. 504p. 1988. 39.95 (ISBN 0-252-01334-4). U of Ill Pr.

Records of the UNESCO General Conference: 20th Session, Paris, Oct. 24-Nov. 28, 1978, 2 vols. (Eng., Fr., Rus., Span. & Armenian.). 1979. Vol. 1: Resolutions. pap. 6.50 (ISBN 92-3-101703-9, U910, UNESCO); Vol. 2: Reports. pap. 11.50 (U966). UNIPUB.

Records of the Vienna Diplomatic Conference on the Trademark Registration Treaty: 1973. 1975. 55.00 (ISBN 0-686-53028-4, WIPO35, WIPO). UNIPUB.

Records of the Virginia Company of London, 4 vols. Virginia Company of London. Ed. by Susan M. Kingsbury. LC 74-19621. Repr. of 1935 ed. Set. 230.00 (ISBN 0-404-12457-7); each 57.50 (ISBN 0-686-85632-5). AMS Pr.

Records of the Washington Diplomatic Conference on the Patent Cooperation Treaty: 1970. 1972. 69.30 (ISBN 0-686-53029-2, WIPO32, WIPO). UNIPUB.

Records of Trinity Church, Boston, Vol. I: 1728-1830. Ed. by Andrew Oliver & James B. Peabody. LC 80-68230. 519p. 1980. 30.00x (ISBN 0-8139-0950-3, Colonial Soc Ma). U Pr of Va.

Records of Trinity Church, Boston: Vol. II - 1728-1830. Andrew Oliver & James B. Peabody. LC 80-68230. 571p. 1982. 30.00x (ISBN 0-8139-0982-1, Colonial Soc MA). U Pr of Va.

Records of Washington County, Georgia. Marie De Lamar & Elisabeth Rothstein. LC 84-73076. 184p. 1985. Repr. of 1975 ed. 18.50 (ISBN 0-8063-1110-X). Genealog Pub.

Records on the International Conference of States on the Protection of Phonograms: 1971. 1975. pap. 33.00 (ISBN 0-686-53024-1, WIPO36, WIPO). UNIPUB.

Records Relating to the Early History of Boston, 39 vols. Boston Registry Department Staff. LC 74-19611. Repr. of 1909 ed. Set. 1170.00 (ISBN 0-404-12343-0); 30.00 ea. AMS Pr.

Records Relating to the Gold Coast Settlements from 1750 to 1874. J. J. Crooks. 576p. 1973. Repr. of 1923 ed. 38.00x (ISBN 0-7146-1647-8, BHA-01647, F Cass Co). Biblio Dist.

Records Reorganization in a Court for the Idaho Supreme Court. National Center for State Courts Staff. (Paul Reardon Ser.). 16p. 1982. manuscript 0.96 (PRS-034). Natl Ctr St Courts.

Records Retention & Disposition Project, Fifth District, Minnesota: Final Project Report. National Center for State Courts Staff. 38p. 1981. manuscript 2.28 (NCRO-045). Natl Ctr St Courts.

Records Retention & Disposition Recommendations for the Circuit Court of Madison County. National Center for State Courts Staff. 14p. (On loan through the NCSC Library). 1976. write for info. (MAB-143). Natl Ctr St Courts.

Records: Vol. 1, Resolutions. UNESCO General Conference, 21st, Belgrade, 1980. pap. 7.50 (ISBN 92-3-101916-3, U1086, UNESCO). UNIPUB.

Recount. Dominick Abel. 256p. (Orig.). 1987. pap. 2.95 (ISBN 0-8041-0133-7, Pub. by Ivy). Ballantine.

Recourse to Tax Havens: Use & Abuse. (IFA Congress Seminar Ser.: No. 5). 120p. 1982. pap. 15.00 cancelled (ISBN 90-200-0653-3, Pub. by Kluwer Law Netherlands). Kluwer Academic.

Recovered Yesterdays in Literature. William A. Quayle. LC 74-117829. (Essay Index Reprint Ser). 1916. 19.00 (ISBN 0-8369-1678-6). Ayer Co Pubs.

Recoveries. Theodore Weiss. 1982. pap. 6.95 (ISBN 0-02-071050-X, Collier). Macmillan.

Recreation Management & Pricing: The Effects of Charging Policy on Demand at Countryside Recreation Sites. Ed. by Tony Bovaird et al. LC 84-10151. 182p. 1984. text ed. 32.95x (ISBN 0-566-00671-5). Gower Pub Co.

Recreation Management of Water Resources. Roger Warren & Phillip Rea. LC 86-628. (Parks & Recreation Ser.). (Illus.). 79p. (Orig.). 1986. pap. text ed. 15.00x (ISBN 0-942280-28-8); pap. 16.95. Pub Horizons.

Recreation on the Colorado River. 1st ed. D. J. Dirksen & R. A. Reeves. 112p. (Orig.). 1985. pap. 9.95 (ISBN 0-943798-07-8). Recreation Sales Pub.

Recreation Planning & Design. S. M. Gold. 1980. text ed. 49.50 (ISBN 0-07-023644-5). McGraw.

Recreation Planning & Development, 2 Vols. 775p. 1979. pap. 57.00x (ISBN 0-87262-200-2). Am Soc Civil Eng.

Recreation Program Coordinator. (Career Examination Ser.: C-3407). Date not set. pap. 16.00 (ISBN 0-8373-3407-1). Natl Learning.

Recreation Program Planning Today. Richard Kraus. 1985. text ed. write for info. (ISBN 0-673-18141-3). Scott F.

Recreation: Programming & Leadership. 4th ed. Dan Corbin & Ellen Williams. (Illus.). 432p. 1987. text ed. 30.00 (ISBN 0-13-767963-7). P-H.

Recreation Programming for Developmentally Disabled Persons. Paul Wehman. LC 78-14554. (Illus.). 300p. 1979. 21.00x (ISBN 0-936104-79-1, 1134). Pro Ed.

Recreation Programming for Visually Impaired Children & Youth. Ed. by Jerry D. Kelley. (Illus.). 160p. 1981. pap. 12.00 (ISBN 0-89128-106-1, PEP106); training manual o.p. 9.00 (ISBN 0-89128-117-7, PEP117). Am Foun Blind.

Recreation, Reflection & Re-Creation: Perspectives on Rabelais's Pantagruel. Raymond C. La Charite. LC 79-53402. (French Forum Monographs: No. 19). 137p. (Orig.). 1980. pap. 9.95x (ISBN 0-917058-18-6). French Forum.

Recreation Site Survey Manual. Tourism & Recreation Research Unit, Endinburgh University. (Illus.). 150p. 1983. 33.00 (ISBN 0-419-12680-5, NO. 6769, Pub. by Tavistock). Routledge Chapman & Hall.

Recreation Specialist. Jack Rudman. (Career Examination Ser.: C-692). (Cloth bdg. avail. on request). pap. 14.00 (ISBN 0-8373-0692-2). Natl Learning.

Recreation Supervisor. Jack Rudman. (Career Examination Ser.: C-693). (Cloth bdg. avail. on request). pap. 14.00 (ISBN 0-8373-0693-0). Natl Learning.

Recreation Therapist. Jack Rudman. (Career Examination Ser.: C-2698). (Cloth bdg. avail. on request). pap. 14.00 (ISBN 0-8373-2698-2). Natl Learning.

Recreation Today: Program Planning & Leadership. 2d ed. Richard G. Kraus. LC 76-49059. (Illus.). 1977. text ed. write for info. (ISBN 0-673-16201-X). Scott F.

Recreation Vehicle Park Design & Management. 52p. 1977. 5.00 (ISBN 0-318-18047-2). RV Indus Assn.

Recreation, Vol. 1: Current Selected Research. Ed. by James H. Humphrey & Fred Humphrey. 1988. 57.50 (ISBN 0-404-63901-1). AMS Pr.

Recreation Worker. Jack Rudman. (Career Examination Ser.: C-429). (Cloth bdg. avail. on request). pap. 12.00 (ISBN 0-8373-0429-6). Natl Learning.

Recreational Activity Development for the Aging in Homes, Hospitals, & Nursing Homes. Carol Lucas. (Illus.). 68p. 1978. pap. 6.50x (ISBN 0-398-03058-8). C C Thomas.

Recreational Areas. Ed. by Time-Life Books Editors. (Home Repair & Improvement Ser.). (Illus.). 1980. 10.95. Time-Life.

Recreational Development Handbook. J. Eric Smart et al. LC 81-51294. (Community Builders Handbook Ser.). (Illus.). 272p. 1981. 50.00 (ISBN 0-87420-599-9, R13). Urban Land.

Recreational Football: Flag, Touch & Flicker. Mildred J. Little et al. (Physical Education Activities Ser.). 112p. 1980. pap. text ed. write for info. (ISBN 0-697-07092-1). Wm C Brown.

Recreational Geography of the U. S. S. R. V. Preobrazhensky & V. Krivosheyev. 228p. 1982. 6.45 (ISBN 0-686-47689-1, Pub. by Progress Pubs U. S. S. R.). Imported Pubns.

Recreational Jazz Dance. 2nd ed. Ann I. Czompo. Ed. by Andor Czompo. LC 79-26223. (Illus.). 1979. pap. text ed. 9.95 (ISBN 0-935496-00-9). AC Pubns.

Recreational Land Management. C. W. Miles & W. Seabrooke. 1977. 25.00x (ISBN 0-419-11060-7, NO. 6467, Pub. by E & FN Spon). Routledge Chapman & Hall.

Recreational Leadership: Group Dynamics & Interpersonal Behavior. 2nd ed. Jay S. Shivers. 1986. text ed. 29.95 (ISBN 0-916622-41-X). Princeton Bk Co.

Recreational Management Handbook. Ed. by Institute of Recreation Management. 1980. 40.00x (ISBN 0-419-11620-6, NO. 6336, Pub. by E & FN Spon England). Routledge Chapman & Hall.

Recreational Safety: The Standard of Care. Jay S. Shivers. LC 85-47630. (Illus.). 320p. 1986. 38.50x (ISBN 0-8386-3241-6). Fairleigh Dickinson.

Recreational Sports Programming. Richard F. Mull & Kathy G. Bayless. Ed. by F. R. Maradie. 450p. 1983. 25.95 (ISBN 0-87670-093-8). Athletic Inst.

Recreational Surveys: Monographs. Mary Vance. (Public Administration Ser.: P 1889). 33p. 1986. 8.75 (ISBN 0-89028-799-6). Vance Biblios.

Recreational Use of Domestic Water Supply Reservoirs: Perception & Choice. Duane Baumann. LC 69-318025. (Research Papers Ser.: No. 121). 125p. 1969. pap. 12.00 (ISBN 0-89065-028-4). U Chicago Comm Geo.

Recreational Use of Wild Lands. 3rd ed. C. Frank Brockman & Lawrence C. Merriam, Jr. (M-H Series in Forest Resources). (Illus.). 1979. text ed. 42.95 (ISBN 0-07-007982-X). McGraw.

Recreational Vehicle Maintenance. Ed. by Jeff Robinson. (Illus.). 232p. pap. text ed. 8.95 (ISBN 0-89287-081-8, X930). Clymer Pub.

Recreational Vehicle Parks. (Five Hundred Ser.). 1974. pap. 2.00 (ISBN 0-685-58222-1, 501D). Natl Fire Prot.

Recreational Vehicles. National Fire Protection Association Staff. 81p. 1982. 13.50 (ISBN 0-317-63479-8, 501C-82). Natl Fire Prot.

Recreational Vehicles. (Five Hundred Ser.). 96p. 1974. pap. 3.75 (ISBN 0-685-46038-X, 501C). Natl Fire Prot.

Recreational Vehicles & Travel: A Resource Guide. Bernard Mergen. LC 84-28974. (American Popular Culture Ser.). ix, 222p. 1985. lib. bdg. 36.95 (ISBN 0-313-23672-0, MER/). Greenwood.

Recreations in Logic. D. G. Wells. LC 79-51882. (Illus., Orig.). 1980. pap. 2.50 (ISBN 0-486-23895-4). Dover.

Recreations in the Theory of Numbers. Albert H. Beiler. (Orig.). 1964. pap. 6.95 (ISBN 0-486-21096-0). Dover.

Recreations of a Literary Man. Percy Fitzgerald. 1973. Repr. of 1883 ed. 35.00 (ISBN 0-8274-0661-4). R West.

Recreations of a Southern Barrister. facs. ed. A. H. Sands. LC 75-152929. (Black Heritage Library Collection Ser.). 1859. 17.00 (ISBN 0-8369-8774-8). Ayer Co Pubs.

Recreations of an Anthologist. facs. ed. Brander Matthews. LC 67-26766. (Essay Index Reprint Ser.). 1904. 16.75 (ISBN 0-8369-0699-3). Ayer Co Pubs.

Recruit to Revolution: Adventure & Politics in Indonesia. John Coast. LC 76-179179. Repr. of 1952 ed. 29.50 (ISBN 0-404-54809-1). AMS Pr.

Recruiters Handbook. 3rd ed. Ed. by Philip Farish. 30.00 (ISBN 0-318-01037-2). Enterprise IL.

Recruiting an Elite: Admission to Harvard College. Ed. by Frank Freidel et al. (Harvard Dissertations American History & Political Science Ser.). 260p. 1988. lib. bdg. 55.00 (ISBN 0-8240-5123-8). Garland Pub.

Recruiting & Encouraging Friendship Partners. (Church O. F. Ministry Team Booklets Ser.). 23p. (Orig.). 1986. hdbk. 1.00 (ISBN 0-910796-03-3). Intl Students Inc.

Recruiting & Hiring the Computer Professional. David J. Moore. LC 86-11036. (Illus.). 320p. 1987. 32.95 (ISBN 0-442-26443-7). Van Nos Reinhold.

Recruiting & Selection Procedures, No. 146. 1988. 30.00 (ISBN 0-87179-986-3). BNA.

Recruiting & Training Volunteers. Paul Ilsley & John A. Niemi. (Adult Education Association Professional Development Ser.). (Illus.). 176p. 1981. text ed. 24.95 (ISBN 0-07-000556-7). McGraw.

Recruiting & Training Volunteers for Church & Synagogue Libraries. Lorraine E. Burson. LC 86-9682. (Guide Ser.: No. 14). 32p. 1986. pap. 5.95 (ISBN 0-915324-24-5). CSLA.

Recruiting Effective Insurance Agents. Didactic Systems Staff. (Didactic Simulation Game Ser.). 1973. pap. 24.90 (ISBN 0-89401-082-4); pap. 24.90 french ed. (ISBN 0-89401-083-2); pap. 21.50 for 2 or more (ISBN 0-685-77370-1); pap. 0.50 leader's guide (ISBN 0-685-77371-X). Didactic Syst.

Recruiting Evangelism Callers: Enlisting & Coordinating Workers. Walter A. Schmidt. 56p. (Orig.). 1984. pap. 4.95 (ISBN 0-8066-2069-2, 23-1830). Augsburg.

Recruiting Game: Toward a New System of Intercollegiate Sport. 2nd ed. John F. Rooney, Jr. LC 86-19152. xxii, 232p. 1987. 27.95x (ISBN 0-8032-3879-7); pap. 8.95 (ISBN 0-8032-8924-3, Bison). U of Nebr Pr.

Recruiting, Interviewing, Selecting & Orienting New Employees. D. Arthur. 214p. 1986. 35.00 (ISBN 0-8144-5539-5). AMACOM.

Recruiting Minority Students. NAIS Admission & Minority Affairs Committees. 1979. pap. 3.25 (ISBN 0-934338-41-8). NAIS.

Recruiting Officer. George Farquhar. Ed. by John Ross. (New Mermaids Ser.). 1977. pap. 4.95x (ISBN 0-393-90039-8). Norton.

Recruiting Officer. George Farquhar. Ed. by Michael Shugrue. LC 65-15341. (Regents Restoration Drama Ser.). xxii, 137p. 1965. 14.50x (ISBN 0-8032-0358-6); pap. 3.25xo. p. (ISBN 0-8032-5357-5, BB 253, Bison). U of Nebr Pr.

Recruiting Officer. George Farquhar. Ed. & pref. by Peter Dixon. LC 85-3124. (Revels Plays Ser.). (Illus.). 307p. 1985. 50.00 (ISBN 0-7190-1534-0, Pub. by Manchester Univ Pr); pap. 13.50 (ISBN 0-7190-1622-3, Pub. by Manchester Univ Pr). St Martin.

Recruiting Qualified Disabled Workers: An Employer's Directory to Placement Services in the Greater New York Area. Compiled by Lana Smart. LC 79-92836. 160p. 1980. 5.95 (ISBN 0-686-38815-1). Human Res Ctr.

Recruiting Superior Teachers: The Interview Process. William Goldstein. LC 85-63694. (Fastback Ser.: No. 239). 50p. (Orig.). 1986. pap. 0.90 (ISBN 0-87367-239-9). Phi Delta Kappa.

Recruiting, Training, & Compensating Attorney Staff. 38p. 1986. pap. 14.95 (ISBN 0-317-63611-1, 511-0203-01). Amer Bar Assn.

Recruiting, Training, & Compensating Attorney Staff see Corporate Law Department Series.

Recruiting, Training, & Developing Volunteer Adult Workers. John Hendee. (Illus.). 80p. 1988. wkbk. 2.95 (ISBN 0-87403-442-6, 18-88592). Standard Pub.

Recruiting, Training, & Developing Volunteer Youth Workers. David Roadcup. 1987. 9.95 (ISBN 0-87403-220-2, 88590). Standard Pub.

Recruiting, Training & Motivating Volunteer Workers. rev. ed. Arthur R. Pell. LC 71-180210. 62p. 1977. pap. 2.50 (ISBN 0-87576-038-4). Pilot Bks.

Recruiting, Training & Retaining New Employees: Managing the Transition from College to Work. Jack J. Phillips. LC 86-46332. (Management Ser.). 1987. text ed. 29.95x (ISBN 1-55542-042-7). Jossey-Bass.

Recruitment Administrators Job Survey. 25.00 (ISBN 0-318-02093-9); members 5.00 (ISBN 0-318-02094-7). NALP.

Recruitment & Selection in the Labour Market: A Comparative Study of Britain & West Germany. Paul Windolf et al. 210p. 1988. text ed. 43.00x (ISBN 0-566-00937-4, Pub. by Grower Pub England). Gower Pub Co.

Recruitment & Selection of Wholesale-Distributor Sales Personnel. Edgar S. Ellman. 1988. incl. forms 154.00. Natl Assn Wholesale Dists.

Recruitment & Selection Practices in Oklahoma Police Departments. John Pelissero. (Criminal Justice Policy & Administration Research Ser.). 47p. 1978. 3.00 (ISBN 0-686-00897-9). Univ OK Gov Res.

Recruitment & Training of Teacher Interns. Edward C. Meyers & Wendell E. Cannon. 150p. 1960. 3.95 (ISBN 0-88474-008-0). U of S Cal Pr.

Recruitment & Training of the Research Psychiatrist, Vol. 6. GAP Committee on Psychopathology. LC 62-2872. (Report No. 65). 1967. pap. 5.00 (ISBN 0-87318-090-9, Pub. by GAP). Brunner-Mazel.

Recruitment Handbook. 3rd ed. Ed. by Bernard Ungerson. 354p. 1983. text ed. 47.00x (ISBN 0-566-02192-7). Gower Pub Co.

Recruitment of Political Leaders: A Study of Citizen-Politicians. Kenneth Prewitt. LC 81-6344. (Urban Government Ser.). (Illus.). 1981. Repr. of 1970 ed. lib. bdg. 35.00x (ISBN 0-313-22744-6, PRRP). Greenwood.

Recruitment-Selection. American Society for Personnel Administration Staff. 53p. (Orig.). 1986. pap. 20.00 (ISBN 0-939900-24-6). Am Soc Personnel.

Recruitment, Selection & Training of Social Scientists. Elbridge Sibley. LC 48-9155. (Social Science Research Council Bulletin: No. 58). 1948. pap. 15.00 (ISBN 0-527-03286-7). Kraus Repr.

Recruitment, Training & Career Development in the Public Service. Report II. Joint Committee on the Public Service. Third Session, Geneva, 1983. ii, 86p. 1983. pap. 10.50 (ISBN 92-2-103336-8). Intl Labour Office.

Recruits to Labour: The British Labour Party, 1914-1931. Catherine A. Cline. LC 63-13888. 1963. 19.95x (ISBN 0-8156-2046-2). Syracuse U Pr.

Recrystallization & Grain Growth in Metals. P. Cotterill & P. R. Mould. LC 75-33874. 410p. 1976. 31.50 (ISBN 0-470-17527-3). Krieger.

Recsk - Emberek az embertelensegben (Recsk Man in Inhumanity) Zoltan Nyeste. LC 82-82973. (Tanuk Koruknol). (Illus.). 80p. 1982. pap. 6.00 (ISBN 0-910539-00-6). Hungarian Alumni.

Rectal & Anal Cancers: Conservative Treatment by Irradiation; An Alternative to Radical Surgery. Jean Papillon. (Illus.). 220p. 1982. 58.00 (ISBN 0-387-11626-5). Springer-Verlag.

Rectangles. Graham Percy. (Shape Ser.). 16p. (ps). 1986. bds. 3.95 (ISBN 0-915391-18-X, Pub by Mad Hatter Bks). Slawson Comm.

Rectangular Quilt Blocks. Jean Roesler. 136p. pap. 9.95 (ISBN 0-87069-373-5). Wallace-Homestead.

Rectangular Record. Lou Stevens. (Illus.). 44p. (Orig.). 1981. 8.95 (ISBN 0-9606222-2-5); pap. 3.95 (ISBN 0-9606222-1-7). Clone Records.

Rectification of the Birth Time. Gustav Schwickert. 176p. 1954. 5.00 (ISBN 0-86690-158-2, 1457-01). Am Fed Astrologers.

Rectified Lunar Atlas. E. A. Whitaker et al. LC 63-17721. (Photographic Lunar Atlas, Suppl: No. 2). (Illus.). 147p. 1964. 50.00x (ISBN 0-8165-0077-0). U of Ariz Pr.

Rector & the Doctor's Family. Margaret Oliphant. 208p. 1986. pap. 6.95 (ISBN 0-14-016151-1). Penguin.

Rector of Justin. Louis Auchincloss. 1980. pap. 3.95 (ISBN 0-395-29179-8). HM.

Rector of Justin. Louis Auchincloss. (Rediscovery Bks.). 352p. 1987. Repr. 9.95 (ISBN 0-940595-09-5). Hill & Co Pubs.

Rector's Daughter. F. M. Mayor. 224p. 1985. pap. 6.95 (ISBN 0-14-003575-3). Penguin.

Rectory Magazine. facsimile ed. Lewis Carroll. LC 75-37212. 128p. 1976. 12.95 (ISBN 0-292-77010-3). U of Tex Pr.

Rectory Umbrella & Mischmasch. Lewis Carroll. (Illus.). 1932. pap. 3.50 (ISBN 0-486-21345-5). Dover.

Recuecil des Cours. Academie de Droit International Staff. 1985. text ed. 53.50 (ISBN 90-247-3231-X, Pub. by Martinus Nijhoff Netherlands). Kluwer Academic.

Recueil de Chansons Pieuses Du XIIIe Siecle. Edward G. Jarnstrom. LC 80-2162. Repr. of 1910 ed. 29.50 (ISBN 0-404-19024-3). AMS Pr.

Recueil de Chansons Populaires, 6 tomes. Rolland. Set. 85.00 (ISBN 0-685-36691-X). French & Eur.

Recueil de contes populaires de la Kabylie du Djurdjura. J. Riviere. LC 78-20113. (Collection de contes et de chansons populaires: Vol. 4). Repr. of 1882 ed. 21.50 (ISBN 0-404-60354-8). AMS Pr.

Recueil de contes populaires de la Senegambie. L. J. Berenger-Feraud. LC 78-20118. (Collection de contes et de chansons populaires: Vol. 9). Repr. of 1885 ed. 21.50 (ISBN 0-404-60359-9). AMS Pr.

Recueil de Contes Populaires de la Senegambie. Laurent J. Berenger-Feraud. (Fr.). 1885. 23.00 (ISBN 0-8115-2989-4). Kraus Repr.

Recueil de contes populaires grecs. Tr. by E. Legrand. LC 78-20108. (Collection de contes et de chansons populaires: Vol. 1). Repr. of 1881 ed. 21.50 (ISBN 0-404-60351-3). AMS Pr.

Recueil de contes populaires slaves. L. Leger. LC 78-20114. (Collection de contes et de chansons populaires: Vol. 5). Repr. of 1882 ed. 21.50 (ISBN 0-404-60355-6). AMS Pr.

Recueil de Decorations Interieures, Comprenant Tout Ce Qui a l'Ameublement. C. Percier & P. F. Fontaine. 48p. 1812. Repr. text ed. 62.10x (ISBN 0-576-15146-7, Pub. by Gregg Intl Pubs England). Gregg Intl.

Recueil De Farces Francaises Inedites Du XVe Siecle. Ed. by Gustave Cohen. 1949. 20.00x (ISBN 0-910956-21-9). Medieval Acad.

Recueil de Plans d'Eglises Cisterciennes, 2 tomes. Dimier. Set. 100.75 (ISBN 0-685-34012-0). French & Eur.

Recueil de Terminologie Multilinque du Soudage et des Techniques Connexes, 18p. (Fr. & Eng., Multilinqual Collection of Welding Terminology and Terminology of Related Techniques). pap. 49.95 (ISBN 0-686-56760-9, M-6480). French & Eur.

Recueil Des Accords Internationaux Conclus Par les Cantons Suisses, Vol. 8. Yves Lejeune. (Schriften des Forschungsinstituts fur Foderalismus und Regionalstrukturen). 500p. (Fr.). 1982. 47.35 (ISBN 3-261-04736-4). P Lang Pubs.

Recueil des Cours, Vol. 200. Ed. by Academic de Droit International. 1988. lib. bdg. 79.50 (ISBN 90-247-3644-7, Pub. by Martinus Nijhoff Netherlands). Kluwer Academic.

Recueil des Cours. Academie de Droit. 1986. lib. bdg. 62.50 (ISBN 90-247-3373-1, Pub. by Martinus Nijhoff Netherlands). Kluwer Academic.

Recueil des Cours. Academie de Droit International Staff. 1986. lib. bdg. 62.50 (ISBN 90-247-3323-5, Pub. by Martinus Nijhoff Netherlands). Kluwer Academic.

Recueil des Cours. Academie De droit. 1986. lib. bdg. 75.00 (ISBN 90-247-3336-7, Pub. by Martinus Nijhoff Netherlands). Kluwer Academic.

Recueil des Cours, Vol. 194. Ed. by Academic de Droit International. 1988. lib. bdg. 72.50 (ISBN 90-247-3636-6, Pub. by Martinus Nijhoff Netherlands). Kluwer Academic.

Recueil Des Cours De La'academie De Droit International De la Haye: Collected Courses of the Hague Academy of International Law, Vol. 152 (1976-iv) F. Durante et al. 478p. 1980. 40.00x (ISBN 90-286-0590-8, Pub. by Sijthoff & Noordhoff). Kluwer Academic.

Recueil Des Cours De L'academie De Droit International De la Haye-Collected Courses of the Hague Academy of International Law: General Index to Volumes 126 to 151. 1980. 40.00 (ISBN 90-286-0630-0, Pub. by Sijthoff & Noordhoff). Kluwer Academic.

Recueil Des Cours De L'academie De Droit International De la Haye: Collected Courses of the Hague Academy of Int'l Law, Vol. 156 (1977-III) T. Ansay et al. 482p. 1980. 40.00x (ISBN 90-286-0600-9, Sijthoff & Noordhoff). Kluwer Academic.

Recueil Des Cours L'academie De Droit International De la Haye: Collected Courses of the Hague Academy of Int'l Law, Vol. 162 (1979-i) E. Vitta & I. Brownlie. 1980. 40.00x (ISBN 90-286-0530-4, Pub. by Sijthoff & Noordhoff). Kluwer Academic.

Red & Green: The New Politics of the Environment. Joe Weston. Ed. by Neil Middleton. 192p. 1986. pap. 9.50 (ISBN 0-7453-0147-9, Pub. by Pluto Pr). Longwood Pub Group.
Red & Hot: The Fate of Jazz in the Soviet Union. S. Frederick Starr. LC 85-18171. 392p. 1985. pap. 9.95 (ISBN 0-87910-026-5). Limelight Edns.
Red & Hot: The Fate of Jazz in the Soviet Union, 1917-1980. S. Frederick Starr. (Illus.). 1983. 21.95 (ISBN 0-19-503163-6). Oxford U Pr.
Red & the Black see also Scarlet & the Black.
Red & the Black. Stendhal. Tr. by Lloyd C. Parks. (Illus., Orig.). 1970. pap. 3.95 (ISBN 0-451-51793-8, CE1793, Sig Classics). NAL.
Red & the Black. Stendhal. Tr. by C. K. Moncrieff. LC 84-4612. 633p. 1984. 9.95 (ISBN 0-394-60511-X). Modern Lib.
Red & the Black Notes. D. L. Gobert. (Orig.). 1967. pap. 3.95 (ISBN 0-8220-1111-5). Cliffs.
Red & the Blue: A Study in Treason & Intelligence. Andrew Sinclair. 1987. 17.95 (ISBN 0-316-79237-3). Little.
Red & the Green. Richard Dimitt. (Illus., Orig.). (ps-3). 1.75 (ISBN 0-8198-0131-3). Dghtrs St Paul.
Red & the Green. Iris Murdoch. 288p. 1988. pap. 6.95 (ISBN 0-14-002756-4). Penguin.
Red & the White: History of Wine in France & Italy in the 19th Century. Leo Loubere. LC 78-2304. (Illus.). 401p. 1978. 52.50 (ISBN 0-87395-370-3). State U NY Pr.
Red & White: Indian Views of the White Man, 1492-1982. Annette Rosenstiel. LC 82-23901. (Illus.). 192p. 1983. 14.95x (ISBN 0-87663-657-1). Universe.
Red & White on the New York Frontier: A Struggle for Survival, Insights from the Papers of Erastus Granger, Indian Agent, 1807-1819. Charles M. Snyder. LC 78-14239. (Illus.). 1978. 9.50 (ISBN 0-916346-28-5). Harbor Hill Bks.
Red Apache Sun. Robert E. Mills. (Kansan Ser.: No. 3). 1981. pap. 1.95 (ISBN 0-8439-0877-7, Leisure Bks). Leisure NY.
Red Ape: Orang-utans & Human Origins. Jeffrey H. Schwartz. (Illus.). 352p. 1987. 18.95 (ISBN 0-395-38017-0). HM.
Red Are the Embers. Guanetta Gordon. LC 83-66878. 159p. 1980. 8.50 (ISBN 0-8233-0317-9). Golden Quill.
Red Armour. R. E. Simpkin. (Brassey Bk.). 200p. 1984. text ed. 37.00 (ISBN 0-08-028341-1). Pergamon.
Red Army. E. Wollenberg. Tr. by Claud W. Sykes from Ger. LC 73-860. (Russian Studies: Perspectives on the Revolution Ser). 401p. 1973. Repr. of 1940 ed. 30.25 (ISBN 0-88355-056-3). Hyperion Conn.
Red Army & Society: A Sciology of the Soviet Military. Ellen Jones. 230p. 1986. pap. text ed. 14.95x (ISBN 0-04-497016-1). Unwin Hyman.
Red Army & Society: A Sociology of the Soviet Military. Ellen Jones. LC 84-12336. 280p. 1985. text ed. 34.95x (ISBN 0-04-322011-8). Unwin Hyman.
Red Army in Kiangsi: 1931-1934. Peter Donovan. LC 77-376348. (East Asia Papers: No. 10). 216p. 1976. 6.00 (ISBN 0-939657-10-4). Cornell East Asia Pgm.
Red Army Microcosm. Walter S. Dunn. 1985. pap. 3.00 (ISBN 0-317-19915-3). Intl Inst Adv Stud.
Red Army of China. Edgar O'Ballance. 232p. 1962. 80.00x (ISBN 0-317-69444-8, Pub. by Han-Shan Tang Ltd). State Mutual Bk.
Red Army on Pakistan's Border: Policy Implications for the United States. Ed. by T. L. Eliot & R. L. Pfaltzgraff. (IFPA Foreign Policy Reports: No. 8). 100p. 1986. pap. 9.95 (ISBN 0-08-034487-9, PDP). Pergamon.
Red Army Order of Battle: In the Great Patriotic War. Robert G. Poirier & Albert Z. Conner. 416p. 1985. 22.50 (ISBN 0-89141-237-9). Presidio Pr.
Red Army Order of Battle, 1941-1945. LC 83-81813. 200p. 1983. 13.95 (ISBN 0-941052-66-4, 66); pap. 9.95 (ISBN 0-941052-11-7, 16). Valor Pub.
Red Army Resurgent. John Shaw. LC 79-21867. (World War II Ser.). (gr. 7 up). 22.60 (ISBN 0-8094-2519-X, Pub. by Time-Life). Silver.
Red Army Resurgent. John Shaw. Ed. by Time-Life Books. (World War II Ser.). (Illus.). 1980. 14.95 (ISBN 0-8094-2518-1). Time-Life.
Red Army: The Red Army 1918-1945; The Soviet Army 1946 to the Present. Basil H. Liddell-Hart. (Illus.). 13.25 (ISBN 0-8446-0774-6). Peter Smith.
Red Arrow: The First Hundred Years. Ronald DeGraw. Ed. by Mac Sebree. (Interubans Special Ser.: 96). (Illus.). 160p. 1985. 31.95 (ISBN 0-916374-67-X). Interurban.
Red as Blood. Tanith Lee. 208p. 1986. pap. 2.50 (ISBN 0-87997-790-6). DAW Bks.
Red Badge of Courage. Stephen Crane. (Airmont Classics Ser.). (gr. 7 up). 1964. pap. 1.75 (ISBN 0-8049-0003-5, CL-3). Airmont.
Red Badge of Courage. Stephen Crane. (Literature Ser). (gr. 7-12). 1969. pap. text ed. 6.92 (ISBN 0-87720-712-7). AMSCO Sch.
Red Badge of Courage. Stephen Crane. 160p. (Orig.). (gr. 7-12). 1981. pap. 1.50 (ISBN 0-553-21011-4, Bantam Classics). Bantam.
Red Badge of Courage. Stephen Crane. LC 69-13318. (Merrill Standard Ser). 1975. 6.00x (ISBN 0-910294-29-1); pap. 4.00x (ISBN 0-910294-30-5). Brown Bk.
Red Badge of Courage. Stephen Crane. LC 42-36053. 251p. 1942. 6.95 (ISBN 0-394-60493-8); pap. 4.00. Modern Lib.
Red Badge of Courage. Stephen Crane. (Modern Library College Editions). 1951. pap. write for info (T45, RanC). Random.
Red Badge of Courage. Stephen Crane. Ed. by Irwin Shapiro. LC 73-75464. (Now Age Illustrated Ser.). (Illus.). 64p. (Orig.). (gr. 5-10). 1973. 7.50 (ISBN 0-88301-214-6); pap. 2.95 (ISBN 0-88301-101-8). Pendulum Pr.
Red Badge of Courage. Stephen Crane. Adapted by Betty R. Wright. LC 81-2611. (Short Classics Ser.). (Illus.). 48p. (gr. 4 up). 1981. PLB 15.99 (ISBN 0-8172-1670-7). Raintree Pubs.
Red Badge of Courage. rev. ed. Stephen Crane. Ed. by Robert J. Dixson. (American Classics Ser.: Bk. 10). (gr. 9 up). 1974. pap. text ed. 4.75 (ISBN 0-13-024605-0, 18129); cassettes 55.00 (ISBN 0-13-024795-2, 58235). Prentice ESL.
Red Badge of Courage. Stephen Crane. 180p. (gr. 7-12). 1972. pap. 2.25 (ISBN 0-590-02117-6); tchr's. guide 1.25 (ISBN 0-590-40678-7). Scholastic Inc.
Red Badge of Courage. Stephen Crane. LC 67-26616. 1967. Repr. of 1894 ed. 25.00x (ISBN 0-8201-1010-8). Schol Facsimiles.
Red Badge of Courage. Stephen Crane. Ed. by Harry Shefter. (Enriched Classics Edition Ser.). 224p. pap. 2.95 (ISBN 0-671-50132-1). WSP.
Red Badge of Courage. Stephen Crane. Adapted by Betty R. Wright. LC 81-2611. (Short Classics Ser.). (Illus.). 48p. (gr. 4-12). 1983. pap. 9.27 (ISBN 0-8172-2019-4). Raintree Pubs.
Red Badge of Courage. Stephen Crane. 134p. 1983. pap. text ed. 3.95x (ISBN 0-460-01309-2, Pub. by Evman England). Biblio Dist.
Red Badge of Courage. Stephen Crane. Ed. by Henry Binder. 192p. 1983. pap. 6.95 (ISBN 0-380-64113-5, 64113). Avon.
Red Badge of Courage. Stephen Crane. 11.95 (ISBN 0-89190-118-3, Pub. by Am Repr). Amereon Ltd.
Red Badge of Courage. Stephen Crane. LC 86-45561. (Running Press Classics Ser.). 160p. 1986. lib. bdg. 12.90 (ISBN 0-89471-483-X); pap. 3.95 (ISBN 0-89471-482-1). Running Pr.
Red Badge of Courage. Stephen Crane. (Puffin Classics Ser.). 1987. pap. 2.25 (ISBN 0-14-035055-1, Puffin Bks). Penguin.
Red Badge of Courage. Stephen Crane. Ed. by Henry Binder. 208p. 1987. pap. 2.95 (ISBN 0-380-70432-3). Avon.
Red Badge of Courage see Four Classic American Novels.
Red Badge of Courage see Prose & Poetry.
Red Badge of Courage: A Facsimile of the Manuscript. Ed. by Fredson Bowers. 1973. deluxe ed. 175.00 boxed (ISBN 0-89723-035-3). Bruccoli.
Red Badge of Courage: An Annotated Text with Critical Essays. rev. ed. Stephen Crane. (Norton Critical Editors Ser.). 1976. pap. 6.95x (ISBN 0-393-09182-1, NortonC). Norton.
Red Badge of Courage: An Episode of the American Civil War. Stephen Crane. Ed. by Henry Binder. (Norton Critical Edition Ser.). 1982. 14.95 (ISBN 0-393-01345-6). Norton.
Red Badge of Courage: An Episode of the American Civil War. Stephen Crane, Jr. (Penguin American Library). 162p. 1983. pap. 2.95 (ISBN 0-14-039021-9). Penguin.
Red Badge of Courage & Other Favorites. Stephen Crane. LC 80-54131. (Silver Burdett Classics for Kids Ser.). 288p. (gr. 6 up). 1985. pap. 3.67 (ISBN 0-382-09990-7). Silver.
Red Badge of Courage & Other Writings. Stephen Crane. Ed. by Richard Chase. (YA) (gr. 9 up). 1960. pap. 6.95 (ISBN 0-395-05143-6, RivEd). HM.
Red Badge of Courage & Selected Stories. Stephen Crane. 224p. (RL 7). 1952. pap. 1.50 (ISBN 0-451-51592-7, CW1592, Sig Classics). NAL.
Red Badge of Courage by Stephen Crane. 48p. (Orig.). 1987. pap. 9.95 (ISBN 1-55651-777-7); cassette (ISBN 1-55651-778-5). Cram Cassettes.
Red Badge of Courage (Crane) Dixler. (Book Notes Ser.). 1984. pap. 2.50 (ISBN 0-8120-3438-4). Barron.
Red Badge of Courage Notes. J. M. Lybyer. (Orig.). 1964. pap. 3.25 (ISBN 0-8220-1120-4). Cliffs.
Red Badge of Courage: Redefining the Hero. Donald B. Gibson. (Twayne's Masterwork Studies: Vol. 15). 112p. 1988. lib. bdg. 16.95 (ISBN 0-8057-7961-2, Twayne). G K Hall.
Red Badge of Courage: Redefining the Hero. Donald B. Gibson. (Twayne's Masterwork Studies: Vol. 15). 112p. 1988. lib. bdg. 6.95 (ISBN 0-8057-8014-9, Twayne). G K HAll.
Red Badge of Courage: Student Activity Book. Marcia Sohl & Gerald Dackerman. (Now Age Illustrated Ser.). (Illus.). 16p. (gr. 4-10). 1976. pap. 1.25 (ISBN 0-88301-184-0). Pendulum Pr.
Red Badge of Courage, with Reader's Guide. Stephen Crane. (AMSCO Literature Program). (gr. 9-12). 1971. text ed. 11.58 (ISBN 0-87720-837-9); pap. text ed. 7.83 (ISBN 0-87720-811-5); tchr's. ed. 8.16 (ISBN 0-87720-911-1). AMSCO Sch.
Red Baker. Robert Ward. 1986. pap. 5.95 (ISBN 0-671-61747-8). WSP.
Red Balloon. Albert Lamorisse. LC 57-9229. (Illus.). 45p. (gr. 3-7). 1967. pap. 13.95 (ISBN 0-385-00343-9). Doubleday.
Red Balloon. Albert Lamorisse. LC 57-9229. (Illus.). (gr. 3-6). 1978. pap. 5.95 (ISBN 0-385-14297-8, Zephyr BFYR). Doubleday.
Red Baron. Richard A. Boning. (Incredible Ser.). (Illus.). 1975. 7.95 (ISBN 0-87966-111-9). B Loft.
Red Beans & Rice: Recipes for Lesbian Health & Wisdom. Bode Noonan. LC 86-4175. (Feminist Ser.). (Illus.). 78p. (Orig.). 1986. 17.95 (ISBN 0-89594-195-3); pap. 5.95 (ISBN 0-89594-194-5). Crossing Pr.
Red Beans & Ricely Yours. Christopher Blake. 1974. pap. 2.50 (ISBN 0-317-11781-5). Southern U Pr.
Red Beret: The Story of the Parachute Regiment at War 1940-45. 19th ed. Hilary Saunders. (Airborne Ser.). 336p. 1985. 19.95 (ISBN 0-89839-087-7). Battery Pr.
Red Bird of Ireland. Sondra G. Langford. LC 82-13897. 192p. (gr. 4-7). 1983. 10.95 (ISBN 0-689-50270-2, M K McElderry). Macmillan.
Red Blood Cell, 2 vols. 2nd ed. Ed. by Douglas N. Surgenor. Vol. 1, 1974. 113.00 (ISBN 0-12-677201-0); Vol. 2, 1975. 113.00 (ISBN 0-12-677202-9). Acad Pr.
Red Blood Cell & Lens Metabolism. Satish K. Srivastava. (Developments in Biochemistry: Vol. 9). 508p. 1980. 108.00 (ISBN 0-444-00388-6, Biomedical Pr). Elsevier.
Red Blood Cell Substitutes. Chang & Geyer. 486p. 1988. 99.75 (ISBN 0-8247-8027-2). Dekker.
Red Blood Cells As Carriers for Drugs: Potential Therapeutic Applications. Ed. by C. Ropars et al. (Illus.). 272p. 1987. 94.00 (ISBN 0-08-036137-4). Pergamon.
Red Blood Cells As Carriers for Drugs. Ed. by DeLoach et al. (Bibliotheca Haematologica Ser.: No. 51). (Illus.). viii, 162p. 1985. 69.50 (ISBN 3-8055-3940-1). S Karger.
Red Blood Cells of Domestic Animals. Ed. by N. S. Agar & P. G. Board. xviii, 420p. 1983. 203.75 (ISBN 0-444-80455-2). Elsevier.
Red, Blue, Yellow Shoe. Tana Hoban. LC 86-3095. (Illus.). 12p. (ps). 1986. pap. 3.95 (ISBN 0-688-06563-5). Greenwillow.
Red Book of Animal Stories. Ed. by Andrew Lang. LC 72-184815. (Illus.). (gr. 5-10). 1972. pap. 7.25 (ISBN 0-8048-1029-X). C E Tuttle.
Red Book of Appin. Ethan A. Hitchcock. 15.00 (ISBN 0-89314-413-4). Philos Res.
Red Book of Hob Stories. William Mayne. LC 83-15125. (Illus.). 32p. (gr. k-4). 1984. 7.95 (ISBN 0-399-21047-4, Philomel). Putnam Pub Group.
Red Book of Marine Engineering Questions & Answers, Vol. 1: Third & Second Assistant Engineers. 4th ed. William B. Paterson. LC 76-153141. (Illus.). 1972. pap. 15.00x (ISBN 0-87033-088-8). Cornell Maritime.
Red Book of Marine Engineering Questions & Answers, Vol. 2: First Assistant & Chief Engineer. 4th ed. William B. Paterson. LC 76-153141. (Illus.). 1973. pap. 15.00x (ISBN 0-87033-089-6). Cornell Maritime.
Red Book of Ophthalmology 1985. LC 15-6770. 313p. 1985. 50.00 (ISBN 0-87873-060-5). Prof Pr Bks NYC.
Red Book of Opthalmology, 1987-1988. Ed. by Book Research Department, Professional Press Books. 300p. 1987. pap. 60.00 (ISBN 0-87873-074-5). Prof Pr Bks NYC.
Red Book of the Exchequer, 3 vols. Ed. by Hubert Hall. (Rolls Ser.: No. 99). Repr. of 1896 ed. 132.00 (ISBN 0-8115-1178-2). Kraus Repr.
Red Book of the U. S. S. R. (Krasnaya Kniga SSSR) 460p. 1978. 70.00x (Pub. by Collets (UK)). State Mutual Bk.
Red Book on Transportation of Hazardous Materials. 2nd ed. Lawrence W. Bierlein. LC 86-32558. 800p. 1987. 96.95 (ISBN 0-442-21044-2). Van Nos Reinhold.
Red Box. 1987. 15.00 (ISBN 0-86319-043-X, Pub. by New Playwrights Network). State Mutual Bk.
Red Brand. Charles A. Seltzer. 1976. Repr. of 1929 ed. lib. bdg. 18.95x (ISBN 0-88411-116-4, Pub. by Aeonian Pr). Amereon Ltd.
Red Bread: Collectivization in a Russian Village. Maurice Hindus. LC 88-45100. 400p. (Orig.). 1988. 29.95 (ISBN 0-253-34953-2); pap. 12.50 (ISBN 0-253-20485-2). Ind U Pr.
Red Brick Three Flat. Henry Kranz. 72p. (Orig.). 1985. pap. 3.95 (ISBN 0-942582-09-8). Erie St Pr.
Red Brother. R. Ray Baker. 1927. 5.00x (ISBN 0-685-21799-X). Wahr.
Red Bud Women-Four Dramatic Episodes. Mark Odea. LC 76-40391. (One-Act Plays in Reprint Ser.). 1976. 15.00x (ISBN 0-8486-2006-2). Roth Pub Inc.
Red Butterfly: Lupus Patients Can Survive. 2nd ed. Linda R. Bell. (Illus.). 1988. pap. 5.95 (ISBN 0-8283-1880-8). Branden Pub Co.
Red Cabin Cookbook. Pat Harris. (Illus.). 128p. (Orig.). 1981. pap. 8.95 (ISBN 0-939688-05-0). Directed Media.
Red Calypso. Geoffrey Wagner. 1988. pap. 12.95 (ISBN 0-89526-773-X). Regnery Gateway.
Red Capitalism: An Analysis of the Navajo Economy. Kent Gilbreath. LC 72-12547. pap. 41.80 (ISBN 0-317-29296-X, 2055512). Bks Demand UMI.
Red Car Days: Pacific Electric Memories. Raphael Long. Ed. by Jim Walker. (Special Ser.: No. 90). (Illus.). 64p. 1983. pap. 11.95 (ISBN 0-916374-63-7). Interurban.
Red Carnation. V. Morazova. 232p. 1981. 7.00 (ISBN 0-8285-2024-0, Pub. by Progress Pubs USSR). Imported Pubns.
Red Carpet. Rex Parkin. LC 88-5192. (Illus.). 48p. (gr. k-3). 1988. PLB 14.95 (ISBN 0-02-770010-0). Macmillan.
Red Cedar Warrior. S. J. Brito. 86p. (Orig.). 1987. pap. text ed. 9.50 (ISBN 0-936204-50-8). Jelm Mtn.
Red Cell. Ed. by George J. Brewer. LC 78-71. (Progress in Clinical & Biological Research Ser.: Vol. 21). 782p. 1978. 82.00 (ISBN 0-8451-0021-1). A R Liss.
Red Cell Antigens & Antibodies. Ed. by George Garratty. LC 86-22325. 1986. text ed. 19.00 (ISBN 0-915355-32-9). Am Assn Blood.
Red Cell Deformability & Filterability. Ed. by J. A. Dormandy. (Developments in Hematology & Immunology Ser.). 1983. lib. bdg. 40.00 (ISBN 0-89838-578-4, Pub. by Martinus Nijhoff Netherlands). Kluwer Academic.
Red Cell: Fifth Ann Arbor Conference. Ed. by George J. Brewer. LC 81-2653. (Progress in Clinical & Biological Research Ser.: Vol. 55). 840p. 1981. 86.00 (ISBN 0-8451-0055-6). A R Liss.
Red Cell Manual. 5th ed. Robert S. Hillman & Clement A. Finch. LC 85-6796. 162p. 1985. pap. text ed. 11.95 (ISBN 0-8036-4634-8). Davis Co.
Red Cell Membranes: A Methodological Approach. J. C. Ellory & T. Young. (Biological Techniques Ser.). 1982. 69.00 (ISBN 0-12-237140-2). Acad Pr.
Red Cell Metabolism: A Manual of Biochemical Methods. 3rd ed. Ernest Beutler. 208p. 1984. 29.50 (ISBN 0-8089-1672-6, 790582). Grune.
Red Cell: Production, Metabolism, Destruction, Normal & Abnormal. rev. ed. John W. Harris & Robert Kellermeyer. (Commonwealth Fund Publications Ser). 1970. pap. 15.00x (ISBN 0-674-75102-7). Harvard U Pr.
Red Cell Rheology. Ed. by M. Bessis et al. (Illus.). 1978. pap. 68.00 (ISBN 0-387-09001-0). Springer-Verlag.
Red Cell Shape: Physiology, Pathology, Ultrastructure. Ed. by M. Bessis et al. LC 73-77351. (Illus.). 180p. 1973. 35.00 (ISBN 0-387-06257-2). Springer-Verlag.
Red Cell: Sixth Ann Arbor Conference. George J. Brewer. (Progress in Clinical & Biological Research Ser.: Vol. 165). 608p. 1984. 95.00 (ISBN 0-8451-5015-4). A R Liss.
Red Center. Frederick Nolan. 256p. 1987. 15.95 (ISBN 0-312-00179-7). St Martin.
Red Center. Frederick Nolan. 1988. pap. 3.95 (ISBN 0-312-90961-6). St Martin.
Red Chameleon. Stuart Kaminsky. 240p. 1986. pap. 3.50 (ISBN 0-441-71086-7, Pub. by Charter Bks). Ace Bks.
Red Child, White Child: The Strange Disappearance of Casper Partridge. William C. Haygood. (Wisconsin Stories Ser.). (Illus.). 146p. 1979. pap. 1.75 (ISBN 0-87020-185-9). State Hist Soc Wis.
Red Children in White America. Ann H. Beuf. LC 76-49737. 168p. 1977. 19.95x (ISBN 0-8122-7719-8). U of Pa Pr.
Red China in Prophecy. Gordon Lindsay. (Prophecy Ser.). 2.25 (ISBN 0-89985-059-6). Christ Nations.
Red China Today: The Other Side of the River. rev ed. Edgar Snow. (Illus.). 1971. 25.00 (ISBN 0-394-46261-0). Random.
Red China's Fighting Hordes: A Realistic Account of the Chinese Communist Army by a U. S. Army Officer. Robert B. Rigg. LC 70-138177. (Illus.). 378p. 1971. Repr. of 1951 ed. lib. bdg. 35.00x (ISBN 0-8371-5634-3, RIRC). Greenwood.
Red Christmas. Patrick Ruell. 176p. 1987. pap. 3.50 (ISBN 0-445-40642-9). Mysterious Pr.
Red City: Limoges & the French Nineteenth Century. John M. Merriman. (Illus.). 1985. 32.00x (ISBN 0-19-503590-9). Oxford U Pr.
Red City: Limoges & the French Nineteenth Century. John M. Merriman. (Illus.). 336p. 1989. pap. 10.95 (ISBN 0-19-505682-5). Oxford U Pr.
Red Clay. Myldred Hutchins. (Illus.). 132p. 1981. 5.95 (ISBN 0-87797-075-0). Cherokee.
Red Clay & Early Morning Sunshine. John J. Hladczuk. LC 79-84246. 1979. 5.95 (ISBN 0-87212-101-1). Libra.
Red Cloud & the Sioux Problem. James C. Olson. LC 65-10048. (Illus.). xii, 385p. 1965. 28.95x (ISBN 0-8032-0136-2); (Bison). U of Nebr Pr.
Red Cloud: Sioux War Chief. Virginia F. Voight. LC 74-20884. (Indians Ser.). (Illus.). 80p. (gr. 2-5). 1975. PLB 6.69 (ISBN 0-8116-6611-5). Garrard.
Red Cloud's Folk: A History of the Oglala Sioux Indians. George E. Hyde. LC 76-360988. (Civilization of the American Indian Ser.: Vol. 15). (Illus.). 352p. (Orig.). 1984. pap. 9.95 (ISBN 0-8061-1520-3). U of Okla Pr.
Red Colobus Monkey. Thomas T. Struhsaker. LC 74-21339. (Wildlife Behavior & Ecology Ser.). (Illus.). xiv, 312p. 1976. 30.00x (ISBN 0-226-77769-3). U of Chicago Pr.

Red Ice. Nicholas Barker & Anthony Masters. 256p. 1987. 16.95 (ISBN 0-312-01079-6, Pub. by Thomas Dunne Bks). St Martin.

Red Ink II: A Guide to Understanding the Continuing Deficit Dilemma. Alfred J. Watkins. LC 87-36000. 120p. (Orig.). 1988. 16.95 (ISBN 0-8191-6838-6, Pub. by Hamilton Pr Roosevelt); pap. 5.95 (ISBN 0-8191-6839-4, Pub. by Hamilton Pr Roosevelt). U Pr of Amer.

Red Insurrection in Finland in 1918: A Study Based on Documentary Evidence. H. Soderhjelm. Tr. by Anne I. Fausboll. LC 75-39063. (Russian Studies: Perspectives on the Revolution Ser.). 159p. 1976. Repr. of 1919 ed. 17.60 (ISBN 0-88355-443-7). Hyperion Conn.

Red Is My Favorite Color. Phyllis Halloran. (Illus., Orig.). (gr. k up). 1988. pap. 8.95 (ISBN 0-943867-01-0). Reading Inc.

Red Is the Port Light. Joseph Tomelty. 232p. 1983. pap. 5.95 (ISBN 0-85640-299-0, Pub. by Blackstaff Pr). Longwood Pub Group.

Red Is the River. T. V. Olsen. 416p. (Orig.). 1983. pap. 3.50 (ISBN 0-449-12407-X, GM). Fawcett.

Red Is the Valley. Wayne Overholser. 160p. 1988. pap. 2.75 (ISBN 0-380-70680-6). Avon.

Red Jack. Greenberg et al. 1988. pap. 3.95 (ISBN 0-88677-315-6). DAW Bks.

Red Jack's Daughter. Edith Layton. (Regency Romance Ser.). 1986. pap. 2.50 (ISBN 0-451-14488-0, Sig). NAL.

Red Jasmine. Inglis Fletcher. (Albemarle Ser.). 320p. 1976. Repr. of 1932 ed. lib. bdg. 21.95x (ISBN 0-89244-012-0). Queens Hse-Focus Serv.

Red Jenny: A Life with Karl Marx. H. F. Peters. (Illus.). 208p. 1987. 14.95 (ISBN 0-312-00005-7). St Martin.

Red Knife Valley see Confessions of the Barbarian.

Red Knight of Germany: The Story of Baron Von Richthofen, Germany's Great War Bird. Floyd Gibbons. Ed. by James Gilbert. LC 79-7256. (Flight: Its First Seventy-Five Years Ser.). (Illus.). 1979. Repr. of 1927 ed. lib. bdg. 28.50x (ISBN 0-405-12167-9). Ayer Co Pubs.

Red Lady. Katharine N. Burt. Bd. with Hidden Creek. 1979. pap. 2.50 (ISBN 0-451-11596-1, AE1596, Sig). NAL.

Red Lake Court of Indian Offenses: Management Audit. National Center for State Courts Staff. 52p. 1982. manuscript 3.12 (NCRO, T/A-508). Natl Ctr St Courts.

Red Lake Court of Tribal Offenses Court Manual. National Center for State Courts Staff. 450p. (On loan through the NCSC Library). 1982. write for info. (NCRO-067). Natl Ctr St Courts.

Red Lake of the Heart. Mary Logue. (Orig.). 1987. pap. 3.95 (ISBN 0-440-17248-9). Dell.

Red Lamp. Mary R. Rinehart. 336p. 1987. pap. 3.50 (ISBN 0-8217-2017-1). Zebra.

Red Lamp of Incest: An Enquiry into the Origins of Mind & Society. Robin Fox. LC 83-16686. 284p. 1983. pap. text ed. 7.95 (ISBN 0-268-01620-8). U of Notre Dame Pr.

Red Leaves in the Air. Peggy Lyles. 20p. 1979. 7.00 (ISBN 0-913719-38-2); pap. 2.00 (ISBN 0-913719-37-4). High-Coo Pr.

Red Letter Alphabet Book. Ellen Gould. (Illus.). 29p. (gr. k up). 1983. pap. 7.00 (ISBN 0-938017-00-4). Learn Tools.

Red Letter Days. Molly Keane & Snaffles. (Illus.). 96p. 1988. 29.95 (ISBN 0-233-98159-4, Pub. by A Deutsch England). David & Charles.

Red Letter Days. Mekeel McBride. (Poetry Ser.). 1988. 14.95 (ISBN 0-88748-064-0); pap. 7.95 (ISBN 0-88748-065-9). Carnegie Mellon.

Red Letter Days of Samuel Pepys. E. F. Allen. 59.95 (ISBN 0-8490-0937-5). Gordon Pr.

Red Letter Days of Samuel Pepys. Edward F. Allen. 1910. Repr. 15.00 (ISBN 0-8274-3257-7). R West.

Red Letter Nights. James Agate. LC 71-91886. Repr. of 1944 ed. 22.00 (ISBN 0-405-08193-6, Pub. by Blom). Ayer Co Pubs.

Red-Letter Poems: By English Men & Women. facsimile ed. LC 71-167480. (Granger Index Reprint Ser.). Repr. of 1885 ed. 25.00 (ISBN 0-8369-6285-0). Ayer Co Pubs.

Red Level Teacher: Word Attack & Study Skills. 2nd ed. Chicago Board of Education Staff. (Chicago Mastery Learning Reading Ser.). 643p. (gr. 1). 1982. 20.00 (ISBN 0-88106-009-7, 1220). Mastery Ed.

Red Level Word Attack & Study Skills. 2nd ed. Chicago Board of Education Staff. (Chicago Mastery Learning Reading Ser.: Bk. 1). 199p. (gr. 1). 1982. 2.00 (ISBN 0-88106-007-0, 1121). Mastery Ed.

Red Light, Green Light. Dovie D. Sweet. 40p. 1988. Repr. of 1978 ed. 5.00 (ISBN 0-913211-51-6, Am Liberty Pub). Jackson Assocs.

Red Light, Green Light Learning Games. Eunice Magos & Esther Hornnes. Ed. by Ellen Sussman. (Illus.). 48p. (Orig.). (ps-1). 1985. 5.95 (ISBN 0-933606-41-9, 639). Monkey Sisters.

Red Light, Green Light: The Life of Garrett Morgan & His Invention of the Stoplight. Dovie D. Sweet. (gr. k-4). 1978. 5.00 (ISBN 0-682-49088-1). Exposition-Phoenix.

Red Light, Red Light. Harold Schofield. 416p. 1988. pap. 4.95 (ISBN 0-8125-0881-5, Dist. by St Martin's Pr & Warner Pub Servs). Tor Bks.

Red-Light Victim. Lawrence Kinsley. (Orig.). 1981. pap. 2.50 (ISBN 0-505-51649-7, Pub. by Tower Bks). Leisure NY.

Red Lights Out: A Legal History of Prostitution, Disorderly Houses & Vice Districts, 1870-1917. Thomas C. Mackey. Ed. by Harold Hyman & Stuart Bruchey. (American Legal & Constitutional History Ser.). 330p. 1987. lib. bdg. 40.00 (ISBN 0-8240-8286-9). Garland Pub.

Red Lights: Selected Tanka Sequences from Shakko. Mokichi Saito. Tr. by Seishi Shinoda & Sanford Goldstein. (Illus.). 308p. 1988. pap. 19.75 (ISBN 0-911198-90-3). Purdue U Pr.

Red Limit Freeway. John De Chancie. 288p. 1987. pap. 2.95 (ISBN 0-441-71123-5, Pub. by Charter Bks). Ace Bks.

Red Limit: The Search for the Edge of the Universe. rev. ed. Timothy Ferris. LC 83-3068. (Illus.). 288p. 1983. pap. 10.95 (ISBN 0-688-01836-X, Quill NY). Morrow.

Red Lion: A Persian Story. Diane Wolkstein. LC 77-3963. (gr. k-3). 1977. (Crowell Jr Bks); PLB 11.89 (ISBN 0-690-01347-7). HarpJ.

Red Love. Aleksandra M. Kollontai. LC 72-90296. (Soviet Literature in English Translation Ser.). 286p. 1973. Repr. of 1927 ed. 21.65 (ISBN 0-88355-007-5). Hyperion Conn.

Red Mack Truck Massacre. Luana Luther. (Illus.). 64p. (Orig.). 1981. pap. 4.75 (ISBN 0-939470-00-4). Syder Pr.

Red Magician. Lisa Goldstein. (Orig.). 1983. pap. 2.50 (ISBN 0-671-49907-6, Timescape). PB.

Red Man in the United States. Gustavus E. Lindquist. LC 68-56243. (Illus.). 1973. Repr. of 1923 ed. lib. bdg. 45.00x (ISBN 0-678-00798-5). Kelley.

Red Man's America: A History of Indians in the United States. rev. ed. Ruth M. Underhill. LC 79-171345. (Illus.). 398p. 1971. pap. 12.95 (ISBN 0-226-84165-0, P437, Phoen). U of Chicago Pr.

Red Man's America: A History of the Indians in the United States. rev. ed. Ruth M. Underhill. LC 79-171345. (Illus.). 1971. 25.00X (ISBN 0-226-84164-2). U of Chicago Pr.

Red Man's Continent. Ellsworth Huntington. 1919. 8.50x (ISBN 0-686-83728-2). Elliots Bks.

Red Man's Continent see Chronicles of America.

Red Man's Religion: Beliefs & Practices of the Indians North of Mexico. Ruth M. Underhill. LC 65-24985. 1972. pap. 10.95x (ISBN 0-226-84167-7, P481, Phoen). U of Chicago Pr.

Red Market: Industrial Co-operation & Specialisation in Comecon. Vladimir Sobell. LC 83-16316. 265p. 1983. text ed. 36.95x (ISBN 0-566-00647-2). Gower Pub Co.

Red Meekins. William A. Fraser. LC 72-125212. (Short Story Index Reprint Ser). 1921. 18.00 (ISBN 0-8369-3579-9). Ayer Co Pubs.

Red Men. Patrick McGinley. 256p. 1987. 15.95 (ISBN 0-312-00180-0, J Kahn). St Martin.

Red Men of Nigeria: Account of a Lengthy Residence amoung the Fulani. J. R. Wilson-Haffenden. (Illus.). 318p. 1967. Repr. of 1930 ed. 29.50x (ISBN 0-7146-1111-5, F Cass Co). Biblio Dist.

Red Men on the Brandywine. C. A. Weslager. (Illus.). 155p. Date not set. pap. 5.95 (ISBN 0-912608-20-X). Mid Atlantic.

Red Menace. Michael Anania. 150p. (Orig.). 1984. 13.95 (ISBN 0-938410-19-9). Thunder's Mouth.

Red Menace. Michael Anania. 144p. 1986. pap. 3.95 (ISBN 0-380-70053-0, Bard). Avon.

Red Menace. Dick Stivers. (Able Team Gold Eagle Ser.). 1988. pap. 2.95. S&S.

Red Miracle. Edward Podolsky. LC 70-167402. (Essay Index Reprint Ser.). 1947. 22.00 (ISBN 0-8369-2818-0). Ayer Co Pubs.

Red Moon. Warren Murphy. 320p. (Orig.). 1982. pap. 2.95 (ISBN 0-449-14491-7, GM). Fawcett.

Red Moon - Red Lake. Ascher & Straus. 128p. 1988. 16.00 (ISBN 0-914232-96-7); pap. 8.00 (ISBN 0-914232-97-5). McPherson & Co.

Red Moon-Red Lake. Ascher & Straus. 32p. (Orig.). 1984. pap. 3.00 (ISBN 0-917061-21-7). Top Stories.

Red Mountain. Will Comstock. (Orig.). 1981. pap. 1.95 (ISBN 0-505-51688-8, Pub. by Tower Bks). Leisure NY.

Red Mouth. Walasse Ting. 1977. pap. 35.00x (ISBN 0-8150-0901-1). Wittenborn.

Red Multinationals or Red Herrings? The Activities of Enterprises from Socialist Countries in the West. Ed. by Geoffrey Hamilton. LC 85-25102. 200p. 1986. 29.95 (ISBN 0-312-66656-X). St Martin.

Red Napoleon: A Novel. Floyd P. Gibbons. LC 75-26975. (Lost American Fiction Ser.). 494p. 1976. Repr. of 1929 ed. 9.85 (ISBN 0-8093-0764-2). S Ill U Pr.

Red Navy at Sea: Soviet Naval Operations, 1956-1980 on the High Seas. Bruce W. Watson. LC 82-21948. 1982. 36.00x (ISBN 0-86531-204-4). Westview.

Red Neck. McAlister Coleman. LC 74-22772. (Labor Movement in Fiction & Non-Fiction). Repr. of 1936 ed. 30.00 (ISBN 0-404-58412-8). AMS Pr.

Red Network: A "Who's Who" & Handbook of Radicalism for Patriots. Elizabeth K. Dilling. LC 76-46073. (Anti-Movements in America). 1977. Repr. of 1935 ed. lib. bdg. 27.50x (ISBN 0-405-09946-0). Ayer Co Pubs.

Red Nose Readers. Allan Ahlberg. Incl. Big Bad Pig. LC 84-27748. 1985. PLB 3.95 (ISBN 0-394-87194-4); Fee Fi Fo Fum. LC 84-27745. 1985. PLB 3.95 (ISBN 0-394-87193-6); Happy Worm. LC 84-27742. 1985. PLB 3.95 (ISBN 0-394-87196-0); Help! LC 84-27739. 1985. PLB 3.95 (ISBN 0-394-87190-1). (Illus.). 32p. (ps-2). 1985. (BYR). Random.

Red-Nosed Frost. A. Nekrasov. Ed. by V. E. Holttum. (Library of Russian Classics). 144p. pap. text ed. 9.95x (ISBN 0-900186-60-7). Basil Blackwell.

Red Noses. Peter Barnes. LC 85-20456. 112p. (Orig.). 1986. pap. 8.95 (ISBN 0-571-13771-7). Faber & Faber.

Red Notebook of Charles Darwin. Ed. by Sandra Herbert. LC 78-74215. (Illus.). 150p. 1980. 34.95x (ISBN 0-8014-1226-9). Cornell U Pr.

Red Oaks of Rum Village. Anton N. Nyerges. 1988. pap. 17.00 (ISBN 0-9600954-5-4). Nyerges.

Red October: Bolshevik Revolution of 1917. Robert V. Daniels. LC 84-45069. (Illus.). 294p. 1984. 25.00x (ISBN 0-8070-5644-8); pap. 11.95x (ISBN 0-8070-5645-6, BP679). Beacon Pr.

Red Oleanders. Rabindranath Tagore. 105p. Date not set. 4.95. Asia Bk Corp.

Red on Red. Red Holzman & Harvey Frommer. LC 87-47582. 224p. 1987. 17.95 (ISBN 0-553-05225-X). Bantam.

Red on Red. Red Holzman & Harvey Frommer. Date not set. pap. 4.50 (ISBN 0-553-27316-7). Bantam.

Red Orchestra: Instruments of Soviet Policy in Latin America & the Caribbean. Ed. by Dennis Bark. (Publications: No. 308). 250p. 1986. pap. 6.95x (ISBN 0-8179-8082-2). Hoover Inst Pr.

Red Orchestra: The Case of Africa. Ed. by Dennis L. Bark. 240p. 1988. text ed. 12.95 (ISBN 0-8179-8741-X); pap. text ed. 15.95 (ISBN 0-8179-8742-8). Hoover Inst Pr.

Red Orchestra: The Case of the South West Pacific, P-376. Ed. by Dennis L. Bark. 450p. 1988. pap. text ed. 14.95 (ISBN 0-8179-8762-2). Hoover Inst Pr.

Red over Black: Black Slavery among the Cherokee Indians. R. Halliburton, Jr. LC 76-15329. (Illus.). 1977. lib. bdg. 35.00 (ISBN 0-8371-9034-7, HAR/). Greenwood.

Red Overcoat & other Stories. Frank Ananicz. 24p. 1983. pap. 3.00 (ISBN 0-933292-12-0). Arts End.

Red Owl. Robert Morgan. 88p. (Orig.). 1972. pap. 1.95x (ISBN 0-393-04136-0). Norton.

Red Pandas: A Natural History. Dorcas MacClintock. (Illus.). 112p. (gr. 7 up). 1988. 13.95 (ISBN 0-684-18677-2, Pub. by Scribner). Macmillan.

Red Parka. Angela Starr. Ed. by Marily L. Metzger. 1987. 8.95 (ISBN 0-533-07077-5). Vantage.

Red Patriots: The Story of the Seminoles. Charles H. Coe. Intro. by Charlton W. Tebeau. LC 73-5702. (Floridiana Facsimile & Reprint Ser.). 347p. 1974. Repr. of 1898 ed. 12.00 (ISBN 0-8130-0401-2). U Presses Fla.

Red Pavilion. Robert Van Gulik. 184p. 1984. pap. 3.50 rack-size (ISBN 0-684-18142-8, ScribT). Scribner.

Red Peephole Book. Dorothy Savage. (Peephole Bks.). (Illus.). 10p. (ps). 1986. pap. 1.95 (ISBN 0-525-44246-4). Dutton.

Red Peony. Lin Yutang. 400p. 1980. (Pub. by Mei Ya China); pap. 10.95 (ISBN 0-89955-194-7, Pub. by Mei Ya China). Intl Spec Bk.

Red Pepper Burns. Grace S. Richmond. Repr. lib. bdg. 16.95x (ISBN 0-89190-491-3, Pub. by River City Pr). Amereon Ltd.

Red Pepper's Patients. Grace S. Richmond. Repr. lib. bdg. 18.95x (ISBN 0-89190-492-1, Pub. by River City Pr). Amereon Ltd.

Red Petrograd: Revolution in the Factories, 1917-1918. S. A. Smith. (Soviet & East European Studies). 347p. 1985. pap. 15.95 (ISBN 0-521-31618-9). Cambridge U Pr.

Red Phoenix: The Rise of Soviet Air Power, 1941-1945. Von Hardesty. LC 82-600153. (Illus.). 288p. 1982. 24.95 (ISBN 0-87474-510-1, HARP). Smithsonian.

Red Planet. Robert A. Heinlein. 1981. pap. 2.95 (ISBN 0-345-34039-6, Del Rey Bks). Ballantine.

Red Plot Against America. Robert E Stripling. Ed. by Bob Considine & Gerald Grob. LC 76-46105. (Anti-Movements in America). 1977. Repr. of 1949 ed. lib. bdg. 23.50x (ISBN 0-405-09976-2). Ayer Co Pubs.

Red Pony. reissue ed. John Steinbeck. (Illus.). (gr. 7 up). 1959. lib. bdg. 11.95 (ISBN 0-670-59184-X). Viking.

Red Pony. John Steinbeck. 112p. 1986. 15.95 (ISBN 0-670-81285-4). Viking.

Red Pony. John Steinbeck. 1986. pap. 2.50 (ISBN 0-553-26444-3). Bantam.

Red Pony see Short Novels of John Steinbeck.

Red Pony "Chrysanthemums" "Flight" Notes. Gary K. Carey. (Orig.). 1978. pap. text ed. 3.25 (ISBN 0-8220-1135-2). Cliffs.

Red Pottage. Mary Cholmondeley. (Virago Modern Classics Ser.). 392p. 1986. pap. 6.95 (ISBN 0-14-016115-5). Penguin.

Red Pottage, 1899 see In Deacon's Orders, 1895.

Red Power: The American Indians' Fight for Freedom. Alvin M. Josephy, Jr. LC 84-20821. viii, 247p. 1985. pap. 7.50 (ISBN 0-8032-7563-3, BB 909, Bison). U of Nebr Pr.

Red Prelude see Alexander Conspiracy: A Life of A. I. Zhelybov.

Red Prelude: The Life of the Russian Terrorist Zhelyabov. David Footman. LC 78-14119. (Illus.). 1984. Repr. of 1945 ed. 24.00 (ISBN 0-88355-792-4). Hyperion Conn.

Red Prophet. Orson S. Card. 320p. 1988. pap. 3.95 (ISBN 0-8125-3359-3). Tor Bks.

Red Prophet: The Tales of Alvin Maker II. Orson S. Card. 320p. 1988. 17.95x (ISBN 0-312-93043-7). Tor Bks.

Red Rackham's Treasure. Herge. (Illus.). 62p. 15.95 (ISBN 0-416-92540-5); pap. 4.95 (ISBN 0-416-80010-6). French & Eur.

Red Rackham's Treasure. Herge. LC 73-21253. (Adventures of Tintin Ser.). (Illus.). 64p. (Orig.). (gr. k up). 1974. pap. 6.95 (ISBN 0-316-35834-7, Joy St Bks). Little.

Red Raiders: Texas Tech Football. Ralph Sellmeyer & James Davidson. LC 77-79554. (College Sports Ser.). 1978. 9.95 (ISBN 0-87397-123-X). Strode.

Red Record of the Sioux. Willis F. Johnson. LC 76-43757. Repr. of 1891 ed. 64.50 (ISBN 0-404-15598-7). AMS Pr.

Red Redmaynes. Eden Phillpotts. (Illus.). 384p. 1982. pap. 5.95 (ISBN 0-486-24255-2). Dover.

Red Republican & Friend of the Good People: Eighteen Fifty to Eighteen Fifty-One, 2 vols. Ed. by George J. Harney. 472p. 1966. 21.50 (ISBN 0-85036-096-X, Pub. by Merlin Pr UK). Longwood Pub Group.

Red Ribbon Rosie. Jean Marzollo. LC 87-29641. (Stepping Stone Bks.). (Illus.). 64p. (Orig.). (gr. 2-4). 1988. lib. bdg. 5.99 (ISBN 0-394-99608-9, BYR); pap. 1.95 (ISBN 0-394-89608-4). Random.

Red Ribbons for Emma. New Mexico People & Energy Collective et al. LC 80-83883. (Illus.). 48p. (Orig.). (gr. 3 up). 1981. 8.00 (ISBN 0-938678-07-8). New Seed.

Red Riding Hood. Beatrice S. De Regniers. LC 79-175561. (Illus.). (ps-3). 1977. pap. 1.95 (ISBN 0-689-70435-6, Aladdin). Macmillan.

Red Riding Hood. James Marshall. LC 86-16722. (Illus.). 32p. (ps-3). 1987. 10.95 (ISBN 0-8037-0344-9, 01063-320); PLB 9.89 (ISBN 0-8037-0345-7). Dial Bks Young.

Red Riding Hood. Lee Mendelson et al. write for info. P-H.

Red Riding Hood. (Derrydale Fairytale Library). (Illus.). (ps-3). 1985. 2.98 (ISBN 0-517-28810-9). Outlet Bk Co.

Red Riding Hood. (Diamond Series Pop-Ups). (Illus.). (ps-1). 1.29 (ISBN 0-517-47346-1). Outlet Bk Co.

Red Right Hand. Joel Townsley Rogers. 198p. pap. 3.50 (ISBN 0-88184-008-4). Carroll & Graf.

Red River. Jack Hawkins. (Chopper I Ser.). 368p. (Orig.). 1987. pap. 3.95 (ISBN 0-8041-0030-6, Pub. by Ivy). Ballantine.

Red River Blues: The Blues Tradition in the Southeast. Bruce Bastin. LC 85-8571. (Music in American Life Ser.). (Illus.). 398p. 1986. 24.95 (ISBN 0-252-01213-5). U of Ill Pr.

Red River Campaign: Politics & Cotton in the Civil War. Ludwell H. Johnson. LC 58-59976. pap. 82.30 (2001834). Bks Demand UMI.

Red River Controversy. C. A. Welborn. 6.95 (ISBN 0-89015-026-5). Eakin Pr.

Red River Expedition. LC 76-42128. (Civil War Monographs). 1977. Repr. of 1865 ed. lib. bdg. 30.00 (ISBN 0-527-17560-9); 23.00 (ISBN 0-527-17561-7). Kraus Repr.

Red River in Southwestern History. Carl N. Tyson. LC 81-40292. (Illus.). 240p. 1981. 18.95 (ISBN 0-8061-1659-5). U of Okla Pr.

Red River Journal & Other Papers Relative to the Red River Resistance of 1869-1870. Alexander Begg. Ed. by W. L. Morton. LC 69-14506. 1969. Repr. of 1956 ed. lib. bdg. 36.75x (ISBN 0-8371-5074-4, BERR). Greenwood.

Red River Settlers: Records of the Settlers of Northern Montgomery, Robertson & Sumner Counties, Tennessee. Edythe R. Whitley. LC 80-66829. (Illus.). 189p. 1980. 15.00 (ISBN 0-8063-0897-4). Genealog Pub.

Red River Story. Alfred Silver. 1988. pap. 8.95 (ISBN 0-345-32692-X). Ballantine.

Red River Trails: Oxcart Routes Between St. Paul & the Selkirk Settlement, 1820-1870. Rhoda R. Gilman et al. LC 78-11045. (Illus.). 104p. 1979. pap. 7.95 (ISBN 0-87351-133-6). Minn Hist.

Red River-Twining Area: A New Mexico Mining Story. Jim B. Pearson. LC 85-2882. (Historical Society of New Mexico Publications Ser.). (Illus.). 231p. 1986. 19.95x (ISBN 0-8263-0875-9); pap. 10.95 (ISBN 0-8263-0876-7). U of NM Pr.

Red Roads. Charlie Smith. (National Poetry Ser.). 1987. 13.95 (ISBN 0-525-24509-X, 01354-410); pap. 7.95 (ISBN 0-525-48282-2, 0772-230). Dutton.

Red Robins: A Play. Kenneth Koch. LC 79-49439. 1979. 8.95 (ISBN 0-933826-05-2); pap. 3.95 (ISBN 0-933826-04-4). PAJ Pubns.

Red Rock, a Chronicle of Reconstruction. Thomas N. Page. LC 67-29275. (Americans in Fiction Ser.). (Illus.). 599p. Repr. of 1898 ed. lib. bdg. 22.00 (ISBN 0-8398-1551-4). Irvington.

Red Rock: A Chronicle of Reconstruction. Thomas N. Page. 584p. 1982. Repr. of 1899 ed. lib. bdg. 25.00 (ISBN 0-89987-668-4). Darby Bks.

Red Years-Black Years: A Political History of Spanish Anarchism, 1911-1937. Robert W. Kern. LC 77-13595. pap. 93.50 (ISBN 0-317-42090-9, 2025711). Bks Demand UMI.

Red, Yellow, Black, White, & Brown. David Telfer. 1981. pap. 3.95 (ISBN 0-87162-250-5, D6460). Warner Pr.

Red, Yellow, Blue: A Wrinkles Book of Colors. Anita Shevett & Steve Shevett. LC 86-70326. (Illus.). 12p. (ps-k). 1986. 2.95 (ISBN 0-394-88427-2, BYR). Random.

Redaccion Comercial Estructurada. 2nd ed. Rojas. 200p. 1982. text ed. 15.36 (ISBN 0-07-053566-3). McGraw.

Redaction of Genesis. Gary A. Rendsburg. xii, 132p. 1986. text ed. 12.50x (ISBN 0-931464-25-0). Eisenbrauns.

Redactional Style in the Marcan Gospel: A Study of Syntax & Vocabulary as Guides to Redaction in Mark. E. J. Pryke. LC 76-52184. (Society for New Testament Studies. Monograph Ser.: No. 33). pap. 53.60 (2031714). Bks Demand UMI.

Redating the New Testament. John A.. Robinson. LC 76-17554. 384p. 1976. 15.00 (ISBN 0-664-21336-7). Westminster John Knox.

Redating the Teacher of Righteousness. B. E. Thiering. (Austrailian & New Zealand Studies in Theology & Religion). 238p. (Orig.). 1979. pap. 19.95 (ISBN 0-85821-305-2, Pub. by Theol Explor). ANZ Religious Pubns.

Redback. Howard Jacobson. 1987. 17.95 (ISBN 0-670-81541-1). Viking.

Redbeans & Rice, Good Ole Grits, & Other Southern Foods: A Celebration of the Dishes of Dixie. Lillie P. Gallagher. (Illus.). 128p. 1986. 6.95 (ISBN 0-9610174-4-9). Petit Press.

Redbird. Patrick Fort. LC 87-23591. (Illus.). 32p. (ps-5). 1988. 19.95 (ISBN 0-531-05746-1). Orchard Bks Watts.

Redbook: The Consumer's Automobile Purchasing Guide and Reference Manual. Michael L. Van Natten. 1988. 12.95 (ISBN 0-533-07360-X). Vantage.

Redbook's Guide to Buying Your First Home. Ruth Pomeroy. 1980. pap. 4.95 (ISBN 0-686-60934-4, 24716, Fireside, 25385). S&S.

Redbook's Wise Woman's Diet Cookbook. Ed. by Ruth F. Pomeroy. LC 82-22467. 368p. 1984. pap. 5.95 (ISBN 0-452-25532-5, Plume); 14.95 (ISBN 0-453-00436-9). NAL.

Redbud. Jilla Y. Smith. (Chapbook Ser.: No. 1). 28p. (Orig.). 1987. pap. 3.00 (ISBN 0-933573-09-X). Wayland Pr.

Redburn. Herman Melville. (Writings of Herman Melville Ser.). 1972. 36.95x (ISBN 0-8101-0013-4); pap. 12.95 (ISBN 0-8101-0016-9). Northwestern U Pr.

Redburn. Herman Melville. Ed. by Harold Beaver. (English Library). 448p. 1977. pap. 4.95 (ISBN 0-14-043105-5). Penguin.

Redburn, White-Jacket, Moby-Dick. Herman Melville. Ed. by G. Thomas Tanselle. Incl. White-Jacket; Or the World in a Man-of-War; Moby-Dick; Or the Whale. LC 82-18677. 1436p. 1983. 27.50 (ISBN 0-940450-09-7). Library of America.

Redcoat. Bernard Cornwell. 1988. 18.95 (ISBN 0-670-81681-7). Viking.

Redder Blood. William M. Ashby. LC 73-18570. Repr. of 1915 ed. 17.00 (ISBN 0-404-11380-X). AMS Pr.

Redding & Shasta County: Gateway to the Cascades. John D. Lawson. Ed. by Gail Koffman. LC 86-22375. (Illus.). 184p. 1986. 27.95 (ISBN 0-89781-187-9). Windsor Pubns Inc.

Rede an Den Kleinen Mann. Wilhelm Reich. 1973. 25.00 (ISBN 0-374-24851-6). FS&G.

Rede Me & Be Nott Wrothe for I Say No Thynge but Trothe. William Roy. LC 76-38221. (English Experience Ser.: No. 485). 144p. 1972. Repr. of 1528 ed. 25.00 (ISBN 90-221-0485-0). Walter J Johnson.

Rede und Redeszene in der Deutschen Erzahlung Bis Wolfram Von Eschenbach. pap. 13.00 (ISBN 0-685-02059-2). Johnson Repr.

Rededication of Fondren Library of Rice University. Ed. by Hardin Craig, Jr. (Rice University Studies: Vol. 55, No. 4). 112p. 1969. pap. 10.00x (ISBN 0-89263-202-X). Rice Univ.

Redeem the Time: The Puritan Sabbath in Early America. Winton U. Solberg. (Illus.). 1977. 27.00x (ISBN 0-674-75130-2). Harvard U Pr.

Redeemed Captive. John Williams. Date not set. pap. 8.95 (ISBN 1-55709-118-8). Applewood.

Redeemed Captive Returning to Zion. J. Williams. 1908. 23.00 (ISBN 0-527-96920-6). Kraus Repr.

Redeemed Captive Returning to Zion: Or, a Faithful History of Remarkable Occurrences in the Captivity & Deliverance of Mr. John Williams. facs. ed. Ed. by Stephen W. Williams. LC 78-109637. (Select Bibliographies Reprint Ser). 1853. 19.00 (ISBN 0-8369-5246-4). Ayer Co Pubs.

Redeemed Creation: The Sacramentals Today. Laurence Brett. LC 84-80347. (Message of the Sacraments Ser.: Vol. 8). 12.95 (ISBN 0-89453-398-3); pap. 8.95 (ISBN 0-89453-234-0). M Glazier.

Redeemed from Poverty, Sickness, & Death. Kenneth E. Hagin. 1966. pap. 1.00 (ISBN 0-89276-001-X). Hagin Ministries.

Redeemed from the Curse. Perry A. Gaspard. 64p. 1983. pap. 2.25 (ISBN 0-931867-03-7). Abundant Life Pubns.

Redeemer Nation: The Idea of America's Millenial Role. Ernest L. Tuveson. LC 68-14009. (Midway Reprint Ser.). 1980. pap. 14.95x (ISBN 0-226-81921-3). U of Chicago Pr.

Redeemer of Man. Pope John Paul II. 103p. (Orig.). 1979. pap. 3.95 (ISBN 1-55586-003-6). US Catholic.

Redeemers, Bourbons & Populists: Tennessee, 1870-1896. Roger L. Hart. LC 73-91776. 240p. 1975. 30.00 (ISBN 0-8071-0079-X). La State U Pr.

Redeeming Creation: A Christian World Evolving. John Morton. (Illus.). 84p. (Orig.). 1984. pap. 5.95 (ISBN 0-318-20036-8, Pub. by Zealandia Pubns). ANZ Religious Pubns.

Redeeming Eve: Women Writers of the English Renaissance. Elaine V. Beilin. 352p. 1987. text ed. 33.00 (ISBN 0-691-06715-5). Princeton U Pr.

Redeeming Higher Education: India. Ed. by Amrik Singh. 1986. 18.50x (ISBN 0-8364-1527-2, Pub. by Ajanta). South Asia Bks.

Redeeming Marriage. Edward S. Gleason. LC 87-29960. 158p. (Orig.). 1988. pap. 7.95 (ISBN 0-936384-55-7). Cowley Pubns.

Redeeming Shakespeare's Words. Paul A. Jorgensen. 1985. Repr. of 1962 ed. 25.00x (ISBN 0-520-05470-9). U of Cal Pr.

Redeeming State: A Handbook-Leader's Guide for Couples Planning Remarriage in the Church. Judith T. O'Brien & Gene O'Brien. 1984. leader's guide pamphlet 2.95 (ISBN 0-8091-5183-9); pap. 3.95 handbook-pamphlet (ISBN 0-8091-5182-0). Paulist Pr.

Redeeming the Time: A People's History of the 1920's & the New Deal. Page Smith. 1232p. 1987. text ed. 34.95 (ISBN 0-07-058575-X). McGraw.

Redefining American Policy in Southeast Asia. Lucian W. Pye. 1982. pap. 6.00 (ISBN 0-8447-1095-4). Am Enterprise.

Redefining Corporate-Federal Relations. Phyllis S. McGrath. LC 79-52413. (Report Ser.: No. 757). (Illus.). 102p. 1979. pap. 30.00 (ISBN 0-8237-0193-X). Conference Bd.

Redefining Death. Karen G. Gervais. LC 86-10978. 320p. 1987. 25.00x (ISBN 0-300-03616-7). Yale U Pr.

Redefining Death. Karen G. Gervais. LC 86-10978. 231p. 1988. pap. 9.95x (ISBN 0-300-04197-7). Yale U Pr.

Redefining Death: Midrash & Literature. Geoffrey Hartman. LC 85-17898. 415p. 1988. pap. 16.95x (ISBN 0-300-04198-5). Yale U Pr.

Redefining General Education in the American High School. Arthur D. Roberts & Gordon Cawelti. LC 84-71655. 160p. (Orig.). 1984. pap. text ed. 8.50 (ISBN 0-87120-126-7, 611-84332). Assn Supervision.

Redefining Government's Role in the Market System. Committee for Economic Development. 1979. lib. bdg. 6.50 (ISBN 0-87186-768-0); pap. 5.00 (ISBN 0-87186-068-6). Comm Econ Dev.

Redefining Human Life: Reproductive Technologies & Social Policy. Robert H. Blank. (Special Studies in Science, Technology, & Public Policy-Society). 280p. 1983. lib. bdg. 35.50x (ISBN 0-86531-665-1). Westview.

Redefining Politics: People, Resources & Power. Adrian Leftwich. 320p. 1983. 32.00 (ISBN 0-416-73590-8, NO. 3950); pap. 14.95 (ISBN 0-416-73600-9, NO. 3951). Routledge Chapman & Hall.

Redefining Remedial Education: Policies & Practice in Secondary Schools. Hazel Bines. 200p. 1986. 29.00 (ISBN 0-7099-3984-1, Pub. by Croom Helm Ltd); pap. 13.50 (ISBN 0-7099-5028-4). Routledge Chapman & Hall.

Redefining Revolution. 2nd ed. Cornelius Castoriadis. 200p. 1988. 29.95 (ISBN 0-920057-18-7, Dist. by U of Toronto Pr); pap. 14.95 (ISBN 0-920057-19-5, Dist. by U of Toronto Pr). Black Rose Bks.

Redefining Social Problems. Ed. by Edward Seidman & Julian Rappaport. (Perspectives in Social Psychology Ser.). 334p. 1986. 35.00x (ISBN 0-306-42052-X, Plenum Pr). Plenum Pub.

Redefining the American Gothic: From Wieland to Day of the Dead. Louis Gross. Ed. by Robert Scholes. (Studies in Speculative Fiction: No. 20). 1988. price not set (ISBN 0-8357-1901-4). UMI Res Pr.

Redefining the Discipline of Adult Education. Robert D. Boyd et al. LC 80-8006. (Higher Education Ser.). 1980. text ed. 25.95x (ISBN 0-87589-482-8). Jossey-Bass.

Redefining the Environment. Jerome Abarbanel. (Key Issues Ser.: No. 9). 40p. 1972. pap. 2.00 (ISBN 0-87546-200-6). ILR Pr.

Redefining the Manager's Job: The Proactive Manager in a Reactive World. Merritt Kastens. 256p. 1980. 14.95 (ISBN 0-8144-5619-7). AMACOM.

Redefining the New Federalism: Impact on Low-Income & Other Older Americans. William E. Oriol. (Illus.). 150p. 1983. 13.50 (ISBN 0-910883-03-3). Natl Coun Aging.

Redefining the Past: Essays in Diplomatic History in Honor of William Appleman Williams. Ed. by Lloyd C. Gardner. LC 86-8427. (Illus.). 272p. 1986. text ed. 27.95x (ISBN 0-87071-348-5). Oreg St U Pr.

Redefining the Supreme Court's Role: A Theory of Managing the Federal Judicial Process. Samuel Estreicher & John Sexton. LC 86-9247. 224p. 1987. 20.00x (ISBN 0-300-03733-3). Yale U Pr.

Redefining the Supreme Court's Role: A Theory of Managing the Federal Judicial Process. Samuel Estreicher & John E. Sexton. LC 86-9247. 206p. 1988. Repr. of 1986 ed. 11.95 (ISBN 0-300-03734-1). Yale U Pr.

Redefinition of Conservatism: Politics & Doctrine. Charles Covell. LC 85-8296. 272p. 1986. 27.50 (ISBN 0-312-66725-6). St Martin.

Redefinition of the Gifted: A Paradigm for Teachers & Mentors, Brief No. 7. Paul Brandwein & Evelyn Morholf. 1986. 8.95 (ISBN 0-318-18971-2). NSLTIGT.

Redelyke Argumenten. P. J. Schellens. viii, 291p. 1985. pap. write for info. (ISBN 90-6765-132-X). Foris Pubns.

Redemocratization in Bolivia: A Political-Economic Analysis of the Siles Zuazo Government, 1982-1985. Ed. by Jerry R. Ladman & Juan A. Morales. 150p. 1988. text ed. 30.00 (ISBN 0-87918-065-X). ASU Lat Am St.

Redemption. Chet Hagan. 1987. 17.95 (ISBN 0-931933-63-3). Richardson & Steirman.

Redemption. Chet Hagen. 1989. pap. price not set. Tor Bks.

Redemption Accomplished & Applied. Donald W. Bowdle. 1972. 5.25 (ISBN 0-87148-726-8); pap. 4.25 (ISBN 0-87148-727-6). Pathway Pr.

Redemption: Accomplished & Applied. John Murray. 1961. pap. 6.95 (ISBN 0-8028-1143-4). Eerdmans.

Redemption by War: The Intellectuals & 1914. Roland N. Stromberg. LC 81-10715. viii, 252p. 1982. 27.50x (ISBN 0-7006-0220-8). U Pr of KS.

Redemption, Conceived & Revealed. H. P. Robinson. 3.95 (ISBN 0-911866-59-0); pap. 2.95 (ISBN 0-911866-89-2). Advocate.

Redemption, Hindu & Christian: The Religious Quest of India. facsimile ed. Sydney Cave. LC 73-102230. (Select Bibliographies Reprint Ser). 1919. 24.50 (ISBN 0-8369-5115-8). Ayer Co Pubs.

Redemption in Black Theology. Olin P. Moyd. LC 78-23816. 1979. soft cover 8.95 (ISBN 0-8170-0806-3). Judson.

Redemption of Africa & Black Religion. St. Claire Drake. LC 70-171226. (Orig.). 1970. pap. 6.95 (ISBN 0-88378-017-8). Third World.

Redemption of Elsdon Bird. Noel Virtue. 128p. 1987. 15.95 (ISBN 0-8021-0022-8). Grove.

Redemption of God: A Theology of Mutual Relation. Isabel C. Heyward. LC 81-43706. 266p. (Orig.). 1982. lib. bdg. 30.75 (ISBN 0-8191-2389-7); pap. text ed. 13.00 (ISBN 0-8191-2390-0). U Pr of Amer.

Redemption of Howard Gray. C. W. Naylor. 72p. pap. 0.50 (ISBN 0-686-29162-X). Faith Pub Hse.

Redemption of Matter: Towards the Rapprochment of Science & Religion. James W. Jones. 154p. (Orig.). 1984. lib. bdg. 24.25 (ISBN 0-8191-3675-1); pap. text ed. 9.75 (ISBN 0-8191-3676-X). U Pr of Amer.

Redemption of Ruth. Leslie Madison. 96p. (Orig.). 1982. pap. 2.50 (ISBN 0-89323-038-3). Bible Memory.

Redemption of the Unwanted: From the Liberation of the Death Camps to the Founding of Israel. Abram L. Sachar. LC 83-3025. (Illus.). 320p. 1983. 19.95 (ISBN 0-312-66729-9, Pub. by Marek). St Martin.

Redemption of the Unwanted: The Post-Holocaust Years. Abram L. Sachar. 334p. 1985. pap. 9.95 (ISBN 0-312-66730-2, Pub. by Marek). St Martin.

Redemption of Thinking: A Study in the Philosophy of Thomas Aquinas. Rudolf Steiner. Tr. by A. P. Sheperd & Mildred R. Nicoll. Orig. Title: Philosophie des Thomas von Aquino. 191p. 1983. pap. text ed. 8.95 (ISBN 0-88010-044-3). Anthroposophic.

Redemption Song, The Boot Dance, Les Femmes Noires: Three Plays. Edgar White. 192p. 1986. pap. 9.95 (ISBN 0-7145-2837-4, Dist. by Kampmann & Co). M Boyars Pubs.

Redemption Song: The Story of Operation Moses. Louis Rapoport. LC 85-30489. (Illus.). 320p. 1986. 18.95 (ISBN 0-15-176120-5). HarBraceJ.

Redemption: The Exodus from Egypt see Torah Anthology: Mem Lo'ez.

Redemption: Three Sermons, 1637-1656. Thomas Hooker. LC 56-9145. 1977. Repr. 30.00x (ISBN 0-8201-1234-8). Schol Facsimiles.

Redemption Truths. Robert Anderson. LC 80-16161. (Sir Robert Anderson Library). Orig. Title: For Us Men. 192p. 1980. pap. 4.95 (ISBN 0-8254-2131-4). Kregel.

Redemptioners & Indentured Servants in the Colony & Commonwealth of Pennsylvania. Karl F. Geiser. 1901. 75.00x (ISBN 0-686-51298-7). Elliots Bks.

Redemptions: A Novel of Costa Rica. Carlos Gagini. Tr. by E. Bradford Burns from Span. (Illus.). 144p. (Orig.). 1984. 14.00x (ISBN 0-916304-66-3); pap. 6.50x (ISBN 0-916304-67-1). SDSU Press.

Redemptive Dancing: Prayer Dance & Congregational Dance in the Life of the Contemporary Church. Janet Skidmore. Ed. by Doug Adams. pap. 2.50 (ISBN 0-941500-46-2). Sharing Co.

Redemptive Encounters: Three Modern Styles in the Hindu Tradition. Lawrence A. Babb. (Comparative Studies in Religion & Society: Vol. 1). 1987. 29.95x (ISBN 0-520-05645-0). U of Cal Pr.

Redemptive History & Biblical Interpretation. Geerhardus Vos. Ed. by Richard B. Gaffin, Jr. 584p. 1981. 17.50 (ISBN 0-8010-9286-8). Baker Bk.

Redemptive History & the New Testament Scriptures. Herman Ridderbos. Tr. by H. De Jongste & Richard B. Graffin, Jr. LC 87-32875. Orig. Title: Authority of the New Testment Scriptures. 110p. (Dutch.). 1988. pap. 6.95 (ISBN 0-87552-416-8). Presby & Reformed.

Redemptive Intimacy: A New Perspective for the Journey to Adult Faith. Dick Westley. LC 80-54810. 176p. 1981. pap. 5.95 (ISBN 0-89622-123-7). Twenty-Third.

Redemptive Responses of Jesus. Howard W. Roberts. (Orig.). 1987. pap. 5.95 (ISBN 0-8054-5715-1). Broadman.

Redemptive Suffering in Islam. Mahmoud Ayoub. (Religion & Society Ser.: No. 10). 1978. 35.25 (ISBN 90-279-7948-0). Mouton.

Redemptorama: Culture, Politics & the New Evangelicalism. Carol Flake. (Nonfiction Ser.). 320p. 1985. pap. 7.95 (ISBN 0-14-008265-4). Penguin.

Redemptorist on the American Missions, 3 vols. In 2. Joseph Wissel. 115.00 (ISBN 0-405-10867-2). Ayer Co Pubs.

Reden Gehalten in Wissenschaftlichen Versammlungen und Kleinere Aufsatze Vermischten Inhalts, 3 vols. in two. Karl E. Von Baer. Ed. by Keir B. Sterling. LC 77-81114. (Biologists & Their World Ser.). (Ger.). 1978. Repr. of 1876 ed. Set. lib. bdg. 93.00x (ISBN 0-405-10700-5); lib. bdg. 46.50x ea. Vol. 1 (ISBN 0-405-10701-3). Vol. 2 (ISBN 0-405-10702-1). Ayer Co Pubs.

Reden Gotamo Buddhos. Karl E. Neumann. 344p. 1907. 48.00x (ISBN 0-317-69445-6, Pub. by Han-Shan Tang Ltd). State Mutual Bk.

Reden, Mitreden, Dazwischenreden. C. Kramsch & E. Crocker. 256p. (Orig.). 1985. pap. 23.75 (text tape pkg.) (ISBN 0-8384-1332-3); instr's. manual avail. (ISBN 0-8384-1323-4). Heinle & Heinle.

Reden und Schriften see Essays & Speeches on Various Subjects.

Redencion Lograda y Aplicada. Ed. by Donald N. Bowdle. 126p. (Span.). 1979. pap. 3.95 (ISBN 0-87148-521-4). Pathway Pr.

Redescription of Etheostoma Australe & a Key for the Identification of Mexican Etheostoma Percidae. Lawrence M. Page. (Occasional Papers: No. 89). 10p. 1981. 1.25 (ISBN 0-317-04828-7). U of KS Mus Nat Hist.

Redesign of Catalogs & Indexes for Improved Online Subject Access: Selected Papers of Pauline A. Cochrane. Pauline A. Cochrane. LC 85-42722. (Illus.). 496p. 1985. lib. bdg. 47.50 (ISBN 0-89774-158-7). Oryx Pr.

Redesigning Rural Development: A Strategic Perspective. Bruce F. Johnston & William C. Clark. LC 81-17138. 336p. 1982. text ed. 32.50x (ISBN 0-8018-2731-0); pap. text ed. 12.95x (ISBN 0-8018-2732-9). Johns Hopkins.

Redesigning School Health Services. Annette Lynch. LC 82-12178. (Illus.). 272p. 1983. 39.95x (ISBN 0-89885-102-5). Human Sci Pr.

Redesigning Science & Technology Education: 1984 NSTA Yearbook. Ed. by Rodger Bybee et al. 248p. (Orig.). 1984. pap. text ed. 7.50 (ISBN 0-87355-042-0). Natl Sci Tchrs.

Redesigning the American Dream: The Future of Housing, Work, & Family Life. Dolores Hayden. LC 83-9339. (Illus.). 270p. 1984. 17.95 (ISBN 0-393-01779-6). Norton.

Redesigning the American Dream: The Future of Housing, Work, & Family Life. Dolores Hayden. (Illus.). 288p. 1986. pap. 8.95 (ISBN 0-393-30317-9). Norton.

Redesigning the Future: A Systems Approach to Societal Problems. Russell L. Ackoff. LC 74-10627. 260p. 1974. 29.95 (ISBN 0-471-00296-8). Wiley.

Redesigning the Molecules of Life. Ed. by S. A. Benner. (Illus.). vii, 175p. Date not set. pap. 32.50 (ISBN 0-387-19166-6). Springer-Verlag.

Redesigning the State: The Politics of Constitutional Change. Ed. by Keith Banting & Richard Simeon. 269p. 1985. 14.95c (ISBN 0-8020-5665-2); pap. 14.95 (ISBN 0-8020-6569-4). U of Toronto Pr.

Redesigning the World: William Morris, the 1880's, & the Arts & Crafts. Peter Stansky. LC 84-42558. (Illus.). 288p. 1984. text ed. 29.00 (ISBN 0-691-06616-7); pap. 12.95 (ISBN 0-691-01411-6). Princeton U Pr.

Redesigning Work: A Strategy for Change. Mary D. Lee & J. Richard Hackman. (Studies in Productivity: Vol. 9). 43p. 1979. pap. 39.00 (ISBN 0-08-029490-1). Work in Amer.

Redeye. Richard Aellen. LC 87-46266. 352p. 1988. 18.95 (ISBN 1-55611-082-0). D I Fine.

Redgate Gold. Jack Slade. (Lassiter Ser.: No. 28). (Orig.). 1981. pap. 1.95 (ISBN 0-505-51724-8, Pub. by Tower Bks). Leisure NY.

Redgauntlet. Walter Scott. 1970. Repr. of 1906 ed. 12.95x (ISBN 0-460-00141-8, Evman). Biblio Dist.

Redgauntlet. Walter Scott. 1982. pap. 4.95x (ISBN 0-460-01141-3, Evman). Biblio Dist.

Redgauntlet. 2nd ed. Walter Scott. Ed. by Kathryn Sutherland. (WC-P Ser.). 1985. pap. 6.95 (ISBN 0-19-281668-3). Oxford U Pr.

Redhead Book: A Book for & about Redheads. rev. ed. Allen P. Sacharov. LC 85-51636. (Illus.). 160p. 1985. pap. 7.95 (ISBN 0-910027-04-8). Word of Mouth.

Redheaded Woman. Helen Eustis. LC 84-145828. (Illus.). 36p. (Orig.). (gr. 7 up). 1983. pap. 6.95 (ISBN 0-88138-013-X). Green Tiger Pr.

Redhead's Handbook. Pat Doran et al. (Illus.). 1984. pap. 5.95 (ISBN 0-452-25509-0, Plume). NAL.

Redhouse English-Turkish Dictionary. (Eng. & Turkish.). 1974. 33.00x (ISBN 0-686-16859-3). Intl Learn Syst.

Redhouse Turkish-English Dictionary. (Turkish & Eng.). 1968. 41.00x (ISBN 0-686-16860-7). Intl Learn Syst.

Redi-Reference. Bob Phillips. 1975. pap. 1.95 (ISBN 0-89081-043-5). Harvest Hse.

Redigging the Wells. Monroe E. Hawley. 1976. 8.95 (ISBN 0-89137-513-9); pap. 5.95 (ISBN 0-89137-512-0). Quality Pubns.

Redimido De La Pobreza, La Enfermedad, La Muerte. 2nd ed. Kenneth E. Hagin. 1982. pap. 1.00 (ISBN 0-89276-101-6). Hagin Ministries.

Redirecting Children's Misbehavior. Bill Kvols-Riedler & Kathy Kvols-Riedler. (Illus.). 255p. (Orig.). 1979. pap. 10.95 (ISBN 0-933450-00-1). RDIC Pubns.

Redirecting Education, 2 Vols. facs. ed. Ed. by Rexford G. Tugwell & Leon H. Keyserling. LC 74-128323. (Essay Index Reprint Ser). 1935. Set. 44.00 (ISBN 0-8369-2031-7). Ayer Co Pubs.

Redirecting Public Funds: A Strategy for the City of Berkeley. Citizens Committee on Responsible Investments. 50p. 1980. 4.95 (ISBN 0-318-13771-2); inst. 9.95 (ISBN 0-318-13772-0). NCPA Washington.

Redirections in Organizational Analysis. Michael Reed. 180p. 1986. pap. 17.95 (ISBN 0-422-78940-2, 9589, Pub. by Tavistock England). Routledge Chapman & Hall.

Rediscover America. James Piety. 155p. 1986. wkbk. 10.80 (ISBN 0-87563-286-6). Stipes.

Rediscovered Artists of Essex County (1865-1915) Frederic Sharf & John Wright. 15p. 1987. pap. 2.00 (ISBN 0-88389-094-1). Essex Inst.

Rediscovered Country. S. E. White. (Illus.). 440p. 1987. Repr. of 1914 ed. 25.00 (ISBN 0-935632-51-4). Wolfe Pub Co.

Rediscovered Fiction by American Women: A Personal Selection, 18 bks. Ed. by Elizabeth Hardwick. (Illus.). 1977. Set. lib. bdg. 496.00x (ISBN 0-405-10060-4). Ayer Co Pubs.

Rediscovered Masterpieces of Mesoamerica: Mexico-Guatemala-Honduras. Ed. by Gerald Berjonneau & Jean-Louis Sonnery. (Illus.). 288p. 1986. 75.00 (ISBN 0-8478-0709-6). Rizzoli Intl.

Rediscoverers: Major Writers in the Portuguese Literature of National Regeneration. Ronald W. Sousa. LC 80-21453. (Illus.). 208p. 1981. 22.50x (ISBN 0-271-00300-6). Pa St U Pr.

Rediscoveries. Ed. by John A. Hall. 226p. 1986. 34.50x (ISBN 0-19-824794-X); pap. 11.95x (ISBN 0-19-824793-1). Oxford U Pr.

Rediscoveries II. Ed. by David Madden & Peggy Bach. 288p. 1988. 18.95 (ISBN 0-88184-391-1). Carroll & Graf.

Rediscoveries in American Sculpture: Studio Works, 1893-1939. Janis Conner & Joel Rosenkrantz. (Illus.). 176p. 1989. 39.95 (ISBN 0-292-70401-1). U of Tex Pr.

Rediscoveries in Art: Some Aspects of Taste, Fashion, & Collecting in England & France. Francis Haskell. (Wrightsman Lectures). 340p. 1980. pap. 16.95 (ISBN 0-8014-9187-8). Cornell U Pr.

Rediscoveries: Literature & Places in Illinois. Robert C. Bray. LC 81-3353. 184p. 1982. 19.95 (ISBN 0-252-00911-8). U of Ill Pr.

Rediscovering America. Frederick W. Turner. 416p. 1985. 25.00 (ISBN 0-670-80774-5). Viking.

Rediscovering America: John Muir in His Time & Ours. Frederick Turner. LC 86-24885. (Illus.). 432p. 1987. pap. 10.95 (ISBN 0-87156-704-0). Sierra.

Rediscovering Brooklyn History: A Guide to Research Collections. Thomas Mills. LC 78-65791. (Brooklyn Rediscovery Booklet Ser.). (Illus.). 35p. 1978. pap. 2.50 (ISBN 0-933250-00-2). Bklyn Educ.

Rediscovering Fatima. Robert J. Fox. LC 82-60667. (Illus.). 144p. (Orig.). 1982. pap. 5.95 (ISBN 0-87973-657-7, 657). Our Sunday Visitor.

Rediscovering French Film. Ed. by Mary Lea Bandy. (Illus.). 240p. 1983. pap. 15.00 (ISBN 0-87070-335-8, 729353, Pub. by Museum Mod Art). NYGS.

Rediscovering Governance: A Guide to "Nonservice" Approaches to Address Neighborhood Problems. annual 80p. 1980. 5.00 (ISBN 0-318-16231-8, P180900). Pub Tech Inc.

Rediscovering Hawthorne. Kenneth Dauber. LC 76-45893. Repr. of 1977 ed. 47.20 (ISBN 0-8357-9510-1, 2014030). Bks Demand UMI.

Rediscovering Illinois: Archaeological Explorations in & Around Fulton County. Fay-Cooper Cole & Thorne Deuel. (Midway Reprint Ser.). (Illus.). xvi, 296p. 1975. pap. text ed. 12.50x (ISBN 0-226-11336-1). U of Chicago Pr.

Rediscovering India. (Illus.). 150p. 1983. text ed. 50.00x (ISBN 0-7069-2277-8, Pub. by Vikas India). Advent NY.

Rediscovering Japanese Space. Kisho Kurokawa. (Illus.). 224p. 42.50 (ISBN 0-8348-0224-4). Weatherhill.

Rediscovering Jesus: Challenge of Discipleship. Eamonn Bredin. LC 86-50244. 300p. 1986. pap. 9.95 (ISBN 0-89622-300-0). Twenty-Third.

Rediscovering Love. Willard Gaylin. 240p. 1986. 15.95 (ISBN 0-670-81120-3). Viking.

Rediscovering Love. Willard Gaylin. 304p. 1987. pap. 4.50 (ISBN 0-14-010431-3). Penguin.

Rediscovering Mantua (Portage County, Ohio) Elmer F. Pfaff. (Illus.). 212p. (Orig.). 1985. pap. 10.00 (ISBN 0-9615749-0-9). Mage In Nation.

Rediscovering Mathematics. A. H. Hackert. 1982. text ed. 27.95 (ISBN 0-8053-3660-5); pap. text ed. 4.95 instr' s guide (ISBN 0-8053-3661-3). Benjamin-Cummings.

Rediscovering Mathematics. Adelbert F. Hackert. 501p. 1982. pap. text ed. 21.95x (ISBN 0-935920-41-2). Natl Pub Black Hills.

Rediscovering Myself & Others in God: The Never-Ending Dialogue. Robert E. Lauder. LC 86-32171. 73p. (Orig.). 1987. pap. 4.95 (ISBN 0-8189-0517-4). Alba.

Rediscovering Passover: A Complete Guide to Passover for Christians. Joseph Stallings. LC 87-62531. 286p. (Orig.). 1988. pap. 9.95 (ISBN 0-89390-106-7). Resource Pubns.

Rediscovering Pastoral Care. Alastair V. Campbell. LC 81-7547. 132p. 1981. pap. 7.95 (ISBN 0-664-24381-9). Westminster John Knox.

Rediscovering Paul: Philemon & the Sociology of Paul's Narrative World. Norman Petersen. LC 84-48730. 320p. 1985. 24.95 (ISBN 0-8006-0741-4, 1-741). Fortress.

Rediscovering Prophecy: A New Song for a New Kingdom. Ronald B. Allen. 1987. pap. 7.95 (ISBN 0-88070-187-0). Multnomah.

Rediscovering Self-Help: Its Role in Social Care. Ed. by Diane L. Pancoast et al. (Social Service Delivery Systems Annual: Vol. 6). 296p. 1983. 39.95 (ISBN 0-8039-1990-5); pap. 17.95 (ISBN 0-8039-1993-X). Sage.

Rediscovering Some New England Artists: 1875-1900. Rolf H. Kristiansen & John J. Leahy. LC 86-60495. (Illus.). 316p. (Orig.). 1987. pap. 16.95 (ISBN 0-9616580-0-2). Gardner-O'Brien.

Rediscovering the Angels & Natives of Eternity. 8th ed. Flower A. Newhouse. (Illus.). 11.00 (ISBN 0-910378-02-9). Christward.

Rediscovering the Charismata: Building up the Body of Christ Through Spiritual Gifts. Charles Bryant. 192p. 1986. 11.95 (ISBN 0-8499-0539-7). Word Bks.

Rediscovering the Constitution. Jefferson Foundation Staff & Congressional Quarterly Staff. 221p. 1987. pap. 9.95 (ISBN 0-87187-407-5). Congr Quarterly.

Rediscovering the Gift of Healing. 2nd ed. Lawrence Althouse. 144p. 1983. pap. 5.95 (ISBN 0-87728-604-3). Weiser.

Rediscovering the I Ching: The First Translation to Reflect Contemporary Scholarship Regarding This Ancient Chinese Oracle. Greg Whincup. LC 85-20595. (Illus.). 256p. 1986. pap. 18.95 (ISBN 0-385-19667-9). Doubleday.

Rediscovering the Impact of Jesus' Death. Joseph A. Grassi. LC 87-60873. 130p. (Orig.). 1987. pap. 6.95 (ISBN 1-55612-065-6). Sheed & Ward MO.

Rediscovering the Lord's Supper: Communion with Israel, with Christ & Among the Guests. Markus Barth. LC 87-46294. 1988. pap. 11.95 (ISBN 0-8042-3749-2, John Knox). Westminster John Knox.

Rediscovering the Parables. Joachim Jeremias. LC 67-13197. 187p. 1977. pap. text ed. write for info. (ISBN 0-02-360490-5, Pub. by Scribner). Macmillan.

Rediscovering the Past at Mexico's Periphery: Essays on the History of Modern Yucatan. Gilbert M. Joseph. LC 85-1185. (Illus.). 208p. 1986. 28.95 (ISBN 0-8173-0268-9). U of Ala Pr.

Rediscovering the Power of the Gospel: Jesus' Theology of the Kingdom. J. Arthur Baird. LC 82-83623. 1982. pap. 9.95 (ISBN 0-910789-00-2). Iona Pr.

Rediscovering the Sacraments: Approaches to the Sacrament. Brennan Hill. 126p. (Orig.). 1982. 4.95 (ISBN 0-8215-9882-1). Sadlier.

Rediscovering the Social Group: A Self-Categorization Theory. John C. Turner. 216p. 1987. text ed. 34.95 (ISBN 0-631-14806-X). Basil Blackwell.

Rediscovering the Teachings of Jesus. Norman Perrin. LC 67-11510. 1976. pap. 8.95 (ISBN 0-06-066493-2, RD 151, HarpR). Har-Row.

Rediscovering the Traditions of Israel. Douglas A. Knight. LC 75-6868. (Society of Biblical Literature. Dissertation Ser.: No. 9). pap. 86.50 (ISBN 0-317-07884-4, 2017515). Bks Demand UMI.

Rediscovering the Wheel: Contrary Thinking & Investment Strategy. Bradbury K. Thurlow. LC 81-68904. 1981. flexible cover 12.00 (ISBN 0-87034-062-X). Fraser Pub Co.

Rediscovering the Woodburning Cookstove. Robert Bobrowski. LC 76-4680. (Illus.). 98p. 1976. pap. 7.95 (ISBN 0-85699-130-9). Chatham Pr.

Rediscovery of Black Nationalism. Theodore Draper. 1970. write for info. Viking.

Rediscovery of Greece: Travellers & Painters of the Romantic Era. Fani-Maria Tsigakou. (Illus.). 208p. 1981. 50.00 (ISBN 0-89241-354-9). Caratzas.

Rediscovery of Inner Experience. Lucy Bregman. LC 81-22600. 200p. 1982. text ed. 18.95x (ISBN 0-88229-686-8). Nelson-Hall.

Rediscovery of John Wesley. George C. Cell. LC 83-6505. 438p. 1983. pap. text ed. 16.50 (ISBN 0-8191-3222-5). U Pr of Amer.

Rediscovery of Jones, Studies in the Obvious. facs. ed. Simeon Strunsky. LC 67-22064. (Essay Index Reprint Ser). 1931. 17.00 (ISBN 0-8369-0911-9). Ayer Co Pubs.

Rediscovery of Meaning & Other Essays. Owen Barfield. vi, 260p. 1985. pap. 10.95 (ISBN 0-8195-6124-X). Wesleyan U Pr.

Rediscovery of Newman: An Oxford Symposium. Ed. by John Coulson & Arthur M. Allchin. LC 68-84451. 1967. text ed. 15.00x (ISBN 0-8401-0458-8). A R Allenson.

Rediscovery of Sir John Mandeville. Josephine W. Bennett. (MLA Mono Ser.: 19). 1954. 32.00 (ISBN 0-527-06700-8). Kraus Repr.

Rediscovery of the Business Cycle. Paul A. Volcker. LC 78-19850. 1978. 14.95 (ISBN 0-02-933430-6). Free Pr.

Rediscovery of the Family & Other Lectures: Sister Marie Hilda Memorial Lectures 1954-1973. 112p. 1981. pap. text ed. 10.00 (ISBN 0-08-025754-2). Pergamon.

Rediscovery of the Frontier. Percy H. Boynton. LC 31-28011. (Illus.). 1969. Repr. of 1931 ed. lib. bdg. 35.00x (ISBN 0-8371-0480-7, BORE). Greenwood.

Rediscovery of the Holy Land in the Nineteenth Century. Yehoshua Ben-Arieh. LC 79-67619. (Illus.). 266p. 1980. 24.95x (ISBN 0-8143-1654-9, Co-Pub by Magnes Press, Hebrew University, & Israel Exploration Society). Wayne St U Pr.

Rediscovery of the New World. (Eng. & Span.). 1972. pap. 1.00 Eng. ed. (ISBN 0-8270-4545-X); pap. 1.00 Span. ed. (ISBN 0-8270-4550-6). OAS.

Rediscovery of the Old Testament. H. H. Rowley. 224p. 1946. 14.00 (ISBN 0-227-67576-2). Attic Pr.

Rediscovery: Three Hundred Years of Stories by & about Women. Ed. by Betzy Dinesen. 272p. 1982. pap. 3.50 (ISBN 0-380-60756-5, 60756-5, Bard). Avon.

Redistribution & the Welfare System. Edgar K. Browning. LC 75-15155. (Orig.). 1975. pap. 8.50 (ISBN 0-8447-3170-6). Am Enterprise.

Redistribution of Income in Postwar Britain. Allan M. Cartter. LC 72-86540. 256p. 1973. Repr. of 1955 ed. 26.50x (ISBN 0-8046-1750-3, Pub. by Kennikat). Assoc Faculty Pr.

Redistribution of Population in Africa. John I. Clarke & Leszek A. Kosinski. xii, 212p. 1982. text ed. 50.00x (ISBN 0-435-95030-4); pap. text ed. 22.50x (ISBN 0-435-95031-2). Heinemann Ed.

Redistribution Through Public Choice. Harold M. Hochman & George E. Peterson. LC 73-19748. 1974. 37.50x (ISBN 0-231-03775-9). Columbia U Pr.

Redistribution Through the Financial System: The Grants Economics of Money & Credit. Ed. by Kenneth E. Boulding & Thomas F. Wilson. LC 78-18017. 336p. 1978. 56.95 (ISBN 0-275-90286-2, C0286). Praeger.

Redistribution with Growth: An Approach to Policy. Hollis Chenery et al. 1974. pap. 10.95x (ISBN 0-19-920070-X). Oxford U Pr.

Redistributive Effects of Government Programmes: The Chilean Case. A. Foxley et al. (Illus.). 1979. 50.00 (ISBN 0-08-023130-6). Pergamon.

Redistricting Arkansas Circuit & Chancery Courts. National Center for State Courts Staff. 87p. 1976. manuscript 5.22 (MAB-099). Natl Ctr St Courts.

Redivision of Labor: Women & Economic Choice in Four Guatemalan Communities. Laurel H. Bossen. LC 83-426. (SUNY Series in the Anthropology of Work). (Illus.). 396p. 1984. 59.50 (ISBN 0-87395-740-7); pap. 19.95 (ISBN 0-87395-741-5). State U NY Pr.

Redland Family. G. T. Ridlon. LC 70-138071. (Saco Valley Settlements Ser). 1970. pap. 1.75 (ISBN 0-8048-0828-7). C E Tuttle.

Redland Park Recorded. Peggy Thomas. 240p. 1986. pap. 30.00x (ISBN 0-947939-03-2, Pub. by Elmcrest Uk). State Mutual Bk.

Redland Park Recorded. Peggy Thomas. 240p. 1987. pap. 35.00x (ISBN 0-317-62094-0, Michael Gardener Pubs). State Mutual Bk.

Redlands, Our Town. Frank E. Moore. (Illus.). 256p. 1987. 14.95 (ISBN 0-914167-04-9); pap. 7.95 (ISBN 0-914167-05-7). Moore Hist.

Redlight Ladies of Virginia City, Nevada. George J. Williams, III. (Nevada Prostitution Ser.). (Illus., Orig.). 1984. 10.95 (ISBN 0-935174-13-3); pap. 5.95 (ISBN 0-935174-12-5). Tree by River.

Redlining: A Selective Bibliography. Lorna Peterson. (Public Administration Ser.: P 1952). 6p. 1986. 3.00 (ISBN 0-89028-892-5). Vance Biblios.

Redmire Pool. Kevin Clifford & Len Arbery. 1985. 60.00x (ISBN 0-317-39161-5, Pub. by BeeKay Pubs Ltd). STate Mutual Bk.

Redmond: Where the Desert Blooms. Keith Clark. (Illus.). 128p. 1986. pap. 8.95 (ISBN 0-87595-178-3). Oregon Hist.

Redneck Bride. John F. Ryan. LC 86-3350. (Illus.). 176p. 1986. pap. 7.95 (ISBN 0-87483-005-2). August Hse.

Redneck Country Cookin' 2nd ed. Billie T. Signer. LC 82-40404. 110p. 1985. pap. 7.95 (ISBN 0-941186-06-7). J & B Bks.

Redneck Exercise Book. Paul Johnson & Nell Weaver. LC 84-62351. (Illus.). 50p. 1984. pap. 4.95 (ISBN 0-914546-58-9). Rose Pub.

Redneck Liberal: Theodore G. Bilbo & the New Deal. Chester M. Morgan. LC 85-11023. (Illus.). 274p. 1985. text ed. 30.00 (ISBN 0-8071-1243-7). La State U Pr.

Redneck Waltz. Howard Smead. Date not set. 17.95 (ISBN 0-942597-03-6). White Mane Pub.

Redneck Way of Knowledge. Blanche M. Boyd. 176p. 1983. pap. 5.95 (ISBN 0-14-006725-6). Penguin.

Redneck Way of Knowledge: Down-Home Tales. Blanche Boyd. LC 81-48138. 160p. 1982. 10.45 (ISBN 0-394-51050-X). Knopf.

Redneckin' Made Easy. Bo Whaley. 1988. pap. 2.95 (ISBN 0-934395-94-2). Rutledge Hill Pr.

Rednecks & Other Bonafide Americans. Bo Whaley. LC 86-21917. 176p. 1986. 9.95 (ISBN 0-934395-41-1). Rutledge Hill Pr.

Redney: A Life of Sara Jeannette Duncan. Marian Fowler. (Illus.). 336p. 1983. 9.95 (ISBN 0-88784-099-X, Pub. by Hse Anansi Pr Canada). U of Toronto Pr.

Redoute Treasury: Four Hundred & Sixty-Eight Watercolors from Les Liliacees. Frances Mallary & Peter Mallary. (Illus.). 468p. 1986. 50.00 (ISBN 0-86565-067-5). Vendome.

Redoute's Fairest Flowers. Martyn Rix & William T. Stern. (Illus.). 320p. 1987. 35.00 (ISBN 0-13-769845-3). P-H.

Redress for Success: Using the Law to Enforce Your Rights As a Woman. Dana Shilling. 336p. 1985. 22.95 (ISBN 0-670-80809-1). Viking.

Redress for Success: Using the Law to Enforce Your Rights As a Woman. Dana Shilling. (Nonfiction Ser.). 336p. (Orig.). 1985. pap. 8.95 (ISBN 0-14-008419-3). Penguin.

Redressing the Balance: American Women's Literary Humor from Colonial Times to the 1980s. Ed. by Nancy Walker & Zita Dresner. (Orig.). 1988. text ed. 35.00x (ISBN 0-87805-363-8); pap. 17.95x (ISBN 0-87805-364-6). U Pr of Miss.

Reds Bring Reaction. W. J. Ghent. 1977. lib. bdg. 59.95 (ISBN 0-8490-2505-2). Gordon Pr.

Reds Bring Reaction. William J. Ghent. 17.00 (ISBN 0-405-09952-5, 10047). Ayer Co Pubs.

Reds, Reds, Copper Reds. Robert Tichane. Tr. by Thomas Elmer. LC 84-62546. (Oriental Glaze Ser.). (Illus.). 306p. 1985. 25.00x (ISBN 0-914267-04-3). NYS Inst Glaze.

Redskin Country: An Inside Look at Washington Redskins' Football. 2nd ed. Ken Denlinger & Paul Attner. LC 83-80699. (Illus.). 192p. 1983. cancelled (ISBN 0-88011-191-7). Leisure Pr.

Redskin Morning, & Other Stories. Joan M. Grant & Ralph Layers. 19.00 (ISBN 0-405-11787-6). Ayer Co Pubs.

Redskins, Ruffleshirts & Rednecks: Indian Allotments in Alabama & Mississippi 1830-1860. Mary E. Young. LC 61-15150. (Civilization of the American Indian Ser: No. 61). (Illus.). Repr. of 1961 ed. 58.30 (ISBN 0-8357-9739-2, 2016284). Bks Demand UMI.

Redskins Trivia. Jim Perry. (Illus.). 184p. Date not set. pap. 7.95 (ISBN 0-933341-64-4). Quinlan Pr.

Redthroats. David Cale. (Orig.). 1989. 6.95 (ISBN 0-679-73961-0, Vin). Random.

Reduce: Software for Algebraic Computation. Gerhard Rayna. LC 87-20535. 335p. 1988. pap. 29.80 (ISBN 0-387-96598-X). Springer-Verlag.

Reduce Your Tax Byte. Donald R. Woodwell. 230p. 1986. cancelled (ISBN 0-917253-42-6). Probus Pub Co.

Reduced Enrichment for Research & Test Reactors. Ed. by P. Von der Hardt & A. Travelli. 1986. lib. bdg. 74.50 (ISBN 90-277-2233-1, Pub. by Reidel Holland). Kluwer Academic.

Reduced Instruction Set Computer Architectures For VLSI. Manolis G. H. Katevenis. (Association for Computing Machinery Doctoral Dissertation Award Ser.). (Illus.). 225p. 1985. text ed. 30.00x (ISBN 0-262-11103-9). MIT Pr.

Reduced Instruction Set: Computer RISK Architecture. Daniel Tabak. 161p. 1987. 39.95 (ISBN 0-471-91302-2). Wiley.

Reduced Instruction Set Computers. William Stallings. (Tutorial Text Ser.). 376p. 1986. 44.00 (ISBN 0-8186-0713-0, FE713). IEEE Comp Soc.

Reduced Terms of Jury Service in the Federal Courts. National Center for State Courts Staff. 41p. 1986. manuscript 3.00 (CJS-003). Natl Ctr St Courts.

Reducing Adolescent Prejudice: A Handbook. Nina H. Gabelko & John U. Michaelis. 226p. pap. 15.95 (ISBN 0-686-95038-0). ADL.

Reducing Adolescent Prejudice: A Handbook, Grades 9-12. Nina H. Gabelko & John U. Michaelis. 230p. 1981. pap. text ed. 15.95x (ISBN 0-8077-2601-X); dup. masters 17.95x (ISBN 0-8077-2639-7). Tchrs Coll.

Reducing Adolescent Prejudice: Duplicating Masters. 83p. pap. 17.95 (ISBN 0-686-95039-9). ADL.

Reducing & Eliminating Behavior. Ellsworth Community College Staff. Ed. by Michael Davis. (RATES Ser.: No. 9). (Illus.). 84p. (Orig.). 1983. pap. 3.00x (ISBN 0-916671-45-3). Material Dev.

Reducing Cost of Space Transportation: Proceedings of the Goddard Memorial Symposium, 7th, Washington, D.C., 1969. (Science & Technology Ser.: Vol. 21). (Illus.). 1969. 25.00x (ISBN 0-87703-049-9, Pub. by Am Astronaut). Univelt Inc.

Reducing Court Recording Cost. National Center for State Courts Staff. (Paul Reardon Ser.). 25p. 1983. manuscript 1.50 (PRS-044). Natl Ctr St Courts.

Reducing Crime & Assuring Justice. Committee for Economic Development. LC 72-81298. 86p. 1972. lib. bdg. 2.50 (ISBN 0-87186-746-X); pap. 1.50 (ISBN 0-87186-046-5). Comm Econ Dev.

Reducing Diarrhea in Tube Fed Patients. Ed. by Jo-Ann Horsley. (Using Research to Improve Nursing Practice Ser.). 99p. 1981. 12.50 (ISBN 0-8089-1326-3, 792066). Grune.

Reducing Diet & Medical Processes: A Research Subject Analysis with Bibliography. Chester D. Donovan. LC 84-45734. 150p. 1987. 34.50 (ISBN 0-88164-246-0); pap. 26.50 (ISBN 0-88164-247-9). ABBE Pubs Assn.

Reducing Disparity in Judicial Sentencing: A Social-Psychological Approach. Siegfried L. Sporer. (European University Studies-Ser. 6, Psychology: Vol. 97). 114p. 1982. 14.20 (ISBN 3-8204-7208-8). P Lang Pubs.

Reducing Earthquake Hazards: Lessons Learned from Earthquakes. 208p. 1986. 10.00 (ISBN 0-943198-27-5). Earthquake Eng.

Reducing Earthquake Risks: A Planner's Guide. (PAS Reports: No. 364). 82p. 1981. 18.00 (ISBN 0-318-13071-8). Am Plan Assn.

Reducing Educational Disadvantage. Paul Widlake. LC 86-8676. 160p. 1987. 65.00x (ISBN 0-335-15241-4, Open Univ Pr); pap. 21.00x (ISBN 0-335-15240-6). Taylor & Francis.

Reducing Energy Consumption in Buildings. Seymour Jarmul. 80p. 1988. 13.75 (ISBN 0-86619-178-X); French ed. 13.75 (ISBN 0-86619-177-1). Vols Tech Asst.

Reducing Energy Costs in Nursing Homes. 55p. 4.50 (ISBN 0-318-17110-4, 110112); o.p 7.50 (ISBN 0-318-17111-2). Am Health Care Assn.

Reducing Energy Costs in Small Businesses. IMR Corporation. 1983. text ed. 30.00 (ISBN 0-8359-6615-1, Reston). P-H.

Reducing Energy Costs in Wholesale Distribution. 122p. 30.00 (ISBN 0-318-15149-9); members 22.00 (ISBN 0-318-15150-2); commodity line association members 25.00 (ISBN 0-318-15151-0). Natl Assn Wholesale Dists.

Reducing Failures of Engineered Facilities: Proceedings of a Workshop Sponsored by the National Science Foundation & ASCE. 108p. 1985. 13.00x (ISBN 0-87262-485-4). Am Soc Civil Eng.

Reducing Fertility in Developing Countries: A Review of Determinants & Policy Levers. Rodolfo Bulatao. (Working Paper: No. 680). 136p. 1984. 8.00 (ISBN 0-8213-0444-5, WP 0680). World Bank.

Reducing Hazardous Waste Generation. National Research Council. 88p. 1985. pap. text ed. 4.95x (ISBN 0-309-03498-1). Natl Acad Pr.

Reducing Inappropriate Use of Juvenile Detention in Los Angeles County. 1987. 7.00 (ISBN 0-318-23566-8). Natl Coun Crime.

Reducing Industrial Oil Costs. John Hall. 1987. 90.50 (ISBN 0-291-39740-9, Pub. by Gower Pub England). Gower Pub Co.

Reducing Infant Mortality in the Ten Largest Cities in the United States, New York 1912. New York Milk Committee. Ed. by David J. Rothman & Sheila M. Rothman. (Women & Children First Ser.). 176p. 1986. lib. bdg. 30.00 (ISBN 0-8240-7668-0). Garland Pub.

Reducing Input Subsidies to Livestock Producers in Cyprus: An Economic Analysis. Avishay Braverman et al. (Working Paper: No. 782). 62p. 1986. 5.00 (ISBN 0-8213-0672-3). World Bank.

Reducing Labor Turnover in Financial Institutions. Presley T. Creery & Katherine W. Creery. LC 87-37572. (Illus.). 176p. 1988. lib. bdg. 39.95 (ISBN 0-89930-296-3, CYR/, Quorum Bks). Greenwood.

Reducing Malnutrition in Developing Countries: Increasing Rice Production in South & Southeast Asia see Trilateral Commission Task Force Reports.

Reducing Personal Income Tax: A Guide to Deductions & Credits. John E. Davidian & Jacob L. Todres. 1988. looseleaf 70.00 (ISBN 0-318-23689-3). NY Law Pub.

Reducing Pollution from Selected Energy Transformation Sources. Chem Systems International, Ltd. Staff. 230p. 1976. 35.00 (ISBN 0-86010-036-7). Graham & Trotman.

Reducing Regulatory & Financial Impediments to Energy Conservation. 120p. 1982. 20.00 (ISBN 0-318-17714-5, DG82-316). Pub Tech Inc.

Reducing Risk & Liability Through Better Specifications & Inspections. Compiled by American Society of Civil Engineers Staff. LC 82-70874. 165p. 1982. pap. 19.00x (ISBN 0-87262-301-7). Am Soc Civil Eng.

Reducing Risks to Life: Measurement of the Benefits. Martin J. Bailey. 66p. 1980. pap. 7.00 (ISBN 0-8447-3346-6). Am Enterprise.

Reducing Stress in Children Through Creative Relaxation. James H. Humphrey & Joy N. Humphrey. 136p. 1981. 18.75x (ISBN 0-398-04567-4). C C Thomas.

Reducing Stress in Young Children's Lives. Janet B. McCracken. LC 86-62564. (Illus.). 1986. pap. 7.00 (ISBN 0-935989-03-X, NAEYC 216). Natl Assn Child Ed.

Reducing the Carcinogenic Risks in Industry. Paul F. Deisler, Jr. (Occupation Safety & Health Ser.). 288p. 1984. 65.00 (ISBN 0-8247-7250-4). Dekker.

Reducing the Cost of Dental Care. Ed. by Robert T. Kudrle & Lawrence Meskin. 240p. 1983. 25.00x (ISBN 0-8166-1118-1). U of Minn Pr.

Reducing the Cost of Surveys. Seymour Sudman. LC 67-17611. (NORC Monographs in Social Research Ser.: No. 10). 1967. 9.95x (ISBN 0-202-30030-7). NORC.

Reducing the Energy Cost Burden on Low Income Residents. 87p. 1982. 15.00 (ISBN 0-318-17347-6, DG/82-308). Pub Tech Inc.

Reducing the Frequency of Nuclear Reactor Scrams. OECD. 692p. (Orig., Eng. & Fr.). 1987. pap. 44.00x (ISBN 92-64-02937-0). OECD.

Reducing the Paperwork Overload in Hudson County, New Jersey, Superior Court Law Division (Criminal) National Center for State Courts Staff. 29p. 1981. manuscript 1.74 (NERO-089). Natl Ctr St Courts.

Reducing the Risk of Nuclear War. Ed. by Robert J. Einhorn & Patrick J. Garrity. 63p. 1985. 14.95 (ISBN 0-89206-077-8). CSI Studies.

Reducing the Risk of Nuclear War: A Report of the CSIS Group on Strategy & Arms Control. Ed. by Robert J. Einhorn & Patrick J. Garrity. (CSIS Panel Report). (Orig.). 1985. pap. text ed. 14.95 (ISBN 0-8191-5945-X, Pub. by CSIS). U Pr of Amer.

Reducing the Storm to a Whisper: The Story of a Breakdown. Patrick Howell. 228p. 1985. 15.95 (ISBN 0-88347-183-3). Thomas More.

Reducing the Time & Cost of the Appellate Process: Arizona Appellate Project Report. National Center for State Courts Staff. 40p. 1976. manuscript 2.40 (MAB-100). Natl Ctr St Courts.

Reducing Workweeks to Prevent Layoffs: The Economic & Social Impacts of Unemployment Insurance Supported Work Sharing. Fred Best. LC 87-10097. 228p. 1988. 39.95 (ISBN 0-87722-506-0). Temple U Pr.

Reducing Writing Apprehension. Michael W. Smith. (Theory & Research into Practice Ser.). (Orig.). 1984. pap. 6.00 (ISBN 0-8141-3967-1). NCTE.

Reduction. Ed. by R. L. Augustine. (Techniques & Applications in Organic Synthesis Ser.: Vol. 2). 1968. 75.00 (ISBN 0-8247-1026-6). Dekker.

Reduction & Control of Unaccounted-for Water: Working Guidelines. Ed. by P. Jeffecoate & A. Saravanapavan. (World Bank Technical Paper Ser.: No. 72). 1987. pap. text ed. 10.00 (ISBN 0-8213-0951-X, WB218, Pub. by Wrld Bank). UNIPUB.

Reduction in Fleet Fuel Consumption. 76p. 1981. 15.00 (ISBN 0-318-16232-6, DG81801). Pub Tech Inc.

Reduction in Force: Legal Issues & Recommended Policy. Robert E. Phay. 54p. 1980. 6.95 (ISBN 0-686-39474-7). U of NC Inst Gov.

Reduction in the Abstract Sciences. Daniel A. Bonevac. 184p. 1982. 18.50 (ISBN 0-915145-14-6). Hackett Pub.

Reduction of Animal Usage in the Development & Control of Biological Products. Ed. by I. Davidson & W. Hennessen. (Developments in Biological Standardization Ser.: Vol. 64). (Illus.). x, 330p. 1986. pap. 80.00 (ISBN 3-8055-4460-X). S Karger.

Reduction of Gold & Silver Ore. L. K. Hodges. (Prospecting Ser.). 24p. pap. 2.95 (ISBN 0-8466-1993-8, S134D). Shorey.

Reduction of Impediments to Alternative Energy Use. 120p. 1982. 20.00 (ISBN 0-318-17718-8, DG 82-316). Pub Tech Inc.

Reduction of Mayan Dates. Herbert J. Spinden. (HU PMM). 1924. 26.00 (ISBN 0-527-01209-2). Kraus Repr.

Reduction of Military Budgets. (Disarmament Study Ser.: No. 10). 99p. 1983. pap. 8.50x (ISBN 0-8002-3452-9). Intl Pubns Serv.

Reduction of Military Budgets. (Disarmament Study Ser.: No. 4). 197p. 1981. pap. 15.00x (ISBN 0-8002-3457-X). Intl Pubns Serv.

Reduction of Military Budgets. (Disarmament Study Ser.: No. 10). 99p. 1983. pap. text ed. 8.50 (ISBN 92-1-142037-7, E.83.IX.4). UN.

Reduction of Regional Disparities: The Role of Educational Planning. Gabriel Carron & Ta Ngoc Chau. (Illus.). 126p. (Co-published with Kogan Page Ltd.). 1981. pap. 15.00 (ISBN 92-803-1100-X, U1195, UNESCO). UNIPUB.

Reduction of the Product of Two Irreducible Unitary Representations of the Proper Orthochronous Quantummechanical Poincare Group. M. Schaaf. LC 72-139677. (Lecture Notes in Physics: Vol. 5). 1970. pap. 10.70 (ISBN 0-387-05194-5). Springer-Verlag.

Reduction of Working Time: Scope & Implications in Industrialised Market Economies. Rolande Cuvillier. 150p. 1984. text ed. 24.50 (ISBN 92-2-103817-3); pap. 17.50 (ISBN 92-2-102702-3). Intl Labour Office.

Reduction of Working Time: Scope & Implications in Industrialized Market Economies. Rolande Cuvillier. 150p. 1985. pap. 17.50 (ILO346, ILO). UNIPUB.

Reduction on Vehicle Fuel Consumption. 76p. 1981. 15.00 (ISBN 0-318-17351-4, DG/81-801). Pub Tech Inc.

Reduction, Time & Reality: Studies in the Philosophy of the Natural Sciences. Richard Healey. 208p. 1981. 34.50 (ISBN 0-521-23708-4). Cambridge U Pr.

Reductionism & Cultural Being. Joseph W. Smith. 1984. lib. bdg. 56.00 (ISBN 90-247-2884-3, Pub. by Martinus Nijhoff Netherlands). Kluwer Academic.

Reductionism in Academic Disciplines. Ed. by Arthur Peacocke. 1985. 33.00x. Taylor & Francis.

Reductionist Poem. Anthony Cronin. 39p. 1980. pap. 6.95 (ISBN 0-906897-12-2). Dufour.

Reductions in Organic Chemistry. M. Hudlicky. LC 84-3768. (Chemical Science Ser.). 309p. 1984. 49.95x (ISBN 0-470-20018-9). Halsted Pr.

Reductions in U. S. Domestic Spending: How They Affect State & Local Governments. Ed. by John W. Ellwood. LC 82-10975. (Illus.). 401p. 1982. pap. 9.95 (ISBN 0-87855-923-X). Transaction Bks.

Reductive Object. (Illus.). 1979. 3.00 (ISBN 0-910663-22-X). ICA Inc.

Redundancy & Recession: In South Wales. C. C. Harris & The Redundancy & Unemployment Research Group, School of Social Studies, University College of Swansea. 256p. Date not set. text ed. 55.00 (ISBN 0-631-15106-0). Basil Blackwell.

Redundancy: Case Studies in Co-operation & Conflict. Stephen Wood & Ian Dey. 128p. 1983. text ed. 33.00x (ISBN 0-566-00571-9). Gower Pub Co.

Redundancy in Mathematical Programming: A State-of-the-Art Survey. M. H. Karwan et al. (Lecture Notes in Economics & Mathematical Systems: Vol. 206). (Illus.). 286p. 1983. pap. 22.00 (ISBN 0-387-11552-8). Springer-Verlag.

Redundancy in the Nineteen Eighties: The Take-Up of Voluntary Schemes. Alan Gordon. LC 84-21052. (Institute of Manpower Studies: No. 6). 112p. 1984. pap. text ed. 27.00 (ISBN 0-566-00826-2). Gower Pub Co.

Redundancy, Layoffs & Plant Closures: Their Nature & Social Impact. Ed. by Raymond M. Lee. 352p. 1986. 55.00 (ISBN 0-7099-4129-3, Pub. by Croom Helm Ltd). Routledge Chapman & Hall.

Redundant Counties? Participation & Electoral Choice in England's Metropolitan Countries. S. Bristow et al. 1984. 32.00x (ISBN 0-905777-41-7, Pub. by Hesketh UK). State Mutual Bk.

Redundant Male: Is Sex Irrelevant in the Modern World? Jeremy Cherfas & John Gribbin. LC 84-42971. 208p. 15.45 (ISBN 0-394-53030-6); pap. 7.95 (ISBN 0-394-74005-X). Pantheon.

Redundant Space. Howard Green & Paul Foley. 1986. text ed. 22.50 (ISBN 0-06-318344-7, IntlDept). Har-Row.

Redundant Women. Angela Coyle. 160p. 1984. pap. 7.95 (ISBN 0-7043-3923-4, Pub. by Quartet Bks.). Salem Hse Pubs.

Redville Wanderer. 1982. 15.00x (ISBN 0-906660-95-5, Pub. by New Playwrights Network). State Mutual Bk.

Redwall. Brian Jacques. (gr. k up). 1987. 15.95 (ISBN 0-399-21424-0, Philomel). Putnam Pub Group.

Redward Edward Papers. Avram Davidson. LC 74-27578. 208p. 1978. 15.00. Ultramarine Pub.

Redwing Blackbird. Paul Foreman. 1973. pap. 2.50x (ISBN 0-914476-15-7). Thorp Springs.

Redwings. Robert Nero. LC 83-10486. (Smithsonian Nature Bks.). (Illus.). 160p. 1984. pap. 12.95 (ISBN 0-87474-677-9, NEREP). Smithsonian.

Redwood: A Tale. Catherine M. Sedgwick. 1972. Repr. of 1824 ed. lib. bdg. 29.50 (ISBN 0-8422-8108-8). Irvington.

Redwood Classic. Ralph W. Andrews. (Illus.). 174p. 1985. pap. 12.95 (ISBN 0-88740-049-3). Schiffer.

Redwood Country. Lynwood Carranco. (Illus.). 360p. (Orig.). 1986. pap. 14.95 (ISBN 0-89863-097-5). Star Pub CA.

Redwood Country: A Pictorial Guide Through California's Magnificent Redwood Forests. rev. ed. Harriet Weaver. LC 83-2098. (Illus.). 132p. (Orig.). 1983. pap. 8.95 (ISBN 0-87701-279-2). Chronicle Bks.

Redwood Delta. Ron Flesch. 1988. pap. 3.95. Berkley Pub.

Redwood Empire. A. E. Maxwell. 416p. Date not set. pap. 3.95 (ISBN 0-373-97049-8, Pub. by Worldwide). Harlequin Bks.

Redwood Empire. 14.95 (ISBN 0-933692-32-3). A R Collings.

Redwood Empire, Wildflower Jewels see Wildflowers of the Redwood Empire.

Redwood Forest & Native Grasses & Their Stories. Craig C. Dremann. (Orig.). 1987. pap. 1.00 (ISBN 0-933421-19-2). Redwood Seed.

Redwood Lumber Industry. Lynwood Carranco. (Illus.). 218p. 17.50 (ISBN 0-87095-084-3). Gldn West Bks.

Redwood Railways. Gilbert H. Kneiss. LC 57-671. (Illus.). 1956. 14.95 (ISBN 0-8310-7005-6). Howell-North.

Redwood Region Flower Finder. Phoebe Watts. (Illus.). 1979. pap. 1.50 (ISBN 0-912550-08-2). Nature Study.

Redwood Seed. Kelsey Morton. (Wellspring Bk.). (Illus.). 128p. 1988. pap. 8.95 (ISBN 0-916349-45-4). Amity Hse Inc.

Redwood: The Story Behind the Scenery. Richard A. Rasp. LC 88-80122. (Illus.). 48p. 1988. pap. 4.50 (ISBN 0-88714-022-X). KC Pubns.

Redwoods & California's North Coast. Bob Von Normann. Ed. by George Castaldo. 32p. (Orig.). 1988. 5.95 (ISBN 0-915687-01-1). FVN Corp.

Redwoods Are the Tallest Trees in the World. David A. Adler. LC 77-4713. (Let's-Read-&-Find Out Science Bks.). (Illus.). (gr. k-3). 1978. PLB 12.89 (ISBN 0-690-01368-X, Crowell Jr Bks). HarpJ.

Reed Ferris' Nineteen-Thirty to Nineteen Forty-Three Bird Banding Records & Birds Observations for Tillamook County, Oregon. Range D. Bayer & Reed W. Ferris. LC 87-81812. (Studies in Oregon Ornithology: No. 3). (Illus.). ix, 131p. (Orig.). 1987. pap. 6.50 (ISBN 0-939819-02-3). Gahmken Pr.

Reed Organ: Its Design & Construction. H. F. Milne. (Illus.). pap. 7.50x (ISBN 0-913746-02-9). Organ Lit.

Reed, Pen & Brush Alphabets for Writing & Lettering. Edward M. Catich. LC 80-15498. (Visual Communications Bks.). (Illus.). 64p. (Orig.). 1980. pap. 9.95 (ISBN 0-8038-5891-4). Hastings.

Reed Smoot: Apostle in Politics. Milton R. Merrill. (Western Experience Ser.). 500p. Date not set. PLB 37.50 (ISBN 0-87421-127-1). Utah St U Pr.

Reed Town, Japan: A Study in Community Power Structure & Political Change. Yasumasa Kuroda. LC 73-85580. 297p. 1974. text ed. 17.50x (ISBN 0-8248-0292-6). UH Pr.

Reed Trio: An Annotated Bibliography of Original Published Works. James E. Gillespie, Jr. LC 74-174729. (Detroit Studies in Music Bibliography Ser.: No. 20). 1971. pap. 6.00 (ISBN 0-911772-42-1). Harmonie Pk Pr.

Reeds. Gibbons Ruark. LC 78-90515. 571p. (Orig.). 1978. 5.95 (ISBN 0-89672-058-6); pap. 2.95 (ISBN 0-89672-057-8). Tex Tech Univ Pr.

Reeds & Mud. Vicente Blasco-Ibanez. Tr. by Lester Beberfall. (Orig.). 1966. pap. 3.95 (ISBN 0-8283-1470-5). Branden Pub Co.

Reed's Marine Distance Tables. 6th ed. Compiled by R. W. Caney & J. E. Reynolds. Date not set. pap. 32.50 (ISBN 0-947637-80-X). Heinman.

Reeds of Rainbows. Mackenzie Munro. 64p. 1985. 9.50 (ISBN 0-908175-25-6, Pub. by Boolarong Pubn Australia). Intl Spec Bk.

Reef. Edith Wharton. 384p. 1984. 20.00 (ISBN 0-684-15557-5); pap. 9.95 (ISBN 0-684-18249-1). Scribner.

Reef. Edith Wharton. (Twentieth Century Classics Ser.). 400p. 1987. pap. 4.95 (ISBN 0-02-055410-9, Collier). Macmillan.

Reef see Novels.

Reef & Shore Fauna of Hawaii: Protozoa Through Ctenophora. Ed. by D. M. Devaney & L. G. Eldredge. LC 77-89747. (Special Publication Ser: No. 64 (1)). (Illus.). 290p. 1977. pap. 22.50 (ISBN 0-910240-22-1). Bishop Mus.

Reef & the Wrasse. Susan Steere & Kathryn M. Ring. (Juvenile Natural History Ser.). (Illus.). 32p. (Orig.). (gr. 4-6). 1988. PLB 12.95 (ISBN 0-943173-05-1); pap. 6.95 (ISBN 0-943173-24-8). Harbinger AZ.

Reef Diagenesis. Ed. by J. Schroeder & B. H. Purser. (Illus.). 450p. 1986. 59.00 (ISBN 0-387-16594-0). Springer-Verlag.

Reef Fishes of the Indian Ocean. Gerald R. Allen & Roger C. Steene. (Pacific Marine Fishes Ser.: Bk. 10). (Illus.). 240p. 1987. 34.95 (ISBN 0-86622-386-X, H1084). TFH Pubns.

Reef Fishes of the Sea of Cortez: The Rocky-Shore Fishes of the Gulf of California. Donald A. Thomson et al. LC 86-24996. (Illus.). 302p. 1987. pap. 19.95 (ISBN 0-8165-0984-0). U of Ariz Pr.

Reef Lights: Seaswept Lighthouses of the Florida Keys. Dean Love. LC 82-83206. (Illus.). 134p. 1982. pap. 9.95 (ISBN 0-943528-03-8). Hist Fl Keys.

Reefcomber's Field Guide. Idaz Greenberg. (Illus.). 1986. plastic card 5.00x (ISBN 0-913008-17-6). Seahawk Pr.

Reefer Madness: Marijuana in America. Larry Sloman. (Illus.). 360p. 1983. pap. 8.95 (ISBN 0-394-62446-7, E851, Ever). Grove.

Reefs. Kevin O'Donnell, Jr. 224p. (Orig.). 1982. pap. 2.50 (ISBN 0-425-06235-X). Berkley Pub.

Reefs. Ruth Radlauer & Henry M. Anderson. LC 82-17862. (Geo Bks.). (Illus.). 48p. (gr. 4 up). 1983. PLB 13.27 (ISBN 0-516-07836-4); pap. 3.95 (ISBN 0-516-47836-2). Childrens.

Reference Guide to Fantastic Films, Science Fiction, Fantasy, & Horror, Vol. 3: P-Z. Ed. by Walt Lee. LC 72-88775. (Illus.). 270p. (Orig.). 1974. pap. 17.95 (ISBN 0-913974-03-X). Chelsea-Lee Bks.

Reference Guide to Fantastic Films, Science Fiction, Fantasy, & Horror, Vol. 2: G-O. Ed. by Walt Lee. LC 72-88775. (Illus.). 242p. (Orig.). 1973. pap. 17.95 (ISBN 0-913974-02-1). Chelsea-Lee Bks.

Reference Guide to Fantastic Films, Science Fiction, Fantasy, & Horror, Vol. 1: A-F. Ed. by Walt Lee. LC 72-88775. (Illus.). 230p. (Orig.). 1972. pap. 17.95 (ISBN 0-913974-01-3). Chelsea-Lee Bks.

Reference Guide to Fantastic Films, Science Fiction, Fantasy, & Horror, 3 vols. Ed. by Walt Lee. LC 72-88775. (Illus.). 742p. (Orig.). 1974. pap. 53.85 set (ISBN 0-913974-04-8). Chelsea-Lee Bks.

Reference Guide to Georgia Legal History & Legal Research. Leah F. Chanin. 177p. 1980. 20.00x (ISBN 0-87215-315-0); 1983 supplement 7.50x (ISBN 0-87215-711-3). Michie Co.

Reference Guide to Handbooks & Annuals. 1985 ed. Ed. by J. William Pfeiffer. LC 75-14661. 206p. 1985. pap. 14.95 (ISBN 0-88390-065-3). Univ Assocs.

Reference Guide to Historical Fiction for Children & Young Adults. Lynda G. Adamson. LC 87-7533. 420p. 1987. lib. bdg. 49.95 (ISBN 0-313-25002-2, ARH/). Greenwood.

Reference Guide to Indiana. Ingrid E. Jonsson. LC 77-80566. 1977. lib. bdg. 39.00x (ISBN 0-403-07220-4). Somerset Pub.

Reference Guide to International Taxation Profiting from Your International Operations. Michel W. Glautier & Frederick W. Bassinger. LC 86-45754. 448p. 1987. 59.95 (ISBN 0-669-14292-1). Lexington Bks.

Reference Guide to Management Techniques & Activities. I. G. Bloor. 114p. 1987. 19.95 (ISBN 0-08-034268-X, PBL); pap. 9.75 (ISBN 0-08-034269-8, PBL). Pergamon.

Reference Guide to Minnesota History: A Subject Bibliography of Books, Pamphlets & Articles in English. Compiled by Michael Brook. LC 74-4222. 132p. 1974. pap. 8.95 (ISBN 0-87351-082-8). Minn Hist.

Reference Guide to Modern Fantasy for Children. Pat Pflieger. LC 83-10692. 768p. 1984. lib. bdg. 67.95 (ISBN 0-313-22886-8, PFC/). Greenwood.

Reference Guide to Real Estate. 192p. 4.95 (ISBN 0-8092-5682-7). Contemp Bks.

Reference Guide to Science Fiction & Fantasy. Michael Burgess. 125p. 1988. lib. bdg. 28.50 (ISBN 0-87287-611-X). Libs Unl.

Reference Guide to SURVEYS. Randall L. Voight & George Franklin, Jr. (Decision Support Ser.). 448p. 1981. 125.00 (ISBN 0-930318-11-0). Intl Res Eval.

Reference Guide to Texas Law & Legal History: Sources & Documentation. Marian Boner. LC 75-19408. 118p. 1976. 12.50x (ISBN 0-292-77007-3). U of Tex Pr.

Reference Guide to Texas Law & Legal History: Sources & Documentation. 2nd ed. Karl T. Gruben & James E. Hambleton. LC 87-21731. 1987. 27.50 (ISBN 0-409-25201-8). Butterworth TX.

Reference Guide to the American Film Noir: 1940-1958. Robert Ottoson. LC 80-23176. 290p. 1981. 19.00 (ISBN 0-8108-1363-7). Scarecrow.

Reference Guide to the Iranian Oral History Project. Habib Ladjevardi. (Orig.). 1988. monograph 4.95 (ISBN 0-932885-04-7). Harvard CMES.

Reference Guide to the Literature of Travel, Including Voyages, Geographical Descriptions, Adventures, Shipwrecks & Expeditions, 3 vols. Edward G. Cox. LC 70-90492. 1935-1949. Repr. Vol. 2. lib. bdg. 35.00 (ISBN 0-8371-2162-0, COLV). Greenwood.

Reference Guide to the Study of Public Opinion. Harwood L. Childs. LC 73-12777. 118p. Repr. of 1934 ed. 40.00x (ISBN 0-8103-3704-5). Gale.

Reference Guide to the United States Supreme Court. Ed. by Stephen Elliott. (Illus.). 480p. 1986. 60.00x (ISBN 0-8160-1018-8). Facts On File.

Reference Guide to United States Department of State Special Files. Gerald K. Haines. LC 84-4483. (Illus.). xliv, 394p. 1985. lib. bdg. 50.95 (ISBN 0-313-22750-0, HUS/). Greenwood.

Reference Handbook: Basic Science Concepts & Applications. American Water Works Association Staff. (General References Ser.). (Illus.). 756p. 1980. text ed. 24.00 (ISBN 0-89867-202-3). Am Water Wks Assn.

Reference Handbook of Cosmetology & Related Fields. Violet B. Jones. LC 85-51719. (Illus.). 91p. (Orig.). 1986. pap. 10.00 (ISBN 0-933675-00-3). Visible Diff.

Reference Handbook of Grammar & Usage. Porter G. Perrin. (Derived from Writer's guide & Index to English). 1972. 12.95 (ISBN 0-688-00061-4). Morrow.

Reference Handbook on the Deserts of North America. Ed. by Gordon L. Bender. LC 80-24791. (Illus.). xiii, 594p. 1982. lib. bdg. 76.95 (ISBN 0-313-21307-0, BRD/). Greenwood.

Reference Index to Collected Works of V. I. Lenin, Pt. 1. 334p. 1980. 2.90 (ISBN 0-8285-0165-3, Pub. by Progress Pubs USSR). Imported Pubns.

Reference Index to Collected Works of V. I. Lenin, Part 2. 664p. 1980. 4.75 (ISBN 0-8285-1795-9, Pub. by Progress Pubs USSR). Imported Pubns.

Reference Index to Twelve Thousand Spanish American Authors. Raymond L. Grismer. LC 79-123600. (Bibliography & Reference Ser.: No. 287). 1970. Repr. of 1939 ed. lib. bdg. 19.00 (ISBN 0-8337-1460-0). B Franklin.

Reference Interview As a Creative Art. Elaine Z. Jennerich & Edward J. Jennerich. 200p. 1987. lib. bdg. 24.50 (ISBN 0-87287-445-1). Libs Unl.

Reference Interviews & Questions. Thomas P. Slavens. 1970. pap. 6.90 (ISBN 0-87506-044-7). Campus.

Reference Interviews, Questions, & Materials. 2nd ed. Ed. by Thomas P. Slavens. LC 85-1968. 152p. 1985. 15.00 (ISBN 0-8108-1797-7). Scarecrow.

Reference Library, 4 vols. pap. 10.45 boxed set (ISBN 0-345-32965-1, Del Rey). Ballantine.

Reference Man. International Commission on Radiological Protection. (ICRP Publication Ser: No. 23). 1975. 98.00 (ISBN 0-08-017024-2). Pergamon.

Reference Manual for Office Personnel. 6th ed. Clifford R. House & Kathie Sigler. 233p. 1981. pap. text ed. write for info. (ISBN 0-538-11452-5, K45U). SW Pub.

Reference Manual for Telecommunications. Roger L. Freeman. LC 84-13207. 1504p. 1985. pap. 88.95 (ISBN 0-471-86753-5). Wiley.

Reference Manual for the Ada Programming Language. 331p. 1983. pap. 18.50 (ISBN 0-387-90887-0). Springer-Verlag.

Reference Manual for the Ada Programming Language. (MIL STD 1815A 1983 Ser.). 344p. (Orig.). 1983. pap. 8.00 (ISBN 0-318-11823-8, S/N 008-000-00394-7). USGPO.

Reference Manual: For the Office. 7th ed. Clifford R. House & Kathie Sigler. 1989. pap. text ed. price not set (ISBN 0-538-11461-4, K46U). SW Pub.

Reference Manual of Countermeasures for Hazardous Substance Releases. W. Unterberg et al. 304p. 1988. 50.00 (ISBN 0-89116-066-3). Hemisphere Pub.

Reference Manual of Woody Plant Propagation: From Seed to Tissue Culture. Michael A. Dirr & Charles W. Heuser. (Illus.). 240p. 1987. pap. text ed. 29.95x (ISBN 0-942375-00-9). Varsity Pr.

Reference Manual on Doing Business in Latin America. 2nd ed. Ed. by Donald R. Shea et al. LC 79-22412. 206p. 1980. 30.00 (ISBN 0-930450-12-4); pap. 20.00 (ISBN 0-930450-13-2). U Wis-Mil Ctr Latin Am.

Reference Manual on Electronic Manuscript Preparation Markup: Version 2.0. 1988. 5.00. AAP.

Reference Materials. (Basic Academics Ser.: Module 10). (Illus.). 60p. 1982. spiral bdg. 17.50x (ISBN 0-87683-234-6). GP Pub.

Reference Materials. (Principles of Steam Generation Ser.: Module 20). 45p. 1982. spiral bdg. 17.50x (ISBN 0-87683-270-2). GP Pub.

Reference Materials. Peggy Yarbo. (Language Arts Ser.). 24p. (gr. 5-9). 1980. wkbk. 5.00 (ISBN 0-8209-0314-0, RM-1). ESP.

Reference Materials in Ethnomusicology. 2nd,rev. ed. B. Nettl. (Detroit Studies in Music Bibliography Ser.: No. 1). 1967. pap. 6.00 (ISBN 0-911772-21-9). Harmonie Pk Pr.

Reference Materials on Latin America in English: The Humanities. Richard D. Woods. LC 80-11412. 651p. 1980. 45.00 (ISBN 0-8108-1294-0). Scarecrow.

Reference Materials on Mexican Americans: An Annotated Bibliography. Richard D. Woods. LC 76-10663. 197p. 1976. 16.50 (ISBN 0-8108-0963-X). Scarecrow.

Reference Methods for Marine Radioactivity Studies. (Technical Reports Ser.: No. 118). (Illus.). 284p. (Orig.). 1970. pap. 27.00 (ISBN 92-0-125470-9, IDC118, IAEA). UNIPUB.

Reference Methods for Marine Radioactivity Studies - 2. (Technical Reports Ser.: No. 169). (Illus.). 240p. 1975. pap. 30.00 (ISBN 92-0-125275-7, IDC169, IAEA). UNIPUB.

Reference Notebook Set, 3 bks. Harry Busby & Timothy Zurick. Set. 15.95 (ISBN 0-912524-28-6). Busn News.

Reference on Fundraising. Bibliotheca Press Research Staff. 50p. 1982. pap. text ed. 2.75 (ISBN 0-939476-73-8, Pub. by Bibio Pr GA). Prosperity & Profits.

Reference Other Orientation: An Extension of the Reference Group Concept. Raymond L. Schmitt. LC 76-156789. (Perspectives in Sociology Ser.). 256p. 1972. 12.50x (ISBN 0-8093-0564-X). S Ill U Pr.

Reference Point. Candy Edwards. LC 82-83712. (Illus.). 80p. (gr. 3-6). 1983. pap. text ed. 6.95 (ISBN 0-86530-042-9, IP 42-9). Incentive Pubns.

Reference Procedure for the Human Erythrocyte Sedimentation Rate (E.S.R.) Test: Tentative Standard. National Committee for Clinical Laboratory Standards. 1983. 20.00 (H2-T2) (ISBN 0-318-19391-4). Natl Comm Clin Lab Stds.

Reference Procedure for the Quantitative Determination of Hemoglobin in Blood: Approved Standard, Vol. 4. National Committee for Clinical Laboratory Standards. 1984. 20.00 (ISBN 0-318-19442-2, H15-A). Natl Comm Clin Lab Stds.

Reference Radiographs, Discontinuities in Aluminum Welds: RRS-P. 440.00 (ISBN 0-317-37068-5). Am Welding.

Reference Readiness: A Manual for Librarians & Students. 3rd ed. Agnes A. Hede. LC 84-5766. xv, 352p. 1984. 25.00 (ISBN 0-208-02001-2, Lib Prof Pubns); pap. 19.50x (ISBN 0-208-02002-0, Lib Prof Pubns). Shoe String.

Reference Seismic Ground Motions in Nuclear Safety Assessments. OECD-Nuclear Energy Agency. (Illus.). 171p. (Orig.). 1980. pap. text ed. 16.00x (ISBN 92-64-12100-5). OECD.

Reference Service. 3rd, rev. ed. Krishan Kumar. x, 431p. 1988. text ed. 35.00x (ISBN 0-7069-3765-1, Pub. by Vikas India). Advent NY.

Reference Service: A Perspective. Ed. by Sul H. Lee. LC 83-60917. (Library Management Ser.: No. 6). 1983. 35.00 (ISBN 0-87650-150-1). Pierian.

Reference Service in the Small Library. Geraldine B. King. LC 85-20083. (L A M A Small Libraries Publications: No. 12). 12p. 1985. pap. 3.50x (ISBN 0-8389-3323-8). ALA.

Reference Services Administration & Management. Ed. by Bill Katz & Ruth A. Fraley. LC 82-1085. (Reference Librarian Ser.: No. 3). 147p. 1982. text ed. 32.95 (ISBN 0-86656-164-1, B164). Haworth Pr.

Reference Services & Library Instruction: A Handbook for Library Management. David F. Kohl. LC 85-13431. (Handbooks for Library Management Ser.). 324p. 1985. lib. bdg. 37.75 (ISBN 0-87436-432-9). ABC-Clio.

Reference Services & Public Policy. Ed. by Richard D. Irving & Bill Katz. LC 87-35779. (Reference Librarian Ser.: Vol. 20). (Illus.). 230p. 1988. text ed. 29.95 (ISBN 0-86656-742-9). Haworth Pr.

Reference Services & Technical Services: Interactions in Library Practice. Ed. by Gordon Stevenson & Sally Stevenson. LC 83-22790. (Reference Librarian Ser.: No. 9). 176p. 1984. text ed. 33.95 (ISBN 0-86656-174-9). Haworth Pr.

Reference Services for Children & Young Adults. Ed. by Bill Katz & Ruth A. Fraley. LC 83-325. (Reference Librarian Ser.: Nos. 7 & 8). 215p. 1983. text ed. 24.95 (ISBN 0-86656-201-X, B201). Haworth Pr.

Reference Services in Archives. Ed. by Lucille Whalen & Bill Katz. LC 85-17534. (Reference Librarian Ser.: No. 13). 210p. 1986. text ed. 34.95 (ISBN 0-86656-521-3, B521); pap. text ed. 24.95 (ISBN 0-86656-522-1, B522). Haworth Pr.

Reference Services in the 1980s. Ed. by Bill Katz. LC 81-20196. (Reference Librarian Ser.: Nos. 1-2). 188p. 1982. pap. 29.95 (ISBN 0-86656-110-2, B110). Haworth Pr.

Reference Services Review, Vol. 15, 1987. (Quarterly, Standing orders accepted). per year 55.00 (ISBN 0-685-44107-5). Pierian.

Reference Services Today: From Interview to Burnout. Ed. by Bill Katz & Ruth Fraley. LC 86-29481. 300p. 1987. 34.95 (ISBN 0-86656-572-8). Haworth Pr.

Reference Shelf 1987, 6 vols. 1987. Set. 48.00 (ISBN 0-317-55847-1); 10.00 ea. Wilson.

Reference Software Products Handbook. Intel Staff. 352p. (Orig.). 1985. pap. 10.00 (ISBN 0-917017-24-2, 231195). Intel Corp.

Reference Sources: A Brief Guide. 9th ed. Eleanor A. Swidan. 1988. pap. 8.95 (ISBN 0-910556-26-1). Enoch Pratt.

Reference Sources for Small & Medium-Sized Libraries. 4th ed. Ed. by Jovian Lang & Deborah Masters. LC 84-6513. 268p. 1984. pap. text ed. 20.00x (ISBN 0-8389-3293-2). ALA.

Reference Sources in English & American Literature: An Annotated Bibliography. Robert C. Schweik & Dieter Riesner. 1977. pap. 10.95x (ISBN 0-393-09104-X). Norton.

Reference Sources in Library & Information Services: A Guide to the Literature. Gary R. Purcell & Gail A. Schlachter. LC 83-19700. 359p. 1984. lib. bdg. 46.75 (ISBN 0-87436-355-1). ABC-Clio.

Reference Sources in Social Work: An Annotated Bibliography. James H. Conrad. LC 81-21219. 207p. 1982. 17.50 (ISBN 0-8108-1503-6). Scarecrow.

Reference Sources 1977. Ed. by Linda Mark. 1977. 75.00 (ISBN 0-87650-084-X). Pierian.

Reference Sources 1978. Ed. by Linda Mark. 1978. 75.00 (ISBN 0-87650-096-3). Pierian.

Reference Sources 1979. Ed. by Linda Mark. 1980. 75.00. Pierian.

Reference Sources 1980. Ed. by S. Balachandran & M. Balachandran. 1981. 75.00 (ISBN 0-87650-127-7). Pierian.

Reference Sources: 1981. S. Balachandran & M. Balachandran. 1982. 75.00 (ISBN 0-686-47138-5). Pierian.

Reference Sources, 1982. Terry Silver. 1984. 75.00 (ISBN 0-87650-167-6). Pierian.

Reference Sources, 1983. Terry Silver. 1985. 75.00 (ISBN 0-87650-165-X). Pierian.

Reference to Kinds in English. Greg N. Carlson. Ed. by Jorge Hankamer. LC 79-6619. (Outstanding Dissertations in Linguistics Ser.). 300p. 1985. text ed. 42.00 (ISBN 0-8240-4551-3). Garland Pub.

Reference to the Present. Ilija Poplasen. 241p. 1982. 20.00 (ISBN 0-935352-11-2). MIR PA.

Reference Tools for Fine Arts Visual Resources Collections. Ed. by Christine Bunting. (Occasional Papers: 4). 56p. 1984. pap. 12.00 (ISBN 0-942740-02-5). Art Libs Soc.

Reference, Truth & Reality: Essays on the Philosophy of Language. Ed. by Mark Platts. 1980. pap. 12.95x (ISBN 0-7100-0406-0). Routledge Chapman & Hall.

Reference Update 80: Selected Recent Works in the Social Sciences. Ed. by Kathy Jursik & Grace Waibel. (CPL Bibliographies Ser.: No. 50). 69p. 1981. 10.00 (ISBN 0-86602-050-0). Coun Plan Librarians.

Reference Values in Human Chemistry: Proceedings. International Colloquium, Automatisation & Prospective Biology Symposium, 2nd, Pont-a-Mousson, October 1972. Ed. by G. Siest. 1973. 86.00 (ISBN 3-8055-1622-3). S Karger.

Reference Values in Laboratory Medicine: The Current State of the Art. Ed. by R. Graesbeck & T. Alstroem. LC 80-42312. 413p. 1982. 73.95x (ISBN 0-471-28025-9, Pub. by Wiley-Interscience). Wiley.

Reference VI. rev. ed. Cscapes. 10p. 1987. pap. 3.00 (ISBN 0-916151-19-0). Specialized Sys.

Reference Work in the Humanities. Edmund F. Santa Vicca. LC 80-18783. 173p. 1980. 16.50 (ISBN 0-8108-1342-4). Scarecrow.

Reference Work in the Public Library. Rolland E. Stevens & Joan M. Walton. LC 82-17147. 269p. 1983. 28.50 (ISBN 0-87287-332-3). Libs Unl.

Reference Work in the University Library. Rolland E. Stevens & Linda C. Smith. LC 86-173. 530p. 1986. 37.50 (ISBN 0-87287-449-4). Libs Unl.

Reference Works for Theological Research: An Annotated Selective Bibliographical Guide. 2nd ed. Robert J. Kepple. LC 81-40350. 298p. 1981. lib. bdg. 30.50 (ISBN 0-8191-1679-3); pap. text ed. 14.50 (ISBN 0-8191-1680-7). U Pr of Amer.

Reference Works in the Field of Religion 1977-1985. Elsie Freudenberger. (Orig.). 1986. pap. 15.00 (ISBN 0-87507-037-X). Cath Lib Assn.

References & Conference Proceedings Toward the Understanding of Fracture Mechanics. Ed. by Pir M. Toor & C. Michael Hudson. LC 85-26713. (ASTM Data Series Publication). (Illus.). 54p. 1985. text ed. 12.00 (ISBN 0-8031-0466-9, 05-063000-30). ASTM.

References for Students of Language Planning. Joan Rubin & Bjorn H. Jernudd. LC 79-17656. 132p. 1979. pap. text ed. 6.00x (ISBN 0-8248-0686-7, Eastwest Ctr). UH Pr.

References on Fatigue, 1965-1966 - STP 9P. 1968. microfiche 11.00 (ISBN 0-8031-0132-5, 04-009160-30). ASTM.

Referendum Device. Ed. by Austin Ranney. 1981. 23.00 (ISBN 0-8447-2196-4); pap. 12.50 (ISBN 0-8447-2195-6). Am Enterprise.

Referendum Experience, Scotland 1979. Ed. by J. M. Bochel et al. (Illus.). 224p. 1981. text ed. 22.00 (ISBN 0-08-025734-8, R120). Pergamon.

Referendum Impact Committee Report. 22.00 (ISBN 0-317-62721-X). DC Bar Assn.

Referendum in America. facsimile ed. Ellis P. Oberholtzer. LC 71-119939. (Select Bibliographies Reprint Ser). Repr. of 1893 ed. 18.00 (ISBN 0-8369-5382-7). Ayer Co Pubs.

Referendum in America. Ellis P. Oberholtzer. LC 70-153370. (American Constitutional & Legal History Ser). 1971. Repr. of 1912 ed. lib. bdg. 59.50 (ISBN 0-306-70149-9). Da Capo.

Referendum Voting: Social Status & Policy Preferences. Harlan Hahn & Sheldon Kamieniecki. LC 87-8419. (Contributions in Political Science Ser.: No. 190). 184p. 1987. lib. bdg. 35.00 (ISBN 0-313-25611-X, KRM/). Greenwood.

Referendums: A Comparative Study of Practice & Theory. Ed. by David Butler & Austin Ranney. 1978. pap. 12.50 (ISBN 0-8447-3318-0). Am Enterprise.

Referential Communication: Barrier Activities for Speakers & Listeners, 2 pts. Nancy L. McKinley & Linda Schwartz. 100p. (Orig.). 1985. Pt. I. pap. text ed. 80.00x (ISBN 0-930599-00-4); Pt. II. 87.00x (ISBN 0-930599-01-2). Thinking Pubns.

Referential-Semantic Analysis. T. Thrane. LC 79-17405. (Cambridge Studies in Linguistics Monograph: No. 28). 1980. 47.50 (ISBN 0-521-22791-7). Cambridge U Pr.

Referral Process in Libraries: A Characterization & an Exploration of Related Factors. George S. Hawley. LC 87-9201. 196p. 1987. 22.50 (ISBN 0-8108-2010-2). Scarecrow.

Refiguring Anthropology: First Principles of Probability & Statistics. David H. Thomas. (Illus.). 532p. 1986. Repr. of 1976 ed. text ed. 19.95x (ISBN 0-88133-223-2). Waveland Pr.

Refillable Steamy. Greg Stewart & Nolan Palmer. LC 76-21596. 1976. perfect bdg 3.00 (ISBN 0-915214-17-2). Litmus.

Refined Carbohydrate Foods & Disease: Some Implications of Dietary Fibre. Ed. by D. P. Burkitt & H. C. Trowell. 1975. 75.00 (ISBN 0-12-144750-2). Acad Pr.

Refined Dynamical Theories of Beams, Plates & Shells & Their Applications: Proceedings of the Euromech-Colloquium 219. Ed. by I. Elishakoff & H. Irretier. (Lecture Notes in Engineering Ser.: Vol. 28). 435p. 1987. pap. 54.40 (ISBN 0-387-17573-3). Springer-Verlag.

Reflections of Joy: Acrylic Painting Techniques. Joyce Beebe. (Designer Ser.). (Illus.). 32p. (Orig.). 1986. pap. 6.95 (ISBN 0-917121-13-9, 50-100). M F Weber Co.

Reflections of Leisure: A Tribute. Robert L. Wilder. 96p. 1980. 12.50 (ISBN 0-943272-15-7); autographed ed. 20.00 (ISBN 0-943272-16-5). Inst Recreation Res.

Reflections of Life: A Family Album in Poetry & Prose. Margaret W. Taylor. 1988. 5.95 (ISBN 0-533-07876-8). Vantage.

Reflections of Life & Love. Gertrude J. Black & Don J. Black. 54p. (Orig.). 1976. pap. 2.00 (ISBN 0-317-59298-X, 8657). Pubs Bk Sales.

Reflections of Light. Jacquelyn Poen. 33p. 1986. 5.95 (ISBN 0-533-07022-8). Vantage.

Reflections of Love. Carol A. Osley. 42p. (Orig.). 1982. pap. 4.25 (ISBN 0-910119-01-5). SOCO Pubns.

Reflections of Mind: Western Psychology Meets Tibetan Buddhism. Tarthang Tulku. LC 75-5254. (Illus.). 1975. 17.95 (ISBN 0-913546-15-1); pap. 8.95 (ISBN 0-913546-14-3). Dharma Pub.

Reflections of My Grandparents. Sylvia Healy. (Illus.). 80p. 1985. 24.95 (ISBN 0-939688-13-1). Directed Media.

Reflections of My Life: The Apology of John the Baptist. Dennis Dallison. Ed. by Ruth Norman. 77p. (Orig.). 1982. pap. text ed. 2.50 (ISBN 0-932642-75-6). Unarius Pubns.

Reflections of Myself: Who I Was Then, Who I Am Now, & Who I Will Become. Cheryl A. Hebert. 1987. 10.95 (ISBN 0-533-06319-1). Vantage.

Reflections of Nazism. Saul Friedlander. 112p. 1986. pap. 3.95 (ISBN 0-380-70090-5, Discus). Avon.

Reflections of Portland, Maine. Ed. by Frederic Thompson & Dennis Griggs. (Illus.). 124p. 1986. 29.95 (ISBN 0-9611320-1-9). Congress Sq.

Reflections of Reality in Japanese Art. Sherman Lee. (Illus.). 161p. 1972. pap. 100.00x (Pub. by Han-Shan Tang Ltd). State Mutual Bk.

Reflections of Reality in Japanese Art. Ed. by Sherman Lee & Michael R. Cunningham. 292p. 1983. 510.00x (Pub. by Han-Shan Tang Ltd). State Mutual Bk.

Reflections of Reality in Japanese Art. Sherman E. Lee. LC 82-45940. (Illus.). 304p. (Catalogue by Michael R. Cunningham). 1983. 15.00x (ISBN 0-910386-70-6, Pub. by Cleveland Mus Art). Ind U Pr.

Reflections of Renaissance England: Life, Thought, & Religion Mirrored in Illustrated Pamphlets. Marie-Helene Davies. LC 85-32028. (Princeton Theological Monographs: No. 1). 1986. pap. 33.00 (ISBN 0-915138-68-9). Pickwick.

Reflections of Romantic Love: Pictures from the Tate Gallery. Compiled by John Hadfield. (Illus.). 48p. 1987. 11.95 (ISBN 0-7153-8847-9). David & Charles.

Reflections of Salem's Past. Dale E. Shaffer. (Illus.). 80p. (Orig.). 1984. pap. 3.95 (ISBN 0-915060-21-3). D E Shaffer.

Reflections of Social Life in the Navaho Origin Myth. Katherine Spencer. LC 76-43850. (Univ. of New Mexico. Publications in Anthropology: No. 3). 1983. Repr. of 1947 ed. 20.00 (ISBN 0-404-15705-X). AMS Pr.

Reflections of Southern Jewry: The Letters of Charles Wessolowsky. Ed. by Louis Schmier. LC 81-16995. viii, 184p. 1982. 12.95 (ISBN 0-86554-020-9, MUP-H15). Mercer Univ Pr.

Reflections of Success. Janet Trout & Diane Walter. 1984. pap. 5.95 (ISBN 0-912315-81-4). Word Aflame.

Reflections of Tantras. Sudhakar Chattopadhyaya. 106p. 1979. 11.95. Asia Bk Corp.

Reflections of the Heart. Jacquelyn Brown. 64p. 1989. 6.95 (ISBN 0-89962-784-6). Todd & Honeywell.

Reflections of the Inward Silence. Ed. by Salvatore S. Buttaci & Susan L. Gerstle. LC 76-19240. 1976. 9.95 (ISBN 0-917398-03-3); pap. 7.95 (ISBN 0-917398-04-1). New Worlds.

Reflections of the Law in Literature. Francis L. Windolph. LC 71-117863. (Essay Index Reprint Ser). 1956. 13.00 (ISBN 0-8369-1739-1). Ayer Co Pubs.

Reflections of the Outer Banks. Donald E. McAdoo & Carol McAdoo. LC 75-23489. 104p. 1976. 19.95 (ISBN 0-916424-00-6). Island Pub.

Reflections of the Sea: Pictures from the Tate Gallery. Compiled by John Hadfield. (Illus.). 48p. 1987. 11.95 (ISBN 0-7153-8854-1). David & Charles.

Reflections of the Self: Poems of Spiritual Life. Swami Muktananda. LC 80-50391. (Illus.). 200p. (Orig.). 1980. pap. 6.50 (ISBN 0-914602-50-0). SYDA Found.

Reflections of Women in Antiquity. Helene P. Foley. 420p. 1982. 50.00 (ISBN 0-677-16370-3). Gordon & Breach.

Reflections of Yesterday, Vol. 1. Jesse Sarmiento. (Illus.). 88p. pap. 5.95 (ISBN 0-9615290-1-6). Rainy Day Fl.

Reflections on a Century of United States-Korean Relations. Academy of Korean Studies Wilson Center. LC 83-3644. (Illus.). 382p. (Orig.). 1983. lib. bdg. 39.50 (ISBN 0-8191-3109-1); pap. text ed. 20.75 (ISBN 0-8191-3110-5). U Pr of Amer.

Reflections on a Gift of Watermelon Pickle & Other Modern Verse. Ed. by Stephen Dunning et al. LC 66-8763. (Illus.). 144p. (gr. 7 up). 1966. 14.95 (ISBN 0-688-41231-9); PLB 12.88 (ISBN 0-688-51231-3). Lothrop.

Reflections on a Literary Revolution. Graham G. Hough. LC 60-2451. pap. 33.30 (2029509). Bks Demand UMI.

Reflections on a Philosophy. Forrest C. Shaklee, Sr. LC 73-10833. 3.95 (ISBN 0-87502-037-2); pap. 1.25 (ISBN 0-87502-038-0). Benjamin Co.

Reflections on a Troubled World Economy. Ed. by Fritz Machlup et al. (Essays in Honor of Herbert Giersch). 350p. 1983. 33.50x (ISBN 0-312-66741-8). St Martin.

Reflections on Afro-American Music. With Contributions from Richard L. Abrams & Others. Dominique-Rene De Lerma. LC 72-619703. pap. 69.80 (2027301). Bks Demand UMI.

Reflections on America. Jacques Maritain. LC 74-26882. 205p. 1975. Repr. of 1958 ed. 20.00x (ISBN 0-87752-166-2). Gordian.

Reflections on America, Nineteen Eighty-Four: An Orwell Symposium. Ed. by Robert Mulvihill. LC 85-2538. (Illus.). 232p. 1986. o. p. 25.00x (ISBN 0-8203-0778-5); pap. 12.95 (ISBN 0-8203-0780-7). U of Ga Pr.

Reflections on Art. Susanne K. Langer. 1979. 30.50 (ISBN 0-405-10611-4). Ayer Co Pubs.

Reflections on Behaviorism & Society. B. F. Skinner. (Century Psychology Ser.). (Illus.). 1978. ref. 29.00 (ISBN 0-13-770057-1). P-H.

Reflections on Biochemistry. A. Kornberg et al. 1976. 69.00 (ISBN 0-08-021011-2); pap. 20.00 (ISBN 0-08-021010-4). Pergamon.

Reflections on Biologic Research. Giulio Gabbiani et al. LC 67-26012. (Illus.). 256p. 1967. 10.50 (ISBN 0-87527-035-2). Green.

Reflections on British Painting. Roger E. Fry. LC 76-99695. (Essay Index Reprint Ser.). 1934. 20.00 (ISBN 0-8369-1350-7). Ayer Co Pubs.

Reflections on Celibacy & Marriage in Four Letters to a Friend. F. Douglas. LC 83-48585. (Marriage, Sex & the Family in England Ser.). 87p. 1984. lib. bdg. 20.00 (ISBN 0-8240-5907-7). Garland Pub.

Reflections on Community Building. Marjorie Spock. 1984. pap. 3.25 (ISBN 0-916786-67-6). St George Bk Serv.

Reflections on Composing: Four American Composers. Frederick Koch. LC 78-59839. 1986. pap. 12.95 (ISBN 0-915604-20-5). Carnegie-Mellon.

Reflections on De Gaulle: Political Founding in Modernity. Will Morrisey. LC 83-1225. 222p. (Orig.). 1983. lib. bdg. 30.25 (ISBN 0-8191-3095-8); pap. text ed. 14.00 (ISBN 0-8191-3096-6). U Pr of Amer.

Reflections on Death & Grief. Albert J. Walsh. 96p. 1986. pap. 4.50 (ISBN 0-8010-9673-1). Baker Bk.

Reflections on Door County. Grace Samuelson. 192p. 1986. 14.95 (ISBN 0-89658-062-8). Voyageur Pr Inc.

Reflections on Economic Development & Social Change. Hanumantha Rao et al. 1979. 22.50x (ISBN 0-8364-0522-6). South Asia Bks.

Reflections on Equestrian Art. Nuno Oliveira. Tr. by Phyllis Fields from Port. (Illus.). 12.25 (ISBN 0-85131-257-8, Pub. by J A Allen U K). S R Smith Sporting Bks.

Reflections on Fieldwork in Morocco. Paul Rabinow. LC 77-71066. (Quantum Bks.: No. 11). 1977. 19.50x (ISBN 0-520-03450-3); pap. 9.95x (ISBN 0-520-03529-1). U of Cal Pr.

Reflections on Finance, Education & Society. C. D. Deshmukh. 1972. 9.95 (ISBN 0-8426-0416-2). Orient Bk Dist.

Reflections on Frege's Philosophy. Reinhardt Grossmann. LC 77-78328. (Northwestern University Publications in Analytic Philosophy Ser). Repr. of 1969 ed. 52.70 (ISBN 0-8357-9468-7, 2010264). Bks Demand UMI.

Reflections on Gender & Science. Evelyn F. Keller. LC 84-17327. 176p. 1985. 24.00x (ISBN 0-300-03291-9). Yale U Pr.

Reflections on Gender & Science. Evelyn F. Keller. LC 84-17327. 176p. 1986. pap. 8.95 (ISBN 0-300-03636-1, Y-581). Yale U Pr.

Reflections on Growing up Disabled. Ed. by Reginald Jones. 103p. 1983. pap. 10.50 (ISBN 0-86586-134-X). Coun Exc Child.

Reflections on Hanging. Arthur Koestler. LC 82-45670. Date not set. Repr. of 1957 ed. 30.00 (ISBN 0-404-62423-5). AMS Pr.

Reflections on History. Jacob Burckhardt. LC 78-24385. Orig. Title: Force & Freedom. 1979. 9.00 (ISBN 0-913966-37-1, Liberty Clas); pap. 5.00 (ISBN 0-913966-38-X). Liberty Fund.

Reflections on History & Historians. Theodore S. Hamerow. LC 86-22451. 288p. 1986. text ed. 25.00x (ISBN 0-299-10930-5). U of Wis Pr.

Reflections on Human Nature. Arthur O. Lovejoy. LC 61-15700. 281p. 1961. pap. 8.95x (ISBN 0-8018-0395-0). Johns Hopkins.

Reflections on Humanae Vitae. Pope John Paul II. 96p. 1984. 3.75 (ISBN 0-8198-6409-9); pap. 2.75 (ISBN 0-8198-6410-2). Dghtrs St Paul.

Reflections on Islamic History & Civilization: The Complete Collected Essays of Sir Hamilton Gibb, 5 vols. Ed. by Lawrence I. Conrad. (Illus.). Set, 2500p. 125.00; Vol. 1. 25.00 (ISBN 0-87850-055-3). Darwin Pr.

Reflections on JFK's Assasination: 250 Famous Americans Remember November 22, 1963. John Jovich. (Illus.). 275p. (Orig.). 1988. pap. 9.95 (ISBN 0-933149-29-8). Woodbine House.

Reflections on Kant's Philosophy. Ed. by William H. Werkmeister. LC 75-20376. 181p. 1975. 20.00x (ISBN 0-8130-0541-8). U Presses Fla.

Reflections on Kashimir Politics. Syed T. Hussain. 1987. 31.00x (ISBN 0-8364-2139-6, Pub. by Usha). South Asia Bks.

Reflections on Kashmir Politics. Syed T. Hussain. 1987. 31.00x (ISBN 0-8364-2231-7, Pub. by Sundeep), South Asia Bks.

Reflections on Kurt Godel. Hao Wang. LC 86-21095. (Illus.). 376p. 1987. 25.00x (ISBN 0-262-23127-1). MIT Pr.

Reflections on Lace. Nenia Lovesey. (Illus.). 122p. 1988. 29.95 (ISBN 0-85219-750-0, Pub. by Batsford England). David & Charles.

Reflections on Landscape: The Lives & Work of Six British Landscape Architects. Sheila Harvey. 200p. 1987. text ed. 53.95 (ISBN 0-291-39708-5, Pub. by Gower Pub England). Gower Pub Co.

Reflections on Language. Noam Chomsky. 1975. pap. 7.95 (ISBN 0-394-73123-9). Pantheon.

Reflections on Learning. facs. ed. Howard M. Jones. LC 69-17580. (Essay Index Reprint Ser). 1958. 12.00 (ISBN 0-8369-0022-7). Ayer Co Pubs.

Reflections on Liberation. Daryl R. Grigsby. LC 84-72421. (Illus.). 176p. (Orig.). 1985. pap. 5.95 (ISBN 0-9614210-0-2). Asante Pubns.

Reflections on Liberty. Laurance Labadie. (Men & Movements in the History & Philosophy of Anarchism Ser.). 1979. lib. bdg. 59.95 (ISBN 0-685-96413-2). Revisionist Pr.

Reflections on Life. Raymond Nelson. LC 87-50264. 58p. 1987. 6.95 (ISBN 1-55523-072-5). Winston-Derek.

Reflections on Life after Life. Raymond A. Moody, Jr. 1985. pap. 3.95 (ISBN 0-553-25227-5). Bantam.

Reflections on Life & Death. Joseph Chiari. LC 77-4054. 141p. 1977. 20.00x (ISBN 0-87752-212-X). Gordian.

Reflections on Life Long Education & the School. (UIE Monographs: Unesco Institute for Education: No. 3). 80p. 1975. pap. 5.00 (ISBN 92-820-1006-6, U541, UNESCO). UNIPUB.

Reflections on Literature for Children. Ed. by Francelia Butler & Richard W. Rotert. LC 84-12554. xi, 281p. 1984. lib. bdg. 29.50 (ISBN 0-208-02054-3, Lib Prof Pubns); pap. 20.00x (ISBN 0-208-02075-6, Lib Prof Pubns). Shoe String.

Reflections on Love, Religion, & Beyond. 2nd, rev. ed. Donald W. Garner. LC 87-62644. 92p. 1988. pap. 3.95 (ISBN 0-9618970-1-5). Sea Crow Prodn.

Reflections on Malraux: Cultural Foundings in Modernity. Will Morrisey. 346p. (Orig.). 1985. lib. bdg. 31.00 (ISBN 0-8191-4240-9); pap. text ed. 15.50 (ISBN 0-8191-4241-7). U Pr of Amer.

Reflections on Marriage. Rosemarie De Haan. (Illus.). 48p. 1972. pap. 1.95 (ISBN 0-917814-04-5). Astroart Ent.

Reflections on Marriage. Reverend William P. Steinhauser & Laurie A. Boyce. LC 84-71173. (Marriage & Marriage Preparation Ser.). (Illus.). 72p. (Orig.). 1984. 2.95 (ISBN 0-940679-00-0). CCOC.

Reflections on Mary's Help Hospital & Seton Medical Center, 1893-1985. Marie M. Mahoney. 180p. 1986. 25.00 (ISBN 0-9616516-0-1). Seton Med Ctr.

Reflections on Medicine, Biotechnology & the Law. Zelman Cowen. LC 86-1492. viii, 62p. 1986. 10.95x (ISBN 0-8032-1436-7). U of Nebr Pr.

Reflections on Modern History: The Historian & Human Responsibility. Hans Kohn. LC 77-28495. 1978. Repr. of 1963 ed. lib. bdg. 35.00x (ISBN 0-313-20232-X, KORM). Greenwood.

Reflections on Muscle. Andrew Huxley. LC 79-5480. (Illus.). 120p. 1980. 32.00x (ISBN 0-691-08255-3). Princeton U Pr.

Reflections on Nazism: An Essay on Death & Kitsch. Saul Friedlander. Tr. by Thomas Weyr from Fr. LC 82-48117. 160p. 1984. 13.45i (ISBN 0-06-015097-1, HarpT). Har-Row.

Reflections on Nikolai Gogol. Marrianne Bogojavlensky. 69p. 1968. pap. 3.00 (ISBN 0-317-30452-6). Holy Trinity.

Reflections on Our Age: UNESCO. facs. ed. Intro. by David Hardman. LC 74-128295. (Essay Index Reprint Ser). 1949. 22.00 (ISBN 0-8369-2024-4). Ayer Co Pubs.

Reflections on Our Times. P. N. Haksar. 119p. 1982. 19.95. Asia Bk Corp.

Reflections on Political Identity. Anne Norton. LC 88-45400. (Constitutional Thought Ser.). 192p. 1988. text ed. 24.50x (ISBN 0-8018-3694-8). Johns Hopkins.

Reflections on Population. 2nd ed. Rafael M. Salas. 256p. 1985. 48.00 (ISBN 0-08-032406-1). Pergamon.

Reflections on Puebla. CIIR Staff. 56p. 1980. 15.00x (ISBN 0-904393-49-6, Pub. by CIIR). State Mutual Bk.

Reflections on Reasoning. Raymond S. Nickerson. 200p. 1986. 19.95 (ISBN 0-89859-762-5); pap. 12.50 (ISBN 0-89859-763-3). L Erlbaum Assocs.

Reflections on Rebellion: Indonesian Stories from the Communist Rebellions of 1949 & 1965. John McGlynn & William Frederick. (Papers in International Studies: Southeast Asia Ser.: No. 60). 160p. 1983. pap. 9.00x (ISBN 0-89680-111-X, Ohio U Ctr Intl). Ohio U Pr.

Reflections on Relationships. (gr. 11-12). 1978. wkbk. 9.64 (ISBN 0-13-770081-4). P-H.

Reflections on Resemblance, Ritual, & Religion. Brian K. Smith. 256p. 1988. 32.50 (ISBN 0-19-505545-4). Oxford U Pr.

Reflections on Revival. Charles G. Finney. LC 78-26527. 160p. 1979. pap. 4.95 (ISBN 0-87123-157-3, 210157). Bethany Hse.

Reflections on Revolution in France. Edmund Burke. 1982. pap. 5.95 (ISBN 0-14-043204-3). Penguin.

Reflections on St. Paul. Burns K. Seeley. Ed. by Jerome F. Coniker. LC 82-72202. (Living Meditation & Prayerbook Ser.). (Illus.). 270p. (Orig.). 1982. pap. text ed. 5.00 (ISBN 0-932406-07-6). AFC.

Reflections on Samson. Lou Lipsitz. (Illus.). 1977. pap. 5.00 (ISBN 0-87711-071-9). Story Line.

Reflections on Science & Human Affairs. Hudson Hoagland. 100p. 1974. text ed. 18.95 (ISBN 0-87073-814-3). Schenkman Bks Inc.

Reflections on Science & the Media. June Goodfield. LC 81-66420. 114p. 1981. 9.00 (ISBN 0-87168-252-4). AAAS.

Reflections on Self Psychology. Ed. by Joseph D. Lichtenberg & Samuel Kaplan. 448p. 1983. text ed. 39.95 (ISBN 0-88163-001-2). Analytic Pr.

Reflections on Shamanism: The Tribal Healer & the Technological Trance. John Grim. (Teilhard Studies: No. 6). 20p. (Orig.). 1981. pap. 3.00 (ISBN 0-89012-029-3). Anima Pubns.

Reflections on Shattered Windows: Promises & Prospects for Asian American Studies. Ed. by Gary Y. Okihiro et al. 239p. 1988. 25.00 (ISBN 0-87422-051-3); pap. 14.95 (ISBN 0-87422-039-4). Wash St U Pr.

Reflections on Simplicity. Elaine Prevallet. LC 82-80439. 31p. 1982. pap. 2.50x (ISBN 0-87574-244-0). Pendle Hill.

Reflections on Suicide. Anne L. Stael-Holstein. LC 77-37724. Repr. of 1813 ed. 24.50 (ISBN 0-404-56838-6). AMS Pr.

Reflections on Texas. (Illus.). 30p. pap. 2.95 (ISBN 0-933164-42-4). U of Tex Inst Tex Culture.

Reflections on the African Refugee Problem. Gaim Kibreab. LC 84-81772. 140p. 1985. 25.00 (ISBN 0-86543-006-3); pap. 7.95 (ISBN 0-86543-007-1). Africa World.

Reflections on the American Institutions: Selections from the American Commonwealth. James Bryce. 12.00 (ISBN 0-8446-0517-4). Peter Smith.

Reflections on the Beginnings of Prestressed Concrete in America. 368p. 1981. soft cover 30.00x (ISBN 0-937040-18-5, JR-H-81). Prestressed Concrete.

Reflections on the Brazilian Counterrevolution. Florestan Fernandes. Pref. by Warren Dean. Tr. by Michel Vale & Patrick M. Hughes. LC 80-5456. 200p. 1981. 35.00 (ISBN 0-87332-177-4). M E Sharpe.

Reflections on the Causes of Human Misery. Barrington Moore, Jr. 208p. 1972. pap. 7.95x (ISBN 0-8070-1531-8, BP456). Beacon Pr.

Reflections on the Civil War. Bruce Catton. Ed. by John Leekley. 272p. 1984. pap. 3.95 (ISBN 0-425-10495-8). Berkley Pub.

Reflections on the Creed. Daniel Overduin. 1980. pap. 0.75 (ISBN 0-570-03814-6, 12-2782). Concordia.

Reflections on the Cuban Missile Crisis. Raymond L. Garthoff. LC 87-27824. 159p. 1987. 18.95 (ISBN 0-8157-3052-7); pap. 8.95t (ISBN 0-8157-3051-9). Brookings.

Reflections on the Death of a Porcupine & Other Essays. D. H. Lawrence. Ed. by Michael Herbert. (Cambridge Edition of the Works of D. H. Lawrence). 400p. 1988. 69.50 (ISBN 0-521-26622-X); pap. 24.95 (ISBN 0-521-35847-7). Cambridge U Pr.

Reflections on the Decline of Science in England. Charles Babbage. LC 77-115928. 1970. Repr. of 1830 ed. 29.50x (ISBN 0-678-00645-8). Kelley.

Reflections on the Decline of Science in England & on Some of Its Causes. C. Babbage. 256p. 1971. Repr. of 1830 ed. 27.50x (ISBN 0-7165-1578-4, BBA 02134, Pub. by Irish Academic Pr Ireland). Biblio Dist.

Reflections on the Failure of Socialism. Max Eastman. LC 82-2957. 128p. 1982. Repr. of 1955 ed. lib. bdg. 35.00x (ISBN 0-313-23534-1, EARE). Greenwood.

Reflections on the Failure of the First West Indian Federation. Hugh W. Springer. LC 70-38762. (Harvard University. Center for International Affairs. Occasional Papers in International Affairs: No. 4). Repr. of 1962 ed. 11.50 (ISBN 0-404-54604-8). AMS Pr.

Reflections on the Fantastic: Selected Essays from the Fourth International Conference on the Fantastic in the Arts. Ed. by Michael R. Collings. LC 86-12123. (Contributions to the Study of Science Fiction & Fantasy Ser.: No. 24). 124p. 1986. lib. bdg. 35.00 (ISBN 0-313-25555-5, CRF/). Greenwood.

Reform & Punishment: Essays on Criminal Sentencing. Michael H. Tonry & Franklin E. Zimring. LC 83-6504. (Studies in Crime & Justice). 1983. 25.00x (ISBN 0-226-80816-5). U of Chicago Pr.

Reform & Reaction in the Platine Provinces, 1810-1852. David Bushnell. LC 83-10490. (University of Florida Social Sciences Monographs: No. 69). viii, 182p. (Orig.). 1983. 18.00x (ISBN 0-8130-0757-7). U Presses Fla.

Reform & Reaction: The Big City Public Library in American Life. Rosemary R. DuMont. LC 77-71864. (Contributions in Librarianship & Information Science: No. 21). 1977. lib. bdg. 45.00 (ISBN 0-8371-9540-3, DRR/). Greenwood.

Reform & Rebellion in Afghanistan, 1919-1929: King Amanullah's Failure to Modernize a Tribal Society. Leon B. Poullada. LC 72-12291. (Illus.). 318p. 1973. 35.00x (ISBN 0-8014-0772-9). Cornell U Pr.

Reform & Reformation: England & the Continent c.1500-c.1750. Ed. by Derek Baker. (Studies in Church History: Subsidia 2). (Illus.). 336p. 1980. 45.00x (ISBN 0-631-19270-0). Basil Blackwell.

Reform & Reformation: England, 1509-1558. G. R. Elton. LC 77-6464. (Harvard Paperback Ser.: No. 146, The New History of England). 1979. 29.50x (ISBN 0-674-75245-7); pap. 9.95x (ISBN 0-674-75248-1). Harvard U Pr.

Reform & Reformers in the Progressive Era. Ed. by David R. Colburn & George E. Pozzetta. LC 82-6140. (Contributions in American History: No. 101). (Illus.). xi, 196p. 1982. lib. bdg. 35.00 (ISBN 0-313-22907-4, CRP/). Greenwood.

Reform & Regret: The Story of Federal Judicial Involvement in the Alabama Prison System. Larry W. Yackle. 336p. 1989. 34.95 (ISBN 0-19-505737-6). Oxford U Pr.

Reform & Regulation: American Politics from Roosevelt to Wilson. 2nd ed. Lewis L. Gould. 200p. 1986. pap. 9.00 (ISBN 0-394-35413-3, KnopfC). Knopf.

Reform & Regulation in Long Term Care. Ed. by Valerie LaPorte & Jeffrey Rubin. LC 79-9761. 230p. 1979. 40.95 (ISBN 0-275-90379-6, C0379). Praeger.

Reform & Renewal in Higher Education: Implications for Library Instruction. Ed. by Carolyn Kirkendall. LC 80-81485. (Library Orientation Ser.: No. 10). 1980. 19.50 (ISBN 0-87650-124-2). Pierian.

Reform & Renewal, Thomas Cromwell & the Common Weal. Geoffrey R. Elton. (Wiles Lectures, 1972). 230p. 1973. pap. 12.95 (ISBN 0-521-09809-2). Cambridge U Pr.

Reform & Repression: U. S. Policy in El Salvador. Robert Armstrong & Philip Wheaton. (Illus.). 14p. 1983. pap. 1.50 (ISBN 0-942638-01-8, 14L). New Amer Pr.

Reform & Resistance in the International Order. Ian Clark. LC 79-54017. 1980. pap. 13.95 (ISBN 0-521-29763-X). Cambridge U Pr.

Reform & Revival: English Government in Ireland 1470-1534. Steven G. Ellis. 272p. 1986. 32.50 (ISBN 0-312-66751-5). St Martin.

Reform & Revolution in Asia. Ed. by G. F. Hudson. LC 72-85550. 300p. 1973. 27.50 (ISBN 0-312-66780-9). St Martin.

Reform & Revolution in China: The 1911 Revolution in Hunan & Hubei. Joseph W. Esherick. LC 75-17297. (Center for Chinese Studies, University of Michigan: No. 5). 1976. pap. 12.95x (ISBN 0-520-05734-1). U of Cal Pr.

Reform & Revolution: Transformation of Hungary's Agriculture, 1945-1970. Ferenc Donath. 490p. 1980. 20.00x (Pub. by Collets (UK)). State Mutual Bk.

Reform As Reorganization: Papers. Royce Hanson & Julius Margolis. LC 73-19348. (Governance of Metropolitan Regions Ser.: No. 4). pap. 34.80 (ISBN 0-317-09382-7, 2020967). Bks Demand UMI.

Reform by Statues: Thomas Starkey's Dialogue & Thomas Cromwell's Policy. G. R. Elton. (Raleigh Lectures on History). 1968. pap. 5.50 (ISBN 0-85672-319-3, Pub. by British Acad). Longwood Pub Group.

Reform Impulse, 1825-1850. Ed. by Walter Hugins. LC 76-187905. (Documentary History Ser.). x, 262p. 1972. 24.95x (ISBN 0-87249-264-8). U of SC Pr.

Reform in Administration of Justice. American Academy of Political & Social Science Staff. LC 79-156961. (Foundations of Criminal Justice Ser.). Repr. of 1914 ed. 16.00 (ISBN 0-404-09101-6). AMS Pr.

Reform in America: The Continuing Frontier. Robert H. Walker. LC 85-15711. (Illus.). 280p. 1985. 25.00 (ISBN 0-8131-1549-3). U Pr of Ky.

Reform in China: Challenges & Choices - A Summary & Analysis of the CESRRI Survey. Chinese Economic System Reform Research Institute Staff. Ed. by Bruce L. Reynolds. 250p. 1987. text ed. 39.95 (ISBN 0-87332-458-7, Pub. by East Gate Bk); pap. text ed. 15.95 (ISBN 0-87332-459-5). M E Sharpe.

Reform in China: Huang Tsun-Husien & the Japanese Model. Noriko Kamachi. (Harvard East Asian Monographs: No. 95). 350p. 1981. text ed. 21.00x (ISBN 0-674-75278-3). Harvard U Pr.

Reform in Detroit: Hazen S. Pingree & Urban Politics. Melvin G. Holli. LC 81-6347. xvi, 269p. 1981. Repr. of 1969 ed. lib. bdg. 35.00x (ISBN 0-313-22671-7, HORI). Greenwood.

Reform in Graduate & Professional Education. Lewis B. Mayhew & Patrick J. Ford. LC 73-20968. (Jossey-Bass Series in Higher Education). pap. 67.50 (2027762). Bks Demand UMI.

Reform in Nineteenth-Century China. Ed. by Paul A. Cohen & John E. Schrecker. (East Asian Monographs: No. 72). 1976. pap. 11.00x (ISBN 0-674-75281-3). Harvard U Pr.

Reform in Oaxaca, 1856-76: A Microhistory of the Liberal Revolution. Charles R. Berry. LC 80-15378. xx, 282p. 1981. 25.95x (ISBN 0-8032-1158-9). U of Nebr Pr.

Reform in Soviet Politics: The Lessons of Recent Policies on Land & Water. Thane Gustafson. LC 80-24286. (Illus.). 224p. 1981. 39.50 (ISBN 0-521-23377-1). Cambridge U Pr.

Reform in Sung China: Wang An-Shih, 1021-1086, & His New Policies. James T. Liu. LC 59-9281. (East Asian Ser: No. 3). 1959. 5.00x (ISBN 0-674-75300-3). Harvard U Pr.

Reform in the Ottoman Empire, 1856-1876. Roderic H. Davison. LC 73-148618. 503p. 1973. Repr. of 1963 ed. 50.00x (ISBN 0-87752-135-2). Gordian.

Reform in the Ottoman Empire, 1856-1876. Roderic H. Davison. LC 63-12669. pap. 123.30 (ISBN 0-317-09287-1, 2000890). Bks Demand UMI.

Reform in the Provinces: The Government of Stuart England. Anthony Fletcher. LC 86-1684. 352p. 1986. text ed. 35.00t (ISBN 0-300-03673-6). Yale U Pr.

Reform in the Royal Navy: A Social History of the Lower Deck, 1850-80. Eugene L. Rasor. LC 76-20689. 210p. 1976. 22.50 (ISBN 0-208-01595-7, Archon). Shoe String.

Reform in Trade Union Discrimination in the Construction Industry: Operation Dig & Its Legacy. Irwin Dubinsky. LC 72-12974. (Special Studies in U. S. Economic, Social, & Political Issues). 1973. 49.50x (ISBN 0-275-07080-8). Irvington.

Reform in Tsarist Russia: The State Bureaucracy & Local Government, 1900-1914. Neil B. Weissman. 288p. 1981. 35.00x (ISBN 0-8135-0926-2). Rutgers U Pr.

Reform Jewish Practice. S. Freehof. 9.95x (ISBN 0-87068-750-6). Ktav.

Reform Judaism Today. Eugene B. Borowitz. 800p. 1983. pap. text ed. 14.95x (ISBN 0-87441-364-8). Behrman.

Reform, Labor & Feminism: Margaret Dreier Robins & the National Women's Trade Union League. Elizabeth A. Payne. LC 87-10794. (Women in American History Ser.). (Illus.). 200p. 21.95 (ISBN 0-252-01445-6). U of Ill Pr.

Reform Movement in China: 1898-1912. Meribeth E. Cameron. LC 78-161506. (Standford University. Standford Studies in History, Economics & Political Science Ser. 3: No. 1). Repr. of 1931 ed. 22.00 (ISBN 0-404-50959-2). AMS Pr.

Reform of Criminal Law in Pennsylvania: Selected Enquiries 1787-1819. Ed. by Morton Hortwitz et al. LC 73-37983. 1972. 31.00 (ISBN 0-405-04026-1). Ayer Co Pubs.

Reform of Education. Giovanni Gentile. Tr. by Dino Bigongiari. LC 78-63672. (Studies in Fascism: Ideology & Practice). 264p. Repr. of 1922 ed. 25.00 (ISBN 0-404-16935-X). AMS Pr.

Reform of Environmental Regulation. Ed. by Wesley A. Magat. LC 82-1604. 208p. 1982. prof. ref. 32.00x (ISBN 0-88410-908-9). Ballinger Pub.

Reform of Girls' Secondary & Higher Education in Victorian England: A Study of Elites & Educational Change. Joyce S. Pedersen. Ed. by William H. McNeill & Peter Stansky. (Modern European History Ser.). 475p. 1987. lib. bdg. 70.00 (ISBN 0-8240-7828-4). Garland Pub.

Reform of Industrial Relations. Ed. by Hugh M. Pollock. (Issues in Industrial Relations Ser.). 100p. 1982. 14.95 (ISBN 0-86278-026-8, Pub. by O'Brien Pr Ireland); pap. 7.95 (ISBN 0-86278-027-6, Pub. by O'Brien Pr Ireland). Irish Bks Media.

Reform of International Institutions. C. Fred Bergsten et al. 1978. 15.00 (ISBN 0-318-02786-0); pap. 4.95 (ISBN 0-318-02787-9). Trilateral Comm.

Reform of International Institutions see Trilateral Commission Task Force Reports.

Reform of Joint Military Management: A Selected Bibliography. Anthony G. White. (Public Administration Ser.: P 1966). 7p. 1986. 3.00 (ISBN 0-89028-926-3). Vance Biblios.

Reform of Legal Procedure. Moorfield Storey. 263p. 1986. Repr. of 1912 ed. lib. bdg. 27.50x (ISBN 0-8377-1140-1). Rothman.

Reform of Local Government Finance in Britain. S. J. Bailey & R. Paddison. 208p. 1988. lib. bdg. 55.00 (ISBN 0-415-00530-2). Routledge Chapman & Hall.

Reform of Prisoners, 1830-1900. W. J. Forsythe. LC 86-28022. 256p. 1987. 35.00 (ISBN 0-312-00466-4). St Martin.

Reform of Social Security. A. W. Dilnot. 1984. 21.00x (ISBN 0-19-877226-2); pap. 8.95x (ISBN 0-19-877225-4). Oxford U Pr.

Reform of Social Security & Federal Pension Cost-of-Living Adjustments. American Enterprise Institute for Public Policy Research Staff. 1985. 15.75 (ISBN 0-8447-0264-1). Am Enterprise.

Reform of the Criminal Law & Procedure. facsimile ed. Ed. by Robert M. Fogelson. LC 74-3816. (Criminal Justice in America). 1974. Repr. of 1911 ed. 18.00 (ISBN 0-405-06165-X). Ayer Co Pubs.

Reform of the Fallen World: The 'Virtuous Prince' in Jonsonian Tragedy & Comedy. William D. Wolf. Ed. by James Hogg. (Jacobean Drama Studies). 154p. (Orig.). 1973. pap. 15.00 (ISBN 0-317-40087-8, Pub. by Salzburg Studies). Longwood Pub Group.

Reform of the FBI Intelligence Activities. John T. Elliff. LC 78-70290. 1979. 29.00 (ISBN 0-691-07607-3). Princeton U Pr.

Reform of the Hebrew Alphabet. Michael Landmann. Tr. by David J. Parent. LC 76-14595. (Illinois Language & Culture Ser.: Vol. 1). pap. 86.30 (ISBN 0-317-09443-2, 2013715). Bks Demand UMI.

Reform of the Liturgy, 1948-1975. Annibale Bugnini. Tr. by Matthew J. O'Connell from Ital. 1200p. 1988. pap. 24.95 (ISBN 0-8146-1571-6). Liturgical Pr.

Reform of the Public Delivery of Education Systems, 1982-1986. Dale E. Casper. (Public Administration Ser.: P 2245). 12p. 1987. 3.75 (ISBN 1-55590-485-8). Vance Biblios.

Reform of the Venezuelan Fiscal System. Ed. by T. E. Batalla. 432p. 1988. text ed. 38.95xt (ISBN 0-8138-0021-8). Iowa St U Pr.

Reform of Undergraduate Education. Arthur E. Levine & John R. Weingart. LC 73-7154. (Jossey-Bass Higher Education Ser.). Repr. of 1974 ed. 44.00 (ISBN 0-8357-9343-5, 2013960). Bks Demand UMI.

Reform of Workplace Industrial Relations: Theory, Myth & Evidence. rev. ed. Eric Batstone. 272p. 1988. 49.95 (ISBN 0-19-827585-4); pap. 24.95 (ISBN 0-19-827282-0). Oxford U Pr.

Reform or Revolution. Daniel De Leon. 1977. pap. 0.50 (ISBN 0-935534-37-7). NY Labor News.

Reform or Revolution. Rosa Luxemburg. 69.95 (ISBN 0-87968-069-5). Gordon Pr.

Reform or Revolution. Rosa Luxemburg. Tr. by Integer. LC 73-79783. 1973. 12.00 (ISBN 0-87348-302-2); pap. 2.95 (ISBN 0-87348-303-0). Path Pr NY.

Reform, Orthodoxy, Conservatism, & Reconstruction see Understanding American Judaism: Toward the Description of Modern Religion.

Reform Papers see Writings of Henry D. Thoreau.

Reform, Planning & City Politics: Montreal, Winnipeg, Toronto. Harold Kaplan. 768p. 1981. 47.50x (ISBN 0-8020-5543-5). U of Toronto Pr.

Reform, Protest & Social Transformation. Satish K. Sharma. 1987. 31.50x (ISBN 81-7024-098-0, Pub. by Ashish India). South Asia Bks.

Reform Rabbi in the Progressive Era: The Early Career of Stephen S. Wise. Ed. by Frank Feidel & Ernest May. (Harvard Dissertations in American History & Political Science). 440p. 1988. lib. bdg. 75.00 (ISBN 0-8240-5146-7). Garland Pub.

Reform, Rebellion & the Heavenly Way. Benjamin Weems. LC 64-17267. (Association for Asian Studies Monograph: No. 15). 122p. 1964. 7.95x (ISBN 0-8165-0144-0). U of Ariz Pr.

Reform Responsa for Our Time. S. B. Freehof. 15.00x (ISBN 0-87820-111-4, HUC Pr). Ktav.

Reform Response: Recent Reform Responses. Solomon B. Freehof. LC 72-12300. pap. 61.50 (ISBN 0-317-41851-3, 2026179). Bks Demand UMI.

Reform Rule in Czechoslovakia: The Dubcek Era, 1968-1969. Galia Golan. LC 72-83587. pap. 83.80 (ISBN 0-317-26401-X, 2024458). Bks Demand UMI.

Reform Spirit in America: A Documentation of the Pattern of Reform in the American Republic. Robert H. Walker. LC 85-4317. 704p. 1985. Repr. of 1976 ed. lib. bdg. 42.50 (ISBN 0-89874-724-4). Krieger.

Reform Thought in Sixteenth Century Italy. Elisabeth G. Gleason. Ed. by James A. Massey. LC 81-5648. (American Academy of Religion Texts & Translations Ser.). 1981. pap. text ed. 10.95 (ISBN 0-89130-498-3, 01-02-04). Scholars Pr GA.

Reform, War & Reaction: 1912-1932. Ed. by Stanley Coben. LC 72-12667. (Documentary History of the United States). xxii, 466p. 1973. 24.95x (ISBN 0-87249-277-X). U of SC Pr.

Reforma Mexico & the United States: A Search for Alternatives to Annexation, 1854-1861. Donathon C. Olliff. LC 81-3322. 256p. 1981. 21.50 (ISBN 0-8173-0070-8). U of Ala Pr.

Reforma Universitaria. (Ayacucho Library Collection Ser.: Vol. 39). (Span.). 19.95 (ISBN 0-317-56400-5, Pub. by Biblioteca Ayacucho); pap. 8.50 (ISBN 0-317-56401-3, Pub. by Biblioteca Ayacucho). Humanities.

Reformatio Perennis: Essays on Calvin & the Reformation in Honor of Ford Lewis Battles. Ed. by Brian Gerrish. (Pittsburgh Theological Monograph Ser.: No. 32). 1981. pap. 15.00 (ISBN 0-915138-41-7). Pickwick.

Reformation. J. A. Babington. LC 71-118513. 1971. Repr. of 1901 ed. 28.75x (ISBN 0-8046-1135-1, Pub. by Kennikat). Assoc Faculty Pr.

Reformation. Will Durant. (Story of Civilization: Vol. 6). (Illus.). 1957. 29.95 (ISBN 0-671-61050-3). S&S.

Reformation. George P. Fisher. LC 83-45660. Repr. of 1906 ed. 54.50 (ISBN 0-404-19810-4). AMS Pr.

Reformation. Harold J. Grimm. LC 72-76717. (AHA Pamphlets: No. 403). 1972. pap. text ed. 1.50 (ISBN 0-87229-003-4). Am Hist Assn.

Reformation. Peter Klassen. LC 79-54030. (Problems in Civilization Ser.). (Orig.). 1980. pap. text ed. 6.95x (ISBN 0-88273-408-3). Forum Pr IL.

Reformation, Vol. 3. Owen Chadwick. (History of the Church Ser.). (Orig.). 1964. pap. 5.95 (ISBN 0-14-020504-7, Pelican). Penguin.

Reformation see Renaissance & Reformation.

Reformation: A Narrative History Related by Contemporary Observers & Participants. Ed. by Hans J. Hillerbrand. (Twin Brooks Ser). (Illus.). 1978. pap. 13.95 (ISBN 0-8010-4185-6). Baker Bk.

Reformation: A Picture Story of Martin Luther. Dietrich Steinwede. Tr. by Edward A. Cooperrider from Ger. LC 82-49055. (Illus.). 56p. 1983. pap. 0.95 (ISBN 0-8006-1710-X, 1-1710). Fortress.

Reformation & Counter-Reformation. Ed. by Hubert Jedin & John Dolan. 1980. 59.50x (ISBN 0-686-95526-9). Crossroad NY.

Reformation & Reaction in Tudor Cambridge. H. C. Porter. LC 77-179573. (Illus.). xv, 462p. 1972. Repr. of 1958 ed. 38.50 (ISBN 0-208-01228-1, Archon). Shoe String.

Reformation & Renaissance. Jean M. Stone. LC 83-45670. (Illus.). Date not set. Repr. of 1904 ed. 76.50 (ISBN 0-404-19820-1). AMS Pr.

Reformation & Resistance in Tudor Lancashire. Christopher Haigh. LC 73-88308. pap. 97.80 (ISBN 0-317-29372-9, 2024476). Bks Demand UMI.

Reformation & Revolution 1558-1660. Robert Ashton. 503p. pap. 7.95 (ISBN 0-586-08449-5). Academy Chi Pubs.

Reformation & Society in Sixteenth Century Europe. A. G. Dickens. (History of European Civilization Library). (Illus., Orig.). 1966. pap. text ed. 11.00 net (ISBN 0-15-576455-1, HC). HarBraceJ.

Reformation & the Advent Movement. Walter L. Emmerson. 224p. pap. 12.95 (ISBN 0-8280-0168-5). Review & Herald.

Reformation & the People. Thomas A. Lacey. LC 83-45583. Date not set. Repr. of 1929 ed. 22.00 (ISBN 0-404-19901-1). AMS Pr.

Reformation & Utopia: The Marxist Interpretation of the Reformation & Its Antecedents. Abraham Friesen. 287p. 1974. pap. 48.50x (ISBN 3-515-01818-2, Pub by Franz Steiner). Coronet Bks.

Reformation: Basic Interpretations. 2nd ed. Ed. by Lewis W. Spitz. (Problems in European Civilization Ser.). 1972. pap. text ed. 7.50 (ISBN 0-669-81620-5). Heath.

Reformation Debate. Ed. by John Calvin & Jacopo Sadoleto. 1976. pap. 4.95 (ISBN 0-8010-2390-4). Baker Bk.

Reformation Era: 1500-1650. 2nd ed. Harold J. Grimm. (Illus.). 700p. 1973. text ed. write for info. (ISBN 0-02-347270-7, 34727). Macmillan.

Reformation Europe: A Guide to Research. Ed. by Steven E. Ozment. 390p. 1982. 18.50x (ISBN 0-910345-01-5); pap. 13.50x (ISBN 0-686-82436-9). Center Reform.

Reformation Europe: Age of Reform & Revolution. De Lamar Jensen. 480p. 1981. pap. text ed. 14.50 (ISBN 0-669-03626-9). Heath.

Reformation in England. Gustave L. Constant. Tr. by R. E. Scantlebury. LC 83-45576. Date not set. Repr. of 1934 ed. 85.00 (ISBN 0-404-19895-3). AMS Pr.

Reformation in England, 2 vols. Merle D'Aubigne. 1977. Vol. 1. pap. 17.95 (ISBN 0-85151-486-3); Vol. 2. pap. 17.95 (ISBN 0-85151-487-1); Set. 33.95 (ISBN 0-85151-488-X). Banner of Truth.

Reformation in England to the Accession of Elizabeth 1. Arthur G. Dickens & Dorothy Carr. (Documents of Modern History Ser). (Orig.). 1968. pap. write for info. (ISBN 0-312-66815-5). St Martin.

Reformation in Germany. H. C. Vedder. 1977. lib. bdg. 59.95 (ISBN 0-8490-2506-0). Gordon Pr.

Reformation in Germany. Henry C. Vedder. LC 83-45671. Date not set. Repr. of 1914 ed. 52.50 (ISBN 0-404-19821-X). AMS Pr.

Reformation in Historical Thought. A. G. Dickens et al. 456p. 1985. text ed. 35.00x (ISBN 0-674-75311-9). Harvard U Pr.

Reformation in Its Literature. Arthur Smellie. LC 83-45669. Date not set. Repr. of 1925 ed. 38.00 (ISBN 0-404-19819-8). AMS Pr.

Reformation in Lithuania: Religious Fluctuations in the Sixteenth Century. Antanas Musteikus. (East European Monographs: No. 246). 160p. 1988. 20.00 (ISBN 0-88033-143-7). East Eur Quarterly.

Reformation in Northern England. J. S. Fletcher. LC 71-118469. 1971. Repr. of 1925 ed. 23.50x (ISBN 0-8046-1218-8, Pub. by Kennikat). Assoc Faculty Pr.

Reformation in Poland. Paul Fox. LC 72-136395. Repr. of 1924 ed. 24.50 (ISBN 0-404-02544-7). AMS Pr.

Refractories: Production & Properties. J. H. Chesters. 562p. (Orig.). 1973. pap. text ed. 50.00x (ISBN 0-900497-84-X, Pub. by Inst Metals). Brookfield Pub Co.

Refractories: The Hidden Industry. Corrinne Krause. 256p. 1987. 38.00 (ISBN 0-916094-94-4). Am Ceramic.

Refractory Carbides. Edmund K. Storms. 1967. 77.00 (ISBN 0-12-672850-X). Acad Pr.

Refractory Concrete. 1978. 39.75 (ISBN 0-686-71024-X, SP-57) (ISBN 0-686-71025-8). ACI.

Refractory Concrete: State-of-the Art Report. 224p. 1979. 38.75 (ISBN 0-317-32086-6, 547R-79). ACI.

Refractory Husbands. Mary S. Cutting. LC 79-128729. (Short Story Index Reprint Ser). 1913. 14.00 (ISBN 0-8369-3620-5). Ayer Co Pubs.

Refractory Metals & Alloys III: Applied Aspects. Ed. by Robert I. Jaffee. LC 65-24869. (Metallurgical Society Conference Ser.: Vol. 30). pap. 160.00 (ISBN 0-317-10849-2, 2001518). Bks Demand UMI.

Refractory Metals & Alloys IV: Research & Development. Ed. by R. I. Jaffee et al. LC 68-21965. (Metallurgical Society Conferences: Vol. 41). pap. 160.00 (ISBN 0-317-10586-8, 2001530). Bks Demand UMI.

Refractory Metals & Alloys: Proceedings. Ed. by M. Semchyshen. LC 61-9444. (Metallurgical Society Conferences: Vol. 11). pap. 158.80 (ISBN 0-317-10265-6, 2000674). Bks Demand UMI.

Refractory Metals & Their Industrial Applications-STP 849. ASTM Committee B-10. Ed. by Robert E. Smallwood. LC 84-70136. (Illus.). 115p. 1984. pap. text ed. 19.00 (ISBN 0-8031-0203-8, 04-849000-05). ASTM.

Refrainformen im Chansonnier de L'arsenal. Herta Orenstein. (Wissenschaftliche Abhandlungen-Musicological Studies Ser.: Vol. 19). 120p. (Ger.). 1972. lib. bdg. 40.00 (ISBN 0-912024-89-5). Inst Mediaeval Mus.

Refrains chez les trouveres du XIIe siecle au debut du XIVe. Eglal Doss-Quinby. LC 84-47878. (American University Studies II (Romance Languages & Literature): Vol. 17). 316p. 1984. text ed. 32.00 (ISBN 0-8204-0153-6). P Lang Pubs.

Reframing: Neuro-Linguistic Programming & the Transformation of Meaning. Richard Bandler & John Grinder. Ed. by Steve Andreas & Connirae Andreas. 215p. (Orig.). 1982. 10.00 (ISBN 0-911226-24-9); pap. 6.50 (ISBN 0-911226-25-7). Real People.

Refranes: Southwestern Spanish Proverbs. rev., bilingual ed. Ruben Cobos. (Illus.). 128p. 1985. pap. 8.95 (ISBN 0-89013-177-5). Museum NM Pr.

Refrano General Ideologico Espanol. Luis Martinez Kleiser. 814p. (Span.). 1978. pap. 95.00 (ISBN 84-7155-268-X, S-50174). French & Eur.

Refresh Your Marriage with Self Talk. David Stoop & Jan Stoop. 160p. (Orig.). 1984. pap. 6.95 (ISBN 0-8007-5164-7, Power Bks). Revell.

Refresher Course in Gregg Shorthand. Madeline S. Strony et al. (Diamond Jubilee Ser.). 1970. text ed. 23.45 (ISBN 0-07-062205-1). McGraw.

Refresher Course in Gregg Shorthand. Madeline S. Strony et al. 128p. 1985. pap. text ed. 7.95 (ISBN 0-07-062289-2). McGraw.

Refresher Course in Gregg Shorthand Simplified. Madeline S. Strony et al. 1962. text ed. 23.50 (ISBN 0-07-062248-5). McGraw.

Refresher Guide for the Safety Professional. 110.00 (ISBN 0-939874-48-2). ASSE.

Refreshing Grammar. James B. Hogins. 272p. (Orig.). 1985. pap. text ed. write for info. (ISBN 0-574-22095-X, 13-5095); instr's. guide avail. (ISBN 0-574-22096-8, 13-5096). SRA.

Refreshing Pauses: Coca-Cola & Human Rights in Guatemala. Henry J. Frundt. LC 87-16001. 288p. 1987. lib. bdg. 34.95 (ISBN 0-275-92764-4, C2764). Praeger.

Refreshment in the Desert: Spiritual Connections in Daily Life. Gilbert Padilla. LC 85-50663. 144p. (Orig.). 1985. pap. 7.95 (ISBN 0-89622-228-4). Twenty-Third.

Refrigerant Line Sizing. 48p. 1977. 18.00 (ISBN 0-910110-23-9). Am Heat Ref & Air Eng.

Refrigerating Machine Mechanic. Jack Rudman. (Career Examination Ser.: C-1451). (Cloth bdg. avail. on request). pap. 14.00 (ISBN 0-8373-1451-8). Natl Learning.

Refrigerating Machine Operator. Jack Rudman. (Career Examination Ser.: C-670). (Cloth bdg. avail. on request). pap. 14.00 (ISBN 0-8373-0670-1). Natl Learning.

Refrigeration, Pt. I. Ed. by A. Ross Sabin. (Illus.). 144p. (gr. 11). 1974. 20.00 (ISBN 0-938336-01-0). Whirlpool.

Refrigeration, Pt. II. Ed. by A. Ross Sabin. (Illus.). 208p. (gr. 11). 1974. 20.00 (ISBN 0-938336-02-9). Whirlpool.

Refrigeration: A Practical Manual for Apprentices. 3rd ed. G. H. Reed. (Illus.). 153p. 1984. Repr. of 1974 ed. 27.00 (ISBN 0-85334-605-4, Pub. by Elsevier Applied Sci England). Elsevier.

Refrigeration: A Practical Manual for Mechanics. 2nd Ed. ed. Ed. by G. H. Reed. (Illus.). 232p. 1981. 39.75 (ISBN 0-85334-964-9, Pub. by Elsevier Applied Sci England). Elsevier.

Refrigeration & Air-Conditioning. 2nd ed. Air Conditioning & Refrigeration Institute Staff. (Illus.). 992p. 1987. text ed. 32.00 (ISBN 0-13-770181-0); By Lee Miles. write for info. lab manual (ISBN 0-13-770223-X). P-H.

Refrigeration & Air Conditioning. (Illus.). 863p. 32.95 (ISBN 0-318-12212-X). ACR Inst.

Refrigeration & Air Conditioning. (Equipment Planning Guides: No. 14). 1978. pap. 28.00 (ISBN 92-2-101895-4, ILO1077, ILO). UNIPUB.

Refrigeration & Air Conditioning. 1985. 5.00 (ISBN 0-471-63946-X). Wiley.

Refrigeration & Air Conditioning. 2nd ed. W. F. Stoecker & J. W. Jones. 464p. 1982. text ed. 49.95x (ISBN 0-07-061619-1). McGraw.

Refrigeration & Air Conditioning: Operation & Analysis Servicing. Wayne Long. 832p. 1985. text ed. 31.95 scp (ISBN 0-672-97994-2); scp instr's guide 7.33 (ISBN 0-672-97995-0). Bobbs.

Refrigeration & Air Conditioning Technology: Concepts, Procedures & Troubleshooting Techniques. William Whitman & William Johnson. LC 86-16506. 960p. 1986. text ed. 34.95 (ISBN 0-8273-2416-2). Delmar.

Refrigeration & Air-Conditioning Technology. Rex Miller. 1983. text ed. 26.00 (ISBN 0-02-665540-3); student ed. 6.64 (ISBN 0-02-665560-8); tchr's. ed. 6.64 (ISBN 0-02-665550-0). Bennett IL.

Refrigeration & Conditioning Dictionary. Abd-El-Wahed. 395p. (Eng., Fr., Ger. & Arabic.). 1979. 75.00 (ISBN 0-686-97399-2, M-9756). French & Eur.

Refrigeration & Controlled Atmosphere Storage for Horticultural Crops. 42p. 3.50 (ISBN 0-317-59103-7, NRAES-22). NE Agri Engineer.

Refrigeration at Sea. 2nd ed. R. Munton & J. R. Stott. (Illus.). 238p. 1978. 66.75 (ISBN 0-85334-766-2, Pub. by Elsevier Applied Sci England). Elsevier.

Refrigeration: Home & Commercial, 2 vols. Edwin P. Anderson. Ed. by Rex Miller. (Illus.). 1984. Set. 17.95 (Pub. by Audel). Macmillan.

Refrigeration License Manual. 2nd ed. Sylvan Harfenist. LC 74-24888. (Illus.). 1975. pap. 12.00 (ISBN 0-668-02726-6). Arco.

Refrigeration Licenses: (Contractor-Journeyman-Operator) Unlimited. Clayton H. Carrico. 1980. text ed. 29.95x (ISBN 0-912524-20-0). Busn News.

Refrigeration Oil Description, 1981. (ASHRAE Standards Ser.: No. 99). 16.00 (ISBN 0-317-58743-9). Am Heat Ref & Air Eng.

Refrigeration on Fishing Vessels. 2nd ed. John Merritt. (Illus.). 164p. 1979. pap. 20.50 (ISBN 0-85238-095-X, FN24, Pub. by FNB). UNIPUB.

Refrigeration on Fishing Vessels. John H. Merritt. 1978. 40.00 (ISBN 0-685-63449-3). State Mutual Bk.

Refrigeration Principles & Systems: An Energy Approach. Edward G. Pita. LC 83-21780. 148p. 1984. 31.95 (ISBN 0-471-87611-9); write for info. tchrs. ed. (ISBN 0-471-89758-2). Wiley.

Refrigeration Processes: A Practical Handbook on the Physical Properties of Refrigerants & Their Applications. M. H. Meacock. (International Series in Heating, Ventilation & Refrigeration: Vol. 12). 1979. text ed. 63.00 (ISBN 0-08-024211-1); pap. text ed. 25.00 (ISBN 0-08-024234-0). Pergamon.

Refrigeration Reference Notebook. Harry Busby. 160p. 1969. 6.95 (ISBN 0-912524-29-4). Busn News.

Refrigeration Servicing. Paul F. Goliber. LC 75-6064. 91p. 1976. pap. 10.95 (ISBN 0-8273-1005-6). Delmar.

Refrigeration Terms & Definitions, 1975. (ASHRAE Standards Ser.: No. 12). 19.00 (ISBN 0-317-58651-3). Am Heat Ref & Air Eng.

Refrigerator Perry & the Super Bowl Bears. Bill Gutman. (gr. 4 up). 1987. pap. 2.50 (ISBN 0-671-63127-6). Archway.

Refuge. Liane I. Brown. (Illus.). 211p. (Orig.). 1987. pap. write for info. (ISBN 0-89084-392-9). Bob Jones Univ Pr.

Refuge. Sami Michael. Tr. by Edward Grossman from Hebrew. 376p. 1988. 19.95 (ISBN 0-8276-0308-8). JPS Phila.

Refugee. Piers Anthony. (Bio of a Space Tyrant Ser.: Vol. I). 320p. 1985. pap. 3.50 (ISBN 0-380-84194-0). Avon.

Refugee. Asif Currimbhoy. (Writers Workshop Bluebird Ser.). 38p. 1971. flexible cloth 4.80 (ISBN 0-317-42486-6). Ind-US Inc.

Refugee Community Health Care. Stephanie Simmonds et al. (Illus.). 1983. pap. 9.95x (ISBN 0-19-261407-X). Oxford U Pr.

Refugee Enterprise: It Can Be Done. Chris Rolfe et al. (Illus.). 150p. (Orig.). 1987. pap. 13.50x (ISBN 0-946688-59-1, Pub. by Intermed Tech England). Intermediate Tech.

Refugee in International Law. Guy S. Goodwin-Gill. 1984. 49.95x (ISBN 0-19-825372-9); pap. 16.95x (ISBN 0-19-825518-7). Oxford U Pr.

Refugee Mental Health in Resettlement Countries. Ed. by Carolyn L. Williams & Joseph Westermeyer. (Clinical & Community Psychology Ser.). 267p. 1986. text ed. 44.95 (ISBN 0-89116-445-6). Hemisphere Pub.

Refugee Problems in Africa. Ed. by Sven Hamrell. (Scandinavian Institute of African Studies). 123p. 1967. pap. 14.50 (ISBN 0-8419-9700-4, Africana). Holmes & Meier.

Refugee Protection: An Analysis & Action Proposal. 1983. write for info. US Comm Refugees.

Refugee Protection in Africa: Current Trends. 1985. write for info. US Comm Refugees.

Refugee Question in Mid-Victorian Politics. Bernard Porter. LC 78-73947. (Illus.). 1980. 47.50 (ISBN 0-521-22638-4). Cambridge U Pr.

Refugee Question in Mid-Victorian Politics. Bernard Porter. LC 78-73947. pap. 63.50 (ISBN 0-317-55484-0, 2029224). Bks Demand UMI.

Refugee Scholars in America: Their Impact & Their Experiences. Lewis A. Coser. LC 84-40193. 384p. 1984. 29.50x (ISBN 0-300-03193-9). Yale U Pr.

Refugee Summer. Edward Fenton. LC 81-12593. 272p. (gr. 7 up). 1982. pap. 10.95 (ISBN 0-385-28854-9). Delacorte.

Refugees. W. Lewis. write for info. (ISBN 0-275-90020-7, C0020). Praeger.

Refugees: A Tale of Two Continents. Arthur Conan Doyle. 8.95 (ISBN 0-685-20618-1). Transatl Arts.

Refugees: A Third World Dilemma. John Rogge. LC 87-9605. 384p. 1987. text ed. 43.50 (ISBN 0-8476-7557-2). Rowman.

Refugees & Development in Africa. Ed. by Peter Nobel. (Scandinavian Institute of African Studies: No. 19). 121p. 1987. 26.50 (ISBN 91-7106-272-6, Pub. by Nordiska Afrikainstitutet (Uppsala Sweden)). Coronet Bks.

Refugees & Development in Africa: The Case of Eritrea. Gaim Kibreab. LC 86-63776. (Illus.). 300p. 1987. 35.00 (ISBN 0-932415-26-1); pap. 11.95 (ISBN 0-932415-27-X). Red Sea Pr.

Refugees & World Politics. Ed. by Elizabeth Ferris. LC 85-495. 240p. 1985. 38.95 (ISBN 0-275-90099-1, C0099). Praeger.

Refugees: Extended Exile. W. R. Smyser. LC 87-20957. (Washington Papers: No. 129). 158p. 1987. lib. bdg. 31.95 (ISBN 0-275-92877-2, C2877); pap. 9.95 (ISBN 0-275-92878-0, B2878). Praeger.

Refugees from Irian Jaya in Papua New Guinea: A Trip Report. 1985. write for info. US Comm Refugees.

Refugees from Laos-In Harm's Way. Joseph Cerquone. Ed. by Virginia Hamilton. (Issue Brief Ser.). 1986. pap. 2.00. US Comm Refugees.

Refugees from Militarism: Draft-Age Americans in Canada. Renee G. Kasinsky. LC 75-46232. 350p. 1976. 24.95 (ISBN 0-87855-113-1). Transaction Bks.

Refugees from Nowhere. George Bourland. pap. 0.75 (ISBN 0-912136-04-9); pap. 5.00x signed ed. (ISBN 0-685-01070-8). Twowindows Pr.

Refugees from Slavery in Canada West: Report to the Freedmen's Inquiry Commission. Samuel G. Howe. LC 69-18540. (American Negro: His History & Literature Ser., No. 2). Repr. of 1864 ed. 10.00 (ISBN 0-405-01872-X). Ayer Co Pubs.

Refugees in America: Committee for the Study of Recent Immigration from Europe. Ed. by Maurice Davie. LC 74-1513. (Illus.). 453p. 1974. Repr. of 1947 ed. lib. bdg. 35.00x (ISBN 0-8371-7390-6, DARA). Greenwood.

Refugees in International Politics. Leon Gordenker. LC 87-11688. 256p. 1987. 30.00 (ISBN 0-231-06624-4). Columbia U Pr.

Refugees in the Age of Total War. Ed. by Anna C. Bramwell. 432p. 1988. text ed. 75.00 (ISBN 0-04-445194-6). Unwin Hyman.

Refugees in the United States: A Reference Handbook. Ed. by David W. Haines. LC 84-12794. (Illus.). viii, 243p. 1985. lib. bdg. 46.95 (ISBN 0-313-24068-X, HRU/). Greenwood.

Refugees in Uganda & Rwanda: The Banyarwandan Tragedy. 1983. write for info. US Comm Refugees.

Refugees: Issues & Directions. (IMR Special Issues Ser.). 1986. pap. 14.95 (A2). Ctr Migration.

Refugees of a Hidden War: The Aftermath of Counterinsurgency in Guatemala. Beatriz Manz. LC 87-10169. (Anthropological Studies of Contemporary Issues). (Illus.). 288p. 1987. 49.50 (ISBN 0-88706-675-5); pap. 16.95 (ISBN 0-88706-676-3). State U NY Pr.

Refugees of Revolution. Carl F. Wittke. Repr. of 1952 ed. lib. bdg. 35.00 (ISBN 0-8371-2988-5, WIRR). Greenwood.

Refugees: Search for a Haven. Judith Bentley. LC 85-21451. 160p. (YA) (gr. 7 up). 1986. 9.79 (ISBN 0-671-50819-9). Messner.

Refugees South of the Sahara: An African Dilemma. Ed. by Hugh C. Brooks & Yassin El-Ayouty. LC 71-105994. (Contributions in Afro-American & African Studies: No. 14). 1970. 56.95 (ISBN 0-8371-3324-6, BSS&). Greenwood.

Refugees: The Dynamics of Displacement. ICIHI Staff. (Report for the Independent Commission on International Humanitarian Issues). 180p. 1986. 29.95 (ISBN 0-86232-696-6, Pub. by Zed Pr UK); pap. 7.95 (ISBN 0-86232-697-4, Pub. by Zed Pr UK). Humanities.

Refugees: The New International Politics of Displacement. Kathleen Newland. LC 81-50523. (Worldwatch Papers). 1981. pap. 4.00 (ISBN 0-916468-42-9). Worldwatch Inst.

Refugiados. Angel Castro. 1971. pap. text ed. 4.00 (ISBN 0-685-48630-3). E Torres & Sons.

Refugium Botanicum or Figurs & Descriptions from Living Specimens of Little Known or New Plants of Botanical Interest, Vol. II. Illus. by W. H. Fitch. (Orchid Ser.). (Illus.). 1980. Repr. text ed. 27.50 (ISBN 0-930576-19-5). E M Coleman Ent.

Refunding of International Debt. Henry J. Bittermann. LC 72-93542. xii, 252p. 1973. 28.50 (ISBN 0-8223-0280-2). Duke.

Refunding Periodicals, Books, Clubs, Associations: A How to Find or Locate Reference. Data Notes Publishing Staff. LC 83-90727. 200p. 1983. text ed. 3.75 (ISBN 0-911569-06-5, Pub. by Data Notes). Prosperity & Profits.

Refurbishing Our Foundations: Elementary Linguistics from an Advanced Point of View. C. F. Hockett. LC 87-29961. (Current Issues in Linguistic Theory Ser.: Vol. 56). ix, 181p. 1987. 26.00x (ISBN 90-272-3550-3). Benjamins North Am.

Refusals to Deal & Exclusive Distributorships. Antitrust Law Section Members. 64p. 1983. pap. 20.00 (ISBN 0-317-16856-8). Amer Bar Assn.

Refuse-Derived Fuel Processing. Floyd Hasselriis. LC 83-12968. (Vol. 4). 400p. 1984. 42.95 (ISBN 0-250-40314-5). Butterworth.

Refuse Derived Fuels. A. Porteous. (Illus.). xi, 138p. 1981. 30.00 (ISBN 0-85334-937-1, Pub. by Elsevier Applied Sci England). Elsevier.

Refuse Recycling & Recovery. John R. Holmes. LC 80-42145. (Institution of Environmental Science Ser.). (Illus.). 196p. pap. 51.00 (2030465). Bks Demand UMI.

Refuse to Burn. Robert W. Lockerby. (Public Administration Ser.: P 2019). 17p. 1986. 5.00 (ISBN 1-55590-039-9). Vance Biblios.

Refusenik: Trapped in the Soviet Union. Mark Y. Azbel. LC 86-30307. (Illus.). 512p. 1987. pap. 10.95 (ISBN 0-913729-65-5). Paragon Hse.

Refusenik; Voices of Struggle & Hope. Albert S. Axelrad. LC 87-50034. 75p. (Orig.). 1986. pap. text ed. 9.95x (ISBN 0-932269-56-7). Wyndham Hall.

Refusers. Stanley Burnshaw. 1981. 14.95 (ISBN 0-8180-0630-7). Horizon.

Refutation of Machiavelli's Prince or Anti-Machiavel. Frederick Of Prussia. Tr. by Paul Sonnino. LC 80-15801. viii, 174p. 1981. 16.95x (ISBN 0-8214-0559-4); pap. 7.95 (ISBN 0-8214-0598-5). Ohio U Pr.

Refutation of Scepticism. Anthony C. Grayling. LC 85-5032. 150p. 1985. cloth 22.95 (ISBN 0-87548-314-3). Open Court.

Refutation of the 'Apology for Actors' see Apology for Actors.

Refutation of the Apology for Actors see Apology for Actors.

Refutation of the Sects. Yeznik Koghbatsi. Ed. by Thomas J. Samuelian. (Armenian Church Classics Ser.). (Illus.). 1986. pap. 5.00 (ISBN 0-934728-13-5). D O A C.

Reg Butler. John Davies. (Illus.). 88p. pap. 9.95 (ISBN 0-905005-99-6). Salem Hse Pubs.

Reg-Words Keyword Index to Drug Labeling Regulations. D. Snyder & M. Anisfeld. 60p. 1986. 85.00x (ISBN 0-935184-05-8). Interpharm.

Regain. Jean Giono. 192p. 1958. 18.95 (ISBN 0-686-53986-9). French & Eur.

Regain. Marcel Pagnol. 254p. 1973. 22.50 (ISBN 0-686-54841-8). French & Eur.

Regain see Oeuvres Romanesques.

Regaining Competitiveness: Putting The Goal To Work. Mokshagundam L. Srikanth & Harold E. Cavallaro. 200p. 1987. pap. 11.00 (ISBN 0-943953-00-6). Spectrum CT.

Regaining Excellence in Education. Mario D. Fantini. 320p. 1986. pap. text ed. 23.95 (ISBN 0-675-20501-8); text ed. 28.95 (ISBN 0-675-20076-8). Merrill.

Regaining Life's Amenities. Gary Hanson. 1983. 5.95 (ISBN 0-934860-27-0). Adventure Pubns.

Regaining Paradise: Milton & the Eighteenth Century. Dustin Griffin. (Illus.). 300p. 1986. 29.95 (ISBN 0-521-30913-1). Cambridge U Pr.

Regal see History of Roman Private Law.

Regal Reports: Super Money Making Ideas. 1987. lib. bdg. 64.00 (ISBN 0-8490-3910-X). Gordon Pr.

Regal: The Golden Eagle. Lars Klinting. Tr. by Alan Bernstein. (Illus.). 32p. (ps up). 1988. 6.95 (ISBN 91-29-58774-3, Pub. by R & S Bks). FS&G.

Regality of Kirriemuir. Alan Reid. (Illus.). 1987. 75.00x (Pub. by Wm Culross & Son Ltd UK). State Mutual Bk.

Regalo del Cesar. Rene De Goscinny. (Asterix Ser.). (Illus., Span.). 1976. 5.95x (ISBN 0-686-34393-X). Intl Learn Syst.

Regalo del Cesar. R. Goscinny & M. Uderzo. (Illus., Span.). 15.95 (ISBN 0-686-56238-0). French & Eur.

Regalo del Cesar. Rene Goscinny & Albert Uderzo. (Asterix the Gaul Ser.). (Illus.). 48p. 7.95. Dargaud Pub.

Regan's Raiders. Rich Buckler & Monroe Arnold. (Illus.). 96p. 1987. 6.95 (ISBN 1-55601-005-2). Solson Pubns.

Regard et L'excedent. Jacques Taminiaux. (Phaenomenologica Ser. 75). 1978. lib. bdg. 35.50 (ISBN 90-247-2028-1, Pub. by Martinus Nijhoff Netherlands). Kluwer Academic.

Regional & Interregional Co-Operation: Co-Operation for Development in Asia. 250p. 1986. pap. 15.00 (ISBN 1-85148-015-3). Tycooly Pub.

Regional & Interregional Co-Operation: Co-Operation in the 1980s: Principles & Prospects, Vo. 1. 1984. pap. 15.00 (ISBN 0-318-20393-6). Tycooly Pub.

Regional & Interregional Co-Operation, 6 vols. Ed. by Ervin Laszlo. 1984. Set. lib. bdg. 175.00 (ISBN 1-85148-014-5). Tycooly Pub.

Regional & Interregional Co-Operation: Latin American & Caribbean Co-Operation for Development, Vol. 2. 250p. 1986. pap. 15.00 (ISBN 1-85148-014-5). Tycooly Pub.

Regional & Interregional Co-Operation: Regional & Interregional Co-Operation in the 80s: Policies & Strategies, Vol. 6. 150p. 1986. pap. 15.00 (ISBN 1-85148-016-1). Tycooly Pub.

Regional & Interregional Co-operation: World Leadership & International Development, Vol. 5. Ed. by John O'Manique & Michael Lerner. (Illus.). 138p. 1984. 15.00 (ISBN 0-318-20396-0). Tycooly Pub.

Regional & Interregional Input-Output Analysis: An Annotated Bibliography. Frank Giarrantani. LC 75-45868. 1976. 6.00 (ISBN 0-89092-008-7). West Va U Pr.

Regional & Local Economic Analysis for Practitioners. new ed. Avron Bendavid-Val. LC 82-16695. (Illus.). 208p. 1983. 36.95 (ISBN 0-275-90947-6, C0947). Praeger.

Regional & Long-Range Transport of Air Pollution. Ed. by S. Sandroni. 510p. 1987. 170.75 (ISBN 0-444-42818-6). Elsevier.

Regional & Metropolitan Growth & Decline in the United States. William Frey & Alden Speare, Jr. LC 87-43098. (Population of the United States in the 1980s: A Census Monograph Ser.). 400p. 1987. text ed. 37.50 (ISBN 0-87154-293-5). Russell Sage.

Regional & Urban Development Policies: A Latin American Perspective. Guillermo Geisse. LC 78-103483. (Latin American Urban Research Ser.: Vol. 2). pap. 74.50 (ISBN 0-317-29678-7, 2021904). Bks Demand UMI.

Regional & Urban Location. Colin Clark. LC 81-21510. 1982. 32.50x (ISBN 0-312-66903-8). St Martin.

Regional Anesthesia: Journal of the American & European Societies of Regional Anesthesia. Ed. by Phillip Bridenbaugh. 1987. 58.00 (Lippincott Medical). Lippincott.

Regional Anesthesia: Techniques & Clinical Applications. Harold Carron et al. 208p. 1984. 42.50 (ISBN 0-8089-1654-8, 790797). Grune.

Regional Archaeology in the Valle de la Plata, Colombia. Robert Drennan. Tr. by Veronica Kennedy. (Technical Reports: No. 16). (Illus.). 195p. (Orig., Eng. & Span.). 1985. pap. 8.00 (ISBN 0-915703-06-8). U Mich Mus Anthro.

Regional Architecture of the Early South. Ed. by Lisa C. Mullins. (Architectural Treasures of Early America Ser.). (Illus.). 245p. 1987. 19.95 (ISBN 0-918678-21-8). Historical Times.

Regional Aspects of Carbonate Deposition: A Symposium. Ed. by Rufus J. Le Blanc & Julia G. Breeding. LC 57-2837. (Society of Economic Paleontologists & Mineralogists, Special Publication: No. 5). pap. 53.80 (ISBN 0-317-27104-0, 2024732). Bks Demand UMI.

Regional Aspects of Family Planning & Fertility Behavior in Indonesia. Dov Chernichovsky & Oey Astra Meesook. (Working Paper: No. 462). 62p. 1981. 5.00 (ISBN 0-686-36192-X, WP-0462). World Bank.

Regional Bell Holding Companies: Strategic Expansion Programs, Policies, & Issues. Market Intelligence Research Company Staff. Ed. by W. Hammersky. 501p. (Orig.). 1987. pap. text ed. 995.00x (ISBN 0-916483-23-1). Market Res Co.

Regional Block: A Handbook for Use in the Clinical Practice of Medicine & Surgery. 4th ed. Daniel C. Moore. (Illus.). 532p. 1981. 32.75x (ISBN 0-398-01337-3). C C Thomas.

Regional Blood Flow & Clinical Considerations. Ed. by B. M. Altura & S. Halevy. (Cardiovascular Actions of Anesthetics & Drugs Used in Anesthesia Ser.: Vol. 2). (Illus.). viii, 296p. 1987. 143.50 (ISBN 3-8055-4158-9). S Karger.

Regional Bus Transportation: Five Reports. (Transportation Research Record Ser.). 58p. 1975. 2.60 (ISBN 0-309-02451-X). Transport Res Bd.

Regional Cancer Treatment. Ed. by K. R. Aigner et al. (Beitraege zur Onkologie. Contributions to Oncology: Vol. 29). (Illus.). viii, 312p. 1988. 50.00t (ISBN 3-8055-4762-5). S Karger.

Regional Centers in Archaeology: Prospects & Problems. Ed. by William H. Marquardt. LC 77-82743. (Research Ser.: No. 14). (Illus.). 40p. 1977. pap. 4.00 (ISBN 0-943414-15-6). MO Arch Soc.

Regional Cerebal Blood Flow in Neurological Patients: Clinical Significance & Correlation with EEG. P. C. Mosmans. 282p. (Orig.). 1974. pap. text ed. 42.50x (ISBN 90-232-1194-4, Pub. by Van Gorcum Holland). Coronet Bks.

Regional Change in the U. S. Brewing Industry. Joseph E. Pluta. (Industry Ser.). 85p. (Orig.). 1983. pap. 8.00 (ISBN 0-87755-283-5). Bureau Busn UT.

Regional Chemotherapy. Ed. by U. Laffer. (Antibiotics & Chemotherapy Ser.: Vol. 40). (Illus.). viii, 100p. 1988. 59.50 (ISBN 3-8055-4670-X). S Karger.

Regional Co-Operation in Development Research & Training. OECD Staff. (Liaison Bulletin: No. 6). 95p. (Orig.). 1981. pap. 6.00x (ISBN 92-64-12157-9). OECD.

Regional Compendium of Fisheries Legislation: Indian Ocean Region. (FAO Legislative Study: No. 42/1). 503p. 1987. pap. text ed. 45.75 (ISBN 92-5-102567-3, F3067, FAO). UNIPUB.

Regional Compendium of Fisheries Legislation (Indian Ocean Region, Vol. II. (FAO Legislative Studies: No. 42/2). 543p. 1987. pap. 49.50 (ISBN 92-5-102568-1, F3122, FAO). UNIPUB.

Regional Compendium of Fisheries Legislation: West Africa (CECAR Region) Norway Funds-in-Trust. (Legislative Studies: No. 27). 530p. (Eng. & Fr.). 1983. pap. text ed. 35.75 (ISBN 92-5-001307-8, F2434, FAO). UNIPUB.

Regional Compendium of Fisheries Legislation Western Pacific Region, Vol. 1. (Legislative Study Ser.: No. 35). 576p. 1985. pap. 59.00 (ISBN 92-5-102202-X, F2704 5071, FAO). UNIPUB.

Regional Computer Cooperation in Developing Countries. Ed. by R. E. Kalman. 1985. 58.00 (ISBN 0-444-87579-4). Elsevier.

Regional Conflict & National Policy. Ed. by Kent A. Price. xviii, 142p. 1982. 21.00 (ISBN 0-8018-2918-6); pap. 9.95 (ISBN 0-8018-2919-4). Resources Future.

Regional Conflict & U. S. Policy: Angola & Mozambique. Ed. by Richard J. Bloomfield. (Illus.). 1988. text ed. 24.95 (ISBN 0-917256-45-X); pap. 12.95 (ISBN 0-917256-46-8). Ref Pubns.

Regional Conflicts Around Geneva. Adda B. Bozeman. LC 49-10185. (Augustana College Library Ser.: No. 20). 432p. 1949. 7.00x (ISBN 0-910182-15-9). Augustana Coll.

Regional Control of Ocean Pollution: Legal & Institutional Problems & Prospects. C. O. Okidi. 292p. 1978. 34.00x (ISBN 90-286-0367-0, Pub. by Sijthoff & Noordhoff). Kluwer Academic.

Regional Cookbook, Recipe & Cookbook Research Correspondence Course. Cookbook Consortium Educational Division Staff. 1985. pap. text ed. 9.95 (ISBN 0-318-04321-1, Pub. by Cookbk Consorts). Prosperity & Profits.

Regional Cooking of China. rev. ed. Maggie Gin. LC 84-5269. (Illus.). 192p. 1984. pap. 7.95 (ISBN 0-89286-242-4). One Hund One Prods.

Regional Cooperation & Development in South Asia, Vol. I. Bhabani S. Gupta. 1986. 19.00x (ISBN 81-7003-065-X). South Asia Bks.

Regional Cooperation & Development in South Asia, Vol. II. Bhabani S. Gupta. 1986. 19.00x (ISBN 81-7003-066-8). South Asia Bks.

Regional Cooperation for Development & the Peaceful Settlement of Disputes in Latin America. Ed. by Jack Child. (Report Ser.: No. 26). 1987. write for info. Intl Peace.

Regional Cooperation for Development & the Peaceful Settlement of Disputes in Latin American. Ed. by International Peace Academy. 1988. lib. bdg. 49.90 (ISBN 0-317-67385-8, Pub. by Martinus Nijhoff Netherlands). Kluwer Academic.

Regional Cooperation in Industry. (UNIDO Monographs on Industrialization of Developing Countries: Problems & Prospects: 18). pap. 4.00 (ISBN 92-1-106050-8, E.69.II.B.39, VOL. 18). UN.

Regional Cooperation in the Development of Coarse Grains, Pulses, Roots & Tuber (CGPRT) Crops in Asia & the Pacific. 242p. 1979. pap. 14.00 (ISBN 92-1-119207-2, E.78.II.F.7). UN.

Regional Creative Ojo Book. Diane Thomas. LC 75-44654. 1976. pap. 2.95 (ISBN 0-918126-02-9). Hunter Ariz.

Regional Cross Sections of the Texas Panhandle: Precambrian to Mid-Permian. C. Robertson Handford et al. (Illus.). 1984. Repr. of 1981 ed. 3.00 (ISBN 0-686-36995-5). Bur Econ Geology.

Regional Cults, No. 16. R. P. Werbner. 1977. 55.50 (ISBN 0-12-744950-7). Acad Pr.

Regional Cults & Rural Traditions: An Interacting Pattern of Divinity & Humanity in Rural Bengal. R. M. Sarkar. (Illus.). xx, 351p. 1986. text ed. 50.00x (ISBN 81-210-0095-5, Pub. by Inter India Pubns N Delhi). Apt Bks.

Regional, Cultures, Managerial Behavior, & Entrepreneurship: An International Perspective. Ed. by Joseph W. Weiss. 216p. 1988. lib. bdg. 39.95 (ISBN 0-89930-327-7, WRI/, Quorum Bks). Greenwood.

Regional Dances of the Mexico. Edith Johnston. (Illus.). 64p. (gr. 3 up). 1983. pap. 6.60 (ISBN 0-8442-7509-3, Passport Bks.). Natl Textbk.

Regional Decentralization for Agricultural Development Planning in the Near East & North Africa. (FAO Economic & Social Development Paper Ser.: No. 73). 73p. 1988. pap. 9.00 (ISBN 92-5-102636-X, F3206, FAO). UNIPUB.

Regional Decline of a National Party: Liberals on the Prairies. David E. Smith. (Canadian Government Ser.). 184p. 1981. pap. 9.95 (ISBN 0-8020-6430-2). U of Toronto Pr.

Regional Demand & Supply Behavior by Sectors of the U. S. Coal Industry. Curt Harvey. 45p. 1982. pap. text ed. 5.00 (ISBN 0-86607-009-5). KY Energy Cabnt Lab.

Regional Dermatology: A System of Diagnosis for Nondermatologists. 2nd ed. Erwin Epstein, Sr. 464p. 1984. 64.00 (ISBN 0-8089-1674-2, 791167); pap. 24.50 (ISBN 0-8089-1695-5, 791166). Grune.

Regional Development Agencies in Europe. Ed. by Douglas Yuill. 458p. 1982. text ed. 44.50x (ISBN 0-566-00589-1). Gower Pub Co.

Regional Development & Family Planning. S. Siva Raju. xix, 231p. 1988. text ed. 32.50x (ISBN 81-7035-036-0, Pub. by Daya Pub Hse India). Apt Bks.

Regional Development & Planning. P. A. Compton & M. Pecsi. (British & Hungarian Case Studies). 234p. 1976. 52.50x (ISBN 0-317-53863-2, Pub. by Collets (UK)). State Mutual Bk.

Regional Development & Planning in Indonesia: A Review of Methodology. (Working Papers Ser.: No. 76-4). 64p. 1979. pap. 6.00 (ISBN 0-686-78250-X, CRD031, UNCRD). UNIPUB.

Regional Development & Settlement Policy. D. Dewar et al. 192p. 1986. text ed. 34.95x (ISBN 0-04-333023-1). Unwin Hyman.

Regional Development & the European Economic Community: A Canadian Perspective. Ian McAllister. 243p. 1982. pap. 13.95x (ISBN 0-920380-59-X, Pub. by Inst Res Pub Canada). Brookfield Pub Co.

Regional Development & the Local Community: Planning, Politics & Social Context. Clyde Weaver. LC 83-21640. 750p. 1984. text ed. 42.95x (ISBN 0-471-90067-2, Pub. by Wiley). Wiley.

Regional Development & Transportation in Argentina: Mendoza & the Gran Oeste Argentino Railroad, 1885-1914. William J. Fleming & Stuart Bruchey. (South American & Latin American Economic History Ser.). 330p. 1987. lib. bdg. 50.00 (ISBN 0-8240-1360-3). Garland Pub.

Regional Development at the International Level, Vol. II: African & Canadian Perspectives. Timothy M. Shaw & Yash Tandon. (Illus.). 288p. (Orig.). 1985. lib. bdg. 30.00 (ISBN 0-8191-4848-2); pap. text ed. 14.25 (ISBN 0-8191-4849-0). U Pr of Amer.

Regional Development at the International Level, Vol. I: Canadian & African Perspectives. Ed. by Timothy M. Shaw & Yash Tandon. (Illus.). 338p. (Orig.). 1985. lib. bdg. 31.00 (ISBN 0-8191-4850-4); pap. text ed. 15.25 (ISBN 0-8191-4851-2). U Pr of Amer.

Regional Development: Experiences & Prospects in Eastern Europe. Kosta Mihailovic. Ed. by Antoni Kuklinski. LC 71-163631. (Illus.). 225p. 1972. text ed. 21.50x (ISBN 90-2797-945-6). Mouton.

Regional Development: Experiences & Prospects in South & Southeast Asia. Louis Lefeber & Mrinal Datta-Chaudhuri. LC 72-152080. (Regional Planning Ser: No. 1). 278p. 1971. text ed. 23.25x (ISBN 90-2796-914-0). Mouton.

Regional Development: Experiences & Prospects in the United States of America. John H. Cumberland. 170p. 1971. text ed. 13.00x (ISBN 90-2797-266-4). Mouton.

Regional Development in a Global Economy. Mytelka. LC 79-10192. 1979. text ed. 29.00t (ISBN 0-300-02342-1). Yale U Pr.

Regional Development in Britain. 2nd ed. Gerald Manners et al. LC 79-42901. (Illus.). 440p. pap. 114.40 (2030529). Bks Demand UMI.

Regional Development in Britain. 2nd ed. Gerald Manners et al. LC 79-42901. 432p. 1980. 100.00x (ISBN 0-471-27636-7, Pub. by Wiley-Interscience). Wiley.

Regional Development in the U. S. S. R. Modelling the Formation of Soviet Territorial-Production Complexes. Ed. by M. K. Bandman. (Urban & Regional Planning Ser.). (Illus.). 332p. 1984. text ed. 67.00 (ISBN 0-08-023341-4). Pergamon.

Regional Development in the U. S. S. R. Trends & Prospects. LC 79-91195. (NATO Colloquium Publications). 1979. 30.00 (ISBN 0-89250-115-4). Orient Res Partners.

Regional Development in Western Europe. 3rd ed. Hugh Clout. LC 86-28933. 1987. write for info. (ISBN 0-471-91428-2). Wiley.

Regional Development Modelling Theory & Practice. Albegov. (Studies in Regional Science: Vol. 8). 1982. 84.25 (ISBN 0-444-86473-3). Elsevier.

Regional Development Planning in India: A New Strategy. R. P. Misra et al. 1975. 22.50x (ISBN 0-7069-0323-4). Intl Bk Dist.

Regional Development Policy: The Struggle for Rural Progress in Low Income Nations. Robert Riddell. LC 84-17774. 300p. 1985. 29.95 (ISBN 0-312-66904-6). St Martin.

Regional Development: Problems & Policies in Eastern & Western Europe. Ed. by George Demko. LC 84-40039. 283p. 1984. 27.95 (ISBN 0-312-66905-4). St Martin.

Regional Development: Problems & Policy Responses in Five Asian & Pacific Countries. Ed. by E. B. Prantilla. 339p. 1985. pap. 25.00 (CRD175, UNCRD). UNIPUB.

Regional Dictionary of Chicano Slang. Librado K. Vasquez & Maria E. Vasquez. 111p. 1975. 13.50 (ISBN 0-8363-0083-1). Jenkins.

Regional Differences in Family Structure in India. Pauline Kolenda. 1987. 40.00x (ISBN 81-7033-029-7, Pub. by Rawat). South Asia Bks.

Regional Differences in Family Structure in India. Pauline Kolenda. 400p. 1987. 49.95. Asia Bk Corp.

Regional Dimensions of Industrial Policy. Ed. by Michael E. Bell & Paul S. Lande. LC 80-8994. 224p. 1981. 26.50x (ISBN 0-669-04491-1). Lexington Bks.

Regional Directory of Minority & Women-Owned Business Firms: Northeastern Region. Ed. by Pamela G. Osbourne. 280p. 1988. 95.00 (ISBN 0-933527-14-4). Business Research.

Regional Directory of Minority & Women-Owned Business Firms: South Central Region. Ed. by Pamela G. Osbourne. 200p. 1988. 95.00 (ISBN 0-933527-15-2). Business Research.

Regional Disaggregation of National Policies & Plans. Ed. by A. Kuklinski. (Regional Planning Ser.: No. 8). 1975. text ed. 30.00x (ISBN 90-2797-921-9). Mouton.

Regional Disparities in Educational Development: A Controversial Issue. Ed. by Gabriel Carron & Ta Ngoc Chau. (Illus.). 257p. 1980. pap. 10.50 (ISBN 92-803-1085-2, U1048, UNESCO). UNIPUB.

Regional Disparities in Educational Development: Diagnosis & Policies for Reduction. Ed. by Gabriel Carron & Ta Ngoc Chau. (Illus.). 409p. 1980. pap. 10.50 (ISBN 92-803-1086-0, U1049, UNESCO). UNIPUB.

Regional Disparity & Economic Development in the European Community. W. Molle et al. LC 79-91668. 428p. 1980. text ed. 42.00x (ISBN 0-916672-50-6, Pub. by Allanheld). Rowman.

Regional Distribution of Federal Receipts & Expenditures in the 19th Century: A Quantative Study. John B. Legler. Ed. by Stuart Bruchey. LC 76-39833. (Nineteen Seventy-Seven Dissertations Ser.). (Illus.). 1977. lib. bdg. 21.00x (ISBN 0-405-09913-4). Ayer Co Pubs.

Regional Diversity of Political Values: Idaho Political Culture. Robert H. Blank. LC 78-62742. 1978. pap. text ed. 11.00 (ISBN 0-8191-0590-2). U Pr of Amer.

Regional Dynamics: Burgundian Landscapes in Historical Perspective. Ed. by Carole E. Crumley & William H. Marquadt. 630p. 1987. 95.00 (ISBN 0-12-198380-3); 39.95 (ISBN 0-12-198381-1). Acad Pr.

Regional Dynamics of Language Differentiation in Belgium: A Study in Cultural-Political Geography. Alexander B. Murphy. (Research Papers: No. 227). 1988. pap. 12.00 (ISBN 0-89065-132-9). U Chicago Comm Geo.

Regional Dynamics of the Indonesian Revolution: Unity from Diversity. Ed. by Audrey R. Kahin. LC 85-8532. 312p. 1985. text ed. 25.00x (ISBN 0-8248-0982-3). UH Pr.

Regional Dynamics: Studies in Adjustment Theory. Gordon L. Clark et al. 350p. 1986. text ed. 44.95x (ISBN 0-04-330353-6); pap. text ed. 19.95x (ISBN 0-04-330354-4). Unwin Hyman.

Regional Earth Science Information in Local Water Management. Murray B. McPherson. 185p. 1975. pap. 13.00x (ISBN 0-87262-151-0). Am Soc Civil Eng.

Regional Econometric Forecasting System: Major Economic Areas of Michigan. Harold T. Shapiro & George A. Fulton. 1983. 39.50 (ISBN 0-472-10035-1). U of Mich Pr.

Regional Economic Co-Operation in South Asia. M. R. Aggarwal. 155p. 1979. 16.95. Asia Bk Corp.

Regional Economic Cooperation in Asia: Bangladesh, India, Pakistan & Sri Lanka. Ed. by Charan Wadhva. 380p. 1987. 26.00x (ISBN 0-8364-2058-6, Pub. by Allied India). South Asia Bks.

Regional Economic Cooperation in South Asia. M. R. Aggarwal. 176p. 1979. text ed. 22.00x. Coronet Bks.

Regional Economic Development: Canada's Search for Solutions. Donald J. Savoie. 224p. 1986. pap. 13.95c (ISBN 0-8020-6614-3). U of Toronto Pr.

Regional Economic Development: Essays in Honour of Francois Perroux. Ed. by B. Higgins & D. J. Savoie. (Illus.). 352p. 1987. text ed. 29.95x (ISBN 0-04-338155-3). Unwin Hyman.

Regional Economic Development in Italy. Lloyd B. Saville. LC 67-21707. pap. 51.30 (ISBN 0-317-20419-X, 2023444). Bks Demand UMI.

Regional Economic Development in the Middle East: A Survey. James Prescott & Bakir Abu-Kishk. (Studies in Technology & Social Change: No. 3). 61p. (Orig.). 1988. pap. text ed. 6.00 (ISBN 0-945271-03-4). ISU-TSCP.

Regional Economic Development: The Federal Role. Gordon C. Cameron. LC 77-86390. (Resources for the Future Ser.). Repr. of 1970 ed. 27.50 (ISBN 0-404-60329-7). AMS Pr.

Regional Economic History: The Mid-Alantic Area since 1700. Glenn Porter. 92p. 1976. pap. write for info. (ISBN 0-914650-13-0). Hagley Museum.

Regional Economic Impact from Construction of a Nuclear Electric Generating Plant. Gene Steiker & James Strathman. (Discussion Paper Ser.: No. 91). 1976. pap. 5.50 (ISBN 0-686-32257-6). Regional Sci Res Inst.

Regional Economic Impact of Technological Change. A. T. Thwaites & R. P. Oakey. LC 83-13851. 256p. 1985. 29.95 (ISBN 0-312-66906-2). St Martin.

Regional Economic Modeling in Theory & in Practice. Curtis C. Harris, Jr. & Mehrzad Nadji. LC 87-10444. 174p. (Orig.). 1987. lib. bdg. 24.00 (ISBN 0-8191-6389-9); pap. text ed. 12.75 (ISBN 0-8191-6390-2). U Pr of Amer.

TITLE INDEX REGIONAL SHIFTS & METROPOLITAN

Regional Economic Policy. H. Folmer. 1986. lib. bdg. 44.50 (ISBN 90-247-3308-1, Pub. by Martinus Nijhoff Netherlands). Kluwer Academic.

Regional Economic Structure & Environmental Pollution. B. E. Coupe. (Studies in Applied Science: No. 5). 1977. pap. 15.50 (ISBN 90-207-0646-2, Pub. by Martinus Nijhoff Netherlands). Kluwer Academic.

Regional Economics. Harry W. Richardson. LC 79-11913. 328p. 1979. 24.95 (ISBN 0-252-00748-4). U of Ill Pr.

Regional Economics: Monographs. Mary Vance. (Public Administration Ser.: P 2124). 22p. 1987. 6.25 (ISBN 1-55590-244-8). Vance Biblios.

Regional Economy of West Bengal: A Study in Urbanization, Growth, Potential & Optimization of Industrial Location. D. S. Ganguly. cancelled (ISBN 0-8364-0521-8, Orient Longman). South Asia Bks.

Regional Emigration & Remittances in Developing Countries: The Portuguese Experience. Rick L. Chaney. LC 85-19382. 270p. 1986. 40.95 (ISBN 0-275-92018-6, C2018). Praeger.

Regional Employment Programme for Latin America & the Caribbean: Employment in Latin America. LC 78-19459. (Praeger Special Studies). 208p. 1978. 40.95 (ISBN 0-275-90309-5, C0309). Praeger.

Regional Energy Self-Sufficiency: Some Public Policy Implications. C. S. Papacostas. (Working Papers Ser.: No. 83-5). 22p. 1983. pap. text ed. 7.50 (ISBN 0-686-88340-3, CRD157, UNCRD). UNIPUB.

Regional English Accents: Belfast. James Milroy. 128p. 1981. pap. 5.95 (ISBN 0-85640-241-9, Pub. by Blackstaff Pr). Longwood Pub Group.

Regional Experiences in a Developing Economy. 1983. 8.00 (ISBN 0-471-63959-1). Wiley.

Regional Factors in National Planning & Development. United States, National Resources Committee. LC 72-174478. (FDR & the Era of the New Deal Ser). 223p. 1975. Repr. of 1935 ed. lib. bdg. 27.50 (ISBN 0-306-70387-4). Da Capo.

Regional Flood Frequency Analysis. Ed. by Vijay P. Singh. 1987. lib. bdg. 68.00 (ISBN 90-277-2575-6, Pub. by Reidel). Kluwer Academic.

Regional Framework for Resource Allocation & Public Sector Programmes: A Malaysian Example. (Working Papers Ser.: No. 76-10). 38p. 1979. pap. 6.00 (ISBN 0-686-79206-8, CRD118, UNCRD). UNIPUB.

Regional French of County Beauce, Quebec. Raleigh Morgan, Jr. LC 74-78061. (Janua Linguarum, Series Practica: No. 177). 128p. 1975. pap. text ed. 16.80x (ISBN 90-2793-107-0). Mouton.

Regional Geography: Global Patterns. 2nd ed. Pontius-Woodward. 208p. 1987. pap. text ed. 14.95 (ISBN 0-8403-4534-8). Kendall-Hunt.

Regional Geography of Anglo-America. 6th ed. C. Langdon White et al. (Illus.). 624p. 1985. text ed. write for info. (ISBN 0-13-770892-0). P-H.

Regional Geology Series. 1979. 6.25 (ISBN 0-318-23037-2). Natl Water Well.

Regional Government & Political Integration in Southwest China, 1949-1954: A Case Study. Dorothy J. Solinger. LC 75-22662. (Center for Chinese Studies, UC Berkeley: No. 16). 1977. 43.00x (ISBN 0-520-03104-0). U of Cal Pr.

Regional Government in England. Ed. by Brian W. Hogwood & Michael Keating. (Illus.). 1982. 49.00x (ISBN 0-19-827434-3). Oxford U Pr.

Regional Growth & Decline in the United States. 2nd ed. Bernard L. Weinstein & John Rees. 176p. 1985. 35.00 (ISBN 0-275-90184-X, C0184). Praeger.

Regional Guide to Human Anatomy. T. Alan Twietmeyer & Thomas O. McCracken. LC 87-16944. (Illus.). 194p. (Orig.). 1988. pap. text ed. 12.95 (ISBN 0-8121-1103-6). Lea & Febiger.

Regional Guide to Informational Sources on the Irish in the United States & Canada. Seamus Metress. (Public Administration Ser.: P 1841). 123p. 1986. 25.00 (ISBN 0-89028-711-2). Vance Biblios.

Regional Health Facility System Planning: An Access Opportunity Approach. Jerry B. Schneider & John G. Symons, Jr. (Discussion Paper Ser.: No. 48). 1971. pap. 6.50 (ISBN 0-686-32216-9). Regional Sci Res Inst.

Regional History of the Railway of Great Britain, Vol. 2: Southern England. H. P. White. (Illus.). 260p. 1982. 32.95 (ISBN 0-7153-8365-5). David & Charles.

Regional History of the Railways of Great Britain: North & Mid Wales, Vol. 11. Peter E. Baughan. LC 79-56255. (Illus.). 208p. 1980. 24.95 (ISBN 0-7153-7850-3). David & Charles.

Regional History of the Railways of Great Britain: The North East, Vol. 4. K. Hoole. (Illus.). 260p. 1986. 32.95 (ISBN 0-946537-31-3). David & Charles.

Regional History of the Railways of Great Britain, Vol. 13: Thames & Severn. R. Christiansen. LC 80-68696. (Illus.). 224p. 1981. 32.95 (ISBN 0-7153-8004-4). David & Charles.

Regional History of the Railways of Great Britain: Vol. 14: The Lake Counties. David Joy. (Illus.). 240p. 1983. 32.95 (ISBN 0-946537-02-X). David & Charles.

Regional History of the Railways of Great Britain, Vol. 6: Scotland - Lowlands & Borders. John Thomas & Alan Paterson. (Regional Histories of the Railways of Great Britain Ser.). (Illus.). 288p. 1984. 32.95 (ISBN 0-946537-12-7). David & Charles.

Regional History of the Railways of Great Britain, Vol. 8: South & West Yorkshire. David Joy. (Regional Histories of the Railways of Great Britain Ser.). (Illus.). 304p. 1984. 29.95 (ISBN 0-946537-11-9). David & Charles.

Regional History of the Railways of Great Britain. Ed. by David J. Thomas. Incl; Vol. 5. Eastern Counties. Donald I. Gordon. LC 76-385595. (Illus.). 256p. 1968. 24.95x (ISBN 0-678-05734-6). Kelley.

Regional Housing Assistance Allocations & Regional Housing Needs. John Goodman, Jr. 50p. 1979. pap. text ed. 6.00 (ISBN 0-87766-263-0). Urban Inst.

Regional Housing Plan. 60p. 1978. 3.00 (ISBN 0-318-22726-6). Assn Bay Area.

Regional Hydrology Fundamentals. Raul A. Deju. (Illus.). 222p. 1971. 78.00 (ISBN 0-677-03860-7). Gordon & Breach.

Regional Imagination: The South & Recent American History. Dewey W. Grantham. LC 78-26556. pap. 70.80 (2029468). Bks Demand UMI.

Regional Imbalance & Fiscal Equalization. R. K. Sinha. 1985. 22.50x (ISBN 0-8364-1420-9, Pub. by South Asia Pubs.). South Asia Bks.

Regional Immunology. Streilein. 1988. pap. write for info. (ISBN 0-471-61047-X). Wiley.

Regional Impact of Community Policies in Europe. Willem Molle & Riccardo Cappellin. 210p. 1988. text ed. 60.00 (ISBN 0-566-05587-2, Pub. by Gower Pub England). Gower Pub Co.

Regional Impacts of Resource Developments. Ed. by Chris Kissling et al. 285p. 1984. 24.95 (ISBN 0-949614-08-4, Pub. by Croom Helm Ltd). Routledge Chapman & Hall.

Regional Impacts of U. S. - Mexican Relations. Intro. by Ina Rosenthal-Urey. Tr. by Sandra Del Castillo from Span. (Monograph: No. 16). xviii, 154p. (Orig.). 1986. pap. 14.00 (ISBN 0-935391-67-3). Ctr Mex Studies.

Regional Imperatives in Utilization & Management of Resources: India & the USSR. Manzoor Alam & Atiya H. Kidwai. 1987. 58.50 (ISBN 0-8364-2256-2, Pub. by Concept). South Asia Bks.

Regional Incomes in the United States 1929-1967: Level, Distribution, Stability, & Growth. Philip M. Lankford. LC 72-91224. (Research Papers Ser.: No. 145). (Illus.). 137p. 1973. pap. 12.00 (ISBN 0-89065-052-7). U Chicago Comm Geo.

Regional Industrial Analysis & Development. Geoffrey J. Hewings. LC 77-76803. (Illus.). 1977. 19.95x (ISBN 0-312-66910-0). St Martin.

Regional Industrial Co-Operation: Experiences & Perspectives of ASEAN & the Andean Pact. 102p. 1986. 9.00 (ISBN 92-1-106204-7, E.85.II.B.5). UN.

Regional Industrial Information Transfer: Papers Delivered at the First European Symposium of Regional Industrial Information Transfer. Ed. by J. M. Gibb. LC 82-62307. 240p. 1983. 31.50 (ISBN 0-86187-324-6, Pub. by Frances Pinter). Longwood Pub Group.

Regional Inequality & Development: A Case Study of Kenya. Arne Bigsten. 200p. 1980. text ed. 44.00x (ISBN 0-566-00382-1). Gower Pub Co.

Regional Information & Regional Planning. A. Kuklinski. (Regional Planning Ser: No. 6). (Illus.). 390p. 1974. text ed. 28.50x (ISBN 0-686-22596-1). Mouton.

Regional Input-Output Analysis. Geoffrey Hewings. Ed. by Grant I Thrall. LC 85-14220. (Scientific Geography Ser.: Vol. 6). 96p. 1985. pap. text ed. 7.95 (ISBN 0-8039-2521-2); 16.95 (ISBN 0-8039-2740-1). Sage.

Regional Input Output Model & Economic Multipliers for the San Francisco Bay Region: 1982. 40p. 1986. 35.00 (ISBN 0-318-22684-7). Assn Bay Area.

Regional Input-Output Study: Recollections, Reflections & Diverse Notes on the Philadelphia Experience. Walter Isard & Thomas W. Langford. (Regional Science Studies Ser: No. 10). 1971. 30.00x (ISBN 0-262-09013-9). MIT Pr.

Regional Integration & the Trade of Latin America. Roy Blough & Jack N. Behrman. LC 68-19545. 184p. 1968. pap. 2.50 (ISBN 0-87186-222-0). Comm Econ Dev.

Regional Integration in East & West. Christopher T. Saunders. LC 83-9796. 280p. 1983. 32.50 (ISBN 0-312-66917-8). St Martin.

Regional Integration: The Latin American Experience. Ed. by Altaf Gauhar. 1985. 34.00x (ISBN 0-8133-0290-0). Westview.

Regional Integration: Theory & Research. Ed. by Leon N. Lindberg & Stuart A. Scheingold. LC 77-139717. (Illus.). 1970. 29.50x (ISBN 0-674-75326-7); pap. 8.95x (ISBN 0-674-75327-5). Harvard U Pr.

Regional Integrations in the New World Economic Environment. Andras Inotai. Tr. by Karoly Kerepesi from Hungarian. 296p. 1986. text ed. 35.00 (ISBN 963-05-4353-2, Pub. by Akademiai Kiado Hungary). Humanities.

Regional Italian Cooking. Valentina Harris. LC 86-30509. 1987. 12.95 (ISBN 0-394-56173-2). Pantheon.

Regional Italian Kitchen. Nika Hazelton. LC 78-3717. (Illus.). 370p. 1978. 14.95 (ISBN 0-87131-252-2). M Evans.

Regional Italian Kitchen. Nika Hazelton. LC 78-3717. (Illus.). 370p. 1983. pap. 7.95 (ISBN 0-87131-413-4). M Evans.

Regional Labour Markets: Analytical Contributions & Cross-National Comparisons. M. M. Fischer & P. Nijkamp. 1987. 92.75 (ISBN 0-444-70323-3). Elsevier.

Regional Landscapes of the United States & Canada. 3rd ed. Stephen S. Birdsall & John W. Florin. LC 84-22086. 457p. 1985. write for info. (ISBN 0-471-88490-1). Wiley.

Regional Language in France. Ed. by Andree Tabouret-Keller. (International Journal of the Sociology of Language: No. 29). 1980. pap. text ed. 14.40x (ISBN 90-279-3068-6). Mouton.

Regional Learning Service: An Experiment in Freeing Up Lives. Jean Kordalewski. pap. 4.00 (ISBN 0-317-38478-3). Natl Ctr Educ Broker.

Regional Long Waves, Uneven Growth & the Cooperative Alternative. Douglas E. Booth. LC 87-2348. 126p. 1987. lib. bdg. 32.95 (ISBN 0-275-92567-6, C2567). Praeger.

Regional Model Life Tables & Stable Populations: Monograph. Ansley J. Coale & Paul Demeny. (Studies in Population). 1983. 49.50 (ISBN 0-12-177080-X). Acad Pr.

Regional Models of Trade & Development. B. S. M. Berendsen. (Studies in Developing & Planning: Vol. 7). 1978. lib. bdg. 20.50 (ISBN 90-207-0753-1, Pub. by Martinus Nijhoff Netherlands). Kluwer Academic.

Regional Myocardial Metabolism by Positron Tomography. Ed. by H. W. Heiss. (Advances in Clinical Cardiology Ser.: Vol. 3). (Illus.). 400p. 1987. 125.00 (ISBN 0-930379-00-4). Found Advances.

Regional National Econometric Modeling with an Application to the Italian Economy. Ed. by Murray Brown et al. 204p. 1978. 24.00x (ISBN 0-85086-064-4, NO. 2932, Pub. by Pion England). Routledge Chapman & Hall.

Regional Nuclear Fuel Cycle Centres, 2 vols. (Illus.). 1977. pap. 17.25 (ISBN 92-0-159177-2, ISP445-1, IAEA); pap. 36.50 (ISBN 92-0-159277-9, ISP445-2). UNIPUB.

Regional Organization & Order in South-East Asia. Arnfinn Jorgensen-Dahl. LC 81-18465. 1982. 29.95 (ISBN 0-312-66924-0). St Martin.

Regional Organization of the Social Security Administration. John A. Davis. LC 68-59254. (Columbia University Studies in the Social Sciences: No. 571). Repr. of 1950 ed. 24.50 (ISBN 0-404-51571-1). AMS Pr.

Regional Patterns of Intercensal & Lifetime Migration in Sri Lanka. Dayalal Abeysekera. LC 81-12540. (Papers of the East-West Population Institute: No. 75). v, 46p. (Orig.). 1981. pap. text ed. 1.25 (ISBN 0-86638-016-7). EW Ctr HI.

Regional Patterns of Manufacturing Foreign Direct Investment in the United States. (Special Project Report Ser.). 88p. 1987. 7.00 (ISBN 0-89940-856-7). LBJ Sch Pub Aff.

Regional Perspectives on Energy Issues. Ed. by Helen Axel. (Report Ser.: No. 825). (Illus.). vii, 63p. (Orig.). 1982. pap. 75.00 (ISBN 0-8237-0264-2). Conference Bd.

Regional Perspectives on the Puerto Rican Experience. Ed. by Carlos E. Cortes. LC 79-6231. (Hispanics in the United States Ser.). lib. bdg. 74.50x (ISBN 0-405-13178-X). Ayer Co Pubs.

Regional Plan Amendments, 1981: Economic Development, Energy, Flooding, Transportation, Urban Development & Open Space. 73p. Pgs. avail. for insertion in 3-hole punched bndr. 8.00 (ISBN 0-318-22732-0); Amended chapters also avail. sep. write for info. Assn Bay Area.

Regional Plan for Small Quantity Generators of Hazardous-Waste. 55p. 1985. pap. 9.50 (ISBN 0-318-22709-6). Assn Bay Area.

Regional Plan of New York & Its Environs: The Graphic Regional Plan, Vol. 1. Ed. by Richard C. Wade. Incl. The Building of the City by Thomas Adams. LC 73-2914. (Metropolitan America Ser.). 930p. 1974. Repr. Set. 38.50x (ISBN 0-405-05413-0). Ayer Co Pubs.

Regional Planner. Jack Rudman. (Career Examination Ser.: C-694). (Cloth bdg. avail. on request). pap. 14.00 (ISBN 0-8373-0694-9). Natl Learning.

Regional Planning: Evolution, Crisis & Prospects. Ed. by Gill C. Lim. LC 82-13839. (Illus.). 198p. 1983. text ed. 24.95x (ISBN 0-86598-097-7, Pub. by Allanheld). Rowman.

Regional Planning in Europe. Ed. by R. Hudson & J. Lewis. 1982. pap. 17.95x (ISBN 0-85086-097-0, 8008, Pub. by Pion Ltd.). Routledge Chapman & Hall.

Regional Planning in India. Chand et al. LC 83-3146. 1984. 12.00x (Pub. by Allied India). South Asia Bks.

Regional Planning: Introduction and Explanation. Melville C. Branch. LC 87-27314. 222p. 1988. lib. bdg. 45.00 (ISBN 0-275-92403-3, C2403); pap. 19.95 (ISBN 0-275-92539-0, B2539). Praeger.

Regional Policies in Canada. 80p. 1980. 5.00 (ISBN 92-64-12104-8). OECD.

Regional Policies in Nigeria, India & Brazil. Ed. by Antoni Kuklinski. (Regional Planning Ser.: Vol. 9). 1978. text ed. 30.00 (ISBN 90-279-7842-5). Mouton.

Regional Policies in the United States. OECD Staff. (Document Ser.). (Illus.). 97p. (Orig.). 1980. pap. 5.50x (ISBN 92-64-12086-6). OECD.

Regional Policy: A European Approach. 2nd ed. Norbert Vanhove & Leo Klaassen. 450p. 1987. text ed. 50.00x (ISBN 0-566-05413-2, Pub. by Gower Pub England). Gower Pub Co.

Regional Policy: A European Approach. Norbert Vanhove & Leo H. Klaassen. LC 79-55648. 540p. 1980. text ed. 25.00x (ISBN 0-916672-49-2, Pub. by Allanheld). Rowman.

Regional Policy Evalution: Methodological Review & the Scottish Example. D. R. Diamond & N. A. Spence. 170p. 1984. text ed. 33.50x (ISBN 0-566-00644-8). Gower Pub Co.

Regional Policy for Ever? Graham Hellett et al. (Institute of Economic Affairs, Readings in Political Economy Ser.: No. 11). 152p. 1973. pap. 6.95 technical (ISBN 0-255-36041-X). Transatl Arts.

Regional Policy in the European Community. Douglas Yuill et al. 1980. 29.95 (ISBN 0-312-66931-3). St Martin.

Regional Political Parties & State. Gopa Kumar. 1986. 18.50 (ISBN 0-8364-1910-3, Pub. by Deep). South Asia Bks.

Regional Political Parties in India. K. Banerjee. 375p. 1984. text ed. 45.00x (ISBN 0-86590-293-3, Pub. by B R Pub Corp Indian). Apt Bks.

Regional Population Projection Models. Andrei Rogers. (Scientific Geography Ser.: Vol. 4). 96p. (Orig.). 1985. text ed. 16.95 (ISBN 0-8039-2567-0); pap. text ed. 7.95 (ISBN 0-8039-2374-0). Sage.

Regional Postgraduate Program in Information Science in Anglophone Africa: Identification of an Appropriate Location (Report of a Joint UNESCO/IDRC Mission) Ed. by Kenneth H. Roberts. 61p. (Orig.). 1986. pap. 7.00 (ISBN 0-88936-466-4, IDRCTS53, Pub by IDRC). UNIPUB.

Regional Price Formation in Eastern Europe. Jozef M. Van Brabant. 1987. lib. bdg. 83.50 (ISBN 90-247-3540-8). Kluwer Academic.

Regional Problem. Stuart Holland. LC 77-70276. 1977. 19.95x (ISBN 0-312-66935-6). St Martin.

Regional Problem in Western Europe. H. Clout. LC 75-7216. (Topics in Geography Ser.). (Illus.). 64p. 1976. 16.95 (ISBN 0-521-20909-9); pap. text ed. 7.95 (ISBN 0-521-09997-8). Cambridge U Pr.

Regional Problems & Policies in Greece. OECD Staff. 87p. (Orig.). 1981. pap. text ed. 7.50x (ISBN 92-64-12208-7). OECD.

Regional Problems, Problem Regions & Public Policy in the U. K. Ed. by Peter Damesick & Peter Wood. (Illus.). 288p. 1987. 64.00 (ISBN 0-19-823257-8). Oxford U Pr.

Regional Pulmonary Function in Health & Disease. Ed. by B. L. Holman & J. F. Lindeman. (Progress in Nuclear Medicine Ser.: Vol. 3). 196p. 1973. 46.75 (ISBN 3-8055-1425-5). S Karger.

Regional Reporter Citations. Shepard's Editorial Staff. (Specialized Citations). write for info. Shepards-McGraw.

Regional Reporters. write for info. West Pub.

Regional Residuals Environmental Quality Management Modeling. Ed. by Blair T. Bower. LC 77-92413. (Resources for the Future, RFF Research Paper Ser.: NO. R-7). pap. 61.00 (ISBN 0-317-26044-8, 2023786). Bks Demand UMI.

Regional Restructuring under Advanced Capitalism. Ed. by Philip O'Keefe. (Geography & Environment Ser.). 134p. 1984. 26.00 (ISBN 0-7099-1943-3, Pub. by Croom Helm Ltd). Routledge Chapman & Hall.

Regional Restructuring under Apartheid: Urban & Regional Policies in Contemporary South Africa. Ed. by Richard Tomlinson & Mark Addleson. 330p. 1988. pap. text ed. 27.95x (ISBN 0-86975-327-4, Pub. by Ravan Pr). Ohio U Pr.

Regional Science: New Concepts & Old Problems. E. L. Cripps. (London Papers in Regional Science). 210p. 1980. pap. text ed. 15.50x (ISBN 0-85086-048-2, ?NO. 2958, Pub. by Pion England). Routledge Chapman & Hall.

Regional Security & Anti-Tactical Ballistic Missiles: Political & Technical Issues. W. A. Davis, Jr. (IFPA Special Reports). (Illus.). 72p. 1987. pap. 9.95 (PDP). Pergamon.

Regional Security & ATBM. William A. Davis. LC 86-30349. (Special Report). 9.95. Inst Foreign Policy Anal.

Regional Security Developments & Stability in Southeast Asia. Lee S. Ann. 60p. (Orig.). 1980. pap. text ed. 10.00x (ISBN 0-566-04010-7, Pub. by Inst Southeast Asian). Gower Pub Co.

Regional Security in the Middle East. Ed. by Charles Tripp. LC 83-40155. (Adelphi Library). 192p. 1984. 22.50 (ISBN 0-312-66940-2). St Martin.

Regional Security in the Third World. Ed. by Mohammed Ayoob. 284p. 1986. 41.50 (ISBN 0-8133-0375-3). Westview.

Regional Shifts & Metropolitan Reversal in the U. S. Charles L. Leven. 1981. pap. 2.00 (ISBN 0-318-00031-8, INS 20). Inst for Urban & Regional.

Regional Shifts in Population & Changes in Metro-Nonmetro Boundaries in the U. S. rev. ed. Charles L. Leven & Stephen Sheppard. (Regional Population Studies: RPS 1). 1982. pap. 2.00. Inst for Urban & Regional.

Regional Silviculture of the United States. 2nd ed. Ed. by John W. Barrett. LC 80-17129. 551p. 1980. 46.95 (ISBN 0-471-05645-6). Wiley.

Regional Sketches. Harriet Beecher Stowe. Ed. by John R. Adams. (Masterworks of Literature Ser.). 1972. 10.95x (ISBN 0-8084-0024-X); pap. 6.95x (ISBN 0-8084-0025-8). New Coll U Pr.

Regional Specialization, Employment & Economic Growth in Belgium from 1846 to 1970. Guido L. De Brabander. Ed. by Stuart Bruchey. LC 80-2797. (Dissertations in European Economic History II). (Illus.). 1981. lib. bdg. 27.50x (ISBN 0-405-13981-0). Ayer Co Pubs.

Regional, State, & Local Associations, Vol. 3: Middle Atlantic States. Ed. by Denise M. Allard & Katherine Gruber. (Encyclopedia of Associations Ser.). 421p. 1988. 85.00x (ISBN 0-8103-2085-1). Gale.

Regional, State & Local Organizations, 1988-89, Vol. 4: Western States. Susan B. Martin. 1988. 85.00 (ISBN 0-8103-2089-4). Gale.

Regional, State & Local Organizations, 1988-89, Vol. 5: Southeastern States. Ed. by Susan B. Martin. 1988. 85.00 (ISBN 0-8103-2086-X). Gale.

Regional, State & Local Organizations, 1988-89 Vol. 6: Southwest & South Central States. Ed. by Susan B. Martin. 1988. 85.00 (ISBN 0-8103-2088-6). Gale.

Regional, State & Local Organizations, 1988-89, Vol. 7: Northwestern & Great Plains States. Ed. by Susan B. Martin. 1988. 85.00 (ISBN 0-8103-2090-8). Gale.

Regional Statistics: A Guide to Information Sources. Ed. by M. Balachandran. LC 80-14260. (Economics Information Guide Ser.: Vol. 13). 272p. 1980. 68.00x (ISBN 0-8103-1463-0). Gale.

Regional Stratigraphy of North America. W. J. Frazier & D. R. Schwimmer. LC 87-7019. (Illus.). 744p. 1987. 110.00x (ISBN 0-306-42324-3, Plenum Pr). Plenum Pub.

Regional Structure of Development & Growth in India, 2 vols. Ed. by G. P. Mishra & A. Joshi. 1985. Vol. 1. 38.00 (ISBN 0-8364-1446-2, Pub. by Ashish India); Vol. 2. 38.00 (ISBN 0-8364-1445-4); Set. 76.00 (ISBN 0-317-38615-8). South Asia Bks.

Regional Studies - Methods & Analyses. I. Bencze & G. Bora. (Selected Papers). 416p. 1974. 60.00x (ISBN 0-317-53862-4, Pub. by Collets (UK)). State Mutual Bk.

Regional Studies for Planning & Projection: The Siberian Experience. A. G. Aganbegyan. (Regional Planning Ser.: No. 7). 1979. text ed. 46.25 (ISBN 90-279-7888-3). Mouton.

Regional Studies: The Geneva Programme. Stanislaw Komorowski. (Working Papers Ser.: No. 82-1). 98p. 1982. pap. 6.00 (ISBN 0-686-43302-5, CRD146, UNCRD). UNIPUB.

Regional Study on Rainfed Agriculture & Agro-Climatic Inventory of Eleven Countries in the Near East Region. (Illus.). 174p. 1982. pap. 17.00 (ISBN 92-5-101222-9, F2369, FAO). UNIPUB.

Regional Styles In Cypriote Sculpture: The Sculpture from Idalion. Pamela Gaber-Saletan. Ed. by S. J. Freedberg. (Outstanding Dissertations in Fine Arts Ser.). (Illus.). 255p. 1985. Repr. of 1982 ed. 35.00 (ISBN 0-8240-6855-6). Garland Pub.

Regional Survey of New York & Its Environs, 10 vols. Ed. by Richard C. Wade. (Metropolitan America Ser.). (Illus.). 1974. Set. 224.00x (ISBN 0-405-05439-4). Ayer Co Pubs.

Regional Tectonic Synthesis of Northwestern New England & Adjacent Quebec. Wallace M. Cady. LC 77-98020. (Geological Society of America Memoir Ser.: No. 120). pap. 62.00 (ISBN 0-317-28385-5, 2025466). Bks Demand UMI.

Regional Theatre Directory, 1987-1988. Ed. by Jill Charles. 166p. 1987. pap. 10.95 (ISBN 0-317-61877-6). Theatre Directories.

Regional Theatre Directory, 1988-89. Ed. by Jill Charles. 180p. 1988. pap. text ed. 11.95 (ISBN 0-933919-10-7). Theatre Directories.

Regional Theatre: The Revolutionary Stage. Joseph W. Zeigler. LC 76-51780. (Quality Paperbacks Ser.). 1977. pap. text ed. 6.95 (ISBN 0-306-80056-X). Da Capo.

Regional Theory of World Trade. Andreas Grotewold. LC 79-83769. (Illus.). 86p. 1979. 10.50x (ISBN 0-933550-00-6). Ptolemy Pr.

Regional Training Course in Agricultural Project Analysis Held at New Delhi, India 2-28 November 1970. pap. 7.50 (F697, FAO). UNIPUB.

Regional Transformation & Industrial Revolutions: A Geography of the Yorkshire Woollen Industry. Derek Gregory. (Illus.). 1983. 39.50x (ISBN 0-8166-1139-4); pap. 15.95 (ISBN 0-8166-1140-8). U of Minn Pr.

Regional Transit Authorities: A Policy Analysis of Massachusetts. Barbara P. Glacel. 300p. 1983. 44.95 (ISBN 0-275-90987-5, C0987). Praeger.

Regional Trends, 1988, No. 23. Ed. by T. Griffin. (Illus.). 160p. 1988. pap. 43.00 (ISBN 0-11-620344-7, HM3512, Pub. by Her Maj Station Offc). UNIPUB.

Regional Unemployment Differences in Great Britain Bound with Interregional Migration Models & Their Application to Great Britain. R. Weeden. LC 73-86048. (National Institute of Economic & Social Research - Regional Studies: No. 2). (Illus.). 200p. 1973. 15.95 (ISBN 0-521-20376-7). Cambridge U Pr.

Regional Urban Centres: Structure & Interaction. Kalpana Markandey. xviii, 214p. 1986. text ed. 35.00x (ISBN 81-210-0096-3, Pub. by Inter India Pubns N Delhi). Apt Bks.

Regional Variation in Indian Ocean Coral Reefs. Zoological Society of London - 28th Symposium. Ed. by D. R. Stoddart & Maurice Yonge. 1972. 107.50 (ISBN 0-12-613328-X). Acad Pr.

Regional Variations in Metropolitan Growth & Development. Charles L. Leven. 1977. pap. 2.00 (ISBN 0-318-00026-1, INS 13). Inst for Urban & Regional.

Regional Variations in the Economic Development of Germany During the Nineteenth Century. Frank B. Tipton, Jr. LC 76-6857. 270p. 1976. lib. bdg. 25.00x (ISBN 0-8195-4096-X). Wesleyan U Pr.

Regional Variations in Western Europe. Hugh Clout. (Cambridge Topics in Geography: Second Ser.). (Illus.). 128p. 1986. 14.95 (ISBN 0-521-30547-0); pap. 6.95 (ISBN 0-521-27774-4). Cambridge U Pr.

Regional Vocabulary of Texas. 1962 ed ed. E. Bagby Atwood. LC 62-9784. (Illus.). 286p. 1969. pap. 10.95 (ISBN 0-292-77008-1). U of Tex Pr.

Regional Volume Table for Gmelina Arborea. A. Greaves. 1978. 30.00x (ISBN 0-85074-044-4, Pub. by For Lib Comm England). State Mutual BK.

Regional Wage Inflation & Unemployment. Ed. by R. L. Martin. 235p. 1981. 25.00x (ISBN 0-85086-090-3, NO. 8003, Pub. by Pion England). Routledge Chapman & Hall.

Regionale Chemotherapie der Leber. Ed. by K. Aigner. (Beitraege zur Onkologie. Contributions to Oncology: Vol. 21). (Illus.). viii, 140p. 1985. 52.75 (ISBN 3-8055-4014-0). S Karger.

Regionalisation of Transport & Regional Planning in Practice: An Examination Based on Case Studies. OECD & Council of Europe. (Orig.). 1984. pap. 20.00x (ISBN 92-821-1091-5). OECD.

Regionalism & National Unity in Nepal. Frederick H. Gaige. LC 74-30520. 1975. 36.50x (ISBN 0-520-02728-0). U of Cal Pr.

Regionalism & Regional Devolution in Comparative Perspective. Mark O. Rousseau & Raphael Zariski. LC 87-47735. 303p. 1987. lib. bdg. 45.95 (ISBN 0-275-92546-3, C2546). Praeger.

Regionalism & State Politics in India. R. N. Mishra. 1985. 27.50x (ISBN 0-8364-1370-9, Pub. by Ashish India). South Asia Bks.

Regionalism & Supranationalism. David M. Cameron. 136p. 1981. pap. text ed. 9.95x (ISBN 0-920380-74-3, Pub.by Inst Res Pub Canada). Brookfield Pub Co.

Regionalism & the Female Imagination. Ed. by Emily Toth. 176p. 1985. text ed. 34.95 (ISBN 0-89885-168-8); pap. text ed. 16.95 (ISBN 0-89885-169-6). Human Sci Pr.

Regionalism & the Musical Heritage of Latin America. Joseph Arbena et al. (Latin American Curriculum Units for Junior & Community Colleges Ser.). v, 84p. (Orig.). 1980. pap. text ed. 4.95x (ISBN 0-86728-006-9). U TX Inst Lat Am Stud.

Regionalism & the New International Economic Order: Studies Presented to the UNITAR-CEESTEM Club of Rome Conference at the United Nations. Ed. by Davidson Nicol & Luis Echeverria. LC 80-23706. (Pergamon Policy Studies on International Development). 448p. 1981. text ed. 70.00 (ISBN 0-08-026318-6); pap. text ed. 29.00 (ISBN 0-08-026331-3). Pergamon.

Regionalism & the Pacific Northwest. Ed. by William G. Robbins & Robert J. Frank. LC 83-2416. 256p. 1983. 18.95x (ISBN 0-87071-337-X); pap. 11.95x (ISBN 0-87071-338-8). Oreg St U Pr.

Regionalism & the South: Selected Papers of Rupert Vance. Ed. by John Reed & Daniel J. Singal. LC 81-16235. 300p. 1982. 30.00x (ISBN 0-8078-1513-6). U of NC Pr.

Regionalism & the United Nations. B. Andemichael. 623p. 1979. 45.00x (ISBN 90-286-0109-0, Pub. by Sijthoff & Noordhoff). Kluwer Academic.

Regionalism & the U. N. System. Ed. by Berhanykun Andemicael. LC 79-14018. 603p. 1979. lib. bdg. 54.00. Oceana.

Regionalism in America. Ed. by Merrill Jensen. 442p. 1964. pap. 12.50x (ISBN 0-299-00794-4). U of Wis Pr.

Regionalism in America. Steiner. 1985. lib. bdg. 26.00 (ISBN 0-8240-9048-9). Garland Pub.

Regionalism in India: A Study of Telangana. G. Ram Reddy. 1979. 20.00x (ISBN 0-8364-0332-0). South Asia Bks.

Regionalism: Monographs. Mary Vance. (Public Administration Ser.: P 2125). 56p. 1987. 14.50 (ISBN 1-55590-245-6). Vance Biblios.

Regionalist Art, Thomas Hart Benton, John Steuart Curry, Grant Wood: A Guide to the Literature. Mary S. Guedon. LC 82-3334. 199p. 1982. 16.50 (ISBN 0-8108-1543-5). Scarecrow.

Regionalization: Issues in Intensive Care for High Risk Newborns & their Families. Claire S. Rudolph & Susan R. Borker. LC 87-15136. 208p. 1987. lib. bdg. 42.95 (ISBN 0-275-92547-1, C2547). Praeger.

Regionalization of Warfare: The Falkland Islands, Lebanon & the Iran-Iraq Conflict. Ed. by James Brown & William P. Snyder. (Illus.). 266p. 1984. 34.95 (ISBN 0-88738-022-0); pap. 14.95 (ISBN 0-87855-985-X). Transaction Bks.

Regionalization of Water Management: A Revolution in England & Wales. Daniel A. Okun. (Illus.). 377p. 1977. 55.00 (ISBN 0-85334-738-7, Pub. by Elsevier Applied Sci England). Elsevier.

Regionalized Systems as an Approach to Perinatal Health Care: Annotated Bibliography. Barbara Pearce. (CPL Bibliographies Ser: No. 54). 81p. 1981. 13.00 (ISBN 0-86602-054-3). Coun Plan Librarians.

Regions & Locales. Ed. by Richard Grossinger & Lindy Hough. (Earth Geography Booklet Ser: No. 2). (Illus.). 312p. (Orig.). 1973. pap. 4.00 (ISBN 0-913028-13-4). North Atlantic.

Regions & Regionalism in the United States. Michael Bradshaw. LC 87-17917. 1988. 27.50 (ISBN 0-87805-339-5); pap. 12.95 (ISBN 0-87805-340-9). U Pr of Miss.

Regions & Resources: Strategies for Development. David Kresge et al. (Joint Center for Urban Studies Ser.). (Illus.). 264p. 1984. text ed. 32.50x (ISBN 0-262-11091-1). MIT Pr.

Region's Growth. (Illus.). 143p. (B). 1967. 10.00 (ISBN 0-318-16380-2); members 7.00 (ISBN 0-318-16381-0, 105). Regional Plan Assn.

Regions in Crisis: New Perspectives in European Regional Theory. Ed. by J. Carney et al. 1980. 26.00 (ISBN 0-312-66944-5). St Martin.

Regions in Question: Space Development Theory & Regional Policy. C. G. Gore. (Development & Underdevelopment Ser.). 304p. 1984. text ed. 29.95 (ISBN 0-416-31410-4, 4031); pap. text ed. 14.95 (ISBN 0-416-31420-1, 4021). Routledge Chapman & Hall.

Regions in the European Community. Michael Keating & Barry Jones. (Illus.). 262p. 1985. 39.95x (ISBN 0-19-827476-9). Oxford U Pr.

Region's Money Flows: The Government Accounts, Vol. 1. 88p. (B). 1977. 10.00 (ISBN 0-318-16382-9, 127); members 7.00 (ISBN 0-318-16383-7). Regional Plan Assn.

Regions of Memory: Uncollected Prose, 1949-1982. W. S. Merwin. Ed. by Ed Folsom & Cary Nelson. LC 86-1358. 376p. 1987. 24.95 (ISBN 0-252-01241-0). U of Ill Pr.

Regions of Recent Star Formation. Ed. by R. S. Roger & P. E. Dewdney. 1982. lib. bdg. 59.50 (ISBN 90-277-1383-9, Pub. by Reidel Holland). Kluwer Academic.

Regions of Silence: Studies on the Difficulty of Communicating. Maria G. Ciani. (London Studies in Classical Philology: Vol. 17). viii, 160p. 1987. 41.00x (ISBN 90-70265-17-6, Pub. by Gieben Amsterdam). Benjamins North Am.

Regions of Silence: Studies on the Difficulty of Communicating. Ed. by Maria G. Ciani. Tr. by Cathleen Arthur from Ital. (London Studies in Classical Philology: Vol. 17). 172p. 1987. text ed. 75.00 (ISBN 90-70265-17-6, Pub. by J. C. Grieber). Humanities.

Regions of the World Today. Benhart-Scull. 272p. 1985. pap. text ed. 18.95 (ISBN 0-8403-3599-7). Kendall Hunt.

Regis Debray & the Latin American Revolution: A Collection of Essays. Ed. by Leo Huberman & Paul M. Sweezy. LC 68-8077. pap. 37.50 (2030767). Bks Demand UMI.

Regis Touch: Million-Dollar Advice from America's Top Marketing Consultant. Regis McKenna. LC 84-28374. (Illus.). 256p. 1985. pap. text ed. 9.95 (ISBN 0-201-13964-2). Addison-Wesley.

Register Allocation in Optimizing Compilers. Bruce W. Leverett. LC 83-18297. (Computer Science: Systems Programming Ser.: No. 19). 234p. pap. 60.90 (2070313). Bks Demand UMI.

Register Book for the Parish Prince Frederick Winyaw: Anno Domini 1713. National Association Colonial Dames of America. (Illus.). 270p. 1982. Repr. of 1916 ed. 25.00 (ISBN 0-89308-299-6). Southern Hist Pr.

Register Cliff & the Guernsey Ruts on the Oregon Trail. Bert Webber. (Illus., Orig.). Date not set. pap. write for info (ISBN 0-936738-17-0). Webb Research.

Register Development Research Projects in Africa. OECD. 524p. (Orig.). 1987. pap. 48.00x (ISBN 92-64-02872-2). OECD.

Register in Puerto Rico, Nineteen Hundred & Three to Nineteen Hundred & Five, 2 vols. Charles Hartzell. (Puerto Rico Ser.). 1979. Set. lib. bdg. 200.00 (ISBN 0-8490-2994-5). Gordon Pr.

Register-Index for the Gmelin Handbuch Dev Anorganischen Chemie. Max Planck for the Advancement of Science, Gmelin Institute for Inorgaic Chemistry. (Gmelin Handbuch der Anorganischen Chemie, 8th Ed., Formula Index: Vol. 1, Ac-Au). 254p. 1975. 216.00 (ISBN 0-387-93295-X). Springer-Verlag.

Register Innocenz' 3rd Uber Die Reichsfrage, 1198-1209. Pope Innocent Third. Ed. by Georgine Tangl. 1923. 23.00 (ISBN 0-384-07885-0). Johnson Repr.

Register of Albemarle Parish, Surry & Sussex Counties, 1739-1788. National Society of Colonial Dames of America in the Commonwealth of Virginia Staff. Ed. by Gertrude R. Richards. (Illus.). 275p. 1984. Repr. of 1958 ed. 32.50 (ISBN 0-89308-545-6). Southern Hist Pr.

Register of American Malacologists. R. Tucker Abbott. LC 86-72678. 180p. 1987. 21.00 (ISBN 0-915826-18-6). Am Malacologists.

Register of Americans of Prominent Descent, Vol. I. Compiled by Sue M. O'Brien. LC 81-69243. 545p. 1982. 35.00 (ISBN 0-686-36318-3). Morten Pub.

Register of Baptisms in the Dutch Church at Colchester from 1645-1728 see Registers of the Church Known As La Patente in Spittlefields from 1689-1785.

Register of Baptisms of the French Protestant Refugees Settled at Thorney, Cambridgeshire, 1654-1727. Ed. by Henry Peet. Bd. with Letters of Denization. Ed. by William A. Shaw. Repr. of 1911 ed; Registers of the French Church of Portarlington, Ireland. Ed. by Thomas P. Le Fanu. Repr. of 1908 ed; Registers of the French Churches of Bristol. Ed. by Charles E. Lart. Repr. of 1912 ed; Register of the French Church at Thorpe-le-Spoken. Ed. by William C. Waller. Repr. of 1912 ed. (Huguenot Society of London Publications Ser.: Vols. 17-20). Repr. of 1903 ed. 144.00 (ISBN 0-8115-1650-4). Kraus Repr.

Register of Black, Mulatto & Poor Person in Four Ohio Countries, 1791-1861. Joan Turpin. 50p. (Orig.). 1985. pap. 8.00 (ISBN 0-917890-46-9). Heritage Bk.

Register of Consulting Scientists. 6th ed. D. J. B. Copp. 100p. 1984. 48.00x (ISBN 0-85274-751-9, Pub. by A Hilger UK). Taylor & Francis.

Register of Development Research Projects Concerning the English-Speaking Caribbean. OECD. 320p. (Orig.). 1987. pap. 25.00x (ISBN 92-64-02963-X). OECD.

Register of Development Research Projects in Latin America. OECD. (Orig.). 1984. pap. 60.00x (ISBN 92-64-02612-6). OECD.

Register of Development Research Projects in Asia. OECD. (Liason Bulletin Ser.). 350p. (Orig.). 1980. pap. text ed. 17.50x (ISBN 92-64-02096-9, 40-80-01-3). OECD.

Register of Education & Training Activites in Librarianship, Information Science & Archives. 61p. (Eng., Fr. & Span.). 1982. pap. 5.00 (ISBN 92-3-002022-2, U1264, UNESCO). UNIPUB.

Register of Environmental Engineering Graduate Programs. 5th ed. Ed. by Gary L. Amy & William R. Knocke. LC 84-70854. 626p. 1984. pap. 30.00 (ISBN 0-917567-00-5). Assn Environ Eng.

Register of Federal United States Military Records, Vol. 3: 1866 - World War II & Records of Various Branches of the Military. U. S. - Canada Reference Staff & Volunteers et al. xvi, 176p. (Orig.). 1986. pap. 17.00 (ISBN 0-917890-94-9). Heritage Bk.

Register of Federal United States Military Records: 1775-1860, Vol. 1. Marilyn Deputy et al. 249p. (Orig.). 1986. pap. 20.00 (ISBN 0-917890-74-4). Heritage Bk.

Register of Holy Trinity, Coventry, Warickshire. 1987. 35.00x (Pub. by Birmingham Midland Soc UK). State Mutual Bk.

Register of International Rivers. United Nations Centre for Natural Resources, Energy & Transport. 1978. 51.00 (ISBN 0-08-022408-3). Pergamon.

Register of International Transfers of Inland Fish Species. R. L. Welcomme. (Fisheries Technical Papers: No. 213). 130p. 1981. pap. 9.50 (ISBN 92-5-001098-2, F2196; FAO). UNIPUB.

Register of Invalid Pensions, Revolutionary Service, 1789. Bob Closson & Mary Closson. 16p. 1987. pap. text ed. 2.50 (ISBN 0-933227-67-1). Closson Pr.

Register of Marriages & Baptisms Performed by Rev. John Cuthbertson, Covenantor Minister, 1751-1791. John Cuthbertson. Ed. by S. Helen Fields. LC 83-81655. (Illus.). 301p. 1983. Repr. of 1934 ed. 20.00 (ISBN 0-8063-1047-2). Genealog Pub.

Register of Middle English Religious & Didactic Verse. Carleton F. Brown. 52.00 (ISBN 0-8369-7155-8, 7987). Ayer Co Pubs.

Register of Ministers, Exhorters & Readers & of Their Stipends. Church of Scotland Staff. LC 71-174310. (Maitland Club, Glasgow. Publications: No. 5). Repr. of 1830 ed. 15.00 (ISBN 0-404-52929-1). AMS Pr.

Register of National Bibliography, 3 vols in 2. William P. Courtney. (Bibliography & Reference Ser.: No. 135). 1968. Repr. of 1912 ed. Set. 50.00 (ISBN 0-8337-0704-3). B Franklin.

Register of Naval Officers of the Confederate Navy. John M. Carroll. 24.95 (ISBN 0-8488-0011-7, Pub. by J M C & Co); pap. 14.95 (ISBN 0-8488-0046-X). Amereon Ltd.

Register of New Fruit & Nut Varieties. 2nd rev. & enl. ed. Reid M. Brooks & Harold P. Olmo. LC 76-100017. 512p. 1972. 45.00x (ISBN 0-520-01638-6). U of Cal Pr.

Register of One Name Studies. 5th ed. 1987. 30.00x (Pub. by Birmingham Midland Soc UK). State Mutual Bk.

Register of Overwharton Parish, Stafford County, Virginia, 1723-1758. George H. King. (Illus.). 296p. 1985. Repr. of 1961 ed. 30.00 (ISBN 0-89308-576-6). Southern Hist Pr.

Register of Oxyrhynchites 30 BC - AD 96. John Whitehorne & Brian Jones. LC 81-18494. (BASP Supplements). 296p. 1983. 33.50 (ISBN 0-89130-529-7, 31-00-25). Scholars Pr GA.

Register of Polish American Scholars, Scientists, Writers & Artists. Ed. by Damian Wandycz. 80p. 1969. pap. 4.00 (ISBN 0-940962-38-1). Polish Inst Art & Sci.

Register of Reporting Labor Organizations, 1986. 2nd ed. 357p. 1986. pap. 17.00 (ISBN 0-318-21555-1, S/N 029-011-00011-7). USGPO.

Register of Research: Investigation in Adult Education. ERIC Staff & Adult Education Association of the U. S. A. Staff. 1968 2.30 (ISBN 0-88379-012-2); 1970 6.90 (ISBN 0-88379-013-0); 8.00 (ISBN 0-88379-030-0). A A A C E.

Register of Revolutionary Soldiers & Patriots Buried in Litchfield County. LC 76-42089. 1976. 9.65x (ISBN 0-914016-32-6). Phoenix Pub.

Register of Royal & Baronial Domestic Minstrels, 1272-1327. Constance Bullock-Davies. 320p. 1986. 54.00 (ISBN 0-85115-431-X, Pub. by Boydell & Brewer). Longwood Pub Group.

Register of St. Augustine's Abbey, Canterbury: Commonly Called the Black Book, 2 pts. Ed. by G. J. Turner & H. E. Salter. (British Academy, London, Record of the Social & Economic History of England & Wales Ser.: Vol. 2). Pt. 1, Reprint of 1915 Edition. pap. 45.00 (ISBN 0-8115-1242-8); Pt. 2, Reprint of 1924 Ed. pap. 36.00 (ISBN 0-8115-1243-6). Kraus Repr.

Register of St. Kenelm's Clifton upon Teme Worcestershire. 1987. 35.00x (Pub. by Birmingham Midland Soc UK). State Mutual Bk.

Register of St. Mary, Oldswinford, Worcestershire. 1987. 35.00x (Pub. by Birmingham Midland Soc UK). State Mutual Bk.

Register of St. Michael & All Angels, Adbaston, Staffs. 1987. 35.00x (Pub. by Birmingham Midland Soc UK). State Mutual Bk.

Register of St. Modwen, Burton-on-Trenton Staffs. 1987. 35.00x (Pub. by Birmingham Midland Soc UK). State Mutual Bk.

Register of Saint Paul's Parish 1715-1776, Stafford County 1715-1776, King George County, Virginia, 1777-1798. George H. King. (Illus.). 192p. 1985. Repr. of 1960 ed. 30.00 (ISBN 0-89308-577-4). Southern Hist Pr.

Register of St. Peter de Witton, Droitwich, Worcestershire. 1987. 35.00x (Pub. by Birmingham Midland Soc UK). State Mutual Bk.

Register of St. Philip's Parish, Charles Town, or Charleston, S. C. 1754-1810. Ed. by D. E. Smith & A. S. Salley, Jr. 1971. 31.95x (ISBN 0-87249-217-6). U of SC Pr.

Register of St. Philip's Parish, Charles Town, South Carolina, 1720-1758. Ed. by A. S. Salley, Jr. 1971. 31.95x (ISBN 0-87249-216-8). U of SC Pr.

Register of St. Philip's the Cathedral Church of Birmingham. 1987. 35.00x (Pub. by Birmingham Midland Soc UK). State Mutual Bk.

Register of the Abbey of St. Thomas, Dublin. Ed. by John T. Gilbert. (Rolls Ser.: No. 94). Repr. of 1889 ed. 44.00 (ISBN 0-8115-1171-5). Kraus Repr.

Register of the Charterhouse of London: Land Rev. Misc Book 61 of the London Public Record Office. James Hogg. (Analecta Cartusiana Ser.: No. 89). (Orig.). 1987. 25.00 (ISBN 3-7052-0146-8, Pub. by Salzburg Studies). Longwood Pub Group.

Register of the Church of St. Giles, Sheldon, Pt. 2. 1987. 35.00x (Pub. by Birmingham Midland Soc UK). State Mutual Bk.

Register of the Department of State. U. S. Department Of State. Repr. of 1874 ed. 14.00 (ISBN 0-384-62952-0). Johnson Repr.

Register of the French Church at Thorpe-le-Spoken see Register of Baptisms of the French Protestant Refugees Settled at Thorney, Cambridgeshire, 1654-1727.

Register of the Marriages Celebrated in Greenbrier County (West) Virginia from 1781-1849. Compiled by Norma P. Evans. LC 82-82599. 84p. 1983. pap. 15.00x (ISBN 0-937418-07-2). N P Evans.

Register of the United Nations Serial Publications. pap. 15.00 (E.82.O.8). UN.

Register of the Visitors of the University of Oxford, from A.D. 1647 to A.D. 1658. Oxford University Staff. Ed. by M. Burrows. Repr. of 1881 ed. 60.00 (ISBN 0-384-44210-2). Johnson Repr.

Register of U. S. Military Records: The Civil War, Vol. 2. The U. S. Canada Reference Staff & Voluteers & Marilyn Deputy. xix, 456p. (Orig.). 1986. pap. 30.00 (ISBN 0-917890-83-3). Heritage Bk.

Register of Vital Records of Roman Catholic Parishes from the Region Beyond the Bug River. Edward A. Peckwas. 44p. 5.95 (ISBN 0-317-57777-8). Polish Genealog.

Register over Dast Magazin, Vol. I-XV, Sept. 1968-Dec. 1982. Iwan Erichsson. LC 85-11366. 146p. 1985. Repr. lib. bdg. 19.95x (ISBN 0-89370-875-5). Borgo Pr.

Register to "Genera Siphonogamarum". K. W. Von Dalla Torre & H. Harms. 1958. Repr. of 1907 ed. 42.50x (ISBN 3-7682-0072-8). Lubrecht & Cramer.

Registered & Graduate Nurses. Jack Rudman. (Admission Test Ser.: ATS-19). 300p. (Cloth bdg. avail. on request). pap. 13.95. Natl Learning.

Registered Nurse Consultant to the Intermediate Care Facility. (NO. GE-6). 219p. 1977. 5.00 (ISBN 0-686-40477-7). ANA.

Registered Professional Nurse. Jack Rudman. (Career Examination Ser.: C-671). (Cloth bdg. avail. on request). pap. 14.00 (ISBN 0-8373-0671-X). Natl Learning.

Registered Representative. Jack Rudman. (Admission Test Ser.: ATS-1). 300p. (Cloth bdg. avail. on request). pap. 13.95 (ISBN 0-8373-5001-8). Natl Learning.

Registered Technologist - R.T.(AR-RT) Jack Rudman. (Career Examination Ser.: C-680). (Cloth bdg. avail. on request). pap. 14.00 (ISBN 0-8373-0680-9). Natl Learning.

Registered Timber Marks of Eastern Canada, 1870-1984. Diane Aldred. 841p. 1985. text ed. 78.00x (ISBN 0-919868-24-X, Pub. by Multisci Canada). Brookfield Pub Co.

Registering Agents Services for Delaware Incorporators: A Directory. Compiled by Bibliotheca Press Research Division Staff. 150p. 1983. pap. text ed. 2.95 (ISBN 0-939476-87-8, Pub. by Biblio Pr GA). Prosperity & Profits.

Registering Title to Land: A Series of Lectures Delivered at Yale. Jacques Dumas. 106p. 1985. Repr. of 1900 ed. lib. bdg. 20.00x (ISBN 0-8377-0522-3). Rothman.

Registers of Hanbury, Worcestershire. 1987. 35.00x (Pub. by Birmingham Midland Soc UK). State Mutual Bk.

Registers of North Farnham Parish, 1663-1814, & Lunenburg Parish, 1783-1800, Richmond County, Virginia. George H. King. (Illus.). 240p. 1985. Repr. of 1966 ed. 28.50 (ISBN 0-89308-580-4). Southern Hist Pr.

Registers of Park Lane Presbyterian Church, Cradley, Worcestershire. 1987. 35.00x (Pub. by Birmingham Midland Soc UK). State Mutual Bk.

Registers of St. John the Baptist, Halesowen Worcestershire. 1987. 35.00x (Pub. by Birmingham Midland Soc UK). State Mutual Bk.

Registers of St. John the Baptist, Wasperton. 1987. 35.00x (Pub. by Birmingham Midland Soc UK). State Mutual Bk.

Registers of St. Mary Kingswinford, Staffs. 1987. 35.00x (Pub. by Birmingham Midland Soc UK). State Mutual Bk.

Registers of St. Mary, Swynnerton, Staffs. 1987. 35.00x (Pub. by Birmingham Midland Soc UK). State Mutual Bk.

Registers of St. Michael & All Angels, GT Witley, Worcestershire. 1987. 35.00x (Pub. by Birmingham Midland Soc UK). State Mutual Bk.

Registers of St. Nicholas, Kings Norton Worcestershire. 1987. 35.00x (Pub. by Birmingham Midland Soc UK). State Mutual Bk.

Registers of the Chapelry of St. Michael & All Angles, Little Witley, Worcestershire. 1987. 35.00x (Pub. by Birmingham Midland Soc UK). State Mutual Bk.

Registers of the Church Known As La Patente in Spittlefields from 1689-1785. Ed. by William Minet & William C. Waller. Bd. with Register of Baptisms in the Dutch Church at Colchester from 1645-1728. Ed. by William J. Moens. Repr. of 1905 ed; Pt. 2. Registers of the French Church. Ed. by W. J. Moens. Repr. of 1899 ed. (Hugenot Society of London Publications Ser.: Vols. 11-13). Repr. of 1898 ed. 135.00 (ISBN 0-8115-1648-2). Kraus Repr.

Registers of the Church of St. Augustine the Less, Bristol, 1577-1700. Adapted by Arthur Sabin. 1987. 59.00x (Pub. by Cheltenham Art Gallery & Mus UK). State Mutual Bk.

Registers of the Church of St. Editha, Church Eaton, Staffs. 1987. 30.00x (Pub. by Birmingham Midland Soc UK). State Mutual Bk.

Registers of the French Church see Letters of Denization & Acts of Naturalization for Aliens in England, 1509-1603.

Registers of the French Church see Registers of the Church Known As La Patente in Spittlefields from 1689-1785.

Registers of the French Church see Registers of the French Non-Conformist Churches of Lucy Lane & Peter Street, Dublin.

Registers of the French Church of Portarlington, Ireland see Register of Baptisms of the French Protestant Refugees Settled at Thorney, Cambridgeshire, 1654-1727.

Registers of the French Churches of Bristol see Register of Baptisms of the French Protestant Refugees Settled at Thorney, Cambridgeshire, 1654-1727.

Registers of the French Conformed Churches of St. Patrick & St. Mary, Dublin see Despatches of Michele Suriand & Marc'Antonio Barbaro, Venetian Ambassadors at the Court of France, 1560-1563.

Registers of the French Non-Conformist Churches of Lucy Lane & Peter Street, Dublin. Ed. by Thomas P. Le Fanu. Bd. with History of the Walloon & Huguenot Church at Canterbury. F. W. Cross. Repr. of 1898 ed; Pt. 3. Registers of the French Church. Ed. by T. C. Colyer-Fergusson. Repr. of 1906 ed. (Hugenot Society of London Publication Ser.: Vols. 14-16). Repr. of 1901 ed. 135.00 (ISBN 0-8115-1649-0). Kraus Repr.

Registers of the Independent, Baptists & Wesl-eyan, Bromsgrove, Worcestershire. up to 1837. 1987. 35.00x (Pub. by Birmingham Midland Soc UK). State Mutual Bk.

Registers of the Walloon or Strangers' Church in Canterbury, 3 pts. Ed. by Robert Hovenden. (Huguenot Society of London Publications Ser.: Vol. 5). Repr. of 1891 ed. Set. 107.00 (ISBN 0-8115-1644-X). Kraus Repr.

Registers of Wednesfield, Staff: Baptists. & Burials, 1751 to 1837. 1987. 35.00x (Pub. by Birmingham Midland Soc UK). State Mutual Bk.

Registrar. Jack Rudman. (Career Examination Ser.: C-1452). (Cloth bdg. avail. on request). pap. 12.00 (ISBN 0-8373-1452-6). Natl Learning.

Registrar's Guide to Facilities Planning & Management. American Association of Collegiate Registrars & Admissions Officers Staff. pap. 20.00 (ISBN 0-317-26608-X, 2024074). Bks Demand UMI.

Registration & the Draft. Martin Anderson. 424p. 1982. 19.95 (ISBN 0-8179-7421-0, P242). Hoover Inst Pr.

Registration & the Military Selective Service Act. 3.50. Natl Lawyers Guild.

Registration Examination for Dieticians (RED) Jack Rudman. (Admission Test Ser.: ATS-41). (Cloth bdg. avail. on request). pap. 17.95 (ISBN 0-8373-5041-7). Natl Learning.

Registration of City School Children: A Consideration of the Subject of the City School Census. John D. Haney. LC 76-176836. (Columbia University. Teachers College. Contributions to Education: No. 30). Repr. of 1910 ed. 22.50 (ISBN 0-404-55030-4). AMS Pr.

Registration Techniques. 26p. 10.95 (ISBN 0-914951-18-1). LERN.

Registrator. Filipp Berman. 140p. (Rus.). 1984. pap. 8.00 (ISBN 0-88233-730-0). Ardis Pubs.

Registres De l'Hotel de Ville de Paris Pendant la Fronde, 3 vols. 1481p. 1846-48. Set. pap. 110.00 (ISBN 0-685-27512-4). Johnson Repr.

Registrum Cartarum Ecclesie Sancti Egidii De Edinburgh. Ed. by David Laing. LC 76-174803. (Bannatyne Club, Edinburgh. Publications: No. 105). Repr. of 1859 ed. 47.50 (ISBN 0-404-52860-0). AMS Pr.

Registrum De Dunfermelyn. Ed. by Cosmo Innes. LC 70-164810. (Bannatyne Club, Edinburgh. Publications: No. 74). Repr. of 1842 ed. 55.00 (ISBN 0-404-52793-0). AMS Pr.

Registrum Domus De Soltre. Ed. by David Laing. LC 77-171638. (Bannatyne Club, Edinburgh. Publications: No. 109). Repr. of 1861 ed. 42.50 (ISBN 0-404-52863-5). AMS Pr.

Registrum Episcopatus Aberdonensis: Ecclesie Cathedralis Aberdonensis Regesta Que Extant in Unum Collecta, 2 Vols. Aberdeen, Scotland (Diocese Staff) Ed. by Cosmo Innes. LC 77-38504. (Maitland Club, Glasgow. Publications: No. 63). 1845. Set. 75.00 (ISBN 0-404-53065-6). AMS Pr.

Registrum Episcopatus Brechinensis, 2 Vols. Ed. by Patrick Chalmers & John I. Chalmers. LC 72-39524. (Bannatyne Club, Edinburgh. Publications: No. 102). Repr. of 1856 ed. Set. 110.00 (ISBN 0-404-52855-4). AMS Pr.

Registrum Episcopatus Glasguensis, 2 Vols. Ed. by Cosmo Innes. LC 70-168151. (Maitland Club, Glasgow. Publications: No. 61). Repr. of 1843 ed. Set. 95.00 (ISBN 0-685-05956-1). AMS Pr.

Registrum Episcopatus Moraviensis. Moray Scotland. Ed. by Cosmo N. Innes. LC 71-172742. (Bannatyne Club, Edinburgh. Publications: No. 58). Repr. of 1837 ed. 47.50 (ISBN 0-404-52768-X). AMS Pr.

Registrum Epistolarum Fratris Johannis Peckham, Archiepiscopi Cantuanriensis, 3 vols. Ed. by Charles Martin. (Rolls Ser.: No. 77). Repr. of 1886 ed. Set. 132.00 (ISBN 0-8115-1147-2). Kraus Repr.

Registrum epistolarum Stephani de Lexinton abbatis de Stannlegia et de Saviagnaco see Letters from Ireland, 1228-1229.

Registrum Honoris De Morton, 2 Vols. Ed. by Thomas Thomson et al. LC 76-173002. 1853. Set. 95.00 (ISBN 0-404-52836-8). AMS Pr.

Registrum Malmesburiense: The Register of Malmesbury Abbey, 2 vols. Ed. by J. S. Brewer & Charles T. Martin. (Rolls Ser.: No. 72). Repr. of 1880 ed. 88.00 (ISBN 0-8115-1140-5). Kraus Repr.

Registrum Metellanum, I. Maitland Club. LC 72-967. (Maitland Club. Glasgow. Publications: No. 11). Repr. of 1831 ed. 10.00 (ISBN 0-404-52941-0). AMS Pr.

Registrum Monasterii De Passelet. Paisley Abbey. Ed. by Cosmo Innes. LC 75-174311. (Maitland Club. Glasgow. Publications: No. 17). Repr. of 1832 ed. 52.50 (ISBN 0-404-52954-2). AMS Pr.

Registrum Palatinum Dunelmense: The Register of Richard de Kellawe...1311-1316, 4 vols. Ed. by Thomas D. Hardy. (Rolls Ser.: No. 62). Repr. of 1878 ed. 240.00 (ISBN 0-8115-1130-8). Kraus Repr.

Registrum S. Marie De Neubotle. Newbattle Abbey. Ed. by Cosmo Innes. LC 74-173074. (Bannatyne Club, Edinburgh. Publications: No. 89). Repr. of 1849 ed. 42.50 (ISBN 0-404-52819-8). AMS Pr.

Registrum Sive Liber Irrotularius Et Consuetudinarius Prioratus Beatae Mariae Wigorniensis. William H. Hale. LC 17-1258. (Camden Society, London. Publications, First Ser.: No. 91). Repr. of 1865 ed. 37.00 (ISBN 0-404-50191-5). AMS Pr.

Registrum, Sive, Liber Irrotularius et Consuetudinarius Prioratus Beatae Mariae Wigorniensis. Worcester Cathedral. 37.00 (ISBN 0-384-69240-0). Johnson Repr.

Registry of Certified Interpreters, 1988. Ed. by Mel Broswell & Don D. Roose. 123p. (Orig.). Date not set. pap. text ed. 24.95. RID Pubns.

Registry of Mass Spectral Data. 2nd ed. Fred W. McLafferty & Douglas B. Stauffer. LC 87-31645. 1000p. 1988. 700.00 (ISBN 0-471-62886-7). Wiley.

Registry of Mass Spectral Data Including PBMSTIRS & Find-it, 1988. Fred W. McLafferty. 1988. 2895.00 (ISBN 0-471-61660-5). Wiley.

Registry of Mass Spectral Data 4E Database. McLafferty. 1986. 85.00 (ISBN 0-471-85090-X). Wiley.

Registry of Professional Reporters & Membership Directory. 350p. pap. 10.50 (ISBN 0-318-15866-3, 184). Natl Shorthand Rptr.

Registry of Women in Religious Studies, 1981-1982. Compiled by Carol Bohn & Lorine Getz. 1982. pap. 9.95x (ISBN 0-88946-277-1). E Mellen.

Regla Kimbisa del Santo Cristo del Buen Viaje. 2nd ed. Lydia Cabrera. (Coleccion del Chichereku en el Exilio Ser.). 85p. (Span.). 1986. pap. 6.95 (ISBN 0-89729-396-7). Ediciones.

Reglamento de las construcciones de concreto reforzado: Aci 318-77S y commentarios. (Span.). 1975. 37.25 (ISBN 0-685-85085-4, 318-71S) (ISBN 0-685-85086-2). ACI.

Reglas De Catalogacion Angloamericanas. 395p. (Span.). 1970. 8.00 (ISBN 0-8270-3075-4). OAS.

Reglas de Catalogacion Angloamericanas. 2nd ed. University of Costa Rica. 771p. 1983. pap. 30.00 (ISBN 0-8389-2038-1). ALA.

Reglas De Congo: Palo Monte-Mayombe. Lydia Cabrera. LC 79-50627. (Coleccion Del Chichereku). 1979. pap. 15.00 (ISBN 0-686-59741-9). Ediciones.

Reglas de Congo: Palo Monte-Mayombe. Lydia Cabrera. LC 79-50627. (Coleccion del Chichereku Ser.). 225p. (Orig., Span.). 1986. pap. 18.00 (ISBN 0-89729-398-3). Ediciones.

Reglas de los Buenos Principios de Fabricacion para Fabricacion, el Empacar, el Almacenaje, y la Instalacion de Aparatos Medicos (BPFs de Aparatos) LC 87-3898. 1987. 3.85 (ISBN 0-940701-07-3). Keystone PA.

Reglas Para la Ordenacion Alfabetica De los Catalogos. (Manuales Del Bibliotecario Ser.: No. 8). 1978. pap. text ed. 3.00 (ISBN 0-8270-3080-0). OAS.

Reglas Parlamentarias. H. F. Kerfoot. Tr. by Jose M. Sanchez from Eng. 88p. (Span.). 1986. Repr. of 1984 ed. 1.95 (ISBN 0-311-11012-6). Casa Bautista.

Reglementation des Activites Nucleaires: Communications Presentees au Seminaire Interregional sur le Droit Nucleaire Rabat, Maroc, 30 May-4 June, 1983. (Collection Juridique Ser.: No. 13). (Illus.). 333p. (Orig., Fr.). 1986. pap. text ed. 54.50 (ISBN 92-0-276086-1, ISP703, IAEA). UNIPUB.

Reglements Miniers, 1390-1512 see Actes Des Premiers Sultans Conserves Dans le Manuscrits Turcs De la Bibliotheque Nationale a Paris.

Regles pour la Direction de l'Esprit. Rene Descartes. 152p. 1966. 9.95 (ISBN 0-686-55679-8). French & Eur.

Regles Utiles et Claires Pour la Direction De L'Esprit et la Recherche De la Verite. Rene Descartes. (Archives Internationales D'Histoire Des Idees: No. 88). 1977. lib. bdg. 60.50 (ISBN 90-247-1907-0, Pub. by Martinus Nijhoff Netherlands). Kluwer Academic.

Regnal Formulas in Byzantine Egypt. Roger S. Bagnall & K. A. Worp. LC 79-1316. (Supplements to the Bulletin of American Society of Papyrologists). 1979. pap. 10.00 (ISBN 0-89130-280-8, 311102). Scholars Pr GA.

Regne de Phillippe III le Hardi: Etude sur le Pouvoir de 1287 a 1285. Chares-Victor Langlois. 480p. (Orig.). pap. text ed. 87.50x. Coronet Bks.

Regnum & Sacerdotium: An Irish Tradition. P. MacCana. (Sir John Rhys Memorial Lectures in Celtic Studies). 1979. pap. 5.50 (ISBN 0-85672-208-1, Pub. by British Acad). Longwood Pub Group.

Regnum, Religio et Ratio: Essays Presented to Robert M. Kingdon. Ed. by Jerome Friedman. (Essays & Studies). (Illus.). 200p. 1987. 30.00x (ISBN 0-940474-08-5). Sixteenth Cent.

Regreso al Colegio. Charles M. Schulz. 1.50 (ISBN 0-686-56189-9). French & Eur.

Regressed Patient. L. B. Boyer. LC 82-24363. 368p. 1983. 30.00x (ISBN 0-87668-626-9). Aronson.
Regression: A Second Course in Statistics. Thomas H. Wonnacott & Ronald J. Wonnacott. LC 80-271. (Probability & Mathematical Statistics: Applied & Probability & Statistics Ser.). 556p. 1981. 45.50 (ISBN 0-471-95974-X). Wiley.
Regression: A Second Course on Statistics. Thomas H. Wonnacott & Ronald J. Wonnacott. LC 86-14384. 576p. 1986. Repr. of 1981 ed. text ed. 44.00 (ISBN 0-89874-970-0). Krieger.
Regression Analysis & Its Application: A Data Oriented Approach. R. F. Gunst & R. L. Mason. (Statistics: Textbooks & Monographs Ser.: Vol. 34). 49.75 (ISBN 0-8247-6993-7). Dekker.
Regression Analysis by Example. 2nd ed. Chatterjee. (Probability & Mathematical Statistics Ser.). 1985. write for info. (ISBN 0-471-88479-0). Wiley.
Regression Analysis by Example. Samprit Chatterjee & Bertram Price. LC 77-24510. (Probability & Mathematical Statistics Ser.). 228p. 1977. 37.50 (ISBN 0-471-01521-0, Pub. by Wiley-Interscience). Wiley.
Regression Analysis of Prior Experiences of Key Production Personnel As Predictors of Revenues from High-Grossing Motion Pictures in American Release. Thomas S. Simonet. Ed. by Garth S. Jowett. LC 79-6685. (Dissertations on Film, 1980 Ser.). 1980. lib. bdg. 33.00x (ISBN 0-405-12917-3). Ayer Co Pubs.
Regression Analysis with Application. Ed. by G. Barrie Wetherill. (Monographs on Statistics & Applied Probability). 250p. 1987. pap. 34.50 (ISBN 0-412-27490-6, 9984, Pub. by Chapman & Hall England). Routledge Chapman & Hall.
Regression & Econometric Methods. David S. Huang. LC 80-12646. 288p. 1980. Repr. of 1970 ed. lib. bdg. 23.50 (ISBN 0-89874-181-5). Krieger.
Regression & Factor Analysis in Econometrics. H. F. Schilderinck. (Tilburg Studies in Econometrics: No. 1). 1977. lib. bdg. 23.00 (ISBN 90-207-0664-0, Pub. by Martinus Nijhoff Netherlands). Kluwer Academic.
Regression & the Moore-Penrose Pseudo-Inverse. Arthur Albert. (Mathematics in Science & Engineering Ser.: Vol. 94). 1972. 46.00 (ISBN 0-12-048450-1). Acad Pr.
Regression Diagnostics: Identifying Influential Data & Sources of Collinearity. David A. Belsley et al. LC 79-19876. (Probability & Mathematical Statistics Ser.). 292p. 1980. 41.95x (ISBN 0-471-05856-4). Wiley.
Regression Estimation from Grouped Observation. Y. Haitovsky. (Griffin Monograph: No. 33). (Illus., Orig.). 1973. pap. 12.00x (ISBN 0-02-845640-8). Hafner.
Regression Estimation from Grouped Observations. Y. Haitovsky. 1973. 17.95x (ISBN 0-85264-219-9). Lubrecht & Cramer.
Regression Methods. R. Freund & P. Minton. (Statistics Ser.: Vol. 30). 1979. 34.75 (ISBN 0-8247-6647-4). Dekker.
Regression of Atheroschlerotic Lesions: Experimental Studies & Observations in Humans. Ed. by M. Rene Malinow & Victor H. Blaton. LC 84-9952. (NATO ASI Ser. A, Life Sciences: Vol. 79). 364p. 1984. 65.00x (ISBN 0-306-41732-4, Plenum Pr). Plenum Pub.
Regressions in Mental Development: Basic Phenomena & Theories. Ed. by Thomas G. Bever. 336p. 1982. text ed. 39.95x (ISBN 0-89859-096-5). L Erlbaum Assocs.
Regressive Ego Phenomena in Psychoanalysis see Beating Fantasies.
Regrets. Joachim du Bellay. Tr. by C. H. Sisson from Fr. 147p. 1984. pap. 8.50 (ISBN 0-85635-471-6). Carcanet.
Regrets et autres oeuvres poetiques. Joachim Du Bellay. Ed. by Jolliffe. Bd. with Antiquitez de Rome Plus un Songe ou Vision sur le Mesme Subject. (Textes Litteraires Francais). 8.75 (ISBN 0-685-34184-4). French & Eur.
Regrets Only. Sally Quinn. 525p. 1986. 18.45 (ISBN 0-671-24973-8). S&S.
Regrets Only. Sally Quinn. 672p. 1987. pap. 4.95 (ISBN 0-345-34459-6). Ballantine.
Regrowing the American Economy. American Assembly Staff. LC 83-3171. 191p. pap. 49.70 (2029866). Bks Demand UMI.
Regrowing the American Economy. Ed. by G. William Miller. LC 83-3171. (Illus.). 192p. 1983. 11.95 (ISBN 0-13-771022-4); pap. 4.95 (ISBN 0-13-771014-3). Am Assembly.
Regula Musice Plane. Bonaventura Da Brescia. (Monuments of Music & Music Literature in Facsimile Series II: Vol. 77). (Illus.). 46p. (Ital.). 1975. Repr. of 1497 ed. 20.00x (ISBN 0-8450-2277-6). Broude.
Regular & Chaotic Motions in Dynamic Systems. Ed. by A. S. Wightman & G. Velo. (NATO ASI Series B, Physics: Vol. 118). 318p. 1985. 55.00x (ISBN 0-306-41896-7, Plenum Pr). Plenum Pub.
Regular & Related Solutions: The Solubility of Gases, Liquids & Solids. Joel Hildebrand et al. LC 79-122670. 230p. 1970. Repr. of 1970 ed. 19.50 (ISBN 0-442-15665-0, (JW), VN). Krieger.
Regular & Stochastic Motion. A. J. Lichtenberg & M. A. Lieberman. (Applied Mathematical Sciences Ser.: Vol. 38). (Illus.). 499p. 1983. 48.00 (ISBN 0-387-90707-6). Springer-Verlag.
Regular Boundary Value Problems Associated with Pairs of Ordinary Differential Expressions. E. A. Coddington & H. S. De Snoo. (Lecture Notes in Mathematics Ser.: Vol. 858). 225p. 1981. pap. 16.00 (ISBN 0-387-10706-1). Springer-Verlag.
Regular Cycles of Money, Inflation, Regulation & Depression. Ravi Batra. LC 85-50598. (Illus.). 192p. 1985. 20.00x (ISBN 0-939352-04-4). Venus Bks.
Regular Dad: Making Fatherhood Fun. Ron G. Woods. LC 86-81572. 175p. (Orig.). 1986. pap. 9.95x (ISBN 0-88290-313-6). Horizon Utah.
Regular Dirichlet-Voronoi Partitions for the Second Triclinic Group: Proceedings. Steklov Institute of Mathematics, Academy of Sciences, USSR & M. I. Stogrin. LC 75-23284. (Proceedings of the Steklov Institute of Mathematics: No.123). 116p. 1975. 43.00 (ISBN 0-8218-3023-6, STEKLO-123). Am Math.
Regular Polytopes. H. S. Coxeter. (Illus.). 321p. 1973. pap. 7.95 (ISBN 0-486-61480-8). Dover.
Regular Rolling Noah. George E. Lyon. LC 86-8312. (Illus.). 32p. (ps-2). 1986. 13.95 (ISBN 0-02-761330-5). Bradbury Pr.
Regular Semigroups As Extensions. F. Pastijn. (Pitman Research Notes in Mathematics Ser.). 256p. 1986. pap. 33.95 (ISBN 0-470-20557-1, Co-Pub. with Longman). Wiley.
Regular Solids & Isolated Singularities. K. Lamotke. (Advanced Lectures in Mathematics Ser.). 224p. 1986. pap. 21.50 (ISBN 3-528-08958-X, Pub. by Vieweg & Sohn). IPS.
Regular Structures: Lectures in Pattern Theory III. U. Gronander. (Applied Mathematical Sciences Ser: Vol. 33). 569p. 1981. pap. 35.00 (ISBN 0-387-90560-X). Springer-Verlag.
Regularity. (Tops Cards Ser.: No. 7). 1978. pap. 10.50 (ISBN 0-941008-07-X). Tops Learning.
Regularity of Capillary Movement of Water & of Salt Solutions in Stratified Soils: An Experimental Study. I. N. Felitsiant. 96p. 1966. text ed. 23.00x (ISBN 0-7065-0421-6, Pub. by Keter Pub Jerusalem). Coronet Bks.
Regularity of Solutions of Quasilinear Elliptic Systems. Ed. by Collet's Holdings, Ltd. Staff. 1986. 49.00x (ISBN 0-317-46709-3, Pub. by Collets (UK)). State Mutual Bk.
Regularization for Applied Inverse & Ill-Posed Problems. Ed. by Collet's Holdings, Ltd. Staff. 1986. 42.00x (ISBN 0-317-46710-7, Pub. by Collets (UK)). State Mutual Bk.
Regularly Varying Functions. (Lecture Notes in Mathematics: Vol. 508). 112p. 1976. pap. 13.00 (ISBN 0-387-07618-2). Springer-Verlag.
Regulars. Stephen Lewis. 480p. 1985. pap. 3.95 (ISBN 0-8439-2197-8, Leisure Bks). Leisure NY.
Regulated Children-Liberated Children: Education in Psychohistorical Perspective. Ed. by Barbara Finkelstein. 230p. 1979. 19.95 (ISBN 0-914434-08-X); pap. 9.95 (ISBN 0-914434-10-1). Psychohistory Pr.
Regulated Consumer. Mary B. Peterson. LC 71-153200. 185p. 1976. pap. 2.95 (ISBN 0-916054-10-1, Dist. by Kampmann). Green Hill.
Regulated Emigration of the German Proletariat with Special Reference to Texas, a Translation. Ferdinand Von Herff. Tr. by Arthur L. Finck, Jr. from Ger. LC 78-53527. 75p. 1978. 10.00 (ISBN 0-911536-72-8). Trinity U Pr.
Regulated Industries. Paul W. MacAvoy. 1979. 14.95 (ISBN 0-393-01280-8); pap. 4.95x (ISBN 0-393-95094-8). Norton.
Regulated Industries in a Nutshell. 2nd ed. Ernest Gellhorn & Richard J. Pierce. (Nutshell Ser.). 384p. 1986. pap. 11.95 (ISBN 0-314-34697-X). West Pub.
Regulated Power Supplies. 3rd ed. Irving M. Gottlieb. LC 81-52157. 424p. 1981. pap. 19.95 (ISBN 0-672-21808-9). Sams.
Regulated Rivers. Ed. by Albert Lillehammer & Svein J. Saltveit. 580p. 1985. 60.00x (ISBN 82-00-07315-7). Oxford U Pr.
Regulated Rivers: Research & Management. 1987. write for info. Wiley.
Regulated Streams. Ed. by J. F. Craig & J. B. Kemper. LC 87-16596. (Advances in Ecology Ser.). (Illus.). 444p. 1987. 79.50x (ISBN 0-306-42674-9, Plenum Pr). Plenum Pub.
Regulating America, Regulating Sweden: A Comparative Study of Occupational Safety & Health Policy. Steven Kelman. 280p. 1981. text ed. 32.50x (ISBN 0-262-11076-8). MIT Pr.
Regulating Birth: Midwives, Medicine, & the Law. Raymond G. DeVries. LC 84-16196. (Health, Society & Policy Ser.). 29.95 (ISBN 0-87722-379-3). Temple U Pr.
Regulating Business by Independent Commission. Marver H Bernstein. LC 77-2985. 1977. Repr. of 1955 ed. lib. bdg. 35.00x (ISBN 0-8371-9563-2, BERB). Greenwood.
Regulating Campaign Finance. Ed. by Lloyd N. Cutler et al. LC 85-72102. (Annals of the American Academy of Political & Social Science: Vol. 486). 200p. (Orig.). 1986. text ed. 15.00 (ISBN 0-8039-2542-5); pap. text ed. 7.95 (ISBN 0-8039-2543-3). Sage.
Regulating Competition in Oil: Government Intervention in the U. S. Refining Industry, 1948-1975. E. Anthony Copp. LC 76-19795. (Texas A&M University Economics Ser.: No. 1). 304p. 1976. 24.50x (ISBN 0-89096-014-3). Tex A&M Univ Pr.
Regulating Consumer Product Safety. W. Kip Viscusi. LC 84-2865. (AEI Studies: No. 400). 116p. 1984. 14.95 (ISBN 0-8447-3548-5); pap. 7.00 (ISBN 0-8447-3547-7). Am Enterprise.
Regulating Excellence: Examining Strategies for Improving Student & Teacher Performance. 73p. 1985. 9.00 (ISBN 0-318-18981-X). NASBE.
Regulating Fraud: White-collar Crime & the Criminal Process. Michael Levi. 416p. 1987. lib. bdg. 49.95x (ISBN 0-422-61160-3, Pub. by Routledge UK). Routledge Chapman & Hall.
Regulating Government: The Positive-Sum Solution. Dwight R. Lee & Richard B. McKenzie. 208p. 1986. 22.95 (ISBN 0-669-13443-0). Lexington Bks.
Regulating Health Care, Vol. 33, No. 4. LC 79-57402. 1980. 6.50 (ISBN 0-318-01785-7). Acad Poli Sci.
Regulating Industrial Risks: Public, Experts, & Media. Harry J. Otway & Malcolm Peltu. LC 85-14946. 192p. 1986. pap. text ed. 59.95 (ISBN 0-408-00740-0). Butterworth.
Regulating International Business Through Codes of Conduct. Raymond J. Waldman. 139p. 1980. 22.50 (ISBN 0-8447-3392-X); pap. 11.00 (ISBN 0-8447-3424-1). Am Enterprise.
Regulating Land Use: The Law of Zoning. Irving J. Sloan. (Legal Almanac Ser.: No. 78). 160p. 1988. lib. bdg. 10.00 (ISBN 0-379-11165-9). Oceana.
Regulating Paradise: Land Use Control in Hawaii. David L. Callies. LC 84-8718. 253p. 1984. pap. text ed. 14.95x (ISBN 0-8248-0891-6). UH Pr.
Regulating Pesticides. National Research Council. xiii, 288p. 1980. pap. text ed. 12.50x (ISBN 0-309-02946-5). Natl Acad Pr.
Regulating Pesticides in Food: The Delaney Paradox. National Research Council Staff. 288p. 1987. pap. text ed. 19.95x (ISBN 0-309-03746-8). Natl Acad Pr.
Regulating Pesticides in Texas. LC 84-82118. (Policy Reserach Project Ser.: No. 66). 283p. 1984. 8.50 (ISBN 0-89940-668-8). LBJ Sch Pub Aff.
Regulating Prospective Payment: An Analysis of the New Jersey Hospital Rate-setting Commission. Mindy Widman & Donald W. Light. LC 87-29730. 180p. 1988. pap. 20.00x (ISBN 0-910701-28-8, 0891). Health Admin Pr.
Regulating Safety: A Economic & Political Analysis of Occupational Safety & Health Policy. John Mendeloff. (Illus.). 1979. text ed. 35.00x (ISBN 0-262-13147-1). MIT Pr.
Regulating Safety & Health: A Working Model. Leo Teplow. 270p. 1988. pap. 37.50. ASSE.
Regulating Society: Beguines, Bohemians, & Other Marginals. Ephraim H. Mizruchi. LC 82-48161. xiv, 208p. 1987. pap. 10.95 (ISBN 0-226-53284-4). U of Chicago Pr.
Regulating Society: Marginality & Social Control in Historical Perspective. Ephraim H. Mizruchi. 224p. 1982. text ed. 29.95 (ISBN 0-02-921660-5). Free Pr.
Regulating the Airlines: Administrative Justice & Agency Discretion. Robert Baldwin. 1985. 45.00x (ISBN 0-19-827515-3); pap. 18.95x (ISBN 0-19-827516-1). Oxford U Pr.
Regulating the Automobile. Robert W. Crandall et al. LC 85-48171. (Studies in the Regulation of Economic Activity). 202p. 1986. 28.95 (ISBN 0-8157-1594-3); pap. 10.95 (ISBN 0-8157-1593-5). Brookings.
Regulating the City: Competition, Scandal & Reform. Michael Clarke. LC 85-29715. 192p. 1986. 65.00x (ISBN 0-335-15381-X, Pub. by Open Univ Pr); pap. 24.00x (ISBN 0-335-15382-8). Taylor & Francis.
Regulating the Intellectuals: Perspectives on Academic Freedom in the 1980's. Ed. by Craig Kaplan & Ellen Schrecker. LC 83-17836. 272p. 1984. 35.00 (ISBN 0-275-91021-0, C1021). Praeger.
Regulating the Lives of Women: Social Welfare Policy from Colonial Times to the Present. Mimi Abramovitz. 400p. 1988. lib. bdg. 35.00 (ISBN 0-89608-330-6); pap. 15.00 (ISBN 0-89608-329-2). South End Pr.
Regulating the Multinational Enterprise: National & International Challenges. Ed. by Bart S. Fisher & Jeff Turner. LC 83-11002. 192p. 1983. 35.00x (ISBN 0-275-90978-6, C0978). Praeger.
Regulating the New Financial Services Industry. Cynthia A. Glassman et al. LC 88-14085. 96p. (Orig.). 1988. lib. bdg. 18.50 (ISBN 0-944237-26-6); pap. text ed. 8.75 (ISBN 0-944237-25-8). Ctr National Policy.
Regulating the Poor: The Functions of Public Relief. Frances F. Piven & Richard A. Cloward. 416p. 1972. pap. 5.95 (ISBN 0-394-71743-0, V743, Vin). Random.
Regulating U. S. Intelligence Operations: A Study in Definition of the National Interest. John M. Oseth. LC 84-22105. 256p. 1985. 24.00 (ISBN 0-8131-1534-5). U Pr of KY.
Regulating Utilities in an Era of Deregulation. Ed. by Michael A. Crew. LC 86-26939. 216p. 1987. 35.00 (ISBN 0-312-00527-X). St Martin.
Regulation: A Case Approach. 2nd ed. Leonard W. Weiss & Allyn D. Strickland. 1982. text ed. 25.95 (ISBN 0-07-069098-7). McGraw.
Regulation & Contraction of Smooth Muscle. Ed. by Marion J. Siegman et al. LC 87-16966. (Progress in Clinicl & Biological Research Ser.: Vol. 245). 526p. 1987. 96.00 (ISBN 0-8451-5095-2, 5095). A R Liss.
Regulation & Control of Cell Proliferation. K. Lapis & A. Jeney. 512p. 1984. 270.00x (ISBN 0-569-08824-0, Pub. by Collets (UK)). State Mutual Bk.
Regulation & Control of Cell Proliferation. Ed. by K. Lapis & A. Jenery. 506p. 1984. text ed. 63.00 cancelled (ISBN 963-05-3246-8, Pub. by Akademiai Kaido Hungary). IPS.
Regulation & Deregulation. Jules Backman. (ITT Key Issues Lecture Ser.). 188p. (Orig.). 1981. pap. text ed. 8.40 scp (ISBN 0-672-97879-2). Bobbs.
Regulation & Deregulation of the Motor Carrier Industry. Ed. by John R. Felton & Dale G. Anderson. (Illus.). 232p. 1988. text ed. 24.95xt (ISBN 0-8138-0071-4). Iowa St U Pr.
Regulation & Development of Membrane Transport Processes. Ed. by James S. Graves. LC 84-11987. (Society of General Physiologists Ser.: Vol. 39). 287p. 1985. text ed. 39.95 (ISBN 0-471-81038-X, Pub. by Wiley-Interscience). Wiley.
Regulation & Its Reform. Stephen Breyer. LC 81-6753. (Illus.). 480p. 1982. text ed. 27.95x (ISBN 0-674-75375-5). Harvard U Pr.
Regulation & Its Reform. Stephen Breyer. 488p. 1984. pap. text ed. 9.95x (ISBN 0-674-75376-3). Harvard U Pr.
Regulation & Planning: The Case of Environmental Politics. Guy Benveniste. LC 80-70765. 250p. 1980. pap. text ed. 12.50x (ISBN 0-87835-075-6). Boyd & Fraser.
Regulation & Policies of American Shipping. Ernst G. Frankel. 352p. 1982. 28.00 (ISBN 0-86569-099-5). Auburn Hse.
Regulation & Reform of the America Banking System, 1900-1929. Eugene N. White. LC 82-61395. 256p. 1983. 31.00x (ISBN 0-691-04232-2). Princeton U Pr.
Regulation & Science. Jurgen Schmandt. (Working Paper Ser.: No. 25). 1983. 3.50 (ISBN 0-318-01669-9). LBJ Sch Pub Aff.
Regulation & Supervision of Financial Institutions. D. T. Llewellyn. 1986. 59.00x (ISBN 0-85297-174-5, Pub. by Inst of Bankers). State Mutual Bk.
Regulation & the Accounting Profession. UCLA Extension. Ed. by John W. Buckley & J. Fred Weston. LC 79-28661. (UCLA Conference Ser.). 244p. 1980. 27.95 (ISBN 0-534-97983-1, Lifetime Learn). Van Nos Reinhold.
Regulation & the Courts: The Case of the Clean Air Act. R. Shep Melnick. LC 83-7694. 404p. 1983. 32.95 (ISBN 0-8157-5662-3); pap. 12.95 (ISBN 0-8157-5661-5). Brookings.
Regulation & the Quality of Dental Care. Peter Milgrom. LC 78-1922. 258p. 1978. text ed. 56.95 (ISBN 0-89443-034-3). Aspen Pub.
Regulation & the Reagan Era. Ed. by Roger Meiners & Bruce Yandle. (Independent Studies in Political Economy). 1988. price not set (ISBN 0-8419-1174-6). Holmes & Meier.
Regulation B - Equal Credit Opportunity Act Comprehensive Compliance Manual. 193p. 1980. 34.00 (ISBN 0-317-32407-1, 048700); members 27.50 (ISBN 0-317-32408-X). Am Bankers.
Regulation by Municipal Licensing. John Bossons et al. (Ontario Economic Council Research Studies: No. 30). 120p. 1984. pap. 5.95x (ISBN 0-8020-3390-3). U of Toronto Pr.
Regulation D. Randolph H. Elkins & Larry M. Meeks. (Corporate Practice Ser.: No. 51). 1986. 92.00. BNA.
Regulation E: Comprehensive Compliance Manual. William J. O'Connor & American Bankers Association. LC 82-227487. (Illus.). Date not set. price not set. Am Bankers.
Regulation, Federalism & Interstate Commerce. Edmund W. Kitch. Ed. by A. Dan Tarlock. LC 80-23166. 176p. 1981. text ed. 35.00 (ISBN 0-89946-065-8). Oelgeschlager.
Regulation Game: How British & West German Companies Bargain with Government. Ed. by Alan Peacock. 220p. 1985. 39.95x (ISBN 0-631-13785-8). Basil Blackwell.
Regulation Governing the Transport of Radioactive Materials. OECD Nuclear Energy Agency. 202p. (Orig.). 1981. pap. 21.00x (ISBN 92-64-12158-7). OECD.
Regulation in Perspective: Historical Essays. Ed. by Thomas K. McCraw. (Harvard Graduate School of Business Administration, Division of Research). 225p. 1981. 18.50 (ISBN 0-87584-121-X). Harvard U Pr.
Regulation in Perspective: Historical Essays. Ed. by Thomas K. McCraw. 246p. 1983. pap. text ed. 9.95x (ISBN 0-87584-124-4). Harvard U Pr.
Regulation in Texas: Its Impact, Processes & Institutions, 2 Vols. (Policy Research Project Reports: No. 76). 1986. Set. 18.00 (ISBN 0-89940-678-5); Vol. 1: Overview, 271pps. 10.00 (ISBN 0-89940-679-3); Vol. 2: Case Studies, 221 pps. 10.00 (ISBN 0-89940-680-7). LBJ Sch Pub Aff.
Regulation of Accounting. Peter Taylor & Stuart Turley. 232p. 1987. text ed. 45.00 (ISBN 0-631-13878-1). Basil Blackwell.

Regulation of Transnational Communications: Michigan Yearbook of International Studies. LC 84-9223. 1984. text ed. 55.00 (ISBN 0-87632-437-5). Clark Boardman.

Regulation of Vertebrate Limb Regeneration. Ed. by Raymond Sicard. (Illus.). 1985. 35.00x (ISBN 0-19-503604-2). Oxford U Pr.

Regulation on the Organization & Operations of the Illinois Administrative Office of the Courts. 93p. 1987. 6.00 (NERO-213). Natl Ctr St Courts.

Regulation: Politics, Bureaucracy, & Economics. Kenneth J. Meier. LC 84-51842. 400p. 1985. write for info. (ISBN 0-312-66971-2); pap. text ed. write for info. (ISBN 0-312-66972-0). St Martin.

Regulation Reporter on Prepaid Legal Services. 1240p. ann. subscr. 275.00, incl. 6 supplements (ISBN 0-317-46497-3); ann. supplements 125.00 ea. Am Prepaid.

Regulation, Service Quality, & Market Performance: A Model of Airline Rivalry. John C. Panzar. LC 78-75053. (Outstanding Dissertations in Economics Ser.). 1979. lib. bdg. 20.00 (ISBN 0-8240-4131-3). Garland Pub.

Regulation State-Pak. LC 2-15. Date not set. 17.50 (ISBN 0-317-65823-9). Am Prepaid.

Regulation: The Politics of Policy. Michael D. Reagan. 1987. pap. text ed. write for info. (ISBN 0-673-39471-9). Scott F.

Regulation, Values & the Public Interest. Kenneth M. Sayre et al. Ed. by James B. Stewart. LC 80-451. 224p. (Orig.). 1980. pap. text ed. 3.60 (ISBN 0-268-01607-0). U of Notre Dame Pr.

Regulation Z Handbook. Stuart M. Bloch & William B. Ingersoll. 44p. 1982. 19.95 (ISBN 0-318-19283-7). Land Dev Inst.

Regulation Z, Truth-in-Lending: Comprehensive Compliance Manual. Robert P. Chamness & William J. O'Connor. LC 86-136774. Date not set. price not set. Am Bankers.

Regulation Z, Truth-in-Lending: Comprehensive Compliance Manual. William J. O'Connor & Phillip S. Toohey. LC 83-166229. vii, 118p. 1982. 82.50. Am Bankers.

Regulations & Legislation on Food Additives & Chemicals for Food Packaging. UN Economic Commission for Europe. 42p. 1985. pap. 7.00 (ISBN 92-1-116326-9, E.84.II.E.30). UN.

Regulations for Electrical Installations. 15th ed. Institution of Electrical Engineers (UK) Staff & Peter Peregrinus, Ltd. Staff. 232p. 1981. pap. 44.00 (ISBN 0-85296-235-5, WRR04). Inst Elect Eng.

Regulations for Electrical Installations: 15th Edition of the IEE Wiring Regulations. 232p. 1986. pap. 70.00 casebound (ISBN 0-85296-324-6, WR004). Inst Elect Eng.

Regulations for the Control of Pollution by Noxious Liquid Substances in Bulk: Articles of the International Convention for the Prevention of Pollution from Ships, 1973, & the Protocol of 1978 Relating Thereto. (Annex II of Marpol Ser.: No. 73/78). (Illus.). 144p. (Orig.). 1986. pap. text ed. 15.75 (ISBN 92-801-1206-6, IMC0512 86 13E, Pub. by Intl Maritime Orgn). UNIPUB.

Regulations for the Prussian Infantry: To Which Is Added the Prussian Tactick. Prussia Kriegsministerium. LC 68-54803. Repr. of 1759 ed. lib. bdg. 35.00x (ISBN 0-8371-0625-7, PRPI). Greenwood.

Regulations Made Easy for Instrument Pilots. Dick Doberstein. Date not set. pap. text ed. 6.95 (ISBN 0-9607866-1-9). Simplified Reg.

Regulations Made Easy for Private Pilots. Dick Doberstein. Date not set. pap. text ed. 6.95 (ISBN 0-9607866-4-3). Simplified Reg.

Regulations of Advertising by Lawyers: Comparisons of ABA Model Code of Professional Responsibility, ABA Proposal B & State Codes. 137p. 1978. 25.00 (ISBN 0-686-47769-3). Amer Bar Assn.

Regulations of International Economic Relations Through Law. Palitha T. Kohona. 1985. lib. bdg. 49.50 (ISBN 90-247-3104-6, Pub. by Martinus Nijhoff Netherlands). Kluwer Academic.

Regulations on Accounting & Internal Controls. New Jersey Casino Control Commission. 140p. 1987. write for info. Am Inst CPA.

Regulations, Recommendations & Assessments Extracted from the Registry of Toxic Effects of Chemical Substances. Richard J. Lewis, Sr. & Doris V. Sweet. (DHHS Publication NIOSH Ser.: No. 86-120). 436p. 1986. pap. 20.00 (ISBN 0-318-21667-1, S/N 017-033-00424-2). USGPO.

Regulators. William Degenhard. 598p. 1981. pap. 11.95 (ISBN 0-933256-23-X). Second Chance.

Regulators. William Degenhard. LC 80-54849. 598p. 1981. Repr. of 1943 ed. 22.50 (ISBN 0-933256-22-1). Second Chance.

Regulatory & Institutional Framework for Nuclear Activities: Nuclear Legislation Analytical Study, Vol. II. OECD. 230p. (Orig.). 1984. pap. 30.00x (ISBN 92-64-12602-3). OECD.

Regulatory & Institutional Framework for Nuclear Activities: Vol. I. OECD-Nuclear Energy Agency. (Nuclear Legislation Analytical Study). 219p. 1983. pap. 25.00 (ISBN 92-64-12534-5). OECD.

Regulatory Approach to Air Quality Management: A Case Study of New Mexico. Winston Harrington. 132p. 1981. 10.00 (ISBN 0-8018-2700-0). Resources Future.

Regulatory Aspects of Carcinogenesis & Food Additives: The Delaney Clause. Ed. by Frederick Coulston. (Ecotoxicology & Environmental Quality Ser.). 1979. 64.00 (ISBN 0-12-192750-4). Acad Pr.

Regulatory Biochemistry in Neural Tissues. Ed. by Louis Sokoloff. 1976. pap. text ed. 8.95x (ISBN 0-262-69052-7). MIT Pr.

Regulatory Bureaucracy: The Federal Trade Commission & Antitrust Policy. Robert A. Katzmann. (Studies in American Politics & Public Policy: No. 6). 1979. 32.50x (ISBN 0-262-11072-5). MIT Pr.

Regulatory Chemicals of Health & Environmental Concern. Lederer. 1985. 38.50 (ISBN 0-317-43523-X). Van Nos Reinhold.

Regulatory Chemicals of Health Environment Concern. Lederer. 1985. 41.95 (ISBN 0-442-26018-0). Van Nos Reinhold.

Regulatory Compliance Monitoring by Atomic Absorption Spectroscopy. Sidney A. Katz & Stephen W. Jenniss. (Illus.). 278p. 1984. 41.00 (ISBN 0-89573-114-2). VCH Pubs.

Regulatory Control & Standardization of Allergenic Extracts. H. D. Brede & E. A. Stevens. 356p. 1985. pap. 42.00 (ISBN 0-89574-217-9, Pub. by Gustav Fischer Verlag). VCH Pubs.

Regulatory Decision Making: The Virginia State Corporation Commission. Lawrence J. O'Toole, Jr. & Robert S. Montjoy. LC 84-5146. 389p. 1984. text ed. 32.50x (ISBN 0-8139-1034-X). U Pr of Va.

Regulatory Environment of Business. James E. Inman. LC 83-21845. 684p. 1984. write for info. (ISBN 0-471-87707-7, Pub by Wiley). Wiley.

Regulatory Executives. Robert H. Miles & Arvind Bhambri. LC 83-8641. 1983. 28.00 (ISBN 0-8039-2026-1). Sage.

Regulatory Framework for the Storage & Disposal of Radioactive Waste in the Member States of the European Community. Associated Nuclear Services for the European Commission. 1988. lib. bdg. 68.00 (ISBN 0-86010-929-1, Pub. by Graham & Trotman UK). Humanities.

Regulatory Function of Adenosine. Ed. by Robert M. Berne et al. 1983. lib. bdg. 93.50 (ISBN 90-247-2779-0, Pub. by Martinus Nijhoff Netherlands). Kluwer Academic.

Regulatory Functions - Mechanisms of Hormone Action see Comprehensive Biochemistry, Section 5: Chemical Biology.

Regulatory Functions of Interferons, Vol. 350. Ed. by Jan Vilcek et al. LC 80-25207. (Annals of the New York Academy of Sciences). 641p. 1980. 126.00x (ISBN 0-89766-089-7); pap. 126.00x (ISBN 0-89766-090-0). NY Acad Sci.

Regulatory Functions of the CNS - Motion & Organization Principles: Proceedings of the 28th International Congress of Physiological Sciences, Budapest, 1980. J. Szentagothai et al. LC 80-4188. (Advances in Physiological Sciences: Vol. 1). (Illus.). 300p. 1981. 50.00 (ISBN 0-08-026814-5). Pergamon.

Regulatory Functions of the CNS Subsystems: Proceedings of the 28th International Congress of Physiological Sciences, Budapest, 1980. J. Szentagothai et al. LC 80-41884. (Advances in Physiological Sciences: Vol. 2). (Illus.). 293p. 1981. 50.00 (ISBN 0-08-027371-8). Pergamon.

Regulatory Impact Analysis. Ed. by Law & Business Inc. Staff & Legal Times Seminars Staff. (Seminar Course Handbooks). 1983. pap. 30.00 (ISBN 0-686-89378-6, C00982, Law & Business). HarBraceJ.

Regulatory Impact on Pensions. Wayne Wendling et al. 91p. (Orig.). 1986. pap. 20.00 (ISBN 0-89154-314-7). Intl Found Employ.

Regulatory Interventionism in the Utility Industry: Fairness, Efficiency, & the Pursuit of Energy Conservation. Barbara R. Barkovich. 1989. 39.85 (ISBN 0-89930-383-8, BVY/, Quorum Bks). Greenwood.

Regulatory Justice: Implementing a Wage-Price Freeze. Robert A. Kagan. LC 77-72498. 200p. 1978. 17.95x (ISBN 0-87154-425-3). Russell Sage.

Regulatory Language Behavior. Betty L. Dubois & Isabel Crouch. (Edward Sapir Monograph Series in Language, Culture, & Cognition: No. 13). xii, 96p. (Orig.). 1985. pap. 8.00x (ISBN 0-933104-19-7). Jupiter Pr.

Regulatory Mechanisms Affecting Gonadal Hormone Action. Ed. by J. A. Thomas & R. L. Singhal. (Advances in Sex Hormone Research Ser.: Vol. 3). pap. 89.00 (ISBN 0-317-27715-4, 2052098). Bks Demand UMI.

Regulatory Mechanisms for Nursing Training & Practice: Meeting Primary Health Care Needs. (Technical Report Ser.: No. 738). 71p. 1986. pap. 6.00 (ISBN 92-4-120738-8). World Health.

Regulatory Mechanisms of Synaptic Transmission. Ed. by R. Tapia & C. W. Cotman. 430p. 1981. 69.50x (ISBN 0-306-40740-X, Plenum Pr). Plenum Pub.

Regulatory Peptides. Julia M. Polak. (BioSeries-EXS). 150p. 1988. 45.95 (ISBN 0-8176-1976-3). Birkhauser.

Regulatory Peptides & Amines During Ontogeny & in Non-Endocrine Cancers: Occurence & Possible Functional Significance. Lars-Inge Larsson. (Progress in Histochemistry & Cytochemistry Ser.: V. 17/4). 190p. 1988. pap. 90.00 (ISBN 0-89574-263-2, Pub. by Gustav Fischer Verlag). VCH Pubs.

Regulatory Peptides: From Molecular Biology to Function. Ed. by E. Costa & M. Trabucci. (Advances in Biochemical Psychopharmacology Ser.: Vol. 33). 588p. 1982. text ed. 103.00 (ISBN 0-89004-797-9). Raven.

Regulatory Peptides in Digestive, Nervous & Endocrine Systems: Proceedings of the International Symposium on Regulatory Peptides, Mode of Action on Digestive, Nervous & Endocrine Systems held in Gouvieux-Chantilly, France, 9-11 May. 1985. Ed. by M. Lewin & S. Bonfils. (INSERM Symposium Ser.: No. 25). 434p. 1985. 131.75 (ISBN 0-444-80717-9). Elsevier.

Regulatory Policy Analysis. Ed. by Mel Dubnick & Alan Gitelson. (Orig.). 1982. pap. 8.00 (ISBN 0-918592-51-8). Policy Studies.

Regulatory Policy & Practices: Regulating Better & Regulating Less. Fred Thompson. LC 82-13131. 270p. 1982. 36.95 (ISBN 0-275-90916-6, C0916). Praeger.

Regulatory Policy & the Social Sciences. Roger G. Noll. (California Series on Social Choice & Political Economy: No. 5). 1985. 42.50x (ISBN 0-520-05187-4). U of Cal Pr.

Regulatory Politics & Electric Utilities. Douglas D. Anderson. 191p. 1981. 26.00 (ISBN 0-86569-058-8). Auburn Hse.

Regulatory Problems & Regulatory Reform: The Perceptions of Business. James Greene. (Report Ser.: No. 769). vi, 50p. (Orig.). 1980. pap. 15.00 (ISBN 0-8237-0205-7). Conference Bd.

Regulatory Process & Labor Earnings. Ronald G. Ehrenberg. LC 79-6953. (Studies in Labor Economics). 1979. 29.95 (ISBN 0-12-233250-4). Acad Pr.

Regulatory Process: With Illustrations from Commercial Aviation. Emmette S. Redford. 346p. 1969. 20.00x (ISBN 0-292-78413-9). U of Tex Pr.

Regulatory Processes & Jurisdictional Issues in the Regulation of Hazardous Products in Canada. (Science Council of Canada Background Studies: No. 41). 1978. pap. 10.25 (ISBN 0-660-01490-4, SSC108, SSC). UNIPUB.

Regulatory Processes in Clinical Endocrinology. Ed. by Walter B. Essman. 300p. 1982. text ed. 40.00 (ISBN 0-88331-193-3). Luce.

Regulatory Reform & Public Utilities. Ed. by Michael A. Crew. LC 81-47749. 288p. 1982. 31.50x (ISBN 0-669-04834-8). Lexington Bks.

Regulatory Reform in Canada. W. T. Stanbury & Fred Thompson. 139p. (Orig.). 1982. pap. text ed. 7.95x (ISBN 0-920380-71-9, Pub. by Inst Res Pub Canada). Brookfield Pub Co.

Regulatory Reform: New Vision or Old Curse. Margaret N. Maxey & Robert L. Kuhn. LC 84-26261. 1985. 40.95 (ISBN 0-275-90145-9, C0145). Praeger.

Regulatory Reform: Politics & the Environment. Peter W. House & Roger D. Shull. LC 85-20282. 232p. (Orig.). 1986. lib. bdg. 29.50 (ISBN 0-8191-5013-4, ABT Bks); pap. text ed. 13.50 (ISBN 0-8191-5014-2). U Pr of Amer.

Regulatory Reform Reconsidered. Ed. by Gregory A. Daneke & David J. Lemak. 1985. pap. 21.50x (ISBN 0-8133-7143-0). Westview.

Regulatory Reform since Nineteen Seventy-Seven: A Bibliographic Overview. Clarence E. Chisholm & Alva W. Stewart. (Public Administration Ser.: Bibliography P 1619). 1985. pap. 2.00 (ISBN 0-89028-289-7). Vance Biblios.

Regulatory Reform: What Actually Happened? Leonard W. Weiss & Michael Klass. LC 85-23796. 1986. pap. text ed. write for info. (ISBN 0-673-39141-8). Scott F.

Regulatory Regimes in Conflict: Problems of Regulation in a Continental Perspective. Ed. by Fred Thompson. LC 84-17316. (Illus.). 170p. 1985. 25.50 (ISBN 0-8191-4269-7, Pub. by CN Stud Pro Inst); pap. 12.25 (ISBN 0-8191-4270-0, Pub. by CN Stud Pro Inst). U Pr of Amer.

Regulatory Role of the Nervous System in Aging. Ed. by H. T. Blumenthal. (Interdisciplinary Topics in Gerontology Ser.: Vol. 7). 1970. 34.75 (ISBN 3-8055-0508-6). S Karger.

Regulatory Roles of Opiad Peptides: Symposium to the Second World Congress of Neuroscience, Budapest, 1987. Ed. by P. Illes & C. Farsang. 522p. 1988. lib. bdg. 98.00 (ISBN 0-89573-818-X, Pub. by Gustav Fischer Verlag). VCH Pubs.

Regulatory Rulemaking to Implement Congressional Legislation: Lessons from the Powerplant & Industrial Fuel Use Act of 1978. Frank A. Camm. LC 83-11010. 1983. 7.50 (ISBN 0-8330-0510-3, R-2982-DOE-RC). Rand Corp.

Regulatory T Lymphocytes. Ed. by Benvenuto Pernis & Henry J. Vogel. (P & S Biomedical Science Ser.). 1980. 77.00 (ISBN 0-12-551860-9). Acad Pr.

Regulus vel Pueri Soli Sapiunt: (The Little Prince) Antoine de Saint-Exupery. Tr. by Augusto Haury from Fr. (Illus.). 96p. (Lat.). 1985. pap. 3.95 (ISBN 0-15-676300-1, Harv). HarBraceJ.

Rehab Right. City of Oakland Planning Department Staff. LC 86-5945. (Illus.). 144p. (Orig.). 1986. pap. 9.95 (ISBN 0-89815-172-4). Ten Speed Pr.

Rehabbing for Profit. Jerry C. Davis. (Illus.). 224p. 1987. text ed. 39.95 (ISBN 0-07-015695-6). McGraw.

Rehabilitated AASHTO Road Test. (Quality Improvement Program Ser.: No. 101). 24p. 1981. 20.00 (ISBN 0-317-58389-1). Natl Asphalt Pavement.

Rehabilitating America. Frank Bowe. 1980. 13.45x (ISBN 0-06-010436-8). Har-Row.

Rehabilitating Damaged Ecosystems. Ed. by John Cairns, Jr. 1988. 99.50 ea. Vol. I, 192 pgs (ISBN 0-8493-4391-7, 4391). Vol. II, 224 pgs (ISBN 0-8493-4392-5, 4392). CRC Pr.

Rehabilitating Historic Properties 1984. (Real Estate Law & Practice Ser.). 427p. 1984. 45.00 (ISBN 0-317-15188-6, N44433). PLI.

Rehabilitating Juvenile Justice. Charles H. Shireman & Frederic G. Reamer. LC 86-6788. 224p. 1986. 25.00 (ISBN 0-231-06328-8). Columbia U Pr.

Rehabilitating Oiled Seabirds: A Field Manual. Anne S. Williams. Ed. by Jeff Burridge & Meryl Kane. LC 85-73815. (Illus.). 50p. (Orig.). 1986. pap. text ed. 25.00 (ISBN 0-89364-056-5, 841-44070). Am Petroleum.

Rehabilitating Older & Historic Buildings: Guidelines for Design. Vonier. 1987. write for info. (ISBN 0-471-83134-4). Wiley.

Rehabilitating Older & Historic Buildings: Law Taxation Strategies. Stephen L. Kass et al. LC 85-18370. 440p. 1985. 95.00 (ISBN 0-471-80154-2). Wiley.

Rehabilitating Older & Historic Buildings: Law Taxation Strategies, 1988 Cumulative Supplement. Stephen L. Kass et al. 1988. pap. 35.00 (ISBN 0-471-60147-0). Wiley.

Rehabilitating People with Disabilities into the Mainstream of Society. Allen D. Spiegel & Simon Podair. LC 80-26497. (Noyes Medical Publications). (Illus.). 350p. 1981. 28.00 (ISBN 0-8155-0839-5). Noyes.

Rehabilitating Residential & Commercial Properties. (Journal Reprint Ser.). 8.75 (ISBN 0-686-46402-8, 860). Inst Real Estate.

Rehabilitating the Narcotics Addict; Report. Institute on New Developments in the Rehabilitation of the Narcotics Addict et al. Ed. by United States Public Health Service Division of Hospitals. Tr. by United States Dept. of Health, Education, & Welfare Vocational Rehabilitation Administration. (Illus.). 1968. Repr. of 1966 ed. 11.00 (ISBN 0-405-00056-1, 16411). Ayer Co Pubs.

Rehabilitation: A Component of Comprehensive Cardiac Care. Ed. by Nanette K. Wenger. (Bibliotheca Cardiologica Ser.: No. 40). (Illus.). xii, 132p. 1986. 88.75 (ISBN 3-8055-4359-X). S Karger.

Rehabilitation after Myocardial Infarction. C. T. Kappagoda. LC 84-4623. (Other Medical Bks.: Vol. 7). 1984. pap. text ed. 33.25 (ISBN 0-87488-539-6). Med Exam.

Rehabilitation after Myocardial Infarction: The European Experience. Ed. by Veikko Kallio & Elizabeth Clay. (Public Health in Europe Ser.: No. 24). 148p. 1985. pap. 7.80 (ISBN 92-890-1160-2). World Health.

Rehabilitation & Acquired Deafness. Ed. by William J. Watts. 288p. 1983. text ed. 35.00x (ISBN 0-7099-2746-0, Pub. by Croom Helm England). Sheridan.

Rehabilitation & Human Services: Critical Issues for the Eighties. Intro. by G. Douglas Tyler. (Readings in Deafness Ser.: No. 6). (Illus.). 204p. (Orig.). 1983. pap. text ed. 7.00 (ISBN 0-914494-07-4). Am Deaf & Rehab.

Rehabilitation & the Chronic Renal Disease Patient. Ed. by Nancy G. Kutner et al. LC 85-1866. 200p. 1985. text ed. 27.50 (ISBN 0-89335-222-5). PMA Pub Corp.

Rehabilitation Approaches to Drug & Alcohol Dependence. 2nd ed. Behrouz Shahandeh. 1987. pap. 10.50. Intl Labour Office.

Rehabilitation Aspects of Drug Dependence. Ed. by Arnold Schecter. 1977. 55.00 (ISBN 0-8493-5475-7). CRC Pr.

Rehabilitation Assistant. Jack Rudman. (Career Examination Ser.: C-545). (Cloth bdg. available on request). pap. 12.00 (ISBN 0-8373-0545-4). Natl Learning.

Rehabilitation Caseload Management. Jack L. Cassell & S. Wayne Mulkey. LC 85-3385. 350p. 1985. pap. text ed. 21.00x (ISBN 0-936104-67-8, 1275). Pro Ed.

Rehabilitation Cost Analyst. Jack Rudman. (Career Examination Ser.: C-3121). 1988. pap. 16.00 (ISBN 0-8373-3121-8). Natl Learning.

Rehabilitation Counseling & Services: Profession & Process. Ed. by Gerald L. Gandy et al. (Illus.). 376p. 1987. 39.75X (ISBN 0-398-05282-4). C C Thomas.

Rehabilitation Counseling: Basics & Beyond. Ed. by Randall M. Parker. LC 86-18729. (Illus.). 348p. (Orig.). 1987. pap. text ed. 21.00x (ISBN 0-89079-142-2, 1411). Pro Ed.

Rehabilitation Counseling: Collected Papers. C. H. Patterson. 1969. pap. 7.80x (ISBN 0-87563-015-4). Stipes.

Rehabilitation Counseling of the Blind. Thomas A. Routh. 100p. 1970. 9.25x (ISBN 0-398-01619-4). C C Thomas.

Rehabilitation Counselor. Jack Rudman. (Career Examination Ser.: C-672). (Cloth bdg. avail. on request). pap. 14.00 (ISBN 0-8373-0672-8). Natl Learning.

Rehabilitation Counselor Certification Examination (CRC) Jack Rudman. (Admission Test Ser.: ATS-92). 300p. (Cloth bdg. avail. on request). 1988. pap. 19.95 (ISBN 0-8373-5092-1). Natl Learning.

Rehabilitation Counselor Preparation & Development: Selected Critical Issues. Ed. by William G. Emener. 360p. 1986. 40.25x (ISBN 0-398-05173-9). C C Thomas.

Rehabilitation Counselor Supervisor. Jack Rudman. (Career Examination Ser.: C-1980). (Cloth bdg. avail. on request). pap. 14.00 (ISBN 0-8373-1980-3). Natl Learning.

Rehabilitation Counselor Trainee. Jack Rudman. (Career Examination Ser.: C-1783). (Cloth bdg. avail. on request). pap. 12.00 (ISBN 0-8373-1783-5). Natl Learning.

Rehabilitation Detectives. Paul C. Higgins. 240p. 1985. 29.95 (ISBN 0-8039-2450-X); pap. 14.95 (ISBN 0-8039-2451-8). Sage.

Rehabilitation Evaluation: Some Application Guidelines. Ed. by James A. Bitter & Don L. Goodyear. LC 75-9719. 1975. text ed. 29.50x (ISBN 0-8422-5223-1); pap. text ed. 9.95x (ISBN 0-8422-0502-0). Irvington.

Rehabilitation Exercises for the Cancer Patient. Ernest H. Rosenbaum et al. LC 79-54996. (Illus., Orig.). 1980. pap. 4.95 (ISBN 0-915950-37-5). Bull Pub.

Rehabilitation for the Unwanted. Julius A. Roth & Elizabeth M. Eddy. 232p. text ed. 39.50x cancelled (ISBN 0-8290-0904-3); pap. text ed. 18.95x cancelled (ISBN 0-8290-0905-1). Irvington.

Rehabilitation in Australia & New Zealand: U. S. Observation. (International Exchange of Experts & Information in Rehabilitation Ser.: No. 21). 189p. 1983. 3.00 (ISBN 0-939986-33-7). World Rehab Fund.

Rehabilitation in Community Mental Health. H. Richard Lamb. LC 76-168989. (Jossey-Bass Behavioral Science Ser.). pap. 55.50 (2027760). Bks Demand UMI.

Rehabilitation in Industry: A Modern Monograph in Industrial Medicine. Ed. by Donald A. Covalt. LC 58-10361. (Illus.). 166p. 1958. 44.50 (ISBN 0-8089-0104-4, 790925). Grune.

Rehabilitation in Ischemic Heart Disease. Ed. by William Blocker, Jr. & David Cardus. LC 80-22840. (Illus.). 500p. 1983. text ed. 80.00 (ISBN 0-88331-194-1). Luce.

Rehabilitation in Psychiatry: An Introductory Handbook. Clephane Hume & Ian Pullen. LC 85-11677. (Illus.). 230p. (Orig.). 1986. pap. text ed. 22.00 (ISBN 0-443-02509-6). Churchill.

Rehabilitation in the Aging. Ed. by T. Franklin Williams. (Illus.). 390p. 1984. 60.50 (ISBN 0-89004-417-1, 471). Raven.

Rehabilitation: Index of Modern Information with Bibliography. Keith S. Pittham. LC 88-47796. 150p. (Orig.). 1988. 34.50 (ISBN 0-88164-884-1); pap. 26.50 (ISBN 0-88164-885-X). ABBE Pubs Assn.

Rehabilitation Inspector. Jack Rudman. (Career Examination Ser.: C-2639). (Cloth bldg. avail. on request). pap. 14.00 (ISBN 0-8373-2639-7). Natl Learning.

Rehabilitation International: Proceedings of the Fifteenth World Congress of Rehabilitation International, Held June 1984 in Lisbon, Portugal. 350p. 1984. 30.00 (ISBN 0-317-19041-5). Rehab Intl.

Rehabilitation International Vocational Seminar, Toronto, Canada, 1980. Rehabilitation International Vocational Commission. 9.00 (ISBN 0-686-94892-0). Rehab Intl.

Rehabilitation Interventions for the Institutionalized Elderly. Ed. by Ellen D. Taira. (Physical & Occupational Therapy in Geriatrics Ser.: Vol. 6, No. 2). (Illus.). 80p. 1988. text ed. 17.95 (ISBN 0-86656-833-6). Haworth Pr.

Rehabilitation Interviewer. Jack Rudman. (Career Examination Ser.: C-2708). (Cloth bdg. avail. on request). 1988. pap. 14.00 (ISBN 0-8373-2708-3). Natl Learning.

Rehabilitation Literature, 1950 to 1955: A Bibliographic Review of the Medical Care, Education, Employment, Welfare & Psychology of Handicapped Children & Adults. Earl C. Graham & Marjorie Mullen. Ed. by William R. Phillips & Janet Rosenberg. LC 79-6901. (Physically Handicapped in Society Ser.). 1980. Repr. of 1956 ed. lib. bdg. 55.50x (ISBN 0-405-13112-7). Ayer Co Pubs.

Rehabilitation Management of Rheumatic Conditions. 2nd ed. George E. Ehrlich. 400p. 1985. 41.95 (ISBN 0-683-02792-1). Williams & Wilkins.

Rehabilitation Medicine. 2nd ed. P. J. Nichols. LC 79-42891. 1980. text ed. 55.00 (ISBN 0-407-00175-1). Butterworth.

Rehabilitation Medicine & Psychiatry. Jack Meislin. (Illus.). 564p. 1976. 36.25 (ISBN 0-398-03432-X). C C Thomas.

Rehabilitation Medicine: Principles & Practice. DeLisa. LC 65-9285. 1988. 75.00 (ISBN 0-397-50764-X, Lippincott Medical). Lippincott.

Rehabilitation Nursing: Perspectives & Applications. Victor A. Christopherson et al. (Illus.). 512p. (Orig.). 1973. text ed. 29.95 (ISBN 0-07-010815-3). McGraw.

Rehabilitation Nursing: Process & Application. Dittmar. (Illus.). 850p. 1989. 29.95 (ISBN 0-8016-1319-1). Mosby.

Rehabilitation of a Child with a Traumatic Brain Injury. Robert A. Hock. (Illus.). 324p. 1984. 40.50x (ISBN 0-398-04896-7). C C Thomas.

Rehabilitation of Arm Amputees & Limb Deficient Children. Elizabeth Robertson. (Illus.). 1982. text ed. 27.95 (ISBN 0-7216-0759-4, Bailliere-Tindall). Saunders.

Rehabilitation of Athletic Injuries: An Atlas of Therapeutic Exercise. Joseph S. Torg. (Illus.). 288p. 1987. text ed. 35.50 (ISBN 0-8151-8820-X). Year Bk Med.

Rehabilitation of Brain Functions: Principles, Procedures & Techniques of Neurotraining. James F. Craine & Howard E. Gudeman. 358p. 1981. spiral bdg. 35.75x (ISBN 0-398-04605-0). C C Thomas.

Rehabilitation of Clergy Alcoholics: Ardent Spirits Subdued. Joseph H. Fichter. LC 80-28447. 203p. 1982. 26.95 (ISBN 0-89885-009-6). Human Sci Pr.

Rehabilitation of Cognitive Disabilities. Ed. by J. Michael Williams & Charles J. Long. (Illus.). 246p. 1987. 49.50x (ISBN 0-306-42594-7, Plenum Pr). Plenum Pub.

Rehabilitation of Criminal Offenders: Problems & Prospects. National Research Council. 1979. pap. 15.25x (ISBN 0-309-02895-7). Natl Acad Pr.

Rehabilitation of Criminals: A Bibliography. Mary Vance. 33p. 1988. pap. 7.50 (ISBN 1-55590-674-5). Vance Biblios.

Rehabilitation of Juvenile Offenders: A Bibliography. Mary Vance. 28p. 1988. pap. 6.25 (ISBN 1-55590-673-7). Vance Biblios.

Rehabilitation of Marginal Housing Stock in Urban Areas: A Selected Annotated Bibliography, No. 929-930. Ila M. Hallowell & Marilyn Gehr. 1975. 6.50 (ISBN 0-686-20378-X). CPL Biblios.

Rehabilitation of Memory. Barbara A. Wilson. LC 86-7636. 259p. 1986. lib. bdg. 30.00 (ISBN 0-89862-678-1). Guilford Pr.

Rehabilitation of Memory. Barbara A. Wilson. 259p. 1988. lib. bdg. 15.00 (ISBN 0-89862-513-0, 2513). Guilford Pr.

Rehabilitation of Sports Injuries. Moynes et al. (Illus.). 300p. 1989. 40.00 (ISBN 0-8016-3580-2). Mosby.

Rehabilitation of the Brain-Damaged Adult. Gerald Goldstein & Leslie Ruthven. (Applied Clinical Psychology Ser.). 280p. 1983. 35.00x (ISBN 0-306-40498-2, Plenum Pr.). Plenum Pub.

Rehabilitation of the Burn Patient. Vincent Degreggorio. 1983. 25.00 (ISBN 0-318-23306-1). Phoenix Soc.

Rehabilitation of the Burn Patient. Ed. by Vincent R. DiGregorio. (Clinics in Physical Therapy Ser.: Vol. 5). (Illus.). 178p. 1984. text ed. 30.00 (ISBN 0-443-08200-6). Churchill.

Rehabilitation of the Cardiac Patient. Ed. by Nanette K. Wenger et al. (Advances in Cardiology Ser.: Vol. 33). (Illus.). xvi, 192p. 1987. 109.50 (ISBN 3-8055-4339-5). S Karger.

Rehabilitation of the Coronary Patient. Ed. by Nanette K. Wenger & Herman K. Hellerstein. LC 78-12531. 336p. Repr. of 1978 ed. 38.95 (ISBN 0-471-93369-4, JW). Krieger.

Rehabilitation of the Drunken Driver: A Corrective Course in Phoenix, Arizona for Persons Convicted of Drinking under the Influence of Alcohol. Ernest Stewart & James L. Malfetti. LC 73-137738. pap. 66.30 (ISBN 0-317-28974-8, 2020326). Bks Demand UMI.

Rehabilitation of the Elderly: A Tale of Two Hospitals. Morris W. Stroud, III & Sidney Katz. LC 84-62817. 172p. 1985. 19.95 (ISBN 0-87013-240-7). Mich St U Pr.

Rehabilitation of the Hand. 3rd ed. Hunter et al. (Illus.). 1200p. 1989. 110.00 (ISBN 0-8016-2472-X). Mosby.

Rehabilitation of the Hand. 2nd ed. James M. Hunter. 800p. 1984. 110.00 (ISBN 0-8016-2355-3). Mosby.

Rehabilitation of the Hand. 4th rev. ed. C. B. Wynn-Parry. LC 80-41761. (Illus.). 1981. text ed. 120.00 (ISBN 0-407-38503-7). Butterworth.

Rehabilitation of the Head & Neck Cancer Patient: Psychosocial Aspects. Ed. by Andrew Blitzer et al. 250p. 1985. 29.50x (ISBN 0-398-05156-9). C C Thomas.

Rehabilitation of the Head Injured Adult. Mitchell Rosenthal et al. LC 82-23504. 454p. 1983. 45.00 (ISBN 0-8036-7625-5). Davis Co.

Rehabilitation of the Injured Knee. Hunter & Funk. 1984. 67.00 (ISBN 0-8016-2318-9). Mosby.

Rehabilitation of the Older Patient. Ed. by Amanda J. Squires. (Therapy in Practice Ser.). (Illus.). 288p. 1988. pap. text ed. 29.50x (ISBN 0-7099-5423-9, Pub. by Croom Helm UK). Sheridan Med Bks.

Rehabilitation of the Other Adult. Keith Andrews. (Illus.). 388p. 1987. text ed. 49.95 (Pub. by E Arnold UK). Williams & Wilkins.

Rehabilitation of the Physically Disabled Adult. Ed. by C. John Goodwill & M. Anne Chamberlain. (Illus.). 880p. 1988. text ed. 89.50x (ISBN 0-7099-3874-8, Pub. by Croom Helm UK); pap. text ed. 45.00x (ISBN 0-7099-3883-7). Sheridan Med Bks.

Rehabilitation of the Severely Brain-Injured Adult: A Practical Approach. Ed. by Ian Fussey & Gordon M. Giles. (Therapy in Practice Ser.). 221p. (Orig.). 1988. pap. text ed. 29.00 (ISBN 0-7099-1904-2, 049, Pub. by Croom Helm). P H Brookes.

Rehabilitation of the Surgical Knee. Ed. by George J. Davies. 100p. (Orig.). 1984. pap. 25.00 (ISBN 0-930269-00-4). CyPr NY.

Rehabilitation of the Wounded. Ed. by Carl Kelsy & William R. Phillips. LC 79-6910. (Physically Handicapped in Society Ser.). 1980. Repr. of 1918 ed. lib. bdg. 17.00x (ISBN 0-405-13120-8). Ayer Co Pubs.

Rehabilitation of Workers' Compensation & Other Insurance Claimants: Case Management, Forensic, & Business Aspects. John D. Rasch. (Illus.). 222p. 1985. 29.50 (ISBN 0-398-05087-2). C C Thomas.

Rehabilitation Oncology. J. Herbert Dietz, Jr. LC 80-22911. 194p. 1981. 32.50 (ISBN 0-471-08414-X). Krieger.

Rehabilitation Outcomes: Analysis & Measurement. Ed. by Marcus J. Fuhrer. LC 87-894. 320p. 1987. text ed. 35.00 (ISBN 0-933716-77-X, 77X). P H Brookes.

Rehabilitation Policies & Programmes. S. D. Gokhale. 126p. 1986. 14.00X (ISBN 0-8364-1872-7, Pub. by Somaiya). South Asia Bks.

Rehabilitation Practices with the Physically Disabled. James Garrett & Edna Levine. LC 72-13875. 569p. 1973. 44.00x (ISBN 0-231-03523-3). Columbia U Pr.

Rehabilitation Profession. Adrienne Levatino-Donoghue. 140p. 1979. 9.00 (ISBN 0-318-14957-5, N602); members 7.00 (ISBN 0-318-14958-3). NAHRO.

Rehabilitation Programming in Production. Ronald R. Fry. 280p. (Orig.). Date not set. pap. text ed. cancelled (ISBN 0-916671-77-1). Material Dev.

Rehabilitation Psychology: A Comprehensive Textbook. Ed. by David W. Krueger. LC 83-15703. 406p. 1984. 40.00 (ISBN 0-89443-946-4). Aspen Pub.

Rehabilitation Psychology Desk Reference. Bruce Caplan. 1987. 49.00 (ISBN 0-87189-620-6). Aspen Pub.

Rehabilitation, Recidivism & Research. Robert Martinson & Ted Palmer. 96p. 1976. 6.00 (ISBN 0-318-15372-6). Natl Coun Crime.

Rehabilitation, Renovation, & Preservation of Concrete & Masonry Structures. 276p. pap. 51.50 (ISBN 0-317-39822-9). ACI.

Rehabilitation, Renovation, & Reconstruction of Buildings: Proceedings of a Workshop Sponsored by the National Science Foundation & ASCE. 105p. 1985. 14.00x (ISBN 0-87262-493-5). Am Soc Civil Eng.

Rehabilitation Strategies for Sensorineural Hearing Loss: Proceedings of the Second Conference on Auditory Techniques. Ed. by Paul Yanick, Jr. 240p. 1979. 29.50 (ISBN 0-8089-1215-1, 794946). Grune.

Rehabilitation Techniques in Rheumatology. Anthony Clarke. 288p. 1987. 30.50 (ISBN 0-683-01704-7). Williams & Wilkins.

Rehabilitation Techniques: Vocational Adjustment for the Handicapped. James S. Payne. 208p. 1984. text ed. 29.95 (ISBN 0-89885-159-9). Human Sci Pr.

Rehabilitation Technology Sourcebook. Alexandra Enders & Marion G. Hall. 300p. 1988. 29.95 (ISBN 0-939957-12-4). Demos Pubns Inc.

Rehabilitation: The Federal Government's Response to Disability, 1935 to 1954. Edward D. Berkowitz. Ed. by William R. Phillips & Janet Rosenberg. LC 79-6896. (Physically Handicapped in Society Ser.). 1980. lib. bdg. 33.50x (ISBN 0-405-13107-0). Ayer Co Pubs.

Rehabilitation Through Learning: Energy Conservation & Joint Protection: A Workbook for Persons with Rheumatoid Arthritis with Instructor's Guide. Gloria Furst. v, 181p. 1985. pap. 10.50 (ISBN 0-318-19920-3, S/N 017-045-00104-7, S/N 017-045-00103-9). USGPO.

Rehabilitation: Twenty-Five Years of Concepts, Principles, Perspectives. Ed. by Stephen J. Regnier & Marian Petkovsek. (Illus.). 192p. (Orig.). 1985. pap. 9.95 (ISBN 0-933851-00-6). Natl Easter Seal.

Rehabilitations. Clive S. Lewis. 1973. Repr. of 1939 ed. 40.00 (ISBN 0-8274-1286-X). R West.

Rehabilitations & Other Essays. facsimile ed. Clive S. Lewis. LC 71-167377. (Essay Index Reprint Ser). Repr. of 1939 ed. 15.00 (ISBN 0-8369-2559-9). Ayer Co Pubs.

Rehabilitations & Other Essays. Clive S. Lewis. LC 73-684. 1939. Repr. of 1980 ed. lib. bdg. 42.00 (ISBN 0-8414-2250-8). Folcroft.

Rehabilitations & Other Essays. Clive S. Lewis. Repr. of 1939 ed. 14.00x (ISBN 0-403-04233-X). Somerset Pub.

Rehabilitative Audiology. Ed. by Raymond Hull. 542p. 1982. 44.50 (ISBN 0-8089-1434-0, 792079). Grune.

Rehabilitative Audiology for Children & Adults. Jerome Alpiner & Patricia McCarthy. (Illus.). 496p. 1987. 32.95 (ISBN 0-683-00077-2). Williams & Wilkins.

Rehabilitative Audiology for Children & Adults. Julia M. Davis & Edward J. Hardick. LC 81-7427. 509p. 1981. write for info. (ISBN 0-02-327860-9). Macmillan.

Rehabilitative Surgery see Plastic & Reconstructive Surgery of the Face & Neck.

Rehearsal. George Villiers. LC 76-39791. 1976. Repr. of 1869 ed. lib. bdg. 25.50 (ISBN 0-8414-2965-0). Folcroft.

Rehearsal see Restoration Plays.

Rehearsal Copies of Bernard Shaw's Plays. Fritz E. Lowenstein. 1979. Repr. of 1950 ed. lib. bdg. 16.50 (ISBN 0-8492-1616-8). R West.

Rehearsal Copies of Bernard Shaw's Plays. Ed. by Fritz E. Lowenstein. LC 77-5396. Repr. of 1950 ed. lib. bdg. 17.00 (ISBN 0-8414-5823-5). Folcroft.

Rehearsal for Love. Faith Baldwin. 1976. Repr. of 1940 ed. lib. bdg. 19.95x (ISBN 0-88411-612-3, Pub. by Aeonian Pr). Amereon Ltd.

Rehearsal for Love. W. E. Ross. (YA) (gr. 7 up). 1984. 9.95 (ISBN 0-8034-8418-6, Avalon). Bouregy.

Rehearsal for Murder. P. M. Carlson. 224p. 1988. pap. 3.50 (ISBN 0-553-27234-9). Bantam.

Rehearsal for Reconstruction: The Port Royal Experiment. Willie L. Rose. 1976. pap. 12.95x (ISBN 0-19-519882-4). Oxford U Pr.

Rehearsal for Republicanism: Free Soil & the Politics of Antislavery. John Mayfield. (National University Publications, Political Science Ser.). 224p. 1980. 24.50x (ISBN 0-8046-9253-X, Pub. by Kennikat). Assoc Faculty Pr.

Rehearsal for the Bigtime. Berniece Rabe. Ed. by Frank Sloan. (Illus.). 144p. (YA) (gr. 7-9). 1988. 12.90 (ISBN 0-531-10504-0). Watts.

Rehearsal Guide for the Choral Director. Jack Boyd. LC 77-2051. 1977. pap. text ed. 11.95 (ISBN 0-916656-03-9). Mark Foster Mus.

Rehearsal: The Principles & Practice of Acting for the Stage. 6th ed. Miriam A. Franklin & James G. Dixon, III. (Illus.). 272p. 1983. pap. write for info. (ISBN 0-13-771550-1). P-H.

Rehearsal, 1671. George Villiers. Ed. by Edward Arber. 132p. pap. 15.00 (ISBN 0-87556-342-2). Saifer.

Rehearsal, 1671, 1672. large type ed. Ed. by Edward Arber. 132p. 1983. pap. 15.00 (ISBN 0-686-89438-3). Saifer.

Rehearsals for Change. Dennis Altman. 215p. 1982. pap. 6.95 (ISBN 0-00-635716-4, Pub by W Collins). Intl Spec Bk.

Rehearsals of Revolution: The Political Theater of Bengal. Rustom Bharucha. LC 83-10470. (Illus.). 276p. 1983. text ed. 25.00x (ISBN 0-8248-0845-2). UH Pr.

Rehearse Before You Retire. 3rd, rev. ed. Elmer Otte. LC 77-79286. 208p. 1977. pap. 5.50 (ISBN 0-9602938-1-7). Retirement Res.

Rehearsing the Audience: Ways to Develop Student Perceptions of Theatre. Ken Davis. (Illus.). 95p. 1988. pap. 6.50 (ISBN 0-8141-3986-8). NCTE.

Rehearsing the Revolution: The Staging of Marat's Death, 1793-1797. Marie-Helene Huet. Tr. by Robert Hurley from Fr. LC 81-21965. (Quantum Books: No. 25). 150p. 1982. 25.00x (ISBN 0-520-04321-9). U of Cal Pr.

Rehumanization or Dehumanization: Essays on Alexander Solzhenitsyn, Arnost Kolman, Gyorgy Lukacs, Adam Schaff. Pavel Kovaly. 260p. 1974. 10.00 (ISBN 0-8283-1536-1). Branden Pub Co.

Rehumanizing Housing. Necdet Teymur et al. (Illus.). 200p. 1988. text ed. 90.00 (ISBN 0-408-02039-3). Butterworth.

Reich for Beginners. David Z. Mairowitz. (Writers & Readers Documentary Comic Bks). (Illus.). 176p. 1986. pap. 6.95 (ISBN 0-86316-031-X). Writers & Readers.

Reichard Collection of Early Pennsylvania German Dialogues & Plays. Ed. by Albert F. Buffington. (Penn. German Ser.: Vol. 61). 1962. 20.00 (ISBN 0-911122-15-X). Penn German Soc.

Reichian Growth: Melting the Blocks to Life & Love. Nick Totten & Em Edmondson. 160p. (Orig.). 1988. pap. 15.95 (ISBN 1-85327-016-4, Pub. by Prism Pr). Avery Pub.

Reichstag Fire Trial: The Second Brown Book of the Hitler Terror. World Committee For The Relief Of The Victims Of German Fascism. LC 68-9605. 1969. Repr. of 1934 ed. 32.50 (ISBN 0-86527-165-8). Fertig.

Reichswehr & Politics: Nineteen Eighteen to Nineteen Thirty-Three. F. L. Carsten. 1974. pap. 10.95x (ISBN 0-520-02492-3). U of Cal Pr.

Reid's Branson Instruction to Juries, 7 Vols. 3rd ed. 1960p. Set. with 1986 suppl. 250.00x (ISBN 0-672-84048-0, Bobbs-Merrill Law); 1986 suppl. 100.00x (ISBN 0-87215-879-9). Michie Co.

Reid's Controversy in Obstetrics & Gynecology 3. Frederick P. Zuspan & C. Donald Christian. (Illus.). 672p. 1983. 89.00 (ISBN 0-7216-2565-7). Saunders.

Reign of Andrew Jackson. Frederic A. Ogg. 1919. 8.50x (ISBN 0-686-83729-0). Elliots Bks.

Reign of Andrew Jackson see Chronicles of America.

Reign of Charles V, 1516-1558. William L. McElwee. LC 83-45657. Date not set. Repr. of 1936 ed. 36.00 (ISBN 0-404-19807-4). AMS Pr.

Reign of Conscience: Individual, Church & State in Lord Acton's History of Liberty. John Nurser. Ed. by William H. McNeill & Peter Stansky. (Modern European History Ser.). 225p. 1987. lib. bdg. 40.00 (ISBN 0-8240-7826-8). Garland Pub.

Reign of Doctor Joseph Gaspard Roderick De Francia in Paraguay: Being an Account of a Six Years' Residence in That Republic from July 1819 to May 1825. J. R. Rengger & M. Longchamps. Tr. by J. R. Rengger from Fr. 1970. Repr. of 1827 ed. lib. bdg. 14.95x (ISBN 0-89712-004-3). Documentary Pubns.

Reign of Doctor Joseph Gaspard Roderick De Francia, in Paraguay. Johann R. Rengger & M. Longchamps. LC 70-130334. (Latin-American History & Culture Ser). 1971. Repr. of 1827 ed. 27.00x (ISBN 0-8046-1394-X, Pub. by Kennikat). Assoc Faculty Pr.

Reign of Elizabeth, Fifteen Fifty-Eight to Sixteen Three. 2nd ed. J. B. Black. (Oxford History of England Ser.). 1959. 45.00x (ISBN 0-19-821701-3). Oxford U Pr.

Reign of Elizabeth I. Ed. by Christopher Haigh. LC 94-16305. 307p. 1985. 27.50x (ISBN 0-8203-0757-2). U of Ga Pr.

Reign of ETS: The Corporation That Makes up Minds. Ed. by Nairn, Allan & Associates Staff. LC 80-107761. (Ralph Nader Report on the Educational Testing Service). 554p. (Orig.). 1980. pap. 30.00 (ISBN 0-936486-00-7). R Nader.

Reign of Fear: Fiction & Film of Stephen King. Ed. by Don Herron. 272p. 1988. 25.00 (ISBN 0-88733-062-2). Underwood-Miller.

Reign of Fire. M. Bradley Kellogg. (Lears Daughters Ser.: Pt. 2). 1986. pap. 3.50 (ISBN 0-451-14526-7, Sig). NAL.

Reign of George Third, Seventeen Sixty to Eighteen Fifteen. J. Steven Watson. (Oxford History of England Ser). 1960. 42.00x (ISBN 0-19-821713-7). Oxford U Pr.

Reign of God: An Introduction to Christian Theology from a Seventh-Day Adventist Perspective. Richard Rice. LC 85-70344. 400p. 1985. text ed. 23.95 (ISBN 0-943872-90-1). Andrews Univ Pr.

Reign of Grace. Abrh Booth. 5.95 (ISBN 0-685-88390-6). Reiner.

Reign of Guilt. David C. Phillips. (Collected Works of David G. Phillips). 1988. Repr. of 1981 ed. lib. bdg. 59.00x. Am Biog Serv.

Reign of Guilt. David G. Phillips. (American Author Ser.). 1981. Repr. lib. bdg. 29.00 (ISBN 0-686-71939-5). Scholarly.

Reign of Henry Eighth from His Accession to the Death of Wolsey, 2 Vols. John S. Brewer. Ed. by James Gairdner. LC 70-52901. Repr. of 1884 ed. Set. 65.00 (ISBN 0-404-01072-5). AMS Pr.

Reign of Henry Seventh from Contemporary Sources, 3 Vols. Ed. by Albert F. Pollard. LC 73-181970. Repr. of 1914 ed. Set. 95.00 (ISBN 0-404-05140-5). AMS Pr.

Reign of Henry the Fifth, 3 vols. James H. Wylie. 1914-1929. Repr. Vol. 1. lib. bdg. 24.75 (ISBN 0-8371-1786-0, WYHA); Vol. 2. lib. bdg. 24.75 (ISBN 0-8371-0864-0, WYHB); Vol. 3. lib. bdg. 24.75 (ISBN 0-8371-0865-9, WYHC). Greenwood.

Reign of Henry VI. Ralph A. Griffiths. LC 80-53771. (Illus.). 604p. 1981. 45.00x (ISBN 0-520-04356-1). U of Cal Pr.

Reign of Henry VIII: Personalities & Politics. David Starkey. (Illus.). 174p. 1986. 17.95 (ISBN 0-531-15014-3). Watts.

Reign of James VI & I. Ed. by Alan G. Smith. LC 73-79379. (Problems in Focus Ser.). 275p. 1973. 25.00 (ISBN 0-312-67025-7). St Martin.

Reign of Jesus Thru Mary. Gabriel Denis. 6.00 (ISBN 0-910984-03-4). Montfort Pubns.

Reign of King Edward the Third (1596) & Shakespeare. Richard Proudfoot. 1985. pap. 5.50 (ISBN 0-85672-539-0, Pub. by British Acad). Longwood Pub Group.

Reign of King John. Sidney Painter. 1979. 30.50 (ISBN 0-405-10619-X). Ayer Co Pubs.

Reign of King Pym. Jack H. Hexter. (Historical Studies: No. 48). 1941. 15.00x (ISBN 0-674-75401-8). Harvard U Pr.

Reign of Law: A Tale of the Kentucky Hemp Fields. facsimile ed. James L. Allen. LC 77-164556. (American Fiction Reprint Ser). Repr. of 1900 ed. 31.00 (ISBN 0-8369-7032-2). Ayer Co Pubs.

Reign of Law (Buddhist Essays) Curuppumullage Jinarajadasa. LC 78-72902. Repr. of 1923 ed. 22.50 (ISBN 0-404-17314-4). AMS Pr.

Reign of Patti. Herman Klein. Ed. by Andrew Farkas. LC 76-29944. (Opera Biographies). (Illus.). 1977. Repr. of 1920 ed. lib. bdg. 42.00x (ISBN 0-405-09686-0). Ayer Co Pubs.

Reign of Patti. Herman Klein. LC 77-17874. (Music Reprint Ser.: 1978). (Illus.). 1978. Repr. of 1920 ed. lib. bdg. 55.00 (ISBN 0-306-77530-1). Da Capo.

Reign of Rabble: The St. Louis General Strike of 1877. David T. Burbank. LC 66-21658. 1966. 25.00x (ISBN 0-678-00186-3). Kelley.

Reign of Reality: A Fresh Start for the Earth. Joyce Marshall & Gene Marshall. LC 87-90621. (Illus.). 267p. 1987. 10.00 (ISBN 0-9611552-2-1). Realistic Living.

Reign of Relativity. Viscount Haldane. 434p. 1981. Repr. lib. bdg. 35.00 (ISBN 0-8495-2354-0). Arden Lib.

Reign of Stalin. Abdurakham Avtorkhanov. pseud. Tr. by L. J. Smith from Fr. LC 74-10074. (Russian Studies: Perspectives on the Revolution Ser). 256p. 1974. Repr. of 1953 ed. 23.00 (ISBN 0-88355-182-9). Hyperion Conn.

Reign of the Ayatollahs: Iran & the Islamic Revolution. Shaul Bakhash. LC 83-46078. 276p. 1986. pap. 10.95 (ISBN 0-465-06888-X, PL-5152). Basic.

Reign of the Fortunate King: Manuel First of Portugal. Elaine Sanceau. 184p. 1970. 21.50 (ISBN 0-208-00968-X, Archon). Shoe String.

Reign of the House of Rothschild. E. Corti. 75.00 (ISBN 0-87968-171-3). Gordon Pr.

Reign of the Phallus: Sexual Politics in Ancient Athens. Eva C. Keuls. LC 83-48793. (Illus.). 352p. 1985. 27.00i (ISBN 0-06-015300-8, HarpT). Har-Row.

Reign of the Phallus: Sexual Politics in Ancient Athens. Eva C. Keuls. LC 83-48793. (Illus.). 464p. 1986. pap. 14.95 (ISBN 0-06-091129-8, PL 1129, PL). Har-Row.

Reign of the Pirates. Archibald Hurd. 1979. Repr. of 1925 ed. lib. bdg. 35.00 (ISBN 0-8495-2347-8). Arden Lib.

Reign of the Pirates of British Origin: Twelve Buccaneers of the East & West Indies, 1670-1750. Archibald Hurd. 1977. pap. text ed. write for info. (ISBN 0-8490-2508-7). Gordon Pr.

Reign of the Theatrical Director: French Theatre, 1887-1924. Bettina Knapp. LC 87-51204. viii, 365p. 1988. 30.00x (ISBN 0-87875-358-3). Whitston Pub.

Reign of William Rufus & the Accession of Henry the First, 2 Vols. Edward A. Freeman. Repr. of 1882 ed. Set. 85.00 (ISBN 0-404-00620-5); 42.50 ea. Vol. 1 (ISBN 0-404-00621-3). Vol. 2 (ISBN 0-404-00622-1). AMS Pr.

Reign of Wizardry. Jack Williamson. (Illus.). 1979. Repr. of 1964 ed. 15.00 (ISBN 0-932096-01-8). Phantasia Pr.

Reign of Women in Eighteenth Century France. Vera Lee. (Illus.). 140p. 1976. 18.95x (ISBN 0-87083-990-X); pap. 11.95x (ISBN 0-87073-992-1). Schenkman Bks Inc.

Reigning Cats & Dogs. Ed. by Lois L. Kaufman. LC 87-63106. (Illus.). 64p. 1988. 5.95 (ISBN 0-88088-479-7). Peter Pauper.

Reigning in Life As a King. John Osteen. 140p. (Orig.). 1984. pap. 4.95 (ISBN 0-912631-01-5). J O Pubns.

REIKI - Universal Life Energy: Heals Body, Mind & Spirit - A Holistic Method Suitable for Self-Treatment & the Home, Professional Practice, Teleotherapeutics-Spiritual Healing. Bodo Baginski & Shalila Sharamon. Tr. by Chris Baker & Judith Harrison. (Illus.). 224p. (Orig.). 1988. 10.95x (ISBN 0-940795-02-7). LifeRhythm.

Reiki Factor. 2nd ed. Barbara Ray. 134p. 1985. pap. 10.00 (ISBN 0-933267-00-2). Radiance Assocs.

Reilgion En Chine. J. Edkins. 315p. 1882. 315.00x (Pub. by Han-Shan Tang Ltd). State Mutual Bk.

Reilly: Ace of Spies. TV tie-in ed. Robin B. Lockhart. 224p. 1984. pap. 4.95 (ISBN 0-14-006895-3). Penguin.

Reilly: The First Man. Robin B. Lockhart. 160p. 1987. pap. 3.95 (ISBN 0-14-010027-X). Penguin.

Reilly's Luck. Louis L'Amour. 224p. (Orig.). 1985. pap. 2.95 (ISBN 0-553-25305-0). Bantam.

Reima Pietila: Architecture, Context & Modernism. Malcolm Quantrill. (Illus.). 248p. 1985. pap. 29.95 (ISBN 0-8478-0635-9). Rizzoli Intl.

Reimagining America: A Theological Critique of the American Mythos & Biblical Hermeneutics. Charles Mabee. LC 84-27335. xvi, 156p. 1985. 13.95 (ISBN 0-86554-148-5, MUP/H139). Mercer Univ Pr.

Reimann Problem & Interaction of Waves in Gas Dynamics. Tong Chang & Ling Hsiao. (Pitman Monographs & Surveys in Pure & Applied Mathematics). 240p. 1988. 135.00 (ISBN 0-470-21014-1). Wiley.

Reimarus: Fragments. Ed. by Charles H. Talbert. Tr. by Ralph S. Fraser. (Reprints & Translations). 1985. pap. 13.95 (ISBN 0-89130-858-X, 00-07-07). Scholars Pr Ga.

Reimos en Serio. Charles Whitehead et al. 132p. 1984. pap. 6.50 (ISBN 0-88334-179-4). Ind Sch Pr.

Reina del Amor. Wilson Ferranti. (Pimienta Collection Ser). (Orig., Span.). 1977. pap. 1.00 (ISBN 0-88473-269-X). Fiesta Pub.

Reina the Galgo. Nicole De Messieres. 224p. (gr. 7 up). 1981. 9.95 (ISBN 0-525-66749-0). Lodestar Bks.

Reincarnation. Swami Abhedananda. 4.95 (ISBN 0-87481-604-1). Vedanta Pr.

Reincarnation. 11th ed. Annie Besant. 1975. 5.25 (ISBN 0-8356-7019-8). Theos Pub Hse.

Reincarnation. George B. Brownell. 153p. 1981. pap. 9.00 (ISBN 0-89540-107-X, SB-107). Sun Pub.

Reincarnation. David C. Murray. 288p. (Orig.). 1988. pap. 14.95 (ISBN 1-85327-013-X, Pub. by Prism Pr). Avery Pub.

Reincarnation. Katherine Tingley. 72p. 1981. pap. 6.00 (ISBN 0-89540-111-8, SB-111). Sun Pub.

Reincarnation. Leoline L. Wright. LC 74-18350. pap. 3.25 (ISBN 0-8356-0453-5, Quest). Theos Pub Hse.

Reincarnation: A Christian Critique of a New Age Doctrine. 2nd. rev. ed. Mark Albrecht. 135p. (Orig.). 1987. pap. 5.95 (ISBN 0-317-59754-X). Inter-Varsity.

Reincarnation: A Hope of the World. Irving S. Cooper. LC 79-11475. 1979. pap. 3.95 (ISBN 0-8356-0528-0, Quest). Theos Pub Hse.

Reincarnation: A Lost Chord in Modern Thought. Leoline L. Wright et al. Ed. by Emmett Small & Helen Todd. (Theosophical Manual). 122p. 1975. pap. 3.25. Point Loma Pub.

Reincarnation: A New Horizon in Science, Religion & Society. Sylvia Cranston & Carey Williams. 1984. 16.95 (ISBN 0-517-55496-8, Harmony). Crown.

Reincarnation: An East-West Anthology. Joseph Head & S. L. Cranston. LC 68-146. 1968. pap. 5.50 (ISBN 0-8356-0035-1, Quest). Theos Pub Hse.

Reincarnation & Christianity. Robert A. Morey. LC 80-24497. 60p. 1980. pap. 2.95 (ISBN 0-87123-493-9, 210493). Bethany Hse.

Reincarnation & Immortality. 2nd ed. Swami Paramananda. 1961. 4.50 (ISBN 0-911564-05-5). Vedanta Ctr.

Reincarnation & Immortality. 3rd ed. Rudolf Steiner. LC 77-130817. 224p. 1970. pap. 5.00 (ISBN 0-89345-221-1, Steinerbks). Garber Comm.

Reincarnation & Karma: Their Significance in Modern Culture. Rudolf Steiner. Tr. by D. S. Osmond & Charles Davy. 95p. (Ger.). 1977. pap. 6.50 (ISBN 0-919924-06-9, Pub. by Steiner Book Centre Canada). Anthroposophic.

Reincarnation & Law of Karma. William W. Atkinson. 8.00 (ISBN 0-911662-26-X). Yoga.

Reincarnation & Other Essays. Eugen Kolisko. 1979. Repr. of 1940 ed. 9.50 (ISBN 0-906492-14-9, Pub. by Kolisko Archives). St George Bk Serv.

Reincarnation & Translation. Jim Lewis. 31p. (Orig.). 1981. pap. 3.00 (ISBN 0-942482-02-6). Unity Church Denver.

Reincarnation As a Christian Hope. Geddes MacGregor. LC 81-8013. (Library of Philosophy & Religion). 174p. 1982. 28.50x (ISBN 0-389-20220-7). B&N Imports.

Reincarnation: Cycle of Opportunity. Robert G. Chaney. LC 84-72387. (Adventures in Esoteric Learning Ser.). (Illus.). 56p. 1984. pap. 4.25. Astara.

Reincarnation Explained. Chris Butler. LC 83-61000. 288p. 1984. 12.95 (ISBN 0-88187-000-5). Science Identity.

Reincarnation Explored. John Algeo. LC 87-40130. 166p. (Orig.). 1987. pap. 6.95 (ISBN 0-8356-0624-4, Quest). Theos Pub Hse.

Reincarnation, Fact or Fallacy. rev. ed. Geoffrey Hodson. LC 67-4405. 1967. pap. 2.95 (ISBN 0-8356-0046-7, Quest). Theos Pub Hse.

Reincarnation Five Keys to Past Lives. J. H. Brennan. (Paths to Inner Power Ser.). 1981. pap. 3.50 (ISBN 0-85030-275-7, Pub. by Thorsons UK). Weiser.

Reincarnation for the Christian. 2nd ed. Quincy Howe, Jr. LC 87-40132. 114p. 1987. pap. 5.75 (ISBN 0-8356-0626-0, Quest). Theos Pub Hse.

Reincarnation: Illusion or Reality. Edmond Robillard. LC 82-1638. 182p. (Orig.). 1982. pap. 5.95 (ISBN 0-8189-0432-1). Alba.

Reincarnation in Christianity. Geddes MacGregor. LC 77-20925. (Orig.). 1978. 9.75 (ISBN 0-8356-0504-3). Theos Pub Hse.

Reincarnation, Key to Immortality. Marcia Moore & Mark Douglas. LC 67-19603. 1968. 10.00 (ISBN 0-912240-02-4). Arcane Pubns.

Reincarnation of Bridgett. Joseph F. Coscia. 139p. 1981. 6.00 (ISBN 0-682-49699-5). Exposition-Phoenix.

Reincarnation of John Wilkes Booth. Dell Leonardi. LC 74-27952. 1975. 6.95 (ISBN 0-8159-6716-0). Devin.

Reincarnation of John Wilkes Booth: A Study in Hypnotic Regression. Dell Leonardi. LC 74-27952. 1975. pap. 45.00 (ISBN 0-317-08182-9, 2022710). Bks Demand UMI.

Reincarnation of Reece Erikson. Raymond Obstfeld. 320p. 1988. pap. 3.95 (ISBN 0-8125-8658-1). Tor Bks.

Reincarnation of Robert Macready. Robert Macready. 336p. (Orig.). 1981. pap. 2.75 (ISBN 0-89083-703-1). Zebra.

Reincarnation Sensation. Norman L. Geisler & J. Yutaka Amano. 224p. 1986. pap. 6.95 (ISBN 0-8423-5404-2). Tyndale.

Reincarnation: The Cycle of Necessity. Manly P. Hall. 1978. pap. 7.95 (ISBN 0-89314-387-1). Philos Res.

Reincarnation: the Phoenix Fire Mystery. Joseph Head & S. L. Cranston. 1977. 10.95 (ISBN 0-517-52893-2). Crown.

Reincarnation: The Phoenix Fire Mystery. Ed. by Joseph Head & S. L. Cranston. 1986. pap. 12.95 (ISBN 0-517-56101-8, Harmony). Crown.

Reincarnation Through the Zodiac. Joan Hodgson. LC 79-444. (Illus.). 137p. 1979. pap. 6.50 (ISBN 0-916360-11-3). CRCS Pubns CA.

Reincarnation Unnecessary. Violet M. Shelley. 1979. pap. 5.95 (ISBN 0-87604-112-8). ARE Pr.

Reincarnation vs. Resurrection. John Snyder. (Orig.). 1984. pap. 4.95 (ISBN 0-8024-0321-2). Moody.

Reincarnations. Richard Kostelanetz. 1981. pap. 5.00 (ISBN 0-686-84602-8); signed 50.00 (ISBN 0-686-84603-6). Future Pr.

Reindeer & Caribou. facs. ed. C. C. Georgeson. (Shorey Historical Ser.). (Illus.). 24p. pap. 2.95 (ISBN 0-8466-0159-1, S159). Shorey.

Reindeer & Caribou Hunters: An Archaeological Study. Arthur E. Spiess. LC 79-17697. (Studies in Archaeology Ser.). 1979. 24.95 (ISBN 0-12-657950-4). Acad Pr.

Reindeer & Its Domestication. Berthold Laufer. LC 18-12075. (Amer Anthro Assn Memoirs). 1917. pap. 15.00 (ISBN 0-527-00517-7). Kraus Repr.

Reindeer & the Easter Bunny. Jim Olson. Ed. by Jane Van Vleck & Sally Olson. (Illus.). 18p. (Orig.). (gr. 1-4). 1981. pap. 3.95 (ISBN 0-943806-00-3). Neahtawanta Pr.

Reindeer, Dogs, & Snow-Shoes: A Journal of Siberian Travel & Explorations Made in the Years 1865, 1866 & 1867. Richard J. Bush. LC 72-115514. (Russia Observed Ser., No. 1). (Illus.). 1970. Repr. of 1871 ed. 26.50 (ISBN 0-405-03011-8). Ayer Co Pubs.

Reindeer Moon. Elizabeth M. Thomas. 1987. 17.95 (ISBN 0-395-42112-8). HM.

Reindeer Moon. Elizabeth M. Thomas. 1988. pap. 4.50 (ISBN 0-671-64886-1). PB.

Reindeer on South Georgia: The Ecology of an Introduced Population. N. Leader-Williams. (Studies in Polar Research). (Illus.). 275p. Date not set. price not set (ISBN 0-521-24271-1). Cambridge U Pr.

Reindeer People. Megan Lindholm. 1988. pap. 3.50 (ISBN 0-441-71233-9). Ace Bks.

Reindeer Round-Up: A Merry Christmas at the North Pole. Walt Disney Company Staff. (Illus.). 26p. (ps up). 1988. 19.95 (ISBN 1-55578-313-9). Worlds Wonder.

Reindeer's Shoe & Other Stories. Karle B. Wilson. LC 88-2292. (Illus.). 112p. (ps-12). 1988. casebound 17.95 (ISBN 0-936650-07-9). E C Temple.

Reindustrialization & Technology. Roy R. Rothwell & Walter Zegveld. 300p. (Orig.). 1985. 35.00 (ISBN 0-87332-330-0); pap. 15.95 (ISBN 0-87332-331-9). M E Sharpe.

Reindustrialization: Implication for U. S. Industrial Policy. Robert J. Thornton. LC 84-47777. (Contemporary Studies in Economic & Financial Analysis: Vol. 46). 160p. 1984. 52.50 (ISBN 0-89232-485-6). Jai Pr.

Reindustrialization: Implications for Voc Ed. James A. Leach. 50p. 1982. 4.95 (ISBN 0-318-22187-X, IN233). Natl Ctr Res Voc Ed.

Reindustrialization of America. Business Week Magazine Staff. 1982. text ed. 23.50 (ISBN 0-07-009324-5). McGraw.

Reindustrialization of America. The Business Week Team Staff. pap. cancelled (ISBN 0-671-45617-2). WSP.

Reindustrialization Policy: Implications for Large Cities. 130p. 1981. 18.00 (ISBN 0-318-17321-2, IB/81-908). Pub Tech Inc.

Reindustrialization: The Menace Behind the Promise. Sam Marcy. 56p. 1981. pap. 2.00 (ISBN 0-89567-045-3). World View Forum.

Reindustrializing New York State: Strategies, Implications, Challenges. Ed. by Morton Schoolman & Alvin Magid. LC 85-14771. 448p. 1986. 59.50 (ISBN 0-88706-177-X); pap. 19.95x (ISBN 0-88706-178-8). State U NY Pr.

Reine Land: Zur Begegnung von Amida-Buddhismus und Christentum. Christiane Langer-Kaneko. (Zeitschrift fur Religions- und Geistesgeschichte, Beiheft Ser.: Vol. 29). xii, 194p. 1986. 31.75 (ISBN 90-04-07786-3, Pub. by E J Brill). Heinman.

Reine Margot see Oeuvres Illustrees.

Reine Morte. Henry De Montherlant. (Folio Ser.: No. 12). 1957. 5.95 (ISBN 0-685-11525-9). Schoenhof.

Reine Morte. Henry De Montherlant. 1957. write for info. French & Eur.

Reines de la France. Jean Cocteau. 168p. 1952. 18.95 (ISBN 0-686-54557-5). French & Eur.

Reinforced & Prestressed Concrete. 3rd ed. Kong & Evans. 1987. pap. 41.95 (ISBN 0-278-00016-9). Van Nos Reinhold.

Reinforced & Prestressed Concrete. 3rd ed. Kong & Evans. 41.95 (ISBN 0-317-64267-7). Van Nos Reinhold.

Reinforced & Prestressed Masonry: Proceedings of a Conference Sponsored by the Institution of Civil Engineers & the Institution of Structural Engineers. 167p. 1982. 30.00 (ISBN 0-7277-0161-4, Pub. by T Telford UK). Am Soc Civil Eng.

Reinforced Concrete. E. E. Sigalov & S. G. Strongin. Tr. by S. Kline. (Illus.). 396p. 1963. 115.00 (ISBN 0-677-20500-7). Gordon & Breach.

Reinforced Concrete: A Fundamental Approach. Edward G. Nawy. (Illus.). 688p. 1985. text ed. write for info. (ISBN 0-13-771643-5). P-H.

Reinforced Concrete Chimneys & Towers. 2nd ed. G. M. Pinford. (Viewpoint Ser.). (Illus.). 176p. 1985. text ed. 45.00x (ISBN 0-86310-016-3, Pub. by Viewpoint). Scholium Intl.

Reinforced Concrete Columns. American Concrete Institute Staff. LC 75-8454. (American Concrete Institute Publication Ser: SP-50). (Illus.). pap. 80.00 (ISBN 0-317-10048-3, 2022761). Bks Demand UMI.

Reinforced Concrete Design. Everard & J. L. Tanner. (Schaum Outline Ser.). 1966. pap. text ed. 11.50 (ISBN 0-07-019770-9). McGraw.

Rejoice in Me: A Pocket Guide to Daily Scriptural Prayer. David Rosage. 256p. 1986. pocket-size 3.95 (ISBN 0-89283-298-3). Servant.
Rejoice in Me: A Pocket Guide to Daily Spritual Prayer. David Rosage. 256p. 1987. 7.95 (ISBN 0-89283-364-5). Servant.
Rejoice in the Lord. James D. Craig. 32p. 1981. pap. 2.49 (ISBN 0-88151-018-1). Lay Leadership.
Rejoice in the Lord: A Hymn Companion to the Scriptures. The Reformed Church in America. Ed. by Erik Routley. 608p. 1985. 12.95x (ISBN 0-8028-9009-1). Eerdmans.
Rejoice! Jesus Is Alive! Pat Floyd. (Little Lamb Christian Storybooks Ser.). (Illus.). 24p. (gr. k-2). 1987. pap. 6.95 (ISBN 0-939697-39-4). Graded Pr.
Rejoice with Jerusalem. Ed. by Dov P. Elkins. 1972. pap. 1.95 (ISBN 0-87677-065-0). Prayer BK.
Rejoice, You're a Sunday School Teacher. John T. Sisemore. LC 76-20053. 1977. 7.95 (ISBN 0-8054-5147-1). Broadman.
Rejoicing Heart. Joyce M. Smith. 1979. pap. 2.95 (ISBN 0-8423-5418-2). Tyndale.
Rejoicings. Gerald Stern. LC 83-63291. 80p. 1984. 13.95 (ISBN 0-915371-00-6); pap. 6.95 (ISBN 0-915371-01-4). Metro Bk Co.
Rejuvenating Introductory Courses. Ed. by Karen I. Spear. LC 84-82086. (Teaching & Learning Ser.: No. 20). (Orig.). 1984. pap. text ed. 12.95x (ISBN 0-87589-793-2). Jossey-Bass.
Rejuvenating the Body Through Fasting with Spirulina Plankton. 2nd ed. Christopher Hills. (Illus.). 64p. 1980. pap. text ed. 2.50 (ISBN 0-916438-35-X). Univ of Trees.
Rejuvenation. Linda Clark. 1978. 12.95 (ISBN 0-8159-6718-7). Devin.
Rejuvenation. Horst Rechelbacher. (Illus.). 224p. 1987. pap. 10.95 (ISBN 0-89281-248-6). Inner Tradit.
Rejuvenation Strategy. Rene Cailliet & Leonard Gross. 320p. (Orig.). Date not set. pap. 4.50 (ISBN 0-671-65249-4). PB.
Rekindled. Pat Williams et al. 160p. 1985. 10.95 (ISBN 0-8007-1417-2). Revell.
Rekindling Desire: Bringing Your Sexual Relationship to Life. Warwick Williams. 191p. 1988. pap. 10.95 (ISBN 0-934986-47-9). New Harbinger.
Rekindling Development: Multinational Firms & Third World Debt. Ed. by Lee A. Tavis. LC 87-40619. 352p. 1988. text ed. 26.95x (ISBN 0-268-01634-8). U of Notre Dame Pr.
Rekindling the Flame: Strategies for a Vital United Methodism. William H. Willimon & Robert L. Wilson. 128p. 1987. 9.95 (ISBN 0-687-35932-5). Abingdon.
Relacion de Acuerdos Bilaterales: OEA Ser. B/II 1, 1949-1980. OAS General Secretariat for Legal Affairs. (Ser. Sobre Tratados: No. 59). 74p. (Span., Eng., Fr. & Port.). 1980. 4.00 (ISBN 0-8270-1283-7). OAS.
Relacion de las Cosas de Yucatan. D. De Landa. Tr. by A. Tozzer. (Harvard University Peabody Museum of Archaeology & Ethnology Papers). Repr. of 1941 ed. 72.00 (ISBN 0-527-01245-9). Kraus Repr.
Relacion del Viaje por el Mar del Sur. Amadeo Frezier. (Ayacucho Library Collection Ser.: Vol.99). (Span.). 1982. 25.00 (ISBN 0-317-56718-7, Pub. by Biblioteca Ayacucho); pap. 12.50 (ISBN 0-317-56719-5, Pub. by Biblioteca Ayacucho). Humanities.
Relacion Hospedante-Parasito Mecanismo De Patogenicidad De los Microorganismos. Manuel R. Leiva. (Serie Biologia: No. 14). 91p. 1981. pap. 3.50 (ISBN 0-8270-1322-1). OAS.
Relacion o Naugragios de Alvar Nunez Cabeza de Vaca. Ed. by Martin A Favata & Jose B. Fernandez. 27.50 (ISBN 0-916379-35-3). Scripta.
Relacion Perfecta. Swami Muktananda. LC 81-84261. 218p. 1982. pap. 7.00 (ISBN 0-914602-84-5). SYDA Found.
Relaciones. Geronimo Zarate Salmeron. LC 66-27660. 122p. 1982. lib. bdg. 29.95x (ISBN 0-89370-728-7). Borgo Pr.
Relaciones Humanas. Rosemary T. Fruehling. 141p. 1982. text ed. 12.96 (ISBN 0-07-022540-0). McGraw.
Relaciones Humanas en Prevencion de Accidentes. 383p. 35.00 (ISBN 0-318-17995-4). Inter-Am Safety.
Relais & Chateaux, 1988. 200p. (Orig.). 1988. pap. 6.95 (ISBN 0-317-66607-X). Hunter Pub NY.
Relapse. John Vanbrugh. Ed. by Bernard Harris. (New Mermaid Ser.). 1976. pap. 2.95x (ISBN 0-393-90032-0). Norton.
Relapse. John Vanbrugh. Ed. by Curt A. Zimansky. LC 70-107279. (Regents Restoration Drama Ser.). (Illus.). 183p. pap. 47.60 (2029927). Bks Demand UMI.
Relapse see Restoration Plays.
Relapse: A Guide to Successful Recovery. Dennis C. Daley. Ed. by Lee M. Joiner. LC 87-24385. 48p. (Orig.). 1987. pap. text ed. 3.95 (ISBN 0-943519-02-0, B1902). Human Servs Inst.
Relapse for Eating Disorder Sufferers. Judi Hollis. 28p. (Orig.). 1985. pap. 1.25 (ISBN 0-89486-298-7). Hazelden.
Relapse Prevention: Maintenance Strategies in the Treatment of Addiction. Ed. by G. Alan Marlatt & Judith R. Gordon. LC 84-19319. (Guilford Clinical Psychology & Psychotherapy Ser.). 558p. 1985. text ed. 39.50 (ISBN 0-89862-009-0). Guilford Pr.
Relapse Prevention: Treatment Alternatives & Counseling Aids. Dennis C. Daley. Ed. by Lee M. Joiner. LC 88-873. 144p. (Orig.). 1988. pap. text ed. write for info. (ISBN 0-943519-06-3, B1906). Human Servs Inst.
Relapse Prevention Workbook: For Recovering Alcoholics & Drug Dependent Persons. Dennis C. Daley. 32p. (Orig.). 1986. wkbk. pkg. of 4 11.50 (ISBN 0-918452-88-0). Learning Pubns.
Related Beverages. R. J. Clarke & R. Macrae. (Coffee Ser.: Vol. 5). 1987. 63.00 (ISBN 1-85166-103-4). Elsevier.
Related Mathematics for Carpenters. 2nd ed. P. Reband. (Illus.). 218p. 1973. pap. 8.96 (ISBN 0-8269-2332-1). Am Technical.
Related Sermons see Commentary on the Lord's Sermon on the Mount with Seventeen Related Sermons.
Related Services for Handicapped Children. Ed. by Morton M. Esterson & Linda F. Bluth. LC 86-14804. 176p. (Orig.). 1986. pap. text ed. 24.50 (ISBN 0-316-10045-5, 100455). College-Hill.
Related Technical Subjects (Biological & Chemical) Chairman - Sr. H.S. Jack Rudman. (Teachers License Examination Ser.: CH-20). (Cloth bdg. avail. on request). pap. 15.95 (ISBN 0-8373-8170-3). Natl Learning.
Related Technical Subjects (Biological & Chemical) Sr. H.S. Jack Rudman. (Teachers License Examination Ser.: T-50). (Cloth bdg. avail. on request). pap. 13.95 (ISBN 0-8373-8050-2). Natl Learning.
Related Technical Subjects (Mechanical, Structural, Electrical) Chairman - Sr. H.S. Jack Rudman. (Teachers License Examination Ser.: CH-21). (Cloth bdg. avail. on request). pap. 15.95 (ISBN 0-8373-8171-1). Natl Learning.
Related Technical Subjects (Mechanical, Structural, Electrical) Sr. H.S. Jack Rudman. (Teachers License Examination Ser.: T-51). (Cloth bdg. avail. on request). pap. 13.95 (ISBN 0-8373-8051-0). Natl Learning.
Relatedness: Essays in Metaphysics & Theology. Harold H. Oliver. LC 84-1152. xvi, 178p. 1984. 14.50 (ISBN 0-86554-141-8, MUP/H132). Mercer Univ Pr.
Relating. Judy Bisignano. 64p. (gr. 3-8). 1985. wkbk. 6.95 (ISBN 0-86653-331-1). Good Apple.
Relating: An Astrological Guide to Living with Others on a Small Planet. Liz Greene. LC 83-145084. (Orig.). 1978. pap. 8.95 (ISBN 0-87728-418-0). Weiser.
Relating & Interacting: An Introduction to Interpersonal Communication. Ray Ross & Mark Ross. (Illus.). 320p. 1981. pap. text ed. write for info. (ISBN 0-13-771923-X). P-H.
Relating: Reflections of a Psychologist. Alan Rauchway. (Illus.). 116p. 1985. pap. 8.95 (ISBN 0-89529-290-4). Avery Pub.
Relating to Readers in the 'Eighties. Clark, Martire & Bartolomeo, Inc. Staff. 54p. Date not set. 6.00. Am News Pubs.
Relation & Consciousness. Eric Toms. 56p. (Orig.). 1984. pap. 7.50 (ISBN 0-7073-0435-0, Pub. by Scot Acad Pr). Longwood Pub Group.
Relation Between Association & the Higher Mental Processes. John W. Tilton. LC 71-177706. (Columbia University. Teachers College. Contributions to Education: No. 218). Repr. of 1926 ed. 22.50 (ISBN 0-404-55218-8). AMS Pr.
Relation Between Early Language Habits & Early Habits of Conduct Control. Ethel M. Waring. LC 72-177662. (Columbia University. Teachers College. Contributions to Education: No. 260). Repr. of 1927 ed. 22.50 (ISBN 0-404-55260-9). AMS Pr.
Relation Between Final Demand & Income Distribution. C. Grootaert. (Lecture Notes in Economics & Mathematical Systems Ser.: Vol. 217). 105p. 1983. pap. 12.00 (ISBN 0-387-12307-5). Springer-Verlag.
Relation Between Grade School Record & High School Achievement: A Study of the Diagnostic Value of Individual Record Cards. Clay C. Ross. LC 70-177211. (Columbia University. Teachers College. Contributions to Education: No. 166). Repr. of 1925 ed. 22.50 (ISBN 0-404-55166-1). AMS Pr.
Relation Between Laboratory & Space Plasmas. K. Kikuchi. 1982. 58.00 (ISBN 90-277-1248-4, Pub. by Reidel Holland). Kluwer Academic.
Relation Between Linguistic Structure & Associative Interference in Artificial Linguistic Material. Dael L. Wolfle. (LM). 1932. pap. 16.00 (ISBN 0-527-00815-X). Kraus Repr.
Relation Between Major World Problems & Systems Learning: Proceedings of the Society for General Systems Research, 1983, Vols. 1 & 2. George E. Lasker. 800p. 1983. Set. pap. text ed. 66.00x (ISBN 0-914105-28-0). Intersystems Pubns.
Relation Between Morality & Intellect: A Compendium of Evidence Contributed by Psychology, Criminology, & Sociology. Clara Cooper. LC 71-176638. (Columbia University. Teachers College. Contributions to Education: No. 607). Repr. of 1935 ed. 22.50 (ISBN 0-404-55607-8). AMS Pr.
Relation Between Physical & Mental Illness: The Physical Status of Psychiatric Patients at a Multiphasic Screening Survey. Ed. by Michael R. Eastwood. LC 74-76877. (Clarke Institute of Psychiatry, Monograph Ser.: No. 4). pap. 33.30 (ISBN 0-317-26915-1, 2023611). Bks Demand UMI.
Relation Between the Lord of a Mannor & the Coppy-Holder His Tenent, Etc. Charles Calthorpe. LC 74-38163. (English Experience Ser.: No. 440). 100p. 1972. Repr. of 1635 ed. 15.00 (ISBN 90-221-0440-0). Walter J Johnson.
Relation des Voyages a la Cote Occidentale d'Afrique d'Alvise de Ca' da Mosto 1455-1457. Charles M. Schefer. (Fr.). 1895. 18.00 (ISBN 0-8115-3077-9). Kraus Repr.
Relation Modules of Finite Groups. Karl W. Gruenberg. LC 76-3645. (CBMS Regional Conference Ser. in Mathematics: Vol. 25). 82p. 1976. pap. 17.00 (ISBN 0-8218-1675-6, CBMS-25). Am Math.
Relation of a Voyage to Guiana by Robert Harcourt. Ed. by Charles Harris. (Hakluyt Society Works Ser.: No. 2, Vol. 60). (Illus.). Repr. of 1926 ed. 25.00 (ISBN 0-8115-0363-1). Kraus Repr.
Relation of Accelerated Normal & Retarded Puberty to the Height & Weight of School Children. Herman G. Richard. (SRCD M). 1937. pap. 15.00 (ISBN 0-527-01494-X). Kraus Repr.
Relation of Aging to Immunity. R. L. Walford et al. (Illus.). 220p. 1973. text ed. 29.75x (ISBN 0-8422-7106-6). Irvington.
Relation of Apparitions of Spirits: In the Principality of Wales. 2nd ed. Edmund Jones. LC 77-87687. Repr. of 1780 ed. 18.50 (ISBN 0-404-16485-4). AMS Pr.
Relation of Biology to Astronomy. Fred Hoyle. (Illus.). 26p. (Orig.). 1980. pap. 2.25 (ISBN 0-906449-20-0, Pub. by UC Cardiff Pr). Longwood Pub Group.
Relation of Certain Anomalies of Vision & Lateral Dominance to Reading Disability. Philip W. Johnston. (SRCD M). 1942. 13.00 (ISBN 0-527-01523-7). Kraus Repr.
Relation of Certain Formal Attributes of Siblings to Attitudes Held Toward Each Other & Toward Their Parents. H. L. Koch. (SRCD M Ser.). 1960. 16.00 (ISBN 0-527-01586-5). Kraus Repr.
Relation of Coal Properties to Gasification Reactivity. J. L. Johnson & Institute of Gas Technology. 270p. 1975. softcover 8.50 (ISBN 0-318-12688-5, M60677). Am Gas Assn.
Relation of Corbordism to K-Theories. Pierre E. Conner & E. E. Floyd. (Lecture Notes in Mathematics: Vol. 28). 1966. pap. 10.70 (ISBN 0-387-03610-5). Springer-Verlag.
Relation of Custom to Law. Gilbert T. Sadler. (Legal Reprint Ser.). viii, 86p. 1986. Repr. of 1919 ed. lib. bdg. 20.00x (ISBN 0-8377-2610-7). Rothman.
Relation of Diu Krone to La Mule Sanz Frain. Lawrence L. Boll. LC 77-140018. (Catholic University Studies in German Ser.: No. 2). Repr. of 1929 ed. 18.00 (ISBN 0-404-50222-9). AMS Pr.
Relation of Educational Plans to Economic & Social Planning. Raymond Poignant. (Fundamentals of Educational Planning: No. 2). (Illus.). 51p. (2nd Printing 1982). 1967. pap. 5.00 (ISBN 92-803-1007-0, U543, UNESCO). UNIPUB.
Relation of Engineering Mechanics Research to the Practice of Civil Engineering: Engineering Mechanics Division Specialty Conference, Washington, D.C., October 12-14, 1966. American Society of Civil Engineers, Engineering Mechanics Division Staff. LC 67-1660. (Illus.). pap. 160.00 (ISBN 0-317-11018-7, 2004904). Bks Demand UMI.
Relation of Hormones to Development: Proceedings, Vol. 10. Cold Spring Harbor Symposia on Quantitative Biology Staff. Repr. of 1942 ed. 27.00 (ISBN 0-384-50250-4). Johnson Repr.
Relation of Language Difficulty to Intelligence & School Retardation in a Group of Spanish-Speaking Children. Zella K. Flores. LC 74-833371. 1975. Repr. of 1926 ed. soft bdg. 10.95 (ISBN 0-88247-355-7). R & E Pubs.
Relation of Literature to Life. Charles D. Warner. 15.25 (ISBN 0-8369-7237-6, 8036). Ayer Co Pubs.
Relation of Maryland, 2 pts. LC 76-57399. (English Experience Ser.: No. 815). 1977. Repr. of 1635 ed. lib. bdg. 20.00 (ISBN 90-221-0815-5). Walter J Johnson.
Relation of Moliere to the Restoration Comedy. John Wilcox. LC 64-14719. 1938. 20.00 (ISBN 0-405-09078-1). Ayer Co Pubs.
Relation of My Imprisonment. Russell Banks. LC 83-17873. (Contemporary Literature Ser.: No. 19). 128p. 1984. 12.95 (ISBN 0-940650-25-8); ltd. signed edition 20.00 (ISBN 0-940650-24-X). Sun & Moon CA.
Relation of My Imprisonment. Russell Banks. 1987. pap. 3.95 (ISBN 0-345-33076-5). Ballantine.
Relation of Nature to Man in Aboriginal America. Clark Wissler. LC 75-160133. Repr. of 1926 ed. 22.00 (ISBN 0-404-07005-1). AMS Pr.
Relation of Ore Deposition to Doming in the North American Cordillera. LC 60-2730. (Geological Society of America, Memoir Ser.: No. 77). pap. 32.80 (ISBN 0-317-10779-8, 2007960). Bks Demand UMI.
Relation of Parental Authority to Children's Behavior & Attitudes. Marian J. Yarrow. Repr. of 1946 ed. lib. bdg. 18.75x (ISBN 0-8371-2701-7, YAPA). Greenwood.
Relation of Proceedings Concerning the Affairs of the Kirk of Scotland. John L. Rothes. LC 79-174966. (Bannatyne Club, Edinburgh. Publications: No. 37). Repr. of 1830 ed. 28.00 (ISBN 0-404-52743-4). AMS Pr.
Relation of Ralph Waldo Emerson to Public Affairs. Raymer Mc Quiston. LC 73-15040. 1923. Repr. lib. bdg. 19.00 (ISBN 0-8414-6072-8). Folcroft.
Relation of Religion to Civil Government in the United States. Isaac J. Cornelison. LC 75-107409. (Civil Liberties in American History Ser). 1970. Repr. of 1895 ed. lib. bdg. 45.00 (ISBN 0-306-71890-1). Da Capo.
Relation of Seneca False Face Masks to Seneca & Ontario Archeology. Zena P. Mathews. LC 77-94707. (Outstanding Dissertations in the Fine Arts Ser.). 1978. lib. bdg. 44.00x (ISBN 0-8240-3239-X). Garland Pub.
Relation of Sensation to Other Categories in Contemporary Psychology. Carl Rahn. Bd. with Effect of Adaptation on the Temperature Difference. E. Abbott. Repr. of 1913 ed; No. 6. Iowa University Studies in Psychology. C. E. Seashore. Repr. of 1914 ed; Exp'l & Introspective Study of the Human Learning Process in the Maze. F. A. Perrin. Repr. of 1914 ed; On the Psychophysiology of a Prolonged Past. Herbert S. Langfeld. Repr. of 1914 ed. (Psychology Monographs General & Applied: Vol. 16). pap. 36.00 (ISBN 0-8115-1415-3). Kraus Repr.
Relation of Shell Form to Life Habits of the Bivalvia (Mollusca) Steven M. Stanley. LC 71-111441. (Geological Society of America Memoir Ser.: No. 125). pap. 77.50 (ISBN 0-317-28382-0, 2025463). Bks Demand UMI.
Relation of Social, Economic, & Personal Characteristics to Reading Ability. Margaret R. Ladd. LC 78-176968. (Columbia University. Teachers College. Contributions to Education: No. 582). Repr. of 1933 ed. 22.50 (ISBN 0-404-55582-9). AMS Pr.
Relation of Some Yeares Travaile Begunne Anno 1626, into Afrique & the Greater Asia. Sir Thomas Herbert. LC 76-25706. (English Experience Ser.: No. 349). 1971. Repr. of 1634 ed. 50.00 (ISBN 90-221-0349-8). Walter J Johnson.
Relation of Supervision & Other Factors to Certain Phases of Musical Achievement in the Rural Schools of Utah. Nels W. Christiansen. LC 79-176699. (Columbia University. Teachers College. Contributions to Education: No. 934). Repr. of 1948 ed. 22.50 (ISBN 0-404-55934-4). AMS Pr.
Relation of the Bible to Learning. E. H. Runner. 1974. pap. 4.95 (ISBN 0-686-11988-6). Wedge Pub.
Relation of the Discovery & Conquest of the Kingdoms of Peru, 2 Vols. in 1. P. Pizarro. Tr. by Philip A. Means. (Cortez Society). Repr. of 1921 ed. 45.00 (ISBN 0-527-19724-6). Kraus Repr.
Relation of the Discovery & Conquest of the Kingdoms of Peru. Pedro Pizarro. LC 77-88577. 1977. Repr. of 1917 ed. lib. bdg. 45.00 (ISBN 0-89341-283-X). Longwood Pub Group.
Relation of the Executive Power to Legislation. Henry C. Black. LC 73-19130. (Politics & People Ser.). 192p. 1974. Repr. 12.00x (ISBN 0-405-05855-1). Ayer Co Pubs.
Relation of the Expongnable Attempt & Conquest of the Ylande of Tercera. Alvaro De Bacan. LC 76-57352. (English Experience Ser.: No. 772). 1977. Repr. of 1584 ed. lib. bdg. 20.00 (ISBN 90-221-0772-8). Walter J Johnson.
Relation of the Judiciary to the Constitution. William M. Meigs. LC 73-124896. (American Constitutional & Legal History Ser). 1971. Repr. of 1919 ed. lib. bdg. 35.00 (ISBN 0-306-71988-6). Da Capo.
Relation of the Lord De-la-Warre, Lord Governour of the Colonie Planted in Virginea. Thomas West. LC 77-25508. (English Experience Ser.: No. 249). 20p. 1970. Repr. of 1611 ed. 7.00 (ISBN 90-221-0249-1). Walter J Johnson.
Relation of the People to the Land in Southern Iraq. Fuad Baali. LC 66-64914. (University of Florida Social Sciences Monographs: No. 31). 1966. pap. 5.50x (ISBN 0-8130-0010-6). U Presses Fla.
Relation of the Rate of Response to Intelligence see Influence of Intuition in the Acquisition of Skill.
Relation of the Second Voyage to Guiana. Lawrence Keymis. LC 76-6258. (No. 65). 48p. 1968. Repr. of 1596 ed. 11.50 (ISBN 90-221-0065-0). Walter J Johnson.

Relation of the State to Private Education in Norway: A Study of the Historical Development of State Regulations Governing the Various Types of Private Education in Norway. Emma Arent. LC 74-176522. (Columbia University. Teachers College. Contributions to Education: No. 235). Repr. of 1926 ed. 22.50 (ISBN 0-404-55235-8). AMS Pr.

Relation of the Successful Beginnings of the Lord Baltimore's Plantation in Mary-Land. Cecil Calvert & Baron Baltimore. LC 77-6864. (English Experience Ser.: No. 857). 1977. Repr. of 1634 ed. lib. bdg. 3.50 (ISBN 90-221-0857-0). Walter J Johnson.

Relation of the Swedish-American Newspaper to the Assimilation of Swedish Immigrants. Albert F. Schersten. LC 36-19550. (Augustana College Library Publication Ser.: No. 15). 102p. 1935. pap. 3.00x (ISBN 0-910182-10-8). Augustana Coll.

Relation of the Synodical Month & Eclipses to the Maya Correlation Problem see Studies in Middle America.

Relation of the Teacher's Education to Her Effectiveness. C. L. Jacobs. LC 79-176901. (Columbia University. Teachers College. Contributions to Education: No. 277). Repr. of 1928 ed. 22.50 (ISBN 0-404-55277-3). AMS Pr.

Relation of the Troubles Which Have Happened in New-England, by Reason of the Indians There from the Year 1614 to the Year 1675. Increase Mather. LC 78-141093. (Research Library of Colonial Americana). 1971. Repr. of 1677 ed. 13.00 (ISBN 0-405-03298-6). Ayer Co Pubs.

Relation of Theoretical & Applied Linguistics. Ed. by O. M. Tomic & R. W. Shuy. LC 87-16198. (Topics in Language & Linguistics Ser.). (Illus.). 216p. 1987. 34.50x (ISBN 0-306-42630-7, Plenum Pr). Plenum Pub.

Relation of Theory to Practice in Psychotherapy. Ed. by Leonard D. Eron & Robert Callahan. LC 69-13705. 1969. 39.50 (ISBN 0-202-26017-8). Irvington.

Relation of Thomas Jefferson to American Foreign Policy, 1783-1793. William K. Woolery. LC 78-64123. (Johns Hopkins University. Studies in the Social Sciences. Forty-Fifth Ser. 1927: 2). Repr. of 1927 ed. 13.50 (ISBN 0-404-61237-7). AMS Pr.

Relation of Thomas Jefferson to American Policy, 1783-1793. William K. Woolery. LC 70-131863. 1971. Repr. of 1927 ed. 9.00x (ISBN 0-403-00750-X). Scholarly.

Relation of Tristram Shandy to the Life of Sterne. Overyon P. James. 1966. text ed. 11.20x (ISBN 0-686-22455-8). Mouton.

Relation of Two Trips to Peten: Made for the Conversion of the Heathen Ytzaex & Cehaches. Fray A. De Avendano y Loyola. Ed. by Frank E. Comparato. Tr. by Charles P. Bowditch & Guillermo Rivera. LC 86-80968. (Ethnographic Ser.). 72p. (Orig.). 1987. pap. 16.00x (ISBN 0-911437-06-1). Labyrinthos.

Relation of Various Anthropometric Measurements of Selected College Women to Success in Certain Physical Activities. Elizabeth Beall. LC 77-176547. (Columbia University. Teachers College. Contributions to Education: No. 774). Repr. of 1939 ed. 22.50 (ISBN 0-404-55774-0). AMS Pr.

Relation, or Journal, of a Late Expedition to the Gates of St. Augustine, on Florida: Conducted by the Hon. General James Oglethorpe, with a Detachment of His Regiment & from Georgia. Edward Kimber. Intro. by John J. TePaske. LC 75-45209. (Floridiana Facsimile & Reprint Ser.). 1976. Repr. of 1744 ed. 6.00 (ISBN 0-8130-0412-8). U Presses Fla.

Relation or Journal of the Beginning of the English Plantation at Plymouth. LC 74-80210. (English Experience Ser.: No. 683). 1974. Repr. of 1622 ed. 20.00 (ISBN 90-221-0683-7). Walter J Johnson.

Relation, or Rather a True Account, of the Island of England. 1847. 19.00 (ISBN 0-384-50260-1). Johnson Repr.

Relation, or Rather a True Account of the Isle of England. Ed. by Charlotte A. Sneyd. Repr. of 1847 ed. 19.00 (ISBN 0-404-50137-0). AMS Pr.

Relational Concepts in Psychoanalysis: An Integration. Stephen A. Mitchell. 1988. text ed. 25.00. Harvard U Pr.

Relational Data Base Management System. A. T. Hutt. LC 79-40516. (Wiley Computing Ser.). 226p. 1979. 57.95 (ISBN 0-471-27612-X, Pub. by Wiley-Interscience). Wiley.

Relational Database. Luther Larue. Ed. by William Steele. 295p. 1985. pap. 39.95 (ISBN 0-935506-37-3). Carnegie Pr.

Relational Database Design with Microcomputer Applications. Glenn A. Jackson. (Illus.). 256p. 1988. text ed. 27.00 (ISBN 0-13-771841-1). P-H.

Relational Database Management in the Unix Environment. Rod Manis et al. (Illus.). 576p. 1988. pap. text ed. 28.00 (ISBN 0-13-771833-0). P-H.

Relational Database: Selected Writings. C. J. Date. 1986. text ed. 37.75 (ISBN 0-201-14196-5). Addison-Wesley.

Relational Database Systems. D. Bell. (INFO Ser.: No. 14.5). (Illus.). 470p. 1986. 428.00 (ISBN 0-08-034094-6). Pergamon.

Relational Database Systems. C. Delobel & M. Adiba. Tr. by M. L. Hollett. 470p. 1985. 65.00 (ISBN 0-444-87718-5, North-Holland). Elsevier.

Relational Database Systems: Analysis & Comparison. Ed. by J. W. Schmidt & M. L. Brodie. 618p. 1983. 27.00 (ISBN 0-387-12032-7). Springer-Verlag.

Relational Database Technology. S. Alagic. (Texts & Monographs in Computer Science). (Illus.). 275p. 1986. 33.00 (ISBN 0-387-96276-X). Springer-Verlag.

Relational Databases. Chao-Chih Yang. (Illus.). 256p. 1986. text ed. 43.00 (ISBN 0-13-771858-6). P-H.

Relational Databases: Concepts & Systems. Georges Gardarin & Patrick Valduriez. (Illus.). 480p. 1988. text ed. price not set (ISBN 0-201-09955-1). Addison-Wesley.

Relational Diagramming: Enchancing the Software Development Process. Daniel C. Morris & Joel S. Brandon. 320p. 1988. text ed. 44.95 (ISBN 0-07-043198-1). McGraw.

Relational Information Systems. T. H. Merrett. 1983. text ed. 39.00 (ISBN 0-8359-6642-9, Reston). P-H.

Relational Metaphysics. Harold H. Oliver. (Studies in Philosophy & Religion: No. 4). 224p. 1981. 32.00 (ISBN 90-247-2457-0, Pub. by Martinus Nijhoff Netherlands). Kluwer Academic.

Relational Self: Ethics & Therapy from a Black Church Perspective. John Smith, Jr. 256p. (Orig.). 1982. pap. 11.95 (ISBN 0-687-35945-7). Abingdon.

Relational Theory of Computing. J. G. Sanderson. (Lecture Notes in Computer Science: Vol. 82). 147p. 1980. pap. 15.00 (ISBN 0-387-09987-5). Springer-Verlag.

Relational Typology. Ed. by Frans Plank. (Trends in Linguistics, Studies & Monographs: No. 28). xii, 443p. 1985. 126.50 (ISBN 3-11-009591-2). Mouton.

Relations Between Ancient Russia & Scandinavia & the Origin of the Russian State. Vilhelm L. Thomsen. 1964. Repr. of 1876 ed. 20.50 (ISBN 0-8337-3533-0). B Franklin.

Relations Between Arabs & Israelis Prior to the Rise of Islam. D. S. Margoliouth. (British Academy, London, Schweich Lectures on Biblical Archaeology Series, 1921). pap. 19.00 (ISBN 0-8115-1263-0). Kraus Repr.

Relations Between Combinatorics & Other Parts of Mathematics. Ed. by D. K. Ray-Chaudhuri. LC 78-25979. (Proceedings of Symposia in Pure Mathematics: Vol. 34). 378p. 1986. pap. 35.00 (ISBN 0-8218-1434-6, PSPUM-34). Am Math.

Relations Between Federal & State Courts. Mitchell Wendell. LC 68-58637. (Columbia University. Studies in the Social Sciences: No. 555). Repr. of 1949 ed. 22.50 (ISBN 0-404-51555-X). AMS Pr.

Relations Between Freedom & Responsibility in the Evolution of Democratic Government. Arthur T. Hadley. LC 73-19151. (Politics & People Ser.). 186p. 1974. Repr. 10.00x (ISBN 0-685-49686-4). Ayer Co Pubs.

Relations Between Normal Aging & Disease. Ed. by Horton A. Johnson. (Aging Ser.: Vol. 28). 270p. 1985. text ed. 87.00 (ISBN 0-88167-063-4). Raven.

Relations Between Northern & Southern Baptists. rev. ed. Robert A. Baker. Ed. by Edwin S. Gaustad. LC 79-52590. (Baptist Tradition Ser.). 1980. Repr. of 1954 ed. lib. bdg. 23.00x (ISBN 0-405-12457-0). Ayer Co Pubs.

Relations Between Psychopathological & Socio-Professional Factors in Out-Patient Department Psychiatry. Ed. by G. Leresche & J. Bovet. (Journal: Psychopathology: Vol. 19, Suppl. 1, 1986). (Illus.). 260p. 1986. pap. 52.00 (ISBN 3-8055-4332-8). S Karger.

Relations Between Religion & Science: Eight Lectures Preached Before the University of Oxford in Eighteen Eighty-Four on the Foundation of the Late Reverend John Bampton Ma. Frederick Temple. 264p. Repr. of 1884 ed. text ed. 41.40x (ISBN 0-576-29206-0, Pub. by Gregg Intl Pubs England). Gregg Intl.

Relations Between Scholastic Achievement in a School of Social Work & Six Factors in Students Background. Thornton W. Merriam. LC 70-177072. (Columbia University. Teachers College. Contributions to Education: No. 616). Repr. of 1934 ed. 22.50 (ISBN 0-404-55616-7). AMS Pr.

Relations Between Structure & Function in the Prokaryotic Cell. Ed. by R. Y. Stanier & H. J. Rogers. LC 77-21093. (Society for General Microbiology Symposium: No. 28). (Illus.). 1978. 67.50 (ISBN 0-521-21909-4). Cambridge U Pr.

Relations Between Structure & Relations in Nuclear Physics: Proceedings. Ed. by D. Feng et al. 428p. 1987. 64.00x (ISBN 9971-50-264-X). World Scientific Pub.

Relations Between the Council of Europe & the U. N. (Regional Studies Ser.). pap. 3.00 (ISBN 92-1-157036-0, E.75XV.RS-1). UN.

Relations Between the Laws of Babylonia & the Laws of the Hebrew Peoples. C. H. Johns. (British Academy, London, Schweich Lectures on Biblical Archaeology Series, 1912). pap. 19.00 (ISBN 0-8115-1254-1). Kraus Repr.

Relations Between the Spanish-Americans & Anglo-Americans in New Mexico. Carolyn Zeleny. LC 73-14219. (Mexican American Ser.). (Illus.). 370p. 1974. 29.00x (ISBN 0-405-05692-3). Ayer Co Pubs.

Relations Between the United Nations & Non-United Nations Regional Intergovernmental Organizations. pap. 1.00 (ISBN 92-1-157016-6, E.75.XV.CR-3). UN.

Relations de voyages du Dixieme siecle a l'evolution des idees. Geoffrey Atkinson. LC 79-166450. (Research & Source Works Ser.: No. 785). 1971. Repr. of 1924 ed. lib. bdg. 22.50 (ISBN 0-8337-3948-4). B Franklin.

Relations Humaines Dans L'Entreprise see Cahiers de l'Institut de Science Economique Appliquee.

Relations in Public. Erving Goffman. 390p. 1972. pap. 9.95x (ISBN 0-06-131957-0, TB 1957, Torch). Har-Row.

Relations of Carlyle to Kant & Fichte. Margaret Storrs. LC 77-9971. 1929. lib. bdg. 25.00 (ISBN 0-8414-7562-8). Folcroft.

Relations of Development & Aging. Ed. by James E. Birren & Leon Stein. LC 79-8659. (Growing Old Ser.). (Illus.). 1980. Repr. of 1964 ed. lib. bdg. 27.50x (ISBN 0-405-12775-8). Ayer Co Pubs.

Relations of General Intelligence to Certain Mental & Physical Traits. Cyrus D. Mead. LC 77-177063. (Columbia University. Teachers College. Contributions to Education). Repr. of 1916 ed. 22.50 (ISBN 0-404-55076-2). AMS Pr.

Relations of Golconda in the Early Seventeenth Century. Ed. by W. H. Moreland. (Hakluyt Society Works Ser.: No. 2, Vol. 66). (Illus.). Repr. of 1930 ed. 21.00 (ISBN 0-8115-0370-4). Kraus Repr.

Relations of Literature & Science: An Annotated Bibliography of Scholarship, 1880-1980. Ed. by Walter Schatzberg et al. LC 87-26241. 527p. 1987. 40.00 (ISBN 0-87352-172-2); pap. 19.75 (ISBN 0-87352-173-0). Modern Lang.

Relations of Literature & Science: A Selected Bibliography, 1930-1949. Ed. by Fred A. Dudley. LC 50-4895. pap. 36.50 (ISBN 0-317-10401-2, 2000294). Bks Demand UMI.

Relations of Nations. 6th ed. Frederick N. Hartmann. 736p. 1983. text ed. write for info. (ISBN 0-02-351350-0). Macmillan.

Relations of Pennsylvania with the British Government, 1696-1765. Winfred T. Root. LC 71-99249. Repr. of 1912 ed. 28.50 (ISBN 0-404-00608-6). AMS Pr.

Relations of Pennsylvania with the British Government, 1696-1765. Winfred T. Root. 1912. 24.00 (ISBN 0-8337-3054-1). B Franklin.

Relations of Production: Marxist Approaches to Economic Anthropology. Ed. by David Seddon. 414p. 1978. 32.50x (ISBN 0-7146-3000-4, F Cass Co); pap. 12.50x (ISBN 0-7146-4024-7, F Cass Co). Biblio Dist.

Relations of Religious Training & Life Patterns to the Adult Religious Life. Luther E. Woodward. LC 71-177627. (Columbia University. Teachers College. Contributions to Education: No. 527). Repr. of 1932 ed. 22.50 (ISBN 0-404-55527-6). AMS Pr.

Relations of Shirley's Plays to the Elizabethan Drama. Robert S. Forsythe. LC 65-19615. 1914. 27.50 (ISBN 0-405-08528-1, Blom Pubns). Ayer Co Pubs.

Relations of the Sexes. Eliza B. Duffey. LC 73-20619. (Sex, Marriage & Society Ser.). 320p. 1974. Repr. of 1876 ed. 24.50x (ISBN 0-405-05824-1, Blom Pubns). Ayer Co Pubs.

Relations of the United States & Spain: Diplomacy. French E. Chadwick. LC 68-25054. 610p. 1968. Repr. of 1909 ed. 16.00x (ISBN 0-8462-1230-7). Russell.

Relations Politiques de la France et de l' Espagne avec l' Ecosse au Seizieme Siecle, 5 vols. Ed. by Jean B. Teulet. Incl. Vol. 1. Correspondences Francais 1515-1560. 47.50 (ISBN 0-404-52891-0); Vol. 2. Correspondences Francaises 1559-1573. 47.50 (ISBN 0-404-52892-9); Vol. 3. Correspondences Francaises 1575-1585. 47.50 (ISBN 0-404-52893-7); Vol. 4. Correspondences Francaises 1585-1603. 47.50 (ISBN 0-404-52894-5); Vol. 5. Correspondences Espagnoles 1562-1588. 47.50 (ISBN 0-404-52895-3). LC 77-176145. (Bannatyne Club, Edinburgh. Publications: No. B). (Fr.). Repr. of 1862 ed. 237.50 set (ISBN 0-404-52890-2). AMS Pr.

Relations Politiques et Commerciales De l'Empire Romain Avec l'Asie Orientale. Joseph T. Reinaud. LC 72-10083. (Illus.). 339p. 1973. Repr. of 1863 ed. 29.00 (ISBN 0-8337-2933-0). B Franklin.

Relations: Selected Poems, 1950-1985. Philip Booth. 272p. 1986. 25.00 (ISBN 0-670-80943-8). Viking.

Relations: Selected Poems 1950-1985. Philip Booth. 272p. 1986. pap. 12.95 (ISBN 0-14-058560-5). Penguin.

Relations sur le Quietisme see Oeuvres.

Relations with Children. Shelley Dr. Phillips. 256p. (Orig.). 1986. pap. 12.95 (ISBN 0-86417-057-2, Pub. by Kangaroo Pr). Intl Spec Bk.

Relationshift. Jacinth I. Baublitz. 216p. (Orig.). 1983. pap. 13.95 (ISBN 0-9610316-0-3). J I Baublitz.

Relationship--Success. H. Lee Ashwood & Gloria J. Gordon. 195p. (Orig.). 1988. pap. 6.97 (ISBN 0-937905-04-6). Relation Family Comns.

Relationship Between Attitude & Information Concerning the Japanese in America. Gwynne Nettler. Ed. by Harriet Zuckerman & Robert K. Merton. LC 79-9016. (Dissertations in Sociology Ser.). 1980. lib. bdg. 19.00x (ISBN 0-405-12984-X). Ayer Co Pubs.

Relationship Between Certain Psychological Tests & Shorthand Achievement. Agnes E. Osborne. LC 78-177137. (Columbia University Studies: No. 873). Repr. of 1943 ed. 22.50 (ISBN 0-404-55873-9). AMS Pr.

Relationship Between Content of an Adult Intelligence Test & Intelligence Test Score As a Function of Age. R. E. Kushner. LC 75-176935. (Columbia University. Teachers College. Contributions to Education: No. 933). Repr. of 1947 ed. 22.50 (ISBN 0-404-55933-6). AMS Pr.

Relationship Between Disarmament & Development. (Disarmament Study Ser.: No. 5). 189p. 1982. pap. 14.00x. Intl Pubns Serv.

Relationship Between Disarmament & International Security. (Disarmament Study Ser.: No. 8). 7.00 (ISBN 92-1-142032-6, E.82.IX.4). UN.

Relationship Between Engine Oil Viscosity & Engine Performance - STP 621. 116p. 1977. pap. 15.00 (ISBN 0-8031-0549-5, 04-621000-12); Suppl. No. 1. pap. 12.00 (ISBN 0-8031-0550-9, 04-621010-12); Suppl. No. 2. pap. 15.00 (ISBN 0-8031-0551-7, 04-621030-12); Suppl. No. 3. pap. 15.00 (ISBN 0-8031-0552-5, 04 621030 12); Suppl. 4. pap. 18.00 (ISBN 0-8031-0553-3). ASTM.

Relationship Between Engine Oil Viscosity & Engine Performance, Pts. V & VI. LC 77-150198. 204p. 1980. cancelled (ISBN 0-89883-231-4, SP460). Soc Auto Engineers.

Relationship Between Experimental Embryology & Molecular Biology. E. Wolff. 170p. 1967. 64.00 (ISBN 0-677-12800-2). Gordon & Breach.

Relationship Between High-Temperature Oil Rheology & Engine Operation: A Status Report DS-62. Ed. by J. A. Spearot. LC 85-15747. (Illus.). 140p. 1985. pap. text ed. 16.00 (ISBN 0-8031-0448-0, 05-894000-12). ASTM.

Relationship Between Homosexuality & Psychological Functioning in a Perspective of Personality Types. Lena N. Schonnesson. 283p. (Orig.). 1983. 30.00 (ISBN 91-22-00634-6, Pub. by Almqvist & Wiksell). Coronet Bks.

Relationship Between Housing & the National Economy: Synthesis Report on the Seminar Held in Prague (Czechoslovakia) 10-14 May 1982. 60p. 1986. 8.50 (ISBN 92-1-116325-0, E.85.II.E.16). UN.

Relationship Between Item Validity & Test Validity. Max Smith. LC 79-177767. (Columbia University. Teachers College. Contributions to Education Ser.: No. 621). Repr. of 1934 ed. 22.50 (ISBN 0-404-55621-3). AMS Pr.

Relationship Between Learning Disabilities & Juvenile Delinquency: Executive Summary. 35p. 1982. pap. 4.50 manuscript (ISBN 0-89656-066-X, R-072). Natl Ctr St Courts.

Relationship Between Microsomal Enzyme Induction & Liver Tumour Formation. (Agricultural Research Reports: No. 890). 1979. pap. 18.00 (ISBN 90-220-0707-3, PDC205, PUDOC). UNIPUB.

Relationship Between Milk & Beef Production in Europe. pap. 12.50 (F1085, FAO). UNIPUB.

Relationship Between Monetary & Fiscal Policy. Alec Cairncross. (Keynes Lectures in Economics). 10p. 1981. pap. 5.50 (ISBN 0-85672-291-X, Pub. by British Acad). Longwood Pub Group.

Relationship Between Numerical Computation & Programming Language. K. Reid. 378p. 1982. 44.75 (ISBN 0-444-86377-X, North-Holland). Elsevier.

Relationship Between Prefrontal & Limbic Cortex: A Comparative Anatomical Review. Ed. by R. Reep. (Journal: Brain, Behavioral & Evolution: Vol. 25, Nos. 1-2). (Illus.). 80p. 1985. pap. 36.75 (ISBN 3-8055-4033-7). S Karger.

Relationship Between Scholars & Rulers in Imperial China: A Comparison Between China & the West. Kai-fu Tsao. LC 83-19813. 260p. (Orig.). 1984. lib. bdg. 27.75 (ISBN 0-8191-3631-X); pap. text ed. 13.50 (ISBN 0-8191-3632-8). U Pr of Amer.

Relationship Between Social & Cognitive Development. Ed. by Willis F. Overton. (Jean Piaget Society Ser.). 272p. 1983. text ed. 29.95x (ISBN 0-89859-249-6). L Erlbaum Assocs.

Relationship Between Taxation & Financial Reporting: Income Tax Accounting. OECD. (Accounting Standards Harmonization Ser.: No. 3). 144p. (Orig., Eng. & Fr.). 1987. pap. 11.00x (ISBN 92-64-02938-9). OECD.

Relationship Between the Church & the Theatre: Exemplified by Selected Writings of the Church Fathers & by Liturgical Texts Until Amalarius of Metz - 775-852 A.D. Christine C. Schnusenberg. LC 86-24637. 452p. (Orig.). 1988. lib. bdg. 34.50 (ISBN 0-8191-5733-3). U Pr of Amer.

Relationship Between the Development of Fishing Gear & the Study of It: Bibliography. M. E. Merdinyan & C. D. Mortimer. (Marine Memo Ser.: No. 59). 43p. Date not set. cancelled 1.00 (ISBN 0-686-36965-3, P828). Sea Grant Pubns.

Relationship Between the Rate of Economic Growth & the Rate, Allocation, & Efficiency of Investment. Dennis Anderson. 44p. 1983. 5.00 (ISBN 0-8213-0186-1, WP 0591). World Bank.

Relationship Between Theory & Practice in Social Casework. Bernece K. Simon. 56p. (Orig.). 1960. pap. text ed. 2.95x (ISBN 0-87101-337-1). Natl Assn Soc Wkrs.

Relationship Between Yugoslavia & Albania. Collets Staff. 304p. 1984. 32.50x (ISBN 0-317-53817-9, Pub. by Collets (UK)). State Mutual Bk.

Relationship Book: The Adolescent's Guide for Learning the Relationship Skills. Richard D. Solomon & Elaine C. Solomon. 125p. 1987. pap. text ed. 12.95 (ISBN 0-9617198-4-2). NIRt Inc.

Relationship Enhancement: Skill-Training Programs for Therapy, Problem Prevention, & Enrichment. Bernard G. Guerney, Jr. LC 76-11884. (Social & Behavioral Science Ser.). (Illus.). 1977. 29.95x (ISBN 0-87589-310-4). Jossey-Bass.

Relationship Ideal & Family Forever. H. Lee Ashwood. 236p. 1986. pap. 10.95 (ISBN 0-937905-00-3). Relation Family Comns.

Relationship of Adaptation & Fun & Pleasure to Psychological Growth (An Appendix to Homosexuality: The Psychology of the Creative Process) Paul Rosenfels. LC 86-142926. (Ninth Street Center Monographs). (Orig.). 1975. pap. 3.95 (ISBN 0-932961-01-0). Ninth St Ctr.

Relationship of Advertising Expenditures to Sales: An Anthology of Classic Articles. Ed. by Avijit Ghosh & Samuel Craig. LC 84-46070. (History of Advertising Ser.). 400p. 1985. lib. bdg. 50.00 (ISBN 0-8240-6764-9). Garland Pub.

Relationship of City Planning to School Plant Planning. R. A. Holy. LC 73-176877. (Columbia University. Teachers College. Contributions to Education Ser.: No. 662). Repr. of 1935 ed. 22.50 (ISBN 0-404-55662-0). AMS Pr.

Relationship of Esteem Values with Intelligence Quotient & Grade Point Averages. James W. Simmons. LC 76-24726. 1977. soft cover 10.95 (ISBN 0-88247-427-8). R & E Pubs.

Relationship of External Debt & Growth: Sudan's Experience, 1975-1984. Y. Hossein Farzin. (Discussion Paper Ser.: No. 24). 38p. 1988. 5.00 (ISBN 0-8213-1025-9, DP0024). World Bank.

Relationship of Histology to Cancer Treatment: Proceedings. West Coast Cancer Symposium, 9th Annual, San Francisco, 1973. Ed. by J. M. Vaeth. (Frontiers of Radiation Therapy & Oncology: Vol. 9). 200p. 1974. 94.75 (ISBN 3-8055-1748-3). S Karger.

Relationship of Library User Studies to Performance Measures: A Review of the Literature. Ronald R. Powell. (Occasional Papers: No. 181). (Orig.). 1988. pap. text ed. 3.00. U IL BD Trustees.

Relationship of Organic Matter & Mineral Diagenesis. Donald L. Gautier et al. (Short Course Notes Ser.: No. 17). 279p. 1985. pap. 22.00 (ISBN 0-918985-51-X). SEPM.

Relationship of Painting & Literature: A Guide to Information Sources. Ed. by Eugene L. Huddleston & Douglas A. Noverr. LC 78-53436. (American Studies Information Guide: Vol. 4). 208p. 1978. 68.00x (ISBN 0-8103-1394-4). Gale.

Relationship of Prices to Economic Stability & Growth. U. S. Congress - Joint Economic Committee. LC 79-90718. 1958-1959. Repr. lib. bdg. 29.50x (ISBN 0-8371-2897-8, REOP). Greenwood.

Relationship of Reading to the Social Acceptability of Sixth Grade Children. Mary A. McAlpin. LC 75-177076. (Columbia University. Teachers College. Contributions to Education Ser.: No. 953). Repr. of 1949 ed. 22.50 (ISBN 0-404-55953-0). Ams Pr.

Relationship of Renaissance Concepts of Honour to Shakespeares Problem Plays. Alice Shalvi. Ed. by James Hogg. (Jacobean Drama Studies). 362p. (Orig.). 1972. pap. 15.00 (ISBN 3-7052-0306-1, Pub. by Salzburg Studies). Longwood Pub Group.

Relationship of Self Concept & the Other Variables to the Work Value Orientation of Black Females Enrolled in Inner City Schools. Sandra E. Yates. Ed. by R. Reed. LC 81-83609. (Orig.). 1982. 13.95 (ISBN 0-88247-651-3); pap. 9.95 (ISBN 0-88247-629-7). R & E Pubs.

Relationship of Stock Market Fluctuations to Lunar Cycles. Frank J. Guarino. LC 78-56416. 80p. 1978. 5.00 (ISBN 0-86690-112-4, 1163-01). Am Fed Astrologers.

Relationship of the Library to Instructional Systems. James Brown et al. Ed. by John T. Corrigan. (Catholic Library Association Studies in Librarianship: No. 2). 1978. pap. 3.00 (ISBN 0-87507-006-X). Cath Lib Assn.

Relationship of the Prison Program to Changes in Attitudes & Self Concepts of Inmates. Howard M. Cohen. LC 74-28609. 1975. soft cover 12.95 (ISBN 0-88247-330-1). R & E Pubs.

Relationship of the Professed Philosophy to the Suggested Educational Experiences. Nancy G. Milligan. LC 78-177074. (Columbia University. Teachers College. Contributions to Education Ser.: No. 729). Repr. of 1937 ed. 22.50 (ISBN 0-404-55729-5). AMS Pr.

Relationship of the Spanish Libro De Alexandre to the Alexandreis of Gautier De Chatillon. Raymond S. Willis, Jr. (Elliott Monographs: Vol. 31). 1934. 12.00 (ISBN 0-527-02634-4). Kraus Repr.

Relationship of Theory & Research. Fawcett & Downs. 208p. 1985. pap. 23.95 (ISBN 0-8385-8365-2). Appleton & Lange.

Relationship of Verbal & Non-Verbal Communication. Ed. by Mary R. Key. (Contributions to the Sociology of Language Ser.: No. 25). 1980. text ed. 49.50x (ISBN 90-279-7878-6); pap. text ed. 12.50x (ISBN 90-279-7637-6). Mouton.

Relationship Restored: Trends in U. S. - China Educational Exchanges, 1978-1984. David M. Lampton et al. 288p. 1986. pap. text ed. 19.95x (ISBN 0-309-03678-X). Natl Acad Pr.

Relationship Selling: How to Get & Keep Customers. Jim Cathcart. (Illus.). 128p. (Orig.). 1987. pap. 14.95 (ISBN 0-937359-25-4). HDL Pubs.

Relationship Systems of the Tlingit, Haida, & Tsimshian. Theresa M. Durlach. LC 73-3547. (American Ethnological Society. Publications: No. 11). Repr. of 1928 ed. 27.50 (ISBN 0-404-58161-7). AMS Pr.

Relationship: The Heart of Helping People. Helen H. Perlman. LC 78-19064. x, 236p. 1979. lib. bdg. 16.00x (ISBN 0-226-66035-4); pap. 8.95 (ISBN 0-226-66036-2). U of Chicago Pr.

Relationship: The Key to Fulfillment: In the Song of Solomon. Violet Kiteley. 145p. (Orig.). 1987. pap. 4.95 (ISBN 0-914903-29-2). Destiny Image.

Relationships. Gladys Hunt. (Fisherman Bible Studyguide Ser.). 64p. 1983. saddle stitched 2.95 (ISBN 0-87788-721-7). Shaw Pubs.

Relationships: A Study Guide. Dean Sherman. (Illus.). 80p. 1985. wkbk. 5.50 (ISBN 0-935779-06-X); audio album 24.95 (ISBN 0-935779-07-8); video series 150.00 (ISBN 0-935779-08-6). Crown Min.

Relationships: Adult Children of Alcoholics. Joseph Perez. 1988. 19.95 (ISBN 0-89876-150-6). Gardner Pr.

Relationships among Hearing Acuity, Speech Production, & Reading Performance in Grades 1a, 1b, & 2a. Lois J. Rossignol. LC 73-177212. (Columbia University. Teachers College. Contributions to Education Ser.: No. 936). Repr. of 1948 ed. 22.50 (ISBN 0-404-55936-0). AMS Pr.

Relationships among the Gospels: An Interdisciplinary Dialogue. Albert C. Outler et al. Ed. by William O. Walker, Jr. LC 78-52845. (Monograph Series in Religion). 359p. 1978. text ed. 15.00 (ISBN 0-911536-73-6). Trinity U Pr.

Relationships & Communication: A Book for Friends, Co-Workers & Lovers. 2nd ed. Jerry L. Buley. 208p. 1982. pap. text ed. 13.95 (ISBN 0-8403-2945-8, 40294501). Kendall-Hunt.

Relationships & Development. Ed. by W. Hartup & Z. Rubin. 240p. 1986. text ed. 27.50 (ISBN 0-89859-621-1). L Erlbaum Assocs.

Relationships & Life Cycles: Modern Dimensions of Astrology. Stephen Arroyo. LC 79-53979. 1979. pap. 8.95 (ISBN 0-916360-12-1). CRCS Pubns CA.

Relationships Between Expressed Preferences & Curricular Abilities of Ninth Grade Boys. Oliver K. Garretson. LC 76-176976. (Columbia University. Teachers College. Contributions to Education Ser.: No. 396). Repr. of 1930 ed. 22.50 (ISBN 0-404-55396-6). AMS Pr.

Relationships Between Health & Social Education PSSC & HEc. 1976. 22.00x (ISBN 0-317-05771-5, Pub. by Natl Inst Social Work). State Mutual Bk.

Relationships Between Mental & Physical Growth. E. M. Abernethy. (Society for Research in Child Development Monographs: Vol. 1, No. 7). pap. 12.00 (ISBN 0-527-01492-3). Kraus Repr.

Relationships Between Physiographic Units & Highway Design Factors. 161p. 1972. 7.20. Transport Res Bd.

Relationships Between School Taxes & Town Taxes in Vermont Local Government. Leonard J. Tashman & Michael J. Munson. (Occasional Papers: No. 8). (Illus.). 38p. (Orig.). 1984. pap. text ed. 2.50x (ISBN 0-944277-13-6). U VT Ctr Rsch VT.

Relationships: Face to Face. Carolyn Nystrom & Matthew Floding. (Young Fisherman Bible Studyguide Ser.). 64p. (Orig.). (YA) (gr. 7 up). 1986. pap. 2.95 student ed. (ISBN 0-87788-722-5); tchr's ed. 4.95 (ISBN 0-87788-723-3). Shaw Pubs.

Relationships in Marriage & the Family. 2nd ed. Nick Stinnett & James Walters. 544p. 1984. text ed. write for info. (ISBN 0-02-417560-9). Macmillan.

Relationships in the New Age of AIDS. Betty Bethards. 56p. (Orig.). 1988. pap. 4.95 (ISBN 0-918915-12-0). Inner Light Found.

Relationships: Issues of Emotional Living in an Age of Stress for Clergy & Religious. Martin C. Helldorfer & Anna Polcino. Ed. by Sean D. Sammon. LC 83-2706. 144p. (Orig.). 1983. pap. 8.00 (ISBN 0-89571-015-3). Affirmation.

Relationships: Marriage & Family Reader. Jeffrey P. Rosenfeld. LC 81-8941. 1982. pap. text ed. write for info (ISBN 0-394-33293-8, RanC). Random.

Relationships of Chrysemyd Turtles of North America: Testudines: Emydidae. Joseph P. Ward. (Special Publications of the Museum Ser.: No. 21). (Illus.). 50p. 1984. pap. 9.00 (ISBN 0-89672-121-3). Tex Tech Univ Pr.

Relationships of the Amphiberingian Marmots (Mammalia: Sciuridae) Robert S. Hoffman et al. (Occasional Papers: No. 83). 56p. 1979. pap. 3.00 (ISBN 0-317-04825-2). U of KS Mus Nat Hist.

Relationships of the Superorders Alectoromorphae & Charadriomorphae (Aves) A Comparative Study of the Avian Hand. Boris C. Stegmann. (Publications: No. 17). (Illus.). 119p. 1978. 10.00 (ISBN 0-686-35806-6). Nuttall Ornith.

Relationships: Parents, Peers, & Pests. Ed. by Paul Woods. (Bible Basics Youth Electives Ser.). 96p. (Orig.). 1988. tchr's ed. 9.95 (ISBN 1-55513-877-2, 68775). Cook.

Relationships: The Art of Making Life Work. John-Roger. 200p. 1986. 15.00 (ISBN 0-914829-50-5). Mandeville LA.

Relationships Within Families. Ed. by Robert A. Hinde & Joan Stevenson-Hinde. (Illus.). 370p. 1988. 70.00 (ISBN 0-19-852170-7). Oxford U Pr.

Relative Analgesia in Dental Practice: Inhalation Analgesia & Sedation with Nitrous Oxide. 2nd ed. Harry Langa. LC 76-1223. (Illus.). 1976. text ed. write for info. (ISBN 0-7216-5621-8). Saunders.

Relative Baseball II. Merritt Clifton & Pete Palmer. 80p. 1985. 5.00 (ISBN 0-317-19196-9). Samisdat.

Relative Clauses in Spanish Without Overt Antecedents & Related Constructions. Susan Plann. (UC Publications in Linguistics: Vol. 93). 1980. pap. 20.50x (ISBN 0-520-09608-8). U of Cal Pr.

Relative Contributions of Mantle, Oceanic Crust & Continental Crust to Magma Genesis: Proceedings of a Royal Society Discussion Meeting Held March 23-24, 1983. Royal Society. Ed. by S. Moorbath et al. (Philosophical Transactions of the Royal Society, Series A: Vol. 310). (Illus.). 342p. 1984. lib. bdg. 102.00x (ISBN 0-85403-230-4, Pub. by Royal Soc London). Scholium Intl.

Relative Deprivation & Social Comparison: The Ontario Symposium, Vol. 4. Ed. by James M. Olson et al. (Ontario Symposium Ser.). 288p. 1986. text ed. 32.50 (ISBN 0-89859-704-8). L Erlbaum Assocs.

Relative Deprivation & Working Women. Faye J. Crosby. (Illus.). 1982. pap. text ed. 10.95x (ISBN 0-19-503147-4). Oxford U Pr.

Relative Difficulty of Certain Topics in Mathematics for Slow-Moving Ninth Grade Pupils. Virgil S. Mallory. LC 79-177050. (Columbia University. Teachers College. Contributions to Education: No. 769). Repr. of 1939 ed. 22.50 (ISBN 0-404-55769-4). AMS Pr.

Relative Duties of Parents & Children, Husbands & Wives, Masters & Servants. William Fleetwood. LC 83-48607. (Marriage, Sex & the Family in England Ser.). 495p. 1985. lib. bdg. 61.00 (ISBN 0-8240-5933-6). Garland Pub.

Relative Frequency of English Speech Sounds. rev. ed. Godfrey Dewey. (Studies in Education: No. 4). 1950. 15.00x (ISBN 0-674-75450-6). Harvard U Pr.

Relative Frequency Tables, 1900-1949. LC 78-61158. 312p. 1978. 15.00 (ISBN 0-86690-053-5, 1004-01). Am Fed Astrologers.

Relative Humidity: Thermodynamic Charts. Technical Association of the Pulp & Paper Industry. pap. 20.00 (ISBN 0-317-26870-8, 2025293). Bks Demand UMI.

Relative Identity. Nicholas Griffin. (Clarendon Library of Logic & Philosophy Ser.). 1977. 37.00x (ISBN 0-19-824409-6). Oxford U Pr.

Relative Importance of Factors of Interest in Reading Materials for Junior High School Pupils. Dale Zeller. LC 77-177607. (Columbia University. Teachers College. Contributions to Education Ser.: No. 841). Repr. of 1941 ed. 22.50 (ISBN 0-404-55841-0). AMS Pr.

Relative Inefficiency of Quotas. James E. Anderson. 240p. 1988. text ed. 25.00x (ISBN 0-262-01103-4). MIT Pr.

Relative Invariants of Rings: The Commutative Theory. A. Verschoren & F. Van Oystaeyen. (Pure & Applied Mathematics: A Series of Monographs & Textbooks: Vol. 79). 272p. 1983. 49.75 (ISBN 0-8247-7043-9). Dekker.

Relative Invariants of Rings: The Noncommutative Theory. F. Van Oystaeyen & A. Verschoren. (Pure & Applied Mathematics: A Series of Monographs & Textbooks: Vol. 86). (Illus.). 312p. 1984. 65.00 (ISBN 0-8247-7281-4). Dekker.

Relative Merits: A Personal View of the Bandaranaike Family of Sri Lanka. Yasmine Gooneratne. LC 85-18386. (Illus.). 272p. 1986. 25.00 (ISBN 0-312-67037-0). St Martin.

Relative Merits of Conventional & Imaginative Types of Problems in Arithmetic. Harry G. Wheat. LC 71-177643. (Columbia University. Teachers College. Contributions to Education: No. 359). Repr. of 1929 ed. 22.50 (ISBN 0-404-55359-1). AMS Pr.

Relative Merits of Three Methods of Subtraction: An Experimental Comparison of the Decomposition Method of Subtraction with the Equal Additions Method & the Austrian Method. J. T. Johnson. LC 77-176914. (Columbia University. Teachers College. Contributions to Education Ser.: No. 738). Repr. of 1938 ed. 22.50 (ISBN 0-404-55738-4). AMS Pr.

Relative Motions Between Oceanic & Continental Plates In the Pacific Basin. Ed. by David C. Engebretson et al. (Special Paper: No. 206). (Illus.). 1986. pap. 12.50 (ISBN 0-8137-2206-3). Geol Soc.

Relative National Accounts: A Statistical Basebook - 1976 Edition. Lucie R Blau. LC 77-70217. (Report Ser.: No. 708). (Illus.). 79p. (Orig.). 1977. 30.00 (ISBN 0-8237-0142-5). Conference Bd.

Relative National Accounts: A Statistical Basebook. Lucie R. Blau. (Report Ser: No. 620). 77p. (Orig.). 1974. pap. 17.50 (ISBN 0-8237-0048-8). Conference Bd.

Relative Permeability of Petroleum Reservoirs. Mehdi M. Honarpour et al. 152p. 1986. 69.00 (ISBN 0-8493-5739-X). CRC Pr.

Relative Productivity, Factor Intensity & Technology in the Manufacturing Sectors of the U. S. & the U. K. During the Nineteenth Century. Asher Ephraim. Ed. by Stuart Bruchey. LC 76-39822. (Nineteen Seventy-Seven Dissertations Ser.). (Illus.). 1977. lib. bdg. 21.00x (ISBN 0-405-09902-9). Ayer Co Pubs.

Relative Strangers. Maureen Rissik. LC 86-21749. 1987. 18.95 (ISBN 0-688-06597-X). Morrow.

Relative Strangers. Maureen Rissik. 416p. 1988. pap. 3.95 (ISBN 0-345-35238-6). Ballantine.

Relative Strangers. Jessica Steele. (Romances Ser.: No. 2861). 192p. Date not set. pap. 1.95 (ISBN 0-317-63918-8). Harlequin Bks.

Relative Values: Determining Attorneys' Fees. 300p. 1985. text ed. 65.00 (ISBN 0-07-021162-0). Shepards McGraw.

Relative Values for Physicians. Relative Value Studies, Inc. Staff. 64p. 1985. write for info. (ISBN 0-07-073965-X). McGraw.

Relative Values for Physicians. 2nd ed. Relative Value Studies, Inc. Staff. 544p. 1986. text ed. 150.00 (ISBN 0-07-073969-2). McGraw.

Relatively Dangerous. Roderic Jeffries. 192p. 1987. 13.95 (ISBN 0-312-01080-X). St Martin.

Relatively Dangerous. Roderic Jeffries. (Nightingale Ser.). 302p. 1988. pap. 12.95x (ISBN 0-8161-4393-5, Large Print Bks). G K Hall.

Relatively Speaking see Your Family Tree Connection.

Relatively Speaking: Relativity, Black Holes, & the Fate of the Universe. Eric Chaisson. (Illus.). 1988. 15.95 (ISBN 0-393-02536-5). Norton.

Relatives. Tracy Voigt. (Orig.). (gr. 10 up). 1982. pap. write for info. T Voigt.

Relatives at Risk for Mental Disorder. Ed. by David L. Dunner et al. (American Psychopathological Association Ser.). (Illus.). 336p. 1988. text ed. 79.00 (ISBN 0-88167-381-1). Raven.

Relatives Came. Cynthia Rylant. LC 85-10929. (Illus.). 32p. (ps-2). 1985. 12.95 (ISBN 0-02-777220-9). Bradbury Pr.

Relatives in Orbit. Corine Holschbach. (Illus.). 64p. 1986. 7.95 (ISBN 0-89962-514-2). Todd & Honeywell.

Relativism & Realism in Science. Ed. by Robert Nola. 1988. lib. bdg. 79.00 (ISBN 90-277-2647-7, Pub. by Reidel Holland). Kluwer Academic.

Relativism & the Natural Left. William P. Kreml. 192p. 1984. 25.00x (ISBN 0-8147-4584-9); pap. 10.00x (ISBN 0-8147-4585-7). NYU Pr.

Relativism & the Social Sciences. Ernest Gellner. 200p. 1985. 47.50 (ISBN 0-521-26530-4). Cambridge U Pr.

Relativism & the Social Sciences. Ernest Gellner. 212p. 1987. pap. 10.95 (ISBN 0-521-33798-4). Cambridge U Pr.

Relativism: Cognitive & Moral. Ed. by Jack W. Meiland & Michael Krausz. LC 81-19834. 272p. 1982. 22.95 (ISBN 0-268-01611-9); pap. 9.95 (ISBN 0-268-01612-7). U of Notre Dame Pr.

Relativism in the Arts. Ed. by Betty J. Craige. LC 82-4726. 216p. 1983. 21.00x (ISBN 0-8203-0625-8). U of Ga Pr.

Relativism: Interpretation & Confrontation. Ed. by Michael Krausz. 1988. text ed. 34.95x (ISBN 0-268-01636-4). U of Notre Dame Pr.

Relativism, Knowledge, & Faith. Gordon D. Kaufman. LC 59-11620. pap. 38.80 (2026778). Bks Demand UMI.

Relativism Refuted. Harvey Siegel. 1987. lib. bdg. 64.00 (ISBN 90-277-2469-5, Pub. by Reidel Holland). Kluwer Academic.

Relativism: Thoughts & Aphorisms. W. J. Stankiewicz. (Illus.). 1972. buckram 25.00 (ISBN 0-686-09043-8). Girs Pr.

Relativist & Absolutist: The Early Neoclassical Debate in England. Emerson R. Marks. LC 75-23348. 171p. 1975. Repr. of 1955 ed. lib. bdg. 35.00x (ISBN 0-8371-8348-0, MARAB). Greenwood.

Relativistic Action at a Distance: Classical & Quantum Aspects, Barcelona, Spain 1981, Proceedings. Ed. by J. Llosa. (Lecture Notes in Physics Ser.: Vol. 162). 263p. 1982. pap. 18.00 (ISBN 0-387-11573-0). Springer-Verlag.

Relativistic Astrophysics. M. Demianski. (International Studies of Natural Philosophy: Vol. 110). (Illus.). 300p. 1985. text ed. 55.00 (ISBN 0-08-025042-4). Pergamon.

Relativistic Astrophysics & Cosmology: Proceedings of the Sir Arthur Eddington Centenary Symposium, Vol. 1. Ed. by V. De Sabbata & T. M. Karade. 284p. 1984. 44.00 (ISBN 9971-966-99-9). World Scientific Pub.

Relativistic Astrophysics & Cosmology: Proceedings of the XIV Gift International Seminar Sant Feliu de Guixols, Spain, June 27-July 1, 1983. X. Fustero & E. Verdaguer. 320p. 1984. 41.00 (ISBN 9971-966-60-3). World Scientific Pub.

Relativistic Astrophysics Eighth Symposium, Texas, Vol. 302. Ed. by Michael D. Papagiannis. (Annals of the New York Academy of Sciences). 689p. 1977. 47.00x (ISBN 0-89072-048-7). NY Acad Sci.

Relativistic Astrophysics: First Italian-Korean Symposium on Relativistic Astrophysics. Ed. by Y. D. Kim et al. 250p. 1988. 35.00 (ISBN 9971-50-576-2). World Scientific Pub.

Relativistic Astrophysics: Proceedings of the 13th Texas Symposium. Ed. by M. Ulmer. 656p. 1987. 90.00 (ISBN 9971-50-307-7); pap. 46.00 (ISBN 9971-50-310-7). World Scientific Pub.

Relativistic Astrophysics, Vol. 1: Stars & Relativity. Ya. B. Zeldovich & I. D. Novikov. Ed. by Kip Thorne & W. David Arnett. Tr. by Eli Arlock. LC 77-128549. 1982. text ed. 55.00x cloth (ISBN 0-226-97955-5). U of Chicago Pr.

Relativistic Astrophysics: Vol. 2, The Structure & Evolution of the Universe. Ya. B. Zel'dovich & I. D. Novikov. Ed. by Gary Steigman. Tr. by Leslie Fishbone. LC 77-128549. (Illus.). 768p. 1983. Repr. of 1971 ed. lib. bdg. 80.00x (ISBN 0-226-97957-1). U of Chicago Pr.

Relativistic Channeling. Ed. by R. Carrigan & J. Ellison. LC 87-7318. (NATO ASI Series B, Physics: Vol. 165). (Illus.). 538p. 1987. 95.00x (ISBN 0-306-42689-7, Plenum Pr). Plenum Pub.

Relativistic Cosmology: An Introduction. J. Heidmann. (Illus.). 168p. 1980. pap. 28.00 (ISBN 0-387-10138-1). Springer-Verlag.

Relativistic Deduction: Epistemological Implications of the Theory of Relativity with a Review by Albert Einstein. Emile Meyerson. Tr. by David A. Sipfle & Mary A. Sipfle. 290p. 1984. lib. bdg. 49.00 (ISBN 90-277-1699-4, Pub. by Reidel Holland). Kluwer Academic.

Relativistic Dynamics & Quark-Nuclear Physics. Ed. by Mikkel B. Johnson & Alan Picklesimer. LC 86-15814. 861p. 1986. 47.95 (ISBN 0-471-85327-5). Wiley.

Relativistic Effects in Atoms, Molecules, & Solids. Ed. by G. L. Malli. LC 82-16714. (NATO ASI Series B, Physics: Vol. 87). 554p. 1983. 89.50x (ISBN 0-306-41169-5, Plenum Press). Plenum Pub.

Relativistic Electrodynamics & Differential Geometry. S. Parrott. (Illus.). 320p. 1986. 48.00 (ISBN 0-387-96435-5). Springer-Verlag.

Relativistic Kinetic Theory: Principles & Applications. S. R. De Groot et al. 418p. 1980. 121.00 (ISBN 0-444-85453-3, North-Holland). Elsevier.

Relativistic Mechanics, Time & Inertia. E. Tocaci. 1984. lib. bdg. 54.00 (ISBN 90-277-1769-9, Pub. by Reidel Holland). Kluwer Academic.

Relativistic Models of Extended Hadrons Obeying a Mas-Spin Trajectory Constraint. N. Mukunda et al. (Lecture Notes in Physics: Vol. 165). 163p. 1982. pap. 11.00 (ISBN 0-387-11586-2). Springer-Verlag.

Relativistic Nuclear Many-Body Physics: Proceedings. Ed. by Buny C. Clark et al. 700p. 1989. 84.00 (ISBN 9971-50-680-7). World Scientific Pub.

Relativistic Nuclear Physics: Theories of Structure & Scattering. L. C. Celenza & C. M. Shakin. LC 85-29634. (Lecture Notes on Physics Ser.). 300p. 1986. 41.00 (ISBN 9971-50-010-8, Z0207P-B); pap. 23.00x (ISBN 9971-50-011-6). World Scientific Pub.

Relativistic Particle Physics. H. Pilkuhn. LC 79-10666. (Texts & Monographs in Physics). (Illus.). 1979. 67.00 (ISBN 0-387-09348-6). Springer-Verlag.

Relativistic Point Dynamics. H. Arzelies. LC 72-142173. 416p. 1972. 93.00 (ISBN 0-08-015842-0). Pergamon.

Relativistic Propagation of Light. Wallace Kantor. 1976. 10.00x (ISBN 0-87291-084-9); pap. 6.95x (ISBN 0-685-74222-9). Coronado Pr.

Relativistic Quantum Fields. James D. Bjorken & S. D. Drell. (International Pure & Applied Physics Ser.). 1965. text ed. 48.95 (ISBN 0-07-005494-0). McGraw.

Relativistic Quantum Fields. C. Nash. 1979. 69.00 (ISBN 0-12-514350-8). Acad Pr.

Relativistic Quantum Mechanics. James D. Bjorken & S. D. Drell. (International Series in Pure & Applied Physics). 1964. text ed. 48.95 (ISBN 0-07-005493-2). McGraw.

Relativistic Theories of Materials. A. Bressan. LC 77-2632. (Springer Tracts in Natural Philosophy: Vol. 29). 1978. 62.00 (ISBN 0-387-08177-1). Springer-Verlag.

Relativistic Theory of Atoms & Molecules. P. Pyykko. (Lecture Notes in Chemistry: Vol. 41). ix, 389p. 1986. pap. 41.10 (ISBN 0-387-17167-3). Springer-Verlag.

Relativity: A Point of View: Poems. Kelly Cherry. LC 76-45643. x, 59p. 1977. 13.95x (ISBN 0-8071-0276-8); pap. 6.95 (ISBN 0-8071-0277-6). La State U Pr.

Relativity & Common Sense: A New Approach to Einstein. Hermann Bondi. (Illus.). 177p. 1980. pap. 3.95 (ISBN 0-486-24021-5). Dover.

Relativity & Consciousness: A New Approach to Evolution. Kate Flores. LC 84-24674. 186p. (Orig.). 1985. pap. 10.00x (ISBN 0-87752-230-8). Gordian.

Relativity & Engineering. J. Van Bladel. (Springer Series in Electrophysics: Vol. 15). (Illus.). 420p. 1984. 40.00 (ISBN 0-387-12561-2). Springer-Verlag.

Relativity & Geometry. R. Torretti. (Foundations & Philosophy of Science & Technology Ser.). (Illus.). 400p. 1983. text ed. 61.00 (ISBN 0-08-026773-4). Pergamon.

Relativity & Gravitation. C. G. Kuper & A. Peres. 336p. 1971. 124.00 (ISBN 0-677-14300-1). Gordon & Breach.

Relativity & High Energy Physics. W. G. Roser. (Wykeham Science Ser.: No. 7). 160p. 1969. pap. cancelled (ISBN 0-85109-080-X). Taylor & Francis.

Relativity & High Energy Physics. W. G. Rosser & R. K. McCulloch. (Wykeham Science Ser.: No. 7). 160p. 1969. 18.00x (ISBN 0-8448-1109-2, Pub. by Crane Russak & Co). Taylor & Francis.

Relativity & Its Roots. Banesh Hoffmann. (Illus.). 184p. 1983. pap. text ed. 11.95 (ISBN 0-7167-1510-4). W H Freeman.

Relativity & the Question of Discretization in Astronomy. D. G. Edelen & A. G. Wilson. LC 79-108675. (Springer Tracts in Natural Philosophy: Vol. 20). (Illus.). 1970. 32.00 (ISBN 0-387-05254-2). Springer-Verlag.

Relativity, Astrophysics & Cosmology: Proceedings. Conference of the Summer School, Banff Centre, Banff, Alberta, Canada, August 14-26, 1972. Ed. by Werner Israel. LC 72-97957. (Astrophysics & Space Science Library: Vol. 38). 340p. 1973. lib. bdg. 52.65 (ISBN 90-277-0369-8, Pub. by Reidel Holland). Kluwer Academic.

Relativity, Cosmology, Topological Mass & Supergravity: Proceedings of the Silarg Symposium on Gravity, Gauge Theories & Supergravity, USB Campus, Caracas, Dec. 5-11, 1982. Ed. by C. Aragone. 400p. 1984. 48.00 (ISBN 9971-950-95-2). World Scientific Pub.

Relativity Electromagnetism & Quantum Physics see Physics.

Relativity Explosion: A Lucid Account of Why Quasars, Pulsars, Black Holes & the New Atomic Clocks Are Vindicating Einstein's Revolutionary Theory. Martin Gardner. LC 76-10588. 1976. pap. 6.95 (ISBN 0-394-72104-7, Vin). Random.

Relativity for Scientists & Engineers. rev. ed. Ray Skinner. (Illus.). 352p. pap. 10.95 (ISBN 0-486-64215-1). Dover.

Relativity: From Einstein to Black Holes. Gerald E. Tauber. Ed. by M. Kline. (Venture Ser.). (Illus.). 128p. (gr. 6-12). 1988. 11.90 (ISBN 0-531-10482-6). Watts.

Relativity, Groups & Topology, II: Proceedings of the Les Houches Summer School, Session XL, 27 June-4 August, 1983, 3 Pts, Vol. 40. Les Houches Summer School. Ed. by B. DeWitt & R. Stora. 1986. Pt. I, 380p. 31.75 (ISBN 0-444-87019-9, North Holland); Pt. II, 406p. 31.75 (ISBN 0-444-87021-0); Pt. 3, 538p. 93.00 (ISBN 0-317-55238-4); Set. 90.00 (ISBN 0-444-87017-2). Elsevier.

Relativity in Celestial Mechanics & Astrometry. Ed. by J. Kovalevsky & V. A. Brumberg. (Publications of The International Astronomical Union-Proceedings of Symposia). (Orig.). 1986. 64.95 (ISBN 0-318-18941-0, Pub. by Reidel Holland); pap. text ed. 29.50 (ISBN 0-318-18942-9). Kluwer Academic.

Relativity in Man & Society. Arthur F. Bentley. 1967. lib. bdg. 26.00 (ISBN 0-374-90589-4, Octagon). Hippocrene Bks.

Relativity Mechanics & Statistical Physics. 1983. 2.25 (ISBN 0-471-63897-8). Wiley.

Relativity of Wrong. Isaac Asimov. LC 87-24141. 216p. 1988. 17.95 (ISBN 0-385-24473-8). Doubleday.

Relativity, Philosophy & Mind: The Notebooks of Paul Brunton, Vol. 13. Paul Brunton. Ed. by Paul Cash & Timothy Smith. (Illus.). 550p. 1988. 22.50 (ISBN 0-943914-38-8, Dist. by Kampmann & Co); pap. 14.95 (ISBN 0-943914-39-6, Dist. by Kampmann & Co). Larson Pubns Inc.

Relativity Physics. R. Turner. (Student Physics Ser.). (Illus.). 128p. (Orig.). 1984. pap. text ed. 9.95x (ISBN 0-7102-0001-3). Routledge Chapman & Hall.

Relativity, Quanta & Cosmology in the Development of the Scientific Thought of Albert Einstein. Mario Pantaleo & Francesco De Finis. 240.00 (ISBN 0-384-14090-4). Johnson Repr.

Relativity Reexamined. Leon Brillouin. 1970. 30.50 (ISBN 0-12-134945-4). Acad Pr.

Relativity, Supersymmetry & Cosmology: Proceedings of the Fifth Latin-American Symposium on Relativity & Gravity - SILARG V, Bariloche, Argentina, January 1985. Ed. by O. Bressan et al. 300p. 1985. 41.00 (ISBN 9971-50-003-5). World Scientific Pub.

Relativity, Supersymmetry, & Strings. Ed. by A. Rosenblum. (Illus.). 192p. 1988. 55.00x (ISBN 0-306-42680-3, Plenum Pr). Plenum Pub.

Relativity: The General Theory. J. L. Synge. 1960. 105.25 (ISBN 0-444-10279-5, North-Holland). Elsevier.

Relativity: The Golden Cloak. Rudy Ydur. LC 77-89035. 64p. 1980. pap. 4.95 (ISBN 0-930592-04-2). Lumeli Pr.

Relativity: The Special & General Theory. Albert Einstein. Tr. by Robert W. Lawson. 1961. pap. 3.95 (ISBN 0-517-02530-2). Crown.

Relativity: The Special & General Theory. Albert Einstein. 14.25 (ISBN 0-8446-1169-7). Peter Smith.

Relativity: The Special Theory. 2nd ed. J. L. Synge. 1965. 105.25 (ISBN 0-444-10280-9, North-Holland). Elsevier.

Relativity: The Theory & Its Philosophy. Roger B. Angel. (Foundations & Philosophy of Science & Technology Ser.). (Illus.). 320p. 1980. pap. text ed. 31.00 (ISBN 0-08-025196-X). Pergamon.

Relativity Theory & Astrophysics: Galactic Structure, Proceedings of the Cornell University, Summer Seminar, 1965, Vol. 9. Cornell University, Summer Seminar Staff. Ed. by J. Ehlers. LC 62-21481. (Lectures in Applied Mathematics). 220p. 1974. Repr. of 1967 ed. 27.00 (ISBN 0-8218-1109-6, LAM-9). Am Math.

Relativity Theory & Astrophysics: Relativity & Cosmology. Ed. by J. Ehlers. LC 62-21481. (Lectures in Applied Mathematics Ser.: Vol. 8). 292p. 1979. pap. 28.00 (ISBN 0-8218-1108-8, LAM-8). Am Math.

Relativity Theory & Astrophysics: Stellar Structure. Ed. by J. Ehlers. LC 62-21481. (Lectures in Applied Mathematics Ser.: Vol. 10). 136p. 1967. 26.00 (ISBN 0-8218-1110-X, LAM-10). Am Math.

Relativity Theory: Its Origins & Impact on Modern Thought. Ed. by Pearce Williams. LC 79-9774. 174p. 1979. Repr. of 1968 ed. 13.50 (ISBN 0-88275-959-0). Krieger.

Relativity, Thermodynamics, & Cosmology. Richard C. Tolman. LC 83-45477. 1934. 49.50 (ISBN 0-404-20262-4, QC6). AMS Pr.

Relativity, Thermodynamics & Cosmology. Richard C. Tolman. xv, 501p. 1987. pap. text ed. 11.95 (ISBN 0-486-65383-8). Dover.

Relativity Today: Proceedings of the 2nd Hungarian Relativity Workshop. Ed. by Z. Peries. 400p. (Orig.). 1988. 63.00 (ISBN 9971-50-513-4); pap. 37.00 (ISBN 9971-50-517-7). World Scientific Pub.

Relativity Visualized. Lewis Carroll Epstein. LC 82-84280. (Illus.). 210p. 1987. pap. 15.95 (ISBN 0-935218-05-X). Insight Pr CA.

Relativization & Nominalized Clauses in Huallaga (Huanuco) Quechua. David J. Weber. LC 83-1094. (UC Publications in Linguistics: Vol. 103). 144p. 1984. pap. text ed. 12.00x (ISBN 0-520-09666-5). U of Cal Pr.

Relativization in Hebrew: A Transformational Approach. Yehiel Hayon. (Janua Linguarum Ser. Practica: No. 189). (Illus.). 238p. (Orig.). 1973. pap. text ed. 36.00x (ISBN 90-2792-391-4). Mouton.

Relatorio Anual Da Corte Interamericana De Direitos Humanos a Assembleia General 1980. Inter-American Court of Human Rights. (OEA Ser.: No. L/V/III.3. Doc. 13. 15 Outubro). 56p. 1980. pap. 5.00 (ISBN 0-8270-1292-6). OAS.

Relatos Escogidos. Konstantin Paustovski. 335p. (Span.). 1975. 6.45 (ISBN 0-8285-1326-0, Pub. by Progress Pubs USSR). Imported Pubns.

Relatos Simbolicos: Reading for Skill Development & Communication. K. Chastain. 1983. 20.00 (ISBN 0-8384-1181-9). Heinle & Heinle.

Relax & Enjoy Your Baby. Loraine Stern & Kathleen Mackay. Orig. Title: Off to a Great Start. 1988. pap. 7.95 (ISBN 0-393-30531-7). Norton.

Relax, It's Good for You. Ed Bernd, Jr. 2.95 (ISBN 0-913343-35-8). Inst Psych Inc.

Relax One, Two, Three. rev. ed. Carol Healy. (Illus.). 30p. 1985. pap. text ed. 4.95 (ISBN 0-932491-06-5). Res Appl Inc.

Relax, Recover: Stress Management for Recovering People. Patricia Wuertzer & Lucinda May. LC 87-46219. 144p. (Orig.). 1988. pap. 7.95 (ISBN 0-06-255482-4, PL 4287, HarpR). Har-Row.

Relax! This Book Is Only a Phase You're Going Through: Gay Cartoons from Christopher Street Magazine. Charles Ortleb & Richard Fiala. LC 78-3978. (Illus.). 1978. 4.95 (ISBN 0-312-67046-X); prepack 49.50 (ISBN 0-312-67047-8). St Martin.

Relax! with Self-Therap-Ease. Bonnie Pendleton & Betty Mehling. (Illus.). metal bdg. 15.00 (ISBN 0-917306-01-5). Calif Pubns.

Relax! With Self Therap-Ease: A Simple Illustrated Course. Bonnie Pendleton & Betty Mehling. (Illus.). 176p. 1984. O.p. 13.95 (ISBN 0-13-772195-1); pap. 7.95 (ISBN 0-13-772187-0). P-H.

Relax with Vernon Sechriest. Vernon Sechriest. Intro. by Mae Woods Bell. LC 85-81255. 100p. (Orig.). 1985. pap. 5.95 (ISBN 0-938828-02-9). Falls Tar.

Relaxation. James Hewitt. (Teach Yourself Ser.). 184p. 1988. pap. 7.95 (ISBN 0-679-72117-7). Random.

Relaxation: A Comprehensive Manual for Adults, Children, & Children with Special Needs. Joseph R. Cautela & June Groden. LC 78-62906. (Illus., Orig.). 1978. spiral 13.95 (ISBN 0-87822-186-7, 1867). Res Press.

Relaxation: A Natural High. Sue Gentry. 36p. 1982. inc. audio cassette 6.95 (ISBN 0-89486-142-5). Hazelden.

Relaxation & Imagery: Tools for Therapeutic Communication & Intervention. Zahourek. 272p. 1988. 29.95 (ISBN 0-7216-2589-4). Saunders.

Relaxation & (Re-, or) De-Sensitization Training, Set-RD. Russell E. Mason. 1975. pap. 55.00x (ISBN 0-89533-006-7); incl. tape-1a, t-1, t-2, t-5a, t-6, t-9, Brief Outlines 1, Relaxation Training 45.00x, Clinical Applications, rev. ed., 1979, & Hierarchy incl.; tapes only 45.00x. F I Comm.

Relaxation & Stress Reduction Workbook. 2nd ed. Davis et al. (Illus.). 208p. 1982. 22.50 (ISBN 0-934986-08-8); pap. 12.50 (ISBN 0-934986-04-5). New Harbinger.

Relaxation Dynamics: Nine World Approaches to Self-Relaxation. Jonathan C. Smith. LC 85-61470. 350p. (Orig.). 1985. pap. text ed. 18.95 (ISBN 0-87822-244-8). Res Press.

Relaxation in Glass & Composites. George W. Scherer. LC 85-17871. 331p. 1986. 54.95 (ISBN 0-471-81991-3). Wiley.

Relaxation in Magnetic Resonance: Dielectric & Mossbauer Applications. Charles P. Poole et al. 1971. 84.00 (ISBN 0-12-561450-0). Acad Pr.

Relaxation in Viscous Liquids & Glasses. Steven A. Brawer. 232p. 1985. 50.00 (ISBN 0-916094-68-5). Am Ceramic.

Relaxation Kinetics. C. F. Bernasconi. 1976. 70.00 (ISBN 0-12-092950-3). Acad Pr.

Relaxation Phenomena in Condensed Matter Physics. Sushanta Dattagupta. 302p. 1987. 39.50 (ISBN 0-12-203610-7). Acad Pr.

Relaxation Phenomena in Polymers. Ed. by G. M. Bartenev & y. V. Zelenev. 360p. 1974. text ed. 70.00x (ISBN 0-7065-1485-8, Pub. by Keter Pub Jerusalem). Coronet Bks.

Relaxation Principle: Freedom Through a Change in Viewpoint. William F. McLaughlin. LC 87-82451. 208p. 1988. pap. 9.95 (ISBN 0-9619540-0-0). Joy Pub NM.

Relaxation Processes in Glasses: Special Journal Issue. D. E. Day. 1974. Repr. 71.00 (ISBN 0-444-10613-8, North-Holland). Elsevier.

Relaxation Response. Herbert Benson & Miriam Z. Klipper. 1976. pap. 3.95 (ISBN 0-380-00676-6). Avon.

Relaxation Sensation: The Number One Success Factor in Life. Lorenzo. (Illus.). 128p. (Orig.). 1981. pap. 9.95 (ISBN 0-941122-00-X). Prema Bks.

Relaxation Techniques & Health Sciences: Medical Subject Analysis with Reference Bibliography. Sally M. Frost. LC 85-47860. 150p. 1987. 34.50 (ISBN 0-88164-396-3); pap. 26.50 (ISBN 0-88164-397-1). ABBE Pubs Assn.

Relaxation Techniques for the Simulation of VLSI Circuits. Jacob K. White & Alberto Sangiovanni-Vincentelli. 1986. lib. bdg. 35.95 (ISBN 0-89838-186-X). Kluwer Academic.

Relaxin: Structure, Function & Evolution, Vol. 380. Ed. by Bernard G. Steinetz. 246p. 1982. 54.00 (ISBN 0-89766-149-4); pap. 54.00 (ISBN 0-89766-150-8). NY Acad Sci.

Relay Control Systems. Yakov Z. Tsypkin. Tr. by C. Constanda. (Illus.). 450p. 1985. 90.00 (ISBN 0-521-24390-4). Cambridge U Pr.

Release. Michael Hewlings. 1972. pap. 1.95 (ISBN 0-685-27679-1, Pub. by Anvil Pr); pap. 5.00 signed ltd. ed. (ISBN 0-685-27680-5). Small Pr Dist.

Release & Uptake Functions in Adrenergic Nerve Granules. U. Von-Euler. (Sherrington Lectures: Vol. XV). 99p. 1980. text ed. 15.00x (ISBN 0-85323-084-6, Pub. by Liverpool U Pr). Humanities.

Release from Isolation: How to Find Friendship, Love, & Happiness. J. S. Martindale. LC 79-162932. 1971. 19.95x (ISBN 0-911012-08-7). Nelson-Hall.

Release from Your Problems. David Seabury. 96p. 1966. pap. 4.95 (ISBN 0-911336-15-X). Sci of Mind.

Release of Catecholamines from Adrenergic Neurons. new ed. Ed. by David M. Paton. 1979. 93.00 (ISBN 0-08-021536-X); pap. 39.00 (ISBN 0-08-023755-X). Pergamon.

Release of Genetically Engineered Microorganisms. Ed. by M. Sussman et al. 300p. 1988. price not set (ISBN 0-12-677521-4); pap. price not set (ISBN 0-12-677522-2). Acad Pr.

Release of Neural Transmitter Substances. B. Katz. (Sherrington Lectures: Vol. X). 70p. 1969. text ed. 7.95x (ISBN 0-85323-060-9, Pub. by Liverpool U Pr). Humanities.

Release to Those in Prison. William Klassen. (Focal Pamphlet: No. 26). pap. 20.00 (ISBN 0-317-55620-7, 2029248). Bks Demand UMI.

Release Your Brakes! James W. Newman. 1978. pap. 3.95 (ISBN 0-446-30978-8). Warner Bks.

Release Your Brakes. James W. Newman. (Illus.). 288p. 1988. pap. 14.95 (ISBN 0-937359-44-0). HDL Pubs.

Release Your Business Potential: Using the A. I. M. Strategy to Achieve a Hyper-Performer. Errol R. Korn & George J. Pratt. 1988. cassette 15.95 (ISBN 0-471-62908-1). Wiley.

Released into Dawn. Kelly Adams. (Second Chance at Love Ser.: No. 440). 1988. pap. 2.50 (ISBN 0-425-10836-8). Berkley Pub.

Released to Reign. Charles Trombley. LC 79-90266. 1979. pap. 4.95 (ISBN 0-89221-064-8). New Leaf.

Releasement: Spirituality for Ministry. Barbara Fiand. 112p. 1987. 11.95 (ISBN 0-8245-0813-0). Crossroad NY.
Releasing Anger. S. Richard. 20p. 1985. pap. 0.85 (ISBN 0-89486-249-9). Hazelden.
Releasing Hormones: And Genetics & Immunology. Ed. by Eng-Soon Teoh et al. (Advances in Fertility & Sterility Ser.). (Illus.). 250p. 1987. 55.00 (ISBN 0-940813-18-1). Parthenon NJ.
Releasing My Files. Shirley Aycock. 46p. 1986. Stapled Chapbook 2.25 (ISBN 0-942432-11-8). M O P Pr.
Releasing the Ability of God Through Prayer. Charles Capps. 159p. 1978. pocketbook 3.50 (ISBN 0-89274-075-2). Harrison Hse.
Releasing: The New Behavioral Science Method for Dealing with Pressure Situations. Patricia Carrington. LC 83-15143. 264p. Repr. of 1984 ed. 20.00 (ISBN 0-935385-00-2). Pace Educ Systems.
Releasing the Potential of the Older Volunteer. Ed. by Mary M. Seguin & Beatrice O'Brien. (Andrus Gerontology Center Bk.). (Illus.). 96p. 1976. pap. 7.00x (ISBN 0-317-06886-5, 05749-5). Lexington Bks.
Releasing the Power of the Holy Spirit. Brick Bradford. 32p. 1983. 2.95x (ISBN 0-934421-00-5). Presby Renewal Pubns.
Relentless Gun. Giles A. Lutz. 144p. 1981. pap. 1.75 (ISBN 0-449-13996-4, GM). Fawcett.
Relevance: Communication & Cognition. Dan Sperber & Deirdre Wilson. (Language & Thought Ser.). (Illus.). 288p. 1986. text ed. 27.00x (ISBN 0-674-75475-1); pap. text ed. 10.95x (ISBN 0-674-75476-X). Harvard U Pr.
Relevance in Social Science Research: A Colloquium. Ed. by P. C. Joshi. 368p. 1982. text ed. 37.50x (ISBN 0-7069-1439-2, Pub. by Vikas India). Advent NY.
Relevance in the Education of Today's Business Student, 1973. (Yearbooks). 292p. 7.50 (ISBN 0-933964-10-2). Natl Busn Ed Assoc.
Relevance Lost: The Rise & Fall of Management Accounting. H. Thomas Johnson & Robert S. Kaplan. 288p. 1987. 24.95 (ISBN 0-87584-138-4, Dist. by Harper & Row Pubs., Inc.). Harvard Busn.
Relevance of Ancient Social & Political Philosophy for Our Times: A Short Introduction to the Problem. Kurt Von Fritz. LC 74-78098. iv, 57p. 1974. pap. 5.20x (ISBN 3-11-004859-0). De Gruyter.
Relevance of Apocalyptic. 3rd, rev. ed. H. H. Rowley. LC 64-12221. 240p. 1980. pap. text ed. 9.50 (ISBN 0-87921-061-3). Attic Pr.
Relevance of Bliss. Nona Coxhead. 192p. 1986. pap. 6.95 (ISBN 0-312-67055-9). St Martin.
Relevance of Canadian History: U. S. & Imperial Perspectives. Robin W. Winks. 116p. 1988. Repr. of 1979 ed. lib. bdg. 8.75 (ISBN 0-8191-6831-9). U Pr of Amer.
Relevance of Charles Peirce. Ed. by Eugene Freeman. (Monist Library of Philosophy). 412p. 1983. cloth 29.95 (ISBN 0-914417-00-2). Hegeler Inst.
Relevance of Culture. Morris Freilich et al. 352p. (Orig.). 1989. lib. bdg. 49.95 (ISBN 0-89789-181-3); pap. text ed. 18.95 (ISBN 0-89789-180-5). Bergin & Garvey.
Relevance of Economic Theories. Josef Pajestka & C. H. Feinstein. 1980. 36.00 (ISBN 0-312-67054-0). St Martin.
Relevance of Education. Jerome S. Bruner. LC 74-139376. 192p. 1971. 5.95x (ISBN 0-393-04334-7, Norton Lib.); pap. 4.95x (ISBN 0-393-00690-5, Norton Lib). Norton.
Relevance of Education to Rural Development: Regional Study Group Meeting on Identification of Causes of Educational Underdevelopment in Rural Areas & on Relevance of Education to the Rural Environment, Bangkok, Oct. 22-Nov. 8, 1985. (APEID Ser.). 53p. 1986. pap. text ed. 10.00 (ISBN 0-318-21535-7, UB218, UB). UNIPUB.
Relevance of General Systems Theory. Ed. by Ervin Laszlo. LC 72-81355. 192p. 1972. 8.95 (ISBN 0-8076-0659-6); pap. 3.45 (ISBN 0-8076-0658-8). Braziller.
Relevance of International Adjudication. Milton Katz. LC 68-21974. 1968. 15.00x (ISBN 0-674-75500-6). Harvard U Pr.
Relevance of John's Apocalypse. Donald Guthrie. 96p. (Orig.). 1987. pap. 6.95 (ISBN 0-8028-0329-6). Eerdmans.
Relevance of Metaethics to Ethics. T. Tannsjo. (Stockholm Studies in Philosophy: No. 5). 226p. (Orig.). 1976. pap. 24.50x (ISBN 0-317-65788-7). Coronet Bks.
Relevance of N-Nitroso Compounds to Human Cancer: Exposures & Mechanisms. Ed. by H. Bartsch et al. (IARC Scientific Ser. 84). (Illus.). 688p. 1987. 98.00 (ISBN 92-832-1184-7). Oxford U Pr.
Relevance of Natural Science to Theology. William H. Austin. LC 75-43222. (Library of Philosophy & Religion). 132p. 1976. text ed. 28.50x (ISBN 0-06-490240-4, 06321). B&N Imports.
Relevance of Physics. Stanley L. Jaki. LC 66-20583. 1967. 25.00x (ISBN 0-226-39143-4). U of Chicago Pr.
Relevance of Prepaid Group Practice to the Effective Delivery of Health Services. Ernest Saward. Ed. by T. Bell. 12p. 1968. pap. text ed. 1.00 (ISBN 0-936164-04-2). Group Health Assoc of Amer.
Relevance of Public Finance for Policy Making: Proceedings of the Congress of International Institute of Public Finance, 41st. Hans M. Van de Kar & Barbara L. Wolfe. LC 87-6197. 341p. 1987. 45.00x (ISBN 0-8143-1910-6). Wayne St U Pr.
Relevance of Ranganathan's Contributions to Library Science in a Changing Context. R. S. Rajagopalan. 1988. text ed. 35.00x (ISBN 0-7069-4012-1, Pub. by Vikas India). Advent NY.
Relevance of the Beautiful & Other Essays. Hans-Georg Gadamer. Ed. by Robert Bernasconi. 190p. 1987. 39.50 (ISBN 0-521-24178-2); pap. 10.95 (ISBN 0-521-33953-7). Cambridge U Pr.
Relevancy of Torah to the Social & Ethical Issues of Our Time. Dovid Cohen. (Annual Fryer Memorial Lecture Ser.). 0.50 (ISBN 0-914131-57-5, 136). Torah Umesorah.
Relevant Financial Statements: Original Anthology. new ed. Joshua Ronen & George H. Sorter. Ed. by Richard P. Brief. LC 77-87318. (Development of Contemporary Accounting Thought Ser). 1978. lib. bdg. 20.00x (ISBN 0-405-10930-X). Ayer Co Pubs.
Relevant Logic: A Philosophical Examination of Inference. Stephen Read. 208p. Date not set. text ed. 55.00 (ISBN 0-631-16184-8). Basil Blackwell.
Relevant Logics & Their Rivals, One. Richard Routley. 460p. 1983. 33.00 (ISBN 0-917930-80-0); pap. 19.00 (ISBN 0-917930-66-5). Ridgeview.
Relevant Mathematics. George N. Stone & Lawrence W. Becker. Incl. Algebra I. (gr. 9). 1970 (ISBN 0-88334-024-0); Geometry. (gr. 10). 1971 (ISBN 0-88334-043-7); Advanced Algebra & Trigonometry. (gr. 11-12). 1971 (ISBN 0-88334-044-5). pap. text ed. 8.00 ea. Ind Sch Pr.
Relevant Memoir: The Story of the Equinox Cooperative Press. Henry Hart. (Illus.). 1977. 10.95 (ISBN 0-930986-00-8). Three Mtn Pr.
Relevant Methods in Comparative Education: Report of a Meeting of International Experts. Ed. by Reginald Edwards et al. (International Studies in Education: No. 33). (Illus.). 270p. 1973. pap. 12.75 (ISBN 92-820-1003-1, U544, UNESCO). UNIPUB.
Relevant Problems for Chemical Principles. 4th, rev. ed. I. S. Butler & A. E. Grosser. 1984. pap. 15.95 (ISBN 0-8053-1230-7). Benjamin-Cummings.
Relevant Record. Charles P. Conn & Charles W. Conn. LC 76-2969. (Illus.). (YA) (gr. 7-12). 1976. pap. 1.99 (ISBN 0-87148-732-2). Pathway Pr.
Relevant Topics in Athletic Training. Kent Scriber & Edmund J. Burke. 1978. text ed. 19.95; pap. 14.95 (ISBN 0-932392-02-4). Mouvement Pubns.
Relevants. Edward G. Quinn & Paul J. Dolan. 1970. pap. text ed. 5.95 (ISBN 0-02-925600-3). Free Pr.
Releves de Touen Houang. Musee Cernuschi. 25p. 1956. 105.00x (ISBN 0-317-68488-4, Pub. by Han-Shan Tang Ltd). State Mutual Bk.
Relexions Sur la Nature Des Choses et la Logique Du Droit: Contribution a L'ontologie & a L'epistemologie Juridiques. H. A. Schwarz-Liebermann Von Wahlendorf. 1973. 20.80x (ISBN 90-2797-168-4). Mouton.
Reliability & Biometry: Statistical Analysis of Lifelength. Ed. by Frank Proschan & R. J. Serfling. LC 74-78907. (Proceeding Ser.). x, 815p. 1974. text ed. 44.00 (ISBN 0-89871-159-2). Soc Indus-Appl Math.
Reliability & Degradation: Semiconductor Devices & Circuits. M. J. Howes & D. V. Morgan. LC 80-42310. (Solid State Devices & Circuits Ser.). 424p. 1981. 84.95x (ISBN 0-471-28028-3, Pub. by Wiley-Interscience). Wiley.
Reliability & Fault Tree Analysis: Theoretical & Applied Aspects of System Reliability & Safety Assessment. Ed. by Richard E. Barlow et al. LC 75-22580. (Proceeding Ser.). (Illus.). xxxix, 927p. 1975. Repr. of 1982 ed. text ed. 46.50 (ISBN 0-89871-033-2). Soc Indus-Appl Math.
Reliability & Life Testing. S. K. Sinha. 1986. 24.95 (ISBN 0-470-20701-9). Wiley.
Reliability & Maintainability in Perspective: Practical, Contractual, Commercial & Software Aspects. David J. Smith. 1985. 29.95 (ISBN 0-470-20175-4). Halsted Pr.
Reliability & Maintainability Management. Balbir S. Dhillon & Hans Reiche. (Illus.). 288p. 1985. 39.95 (ISBN 0-442-27637-0). Van Nos Reinhold.
Reliability & Maintainability of Electronic Systems. Ed. by J. E. Arsenault & J. A. Roberts. LC 79-10543. (Digital Systems Design ser.). (Illus.). 584p. 1980. text ed. 44.95 (ISBN 0-914894-24-2, Computer Sci Pr). W H Freeman.
Reliability & Optimization of Structural Systems. Ed. by P. Thoft-Christensen. (Lecture Notes in Engineering Ser.: Vol. 33). (Illus.). vi, 474p. 1987. pap. 71.50 (ISBN 0-387-18570-4). Springer-Verlag.
Reliability & Quality Control. Ed. by A. P. Basu. 416p. 1986. 80.00 (ISBN 0-444-87925-0, North-Holland). Elsevier.
Reliability & Risk Analysis: Methods & Nuclear Power Applications. Norman J. McCormick. LC 81-2758. 1981. 42.50 (ISBN 0-12-482360-2). Acad Pr.
Reliability & Robustness of Engineering Software. C. A. Brebbia. 1987. 175.75 (ISBN 0-444-98948-X). Elsevier.
Reliability & Robustness of Engineering Software. C. A. Brebbia & G. Keramidas. LC 87-62015. 450p. 1987. 138.00 (ISBN 0-931215-61-7). Computational Mech MA.
Reliability & Safety of Pressure Components. Ed. by C. Sundararajan. (PVP Ser.: Vol. 62). 254p. 1982. 50.00 (H00219). ASME.
Reliability & Validity Assessment. Edward G. Carmines & Richard A. Zeller. LC 79-67629. (Quantitative Applications in the Social Sciences: No. 17). (Illus.). 70p. 1979. pap. 6.50 (ISBN 0-8039-1371-0). Sage.
Reliability & Validity in Neuropsychological Assessment. M. D. Franzen. (Critical Issues in Neuropsychology Ser.). (Illus.). 280p. Date not set. price not set (ISBN 0-306-43065-7, Plenum Pr). Plenum Pub.
Reliability & Validity in Qualitative Research. Jerome Kirk & Marc L. Miller. (Qualitative Research Methods Ser.: Vol. 1). 96p. 1985. text ed. 12.50 (ISBN 0-8039-2560-3); pap. text ed. 6.00 (ISBN 0-8039-2470-4). Sage.
Reliability Assessment of Large Electric Power Systems. Roy Billinton & Ronald N. Allen. 1988. lib. bdg. 52.50 (ISBN 0-89838-266-1). Kluwer Academic.
Reliability, Availability & Maintainability: RAM. Joseph W. Foster, 3rd et al. LC 80-81873. 272p. 1982. Repr. of 1981 ed. 25.95 (ISBN 0-930206-05-3). Weber Systems.
Reliability Considerations in Fiber Optic Applications. Ed. by Paul. 174p. 1986. 36.00 (ISBN 0-89252-752-8, 717). SPIE.
Reliability Data Bases. Aniello Amendola & Alfred Z. Keller. 1987. lib. bdg. 74.00 (ISBN 90-277-2549-7, Pub. by Reidel Holland). Kluwer Academic.
Reliability Data Collection & Use in Risk & Availabilty Assessement. Ed. by H. J. Wingender. xvi, 720p. 1986. 89.00 (ISBN 0-387-16365-4). Springer-Verlag.
Reliability Data for Pumps & Drivers Valve Actuator & Valves: Standard 500-1984. (IEEE Standards Publications). 488p. 1987. for info. 53.00 (ISBN 0-471-85686-X). Wiley.
Reliability Engineering. ARINC Research Corporation Staff. 1964. ref. ed. 59.00 (ISBN 0-13-773127-2). P-H.
Reliability Engineering. Ed. by Patrick D. T. O'Connor. (Arab School of Science & Technology Ser.). 305p. 1987. 49.50 (ISBN 0-89116-684-X). Hemisphere Pub.
Reliability Engineering for Electrical Design. Fuqua. (Electrical Engineering Ser.). 392p. 1986. 69.75 (ISBN 0-8247-7571-6). Dekker.
Reliability Engineering for Nuclear & Other High Technology Systems: A Practical Guide. Armand A. Lakner & Ronald T. Anderson. (Illus.). 418p. 1985. 120.75 (ISBN 0-85334-286-5, Pub. by Elsevier Applied Sci England). Elsevier.
Reliability Engineering in Systems Design & Operation. B. Dhillion. 336p. 1982. 45.95 (ISBN 0-442-27213-8). Van Nos Reinhold.
Reliability Evaluation of Engineering Systems. R. Billinton & R. N. Allan. LC 82-18578. 360p. 1983. 45.00x (ISBN 0-306-41296-9, Plenum Press). Plenum Pub.
Reliability Evaluation of Power Systems. Ed. by Roy Billinton & Ronald N. Allan. 436p. 1984. 59.50x (ISBN 0-306-41450-3, Plenum Pr). Plenum Pub.
Reliability Evaluation of Some Fault-Tolerant Computer Architectures. S. Osaki & T. Nishio. (Lecture Notes in Computer Science Ser.: Vol. 97). 129p. 1980. pap. 13.00 (ISBN 0-387-10274-4). Springer-Verlag.
Reliability for the Technologies. Leonard Doty. LC 85-14423. 242p. 1985. 24.95x (ISBN 0-8311-1169-0). Indus Pr.
Reliability Handbook. William G. Ireson. 1966. text ed. 75.50 (ISBN 0-07-032040-3). McGraw.
Reliability-Heavy Duty. 1983. 10.00 (ISBN 0-89883-304-3, SP533). Soc Auto Engineers.
Reliability in Computer System Design. B. S. Dhillon. Ed. by Marvin Zelkowitz. LC 87-1164. (Ablex Series in Software Engineering). 336p. 1987. text ed. 45.00 (ISBN 0-89391-412-6). Ablex Pub.
Reliability in Computing: The Role of Interval Methods in Scientific Computing. Ed. by Ramon E. Moore. (Perspectives in Computing Ser.: Vol. 19). 428p. 1988. 49.95 (ISBN 0-12-505630-3). Acad Pr.
Reliability in Electrical & Electronic Components & Systems. Ed. by E. Lauger & J. Moltoft. 1172p. 1982. 142.00 (ISBN 0-444-86419-9, North-Holland). Elsevier.
Reliability in Engineering Design. K. C. Kapur & L. R. Lamberson. LC 76-1304. 586p. 1977. text ed. write for info. (ISBN 0-471-51191-9). Wiley.
Reliability in the Acquisitions Process. Launder Depriest. (Statistics Lecture Notes). 296p. 1983. 45.00 (ISBN 0-8247-1792-9). Dekker.
Reliability in Water Resources Management. Ed. by Edward A. McBean et al. LC 79-64191. 1979. 18.00 (ISBN 0-918334-30-6). WRP.
Reliability: Management, Methods & Mathematics. 2nd. ed. Lloyd & Lipow. 240p. 1985. pap. 25.00 (ISBN 0-87389-000-0). ASQC Qual Pr.
Reliability: Management, Methods & Mathematics. 2nd ed. D. K. Lloyd & M Lipow. 616p. 1977. 22.50 (ISBN 0-318-13241-9, P 140). Am Soc QC.
Reliability: Management, Methods & Mathematics. 2nd rev. ed. David K. Lloyd & Myron Lipow. LC 77-80554. 1977. Repr. of 1962 ed. 22.50 (ISBN 0-9601504-1-2). Lloyd & Lipow.
Reliability Modeling in Electric Power Systems. J. Endrenyi. LC 78-6222. 352p. 1978. 97.95x (ISBN 0-471-99664-5, Pub. by Wiley-Interscience). Wiley.
Reliability Modelling & Applications. A. G. Colombo & A. Z. Keller. 1987. lib. bdg. 72.00 (ISBN 90-277-2566-7, Pub. by Reidel Holland). Kluwer Academic.
Reliability of Analogue Electronic Systems. K. B. Klaasen. (Studies in Electrical & Electronic Engineering: Vol. 13). 278p. 1984. 92.00 (ISBN 0-444-42388-5). Elsevier.
Reliability of Engineering Materials. Alrick L. Smith. (Illus.). 160p. (Orig.). 1985. pap. text ed. 24.95 (ISBN 0-408-01507-1). Butterworth.
Reliability of Hydro-Reclamation Installations. Te E. Mirtskhulava. Tr. by V. S. Kothekar from Rus. 308p. 1987. text ed. 48.50 (ISBN 90-6191-491-4, Pub. by A A Balkema). Brookfield Pub Co.
Reliability of Instrumentation Systems for Safeguarding & Control: Proceedings of the IFAC Workshop, the Hague, the Netherlands, 12-14 May, 1986. Ed. by J. P. Jansen. (IFAC Publication Ser.). (Illus.). 250p. 1987. 65.00 (ISBN 0-08-034063-6, PBL). Pergamon.
Reliability of Large Machines. 116p. (Orig.). 1982. pap. text ed. 37.50x (ISBN 0-85825-170-1, Pub. by Inst Engineering Australia). Brookfield Pub Co.
Reliability of Mental Tests in the Division of an Academic Group see Two Studies in Mental Tests.
Reliability of Non-Destructive Inspection: Assessing the Assessment of Structures Under Stress. M. G. Silk et al. 232p. 1987. 66.00x (ISBN 0-85274-533-8, Pub. by A Hilger UK). Taylor & Francis.
Reliability of Nuclear Power Plants. (Proceedings Ser.). (Illus.). 751p. 1976. pap. 80.00 (ISBN 92-0-050075-7, ISP403, IAEA). UNIPUB.
Reliability of Power Supply Systems. Institution of Electrical Engineers (UK) & Peter Peregrinus, Ltd. (Conference Publications: No. 225). 166p. 1983. pap. 64.00 (ISBN 0-85296-278-9, IC225). Inst Elect Eng.
Reliability of Randomly Excited Hysteretic Structures. B. F. Spencer. (Lecture Notes in Engineering Ser.: Vol. 21). 155p. 1986. pap. 18.70 (ISBN 0-387-16863-X). Springer-Verlag.
Reliability of Reactor Pressure Components: Proceedings of a Symposium, Stuttgart 21-25 March 1983. (Proceedings Ser.). 414p. 1983. pap. text ed. 80.00 (ISBN 92-0-050883-9, ISP645, IAEA). UNIPUB.
Reliability of Shell Buckling Predictions. William A. Litle. (Press Research Monographs: No. 25). 1964. 25.00x (ISBN 0-262-12013-5). MIT Pr.
Reliability of Sub-Seabed Disposal Operations for High Level Waste. M. M. Sarshar. 1986. pap. 61.00 (ISBN 0-86010-835-X, Pub. by Graham & Trotman UK). Kluwer Academic.
Reliability Problems of Reactor Pressure Components, 2 vols. (Proceedings Ser.). 1978. Vol. 1. pap. 61.00 (ISBN 92-0-050078-1, ISP467-1, IAEA); Vol.2. pap. 45.75 (ISP-467-2). UNIPUB.
Reliability Specification. EEMUA Staff. 1987. 75.00x (ISBN 0-85931-118-X, Pub. by EEMUA). State Mutual Bk.
Reliability, Stress Analysis & Failure Prevention Methods in Mechanical Design: International Conference on Reliability, Stress Analysis & Failure Prevention, 1980 San Francisco, CA. Ed. by Wayne D. Milestone. LC 80-66039. 1980. pap. 85.10 (ISBN 0-317-58253-4, 2056393). Bks Demand UMI.
Reliability Technology. Green & Bourne. 636p. 99.95 (ISBN 0-318-13243-5). Am Soc QC.
Reliability Technology. A. E. Green & A. J. Bourne. LC 73-161691. 636p. 1972. 146.00 (ISBN 0-471-32480-9). Wiley.
Reliability Technology: Theory & Applications. Ed. by J. Moltoft & F. Jensen. 450p. 1986. 105.25 (ISBN 0-444-70039-0, North-Holland). Elsevier.
Reliability Test Plans & Facilities Workshop Proceedings. LC 62-38584. 33p. 1977. pap. text ed. 4.50 (ISBN 0-915414-51-1). Inst Environ Sci.
Reliability: The User-Maker Partnership: Papers Presented at the 9th International Technical Conference of British Pump Manufacturers Association. 304p. 1985. softcover 60.00 (ISBN 0-947711-00-7, Dist. by Air Science Co.). BHRA Fluid.
Reliability Theory & Applications: Proceedings of China-Japan Symposium. Ed. by S. Osaki & J. Cao. 448p. 1987. 55.00 (ISBN 9971-50-347-6). World Scientific Pub.
Reliability Theory & Its Application in Structural & Soil Mechanics. Ed. by P. Thoft-Christensen. (NATO, E Ser.). 1983. lib. bdg. 87.00 (ISBN 90-2472-859-2, Pub. by Martinus Nijhoff Netherlands). Kluwer Academic.
Reliability Theory & Models: Stochastic Failure Models, Optimal Maintenance Policies, Life Testing, & Structure. Ed. by M. Abdel-Hameed et al. (Notes & Reports in Computer & Applied Mathematics Ser.). 1984. 49.00 (ISBN 0-12-041420-1). Acad Pr.
Reliability vs. Reality: Proceedings of the Annual Meeting of the Institute of Environmental Sciences, 10th, 1964. Annual Meeting of the Institute of Environmental Sciences Staff. LC 62-38584. (Illus.). 1964. pap. text ed. 7.00 (ISBN 0-915414-04-X). Inst Environ Sci.

Reliable Computer Systems. S. K. Shrivastava. (Texts & Monographs in Computer Science). (Illus.). 620p. 1985. 45.00 (ISBN 0-387-15256-3). Springer-Verlag.

Reliable Data Structures in C. Thomas Plum. 200p. 1985. pap. text ed. 25.00x (ISBN 0-911537-04-X). Plum Hall.

Reliable Distributed Real-Time Operating Systems: The Alpha Kernel. J. Duane Northcutt. (Perspectives in Computing Ser.). 246p. 1987. 25.00 (ISBN 0-12-521690-4). Acad Pr.

Reliable Distributed System Software. John A. Stankovic. (Tutorial Text Ser.). 400p. 1985. 36.00 (ISBN 0-8186-0570-7, EZ570). IEEE Comp Soc.

Reliable Fuels for Liquid Metal Reactors: International Conference Proceedings, Tucson, AZ September 7-11, 1986. 919p. 1986. 75.00 (ISBN 0-318-22500-X). Am Nuclear Soc.

Reliable Healthcare Companion: Understanding & Managing Arthritis. Ed. by John Decker. 192p. (Orig.). 1987. pap. 6.95 (ISBN 0-380-75011-2). Avon.

Reliable Healthcare Companions: Understanding & Managing Asthma. John L. Decker. Ed. by Michael Kaliner. 192p. 1988. pap. 6.95 (ISBN 0-380-75427-4). Avon.

Reliable Healthcare Companions: Understanding & Managing Diabetes. Ed. by John L. Decker & Phillip Gorden. 192p. 1987. pap. 6.95 (ISBN 0-380-75247-6). Avon.

Reliable Healthcare Companions: Understanding & Managing Hypertension. John L. Decker & Harry R. Keiser. 224p. 1987. pap. 6.95 (ISBN 0-380-75248-4). Avon.

Reliable Healthcare Companions: Understanding & Managing Osteoporosis. Ed. by John L. Decker. 176p. 1988. pap. 6.95 (ISBN 0-380-75429-0). Avon.

Reliable Knowledge. John M. Ziman. LC 78-3792. (Illus.). 1979. 34.50 (ISBN 0-521-22087-4). Cambridge U Pr.

Reliable Nuclear Power Today: Proceedings, American Nuclear Society Topical Meeting, Charlotte NC, April 10-13, 1978. 172p. softcover 23.00 (ISBN 0-317-33039-X, 700036). Am Nuclear Soc.

Relic of the Revolution. Charles Herbert. LC 67-29023. (Eyewitness Accounts of the American Revolution Ser.: No. 1). 1968. Repr. of 1847 ed. 9.50 (ISBN 0-405-01114-8). Ayer Co Pubs.

Relics. Joan C. Cruz. LC 84-60744. (Illus.). 352p. 1984. pap. 10.95 (ISBN 0-87973-701-8, 701). Our Sunday Visitor.

Relics. Elton Glaser. 51p. 1984. 17.00x (ISBN 0-8195-2118-3); pap. 8.95 (ISBN 0-8195-1119-6). Wesleyan U Pr.

Relics. Allen Hoey. 16p. pap. 2.50 (ISBN 0-918092-10-8). Tamarack Edns.

Relics of Ancient China, from the Collection of Dr. Paul Singer. Asia Society & Paul Singer. Ed. by Asia House Gallery, New York. 35.50 (ISBN 0-405-06566-3, 10761). Ayer Co Pubs.

Relics of Literature. Stephen Collet. 1973. Repr. of 1823 ed. 45.00 (ISBN 0-8274-1664-4). R West.

Relics of Sherlock Holmes. Gary Lovisi. 48p. (Orig.). 1987. pap. 3.00 (ISBN 0-936071-05-2). Gryphon Pubns.

Relics of the Road. Gini Rice. Incl. GMC Truck Gems, 1900-1950 (ISBN 0-8038-6326-8). o.p. 10.95 ea. Hastings.

Relics Recycled on Cloud Nine. Margaret R. Otis. LC 81-18286. (Illus.). 96p. 1981. pap. 4.95 (ISBN 0-915010-30-5). Sutter House.

Relics Salvaged from the Seabed off Sinan. Bureau of Cultural Properties. 339p. 1985. 420.00x (ISBN 0-317-68999-1, Pub. by Han-Shan Tang Ltd). State Mutual Bk.

Relics, Water & the Kitchen Sink: A Diver's Guide to Underwater Archeology. 2nd ed. Alan R. Rowe. 56p. 1988. pap. 6.95 (ISBN 0-9616399-1-1). Sea Sports Pubns.

Relief & Reconstruction. Roger Wilson. 1943. pap. 2.50x (ISBN 0-87574-022-7, 022). Pendle Hill.

Relief & Rescue of Jews from Nazi Oppression, 1943-1945. J. Mendelsohn. LC 81-80322. (Holocaust Ser.). 264p. 1982. lib. bdg. 61.00 (ISBN 0-8240-4888-1). Garland Pub.

Relief at Last! Neutralization for Food Allergy & Other Illnesses. Joseph B. Miller. (Illus.). 352p. 1987. 41.25 (ISBN 0-398-05283-2). C C Thomas.

Relief Book for Pressured Cookers. Leola Skeen. 100p. 1984. pap. 12.95 (ISBN 0-930047-00-1). Goldenleaf Pub Co.

Relief from Back Pain: The Tollison Program. C. David Tollison. 253p. 1987. text ed. 21.95 (ISBN 0-89876-140-9). Gardner Pr.

Relief from Headache. Donald I. Peterson. LC 83-71941. (Illus.). 153p. 1983. pap. 7.50 (ISBN 0-913657-00-X). D E Donel.

Relief from Premenstrual Syndrome. Celia M. Halas. 145p. 1984. 13.95 (ISBN 0-8119-0691-4). Fell.

Relief in Hungary & the Failure of the Joel Brand Mission. J. Mendelsohn. LC 81-80323. (Holocaust Ser.). 256p. 1982. lib. bdg. 61.00 (ISBN 0-8240-4889-X). Garland Pub.

Relief-Moulded Jugs, 1820-1900. R. K. Henrywood. (Illus.). 1984. 49.50. Antique Collect.

Relief Moulded Jugs, 1820-1900. R. K. Henrywood. 1985. 49.50 (ISBN 0-907462-58-8). Apollo.

Relief of Intractable Pain. 3rd. rev. ed. M. Swerdlow. (Monographs in Anaesthesiology: Vol. 13). 1984. 133.25 (ISBN 0-444-80512-5, 1-068-84). Elsevier.

Relief of Pain by T. E. N. S. Transcutaneous Electrical Nerve Stimulation. Bengt Sjolund & Margareta Eriksson. LC 85-16935. 116p. 1985. pap. 17.50 (ISBN 0-471-90753-7, Dist. by A R Liss). Wiley.

Relief of Poverty: 1834-1914. 2nd, rev. ed. Michael E. Rose. (Studies in Economic & Social History). (Illus.). 80p. 1986. pap. text ed. 9.95x (ISBN 0-333-11236-9). Humanities.

Relief or Reform? Reagan's Regulatory Dilemma. George C. Eads & Michael Fix. LC 84-5283. (Changing Domestic Priorities Ser.). 283p. 1984. pap. 12.95x (ISBN 0-87766-333-5). Urban Inst.

Relief Printmaking. Gerald F. Brommer. LC 77-113860. (Illus.). (YA) (gr. 7-12). 12.95 (ISBN 0-87192-034-4). Davis Mass.

Relief Sculpture for the Facade of the Certosa di Pavia, 1473-1499. Charles R. Morscheck, Jr. LC 77-94727. (Outstanding Dissertations in the Fine Arts Ser.). 1978. lib. bdg. 69.00x (ISBN 0-8240-3243-8). Garland Pub.

Relief Woodcarving & Lettering. Ian Norbury. (Illus.). 157p. 1988. pap. 15.95 (ISBN 0-941936-12-0). Linden Pub Fresno.

Reliefers. Rosetta Daily. 240p. 1986. 14.95 (ISBN 0-8059-3015-9). Dorrance.

Reliefs & Inscriptions at Karnak, IV: The Battle Reliefs of King Sety I. Epigraphic Survey Staff. LC 84-61870. (Oriental Institute Publications Ser.: No. 107). 1986. portfolio 125.00 (ISBN 0-918986-42-7). Oriental Inst.

Religieuse. Denis Diderot. (Folio Ser.: No. 57). 1972. 7.95 (ISBN 0-686-56027-2). Schoenhof.

Religieuse. Denis Diderot. 1972. write for info. French & Eur.

Religieuse see Oeuvres.

Religio Medici, Hydriotaphia & the Garden of Cyrus. Thomas Browne. Ed. by R. H. Robbins. 1972. pap. 11.95x (ISBN 0-19-871064-X). Oxford U Pr.

Religio-Political Ferment in North-West Frontier During the Mughal Period. Tariq Ahmed. 1983. 12.50x (ISBN 0-8364-1081-5, Pub. by Idarah). South Asia Bks.

Religioese Existenz und Literarische Produktion. Albrecht Willert. 316p. (Ger.). 1982. 43.70 (ISBN 3-8204-5994-4). P Lang Pubs.

Religion. Gilda Berger. (Reference First Bk.). 96p. (gr. 4 up). 1983. PLB 10.40 (ISBN 0-531-04538-2). Watts.

Religion. Leszek Kolakowski. LC 81-85135. 1982. 24.95x (ISBN 0-19-520372-0). Oxford U Pr.

Religion. Desmond Painter & John Shepard. Ed. by Malcolm Yapp & Margaret Killinger. (World History Ser.). (Illus.). 32p. (gr. 6-11). 1980. lib. bdg. 6.95 (ISBN 0-89908-145-2); pap. text ed. 2.45 (ISBN 0-89908-120-7). Greenhaven.

Religion, 3 vols. (British Parliamentary Papers Ser.). 1971. Set. 284.00x (ISBN 0-7165-1498-2, Pub. by Irish Academic Pr Ireland). Biblio Dist.

Religion, Vol. 1 (incl. 1978-1980 Supplements) Ed. by Eleanor C. Goldstein. (Social Issues Resources Ser.). 1981. 75.00 (ISBN 0-89777-021-8). Soc Issues.

Religion, Vol. 2 (incl. 1981-1985 Supplements) Ed. by Eleanor C. Goldstein. 1986. 75.00 (ISBN 0-89777-053-6). Soc Issues.

Religion: A Dialogue, & Other Essays. 3rd ed. Arthur Schopenhauer. Tr. by T. Bailey Saunders. LC 72-488. (Essay Index Reprint Ser.). Repr. of 1891 ed. 13.00 (ISBN 0-8369-2820-2). Ayer Co Pubs.

Religion: A Dialogue, & Other Essays. Arthur Schopenhauer. Tr. by T. Bailey Saunders. LC 72-11305. 140p. 1973. Repr. of 1899 ed. lib. bdg. 35.00x (ISBN 0-8371-6652-7, SCRE). Greenwood.

Religion: A Preface. John F. Wilson. (Illus.). 240p. 1982. pap. text ed. write for info. (ISBN 0-13-773192-2). P-H.

Religion: A Secular Theory. Andrew M. Greeley. 144p. 1982. text ed. 19.95 (ISBN 0-02-912870-6); pap. text ed. 8.95x (ISBN 0-02-912880-3). Free Pr.

Religion: A Sociological View. Elizabeth K. Nottingham. LC 81-40769. 348p. 1981. pap. text ed. 14.25 (ISBN 0-8191-1813-3). U Pr of Amer.

Religion Across Cultures. Eugene A. Nida. LC 68-11733. (Applied Cultural Anthropology Ser). 111p. 1979. pap. text ed. 3.95x (ISBN 0-87808-738-9). William Carey Lib.

Religion, Aging & Health: A Global Perspective. Ed. by William M. Clements. (Journal of Religion & Aging: Vol. 4, Nos. 3-4). (Illus.). 156p. 1988. text ed. 22.95 (ISBN 0-86656-803-4). Haworth Pr.

Religion, Altered States of Consciousness, & Social Change. Ed. by Erika Bourguignon. LC 72-8448. (Illus.). 399p. 1973. 12.50 (ISBN 0-8142-0167-9). Ohio St U Pr.

Religion: An Anthropological View. Anthony F. Wallace. 1966. text ed. write for info (ISBN 0-394-30543-4, RanC). Random.

Religion: An Introduction. T. William Hall et al. LC 85-42777. 288p. (Orig.). 1986. pap. 14.95 (ISBN 0-06-063573-8, HarpR). Har-Row.

Religion & Aging: An Annotated Bibliography. Vincent J. Fecher. LC 82-81019. 119p. 1982. 16.00 (ISBN 0-911536-96-5); pap. 9.00 (ISBN 0-911536-97-3). Trinity U Pr.

Religion & Aging: The Behavioral & Social Sciences Look at Religion & Aging. Ed. by Richard H. Davis. 84p. 1967. pap. 3.00 (ISBN 0-88474-009-9). U of S Cal Pr.

Religion & Alienation: A Theological Reading of Sociology. Ed. by Gregory Baum. LC 75-28652. 304p. 1976. pap. 9.95 (ISBN 0-8091-1917-X). Paulist Pr.

Religion & America: Spirituality in a Secular Age. Ed. by Mary Douglas & Steven M. Tipton. LC 82-72500. 256p. 1983. 25.00x (ISBN 0-8070-1106-1); pap. 14.95x (ISBN 0-8070-1107-X, BP648). Beacon Pr.

Religion & Art. Paul Weiss. (Aquinas Lecture). 1963. 7.95 (ISBN 0-87462-128-3). Marquette.

Religion & Art see Richard Wagner's Prose Works.

Religion & Art, & Other Essays. facs. ed. John L. Spalding. LC 72-86785. (Essay Index Reprint Ser). 1905. 17.00 (ISBN 0-8369-1195-4). Ayer Co Pubs.

Religion & Art in Ashanti. Robert S. Rattray. LC 76-44781. Repr. of 1927 ed. 34.50 (ISBN 0-404-15878-1). AMS Pr.

Religion & Art of William Hale White (Mark Rutherford) Wilfred Stone. 1979. Repr. of 1954 ed. lib. bdg. 30.00 (ISBN 0-8492-8233-0). R West.

Religion & Art of William Hale White. Wilfred H. Stone. LC 79-176447. Repr. of 1954 ed. 28.00 (ISBN 0-404-51822-2). AMS Pr.

Religion & Artificial Reproduction: An Inquiry into the Vatican Instruction, On Respect for Human Life. Thomas A. Shannon & Lisa S. Cahill. 144p. 1988. 17.95 (ISBN 0-8245-0860-2). Crossroad NY.

Religion & Ceremonies of the Lenape. Mark R. Harrington. LC 76-43731. (MAI Indian Notes & Monographs. Miscellaneous). Repr. of 1921 ed. 31.50 (ISBN 0-404-15572-3). AMS Pr.

Religion & Churches in Eastern Europe. Ed. by Virgil Elizondo & Norbert Greinacher. (Concilium Ser.: Vol. 154). 128p. (Orig.). 1982. pap. 6.95 (ISBN 0-8164-2385-7, HarpR). Har-Row.

Religion & Civilization. A. H. Nadvi. 4.00 (ISBN 0-686-18566-8). Kazi Pubns.

Religion & Communism. Julius F. Hecker. LC 73-842. (Russian Studies: Perspectives on the Revolution Ser.). 302p. 1987. Repr. of 1934 ed. 26.75 (ISBN 0-88355-037-7). Hyperion Conn.

Religion & Communist Society: Selected Papers from the Second World Congress for Soviet & East European Studies. Ed. by Dennis J. Dunn. 165p. (Orig.). 1983. pap. 14.00 (ISBN 0-933884-29-X). Berkeley Slavic.

Religion & Conscience in Ancient Egypt. William F. Petrie. LC 72-83176. Repr. of 1898 ed. 24.50 (ISBN 0-405-08854-X). Ayer Co Pubs.

Religion & Constitutional Government in the United States: A Historical Overview with Sources. John E. Semonche. (Constitutional Bookshelf Ser.). 250p. (Orig.). 1985. pap. 14.95 (ISBN 0-930095-09-X). Signal Bks.

Religion & Cult. John Sheehan. 240p. pap. 6.95 (ISBN 0-87462-446-0). Marquette.

Religion & Culture. Christopher H. Dawson. LC 77-27183. (Gifford Lectures Ser.: 1947). 232p. Repr. of 1948 ed. 27.50 (ISBN 0-404-60498-6). AMS Pr.

Religion & Culture: Essays in Honor of Bernard Lonergan, S.J. Ed. by Timothy P. Fallon & Philip B. Riley. LC 86-30153. 395p. 1987. 49.50x (ISBN 0-88706-289-X). State U NY Pr.

Religion & Culture: Essays in Honor of Paul Tillich. facsimile ed. Walter Leibrecht. LC 78-167376. (Essay Index Reprint Ser). Repr. of 1959 ed. 24.50 (ISBN 0-8369-2558-0). Ayer Co Pubs.

Religion & Dance. Ed. by Dennis J. Fallon & Mary J. Wolbers. LC 83-189712. (Focus on Dance Ser.: No. 10). pap. 24.00 (ISBN 0-317-55536-7, 2029558). Bks Demand UMI.

Religion & Doubt: Toward a Faith of Your Own. Richard Creel. 1977. write for info. (ISBN 0-13-771931-0). P-H.

Religion & Education Under the Constitution. James Milton O'Neill. LC 72-171389. (Civil Liberties in American History Ser). 338p. 1972. Repr. of 1949 ed. lib. bdg. 39.50 (ISBN 0-306-70228-2). Da Capo.

Religion & Empire. Louis B. Wright. 1965. lib. bdg. 18.50x (ISBN 0-374-98816-1, Octagon). Hippocrene Bks.

Religion & Empire: The Dynamics of Aztec & Inca Expansionism. Geoffrey W. Conrad & Arthur A. Demarest. LC 83-14414. (New Studies in Archaeology). 256p. 1984. 72.50 (ISBN 0-521-24357-2); pap. 18.95 (ISBN 0-521-31896-3). Cambridge U Pr.

Religion & Empiricism. John E. Smith. (Aquinas Lecture Ser.). 1967. 7.95 (ISBN 0-87462-132-1). Marquette.

Religion & Environmental Crisis. Ed. by Eugene C. Hargrove. LC 86-7019. 248p. 1986. 25.00x (ISBN 0-8203-0845-5); pap. 12.00x (ISBN 0-8203-0846-3). U of GA Pr.

Religion & Ethnicity. Ed. by Harold Coward & Leslie Kawamura. 181p. 1978. pap. text ed. 9.95 (ISBN 0-88920-064-5, Pub. by Wilfrid Laurier Canada). Humanities.

Religion & Fertility: Arab Christian-Muslim Differentials. Joseph Chamie. LC 80-19787. (ASA Rose Monograph). (Illus.). 176p. 1981. 29.95 (ISBN 0-521-23677-0); pap. 9.95 (ISBN 0-521-28147-4). Cambridge U Pr.

Religion & Freedom in the Modern World. Herbert J. Muller. LC 63-20911. 1963. pap. 1.50x (ISBN 0-226-54815-5, P193, Phoen). U of Chicago Pr.

Religion & Freedom of Thought. facs. ed. Perry Miller et al. LC 78-128296. (Essay Index Reprint Ser). 1954. 10.00 (ISBN 0-8369-2199-2). Ayer Co Pubs.

Religion & Human Experience. Andrew Panzarella. LC 73-87024. 110p. 1974. pap. 5.20x (ISBN 0-88489-058-9); tchr's. guide 3.00x (ISBN 0-88489-080-5). St Marys.

Religion & Human Purpose. Ed. by William Horosz & Tad Clements. 1987. lib. bdg. 64.50 (ISBN 90-247-3000-7, Pub. by Martinus Nijhoff Netherlands). Kluwer Academic.

Religion & Humanism: Papers Read at the Eighteenth Summer Meeting & the Nineteenth Winter Meeting of the Ecclesiastical History Society. Ed. by Keith Robbins. (Studies in Church History: Vol. 17). (Illus.). 378p. 1981. 45.00x (ISBN 0-631-18050-8). Basil Blackwell.

Religion & Imagination. John Coulson. 1981. 45.00x (ISBN 0-19-826656-1). Oxford U Pr.

Religion & Industrial Society: The Protestant Social Congress in Wilhelmine Germany. Harry Liebersohn. LC 86-71421. (Transactions Ser.: Vol. 76, Pt. 6). 1986. 15.00 (ISBN 0-87169-766-1). Am Philos.

Religion & Judgment: An Essay on the Method & Meaning of Religion. Willard E. Arnett. LC 66-11680. (Century Philosophy Ser.). 1966. 49.50x (ISBN 0-89197-377-X). Irvington.

Religion & Law: Biblical-Judaic & Islamic Perspectives. Ed. by Edwin B. Firmage et al. 450p. 1988. text ed. price not set (ISBN 0-931464-39-0). Eisenbrauns.

Religion & Learning at Yale: Church of Christ in the College & University, 1757-1957. Ralph H. Gabriel. 1958. 49.50x (ISBN 0-685-69820-3). Elliots Bks.

Religion & Legitimation of Power in Sri Lanka. Ed. by Bardwell L. Smith. LC 77-7449. 1978. pap. 7.95 (ISBN 0-89012-008-0). Anima Pubns.

Religion & Legitimation of Power in Thailand, Laos & Burma. Ed. by Bardwell L. Smith. LC 77-7444. 1978. pap. 7.95 (ISBN 0-89012-009-9). Anima Pubns.

Religion & Life in the Early Victorian Age. Ernest E. Kellett. LC 76-6509. 1976. Repr. of 1938 ed. lib. bdg. 32.50 (ISBN 0-8414-5522-8). Folcroft.

Religion & Life: The Foundations of Personal Religion. facs. ed. W. R. Inge et al. LC 68-22940. (Essay Index Reprint Ser). 1923. 13.00 (ISBN 0-8369-0819-8). Ayer Co Pubs.

Religion & Literature. Dame H. Gardner. 1983. pap. text ed. 9.95x (ISBN 0-19-812824-X). Oxford U Pr.

Religion & Literature: The Convergence of Approaches. Ed. by John R. Mulder. (AAR Thematic Studies). pap. 8.95_o.s. (ISBN 0-89130-676-5, 01-24-72). Scholars Pr GA.

Religion & Love in Dante. Charles W. Williams. LC 74-32204. lib. bdg. 17.50 (ISBN 0-8414-9384-7). Folcroft.

Religion & Man: Indian & Far Eastern Religious Traditions. Robert D. Baird & Alfred Bloom. (Religion & Man: An Introduction, Pts. 2 & 3). 1972. pap. text ed. 18.50 scp (ISBN 0-06-040448-5, HarpC). Har-Row.

Religion & Medicine: A Medical Subject Analysis & Research Index with Bibliography. Patricia S. Hurley. LC 83-71656. 148p. 1985. 34.50 (ISBN 0-88164-032-8); pap. 26.50 (ISBN 0-88164-033-6). ABBE Pubs Assn.

Religion & Medicine of the Ga People. Margaret J. Field. LC 76-44718. 1977. Repr. of 1937 ed. 37.50 (ISBN 0-404-15923-0). AMS Pr.

Religion & Mental Illness. Carol Murphy. 1955. pap. 2.50x (ISBN 0-87574-082-0, 082). Pendle Hill.

Religion & Modern Life. Harvard University, Phillips Brooks House Association Staff. LC 75-39104. (Essay Index Reprint Ser.). Repr. of 1927 ed. 21.00 (ISBN 0-8369-2713-3). Ayer Co Pubs.

Religion & Modernization in Southeast Asia. Fred Von Der Mehden. 232p. 1986. text ed. 29.95x (ISBN 0-8156-2360-7); pap. text ed. 14.95x (ISBN 0-8156-2361-5). Syracuse U Pr.

Religion & Moral Reason: A New Method for Comparative Study. Ronald M. Green. 302p. 1988. 29.95 (ISBN 0-19-504340-5); pap. text ed. 10.95 (ISBN 0-19-504341-3). Oxford U Pr.

Religion & Morality: Their Nature & Mutual Relations. James J. Fox. 334p. 1983. Repr. of 1899 ed. 20.00x (ISBN 0-939738-09-0). Zubal Inc.

Religion & Myth. James MacDonald. LC 74-82059. Repr. of 1893 ed. 25.00x (ISBN 0-8371-1550-7, MAR&, Pub. by Negro U Pr). Greenwood.

Religion & National Identity. Ed. by Stuart Mews. (Studies in Church History: Vol. 18). 500p. 1982. 45.00x (ISBN 0-631-18060-5). Basil Blackwell.

Religion & Nationalism in Eastern Europe & the Soviet Union. Ed. by Dennis J. Dunn. LC 87-10038. 125p. 1987. lib. bdg. 22.00x (ISBN 1-55587-069-4). Lynne Rienner.

Religion & Nationalism in Southeast Asia: Burma, Indonesia, & the Philippines. Fred R. Von der Mehden. (Illus.). 272p. 1968. pap. 7.95 (ISBN 0-299-02944-1). U of Wis Pr.

Religion & Nationalism in Soviet & East European Politics. rev. & enl. ed. Ed. by Pedro Ramet. 560p. 1989. lib. bdg. 69.50 (ISBN 0-8223-0854-1); pap. text ed. 24.95 (ISBN 0-8223-0891-6). Duke.

Religion & Nature: With Charles Birch & Others. Ed. by K. J. Sharpe & J. M. Ker. (Illus.). 116p. (Orig.). 1984. pap. 11.95 (ISBN 0-9597672-0-7, Pub. by Auckland Univ Chaplaincy). ANZ Religious Pubns.

Religion and: New Zealand's Future: Proceedings of the Seventh Auckland Religious Studies Colloquim, May 2-3, 1981. Ed. & pref. by Kevin J. Sharpe. 148p. (Orig.). 1982. pap. 11.95 (ISBN 0-908564-86-4, Pub. by Dunmore NZ). ANZ Religious Pubns.

Religion & Nothingness. Keiji Nishitani. Tr. by Jan Van Bragt from Japanese. LC 81-4084. (Mazan Studies in Religion & Culture: No. 1). 366p. 1982. 37.50x (ISBN 0-520-04329-4); pap. 11.95x (ISBN 0-520-04946-2). U of Cal Pr.

Religion & Our Divided Denominations. facs. ed. Ed. by Willard L. Sperry. LC 74-128315. (Essay Index Reprint Ser). 1945. 14.00 (ISBN 0-8369-2201-8). Ayer Co Pubs.

Religion & Pain: The Spiritual Dimensions of Health Care. Joseph H. Fichter. 128p. 1981. 9.95 (ISBN 0-8245-0102-0). Crossroad NY.

Religion & Pastoral Care: Information Index with Bibliography. Louis D. Sankaran. LC 88-47620. 150p. 1988. 34.50 (ISBN 0-88164-724-1); pap. 26.50 (ISBN 0-88164-725-X). ABBE Pubs Assn.

Religion & Personality in the Spiral of Life. David Belgum. LC 79-66478. 1979. pap. text ed. 15.00 (ISBN 0-8191-0832-4). U Pr of Amer.

Religion & Personality in the Spiral of Life. enl. ed. David Belgum. LC 88-19018. (Illus.). 426p. (Orig.). 1988. pap. text ed. 23.75 (ISBN 0-8191-7101-8). U Pr of Amer.

Religion & Personality Integration. Nilsen Anker. (Psycholgia Religionum Ser.: No. 8). 174p. (Orig.). 1980. pap. 18.00x (ISBN 91-554-0991-1, Pub. by Uppsala Univ Acta Univ Uppsaliensis (Uppsala Sweden)). Coronet Bks.

Religion & Philosophy in Germany. Heinrich Heine. Tr. by John Snodgrass from Ger. LC 85-27675. 177p. (Orig.). 1986. 39.50 (ISBN 0-88706-282-2); pap. 12.95x (ISBN 0-88706-283-0). State U NY Pr.

Religion & Philosophy in the Histories of Tacitus. R. T. Scott. (Papers & Monographs: No. 22). 139p. 1968. 7.50 (ISBN 0-318-12330-4). Am Acad Rome.

Religion & Philosophy in the Histories of Tacitus. R. T. Scott. 141p. 1968. 22.00x (ISBN 0-271-00470-3). Pa St U Pr.

Religion & Philosophy of the Veda & Upanishads, 2 vols. A. B. Keith. 1976. Repr. Set. 30.00 (ISBN 0-89684-304-1). Orient Bk Dist.

Religion & Pilgrim Taxes under the Company Raj. Nancy Cassels. LC 87-61956. (Illus.). 207p. 1988. 34.00 (ISBN 0-913215-26-0). Riverdale Co.

Religion & Political Conflict in Latin America. Ed. by Daniel H. Levine. LC 85-24525. xiii, 266p. 1986. 24.95x (ISBN 0-8078-1689-2); pap. 9.95x (ISBN 0-8078-4150-1). U of NC Pr.

Religion & Political Culture in Kano. John N. Paden. LC 74-153548. 1973. 46.50x (ISBN 0-520-02020-0). U of Cal Pr.

Religion & Political Modernization. Ed. by Donald E. Smith. LC 73-86917. pap. 87.50 (ISBN 0-317-29714-7, 2022041). Bks Demand UMI.

Religion & Political Society. Jurgen Moltmann et al. LC 73-18424. (Symposium Ser.: Vol. 1). xi, 209p. 1976. Repr. of 1974 ed. 19.95x (ISBN 0-88946-953-9). E Mellen.

Religion & Politics. Ed. by Myron J. Aronoff. (Political Anthropology Ser.: Vol. III). 145p. 1983. 29.95 (ISBN 0-87855-459-9); pap. 12.95 (ISBN 0-87855-977-9). Transaction Bks.

Religion & Politics. F. W. Sollmann. 1983. pap. 2.50x (ISBN 0-87574-014-6, 014). Pendle Hill.

Religion & Politics: Bishop Valerian Trifa & His Times. Gerald J. Bobango. (East European Monograph: No. 92). 299p. 1981. 25.00x (ISBN 0-914710-86-9). East Eur Quarterly.

Religion & Politics in America. Robert Booth Fowler. LC 84-20237. (Atla Monograph: No. 21). 365p. 1984. 25.00 (ISBN 0-8108-1752-7). Scarecrow.

Religion & Politics in Chile: An Analysis of Religious Models. Orlando Mella. (Studia Sociologica Upsaliensia: No. 27). (Illus.). 202p. (Orig.). 1987. pap. text ed. 24.00x (ISBN 91-554-2078-8). Coronet Bks.

Religion & Politics in Colonial South Carolina. John W. Brinsfield. (Illus.). 204p. 1983. 25.00 (ISBN 0-89308-333-X, SC 69). Southern Hist Pr.

Religion & Politics in Contemporary Iran. Shahrough Akhavi. LC 79-22084. 255p. 1980. 54.50 (ISBN 0-87395-408-4); pap. 16.95x (ISBN 0-87395-456-4). State U NY Pr.

Religion & Politics in Haiti. Harold Courlander & Remy Bastien. LC 66-26633. (Illus.). 1970. 3.95 (ISBN 0-911976-00-0). ICR.

Religion & Politics in Iran: Shi'ism from Quiestism to Revolution. Nikki R. Keddie. LC 82-17351. 288p. 1983. text ed. 30.00x (ISBN 0-300-02874-1). Yale U Pr.

Religion & Politics in Iran: Shi'ism from Quietism to Revolution. Ed. by Nikki R. Keddie. LC 82-17351. 288p. 1984. pap. 11.95x (ISBN 0-300-03245-5, Y-504). Yale U Pr.

Religion & Politics in Israel. Charles S. Liebman & Eliezer Don-Yehiya. LC 83-48172. (Jewish Political & Social Studies Ser.). 160p. 1984. 17.50x (ISBN 0-253-34497-2). Ind U pr.

Religion & Politics in Israel: The Interplay of Judaism & Zionism. Daniel J. Elazar & Janet Aviad. 32p. 1981. pap. 2.50 (ISBN 0-87495-033-3). Am Jewish Comm.

Religion & Politics in Korea under the Japanese Rule. Wi J. Kang. LC 86-18262. (Studies in Asian Thought & Religion: Vol. 5). 1987. lib. bdg. 39.95x (ISBN 0-88946-056-6). E Mellen.

Religion & Politics in Latin America: The Catholic Church in Venezuela & Columbia. Daniel H. Levine. LC 80-7542. 356p. 1981. pap. 13.95x (ISBN 0-691-02200-3). Princeton U Pr.

Religion & Politics in Mid-Eighteenth Century Anglesey. G. Nesta Evans. 251p. 1953. text ed. 17.50x (ISBN 0-7083-0071-5, Pub. by U of Wales). Humanities.

Religion & Politics in Muslim Society: Order & Conflict in Pakistan. Abkar S. Ahmed. LC 82-14774. (Illus.). 225p. 1983. 47.50 (ISBN 0-521-24635-0). Cambridge U Pr.

Religion & Politics in the Age of the Counterreformation: Emperor Ferdinand II, William Lamormaini, S.J., & the Formation of Imperial Policy. Robert S. J. Bireley. LC 80-27334. xiii, 311p. 1981. 32.50x (ISBN 0-8078-1470-9). U of NC Pr.

Religion & Politics in the Modern World. Ed. by Peter H. Merkl. Ninian Smart. 296p. 1983. 40.00x (ISBN 0-8147-5389-2); pap. 12.50x (ISBN 0-8147-5393-0). NYU Pr.

Religion & Politics in the Punjab. Boginer Singh. 1986. 36.00 (ISBN 0-8364-1911-1, Pub. by Deep). South Asia Bks.

Religion & Politics in the Punjab in the 1920's. Prem R. Uprety. 1981. 20.00x (ISBN 0-8364-0757-1, Pub. by Sterling). South Asia Bks.

Religion & Politics in the South: Mass & Elite Perspectives. Ed. by Tod A. Baker & Robert P. Steed. LC 83-21155. 208p. 1983. 35.00 (ISBN 0-275-90940-9, C0940). Praeger.

Religion & Politics in the United States. Kenneth D. Wald. LC 86-60659. 304p. 1986. 29.95 (ISBN 0-312-67058-3); pap. write for info. (ISBN 0-312-67056-7). St Martin.

Religion & Politics in the 1980's: A Selective Bibliography. Clarence Chisholm & Alva W. Stewart. (Public Administration Ser.: P 2214). 12p. 1987. 3.75 (ISBN 1-55590-414-9). Vance Biblios.

Religion & Politics in Tibet. B. R. Burman. 180p. 1979. 14.95. Asia Bk Corp.

Religion & Politics: Institute of Church-State Studies. Ed. by James E. Wood, Jr. LC 83-71725. 122p. (Orig.). 1983. pap. 6.95 (ISBN 0-918954-39-8). Baylor Univ Pr.

Religion & Politics: The Intentions of the Authors of the First Amendment. Michael J. Malbin. 40p. 1978. pap. 6.00 (ISBN 0-8447-3302-4). Am Enterprise.

Religion & Power: The Case of Methodism in Norway. Anne Hassing. 323p. 10.00 (ISBN 0-318-14178-7). Gen Comm Arch.

Religion & Power: The Case of Methodism in Norway. Arne Hassing. (Jesse Lee Prize Ser.). (Illus.). 300p. 1980. 15.00 (ISBN 0-915466-03-1). United Meth Archives.

Religion & Psychology: A Medical Subject Analysis & Research Index with Bibliography. Nancy L. Alpert. LC 83-71657. 150p. 1985. 34.50 (ISBN 0-88164-034-4); pap. 26.50 (ISBN 0-88164-035-2). ABBE Pubs Assn.

Religion & Public Doctrine in Modern England: Assaults, Vol. 2. Maurice Cowling. (Cambridge Studies in the History & Theory of Politics). 403p. 1985. 54.50 (ISBN 0-521-25959-2). Cambridge U Pr.

Religion & Public Doctrine in Modern England. Maurice Cowling. (Cambridge Studies in the History & Theory of Politics). 498p. 1981. 65.00 (ISBN 0-521-23289-9). Cambridge U Pr.

Religion & Radical Empiricism. Nancy Frankenberry. LC 86-16558. (SUNY Series in Religious Studies). 226p. 1987. 49.50 (ISBN 0-88706-408-6); pap. 14.95x (ISBN 0-88706-409-4). State U NY Pr.

Religion & Rational Choice. Shivesh C. Thakur. (Library of Philosophy & Religion). 132p. 1981. 29.50x (ISBN 0-389-20047-6). B&N Imports.

Religion & Rational Outlook. S. N. Dasgupta. 1974. Repr. 16.95x (ISBN 0-8426-0661-0). Orient Bk Dist.

Religion & Reality. James H. Tuckwell. LC 77-118552. 1971. Repr. of 1915 ed. 25.00x (ISBN 0-8046-1177-7, Pub. by Kennikat). Assoc Faculty Pr.

Religion & Rebellion in Iran: The Iranian Tobacco Protest of 1891-1892. Nikki R. Keddie. 163p. 1966. 27.50x (ISBN 0-7146-1971-X, F Cass Co). Biblio Dist.

Religion & Religions: A Speech Given at "Het Oude Loo" May 27th, 1956. J. W. Kaiser. 37p. 1987. pap. 10.00 (ISBN 0-943185-00-9). JWK Pubns.

Religion & Religiosity in America. Ed. by Jeffrey K. Hadden & Theodore E. Long. LC 82-23605. (Studies in Honor of Joseph H. Fichter). 192p. 1983. 15.95 (ISBN 0-8245-0555-7). Crossroad NY.

Religion & Republic: The American Circumstance. Martin E. Marty. LC 86-47755. 320p. 1987. 25.00 (ISBN 0-8070-1206-8). Beacon Pr.

Religion & Respectability: Sunday Schools & English Working Class Culture, 1780-1850. Thomas W. Laqueur. LC 74-29728. 1976. 40.00x (ISBN 0-300-01859-2). Yale U Pr.

Religion & Revolution in Peru, 1824-1976. Jeffrey L. Klaiber. LC 76-51616. 1977. text ed. 22.95x (ISBN 0-268-01599-6). U of Notre Dame Pr.

Religion & Ritual in Chinese Society. Ed. by Arthur P. Wolf. LC 73-89863. (Studies in Chinese Society). xiv, 378p. 1974. 32.50x (ISBN 0-8047-0858-4). Stanford U Pr.

Religion & Ritual in Korean Society. Ed. by Laurel Kendall & Griffin Dix. LC 86-82390. (Korea Research Monograph: No. 12). xii, 223p. 1987. pap. 15.00x (ISBN 0-317-54483-7). IEAS.

Religion & Rural Life: A Mission Statement for the Religion & Rural Life Council of Rural America. Patrick J. Ronan. 1982. 1.90 (ISBN 0-318-01734-2). Rural America.

Religion & Rural Revolt. Ed. by Janos M. Bak & Gerhardt Benecke. LC 83-18698. 464p. 1984. 90.00 (ISBN 0-7190-0990-1, Pub. by Manchester Univ Pr); pap. 9.95 (ISBN 0-7190-0991-X). St Martin.

Religion & Science. Joseph Le Conte. LC 75-3239. Repr. of 1874 ed. 21.50 (ISBN 0-404-59231-7). AMS Pr.

Religion & Science. Bertrand Russell. 1961. pap. 8.95 (ISBN 0-19-500228-8). Oxford U Pr.

Religion & Science. F. V. Verbitsky. 1959. pap. 1.00 (ISBN 0-317-30432-1). Holy Trinity.

Religion & Scientific Method. G. Schlesinger. 1977. lib. bdg. 29.00 (ISBN 90-277-0815-0, Pub. by Reidel Holland); pap. 10.50 (ISBN 90-277-0816-9, Pub. by Reidel Holland). Kluwer Academic.

Religion & Self-Acceptance: A Study of the Relationship Between Belief in God & the Desire to Know. John F. Haught. LC 80-5872. 195p. 1980. lib. bdg. 26.00 (ISBN 0-8191-1296-8); pap. text ed. 11.25 (ISBN 0-8191-1297-6). U Pr of Amer.

Religion & Sex. Chapman Cohen. LC 72-9631. Repr. of 1919 ed. 40.00 (ISBN 0-404-57430-0). AMS Pr.

Religion & Sexism. Rosemary R. Ruether. 1974. pap. 10.95 (ISBN 0-671-21693-7, Touchstone Bks). S&S.

Religion & Sexuality: Judaic-Christian Viewpoints in the U. S. A. John M. Holland et al. LC 81-66867. (Association of Sexologists Monographs: No. 1). 80p. 1981. pap. 5.95 (ISBN 0-939902-00-1). Assn Sexologists.

Religion & Sexuality: The Shakers, the Mormons, & the Oneida Community. Lawrence Foster. LC 83-18315. 354p. 1984. pap. 9.95 (ISBN 0-252-01119-8). U of Ill Pr.

Religion & Sexuality: Three American Communal Experiments of the Nineteenth Century. Lawrence Foster. 1981. 24.95x (ISBN 0-19-502794-9). Oxford U Pr.

Religion & Social Conflicts. Otto Maduro. Tr. by Robert R. Barr from Span. LC 82-3439. Orig. Title: Religion y Lucha de Clase. 192p. (Orig.). 1982. pap. 8.95 (ISBN 0-88344-428-3). Orbis Bks.

Religion & Social Organization in Central Polynesia. Robert W. Williamson. Ed. by Ralph Piddington. LC 75-35218. Repr. of 1937 ed. 38.00 (ISBN 0-404-14241-9). AMS Pr.

Religion & Social Responsibility. T. B. Irving. pap. 1.00 (ISBN 0-686-18445-9). Kazi Pubns.

Religion & Social Work Practice in Contemporary American Society. Frank M. Loewenberg. 184p. 1988. 22.00x (ISBN 0-231-06452-7). Columbia U Pr.

Religion & Societies: Asia & the Middle East. Ed. by Carlo Caldarola. (Religion & Society: No. 22). 688p. 1982. text ed. 80.75 (ISBN 90-279-3259-X); Pub. 1984. pap. 34.95 (ISBN 3-11-010021-5). Mouton.

Religion & Society in Central Africa: The BaKongo of Lower Zaire. Wyatt MacGaffey. LC 85-31805. (Illus.). xii, 296p. 1986. lib. bdg. 45.00x (ISBN 0-226-50029-2); pap. text ed. 16.95x (ISBN 0-226-50030-6). U of Chicago Pr.

Religion & Society in Maharashtra. Ed. by Milton Israel & N. K. Wagle. 1987. 36.00x (ISBN 0-9692907-0-5, Pub. by Ctr South Asian); pap. 16.00x (ISBN 0-9692907-1-3, Pub. by Ctr South Asian). South Asia Bks.

Religion & Society in Modern Japan. Edward Norbeck. (Rice University Studies: Vol. 56, No. 1). 232p. 1970. pap. 10.00x (ISBN 0-89263-203-8). Rice Univ.

Religion & Society in North America: An Annotated Bibliography. Ed. by Robert de V. Brunkow. LC 82-24304. (Clio Bibliography Ser.: No. 12). 515p. 1983. lib. bdg. 69.00 (ISBN 0-87436-042-0). ABC-Clio.

Religion & Society in South India. V. Sudarsen et al. xvi, 280p. 1987. text ed. 35.00x (ISBN 81-7018-435-5, Pub. by B R Pub Corp Delhi), Apt Bks.

Religion & Society in the American West: Historical Essays. Ed. by Carl Guarneri & David Alvarez. LC 87-10591. (Illus.). 508p. (Orig.). 1987. lib. bdg. 36.50 (ISBN 0-8191-6431-3); pap. text ed. 23.75 (ISBN 0-8191-6432-1). U Pr of Amer.

Religion & Society in Transition: The Church & Social Change in England, 1560-1850. Ernest E. Best. LC 82-21699. (Texts & Studies in Religion: Vol. 15). 353p. 1983. lib. bdg. 59.95x (ISBN 0-88946-804-4). E Mellen.

Religion & State in Iran, 1785-1906: The Role of the 'Ulama in the Qajar Period. Hamid Algar. LC 72-79959. (Near Eastern Center Series, UCL A: No. 17). 1980. 34.50x (ISBN 0-520-04100-3). U of Cal Pr.

Religion & State in the Kingdom of Saudi Arabia. Ayman Al-Yassini. (WVSS on the Middle East Ser.). 190p. 1985. 39.00x (ISBN 0-8133-0058-4). Westview.

Religion & Statecraft among the Romans. Alan Wardman. LC 82-47928. pap. 55.80 (2026708). Bks Demand UMI.

Religion & Superstition in the Plays of Ben Johnson & Thomas Middleton. B. Johansson. (Essays & Studies on English Language & Literature: Vol. 7). pap. 28.00 (ISBN 0-8115-0205-8). Kraus Repr.

Religion & Superstition in the Plays of Ben Johnson & Thomas Middleton. Berril Johansson. LC 68-1346. 1970. Repr. of 1950 ed. 75.00x (ISBN 0-8383-0667-5). Haskell.

Religion & the Ameican Revolution in North Carolina. Robert M. Calhoon. (Illus.). x, 81p. 1976. pap. 3.00 (ISBN 0-86526-120-2). NC Archives.

Religion & the American Revolution. Jerald Brauer. LC 76-9718. pap. 22.30 (2026888). Bks Demand UMI.

Religion & the Artifice of Jacobean & Caroline Drama. Peter F. Mullany. Ed. by James Hogg. (Jacobean Drama Studies). 185p. (Orig.). 1977. pap. 15.00 (ISBN 0-317-40088-6, Pub. by Salzburg Studies). Longwood Pub Group.

Religion & the Challenge of Philosophy. J. E. Barnhart. (Quality Paperback Ser.: No. 291). 400p. (Orig.). 1975. pap. 8.95 (ISBN 0-8226-0291-1). Littlefield.

Religion & the Constitution. Walter Berns et al. 34p. 1984. pap. 5.00 (ISBN 0-8447-2249-9). Am Enterprise.

Religion & the Constitution. Paul G. Kauper. LC 64-7898. pap. 36.80 (ISBN 0-317-29869-0, 2051881). Bks Demand UMI.

Religion & the Constitution: A Reinterpretation. Peter J. Ferrara. LC 83-81643. 172p. (Orig.). 1983. pap. text ed. 10.75 (ISBN 0-942522-06-0). Free Congr Res.

Religion & the Decline of Magic. Keith Thomas. 716p. 1975. pap. text ed. write for info. (ISBN 0-02-420200-2, Pub. by Scribner). Macmillan.

Religion & the Decline of Magic. Keith Thomas. 736p. 1986. pap. 19.95 (ISBN 0-684-14542-1). Scribner.

Religion & the Family in East Asia. Ed. by George A. De Vos & Takao Sofue. 1986. pap. 15.95x (ISBN 0-520-05762-7). U of Cal Pr.

Religion & the Law. 64p. 1975. pap. 1.00 (ISBN 0-686-47944-0). Amer Bar Assn.

Religion & the Life Cycle. Robert C. Fuller. LC 88-45237. 176p. 1988. pap. 10.95 (ISBN 0-8006-2306-1). Fortress.

Religion & the Modern Mind. Walter T. Stace. LC 80-24093. 285p. 1980. Repr. of 1952 ed. lib. bdg. 27.50x (ISBN 0-313-22662-8, STRM). Greenwood.

Religion & the Modern World. Pennsylvania University Bicentennial Conference. Ed. by Jacques Maritain & Joseph Hromadka. LC 68-26204. Repr. of 1941 ed. 22.50x (ISBN 0-8046-0360-X, Pub. by Kennikat). Assoc Faculty Pr.

Religion & the Northern Ireland Problem. John Hickey. LC 83-26612. 162p. 1984. 24.50x (ISBN 0-389-20448-X, 08012). B&N Imports.

Religion & the One: Philosophies East & West. Frederick Copleston. LC 81-5372. (Gifford Lectures, 1980 Ser.). 320p. 1981. 24.50x (ISBN 0-8245-0092-X). Crossroad NY.

Religion & the People of Western Europe, 1789-1970. Hugh McLeod. (Oxford Paperbacks University Ser.). 1981. 17.95x (ISBN 0-19-215832-5); pap. 9.95x (ISBN 0-19-289101-4). Oxford U Pr.

Religion & the People, 800-1700. Ed. by James Obelkevich. LC 78-7847. v, 336p. 1979. 32.50x (ISBN 0-8078-1332-X). U of NC Pr.

Religion & the Persistence of Capitalism. Preston. Date not set. 12.95 (Pub. by SCM Pr England). Fortress.

Religion & the Presidential Election. Paul Lopatto. LC 84-26281. (American Political Parties & Elections Ser.). 192p. 1985. 36.95 (ISBN 0-275-90138-6, C0138). Praeger.

Religion & the Public Order: An Annual Review of Church & State & of Religion, Law, & Society. Ed. by Donald A. Giannella. LC 64-17164. pap. 72.00 (ISBN 0-317-20699-0, 2024114). Bks Demand UMI.

Religion & the Public Schools. Incl. The Legal Issue. Paul A. Freund. (Burton Lectures Ser: 1965); The Educational Issue. Robert Ulich. (Inglis Lectures Ser: 1965). LC 65-26011. vi, 56p. 1965. 2.00x (ISBN 0-674-75600-2). Harvard U Pr.

Religion & the Rebel. Colin Wilson. LC 74-9134. 338p. 1974. Repr. of 1957 ed. lib. bdg. 35.00 (ISBN 0-8371-7596-8, WIRA). Greenwood.

Religion & the Rebel. Rev. ed. Colin Wilson. 352p. 1984. pap. 9.95 (ISBN 0-88162-050-5). Salem Hse Pubs.

Religion & the Rise of Capitalism. Richard H. Tawney. 12.75 (ISBN 0-8446-1446-7). Peter Smith.

Religion & the Rise of Western Culture. Christopher H. Dawson. LC 77-27181. (Gifford Lectures: 1948-49). Repr. of 1950 ed. 26.50 (ISBN 0-404-60499-4). AMS Pr.

Religion & the Schools: Significant Court Decisions in the 1980s. Eugene T. Connors. LC 88-60070. (Fastback Ser.: No. 272). 50p. (Orig.). 1988. pap. 0.90 (ISBN 0-87367-272-0). Phi Delta Kappa.

Religion & the Sciences of Life: With Other Essays on Allied Topics. William McDougall. LC 70-39108. (Essay Index Reprint Ser.). Repr. of 1934 ed. 20.00 (ISBN 0-8369-2700-1). Ayer Co Pubs.

Religion & the Scientific Future. Langdon Gilkey. LC 81-18934. (Reprints of Scholarly Excellence (ROSE)). xii, 193p. Repr. of 1970 ed. text ed. 13.95 (ISBN 0-86554-030-6, MUP-H21). Mercer Univ Pr.

Religion & the Sociology of Knowledge: Modernization & Pluralism in Christian Thought & Structure. Ed. by Barbara Hargrove. LC 83-22149. (Studies in Religion & Society: Vol. 8). 412p. 1984. lib. bdg. 59.95x (ISBN 0-88946-872-9). E Mellen.

Religion & the State: Essays in Honor of Leo Pfeffer. Ed. by James E. Wood, Jr. 596p. 1985. 39.95x (ISBN 0-918954-29-0). Baylor Univ Pr.

Religion & the State in Georgia in the Eighteenth Century. Reba C. Strickland. LC 40-4840. (Columbia University Studies in the Social Sciences: No. 460). Repr. of 1939 ed. 18.50 (ISBN 0-404-51460-X). AMS Pr.

Religion & the State: The Making & Testing of an American Tradition. Evarts B. Greene. LC 75-41122. Repr. of 1941 ed. 17.25 (ISBN 0-404-14548-5). AMS Pr.

Religion & the State: The Struggle for Legitimacy & Power. Ed. by Robert J. Myers. LC 85-72100. (Annals of the American Academy of Political & Social Science Ser.: Vol. 483). 1986. text ed. 15.00 (ISBN 0-8039-2538-7); pap. text ed. 7.95 (ISBN 0-8039-2539-5). Sage.

Religion & the Transformation of Society: A Study in Social Change in Africa. Monica H. Wilson. LC 73-134622. (Scott Holland Memorial Lectures: 15; 1969). pap. 43.30 (ISBN 0-317-27081-8, 2024562). Bks Demand UMI.

Religion & the Unconscious. 2nd ed. Ann Ulanov & Barry Ulanov. LC 75-16302. 288p. 1985. pap. 14.95 (ISBN 0-664-24657-5). Westminster John Knox.

Religion & the Western Mind. Ninian Smart. LC 86-10578. 142p. 1987. 39.50x (ISBN 0-88706-382-9); pap. 14.95x (ISBN 0-88706-383-7). State U NY Pr.

Religion & the Working Class in Nineteenth Century Britain. H. McLeod. (Studies in Economic & Social History). 72p. 1984. pap. text ed. 9.95 (ISBN 0-333-28115-2, Pub. by Macmillan UK). Humanities.

Religion & the World. Morteza Mutahhari. Tr. by Mohammad S. Tawheedi. 44p. 1984. pap. 3.95 (ISBN 0-940368-34-X). Tahrike Tarsile Quran.

Religion & the World Order. Ed. by F. Ernest Johnson. LC 68-26189. (Essay & General Literature Index Reprint Ser). 1969. Repr. of 1944 ed. 22.50x (ISBN 0-8046-0221-2, Pub. by Kennikat). Assoc Faculty Pr.

Religion & Theatre. M. L. Varadpande. 100p. 1982. text ed. 15.00x (ISBN 0-391-02794-8). Humanities.

Religion & Truth. Donald Wiche. 295p. 1981. text ed. 44.50 (ISBN 90-279-3149-6). Mouton.

Religion & Ultimate Well-Being: An Explanatory Theory. Martin Prozesky. LC 84-3340. 224p. 1984. 25.00 (ISBN 0-312-67057-5). St Martin.

Religion & Violence. 2nd ed. Robert McAfee Brown. LC 87-10476. (Illus.). 144p. (Orig.). 1987. pap. 8.95 (ISBN 0-664-24078-X). Westminster John Knox.

Religion & Welsh Literature in the Age of the Reformation. Glanmor Williams. (Sir John Rhys Memorial Lectures in Celtic Studies). 1985. pap. 4.25 (ISBN 0-85672-497-1, Pub. by British Acad). Longwood Pub Group.

Religion As a Bar to Progress. Charles T. Gorham. 31p. 1988. pap. 3.00 saddle-stitched (5128). Am Atheist.

Religion As Anxiety & Tranquillity: An Essay in Comparative Phenomenology of the Spirit. J. G. Arapura. (Religion & Reason Ser.: No. 5). 1973. 19.00x (ISBN 90-2797-180-3). Mouton.

Religion As Art. T. R. Martland. LC 80-27104. (Series in Philosophy). 221p. 1981. 49.50x (ISBN 0-87395-520-X); pap. 16.95x (ISBN 0-87395-521-8). State U NY Pr.

Religion As Creative Insecurity. Peter A. Bertocci. LC 73-1836. 128p. 1973. Repr. of 1958 ed. lib. bdg. 25.00x (ISBN 0-8371-6803-1, BECI). Greenwood.

Religion As Critique. Robert J. Ackermann. LC 84-16471. 184p. 1985. lib. bdg. 20.00x (ISBN 0-87023-462-5); pap. 9.95x (ISBN 0-87023-463-3). U of Mass Pr.

Religion As Language-Game: A Critical Study with Special Regard to D. Z. Phillips. Lars Haikola. (Studia Philosophiae Religionis: Vol. 4). 1977. pap. 24.00x (ISBN 91-40-04596-X). Coronet Bks.

Religion As Social Vision: The Movement Against Untouchability in 20th-Century Punjab. Mark Juergensmeyer. LC 80-24187. (Center for South & Southeast Asia Studies, UC Berkeley: No. 34). (Illus.). 350p. 1982. 37.50x (ISBN 0-520-04301-4). U of Cal Pr.

Religion As Story. Ed. by James B. Wiggins. 218p. 1985. pap. text ed. 10.25 (ISBN 0-8191-4682-X). U Pr of Amer.

Religion As Structure & Process: A Sociological View. Lee Braude. 1988. price not set (ISBN 0-89874-993-X). Krieger.

Religion at Bowdoin College: A History. Ernst C. Helmreich. LC 81-71331. (Illus.). 1981. pap. 7.50 (ISBN 0-916606-03-1). Bowdoin Coll.

Religion Auf Ostflores, Adonare und Solor. Paul Arndt. 28.00 (ISBN 0-384-02115-8). Johnson Repr.

Religion Behind the Iron Curtain. George N. Shuster. LC 78-13547. 1978. Repr. of 1954 ed. lib. bdg. 35.00x (ISBN 0-313-20634-1, SHRB). Greenwood.

Religion, BL-BX. Ed. by James Larrabee. LC 85-6863. (LC Cumulative Classification Ser.). 1000p. 1985. loose-leaf set 105.00 (ISBN 0-933949-11-1); vol. 1 0.00 (ISBN 0-933949-12-X); vol. 2 0.00 (ISBN 0-933949-13-8); fiche set 0.00 (ISBN 0-933949-15-4); fiche vol. 1 0.00 (ISBN 0-933949-16-2); fiche vol. 2 0.00 (ISBN 0-933949-17-0). Livia Pr.

Religion Coming of Age. Roy W. Sellars. LC 75-3362. Repr. of 1928 ed. 20.50 (ISBN 0-404-59359-3). AMS Pr.

Religion Cristiana En Su Expresion Doctrinal. Edgar Y. Mullins. Tr. by Sara A. Hale. Orig. Title: Christian Religion in Its Doctrinal Expression. 522p. 1983. pap. 9.95 (ISBN 0-311-09042-7). Casa Bautista.

Religion, Critique et Philisophique Positive Chez Pierre Bayle. Jean Delvolve. (Research & Source Works Ser.: No. 836). 1971. Repr. of 1906 ed. lib. bdg. 29.50 (ISBN 0-8337-4073-3, 74-166962). B Franklin.

Religion, Cults & the Law. 2nd ed. A. Burstein. (Legal Almanac Ser.: No. 23). 128p. 1980. 6.95 (ISBN 0-379-11133-0). Oceana.

Religion, Culture & Methodology: Papers of the Groningen Working-Group for the Study of Fundamental Problems & Methods of Science of Religion. Ed. by T. P. Van Baaren & H. J. Driljvers. 1973. text ed. 14.00x (ISBN 90-2797-249-4). Mouton.

Religion, Culture & Society in the Early Middle Ages. Ed. by Thomas F. Noble & John J. Contreni. LC 87-5709. (Studies in Medieval Culture: No. 23). 1987. 32.95 (ISBN 0-918720-83-4); pap. 15.95 (ISBN 0-918720-84-2). Medieval Inst.

Religion, Culture & Values: A Cross-Cultural Analysis of Motivational Factors in Native Irish & American Irish Catholicism. Bruce F. Biever. LC 76-6322. (Irish Americans Ser). 1976. 62.00 (ISBN 0-405-09319-5). Ayer Co Pubs.

Religion der Aegypter. Erman Adolf. (Illus.). 1978. Repr. of 1934 ed. 19.20x (ISBN 3-11-005187-7). De Gruyter.

Religion des Cathares: Etude sur le Gnosticisme de la Basse Antiquite et du Moyen Age. Hans Soderberg. LC 77-84720. Repr. of 1949 ed. 32.00 (ISBN 0-404-16124-3). AMS Pr.

Religion des Geistes. Salomon Formstecher. Ed. by Steven Katz. LC 79-7129. (Jewish Philosophy, Mysticism & History of Ideas Ser.). 1980. Repr. of 1841 ed. lib. bdg. 40.00x (ISBN 0-405-12251-9). Ayer Co Pubs.

Religion Des Romischen Heeres. facsimile ed. Alfred Von Domaszewski. LC 75-10634. (Ancient Religion & Mythology Ser.). (Illus., Ger.). 1976. Repr. of 1895 ed. 12.00 (ISBN 0-405-07012-8). Ayer Co Pubs.

Religion, Developement & African Identity. Kirsten Holst Petersen. (Scandinavian Institute of African Studies, Seminar Proceedings: No. 17). 163p. 1987. text ed. 32.00x (ISBN 91-7106-263-7, Pub. by Nordisken Afrikainstitutet (Uppsala Sweden)). Coronet BKs.

Religion, Dynamique Sociale et Dependance: Les Mouvements Protestants En Argentine et Au Chili. Christian Lalive D'Epinay. (Interaction Ser: L'homme et Son Environnementsocial, No. 4). (Illus.). 368p. (Fr.). 1976. pap. text ed. 36.40x (ISBN 90-2797-922-7). Mouton.

Religion et Culture. Jacques Maritain. 176p. 1968. 9.95 (ISBN 0-686-56366-2). French & Eur.

Religion Experience & Christian Faith. Dillistone. Date not set. 9.95 (Pub. by SCM Pr England). Fortress.

Religion Faces the World Crisis. Leroy Waterman. 1943. 5.00x (ISBN 0-685-21800-7). Wahr.

Religion for a New Generation. 2nd ed. Jacob Needleman et al. Ed. by Kenneth J. Scott. 576p. 1977. pap. text ed. write for info. (ISBN 0-02-385990-3). Macmillan.

Religion for Every Day, 2 vols. William Booth. 300p. 1987. Set. 9.95 (ISBN 0-86544-045-X). Salv Army Suppl South.

Religion for Free Minds. Julius S. Bixler. LC 75-3048. (Philosophy in America Ser.). 1976. Repr. of 1939 ed. 18.00 (ISBN 0-404-59045-4). AMS Pr.

Religion for Little Children: A Parent's Guide. Christiane Brusselmans & Edward Wakin. LC 76-140110. 1977. pap. 6.95 (ISBN 0-87973-825-1). Our Sunday Visitor.

Religion for Mankind. Horace Holley. 248p. 1956. 16.50 (ISBN 0-87743-011-X); pap. 7.50 (ISBN 0-85398-000-4). G Ronald Pub.

Religion for Peace: Unabridged Proceedings. World Conference on Religion & Peace, 1st Assembly. Ed. by Jack A. Homer. 391p. 1973. pap. 4.50 (ISBN 0-317-61731-1); 6.00 (ISBN 0-317-61732-X). World Confer Rel & Peace.

Religion for the People of Today. Daughters of St. Paul. LC 78-160576. (Illus.). 1971. pap. 1.25 (ISBN 0-8198-0345-6). Dghtrs St Paul.

Religion for Tomorrow. Theron D. Wilson. LC 62-9776. 148p. 1963. 5.95 (ISBN 0-8022-1897-0). Philos Lib.

Religion, Ideology & Heidegger's Concept of Falling. Gregory Tropea. LC 87-17685. (American Academy of Religion Academy Ser.). 261p. 1987. 18.95 (ISBN 1-55540-041-8, 01-01-54); pap. 13.95 (ISBN 1-55540-042-6). Scholars Pr GA.

Religion: If There Is No God.. On God, the Devil, Sin & Other Worries of the So-Called Philosophy of Religion. Leszek Kolakowski. Ed. by Frank Kermode. 1982. pap. 8.95 (ISBN 0-19-520429-8). Oxford U Pr.

Religion in a Chinese Town. Philip C. Baity. (Asian Folklore & Social Life Monographs: No. 64). 318p. 1975. 17.00x (ISBN 0-89986-059-1). Oriental Bk Store.

Religion in a Free Society. Sidney Hook. LC 67-11242. xii, 120p. 1967. 11.95x (ISBN 0-8032-0077-3). U of Nebr Pr.

Religion in a Religious Age. Ed. by S. D. Goitein. 12.50x (ISBN 0-87068-268-7, Pub. by an Academic Inst); pap. 8.95. Ktav.

Religion in a Revolutionary Society. Peter L. Berger. (Bicentennial Lecture Ser.). 16p. 1974. pap. 5.00 (ISBN 0-8447-1306-6). Am Enterprise.

Religion in a Technical Age. Samuel H. Miller. LC 68-17628. 1968. 9.95x (ISBN 0-674-75650-9). Harvard U Pr.

Religion in a Tswana Chiefdom. Berthold A. Pauw. LC 85-21881. (Illus.). xii, 274p. 1985. Repr. of 1960 ed. lib. bdg. 79.50x (ISBN 0-313-24974-1, PRTC). Greenwood.

Religion in Aboriginal Australia: An Anthology. Ed. by Max Charlesworth et al. LC 83-23437. (Illus.). 458p. 1984. text ed. 39.50x (ISBN 0-7022-1754-9). U of Queensland Pr.

Religion in America. Ed. by Julie Bach & Tom Modl. (Opposing Viewpoints Sources Ser.). (Illus.). 250p. (gr. 5-11). 1988. PLB 13.95 (ISBN 0-89908-437-0); pap. text ed. 6.95 (ISBN 0-89908-412-5). Greenhaven.

Religion in America. 2nd ed. George C. Bedell et al. LC 81-8239. 1982. text ed. write for info. (ISBN 0-02-307810-3). Macmillan.

Religion in America, 38 vols. Ed. by Edwin S. Gaustad. 1969. Repr. Set. 2510.50 (ISBN 0-405-00229-7). Ayer Co Pubs.

Religion in America. Ed. by Gillian Lindt. LC 75-54571. (Great Contemporary Issues Ser.). 1977. lib. bdg. 35.00x (ISBN 0-405-09865-0). Ayer Co Pubs.

Religion in America: A Critical Abridgment. Robert Baird. 11.25 (ISBN 0-8446-0471-2). Peter Smith.

Religion in America: An Historical Account of the Development of American Religious Life. 4th ed. Winthrop Hudson. 512p. 1987. text ed. write for info. (ISBN 0-02-357820-3). Macmillan.

Religion in America: History & Historiography. Edwin S. Gaustad. LC 73-91240. (AHA Pamphlets: No. 260). 60p. 1974. pap. text ed. 1.50 (ISBN 0-87229-016-6). Am Hist Assn.

Religion in America: Ser. 2, 40 vols. Ed. by Edwin S. Gaustad. 1972. Repr. 830.00 set (ISBN 0-405-04050-4). Ayer Co Pubs.

Religion in American History: Interpretive Essays. John F. Wilson & John M. Mulder. 448p. 1978. pap. text ed. write for info. (ISBN 0-13-771980-9). P-H.

Religion in American Life. Compiled by Nelson R. Burr. LC 70-136219. (Goldentree Bibliographies in American History Ser.). (Orig.). 1971. 15.95x (ISBN 0-88295-507-1). Harlan Davidson.

Religion in American Politics. Ed. by Charles Dunn. 1988. price not set (ISBN 0-87187-486-5). Congr Quarterly.

Religion in American Public Life. A. James Reichley. LC 85-21312. 402p. 1985. 31.95 (ISBN 0-8157-7378-1); pap. 11.95 (ISBN 0-8157-7377-3). Brookings.

Religion in an African City. Geoffrey Parrinder. LC 74-142921. (Illus.). 1973. Repr. of 1953 ed. 35.00x (ISBN 0-8371-5947-4, PAC&, Pub. by Negro U Pr). Greenwood.

Religion in Antebellum Kentucky. John B. Boles. LC 76-4434. (Kentucky Bicentennial Bookshelf Ser.). 160p. 1976. 6.95 (ISBN 0-8131-0227-8). U Pr of Ky.

Religion in Appalachia. Ed. by John D. Photiadis. 1979. 10.75 (ISBN 0-686-26337-5). W Va U Ctr Exten.

Religion in Australian Life: A Bibliography of Social Research. Georgina Fitzpatrick. Ed. by Michael Mason. 264p. (Orig.). 1982. pap. 19.95 (ISBN 0-908083-10-6, Pub. by AASR Australia). ANZ Religious Pubns.

Religion in China. Robert Orr. 144p. 1980. 4.95 (ISBN 0-318-16788-3). US-China Peoples Friendship.

Religion in China. Robert G. Orr. (Orig.). 1980. pap. 4.95 (ISBN 0-377-00103-1). Friendship Pr.

Religion in Context: Cults & Charisma. I. M. Lewis. (Essays in Social Anthropology Ser.). (Illus.). 160p. 1986. 39.50 (ISBN 0-521-30616-7); pap. 10.95 (ISBN 0-521-31596-4). Cambridge U Pr.

Religion in Dialogue: East & West Meet. Ed. by Zacharias P. Thundy et al. 336p. (Orig.). 1985. lib. bdg. 31.25 (ISBN 0-8191-4466-5); pap. text ed. 15.50 (ISBN 0-8191-4467-3). U Pr of Amer.

Religion in Economics: A Study of John B. Clark, Richard T. Ely & Simon N. Patten. J. Rutherford Everett. xiii, 160p. 1982. Repr. of 1946 ed. lib. bdg. 25.00x (ISBN 0-87991-866-7). Porcupine Pr.

Religion in England: 1688-1781. Gordon Rupp. LC 85-23886. (History of the Christian Church Ser.). 520p. 1987. 79.00x (ISBN 0-19-826918-8). Oxford U Pr.

Religion in Essence & Manifestation. G. Van der Leeuw. Tr. by J. E. Turner. LC 85-43382. 1986. text ed. 66.50x (ISBN 0-691-07272-8); pap. 12.50x (ISBN 0-691-02038-8). Princeton U Pr.

Religion in Essence & Manifestation, 2 vols. Gerardus Van Der Leeuw. 26.50 set (ISBN 0-8446-1457-2). Peter Smith.

Religion in Film. Ed. by John R. May & Michael Bird. LC 81-23983. (Illus.). 232p. 1982. text ed. 19.95x (ISBN 0-87049-352-3); pap. text ed. 9.95x (ISBN 0-87049-368-X). U of Tenn Pr.

Religion in Greek Literature: A Sketch in Outline. facsimile ed. Lewis Campbell. LC 79-148874. (Select Bibliographies Reprint Ser). Repr. of 1898 ed. 22.00 (ISBN 0-8369-5645-1). Ayer Co Pubs.

Religion in Higher Education among Negroes. Richard I. McKinney. LC 75-38785. (Religion in America, Ser. 2). 186p. 1972. Repr. of 1945 ed. 15.00 (ISBN 0-405-04075-X). Ayer Co Pubs.

Religion in Higher Education among Negroes. Richard I. McKinney. 1945. 13.50x (ISBN 0-686-51299-5). Elliots Bks.

Religion in Human Experience: A Comparative Study. John R. Everett. 1977. lib. bdg. 59.95 (ISBN 0-8490-2509-5). Gordon Pr.

Religion in Human Life: Anthropological Views. Edward Norbeck. 74p. 1988. pap. text ed. 5.95x (ISBN 0-88133-354-9). Waveland Pr.

Religion in Indiana: A Guide to Historical Resources. L. C. Rudolph & Judith E. Endelman. LC 84-43186. 224p. 1986. 22.50x (ISBN 0-253-34960-5). Ind U Pr.

Religion in Japanese History. Joseph M. Kitagawa. LC 65-23669. 475p. 1966. 37.50x (ISBN 0-231-02834-2). Columbia U Pr.

Religion in Judah under the Assyrians. John McKay. LC 72-97460. (Studies in Biblical Theology, 2nd Ser.: No. 26). 1973. pap. text ed. 10.00x (ISBN 0-8401-3076-7). A R Allenson.

Religion in Life at Louisbourg, 1713-1758. A. J. Johnston. 288p. 1984. 32.50x (ISBN 0-7735-0427-3). McGill-Queens U pr.

Religion in Life Founders, Prophets & Sacred Books. John R. Bailey. 1987. 39.00x (ISBN 0-7217-3034-5, Pub. by Schofield & Sims). State Mutual Bk.

Religion in Life: Religious Beliefs & Moral Codes. John R. Bailey. 1987. 39.00x (ISBN 0-7217-3037-X, Pub. by Schofield & Sims). State Mutual Bk.

Religion in Life: Religious Buildings & Festivals. John R. Bailey. 1987. 39.00x (ISBN 0-7217-3033-7, Pub. by Schofield & Sims). State Mutual Bk.

Religion in Life: Religious Leaders & Places of Pilgrimage Today. John R. Bailey. 1987. 39.00x (ISBN 0-7217-3036-1, Pub. by Schofield & Sims). State Mutual Bk.

Religion in Life: Worship, Cermonial & Rites of Passage. John R. Bailey. 1987. 39.00x (ISBN 0-7217-3035-3, Pub. by Schofield & Sims). State Mutual Bk.

Religion in Modern India. Ed. by Robert D. Baird. 1982. 36.00x (ISBN 0-8364-0826-8); 19.00x (ISBN 0-8364-0830-6). South Asia Bks.

Religion in New Zealand Society. Ed. by Brian Colless & Peter Donovan. 216p. 1980. 21.95 (ISBN 0-567-09303-4, Pub. by T & T Clark Uk). Fortress.

Religion in Overalls. William Johnsson. LC 77-22464. (Anvil Ser.). 1977. pap. 8.95 (ISBN 0-8127-0143-7). Review & Herald.

Religion in Plato & Cicero. John E. Rexine. LC 68-28581. 72p. Repr. of 1959 ed. lib. bdg. 35.00x (ISBN 0-8371-0198-0, RERP). Greenwood.

Religion in Politics. Arun Shourie. 1987. 16.50x (ISBN 0-8364-2149-3, Pub. by Roli Books). South Asia Bks.

Religion in Practice. Swami Prabhavananda. 6.95 (ISBN 0-87481-016-7). Vedanta Pr.

Religion in Primitive Culture. Edward Tylor. (Primitive Culture - Part 2). 18.75 (ISBN 0-8446-0946-3). Peter Smith.

Religion in Primitive Cultures: A Study in Ethnophilosophy. Wilhelm Dupre. (Religion & Reason: No. 9). 366p. 1975. text ed. 39.00x (ISBN 0-686-22610-0). Mouton.
Religion in Public Education. Vivian T. Thayer. LC 78-12385. 1979. Repr. of 1947 ed. lib. bdg. 35.00x (ISBN 0-313-21212-0, THRP). Greenwood.
Religion in Radical Transition. Ed. by Jeffrey K. Hadden. 166p. 1973. 17.95 (ISBN 0-87855-070-4); pap. 8.95x (ISBN 0-87855-567-6). Transaction Bks.
Religion in Recent Art. 3rd ed. Peter T. Forsyth. LC 73-148780. Repr. of 1905 ed. 24.50 (ISBN 0-404-02515-3). AMS Pr.
Religion in Roman Britain. Martin Henig. LC 84-6914. 256p. 1984. 29.95 (ISBN 0-312-67059-1). St Martin.
Religion in Schools: A Philosophical Examination. John A. Sealey. (Studia Philophiae Religionis: No. 9). (Orig.). 1982. pap. 28.50x (ISBN 0-317-65790-9). Coronet Bks.
Religion in Shreds. C. Brandon Rimmer. LC 73-82861. pap. 1.25 (ISBN 0-88419-046-3, Co-Pub by Crection Hse). Aragorn Bks.
Religion in Society: A Sociology of Religion. 2nd ed. Ronald L. Johnstone. (Illus.). 320p. 1983. text ed. write for info. (ISBN 0-13-773077-2). P-H.
Religion in Society: A Sociology of Religion. 3rd ed. Ronald L. Johnstone. (Illus.). 320p. Date not set. text ed. price not set (ISBN 0-13-773102-7). P-H.
Religion in Sociological Perspective. Keith A. Roberts. 466p. 1984. 36.00x (ISBN 0-256-03127-4). Dorsey.
Religion in Sociological Perspective. Bryan Wilson. 1982. pap. 7.95x (ISBN 0-19-826664-2). Oxford U Pr.
Religion in South Asia. Ed. by G. A. Oddie. 204p. 1977. 14.95. Asia Bk Corp.
Religion in Soviet Russia, Nineteen Seventeen to Nineteen Forty-Two. Nicholas S. Timasheff. LC 78-23615. 1980. Repr. of 1942 ed. lib. bdg. 35.00x (ISBN 0-313-21040-3, TIRS). Greenwood.
Religion in Strange Times: The 1960s & 1970s. Ronald B. Flowers. LC 84-1062. xiv, 242p. 1984. 19.95 (ISBN 0-86554-127-2, MUP-H118). Mercer Univ Pr.
Religion in Tennessee, Seventeen Seventy-Seven to Nineteen Forty-Five. Herman A. Norton. LC 81-1562. (Tennessee Three Star Ser.). (Illus.). 136p. 1981. pap. 3.50 (ISBN 0-87049-318-3). U of Tenn Pr.
Religion in the Age of Romanticism: Studies in Early Nineteenth Century Thought. Bernard M. Reardon. 320p. 1985. 44.50 (ISBN 0-521-30088-6); pap. 15.95 (ISBN 0-521-31745-2). Cambridge U Pr.
Religion in the American Novel: The Search for Belief, 1860-1920. Leo F. O'Connor. LC 83-21842. 364p. (Orig.). 1984. lib. bdg. 32.75 (ISBN 0-8191-3683-2); pap. text ed. 15.25 (ISBN 0-8191-3684-0). U Pr of Amer.
Religion in the Curriculum. ASCD, Panel on Religion in the Curriculum Staff. LC 87-81861. 36p. 1987. pap. text ed. 6.00 (ISBN 0-87120-149-6, 611-87052). Assn Supervision.
Religion in the Eighteenth Century. John Browning & Richard Morton. LC 79-17715. (McMaster University Eighteenth Century Studies). 145p. 1979. lib. bdg. 22.00 (ISBN 0-8240-4005-8). Garland Pub.
Religion in the Japanese Experience: Sources & Interpretations. Ed. by H. Byron Earhart. (Religious Life of Man Ser.). 270p. 1974. pap. text ed. write for info. (ISBN 0-8221-0104-1). Wadsworth Pub.
Religion in the Lives of English Women, 1760-1930. Ed. by Gail Malmgreen. LC 86-45172. 224p. 1986. 29.95x (ISBN 0-253-34973-7). Ind U Pr.
Religion in the Making. Alfred N. Whitehead. pap. 5.95 (ISBN 0-452-00723-2, Mer). NAL.
Religion in the Middle East, 2 vols. Arthur J. Arberry. LC 68-21187. (Illus.). 1969. Vol. 1. 62.50 (ISBN 0-521-20543-3). Cambridge U Pr.
Religion in the Middle East: Three Religions in Concord & Conflict, Vol. 2: Islam. Ed. by Arthur J. Arberry. LC 76-11080. pap. 160.00 (2031615). Bks Demand UMI.
Religion in the New Netherland, 1623-1664. Frederick K. Zwierlein. LC 72-120851. (Civil Liberties in American History Ser.). 1971. Repr. of 1910 ed. lib. bdg. 39.50 (ISBN 0-306-71960-6). Da Capo.
Religion in the Old South. Donald G. Mathews. LC 77-587. 1979. pap. 11.00x (ISBN 0-226-51002-6, P819, Phoen). U of Chicago Pr.
Religion in the Pacific Era. Ed. by Frank K. Flinn & Tyler Hendricks. LC 85-12028. 228p. (Orig.). 1985. (Pub. by New Era Bks.); pap. text ed. 12.95 (ISBN 0-913757-19-5, Pub. by New Era Bks.). Paragon Hse.
Religion in the Philosophy of William James. Julius S. Bixler. LC 75-3049. Repr. of 1926 ed. 24.50 (ISBN 0-404-59046-2). AMS Pr.
Religion in the Popular Prints 1600-1832. J. Miller. LC 85-5938. (The English Satirical Print Ser.). 372p. 1986. lib. bdg. 65.00 (ISBN 0-85964-170-8). Chadwyck-Healey.
Religion in the Post-War World. facsimile ed. Ed. by Willard L. Sperry et al. LC 76-142698. (Essay Index Reprints - Religion & Education Ser.: Vol. 4). Repr. of 1945 ed. 14.00 (ISBN 0-8369-2202-6). Ayer Co Pubs.
Religion in the Public Realm. David Tracy. 176p. 1987. 12.95 (ISBN 0-8245-0666-9). Crossroad NY.
Religion in the Public Schools. American Association of school Administrators Staff. 61p. (Orig.). 1986. pap. text ed. 12.95 (ISBN 0-87652-109-X, 21-00174). Am Assn Sch Admin.
Religion in the Public Schools: An Introduction. Richard C. McMillan. LC 84-9147. x, 301p. 1984. 21.95 (ISBN 0-86554-093-4, H85). Mercer Univ Pr.
Religion in the Public Square: Proceedings of a Symposium on the Separation Between Church & State. Richard J. Neuhaus et al. Ed. by James J. Cox. 67p. (Orig.). 1986. pap. text ed. 3.95. WIOCP.
Religion in the Rebel Ranks. Sidney J. Romero. (Illus.). 226p. (Orig.). 1983. lib. bdg. 28.50 (ISBN 0-8191-3327-2); pap. text ed. 13.25 (ISBN 0-8191-3328-0). U Pr of Amer.
Religion in the Reich. Michael Power. LC 78-63706. (Studies in Fascism: Ideology & Practice). 1979. Repr. of 1939 ed. 28.00 (ISBN 0-404-16976-7). AMS Pr.
Religion in the Secular City: Toward a Post-Modern Theology. Harvey Cox. 320p. 1984. 16.95 (ISBN 0-671-45344-0). S&S.
Religion in the Secular City: Toward a Postmodern Theology. Harvey Cox. 304p. 1985. pap. 7.95 (ISBN 0-671-52805-X, Touchstone Bks). S&S.
Religion in the South. Ed. by Charles R. Wilson. LC 85-5361. (Chancellor's Symposium Ser.). (Orig.). 1985. 15.00x (ISBN 0-87805-256-9); pap. 8.95 (ISBN 0-87805-257-7). U Pr of Miss.
Religion in the Soviet Union. Albert Boiter. (Washington Papers: Vol. VIII, No. 78). 88p. (Orig.). 1980. pap. text ed. 7.95 (ISBN 0-8191-6022-9, Pub. by CSIS). U Pr of Amer.
Religion in the Struggle for Power: A Study in the Sociological Study of Religion. Milton J. Yinger. Ed. by Harriet Zuckerman & Robert K. Merton. LC 79-9040. (Dissertations in Sociology Ser.). 1980. Repr. of 1946 ed. lib. bdg. 26.50x (ISBN 0-405-13007-4). Ayer Co Pubs.
Religion in the Struggle for World Community: Unabridged Proceedings. World Conference on Religion & Peace, 3rd Assembly. Ed. by Homer A. Jack. (Orig.). 1980. pap. 6.95 (ISBN 0-935934-05-7). World Confer Rel & Peace.
Religion in the Twentieth Century. Ed. by Vergilius T. Ferm. Repr. of 1948 ed. lib. bdg. 35.00x (ISBN 0-8371-2290-2, FERT). Greenwood.
Religion in the U. S. A, 2 vols. Robert Baird. (Works of Rev. Robert Baird). 1985. Repr. Set. lib. bdg. 89.00 (ISBN 0-932051-57-X, Pub. by Am Repr Serv). Am Biog Serv.
Religion in the United States of America. Robert Baird. LC 70-83411. (Religion in America, Ser. 1). 1969. Repr. of 1844 ed. 38.50 (ISBN 0-405-00232-7). Ayer Co Pubs.
Religion in the West. Ed. by Ferenc M. Szasz. (Illus.). 108p. 1984. pap. text ed. 9.95x (ISBN 0-89745-050-7). Sunflower U Pr.
Religion in the World Today. Miran Mchdelov. 237p. 1987. pap. 4.95 (ISBN 0-8285-3728-3, Pub. by Progress Pubs USSR). Imported Pubns.
Religion in Today's World. Ed. by Frank Whaling. 392p. Date not set. 35.95 (ISBN 0-567-09452-9, Pub. by T & T Clark Ltd UK). Fortress.
Religion in Transition. facs. ed. Ed. by Vergilius T. Ferm. LC 68-29204. (Essay Index Reprint Ser). 1937. 15.50 (ISBN 0-8369-0074-X). Ayer Co Pubs.
Religion in Victorian Society: A Sourcebook of Documents. Ed. by Richard J. Helmstadter & Paul T. Phillips. 484p. (Orig.). 1986. lib. bdg. 38.00 (ISBN 0-8191-4994-2); pap. text ed. 18.75 (ISBN 0-8191-4995-0). U Pr of Amer.
Religion in West European Politics. Ed. by Suzanne Berger. (Illus.). 200p. 1982. text ed. 29.50x (ISBN 0-7146-3218-X, F Cass Co). Biblio Dist.
Religion in Western Civilization Since the Reformation: Select Readings. Ed. by Jon Alexander & Giles Dimock. 184p. 1983. pap. text ed. 7.25 (ISBN 0-8191-3391-4). U Pr of Amer.
Religion Inc. S. Lamont. 1986. 49.75X (ISBN 0-245-54334-1, Pub. by Harrap Ltd England). State Mutual Bk.
Religion: Innocent or Guilty. Ron Yerman. LC 85-90019. 180p. 1985. 11.95 (ISBN 0-533-06540-2). Vantage.
Religion, Intergroup Relations, & Social Change in South Africa. G. C. Oosthuizen et al. LC 88-15430. (Contributions in Ethnic Studies: No. 24). 256p. 1988. lib. bdg. 35.95 (ISBN 0-313-26360-4, HSG/). Greenwood.
Religion Journals & Serials: An Analytical Guide. Compiled by Eugene C. Fieg, Jr. LC 87-32276. (Annotated Bibliographies of Serials: A Subject Approach Ser.: No. 13). 232p. 1988. lib. bdg. 45.00 (ISBN 0-313-24513-4, FRJ/). Greenwood.
Religion, Law & the Growth of Constitutional Thought, 1150-1650. Brian Tierney. LC 81-12265. 128p. 1982. 27.95 (ISBN 0-521-23495-6). Cambridge U Pr.
Religion Lessings. Gottfried Fittbogen. 1967. 36.00; pap. 31.00 (ISBN 0-685-13575-6). Johnson Repr.
Religion, Literature, & Society in Ancient Israel, Formative Christianity & Judaism: Formative Judaism. Ed. by Jacob Neusner et al. (New Perspectives on Ancient Judaism Ser.: Vol. I). 170p. (Orig.). 1987. lib. bdg. 25.00 (ISBN 0-8191-6513-1, Pub. by Studies in Judaism); pap. text ed. 12.75 (ISBN 0-8191-6514-X, Pub. by Studies in Judaism). U Pr of Amer.
Religion, Morality, & the Law. Ed. by J. Roland Pennock & John W. Chapman. (Nomos Ser.: Vol. XXX). 356p. 1988. 42.50x (ISBN 0-8147-6606-4). NYU Pr.
Religion, Morality & "the New Right". Ed. by Melinda Maidens. 224p. 1982. 24.95x (ISBN 0-87196-639-5). Facts on File.
Religion, Morality & the Person: Essays on Tallensi Religion. Meyer Fortes. Ed. by Jack Goody. (Illus.). 400p. 1987. 49.50 (ISBN 0-521-33505-1); pap. 14.95 (ISBN 0-521-33693-7). Cambridge U Pr.
Religion, My Own: The Literary Works of Najib Mahfuz. Mattityahu Peled. LC 82-17582. 268p. 1983. 39.95 (ISBN 0-87855-135-2). Transaction Bks.
Religion, Nationalism & Economic Action: Critical Questions on Durkheim & Weber. Matthew Schoffeleers & Daniel Meijers. 96p. 1978. pap. text ed. 7.50 (ISBN 90-232-1614-8, Pub. by Van Gorcum Holland). Longwood Pub Group.
Religion o Cristo? Martin R. DeHaan. Orig. Title: Religion or Christ. 64p. (Span.). 1970. pap. 2.25 (ISBN 0-8254-1153-X). Kregel.
Religion of a Literary Man. Richard Le Gallienne. 1894. Repr. lib. bdg. 29.00 (ISBN 0-8414-5796-4). Folcroft.
Religion of Ancient Greece. Jane E. Harrison. 1979. Repr. of 1905 ed. lib. bdg. 29.00 (ISBN 0-8495-2325-7). Arden Lib.
Religion of Ancient Greece. T. Zielinski. x, 235p. pap. 10.00 (ISBN 0-89005-090-2). Ares.
Religion of Ancient Greece. facsimile ed. Thaddeus Zielinski. Tr. by George R. Noyes. LC 76-107838. (Select Bibliographies Reprint Ser). 1926. 17.00 (ISBN 0-8369-5222-7). Ayer Co Pubs.
Religion of Ancient Palestine in the Light of Archaeology. S. A Cook. (British Academy, London, Schweich Lectures on Biblical Archaeology Series, 1925). pap. 28.00 (ISBN 0-8115-1267-3). Kraus Repr.
Religion of Ancient Scandinavia. W. A. Craigie. 59.95 (ISBN 0-8490-0939-1). Gordon Pr.
Religion of Ancient Scandinavia. facsimile ed. William A. Craigie. LC 74-99657. (Select Bibliographies Reprint Ser). 1906. 14.50 (ISBN 0-8369-5086-0). Ayer Co Pubs.
Religion of Art in Proust. Barbara J. Bucknall. LC 78-83546. (Studies in Language & Literature, Vol. 60). 222p. 1970. 22.95 (ISBN 0-252-00022-6). U of Ill Pr.
Religion of Beauty in Woman: Essays on Platonic Love in Poetry & Society. Jefferson B. Fletcher. LC 68-925. (Studies in Poetry, No. 38). 1969. Repr. of 1911 ed. lib. bdg. 75.00x (ISBN 0-8383-0550-4). Haskell.
Religion of Burma & Other Papers. Ananda-Maitreya. LC 77-87482. Repr. of 1929 ed. 31.50 (ISBN 0-404-16790-X). AMS Pr.
Religion of Capital. 9th ed. Paul Lafargue. 1967. pap. 0.50 (ISBN 0-935534-38-5). NY Labor News.
Religion of China. Max Weber. 1968. 14.95 (ISBN 0-02-934440-9); text ed. 14.95 (ISBN 0-02-934450-6). Free Pr.
Religion of Dr. Johnson. facsimile ed. William T. Cairns. LC 71-93324. (Essay Index Reprint Ser). 1946. 17.00 (ISBN 0-8369-1279-9). Ayer Co Pubs.
Religion of Dostoevsky. Boyce Gibson. 214p. 6.95 (ISBN 0-664-20989-0). Brown Bk.
Religion of Ethical Nationhood. Mordecai M. Kaplan. 1970. pap. 11.50 (ISBN 0-935457-22-4). Reconstructionist Pr.
Religion of George Fox: As Revealed in His Epistles. Howard H. Brinton. LC 68-57978. (Orig.). 1968. pap. 2.50x (ISBN 0-87574-161-4). Pendle Hill.
Religion of Humanity: The Impact of Comtean Positivism on Victorian Britain. T. R. Wright. (Illus.). 325p. 1986. 44.50 (ISBN 0-521-30671-X). Cambridge U Pr.
Religion of Isaac Newton: The Fremantle Lectures 1973. Frank E. Manuel. 1974. 24.95x (ISBN 0-19-826640-5). Oxford U Pr.
Religion of Islam. F. A. Klein. 248p. 1985. text ed. 17.95x (ISBN 0-7007-0010-2, Pub. by Curzon Pr England); pap. text ed. 8.95. Apt Bks.
Religion of Islam. F. A. Klein. 241p. 1978. Repr. of 1906 ed. 16.50 (ISBN 0-89684-153-7). Orient Bk Dist.
Religion of Islam. F. A. Klein. 248p. 1985. pap. text ed. 12.50x (Pub by Curzon Pr UK). Humanities.
Religion of Islam. F. A. Klein. 248p. 1988. pap. 40.00x (ISBN 0-7007-0190-7, Pub. by Curzon Pr Ltd UK). State Mutual Bk.
Religion of Islam. Maulana-Muhammad-Ali. 1978. 48.50x (ISBN 0-89684-447-1). Orient Bk Dist.
Religion of Israel. Yehezkel Kaufmann. Tr. by Moshe Greenberg. LC 60-5466. 1960. 36.00x (ISBN 0-226-42728-5). U of Chicago Pr.
Religion of Israel: From Its Beginnings to the Babylonian Exile. Yehezkel Kaufmann. Tr. by Moshe Greenberg. LC 60-5466. 304p. 1972. pap. 13.95 (ISBN 0-8052-0364-8). Schocken.
Religion of Japan's Korean Minority: The Preservation of Ethnic Identity. Helen Hardacre. LC 84-80604. (Korea Research Monographs: No. 9). (Illus.). 74p. (Orig.). 1985. pap. text ed. 6.00x (ISBN 0-912966-67-X). IEAS.
Religion of Java. Clifford Geertz. LC 75-18746. xvi, 396p. 1976. pap. 14.00x (ISBN 0-226-28510-3, P658, Phoen). U of Chicago Pr.
Religion of Love. Swami Vivekananda. 114p. pap. 1.95 (ISBN 0-87481-129-5). Vedanta Pr.
Religion of Love. Swami Vivekananda. Ed. by Robert Adjemian & Cecile Guenther. 1988. pap. 7.95 (ISBN 0-87481-045-0). Vedanta Pr.
Religion of Man. Rabindranath Tagore. LC 77-27145. (Hibbert Lectures: 1930). 248p. Repr. of 1931 ed. 27.50 (ISBN 0-404-60426-9). AMS Pr.
Religion of Man. Rabindranath Tagore. 128p. 1988. pap. 9.95 (ISBN 0-04-200014-9). Unwin Hyman.
Religion of Manipur. Saroj Nalini Parratt. 1980. 13.00x (ISBN 0-8364-0594-3, Pub. by Mukhopadhyaya India). South Asia Bks.
Religion of Nature. Basil Willey. LC 76-40105. 1957. lib. bdg. 17.50 (ISBN 0-8414-9506-8). Folcroft.
Religion of Nature Delineated. William Wollaston. Ed. by Rene Wellek. LC 75-11267. (British Philosophers & Theologians of the 17th & 18th Centuries Ser.). 1978. Repr. of 1722 ed. lib. bdg. 51.00 (ISBN 0-8240-1816-8). Garland Pub.
Religion of Nature Delineated, 1724 & Related Commentaries. William Wollaston. LC 74-1469. 1974. 45.00x (ISBN 0-8201-1127-9). Schol Facsimiles.
Religion of Philosophers. facs. ed. James H. Dunham. LC 78-80386. (Essay Index Reprint Ser). 1947. 21.50 (ISBN 0-8369-1059-1). Ayer Co Pubs.
Religion of Plato. P. E. More. (Greek Tradition: Vol. 1). Repr. of 1921 ed. 35.00 (ISBN 0-527-64950-3). Kraus Repr.
Religion of Power. 2nd ed. Cheryl Forbes. 144p. 1988. 6.95 (ISBN 0-310-45771-8, 12396P). Zondervan.
Religion of Protestants: The Church in English Society 1559-1625. Patrick Collinson. 1982. pap. 15.95x (ISBN 0-19-820053-6). Oxford U Pr.
Religion of Science Fiction. Frederick A. Kreuziger. LC 86-72543. 166p. 1986. 19.95 (ISBN 0-87972-366-1); pap. 9.95 (ISBN 0-87972-367-X). Bowling Green Univ.
Religion of Shakespeare. Richard Simpson. Ed. by Henry S. Bowden. LC 74-176025. Repr. of 1899 ed. 47.50 (ISBN 0-404-00961-1). AMS Pr.
Religion of Shakespeare. Richard Simpson. 1973. Repr. of 1899 ed. 17.45 (ISBN 0-8274-1094-8). R West.
Religion of Socialism: Being Essays in Modern Socialist Criticism. Ernest B. Bax. LC 74-39668. (Essay Index Reprint Ser.). Repr. of 1886 ed. 18.00 (ISBN 0-8369-2743-5). Ayer Co Pubs.
Religion of Soldier & Sailor. Paul D. Moody et al. LC 45-3352. 1945. 9.50x (ISBN 0-674-75750-5). Harvard U Pr.
Religion of Solidarity. Edward Bellamy. LC 73-9680. 1940. lib. bdg. 12.50 (ISBN 0-8414-3139-6). Folcroft.
Religion of Solidarity. Edward Bellamy. (Institute of World Culture Ser.). 132p. 1984. pap. 8.75 (ISBN 0-88695-029-5). Concord Grove.
Religion of the Ancient Celts. John A. MacCulloch. LC 77-4127. 1977. lib. bdg. 57.50 (ISBN 0-8414-5998-3). Folcroft.
Religion of the Chinese. Jan J. Groot. LC 79-2824. 230p. 1981. Repr. of 1910 ed. 21.50 (ISBN 0-8305-0004-9). Hyperion Conn.
Religion of the Crow Indians. Robert H. Lowie. LC 74-7986. Repr. of 1922 ed. 15.00 (ISBN 0-404-11876-3). AMS Pr.
Religion of the Future see Modern Essays.
Religion of the Heart: Anglican Evangelicalism & the Nineteenth-Century Novel. Elisabeth Jay. 1979. 49.00x (ISBN 0-19-812092-3). Oxford U Pr.
Religion of the Hindus. Kenneth Morgan. 1987. Repr. of 1953 ed. 26.00x (ISBN 81-208-0387-6, Pub. by Motilal Banarsidass). South Asia Bks.
Religion of the Hindus. H. H. Wilson. 416p. 1978. Repr. of 1862 ed. 13.95x (ISBN 0-89684-135-9). Orient Bk Dist.
Religion of the Hindus: Interpreted by Hindus. Ed. by Kenneth W. Morgan. LC 53-10466. Repr. of 1953 ed. 112.00 (ISBN 0-8357-9975-1, 2015620). Bks Demand UMI.
Religion of the Ifugaos. R. F. Barton. LC 48-3664. (American Anthropological Association Memoirs Ser). Repr. of 1946 ed. 23.00 (ISBN 0-527-00564-9). Kraus Repr.
Religion of the Kwakiutl Indians, 2 Vols. Franz Boas. LC 72-82368. (Columbia Univ. Contributions to Anthropology Ser.: No. 10). Repr. of 1930 ed. Set. 60.00 (ISBN 0-404-50560-0); 30.00 ea. AMS Pr.
Religion of the Machine Age. Dora Russell. 232p. 1985. 27.95 (ISBN 0-7100-9547-3). Routledge Chapman & Hall.
Religion of the Manichees: Donnellan Lectures for 1924. Francis C. Burkitt. LC 77-84698. Repr. of 1925 ed. 29.00 (ISBN 0-404-16105-7). AMS Pr.
Religion of the Republic. Elwyn A. Smith. LC 70-130326. pap. 76.00 (2026890). Bks Demand UMI.

Religionswissenschaft Joachim Wachs. Rainer Flasche. (Theologische Bibliothek Toeelmann: Vol. 35). 1978. 35.20x (ISBN 3-11-007238-6). De Gruyter.
Religiose Poesie der Juden in Spanien. Michael Sachs. Ed. by Steven Katz. LC 79-7150. (Jewish Philosophy, Mysticism & History of Ideas Ser.). 1980. Repr. of 1901 ed. lib. bdg. 37.00x (ISBN 0-405-12285-3). Ayer Co Pubs.
Religiose Reden. Paul Tillich. 518p. 1987. lib. bdg. 44.00x (ISBN 3-11-011486-0). De Gruyter.
Religiose Stromungen Judentum: Mit besondered Berucksichtigung des Chassidismus. Samuel A. Horodezky. Ed. by Steven Katz. LC 79-7137. (Jewish Philosophy, Mysticism & History of Ideas Ser.). 1980. Repr. of 1920 ed. lib. bdg. 23.00x (ISBN 0-405-12263-2). Ayer Co Pubs.
Religious Accommodation in the Workplace: A Legal & Practical Handbook. 150p. 1987. 60.00 (ISBN 0-87179-949-9). BNA.
Religious Affections. Jonathan Edwards. Ed. by John E. Smith. LC 59-12702. (Works of Jonathan Edwards Ser.: Vol. 2). (Illus.). 1959. 65.00x (ISBN 0-300-00966-6). Yale U Pr.
Religious Affections. Jonathan Edwards. Ed. by James M. Houston. LC 84-14863. (Classics of Faith & Devotion Ser.). 1984. 14.95 (ISBN 0-88070-064-5). Multnomah.
Religious Affections. Jonathan Edwards. 382p. 1986. pap. 11.95 (ISBN 0-85151-485-5). Banner of Truth.
Religious & Anti-Religious Thought in Russia. George L. Kline. LC 68-54484. (Weil Lectures). Repr. of 1968 ed. 47.30 (ISBN 0-317-09813-6, 2020097). Bks Demand UMI.
Religious & Cosmic Beliefs of Central Polynesia, 2 vols. Robert W. Williamson. LC 75-35220. Repr. of 1933 ed. Set. 87.50 (ISBN 0-404-14300-8). AMS Pr.
Religious & Educational Philosophy of the Young Women's Christian Association. Grace H. Wilson. LC 70-177632. (Columbia University. Teachers College. Contributions to Education: No. 554). Repr. of 1933 ed. 22.50 (ISBN 0-404-55554-3). AMS Pr.
Religious & Inspirational Books & Serials in Print 1987. Ed. by Bowker, R. R., Co. Staff. 1700p. 1987. 89.00 (ISBN 0-8352-2320-5). Bowker.
Religious & Inspirational Books & Serials in Print 1989. Ed. by Bowker, R. R., Co. Staff. 1900p. 1989. price not set (ISBN 0-8352-2509-7). Bowker.
Religious & Inspirational: Prophesying the Visitation of Destruction in Our Nation. Alex Riley & Diane Riley. LC 87-91668. (Illus.). 144p. (Orig.). 1988. pap. 12.00 (ISBN 0-9619016-0-8). Alexian Pr.
Religious & Moral Values In Public Schools: A Constitutional Analysis. 61p. 1981. 5.00 (ISBN 0-318-17962-8, LEC-81-1). Ed Comm States.
Religious & Spiritual Groups in Modern America. 2nd ed. Robert S. Ellwood & Harry Partin. 384p. 1988. pap. text ed. 22.67 (ISBN 0-13-773045-4). P-H.
Religious & Spiritual Groups in Modern America. Robert S. Ellwood, Jr. 352p. 1973. pap. 24.00 (ISBN 0-13-773309-7). P-H.
Religious Archives, a Complete Technical Look for the Layman. Kevin Sandifer. Ed. by Rowland P. Gill. 96p. (Orig.). 1985. pap. text ed. 8.30 (ISBN 0-910653-03-8, 8101-C). Archival Servs.
Religious Archives: An Introduction. August R. Suelflow. LC 80-17159. (SAA Basic Archival Manual Ser.). 1980. pap. text ed. 7.00 (ISBN 0-931828-20-1). Soc Am Archivists.
Religious Art: A Workbook for Artists & Designers. Robin Landa. 272p. 1985. 29.95 (ISBN 0-13-773037-3); pap. 16.95 (ISBN 0-13-773029-2). P-H.
Religious Art from the Twelfth to the Eighteenth Century. Emile Male. LC 82-47903. (Illus.). 256p. 1982. 35.50x (ISBN 0-691-04000-1); pap. 11.95x (ISBN 0-691-00347-5). Princeton U Pr.
Religious Art in France: The Late Middle Ages: A Study of Medieval Iconography & Its Sources, Vol. 3. Emile Male. Ed. by Harry Bober. Tr. by Marthiel Mathews. (Bollingen Ser. XC: No. 3). 600p. 1987. text ed. 89.50x (ISBN 0-691-09914-6). Princeton U Pr.
Religious Art in France: The Thirteenth Century-A Study of the Origins of Medieval Iconography. Emile Male. Ed. by Harry Bober. Tr. by Marthiel Mathews from Fr. LC 82-11210. (Bollingen Ser.: XC). (Illus.). 576p. 1984. 75.00x (ISBN 0-691-09913-8). Princeton U Pr.
Religious Art in France: The Twelfth Century. Emile Male. LC 72-14029. (Bollingen Ser.: No. 90). 1978. 73.50x (ISBN 0-691-09912-X). Princeton U Pr.
Religious Aspects of Swedish Immigration: A Study of Immigrant Churches. George M. Stephenson. LC 69-18790. (American Immigration Collection Ser., No. 1). (Illus.). 1969. Repr. of 1932 ed. 22.50 (ISBN 0-405-00539-3). Ayer Co Pubs.
Religious Aspects of Swedish Immigration. George M. Stephenson. LC 71-137294. Repr. of 1932 ed. 14.00 (ISBN 0-404-06257-1). AMS Pr.
Religious Aspects of the Conquest of Mexico. C. S. Braden. 1976. lib. bdg. 59.95 (ISBN 0-8490-2510-9). Gordon Pr.
Religious Aspects of the Conquest of Mexico. Charles S. Braden. LC 74-181914. Repr. of 1930 ed. 37.50 (ISBN 0-404-00925-5). AMS Pr.
Religious Aspects of the Unconscious. James Kirsch. 1985. 10.00x (ISBN 0-317-62128-9, Guild of Pastoral Psych). State Mutual Bk.
Religious Assortative Marriage in the United States. Robert A. Johnson. LC 80-978. (Studies in Population). 1980. 41.50 (ISBN 0-12-386580-8). Acad Pr.
Religious Attitude & Life in Islam. D. B. MacDonald. 336p. 1985. 220.00x (ISBN 1-85077-050-6, Pub. by Darf Pubs Ltd). State Mutual Bk.
Religious Attitude & Life in Islam. Duncan B. Macdonald. LC 70-121277. Repr. of 1909 ed. 20.50 (ISBN 0-404-04125-6). AMS Pr.
Religious Attitudes of Japanese Men. Fernando M. Basabe. LC 68-57415. 1969. bds. 15.00 (ISBN 0-8048-0651-9). C E Tuttle.
Religious Attitudes Toward Usury: Two Early Polemics. Ed. by Arno Press Staff & Leonard Silk. LC 79-38471. (The Evolution of Capitalism Ser.). 1972. 25.50 (ISBN 0-405-04135-7). Ayer Co Pubs.
Religious Basis of Spenser's Thought. Virgil K. Whitaker. LC 76-182732. Repr. of 1950 ed. 18.00 (ISBN 0-404-51815-X). AMS Pr.
Religious Belief & Character among Jewish Adolescents. Abraham N. Franzblau. LC 78-176783. (Columbia University. Teachers College. Contributions to Education: No. 634). Repr. of 1934 ed. 22.50 (ISBN 0-404-55634-5). AMS Pr.
Religious Belief & Religious Skepticism. Gary Gutting. LC 82-50287. xi, 192p. 1983. pap. text ed. 9.95x (ISBN 0-268-01618-6, 85-16189). U of Notre Dame Pr.
Religious Belief & the Will. Louis P. Pojman. (Problems of Philosophy Ser.). 256p. 1986. text ed. 32.50 (ISBN 0-7102-0399-3). Routledge Chapman & Hall.
Religious Beliefs & White Prejudice. Robert Buis. 71p. 1975. pap. text ed. 7.95x (ISBN 0-86975-044-5, Pub. by Ravan Pr). Ohio U Pr.
Religious Bibliographies in Serial Literature: A Guide. Michael J. Walsh et al. LC 81-312. 224p. 1981. lib. bdg. 40.95 (ISBN 0-313-22987-2, WRB/). Greenwood.
Religious Bodies of America. F. E. Mayer. 616p. 1987. 18.95 (ISBN 0-570-03294-6, 15-1714). Concordia.
Religious Books for Children: An Annotated Bibliography. Patricia Pearl. LC 83-7339. 36p. (Orig.). 1983. pap. 5.95 (ISBN 0-915324-21-0); pap. 4.75 members. CSLA.
Religious Books, 1876-1982, 4 vol. set. 4389p. 1983. 245.00x (ISBN 0-8352-1602-0). Bowker.
Religious Broadcast Management Handbook. Thomas C. Durfey & James A. Ferrier. 1986. pap. 15.95 (ISBN 0-310-39741-3, 12258P). Zondervan.
Religious Broadcasting, Nineteen Twenty to Nineteen Eighty-Three: A Selectively Annotated Bibliography. Lenwood Davis & George H. Hill. (Reference Library of Social Science). 1984. lib. bdg. 40.00 (ISBN 0-8240-9015-2). Garland Pub.
Religious Buildings. Architectural Record Magazine Editors. 1980. text ed. 45.50 (ISBN 0-07-002342-5). McGraw.
Religious Care of the Psychiatric Patient. Wayne E. Oates. LC 78-18454. 252p. 1978. 13.95 (ISBN 0-664-21365-0). Westminster John Knox.
Religious Change & Continuity: Sociological Perspectives. Ed. by Harry M. Johnson. LC 79-83574. (Jossey-Bass Social & Behavioral Science Ser.). pap. 94.80 (2027756). Bks Demand UMI.
Religious Change in Zambia: Exploratory Studies. Wim M. Van Binsbergen. 424p. 1984. pap. 14.95x (ISBN 0-7103-0012-3, Kegan Paul). Routledge Chapman & Hall.
Religious Change in Zambia: Exploratory Studies. Wim M. J. Van Binsbergen. (Monographs from the African Studies Centre, Leiden). (Illus.). 416p. 1981. 50.00x (ISBN 0-7103-0000-X). Routledge Chapman & Hall.
Religious Changes in Contemporary Poland: Secularization & Politics. Maciej Pomian-Srzednicki. (International Library of Sociology). 227p. 1982. 27.95x (ISBN 0-7100-9245-8). Routledge Chapman & Hall.
Religious Chastity: An Ethnological Study, by John Main (Pseud.) Elsie W. Parsons. LC 72-9672. Repr. of 1913 ed. 52.00 (ISBN 0-404-57489-0). AMS Pr.
Religious Concerns in Contemporary Education. Philip H. Phenix. LC 59-11329. Repr. of 1959 ed. 29.50 (ISBN 0-8357-9605-1, 2016949). Bks Demand UMI.
Religious Confessions & Confessants. Anna R. Burr. 1977. lib. bdg. 59.95 (ISBN 0-8490-2511-7). Gordon Pr.
Religious Conflict in America: A Bibliography. Albert J. Menendez. LC 84-48078. (Reference Library of Social Science). 500p. 1984. lib. bdg. 20.00 (ISBN 0-8240-8904-9). Garland Pub.
Religious Conflict in Social Context: The Resurgence of Orthodox Judaism in Frankfurt Am Main, 1838-1877. Robert Liberles. LC 84-27981. (Contributions to the Study of Religion Ser.: No. 13). xvi, 297p. 1985. lib. bdg. 35.00 (ISBN 0-313-24806-0, LRX/). Greenwood.
Religious Congregations & Health Care Facilities: Accountability & Adaptation. LC 83-5228. 86p. (Orig.). 1983. pap. 7.00 (ISBN 0-87125-083-7). Cath Health.
Religious Congregations & Health Care Facilities: Commitment & Collaboration. LC 81-18064. 100p. 1982. pap. 6.00 (ISBN 0-87125-073-X). Cath Health.
Religious Congregations & Health Care Facilities: Competition & Cooperation. LC 85-17155. 85p. (Orig.). 1985. pap. 9.00 (ISBN 0-87125-107-8). Cath Health.
Religious Congregations & Health Facilities: Tradition & Transition. LC 84-7692. 100p. (Orig.). 1984. pap. 9.00 (ISBN 0-87125-095-0). Cath Health.
Religious Consciousness. G. S. Ghurye. 383p. 1965. 16.95. Asia Bk Corp.
Religious Consciousness: A Psychological Study. James B. Pratt. 1971. Repr. of 1920 ed. 21.95x (ISBN 0-02-850350-3). Hafner.
Religious Controversies of the Elizabethan Age: A Survey of Printed Sources. Peter Milward. LC 77-80038. xvi, 202p. 1977. 21.00x (ISBN 0-8032-0923-1). U of Nebr Pr.
Religious Controversies of the Jacobean Age: A Survey of Printed Sources. Peter Milward. xii, 264p. 1978. 29.50x (ISBN 0-8032-3058-3). U of Nebr Pr.
Religious Controversies of the Nineteenth Century: Selected Documents. Ed. by A. O. Cockshut. LC 66-18225. vi, 265p. 1966. 22.50x (ISBN 0-8032-0019-6). U of Nebr Pr.
Religious Conversions in India. Brojendra N. Bannerjee. 384p. 1982. 29.95x (ISBN 0-940500-28-0, Pub. by Harnam Pub India). Asia Bk Corp.
Religious Convictions & Political Choice. Kent Greenawalt. 288p. 1987. 29.95 (ISBN 0-19-504913-6). Oxford U Pr.
Religious Crises in Modern America. Martin E. Marty. LC 81-80740. (Charles Edmondson Historical Lectures Ser.). 40p. (Orig.). 1981. pap. 4.50x (ISBN 0-918954-26-6). Baylor Univ Pr.
Religious Cults Associated with the Amazons. Florence M. Anderson. LC 73-158253. Repr. of 1912 ed. 16.00 (ISBN 0-404-00749-X). AMS Pr.
Religious Cults Associated with the Amazons. F. M. Bennett. v, 79p. 1985. Repr. of 1912 ed. lib. bdg. 25.00x (ISBN 0-89241-204-6). Caratzas.
Religious Cults of the Pai-i along the Burma-Yunnan Border. T'ien Ju-K'ang. (Southeast Asia Program Ser.: No. 1). 144p. (Orig.). 1986. pap. text ed. 7.50 (ISBN 0-87727-117-8). Cornell SE Asia.
Religious Currents in the Nineteenth Century. Vilhelm Gronbech. Tr. by P. M. Mitchell & W. D. Paden. LC 72-11829. (Arcturus Bks. Paperbacks). 206p. 1973. lib. bdg. 7.00x (ISBN 0-8093-0629-8); pap. 2.45x (ISBN 0-8093-0630-1). S Ill U Pr.
Religious Dances in the Christian & in Popular Medicine. Eugene L. Backman. Ed. by E. Classen. LC 77-8069. 1977. Repr. of 1952 ed. 35.00x (ISBN 0-8371-9678-7, BARD). Greenwood.
Religious Data: Recurrent Christian Sources, Non-Recurrent Christian Data, Judaism, Other Religions. L. M. Barley et al. (Reviews of U. K. Statistical Sources: No. 20). 635p. 1987. 115.00 (ISBN 0-08-034778-9, PBL). Pergamon.
Religious Denominations in the United States: Their Past History, Present Condition, & Doctrines. Israel D. Rupp. LC 72-2943. Repr. of 1861 ed. 67.50 (ISBN 0-404-10709-5). AMS Pr.
Religious Design of Hemingway's Early Fiction. Larry E. Grimes. Ed. by A. Walton Litz. LC 85-1183. (Studies in Modern Literature: No. 50). 166p. 1985. 34.95 (ISBN 0-8357-1635-X). UMI Res Pr.
Religious Development in the Province of North Carolina. S. B. Weeks. pap. 9.00 (ISBN 0-384-66390-7). Johnson Repr.
Religious Development in the Province of North Carolina. Stephen B. Weeks. LC 78-63811. (Johns Hopkins University. Studies in the Social Sciences. Tenth Ser. 1892: 5-6). Repr. of 1892 ed. 11.50 (ISBN 0-404-61074-9). AMS Pr.
Religious Dimension in Hegel's Thought. Emil L. Fackenheim. LC 81-21914. xiv, 274p. 1982. pap. 10.00x (ISBN 0-226-23350-2). U of Chicago Pr.
Religious Dimension in Hegel's Thought. Emil L. Fackenheim. 1984. 16.25 (ISBN 0-8446-5997-5). Peter Smith.
Religious Dimension in Hispanic Los Angeles: A Protestant Case Study. Clifton L. Holland. LC 74-5123. 541p. (Orig.). 1974. pap. 10.95 (ISBN 0-87808-309-X). William Carey Lib.
Religious Dimension: New Directions in Quantitative Research. Ed. by Robert Wuthnow. LC 79-6948. 1979. 29.95 (ISBN 0-12-766050-X). Acad Pr.
Religious Dimension of Jane Austen's Novels. Gene Koppel. Ed. by Juliet McMaster. LC 87-25540. (Nineteenth-Century Studies). 154p. 1987. 39.95 (ISBN 0-8357-1858-1). UMI Res Pr.
Religious Discourse: Thanksgiving Day Sermon, November 26, 1789. Gershom M. Seixas. LC 77-7298. (Illus.). 1977. pap. 2.00 (ISBN 0-916790-00-2). Jewish Hist.
Religious Diversity. Wilfred C. Smith. (Crossroad Paperback Ser.). 224p. 1982. pap. 9.95 (ISBN 0-8245-0458-5). Crossroad NY.
Religious Diversity & Social Change: American Cities, 1890-1906. Kevin J. Christiano. (Illus.). 272p. 1988. 34.50 (ISBN 0-521-34145-0). Cambridge U Pr.
Religious Dogmatics & the Evolution of Societies. Niklas Luhmann. Tr. by Peter Beyer. LC 84-8976. (Studies in Religion & Society: Vol. 9). 192p. 1984. lib. bdg. 49.95x (ISBN 0-88946-866-4). E Mellen.
Religious Doubt: Its Nature, Treatment, Causes, Difficulties, Consequences & Dissolution. John W. Diggle. 1978. Repr. of 1895 ed. lib. bdg. 25.00 (ISBN 0-8495-1030-9). Arden Lib.
Religious Drama: Ends & Means. Harold A. Ehrensperger & Stanley Lehrer. LC 77-22986. (Illus.). 1977. Repr. of 1962 ed. lib. bdg. 35.00x (ISBN 0-8371-9744-9, EHRD). Greenwood.
Religious Drama, Vol. 1: Five Plays. Ed. by Marvin Halverson. 11.25 (ISBN 0-8446-2792-5). Peter Smith.
Religious Drama, Vol. 2: 21 Medieval Mystery & Morality Plays. Ed. by E. Martin Browne. 17.75 (ISBN 0-8446-2793-3). Peter Smith.
Religious Drama, Vol. 3. Ed. by Marvin Halverson. 11.25 (ISBN 0-8446-2794-1). Peter Smith.
Religious Ecstasy. Ed. by Nils G. Holm. (Scripta Instituti Donnerain Aboensis: No. XI). 306p. 1982. pap. text ed. 25.00x (ISBN 91-22-00574-9, Pub. by Almqvist & Wiksell). Humanities.
Religious Education & Our Ultimate Committment: An Application of Henry Nelson Wieman's Philosophy of Creative Interchange. Harold Rosen. LC 84-19651. 196p. (Orig.). 1985. lib. bdg. 25.50 (ISBN 0-8191-4341-3, Unitarian Univ Assn); pap. text ed. 11.50 (ISBN 0-8191-4342-1, Unitarian Univ. Assn.). U Pr of Amer.
Religious Education & the Future. Ed. by Dermot Lane. 240p. (Orig.). 1987. pap. 9.95 (ISBN 0-8091-2877-2). Paulist Pr.
Religious Education & Theology. Ed. by Norma H. Thompson. LC 81-17852. 254p. 1982. pap. 12.95 (ISBN 0-89135-029-2). Religious Educ.
Religious Education, Catechesis & Freedom. Kenneth Barker. LC 81-13962. 255p. (Orig.). 1981. pap. 12.95 (ISBN 0-89135-028-4). Religious Educ.
Religious Education: Chicago, 1906-1955, Vols. 1-50. Set. lib. bdg. 2250.00 (ISBN 0-685-77259-4); lib. bdg. 45.00 ea.; Set. pap. 2000.00; pap. 40.00 ea. AMS Pr.
Religious Education Development. Gabriel Moran. (Images for the Future). 204p. 1983. pap. 12.95 (ISBN 0-86683-692-6, AY8272, HarpR). Har-Row.
Religious Education Encounters Liberation Theology. Daniel S. Schipani. 300p. (Orig.). 1988. pap. 14.95 (ISBN 0-89135-064-0). Religious Educ.
Religious Education Five-Twelve. Derek Bastide. 33.00x (ISBN 1-85000-149-9, Falmer Press); pap. 17.00x (ISBN 1-85000-150-2). Taylor & Francis.
Religious Education Handbook: A Practical Parish Guide. James P. Enswiler. LC 79-26008. 108p. (Orig.). 1980. pap. 4.95 (ISBN 0-8189-0398-8). Alba.
Religious Education in a Pluralistic Society. M. C. Felderhof. 160p. 1985. pap. text ed. 20.95 (ISBN 0-340-35413-5). Princeton Bk Co.
Religious Education in a Psychological Key. John H. Peatling. LC 81-8678. 439p. (Orig.). 1981. pap. 14.95 (ISBN 0-89135-027-6). Religious Educ.
Religious Education in German Schools: An Historical Approach. Ernst C. Helmreich. LC 59-11509. 1959. 27.00x (ISBN 0-674-75850-1). Harvard U Pr.
Religious Education: Its Effects, Its Challenges Today. Robert J. Fox. 1972. pap. 0.95 (ISBN 0-8198-0344-8). Dghtrs St Paul.
Religious Education Ministry with Youth. Ed. by D. Campbell Wyckoff & Don Richter. LC 81-19239. 257p. (Orig.). 1982. pap. 12.95 (ISBN 0-89135-030-6). Religious Educ.
Religious Education, Nineteen Forty-Four to Nineteen Eighty-Four. Ed. by A. G. Wedderspoon. 238p. 1968. 4.95 (ISBN 0-87921-063-X); pap. 2.50 (ISBN 0-87921-064-8). Attic Pr.
Religious Education of Adults. Leon McKenzie. LC 81-19926. 256p. 1982. pap. 12.95 (ISBN 0-89135-031-4). Religious Educ.
Religious Education of Older Adults. Linda J. Vogel. LC 83-21109. 217p. (Orig.). 1984. pap. 12.95 (ISBN 0-89135-040-3). Religious Educ.
Religious Education of Preschool Children. Lucie W. Barber. LC 80-27623. 196p. (Orig.). 1981. pap. 12.95 (ISBN 0-89135-026-8). Religious Educ.
Religious Education of the Deaf. Ed. by J. Van Eijndhoven. (Modern Approaches to the Diagnosis & Instruction of Multi-Handicapped Children Ser.: Vol. 11). 168p. 1973. text ed. 14.75 (ISBN 90-237-4111-0, Pub. by Swets & Zeitlinger Netherlands). Hogrefe Intl.
Religious Education: Philosophical Perspectives. John Sealey. Ed. by Philip Snelders & Colin Wringe. (Introductory Studies in the Philosophy of Education). 120p. 1985. text ed. 29.95x (ISBN 0-04-370130-2); pap. text ed. 10.95x (ISBN 0-04-370131-0). Unwin Hyman.
Religious Enthusiasm in the New World: Heresy to Revolution. David S. Lovejoy. 336p. 1985. text ed. 27.00x (ISBN 0-674-75864-1). Harvard U Pr.
Religious Ethics & Pastoral Care. Don S. Browning. LC 83-5589. (Theology & Pastoral Care Ser.). 128p. 1983. pap. 7.95 (ISBN 0-8006-1725-8, 1-1725). Fortress.
Religious Experience. Wayne Proudfoot. LC 84-23928. 1985. 32.00x (ISBN 0-520-05143-2). U of Cal Pr.

Religious Postures: Essays on Modern Christian Apologists & Religious Problems. G. A. Wells. LC 88-1526. 277p. (Orig.). 1988. 28.95 (ISBN 0-8126-9070-2); pap. 14.95 (ISBN 0-8126-9071-0). Open Court.

Religious Potential of the Child. Sofia Cavalletti. 224p. 1982. pap. 10.95 (ISBN 0-8091-2389-4). Paulist Pr.

Religious Poverty & the Profit Economy in Medieval Europe. Lester K. Little. LC 78-58630. (Paperback Ser.). 268p. 1983. pap. 10.95x (ISBN 0-8014-9247-5). Cornell U Pr.

Religious Press in America. Martin E. Marty et al. LC 72-6844. 184p. 1973. Repr. of 1963 ed. lib. bdg. 35.00x (ISBN 0-8371-6500-8, MARP). Greenwood.

Religious Press in the South Atlantic States, 1802-1865. Henry S. Stroupe. (Duke University. Trinity College Historical Socity. Historical Papers: No. 32). Repr. of 1956 ed. 24.50 (ISBN 0-404-51782-X). AMS Pr.

Religious Progress on the Pacific Slope: Addresses & Papers at the Celebration of the Semi-Centennial Anniversary of Pacific School of Religion, Berkeley, California. facs. ed. Pacific School Of Religion. LC 68-22941. (Essay Index Reprint Ser). 1968. Repr. of 1917 ed. 19.00 (ISBN 0-8369-0820-1). Ayer Co Pubs.

Religious Quests of the Graeco-Roman World. S. Angus. 1929. 30.00 (ISBN 0-686-20108-6). Quality Lib.

Religious Quests of the Graeco-Roman World: A Study in the Historical Background of Early Christianity. Samuel Angus. LC 66-30791. 1929. 20.00 (ISBN 0-8196-0196-9). Biblo.

Religious Reason: The Rational & Moral Basis of Religious Belief. Ronald M. Green. 1978. text ed. 18.95x (ISBN 0-19-502388-9); pap. text ed. 7.95x (ISBN 0-19-502389-7). Oxford U Pr.

Religious Repression in Cuba. Juan Clark. 115p. (Orig.). 1986. pap. 8.95 (ISBN 0-935501-04-5). U Miami N-S Ctr.

Religious Resurgence: Comtemporary Cases in Islam, Christianity, & Judaism. Ed. by Richard T. Antoun & Mary C. Hegland. 288p. 1987. text ed. 27.50 (ISBN 0-8156-2409-3). Syracuse U Pr.

Religious Revolt in the Seventeenth Century: The Schism of the Russian Church. Nickolas B. Lupinin. 220p. 1984. 24.00 (ISBN 0-940670-12-7). Kingston Pr.

Religious Revolution in the Ivory Coast: The Prophet Harris & the Harris Church. Sheila S. Walker. LC 81-13010. (Studies in Religion). xvii, 206p. 1983. 32.00x (ISBN 0-8078-1503-9). U of NC Pr.

Religious Right & Israel: The Politics of Armageddon. Ruth W. Mouly. (Midwest Research Monograph: No. 2). 47p. 1985. pap. 3.00 (ISBN 0-915987-01-5). Political Rsch Assocs.

Religious Rock'n'Roll, A Wolf in Sheep's Clothing. Jimmy Swaggart & Robert P. Lamb. 1987. 12.95 (ISBN 0-935113-05-3). Swaggart Ministries.

Religious Roots of Rebellion: Christians in Central American Revolutions. Philip Berryman. LC 83-19343. 480p. (Orig.). 1984. pap. 19.95 (ISBN 0-88344-105-5). Orbis Bks.

Religious School Board: A Manual. Louis Lister & Rebecca Lister. 1978. pap. 5.00 (ISBN 0-8074-0014-9, 243870). UAHC.

Religious Schooling in America. Ed. by James C. Carper & Thomas C. Hunt. LC 84-1942. 257p. (Orig.). 1984. pap. 14.95 (ISBN 0-89135-043-8). Religious Educ.

Religious Schools in America: A Selected Bibliography. Thomas C. Hunt et al. LC 86-12118. (Reference Library of Social Science: Vol. 338). 416p. 1986. lib. bdg. 47.00 (ISBN 0-8240-8583-3). Garland Pub.

Religious Science Book. Parker L. Johnstone. 212p. 1984. 7.95 (ISBN 0-917802-13-6). Theoscience Found.

Religious Science for Youth. Docia W. Norris. pap. 1.50 (ISBN 0-87516-153-7). DeVorss.

Religious Science Hymnal. 3rd ed. Ed. by Irma Glen. 225p. 1982. Repr. of 1956 ed. 8.00 (ISBN 0-87516-489-7). DeVorss.

Religious Seekers & the Advent of Mormonism. Dan Vogel. 300p. 1988. pap. 9.95 (ISBN 0-941214-64-8). Signature Bks.

Religious Sentimentalism in the Age of Johnson: 1740-1780 see Religious Trends in English Poetry.

Religious Sentiments of Charles Dickens: Collected from His Writings. Charles Dickens. Ed. by C. McKenzie. LC 73-7504. (Studies in Dickens, No. 52). 1973. Repr. of 1884 ed. lib. bdg. 39.95x (ISBN 0-8383-1697-2). Haskell.

Religious Significance of Atheism. Alasdair MacIntyre & Paul Ricoeur. LC 68-28398. (Bampton Lectures in America Ser.: No. 18). 98p. 1969. 20.00 (ISBN 0-231-03139-4). Columbia U Pr.

Religious Significance of Atheism. Alasdair MacIntyre & Paul Ricoeur. LC 68-28398. (Bampton Lectures in America: No. 18). 98p. 1986. pap. 10.00 (ISBN 0-231-06367-9). Columbia U Pr.

Religious Signing. Elaine Costello. (Illus.). 176p. 1986. pap. 9.95 (ISBN 0-553-34244-4). Bantam.

Religious Solution to the Social Problem. Howard H. Brinton. 1934. pap. 2.50x (ISBN 0-87574-002-2, 002). Pendle Hill.

Religious Songs & Other Items see Ozark Folksongs.

Religious Sonnets of Dylan Thomas. H. H. Kleinman. 1979. Repr. of 1963 ed. lib. bdg. 17.00x (ISBN 0-374-94589-6, Octagon). Hippocrene Bks.

Religious Spectrum. Margaret Chatterjee. (Studies in an Indian Context). 196p. 1984. 24.95 (ISBN 0-317-39860-1, Pub. by Allied Pubs India). Asia Bk Corp.

Religious Spectrum. 196p. 1984. 24.95. Asia Bk Corp.

Religious Speeches of Bernard Shaw. Ed. by Warren S. Smith. LC 63-18890. 1963. 19.95x (ISBN 0-271-73095-1). Pa St U Pr.

Religious Strife in Egypt: Crisis & Ideological Conflict in the Seventies. Nadia R. Farah. 144p. 1986. text ed. 42.00 (ISBN 2-88124-092-5). Gordon & Breach.

Religious Studies in Alberta: A State-of-the-Art Review. Ronald Neufeldt. (Study of Religion in Canada Ser.). 145p. 1983. pap. text ed. 10.00x (ISBN 0-317-03613-0, Pub. by Wilfrid Laurier Canada). Humanities.

Religious Study of Judaism: Context, Text, Circumstance, Vol. 3. Jacob Neusner. (Studies in Judaism). 234p. (Orig.). 1987. lib. bdg. 25.50 (ISBN 0-8191-6047-4, Pub. by Studies in Judaism); pap. 13.75 (ISBN 0-8191-6048-2, Pub. by Studies in Judaism). U Pr of Amer.

Religious Study of Judaism: Description, Analysis & Interpretation. Jacob Neusner. LC 85-30411. (Studies in Judaism Ser.: Vol. 1). 188p. (Orig.). 1986. lib. bdg. 23.75 (ISBN 0-8191-5393-1, Pub. by Studies in Judaism); pap. text ed. 10.25 (ISBN 0-8191-5394-X). U Pr of Amer.

Religious Study of Judaism: Description, Analysis, Interpretation-The Centrality of Context. Jacob Neusner. LC 85-30411. (Studies in Judaism: Vol. 2). 230p. (Orig.). 1986. lib. bdg. 25.75 (ISBN 0-8191-5450-4, Pub. by Studies in Judaism); pap. text ed. 13.50 (ISBN 0-8191-5451-2). U Pr of Amer.

Religious Symbols & Their Functions. Ed. by Haralds Biezais. 178p. (Orig.). 1979. pap. text ed. 22.50 (ISBN 91-22-00199-9, Pub. by Almqvist & Wiksell). Coronet Bks.

Religious System of China, 6 vols. J. J. DeGroot. 1982. Repr. of 1892 ed. 160.00x (ISBN 0-89986-346-9). Oriental Bk Store.

Religious System of the Amazulu. (Folk Lore Society, London Ser.: Vol. 15). Repr. of 1884 ed. 43.00 (ISBN 0-8115-0506-5). Kraus Repr.

Religious Systems of the Mahanubhava Sect. Anne Feldhaus. 1983. 26.00x (ISBN 0-8364-1005-X). South Asia Bks.

Religious Teachers of Greece. James Adam. LC 72-2565. (Select Bibliographies Reprint Ser). 1972. Repr. of 1908 ed. 26.00 (ISBN 0-8369-6843-3). Ayer Co Pubs.

Religious Teachers of Greece. James Adam. LC 65-22806. (Library of Religious & Philosophical Thought). 1966. Repr. of 1908 ed. lib. bdg. 45.00x (ISBN 0-678-09950-2, Reference Bk Pubs). Kelley.

Religious Teachings for Children, Bk. 1. Shaikh M. Sarwar. 44p. pap. 5.00 (ISBN 0-941724-03-4). Islamic Seminary.

Religious Teachings for Children, Bk. 2. Shaikh M. Sarwar. 66p. pap. 5.00 (ISBN 0-941724-04-2). Islamic Seminary.

Religious Teachings for Children, Bk. 3. Shaikh M. Sarwar. 80p. pap. 5.00 (ISBN 0-941724-05-0). Islamic Seminary.

Religious Teachings for Children, Bk. 4. Shaikh M. Sarwar. 72p. 1981. pap. 5.00 (ISBN 0-941724-06-9). Islamic Seminary.

Religious Television: The Experience in America. Peter Horsfield. LC 83-11313. (Communication & Human Values Ser.). (Illus.). 192p. 1984. text ed. 17.95 (ISBN 0-582-28432-5). Longman.

Religious Thinking from Childhood to Adolescence. Ronald Goldman. 1968. pap. text ed. 6.95 (ISBN 0-8164-2061-0, SP53, HarpR). Har-Row.

Religious Thought & Economic Society: Four Chapters of an Unfinished Work. Jacob Viner. Ed. by Jacques Melitz & Donald Winch. LC 77-93857. vi, 211p. 1978. 21.95 (ISBN 0-8223-0398-1). Duke.

Religious Thought & the Modern Psychologies: A Critical Conversation in the Theology of Culture. Don S. Browning. LC 86-45205. 288p. 1986. 22.50 (ISBN 0-8006-0784-8). Fortress.

Religious Thought & the Modern Psychologies: A Critical Conversation in the Theology of Culture. Don S. Browning. LC 86-45205. 1988. pap. 12.95 (ISBN 0-8006-2322-3). Fortress.

Religious Thought in England from the Reformation to the End of the Last Century, 3 Vols. John Hunt. LC 72-153593. Repr. of 1873 ed. Set. 125.00 (ISBN 0-404-09480-5). AMS Pr.

Religious Thought in England in the Nineteenth Century. John Hunt. 424p. Repr. of 1896 ed. text ed. 62.10x (ISBN 0-576-29211-7, Pub. by Gregg Intl Pubs England). Gregg Intl.

Religious Thought in India. T. N. Sharma. 1980. 11.00x (ISBN 0-8364-0619-2, Pub. by Ramneek). South Asia Bks.

Religious Thought in the Greater American Poets. facs. ed. Elmer J. Bailey. LC 68-8436. (Essay Index Reprint Ser). 1968. Repr. of 1922 ed. 16.00 (ISBN 0-8369-0167-3). Ayer Co Pubs.

Religious Thought in the Last Quarter-Century. Ed. by Gerald B. Smith. LC 71-107739. (Essay Index Reprint Ser). 1927. 12.00 (ISBN 0-8369-1583-6). Ayer Co Pubs.

Religious Thought of H. Richard Niebuhr. Jerry A. Irish. LC 83-6202. pap. 32.30 (2027155). Bks Demand UMI.

Religious Thought of Jose Rizal. rev. ed. Eugene A. Hessel. 354p. (Orig.). 1984. pap. 12.25x (ISBN 0-318-01161-1, Pub. by New Day Philippines). Cellar.

Religious Thoughts in the Reformation. Bernard Reardon. 1981. pap. text ed. 16.95 (ISBN 0-582-49031-6). Longman.

Religious Thoughts of Some of Our Poets. Alfred C. Fryer. 1911. Repr. 17.50 (ISBN 0-8274-3263-1). R West.

Religious Toleration & Persecution in Ancient Rome. Simeon L. Guterman. LC 70-104269. 160p. Repr. of 1951 ed. lib. bdg. 22.50x (ISBN 0-8371-3936-8, GURT). Greenwood.

Religious Toleration & Social Change in Hamburg, 1529-1819. Joachim Whaley. (Cambridge Studies in Early Modern History). 290p. 1985. 52.50 (ISBN 0-521-26189-9). Cambridge U Pr.

Religious Traditions & the Limits of Tolerance. Ed. by Louis Hammann & Harry M. Buck. 1987. 12.95 (ISBN 0-89012-047-1). Anima Pubns.

Religious Trends in Early Islamic Iran. Wilfred Madelung. (Columbia Lecture Series on Iranian Studies). 128p. 1988. 32.50x (ISBN 0-88706-700-X); pap. 9.95x (ISBN 0-88706-701-8). State U NY Pr.

Religious Trends in English Poetry, 6 vols. Hoxie N. Fairchild. Incl. Vol. 1. Protestantism & the Cult of Sentiment: 1700-1740 (ISBN 0-231-08821-3); Vol. 2. Religious Sentimentalism in the Age of Johnson: 1740-1780. 1942 (ISBN 0-231-08822-1); Vol. 3. Romantic Faith: 1780-1830. 1949 (ISBN 0-231-08823-X); Vol. 4. Christianity & Romanticism in the Victorian Era: 1830-1880. 1957 (ISBN 0-231-08824-8); Vol. 5. Gods of a Changing Poetry: 1880-1920. 1962 (ISBN 0-231-08825-6); Vol. 6. Valley of Dry Bones: 1920-1965. 1968 (ISBN 0-231-08826-4). LC 39-12839. 45.00x ea. Columbia U Pr.

Religious Urge-Reverential Life: The Notebooks of Paul Brunton, Vol. 12. Paul Brunton. 384p. 1988. 22.50 (ISBN 0-943914-36-1); pap. 12.50 (ISBN 0-943914-37-X). Larson Pubns Inc.

Religious Values. Edgar S. Brightman. Repr. of 1925 ed. 29.00 (ISBN 0-527-11010-8). Kraus Repr.

Religious Values & Development. Ed. by Kenneth P. Jameson & Charles K. Wilber. (Illus.). 154p. 1981. 53.00 (ISBN 0-08-026107-8). Pergamon.

Religious Values in an Age of Violence. Marc H. Tanenbaum. (Pere Marquette Theology Lectures). 1976. 7.95 (ISBN 0-87462-508-4). Marquette.

Religious Women in the United States: A Survey of the Literature from 1950 to 1983. Elizabeth Kolmer. LC 84-81252. (Consecrated Life Studies Ser.: Vol. 4). 1984. pap. 6.95 (ISBN 0-89453-445-9). M Glazier.

Religious Word. 2nd ed. Richard C. Bush et al. 1982. text ed. write for info. (ISBN 0-02-317530-3). Macmillan.

Religious Worlds: The Comparative Study of Religion. William E. Paden. LC 88-47658. 240p. 1988. 19.95 (ISBN 0-8070-1210-6); pap. 9.95 (ISBN 0-8070-1211-4, BP 806). Beacon Pr.

Religious Writer's Marketplace: The Definitive Sourcebook. rev. & updated ed. Ed. by William H. Gentz. LC 84-27691. 221p. 1985. pap. 17.95 (ISBN 0-89471-305-1). Running Pr.

Religious Writers of England. Pearson M. Muir. 1901. 20.00 (ISBN 0-8274-3264-X). R West.

Religiously Mixed Marriage. Gary Beauchamp & Deanna Beauchamp. 4.95 (ISBN 0-89137-528-7). Quality Pubns.

Religiousness in Yoga: Lectures on Theory & Practice. T. K. Desikachar. Ed. by Mary L. Skelton & J. R. Carter. LC 79-9643. (Illus.). 314p. 1980. text ed. 28.50 (ISBN 0-8191-0966-5); pap. text ed. 12.50 (ISBN 0-8191-0967-3). U Pr of Amer.

Religioznaya Tchuvstvo, Promisl Bozhil i Dukovnoje Prizvanije. Archbishop Athanasius Martos. 30p. 1983. pap. 2.00 (ISBN 0-317-29069-X). Holy Trinity.

Religya i Literatura: Religion & Literature. Sergei Averintsev. LC 81-4115. 140p. (Rus.). 1981. pap. 7.00 (ISBN 0-938920-02-2). Hermitage.

Relinking with Witchcraft: Cooperation with Nature Spirits. Rhuddlwm Gawr. LC 85-73745. (Illus.). 140p. 1988. 12.95 (ISBN 0-931760-37-2, CP 10115); pap. 10.95 (ISBN 0-931760-15-1). Camelot GA.

Reliquare. William L. Fox et al. LC 87-70382. (Windriver Ser.). (Illus.). 32p. (Orig.). 1987. pap. 10.00 (ISBN 0-916918-36-X); 26 lettered ed. 25.00 (ISBN 0-916918-37-8). Duck Down.

Reliques of Ancient English Poetry, 3 vols. Thomas Percy. Ed. by Henry B. Wheatley. 1885. Repr. Set. 100.00 (ISBN 0-8274-3265-8). R West.

Reliques of Ancient English Poetry: Consisting of Old Heroic Ballads, Songs, & Other Pieces of Our Earlier Poets, 2 vols. Thomas Percy. Ed. by J. V. Prichard. 434p. 1983. Repr. of 1892 ed. Set. lib. bdg. 100.00 (ISBN 0-89984-836-2). Century Bookbindery.

Reliques of Irish Poetry, 1789. Ed. by Charlotte Brooke. Bd. with Memoir of Miss Brooke. 1816. A. C. Seymour. LC 76-133327. 544p. 1970. 75.00x (ISBN 0-8201-1082-5). Schol Facsimiles.

Reliques of Robert Burns: Consisting Chiefly of Original Letters, Poems, & Critical Observations on Scottish Songs, Collected & Published by Robert Cromek (1780-1812) Robert Burns. LC 78-72777. Repr. of 1808 ed. AMS Pr.

Reliquiae, 2 vols. A. D. Godley. Ed. by C. R. Fletcher. 1973. Repr. of 1926 ed. 75.00 (ISBN 0-8274-0201-5). R West.

Reliquiae Antiquae, 2 Vols. Ed. by Thomas Wright & James O. Halliwell. LC 13-3962. Repr. of 1843 ed. Set. 65.00 (ISBN 0-404-07047-7). AMS Pr.

Reliquiae Celticae, 2 vols. Alexander Cameron. Ed. by Alexander MacBain & John K. Kennedy. LC 78-72621. (Celtic Language & Literature: Goidelic & Brythonic). Repr. of 1894 ed. Set. 84.50 (ISBN 0-404-17543-0). AMS Pr.

Reliquiae Diluvianae: Observations on the Organic Remains Contained in Caves Fissures, & Diluvial Gravel. William Buckland. Ed. by Claude C. Albritton, Jr. LC 77-6510. (History of Geology Ser.). (Illus.). 1978. Repr. of 1823 ed. lib. bdg. 30.00x (ISBN 0-405-10433-2). Ayer Co Pubs.

Reliquiae Juveniles: Miscellaneous Thoughts in Prose & Verse. Isaac Watts. LC 68-17018. 1968. Repr. of 1734 ed. 50.00x (ISBN 0-8201-1049-3). Schol Facsimiles.

Reliquiae Selectae. Menander. Ed. by F. H. Sandbach. (Oxford Classical Texts Ser.). 1972. text ed. 17.50x (ISBN 0-19-814571-3). Oxford U Pr.

Reliquien als Kultobjekt: Geschichte des Reliquienkultes see Reliquienkult im Altertum.

Reliquienkult im Altertum, 2 vols. in 1. Friedrich Pfister. Incl. Vol. 1. Das Objekt des Reliquienkultes; Vol. 2. Reliquien als Kultobjekt: Geschichte des Reliquienkultes. xii, 686p. (Ger.). 1974. Repr. of 1909 ed. 76.00x (ISBN 3-11-002453-5). De Gruyter.

Relish for Eternity: The Process of Divinization in the Poetry of John Clare. Greg Crossan. Ed. by James Hogg. (Romantic Reassessment Ser.). 267p. (Orig.). 1976. pap. 15.00 (ISBN 3-7052-0508-0, Pub. by Salzburg Studies). Longwood Pub Group.

Reliving Past Lives. Helen Wambach. 208p. 1984. pap. 6.95 (ISBN 0-06-464080-9, BN 4080, B&N Bks). Har-Row.

Reliving the Past: The Worlds of Social History. Ed. by Olivier Zunz. LC 85-1065. x, 336p. 1985. 33.00x (ISBN 0-8078-1658-2); pap. 10.95x (ISBN 0-8078-4137-4). U. of NC Pr.

Re'lize Whut Ahm Talkin' 'Bout. Steve Chenault. softcover 7.95 (ISBN 0-912216-24-7). Angel Pr.

Reloader's Bible: The Complete Guide To Making Ammunition at Home. Don Geary. (Illus.). 256p. 1986. 17.95 (ISBN 0-668-06025-5). P-H.

Reloader's Guide. 3rd ed. R. A. Steindler. (Illus.). 224p. pap. 9.95 (ISBN 0-88317-021-3). Stoeger Pub Co.

Reloading for Shotgunners. 2nd ed. Ed. by Robert S. Anderson. (Illus.). 256p. (Orig.). 1985. pap. 12.95 (ISBN 0-910676-92-5). DBI.

Relocating Spouse's Guide to Employment: Options & Strategies in the U. S. & Abroad. Frances Bastress. LC 86-19230. (Illus.). 265p. (Orig.). 1986. pap. 12.95 (ISBN 0-937623-00-8). Woodley Pubns.

Relocating Spouse's Guide to Employment: Options & Strategies in the U. S. & Abroad. rev. ed. Frances Bastress. 265p. 1987. pap. 12.95 (ISBN 0-937623-01-6). Woodley Pubns.

Relocation Assistant. Jack Rudman. (Career Examination Ser.: C-1988). (Cloth bdg. avail. on request). pap. 12.00 (ISBN 0-8373-1988-9). Natl Learning.

Relocation Program see U. S. War Relocation Authority.

Relocation Program: A Guidebook for the Residents of Relocation Centers see U. S. War Relocation Authority.

Relocation Supervisor. Jack Rudman. (Career Examination Ser.: C-3057). 1988. pap. 14.00 (ISBN 0-8373-3057-2). Natl Learning.

Relocations: The Churches' Report on Forced Removals in South Africa. CIIR Staff. 64p. 1984. 12.00x (ISBN 0-946848-25-4, Pub. by CIIR). State Mutual Bk.

Reluctant Abigail. Miranda Cameron. 1984. pap. 2.50 (ISBN 0-451-13162-2, Sig). NAL.

Reluctant Admiral: Yamamoto & the Imperial Navy. Hiroyuki Agawa. Tr. by John Bester. LC 79-84652. 397p. 1982. 16.95x (ISBN 0-87011-355-0); pap. 7.95 (ISBN 0-87011-512-X). Kodansha.

Reluctant Adventuress. Sylvia Thorpe. 224p. 1977. pap. 1.50 (ISBN 0-449-23426-6, Crest). Fawcett.

Reluctant Ally: Austria's Policy in the Austro-Turkish War, 1737-1739. Karl A. Roider, Jr. LC 72-79336. (Illus.). vi, 198p. 1972. 25.00 (ISBN 0-8071-0237-7). La State U Pr.

Reluctant Ally: France & Atlantic Security. Michael M. Harrison. LC 80-8865. 320p. 1981. text ed. 37.50x (ISBN 0-8018-2474-5). Johns Hopkins.

Reluctant Angel. Jon L. Joyce. (Orig.). 1983. pap. 2.25 (ISBN 0-937172-53-7). JLJ Pubs.

Reluctant Art: The Growth of Jazz. Benny Green. (New Reprints in Essay & General Literature Index Ser.). 1975. Repr. of 1963 ed. 20.25 (ISBN 0-518-10199-1, 10199). Ayer Co Pubs.

Reluctant Beligerent: American Entry into World War II. 2nd ed. Robert A. Divine. 179p. 1979. pap. text ed. write for info (ISBN 0-394-34171-6, RanC). Random.

Reluctant Belligerent: American Entry into World War II. Robert A. Divine. LC 75-31695. (America in Crisis Ser.). 186p. 1976. Repr. of 1965 ed. 12.50 (ISBN 0-88275-346-0). Krieger.

Reluctant Colonists. Doreen Greig. (Illus.). 368p. 1986. 30.00 (ISBN 90-232-2227-X, Pub. by Van Gorcum Holland). Longwood Pub Group.

Reluctant Confederates: Upper South Unionists in the Secession Crisis. Daniel W. Crofts. LC 88-6927. (Fred W. Morrison Series in Southern Studies). (Illus.). 540p. 1989. 45.00x (ISBN 0-8078-1809-7). U of NC Pr.

Reluctant Crusade: American Foreign Policy in Korea, 1941-1950. James A. Matray. LC 85-1079. 368p. 1985. text ed. 30.00x (ISBN 0-8248-0973-4). UH Pr.

Reluctant Debutante. Marilyn Carter. 256p. (Orig.). 1988. pap. 2.95 (ISBN 0-446-34450-8). Warner Bks.

Reluctant Doctor. Moliere, pseud. Tr. by W. Hannan. (Orig.). 1963. pap. 3.50x (ISBN 0-87830-535-1). Theatre Arts.

Reluctant Dragon. Kenneth Grahame. (Illus.). 58p. (gr. 3-6). 1953. 6.95 (ISBN 0-8234-0093-X). Holiday.

Reluctant Dragon. Kenneth Grahame. LC 83-209. (Illus.). 48p. (gr. 4-6). 1983. 11.50 (ISBN 0-03-064031-8). H Holt & Co.

Reluctant Dragon. Kenneth Grahame. Ed. by I. M. Richardson. LC 87-10906. (Illus.). 32p. (gr. k-4). 1987. lib. bdg. 9.79 (ISBN 0-8167-1059-7); pap. text ed. 1.95 (ISBN 0-8167-1060-0). Troll Assocs.

Reluctant Dragon. Kenneth Grahame. LC 83-209. (Illus.). 32p. (gr. 3-6). 1988. pap. 4.95 (ISBN 0-8050-0802-0). H Holt & Co.

Reluctant Duke. Philippa Castle. 256p. 1986. pap. 2.95 (ISBN 0-446-30097-7). Warner Bks.

Reluctant Empress: A Biography of Elisabeth of Austria. Brigitte Hamann. LC 86-45512. 432p. 1986. 25.00 (ISBN 0-394-53717-3). Knopf.

Reluctant Exhibitionist. Martin Shepard. LC 83-63255. 280p. 1985. pap. 5.95 (ISBN 0-932966-57-8). Permanent Pr.

Reluctant Farewell: An American Report's Candid Look Inside the Soviet Union. Andrew Nagorski. 1987. pap. 8.95 (ISBN 0-8050-0454-8, Owl Bks). HR&W.

Reluctant Farmer see Strength of the Hills.

Reluctant Farmer: The Rise of Agricultural Extension to 1914. Roy V. Scott. LC 70-102023. pap. 93.50 (ISBN 0-317-28992-6, 2020235). Bks Demand UMI.

Reluctant Feminists in German Social Democracy 1885-1917. Jean H. Quataert. LC 79-84011. (Illus.). 1979. 37.00 (ISBN 0-691-05276-X). Princeton U Pr.

Reluctant Flirt. Elizabeth Mansfield. 208p. 1987. pap. 2.50 (ISBN 0-515-08937-0). Jove Pubns.

Reluctant Followers: A Chosen People? Ronald R. Hamilton. Ed. by Michael L. Sherer. (Orig.). 1986. pap. 6.25 (ISBN 0-89536-824-2, 6833). CSS of Ohio.

Reluctant God. Pamela F. Service. LC 87-16840. 224p. (gr. 5-8). 1988. 13.95 (ISBN 0-689-31404-3, Atheneum Childrens Bks). Macmillan.

Reluctant Guru. R. K. Narayan. 173p. 1975. pap. 2.50 (ISBN 0-88253-729-6). Ind-US Inc.

Reluctant Heiress. Janet Templeton. LC 86-24142. 336p. 1987. 16.95 (ISBN 0-385-23982-3, GC Large Print). Doubleday.

Reluctant Hero. Francoise Sagan. Tr. by Christine Donougher. 1987. 16.95 (ISBN 0-525-24550-2, 01646-490). Dutton.

Reluctant Hunter. Joyce P. Hardy. 1988. pap. 8.00 (ISBN 0-941179-22-2). Latitudes Pr.

Reluctant Imperialists: Calhoun, the South Carolinians, & the Mexican War. Ernest M. Lander, Jr. LC 79-16879. 207p. 1980. 22.50 (ISBN 0-8071-0594-5). La State U Pr.

Reluctant Little Astronaut. P. Mae Malone. (Illus.). 32p. (gr. 3). 1985. Repr. of 1967 ed. 4.00. Exposition-Phoenix.

Reluctant Memory. Dorothy L. Gray. 1977. 4.00 (ISBN 0-682-48897-6). Exposition-Phoenix.

Reluctant Missionary. Ken Miller. (YA) (gr. 9 up). 1987. write for info. (ISBN 0-942241-01-0). Pubs Bk Sales.

Reluctant Naturalist: A Study of G.E. Moore's Principia Ethica. Dennis Rohatyn. 150p. (Orig.). 1987. lib. bdg. 22.50 (ISBN 0-8191-5767-8); pap. text ed. 9.75 (ISBN 0-8191-5768-6). U Pr of Amer.

Reluctant Paragon. Catherine George. (Harlequin Romances Ser.). 192p. 1983. pap. 1.75 (ISBN 0-373-02535-1). Harlequin Bks.

Reluctant Partners: Nashville & the Union, July 1, 1863, to June 30, 1865. Walter T. Durham. (Illus.). 320p. 1987. 19.95x (ISBN 0-9615966-1-9). TN His Soc.

Reluctant Patron. Peter Alter. LC 86-32062. 1988. 50.00 (ISBN 0-907582-67-2, Pub. by Berg Pubs). St Martin.

Reluctant Patron: The United States Government & the Arts, 1943-1965. Gary O. Larson. LC 82-40492. (Illus.). 320p. (Orig.). 1983. pap. 15.95 (ISBN 0-8122-1144-8). U of Pa Pr.

Reluctant Pilgrim: Defoe's Emblematic Method & Quest for Form in Robinson Crusoe. J. Paul Hunter. 288p. 1966. 32.50x (ISBN 0-8018-0286-5). Johns Hopkins.

Reluctant Pioneers: Village Development in Israel. Alex Weingrod. LC 78-159987. 1971. Repr. of 1966 ed. 24.50x (ISBN 0-8046-1686-8, Pub. by Kennikat). Assoc Faculty Pr.

Reluctant Rake. Jane Ashford. 224p. 1987. pap. 2.50 (ISBN 0-451-14808-8, Sig). NAL.

Reluctant Rapture. Marjorie Shoebridge. 480p. (Orig.). 1986. pap. 3.95 (ISBN 0-8439-2308-3, Leisure Bks). Leisure NY.

Reluctant Ratifiers: Virginia Considers the Federal Constitution. Edwin L. Shepard. (Illus.). 48p. (Orig.). 1988. pap. text ed. 1.00 (ISBN 0-945015-01-1). VA Hist Soc.

Reluctant Rebel in Air Force Blues. J. Remy Theberge. LC 77-74192. (Illus.). 1977. 7.95 (ISBN 0-918862-01-9). Golden Gambit.

Reluctant Rebels see Lawful Revolution: Louis Kossuth & the Hungarians, 1848-1849.

Reluctant Rebels: Comparative Studies of Revolution & Underdevelopment. John Walton. LC 83-7698. 1984. 32.00x (ISBN 0-231-05728-8); pap. 12.50x (ISBN 0-231-05729-6). Columbia U Pr.

Reluctant Reformers: The Impact of Racism on American Social Reform Movements. Robert Allen. LC 73-85495. 1974. 10.95 (ISBN 0-88258-002-7); pap. 6.95 (ISBN 0-88258-026-4). Howard U Pr.

Reluctant Relative. Jessica Steele. (Harlequin Presents Ser.). 192p. 1984. pap. 1.95 (ISBN 0-373-10661-0). Harlequin Bks.

Reluctant Resister. Jeff Deitrich. (Illus.). 1983. 17.00 (ISBN 0-87775-156-0); pap. 8.00 (ISBN 0-87775-157-9). Unicorn Pr.

Reluctant Revolutionaries: Englishmen & the Revolution of 1688. W. A. Speck. (Illus.). 250p. 1988. 39.95 (ISBN 0-19-822768-X). Oxford U Pr.

Reluctant Revolutionary. Edward Teller. LC 64-25274. 85p. 1964. 10.00x (ISBN 0-8262-0032-X). U of Mo Pr.

Reluctant Ronin: A Superintendent Otani Mystery. James Melville. 192p. 1988. 15.95 (ISBN 0-684-18947-X). Scribner.

Reluctant Supplier: U. S. Decision-Making for Arms Sales. Paul Y. Hammond & David J. Louscher. LC 82-22514. 336p. 1983. 30.00 (ISBN 0-89946-149-2). Oelgeschlager.

Reluctant Swordsman. Dave Duncan. 1988. pap. 3.50 (ISBN 0-345-35291-2, Del Rey). Ballantine.

Reluctant to Read? Ed. by John L. Foster. 176p. 1981. 20.00x (ISBN 0-7062-3642-4, Pub. by Ward Lock Educ Co Ltd). State Mutual Bk.

Reluctant Union: Alsace-Lorraine & Imperial Germany, 1871-1918. Dan P. Silverman. LC 73-180693. (Illus.). 272p. 24.95x (ISBN 0-271-01111-4). Pa St U Pr.

Reluctant Vegetarian Cookbook. Simon Hope. (Illus.). 192p. 1985. 20.95 (ISBN 0-434-34667-5, Pub. by W Heinemann Ltd). David & Charles.

Reluctant Vision: An Essay in the Philosophy of Religion. Thomas P. Burke. LC 73-88354. pap. 35.50 (2026883). Bks Demand UMI.

Reluctant Warrior: The Challenge of Arms Control. Coit D. Blacker. LC 86-32011. (Political Science Ser.). (Illus.). 208p. 1987. text ed. 12.95 (ISBN 0-7167-1862-6). W H Freeman.

Reluctant Welfare State: A History of American Social Welfare Policies. Bruce S. Jansson. 278p. 1988. text ed. write for info. (ISBN 0-534-08490-7). Wadsworth Pub.

Reluctant Widow. Georgette E. Heyer. 1988. pap. 3.50 (ISBN 0-425-10884-8). Berkley Pub.

Reluctant Witness. Kenneth L. Chaffin. LC 74-84548. 1975. 8.50 (ISBN 0-8054-5550-7). Broadman.

Rem Khokhlov. V. I. Grigoryev. 109p. 1985. pap. 2.95 (ISBN 0-8285-3072-6, Pub. by Mir Pubs USSR). Imported Pubns.

REM Sleep: Its Temporal Distribution. Ed. by Charles A. Czeisler & Christian Guilleminault. (Sleep Journal Reprint: Vol. 2, Nos. 3-4, 1980). 126p. 1980. pap. text ed. 23.50 (ISBN 0-89004-527-5). Raven.

Remaines Concerning Britain. William Camden. LC 77-113572. (Illus.). Repr. of 1657 ed. 46.50 (ISBN 0-404-01367-8). AMS Pr.

Remaines of Gentilisme & Judaisme see Three Prose Works.

Remaines of Gentilisme & Judaisme, Sixteen Hundred Eighty-Six to Eighty-Seven. John Aubrey. Ed. by James Britten. (Folk-Lore Society, London, Monograph Ser.: Vol. 4). pap. 29.00 (ISBN 0-8115-0501-4). Kraus Repr.

Remains Concerning Britain. William Camden. Ed. by R. D. Dunn. 632p. 1984. 75.00x (ISBN 0-8020-2457-2). U of Toronto Pr.

Remains of Animals in Quaternary Lake & Bog Sediments & Their Interpretation. Ed. by David G. Frey. (Limnology Report). (Illus.). 116p. (Orig.). 1964. pap. text ed. 20.00x (ISBN 3-510-47002-8, Pub. by E Schweizerbartsche). Coronet Bks.

Remains of Christopher Columbus. Joseph R. Muratore. (Illus.). 91p. 1973. pap. 3.00 (ISBN 0-686-09021-7). Muratore.

Remains of Edmund Grindal, Successively Bishop of London, & Archbishop of York & Canterbury. Edmund Grindal. Repr. of 1843 ed. 41.00 (ISBN 0-384-20090-7). Johnson Repr.

Remains of Elmet. Ted Hughes. LC 78-24817. (Illus.). 1979. 17.00 (ISBN 0-06-011953-5, HarpT). Har-Row.

Remains of Kirke White, with an Account of His Life. Robert Southey. Ed. by Donald H. Reiman. LC 75-31271. (Romantic Context Ser.: Poetry 1789-1830). 1978. lib. bdg. 113.00 (ISBN 0-8240-2217-3). Garland Pub.

Remains of Myles Coverdale, Bishop of Exeter. Myles Coverdale. 1846. 51.00 (ISBN 0-384-09950-5). Johnson Repr.

Remains of Old Latin, 4 vols. Ed. by E. H. Warmington. Incl. Vol. 1. Ennius. Caecilius (ISBN 0-674-99324-1); Vol. 2. Livius Andronicus, Naevius, Pacuvius, Accius (ISBN 0-674-99347-0); Vol. 3. Lucilius. Laws of the XII Tables (ISBN 0-674-99363-2); Vol. 4. Archaic Inscriptions (ISBN 0-674-99396-9). (Loeb Classical Library: No. 294, 314, 329, 359). (Lat. & Eng.). 13.95x ea. Harvard U Pr.

Remains of the Early Popular Poetry of England, 4 Vols. Ed. by William C. Hazlitt. Repr. of 1866 ed. 95.00 (ISBN 0-404-03240-0). AMS Pr.

Remains of the Rev. James Marsh, D. D. James Marsh. Ed. by Joseph Torrey. LC 77-122659. 1971. Repr. of 1843 ed. 42.00x (ISBN 0-8046-1308-7, Pub. by kennikat). Assoc Faculty Pr.

Remains of Thomas Hearne. Ed. by Centaur Books Staff. 1985. 75.00x (ISBN 0-900000-30-9, Pub. by Centaur Bks). State Mutual Bk.

Remains of Thomas Hearne: Reliquiae Hearnianae, Being Extracts from His MS Diaries. Thomas Hearne. Ed. by John Buchanan-Brown. LC 67-13936. (Centaur Classics Ser.). 489p. 1966. 22.50x (ISBN 0-8093-0239-X). S Ill U Pr.

Remains: Stories of Vietnam. William Crapser. LC 88-6667. 175p. 1988. 18.95 (ISBN 0-937584-13-4); pap. 9.95 (ISBN 0-937584-14-2). Sachem Pr.

Remaking America: New Uses, Old Places. Barbaralee Diamonstein. (Illus.). 1986. 30.00 (ISBN 0-517-56287-1). Crown.

Remaking American Politics. Richard A. Harris & Sidney M. Milkis. 374p. 1988. 33.00 (ISBN 0-8133-0495-4); pap. 15.95 (ISBN 0-8133-0496-2). Westview.

Remaking China Policy: U. S.-China Relations & Governmental Decisionmaking. Richard Moorsteen & Morton Abramowitz. LC 74-164428. (Rand Corporation Research Studies). 127p. 1971. 12.00x (ISBN 0-674-75981-8). Harvard U Pr.

Remaking Cities: Contradictions of the Recent Urban Environment. Alison Ravetz. 375p. 1980. 29.95 (ISBN 0-85664-293-2, Pub. by Croom Helm Ltd); pap. 13.00 (ISBN 0-7099-2220-5). Routledge Chapman & Hall.

Remaking Ibieca: Rural Life in Aragon under Franco. Susan F. Harding. LC 83-21884. (Illus.). vii, 348p. 1984. 27.50x (ISBN 0-8078-1594-2). U of NC Pr.

Remaking Japan: The American Occupation As New Deal. Theodore Cohen. Ed. by Herbert Passin. 553p. 1987. 27.50 (ISBN 0-317-62616-7). Free Pr.

Remaking Motherhood. Julius Held & Anita Shreve. 1987. 18.95 (ISBN 0-670-80722-2). Viking.

Remaking Motherhood: How Working Mothers Are Shaping Our Children's Future. Anita Shreve. 1988. pap. 7.95 (ISBN 0-449-90300-1, Columbine). Fawcett.

Remaking of a City: Rochester, New York 1964-1984. Buttino-Hare. 464p. 1984. pap. text ed. 18.95 (ISBN 0-8403-3451-6). Kendall-Hunt.

Remaking of a Land Surveyor. Michael J. Schmitz. Ed. by Roy Minnick. (Illus.). 223p. (Orig.). 1978. pap. 22.00 (ISBN 0-910845-03-4, 715). Landmark Ent.

Remaking of Istanbul: Portrait of an Ottoman City in the Nineteenth Century. Zeynep Celik. LC 85-26536. (Illus.). 200p. 1986. 25.00x (ISBN 0-295-96364-6). U of Wash Pr.

Remaking of Modern Armies. B. H. Liddell Hart. 1980. lib. bdg. 64.95 (ISBN 0-8490-3189-3). Gordon Pr.

Remaking of Modern Armies. Basil H. Liddell Hart. LC 79-24497. 1980. Repr. of 1928 ed. lib. bdg. 35.00x (ISBN 0-313-22174-X, LHRM). Greenwood.

Remaking of Pittsburgh: Class & Culture in an Industrializing City, 1877-1919. Francis G. Couvares. LC 83-5044. (American Social History Ser.). 187p. 1984. 49.50 (ISBN 0-87395-778-4); pap. 16.95x (ISBN 0-87395-779-2). State U NY Pr.

Remaking of Sigmund Freud. Barry N. Malzberg. 288p. 1985. pap. 2.95 (ISBN 0-345-31861-7, Del Rey). Ballantine.

Remaking of the English Navy by Admiral St. Vincent - Key to the Victory over Napoleon: The Great Unclaimed Naval Revolution (1795-1805) Charles B. Arthur. (Illus.). 278p. (Orig.). 1986. lib. bdg. 27.00 (ISBN 0-8191-5309-5); pap. text ed. 14.50 (ISBN 0-8191-5310-9). U Pr of Amer.

Remaking of Wales in the Eighteenth Century. Ed. by Trevor Herbert & Gareth E. Jones. (Welsh History & Its Sources Ser.). 1988. pap. text ed. 19.95 (ISBN 0-7083-1024-9, Pub. by U of Wales). Humanities.

Remaking Society. Murray Bookchin. 200p. 1989. 34.95 (ISBN 0-921689-03-9, Dist. by U of Toronto Pr); pap. 14.95 (ISBN 0-921689-02-0, Dist. by U of Toronto Pr). Black Rose Bks.

Remaking the International Monetary System - the Rio Agreement & Beyond. Fritz Machlup. LC 68-31419. 176p. 1968. pap. 3.00 (ISBN 0-87186-224-7). Comm Econ Dev.

Remaking the International Monetary System: The Rio Agreement & Beyond. Fritz Machlup. LC 68-31419. (Committee for Economic Development. CED Supplementary Paper: No. 24). pap. 42.80 (ISBN 0-317-19923-4, 2023125). Bks Demand UMI.

Remaking the Welfare State: Retrenchment & Social Policy in America & Europe. Ed. by Michael K. Brown. 320p. 1988. 34.95 (ISBN 0-87722-541-9). Temple U Pr.

Remaking the World Bank. Barend A De Vries. 200p. (Orig.). 1988. pap. 14.95 (ISBN 0-932020-49-6). Seven Locks Pr.

Remaking Urban Scotland: Strategies for Local Economic Development. Michael Keating & Robin Boyle. (Scottish Economic Policy: Vol. 3). 175p. 1987. 25.00 (ISBN 0-85224-531-9, Pub. by Edinburgh U Pr Scotland). Columbia U Pr.

Remanufacturing: The Experience of the of the United States & Implications for Developing Countries. Robert T. Lund. (Technical Paper: No. 31). 120p. 1985. 5.00 (ISBN 0-8213-0448-8, BK 0448). World Bank.

Remar Sutton's Body Worry. Remar Sutton. Orig. Title: Body Worry. 304p. 1987. 17.95 (ISBN 0-670-81653-1). Viking.

Remarkable Aerial Voyage. Willem Bilderdijk. Tr. & intro. by Paul Vincent. LC 87-70814. 88p. 1988. pap. 13.95 (ISBN 0-905075-24-2, Pub. by Wilfion Bks Scotland). Dufour.

Remarkable & Unknown Health Properties of Wine & Spirits. William Sanford. (Illus.). 117p. Repr. of 1799 ed. 117.75 (ISBN 0-89901-046-6). Found Class Reprints.

Remarkable Animals. David Christie et al. (Illus.). 240p. 1987. 19.95 (ISBN 0-85112-867-X, Pub. by Guinness Superlatives). Sterling.

Remarkable Birth of Planet Earth. Henry M. Morris. LC 73-166083. 112p. 1972. pap. 3.50 (ISBN 0-87123-485-8, 200485). Bethany Hse.

Remarkable Children: Twenty Who Made History. Dennis B. Fradin. 208p. (YA) (gr. 4-7). 1987. 14.95 (ISBN 0-316-29126-9). Little.

Remarkable Egg. Adelaide Holl. LC 68-24455. (Illus.). (gr. k-3). 1968. PLB 11.88 (ISBN 0-688-51090-6). Lothrop.

Remarkable Expedition: The Story of Stanley's Rescue of Emin Pasha from Equatorial Africa. Olivia Manning. LC 85-47607. (Illus.). 288p. 1985. 12.95 (ISBN 0-689-11627-6). Atheneum.

Remarkable GG-1. Karl Zimmermann. 1977. pap. 6.95 (ISBN 0-915276-16-X). Quadrant Pr.

Remarkable History of the Hudson's Bay Company: Induding That of the French Traders of Northwestern Canada, & of the Astor Fur Companies. George Bryce. (Research & Source Works Ser.: No. 171). (Illus.). 1968. 29.50 (ISBN 0-8337-0407-9). B Franklin.

Remarkable Iowa Women. Ethel W. Hanft. Tr. by Linda L. Dagel. LC 80-139767. (Illus.). 130p. 1983. 6.95 (ISBN 0-9605162-2-0). River Bend.

Remarkable Medicine Has Been Overlooked. rev. ed. Jack Dreyfus. 1983. pap. 4.95 (ISBN 0-671-47673-4). PB.

Remarkable Mr. Featherstonhaugh: The First U. S. Government Geologist. Edmund Berkeley & Dorothy S. Berkeley. LC 87-5006. (History of American Science & Technology Ser.). 352p. 1988. 39.95 (ISBN 0-8173-0365-0). U of Ala Pr.

Remarkable Providences Illustrative of the Earlier Days of American Colonisation. Increase Mather. Ed. by Richard M. Dorsen. LC 77-70610. (International Folklore Ser.). 1977. Repr. of 1856 ed. lib. bdg. 24.50x (ISBN 0-405-10107-4). Ayer Co Pubs.

Remarkable Ramsey. Barbara Rinkoff. (Illus.). (gr. 2-6). 15.25 (ISBN 0-8446-6195-3). Peter Smith.

Remarkable Recipes. Antoinette K. Hatfield. Ed. by Thomas K. Worcester. (Illus.). 156p. 7.95 (ISBN 0-911518-04-5). Touchstone Oregon.

Remarkable Record of Job. Henry Morris. 180p. 1988. 12.95 (ISBN 0-89051-140-3). Master Bks.

Remarkable Record of Job: The Ancient Wisdom, Scientific Accuracy, & Life-Changing Message of an Amazing Book. Henry M. Morris. 1988. 9.95 (ISBN 0-8010-6238-1). Baker Bk.

Remarkable Red Raspberry Recipes. Sibyl Kile. (Illus.). 170p. (Orig.). 1985. pap. 7.95 (ISBN 0-9615201-2-4). BCG Ltd.

Remarkable Relations: The Story of the Pearsall Smith Women. Barbara Strachey. LC 82-8429. (Illus.). 370p. 1982. 15.95x (ISBN 0-87663-396-3). Universe.

Remarkable Return of Winston Potter Crisply. Eve Rice. LC 77-28101. 224p. (gr. 5-9). 1978. PLB 11.88 (ISBN 0-688-84145-7). Greenwillow.

Remarkable Riderless Runaway Tricycle. rev. ed. Bruce McMillan. (Illus.). 48p. (gr. k-4). 1985. pap. 6.95 (ISBN 0-934313-00-8). Apple Isl Bks.

Remarkable Trials of All Countries; Particularly of the United States, Great Britain, Ireland & France: With Notes & Speeches of Counsel. Containing Thrilling Narratives of Fact from the Court-Room, Also Historical Reminiscences of Wonderful Events. Compiled by Thomas Dunphy & Thomas J. Cummins. 464p. 1981. Repr. of 1867 ed. lib. bdg. 35.00x (ISBN 0-8377-0512-6). Rothman.

Remarkable Woman. Anne Edwards. Date not set. pap. 4.50 (ISBN 0-671-62574-8). PB.

Remarkable Woman: A Biography of Katharine Hepburn. Anne Edwards. LC 85-11523. (Illus.). 472p. 1985. 18.95 (ISBN 0-688-04528-6). Morrow.

Remarkable Woman: A Biography of Katherine Hepburn. Anne Edwards. (Large Print Bks.). (Illus.). 652p. 1986. lib. bdg. 21.95 (ISBN 0-8161-4064-2, Large Print Bks). G K Hall.

Remarkable Women of Ancient Egypt. 2nd, rev. ed. Barbara S. Lesko. (Illus.). 1987. pap. 8.95 (ISBN 0-930548-09-4). B C Scribe.

Remarkable World of John Wesley: Pioneer in Mental Health. Franklin Wilder. (Illus.). 1978. 7.00 (ISBN 0-682-49129-2). Exposition-Phoenix.

Remarkable Year. M. Prilezhayeva. 265p. 1980. 9.45 (ISBN 0-8285-2324-X, Pub. by Progress Pubs USSR). Imported Pubns.

Remarks about Academic Matters. Rudolf Kurth. LC 81-40177. 124p. (Orig.). 1982. lib. bdg. 21.75 (ISBN 0-8191-1855-9); pap. text ed. 10.00 (ISBN 0-8191-1856-7). U Pr of Amer.

Remarks Concerning the Government & the Laws of the United States of America, in Four Letters, Addressed to Mr. Adams, from the French, of the Abbe De Mably. Gabriel Bonnot De Mably. LC 72-6273. Repr. of 1785 ed. 23.50 (ISBN 0-8337-2160-7). B Franklin.

Remarks, Critical & Illustrative, on the Text & Notes of the Last Edition of Shakspeare. Joseph Ritson. LC 73-174324. Repr. of 1783 ed. 14.50 (ISBN 0-404-05348-3). AMS Pr.

Remarks, Critical, Conjectural & Explanatory upon the Plays of Shakespeare, 2 vols. E. H. Seymour. LC 74-175848. 1976. Repr. of 1805 ed. Set. 52.50 (ISBN 0-404-05754-3). AMS Pr.

Remarks Made on a Tour to Prairie du Chien: Thence to Washington City in 1829. fascimile ed. Caleb Atwater. LC 75-82. (Mid-American Frontier Ser.). 1975. Repr. of 1831 ed. 25.50x (ISBN 0-405-06851-4). Ayer Co Pubs.

Remarks of Henry Brewster Stanton in the Representatives Hall. Henry B. Stanton. LC 77-82223. (Anti-Slavery Crusade in America). 1969. Repr. of 1837 ed. 7.50 (ISBN 0-405-00662-4). Ayer Co Pubs.

Remarks on Colour. Ludwig Wittgenstein. Ed. by G. E. Anscombe. Tr. by Linda L. McAlister & Margarete Schattle. 1977. 27.50x (ISBN 0-520-03357-4); pap. 7.95x (ISBN 0-520-03727-8). U of Cal Pr.

Remarks on Don Juan. C. C. Colton. 1978. Repr. of 1826 ed. lib. bdg. 15.00 (ISBN 0-8495-0908-4). Arden Lib.

Remarks on Don Juan. Charles C. Colton. LC 75-33020. 1975. Repr. of 1826 ed. lib. bdg. 15.00 (ISBN 0-8414-3641-X). Folcroft.

Remarks on Frazer's Golden Bough. Ludwig Wittgenstein. Tr. by A. C. Miles & R. Rhees. LC 79-4038. 1987. Repr. of 1971 ed. text ed. 6.95 (ISBN 0-391-02952-5). Humanities.

Remarks on Mister J. P. Collier's & Mister C. Knight's Edition of Shakespeare. Alexander Dyce. LC 79-164815. Repr. of 1844 ed. 24.00 (ISBN 0-404-02230-8). AMS Pr.

Remarks on Pacific Fishes. V. Pietschmann. (BMB). pap. 10.00 (ISBN 0-527-02179-2). Kraus Repr.

Remarks on Prison & Prison Discipline in the United States: With Intro. & Index Added. 2nd ed. Dorothea L. Dix. LC 84-7714. (Patterson Smith Series in Criminology, Law Enforcement, & Social Problems: Publication No. 4). iv, 113p. 1984. Repr. of 1845 ed. lib. bdg. 13.50 (ISBN 0-87585-705-1). Patterson Smith.

Remarks on Scottish Songs & Ballads, Ancient & Modern: With Anecdotes of Their Authors. Allan Cunningham & Robert Burns. 384p. 1982. Repr. of 1841 ed. lib. bdg. 100.00 (ISBN 0-8495-0607-7). Arden Lib.

Remarks on Several Acts of Parliament Relating More Especially to the Colonies Abroad. Jonathan Blenman. LC 70-141127. (Research Library of Colonial Americana). 1971. Repr. of 1742 ed. 13.00 (ISBN 0-405-03331-1). Ayer Co Pubs.

Remarks on Some Fundamental Doctrines of Political Economy. John Craig. LC 70-121321. 1970. Repr. of 1821 ed. lib. bdg. 35.00x (ISBN 0-678-00684-9). Kelley.

Remarks on Some of the Characters of Shakespere. 3rd ed. Thomas Whately. Repr. of 1839 ed. 25.00 (ISBN 0-404-06917-7). AMS Pr.

Remarks on Some of the Characters of Shakespeare. 3rd ed. Thomas Whately. Ed. by Richard Whately. 152p. 1970. Repr. of 1839 ed. bds. 27.50x (ISBN 0-7146-2518-3, F Cass Co). Biblio Dist.

Remarks on Some of the Characters of Shakespeare. 3rd ed. Thomas Whately. LC 76-96362. (Eighteenth Century Shakespeare). 1970. Repr. of 1839 ed. lib. bdg. 27.50x (ISBN 0-678-05129-1). Kelley.

Remarks on the Character & Writings of John Milton. 3rd ed. William E. Channing. LC 72-966. Repr. of 1828 ed. 12.50 (ISBN 0-404-01448-8). AMS Pr.

Remarks on the Country Extending from Cape Palmas to the River Congo. John Adams. 265p. 1966. Repr. of 1823 ed. 25.00x (ISBN 0-7146-1783-0, BHA 01783, F Cass Co). Biblio Dist.

Remarks on the Differences in Shakespeare's Versification in Different Periods of His Life. Charles Bathurst. LC 75-113550. 1970. Repr. of 1857 ed. 18.00 (ISBN 0-404-00692-2). AMS Pr.

Remarks on the Foundations of Mathematics. rev. ed. Ludwig Wittgenstein. Ed. by G. H. Von Wright & R. Rhees. Tr. by G. E. Anscombe. 448p. 1983. pap. text ed. 13.95x (ISBN 0-262-73067-7). MIT Pr.

Remarks on the Life & Writing of Dr. Jonathan Swift. John Orrery. 1968. Repr. of 1752 ed. cancelled (ISBN 3-4870-1960-4). Adlers Foreign Bks.

Remarks on the Life & Writings of William Shakespeare. John Britton. LC 79-39531. Repr. of 1818 ed. 19.00 (ISBN 0-404-01086-5). AMS Pr.

Remarks on the Philosophy of Psychology, Vol. 1. Ludwig Wittgenstein. Ed. by G. E. Anscombe & G. H. Von Wright. LC 80-52781. 408p. 1980. lib. bdg. 40.00x (ISBN 0-226-90433-4). U of Chicago Pr.

Remarks on the Philosophy of Psychology, Vol. 1. Ludwig Wittgenstein. Ed. by G. E. M. Anscombe & G. H. Von Wright. Tr. by G. E. M. Anscombe. vi, 416p. 1988. pap. 17.95 (ISBN 0-226-90436-9). U of Chicago Pr.

Remarks on the Philosophy of Psychology, Vol. 2. Ludwig Wittgenstein. Ed. by G. H. Von Wright & Heikki Nyman. Tr. by C. G. Luckhardt & A. E. Aue. LC 80-52781. 1980. lib. bdg. 27.50x (ISBN 0-226-90434-2). U of Chicago Pr.

Remarks on the Philosophy of Psychology, Vol. 2. Ludwig Wittgenstein. Ed. by G. H. Von Wright & Heikki Nyman. Tr. by C. G. Luckhardt & M. A. E. Aue. vi, 263p. 1988. pap. 13.95 (ISBN 0-226-90437-7). U of Chicago Pr.

Remarks on the Review of Inchiquin's Letters. Timothy Dwight. 1972. Repr. of 1815 ed. text ed. 29.00 (ISBN 0-8422-8040-5). Irvington.

Remarks on the Review of Inchiquin's Letters. Timothy Dwight. 1986. pap. text ed. 6.95x (ISBN 0-8290-1921-9). Irvington.

Remarks on the Statistics & Political Institutions of the United States. facsimile ed. William G. Ouseley. LC 70-117887. (Select Bibliographies Reprint Ser). Repr. of 1832 ed. 19.00 (ISBN 0-8369-5340-1). Ayer Co Pubs.

Remarks upon Alchemy & the Alchemists: Indicating a Method of Discovering the True Nature of Hermetic Philosophy. Ethan A. Hitchcock. LC 75-36842. (Occult Ser.). 1976. Repr. of 1857 ed. 24.50x (ISBN 0-405-07955-9). Ayer Co Pubs.

Remarks upon an Essay Concerning Humane Understanding: In a Letter Address'd to the Author. Thomas Burnet. LC 83-48565. 92p. 1984. lib. bdg. 20.00 (ISBN 0-8240-5600-0). Garland Pub.

Remarks upon Milton's Paradise Lost. William Massey. LC 77-4961. 1751. lib. bdg. 35.50 (ISBN 0-8414-6194-5). Folcroft.

Remarks upon Milton's Paradise Lost. William Massey. 276p. 1980. Repr. of 1761 ed. lib. bdg. 35.00 (ISBN 0-8492-6755-2). R West.

Remarques sur les Memoires Imaginaires. Georges Duhamel. 96p. 1934. 9.95 (ISBN 0-686-55194-X). French & Eur.

Remarques Sur les Spacelariacees. C. Sauvageau. 1971. Repr. of 1904 ed. 90.00x (ISBN 3-7682-0717-X). Lubrecht & Cramer.

Remarriage. Marilyn Ihinger-Tallman & Kay Pasley. (Family Studies Text Ser.: Vol. 7). 160p. 1987. text ed. 19.95 (ISBN 0-8039-2628-6); pap. text ed. 9.95 (ISBN 0-8039-2629-4). Sage.

Remarriage: A Family Affair. Lillian Messinger. 274p. 1984. 16.95 (ISBN 0-306-41770-7, Plenum Pr). Plenum Pub.

Remarriage: A Review & Annotated Bibliography. Benjamin Schlesinger. (CPL Bibliographies Ser.: No. 115). 69p. 1983. 12.00 (ISBN 0-86602-115-9). Coun Plan Librarians.

Remarriage & Blended Families. Stephen R. Treat. 24p. 1988. pap. 1.25 (ISBN 0-8298-0775-6). Pilgrim NY.

Remarriage & God's Renewing Grace. Dwight H. Small. 184p. 1986. pap. 7.95 (ISBN 0-8010-8264-1). Baker Bk.

Remarriage & Stepparenting: Current Research & Theory. Ed. by Kay Pasley & Marilyn Ihinger-Tallman. (Guilford Perspectives on Marriage & Family Ser.). 323p. 1987. lib. bdg. 35.00 (ISBN 0-89862-697-8); pap. 19.95 (ISBN 0-89862-922-5). Guilford Pr.

Remarriage: Opportunity to Grow. Charles Cerling. 192p. (Orig.). 1988. pap. 6.95 (ISBN 0-8007-5278-3). Revell.

Remarriage Reality: What You Can Learn From It. Elaine S. Mynatt. LC 84-80873. (Illus.). 225p. (Orig.). 1984. pap. 10.00 (ISBN 0-911175-04-0). Elm Pubns.

Remarriages & Subsequent Divorces: United States, 1970-83. Barbara F. Wilson. Ed. by Klaudia Cox. LC 88-1923. (Series 21: No. 45). 41p. Date not set. pap. text ed. 1.22 (ISBN 0-8406-0399-1). Natl Ctr Health Stats.

Remarried Divorcees & Eucharistic Communion. Bertrand De Margerie. 1980. pap. 1.95 (ISBN 0-8198-6401-3). Dghtrs St Paul.

Remarried Family: Challenge & Promise. Esther Wald. LC 80-205980. 254p. 1981. 21.00 (ISBN 0-87304-184-4); pap. 16.95 (ISBN 0-87304-183-6). Family Serv.

Rembrandt. Bob Haak. (Pocket Art Ser.). (Illus.). 1981. pap. 6.95 (ISBN 0-8120-2103-7). Barron.

Rembrandt. Michael Kitson. (Phaidon Color Library). (Illus.). 84p. 1983. pap. 18.95 (ISBN 0-7148-2241-8). Salem Hse Pubs.

Rembrandt. Charles Mee. 1988. 19.95 (ISBN 0-671-62213-7). S&S.

Rembrandt, 2 vols. Emile Michel. 200.00 (ISBN 0-8490-0943-X). Gordon Pr.

Rembrandt. Ludwig Munz & B. Haak. (Library of Great Painters Ser). 1966. 45.00 (ISBN 0-8109-0437-3). Abrams.

Rembrandt. Ludwig Munz & Bob Haak. (Masters of Art Ser.). 164p. 1984. 19.95 (ISBN 0-8109-1594-4). Abrams.

Rembrandt. Ernest Raboff. LC 87-45157. (Art for Children Ser.). (Illus.). 32p. (gr. 1 up). 1987. 11.95i (ISBN 0-397-32228-3, Lipp Jr Bks). HarpJ.

Rembrandt. Ernest Raboff. LC 87-45148. (Trophy Nonfiction Art for Children Bks.). (Illus.). 32p. (gr. 1 up). 1987. pap. 5.95 (ISBN 0-06-446072-X, Trophy). HarpJ.

Rembrandt. Christopher White. LC 83-51330. (World of Art Ser.). (Illus., Orig.). 1984. text ed. 11.95 (ISBN 0-500-20195-1). Thames Hudson.

Rembrandt. Xenia Yegorova. 1986. 30.00x (ISBN 0-317-61363-4, Pub. by Collets (UK)). State Mutual Bk.

Rembrandt & His Century: Dutch Drawings of the Seventeenth Century. Pref. by Charles Ryskamp. (Illus.). 1978. pap. 15.95 (ISBN 0-685-46543-8). Pierpont Morgan.

Rembrandt & His Critics Sixteen Thirty to Seventeen Thirty. Seymour Slive. LC 86-81978. (Illus.). xii, 240p. 1988. Repr. of 1953 ed. lib. bdg. 40.00 (ISBN 0-87817-311-0). Hacker.

Rembrandt & Persia. Leonard J. Slatkes. (Illus.). 120p. 1983. 20.00 (ISBN 0-89835-241-X). Abaris Bks.

Rembrandt & the Italian Renaissance. Kenneth Clark. LC 66-13550. (Illus.). 1966. 50.00 (ISBN 0-8147-0080-2). NYU Pr.

Rembrandt Bible Drawings. Rembrandt Van Rijn. LC 79-52975. (Fine Art Library). (Illus.). 64p. (Orig.). 1980. pap. 3.50 (ISBN 0-486-23878-4). Dover.

Rembrandt Documents. Marjon Van Der Meulen & Walter L. Strauss. LC 78-53627. (Illus.). 1979. 115.00 (ISBN 0-913870-68-4). Abaris Bks.

Rembrandt Drawings. B. Haak. Tr. by Elizabeth Willems-Treeman. LC 76-10073. (Illus.). 1976. 22.50 (ISBN 0-87951-047-1). Overlook Pr.

Rembrandt Drawings. B. Haak. Tr. by Elizabeth Willems-Treeman. LC 76-10073. (Illus.). 1977. pap. 10.95 (ISBN 0-87951-051-X). Overlook Pr.

Rembrandt Etchings: Forty-Five Plates. Rembrandt Van Rijn. (Illus.). 48p. 1988. pap. 3.50t (ISBN 0-486-25677-4). Dover.

Rembrandt: Experimental Etcher. Ed. by Museum of Fine Arts Staff. LC 87-80024. 1987. Repr. of 1969 ed. lib. bdg. 60.00 (ISBN 0-87817-320-X). Hacker.

Rembrandt Fecit: A Selection of Rembrandt's Etchings. Ed. by Julius S. Held. (Illus.). 32p. 1981. pap. 4.00 (ISBN 0-931102-05-7). S & F Clark Art.

Rembrandt, Harmensz Van Rijn: Paintings from Soviet Museums. 4th, rev. ed. by V. Loewinson-Lessing. 67p. 1975. 83.00x (ISBN 0-317-14284-4, Pub. by Collets (UK)). State Mutual Bk.

Rembrandt: His Life, His Paintings. Gary Schwartz. LC 85-40546. (Illus.). 380p. 1985. 50.00 (ISBN 0-670-80876-8). Viking.

Rembrandt Landscape Drawings. Rembrandt Van Rijn. (Dover Art Library). (Illus.). 64p. (Orig.). 1981. pap. 3.50 (ISBN 0-486-24160-2). Dover.

Rembrandt: Life & Work. rev. ed. Jakob Rosenberg. (Landmarks in the History of Art Ser.). (Illus.). 398p. 1980. pap. 16.95 (ISBN 0-8014-9198-3). Cornell U Pr.

Rembrandt nel Seicento Toscano. Bert W. Meijer. (Halia ei Paesi Bassi). 63p. (Orig., Ital.). 1983. pap. 16.00x (ISBN 88-7038-068-8, Pub. by Centro Di Italia). Benjamins North Am.

Rembrandt: Paintings from Soviet Museums. V. Lowensohn-Lessing. 184p. 1987. 45.00 (ISBN 0-8285-3810-7, Pub. by Aurora Pubs USSR). Imported Pubns.

Rembrandt Peale 1778-1860: A Life in the Arts. Carol Herner. 121p. 1985. 10.00 (ISBN 0-910732-19-1). Pa Hist Soc.

Rembrandt Returns. Robert R. Leichtman. (From Heaven to Earth Ser.). (Illus.). 96p. (Orig.). 1981. pap. 3.50 (ISBN 0-89804-064-7). Ariel OH.

Rembrandt Self-Portraits. Pascal Bonafoux. LC 85-42921. (Illus.). 140p. 1985. 60.00 (ISBN 0-8478-0629-4). Rizzoli Intl.

Rembrandt: Self-Portraits. Christopher Wright. 136p. 1982. 78.00x (ISBN 0-86092-054-2, Pub. by Gordon Fraser). State Mutual Bk.

Rembrandt Takes a Walk. Mark Strand. (Illus.). (gr. 3 up). 1986. 14.95 (ISBN 0-517-56293-6). Crown.

Rembrandt: The Human Form & Spirit. Jacqueline Guillaud & Maurice Guillaud. (Illus.). 700p. 1986. 75.00 (ISBN 0-517-56341-X, C N Potter Bks). Crown.

Rembrandt: The Nightwatch. E. Haverkamp-Begemann. LC 81-47921. (Illus.). 204p. 1982. cloth 37.00x (ISBN 0-691-03991-7); pap. 14.50x (ISBN 0-691-00341-6). Princeton U Pr.

Rembrandt: Werk und Forschung. Otto Benesch. Repr. 17.00 (ISBN 0-384-03899-9). Johnson Repr.

Rembrandt's Enterprise: The Studio & the Market. Svetlana Alpers. (Illus.). 308p. 1988. 29.95 (ISBN 0-226-01514-9). U of Chicago Pr.

Rembrandt's Etchings: States & Values. G. W. Nowell-Usticke. LC 87-80028. (Illus.). 379p. 1988. Repr. lib. bdg. 60.00 (ISBN 0-87817-300-5). Hacker.

Rembrandt's Etchings True & False. George Biorklund & Osbert H. Barnard. LC 87-80027. (Illus.). 200p. 1988. Repr. of 1968 ed. lib. bdg. 50.00 (ISBN 0-87817-319-6). Hacker.

Rembrandt's Hat. Bernard Malamud. 224p. 1973. 11.95 (ISBN 0-374-24909-1); pap. 8.95. FS&G.

Rembrandt's Hat. Bernard Malamud. 204p. 1986. pap. 8.95 (ISBN 0-374-52034-8). FS&G.

Rembrandt's Mirror. Laurence Lerner. 72p. 1987. pap. 9.95 (ISBN 0-8265-1223-2). Vanderbilt U Pr.

Rembrandt's Portrait: A Biography. Charles L. Mee, Jr. 1988. 19.95 (ISBN 0-671-62113-0). S&S.

Remedia Amoria see Amores.

Remedia Amoris. Ed. by A. A. Henderson. 160p. 1980. pap. 10.00x (ISBN 0-7073-0246-3, Pub. by Scot Acad Pr). Longwood Pub Group.

Remedial Action Technology for Waste Disposal Sites. 2nd ed. Kathleen Wagner et al. LC 86-17992. (Pollution Technology Review Ser.: No. 135). (Illus.). 642p. 1987. 54.00 (ISBN 0-8155-1100-0). Noyes.

Remedial & Clinical Reading Instruction. Sandra McCormick. 544p. 1987. text ed. 33.95 (ISBN 0-675-20284-1). Merrill.

Remedial Arithmetic. Fred Justus. (Math Ser.). 24p. (gr. 3-5). 1979. wkbk. 5.00 (ISBN 0-8209-0112-1, A-22). ESP.

Remedial Arithmetic 1A. Fred Justus. (Math Ser.). 24p. (gr. 2-3). 1978. wkbk. 5.00 (ISBN 0-8209-0109-1, A-19). ESP.

Remedial Arithmetic 1B. Fred Justus. (Math Ser.). 24p. (gr. 2-4). 1978. wkbk. 5.00 (ISBN 0-8209-0110-5, A-20). ESP.

Remedial Arithmetic 1C. Fred Justus. (Math Ser.). 24p. (gr. 3-5). 1978. wkbk. 5.00 (ISBN 0-8209-0111-3, A-21). ESP.

Remedial Drama. Sue Jennings. LC 74-77191. 1978. pap. 8.95 (ISBN 0-87830-563-7). Theatre Arts.

Remedial English. Evan Smith. 32p. 1987. pap. 1.95. Dramatists Play.

Remedial Mathematics for Science & Engineering. Felix Arscott et al. 152p. 1983. pap. text ed. 10.50 (ISBN 0-8403-3740-X). Kendall-Hunt.

Remedial Painting of Weathering Steel: State of the Art Survey. John D. Keane et al. 22p. 1984. 30.00 (ISBN 0-938477-08-0). SSPC.

Remedial Reading: A Text-Workbook. Alice D. Lorenz. (Illus.). (gr. 4-12). 1973. pap. text ed. 3.24, five or more 2.22 ea.; tchr's manual 0.50. Modern Curr.

Remedial Reading Drills with Directions. Kirk Hegge. 1965. 5.00x (ISBN 0-685-21801-5). Wahr.

Remedial Reading Handbook. Bonnie Lass & Beth Davis. (Illus.). 224p. 1985. text ed. write for info. (ISBN 0-13-773482-4); pap. text ed. write for info. (ISBN 0-13-773474-3). P-H.

Remedial Techniques in Basic School Subjects. Grace M. Fernald. Ed. by Lorna Idol. LC 87-9852. (The Pro-Ed Classic Ser.). (Illus.). 276p. 1988. text ed. 24.00x (ISBN 0-89079-149-X, 1419). Pro Ed.

Remedial Technologies for Underground Storage Tanks. L. M. Preslo et al. LC 87-34251. (Illus.). 220p. 1988. 49.95 (ISBN 0-87371-125-4). Lewis Pubs Inc.

Remediarium Conversorum: A Synthesis in Latin of "Moralia in Job". Gregory the Great. Compiled by Peter of Waltham & Joseph Gildea. LC 84-3693. 504p. 1984. 25.00 (ISBN 0-8453-4507-9). Assoc Univ Prs.

Remediating Children's Language: Behavioral & Naturalistic Approaches. Ed. by Dave J. Muller. LC 84-7810. (Illus.). 255p. 1984. text ed. 31.00 (ISBN 0-316-58926-8, 589268). College-Hill.

Remediation of Learning Disabilities: A Handbook of Psychoeducational Resource Programs. 2nd ed. Robert E. Valett. LC 67-26847. 1974. pap. 22.50 (ISBN 0-8224-5851-9). D S Lake Pubs.

Remedies. (Sum & Substance Ser.). 1981. write for info. (ISBN 0-940366-10-X). Herbert Legal Ser.

Remedies: Adaptable to Courses Utilizing Laycock's Casebook on Modern American Remedies. Casenotes Publishing Co., Inc. Staff et al. Ed. by Norman S. Goldenberg. (Casenote Legal Briefs Ser.). (Orig.). 1987. pap. text ed. write for info. (ISBN 0-87457-149-9, 1254). Casenotes Pub.

Remedies: Adaptable to Courses Utilizing Leavell, Love & Nelson's Casebook on Equitable Remedies & Restitution. Casenotes Publishing Co., Inc. Staff. Ed. by Norman S. Goldenberg et al. (Legal Briefs Ser.). 1986. pap. write for info. (ISBN 0-87457-120-0, 1253). Casenotes Pub.

Remedies: Adaptable to Courses Utilizing Re's Casebook on Remedies. Casenotes Publishing Co., Inc. Staff. Ed. by Norman S. Goldenberg et al. (Legal Briefs Ser.). 1983. pap. write for info. (ISBN 0-87457-121-9, 1252). Casenotes Pub.

Remedies: Adaptable to Courses Utilizing York, Bauman & Rendleman's Casebook on Remedies. Casenotes Publishing Co., Inc. Staff. Ed. by Norman S. Goldenberg et al. (Legal Briefs Ser.). 1985. pap. write for info. (ISBN 0-87457-122-7, 1250). Casenotes Pub.

Remedies Against the Plague. Arnold C. Klebs & Eugene Droz. LC 75-23732. Repr. of 1925 ed. 35.00 (ISBN 0-404-13290-1). AMS Pr.

Remedies & Rackets: The Truth About Patent Medicines Today. James Cook. LC 75-39284. (Getting & Spending: the Consumer's Dilemma). 1976. Repr. of 1958 ed. 20.00x (ISBN 0-405-08059-X). Ayer Co Pubs.

Remedies, Cases & Materials On. 2nd ed. Edward D. Re. (University Casebook Ser.). 1385p. 1987. text ed. 34.00 (ISBN 0-88277-558-8); write for info. tchr's manual (ISBN 0-88277-628-2). Foundation Pr.

Remedies: Cases & Materials On. 4th ed. Kenneth H. York et al. (American Casebook Ser.). 1029p. 1985. pap. text ed. 34.95 (ISBN 0-314-84584-4). West Pub.

Remedies, Cases & Materials on: Successor Edition. Edward D. Re. LC 81-17400. (University Casebook Ser.). 1252p. 1982. text ed. 26.75 (ISBN 0-88277-044-6). Foundation Pr.

Remedies, Cases & Materials: Successor Edition, 1984 Supplement. Edward D. Re. (University Casebook Ser.). 151p. 1984. pap. text ed. 5.95 (ISBN 0-88277-201-5). Foundation Pr.

Remedies: Damages, Equity, & Restitution. Robert S. Thompson & John A. Sebert. LC 83-72025. (Analysis & Skills Ser.). 1983. 33.50. Bender.

Remedies for Breach of Contract: A Comparative Account. Guenter H. Treitel. 400p. 1988. 85.00 (ISBN 0-19-825500-4). Oxford U Pr.

Remedies in a Nutshell. John F. O'Connell. LC 84-19705. (Nutshell Ser.). 320p. 1984. pap. text ed. 9.95 (ISBN 0-314-85066-X). West Pub.

Remedies in Arbitration. Marvin Hill, Jr. & Anthony V. Sinicropi. 372p. 1981. text ed. 30.00 (ISBN 0-87179-359-8, 0359). BNA.

Remedies in Employment Discrimination Cases. Belton. 1988. write for info. (ISBN 0-471-80051-1). Wiley.

Remedies Phase of an EEO Case: A Study Guide for the ABA Videolaw Seminar. American Bar Association Staff. 537p. Date not set. price not set. Amer Bar Assn.

Remedies, Recipes & Rhymes: Good Health, Good Food, Good Humor - Ingredients for a Great Life! Jonathan T. Cook. Ed. by Jack Thomas. (Illus.). 504p. 1988. 16.95 (ISBN 0-945380-00-3). Salient Prodns.

Remedies, Teacher's Manual to Accompany Cases & Materials on: Successor Edition. Edward D. Re. (University Casebook Ser.). 260p. 1983. pap. text ed. write for info (ISBN 0-88277-142-6). Foundation Pr.

Remedy for Overproduction & Unemployment. Hugo Bilgram. 1979. lib. bdg. 39.95 (ISBN 0-87700-287-8). Revisionist Pr.

Remember. O. P. Kretzmann. 1957. 2.25 (ISBN 0-570-03300-4, 12-2632). Concordia.

Remember Anything You Want. Virginia P. Krymow. LC 77-75039. 1977. pap. 3.00 (ISBN 0-918838-00-2). Arlotta.

Remember Betsy Floss & Other Colonial American Riddles. David A. Adler. LC 87-45333. (Illus.). 64p. (gr. 1-4). 1987. reinforced 9.95 (ISBN 0-8234-0664-4). Holiday.

Remember Betsy Floss & Other Colonial American Riddles. David A. Adler. (Illus.). 64p. 1989. pap. 2.50 (ISBN 0-553-15671-3, Skylark). Bantam.

Remember Cambodia. Helen Penfold. 1979. pap. 3.75 (ISBN 0-85363-129-8). OMF Bks.

Remember Gettysburg! Kevin Randle & Robert Cornett. 1988. pap. 3.50 (ISBN 1-55773-089-X, Pub. by Charter Bks). Ace Bks.

Remember Goliad Fannin. Jean Flynn. 64p. (gr. 4-7). 1984. 6.95 (ISBN 0-89015-444-9). Eakin Pr.

Remember Hungary 1956: A Pictorial History of the Hungarian Revolution. Francis Laping & Hans Knight. 300p. 1975. 35.00 (ISBN 0-912404-01-9). Alpha Pubns.

Remember Kirkland Lake: The Gold-Miners' Strike of 1941-42. Laurel S. MacDowell. (The State & Economic Life Ser.). 308p. 1983. 30.00x (ISBN 0-8020-5585-0); pap. 13.95 (ISBN 0-8020-6457-4). U of Toronto Pr.

Remember Maine. Keith Jennison. LC 72-106943. (Illus., Orig.). 1978. pap. 5.95 (ISBN 0-911764-05-4). Durrell.

Remember Maine. Keith W. Jennison. (Illus.). 96p. 1987. pap. 7.95 (ISBN 0-88150-071-2). Countryman.

Remember March. M. J. Adamson. (Mystery Ser.). 224p. (Orig.). 1987. pap. 2.95 (ISBN 0-553-26797-3). Bantam.

Remember Me. Fay Weldon. 1985. pap. 3.50 (ISBN 0-345-32976-7). Ballantine.

Remember Me to Harold Square. Paula Danziger. LC 87-6844. 160p. (YA) (gr. 5-9). 1987. pap. 14.95 (ISBN 0-385-29610-X). Delacorte.

Remember Me to Harold Square. Paula Danziger. (gr. k-12). 1988. pap. 2.95 (ISBN 0-440-20153-5). Dell.

Remember Me to Marcie. Martin Yoseloff. 6.95 (ISBN 0-8453-7696-9, Cornwall Bks). Assoc Univ Prs.

Remember Me When I Am Dead. Carol B. York. LC 80-13461. (gr. 5-8). 1980. 8.95 (ISBN 0-525-66694-X). Lodestar Bks.

Remember Me: Women & Their Friendship Quilts. Linda O. Lipsett. LC 85-9525. (Illus.). 136p. 1985. 29.95 (ISBN 0-913327-04-2); pap. 19.95 (ISBN 0-913327-03-4). Quilt Digest Pr.

Remember Mobile. Caldwell Delaney. (Illus.). 242p. 1980. Repr. of 1948 ed. 15.00 (ISBN 0-940882-13-2). Haunted Bk Shop.

Remember Murder. Patricia Manning. (Private Library Collection). 1986. 6.95 (ISBN 0-938422-37-5). SOS Pubns CA.

Remember Not to Forget: A Memory of the Holocaust. Norman Finkelstein. LC 84-17315. (Illus.). 32p. (gr. 1-3). 1985. lib. bdg. 8.90 (ISBN 0-531-04892-6). Watts.

Remember Pearl Harbor. 6th ed. Blake Clark. (Tales of the Pacific). 256p. 1987. pap. 3.95 (ISBN 0-935180-49-4). Mutual Pub HI.

Remember Ruben. Mongo Beti. Tr. by Gerald Moore from Fr. (African Writers Ser.). 252p. pap. 9.00 (ISBN 0-435-90214-8). Heinemann Ed.

Remember Santiago. Douglas C. Jones. 1988. 18.95 (ISBN 0-8050-0776-8). H Holt & Co.

Remember Scarborough Nineteen Fourteen. Hendon Publishing Co., Ltd. Staff. 1986. 3.50x (ISBN 0-317-54158-7, Pub. by Hendon Pub UK). State Mutual Bk.

Remember the a la Mode! Riddles & Puns. Ed. by Charles Keller. LC 83-13832. (Illus.). 64p. (gr. 3-5). 1983. 10.95 (ISBN 0-13-773358-5). P-H.

Remember the Ala Mode: Riddles & Puns. Charles Keller. 64p. (gr. 3-7). 1986. pap. 5.95 (ISBN 0-13-773342-9). P-H.

Remember the Alamo. Amelia Barr. 329p. 1980. Repr. of 1880 ed. lib. bdg. 11.95x (ISBN 0-89968-215-4). Lightyear.

Remember the Alamo. Amelia E. Barr. 1888. 35.00 (ISBN 0-932062-10-5). Sharon Hill.

Remember the Alamo! Kevin Randle & Robert Cornett. 240p. 1986. pap. 3.50 (ISBN 0-441-71325-4, Pub. by Charter Bks). Ace Bks.

Remember the Alamo! Robert Penn Warren. (Landmark Ser.: No. 79). (Illus.). (gr. 4-6). 1963. Random.

Remember the Days see This Rough New Land.

Remember the Days of Old. Isidore Fishman. (Illus.). (gr. 4-9). 1970. 4.95. Prayer Bk.

Remember the Days of Old. Isidore Fishman. LC 79-100058. 1969. 4.95 (ISBN 0-87677-000-6). Hartmore.

Remember the Dream. Harold Gershowitz. 560p. (Orig.). 1988. pap. 4.50 (ISBN 0-553-26933-X). Bantam.

Remember the Eagle Day. Guenn Martin. LC 83-26376. (Illus.). 128p. (gr. 7-9). 1983. pap. 4.95 (ISBN 0-8361-3351-X). Herald Pr.

Remember the Future: The Apollo Legacy. Ed. by Stan Kent. (Science & Technology Ser.: Vol. 50). 218p. 1980. lib. bdg. 25.00x (ISBN 0-87703-126-6, Pub. by Am Astronaut); pap. 15.00x (ISBN 0-87703-127-4). Univelt Inc.

Remember the Golden Rule. Johnny Hart & Brant Parker. (Wizard of Id Ser.). (Illus.). 1984. pap. 1.95 (ISBN 0-449-12745-1, GM). Fawcett.

Remember the Ladies. Lyn Lifshin. 1985. pap. 1.50 (ISBN 0-317-19794-0). Ghost Dance.

Remember the Ladies: A Woman's Book of Days. Kirstin Olsen. (Illus.). 224p. 1988. 20.00 (ISBN 1-55562-070-1). Main Street.

Remember the Ladies: New Perspectives on Women in American History. Ed. by Carol George. (Illus.). 256p. 1975. 14.95x (ISBN 0-8156-0110-7). Syracuse U Pr.

Remember the Light. Mary P. Fisher. (Illus.). 32p. (Orig.). (gr. k-4). 1986. pap. 4.50 (ISBN 0-9615149-7-3). Fenton Valley Pr.

Remember the Maine: A Pictorial History. James F. Muche. (Orig.). 1984. pap. 5.95x (ISBN 0-910651-07-8). Fathom Eight.

Remember the Prisoners: Current Accounts of Believers in Russia. Ed. by Peter Masters. pap. 6.95 (ISBN 0-8024-7388-1). Moody.

Remember the Promise. Alvin N. Rogness. LC 76-27082. 1977. kivar 3.50 (ISBN 0-8066-1567-2, 10-5480). Augsburg.

Remember the Promise. Alvin N. Rogness. LC 76-27082. 1977. gift ed. 7.95 (ISBN 0-8066-1619-9, 10-5481). Augsburg.

Remember the Rainbow. Jacqueline Mehrabi. (Illus.). 40p. (ps-2). 1985. G Ronald Pub.

Remember the Rock. Philip Hastings. pap. 9.95 (ISBN 0-944119-02-6). Andover Junction.

Remember the Secret. Elisabeth Kubler-Ross. LC 81-68454. (Illus.). 64p. (gr. 5 up). 1981. 8.95 (ISBN 0-89087-332-1). Celestial Arts.

Remember the Secret. Elisabeth Kubler-Ross. (Illus.). 32p. (ps up). 1988. pap. 8.95 (ISBN 0-89087-524-3). Celestial Arts.

Remember This Time. Gloria K. Broder & Bill Broder. LC 83-4249. 336p. 1983. 14.95 (ISBN 0-937858-23-4). Newmarket.

Remember This Time. Gloria K. Broder & Bill Broder. LC 83-4249. 325p. Date not set. pap. cancelled (ISBN 0-937858-91-9). Newmarket.

Remember to Kill Me. Hugh Pentecost. 224p. 1988. pap. 3.50 (ISBN 0-373-26010-5, Pub. by Worldwide). Harlequin Bks.

Remember to Love. Dorothy Bastien. (YA) (gr. 7 up). 1979. pap. 1.95 (ISBN 0-590-32398-9, Wishing Star Bks). Scholastic Inc.

Remember to Remember. Henry Miller. LC 45-11390. 10.00 (ISBN 0-8112-0113-9, NDP111). New Directions.

Remember to Remember Me. Marilyn Levy. (gr. 5 up). 1988. pap. 2.95 (ISBN 0-449-70278-2, Juniper). Abrams.

Remember to Remember Me. Marilyn Levy. (gr. 5 up). Date not set. pap. 2.95 (Juniper). Fawcett.

Remember Today. Elswyth Thane. Repr. lib. bdg. 16.95x (ISBN 0-88411-973-4, Pub. by Aeonian Pr). Amereon Ltd.

Remember Us. Lucien T. Martin & Melba B. Martin. (Illus.). 298p. 1987. 30.00 (ISBN 0-9620005-0-7). Martin Pubs.

Remember When...? Marjorie Daniels. (Illus.). 157p. (Orig.). 1988. pap. 4.95 (ISBN 0-940828-17-0). Olympic Pub.

Remember When, Vol. I. Jerome M. Hall. 150p. 1985. 14.95x (ISBN 0-9614356-0-7). Creative Concepts.

Remember Who You Are: Baptism, a Model for Christian Life. William H. Willimon. LC 79-93359. (Illus.). 128p. (Orig.). 1980. pap. 4.50x (ISBN 0-8358-0399-6). Upper Room.

Remember Your Confirmation. 1977. pap. 2.10 (ISBN 0-570-03751-4, 12-2655). Concordia.

Remember Your Essence. Paul Williams. 176p. 1987. 12.95 (ISBN 0-517-56524-2, Harmony). Crown.

Remembered Death. Agatha Christie. 1986. pap. 3.50 (ISBN 0-671-54320-2). PB.

Remembered Drums: A History of the Puget Sound Indian War. J. A. Eckrom. 220p. 1988. 17.95 (ISBN 0-936546-14-X). Pioneer Pr Bks.

Remembered Earth: An Anthology of Contemporary Native American Literature. Ed. by Geary Hobson. LC 80-54561. 428p. 1981. pap. 11.95x (ISBN 0-8263-0568-7). U of NM Pr.

Remembered Future: A Study in Literary Mythology. Harold Fisch. LC 83-48899. 208p. 1985. 22.50x (ISBN 0-253-35003-4). Ind U Pr.

Remembered Gate: Origins of American Feminism - the Woman & the City, 1800-1860. Barbara J. Berg. (Urban Life in America Ser.). (Illus.). 1978. pap. 8.95 (ISBN 0-19-502704-3). Oxford U Pr.

Remembered Image: Prendergast Watercolors 1896-1906. Coe K. Gallery. (Illus.). 52p. 1987. pap. 12.95 (ISBN 0-87663-509-5). Universe.

Remembered Light. Albert Huffstickler. 32p. pap. 4.95 (ISBN 0-941720-05-5). Slough Pr TX.

Remembered Magic. Marisa Caroll. (Superromance Ser.: No. 268). 308p. Date not set. pap. 2.75 (ISBN 0-317-63886-6). Harlequin Bks.

Remembered Village. M. N. Srinivas. (Center for South & Southeast Asia Studies: No. 26). 1977. 35.00x (ISBN 0-520-02997-6); pap. 10.95x (ISBN 0-520-03948-3). U of Cal Pr.

Remembering. Wendell Berry. LC 88-61166. 160p. 1988. 14.95 (ISBN 0-86547-330-7). N Point Pr.

Remembering. Art Fettig. LC 81-90188. (Illus.). 1982. pap. 3.95 (ISBN 0-9601334-2-9). Growth Unltd.

Remembering. Dandi Knorr. 64p. 1985. 14.95 (ISBN 0-8423-5475-1). Tyndale.

Remembering: A Phenomenological Study. Edward S. Casey. (Studies in Phenomenology & Existential Philosophy). 1987. 47.50x (ISBN 0-253-34942-7); pap. 18.50x (ISBN 0-253-20409-7). Ind U Pr.

Remembering Alamo: And Other Things Along the Way. Virgie V. Jones. (Illus.). 229p. 1975. 20.00 (ISBN 0-9600890-1-2). Morris-Burt Pr.

Remembering America: A Sampler of the WPA American Guide Series. Ed. by Archie Hobson. (Illus.). 478p. 1985. 25.00 (ISBN 0-231-06050-5). Columbia U Pr.

Remembering America: A Sampler of the WPA American Guide Series. Ed. by Archie Hobson. (Illus.). 411p. 1987. pap. 11.95 (ISBN 0-02-033280-7, Collier). Macmillan.

Remembering America: A Voice from the Sixties. Richard N. Goodwin. 560p. 1988. 19.95 (ISBN 0-316-32024-2). Little.

Remembering & Forgetting: An Inquiry into the Nature of Memory. Edmund B. Bolles. 1988. 22.95 (ISBN 0-8027-1004-2). Walker & Co.

Remembering & Repeating: Biblical Creation in Paradise Lost. Regina M. Schwartz. (Illus.). 160p. Date not set. price not set (ISBN 0-521-34357-7). Cambridge U Pr.

Remembering Box. Eth Clifford. (Illus.). 64p. (gr. 2-5). 1985. 12.95 (ISBN 0-395-38476-1). HM.

Remembering Buddy: The Definitive Biography of Buddy Holly. John Goldrosen & John Beecher. (Illus.). 208p. 1987. pap. 12.95 (ISBN 0-14-010363-5). Penguin.

Remembering Carlos Bulosan. P. C. Morantte. 164p. (Orig.). 1984. pap. 11.50 (ISBN 971-10-0184-5, Pub. by New Day Philippines). Cellar.

Remembering E. G. Peterson: His Life & Our Story. E. G. Peterson. (Illus.). 137p. 1974. 8.95 (ISBN 0-87421-070-4). Utah St U Pr.

Remembering Franz Liszt. rev. ed. Ed. by Mark N. Grant. Incl. My Memories of Liszt. Alexander Siloti. Repr; Life & Liszt. Arthur Friedheim. Repr. of 1961 ed. LC 86-145. (Illus.). 384p. 1986. 32.50 (ISBN 0-87910-113-X); pap. 14.95 (ISBN 0-87910-058-3). Limelight Edns.

Remembering God in Youth. Robert Taylor. 2.50 (ISBN 0-89315-238-2). Lambert Bk.

Remembering Greatness & Other Short Stories. Myrna Chase. LC 85-91415. 90p. 1987. 7.95 (ISBN 0-533-06940-8). Vantage.

Remembering His Benefit. Daniel Nicholoson. 48p. 1988. pap. text ed. 2.95 (ISBN 0-88144-074-4). Christian Pub.

Remembering James Agee. Ed. by David Madden. LC 74-77326. (Illus.). 172p. 1974. 20.00 (ISBN 0-8071-0086-2). La State U Pr.

Remembering John Masefield. Corliss Lamont. LC 73-139992. 119p. 1971. 14.50 (ISBN 0-8386-7836-X). Fairleigh Dickinson.

Remembering Made Easy. Arthur L. Logan. LC 65-27668. 1965. pap. 1.95 (ISBN 0-668-01402-4). Arco.

Remembering Me: A Journal for You & Your Loved Ones. Danielle Light. 136p. 1986. pap. 7.95 (ISBN 0-9616478-0-9). Mt Shasta Pubns.

Remembering Milton: Essays on the Texts & Traditions. Ed. by Margaret Ferguson & Mary Nyquist. 440p. 1988. text ed. 45.00 (ISBN 0-416-39730-1); pap. text ed. 14.95 (ISBN 0-416-39740-9). Routledge Chapman & Hall.

Remembering Names: Improvement Is Easy. Arthur A. Merrill. (Illus.). 57p. 1985. 9.75 (ISBN 0-911894-50-0). Analysis.

Remembering Reconsidered: Ecological & Traditional Approaches to the Study of Memory. Ulric Neisser & Eugene Winograd. (Emory Symposia in Cognition Ser.: No. 2). (Illus.). 420p. 1988. 44.50 (ISBN 0-521-33031-9). Cambridge U Pr.

Remembering Srila Prabhupada. Satsvarupa Das Goswami. Ed. by Mandalesvara Dasa. 1983. Bk. 1 & 2, 108p. pap. text ed. 5.95 (ISBN 0-911233-13-X); Bk. 3 & 4, 100p. pap. text ed. 4.95 (ISBN 0-911233-14-8); Set. (ISBN 0-911233-12-1); Bk. 5, 101p. pap. text ed. 3.95 (ISBN 0-911233-15-6); Bk. 6, 98p. pap. text ed. 3.95 (ISBN 0-911233-16-4). Gita Nagari.

Remembering the God to Come. Antonio De Nicolas. 112p. 1988. 21.95 (ISBN 1-55778-012-9); pap. 9.95 (ISBN 1-55778-101-X). Paragon Hse.

Remembering the Good Times. Richard Peck. LC 84-19962. 192p. (gr. 7 up). 1985. pap. 14.95 (ISBN 0-385-29396-8). Delacorte.

Remembering the Good Times. Richard Peck. (gr. 5-12). 1986. pap. 2.95 (ISBN 0-440-97339-2, LFL). Dell.

Remembering the Soos. David Evans. 102p. 1986. pap. 5.95 (ISBN 0-317-54062-9). Plains Press.

Remembering: The University of Utah. Ed. by Elizabeth Haglund. (Illus.). 250p. 1981. 24.95 (ISBN 0-87480-191-5). U of Utah Pr.

Remembering the Yellow Journal. Hal Z. Bennett. (Orig.). 1978. pap. 3.95 (ISBN 0-686-24532-6). Hal Z Bennett.

Remembering Vernon. Juliet Fox-Hutchinson. 112p. (Orig.). 1984. pap. 12.95x (ISBN 0-85362-209-4, Oriel). Routledge Chapman & Hall.

Remembering Who We Are: Observations of a Southern Conservative. M. E. Bradford. LC 84-22225. 200p. 1985. 15.95 (ISBN 0-8203-0766-1). U of Ga Pr.

Remembering with Love. Helen S. Rice. (Illus.). 128p. 1985. 13.95 (ISBN 0-8007-1434-2). Revell.

Remembering Yesterday's Hits. Ed. by Reader's Digest Editors. (Illus.). 252p. 1986. lie-flat spiral bdg. 26.95 (ISBN 0-89577-249-3, Pub. by RD Assn). Random.

Remembrance. Graham Reid. LC 85-10117. 96p. (Orig.). 1985. pap. 8.95 (ISBN 0-571-13549-8). Faber & Faber.

Remembrance. Danielle Steel. 1981. 19.95. Delacorte.

Remembrance. Danielle Steel. 544p. 1983. pap. 4.95 (ISBN 0-440-17370-1). Dell.

Remembrance see Danielle Steel.

Remembrance: An Autobiography. G. J. Massingham. 1941. Repr. 20.00 (ISBN 0-8274-3267-4). R West.

Remembrance & Light: Images of Martha's Vineyard. Henry B. Hough. LC 84-4595. (Illus.). 112p. 1984. deluxe ed. 250.00 slip case ltd ed. o.p. (ISBN 0-916782-56-5); pap. 12.95 (ISBN 0-916782-54-9). Harvard Common Pr.

Remembrance & Pantomime. Derek Walcott. 176p. 1980. 15.95 (ISBN 0-374-24912-1); pap. 7.95 (ISBN 0-374-51569-7). FS&G.

Remembrance of Christ. C. H. Spurgeon. 1977. pap. 0.95 (ISBN 0-686-23223-2). Pilgrim Pubns.

Remembrance of Games Past: On Tour with the Tennis Grand Masters. John Sharnik. (Illus.). 384p. 1986. 19.95 (ISBN 0-02-610040-1). Macmillan.

Remembrance of Patria: Dutch Arts & Culture in Colonial America, 1609-1776. Roderic H. Blackburn. (Illus.). Date not set. 39.95 (ISBN 0-939072-06-8). Albany Hist & Art.

Remembrance of Swings Past. Ron Luciano & David Fisher. LC 87-47914. 320p. 1988. 17.95 (ISBN 0-553-05262-4). Bantam.

Remembrance of the Sun. Kate Gilmore. LC 86-15393. 256p. (YA) (gr. 7 up). 1986. 13.95 (ISBN 0-395-41104-1). HM.

Remembrance of Things Past. Marcel Proust. 1981. Boxed Set. 75.00 (ISBN 0-394-50643-X); Vol. 1. 25.00 (ISBN 0-394-50644-8); Vol. 2. 25.00 (ISBN 0-394-50645-6); Vol. 3. 25.00 (ISBN 0-394-50646-4). Random.

Remembrance of Things Past, 3 vols. Marcel Proust. Tr. by C. Scott Moncrieff & Terence Kilmartin. LC 82-40052. Orig. Title: A La Recherche Du Temps Perdu. 1982. Set. pap. 40.00 (ISBN 0-394-71243-9, Vin); pap. 40.00 ea. Vol. 1, 1056p. Vol. 2, 1216p. Vol. 3, 1144p. Random.

Remembrance of Tucson's Past: Century Ago & More, & Less in Tucson Arizona. Kerson D. Diamos. 150p. (Orig.). 1985. pap. 14.00 (ISBN 0-9614985-1-X). El Siglo Bks.

Remembrance, Reunion, & Revival: Celebrating a Decade of Appalachian Studies. Dorgan et al. Intro. by Helen Roseberry. (Proceedings of the Appalachian Studies Conference). (Orig.). 1988. pap. text ed. 10.95 (ISBN 0-913239-52-6). Appalach Consortium.

Remembrance Rock. Carl Sandburg. LC 48-8509. 1067p. 1948. 15.00 (ISBN 0-15-176799-8). HarBraceJ.

Remembrances. Eleanora Brownleigh. 480p. 1988. pap. 4.50 (ISBN 1-55817-112-6). Windsor NY.

Remembrances. Ben Burroughs. (Sketches Ser.). 144p. (Orig.). 1986. pap. 8.50 (ISBN 0-8303-0168-2). Fleet.

Remembrances. William Corbett. 1987. 4.00 (ISBN 0-935724-29-X). Figures.

Remembrances of Concord & the Thoreaus: Letters of Horace Hosmer to Dr. S. A. Jones. Horace Hosmer. Ed. by George Hendrick. LC 77-24232. 183p. 1977. 14.50 (ISBN 0-252-00660-7). U of Ill Pr.

Remembrances of Emerson. J. Albee. 1985. 62.50 (ISBN 0-317-19973-0). Bern Porter.

Remembrances of Emerson. John Albee. LC 73-11303. 1974. Repr. of 1903 ed. lib. bdg. 12.50 (ISBN 0-8414-2877-8). Folcroft.

Remembrances of Rivers Past. Ernest Schwiebert. LC 84-45099. (Illus.). 288p. 1984. pap. 8.95 (ISBN 0-916870-71-5, A Donald S. Ellis Book). Creative Arts Bk.

Remembrances: The Experience of the Past in Classical Chinese Literature. Stephen Owen. 160p. 1986. text ed. 18.50x (ISBN 0-674-76015-8). Harvard U Pr.

Remeslo. Sergei Dovlatov. 183p. (Rus.). 1985. 21.50 (ISBN 0-88233-563-4); pap. 7.50 (ISBN 0-88233-523-5). Ardis Pubs.

Remf Diary. David Willson. 313p. 1988. 18.95 (ISBN 0-930773-05-5); pap. 8.95 (ISBN 0-930773-06-3). Black Heron Pr.

Remind Me Not to Fall in Love. Hila Coleman. (YA) (gr. 7 up). 1987. pap. 2.50 (ISBN 0-671-60123-7). Archway.

Remind Me to Murder You Later: Short Stories. James Boylan. LC 88-45417. 144p. 1988. 15.95 (ISBN 0-8018-3728-6). Johns Hopkins.

Reminded of His Goodness Songbook. Gary L. Johnson. 32p. 1981. pap. 2.50 (ISBN 0-87123-779-2, 280779). Bethany Hse.

Reminder List of Eligible Releases--60th Annual Academy Awards for Distinguished Achievements During 1987. Ed. by Byerly Woodward. 40p. 1988. pap. 5.00 (ISBN 0-942102-06-1). Acad Motion Pic.

Reminders for Company Secretaries. 25th ed. John Birds. 1986. pap. 49.00x (ISBN 0-85308-077-1, Pub. by Jordon & Sons UK). State Mutual Bk.

Remington & Russell: The Sid Richardson Collection. Brian W. Dippie. (Illus.). 188p. 1982. 29.95 (ISBN 0-292-77027-8). U of Tex Pr.

Remington Arms & History. Vol. 1, 1816-1934. 42.00 (ISBN 0-911614-17-6); Vol. 2, 1934-1989. 42.00 (ISBN 0-911614-18-4). B West.

Remington Arms & History, 1816-Date. Bill West. LC 71-121899. (West Arms Library). (Illus.). 1972. 48.00x (ISBN 0-911614-08-7). B West.

Remington Arms Catalogues, 1877-1899. Bill West. (West Arms Library). (Illus.). 1971. 10.00x (ISBN 0-911614-09-5). B West.

Remington Bullet Knives. Melvin Brewster & George A. Hoyem. (Illus.). 50p. (Orig.). 1985. pap. 9.95 (ISBN 0-9604982-5-7). Armory Pubns.

Remington Contract. Raymond Obstfeld. 304p. (Orig.). 1988. pap. 3.95 (ISBN 0-373-97095-1, Pub. by Worldwide). Harlequin Bks.

Remington: Dash for the Timber. (Let's Get Lost in a Painting Ser.). 1983. write for info. Garrard.

Remington Factor. Raymond Obstfeld. 272p. 1985. pap. 3.50 (ISBN 0-441-71344-0). Ace Bks.

Remington Gun Catalog 1877. 1.50 (ISBN 0-913150-17-7). Pioneer Pr.

Remington No. One: West of the Pecos. James C. Boone. 176p. 1987. pap. 2.50 (ISBN 0-380-75265-4). Avon.

Remington, No. 3: Showdown at Comanche Butte. James C. Boone. 160p. (Orig.). 1987. pap. 2.50 (ISBN 0-380-75268-9). Avon.

Remington, No. 4: Lawman's Justice. James C. Boone. 160p. 1987. pap. 2.50 (ISBN 0-380-75269-7). Avon.

Remington, No. 5: Wyoming Blood Trail. James C. Boone. 176p. 1987. pap. 2.75 (ISBN 0-380-75270-0). Avon.

Remington, No. 6: Border Trouble. James C. Boone. 176p. 1988. pap. 2.75 (ISBN 0-380-75271-9). Avon.

Remington, No. 7: Red River Revenge. James C. Boone. 160p. 1988. pap. 2.75 (ISBN 0-380-75559-9). Avon.

Remington, No. 8: Six-Guns at Spanish Peak. James C. Boone. 176p. 1988. pap. 2.75 (ISBN 0-380-75560-2). Avon.

Remington, No. 9: The Lawless Clan. James C. Boone. 160p. 1988. pap. 2.75 (ISBN 0-380-75612-9). Avon.

Remington One Thousand One Hundred Exotic Weapon System. (Weaponry Ser.). 1986. lib. bdg. 79.95 (ISBN 0-8490-3716-6). Gordon Pr.

Remington Ridge. Kit Dalton. (Buckskin Ser.: No. 18). 208p. (Orig.). 1987. pap. 2.50 (ISBN 0-8439-2509-4, Leisure Bks). Leisure NY.

Remington Rolling Block Firearms. Konrad F. Schreier, Jr. Ed. by Pioneer Press. (Illus.). pap. 6.95 (ISBN 0-913150-39-8). Pioneer Pr.

Remington Rolling Block Pistols. Jerry Landskron. LC 81-50481. (Illus.). 304p. 1981. 34.95 (ISBN 0-940028-01-8); deluxe ed. 39.95 (ISBN 0-940028-00-X). Rolling Block.

Remington Tips. E. Dixon Larson. 4.95 (ISBN 0-913150-34-7). Pioneer Pr.

Remington Warm-up Studies for Trombone. Donald Hunsberger. LC 80-67541. (Illus.). 1980. 8.95 (ISBN 0-918194-10-5). Accura.

Remington 1100 Exotic Weapon System. (Illus.). 88p. 1983. 15.00 (ISBN 0-87364-262-7). Paladin Pr.

Remington's Frontier Sketches. Frederic Remington. LC 70-101992. (Research & Source Works Ser.: No. 398). (Illus.). 1970. Repr. of 1898 ed. 25.50 (ISBN 0-8337-2936-5). B Franklin.

Remington's Pharmaceutical Sciences. 17th ed. 1985. 85.00 (ISBN 0-912734-03-5). Mack Pub.

Reminiscence & Rote Learning see Studies in Clinical Psychology.

Reminiscence of the Indians. Cephas Washburn. LC 7-19591. Repr. of 1869 ed. 27.00 (ISBN 0-384-65970-5). Johnson Repr.

Reminiscences, 2 vols. Thomas Carlyle. Ed. by James A. Froude. 1881. 21.50 set (ISBN 0-8274-3268-2). R West.

Reminiscences, 2 vols. Thomas Carlyle. Ed. by James A. Froude. LC 71-144936. (Literature Ser.). 1972. Repr. of 1881 ed. 29.00x (ISBN 0-403-00898-0). Scholarly.

Reminiscences. Thomas Carlyle. Ed. by James A. Froude. 352p. 1983. Repr. of 1881 ed. lib. bdg. 30.00. Darby Bks.

Reminiscences. Douglas MacArthur. (Quality Paperbacks Ser.). (Illus.). 1985. pap. 10.95 (ISBN 0-306-80254-6). Da Capo.

Reminiscences, 2 vols. Justin McCarthy. 1973. Repr. of 1899 ed. 50.00 set (ISBN 0-8274-0751-3). R West.

Reminiscences. Nicholas Poppe. Ed. by Henry G. Schwarz. LC 82-4544. (Studies on East Asia: Vol. 16). (Illus.). vii, 330p. 1983. 20.00 (ISBN 0-914584-16-2, Center for East Asian Studies). WWUCEAS.

Reminiscences. Rabindranath Tagore. 272p. 1912. 5.50. Asia Bk Corp.

Reminiscences. Gerald Van De Linde. Ed. by Richard P. Brief. LC 77-87290. (Development of Contemporary Accounting Thought Ser.). 1978. Repr. of 1917 ed. lib. bdg. 34.50x (ISBN 0-405-10917-2). Ayer Co Pubs.

Reminiscences. Isaac Wise. Ed. by David Philipson. LC 73-2233. (Jewish People; History, Religion, Literature Ser.). Repr. of 1901 ed. 30.00 (ISBN 0-405-05294-4). Ayer Co Pubs.

Reminiscences see Recollections.

Reminiscences: A Lifetime of Spiritualism. Ursula Roberts. 115p. 1985. 20.00x (ISBN 0-7212-0726-X, Pub. by Regency Pr). State Mutual Bk.

Reminiscences &... Solomon Oudel & Owen Barfield. 1986. pap. 3.95 (ISBN 0-916786-89-7). St George Bk Serv.

Reminiscences & Gospel Hymn Stories. George C. Stebbins. LC 74-144689. Repr. of 1924 ed. 24.50 (ISBN 0-404-07203-8). AMS Pr.

Reminiscences & Memorials of Men of the Revolution. Artemas B. Muzzey. LC 70-142542. 444p. 1971. Repr. of 1883 ed. 51.00x (ISBN 0-8103-3629-4). Gale.

Reminiscences & Reflection of a Chief Justice. B. P. Sinha. 234p. 1986. text ed. 35.00x (ISBN 0-86590-797-8, Pub. by B R Pub Corp Delhi). Apt Bks.

Reminiscences & Reflections. Hans Krebs. (Illus.). 1982. 24.95x (ISBN 0-19-854702-1). Oxford U Pr.

Reminiscences & Reflections, 2 vols. George K. Zhukov. Tr. by Vic Schneierson et al. 940p. 1985. 18.95 (ISBN 0-8285-3034-3, Pub. by Progress Pubs USSR). Imported Pubns.

Reminiscences & Reflexions of a Mid & Late Victorian. E. Belfort Bax. LC 67-27466. 1967. Repr. of 1918 ed. 35.00x (ISBN 0-678-00313-0). Kelley.

Reminiscences & Souvenirs of the Assassination of Abraham Lincoln. J. E. Buckingham, Sr. LC 80-128964. (Illus.). 89p. 22.50 (ISBN 0-939128-01-2); pap. 17.50 (ISBN 0-939128-02-0). J L Barbour.

Reminiscences, Biographical & Historical. Randolph Clark. LC 86-1286. 96p. 1986. Repr. of 1919 ed. 25.00x (ISBN 0-87565-064-3). Tex Christian.

Reminiscences: Discreet & Indiscreet. T. N. Kaul. (Illus.). 312p. 1982. 43.95 (ISBN 0-940500-84-1, Pub by Lancer India). Asia Bk Corp.

Reminiscences, Eighteen Twenty-Seven to Eighteen Ninety-Seven. Robert M. McLane. LC 72-79831. (China Library). 1972. Repr. of 1903 ed. lib. bdg. 21.00 (ISBN 0-8420-1375-X). Scholarly Res Inc.

Reminiscences (Mainly Personal) of William Graham Sumner. Albert G. Keller. 1933. 39.50x (ISBN 0-686-51300-2). Elliots Bks.

Reminiscences of a Bungle & Two Other Northwest Rebellion Diaries. Ed. by R. C. MacLeod. 1324p. 1983. pap. 9.95x (ISBN 0-88864-077-3, Pub. by Univ of Alta Pr Canada). U of Nebr Pr.

Reminiscences of a Dramatic Critic: With an Essay on the Art of Henry Irving. Henry A. Clapp. LC 72-5536. (Select Bibliographies Reprint Ser). 1972. Repr. of 1902 ed. 21.00 (ISBN 0-8369-6902-2). Ayer Co Pubs.

Reminiscences of a Fiddle Dealer. David Laurie. (Illus.). 1977. Repr. of 1924 ed. text ed. 22.00 (ISBN 0-918624-01-0). Virtuoso.

Reminiscences of a Manchester Woman. Gladys Allsop. 1987. 35.00x (ISBN 0-9512406-0-9, Pub. by Janice Owen UK). State Mutual Bk.

Reminiscences of a Marine. John A. Lejeune. Ed. by Richard H. Kohn. LC 78-22384. (American Military Experience Ser.). (Illus.). 1979. Repr. of 1930 ed. lib. bdg. 34.50x (ISBN 0-405-11860-0). Ayer Co Pubs.

Reminiscences of a Marine. John A. Lejeune. (Illus.). 488p. Date not set. Repr. of 1930 ed. 8.95 (ISBN 0-686-30999-5). Marine Corps.

Reminiscences of a Newburyport Nonagenarian. Sarah A. Emery. LC 78-5010. (Illus.). 1978. Repr. of 1879 ed. 27.50 (ISBN 0-917890-09-4). Heritage Bk.

Reminiscences of a Pastorial Ministry. Horace M. Taylor. 67p. (Orig.). 1987. pap. 5.00 (ISBN 0-9617424-1-0). H M Taylor.

Reminiscences of a Portrait Painter. G. P. A. Healy. LC 78-96439. (Library of American Art Ser). (Illus.). 1970. Repr. of 1894 ed. lib. bdg. 39.50 (ISBN 0-306-71829-4). Da Capo.

Reminiscences of a Ranchman. Edgar B. Bronson. LC 62-8407. xvi, 370p. 1962. 28.95x (ISBN 0-8032-0886-3); pap. 6.95 (ISBN 0-8032-5023-1, BB 127, Bison). U of Nebr Pr.

Reminiscences of a Stock Operator. Edwin Lefevre. LC 76-41491. 1980. pap. 12.00 (ISBN 0-87034-058-1). Fraser Pub Co.

Reminiscences of a Stock Operator. Edwin Lefevre. LC 76-41491. 1982. Repr. of 1923 ed. text ed. 20.00 (ISBN 0-87034-065-4). Fraser Pub Co.

Reminiscences of a Stock Operator. Edwin LeFevre. 316p. 1985. Repr. of 1923 ed. 18.95 (ISBN 0-934380-11-2). Traders Pr.

Reminiscences of a Trip Across the Plains in 1846 & Early Days in California. Luella Dickenson. 48p. 1977. 12.00 (ISBN 0-87770-180-6). Ye Galleon.

Reminiscences of a Very Old Man. John Sartain. LC 74-81559. (Illus.). Repr. of 1899 ed. 24.50 (ISBN 0-405-08916-3). Ayer Co Pubs.

Reminiscences of a Very Old Man: 1808-1897. John Sartain. 297p. Repr. of 1899 ed. text ed. cancelled (ISBN 0-8290-1441-1). Irvington.

Reminiscences of a Viennese Psychoanalyst. Richard F. Sterba. LC 82-11149. (Illus.). 185p. 1982. 24.95x (ISBN 0-8143-1716-2). Wayne St U Pr.

Reminiscences of a Yarmouth, Maine Schoolboy. Edward C. Plummer. (Illus.). 263p. 1926. 5.00x (ISBN 0-686-00235-0). O'Brien.

Reminiscences of Abraham Lincoln. Ed. by Allen T. Rice. LC 72-13766. (Concordance Ser., No. 37). 1971. Repr. of 1888 ed. lib. bdg. 69.95x (ISBN 0-8383-1227-6). Haskell.

Reminiscences of Adams, Jay & Randolph Cos., Ind., 1896. Martha Lynch. 363p. 1979. 19.00 (ISBN 0-686-27819-4). Bookmark.

Reminiscences of an Active Life: The Autobiography of John Roy Lynch. John R. Lynch. Ed. by John H. Franklin. LC 70-110669. (Negro American Biographies & Autobiographies Ser). 1970. 30.00x (ISBN 0-226-49818-2). U of Chicago Pr.

Reminiscences of an American Scholar. John W. Burgess. LC 34-2217. Repr. of 1934 ed. 18.00 (ISBN 0-404-01236-1). AMS Pr.

Reminiscences of an Army Chaplain. Horace M. Taylor. LC 86-1472. 123p. 1987. 4.50 (ISBN 0-9617424-0-2). H M Taylor.

Reminiscences of an Old Georgia Lawyer. Garnett Andrews, Jr. LC 84-12652. 112p. 1984. Repr. of 1870 ed. 9.95 (ISBN 0-87797-078-5). Cherokee.

Reminiscences of an Unlettered Man: Robert Barclay 1850-1924: Farm Servant, Tailor & Postman in Forgue & Auchterless. Ed. by D. Stevenson. (Centre for Scottish Studies). 96p. 1986. pap. text ed. 6.50 (ISBN 0-08-032442-8, Pub. by AUP). Pergamon.

Reminiscences of Carl Schurz, 3 vols. Carl Schurz. 1988. Repr. of 1907 ed. Set. lib. bdg. 150.00x. Am Biog Serv.

Reminiscences of Colonel Henry Ernst Dosch. Fred Lockley. 19p. 1972. pap. 2.50 (ISBN 0-87770-081-8). Ye Galleon.

Reminiscences of Company "H", First Arkansas Mounted Rifles. Robert H. Dacus. 47p. 7.50 (ISBN 0-89029-005-9). Pr of Morningside.

Reminiscences of Confederate Service, 1861-1865. Francis W. Dawson. Ed. by Bell I. Wiley. LC 79-26720. (Library of Southern Civilization). xii, 220p. 1980. 25.00 (ISBN 0-8071-0689-5). La State U Pr.

Reminiscences of D. H. Lawrence. facsimile ed. John M. Murry. LC 75-157349. (Select Bibliographies Reprint Ser). Repr. of 1933 ed. 17.00 (ISBN 0-8369-5810-1). Ayer Co Pubs.

Reminiscences of Edgar Allan Poe. Mary Nichols. LC 74-4041. (Studies in Poe, No. 23). 1974. lib. bdg. 22.95x (ISBN 0-8383-2068-6). Haskell.

Reminiscences of Edgar Allan Poe. Mary G. Nichols. LC 73-1138. Repr. of 1931 ed. lib. bdg. 25.50 (ISBN 0-8414-2350-4). Folcroft.

Reminiscences of Edmund Evans. Edmund Evans. Ed. by Ruari McLean. 1967. 10.40x (ISBN 0-19-818126-4). Oxford U Pr.

Reminiscences of Felix Mendelssohn-Bartholdy. Elise Polko. (Music Reprint Ser.). 1989. 35.00 (ISBN 0-306-76297-8). Da Capo.

Reminiscences of Fifty Years in Texas. facsimile ed. John J. Linn. LC 86-60968. (Illus.). 397p. 1986. Repr. of 1883 ed. 19.95 (ISBN 0-938349-00-7). State House Pr.

Reminiscences of Friedrich Froebel. B. von Marenholz Bulow. Tr. by Mrs. Horace Mann. 359p. 1980. Repr. of 1877 ed. lib. bdg. 30.00 (ISBN 0-8492-2833-6). R West.

Reminiscences of Frontier Life. 2nd ed. I. B. Hammond. LC 23-939860. (Illus.). 100p. 1980. pap. text ed. 4.95 (ISBN 0-939860-04-X). Tremaine Graph & Pub.

Reminiscences of Fugitive Slave Law Days in Boston. Austin Bearse. LC 74-82170. (Anti-Slavery Crusade in America Ser). 1969. Repr. of 1880 ed. 13.00 (ISBN 0-405-00609-8). Ayer Co Pubs.

Reminiscences of General Basil W. Duke, C. S. A. Basil W. Duke. (Select Bibliographies Reprint Ser). 1911. 33.00 (ISBN 0-8369-5150-6). Ayer Co Pubs.

Reminiscences of General Herman Haupt. Herman Haupt. LC 80-1314. (Railroads Ser.). (Illus.). 1981. Repr. of 1901 ed. lib. bdg. 30.00x (ISBN 0-405-13786-9). Ayer Co Pubs.

Reminiscences of Golf on St. Andrews. James Balfour. Date not set. 17.95x (ISBN 0-940889-14-5). Classics Golf.

Reminiscences of Gov. R. J. Walker: With the True Story of the Rescue of Kansas from Slavery. facsimile ed. George W. Brown. LC 79-38010. (Black Heritage Library Collection). Repr. of 1902 ed. 17.50 (ISBN 0-8369-8978-3). Ayer Co Pubs.

Reminiscences of H. P. Blavatsky. rev. new ed. Constance Wachtmeister. LC 76-44810. 1977. pap. 3.75 (ISBN 0-8356-0488-8, Quest). Theos Pub Hse.

Reminiscences of Henry Angelo, 2 vols. Henry Angelo. LC 77-81198. (Illus.). 1904. 55.00 (ISBN 0-405-08207-X). Ayer Co Pubs.

Reminiscences of Henry Clay Barnabee. facsimile ed. Henry C. Barnabee. Ed. by George L. Varney. LC 73-169779. (Select Bibliographies Reprint Ser). Repr. of 1913 ed. 42.00 (ISBN 0-8369-5999-X). Ayer Co Pubs.

Reminiscences of Horsham. Henry Burstow. LC 75-19030. 1975. Repr. of 1911 ed. lib. bdg. 32.50 (ISBN 0-8414-3125-6). Folcroft.

Reminiscences of James Burrill Angell. facsimile ed. James B. Angell. LC 79-152970. (Select Bibliographies Reprint Ser.). 1972. Repr. of 1911 ed. 18.00 (ISBN 0-8369-5722-9). Ayer Co Pubs.

Reminiscences of James N. Glover. James N. Glover. (Illus.). 1985. 14.95 (ISBN 0-87770-356-6); pap. 9.95. Ye Galleon.

Reminiscences of John B. Jervis: Engineer of the Old Croton. John B. Jervis. Ed. by Neal FitzSimons. LC 70-145552. (New York State Studies). 1971. 7.75x (ISBN 0-8156-0077-1). Syracuse U Pr.

Reminiscences of John Montgomery. John Montgomery. 208p. 1981. text ed. 36.00 (ISBN 0-86961-113-5, Pub. by A A Balkema). Brookfield Pub Co.

Reminiscences of Joseph B. Cumming 1893-1983. LC 84-206046. 1983. pap. 6.00 (ISBN 0-937044-09-1). Richmond Cty Hist Soc.

Reminiscences of Lady Randolph Churchill. J. J. Churchill. Repr. of 1908 ed. 31.00 (ISBN 0-527-17100-X). Kraus Repr.

Reminiscences of Lafcadio Hearn. LC 78-16202. 1978. Repr. of 1918 ed. lib. bdg. 40.00 (ISBN 0-8414-2226-5). Folcroft.

Reminiscences of Lenin. N. K. Krupskaya. LC 67-27253. (Illus.). 576p. 1970. 7.50 (ISBN 0-7178-0253-1); pap. 4.95 (ISBN 0-7178-0254-X). Intl Pubs Co.

Reminiscences of Leo Nikilaevich Tolstoy. Maxim Gorky. Tr. by S. S. Koteliansky & Leonard Woolf. LC 77-23858. 1977. Repr. of 1920 ed. lib. bdg. 27.00 (ISBN 0-8414-4455-2). Folcroft.

Reminiscences of Leo Nikolaevich Tolstoy. Maxim Gorky. 86p. 1981. Repr. of 1920 ed. lib. bdg. 17.00 (ISBN 0-8495-2048-7). Arden Lib.

Reminiscences of Levi Coffin. Levi Coffin. LC 79-113578. Repr. of 1876 ed. 15.00 (ISBN 0-404-00143-2). AMS Pr.

Reminiscences of Levi Coffin. Levi Coffin. LC 68-55510. 1968. Repr. of 1876 ed. 49.50x (ISBN 0-678-00430-7). Kelley.

Remote Sensing: Proceedings of the 27th International Geological Congress, Vol. 18. International Geological Congress Staff. 236p. 1984. lib. bdg. 74.00x (ISBN 90-6764-027-1). Coronet Bks.
Remote Sensing: The Quantitative Approach. Philip H. Swain & Shirley M. Davis. (Illus.). 1978. text ed. 60.95 (ISBN 0-07-062576-X). McGraw.
Remote Sensing Using Infrared Radiation: A Special Issue of the International Journal of Remote Sensing, Vol. 5, No. 1. 1984. 33.00x (ISBN 0-85066-983-9). Taylor & Francis.
Remote Sensing, Vol. I: ASPRS-ACSM Annula Convention, Baltimore, MD. American Society of Photogrammetry & Remote Sensing Staff & American Congress on Surveying & Mapping. 451p. 1987. 15.00 (ISBN 0-317-59920-8, T674). Am Congrs Survey.
Remote Sensing Yearbook Nineteen Eighty-Six. Ed. by Arthur Cracknell. 300p. 1986. 110.00x (ISBN 0-85066-313-X). Taylor & Francis.
Remote Sensing Yearbook 1987, Vol. 2. Ed. by A. P. Cracknell & L. W. Hayes. 690p. 1987. 154.00x (ISBN 0-85066-378-4). Taylor & Francis.
Remote Sensing Yearbook 1988. Ed. by A. P. Cracknell & L. W. Hayes. 600p. 1988. 154.00x (ISBN 0-85066-407-1). Taylor & Francis.
Remote Site Power Systems. 400p. 1985. 1900.00 (ISBN 0-86621-658-8, W730). Frost & Sullivan.
Remote Sounding of Atmospheres. John T. Houghton et al. (Cambridge Planetary Science Ser.: No. 3). (Illus.). 343p. 1986. pap. 24.95 (ISBN 0-521-31065-2). Cambridge U Pr.
Remote Sounding of the Atmosphere from Space: Proceedings of the Committee on Space Research, 21st Plenary Meeting, Innsbruck, Austria, 1978. Ed. by H. J. Bolle. (Illus.). 1979. 76.00 (ISBN 0-08-023419-4). Pergamon.
Remote Station Protective Signaling Systems. (Seventy Ser.). 1974. pap. 3.00 (ISBN 0-685-58065-2, 72C). Natl Fire Prot.
Remote Systems & Robotics in Hostile Environments: Proceedings. 669p. 1987. 70.00 (ISBN 0-89448-131-2, 700120). Am Nuclear Soc.
Remote the Land's Heart: Wildlife & Landscape in Southern New Zealand. Chris Gaskin. (Illus.). 176p. (Orig.). 1987. pap. 34.95 (ISBN 0-86868-076-1, Pub. by J McIndoe Ltd New Zealand). Intl Spec Bk.
Remotely Operated Vehicles: Technology Requirements Present & Future (ROV'86) Ed. by Society for Underwater Technology (SUT) Staff. 1986. lib. bdg. 63.00 (ISBN 0-86010-815-5, Pub. by Graham & Trotman). Kluwer Academic.
Removable Appliance Fabrication. Witt et al. (Illus.). 266p. 1988. text ed. 72.00 (ISBN 0-86715-180-3, 1803). Quint Pub Co.
Removable Closure of the Interdental Space. Arnold Gaerny. (Illus.). 196p. 1972. 38.00 (ISBN 0-931386-62-4). Quint Pub Co.
Removable Orthodontic Appliances. 2nd ed. T. M. Graber & Bedrich Neumann. (Illus.). 631p. 1984. 67.00 (ISBN 0-7216-1238-5). Saunders.
Removable Partial Dentures. Renner & Boucher. 1987. text ed. 56.00 (ISBN 0-317-56217-7, 1897). Quint Pub Co.
Removable Partial Prosthodontics. 2nd ed. Ernest L. Miller & Joseph E. Grasso. (Illus.). 424p. 1981. 39.50 (ISBN 0-683-05990-4). Williams & Wilkins.
Removable Prosthodontic Techniques. rev. ed. John B. Sowter. Ed. by Roger M. Barton. LC 86-7065. (Dental Laboratory Technology Manuals Ser.). (Illus.). viii, 248p. 1987. pap. text ed. 20.00x (ISBN 0-8078-4166-8). U of NC Pr.
Removal & Return: The Socio-Economic Effects of the War on Japanese Americans. Leonard Bloom & Ruth Riemer. LC 49-9867. (University of California Publications in Culture & Society: Vol. 4). pap. 69.00 (ISBN 0-317-29103-3, 2021393). Bks Demand UMI.
Removal & Return: The Socio-Economic Effects of the War on Japanese Americans. Leonard Broom & Ruth Riemer. (UC Publications in Culture & Society: Vol. 4). 1974. 32.50x (ISBN 0-520-02522-9). U of Cal Pr.
Removal of Causes from State Courts to Federal Courts, with Forms Adapted to the Several Acts of Congress on the Subject. 3rd ed. John F. Dillon. xxiii, 168p. 1981. Repr. of 1881 ed. lib. bdg. 22.00x (ISBN 0-8377-0514-2). Rothman.
Removal of Hazardous Waste in Wastewater Facilities - Halogenated Organics. Water Pollution Control Federation Staff. (Manual of Practice Ser.: MFD11). 111p. 1986. pap. 41.50 (ISBN 0-943244-65-X). Water Pollution.
Removal of Metals from Wastewater: Neutralization & Precipitation. G. C. Cushnie, Jr. LC 83-22142. (Pollution Technology Review Ser.: No. 107). (Illus.). 232p. 1984. 32.00 (ISBN 0-8155-0976-6). Noyes.
Removal of Smoke & Grease-Laden Vapors from Commercial Cooking Equipment. National Fire Protection Association Staff. 1984. 10.50 (ISBN 0-317-63298-1, 96-84). Natl Fire Prot.
Removal of Teeth: A Self-Instructional Guide, Bk. 2. 3rd, rev. ed. James R. Hooley & Robert J. Whitacre. (Illus.). 117p. 1983. pap. 19.95x (ISBN 0-89939-021-8). Stoma Pr.
Removal of the Cherokee Indians from Georgia. Wilson Lumpkin. LC 79-90182. (Mass Violence in America Ser). Repr. of 1907 ed. 32.00 (ISBN 0-405-01325-6). Ayer Co Pubs.
Removal of the Cherokee Indians from Georgia, 2 vols. in 1. Wilson Lumpkin. LC 76-123200. 1971. Repr. of 1907 ed. lib. bdg. 45.00x (ISBN 0-678-00710-1). Kelley.
Removal of the Cherokee Nation: Manifest Destiny or National Dishonor? Ed. by Louis Filler & Allen Guttmann. LC 76-53820. 128p. 1988. text ed. 9.50 (ISBN 0-88275-482-3); pap. 7.50 (ISBN 0-89464-281-2). Krieger.
Removal of Volatile Organic Chemicals from Potable Water: Technologies & Costs. LC 86-17962. (Pollution Technology Review Ser.: No. 134). (Illus.). 231p. 1987. 36.00 (ISBN 0-8155-1099-3). Noyes.
Remove Protective Coating a Little at a Time. John Donovan. LC 73-4977. 112p. (YA) (gr. 7 up). 1973. PLB 12.89 (ISBN 0-06-021720-0). HarpJ.
Remove the Bodies. Elizabeth Ferrars. (Black Dagger Crime Ser.). 192p. 1988. text ed. 14.95x (ISBN 0-86220-726-6, Pub. by Firecrest Pub Ltd). Prescott Pr NH.
Remove Your Shoes. Jim Hogan. 128p. (Orig.). pap. text ed. 5.95 (ISBN 0-934318-34-4). Falcon Pr MT.
Removing Obstacles to Economic Growth. Ed. by Michael L. Wachter & Susan M. Wachter. 560p. 1984. 35.95x (ISBN 0-8122-7923-9). U of Pa Pr.
Removing Roadblocks in Reading. new ed. Katherine H. O'Connor. LC 72-96305. (Illus.). 200p. 1976. pap. text ed. 8.85 (ISBN 0-910812-11-X). Johnny Reads.
Removing the Obstacles. Institute for Food & Develop Policy. Ed. by Brent Millikan & David Kinley. 45p. (Orig.). 1984. pap. 2.95 (ISBN 0-935028-15-3). Inst Food & Develop.
Removing the Stones. Mary Hajos. 1976. pap. 2.95 (ISBN 0-87508-264-5). Chr Lit.
Rempart. Jacques Audiberti. 144p. 1953. 9.95 (ISBN 0-686-54503-6). French & Eur.
Rempart des Beguines. Francoise Mallet-Joris. 1951. 8.95 (ISBN 0-686-56312-3); pap. 3.95 (ISBN 0-686-56313-1). French & Eur.
Remy de Gourmont. Paul E. Jacob. 176p. 1980. Repr. of 1931 ed. lib. bdg. 25.00 (ISBN 0-89984-260-7). Century Bookbindery.
Remy De Gourmont: A Modern Man of Letters. Richard Aldington. LC 74-28305. 1928. 12.50 (ISBN 0-8414-2855-7). Folcroft.
Remy De Gourmont: His Ideas & Influence in England & America. Glenn S. Burne. LC 63-14295. (Crosscurrents-Modern Critiques Ser.). 205p. 1963. 7.95x (ISBN 0-8093-0105-9). S Ill U Pr.
Remy De Gourmont, Selections from All His Works. Remy de Gourmont. Ed. by Richard Aldington. Tr. by Richard Aldington from Fr. LC 77-10269. (Illus.). Repr. of 1928 ed. 49.50 (ISBN 0-404-16321-1). AMS Pr.
Remz-It! A Simple Method for Developing Inexpensive & Effective Training. Carol L. Remz. (Remz-It! Training System Ser.: No. 1). 135p. 1987. 295.00 (ISBN 0-941999-01-7). Human Resc.
Remz-It! How to Easily Create Non-Computereze Documentation that End Users Love. Carol L. Remz & Judith E. Blumberg. (Remz-It! Training System Ser.: No. 2). 100p. 1987. 295.00 (ISBN 0-941999-02-5). Human Resc.
Remz-It! Professional Trainer Skills. 1987. 295.00 (ISBN 0-941999-03-3); wkbk. 25.00 (ISBN 0-941999-04-1). Human Resc.
Renaissance. Peter Burke. LC 86-18571. (Studies in European History). 96p. 1987. pap. text ed. 8.50 (ISBN 0-391-03484-7). Humanities.
Renaissance. 2nd ed. Ed. by Karl H. Dannenfeldt. (Problems in European Civilization Ser). 1974. pap. text ed. 7.50 (ISBN 0-669-90530-5). Heath.
Renaissance. Will Durant. (Story of Civilization: Vol. 5). 1953. 29.95 (ISBN 0-671-61600-5). S&S.
Renaissance. Ernest Jacob. LC 74-23590. 1974. Repr. of 1930 ed. lib. bdg. 27.00 (ISBN 0-8414-5327-6). Folcroft.
Renaissance. Rosa M. Letts. (Cambridge Introduction to the History of Art Ser.: No. 3). (Illus.). 100p. 1981. pap. 9.95 (ISBN 0-521-29957-8). Cambridge U Pr.
Renaissance. Walter Pater. LC 77-12308. 239p. 1977. pap. 6.95 (ISBN 0-915864-35-5). Academy Chi Pubs.
Renaissance. Walter Pater. Intro. by Adam Philips. (World's Classics Ser.). 192p. 1987. pap. 4.95 (ISBN 0-19-281737-X). Oxford U Pr.
Renaissance. Walter H. Pater. LC 77-14040. 1977. Repr. of 1917 ed. lib. bdg. 57.50 (ISBN 0-8414-6846-X). Folcroft.
Renaissance. Michel Pierre. Ed. by Walter Kossmann. LC 86-42665. (Events of Yesteryear Ser.). (Illus.). 69p. (gr. 6 up). 1987. 12.96 (ISBN 0-382-09295-3). Silver.
Renaissance. LC 79-10210. (Living Past Ser.). (Illus.). 64p. (gr. 4 up). 1979. 7.95 (ISBN 0-668-04787-9, 4787-9). Arco.
Renaissance. Francene Sabin. LC 84-2695. (Illus.). 32p. (gr. 3-6). 1985. PLB 8.45 (ISBN 0-8167-0246-2); pap. text ed. 1.95 (ISBN 0-8167-0247-0). Troll Assocs.
Renaissance. Edith Sickel. 256p. Repr. of 1984 ed. lib. bdg. 40.00 (ISBN 0-918377-48-X). Russell Pr.
Renaissance. Gloria Verges & Oriol Verges. (Journey Through History Ser.). (Illus.). 32p. (gr. 2-4). 1988. pap. 3.95 (ISBN 0-8120-3396-5); El Renacimiento. pap. 3.95 (ISBN 0-8120-3397-3). Barron.
Renaissance see Renaissance & Reformation.
Renaissance: A Reconsideration of the Theories & Interpretations of the Age. Symposium on the Renaissance, University of Wisconsin, 1959. Ed. by Tinsley Helton. LC 80-21869. xiii, 160p. 1980. Repr. of 1961 ed. lib. bdg. 35.00 (ISBN 0-313-22797-7, SYRE). Greenwood.
Renaissance Alphabet: Il perfetto scrittore, parte seconda. Giovan F. Cresci. LC 77-121765. (Illus.). 74p. 1971. 27.50x (ISBN 0-299-05761-5). U of Wis Pr.
Renaissance: An Illustrated Encyclopedia. Ilan Rachum. LC 79-13631. (Octopus Bk.). (Illus.). 1980. 24.95 (ISBN 0-7064-0857-8, Mayflower Bks). Smith Pubs.
Renaissance & Baroque. Heinrich Wolfflin. Tr. by Kathrin Simon. (Paperback Ser.). (Illus.). 197p. 1967. pap. 8.95x (ISBN 0-8014-9046-4). Cornell U Pr.
Renaissance & Baroque Bronzes from the Abbott Guggenheim Collection. Laura Camins. LC 87-83424. (Illus.). 152p. 1988. pap. 14.95 (ISBN 0-88401-056-2). Fine Arts Mus.
Renaissance & Baroque Music, a Comprehensive Survey. Friedrich Blume. Tr. by M. Herter Norton. (Illus., Orig.). 1967. pap. 7.95x (ISBN 0-393-09710-2, NortonC). Norton.
Renaissance & Baroque Paintings from the Sciarra & Fiano Collections. Richard E. Spear. LC 72-1141. (Illus.). 112p. 1973. 29.75x (ISBN 0-271-01156-4). Pa St U Pr.
Renaissance & Golden Age Essays in Honor of D. W. McPheeters. Ed. by Bruno M. Damiani. (Span.). 1984. 25.00 (ISBN 0-916379-10-8). Scripta.
Renaissance & Mannerism in Italy. Alastair Smart. (History of Art Ser.). (Illus.). 252p. 1971. pap. text ed. 11.00 net (ISBN 0-15-576595-7, HC). HarBraceJ.
Renaissance & Mannerism in Northern Europe & Spain. Alastair Smart. (History of Art Ser.). (Illus.). 224p. 1972. pap. text ed. 11.00 net (ISBN 0-15-576596-5, HC). HarBraceJ.
Renaissance & Modern Art. W. H. Goodyear. 1978. Repr. of 1908 ed. lib. bdg. 30.00 (ISBN 0-8495-1945-4). Arden Lib.
Renaissance & Modern: Essays in Honor of Edwin M. Moseley. Ed. by Murray J. Levith. 180p. 1976. 11.95x (ISBN 0-8156-2177-9). Syracuse U Pr.
Renaissance & Reaction in 19th Century Bengal: Bankim Chandra Chatterjee. M. K. Haldar. LC 76-52204. 1977. 12.50x (ISBN 0-88386-900-4). South Asia Bks.
Renaissance & Reform: The Italian Contribution. Frances A. Yates. Ed. by J. Trapp. (Collected Essays Ser.: Vol. II). (Illus.). 288p. 1983. 31.50 (ISBN 0-7100-9530-9). Routledge Chapman & Hall.
Renaissance & Reformation. Trevor Cairns. (Cambridge Introduction to World Histroy Ser.). (Illus.). 96p. 1987. pap. 7.95 (ISBN 0-521-33685-6). Cambridge U Pr.
Renaissance & Reformation. William R. Estep. 320p. (Orig.). pap. text ed. 21.95 (ISBN 0-8028-0050-5). Eerdmans.
Renaissance & Reformation. 2nd ed. Vivian H. Green. (Illus.). 1974. pap. text ed. write for info. (ISBN 0-312-67305-1). St Martin.
Renaissance & Reformation, 2 vols. Lewis W. Spitz. Incl. Vol. 1. Renaissance. LC 12-2759 (ISBN 0-570-03818-9); Vol. 2. Reformation. LC 12-2760 (ISBN 0-570-03819-7). 1980. pap. 16.95 ea. Concordia.
Renaissance & Reformation: A Short History. 2nd ed. John F. New. 201p. 1977. pap. text ed. 11.00 (ISBN 0-394-34199-6, RanC). Random.
Renaissance & Reformation England: 1509-1714 see Harbrace History of England.
Renaissance & Reformation in Germany: An Introduction. Gerhart Hoffmeister. LC 77-5429. 1977. 25.00x (ISBN 0-8044-1391-6); pap. 9.95 (ISBN 0-8044-6272-0). Ungar.
Renaissance & Reformation in Scotland. Ed. by Ian B. Cowan & Duncan Shaw. 220p. 1983. 22.50x (ISBN 0-7073-0261-7, Scot Acad Pr). Longwood Pub Group.
Renaissance & Reformation, Thirteen Hundred to Sixteen Forty-Eight. 3rd ed. Gelffrey R. Elton. (Ideas & Institutions in Western Civilization: Vol. 3). 1976. pap. text ed. write for info. (ISBN 0-02-332840-1). Macmillan.
Renaissance & Reformation Times. Dorothy Mills. LC 83-45667. Date not set. Repr. of 1939 ed. 55.00 (ISBN 0-404-19817-1). AMS Pr.
Renaissance & Renascences in Western Art. Erwin Panofsky. (Icon Edition). (Illus.). 380p. 1972. pap. 10.95 (ISBN 0-06-430026-9, IN-26, HarpT). Har-Row.
Renaissance & Renewal in Christian History. Derek Baker. (Studies in Church History: Vol. 14). 428p. 1977. 45.00x (ISBN 0-631-17780-9). Basil Blackwell.
Renaissance & Renewal in the Twelfth Century. Ed. by Robert L. Benson & Giles Constable. (Illus.). 832p. 1983. text ed. 70.00x (ISBN 0-674-76085-9). Harvard U Pr.
Renaissance & Renewal in the Twelfth Century. Ed. by Robert L. Benson & Giles Constable. 816p. 1985. pap. text ed. 17.95x (ISBN 0-674-76086-7). Harvard U Pr.
Renaissance & Revolt: Essays in the Intellectual & Social History of Early France. J. H. Salmon. (Cambridge Studies in Early Modern History). 380p. 1987. 49.50 (ISBN 0-521-32769-5). Cambridge U Pr.
Renaissance & Romanticism: Tieck's Conception of Cultural Decline as Portrayed in his "Vittoria Accorombona". Christiane Keck. (Germanic Studies in America: Vol. 20). 120p. 1976. 19.60 (ISBN 3-261-01699-X). P Lang Pubs.
Renaissance & the New World. Giovanni Caselli. LC 85-22900. (History of Everyday Things Ser.). (Illus.). 48p. (YA) (gr. 6-8). 1986. 14.95 (ISBN 0-87226-050-X). P Bedrick Bks.
Renaissance & the Reformation. Henry S. Lucas. LC 83-45665. Date not set. Repr. of 1934 ed. 67.50 (ISBN 0-404-19815-5). AMS Pr.
Renaissance Architecture. Bates Lowry. LC 61-13691. (Great Ages of World Architecture Ser). (Illus.). 128p. 1962. pap. 9.95 (ISBN 0-8076-0335-X). Braziller.
Renaissance Architecture. Peter Murray. LC 70-149850. (History of World Architecture). (Illus.). 1971. 50.00 (ISBN 0-8109-1000-4). Abrams.
Renaissance Architecture. Peter Murray. LC 82-62749. (History of World Architecture Ser.). (Illus.). 220p. pap. 25.00 (ISBN 0-8478-0474-7). Rizzoli Intl.
Renaissance Architecture. Roger T. Smith. (Illus.). 143p. 1983. 127.25 (ISBN 0-86650-081-2). Gloucester Art.
Renaissance Architecture in Venice. Ralph Lieberman. LC 82-22606. (Illus.). 144p. 1982. 45.00 (ISBN 0-89659-310-X). Abbeville Pr.
Renaissance Architecture: Monographs Published 1976-1987. Mary Vance. (Architecture Ser.: A 1949). 15p. 1987. 3.75 (ISBN 1-55590-579-X). Vance Biblios.
Renaissance Architecture of Central & Northern Spain. A. Whittlesey. 1976. lib. bdg. 75.00 (ISBN 0-8490-2514-1). Gordon Pr.
Renaissance Art. Ed. by Creighton Gilbert. LC 70-92848. (Icon Editions). (Illus.). 270p. 1973. pap. 7.95 (ISBN 0-06-430033-1, IN-33, HarpT). Har-Row.
Renaissance Art: A Topical Dictionary. Irene Earls. LC 87-250. 345p. 1987. lib. bdg. 55.00 (ISBN 0-313-24658-0, ERT/). Greenwood.
Renaissance Artist at Work: From Pisano to Titian. Bruce Cole. LC 82-48102. (Icon Editions). (Illus.). 208p. 1983. 19.50i (ISBN 0-06-430902-9, HarpT). Har-Row.
Renaissance Artists. Franciscus Junius. (Printed Sources of Western Art Ser.). 332p. (Lat.). 1981. pap. 40.00 (ISBN 0-915346-68-0). A Wofsy Fine Arts.
Renaissance Artists & Antique Sculpture: A Handbook of Sources. Phyllis P. Bober & Ruth Rubenstein. (Harvey Miller Publication Ser.). (Illus.). 1985. 65.00x (ISBN 0-19-921029-2). Oxford U Pr.
Renaissance Bronzes in the Walters Art Gallery. Edgar P. Bowron. (Walters Art Gallery Picture Book). (Illus.). 1978. pap. 4.00 (ISBN 0-911886-16-8). Walters Art.
Renaissance Cardinal's Ideal Palace. Kathleen Weil-Garris & John D'Amico. 105p. 1980. 22.00x (ISBN 0-271-00458-4). Pa St U Pr.
Renaissance City. Giulio Argan. LC 70-90409. (Planning & Cities Ser). (Illus.). 1969. pap. 7.95 (ISBN 0-8076-0521-2). Braziller.
Renaissance Concepts of the Commonplaces. Sr. Joan M. Lechner. LC 74-6153. 268p. 1974. Repr. of 1962 ed. lib. bdg. 69.50x (ISBN 0-8371-7491-0, LERC). Greenwood.
Renaissance Cuisine. Fontbonne Auxiliary of St. John Hospital Staff. 1982. 10.00x (ISBN 0-317-07269-2). Intl Bk Ctr.
Renaissance Curiosa. Wayne Shumaker. LC 81-14177. (Medieval & Renaissance Texts & Studies: Vol. 8). (Illus.). 208p. 1982. 15.00 (ISBN 0-86698-014-8). Medieval & Renaissance NY.
Renaissance Des Arts a la Cour De France, 2 Vols. Leon E. Laborde. (Illus.). 1890. 55.50 (ISBN 0-8337-1974-2). B Franklin.
Renaissance des Eros Uranios. Benedict Friedlaender. LC 75-12316. (Homosexuality: Lesbians & Gay Men in Society, History & Literature). (Ger.). 1975. Repr. of 1904 ed. 30.00x (ISBN 0-405-07362-3). Ayer Co Pubs.
Renaissance des Hausarztes. E. Sturm. (Patient Allgemeinmedizin: Band 1). (Illus.). 290p. 1983. 29.00 (ISBN 3-540-12374-1). Springer-Verlag.
Renaissance Dialectic & Renaissance Piety: Benet of Canfield's Rule of Perfection. Tr. & intro. by Kent Emery. (Medieval & Renaissance Texts & Studies: Vol. 50). (Illus.). 320p. 1987. 25.00 (ISBN 0-86698-034-2). Medieval & Renaissance NY.
Renaissance Diplomacy. Garrett Mattingly. 284p. 1988. pap. 7.95 (ISBN 0-486-25570-0). Dover.

Renaissance Discovery of Classical Antiquity. Roberto Weiss. (Illus.). 240p. Date not set. pap. text ed. 15.95 (ISBN 0-631-16077-9). Basil Blackwell.

Renaissance Drama, 1 of 7 vols. Intro. by Derek Traversi. (Great Writers Library). 122p. pap. 7.95 (ISBN 0-312-34702-2). Academy Chi Pubs.

Renaissance Drama, No. 7. Ed. by Samuel Schoenbaum. 157p. 1964. 32.95x (ISBN 0-8101-0219-6). Northwestern U Pr.

Renaissance Drama, No. 8. Ed. by Samuel Schoenbaum. xi, 232p. 1965. 32.95x (ISBN 0-8101-0220-X). Northwestern U Pr.

Renaissance Drama, No. 9. Ed. by Samuel Schoenbaum. viii, 317p. 1966. 32.95x (ISBN 0-8101-0221-8). Northwestern U Pr.

Renaissance Drama & the English Church Year. R. Chris Hassel, Jr. LC 78-24233. (Illus.). xii, 215p. 1979. 19.95x (ISBN 0-8032-2304-8). U of Nebr Pr.

Renaissance Drama in England & Spain: Topical Allusion & History Plays. John Loftis. (Illus.). 296p. 1987. text ed. 34.50 (ISBN 0-691-06706-6). Princeton U Pr.

Renaissance Drama in the Theater. Ed. by Leonard Barkan. (Renaissance Drama New Ser.: IX). 1979. lib. bdg. 32.95x (ISBN 0-8101-0524-1). Northwestern U Pr.

Renaissance Drama New Series, Vol. X. Leonard Barkan. LC 67-29872. 216p. 1981. 32.95x (ISBN 0-8101-0545-4). Northwestern U Pr.

Renaissance Drama New Series XI: Tragedy. Leonard Barkan. 210p. 1984. 42.95x. Northwestern U Pr.

Renaissance Drama New Series XII: Essays on Dramatic Technique. Leonard Barkan. 210p. 1981. 42.95x. Northwestern U Pr.

Renaissance Drama New Series XV: Modes, Motifs, & Genres, Vol. xv. Ed. by Leonard Barkan. (Renaissance Drama New Ser.). 220p. 1985. 42.95x (ISBN 0-8101-0676-0). Northwestern U Pr.

Renaissance Drama New Series XVI: Relations & Influences - Literary & Dramatic. 220p. 1984. 42.95x (ISBN 0-8101-0549-7). Northwestern U Pr.

Renaissance Drama XVI: New Readings & Rereadings. Ed. by Leonard Barkan. (Renaissance Drama New Ser.). 220p. 1987. 42.95x (ISBN 0-8101-0677-9). Northwestern U Pr.

Renaissance Drama XVII: Renaissance Drama & Cultural Change. Ed. by Mary B. Rose. (Renaissance Drama New Ser.). 250p. 1987. 42.95 (ISBN 0-8101-0678-7). Northwestern U Pr.

Renaissance Drama XVIII: Essays on Sexuality, Influence, & Performance. Ed. by Mary B. Rose. (Renaissance Drama New Ser.). (Illus.). 200p. 1988. 42.95x (ISBN 0-8101-0679-5). Northwestern U Pr.

Renaissance Dramatic Bawdy (Exclusive of Shakespeare) An Annotated Glossary & Critical Essays, 2 vols. James T. Henke. Ed. by James Hogg. (Jacobean Drama Studies). 345p. (Orig.). 1974. pap. 30.00 (ISBN 0-317-40089-4, Pub. by Salzburg Studies). Longwood Pub Group.

Renaissance Dramatists. Kate McLuskie. (Feminist Readings Ser.). 160p. 1989. text ed. 29.95 (ISBN 0-391-03520-7); pap. text ed. 12.50 (ISBN 0-391-03521-5). Humanities.

Renaissance, Eighteenth Century & Modern Language in English Poetry. Josephine Miles. LC 77-16356. 1960. 15.00 (ISBN 0-8492-1750-4). R West.

Renaissance Eloquence: Studies in the Theory and Practice of Renaissance Rhetoric. Ed. by James J. Murphy. LC 81-13128. 528p. 1983. text ed. 35.00x (ISBN 0-520-04543-2). U of Cal Pr.

Renaissance English Translations of Erasmus: A Bibliography to 1700. E. J. Devereux. (Erasmus Ser.). 256p. 1983. 35.00x (ISBN 0-8020-2411-4). U of Toronto Pr.

Renaissance Entertainment: Festivities for the Marriage of Cosimo I, Duke of Florence, in 1539. Ed. by Andrew C. Minor & M. Bonner Mitchell. LC 68-11348. (Illus.). 389p. 1968. 39.00x (ISBN 0-8262-8522-8). U of Mo Pr.

Renaissance Essays. Denys Hay. 435p. 1988. 45.00 (ISBN 0-907628-96-6). Hambledon Press.

Renaissance Essays. Hugh Trevor-Roper. LC 85-2775. viii, 312p. 1985. lib. bdg. 22.50x (ISBN 0-226-81225-1). U of Chicago Pr.

Renaissance Essays. Hugh Trevor-Roper. viii, 312p. 1989. pap. 16.95 (ISBN 0-226-81227-8). U of Chicago Pr.

Renaissance: Essays in Interpretation. Andre Chastel & Cecil Grayson. 336p. 1982. 46.00 (ISBN 0-416-31130-X, NO. 3770). Routledge Chapman & Hall.

Renaissance Europe: Age of Recovery & Reconciliation. De Lamar Jensen. 416p. 1981. pap. text ed. 14.50 (ISBN 0-669-51722-4). Heath.

Renaissance Europe: The Individual & Society, 1480-1520. J. R. Hale. LC 77-73495. 1978. pap. 10.95x (ISBN 0-520-03471-6, CAMPUS 194). U of Cal Pr.

Renaissance Exploration. J. R. Hale. (Illus.). 112p. (Orig.). 1972. pap. 6.95 (ISBN 0-393-00635-2, Norton Lib, Norton Lib). Norton.

Renaissance Fictions of Anatomy. Devon L. Hodges. LC 84-16343. (Illus.). 160p. 1985. lib. bdg. 17.50x (ISBN 0-87023-470-6). U of Mass Pr.

Renaissance Florence. Gene A. Brucker. LC 74-10921. 320p. 1975. Repr. of 1969 ed. lib. bdg. 16.50 (ISBN 0-88275-184-0). Krieger.

Renaissance Florence. updated ed. Gene A. Brucker. LC 82-40097. (Illus.). 320p. 1983. text ed. 36.50x (ISBN 0-520-04919-5); pap. 10.95x (ISBN 0-520-04695-1). U of Cal Pr.

Renaissance: From the World of Fear to the World of Love. Patricia Grabow. 331p. (Orig.). 1984. pap. 9.95 (ISBN 0-942494-82-2). Coleman Pub.

Renaissance Garden in England. Roy Strong. (Illus.). 1979. 24.95 (ISBN 0-500-01209-1). Thames Hudson.

Renaissance Genres. Ed. by Barbara K. Lewalski. (English Studies: No. 14). 512p. 1986. text ed. 27.50x (ISBN 0-674-76040-9); pap. text ed. 8.95x (ISBN 0-674-76041-7). Harvard U Pr.

Renaissance Hamlet: Issues & Responses in 1600. Roland M. Frye. LC 83-4255. (Illus.). 368p. 1984. 28.50x (ISBN 0-691-06579-9). Princeton U Pr.

Renaissance Historicism: Selections from "English Literary Renaissance". Ed. by Arthur F. Kinney & Dan S. Collins. LC 87-6052. 432p. (Orig.). 1988. pap. text ed. 12.95x (ISBN 0-87023-598-2). U of Mass Pr.

Renaissance Humanism: Foundations, Forms & Legacy, 3 vols. Ed. by Albert Rabil, Jr. (Illus.). 1841p. 1988. Vol. 1. text ed. 46.95x (ISBN 0-8122-8063-6); Vol. 2. text ed. 37.95x (ISBN 0-8122-8064-4); Vol. 3. text ed. 51.95x (ISBN 0-8122-8065-2); Set. text ed. 129.95x (ISBN 0-8122-8066-0). U of Pa Pr.

Renaissance Humanism in Papal Rome: Humanists & Churchmen on the Eve of the Reformation. John F. D'Amico. LC 82-49059. (Studies in Historical & Political Science). 352p. 1983. text ed. 37.50x (ISBN 0-8018-2860-0). Johns Hopkins.

Renaissance Humanism: Studies in Philosophy & Poetics. Ernesto Grassi. (Medieval & Renaissance Texts & Studies: Vol. 51). 163p. 1988. text ed. 18.00 (ISBN 0-86698-035-0). Medieval & Renaissance NY.

Renaissance Imagination: Essays & Lectures. P. J. Gordon. Ed. by Stephen Orgel. LC 74-81432. 1976. pap. 10.95x (ISBN 0-520-04092-9). U of Cal Pr.

Renaissance in Bengal: Search for Identity. Arabinda Poddar. LC 77-903412. 152p. 1977. 10.00x (ISBN 0-89684-448-X). Orient Bk Dist.

Renaissance in Business. Alan D. Hammond. 15p. (Orig.). 1985. pap. 2.00 (ISBN 0-935427-02-3). Foundation Hse.

Renaissance in England. Hyder E. Rollins & Herschel Baker. 1954. text ed. 31.00 (ISBN 0-669-21352-7). Heath.

Renaissance in Ferrara & Its European Horizons. J. Salmons & W. Moretti. 332p. 1984. pap. text ed. 32.50x (ISBN 0-7083-0877-5, Pub. by U of Wales). Humanities.

Renaissance in Haiti: Popular Painters in the Black Republic. Selden Rodman. LC 83-45788. 57.50 (ISBN 0-404-20221-7, ND306). AMS Pr.

Renaissance in Historical Thought: Five Centuries of Interpretation. Wallace K. Ferguson. LC 77-74812. Repr. of 1948 ed. 32.50 (ISBN 0-404-14887-5). AMS Pr.

Renaissance in Japan: A Cultural Survey of the Seventeenth Century. Kenneth P. Kirkwood. LC 72-120389. (Illus.). 1970. Repr. bds. 6.50 (ISBN 0-8048-0916-X). C E Tuttle.

Renaissance in Rome. Charles L. Stinger. LC 83-49337. (Illus.). 464p. 1985. 37.50x (ISBN 0-253-35002-6). Ind U Pr.

Renaissance in the North. facsimile ed. W. Gore Allen. LC 79-111810. (Essay Index Reprint Ser.). 1946. 18.00 (ISBN 0-8369-1590-9). Ayer Co Pubs.

Renaissance Influences & Religious Reforms in Russia: Western & Post-Byzantine Impacts on Culture & Education, (16th-17th Centuries) W. K. Medlin & C. G. Patrinelis. 184p. (Orig.). 1970. pap. text ed. 22.00x (ISBN 0-317-56037-9, Pub. by Droz Switzerland). Coronet Bks.

Renaissance: Its Nature & Origins. George C. Sellery. 304p. 1962. pap. 5.95X (ISBN 0-299-00644-1). U of Wis Pr.

Renaissance Jewellery. Yvonne Hackenbroch. (Illus.). 488p. 1979. 95.00 (ISBN 0-85667-056-1). Sotheby Pubns.

Renaissance Jewels, Gold Boxes, & Objects de Vertu from the Thyssen-Bornemisza Collection. Anna S. Cocks & Charles Truman. Ed. by Simon De Pury. LC 84-7342. (Illus.). 384p. 1984. 95.00 (ISBN 0-86565-044-6). Vendome.

Renaissance Landscapes: English Lyrics in a European Tradition. H. M. Richmond. 1973. pap. text ed. 17.60x (ISBN 90-2792-470-8). Mouton.

Renaissance Latin Drama in England: A Collection of the Surviving Books & Manuscripts Reproduced in Facsimile with Introductions & Plot Summaries. Ed. by Marvin Spevack & J. W. Binns. (First Series: Plays Associated with the University of Oxford: 13 Vols.). 1983. Set. pap. 495.00x. Coronet Bks.

Renaissance Latin Poetry. Ed. by I. D. McFarlane. LC 79-55022. (Literature in Context Ser.). 246p. 1980. text ed. 27.50x (ISBN 0-06-494702-5). B&N Imports.

Renaissance Latin Verse: An Anthology. Ed. by Alessandro Perosa & John Sparrow. LC 78-10969. xxix, 562p. 1979. 37.50x (ISBN 0-8078-1350-8). U of NC Pr.

Renaissance Library, 3 Vols. Ed. by Edward Hutton. LC 78-170057. Repr. of 1912 ed. Set. 25.00 (ISBN 0-404-07870-2). AMS Pr.

Renaissance Lieder. Thomas Stolzer et al. Ed. by Edwin Gamble. LC 64-15072. (Penn State Music Series, No. 4). 22p. 1964. pap. 3.00x (ISBN 0-271-73096-X). Pa St U Pr.

Renaissance Light. Paul Hills. LC 86-22454. 168p. 1987. 30.00x (ISBN 0-300-03617-5). Yale U Pr.

Renaissance Likeness: Art & Culture in Raphael's Julius II. Loren Partridge & Randolph Starn. LC 79-63549. (Quantum Bks.: No. 16). (Illus.). 1979. 25.00x (ISBN 0-520-03901-7); pap. 8.95x (ISBN 0-520-04172-0). U of Cal Pr.

Renaissance Literary Theory & Practice. C. S. Baldwin. 1959. 11.25 (ISBN 0-8446-1042-9). Peter Smith.

Renaissance Man, Medieval or Modern? 3rd ed. Ed. by Brian Tierney et al. (Historical Pamphlets). 1977. pap. text ed. write for info (ISBN 0-394-32054-9, RanC). Random.

Renaissance Master Bronzes from the Kunsthistorisches Museum, Vienna. Manfred Leithe-Jasper. (Illus.). 288p. 1986. lib. bdg. 29.95 (ISBN 0-935748-69-5). Scala Books.

Renaissance Minds & Their Fictions. Ronald Levao. LC 84-8756. 1985. 45.00x (ISBN 0-520-05275-7). U of Cal Pr.

Renaissance Miniature Painters & Classical Imagery: The Master of the Putti & His Venetian Workshop. Lilian Armstrong. (Harvey Miller Publications). (Illus.). 1981. 55.00x (ISBN 0-19-921023-3). Oxford U Pr.

Renaissance Music, Vol. 1. Ed. by Ellen Rosand. (Garland Library of the History of Western Music). 350p. 1986. lib. bdg. 50.00 (ISBN 0-8240-7452-1). Garland Pub.

Renaissance Music, Vol. 2. Ed. by Ellen Rosand. (Garland Library of the History of Western Music). 350p. 1986. lib. bdg. 50.00 (ISBN 0-8240-7453-X). Garland Pub.

Renaissance Music for the Harp. Deborah Friou. (Illus.). 32p. (Orig.). 1985. pap. 7.95 (ISBN 0-9602990-9-2). Woods Mus Bks Pub.

Renaissance New Testament, Vols. 1-9. Randolph O. Yaeger. Incl. Vol. 1. 25.00 (ISBN 0-88289-957-0); Vol. 2 (ISBN 0-88289-657-1); Vol. 3 (ISBN 0-88289-357-2); Vol. 4 (ISBN 0-88289-857-4); Vol. 5 (ISBN 0-88289-257-6); Vol. 6 (ISBN 0-88289-757-8); Vol. 7. 1982. 22.50 (ISBN 0-88289-457-9); Vol. 8. 1982. 22.50 (ISBN 0-88289-358-0); Vol. 9. 1982. 22.50 (ISBN 0-88289-858-2). 590p. 1980. each 22.50 (ISBN 0-686-77622-4). Pelican.

Renaissance New Testament, Vol. 10. Randolph O. Yeager. LC 79-28652. 660p. 1982. 22.50 (ISBN 0-88289-258-4). Pelican.

Renaissance New Testament, Vol. 11. Randolph O. Yeager. 660p. 22.50 (ISBN 0-88289-758-6). Pelican.

Renaissance New Testament, Vol. 12. Randolph Yeager. 660p. 1983. 22.50 (ISBN 0-88289-458-7). Pelican.

Renaissance New Testament, Vol. 13. Randolph Yeager. 660p. 1983. 22.50 (ISBN 0-88289-958-9). Pelican.

Renaissance New Testament, Vol. 14. Randolph Yeager. 660p. 1983. 22.50 (ISBN 0-88289-859-0). Pelican.

Renaissance New Testament, Vol. 15. Randolph O. Yeager. (Renaissance New Testament Ser.). 660p. 1985. 22.50 (ISBN 0-88289-259-2). Pelican.

Renaissance New Testament, Vol. 16. Randolph O. Yeager. (Renaissance New Testament Ser.). 660p. 1985. 22.50 (ISBN 0-88289-759-4, 759-4). Pelican.

Renaissance New Testament, Vol. 17. Randolph O. Yeager. (Renaissance New Testament Ser.). 660p. 1985. 22.50 (ISBN 0-88289-459-5). Pelican.

Renaissance New Testament, Vol. 18. (Renaissance New Testament Ser.). 660p. 1985. 22.50 (ISBN 0-88289-159-6). Pelican.

Renaissance Notion of Woman: A Study in the Fortunes of Scholasticism & Medical Science in European Intellectual Life. Ian Maclean. LC 79-52837. (Cambridge Monographs in the History of Medicine). 119p. 1983. pap. 12.95 (ISBN 0-521-27436-2). Cambridge U Pr.

Renaissance of Art in France, 2 vols. Emilia F. Dilke. LC 78-16227. 1978. Repr. of 1879 ed. lib. bdg. 65.00 (ISBN 0-89341-362-3). Longwood Pub Group.

Renaissance of Canadian History: A Biography of A. L. Burt. Lewis H. Thomas. LC 74-79988. Repr. of 1975 ed. 51.30 (ISBN 0-8357-9770-8, 2019425). Bks Demand UMI.

Renaissance of Carbon & Carbro - The Pictorial Photographer's Handbook. Tracy Diers. (Illus.). 1980. write for info. (ISBN 0-9617656-1-5). Tracy Diers.

Renaissance of Gravure: The Art of S. W. Hayter. Ed. by P. M. Hacker. (Illus.). 104p. 1988. pap. 26.00 (ISBN 0-19-952111-5). Oxford U Pr.

Renaissance of Interstitial Brachytherapy: Proceedings of the Annual San Francisco Cancer Symposium, 12th, March 4-5, 1977. Annual San Francisco Cancer Symposium Staff. Ed. by J. M. Vaeth. (Frontiers of Radiation Therapy and Oncology: Vol. 12). (Illus.). 1977. 78.75 (ISBN 3-8055-2706-3). S Karger.

Renaissance of Islam. S. K. Bukhsh. 1981. 29.00 (ISBN 0-686-97863-3). Kazi Pubns.

Renaissance of Islam. Adam Mez. Tr. by Salahuddin K Bukhsl & D. S. Margoliovth. LC 70-180361. Repr. of 1937 ed. 27.00 (ISBN 0-404-56293-0). AMS Pr.

Renaissance of Islam: Art of the Mamluks. Esin Atil. LC 80-607866. (Illus.). 288p. (Orig.). 1981. 55.00 (ISBN 0-87474-214-5, ATRI). Smithsonian.

Renaissance of Italian Cooking. Lorenza De'Medici. 1989. price not set (Studio Bks). Viking.

Renaissance of Mark Twain's House. Wilson H. Faude. 1977. lib. bdg. 23.00x (ISBN 0-89244-074-0, Pub. by Queens Hse). Amereon Ltd.

Renaissance of Medicine in Italy. Arturo Castiglioni. LC 79-114967. 1979. 14.00 (ISBN 0-405-10587-8). Ayer Co Pubs.

Renaissance of Modern Hebrew & Modern Standard Arabic: Parallels & Differences in the Revival of Two Semitic Languages. Joshua Blau. (UC Publications in Near East Studies: Vol. 18). 1982. pap. 30.00x (ISBN 0-520-09548-0). U of Cal Pr.

Renaissance of the Greek Ideal. Diana Watts. 1976. lib. bdg. 59.95 (ISBN 0-8490-2515-X). Gordon Pr.

Renaissance of the Lyric in French Romanticism: Elegy, "Poeme," & Ode. Laurence M. Porter. LC 78-52832. (French Forum Monographs: No. 10). 143p. (Orig.). 1978. pap. 9.95x (ISBN 0-917058-09-7). French Forum.

Renaissance of the Marxian System see Economics & Marxism.

Renaissance of the Nineties. W. G. Murdoch. LC 72-194080. 1911. lib. bdg. 32.50 (ISBN 0-8414-6686-6). Folcroft.

Renaissance of the Spirit. Mary Scott. LC 87-40525. 172p. (Orig.). 1988. pap. 6.95 (ISBN 0-8356-0632-5). Theos Pub Hse.

Renaissance of the State Psychiatric System: A Special Issue of Psychiatric Quarterly. Ed. by Stephen L. Katz. 102p. 1987. 12.95 (ISBN 0-89885-346-X). Human Sci Pr.

Renaissance of the Torah Jew. Saul Bernstein. 1986. text ed. 20.00x (ISBN 0-88125-090-2). Ktav.

Renaissance of the Twelfth Century. Charles H. Haskins. x, 437p. 1971. pap. 8.95x (ISBN 0-674-76075-1). Harvard U Pr.

Renaissance of the Twelfth Century. Ed. by Stephen K. Scher. LC 68-56467. (Illus.). 1969. pap. 6.00 (ISBN 0-911517-32-4). Mus of Art RI.

Renaissance Orientale. Raymond Schwab. LC 75-30012. Repr. of 1950 ed. 47.50 (ISBN 0-404-14018-1). AMS Pr.

Renaissance Ornament Prints & Drawings. Janet S. Byrne. Ed. by Amy Horbar. LC 81-18806. (Illus.). 144p. 1981. 35.00 (ISBN 0-87099-288-0). Metro Mus Art.

Renaissance Painting. Paul Stirton. LC 78-25564. (Mayflower Gallery). (Illus.). 1979. 12.50 (ISBN 0-8317-7376-6, Mayflower Bks); pap. 6.95 (ISBN 0-8317-7377-4). Smith Pubs.

Renaissance Painting in Manuscripts: Treasures from the British Library. Thomas Kren. (Illus.). 210p. 1983. 50.00 (ISBN 0-7123-0024-4); pap. 25.00 (ISBN 0-7123-0016-3). J P Getty Mus.

Renaissance Painting in Manuscripts: Treasures from the British Library. Ed. by Thomas Kren. Janet Backhouse et al. LC 83-12591. (Illus.). 217p. 1983. 39.50 (ISBN 0-933920-51-2, Co-pub. by Hudson Hill Pr); pap. 25.00 (ISBN 0-933920-52-0). Hudson Hills.

Renaissance Papers, 1983. Southeastern Renaissance Conference. Ed. by A. Leigh Deneef & M. Thomas Hester. LC 55-3551. pap. 29.30 (2052203). Bks Demand UMI.

Renaissance Paris: Architecture & Growth, 1475-1600. David Thomson. LC 84-40286. (Illus.). 216p. 1984. text ed. 42.50x (ISBN 0-520-05347-8); pap. 15.95x (ISBN 0-520-05359-1). U of Cal Pr.

Renaissance Patterns for Lace & Embroidery. Federico Vinciolo. (Illus.). 1971. pap. 3.50 (ISBN 0-486-22438-4). Dover.

Renaissance Perspectives in Literature & the Visual Arts. Murray Roston. LC 86-18681. (Illus.). 448p. 1987. text ed. 45.00 (ISBN 0-691-06683-3). Princeton U Pr.

Renaissance Philosophy: New Translations of Lorenz Valla, Paul Cortese, Cajetan, T. Bacciliere, Juan Luis Vives, Peter Ramus. Ed. by Leonard A. Kennedy. 1973. pap. text ed. 14.00x (ISBN 90-2797-193-5). Mouton.

Renaissance Philosophy of Giordano Bruno. Irving L. Horowitz. LC 52-14845. 160p. pap. 41.60 (AU00355). Bks Demand UMI.

Renaissance Philosophy of Man. Ed. by Ernst Cassirer et al. LC 48-9358. 1956. pap. 10.95 (ISBN 0-226-09604-1, P1, Phoen). U of Chicago Pr.

Renaissance Reconsidered: Proceedings. Ed. by Leona Gabel. LC 64-5397. (Studies in History: No. 44). 1964. pap. 10.80 (ISBN 0-87391-004-4). Smith Coll.

Renaissance Rediscovery of Linear Perspective. Samuel Y. Edgerton, Jr. (Icon Editions). 1976. pap. 7.95 (ISBN 0-06-430069-2, IN-69, HarpT). Har-Row.

Renaissance, Reformation, & Absolutism Fourteen Hundred to Sixteen Sixty, Vol. I. Ed. by Thomas G. Barnes & Gerald D. Feldman. LC 79-66685. 1979. pap. text ed. 11.25 (ISBN 0-8191-0847-2). U Pr of Amer.

Renaissance, Reformation, & Absolutism: 1450 to 1650. 2nd ed. Ed. by Norman F. Cantor & Michael S. Werthman. LC 72-76355. (Structure of European History Ser.: Vol. 3). 319p. 1972. pap. text ed. 7.95x (ISBN 0-88295-712-0). Harlan Davidson.
Renaissance Rereadings: Intertext & Context. Ed. by Maryanne C. Horowitz et al. LC 87-27228. 304p. 1988. 29.95 (ISBN 0-252-01489-8); pap. 12.50 (ISBN 0-252-06009-1). U of Ill Pr.
Renaissance Revisited. Sutton. 409p. 1987. write for info. (ISBN 0-932582-55-9). Dance Notation.
Renaissance Revivals: City Comedy & Revenge Tragedy in the London Theatre, 1576-1980. Wendy Griswold. LC 86-7059. (Illus.). xviii, 288p. 1986. lib. bdg. 24.95x (ISBN 0-226-30923-1). U of Chicago Pr.
Renaissance Rhetoric: A Short Title Catalogue. James J. Murphy. LC 80-8501. 375p. 1981. lib. bdg. 61.00 (ISBN 0-8240-9487-5). Garland Pub.
Renaissance Rome: A Portrait of a Society, 1500-1559. Peter Partner. 1976. pap. 10.95x (ISBN 0-520-03945-9). U of Cal Pr.
Renaissance Sackbut & Its Use Today: Further or Amended Information. 1985. 4.50 (05-016522). Henry Fischer.
Renaissance Sackbut & Its Use Today. Henry G. Fischer. LC 84-62233. 61p. 1984. pap. 4.50 (ISBN 0-87099-412-3). Metro Mus Art.
Renaissance, Savonarola - Cesare - Borgia -Julius II - Leo X - Michael Angelo. Arthur Gobineau. Ed. by Oscar Levy. 349p. 1981. Repr. of 1903 ed. lib. bdg. 50.00 (ISBN 0-89984-235-6). Century Bookbindery.
Renaissance Self-Fashioning: From More to Shakespeare. Stephen Greenblatt. LC 80-13837. (Illus.). x, 322p. 1983. pap. 12.95x (ISBN 0-226-30654-2). U of Chicago Pr.
Renaissance Singer. Ed. by Thomas Dunn. LC 75-20077. 1976. 9.00 (ISBN 0-911318-10-0). E C Schirmer.
Renaissance Small Bronze Sculpture & Associated Decorative Arts at the NGA. Carolyn C. Wilson. pap. 4.95 (ISBN 0-89468-067-6, 83-8018). Natl Gallery Art.
Renaissance: Studies in Art & Poetry. Walter Pater. Ed. by Donald L. Hill. 1980. 42.00x (ISBN 0-520-03325-6); pap. 10.95x (ISBN 0-520-03664-6). U of Cal Pr.
Renaissance Studies in Honor of Carroll Camden. Ed. by J. A. Ward. (Rice University Studies: Vol. 60, No. 2). 169p. 1974. pap. 10.00x (ISBN 0-89263-220-8). Rice Univ.
Renaissance Studies in Honor of Hardin Craig. Baldwin Maxwell. LC 72-187877. 1941. lib. bdg. 52.00 (ISBN 0-8414-0487-9). Folcroft.
Renaissance Tapestry: The Gonzaga of Mantua. Kate Simon. LC 87-45669. (Illus.). 288p. 1988. 22.50 (ISBN 0-06-015847-6). Har-Row.
Renaissance, the Protestant Revolution & the Catholic Reformation in Continental Europe. Edward M. Hulme. LC 83-45662. Repr. of 1915 ed. 62.50 (ISBN 0-404-19812-0). AMS Pr.
Renaissance Theatre: A Historiographical Handbook. Ronald W. Vince. LC 83-13031. 224p. 1984. lib. bdg. 36.95 (ISBN 0-313-24108-2, VRE/). Greenwood.
Renaissance Theory of Love: The Context of Giordano Bruno's Eroici Furori. John C. Nelson. LC 58-7170. pap. 72.00 (ISBN 0-317-09244-8, 2005782). BKs Demand UMI.
Renaissance Thought, Vol. 1. Paul Kristeller. pap. 6.95x (ISBN 0-06-131048-4, TB1048, Torch). Har-Row.
Renaissance Thought & Its Sources. Paul O. Kristeller. Ed. by Michael Mooney. LC 79-15521. 352p. 1979. 39.00x (ISBN 0-231-04512-3); pap. 16.50x (ISBN 0-231-04513-1). Columbia U Pr.
Renaissance Thought & the Arts: Collected Essays. Paul O. Kristeller. LC 79-5485. 1980. 25.00 (ISBN 0-691-07253-1); pap. 8.50x (ISBN 0-691-02010-8). Princeton U Pr.
Renaissance Tragedy & the Senecan Tradition: Anger's Privilege. Gordon Braden. LC 84-21029. 256p. 1985. text ed. 25.00t (ISBN 0-300-03253-6). Yale U Pr.
Renaissance Tragicomedy: Explorations in Genre & Politics. Ed. by Nancy K. Maguire. LC 85-48060. (Studies in the Renaissance: No. 20). 1986. 34.50 (ISBN 0-404-62290-9). AMS Pr.
Renaissance Views of Man. Ed. by S. Davies. 214p. 1978. pap. 14.00 (ISBN 0-7190-0726-7, Pub. by Manchester Univ Pr). St Martin.
Renaissance Views of Man. Stevie Davies. (Literature in Context Ser.). 203p. 1979. text ed. 27.50x (ISBN 0-06-491621-9). B&N Imports.
Renaissance Vistas. facs. ed. Maude Barnes. LC 68-55838. (Essay Index Reprint Ser). 1930. 17.00 (ISBN 0-8369-0178-9). Ayer Co Pubs.
Renaissance War Studies. J. R. Hale. (Illus.). 624p. 1983. 50.00 (ISBN 0-907628-02-8). Hambledon Press.
Renaissance Woman: Helisenne's Personal & Invective Letters. Ed. by Marianna M. Mustacchi & Paul J. Archambault. Tr. by Marianna M. Mustacchi & Paul J. Arcambault. 96p. (Orig.). 1986. text ed. 19.95x (ISBN 0-8156-2347-X); pap. 8.95X (ISBN 0-8156-2348-8). Syracuse U Pr.
Renaissance, 1493-1520 see Cambridge New Modern History.

Renaissances Before the Renaissance: Cultural Revivals of Late Antiquity & the Middle Ages. Ed. by Warren Treadgold. LC 83-42793. (Illus.). 256p. 1984. 29.50x (ISBN 0-8047-1198-4). Stanford U Pr.
Renal Ammonia Metabolism. Ed. by R. L. Tannen et al. (Contributions to Nephrology Ser.: Vol. 31). (Illus.). x, 154p. 1982. 64.75 (ISBN 3-8055-3481-7). S Karger.
Renal & Adrenal Tumors. 2nd, rev. ed. Ed. by E. Lohr. L. D. Leder. (Illus.). 340p. 1987. 165.50 (ISBN 0-387-16554-1). Springer-Verlag.
Renal & Electrolyte Disorders. 3rd ed. Ed. by Robert W. Schrier. 1986. text ed. 30.00 (ISBN 0-316-77479-0). Little.
Renal & Genitourinary Disorders. Brundage & Gray. (Illus.). 300p. 1991. text ed. 29.95 (ISBN 0-8016-1685-9). Mosby.
Renal & Urologic Emergencies. Ed. by Allan B. Wolfson & Ann Harwood-Nuss. (Clinics in Emergency Medicine Ser.: Vol. 8). (Illus.). 291p. 1986. text ed. 35.00 (ISBN 0-443-08454-8). Churchill.
Renal Basement Membranes in Health & Disease. Ed. by Robert G. Price & Billy G. Hudson. 456p. 1987. 59.00 (ISBN 0-12-564725-5). Acad Pr.
Renal Biochemistry: Cells, Membranes, Molecules. Ed. by R. K. Kinne. 476p. 1985. 195.25 (ISBN 0-444-80627-X). Elsevier.
Renal Biopsy in Glomerular Disease. E. Beregi & I. Varga. 335p. 1978. 143.00x (ISBN 0-569-08469-5, Pub. by Collets (UK)). State Mutual Bk.
Renal Biopsy in Glomerular Diseases. E. Beregi & I. Varga. 1978. cancelled 34.50 (ISBN 963-05-1356-0, Pub. by Akademiai Kaido Hungary). IPS.
Renal Calculus. L. N. Pyrah. (Illus.). 1979. 58.00 (ISBN 0-387-09080-0). Springer-Verlag.
Renal Carcinoma. James L. Bennington & Robert M. Kradjian. LC 67-10430. pap. 92.30 (ISBN 0-317-07919-0, 2001766). Bks Demand UMI.
Renal Cells in Culture. Ed. by L. G. Fine. (Journal: Mineral & Electrolyte Metabolism: Vol. 12, No. 1, 1986). (Illus.). 84p. 1986. pap. 62.75 (ISBN 3-8055-4160-0). S Karger.
Renal Complications of Neoplasia. Ed. by Thurman D. McKinney. 288p. 1985. 50.95 (ISBN 0-275-92031-3, C2031). Praeger.
Renal Cortical Necrosis. F. A. Laszlo. (Contributions to Nephrology Ser.: Vol. 28). (Illus.). viii, 216p. 1981. pap. 50.00 (ISBN 3-8055-2109-X). S Karger.
Renal Cystic Disease. Hartman. 240p. 1988. price not set (ISBN 0-7216-2343-3). Saunders.
Renal Disease. P. Sweny & Z. Varghese. (Clinical Tests Ser.). (Illus.). 225p. 1988. pap. 48.00x (ISBN 0-7234-0873-4, Pub. by Wolfe Pub UK). Sheridan Med Bks.
Renal Disease: A Conceptual Approach. E. Kinsey & M. Smith. Ed. by Elizabeth A. Brain. LC 86-26835. (Illus.). 143p. (Orig.). 1987. pap. text ed. 12.50 (ISBN 0-443-08504-8). Churchill.
Renal Disease: A Manual of Patient Care. Lynn W. Kagan. (Illus.). 1979. text ed. 33.95 (ISBN 0-07-033190-1). McGraw.
Renal Disease: An Illustrated Guide. D. Gwynn Williams. (Topics in Renal Disease Ser.). 96p. 1982. 17.95 (ISBN 0-85200-421-4, Pub. by MTP Pr England). Kluwer Academic.
Renal Disease-Classification & Atlas of Glomerular Diseases. Jacob Churg et al. LC 81-13444. (Illus.). 372p. 1982. text ed. 75.00 (ISBN 0-89640-066-2). Igaku-Shoin.
Renal Disease: Classification & Atlas of Infectious & Tropical Diseases. Jacob Churg et al. (Renal Diseases Ser.). (Illus.). 264p. 1988. text ed. 105.00 (ISBN 0-89189-258-3). Am Soc Clinical.
Renal Disease: Classification & Atlas of Tubulo-Interstitial Diseases. Jacob Churg et al. LC 84-9118. (Illus.). 225p. 1985. 93.50 (ISBN 0-89640-104-9). Igaku-Shoin.
Renal Disease: Vascular & Developmental & Hereditary Diseases. Jacob Churg et al. LC 85-11887. 304p. (Orig.). text ed. 98.50 (ISBN 0-89640-116-2). Igaku-Shoin.
Renal Dysfunction: Mechanisms Involved in Fluid & Solute Imbalance. Heinz Valtin. 1979. text ed. 19.50 (ISBN 0-316-89553-9); pap. text ed. 19.50 (ISBN 0-316-89554-7). Little.
Renal Failure: Who Cares? Ed. by F. M. Parsons & C. Ogg. 200p. 1982. text ed. write for info. (ISBN 0-85200-476-1, Pub. by MTP Pr England). Kluwer Academic.
Renal Function & Disease in the Elderly. Ed. by J. S. Cameron & J. F. Nunez. (Illus.). 352p. 1987. text ed. 160.00 (ISBN 0-407-00395-9). Butterworth.
Renal Function in Anaesthesia & Surgery. David Bevan. 240p. 1979. 56.00 (ISBN 0-8089-1160-0, 790581). Grune.
Renal Function: Mechanisms Preserving Fluid & Solute Balance in Health. 2nd ed. Heinz Valtin. 1983. pap. 19.50 (ISBN 0-316-89557-1). Little.
Renal Glomerular Disease. P. Sharpstone & J. A. Trafford. (Topics in Renal Disease Ser.). 108p. 1982. 17.95 (ISBN 0-85200-422-2, Pub. by MTP Pr England). Kluwer Academic.
Renal Handling of Phosphate. Ed. by Shaul G. Massry & Herbert Fleisch. LC 79-18651. (Illus.). 398p. 1980. 65.00x (ISBN 0-306-40368-4, Plenum Med Bk). Plenum Pub.

Renal Histopathology: A Light, Electron, & Immunofluorescent Microscopy Study of Renal Disease. 2nd ed. Robert Meadows. (Illus.). 1978. text ed. 95.00x (ISBN 0-19-261213-1). Oxford U Pr.
Renal Immunology. G. Lubec. (Contributions to Nephrology: Vol. 35). (Illus.). vi, 194p. 1983. pap. 64.75 (ISBN 3-8055-3587-2). S Karger.
Renal Insufficiency in Children, Cologne, Germany, 1981: Proceedings. Ed. by Monika Bulla. (Illus.). 280p. 1982. pap. 48.00 (ISBN 0-387-10902-1). Springer-Verlag.
Renal Medicine: Concise Medical Textbook. 2nd ed. Roger Gabriel. (Illus.). 288p. 1982. pap. text ed. 19.95 (ISBN 0-7216-0727-6, Bailliere-Tindall). Saunders.
Renal Nerves. Ed. by G. F. DiBona. (Journal: Mineral & Electrolyte Metabolism Ser.: Vol. 15 No. 1). (Illus.). 92p. 1989. pap. 50.00 (ISBN 3-8055-4887-7). S Karger.
Renal Nursing. Uldall. 1986. 15.00 (ISBN 0-8016-5172-7). Mosby.
Renal Papilla & Hypertension. Ed. by Anil K. Mandal & Sven-Olof Bohman. LC 80-15989. (Illus.). 262p. 1980. 52.50x (ISBN 0-306-40506-7, Plenum Med Bk). Plenum Pub.
Renal Pathology. E. M. Darmady & A. MacIver. LC 79-42838. (Postgraduate Pathology Ser.). 560p. 1980. 125.00 (ISBN 0-407-00119-0). Butterworth.
Renal Pathology. Ed. by C. Craig Tisher et al. LC 65-9434. (Illus.). 1728p. 1988. price not set (ISBN 0-397-50779-8, Lippincott Medical). Lippincott.
Renal Pathology in Biopsy: Light, Electron & Immunofluorescent Microscopy & Clinical Aspects. H. U. Zollinger et al. Tr. by E. Castagnoli. LC 77-23922. (Illus.). 1977. 120.00 (ISBN 0-387-08382-0). Springer-Verlag.
Renal Pathophysiology. 3rd ed. Alexander Leaf & Ramzi Cotran. (Illus.). 1985. text ed. 35.00x (ISBN 0-19-503487-2); pap. text ed. 18.95x (ISBN 0-19-503488-0). Oxford U Pr.
Renal Pathophysiology: Recent Advances. Ed. by Alexander Leaf et al. 293p. 1980. text ed. 65.00 (ISBN 0-89004-399-X). Raven.
Renal Physiology. 2nd ed. E. Koushanpour & W. Kriz. (Illus.). xii, 390p. 1986. 49.00 (ISBN 0-387-96304-9). Springer-Verlag.
Renal Physiology. Donald J. Marsh. (Illus.). 164p. 1983. pap. 16.50 (ISBN 0-89004-992-0). Raven.
Renal Physiology. 3rd, rev. ed. Arthur J. Vander. (Illus.). 1985. text ed. 18.95 (ISBN 0-07-066959-7). McGraw.
Renal Physiology in Health and Disease. Barry M. Brenner et al. (Illus.). 190p. 1987. 20.95 (ISBN 0-7216-1973-8). Saunders.
Renal Physiology: People & Ideas. Ed. by Carl W. Gottschalk et al. (American Physiological Society Book). (Illus.). 520p. 1987. 84.50 (ISBN 0-19-520702-5). Oxford U Pr.
Renal Physiology: Principles & Functions. Esmail Koushanpour. LC 75-12489. (Illus.). Repr. of 1976 ed. 112.00 (ISBN 0-8357-9558-6, 2012275). Bks Demand UMI.
Renal Problems in Critical Care. Ed. by Lynn Schoengrund & Pamela Balzer. LC 84-27075. (Critical Care Nursing Ser.). 309p. 1985. pap. 23.00 (ISBN 0-471-88801-X). Wiley.
Renal Radiology & Imaging. O. P. Fitzgerald-Finch. (Topics in Renal Disease Ser.). 96p. 1982. 17.95 (ISBN 0-85200-423-0, Pub. by MTP Pr England). Kluwer Academic.
Renal Research: Clinical & Experimental Contributions from Japan. Ed. by K. Kobayashi et al. (Contributions to Nephrology Ser.: Vol. 6). 1977. 46.00 (ISBN 3-8055-2402-1). S Karger.
Renal Sonography. 2nd, rev. ed. F. S. Weill et al. (Illus.). 225p. 1986. 95.00 (ISBN 0-387-15343-8). Springer-Verlag.
Renal Stone Disease: Pathogenesis, Prevention, & Treatment. Ed. by Charles Y. Pak. (Topics in Renal Medicine Ser.). 1987. lib. bdg. 77.50 (ISBN 0-89838-886-4, Pub. by Martinus Nijhoff Netherlands). Kluwer Academic.
Renal Stones: Etiology, Management, & Treatment. U. Backman et al. 206p. (Orig.). 1985. 52.00x (ISBN 91-22-00764-4, Pub. by Almqvist & Wiksell). Coronet Bks.
Renal System Course. Competence Assurance Systems Staff. (Illus.). 1981. pap. text ed. 50.00 (ISBN 0-89147-074-3). CAS.
Renal Transplantation. Ed. by Marvin R. Garovoy & Ronald D. Guttmann. (Illus.). 446p. 1986. text ed. 65.00 (ISBN 0-443-08263-4). Churchill.
Renal Transplantation: A Clinical Handbook. Richard F. Wood. (Illus.). 200p. 1984. pap. 15.95 (ISBN 0-7216-0944-9, Bailliere-Tindall). Saunders.
Renal Transport of Organic Substances. Ed. by R. Greger et al. (Proceedings of Life Sciences Ser.). (Illus.). 330p. 1981. 39.00 (ISBN 0-387-10904-8). Springer-Verlag.
Renal Tumors: Proceedings of the First International Symposium on Kidney Tumors. Ed. by Rene Kuss & Gerald P. Murphy. LC 82-14008. (Progress in Clinical & Biological Research Ser.: Vol. 100). 722p. 1982. 80.00 (ISBN 0-8451-0100-5). A R Liss.
Renal Vein Thrombosis. Francisco Llach. LC 82-83041. (Illus.). 224p. 1983. pap. 29.50 monograph (ISBN 0-87993-186-8). Futura Pub.

Renald, the Adventurer. Robert Duc. Ed. by Sylvia Ashton. LC 77-70428. 1977. 12.95 (ISBN 0-87949-069-1). Ashley Bks.
Renaming the Streets, Poems. John Stone. LC 85-11289. 49p. 1985. text ed. 13.95 (ISBN 0-8071-1271-2); pap. 6.95 (ISBN 0-8071-1272-0). La State U Pr.
Renard et la Boussole. 2nd ed. Robert Pinget. 245p. 1971. 12.95 (ISBN 0-686-54880-9). French & Eur.
Renard the Fox. Rachel Anderson & David Bradby. (Myths & Legends Ser.). (Illus.). 80p. (gr. 5-8). 1987. 13.95 (ISBN 0-19-274129-2). Oxford U Pr.
Renard the Fox: The Misadventures of an Epic Hero. Tr. by Patricia Terry. LC 83-8128. (Illus.). 186p. 1983. text ed. 21.95x (ISBN 0-930350-47-2); pap. 11.95x (ISBN 0-930350-48-0). NE U Pr.
Renascence & Other Poems. Edna St. Vincent Millay. LC 72-3092. (Granger Index Reprint Ser.). Repr. of 1917 ed. 10.75 (ISBN 0-8369-8245-2). Ayer Co Pubs.
Renascence of the English Drama. facsimile ed. Henry A. Jones. LC 75-3126. (Essay Index Reprint Ser). Repr. of 1895 ed. 23.50 (ISBN 0-8369-2511-4). Ayer Co Pubs.
Renascence Portraits. facs. ed. Paul Van Dyke. LC 69-17593. (Essay Index Reprint Ser). 1905. 19.00 (ISBN 0-8369-0096-0). Ayer Co Pubs.
Renascent Africa. Nnamdi Azikiwe. LC 79-94488. Repr. of 1937 ed. 35.00x (ISBN 0-8371-2365-8, AZR&). Greenwood.
Renascent Mexico. Hubert Herring. 1976. lib. bdg. 59.95 (ISBN 0-8490-0944-8). Gordon Pr.
Renata Tebaldi: The Woman & the Diva. Victor I. Seroff. LC 70-136653. (Biography Index Reprint Ser.). Repr. of 1961 ed. 21.00 (ISBN 0-8369-8048-4). Ayer Co Pubs.
Renata, Whizbrain, & the Ghost. Caron Lee Cohen. LC 86-22330. (Illus.). 32p. (gr. k-3). 1987. 12.95 (ISBN 0-689-31271-7, Atheneum Childrens Bks). Macmillan.
Renate Ponsold - Robert Motherwell: Apropos Robinson Jeffers. Ed. by Constance W. Glenn. (Illus.). 50p. 1980. pap. 45.00 (ISBN 0-936270-18-7). CA St U LB Art.
Renato Beluche: Smuggler, Privateer, & Patriot, 1780-1860. Jane L. De Grummond. LC 82-14969. (Illus.). 328p. 1983. text ed. 35.00 (ISBN 0-8071-1054-X). La State U Pr.
Renaud. Antonio Sacchini. Ed. by Eugene Gigout. (Chefs-d'oeuvre classiques de l'opera francais Ser.: Vol. 38). (Illus.). 296p. (Fr.). 1972. pap. 27.50x (ISBN 0-8450-1138-3). Broude.
Renault R5 & Le Car: 1975-1983 Shop Manual. Jim Combs. (Illus.). 232p. (Orig.). pap. text ed. 14.95 (ISBN 0-89287-293-4, A187). Clymer Pub.
Renault 1975-85. Chilton Automotives Editorial Staff. LC 84-45489. 224p. (Orig.). 1985. pap. 13.95 (ISBN 0-8019-7561-1). Chilton.
Renbukai: Ultimate Martial Art, Vol. 1. Ronald L. Marchini. (Illus.). 128p. (Orig.). 1981. pap. 6.95 (ISBN 0-86568-030-2, 520). Unique Pubns.
Renbukai: Ultimate Martial Art, Vol. 2. Ronald L. Marchini. (Illus.). 144p. (Orig.). 1982. pap. 7.95 (ISBN 0-86568-041-8, 521). Unique Pubns.
Renbukai: Ultimate Martial Art, Vol. 3. Ronald L. Marchini. (Illus.). 152p. (Orig.). 1982. pap. 7.95 (ISBN 0-86568-043-4, 522). Unique Pubns.
Rencontres: French Grammar in Action. Jean-Paul Valette & Rebecca M. Valette. LC 84-81479. 484p. 1985. pap. text ed. 18.00 (ISBN 0-669-07648-1); wkbk. 12.00 (ISBN 0-669-07649-X); 9 cassettes 35.00 (ISBN 0-669-07650-3); traescript 2.00 (ISBN 0-669-07651-1); demo tape 2.00 (ISBN 0-669-07652-X). Heath.
Rendall Family. G. T. Ridlon. LC 74-138072. (Saco Valley Settlements Ser). 1970. pap. 1.50 (ISBN 0-8048-0829-5). C E Tuttle.
Rendement Hospitalier (II) see Cahiers de l'Institut de Science Economique Appliquee.
Render Them Submissive: Responses to Poverty in Philadelphia, 1760-1800. John K. Alexander. LC 79-22638. 248p. 1980. lib. bdg. 17.50x (ISBN 0-87023-289-4). U of Mass Pr.
Render unto Caesar. Nancy Fairweather. 1978. pap. 1.95 (ISBN 0-8439-0515-8, Leisure Bks). Leisure NY.
Rendered Infamous: A Book of Political Reality. Stephen Gaskin. 268p. 1985. 11.95 (ISBN 0-89789-099-X). Bergin & Garvey.
Rendering from Worcester's Past: Nineteenth-Century Architectural Drawings from the American Antiquarian Society. Lisa Koenigsberg. (Illus.). 68p. 1987. pap. 13.50 (ISBN 0-912296-91-7, Dist. by U Pr of Virginia). Am Antiquarian.
Rendering Highlights. (Airbrush Artist's Library). (Illus.). 144p. 1988. 12.95 (ISBN 0-89134-262-1). North Light Bks.
Rendering in Mixed Media. Joseph Ungar. (Illus.). 160p. 1985. 27.50 (ISBN 0-8230-7426-9); pap. 16.95 (ISBN 0-8230-7427-7). Watson-Guptill.
Rendering in Pen & Ink. Arthur L. Guptill. Ed. by Susan E. Meyer. (Illus.). 256p. 1976. 24.95 (ISBN 0-8230-4530-7). Watson-Guptill.
Rendering in Pencil. rev. ed. Arthur L. Guptill. Ed. by Susan E. Meyer. (Illus.). 272p. 1977. 27.50 (ISBN 0-8230-4531-5). Watson-Guptill.
Rendering with Markers: Definitive Techniques for Designers, Illustrators & Architects. Ronald B. Kemnitzer. (Illus.). 144p. 1983. pap. 16.95 (ISBN 0-8230-4532-3). Watson-Guptill.

Renderings of Stefanos: Book I, Science & Technology. Stefan Grunwald. LC 79-10680. 1980. pap. 4.95 (ISBN 0-915442-91-4, Unilaw). Donning Co.

Renders Their Relatives: Joshua Render of Charles County, Maryland; Orange County, Virginia, & His Descendants, 1720-1985. Pearl O. Smith. LC 85-50210. 1985. 20.00 (ISBN 0-9614492-0-9). Weeks Pubs.

Rendez-Vous see Djinn.

Rendez-Vous: An Invitation to French. 2nd ed. Judith A. Muyskens et al. 608p. 1982. write for info (ISBN 0-394-32638-5, RanC). Random.

Rendez-vous: An Invitation to French. 2nd ed. Judith A. Nuyskens & Alice C. Omaggio. 549p. 1986. text ed. 23.00 (ISBN 0-394-34267-4); wkbk. 9.00 (ISBN 0-394-34265-8); lab. manual 9.00 (ISBN 0-394-34264-X). Random.

Rendez-Vous De Senlis. Jean Anouilh. (Folio Ser.: No. 375). pap. 6.95 (ISBN 0-685-37162-X). Schoenhof.

Rendez-vous de Senlis see Pieces Roses.

Rendez-Vous en France. Sten-Gunnar Hellstrom et al. 1972. pap. text ed. 6.95 (ISBN 0-912022-28-0, 40252); exercise bk 5.95 (ISBN 0-912022-29-9, 40652). EMC.

Rendez-Vous: La France et la Francophonie. Eloise A. Briere et al. 250p. 1982. pap. text ed. write for info (ISBN 0-394-32883-3, RanC). Random.

Rendez-Vous sur L'Ile. Flora Kidd. (Collection Harlequin Ser.). 192p. 1983. pap. 1.95 (ISBN 0-373-49362-2). Harlequin Bks.

Rendezuous in Black. Cornell Woolrich. 16.95 (ISBN 0-88411-889-4, Pub. by Aeonian Pr). Amereon Ltd.

Rendezvous at the Alamo: Highlights in the Lives of Bowie, Crockett, & Travis. Virgil E. Baugh. LC 85-8570. (Illus.). x, 251p. 1985. 19.95x (ISBN 0-8032-1190-2); pap. 7.95 (ISBN 0-8032-6074-1, BB 929, Bison). U of Nebr Pr.

Rendezvous in Averoigne: The Best Fantastic Tales of Clark Ashton Smith. Clark A. Smith. (Illus.). 480p. 1988. 22.95 (ISBN 0-87054-156-0). Arkham.

Rendezvous in Black. Cornell Woolrich. 224p. 1982. pap. 2.25 (ISBN 0-345-30489-6). Ballantine.

Rendezvous in Haiti. Stephen Becker. 1987. 14.95 (ISBN 0-393-02367-2). Norton.

Rendezvous in Singapore. Cora Cheney & Ben Partridge. (Illus.). (gr. 4-6). 1962. PLB 4.99 (ISBN 0-394-91538-0). Knopf.

Rendezvous of Western Art, 1975. Ed. by Vivian A. Paladin. 1975. pap. 6.00 (ISBN 0-917298-07-1). MT Hist Soc.

Rendezvous: Selected Papers of the Fourth North American Fur Trade Conference, 1981. Ed. by Thomas C. Buckley & Ellen Green. LC 84-5985. (Illus.). 231p. (Orig.). 1984. pap. 7.50 (ISBN 0-9613451-0-1). Minn Hist.

Rendezvous with Destiny. Leonard Rapport & Arthur Northwood, Jr. (Illus.). 1977. 14.00 (ISBN 0-686-26296-4). One Hund First Air.

Rendezvous with Destiny: A History of Modern American Reform. Eric F. Goldman. (YA) (gr. 9 up). 1978. pap. 5.95 (ISBN 0-394-72538-7, Vin). Random.

Rendezvous with Destiny: Addresses & Opinions of Franklin Delano Roosevelt. Franklin D. Roosevelt. Ed. by J. B. Hardman. LC 44-3917. 1968. Repr. of 1944 ed. 29.00 (ISBN 0-527-76712-3). Kraus Repr.

Rendezvous with Halley's Comet. Sam S. Mims. (Illus.). 44p. (Orig.). 1985. pap. text ed. 4.95 (ISBN 0-936591-00-5). Space News Pub.

Rendezvous with Rama. Arthur C. Clarke. 1988. pap. 3.50 (ISBN 0-345-35056-1, Del Rey). Ballantine.

Rendezvous with Reality: The American Economy after Reagan. Murray Weidenbaum. LC 88-47671. 336p. 1988. 19.95 (ISBN 0-465-06914-2). Basic.

Rendezvous with the Unknown. Adolph H. Parr. pap. 0.95 (ISBN 0-8198-0133-X). Dghtrs St Paul.

Rendicion de Breda en la Literatura Y el Arte de Espana. Simon A. Vosters. (Serie A: Monagrafias, XXIX). (Illus.). 217p. (Orig., Span.). 1973. pap. 20.00 (ISBN 0-900411-67-8, Pub. by Tamesis Bks Ltd). Longwood Pub Group.

Rene. Rene de Chateaubriand. 128p. 1970. 5.95 (ISBN 0-686-54374-2). French & Eur.

Rene see Atala.

Rene see Oeuvres Romanesques et Voyages.

Rene Char. Mary A. Caws. (Twayne's World Authors Ser.). 1977. lib. bdg. 17.95 (ISBN 0-8057-6268-X). Irvington.

Rene Char: The Myth & the Poem. James R. Lawler. LC 77-85547. (Essays in Literature Ser). 1978. 21.00x (ISBN 0-691-06355-9). Princeton U Pr.

Rene Clair: A Guide to References & Resources. Naomi Greene. (Performing Arts: Film-Directors Ser.). 1985. lib. bdg. 53.00 (ISBN 0-8161-8503-4). G K Hall.

Rene Crevel: Le Pays des Miroirs Absolus. Myrna B. Rochester. (Stanford French & Italian Studies: No. 12). x, 174p. 1979. pap. 29.50 (ISBN 0-915838-25-7). Anma Libri.

Rene Descartes: The Story of a Soul. Herman R. Reith. 212p. (Orig.). 1986. lib. bdg. 23.75 (ISBN 0-8191-5669-8); pap. text ed. 13.25 (ISBN 0-8191-5670-1). U Pr of Amer.

Rene Etiemble: The Crisis in Comparative Literature. Herbert Weisinger & Georges Joyaux. xxiv, 62p. 1966. 3.00 (ISBN 0-87013-099-4). Mich St U Pr.

Rene Fernandat, Poet & Critic. Sr. Mary H. Konkel. LC 71-128928. (CarL Ser.: No. 45). Repr. of 1952 ed. 29.00 (ISBN 0-404-50345-4). AMS Pr.

Rene Guenon & the Future of the West: The Life & Writings of a 20th Century Metaphysician. Robin Waterfield. 160p. (Orig.). 1988. pap. 12.95 (ISBN 0-85030-545-4, Pub. by Aquarian Pr England). Sterling.

Rene Leys. Victor Segalen. Tr. by J. A. Underwood. 222p. Date not set. 17.95 (ISBN 0-87951-324-1). Overlook Pr.

Rene Leys. Victor Segalen. 1988. 17.95 (ISBN 0-87951-293-8). Overlook Pr.

Rene Magritte. Schneede. (Pocket Art Ser.). 1982. pap. 6.95 (ISBN 0-8120-2187-8). Barron.

Rene Maran. Keith Cameron. (World Author Ser.). 1985. lib. bdg. 27.95 (ISBN 0-8057-6604-9, Twayne). G K Hall.

Rene Maran: The Black Frenchman: A Biocritical Study. Femi Ojo-Ade. LC 81-51663. (Illus.). 277p. 1984. 25.00 (ISBN 0-914478-93-1); pap. 12.00 (ISBN 0-914478-94-X). Three Continents.

Rene ou La Vie de Chateaubriand. Andre Maurois. (Coll. Diamant). 25.50 (ISBN 0-685-36957-9). French & Eur.

Rene ou la Vie de Chateaubriand. Andre Maurois. 445p. 1977. 14.95 (ISBN 0-686-55497-3). French & Eur.

Rene Spitz: Dialogues from Infancy. Ed. by Robert N. Emde. LC 83-26461. 495p. 1984. text ed. 52.50x (ISBN 0-8236-5787-6). Intl Univs Pr.

Renealmia (Zingiberaceae-Zingiberoideae) Costoideae (Additions) (Zingiberaceae) P. J. M. Mass. LC 77-72241. (Flora Neotropica Monograph: No. 18). 1977. pap. 21.00x (ISBN 0-89327-192-6). NY Botanical.

Renegade. Judy Gill. (Loveswept Ser.: No. 282). 192p. (Orig.). 1988. pap. 2.50 (ISBN 0-553-21936-7). Bantam.

Renegade. Donald C. Porter. (Colonization of America Ser.: No. 2). (Orig.). 1984. pap. 3.95 (ISBN 0-553-25020-5). Bantam.

Renegade. Jack Slade. (Sundance Ser.: No. 12). 192p. 1982. pap. 2.25 (ISBN 0-8439-1146-8, Leisure Bks). Leisure NY.

Renegade Agent. Don Pendleton. (Executioner Ser.: No. 47). 192p. 1982. pap. 1.95 (ISBN 0-373-61047-5, Pub. by Worldwide). Harlequin Bks.

Renegade & Other Tales. Martha Wolfenstein. LC 79-101824. (Short Story Index Reprint Ser.). 1905. 19.00 (ISBN 0-8369-3212-9). Ayer Co Pubs.

Renegade Christmas. William Everson. 30p. 1984. deluxe ed. 150.00 signed (ISBN 0-935716-29-7). Lord John.

Renegade: Costa Rican Carnage, No. 33. Ramsay Thorne. 160p. 1985. pap. 2.75 (ISBN 0-446-32408-6). Warner Bks.

Renegade: Death over Darien, No. 32. Ramsay Thorne. (Orig.). 1985. pap. 2.50 (ISBN 0-446-32407-8). Warner Bks.

Renegade Girl. Mary A. Gibbs. 224p. 1981. pap. 1.50 (ISBN 0-449-50198-1, Crest). Fawcett.

Renegade: Guns for Garcia, No. 36. Ramsay Thorne. 160p. (Orig.). 1986. pap. 2.95 (ISBN 0-446-34049-9). Warner Bks.

Renegade Heart. Peggy Hanchai. 1987. pap. 3.95 (ISBN 0-451-40020-8, Onyx). NAL.

Renegade Heart. Marjorie Price. 448p. 1987. pap. 3.75 (ISBN 0-8217-2244-1). Zebra.

Renegade Love. Katherine Sutcliffe. 352p. 1988. pap. 3.95 (ISBN 0-380-75402-9). Avon.

Renegade MIA's. Jack Hawkins. 368p. (Orig.). 1987. pap. 3.95 (ISBN 0-317-58572-X, Pub. by Ivy). Ballantine.

Renegade No. 1. Ramsey Thorne. (Orig.). 1979. pap. 2.25 (ISBN 0-446-30827-7). Warner Bks.

Renegade No. 10: The Great Game. Ramsay Thorne. 192p. (Orig.). 1981. pap. 2.25 (ISBN 0-446-30830-7). Warner Bks.

Renegade No. 11: Citadel of Death. Ramsay Thorne. 192p. (Orig.). 1981. pap. 2.25 (ISBN 0-446-30778-5). Warner Bks.

Renegade No. 13: Mahogany Pirates. Ramsay Thorne. (Orig.). 1982. pap. 1.95 (ISBN 0-446-30123-X). Warner Bks.

Renegade, No. 14: Harvest of Death. Ramsay Thorne. 192p. (Orig.). 1982. pap. 1.95 (ISBN 0-446-30124-8). Warner Bks.

Renegade, No. 16: Mexican Marauder. Ramsay Thorne. 192p. (Orig.). 1983. pap. 2.50 (ISBN 0-446-32253-9). Warner Bks.

Renegade, No. 17: Slaughter in Sinaloa. Ramsay Thorne. 192p. (Orig.). 1983. pap. 2.25 (ISBN 0-446-30257-0). Warner Bks.

Renegade No. 20: Shots at Sunrise. Ramsay Thorne. 192p. (Orig.). 1983. pap. 2.25 (ISBN 0-446-30631-2). Warner Bks.

Renegade No. 21: River of Revenge. Ramsay Thorne. 192p. (Orig.). 1983. pap. 2.50 (ISBN 0-446-30632-0). Warner Bks.

Renegade No. 22: Payoff in Panama. Ramsay Thorne. 192p. (Orig.). 1984. pap. 2.50 (ISBN 0-446-30984-2). Warner Bks.

Renegade No. 23: Volcano of Violence. Ramsay Thorne. 192p. (Orig.). 1984. pap. 2.50 (ISBN 0-446-30986-9). Warner Bks.

Renegade No. 24: Guatemala Gunman. Ramsay Thorne. 192p. 1984. pap. 2.50 (ISBN 0-446-30988-5). Warner Bks.

Renegade, No. 25: High Sea Showdown. Ramsay Thorne. 192p. (Orig.). 1984. pap. 2.50 (ISBN 0-446-30990-7). Warner Bks.

Renegade, No. 26: Blood on the Border. Ramsay Thorne. 176p. (Orig.). 1984. pap. 2.50 (ISBN 0-446-30992-3). Warner Bks.

Renegade, No. 27: Savage Safari. Ramsay Thorne. 176p. (Orig.). 1984. pap. 2.50 (ISBN 0-446-30995-8). Warner Bks.

Renegade, No. 28: The Slave Raiders. Ramsay Thorne. 192p. (Orig.). 1985. pap. 2.50 (ISBN 0-446-32398-5). Warner Bks.

Renegade, No. 29: Murder in Merida. Ramsay Thorne. 224p. (Orig.). 1985. pap. 2.50 (ISBN 0-446-32400-0). Warner Bks.

Renegade No. 30: Mayhem at Mission Bay. Ramsay Thorne. (Renegade Ser.). 193p. (Orig.). 1985. pap. 2.50 (ISBN 0-446-32402-7). Warner Bks.

Renegade No. 5: Macumba Killer. Ramsay Thorne. 224p. (Orig.). 1980. pap. 2.25 (ISBN 0-446-30775-0). Warner Bks.

Renegade No. 6: Panama Gunner. Ramsay Thorne. 256p. (Orig.). 1980. pap. 2.25 (ISBN 0-446-30829-3). Warner Bks.

Renegade No. 8: Over the Andes to Hell. Ramsay Thorne. 192p. (Orig.). 1981. pap. 2.25 (ISBN 0-446-30781-5). Warner Bks.

Renegade No. 9: Hell Raider. Ramsay Thorne. 208p. (Orig.). 1981. pap. 2.25 (ISBN 0-446-30777-7). Warner Bks.

Renegade: Number 35, Standoff in the Sky. Ramsay Thorne. (Orig.). 1986. pap. 2.95 (ISBN 0-446-34047-2). Warner Bks.

Renegade, Outcast & Maverick: Three Pioneer California Clergy 1847-1893. Lionel J. Ridout. 1973. 7.95x (ISBN 0-916304-10-8). SDSU Press.

Renegade Player. Dixie Browning. (Nightingale Ser.). 256p. (Orig.). 1985. pap. 9.95 (ISBN 0-8161-3917-2, Large Print Bks). G K Hall.

Renegade Poet, & Other Essays. facs. ed. Francis Thompson. LC 67-22122. (Essay Index Reprint Ser). 1910. 15.00 (ISBN 0-8369-0934-8). Ayer Co Pubs.

Renegade Preacher. Syd Kingston. 1985. 24.95x (ISBN 0-7090-1926-2, Pub. by R Hale Ltd UK). State Mutual Bk.

Renegade Psychiatrist's Story: An Introduction to the Science of Human Nature. Paul Rosenfels. LC 86-142970. (Ninth Street Center Monographs). (Orig.). 1979. pap. 3.95 (ISBN 0-932961-05-3). Ninth St Ctr.

Renegade Ramrod. Leslie Ernenwein. 1976. pap. 0.95 (ISBN 0-685-64016-7, LB345, Leisure Bks). Leisure NY.

Renegade Rebellion. Jon Sharpe. (Trailsman Ser.: No. 71). 176p. 1987. pap. 2.75 (ISBN 0-451-15051-1, Sig). NAL.

Renegade Riders. Donald McGregor. (Orig.). 1980. pap. 1.75 (ISBN 0-505-51549-0, Pub. by Tower Bks). Leisure NY.

Renegade Saint. Phil E. Quinn. 1988. write for info. Abingdon.

Renegade Saint: A Story of Hope by a Child Abuse Survivor. Phil E. Quinn. 1986. 12.95 (ISBN 0-687-36130-3). Abingdon.

Renegade: Shoot-out in Segovia, No. 31. Ramsay Thorne. 1985. pap. 2.75 (ISBN 0-446-32404-3). Warner Bks.

Renegade: The Golden Express, No. 34. Ramsay Thorne. 176p. 1986. pap. 2.75 (ISBN 0-446-34045-6). Warner Bks.

Renegade Tribe: The Palouse Indians & the Invasion of the Inland Pacific Northwest. Clifford E. Trafzer & Richard D. Scheuerman. LC 86-23398. 224p. 1986. 25.00 (ISBN 0-87422-028-9); pap. 15.95 (ISBN 0-87422-027-0). Wash St U Pr.

Renegades. Mary Canon. (O'Hara Dynasty Ser.). 1982. pap. 2.95 (ISBN 0-373-89003-6). Harlequin Bks.

Renegade's Honor: A Renegade Legion Novel. 1988. pap. 4.95 (ISBN 1-55560-057-3). FASA Corp.

Renegades of Gor, No. 23. John Norman. 1986. pap. 3.95 (ISBN 0-88677-112-9). DAW Bks.

Renegades of Luntar. Roger E. Moore. LC 85-51049. (Crimson Crystal Adventures Ser.). (Illus.). 160p. (gr. 4-6). 1985. pap. 2.95 (ISBN 0-394-74164-1). Random.

Renegade's Trail. Gordon D. Shireffs. 1988. pap. 2.95 (ISBN 0-449-44511-9, GM). Fawcett.

Renegotiable Rate: Mortgage Handbook. Financial Publishing Co. Staff. 384p. 1981. pap. 16.50 (ISBN 0-87600-557-1). Finan Pub.

Renegotiating Secondary School Mathematics: A Study of Curriculum Change & Stability. Barry Cooper. (Studies in Curriculum History Ser.: Vol. 3). 300p. 1985. 36.00x (ISBN 1-85000-014-X, Falmer Pr); pap. 20.00x (ISBN 1-85000-013-1, Falmer Pr). Taylor & Francis.

Renegotiation of the Social Contract. Nelson W. Polsby. 1976. 1.00 (ISBN 1-55614-106-8). U of SD Gov Res Bur.

Renegotiations in International Business Transactions: The Process of Dispute-Resolution Between Multinational Investors & Host Societies. William A. Stoever. LC 79-4727. 400p. 1981. 35.00x (ISBN 0-669-03057-0). Lexington Bks.

Renew, Leadership Book, No. 1. Archdiocese of Newark, Office of Pastoral Renewal Staff. 1980. 10.00 (ISBN 0-8091-9195-4). Paulist Pr.

Renew My Church see Renueva Mi Iglesia.

Renew, Pastoral Staff Book, No. 1. Archdiocese of Newark, Office of Pastoral Renewal Staff. 1980. 3.95 (ISBN 0-8091-9196-2). Paulist Pr.

Renew the Earth: A Guide to the Second Draft of the U. S. Bishops' Pastoral Letter on Catholic Social Teachings & the U. S. Economy. James E. Hug. (Illus.). 32p. (Orig.). 1985. pap. text ed. 1.50 (ISBN 0-934255-02-4). Center Concern.

Renew Your Mind. Charles Plunkett. 111p. (Orig.). 1985. pap. 5.95 (ISBN 0-9618786-0-6). JC Pub.

Renewable Energies: Sources, Conversion & Application. Ed. by P. D. Dunn et al. (Energy Ser.). 373p. 1986. casebound 74.00 (ISBN 0-86341-039-1, EN002). Inst Elect Eng.

Renewable Energy. Bent Sorensen. LC 79-50306. 1980. 82.50 (ISBN 0-12-656150-8). Acad Pr.

Renewable Energy Alternative: How the United States & the World Can Prosper Without Nuclear Energy or Coal. John O. Blackburn. LC 86-29273. xi, 201p. 1987. lib. bdg. 34.95 (ISBN 0-8223-0687-5); pap. text ed. 13.95 (ISBN 0-8223-0744-8). Duke.

Renewable Energy Assessments: An Energy Planner's Manual. Marcia Gowen. 250p. 1985. pap. 17.00 (ISBN 0-86638-065-5). EW Ctr HI.

Renewable Energy Dictionary. Ed. by Margaret Crouch. 500p. 1982. 27.50 (ISBN 0-86619-161-5, 11073-BK). Vols Tech Asst.

Renewable Energy for Industrialization & Development. David J. Jhirad. (Energy Management Training Program Monograph Ser.). 200p. 1985. softcover 20.00x (ISBN 0-86531-766-6). Westview.

Renewable Energy for the Future. 33p. 1981. 3.00 (ISBN 0-318-22699-5). Assn Bay Area.

Renewable Energy in Cities. Center for Renewable Resources Staff. LC 83-23455. (Illus.). 376p. 1984. 43.95 (ISBN 0-442-21654-8). Van Nos Reinhold.

Renewable Energy: Progress, Prospects. Stephen W. Sawyer. (Resource Publications in Geography). 90p. (Orig.). 1986. pap. 6.00 (ISBN 0-89291-192-1). Assn Am Geographers.

Renewable Energy Resources. Tony Twidell & Tony Weir. 500p. 1986. text ed. 59.95 (ISBN 0-419-12000-9, NO. 6832, Pub. by E & FN Spon England); pap. text ed. 29.95. Routledge Chapman & Hall.

Renewable Energy Resources in Asean. Jurgen Steiger. (Research Notes & Discussions Paper Ser.: No. 64). 54p. 1988. pap. 8.00 (ISBN 9971-988-82-8, Pub. by Inst Southeast Asian Stud). Gower Pub Co.

Renewable Energy Resources in the Developing Countries. iv, 33p. 1980. pap. 5.00 (ISBN 0-686-39735-5, BK-9176). World Bank.

Renewable Energy Sources: International Progress, Vols. 4 A & B. Ed. by T. Nejat Veziroglu. (Energy Research Ser.). 1984. Set. 331.75 (ISBN 0-444-42363-X); Vol. A, 456 pgs. 194.75 (ISBN 0-444-42361-3, I-313-84); Vol. B, 498 pgs. 194.75 (ISBN 0-444-42362-1). Elsevier.

Renewable Energy Technologies. Ed. by M. J. Chadwick & L. A. Kristoferson. 1986. 84.00 (ISBN 0-08-034061-X, Pub. by PPL). Pergamon.

Renewable Energy: The Power to Choose. Daniel Deudney & Christopher Flavin. 448p. 1984. pap. 8.95 (ISBN 0-393-30201-6). Norton.

Renewable Energy: Today's Contribution, Tomorrow's Promise. Cynthia P. Shea. (Worldwatch Papers). 68p. (Orig.). 1988. pap. 4.00 (ISBN 0-916468-82-8). Worldwatch Inst.

Renewable Resource Economy. Robert D. Hamrin. 208p. 1983. 35.00 (ISBN 0-275-90995-6, C0995). Praeger.

Renewable Resource Management: Proceedings. Ed. by T. L. Vicent & J. M. Skowronski. (Lecture Notes in Biomathematics Ser.: Vol. 40). 236p. 1981. pap. 17.00 (ISBN 0-387-10566-2). Springer-Verlag.

Renewable-Resource Materials: New Polymer Sources. Ed. by Charles E. Carraher, Jr. & L. H. Sperling. (Polymer Science & Technology Ser.: Vol. 33). 342p. 1986. 59.50x (ISBN 0-306-42271-9, Plenum Pr). Plenum Pub.

Renewable Resource Utilization for Development. Robert P. Morgan & Larry J. Icerman. (PPS on International Development Ser.). 325p. 1981. 60.00 (ISBN 0-08-026338-0). Pergamon.

Renewable Resources: A Systematic Approach. Ed. by Enrique Campos-Lopez. 1980. 53.50 (ISBN 0-12-158350-3). Acad Pr.

Renewable Resources & Recreation. Date not set. 5.00 (ISBN 0-317-59275-0). Am Forestry.

Renewable Resources in Our Future. A. D. Hinckley. (Environmental Sciences & Applications Ser.: Vol. 8). 1980. 23.00 (ISBN 0-08-023432-1); pap. 12.50 (ISBN 0-08-023433-X). Pergamon.

Renewable Resources in the Pacific: Proceedings of the Twelfth Pacific Trade & Development Conference, Held in Vancouver, Canada, September 7-11, 1981. Ed. by H. E. English & Anthony Scott. 293p. 1982. pap. 15.00 (ISBN 0-88936-312-9, IDRC181, IDRC). UNIPUB.

Renewable Sources of Energy: IEA. OECD. 334p. (Orig., Eng. & Fr.). 1987. pap. 44.00x (ISBN 92-64-12942-1). OECD.

Renewable Virgin. Barbara Paul. (Nightingale Ser.). 360p. (Orig.). 1985. pap. 9.95 (ISBN 0-8161-3888-5, Large Print Bks). G K Hall.

Renewable Virgin. Barbara Paul. (Mystery Ser.). 192p. 1986. pap. 2.95 (ISBN 0-553-26234-3). Bantam.
Renewal. Russell Shaw. LC 86-81998. 328p. 1986. pap. 11.95 (ISBN 0-89870-109-0). Ignatius Pr.
Renewal. Carol S. Smith. 1982. pap. 1.75 (ISBN 0-345-29755-5). Ballantine.
Renewal & Improvement of Secondary Education: Concepts & Practices. Herbert J. Klausmeier et al. (Illus.). 362p. (Orig.). 1984. lib. bdg. 30.50 (ISBN 0-8191-3609-3); pap. text ed. 14.25 (ISBN 0-8191-3610-7). U Pr of Amer.
Renewal & Recognition of Teachers: Fellowships for Independent Study. Council for Basic Education Staff. 22p. 1985. pap. 4.95 (ISBN 0-931989-26-4). Coun Basic Educ.
Renewal & Reconciliation. James O'Reilly. (Synthesis Ser). 36p. 1974. pap. 0.75 (ISBN 0-8199-0361-2). Franciscan Herald.
Renewal & Reform of Canon Law. Teodoro J. Urresti et al. Ed. by Neophytos Edelby. LC 67-30868. (Concilium Ser.: Vol. 28). 191p. 1967. 7.95 (ISBN 0-8091-0125-4). Paulist Pr.
Renewal As a Way of Life. Richard F. Lovelace. LC 85-10029. 216p. 1985. pap. 9.95 (ISBN 0-87784-594-8). Inter-Varsity.
Renewal Factor: How the Best Get & Keep the Competitive Edge. Robert H. Waterman, Jr. LC 87-47588. 352p. 1987. 19.95 (ISBN 0-553-05226-8). Bantam.
Renewal Factor: How the Best Get & Keep the Competitive Edge. Robert H. Waterman, Jr. 352p. (Orig.). 1988. pap. 4.95 (ISBN 0-553-27304-3). Bantam.
Renewal in the Spirit. Pius R. Regamey. 1980. 5.95 (ISBN 0-8198-6402-1); pap. 4.95 (ISBN 0-8198-6403-X). Dghtrs St Paul.
Renewal in Worship. rev. ed. Michael E. Marshall. 120p. 1985. pap. 7.95 (ISBN 0-8192-1374-8). Morehouse.
Renewal of Buddhism in China: Chu-Hung & the Late Ming Synthesis. Chun-fang Yu. LC 79-28073. (Buddhist Studies). (Illus.). 1981. 37.50x (ISBN 0-231-04972-2). Columbia U Pr.
Renewal of Civilization. rev. ed. David Hofman. 144p. 1969. pap. 2.95; 14.50 (ISBN 0-85398-106-X). G Ronald Pub.
Renewal of Education. Rudolf Steiner. 1982. 16.95 (ISBN 0-317-65187-0); pap. 12.95 (ISBN 0-317-65188-9, Pub. by Kolisko Archive). St George Bk Serv.
Renewal of Faith. Thomas White & Desmond O'Donnell. LC 74-76320. 240p. 1974. pap. 2.95 (ISBN 0-87793-068-6). Ave Maria.
Renewal of Literature: Emersonian Reflections. Richard Poirer. LC 86-10232. 256p. Date not set. 19.95 (ISBN 0-394-50140-3). Random.
Renewal of Literature: Emersonian Reflections. Richard Poirier. 1988. pap. 9.95 (ISBN 0-300-04086-5). Yale U Pr.
Renewal of Mathematics Teaching in Primary Education. Ed. by Secretariat of the Council of Europe. (Reports of European Contact Workshops Organized under the Auspices of the Council of Europe). 225p. 1985. pap. text ed. 21.50 (ISBN 90-265-0599-X, Pub. by Swets Zeitlinger Natherlands). Hogrefe Intl.
Renewal of Our Salesian Life, 2 vols. Joseph Aubry. Tr. by Paul Bedard & Kenneth Whitehead. LC 84-70210. Orig. Title: Rinnovare la Nostra Vita Salesiana. 426p. 1984. pap. text ed. cancelled (ISBN 0-89944-071-1); Vol. I:The Active Apostolate. pap. 5.00; Vol. II:The Salesian Community & Family. pap. 5.50 (ISBN 0-89944-077-0). Don Bosco Multimedia.
Renewal of Preaching. Ed. by Karl Rahner. LC 68-22795. (Concilium Ser.: Vol. 33). 204p. 7.95 (ISBN 0-8091-0126-2). Paulist Pr.
Renewal of the Generalized System of Preferences: Legislative Analysis. 31p. 1984. 6.00 (ISBN 0-8447-0257-9). Am Enterprise.
Renewal of the Price-Anderson Act: 1985, 99th Congress, 1st Session. American Enterprise Institute for Public Policy Research Staff. LC 85-203977. 204p. 1985. 6.00 (ISBN 0-8447-0265-X). Am Enterprise.
Renewal of the Social Organism. Rudolf Steiner. 180p. (Orig.). 1985. 20.00 (ISBN 0-88010-126-1, 582413); pap. 8.95 (ISBN 0-88010-125-3). Anthroposophic.
Renewal of the Teacher-Scholar: Faculty Development in the Liberal Arts College. William C. Nelsen. vi, 110p. (Orig.). 1981. pap. 7.00 (ISBN 0-911696-06-7). Assn Am Coll.
Renewal Parts for Motors & Generators (Performance, Selection, & Maintenance) 1981. 5.50 (ISBN 0-318-18027-8, RP 1-1981). Natl Elec Mfrs.
Renewal Theology: God, the World, & Redemption. Rodman Williams. 432p. 1988. 19.95 (ISBN 0-310-24290-8, 18427). Zondervan.
Renewal Theory. D. R. Cox. (Monographs on Statistic & Applied Probability). 1967. pap. 8.95 (ISBN 0-412-20570-X, NO. 6068, Pub. by Chapman & Hall). Routledge Chapman & Hall.
Renewal Time. Es'kia Mphahlele. (Readers International Ser.). 225p. (Orig.). 1988. 16.95 (ISBN 0-930523-55-5); pap. 8.95 (ISBN 0-930523-56-3). Readers Intl.
Renewals. Eliot DeY. Schein. 1984. 49.95 (ISBN 0-918110-10-6). Folio.
Renewed at Each Awakening: The Formative Power of Sacred Words. Susan Muto. 1985. pap. 4.95 (ISBN 0-87193-147-8). Dimension Bks.
Renewed Day by Day. Aiden W. Tozer. LC 80-69301. 380p. 12.95 (ISBN 0-87509-252-7); pap. 8.95 kivar (ISBN 0-87509-292-6). Chr Pubns.
Renewed Mind. Larry Cristenson. LC 74-12770. 143p. (Orig.). 1981. pap. 4.95 (ISBN 0-87123-479-3, 210479). Bethany Hse.
Renewed Power for Preaching. Glenn H. Asquith. 128p. 1983. pap. 3.95 (ISBN 0-8170-1003-3). Judson.
Renewing America: Natural Resource Assets & State Economic Development. William E. Nothdurft. Ed. by Barbara Dyer. 190p. 1984. 16.95 (ISBN 0-934842-32-9). CSPA.
Renewing American Industry. Paul R. Lawrence & Davis Dyer. LC 82-72096. 400p. 1983. 22.95 (ISBN 0-02-918170-4). Free Pr.
Renewing American Industry. Paul R. Lawrence & Davis Dyer. LC 82-72096. 400p. 1984. pap. text ed. 14.95x (ISBN 0-02-918220-4). Free Pr.
Renewing America's Cities. Thomas F. Johnson et al. LC 73-11854. (Illus.). 130p. 1973. Repr. of 1962 ed. lib. bdg. 35.00x (ISBN 0-8371-7073-7, JORA). Greenwood.
Renewing Family Life. Abraham Schmitt & Dorothy Schmitt. LC 84-22504. (Orig.). 1985. pap. 6.95 (ISBN 0-8361-3384-6). Herald Pr.
Renewing Italian Socialism: Nenni to Craxi. Spenser M. Di Scala. 336p. 1988. 39.95 (ISBN 0-19-505235-8). Oxford U Pr.
Renewing Our Cities. Miles L. Colean. LC 53-9616. 1975. Repr. of 1953 ed. 21.00 (ISBN 0-527-02802-9). Kraus Repr.
Renewing Our Infrastrucutre: Workable Ways to Build & Maintain Public Facilities. 78p. 1983. 4.00 (ISBN 0-318-22693-6). Assn Bay Area.
Renewing Resources: A Critique of the Issues. 133p. 1984. 20.00 (ISBN 1-55516-441-2). Natl Conf State Legis.
Renewing the American Community College: Priorities & Strategies for Effective Leadership. William L. Deegan & Dale Tillery. LC 85-45052. (Higher Education Ser.). 1985. text ed. 26.95x (ISBN 0-87589-664-2). Jossey-Bass.
Renewing the Baptismal Promises. William E. Reiser. 150p. (Orig.). Date not set. pap. 7.95 (ISBN 0-916134-89-X). Pueblo Pub Co.
Renewing the Dream: National Archives Bicentennial '87 Lectures on Contemporary Constitutional Issues. Ed. by Ralph S. Pollock. LC 86-19103. (Illus.). 194p. (Orig.). 1987. 21.50 (ISBN 0-8191-5664-7, Pub. by Natl Archives UCSG); pap. text ed. 12.25 (ISBN 0-8191-5665-5). U Pr of Amer.
Renewing the Judeo-Christian Wellsprings. Ed. by Val A. McInnes. LC 86-24909. 160p. 1987. 16.95x (ISBN 0-8245-0832-7). Crossroad NY.
Renewing the Mind. Casey Treat. 142p. 1984. pap. 5.95 (ISBN 0-88144-112-0). Christian Pub.
Renewing the Promise: Medicare & Its Reform. Ed. by David Blumenthal et al. (Illus.). 256p. 1988. 29.95 (ISBN 0-19-504304-9). Oxford U Pr.
Renewing the Sunday School & the CCD. Ed. by D. Campbell Wyckoff. LC 85-19419. 254p. (Orig.). 1986. pap. 14.95 (ISBN 0-89135-053-5). Religious Educ.
Renewing the World: Plains Indian Religion & Morality. Howard L. Harrod. LC 87-5010. 213p. 1987. 22.50x (ISBN 0-8165-0958-1). U of Ariz Pr.
Renewing Your Mind. Mona Johnian. (Orig.). 1986. pap. text ed. 3.95 (ISBN 0-88368-182-X). Whitaker Hse.
Renewing Your Mind in a Secular World. Ed. by John Woodbridge et al. (Orig.). 1985. pap. 7.95 (ISBN 0-8024-0384-0). Moody.
Renewing Your Program. Jerry D. 20p. (Orig.). 1986. pap. 0.95 (ISBN 0-89486-354-1). Hazelden.
Renfrew Park: A Pennslyvania German Farmstead. Daniel Arthur & Ronald R. Keiper. LC 87-91492. (Illus.). 160p. 1988. smyth sewn 21.00 (ISBN 0-9618407-0-6). Daniel W Arthur.
Renga: A Chain of Poems. Octavio Paz et al. LC 76-18475. 97p. 1972. 5.95 (ISBN 0-8076-0640-5); pap. 2.95 (ISBN 0-8076-0639-1). Braziller.
Rengma Nagas. James P. Mills. LC 76-44761. Repr. of 1937 ed. 46.00 (ISBN 0-404-15870-6). AMS Pr.
Renifleur's Daughter. Candida Fraze. LC 86-26945. 1987. 16.95 (ISBN 0-8050-0381-9). H Holt & Co.
Renin Angiotensin System: A Model for the Synthesis of Peptides in the Brain. Ed. by D. Ganten et al. (Experimental Brain Research Ser.: Supplement 4). (Illus.). 385p. 1982. pap. 49.00 (ISBN 0-387-11344-4). Springer-Verlag.
Renmin de Taodu: Yixing Dingshuzhen. 28p. 1959. 80.00x (ISBN 0-317-45189-8, Pub. by Han-Shan Tang Ltd). State Mutual Bk.
Renno. Donald C. Porter. (Orig.). 1985. pap. 3.95 (ISBN 0-553-25154-6). Bantam.
Renny Darling's Diet Gourmet: The Yes, Yes, Yes Cookbook. Renny Darling. (Illus.). 1982. pap. 9.95 (ISBN 0-930440-16-1). Royal Hse.
Renny Darling's Party Planner. Renny Darling. (Illus.). 1978. 15.95 (ISBN 0-930440-02-1); pap. 9.95 (ISBN 0-930440-03-X). Royal Hse.
Reno Court of Inquiry: Proceedings of a Court of Inquiry in the Case of Major Marcus A. Reno, January 13, 1879, Chicago, Illinois, Concerning His Conduct at the Battle of the Little Big Horn River, June 25-26, 1876. Ed. by John M. Carroll & Robert Aldrich. (Illus.). 1985. 67.00 (ISBN 0-317-28326-X, Pub. by J M C & Co). Amereon Ltd.
Reno-Sparks Nevada. Phyllis Zauner & Lou Zauner. LC 84-50319. (Western Mini-Histories). (Illus.). 64p. (Orig.). 1984. pap. 4.50 (ISBN 0-936914-01-7). Zanel Pubns.
Reno Two: The National Championship Air Races. Mike Jerram. (Osprey Color Library Ser.). (Illus.). 120p. (Orig.). 1986. pap. 14.95 (ISBN 0-85045-702-5, Pub. by Osprey England). Motorbooks Intl.
Renoir. William Gaunt. (Phaidon Color Library). (Illus.). 84p. 1983. pap. 18.95 (ISBN 0-7148-2242-6). Salem Hse Pubs.
Renoir. John House et al. (Illus.). 304p. 1985. 40.00 (ISBN 0-8109-1575-8). Abrams.
Renoir. Walter Pach. (Library of Great Painters Ser). (Illus.). 1950. 45.00 (ISBN 0-8109-0446-2). Abrams.
Renoir. Walter Pach. (Masters of Art Ser.). 1984. 19.95 (ISBN 0-8109-1593-6). Abrams.
Renoir. Denis Rouart. (Illus.). 160p. 1985. 19.95 (ISBN 0-8478-0585-9). Rizzoli Intl.
Renoir. Bruno F. Schneider. (Q L P Art Ser.). (Illus.). 1958. 12.95 (ISBN 0-517-00498-4). Crown.
Renoir: A Retrospective. Ed. by Nicholas Wadley. (Illus.). 384p. 1987. 75.00 (ISBN 0-88363-387-6) (ISBN 0-317-59072-3). H L Levin.
Renoir & Company. Charles Getchell. (Illus.). 44p. (Orig.). 1985. pap. 4.95 (ISBN 0-938864-09-2). Ipswich Pr.
Renoir Drawings. Auguste Renoir. Ed. by John Rewald. LC 83-45845. Repr. of 1946 ed. 50.00 (ISBN 0-404-20213-6). AMS Pr.
Renoir: Girl with a Watering Can. (Let's Get Lost in a Painting Ser.). 1983. write for info. Garrard.
Renoir, My Father. Jean Renoir. Tr. by Randolph Weaver & Dorothy Weaver. LC 87-30164. (Lively Arts Ser.). (Illus.). 448p. 1988. pap. 9.95 (ISBN 0-916515-39-7). Mercury Hse Inc.
Renoir, My Father. Jean Renoir. 1988. 39.00x (ISBN 0-86287-394-0, Pub. by Harrap Ltd England). State Mutual Bk.
Renormalization: An Introduction to Renormalization, the Renormalization Group, & the Operator-Product Expansion. John C. Collins. (Monographs on Mathematical Physics). (Illus.). 400p. 1984. 80.00 (ISBN 0-521-24261-4). Cambridge U Pr.
Renormalization: An Introduction to Renormalization, the Renormalization Group, & the Operator-Product Expansion. John C. Collins. (Monographs on Mathematical Physics). (Illus.). 380p. 1986. pap. 24.95 (ISBN 0-521-31177-2). Cambridge U Pr.
Renormalization Group: Proceedings of the 1st Conference on Renormalization Group. Ed. by P. V. Shirkov. 472p. 1988. 68.00 (ISBN 9971-50-573-8); pap. 42.00 (ISBN 9971-50-574-6). World Scientific Pub.
Renormalization Group Theory of Macromolecules. Karl F. Freed. (Physical Chemistry Ser.). 1986. 39.95 (ISBN 0-471-82845-9). Wiley.
Renormalization in Quantum Field Theory with a Cut-Off. R. L. Ingraham. 196p. 1967. 79.00 (ISBN 0-677-01410-4). Gordon & Breach.
Renormalization of Quantum Field Theories with Non-Linear Field Transformations. Ed. by P. Breitenlohner et al. (Lecture Notes in Physics Ser.: Vol. 303). vi, 239p. 1988. 24.20 (ISBN 0-387-19263-8). Springer-Verlag.
Renormalization Theory. Ed. by A. S. Wightman & G. Velo. LC 75-45277. (NATO Advanced Study Institute: No. 23). 1976. lib. bdg. 39.50 (ISBN 9-0277-0668-9). Kluwer Academic.
Renormalized Supersymmetry: The Perturbation Theory of N-1 Supersymmetric Theories in Flat Space-Time. O. Piquet & K. Sibold. (Progress in Physics Ser.: Vol. 12). 368p. 1986. 45.50 (ISBN 0-8176-3346-4). Birkhauser.
Renouveau 1958-1962 see Memoires d'Espoir.
Renovascular Hypertension. James C. Stanley et al. (Illus.). 400p. 1984. write for info. (ISBN 0-7216-8551-X). Saunders.
Renovascular Hypertension. Ed. by W. Vetter et al. (Journal: Nephron Ser.: Vol. 44, Suppl. 1, 1986). (Illus.). iv, 116p. 1986. pap. 28.00 (ISBN 3-8055-4387-5). S Karger.
Renovascular Hypertension: Pathophysiology, Diagnosis, & Treatment. Ed. by Nicola Glorioso et al. (Illus.). 524p. 1987. text ed. 67.50 (ISBN 0-88167-269-6). Raven.
Renovated Waste Water: An Alternative Source of Municipal Water Supply in the United States. James F. Johnson. LC 72-182155. (Research Papers: No. 135). (Illus.). 155p. (Orig.). 1971. pap. 12.00 (ISBN 0-89065-042-X). U Chicago Comm Geo.
Renovating the Victorian House: A Guide for Aficionados of Old Houses. Katherine Rusk. LC 82-12397. (Illus.). 200p. (Orig.). 1983. 24.95 (ISBN 0-89286-217-3); pap. 12.95 (ISBN 0-89286-187-8). One Hund One Prods.
Renovation & Counter-Reformation: Vasari & Duke Cosimo in Sta Maria Novella & Sta Croce 1565-1577. Marcia B. Hall. (Oxford-Warburg Studies). (Illus.). 1979. 59.00x (ISBN 0-19-817352-0). Oxford U Pr.
Rent-a-Star. Susan Saunders. LC 87-33116. (Fifth Grade S.T.A.R.S Ser.). 128p. (Orig.). (gr. 3-6). 1988. lib. bdg. 5.99 (ISBN 0-394-99605-4); pap. 2.95 (ISBN 0-394-89605-X). Knopf.
Rent a Third Grader. B. B. Hiller. 192p. (gr. 2-4). Date not set. pap. 2.50 (ISBN 0-590-40966-2). Scholastic Inc.
Rent Control. Robert Albon & David Stafford. 144p. 1987. lib. bdg. 52.50x (ISBN 0-7099-5411-5, Pub. by Croom Helm UK). Routledge Chapman & Hall.
Rent Control. Robert A. Carter. 30p. 1982. 5.00 (ISBN 0-318-22974-9). NYS Library.
Rent Control: A Non Solution. 56p. 3.50 (ISBN 0-318-15193-6, NO. 111-116). Natl Assoc Realtors.
Rent Control: A Source Book. 2nd ed. Ed. by John I. Gilderbloom et al. LC 80-70624. 320p. 1981. 11.95 (ISBN 0-938806-01-7). Foun Natl Prog.
Rent Control: A Trap for Apartment Residents & Homeowners. (Public Service Brochure Ser.). One hundred copies. 21.95 (ISBN 0-686-46401-X, 873). Inst Real Estate.
Rent Control: An International Bibliography on Economics & Public Policy. Robert M. Clatanoff & Marc A. Levin. (Bibliographic Ser.: No. 11). 107p. 1985. pap. 19.00 (ISBN 0-88329-143-6). IAAO.
Rent Control: Case Histories. 50p. 8.00 (ISBN 0-318-15194-4, NO. 186-108). Natl Assoc Realtors.
Rent Control Debate. Ed. by Paul L. Niebanck. LC 85-1181. (Urban & Regional Policy & Development Studies). xii, 148p. 1986. 30.00x (ISBN 0-8078-1670-1); pap. 12.95x (ISBN 0-8078-4142-0). U of NC Pr.
Rent Control in North America & Four European Countries. Joel F. Brenner & Herbert M. Franklin. 78p. 1977. pap. 6.95 (ISBN 0-87855-733-4). Transaction Bks.
Rent Control: The Perennial Folly. Charles Baird. LC 80-16317. (Cato Public Policy Research Cato Monograph: No. 2). 110p. (Orig.). 1980. pap. 5.00x (ISBN 0-932790-22-4). Cato Inst.
Rent Examiner. Jack Rudman. (Career Examination Ser.: C-695). (Cloth bdg. avail. on request). pap. 12.00 (ISBN 0-8373-0695-7). Natl Learning.
Rent Inspector. Jack Rudman. (Career Examination Ser.: C-673). (Cloth bdg. avail. on request). pap. 12.00 (ISBN 0-8373-0673-6). Natl Learning.
Rent Research Assistant. Jack Rudman. (Career Examination Ser.: C-696). (Cloth bdg. avail. on request). pap. 12.00 (ISBN 0-8373-0696-5). Natl Learning.
Rent Stabilization & Control Laws in N. Y. Jeffrey H. Gallet et al. (Supplemented annually). 25.00 (ISBN 0-87526-082-9). Gould.
Rent: What Every Tenant & Landlord Must Know. J. James Hasenau. LC 70-150794. (Illus., Orig.). 1973. 9.95 (ISBN 0-913042-00-5). Holland Hse Pr.
Rental Homes: The Tax Shelter That Works & Grows for You. Zucchero. 1983. text ed. 13.95 (ISBN 0-8359-6644-5, Reston). P-H.
Rental Housing. W. Paul O'Mara & Cencil E. Sears. 176p. 1984. 38.00 (ISBN 0-87420-631-6, RH1). Urban Land.
Rental Housing in California: Market Forces & Public Policies. Ed. by LeRoy Graymer et al. LC 86-28540. (Lincoln Institute of Land Policy-OG&H Ser.). (Illus.). 128p. 1987. text ed. 30.00x (ISBN 0-89946-220-0, 220-0). Oelgeschlager.
Rental Housing in the 1980s. Anthony Downs. LC 83-10124. 202p. 1983. 26.95 (ISBN 0-8157-1922-1); pap. 9.95 (ISBN 0-8157-1921-3). Brookings.
Rental Housing: Is There a Crisis? John Weicher et al. LC 81-53063. 113p. 1981. text ed. 18.95 (ISBN 0-87766-307-6, URI 33400). Urban Inst.
Rente Fonciere see Cahiers de l'Institut de Science Economique Appliquee.
Rented Tuxedo. Jim Tyack. 1976. 4.00 (ISBN 0-935252-03-7); signed ed. 10.00. Street Pr.
Renting Mailing Lists. 1987. lib. bdg. 79.95 (ISBN 0-8490-3929-0). Gordon Pr.
Rents. Michael Wilcox. (New Theatrescripts Ser.). 80p. 1983. pap. 4.95 (ISBN 0-413-51810-8, NO. 3806). Heinemann Ed.
Rentsch: Herold Families in America. Mary B. Matreyek. Ed. by Bunkhouse Publishers, Inc. Staff. 743p. 1986. 125.00 (ISBN 0-937594-10-5). Bunkhouse.
Renueva Mi Iglesia. David Haney. Ed. by Jose Luis Martinez. Tr. by Guillermo Kratzig. Orig. Title: Renew My Church. 104p. (Span.). 1983. pap. 3.50 (ISBN 0-311-17025-0). Casa Bautista.
Renunciation & Reformulation: A Study of Conversion in an American Sect. Harriet Whitehead. LC 86-16211. (Anthropology of Contemporary Issues Ser.). (Illus.). 304p. 1987. 32.50x. Cornell U Pr.
Renunciation As a Tragic Focus: A Study of Five Plays. Eugene H. Falk. LC 72-78701. (American Guidebook Ser.). 1954. Repr. 29.00x (ISBN 0-403-04236-4). Somerset Pub.
Renunciation As a Tragic Focus: A Study of Five Plays. Eugene H. Falk. 1988. Repr. of 1954 ed. lib. bdg. 49.00x. Am Biog Serv.
Renunciation of War see Origin & Conclusion of the Paris Pact.

Renzo Piano: A Bibliography. Mary E. Huls. (Architecture Ser.: A 1673). 8p. 1986. 3.00 (ISBN 1-55590-023-2). Vance Biblios.

Renzoni on Baccarat. Tommy Rezoni. LC 72-76844. 160p. 1974. 7.00 (ISBN 0-8184-0067-6). Lyle Stuart.

Reoperative Arterial Surgery. Ed. by John Bergan & James S. Yao. 640p. 1986. 99.50 (ISBN 0-8089-1789-7, 790563). Grune.

Reoperative Surgery. Ronald K. Tompkins. LC 65-9194. (Illus.). 1988. 65.00 (ISBN 0-397-50755-0, Lippincott Medical). Lippincott.

Reoperative Surgery of the Abdomen. Fry. (Science & Practice in Surgery Ser.). 496p. 1986. 69.75 (ISBN 0-8247-7369-1). Dekker.

Reoperative Vascular Surgery. Trout & DePalma. (Science & Practice of Surgery Ser.). 416p. 1987. 89.00 (ISBN 0-8247-7723-9). Dekker.

Reordering of Power: A Socio-Political Reading of Mark's Gospel. Herman Waetjen. LC 88-45251. 224p. (Orig.). 1989. pap. 19.95 (ISBN 0-8006-2319-3). Fortress.

Reorganised National Health Service. 2nd ed. Ruth Levitt. 256p. 1979. pap. 9.00 (ISBN 0-85664-683-0, Pub. by Croom Helm Ltd). Routledge Chapman & Hall.

Reorganised National Health Service. 3rd ed. Ruth Levitt & Andrew Wall. LC 84-12745. 296p. 1984. 31.00 (ISBN 0-7099-1673-6, Pub. by Croom Helm Ltd); pap. 15.50 (ISBN 0-7099-1674-4). Routledge Chapman & Hall.

Reorganization & Reform in the Soviet Economy. Ed. by Susan Linz & William Moskoff. 200p. 1988. 32.50 (ISBN 0-87332-472-2). M E Sharpe.

Reorganization in the Public Library. Terry D. Webb. LC 82-42917. (Illus.). 144p. 1985. lib. bdg. 36.50x (ISBN 0-89774-074-2). Oryx Pr.

Reorganization of British Local Government. John Dearlove. LC 78-18092. 1979. o. p. 44.50 (ISBN 0-521-22341-5); pap. 13.95 (ISBN 0-521-29456-8). Cambridge U Pr.

Reorganization of the American Railroad System, 1893-1900. Edward G. Campbell. LC 76-76643. (Columbia University Studies in the Social Sciences: No. 434). Repr. of 1938 ed. 26.00 (ISBN 0-404-51434-0). AMS Pr.

Reorganization of the Federal Judiciary, 6 vols. in 3. United States Senate Committee on the Judiciary, 75th Congress, 1st Session. LC 73-124924. (American Constitutional & Legal History Ser.). 1970. Repr. of 1937 ed. lib. bdg. 195.00 (ISBN 0-306-71991-6). Da Capo.

Reorganization of the Joint Chiefs of Staff: A Critical Analysis. Allen R. Miller et al. LC 86-28384. (Foreign Policy Report). 1986. 9.95. Inst Foreign Policy Anal.

Reorganization of the Joint Chiefs of Staff: A Critical Analysis. A. R. Millett et al. (IFPA Foreign Policy Reports). 100p. 1987. pap. 9.95 (PDP). Pergamon.

Reorganizations under Chapter of the Bankruptcy Code. Richard F. Broude. 500p. 1986. looseleaf 70.00 (ISBN 0-318-19265-9, 00595). NY Law Pub.

Reorganizations under Chapter 11 of the Bankruptcy Code. Richard F. Broude. 500p. 1986. 70.00. NY Law Pub.

Reorganizing America's Defense: Leadership in War & Peace. Ed. by Robert J. Art et al. (Illus.). 400p. 1985. 41.00 (ISBN 0-08-031973-4, Pub. by Aberdeen Scotland); pap. 16.95 (ISBN 0-08-031972-6, Pub. by Aberdeen Scotland). Pergamon.

Reorienting Health Services: Application of a Systems Approach. Ed. by Charles O. Panneborg et al. LC 83-17750. (NATO Conference Series II, Systems Science: Vol. 15). 386p. 1984. 75.00x (ISBN 0-306-41481-3, Plenum Pr). Plenum Pub.

Reorienting the Federal - State Employment Service. Arnold L. Nemore & Garth L. Mangum. (Policy Papers in Human Resources & Industrial Relations Ser.: No. 8). (Orig.). 1968. pap. 5.00x (ISBN 0-87736-108-8). U of Mich Inst Labor.

Reoviridae. Ed. by Wolfgang K. Joklik. LC 83-6276. (Viruses Ser.). 588p. 1983. 89.50x (ISBN 0-317-59944-5, Plenum Pr). Plenum Pub.

Repair Aide. Jack Rudman. (Career Examination Ser.: C-1453). (Cloth bdg. avail. on request). pap. 12.00. Natl Learning.

Repair & Maintenance of Large Appliances. John E. Traister. (Illus.). 224p. 1986. text ed. 32.00 (ISBN 0-13-773458-1). P-H.

Repair & Reconstruction in the Orbital Region. 2nd ed. John C. Mustarde. (Illus.). 1980. text ed. 130.00 (ISBN 0-443-01698-4). Churchill.

Repair & Regeneration of the Nervous System: Berlin, 1981 Proceedings. J. G. Nicholls. (Dahlem Workshop Reports Ser.: Vol. 24). 411p. 1982. 29.00 (ISBN 0-387-11649-4). Springer-Verlag.

Repair & Renewal of Buildings: Proceedings of a Conference Organized by the Institution of Civil Engineers. 119p. 1983. 33.00 (ISBN 0-7277-0172-X, Pub. by T Telford UK). Am Soc Civil Eng.

Repair & Strengthening of Old Steel Truss Bridges. 141p. 1979. pap. 16.80 (ISBN 0-87262-194-4). Am Soc Civil Eng.

Repair & Tune-up Guide For: MG 1961-1980. LC 81-70232. 240p. 1982. 13.95 (ISBN 0-8019-7173-X). Chilton.

Repair Crew Chief. Jack Rudman. (Career Examination Ser.: C-1454). (Cloth bdg. avail. on request). pap. 16.00 (ISBN 0-8373-1454-2). Natl Learning.

Repair Crew Worker. Jack Rudman. (Career Examination Ser.: C-2004). (Cloth bdg. avail. on request). pap. 14.00 (ISBN 0-8373-2004-6). Natl Learning.

Repair Garages. National Fire Protection Association Staff. 1985. 10.50 (ISBN 0-317-63291-4, 88B-85). Natl Fire Prot.

Repair Garages. (Eighty-Ninety Ser.). 1973. pap. 6.50 (ISBN 0-685-58141-1, 88B). Natl Fire Prot.

Repair, Maintain & Store Lawn Mowers & Garden Equipment. Richard V. Nunn. Ed. by Roundtable Press. (Illus.). 160p. (Orig.). 1984. pap. 7.95 (ISBN 0-932944-64-7). Creative Homeowner.

Repair of Buildings Damaged by Earthquakes. pap. 9.50 (ISBN 92-1-130032-0, E.77.IV.8). UN.

Repair of DNA Lesions Introduced by N-Nitroso Compounds. Ed. by Bjornar Myrnes & Hans Krokan. (Illus.). 292p. 1986. 45.00 (ISBN 82-00-18332-7). Oxford U Pr.

Repair of Gypsum Board Joint Ridging. write for info. (GA-221). Gypsum Assn.

Repair or Install Your Own Telephone or Intercom. Orig. Title: Grow Your Own Phone. 144p. (Orig.). 1989. pap. 7.95 (ISBN 0-89709-162-0). Liberty Pub.

Repair, Protection & Waterproofing of Concrete Structures. P. H. Perkins. 324p. 1986. 57.75 (ISBN 1-85166-008-9, Pub. by Elsevier Applied Sci England). Elsevier.

Repair Shop Manager. Jack Rudman. (Career Examination Ser.: C-1801). (Cloth bdg. avail. on request). pap. 16.00 (ISBN 0-8373-1801-7). Natl Learning.

Repair Supervisor. Jack Rudman. (Career Examination Ser.: C-2615). (Cloth bdg. avail. on request). pap. 14.00 (ISBN 0-8373-2615-X). Natl Learning.

Repairable Lesions in Microorganisms. Ed. by A. Hurst & A. Nasim. 1985. 71.50 (ISBN 0-12-362690-0). Acad Pr.

Repairable Systems Reliability: Modelling, Inference, Misconceptions & Their Causes. Harold Asher & Harry Feingold. 240p. 1984. 45.00 (ISBN 0-8247-7276-8). Dekker.

Repairing America: An Account of the Movement for Japanese-American Redress. William M. Hohri. (Illus.). 1988. 25.00 (ISBN 0-87422-033-5); pap. 15.00 (ISBN 0-87422-034-3). Wash St U Pr.

Repairing & Maintaining Your Own Stereo System. Matthew Mandl. (Illus.). 176p. 1983. 36.00 (ISBN 0-13-773515-4). P-H.

Repairing & Restoring Antique Furniture. John Rodd. (Illus.). 200p. 1987. 29.95 (ISBN 0-7153-6962-8). David & Charles.

Repairing Appliances. LC 81-9279. (Home Repair & Improvement Ser.). lib. bdg. 15.94 (ISBN 0-8094-3483-0, Pub. by Time-Life). Silver.

Repairing Appliances. Time-Life Books Editors. (Home Repair & Improvement Ser.). (Illus.). 128p. 1982. 11.95 (ISBN 0-8094-3482-2). Time-Life.

Repairing Body Fluids: Principles & Practice. Kassirer et al. 176p. 1988. 38.50 (ISBN 0-7216-1149-4). Saunders.

Repairing Christian Lifestyles. 2nd ed. Steve Clapp & Sue I. Mauck. (Repairing Christian Lifestyles Ser.). (Illus.). 174p. (YA) (gr. 7-12). 1983. pap. 6.00 (ISBN 0-914527-26-6); pap. 5.00 leader's guide (ISBN 0-914527-27-4). C-Four Res.

Repairing Furniture. Time-Life Books Editors. (Home Repair & Improvement). (Illus.). 128p. 1981. 11.95 (ISBN 0-8094-2438-X). Time-Life.

Repairing Nails Pops in Gypsum Board Surfaces. write for info. (GA-222). Gypsum Assn.

Repairing Old China & Ceramic Tile. Jeff Oliver. 1986. 9.70 (ISBN 0-316-65007-2). Little.

Repairing Quartz Watches. Henry B. Fried. 1983. 22.95 (ISBN 0-918845-06-8). Am Watchmakers.

Repairing the Breach: Ministering in Community Conflict. Ronald S. Kraybill. LC 82-80586. 95p. 1982. pap. 3.95 (ISBN 0-8361-3302-1). Herald Pr.

Repairing the Reed Organ & Harmonium. S. G. Earl. (Illus.). pap. 3.00x (ISBN 0-913746-06-1). Organ Lit.

Repairing Watch Cases: Schwanatus & Fenimore 1909. 1981. pap. 4.00 (ISBN 0-915706-14-8). Am Reprints.

Repairs at Sea. Nigel Calder. (International Marine Seamanship Ser.). (Illus.). 224p. 1988. pap. 12.95 (ISBN 0-87742-249-4). Intl Marine.

Repairs: Poems. G. E. Murray. LC 79-5379. (Devins Award Ser.). 96p. 1979. text ed. 8.95 (ISBN 0-8262-0290-X). U of Mo Pr.

Reparation at the Paris Peace Conference, 2 Vols. Philip M. Burnett. 1965. lib. bdg. 86.00x (ISBN 0-374-91102-9, Octagon). Hippocrene Bks.

Reparation in World Politics: France & European Economic Diplomacy, 1916-1923. Marc Trachtenberg. LC 79-26898. 1980. 38.00x (ISBN 0-231-04786-X). Columbia U Pr.

Reparative Motif in Child & Adult Therapy. Hugh G. Clegg. LC 84-2901. (Illus.). 240p. 1984. 25.00x (ISBN 0-87668-704-4). Aronson.

Reparenting Schizophrenics. Elaine Childs-Gowell. LC 78-66873. (Illus.). 1979. 12.95 (ISBN 0-8158-0372-9). Chris Mass.

Repartition Modulo 1. Ed. by G. Rauzy. LC 75-20300. (Lecture Notes in Mathematics: Vol. 475). 258p. 1975. pap. 14.70 (ISBN 0-387-07388-4). Springer-Verlag.

Repase y Escriba: Curso de Gramatica Avanzada y Composicion. Maria C. Dominicis & John J. Reynolds. 368p. (Span.). 1987. write for info. (ISBN 0-471-85021-7); answer key avail. (ISBN 0-471-85459-X). Wiley.

Repaso de Espanol. 3rd ed. J. Sobrino et al. 1984. text ed. 21.75 (ISBN 0-8384-1215-7); wkbk. 15.50 (ISBN 0-8384-1216-5); cassette 110.00x (ISBN 0-8384-1217-3). Heinle & Heinle.

Repaso Pratico y Cultural. 4th ed. Vincenzo Cioffari & Emilio Gonzalez. 1977. text ed. 22.00 (ISBN 0-669-96461-1); wkbk. 11.00 (ISBN 0-669-96479-4); 6 cassette set 30.00 (ISBN 0-669-00333-6); 6 reel set 60.00 (ISBN 0-669-97782-9). Heath.

Repatriates & Refugees in a Colonial Society: The Case of Kenya. Joseph E. Harris. (Illus.). 256p. 1987. 17.95 (ISBN 0-88258-148-1). Howard U Pr.

Repeal of Contemporaneous Travel, Entertainment, & Mixed-Use Property Recordkeeping Requirements: As Approved by Congress, May 16, 1985: Explanation, Code Sections as Amended, Committee Reports. LC 86-132770. 35p. Date not set. price not set. P-H.

Repeal of the Blues: How Black Entertainers Influenced Civil Rights. Alan Pomerance. (Illus.). 288p. 1988. 17.95 (ISBN 0-8065-1105-2, Citadel Pr). Lyle Stuart.

Repeal of the Combination Acts: 1825. LC 72-2540. (British Labor Struggles Ser). (5 pamphlets & one broadside). 1972. 20.00 (ISBN 0-405-04432-1). Ayer Co Pubs.

Repeal of the Missouri Compromise. P. Orman Ray. 1965. Repr. of 1909 ed. 12.50x (ISBN 0-910324-07-7). Canner.

Repealing National Prohibition. David E. Kyvig. LC 79-13516. (Illus.). 1980. lib. bdg. 26.00x (ISBN 0-226-46641-8). U of Chicago Pr.

Repeat after Me. Claudia Black. 154p. (Orig.). 1985. pap. 13.95 (ISBN 0-910223-04-1). MAC Pub.

Repeat-Buying. 2nd ed. Andrew S. Ehrenberg. (Charles Griffin Book). 300p. 1988. 49.95 (ISBN 0-19-520634-7). Oxford U Pr.

Repeat Performance. William O'Farrell. LC 87-82446. 248p. 1987. pap. 4.95 (ISBN 0-930330-71-4). Intl Polygonics.

Repeatability Problem in Parapsychology. Ed. by Betty Shapin & Lisette Coly. LC 84-62647. (Proceedings of an International Conference Held in San Antonio, Texas, October 28-29 1983). 264p. 1985. 18.00 (ISBN 0-912328-38-X). Parapsych Foun.

Repent & Believe. Derek Prince. (Foundation Ser.: Bk. II). 1965-66. pap. 2.95 (ISBN 0-934920-01-X, B-11). Derek Prince.

Repent, O Graduate. Harold T. Toolsie. 1980. 7.50 (ISBN 0-682-49060-1). Exposition-Phoenix.

Repentance. Bishop Chrysostomos. (Themes in Orthodox Patristic Psychology Ser.: Vol. III). 75p. (Orig.). 1986. pap. 5.00 (ISBN 0-911165-09-6). Ctr Trad Orthodox.

Repentance. Saint Ephraem. pap. 1.95 (ISBN 0-686-18718-0). Eastern Orthodox.

Repentance & Reconciliation in the Church. Doris Donnelly et al. Ed. & intro. by Michael J. Henchal. (Orig.). 1987. pap. 4.95 (ISBN 0-8146-1572-4). Liturgical Pr.

Repentance & Retribution in Early English Drama. James A. Reynolds. Ed. by James Hogg. (Jacobean Drama Studies). 116p. (Orig.). 1982. pap. 15.00 (ISBN 3-7052-0398-3, Salzburg Studies). Longwood Pub Group.

Repentance & Revolt: A Psychological Approach to History. Richard Freeman. 247p. 22.50 (ISBN 0-8386-7471-2). Fairleigh Dickinson.

Repentance & Twentieth Century Man. C. John Miller. (Orig.). 1980. pap. 2.95 (ISBN 0-87508-334-X). Chr Lit.

Repentance of Mary Magdalene. Lewis Wager. LC 70-133754. (Tudor Facsimile Texts. Old English Plays: No. 36). Repr. of 1908 ed. 49.50 (ISBN 0-404-53336-1). AMS Pr.

Repentance: The Joy Filled Life. Basilea Schlink. LC 83-23774. 96p. 1984. pap. 4.95 (ISBN 0-87123-592-7, 210592). Bethany Hse.

Repercussions of the Kalam in Jewish Philosophy. Harry A. Wolfson. LC 78-9798. 1979. 19.50x (ISBN 0-674-76175-8). Harvard U Pr.

Repertoire, Vol. 1. Ed. by Wolfgang Hageney. (Illus.). 88p. (Eng., Ital., Ger., Span. & Fr.). 1987. pap. 19.95 (ISBN 88-7070-096-8). R Silver.

Repertoire, Vol. 2. Ed. by Wolfgang Hageney. (Illus.). 88p. (Eng., Ital., Ger., Span. & Fr.). 1987. pap. 19.95 (ISBN 88-7070-097-6). R Silver.

Repertoire, Vol. 3. Ed. by Wolfgang Hageney. (Illus.). 88p. (Eng., Ital., Ger., Span. & Fr.). 1987. pap. 19.95 (ISBN 88-7070-098-4). R Silver.

Repertoire, Vol. 4. Ed. by Wolfgang Hageney. (Illus.). 88p. (Eng., Ital., Ger., Span. & Fr.). 1987. pap. 19.95 (ISBN 88-7070-099-2). R Silver.

Repertoire, Vol. 5. Ed. by Wolfgang Hageney. (Illus.). 88p. (Eng., Ital., Ger., Span. & Fr.). 1987. pap. 19.95 (ISBN 88-7070-100-X). R Silver.

Repertoire Analytique et Chronologique De la Correspondance De Guillaume Bude. Louis Delaruelle. 1963. Repr. of 1907 ed. 22.50 (ISBN 0-8337-0812-0). B Franklin.

Repertoire Bibliographique De la Litterature Francaise Des Origines a 1911, 2 vols. Robert Federn. 612p. Repr. of 1913 ed. 58.00 (ISBN 0-384-15401-8). Johnson Repr.

Repertoire de la Cuisine. Louis Saulnier. 1977. text ed. 16.95 (ISBN 0-8120-5108-4); text ed. 19.95 deluxe ed. (ISBN 0-8120-5109-2). Barron.

Repertoire de la Cuisine. Louis Saulnier. 239p. 1970. text ed. 19.95 thumb indexed (ISBN 0-911202-14-5). Radio City.

Repertoire de peintures du Moyen Age et de la renaissance (1280-1580, 6 Vols. Salomon Reinach. 456.00 (ISBN 0-8115-0047-0). Kraus Repr.

Repertoire des Articles Relatifs a l'Histoire et a la Litterature Juives Parus dans les Periodiques De 1665 a 1900. rev. ed. Moise Schwab. (Fr.). 1971. 79.50 (ISBN 0-87068-163-X). Ktav.

Repertoire Des Imprimeurs Parisiens, Libraires, Foundeurs De Caracteres et Correcteurs De l'Imprimerie Depius l'Introduction De l'Imprimerie (1470) Jusqu'a la Fin Du Xvie Siecle. Renouard. 61.95 (ISBN 0-685-35952-2). French & Eur.

Repertoire Des Index et Lexiques D'Auteurs Latins. Paul Faider. LC 77-150150. (Fr). 1971. Repr. of 1926 ed. lib. bdg. 16.50 (ISBN 0-8337-1097-4). B Franklin.

Repertoire des Livres de Langue Francaise Disponibles (1972, 2 tomes. Set. 95.00 (ISBN 0-685-35972-7). French & Eur.

Repertoire Des Sources Historiques Du Moyen Age: Bio-Bibliographie, 2 vols. 2nd ed. C. Ulysse Chevalier. 1905-07. Set. 275.00 (ISBN 0-527-16700-2). Kraus Repr.

Repertoire des Sources Historiques du Moyen Age: Topo Bibliographie, 1894-1903, 2 vols. Cyr U. Chevalier. (Fr.). 225.00 (ISBN 0-527-16710-X). Kraus Repr.

Repertoire Des Traites De Paix, De Commerce, D'alliance Etc, 2 Vols. Tetot. LC 10-16452. 1866-1873. Set. 72.00 (ISBN 0-527-89200-9). Kraus Repr.

Repertoire Des Traites De Paix, de Commerce, D'alliance, Etc., Conventions et Autres Actes Conclus Entre Toutes les Puissances Du Globe, Depuis 1867 Jusqua Nos Jours, 2 vols. in 1. Gabriel De Ribier. Repr. of 1899 ed. 69.00 (ISBN 0-527-75160-X). Kraus Repr.

Repertoire des Vases Peints Grecs et Etrusques, 2 Vols. Salomon Reinach. 113.00. Kraus Repr.

Repertoire for the Solo Voice: A Fully Annotated Guide to Works for the Solo Voice Published in Modern Editions and Covering Material from the 13th Century to the Present, Vols. 1&2. Noni Espina. LC 76-30441. 1341p. 1977. 85.00 (ISBN 0-8108-0943-5). Scarecrow.

Repertoire: Modern Interior Design 1928-1929. Ed. by Wolfgang Hageney. (Illus.). 312p. (Eng., Ital., Ger., Span. & Fr.). 1986. 69.95 (ISBN 88-7070-068-2). R Silver.

Repertoire of League of Nations Documents, 1919-1947, 2 vols. Carnegie Endowment for International Peace Staff. Ed. by Victor-Yves Ghebali. LC 73-7839. 773p. 1973. lib. bdg. 85.00 (ISBN 0-379-00371-6); lib. bdg. 42.50 ea. Oceana.

Repertoire of the Practice of the Security Council. Incl. 1946-1951. pap. 6.00 (E.54.VII.1); 1952-1955. 3.00 (E.57.VII.1); 1956-1958. pap. 3.00 (E.59.VII.1); 1959-1963. pap. 6.00 (E.65.VII.1); 1964-1965. pap. 6.00 (E.68.VII.1); 1966-1968. pap. 5.50 (E.71.VII.1); 1969-1971. pap. 17.00 (E.76.VII.1); 1972-1974. pap. 17.00 (E.79.VII.1). UN.

Repertoire of the Practice of the Security Council: Supplement, 1975-1980. 458p. 1986. pap. 29.00 (ISBN 92-1-137026-4, E.86.VII.1). UN.

Repertorio de Navidad. Francisco Ordonez. 80p. 1986. pap. 1.95 (ISBN 0-311-08211-4). Casa Bautista.

Repertorio dei Sinonimi della Lingua Italiana. R. Ferrari. 463p. (Ital.). 1980. Leatherette 19.95 (ISBN 0-686-97411-5, M-9181). French & Eur.

Repertorio Selecto del Teatro Hispanoamericano Contemporaneo. Erminio Neglia & Luis Ordaz. LC 79-15199. 111p. 1982. 22.50x (ISBN 0-87918-042-0). ASU Lat Am St.

Repertorium Commentationuma Societatibus Litterariis Editarum Secundum Disciplinarum Ordinem, 16 vols. Jeremias D. Reuss. 1962. 550.00 (ISBN 0-8337-2966-7). B Franklin.

Repertorium der Griechischen Christlichen Papyri, Pt.1: Biblische Papyri, Altes Testament, Neues Testament, Varia, Apokryphen. Ed. by Kurt Aland. (Patristische Texte und Studien, Vol. 18). 473p. 1976. 63.20x (ISBN 3-11-004674-1). De Gruyter.

Repertorium fuer Kunstwissenschaft, 52 vols. Ed. by Wilhelm Waetzold et al. (Ger.). 1968-69. Set. 6275.00 (ISBN 3-11-002641-4). De Gruyter.

Repertorium Organorum Recentioris et Motetorum Vetustissimi Stili, Band I, 2: Handschiften in Mensuralnotation. Fredrich Ludwig. (Wissenschaftliche Abhandlungen-Musicological Studies Ser.: Vol. 26). 350p. (Ger.). 1979. lib. bdg. 100.00 (ISBN 0-912024-37-2). Inst Mediaeval Mus.

Repertorium Organorum Recentioris et Motetorum Vetussissimi Stili, Katalog. Friedrich Ludwig. Ed. by Luther Dittmer. (Wissenschaftliche Abhandlungen-Musicological Studies Ser.: Vol. 17). 128p. (Ger.). 1971. lib. bdg. 40.00 (ISBN 0-912024-87-9). Inst Mediaeval Mus.

Repertory Grid Technique & Personal Constructs: Applications in Clinical & Educational Settings. Ed. by Nigel Beail. (Illus.). 407p. 1985. 39.95 (ISBN 0-914797-16-6, Co-Pub. by Croom Helm Ltd.). Brookline Bks.

Repertory Movement: A History of Regional Theatre in Britain. George Rowell & Anthony Jackson. (Illus.). 234p. 1984. 44.50 (ISBN 0-521-23739-4); pap. 14.95 (ISBN 0-521-31919-6). Cambridge U Pr.

Repertory of Homoeopathic Materia Medica. J. T. Kent. 1975. 40.00 (ISBN 0-685-76570-9, Pub. by Harjeet). Formur Intl.

Repertory of Practice of United Nations Organs: Articles 1-111 of the Charter, Table of Contents & Subject Index, Suppl. Nos. 1-3. 11.00 (ISBN 0-317-52083-0, E.79.V.2). UN.

Repertory of Practice of United Nations Organs: Articles 55-111 of the Charter, Suppl. No. 4, Vol. 2. 26.00 (ISBN 92-1-133199-4, E.82.V.7). UN.

Repertory of Practice of United Nations Organs: Articles 92-111 of the Charter, Suppl. No. 5, vol. 5. 1986. pap. 19.00 (ISBN 92-1-133283-4, E.86.V.7). UN.

Repertory of Practice of United Nations Organs, Suppl. No. 5, Vol. 2. 1986. 17.50 (ISBN 92-1-133270-2, E.85.V.8). UN.

Repertory of Practice of United Nations Organs: Suppl. No. 4, Vol. 6. 27.00 (ISBN 0-317-66198-1, E.86.V.6). UN.

Repertory of Practice of United Nations Organs: Suppl. No. 5 Vol. 1 Articles 1-22 of the Charter Covering the Period 1 Jan. 1970 to 31 Dec. 1978. 288p. 1987. 27.00 (ISBN 92-1-133282-6, E.86.V.6). UN.

Repertory of Practices of United Nations Organs: Articles 1-54 of the Charter, Suppl. No. 4, Vol. 1. 26.00 (ISBN 0-317-52084-9, E.80.V.13). UN.

Repertory of the Comedies Humaines of Balzac. Anatole Cerfberr & Jules Christophe. 75.00 (ISBN 0-87968-319-8). Gordon Pr.

Repertory of Tropes at Winchester, 2 vols. Alejandro Planchart. LC 76-3033. 1976. text ed. 63.00x (ISBN 0-691-09121-8). Princeton U Pr.

Reperusals & Re-Collections. facs. ed. Logan P. Smith. LC 68-29249. (Essay Index Reprint Ser). 1968. Repr. of 1937 ed. 20.00 (ISBN 0-8369-0884-8). Ayer Co Pubs.

Repetition. Peter Handke. Tr. by Ralph Manheim from Ger. LC 87-33065. 225p. 1987. 18.95 (ISBN 0-374-24934-2). FS&G.

Repetition & Semiotics: Interpreting Prose Poems. Stamos Metzidakis. LC 86-60801. 175p. 1986. 21.95 (ISBN 0-917786-41-6). Summa Pubns.

Repetition & Trauma: Toward a Teleonomic Theory of Psychoanalysis. Max M. Stern. Ed. by Liselotte B. Stern. 144p. 1988. text ed. 19.95 (ISBN 0-88163-073-X). Analytic Pr.

Repetition Effects over the Years: An Anthology of Classic Articles. Ed. by C. Samuel Craig & Brian Sternthal. LC 84-46069. 290p. 1986. lib. bdg. 35.00 (ISBN 0-8240-6763-0). Garland Pub.

Repetition in Shakespeare's Plays. Paul V. Kreider. 1972. lib. bdg. 20.50x (ISBN 0-374-94643-4, Octagon). Hippocrene Bks.

Repetition ou l'Amour Puni. Jean Anouilh. (Folio Ser.: No. 444). pap. 5.95 (ISBN 0-685-23917-9, 2383, Pub. by Livre de poche). Schoenhof.

Repetition ou l'Amour Puni. Jean Anouilh. write for info. (2383, Pub. by Livre de Poche). French & Eur.

Repetition ou L'amour Puni see Pieces Brillantes.

Repetitions: The Postmodern Occasion in Literature & Culture. William V. Spanos. LC 86-20041. 376p. 1987. text ed. 37.50 (ISBN 0-8071-1316-6). La State U Pr.

Repetitive Manufacturing Production Planning. Robert A. Gessner. LC 87-21067. 198p. 1988. 39.95 (ISBN 0-471-84836-0). Wiley.

Repha. Repha Buckman. Ed. & intro. by Robert Lawson. (Illus.). 68p. (Orig.). 1986. Set. 15.99 (ISBN 0-940559-03-X); pap. 5.00 (ISBN 0-940559-00-5); record 6.95 (ISBN 0-940559-02-1); cassette 6.95 (ISBN 0-940559-01-3). Tri Crown Pr.

Replacement Cost Accounting. Lawrence Revsine. (Contemporary Topics in Accounting Ser.). (Illus.). 224p. (Ref. ed). 1973. 22.33 (ISBN 0-13-773630-4). P-H.

Replacement Costs for Managerial Purposes. J. Klaassen & P. Verburg. (Advanced Management Ser.: Vol. 6). 1984. 63.25 (ISBN 0-444-86670-1, I-547-83). Elsevier.

Replacement of Renal Function by Dialysis. 2nd ed. Ed. by W. Drukker & F Parsons. lib. bdg. 160.00 (ISBN 0-89838-553-9, Pub. by Martinus Nijhoff Netherlands). Kluwer Academic.

Replacement of Renal Function by Dialysis. Ed. by William Drukker et al. (Illus.). 1978. lib. bdg. 115.80 (ISBN 90-247-2042-7, Pub. by Martinus Nijhoff Netherlands); pap. 49.50 (ISBN 0-686-28552-2). Kluwer Academic.

Replacement of Renal Function by Dialysis. rev., 2nd, & enlarged ed. Ed. by William Drukker et al. 1985. pap. text ed. 79.95 (ISBN 0-89838-770-1, Pub. by Martinus Nijhoff Netherlands). Kluwer Academic.

Replacement of the Knee. R. S. Laskin et al. (Illus.). 225p. 1984. 85.00 (ISBN 0-387-12943-X). Springer-Verlag.

Replacement Parts for Agricultural Machinery. (Agricultural Services Bulletins: No. 44). 33p. (Eng. & Fr.). 1981. pap. 7.50 (ISBN 92-5-101045-5, F2173, FAO). UNIPUB.

Replacing the Warrior: Cultural Ideals & Militarism. William A. Myers. LC 85-81253. 32p. (Orig.). 1985. pap. 2.50x (ISBN 0-87574-263-7). Pendle Hill.

Replay. Ken Grimwood. LC 86-13986. 311p. 1987. 17.95 (ISBN 0-87795-781-9). Morrow.

Replay. Ken Grimwood. Ed. by Damaris Rowland. 320p. 1988. pap. 3.95 (ISBN 0-425-10640-3). Berkley Pub.

Replay: Murder. John Logue. pap. 2.50 (ISBN 0-345-30304-0). Ballantine.

Replenishing Jennifer. John Colleton. (Orig.). 1975. pap. 2.50 (ISBN 0-451-11585-6, AE1585, Sig). NAL.

Replenishing Jessica. Maxwell Bodenheim. LC 73-18548. (BCL Ser.: II). Repr. of 1949 ed. 16.50 (ISBN 0-404-11363-X). AMS Pr.

Replica. Richard Bowker. 304p. (Orig.). 1987. pap. 3.95 (ISBN 0-553-26043-X). Bantam.

Replica Shadowing & Freeze-Etching Techniques. rev. ed. M. Willison & A. J. Rowe. (Practical Methods in Electron Microscopy Ser.: Vol. 8). 302p. 1980. 109.50 (ISBN 0-444-80166-9, Biomedical Pr); pap. 24.00 (ISBN 0-444-80165-0). Elsevier.

Replication & Molding of Optical Components. Ed. by Riedl. 1988. 43.00 (ISBN 0-89252-931-8, 896). SPIE.

Replication of DNA. David T. Denhardt. Ed. by John J. Head. LC 83-71256. (Carolina Biology Readers Ser.). 16p. (gr. 10 up). 1983. pap. 1.65 (ISBN 0-89278-320-6, 45-9720). Carolina Biological.

Replication of DNA & RNA. (Landmark Ser.). 1979. 22.50x (ISBN 0-8422-4124-8). Irvington.

Replication of Habitat Profiles for Birds. Richard F. Johnston. (Occasional Papers: No. 82). 11p. 1979. pap. 1.25 (ISBN 0-317-04610-1). U of KS Mus Nat Hist.

Replication of Mammalian Parvoviruses. Ed. by D. C. Ward & P. Tattersall. LC 77-90839. (Illus.). 547p. 1978. 67.00x (ISBN 0-87969-120-4). Cold Spring Harbor.

Replication of Negative Strand Viruses. Ed. by D. H. Bishop & R. W. Compans. (Developments in Cell Biology Ser.: Vol. 7). 990p. 1981. 258.50 (ISBN 0-444-00606-0, Biomedical Pr). Elsevier.

Replication of Viral & Cellular Genomes. Ed. by Yechiel Becker. (Developments in Molecular Virology Ser.). 1983. lib. bdg. 61.00 (ISBN 0-89838-589-X, Pub. by Martinus Nijhoff Netherlands). Kluwer Academic.

Reply from Wilderness Island. Peter Balakian. 96p. 1988. pap. 10.95 (ISBN 0-935296-73-5). Sheep Meadow.

Reply of Feargus O'Connor Esq. M. P. to the Charges Against His Land & Labour Scheme see Employer & the Employed, the Chambers' Philosophy Refuted.

Reply of the Orthodox Church to Roman Catholic Overtures on Reunion. rev., enl. ed. Anthimos. 64p. 1986. pap. 2.00 (ISBN 0-913026-62-X). St Nectarios.

Reply of the Orthodox Church to Roman Catholic Overtures on Reunion. Holy Synod of the Ecumenical Patriarchate Staff. Ed. by Orthodox Christian Educational Society Staff. Anthimus. (Orig., Gr.). 1978. pap. 0.50x (ISBN 0-938366-35-1). Orthodox Chr.

Reply Requested: Thirty Letters of Advice. R. Yerkey. 1981. write for info. (ISBN 0-201-10078-9). Addison-Wesley.

Reply to J. A. Hobson. C. H. Douglas. 59.95 (ISBN 0-8490-0945-6). Gordon Pr.

Reply to Myth: Perspectives on Intimacy. John F. Crosby. 669p. 1985. pap. write for info. (ISBN 0-02-325370-3). Macmillan.

Reply to the Essay on Population by the Rev. T. R. Malthus. William Hazlitt. LC 66-21678. 1969. Repr. of 1807 ed. 45.00x (ISBN 0-678-00203-7). Kelley.

Reply to the Headlines: Poems 1965-1970. Martin Robbins. LC 73-115028. 70p. 1970. 6.00 (ISBN 0-8040-0260-6, Pub. by Swallow). Ohio U Pr.

Reply to the Observations of Lieut. Gen. Sir William Howe, on a Pamphlet, Entitled "Letters to a Nobleman" In Which His Misrepresentations Are Detected. Joseph Galloway. LC 72-8751. (American Revolutionary Ser.). 1781. lib. bdg. 26.50 (ISBN 0-8398-0669-8). Irvington.

Repo & Reverse Markets. Marcia Stigum. 1988. 62.50 (ISBN 0-87094-988-8). Dow Jones-Irwin.

Repo Man. Alex Cox. Intro. by Dick Rude. (Illus.). 128p. (Orig.). 1988. pap. 9.95 (ISBN 0-571-12977-3). Faber & Faber.

Reponses. Francoise Sagan. 192p. 1974. 14.95 (ISBN 0-686-55395-0); pap. 3.95 (ISBN 0-686-55396-9). French & Eur.

Reponses a Paul Claudel: Avec: Lettres Ouvertes. Francois Mauriac. (Illus.). 12.50 (ISBN 0-686-55476-0). French & Eur.

Report. American Psychological Association, Committee on the Standardizing of Procedure in Experimental Tests. Ed. by R. S. Woodworth. Bd. with Tests of Practical Mental Classification. W. H. Healy. Repr. of 1911 ed; Some Types of Attention. H. C. McComas. Repr. of 1911 ed; On the Functions of the Cerebrum. S. I. Franz. Repr. of 1911 ed. (Psychology Monographs General & Applied: Vol. 13). pap. 29.00 (ISBN 0-8115-1412-9). Kraus Repr.

Report, 7 vols. India. Hemp Drugs Commission, 1893-1894. 3394p. pap. 350.00 (ISBN 0-685-27598-1). Johnson Repr.

Report. International Agency for Research on Cancer. Incl. 1970. pap. 1.20 (ISBN 0-686-16946-8); 1971. pap. 1.20 (ISBN 0-686-16947-6); 1972-73. pap. 2.40 (ISBN 0-686-16948-4); 1974. pap. 4.00 (ISBN 0-686-16949-2); 1975. pap. 4.80 (ISBN 0-686-16950-6). (Also avail. in French). pap. World Health.

Report. facsimile ed. South Carolina General Assembly Joint Committee to Investigate Law Enforcement. LC 74-3855. (Criminal Justice in America Ser.). 1974. Repr. of 1937 ed. 63.00x (ISBN 0-405-06168-4). Ayer Co Pubs.

Report. facsimile ed. U. S. Advisory Committee on Education. LC 74-1711. (Children & Youth Ser.). 260p. (February, 1938). 1974. Repr. of 1938 ed. 23.50x (ISBN 0-405-05987-6). Ayer Co Pubs.

Report. WHO Expert Committee on Biological Standardization, 21st, Geneva, 1968. (Technical Report Ser: No. 413). 106p. (Eng., Fr., Rus. & Span.). 1969. pap. 2.80 (ISBN 92-4-120413-3, 176). World Health.

Report. WHO Expert Committee on Biological Standardization, 20th, Geneva, 1967. (Technical Report Ser: No. 384). 100p. (Eng., Fr., Rus. & Span.). 1968. pap. 2.80 (ISBN 92-4-120384-6, 175). World Health.

Report. WHO Expert Committee on Biological Standardization, 23rd, Geneva, 1970. (Technical Report Ser: No. 463). 91p. 1971. pap. 2.80 (ISBN 92-4-120463-X, 178). World Health.

Report. WHO Expert Committee on Biological Standardization, 22nd, Geneva, 1969. (Technical Report Ser: No. 444). 132p. 1970. pap. 2.80 (ISBN 92-4-120444-3, 177). World Health.

Report. WHO Expert Committee on Biological Standardization, 17th, Geneva, 1964. (Technical Report Ser: No. 293). 86p. (Eng., Fr., Rus. & Span.). 1964. pap. 2.00 (ISBN 92-4-120293-9). World Health.

Report. WHO Expert Committee on Biological Standardization, 19th, Geneva, 1966. (Technical Report Ser: No. 361). 120p. (Eng., Fr & Span.). 1967. pap. 2.80 (ISBN 92-4-120361-7). World Health.

Report. WHO Expert Committee on Filariasis, Geneva, 1961. (Technical Report Ser: No. 233). 49p. (Eng., Fr., Rus. & Span.). 1962. pap. 1.20 (ISBN 92-4-120233-5). World Health.

Report. WHO Expert Committee on Gonococcal Infections, 1st, Geneva, 1962. (Technical Report Ser: No. 262). 70p. (Eng., Fr., Rus. & Span.). 1963. pap. 2.00 (ISBN 92-4-120262-9). World Health.

Report. WHO Expert Committee on Malaria. Incl. 15th Report, Geneva, 1970. (Technical Report Ser: No. 467). 59p. (Eng., Fr. & Span.). 1971. pap. 2.00 (ISBN 92-4-120467-2, 1078); 14th Report, Geneva, 1967. (Technical Report Ser: No. 382). 50p. (Eng., Fr. Rus. & Span.). 1968. pap. 2.00 (ISBN 92-4-120382-X, 1077). pap. World Health.

Report. WHO Expert Committee on Onchocerciasis, 2nd, Geneva, 1965. (Technical Report Ser: No. 335). 96p. (Eng., Fr., Rus. & Span.). 1966. pap. 2.00 (ISBN 92-4-120335-8). World Health.

Report. WHO Expert Committee on Respiratory Virus Diseases, 1st, Stockholm, 1958. (Technical Report Ser: No. 170). 59p. (Eng., Fr. & Span.). 1959. pap. 1.20 (ISBN 92-4-120170-3). World Health.

Report. WHO Expert Committee on Smallpox Eradication, 2nd, 1972. (Technical Report Ser: No. 493). 64p. pap. 2.80 (ISBN 92-4-120493-1, 1462). World Health.

Report. WHO Expert Committee on Yellow Fever, 3rd, 1971. (Technical Report Ser: No. 479). 56p. pap. 2.00 (ISBN 92-4-120479-6, 1621). World Health.

Report, Vol. 10. Ed. by Lida F. Harshman. 1970. 5.00 (ISBN 0-935057-25-0). OH Genealogical.

Report, Vol. 11. Ed. by Lida F. Harshman. 1971. 5.00 (ISBN 0-935057-26-9). OH Genealogical.

Report, Vol. 12. Ed. by Lida F. Harshman. 1972. 5.00 (ISBN 0-935057-27-7). OH Genealogical.

Report, Vol. 13. Ed. by Lida F. Harshman. 1973. 5.00 (ISBN 0-935057-28-5). OH Genealogical.

Report, Vol. 14. Ed. by Lida F. Harshman. 1974. 7.00 (ISBN 0-935057-29-3). OH Genealogical.

Report, Vol. 15. Ed. by Lida F. Harshman. 1975. 10.00 (ISBN 0-935057-30-7). OH Genealogical.

Report, Vol. 16. Ed. by Lida F. Harshman. 1976. 10.00 (ISBN 0-935057-31-5). OH Genealogical.

Report, Vol. 17. Ed. by Lida F. Harshman. 1977. 12.00 (ISBN 0-935057-32-3). OH Genealogical.

Report, Vol. 18. Ed. by Cora H. Bartholow. 1978. 12.00 (ISBN 0-935057-33-1). OH Genealogical.

Report, Vol. 19. Ed. by Cora H. Bartholow. 1979. 12.00 (ISBN 0-935057-34-X). OH Genealogical.

Report, Vol. 20. Ed. by Cora H. Bartholow. 1980. 12.00 (ISBN 0-935057-35-8). OH Genealogical.

Report, Vol. 21. Ed. by Cora H. Bartholow. 1981. 15.00 (ISBN 0-935057-36-6). OH Genealogical.

Report, Vol. 22. Ed. by Cora H. Bartholow. 1982. 15.00 (ISBN 0-935057-37-4). OH Genealogical.

Report, Vol. 23. Ed. by Carol W. Bell. 1983. 15.00 (ISBN 0-935057-38-2). OH Genealogical.

Report, Vol. 24. Ed. by Carol W. Bell. 1984. 16.00 (ISBN 0-935057-39-0). OH Genealogical.

Report, Vol. 25. Ed. by Carol W. Bell. 1985. 16.00 (ISBN 0-935057-40-4). OH Genealogical.

Report, Vol. 26. Ed. by Carol W. Bell. 1986. 16.00 (ISBN 0-935057-42-0). OH Genealogical.

Report, Vol. 27. Ed. by Carol W. Bell. 1987. 16.00 (ISBN 0-317-69993-8). Oh Genealogical.

Report about the Dispute of a Man with His Ba: Papyrus Berlin 3024. Hans Goedicke. LC 70-131472. pap. 64.00 (ISBN 0-317-09898-5, 2002277). Bks Demand UMI.

Report Analyzes Telecommunications Brokering Business. 250p. write for info. C C M I.

Report & Interim Report, 2 vols. in 1. League of Nations, Financial Committee, Gold Delegation. Ed. by Mira Wilkins. LC 78-3929. (International Finance Ser.). 1978. Repr. of 1930 ed. lib. bdg. 20.00x (ISBN 0-405-11232-7). Ayer Co Pubs.

Report & Proceedings of the Expert Consulation on Shared Fishery Resources. Ed. by R. Mahon. 278p. (Orig.). 1987. pap. 27.00 (ISBN 92-5-102577-0, F3121, FAO). UNIPUB.

Report & Proceedings of the Investigation of the New York City Police. 1971. 325.00 (713). Ayer Co Pubs.

Report & Proceedings of the Senate Committee Appointed to Investigate the Police Department of the City of New York: The Lexow Committee Report, 6 vols. LC 75-154600. 1971. Repr. of 1895 ed. 300.00 set (ISBN 0-405-03399-0). Ayer Co Pubs.

Report & Recommendations of the In-Rem Housing Task Force: Committee on Housing & Urban Development. Terence Benbow. 1981. pap. 2.50 (ISBN 0-88156-082-0). Comm Serv Soc NY.

Report & Recommendations to the President of the United States on Americans Outdoors. 218p. (Orig.). 1986. pap. 11.00 (ISBN 0-317-62879-8, S-N 040-000-00515-3). USGPO.

Report by the Tariff Board Pursuant to the Inquiry by the Minister of Finance Respecting Fresh & Processed Fruits & Vegetables, 2 vols. 1978. pap. 27.75 set (SSC121, SSC) (ISBN 0-660-01786-5). UNIPUB.

Report Card. 12/1987 ed. Terry Thortnton & Sandy Thornton. (Illus.). 32p. (gr. 2-5). pap. 5.95 (ISBN 0-687-36140-0). Abingdon.

Report Card in Nutrition: A Personalized Diet Evaluation. 2nd ed. B. L. Frye. 138p. 1986. pap. text ed. 11.00x (ISBN 0-89787-121-9). Gorsuch Scarisbrick.

Report Card on Reaganomics. Murray L. Weidenbaum. (Seventeenth Annual William K. McInally Memorial Lecture Ser.). 15p. pap. 1.00 (ISBN 0-87712-235-0). UMI Div Res GSBA.

Report Card Trap: How to Avoid It. Beverly A. Haley. LC 85-13506. 152p. (Orig.). 1985. pap. 5.95 (ISBN 0-932620-55-8). Betterway Pubns.

Report for Controlling the Desert Locust in the Eastern Region of Southwest Asia: Commission Meeting, 12th Session. 28p. 1978. pap. 7.50 (ISBN 0-685-20385-9, F1266, FAO). UNIPUB.

Report for the Thirteenth FAO Regional Conference for Asia & the Far East, Manila, Philippines 5-13 August, 1976. pap. 7.50 (F1119, FAO). UNIPUB.

Report for the Thirteenth FAO Regional Conference for the Near East, Tunis, Tunisia, October 4-11, 1976. pap. 7.50 (F1124, FAO). UNIPUB.

Report Four-Metes & Bounds Descriptions. rev. ed. Jesse E. Fant et al. (Illus.). 161p. (Orig.). 1980. 22.10 (ISBN 0-87518-207-0). Fant-Freeman-Madson.

Report from a Chinese Village. Jan Myrdal. (Pantheon Village Ser.). (Illus.). 1981. pap. 7.95. Pantheon.

Report from a Town under Siege. Herbert Zbigniew. Tr. by Buguslaw Rostworowski from Pol. (Poetry Ser.). (Illus.). 16p. (Orig.). 1984. pap. 6.50 (ISBN 0-317-39888-1); limited paper with original drawing 10.00 (ISBN 0-317-39889-X). Seluzicki Fine Bks.

Report from AI to the Government of the Syrian Arab Republic. 1983. 4.95 (ISBN 0-86210-058-5). Amnesty Intl USA.

Report from Banaran: The Story of the Experiences of a Soldier During the War of Independence. T. B. Simatupang. Tr. by Benedict Anderson & Elizabeth Graves. 186p. 1972. pap. 6.50 (ISBN 0-87763-005-4). Cornell Mod Indo.

Report from Formosa. H. Maclear Bate. 1952. cancelled. Century Bookbindery.

Report from Hokkaido: The Remains of Russian Culture in Northern Japan. George A. Lensen. LC 73-2878. (Illus.). 216p. 1973. Repr. of 1954 ed. lib. bdg. 35.00x (ISBN 0-8371-6818-X, LERH). Greenwood.

Report from Israel. Arnold Forster. 72p. pap. 1.25 (ISBN 0-686-74976-6). ADL.

Report from Jerusalem: City at the Crossroads. J. Robert Moskin. LC 77-79877. (Illus.). 64p. 1977. pap. 1.50 (ISBN 0-87495-013-9). Am Jewish Comm.

Report of the Commissioner of Indian Affairs for the Territories of Washington & Idaho & the State of Oregon for the Year of 1870. 75p. 1981. 12.50 (ISBN 0-87770-247-0). Ye Galleon.

Report of the Commissioner of Indian Affairs: Reports for the Years 1824-1899, 65 vols. U. S. Office Of Indian Affairs. Repr. of 1899 ed. Set. write for info. (ISBN 0-404-07550-9). AMS Pr.

Report of the Commissioner (Ombudsman) for Local Administration in Scotland for the Year Ended 31 March 1987. 28p. (Orig.). 1987. pap. text ed. 5.00 (ISBN 0-11-887434-9, HM709, Pub. by Her Maj Station Ofc). UNIPUB.

Report of the Committee Appointed Pursuant to House Resolutions 429 & 504 to Investigate the Concentration of Control of Money & Credit. facsimile ed. Banking & Currency Committee. LC 75-2677. (Wall Street & the Security Market Ser.). 1975. Repr. of 1913 ed. 20.00x (ISBN 0-405-07239-2). Ayer Co Pubs.

Report of the Committee of Experts on the Application of Conventions & Recommendations (Articles 19, 22 & 35 of the Constitution) Vol. A: General Report & Observations Concerning Particular Countries Report III, Part 4a. International Labour Conference, 66th Session. International Labour Office Staff. xv, 242p. (Orig.). 1980. pap. 21.00 (ISBN 92-2-102092-4). Intl Labour Office.

Report of the Committee of Experts on the Application of Conventions & Recommendations: International Labour Conference 67th Session, 1981, Report III (pt. 4a) xv, 244p. (Orig.). 1981. pap. 21.00 (ISBN 92-2-102401-6). Intl Labour Office.

Report of the Committee of Experts on the Application of Conventions & Recommendations, Report III, Pt. 4A. (International Labour Conference reports Ser.). 487p. (Orig.). 1987. pap. text ed. 35.00 (ISBN 92-2-105572-8, ILO628, ILO). UNIPUB.

Report of the Committee of Fifteen on the Elementary School. William T. Harris. LC 73-89188. (American Education: Its Men, Institutions & Ideas, Ser. 1). 1969. Repr. of 1895 ed. 13.00 (ISBN 0-405-01426-0). Ayer Co Pubs.

Report of the Committee of the Senate upon the Relations Between Labor & Capital & Testimony Taken by the Committee, 4 vols. United States Congress Senate Committee on Education & Labor. 297.00 (ISBN 0-405-07518-9, 18381). Ayer Co Pubs.

Report of the Committee on Condemnation & Condemnation Procedure, 1980. 279p. 1980. pap. 20.00 (ISBN 0-686-48106-2). Amer Bar Assn.

Report of the Committee on Conferences: 40th Session, Supplement No. 32. 87p. 9.50 (ISBN 0-317-41399-6). UN.

Report of the Committee on Economic Security of 1935. Intro. by Forrest Chisman & Alan Pifer. LC 85-60612. 304p. 1985. 35.00 (ISBN 0-933597-02-9); pap. 9.95 (ISBN 0-933597-03-7). Natl Conf Soc Welfare.

Report of the Committee on Fisheries. Incl. Fourteenth Session, Rome, May 26-30, 1981. (No. 256). 43p. (Eng., Fr & Span.). 1981. pap. 7.50 (ISBN 92-5-101106-0, F2209). UNIPUB; Twelfth Session. (No. 208). 32p. 1979. pap. 7.50 (ISBN 92-5-100656-3, F1518). UNIPUB. (Fisheries Reports, FAO). UNIPUB.

Report of the Committee on Fisheries. (Fisheries Reports). 17p. 1967. pap. 7.50 (ISBN 0-686-93093-2, F1667, FAO). UNIPUB.

Report of the Committee on Infectious Diseases, 1988. 21th ed. American Academy of Pediatrics, Committee on Infectious Diseases Staff. 624p. 1988. pap. text ed. 30.00 (ISBN 0-910761-20-5). Am Acad Pediat.

Report of the Committee on Information: 40th Session, Supplement No. 21. 48p. 7.00 (ISBN 0-317-41525-5). UN.

Report of the Committee on Police Conditions of Service. Police Conditions of Service Committee. LC 76-156281. (Police in Great Britain Ser). 1971. Repr. of 1949 ed. 19.00 (ISBN 0-405-03392-3). Ayer Co Pubs.

Report of the Committee on Pornography & Prostitution, Vols. 1 & 2. 784p. 1985. pap. text ed. 45.95x Set (ISBN 0-660-11809-2). Brookfield Pub Co.

Report of the Committee on Secondary School Studies, Appointed at the Meeting of the National Education Association. National Education Association, Committee on Secondary School Studies. LC 70-89222. (American Education: Its Men, Institutions & Ideas, Ser. 1). 1969. Repr. of 1893 ed. 19.00 (ISBN 0-405-01403-1). Ayer Co Pubs.

Report of the Committee on Sexual Offences Against Children & Youths: Sexual Offences Against Children, 2 vols. Canadian Government Publishing Centre Staff. 1314p. 1985. Set. pap. 46.50 (ISBN 0-660-11639-1, SSC193, SSC). UNIPUB.

Report of the Committee on the Criteria & Nomenclature of the Major Divisions of the Ocean Bottom. (Publications Scientifique Ser.). 124p. 1940. 2.00 (ISBN 0-318-14529-4). Intl Assoc Phys Sci Ocean.

Report of the Committee on the Drafting of an International Convention Against Apartheid in Sports: 40th Session, Supplement No. 36. 15p. 4.00 (ISBN 0-317-41400-3). UN.

Report of the Committee on the Elimination of Discrimination Against Women: 41st Session, Supplement No. 45. 57p. 7.00. UN.

Report of the Committee on the Elimination of Racial Discrimination: 40th Session, Supplement No. 18. 146p. 15.00 (ISBN 0-317-41387-2). UN.

Report of the Committee on the Exercise of the Inalienable Rights of the Palestinian People: 40th Session, Supplement No. 35. 82p. 9.50 (ISBN 0-317-41527-1). UN.

Report of the Committee on the Future of the College. M. Bressler. 1974. 3.95x (ISBN 0-691-09361-X). Princeton U Pr.

Report of the Conference of see Report of FAO Conference.

Report of the Conference of FAO. 222p. (Orig.). 1987. pap. 27.00 (F3176, FAO). UNIPUB.

Report of the Conference on Disarmament: 40th Session, Supplement No. 27. 190p. 17.50 (ISBN 0-317-41526-3). UN.

Report of the Consultation on the Establishment of the European Research Network on Trace Elements. 1978. pap. 7.50 (ISBN 92-5-100342-4, F1234, FAO). UNIPUB.

Report of the Council of FAO. (Orig.). 1987. pap. text ed. 9.00 (ISBN 92-5-102632-7, F3148/1, FAO). UNIPUB.

Report of the Council of FAO: Eighty-Eighth Session, Rome November 1985. 24p. 1986. pap. text ed. 7.50 (ISBN 92-5-102348-4, F2834, FAO). UNIPUB.

Report of the Council of FAO, Ninety-First Session, Rome, 15-26 June 1987. 100p. (Orig.). 1987. pap. text ed. 11.25 (ISBN 92-5-102597-5, F3112, FAO). UNIPUB.

Report of the Council of FAO: Ninety-Third Session, Rome, 27 November 1987. (Orig.). 1987. pap. 9.00 (ISBN 92-5-102643-2, F3171, FAO). UNIPUB.

Report of the Council of FAO, 90th Session, Rome: 17-28 November, 1986. (Illus.). 75p. (Orig.). 1987. pap. text ed. 8.75 (ISBN 92-5-102539-8, F3021, FAO). UNIPUB.

Report of the Council of Hygiene & Public Health of the Citizens' Association of New York Upon the Sanitary Condition of the City. Citizens' Association of New York Staff. LC 77-112532. (Rise of Urban America). (Illus.). 1970. Repr. of 1866 ed. 46.50 (ISBN 0-405-02443-6). Ayer Co Pubs.

Report of the Council of the Shakespeare Society to the Second Annual Meeting, 1843 see English Fairy Mythology: Illustrations of the Fairy Mythology of a Midsummer Night's Dream; with Oberon's Vision in the Midsummer Night's Dream, Illusustrated by a Comparison with Lylie's Endymion,.

Report of the County of Lanark of a Plan for Relieving Public Distress & Removing Discontent by Giving Permanent, Productive Employment to the Poor & Working Classes. Robert Owen. LC 72-2942. Repr. of 1821 ed. 29.00 (ISBN 0-404-10708-7). AMS Pr.

Report of the Crime Commission. 48.00. Ayer Co Pubs.

Report of the CSIS Congressional Study Group on Mexico. Pete Wilson & Lloyd Bentsen. (CSIS Panel Report Ser.). 1988. write for info. CSI Studies.

Report of the Debates & Proceedings of the Peace Convention Held in Washington, D.C., Feb. 1861. L. E. Chittenden. LC 70-158578. 626p. 1971. Repr. of 1864 ed. lib. bdg. 79.50 (ISBN 0-306-70190-1). Da Capo.

Report of the Debates in the Convention of California on the Formation of the State Constitution, in Sept. & Oct., 1849. John R. Browne. LC 72-9431. (Far Western Frontier Ser.). 532p. 1973. Repr. of 1850 ed. 36.50 (ISBN 0-405-04962-5). Ayer Co Pubs.

Report of the Decision of the Supreme Court of the United States & the Opinions of Judges Thereof, in the Case of Dred Scott vs. John F. A. Sanford. facsimile ed. LC 69-11323. (Law, Politics & History Ser.). 240p. 1970. Repr. of 1857 ed. lib. bdg. 29.50 (ISBN 0-306-71183-4). Da Capo.

Report of the Director General: Activities of the ILO, Report 1. (Maritime Session: No. 74). 97p. (Orig.). 1987. pap. text ed. 12.25 (ISBN 92-2-105787-9, ILO669, ILO). UNIPUB.

Report of the Director General: Activities of the ILO, 1986. 79p. (Orig.). 1987. pap. text ed. 12.25 (ISBN 92-2-105566-3, ILO612, ILO). UNIPUB.

Report of the Director-General: Appendices. International Labour Conference, 67th Session, 1981. iii, 49p. (Orig.). 1981. pap. 10.50 (ISBN 92-2-102394-X). Intl Labour Office.

Report of the Director-General. Application of ILO Standards, Report I, Pt. 2: Ninth Asian Regional Conference, Manila, December 1980. iii, 45p. (Orig.). 1980. pap. text ed. 8.75 (ISBN 92-2-102498-9). Intl Labour Office.

Report of the Director-General. Asian Development in the 1980s - Growth, Employment & Working Conditions, Report I, Pt. 1: Ninth Asian Regional Conference, Manila, December, 1980. iii, 100p. (Orig.). 1980. pap. 12.25 (ISBN 92-2-102497-0). Intl Labour Office.

Report of the Director-General: International Labour Conference, 68th Session 1982. International Labour Office Staff. 133p. (Orig.). 1982. pap. 14.00 (ISBN 92-2-102783-X). Intl Labour Office.

Report of the Director-General International Labour Conference 70th Session 1984. International Labour Office Staff. viii, 139p. (Orig.). 1984. pap. 14.00 (ISBN 92-2-103433-X). Intl Labour Office.

Report of the Director-General: International Labour Conference 71st Session 1985. 131p. 1986. pap. 14.00 (ISBN 92-2-103719-3, ILO488, ILO). UNIPUB.

Report of the Director-General on the Application of the Declaration Concerning the Policy of Apartheid in South Africa: International Labour Conference, 73rd Session, 1987. (Apartheid in South Africa Ser.). 180p. (Orig.). 1987. pap. text ed. 17.50 (ISBN 92-2-105568-X, ILO630, ILO). UNIPUB.

Report of the Director-General, Report One: Twelfth Conference of American States. 95p. 1986. pap. text ed. 12.25 (ISBN 92-2-105334-2). Intl Labour Office.

Report of the EIFAC Consultation on Eel Fishing Gear & Techniques: Hamburg, 1970. (European Inland Fisheries Advisory Commission (EIFAC): Technical Papers: No. 14). 192p. (Eng. & Fr.). 1971. pap. 12.00 (ISBN 92-5-002064-3, F757, FAO). UNIPUB.

Report of the EIFAC Working Party on Stock Enhancement. (EIFAC Technical Papers: No. 44). 49p. (Eng. & Fr.). 1985. pap. 7.50 (ISBN 92-5-002136-4, F2682, FAO). UNIPUB.

Report of the EIFAC Workshop on Fish-Farm Effluents: Silkeborg, Denmark, May 26-28, 1981. John S. Alabaster. (European Inland Fisheries Advisory Commission (EIFAC): Technical Papers: No. 41). 174p. 1982. pap. 12.00 (ISBN 92-5-101162-1, F2285, FAO). UNIPUB.

Report of the Eighteenth Conference on International Organizations for the Joint Study of Programmes. 28p. 1976. pap. 7.50 (ISBN 92-5-100037-9, F2063, FAO). UNIPUB.

Report of the Eighteenth FAO Regional Conference for Latin America & the Caribbean: Buenos Aires, 6-15 August 1984. 11p. 1985. pap. 7.50 (ISBN 92-5-102212-7, F2746 5111, FAO). UNIPUB.

Report of the Eighteenth FAO Regional Conference for the Near East, Istanbul, Turkey, March 17-21 1986) FAO Staff. 32p. (Orig.). 1987. pap. text ed. 7.5001635515x (ISBN 92-5-102468-5, F2990, FAO). UNIPUB.

Report of the Eighteenth Session of the Joint FAO-WHO Committee of Government Experts on the Code of Principles Concerning Milk & Milk Products. 1977. pap. 8.25 (ISBN 0-685-80150-0, F653, FAO). UNIPUB.

Report of the Eighth Session of the Conference. pap. 6.25 (F357, FAO). UNIPUB.

Report of the Eighth Session of the Fishery Committee for the Eastern Central Atlantic (CECAF) Lome, Tago, Sept. 1982. (Fisheries Reports: No. 282). 44p. (Eng & Fr.). 1983. pap. text ed. 7.50 (ISBN 92-5-101357-8, F2451, FAO). UNIPUB.

Report of the Eighth Session of the Indian Ocean Fishery Commission. (FAO Fisheries Report Ser.: No. 341). 24p. 1986. pap. text ed. 7.50 (ISBN 92-5-102305-0, F2831, FAO). UNIPUB.

Report of the Eighth Session of the Indian Ocean Fishery Commission Executive Committee for the Implementation of the International Indian Ocean Fishery Survey & Development Programme: Rome, 23-24 April 1979. (Fisheries Reports: No. 221). 18p. (Eng & Fr.). 1979. pap. 7.50 (ISBN 92-5-100776-4, F1828, FAO). UNIPUB.

Report of the Eleventh FAO Regional Conference for Europe. 1979. pap. 7.50 (ISBN 92-5-100726-8, F1580, FAO). UNIPUB.

Report of the Eleventh Session of the Advisory Committee of Experts on Marine Research. (FAO Fisheries Report Ser.: No. 338). 20p. (Orig.). 1986. pap. text ed. 7.50 (ISBN 92-5-102308-5, F2851, FAO). UNIPUB.

Report of the Eleventh Session of the Committee on Fisheries: Rome, 9-26 April 1977. (Fisheries Reports: No. 196). 58p. (Eng., Fr & Span.). 1977. pap. 7.50 (ISBN 92-5-100336-X, F1178, FAO). UNIPUB.

Report of the Eleventh Session of the Coordinating Working Party on Atlantic Fishery Statistics: Luxembourg, July 1982. (Fisheries Reports: No. 274). 46p. 1982. pap. 7.50 (ISBN 92-5-101257-1, F2370, FAO). UNIPUB.

Report of the Eleventh Session of the European Inland Fisheries Advisory Commission: Stavanger, Norway, 28 May - 3 June 1980. (Fisheries Reports: No. 248). 63p. (Eng. & Fr.). 1981. pap. 7.50 (ISBN 92-5-101062-5, F2181, FAO). UNIPUB.

Report of the Ellis Island Committee. Carleton H. Palmer. LC 78-145478. (American Immigration Library). 149p. 1971. Repr. of 1934 ed. lib. bdg. 12.95x (ISBN 0-89198-021-0). Ozer.

Report of the European Seminar on Evaluation of Home Economics Extension Programs. pap. 5.75 (F371, FAO). UNIPUB.

Report of the Experiments on Animal Magnetism: Proceedings of the Committee of the Medical Section of the French Royal Academy of Sciences, June 21-28, 1831. French Royal Academy of Sciences, Medical Section Committee & J. C. Colquhoun. LC 75-7371. (Perspectives in Psychical Research Ser.). 1975. Repr. of 1833 ed. 23.50x (ISBN 0-405-07022-5). Ayer Co Pubs.

Report of the Expert Committee on the Public Health Aspects of Housing, 1st, Geneva, 1961. Expert Committee on the Public Health Aspects of Housing. (Technical Report Ser: No. 225). 60p. (Eng., Fr. & Span.). 1961. pap. 1.20 (ISBN 92-4-120225-4). World Health.

Report of the Expert Consulation on the Use of Microcomputers for Processing Statistical & Biological Data. (FAO Fisheries Report: No. 381). 27p. 1987. pap. text ed. 9.00 (ISBN 92-5-002561-0, F3117, FAO). UNIPUB.

Report of the Expert Consultation on Quantitative Analysis in Fishery Industries Development. Rome, Italy, January 16-24 1975: A Review of Quantitative Methods for Marketing Management, Vol. 6. pap. 7.50 (F814, FAO). UNIPUB.

Report of the Expert Consultation on Strategies for Fisheries Development: FAO Fisheries Report, No. 295. 35p. 1983. pap. text ed. 7.50 (ISBN 92-5-101408-6, F2511, FAO). UNIPUB.

Report of the Expert Consultation on the Aquisition of Socio-Economic Information in Fisheries: (With Particular Reference to Small-Scale Fisheries) (FAO Fisheries Ser.: No. 344). 21p. (Orig.). 1986. pap. text ed. 7.50 (ISBN 92-5-102316-6, F2852, FAO). UNIPUB.

Report of the Expert Consultation on the Development of Quicker Methods of Resource Appraisal of Inland Waters, Ghana, 1975. (Fisheries Reports: No. 179). 1976. pap. 7.50 (ISBN 0-685-74521-X, F827, FAO). UNIPUB.

Report of the Expert Consultation on Training in the Fisheries Investment Project Cycle. (FAO Fisheries Report Ser.: No. 378). 13p. 1987. pap. text ed. 9.00 (ISBN 92-5-102585-1, F3097, FAO). UNIPUB.

Report of the Expert Consultation on the Regulation of Fishing Effort (Fishing Mortality) Rome, January 1983. Ed. by W. C. MacKenzie. (Fisheries Reports: No. 289). 39p. (Eng., Fr. & Span.). 1984. pap. 7.50 (ISBN 92-5-101394-2, F2488, FAO); Suppl. 1. pap. 11.50 (ISBN 92-5-002120-8, F2638); Suppl. 2. pap. 15.00 (ISBN 92-5-101493-0, F2575); Suppl. 3. pap. 19.75 (ISBN 92-5-102257-7, F2796). UNIPUB.

Report of the FAO Conference. Incl. Ninth Session. pap. 7.50 (F359). UNIPUB; Tenth Session, Rome, 1959. 1960. pap. 5.50 (ISBN 0-685-36330-9, F360). UNIPUB. FAO. UNIPUB.

Report of the FAO Council: 78th Session, Rome, November 24 - December 4, 1980. 119p. (Eng., Fr. & Span.). 1980. pap. 11.00 (ISBN 92-5-101032-3, F2136, FAO). UNIPUB.

Report of the FAO-Danida Regional Seminar on Small-Scale Water Resources Development in Africa (West) 29p. 1978. pap. 7.50 (ISBN 92-5-100449-8, F1320, FAO). UNIPUB.

Report of the FAO Desert Locust Control Committee: 19th Session, Rome, 1975. 32p. 1976. pap. 7.50 (ISBN 0-685-66347-7, F1127, FAO). UNIPUB.

Report of the FAO Expert Consultation on Fish Technology in Africa: Dar-es-Salaam, Tanzania, 11-15 Feb. 1980. (Fisheries Reports: No. 237). 23p. (Eng. & Fr.). 1981. pap. 7.50 (ISBN 92-5-100981-3, F2101, FAO). UNIPUB.

Report of the FAO Expert Consultation on Fish Technology in Africa: Casablanca, Morocco, 7-11 June 1982. (Fisheries Reports: No. 268). 24p. (Eng. & Fr.). 1982. pap. 7.50 (ISBN 92-5-101236-9, F2337, FAO). UNIPUB.

Report of the FAO Expert Consultation on Fish Technology in Africa: Lusaka, Zambia, 21-25 January 1985. (Fisheries Reports: No. 329). 20p. 1985. pap. 7.50 (ISBN 92-5-102252-6, F2765, FAO). UNIPUB.

Report of the FAO Global Survey of Pesticide Susceptibility of Stored Grain Pests. B. R. Champ & C. E. Dyte. (Plant Production & Protection Papers: No. 5). 297p. 1976. pap. 17.00 (ISBN 92-5-100022-0, F1394, FAO). UNIPUB.

Report of the FAO-ILO-WHO Joint Symposium of Industrial Feeding & Canteen Management in Europe: Rome, 1963. (Nutrition Meetings Reports: No. 36). 44p. 1965. pap. 5.75 (ISBN 0-686-92864-4, F375, FAO). UNIPUB.

Report of the FAO-LKIM Workshop on Strategic Fisheries Development & Manpower Planning in Malaysia: Kuala Lampur, Malaysia, October 1982. (Fisheries Reports: No. 286). 65p. 1984. pap. 7.50 (ISBN 92-5-101376-4, F2490, FAO). UNIPUB.

Report of the Informal Consultation on Antarctic Kill, 1974. (Fisheries Reports: No. 153). 153p. 1974. pap. 7.50 (ISBN 0-686-93980-8, F794, FAO). UNIPUB.

Report of the Intergovermental Group on Hard Fibres to the Committee on Commodity Problems. Incl. Eleventh Session. 13p. 1976. pap. 7.50 (ISBN 92-5-100074-3, F1118). UNIPUB; Thirteenth Session, Rome, 1978. 13p. 1978. pap. 7.50 (ISBN 92-5-100571-0, F1408). UNIPUB; Sixteenth Session, Salvador, Bahia, Brazil, 25-30 March 1981. 14p. (Eng., Fr. & Span.). 1981. pap. 10.00 (ISBN 92-5-101072-2, F2111). UNIPUB. FAO). UNIPUB.

Report of the Intergovernmental Group on Hard Fibres: 12th Session. 13p. 1977. pap. 7.50 (ISBN 92-5-100302-5, F1125, FAO). UNIPUB.

Report of the Intergovernmental Group on Jute, Kenaf & Allied Fibres. Incl. Twelfth Session. 17p. 1977. pap. 7.50 (ISBN 92-5-100125-1, F1121). UNIPUB; Thirteenth Session, Rome, 19-21 October 1977. 1977. pap. 7.50 (ISBN 92-5-100451-X, F1336). UNIPUB; Fourteenth Session. 1979. pap. 7.50 (ISBN 92-5-100669-5, F1533). UNIPUB; Seventeenth Session, Rome, 9-11 December 1981. 8p. pap. 7.50 (F2318). UNIPUB. FAO). UNIPUB.

Report of the Intergovernmental Group on Oilseeds, Oils, & Fats to the Committee on Commodity Problems. Incl. Tenth Session. 19p. 1976. pap. 7.50 (ISBN 0-685-68966-2, F1117). UNIPUB; Eleventh Session. (Illus.). 29p. 1978. pap. 7.50 (ISBN 0-685-20384-0, F1143). UNIPUB; Thirteenth Session. 34p. 1979. pap. 7.00 (ISBN 0-686-93098-3, F1639). UNIPUB; Fourteenth Session, Rome, April 1980. 38p. 1981. pap. 7.50 (ISBN 92-5-100937-6, F2044). UNIPUB. FAO). UNIPUB.

Report of the Intergovernmental Group on Rice to the Committee on Commodity Problems. Incl. Nineteenth Session. 1976. pap. 7.50 (ISBN 92-5-100028-X, F1129). UNIPUB; Twentieth Session. pap. 7.50 (ISBN 92-5-100301-7, F1247). UNIPUB; Twenty-First Session. 36p. 1978. pap. 7.50 (ISBN 92-5-100576-1, F1409). UNIPUB; Twenty-Third Session, Rome, 17-21 March 1980. 2nd ed. 31p. (Eng., Fr. & Span.). 1980. pap. 7.50 (ISBN 92-5-100926-0, F2043). UNIPUB; Twenty-Fourth Session, Rome, March 1981. 14p. (Eng., Fr. & Span.). 1981. pap. 7.50 (ISBN 92-5-101067-6, F2183). UNIPUB. FAO). UNIPUB.

Report of the International Civil Service Commission: 40th Session, Supplement No. 30. 87p. 9.50 (ISBN 0-317-41394-5). UN.

Report of the International Conference for the Immediate Independence of Namibia: Vienna, 7-11 July 1986. 99p. 1986. 11.00 (ISBN 92-1-100300-8, E.86.I.16). UN.

Report of the International Conference on Drug Abuse & Illicit Trafficking, Vienna, 17-26 June 1987. 143p. 1987. 17.00 (ISBN 92-1-100320-2, E. 87.I.18). UN.

Report of the International Conference on Investment in Fisheries: Rome, 1969, Vol. 1. (Fisheries Reports: No. 83,). 78p. 1970. pap. 7.50 (ISBN 0-686-93042-8, F1685, FAO). UNIPUB.

Report of the International Conference on Population, 1984: Mexico City, 6-14 August 1984. 101p. 11.00 (ISBN 92-1-151100-3, E.84.XIII.8). UN.

Report of the International Court of Justice: 40th Session, Supplement No. 4. 8p. 3.00 (ISBN 0-317-41519-0). UN.

Report of the International Law Commission on the Work of Its Thirty-Seventh Session: 40th Session, Supplement No. 10. 187p. 17.50 (ISBN 0-317-41384-8). UN.

Report of the International Narcotics Control Board for 1985: Demand & Supply of Opiates for Medical & Scientific Needs. 40p. 1986. 6.00 (ISBN 92-1-148072-8, E.85.XI.7). UN.

Report of the International Narcotics Control Board for 1986. 35p. 1987. 9.00 (ISBN 92-1-148073-6, E.86.XI.2). UN.

Report of the International Narcotics Control Board for 1987. 40p. 1987. pap. 12.00 (ISBN 92-1-148074-4, E.87.XI.3). UN.

Report of the International Narcotics Control Board on Its Work in 1974. pap. 3.50 (E.75.II.3). UN.

Report of the International Rice Commission, Working Party on Fertilizers: 3rd Meeting, Bangkok,1953. (Agricultural Development Papers: No. 39). 46p. 1953. pap. 5.75 (ISBN 0-686-92869-5, F1920, FAO). UNIPUB.

Report of the Interregional Seminar to Promote the Implementation of the International Plan of Action on Aging. 46p. 1986. pap. 7.00 (ISBN 92-1-130111-4, E.86.IV.5). UN.

Report of the IPFC Ad Hoc Committee to Review the Functions & Responsibilities of IPFC: Bagnou, 1975. (Fisheries Reports: No. 181). 21p. 1976. pap. 7.50 (ISBN 0-686-93991-3, F829, FAO). UNIPUB.

Report of the IPFC Group of Experts on the Indian Ocean. 1967. pap. 7.50 (F1670, FAO). UNIPUB.

Report of the IPFC-IOFC Ad Hoc Working Party of Scientists on Assessment of Tuna. Incl. First Session, Rome, 1972. (No. 137). 20p. 1973. pap. 7.50 (ISBN 0-686-93097-5, F783). UNIPUB; Second Session, Nates, 1974. (No. 152). 22p. 1974. pap. 7.50 (ISBN 0-686-93979-4, F793). UNIPUB. (Fisheries Reports, FAO). UNIPUB.

Report of the IPFC-IOFC Joint Working Party of Experts on Indian Ocean & Western Pacific Fishery Statistics. Incl. First Session, Bangkok. (No. 120). 14p. 1971. pap. 5.75 (ISBN 0-686-93077-0, F1703). UNIPUB; Third Session. (No. 157). (Illus.). 1976. pap. 7.50 (ISBN 0-685-74970-3, F798). UNIPUB; Fourth Session, Colombo, Sri Lanka, 1976. (No. 189). 19p. (Eng. & Fr.). 1977. pap. 7.50 (ISBN 92-5-100260-6, F837). UNIPUB. (Fisheries Reports, FAO). UNIPUB.

Report of the Joint Committee of the General Assembly Appointed to Investigate the Police Department of the City of St. Louis. Missouri Joint Committee Of The General Assembly. LC 70-154587. (Police in America Ser). 1971. Repr. of 1868 ed. 22.00 (ISBN 0-405-03384-2). Ayer Co Pubs.

Report of the Joint Committee on Reconstruction at the First Session: Proceedings. U. S. Congress. Repr. of 1866 ed. 63.00 (ISBN 0-384-62895-8). Johnson Repr.

Report of the Joint Committee on Reconstruction, 4 pts. facsimile ed. U. S. 39th Congress 1st Session. Ed. by W. P. Fessenden et al. LC 78-168523. (Black Heritage Library Collection). Repr. of 1866 ed. 37.00 (ISBN 0-8369-8875-2). Ayer Co Pubs.

Report of the Joint Committee on the Conduct of the War Upon Fort Pillow Massacre. Joint Committee on the Conduct of the War, U. S. 38th Congress. Bd. with Returned Prisoners. (House of representatives, report no. 67). (Basic Afro-American Reprint Library). (Illus.). 162p. (House of representatives, report no. 65). Repr. of 1864 ed. 17.00 (ISBN 0-384-62900-8). Johnson Repr.

Report of the Joint Committee on the Investigation of the Pearl Harbor Attack. United States, 79th Congress, 2nd Session. LC 74-166954. (FDR & the Era of the New Deal Ser.). (Illus.). 1972. Repr. of 1946 ed. lib. bdg. 59.50 (ISBN 0-306-70331-9). Da Capo.

Report of the Joint FAO-WHO Expert Committee on Nutrition: Rome, 11-20 December 1974. pap. 7.25 (F184, FAO). UNIPUB.

Report of the Joint FAO-WHO Food Standards Regional Conference for Latin America. (Codex Alimentarius Commission Reports). 1979. pap. 13.00 (ISBN 92-5-100682-2, F1618, FAO). UNIPUB.

Report of the Joint ICES-EIFAC Symposium on Eel Research & Management: Helsinki, Finland, 9-11 June 1976 (Anguilla Spp.) (European Inland Fisheries Advisory Commission (EIFAC): Technical Papers: No. 28). 49p. (Eng. & Fr.). 1976. pap. 7.50 (ISBN 92-5-000121-5, F769, FAO). UNIPUB.

Report of the Joint Meeting of the Western Central Atlantic Fishery Commission Working Party on Assessment of Fishery Resources & Working Party on Stock Assessment of Shrimp & Lobster Resources: Cartagena, Columbia, 18-23 Nov. 1977. (Fisheries Reports: No. 211). 108p. (Eng., Fr. & Span.). 1978. pap. 7.50 (ISBN 92-5-100675-X, F1543, FAO). UNIPUB.

Report of the Joint Session of the Indian Ocean Fishery Commission (7th Session) & the Indo-Pacific Fishery Commission (20th Session) (FAO Fisheries Report Ser.: No. 281, Rev. 1). 190p. 1986. pap. text ed. 12.00 (ISBN 92-5-002287-5, F2833, FAO). UNIPUB.

Report of the Joint Special Committee on Investigation of the Affairs of the Maine State Prison: Made to the Fifty-Third Legislature. facsimile ed. Maine Joint Special Committee. LC 74-3832. (Criminal Justice in America Ser.). 1974. Repr. of 1874 ed. 12.00x (ISBN 0-405-06152-8). Ayer Co Pubs.

Report of the Joint Special Committee to Investigate Chinese Immigration. U.S. Senate Joint Special Committee. Ed. by Roger Daniels. LC 78-54836. (Asian Experience in North America Ser.). 1979. Repr. of 1877 ed. lib. bdg. 85.00x (ISBN 0-405-11294-7). Ayer Co Pubs.

Report of the Kansas Judicial Study Advisory Committee: Recommendations for Improving the Kansas Judicial System. 120p. (Reprinted from Washburn Law Journal, Vol. 13, No. 2). 1974. 1.00 (ISBN 0-318-14443-3). IJA NYU.

Report of the Kingdom of Congo & of the Surroundings: Countries Drawn Out of the Writings of the Portuguese Duarte Lopez. Filippo Pigafetta. Ed. by Margarite Hutchinson. (Illus.). 174p. 1970. Repr. of 1591 ed. 34.00x (ISBN 0-7146-1847-0, F Cass Co). Biblio Dist.

Report of the Kingdome of Congo, Gathered by P. Pigafetta. Duarte Lopes. Tr. by A. Hartwell. LC 75-25675. (English Experience Ser.: No. 260). 1970. Repr. of 1597 ed. 65.00 (ISBN 90-221-0260-2). Walter J Johnson.

Report of the Land Planning Committee, Pt. 2. Land Planning Committee, U.S. National Resources Board. LC 75-26322. (World Food Supply Ser). (Illus.). 1976. Repr. of 1934 ed. 18.00x (ISBN 0-405-07798-X). Ayer Co Pubs.

Report of the Man-Made Lakes Stock Assessment Working Group: Jinji, Uganda, 1970. (Fisheries Reports: No. 87). 13p. 1970. pap. 7.50 (ISBN 0-686-93051-7, F1688, FAO). UNIPUB.

Report of the Manuscripts of Mrs. Stopford-Sackville of Drayton House, Northamptonshire, 2 vols. Great Britain Historical Manuscripts Commission. Ed. by George Billias. LC 72-8813. (American Revolutionary Ser.). Repr. of 1910 ed. Set. lib. bdg. 100.00 (ISBN 0-8398-0803-8). Irvington.

Report of the Meeting for Consultations on Underwater Noise: Rome, 1968. (Fisheries Reports: No. 76). 35p. 1970. pap. 7.50 (ISBN 0-686-93032-0, F1682, FAO). UNIPUB.

Report of the Meeting of Experts on the Mechanization of Rice Production & Processing, Paramaribo, 1971. (Illus.). 203p. (Orig.). 1973. pap. 5.75 (ISBN 0-685-32468-0, F374, FAO). UNIPUB.

Report of the Meetings on Fertilizer Production, Distribution & Utilization in Latin America: Rio de Janeiro, 1951. (Agricultural Development Papers: No. 36). 52p. 1953. pap. 5.75 (ISBN 0-686-92856-3, F1919, FAO). UNIPUB.

Report of the Miller Center Commission on Presidential Disability & the Twenty-Fifth Amendment. Miller, White Burkett, Center of Public Affairs Staff & University of Virginia Staff. 44p. (Orig.). 1988. pap. text ed. 4.75 (ISBN 0-8191-6893-9, Co-pub. by White Miller Center). U Pr of Amer.

Report of the NAEA Commission on Art Education. Ed. by NAEA Commission on Art Education. 1977. 5.00 (ISBN 0-937652-22-9). Natl Art Ed.

Report of the National Bipartisan Commission on Central America. Henry Kissinger. 132p. 1984. pap. 4.75 (ISBN 0-318-11825-4, S/N 040-000-00477-7). USGPO.

Report of the National Conservation Commission, 3 vols. Ed. by Henry Gannett. LC 72-2837. (Use & Abuse of America's Natural Resources Ser). (Illus.). 1960p. 1972. Repr. of 1909 ed. Set. 127.00, 42.00, 42.00, 43.00 (ISBN 0-405-04506-9). Vol. 1 (ISBN 0-405-04543-3). Vol. 2 (ISBN 0-405-04544-1). Vol. 3 (ISBN 0-405-04545-X). Ayer Co Pubs.

Report of the New York State Commission on Relief for Widowed Mothers. New York State Commission on Relief for Widowed Mothers. LC 74-1696. (Children & Youth Ser.: Vol. 18). 602p. 1974. Repr. of 1914 ed. 44.00x (ISBN 0-405-05973-6). Ayer Co Pubs.

Report of the Ninth FAO Regional Conference for Africa: Freetown, Sierra Leone 2-12. pap. 7.50 (ISBN 92-5-100246-0, F1113, FAO). UNIPUB.

Report of the Ninth Session of European Inland Fisheries Commission. (Fisheries Reports: No. 178). 1977. pap. 7.50 (ISBN 92-5-000120-7, F826, FAO). UNIPUB.

Report of the Ninth Session of the Advisory Committee of Experts on Marine Resources Research: Supplement No. 1, Selected Working Papers, Rome, June 5-9, 1978. 2nd ed. (Fisheries Reports: No. 206). 61p. 1979. pap. 7.50 (ISBN 92-5-100646-6, F1523, FAO). UNIPUB.

Report of the Ninth Session of the Fishery Committee for the Eastern Central Atlantic (CECAF) Banjul, the Gambia, 15-18 October 1984. (Fisheries Reports: No. 322). 46p. 1985. pap. 7.50 (ISBN 92-5-102204-6, F2760, FAO). UNIPUB.

Report of the North American Forestry Commission: 8th Session. (Illus., Orig.). 1976. pap. 7.50 (ISBN 92-5-100025-5, F1111, FAO). UNIPUB.

Report of the North Carolina Geological Survey see Bulletins of American Paleontology.

Report of the Nutrition Committee for South & East Asia: 4th Session, Tokyo, 1956. (Nutrition Meetings Reports: No. 14). 50p. 1957. pap. 5.75 (ISBN 92-5-101828-6, F361, FAO). UNIPUB.

Report of the Nutrition Committee for the Middle East: First Session. pap. 5.75 (F382, FAO). UNIPUB.

Report of the Nutrition Problems in Latin America: 4th Conference, Guatemala City, 1957. 1959. pap. 6.00 (ISBN 0-685-36327-9, F370, FAO). UNIPUB.

Report of the of the Indian Ocean Fishery Commission: 5th Session, Cohin, India, 1977. (Fisheries Reports: No. 199). 41p. (Eng. & Fr.). 1977. pap. 7.50 (ISBN 92-5-100549-4, F1420, FAO). UNIPUB.

Report of the Organization & Campaigns of the Army of the Potomac: To Which Is Added an Account of the Campaign in Western Virginia, with Plans of Battle-Fields. George B. McClellan. LC 78-109629. (Select Bibliographies Reprint Ser). 1864. 32.00 (ISBN 0-8369-5238-3). Ayer Co Pubs.

Report of the PAK-FAO Seminar on Agricultural Perspective Planning: Jan. 10-19, 1977, Islamabad. 588p. 1983. pap. 44.50 (ISBN 92-5-100334-3, F1230, FAO). UNIPUB.

Report of the Pennsylvania State Parole Commission to the Legislature, 1927 Part I, & Part Ii. facsimile ed. Parole Commission, Commonwealth of Pennsylvania. LC 74-3849. (Criminal Justice in America Ser.). 1974. Repr. of 1927 ed. 25.50x (ISBN 0-405-06163-3). Ayer Co Pubs.

Report of the Preparatory Committee for the International Conference on the Relationship Between Disarmament & Development: 40th Session, Supplement No. 51. 22p. 4.00. UN.

Report of the President's Commission on Campus Unrest: Including the Killings at Jackson State & Kent State Tragedy. LC 71-139710. 537p. 1970. 5.95 (ISBN 0-405-01712-X). Ayer Co Pubs.

Report of the President's Special Review Board. (Illus.). 294p. (Orig.). 1987. pap. 14.00 (S/N 040-000-00514-5). USGPO.

Report of the President's Special Review Board. John Tower et al. 280p. pap. 14.00 (ISBN 0-318-22669-3). USGPO.

Report of the Proceedings & Papers Read in Prince's Hall. Industrial Remuneration Conference. LC 67-30064. 1968. Repr. of 1885 ed. 49.50x (ISBN 0-678-00350-5). Kelley.

Report of the Public Lands Commission. U.S. House of Representatives, 46th Congress. LC 72-2865. (Use & Abuse of America's Natural Resources Ser). 796p. 1972. Repr. of 1880 ed. 55.00 (ISBN 0-405-04532-8). Ayer Co Pubs.

Report of the Public Lands Commission with Appendix. LC 72-2864. (Use & Abuse of America's Natural Resources Ser). 402p. 1972. Repr. of 1905 ed. 19.00 (ISBN 0-405-04531-X). Ayer Co Pubs.

Report of the Railroads Committee upon Several Petitions for Legislative Aid to the Canajoharie & Catskill Railroad. 1973. pap. 2.00 (ISBN 0-685-32729-9). Hope Farm.

Report of the Regional Conference for Asia & the Far East. Incl. Twelfth, Tokyo, Japan, 17-27 Sept. 1974. 76p. 1976. pap. 7.50 (ISBN 0-685-66334-5, F1122). UNIPUB; Third, Bandung, 1956. 94p. 1957. pap. 6.00 (ISBN 0-686-92902-0, F390). UNIPUB. FAO). UNIPUB.

Report of the Regional Conference for Latin America: 4th Session, Santiago, 1956. 89p. 1957. pap. 6.00 (ISBN 0-686-92898-9, F378, FAO). UNIPUB.

Report of the Round Tables & General Conferences at the Twelfth Session (Institute of Politics, Williams College) Ed. by John Bakeless. 1932. 75.00x (ISBN 0-686-51301-0). Elliots Bks.

Report of the Royal Commision on Capital Punishment: Presented to Parliament by Command of Her Majesty, Sept. 1953. Great Britain, Royal Commission on Capital Punishment. LC 79-25707. 505p. 1980. Repr. of 1953 ed. lib. bdg. 45.50x (ISBN 0-313-22121-9, GBCP). Greenwood.

Report of the Royal Commission of 1552. Walter C. Richardson. LC 72-86893. 1974. 16.00 (ISBN 0-937058-08-4). West Va U Pr.

Report of the Royal Commission on Capital Punishment. Royal Commission on Capital Punishment (1949-1953), Great Britain. LC 82-45646. Date not set. Repr. of 1953 ed. 57.50 (ISBN 0-404-62419-7). AMS Pr.

Report of the Royal Commission on Chinese & Japanese Immigration. Canada Royal Commission on Chinese & Japanese Immigration. Ed. by Roger Daniels. LC 78-54812. (Asian Experience in North America Ser.). 1979. Repr. of 1902 ed. lib. bdg. 30.50x (ISBN 0-405-11268-8). Ayer Co Pubs.

Report of the Royal Commission on Corporate Concentration. 1979. pap. 28.00 (ISBN 0-660-01456-4, SSC119, SSC). UNIPUB.

Report of the Royal Commission on Police Powers & Procedure. Royal Commission On Police Powers & Procedures. LC 73-156283. (Police in Great Britain Ser). 1971. Repr. of 1929 ed. 13.00 (ISBN 0-405-03394-X). Ayer Co Pubs.

Report of the Royal Commission on the Status of Women in Canada. pap. 10.20 (SSC75, SSC). UNIPUB.

Report of the Second Joint Meeting of the Working Party on Assessment of Fish Resources & the Working Party on Stock Assessment of Shrimp & Lobster Resources (WECAF) Mexico City, Mexico, 26-29 Nov. 1979. (Fisheries Reports: No. 235). 49p. (Eng. & Span.). 1981. pap. 7.50 (ISBN 92-5-101049-8, F2143, FAO). UNIPUB.

Report of the Second Meeting of the Eastern African Sub-Committee for Soil Correlation & Land Evaluation: Addis-Ababa, Ethiopia, 25-30 October 1976. East African Subcommittee for Soil Correlation & Land Evaluation. (World Soil Resources Reports: No. 47). 131p. 1978. pap. 8.50 (ISBN 92-5-100408-0, F1318, FAO). UNIPUB.

Report of the Second Session of the Commission for Island Fisheries of Latin America: Santo Domingo, Dominican Republic, December 2-4, 1981. (Fisheries Reports: No. 261). 46p. (Eng. & Span.). 1982. pap. 7.50 (ISBN 92-5-101191-5, F2309, FAO). UNIPUB.

Report of the Second Session of the Committee for the Development & Management of Fisheries in the Southwest Indian Ocean: Indian Ocean Fisheries Commission (IOFC), Make, Seychelles, Dec. 1982. (Fisheries Reports: No. 285). 56p. (Eng. & Fr.). 1983. pap. text ed. 7.50 (ISBN 92-5-101352-7, F2453, FAO). UNIPUB.

Report of the Third Session of the Standing Committee on Resources Research and Development, Indo-Pacific Fishery Committee (IPFC) (Fisheries Reports: No. 275). pap. 9.50 (ISBN 92-5-101256-3, F2354, FAO). UNIPUB.

Report of the Third Session of the Western Central Atlantic Fishery Commission: Havana, Cuba, 18-22 Nov. 1980. (Fisheries Reports: No. 246). 52p. (Eng., Fr. & Span.). 1981. pap. 7.50 (ISBN 92-5-101044-7, F2182, FAO). UNIPUB.

Report of the Third Session of the Working Party on Fishery Statistics: Paipa, Department of Boyaca, Colombia, 22-26 October 1984. 53p. (Eng., Fr. & Span.). 1985. pap. 7.50 (ISBN 92-5-002238-7, F2773, FAO). UNIPUB.

Report of the Thirteenth FAO Regional Conference for Africa: Harare, 16-29 July 1984. 26p. 1985. pap. 7.50 (ISBN 92-5-102207-0, F2733, FAO). UNIPUB.

Report of the Thirteenth FAO Regional Conference for Europe: Sofia, Bulgaria, 4-8 Oct. 1982. 33p. (Eng., Fr. & Span.). 1983. pap. text ed. 7.50 (ISBN 92-5-101334-9, F2440, FAO). UNIPUB.

Report of the Trial of James H. Peck. Arthur Joseph Stansbury. LC 70-38789. (Law, Politics & History Ser). 592p. 1972. Repr. of 1833 ed. lib. bdg. 65.00 (ISBN 0-306-70443-9). Da Capo.

Report of the Truth of the Fight about the Iles of Acores. Walter Raleigh. LC 72-26280. (English Experience Ser.: No. 183). 32p. 1969. Repr. of 1591 ed. 30.00 (ISBN 90-221-0183-5). Walter J Johnson.

Report of the Twelfth FAO Regional Conference for Africa: Algiers, Sept. 22-Oct. 2, 1982. 48p. (Eng. & Fr.). 1983. pap. text ed. 7.50 (ISBN 92-5-101316-0, F2404, FAO). UNIPUB.

Report of the Twelfth Session of the Coordinating Working Party on Atlantic Fishery Statistics: Copenhagen, Denmark, 25 July - 1 August 1984. (Fisheries Reports: No. 316). 60p. 1985. pap. 7.50 (ISBN 92-5-102156-2, F2685, FAO). UNIPUB.

Report of the Twelfth Session of the European Inland Fisheries Advisory Commission: Budapest, Hungary, May-June 1982. (Fisheries Reports: No. 267). 47p. (Eng. & Fr.). 1982. pap. 7.50 (ISBN 92-5-101250-4, F2353, FAO). UNIPUB.

Report of the Twelfth Session of the FAO: Rome, Italy, 1963. FAO Conference Staff. 1964. pap. 5.75 (ISBN 0-685-36332-5, F366, FAO). UNIPUB.

Report of the Twentieth Session of the FAO Desert Locust Control Committee. 41p. 1977. pap. 7.50 (ISBN 92-5-100191-X, F1128, FAO). UNIPUB.

Report of the Twentieth Session of the Intergovernmental Group on Grains to the Committee on Commodity Problems. 30p. 1980. pap. 6.00 (ISBN 92-5-100919-8, F1953, FAO). UNIPUB.

Report of the Twentieth Session of the United Nations-FAO Committee on Food Aid Policies & Programmes: World Food Programme, Rome, 30 September - 10 October, 1985. 79p. 1986. pap. text ed. 7.50 (ISBN 92-5-102323-9, F2838, FAO). UNIPUB.

Report of the Twenty-First Session of the FAO Desert Locust Control Committee. 41p. 1978. pap. 7.50 (ISBN 92-5-100492-7, F1344, FAO). UNIPUB.

Report of the Twenty-Second Session of the European Commission for the Control of Foot & Mouth Disease. (Illus.). 1978. pap. 9.50 (ISBN 92-5-100319-X, F1245, FAO). UNIPUB.

Report of the United Nations University Expert Group on Human & Social Development. 36p. 1980. pap. 5.00 (ISBN 92-808-0145-7, TUNU082, UNU). UNIPUB.

Report of the United Nations Water Conference. pap. 8.50 (ISBN 92-1-104107-4, E.77.II.A.12). UN.

Report of the United States & Mexican Boundry Survey, 3 vols. William H. Emory. 1987. Repr. limited ed. of 750 175.00 (ISBN 0-87611-085-5). Tex St Hist Assn.

Report of the United States Education Mission to Japan. U. S. Education Mission to Japan. LC 83-45480. 1946. 18.00 (ISBN 0-404-20270-5, LA1312). AMS Pr.

Report of the Western Central Atlantic Fishery Commission. Incl. First Session, Port of Spain, Trinidad & Tobago, 1975. (No. 172). 31p. 1976. pap. 7.50 (ISBN 0-685-66354-X, F822). UNIPUB; Second Session, Panama, May 22-26, 1978. (No. 209). 54p. (Eng., Fr. & Span.). 1978. pap. 7.50 (ISBN 92-5-100665-2, F1537). UNIPUB; Fourth Session, Managua, Nicaragua, May 1983. (No. 292). 39p. (Eng. & Span.). 1984. pap. 7.50 (ISBN 92-5-101391-8, F2498). UNIPUB. (Fisheries Reports, FAO). UNIPUB.

Report of the Working Group on the Management of Diabetes. 110p. (Orig.). 1987. pap. 11.95 (ISBN 0-11-493405-3, HM1270, Pub. by Her Maj Station Ofc). UNIPUB.

Report of the Working Party on Courses for Animal Licensees. M. W. Smith. 1984. 16.00x (Pub. by Univ Federation Animal). State Mutual Bk.

Report of the Working Party on Resources Appraisal & Fishery Statistics of the General Fisheries Council for the Mediterranean: 6th Session. (Fisheries Reports: No. 182). (Illus.). 1976. pap. 8.75 (ISBN 92-5-100027-1, F203, FAO). UNIPUB.

Report of the Working Party on the Principles for Fisheries Management in the New Ocean Regime: Advisory Committee of Experts on Marine Resources Research, Nantes, France, Mar. 14-18, 1983. (Fisheries Report: No. 299). 13p. 1984. pap. 7.50 (ISBN 92-5-101428-0, F2550, FAO). UNIPUB.

Report of the Working Party on the Promotion of Fishery Resources Research in Developing Countries: Floro, Norway, Sept. 1979 & Rome, Italy, Sept. 1980. (Fisheries Reports: No. 251). 245p. 1981. pap. 17.00 (F2226, FAO). UNIPUB.

Report of the Workshop on Aquaculture Planning in the SADCC Countries. Ed. by Andre G. Coche & Francois Demoulin. (CIFA Technical Paper: No. 15). 22p. (Orig.). 1986. pap. text ed. 7.50 (ISBN 92-5-102394-8, F2927, FAO). UNIPUB.

Report of the Workshop on Fisheries Development Planning in the WECAFC Region: Castries, St. Lucia, 15-16 July, 1985. (FAO Fisheries Report: No. 359). 22p. (Orig., Eng., Fr. & Span.). 1986. pap. text ed. 7.50 (ISBN 92-5-002425-8, F2945, FAO). UNIPUB.

Report of the Workshop on the Phenomenon Known as "El Nino" Ecuador, 1974. (Fisheries Reports: No. 163). 24p. 1975. pap. 7.50 (ISBN 0-686-93985-9, F806, FAO). UNIPUB.

Report of the World Assembly on Aging: Vienna, 26 July to 6 August 1982. 101p. 1983. pap. 9.00 (ISBN 92-1-100200-1, E.82.I.16). UN.

Report of the World Conference on Sanctions Against Racist South Africa: Paris, June 16-20, 1986. 79p. pap. 11.00 (ISBN 92-1-100305-9, E.86.I.23). UN.

Report of the World Food Congress: 2nd, The Hague, 1970, Vol. 2. (Illus.). 141p. (Orig.). 1971. pap. 13.75 (ISBN 0-685-02921-2, F379, FAO). UNIPUB.

Report of the 10th Regional Conference for Europe: Bucharest, Romania 20-25 Sept., 1976. pap. 7.50 (F1116, FAO). UNIPUB.

Report of the 11th Regional Conference for Africa. pap. 7.50 (ISBN 92-5-100996-1, F2098, FAO). UNIPUB.

Report of the 14th Session of the European Inland Fisheries Advisory Commission, Bordeaux France, May 27-June 3 1986. (FAO Fisheries Report Ser.: No. 364). (Illus.). 71p. (Orig.). 1987. pap. text ed. 7.50 (ISBN 92-5-102229-1, F2986, FAO). UNIPUB.

Report of the 15th FAO Regional Conference for Europe: Istanbul, Turkey 28 April - 2 May 1986. 25p. (Orig.). 1987. pap. text ed. 7.50 (ISBN 92-5-102491-X, F3000, FAO). UNIPUB.

Report of the 18th FAO Regional Conference for Asia & the Pacific: Rome 8-17 July 1986. 50p. (Orig.). 1987. pap. 7.50 (ISBN 0-317-57584-8, F2994, FAO). UNIPUB.

Report of the 1960 World Census of Agriculture: Census Results by Countries. Vol. 1, pt. A. pap. 9.50 (F388, FAO); Vol. 1, pt. B. pap. 18.75 (F391); Vol. 1, pt. C. pap. 34.50 (F394). UNIPUB.

Report of the 26th Session of the European Commission for the Control of Foot & Mouth Disease: Rome, April 23-36, 1985. (Illus.). 100p. (Orig.). 1986. pap. text ed. 7.50 (ISBN 0-317-46068-4, F2837, FAO). UNIPUB.

Report of the 4th Session of the Committee for the Development & Management of Fisheries in the Bay of Bengal & Tenth Meeting of the Advisory Committee for the Development of Small-Scale Fisheries of the Bengal Programme. (FAO Fisheries Report Ser.: No. 363). 26p. (Orig.). 1986. pap. text ed. 7.50 (ISBN 92-5-102453-7, F2969, FAO). UNIPUB.

Report of U. S. Select Commission on Immigration & Refugee Policy: A Critical Analysis. Pref. by Wayne A. Cornelius & Ricardo Anzaldua. (Research Report Ser.: No. 32). 34p. (Orig.). 1983. pap. 5.00 (ISBN 0-935391-31-2, RR-32). Ctr Mex Studies.

Report of Wenamum. Hans Goedicke. LC 74-6823. (Johns Hopkins Near Eastern Studies). pap. 50.00 (ISBN 0-317-41825-4, 2025625). Bks Demand UMI.

Report of Working Party on Crop & Livestock Insurance: Bangkok, 1956. 44p. 1957. pap. 5.75 (ISBN 0-686-93273-0, F389, FAO). UNIPUB.

Report of 16th Session of Joint FAO-WHO Committee of Government Experts on the Code of Principles Concerning Milk & Milk Products. pap. 7.50 (ISBN 92-5-100531-1, F2110, FAO). UNIPUB.

Report of 4th Meeting of the International Rice Commission's Working Party on Fertilizers. 1954. pap. 5.75 (F1921, FAO). UNIPUB.

Report on a Further Study of Current Developments in Office Automation. Tom Wilson. (British Library Reseach Paper: N0. 12). 1987. pap. 7.50 (ISBN 0-7123-3102-6, Pub. by British Lib). Longwood Pub Group.

Report on a Journey to Riyadh (1865) Lewis Pelly. (Arabia Past & Present Ser.: Vol. 6). (Illus.). 1978. Repr. 21.00 (ISBN 0-902675-64-8). Oleander Pr.

Report on a Melanau Sago Producing Community in Sarawak. H. S. Morris. (Illus.). vi, 184p. Repr. of 1953 ed. 32.00 (ISBN 0-384-40158-9). Johnson Repr.

Report on a National Study of Parental Leaves. 1986. 30.00 (ISBN 0-89584-153-3). Catalyst.

Report on a Negotiation: Helsinki-Geneva-Helsinki Nineteen Seventy-Two to Nineteen Seventy-Five. Ed. by Luigi V. Ferraris. Tr. by Marie-Claire Barber from Ital. (Collections De Relations Internationales Ser.). 439p. 1980. 46.00x (ISBN 9-0286-0779-X, Pub. by Sijthoff & Noordhoff). Kluwer Academic.

Report on a Workshop on Multilingual Systems. Verina Horsnell. (R&D Report 5265). 40p. (Orig.). 1976. pap. 8.25 (ISBN 0-85350-137-8, Pub. by British Lib). Longwood Pub Group.

Report on a Workshop on Technology Choices, Work & Society's Future. Ed. by Aspen Institute Staff. 136p. (Orig.). 1979. pap. text ed. 8.00 (ISBN 0-8191-5836-4, Pub. by Aspen Inst for Humanistic Studies). U Pr of Amer.

Report on Afghanistan. Kuldip Nayar. 1981. 12.00x (ISBN 0-8364-0690-7, Pub. by Allied India). South Asia Bks.

Report on Afghanistan. Kuldip Nayyar. 212p. 1980. 15.95. Asia Bk Corp.

Report on American Manuscripts in the Royal Institution of Great Britain, 4 vols. Great Britain Historical Manuscripts Commission. Ed. by George Billias. LC 72-8703. (American Revolutionary Ser.). 1979. Repr. of 1909 ed. Set. lib. bdg. 200.00 (ISBN 0-8398-0801-1). Irvington.

Report on an Analysis of the Office of Pipeline Safety Annual Report Data for the Natural Gas Distribution Companies 1970-1975. John F. Kiefner et al. 83p. 1977. pap. 2.00 (ISBN 0-318-12690-7, X50577). Am Gas Assn.

Report on an Income Tax in Texas. Melvin Greenhut. Ed. by Svetozar Pejovich & Henry Dethloff. (Public Issues Ser.: No. 21). 1986. pap. 2.00 (ISBN 0-86599-057-3). Ctr Educ Res.

Report on an Investigation of the Feasibility of Establishing a National Civil Engineering Software Center to the American Society of Civil Engineers for the Research Council on Computer Practices. Kenneth Medearis. LC 79-302366. pap. 32.00 (ISBN 0-317-20732-6, 2023822). Bks Demand UMI.

Report on Archaeological Work at Suwannet eth-Thaniya, Tananir, & Khirbet Minha. Ed. by George M. Landes. LC 75-30540. (American Schools of Oriental Research, Supplement Ser.: Vol. 21). 117p. text ed. 13.50 (ISBN 0-89757-317-X, Am Sch Orient Res); pap. text ed. 10.00 (ISBN 0-89757-321-8). Eisenbrauns.

Report on Atlantic Fishery Statistics: Coordinating Working Party, 8th Session. (Fisheries Reports: No. 156). (Illus.). 39p. 1976. pap. 7.50 (ISBN 0-685-74969-X, F797, FAO). UNIPUB.

Report on Available Standard Samples, Reference Samples, & High-Purity Materials for Spectrochemical Analysis - DS 2. 156p. 1963. pap. 4.50 (05-002000-39). ASTM.

Report on Bengal. Famine Inquiry Commission of India. LC 75-26302. (World Food Supply Ser). 1976. Repr. of 1945 ed. 20.00x (ISBN 0-405-07781-5). Ayer Co Pubs.

Report on Blacklisting: Part One, the Movies. John Cogley. LC 79-169349. (Arno Press Cinema Program). 326p. 1972. Repr. of 1956 ed. 24.50 (ISBN 0-405-03915-8). Ayer Co Pubs.

Report on Brunei in Nineteen Hundred Four. M. S. McArthur. (CIS Southeast Asia Ser.: No. 74). 216p. 1986. pap. text ed. 13.50x (ISBN 0-89680-135-7, Ohio U Ctr Intl). Ohio U Pr.

Report on Cameras in the Courtroom: Courts, Lawyers & the Adminstration of Justice Section. 10.00 (ISBN 0-317-62689-2). DC Bar Assn.

Report on Codes of Practice for Fish & Fishery Products: Ad Hoc Consultation, 2nd, Rome, 1969. (Fisheries Reports: No. 73). 6p. 1969. pap. 7.50 (ISBN 0-686-93029-0, F1680, FAO). UNIPUB.

Report on Computer Crime. Criminal Justice Section. 69p. 1984. pap. 5.00. Amer Bar Assn.

Report on Cooperation in American Export Trade. U. S. Federal Trade Commission. LC 82-48327. (World Economy Ser.). 984p. 1982. lib. bdg. 121.00 (ISBN 0-8240-5382-6). Garland Pub.

Report on County Consolidation in South Dakota with Special Reference to Buffalo & Jerauld Counties. W. O. Farber & William H. Cape. 1968. 5.00 (ISBN 1-55614-107-6). U of SD Gov Res Bur.

Report on Credit for Artisanal Fishermen in Southeast Asia. (Fisheries Reports: No. 122). 67p. 1972. pap. 7.50 (ISBN 0-686-93018-5, F1705, FAO). UNIPUB.

Report on Diesel & Gas Engines Power Costs, 1974: Data for 1972 & Previous Years. American Society of Mechanical Engineers Staff. pap. 20.00 (ISBN 0-317-08172-1, 2013318). Bks Demand UMI.

Report on Domestic & International Loan Charge-offs, 1985. Ed. by Marlene Granitz. (Illus.). 40p. 1986. pap. text ed. 18.00 (ISBN 0-936742-34-8). Robt Morris Assocs.

Report on Drug Abuse & Alcoholism, 1982. Joseph A. Califano, Jr. (Illus.). 312p. (Orig.). pap. 3.95 (ISBN 0-446-30625-8). Warner Bks.

Report on Economic Conditions of the South: FDR & the Era of the New Deal. U. S. Emergency Council. LC 70-172009. 1972. Repr. lib. bdg. 15.00 (ISBN 0-306-70438-2). Da Capo.

Report on Education. Edward Seguin. LC 76-39942. (History of Psychology Ser.). 1976. Repr. of 1880 ed. 35.00x (ISBN 0-8201-1282-8). Schol Facsimiles.

Report on Effective Psychotherapy: Legislative Testimony. Roberta Russell. Ed. by Suzanne Smith. LC 81-90112. 81p. 1981. 30.00x (ISBN 0-940106-00-0). Latin Assoc.

Report on Elevated-Temperature Properties of Selected Superalloys, DS7-S1. 1968. pap. 11.00 (ISBN 0-8031-0814-1, 05-007001-40). ASTM.

Report on Equal Employment Opportunity & Affirmative Action, 1980: The Roots Grow Deeper. Geraldine Leshin. 526p. 1980. pap. text ed. 10.00 (ISBN 0-89215-110-2). U Cal LA Indus Rel.

Report on Equipment Availability for the Ten-Year Period, 1967-1976. 50p. 1977. 18.75 (ISBN 0-317-34109-X, 047764). Edison Electric.

Report on Fish Toxicity Testing Procedures: Prepared by the EIFAC Working Party on Toxicity Testing Procedures. (European Inland Fisheries Advisory Commission (EIFAC): Technical Papers: No. 24). (Eng. & Fr.). 1975. pap. 7.50 (ISBN 92-5-102076-0, F765, FAO). UNIPUB.

Report on Fisheries: Committee on Fisheries, Rome, 1967. 2nd ed. (Fisheries Reports: No. 46). 44p. 1967. pap. 7.50 (ISBN 0-686-93005-3, F1666, FAO). UNIPUB.

Report on Fisheries: Committee on Fisheries, 10th Session, Rome, 1975. (Fisheries Reports: No. 162). 45p. 1975. pap. 7.50 (ISBN 0-686-93983-2, F805, FAO). UNIPUB.

Report on Fisheries: Committee on Fisheries, 9th Session, Rome, October 15-22, 1974. (Fisheries Reports: No. 154). 39p. 1976. pap. 7.50 (ISBN 0-685-68359-1, F795, FAO). UNIPUB.

Report on Fisheries Education Problems in the Near East Region. (Fisheries Reports: No. 48). pap. 5.75 (F1668, FAO). UNIPUB.

Report on Fisheries Legislation & Administration in the United Kingdom (England & Wales) (Fisheries Reports: No. 98). 33p. 1971. pap. 5.75 (ISBN 0-686-93039-8, F1692, FAO). UNIPUB.

Report on Fisheries: 5th Session, Committee on Fisheries, Rome, 1970. (Fisheries Reports: No. 86). 44p. 1970. pap. 7.50 (ISBN 0-686-93050-9, F1687, FAO). UNIPUB.

Report on Fisheries: 6th Session, Committee on Fisheries, Rome, 1971. (Fisheries Reports: No. 103). 50p. 1971. pap. 7.50 (ISBN 0-686-93054-1, F1694, FAO). UNIPUB.

Report on Fisheries: 8th Session, Committee on Fisheries, Rome, 1973. (Fisheries Reports: No. 135). 47p. 1973. pap. 5.75 (ISBN 0-686-93094-0, F1711, FAO). UNIPUB.

Report on Fishery Administration & Services: Conference, Rome, 1966, 3 vols. (Fisheries Reports: No. 43, Vols. 1-3). 1967. Vol. 1, 169p. pap. 11.25 (ISBN 0-686-92992-6, F1661, FAO); Vol. 2, 310p. pap. 19.50 (ISBN 0-686-98836-1, F1662). UNIPUB.

Report on Fishery Statistics in the North Atlantic Area: Continuing Working Party on Fishery Statistics, 5th Session, 1967. (Fisheries Reports: No. 45). 33p. 1967. pap. 7.50 (ISBN 0-686-93002-9, F1665, FAO). UNIPUB.

Report on Fishing for Squid & Other Cephalopods: Expert Consultation on Fishing, Tokyo & Hakodat, Japan, 1975. (Fisheries Reports: No. 170). 11p. 1976. pap. 7.50 (ISBN 0-685-66350-7, F817, FAO). UNIPUB.

Report on Forest Research Nineteen Eighty-Seven. 108p. (Orig.). 1987. pap. text ed. 20.00 (ISBN 0-11-710255-5, HM1480, Pub. by Her Maj Station Ofc). UNIPUB.

Report on Forestry Education: Advisory Commission, 9th Session, Jakarta, 1978. (Forestry Papers: No. 48). 139p. 1979. pap. 9.50 (ISBN 92-5-100772-1, F1848, FAO). UNIPUB.

Report on Government Procurement Practices. LC 87-92178. 144p. 1988. 13.95 (ISBN 0-9606848-2-4). Fishner Bks.

Report on Highway & Bridge Surveys. (Manual & Report on Engineering Practice Ser.: No. 44). 159p. 1962. pap. 9.60 (ISBN 0-87262-219-3). Am Soc Civil Eng.

Report on Human Rights in Chile. 1986. 5.00. Natl Lawyers Guild.

Report on Human Rights in Chile: February, March, April 1985. Comision Chilena de Derechos Humanos Staff & Lawyers Committee for Human Rights, U. S. Staff. LC 86-157400. 28p. Date not set. price not set. Lawyers Comm Human.

Report on Human Rights in Chile, May-July 1985 from the Chilean Commission on Human Rights. LC 87-101315. 32p. Date not set. price not set (Pub. by America's Watch). Fund Free Expression.

Report on Human Rights in El Salvador, January 26, 1982. Americas Watch Staff & American Civil Liberties Union Staff. 312p. 1982. pap. 3.95 (ISBN 0-394-71141-6, Vin). Random.

Report on Indian Constitutional Reforms. 243p. 1985. Repr. of 1918 ed. text ed. 40.00x (ISBN 0-86590-707-2, Pub. by Daya Pub Hse India). Apt Bks.

Report on India's Food Crisis & Steps to Meet It. Agricultural Production Team Staff. LC 75-26294. (World Food Supply Ser). 1976. Repr. of 1959 ed. 21.00x (ISBN 0-405-07767-X). Ayer Co Pubs.

Report on the Situation of Human Rights in Paraguay-Informe Sobre la Situacion De los Derechos Humanos En Paraguay. (Eng. & Span.). 1978. pap. 3.00 Eng. ed. (ISBN 0-8270-2595-5); pap. 3.00 Span. ed. (ISBN 0-8270-2565-3). OAS.

Report on the Situation of Human Rights in the Republic of Bolivia. OAS General Secretariat Inter-American Commision of Human Rights. 117p. (Span.). 1981. pap. 5.00. OAS.

Report on the Situation of Human Rights in the Republic of Guatemala. OAS General Secretariat Inter-American Commission of Human Rights. (OAS Ser. L V II.53: Doc. 21, Rev. 3). 133p. (Span.). 1981. pap. 6.00 (ISBN 0-8270-1428-7). OAS.

Report on the Situation of Human Rights in the Republic of Colombia. OAS General Secretariat Inter-American Commmission of Human Rights. 222p. (Span.). 1981. pap. 8.00 (ISBN 0-8270-1374-4). OAS.

Report on the Situation of Human Rights in the Republic of Nicaragua. OAS General Secretariat Inter-American Commission of Human Rights. 171p. (Span.). 1981. pap. 7.00 (ISBN 0-8270-1373-6). OAS.

Report on the Situation of Human Rights in Uruguay-Informe Sobre la Situacion de los Derechos Humanos en Uruguay. 1978. Eng. & Span eds. 3.00 ea. (ISBN 0-685-67897-0); Eng. Ed. pap. 3.00 Span. ed. (ISBN 0-8270-2585-8). Span Ed (ISBN 0-8270-2570-X). OAS.

Report on the Social Statistics of Cities. George E. Waring & United States Census Office 10th Census, 1880 Census Reports Vols. 18-19 1970. 1970. 80.50 (18805). Ayer Co Pubs.

Report on the Social Statistics of Cities, 2vols. George E. Waring, Jr. Incl. New England & the Middle States. Vol. 1 (ISBN 0-405-02482-7); Southern of the Western States. Vol. 2 (ISBN 0-405-02483-5). LC 70-112577. (Rise of Urban America Ser). (Illus). 1970. Repr. of 1886 ed. Set. 161.00 (ISBN 0-405-02481-9). Ayer Co Pubs.

Report on the Steel Plate Sector. 144p. (Orig.). 1982. pap. 8.50x (ISBN 92-64-12261-3). OECD.

Report on the Steel Strike of 1919. Interchurch World Movement. LC 73-139200. (Civil Liberties in American History Ser). (Illus.). 1971. Repr. of 1920 ed. lib. bdg. 37.50 (ISBN 0-306-70081-6). Da Capo.

Report on the Stoney Corals from the Red Sea. Scheer Georg & Gopinadha Pillai. (Zoologica Ser.: Heft 133). 198p. 1983. pap. text ed. 175.00x (ISBN 3-510-55019-6). Lubrecht & Cramer.

Report on the Study of EDP-Related Fraud in the Banking & Insurance Industry. 27p. 1984. 3.50 (ISBN 0-317-37104-5). Am Inst CPA.

Report on the Swanscombe Skull see Swanscombe Skull.

Report on the "The Star Spangled Banner". Oscar G. Sonneck. LC 75-145993. 1972. pap. 4.50 (ISBN 0-486-22237-3). Dover.

Report on the Theory of Numbers. Henry J. Smith. LC 64-8080. 1966. 15.95 (ISBN 0-8284-0186-1). Chelsea Pub.

Report on the Trial...Against the Directors & the Manager of the City of Glasgow Bank. Charles T. Couper. LC 83-49106. (Accounting History & the Development of a Profession Ser.). 467p. 1984. lib. bdg. 60.00 (ISBN 0-8240-6320-1). Garland Pub.

Report on the UNESCO La Breviere Seminar on Workers. Ed. by G. D. Cole & Andre Philip. (UNESCO Education Studies & Documents: No. 1). pap. 16.00 (ISBN 0-8115-1325-4). Kraus Repr.

Report on the United Nations Conference on New & Renewable Sources of Energy, Nairobi, 10-21 August 1981. 126p. 1981. pap. 11.00 (ISBN 92-1-100204-4, E.81.I.24). UN.

Report on the U. S. & the U. N. A Balance Sheet. U. N. Assessment Project. 62p. 1984. pap. 4.00. Heritage Found.

Report on the United States-Japan Trade Law Conference: Proceedings of the Federal BAr Association, Conference, June 1979. Federal Bar Association Staff. 197p. 35.00 (ISBN 0-318-14090-X). Federal Bar.

Report on the West Coast Women's Studies Conference. Ed. by Women's Studies Committee & Joan H. Wilson. 1974. pap. 5.00 (ISBN 0-912786-35-3). Know Inc.

Report on the Withdrawal by the United States of a Tariff Concession under Article 19 of the General Agreement on Tariffs & Trade. pap. 5.00 (G63, GATT). UNIPUB.

Report on the Work of the Prison Department 1986-87. 90p. (Orig.). 1987. pap. text ed. 35.00 (ISBN 0-10-102462-2, HM1442, Pub. by Her Maj Station Ofc). UNIPUB.

Report on the World Food Program. FAO Executive Director Staff. 1965. pap. 5.75 (ISBN 0-685-36329-5, F397, FAO). UNIPUB.

Report on the 11th Session of the FAO Conference: Rome, Italy, 1961. FAO Conference Staff. 1962. pap. 5.75 (ISBN 0-685-36331-7, F358, FAO). UNIPUB.

Report on the 1931 Powell Mound Excavations, Madison County, Illinois. Steven R. Ahler & Peter J. DePuydt. (Reports of Investigations: No. 43). (Illus.). 1987. pap. 5.00 (ISBN 0-89792-111-9). Ill St Museum.

Report on the 1950 World Census of Agriculture. (Census Bulletins: Vol. 2). 168p. 1958. pap. 9.50 (ISBN 0-686-93071-1, F1929, FAO). UNIPUB.

Report on the 1960 World Census of Agriculture: Analysis & International Comparison of Census, Vol. 5. 239p. 1971. pap. 17.50 (ISBN 92-5-101730-1, F395. FAO). UNIPUB.

Report on the 1960 World Census of Agriculture: Methodology, Vol. 3. 414p. 1969. pap. 23.50 (ISBN 92-5-101728-X, F392, FAO). UNIPUB.

Report on the 1960 World Census of Agriculture: Processing & Tabulation, Vol. 4. 147p. 1968. pap. 10.00 (ISBN 92-5-101729-8, F396, FAO). UNIPUB.

Report on the 1960 World Census of Agriculture: Programme, Concepts & Scope, Vol. 2. 186p. 1969. pap. 21.25 (ISBN 92-5-101727-1, F393, FAO). UNIPUB.

Report on the 1970 World Census of Agriculture - Jordan. (Census Bulletins: No. 23). 1979. pap. 7.50 (ISBN 0-685-96684-4, F1563, FAO). UNIPUB.

Report on the 1970 World Census of Agriculture. (Statistics Ser.: No 10). (Illus.). 1977. pap. 25.00 (ISBN 92-5-100427-7, F1444, FAO). UNIPUB.

Report on the 1970 World Census of Agriculture. Incl. Botswana, Surinam. (No. 1, o. p.). 1973 (F1051). UNIPUB; Japan, Malta. (No. 2, o. p.). 1973 (F1052). UNIPUB; Czechoslovakia, Luxembourg. (No. 3, o.p.). 1973 (F1053). UNIPUB; Canada, Sweden. (No. 4, o. p.). 1973 (F1054). UNIPUB; Fiji, Norway, Portugal. (No. 5, o. p.). 1974 (F1055). UNIPUB; American Samoa, Guam, Pacific Islands (Trust Territory), Puerto Rico, Virgin Islands (U. S.) (No. 6, o. p.). 1974 (F1056). UNIPUB; Finland, U. S. A. (No. 7, o. p.). 1974 (F1057). UNIPUB; Ghana, Iraq, Uruguay. (No. 8, o. p.). 1974 (F1058). UNIPUB; France, Lesotho, Malawi. (No. 9, o. p.). 1975 (F1059). UNIPUB; Costa Rica, Korea, Republic of Swaziland. (No. 10, o. p.). 1975 (F1060). UNIPUB; New Zealand, Zambia. (No. 11, o. p.). 1975 (F1061). UNIPUB; Greece, Jamaica. (No. 13). 1976 (F1079). UNIPUB; Denmark, Netherlands, Switzerland. (No. 14). 1976 (F1080). UNIPUB; Bahrain, Italy, Peru. (No. 16, o. p.). 1977 (F1274). UNIPUB; Saudi Arabia, Yugoslavia. (No. 17). 1977 (F1273). UNIPUB. (Census Bulletin Ser.). pap. 7.50 ea. (FAO). UNIPUB.

Report on the 1970 World Census of Agriculture: Results by Countries. (Census Bulletins: No. 19). 50p. 1979. pap. 9.50 (ISBN 0-686-59471-1, F1493, FAO). UNIPUB.

Report on Theosophical Society. Society for Psychical Report. LC 75-36920. (Occult Ser.). (Illus.). 1976. 26.50x (ISBN 0-405-07975-3). Ayer Co Pubs.

Report on Title XX Social Services Block Grant Expenditures: July 1, 1981-June 30, 1982. Illinois Office of the Governor. LC 84-620983. Date not set. price not set. Illinois Governor.

Report on Trade Conditions in China. Harry Burrill & Raymond F. Crist. LC 78-74353. (Modern Chinese Economy Ser.). 130p. 1980. lib. bdg. 20.00 (ISBN 0-8240-4265-4). Garland Pub.

Report on United States Catholic Schools, 1972-73. 98p. 1973. 2.40 (ISBN 0-686-29263-4). Natl Cath Educ.

Report on University Adult Education in Australia & New Zealand. P. Sheats. 1967. 2.50 (ISBN 0-8156-7013-3, NES 27). Syracuse U Cont Ed.

Report on Unpublished Opinions of the California Courts of Appeal. National Center for State Courts Staff. 23p. 1976. manuscript 1.38 (MAB-106). Natl Ctr St Courts.

Report Prepared for the Sixth International Conference of Labour Statisticians: Montreal, 4 to 12 August, 1948. Incl. Pt. I. Employment, Unemployment & Labor Force Statistics, a Study of Methods. 1948; Pt. II. Cost-of-Living Statistics, Methods & Techniques of the Post-War Period. 1947; Pt. III. Methods of Statistics of Industrial Injuries. 1947; Final Report: The Sixth International Conference of Labour Statisticians, Montreal, 4-12 August, 1948. (I.L.O. Studies & Reports New Ser.: No. 7). Repr. of 1947 ed. 51.00 (ISBN 0-8115-3332-8). Kraus Repr.

Report Presented 1909 see Study of Sensory Control in the Rat.

Report Series Code Dictionary. 3rd ed. Ed. by Eleanor J. Aronson & Asta V. Kane. 647p. 1986. 175.00x (ISBN 0-8103-2147-5). Gale.

Report: Submitted to the Supreme Commander for the Allied Powers, Tokyo, March 30, 1946. United States. Education Mission to Japan Staff. LC 76-48977. (U. S. Dept. of State, Pub. 2579 Far Eastern Ser.: No. 11). 1977. Repr. of 1946 ed. lib. bdg. 35.00x (ISBN 0-8371-9331-1, USRU). Greenwood.

Report That Dr. Miguel Ramos de Arizpe, Priest of Borbon, & Deputy in the Present General & Special Cortes of Spain for the Province of Coahuila, One of the Four Eastern Interior Provinces of the Kingdom of Mexico, Presents to the August Congress. Miguel Ramos-Arizpe. Tr. & intro. by Nettie L. Benson. LC 69-19011. xiii, 61p. 1970. Repr. of 1950 ed. lib. bdg. 35.00 (ISBN 0-8371-1036-X, TLRR). Greenwood.

Report to Congress & the Secretary by the Task Force on Long-Term Health Care Policies. Daniel P. Bourque. LC 87-2170. (DHHS Publication HCFA). 340p. 1987. pap. 18.00 (ISBN 0-318-23757-1, 017-060-00202-6). USGPO.

Report to Congress: Civil Rights Attorneys Fees Awards Act of 1976. 56p. 1984. 10.00 (ISBN 0-318-17613-0). Natl Attys General.

Report to Greco. Nikos Kazantzakis. 1975. pap. 10.75 (ISBN 0-671-22027-6, Touchstone Bks). S&S.

Report to Honorable Vivian Sue Shields, Superior Court Judge, Hamilton County, Indiana. 36p. 1986. manuscript 2.16 (ISBN 0-317-59196-7, MAB-103). Natl Ctr St Courts.

Report to the Attorney General: Department of Law Reorganization Study. 326p. 1979. 23.00 (ISBN 0-318-14444-1). IJA NYU.

Report to the California Judicial Council on Ways to Improve Trial Jury Selection & Management. National Center for State Courts Staff. 362p. (On loan through the NCSC Library). 1978. pap. write for info. (WRO-063). Natl Ctr St Courts.

Report to the California Judicial Council on Ways to Improve Trial Jury Selection & Management: Executive Summary. National Center for State Courts Staff. 35p. (On loan through the NCSC Library). 1978. pap. write for info. (WRO-064). Natl Ctr St Courts.

Report to the Committee of the City Council Appointed to Obtain the Census of Boston for the Year 1845. Lemuel Shattuck. LC 75-17243. (Social Problems & Social Policy Ser.). (Illus.). 1976. Repr. of 1846 ed. 23.50x (ISBN 0-405-07514-6). Ayer Co Pubs.

Report to the Congress on the Strategic Defense Initiative, April 1987. 3rd ed. (Illus.). 270p. 1987. pap. 13.00 (ISBN 0-318-22936-6, S/N 008-000-00480-3). USGPO.

Report to the Dade County Grand Jury Regarding Guardianship. W. Schmidt. 1982. write for info. FSU CSP.

Report to the Governor the Committee to Study P.R's Finances see Informe al Gobernador del Comite Para el Estudio de las Finanzas de Puerto Rico (Informe Tobin).

Report to the House of Delegates of the Nebraska State Bar Association from the Special Committee to Study the Nebraska Court System. National Center for State Courts Staff. 175p. (On loan through the NCSC Library). 1978. write for info. (NCRO-068). Natl Ctr St Courts.

Report to the King: Colonel Juan Camargo y Cavallero's Account of New Spain, 1815. John S. Leiby. (American University Studies IX: Vol. 3). 227p. (Orig.). 1984. pap. text ed. 22.70 (ISBN 0-8204-0050-5). P Lang Pubs.

Report to the Nation on Crime & Justice. 2nd ed. (NCJ-105506 Ser.). (Illus.). 138p. (Orig.). 1988. pap. 8.50 (S/N 027-000-01295-7). USGPO.

Report to the President for Transmittal to the Congress. U.S. Commission on Intergovernmental Relations. LC 77-74962. (American Federalism-the Urban Dimension). (Illus.). 1978. Repr. of 1955 ed. lib. bdg. 26.50x (ISBN 0-405-10505-3). Ayer Co Pubs.

Report to the Secretary of War of the United States, on Indian Affairs. Jedidiah Morse. LC 68-27675. (Illus.). 1970. Repr. of 1822 ed. 45.00x (ISBN 0-678-00548-6). Kelley.

Report to the Secretary of War of the U. S. on Indian Affairs. Jedidiah Morse. LC 70-108516. (Illus.). 400p. 1972. Repr. of 1822 ed. 25.00x (ISBN 0-403-00345-8). Scholarly.

Report to the Secretary on the Homeless & Emergency Shelters. 67p. 1984. 6.25 (37,514). NCLS Inc.

Report to the Stockholders & Other Poems. 3rd ed. John Beecher. LC 62-6046. (Illus.). 1971. 5.00 (ISBN 0-911234-02-0). Red Mtn.

Report: Under Chapter Sixty-Two of the Resolves of 1935. facsimile ed. Special Commission on Investigation of the Judicial System, Commonwealth of Massachusetts. LC 74-3833. (Criminal Justice in America Ser.). 1974. Repr. of 1936 ed. 14.00x (ISBN 0-405-06153-6). Ayer Co Pubs.

Report upon Pile-Structures in Naaman's Creek, Near Claymont, Delaware. H. T. Cresson. (Harvard University Peabody Museum of Archaeology & Ethnology Papers Ser: HU. PMP Vol. 1, No. 4). pap. 14.00 (ISBN 0-527-01186-X). Kraus Repr.

Report upon the Colorado River of the West. Joseph C. Ives. LC 69-18459. (American Scene Ser). (Illus.). 1969. Repr. of 1861 ed. lib. bdg. 52.50 (ISBN 0-686-85847-6). Da Capo.

Report Upon the Illegal Practices of the United States Department of Justice. R. G. Brown et al. LC 73-90206. (Mass Violence in America Ser). Repr. of 1920 ed. 14.00 (ISBN 0-405-01301-9). Ayer Co Pubs.

Report... Upon the Settlement of the Revenues of Excise & Customs in Scotland A.D. MDCLVI. Thomas Tucker. LC 79-177574. (Bannatyne Club, Edinburgh. Publications: No. 7). Repr. of 1824 ed. 17.50 (ISBN 0-404-52708-6). AMS Pr.

Report, Vol. 28. Ed. by Carol W. Bell. 1988. 19.00. OH Genealogical.

Report with Findings & Recommendations to the Conference of Chief Justices from Its Task Force on Lawyer Competence. National Center for State Courts Staff. 84p. 1982. manuscript 5.04 (NCSC-021). Natl Ctr St Courts.

Report Writer. Steve Eckols. LC 80-82868. 106p. 1980. pap. 13.50. M Murach & Assoc.

Report Writing: A Practical Guide to Effective Report Writing Presented in Report Form. Ed. by Management Update, Ltd. Staff. 112p. 1985. 49.00x (ISBN 0-946679-02-9, Pub. by Mgmt Update UK); pap. 30.00x (ISBN 0-946679-01-0). State Mutual Bk.

Report Writing Correspondence Course. American Correctional Association Staff. Ed. by Diane Geiman & Rosalie Rosetti. (Correspondence Courses Ser.). 250p. (Orig.). 1987. Set (Bks. I & II) pap. 35.00 (ISBN 0-942974-90-5). Am Correctional.

Report Writing for Architects. Chappell. 1987. 18.95 (ISBN 0-85139-966-5). Van Nos Reinhold.

Report Writing for Architects. David Chappell. 128p. 1984. 28.50 (ISBN 0-89397-189-8). Nichols Pub.

Report Writing for Business & Industry. Steven P. Golen et al. LC 84-17256. (Business Communications Ser.). 526p. 1985. write for info. (ISBN 0-471-80822-9). Wiley.

Report Writing for Management. William J. Gallagher. (Orig.). 1969. pap. write for info. (ISBN 0-201-02256-7). Addison-Wesley.

Report Writing for Quality Assurance Analysts. William E. Perry. (Illus.). 1981. pap. 24.95 (ISBN 0-318-20494-0). Quality Assurance.

Report Writing in Assessment & Evaluation. Stephen W. Thomas. (Illus.). 188p. (Orig.). 1986. pap. 17.75x (ISBN 0-916671-56-9). Material Dev.

Report Writing in dBASE II. Marilyn McMahon et al. 15.95 (ISBN 0-317-06186-0). P-H.

Report Writing in Special Education. Norman Tallent. (Illus.). 1980. text ed. write for info. (ISBN 0-13-773606-1). P-H.

Report Writing Reference: Detailed Outlines & Examples for Writing Better Crime Reports. Gary C. Benthin. 118p. 1987. pap. text ed. 10.00 (ISBN 0-940551-00-4). Pumpernickel Pub.

Report Writing Skills. 88p. 12.95 (ISBN 0-911703-08-X). CDS Assocs.

Report 1987: Hospital Pharmacy Computer Systems. William A. Gouveia et al. iv, 127p. 1987. pap. text ed. 20.00 (ISBN 0-930530-75-6). Am Soc Hosp Pharm.

Reportazhi V. A. Giliarovskogo. B. I. Esom. 110p. (Rus.). 1985. 29.00x (ISBN 0-317-42756-3, Pub by Collets (UK)). State Mutual Bk.

Reporte of a Discourse Concerning Supreme Power in Affaires of Religion. John Hayward. LC 79-84116. (English Experience Ser.: No. 935). 64p. 1979. Repr. of 1606 ed. lib. bdg. 8.00 (ISBN 90-221-0935-6). Walter J Johnson.

Reporter. Jake Highton. (Illus.). 1978. pap. 27.95 (ISBN 0-07-028771-6). McGraw.

Reporter & the Law: Techniques of Covering the Courts. Lyle W. Denniston. LC 79-24051. 1980. 18.00x (ISBN 0-8038-6341-1). Hastings.

Reporter As Artist: A Look at the New Journalism Controversy. Ed. by Ronald Weber. LC 73-19898. (Communications Arts Bks.). 312p. 1974. 12.00 (ISBN 0-8038-6330-6). Hastings.

Reporter on the Job, Vol. III. rev. ed. Beverly L. Ritter & Michael LaBorde. (Computer-Compatible Machine Shorthand for Expanding Careers Ser.). 166p. 1986. pap. text. ed. 27.00 (ISBN 0-938643-09-6); tchr's. ed. 15.00 (ISBN 0-938643-11-8). Stenotype Educ.

Reporter Reader. Reporter. Ed. by Max Ascoli. LC 74-93373. (Essay Index Reprint Ser.). 1956. 25.50 (ISBN 0-8369-1428-7). Ayer Co Pubs.

Reporter Services & Their Use. Ed. by Sanford M. Morse. 126p. 1980. pap. 5.00 (ISBN 0-87179-340-7). BNA.

Reporter vs. Publisher: What Journalism Professors Don't Tell You. Janice Brownfield. LC 85-70671. 256p. (Orig.). 1986. pap. 14.95 (ISBN 0-9614521-7-X). Alpenstock.

Reporters & Officials: The Organization & Politics of Newsmaking. Leon V. Sigal. 1973. pap. text ed. 10.00 (ISBN 0-669-89276-9). Heath.

Reporters Arranged & Characterized with Incidental Remarks. 4th ed. John W. Wallace. LC 16-9001. 654p. 1961. Repr. of 1882 ed. lib. bdg. 45.00 (ISBN 0-89941-355-2). W S Hein.

Reporter's Desk Reference. 161p. 1982. pap. 13.75 (ISBN 0-318-01724-5). Natl Shorthand Rptr.

Reporters' Ethics. Bruce M. Swain. 1978. text ed. 13.50x (ISBN 0-8138-1280-1). Iowa St U Pr.

Reporter's Handbook: An Investigator's Guide to Documents & Techniques. Ed. by John H. Ullmann et al. (Illus.). 592p. 1983. 19.95 (ISBN 0-312-67394-9); pap. write for info. (ISBN 0-312-67393-0). St Martin.

Reporter's Notes to Code of Judicial Conduct. E. Wayne Thode. ii, 104p. 1973. 4.50 (ISBN 0-317-33355-0). Amer Bar Assn.

Reporters Report Reporters. Curtis D. MacDougall. LC 68-15283. (Illus.). 193p. pap. 50.20 (2029781). Bks Demand UMI.

Reporters under Fire: U. S. Media Coverage of Conflicts in Lebanon & Central America. Landrum R. Bolling. (Replica Edition-Softcover Ser.). 170p. 1985. pap. 22.50x (ISBN 0-8133-7006-X). Westview.

Reporting: A Street Cops Guide - Pennsylvania Edition. David A. Varrelman. 80p. pap. text ed. 5.95 (ISBN 0-940438-02-X). Innovations Pr.

Reporting Africa. Ed. by Olav Stokke. LC 76-163923. 250p. 1971. 25.00 (ISBN 0-8419-0090-6, Africana). Holmes & Meier.

Reporting: An Inside View. Lou Cannon. LC 77-79691. 1977. 9.95 (ISBN 0-930302-12-5); pap. 4.95 (ISBN 0-930302-13-3). Cal Journal.

Reporting & Disclosure Requirements. Thomas S. Monfried, Jr. & James N. Karas. (Rules for Operation of Qualified Plans Ser.). 41p. 1979. pap. 2.00 (ISBN 0-317-31179-4, B362). Am Law Inst.

Reporting & Documenting Patient Care: OR. (Modular Independent Learning Systems). 49p. 1980. 7.00 (ISBN 0-939583-17-8). Assn Oper Rm Nurses.

Reporting & Writing the News. Evan Hill & John J. Breen. (Illus.). 318p. 1988. pap. 15.95x (ISBN 0-88133-380-8). Waveland Pr.

Reporting by Key Informants on Labour Markets: An Operational Manual. W. Mason & L. Richter. vi, 41p. (Orig.). 1985. pap. 8.75 (ISBN 92-2-105109-9). Intl Labour Office.

Reporting Child Abuse & Neglect: A Guide for Professionals, the Public & Accused Parents. Douglas J. Besharov. LC 86-17466. Date not set. cancelled (ISBN 0-917561-27-9); pap. cancelled (ISBN 0-917561-28-7). Adler & Adler.

Reporting Chronic Conditions in the National Health Interview Survey: A Review of Findings from Evaluation Studies & Methodological Tests. Thomas B. Jabine. Ed. by Klaudia Cox. LC 87-1379. (Series 2: No. 105). 113p. Date not set. pap. 3.50 (ISBN 0-317-57596-1). Natl Ctr Health Stats.

Reporting for Television. Carolyn Diana Lewis. LC 83-7568. (Illus.). 192p. 1983. 22.50x (ISBN 0-231-05538-2). Columbia U Pr.

Reporting for the Print Media. 3rd ed. Fred Fedler. 641p. 1984. pap. text ed. 17.00 net (ISBN 0-15-576625-5, HC); instr's. manual avail. (ISBN 0-15-576626-0). HarBraceJ.

Reporting Foreign Operations. Samuel R. Hepworth. Ed. by Richard P. Brief. LC 80-1494. (Dimensions of Accounting Theory & Practice Ser.). 1981. Repr. of 1956 ed. lib. bdg. 23.00x (ISBN 0-405-13524-6). Ayer Co Pubs.

Reporting from Corinth. Alice Friman. LC 83-173208. 88p. (Orig.). 1984. pap. 6.95 (ISBN 0-935306-24-2). Barnwood Pr.

Reporting India, 1973. annual G. G. Mirchandani. LC 75-903643. 1975. 10.00 (ISBN 0-88386-591-2). South Asia Bks.

Reporting India, 1975. G. Mirchandani. 1977. 11.50 (ISBN 0-88386-952-7). South Asia Bks.

Reporting India, 1976. G. C. Mirchandani. 1977. 12.50x (ISBN 0-8364-0062-3). South Asia Bks.

Reporting India, 1977-78. G. G. Mirchandani. 1978. 14.00x (ISBN 0-8364-0271-5). South Asia Bks.

Reporting Manual. Larry L. Perry. 248p. 1987. ring binder 95.00 (ISBN 0-13-773490-5, Busn). P-H.

Reporting of Service Efforts & Accomplishments. Paul K. Brace et al. LC 80-84887. (Financial Accounting Standards Board Research Report). (Illus.). 114p. (Orig.). 1980. pap. 6.50 (ISBN 0-910065-09-8). Finan Acct Found.

Reporting of Social Science in the National Media. Carol Weiss & Eleanor Singer. LC 87-43099. 320p. 1988. text ed. 29.95 (ISBN 0-87154-802-X). Russell Sage.

Reporting of Summary Indicators: An Investigation of Research & Practice. Paul Frishkoff. LC 81-70208. (Financial Accounting Standards Board Research Report). 74p. (Orig.). 1981. pap. 6.00 (ISBN 0-910065-13-6). Finan Acct Found.

Reporting Public Affairs: Problems & Solutions. Ronald P. Lovell. 417p. 1983. text ed. write for info. (ISBN 0-534-01126-8). Wadsworth Pub.

Reporting Science: The Case of Aggression. Ed. by Jeffrey H. Goldstein. 144p. 1985. text ed. 19.95 (ISBN 0-89859-608-4); pap. 9.95 (ISBN 0-89859-671-8). L Erlbaum Assocs.

Reporting Southern Africa: Western News Agencies Reporting from Southern Africa. Phil Harris. 168p. 1981. pap. 6.00 (ISBN 92-3-101700-4, U1097, UNESCO). UNIPUB.

Reporting Stenographer. Jack Rudman. (Career Examination Ser.: C-2125). (Cloth bdg. avail. on request). 1988. pap. 12.00 (ISBN 0-8373-2125-5). Natl Learning.

Reporting System for Hospital Social Work. Society for Hospital Social Work Directors of the American Hospital Association. LC 84-245156. 32p. 1978. pap. 11.25 (ISBN 0-939450-58-5, 187118). AHA.

Reporting Systems for Bank Management. John R. Walker. LC 87-17424. (Illus.). 304p. 1987. text ed. 59.00 (ISBN 0-87267-106-2). Bank Admin Inst.

Reporting Technical Information. 6th ed. Kenneth W. Houp & Thomas E. Pearsall. 770p. 1988. pap. text ed. write for info. (ISBN 0-02-357220-5). Macmillan.

Reporting the Citizen's News. Ralph S. Izard. 1982. text ed. 23.95 (ISBN 0-03-057366-1). HR&W.

Reporting U. S.-European Relations: Four Nations, Four Newspapers. Ed. by Michael Rice & James A. Cooney. LC 81-19266. 168p. 1982. text ed. 28.00 (ISBN 0-08-027525-7, K125); pap. text ed. 12.75 (ISBN 0-08-027524-9). Pergamon.

Reporting: Violence & Vandalism. 4.95 (ISBN 0-318-01765-2, 021-00882). Am Assn Sch Admin.

Reporting with Understanding. Gary Atkins & William Rivers. 240p. 1987. text ed. 24.95x (ISBN 0-8138-1517-7). Iowa St U Pr.

Reportorie of Records at Westminster. A. Agard. LC 72-225. (English Experience Ser.: No. 291). 1971. Repr. of 1631 ed. 22.00 (ISBN 90-221-0291-2). Walter J Johnson.

Reportorio de Todos los Caminos de Espana. facsimile ed. Pedro J. Villuga. 1950. 20.00 (ISBN 0-527-93180-2). Kraus Repr.

Reportpack Simplified. Donald C. Scot. 250p. 1983. 44.95 (ISBN 0-442-28111-0). Van Nos Reinhold.

Reports. Midwest Category Seminar, 1st. Ed. by J. Benabou et al. (Lecture Notes in Mathematics: Vol. 47). (Orig.). 1967. pap. 10.70 (ISBN 0-387-03918-X). Springer-Verlag.

Reports. Midwest Category Seminar, 2nd. Ed. by S. MacLane. (Lecture Notes in Mathematics: Vol. 61). (Orig.). 1968. pap. 10.70 (ISBN 0-387-04231-8). Springer-Verlag.

Reports. Midwest Category Seminar, 4th. Ed. by S. MacLane. LC 78-126772. (Lecture Notes in Mathematics: Vol. 137). 1970. pap. 10.70 (ISBN 0-387-04926-6). Springer-Verlag.

Reports. Midwest Category Seminar, 5th. Ed. by J. W. Gray & S. MacLane. (Lecture Notes for Mathematics: Vol. 195). 1971. pap. 14.00 (ISBN 0-387-05442-1). Springer-Verlag.

Reports, 19 vols. U. S. Industrial Commission, Washington, D. C., 1900-1902. Incl. Vol. 1. lib. bdg. 40.00 (ISBN 0-8371-9921-2, RICA); Vol. 2, 3 & 4, 3 vols. lib. bdg. 40.00 (ISBN 0-8371-9922-0, RICB); Vol. 5 & 6. lib. bdg. 40.00 (ISBN 0-8371-9923-9, RICC); Vol. 7. lib. bdg. 40.00 (ISBN 0-8371-9924-7, RICD); Vol. 8. lib. bdg. 40.00 (ISBN 0-8371-9925-5, RICE); Vol. 9. lib. bdg. 40.00 (ISBN 0-8371-9926-3, RICF); Vol. 10. lib. bdg. 40.00 (ISBN 0-8371-9927-1, RICG); Vol. 11. lib. bdg. 40.00 (ISBN 0-8371-9928-X, RICH); Vol. 12. lib. bdg. 40.00 (ISBN 0-8371-9929-8, RICI); Vol. 13. lib. bdg. 40.00 (RICJ); Vol. 14. lib. bdg. 40.00 (ISBN 0-8371-9931-X, RICK); Vol. 15. lib. bdg. 40.00 (ISBN 0-8371-9932-8, RICL); Vol. 16. lib. bdg. 40.00 (ISBN 0-8371-9933-6, RICM); Vol. 17. lib. bdg. 40.00 (ISBN 0-8371-9934-4, RICN); Vol. 18. lib. bdg. 40.00 (ISBN 0-8371-9935-2, RICO); Vol. 19. lib. bdg. 40.00 (ISBN 0-8371-9936-0, RICP). LC 73-103309. (Illus.). 1900-02. Repr. Greenwood.

Reports & Observations on the Discipline & Management of Prisons. Joshua Jebb. (Crime & Punishment in England, 1850-1922 Ser.). 223p. 1984. lib. bdg. 30.00. Garland Pub.

Reports & Opinions of the Attorney General of the Republic of Liberia: December 1922-July 1930. Liberia, Republic of. 448p. 1969. 40.00x (ISBN 0-8014-0530-0). Cornell U Pr.

Reports & Papers on Botany. Ed. by Arthur Henfrey. Repr. of 1849 ed. 37.00 (ISBN 0-384-22312-5). Johnson Repr.

Reports & Papers Presented at the Indo-Pacific Fishery Commission Expert Consultation on Inland Fisheries of the Larger Indo-Pacific Islands, Bangkok, Thailand, 4-9 August 1986. Ed. by T. Petr. (FAO Fisheries Report: No. 371 Supplement). 258p. (Orig.). 1987. pap. 24.75 (ISBN 92-5-102639-4, F3173, FAO). UNIPUB.

Reports by Management. 27p. 1981. pap. 1.25 (ISBN 0-317-30646-4). Amer Bar Assn.

Reports Comprising the Survey of the Cook County Jail. facsimile ed. Chicago Community Trust Staff. LC 73-3818. (Criminal Justice in America Ser.). (Illus.). 1974. Repr. of 1923 ed. 24.50x (ISBN 0-405-06139-0). Ayer Co Pubs.

Reports for Government: Writing Workshop Workbook. James S. Hanna, Jr. (Illus.). 104p. 1981. pap. text ed. 10.00 (ISBN 0-9607024-0-7). J S Hanna.

Reports from a Wilderness: A Spiral of Poems. Christine F. Heffner. Ed. by Bonnie B. Langenhahn. 60p. 1987. pap. 5.95 (ISBN 0-9618212-0-5). McCormick & Schilling.

Reports from the Select Committee on Police & Minutes of Evidence, Vol. 36. Select Committee On Police. LC 77-156284. (Police in Great Britain Ser). 1971. Repr. of 1853 ed. 24.50 (ISBN 0-405-03395-8). Ayer Co Pubs.

Reports of Cases Decided by Chief Justice Chase in the Circuit Court of the United States for the Fourth Circuit: 1865-1869. facsimile ed. Bradley T. Johnson. LC 75-75292. (American Constitutional & Legal History Ser.). 1972. Repr. of 1876 ed. lib. bdg. 75.00 (ISBN 0-306-71291-1). Da Capo.

Reports of Cases Determined in the General Court of Virginia From 1730-1740, 1768-1772. Thomas Jefferson. LC 81-84431. viii, 145p. 1981. Repr. of 1829 ed. lib. bdg. 35.00 (ISBN 0-89941-143-6). W S Hein.

Reports of Cases in Courts of Star Chamber & High Commission. Great Britain, Court of the Star Chamber Staff. Ed. by Samuel R. Gardiner. 1886. 27.00 (ISBN 0-384-19760-4). Johnson Repr.

Reports of Cases in the Vice Admiralty of the Province of New York & in the Courts of Admiralty of the State of New York, 1715-1788. Charles M. Hough. (Yale Historical Pubs., Manuscripts & Edited Texts Ser.: No. VIII). 1925. 85.00x (ISBN 0-685-89777-X). Elliots Bks.

Reports of Current Work on Behavior of Materials at Elevated Temperatures: November 18-21, 1974, New York, N. Y. Held as Part of the 1974 ASME Winter Annual Meeting. Ed. by A. O. Schaefer. LC 74-22198. pap. 48.30 (ISBN 0-317-08567-0, 2016882). Bks Demand UMI.

Reports of Economic Missions, 5 vols. International Bank for Reconstruction & Development. Repr. of 1961 ed. Set. 287.50 (ISBN 0-404-60300-9); 57.50 ea. AMS Pr.

Reports of European Communities: 1952-77 Index to Authors & Chairmen. Ed. by June Neilson. 576p. 1981. text ed. 64.00x (ISBN 0-7201-1592-2). Mansell.

Reports of Explorations Printed in the Documents of the United States Government. U. S. Supt. of Documents. 1969. 19.00 (ISBN 0-8337-1593-3). B Franklin.

Reports of Inspection Made in the Summer of 1877. William T. Sherman & Philip H. Sheridan. 1985. 17.95 (ISBN 0-87770-329-9). Ye Galleon.

Reports of International Arbitral Awards, Vol. 18. 33.00 (ISBN 92-1-033009-9, EF.80.V.7). UN.

Reports of Judgements, Advisory Opinions & Orders: Frontier Dispute. (Eng. & Fr.). 2.00 (ISBN 0-317-52091-1, ICJ NO. 518). UN.

Reports of Ministers on the Secrete Meeting of the So Called "Chroncommittee" of the Government of Szalasi. Hungarian Historical Research Society Staff. LC 77-85228. 194p. 1980. pap. 11.95 (ISBN 0-935484-05-1). Universe Pub Co.

Reports of Officers in Relation to Recent Battles at Pittsburgh Landing. LC 76-43153. (Civil War Monographs). 1977. lib. bdg. 24.00 (ISBN 0-527-17573-0); pap. 17.00 (ISBN 0-527-17574-9). Kraus Repr.

Reports of ORCA on Water Fluoridation. Ed. by European Organization for Caries Research, Board. (Caries Research Ser.: Vol. 8, Suppl. 1). 36p. 1974. 11.50 (ISBN 3-8055-1707-6). S Karger.

Reports of Special Assistant Poor Law Commissioners on the Employment of Women & Children in Agriculture. Great Britain Poor Law Board Staff. LC 68-141609. 378p. 1968. Repr. of 1843 ed. PLB 45.00x (ISBN 0-678-05232-8). Kelley.

Reports of the Ayacucho Archaeological-Botanical Project. Incl. First Annual Report of the Ayacucho Project. R. MacNeish. 1969. 3.00 (ISBN 0-939312-15-8); Second Annual Repoert of the Ayacucho Project. R. MacNeish et al. 1970. 3.00 (ISBN 0-939312-16-6). Peabody Found.

Reports of the Cambridge Anthropological Expedition to Torres Straits, 6 vols. Ed. by A. C. Haddon. Incl. General Ethnography. Repr. of 1935 ed. 53.00 (ISBN 0-685-27602-3); Physiology & Psychology. Repr. of 1901 ed. 35.00 (ISBN 0-685-27603-1); Linguistics. S. H. Ray. Repr. of 1907 ed. 53.00 (ISBN 0-685-27604-X); Arts & Crafts. Repr. of 1912 ed. Vols. 4-6. 44.00 ea.; Sociology, Magic & Religion of the Western Islanders. Repr. of 1904 ed. 33.00 (ISBN 0-685-27606-6); Sociology, Magic & Religion of the Eastern Islanders. Repr. of 1908 ed. 26.00 (ISBN 0-685-27607-4). (Landmarks in Anthropology Ser). 2242p. Set. 260.00 (ISBN 0-686-57612-8). Johnson Repr.

Reports of the Coxcatlan Project. Edward B. Sisson. Incl. First Annual Report. 1973; Second Annual Report. 1974. Peabody Found.

Reports of the Delegates of the Mosely Industrial Commission to the United States of America, Oct.-Dec., 1902. Mosely Industrial Commission. LC 73-2526. (Big Business; Economic Power in a Free Society Ser.). Repr. of 1903 ed. 17.00 (ISBN 0-405-05105-0). Ayer Co Pubs.

Reports of the Fourth Session of the Committee on Resource Management: Rome, 17-18 June 1982 & the Technical Consultation on Regulation of Efforts in Trawl Fisheries in the Mediterranean. (Fisheries Reports: No. 270). 83p. (Eng. & Fr.). 1983. pap. text ed. 7.50 (ISBN 92-5-001266-7, F2376, FAO). UNIPUB.

Reports of the General Conference, 15th Session: Proceedings. pap. 11.00 (U526, UNESCO). UNIPUB.

Reports of the House of Commons on the Education & on the Health of the Poorer Classes in Large Towns, with Some Suggestions for Their Improvement. Robert A. Slaney. LC 84-48284. (Rise of Urban Britain Ser.). 222p. 1985. 35.00 (ISBN 0-8240-6286-8). Garland Pub.

Reports of the Immigration Commission, 41 Vols. United States Immigration Commission. LC 76-85474. Repr. of 1910 ed. Set. 1006.00 (ISBN 0-405-00390-0). Ayer Co Pubs.

Reports of the Industrial Commission on Immigration Including Testimony, with Review & Digest, & Special Reports on Education Including Testimony with Review & Digest. United States Industrial Commission - 57th Congress - 1st Session. LC 70-129417. (American Immigration Collection, Ser. 2). 1970. Repr. of 1901 ed. 45.00 (ISBN 0-405-00571-7). Ayer Co Pubs.

Reports of the Law of Civil Government in Territory Subject to Military Occupation by the Military Forces of the United States. 3rd. ed. Charles E. Magoon. Ed. by Igor I. Kavass & Adolf Sprudzs. LC 72-75029. (International Military Law & History Ser.: Vol. 2). 808p. 1972. Repr. of 1903 ed. lib. bdg. 45.00 (ISBN 0-930342-39-9). W S Hein.

Reports of the Magicians & Astrologers of Nineveh & Babylon in the British Museum, 2 vols. Reginald C. Thompson. LC 73-18857. (Luzac's Semitic Text & Translation Ser.: Nos. 6-7). Repr. of 1900 ed. Set. 30.00 (ISBN 0-404-11358-3); Vol. 1. (ISBN 0-404-11359-1); Vol. 2. (ISBN 0-404-11360-5). AMS Pr.

Reports of the Mosely Education Commission to the United States of America, October-December, 1903. Mosely Education Commission. LC 73-89223. (American Education: Its Men, Institutions & Ideas, Ser. 1). 1969. Repr. of 1904 ed. 18.00 (ISBN 0-405-01445-7). Ayer Co Pubs.

Reports of the Princeton University Expeditions to Patagonia, 1896-1899, 8 vols. & supp. Ed. by W. B. Scott. (Illus.). 4948p. 1914. PLB 995.00x set (ISBN 3-510-99068-4, Pub. by E Schweizerbartsche). Coronet Bks.

Reports of the Prison Discipline Society, Boston: Reports 1-29, 1826-1854 (With Intro. essay & Analytical Index Added, 6 vols. Prison Discipline Society. LC 71-129322. (Criminology, Law Enforcement, & Social Problems Ser.: No. 155). (Illus.). 1972. Set. 175.00x (ISBN 0-87585-155-X). Patterson Smith.

Reports of the Proceedings & Debates. New York Constitutional Convention, 1821. LC 72-133168. (Law, Politics & History Ser.). 1970. Repr. of 1821 ed. lib. bdg. 85.00 (ISBN 0-306-70069-7). Da Capo.

Reports of the Proceedings of the Annual Conventions of the American Federation of Labor, 74 vols. in 58. American Federation of Labor Staff. Repr. of 1881 ed. Set. 2480.00 (ISBN 0-685-56820-2). AMS Pr.

Reports of the Royal Commission on Chinese Immigration. Ed. by Roger Daniels. LC 78-54810. (Asian Experience in North America Ser.). 1979. Repr. of 1885 ed. lib. bdg. 47.50x (ISBN 0-405-11267-X). Ayer Co Pubs.

Reports of the Special Committee Appointed to Investigate the Official Conduct of the Members of the Board of Police Commissioners: City of Boston, Document No. 166. Joint Special Committee. LC 78-156279. (Police in America Ser). 1971. Repr. of 1882 ed. 13.00 (ISBN 0-405-03372-9). Ayer Co Pubs.

Reports of the Trials of Colonel Aaron Burr, 2 Vols. Aaron Burr. LC 69-11321. (Law, Politics & History Ser). 1969. Repr. of 1808 ed. lib. bdg. 89.50 (ISBN 0-306-71182-6). Da Capo.

Reports of the United States Delegation to the Third United Nations Conference on the Law of the Sea: OP33, Occasional Paper, No. 33. Ed. by M. Nordquist & C. H. Park. 1983. 16.00 (ISBN 0-911189-07-6). Law Sea Inst.

Reports of the United States Tax Court, Vol. 84: Jan. 1, 1985 to June 30, 1985. Ed. by Mary Pittman. 1404p. 1985. 38.00 (ISBN 0-318-19893-2, S/N 028-005-00154-3). USGPO.

Reports of the XIV International Congress of the Historical Sciences Series. LC 77-81885. 1977. lib. bdg. 125.00 set (ISBN 0-405-10517-7). Ayer Co Pubs.

Reports on Astronomy, 3 pts. Ed. by G. Contopoulos. (Transactions of the International Astronomical Union: Vol. XVIA). 1976. Pt. 1. lib. bdg. 47.50 (ISBN 90-277-0739-1, Pub. by Reidel Holland); Pt. 2. lib. bdg. 47.50 (ISBN 90-277-0740-5); Pt. 3. lib. bdg. 47.50 (ISBN 90-277-0741-3); Set. lib. bdg. 126.00 (ISBN 90-277-0703-0). Kluwer Academic.

Reports on Astronomy, 3 pts. Ed. by Edith A. Muller. (Transactions of the International Astronomical Union Ser.: Vol. XVII A). 1979. lib. bdg. 29.50 ea. (Pub. by Reidel Holland); Pt. 1. (ISBN 90-277-1005-8). Pt. 2. (ISBN 90-277-1006-6); Pt. 3. (ISBN 90-277-1007-4). Kluwer Academic.

Reports on Astronomy. Ed. by Jean-Pierre Swings. 1988. lib. bdg. 149.00 (ISBN 90-277-2734-1). Kluwer Academic.

Reports on Astronomy. P. Wayman. 1982. 67.50 (ISBN 90-277-1423-1, Pub. by Reidel Holland). Kluwer Academic.

Reports on Astronomy: Transactions of the International Astronomical Union Volume XIXA. Ed. by Richard M. West. 1985. lib. bdg. 69.00 (ISBN 90-277-2039-8, Pub. by Reidel Netherlands). Kluwer Academic.

Reports on Ceftriaxone (RocephinR) Ed. by H. Schoenfeld. (Journal Chemoptherapy: Vol. 27, Suppl. 1). (Illus.). iv, 104p. 1981. pap. 19.50 (ISBN 3-8055-3034-X). S Karger.

Reports on Crime Investigation: 82nd Congress, First Session, Senate Reports. Special Committee of the Senate to Investigate Organized Crime in Interstate Commerce. LC 77-90207. (Mass Violence in America Ser). Repr. of 1951 ed. 12.00 (ISBN 0-405-01336-1). Ayer Co Pubs.

Reports on Happiness: A Pilot Study of Behavior Related to Mental Health. Norman M. Bradburn & David Caplovitz. LC 64-15605. (NORC Monographs in Social Research Ser.: No. 3). 1965. 9.95x (ISBN 0-202-30020-X). NORC.

Reports on International Trade: International Trade. 1969. pap. 13.00 (G12, GATT). UNIPUB.

Reports on Medical Applications of Ozone. 1985. 80.00 (ISBN 0-317-18827-5). Pan Am Intl Ozone.

Reports on Nationalism by a Study Group of Members of the Royal Institute of International Affairs: Proceedings. Royal Institute of International Affairs. 360p. 1963. 30.00x (ISBN 0-7146-1571-4, F Cass Co). Biblio Dist.

Reports on Taxation I: Collected Economic Essays, Vol.7. Nicholas Kaldor. LC 78-31926. 242p. 1980. 44.50 (ISBN 0-8419-0296-8). Holmes & Meier.

Reports on Taxation II: Collected Economic Essays, Vol. 8. Nicholas Kaldor. LC 78-31926. 297p. 1980. 44.50 (ISBN 0-8419-0297-6). Holmes & Meier.

Reports on the Discovery of Peru. Clements R. Markham. LC 70-134711. (Hakluyt Soc. Ser.: No. 47). 1970. Repr. of 1872 ed. lib. bdg. 24.00 (ISBN 0-8337-2227-1). B Franklin.

Reports on the Northeastern Part of the Quinghai-Xizang Plateau (Tibet) by Sino-West German Scientific Expedition. Ed. by J. Hoeverman & Wang Wenying. 510p. 1987. 37.50x (ISBN 3-443-39075-7). Lubrecht & Cramer.

Reports on the Second INCRA International Symposium on Automotive Radiators. 266p. 1967. 39.90 (ISBN 0-317-34542-7, 99). Intl Copper.

Reports on the State of Certain Parishes in Scotland. Ed. by Alexander Macdonald. LC 79-175588. (Maitland Club, Glasgow. Publications: No. 34). Repr. of 1835 ed. 24.50 (ISBN 0-404-53003-6). AMS Pr.

Reports on the Work of the Five Main Committees on the Intellectual Property Conference of Stockholm: 1967. 1967. pap. 7.50 (ISBN 0-686-53030-6, WIPO29, WIPO). UNIPUB.

Reports Presented at May 9, 1986 CMA Production Seminar on Unit Production Systems, PCT & S Research Projects, & Update on Air Jet Loom Linings. 20.00 (ISBN 0-318-21997-2). Clothing Mfrs.

Reports to the Hon. George Stoneman, Governor of California, on Certain Claims of the State of California Against the United States, November 1, 1878, to November 1, 1886. John Mullin. Ed. by Stuart Bruchey. LC 78-56670. (Management of Public Lands in the U. S. Ser.). (Illus.). 1979. Repr. of 1886 ed. lib. bdg. 40.00x (ISBN 0-405-11345-5). Ayer Co Pubs.

Reports Upon Insects Collected During Geographical & Geological Explorations & Surveys West of the One Hundredth Meridian, During the Years 1872, 1873, & 1874. Ed. by George M. Wheeler & Keir B. Sterling. LC 77-81109. (Biologists & Their World Ser.). (Illus.). 1978. Repr. of 1875 ed. lib. bdg. 22.40x (ISBN 0-405-10693-9). Ayer Co Pubs.

Repos du Guerrier. Christiane Rochefort. (Idees Ser.). 280p. 1958. 12.50 (ISBN 0-686-55228-8). French & Eur.

Repos du Guerrier. Christiane Rochefort. 1960. 9.95 (ISBN 0-686-55229-6). French & Eur.

Repos du Guerrier. Christiane Rocherfort. 280p. 1958. write for info. French & Eur.

Repos Du Septieme Jour. Paul Claudel. 1973. 14.95 (ISBN 0-686-54429-3). French & Eur.

Repossessing & Renewing: Essays in the Green American Tradition. Sherman Paul. LC 75-5351. xviii, 294p. 1976. 32.50 (ISBN 0-8071-0179-6). La State U Pr.

Repossession & You. 3.50 (ISBN 0-944253-77-6). Inst Dev Indian Law.

Repossessions. 2nd ed. National Consumer Law Center, Inc. Staff. LC 88-61108. (Consumer Credit & Sales Legal Practice Ser.). 350p. 1988. pap. 60.00x. Nat Consumer Law.

Repossessions: 1982 & 1987 Supplement. LC 82-60508. 141p. 1982. pap. 48.00 (ISBN 0-943116-09-0). Nat Consumer Law.

Repraesentation in der Demokratie. Gerhard Leibholz. (Sammlung Goeschen 6001). Orig. Title: Wesen der Repraesentation und der Gestaltwandel der Demokratie im 20. Jahrhundert. 275p. 1973. pap. 5.90 (ISBN 3-11-004544-3). De Gruyter.

Representaciones en la Ensenanza de las Matematicas. Ana H. Quintero. LC 87-25573. 1988. pap. write for info. (ISBN 0-8477-2750-5). U of PR Pr.

Representaciones Palaciegas: Sixteen Three to Sixteen Ninety-Nine Estudio Y Documentos. Ed. by N. D. Shergold & J. E. Varey. (Serie C: Fuentes para la Historia del Teatro en Espana, I). 276p. (Orig., Span.). 1982. 22.50 (ISBN 0-7293-0132-X, Pub. by Tamesis Bks Ltd). Longwood Pub Group.

Representation & Development in Brazil, 1972-1973. 2nd ed. Youseff Cohen et al. LC 80-84095. 1980. write for info., codebk (ISBN 0-89138-950-4). ICPSR.

Representation & Exchange of Knowledge As a Basis of Information Processes: Proceedings of the 5th International Research Forum in Information Science (IRFIS 5) Heidelberg, 5-7 Sept., 1983. Ed. by Hans J. Dietschmann. 434p. 1984. 79.00 (ISBN 0-444-87563-8, I-302-84, North Holland). Elsevier.

Representation & Form. Walter Abell. LC 79-138573. (Illus.). 1971. Repr. of 1936 ed. lib. bdg. 25.00x (ISBN 0-8371-5772-2, ABRF). Greenwood.

Representation & Form: A Study of Aesthetic Values in Representational Art. Walter Abell. LC 36-17784. 172p. 1936. Repr. 16.00x (ISBN 0-403-08900-X). Somerset Pub.

Representation & Form: A Study of Aesthetic Values in Representational Art. Walter Abell. 1988. Repr. of 1936 ed. lib. bdg. 49.00x. Am Biog Serv.

Representation & Legislative Culture in Constituencies: A Study of Linkage Forms in Korea, No. 13. Chong L. Kim & Young W. Kihl. LC 83-620939. 30p. 1983. write for info. U Iowa Law.

Representation & Manipulation of Objects & Environments, Vol. 2. Kalay. 1988. write for info. (ISBN 0-471-85388-7). Wiley.

Representation & Misrepresentation of the Puritan in Elizabethan Drama. Aaron M. Myers. LC 76-20654. 1976. Repr. of 1931 ed. lib. bdg. 35.50 (ISBN 0-8414-6141-4). Folcroft.

Representation & Presidential Primaries: The Democratic Party in the Post-Reform Era. James I. Lengle. LC 80-1791. (Contributions in Political Science Ser.: No. 57). (Illus.). xv, 133p. 1981. lib. bdg. 35.00 (ISBN 0-313-22482-X, LEP/). Greenwood.

Representation & Redistricting Issues. Bernard Grofman et al. LC 81-47783. (Policy Studies Organization Bk.). 304p. 1982. 33.00x (ISBN 0-669-04718-X). Lexington Bks.

Representation & Responsibility: Exploring Legislative Ethics. Ed. by Bruce Jennings & Daniel Callahan. 348p. 1985. 42.50X (ISBN 0-306-41994-7, Plenum Pr.). Plenum Pub.

Representation & Revelation: Victorian Realism from Carlyle to Yeats. John P. McGowan. LC 85-20117. 272p. 1986. text ed. 26.00 (ISBN 0-8262-0492-9). U of Mo Pr.

Representation & Suffrage in Massachusetts: 1620-1691. G. H. Haynes. 1973. Repr. of 1894 ed. 11.00 (ISBN 0-384-21865-2). Johnson Repr.

Representation & Suffrage in Massachusetts; 1620-1691. George H. Haynes. LC 78-63832. (Johns Hopkins University. Studies in the Social Sciences. Twelfth Ser. 1894: 8-9). Repr. of 1894 ed. 11.50 (ISBN 0-404-61092-7). AMS Pr.

Representation & the Imagination: Beckett, Kafka, Nabokov, & Schoenberg. Daniel Albright. LC 80-26976. (Chicago Originals Ser.). viii, 222p. 1981. lib. bdg. 20.00x (ISBN 0-226-01252-2). U of Chicago Pr.

Representation, Comprehension & Communication of Sets: The Role of Number. 32p. 1980. pap. 5.00 (ISBN 92-808-0133-3, TUNU055, UNU). UNIPUB.

Representation in Contemporary French Fiction. Dina Sherzer. LC 85-5882. xviii, 205p. 1986. 21.50x (ISBN 0-8032-4158-5). U of Nebr Pr.

Representation in Italy: Institutionalized Tradition & Electoral Choice. Samuel H. Barnes. LC 76-51819. (Illus.). 1977. 20.00x (ISBN 0-226-03726-6). U of Chicago Pr.

Representation in State Legislatures. Malcolm E. Jewell. LC 82-40174. 216p. 1982. 18.00x (ISBN 0-8131-1463-2). U Pr of Ky.

Representation in Virginia. J. A. Chandler. 1973. pap. 9.00 (ISBN 0-384-08462-1). Johnson Repr.

Representation in Virginia. Julian A. Chandler. LC 78-63850. (Johns Hopkins University. Studies in the Social Sciences. Fourteenth Ser. 1896: 6-7). Repr. of 1896 ed. 11.50 (ISBN 0-404-61107-9). AMS Pr.

Representation of Blacks in Elective Offices in Majority Black Southern Counties. K. Farouk Brimah. 1983. write for info. Voter Ed Proj.

Representation of Deities of the Maya Manuscripts. P. Schellhas. (Harvard University Peabody Museum: Vol. 4, No. 1). (Illus.). 1904. pap. 15.00 (ISBN 0-527-01198-3). Kraus Repr.

Representation of Implicit & Dethematized Subjects. G. J. Roberts. (Linguistic Models Ser.). x, 300p. 1987. pap. write for info. Foris Pubns.

Representation of Indefiniteness. Ed. by Eric J. Reuland & Alice G. Ter Meulen. 320p. 1987. 35.00x (ISBN 0-262-18126-6). MIT Pr.

Representation of Indigent Criminal Defendants in the Courts of Hamilton County, Ohio: Evaluation Report for the Ohio Public Defender Commission. 134p. 1987. manuscript 8.00 (ISBN 0-317-59198-3, NERO-201). Natl Ctr St Courts.

Representation of Indigent Felony Defendants in the Cuyahoga County (OH) Court of Common Pleas. National Center for State Courts Staff. 144p. 1984. manuscript 8.64 (NERO-138). Natl Ctr St Courts.

Representation of Indigent Persons in the Courts of Lawrence County, Ohio. National Center for State Courts Staff. 62p. 1985. manuscript 4.00 (NERO-166). Natl Ctr St Courts.

Representation of Indigent Persons in the Courts of Scioto County, Ohio. National Center for State Courts Staff. 79p. 1985. manuscript 5.00 (NERO-165). Natl Ctr St Courts.

Representation of Knowledge & Belief. Myles Brand & Robert M. Harnish. LC 86-24961. (Arizona Colloquim on Cognition Ser.: No. 1). 368p. 1986. 39.95x (ISBN 0-8165-0971-9). U of Ariz Pr.

Representation of Lie Groups & Lie Algebras. Ed. by A. Kirillov. 226p. 1985. 30.00 (ISBN 963-05-3542-4, Pub. by Akademiai Kiado Hungary). Humanities.

Representation of Meaning in Memory. W. Kintsch. 280p. 1974. text ed. 24.95x (ISBN 0-89859-130-9). L Erlbaum Assocs.

Representation of Real Reductive Lie Groups. D. Vogan. 1981. text ed. 45.50x (ISBN 0-8176-3037-6). Birkhauser.

Representation of Rings by Sections. John Dauns & Karl Hofmann. LC 52-42839. (Memoirs: No. 83). 180p. 1983. pap. 12.00 (ISBN 0-8218-1283-1, MEMO-83). Am Math.

Representation of Speech in the Peripheral Auditory System: Proceedings of the Symposium, Stockholm, Sweden, May, 1982. Ed. by R. Carlson & B. Granstrom. 294p. 1982. 98.50 (ISBN 0-444-80447-1, Biomedical Pr). Elsevier.

Representation of State Agencies. 71p. 1979. 4.50 (ISBN 0-318-15225-8). Natl Attys General.

Representation of the Self in the American Renaissance. Jeffrey Steele. LC 87-4050. xviii, 218p. 1987. 27.95X (ISBN 0-8078-1750-3). U of NC Pr.

Representation of Witnesses Before Federal Grand Juries. Grand Jury Project. 85.00. Natl Lawyers Guild.

Representation of Witnesses Before Federal Grand Juries. 3rd ed. National Lawyers Guild. LC 83-15607. 1984. looseleaf 85.00 (ISBN 0-87632-426-X). Clark Boardman.

Representation of Women in Fiction. Ed. by Carolyn G. Heilbrun & Margaret R. Higonnet. LC 82-12685. (Selected Papers from the English Institute; 1981, New Ser.: No. 7). 214p. pap. 55.70 (2030574). Bks Demand UMI.

Representation Problem for Frechet Surfaces. J. W. Youngs. LC 52-42839. (Memoirs: No. 8). 143p. 1980. pap. 15.00 (ISBN 0-8218-1208-4, MEMO-8). Am Math.

Representation Theorems on Banach Function Spaces. Neil E. Gretsky. LC 52-42839. (Memoirs: No. 84). 56p. 1968. pap. 11.00 (ISBN 0-8218-1284-X, MEMO-84). Am Math.

Representation Theory & Harmonic Analysis of Semisimple Lie Groups. Sally & Vogan. (SURV Ser.: No. 30). 350p. 1988. write for info. (ISBN 0-8218-1526-1). Am Math.

Representation Theory I. Ed. by V. Dlab & P. Gabriel. (Lecture Notes in Mathematics Ser.: Vol. 831). 373p. 1980. pap. 26.00 (ISBN 0-387-10263-9). Springer-Verlag.

Representation Theory I: Finite Dimensional Algebras. Ed. by V. Dlab et al. (Lecture Notes in Mathematics Ser.: Vol. 1177). xv, 340p. 1986. pap. 28.80 (ISBN 0-387-16432-4). Springer-Verlag.

Representation Theory II. Ed. by V. Dlab & P. Gabriel. (Lecture Notes in Mathematics: Vol. 832). 673p. 1980. pap. 45.00 (ISBN 0-387-10264-7). Springer-Verlag.

Representation Theory II: Groups & Orders. Ed. by V. Dlab et al. (Lecture Notes in Mathematics Ser.: Vol. 1178). xv, 370p. 1986. pap. 28.80 (ISBN 0-387-16433-2). Springer-Verlag.

Representation Theory of Algebras. Robert Gordon. (Lecture Notes in Pure & Applied Math Ser.: Vol. 37). 1978. 75.00 (ISBN 0-8247-6714-4). Dekker.

Representation Theory of Finite Groups & Associative Algebras. Charles W. Curtis & Irving Reiner. (Classics Library). 689p. 1988. pap. 29.95 (ISBN 0-471-60845-9). Wiley.

Representation Theory of Finite Groups & Related Topics: Proceedings of the Symposia in Pure Mathematics-Madison, Wis.-1970. Ed. by I. Reiner. LC 79-165201. (Vol. 21). 1971. 32.00 (ISBN 0-8218-1421-4, PSPUM-21). Am Math.

Representation Theory of Finite Groups. W. Feit. (Mathematical Library: Vol. 25). 502p. 1982. 84.25 (ISBN 0-444-86155-6, North Holland). Elsevier.

Representation Theory of Lie Groups. M. F. Atiyah et al. LC 78-73820. (London Mathematical Society Lecture Note: No. 34). 1980. pap. 37.50 (ISBN 0-521-22636-8). Cambridge U Pr.

Representation Theory of Reductive Groups. Ed. by Peter C. Trombi. (Progress in Mathematics). 1983. text ed. 28.50 (ISBN 0-8176-3135-6). Birkhauser.

Representation Theory of Semisimple Groups: An Overview Based on Examples. Anthony W. Knapp. LC 85-43295. (Princeton Mathematical Ser.: No. 36). 912p. 1986. text ed. 75.00 (ISBN 0-691-08401-7). Princeton U Pr.

Representation Theory of the Symmetric Group. Gilbert Robinson. LC 63-424. (Mathematical Expositions Ser.: No. 12). pap. 53.50 (ISBN 0-317-09069-0, 2014385). Bks Demand UMI.

Representation Theory: Selected Papers. I. M. Gelfand. LC 82-4440. (London Mathematical Society Lecture Notes Ser. 69). 330p. 1982. pap. 34.50 (ISBN 0-521-28981-5). Cambridge U Pr.

Representation Versus Direct Democracy in Fighting about Taxes. Lewis A. Dexter. 155p. 1982. 18.95 (ISBN 0-87073-425-3); pap. 11.95 (ISBN 0-87073-426-1). Schenkman Bks Inc.

Representational Approach to the Joint Determination of Housing Market Segmentation & Housing Preferences. Tony E. Smith. (Discussion Paper Ser.: No. 116). 1980. pap. 5.50 (ISBN 0-686-32281-9). Regional Sci Res Inst.

Representational Mind: A Study of Kant's Theory of Knowledge. Richard E. Aquila. LC 83-47918. (Studies in Phenomenology & Existential Philosophy Ser.). 224p. 1984. 22.50x (ISBN 0-253-35005-0). Ind U Pr.

Representations of Algebraic Groups. Ed. by Jens C. Jantzen. (Pure & Applied Mathematics Ser.). 443p. 1987. 59.50 (ISBN 0-12-380245-8). Acad Pr.

Representations of Algebras, Locally Compact Groups, & Banach - Algebraic Bundles, Vol. 1: Basic Representation Theory of Groups & Algebras. Ed. by James M. Fell & Robert S. Doran. (Pure & Applied Mathematics Ser.). 746p. 1988. 99.00 (ISBN 0-12-252721-6). Acad Pr.

Representations of Algebras, Locally Compact Groups, & Banach Algebraic Bundles, Vol. 2: Induced Representations, the Imprivitivity Theorem, & the Generalized Mackey Analysis. Ed. by James M. Fell & Robert S. Doran. (Pure & Applied Mathematics Ser.). 738p. 1988. 99.00 (ISBN 0-12-252722-4). Acad Pr.

Representations of Algebras, Mexico Nineteen Eighty: Proceedings. Ed. by M. Auslander & E. Lluis. (Lecture Notes in Mathematics Ser.: Vol. 903). 371p. 1981. pap. 22.00 (ISBN 0-387-11179-4). Springer-Verlag.

Representations of Algebras: Proceedings. International Conference, Ottawa, 1974. Ed. by V. Dlab & P. Gabriel. (Lecture Notes in Mathematics: Vol. 488). xii, 378p. 1975. pap. 20.00 (ISBN 0-387-07406-6). Springer-Verlag.

Representations of Algebras: Proceedings of the Durham Symposium 1985. Ed. by P. J. Webb. (London Mathematical Society Lecture Note Ser.: No. 116). 275p. 1987. pap. 29.95 (ISBN 0-521-31288-4). Cambridge U Pr.

Representations of Algebras, Workshopnotes, Puebla, Mexico 1980. Ed. by M. Auslander & E. Lluis. (Lecture Notes in Mathematics: Vol. 944). 258p. 1982. pap. 17.00 (ISBN 0-387-11577-3). Springer-Verlag.

Representations of Compact Lie Groups. T. Brocker & Tom T. Dieck. (Graduate Texts in Mathematics Ser.: Vol. 98). (Illus.). x, 313p. 1985. 45.00 (ISBN 0-387-13678-9). Springer-Verlag.

Representations of Finite Classical Groups: A Hopf Algebra Approach. A. V. Zelevinsky. (Lecture Notes in Mathematics Ser.: Vol. 869). 184p. 1981. pap. 14.00 (ISBN 0-387-10824-6). Springer-Verlag.

Representations of Finite Groups. Hirosi Nagao & Yukio Tsushima. 418p. 1988. price not set (ISBN 0-12-513660-9). Acad Pr.

Representations of General Linear Groups. G. D. James. (London Mathematical Society Lecture Note Ser.: No. 94). 160p. 1984. pap. 19.95 (ISBN 0-521-26981-4). Cambridge U Pr.

Representations of Integers As Sums of Squares. Ed. by E. Grosswald. (Illus.). 200p. 1985. 49.50 (ISBN 0-387-96126-7). Springer-Verlag.

Representations of Permutation Groups, Part 2. A. Kerber. (Lecture Notes in Mathematics Ser: Vol. 495). v, 175p. 1975. 14.00 (ISBN 0-387-07535-6). Springer-Verlag.

Representations of Rank One Lie Groups. D. H. Collingwood. LC 85-19375. (Pitman Research Notes in Mathematics Ser.). 244p. 1986. pap. 41.95 (ISBN 0-470-20649-7, Co-Pub. with Longman). Wiley.

Representations of Rank One Lie Groups 2: N-Cohomology. D. H. Collingwood. (MEMO Ser.: No. 387). 108p. 1988. write for info. (ISBN 0-8218-2450-3). Am Math.

Representations of Revolution. Michelle Perrot. LC 86-26753. 356p. 1987. text ed. 27.50 (ISBN 0-300-03849-6). Yale U Pr.

Representations of Revolution, 1789-1820. Ronald Paulson. LC 82-13458. (Illus.). 416p. 1983. text ed. 40.00t (ISBN 0-300-02864-4). Yale U Pr.

Representations of Rings over Skew Fields. A. H. Schofield. (London Mathematical Society Lecture Note Ser.: No. 92). (Illus.). 240p. 1985. pap. 27.95 (ISBN 0-521-27853-8). Cambridge U Pr.

Representations of the Rotation & Lorentz Groups: An Introduction. Moshe Carmelli & Shimon Malin. (Lecture Notes in Pure & Applied Mathematics Ser.: Vol. 16). 1976. 39.75 (ISBN 0-8247-6449-8). Dekker.

Representations of Women: Nineteenth-Century British Women's Poetry. Kathleen Hickok. LC 83-13029. (Contributions in Women's Studies: No. 49). ix, 277p. 1984. lib. bdg. 35.00 (ISBN 0-313-23837-5, HIR/). Greenwood.

Representations: Philosophical Essays on the Foundations of Cognitive Science. Jerry A. Fodor. LC 81-24313. (Illus.). 384p. 1981. 33.00x (ISBN 0-262-06079-5, Pub. by Bradford); pap. 10.95x (ISBN 0-262-56027-5). MIT Pr.

Representations: Social Constructions of Gender. Ed. by R. Unger. Date not set. price not set (ISBN 0-89503-052-7). Baywood Pub.

Representative Actors: A Collection of Criticisms, Anecdotes, Personal Descriptions Referring to Many Celebrated British Actors from the Sixteenth to the Present Century. W. Clark Russell. 1975. Repr. 40.00 (ISBN 0-8274-4030-8). R West.

Representative Actors, Collection of Criticisms, Anecdotes, Personal Descriptions: Referring to British Actors from the Sixteenth to the Present Century. W. Clark Russell. 1978. Repr. lib. bdg. 45.00 (ISBN 0-8495-4554-4). Arden Lib.

Representative American Short Stories. Alexander Jessup. 1979. Repr. of 1923 ed. lib. bdg. 40.00 (ISBN 0-8492-1271-5). R West.

Representative American Speeches, 1986-1987. Ed. by Owen Peterson. (Reference Shelf Ser.: Vol. 59, No. 4). 171p. 1987. pap. text ed. 10.00. Wilson.

Representative Americans: The Colonists, Vol. I. Norman K. Risjord. (Representative Americans Ser.). 272p. 1981. pap. text ed. 11.50 (ISBN 0-669-02831-2). Heath.

Representative Americans: The Revolutionary Generation, Vol. 2. Norman Risjord. 1980. pap. text ed. 11.50 (ISBN 0-669-02710-3). Heath.

Representative & Responsible Government: An Essay on the British Constitution. Anthony H. Birch. LC 71-465276. pap. 63.00 (2026509). Bks Demand UMI.

Representative Art & Artist of New Mexico: School of America Research. 1976. 20.00 (ISBN 0-686-43122-7). Apollo.

Representative Bibliography of American Labor History. Maurice F. Neufeld. LC 64-63608. (ILR Bibliography Ser.: No. 6). 160p. 1964. 4.50 (ISBN 0-87546-021-6); pap. 2.00 (ISBN 0-87546-261-8). ILR Pr.

Representative Biographies of English Men of Letters. Charles T. Copeland. 1973. Repr. of 1910 ed. 30.00 (ISBN 0-8274-1658-X). R West.

Representative British Architects of the Present Day. facs. ed. Charles H. Reilly. LC 67-26774. (Essay Index Reprint Ser). 1967. Repr. of 1931 ed. 20.00 (ISBN 0-8369-0818-X). Ayer Co Pubs.

Representative Bureaucracy & the American Political System. Samuel Krislov & David H. Rosenbloom. LC 81-10625. 222p. 1981. 36.95 (ISBN 0-275-90663-9, C0663). Praeger.

Representative Bureaucracy in Oklahoma: A Comparison of Citizens' & Administrators' Characteristics & Attitudes. Elizabeth Gunn. 58p. 1982. 4.00 (ISBN 0-318-01377-0). Univ OK Gov Res.

Representative Democracy: Public Policy & Midwestern Legislatures in the Late Nineteenth Century. Ballard C. Campbell. 267p. 1980. text ed. 24.50x (ISBN 0-674-76275-4). Harvard U Pr.

Representative English Comedies, 4 Vols. Ed. by Charles M. Gayley. LC 76-88240. Repr. of 1936 ed. Set. 160.00 (ISBN 0-404-01950-1); 40.00 ea. Vol. 1 (ISBN 0-404-01951-X). Vol. 2 (ISBN 0-404-01952-8). Vol. 3 (ISBN 0-404-01953-6). Vol. 4 (ISBN 0-404-01954-4). AMS Pr.

Representative English Comedies. Ed. by Gayley C. Mills. 1978. Repr. of 1903 ed. lib. bdg. 35.00 (ISBN 0-8492-0991-9). R West.

Representative English Dramas from Dryden to Sheridan. Frederick Tupper & James W. Tupper. 1975. Repr. of 1914 ed. 40.00 (ISBN 0-8274-4042-1). R West.

Representative English Literature from Chaucer to Tennyson. Henry S. Pancoast. 514p. 1981. Repr. of 1898 ed. lib. bdg. 25.00 (ISBN 0-89984-395-6). Century Bookbindery.

Representative English Literature from Chaucer to Tennyson. Henry S. Pancoast. 1973. Repr. of 1893 ed. 20.00 (ISBN 0-8274-1248-7). R West.

Representative English Novelists: Defoe to Conrad. Bruce McCullough. LC 72-5807. (Essay Index Reprint Ser). 1972. Repr. of 1946 ed. 21.00 (ISBN 0-8369-7298-8). Ayer Co Pubs.

Representative Essays: English & American. Ed. by John R. Moore. LC 72-284. (Essay Index Reprint Ser.). Repr. of 1930 ed. 20.00 (ISBN 0-8369-2808-3). Ayer Co Pubs.

Representative Essays of Borden Parker Bowne. Borden P. Bowne. Ed. by Warren E. Steinkraus. LC 80-82504. 1980. 12.50 (ISBN 0-86610-066-0). Meridian Pub.

Representative French Lyrics of the Nineteenth Century. George Henning. 1977. Repr. of 1935 ed. 15.00. Century Bookbindery.

Representative German Poems. K. Knortz. 59.95 (ISBN 0-8490-0946-4). Gordon Pr.

Representative Government & Economic Power. David Coombes. (Policy Studies Institute Ser.). vi, 208p. 1982. text ed. 30.50x (ISBN 0-435-83180-1). Gower Pub Co.

Representative Government & Environmental Management. Edwin T. Haefele. 202p. 1974. 17.50 (ISBN 0-8018-1571-1). Resources Future.

Representative Government & the Revolution: The Maryland Constitutional Crisis of 1787. Ed. by Melvin Yazawa. LC 75-6546. pap. 50.00 (2026705). Bks Demand UMI.

Representative Government in Early Modern France. J. Russell Major. LC 79-14711. 800p. 1980. text ed. 59.00t (ISBN 0-300-02300-6). Yale U Pr.

Representative Governments & the Degeneration of Democracy. John S. Mill. 375p. 1985. 2 vols. 187.95 (ISBN 0-86722-098-8). Inst Econ Pol.

Representative Institutions in Renaissance France, 1421-1559. James R. Major. LC 82-25305. ix, 182p. 1983. Repr. of 1960 ed. lib. bdg. 38.50x (ISBN 0-313-23569-4, MAJR). Greenwood.

Representative Institutions in Theory & Practice. 217p. 1982. 25.25. P Lang Pubs.

Representative Irish Tales. Ed. by William B. Yeats. 1979. 30.00 (ISBN 0-901072-83-4, Pub. by Colin Smythe Ltd Britain); pap. 9.95 (ISBN 0-901072-84-2, Pub. by Colin Smythe Ltd Britain). Dufour.

Representative Man: Ralph Waldo Emerson in His Time. Joel Porte. (Illus.). 1979. 25.00x (ISBN 0-19-502436-2). Oxford U Pr.

Representative Man: Ralph Waldo Emerson in His Time. Joel Porte. (Illus.). 361p. Date not set. 42.50 (ISBN 0-231-06741-0); pap. 16.50 (ISBN 0-231-06740-2). Columbia U Pr.

Representative Medieval & Tudor Plays. Ed. by Roger S. Loomis & Henry W. Wells. LC 77-111109. (Play Anthology Reprint Ser). 1942. 22.50 (ISBN 0-8369-8202-9). Ayer Co Pubs.

Representative Men. Ralph Waldo Emerson. Ed. by Myron Simon. LC 79-92838. (Mind of Man Ser.). (Illus.). 224p. 1980. text ed. 30.00 (ISBN 0-934710-02-3). J Simon.

Representative Men see Essays & Lectures.

Representative Men of Puerto Rico. F. E. Jackson. (Puerto Rico Ser.). 1979. lib. bdg. 75.00 (ISBN 0-8490-2995-3). Gordon Pr.

Representative Men of the Bible see Portraits of Bible Men.

Representative Men: The Biographical Essays of John Clellon Holmes. John C. Holmes. LC 87-31681. 232p. (Orig.). 1988. 22.95 (ISBN 1-55728-007-X); pap. 12.95 (ISBN 1-55728-008-8). U of Ark Pr.

Representative Modern Plays British & American from Robertson to O'Neill. Richard A. Corell. 654p. Repr. of 1929 ed. lib. bdg. 75.00 (ISBN 0-8492-7309-9). R West.

Representative Modern Plays: Ibsen to Tennessee Williams. Robert Warnock. 1964. pap. write for info. (ISBN 0-673-05415-2). Scott F.

Representative Modern Preachers. facs. ed. Lewis O. Brastow. LC 68-57306. (Essay Index Reprint Ser). 1904. 20.00 (ISBN 0-8369-0101-0). Ayer Co Pubs.

Representative of the People? D. Hirst. LC 75-9283. 320p. 1975. o. p. 42.50 (ISBN 0-521-20810-6). Cambridge U Pr.

Representative One-Act Plays by American Authors. 1931. 30.00 (ISBN 0-8495-6266-X). Arden Lib.

Representative Opinions of Mr. Justice Holmes. Oliver W. Holmes, Jr. Compiled by Alfred Lief. LC 76-156194. 319p. 1972. Repr. of 1931 ed. lib. bdg. 35.00x (ISBN 0-8371-6143-6, HORO). Greenwood.

Representative Passages from English Literature. William Hudson. 1977. Repr. of 1926 ed. 15.00 (ISBN 0-89984-203-8). Century Bookbindery.

Representative Phi Beta Kappa Orations, Ser. 1. 2nd ed. Ed. by Clark S. Northup. Repr. of 1930 ed. 31.50 (ISBN 0-404-04795-5). AMS Pr.

Representative Phi Beta Kappa Orations, Ser. 2. Ed. by Clark S. Northup. LC 74-173800. Repr. of 1927 ed. 31.50 (ISBN 0-404-04796-3). AMS Pr.

Representative Photoplays Analyzed. Scott O'Dell. 44.95 (ISBN 0-8490-0947-2). Gordon Pr.

Representative Plays, 4 vols. Henry A. Jones. LC 72-145116. 1925. Repr. Set. 295.00x (ISBN 0-403-01054-3); 75.00x ea. Scholarly.

Representative Plays, 4 vols. Henry A. Jones. 1988. Repr. of 1925 ed. Set. lib. bdg. 295.00x. Am Biog Serv.

Representative Plays by American Dramatists. Montrose J. Moses. 1972. 132.00 (1026). Ayer Co Pubs.

Representative Plays by American Dramatists, 3 vols. Ed. by Montrose J. Moses. Incl. Vol. 1. 1765-1819. 678p (ISBN 0-405-08803-5); Vol. 2. 1815-1858. 823p (ISBN 0-405-08805-1); Vol. 3. 1856-1911. 926p (ISBN 0-405-08806-X). LC 64-14707. 1911. 35.00 ea.; 100.00 set (ISBN 0-685-24466-0). Ayer Co Pubs.

Representative Short Story Cycles of the Twentieth Century: Studies in a Literary Genre. Forrest L. Ingram. LC 75-159465. (De Proprietatibus Litterarum, Ser. Major: No. 15). 234p. 1971. text ed. 24.00x (ISBN 90-2791-848-1). Mouton.

Representative Spanish Authors, Vol. 1: From the Middle Ages Through the Eighteenth Century. 3rd ed. Ed. by Walter T. Pattison & Donald W. Bleznick. 1971. text ed. 22.00x (ISBN 0-19-501326-3). Oxford U Pr.

Representative Spanish Authors, Vol. 2: The Nineteenth Century to the Present. 3rd ed. Ed. by Walter T. Pattison & Donald W. Bleznick. 1971. text ed. 24.00x (ISBN 0-19-501433-2). Oxford U Pr.

Representative Women of the Bible (Eve to Mary Magdalene) see Portraits of Bible Women.

Representative Works, Nineteen Thirty-Eight-Nineteen Eighty-Five. Jackson MacLow. LC 85-61392. 350p. (Orig.). 1985. 18.95 (ISBN 0-937804-19-3); pap. 12.95 (ISBN 0-937804-18-5). Segue NYC.

Representative Works of Contemporary American Artists. Alfred Trumble. Ed. by H. Barbara Weinberg. LC 75-28879. (Art Experience in Late 19th Century America Ser.: Vol. 13). (Illus.). 1976. Repr. of 1887 ed. lib. bdg. 88.00 (ISBN 0-8240-2237-8). Garland Pub.

Representative Writings of the Early Nineteenth Century (1800-1839) see Millennium in America: From the Puritan Migration to the Civil War.

Representative Writings of the Eighteenth Century: Applications of Prophecy see Millennium in America: From the Puritan Migration to the Civil War.

Representative Writings of the Eighteenth Century: Scriptural Interpretations see Millennium in America: From the Puritan Migration to the Civil War.

Representative Writings, 1840-1860 see Millennium in America: From the Puritan Migration to the Civil War.

Representatives & Represented: Bases of Public Support for the American Legislatures. Samuel C. Patterson & Ronald D. Hedlund. LC 75-20232. (Wiley-Interscience Publication Ser.). (Illus., Orig.). pap. 57.50 (ISBN 0-317-09252-9, 2012590). Bks Demand UMI.

Representatives of Revolution. Ronald Paulson. LC 82-13458. 416p. 1987. pap. 15.95 (ISBN 0-300-03930-1, Y-634). Yale U Pr.

Representatives of the Lower Clergy in Parliament, 1295-1340. Jeffrey H. Denton & John P. Dooley. (Royal Historical Society Studies in History). 160p. 1987. 45.00 (ISBN 0-86193-207-2, Pub. by Boydell & Brewer). Longwood Pub Group.

Representatives of the People. Vernon Bogdanor. 350p. 1985. text ed. 38.50 (ISBN 0-566-00878-5). Gower Pub Co.

Representatives: The Real Nature & Function of Papal Legates. Mario Oliveri. LC 81-108272. 192p. (Orig.). 1981. pap. 4.95 (ISBN 0-905715-20-9). Wanderer Pr.

Represented Discourse in the Novels of Francois Mauriac. Sr. Anne G. Landry. LC 70-128933. (Carl Ser.: No. 44). Repr. of 1953 ed. 19.00 (ISBN 0-404-50344-6). AMS Pr.

Representing America: Experiences of U. S. Diplomats in the U. N. Linda M. Fasulo. (Illus.). 344p. 1985. pap. 10.95 (ISBN 0-8160-1304-7). Facts on File.

Representing America, Nineteen Hundred to Nineteen Hundred Forty: Paintings form the Permanent Collection of the Whitney Museum of American Art. LC 86-80643. (Illus.). 29p. 1986. pap. 4.00 (ISBN 0-939896-08-7). Flint Inst Arts.

Representing & Acquiring Geographic Knowledge. Ernest Davis. LC 86-10673. (Research Notes in Artificial Intelligence Ser.). (Illus.). 223p. 1986. pap. text ed. 22.95 (ISBN 0-934613-22-2). Morgan Kaufmann.

Representing & Intervening: Introductory Topics in the Philosophy of Natural Science. Ian Hacking. LC 83-5132. 272p. 1983. 47.50 (ISBN 0-521-23829-3); pap. 13.95 (ISBN 0-521-28246-2). Cambridge U Pr.

Representing Artists, Collectors, & Dealers 1985: A Course Handbook. Ralph E. Lerner. 1024p. 1985. pap. 15.00 (G4-3768). PLI.

Representing Battered Women in Custody Disputes in the District of Columbia: Litigating Custody As a Part of a Civil Protection Order. Women's Legal Defense Fund Staff. 12p. 1986. 5.00 (ISBN 0-317-67860-4). Women's Legal Defense.

Representing Children in the Family Division of the District of Columbia Superior Court. 25.00 (ISBN 0-317-62728-7). DC Bar Assn.

Representing Clients with Tax Problems. National Consumer Law Center. 124p. 1985. 10.00 (39,833). NCLS Inc.

Representing Corporate Officers & Directors. Marc J. Lane. LC 87-10044. (Business Practice Library Ser.). Date not set. price not set (ISBN 0-471-81788-0, Pub. by Wiley Law Pubns). Wiley.

Representing Disability Claimants Before the Social Security Administration: A Primer for New Advocates. Greater Upstate Law Project & Monroe County Legal Assitance Coproration. 154p. 1985. 12.00 (40,208). NCLS Inc.

Representing God in Washington: The Role of Religious Lobbies in the American Polity. Allen D. Hertzke. LC 87-15144. 278p. 1988. lib. bdg. 29.50x (ISBN 0-87049-553-4); pap. 14.95 (ISBN 0-87049-570-4). U of Tenn Pr.

Representing Kenneth Burke: Selected Papers from the English Institute. Ed. by Hayden White & Margaret Brose. LC 82-47972. (New Ser.: No. 6). 224p. 1983. 22.50x (ISBN 0-8018-2877-5). Johns Hopkins.

Representing Learning Disabled Children: A Manual for Attorneys. National Legal Resources Center for Child Advocacy & Protection Staff. 152p. 1985. pap. 10.00 (ISBN 0-317-63395-3, 549-0020-01). Amer Bar Assn.

Representing Lesbian Mothers & Gay Fathers in the District of Columbia, Maryland, & Virginia. Women's Legal Defense Fund Staff. 1986. 4.00 (ISBN 0-317-67859-0). Women's Legal Defense.

Representing Older Persons: An Advocates Manual. Burton Fretz et al. Ed. by Bruce Fried. (Orig.). 1985. pap. 25.00 (ISBN 0-932605-00-1). Natl Sen Citizens.

Representing Older Persons: An Advocates Manual. National Senior Citizen Law Center Staff. 124p. 1986. Repr. of 1985 ed. 15.00 (ISBN 0-941077-10-1, 38,950). NCLS Inc.

Representing Primary Caretaker Parents in Custody Disputes: A Manual for Attorneys. Women's Legal Defense Fund. 69p. (Orig.). 1984. pap. 15.00 (ISBN 0-932689-01-9). Women's Legal Defense.

Representing Professional Athletes & Teams 1986: A Course Handbook. 894p. 1986. pap. 45.00 (G4-3793). PLI.

Representing Publicly Traded Corporations 1987: Advising Corporate Management in a High Risk Environment, Vol 562. (Corporate Law & Practice Course Handbook Ser., 1986-1987). 655p. 1987. Set. pap. 45.00 (ISBN 0-685-85304-7, B4-6793). PLI.

Representing Residential Landlords & Tenants, 2 vols. Pennsylvania Bar Institute. 469p. 1984. 30.00 (ISBN 0-318-02179-X, 242). PA Bar Inst.

Representing Shakespeare: New Psychoanalytic Essays. Murray M. Schwartz & Coppelia Kahn. LC 79-3682. 320p. 1982. pap. text ed. 9.95x (ISBN 0-8018-2825-2). Johns Hopkins.

Representing Start-Up & High-Tech Companies. Pennsylvania Bar Institute. 132p. 1985. 30.00 (ISBN 0-318-19071-0, 297). PA Bar Inst.

Representing Super Doll. Richard Peck. 192p. (YA) (gr. 7 up). 1982. pap. 2.75 (ISBN 0-440-97362-7, LFL). Dell.

Representing Tax-Exempt Organizations: Program Materials, April 25-26, 1985, Washington, D.C. Georgetown University, Law Center Staff. LC 85-242755. Date not set. price not set. Grgtwn U Law Ctr.

Representing Tax-Exempt Organizations. Pennsylvania Bar Institute. 207p. 1985. 35.00 (ISBN 0-318-19072-9, 287). PA Bar Inst.

Representing the Child Client, No. 584. M. I. Soler et al. 1987. 85.00 (ISBN 0-317-67054-9). Bender.

Representing the English Renaissance. Ed. by Stephen Greenblatt. (Representation Bks.: No. 2). 360p. 1988. 42.00x (ISBN 0-520-06129-2); pap. 12.95x (ISBN 0-520-06130-6). U of Cal Pr.

Representing the Growing Technology Company. American Law Institute-American Bar Association Committee for Continuing Professional Education. LC 87-107673. (ALI-ABA Course of Study Materials Ser.). 877p. Date not set. price not set. Am Law Inst.

Representing the Lender in Litigation. Helen D. Chaitman & Practising Law Institute Staff. LC 86-60578. (Commercial Law & Practise Handbook Ser.: No. 385). 968p. 1986. 45.00 (A4-4148). PLI.

Representing the Nonprofit Organization. Marilyn E. Phelan. LC 87-23901. 368p. (Orig.). 1987. pap. 24.95 (ISBN 0-8366-0008-8). Callaghan.

Representing the Residential Real Estate Client. Frank Taddeo, Jr. 144p. 1987. 29.95 (ISBN 0-13-773763-7, Busn). P-H.

Representing the Respondent in Civil Commitment Proceedings. Donald H. Hermann. LC 85-194191. (Problems in Professional Responsibility). 35p. Date not set. price not set. Amer Bar Assn.

Representing Trade Associations, 1985. Practising Law Institute Staff & Roger A. Clark. LC 85-19017. (Commercial Law & Practice Course Handbook Ser.: No. 362). 544p. 1985. 15.00 (A4 4131). PLI.

Representing Yourself: What You Can Do Without a Lawyer. Kenneth Lasson & The Public Citizen Litigation Group. LC 83-1406. 270p. 1983. pap. 8.25 (ISBN 0-374-51726-6). FS&G.

Represion Religiosa en Cuba. Juan Clark. 124p. (Orig., Span.). pap. cancelled (ISBN 0-917049-05-5). Saeta.

Repressible Conflict, 1830-1861. Avery O. Craven. LC 83-45425. Repr. of 1939 ed. 19.00 (ISBN 0-404-20070-2). AMS Pr.

Repression & Revolt: The Origins of the 1948 Communist Insurrection in Malaya & Singapore. Michael R. Stenson. LC 75-631242. (Papers in International Studies: Southeast Asia Ser.: No. 10). pap. 20.00 (ISBN 0-317-09490-4, 2005116). Bks Demand UMI.

Repression: Basic & Surplus Repression in Psychoanalytic Theory: Freud, Reich, & Marcuse. Gad Horowitz. LC 77-5006. pap. 59.30 (ISBN 0-317-27027-3, 2023638). Bks Demand UMI.

Repression Disguised As Law: Human Rights in Poland. 1987. 8.00 (ISBN 0-317-62858-5). Lawyers Comm Human.

Repression in Taiwan: A Look at the Kaohsiung Rally & Trials. 34p. 2.00 (ISBN 0-686-36618-2). Asia Resource.

Repression in Victorian Fiction: Charlotte Bronte, George Eliot, & Charles Dickens. John Kucich. LC 86-25087. 320p. 1987. 32.00x (ISBN 0-520-05980-8). U of Cal Pr.

Repression of Crime, Studies in Historical Penology. Harry E. Barnes. LC 69-14911. (Criminology, Law Enforcement, & Social Problems Ser.: No. 56). 1969. Repr. of 1926 ed. 16.00x (ISBN 0-87585-056-1). Patterson Smith.

Repression of Psychoanalysis: Otto Fenichel & the Political Freudians. Russell Jacoby. LC 83-70756. 250p. 1983. text ed. 16.95 (ISBN 0-465-06916-9). Basic.

Repression of Psychoanalysis: Otto Fenichel & the Political Freudians. Russell Jacoby. LC 86-11358. xiv, 202p. 1986. pap. 10.95 (ISBN 0-226-39069-1). U of Chicago Pr.

Repressor of Overmuch Blaming of the Clergy, by Sometime Bishop of Chichester, 2 vols. Reginald Peacock. Ed. by Churchill Babington. (Roll Ser.: No. 19). Repr. of 1860 ed. 88.00 (ISBN 0-8115-1025-5). Kraus Repr.

Reprieve. Jean-Paul Sartre. LC 72-4475. 1972. pap. 6.95 (ISBN 0-394-71839-9, Vin). Random.

Reprieve for the Iron Horse: Amtrack. William E. Thomas. 1974. 6.25 (ISBN 0-87511-120-3). Claitors.

Reprieve: The Testament of John Resko. John Resko. LC 75-17464. 285p. 1975. Repr. of 1956 ed. lib. bdg. 35.00x (ISBN 0-8371-8311-1, RERE). Greenwood.

Reprint of Status of the Safety Professional. 1981. 25.00 (ISBN 0-939874-43-1). ASSE.

Reprinted Pieces. Charles Dickens. 1970. Repr. of 1921 ed. 12.95x (ISBN 0-460-00744-0, Evman). Biblio Dist.

Reprinted Selected Top Articles Published 1977, No. 1. H. M Myers. (Karger Highlights, Oral Science One Ser.). 1979. 10.00 (ISBN 3-8055-3028-5). S Karger.

Reprinted Selected Top Articles Published 1976 - 1977. Ed. by G. H. Berlyne. (Karger Highlights, Nephrology One Ser.). (Illus.). 1978. pap. 10.00 (ISBN 3-8055-2938-4). S Karger.

Reprints of Articles on Drug Therapy, 6 Vols. Ed. by Jan Koch-Weser. Incl. Vol. 6. (Illus.). 215p. 1980. Repr. of 1980 ed. pap. 7.50 (ISBN 0-910133-12-3); Vol. 5. (Illus.). 232p. 1980. Repr. of 1980 ed. pap. 7.50 (ISBN 0-910133-11-5); Vol. 4. (Illus.). 141p. 1977. Repr. of 1976 ed. pap. 6.00 (ISBN 0-910133-10-7); Vol. 3. (Illus.). 197p. 1976. Repr. of 1975 ed. pap. 6.00 (ISBN 0-910133-09-3); Vol. 2. (Illus.). 167p. 1976. Repr. of 1975 ed. pap. text ed. 6.00 (ISBN 0-910133-08-5); Vol. 1. (Illus.). 163p. 1976. Repr. of 1974 ed. pap. text ed. 6.00 (ISBN 0-910133-07-7). (Orig.). pap. MA Med Soc.

Reprints of Bette Hochberg's Textile Articles. 36p. 1982. pap. 4.95 (ISBN 0-9600990-7-7). B Hochberg.

Reprints of Selected Methods for the Analysis of Vitamin A & Carotenoids in Nutrition Surveys. Ed. by Guillermo Arroyave et al. 186p. 1982. pap. text ed. 9.00 (ISBN 0-935368-30-2). Nutrition Found.

Reprints of Welsh Manuscripts, 7 vols. Ed. by E. Stanton Roberts et al. Incl. Vol. 1. Llanstephan, Ms. 6 (ISBN 0-404-18241-0); Vol. 2. Peniarth, Ms. 67 (ISBN 0-404-18242-9); Vol. 3. Peniarth, Ms. 57 (ISBN 0-404-18243-7); Vol. 4. Peniarth, Ms. 76 (ISBN 0-404-18244-5); Vol. 5. Peniarth, Ms. 53 (ISBN 0-404-18245-3); Vol. 6. Peniarth, Ms. 49 (ISBN 0-404-18246-1); Vol. 7. Gwyneddon, Ms. 3 (ISBN 0-404-18247-X). LC 78-72656. (Celtic Language & Literature: Goidelic & Brythonic). Repr. Set. 171.50 (ISBN 0-404-18240-2); 24.50 ea. AMS Pr.

Reprise. Leslie Stephan. 176p. 1988. 14.95 (ISBN 0-312-02272-7, Pub. by Thomas Dunne Bks). St Martin.

Reprise: A Review of Basic Writing Skills. 2nd ed. C. Jeriel Howard & Eileen Lundy. 1979. pap. text ed. write for info. (ISBN 0-673-16220-6). Scott F.

Repro Lab: A Laboratory Manual for Animal Reproduction. 4th ed. A. M. Sorensen, Jr. (Illus.). 151p. 1979. pap. text ed. 9.95x (ISBN 0-89641-011-0). American Pr.

Reproach of the Gospel: An Inquiry into the Apparent Failure of Christianity As a General Rule of Life & Conduct. James H. Peile. 1977. lib. bdg. 59.95 (ISBN 0-8490-2516-8). Gordon Pr.

Reprobation Asserted. John Bunyan. pap. 1.25 (ISBN 0-685-19841-3). Reiner.

Reproducibility & Accuracy of Mechanical Tests, STP- 626. Ed. by H. E. Bennett et al. (NBS Special Publication Ser.: No. 568). 152p. 1977. pap. 15.00 (ISBN 0-8031-0556-8, 04-626000-23). ASTM.

Reproducible Blank Holiday Patterns. Janet Dellosa & Patti Carson. (Stick-Out-Your-Neck Ser.). (Illus.). 32p. (gr. k-6). 1984. pap. 1.98 (ISBN 0-88724-032-1, CD-0913). Carson-Dellos.

Reproducible Exercises for Blue Northers to Sea Breezes: Texas Weather & Climate. Donald R. Haragan. (Illus.). 58p. 1984. pap. 8.95x (ISBN 0-937460-16-8). Hendrick-Long.

Reproducing Families: The Political Economy of English Population History. David Levine. (Themes in Social Sciences Ser.). 272p. 1987. 34.50 (ISBN 0-521-33256-7); pap. 9.95 (ISBN 0-521-33785-2). Cambridge U Pr.

Reproducing Order: A Study of Police Patrol Work. Richard V. Ericson. (Canadian Studies in Criminology). 256p. 1982. 30.00x (ISBN 0-8020-5569-9); pap. 14.95 (ISBN 0-8020-6475-2). U of Toronto Pr.

Reproducing the World: Essays in Feminist Theory. Mary O'Brien. (Feminist Theory & Politics Ser.). 224p. 1988. 28.50 (ISBN 0-8133-0761-9); 13.50 (ISBN 0-8133-0760-0). Westview.

Reproduction, Vol 7. Ed. by Norman Adler et al. (Handbook of Behavioral Neurobiology). 784p. 1985. 95.00x (ISBN 0-306-41768-5, Plenum Pr). Plenum Pub.

Reproduction & Aging. Andras Balazs et al. 331p. 1974. text ed. 29.50x (ISBN 0-8422-7159-7). Irvington.

Reproduction & Breeding Techniques for Laboratory Animals. Ed. by E. S. Hafez. LC 70-98498. pap. 108.30 (ISBN 0-317-29300-1, 2055677). Bks Demand UMI.

Reproduction & Culture of Milkfish. Ed. by Cheng-Sheng Lee & I-Chiu Liao. (Illus.). 226p. (Orig.). 1985. pap. write for info. (ISBN 0-9617016-1-7). Oceanic Inst.

Reproduction & Development of Pacific Coast Marine Invertebrates. Megumi F. Strathmann. (Illus.). 640p. 1987. 35.00 (ISBN 0-295-96523-1). U of Wash Pr.

Reproduction & Development: Proceedings of the 28th International Congress of Physiological Sciences, Budapest, 1980. Ed. by B. Flerko et al. LC 80-41877. (Advances in Physiological Sciences: Vol. 15). (Illus.). 200p. 1981. 34.00 (ISBN 0-08-027336-X). Pergamon.

Reproduction & Disease in Captive & Wild Animals. Ed. by G. R. Smith & J. P. Hearn. (Zoological Society of London Symposia Ser.). (Illus.). 250p. 1988. 70.00 (ISBN 0-19-854007-8). Oxford U Pr.

Reproduction & Environment. R. L. Holmes. (Contemporary Science Library). (Illus.). 1971. pap. 1.65x (ISBN 0-393-00588-7, Norton Lib). Norton.

Reproduction & Human Welfare: A Challenge to Research-A Review of the Reproductive Sciences & Contraceptive Development. Roy O. Greep et al. 1976. text ed. 32.50x (ISBN 0-262-07067-7). MIT Pr.

Reproduction & Man. Richard J. Harrison. (Contemporary Science Library). (Illus.). 1971. pap. 1.65x (ISBN 0-393-00581-X, Norton Lib). Norton.

Reproduction Growth & Development in Two Species of Cloud Forest Peromycus from Southern Mexico. Eric A. Rickart. (Occasional Papers: No. 67). 22p. 1977. pap. 1.25 (ISBN 0-317-04907-0). U of Ks Mus Nat Hist.

Reproduction in Cattle. A. R. Peters & P. J. Ball. (Illus.). 256p. 1987. text ed. cancelled (ISBN 0-408-10866-5); pap. text ed. 24.95 (ISBN 0-408-10867-3). Butterworth.

Reproduction in Domestic Animals. 3rd ed. Ed. by H. H. Cole & P. T. Cupps. 1977. 54.00 (ISBN 0-12-179252-8). Acad Pr.

Reproduction in Domestic Ruminants. Ed. by G. D. Niswender et al. (Journals of Reproduction & Fertility, Supplement: No. 34). 270p. 1987. 67.00x (ISBN 0-906545-12-9, Biochemical Society). Rsrch Bks CT.

Reproduction in Farm Animals. 5th ed. Ed. by E. S. Hafez. LC 85-19910. (Illus.). 649p. 1987. text ed. 42.50 (ISBN 0-8121-1013-7). Lea & Febiger.

Reproduction in Humans see Anatomy & Physiology: A Programmed Approach.

Reproduction in Marginal Populations of the Hispid Cotton Rat (Sigmodon Hispidus) in Northern Kansas. Leroy R. McClenaghan & Michael S. Gaines. (Occasional Papers: Vol. 74). 16p. 1978. pap. 1.25 (ISBN 0-317-04888-0). U of KS Mus Nat Hist.

Reproduction in New World Primates: Animal Models for Medical Research. Ed. by J. P. Hearn. (Illus.). 350p. 1982. text ed. 55.00 (ISBN 0-85200-407-9, Pub. by MTP Pr England). Kluwer Academic.

Reproduction in Reef Fishes. R. E. Thresher. (Illus.). 400p. 1984. 39.95 (ISBN 0-87666-808-2, H-1048). TFH Pubns.

Reproduction in Sheep. Ed. by D. R. Lindsay & D. T. Pearce. 427p. 1985. 85.00 (ISBN 0-521-30659-0). Cambridge U Pr.

Reproduction in the Dog & Cat. J. Christiansen. (Illus.). 225p. 1984. pap. 27.95 (ISBN 0-7216-0974-0, Bailliere-Tindall). Saunders.

Reproduction in the Female Mammal: Proceedings. Easter School in Agricultural Science (13th 1966, University of Nottingham) Ed. by G. E. Lamming & E. C. Amoroso. pap. 148.80 (ISBN 0-317-42116-6, 2025756). Bks Demand UMI.

Reproduction in the Pig. Paul Hughes & Mike Varley. LC 80-40241. 254p. 1980. pap. text ed. 27.50 (ISBN 0-408-70921-9). Butterworth.

Reproduction in the United States: 1965. Norman B. Ryder & Charles F. Westoff. LC 78-120760. (Office of Population Research Ser.). 1971. 45.00x (ISBN 0-691-09318-0). Princeton U Pr.

Reproduction, Medicine & the Socialist State. Alena Hietlinger. 256p. 1987. 27.50x (ISBN 0-312-67403-1). St Martin.

Reproduction of Colour. 4th ed. R. W. Hunt. (Illus.). 663p. 1988. 89.95 (ISBN 0-86343-088-0). Van Nos Reinhold.

Reproduction of Daily Life. F. Perlman. 1969. 1.00x (ISBN 0-934868-17-4). Black & Red.

Reproduction of Eukaryotic Cells. D. M. Prescott. 1976. 39.50 (ISBN 0-12-564150-8). Acad Pr.

Reproduction of Eukaryotic Cells. D. M. Prescott. Ed. by J. J. Head. LC 76-62968. (Carolina Biology Readers Ser.). (Illus.). 16p. (gr. 10 up). 1978. pap. 1.65 (ISBN 0-89278-296-X, 45-9696). Carolina Biological.

Reproduction of Marine Invertebrates: Acoelomate & Pseudocoelomate Metazoans, Vol. 1. Ed. by Arthur C. Giese & John S. Pearse. 1974. 93.50 (ISBN 0-12-282501-2). Acad Pr.

Reproduction of Marine Invertebrates: Entoprocts: Lesser Callomates. Pearse Giese. 1975. Vol. 2. 93.50. Acad Pr.

Reproduction of Marine Invertebrates: General Aspects: Seeking Unity in Diversity, Vol. IX. Ed. by A. C. Giese et al. 1987. text ed. 45.00 (ISBN 0-940168-08-1). Boxwood.

Reproduction of Marine Invertebrates: Lophorphorates, Echinoderms, Vol. VI. Ed. by A. C. Giese et al. 1988. Repr. of 1976 ed. text ed. 45.00 (ISBN 0-940168-09-X). Boxwood.

Reproduction of Marine Invertebrates: Molluscs: Pelecypods & Lesser Classes, Vol. 5. Ed. by Arthur C. Giese & John S. Pearse. LC 72-84365. 1979. 93.50 (ISBN 0-12-282505-5). Acad Pr.

Reproduction of Marine Invertebrates, Vol. 2: Entoprocts: Lesser Coelomates. Ed. by Arthur C. Giese & John S. Pearse. 344p. 1975. 93.50 (ISBN 0-12-282502-0). Acad Pr.

Reproduction of Marine Invertebrates, Vol. 3: Annelids: Echiurans. Ed. by Arthur C. Giese & John S. Pearse. 343p. 1975. 93.50 (ISBN 0-12-282503-9). Acad Pr.

Reproduction of Marine Invertebrates, Vol. 4: Molluscs: Gastropods & Cephalopods. Ed. by Arthur C. Giese & John S. Pearse. 369p. 1977. 93.50 (ISBN 0-12-282504-7). Acad Pr.

Reproduction of Mothering: Psychoanalysis & the Sociology of Gender. Nancy Chodorow. 263p. 1978. pap. 8.95x (ISBN 0-520-03892-4); cloth 28.00x. U of Cal Pr.

Reproduction of Profiles. Rosmarie Waldrop. LC 87-110380. 96p. 1987. 19.95 (ISBN 0-8112-1044-8); pap. 9.95 (ISBN 0-8112-1045-6, NDP649). New Directions.

Reproduction of Social Control: A Study of Prison Workers at San Quentin. Barbara A. Owen. 172p. 1988. lib. bdg. 37.95 (ISBN 0-275-92818-7, C2818, Praeger). Greenwood.

Reproduction of Sound in High Fidelity & Stereo Phonographs. Edgar Villchur. (Illus.). 1966. pap. text ed. 2.95 (ISBN 0-486-21515-6). Dover.

Reproduction Photography for Lithography. Eric Chambers. (Illus.). 340p. 1979. 37.00 (1504) (ISBN 0-88362-057-X). Graphic Arts Tech Found.

Reproduction, Sex, & Preparation for Marriage. 2nd ed. Lawrence Crawley et al. (Illus.). 256p. 1973. pap. 25.00 (ISBN 0-13-773937-0). P-H.

Reproduction: The New Frontier in Occupational & Environmental Health Research. James E. Lockey et al. LC 84-7871. (Progress in Clinical & Biological Research Ser.: Vol. 160). 632p. 1984. 75.00 (ISBN 0-8451-5010-3). A R Liss.

Reproductions. LC 87-80120. 448p. 1987. 40.00 (ISBN 0-88445-018-X). Haddad's Fine Arts.

Reproductions from Illuminated Manuscripts: Series V. British Library Staff. (Illus.). 30p. 1965. Boxed prints 7.50 (ISBN 0-7141-0448-5, Pub. by British Lib). Longwood Pub Group.

Reproductions of Banality: Fascism, Literature & French Intellectual Life. Alice Y. Kaplan. LC 86-1425. (Theory & History of Literature Ser.: Vol. 36). 243p. (Orig.). 1986. 35.00x (ISBN 0-8166-1494-6); pap. 14.95 (ISBN 0-8166-1495-4). U of Minn Pr.

Reproductive & Developmental Behavior in Sheep: An Anthology from "Applied Animal Ethology". Ed. by A. F. Fraser. (Developments in Animal & Veterinary Sciences Ser.: Vol. 18). 478p. 1985. 84.25 (ISBN 0-444-42444-X). Elsevier.

Reproductive & Developmental Toxicity of Metals. Ed. by Tom W. Clarkson et al. 850p. 1983. 125.00x (ISBN 0-306-41396-5, Plenum Pr). Plenum Pub.

Reproductive Behavior & Evolution. Ed. by J. S. Rosenblatt & B. R. Komisaruk. LC 77-10855. (Evolution, Development, & Organization of Behavior Ser.: Vol. 1). (Illus.). 182p. 1977. 39.50x (ISBN 0-306-34481-5, Plenum Pr). Plenum Pub.

Reproductive Behaviour in Ungulates. Andrew F. Fraser. 1968. 60.00 (ISBN 0-12-266450-7). Acad Pr.

Reproductive Biology. Ed. by H. Balin & S. Glasser. 1973. 92.00 (ISBN 0-444-15004-8, Excerpta Medica). Elsevier.

Reproductive Biology of Invertebrates: Oogenesis, Oviposition & Oosorption, Vol. 1. Ed. by K. G. Adiyodi & Rita G. Adiyodi. LC 81-16355. (Reproductive Biology of Invertebrates Ser.). 770p. 1983. 169.00 (ISBN 0-471-10128-1, Pub. by Wiley-Interscience). Wiley.

Reproductive Biology of Invertebrates: Spermatogenesis & Sperm Function, Vol. 2. Ed. by K. G. Adiyodi & Rita G. Adiyodi. LC 81-16355. 692p. 1984. 151.95 (ISBN 0-471-90071-0, Pub. Wiley-Interscience). Wiley.

Reproductive Biology of Lizards on the American Samoan Islands. Terry D. Schwaner. (Occasional Papers: No. 86). 53p. 1980. 3.00 (ISBN 0-317-04887-2). U of KS Mus Nat Hist.

Reproductive Biology of the Great Apes: Comparative & Biomedical Perspectives. Ed. by Charles E. Graham. LC 80-89417. 1981. 78.50 (ISBN 0-12-295020-8). Acad Pr.

Reproductive Biology of the Primates. Ed. by P. Luckett. (Contributions to Primatology Ser.: Vol. 3). 284p. 1974. pap. 86.00 (ISBN 3-8055-1671-1). S Karger.

Reproductive Change in Developing Countries: Insights from the World Fertility Survey. Ed. by John Cleland & John Hobcraft. (Illus.). 301p. 1985. 28.00x (ISBN 0-19-828465-9). Oxford U Pr.

Reproductive Cycles in Tropical Reptiles. Henry S. Fitch. (Occasional Papers: No. 96). 53p. 1982. 3.25 (ISBN 0-317-04861-9). U of KS Mus Nat Hist.

Reproductive Decisions. R. I. Dunbar. LC 84-42584. (Monographs in Behavior & Ecology). (Illus.). 256p. 1984. text ed. 40.00x (ISBN 0-691-08360-6); pap. text ed. 14.50x (ISBN 0-691-08361-4). Princeton U Pr.

Reproductive Ecology of Marine Invertebrates. Ed. by Stephen E. Stancyk. LC 79-13841. (Belle W. Baruch Library in Marine Science Ser.). xvi, 284p. 1979. lib. bdg. 42.95x (ISBN 0-87249-379-2). U of SC Pr.

Reproductive Efficiency in Cattle: A Guideline for Projects in Developing Countries. M. Vanderplassche. (Animal Production & Health Papers: No. 25). 126p. 1982. pap. 8.50 (ISBN 92-5-101163-X, F2303, FAO). UNIPUB.

Reproductive Endocrinology: Physiology, Pathophysiology & Clinical Management. 2nd ed. Samuel S. Yen & Robert B. Jaffe. (Illus.). 806p. 1986. 99.00 (ISBN 0-7216-9630-9). Saunders.

Reproductive Energetic in Mammals. Ed. by A. S. Loudon & P. A. Racey. (Symposia of the Zoological Society of London Ser.: No. 57). (Illus.). 400p. 1987. 95.00 (ISBN 0-19-854005-1). Oxford U Pr.

Reproductive Ethics. Michael Bayles. 192p. 1984. pap. text ed. write for info. (ISBN 0-13-773904-4). P-H.

Reproductive Failure. Ed. by Alan H. DeCherney. (Illus.). 308p. 1986. text ed. 46.00 (ISBN 0-443-08346-0). Churchill.

Reproductive Fitness. 2nd ed. Ed. by C. R. Austin & R. V. Short. (Reproduction in Mammals Ser.: Bk. 4). (Illus.). 225p. 1985. 42.50 (ISBN 0-521-26649-1); pap. 14.95 (ISBN 0-521-31984-6). Cambridge U Pr.

Reproductive Function in the Human Male: Report. WHO Scientific Group. Geneva, 1972. (Technical Report Ser.: No. 520). (Also avail. in French & Spanish). 1973. pap. 1.60 (ISBN 92-4-120520-2). World Health.

Reproductive Genetics & the Law. Sherman Elias & George J. Annas. LC 86-28185. 1987. 41.50 (ISBN 0-8151-3062-7). Year Bk Med.

Reproductive Hazards of Industrial Chemicals. Ed. by S. M. Barlow & F. M. Sullivan. 610p. 1982. 103.50 (ISBN 0-12-078960-4). Acad Pr.

Reproductive Health Care Manual. Elizabeth Connell-Tatum & Howard Tatum. LC 84-70995. 1985. 8.65 (ISBN 0-917634-12-8). Creative Infomatics.

Reproductive Health Hazards in the Workplace. LC 85-600559. (OTA-BA-266 Ser.). (Illus.). 436p. (Orig.). 1985. pap. 15.00 (ISBN 0-318-19895-9, S/N 052-003-01001-1). USGPO.

Reproductive Health in Africa: Issues & Options. Ed. by Barbara Janowitz et al. (Illus.). 70p. (Orig., Also avail. in French). 1984. write for info. (ISBN 0-939704-04-8). Fam Health Intl.

Reproductive Immunology. Norbert Gleicher. LC 81-11812. (Progress in Clinical & Biological Research Ser.: Vol. 70). 510p. 1981. 95.00 (ISBN 0-8451-0070-X). A R Liss.

Reproductive Immunology 1983: Proceedings of the Second International Congress of Reproductive Immunology, Kyoto, Japan, August 17-20, 1983. Ed. by S. Isojima & W. D. Billington. 276p. 1984. 109.00 (ISBN 0-444-80551-6). Elsevier.

Reproductive Immunology 1986. Ed. by D. A. Clark & B. A. Croy. 310p. 1986. 108.00 (ISBN 0-444-80835-3). Elsevier.

Reproductive Impairments among Married Couples: United States. William D. Mosher et al. (Ser. 23: No. 11). 51p. 1982. pap. text ed. 4.75 (ISBN 0-8406-0252-9). Natl Ctr Health Stats.

Reproductive Medicine. Ed. by E. Steinberger et al. (Serono Symposia Publications from Raven Press: Vol. 29). 520p. 1986. text ed. 79.50. Raven.

Reproductive Pasts, Reproductive Futures: Genetic Counseling & Its Effectiveness. James R. Sorenson et al. LC 81-19322. (Birth Defects: Original Article Ser.: Vol. XVII, No. 4). 214p. 1981. 39.00 (ISBN 0-8451-1044-6). A R Liss.

Reproductive Physiology in Clinical Practice. Daniel H. Riddick. (Illus.). 256p. 1987. text ed. 65.00 (ISBN 0-86577-218-5). Thieme Med Pubs.

Reproductive Physiology of Fish. 256p. 1983. 27.75 (ISBN 90-220-0818-5, PDC251, Pudoc). UNIPUB.

Reproductive Physiology of Marsupials. Hugh Tyndale-Biscoe & Marilyn Renfree. (Monographs in Marsupial Biology Ser.). (Illus.). 507p. 1987. 75.00 (ISBN 0-521-25285-7); pap. 27.95 (ISBN 0-521-33792-5). Cambridge U Pr.

Reproductive Physiology of Teleost Fishes: A Review of Present Knowledge & Needs for Future Research. (Agricultural Development & Coordination Programme). 89p. 1981. pap. 7.50 (ISBN 92-5-101145-1, F2257, FAO). UNIPUB.

Reproductive Physiology of Vertebrates. 2nd ed. Ari Van Tienhoven. (Comstock Bk). (Illus.). 491p. 1983. 49.50x (ISBN 0-8014-1281-1). Cornell U Pr.

Reproductive Processes & Contraception. Ed. by Kenneth W. McKerns. LC 80-20744. (Biochemical Endocrinology Ser.). 752p. 1981. 89.50x (ISBN 0-306-40534-2, Plenum Pr). Plenum Pub.

Reproductive Rights: A Bibliography. Ed. by Joan Nordquist. (Contemporary Social Issues: A Bibliographic Ser.: No. 9). 60p. 1988. pap. 15.00 (ISBN 0-937855-17-0). Ref Rsch Serv.

Republican Heyday: Republicanism Through the McKinley Years. Clarence A. Stern. 1969. pap. 1.25 (ISBN 0-9600116-2-5). Stern.

Republican Humor. Stephen J. Skubik & Hal E. Short. 200p. 1976. 9.95 (ISBN 0-87491-033-1); pap. 5.95 (ISBN 0-87491-034-X). Acropolis.

Republican Iraq: A Study in Iraqi Politics Since the Revolution of 1958. Majid Khadduri. LC 80-1923. Repr. of 1969 ed. 37.00 (ISBN 0-404-18973-3). AMS Pr.

Republican Letters. Samuel Langhorne Clemens. LC 77-787. 1977. Repr. of 1941 ed. lib. bdg. 30.00 (ISBN 0-8414-3417-4). Folcroft.

Republican Letters. Mark Twain. 1941. lib. bdg. 39.00 (ISBN 0-685-10535-0). Folcroft.

Republican Looks at His Party. Arthur Larson. LC 74-12630. 210p. 1974. Repr. of 1956 ed. lib. bdg. 25.00x (ISBN 0-8371-7737-5, LARE). Greenwood.

Republican Party: A History. William S. Myers. (Government & Political Science Ser). 1968. Repr. of 1928 ed. 35.00 (ISBN 0-384-40741-2); with Democratic Party by Kent 68.00 (ISBN 0-384-40743-9). Johnson Repr.

Republican Party: A History of Its Fifty Years Existence, 2 vols. Francis Curtis. LC 75-41070. (BCL Ser. II). Repr. of 1904 ed. Set. 69.50 (ISBN 0-404-14870-0). AMS Pr.

Republican Party: A Short History. 2nd ed. Franklin L. Burdette. LC 72-2352. 214p. 1972. pap. 7.50 (ISBN 0-686-47404-X). Krieger.

Republican Party & Black America: From McKinley to Hoover, 1896-1933. Richard B. Sherman. LC 72-96714. 274p. 1973. 20.00x (ISBN 0-8139-0467-6). U Pr of Va.

Republican Party & the South, 1855-1877. Richard H. Abbott. LC 85-16557. (Fred W. Morrison Series in Southern Studies). xiv, 303p. 1986. 27.50x (ISBN 0-8078-1680-9). U of NC Pr.

Republican Party & Wendell Wilkie. Donald B. Johnson. LC 81-4168. ix, 354p. 1981. Repr. of 1960 ed. lib. bdg. 35.00x (ISBN 0-313-22876-0, JORP). Greenwood.

Republican Party As a Minority Party in Wartime, 1943-1944. Jeffrey Harry. Ed. by Robert E. Burke & Frank Freidel. (Modern American History Ser.). 45.00 (ISBN 0-8240-5668-X). Garland Pub.

Republican Party in the U. S. Senate, 1974-84: Party Change & Institutional Development. Christopher J. Bailey. LC 87-31397. 160p. 1988. 35.00 (ISBN 0-7190-2582-6, Pub. by Manchester Univ Pr). St Martin.

Republican Party: Its Heritage & History. Fred Schwengel. (Illus.). 160p. 1988. 18.95 (ISBN 0-87491-882-0); pap. 12.95 (ISBN 0-87491-883-9). Acropolis.

Republican Party Reptile. P. J. O'Rourke. LC 86-26504. 256p. 1987. 6.95 (ISBN 0-87113-145-5). Atlantic Monthly.

Republican Portugal: A Political History, 1910-1926. Douglas L. Wheeler. LC 77-15059. (Illus.). 352p. 1978. 37.50x (ISBN 0-299-07450-1). U of Wis Pr.

Republican Protestantism in Aztlan. E. C. Orozco. LC 80-82906. 261p. 1980. 24.00x (ISBN 0-9606102-1-9); pap. 14.00x (ISBN 0-9606102-2-7). Petereins Pr.

Republican Revolt. Nazaruddin Sjamsuddin. 376p. 1986. 37.00 (ISBN 9971-988-15-1, Pub. by Inst Southeast Asian Stud). Gower Pub Co.

Republican Right since Nineteen Forty-Five. David W. Reinhard. LC 82-40460. 304p. 1983. 25.00 (ISBN 0-8131-1484-5). U Pr of Ky.

Republican Rome, the Army & the Allies. Emilio Gabba. Tr. by P. J. Cuff. LC 76-14307. 1977. 46.00x (ISBN 0-520-03259-4). U of Cal Pr.

Republican Roosevelt. 2nd ed. John M. Blum. LC 54-5182. 177p. 1954. 13.50x (ISBN 0-674-76301-7); pap. 6.95x (ISBN 0-674-76302-5). Harvard U Pr.

Republican Tradition in Europe. facsimile ed. Herbert A. Fisher. LC 75-179519. (Select Bibliographies Reprint Ser). Repr. of 1911 ed. 21.00 (ISBN 0-8369-6648-1). Ayer Co Pubs.

Republicanism & Socialism in Ireland: A Study in the Relationship of Politics & Ideology from the United Irishmen to James Connolly. Priscilla Metscher. (Bremer Beitrage zur Literatur und Ideologiegeschichte Ser.: Vol. 2). 617p. 1986. pap. 48.55 (ISBN 3-8204-8520-1). P Lang Pubs.

Republicanism in New Orleans see New Orleans Voter: A Handbook of Political Description.

Republicanism in Reconstruction Texas. Carl H. Moneyhon. (Illus.). 335p. 1980. text ed. 22.50x (ISBN 0-292-77553-9). U of Tex Pr.

Republicanism, Representation, & Consent: Views of the Founding Era. Ed. by Daniel J. Elazar. LC 79-5466. 137p. (Orig.). 1979. pap. 14.95 (ISBN 0-87855-807-1). Transaction Bks.

Republicans & Federalists in Pennsylvania: 1790-1801. Harry M. Tinkcom. LC 50-9356. (Orig.). 1950. pap. 4.95 (ISBN 0-911124-24-1). Pa Hist & Mus.

Republicans & Imperialists: Anglo-Irish Relations in the 1930s. Deirdre McMahon. LC 83-51121. 352p. 1984. 36.00t (ISBN 0-300-03071-1). Yale U Pr.

Republicans & Vietnam, 1961-1968. Terry Dietz. LC 85-24764. (Contributions in Political Science: No. 146). (Illus.). 199p. 1986. lib. bdg. 35.00 (ISBN 0-313-24892-3, DRV/). Greenwood.

Republicans Face the Southern Question: The New Departure Years, 1877-1897. Vincent P. De Santis. LC 78-64231. (Johns Hopkins University. Studies in the Social Sciences. Seventy-Seventh Ser. 1959: 1). Repr. of 1959 ed. 13.00 (ISBN 0-404-61336-5). AMS Pr.

Republicans, Negroes, & Progressives in the South, Nineteen Twelve to Nineteen Sixteen. Paul D. Casdorph. LC 80-15398. (Illus.). ix, 262p. 1981. text ed. 19.75 (ISBN 0-8173-0048-1). U of Ala Pr.

Republic's Private Navy: The American Privateering Business As Practiced by Baltimore During the War of 1812. Jerome R. Garitee. LC 76-41487. (American Maritime Library: Vol. 8). (Illus.). xx, 356p. 1977. 10.00 (ISBN 0-8195-5004-3); limited ed. 35.00 (ISBN 0-8195-5005-1). Mystic Seaport.

Republikanische Richterbund (1921-1933) Birger Schulz. (Rechtshistorische Reihe: Vol. 21). 211p. (Ger.). 1982. 24.75 (ISBN 3-8204-7122-7). P Lang Pubs.

Republique Des Lacedemoniens. Xenophon. Ed. by W. R. Connor. LC 78-18589. (Greek Texts Commentaries Ser.). (Illus.). 1979. Repr. of 1934 ed. lib. bdg. 14.00x (ISBN 0-405-11431-1). Ayer Co Pubs.

Republique en Marche. Emile Zola. 660p. 1956. 8.95 (ISBN 0-686-55799-9). French & Eur.

Republique Imperiale; les Etats-Unis Dans le Monde, 1945-1972 see Imperial Republic: The United States & the World 1945-1973.

Republique... Notre Royaume de France. Charles Peguy. pap. 7.95 (ISBN 0-685-37037-2). French & Eur.

Republique Universelle, ou Adresse aux Tyrannicides. Jean-Baptiste Cloots. LC 72-147425. (Library of War & Peace; Proposals for Peace, a History). lib. bdg. 46.00 (ISBN 0-8240-0217-2). Garland Pub.

Repudiation of State Debts. William A. Scott. LC 77-137282. Repr. of 1893 ed. 12.50 (ISBN 0-404-05642-3). AMS Pr.

Repulsion: Aesthetics of the Grotesque. Alternative Museum Staff. LC 86-72479. (Illus., Orig.). 1986. pap. 6.00 (ISBN 0-932075-12-6). Alternative Mus.

Repunits & Repetends. Samuel Yates. LC 82-50241. 215p. 1982. pap. 13.00 (ISBN 0-9608652-0-9). S Yates.

Repurchase & Reverse Repurchase Agreements 1985. 715p. 1985. 15.00 (A4-4135). PLI.

Reputation & Influence of William Godwin in America. O. Earle. 59.95 (ISBN 0-8490-0948-0). Gordon Pr.

Reputation Dies. Alice C. Ley. 176p. 1986. pap. 2.95 (ISBN 0-446-34117-7). Warner Bks.

Reputation for a Song. Edward Grierson. 272p. 1987. pap. 5.95 (ISBN 0-14-008241-7). Penguin.

Reputation of Abraham Cowley: Sixteen Sixty - Eighteen Hundred. Arthur H. Nethercott. (English Literature Ser., No. 33). 1970. pap. 22.95x (ISBN 0-8383-0057-X). Haskell.

Reputation of John Donne 1779-1873. Raoul Granqvist. (Illus.). 212p. (Orig.). 1975. pap. text ed. 20.00x (ISBN 91-554-0331-X, Pub. by Almqvist & Wiksell). Coronet Bks.

Reputation of Jonathan Swift 1781-1882. Donald M. Berwick. LC 65-21096. (Studies in Irish Literature, No. 16). 1969. Repr. of 1941 ed. lib. bdg. 39.95x (ISBN 0-8383-0508-3). Haskell.

Reputation of the American Businessman. Sigmund Diamond. 16.50 (ISBN 0-8446-0581-6). Peter Smith.

Reputation of the Metaphysical Poets During the Age of Johnson & the Romantic Revival. Arthur H. Nethercott. LC 72-98993. (English Literature Ser., No. 33). 1970. pap. 22.95x (ISBN 0-8383-0058-8). Haskell.

Reputation of Trollope. John C. Olmsted & Jeffrey Welch. LC 76-52683. (Library of Humanities Reference Bks.: No. 88). lib. bdg. 36.00 (ISBN 0-8240-9885-4). Garland Pub.

Reputations. Douglas Goldring. LC 68-16294. 1968. Repr. of 1920 ed. 23.00x (ISBN 0-8046-0174-7, Pub. by Kennikat). Assoc Faculty Pr.

Reputations Live on: An Early Malay Autobiography. Amin Sweeney. 150p. 1980. 30.00x (ISBN 0-520-04073-2). U of Cal Pr.

Reputations Ten Years After. facs. ed. Basil H. Liddell Hart. LC 68-8478. (Essay Index Reprint Ser). (Illus.). 1968. Repr. of 1928 ed. 20.00 (ISBN 0-8369-0619-5). Ayer Co Pubs.

Request Presented to the King of Spayn by the Inhabitants of the Lowe Countreyes, Protesting That They Will Live According to the Reformation of the Gospell. LC 71-26044. (English Experience Ser.: No. 266). 1970. Repr. of 1578 ed. 7.00 (ISBN 90-221-0266-1). Walter J Johnson.

Requiem. Jean Cocteau. 180p. 1962. 8.95 (ISBN 0-686-54558-3). French & Eur.

Requiem. Sam Hamill. 32p. 1983. 36.00x (ISBN 0-914742-68-X). Copper Canyon.

Requiem. Jerome McDonough. (Illus.). 41p. (Director's Production Script). 1977. pap. 7.50 (ISBN 0-88680-164-8). I E Clark.

Requiem: A Novel. Shizuko Go. LC 84-48698. 120p. 1985. 14.95 (ISBN 0-87011-716-5). Kodansha.

Requiem, & Its Maquettes. Francis Warner. 1978. 8.95 (ISBN 0-86140-063-1, Pub. by Colin Smythe Ltd Britain). Dufour.

Requiem for a Dream. Hubert Selby, Jr. (Classic Reprint Ser.). 278p. 1988. lib. bdg. 20.00 (ISBN 0-938410-57-1); pap. 9.95 (ISBN 0-938410-56-3). Thunder's Mouth.

Requiem for a Fleet. Robert H. Freeman. 260p. 1984. 15.00 (ISBN 0-931099-00-5). Shellback Pr.

Requiem for a Kingfish. Ed Reed. LC 86-71787. 250p. 1986. 24.95 (ISBN 0-9617384-0-5). Award Pubns.

Requiem for a Nun. William Faulkner. 1951. 13.95 (ISBN 0-394-44274-1). Random.

Requiem for a Nun. William Faulkner. LC 74-17145. 1975. pap. 5.95 (ISBN 0-394-71412-1, Vin). Random.

Requiem for a Nun: Preliminary Material, 2 vols. William Faulkner. Ed. by Blotner et al. (William Faulkner Manuscripts Ser.). 1987. 200.00 (ISBN 0-8240-6825-4). Garland Pub.

Requiem for a Nun: Revised Galley Proofs. William Faulkner. Ed. by Blotner et al. (William Faulkner Manuscripts Ser.). 100.00 (ISBN 0-8240-6827-0). Garland Pub.

Requiem for a Nun: Typescript. William Faulkner. Ed. by Blotner et al. (William Faulkner Manuscripts Ser.). 100.00 (ISBN 0-8240-6826-2). Garland Pub.

Requiem for a People: The Rogue Indians & the Frontiersmen. Stephen D. Beckham. LC 79-145497. (Civilization of the American Indian Ser.: Vol. 108). (Illus.). 1978. 16.95 (ISBN 0-8061-0942-4); pap. 9.95 (ISBN 0-8061-1036-8). U of Okla Pr.

Requiem for a River Rat. Neal Ekker. LC 85-4566. 1985. 15.95 (ISBN 0-934878-58-7). Dembner Bks.

Requiem for a Ruler of Worlds. Brian Daley. 304p. (Orig.). 1986. pap. 3.50 (ISBN 0-345-31487-5, Del Rey). Ballantine.

Requiem for a Woman's Soul. Omar Rivabella. LC 85-10765. 128p. 1986. 14.45 (ISBN 0-394-54917-1). Random.

Requiem for a Women's Soul. Omar Rivabella. Tr. by Paul Riveiera. 128p. 1987. pap. 4.95 (ISBN 0-14-009773-2). Penguin.

Requiem for Astounding. Alva Rogers. LC 64-57082. (Illus.). 1964. pap. 6.00 (ISBN 0-911682-16-3). Advent.

Requiem for Battleship Yamato. Mitsuru Yoshida. Tr. by Richard Minear from Japanese. LC 84-40661. (Illus.). 204p. 1985. 16.95 (ISBN 0-295-96216-X). U of Wash Pr.

Requiem for Heurtebise: Homage to Jean Cocteau. David L. Fisher. 1974. pap. 1.00 (ISBN 0-686-18853-5); signed ed. 2.00 (ISBN 0-686-18854-3). Man-Root.

Requiem for Idols. Norah Lofts. 208p. 1982. pap. 2.50 (ISBN 0-449-24507-1, Crest). Fawcett.

Requiem for Innocence. Frank J. Foley, Jr. LC 75-9425. 61p. 1975. 5.00 (ISBN 0-8233-0221-0). Golden Quill.

Requiem for Sugar. George Grace. (Illus.). 1986. 2.00 (ISBN 0-938838-28-8). Textile Bridge.

Requiem for the Card Catalog: Management Issues in Automated Cataloging. Ed. by Daniel Gore et al. LC 78-7129. (New Directions in Librarianship Ser.: No. 2). 1979. lib. bdg. 35.00 (ISBN 0-313-20608-2, GMI/). Greenwood.

Requiem for the Narrow Gauge. Ross B. Grenard. 125p. 1984. 24.95 (ISBN 0-912113-13-8); pap. 12.95 (ISBN 0-912113-12-X). Railhead Pubns.

Requiem in Full Score. Giuseppe Verdi. 1978. pap. 8.95 (ISBN 0-486-23682-X). Dover.

Requiem on Cerro Maravilla: The Police Murders in Puerto Rico & the Federal Government Coverup. Manuel Suarez. (Illus.). 278p. 1987. 18.95 (ISBN 0-943862-35-3); pap. 9.95 (ISBN 0-943862-36-1). Waterfront NJ.

Requiem por un Campesino. Sender. (EMC Easy Readers: Series C). (YA) (gr. 7-12). 1972. pap. 4.95 (ISBN 0-88436-055-5, 70273). EMC.

Requiem Por Yarini. Carlos Felipe. 1978. pap. 3.00 (ISBN 0-685-95271-1). Ediciones.

Requiem: Variations on Eighteenth-Century Themes. Forrest McDonald & Ellen S. McDonald. 192p. 1988. 19.95 (ISBN 0-7006-0370-0). U Pr of Ks.

Required Photographic Documentation & Equipment. William Leisher & Richard Amt. 1980. 9.00 (ISBN 0-318-18701-9). Am Inst Conser Hist.

Required Reading: A Decade of Political Wit & Wisdom. Eugene McCarthy. 256p. 1988. 16.95 (ISBN 0-15-176880-3). HarBraceJ.

Required Writing: Miscellaneous Pieces 1955-1982. Philip Larkin. LC 84-4099. 336p. 1984. 17.95 (ISBN 0-374-24948-2); pap. 9.95 (ISBN 0-374-51840-8). FS&G.

Requirements Analysis for Computerization of the New Jersey Courts, 2 vols. National Center for State Courts Staff. 1982. Vol. I, 498 pgs. manuscript 29.88 (R-075); Vol. II, 692 pgs. manuscript 41.52 (R-076). Natl Ctr St Courts.

Requirements Analysis for Lorain County (Ohio) Child Support Enforcement System. 50p. 1986. manuscript 3.00 (NERO-186). Natl Ctr St Courts.

Requirements Definition Study of the San Mateo County Municipal Court. National Center for State Courts Staff. 290p. 1985. manuscript 18.00 (WRO-065). Natl Ctr St Courts.

Requirements-Driven Software Design. Mack Alford. (Illus.). 400p. 1988. 44.95 (ISBN 0-07-001051-X). McGraw.

Requirements Engineering Environments: Proceedings of the International Symposium on Current Issues of Requirements Engineering Environments, Sept. 20-21, 1982, Kyoto, Japan. Ed. by Y. Ohno. 174p. 1983. 73.75 (ISBN 0-444-86533-0, North Holland). Elsevier.

Requirements for a Software Engineering Environment. Marvin Zelkowitz. (Software Engineering Ser.: Vol. 2). (Illus.). 192p. 1988. text ed. 32.50 (ISBN 0-89391-447-9). Ablex Pub.

Requirements for Biological Substances: Manufacturing Establishments & Control Laboratories, a Report. WHO Expert Group, Geneva, 1965. (Technical Report Ser: No. 323). 71p. (Eng., Fr., Rus. & Span.). 1966. pap. 2.00 (ISBN 92-4-120323-4). World Health.

Requirements for Certification of Teachers, Counselors, Librarians, Administrators: For Elementary Schools, Secondary Schools....(Etc) 51st ed. Mary P. Burks. x, 240p. 1986. lib. bdg. 28.00x (ISBN 0-226-08105-2). U of Chicago Pr.

Requirements for Certification of Teachers, Counselors, Librarians, Administrators for Elementary Schools, Secondary Schools, Junior Colleges, 1987-1988. 52nd ed. Mary P. Burks. 250p. text ed. 29.00x (ISBN 0-226-08106-0, A43-1905). U of Chicago Pr.

Requirements for Certification of Teachers, Counselors, Librarians, Administrators for Elementary Schools, Secondary Schools, Junior Colleges Fifty-Third Edition, 1988-89. Mary P. Burks. 272p. 1988. 30.00x (ISBN 0-226-08107-9). U of Chicago Pr.

Requirements for Faithfulness. 1981. 1.25 (ISBN 0-89858-030-7). Fill the Gap.

Requirements for Land Surveyor Registration: Summaries by State. 75p. 1980. 15.00 (ISBN 0-317-32469-1, S230); members 10.00 (ISBN 0-317-32470-5). Am Congrs Survey.

Requirements for Poultry Virus Vaccines: Proceedings. International Symposium on Requirements for Poultry Virus Vaccines, Lyon, 1973. Ed. by Ch Merieux et al. (Developments in Biological Standardization: Vol. 25). 1976. 25.50 (ISBN 3-8055-2413-7). S Karger.

Requirements for the Irradiaton of Food on a Commercial Scale: Proceedings. Panel, Vienna, March 18-22, 1974. (Illus.). 219p. 1975. pap. 22.75 (ISBN 92-0-111275-0, ISP394, IAEA). UNIPUB.

Requirements of Ascorbic Acid, Vitamin D, Vitamin B12, Folate & Iron. WHO-FAO Joint Expert Group, Geneva, 1969. (Technical Report Ser: No. 452). 75p. 1970. pap. 2.00 (ISBN 92-4-120452-4, 669). World Health.

Requirements of Laws & Regulations Enforced by the U. S. Food & Drug Administration. 85p. 1984. pap. 2.50 (ISBN 0-318-18826-0, S/N 017-012-00321-4). USGPO.

Requirements of Vitamin A, Thiamine, Riboflavin & Niacin: Report of a Joint FAO-WHO Expert Group. (Nutrition Meetings Reports: No. 41). 86p. (3rd Printing 1978). 1967. pap. 7.50 (ISBN 92-5-100453-6, F1467, FAO). UNIPUB.

Requisitions De Grains Sous la Terreur. Albert Mathiez. (Revue D'histoire Economique et Sociale: Vol. 8). (Fr.). 1973. Repr. of 1920 ed. lib. bdg. 15.00 (ISBN 0-8337-2298-0). B Franklin.

Rereading Capital. Ben Fine & Laurence Harris. LC 78-20912. 1979. 24.00x (ISBN 0-231-04792-4). Columbia U Pr.

Rereading Doris Lessing: Narrative Patterns of Doubling & Repetition. Claire Sprague. LC 86-30879. xii, 210p. 1987. 22.00x (ISBN 0-8078-1747-3); pap. 9.95x (ISBN 0-8078-4187-0). U of NC Pr.

Rereading Russell: Essays on Bertrand Russell's Metaphysics & Epistemology. Ed. by C. Wade Savage & C. Anthony Anderson. (Minnesota Studies in the Philosophy of Science: Vol. XII). 350p. 1988. text ed. 29.50x (ISBN 0-8166-1649-3). U of Minn Pr.

Rereadings: Eight Early French Novels. Philip Stewart. 315p. 1984. pap. 17.00 (ISBN 0-917786-32-7). Summa Pubns.

Rerum Anglicarum Scriptores Post Bedam Praecipui Ex Vetustissimis Codicibus Manuscriptis Nunc Primun in Lucem Editi. H. Savile. 1006p. Date not set. Repr. of 1601 ed. text ed. 155.00x (ISBN 0-576-72245-6, Pub. by Gregg Intl Pubs England). Gregg Intl.

Reruns. Jonathan Baumbach. LC 74-77780. 170p. 1974. 9.95 (ISBN 0-914590-00-6); pap. 5.95 (ISBN 0-914590-01-4). Fiction Coll.

Res Cogitans: An Essay in Rational Psychology. Zeno Vendler. LC 72-3182. (Contemporary Philosophy Ser.). 273p. 1972. 29.95x (ISBN 0-8014-0743-5). Cornell U Pr.

Res Gestae Divi Augusti. Augustus. Ed. by P. A. Brunt & J. M. Moore. 1967. pap. 7.95x (ISBN 0-19-831772-7). Oxford U Pr.

Res Gestae Divi Augusti. Paterculus Velleius. (Loeb Classical Library: No. 152). 13.95x (ISBN 0-674-99168-0). Harvard U Pr.

Res Judicata. Robert C. Casad. (Nutshell Ser.). 310p. 1976. 7.95 (ISBN 0-317-00004-7). West Pub.

Res Judicata & Collateral Estoppel: Tools for Plaintiffs & Defendants. Warren Freedman. LC 87-7307. 1988. 39.95 (ISBN 0-89930-277-7, FJD/, Quorum Bks). Greenwood.

Research & Instruction in Written Language. (Exceptional Children Ser.: Vol. 54, No. 6). 96p. 1988. 7.00 (B710). Coun Exc Child.

Research & Issues in Psychology. Winston-Mottin. 352p. 1984. pap. text ed. 19.95 (ISBN 0-8403-3460-5). Kendall-Hunt.

Research & Language Learning see Language Teaching: Broader Contexts.

Research & Lawmakers: A Student Perspective. Barry Salussolia & David Rider. LC 84-621357. (Occasional Papers: No. 4). (Illus.). 1981. pap. text ed. 2.50 (ISBN 0-944277-05-5). U of VT Dept Hist.

Research & Lawmakers: A Student Perspective. Ed. by Barry Salussolia & David Rider. (Occasional Papers: No. 4). (Illus.). 66p. (Orig.). 1981. pap. text ed. 2.50x. U VT Ctr Rsch VT.

Research & Medical Practice: Their Interaction. Ciba Foundation Staff. LC 76-24846. (Ciba Foundation Symposium, New Ser.: 44). pap. 57.00 (ISBN 0-317-29782-1, 2022172). Bks Demand UMI.

Research & Methodology in General Pediatrics: A Swiss Experience. Ed. by P. Girardet. (Journal: Paediatrician: Vol. 9, Nos. 5-6). (Illus.). 128p. 1981. pap. 46.75 (ISBN 3-8055-2661-X). S Karger.

Research & Policy-Making: The Case of Regional Policy. 106p. (Orig.). 1982. pap. 8.00x (ISBN 92-64-12269-9). OECD.

Research & Policy: The Uses of Qualitative Methods in Social & Educational Research. Janet Finch. (Social Research & Educational Studies: Vol. 2). 260p. 1986. 38.00x (ISBN 1-85000-098-0, Pub. by Falmers Pr); pap. 21.00x (ISBN 1-85000-099-9). Taylor & Francis.

Research & Practice in Physical Education: Selected Papers from the 1976 Research Symposia of the AAHPER National Convention. Ed. by Robert E. Stadulis. LC 77-150410. pap. 74.30 (ISBN 0-317-55500-6, 2029534). Bks Demand UMI.

Research & Practice In Social Skills Training. Ed. by Arno S. Bellack & M. Hersen. LC 79-12118. (Illus.). 370p. 1979. 42.50x (ISBN 0-306-40233-5, Plenum Pr). Plenum Pub.

Research & Practice: Twenty-One of Library Research in the U. K. Nick Moore. (Library & Information Report: No. 55). 1987. pap. 24.75 (ISBN 0-7123-3088-7, Pub. by British Lib). Longwood Pub Group.

Research & Productivity: Endogenous Technical Change. Ryuzo Sato & Gilbert Suzawa. 200p. 1983. 26.00 (ISBN 0-86569-068-5). Auburn Hse.

Research & Project Funding for the Uninitiated. Robert E. McAdam et al. (Illus.). 82p. 1982. spiral bdg. 19.75x (ISBN 0-398-04635-2). C C Thomas.

Research & Reference Guide to French Studies. 2nd ed. Charles B. Osburn. LC 81-5637. 570p. 1981. 37.50 (ISBN 0-8108-1440-4). Scarecrow.

Research & Reflections in Archaeology & History: Essays in Honor of Doris Stone. E. W. Andrews. (Publication: No. 57). 217p. 1986. 35.00 (ISBN 0-939238-87-X). Tulane MARI.

Research & Report Writing for Business & Economics. Conrad Berenson & Raymond Colton. (Orig.). 1970. pap. text ed. write for info (ISBN 0-394-30318-0, RanC). Random.

Research & Results in Plant Breeding. Ed. by Gosta Olsson. (Illus.). 292p. (Orig.). pap. text ed. 42.50x (ISBN 91-36-88705-6, Pub. by LTs Forlag A B (Stockholm Sweden)). Coronet Bks.

Research & Source Guide for Students in Speech Pathology & Audiology. Gordon F. Holloway & L. Michael Webster. LC 73-571. 112p. 1978. 9.50 (ISBN 0-87527-154-5). Green.

Research & Technical Writing. E. Pokress. 8.60x (ISBN 0-685-22754-5). Aurea.

Research & Technology. Ed. by I. Bernard Cohen. LC 79-7982. (Three Centuries of Science in America Ser.). (Illus.). 1980. lib. bdg. 23.00x (ISBN 0-405-12564-X). Ayer Co Pubs.

Research & the Ageing Population: Symposium No. 134. Ciba Foundation Symposium Staff. LC 87-29440. (CIBA Foundation Symposia Ser.). 264p. 1988. 49.95 (ISBN 0-471-91420-7). Wiley.

Research & the Complex Causality of the Schizophrenias. Group for the Advancement of Psychiatry Staff. LC 84-9535. (Report Ser.: No. 116). 104p. 1984. pap. text ed. 13.95 (ISBN 0-87630-373-4). Brunner-Mazel.

Research & the Health of Americans: Priorities, Process & Strategies. Stephen P. Strickland. 20p. (Orig.). 1978. pap. text ed. 5.00 (ISBN 0-8191-5905-0, Pub. by Aspen Inst for Humanistic Studies). U Pr of Amer.

Research & the Library: A Student Guide to Basic Techniques. Alan L. Whipple. 120p. (Orig.). (gr. 8-11). 1974. pap. text ed. 3.95x (ISBN 0-88334-062-3). Ind Sch Pr.

Research & the Practice of Librarianship: An International Symposium. G. G. Allen & F. C. Exon. (Western Library Studies: No. 7). 220p. 1986. text ed. 35.00 (ISBN 0-908155-61-1, W561-1, Pub. by W A Inst Tech Australia). ALA.

Research & Theory in Current Archeology. Ed. by Charles L. Redman. LC 80-16701. 400p. 1983. Repr. of 1973 ed. lib. bdg. 21.50 (ISBN 0-89874-226-9). Krieger.

Research & Theory in Developmental Psychology: Awards Papers of the New York State Psychological Association. Ed. by Marguerite F. Levy. 1983. 27.50x (ISBN 0-8290-1067-X). Irvington.

Research & Thought in Administrative Theory: Developments in the Field of Educational Administration. Ed. by Gladys S. Johnston & Carol C. Yeakey. LC 86-20196. (Illus.). 236p. (Orig.). 1986. lib. bdg. 25.75 (ISBN 0-8191-5622-1); pap. text ed. 13.25 (ISBN 0-8191-5623-X). U Pr of Amer.

Research & Training for Management of Arid Lands. J. A. Mabbutt. 48p. 1981. pap. 10.00 (ISBN 92-808-0198-3, TUNU129, UNU). UNIPUB.

Research & Training in Literacy in Asia & Oceania. (Illus.). 73p. 1979. pap. 5.00 (ISBN 0-686-59436-3, UB077, UB). UNIPUB.

Research Animals & Concepts of Applicability to Clinical Medicine: Experimental Biology & Medicine, Vol. 7. Ed. by K. Gaertner & H. Hackbarth. (Illus.). x, 234p. 1982. pap. 98.75 (ISBN 3-8055-3492-2). S Karger.

Research Animals & Experimental Design in Nephrology. H. Stolte & Jeannette Alt. (Contributions to Nephrology Ser.: Vol. 19). (Illus.). x, 250p. 1980. soft cover 54.75 (ISBN 3-8055-3075-7). S Karger.

Research, Application, & Experience with Precast Prestressed Bridge Deck Panels. (PCI Journal Reprints Ser.). 24p. pap. 5.00 (ISBN 0-318-19843-6, JR167). Prestressed Concrete.

Research Applications of Nuclear Pulsed Systems. (Panel Proceedings Ser.). (Illus.). 234p. 1967. pap. 16.25 (ISBN 92-0-151067-5, ISP144, IAEA). UNIPUB.

Research Approaches to Movement & Personality. Philip Eisenberg & Irmgard Bartenieff. 1979. 24.50 (ISBN 0-405-03146-7, 11041). Ayer Co Pubs.

Research As a Basis for Teaching. Ed. by Jean Rudduck & David Hopkins. LC 84-28989. 142p. (Orig.). 1985. pap. text ed. 12.50x (ISBN 0-435-80785-4). Heinemann Ed.

Research Assistant. Jack Rudman. (Career Examination Ser.: C-674). (Cloth bdg. avail. on request). pap. 14.00 (ISBN 0-8373-0674-4). Natl Learning.

Research at the Hampstead Child-Therapy Clinic & Other Papers. Anna Freud. LC 67-9514. (Writings of Anna Freud Ser.: Vol. 5). 575p. 1969. text ed. 55.00x (ISBN 0-8236-6874-6). Intl Univs Pr.

Research Balloons: Exploring Hidden Worlds. Carole S. Briggs. (Lerner Discovery! Ser.). (Illus.). 64p. (gr. 5 up). 1988. PLB 12.95 (ISBN 0-8225-1585-7). Lerner Pubns.

Research, Bibliographic, & Resource Guide on the Hispanic Elderly. Carmela G. Lacayo. 421p. 1981. 20.00; pap. text ed. write for info. Assn Personas Mayores.

Research Book for Gifted Programs K-8. Nancy Polette. 14.95 (ISBN 0-8108-1857-4). Scarecrow.

Research Booklet: A Directory of Projects & People Involved in Psychosocially-Oriented Child Health Research. 50p. 1988. 7.50 (ISBN 0-318-17767-6); members 5.00 (ISBN 0-318-17768-4). Assn Care Child.

Research, Breeding & Production of Crop Plants: Proceedings of the First Nordic Cell & Tissue Culture Symposium. Chris H. Bornman et al. (Illus.). 170p. (Orig.). 1985. pap. text ed. 57.50x (Pub. by Almqvist & Wiksell). Coronet Bks.

Research Briefings, 1985. National Academy of Sciences Staff et al. 112p. 1985. pap. text ed. 9.95x (ISBN 0-309-03585-6). Natl Acad Pr.

Research Briefings, 1986. Committee on Science, Engineering & Public Policy et al. 62p. 1986. pap. text ed. 7.50x (ISBN 0-309-03689-5). Natl Acad Pr.

Research Briefings 1987. National Academy of Sciences et al. 72p. 1988. pap. text ed. 9.95x (ISBN 0-309-03828-6). Natl Acad Pr.

Research Center Directory, 1989, 2 vols. 13th ed. Ed. by Peter Dresser. 1500p. 1988. 380.00 (ISBN 0-8103-2591-8). Gale.

Research Centers Directory, 2 vols. 12th ed. Ed. by Peter D. Dresser. 2000p. 1987. 365.00x (ISBN 0-8103-0678-6). Gale.

Research Centers: The Pentagon Moves the High-Tech Battlefield on Campus. Greg LeRoy. (Illus.). 22p. (Orig.). 1988. pap. text ed. 3.00 (ISBN 0-945210-01-9). Public Search.

Research Challanges. Melissa Donovan. (Illus.). 168p. (gr. 4-8). 1985. wkbk. 10.95 (ISBN 0-86653-271-4). Good Apple.

Research, Comparisons & Medical Applications of Ericksonian Techniques. Ed. by Stephen Lankton & Jeffrey K. Zeig. LC 88-2896. (Ericksonian Monographs: No. 4). 1988. 25.00 (ISBN 0-87630-510-9). Brunner-Mazel.

Research Conference on Labor Relations: Proceedings, Annual Research Conference, 8th, UCLA, 1965. Annual Research Conference Staff. 2.00 (ISBN 0-89215-028-9). U Cal LA Indus Rel.

Research Conference, 1980: Proceedings. 35.00 (ISBN 0-318-01803-9, PREZ). Bank Mktg Assn.

Research Conference, 1981: Proceedings. 45.00 (ISBN 0-318-01802-0, PREO). Bank Mktg Assn.

Research Councils in the Social Sciences see Survey on the Ways in Which States Interpret Their International Obligations.

Research Councils in the Social Sciences Addenda see Survey on the Ways in Which States Interpret Their International Obligations.

Research Craft: An Introduction to Social Research Methods. 2nd ed. John B. Williamson et al. 1982. text ed. write for info. (ISBN 0-673-39606-1). Scott F.

Research Data Management in the Ecological Sciences. Ed. by William K. Michener. (Belle W. Baruch Library in Marine Science: No. 16). 448p. 1986. text ed. 42.95x (ISBN 0-87249-476-4). U of SC Pr.

Research Department Report, 1983-1984. 1985. 100.00 (ISBN 0-88362-113-4, 8562). Graphic Arts Tech Found.

Research Department Report, 1984-1985. 1985. 100.00 (8563). Graphic Arts Tech Found.

Research Design & Evaluation in Speech-Language Pathology & Audiology. 2nd ed. Franklin H. Silverman. (Illus.). 368p. 1985. text ed. write for info. (ISBN 0-13-774126-X). P-H.

Research Design & Methods: A Process Approach. Kenneth S. Bordens & Bruce B. Abbott. 608p. 1988. text ed. 33.95 (ISBN 0-87484-794-X). Mayfield Pub.

Research Design & Statistics for Applied Linguistics. Evelyn Hatch & Hossein Farhady. 312p. 1982. pap. text ed. 19.95 (ISBN 0-88377-202-7). Newbury Hse.

Research Design & Statistics for Physical Education. Anne L. Rothstein. (Illus.). 320p. 1985. text ed. 31.67 (ISBN 0-13-774142-1). P-H.

Research Design in Anthropology: Paradigms & Pragmatics in the Testing of Hypotheses. John A. Brim & David H. Spain. 123p. 1982. pap. text ed. 7.95x (ISBN 0-8290-0583-8). Irvington.

Research Design in Clinical Psychology & Psychiatry. J. B. Chassan. 496p. 1982. text ed. 19.50x (ISBN 0-8290-1009-2). Irvington.

Research Design in the Behavioral Sciences: Multiple Regression Approach. Francis J. Kelly et al. LC 69-15324. 367p. 1969. 6.00x (ISBN 0-8093-0341-8). S Ill U Pr.

Research Design: Strategies & Choices in the Design of Social Research. Catherine Hakim. (Comtemporary Social Research Ser.: No. 13). 240p. 1987. text ed. 34.95x (ISBN 0-04-312031-8); pap. text ed. 14.95x (ISBN 0-04-312032-6). Unwin Hyman.

Research Design: Women: Domains of Decisions: Report of a Meeting of Researchers 1-5 April 1985 Bangkok, Thailand. 46p. 1986. pap. 7.50 (UB192, UNESCO). UNIPUB.

Research Designs. Paul Spector. (University Papers: No. 23). (Illus.). 88p. 1981. pap. 6.50 (ISBN 0-8039-1709-0). Sage.

Research Designs in General Semantics. Ed. by Kenneth G. Johnson. 298p. 1974. 90.00 (ISBN 0-677-14370-2). Gordon & Breach.

Research Developments in Drug & Alcohol Use, Vol. 362. LC 81-3973. 244p. 1981. 49.00x (ISBN 0-89766-117-6, Millman Pub); pap. 49.00x (ISBN 0-89766-118-4). NY Acad Sci.

Research Dilemmas in Administration & Policy Settings. Ed. by Catherine Marshall. (Special Issues of the Anthropological & Education Quarterly Ser.: Vol. 15, No. 3). 1984. 7.50 (ISBN 0-317-66345-3). Am Anthro Assn.

Research Directions in Computer Control of Urban Traffic Systems. 393p. 1979. pap. 20.00x (ISBN 0-87262-179-0). Am Soc Civil Eng.

Research Directions in Object-Oriented Programming. Ed. by Bruce Shriver & Peter Wegner. (Computer Systems Ser.). 500p. 1987. 40.00x (ISBN 0-262-19264-0). MIT Pr.

Research Directions in Software Technology. Ed. by Peter Wegner. (MIT Computer Science & Artificial Intelligence Ser.: No. 2). (Illus.). 1979. text ed. 50.00x (ISBN 0-262-23090-9). MIT Pr.

Research Directions of Black Psychologists. Ed. by A. Wade Boykin et al. Anderson J. Franklin & J. Frank Yates. LC 79-7348. 440p. 1980. 40.00x (ISBN 0-87154-254-4). Russell Sage.

Research Essentials of Administrative Law. H. B. Jacobini et al. LC 83-60926. 1983. text ed. 5.95x (ISBN 0-913530-35-2). Palisades Pub.

Research Ethics. Kare Berg et al. LC 83-9885. (Progress in Clinical & Biological Research Ser.: Vol. 128). 432p. 1983. 75.00 (ISBN 0-8451-0128-5). A R Liss.

Research Evaluating a Child Study Program. R. M. Brandt & H. V. Perkins. (SRCD.M). 1956. pap. 15.00 (ISBN 0-527-01566-0). Kraus Repr.

Research Evidence for the Effectiveness of Bilingual Education. Rudolph C. Troike. LC 79-103425. 18p. 1978. pap. 2.15 (ISBN 0-89763-006-8). Natl Clearinghse Bilingual Ed.

Research Experience. Ed. by M. Patricia Golden. LC 75-17321. 1976. pap. text ed. 18.95 (ISBN 0-87581-188-4). Peacock Pubs.

Research Experiences in Plant Physiology: A Laboratory Manual. 2nd ed. T. C. Moore. (Illus.). 348p. 1981. pap. 24.80 (ISBN 0-387-90606-1). Springer-Verlag.

Research-Extension-Farmer: A Two-Way Continuum for Agricultural Development. Ed. by Michael M. Cernea et al. (Symposium Ser.). 192p. 1985. 14.00 (ISBN 0-8213-0652-9, BK 0652). World Bank.

Research Fields in Physics at United Kingdom & Irish Universities & Polytechnics. 8th ed. Compiled by The Institute of Physics. 364p. 1987. pap. 110.00x (ISBN 0-85498-043-1, Pub. by A Hilger UK). Taylor & Francis.

Research Fleet of the World 1969: Fish Technical Paper, No. 93. pap. 12.25 (F851, FAO). UNIPUB.

Research for Decision Making: Methods for Librarians. Robert Swisher & Charles R. McClure. LC 84-12381. 210p. 1984. 25.00x (ISBN 0-8389-0398-3). ALA.

Research for Educational Planning: Notes on Emergent Needs. William J. Platt. 67p. (Orig.). 1970. pap. 5.00 (ISBN 92-803-1039-9, U552, UNESCO). UNIPUB.

Research for Forest Management. Ed. by J. J. Landsberg & W. L. Parsons. 200p. 1985. 25.00 (ISBN 0-643-03783-7, Pub. by CSIRO). Intl Spec Bk.

Research for Health Professionals: Design, Analysis, & Ethics. Robert P. Heaney & Charles J. Dougherty. (Illus.). 216p. 1988. text ed. 24.95x (ISBN 0-8138-1712-9). Iowa St U Pr.

Research for Marketing Decisions. 4th ed. Paul E. Green & Donald S. Tull. (Illus.). 1978. ref. 42.00 (ISBN 0-13-774158-8). P-H.

Research for Marketing Decisions. 5th ed. Paul E. Green et al. (Illus.). 768p. 1988. text ed. 40.33 (ISBN 0-13-774175-8). P-H.

Research for Nursing: A Guide for the Enquiring Nurse. Jill C. MacLeod & Lisbeth Hockey. (Nursing Modules for Student Nurses Ser.). 1979. 10.95 (ISBN 0-471-25642-0, Pub. by Wiley Hayden). Wiley.

Research for Profit. O. A. Battista. 1988. 39.95 (ISBN 0-915074-12-5). Knowledge TX.

Research for Profit: The Problem, the Solution, a Case History. Paul W. Bachman. LC 78-75633. (Illus.). pap. 50.50 (ISBN 0-317-09730-X, 2012403). Bks Demand UMI.

Research for Romance. Erin Phillips. (First Love Ser.). 186p. (YA) (gr. 7 up). 1984. pap. 1.95 (ISBN 0-671-53396-7). PB.

Research for Tomorrow: Yearbook of Agriculture, 1986. John J. Crowley. (Illus.). 344p. 1986. 9.50 (ISBN 0-318-21889-5, S/N 001-000-04472-9). USGPO.

Research Framework for Traditional Fisheries. Ian R. Smith. (Illus.). 40p. 1983. pap. text ed. 6.50x (ISBN 0-89955-391-5, Pub. by ICLARM Philippines). Intl Spec Bk.

Research Frontiers in Fluid Dynamics. Ed. by Raymond J. Seeger & G. Temple. LC 65-14246. (Interscience Monographs & Texts in Physics & Astronomy: Vol. 15). pap. 160.00 (ISBN 0-317-08477-1, 2051478). Bks Demand UMI.

Research Frontiers in Marketing: Dialogues & Directions: 1978 Educator's Proceedings. American Marketing Association Staff. Ed. by Subhash C. Jain. LC 78-8596. (American Marketing Association Proceedings Ser.: 43). pap. 113.80 (ISBN 0-317-39638-2, 2023364). Bks Demand UMI.

Research Fundamentals in Home Economics. 3rd ed. Marjory L. Joseph & William D. Joseph. (Illus.). 1986. pap. 24.95x (ISBN 0-916434-33-8). Plycon Pr.

Research Funding As an Investment: Can we Measure the Return? A Technical Memorandum. LC 86-600525. (OTA-TM-SET-36). 78p. (Orig.). 1986. pap. 3.75 (ISBN 0-318-20387-1, S/N 052-003-01039-9). USGPO.

Research Games. K. C. Bowen. 126p. 1978. 31.00x (ISBN 0-85066-169-2). Taylor & Francis.

Research Guide & Handbook. Richard Veit. 326p. 1989. text ed. price not set (ISBN 0-02-423030-8). Macmillan.

Research Guide for China's Response to the West: A Documentary Survey, 1839-1923. Teng Ssu-Ya et al. LC 53-5061. 1954. 5.95x (ISBN 0-674-76350-5). Harvard U Pr.

Research Guide for Law Enforcement & the Criminal Justice System. Jack E. Whitehouse. LC 81-86247. 150p. 1983. lib. bdg. 20.95 (ISBN 0-88247-666-1). R & E Pubs.

Research Guide for Psychology. Raymond G. McInnis. LC 81-1377. (Reference Sources for Social Sciences & Humanities: No. 1). (Illus.). xxvi, 604p. 1982. lib. bdg. 50.95x (ISBN 0-313-21399-2, MCR/). Greenwood.

Research Guide for Studies in Early Childhood. Enid E. Haag. (Reference Sources for the Social Sciences & Humanities Ser.: No. 8). 1988. price not set (ISBN 0-313-24763-3, HRC/). Greenwood.

Research Guide for Undergraduate Students: English & American Literature. 2nd ed. Nancy L. Baker. LC 85-15558. 61p. 1985. pap. 7.50x (ISBN 0-87352-147-1). Modern Lang.

Research Guide: Surrogate Motherhood. Kathleen K. Bach. LC 87-37863. (Legal Research Guides Ser.: Vol. 6). 46p. 1988. lib. bdg. 25.00 (ISBN 0-89941-588-1). W S Hein.

Research Guide to American Historical Figures, 3 vols. Ed. by Robert Muccigrosso. 1800p. 1988. lib. bdg. 189.00 (ISBN 0-933833-09-1). Beacham Pub.

Research Guide to Andean History: Bolivia, Chile, Ecuador, & Peru. Ed. by John J. TePaske. LC 80-29365. xiii, 346p. 1981. 32.50 (ISBN 0-8223-0450-3). Duke.

Research in Institutional Advancement: A Selected, Annotated Compendium of Doctoral Dissertations. Ed. by A. Westley Rowland & Robert Carbone. 188p. 1986. 14.50 (ISBN 0-89964-215-2). Coun Adv & Supp Ed.

Research in International Business & Finance: International Business Strategies in the Asia-Pacific Region, Vol. 4. Ed. by Richard W. Moxon & Thomas W. Roehl. 1983. 113.00 (ISBN 0-89232-308-6). Jai Pr.

Research in International Business & Finance: Uncle Sam As Host, Vol. 5. H. Peter Gray. 1986. 56.50 (ISBN 0-89232-588-7). Jai Pr.

Research in International Business & International Relations, Vol. 3. Ed. by Anant R. Negandhi. 1988. price not set (ISBN 0-89232-649-2). Jai Pr.

Research in International Business & International Relations, Vol. 1: Multinational Corporations & State-Owned Enterprises: A New Challenge in International Business. Ed. by Anant R. Negandhi & Howard Thomas. 1986. 56.50 (ISBN 0-89232-529-1). Jai Pr.

Research in International Business & Finance, Vol. 3. Ed. by Robert G. Hawkins. 300p. 1981. 56.50 (ISBN 0-89232-245-4). Jai Pr.

Research in International Business & Finance, Vol. 7. Ed. by H. Peter Gray. 1988. 56.50 (ISBN 0-89232-906-8). Jai Pr.

Research in International Marketing. Ed. by Peter W. Turnbull & Stanley J. Paliwoda. 400p. 1986. 50.00 (ISBN 0-7099-4313-X, Pub. by Croom Helm Ltd). Routledge Chapman & Hall.

Research in Japan in History of Eastern & Western Cultural Contacts. Japanese National Comm. for Unesco Staff. 154p. 1957. 250.00x (Pub. by Han-Shan Tang Ltd). State Mutual Bk.

Research in Labor Economics, Vol. 1. Ed. by Ronald G. Ehrenberg. (Orig.). 1977. lib. bdg. 56.50 (ISBN 0-89232-017-6). Jai Pr.

Research in Labor Economics, Vol. 2. Ed. by Ronald G. Ehrenberg. 381p. 1979. 56.50 (ISBN 0-89232-097-4). Jai Pr.

Research in Labor Economics, Vol. 3. Ed. by Ronald G. Ehrenberg. 410p. 1980. lib. bdg. 56.50 (ISBN 0-89232-157-1). Jai Pr.

Research in Labor Economics, Vol. 4. Ed. by Ronald G. Ehrenberg. 350p. 1981. 56.50 (ISBN 0-89232-243-8). Jai Pr.

Research in Labor Economics, Vol. 5. Ed. by Ronald G. Ehrenberg. 1982. 56.50 (ISBN 0-89232-312-4). Jai Pr.

Research in Labor Economics, Vol. 6. Ed. by Ronald G. Ehrenberg. 450p. 1984. 56.50 (ISBN 0-89232-418-X). Jai Pr.

Research in Labor Economics, Vol. 9. Ed. by Ronald G. Ehrenberg. 1988. 63.50 (ISBN 0-89232-746-4). Jai Pr.

Research in Labor Economics: New Approaches to Labor Unions, Suppl. 2. Ed. by Joseph Reid. 350p. 1983. 56.50 (ISBN 0-89232-265-9). Jai Pr.

Research in Labor Economics, Supplement 1: Evaluating Manpower Training Programs. Ed. by Farrell Bloch. 1979. lib. bdg. 56.50 (ISBN 0-89232-046-X). Jai Pr.

Research in Law & Economics, Vol. 1. Ed. by Richard O. Zerbe. (Orig.). 1979. lib. bdg. 56.50 (ISBN 0-89232-028-1). Jai Pr.

Research in Law & Economics, Vol. 2. Ed. by Richard Zerbe, Jr. (Orig.). 1980. lib. bdg. 56.50 (ISBN 0-89232-131-8). Jai Pr.

Research in Law & Economics, Vol. 3. Ed. by Richard O. Zerbe. 275p. 1981. 56.50 (ISBN 0-89232-231-4). Jai Pr.

Research in Law & Economics, Vol. 5. Ed. by Richard O. Zebra, Jr. 1983. 56.50 (ISBN 0-89232-419-8). Jai Pr.

Research in Law & Economics, Vol. 9. Ed. by Richard O. Zerbe, Jr. 207p. 1986. 56.50 (ISBN 0-89232-657-3). Jai Pr.

Research in Law & Economics, Vol. 11. Ed. by Richard O. Zerbe, Jr. 1987. 56.50 (ISBN 0-89232-830-4). Jai Pr.

Research in Law & Economics: Antitrust & Regulation, Vol. 6. Richard O. Zerbe. 56.50 (ISBN 0-89232-474-0). Jai Pr.

Research in Law & Economics: Normative Law & Economics, Vol. 7. Richard O. Zerbe. 1985. 56.50 (ISBN 0-89232-590-9). Jai Pr.

Research in Law & Economics: The Economics of Patents & Copyrights, Vol. 8. Richard O. Zerbe, Jr. 1986. 56.50 (ISBN 0-89232-654-9). Jai Pr.

Research in Law & Policy Studies, Vol. 1. Ed. by Stuart S. Nagel. 1987. 52.50 (ISBN 0-89232-525-9). Jai Pr.

Research in Law & Policy Studies, Vol. 2. Ed. by Stuart S. Nagel. 1988. 52.50 (ISBN 0-89232-662-X). Jai Pr.

Research in Law & Sociology, Vol. 2. Ed. by Steven Spitzer. 1979. lib. bdg. 56.50 (ISBN 0-89232-111-3). Jai Pr.

Research in Law & Sociology, Vol. 3. Ed. by Steven Spitzer. 368p. 1980. 56.50 (ISBN 0-89232-186-5). Jai Pr.

Research in Law & Sociology: An Annual Compilation of Research, Vol. 1. Ed. by Rita J. Simon. 1978. lib. bdg. 56.50 (ISBN 0-89232-024-9). Jai Pr.

Research in Law, Deviance & Social Control, Vol. 4. Ed. by Rita J. Simon & Steven Spitzer. 325p. (Orig.). 1981. 56.50 (ISBN 0-89232-241-1). Jai Pr.

Research in Law, Deviance & Social Control, Vol. 6. S. Spitzer & A. Scull. 1985. 56.50 (ISBN 0-89232-512-7). Jai Pr.

Research in Law, Deviance & Social Control, Vol. 7. Ed. by Steven Spitzer & Andrew T. Scull. 1985. 56.50 (ISBN 0-89232-528-3). Jai Pr.

Research in Law, Deviance & Social Control, Vol. 8. Ed. by Steven Spitzer. 1986. 56.50 (ISBN 0-89232-536-4). Jai Pr.

Research in Law, Deviance & Social Control, Vol. 9. Ed. by Steven Spitzer. 1987. 56.50 (ISBN 0-89232-747-2). Jai Pr.

Research in Learning Disabilities: Issues & Future Directions. Ed. by Sharon Vaughn & Candace Bos. LC 87-4233. 288p. (Orig.). 1987. pap. text ed. 26.50 (ISBN 0-316-10305-5, 103055). College-Hill.

Research in Library & Information Science in India. P. S. Kumar. 1987. 38.50x (ISBN 81-7022-016-5, Pub. by Concept). South Asia Bks.

Research in Library Management. M. J. O'Connor. (R&D Report 5550). (Illus.). 94p. (Orig.). 1980. pap. 12.75 (ISBN 0-905984-54-4, Pub. by British Lib). Longwood Pub Group.

Research in Man-Machine Communications Using Time Shared Computer Systems. Butler W. Lampson. LC 77-131392. 73p. 1969. 19.00. Scholarly.

Research in Marketing, Vol. 2. Ed. by Jagdish N. Sheth. 357p. 1979. 56.50 (ISBN 0-89232-059-1). Jai Pr.

Research in Marketing, Vol. 3. Ed. by Jagdish N. Sheth. (Orig.). 1979. lib. bdg. 56.50 (ISBN 0-89232-060-5). Jai Pr.

Research in Marketing, Vol. 4. Ed. by Jagdish N. Sheth. 300p. 1981. 56.50 (ISBN 0-89232-169-5). Jai Pr.

Research in Marketing, Vol. 5. Ed. by Jagdish N. Sheth. 325p. 1981. 56.50 (ISBN 0-89232-211-X). Jai Pr.

Research in Marketing, Vol. 6. Ed. by Jagdish N. Sheth. 300p. 1982. 56.50 (ISBN 0-89232-315-9). Jai Pr.

Research in Marketing, Vol. 7. Ed. by Jagdish N. Sheth. 1984. 56.50 (ISBN 0-89232-420-1). Jai Pr.

Research in Marketing, Vol. 9. Ed. by Jagdish N. Sheth. 1987. 56.50 (ISBN 0-89232-831-2). Jai Pr.

Research in Marketing, Vol. 10. Ed. by Jagdish N. Sheth. 1988. price not set (ISBN 0-89232-920-3). Jai Pr.

Research in Marketing: An Annual Compilation of Research, Vol. 1. Ed. by Jagdish N. Sheth. (Annual Ser.). (Orig.). 1978. lib. bdg. 56.50 (ISBN 0-89232-041-9). Jai Pr.

Research in Marriage. Hamilton. (Women-Children First Ser.). 570p. 1986. lib. bdg. 70.00 (ISBN 0-8240-7657-5). Garland Pub.

Research in Mathematics Education. Ed. by Richard J. Shumway. National Council of Teachers of Mathematics. LC 80-4. (Illus.). 480p. 1980. 27.00 (ISBN 0-87353-163-9). NCTM.

Research in Mental Health Computing: The Next Five Years. Ed. by John H. Greist et al. LC 87-35269. (Computers in Human Services Ser.). 180p. 1988. text ed. 29.95 (ISBN 0-86656-648-1). Haworth Pr.

Research in Mexican History: Topics, Methodology, Sources, & a Practical Guide to Field Research. Ed. by Richard E. Greenleaf & Michael C. Meyer. LC 72-86020. (Illus.). xiv, 226p. 1973. pap. 4.95x (ISBN 0-8032-5773-2, BB 516, Bison). U of Nebr Pr.

Research in Micropolitics, Vol. 3. Ed. by Samuel Long. 1988. 54.50 (ISBN 0-89232-791-X). Jai Pr.

Research in Micropolitics: Voting Behavior, Vol. 1. Samuel Long. 1986. 52.50 (ISBN 0-89232-365-5). Jai Pr.

Research in Music Behavior: Modifying Music Behavior in the Classroom. Clifford K. Madsen et al. LC 74-16362. (Illus.). pap. 71.30 (ISBN 0-317-09961-2, 2020325). Bks Demand UMI.

Research in Music Education: An Introduction to Systematic Inquiry. Edward L. Rainbow & Hildegard C. Froehlich. (Illus.). 330p. 1987. pap. text ed. 32.95 (ISBN 0-02-870320-0). Schirmer Bks.

Research in Numerical Fluid Mechanics. Ed. by P. Wesseling. (Notes on Numerical Fluid Mechanics Ser.: Vol. 17). 180p. 1987. pap. 29.50 (ISBN 3-528-08090-6, Pub. by Vieweg & Sohn). IPS.

Research in Nursing & Health. 1987. write for info. Wiley.

Research in Organizational Behavior, Vol. 1. Ed. by Barry H. Staw. 1979. lib. bdg. 59.50 (ISBN 0-89232-045-1). Jai Pr.

Research in Organizational Behavior, Vol. 2. Ed. by Barry M. Staw & Larry L. Cummings. (Orig.). 1980. lib. bdg. 59.50 (ISBN 0-89232-099-0). Jai Pr.

Research in Organizational Behavior, Vol. 3. Ed. by L. L. Cummings & Barry Staw. 356p. 1981. 59.50 (ISBN 0-89232-151-2). Jai Pr.

Research in Organizational Behavior, Vol. 4. Ed. by Barry Staw & L. L. Cummings. 425p. 1981. 59.50 (ISBN 0-89232-147-4). Jai Pr.

Research in Organizational Behavior, Vol. 5. Ed. by L. L. Cummings. 350p. 1983. 59.50 (ISBN 0-89232-271-3). Jai Pr.

Research in Organizational Behavior, Vol. 6. Ed. by Barry M. Staw. 1984. 59.50 (ISBN 0-89232-351-5). Jai Pr.

Research in Organizational Behavior, Vol. 7. L. L. Cummings & B. Staw. 59.50 (ISBN 0-89232-497-X). Jai Pr.

Research in Organizational Behavior, Vol. 8. Ed. by Barry M. Staw. 1986. 59.50 (ISBN 0-89232-551-8). Jai Pr.

Research in Organizational Behavior, Vol. 9. Ed. by Barry M. Staw. 1987. 59.50 (ISBN 0-89232-636-0). Jai Pr.

Research in Organizational Behavior, Vol. 10. Ed. by Barry M. Staw. 1988. 59.50 (ISBN 0-89232-748-0). Jai Pr.

Research in Organizational Behavior, Vol. 11. Ed. by Barry M. Staw. 1988. price not set (ISBN 0-89232-921-1). Jai Pr.

Research in Organizational Change & Development, Vol. 1. Ed. by Richard W. Woodman & William A. Pasmore. 1987. 56.50 (ISBN 0-89232-749-9). Jai Pr.

Research in Organizational Change & Development, Vol. 2. Ed. by Richard W. Woodman & William A. Pasmore. 1988. 58.50 (ISBN 0-89232-772-3). Jai Pr.

Research in Parapsychology Nineteen Eighty: Abstracts & Papers from the Twenty-Third Annual Convention of the Parapsychological Association, 1980. Ed. by Parapsychological Association et al. LC 66-28580. 173p. 1981. 16.00 (ISBN 0-8108-1425-0). Scarecrow.

Research in Parapsychology 1972: Abstracts & Papers from the 15th Annual Convention of the Parapsychological Association, 1972. Parapsychological Association. Ed. by W. G. Roll et al. LC 66-28580. 249p. 1973. 16.00 (ISBN 0-8108-0666-5). Scarecrow.

Research in Parapsychology 1973: Abstracts & Papers from the 16th Annual Convention of the Parapsychological Association, 1973. Parapsychological Association. Ed. by W. G. Roll et al. LC 66-28580. 249p. 1974. 16.00 (ISBN 0-8108-0708-4). Scarecrow.

Research in Parapsychology 1974: Abstracts & Papers from the 17th Annual Convention of the Parapsychological Association, 1974. Parapsychological Association. Ed. by J. D. Morris & W. G. Roll. LC 66-28580. 272p. 1975. 16.50 (ISBN 0-8108-0850-1). Scarecrow.

Research in Parapsychology 1975: Abstracts & Papers from the 18th Annual Convention of the Parapsychological Association, 1975. Parapsychological Association. Ed. by J. D. Morris et al. LC 66-28580. 277p. 1976. 16.50 (ISBN 0-8108-0895-1). Scarecrow.

Research in Parapsychology 1976: Abstracts & Papers from the 19th Annual Convention of the Parapsychological Association, 1976. Parapsychological Association. Ed. by J. D. Morris et al. LC 66-28580. 285p. 1977. 16.50 (ISBN 0-8108-1080-8). Scarecrow.

Research in Parapsychology 1977: Abstracts & Papers from the 20th Annual Convention of the Parapsychological Association, 1977. Parapsychological Association. Ed. by William G. Roll. LC 66-28580. 279p. 1978. lib. bdg. 16.00 (ISBN 0-8108-1131-6). Scarecrow.

Research in Parapsychology 1978. Parapsychological Association. Ed. by William G. Roll. LC 66-28580. 238p. 1979. 16.00 (ISBN 0-8108-1195-2). Scarecrow.

Research in Parapsychology 1979: Abstracts & Papers from the 22nd Annual Convention of the Parapsychological Association. Parapsychological Association. Ed. by William G. Roll. LC 66-2858. 238p. 1980. 16.00 (ISBN 0-8108-1327-0). Scarecrow.

Research In Parapsychology 1981: Abstracts & Papers from the Twenty-fourth Annual Convention of the Parapsychological Association, 1981. Ed. by William G. Roll et al. LC 66-28580. 252p. 1982. 16.00 (ISBN 0-8108-1550-8). Scarecrow.

Research in Parapsychology 1982: Jubilee Centenary Issue: Abstracts & Papers from the Twenty-Fifth Annual Convention of the Parapsychological Association, 1982. Ed. by Parapsychological Association et al. LC 66-28580. 382p. 1983. 25.00 (ISBN 0-8108-1627-X). Scarecrow.

Research in Parapsychology, 1983: Abstracts & Papers from the Twenty-Sixth Annual Convention of the Parapsychological Association, 1983. Rhea A. White & Richard S. Broughton. LC 66-28580. 196p. 1984. 17.50 (ISBN 0-8108-1695-4). Scarecrow.

Research in Parapsychology 1984: Abstracts & Papers from the Twenty-Seventh Annual Convention of the Parapsychological Association, 1984. Ed. by Rhea A. White & Jerry Solfvin. LC 66-28580. 215p. 1985. 17.50 (ISBN 0-8108-1812-4). Scarecrow.

Research in Parapsychology 1985: Abstracts & Papers from the Twenty-Eighth Annual Convention of the Parapsychological Association, 1985. Debra H. Weiner & Dean I. Radin. LC 66-28580. (Illus.). 256p. 1987. 22.50 (ISBN 0-8108-1936-8). Scarecrow.

Research in Parapsychology 1986: Abstracts & Papers from the Annual Convention of the Parapsychological Association 1986 29th. Ed. by Debra H. Weiner & Roger D. Nelson. LC 66-28580. 256p. 1987. 25.00 (ISBN 0-8108-2068-4). Scarecrow.

Research in Pennsylvania Law. 2nd ed. Carroll C. Moreland & Erwin C. Surrency. LC 65-27629. 118p. 1965. 11.00 (ISBN 0-379-11651-0). Oceana.

Research in Perinatal Medicine. Ed. by Peter W. Nathanielsz & Julian T. Parer. (Research in Perinatal Medicine Ser.: (I)). (Illus.). 246p. 1984. 54.00x (ISBN 0-916859-03-7). Perinatology.

Research in Personnel & Human Resources Management, Vol. 1. Ed. by Kendrith M. Rowland & Gerald R. Ferris. 450p. 1983. 56.50 (ISBN 0-89232-268-3). Jai Pr.

Research in Personnel & Human Resources Management, Vol. 2. Kendrith Rowland & Gerald R. Ferris. 56.50 (ISBN 0-89232-483-X). Jai Pr.

Research in Personnel & Human Resources Management, Vol. 3. Kendrith M. Rowland & Gerald Ferris. 1985. 56.50 (ISBN 0-89232-498-8). Jai Pr.

Research in Personnel & Human Resources Management, Vol. 4. Kendrith M. Rowland & Gerald Ferris. 1986. 56.50 (ISBN 0-89232-606-9). Jai Pr.

Research in Personnel & Human Resorces Management, Vol. 5. Ed. by Kendrith M. Rowland & Gerald R. Ferris. 1987. 56.50 (ISBN 0-89232-750-2). Jai Pr.

Research in Personnel & Human Resources Management, Vol. 6. Ed. by Kendrith M. Rowland. 1988. price not set (ISBN 0-89232-856-8). Jai Pr.

Research in Phenomenology: 1987, Vol. 17. Ed. by John Sallis. 336p. 1988. pap. text ed. 28.00 (0085-5553). Humanities.

Research in Philosophy & Technology: Ethics & Technology, Vol. 9. Ed. by Frederick Ferre. 1987. 54.50 (ISBN 0-89232-609-3). Jai Pr.

Research in Philosophy & Technology: Supplement 1 - Jacques Ellul. Joyce M. Hanks & Asal Rolf. 54.50 (ISBN 0-89232-478-3). Jai Pr.

Research in Philosophy & Technology, Vol. 1. Ed. by Paul T. Durbin. 350p. (Orig.). 1979. lib. bdg. 54.50 (ISBN 0-89232-022-2). Jai Pr.

Research in Philosophy & Technology, Vol. 2. Ed. by Paul T. Durbin. (Orig.). 1979. lib. bdg. 54.50 (ISBN 0-89232-101-6). Jai Pr.

Research in Philosophy & Technology, Vol. 3. Ed. by Frederick Ferre & Carl Mitcham. 412p. 1980. 54.50 (ISBN 0-89232-102-4). Jai Pr.

Research in Philosophy & Technology, Vol. 4. Ed. by Paul T. Durbin. 450p. 1981. 54.50 (ISBN 0-89232-181-4). Jai Pr.

Research in Philosophy & Technology, Vol. 5. Ed. by Frederick Ferre. 339p. 1982. 54.50 (ISBN 0-89232-322-1). Jai Pr.

Research in Philosophy & Technology, Vol. 6. Ed. by Paul T. Durbin & Carl Mitcham. 1983. 54.50 (ISBN 0-89232-352-3). Jai Pr.

Research in Philosophy & Technology, Vol. 7. Paul Durbin. 52.50 (ISBN 0-89232-505-4). Jai Pr.

Research in Philosophy & Technology, Vol. 8. Ed. by Paul T. Durbin & Carl Mitcham. 1985. 54.50 (ISBN 0-89232-593-3). Jai Pr.

Research in Physics & Chemistry. F. J. Malina. 1969. 81.00 (ISBN 0-08-013400-9). Pergamon.

Research in Political Economy, Vol. 1. Ed. by Paul Zarembka. (Orig.). 1978. lib. bdg. 56.50 (ISBN 0-89232-020-6). Jai Pr.

Research in Political Economy, Vol. 2. Ed. by Paul Zarembka. 289p. 1979. 56.50 (ISBN 0-89232-120-2). Jai Pr.

Research in Political Economy, Vol. 3. Ed. by Paul Zarembka. 329p. 1980. lib. bdg. 56.50 (ISBN 0-89232-156-3). Jai Pr.

Research in Political Economy, Vol. 4. Ed. by Paul Zarembka. 300p. 1981. 56.50 (ISBN 0-89232-205-5). Jai Pr.

Research in Political Economy, Vol. 5. Ed. by Paul Zarembka. 298p. 1982. 56.50 (ISBN 0-89232-269-1). Jai Pr.

Research in Political Economy, Vol. 6. Ed. by Paul Zarembka. 1983. 56.50 (ISBN 0-89232-350-7). Jai Pr.

Research in Political Economy, Vol. 7. Paul Zarembka. 56.50 (ISBN 0-89232-490-2). Jai Pr.

Research in Political Economy, Vol. 8. Ed. by Paul Zarembka. 289p. 1985. 56.50 (ISBN 0-89232-595-X). Jai Pr.

Research in Political Economy, Vol. 9. Ed. by Paul Zarembka. 252p. 1986. 56.50 (ISBN 0-89232-661-1). Jai Pr.

Research in Political Economy, Vol. 10. Ed. by Paul Zarembka. 1987. 56.50 (ISBN 0-89232-751-0). Jai Pr.

Research in Political Economy, Vol. 11. Ed. by Paul Zarembka. 1988. price not set (ISBN 0-89232-922-X). Jai Pr.

Research in Political Science. Ed. by Ernest S. Griffith. LC 77-86021. (Essay & General Literature Index Reprint Ser). 1969. Repr. of 1948 ed. 22.50x (ISBN 0-8046-0563-7, Pub. by Kennikat). Assoc Faculty Pr.

Research in Political Sociology, Vol. 1. Ed. by Richard Braungart. 1985. 52.50 (ISBN 0-89232-557-7). Jai Pr.

Research Institutions & Learned Societies. Ed. by Joseph C. Kiger. LC 81-6651. (Encyclopedia of American Institutions Ser.: No. 5). xxv, 551p. 1982. lib. bdg. 46.95 (ISBN 0-313-22061-1, KRE/). Greenwood.

Research Instrumentation for the 21st Century. Ed. by Gary R. Beecher. (Beltsville Symposia in Agricultural Research). 1988. lib. bdg. 122.00 (ISBN 90-247-3595-5, Pub. by Martiinus Nijhoff). Kluwer Academic.

Research Instruments in Social Gerontology: Clinical & Social Psychology, Vol. 1. David Mangen & Warren A. Peterson. LC 81-16449. 666p. 1982. 35.00x (ISBN 0-8166-0991-8). U of Minn Pr.

Research Instruments in Social Gerontology: Social Roles & Social Participation, Vol. 2. Ed. by David J. Mangen & Warren A. Peterson. LC 81-16449. 569p. 1982. 35.00x (ISBN 0-8166-1096-7). U of Minn Pr.

Research Instruments in Social Gerontology, Vol. 3: Health, Program Evaluation, & Demography. Ed. by David J. Mangen & Warren A. Peterson. LC 81-16449. 469p. 1984. 35.00x (ISBN 0-8166-1112-2). U of Minn Pr.

Research Interview: Uses & Approaches. Ed. by Michael Brenner et al. 1985. 55.00 (ISBN 0-12-131580-0). Acad Pr.

Research Interviewing. Elliot G. Mishler. LC 86-9798. 208p. 1986. text ed. 21.00x (ISBN 0-674-76460-9). Harvard U Pr.

Research into Environmental Pollution: A Report of 5 WHO Scientific Groups. (Technical Report Ser: No. 406). 83p. 1968. pap. 2.40 (ISBN 92-4-120406-0, 73). World Health.

Research into Health & Illness: Issues in Design, Analysis & Practice. Andrew F. Long. LC 84-18791. 204p. 1984. text ed. 34.50x (ISBN 0-566-00755-X). Gower Pub Co.

Research into Illustration: An Approach & a Review. Evelyn Goldsmith. (Illus.). 272p. 1984. 44.50 (ISBN 0-521-25674-7). Cambridge U Pr.

Research into Marriage. Penny Jordan. (Harlequin Presents Ser.: No. 994). 192p. Date not set. pap. 1.95 (ISBN 0-317-63735-5). Harlequin Bks.

Research into Nurse Education. Ed. by Bryn D. Davis. 208p. 1983. pap. 17.50 (ISBN 0-7099-0825-3, Pub. by Croom Helm Ltd). Routledge Chapman & Hall.

Research into Personal Development: Educational & Vocational Choice. Ed. by Anders Duner. 192p. 1978. pap. text ed. 18.50 (ISBN 90-265-0284-2, Pub. by Swets & Zeitlinger Netherlands). Hogrefe Intl.

Research into Primary Education: Third All-European Conference of Directors of Educational Research Institutions, Neusiedl (Austria), 4-7 December, 1983. Ed. by Secretariat of the Council of Europe. 204p. 1985. pap. text ed. 19.00 (ISBN 90-265-0616-3, Pub. by Swets Zeitlinger Netherlands). Hogrefe Intl.

Research into the Origin & Treatment of Muscular Dystrophy: Proceedings of a Workshop Held at De Hooge Vuursche, Baarn, Holland 24-27 February, 1984. Ed. by L. P. Ten Kate et al. (Current Clinical Practice Ser.: Vol. 20). 170p. 1985. 51.75 (ISBN 0-444-90405-0). Elsevier.

Research Inventory for the Multilateral Trade Negotiations, 1988, Pts. 1 & 2. Ed. by Jalaleddin Jalali. (World Bank Papers for the Uruguay Round). 294p. 1988. 17.00 (ISBN 0-8213-1070-4, BK1070). World Bank.

Research Issues in Child Development. Ed. by Chris Pratt et al. 208p. 1986. pap. text ed. 17.95x (ISBN 0-86861-414-9). Unwin Hyman.

Research Issues in Irrigation Systems in Developing Countries: Proceedings. (Lincoln Institute Monograph: No. 78-6). 1978. pap. 4.00 (ISBN 0-686-23890-7). Lincoln Inst Land.

Research Issues in Psychological Dimensions of Cancer see Psychosocial Aspects of Cancer.

Research Issues in the Assessment of Birth Settings. Institute of Medicine, Commission on Life Sciences, National Research Council. 181p. 1983. pap. text ed. 15.95x (ISBN 0-309-03337-3). Natl Acad Pr.

Research-Key to the Future for Urethanes: Society of Plastics Industry 24th Annual Urethane Division Technical Conference. LC 79-62906. 139p. 1979. pap. 14.00 (ISBN 0-87762-270-1). Technomic.

Research Libraries & Collections in the United Kingdom: A Selective Inventory & Guide. Stephen Roberts et al. LC 78-11560. 285p. 1978. 30.00 (ISBN 0-208-01667-8, Linnet). Shoe String.

Research Libraries & Their Implementation of AACR2: Foundations in Library & Information Science. Judith Hopkins & John A. Edens. LC 85-23825. (Vol. 22). 360p. 1986. 52.50 (ISBN 0-89232-641-7). Jai Pr.

Research Library Cooperation in the Caribbean: Papers of the First & Second Conferences of the Association of Caribbean University & Research Libraries. Ed. by Alma T. Jordan. LC 73-4218. pap. 39.30 (ISBN 0-317-27849-5, 2024217). Bks Demand UMI.

Research Library of Colonial Americana, 54 bks. Ed. by Richard C. Robey. 1972. 1502.00 (ISBN 0-405-03270-6). Ayer Co Pubs.

Research Made Easy: A Guide for Students & Writers. Robert Matzen. (Orig.). 1987. pap. 2.95 (ISBN 0-553-26473-7). Bantam.

Research Manual for the Medical Record Profession. Margret Amatayakul. 1985. 10.00 (ISBN 0-318-19163-6, 1020). instr's. guide 5.00 (ISBN 0-318-19164-4, 1021). Am Med Record Assn.

Research Materials for the Study of Latin-America at the University of Texas. Lota M. Spell. Repr. of 1954 ed. lib. bdg. 35.00x (ISBN 0-8371-5033-7, TLSR). Greenwood.

Research Materials in the Social Sciences. 2nd ed. Jack A. Clarke. LC 67-25948. pap. 20.00 (ISBN 0-317-27035-4, 2023629). Bks Demand UMI.

Research Matters. Hamp-Lyons & Courter. 1984. pap. text ed. 12.50 (ISBN 0-88377-445-3). Newbury Hse.

Research Memorandum on Crime in the Depression. Thorsten Sellin. LC 79-162837. (Studies in the Social Aspects of the Depression). 1971. Repr. of 1937 ed. 17.00 (ISBN 0-405-00853-8). Ayer Co Pubs.

Research Memorandum on Education in the Depression. Educational Policies Commission. LC 72-162838. (Studies in the Social Aspects of the Depression). 1971. Repr. of 1937 ed. 17.00 (ISBN 0-405-00841-4). Ayer Co Pubs.

Research Memorandum on Internal Migration in the Depression. Warren S. Thompson. LC 70-162840. (Studies in the Social Aspects of the Depression). 98p. 1971. Repr. of 1937 ed. 15.00 (ISBN 0-405-00843-0). Ayer Co Pubs.

Research Memorandum on Minority Peoples in the Depression. Donald Young. LC 74-162841. (Studies in the Social Aspects of the Depression). 1971. Repr. of 1937 ed. 17.00 (ISBN 0-405-00844-9). Ayer Co Pubs.

Research Memorandum on Recreation in the Depression. Jesse F. Steiner. LC 78-162842. (Studies in the Social Aspects of the Depression). 1971. Repr. of 1937 ed. 17.00 (ISBN 0-405-00845-7). Ayer Co Pubs.

Research Memorandum on Religion in the Depression. Samuel C. Kincheloe. LC 71-162843. (Studies in the Social Aspects of the Depression). 1971. Repr. of 1937 ed. 17.00 (ISBN 0-405-00846-5). Ayer Co Pubs.

Research Memorandum on Rural Life in the Depression. Dwight Sanderson. LC 75-162844. (Studies in the Social Aspects of the Depression). 1971. Repr. of 1937 ed. 17.00 (ISBN 0-405-00847-3). Ayer Co Pubs.

Research Memorandum on Social Aspects of Consumption in the Depression. Roland S. Vaile. LC 79-162845. (Studies in the Social Aspects of the Depression). 1971. Repr. of 1937 ed. 17.00 (ISBN 0-405-00848-1). Ayer Co Pubs.

Research Memorandum on Social Aspects of Health in the Depression. Selwyn D. Collins & Clark Tibbitts. LC 72-162846. (Studies in the Social Aspects of the Depression). 1971. Repr. of 1937 ed. 17.00 (ISBN 0-405-00849-X). Ayer Co Pubs.

Research Memorandum on Social Aspects of Reading in the Depression. Douglas Waples. LC 76-162847. (Studies in the Social Aspects of the Depression). 1971. Repr. of 1937 ed. 17.00 (ISBN 0-405-00850-3). Ayer Co Pubs.

Research Memorandum on Social Aspects of Relief Policies in the Depression. R. Clyde White & Mary K. White. LC 70-162848. (Studies in the Social Aspects of the Depression). 1971. Repr. of 1937 ed. 17.00 (ISBN 0-405-00851-1). Ayer Co Pubs.

Research Memorandum on Social Work in the Depression. F. Stuart Chapin & Stuart A. Queen. LC 73-162849. (Studies in the Social Aspects of the Depression). 1971. Repr. of 1937 ed. 17.00 (ISBN 0-405-00852-X). Ayer Co Pubs.

Research Memorandum on the Family in the Depression. Samuel A. Stouffer & Paul F. Lazarsfeld. LC 76-162839. (Studies in the Social Aspects of the Depression). 1971. Repr. of 1937 ed. 17.00 (ISBN 0-405-00842-2). Ayer Co Pubs.

Research Methodology & Business Decisions. John W. Buckley et al. 89p. 9.95 (ISBN 0-86641-039-2, 7581). Natl Assn Accts.

Research Methodology & Quantitative History. Ed. by Charles Stephenson. (Selective Course Outlines & Reading List in History from Leading American Colleges & Universities). 240p. (Orig.). pap. text ed. cancelled (ISBN 0-910129-25-8). Wiener Pub Inc.

Research Methodology for Economists. Glenn L. Johnson. 288p. 1986. 27.50x (ISBN 0-02-948840-0). Macmillan.

Research Methodology for Family Physicians. Ed. by Leif I. Solberg. (Family Practice Research Journal Ser.). 110p. 1984. pap. 12.95 (ISBN 0-89885-221-8). Human Sci Pr.

Research Methodology in Social Sciences. C. R. Reddy. (Illus.). ix, 212p. 1987. text ed. 35.00x (ISBN 81-7035-030-1, Pub. by Daya Pub Hse India). Apt Bks.

Research Methodology in Social Sciences in India. L. P. Vidyarthi & A. Haldar. xiii, 246p. 1985. 25.00 (ISBN 1-55528-049-8, Pub. by Messers Today & Tomorrow Printers & Publishers). Scholarly Pubns.

Research Methodology: Methods & Techniques. 1986. 4.00 (ISBN 0-471-63877-3). Wiley.

Research Methods. R. Dominowski. 1980. write for info. (ISBN 0-13-774315-7). P-H.

Research Methods. Patrick McNeill. (Society Now Ser.). 160p. 1985. pap. text ed. 6.50 (ISBN 0-422-79540-2, 9590, Pub. by Tavistock England). Routledge Chapman & Hall.

Research Methods: A Process of Inquiry. Anthony M. Graziano. 512p. 1988. text ed. 33.95 (ISBN 0-06-042479-6, HarpC). Har-Row.

Research Methods & Statistics. Ronald J. Hy et al. 351p. 1983. 25.95 (ISBN 0-87084-357-5). Anderson Pub Co.

Research Methods & the New Media: The Free Press Series on Communication Technology, Vol. II. Frederick Williams et al. 224p. 1988. 24.95 (ISBN 0-02-935332-7); pap. 14.95 (ISBN 0-02-935331-9). Free Pr.

Research Methods for Community Health & Welfare: An Introduction. Karl E. Bauman. 1980. pap. 10.95x (ISBN 0-19-502699-3). Oxford U Pr.

Research Methods for Counselors: Practical Approaches in Field Settings. Ed. by Leo Goldman. LC 77-10950. (Counseling & Human Development Ser.). 439p. 1978. 39.95x (ISBN 0-471-02339-6). Wiley.

Research Methods for Elite Studies. Ed. by George Moyser & Margaret Wagstaff. (Contemporary Social Research Ser.: No. 14). 240p. 1987. text ed. 34.95x (ISBN 0-04-312035-0); pap. text ed. 16.95x (ISBN 0-04-312036-9). Unwin Hyman.

Research Methods for Managers: A Skill Building Approach. Uma Sekaran. LC 83-6916. (Management Ser.). 336p. 1984. pap. write for info. (ISBN 0-471-87099-4, 1-309); tchr's. manual avail. (ISBN 0-471-88111-2). Wiley.

Research Methods for Multi-Mode Data Analysis. Ed. by Henry G. Law & Conrad W. Snyder, Jr. 272p. 1984. 56.95 (ISBN 0-275-91210-8, C1210). Praeger.

Research Methods for Needs Assessment. John M. Nickens et al. LC 80-5126. 98p. 1980. pap. text ed. 9.00 (ISBN 0-8191-1047-7). U Pr of Amer.

Research Methods for Social Work. Allen Rubin & Earl Babbie. Date not set. text ed. write for info. (ISBN 0-534-10056-2). Wadsworth Pub.

Research Methods in Applied Behavior Analysis: Issues & Advances. Ed. by Alan Poling & R. Wayne Fugua. (Applied Clinical Psychology Ser.). 352p. 1986. 39.50x (ISBN 0-306-42127-5, Plenum Pr). Plenum Pub.

Research Methods in Clinical Oncology. Brigid G. Leventhal & Robert E. Wittes. (Illus.). 256p. 1988. text ed. 69.50 (ISBN 0-88167-382-X). Raven.

Research Methods in Clinical Psychology. Ed. by A. S. Bellack & M. Hersen. (Pergamon General Psychology Ser.: No. 130). (Illus.). 416p. 1984. text ed. 59.00 (ISBN 0-08-029410-3); pap. text ed. 23.50 (ISBN 0-08-029409-X). Pergamon.

Research Methods in Criminal Justice. Jack D. Fitzgerald & Steven M. Cox. 336p. 1986. pap. 14.95x (ISBN 0-8304-1099-6). Nelson-Hall.

Research Methods in Criminal Justice & Criminology. Frank E. Hagan. 1982. text ed. write for info. (ISBN 0-02-477340-9). Macmillan.

Research Methods in Criminal Justice & Criminology. 2nd ed. Frank E. Hagan. 605p. 1989. text ed. price not set (ISBN 0-02-348830-1). Macmillan.

Research Methods in Cultural Anthropology. H. Russell Bernard. 440p. 1988. text ed. 39.95 (ISBN 0-8039-2977-3); pap. text ed. 19.95 (ISBN 0-8039-2978-1). Sage.

Research Methods in Ecology. Frederic E. Clements. Ed. by Frank Egerton, 3rd. LC 77-74210. (History of Ecology Ser.). (Illus.). 1977. Repr. of 1905 ed. lib. bdg. 30.00x (ISBN 0-405-10381-6). Ayer Co Pubs.

Research Methods in Education. Louis Cohen & Lawrence Manion. (Illus.). 328p. 1980. 25.50 (ISBN 0-85664-917-1, Pub. by Croom Helm Ltd). Routledge Chapman & Hall.

Research Methods in Education. 2nd ed. Louis Cohen & Lawrence Manion. LC 85-362. 383p. (Orig.). 1985. pap. 17.00 (ISBN 0-7099-3438-6, Pub. by Croom Helm Ltd). Routledge Chapman & Hall.

Research Methods in Education. Evelyn J. Sowell & Rita J. Casey. 387p. 1982. text ed. write for info. (ISBN 0-534-01025-3). Wadsworth Pub.

Research Methods in Education: A Practical Guide. Robert E. Slavin. (Illus.). 384p. 1984. write for info. (ISBN 0-13-774364-5). P-H.

Research Methods in Human Ecology - Home Economics. John Touliatos & Norma H. Compton. 384p. (Orig.). 1988. text ed. 39.50 (ISBN 0-8138-0719-0). Iowa St U Pr.

Research Methods in Information Systems: Proceedings of the IFIP WG 8.2 Colloquium, Manchester Business School, 1-3 September 1984. Ed. by E. Mumford et al. 320p. 1985. 71.00 (ISBN 0-444-87807-6, North Holland). Elsevier.

Research Methods in Librarianship: Techniques & Interpretation. Ed. by Charles H. Busha & Stephen P. Harter. LC 79-8864. (Library & Information Science Ser.). 432p. 1980. tchrs' ed. 22.50 (ISBN 0-12-147550-6). Acad Pr.

Research Methods in Marine Biology. Ed. by Carl Schlieper. LC 72-6089. (Biology Ser.). (Illus.). 300p. 1972. 20.00x (ISBN 0-295-95234-2). U of Wash Pr.

Research Methods in Mass Communication. Guido H. Stempel, III & Bruce H. Westley. (Illus.). 550p. 1981. text ed. write for info. (ISBN 0-13-774240-1). P-H.

Research Methods In Neurochemistry, Vol. 5. Ed. by Neville Marks & Richard Rodnight. LC 72-222263. 334p. 1981. 62.50x (ISBN 0-306-40583-0, Plenum Pr). Plenum Pub.

Research Methods in Neurochemistry, Vol. 6. Ed. by Neville Marks & Richard Rodnight. 392p. 1985. 62.50x (ISBN 0-306-41751-0, Plenum Pr). Plenum Pub.

Research Methods in Nursing & Health. Sonya I. Shelley. 1984. text ed. 29.75 (ISBN 0-316-78474-5). Scott F.

Research Methods in Organizational Behavior. Eugene Stone. LC 77-18755. (Scott, Foresman Series in Management & Organizations). 1978. pap. text ed. write for info. (ISBN 0-673-16140-4); pap. write for info. (ISBN 0-673-16139-0). Scott F.

Research Methods in Psychology. Philip J. Dunham. 349p. 1988. text ed. 37.50 (ISBN 0-06-041807-9, HarpC). Har-Row.

Research Methods in Psychology. Posavac. 1988. price not set (ISBN 0-471-82186-1). Wiley.

Research Methods in Psychology. John Shaughnessy & Eugene Zechmeister. 450p. 1985. text ed. 23.00 (ISBN 0-394-32834-5, KnopfC). Knopf.

Research Methods in Psychology 2. 2nd ed. David G. Elmes et al. (Illus.). 434p. 1984. 34.50 (ISBN 0-314-85232-8). West Pub.

Research Methods in Social Networks Analysis. Ed. by Linton Freeman. (Illus.). 574p. 1984. lib. bdg. 34.95x (ISBN 0-8304-1094-5). Nelson-Hall.

Research Methods in Social Relations. 5th ed. Louise Kidder & Charles M. Judd. 560p. 1986. text ed. 31.95 (ISBN 0-03-002473-0, HoltC). HR&W.

Research Methods in Social Sciences. B. A. Sharma et al. 280p. 1984. text ed. 27.50X (ISBN 0-86590-211-9, Pub by Sterling Pubs India). Apt Bks.

Research Methods in the Social & Behavioral Sciences. Russell A. Jones. LC 85-14247. (Illus.). 400p. (Orig.). 1985. text ed. 27.95x (ISBN 0-87893-370-0). Sinauer Assocs.

Research Methods in the Social Sciences. 3rd ed. David Nachmias & Chava Nachmias. LC 86-60660. 608p. 1987. text ed. write for info. (ISBN 0-312-67627-1); write for info. (ISBN 0-312-67628-X); write for info. study guide (ISBN 0-312-67629-8). St Martin.

Research Methods: Principles, Practice & Theory for Nurses. 3rd. ed. Catherine Seaman. 432p. 1987. pap. 29.95 (ISBN 0-8385-8275-3). Appleton & lange.

Research Methods: Statistical Concepts & Research Practicum. John H. Behling. 1977. pap. text ed. 8.25 (ISBN 0-8191-0084-6). U Pr of Amer.

Research Monograph. National Art Education Association. Incl. No. 1. Creativity & the Prepared Mind. Ray Hyman; No. 3. Eye More Fantastical. Frank Barron. (065-02292). pap. 2.00 (ISBN 0-937652-24-5). Natl Art Ed.

Research Monograph, 27 vols. United States Works Progress Administration. (FDR & the Era of the New Deal Ser.). 1971. lib. bdg. 385.00 (ISBN 0-306-70359-9). Da Capo.

Research Needs Associated with Toxic Substances. Michael F. Saunders et al. Ed. by Water Pollution Control Federation Staff. (Illus.). 300p. 1982. pap. 40.00 (ISBN 0-943244-02-1, P0002LN). Water Pollution.

Research Needs for Evaluating Urban Public Transportation. (Special Report). 123p. 1975. 5.25 (ISBN 0-309-02383-1). Transport Res Bd.

Research Needs for Unsaturated Zone Transport Modeling of Agricultural Chemicals. Ed. by Thomas J. Gilding. 184p. (Orig.). 1988. pap. text ed. price not set (ISBN 0-944919-01-4). Agri Research Inst.

Research Needs in Civil Engineering Relevant to the Goals of Society. 340p. 1971. pap. 8.00x (ISBN 0-87262-323-8). Am Soc Civil Eng.

Research Needs in Non-Conventional Bioprocesses. Ed. by Linda Curran et al. LC 85-11065. 148p. 1985. 39.50 (ISBN 0-935470-21-2). Battelle.

Research Needs of Organic Farmers. 4p. 1.00 (ISBN 0-317-57599-6). Organic Agri.

Research Needs Related to the Nation's Infrastructure: Proceedings of a Workshop Sponsored by the National Science Foundation & ASCE. 48p. 1984. 13.00x (ISBN 0-87262-433-1). Am Soc Civil Eng.

Research Needs Relating to Performance of Aggregates in Highway Construction. (National Cooperative Highway Research Project Report). 68p. 1970. 3.40 (ISBN 0-309-01887-0). Transport Res Bd.

Research News. Arlene H. Eakle. pap. write for info. Genealog Inst.

Research Notekeeping. Arlene H. Eakle. 11p. 1973. pap. 4.00 (ISBN 0-940764-05-9). Genealog Inst.

Research Objectives in British Archaeology. Ed. by C. Thomas. 56p. 1983. pap. text ed. 6.95 (ISBN 0-906780-32-2, Pub. by Coun Brit Archaeology). Humanities.

Research Odyssey: Developing & Testing a Community Theory. George Hillery, Jr. 250p. 1981. 34.95 (ISBN 0-87855-400-9). Transaction Bks.

TITLE INDEX RESEARCH RESULTS OF THE

Research of Motivation in Education, Vol. 2: The Classroom Milieu. Carole Ames & Russell E. Ames. 1985. 43.00 (ISBN 0-12-056702-4). Acad Pr.

Research on Administration of Physical Education & Athletics, 1971-1982: A Retrieval System. John A. Baker & Mary S. Collins. 88p. (Orig.). 1983. pap. 7.95 (ISBN 0-87881-107-9). Mojave Bks.

Research on Adolescence for Youth Service: An Annotated Bibliography on Adolescent Development, Educational Needs, & Media, 1978-1980. Ed. by Gerald Hodges & Frances B. Bradburn. LC 83-25785. xii, 148p. 1984. pap. text ed. 15.00x (ISBN 0-8389-3297-5). ALA.

Research on Changes of Chinese Society. Albert R. O'Hara. (Asian Folklore & Social Life Monograph: No. 20). 1971. 19.00x (ISBN 0-89986-022-2). Oriental Bk Store.

Research on Composing: Points of Departure. Ed. by Charles R. Cooper & Lee Odell. LC 78-18251. 203p. 1978. pap. 9.75 (ISBN 0-8141-4069-6). NCTE.

Research on Dietary Fibres. Ed. by Ruzsa et al. (Illus.). 238p. 1986. 34.00 (ISBN 963-05-4254-4, Pub. by Akademiai Kiado Hungary). Humanities.

Research on Dolphins. Ed. by M. M. Bryden & Richard Harrison. (Illus.). 400p. 1986. 85.00 (ISBN 0-19-857606-4). Oxford U Pr.

Research on Environments & People: Methods, Quality Assessment, New Directions. Swedish Council for Building Research Staff. Ed. by Roger S. Ulrich & Staffan Hygge. (Illus.). 148p. 1987. pap. 24.00x (ISBN 91-540-4757-9). Coronet Bks.

Research on Exemplary Schools: From Theory to Practice to Policy. Ed. by Gilbert Austin & Herbert Garber. (Educational Psychology Ser.). 1985. 29.95 (ISBN 0-12-068590-6); pap. 19.95 (ISBN 0-12-068591-4). Acad Pr.

Research on Foreign Students & International Study: An Overview & Bibliography. Philip G. Altbach et al. LC 85-3372. 416p. 1985. 38.95 (ISBN 0-275-90052-5, C0052). Praeger.

Research on Grain Legumes in Eastern & Central Africa. 122p. (Orig.). 1987. pap. text ed. 19.20x (ISBN 92-9066-129-1, Pub. by ICRISAT India). Agribookstore.

Research on Health: A Medical Subject Analysis with Bibliography. Mary R. Bartone. LC 84-45738. 150p. 1987. 34.50 (ISBN 0-88164-254-1); pap. 26.50 (ISBN 0-88164-255-X). ABBE Pubs Assn.

Research on Human Subjects: Problems of Social Control in Medical Experimentation. Bernard Barber et al. LC 70-83831. 264p. 1973. 22.50x (ISBN 0-87154-090-8). Russell Sage.

Research on Human Subjects: Problems of Social Control in Medical Experimentation. Bernard Barber et al. LC 78-55938. 263p. 1979. pap. text ed. 15.95x (ISBN 0-87855-649-4). Transaction Bks.

Research on Labor Mobility: An Appraisal of Research Findings in the United States. Herbert S. Parnes. LC 82-6146. xii, 205p. 1982. Repr. of 1954 ed. lib. bdg. 35.00x (ISBN 0-313-23571-6, PARE). Greenwood.

Research on Laser Theory. Ed. by A. N. Orayevskiy. (Proceedings of the Lebedev Physics Institute of the Academy of Sciences of the U. S. S. R. Ser.: Vol. 171). 288p. 1987. text ed. 92.00 (ISBN 0-941743-06-3). Nova Sci Pubs.

Research on Law Students: An Annotated Bibliography. Kenneth H. Barry & Patricia A. Connelly. 54p. (Reprinted from 1978 ABF Res. J., No. 1). 1978. 2.50 (ISBN 0-317-33356-9). Amer Bar Assn.

Research on Measurement Procedures with Individuals with Hearing Impairments. John Reiman & Michael Bollis. Date not set. pap. text ed. price not set (ISBN 0-944232-04-3). Teaching Res.

Research on Men Who Batter: An Overview, Bibliography & Resource Guide. Edward W. Gondolf. Ed. by Lee M. Joiner. LC 87-34229. 104p. (Orig.). 1988. pap. 4.95 (ISBN 0-943519-05-5, B1905). Human Servs Inst.

Research on Men's Vocations to the Priesthood & the Religious Life. Dean R. Hoge et al. 104p. 1984. pap. 6.50 (ISBN 1-55586-904-1). US Catholic.

Research on Modified Fertilizer Materials for Use in Developing-Country Agriculture. D. H. Parish et al. (IFDC Paper Sers. P-2). 1980. 4.00 (ISBN 0-88090-062-8). Intl Fertilizer.

Research on Motivation in Education: Student Motivation, Vol. 1. Russell E. Ames & Carole Ames. LC 83-12315. 1984. 43.00 (ISBN 0-12-056701-6). Acad Pr.

Research on Motivation in Education, Vol. 3: Goals & Cognitions. Ed. by Carole Emes & Russell Ames. 518p. 1988. price not set (ISBN 0-12-056703-2). Acad Pr.

Research on Multiple Sclerosis. 3rd, rev. ed. Byron H. Waksman et al. LC 87-71316. (Illus.). 128p. 1987. pap. 9.50 (ISBN 0-939957-07-8, 0013). Demos Pubns Inc.

Research on Negotiation in Organizations, Vol. 1. Ed. by Ray J. Lewicki et al. 1986. 56.50 (ISBN 0-89232-638-7). Jai Pr.

Research on Negotiation in Organizations, Vol. 2. Ed. by Roy J. Lewicki et al. 1988. 58.50 (ISBN 0-89232-639-5). Jai Pr.

Research on People of Color. 45p. 1984. pap. 5.50 (ISBN 0-87101-125-5). Natl Assn Soc Wkrs.

Research on Psychotherapeutic Approaches: Proceedings, First European Conference on Psychotherapy Research, Trier, 1981, Vol. 4. Ed. by Wolf-Rudiger Minsel & Wolfgang Herff. (Studien zur Padagogischen und Psychologischen Intervention). 312p. 1983. 36.30 (ISBN 3-8204-7744-6). P Lang Pubs.

Research on Reincarnation. Manly P. Hall. pap. 2.50 (ISBN 0-89314-349-9). Philos Res.

Research on Second Language Learning: Focus on the Classroom. James P. Lantolf & Angela Labarca. Ed. by Robert J. DiPietro. LC 86-22300. (Delaware Symposium on Language Studies: Vol. 6). 240p. 1987. text ed. 35.00 (ISBN 0-89391-363-4). Ablex Pub.

Research on Sentencing: The Search for Reform, 2 vols. National Research Council Panel on Sentencing Research & Alfred Blumstein. LC 83-4048. 1983. Vol. I. 19.95x (ISBN 0-309-03347-0); Vol. II. pap. text ed. 24.50x (ISBN 0-309-03383-7); Set. 35.50x. Natl Acad Pr.

Research on Service Delivery to Battered Women & Crime Victims. 1980. 3.00 (ISBN 0-86671-062-0). Comm Coun Great NY.

Research on Steroids. Ed. by A. Klopper et al. 1979. 67.50 (ISBN 0-12-416050-6). Acad Pr.

Research on Steroids, Vol. XI: Steroid Modulation of Neuroendocrine Function-Sterols, Steroids & Bone Metabolism. Ed. by L. Martini et al. (International Congress Ser.: Vol. 633). 1985. 111.75 (ISBN 0-444-80594-X). Elsevier.

Research on Suicide: A Bibliography. Ed. by John L. McIntosh. LC 84-15706. (Bibliographies & Indexes in Psychology Ser.: No. 2). xiii, 323p. 1985. lib. bdg. 39.95 (ISBN 0-313-23992-4, MLR/). Greenwood.

Research on Support for Parents & Infants in the Postnatal Period. C. F. Boukydis. LC 87-1349. 272p. 1987. text ed. 39.50 (ISBN 0-89391-333-2). Ablex Pub.

Research on Teacher Evaluation: The Case for Commitment to Teacher Growth. Richard J. Stiggins & Daniel L. Duke. (Educational Leadership Ser.). 160p. 1988. 44.95 (ISBN 0-88706-669-0); pap. 14.95 (ISBN 0-88706-670-4). State U NY Pr.

Research on Teaching: Concepts, Findings & Implications. Ed. by Penelope L. Peterson & Herbert J. Walberg. LC 78-62102. (Education Ser.). 1979. 25.25x (ISBN 0-8211-1518-9); text ed. 22.50x 10 or more copies. McCutchan.

Research on Technological Innovation, Management & Policy, Vol. 1. Ed. by Richard S. Rosenbloom. 1983. 56.50 (ISBN 0-89232-273-X). Jai Pr.

Research on Technological Innovation, Management & Policy, Vol. 2. Ed. by Richard S. Rosenbloom. 1985. 56.50 (ISBN 0-89232-426-0). Jai Pr.

Research on Technological Innovation, Management & Policy, Vol. 3. Ed. by Richard S. Rosenbloom. 1986. 56.50 (ISBN 0-89232-688-3). Jai Pr.

Research on Technological Innovation, Management & Policy, Vol. 4. Ed. by Richard S. Rosenbloom. 1988. price not set (ISBN 0-89232-798-7). Jai Pr.

Research on Thailand in the Philippines: An Annotated Bibliography of Theses, Dissertations, & Investigation Papers. Sida Chety. LC 77-152541. (Cornell University, Southeast Asia Program, Data Paper: No. 107). pap. 25.00 (ISBN 0-317-29630-2, 2021849). Bks Demand UMI.

Research on the Bureaucracy of Pakistan: A Critique of Sources, Conditions, Issues, with Appended Documents. Ralph J. Braibanti. LC 66-14888. (Duke Univrsity, Commonwealth-Studies Center, Publication: No. 26). pap. 152.50 (ISBN 0-317-20091-7, 2023371). Bks Demand UMI.

Research on the Ethiopian Flora: Proceedings of the First Ethiopian Flora Symposium Held in Uppsala, May 22-26, 1984. Ed. by Inga Hedberg. (Symbolae Botanicae Upsalienses Ser.). (Illus.). 212p. (Orig.). 1986. pap. text ed. 26.50x (ISBN 91-554-1956-9, Pub. by Uppsala Univ Acta Univ Uppsaliensis (Uppsala Sweden)). Coronet Bks.

Research on the Etiology of Schizophrenia. G. IU. Malis. Tr. by Basil Haigh. LC 61-11828. (International Behavioral Science Ser.). (Illus.). pap. 51.80 (ISBN 0-317-10350-4, 2020657). Bks Demand UMI.

Research on the GDR "auf englisch" Researchers of East German Affairs & Their Studies in English-Language Countries. Anita M. Mallinckrodt. (Illus.). 115p. 1984. German-Language Edition. write for info. (ISBN 0-931227-01-1); English-Language Edition. pap. 8.50 (ISBN 0-931227-00-3). Mallinckrodt Comm.

Research on the Legal Profession: A Review of Work Done. 2nd ed. Olavi Maru. LC 86-71978. vii, 106p. (Orig.). 1986. pap. 13.50 (ISBN 0-910059-11-X). Am Bar Foun.

Research on the Propensity for Crime at Different Ages. Adolphe Quetelet. Tr. by Sawyer F. Sylvester from Fr. (Illus.). 100p. 1983. Repr. of 1831 ed. text ed. 18.95 (ISBN 0-87084-749-X). Anderson Pub Co.

Research on the Properties of Line Pipe: Summary Report. G. M. McClure et al. 135p. 1962. softcover 3.00 (ISBN 0-318-12691-5, L00290). Am Gas Assn.

Research on the Quality of Life. Ed. by Frank M. Andrews. LC 86-15179. 384p. 1986. 42.00x (ISBN 0-87944-308-1). Inst Soc Res.

Research on the Viral Hypothesis of Mental Disorders. Ed. by P. V. Morozov. (Advances in Biological Psychiatry: Vol. 12). (Illus.). x, 178p. 1983. pap. 60.75 (ISBN 3-8055-3706-9). S Karger.

Research on Transport Economics: Annual Information Bulletin, Vol. XX, November 1987. OECD. 612p. (Orig., Eng. & Fr.). 1987. pap. 56.00x (ISBN 0-318-23733-4). OECD.

Research on Transport Economics: ECMT. OECD. (Vol. XVII). 534p. (Orig.). 1984. pap. 45.00X (ISBN 0-318-03814-5). OECD.

Research on Transportation Facilities in Cold Regions. Ed. by Orlando B. Andersland & Francis H Sayles. LC 86-25920. 112p. 1986. pap. 15.00x (ISBN 0-87262-568-0). Am Soc Civil Eng.

Research on Urban Hydrology, 3 vols. Ed. by M. B. McPherson. Incl. Vol. 1. State-of-the-Art Reports from Australia, Canada, U. S. S. R., United Kingdom & United States. (No. 15). 185p. 1977. pap. 13.75 (ISBN 92-3-101488-9, U763). UNIPUB; Vol. 2. State-of-the Art Reports from France, the Federal Republic of Germany, India, the Netherlands, Norway, Poland & Sweden. (No. 16). (Illus.). 265p. 1978. pap. 13.75 (ISBN 92-3-101555-9, U849). UNIPUB; Vol. 3. Follow-up Reports from Eleven Countries 1979. (No. 21). 144p. 1981. pap. 14.50 (ISBN 92-3-101984-8, U1230). UNIPUB. (Technical Papers in Hydrology Ser.). (Illus., UNESCO). UNIPUB.

Research on Written Composition: New Directions for Teaching. George Hillocks, Jr. 369p. 1986. 24.75 (ISBN 0-8141-4075-0). NCTE.

Research Opportunities in Renaissance Drama: The Reports of the Modern Language Association Conferences, 20 nos. in 8 vols. Modern Language Association of America. Incl. Vol. 1, No. 1. Chicago Conference, 1955; Vol. 1, No. 2. Washington Conference, 1956; Vol. 1, No. 3. Madison Conference, 1957; Vol. 2, No. 4. New York Conference, 1958; Vol. 2, No. 5. Chicago, 1959 & Philadelphia, 1960, Conferences; Vol. 2, No. 6. Chicago, 1961 & Washington, 1962, Conferences. Repr. of 1962 ed. Set. 335.00 (ISBN 0-404-08063-4); write for info. AMS Pr.

Research Organization & Science Promotion in the Federal Republic of Germany. Ed. by Hildegard & Reinhold Geimer. 217p. 1981. lib. bdg. 18.00 (ISBN 3-598-10357-3). K G Saur.

Research Paper: A Common-Sense Approach. Thomas E. Gaston & Bret H. Smith. (Illus.). 304p. 1987. pap. text ed. write for info. (ISBN 0-13-774100-6). P-H.

Research Paper Guide. new ed. Anthony C. Sherman. Ed. by Robert B. Ewald. 94p. (Orig.). 1970. pap. text ed. 3.95 (ISBN 0-88301-024-0). Pendulum Pr.

Research Paper Manual. Martin H. Skoble. 1977. pap. 2.95 (ISBN 0-89529-008-1). Avery Pub.

Research Paper: Process, Form, & Content. 5th ed. Audrey J. Roth. 305p. 1986. pap. text ed. write for info. (ISBN 0-534-06090-0). Wadsworth Pub.

Research Paper: Process, Form, & Content. 6th ed. Audrey J. Roth. Date not set. pap. text ed. write for info. (ISBN 0-534-09924-6). Wadsworth Pub.

Research Paper: Sources & Resources. John T. Hiers & James O. Williams. LC 85-81378. 189p. 1986. pap. text ed. 9.00 (ISBN 0-669-07152-8). Heath.

Research Paper-the Business Report: A Few Ideas. Sheldon F. Katz. 41p. 1984. pap. text ed. 4.50 (ISBN 0-89917-435-3, Pub. by College Town Pr). Tichenor Pub.

Research Paper Workbook. 2nd ed. Ellen Strenski & Madge Manfred. 256p. 1985. pap. text ed. 13.95 (ISBN 0-582-28542-9). Longman.

Research Papers. 5th ed. William Coyle. LC 79-14110. 1980. pap. 8.40 scp. Bobbs.

Research Papers. 5th ed. William Coyle. LC 79-14110. 1980. pap. 8.48scp. Odyssey Pr.

Research Papers. 6th ed. William Coyle. 240p. (Orig.). 1985. pap. text ed. 8.48scp (ISBN 0-672-61637-8). Bobbs.

Research Papers. 7th ed. William Coyle. 317p. 1987. pap. text ed. write for info. (ISBN 0-02-325410-6). Macmillan.

Research Papers, 5 vols. in 6 bks. Private Philanthropy & Public Need Commission. 1986. Repr. of 1977 ed. Set. lib. bdg. 275.00 (ISBN 0-89941-446-X). W S Hein.

Research Papers: A Guided Writing Experience for Senior High Students. 2nd rev. ed. Richard Corbin & Jonathan Corbin. 1978. pap. text ed. 2.00 (ISBN 0-930348-00-1). NY St Eng Coun.

Research Papers: A New Guide. Samuel Draper. 144p. 1987. pap. text ed. 11.95 (ISBN 0-8403-4271-3). Kendall-Hunt.

Research Paradigms in Psychosomatic Medicine. Ed. by T. N. Wise & G. Fava. (Advances in Psychosomatic Medicine Ser.: Vol. 17). (Illus.). viii, 272p. 1987. 116.75 (ISBN 3-8055-4484-7). S Karger.

Research Parks & Other Ventures: The University-Real Estate Connection. Ed. by Rachelle Levitt. LC 85-52744. 113p. 1985. pap. 36.00 (ISBN 0-87420-633-2, R18). Urban Land.

Research Perspectives on Decision Making under Uncertainty. K. Borcherding et al. 1984. Repr. 84.25 (ISBN 0-444-87574-3). Elsevier.

Research Perspectives on the Transition from School to Work: Report of a European Contact Workshop Organised by the Institute of Education (ECF) under the Auspices of the Commission of the European Communities, Bruges, July 1977. Ed. by Guy Neave. 144p. 1978. pap. text ed. 13.75 (ISBN 90-265-0278-8, Pub. by Swets & Zeitlinger Netherlands). Hogrefe Intl.

Research Philosophy & Techniques: Selected Readings. Ed. by Robert J. Gibbons. LC 82-84587. 244p. (Orig.). 1983. pap. text ed. 15.00 (ISBN 0-89462-015-0). IIA.

Research Planes. David Baker. (Military Aircraft Library). (Illus.). 48p. (gr. 3-8). 1987. PLB 75.96 6 bk. set (ISBN 0-317-60514-3); PLB 12.66 (ISBN 0-86592-354-X). Rourke Corp.

Research Pleasers. Susan S. Petreshene. Ed. by Ellen Sussman. (Illus., Orig.). (gr. 3-6). 1982. pap. text ed. 5.95 (ISBN 0-933606-19-2, MS-618). Monkey Sisters.

Research Potential of Anthropological Museum Collections. Ed. by Anne M. Cantwell et al. (Annals of The New York Academy of Science Ser.: Vol. 376). 585p. 1981. lib. bdg. 115.00x (ISBN 0-89766-141-9); pap. 115.00x (ISBN 0-89766-142-7). NY Acad Sci.

Research Practices in the Study of Kinship. Alan Barnard & Anthony Good. (Research Methods in Social Anthropology Ser.). 1984. 38.00 (ISBN 0-12-078980-9). Acad Pr.

Research Practices in the Study of Kinship. Alan Barnard & Anthony Good. (ASA Research Methods in Social Anthropology Ser.). 226p. 1987. pap. 75.00 (ISBN 0-12-078981-7). Acad Pr.

Research Priorities for the Nineteen-Eighties: Generating a Scientific Basis for Nursing Practice. (No. D-68). 1981p. 1.00 (ISBN 0-686-40490-4). ANA.

Research Priorities in African Literature. Ed. by Bernth Lindfors. 222p. 1984. lib. bdg. 27.00 (ISBN 3-598-10570-3). K G Saur.

Research Priorities in Sentencing. National Center for State Courts Staff, Denver. 82p. 1975. pap. 1.00 (ISBN 0-89656-013-9, R-022). Natl Ctr St Courts.

Research Priorities in Tropical Biology. National Research Council. xii, 116p. 1980. pap. text ed. 9.75x (ISBN 0-309-03043-9). Natl Acad Pr.

Research Priorities on Alcohol: Proceedings of a Symposium. Ed. by Mark Keller. (Journal of Studies on Alcohol: Suppl. No. 8). 1979. 10.00 (ISBN 0-911290-03-6). Rutgers Ctr Alcohol.

Research Process: Essentials of Skill Development. Alberta Kovacs. LC 84-23862. (Illus.). 363p. pap. text ed. 16.95 (ISBN 0-8036-5445-6). Davis Co.

Research Process in Educational Settings: Ten Case Studies. Ed. by Robert G. Burgess. 275p. 1984. 31.00x (ISBN 0-905273-92-3, Falmer Pr); pap. 18.00x (ISBN 0-905273-91-5, Falmer Pr). Taylor & Francis.

Research Process in Nursing. 2nd ed. Patricia A. Dempsey & Arthur D. Dempsey. (Nursing Ser.). 320p. 1986. pap. 21.25 (ISBN 0-86720-350-1). Jones & Bartlett.

Research Process in Political Science. Ed. by W. Phillips Shively. LC 83-62578. 273p. 1984. pap. 13.95 (ISBN 0-87581-300-3). Peacock Pubs.

Research Processes in Physical Education. 2nd ed. David H. Clarke & H. Harrison Clarke. (Illus.). 528p. 1984. pap. write for info. (ISBN 0-13-774513-3). P-H.

Research Program Effectiveness. Ed. by M. C. Yovits et al. 560p. 1966. 118.00 (ISBN 0-677-10680-7). Gordon & Breach.

Research Project on Workfare. Arodel Child & Lynn Johnson. 257p. 1982. 25.00 (32,115). NCLS Inc.

Research Projects for College Students: What to Write Across the Curriculum. Marilyn Lutzker. LC 87-37549. 152p. 1988. lib. bdg. 35.00 (ISBN 0-313-25149-5, LRW/). Greenwood.

Research Reactor Utilization. (Technical Reports Ser.: No. 71). (Illus.). 89p. 1967. pap. 11.50 (ISBN 92-0-155067-7, IDC71, IAEA). UNIPUB.

Research Readings for Discipline-Based Art Education: A Journey Beyond Creating. 1987. 15.00 (ISBN 0-937652-36-9). Natl Art Ed.

Research Readings in Rehabilitation Counseling. H. Moses & C. H. Patterson. 1973. pap. 9.80x (ISBN 0-87563-054-5). Stipes.

Research, Realpolitik, & Development in Korea: The State & the Green Revolution. Larry L. Burmeister. (Rural Studies). 292p. 1988. 29.50 (ISBN 0-8133-7400-6). Westview.

Research Relationship: Practice & Politics in Social Policy Research. Ed. by G. Clare Wenger. (Contemporary Social Research Ser.: No. 15). 240p. 1987. text ed. 34.95x (ISBN 0-04-312037-7); pap. text ed. 16.95x (ISBN 0-04-312038-5). Unwin Hyman.

Research Relevant to Trends in Transport over the Coming Decade. OECD. (ECMT Round Table Ser.: No. 75). 57p. (Orig.). 1987. pap. 11.00x (ISBN 92-821-1118-0). OECD.

Research Results of the National Day Care Study. Jeffrey Travers & Barbara D. Goodson. (National Day Care Study Ser.). (Illus.). 288p. (Orig.). 1981. 35.00x (ISBN 0-89011-554-0). Abt Bks.

Research Review (Ethical) Committees for Animal Experimentation. D. P. Britt. 1985. 16.00x (ISBN 0-317-43890-5, Pub. by Univ Federation Animal). State Mutual Bk.

Research Satellites. D. J. Herda. LC 86-24225. (First Bks.). (Illus.). 72p. (gr. 4-8). 1987. lib. bdg. 10.40 (ISBN 0-531-10311-0). Watts.

Research Scientist. Educational Research Council of America Staff. Ed. by Theodore N. Ferris & John P. Marchak. (Real People at Work Ser.: Series O). (Illus.). 36p. (Orig.). (gr. 5). 1976. pap. text ed. 2.70 (ISBN 0-89247-116-6, 9539). Changing Times.

Research Services Directory. 3rd ed. Ed. by Robert Huffman. 641p. 1986. 290.00x (ISBN 0-8103-0246-2). Gale.

Research Shortcuts. Judi Kesselman-Turkel & Franklynn Peterson. 120p. 1982. pap. 4.95 (ISBN 0-8092-5749-1). Contemp Bks.

Research Society. Ed. by M. W. Shelly & E. Glatt. 564p. 1968. 124.00 (ISBN 0-677-11540-7). Gordon & Breach.

Research, Statistics, Communications: An Anthology. 1977. pap. 2.50 (ISBN 0-912452-18-8). Am Phys Therapy Assn.

Research Strategies for Assessing the Behavioural Effects of Foods & Nutrients: Proceedings of Conference of the Center for Brain Sciences & Metabolism Charitable Trust, Massachusetts Institute of Technology, Cambridge. Ed. by R. J. Wurtman & H. Lieberman. (Illus.). 136p. 1984. 39.00 (ISBN 0-08-030862-7). Pergamon.

Research Strategies in Alcoholism Treatment Assessment. Pref. by Dan J. Lettieri. LC 88-7212. (Drugs & Society Ser.: Vol. 2, No. 2). (Illus.). 120p. 1988. text ed. 19.95 (ISBN 0-86656-782-8). Haworth Pr.

Research Strategies in Historical Archaeology. Ed. by Stanley South. (Studies in Archaeology). 1977. 32.50 (ISBN 0-12-655760-8). Acad Pr.

Research Strategies in Psychotherapy. Edward S. Bordin. LC 74-11272. (Wiley Series on Personality Processes). pap. 71.00 (ISBN 0-317-08426-7, 2051569). Bks Demand UMI.

Research Summary: The Census of Horticultural Specialties. David S. Stump. (Illus.). 76p. 1982. pap. text ed. 10.00 (ISBN 0-935336-01-X). Horticult Research.

Research Support & Federal Government Financing for Medicine with a Dictionary of Subjects, Research Index & Bibliography. Brenda Reynolds. Ed. by John C. Bartone. LC 83-70084. 141p. 1983. 34.50 (ISBN 0-88164-038-7); pap. 26.50 (ISBN 0-88164-039-5). ABBE Pubs Assn.

Research Symposium on the Male Adolescent Voice. Ed. by Maria Runfola & Lee Bash. (Proceedings Ser.). (Illus.). 182p. (Orig.). 1984. pap. 14.95 (ISBN 0-931111-00-5). Suny Buff Music.

Research, Teaching & Learning with the Piaget Model. John W. Renner & Donald G. Stafford. LC 75-17800. (Illus.). 199p. 1976. 16.95x (ISBN 0-8061-1313-8). U of Okla Pr.

Research Teasers. Susan S. Petreshene. Ed. by Ellen Sussman. (Illus., Orig.). (gr. 3-6). 1982. pap. text ed. 5.95 (ISBN 0-933606-18-4, MS-617). Monkey Sisters.

Research Technician. Jack Rudman. (Career Examination Ser.: C-1948). (Cloth bdg. avail. on request). pap. 14.00 (ISBN 0-8373-1948-X). Natl Learning.

Research Techniques for Clinical Social Workers. Ed. by Tony Tripodi & Irwin Epstein. LC 80-15516. 296p. 1980. 22.50x (ISBN 0-231-04652-9). Columbia U Pr.

Research Techniques for High Pressure & High Temperature. Ed. by G. C. Ulmer. (Illus.). 384p. 1971. 31.00 (ISBN 0-387-05594-0). Springer-Verlag.

Research Techniques for Program Planning, Monitoring & Evaluation. Irwin Epstein & Tony Tripodi. LC 76-51825. 178p. 1977. 23.00x (ISBN 0-231-03944-1). Columbia U Pr.

Research Techniques for the Health Sciences. Laurna Rubinson & James J. Neutens. (Illus.). 320p. 1987. text ed. write for info. (ISBN 0-02-404540-3). Macmillan.

Research Techniques for the Social Sciences Manual. Edward Richardson. LC 83-10749. 123p. 1983. pap. 5.00 (ISBN 0-913480-58-4). Inter Am U Pr.

Research Techniques in Human Engineering. Alfred R. E. Chapanis. LC 59-10765. pap. 82.00 (ISBN 0-317-10928-6, 2002276). Bks Demand UMI.

Research Techniques in NDT, 8 vols. Ed. by R. S. Sharpe. 320p. 1982. Vol. 1. 86.00 (ISBN 0-318-21509-8, 140); Vol. 2. 75.60 (ISBN 0-318-21510-1, 141); Vol. 3. 82.95 (ISBN 0-318-21511-X, 142); Vol. 4. 85.00 (ISBN 0-318-21512-8, 143); Vol. 5. 61.40 (ISBN 0-318-21513-6, 144); Vol. 6. 62.45 (ISBN 0-318-21514-4, 145). Am Soc Nondestructive.

Research Techniques in Non-Destructive Testing, Vol. 3. Ed. by R. S. Sharpe. 1978. 99.00 (ISBN 0-12-639053-3). Acad Pr.

Research Techniques in Non-Destructive Testing, Vol. 4. R. S. Sharpe. LC 79-109038. 1980. 99.00 (ISBN 0-12-639054-1). Acad Pr.

Research Techniques in Non-Destructive Testing, Vol. 5. Ed. by R. S. Sharpe. 1983. 90.00 (ISBN 0-12-639055-X). Acad Pr.

Research Techniques in Non-Destructive Testing, Vol. 6. Ed. by R. S. Sharpe. 1983. 90.00 (ISBN 0-12-639056-8). Acad Pr.

Research Techniques in Non-Destructive Testing, Vol. 7. R. S. Sharpe. 1984. 90.00 (ISBN 0-12-639057-6). Acad Pr.

Research Techniques in Nondestructive Testing, Vol. 8. Ed. by R. S. Sharpe. 479p. 1985. 122.50 (ISBN 0-12-639058-4). Acad Pr.

Research Techniques in the Rat. Clayton Petty. (Illus.). 382p. 1982. 40.50 (ISBN 0-398-04595-X). C C Thomas.

Research: The Practical Approach for Occupational Therapy. Alice C. Jantzen. 64p. pap. 6.50 (RAMSCO 00100). Ramsco Pub.

Research: The Validation of Clinical Practice. 2nd, rev. ed. Otto Payton. 311p. 1988. pap. text ed. 19.95 (ISBN 0-8036-6799-X). Davis Co.

Research Through Biotechnology: Institutional Impacts & Societal Concerns. Brian J. Reichel et al. (Bibliographies in Technology & Social Change Ser.: No. 1). viii, 139p. (Orig.). 1987. pap. text ed. 12.00 (ISBN 0-945271-00-X). ISU-TSCP.

Research to Education: A Conceptual Introduction. James H. McMillan & Sally Schumacher. 1984. text ed. write for info. (ISBN 0-673-39167-1). Scott F.

Research to Improve Teaching-Learning Practices. 33p. (Orig.). 1984. pap. 5.00 (UB148, UB). UNIPUB.

Research-To-Practice Dilemma. Ed. by Sharon Merriam. 13p. 1987. 3.00 (ISBN 0-318-23414-9, OC123). Natl Ctr Res Voc Ed.

Research Tools for Latin American Historians: A Select, Annotated Bibliography. David P. Werlich. LC 78-68291. 285p. 1980. lib. bdg. 43.00 (ISBN 0-8240-9762-9). Garland Pub.

Research Tools for the Classics. Ed. by Roger Bagnall. LC 80-25766. (APA Pamphlets). 1980. pap. 7.50 (ISBN 0-89130-452-5, 40-06-06). Scholars Pr GA.

Research Topics in Electromagnetic Wave Theory. Ed. by J. A. Kong. LC 80-28274. 368p. 1981. 45.50x (ISBN 0-471-08782-3, Pub. by John Wiley). Krieger.

Research Tradition in Occupational Therapy. Charlotte B. Royeen. LC 87-43326. 100p. 1988. pap. 19.95 (ISBN 1-55642-035-8). Slack Inc.

Research, Training & Practice in Clinical Medicine of Aging. Ed. by L. Gitman & E. Woodford-Williams. (Interdisciplinary Topics in Gerontology: Vol. 5). 1970. 23.50 (ISBN 3-8055-0505-1). S Karger.

Research, Training, Test & Production Reactor Directory. 2nd ed. LC 83-71582. (Handbook Ser.). 1983. 350.00 (ISBN 0-89448-507-5). Am Nuclear Soc.

Research Trends in Air Pollution Control: Scrubbing, Hot Gas Clean-Up, Sampling & Analysis. Ed. by R. Mahalingam & Alfred J. Engel. LC 81-19133. (AIChE Symposium Ser.: Vol. 77, No. 211). 94p. 1981. pap. 32.00 (ISBN 0-8169-0219-4, S-211). Am Inst Chem Eng.

Research Trends in Graph Theory & Applications. Alavi et al. 1989. price not set (ISBN 0-471-60917-X). Wiley.

Research Universities & Their Patrons. Robert M. Rosenzweig & Barbara Turlington. LC 81-19685. 200p. 1982. 22.50x (ISBN 0-520-04664-1); pap. 6.95x (ISBN 0-520-04735-4). U of Cal Pr.

Research Utilization. Ed. by Carol Weiss. 1976. pap. text ed. 8.00 (ISBN 0-918592-14-3). Policy Studies.

Research Utilization in Social Work Education. Date not set. 7.70. Coun Soc Wk Ed.

Research Utilization Inventory: A Survey of Current Research of Social & Health Agencies in New York City. 1976. pap. 6.00 (ISBN 0-86671-033-7). Comm Coun Great NY.

Research Vessel Data, 4 vols. (Fisheries Reports: No. 29, Vols.1-4). Vol. 1, 1965. 337p. pap. 20.75 (ISBN 0-686-92735-4, F1655, FAO); Vol. 2, 1966. 346p. pap. 21.25 (ISBN 0-686-98611-3, F1656); Vol. 3, 1968. 476p. pap. 27.00 (ISBN 0-686-98612-1, F1657); Vol. 4, 1973. 335p. pap. 20.75 (ISBN 0-686-98613-X, F1658). UNIPUB.

Research with the Locus of Control Construct: Assessment Methods, Vol. I. Ed. by Herbert Lefcourt. LC 81-7876. 1981. 47.00 (ISBN 0-12-443201-8). Acad Pr.

Research with the Locus of Control Construct: Developments & Social Problems, Vol. 2. Ed. by Herbert M. Lefcourt. 1983. 47.00 (ISBN 0-12-443202-6). Acad Pr.

Research with the Locus of Control Construct, Vol. 3: Extensions & Limitations. Ed. by Herbert M. Lefcourt. 1984. 47.00 (ISBN 0-12-443203-4). Acad Pr.

Research Within Reach. Ed. by David Holdzkom & Pamela B. Lutz. (Illus.). 216p. 1984. pap. 6.50 (ISBN 0-317-65975-8). Natl Sci Tchrs.

Research Within Reach: Elementary School Mathematics. Mark J. Driscoll. 141p. 1981. pap. 9.00 (ISBN 0-87353-194-9). NCTM.

Research Within Reach: Secondary School Mathematics. Mark Driscoll. 179p. 1983. 9.00 (ISBN 0-87353-211-2). NCTM.

Research Within Reach: Secondary School Reading. Ed. by Donna Alvermann et al. 200p. 1987. 11.25 (ISBN 0-87207-784-5). Intl Reading.

Research Worker. Jack Rudman. (Career Examination Ser.: C-546). (Cloth bdg. avail. on request). pap. 14.00 (ISBN 0-8373-0546-2). Natl Learning.

Research Workout. Susan Martin & Harriet Green. (Illus.). 144p. (gr. 4-9). 1984. 9.95wkbk (ISBN 0-86653-194-7). Good Apple.

Research Writing: A Complete Guide to Pesearch Papers. W. Dean Memering. (Illus.). 192p. 1983. pap. text ed. write for info. (ISBN 0-13-774430-7). P-H.

Researcher's Guide to American Genealogy. Val D. Greenwood. LC 73-6902. (Illus.). 535p. 1983. 15.00 (ISBN 0-8063-0560-6). Genealog Pub.

Researcher's Guide to American Genealogy. 8th ed. Val D. Greenwood. (Illus.). 535p. 1988. 17.50 (2360). Genealog Pub.

Researchers' Guide to Genealogical & Historical Records in Orange County, New York. Orange County Genealogical Society. (Orig.). 1985. write for info. (ISBN 0-9604116-6-6). Orange County Genealog.

Researcher's Guide to United States Census Availability, 1790-1910. Ann B. Hamilton. iv, 134p. (Orig.). 1987. pap. 15.00 (ISBN 1-55613-066-X). Heritage Bk.

Researcher's Guide to Washington Experts see Who Knows: A Guide to Washington Experts.

Researchers in Powder Metallurgy, Vol. 1. Ed. by B. A. Bork. Tr. by Z. S. Michalewicz from Rus. LC 66-15306. pap. 39.00 (ISBN 0-317-10429-2, 2020675). Bks Demand UMI.

Researchers sur l'Economie Politique de l'Egypte sous les Lagides. G. Lumbroso. 4121p. Repr. of 1870 ed. text ed. 67.50x. Coronet Bks.

Researches Concerning Jean Grolier, His Life & His Library, with a Partial Catalogue of His Books. Antoine J. Leroux De Lincy. Ed. by Roger Portalis. Tr. by Carolyn Shipman. LC 70-80254. (Essays in Literature & Criticism Ser.: No. 137). (Illus.). 1971. Repr. of 1907 ed. lib. bdg. 43.00 (ISBN 0-8337-2078-3). B Franklin.

Researches in Altaic Languages. L. Ligeti. 338p. 1975. 58.00x (ISBN 0-569-08204-8, Pub. by Collets (UK)). State Mutual Bk.

Researches in Anatolia: The Alishar Huyuk, Seasons of 1930-32. Hans H. Von der Osten. LC 30-14678. (Oriental Institution Publications). 1937. No. 29. fiche 14.75 (ISBN 0-226-63939-8); No. 30. fiche 14.75 (ISBN 0-226-63940-1). U of Chicago Pr.

Researches in Geochemistry, Vol. 2. Ed. by Philip H. Abelson. LC 59-6755. 678p. 1967. 47.50 (ISBN 0-471-00167-8, JW). Krieger.

Researches in Indian Epigraphy & Numismatics. Jagannath Agarwal. 1986. 27.00x (ISBN 81-85055-94-7, Pub. by Sundeep). South Asia Bks.

Researches in Indian Epigraphy & Numismatics. Jagannath Agrawal. (Illus.). xii, 133p. 1986. 18.00 (ISBN 0-318-23224-3, Pub. by Sundeep Prakashan India). Nataraj Bks.

Researches in Manichaeism with Special Reference to the Turfan Fragments. Abraham V. Jackson. LC 32-9567. (Columbia University. Indo-Iranian Ser.: No. 13). Repr. of 1932 ed. 31.00 (ISBN 0-404-50483-3). AMS Pr.

Researches in Separation Anxiety: A Third Volume on the Separation Anxiety Test. Henry Hansburg. LC 79-21798. (Adolescent Separation Anxiety Ser.: Vol. 3). 470p. 1986. text ed. 29.95 (ISBN 0-89874-973-5). Krieger.

Researches in Spiritualism. William Crookes. (Illus.). 112p. 1984. Repr. of 1880 ed. photocopy 8.95 (ISBN 0-915554-18-6). Sourcebook.

Researches in the Central Portion of the Usumatsintla Valley. T. Maler. (HU PMM Ser.). Repr. of 1901 ed. 48.00 (ISBN 0-527-01156-8). Kraus Repr.

Researches in the South of Ireland: A Source Book of Irish Folk Tradition. Thomas Croker. 1969. Repr. of 1824 ed. 32.50x (ISBN 0-7165-0077-9, BBA 02154, Pub. by Irish Academic Pr Ireland). Biblio Dist.

Researches in the Uloa Valley, 1898. G. B. Gordon. (HU PMM). Repr. of 1898 ed. 23.00 (ISBN 0-527-01153-3). Kraus Repr.

Researches in the Usumatsintla Valley, Pt. 2. T. Maler. (HU PMM Ser.). Repr. of 1903 ed. 77.00 (ISBN 0-527-01157-6). Kraus Repr.

Researches into the Early History of Mankind & the Development of Civilization. abr. ed. Edward B. Tylor. LC 64-23416. (Classics in Anthropology Ser.). (Orig.). 1964. pap. 2.95X (ISBN 0-226-82122-6, P175, Phoen). U of Chicago Pr.

Researches into the Early History of Mankind & the Development of Civilization. abr. ed. Edward B. Tylor. Ed. by Paul Bohannan. LC 64-23416. 1964. 15.00x (ISBN 0-226-82121-8). U of Chicago Pr.

Researches into the Early History of the Violin Family. Carl Engel. LC 77-75189. 1977. Repr. of 1883 ed. lib. bdg. 20.00 (ISBN 0-89341-094-2). Longwood Pub Group.

Researches into the Laws of Chemical Affinity. 2nd ed. Claude-Louis Berthollet. LC 65-23404. 1966. Repr. of 1809 ed. 27.50 (ISBN 0-306-70914-7). Da Capo.

Researches into the Mathematical Principles of the Theory of Wealth. Augustin Cournot. LC 73-28986. 1971. Repr. of 1927 ed. 27.50x (ISBN 0-678-00066-2). Kelley.

Researches into the Physical History of Man. James C. Prichard. Ed. by George W. Stocking. LC 75-190425. (Classics in Anthropology Ser). 928p. 1973. 25.00x (ISBN 0-226-68120-3). U of Chicago Pr.

Researches on Acupuncture & Moxibustion & Acupuncture Anaesthesia. Ed. by X. Zhang. (Illus.). 1179p. 1986. 60.00 (ISBN 0-387-10901-3). Springer-Verlag.

Researches on Light. Robert Hunt. LC 72-9213. (Literature of Photography Ser.). Repr. of 1844 ed. 24.50 (ISBN 0-405-04921-8). Ayer Co Pubs.

Researches on Ptolemy's Geography of Eastern Asia. G. E. Gerini. LC 90-3098. (Illus.). 974p. 1974. 42.00x (ISBN 0-89684-449-8). Orient Bk Dist.

Researches on the Aura Phenomena. Mahmoud K. Muftic. 29.00x (ISBN 0-317-43576-0, Pub. by Soc of Metaphysicians). State Mutual Bk.

Researches on the I Ching. Iulien Shchutskii. Tr. by William L. Macdonald et al. Ed. by Tsuyoshi Hasegawa & Hellmut Wilhelm. LC 78-63600. (Bollingen Ser.: No. 62). 1979. 25.00 (ISBN 0-691-09939-1). Princeton U Pr.

Researches on the United States. Philip Mazzei. Ed. & tr. by Constance D. Sherman. LC 75-20037. (Illus.). Repr. of 1976 ed. 82.90 (ISBN 0-8357-9814-3, 2016965). Bks Demand UMI.

Researches on Waring's Problem. Leonard E. Dickson. LC 35-19856. (Carnegie Institution of Washington Publication Ser.: No. 464). pap. 66.30 (ISBN 0-317-09159-X, 2015710). Bks Demand UMI.

Researching American Culture: A Guide for Student Anthropologists. Ed. by Conrad P. Kottak. LC 81-23175. 1982. pap. text ed. 10.95x (ISBN 0-472-08024-5). U of Mich Pr.

Researching & Finding Your German Heritage. Marilyn Lind. LC 84-81794. (Illus.). 133p. (Orig.). 1984. pap. text ed. 10.95 (ISBN 0-937463-04-3). Linden Tree.

Researching & Writing: An Interdisciplinary Approach. Christine Hult. 264p. 1986. pap. text ed. write for info. (ISBN 0-534-06150-8). Wadsworth Pub.

Researching & Writing in History: A Practical Handbook for Student. F. N. McCoy. 1974. pap. 8.95x (ISBN 0-520-02621-7). U of Cal Pr.

Researching Arkansas History: A Beginner's Guide. Tom W. Dillard & Valerie Thwing. (Illus.). 64p. 1980. pap. 4.95 (ISBN 0-914546-25-2). Rose Pub.

Researching Industrial Markets: How to Identify, Reach, & Sell to Your Customers. Alan S. Krigman. LC 83-12832. 96p. 1983. pap. text ed. 14.95x (ISBN 0-87664-752-2). Instru Soc.

Researching Information Resources & Developing a Learning Plan: Guidelines. Richard L. Crews. 110p. 1988. pap. text ed. write for info. (ISBN 0-945864-00-0); write for info. wkbk. (ISBN 0-945864-01-9). Columbia Pacific U Pr.

Researching Local History. Mary Reed & Carole Simon-Smolinski. (Local History Technical Leaflets Ser.). (Illus.). 22p. (Orig.). 1985. pap. 1.50 (ISBN 0-931406-08-0). Idaho State Soc.

Researching Oral History Materials: The Case of Earl Warren. G. Edward White. Date not set. price not set. Am Assn Law Libs.

Researching Response to Literature & the Teaching of Literature. Charles Cooper. LC 83-11826. 400p. 1985. text ed. 42.50 (ISBN 0-89391-184-4); pap. 24.50 (ISBN 0-89391-323-5). Ablex Pub.

Researching Social Processes in the Laboratory. John Clark & Carl J Couch. (Contemporary Studies in Sociology: Theoretical & Empiracal Monographs: Vol. 6). 1987. 52.50 (ISBN 0-89232-823-1). Jai Pr.

Researching the Accounting Curriculum: Strategies for Change. William Ferrara. (Studies in Accounting Education). 227p. 1975. 6.00 (ISBN 0-86539-030-4). Am Accounting.

Researching the Development of Lay Leadership in the Roman Catholic Church since Vatican II: Bibliographical Abstracts. L. Thomas Snyderwine. LC 87-12224. (Roman Catholic Studies: Vol. 1). 200p. 1987. lib. bdg. 49.95x (ISBN 0-88946-241-0). E Mellen.

Researching the Old House. Ed. by Greater Portland Landmarks Research Committee. (Illus.). 72p. 1981. pap. 3.95 (ISBN 0-9600612-9-0). Greater Portland.

Researching Writing & Publishing Local History. 2nd ed. Thomas Felt. LC 81-10935. (Illus.). 166p. 1981. pap. 13.50 (ISBN 0-910050-53-8). AASLH Pr.

Researching, Writing & Publishing Your Church's History. Charles W. Deweese. (Resource Kit for Your Church's History ser.). 7p. 1984. pap. 0.50 (ISBN 0-939804-19-0). Hist Comm S Baptist.

Resection & Plastic Surgery of Bronchi. Boris Petrovsky et al. Tr. by MIR Publishers. (Illus.). 375p. 1975. text ed. 22.95x (ISBN 0-8464-0790-6). Beekman Pubs.

Reselection of MPS. Alison Young. vi, 154p. (Orig.). 1983. pap. text ed. 11.95x (ISBN 0-435-83371-5). Gower Pub Co.

Resemblance & Identity: An Examination of the Problem of Universals. Panayot Butchvarov. LC 66-22437. Repr. of 1966 ed. 42.20 (ISBN 0-8357-9239-0, 2015811). Bks Demand UMI.

Residential Development Process: Housing Policy & Theory. Keith N. Morcombe. (Studies in Urban & Regional Policy: No. 1). 160p. 1984. text ed. 32.95x (ISBN 0-566-00731-2). Gower Pub Co.

Residential Displacement in the United States, 1970-1977. Sandra J. Newman & Michael S. Owen. LC 82-12101. (Institute for Social Research Report Ser.). pap. 26.50 (2029469). Bks Demand UMI.

Residential Duct Systems. Ronald K. Yingling et al. (Illus.). 65p. 1981. pap. 17.00 (ISBN 0-86718-000-5). Nat Assn H Build.

Residential Electrical Design. 2nd ed. John E. Traister. LC 75-5407. 192p. 1982. pap. 11.50 (ISBN 0-910460-90-6). Craftsman.

Residential Electrical Wiring. Harry T. Edwards. (Illus.). 240p. 1982. text ed. 29.00 (ISBN 0-8359-6652-6, Reston). P-H.

Residential Electrical Wiring. Rex Miller. (Illus.). 300p. 1981. text ed. 15.96 (ISBN 0-02-665620-5); student guide 6.40 (ISBN 0-02-665640-X); tchr's. ed. 5.60 (ISBN 0-02-665630-2). Bennett IL.

Residential Electrical Wiring: Concepts Applications, & Troubleshooting. Harry M. Hawkins. (Illus.). 192p. 1988. pap. text ed. 18.00 (ISBN 0-13-774787-X). P-H.

Residential Electrical Wiring: Finishing the Installation. Richard Hunter. 1978. wkbk. 8.00 (ISBN 0-8064-0305-5, 804B); audio visual pkg. 169.00 (ISBN 0-8064-0306-3). Bergwall.

Residential Electrical Wiring: Low Voltage & Special Circuits. Richard Hunter. (Orig.). 1978. wkbk. 8.00 (ISBN 0-8064-0307-1, 804C); audio visual pkg. 199.00 (ISBN 0-8064-0308-X). Bergwall.

Residential Electrician's Handbook. John E. Traister. 240p. (Orig.). 1988. pap. 16.75 (ISBN 0-934041-35-0). Craftsman.

Residential Energy Audit Manual. 500p. 1981. text ed. 39.00 (ISBN 0-915586-54-1); pap. text ed. 18.00 (ISBN 0-915586-53-3). Fairmont Pr.

Residential Energy Conservation. Office of Technology Assessment, Congress of the United States. LC 79-55053. 342p. 1980. text ed. 18.95x (ISBN 0-916672-38-7, Pub. by Allanheld). Rowman.

Residential Environmental Preferences & Choice: Some Preliminary Empirical Results Relevant to Urban Form. Mark D. Menchik. (Discussion Ser.: No. 46). 1971. pap. 6.50. Regional Sci Res Inst.

Residential Erosion & Sediment Control: Objectives, Principles & Design Considerations. 64p. 1978. pap. 10.00x (ISBN 0-87262-133-2). Am Soc Civil Eng.

Residential Erosion & Sediment Control: Objectives, Principles & Design Considerations. (Cost Effective Residential Development Standards Ser.). (Illus.). 63p. 1979. pap. 13.00 (ISBN 0-86718-036-6). Nat Assn H Build.

Residential Erosion & Sediment Control: Objectives, Principles & Design Considerations. LC 78-63632. (Illus.). 63p. 1978. pap. 12.50 (ISBN 0-87420-584-0, E09). Urban Land.

Residential Fireplace & Chimney Handbook. 5th ed. J. E. Amrhein. 160p. 1988. pap. text ed. 9.50 (ISBN 0-940116-03-0). Masonry Inst Am.

Residential Foundations: Design, Behavior & Repair. 2nd ed. Robert W. Brown. 128p. 1983. 23.95 (ISBN 0-442-21302-6). Van Nos Reinhold.

Residential Gas Heating. James H. Doolin. 75p. 1982. pap. 15.00 (ISBN 0-914626-06-X). Doolco Inc.

Residential Group Care in Community Context: Insights from the Israeli Experience. Ed. by Zvi Eisikovits & Jerome Beker. LC 85-7682. (Child & Youth Services Ser.: Vol. 7, Nos. 3 & 4). 167p. 1986. text ed. 22.95 (ISBN 0-86656-186-2). Haworth Pr.

Residential Group Therapy for Children. Daphne Lennox. (Residential Social Workers Ser.). 220p. 1982. pap. 10.95 (ISBN 0-422-77550-9, NO. 3782, Pub. by Tavistock England). Routledge Chapman & Hall.

Residential Heat Pumps: Installation & Troubleshooting. S. E. Sutphin. (Illus.). 224p. 1987. text ed. 33.00 (ISBN 0-13-774613-X). P-H.

Residential Heating & Cooling. 228p. 1987. 52.00 (ISBN 0-317-59932-1). Am Heat Ref & Air Eng.

Residential Heating Operations & Troubleshooting. John E. Traister. (Illus.). 240p. 1985. text ed. 37.00 (ISBN 0-13-774696-2). P-H.

Residential Heating Systems & Controls. Howard W. Pennington. LC 84-17598. 94p. 1984. 11.95x (ISBN 0-912524-24-3). Busn News.

Residential Home Management: A Handbook for Managers of Community-Living Facilities. Richard Solomon & Linda L. Solomon. LC 81-6554. 135p. 1982. 34.95x (ISBN 0-89885-037-1). Human Sci Pr.

Residential Hot Water & Steam Heating with Gas, Oil & Solid Fuels. Martin Greenwald. (Illus.). 320p. 1987. text ed. 35.00 (ISBN 0-13-774712-8). P-H.

Residential Hot Water Systems: Repair & Maintenance. John E. Traister. (Illus.). 160p. 1986. text ed. 33.00 (ISBN 0-13-774704-7). P-H.

Residential Housing. Clois E. Kicklighter & Joan C. Kicklighter. (Illus.). 400p. 1986. 24.00 (ISBN 0-87006-590-4). Goodheart.

Residential Housing & Nuclear Attack. Diane Diacon. LC 84-17639. 146p. 1984. 23.50 (ISBN 0-7099-0868-7, Pub. by Croom Helm Ltd). Routledge Chapman & Hall.

Residential Investment & Insurance Practices. Jack Ruff. 54p. (Orig.). 1984. pap. 4.00 (ISBN 1-55719-030-5). U NE Ctr Applied Urban Rsch.

Residential Landlord & Tenant Law. Hamline University Advanced Legal Education Staff. 115p. 1986. 42.40. Hamline Law.

Residential Landscapes: Graphics, Planning & Design. Gregory M. Pierceall. 1983. text ed. 41.00 (ISBN 0-8359-6656-9, Reston). P-H.

Residential Landscaping I: Planning - Design - Construction. Theodore D. Walker. LC 81-18833. (Illus.). 202p. 1982. pap. 16.95 (ISBN 0-914886-15-0). PDA Pubs.

Residential Landscaping II. Philip L. Carpenter. LC 81-18833. (Illus.). 143p. 1983. 21.50 (ISBN 0-914886-21-5); pap. 15.95 (ISBN 0-914886-22-3). PDA Pubs.

Residential Loan Application: ABA RE-2. bulk rates avail. Am Bankers.

Residential Loan Application: ABA RE-2A. bulk orders avail. 12.00 (261201). Am Bankers.

Residential Location & Spatial Behaviour of the Elderly: A Canadian Example. Stephen M. Golant. LC 72-77307. (Research Papers: No. 143). (Orig.). 1972. pap. 12.00 (ISBN 0-89065-050-0). U Chicago Comm Geo.

Residential Location & Urban Housing Markets. Ed. by Gregory K. Ingram. LC 77-10831. (National Bureau of Economic Research. Conference on Research in Income & Wealth. Studies in Income & Wealth: Vol. 43). pap. 107.30 (ISBN 0-317-41723-1, 2052055). Bks Demand UMI.

Residential Location Determinants of the Older Population. Gundars Rudzitis. LC 82-10966. (Research Papers: No. 202). (Illus.). 117p. 1982. pap. text ed. 12.00. U Chicago Comm Geo.

Residential Location Markets & Urban Transportation: Economic Theory, Econometrics & Policy Analysis with Discrete Choice Models. Ed. by Alex Anas. 257p. 1982. 49.50 (ISBN 0-12-057920-0). Acad Pr.

Residential Mobility & Public Policy. Ed. by W. A. Clark & Eric G. Moore. LC 80-12624. (Urban Affairs Annual Reviews: Vol. 19). (Illus.). 320p. 1980. 35.00 (ISBN 0-8039-1447-4); pap. 16.95 (ISBN 0-8039-1448-2). Sage.

Residential Mobility: Monographs. Mary Vance. (Public Administration Ser.: P 1856). 22p. 1986. 6.25 (ISBN 0-89028-726-0). Vance Biblios.

Residential Mobility Patterns in Dallas-Fort Worth & San Antonio: Determinants of Move, Racial Succession & Female-Headed Households. Ardeshir Anjomani et al. 111p. (Orig.). 1985. pap. 15.00 (ISBN 0-936440-59-7). Inst Urban Studies.

Residential Mortgage Foreclosures: Current Developments. Pennsylvania Bar Institute. 252p. 1984. 25.00 (ISBN 0-318-02181-1, 249). PA Bar Inst.

Residential Mortgage Lending. Marshall Dennis. 1985. text ed. 32.00 (ISBN 0-8359-6654-2, Reston); instr's. manual avail. (ISBN 0-8359-6662-3). P-H.

Residential Mortgage Lending. 2nd ed. 254p. 1986. pap. 19.95 (ISBN 0-912857-32-3). Inst Finan Educ.

Residential Mortgage Lending. 1988. 195.00 (ISBN 0-935988-29-7). Todd Pub.

Residential Patterns in American Cities: 1960. Philip H. Rees. LC 78-12169. (Research Papers: No. 189). (Illus.). 1979. pap. 12.00 (ISBN 0-89065-096-9). U Chicago Comm Geo.

Residential Printreading. L. P. Toenjes. (Illus.). 316p. 1987. pap. 20.96 (ISBN 0-8269-0437-8). Am Technical.

Residential Psychiatric Treatment of Children. Ed. by Philip Baker. (Illus.). 351p. 1974. text ed. 24.00 (ISBN 0-8464-1270-5). Beekman Pubs.

Residential Real Estate Appraisal. 2nd ed. George H. Miller & Kenneth W. Gilbeau. (Illus.). 320p. 1988. pap. text ed. 26.00 (ISBN 0-13-762428-X). P-H.

Residential Real Estate Appraisal. 195.00 (ISBN 0-935988-31-9). Todd Pub.

Residential Real Estate Appraisal: An Introduction to Real Estate Appraising. George H. Miller & Kenneth W. Gidbeau. (Illus.). 1980. text ed. 29.67 (ISBN 0-13-774521-4). P-H.

Residential Real Estate: How to Find, Buy, Manage, & Sell for a Profit. Barbara Platt. Ed. by Linda Bowman. LC 87-60697. (Illus.). 206p. 1987. 24.95 (ISBN 0-941089-17-7); pap. 14.95 (ISBN 0-941089-18-5). Roscher Hse.

Residential Real Estate Law & Practice in New Jersey. 2nd ed. Arthur S. Horn. 1986. write for info. NJ Inst CLE.

Residential Remodeling & Renovation: Completing Exterior & Interior of Your Home. Ed. by Frederick U. Hop. (Illus.). 208p. 1988. text ed. 30.00 (ISBN 0-13-775255-5). P-H.

Residential Roof Framing. Alonzo Wass & Saunders. (Illus.). 268p. 1980. text ed. 29.00 (ISBN 0-8359-6655-0, Reston). P-H.

Residential Segregation by Race & Constitutional Conflict in the United States: A Bibliography. Lorna Peterson. (Public Administration Ser.: P 1951). 27p. 1986. 7.50 (ISBN 0-89028-891-7). Vance Biblios.

Residential Site Engineering. Thomas L. Brown. 1988. write for info. (ISBN 0-86718-320-9). Nat Assn H Build.

Residential Special Education: The Current & Future Roles for Special Boarding Schools. Ted Cole. LC 86-8569. 176p. 1986. 59.00x (ISBN 0-335-15125-6, Open Univ Pr); pap. 21.00x (ISBN 0-335-15124-8). Taylor & Francis.

Residential Storm Water Management: Objectives, Principles & Design Considerations. National Association of Home Builders et al. LC 75-34759. 64p. 1975. pap. 8.00 (ISBN 0-86718-038-2). Nat Assn H Build.

Residential Storm Water Management: Objectives, Principles & Design Considerations. 64p. 1975. 7.00x (ISBN 0-87262-160-X). Am Soc Civil Eng.

Residential Teaching Communities: Program Development & Staff Training for Developmentally Disabled Persons. Ralph J. Wetzel & Ronald L. Hoschouer. 1984. text ed. write for info. (ISBN 0-673-15869-1). Scott F.

Residential Treatment of Emotionally Disturbed Children. Ed. by George H. Weber & Bernard J. Haberlein. LC 78-189948. (Child Care Ser). 327p. 1973. text ed. 34.95 (ISBN 0-87705-067-8). Human Sci Pr.

Residential Treatment of Felon Drug Addicts: State Agents As Therapists. Sethard Fisher. (American University Studies XI: Anthropology & Sociology). 209p. 1987. text ed. 32.90 (ISBN 0-8204-0502-7). P Lang Pubs.

Residential Treatment: Past Policies, Present Issues, Future Priorities. Paul S. Pressman. 61p. 1983. pap. 9.95 (ISBN 0-89885-165-3). Human Sci Pr.

Residential Unit Supervisor. (Career Examination Ser.: C-3312). Date not set. pap. 14.00 (ISBN 0-8373-3312-1). Natl Learning.

Residential Utility Problems: A Handbook for Consumers & Advocates. Neighborhod Legal Services. 36p. 1982. 3.50 (33,839). NCLS Inc.

Residential Wastewater Systems. National Association of Home Builders. (Illus.). 110p. 1980. pap. 18.50 (ISBN 0-86718-040-4). Nat Assn H Build.

Residential Wiring. Jeff Markall. 1984. text ed. 32.00 (ISBN 0-8359-6661-5, Reston). P-H.

Residential Wiring. rev. ed. Jeff Markell. 352p. 1987. pap. 18.25 (ISBN 0-934041-19-9). Craftsman.

Residential Wiring. G. Rockis. (Illus.). 260p. 1978. spiral bdg. 17.96 (ISBN 0-8269-1650-3). Am Technical.

Residential Wiring: Concepts & Practices. Harry Hawkins. 1983. text ed. 18.00 (ISBN 0-534-02426-2, PWS-Kent Ser Tech). PWS Kent Pub.

Residential Wraparound Mortgage. Stephen R. Mettling. (Residential Financing Resource Library). 57p. (Orig.). 1981. pap. 6.50 (ISBN 0-88462-128-6, 1905-05, Real Estate Ed). Longman Finan.

Residents As Teachers: A Guide to Educational Practice. Neal A. Whitman & Thomas L. Schwenk. 46p. (Orig.). pap. text ed. 6.00 (ISBN 0-940193-03-5). Univ UT Sch Med.

Resident's Guide to Psychiatric Education. Ed. by M. G. Thompson. LC 78-15961. (Critical Issues In Psychiatry Ser.). 292p. 1979. Spiral bdg. 35.00x (ISBN 0-306-31130-5, Plenum Med Bk). Plenum Pub.

Resident's Recollections. Lloyd E. Klos. LC 87-18918. (Illus.). 192p. (Orig.). 1987. pap. 9.95 (ISBN 0-932334-58-X, Empire State Bks). Heart of the Lakes.

Resident's Recollections, Bk. 2. Lloyd E. Klos. (Illus.). 192p. (Orig.). 1988. pap. 9.95 (ISBN 1-55787-028-4, Empire State Bks.). Heart of the Lakes.

Residua of Thoracic Trauma. Ed. by William Hix & Benjamin Aaron. (Illus.). 280p. 1987. monograph 40.00 (ISBN 0-87993-291-0). Futura Pub.

Residual Deposits: Surface Related Weathering Processes & Materials. R. C. Wilson. (Illus.). 262p. 1983. text ed. 60.00x (ISBN 0-632-01072-X). Blackwell Pubns.

Residual Lease Rates. Financial Publishing Co. Staff. 64p. 1974. pap. 6.50 (ISBN 0-87600-730-2). Finan Pub.

Residual Lease Rates, Sixteen & a Quarter to 25 percent. Ed. by Financial Publishing Co. Staff. (Illus.). 44p. 1973. pap. 6.50 (ISBN 0-87600-729-9). Finan Pub.

Residual Lease Rates: Table III. Financial Publishing Co. Staff. 64p. 1980. pap. 6.50 (ISBN 0-87600-528-8). Finan Pub.

Residual Lease Rates Two to Sixteen Percent. Ed. by Financial Publishing Co. Staff. 64p. 1973. pap. 6.50 (ISBN 0-87600-728-0). Finan Pub.

Residual Stress. I. C. Noyan & J. B. Cohen. (Materials Research & Engineering Ser.). (Illus.). 300p. 1987. 52.00 (ISBN 0-387-96378-2). Springer-Verlag.

Residual Stress & Stress Relaxation. Ed. by Eric Kula & Volker Weiss. LC 82-9803. (Sagamore Army Materials Research Conference Ser.: Vol. 28). 546p. 1982. 89.50x (ISBN 0-306-41102-4, Plenum Pr). Plenum Pub.

Residual Stress Effects in Fatigue-- STP 776. Ed. by H. S. Reemsnyder & J. F. Throop. 241p. 1982. 26.50 (ISBN 0-8031-0711-0, 04-776000-30). ASTM.

Residual Stress for Designers & Metallurgists: Proceedings of a Conference Held 9-10 April 1980, Chicago, IL. American Society for Metals. Ed. by Larry J. Vande Walle. LC 81-4876. (Materials-Metalworking Technology Ser.). pap. 63.80 (2027033). Bks Demand UMI.

Residual Stress Measurement by X-Ray Diffraction. 124p. 1976. 16.00 (ISBN 0-89883-382-5, HS784). Soc Auto Engineers.

Residual Stresses & Their Effect: RSE-P. 55p. 1981. 15.00 (ISBN 0-317-37075-8). Am Welding.

Residual Stresses in CBN & Corundum Ground Gear Tooth Flanks as the Determining Factor in Abrasive Wheel Selections. Peter Moeckli. (Fall Technical Meeting Papers). (Illus.). 14p. 1986. pap. 30.00 (ISBN 1-55589-475-5, 86FTM11). AGMA.

Residual Stresses in Science & Technology, 2 vols. Ed. by E. Macherauch & V. Hauk. 1200p. Set. 142.00 (ISBN 0-317-58409-X, Pub. by DGM Metallurgy Germany). Vol. 1 (ISBN 3-88355-099-X). Vol. 2 (ISBN 3-88355-100-7). IR Pubns.

Residual Stresses: Proceedings. Ed. by E. Macherauch & V. Hauk. Orig. Title: Eigenspannungen. (Ger.). 1986. lib. bdg. 59.00x (ISBN 3-88355-098-1, Pub. by DGM Metallurgy Germany). IR Pubns.

Residual Years. rev. ed. William Everson. LC 68-25585. 1968. 3.95 (ISBN 0-8112-0273-9). New Directions.

Residuals & Influence in Regression. R. D. Cook & S. Weisberg. (Monographs on Statistics & Applied Probability). 200p. 1982. 32.00 (ISBN 0-412-24280-X, NO. 6718, Pub. by Chapman & Hall). Routledge Chapman & Hall.

Residuals Management in Industry: A Case Study of Petroleum Refining. Clifford S. Russell. LC 72-12367. (Resources for the Future Ser.). (Illus.). 208p. 1973. 18.00x (ISBN 0-8018-1497-9). Johns Hopkins.

Residuation Theory. T. S. Blyth & M. F. Janowitz. LC 77-142177. 380p. 1972. text ed. 93.00 (ISBN 0-08-016408-0). Pergamon.

Residue Number System Arithmetic Modern Applications to Digital Signal Processing. M. A. Soderstrand et al. LC 86-10516. 430p. 1986. 54.00 (ISBN 0-87942-204-1, PC01982). Inst Electrical.

Residue of Pesticides & other Contaminants in the Total Environment. R. C. Simms et al. (Residue Reviews: Vol. 88). (Illus.). 164p. 1983. 30.00 (ISBN 0-387-90851-X). Springer-Verlag.

Residue of Song. Marvin Bell. LC 74-80325. (Orig.). 1974. pap. 3.95 (ISBN 0-689-10637-8). Atheneum.

Residue Reviews. Ed. by F. A. Gunther & J. Davies Gunther. (Illus.). 166p. 1982. 38.00 (ISBN 0-387-90750-5). Springer-Verlag.

Residue Reviews, Vols. 1-11. Ed. by F. A. Gunther. Incl. Vol. 1. (Illus.). iv, 162p. 1962; Vol. 2. (Illus.). iv, 156p. 1963; Vol. 3. (Illus.). iv, 170p. 1963; Vol. 4. (Illus.). iv, 175p. 1963; Vol. 5. Instrumentation for the Detection & Determination of Pesticides & Their Residues in Foods. (Illus.). viii, 176p. 1964; Vol. 6. (Illus.). iv, 165p. 1964; Vol. 7. vi, 161p. 1964; Vol. 8. (Illus.). viii, 183p. 1965; Vol. 9. (Illus.). viii, 175p. 1965. o.p. (ISBN 0-387-03391-2); Vol. 10. With Comprehensive Cumulative Contents, Subjectmatter, & Author Indexes of Volume 1-10. (Illus.). viii, 159p. 1965; Vol. 11. (Illus.). viii, 164p. 1965. LC 62-18595. (Eng., Fr. & Ger.). Springer-Verlag.

Residue Reviews, Vols. 13-24. Ed. by F. A. Gunther. Incl. Vol. 13. (Illus.). viii, 136p. 1966; Vol. 14. (Illus.). viii, 131p. 1966. 25.00 (ISBN 0-387-03649-0); Vol. 15. (Illus.). vi, 121p. 1966. 30.30 (ISBN 0-387-03650-4); Vol. 16. (Illus.). viii, 158p. 1966. 35.10 (ISBN 0-387-03651-2); Vol. 17. (Illus.). viii, 184p. 1967. 35.10 (ISBN 0-387-03963-5); Vol. 18. (Illus.). viii, 227p. 1967; Vol. 19. (Illus.). viii, 155p. 1967; Vol. 20. With Cumulative Table of Subjects Covered, Detailed Subject-Matter Index, & Author Index of Volumes 11-20. x, 214p. 1968. 47.20 (ISBN 0-387-04310-1); Vol. 21. (Illus.). viii, 128p. 1968. 43.60 (ISBN 0-387-04311-X); Vol. 22. (Illus.). viii, 120p. 1968; Vol. 23. (Illus.). viii, 152p. 1968. 47.20 (ISBN 0-387-04313-6); Vol. 24. vii, 173p. 1968. 47.20 (ISBN 0-387-04314-4). LC 62-18595. (Eng., Fr. & Ger.). Springer-Verlag.

Resolution of Singularities of Embedded Algebraic Surfaces. S. Abhyankar. (Pure & Applied Mathematics Ser). 1966. 69.50 (ISBN 0-12-041956-4). Acad Pr.

Resolution of Surface Singularities. V. Cossart et al. (Lecture Notes in Mathematics Ser.: Vol. 1101). vii, 132p. 1984. pap. 11.00 (ISBN 0-387-13904-4). Springer-Verlag.

Resolution of the Dominican Crisis, 1965: A Study in Mediation. Audrey Bracey. Martin F. Herz. LC 80-27239. 64p. (Orig.). 1980. pap. 5.00 (ISBN 0-934742-04-9, Inst Study Diplomacy). Geo U Sch For Serv.

Resolution of the Dominican Crisis, 1965: A Study in Mediation. Audrey Bracey. 72p. 1985. pap. text ed. 5.00 (ISBN 0-8191-5067-3, Inst for Study Diplomacy). U Pr of Amer.

Resolution of the Yemen Crisis, 1963: A Case Study in Mediation. Christopher J. McMullen. LC 80-25944. 56p. (Orig.). 1980. pap. 5.00 (ISBN 0-934742-07-3, Inst Study Diplomacy). Geo U Sch For Serv.

Resolution of the Yemen Crisis, 1963: A Case Study in Mediation. Christopher J. McMullen. 60p. 1985. pap. text ed. 5.00 (ISBN 0-8191-5065-7, Inst for Study Diplomacy). U Pr of Amer.

Resolution on CPC History (1949-81) Communist Party of China. 126p. 1981. pap. 6.50 (ISBN 0-317-66867-6). Pergamon.

Resolution Space, Operators & Systems. R. Saeks. (Lecture Notes in Economics & Mathematical Systems: Vol. 82). 267p. 1973. pap. 19.00 (ISBN 0-387-06155-X). Springer-Verlag.

Resolutions & Decisions Adopted by the General Assembly of the United Nations: Thirty-Ninth Session, September 18 Through December 18, 1984. United Nations & Dept. of Public Information. LC 85-1096. 636p. 1985. lib. bdg. 60.00 (ISBN 0-89111-021-6). UNIFO Pubs.

Resolutions & Decisions of the Communist Party of the Soviet Union: 1898-1964, 5 vols. Ed. by Robert H. McNeal. Incl. Vol. 1. Russian Social Democratic Labour Party, 1898-October 1917. Ed. by Ralph C. Elwood; Vol. 2. Early Soviet Period, 1917-1929. Ed. by Richard Gregor; Vol. 3. Stalin Years, 1929-1953. Ed. by Robert H. McNeal; Vol. 4. Khrushchev Years, 1953-1964. Ed. by Grey Hodnett; Vol. 5. Brezhnev Years, 1964-1981. Ed. by Donald V. Schwartz. LC 74-81931. 1974. Set. 150.00x (ISBN 0-8020-2509-9). U of Toronto Pr.

Resolutions & Decisions of the Communist Party of the Soviet Union. Ed. by Robert H. McNeal. Incl. Vol. 1. Russian Social Democratic Labour Party, 1898-October, 1917. Ed. by Ralph C. Elwood. pap. 85.50 (ISBN 0-317-27011-7); Vol. 2. Early Soviet Period, 1917-1929. Ed. by Richard Gregor. pap. 98.50 (ISBN 0-317-27012-5); Vol. 3. Stalin Years, 1929-1953. Ed. by Robert H. McNeal. pap. 72.50 (ISBN 0-317-27013-3). LC 74-81931 (2023650). Bks Demand UMI.

Resolutions & Decisions of the Communist Party of the Soviet Union: Vol. 5, the Brezhnev Years, 1964-1981. Donald V. Schwartz. 296p. 1982. 37.50x (ISBN 0-8020-5552-4). U of Toronto Pr.

Resolutions & Other Decisions of the IMO Assembly, 14th Session, November 11-22, 1985. 220p. (Orig.). 1987. pap. 21.00 (ISBN 92-801-1204-X, IMCO120 86 07E, Pub. by Intl Maritime Orgn). UNIPUB.

Resolutions of the Eighteenth National Convention of the Communist Party, U. S. A. 1967. pap. 1.25 (ISBN 0-87898-018-0). New Outlook.

Resolved to Love: The 1592 Edition of Henry Constable's 'Diana' Ed. by Robert F. Fleissner & James Hogg. (Elizabethan & Renaissance Studies ser.). 89p. (Orig.). 1980. pap. 15.00 (ISBN 3-7052-0758-X, Pub. by Salzburg Studies). Longwood Pub Group.

Resolves, a Duple Century. 3rd ed. Owen Feltham. LC 74-28853. (English Experience Ser.: No. 734). 1975. Repr. of 1628 ed. 55.00 (ISBN 90-221-0734-5). Walter J Johnson.

Resolving Church Conflicts: A Case Study Approach for Local Congregations. Douglass Lewis. LC 80-8347. 192p. (Orig.). 1981. pap. 7.95 (ISBN 0-06-065244-6, RD 342, HarpR). Har-Row.

Resolving Conflict in Africa: The Fermeda Workshop. Ed. by Leonard W. Doob. LC 71-123396. pap. 57.00 (ISBN 0-317-11303-8, 2021995). Bks Demand UMI.

Resolving Conflict in Black Male-Female Relationships. La Francis Rodgers-Rose & James T. Rodgers. 70p. (Orig.). 1985. pap. 8.95 (ISBN 0-934185-00-X). Traces Inst.

Resolving Corrosion Problems in Air Pollution Control Equipment - 1976. LC 75-38373. 117p. 1976. 25.00 (ISBN 0-915567-77-6, 52100). Natl Corrosion Eng.

Resolving Deep-Rooted Conflict: A Handbook. John W. Burton. LC 87-6144. 82p. 1987. lib. bdg. 17.25 (ISBN 0-8191-6284-1, Pub. by GMU Ctr Conflict Resolution); pap. text ed. 7.50 (ISBN 0-8191-6285-X). U Pr of Amer.

Resolving Development Disputes Through Negotiation. Timothy J. Sullivan. (Environment, Development, & Public Policy-Environmental Policy & Planning Ser.). 238p. 1984. 29.50x (ISBN 0-306-41658-1, Plenum Pr). Plenum Pub.

Resolving Disputes: An Alternative Approach. 57p. 1981. pap. 5.00 (ISBN 0-317-63238-8, 478-0006-01). Amer Bar Assn.

Resolving Disputes Between Nations: Coercion or Conciliation? Martin Patchen. xiii, 366p. 1988. lib. bdg. 42.50 (ISBN 0-8223-0764-2); pap. text ed. 14.95 (ISBN 0-8223-0819-3). Duke.

Resolving Employment Disputes Without Litigation. Alan F. Westin & Alfred G. Feliu. LC 87-31989. xvii, 328p. 1988. text ed. 40.00 (ISBN 0-87179-558-2, 0558). BNA.

Resolving Environmental Disputes: A Decade of Experience. Gail Bingham. LC 85-25532. 284p. 1986. pap. 15.00 (ISBN 0-89164-087-8). Conservation Foun.

Resolving Environmental Regulatory Disputes. Lawrence Susskind et al. 260p. 1983. pap. 15.95 (ISBN 0-87073-145-9). Schenkman Bks Inc.

Resolving Faculty Disputes. Jane McCarthy & Irving Ladimer. LC 81-67937. 80p. 1981. pap. 8.00 (ISBN 0-943001-12-9). Am Arbitration.

Resolving Grievances in the Nursing Home: A Study of the Ombudsman Program. Abraham Monk & Howard Litwin. (Social Work & Social Issue, Columbia Studies of Social Gerontology & Aging). 1984. 32.50x (ISBN 0-231-05702-4, King's Crown Paperbacks). Columbia U Pr.

Resolving Grivances in the Nursing Home: A Study of the Ombundsman Program. Abraham Monk et al. LC 83-7606. 247p. 1984. 32.50 (ISBN 0-317-66219-8). Columbia U Pr.

Resolving Internal Management Conflicts for Labor Negotiations see Public Employee Relations Library.

Resolving Labor Management Disputes: A Nine-Country Comparison. Eileen B. Hoffman. (Report Ser: No. 600). (Illus.). 114p. (Orig.). 1973. pap. 17.50 (ISBN 0-8237-0049-6). Conference Bd.

Resolving Language Conflicts: A Study of the World's Constitution. Albert P. Blaustein & Dana Epsten. LC 86-52465. 105p. Date not set. 45.00 (ISBN 0-934833-01-X). USEnglish.

Resolving Locational Conflict. Robert W. Lake. 544p. 1986. pap. text ed. 19.95x (ISBN 0-88285-118-7). Ctr Urban Pol Res.

Resolving Maps & the Dimension Group for Shifts on Finite Type. Boyle et al. (MEMO Ser.: Vol. 377). 156p. 1987. pap. text ed. 19.00 (ISBN 0-8218-2440-6). Am Math.

Resolving Marital Conflicts: A Psychodynamic Perspective. Herbert S. Strean. LC 85-13616. (Personality Processes Ser.). 275p. 1985. 33.95 (ISBN 0-471-82504-2). Wiley.

Resolving Modern Evidence Problems. Frederick B. Lacey. 1985. (ISBN 1-55681-023-7). Natl Inst Trial Ad.

Resolving Nationality Conflicts: The Role of Public Opinion Research. Ed. by W. Phillips Davison & Leon Gordenker. LC 80-15128. 256p. 1980. 42.95 (ISBN 0-275-90467-9, C0467). Praeger.

Resolving Occupational Disease Claims: The Use of Medical Panels. Peter S. Barth. LC 85-20185. (Illus., Orig.). 1985. 15.00 (ISBN 0-935149-00-7). Workers Comp Res Inst.

Resolving Relievances: A Practical Approach. Donald McPherson. 1983. pap. text ed. 21.00 (ISBN 0-8359-6663-1, Reston); instr's. manual avail. (ISBN 0-8359-6664-X). P-H.

Resolving Resistance in Group Psychotherapy. Leslie Rosenthal. LC 85-19940. 216p. 1987. 20.00x (ISBN 0-87668-914-4). Aronson.

Resolving Resistances in Psychotherapy. Herbert S. Strean. LC 84-15174. (Personality Processes Ser.: No. 1-341). 293p. 1985. 33.95x (ISBN 0-471-80709-5, Pub. by Wiley-Interscience). Wiley.

Resolving Securities Disputes: Arbitration & Litigation. David E. Robbins & Practising Law Institute Staff. LC 86-62251. (Corporate Law & Practice Course Handbook Ser.: No. 535). 488p. 1986. 45.00 (ISBN 0-317-59123-1, B46771). PLI.

Resolving Social Conflicts. Kurt Lewin. Ed. by Gertrud W. Lewin. 1978. pap. 4.50 (ISBN 0-285-64718-0, Pub. by Souvenir Pr); 10.95. Intl Spec Bk.

Resolving the Fiscal-Year Dilemma. Kess & Westlin. 72p. (Orig.). 1988. pap. 10.00 (5244). Commerce.

Resolving the Global Economic Crisis: After Wall Street. Intro. by C. Fred Bergsten. (Special Reports: No. 6). 28p. 1987. pap. 3.00 (ISBN 0-88132-070-6). Inst Intl Eco.

Resolving the Housing Crisis: Government Policy, Decontrol, & the Public Interest. Ed. by M. Bruce Johnson. LC 81-22917. (Illus.). 426p. 1982. 34.95 (ISBN 0-88410-381-1); pap. 13.95 (ISBN 0-88410-386-2). PRIPP.

Resolving the Liability Insurance Crisis: State Legislative Activities in 1986 (Collected Papers) 238p. 1986. pap. 65.00 (ISBN 1-55516-935-X). Natl Conf State Legis.

Resolving Transnational Disputes Through International Arbitration. Ed. by Thomas E. Carbonneau. LC 83-25947. (Virginia Legal Ser.-Sokol Colloquium). 301p. 1984. text ed. 30.00x (ISBN 0-8139-1023-4). U Pr of Va.

Resolving Treatment Impasses: The Difficult Patient. Theodore Saretsky. LC 80-24661. 267p. 1981. 34.95 (ISBN 0-87705-088-0). Human Sci Pr.

Resonance Ionization & Its Applications, 1984: Second International Symposium, Knoxville, Tennessee, April 1984. Ed. by G. S. Hurst & M. G. Payne. (Institute of Physics Conference Ser.: No. 71). (Illus.). 374p. 1984. 74.00 (ISBN 0-85498-162-4, Pub. by A Hilger UK). Taylor & Francis.

Resonance Ionization Spectroscopy 1986: Proceedings of the Third International Symposium on Resonance Ionization & Its Applications, Swansea, U. K., September 1986. G. S. Hurst & C. Grey-Morgan. (Institute of Physics Conference Ser.: No. 84). 360p. 1987. 77.00x (ISBN 0-85498-175-6, Pub. by A Hilger UK). Taylor & Francis.

Resonance of Dust: Essays on Holocaust Literature & Jewish Fate. Edward Alexander. LC 79-15515. 276p. 1979. 20.00 (ISBN 0-8142-0303-5). Ohio St U Pr.

Resonance of Grace. James Newcomer. pap. 5.00 (ISBN 0-318-04288-6). Latitudes Pr.

Resonance Oscillations in Mechanical Systems. R. Evan-Wanowski. 1976. 94.75 (ISBN 0-444-41474-6). Elsevier.

Resonance Radiation & Excited Atoms. Allan C. Mitchell & Mark W. Zemansky. LC 62-5588. pap. 91.60 (2031696). Bks Demand UMI.

Resonances in Electron-Molecule Scattering, Van Der Waals Complexes & Reactive Chemical Dynamics. Ed. by Donald G. Truhlar. LC 84-16934. (Symposium Ser.: No. 263). 522p. 1984. lib. bdg. 89.95x (ISBN 0-8412-0865-4). Am Chemical.

Resonances in Heavy Ion Reactions: Bad Honnef, West Germany, 1981 Proceedings. K. A. Eberhard. (Lecture Notes in Physics Ser.: Vol. 156). 448p. 1982. 30.00 (ISBN 0-387-11487-4). Springer-Verlag.

Resonances Models & Phenomena. Ed. by S. Albeverio et al. (Lecture Notes in Physics Ser.: Vol. 211). vi, 359p. 1984. pap. 26.00 (ISBN 0-387-13880-3). Springer-Verlag.

Resonare Christum: The Pittsburgh Years: 1959-1969, Vol. II. John J. Wright. Ed. by R. Stephen Almagno. LC 84-80906. (Illus.). 579p. 1988. 29.95 (ISBN 0-89870-051-5); pap. 19.95 (ISBN 0-89870-194-5). Ignatius Pr.

Resonare Christum: Vol. 1, the Boston & the Worcester Years. John Wright. Pref. by Stephen Almagno. LC 84-80906. 419p. 1985. 16.95 (ISBN 0-89870-050-7). Ignatius Pr.

Resonating Interval: Anticipating the Human Effects of the New Media. Marshall McLuhan. Ed. by Bruce R. Powers. (Communications & Society Ser.). (Illus.). 208p. 1989. 19.95 (ISBN 0-19-505444-X). Oxford U Pr.

Resort & Other Poems. Patricia Hampl. 79p. 1983. 12.95 (ISBN 0-395-34403-4); pap. 6.95 (ISBN 0-395-34932-X). HM.

Resort Architecture: A Bibliography. Mary Vance. (Architecture Ser.: A 1612). 20p. 1986. 5.00 (ISBN 0-89028-902-6). Vance Biblios.

Resort Development: A Network-Related Model for Optimizing Sites & Visits. Fred Glover & Jacques Rogozinski. 1980. 2.50 (ISBN 0-686-64184-1). U CO Busn Res Div.

Resort Development & Management. Chuck Y. Gee. Ed. by Marjorie Harless. LC 81-15282. (Illus.). 1981. 36.95 (ISBN 0-86612-008-4). Educ Inst Am Hotel.

Resort Development & Management. 2nd ed. Chuck Y. Gee. Ed. by Marjorie Harless. (Illus.). 345p. 1988. text ed. 36.95 (ISBN 0-86612-043-2). Educ Inst Am Hotel.

Resort Hotel Photography. 3.95 (ISBN 0-89816-046-4). Embee Pr.

Resort Hotels of the Eastern United States: An Annotated Bibliography. Glenna Dunning. (Architectural Ser.: A 1937). 17p. 1987. 5.00 (ISBN 1-55590-547-1). Vance Biblios.

Resort Hotels of the Western United States: An Annotated Bibliography. Glenna Dunning. (Architecture Ser.: A 1799). 26p. 1987. 7.50 (ISBN 1-55590-269-3). Vance Biblios.

Resort Timesharing Handbook. Steven L. Ingleby & Theodore Boyer. LC 84-2137. (Illus.). 256p. 1984. 39.95 (ISBN 0-88462-450-1, 1991-01, Real Estate Ed). Longman Finan.

Resource: A Pro Bono Manual. Special Commission on Lawyers' Public Service Responsibility. LC 83-72985. 227p. 1983. looseleaf 8.00 (ISBN 0-89707-118-2). Amer Bar Assn.

Resource Acquisition in Corporate Growth. David W. Packer. 1964. 12.00x (ISBN 0-262-16010-2). MIT Pr.

Resource Allocation see Surveys of Economic Theory.

Resource Allocation & Division of Space: Proceedings of an International Symposium Held at Toba Near Nagoya, Japan, 14-17, Dec. 1975. Ed. by T. Fujii & R. Sate. LC 77-14525. (Lecture Notes in Economics & Mathematical Systems: Vol. 147). 1977. pap. text ed. 14.00 (ISBN 0-387-08352-9). Springer-Verlag.

Resource Allocation & Productivity in National & International Agricultural Research. Ed. by Thomas M. Arndt et al. LC 76-44064. (Illus.). 1977. 35.00x (ISBN 0-8166-0805-9). U of Minn Pr.

Resource Allocation in British Universities. Ed. by Michael Shattock & Gwynneth Rigby. 185p. 1983. 28.00x (ISBN 0-900868-97-X). Taylor & Francis.

Resource Allocation Mechanisms. Donald E. Campbell. (Illus.). 192p. 1987. 34.50 (ISBN 0-521-26664-5); pap. 12.95 (ISBN 0-521-31990-0). Cambridge U Pr.

Resource Allocation Model for Child Survival. Howard Barnum et al. LC 80-17933. 216p. 1980. text ed. 45.00 (ISBN 0-89946-052-6). Oelgeschlager.

Resource Allocation Model for Public Health Planning: A Case Study of Tuberculosis Control. M. S. Feldstein et al. (WHO Bulletin Supplement: Vol. 48). (Summary in French). 1973. pap. 6.40 (ISBN 92-4-068481-6). World Health.

Resource Allocation Problems: Algorithmic Problems. Toshihide Ibaraki & Naoki Katoh. (Foundation of Computing Ser.). (Illus.). 338p. 1988. text ed. 37.50x (ISBN 0-262-09027-9). MIT Pr.

Resource & Environmental Economics: Natural Resources & the Environment in Economics. Anthony C. Fisher. LC 81-9951. (Cambridge Surveys of Economic Literature Ser.). 256p. 1981. o. p. 47.50 (ISBN 0-521-24306-8); pap. 14.95 (ISBN 0-521-28594-1). Cambridge U Pr.

Resource & Environmental Effects of U. S. Agriculture. Pierre R. Crosson & Sterling Brubaker. 255p. 1982. 15.00 (ISBN 0-8018-2920-8). Resources Future.

Resource Assistant. Jack Rudman. (Career Examination Ser.: C-1745). (Cloth bdg. avail. on request). 1988. pap. 12.00 (ISBN 0-8373-1745-2). Natl Learning.

Resource Atlas of the Apalachicola Estuary: SGR-55. Robert Livingston. 64p. 1983. write for info. U Fla Law.

Resource Based Learning for Higher & Continuing Education. John Clarke. LC 81-6718. (New Pattern of Learning Ser.). 211p. 1982. 37.95x (ISBN 0-470-27248-1). Halsted Pr.

Resource Based Learning for School Governors. Alan George. LC 84-19965. 198p. 1984. 26.50 (ISBN 0-7099-1184-X, Pub. by Croom Helm Ltd). Routledge Chapman & Hall.

Resource Book: Directory of Organizations, Associations Self Help Groups & Hotlines for Mental Health & Human Services Professionals & Their Clients. Robert L. Barker. LC 86-25765. 176p. 1987. text ed. 17.95 (ISBN 0-86656-622-8). Haworth Pr.

Resource Book for International Communications. Media Institute Transnational Communications Center Staff. LC 83-62433. 68p. 1983. pap. 5.00 (ISBN 0-937790-19-2). Media Inst.

Resource Book for Teaching Reading in the Content Areas. Pauline Hodges-McLain. 96p. 1980. pap. text ed. 9.95 (ISBN 0-8403-2263-1). Kendall-Hunt.

Resource Book for the Kindergarten Teacher. Walter B. Barbe. (Illus.). 1980. 39.95 (ISBN 0-88309-103-8). Zaner-Bloser.

Resource Book for the Special Education Teacher. Virginia H. Lucas & Walter B. Barbe. (Illus.). 1982. 34.95 (ISBN 0-88309-117-8). Zaner-Bloser.

Resource Book of Jewish Music: A Bibliographical & Topical Guide to the Book & Journal Literature & Program Materials. Irene Heskes. LC 84-22435. (Music Reference Collection Ser.: No. 3). xiv, 302p. 1985. lib. bdg. 40.95 (ISBN 0-313-23251-2, HEJ/). Greenwood.

Resource Book of Rural Universities in the Developing Countires. Harold W. Hannah. LC 65-19571. pap. 97.30 (ISBN 0-317-28485-1, 2019049). Bks Demand UMI.

Resource Book on Progressive Pharmaceutical Services. 116p. (Orig.). 1986. pap. text ed. 15.00 (ISBN 0-930530-70-5). Am Soc Hosp Pharm.

Resource Careers: Options & Opportunities in Environmental & Natural Resources Law. LC 79-55232. 107p. 1979. pap. 3.00 (ISBN 0-89707-012-7). Amer Bar Assn.

Resource Communities: A Decade of Disruption. Don D. Detomasi & J. W. Gartrell. 210p. 1984. pap. 36.00x (ISBN 0-8133-0114-9). Westview.

Resource Companion for Curriculum Initiative. Michael Eisenberg & Robert Berkowitz. Ed. by Charles McLure & Peter Hernon. (Information Management, Policies & Service Ser.). 144p. 1988. pap. text ed. 14.95 (ISBN 0-89391-498-3). Ablex Pub.

Resource Competition & Community Structure. David Tilman. Ed. by Robert M. May. LC 81-47954. (Monographs in Population Biology: No. 17). (Illus.). 288p. 1982. 34.50x (ISBN 0-691-08301-0); pap. 11.50x (ISBN 0-691-08302-9). Princeton U Pr.

Resource Conservation & Recovery Act Inspection Manual. U. S. Environmental Protection Agency Staff. 293p. 1982. 48.00 (ISBN 0-86587-107-8). Gov Insts.

Resource Conservation & Recovery Act Orientation Manual. Robert Knox. (Illus.). 186p. 1986. pap. 7.00 (ISBN 0-318-20141-0, S/N 055-000-00255-0). USGPO.

Resource Conservation Glossary. 3rd ed. Pref. by H. Wayne Pritchard. LC 82-5830. 193p. 1982. pap. 7.00 (ISBN 0-935734-09-0). Soil & Water Conserv.

Resource-Constrained Economies: The North American Dilemma. Frwd. By John Fraser. LC 80-16502. xvi, 307p. (Orig.). 1980. pap. text ed. 8.50 (ISBN 0-935734-05-8). Soil & Water Conserv.

TITLE INDEX RESOURCES FOR EARLY CHILDHOOD

Resource Development in the Two-Year College. Ed. by David P. Mitzel. 1988. text ed. 27.95 (ISBN 0-9619545-0-7); pap. text ed. 17.95 (ISBN 0-9619545-1-5). Natl Coun Res Dev.

Resource Developments in the Eighties. Intro. by J. A. Davidson. (Chemeca Ser.). 338p. (Orig.). 1982. pap. text ed. 54.00x (ISBN 0-85825-169-8, Pub. by Inst Engineering Australia). Brookfield Pub Co.

Resource Directory for Youth Workers, 1985. Ed. by Tic Long. 128p. (Orig.). 1985. pap. 8.95 (ISBN 0-687-36167-2). Abingdon.

Resource Directory of Council Innovations: Sixty-Four Reasons Not to Reinvent the Wheel. 56p. 1980. 14.00 (ISBN 0-317-35175-3, 3502); members 7.00 (ISBN 0-317-35176-1). Natl League Cities.

Resource Directory: Organization & Publications That Promote Sex Equity in Postsecondary Education. American Institutes for Research Staff. 73p. 1982. 10.00 (ISBN 0-911696-32-6). Assn Am Coll.

Resource Economics: An Economic Approach. Alan Randal. LC 29-22988. 451p. 1980. 37.95 (ISBN 0-471-87002-1). Wiley.

Resource Economics: An Economic Approach to Natural Resource & Environmental Policy. 2nd ed. Alan Randall. LC 84-15174. 434p. 1987. 33.95 (ISBN 0-471-87468-X). Wiley.

Resource Economics: Selected Works of Orris C. Herfindahl. Ed. by David B Brooks. 348p. 1974. 27.50 (ISBN 0-8018-1645-9). Resources Future.

Resource-Efficient Farming Methods for Tanzania: Proceedings Workshop, University of Dar es Salaam, Morogoro, Tanzania, May 16-20, 1983. Faculty of Agricultural Forestry & Veterinary Science Staff. 128p. 1984. pap. 17.95 (ISBN 0-87857-490-5). Rodale Pr Inc.

Resource Extraction & Market Structure. M. Schafer. (Lecture Notes in Economics & Mathematical Systems Ser.: Vol. 263). xii, 154p. 1986. pap. 17.50 (ISBN 0-387-16081-7). Springer-Verlag.

Resource for Urban Educational Studies. (Urban Education Reports Ser.: No. 2). 1981. 2.00 (ISBN 0-317-13088-9). I N Thut World Educ Ctr.

Resource Guide. 2nd ed. Compiled by Committee on Resource Sharing & Coordinated Acquisitions Staff. x, 56p. 1987. pap. 10.00 (ISBN 0-938435-01-9). LI Lib Resources.

Resource Guide for Drug Management Programs for Older People. 124p. 1986. write for info. US HHS.

Resource Guide for Elementary School Teaching. Richard D. Kellough & Patricia L. Roberts. 448p. 1985. text ed. write for info. (ISBN 0-02-362570-8). Macmillan.

Resource Guide for Fitness Programs for Older Persons. Alan Pardini & Connie Mahoney. 115p. 1986. write for info. US HHS.

Resource Guide for Guatemalan Asylum. 1.50. Natl Lawyers Guild.

Resource Guide for Injury Control Programs for Older Persons. 48p. 1987. write for info. (ISBN 1-55672-023-8). US HHS.

Resource Guide for Introductory Statistics. Robert J. Cruise et al. 360p. 1984. pap. text ed. 26.95 (ISBN 0-8403-3361-7). Kendall-Hunt.

Resource Guide for Mental Health. Richard M. Yarvis. 342p. (Orig.). 1979. pap. text ed. 39.95 (ISBN 0-942888-00-6). Pyramid Systems.

Resource Guide for Nutrition Management for Older Persons. Marjorie Bogaert-Tullis & Sarah Samuels. 101p. 1986. write for info. US HHS.

Resource Guide for Pre-Retirement Planning. Ed. by Eugene H. Seibert & Joanne S. Seibert. 122p. (Orig.). 1986. pap. 39.95 (ISBN 0-939461-00-5). Seibert Assocs.

Resource Guide for Secondary School Teaching. 4th ed. Eugene C. Kim & Richard D. Kellough. 300p. 1986. pap. text ed. write for info. (ISBN 0-02-363850-8). Macmillan.

Resource Guide on Blacks in Higher Education. The National Association for Equal Opportunity in Higher Education Staff. 66p. (Orig.). 1988. pap. text ed. 7.50 (ISBN 0-8191-6949-8, Pub. by NAEOHE). U Pr of Amer.

Resource Guide to Chiropractic: A Bibliography of Chiropractic & Related Areas, 1895-1981. Matthew J. Brennan. 155p. 1981. pap. text ed. 18.00 (ISBN 0-9606618-0-8, K-12). Am Chiro Assn.

Resource Guide to Information on Southern Africa. Margaret C. Lee. 54p. 1988. lab. manual 4.95 (ISBN 1-55523-163-2). Winston-Derek.

Resource Guide to Materials on the Arab World. Audrey Shabbas. (Illus.). 46p. (Orig.). 1987. pap. 6.95 (ISBN 0-937694-74-6). Assn Arab-Amer U Grads.

Resource Guide to People, Places & Programs in Arts & Aging. Priscilla McCutchceon & Cathyrn Wolf. (Illus.). 188p. (Orig.). 1985. pap. 8.00 (ISBN 0-910883-09-2). Natl Coun Aging.

Resource Guide to Preschool & Primary Programs for the Gifted & Talented. Reva C. Jenkins. 86p. 1979. pap. 11.95 (ISBN 0-936386-06-1). Creative Learning.

Resource Guide to Public School Early Childhood Programs. ASCD Early Childhood Education Policy Panel Staff et al. LC 88-70536. 198p. (Orig.). 1988. pap. 11.95 (ISBN 0-87120-151-8, 611-88036). Assn Supervision.

Resource Guide to Special Education: Terms, Laws, Assessment, Procedures, Organizations. 2nd ed. William E. Davis. 329p. 1986. scp. & net 35.95 (ISBN 0-205-08546-6, 248546, Pub. by Longwood Div.). Allyn.

Resource Guide to Themes in Contemporary American Song Lyrics, 1950-1985. B. Lee Cooper. LC 85-21933. (Illus.). 481p. 1986. lib. bdg. 50.95 (ISBN 0-313-24516-9, CPI/). Greenwood.

Resource Handbook for Health Education. Richard K. Means & Phyllis G. Ensor. LC 86-73127. (Illus.). 500p. 1988. pap. text ed. 18.95 (ISBN 0-936157-17-8). Benchmark Pr.

Resource Handbook on Discipline Codes. National School Resource Network Staff. LC 80-17395. 288p. 1980. text ed. 30.00 (ISBN 0-89946-041-0). Oelgeschlager.

Resource Hotline Newsletter. Date not set. 1.00 (ISBN 0-317-59276-9). Am Forestry.

Resource Information on EAPs. ALMACA Staff. pap. 2.00 (ISBN 0-318-22973-0). ALMACA.

Resource Inventory & Baseline Study Methods for Developing Countries. Ed. by Francis Conant. LC 83-15493. (AAAS Publication Ser.: No. 83-3). pap. 146.90 (2031948). Bks Demand UMI.

Resource Kit for Your Church's History. Ed. by Charles W. Deweese. 1984. 11.95 (ISBN 0-939804-12-3). Hist Comm S Baptist.

Resource List for Consumer Lawyers: Antitrust, Trade Regulation & Consumer Affairs Section. 5.00 (ISBN 0-317-62702-3). DC Bar Assn.

Resource Management. M. Mangel. (Lecture Notes in Biomathematics: Vol. 61). v, 138p. 1985. pap. 12.50 (ISBN 0-387-15982-7). Springer-Verlag.

Resource Management & Agricultural Development in Jamaica: Lessons for a Participatory Approach. Harvey Blustain. (Special Series on Resource Management: No. 2). 151p. (Orig.). 1982. pap. text ed. 9.00 (ISBN 0-86731-083-9). Cornell CIS RDC.

Resource Management & Environmental Uncertainty: Lessons from Coastal Upwelling Fisheries. Ed. by Michael H. Glantz & J. Dana Thompson. LC 80-16645. (Advances in Environmental Science & Technology Ser.). 491p. 1981. 77.50x (ISBN 0-471-05984-6, Pub. by Wiley-Interscience). Wiley.

Resource Management & the Oceans: The Political Economy of Deep Seabed Mining. Kurt M. Shusterich. (Westview Replicia Edition Ser.). (Illus.). 280p. 1982. pap. 34.00 (ISBN 0-86531-901-4). Westview.

Resource Management Concepts for Large Systems. R. Suri. (I S Modern Applied Mathematics & Computer Science Ser.: Vol. 3). (Illus.). 94p. 1981. 21.00 (ISBN 0-08-026473-5). Pergamon.

Resource Management Education. Fanatini. write for info. (ISBN 0-275-90006-1, C0006). Praeger.

Resource Management for Community Services. Ed. by An. Cook. 256p. 1988. pap. 42.95 (ISBN 0-317-67217-7). Van Nos Reinhold.

Resource Manual for a Living Revolution. Virginia Coover et al. 330p. 1985. lib. bdg. 19.95 (ISBN 0-86571-015-5); pap. 12.95 (ISBN 0-86571-056-2). New Soc Pubs.

Resource Manual for Guidelines for Exercise Testing & Prescription. Ed. by American College of Sports Medicine Staff. LC 88-3004. (Illus.). 436p. 1988. text ed. 50.00 (ISBN 0-8121-1109-5). Lea & Febiger.

Resource Manual for Typesetting with Your Computer. Al Beechick. LC 86-71983. 48p. 1986. pap. 9.95 (ISBN 0-940319-03-9). Arrow Connection.

Resource Materials: Advanced Tax Planning for Real Estate Transactions. 402p. 1979. pap. 30.00 (ISBN 0-317-32250-8, R117). Am Law Inst.

Resource Materials: Banking & Commercial Lending Law, Vol. VIII. Ed. & intro. by Richard T. Nassberg. 328p. (Orig.). 1987. pap. 40.00 (ISBN 0-8318-0162-X, R161). Am Law Inst.

Resource Materials: Banking & Commercial Lending Law, Vol. II. 633p. 1981. pap. 40.00 (ISBN 0-317-32251-6, R126). Am Law Inst.

Resource Materials: Civil Practice & Litigation in Federal & State Courts Supplement. 2nd ed. Ed. by Sam Pointers. (Resource Materials Ser.). 525p. 1985. pap. 40.00 (ISBN 0-8318-0155-7, R155). Am Law Inst.

Resource Materials: Civil Practice & Litigation in Federal & State Courts, 3 vols. 3rd ed. Ed. by Sol Schreiber. (Resource Materials Ser.). 2705p. 1985. pap. 95.00 (ISBN 0-8318-0154-9, R154). Am Law Inst.

Resource Materials: Civil Practice & Litigation in Federal & State Courts, 2 vols. 4th ed. Ed. by Sol Schrieber. 2450p. 1987. Set. pap. text ed. 95.00 (ISBN 0-8318-0160-3, R160); supplement incl. Am Law Inst.

Resource Materials: Modern Real Estate Transactions. 8th ed. Date not set. pap. text ed. 75.00 (ISBN 0-8318-0167-0). Am Law Inst.

Resource Materials-Partnerships: UPA, ULPA, Securities, Taxation, & Bankruptcy. 7th ed. (Resource Materials Ser.). 817p. 1987. pap. 40.00 (ISBN 0-8318-0161-1, R162). Am Law Inst.

Resource Mobilization in Poor Countries: Implementing Tax Policies. Alex Radian. LC 79-66440. 226p. 1980. 26.95x (ISBN 0-87855-304-5). Transaction Bks.

Resource Notebook on Organization. Duane E. Webster. 147p. 1979. 15.00 (ISBN 0-318-03474-3, ED 191 475). OMS.

Resource Notebook on Planning. Jeffery J. Gardner. 155p. 1979. 15.00 (ISBN 0-318-16099-4). OMS.

Resource Notebook on Staff Development. Jane E. Rosenberg & Maureen Sullivan. 309p. 1983. 25.00 (ISBN 0-318-03475-1). OMS.

Resource of Objectives for Training in Family Medicine: An Atlas. Compiled by STFM Task Force on Objectives. 160p. 1979. 5.00 (ISBN 0-942295-10-2). Soc Tchrs Fam Med.

Resource of War: The Credit of the Government Made Immediately Available-History of the Legal Tender Paper Money Issued During the Great Rebellion Being a Loan Without Interest & a National Currency. Elbridge G. Spaulding. LC 69-19681. (Money Markets Ser.). 1971. Repr. of 1869 ed. lib. bdg. 35.00x (ISBN 0-8371-0662-1, SPRW). Greenwood.

Resource Organization in Primary Schools. 2nd. ed. Cecilia Gordon. (Orig.). 1987. pap. text ed. 17.95X (ISBN 0-86184-164-6). Trans Atl Phila.

Resource Policy: International Perspectives. Ed. by Peter N. Nemetz. (Illus.). 371p. 1980. pap. text ed. 18.95x (ISBN 0-920380-64-6, Pub. by Inst Res Pub Canada). Brookfield Pub Co.

Resource Recovery & Utilization - STP592. 212p. 1975. 20.00 (ISBN 0-8031-0558-4, 04-592000-41). ASTM.

Resource Recovery Economics: Methods for Feasibility Analysis. Stuart H. Russell. (Pollution Engineering & Technology Ser.: Vol. 22). (Illus.). 312p. 1982. 55.00 (ISBN 0-8247-1726-0). Dekker.

Resource Recovery from Municipal Solid Wastes, 2 vols. Luis F. Diaz & George M. Savage. Incl. Vol. I. Primary Processing. 176p. 49.95 (ISBN 0-8493-5613-X); Vol. II. Final Processing. 192p. 49.95 (ISBN 0-8493-5614-8). 1982. 64.00 ea. CRC Pr.

Resource Recovery from Solid Wastes: Proceedings of a Conference in Miami Beach, Florida, May 10-12, 1982. Ed. by Subrata Sengupta & Kau-Fui V. Wong. LC 82-18145. 600p. 1982. 145.00 (ISBN 0-08-028825-1, A125). Pergamon.

Resource-Recovery Plants: A Study of 15 U. S. Facilities. Allen Hershkowitz & Maarten DeKadt. 1989. pap. price not set (ISBN 0-918780-49-7). INFORM.

Resource Recovery Processing Equipment. David Bendersky et al. LC 82-7882. (Pollution Technology Rev. 93). (Illus.). 417p. 1983. 42.00 (ISBN 0-8155-0911-1). Noyes.

Resource Recovery Through Incineration: Proceedings; Papers Presented at 1974 National Incinerator Conference, Miami, Florida, May 12-15, 1974. National Incinerator Conference (1974: Miami,Fla.) LC 70-124402. pap. 95.00 (ISBN 0-317-29795-3, 2016866). Bks Demand UMI.

Resource Regimes: Natural Resources & Social Institutions. Oran R. Young. Ed. by Stephen Krasner. LC 81-21979. (Studies in International Political Economy: Vol. 7). 284p. 1982. 35.00x (ISBN 0-520-04573-4). U of Cal Pr.

Resource Room: A Guide for Special Educators. Barry E. McNamara. 160p. 1989. text ed. 39.50x (ISBN 0-88706-983-5); pap. 12.95x (ISBN 0-88706-984-3). State U NY Pr.

Resource Room Primer. Natalie M. Elman & Janet H. Ginsburg. (Illus.). 320p. 1981. text ed. write for info. (ISBN 0-13-774406-4). P-H.

Resource Scarcity & the Hmong Response. R. G. Cooper. 314p. 1984. text ed. 22.95 (ISBN 9971-69-070-5, Pub. by Singapore U Pr). Ohio U Pr.

Resource Sector in an Open Economy. Ed. by H. Siebert. (Lecture Notes in Economics & Mathematical Systems Ser.: Vol. 200). 161p. 1984. pap. 15.00 (ISBN 0-387-12700-3). Springer-Verlag.

Resource Sharing in Libraries: Why, How, When, Next Action Steps: Based on Papers Presented at the Conference Held April 11-12, 1973 at Pittsburgh, Pennsylvania. Ed. by Allen Kent. LC 73-90724. (Books in Library & Information Science: Vol. 8). (Illus.). pap. 101.30 (ISBN 0-317-07889-5, 2051863). Bks Demand UMI.

Resource Shortages & World Politics. Joanne F. Aviel. 162p. 1977. pap. text ed. 11.00 (ISBN 0-8191-0263-6). U Pr of Amer.

Resource Structure of Agriculture: An Economic Analysis. K. Cowling et al. LC 70-114570. 1970. 36.00 (ISBN 0-08-015585-5). Pergamon.

Resource Teacher: A Guide to Effective Practices. 2nd ed. J. Lee Wiederholt & Donald D. Hammill. LC 83-4642. (Illus.). 414p. 1983. pap. text ed. 22.00x (ISBN 0-936104-33-3, 0085). Pro Ed.

Resource Trends & Population Policy: A Time for Reassessment. Lester R. Brown. LC 79-64839. (Worldwatch Papers). 1979. pap. 4.00 (ISBN 0-916468-28-3). Worldwatch Inst.

Resource Use by Chaparral & Matorral: A Comparison of Vegetation Function in Two Mediterranean Type Ecosystems. Ed. by P. C. Miller. (Ecological Studies: Vol. 39). (Illus.). 416p. 1981. 59.30 (ISBN 0-387-90556-1). Springer-Verlag.

Resource Utilization & Dissemination of Information by REGI Projects. Lawrence M. Stolurow & Myrene R. Hildebrand. (RTF Report Ser.: No. 5). 24p. (Orig.). 1981. pap. text ed. 2.50 (ISBN 0-939984-03-2). U IA Ctr Ed Experiment.

Resourceful Earth: A Response to Global 2000. Ed. by Julian L. Simon & Herman Kahn. (Illus.). 586p. 1984. 14.95 (ISBN 0-631-13467-0). Basil Blackwell.

Resourceful Rehab: A Guide for Historic Buildings in Dade County, Florida. Metropolitan Dade County, Historic Preservation Division, OCED Staff & Charles E. Chase. (Illus., Orig.). 1987. pap. 9.95 (ISBN 0-9618373-0-6). MDC-Hist Preserv Div.

Resourceful Writer. William H. Barnwell. LC 86-81303. 1987. pap. text ed. 22.36 (ISBN 0-395-35915-5); instr's manual 2.36 (ISBN 0-395-42465-8); support pkg. 2.36 (ISBN 0-395-43530-7); transparencies avail. HM.

Resourceful Writer: Readings to Accompany the Harbrace College Handbook. Suzanne S. Webb. 760p. 1987. pap. text ed. 14.00 (ISBN 0-15-576631-7, HC); instr's. manual 3.50 (ISBN 0-15-576632-5). HarBraceJ.

Resources: A Directory of New York City Directories. Ed. by Patricia A. Friedland. 58p. 1988. pap. text ed. 6.50 (ISBN 0-88156-075-8). Comm Serv Soc NY.

Resources & Applications of Industrial Biotechnology. Ed. by R. N. Greenshields. 300p. 1988. 60.00x (ISBN 0-935859-22-5, Stockton Pr). Groves Dict Music.

Resources & Development in the Indian Ocean Region. Ed. by Alex Kerr. 256p. 1981. lib. bdg. 43.00 (ISBN 0-86531-123-4). Westview.

Resources & Development: Natural Resource Policies & Economic Development in an Interdependent World. Ed. by Peter Dorner & Mahmoud A. El-Shafie. (Illus.). 516p. 1980. 34.50x (ISBN 0-299-08250-4). U of Wis Pr.

Resources & Development of Mexico. H. H. Bancroft. 1976. lib. bdg. 59.95 (ISBN 0-8490-2519-2). Gordon Pr.

Resources & Higher Education. Alfred Morris & John Sizer. 226p. 1983. 21.00x (ISBN 0-900868-90-2). Taylor & Francis.

Resources & Needs of American Diplomacy. Smith Simpson. Ed. by Thorsten Sellin. LC 68-57759. (Annals: Vol. 380). 1968. 15.00 (ISBN 0-87761-111-4); pap. 7.95 (ISBN 0-87761-110-6, 380). Am Acad Pol Soc Sci.

Resources & People in East Kentucky: Problems & Potentials of a Lagging Economy. Mary J. Bowman & W. Warren Haynes. LC 83-11766. (Resources for the Future, Inc. Publications). 480p. Repr. of 1963 ed. 78.50 (ISBN 0-404-60328-9). AMS Pr.

Resources & Playing. B. Goodall & A. Kirby. LC 78-40931. (Oxford Geography Ser.). 373p. 1979. 55.00 (ISBN 0-08-023711-8); pap. 24.00 (ISBN 0-08-023710-X). Pergamon.

Resources & Population. Alan Macfarlane. LC 75-13448. (Cambridge Studies in Social Anthropology: No. 12). (Illus.). 352p. 1976. 59.50 (ISBN 0-521-20913-7). Cambridge U Pr.

Resources & Prospects of America: Ascertained During a Visit to the States in the Autumn of 1865. S. Morton Peto. LC 73-2529. (Big Business; Economic Power in a Free Society Ser.). Repr. of 1866 ed. 26.50 (ISBN 0-405-05108-5). Ayer Co Pubs.

Resources & Reimbursement Agent. Jack Rudman. (Career Examination Ser.: C-3157). 1988. pap. 14.00 (ISBN 0-8373-3157-9). Natl Learning.

Resources & Society. J. Zucchetto & A. M. Jansson. (Ecological Studies: Vol. 56). (Illus.). x, 246p. 1985. 76.50 (ISBN 0-387-96151-8). Springer-Verlag.

Resources & the Teacher. Tony Gibson. (Illus.). 160p. 1975. 12.95x (ISBN 0-8464-0792-2). Beekman Pubs.

Resources & World Development: Report of the Dahlem Workshop on Resources & World . Development. Ed. by D. J. McLaren & B. J. Skinner. LC 87-8239. (Physical, Chemical, Earth Science Ser.). 600p. 1987. 168.00 (ISBN 0-471-91568-8). Wiley.

Resources, Environment, & Economics: Applications of the Materials-Energy Balance Principle. R. U. Ayres. LC 77-20049. 207p. 1978. text ed. 40.00 (ISBN 0-471-02627-1, JW). Krieger.

Resources for an Uncertain Future: Papers Presented at a Forum Marking the 25th Anniversary of Resources for the Future, 1977. Ed. by Charles J. Hitch. LC 77-18378. pap. 29.30 (ISBN 0-317-26464-8, 2023800). Bks Demand UMI.

Resources for Christian Leaders. Edward R. Dayton. 3.95 (ISBN 0-912552-45-X). Missions Adv Res Com Ctr.

Resources for Christian Leaders. 8th ed. 1982. 3.95 (ISBN 0-912552-23-9). World Vision Intl.

Resources for Creative Teaching in Early Childhood Education. Bonnie M. Flemming et al. (Illus.). 636p. (Orig., Songs & Parodies by Joanne D. Hicks). 1977. pap. text ed. 27.95 net (ISBN 0-15-576624-4, HC). HarBraceJ.

Resources for Development. Robert J. Yeager. (How to Ser.). 46p. 1986. 8.95. Natl Cath Educ.

Resources for Early Childhood: An Annotated Bibliography & Guide for Educators, Librarians & Parents. Ed. by Hannah N. Scheffler. LC 81-48421. 600p. 1986. lib. bdg. 61.00 (ISBN 0-8240-9390-9); pap. 20.00 (ISBN 0-8240-8769-0). Garland Pub.

Resources for Educating Artistically Talented Students. Gilbert A. Clark & Enid D. Zimmerman. LC 86-23183. (Illus.). 192p. 1987. text ed. 22.00x (ISBN 0-8156-2401-8). Syracuse U Pr.

Resources for Electric Vehicles & Their Infrastructure: Proceedings. 156p. 1980. pap. 15.00 (ISBN 0-906048-22-2, PPL-17). Soc Auto Engineers.

Resources for Every Day in Every Way. Faraday Burditt & Cynthia Holley. (ps) 1989. pap. 8.95 (ISBN 0-8224-2508-4). D S Lake Pubs.

Resources for Freedom: A Report to the President by the President's Materials Policy Commission, June 1952, 2 vols. in 1. United States President's Materials Policy Commission. Bd. with Vol. 1. Foundations for Growth & Security; Vol. 4. The Promise of Technology. LC 72-2863. (Use & Abuse of America's Natural Resources Ser.). 434p. 1972. Repr. of 1952 ed. 29.00 (ISBN 0-405-04533-6). Ayer Co Pubs.

Resources for Future Economic Growth. S. A. Ali. 1979. text ed. 10.95x (ISBN 0-7069-0746-9, Pub. by Vikas India). Advent NY.

Resources for Gifted Children in the New York Area. Darlene Freeman & Virginia Stuart. LC 79-91434. 350p. (Orig.). 1980. pap. 10.00 (ISBN 0-89824-005-0). Trillium Pr.

Resources for Health: Technology Assessment for Policy Makings. Ed. by H. David Banta. LC 81-21079. 256p. 1982. 40.95 (ISBN 0-275-91358-9, C1358). Praeger.

Resources for Latin American Jewish Studies: Essays on Using Jewish Reference Sources for the Study of Latin American Jewry; U. S. Library Collections on L. A. Jews; & U. S. Archival Resources for the Study of Jews in L. A. Thomas Niehaus et al. Ed. by Judith L. Elkin. LC 84-80219. (LAJSA Publication Ser.: No. 1). 59p. (Orig.). 1984. pap. text ed. 10.00 (ISBN 0-916921-00-X). Lat Am Jewish Assn.

Resources for Lifelong Learning. Jane Herzog. (Follet Coping Skills Ser.). 64p. pap. 3.75 (ISBN 0-8428-2337-9); tchr's. guide 1.50 (ISBN 0-8428-2338-7). Cambridge Bk.

Resources for Living. facs. ed. Gaius G. Atkins. LC 77-117756. (Essay Index Reprint Ser.). 1938. 19.00 (ISBN 0-8369-1741-3). Ayer Co Pubs.

Resources for Living. Patricia Thompson et al. 512p. (YA) (gr. 9-12). 1986. text ed. 18.95 (ISBN 0-8219-0185-0, 50451); tchr's ed. 20.00 (ISBN 0-8219-0187-7, 50801); wkbk. 4.95 (ISBN 0-8219-0186-9, 50651). EMC.

Resources for Middle-Grade Reluctant Readers: A Guide for Librarians. Marianne L. Pilla. 130p. 1987. lib. bdg. 18.50 (ISBN 0-87287-547-4). Libs Unl.

Resources for Ministry in Death & Dying. Roger G. Branch & Larry A. Platt. LC 87-14298. (Orig.). 1988. pap. 14.95 (ISBN 0-8054-6945-1). Broadman.

Resources for Personnel Management. Sikes Toni F. 175p. 1984. 15.00 (ISBN 0-318-17638-6). Assn Coll Arts Admin.

Resources for Renewal (Romans) Leader's Guide. 48p. (Orig.). 1982. pap. 1.95 (ISBN 0-89367-080-4). Light & Life.

Resources for Renewal (Romans) Student Guide. 64p. (Orig.). 1982. pap. 2.50 (ISBN 0-89367-079-0). Light & Life.

Resources for Social Change: Race in the United States. James S. Coleman. LC 77-152494. 134p. 1971. 12.75 (ISBN 0-471-16493-3, JW). Krieger.

Resources for South Asian Language Studies in the United States: Report of a Conference Convened by the University of Pennsylvania for the United States Office of Education, January 15-16, 1960. Ed. by William N. Brown. LC 60-15611. pap. 25.80 (ISBN 0-317-11022-5, 2002898). Bks Demand UMI.

Resources for Teaching Home Economics. Virginia L. Clark & Dorothy E. Pomraning. 1986. 5.00 (ISBN 0-911365-26-5, A261-08468). Home Econ Educ.

Resources for Teaching Young Children with Special Needs. Penny L. Deiner. LC 82-84254. 564p. 1983. pap. text ed. 21.95 net (ISBN 0-15-576627-9, HC). HarBraceJ.

Resources for the History of Physics: Guide to Books & Audiovisual Materials, Guide to Original Works of Historical Importance & Their Translations into Other Languages. Ed. by Stephen G. Brush. LC 70-186306. pap. 48.00 (ISBN 0-317-10599-X, 2022324). Bks Demand UMI.

Resources for the Study of Economic History: A Preliminary Guide to Pre-Twentieth Century Printed Material in Collection. Dorothea D. Reeves. (Kress Library of Business & Economics Publication: No. 16). viiii, 62p. 1961. pap. 8.95x (ISBN 0-678-09917-0, Pub. by Kress Lib Business). Kelley.

Resources for the Teaching of Anthropology. Ed. by David G. Mandelbaum et al. LC 81-23204. 316p. 1982. Repr. of 1963 ed. lib. bdg. 59.50x (ISBN 0-313-23441-8, MARTA). Greenwood.

Resources for the Welfare State: An Economic Introduction. John F. Sleeman. LC 78-41314. (Illus.). 197p. pap. 51.30 (2030354). Bks Demand UMI.

Resources for Third World Health Planners: A Selected Subject Bibliography. Singer & Titus. (Traditional Healing Ser.: No. 6). 1980. 17.50 (Trado-Medic Bks); pap. 9.95 (Trado-Medic Bks). Conch Mag.

Resources for Third World Health Planners: A Selected Subject Bibliography. Ed. by Philip Singer & Elizabeth A. Titus. (Traditional Healing Ser.: No. 6). 168p. (Orig.). 1980. 17.50; pap. 9.95. Trado Medic.

Resources for Urban Schools: Better Use & Balance. Ed. by Sterling M. McMurrin. LC 73-158986. 1971. pap. 3.50 (ISBN 0-87186-233-6). Comm Econ Dev.

Resources for Women's Ministries. (Women's Ministries Commission Ser.). 1975. 4.00 (ISBN 0-8309-0258-9). Herald Hse.

Resources for Writing for Publication in Education. Sidney B. Katz et al. LC 79-27127. 1980. pap. text ed. 7.95x (ISBN 0-8077-2579-X). Tchrs Coll.

Resources in America's Future: Patterns of Requirements & Availabilities 1960-2000. Hans H. Landsberg et al. 1037p. 1963. 50.00 (ISBN 0-8018-0357-8). Resources Future.

Resources in Education Annual Cumulation, 3 vols. Ed. by The Oryx Press. 1984. Set. lib. bdg. 237.00; Vols. 1 & 2, Abstracts. lib. bdg. 156.00; Vol. 3, Index. 71.00. Oryx Pr.

Resources in Education-Current Index to Journals in Education, 1983: Annual Update on Microfiche. 1984. cancelled. Oryx Pr.

Resources in Education (RIE), 1982: Abstracts. (Educational Resources Information Clearinghouse Book (ERIC)). 136.00 (ISBN 0-89774-034-3). Oryx Pr.

Resources in Education (RIE), 1982: Index. (Educational Resources Information Clearinghouse Book (ERIC)). 71.00 (ISBN 0-89774-035-1). Oryx Pr.

Resources in Education (RIE), 1983: Abstracts. (Educational Resources Information Clearinghouse Book (ERIC)). 136.00 (ISBN 0-89774-112-9). Oryx Pr.

Resources in Education (RIE), 1983: Index. (Educational Resources Information Clearinghouse Book (ERIC)). 71.00 (ISBN 0-89774-114-5). Oryx Pr.

Resources in Education (RIE), 1984: Index. (Educational Resources Information Clearinghouse Book (ERIC)). 81.00 (ISBN 0-89774-189-7). Oryx Pr.

Resources in Education (RIE), 1985: Abstracts. (Educational Resources Information Clearinghouse Book (ERIC)). 156.00 (ISBN 0-89774-213-3). Oryx Pr.

Resources in Education (RIE), 1985: Index. (Educational Resources Information Clearinghouse Book (ERIC)). 81.00 (ISBN 0-89774-215-X). Oryx Pr.

Resources in Education (RIE), 1986: Abstracts. (Educational Resources Information Clearinghouse Book (ERIC)). 201.00 (ISBN 0-317-67683-0). Oryx Pr.

Resources in Education (RIE) 1986: Index. (Educational Resources Information Clearinghouse Book (ERIC)). 926p. 1987. 101.00 (ISBN 0-89774-239-7). Oryx Pr.

Resources in Education (RIE), 1987: Abstracts. (Education Resources Information Clearinghouse Book (ERIC)). 201.00 (ISBN 0-89774-428-4). Oryx Pr.

Resources in Education (RIE), 1987: Index. (Educational Resources Information Clearinghouse Book (ERIC)). 101.00 (ISBN 0-89774-430-6). Oryx Pr.

Resources in Education, 1983: Annual Cumulation, 2 Vols. 2138p. 1984. Set. lib. bdg. 207.00. Oryx Pr.

Resources in Entomology. Entomological Society of America Staff. 269p. 1987. 15.00 (ISBN 0-938522-32-9). Entomol Soc.

Resources in Theatre & Disability. William Rickert & Jane Bloomquist. LC 88-5545. 208p. (Orig.). 1988. lib. bdg. 27.50 (ISBN 0-8191-5748-1, Pub. by Assn Theatre & Disability); pap. text ed. 14.50 (ISBN 0-8191-5749-X, Pub. by Assn Theatre & Disability). U Pr of Amer.

Resources Management. R. L. Martino. 168p. 1968. 95.00 (ISBN 0-677-61050-5). Gordon & Breach.

Resources Management. Rocco L. Martino. LC 67-30569. (Illus.). pap. 42.00 (ISBN 0-317-10783-6, 2010386). Bks Demand UMI.

Resources of American Music History: A Directory of Source Materials from Colonial Times to World War II. Ed. by D. W. Krummel et al. LC 80-14873. (Music in American Life Ser.). 463p. 1981. 70.00 (ISBN 0-252-00828-6). U of Ill Pr.

Resources of Kind: Genre-Theory in the Renaissance. Rosalie Colie. LC 72-95307. (Una's Lectures: No. 1). 1974. 37.00x (ISBN 0-520-02397-8). U of Cal Pr.

Resources of Merseyside. Ed. by W. Gould & A. Hodgkiss. (Illus.). 212p. 1982. pap. text ed. 12.50x (ISBN 0-85323-384-5, Pub. by Liverpool U Pr). Humanities.

Resources of Music: Introduction & Score. W. Mellers. 8.95x (ISBN 0-521-07263-8). Cambridge U Pr.

Resources of the Earth. Brian J. Skinner et al. (Illus.). 416p. 1988. text ed. price not set (ISBN 0-13-774423-4). P-H.

Resources of the Southern Fields & Forests. Francis P. Porcher. LC 74-125758. (American Environmental Studies). 1970. Repr. of 1869 ed. 46.50 (ISBN 0-405-02684-6). Ayer Co Pubs.

Resources of the United Kingdom. William R. Pettman. LC 68-56563. 1970. Repr. of 1830 ed. 39.50x (ISBN 0-678-00661-X). Kelley.

Resources Papers: Geography, Vol. 1. 1987. 75.00x (ISBN 0-317-62311-7, Pub. by Scientific). State Mutual Bk.

Resources, Power & Women: Proceedings of the African & Asian Inter-Regional Workshop on Strategies for Improving the Employment Conditions of Rural Women, Arusha, United Republic of Tanzania, August 20-25, 1984. Intro. by Dharam Ghai. v, 82p. (Orig.). 1985. pap. 7.00 (ISBN 92-2-105009-2). Intl Labour Office.

Resources Recovery Today & Tomorrow: Proceedings, National Waste Processing Conference, 1980. 621p. 1980. 100.00 (ISBN 0-317-33597-9, 100133). ASME.

Resources, Regimes, World Order. Anthony J. Dolman. (Pergamon Policy Studies on International Development Ser.). 425p. 1981. 58.00 (ISBN 0-08-028080-3); pap. 15.25 (ISBN 0-08-028079-X). Pergamon.

Resources, Society & Future. G. Backstrand. 1980. 63.00 (ISBN 0-08-023266-3); pap. 24.00 (ISBN 0-08-023267-1). Pergamon.

Resources, Values, & Development. Amartya Sen. 512p. 1984. text ed. 32.50x (ISBN 0-674-76525-7). Harvard U Pr.

Respect. Beverly Fiday & Deborah Crowdy. LC 87-36981. (What Is It?--A Values Ser.). (Illus.). 32p. (gr. k-3). 1988. PLB 7.95 (ISBN 0-89565-417-2). Childs World.

Respect. Sally Jordan. (Weathering Storms Ser.). (Illus.). 32p. (gr. 5-9). 1986. saddle stitch 0.79 (ISBN 0-87403-039-0, 3537). Standard Pub.

Respect. Darryl London. 459p. 1984. 14.95 (ISBN 0-917113-00-4). Lloylds Pub.

Respect & Care in Medical Ethics. Ed. by David H. Smith. 340p. (Orig.). 1984. lib. bdg. 28.75 (ISBN 0-8191-4198-4, Poynter Ctr on Ethics & Am Institutions); pap. text ed. 14.50 (ISBN 0-8191-4199-2). U Pr of Amer.

Respect Black: The Writings & Speeches of Henry McNeal Turner. Ed. by Edwin S. Redkey. LC 79-138695. 1971. 9.00 (ISBN 0-405-01984-X). Ayer Co Pubs.

Respect for Acting. Uta Hagen & Haskel Frankel. LC 72-2328. 227p. 1973. 16.95 (ISBN 0-02-547390-5). Macmillan.

Respect for Law. 20p. 1981. pap. 1.40 (ISBN 0-686-47946-7). Amer Bar Assn.

Respect for Life in Medicine, Philosophy, & the Law. Owsei Temkin et al. LC 76-47366. (Thalheimer Lecture Ser.). 1977. text ed. 16.50x (ISBN 0-8018-1942-3). Johns Hopkins.

Respect for Life: The Traditional Upbringing of American Indian Children. Ed. by Sylvester M. Morey & Olivia L. Gilliam. LC 80-83371. (Illus.). 202p. 1980. pap. text ed. 4.95 (ISBN 0-913098-34-5). Myrin Institute.

Respect for Nature: A Theory of Environmental Ethics. Paul W. Taylor. LC 85-43318. (Studies in Moral, Political, & Legal Philosophy). 368p. 1986. text ed. 37.50 (ISBN 0-691-07709-6); pap. 12.50x (ISBN 0-691-02250-X). Princeton U Pr.

Respect Life: Curriculum Guidelines. 109p. 1977. pap. 9.95 (ISBN 1-55586-924-6). US Catholic.

Respect Part II. 1985. write for info. Lloylds Pub.

Respectability of Mr. Bernard Shaw. A. Brinser. LC 75-22167. (Studies in George Bernard Shaw., No. 92). 1975. lib. bdg. 40.95x (ISBN 0-8383-2082-1). Haskell.

Respectability of Mr. Bernard Shaw. Ayers Brinser. LC 72-192026. 1931. lib. bdg. 17.00 (ISBN 0-8414-2542-6). Folcroft.

Respectable Army: The Military Origins of the Republic, 1763-1789. James K. Martin & Mark E. Lender. LC 81-173990. (American History Ser.). (Illus.). 256p. (Orig.). 1982. pap. 8.95x (ISBN 0-88295-812-7). Harlan Davidson.

Respectable Ditch: A History of the Trent-Severn Waterway, 1833-1920. James T. Angus. 460p. 1987. 37.50 (ISBN 0-7735-0597-0). McGill-Queens U Pr.

Respectable Folly: Millenarians & the French Revolution in France and England. Clarke Garrett. LC 74-24378. 252p. 1975. 29.50x (ISBN 0-8018-1618-1). Johns Hopkins.

Respectable Radical: George Howell & Victorian Working Class Politics. F. M. Leventhal. LC 77-135190. 1971. 20.00x (ISBN 0-674-76540-0). Harvard U Pr.

Respectable Rebels: Middle Class Campaigns in Britain in the 1970's. Ed. by Roger King & Neill Nugent. 200p. 1980. 30.00 (ISBN 0-8419-6219-7); pap. 17.50 (ISBN 0-8419-6220-0). Holmes & Meier.

Respected Rebels. Mary A. Kearney & Edward Kearney. Ed. by Jean McConochie. 96p. 1983. pap. text ed. 3.25 (ISBN 0-13-774598-2, 21030). Prentice ESL.

Respected Sir. Naguib Mahfouz. Tr. by Rasheed El-Enany. 164p. 1987. 13.95 (ISBN 0-7043-2596-9, Pub. by Quartet Bks). Salem Hse Pubs.

Respectful Leader. Costa Deir. Ed. by Dick Myhre & Bob Briggs. (Principles of Leadership Ser.). (Orig.). 1988. pap. 3.95 (ISBN 0-939159-11-2). Cityhill Pub.

Respectful Rehabilitation: Answers to Your Questions About Old Buildings. LC 82-15018. (Illus.). 200p. 1986. pap. 12.95 (ISBN 0-89133-103-4). Preservation Pr.

Respectful Treatment: A Practical Handbook of Patient Care. 2nd ed. Martin R. Lipp. 352p. 1986. pap. 20.00 (ISBN 0-444-01001-7). Elsevier.

Respectfully Yours, Mom & Dad. Glenn R. Stouh & Marvyn Womack. Ed. by Kevin Nichols. 224p. (Orig.). 1987. pap. 12.95 (ISBN 0-932471-08-0). Falsoft.

Respecting Life: An Activity Guide. Jane B. Katenkamp. (Illus.). 144p. (Orig.). 1985. pap. 14.95 (ISBN 1-55586-964-5). US Catholic.

Respecting the Pupil, Essays on Teaching Able Students by Members of the Faculty of Phillips Exeter Academy. 2nd 1984 ed. Ed. by Donald B. Cole & Robert H. Cornell. LC 81-81104. (Illus.). 132p. 1981. pap. 6.95 (ISBN 0-939618-01-X). Phillips Exeter.

Respective Roles of State & Local Governments in Land Policy & Taxation. Ed. by George Lefcoe. (Lincoln Institute Monograph: No. 80-7). 271p. 1980. pap. text ed. 12.00 (ISBN 0-686-31827-7). Lincoln Inst Land.

Respighi. (Portraits of Greatness Ser.: No. II). (Eng.). 1987. pap. 12.50 (ISBN 0-918367-09-3). Elite.

Respiration. Ed. by Wallace O. Fenn & Herman Rahn. (Handbook of Physiology: Pt. 3, Vols. 1 & 2). pap. 160.00 ea. (2015381). Bks Demand UMI.

Respiration & Circulation. rev. ed. Ed. by Philip L. Altman & Dorothy S. Dittmer. LC 70-137563. (Biological Handbks). (Illus.). xxv, 930p. 1983. 76.00 (ISBN 0-08-030067-7). Pergamon.

Respiration & Metabolism of Embryonic Vertebrates. Ed. by Roger Seymour. LC 84-9751. (Perspectives in Vertebrate Science Ser.). 1984. lib. bdg. 95.00 (ISBN 90-6193-053-7, Pub. by Junk Pubs Netherlands). Kluwer Academic.

Respiration in Health & Disease. 3rd ed. Reuben M. Cherniack & Louis Cherniack. (Illus.). 480p. 1983. 33.95 (ISBN 0-7216-2527-4). Saunders.

Respiration in Invertebrates. J. P. Mill. LC 72-90019. 1973. 27.50 (ISBN 0-312-67760-X). St Martin.

Respiration in Water & Air: Adaptations, Regulations, Evolution. P. J. Dejours. 179p. 1988. 79.00 (ISBN 0-444-80926-0, Excerpta Medica). Elsevier.

Respiration of Amphibious Vertebrates. Ed. by G. M. Hughes. 1976. 97.00 (ISBN 0-12-360750-7). Acad Pr.

Respiration: Proceedings of the 28th International Congress of Physiological Sciences, Budapest 1980. Ed. by I. Hutas & L. A. Debreczeni. (Advances in Physiological Sciences: Vol. 10). (Illus.). 665p. 1981. 100.00 (ISBN 0-08-026823-4). Pergamon.

Respirators & Protective Clothing. E. C. Hyatt & J. M. White. (Safety Ser.: No. 22). (Illus.). 82p. 1967. pap. 7.75 (ISBN 92-0-123367-1, ISP150, IAEA). UNIPUB.

Respiratory & Alimentary Tract Disease. Ed. by H. S. Rosenberg & J. Bernstein. (Perspectives in Pediatric Pathology Ser.: Vol. 11). (Illus.). x, 218p. 1987. 146.75 (ISBN 3-8055-4435-9). S Karger.

Respiratory & Infectious Disease. LC 87-5396. (Profile of Health & Disease in America Ser.). 240p. 1987. 35.00x (ISBN 0-8160-1458-2). Facts on File.

Respiratory Burst & Its Physiological Significance. Ed. by A. J. Sbarra & R. R. Strauss. (Illus.). 466p. 1988. 85.00x (ISBN 0-306-42883-0, Plenum Pr). Plenum Pub.

Respiratory Care. 1981. 3.50 (ISBN 0-912452-35-8). Am Phys Therapy Assn.

Respiratory Care. Ed. by Susan R. Williams & Barbara McVan. LC 85-17364. (Clinical Pocket Manual Ser.). 187p. 1985. pap. 13.95 (ISBN 0-87434-008-X). Springhouse Pub.

Respiratory Care: A Guide to Clinical Practice. 2nd ed. Ed. by George G. Burton & John E. Hodgkin. (Illus.). 1216p. 1984. text ed. 49.50 (ISBN 0-397-50548-5, 65-06992, Lippincott Medical). Lippincott.

Respiratory Care Case Studies, Vol. 1. 3rd ed. Thomas J. DeKornfeld & Jay S. Finch. (Case Studies Ser.: Vol. 36). (Illus.). 1982. 26.50 (ISBN 0-87488-019-X). Med Exam.

Respiratory Care Examination Review. Raymond S. Edge & Terry L. Forrette. 208p. 1986. pap. 16.95 (ISBN 0-8385-8277-X). Appleton & Lange.

Respiratory Care: National Board Review. C. A. Brainard & M. Wirth. (Illus.). 512p. 1984. pap. 27.50 (ISBN 0-89303-816-4). Appleton & Lange.

Respiratory Care of the Newborn: A Clinical Manual. Claire A. Aloan. LC 65-8329. (Illus.). 368p. 1986. text ed. 27.50 (ISBN 0-397-50666-X, Lippincott Medical). Lippincott.

Respiratory Care Practice. Barnes. 1988. 45.00 (ISBN 0-8151-0490-1). Year Bk Med.

Respiratory Care Sciences: An Integrated Approach. William V. Wojciechowski. LC 84-27076. 324p. 1985. text ed. 22.95 (ISBN 0-471-88523-1). Wiley.

Response of Colleges & Universities to Calls for Divestment. Christopher A. Coons. 148p. (Orig.). 1986. pap. 45.00 (ISBN 0-931035-08-2). IRRC Inc DC.

Response of Different Species to Total Body Irradiation. Ed. by J. J. Broerse & T. J. MacVittie. (Radiology Ser.). 1985. lib. bdg. 40.25 (ISBN 0-89838-678-0, Pub. by Martinus Nijhoff Netherlands). Kluwer Academic.

Response of Fish to Habitat Structure in Standing Water. Ed. by D. L. Johnson & R. A. Stein. LC 79-91186. (AFS North Central Division Special Publication Ser.: No. 6). 77p. 1979. pap. 6.00 (ISBN 0-913235-22-9). Am Fisheries Soc.

Response of Marine Animals to Petroleum & Specific Petroleum Hydrocarbons. Jerry M. Neff & Jack W. Anderson. 177p. 1981. 49.95x (ISBN 0-470-27215-5). Halsted Pr.

Response of Marine Animals to Petroleum & Specific Petroleum Hydrocarbons. Jerry M. Neff & Jack W. Anderson. (Illus.). x, 182p. 1981. 37.00 (ISBN 0-85334-953-3, Pub. by Elsevier Applied Sci England). Elsevier.

Response of Metals to High Velocity Deformation. Ed. by P. G. Shewmon & V. F. Zackay. LC 61-9441. (Metallurgical Society Conferences Ser.: Vol. 9). pap. 125.80 (ISBN 0-317-10938-3, 2000672). Bks Demand UMI.

Response of Multistory Concrete Structures to Lateral Forces. American Concrete Institute Staff. LC 72-93775. (American Concrete Institute Publications Ser.: SP-36). (Illus.). pap. 80.00 (ISBN 0-317-10936-7, 2002352). Bks Demand UMI.

Response of Natural Gas & Crude Oil Exploration & Discovery to Economic Incentives. Robert D. Spooner. Ed. by Stuart Bruchey. LC 78-22749. (Energy in the American Economy Ser.). (Illus.). 1979. lib. bdg. 21.00x (ISBN 0-405-12014-1). Ayer Co Pubs.

Response of Nuclei under Extreme Conditions. Ed. by R. A. Broglia & G. Bertsch. LC 87-32747. (Ettore Majorana International Science Series, Physical Sciences: Vol. 28). (Illus.). 422p. 1988. 79.50x (ISBN 0-306-42571-8, Plenum Pr). Plenum Pub.

Response of Rice to Fertilizer. pap. 5.75 (F413, FAO). UNIPUB.

Response of Social Work to the Depression. Jacob Fisher. 288p. 1980. pap. 11.95x (ISBN 0-87073-891-7). Schenkman Bks Inc.

Response of the Royal Army to the French Revolution: The Role & Development of the Line Army, 1793-1878. Samuel F. Scott. 1978. 39.95x (ISBN 0-19-822534-2). Oxford U Pr.

Response of Wheat to Fertilizers. Mikko Silanpaa. (Soils Bulletins: No. 12). 134p. 1971. pap. 8.50 (ISBN 92-5-100132-4, F1155, FAO). UNIPUB.

Response Set in Personality Assessment. Ed. by Irwin A. Berg. LC 66-28342. 1967. 39.75x (ISBN 0-202-25019-9). Irvington.

Response Surfaces: Design & Analyses. Khuri & Cornell. (Statistics Textbook & Monograph Ser.). 424p. 1987. 45.00 (ISBN 0-8247-7653-4). Dekker.

Response Television: Combat Advertising of the 1980's. John Witek. LC 81-66514. (Illus.). 240p. 1981. text ed. 29.95 (ISBN 0-8442-3064-2, Crain Bks). Natl Textbk.

Response Times: Their Role in Inferring Elementary Mental Organization. R. Duncan Luce. (Psychology Ser.: No. 8). (Illus.). 576p. 1986. 75.00 (ISBN 0-19-503642-5). Oxford U Pr.

Response to Adversity: Higher Education in a Harsh Climate. Gareth Williams & Tessa Blackstone. 153p. 1983. 21.00x (ISBN 0-8002-3886-9). Taylor & Francis.

Response to Contraception. Maxwell Roland. LC 72-93120. (Major Problems in Obstetrics & Gynecology: Vol. 5). pap. 44.50 (ISBN 0-317-26129-0, 2025002). Bks Demand UMI.

Response to Declining Enrollment: School-Closing in Suburbia. Jean Stinchcombe. (Illus.). 296p. (Orig.). 1984. lib. bdg. 30.25 (ISBN 0-8191-3696-4); pap. text ed. 15.50 (ISBN 0-8191-3697-2). U Pr of Amer.

Response to God's Love: A View of the Spiritual Life. Edward Carter. 184p. 1984. 9.95 (ISBN 0-317-14585-1). Loyola.

Response to Government Information Requests. Charles L. Duffney. (Corporate Practice Ser.: No. 29). 1982. 92.00 (ISBN 0-317-55345-3). BNA.

Response to Imperialism: The United States & the Philippine-American War, 1899-1902. Richard E. Welch, Jr. LC 78-11403. (Illus.). xvi, 215p. 1979. 22.00x (ISBN 0-8078-1348-6). U of NC Pr.

Response to Imperialism: The United States & the Philippine-American War, 1899-1902. Richard E. Welch, Jr. LC 78-11403. xvi, 215p. 1987. pap. 9.95x (ISBN 0-8078-4177-3). U of NC Pr.

Response to Industrialism. Samuel P. Hays. LC 57-6981. (Chicago History of American Civilization Ser). 1957. 17.00x (ISBN 0-226-32161-4); pap. 7.00x (ISBN 0-226-32162-2, CHAC9). U of Chicago Pr.

Response to Industrialism: Liberal Businessmen & the Evolving Spectrum of Capitalist Reform, 1886-1960. Kim McQuaid. Ed. by Stuart Bruchey. (American Business History Ser.). 310p. 1986. lib. bdg. 40.00 (ISBN 0-8240-8362-8). Garland Pub.

Response to Innovation: A Study of Popular Argument about New Mass Media. Robert E. Davis. Ed. by Garth S. Loweth. LC 75-21430. (Dissertations on Film Ser.). 1976. lib. bdg. 46.50x (ISBN 0-405-07533-2). Ayer Co Pubs.

Response to Modernity: A History of the Reform Movement in Judaism. Michael A. Meyer. (Studies in Jewish History). 512p. 1988. 39.95 (ISBN 0-19-505167-X). Oxford U Pr.

Response to Need: A Case Study of Adult Education Graduate Program Development in the Southeast. Charles E. Kozoll. LC 72-57. (Occasional Paper Ser.: No. 28). 60p. 1972. pap. 2.25 (ISBN 0-87060-051-6, OCP 28). Syracuse U Cont Ed.

Response to Oil & Chemical Marine Pollution. D. Cormack. (Illus.). 531p. 1983. 104.50 (ISBN 0-85334-182-6, Pub. by Elsevier Applied Sci England). Elsevier.

Response to Progressivism: The Democratic Party & New York Politics, 1902-1918. Robert F. Wesser. LC 86-5415. 288p. 1986. 35.00 (ISBN 0-8147-9213-8). NYU Pr.

Response to Prostitution in the Progressive Era. Mark T. Connelly. LC 79-24038. x, 261p. 1980. 27.50x (ISBN 0-8078-1424-5). U of NC Pr.

Response to Revolution: Imperial Spain & the Spanish American Revolutions, 1810-1840. Michael P. Costeloe. (Cambridge Iberian & Latin American Studies). 256p. 1986. 42.50 (ISBN 0-521-32083-6). Cambridge U Pr.

Response to Revolution: The United States & the Cuban Revolution, 1959-1961. Richard E. Welch, Jr. LC 84-25604. ix, 244p. 1985. 25.00x (ISBN 0-8078-1613-2); pap. 9.95x (ISBN 0-8078-4136-6). U of NC Pr.

Response to Student Writing. Sarah W. Freedman. 223p. 1987. pap. 11.95. NCTE.

Response Variability to Psychotropic Drugs. Ed. by W Janke. (International Series in Experimental Psychology). (Illus.). 272p. 1983. 50.00 (ISBN 0-08-028907-X). Pergamon.

Responses. David Cairns. LC 80-18152. (Music Ser.). 1980. Repr. of 1973 ed. 32.50 (ISBN 0-306-76047-9). Da Capo.

Responses of Oklahoma Urban Officials to Reductions of Federal Aid to Cities. William J. Pammer, Jr. & David R. Morgan. 27p. 1982. 2.00 (ISBN 0-318-01371-1). Univ OK Gov Res.

Responses of Plants to Environmental Stresses. J. Levitt. (Physiological Ecology Ser.). 1972. 85.00 (ISBN 0-12-445560-3). Acad Pr.

Responses of Plants to Environmental Stresses: Vol. I: Chilling, Freezing, & High Temperature Stresses. 2nd ed. J. Levitt. (Physiological Ecology Ser.). 1980. 40.00 (ISBN 0-12-445501-8). Acad Pr.

Responses of Plants to Environmental Stresses, Vol. 2: Water, Radiaton, Salt & Other Stresses. J. Levitt. LC 79-51680. (Physiological Ecology Ser.). 1980. 55.00 (ISBN 0-12-445502-6). Acad Pr.

Responses of the Presidents to Charges of Misconduct. C. Vann Woodward. 1974. pap. 10.00 (ISBN 0-440-05923-2). Delacorte.

Responses: On Paul de Man's Wartime Journalism. Ed. by Werner Hamacher et al. 176p. 1988. 25.00 (ISBN 0-8032-2352-8); pap. 12.95 (ISBN 0-8032-7243-X). U of Nebr Pr.

Responses: Prose Pieces, Nineteen Forty-Eight-Nineteen Seventy-Six. Richard Wilbur. LC 76-24903. 238p. 1976. pap. 3.95 (ISBN 0-15-676550-0, Harv). HarBraceJ.

Responses: Prose Pieces, 1948-1976. Richard Wilbur. LC 76-24903. 238p. 1976. 13.95 (ISBN 0-15-176930-3). HarBraceJ.

Responses to Crime. Lord Windlesham. (Illus.). 368p. 1987. 36.00 (ISBN 0-19-825583-7). Oxford U pr.

Responses to Crime: An Introduction to Swedish Criminal Law & Administration. Alvar Nelson. Tr. by Jerome L. Getz from Swedish. (New York University Criminal Law Education & Research Center Monograph: No. 6). vi, 90p. 1972. pap. text ed. 8.50x (ISBN 0-8377-0900-8). Rothman.

Responses to Elie Wiesel. Ed. by Harry J. Cargas. 286p. 15.00 (ISBN 0-686-95081-X); pap. 5.95 (ISBN 0-686-99458-2). ADL.

Responses to Industrialisation: The British Experience, 1780-1850. Malcolm I. Thomis. LC 75-45331. 194p. (Orig.). 1976. 25.00 (ISBN 0-208-01588-4, Archon). Shoe String.

Responses to Major Findings of Presidential Task Force on Food Assistance. Food Research & Action Center. 25p. 1984. 2.25 (26,017). NCLS Inc.

Responses to Participation at Work. M. Marchington. 232p. 1980. text ed. 37.95x (ISBN 0-566-02148-X). Gower Pub Co.

Responses to Poverty: Lessons from Europe. Ed. by Robert Walker & Roger Lawson. LC 83-25351. 340p. 1984. 32.50 (ISBN 0-8386-3222-X). Fairleigh Dickinson.

Responses to Religion: Studies in the Social Psychology of Religious Belief. Gary M. Maranell. LC 73-19860. xviii, 314p. 1974. 29.95x (ISBN 0-7006-0114-7). U Pr of KS.

Responses to Takeover Bids. 2nd ed. Arthur Fleisher. (Corporate Practice Ser.: No. 6). 1985. 92.00. BNA.

Responses to the Barclay Report, England & Wales, Scotland. Compiled by Janie Thomas. 1984. 25.00x (ISBN 0-317-40613-2, Pub. by Natl Soc Work). State Mutual Bk.

Responsibilities. William B. Yeats. 100p. 1971. Repr. of 1914 ed. 15.00x (ISBN 0-7165-1346-3, BBA 02110, Pub. by Cuala Press Ireland). Biblio Dist.

Responsibilities: A College Reader. Edward Quinn. 396p. 1987. pap. text ed. 14.95 scp (ISBN 0-06-045319-2, HarpC). Har-Row.

Responsibilities & Liabilities of Bank & Bank Holding Company Directors. Robert E. Barnett. 120p. 1985. pap. 10.00 (ISBN 0-317-30610-3, 4763). Commerce.

Responsibilities & Liabilities of Savings Institutions Directors. Robert E. Barnett. 112p. 1984. pap. 10.50 (ISBN 0-317-19244-2, 4828). Commerce.

Responsibilities: Its Sources & Limits. Geoffrey Vickers. (Systems Inquiry Ser.). 142p. (Orig.). 1980. pap. text ed. 10.95x (ISBN 0-914105-18-3). Intersystems Pubns.

Responsibilities of American Advertising: Private Control & Public Influence, 1920-1940. Otis Pease. LC 75-39266. (Getting & Spending: the Consumer's Dilemma). (Illus.). 1976. Repr. of 1958 ed. 20.00x (ISBN 0-405-08039-5). Ayer Co Pubs.

Responsibilities of Colleges & Universities: Proceedings. Pacific Northwest Conference On Higher Education, 1966. Ed. by Boyd A. Martin. LC 48-10303. 1966. pap. 5.00x (ISBN 0-87071-266-7). Oreg St U Pr.

Responsibilities of Corporate Officers & Directors under Federal Securities Laws. Clark. 160p. Date not set. pap. 10.00 (5208). Commerce.

Responsibilities of Corporate Officers & Directors under Federal Securities Law. Commerce Clearing House, Inc. 128p. 1985. 10.00 (ISBN 0-317-30611-1, 4752). Commerce.

Responsibilities of Corporate Officers & Directors under Federal Securities Laws. LC 86-216532. 154p. Date not set. price not set. Commerce.

Responsibilities of Insurance Agents & Brokers, 2 vols. Bertram Harnett. 1974. looseleaf set 195.00 (362); Updates. 1985 170.00; 1986 185.00. Bender.

Responsibilities of Journalism. Ed. by Robert Schmuhl. LC 83-40596. 160p. 1984. text ed. 13.95x (ISBN 0-268-01623-2). U of Notre Dame Pr.

Responsibilities of Journalism. Ed. by Robert Schmuhl. LC 83-40496. 147p. 1984. pap. text ed. 6.95 (ISBN 0-268-01624-0). U of Notre Dame Pr.

Responsibilities of the Novelist & Other Literary Essays. F. Norris. LC 68-26364. (Studies in Fiction, No. 34). 1969. Repr. of 1903 ed. lib. bdg. 49.95x (ISBN 0-8383-0269-6). Haskell.

Responsibilities of Users of Standardized Tests (RUST) write for info. (72179C). Am Assn Coun Dev.

Responsibilities to Future Generations: Environmental Ethics. Ed. by Ernest Partridge. LC 80-84401. 319p. 1981. 19.95 (ISBN 0-87975-153-3); pap. 15.95 (ISBN 0-87975-142-8). Prometheus Bks.

Responsibility. Glenn A. Cheney. LC 85-7321. (American Values First Bk.). (Illus.). 66p. (gr. 4-6). 1985. PLB 10.40 (ISBN 0-531-10045-6). Watts.

Responsibility. Nancy Pemberton & Janet Riehecky. LC 87-37557. (What Is It?--A Values Ser.). (Illus.). 32p. (gr. k-3). 1988. PLB 7.95 (ISBN 0-89565-418-0). Childs World.

Responsibility Accounting. (Financial Information Systems for Community Banks Ser.: Pt. 6). 32p. 1984. 45.00 (ISBN 0-317-66108-6, 386). Bank Admin Inst.

Responsibility & Culture. L. P. Jacks. 1924. 39.50x (ISBN 0-685-89778-8). Elliots Bks.

Responsibility & Liability of Public & Private Interests on Dams. 210p. 1976. pap. 12.00x (ISBN 0-87262-167-7). Am Soc Civil Eng.

Responsibility & Morality: Helping Children Become Responsible & Morally Mature. Larry C. Jensen & Karen M. Hughston. LC 79-10727. (Illus.). 1979. pap. 7.95x (ISBN 0-8425-1679-4). Brigham.

Responsibility, Character, & the Emotions: New Essays in Moral Psychology. Ed. by Ferdinand D. Schoeman. 400p. 1988. 49.50 (ISBN 0-521-32720-2); pap. 17.95 (ISBN 0-521-33951-0). Cambridge U Pr.

Responsibility Factor: Steps Towards Wholeness. Gary L. Holmgren. LC 85-90307. 1985. 15.00 (ISBN 0-932999-00-X). G L Holmgren Pubs.

Responsibility for Child Care: The Changing Role of Family & State in Child Development. Bernard Greenblatt. LC 76-50699. (Jossey-Bass Behavioral Science Ser.). pap. 83.30 (2027754). Bks Demand UMI.

Responsibility for Crime: An Investigation of the Nature & Causes of Crime & a Means of Its Prevention. Philip A. Parsons. LC 75-76683. (Columbia University. Studies in the Social Sciences: No. 91). Repr. of 1909 ed. 16.50 (ISBN 0-404-51091-4). AMS Pr.

Responsibility for Devalued Persons: Ethical Interaction Between Society, the Family, & the Retarded. Stanley Hauerwas. 122p. 1982. 16.25x (ISBN 0-398-04705-7). C C Thomas.

Responsibility for Rural-School Administration: Allocation of Responsibilities in the Administration of Schools in Rural Areas. Frank W. Cyr. LC 70-176703. (Columbia University. Teachers College. Contributions to Education: No. 579). Repr. of 1933 ed. 22.50 (ISBN 0-404-55579-9). AMS Pr.

Responsibility in Business: Issues & Problems. Blair J. Kolasa. LC 72-170645. 1972. pap. text ed. write for info. (ISBN 0-13-773739-4). P-H.

Responsibility in Health Care. George J. Agich. 1982. 39.50 (ISBN 90-277-1417-7, Pub. by Reidell Holland). Kluwer Academic.

Responsibility in Mental Disease. Henry Maudsley. Bd. with Treatise on Insanity. LC 77-72191. (Contributions to the History of Psychology Ser., Vol. III, Pt. C: Medical Psychology). 1978. Repr. of 1876 ed. 30.00 (ISBN 0-89093-167-4). U Pubns Amer.

Responsibility of Forms. Roland Barthes. Tr. by Richard Howard. (Illus.). 320p. 1985. 22.95 (ISBN 0-8090-8075-3); pap. 9.95 (ISBN 0-8090-1522-6). Hill & Wang.

Responsibility of Parent Companies for Their Subsidiaries. 128p. 1980. 6.50x (ISBN 92-64-12068-8). OECD.

Responsibility of States for Acts of Unsuccessful Insurgent Governments. Haig Silvanie. LC 68-58622. (Columbia University Studies in the Social Sciences: No. 457). Repr. of 1939 ed. 18.50 (ISBN 0-404-51457-X). AMS Pr.

Responsibility of States in International Law. C. Eagleton. Repr. of 1928 ed. 31.00 (ISBN 0-527-26050-9). Kraus Repr.

Responsibility of the Artist. Jacques Maritain. LC 70-150415. 120p. 1972. Repr. of 1962 ed. 15.00x (ISBN 0-87752-145-X). Gordian.

Responsibility of the Corporate Parent for Activities of a Subsidiary. Thomas J. Heiden et al. (Course Handbook Ser.). 198p. 1986. pap. 45.00 (B4-6750). PLI.

Responsibility of the Corporate Parent for the Activities of a Subsidiary, 1988. Thomas J. Heiden. 237p. 1988. pap. 45.00 (B4-6834). PLI.

Responsibility of the Individual Within Organizations Environments. Thomas M. Heather. 123p. 1987. pap. text ed. 12.95 (ISBN 0-939303-12-4). Educ Lrn Syst.

Responsibility or a Love Letter to My Son, the Hostage from His Father, the Political Prisoner. (Analysis Ser.: No. 8). 1982. pap. 10.00 (ISBN 0-686-42843-9). Inst Analysis.

Responsibility, Rights & Welfare: The Theory & Practice of the Welfare State. Ed. by J. Donald Moon. 256p. 1988. 30.00 (ISBN 0-8133-0521-7); pap. 14.95 (ISBN 0-8133-0522-5). Westview.

Responsibility Trap: A Blueprint for Treating the Alcoholic Family. Claudia Bepko & Jo A. Krestan. 320p. 1985. 26.95x (ISBN 0-02-902880-9). Free Pr.

Responsibity Accounting. (Financial Information Systems for Community Banks Ser.: Pt. 6). 82p. 1984. 45.00 (ISBN 0-317-66460-3, 386). Bank Admin Inst.

Responsible Administrator: An Approach to Ethics for the Administrative Role. 2nd, rev. ed. Terry L. Cooper. LC 86-3403. (Political Science Ser.). 230p. 1982. 22.50x (ISBN 0-8046-9292-0, 9292, Pub. by Kennikat). Assoc Faculty Pr.

Responsible Assertive Behavior: Cognitive-Behavioral Procedures for Trainers. Arthur J. Lange & Patricia Jakubowski. LC 76-1703. (Orig.). 1976. pap. text ed. 18.95 (ISBN 0-87822-174-3, 1743). Res Press.

Responsible Childbirth: How to Give Birth Normally & Avoid a Cesarean Section. Cynthia L. Duffy & Linda Meyer. LC 83-62295. 120p. (Orig.). 1984. pap. text ed. 9.95 (ISBN 0-88247-713-7). R & E Pubs.

Responsible Christian: A Guide for Moral Decision Making According to Classical Tradition. Vincent E. Rush. 288p. 1984. 10.95 (ISBN 0-8294-0448-1). Loyola.

Responsible Faith: Christian Theology in the Light of 20th-Century Questions. Hans Schwarz. LC 85-26657. 448p. 1986. text ed. 25.95 (ISBN 0-8066-2188-5, 10-5483). Augsburg.

Responsible Government: American & British. Stephen T. Early, Jr. & Barbara B. Knight. LC 80-29601. 336p. 1981. text ed. 24.95x (ISBN 0-88229-658-2); pap. text ed. 12.95x (ISBN 0-88229-776-7). Nelson-Hall.

Responsible Individualism. Wallace Johnson. LC 67-30828. 1967. 5.00 (ISBN 0-8159-6710-1). Devin.

Responsible Journalism. Deni Elliott. LC 86-1759. 1986. 29.95 (ISBN 0-8039-2611-1); pap. 14.95 (ISBN 0-8039-2612-X). Sage.

Responsible Parenthood in the Philippines. Ed. by Vitaliano R. Gorospe. 1970. wrps. 8.75 (ISBN 0-686-09499-9, Pub. by Ateneo Univ. Press). Cellar.

Responsible Parenthood: The Child's Psyche Through the Six-Year Pregnancy. Gilbert M. Kilman & Albert Rosenfeld. LC 79-3437. (Illus.). 348p. 1980. 14.95 (ISBN 0-03-040951-5). H Holt & Co.

Responsible Parenting among Men & Nations: A Challenge for Uncle Sam & the World. Stephen G. Burrows. 96p. 1981. 6.00 (ISBN 0-682-49752-5). Exposition-Phoenix.

Responsible Physician & Thanatology. Ed. by Stewart G. Wolff, Jr. et al. (Current Thanatology Ser.). 100p. 1988. pap. 14.95 (ISBN 0-930194-42-X). Ctr Thanatology.

Responsible Police Administration: Issues & Approaches. Lee W. Potts. LC 82-16059. 232p. 1983. 19.95 (ISBN 0-8173-0140-2). U of Ala Pr.

TITLE INDEX RESTATEMENT OF THE LAW

Responsible Public Speaking. Bobby R. Patton et al. 1983. pap. text ed. write for info. (ISBN 0-673-15363-0). Scott F.
Responsible Reader. Ed. by Linda Ziff. LC 87-60572. 488p. 1987. pap. text ed. write for info. (ISBN 0-312-00262-9); write for info. instr's. manual (ISBN 0-312-00263-7); write for info. instr's. ed. (ISBN 0-312-01309-4). St Martin.
Responsible Reciprocity. Ed. by Julia A. White. LC 83-61311. (Papers on International Issues: No. 5). (Orig.). 1983. pap. text ed. 4.00 (ISBN 0-935082-04-2). Southern Ctr Intl Stud.
Responsible Science: The Impact of Technology on Society. Ed. by Kevin Byrne. LC 86-45013. (Illus.). 160p. 1986. 14.45 (ISBN 0-06-250128-3, HarpR). Har-Row.
Responsible Self. H. Richard Niebuhr. LC 63-15955. 1978. pap. 8.95 (ISBN 0-06-066211-5, RD 266, HarpR). Har-Row.
Responsible Technology: A Christian Perspective. Stephen Monsma et al. 248p. (Orig.). 1986. pap. 12.95 (ISBN 0-8028-0175-7). Eerdmans.
Responsible Vision: The Philosophy of Julian Marfas. Harold Raley. 1980. 20.00x (ISBN 0-89217-004-2); pap. 8.95x (ISBN 0-89217-005-0). American Hispanist.
Responsiblity & Responsiveness. FESC. 1986. 45.00x (ISBN 0-907659-31-4, Pub. by FESC). State Mutual Bk.
Responsio Ad Lutherum, 2 Vols. St. Thomas More. Ed. by John M. Headley. LC 63-7949. (Complete Works of St. Thomas More Ser.: No. 5). 1969. Set. 85.00t (ISBN 0-300-01123-7). Yale U Pr.
Responsive Art. Judy Nagle. 428p. 1980. pap. text ed. 21.95 (ISBN 0-87484-627-7); write for info. instr's manual (ISBN 0-87484-212-3). Mayfield Pub.
Responsive Capitalism: Case Studies in Corporate Social Conduct. Earl A. Molander. (Management Ser.). (Illus.). 432p. 1980. pap. 23.95 (ISBN 0-07-042658-9). McGraw.
Responsive Care: Behavioral Interventions with Elderly Persons. Richard A. Hussian & Ronald L. Davis. LC 85-61467. 256p. (Orig.). 1985. pap. text ed. 16.95 (ISBN 0-87822-245-6). Res Press.
Responsive Communication: Patterns for Making Sense. Ron Scollon & Suzie Scollon. 80p. (Orig.). 1986. pap. 5.95 (ISBN 0-938975-17-X). Black Current.
Responsive Curriculum Development: Theory & Action. Glenys G. Unruh. LC 74-24476. (Illus.). 250p. 1975. 25.25x (ISBN 0-8211-2002-6); text ed. 22.50x 10 or more copies. McCutchan.
Responsive Environments. Bentley et al. 1987. pap. 38.95 (ISBN 0-85139-967-3). Van Nos Reinhold.
Responsive Faith. Millard Erickson. LC 87-81478. 157p. (Orig.). 1987. pap. 4.95 (ISBN 0-935797-29-7). Harvest Il.
Responsive Professional Education: Balancing Outcomes & Opportunities. Joan S. Stark et al. Ed. & frwd. by Jonathan D. Fife. LC 86-82077. (ASHE-ERIC Higher Education Reports, 1986: No. 3). 128p. 1986. pap. 10.00x (ISBN 0-913317-30-6). Assn Study Higher Ed.
Responsive Readings: Versions of Echo in Pastoral, Epic, & the Jonsonian Masque. Joseph Loewenstein. LC 84-40198. (Studies in English: No. 192). 256p. 1984. text ed. 22.00x (ISBN 0-300-03156-4). Yale U Pr.
Responsive Singing: Sabbath Morning Service. Robert Segal. 184p. 1972. 4.50x (ISBN 0-8381-0218-2). United Syn Bk.
Responsive Therapy: A Systematic Approach to Counseling Skills. Sterling Gerber. LC 85-21869. 250p. 1986. text ed. 29.95 (ISBN 0-89885-267-6); pap. text ed. 16.95 (ISBN 0-89885-269-2). Human Sci Pr.
Responsive Workplace: Employers & a Changing Labor Force. Sheila B. Kamerman & Alfred J. Kahn. 320p. 1987. 30.00 (ISBN 0-231-06480-2). Columbia U Pr.
Responsive Workplace: Employers & a Changing Labor Force. Sheila B. Kamerman & Alfred J. Kahn. 329p. 1988. pap. 14.50x (ISBN 0-231-06481-0). Columbia U Pr.
Responsiveness of Kindergarten Children to the Behavior of Their Fellows. Esther K. Harris. (SRCD M). 1946. 16.00 (ISBN 0-527-01538-5). Kraus Repr.
Respublica. LC 79-133727. (Tudor Facsimile Texts. Old English Plays: No. 25). Repr. of 1908 ed. 49.50 (ISBN 0-404-53325-6). AMS Pr.
Respublica Anglicana: The Historie of the Parliament. George Wither. 1966. 24.50 (ISBN 0-8337-3852-6). B Franklin.
Respuesta a La Guerra. Millard Lind. Orig. Title: Answer to War. 188p. 1963. pap. 1.50x (ISBN 0-8361-1149-4). Herald Pr.
Respuestas a Preguntas Dificles. Josh McDowell & Don Stewart. 224p. (Span.). 1986. pap. 4.50 (ISBN 0-8297-0689-5). Life Pubs Intl.
Respuestas Catolicas a Preguntas Fundamentalistas. Philip St. Roman. Tr. by Olimpia Diaz. 96p. (Orig.). 1987. pap. 2.50 (ISBN 0-89243-275-6). Liguori Pubns.
Ressassement Eternel. M. Blanchot. (Reimpressions G & B Ser.). 146p. (Fr.). 1970. 34.00 (ISBN 0-677-50425-X, PAP). Gordon & Breach.
Ressequie Family: 1888. 99p. 5.00 (ISBN 0-940748-41-X). Conn Hist Soc.
Rest & Redemption: A Study of the Biblical Sabbath. Neils-Erik Andreason. (Andrews University Monographs, Studies in Religion: Vol. XI). vii, 137p. 1978. pap. 3.95 (ISBN 0-943872-11-1). Andrews Univ Pr.
Rest Days, the Christian Sunday, the Jewish Sabbath & Their Historical & Anthropological Prototypes. Hutton Webster. LC 68-58165. 344p. 1968. Repr. of 1916 ed. 48.00x (ISBN 0-8103-3342-2). Gale.
Rest from the Quest. Elissa L. McClain. LC 84-80407. 173p. (Orig.). 1985. pap. 5.95 (ISBN 0-910311-13-7). Huntington Hse Inc.
Rest Here, My Heart. Maryhelen Clague. 1979. pap. 1.95 (ISBN 0-449-14284-1, GM). Fawcett.
Rest in Love. 2nd ed. D. H. Melhem. LC 78-58972. 109p. 1978. pap. 10.00x lmtd. ed (ISBN 0-935468-01-3). Dovetail.
Rest in Pieces. Ralph McInerny. (Father Dowling Mystery Ser.). 192p. 1985. 14.95 (ISBN 0-8149-0905-1). Vanguard.
Rest Is Silence. R. P. Jones. (Illus.). 1983. pap. write for info. (ISBN 0-913089-00-1). Broken Moon.
Rest Is Silence. R. P. Jones. (Illus.). 1984. pap. write for info. (ISBN 0-913089-01-X). Broken Moon.
Rest Is Silence. Luigi Pirandello. Tr. by Frederick May. LC 77-3405. 1977. lib. bdg. 25.50 (ISBN 0-8414-6773-0). Folcroft.
Rest Is Silence. Erico Verissimo. Tr. by L. C. Kaplan. Repr. of 1946 ed. lib. bdg. 35.00x (ISBN 0-8371-2318-6, VERS). Greenwood.
Rest Is Silence & Other Stories. Warren Beck. LC 63-12585. 132p. (Orig.). 1963. pap. 5.95 (ISBN 0-8040-0261-4, Pub. by Swallow). Ohio U Pr.
Rest of Faith. J. C. Metcalfe. 1962. pap. 2.95 (ISBN 0-87508-920-8). Chr Lit.
Rest of My Life. Laura R. Hunter & Polly H. Memhard. LC 81-85425. (Illus.). 112p. (Orig.). 1981. pap. 6.95 (ISBN 0-941834-01-8). Growing Pains Pr.
Rest of Our Lives. Bartlett Hall. 1987. 19.95 (ISBN 0-394-56145-7). Random.
Rest of Our Lives. Harvey Jackins. 522p. (Orig.). 1986. 15.00 (ISBN 0-913937-05-3); pap. 12.00 (ISBN 0-913937-06-1). Rational Isl.
Rest of the Afternoon Was Watermelon. Mary Santomauro. LC 78-53081. 1979. 14.95 (ISBN 0-87949-120-5). Ashley Bks.
Rest of the Dream: The Black Odyssey of Lyman Johnson. Wade Hall. 256p. 1988. 23.00 (ISBN 0-8131-1674-0). U Pr of Ky.
Rest of the Story. Finis M. Bruington. LC 87-71127. 1987. write for info. (ISBN 0-9616838-1-3). F M Bruington.
Rest of the Story...About Agriculture Today. 2nd. rev. ed. Harold L. Willis. (Illus.). 221p. (Orig.). 1983. pap. 8.95 (ISBN 0-912311-00-2). H L Willis.
Rest of the Week. Kenneth J. Roberts. LC 73-87984. 191p. Date not set. pap. text ed. 5.95. PAX Tapes.
Rest of Us: The Rise of America's Eastern European Jews. Stephen Birmingham. 384p. 1984. 19.95 (ISBN 0-316-09647-4). Little.
Rest of Us: The Rise of America's Eastern European Jews. Stephen Birmingham. 432p. 1985. pap. 4.50 (ISBN 0-425-08074-9). Berkley Pub.
Rest of Your Life. Allen R. McGinnis. Ed. by Nancy V. Thompson. LC 85-23731. 175p. 1986. 10.00 (ISBN 0-9616042-0-4). J & N Pubs.
Rest Principle: A Neurophysiological Theory of Behavior. John D. Sinclair. LC 80-17396. 240p. 1981. text ed. 29.95x (ISBN 0-89859-065-5). L Erlbaum Assocs.
Rest You Merry. Charlotte MacLeod. 224p. 1979. pap. 2.95 (ISBN 0-380-47530-8). Avon.
Restatement in the Courts, 53 vols. (Restatement of the Law-First Series-Library Edition). Set. 1378.50 (ISBN 0-686-90529-6). Am Law Inst.
Restatement of Economic Liberalism. Samuel Brittan. 1988. text ed. 39.95 (ISBN 0-391-03577-0); pap. text ed. 15.00 (ISBN 0-391-03578-9). Humanities.
Restatement of Judgments, Second, Volumes 1-3. 2nd ed. American Law Institute Staff. 1982. Vol. 1-3, 1415 Pgs. text ed. write for info. (ISBN 0-314-66807-1). Am Law Inst.
Restatement of the Law. write for info. West Pub.
Restatement of the Law - Second Series: Conflict of Laws Proposed Official Draft, 3 Pts. Incl. Pt. 1. 12.00 (ISBN 0-317-31926-4); Pt. 2. 10.00 (ISBN 0-317-31927-2); Pt. 3. 15.00 (ISBN 0-317-31928-0). Am Law Inst.
Restatement of the Law - Second Series: Conflict of Laws Tentative Draft. Incl. No. 9. 6.00 (ISBN 0-317-31931-0); No. 11. 7.25 (ISBN 0-317-31932-9); No. 12. 1.00 (ISBN 0-317-31933-7); No. 13. 3.50 (ISBN 0-317-31934-5). Am Law Inst.
Restatement of the Law, Agency. 63.00 (ISBN 0-686-40946-9). Am Law Inst.
Restatement of the Law-First Series: Agency. 2nd ed. 1983. 63.00 (ISBN 0-686-90430-3). Am Law Inst.
Restatement of the Law-First Series: Conflict of Laws, 4 vols. 1983. Set. 123.00 (ISBN 0-686-90433-8); Vol. 4. 27.50. Am Law Inst.
Restatement of the Law-First Series: Contracts, 3 vols. 2nd ed. 1983. Set. 105.00 (ISBN 0-686-90449-4); Appendix & 3 vols. 108.00. Am Law Inst.
Restatement of the Law-First Series: Judgments. 2nd ed. 1983. write for info. Am Law Inst.
Restatement of the Law-First Series: Restitution Including Reporters' Notes. Warren A. Seavey & Austin W. Scott. xxv, 1033p. 1937. incl. notes 21.00 (ISBN 0-686-90461-3). Am Law Inst.
Restatement of the Law-First Series: Security. xxiv, 596p. 1941. 21.00 (ISBN 0-686-90465-6). Am Law Inst.
Restatement of the Law: Foreign Relations Law of the United States. 2nd ed. American Law Institute. Ed. by Louis Henkin. 985p. 1986. text ed. write for info. (ISBN 0-314-30138-0). Am Law Inst.
Restatement of the Law, Foreign Relations Law of the United States(Revised) Tentative Draft No. 3. rev. ed. LC 82-245125. xxiv, 257p. 1982. 15.00. Am Law Inst.
Restatement of the Law, Foreign Relations Law of the United States: Tentative Draft No. 4. 1983. 15.00 (ISBN 0-317-27318-3). Am Law Inst.
Restatement of the Law, Foreign Relations Law of the United States: Tentative Draft No. 5. 1984. 15.00 (ISBN 0-317-27319-1). Am Law Inst.
Restatement of the Law, Foreign Relations Law of the United States: Tentative Draft No. 6. 1985. 15.00 (ISBN 0-317-27320-5). Am Law Inst.
Restatement of the Law of Restitution, Vols. 2 & 3. American Law Institute Staff. (Restatement of the Law). 855p. 1988. Vol. 2. text ed. 56.50 (ISBN 0-314-61453-2); Vol. 3. text ed. 56.50 (ISBN 0-314-64924-7). Am Law Inst.
Restatement of the Law, Property, 5 Vols. 503p. Vol. 1. 20.00 (ISBN 0-686-40949-3). Vol. 2. 40.00 (ISBN 0-686-40950-7); Vol. 3. 40.00 (ISBN 0-686-40951-5); Vol. 4. 20.00 (ISBN 0-686-40952-3); Vol. 5. 20.00 (ISBN 0-686-40953-1). Am Law Inst.
Restatement of the Law, Restitution. 1033p. 1937. 21.00 (ISBN 0-686-40954-X). Am Law Inst.
Restatement of the Law, Second, Agency, 3 Vols. 622p. 1958. Vol. 1. 63.00 (ISBN 0-686-40963-9). Am Law Inst.
Restatement of the Law, Second, Conflict of Laws, 4 Vols. Willis L. Reese & Austin W. Scott. 1971. 143.00 (ISBN 0-317-30674-X). Am Law Inst.
Restatement of the Law, Second, Conflict of Laws: Proposed Official Draft, Pt. I: Introduction; Domicil; Judicial Jurisdiction; Limitations on the Exercise of Judicial Jurisdiction; Judgments; Procedure. 507p. 1967. 12.00 (ISBN 0-317-30693-6). Am Law Inst.
Restatement of the Law, Second, Conflict of Laws: Proposed Official Draft, Pt. II: Wrongs; Contracts. 402p. 1968. 10.00 (ISBN 0-317-30697-9). Am Law Inst.
Restatement of the Law, Second, Conflict of Laws: Proposed Official Draft, Pt. III: Contracts; Property; Trusts; Status; Agency & Parnerships; Business Corporations; Administration of Estates. 608p. 1969. 15.00 (ISBN 0-317-30700-2). Am Law Inst.
Restatement of the Law, Second, Conflict of Laws: Tentative Draft No. 9: Wrongs. 194p. 1964. 6.00 (ISBN 0-317-30678-2). Am Law Inst.
Restatement of the Law, Second, Conflict of Laws: Tentative Draft No. 11-Recognition of Foreign Country Judgments; Administration of Estates; Procedure. 278p. 1965. 7.25 (ISBN 0-317-30680-4). Am Law Inst.
Restatement of the Law, Second, Conflict of Laws: Tentative Draft No. 12: The Reason for Conflict of Laws; Its Subject Matter & Meaning; Basic Principles. 34p. 1965. 1.00 (ISBN 0-317-30685-5). Am Law Inst.
Restatement of the Law, Second, Conflict of Laws: Tentative Draft No. 13: Property: Trusts (revised) 122p. 1965. 3.50 (ISBN 0-317-30690-1). Am Law Inst.
Restatement of the Law, Second, Contracts: Addition to Chapter 9, Scope of Contractual Obligations, 255 A. Event That Terminates a Duty; Additions to Chapter 10, Performance & Non-Performance, 268A.Effect of Subsequent Events on Duty to Pay Damages; Topic 4. Application of Performances. 452p. 1978. 5.00 (ISBN 0-317-30735-5). Am Law Inst.
Restatement of the Law, Second, Contracts, 6 vols. 1981. plus appendix 108.00 (ISBN 0-686-40965-5). Am Law Inst.
Restatement of the Law, Second, Contracts: Tentative Draft No. 10: Chapter 12. Mistake. 98p. 1975. 5.00 (ISBN 0-317-30723-1). Am Law Inst.
Restatement of the Law, Second, Contracts: Tentative Draft No. 11; Chapter 13, Misrepresentation, Duress & Undue Influence. 1976p. 1985. 8.00 (ISBN 0-317-30727-4). Am Law Inst.
Restatement of the Law, Second, Contracts: Tentative Draft No. 12: Chapter 13. Misrepresentation, Duress, & Undue Influence; Chapter 14. Unenforceability on Grounds of Public Policy. 359p. 1977. 10.00 (ISBN 0-317-30730-4). Am Law Inst.
Restatement of the Law, Second, Contracts: Tentative Draft No. 13: Chapter 15. Discharge by Assent or Alteration: Topic 1. The Requirement of Consideration; Topic 2. Substituted Performance; Substituted Contract, Accord, & Account Stated; Topic 3. Agreement of Rescission; Release & Contract Not to Sue; Topic 4. Alteration. 10.00 (ISBN 0-317-30734-7). Am Law Inst.
Restatement of the Law, Second, Contracts: Tentative Draft No. 14: Chapter 16. Remedies: Topic 1. In General; Topic 2.Enforcement by Specific Performance & Injunction; Topic 4. Restitution; Topic 5. Preclusion by Election & Affirmance. Revisions of: 18C. Mental Illness or Defect; 89292,300. Relief Including Restitution; Supplying a Term; 18B, Infants. Appendix: Pertinent sections of first Restatement. 307p. 1979. 17.50 (ISBN 0-317-30738-X). Am Law Inst.
Restatement of the Law, Second, Contracts: Tentative Draft No. 2: Formation of Contracts-Consideration; Joint & Several Promisors & Promisees. 312p. 1965. 8.00 (ISBN 0-317-30704-5). Am Law Inst.
Restatement of the Law, Second, Contracts: Tentative Draft No. 3: Contract Beneficiaries; Assignment of Contractual Rights & Delegation of Contractual Duties or Conditions. 292p. 1967. 8.00 (ISBN 0-317-30706-1). Am Law Inst.
Restatement of the Law, Second, Contracts: Tentative Draft No. 5: The Scope of Contractual Obligations. 208p. 1970. 7.50 (ISBN 0-317-30707-X). Am Law Inst.
Restatement of the Law, Second, Contracts: Tentative Draft No. 6: The Scope of Contractual Obligations: Effect of Adoption of a Writing, Scope as Affected by Usage. 87p. 1971. 4.00 (ISBN 0-317-30710-X). Am Law Inst.
Restatement of the Law, Second, Contracts: Tentative Draft No. 7: Chapter 9. The Scope of Contractual Obligations: Conditions. 79p. 1972. 5.00 (ISBN 0-317-30713-4). Am Law Inst.
Restatement of the Law, Second, Contracts: Tentative Draft No. 9: Chapter 10. Performance & Non-Performance Topic 3. Effect of Prospective Non-Performance: Chapter 11. Impracticability of Performance & Frustration of Purpose. 119p. 1974. 5.00 (ISBN 0-317-30717-7). Am Law Inst.
Restatement of the Law, Second, Foreign Relations Law of the United States. Adrian S. Fisher & Convey T. Oliver. 679p. 1965. 30.00 (ISBN 0-317-30742-8). Am Law Inst.
Restatement of the Law, Second: Foreign Relations Law of the United States. 679p. 1965. 26.00 (ISBN 0-686-40966-3). Am Law Inst.
Restatement of the Law, Second, Judgments, 3 Vols. Geoffrey C. Hazard & Benjamin Kaplan. 416p. 1982. write for info. Am Law Inst.
Restatement of the Law, Second, Judgments: Tentative Draft No. 1: Chapter 3. Former Adjudication: The Effects of Judicial Judgements Rendered in Civil Cases. 229p. 1973. 8.00 (ISBN 0-317-30760-6). Am Law Inst.
Restatement of the Law, Second, Judgments: Tentative Draft No. 2; Chapter 4. Parties & Other Persons Affected by Judgements: Topic 1. Parties & Persons Represented by Parties. 104p. 1975. 6.00 (ISBN 0-317-30762-2). Am Law Inst.
Restatement of the Law, Second, Judgments: Tentative Draft No. 4: Part I. Chapter 3. Former Adjudication: The Effects of Judicial Judgments Rendered in Civil Actions: Topic 2. Personal Judgments, Title 3. Issue Preclusion. Part II. Chapter 4. Parties & Other Persons Affected by Judgments: Topic 2. Substantive Legal Relationships Resulting in Preclusion. 110p. 1977. 6.00 (ISBN 0-317-30764-9). Am Law Inst.
Restatement of the Law, Second, Judgments: Tentative Draft No. 5: Chapter 2. Validity of Judgments: Topic 1. Notice; Topic 2. Territorial Jurisdiction; Topic 3. Subject Matter Jurisdiction; Chapter 3. Former Adjudication: Topic 2. Personal Judgments. 204p. 1978. 8.00 (ISBN 0-317-30770-3). Am Law Inst.
Restatement of the Law, Second, Judgments: Tentative Draft No. 6: Chapter 5. Relief from a Judgment: Topic 1. Relief Sought by a Party; Topic 2. Relief for Nonparties; Topic 3. Procedure for Obtaining Relief; Revision of 15. Contesting Subject Matter Jurisdiction. 164p. 1979. 10.00 (ISBN 0-317-30772-X). Am Law Inst.
Restatement of the Law, Second, Judgments: Tentative Draft No. 7: Chapter 1 and 6. 104p. 1980. 12.00 (ISBN 0-317-30790-8). Am Law Inst.
Restatement of the Law: Second, Property, Donative Transfers, 2 vols. American Law Institute Staff. Ed. by A. James Casner. 439p. 1985. text ed. write for info. (ISBN 0-314-97073-8). Am Law Inst.
Restatement of the Law, Second, Property: Donative Transfers; Tentative Draft, No. 1, Div. I. 154p. 1978. 7.00 (ISBN 0-686-91057-5). Am Law Inst.
Restatement of the Law, Second, Property: Donative Transfer; Tentative Draft, No. 2, Div. I. 189p. 1979. 12.00 (ISBN 0-686-91058-3). Am Law Inst.
Restatement of the Law, Second, Property: Donative Transfer; Tentative Draft, No. 3, Div. I. 252p. 1980. 14.00 (ISBN 0-686-91059-1). Am Law Inst.
Restatement of the Law, Second, Property: Donative Transfer; Tentative Draft, No. 4, Div I. 85p. 1981. 10.80 (ISBN 0-686-91060-5). Am Law Inst.
Restatement of the Law, Second, Property: Donative Transfer; Tentative Draft, No. 5, Div. I. 261p. 1982. 15.00 (ISBN 0-686-91061-3). Am Law Inst.

Restatement of the Law, Second, Property: Landlord & Tenant, 2 vols. 1977. Vol. 1, xxxix, 514p. 64.00 (ISBN 0-686-40969-8). Vol. 2, xxxv, 477p. Pt. I, xix, 247p. , 1973. 9.00 (ISBN 0-686-40970-1); Pt. II, xxi, 284p. , 1974. tentative draft no. 2 10.00 (ISBN 0-686-40971-X); Pt. IV, xxiv, 233p. , 1975. tentative draft no. 3 8.00 (ISBN 0-686-40972-8); Pt. V, xxxi, 328p. , 1976. tentative draft no. 4 12.00 (ISBN 0-686-40973-6). Am-Law-Inst.

Restatement of the Law, Second, Property: Second, Donative Transfers. American Law Institute Staff & A. James Casner. LC 83-2563. 1983. 50.00 (ISBN 0-314-73634-4); 50.00 (ISBN 0-314-73635-2). Am Law Inst.

Restatement of the Law, Second, Restitution. ALI-ABA Committee on Continuing Professional Education. LC 84-127641. 228p. 1937. 25.00. Am Law Inst.

Restatement of the Law-Second Series, 3 vols. 2nd ed. 1959. Set. 63.00 (ISBN 0-686-90500-8). Vol. 1, xxiv, 655p. Vol. 2, xxii, 516p. Vol. 3, xxviii, 783p. Am Law Inst.

Restatement of the Law-Second Series: Foreign Relations Law of the United States. 26.00 (ISBN 0-686-90431-1). Am Law Inst.

Restatement of the Law, Second, Torts. 1965. 119.00 set (ISBN 0-686-91039-7); 3 vols. 81.00 (ISBN 0-686-91040-0); 2 vols. 69.00 (ISBN 0-686-91041-9). Am Law Inst.

Restatement of the Law, Second, Torts. Tentative & Other Preliminary Drafts. Incl. No. 11. Restatement of the Law, Second, Torts. Tentative & Other Preliminary Drafts: Tentative Drafts. 145p. 1965. 5.00 (ISBN 0-686-91032-X); No. 12. Restatement of the Law, Second, Torts. Tentative & Other Preliminary Drafts: Tentative Draft. 158p. 1966. 5.00 (ISBN 0-686-91033-8); No. 13. Restatement of the Law, Second, Torts. Tentative & Other Preliminary Drafts: Tentative Draft. 172p. 1967. 6.50 (ISBN 0-686-91034-6). 1965. For 4 Vols. 119.00 (ISBN 0-686-91029-X); For 3 Vols. 81.00 (ISBN 0-686-91030-3); For 2 Vols. 69.00 (ISBN 0-686-91031-1). Am Law Inst.

Restatement of the Law, Second, Torts. Tentative & Other Preliminary Drafts: Tentative Drafts see Restatement of the Law, Second, Torts. Tentative & Other Preliminary Drafts.

Restatement of the Law, Second, Torts. Tentative & Other Preliminary Drafts: Tentative Draft see Restatement of the Law, Second, Torts. Tentative & Other Preliminary Drafts.

Restatement of the Law, Second, Torts: Tentative Draft No. 16. 215p. 1970. 7.50 (ISBN 0-317-30791-6). Am Law Inst.

Restatement of the Law, Second, Torts: Tentative Draft No. 17. 180p. 1971. 7.50 (ISBN 0-317-30797-5). Am Law Inst.

Restatement of the Law, Second, Torts: Tentative Draft No. 18. 102p. 1972. 6.50 (ISBN 0-317-30799-1). Am Law Inst.

Restatement of the Law, Second, Torts: Tentative Draft No. 19. 354p. 1973. 10.00 (ISBN 0-317-30805-X). Am Law Inst.

Restatement of the Law, Second, Torts: Tentative Draft No. 20. 321p. 1974. 10.00 (ISBN 0-317-30810-6). Am Law Inst.

Restatement of the Law, Second, Torts: Tentative Draft No. 21. 91p. 1975. 5.00 (ISBN 0-317-30812-2). Am Law Inst.

Restatement of the Law, Second, Torts: Tentative Draft No. 23. 75p. 1977. 5.00 (ISBN 0-317-30813-0). Am Law Inst.

Restatement of the Law, Second, Trusts, 3 Vols. Austin W. Scott. 783p. 1959. 99.00 (ISBN 0-317-30816-5). Am Law Inst.

Restatement of the Law, Security. 596p. 1941. 21.00 (ISBN 0-686-40955-8). Am Law Inst.

Restatement of the Law, Torts. 2nd ed. Vol. 1 & Vol. 2. 54.00 (ISBN 0-686-40956-6); Vol. 3. 32.00 (ISBN 0-686-40957-4); Vol. 4. 33.00 (ISBN 0-686-40958-2); Appendix 3 Vols. 81.00 (ISBN 0-686-40959-0); Appendix 2 Vols. 69.00 (ISBN 0-686-40960-4). Am Law Inst.

Restatement of the Law, Trusts. 2nd ed. 63.00 (ISBN 0-686-40961-2). Am Law Inst.

Restatement of the Laws, Second, Conflict of Laws, 3 Vols. 1971. 123.00 (ISBN 0-686-40964-7). Am Law Inst.

Restatements see Pimsleur's Checklists of Basic American Legal Publications.

Restaurant & Bar Lighting: A Bibliography. Mary E. Huls. (Architecture Ser.: A 1698). 5p. 1986. 3.00 (ISBN 1-55590-068-2). Vance Biblios.

Restaurant & Institutional Food Industry: Update. Business Communications Staff. 1988. pap. 1750.00 (ISBN 0-89336-609-9, GA-039N). BCC.

Restaurant & Institutional Food Service Industry. Business Communications Staff. 97p. 1985. 1250.00 (ISBN 0-89336-426-6, GA-039R). BCC.

Restaurant at the End of the Universe. Douglas Adams. 256p. 1982. 12.95 (ISBN 0-517-54535-7, Harmony). Crown.

Restaurant at the End of the Universe. Douglas Adams. 256p. 1982. pap. 3.95 (ISBN 0-671-53264-2). PB.

Restaurant Book: The Definitive Guide to Starting Your Own Restaurant. Richard Ware & James Rudnick. LC 85-25206. (Illus.). 224p. 1986. 17.95 (ISBN 0-8160-1248-2). Facts on File.

Restaurant Design. Reynaldo Alejandro. LC 87-61168. (Illus.). 256p. 1987. 49.95 (ISBN 0-86636-054-9). PBC Intl Inc.

Restaurant Finance: Handbook for Successful Management & Operations. John Ilich. 142p. Date not set. pap. 6.95 (ISBN 0-935650-08-3). Bengal Pr.

Restaurant Five Hundred: All-American Restaurant & Chef Yearbook. Camaro Editors. (Illus.). 1988. pap. 6.95 (ISBN 0-913290-71-8). Camaro Pub.

Restaurant: From Concept to Operation. Donald E. Lundberg. LC 83-10436. (Tourism-Hospitality Ser.). 308p. 1985. write for info. (ISBN 0-471-84227-3). Wiley.

Restaurant Guide for Lake Tahoe & Vicinity. Mike Parr & Gwen Parr. LC 87-50418. (Illus.). 240p. (Orig.). 1987. pap. 7.95 (ISBN 0-9618573-0-7). Tahoe Pub.

Restaurant Guide to the Finger Lakes. Charles DeMotte & Katherine W. Sundgren. (Illus.). 176p. 1988. pap. 6.95 (ISBN 0-935526-16-1). McBooks Pr.

Restaurant Industry Operations Report, 1986. National Restaurant Association Staff. 80p. 1986. pap. 40.00 (ISBN 0-317-57913-4, CS956). Natl Restaurant Assn.

Restaurant Industry Operations Report, 1985. National Restaurant Association Staff. 80p. 1985. pap. 38.00 (ISBN 0-317-57915-0, CS955). Natl Restaurant Assn.

Restaurant Jobs. Budd & Schwartz. (Career Awareness Plus Ser.). (Illus.). 64p. 1983. pap. text ed. 3.95 (ISBN 0-88102-004-4). Janus Bks.

Restaurant Language. Jim Richey. (Survival Vocabulary Ser.). (Illus.). 48p. (gr. 7-12). 1978. pap. 3.45 (ISBN 0-915510-29-4). Janus Bks.

Restaurant Management Guide. Robert T. Gordon. LC 84-19814. 274p. 1984. 79.50 (ISBN 0-87624-511-4, Inst Busn Plan). P-H.

Restaurant Manager's Waitress Training Resource Manual. Richard C. Ireland. 335p. 1974. 3 ring bdg. 39.95 (ISBN 0-89103-012-3). Ireland Educ.

Restaurant Operations & Controls: A Practical Guide. Marcel R. Escoffier & Shirley D. Escoffier. 256p. 1986. 59.95 (ISBN 0-13-774803-5). P-H.

Restaurant Owner's Handbook: Success Through Management Awareness. Jack C. Drewes. LC 87-32697. 356p. (Orig.). 1988. text ed. 49.95 (ISBN 0-945034-01-6); pap. text ed. 29.95 (ISBN 0-945034-00-8). Posh Pub.

Restaurant Reality: A Manager's Guide. Michael M. Lefever. (Illus.). 304p. (Orig.). 1988. pap. text ed. 29.95 (ISBN 0-442-25938-7). Van Nos Reinhold.

Restaurant Redbook: Los Angeles, Vol. 1. Ed. by Garth W. Bishop. (Illus.). 1988. pap. 4.95 (ISBN 0-913290-89-0). Camaro Pub.

Restaurant Redbook: San Francisco, Vol. 2. Ed. by Garth W. Bishop. (Illus.). 1987. pap. 4.95 (ISBN 0-913290-91-2). Camaro Pub.

Restaurant Server's Guide. rev ed. William B. Martin. LC 85-73177. (Fifty-Minute Ser.). (Illus.). 80p. (Orig.). 1987. pap. 6.95 (ISBN 0-931961-08-4). Crisp Pubns.

Restaurant Server's Guide to Quality Service. William Martin. 1988. 6.95 (110). Am Bartenders.

Restaurant Servers Guide to Quality Service. rev. ed. William B. Martin. (CRISP Publications 50-Minute Ser.). Date not set. 6.95. Human Res Dev Pr.

Restaurant Wordcards. Budd Schwartz & Richey Schwartz. (Career Awareness Plus Ser.). (Illus.). 16p. 1983. pap. text ed. 3.95 (ISBN 0-88102-008-7). Janus Bks.

Restaurant Words. Jim Richey. (Career Awareness Plus Ser.). (Illus.). 48p. 1983. pap. text ed. 3.95 (ISBN 0-88102-000-1). Janus Bks.

Restauranteurs' & Hoteliers' Purchasing Book. H. Berberoglu. 240p. 1981. pap. text ed. 13.95 (ISBN 0-8403-2348-4). Kendall-Hunt.

Restauranteurs & Innkeepers. (Work Throughout History Ser.). (Illus.). 160p. (YA) 1988. 16.95x (ISBN 0-8160-1451-5). Facts on File.

Restaurants, Clubs & Bars. Lawson. 1988. 69.95 (ISBN 0-442-20495-7). Van Nos Reinhold.

Restaurants of New Orleans. Roy F. Guste, Jr. (Illus.). 1987. pap. 12.95 (ISBN 0-393-30430-2). Norton.

Restaurants of New York: 1985 Edition. Seymour Britchky. 352p. 1984. pap. 9.95 (ISBN 0-671-46375-6). S&S.

Restaurants of New York: 1987. Seymour Britchky. 368p. 1986. 10.95 (ISBN 0-671-54457-8, Fireside). S&S.

Restaurants of New York: 1988. Seymour Britchky. 368p. 1987. 10.95 (ISBN 0-671-54458-6, Fireside). S&S.

Restaurants of New York, 1989: The Up-to-Date Guidebook to New York's Best, Most Famous, & Most Underrated Restaurants. Seymour Britchky. 368p. 1988. pap. 10.95 (ISBN 0-671-65823-9, Fireside). S&S.

Restaurants of San Fransisco. rev. ed. Patricia Unterman & Stan Sesser. LC 88-5027. (Orig.). 1988. pap. 9.95 (ISBN 0-87701-495-7). Chronicle Bks.

Restaurants U. S. A. Index of Articles, 1982-85. 32p. 1985. pap. 3.00 (ISBN 0-317-57843-X, NWIND). Natl Restaurant Assn.

Restauration et Gouvernement de Juillet see Histoire de l'Architecture Classique en France.

Restercize. Steven D. Raimondi. Ed. by Vicki Saunders. (Illus.). 50p. (Orig.). 1987. pap. 9.95 (ISBN 0-942491-00-9). Vandenburg Pr.

Resting Bell: Collected Poems. Anthony Barnett. 384p. (Orig.). 1987. 28.00 (ISBN 0-907954-06-5); Agneau 2 Paperbook Ser.: No. 4. pap. 16.00 (ISBN 0-907954-07-3). Small Pr Dist.

Resting Places. Norma L. Woodbridge. (Orig.). 1988. pap. 4.00 (ISBN 0-915541-25-4). Star Bks Inc.

Resting Places in East Anglia. Walter Marsden. 1988. 30.00x (Pub. by Ian Henry Pubns England). State Mutual Bk.

Restitution: A Guidebook for Juvenile Justice Practitioners. Troy Armstrong et al. LC 83-188220. (Juvenile Justice Textbook Ser.: No. 450). (Illus.). xii, 92p. 1983. 7.50 (ISBN 0-318-00254-X). Natl Juv & Family Ct Judges.

Restitution & Community Service as Dispositional Alternatives in Delinquency Cases. John L. Hutzler & Thomas S. Vereb. 57p. 1981. 5.00. Natl Juv & Family Ct Judges.

Restitution As a Criminal Sanction in North Carolina: Its Use & Effects. William N. Trumbull. pap. text ed. write for info. (ISBN 0-89143-021-0). U NC Inst Res Soc Sci.

Restitution As a Criminal Sentence: A Selected Bibliography. Anthony G. White. 1977. 1.50 (ISBN 0-686-19112-9, 1254). CPL Biblios.

Restitution: Background, Program, & Issues. National Center for State Courts Staff. 22p. 1977. manuscript 1.32 (NERO-010). Natl Ctr St Courts.

Restitution of All Things. Andrew Jukes. 194p. 1976. pap. text ed. 5.00 (ISBN 0-910424-65-9). Concordant.

Restitution of Decayed Intelligence: In Antiquities, Concerning the...English Nation. by the Studie & Travaile of R. Verstagen. Dedicated Unto the Kings Most Excellent Majestie. Richard Rowlands. LC 79-84134. (English Experience Ser.: No. 952). 380p. 1979. Repr. of 1605 ed. lib. bdg. 35.00 (ISBN 90-221-0952-6). Walter J Johnson.

Restitution of Man: C. S. Lewis & the Case Against Scientism. Michael D. Aeschliman. 96p. (Orig.). 1983. pap. 5.95 (ISBN 0-8028-1950-8). Eerdmans.

Restitution Program for Uninsured Offenders in Traffic Court. National Center for State Courts Staff. (Paul Reardon Ser.). 20p. 1981. manuscript 1.20 (PRS-020). Natl Ctr St Courts.

Restitution: The Land Claims of the Mashpee, Passamaquoddy, & Penobscot Indians of New England. Paul Brodeur. (Illus.). 155p. 1985. text ed. 18.95x (ISBN 0-939359-69-3). NE U Pr.

Restless Americans: The Challenge of Change in American History, Vol. 1. Edwin C. Rozwenc & Edward C. Martin. LC 76-180833. 336p. 1972. pap. text ed. 9.95 (ISBN 0-536-00734-9, JW). Krieger.

Restless Americans: The Challenge of Change in American History, Vol. 2. Edwin C. Rozwenc & Edward C. Martin. LC 76-180833. 368p. 1972. pap. text ed. 9.95 (ISBN 0-536-00735-7, JW). Krieger.

Restless Angels: The Friendship of Six Victorian Women-Frances Wright, Camilla Wright, Harriet Garnett, Frances Garnett, Julia Garnett Pertz, Frances Trollope. Helen Heineman. LC 82-12421. (Illus.). xvi, 224p. 1983. text ed. 26.95x (ISBN 0-8214-0673-6); pap. 12.95x (ISBN 0-8214-0674-4). Ohio U Pr.

Restless Caribbean: Changing Patterns of International Relations. Ed. by Richard Millett & W. Marvin Will. LC 78-19764. 330p. 1979. 38.95 (ISBN 0-275-90396-6, C0396). Praeger.

Restless Centuries: A History of the American People. 2nd ed. Peter Carroll & David W. Noble. LC 78-67974. 1979. pap. text ed. write for info. (ISBN 0-8087-2920-9). Burgess MN Intl.

Restless City & Christmas Gold. Cyprian Ekwensi. (African Writers Ser.). 1975. pap. text ed. 6.00 (ISBN 0-435-90172-9). Heinemann Ed.

Restless Dead: Ghostly Tales from Around the World. Daniel Cohen. (gr. 4 up). 1987. pap. 2.50 (ISBN 0-671-64373-8). Archway.

Restless Earth: A Report on the New Geology. Nigel Calder. 1978. pap. 9.95 (ISBN 0-14-004902-9). Penguin.

Restless Flames. Emma Merritt. (Hologram Romances Ser.). 1987. pap. 3.95 (ISBN 0-8217-2203-4). Zebra.

Restless Heart: The Life & Influence of St. Augustine. Michael Marshall. (Illus.). 192p. 1987. 19.95 (ISBN 0-8028-3632-1). Eerdmans.

Restless Is the Heart: A Perspective on Love & Violence & Their Intricate Relationships. Robert Kimball. LC 87-51007. 150p. 1987. text ed. 24.95x (ISBN 1-55605-021-6); pap. text ed. 14.95x (ISBN 1-55605-022-4). Wyndham Hall.

Restless Memories: Recollections of the Holocaust Years. rev., 2nd ed. Samuel P. Oliner. LC 85-82084. 215p. (Orig.). 1986. pap. 9.95 (ISBN 0-943376-28-9). Magnes Mus.

Restless Mind. Sam Fishman. 120p. 1982. 6.00 (ISBN 0-8184-0323-3, Pub. by Citadel Pr). Lyle Stuart.

Restless Nights. Dino Buzzati. Tr. & intro. by Lawrence Venuti. LC 82-73713. 144p. 1983. pap. 12.00 (ISBN 0-86547-100-2). N Point Pr.

Restless Oceans. LC 83-624. (Planet Earth Ser.). (gr. 7 up). 1983. lib. bdg. 19.94 (Pub. by Time-Life). Silver.

Restless Oceans. A. B. Whipple. (Planet Earth Ser.). (Illus.). 176p. (YA) (gr. 7 up). 1983. 18.60 (ISBN 0-8094-4340-6); lib. bdg. 22.60 (ISBN 0-8094-4341-4). Time-Life.

Restless Rednecks: Gay Tales of a Changing South. Roy F. Wood. LC 84-25298. 180p. (Orig.). 1985. pap. 7.95 (ISBN 0-912516-90-9). Grey Fox.

Restless Strangers: Nevada's Immigrants & Their Interpreters. Wilbur S. Shepperson. LC 78-117219. (Lancehead Ser). (Illus.). xiv, 287p. 1970. 8.95 (ISBN 0-87417-028-1). U of Nev Pr.

Restless Thoughts. Sandra-Lee Hutt. 32p. 1986. 5.75 (ISBN 0-8062-2833-4). Carlton.

Restless Tide. Georgia Bockoven. (Superromances Ser.). 384p. 1983. pap. 2.95 (ISBN 0-373-70082-2). Harlequin Bks.

Restless Tide. Richard M. Krause. LC 82-116089. 152p. 1981. write for info. NFID.

Restless Universe. 2nd ed. Max Born. (Illus.). viii, 315p. 1951. pap. 6.95 (ISBN 0-486-20412-X). Dover.

Restless Universe. Nigel Henbest & Heather Couper. (Illus.). 214p. 1982. 19.95 (ISBN 0-540-01069-3, Pub. by G Philip). Sheridan.

Restless Wanderers: Shakespeare & the Pattern of Romance. John Dean. Ed. by James Hogg. (Elizabethan & Renaissance Studies). 360p. (Orig.). 1979. pap. 15.00 (ISBN 3-7052-0731-8, Pub. by Salzburg Studies). Longwood Pub Group.

Restless Water. Harriet Door. 70p. (Orig.). 1983. pap. 7.95 (ISBN 0-932662-47-1). St Andrews NC.

Restless Wind. Dorothy Garlock. 384p. (Orig.). 1986. pap. 3.95 (ISBN 0-445-20173-8, Pub. by Popular Lib). Warner Bks.

Restless Yearning. Alison Tyler. (Candlelight Ecstasy Ser.: No. 490). (Orig.). 1987. pap. 2.25 (ISBN 0-440-17452-X). Dell.

Restless Youth. Fedor V. Gladkov. Tr. by R. Parker & V. Scott. LC 75-39000. (Soviet Literature in English Translation Ser.). (Illus.). 265p. 1976. Repr. of 1958 ed. 21.00 (ISBN 0-88355-403-8). Hyperion-Conn.

Reston Directory of Online Data Bases. Jay M. Shafritz & Louis Alexander. 1984. 36.00 (ISBN 0-8359-6668-2, Reston); pap. 26.95 (ISBN 0-8359-6666-6). P-H.

Reston Home Owners Association: A Case Study in New Community Management. Karl J. Ingebritsen. Ed. by Dianne Ader-Brin. 53p. 1977. pap. 10.95 (ISBN 0-912104-26-0, 851). Inst Real Estate.

Restoration. Neva Coyle. 50p. (Orig.). 1985. saddle stitched 2.95 (ISBN 0-87123-851-9). Bethany Hse.

Restoration, Vol. 1. Ruth Norman & Jeff Swanson. (Illus.). 250p. 1981. 8.95 (ISBN 0-932642-66-7). Unarius Pubns.

Restoration, Vol. 2. Ruth Norman. (Illus.). 250p. (Orig.). pap. 8.95 (ISBN 0-932642-67-5). Unarius Pubns.

Restoration: A Political & Religious History of England & Wales 1658-1667. Ronald Hutton. (Illus.). 379p. 1985. 29.95x (ISBN 0-19-822698-5). Oxford U Pr.

Restoration: A Political & Religious History of England & Wales 1658-1667. Ronald Hutton. (Illus.). 400p. 1987. pap. 12.95 (ISBN 0-19-285183-7). Oxford U Pr.

Restoration Adaptations. Ed. by Edward A. Langhans. LC 78-66611. (Eighteenth Century English Drama Ser.). 1980. lib. bdg. 73.00 (ISBN 0-8240-3575-5). Garland Pub.

Restoration Adaptations of Early 17th Century Comedies. Arthur Gewirtz. LC 82-15937. 214p. 1983. lib. bdg. 30.50 (ISBN 0-8191-2722-1); pap. text ed. 13.25 (ISBN 0-8191-2723-X). U Pr of Amer.

Restoration & Early Eighteenth-Century English Literature, 1660-1740: A Selected Bibliography of Resource Materials. Roger D. Lund. LC 79-87585. (Selected Bibliographies in Language & Literature Ser.: No. 1). 42p. 1980. pap. 8.00x (ISBN 0-87352-950-2, SB1). Modern Lang.

Restoration & Eighteenth Century see St. James Reference Guide to English Literature.

Restoration & Eighteenth Century Comedy. Ed. by Scott McMillin. (Critical Editions Ser.). 1973. pap. 12.95x (ISBN 0-393-09997-0). Norton.

Restoration & Eighteenth-Century Poetry 1660-1780. Eric Rothstein. (English Poetry Ser.). 256p. pap. 10.95x (ISBN 0-7102-0552-X). Routledge Chapman & Hall.

Restoration & Eighteenth-Century Theatre Research: Bibliographical Guide, 1900-1968. Carl J. Stratman et al. LC 71-112394. 822p. 1971. 25.00x (ISBN 0-8093-0469-4). S Ill U Pr.

Restoration & Eighteenth Century Theatre Research Bibliography, 1961-68. Carl J. Stratman et al. LC 75-79626. 1969. 10.50x (ISBN 0-87875-000-2). Whitston Pub.

Restoration & Preservation of Vintage & Classic Cars. 2nd ed. Jonathan Wood. 279p. 21.95 (ISBN 0-85429-391-4, 391, Pub. by G T Foulis Ltd). Haynes Pubns.

Restoration & Reaction 1815-1848. Andre Jardin & Andre-Jean Tudesq. Tr. by Elborg Forster. LC 83-5340. (Cambridge History of Modern France: No. 1). (Illus.). 416p. 1984. 77.50 (ISBN 0-521-25241-5). Cambridge U Pr.

Restraint Technologies: Front Seat Occupant Protection. 1987. 58.00 (ISBN 0-89883-961-0, SP690). Soc Auto Engineers.

Restraint Technologies: Rear Seat Occupant Protection. 1987. 36.00 (ISBN 0-89883-962-9, SP691). Soc Auto Engineers.

Restraints on War: Studies in the Limitation of Armed Conflict. Ed. by Michael Howard. 1979. 28.00x (ISBN 0-19-822545-8). Oxford U Pr.

Restricted Advertising & Competition: The Case of Retail Drugs. John F. Cady. 1976. pap. 5.00 (ISBN 0-8447-3207-9). Am Enterprise.

Restricted & General Dimensional Analysis. C. I. Staicu. 303p. 1982. 45.00 (ISBN 0-85626-300-1). Abacus Pr.

Restricted Country. Joan Nestle. 184p. 1987. 18.95 (ISBN 0-932379-38-9); pap. 8.95 (ISBN 0-932379-37-0). Firebrand Bks.

Restricted Orbit Equivalence. D. Rudolph. LC 84-28119. 150p. 1985. pap. text ed. 20.00 (MEMO-323). Am Math.

Restricting the Concept of Free Seas: Modern Maritime Law Re-Evaluated. George P. Smith, 2nd. LC 79-10502. 260p. 1980. 17.50 (ISBN 0-88275-998-1). Krieger.

Restriction Endonucleases & Methylases. J. G. Chirikjian. (Geng Amplification & Analysis Ser.: Vol. 5). 1987. 69.00 (ISBN 0-444-01285-0). Elsevier.

Restriction of Output Among Unorganized Workers. Stanley B. Mathewson. LC 68-25565. (Masterworks in Industrial Relations Ser.). 254p. 1969. 5.95x (ISBN 0-8093-0395-7); pap. 2.45x (ISBN 0-8093-0396-5). S Ill U Pr.

Restrictions of Advertising by Media & Selected Products in 15 Countries of the Middle East & Africa. 43p. 1986. 25.00. Intl Advertising Assn.

Restrictions of Foreign Real Estate Ownership. International Real Estate Institute Staff. (Illus.). 92p. 1988. pap. 28.50 (ISBN 0-935988-28-9). Todd Pub.

Restrictions on Advertising by Media & Selected Products in 14 Countries of Asia. J. Neelankavil. 41p. 1986. 25.00. Intl Advertising Assn.

Restrictions on Advertising by Media & Selected Products in 16 Countries of Europe. James Neelankavil. 44p. 1985. non-members 25.00 (ISBN 0-318-19253-5); members 15.00. Intl Advertising Assn.

Restrictions on Advertising by Media & Selected Products in 12 Countries of the Americas. James P. Neelankavil. 37p. 1986. 25.00 (ISBN 0-318-22261-2). Intl Advertising Assn.

Restrictions on Business Mobility: Political Rhetoric & Economic Reality. Richard B. McKenzie. 1979. pap. 7.00 (ISBN 0-8447-3338-5). Am Enterprise.

Restrictions on the Right to Freedom of Expression in the German Democratic Republic. LC 84-227331. (Amnesty International Briefing). Date not set. price not set. Amnesty Intl USA.

Restrictive Business Practices, Transnational Corporations & Development. Frank Long. (Dimensions of International Business Ser.). 192p. 1981. lib. bdg. 19.00 (ISBN 0-89838-057-X, Pub. by Martinus Nijhoff). Kluwer Academic.

Restrictive Practices in the Building Industry. Frank Knox & Jossleyn Hennessy. (Institute of Economic Affairs Research Monographs: No. 1). (Illus., Orig.). 1969. pap. 2.50 technical (ISBN 0-685-20619-X, OW0039768). Transatl Arts.

Restructuring a Framework for Assessment of Science & Technology as a Driving Power for Social Development: A Biosocial Approach. 22p. 1981. pap. 5.00 (ISBN 92-808-0179-1, TUNU130, UNU). UNIPUB.

Restructuring Alliance Commitments. Amos A. Jordan et al. (CSIS Significant Issues Ser.). 1988. write for info. CSI Studies.

Restructuring American Education: Innovations & Alternatives. Ed. by Ray C. Rist. LC 75-186712. 250p. 1972. 26.95 (ISBN 0-87855-037-2); pap. text ed. 12.95x (ISBN 0-87855-533-1). Transaction Bks.

Restructuring American Foreign Policy. Ed. by John D. Steinbruner. 200p. 1988. 29.95x (ISBN 0-8157-8144-X); pap. 10.95x (ISBN 0-8157-8143-1). Brookings.

Restructuring Domination: Industrialists & the State in Ecuador. Catherine M. Conaghan. LC 88-1335. (Pitt Latin American Ser.). 216p. 1988. 28.95x (ISBN 0-8229-3826-X). U of Pittsburgh Pr.

Restructuring Education: Hightlights of a Conference. Ed. by Melissa A. Berman. (Report Ser.: No. 902). v, 46p. (Orig.). 1987. pap. text ed. 30.00 (ISBN 0-8237-0345-2). Conference Bd.

Restructuring Health Policy: An International Challenge. Ed. by John M. Virgo. 500p. (Orig.). 1986. pap. 25.00 (ISBN 0-914943-02-2). IHEMI.

Restructuring Hospital Quality Assurance: The New Guide for Health Care Providers. Jean G. Carroll. LC 84-71132. 225p. 1984. 27.50 (ISBN 0-87094-541-6). Dow Jones-Irwin.

Restructuring of American Religion: Society & Faith since World War II. Robert Wuthnow. Ed. by John F. Wilson. (Studies in Church & State). 456p. 1988. text ed. 25.00 (ISBN 0-691-07328-7). Princeton U Pr.

Restructuring of Industrial Economies & Trade with Developing Countries. Santosh Mukherjee. (WEP Study Ser.). viii, 110p. 1978. pap. 15.75 (ISBN 92-2-102000-2, ILO1096, ILO). UNIPUB.

Restructuring of Manufacturing Industry: The Experience of the Textile Industry in Pakistan, Philippines, Portugal & Turkey. Barend A. De Vries & Willem Brakel. (Working Paper: No. 558). 59p. 1983. 5.00 (ISBN 0-8213-0151-9, WP 0558). World Bank.

Restructuring of Property Tax Administration. M. A. Muttalib & Mohd A. Kahn. 148p. 1985. text ed. 15.95x (ISBN 0-86590-729-3, Pub. by Sterling Pubs India). APT Bks.

Restructuring of Social & Political Theory. Richard J. Bernstein. LC 76-12544. 310p. 1978. pap. 12.95x (ISBN 0-8122-7742-2). U of Pa Pr.

Restructuring Proposals: Measuring Competition in Numerical Grids. Betty Bock. (Report Ser: No. 619). 177p. (Orig.). 1974. pap. 12.50 (ISBN 0-8237-0050-X). Conference Bd.

Restructuring Steelmills for the '90s. 334p. 1987. pap. text ed. 90.00x (ISBN 0-904357-91-0). IMM-North Am.

Restructuring the Automobile Industry: A Study of Firms & States in Modern Capitalism. Dennis P. Quinn. (Columbia Studies in Business, Government & Society). (Illus.). 416p. 1987. 40.00 (ISBN 0-231-06524-8). Columbia U Pr.

Restructuring the City: The Political Economy of Urban Redevelopment. rev. ed. Norman I. Fainstein & Susan S. Fainstein. (Illus.). 297p. 1986. pap. text ed. 20.95 (ISBN 0-582-28619-0). Longman.

Restructuring the Economic Order: The Role of Law & Lawyers: Proceedings of the Colloquium Organized by the Department of International & Economic Law on June 12 & 13, 1986, on the Occasion of the 350th Anniversary of the University of Utrecht. P. van Dijk. LC 86-33814. 1987. 61.00 (ISBN 9-06-544275-8). Kluwer Academic.

Restructuring the Regions: Analysis, Policy Model & Prognosis. OECD Staff & David Wadley. 172p. (Orig.). 1986. pap. 22.00 (ISBN 92-64-12868-9). OECD.

Restructuring the World Economy. Joyce Kolko. LC 87-46052. 336p. 1988. 24.95 (ISBN 0-394-55920-7); pap. 14.95 (ISBN 0-394-75900-1). Pantheon.

Restructuring Universities: Politics & Power in the Management of Change. Geoffrey Walford. 185p. 1987. 37.95 (ISBN 0-7099-3694-X, Pub. by Croom Helm UK). Routledge Chapman & Hall.

Resuemierende Auswahlbibliographie Zur Neueren Sowjetischen Sprachlehrforschung (Gesteuerter Fremdsprachenerwerb) Rupprecht S. Baur et al. (Language & Literary Ser. in Eastern Europe: No. 3). lxviii, 318p. 1980. 52.00x (ISBN 90-272-1504-9). Benjamins North Am.

Results & Evaluation of New Methodology in Cardiology: Proceedings of the Cardiovascular Disease Conference, 8th, Snowmass at Aspen, Colorado, Jan. 10-14, 1977. Cardiovascular Disease Conference Staff. Ed. by J. H. Vogel. (Advances in Cardiology Ser.: Vol. 22). 1977. 90.00 (ISBN 3-8055-2748-9). S Karger.

Results & Problems in Combinatorial Geometry. Vladimir G. Boltjansky et al. Tr. by B. Bollobas & A. Harris. (Illus.). 112p. 1985. 32.50 (ISBN 0-521-26298-4); pap. 9.95 (ISBN 0-521-26923-7). Cambridge U Pr.

Results Book. Wally Minto. 174p. 1976. 8.95 (ISBN 0-89036-112-6). Coleman Pub.

Results for Retailers. Larry Notman. (Illus.). 1976. pap. 2.50x (ISBN 0-918488-02-8). Newspaper Serv.

Results from the First Mathematics Assessment of the National Assessment of Educational Progress. Thomas Carpenter et al. LC 78-2345. 144p. 1978. pap. 9.00 (ISBN 0-87353-123-X). NCTM.

Results from the Second Mathematics Assessment of the NAEP. Ed. by Mary K. Corbitt. LC 81-4322. 167p. 1981. 9.00 (ISBN 0-87353-172-8). NCTM.

Results from Two National Surveys of Philanthropic Activity. James N. Morgan et al. 204p. (Orig.). 1979. pap. 12.00x (ISBN 0-87944-246-8). Inst Soc Res.

Results in Neuroanatomy, Motor Organization, Cerebral Circulation & Modelling. Ed. by K. Lissak. (Recent Developments of Neurobiology in Hungary Ser.: Vol. 8). 1979. cancellrd 24.50 (ISBN 963-05-1594-6, Pub. by Akademiai Kaido Hungary). IPS.

Results in Neuroanatomy, Motor Organization, Cerebral Circulation & Modelling: Recent Developments in Neurobiology in Hungary, Vol. VIII. Ed. by K. Lissak. 1981. 60.00x (ISBN 0-569-08549-7, Pub. by Collets (UK)). State Mutual Bk.

Results in Neuroanatomy, Neurochemistry, Neurophysiology & Neuropathology. L. Lissak. (Recent Developments in Neurobiology in Hungary Ser.: Vol. 9). 1983. cancelled 28.00 (ISBN 963-05-2947-5, Pub. by Akademiai Kaido Hungary). IPS.

Results in Neuroanatomy, Neurochemistry, Neurophysiology & Neuropathy: Recent Developments of Neurobiology in Hungary 1X. K. Lissak. 234p. 1982. 143.00x (ISBN 0-569-08739-2, Pub. by Collets (UK)). State Mutual Bk.

Results in Neurochemistry, Neuroendocrinology, Neurophysiology & Behavior, Neuropharmacology, Neuropathology, Cybernetics, Vol. 5. Lissak. 1978. cancelled 19.50 (ISBN 963-05-0595-9, Pub. by Akademiai Kaido Hungary). IPS.

Results in Neuroendocrinology, Neurochemistry & Sleep Research. Ed. by K. Lissak. (Recent Developments of Neurobiology in Hungary Ser.: Vol. 7). 1978. cancelled 19.50 (ISBN 963-05-1587-3, Pub. by Akademiai Kaido Hungary). IPS.

Results Kit: How to Hire, Reward & Promote Winners. James J. Kubeck & Thomas J. Doran, Jr. LC 81-65592. (Illus.). 110p. 1981. 99.00 (ISBN 0-939550-00-8). DK Halcyon.

Results of Emancipation. facs. ed. Augustin Cochin. Tr. by Mary L. Booth. LC 76-83942. (Black Heritage Library Collection Ser). 1862. 20.50 (ISBN 0-8369-8544-3). Ayer Co Pubs.

Results of Probation. Ed. by L. Radzinowicz & J. W. Turner. (Cambridge Studies in Criminology: Vol. 10). pap. 16.00 (ISBN 0-8115-0424-7). Kraus Repr.

Results of Slavery. facs. ed. Augustin Cochin. Tr. by Mary L. Booth. LC 73-83960. (Black Heritage Library Collection). 1863. 25.50 (ISBN 0-8369-8698-9). Ayer Co Pubs.

Results of Slavery: Work Crowned by the Institute of France. facsimile ed. Augustin Cochin. Tr. by M. L. Booth. LC 70-109619. (Select Bibliographies Reprint Ser). 1863. 25.50 (ISBN 0-8369-5228-6). Ayer Co Pubs.

Results of the Fifth George Vanderbilt Expedition (1941) Bahamas, Caribbean Sea, Panama, Galapagos Archipelago & Mexican Pacific Islands. George Vanderbilt. (Monograph: No. 6). (Illus.). 583p. (Orig.). 1944. pap. 26.00 (ISBN 0-910006-15-6). Acad Nat Sci Phila.

Results of the First Workshop on Standards in Geothermics. Ed. by R. Haenel & M. Gupta. (Zentralblatt fuer Geologie Ser.). (Illus.). 184p. 1983. pap. text ed. 72.50x (ISBN 0-318-03701-7). Lubrecht & Cramer.

Results of the Nineteen Eighty Bank Postal Survey: Bank Postal Operations & Expenses. 45.00 (ISBN 0-686-95691-5, 064100); members 30.00 (ISBN 0-686-99575-9). Am Bankers.

Results of the Royal Society Joint-Air-Sea Interaction Project (JASIN) Proceedings. Royal Society Discussion Meeting, June 2-3, 1982. Intro. by H. Charnock & R. T. Pollard. (Phil. Trans Royal Society, Series A: Vol. 308). (Illus.). 229p. 1983. Repr. text ed. 70.00x (ISBN 0-85403-206-1, Pub. by Royal Soc London). Scholium Intl.

Results of the School Health Education Evaluation. 68p. (Special Issue of the Journal of School Health). 1985. 5.50. Am Sch Health.

Results of the System of Separate Confinement As Administered at the Pentonville Prison. John T. Burt. LC 83-49229. (Crime & Punishment in England 1850-1912 Ser.). 287p. 1984. lib. bdg. 35.00 (ISBN 0-8240-6203-5). Garland Pub.

Results: Results see Analysis of Emergency Medical Services in Austin, Texas.

Resume & Cover Letter Writing Guide. Carey E. Harbin. 36p. (Orig.). 1988. pap. text ed. 5.95 (ISBN 0-918995-01-9). Voc Offers.

Resume Catalog: 200 Damn Good Examples. Yana Parker. LC 87-7057. 320p. (Orig.). 1988. pap. 9.95 (ISBN 0-89815-219-4). Ten Speed Pr.

Resume de l'Humour. Wilmac. (Fr.). 1962. pap. text ed. 3.45 (ISBN 0-940630-20-6, T-7151 (WRS-660)). Playette Corp.

Resume de Metaphysique Integral Sur les Traces de la Religion Perenne see Survey of Metaphysics & Esoterism.

Resume for Murder. Claire McCormick. 1986. pap. 2.95 (ISBN 0-8027-3165-1). Walker & Co.

Resume Handbook: How to Write Outstanding Resumes & Cover Letters for Every Situation. David V. Hizer & Arthur D. Rosenberg. 144p. 1987. pap. 5.95 (ISBN 0-937860-61-1). Adams Inc MA.

Resume II: Artists, Galleries & Craftspersons of the Door Penisula. Jim Legault. (Illus.). 64p. (Orig.). 1982. 12.75 (ISBN 0-933072-02-3); pap. 6.50 (ISBN 0-933072-03-1). Golden Glow.

Resume Kit. Richard H. Beatty. LC 83-23451. 265p. 1984. pap. 9.95 (ISBN 0-471-88148-1). Wiley.

Resume of a Theory of Language. Louis Hjelmslev. Ed. by Francis J. Whitfield. 312p. 1976. 30.00x (ISBN 0-299-07040-9). U of Wis Pr.

Resume of the Colubrid Snakes of the Genus Tantilla of South America. Larry D. Wilson. (Contributions in Biology & Geology Ser.: No. 68). 32p. 1986. 5.95 (ISBN 0-89326-121-1). Milwaukee Pub Mus.

Resume Power. rev. ed. Tom Washington. 287p. 1988. pap. 8.95 (ISBN 0-931213-04-5). Mount Vernon Pr.

Resume Power: Selling Yourself on Paper. Tom Washington. LC 84-20779. (Orig.). 1985. pap. 8.95 (ISBN 0-931213-03-7). Mount Vernon Pr.

Resume Preparation Manual. 1978. 5.95 (ISBN 0-89584-001-4). Catalyst.

Resume Workbook: A Personal Career File for Job Applications. 5th ed. Carolyn F. Nutter. LC 77-17412. (gr. 9-12). 1978. softcover 6.75 (ISBN 0-910328-00-5). Carroll Pr.

Resume Writer's Handbook. 2nd ed. Michael H. Smith. LC 85-45235. (Illus.). 192p. (Orig.). 1987. pap. 6.95 (ISBN 0-06-463717-4, EH 717, B&N Bks). Har-Row.

Resume Writing: A Comprehensive How-To-Do-It Guide. 3rd ed. Burdette E. Bostwick. LC 85-19698. 323p. 1985. 19.95 (ISBN 0-471-81693-0); pap. 9.95 (ISBN 0-471-81683-3). Wiley.

Resume Writing for the Professional Nurse. Nancy Kuzmich. (Illus.). 110p. 1988. 34.95 (ISBN 0-916780-31-7). CES.

Resume Writing Guide. Ed. by Henry B. Stern. 16p. 1981. 3.50 (ISBN 0-89128-972-0, PVP972). Am Foun Blind.

Resume Writing Made Easy. 2nd ed. Lola M. Coxford. 128p. 1985. pap. 7.95 (ISBN 0-89787-805-1). Gorsuch Scarisbrick.

Resume Writing Made Easy for High Tech Personnel. Lola M. Coxford. 1987. pap. 8.95 (ISBN 0-89787-809-4). Gorsuch Scarisbrick.

Resumen Practico de la Gramatica Inglesa. Robert J. Dixson & Julio I. Andujar. (Orig.). (gr. 9 up). 1967. pap. text ed. 2.95 (ISBN 0-88345-142-5, 17423). Prentice ESL.

Resumes - the Write Stuff: A Quick Guide to Presenting Your Qualifications Effectively. Robbie M. Kaplan. LC 87-45263. 88p. 1987. 8.95 (ISBN 0-912048-47-6). Garrett Pk.

Resumes & How to Write Them see Jobs & How to Get Them.

Resumes for Better Jobs. 3rd ed. Lawrence Brennan et al. (Illus.). 208p. 1987. pap. 6.95 (ISBN 0-13-774936-8). Monarch Pr.

Resumes for Better Jobs. rev. ed. Stanley Strand & Edward C. Gruber. 1973. pap. 5.95 (ISBN 0-671-18708-2). Monarch Pr.

Resumes for College Graduates. William Lewis. 112p. 1984. pap. 7.95 (ISBN 0-671-50422-3). Monarch Pr.

Resumes for Computer Personnel. Adele Lewis & Berl Hartman. 224p. 1984. pap. 9.95 (ISBN 0-8120-2860-0). Barron.

Resumes for Computer Professionals. Arthur R. Pell & George Sadek. 128p. 1985. pap. 7.95 (ISBN 0-671-50338-3, Pub. by Monarch Pr). S&S.

Resumes for Computer Professionals: A Complete Resume Preparation & Job-Getting Guide. William F. Shanahan. LC 83-3914. 144p. (Orig.). 1983. lib. bdg. 6.95 (ISBN 0-668-05785-8); pap. 6.95 (ISBN 0-668-05789-0). Arco.

Resumes for Domestic & Overseas Employment see Resumes for Employment in the U. S. & Overseas.

Resumes for Employment in the U. S. & Overseas. 3rd ed. Ed. by June L. Aulick. Orig. Title: Resumes for Domestic & Overseas Employment. 125p. 1988. pap. 16.50 (ISBN 0-8360-0030-7). World Trade.

Resumes for Engineers. Arthur Pell & George Sadek. (Monarch's Job Finders Ser.). 128p. 1982. pap. 7.95 (ISBN 0-671-44304-6). Monarch Pr.

Resumes for Executive Women. Laurie E. Lico. 128p. (Orig.). 1984. pap. 7.95 (ISBN 0-671-49758-8). S&S.

Resumes for Executives & Professionals. Robert Wilson & Adele Lewis. 192p. 1983. pap. text ed. 9.95 (ISBN 0-8120-0872-3). Barron.

Resumes for Hard Times: How to Make Yourself a Hot Property in a Cold Market. Bob Weinstein. 128p. 1986. pap. 8.95 (ISBN 0-671-45826-4, Fireside). S&S.

Resumes for Secretaries. Leonard Corwen. Date not set. write for info. S&S.

Resumes for Secretaries. Leonard Corwen. 128p. pap. 6.95 (ISBN 0-668-06244-4). Arco.

Resumes for Successful Women. Laurie Lico. 1985. pap. 8.95 (ISBN 0-671-55815-3). PB.

Resumes for Technicians: A Complete Resume Preparation & Job-Getting Guide. William F. Shanahan. LC 82-24444. 144p. 1983. lib. bdg. 12.95 (ISBN 0-668-05748-3); pap. 6.95 (ISBN 0-668-05751-3). Arco.

Resumes Que Consiguen Empleo: Spanish-Language Version of Resumes That Get Jobs. Tr. by Gines Serran-Pagan. 160p. 1988. pap. 8.95 (ISBN 0-13-774977-5). P-H.

Resumes That Get Jobs. 4th ed. Jean Reed. 192p. 1986. pap. text ed. 4.95 (ISBN 0-668-06481-1). Arco.

Resumes That Get Jobs. 3rd ed. Resume Service Staff. LC 80-26456. 192p. 1981. pap. 3.95 (ISBN 0-668-05210-4). Arco.

Resumes That Work. Tom Cowan. LC 83-8332. 192p. 1983. pap. 9.95 (ISBN 0-452-25455-8, Plume). NAL.

Resumes That Work. 2nd ed. Foxman. 1988. price not set (ISBN 0-471-60633-2); pap. price not set (ISBN 0-471-60634-0). Wiley.

Resumes That Work: How to Sell Yourself on Paper. Loretta D. Foxman & Walter L. Polsky. 96p. 1984. pap. 8.95 (ISBN 0-471-80608-0). Wiley.

Resumes: The Nitty Gritty. Joyce L. Kennedy. 28p. 1987. pap. 3.50 (ISBN 0-937238-00-7). Sun Features.

Resuming Green: Selected Poems, 1965-1982. Roland Flint. 12.95 (ISBN 0-931848-73-3, Pub. by Dial); pap. 6.95 (ISBN 0-931848-74-1, Pub. by Dial). Dryad Pr.

Retail Tenant Directory, 1986. Ed. by Donna Wetmore et al. 225.00 (ISBN 0-911790-00-4). Prog Grocers Trade.

Retail Tenant Directory, 1987. Ed. by Denise Anthony et al. 240.00 (ISBN 0-911790-09-8). Prog Grocers Trade.

Retail Tenant Directory 1988. rev. ed. Ed. by Mark Remmer et al. 1988. 250.00 (ISBN 0-911790-10-1). Prog Grocers Trade.

Retail Trade Developments in Great Britain. 4th ed. A. Buckley & C. Swain. 208p. 1980. text ed. 99.95x (ISBN 0-566-02152-8). Gower Pub Co.

Retail Trade in the United Kingdom. 150p. 1985. 150.00x (ISBN 0-686-71956-5, Pub. by Euromonitor). State Mutual Bk.

Retailer's Basic Accounting Handbook: A Manual Retail Accounting System. 80p. pap. 15.00 (ISBN 0-87102-002-5, 26-0150). Natl Ret Merch.

Retailer's Guide to Glass & Pottery. Kenneth Blakemore. (Illus.). 192p. 1984. text ed. 42.95 (ISBN 0-408-01219-6). Butterworth.

Retailer's Guide to Shopping Center Leasing. 15.00 (ISBN 0-87102-007-6, 26-7147). Natl Ret Merch.

Retailer's Guide to Software. Edward Russell. Ed. by Peter Rodwell. (Microcomputing for the Professions Ser.). 163p. 1986. 17.00 (ISBN 0-86187-504-4, Pub. by Frances Pinter). Longwood Pub Group.

Retailer's Guide to Understanding Leases. 200p. 26.00 (ISBN 0-87102-001-7, 26-0065). Natl Ret Merch.

Retailer's Manual. Samuel H. Terry. Ed. by Henry Assael. LC 78-316. (Century of Marketing Ser.). 1978. Repr. of 1869 ed. lib. bdg. 32.00x (ISBN 0-405-11179-7). Ayer Co Pubs.

Retailing. 3rd ed. Mason & Mayer. 1988. 35.95 (ISBN 0-256-05815-6). Business Pubns.

Retailing. 4th ed. Gerald Pintel & Jay Diamond. (Illus.). 560p. 1987. text ed. write for info. (ISBN 0-13-778549-6). P-H.

Retailing: Cases & Applications. Dale Lewison & M. Wayne DeLozier. 544p. 1982. text ed. 28.95 (ISBN 0-675-09920-X); Additional Supplements May Be Obtained from the Publisher. casebook 15.95 (ISBN 0-675-09853-X); study guide 10.95 (ISBN 0-675-09852-1). Merrill.

Retailing: Challenge & Opportunity. 3rd ed. Robert F. Hartley. LC 83-81027. 576p. 1984. text ed. 41.56 (ISBN 0-395-34290-2); instr's manual 3.56 (ISBN 0-395-34291-0). HM.

Retailing Job Analysis & Job Evaluation. National Retail Merchant Association Staff. 17.00 (ISBN 0-87102-032-7, 55-9522). Natl Ret Merch.

Retailing Management: A Planning Approach. L. D. Redinbaugh. 1975. text ed. 34.95 (ISBN 0-07-051366-X). McGraw.

Retailing-Merchandising Trends. Fairchild Market Research Division Staff. (Fairchild Fact File Ser.). (Illus.). 55p. 1984. pap. 17.50 (ISBN 0-87005-488-0). Fairchild.

Retailing: New Perspectives. Dorothy S. Rogers & Mercia Grassi. (Illus.). 672p. 1988. text ed. 36.95 (ISBN 0-03-001997-4); pap. text ed. price not set study guide (ISBN 0-03-014892-8). Dryden Pr.

Retailing: Principles & Practices. 2nd ed. Dale Lewison & Wayne Delozier. 768p. (Additional supplements may be obtained from publisher). 1986. text ed. 37.95 (ISBN 0-675-20474-7); 15.95 (ISBN 0-675-20492-5). Merrill.

Retailing Principles & Practices. 7th ed. Warren G. Meyer et al. LC 80-24885. (Illus.). 560p. (gr. 11-12). 1981. text ed. 24.56 (ISBN 0-07-041693-1). McGraw.

Retailing Principles & Practices. 6th ed. G. H. Richert et al. (Illus.). 592p. (gr. 11-12). 1974. text ed. 24.44 (ISBN 0-07-052325-8). McGraw.

Retailing Strategy: How to Do It! Richard Gentile & Anne Gentile. LC 78-65369. 1978. 20.95 (ISBN 0-86730-505-3). Lebhar Friedman.

Retailing Today. Jay Diamond & Gerald Pintel. (Illus.). 272p. 1988. text ed. write for info. (ISBN 0-13-777509-1). P-H.

Retailing Today. 2nd ed. Don L. James et al. 543p. 1981. text ed. 24.00 net (ISBN 0-15-576672-4, HC). HarBraceJ.

Retained Austenite & Its Measurement by X-Ray Diffraction. 64p. 1980. pap. 15.00 (ISBN 0-89883-224-1, SP453). Soc Auto Engineers.

Retained Common Duct Stones: Prevention & Treatment. Ed. by Robert W. Motson. LC 79-2989. 224p. 1985. 49.50 (ISBN 0-8089-1729-3, 792969). Grune.

Retaining Adult Students. Gordon G. Darkenwald. 23p. 1981. 2.80 (ISBN 0-318-22189-6, IN225). Natl Ctr Res Voc Ed.

Retaining Concepts & Organizing Facts: Advanced Level. James A. Giroux & Glenn R. Williston. Ed. by Edward Spargo. (Comprehension Skills Ser). (Illus.). 64p. (gr. 9 up). 1974. pap. text ed. 4.00x (ISBN 0-89061-019-3, CB-8A). Jamestown Pubs.

Retaining Concepts & Organizing Facts: Middle Level. Glenn R. Williston. (Comprehension Skills Ser.). (Illus.). 64p. (gr. 6-12). 1976. pap. text ed. 4.00x (ISBN 0-89061-071-1, CB-8M). Jamestown Pubs.

Retaining the Original: Multiple Originals, Copies, & Reproductions. (Studies in the History of Art: No. 20). (Illus.). 275p. (Orig.). 1988. pap. 32.00x (ISBN 0-89468-113-3, Dist. by U Pr of New Eng). Natl Gallery Art.

Retaining Wall. Barry Seiler. LC 79-12883. 54p. 1979. pap. 3.75 (ISBN 0-934332-16-9). L'Epervier Pr.

Retaining Wall & Sound Attenuator. (PCI Journal Reprints Ser.). 6p. pap. 4.00 (ISBN 0-686-40146-8, JR242). Prestressed Concrete.

Retaining Walls: A Revision of A-879. Mary Vance. (Architecture Ser.: A 1973). 16p. 1988. 5.00 (ISBN 1-55590-623-0). Vance Biblios.

Retaining Walls, Anchorages & Sheet Piling: Part1. M. Reimbert & A. Reimbert. LC 74-77789. (Series on Rock & Soil Mechanics). Orig. Title: Murs De Soutenements. (Illus.). 284p. 1974. 40.00x (ISBN 0-87849-009-4). Trans Tech.

Retaking the Philippines. William B. Breuer. 1987. pap. 3.95 (ISBN 0-312-90788-5). St Martin.

Retaking the Philippines: America's Return to Corregidor & Bataan, July 1944-March 1945. William B. Breuer. (Illus.). 336p. 1986. 18.95 (ISBN 0-312-67802-9). St Martin.

Retaliators. Donald Hamilton. 224p. 1984. pap. 2.95 (ISBN 0-449-12694-3, GM). Fawcett.

Retardation in Young Children. Sarah Broman et al. 368p. 1987. text ed. 39.95 (ISBN 0-89859-989-X). L Erlbaum Assocs.

Retardation of Aging & Disease by Dietary Restriction. Richard Weindruch & Roy L. Walford. (Illus.). 536p. 1988. text ed. 69.75x (ISBN 0-398-05496-7). C C Thomas.

Retarded Adult in the Community. Elias Katz. (Illus.). 292p. 1977. 32.75x (ISBN 0-398-00981-3). C C Thomas.

Retarded Australians. Clifford Judge. 1975. pap. 16.50x (ISBN 0-522-84082-5, Pub. by Melbourne U Pr). Intl Spec Bk.

Retarded Child: Answers to Questions Parents Ask. Arthur A. Attwell & D. A. Clabby. LC 72-182924. 139p. 1975. pap. 16.50x (ISBN 0-87424-120-0). Western Psych.

Retarded Isn't Stupid, Mom! Sandra Z. Kaufman. LC 87-29915. 256p. 1988. text ed. 15.00 (ISBN 0-933716-96-6, 966). P H Brookes.

Retarded Kids Need to Play: A Manual for Parents & Teachers. Cynthia C. Hirst & Elaine Michaelis. LC 82-83929. (Illus.). 288p. (Orig.). 1983. pap. 14.95 (ISBN 0-88011-097-X, PHIR0097). Leisure Pr.

Retarded Offenders. Santamour. 1982. 44.95 (ISBN 0-275-90895-X, C0895). Praeger.

RETC Proceedings, Nineteen Eighty-One, 2 vols. Ed. by R. L. Bullock & H. J. Jacoby. LC 81-65517. (Illus.). 1759p. Set. 70.00x (ISBN 0-89520-285-9). Soc Mining Eng.

RETC Proceedings, Nineteen Seventy-Four, 2 vols. Ed. by Harry C. Pattison & Elio D'Appolonia. LC 74-84644. (Illus.). 1843p. 1974. Repr. of 1981 ed. 60.00x (ISBN 0-89520-024-4). Soc Mining Eng.

RETC Proceedings, 1985. Ed. by C. David Mann & Martin N. Kelley. LC 85-70960. (Rapid Excavation & Tunneling Ser.). (Illus.). 1278p. 1985. 75.00x (ISBN 0-89520-441-X, 441-X). Soc Mining Eng.

RETC Proceedings, 1987, 2 vols. Intro. by J. M. Jacobs & R. S. Hendricks. LC 87-60888. (Rapid Excavation & Tunneling Conference Ser.). (Illus.). 1379p. 1987. 78.50x (ISBN 0-87335-065-0). Soc Mining Eng.

Retelling the Biblical Story. H. Stephen Shoemaker. LC 85-16650. 1985. pap. 6.95 (ISBN 0-8054-2114-9). Broadman.

Retention. Madeline Hunter. 49p. (Orig.). 1967. pap. 4.95x (ISBN 0-935567-02-X). TIP Pubns.

Retention & Destruction of Bank Records. American Bankers Association Staff. 196p. 1979. 22.00 (ISBN 0-317-32411-X, 062700); members 17.50 (ISBN 0-317-32412-8). Am Bankers.

Retention as a Function of the Method of Measurement. Leo J. Postman & Lucy Rau. LC 57-9951. (California, University, University of California Publications in Psychology Ser.: Vol. 8, No. 3). 1957. pap. 20.00 (ISBN 0-317-08156-X, 2021417). Bks Demand UMI.

Retention of Bank Records. rev. ed. American Bankers Association. LC 85-119139. 171p. write for info. Am Bankers.

Retention of Fillers by Papermaking Fibers. 2nd ed. (Bibliographic Ser.: No. 186-2). 82p. 1959. 8.00 (ISBN 0-317-34437-4); Supplement 1, 1965. 8.00 (ISBN 0-317-34438-2); Supplement 2, 1970. 8.00 (ISBN 0-317-34439-0); Supplement 3, 1975. 10.00 (ISBN 0-317-34440-4). Inst Paper Chem.

Retention of Land for Agriculture: Policy, Practice & Potential in New England. Frank Schnidman et al. LC 87-5580. (Lincoln Institute of Land Policy-OG&H Ser.). (Illus.). 400p. 1987. text ed. 40.00x (ISBN 0-89946-219-7, 219-7). Oelgeschlager.

Retention of Records: A Guide for Retention & Disposal of Student Records. American Association of Collegiate Registrars & Admissions Officers Staff. pap. 20.00 (ISBN 0-317-26604-7, 2024073). Bks Demand uMI.

Retention of Religious Experiences. T. Pettersson. (Illus.). 158p. (Orig.). 1975. pap. text ed. 18.50x (Pub. by Almqvist & Wiksell). Coronet Bks.

Retention of Title. 1987. 200.00x (Pub. by ESC Ltd UK). State Mutual Bk.

Rethinking Active Learning Eight Through Sixteen. Norman Beswick. LC 86-29358. 150p. 1987. 31.00 (ISBN 1-85000-159-6, Falmer Pr); pap. text ed. 15.00x (ISBN 1-85000-160-X, Falmer Pr). Taylor & Francis.

Rethinking Adult Religious Education: A Practical Parish Guide. Jeanne Tighe & Karen Szentkeresti. 144p. (Orig.). 1986. pap. 9.95 (ISBN 0-8091-2829-2). Paulist Pr.

Rethinking Anthropology. E. R. Leach. (London School of Economics Monographs on Social Anthropology: No. 22). 146p. 1966. 34.50 (ISBN 0-485-19522-4, Pub. by Athlone Pr UK); pap. 18.50 (ISBN 0-485-19622-0, Pub. by Athlone Pr UK). Humanities.

Rethinking Architecture: Design Students & Physically Disabled People. Ed. by Raymond Lifchez. 1986. 25.00x (ISBN 0-520-05842-9); pap. 10.95x (ISBN 0-520-05899-2). U of Cal Pr.

Rethinking Artisanal Fisheries Development: Western Concepts, Asian Experiences. Donald K. Emmerson. (Working Paper: No. 423). x, 97p. 1980. 5.00 (ISBN 0-686-36074-5, WP-0423). World Bank.

Rethinking Australia's Defence. Ross Babbage. (Illus.). 312p. 1981. text ed. 37.50x (ISBN 0-7022-1486-8). U of Queensland Pr.

Rethinking Bakhtin. Ed. by Gary S. Morson & Caryl Emerson. 300p. 1988. 34.95 (ISBN 0-8101-0809-7); pap. 9.95 (ISBN 0-8101-0810-0). Northwestern U Pr.

Rethinking Church Music. rev. ed. Paul W. Wohlgemuth. LC 80-85254. 112p. 1981. pap. 5.95 (ISBN 0-916642-15-1). Hope Pub.

Rethinking Cognitive Theory. Jeff Coulter. LC 83-9639. 179p. 1983. 23.95 (ISBN 0-312-67800-2). St Martin.

Rethinking Congregational Development. George E. Morris. LC 84-71366. 144p. (Orig.). 1984. pap. 5.25 (ISBN 0-88177-012-4, DRO12B). Discipleship Res.

Rethinking Congressional Reform. Burton D. Sheppard. LC 84-29833. 211p. (Orig.). 1985. 24.95 (ISBN 0-87073-550-0); pap. 19.95 (ISBN 0-87073-551-9). Schenkman Bks Inc.

Rethinking Crime & Deviance Theory: The Emergence of a Structuring Tradition. Francis T. Cullen. LC 83-17796. 200p. 1984. text ed. 28.50x (ISBN 0-86598-073-X, Rowman & Allanheld); pap. 11.95x. Rowman.

Rethinking Crime & Deviance Theory: The Emergence of a Structuring Tradition. Francis T. Cullen. 200p. 1987. pap. 11.95 (ISBN 0-8476-7551-3). Rowman.

Rethinking Criminal Law. George P. Fletcher. 1978. 28.00 (ISBN 0-316-28592-7). Little.

Rethinking Defense & Conventional Forces. John Glenn et al. LC 83-70039. (Alternatives for the 1980s Ser.). 58p. (Orig.). 1983. pap. text ed. 9.75 (ISBN 0-944237-06-1, Ctr National Policy). U Pr of Amer.

Rethinking Democracy: Freedom & Social Cooperation in Politics, Economy & Society. Carol Gould. Date not set. 39.50. Cambridge U Pr.

Rethinking Democrary: Freedom & Social Cooperation in Politics, Economy & Society. Carol Gould. 432p. 1988. 39.50 (ISBN 0-521-35048-4). Cambridge U Pr.

Rethinking Development. P. W. Preston. 256p. 1987. lib. bdg. 67.50x (ISBN 0-7102-1263-1, Pub. by Routledge UK). Routledge Chapman & Hall.

Rethinking Development: Modernization, Dependency, & Post-Modern Politics. David E. Apter. 312p. 1987. text ed. 35.00 (ISBN 0-8039-2971-4); pap. text ed. 16.95 (ISBN 0-8039-2972-2). Sage.

Rethinking Early Greek Philosophy: Hippolytus of Rome & the Presocratics. Catherine Osborne. LC 87-47719. 400p. 1987. 47.50x (ISBN 0-8014-2103-9). Cornell U Pr.

Rethinking Economic Development. Robert D'A. Shaw. (Development Papers: No. 8). 58p. 1972. pap. 1.00 (ISBN 0-686-28680-4). Overseas Dev Council.

Rethinking Education: The Coming Age of Enlightenment. Roger J. Williams. LC 85-21507. 170p. 1986. pap. 15.00 (ISBN 0-8022-2500-4). Philos Lib.

Rethinking Educational Change. Eric Hewton. 113p. 1983. 24.00x (ISBN 0-900868-93-7). Taylor & Francis.

Rethinking Educational Research. W. B. Dockrell & David Hamilton. 224p. 1980. text ed. 39.95 (ISBN 0-340-20548-2). Princeton Bk Co.

Rethinking Evangelism: A Theological Approach. Ben C. Johnson. LC 86-26787. 142p. (Orig.). 1987. pap. 9.95 (ISBN 0-664-24060-7). Westminster John Knox.

Rethinking Federalism: Block Grants & Federal, State, & Local Responsibilities. Claude E. Barfield. 99p. 1981. pap. 9.00 (ISBN 0-8447-3479-9). Am Enterprise.

Rethinking General Practice: Dilemmas in Primary Care. Margot Jefferys & Bessie Sachs. LC 83-4962. 288p. 1983. pap. 15.95 (ISBN 0-422-78630-6, NO. 3974). Routledge Chapman & Hall.

Rethinking German History: Nineteenth Century Germany & the Origins of the Third Reich. Richard J. Evans. 272p. 1987. text ed. 45.00 (ISBN 0-04-943051-3). Unwin Hyman.

Rethinking History & Myth: Indigenous South American Perspectives on the Past. Ed. by Jonathan D. Hill. (Illus.). 336p. 1988. 39.95 (ISBN 0-252-01543-6); pap. 16.95 (ISBN 0-252-06028-8). U of Ill Pr.

Rethinking How We Age: A New View of the Aging Mind. C. G. Prado. LC 85-9862. (Contributions in Philosophy Ser.: No. 28). 185p. 1986. lib. bdg. 35.00 (ISBN 0-313-24785-4, PRA/). Greenwood.

Rethinking Ideology: A Marxist Debate. Ed. by Sakari Hanninen & Leena Paldan. 160p. 1983. pap. 8.95 (ISBN 0-88477-015-X). Intl General.

Rethinking Indian Law. Committee on Native American Struggles. 1983. 42.00. Natl Lawyers Guild.

Rethinking Intellectual History: Texts, Contexts, Language. Dominick LaCapra. LC 83-7218. (Paperback Ser.). 352p. 1983. pap. 15.95x (ISBN 0-8014-9886-4). Cornell U Pr.

Rethinking Italian Fascism: Capitalism, Populism & Culture. Ed. by David Forgacs. (Illus.). 234p. 1986. text ed. 29.95 (ISBN 0-85315-630-1, Pub. by Lawrence & Wishart Pubs UK). Humanities.

Rethinking Juvenile Justice. Barry Krisberg & Ira Schwartz. 1983. 7.00 (ISBN 0-318-02058-0). Natl Coun Crime.

Rethinking Liberalism. Walter T. Anderson. 1983. pap. 4.95 (ISBN 0-380-84848-1, 84848, Discus). Avon.

Rethinking Marx. Ed. by Sakari Hanninen & Leena Paldan. 200p. 1984. pap. 9.95 (ISBN 0-88477-021-4). Intl General.

Rethinking Mathematical Concepts. R. F. Wheeler. LC 80-42100. (Mathematics & Its Applications Ser.). 314p. 1981. 77.95 (ISBN 0-470-27116-7). Halsted Pr.

Rethinking Mathematical Concepts. Roger F. Wheeler. (Mathematics & Its Applications Ser.). 314p. 1986. pap. 34.95 (ISBN 0-470-20302-1). Halsted Pr.

Rethinking Methodist History. Ed. by Russell E. Richey & Kenneth E. Rowe. (Kingswood Bks.). 1983. pap. 17.95 (ISBN 0-687-36170-2). Abingdon.

Rethinking Military Politics: Brazil & the Southern Cone. Alfred Stepan. 136p. 1988. text ed. 25.00 (ISBN 0-691-07750-9); pap. text ed. 9.95 (ISBN 0-691-02274-7). Princeton U Pr.

Rethinking Modern Political Theory: Essays 1979-1983. John Dunn. 248p. 1985. 37.50 (ISBN 0-521-30130-0); pap. 14.95 (ISBN 0-521-31695-2). Cambridge U Pr.

Rethinking Modernization. Ed. by John J. Poggie, Jr. & Robert N. Lynch. LC 72-826. 352p. 1974. lib. bdg. 56.95 (ISBN 0-8371-6394-3, POM/). Greenwood.

Rethinking Nuclear Strategy. Stephen J. Cimbala. LC 87-28702. 288p. 1988. 40.00 (ISBN 0-8420-2294-5). Scholarly Res Inc.

Rethinking People Management: A New Look at the Human Resources Function. James G. Stockard. 1980. 14.95 (ISBN 0-8144-5576-X). AMACOM.

Rethinking Plato & Platonism. C. J. De Vogel. (Mnemosyne Supplements Ser.: No. 92). x, 254p. 1986. pap. 38.75 (ISBN 90-04-07691-3, Pub. by E J Brill). Heinman.

Rethinking Psychiatry: From Cultural Category to Personal Experience. Arthur Kleinman. 256p. 1988. 25.00x (ISBN 0-02-917441-4). Free Pr.

Rethinking Psychological Anthropology: Continuity & Change in the Study of Human Action. Philip K. Bock. LC 87-27179. 336p. 1988. pap. text ed. 12.95 (ISBN 0-7167-1932-0). W H Freeman.

Rethinking Quaker Principles. Rufus M. Jones. 1940. pap. 2.50x (ISBN 0-87574-008-1, 008). Pendle Hill.

Rethinking Realized Eschatology. Clayton Sullivan. 1988. 19.95 (ISBN 0-86554-302-X, H266). Mercer Univ Pr.

Rethinking Reform: The Principal's Dilemma. NASSP Curiculum Council Staff. 80p. (Orig.). 1986. pap. 7.00 (ISBN 0-88210-193-5). Natl Assn Principals.

Rethinking Regionalism: John Steuart Curry & the Kansas Mural Controversy. M. Sue Kendall. LC 84-40612. (New Directions in American Art Ser.). (Illus.). 164p. (Orig.). 1986. 39.95 (ISBN 0-87474-568-3, KERR); pap. 19.95 (ISBN 0-87474-567-5, KERRP). Smithsonian.

Rethinking Rental Housing. John I. Gilderbloom & Richard P. Appelbaum. 272p. 1987. 34.95 (ISBN 0-87722-498-6). Temple U Pr.

Rethinking Rental Housing. John I. Gilderbloom & Richard P. Appelbaum. LC 87-1958. 296p. 1988. pap. 16.95 (ISBN 0-87722-538-9). Temple U Pr.

Rethinking School Improvement: Research, Craft & Concept. Ed. by Ann Lieberman. 240p. 1986. pap. text ed. 13.95x (ISBN 0-8077-2807-1). Tchrs Coll.

Rethinking Scripture: Essays from a Comparative Perspective. Ed. by Miriam Levering. 288p. 1988. 44.50x (ISBN 0-88706-613-5); pap. 14.95x (ISBN 0-88706-614-3). State U NY Pr.

Rethinking Social Enquiry Reports. Anthony E. Bottoms & Andrew Stelman. (Community Care Practice Handbooks). 110p. 1986. text ed. write for info. (ISBN 0-566-05068-4). Gower Pub Co.

Rethinking Social Inequality. Ed. by David Robbins et al. 272p. 1982. text ed. 36.50x (ISBN 0-566-00557-3). Gower Pub Co.

Rethinking Social Welfare: Why Care for the Stranger? Robert Morris. 256p. 1986. pap. text ed. 17.95 (ISBN 0-582-28589-5). Longman.

Rethinking Socialism: A Theory of Better Practice. Gavin Kitchinag. LC 83-12104. 176p. 1983. pap. 8.95 (ISBN 0-416-35840-3, NO. 3981). Routledge Chapman & Hall.

Retirement Communities: An American Original. Ed. by Michael E. Hunt et al. LC 83-26506. (Journal of Housing for the Elderly Ser.: Vol. 1, Nos. 3-4). 278p. 1984. text ed. 38.95 (ISBN 0-86656-267-2). Haworth Pr.

Retirement Community Places for the Young-Old: A Bibliography. Ina J. Weis. (Public Administration Ser.: P 2113). 13p. 1987. 3.75 (ISBN 1-55590-213-8). Vance Biblios.

Retirement Concepts & Realities of Ethnic Minority Elders. Institute on Minority Aging. Ed. by Percil E. Stanford. (Vol. 5). (Illus., Orig.). 1979. pap. 6.00 (ISBN 0-916304-44-2). SDSU Press.

Retirement: Coping with Emotional Upheavals. Leland Bradford & Martha Bradford. LC 79-4101. 1979. 18.95x (ISBN 0-88229-564-0). Nelson-Hall.

Retirement: Creating Promise out of Threat. Robert K. Kinzel. LC 78-32165. pap. 35.30 (ISBN 0-317-26949-6, 2023584). Bks Demand UMI.

Retirement Dollars for the Self-Employed. pap. 3.95x (ISBN 0-686-05669-8). Dun.

Retirement Edens Outside the Sunbelt. expanded & updated ed. Peter A. Dickinson. 400p. 1987. pap. 10.95 (ISBN 0-673-24836-4). Am Assn Retire.

Retirement Equity Act of 1984: Impact on Your Retirement Plan. LC 85-238526. 40p. Date not set. price not set. P-H.

Retirement Equity Act of 1984: Law-Explanation-Committee Reports. 88p. 1984. pap. 6.00 (ISBN 0-317-19184-5, 4794). Commerce.

Retirement: Everything You Wanted to Know but Didn't Know Who to Ask. Edward Palder. 350p. (Orig.). 1988. pap. 14.95 (ISBN 0-933149-24-7). Woodbine House.

Retirement Guide for Canadians: Planning Now for a Comfortable Future. 8th ed. Henry S. Hunnisett. 295p. 1988. 9.95 (ISBN 0-88908-680-X). ISC Pr.

Retirement Housing: Step by Step Guide for Investors, Developers, Accountants, & Other Professionals. Laughlin. (Real Estate for Professional Practitioners Ser.). 1988. price not set (ISBN 0-471-63476-X). Wiley.

Retirement Income & the Economy: Increasing Income for the Aged. Ed. by Dallas L. Salisbury. 113p. (Orig.). 1980. pap. 10.00 (ISBN 0-86643-024-5). Employee Benefit.

Retirement Income & the Economy: Policy Directions for the 80s. Ed. by Dallas L. Salisbury. LC 81-12632. 305p. 1981. 18.00 (ISBN 0-86643-025-3); pap. 10.00 (ISBN 0-86643-023-7). Employee Benefit.

Retirement Income Opportunities in an Aging America: Income Levels & Adequacy. Employee Benefit Research Institute Staff. (Illus.). 134p. 1986. pap. text ed. 15.75 (ISBN 0-8191-5543-8, Pub. by Employee Benefit Rsch Inst). U Pr of Amer.

Retirement Income Opportunities in an Aging America: Income Levels & Adequacy, Vol. 2. Employee Benefit Research Institute Staff. LC 81-5494. 121p. (Orig.). 1982. pap. 15.00 (ISBN 0-86643-014-8). Employee Benefit.

Retirement Income Opportunities in an Aging America: Pensions & the Economy. Sophie M. Korczyk. LC 81-5494. (Retirement Income Opportunities in an Aging America Ser.: Vol. III). (Orig.). 1982. pap. 15.00 (ISBN 0-86643-015-6). Employee Benefit.

Retirement Income Opportunities in an Aging America: Pensions & the Economy. Sophie M. Korczyk. (Illus.). 152p. 1986. pap. text ed. 15.75 (ISBN 0-8191-5544-6, Pub. by Employee Benefit Rsch Inst). U Pr of Amer.

Retirement Income Opportunities in an Aging America: Vol. 1: Coverage & Benefit Entitlement. Sylvester J. Schieber & Patricia M. George. LC 81-5494. 131p. (Orig.). 1981. pap. 15.00 (ISBN 0-86643-013-X); Set, Vols I, II, III. pap. 25.00 (ISBN 0-86643-012-1). Employee Benefit.

Retirement Income Policy: Considerations for Effective Decision Making. Employee Benefit Research Institute Staff. LC 80-81075. 77p. (Orig.). 1980. pap. 10.00 stapled cover (ISBN 0-86643-007-5). Employee Benefit.

Retirement Income Programs: Directions for Future Research. Employee Benefit Research Institute Staff. 52p. (Orig.). 1980. pap. 10.00 stapled cover (ISBN 0-86643-006-7). Employee Benefit.

Retirement Income, 1975-1985: A Bibliography. Ina J. Weis. (Public Administration Ser.: P 1980). 21p. 1986. 6.25 (ISBN 0-89028-960-3). Vance Biblios.

Retirement Living. Alice Sylliiasen. 126p. pap. 6.95 (ISBN 0-910303-01-0). Writers Pub Serv.

Retirement Living Alternatives U. S. A. the Inside Story. H. Wilson Worley. LC 81-86504. (Illus.). 152p. (Orig.). 1982. pap. 9.95 (ISBN 0-942200-00-4). Columbia Hse Pub.

Retirement Money Book: Ways to Have More Income When You Retire. Ferd Nauheim. LC 81-14940. 250p. 1982. 11.95 (ISBN 0-87491-437-X). Acropolis.

Retirement of National Debts. William Withers. LC 68-58643. (Columbia University. Studies in the Social Sciences: No. 374). Repr. of 1932 ed. 24.50 (ISBN 0-404-51374-3). AMS Pr.

Retirement Paradises of the World. 18th ed. Norman D. Ford. (Illus.). 184p. 5.95 (ISBN 0-686-63828-X). Harian.

Retirement, Pensions, & Social Security. Gary S. Fields & Olivia S. Mitchell. (Illus.). 192p. 1985. text ed. 21.95x (ISBN 0-262-06091-4). MIT Pr.

Retirement Plan Recoveries & Related Issues. Goodman. 24p. (Orig.). 1987. pap. 2.00 (5304). Commerce.

Retirement Planning Alert: Will Your Plans Meet Your Life Style Needs? Richard J. Curtis. LC 87-36488. (Illus.). 62p. (Orig.). 1988. pap. 4.95 (ISBN 0-945298-03-X). Curtis Pubns.

Retirement-Planning & Adjustment: A Selected Bibliography. John J. Miletich. (CPL Bibliographies Ser.: No. 117). 53p. 1983. 9.00 (ISBN 0-86602-117-5). Coun Plan Librarians.

Retirement Planning for a Business & Business Owner. Kenn B. Tacchino. (Huebner School). 420p. (Orig.). 1988. pap. text ed. 22.00 (ISBN 0-943590-19-1). Amer College.

Retirement Planning for Individuals. Edward E. Graves et al. 225p. (Orig.). 1988. pap. text ed. 22.00 (ISBN 0-943590-20-5). Amer College.

Retirement Planning for Professionals. Stuart Hack. LC 86-24559. (Tax & Business Guides for Professionals Ser.). 1988. 85.00 (ISBN 0-471-81458-X). Wiley.

Retirement Planning for Small Business & Professionals Entering the Top-Heavy & Parity Age: ALI-ABA Video Law Review Study Materials. ALI-ABA Committee on Continuing Professional Education. LC 84-166979. (Illus.). xiv, 290p. Date not set. price not set. Am Law Inst.

Retirement Planning Kit, 1984. 2nd ed. Elmer Otte. LC 84-4530. incl. leader's guide & Cassette tape 47.50 (ISBN 0-9602938-0-9). Retirement Res.

Retirement: Planning Tomorrow Today. R. Stadt & J. M. Adams. LC 82-14799. 192p. 1983. pap. text ed. 12.75 (ISBN 0-07-000404-8). McGraw.

Retirement Plans for Employees. John J. McFadden. (Financial Planning & Insurance Ser.). 1988. text ed. 31.95 (ISBN 0-256-05588-2). Irwin.

Retirement Plans in Reorganizations & Liquidations. Isidore Goodman. (Pension & ERISA Ser.). 24p. 1985. pap. 2.00 (ISBN 0-317-44610-X, 5499). Commerce.

Retirement Policy in an Aging Society. Ed. by Robert L. Clark. LC 79-56502. (Illus.). vii, 215p. 1980. 25.00 (ISBN 0-8223-0441-4). Duke.

Retirement Policy: Planning for Change. Jennifer L. Warlick et al. Ed. by Kathryn H. Anderson. 58p. 1982. 5.75 (ISBN 0-318-22190-X, IN242). Natl Ctr Res Voc Ed.

Retirement Policy: The Next Fifty Years. Ed. by Michael Fogarty. (NIESR, PSI, RII A Joint Studies in Public Policy Ser.). viii, 216p. 1982. text ed. 28.50x (ISBN 0-435-83320-0). Gower Pub Co.

Retirement Preparation: What Retirement Specialists Need to Know. Ed. by Helen Dennis. LC 83-48130. 224p. 1984. 29.00x (ISBN 0-669-06949-3); pap. 17.00x (ISBN 0-669-08338-0). Lexington Bks.

Retirement Reconsidered: Economic & Social Roles for Older People. Ed. by Robert Morris & Scott Bass. 272p. 1988. 33.95 (ISBN 0-8261-5870-6). Springer Pub.

Retirement Rehearsal Guidebook. 5th updated & rev. ed. Elmer Otte. LC 84-453. 1984. pap. 9.95 (ISBN 0-9602938-2-5). Retirement Res.

Retirement: Reward or Rejection? J. Roger O'Meara. LC 77-72304. (Report Ser.: No. 713). (Illus.). 69p. 1977. pap. 30.00 (ISBN 0-8237-0145-X). Conference Bd.

Retirement Sample, Vol. 1. Public Employee Retirement Administration. 113p. 1973. 7.00 (ISBN 0-317-34952-X). Municipal.

Retirement Security & Tax Policy. Sophie M. Korczyk. LC 84-7975. 200p. (Orig.). 1984. 30.00 (ISBN 0-86643-040-7); pap. 18.00 (ISBN 0-86643-037-7). Employee Benefit.

Retirement Security & Tax Policy. Sophie M. Korczyk. (Illus.). 156p. 1986. lib. bdg. 31.50 (ISBN 0-8191-5535-7, Pub. by Employee Benefit Rsch Inst); pap. text ed. 19.00 (ISBN 0-8191-5536-5). U Pr of Amer.

Retirement Systems of the American Teacher. W. William Schmid. LC 72-124107. 1970. 16.95x (ISBN 0-8303-0108-9, Acad Edns). Fleet.

Retirement: The Challenge of Change. E. Michael Brady. (Orig.). 1988. pap. 8.00 (ISBN 0-939561-02-6). Univ South ME.

Retirement Tracks: After You Show the Wisdom of Age-Depart in a Hurry. Georgia B. Watson. LC 83-83107. 152p. 1984. 10.50 (ISBN 0-935834-29-X). Rainbow Books.

Retirement: You're in Charge. Eleanor L. Furman. LC 84-3459. 176p. 1984. 35.00 (ISBN 0-275-91159-4, C1159); pap. 8.95 (ISBN 0-275-91804-1, B1804). Praeger.

Retiring in Arizona: Your Onestop Guide to Living, Loving & Lounging under the Sun. Dorothy Tegeler. Ed. by Mary Westheimer. (Illus.). 192p. (Orig.). 1987. pap. 9.95 (ISBN 0-943169-50-X). Fiesta Bks Inc.

Retiring Right: Planning for Your Successful Retirement. 2nd ed. Larry Kaplan. Ed. by Susan Capasso. 376p. 1987. pap. 12.95 (ISBN 0-89529-365-X). Avery Pub.

Reti's Best Games of Chess. Richard Reti & H. Golombek. (Illus.). 173p. 1974. Repr. 4.95 (ISBN 0-486-21636-5). Dover.

Reto en el Paraiso. Alejandro Morales. LC 82-73753. 381p. (Span. & Eng.). 1983. pap. 14.00x (ISBN 0-916950-34-4). Biling Rev-Pr.

Retooling the Science of Mind. B. Bernard Bane. 86p. 1987. pap. 5.00 (ISBN 0-930924-26-6). BMB Pub Co.

Retorno see Aguilas.

Retort: An Anarchist Review, Vols. 1-5, No. 1. 1969. Repr. of 1942 ed. Vols. 1 & 2. lib. bdg. 19.25 (ISBN 0-313-21940-0, RT01); Vols. 3-5. lib. bdg. 19.25 (ISBN 0-313-21941-9, RT03). Greenwood.

Retort Pouch: New Growth Industry. Villy Diernisse. (Illus.). 191p. 1981. 475.00x (ISBN 0-910211-00-0). Laal Co.

Retouches a Mon Retour de l'URSS see Retour De l'URSS.

Retouching from Start to Finish. 2nd ed. Veronica C. Weiss. LC 85-51179. 150p. 1986. Repr. of 1979 ed. 29.95 (ISBN 0-935333-00-2). VC Pub.

Retouching Your Photographs. Jan W. Miller. (Illus.). 144p. 1986. 27.50 (ISBN 0-8174-3831-9, Amphoto); pap. 18.95 (ISBN 0-8174-3832-7, Amphoto). Watson-Guptill.

Retour a Coolabah Creek. Dorothy Cork. (Harlequin Romantique Ser.). 192p. 1983. pap. 1.95 (ISBN 0-373-41205-3). Harlequin Bks.

Retour a Roissy see Story of O: Part Two, Return to the Chateau.

Retour Amont. Rene Char. 96p. 1966. 8.95 (ISBN 0-686-54169-3). French & Eur.

Retour au Palais Farnese: Avec: Choix de Lettres de Romain Rolland a sa Mere (1890-1891) Romain Rolland. (Illus.). 368p. 1956. 5.95 (ISBN 0-686-55268-7). French & Eur.

Retour de l'Enfant Prodigue: Recit. Andre Gide. (Folio Ser.: No. 1044). pap. 6.95 (ISBN 0-685-34155-0). Schoenhof.

Retour De l'URSS. Andre Gide. Incl. Retouches a Mon Retour de l'URSS. (Idees Ser.). pap. 7.95 (ISBN 0-685-34156-9). Schoenhof.

Retracing the Past, 2 Vols. Gary B. Nash. 352p. 1985. Vol. 1. pap. text ed. 17.50 scp (ISBN 0-06-044719-2, HarpC); Vol. 2. pap. text ed. 17.50 scp (ISBN 0-06-044721-4, HarpC). Har-Row.

Retractations. St. Augustine. (Fathers of the Church Ser.: Vol. 60). 451p. 1968. 17.95x (ISBN 0-8132-0060-1). Cath U Pr.

Retractationum Libri Duo. Saint Aurelius Augustinus. (Corpus Scriptorum Ecclesiasticorum Latinorum Ser: Vol. 36). 34.00 (ISBN 0-384-02357-6). Johnson Repr.

Retraining & Tradition: Skilled Worker in an Era of Change. Kentalle Miller & Isobel Miller. 192p. 1975. 22.95 (ISBN 0-8464-1127-X). Beekman Pubs.

Retraining & Upgrading Workers: A Guide for Postsecondary Educators. Catharine Warmbrod & Constance Faddis. 208p. 1983. 12.50 (ISBN 0-318-22191-8, RD235). Natl Ctr Res Voc Ed.

Retraining for the Elderly Disabled. Margaret Mort. LC 84-23761. 458p. (Orig.). 1985. pap. 26.00 (ISBN 0-7099-3532-3, Pub. by Croom Helm Ltd). Routledge Chapman & Hall.

Retraining the Unemployed. Ed. by Gerald Somers. LC 68-19575. pap. 89.80 (ISBN 0-317-39634-X, 2023723). Bks Demand UMI.

Retraite Sentimentale. Sidonie-Gabrielle Colette. (Folio Ser.: No. 135). 12.95 (ISBN 0-685-37284-7); pap. 6.95 (ISBN 0-686-66858-8). Schoenhof.

Retransformation of the School: The Emergence of Contemporary Alternative Schools in the United States. Daniel L. Duke. LC 77-25257. 212p. 1978. 21.95x (ISBN 0-88229-294-3). Nelson-Hall.

Retrato de la Reina: La Historia de Nuestra Senora de Guadalupe. Sr. Mary Amatora. 1972. 7.50 (ISBN 0-682-47542-4, Lochinvar); pap. 5.00 (ISBN 0-682-47548-3, Lochinvar). Exposition-Phoenix.

Retrato de una Epoca. Carlos Cabezas. 212p. (Orig.). 1986. pap. 8.00 (ISBN 0-917049-07-1). Saeta.

Retratos Contemporaneos. Fernando Alegria. 247p. 1979. pap. text ed. 10.00 net (ISBN 0-15-576680-5, HC). HarBraceJ.

Retratos de Hispanoamerica. Ed. by Eugenio Florit & B. P. Patt. (Span.). 1962. text ed. 16.95x (ISBN 0-03-017135-0). Irvington.

Retratos del Salvador. Herbert Lockyer. 192p. (Span.). 1986. pap. 3.50 (ISBN 0-8297-0741-7). Life Pubs Intl.

Retratos Nuevomexicanos: A Collection of Hispanic New Mexican Photography. Steven A. Yates. (Illus.). 1987. pap. text ed. 5.95 (ISBN 0-9609818-1-0). M Rogers Mus.

Retread Shop. T. Jackson King. Date not set. pap. 3.50 (ISBN 0-445-20674-8, Pub. by Popular Lib). Warner Bks.

Retreat. Aharon Appelfeld. (Penguin Fiction Ser.). 176p. 1985. pap. 5.95 (ISBN 0-14-007660-3). Penguin.

Retreat. Henry Denker. 352p. 1988. 18.95 (ISBN 0-688-08306-4). Morrow.

Retreat. Jerrold Mundis. 416p. (Orig.). 1985. pap. 3.95 (ISBN 0-445-20022-7, Pub. by Popular Lib). Warner Bks.

Retreat for Death. Nick Carter. 224p. 1982. pap. 2.50 (ISBN 0-441-71539-7). Ace Bks.

Retreat from China: British Policy in the Far East, 1937-1941. Nicholas Clifford. (China in the 20th Century Ser.). 1976. Repr. of 1967 ed. lib. bdg. 27.50 (ISBN 0-306-70757-8). Da Capo.

Retreat from Doomsday: The Obsolescence of Major War. John Mueller. LC 88-47899. 336p. 1989. 20.95 (ISBN 0-465-06939-8). Basic.

Retreat from Empire? The First Nixon Adminstration. Robert Osgood et al. LC 72-12359. (America & the World Ser: Vol. II). 360p. 1973. 37.50x (ISBN 0-8018-1493-6); pap. 8.95x (ISBN 0-8018-1499-5). Johns Hopkins.

Retreat from Glory. R. H. Lockhart. 348p. 1984. Repr. of 1934 ed. lib. bdg. 25.00 (ISBN 0-89984-945-8). Century Bookbindery.

Retreat from Likeness in the Theory of Painting. facsimile 2nd ed. Frances M. Blanshard. LC 72-37913. (Select Bibliographies Reprint Ser). Repr. of 1945 ed. 20.00 (ISBN 0-8369-6733-X). Ayer Co Pubs.

Retreat from Love. Colette. Tr. by Margaret Crosland. LC 79-19831. 226p. 1980. pap. 5.95 (ISBN 0-15-676588-8, Harv). HarBraceJ.

Retreat from Reconstruction: 1869-1879. William Gillette. LC 79-12450. 1980. text ed. 35.00 (ISBN 0-8071-0569-4); pap. 12.95 (ISBN 0-8071-1006-X). La State U Pr.

Retreat from Reform: Patterns of Political Behavior in Interwar Japan. Sharon Minichiello. LC 84-8535. 186p. 1984. text ed. 18.00x (ISBN 0-8248-0778-2). UH Pr.

Retreat from Reform: The Prohibition Movement in the United States, 1890-1913. Jack S. Blocker, Jr. LC 76-5325. (Contributions in American History: No. 51). 288p. 1976. lib. bdg. 35.00 (ISBN 0-8371-8899-7, BRR/). Greenwood.

Retreat from Safety: Reagan's Attack on America's Health. Public Citizen Staff & Claybrook Joan. 1984. pap. 8.95 (ISBN 0-394-72244-2). Pantheon.

Retreat from Sanity: The Structure of Emerging Psychosis. Malcolm B. Bowers, Jr. LC 73-20296. 245p. 1974. 29.95 (ISBN 0-87705-134-8). Human Sci Pr.

Retreat Guide I. Steve Clapp. 20p. (Orig.). 1981. pap. 2.00 (ISBN 0-914527-04-5). C-Four Res.

Retreat Guide II. Steve Clapp. (C-4 Journals). 29p. (Orig.). 1982. pap. 2.00 (ISBN 0-914527-13-4). C-Four Res.

Retreat Handbook. Sandy Reimer & Larry Reimer. 192p. 1987. pap. 9.95 (ISBN 0-8192-1393-4). Morehouse.

Retreat, Hell! We're Just Fighting in Another Direction. Jim Wilson. (Illus.). 352p. 1988. 19.95 (ISBN 0-688-07576-2). Morrow.

Retreat into Eternity: An Upanishad-Book of Aphorisms. Swami Amar Jyoti. LC 80-54236. (Illus.). 128p. (Orig.). 1981. pap. 12.95 (ISBN 0-933572-03-4). Truth Consciousness.

Retreat into the Mind: Victorian Poetry & the Rise of Psychiatry. Ekbert Faas. 304p. 1989. 34.50 (ISBN 0-691-06748-1). Princeton U Pr.

Retreat of Socialism in India: Two Decades Without Nehru, 1964-1984. R. C. Dutt. 219p. 1987. 20.00x (ISBN 81-7017-217-9, Pub. by Abhinav India). South Asia Bks.

Retreat of Turberculosis Eighteen Fifty to Nineteen Fifty. F. B. Smith. 288p. 1988. lib. bdg. 55.00 (ISBN 0-7099-3383-5, Pub. by Croom Helm UK). Routledge Chapman & Hall.

Retreat Planning Made Easy: A Resource for Christian Retreats. Shirley Harman. 40p. (Orig.). pap. 5.95 (ISBN 0-8066-2155-9, 10-5488). Augsburg.

Retreat: The Dynamic New Answer for Your Firm's Successful Future. Melvin Wallace. LC 79-83673. 1979. 29.95 (ISBN 0-933460-00-7). Wintergreen.

Retreat to Commitment. W. W. Bartley, III. LC 84-14862. 285p. 1984. 21.95 (ISBN 0-87548-420-4). Open Court.

Retreat to Nevada: A Socialist Colony of World War One. Wilbur S. Shepperson. LC 66-63539. (Lancehead Ser). xiv, 204p. 1966. 8.95 (ISBN 0-87417-015-X). U of Nev Pr.

Retreat with Stillwell. Jack Belden. (China in the 20th Century Ser). (Illus.). 368p. 1975. Repr. of 1943 ed. lib. bdg. 32.50 (ISBN 0-306-70734-9). Da Capo.

Retreat with Thomas Merton. M. B. Pennington. (Retreat With Bk.). 128p. 1988. pap. 8.95 (ISBN 0-916349-23-3). Amity Hse Inc.

Retribution, Justice & Therapy. Jeffrie G. Murphy. 1979. lib. bdg. 31.50 (ISBN 90-277-0998-X, Pub. by Reidel Holland); pap. 11.85 (ISBN 90-277-0999-8). Kluwer Academic.

Retribution; or, the Vale of Shadows. Emma D. Southworth. LC 78-64099. Repr. of 1849 ed. 37.50 (ISBN 0-404-17395-0). AMS Pr.

Retrieval & Organizational Strategies in Conceptual Memory: A Computer Model. Janet L. Kolodner. 280p. 1984. 29.95x (ISBN 0-89859-365-4). L Erlbaum Assocs.

Retrieval Bargaining: A Guide for Public Sector Labor Negotations. Richard G. Neal. Ed. by Frances I. Felts. LC 81-90749. 50p. 1982. pap. text ed. 5.00 (ISBN 0-9605018-2-7). Neal Assoc.

Retrieval from Semantic Memory. W. Noordman-Vonk. (Springer Ser. in Language & Communications: Vol. 5). (Illus.). 1979. 21.00 (ISBN 0-387-09219-6). Springer-Verlag.

Retrieval of Geoscience Information: Proceedings, Geoscience Information Society Meeting, Salt Lake City, 1975. Ed. by V. S. Hall. (Proceedings: Vol. 6). 1976. 8.00 (ISBN 0-934485-03-8). Geosci Info.

Retrieval of Information in the Humanities & Social Science. Slavens. (Library Science & Information Ser.: Vol. 37). 136p. 1981. 39.75 (ISBN 0-8247-1542-X). Dekker.

Retrieval of Medicinal Chemical Information. Ed. by W. Jeffrey Howe et al. LC 78-21611. (ACS Symposium Ser.: No. 84). 1978. 26.95 (ISBN 0-8412-0465-9). Am Chemical.

Retrieval System. Maxine Kumin. (Poetry Ser). 1978. pap. 6.95 (ISBN 0-14-042258-7). Penguin.

Retrieval Systems for Lawyers. Kline D. Strong. LC 80-66349. (Illus.). 92p. (Orig.). 1980. pap. 22.00 (ISBN 0-89707-021-6, 5110057). Amer Bar Assn.

Retriever Training. Susan Scales. LC 76-40806. (Illus.). 1977. 18.95 (ISBN 0-7153-7246-7). David & Charles.

Retriever Training - A Better Way. Robert Milner. 59.95 (ISBN 0-935935-01-0). Junction Pr.

Retriever Training for the Duck Hunter. Robert Milner. (Illus.). 150p. 1985. Repr. of 1983 ed. 18.95 (ISBN 0-935935-00-2). Junction Pr.

Retriever Training Tests. James Spencer. LC 83-3709. (Arco Outdoor Ser.). (Illus.). 192p. 1983. 14.95 (ISBN 0-668-05681-9, 5681). Arco.

Retrieving Democracy: In Search of Civic Equality. Philip Green. LC 84-23798. 288p. 1985. 21.95x (ISBN 0-8476-7405-3, Rowman & Allanheld); pap. text ed. 10.95x (ISBN 0-8476-7406-1). Rowman.

Retroactive. Catherine Howe. (Illus.). 20p. (Orig.). 1986. pap. write for info. (ISBN 0-936739-02-9). Hallwalls Inc.

Retroactive Inhibition As Affected by Conditions of Learning. Edward Tolman. Bd. with No. 7. Iowa University Studies in Psychology. Ed. by C. E. Seashore. Repr. of 1918 ed; Higher Scale of Mental Measurement & Its Application to Cases of Insanity. A. J. Rosanoff. Repr. of 1918 ed; Experimental Study of Attention. S. M. Fukuya. Repr. of 1918 ed; Interference of Will-Impluses with Application to Pedagogy. A. A. Roback. Repr. of 1918 ed. (Psychology Monographs General & Applied: Vol. 25). pap. 29.00 (ISBN 0-8115-1424-2). Kraus Repr.

Retroactive Legislation Affecting Interest in Land. John Scurlock. LC 54-62006. (Michigan Legal Publications). xv, 390p. 1982. Repr. of 1953 ed. lib. bdg. 38.00 (ISBN 0-89941-175-4). W S Hein.

Retrofitting of Commercial, Institutional, & Industrial Buildings for Energy Conservation. Milton Meckler. 432p. 1983. 49.95 (ISBN 0-442-26226-4). Van Nos Reinhold.

Retrograde Condensation in Natural Gas Pipelines. American Gas Association Pipeline Research Committee et al. 512p. 1975. 12.00 (ISBN 0-318-12698-2, L22277). Am Gas Assn.

Retrograde Mercury Workbook. C. J. Puotinen. 64p. 1982. pap. 4.95 (ISBN 0-930840-11-9). Ninth Sign.

Retrolental Fibroplasia: A Modern Parable. William A. Silverman. (Monographs in Neonatology). 256p. 1980. 35.50 (ISBN 0-8089-1264-X, 794076). Grune.

Retrolental Fibroplasia & Autistic Symptomatology: An Investigation Into Some Relationships Among Neonatal, Environmental, Developmental & Affective Variables in Blind Prematures. Joan B. Chase. 236p. 1968. pap. 3.00 (ISBN 0-89128-050-2, PCR050). Am Foun Blind.

Retrospect see Fate of French-E in English: The Plural of Nouns Ending in-th.

Retrospect: An Omnibus of Aldous Huxley's Books. 1424p. 1985. Repr. of 1933 ed. lib. bdg. 65.00 (ISBN 0-89987-417-7). Darby Bks.

Retrospect & Prospect. Alfred T. Mahan. LC 68-15831. 1968. Repr. of 1902 ed. 22.00x (ISBN 0-8046-0294-8, Pub. by Kennikat). Assoc Faculty Pr.

Retrospect & Prospect. Ed. by Queensland Art Gallery Staff. 1985. 10.00 (ISBN 0-86917-009-0, Pub. by Boolarong Pubn Australia). Intl Spec Bk.

Retrospect of Fifty Years, 2 vols. in 1. James C. Gibbons. LC 79-38447. (Religion in America, Ser. 2). 720p. 1972. Repr. of 1916 ed. 47.50 (ISBN 0-405-04066-0). Ayer Co Pubs.

Retrospect of Western Travel, 2 Vols. H. Martineau. LC 68-24988. (American History & Americana Ser., No. 47). 1969. Repr. of 1838 ed. lib. bdg. 79.95x (ISBN 0-8383-0165-7). Haskell.

Retrospect of Western Travel, 3 vols. Harriet Martineau. LC 68-57623. (Illus.). 1969. Repr. of 1838 ed. Vol. 2. lib. bdg. 9.00 (ISBN 0-8371-0968-X, MAWV); Vol. 3. lib. bdg. 9.00 (ISBN 0-8371-0969-8, MAWX). Greenwood.

Retrospect of Western Travel, 2 Vols. in 1. Harriet Martineau. Repr. of 1838 ed. 37.00 (ISBN 0-384-35690-7). Johnson Repr.

Retrospection & Introspection. Mary Baker Eddy. pap. 4.50 (ISBN 0-87952-044-2). First Church.

Retrospection & Introspection. Mary Baker Eddy. French 12.50 (ISBN 0-87952-122-8); German 12.50 (ISBN 0-87952-157-0); Italian 12.50 (ISBN 0-87952-182-1); Portugese 12.50 (ISBN 0-87952-207-0); Spanish 7.50 (ISBN 0-87952-231-3); Swedish 12.50 (ISBN 0-87952-252-6). First Church.

Retrospection & Introspection. Mary Baker Eddy. 95p. Braille ed. 68.00 (ISBN 0-87952-051-5). First Church.

Retrospection of America, Seventeen Ninety-Seven to Eighteen Eleven. John Bernard. Ed. by Brander Matthews & Laurence Hutton. LC 73-83401. 1887. 24.50 (ISBN 0-405-08263-0, Blom Pubns). Ayer Co Pubs.

Retrospections of America 1797-1811. Ed. by John Bernard. 380p. 1987. pap. 19.50 (ISBN 1-55613-020-1). Heritage Bk.

Retrospections on Social Psychology. Ed. by Leon Festinger. (Illus.). 1980. text ed. 18.95x (ISBN 0-19-502751-5). Oxford U Pr.

Retrospective. Ed. by Herbert Eimert & Karlheinz Stockhausen. Tr. by Cornelius Cardew & Ruth Koenig. (Reihe: No. 8). 1978. pap. 6.25 (ISBN 3-7024-0152-0, UE26108E). Eur-Am Music.

Retrospective. David B. McCoy. 72p. (Orig.). 1988. pap. 4.00 (ISBN 0-945568-13-4). Spare Change Poetry Pr.

Retrospective Conversion: From Cards to Computer. Anne G. Adler & Elizabeth A. Baber. LC 84-81656. (Library Hi Tech Monograph Ser.: No. 2). 324p. 1984. 45.00 (ISBN 0-87650-177-3). Pierian.

Retrospective Exhibitions of Ernest Meissonier. Ed. by Theodore Reff. (Modern Art in Paris 1855 to 1900 Ser.). 353p. 1981. lib. bdg. 53.00 (ISBN 0-8240-4747-8). Garland Pub.

Retrospective: Lawrence McKinin. Richard G. Baumann. (Illus.). 48p. (Orig.). 1983. pap. 5.00x (ISBN 0-910501-01-7). U of Missouri Mus Art Arch.

Retrospective National Bibliographies: An International Directory. Ed. by Marcelle Beaudiquez. (IFLA Ser.: Vol. 35). 189p. 1986. lib. bdg. 32.00 (ISBN 3-598-20399-3). K G Saur.

Retrospective on the Classical Gold Standard: 1821-1931. Ed. by Michael D. Bordo & Anna J. Schwartz. LC 84-2440. (NBER Conference Report Ser.). 704p. 1984. lib. bdg. 69.00x (ISBN 0-226-06590-1). U of Chicago Pr.

Retrospective Technology Assessement of Submarine Telegraphy: The Transatlantic Cable of 1866. Ed. by V. T. Coates & Bernard Finn. (Illus.). 1979. pap. 12.50 (ISBN 0-911302-39-5). San Francisco Pr.

Retrospective Technology Assessment, 1976. Ed. by J. A. Tarr. (Illus.). 1977. 16.00 (ISBN 0-911302-37-9). San Francisco Pr.

Retrospective Voting in American National Elections. Morris P. Fiorina. LC 80-24454. 288p. 1981. text ed. 49.00t (ISBN 0-300-02557-2); pap. 12.95 (ISBN 0-300-02703-6). Yale U Pr.

Retroversion & Text Criticism: The Predictability Syntax in an Ancient Translation from Greek to Ethropic. John R. Miles. (SBL Septuagint & Cognate Studies). 1985. 16.50 (ISBN 0-89130-878-4, 06-04-17); pap. 10.95 (ISBN 0-89130-879-2). Scholars Pr Ga.

Retrovirus Genes in Lymphocyte Function & Growth. Ed. by E. Wecker & I. Horack. (Current Topics in Microbiology & Immunology Ser.: Vol. 98). (Illus.). 180p. 1982. 38.00 (ISBN 0-387-11225-1). Springer-Verlag.

Retroviruses, Vol. 2. Ed. by P. K. Vogt & H. Koprowski. (Current Topics in Microbiology & Immunology: Vol. 107). (Illus.). 185p. 1983. 62.00 (ISBN 0-387-12384-9). Springer-Verlag.

Retroviruses & Disease. Ed. by Maynard E. Pullman et al. 270p. 1989. price not set (ISBN 0-12-322570-1). Acad Pr.

Retroviruses & Human Pathology. Ed. by Robert C. Gallo et al. LC 85-31692. (Experimental Biology & Medicine Ser.). 576p. 1986. 74.50 (ISBN 0-89603-098-9). Humana.

Retroviruses in Human Lymphoma-Leukemia: Proceedings of the 15th International Symposium of the Princess Takamatsu Cancer Research Fund, Japan, 1984. Ed. by M. Miwa et al. 352p. 1985. lib. bdg. 122.00x (ISBN 90-6764-057-3). Coronet Bks.

Retroviruses, Vol. 3. Ed. by P. K. Vogt & H. Koprowski. (Current Topics in Microbiology & Immunology Ser.: Vol. 112). (Illus.). 135p. 1984. 36.00 (ISBN 0-387-13307-0). Springer Verlag.

Rett Syndrome. Ed. by John M. Opitz et al. LC 86-10282. 432p. 1986. 79.50 (ISBN 0-8451-4215-1, 4215). A R Liss.

Retter. Violet A. Garza. LC 87-40251. (Illus.). 315p. (Orig.). 1987. pap. 11.95 (ISBN 1-55523-092-X). Winston-Derek.

Retting of Jute. (Agricultural Services Bulletins: No. 60). 54p. 1985. pap. 7.50 (ISBN 92-5-101415-9, F2736, FAO). UNIPUB.

Return. Yaw M. Boateng. (African Writers Ser.: No. 186). viii, 120p. (Orig.). 1977. pap. text ed. 6.00 (ISBN 0-435-90186-9). Heinemann Ed.

Return. Herman Branover. Tr. by Ilana Coven from Rus. 190p. 1982. pap. 6.95 (ISBN 0-87306-303-1). Feldheim.

Return. James M. Cody. (Illus.). 1981. lib. bdg. 18.00 (ISBN 0-916908-31-3); pap. 3.50 (ISBN 0-916908-04-6). Place Herons.

Return. Walter De La Mare. Ed. by R. Reginald & Douglas Menville. LC 75-46266. (Supernatural & Occult Fiction Ser.). 1976. Repr. of 1910 ed. lib. bdg. 23.50x (ISBN 0-405-08124-3). Ayer Co Pubs.

Return. Mike Evans. LC 85-31943. 224p. 1986. 12.95 (ISBN 0-8407-5501-5). Nelson.

Return. Evan Innes. (America 2040 Ser.). 384p. (Orig.). 1988. pap. 3.95 (ISBN 0-553-27184-9). Bantam.

Return. Sonia Levitin. LC 86-25891. 224p. (gr. 5 up). 1987. 12.95 (ISBN 0-689-31309-8, Atheneum Children's Bks). Macmillan.

Return. Sonia Levitin. 1988. pap. 2.95 (ISBN 0-449-70280-4, Juniper). Fawcett.

Return. K. S. Maniam. (Writing in Asia Ser.). 185p. (Orig.). 1981. pap. text ed. 7.00x (ISBN 0-686-79036-7, 00263). Heinemann Ed.

Return. Richard Maynard. LC 87-46267. 240p. 1988. 17.95 (ISBN 1-55611-083-9). D I Fine.

Return. Dan O'Neill. 146p. (Orig.). 1984. pap. 2.50 (ISBN 0-931660-05-X). R Oman Pub.

Return. Charles Tomlinson. 64p. 1987. pap. 8.95 (ISBN 0-19-282079-6). Oxford U Pr.

Return. Frederick Turner. LC 81-12545. 48p. 1981. 11.95 (ISBN 0-914378-76-7); pap. 6.95 (ISBN 0-914378-75-9). Countryman.

Return a Stranger. Margaret Mayo. (Harlequin Romances Ser.). 192p. 1984. pap. 1.75 (ISBN 0-373-02602-1). Harlequin Bks.

Return Again, Traveler. Norman Rosten. LC 72-144746. (Yale Ser. of Younger Poets: No. 39). Repr. of 1940 ed. 18.00 (ISBN 0-404-53839-8). AMS Pr.

Return & Reign of Jesus Christ: Zechariah 9-14. John MacArthur, Jr. (John MacArthur's Bible Studies). 1988. pap. 4.95 (ISBN 0-8024-5358-9). Moody.

Return Engagement: Faces to Remember-Then & Now. James Watters. (Illus.). 168p. 1984. 24.95 (ISBN 0-517-55523-9, C N Potter Bks). Crown.

Return from Avalon: A Study of the Arthurian Legend in Modern Fiction. Raymond H. Thompson. LC 84-10853. (Contributions to the Study of Science Fiction & Fantasy Ser.: No. 14). ix, 206p. 1985. lib. bdg. 35.00 (ISBN 0-313-23291-1, THR/). Greenwood.

Return from Darkness. Nina Vida. 400p. (Orig.). 1986. 15.95 (ISBN 0-446-51225-7). Warner Bks.

Return from Darkness. Nina Vida. 400p. 1987. pap. 3.95 (ISBN 0-446-34557-1). Warner BKs.

Return from Death: An Exploration of the Near-Death Experience. Margot Grey. 224p. (Orig.). 1985. pap. 10.95 (ISBN 1-85063-019-4, Ark Paperbks). Routledge Chapman & Hall.

Return from Enlightenment. Forest K. Davis. write for info. (ISBN 0-912362-01-4); pap. write for info. (ISBN 0-912362-02-2). Adamant Pr.

Return from No-Return. Dane Rudhyar. 175p. (Orig.). 1974. pap. 5.00 (ISBN 0-916108-03-1). Seed Center.

Return from Parnassus, Pt 2. LC 72-133728. (Tudor Facsimile Texts. Old English Plays: No. 111). Repr. of 1912 ed. 49.50 (ISBN 0-404-53411-2). AMS Pr.

Return from Parnassus, Part 1 see Pilgrimage to Parnassus.

Return from the Grave. Ed. by Hugh Lamb. LC 76-28598. 1977. 8.95 (ISBN 0-8008-6782-3). Taplinger.

Return from the Stars. Stanislaw Lem. 256p. 1982. pap. 2.95 (ISBN 0-380-58578-2, 58578-2, Bard). Avon.

Return from the U. S. S. R. & Afterthoughts on My Return. Andre Gide. Tr. by Richard Howard from Fr. (Illus.). 192p. 1987. 15.95 (ISBN 0-374-24950-4). FS&G.

Return from Tomorrow. George G. Ritchie & Elizabeth Sherrill. 128p. 1981. pap. 3.95 (ISBN 0-8007-8412-X, Spire Bks). Revell.

Return from Witch Mountain. Alexander Key. 160p. (gr. 5 up). 1984. pap. 2.50 (ISBN 0-671-54131-5). Archway.

Return Indefinite. Gabriele Wohmann. Tr. by James Hawkes from Ger. 192p. Date not set. cancelled (ISBN 0-941324-05-2). Van Vactor & Goodheart.

Return Migration & Regional Economic Problems. Ed. by Russell King. LC 85-24288. 1986. 43.00 (ISBN 0-7099-1578-0, Pub. by Croom Helm Ltd). Routledge Chapman & Hall.

Return Migration & Reintegration Services. Rien Van Gendt & G. Garcia Passigli. 1977. 4.00x (ISBN 92-64-11612-5). OECD.

Return of A. J. Raffles: An Edwardian Comedy in Three Acts Based Somewhat Loosely on E. W. Hornung's Characters in 'The Amateur Cracksman' Graham Greene. 92p. 1975. 9.00 (ISBN 0-317-03942-3). Ultramarine Pub.

Return of a Mad Look at Old Movies. Dick De Bartolo. pap. 1.25 (ISBN 0-451-06835-1, Y6835, Sig). NAL.

Return of a Native Reporter. Robert Chesshyre. 1988. 18.95 (ISBN 0-670-81734-1). Viking.

Return of Arthur Conan Doyle. Grace Cooke & Ivan Cooke. (Illus.). 1963. 12.50 (ISBN 0-85487-037-7). DeVorss.

Return of Astraea: An Astral-Imperial Myth in Calderon. Frederick A. De Armas. LC 86-7758. (Studies in Romance Languages: No. 32). 272p. 1986. 27.00x (ISBN 0-8131-1570-1). U Pr of Ky.

Return of Captain Conquer. Mel Gilden. (gr. 5-8). 1985. 12.95. HM.

Return of Caulfield Blake. G. Clifton Wisler. LC 87-21151. 1987. 14.95 (ISBN 0-87131-530-0). M Evans.

Return of Caulfield Blake. G. Clifton Wisler. 1989. pap. 3.50 (ISBN 0-451-15760-5, Sig). NAL.

Return of Chief Black Foot. Victoria Mauricio. LC 81-2769. (Illus.). 140p. (Orig.). 1981. pap. 5.95 (ISBN 0-89865-053-4, Unilaw). Donning Co.

Return of Christ see Studies in Dogmatics: Theology.

Return of Consciousness. Tawfig Al-Hakim. Tr. by Bayly Winder from Arabic. (Studies in Near Eastern Civilization). 192p. 1985. 35.00x (ISBN 0-8147-9202-2). NYU Pr.

Return of Courage. Jean-Louis Servan-Schreiber. 1987. 12.95 (ISBN 0-201-12207-3). Addison-Wesley.

Return of Dr. Fu Manchu. Sax Rohmer. 1976. lib. bdg. 13.95x (ISBN 0-89968-141-7). Lightyear.

Return of Dr. Sam Johnson, Detector. Lillian De La Torre. 200p. 1985. pap. 4.95 (ISBN 0-930330-34-X). Intl Polygonics.

Return of Eden: Five Essays on Milton's Epics. Northrop Frye. 1975. 15.00x (ISBN 0-8020-1353-8). U of Toronto Pr.

Return of Elijah. Morris Venden. (Harv Ser.). 1983. pap. 4.95 (ISBN 0-8163-0453-X). Pacific Pr Pub Assn.

Return of Eva Peron: Bd. with the Killings in Trinidad. V. S. Naipaul. LC 79-22148. 1980. 13.45 (ISBN 0-394-50968-4). Knopf.

Return of Eva Peron: Bd. with the Killings in Trinidad. V. S. Naipaul. LC 80-6134. 240p. 1981. pap. 4.95 (ISBN 0-394-74675-9, V-675, Vin). Random.

Return of Grand Theory in the Human Sciences. Ed. by Quentin Skinner. 160p. 1985. 34.50 (ISBN 0-521-26692-0); pap. 9.95 (ISBN 0-521-31808-4). Cambridge U Pr.

Return of Halley's Comet. Andrew Fraknoi et al. (Illus.). 36p. 1985. 4.00 (ISBN 0-937707-05-8, IP 700). Astron Soc Pacific.

Return of Halley's Comet. Patrick Moore & John Mason. (Illus.). 1984. 15.95 (ISBN 0-393-01872-5). Norton.

Return of Halley's Comet. Patrick Moore & John Mason. 128p. 1985. pap. 6.95 (ISBN 0-446-38303-1). Warner Bks.

Return of Henry Starr. Richard Slotkin. LC 87-30722. 524p. 1988. 24.95 (ISBN 0-689-11811-2). Atheneum.

Return of Jack the Ripper. Mark Andrews. 1977. pap. 1.75 (ISBN 0-8439-0476-3, Leisure Bks). Leisure NY.

Return of Jeeves. P. G. Wodehouse. LC 85-42606. 224p. 1985. pap. 3.95 (ISBN 0-06-080768-7, P 768, PL). Har-Row.

Return of King Arthur: British & American Arthurian Literature. Beverly Taylor & Elisabeth Brewer. (Arthurian Studies: IX). 390p. 1983. 35.00x (ISBN 0-389-20278-9, 07096). B&N Imports.

Return of Lady Brace. Nancy W. Ross. 242p. 1987. pap. 10.00 (ISBN 0-938077-01-5). Parallax Pr.

Return of Lono. O. A. Bushnell. (Pacific Classics Ser.: No. 1). 290p. 1971. pap. 6.95 (ISBN 0-87022-931-1). UH Pr.

Return of Martin Guerre. Natalie Z. Davis. LC 83-277. 162p. 1984. pap. 7.95 (ISBN 0-674-76691-1). Harvard U Pr.

Return of Martin Guerre. Natalie Zemon Davis. (Illus.). 176p. 1983. 17.50x (ISBN 0-674-76690-3). Harvard U Pr.

Return of Mr. X. Mario Gilbert & Jaime Hernandez. Ed. by Dean Motter. (Limited-Signed Edition Ser.: No. 5). (Illus.). 114p. 1987. signed & limited ed. 34.95 (ISBN 0-936211-03-2); pap. 11.95. Graphitti Designs.

Return of Mr. X. Gilbert Hernandez & Mario Hernandez. Date not set. pap. 8.95 (ISBN 0-446-38698-7). Warner Bks.

Return of Morgette. G. G. Boyer. LC 85-7153. (Morgette Ser.). 1985. 14.95 (ISBN 0-8027-4049-9). Walker & Co.

Return of Morris Schumsky. Steven Schnur. (Illus.). 48p. (gr. 4-6). 1987. pap. 6.95 (ISBN 0-8074-0358-X). UAHC.

Return of Odysseus. Homer. Adapted by I. M. Richardson. LC 83-14234. (Tales from the Odyssey Ser.). (Illus.). 32p. (gr. 4-8). 1984. lib. bdg. 10.79 (ISBN 0-8167-0015-X); pap. text ed. 2.50 (ISBN 0-8167-0016-8). Troll Assocs.

Return of O'Mahony. Harold Frederic. (Collected Works of Harold Frederic). 1988. Repr. of 1892 ed. lib. bdg. 59.00x. Am Biog Serv.

Return of O'Mahony see Collected Works.

Return of Otis. Joseph N. Chappelle. 40p. 1988. 5.75 (ISBN 0-8062-2943-8). Carlton.

Return of Owners of Land in Ireland, 1876. 325p. 1988. Repr. of 1876 ed. 35.00 (2963). Genealog Pub.

Return of Retief. Keith Laumer. 1984. pap. 2.95 (Pub. by Baen Bks). PB.

Return of Service: Stories. Jonathan Baumbach. LC 79-18102. (Illinois Short Fiction Ser.). 140p. 1979. 11.95 (ISBN 0-252-00784-0); pap. 8.95 (ISBN 0-252-00785-9). U of Ill Pr.

Return of Sgt. Hawk. Patrick Clay. (Sgt. Hawk Ser.: No. 2). 1980. pap. 1.95 (ISBN 0-8439-0845-9, Leisure Bks). Leisure NY.

Return of Sherlock Holmes. Arthur Conan Doyle. 320p. 1975. pap. 2.95 (ISBN 0-345-32713-6). Ballantine.

Return of Sherlock Holmes. Arthur Conan Doyle. 320p. 1985. pap. 2.50 (ISBN 0-425-10151-7). Berkley Pub.

Return of Sherlock Holmes. Arthur Conan Doyle. 1987. pap. 3.50 (ISBN 0-14-010026-1). Penguin.

Return of Sherlock Holmes. Arthur Conan Doyle. (Illus.). 320p. 1987. 69.00x (ISBN 0-948397-76-4, Pub. by M O'Mara UK). State Mutual Bk.

Return of Sherlock Holmes. (Classics Ser.). (gr. 4 up). 1988. pap. 3.95 (ISBN 0-582-54155-7). Longman.

Return of Sherlock Holmes see New Method Supplementary Readers.

Return of Silver Chief. Jack O'Brien. 16.95 (ISBN 0-89190-398-4, Pub. by Amereon Hse). Amereon Ltd.

Return of Skull-Face. Robert E. Howard & Richard Lupoff. LC 77-89158. 1977. 9.95x (ISBN 0-913960-17-9). Fax Collect.

Return of Talatu'u. Gary Duckett. LC 86-40285. 150p. (gr. 4-6). 1987. 7.95 (ISBN 1-55523-022-9). Winston-Derek.

Return of Tarzan. Edgar Rice Burroughs. 224p. 1975. pap. 2.50 (ISBN 0-345-31575-8). Ballantine.

Return of the Actor. Alain Touraine. LC 87-13558. 196p. 1985. 29.50x (ISBN 0-8166-1593-4); pap. 13.95 (ISBN 0-8166-1594-2). U of Minn Pr.

Return of the Amasi Bird: Black South African Poetry, 1891-1981. Ed. by Tim Couzens & Essop Patel. 411p. 1982. pap. 12.95 (ISBN 0-86975-195-6, Pub. by Ravan Pr). Ohio U Pr.

Return of the Ancients. F. Edward Butterworth. (Orig.). 1987. pap. 10.00 (ISBN 0-941227-00-6). Cosmic Pr Chico.

Return of the Ayatollah. Mohamed Heikal. 217p. 1986. pap. 16.95 (ISBN 0-233-97660-4, Pub. by A Deutsch England). David & Charles.

Return of the Bird Tribes. Ken Carey. LC 88-50436. 224p. 1988. 16.95 (ISBN 0-912949-19-8, Dist. by Talman Co Inc); pap. 11.95 (ISBN 0-912949-20-1). Uni-Sun.

Return of the Brown Pelican. Photos by Dan E. Guravich. LC 83-901. (Illus.). 118p. 1983. 24.95 (ISBN 0-8071-1114-7). La State U Pr.

Return of the Comet. Dennis Schatz & Yasu Osawa. (Illus.). 42p. (gr. 4-9). 1985. pap. 7.95 (ISBN 0-935051-00-7). Pacific Sci Ctr.

Return of the Crazy Ladies. Joyce Elbert. 1984. pap. 4.50 (ISBN 0-451-15118-6, Sig). NAL.

Return of the Democratic Party to Power in 1884. Harrison C. Thomas. LC 79-82245. (Columbia University Studies in the Social Sciences: No. 203). Repr. of 1919 ed. 21.00 (ISBN 0-404-51203-8). AMS Pr.

Return of the Dinosaurs. Stephan Wilkinson. Ed. by Ernest Dupuy. (Hammond's Captain Atlas & the Globe Riders Ser.). (Illus.). 48p. (gr. 2 up). 1988. pap. 6.95 (ISBN 0-8437-3550-3). Hammond Inc.

Return of the Dragon. Jane Zaring. (Illus.). (gr. 5-8). 1981. 7.95 (ISBN 0-395-30350-8). HM.

Return of the Goddess. Edward Whitmont. 288p. 1984. pap. 12.95 (ISBN 0-8245-0643-X). Crossroad NY.

Return of the Goddess. Edward C. Whitmont. 288p. 1986. pap. 13.00 (ISBN 0-8334-1002-4, Freedeeds Bks). Garber Comm.

Return of the Good Clean Jokes. Bob Phillips. LC 86-62982. 176p. (Orig.). 1986. pap. 3.50 (ISBN 0-89081-568-2). Harvest Hse.

Return of the Great Brain. John D. Fitzgerald. 180p. (gr. 3-5). 1975. pap. 2.95 (ISBN 0-440-45941-9, YB). Dell.

Return of the Great Brain. John D. Fitzgerald. LC 73-15443. (Great Brain Ser.). (Illus.). 176p. (gr. 4-7). 1974. PLB 11.89 (ISBN 0-8037-7413-3). Dial Bks Young.

Return of the Gypsy. Philippa Carr. LC 84-24768. 1985. 16.95 (ISBN 0-399-13064-0, Putnam). Putnam Pub Group.

Return of the Gypsy. Philippa Carr. 1986. pap. 3.95 (ISBN 0-449-20897-4, Crest). Fawcett.

Return of the Headless Horseman. Matt Christopher. LC 81-21936. (Illus.). 96p. (gr. 3-5). 1982. 8.95 (ISBN 0-664-32690-0). Westminster John Knox.

Return of the Inca. Tr. by Grady L. Hillman & Guillermo Delgado. 60p. (Orig.). 1984. lib. bdg. 25.00 (ISBN 0-916908-11-9); pap. 5.95 (ISBN 0-916908-21-6). Place Herons.

Return of the Indian. Lynne R. Banks. LC 85-31119. (Illus.). 192p. (gr. 4-6). 1986. pap. 13.95 (ISBN 0-385-23497-X). Doubleday.

Return of the Indian. Lynne R. Banks. (gr. 3-7). 1987. pap. 2.95 (ISBN 0-380-70284-3, Camelot). Avon.

Return of the Indian. Lynne R. Banks. (Illus.). (gr. k-9). 1988. pap. 2.95. Scholastic Inc.

Return of the Indian Spirit. Vinson Brown. LC 81-65887. (Illus.). 64p. (gr. 5 up). 1982. pap. 5.95 (ISBN 0-89087-401-8). Celestial Arts.

Return of the Individual: Rescue Attempts in a Bureaucratic Age. Wolfgang Kraus. Tr. by John Russell from Ger. 200p. 1985. text ed. 16.60 (ISBN 0-8204-0194-3). P Lang Pubs.

Return of the Irish: A Doctor's Search for the Ultimate Healer. Deepak Chopra. 1989. pap. 7.95 (ISBN 0-395-50077-X). HM.

Return of the Jedi. Illus. by John Gampert. Ed. by Ib Penick. LC 83-60019. (Pop-Up Bks.). (Illus.). 16p. (gr. 1-5). 1983. 5.95 (ISBN 0-394-86016-0). Random.

Return of the Jedi. James Kahn. 224p. 1983. pap. 2.95 (ISBN 0-345-30767-4, Del Rey). Ballantine.

Return of the Jedi. Adapted by Joan D. Vinge. LC 82-20538. (The Storybook Based on the Movie). (Illus.). 64p. (gr. 3-8). 1983. 6.95 (ISBN 0-394-85624-4); lib. bdg. 7.99 (ISBN 0-394-95624-9). Random.

Return of the Jedi Step-Up Movie Adventure. Ed. by Elizabeth Levy. (Return of the Jedi Ser.). (Illus.). 72p. (gr. 1-3). 1983. lib. bdg. 8.99 (ISBN 0-394-96117-X). Random.

Return of the Jesuits. Francis X. Curran. LC 66-29559. 1966. 3.00 (ISBN 0-8294-0018-4). Loyola.

Return of the Kid. Wayne D. Overholser. 192p. 1987. pap. 2.95 (ISBN 0-7701-0623-4). Paperjacks US.

Return of the Killed, Wounded & Missing of the Army under the Immediate Command of Major General Winfield Scott, on the 19th & 20th of August, 1847, During the Mexican-American War. (Stokvis Studies in Historical Chronology & Thought: No. 10). 64p. 1989. lib. bdg. 19.95x (ISBN 0-89370-327-3); pap. text ed. 9.95x (ISBN 0-89370-427-X). Borgo Pr.

Return of the King. J. R. R. Tolkien. 1976. pap. 3.95 (ISBN 0-345-33973-8). Ballantine.

Return of the King. Rev. ed. J. R. R. Tolkien. 1967. 12.95 (ISBN 0-395-08256-0). HM.

Return of the King: Being the Third Part of the Lord of the Rings. J. R. Tolkien. (Illus.). 450p. 1988. 16.95 (ISBN 0-395-48930-X); pap. 7.95 (ISBN 0-395-27221-1). HM.

Return of the Livable City: Learning from America's Best. Partners for Livable Places et al. (Illus.). 320p. 1987. 28.50 (ISBN 0-87491-828-6). Acropolis.

Return of the Lord. Ralph Martin. 118p. (Orig.). 1983. pap. 5.95 (ISBN 0-89283-145-6). Servant.

Return of the Millenium. Ed. by Joseph Bettis & S. K. Johannesen. LC 83-82671. 247p. 1984. pap. 11.95. Rose Sharon Pr.

Return of the Native. Intro. by Harold Bloom. (Modern Critical Interpretations Ser.). 1987. 19.95 (ISBN 0-87754-743-2). Chelsea Hse.

Return of the Native. Thomas Hardy. (Airmont Classics Ser.). (gr. 10 up). 1964. pap. 2.75 (ISBN 0-8049-0038-8, CL-38). Airmont.

Return of the Native. Thomas Hardy. Repr. lib. bdg. 22.95x (ISBN 0-88411-561-5, Pub. by Aeonian Pr). Amereon Ltd.

Return of the Native. Thomas Hardy. (Literature Ser). (gr. 9-12). 1969. pap. text ed. 7.08 (ISBN 0-87720-713-5). AMSCO Sch.

Return of the Native. Thomas Hardy. 384p. (gr. 9-12). 1982. pap. 2.25 (ISBN 0-553-21269-9, Bantam Classics). Bantam.

Return of the Native. Thomas Hardy. Ed. by A. Walton Litz. LC 67-5356. (YA) (gr. 9 up). 1967. pap. 6.50 (ISBN 0-395-05201-7, RivEd). HM.

Return of the Native. Thomas Hardy. 414p. 1973. pap. 2.25 (ISBN 0-451-51974-4, CJ1796, Sig Classics). NAL.

Return of the Native. Thomas Hardy. Ed. by James Gindin. (Critical Ed. Ser). (Illus.). 1969. pap. 10.95x (ISBN 0-393-09791-9). Norton.

Return of the Native. Thomas Hardy. Ed. by Dorothy Calhoun. (Now Age Illustrated IV Ser.). (Illus.). (gr. 4-12). 1978. text ed. 7.50 (ISBN 0-88301-331-2); pap. text ed. 2.95 (ISBN 0-88301-319-3); activity bk. 1.25 (ISBN 0-88301-343-6). Pendulum Pr.

Return of the Native. Thomas Hardy. (English Library Ser.). 1978. pap. 2.95 (ISBN 0-14-043122-5). Penguin.

Return of the Native: American Indian Political Resurgence. Stephen E. Cornell. (Illus.). 288p. 1988. 29.95 (ISBN 0-19-503772-3). Oxford U Pr.

Return of the Native (Hardy) Flowers. (Book Notes Ser.). 1984. pap. 2.50 (ISBN 0-8120-3439-2). Barron.

Return of the Native Notes. Frank Thompson, Jr. (Orig.). 1966. pap. 3.25 (ISBN 0-8220-1138-7). Cliffs.

Return of the Native with Reader's Guide. Thomas Hardy. (AMSCO Literature Program). (gr. 10-12). 1970. text ed. 11.58 (ISBN 0-87720-844-1); pap. 7.83 (ISBN 0-87720-807-7); with model ans. 6.83 (ISBN 0-87720-907-3). AMSCO Sch.

Return of the Nighthawks. Vincent Marzilli, II. (Illus.). 56p. (Orig.). (gr. k-6). 1987. pap. 7.95 (ISBN 0-9617809-1-6). Vincent Marzilli.

Return of the Puritans. 5th ed. LC 87-62433. 208p. 1987. pap. text ed. 5.00 (ISBN 0-932050-38-7). New Puritan.

Return of the Reader: Reader-Response Criticism. Elizabeth Freund. (New Accents Ser.). 192p. 1987. 37.50 (ISBN 0-416-34400-3, 9458); pap. 10.95 (ISBN 0-416-34410-0, 9081). Routledge Chapman & Hall.

Return of the Rishi: A Doctor's Search for the Ultimate Healer. Deepak Chopra. 256p. 1987. 16.95 (ISBN 0-395-45516-2). HM.

Return of the Sea-Eagle. John Love. LC 83-7325. (Illus.). 227p. 1984. 32.50 (ISBN 0-521-25513-9). Cambridge U Pr.

Return of the Seattle Bargain. Howard Hirshman. write for info. Robinson News.

Return of the Seventh Carrier. Peter Albano. 400p. 1987. pap. 3.95 (ISBN 0-8217-2093-7). Zebra.

Return of the Shadow: The History of the Lord of the Rings, Pt. 1. J. R. Tolkien & Christopher Tolkien. 1989. 19.95 (ISBN 0-395-49863-5). HM.

Return of the Shaman. Gene Fowler. (Illus.). 64p. (Orig.). 1981. pap. 4.00 (ISBN 0-915016-29-X). Second Coming.

Return of the Spirit. Al-Hakim. Tr. by William Hutchins from Arabic. 324p. (Orig.). 1989. 30.00 (ISBN 0-89410-425-X); pap. 15.00 (ISBN 0-89410-426-8). Three Continents.

Return of the Star of Bethlehem. Kenneth Boa & William Proctor. 224p. (Orig.). 1985. pap. 4.95 (ISBN 0-310-33631-7, 12770P). Zondervan.

Return of the Texan. Burt Arthur. 1975. pap. 0.95 (ISBN 0-685-61048-9, LB321, Leisure Bks). Leisure NY.

Return of the Time Machine. Egon Friedell. (Hardcover Collection Ser.: Vol. 2). 1987. 19.95x (ISBN 1-55742-045-9). Starmont Hse.

Return of the Twelve. Pauline Clarke. (Orig.). (gr. 3-7). 1986. pap. 4.95 (ISBN 0-440-47536-8). Dell.

Return of the Whistler. Blossom Elfman. 192p. 1982. pap. 2.25 (ISBN 0-449-70027-5, Juniper). Fawcett.

Return of the White Indian see White Indian Boy.

Return of the Whole Number of Persons Within the Several Districts of the United States. U. S. Census Office, 1790. LC 75-22845. (America in Two Centuries Ser.). 1976. Repr. of 1802 ed. 13.00x (ISBN 0-405-07715-7). Ayer Co Pubs.

Return of the Whole Number of Persons Within the Several Districts of the United States. U.S. Census Office, 1800. LC 75-22846. (America in Two Centuries Ser). 1976. Repr. of 1802 ed. 11.00x (ISBN 0-405-07716-5). Ayer Co Pubs.

Return of the Wolf. Martin Bell. 128p. 1983. 12.50 (ISBN 0-8164-0545-X, HarpR); pap. 7.95 (ISBN 0-8164-2470-5). Har-Row.

Return of the Wolf. Martin Bell. 1986. pap. 2.95 (ISBN 0-345-33483-3, Pub. by Ballantine-Epiphany). Ballantine.

Return of William Shakespeare. Hugh Kingsmill. Ed. by R. Reginald & Douglas Melville. LC 77-84240. (Lost Race & Adult Fantasy Ser.). 1978. Repr. of 1929 ed. lib. bdg. 26.50x (ISBN 0-405-10988-1). Ayer Co Pubs.

Return of Zach Stuart. Will C. Knott. 192p. 1984. pap. 2.25 (ISBN 0-441-71818-3). Ace Bks.

Return on Investment: Strategies for Decision Making. Robert Rachlin. 320p. 1987. 24.95 (ISBN 0-531-15528-5). Watts.

Return on Investment: Strategies for Profit. Robert Rachlin. LC 75-44668. 124p. 1976. 14.95 (ISBN 0-938712-00-4). Marr Pubns.

Return Passage of Multi-Stage Turbomachinery. Ed. by P. Nykorowitsch. 66p. 1983. pap. text ed. 20.00 (ISBN 0-317-02644-5, G00225). ASME.

Return: Poems Collected & New. Alurista. LC 81-68424. 176p. (Eng. & Span.). 1982. pap. 12.00x (ISBN 0-916950-24-7). Biling Rev-Pr.

Return Tickets to Southern Europe. L. Grace Dibble. 1981. 25.00x (ISBN 0-7223-1423-X, Pub. by A H Stockwell England). State Mutual Bk.

Return Ties of Existence. Hatef of Isfahan. Ed. & tr. by Mehdi Nakosteen. LC 75-620100. 50p. 1975. lib. bdg. 20.00x. Iran Bks.

Return Ties of Existence of Hatef of Isfahan. Hatefi Isfahan. Tr. by Mehdi Nakosteen from Persian. 70p. 1988. text ed. 20.00. Iran Bks.

Return to a Chinese Village. Jan Myrdal. (Illus.). 1984. 14.45 (ISBN 0-394-53774-2); pap. 7.95 (ISBN 0-394-72453-4). Pantheon.

Return to a Place Lit by a Glass of Milk. Charles Simic. LC 73-92763. 96p. 1974. 5.95 (ISBN 0-8076-0732-0); pap. 4.95 (ISBN 0-8076-0733-9). Braziller.

Return to Anglia. Spike Mays. 192p. 1987. 24.95 (ISBN 0-575-03840-3, Pub. by Gollancz England). David & Charles.

Return to Armageddon. (Phoenix Force Ser.: No. 11). Date not set. pap. 2.25 (Pub. by Worldwide). Harlequin Bks.

Return to Atlantis, Vol. 1. Ruth Norman. 244p. 1987. text ed. 8.95 (ISBN 0-932642-70-5). Unarius Pubns.

Return to Atlantis, Vol. 1. Ruth E. Norman. (Illus.). 1981. 6.95 (ISBN 0-932642-51-9). Unarius Pubns.

Return to Atlantis, Vol. 2. Ruth E. Norman. (Illus.). 170p. (Orig.). 1982. pap. 5.95 (ISBN 0-932642-52-7). Unarius Pubns.

Return to Atlantis, Vol. 3, Pt. 1. Ruth E. Norman. (Illus.). 300p. (Orig.). 1982. 6.95 (ISBN 0-932642-53-5); pap. text ed. 6.95 (ISBN 0-686-87234-7). Unarius Pubns.

Return to Atlantis, Vol. 3, Pt. 2. Ruth E. Norman. (Illus.). 300p. (Orig.). 1982. pap. text ed. 6.95 (ISBN 0-932642-74-8). Unarius Pubns.

Return to Atlantis, Vol. 4. Ruth Norman. 1987. pap. 7.95 (ISBN 0-317-65209-5). Unarius Pubns.

Return to Atlantis, No. 78. R. A. Montgomery. 176p. (Orig.). (gr. 5 up). 1988. pap. 2.50 (ISBN 0-553-27123-7). Bantam.

Return to Auschwitz. Kitt Hart. LC 81-69155. 200p. 1983. pap. 8.95 (ISBN 0-689-70637-5, 283). Atheneum.

Return to Axanar: The Four Years War, 2 bks. John A. Theisen. (Star Trek Ser.). (Illus.). 107p. (Orig.). 1986. Set. pap. 12.00 (ISBN 0-931787-78-5). FASA Corp.

Return to Aztlan: The Social Process of International Migration from Western Mexico. Douglas S. Massey & Rafeal Alarcon. LC 87-5913. (Studies in Demography: Vol. 1). 354p. 1987. 37.50x (ISBN 0-520-06079-2). U of Cal Pr.

Return to Backsight. J. T. Edson. 192p. 1986. pap. 2.50 (ISBN 0-425-09397-2). Berkley Pub.

Return to Big Grass. Ed. by Richard Wentz & Nicoletta Barrie. (Illus.). 188p. 1986. 40.00 (ISBN 0-9617279-0-X); Incl. wildlife art print. deluxe ed. 300.00 (ISBN 0-9617279-1-8). Ducks Unltd.

Return to Bitter Creek. Doris B. Smith. LC 85-40838. (Viking Kestrel Novels). 180p. (gr. 3-7). 1986. 12.95 (ISBN 0-670-80783-4, Viking Kestrel). Viking.

Return to Bitter Creek. Doris B. Smith. (gr. 3-7). 1988. pap. 3.95 (ISBN 0-14-032223-X, Puffin Bks). Penguin.

Return to Black River Camp. Daniel Weber. (Illus.). 60p. (Orig.). 1980. pap. 5.00 (ISBN 0-934996-11-3). American Studies Pr.

Return to Camelot: Chivalry & the English Gentleman. Mark Girouard. LC 81-51343. (Illus.). 320p. 1981. 45.00x (ISBN 0-300-02739-7). Yale U Pr.

Return to Camelot: Chivalry & the English Gentleman. Mark Girouard. LC 81-51343. (Illus.). 320p. 1985. pap. 14.95 (ISBN 0-300-03473-3, Y-549). Yale U Pr.

Return to Center. Bobbie Probstein. LC 85-70723. (Illus.). 256p. (Orig.). 1985. pap. 9.95 (ISBN 0-87516-554-0). DeVorss.

Return to Cheyne Spa. Daisy Vivian. 1988. 16.95 (ISBN 0-8027-1019-0). Walker & Co.

Return to Cosmology: Postmodern Science & the Theology of Nature. Stephen Toulmin. 224p. 1982. pap. 10.95x (ISBN 0-520-05465-2). U of Cal Pr.

Return to Cross Creek. W. Horace Carter. (Illus.). 308p. (Orig.). 1985. pap. text ed. 7.95 (ISBN 0-937866-09-1). Atlantic Pub Co.

Return to Deathwater. Curtis Norris. Ed. by Rick Nayer. (Narnia Solo Adventures Ser.). 192p. 1988. pap. 2.95 (ISBN 0-425-11028-1). Berkley Pub.

Return to Earth. H. M. Hoover. (gr. 5-9). 1988. pap. 3.95 (ISBN 0-14-032610-3, Puffin Bks). Penguin.

Return to Eden. Harry Harrison. LC 87-47985. 400p. 1988. 18.95 (ISBN 0-553-05315-9, Spectra). Bantam.

Return to Eden. Harry Harrison. (Spectra Ser.). 466p. 1989. pap. 4.50 (ISBN 0-553-27700-6, Spectra). Bantam.

Return to Eden. Rosalind Miles. 416p. 1987. pap. 3.95 (ISBN 0-446-30103-5). Warner Bks.

Return to Elysium. Joan Grant. 320p. 1987. pap. 7.95 (ISBN 0-89804-145-7). Ariel OH.

Return to Elysium. Joan M. Grant. 26.50 (ISBN 0-405-11788-4). Ayer Co Pubs.

Return to Fanglith. John Dalmas. 1987. pap. 2.95 (ISBN 0-671-65343-1). Baen Bks.

Return to Free Market Economics. John Jewkes. 1978. 32.50 (ISBN 0-8419-5028-8). Holmes & Meier.

Return to Freedom. Ed. by Thomas H. Johnson. LC 75-134104. (Essay Index Reprint Ser). 1944. 18.00 (ISBN 0-8369-1966-1). Ayer Co Pubs.

Return to Gone-Away. Elizabeth Enright. LC 86-26976. (gr. 3-7). 1987. pap. 4.95 (ISBN 0-15-266376-2, HJ). HarBraceJ.

Return to Gone-Away. Elizabeth Enright. (gr. 3-7). 1988. 15.75 (ISBN 0-8446-6357-3). Peter Smith.

Return to Health. Jess Kraft. Ed. by Barbara A. Kraft. LC 87-60170. 140p. (Orig.). 1987. pap. 6.95 (ISBN 0-9618099-0-6). Red Lantern Pr.

Return to Herbal Medicine. LaDean Griffin. 1979. pap. 6.95 (ISBN 0-89036-073-1). Hawkes Pub Inc.

Return to Jerusalem. Ruth Norman et al. 286p. (Orig.). 1983. pap. 7.95 (ISBN 0-932642-78-0). Unarius Pubns.

Return to Jerusalem. Lois Parker. Ed. by Gerald Wheeler. 160p. (Orig.). 1988. pap. 9.95 (ISBN 0-8280-0426-9). Review & Herald.

Return to Judaism: Religious Renewal in Israel. Janet Aviad. LC 82-17663. xiv, 194p. 1983. lib. bdg. 20.00x (ISBN 0-226-03236-1); pap. 8.95. U of Chicago Pr.

Return to Judaism: Religious Renewal in Israel. Janet Aviad. LC 82-17663. xiv, 194p. 1985. pap. 8.95 (ISBN 0-226-03235-3); 20.00x. U of Chicago Pr.

Return to Kansas. Jim Hamil & Sharon Hamil. LC 84-51557. (Illus.). 112p. 1984. 35.00 (ISBN 0-7006-0268-2). U Pr of KS.

Return to Kashgar. Gunnar Jarring. Tr. by Eva Claeson. (Central Asia Book Ser.). (Illus.). xi, 252p. 1986. 29.75 (ISBN 0-8223-0664-6). Duke.

Return to Laughter. Elenore S. Bowen. 1964. 5.95 (ISBN 0-385-05312-6, N36, Anchor). Natural Hist.

Return to Laughter. Elenore S. Bowen. 1964. 5.95. Doubleday.

Return to Lesbos. Valerie Taylor. 192p. 1982. pap. 3.95 (ISBN 0-930044-33-9, Volute Bks). Naiad Pr.

Return to Life: Two Imaginings of the Lazarus Theme. an original anthology ed. Ed. by Robert Kastenbaum. LC 76-19587. (Death & Dying Ser.). 1977. Repr. of 1976 ed. lib. bdg. 19.00x (ISBN 0-405-09582-1). Ayer Co Pubs.

Return to Lower Cape Cod. A. F. Joy. Ed. by Paul Kemprecos. (Illus.). 100p. (Orig.). 1986. 5.00x (ISBN 0-934703-03-5). Saturscent Pubns.

Return to Main Street: A Journey to Another America. Nancy Eberle. 1983. 4.95 (ISBN 0-393-30114-1). Norton.

Return to Mathematical Circles. Howard W. Eves. 192p. 1988. text ed. 26.50 (ISBN 0-87150-105-8). PWS Kent Pub.

Return to Meaningfulness. Robert Powell. LC 80-54613. 176p. 1982. pap. text ed. 8.50 (ISBN 0-932238-07-6, Pub. by Avant Bks). Slawson Comm.

Revaluations: Studies in Biography. Lascelles Abercrombie. 17.00 (ISBN 0-8369-0821-X). Ayer Co Pubs.
Revaluations: Studies in Biography. Lascelles Abercrombie et al. LC 75-30773. (English Biography Ser., No. 31). 1975. lib. bdg. 49.95x (ISBN 0-8383-2106-2). Haskell.
Revanche De Bozambo see Bozambo's Revenge.
Revant De Maud. Janet Dailey. (Harlequin Romantique Ser.). 192p. 1983. pap. 1.95 (ISBN 0-373-41229-0). Harlequin Bks.
Reve. Emile Zola. (Coll. Diamant). 1954. 14.50 (ISBN 0-685-23955-1). French & Eur.
Reve. Emile Zola. (Folio Ser.: No. 1746). 1976. 6.95 (ISBN 0-686-55800-6). Schoenhof.
Reve. Emile Zola. 1976. write for info. French & Eur.
Reve Apprivoise. Paul Pelckmans. (Faux Titre Ser.: Vol. 26). 168p. (Fr.). 1986. pap. 25.00 (ISBN 90-6203-987-1, Pub. by Rodopi Holland). Humanities.
Reve d'Alembert. 2nd ed. Denis Diderot & Jean Varloot. 248p. 1962. 9.95 (ISBN 0-686-56028-0). French & Eur.
Reve de Ti-Jean: (Ti-Jean's Dream) Oradel N. Morris. (Orig., Fr. & Eng.). 1983. pap. 4.50 (ISBN 0-944064-02-7). Paupieres Pub.
Reve d'une petite fille qui voulut entrer au Carmel see Little Girl Dreams of Taking the Veil.
Reve et la Vie: A Theatrical Experiment by Gustave Flaubert. Katherine S. Kovacs. LC 81-70301. (Harvard Studies in Romance Languages: No. 38). (Orig., Fr.). 1981. pap. 12.50 (ISBN 0-940940-38-8). Harvard U Romance Lang & Lit.
Reve et l'Action: Une Etude de l'Homme a Cheval de Drieu la Rochelle. Thomas M. Hines. 216p. 1978. 12.95 (ISBN 0-917786-02-5). Summa Pubns.
Reve Sans Vie. Susan Alexander. (Collection Harlequin Ser.). 192p. 1983. pap. 1.95 (ISBN 0-373-49343-6). Harlequin Bks.
Reveal & Conceal: Dress in Contemporary Egypt. Andrea B. Rugh. (Contemporary Issues in the Middle East Ser.). (Illus.). 192p. 1986. text ed. 29.95x (ISBN 0-8156-2368-2). Syracuse U Pr.
Revealed Preference in Assignment Housing Markets. James T. Little. 1975. pap. 2.00 (ISBN 0-318-00017-2, HMS 5). Inst for Urban & Regional.
Revealed Preference Model for Analyzing Interneighborhood Mobility. Charles L. Leven & Jonathan Mark. 1975. pap. 2.00 (ISBN 0-318-00018-0, HMS 6). Inst for Urban & Regional.
Revealed Preference of Government. Kaushik Basu. LC 78-67300. pap. 33.10 (2031619). Bks Demand UMI.
Revealing Intimate Memoirs of Marguerite De Valois. Marguerite De Valois. (Illus.). 1978. Repr. of 1831 ed. deluxe ed. 229.75 (ISBN 0-930582-11-X). Gloucester Art.
Revealing Memoirs of Madame de Montespan, 2 vols. Madame de Montespan. (Illus.). 383p. 1987. Repr. of 1897 ed. 247.55 (ISBN 0-89901-338-4). Found Class Reprints.
Revealing Moment & Other Plays. Oscar W. Firkins. LC 33-3099. pap. 77.50 (ISBN 0-317-39687-0, 2055866). Bks Demand UMI.
Revealing the Heart & Mind of Homer. Homer Arnett. Ed. by Helen Graves. LC 85-51972. 150p. 1986. 8.95 (ISBN 1-55523-008-3). Winston-Derek.
Revealing the Universe: Prediction & Proof in Astronomy. Ed. by James Cornell & Alan P. Lightman. (Illus.). 264p. 1981. pap. text ed. 10.95 (ISBN 0-262-53043-0). MIT Pr.
Revealing Word. Charles Fillmore. 1959. 5.95 (ISBN 0-87159-137-5). Unity School.
Reveille for Radicals. Saul D. Alinsky. 1969. pap. 4.95 (ISBN 0-394-70568-8, V568, Vin). Random.
Reveille in Washington, 1860-1865. Margaret Leech. 484p. 1986. pap. 11.95 (ISBN 0-88184-254-0). Carroll & Graf.
Reveille till Taps: Soldier Life at Fort Mackinac, 1780-1895. Keith Widder. LC 73-159625. (Illus.). 116p. (Orig.). 1972. pap. 1.50 (ISBN 0-911872-12-4). Mackinac Island.
Revel, Riot & Rebellion: Popular Politics & Culture in England 1603-1660. David Underdown. (Illus.). 352p. 1987. pap. 10.95 (ISBN 0-19-285193-4). Oxford U Pr.
Revelacion e Inspiracion de las Escrituras. John M. Lewis & Pablo A. Deiros. (Biblioteca de Doctrina Cristiana). 162p. (Span.). 1986. pap. 5.95 (ISBN 0-311-09113-X). Casa Bautista.
Revelaciones Hispanas. Federico Manrique. LC 83-72441. 120p. (Span.). 1983. pap. 6.00 (ISBN 0-9612202-0-1, 001A). Ancla Prods.
Revelation. Albert Barnes. 12.95 (ISBN 0-8010-0849-2). Baker Bk.
Revelation. Bert Beagle. 160p. 1986. 11.95 (ISBN 0-89962-568-1). Todd & Honeywell.
Revelation. Siegbert W. Becker. 1985. 16.95 (ISBN 0-8100-0190-X, 15N0410). Northwest Pub.
Revelation. James L. Blevins. Ed. by John Hayes. LC 84-4387. (Preaching Guides Ser.). 132p. (Orig.). 1984. pap. 6.95 (ISBN 0-8042-3250-4, John Knox). Westminster John Knox.
Revelation. James B. Coffman. 1984. 18.95 (ISBN 0-915547-14-7). Abilene Christ U.
Revelation. Robert H. Conn. Ed. by Lynne M. Deming & Margaret Rogers. (Cokesbury Basic Bible Commentary Ser.). (Illus.). 154p. (Orig.). 1988. pap. text ed. 4.95 (ISBN 0-939697-37-8). Graded Pr.
Revelation. Charles L. Feinberg. 1985. 9.95 (ISBN 0-88469-162-4). BMH Bks.
Revelation. Alger M. Fitch, Jr. (Standard Bible Studies). 112p. 1986. pap. 5.95 (ISBN 0-87403-173-7, 40113). Standard Pub.
Revelation. Tr. by J. Massyngberde Ford. LC 74-18796. (Anchor Bible Ser.: Vol. 38). (Illus.). 504p. 1975. pap. 18.00 (ISBN 0-385-00895-3). Doubleday.
Revelation. Arno C. Gaebelein. LC 61-17225. 1960. 7.95 (ISBN 0-87213-223-4). Loizeaux.
Revelation. Homer Hailey. LC 78-62441. 1979. 14.95 (ISBN 0-8010-4201-1). Baker Bk.
Revelation. Timothy A. Heck. (Standard Bible Study Workbooks Ser.). 64p. 1986. pap. text ed. 1.95 (ISBN 0-87403-193-1, 40213). Standard Pub.
Revelation. H. A. Ironside. 10.95 (ISBN 0-87213-384-2). Loizeaux.
Revelation. Irving L. Jensen. (Bible Self-Study Ser.). 124p. (Orig.). 1971. pap. 3.50 (ISBN 0-8024-1066-9). Moody.
Revelation. Irving L. Jensen. (Irving Jensen's Do-It-Yourself Bible Study Ser.). 110p. (Orig.). 1985. wkbk. 5.95 (ISBN 0-89840-081-3). Heres Life.
Revelation. rev. ed. Leon Morris. (Tyndale New Testament Commentary Ser.). 1987. pap. text ed. 7.95 (ISBN 0-8028-0273-7). Eerdmans.
Revelation. Peggy Payne. LC 87-32621. 1988. 18.95 (ISBN 0-671-65252-4). S&S.
Revelation. Luther Poellot. (Classic Commentary Ser.). 314p. 1987. 14.95 (ISBN 0-570-04235-6, 15-1864). Concordia.
Revelation. (Erdmans Commentaries Ser.). pap. 5.95 (ISBN 0-8010-3405-1). Baker Bk.
Revelation. Charles C. Ryrie. (Everyman's Bible Commentary Ser.). (Orig.). 1968. pap. 5.95 (ISBN 0-8024-2066-4). Moody.
Revelation. Lehman Strauss. LC 64-8641. Orig. Title: Book of the Revelation. 9.95 (ISBN 0-87213-825-9). Loizeaux.
Revelation. J. P. Sweet. LC 78-26383. (Westminster Pelican Commentaries). 378p. 1979. 14.95 (ISBN 0-664-21375-8); softcover 9.95 (ISBN 0-664-24262-6). Westminster John Knox.
Revelation. Geoffrey Wilson. 1985. pap. 7.95 (ISBN 0-87552-977-1, Evangel Pr UK). Presby & Reformed.
Revelation see Commentaries on the New Testament.
Revelation - the Last Book of the Bible. Edwin A. Schick. LC 76-62602. pap. 20.00 (ISBN 0-317-55548-0, 2029617). Bks Demand UMI.
Revelation - the Seer, the Saviour, & the Saved. rev. ed. James D. Strauss. (Bible Study Textbook Ser.). (Illus.). 1972. 15.95 (ISBN 0-89900-048-7). College Pr Pub.
Revelation - Verse by Verse. William R. Newell. (Reference Library Edition). 416p. 1987. Repr. of 1938 ed. text ed. 14.95 (ISBN 0-529-06458-8). World Bible.
Revelation: A Commentary on the Book, Based on the Study of Twenty Four Psychic Discourses of Edgar Cayce. Edgar Cayce. (Twenty-Six Interpretive Readings). 1969. pap. 8.95 (ISBN 0-87604-003-2). ARE Pr.
Revelation: A Study Guide. Edwin Walhout. (Revelation Series for Adults). 1978. pap. text ed. 2.75 (ISBN 0-933140-07-X). CRC Pubns.
Revelation: An Exposition. Carroll Gillis. LC 88-90642. 215p. 1988. 16.95 (ISBN 0-9615673-2-5); pap. 8.95 (ISBN 0-9615673-3-3). Sunburst Pr CA.
Revelation: An Exposition of the First Eleven Chapters. James B. Ramsey. (Geneva Commentary Ser.). 1977. 19.95 (ISBN 0-85151-256-9). Banner of Truth.
Revelation & Divination in Ndembu Ritual. Victor Turner. LC 75-1623. (Symbol, Myth & Ritual Ser). (Illus.). 352p. 1975. cancelled 29.95x (ISBN 0-8014-0863-6); pap. 10.95x (ISBN 0-8014-9158-4). Cornell U Pr.
Revelation & Experience. Carol R. Murphy. LC 64-22765. (Orig.). pap. 2.50x (ISBN 0-87574-137-1). Pendle Hill.
Revelation & Faith: Theological Reflections on the Knowing & Doing of Truth. Theron D. Price. 192p. 1987. 29.95 (ISBN 0-86554-260-0, MUP H-221); pap. 14.95 (ISBN 0-86554-261-9, MUP P-45). Mercer Univ Pr.
Revelation & Its Interpretation. Aylward Shorter. 280p. 1984. pap. text ed. 14.95 (ISBN 0-225-66356-2, AY8482, HarpR). Har-Row.
Revelation & Love's Architecture. Martin C. D'Arcy. 90p. 1976. 8.00 (ISBN 0-89182-010-8). Charles River Bks.
Revelation & Reason. Emil Brunner. 448p. 1984. pap. 14.95 (ISBN 0-913029-01-7). Stevens Bk Pr.
Revelation & Reason in Advaita Vedanta. K. S. Murty. 1974. Repr. 11.25 (ISBN 0-8426-0662-9). Orient Bk Dist.
Revelation & Reason in Islam. Arthur J. Arberry. LC 80-1936. (BCL: Series I & II). Repr. of 1957 ed. 20.00 (ISBN 0-404-18952-0). AMS Pr.
Revelation & Redemption. George W. Buchanan. 1978. text ed. 29.50 (ISBN 0-915948-04-4). Bks Distinction.
Revelation & Religion: Studies in the Theological Interpretation of Religious Types. Herbert H. Farmer. LC 77-27177. (Gifford Lectures: 1950). (Illus.). 256p. Repr. of 1954 ed. 31.00 (ISBN 0-404-60505-2). AMS Pr.
Revelation & Response in the Old Testament. Cuthbert A. Simpson. LC 73-76022. Repr. of 1947 ed. 15.00 (ISBN 0-404-06056-0). AMS Pr.
Revelation & Theology: The Gospel As Narrated Promise. Ronald F. Thiemann. LC 84-40822. 208p. 1985. text ed. 23.95 (ISBN 0-268-01629-1). U of Notre Dame Pr.
Revelation & Theology: The Gospel As Narrated Promise. Ronald F. Thiemann. LC 84-40822. 198p. 1987. pap. text ed. 9.95 (ISBN 0-268-01632-1). U of Notre Dame Pr.
Revelation & Violence: A Study in Contextualization. Walter Brueggemann. LC 86-60473. (Pere Marquette Ser.). 72p. 1986. 7.95 (ISBN 0-87462-541-6). Marquette.
Revelation As Drama. James L. Blevins. LC 84-4986. 1984. pap. 6.95 (ISBN 0-8054-1393-6). Broadman.
Revelation: Bible Study Commentary. Alan F. Johnson. (Bible Study Commentary Ser.). 1986. pap. 7.95 (ISBN 0-310-45173-6, 12386P). Zondervan.
Revelation (Everyman's Bible Commentary) see Apocalipsis (Comentario Biblico Portavoz).
Revelation Explained. F. G. Smith. 464p. Repr. 5.50 (ISBN 0-686-29163-8). Faith Pub Hse.
Revelation Expounded. W. Kelly. 5.95 (ISBN 0-88172-106-9). Believers Bkshelf.
Revelation fo the Christian Age. Ralph F. Brashears. 1988. 18.95 (ISBN 0-533-07412-6). Vantage.
Revelation: For a New Age. Dorothy Elder. LC 81-65477. 320p. (Orig.). 1981. pap. 11.50 (ISBN 0-87516-446-3). DeVorss.
Revelation for Layman. Jim McKeever. 1980. 10.95 (ISBN 0-931608-07-4); pap. 5.95 (ISBN 0-931608-08-2). Omega Pubns OR.
Revelation for Today: Images of Hope. Richard L. Jeske. LC 82-16079. 144p. 1983. pap. 6.95 (ISBN 0-8006-1693-6). Fortress.
Revelation: God & Satan in the Apocalypse. James Kallas. LC 73-78268. 128p. 1973. pap. 7.95 (ISBN 0-8066-1332-7, 10-5490). Augsburg.
Revelation: God's Grand Finale. Hilton Sutton. 280p. (Orig.). 1984. pap. 6.95 (ISBN 0-89274-298-4). Harrison Hse.
Revelation: God's Stamp of Sovereignty. R. Hollis Gause. LC 83-63383. 286p. 1983. pap. text ed. 9.95 (ISBN 0-87148-740-3). Pathway Pr.
Revelation-Illustrated & Made Plain. rev. ed. Tim Lahaye. 456p. 1975. 10.95 (ISBN 0-310-26991-1, 18073P). Zondervan.
Revelation in Indian Thought: A Festschrift in Honor of Professor T. R. V. Murti. Ed. by Harold Coward. LC 77-71192. 1977. 29.95 (ISBN 0-913546-52-6). Dharma Pub.
Revelation in Jewish Wisdom Literature. John C. Rylaarsdam. (Midway Reprint Ser.). pap. 35.00 (ISBN 0-317-26582-2, 2024065). Bks Demand UMI.
Revelation in Religious Belief. George I. Mavrodes. LC 87-26697. 168p. 1988. 24.95 (ISBN 0-87722-545-1). Temple U Pr.
Revelation in the Fourth Gospel: Narrative Mode & Theological Claim. Gail R. O'Day. LC 86-45217. 160p. 1986. pap. 9.95 (ISBN 0-8006-1933-1). Fortress.
Revelation, Inspiration, Scripture. John M. Lewis. LC 83-71822. (Layman's Library of Christian Doctrine Ser.). 1985. 5.95 (ISBN 0-8054-1633-1). Broadman.
Revelation of Baha'u'llah & the Bab: Descartes Theory of Knowledge, Bk. 1. Ruhi Afnan. LC 75-109166. 1970. 8.95 (ISBN 0-8022-2307-9). Philos Lib.
Revelation of Baha'u'llah: Mazra'ih & Bahji 1877-92, Vol. IV. Adib Taherzadeh. (Illus.). 504p. 1988. 29.95 (ISBN 0-85398-269-4); pap. 19.95 (ISBN 0-85398-270-8). G Ronald Pub.
Revelation of Baha'u'llah, Vol. I: Baghdad 1853-1863. Adib Taherzadeh. (Illus.). 384p. 1974. pap. 14.95 (ISBN 0-85398-057-8). G Ronald Pub.
Revelation of Baha'u'llah, Vol. II: Adrianople, 1863-1868. Adib Taherzadeh. (Illus.). 492p. 1977. pap. 17.95 (ISBN 0-85398-071-3). G Ronald Pub.
Revelation of Baha'u'llah Vol. III: Akka',the Early Years 1868-77. Ad. Taherzadeh. (Illus.). 544p. 25.00 (ISBN 0-85398-143-4). G Ronald Pub.
Revelation of Bethlehem. Two Hermits. 1985. pap. 3.50 (ISBN 0-932506-41-0). St Bedes Pubns.
Revelation of Deity. J. E. Turner. Repr. of 1931 ed. 20.00 (ISBN 0-527-91170-4). Kraus Repr.
Revelation of Elchasai: Investigations into the Evidence for a Mesopotamian Jewish Apocalypse of the Second Century & Its Reception by Judeo-Christian Propagandists. Gerard P. Luttikhuizen. 263p. 1985. lib. bdg. 72.50x (ISBN 3-16-144935-5, Pub. by J C B Mohr BRD). Coronet Bks.
Revelation of God in Nature. Bert Thompson & Wayne Jackson. (That You May Believe Ser.). 22p. (Orig.). 1985. pap. 1.50 (ISBN 0-932859-04-6). Apologetic Pr.
Revelation of Hermes. Paracelsus. 1984. pap. 2.95 (ISBN 0-916411-81-8, Pub. by Alchemical Pr). Holmes Pub.
Revelation of Jesus Christ. Ray F. Robbins. LC 75-1739. 240p. 1976. bds. 6.50 (ISBN 0-8054-1354-5). Broadman.
Revelation of Jesus Christ. Ed. by J. B. Smith & J. Otis Yoder. LC 61-7091. 396p. 1961. 14.95 (ISBN 0-8361-1478-7). Herald Pr.
Revelation of Jesus Christ. John F. Walvoord. LC 66-16227. 1966. 17.95 (ISBN 0-8024-7310-5). Moody.
Revelation of John. Ed. by Thomas F. Glasson. (Cambridge Bible Commentary on the New English Bible, New Testament Ser.). (Orig.). 1965. o. p. 16.95 (ISBN 0-521-04208-9); pap. 9.95x (ISBN 0-521-09256-6). Cambridge U Pr.
Revelation of John. James Roberts. 1974. 12.95 (ISBN 0-915547-38-4). Abilene Christ U.
Revelation of John see Daily Study Bible: New Testament.
Revelation of Life Eternal: An Introduction to the Christian Message. Nicholas Arseniev. 144p. 1964. pap. 5.95 (ISBN 0-913836-00-1). St Vladimirs.
Revelation of Purgatory by an Unknown, 15th Century Woman Visionary: Introduction, Critical Text & Translation. Marta P. Harley. LC 85-28390. (Studies in Women & Religion: Vol. 18). 160p. 1986. lib. bdg. 49.95x (ISBN 0-88946-531-2). E Mellen.
Revelation of St. John, Vol. I. Eduard Schick. Ed. by John L. McKenzie. LC 81-605. (New Testament for Spiritual Reading Ser.). 112p. 1981. pap. 4.95. Crossroad NY.
Revelation of St. John, Vol. II. Eduard Schick. Ed. by John L. McKenzie. LC 81-605. (New Testament for Spiritual Reading Ser.). 112p. 1981. 10.00; pap. 4.95. Crossroad NY.
Revelation of Saint John - an Open Book. Irving C. Tomlinson. 285p. 1987. Repr. of 1934 ed. 12.95 (ISBN 0-942910-13-3). Dynapress.
Revelation of St. John, Pt. 1 see New Testament for Spiritual Reading.
Revelation of St. John, Pt. 2 see New Testament for Spiritual Reading.
Revelation of Saint John the Divine. Intro. by Harold Bloom. (Modern Critical Interpretations Ser.). 1987. 19.95 (ISBN 0-87754-916-8). Chelsea Hse.
Revelation of St. John the Divine. G. B. Caird. LC 66-20774. (New Testament Commentaries Ser.). 1966. 19.95 (ISBN 0-06-061296-7, HarpR). Har-Row.
Revelation of the Son of Man. Levi Khamor. (Orig.). 1988. pap. price not set (ISBN 0-932506-51-8). St Bedes Pubns.
Revelation of the True Minerva. Thomas Blenerhasset. LC 42-5954. 1978. Repr. of 1582 ed. 30.00x (ISBN 0-8201-1196-1). Schol Facsimiles.
Revelation of Treasure Hid--Concerning Freedom, Concerning the Motherland, Concerning Justice, Apostolical Canons Respecting Baptism. Apostolos Makrakis. Ed. by Orthodox Christian Educational Society. Tr. by Denver Cummings from Hellenic. 80p. (Orig.). 1952. pap. 2.00x (ISBN 0-938366-23-8). Orthodox Chr.
Revelation Record. Henry M. Morris. 1983. 19.95 (ISBN 0-8423-5511-1). Tyndale.
Revelation Revealed. Jack Van Impe. 282p. 1982. pap. 6.95 (ISBN 0-934803-09-9); 8-cassette set 29.95 (ISBN 0-934803-35-8). J Van Impe.
Revelation, Systematically Studied. Parnell C. Coward. 1983. pap. 6.95 (ISBN 0-87148-739-X). Pathway Pr.
Revelation Taught: The Paraclete in the Gospel of John. Eskil Franck. (New Testament Ser.: No. 14). 168p. (Orig.). 1985. pap. text ed. 32.50x (ISBN 91-40-05114-5, Pub. by Liber Utbildning (Stockholm Sweden)). Coronet Bks.
Revelation Teaching Syllabus. Hilton Sutton. 1985. 10.00 (ISBN 0-89274-318-2). Harrison Hse.
Revelation, the Future Foretold. Keith L. Brooks. (Teach Yourself the Bible Ser.). 1962. pap. 2.95 (ISBN 0-8024-7308-3). Moody.
Revelation: The Lamb Who Is the Lion. Gladys Hunt. (Fisherman Bible Studyguide). 73p. 1973. saddle-stitched 2.95 (ISBN 0-87788-486-2). Shaw Pubs.
Revelation: The Triumph of God. Paul Stevens. (LifeBuilder Bible Studies). 64p. (Orig.). 1987. pap. 2.95 (ISBN 0-8308-1021-8). Inter-Varsity.
Revelation: Three Viewpoints. LC 77-74512. 1977. pap. 10.95 (ISBN 0-8054-1363-4). Broadman.
Revelation Through Reason: Religion in the Light of Science & Philosophy. Errol E. Harris. 1958. 39.50x (ISBN 0-317-27547-X). Elliots Bks.
Revelation to John. Martin H. Franzmann. 148p. 1986. pap. 7.95 (ISBN 0-570-03728-X, 12-2630). Concordia.
Revelation Visualized. Salem Kirban & Gary Cohen. 1971. pap. 14.95 (ISBN 0-912582-08-1). Kirban.
Revelation: Your Future Prophesied. Marjorie H. Russell. (Illus.). 60p. (Orig.). 1985. pap. 7.98 (ISBN 0-9614745-0-5). Arcadia Corp.
Revelations. Carl Hazlewood. (Illus.). 24p. (Orig.). 1987. pap. write for info. (ISBN 0-936739-07-X). Hallwalls Inc.
Revelations: A Collection of Gay Male Coming Out Stories. Wayne Curtis. 200p. (Orig.). 1988. pap. 7.95 (ISBN 1-55583-143-5). Alyson Pubns.
Revelations: As It Is. Patricia Sri. Ed. by Moringland Publications Inc. (Illus.). 635p. (Orig.). 1979. pap. 10.00 (ISBN 0-935146-08-3). Morningland.
Revelations Concerning Napoleon's Escape from St. Helena. Paul P. Ebeyer. 1947. 10.00 (ISBN 0-911116-75-3). Pelican.
Revelations: Diaries of Women. Ed. by Mary J. Moffat & Charlotte Painter. 1975. pap. 5.95 (ISBN 0-394-71151-3, Vin). Random.
Revelations from a Secret Kingdom. Sam Rubin. 48p. 1987. 6.95 (ISBN 0-89962-631-9). Todd & Honeywell.

Revelations from the Half-Seer. C. C. Brown. 1977. pap. 3.00 (ISBN 0-9600378-4-5). C C Brown Pub.

Revelations: Glimpses of Reality. Ronald S. Lello. 152p. 1985. 10.95 (ISBN 0-85683-079-8, Pub. by Shepheard-Walwyn UK). Dufour.

Revelations of a Russian Diplomat: The Memoirs of Dmitrii I. Abrikossow. Dmitrii I. Abrikossow. Ed. by George A. Lensen. LC 64-18426. (Washington Paperbacks on Russia & Asia Ser.: No. 5). (Illus.). 351p. 1968. 20.00x (ISBN 0-295-73911-8); pap. 6.95x (ISBN 0-295-97896-1, WPRA5). U of Wash Pr.

Revelations of a Slave Smuggler. Richard Drake. LC 74-99369. (Illus.). xi, 109p. 1972. Repr. of 1860 ed. lib. bdg. 12.00 (ISBN 0-8411-0040-3). Metro Bks.

Revelations of a Soviet Diplomat. Grigorii Z. Besedovskii. Tr. by M. Norgate. LC 75-39046. (Russian Studies: Perspectives on the Revolution Ser). 276p. 1977. Repr. of 1931 ed. 23.65 (ISBN 0-88355-424-0). Hyperion-Conn.

Revelations of a Spirit Medium. facsimile ed. Harry Price & Eric J. Dingwall. LC 75-7395. (Perspectives in Psychical Research Ser.). 1975. Repr. of 1922 ed. 28.50x (ISBN 0-405-07044-6). Ayer Co Pubs.

Revelations of an International Spy. I. T. Lincoln. 59.95 (ISBN 0-8490-0949-9). Gordon Pr.

Revelations of Antichrist. W. H. Burris. 59.95 (ISBN 0-8490-0950-2). Gordon Pr.

Revelations of Antichrist: Concerning Christ & Christianity. William H. Burr. LC 79-161340. (Atheist Viewpoint Ser). 448p. 1972. Repr. of 1879 ed. 29.00 (ISBN 0-405-03801-1). Ayer Co Pubs.

Revelations of Brimstone: Ominous Portents of the Parousia of Christ. R. Henry Hall. (Illus.). 374p. (Orig.). 1984. pap. 6.95 (ISBN 0-930351-00-2). Spirit Prophecy.

Revelations of Divine Love. Julian of Norwich. Ed. by Roger L. Roberts. LC 82-80471. (Treasures from the Spiritual Classics Ser.). 64p. 1982. pap. 2.95 (ISBN 0-8192-1308-X). Morehouse.

Revelations of Divine Love. Clifton Wolters. 1982. pap. 4.95 (ISBN 0-14-044177-8). Penguin.

Revelations of Divine Love: Juliana of Norwich. Tr. by M. L. Del Mastro. LC 76-52004. 1977. pap. 4.95 (ISBN 0-385-12297-7, Im). Doubleday.

Revelations of Hermes: An Exposition of Adamic Christianity. Robert E. Birdsong. LC 74-84553. (Illus.). 1975. 10.00 (ISBN 0-917108-11-6); pap. 6.95 (ISBN 0-917108-04-3). Sirius Bks.

Revelations of Margaret of Cortona. Ange-Marie Hiral. (Spirit &Life Ser). 1952. 3.00 (ISBN 0-686-11562-7). Franciscan Inst.

Revelations of Prison Life with an Enquiry into Prison Discipline & Secretary Punishments, 2 vols. George L. Chesterton. LC 83-49323. (Crime & Punishment in England, 1850-1922 Ser.). 641p. 1984. Set. lib. bdg. 80.00 (ISBN 0-8240-6206-X). Garland Pub.

Revelations of Saint Birgitta. Ed. by W. P. Cumming. (EETS, OS Ser.: No. 178). Repr. of 1929 ed. 30.00 (ISBN 0-527-00175-9). Kraus Repr.

Revelations of St. Bridget on the Life & Passion of Our Lord & the Life of His Blessed Mother. St. Bridget of Sweden. LC 83-51547. 81p. 1984. pap. 2.50 (ISBN 0-89555-233-7). TAN Bks Pubs.

Revelations of the Nameless One: An Interpretation of the "T" Tarot. Thales. (Illus.). 100p. (Orig.). 1982. pap. 5.95 (ISBN 0-935548-07-6). Santarasa Pubns.

Revelations of the Prophet Joseph Smith: A Historical & Biographical Commentary of the Doctrine & Covenants. Lyndon W. Cook. LC 85-70650. (Illus.). 400p. 1985. Repr. of 1981 ed. 13.95 (ISBN 0-87747-947-X). Deseret Bk.

Revelations of Things to Come. Earlyne C. Chaney. (Illus.). 156p. 1982. pap. 13.95 (ISBN 0-918936-12-8). Astara.

Revelations of Women Mystics: From Middle Ages to Modern Times. Jose D. Vinck. LC 84-24485. 180p. (Orig.). 1985. pap. 5.95 (ISBN 0-8189-0478-X). Alba.

Revelations One: Noah's Flood Was a Result of Nuclear War. Kostis Kandias. (Illus.). 202p. 1981. 10.00 (ISBN 0-682-49672-3). Exposition-Phoenix.

Revelations Revealed. rev. ed. Hal J. Chapel & Richard G. Clark. Ed. by Debbie Danielpour. 1987. pap. 45.00 (ISBN 0-317-62569-1). Paradigm Pub.

Revelatory Positivism? Barth's Earliest Theology & the Marburg School. Simon Fisher. (Theological Monographs). (Illus.). 368p. 1988. 69.00 (ISBN 0-19-826725-8). Oxford U Pr.

Revelliere-Lepeaux, Citizen Director, 1753-1824. Georgia Robison. LC 72-8923. 308p. 1971. Repr. of 1938 ed. lib. bdg. 19.50x (ISBN 0-374-96893-4, Octagon). Hippocrene Bks.

Revels & Jests: Extracts from the Accounts of the Revels at Court in the Reigns of Queen Elizabeth & King James I. Ed. by P. Cunningham & J. O. Halliwell. Bd. with Tarlton's Jests & News Out of Purgatory. (Shakespeare Society of London: Vol. 13). pap. 42.80 (ISBN 0-8115-0175-2). Kraus Repr.

Revels History of Drama in English: Medieval Drama, Vol. I. L. Potter. 1983. 59.95 (ISBN 0-416-13020-8, NO. 6422). Routledge Chapman & Hall.

Revels History of Drama in English, Vol. 2: 1500-1576. Thomas Craik et al. 1980. 59.95x (ISBN 0-416-13030-5, NO. 6365). Routledge Chapman & Hall.

Revels History of Drama in English, Vol. 3: 1576-1613. J. Leeds Barroll et al. LC 74-15177. (Revels History of the Drama in English Ser.). 400p. 1975. 22.00x (ISBN 0-416-13040-2, NO. 2076). Routledge Chapman & Hall.

Revels History of Drama in English, Vol. 5: 1660-1750. Ed. by J. Loftis et al. 335p. 1976. text ed. 22.00x (ISBN 0-416-13060-7, NO. 2299). Routledge Chapman & Hall.

Revels History of Drama in English, Vol. 6: 1750-1880. M. R. Booth et al. LC 74-15178. (Illus.). 250p. 1975. 22.00x (ISBN 0-416-13070-4, NO. 2103). Routledge Chapman & Hall.

Revels History of Drama in English, Vol. 7: 1880 to the Present. Hugh Hunt et al. (Revels History of Drama in English Ser.). (Illus.). 1978. 59.95x (ISBN 0-416-13080-1, NO. 2057); pap. 19.95x (ISBN 0-416-81390-9, NO. 2058). Routledge Chapman & Hall.

Revels History of Drama in English, Vol. 8: American Drama. Travis Bogard et al. (Illus.). 1978. 59.95x (ISBN 0-416-13090-9, NO. 2101); pap. 19.95x (ISBN 0-416-81400-X, NO. 2102). Routledge Chapman & Hall.

Revels History of Drama in English: 1613-1660, Vol. 4. Ed. by Philip Edwards et al. (Illus.). 1982. 59.95x (ISBN 0-416-13050-X, NO. 6423). Routledge Chapman & Hall.

Revels in Jamaica, Sixteen Eighty-Two to Eighteen Thirty-Eight. Richardson Wright. LC 78-81202. (Illus.). 1937. Repr. of 1927 ed. 26.50 (ISBN 0-405-09105-2). Ayer Co Pubs.

Revels of Fancy. facsimile ed. William J. Vandyne. LC 71-179297. (Black Heritage Library Collection). Repr. of 1891 ed. 12.00 (ISBN 0-8369-8933-3). Ayer Co Pubs.

Revenant. Dan Gerber. (Orig.). 1971. 4.95 (ISBN 0-912090-11-1); pap. 2.45 (ISBN 0-912090-10-3). Sumac Mich.

Revenant. Remi Tremblay. (Novels by Franco-Americans in New England 1850-1940 Ser.). 437p. (Fr.). (gr. 10 up). 1980. pap. 4.50 (ISBN 0-911409-21-1). Natl Mat Dev.

Revenant. Hugh Zachary. 240p. 1988. pap. 3.95 (ISBN 0-451-40092-5, Onyx). NAL.

Revenant Christ. Friend Stuart. 1983. pap. 4.95 (ISBN 0-912132-15-9). Dominion Pr.

Revenge. 2nd ed. Howard Brenton. 1982. 6.95 (ISBN 0-413-50010-1, NO. 3652). Heinemann Ed.

Revenge. George Hayduke. 224p. 1984. pap. 9.95 (ISBN 0-8184-0353-5). Lyle Stuart.

Revenge at Blue Valley. W. G. Schreiber. (YA) (gr. 7 up). 1978. 9.95 (ISBN 0-685-86412-X, Avalon). Bouregy.

Revenge at the Spy-Catchers' Picnic. Anne West. LC 84-40774. 1981. 9.70i (ISBN 0-317-56675-X, Lipp Jr Bks). HarpJ.

Revenge Book. B. Smith. 1986. lib. bdg. 79.95 (ISBN 0-8490-3731-X). Gordon Pr.

Revenge Book. Bob Smith. (Illus.). 90p. 1980. pap. 8.00 (ISBN 0-87364-210-4). Paladin Pr.

Revenge for Love. Wyndham Lewis. 342p. 1978. pap. 5.95 (ISBN 0-89526-908-2). Regnery Gateway.

Revenge in Rome. Patricia A. Stewart & Edna H. Maples. (Murder Mystery Parites Ser.). (Illus.). 52p. 1985. 8.00 (ISBN 0-317-38202-0). Univ Games.

Revenge in the Silent Tomb. J. J. Fortune. (Race Against Time Ser.: No. 1). 160p. (Orig.). (YA) (gr. 7-12). 1984. pap. 2.25 (ISBN 0-440-97707-X, LFL). Dell.

Revenge Motive in Websterean Tragedy. Melvin Seiden. Ed. by James Hogg. (Jacobean Drama Studies). 148p. (Orig.). 1973. pap. 15.00 (ISBN 3-7052-0314-2, Pub. by Salzburg Studies). Longwood Pub Group.

Revenge of Bussy D'Ambois by George Chapman. Robert J. Lordi. Ed. by James Hogg. (Jacobean Drama Studies). 229p. (Orig.). 1977. pap. 15.00 (ISBN 3-7052-0366-5, Salzburg Studies). Longwood Pub Group.

Revenge of Dracula. Peter Tremayne. 15.00 (ISBN 0-937986-22-4). D M Grant.

Revenge of Jeremiah Plum. Elizabeth Muskopf. LC 86-27036. (Illus.). 224p. (gr. 4-6). 1987. 12.95 (ISBN 0-8050-0203-0). H Holt & Co.

Revenge of Labyrinthon. Vladimir Koziakin. 64p. 1984. pap. 2.95 (ISBN 0-441-71842-6). Ace Bks.

Revenge of Samuel Stokes. Penelope Lively. 128p. (gr. 4-6). 1981. 9.95 (ISBN 0-525-38205-4). Dutton.

Revenge of the Creature. William R. Sanford & Carl R. Green. Ed. by Howard Schroeder. LC 86-24268. (Movie Monsters Ser.). (Illus.). 48p. (gr. 3-5). 1987. lib. bdg. 9.95 (ISBN 0-89686-313-1). Crestwood Hse.

Revenge of the Creature Features Movie Guide. 3rd, rev. ed. John Stanley. (Illus.). 460p. 1988. deluxe ed. 40.00 slipcase (ISBN 0-940064-05-7); pap. 11.95 (ISBN 0-940064-04-9). Creatures At Large.

Revenge of the Elegant Lady. Alan F. Barton. 1987. 7.95 (ISBN 0-533-06236-5). Vantage.

Revenge of the Falcon Knight. Scott Siegel. (Wizards, Warriors & You Ser.: Bk. 6). 112p. (gr. 4 up). 1985. pap. 2.25 (ISBN 0-380-89524-2). Avon.

Revenge of the Great Magician. Jimmie Davis, Jr. 1984. cancelled (ISBN 0-8062-2331-6). Carlton.

Revenge of the Horseclans. Robert Adams. (Horseclans Ser.: No. 3). 1983. pap. 2.95 (ISBN 0-451-13306-4, AE3306, Sig). NAL.

Revenge of the Hound: The New Sherlock Holmes Novel. Michael Hardwick. LC 87-40188. 320p. 1987. 17.95 (ISBN 0-394-55653-4, Pub. by Villard Bks). Random.

Revenge of the Incredible Dr. Rancid & His Youthful Assistant, Jeffrey. Ellen Conford. 132p. (gr. 1-8). 1980. 14.95 (ISBN 0-316-15288-9). Little.

Revenge of the Incredible Dr. Rancid & His Youthful Assistant, Jeffrey. Ellen Conford. (gr. 4-6). 1983. pap. 2.25 (ISBN 0-590-33746-7, Apple Paperbacks). Scholastic Inc.

Revenge of the Incredible Dr. Rancid & His Youthful Assistant, Jeffrey. Ellen Conford. 128p. (gr. 4-6). 1982. pap. 2.25 (ISBN 0-590-31794-6, Apple Paperbacks). Scholastic Inc.

Revenge of the Incredible Dr. Rancid & His Youthful Assistant, Jeffrey. 120p. (gr. 4-6). 1988. pap. 2.50 (ISBN 0-590-41274-4). Scholastic Inc.

Revenge of the Lawn. Richard Brautigan. (gr. 10 up). 1980. pap. 2.95 (ISBN 0-671-41852-1). PB.

Revenge of the Manitou. Graham Masterton. 272p. 1987. pap. 3.95 (ISBN 0-8125-2181-1). Tor Bks.

Revenge of the Master. (Track Ser.: No. 8). Date not set. pap. 2.50 (ISBN 0-317-64001-1, Pub. by Worldwide). Harlequin Bks.

Revenge of the Mountain Man. William W. Johnston. 256p. 1988. pap. 2.95 (ISBN 0-8217-2356-1). Zebra.

Revenge of the Nerd. John McNamara. 128p. (gr. 5 up). 1985. pap. 2.50 (ISBN 0-440-97353-8, LFL). Dell.

Revenge of the Philistines: Art & Culture 1972-1984. Hilton Kramer. 425p. 1984. 25.00 (ISBN 0-02-918470-3). Free Pr.

Revenge of the Robins Family. Thomas Chastain & Bill Adler. 1985. pap. 3.50 (ISBN 0-446-32533-3). Warner Bks.

Revenge of the Shogun Ninja. Katsumi Toda. LC 84-70702. (Illus.). 125p. 1984. pap. 7.95 (ISBN 0-86568-053-1, 535, Pub. by Dragon Bks Ltd). Unique Pubns.

Revenge of the Wizard's Ghost. John Bellairs. LC 85-4550. (Illus.). 160p. (gr. 5 up). 1985. 11.95 (ISBN 0-8037-0170-5, 01160-350); PLB 11.89 (ISBN 0-8037-0177-2). Dial Bks Young.

Revenge of the Wizard's Ghost. John Bellairs. 160p. 1986. pap. 2.75 (ISBN 0-553-15451-6). Bantam.

Revenge Rider. Jim Wilmeth. 192p. (Orig.). 1981. pap. 1.95 (ISBN 0-505-51738-8, Pub. by Tower Bks). Leisure NY.

Revengers. Donald Hamilton. 352p. (Orig.). 1986. pap. 3.50 (ISBN 0-449-13093-2). Fawcett.

Revenger's Madness: A Study of Revenge Tragedy Motifs. Charles A. Hallett & Elaine S. Hallett. LC 80-13893. xii, 349p. 1980. 26.50x (ISBN 0-8032-2309-9). U of Nebr Pr.

Revenger's Tragedy. Cyril Tourneur. Ed. by Brian Gibbons. (New Mermaid Ser.). 1976. pap. 4.95x (ISBN 0-393-90027-4). Norton.

Revenger's Tragedy. Cyril Tourneur. Ed. by Lawrence J. Ross. LC 66-12744. (Regents Renaissance Drama Ser). xxxii, 130p. 1966. 14.50x (ISBN 0-8032-0283-0); pap. 5.95x (ISBN 0-8032-5284-6, BB 218, Bison). U of Nebr Pr.

Revenger's Tragedy. Cyril Tourneur. Ed. by R. A. Foakes. (Revels Plays Ser.). 152p. 1980. pap. 11.00 (ISBN 0-7190-1612-6, Pub. by Manchester Univ PR). St Martin.

Revenger's Tragedy. Cyril Tourneur. (Swan Theatre Plays). 76p. 1987. pap. 8.95 (ISBN 0-413-16610-4). Heinemann Ed.

Revenger's Tragedy: A Facsimile of the 1607-8 Quarto-Attributed to Thomas Middleton. MacDonald P. Jackson. LC 81-72052. 120p. 1983. 19.50 (ISBN 0-8386-3131-2). Fairleigh Dickinson.

Revenue Act of Nineteen Eighty-Seven: Law & Explanation. 336p. (Orig.). 1987. pap. 7.00 (5259). Commerce.

Revenue Act of 1964. Milton A. Dauber. 160p. 1964. pap. 1.00 (ISBN 0-317-30794-0, B316). Am Law Inst.

Revenue Act of 1978. Lawrence J. Lee & Mervin M. Wilf. 667p. 1979. pap. 10.00 (ISBN 0-686-26715-X, B329). Am Law Inst.

Revenue Administration of the United Provinces. W. H. Moreland. 1984. Repr. of 1911 ed. text ed. 37.50x (ISBN 0-86590-249-6, Pub. by Renaissance New Delhi). Apt Bks.

Revenue Agent. Jack Rudman. (Career Examination Ser.: C-3250). (Cloth bdg. avail. on request). 1988. pap. 14.00 (ISBN 0-8373-3250-8). Natl Learning.

Revenue & Taxation of the Chinese Empire. Joseph Edkins. LC 78-74331. (Modern Chinese Economy Ser.). 240p. 1980. lib. bdg. 32.00 (ISBN 0-8240-4252-2). Garland Pub.

Revenue Enforcement, Tax Amnesty, & the Federal Deficit. Michael Dukakis et al. (Alternatives for the 1980s Ser.). 20p. (Orig.). 1986. pap. text ed. 9.75 (ISBN 0-944237-21-5, Ctr National Policy). U Pr of Amer.

Revenue Patterns in U. S. Cities & Suburbs: A Comparative Analysis. Susan A. MacManus. LC 77-27499. (Praeger Special Studies). 228p. 1978. 42.95 (ISBN 0-275-90304-4, C0304). Praeger.

Revenue Producing Documentation. Jay Blumenthal. 1984. write for info. loose-leaf (ISBN 0-935506-24-1). Carnegie Pr.

Revenue Rulings: Oil, Gas & Minerals. 1983. 240.00 (ISBN 0-88057-035-0). Exec Ent Pubns.

Revenue Sharing & the City. Walter Heller et al. Ed. by Harvey S. Perloff & Richard P. Nathan. LC 77-86396. (Resources for the Future Ser.). 128p. Repr. of 1968 ed. 24.00 (ISBN 0-404-60333-5). AMS Pr.

Revenue Sharing in India. Christine Wallich. 85p. 1982. 5.00 (ISBN 0-317-59152-5, WP 1523). World Bank.

Revenue Sharing Renewal, No. 15. John T. Marlin. (COMP Papers Ser.). 52p. pap. 7.50 (ISBN 0-916450-36-8). Nat Civic League.

Revenue Sharing: The Second Round. Richard P. Nathan & Charles F. Adams, Jr. LC 76-51884. pap. 71.50 (ISBN 0-317-26739-6, 2025391). Bks Demand UMI.

Revenue Sharing: Trick or Treat? William O. Farber. 1973. 1.00 (ISBN 1-55614-108-4). U of SD Gov Res Bur.

Revenue Stamp: An Autobiography. Amrita Pritam. 170p. 1983. pap. text ed. 3.95x (ISBN 0-7069-2210-7, Pub. by Vikas India). Advent NY.

Revenue Stamps of the New England States. Terence Hines. (Illus.). vi, 76p. (Orig.). 1984. pap. 13.00 (ISBN 0-934939-05-5). State Revenue Soc.

Revenue Stamps of the United States. Christopher West. LC 79-67395. (Illus.). 144p. 21.95x (ISBN 0-9603498-0-4). Castenholz Sons.

Revenue Statistics of OECD Member Countries, 1965-1983. OECD. 270p. (Orig., Eng. & Fr.). 1984. pap. 27.00x (ISBN 92-64-02549-9). OECD.

Revenue Statistics of OECD Member Countries, 1965-1986. OECD. 257p. (Orig., Eng. & Fr.). 1987. pap. 34.00x (ISBN 92-64-02966-4, ECD127). OECD.

Revenue Statistics of OECD Member Countries, 1965-1982. OECD Staff. 210p. 1983. pap. 18.00x (ISBN 92-64-02453-0). OECD.

Revenue Statistics of OECD Member Countries 1965-1984. OECD Staff. 258p. (Orig.). 1985. pap. 27.00x (ISBN 92-64-02722-X). OECD.

Revenue Statistics of OECD Member Countries, 1965-1985. OECD Staff. 258p. (Orig.). 1986. pap. 31.00x (ISBN 92-64-02837-4). OECD.

Revenue Systems of ASEAN Countries: An Overview. Mukul G. Asher. 76p. 1980. pap. 5.00x (ISBN 0-8214-0546-2, Pub. by Singapore U Pr). Ohio U Pr.

Revenue Unit Columns from the American Philatelist. Beverly S. King et al. LC 80-53091. 248p. 1981. Repr. of 1942 ed. lib. bdg. 35.00x (ISBN 0-88000-119-4). Quarterman.

Reverberation Machines: The Later Plays & Essays. Richard Foreman. LC 85-17193. (Illus.). 256p. (Orig.). 1985. 19.95 (ISBN 0-88268-001-3); pap. 10.95 (ISBN 0-88268-000-5). Station Hill Pr.

Reverberations: Sound & Structure in the Novels of Virginia Woolf. Kathleen McCluskey. Ed. by A. Walton Litz. LC 85-21015. (Studies in Modern Literature: No. 54). 146p. 1985. 39.95 (ISBN 0-8357-1710-0). UMI Res Pr.

Reverberator. Thomas Hardy. Repr. lib. bdg. 15.95x (ISBN 0-88411-562-3, Pub. by Aeonian Pr). Amereon Ltd.

Reverberator. Henry James. Bd. with Madame de Mauve's; Passionate Pilgrim; Madonna of the Future; Louis Pallant. LC 70-158792. (Novels & Tales of Henry James: Vol. 13). xx, 549p. Repr. of 1908 ed. 37.50x (ISBN 0-678-02813-3). Kelley.

Reverbreration: Refelection of Sound from Submarines & Surface Vessels see Physics of Sound in the Sea.

Revered by All. 2nd ed. Lester Eckman. LC 73-89418. 1976. 10.00 (ISBN 0-88400-002-8). Shengold.

Reverence for Life. Albert Schweitzer. Tr. by Reginald H. Fuller. LC 71-85052. 1980. Repr. of 1969 ed. 18.95 (ISBN 0-89197-920-4). Irvington.

Reverence for Life. William A. Wait. 39p. (Orig.). 1981. pap. 2.95 (ISBN 0-938696-03-3, 8660). Pubs Bk Sales.

Reverence for Wood. Eric Sloane. 1984. pap. 6.95 (ISBN 0-345-31991-5). Ballantine.

Reverence for Wood. Eric Sloane. (Illus.). 112p. 1984. 14.95 (ISBN 0-396-08335-8). Dodd.

Reverend Beecher & Mrs. Tilton: Sex & Class in Victorian America. Altina L. Waller. LC 81-15982. (Illus.). 192p. 1982. lib. bdg. 17.50x (ISBN 0-87023-356-4). U of Mass Pr.

Reverend Charles Owen Rice: Apostle of Contradiction. Patrick J. McGeever. (Illus.). 300p. 1988. 28.95 (ISBN 0-8207-0209-9); pap. 18.00 (ISBN 0-8207-0210-2). Duquesne.

Reverend Colonel Finch. Elizabeth Nitchie. LC 40-33650. Repr. of 1940 ed. 12.50 (ISBN 0-404-04777-7). AMS Pr.

Reverend Devil. Ross Phares. (Illus.). 263p. 1974. 15.00 (ISBN 0-88289-011-5). Pelican.

Reverend Elhanan Winchester: Biography & Letters. LC 72-38464. (Religion in America, Ser. 2). 358p. 1972. Repr. of 1972 ed. 26.50 (ISBN 0-405-04090-3). Ayer Co Pubs.

Reverend John McMillan. Compiled by Ruth C. Weaver. (Illus.). 174p. 1981. pap. text ed. 7.00 (ISBN 0-9607168-0-7). R C Weaver.

Reverend John O'Hanlon's The Irish Emmigrant's Guide to the United States. Ed. by Edward J. Maguire. LC 76-6352. (Irish Americans Ser). 1976. 23.50 (ISBN 0-405-09346-2). Ayer Co Pubs.

Reverend Randolph & Modern Miracles. Terrence L. Smith. 224p. 1988. 16.95 (ISBN 0-399-13358-5). Putnam Pub Group.

Reverend Randolph & the Splendid Samaritan. Charles M. Smith. 256p. 1987. pap. 2.95 (ISBN 0-8041-0141-8, Pub. by Ivy). Ballantine.

Reverend Randolph & the Splendid Samaritan. Charles M. Smith. 1987. 2.95 (ISBN 0-317-61572-6). Ivy Books.

Reverend Smith, Sidney. Osbert Burdett. LC 72-144920. 303p. 1934. Repr. 39.00 (ISBN 0-403-00883-2). Scholarly.

Reverend Sun Myung Moon. Chong Sun Kim. LC 78-52115. 1978. pap. text ed. 10.00 (ISBN 0-8191-0494-9). U Pr of Amer.

Reverend Thomas Bray: His Life & Selected Works Relating to Maryland. Thomas Bray. Ed. by Bernard C. Steiner. LC 72-14420. (Maryland Historical Society. Fund-Publications Ser.: No. 37). Repr. of 1901 ed. 15.00 (ISBN 0-404-57637-0). AMS Pr.

Reverend Thomas Bray: His Life & Selected Works Relating to Maryland. Ed. by Bernard C. Steiner. LC 79-39862. (Religion in America Ser.: No. 2). 256p. 1972. Repr. of 1901 ed. 18.00 (ISBN 0-405-04088-1). Ayer Co Pubs.

Reverent Discipline: Essays in Literary Criticism & Culture. George A. Panichas. LC 73-15749. 488p. 1974. 35.95x (ISBN 0-87049-149-0). U of Tenn Pr.

Reverent Skeptic. J. Wesley Robb. LC 79-83609. 238p. 1979. 12.50 (ISBN 0-8022-2245-5). Philos Lib.

Reverie Jusqu'a Rousseau: Recherches sur un topos Litteraire. Robert J. Morrissey. LC 84-81406. (French Forum Monographs: No. 55). 184p. (Orig.). 1984. pap. 12.95x (ISBN 0-917058-55-0). French Forum.

Reverie; or, a Flight to the Paradise of Fools, 1763, 2 vols. in 1. Charles Johnstone. LC 74-16307. (Novel in England, 1700-1775 Ser). 1974. lib. bdg. 61.00 (ISBN 0-8240-1162-7). Garland Pub.

Reveries du Promeneur Solitaire. Jaen-Jacques Rousseau. Ed. by S. Sylvestre De Sacy. 288p. 1972. write for info. French & Eur.

Reveries du Promeneur Solitaire. Jean-Jacques Rousseau. Ed. by Roddier. (Coll. Prestige). 49.95 (ISBN 0-685-34058-9). French & Eur.

Reveries du Promeneur Solitaire. Jean-Jacques Rousseau. Ed. by S. Sylvestre de Sacy. (Folio Ser.: No. 186). 288p. 1972. 5.95 (ISBN 0-686-55355-1). Schoenhof.

Reveries Du Promeneur Solitaire. Jean-Jacques Rousseau. Ed. by R. Niklaus. (Modern French Texts). 150p. (Fr.). 1946. pap. 11.00 (ISBN 0-7190-0160-9, Pub. by Manchester Univ Pr). St Martin.

Reveries of a Bachelor. Donald G. Mitchell. 59.95 (ISBN 0-8490-0951-0). Gordon Pr.

Reveries of a Solitary. Jean-Jacques Rousseau. LC 73-178094. (Philosophy Monographs: No. 85). 202p. 1972. Repr. of 1927 ed. lib. bdg. 23.50 (ISBN 0-8337-4358-9). B Franklin.

Reveries of Raleigh. Emma S. McPherson. 286p. 1987. 75.00 (ISBN 0-942179-02-1); pap. 35.00. Shelby Hse.

Reveries of the Solitary Walker. Jean-Jacques Rousseau. Ed. by Charles E. Butterworth. LC 78-24806. 1979. 40.00x (ISBN 0-8147-1019-0). NYU Pr.

Reveries of the Solitary Walker. Jean-Jacques Rousseau. Tr. by Peter France from Fr. (Classics Ser.). 1980. pap. 4.95 (ISBN 0-14-044363-0). Penguin.

Reveries over Childhood & Youth. William B. Yeats. 140p. 1971. Repr. of 1915 ed. 15.00x (ISBN 0-7165-1349-8, BBA 02111, Pub. by Cuala Press Ireland). Biblio Dist.

Reversability of Female Sterilization. Ed. by I. Brosens & R. Winston. 204p. 1979. 32.50 (ISBN 0-8089-1150-3, 790685). Grune.

Reversal of Development in Argentina. Carlos H. Waisman. 328p. 1987. text ed. 40.00 (ISBN 0-691-07740-1); pap. text ed. 14.50 (ISBN 0-691-02266-6). Princeton U Pr.

Reversal of Fortune: Inside the Von Bulow Case. Alan M. Dershowitz. LC 85-25722. (Illus.). 1986. 19.45 (ISBN 0-394-53903-6). Random.

Reversal Theory: Applications & Development. Ed. by M. F. Apter et al. 1985. text ed. 29.95 (ISBN 0-906449-74-X). L Erlbaum Assocs.

Reversals. Lia Kraft-Macoy. 272p. 1985. pap. 2.95 (ISBN 0-345-31760-2). Ballantine.

Reversals: A Personal Account of Victory Over Dyslexia. Eileen Simpson. 272p. 1981. pap. 3.95 (ISBN 0-671-49951-3). WSP.

Reversals of the Earth's Magnetic Field. Jacobs. 276p. 1984. 61.00x (ISBN 0-85274-442-0, Pub. by A Hilger UK). Taylor & Francis.

Reverse Acronyms, Initialisms & Abbreviations Dictionary. 12th ed. 304p. 1987. 225.00x (ISBN 0-8103-2507-1). Gale.

Reverse Annuity Mortgages. Stephen R. Mettling. (Residential Financing Resource Library). 14p. (Orig.). 1982. pap. 6.50 (ISBN 0-88462-140-5, 1905-24, Real Estate Ed). Longman Finan.

Reverse Dictionary. Beverly L. Ritter & Steven W. Sharber. (Computer-Compatible Machine Shorthand for Expanding Careers Ser.). 225p. (Orig.). 1987. pap. text ed. 24.00 (ISBN 0-938643-13-4). Stenotype Educ.

Reverse Dictionary of Urdu. Donald Becker. (Urdu.). 1980. 38.00x (ISBN 0-8364-0656-7, Pub. by Manohaar India). South Asia Bks.

Reverse Discrimination. Ed. by Barry R. Gross. LC 76-53643. 401p. 1977. 19.95 (ISBN 0-87975-083-9); pap. 13.95 (ISBN 0-87975-092-8). Prometheus Bks.

Reverse Discrimination: A Resource Guide. Jim Buchanan. LC 85-233321. (Public Administration Ser.: P 1703). 1985. 3.00 (ISBN 0-89028-453-9). Vance Biblios.

Reverse Discrimination Controversy: A Moral & Legal Analysis. Robert K. Fullinwider. (Philosophy & Society Ser.). 300p. 1980. 31.50x (ISBN 0-8476-6273-X); pap. 12.50x (ISBN 0-8476-6901-7). Rowman.

Reverse Effect: How Vitamins & Minerals Promote Health & Cause Disease. Walter A. Heiby. (Illus.). 1216p. (Orig.). 1988. 59.50 (ISBN 0-938869-01-9). MediSci Pubs.

Reverse Hinge Fracture Problem in Fluted Point Manufacture & the Walter Site: A Fluted Point Manifestation in North Central Missouri. George W. Nichols et al. Ed. by Carl H. Chapman. LC 76-178009. (Memoir Ser.: No. 8). (Illus.). 63p. (Orig.). 1970. pap. 2.50 (ISBN 0-943414-23-7). MO Arch Soc.

Reverse Index of Manchu. William Rozycki & Rex Dwyer. Ed. by Denis Sinor. LC 81-52901. (Indiana University Uralic & Altaic Ser.: Vol. 140). vi, 189p. (Orig.). 1981. pap. text ed. 14.00 (ISBN 0-933070-08-X). Ind U Res Inst.

Reverse International Acronyms, Initialisms & Abbreviations Dictionary. 2nd ed. Ed. by Helen E. Sheppard & Julie E. Towell. 907p. 1987. 175.00x (ISBN 0-8103-2197-1). Gale.

Reverse Lexicon of Greek Proper Names. F. Dornseiff & Bernard Hansen. xiv, 340p. (Gr.). 1978. 30.00 (ISBN 0-89005-251-4); pap. 25.00. Ares.

Reverse Licensing: International Technology Transfer to the United States. Manuchehr Shahrokhi. LC 86-25230. 192p. 1987. 32.95 (ISBN 0-275-92258-8, C2258). Praeger.

Reverse Marketing. Michiel R. Leenders & David L. Blenkhorn. 1987. 29.95. Free Pr.

Reverse Micelles: Biological & Technological Relevance of Amphiphilic Structures in Apolar Media. Ed. by P. L. Luisi & B. E. Straub. 364p. 1984. 59.50x (ISBN 0-306-41620-4, Plenum Pr). Plenum Pub.

Reverse Negative. Andre Jute. 1979. 9.95 (ISBN 0-393-01216-6). Norton.

Reverse Osmosis. P. Hoornaert. (EPO Applied Technology Ser.: Vol. 4). 220p. 1984. 77.00 (ISBN 0-08-031144-X). Pergamon.

Reverse Osmosis & Ultrafiltration. Ed. by S. Sourirajann & Takeshi Matsuura. (ACS Symposium Ser.: No. 281). 508p. 1985. lib. bdg. 89.95 (ISBN 0-8412-0921-9). Am Chemical.

Reverse Osmosis Technology: Applications for High-Purity-Water Production. Parekh. (Chemical Industries Ser.). 536p. 1988. 99.75 (ISBN 0-8247-7985-1). Dekker.

Reverse Osmosis Treatment of Drinking Water. Talbert N. Eisenberg & E. Joe Middlebrooks. (Illus.). 271p. 1985. sewn 44.95 (ISBN 0-250-40617-9). Butterworth.

Reverse Paintings on Glass. Mildred L. Ward. LC 78-71881. (Illus.). 128p. 1978. pap. 9.00 (ISBN 0-913689-15-7). Spencer Muse Art.

Reverse Print. Roger Paul. 1987. 16.95 (ISBN 0-533-06996-3). Vantage.

Reverse Side of the Cross. Rufus Moseley. pap. 0.65 ea. 2 for 1.00 (ISBN 0-910924-83-X). Macalester.

Reverse the Charges: How to Save Money on Your Phone Bill. 4th ed. Sam Simon & Joe Waz, Jr. 1983. pap. 2.95 (ISBN 0-394-71490-3). T R A C.

Reverse the Curse in Your Body & Emotions. Annette Capps. 106p. (Orig.). 1987. pap. 3.95 (ISBN 0-9618975-0-3). Annette Capps.

Reverse Thunder. Diane Ackerman. 96p. (Orig.). 1988. pap. 7.95 (ISBN 0-930829-09-3). Lumen Inc.

Reversed-Phase High Performance Liquid Chromatography: Theory, Practice, & Biomedical Applications. Ante M. Krstulovic & Phyllis R. Brown. LC 81-15944. 296p. 1982. 63.00x (ISBN 0-471-05369-4, Pub. by Wiley Interscience). Wiley.

Reversed Thunder: The Revelation of John & the Praying Imagination. Eugene H. Peterson. LC 87-45717. 224p. 1988. 15.95 (ISBN 0-06-066500-9, HarpR). Har-Row.

Reversibility & Stochastic Networks. F. P. Kelly. LC 79-40515. (Wiley Series in Probability & Mathematical Statistics). 230p. 1979. 96.00x (ISBN 0-471-27601-4, Pub. by Wiley-Interscience). Wiley.

Reversible Airway Obstruction: Neurohumoral Mechanisms & Treatment. Ed. by S. Bianco et al. (Journal: Respiration, 1986: Vol. 50, Supplement 2). (Illus.). vi, 326p. 1987. pap. 78.75 (ISBN 3-8055-4524-X). S Karger.

Reversible Polymeric Gels & Related Systems. Ed. by Paul S Russo. LC 87-20305. (Symposium Ser.: No. 350). (Illus.). x, 292p. 1987. 64.95 (ISBN 0-8412-1415-8). AM Chemical.

Reversible Readings: Ambiguity in Four Modern Latin American Novels. Paul B. Dixon. LC 83-5070. (Illus.). 176p. 1985. 19.95x (ISBN 0-8173-0192-5). U of Ala Pr.

Reversible Sex Roles: The Special Case of Benares Sweepers. Mary Searle-Chatterjee. (Women in Development Ser.). (Illus.). 120p. 1981. 38.00 (ISBN 0-08-025780-1). Pergamon.

Reversible Systems. M. B. Sevryuk. (Lecture Notes in Mathematics: Vol. 1211). v, 319p. 1987. pap. 27.80 (ISBN 0-387-16819-2). Springer-Verlag.

Reversible Two-Color Knitting. Jane Neighbors. (Illus.). 224p. 1982. pap. 12.95 (ISBN 0-684-17647-5, ScribT). Scribner.

Reversing Africa's Decline. Lester R. Brown & Edward C. Wolf. LC 85-51311. (Worldwatch Papers). 1985. pap. 4.00 (ISBN 0-916468-65-8). Worldwatch Inst.

Reversing Atherosclerosis. G. A. Gresham. 120p. 1980. 13.00x (ISBN 0-398-03931-3). C C Thomas.

Reversing Diabetes. Julian M. Whitaker. 1988. 19.95 (ISBN 0-446-51304-0). Warner Bks.

Reversing Economic Decline. John C. Carrington & George T. Edwards. LC 79-24035. 224p. 1981. 10.95 (ISBN 0-312-67931-9). St Martin.

Reversing Hair Loss. Mary-Ellen Siegel. (Illus.). 208p. 1985. pap. 6.95 (ISBN 0-671-55469-7). S&S.

Reversing Health Risks. Julian M. Whitaker & June Roth. 288p. 1988. 18.95 (ISBN 0-399-13396-8, Putnam). Putnam Pub Group.

Reversing Heart Disease. Julian M. Whitaker. LC 84-40089. (Illus.). 272p. 1985. 23.00 (ISBN 0-446-51298-2). Warner Bks.

Reversing Heart Disease. Julian M. Whitaker. Date not set. pap. 10.95 (ISBN 0-446-38548-4). Warner Bks.

Reversing Industrial Decline: Industrial Structure in Britain & Her Competitors. Ed. by Paul Hirst & Jonathan Zeitlin. 288p. 1988. 46.75 (ISBN 0-85496-029-5, Pub. by Berg Pubs). St Martin.

Reversing Regional Economic Decline: A Supplement to Exchange Bibliography No. 1193. Nan C. Burg. 1977. 1.50 (ISBN 0-686-19121-8). CPL Biblios.

Reversing the Aging Process. Gene Davis. 332p. (Orig.). 1987. pap. 29.95x (ISBN 0-9618919-0-4). Life Res Found.

Reversing the Nuclear Arms Race. Carla B. Johnston. 180p. (Orig.). 1986. text ed. 18.95 (ISBN 0-87047-032-9); pap. text ed. 11.25 (ISBN 0-87047-033-7). Schenkman Bks Inc.

Reversing the Trend Toward Early Retirement. Robert L. Clark & David T. Barker. 64p. 1981. pap. 7.00 (ISBN 0-8447-3433-0). Am Enterprise.

Reversing Your Blood Profile for Better Health & Longer Life. Whitaker & Roth. 1988. price not set (Putnam). Putnam Pub Group.

Reves et Leur Interpretation. Paul Meunier. Repr. of 1910 ed. 20.00. Darby Bks.

Revi-Lona: A Romance of Love in a Marvelous Land. Frank Cowan. Ed. by R. Reginald & Douglas Melville. LC 77-84216. (Lost Race & Adult Fantasy Ser.). 1978. Repr. of 1890 ed. lib. bdg. 22.00x (ISBN 0-405-10971-7). Ayer Co Pubs.

Review, Vol. 1. Ed. by James O. Hoge & James L. West. 1979. 30.00x (ISBN 0-8139-0760-8). U Pr of Va.

Review, Vol. 2. Ed. by James O. Hoge & James L. West. 1980. 30.00x (ISBN 0-8139-0865-5). U Pr of Va.

Review, Vol. 3. Ed. by James O. Hoge & James L. West. 1981. 30.00x (ISBN 0-8139-0910-4). U Pr of Va.

Review, Vol. 4. Ed. by James O. Hoge, III & James L. W. West. 1983. 30.00x (ISBN 0-8139-0974-0). U Pr of Va.

Review, Vol. 5. Ed. by James O. Hoge & James L. West, III. 300p. 1983. 30.00x (ISBN 0-8139-1005-6). U Pr of Va.

Review, Vol. 6. Ed. by James O. Hoge & James L. West, III. xi, 332p. 1984. 30.00x (ISBN 0-8139-1031-5). U Pr of VA.

Review, Vol. 7. Ed. by James O. Hoge & James L. West, III. xiv, 348p. 1985. 30.00x (ISBN 0-8139-1076-5). U Pr of Va.

Review - Nineteen Seventy Nine Session of the Congress. 35p. 1980. pap. 6.00 (ISBN 0-8447-0228-5). Am Enterprise.

Review- Nineteen Eighty Session of the Congress. 70p. 1981. pap. 6.00 (ISBN 0-8447-0238-2). Am Enterprise.

Review & Abstract of the County Reports to the Board of Agriculture 5 Vols. William Marshall. LC 69-11853. 1968. Repr. of 1818 ed. Set. 195.00x (ISBN 0-678-05613-7). Kelley.

Review & Appraisal of the World Population Plan of Action. 169p. 1986. pap. 14.00 (ISBN 92-1-151158-5, E.86.XIII.2). UN.

Review & Bibliography on Aspects of Fluid Sealing. 1972. text ed. 32.00x (ISBN 0-900983-16-7, Dist. by Air Science Co.). BHRA Fluid.

Review & Essays in English Literature. C. Tovey Duncan. 187p. 1980. Repr. of 1897 ed. lib. bdg. 30.00 (ISBN 0-8492-8427-9). R West.

Review & Evaluation of Appearance: Method & Techniques, STP 914. Ed. by Jay J. Rennilson & W. N. Hale, Jr. LC 86-7999. (Special Technical Publications). (Illus.). 112p. 1986. text ed. 24.00 (ISBN 0-8031-0480-4, 04-914000-36). ASTM.

Review & Evaluation of Smoking Cesation Methods: The United States & Canada, 1978 to 1985. Jerome L. Schwartz. (DHHS Publication). 214p. 1987. pap. 10.00 (ISBN 0-318-23442-4, S/N 017-042-00209-5). USGPO.

Review & Evaluation of the Criminal Justice System Implemented for the ADA County, Idaho Magistrates Division: A Technical Assistance Report. 37p. 1986. manuscript 2.00 (ISBN 0-317-59201-7, WRO, T/A-505). Natl Ctr St Courts.

Review & Index Through 1975 of Genus Candona (Ostracoda) in North America (Exclusive of Pre-Quaternary Species) Larry N. Stout. LC 76-47833. (Microform Publication: No. 6). (Illus.). 1976. 2.40 (ISBN 0-8137-6006-2). Geol Soc.

Review & Synthesis of Research at Historical Sites see Final Report of the New Melones Archeological Project, California.

Review & Synthesis of Research in Trade & Industrial Education. 3rd ed. Curtis R. Finch. 60p. 1983. 4.95 (ISBN 0-318-22193-4, IN260). Natl Ctr Res Voc Ed.

Review Committee on Education for Information Use: Final Report. British Library Staff. (R&D Report 5325). 32p. (Orig.). 1977. pap. 8.25 (ISBN 0-85350-147-5, Pub. by British Lib). Longwood Pub Group.

Review Exercises in Chinese Sentence Structure. Henry C. Fenn. 1.95 (ISBN 0-88710-078-3). Yale Far Eastern Pubns.

Review for NCLEX-PN-VN. 3rd ed. Sandra F. Smith. 500p. 1986. 17.95 (ISBN 0-917010-24-8). Natl Nursing.

Review for the Medical Assistant Examination, ARCO. 3rd ed. John E. Clement. (Illus.). 200p. 1987. pap. text ed. 19.95 (ISBN 0-8385-6197-7, A6197-6). Appleton & Lange.

Review for the Pharmacy Examination, ARCO. 3rd ed. Walter Singer et al. 213p. 1985. pap. text ed. 15.00 (ISBN 0-8385-7839-X, A7839-2). Appleton & Lange.

Review for the Radiologic Technology Examination. 3rd ed. Howard J. Naidech & Lorraine Damon. Date not set. text ed. price not set. Appleton & Lange.

Review Latin Grammar. John K. Colby. (gr. 8-10). 1971. pap. text ed. 3.75x (ISBN 0-88334-034-8). Ind Sch Pr.

Review Manual for Certification in Emergency Nursing. Nedell E. Lanros. 1982. pap. text ed. 17.95 (ISBN 0-89303-244-1). Appleton & Lange.

Review Manual for Immunohematology. Neville J. Bryant. 352p. 1982. write for info. (ISBN 0-7216-2166-X). Saunders.

Review Manual for Operators. William E. Brown & Richard S. Sacks. LC 81-68888. (Illus.). 182p. 1981. pap. text ed. 19.95 (ISBN 0-250-40501-6). Butterworth.

Review Manual for Speech, Language & Hearing. Jerry L. Northern. (Illus.). 480p. 1982. pap. 26.95 (ISBN 0-7216-6874-7). Saunders.

Review Manual for the EMT - Intermediate. 2nd ed. Donald Ptacnik. 240p. 1987. 14.95 (ISBN 0-917010-28-0). Natl Nursing.

Review Manual for the Multi-State & Uniform Exam. Mark L. Levine & Kent J. Levine. Date not set. write for info. Prof Pubns & Educ.

Review Manual for the National Nursing Home Administrators Examination. Robert W. Haacker. 127p. 1987. 25.95. Publicare Pr.

Review: Nineteen Eighty One Session of the Congress. 39p. 1982. pap. 6.00 (ISBN 0-8447-0246-3). Am Enterprise.

Review: Nineteen Eighty-Three Session of the Congress. 42p. 1984. pap. 6.00 (ISBN 0-8447-0253-6). Am Enterprise.

Review: Nineteen Eighty Two Session of the Congress. 62p. 1983. pap. 6.00 (ISBN 0-8447-0247-1). Am Enterprise.

Review of Ada Tasking. A. Burns et al. (Lecture Notes in Computer Science Ser.: Vol. 262). viii, 141p. 1987. pap. 15.40 (ISBN 0-387-18008-7). Springer-Verlag.

Review of African Granulites & Related Rocks. Tom N. Clifford. LC 74-84196. (Geological Society of America Special Papers: No. 156). pap. 20.00 (ISBN 0-317-28368-5, 2025471). Bks Demand UMI.

Review of Agricultural Planning During the Second Postwar Decade. (Agricultural Planning Studies: No. 5). 31p. 1976. pap. 7.50 (ISBN 92-5-101111-7, F689, FAO). UNIPUB.

Review of Agricultural Policies in OECD Member Countries 1980-1982. OECD Staff. 218p. (Orig.). 1983. pap. 15.00x (ISBN 92-64-12504-3). OECD.

Review of Allied Health Education, No. 1. Ed. by Joseph Hamburg. LC 74-7876. (Illus.). 244p. 1974. 20.00x (ISBN 0-8131-1322-9). U Pr of Ky.

Review of Allied Health Education, Vol. 3. Ed. by Joseph Hamburg. LC 74-7876. pap. 41.80 (2027364). Bks Demand UMI.

Review of Allied Health Education, No. 4. Ed. by Joseph Hamburg. LC 74-7876. 160p. 1981. 14.00 (ISBN 0-8131-1455-1). U Pr of Ky.

Review of Allied Health Education, Vol. 5. Ed. by Joseph Hamburg. LC 74-7876. 176p. 1985. 16.00 (ISBN 0-8131-1574-4). U Pr of Ky.

Review of American Colonial Legislation by the King in Council. Elmer B. Russell. 1971. lib. bdg. 18.00x (ISBN 0-374-96994-9, Octagon). Hippocrene Bks.

Review of American Colonial Legislation by the King in Council. Elmer B. Russell. Ed. by R. H. Helmholz & Bernard D. Reams, Jr. LC 80-84869. (Historical Writings in Law & Jurisprudence Ser.: Title No. 21, Bk. 31). 230p. 1981. Repr. of 1915 ed. lib. bdg. 38.00 (ISBN 0-89941-083-9). W S Hein.

Review of American Institute of Chemical Engineers Design Institute for Physical Property Data & Worldwide Affiliated Activities. LC 81-1628. (AIChE Symposium Ser.: Vol. 77, No. 203). 89p. 1981. pap. 24.00 (ISBN 0-8169-0188-0, S-203). Am Inst Chem Eng.

Review of Amino Acid Transport Processes in Animal Cells & Tissues. Joseph Lerner. 1978. text ed. 20.00x (ISBN 0-89101-036-X). U Maine Orono.

Review of Approaches to Viral Chemotherapy. Maxwell Gordon et al. 96p. 1981. 20.00 (ISBN 0-915340-08-9). PJD Pubns.

Review of Austrian Economics, Vol. II. Ed. by Murray N. Rothbard & Walter Block. 304p. 1987. 40.00x (ISBN 0-669-16740-1). Lexington Bks.

Review of Austrian Economics, Vol. 1. Ed. by Murray N. Rothbard. LC 85-460036. 272p. 1986. 35.00x (ISBN 0-669-12892-9). Lexington Bks.

Review of Behavior Therapy, Vol. 11. G. Terence Wilson et al. (Guilford Review of Behavior Therapy Ser.). 404p. 1987. lib. bdg. 37.50 (ISBN 0-89862-751-6). Guilford Pr.

Review of Berkeley's Theory of Vision, Designed to Show the Unsoundness of That Celebrated Speculation. Ed. by George Pitcher. (Philosophy of George Berkeley Ser.). 350p. 1988. lib. bdg. 55.00 (ISBN 0-8240-2435-4). Garland Pub.

Review of Biological Research in Aging, Vol. 1. Morton Rothstein. 424p. 1983. 71.00 (ISBN 0-8451-3500-7). A R Liss.

Review of Biological Research in Aging, Vol. 2. Morton Rothstein. 572p. 1985. 96.00 (ISBN 0-8451-3501-5). A R Liss.

Review of Biological Research in Aging, Vol. 3. Ed. by Morton Rothstein et al. 562p. 1987. 140.00 (ISBN 0-8451-3502-3, 3502). A R Liss.

Review of Biostatisics. 3rd ed. Paul E. Leaverton. 128p. 1986. pap. text ed. 14.50 (ISBN 0-316-51853-0). Little.

Review of Biostatistics: A Program for Self-Instruction. 3rd ed. Paul E. Leaverton. 1986. spiral bdg 12.00 (ISBN 0-316-51852-2, Little Med Div). Little.

Review of Breeding & Propagation Techniques for Grey Mullet Mugil Cephalus L. Ed. by Colin E. Nash & Ziad H. Shahadeh. (Illus.). 87p. 1983. pap. text ed. 11.50x (ISBN 0-89955-392-3, Pub. by ICLARM Philippines). Intl Spec Bk.

Review of Caste in India. J. Murdoch. 110p. 1977. 14.95. Asia Bk Corp.

Review of Child Development Research, 2 Vols. Ed. by Martin L. Hoffman & Lois W. Hoffman. LC 64-20472. Vol. 1, 1964, 548p. 45.00x ea. (ISBN 0-87154-384-2). Vol. 2, 1966, 598p (ISBN 0-87154-385-0). Set of 2 Vols (ISBN 0-87154-383-4). Russell Sage.

Review of Child Development Research, Vol. 3. Bettye Caldwell & Henry N. Ricciuti. 1974. pap. 7.95x (ISBN 0-226-09044-2, P680, Phoen). U of Chicago Pr.

Review of Child Development Research, Vol. 4. Frances D. Horowitz. 1975. 25.00x (ISBN 0-226-35353-2). U of Chicago Pr.

Review of Child Development Research, 9 chapters, Vol. 5. Ed. by E. Mavis Hetherington. Incl. Chap. 1. Your Ancients Revisited: A History of Child Development. Robert S. Sears. 80p; Chap. 2. Ecological Psychology & Children. Paul V. Gump. 64p; Chap. 3. Children's Cooperation & Helping Behaviors. James H. Bryan. 64p; Chap. 4. Impact of Television on Children & Youth. Aletha H. Stein & Lynette K. Friedrich. 80p; Chap. 5. Development of Social Cognition. Carolyn U. Shantz. 72p; Chap. 6. Children's Attention: The Development of Selectivity. Anne D. Pick et al. 72p; Chap. 7. Problems & Prospects in the Study of Learning Disabilities. Joseph Torgeson. 64p; Chap. 9. Interdisciplinary Analysis. Ross D. Parke & Candace W. Collmer. 88p. LC 64-20472. (Review of Child Development Research Ser.). 608p. 1976. PLB 30.00x (ISBN 0-226-33155-5); pap. in indiv. chapters avail. U of Chicago Pr.

Review of Child Development Research, Vol. 6. Ed. by Willard W. Hartup. LC 64-20472. (Review of Child Development Research Ser.). 780p. 1982. lib. bdg. 40.00x (ISBN 0-226-31873-7). U of Chicago Pr.

Review of Child Development Research, Vol. 7. Ed. by Ross D. Parke. LC 64-20472. (Review of Child Development Research Ser.). x, 470p. 1985. lib. bdg. 30.00x (ISBN 0-226-64666-1). U of Chicago Pr.

Review of Clinical Research in Gastroenterology. Masakazu Maruyuama. 270p. 1988. 40.00 (ISBN 0-89640-134-0). Igaku-Shoin.

Review of Cobb County Jury System. National Center for State Courts Staff. 13p. (On loan through the NCSC Library). 1983. write for info. (CJS-005). Natl Ctr St Courts.

Review of Criminal Justice Information Systems, Eleventh Judicial Circuit, Dade County, Florida. 78p. 1987. 5.00 (SERO-032). Natl Ctr St Courts.

Review of Decks, Patios, & Other Outside Construction Projects in the 1980's. Dale E. Casper. (Architecture Ser.: A 1859). 12p. 1987. 3.75 (ISBN 1-55590-389-4). Vance Biblios.

Review of Demand Models: ECMT Round Table Fifty Eight Forecasts-Recorded Traffic Comparisons for Urban And Intercity Transport. OECD Staff. (Orig.). 1982. pap. 9.00x (ISBN 92-821-1078-8). OECD.

Review of Dental Assisting. Hazel O. Torres & Lois E. Mazzucchi. (Illus.). 350p. 1983. 22.95 (ISBN 0-7216-8883-7). Saunders.

Review of Dental Hygiene: Questions & Answers. 3rd ed. Ed. by Pauline F. Steele. LC 85-23876. (Illus.). 280p. 1986. pap. 18.50 (ISBN 0-8121-1029-3). Lea & Febiger.

Review of Developments in Plane Strain Fracture Toughness Testing - STP 463. 275p. 1970. 18.25 (ISBN 0-8031-0037-X, 04-463000-30). ASTM.

Review of Diagnosis, Oral Medicine, Radiology & Treatment Planning. 2nd ed. Wood. (Illus.). 328p. 1987. pap. text ed. 27.95 (ISBN 0-8016-5730-X). Mosby.

Review of Diaphragm Walls. 152p. 1977. 18.00 (ISBN 0-7277-0045-6, Pub. by T Telford UK). Am Soc Civil Eng.

Review of Doctor Johnson's New Edition of Shakespeare. W. Kenrick. LC 78-144647. Repr. of 1765 ed. 12.50 (ISBN 0-404-03659-7). AMS Pr.

Review of Economic Doctrines, 1870-1929. Terence W. Hutchison. LC 74-9273. 456p. 1975. Repr. of 1953 ed. lib. bdg. 41.50x (ISBN 0-8371-7637-9, HURE). Greenwood.

Review of Edwards's "Inquiry into the Freedom of the Will". Henry P. Tappan. LC 75-3412. Repr. of 1839 ed. 35.00 (ISBN 0-404-59406-9). AMS Pr.

Review of Elementary Mathematics. Barnett Rich. (Schaum's Outline Ser.). (Orig.). 1977. pap. text ed. 7.95 (ISBN 0-07-052260-X). McGraw.

Review of Essential Pharmacology with Nursing Implications & Self-Assessment Questions. Stefos. 256p. 1988. pap. text ed. 21.95 (ISBN 0-8385-8417-9). Appleton & Lange.

Review of Essentials of Accounting. Robert N. Anthony. (Illus.). 1988. pap. text ed. write for info. (ISBN 0-201-05905-3). Addison-Wesley.

Review of Fisheries in OECD Member Countries, 1986. OECD. 340p. (Orig.). 1987. pap. 41.00x (ISBN 92-64-13026-8). OECD.

Review of Fisheries in OECD Member Countries, 1984. OECD Staff. 318p. (Orig.). 1985. pap. 22.00x (ISBN 92-64-12750-X). OECD.

Review of Fisheries in OECD Member Countries, 1985. OECD Staff. 338p. (Orig.). 1986. pap. 20.00x (ISBN 92-64-12855-7). OECD.

Review of Food Consumption Survey, 1981: Household Food Consumption by Economic Groups. (Food & Nutrition Papers: No. 27). 292p. 1983. pap. text ed. 22.00 (ISBN 92-5-101320-9, F2435, FAO). UNIPUB.

Review of Food Consumption Surveys 1977: Household Food Consumption by Economic Groups. Incl. Europe, North America, Oceania. (No. 1-1). 162p. (2nd Printing 1981). 1977. pap. 12.25 (ISBN 92-5-100349-1, F1304). UNIPUB; Africa, Latin America, Near East, Far East. (No. 1-2). 292p. (2nd Printing 1981). 1979. pap. 22.00 (ISBN 92-5-100750-0, F1844). UNIPUB. (Food & Nutrition Paper Ser., FAO). UNIPUB.

Review of Forecasts: Scaling & Analysis of Expert Judgments Regarding Cross-Impacts of Assumptions on Business Forecasts & Accounting Measures, Vol. 19. Robert E. Jensen. LC 83-70703. (Studies in Accounting Research). 235p. 1983. 15.00 (ISBN 0-86539-044-4); 11.00. Am Accounting.

Review of General Psychiatry. 2nd ed. Howard Goldman. 1988. pap. 25.00 (ISBN 0-8385-8420-9). Appleton & Lange.

Review of General Psychiatry. Ed. by Howard H. Goldman. LC 84-82084. 696p. 1984. lexotone cover 27.50 (ISBN 0-87041-300-7). Appleton & Lange.

Review of Hamlet. new ed. George H. Miles. LC 77-172730. Repr. of 1907 ed. 12.50 (ISBN 0-404-04324-0). AMS Pr.

Review of Hamlet. George H. Miles. LC 73-475. 1973. lib. bdg. 19.50 (ISBN 0-8414-1512-9). Folcroft.

Review of Hemodialysis for Nurses & Dialysis Personnel. 4th ed. C. F. Gutch & Martha H. Stoner. LC 83-1004. (Illus.). 224p. 1983. pap. text ed. 24.95 (ISBN 0-8016-1991-2). Mosby.

Review of Hogg's "Memoirs of Prince Alexy Haimatoff". 2nd ed. Percy Bysshe Shelley. Ed. by E. Dowden & Thomas J. Wise. Bd. with Extract from "Some Early Writings of Shelley". LC 74-30285. (Shelley Society, Second Ser.: No. 2). Repr. of 1886 ed. 20.00 (ISBN 0-404-11504-7). AMS Pr.

Review of Human Development. Ed. by Tiffany M. Field et al. Gordon Finley. LC 81-21886. 664p. 1982. 67.95x (ISBN 0-471-08116-7). Wiley.

Review of Human Physiology. 2nd ed. H. Frank Winter & Melvin L. Shourd. (Illus.). 563p. 1982. write for info. (ISBN 0-7216-9469-1). Saunders.

Review of Human Physiology. 3rd ed. H. Frank Winter & Melvin L. Shourd. (Illus.). 250p. 1987. pap. 19.95 (ISBN 0-7216-2085-X). Saunders.

Review of Innovative Approaches to College Teaching. Beatrice Gross & Ronald Gross. 68p. 6.00 (ISBN 0-86539-036-3); 3.00. Am Accounting.

Review of Juniperus Chinensis et al. P. J. Van Melle. (Illus.). 1947. pap. 7.50x (ISBN 0-934454-72-8). Lubrecht & Cramer.

Review of Land Policies. Ed. by Otto Koenigsberger et al. 200p. 1981. 94.00 (ISBN 0-08-026078-0). Pergamon.

Review of Legal Education in the United States - Fall 1985: Law School & Bar Admission Requirements. ABA, Legal Education & Admissions to the Bar Section. 84p. 1987. pap. write for info. Amer Bar Assn.

Review of Legal Education in the United States - Fall 1984: Law School & Bar Admission Requirements. 84p. 1985. pap. 3.00 (ISBN 0-317-63633-2, 529-0026-01). Amer Bar Assn.

Review of Legal Education in the United States, Fall, 1983: Law Schools & Bar Admission Requirements. 78p. 1983. pap. 2.00 (ISBN 0-686-48067-8). Amer Bar Assn.

Review of Literature on Herbicides, Including Phenoxy Herbicides & Associated Dioxins; Volume 7, Analysis of Literature on Health Effects Published in 1985 & Volume 8, Annotated Bibliography of Literature on Health Effects Published in 1985, 2 vols. in 1. 149p. (Orig.). 1986. pap. 7.50 (ISBN 0-318-22449-6, S/N 051-000-00186-9). USGPO.

Review of LPG Cargo Quantity Calculations. Sigtto. 1985. 90.00x (ISBN 0-317-61460-6, Pub. by Witherby & Co England). State Mutual Bk.

Review of Lysander Spooner's Essay on the Unconstitutionality of Slavery. Wendell Phillips. LC 76-82220. (Anti-Slavery Crusade in America Ser). 1969. Repr. of 1847 ed. 9.00 (ISBN 0-405-00648-9). Ayer Co Pubs.

Review of Management Information from Computer-Based Circulation Systems in Academic Libraries. C. Mary Overton. (R&D Report 5471). 36p. (Orig.). 1979. pap. 8.25 (Pub. by British Lib). Longwood Pub Group.

Review of Managers in U. S. Industries. Herbert W. Hildebrandt & Edwin L. Millec. (Michigan Management & Executive Development Ser.: No. 6). 1987. pap. text ed. 2.00 (ISBN 0-87712-257-1). UMI Div Res GSBA.

Review of Maritime Transport 1984. 68p. 1986. 9.50 (ISBN 92-1-112206-6, E.85.II.D.18). UN.

Review of Maritime Transport 1985: TD-B-C.4299. 1986. pap. 9.50 (ISBN 92-1-112222-8, E.86.II.D.3). UN.

Review of Maritime Transport, 1986. 92p. 1987. pap. 18.00 (ISBN 92-1-112232-5, E.87.II.D.6). UN.

Review of Maternal Child Nursing. Judith Green. 1978. pap. 17.95 (ISBN 0-07-024302-6). McGraw.

Review of Medical Embryology. Ben Pansky. (Illus.). 527p. 1982. pap. text ed. write for info. (ISBN 0-02-390620-0). Macmillan.

Review of Medical Microbiology. Abraham I. Braude & J. Allen McCutchan. (Illus.). 208p. 1983. pap. 23.95 (ISBN 0-7216-1183-4). Saunders.

Review of Medical Microbiology. 17th ed. Ernest Jawetz et al. 608p. 1986. 22.00 (ISBN 0-8385-8432-2). Appleton & Lange.

Review of Medical Nursing. N. Ercolano. 1979. text ed. 19.95 (ISBN 0-07-019541-2). McGraw.

Review of Medical Physiology. 13th ed. William F. Ganong. 1987. pap. 24.00 (ISBN 0-8385-8435-7). Appleton & Lange.

Review of Mental Health Nursing. P. Haring. 1979. text ed. 20.95 (ISBN 0-07-026415-5). McGraw.

Review of Military Research & Development: 1984. Ed. by Kosta Tsipis. (Illus.). 216p. 1984. text ed. 32.00 (ISBN 0-08-031622-0). Pergamon.

Review of Montana's Office of Court Administrator. 37p. 1986. manuscript 2.00 (ISBN 0-317-59202-5, WRO-072). Natl Ctr St Courts.

Review of National Literatures: India, Vol. 10. Ed. by Anne Paolucci & Ronald Warwick. LC 77-126039. 240p. 1979. 23.00 (ISBN 0-918680-20-4). Griffon Hse.

Review of National Policies for Education: Iceland. OECD. 97p. (Orig.). 1987. pap. 17.00 (ISBN 92-64-13028-4). OECD.

Review of National Policies for Education: Greece. OECD Staff. 122p. (Orig.). 1982. pap. 9.00x (ISBN 92-64-12334-2). OECD.

Review of NCRP Radiation Dose Limit for Embryo & Fetus in Occupationally Exposed Women. LC 77-74778. (NCRP Reports Ser.: No. 53). 1977. 10.00 (ISBN 0-913392-35-9). NCRP Pubns.

Review of Neuroscience. Ben Pansky & Delmas J. Allen. (Illus.). 1980. pap. text ed. write for info. (ISBN 0-02-390610-3). Macmillan.

Review of Nuclear Energy in the United States: Hidden Power. Todd H Otis. LC 81-11859. (Illus.). 192p. 1981. 35.00 (ISBN 0-275-90697-3, C0697). Praeger.

Review of Nursing: Essentials for the State Boards. 2nd ed. Stewart M. Brooks. 1986. pap. text ed. write for info. (ISBN 0-673-39385-2). Scott F.

Review of OBTS & CCH Programs Requirements in the Judiciary. 315p. 1979. manuscript 18.90 (ISBN 0-89656-036-8, F-005). Natl Ctr St Courts.

Review of Organic Functional Groups: Introduction to Medicinal Organic Chemistry. 2nd ed. Thomas L. Lemke. LC 87-22810. (Illus.). 142p. 1988. pap. 12.00 (ISBN 0-8121-1128-1). Lea & Febiger.

Review of Past Research & Test Activities see Monitoring the Outcome of Social Services.

Review of Pathophysiology. Christian E. Kaufman, Jr. & Solomon Papper. (Review Ser.). 1983. pap. text ed. 27.00 (ISBN 0-316-48339-7). Little.

Review of Pediatric Psychology, Vol. 1. Ed. by William J. Burns & John V. LaVigne. 304p. 1984. 49.50 (ISBN 0-8089-1602-5, 790727). Grune.

Review of Pediatrics. 3rd ed. Richard D. Krugman. 144p. 1987. 24.95 (ISBN 0-03-012368-2). Saunders.

Review of Pennsylvania Jury Monitoring, Technical Assistance: Final Report. National Center for State Courts Staff. 44p. 1985. manuscript 3.00 (NERO, T/A-529). Natl Ctr St Courts.

Review of Personality & Social Psychology: Vol. 1. Ed. by Ladd Wheeler. (Illus.). 352p. 1980. 35.00 (ISBN 0-8039-1457-1); pap. 16.95 (ISBN 0-8039-1458-X). Sage.

Review of Personality & Social Psychology, Vol. 2. Wheeler. 352p. 1981. 35.00 (ISBN 0-8039-1667-1); pap. 16.95 (ISBN 0-8039-1668-X). Sage.

Review of Personality & Social Psychology, Vol. 3. Ed. by Ladd Wheeler. (Illus.). 320p. 1982. 35.00 (ISBN 0-8039-1854-2); pap. 16.95 (ISBN 0-8039-1855-0). Sage.

Review of Personality & Social Psychology: Self, Situations, & Social Behavior. Phillip Shaver. (RPSP Ser.: Vol. 6). 312p. (Orig.). 1985. text ed. 35.00 (ISBN 0-8039-2507-7); pap. text ed. 16.95 (ISBN 0-8039-2508-5). Sage.

Review of Personality & Social Psychology, Vol. 5: Emotions, Relationships & Health. Ed. by Phillip Shaver. 320p. 1984. text ed. 35.00 (ISBN 0-8039-2358-9); pap. text ed. 16.95 (ISBN 0-8039-2359-7). Sage.

Review of Personality Theories. Victor J. Drapela. (Illus.). 178p. 1987. 19.75x (ISBN 0-398-05281-6). C C Thomas.

Review of Physiology, Biochemistry & Pharmacology, Vol. 108. 220p. 1987. 61.70 (ISBN 0-387-17778-7). Springer-Verlag.

Review of Pinus Caribaea. A. Greaves. 1980. 30.00x (ISBN 0-85074-052-5, Pub. by For Lib Comm England). State Mutual Bk.

Review of Placement Services Within a Comprehensive Rehabilitation Framework: Survey Report. Richard J. Jacobsen & Pamela B. Avellani. LC 78-72067. 76p. 1978. 8.25 (ISBN 0-686-38818-6). Human Res Ctr.

Review of Placement Services Within a Comprehensive Rehabilitation Framework: Technical Report. David Vandergoot & Jessica Swirsky. LC 78-72067. 60p. 1979. 5.25 (ISBN 0-686-38819-4). Human Res Ctr.

Review of Population Estimates & Projections for Nebraska Cities. Vicki S. Stepp. (Nebraska Economic & Business Report: No. 21). 1978. 5.00 (ISBN 0-686-28412-7). Bur Busn Res U Nrbr.

Review of Private Approaches for Delivery of Public Services. Harry P. Hatry. LC 83-23299. 1983. pap. text ed. 9.95x (ISBN 0-87766-329-7). Urban Inst.

Review of Progress in Quantitative Nondestructive Evaluation, Vol. 1. Ed. by Donald O. Thompson & Dale E. Chimenti. LC 82-9140. 832p. 1982. 125.00x (ISBN 0-306-41024-9, Plenum Pr). Plenum Pub.

Review of Progress in Quantitative Nondestructive Evaluation, Vol. 2. Ed. by Donald O. Thompson & Dale E. Chimenti. 1840p. 1983. 250.00x (ISBN 0-306-41350-7, Plenum Pr). Plenum Pub.

Review of Progress in Quantitative Nondestructive Evaluation, Vol. 3. Ed. by Donald O. Thompson & Dale E. Chimenti. 1516p. 1984. 225.00x (ISBN 0-306-41678-6, Plenum Pr). Plenum Pub.

Review of Progress in Quantitative Nondestructive Evaluation, Vol. 4. Ed. by Donald O. Thompson & Dale E. Chimenti. 1376p. 1985. 195.00x (ISBN 0-306-41927-0, Plenum Pr). Plenum Pub.

Review of Progress in Quantitative Nondestructive Evaluation, Vol. 5. Ed. by Donald O. Thompson & Dale E. Chimenti. 876p. 1986. 235.00x (ISBN 0-306-42269-7, Plenum Pr). Plenum Pub.

Review of Progress in Quantitative Nondistructive Evaluation, Vol. 6. Ed. by Donald O. Thompson & Dale E. Chimenti. (Illus.). 1820p. 1987. 245.00x (ISBN 0-306-42584-X, Plenum Pr). Plenum Pub.

Review of Progress in Quantitative Nondestructive Evaluation, Vol. 7. Ed. by D. O. Thompson & D. E. Chimenti. LC 82-9140. (Illus.). 1882p. 1988. 255.00x (ISBN 0-306-42837-7, Plenum Pr). Plenum Pub.

Review of Published Research on the Relationship of Some Personality Variables to ESP Scoring Level. Gordon L. Mangan. (Parapsychological Monographs, No. 1). 1958. pap. 5.00 (ISBN 0-912328-03-7). Parapsych Foun.

Review of Quantitative Analysis of Vessels & Fishing Operations: Fish Report, Vol. 2, No. 167. pap. 7.50 (F810, FAO). UNIPUB.

Review of Rail Transport Research Needs. (Special Report). 78p. 1980. 4.20 (ISBN 0-309-02985-6). Transport Res Bd.

Review of Relevant National Policies & Programmes in Respect of Rural-Urban Relations in Sri Lanka. (Working Papers Ser.: No. 78-5). 56p. 1978. pap. 6.00 (ISBN 0-686-78251-8, CRD032, UNCRD). UNIPUB.

Review of Research in Education, 3 vols. Incl. Vol. 9. David C. Berliner. 1981 (ISBN 0-935302-01-8); Vol. 10. Ed. by Edmund Gordon. 432p. 1983 (ISBN 0-935302-02-6); Vol. 11. Ed. by Edmund Gordon. 1984 (ISBN 0-935302-04-2); Vol. 12. Ed. by Edmund Gordon. 1985 (ISBN 0-935302-05-0); Vol. 13. Ed. by Ernst Z. Rothkopf. 1986 (ISBN 0-935302-06-9); Vol. 14. Ed. by Ernst Z. Rothkopf. 1987 (ISBN 0-935302-07-7). 18.00 (ISBN 0-317-31936-1); institutional 25.00 (ISBN 0-317-31937-X). Am Educ Res.

Review of Research in Education, No. 4. Ed. by Lee Shulman. LC 72-89719. pap. 90.50 (ISBN 0-8357-9488-1, 2012294). Bks Demand UMI.

Review of Research in Nursing Education. Ed. by William L. Holzemer. 208p. 1986. pap. 19.95 (ISBN 0-88737-340-2, 15-2170). Natl League Nurse.

Review of Research in Social Studies Education: 1976-1983. Ed. by William B. Stanley. (Orig.). 1985. pap. 12.95 (ISBN 0-89994-303-9). Soc Sci Ed.

Review of Research on Modern Problems in Geochemistry. International Association for Geochemistry & Cosmochemistry. Ed. by F. R. Siegel. (Earth Sciences Ser.: No. 16). (Illus.). 290p. 1979. pap. 20.00 (ISBN 92-3-101577-X, U998, UNESCO). UNIPUB.

Review of Research on Parent Influences on Child Personality. Family Service Association of America, Research Department Staff & Ruth V. Frankiel. LC 59-1935. pap. 20.00 (ISBN 0-317-10343-1, 2050172). Bks Demand UMI.

Review of Research on Salt-Affected Soils. I. Szabolcs. (Natural Resources Research Ser.: No. 15). (Illus.). 137p. (Bibliography Compiled by G. Varallyay). 1979. pap. 11.50 (ISBN 92-3-101613-X, U972, UNESCO). UNIPUB.

Review of Research Trends & an Annotated Bibliography: Social & Economic Consequences of the Arms Race & Disarmament. (Reports & Papers in the Social Sciences: No. 39). 44p. 1978. pap. 5.00 (ISBN 92-3-101552-4, U827, UNESCO). UNIPUB.

Review of Resources: Teaching Law & the Constitution. Ed. by Mary E. Glade. 176p. (Orig.). 1987. pap. 14.95 (ISBN 0-89994-320-9). Soc Sci Ed.

Review of Scottish Culture, Vol. 3. Ed. by Alexander Fenton. 120p. 1987. pap. text ed. 15.50 (ISBN 0-85976-183-5, Pub. by John Donald). Humanities.

Review of Scottish Culture Vol. I. A. Fenton. (Review of Scottish Culture Ser.: No. 1). 112p. 1984. pap. text ed. 9.95x (ISBN 0-85976-106-1, Pub. by John Donald Pub UK). Humanities.

Review of Scottish Culture Vol. 2. Ed. by Alexander Fenton. (Review of Scottish Culture Ser.: Vol. 2, 1985). (Illus.). 144p. 1986. text ed. 9.95x (ISBN 0-85976-138-X, Pub. by John Donald Pub UK). Humanities.

Review of Search & Reconnaisance Theory Literature. Michael L. Moore. LC 75-131015. 104p. 1970. 22.00 (ISBN 0-403-04520-7). Scholarly.

Review of "Shall We Splinter?". Robert R. Taylor, Jr. 1985. pap. 3.00 (ISBN 0-934916-08-X). Natl Christian Pr.

Review of Some Aspects of Court Reporting in San Joaquin County, California. National Center for State Courts Staff. 61p. 1986. manuscript 4.00 (WRO-069). Natl Ctr St Courts.

Review of Surgical Nursing. A. Descharnais. 1978. text ed. 21.95 (ISBN 0-07-016560-2). McGraw.

Review of Taxation of Individuals: 1977-1986, 10 vols. Bound set. 450.00x (ISBN 0-686-90034-0). Rothman.

Review of Textile Progress. Manchester & Bradford. 538p. 1972. 75.00x (ISBN 0-686-63796-8). State Mutual Bk.

Review of Textile Progress: A Survey of World Literature, 1965-66, Vol. 17. LC 60-1460. pap. 152.80 (ISBN 0-317-09916-7, 2020708). Bks Demand UMI.

Review of the Accounting Cycle for the IBM-PC. Frederic M. Stiner, Jr. & Annette R. Pearson. 1987. 10.50 (ISBN 0-534-07152-X). PWS Kent Pub.

Review of the Administration & Operation of the Tucson City Court. National Center for State Courts Staff. 162p. 1985. manuscript 10.00 (WRO-054). Natl Ctr St Courts.

Review of the Administration of the Multnomah County Circuit Court. 87p. 1986. manuscript 5.00 (ISBN 0-317-59204-1, WRO-082). Natl Ctr St Courts.

Review of the Andean Leptodactylid Frog Genus Phrynopus. John D. Lynch. (Occasional Papers: No. 35). 51p. 1975. pap. 2.75 (ISBN 0-686-80370-1). U of KS Mus Nat Hist.

Review of the Automated Juror Selection Process in Santa Barbara County, California. National Center for State Courts Staff. 12p. 1985. manuscript 1.00 (CJS-011). Natl Ctr St Courts.

Review of the Broad-Headed Eleutherodactyline Frogs of South America (Leptodactylidae) John D. Lynch. (Occasional Papers: No. 38). 46p. 1975. pap. 2.50 (ISBN 0-686-80371-X). U of KS Mus Nat Hist.

Review of the Calendar Management & Management Information Practices for the Eighteenth Judicial District (Araphoe County) of Colorado: A Technical Assistance Report. National Center for State Courts Staff. 106p. 1985. manuscript 7.00 (WRO, T/A-504). Natl Ctr St Courts.

Review of the Cattle Business in Johnson County Wyoming, Since 1822, & the Causes That Led to the Recent Invasion. Oscar H. Flagg. LC 79-90174. (Mass Violence in America Ser). Repr. of 1892 ed. 6.50 (ISBN 0-405-01309-4). Ayer Co Pubs.

Review of the Causes & Consequences of the Mexican War. William Jay. LC 79-82202. (Anti-Slavery Crusade in America Ser). 1969. Repr. of 1849 ed. 24.50 (ISBN 0-405-00641-1). Ayer Co Pubs.

Review of the Causes & Consequences of the Mexican War. William Jay. (Select Bibliographies Reprint Ser). 1849. 24.50 (ISBN 0-8369-5215-4). Ayer Co Pubs.

Review of the Centrolenid Frogs of Ecuador: With Descriptions of New Species. John D. Lynch & William E. Duellman. (Occasional Papers: No. 16). (Illus.). 66p. 1973. 4.50 (ISBN 0-317-04877-5). U of KS Mus Nat Hist.

Review of the Colonial Slave Registration Acts. facs. ed. African Institution, London Staff. LC 78-149860. (Black Heritage Library Collection). 1820. 14.50 (ISBN 0-8369-8742-X). Ayer Co Pubs.

Review of the Colubrid Snakes of the Genus Tantilla of Central America. Larry D. Wilson. (Contributions in Biology & Geology Ser.: No. 52). 77p. 1982. 10.00 (ISBN 0-89326-082-7). Milwaukee Pub Mus.

Review of the Copepoda Associated with Sea Anemones. Arthur G. Humes. LC 81-71035. (Transactions Ser.: Vol. 72, Pt. 2). 1982. 12.00 (ISBN 0-87169-722-X). Am Philos.

Review of the Criminal Law of the Commonwealth of Kentucky, 3 Vols. Harry Toulmin & James Blair. Incl. Vol. 1. 468p; Vol. 2. 498p; Vol. 3. 310p. LC 83-81437. Set. 225.00x (ISBN 0-912004-23-1). W W Gaunt.

Review of the Deep-Sea Fish Family Platytroctidae: Pisces: Salmoniformes. Tetsuo Matsui & Richard H. Rosenblatt. LC 86-25088. (Bulletin of the Scripps Institution of Oceanography: Vol. 26). (Illus.). 168p. 1987. pap. 17.00x (ISBN 0-520-09708-4). U of Cal Pr.

Review of the Diseases & Treatments of Captive Turtles. James B. Murphy & Joseph T. Collins. LC 82-73100. Date not set. pap. text ed. 16.00. AMS Kansas.

Review of the Fauna of the Marquesas Islands & Discussion of Its Origin. A. M. Adamson. (BMB Ser.: No. 159). Repr. of 1939 ed. 13.00 (ISBN 0-527-02267-5). Kraus Repr.

Review of the Ferns of Northern India: With an Index of the Species & 36 Plates. Charles B. Clarke. (Illus.). 1978. Repr. of 1880 ed. 62.50x (ISBN 0-89955-303-6, Pub. by Intl Bk Dist). Intl Spec Bk.

Review of the Fertilizer Distribution & Handling System in Bangladesh. W. E. Clayton. (IFDC Miscellaneous Publication Ser. A-2). 1981. 10.00 (ISBN 0-88090-063-6). Intl Fertilizer.

Review of the Fiscal Impulse Measure. Peter S. Heller et al. LC 86-3027. (Occasional Papers: No. 44). 45p. 1986. pap. 7.50 (ISBN 0-939934-60-4). Intl Monetary.

Review of the Fishery Resources in the Western Central Atlantic. (WECAF Studies Ser.: No. 3). (Illus.). 1976. pap. 7.50 (ISBN 92-5-100015-8, F1212, FAO). UNIPUB.

Review of the Foreign Press, 1939-1945, 10 Ser. in 27 vols. Great Britain, Royal Institute of International Affairs Staff & Great Britain, Foreign Office Staff. 1980. lib. bdg. 1980.00x (ISBN 0-527-75543-5). Kraus Intl.

Review of the Genus Eucerceris: Hymenoptera Sphecidae. Herman A. Scullen. (Studies in Entomology: No. 1). (Illus.). 80p. 1939. pap. 4.95x (ISBN 0-87071-051-6). Oreg St U Pr.

Review of the Lectures of Wm. A. Smith DD, on the Philosophy & Practice of Slavery. John H. Power. 19.50 (ISBN 0-8369-9172-9, 9046). Ayer Co Pubs.

Review of the Management of Our Affairs in China. Han Shan Tang Ltd. Staff. 217p. 1834. 560.00x (Pub. by Han-Shan Tang Ltd). State Mutual Bk.

Review of the Manual of Personnel Policies for the Judiciary of the State of Delaware: Comments & Suggestions. National Center for State Courts Staff. 18p. 1978. manuscript 1.08 (NCRO-038). Natl Ctr St Courts.

Review of the Marine Resources of the Western Central Atlantic Fisheries Commission (WECAFC) Region. David K. Stevenson. (Fisheries Technical Papers: No. 211). 142p. (Eng. & Span.). 1981. pap. 10.00 (ISBN 92-5-101153-2, F2286, FAO). UNIPUB.

Review of the Mexican War on Christian Principles: And an Essay on the Means of Preventing War. Philip A. Berry. LC 76-143427. (Peace Movement in America Ser). ix, 87p. 1972. Repr. of 1849 ed. lib. bdg. 11.95x (ISBN 0-89198-057-1). Ozer.

Review of the Multilateral Treaty-Making Process. (United Nations Legislative Ser.: No. 21). 521p. 35.00 (ISBN 92-1-133338-5, E.83.V.8). UN.

Review of the Nature & Uses of Examinations in Medical Education. J. Charvat et al. (Public Health Papers Ser: No. 36). 74p. 1968. pap. 4.00 (ISBN 92-4-130036-1, 548). World Health.

Review of the Nearctic Alysiini (Hymenoptera, Braconidae) Robert Wharton. (UC Publications in Entomology: Vol. 88). 122p. 1981. pap. 20.95x (ISBN 0-520-09611-8). U of Cal Pr.

Review of the NLRA Interpretations & Current Case Law - 1984. 342p. 1984. pap. 29.95 (ISBN 0-89707-150-6). Amer Bar Assn.

Review of the North American Eocene & Oligocene Apatemyidae (Mammalia: Insectivora) Robert M. West. (Special Publications: No. 3). (Illus.). 42p. 1973. pap. 5.00 (ISBN 0-89672-028-4). Tex Tech Univ Pr.

Review of the North American Leptoconops (Diptera: Ceratopogonidae) Willis W. Wirth & William R. Atchley. (Graduate Studies: No. 5). (Illus.). 57p. (Orig.). 1973. pap. 3.00 (ISBN 0-89672-012-8). Tex Tech Univ Pr.

Review of the North & Central American Species of Paravilla Painter (Diptera: Bombyliidae) Jack C. Hall. (UC Publications in Entomology: Vol. 92). 192p. 1981. pap. 16.50x (ISBN 0-520-09625-8). U of Cal Pr.

Review of the Ohio Court of Claims Victims of Crime Compensation Program. 87p. 1986. manuscript 5.00 (ISBN 0-317-59205-X, NERO-195). Natl Ctr St Courts.

Review of the Pelycosauria: Geological Society of American Special Papers, No. 28. Alfred S. Romer & Llewellyn I. Price. Ed. by Stephen J. Gould. LC 79-8346. (History of Paleontology Ser.). (Illus.). 1980. Repr. of 1940 ed. lib. bdg. 44.00x (ISBN 0-405-12740-5). Ayer Co Pubs.

Review of the Phyllomedusa Buckleyi Group: (Anura: Hylidae) David C. Cannatella. (Occasional Papers: Vol. 87). 40p. 1980. 2.25 (ISBN 0-317-04840-6). U of KS Mus Nat Hist.

Review of the Principal Questions in Morals. Richard Price. LC 73-179398. 516p. 1974. Repr. of 1787 ed. lib. bdg. 32.50 (ISBN 0-8337-2831-8). B Franklin.

Review of the Principle Questions in Morals. Richard Price. 1986. lib. bdg. 30.00X (ISBN 0-935005-25-0); pap. text ed. 13.00X (ISBN 0-935005-26-9). Ibis Pub VA.

Review of the Report, "Proposal For a Greater New Bedford, MA PCB Health Study". Power Equipment Division NEMA. 15.00 ea. Natl Elec Mfrs.

Review of the Snailfish Genus Paraliparis (Scorpaeniforms: Liparidae) of the Southern Ocean. A. P. Andriashev. (Theses Zoologicae Ser.: No. 7). (Illus.). 204p. 1986. lib. bdg. 57.60x (ISBN 3-87429-264-9). Lubrecht & Cramer.

Review of the Southern African Species of Cyrtanthus. C. Reid & R. Allen Dyer. Ed. by R. Mitchel Beauchamp. (Illus.). 68p. (Orig.). 1984. pap. 12.00 (ISBN 0-930653-00-9). Am Plant Life.

Review of the Species of Exomalopsis Occurring in North America (Hymenoptera, Anthophoridae) P. H. Timberlake. (UC Publications in Entomology: Vol. 86). 164p. 1981. pap. 26.95x (ISBN 0-520-09606-1). U of Cal Pr.

Review of the State of Water Pollution Affecting Inland Fisheries in Southeast Asia. John S. Alabaster. (FAO Fisheries Technical Paper Ser.: No. 260). 25p. (Orig.). 1986. pap. 7.50 (ISBN 92-5-102405-7, F2966, FAO). UNIPUB.

Review of the Structure & Operations of the SEC Practice Section: Report of the SECPS Review Committee. American Institute of Certified Public Accountants Staff. pap. 21.50 (ISBN 0-317-27247-0, 2025097). Bks Demand UMI.

Review of the Taxonomy of the Sorex Vagrans Species Complex from Western North America. Darwen Hennings & Robert S. Hoffmann. (Occasional Papers: No. 68). 35p. 1977. pap. 2.00 (ISBN 0-686-80294-2). U of KS Mus Nat Hist.

Review of the Technological Efficiency of Some Antioxidants & Synergists. FAO-WHO Expert Committee on Food Additives. (WHO Food Additives Ser: No. 3). 144p. 1972. pap. 3.20 (ISBN 92-4-166003-1). World Health.

Review of the Toxicity of the Esters of O-Phthalic Acid (Phthalate Esters) K. N. Woodward et al. (Toxicity Review Ser.: No. 14). 183p. pap. text ed. 27.50 (ISBN 0-11-883859-8, HM654, Pub by Her Maj Station Ofc). UNIPUB.

Review of the United Nations Charter. U. S. Congress - Senate Committee on Foreign Relations. LC 68-55114. (Illus.). 1968. lib. bdg. 35.00x (ISBN 0-8371-3170-7, UNNC). Greenwood.

Review of the United Nations Ground-Water Exploration & Development Programme in the Developing Countries, 1962-1977. (Natural Resources-Water Ser.: No. 7). pap. 7.00 (ISBN 92-1-104072-8, E.79.II.A.4). UN.

Review of the Volutidae. Smith. 3.50 (ISBN 0-87505-252-5). Borden.

Review of the World Resources of Mesopelagic Fish. J. Cjosaeter & K. Kawaguchi. (Fisheries Technical Papers: No. 193). 156p. 1980. pap. 11.25 (ISBN 92-5-100924-4, F2074, FAO). UNIPUB.

Review of Thirty-One Creationist Books. Ed. by Stanley L. Weinberg & Paul Joslin. (Illus.). 74p. (Orig.). 1984. pap. 5.00 (ISBN 0-939873-50-8). Natl Ctr Sci Educ.

Review of Tropical Plant Pathology: Diseases of Cereals, Maize & Millet, Vol. 1. S. P. Raychaudhuri & J. P. Verma. (Illus.). 564p. 1984. 79.00 (ISBN 1-55528-080-3, Pub. by Messers Today & Tomorrow Printers & Publishers). Scholarly Pubns.

Review of Tropical Plant Pathology: Diseases of Fruits, Vol. 2. Ed. by S. P. Raychahduri & J. P. Verma. iv, 406p. 1986. 99.00 (ISBN 1-55528-081-1, Pub. by Messers Today & Tomorrow Printers & Publishers). Scholarly Pubns.

Review of Tropical Plant Pathology: Diseases of Vegetables, Vol. 3. Ed. by S. P. Raychaudhuri & J. P. Verma. (Illus.). 586p. 1987. 95.00 (ISBN 1-55528-144-3, Pub. by Messers Today & Tomorrow Printers & Publishers). Scholarly Pubns.

Review of Undergraduate Physics. Benjamin F. Bayman & Morton Hamermesh. LC 85-26577. 319p. 1986. pap. write for info. (ISBN 0-471-81684-1). Wiley.

Review of United States Competitiveness in Agricultural Trade, a Technical Memorandum. LC 86-600586. (OTA-TM-TET-29 Ser.). (Illus.). 110p. (Orig.). 1986. pap. 5.50 (ISBN 0-318-21556-X, S/N 052-003-01054-2). USGPO.

Review of Vinyl Technology II: Compounding, Processing, & Properties: Sheraton International at O'Hare, October 14-15, 1986. Society of Plastics Engineers Staff. (Illus.). pap. 91.80 (ISBN 0-317-58188-0, 2029713). Bks Demand UMI.

Review of Waste Management Organizations. John Grover. (Radioactive Waste Management & the Nuclear Fuel Cycle Ser. (Special Journal Issue)). 116p. 1984. pap. text ed. 35.00 (ISBN 3-7186-0202-4). Harwood Academic.

Review of Welding Cast Steels & Its Effects on Fatigue & Toughness Properties. 1979. 15.00 (ISBN 0-686-45002-7). Steel Founders.

Review of Wildlife Management. James Peek. (Illus.). 512p. 1986. text ed. 37.00 (ISBN 0-13-780552-7). P-H.

Review Outlines & Materials for Business Law & CPA Law Review. William T. Schantz & Janice E. Jackson. LC 80-13096. 985p. 1980. pap. text ed. 18.50 (ISBN 0-8299-2071-4). West Pub.

Review-Preview 1984-1985. Bookman Publishing Staff. (Yearbook Ser.). (Illus.). 96p. 1984. pap. 8.95 (ISBN 0-934780-42-0). Bookman Pub.

Review-Preview 1985-1986. Bookman Publishing Staff. (Yearbook Ser.). (Illus.). 96p. 1985. pap. 8.95 (ISBN 0-934780-72-2). Bookman Pub.

Review Questions in Analytical Toxicology. J. E. Wallace & N. A. Wade. LC 82-70669. 200p. (Orig.). 1982. pap. text ed. 19.00 (ISBN 0-931890-09-8, Biomed Pubns). PSG Pub Co.

Review Questions in Anatomic Pathology. Ed. by A. M. Ring & S. L. Ostrin. LC 83-73100. (Illus.). 432p. (Orig.). 1985. pap. text ed. 28.00 (ISBN 0-931890-18-7, Biomed Pubns). PSG Pub Co.

Review Questions In Clinical Pathology. Samuel Ostrin & Alvin M. Ring. 399p. 1986. 28.00 (ISBN 0-931890-19-5, Biomed Pubns). PSG Pub Co.

Review Questions in General Vascular Surgery, Vol. 1. William H. Brown & Roy L. Tawes. 288p. 1984. 45.00 (ISBN 0-941022-05-6). Appleton Davies.

Review Questions in General Vascular Surgery, Vol. 2. William H. Brown & Roy L. Tawes. 226p. 1984. 45.00 (ISBN 0-941022-06-4). Appleton Davies.

Review, Sales, Computers see Travel Agent Training Workbook, 1987-88.

Review Seventy-Six. Ed. by Joseph McLaughlin. 48p. 1976. pap. text ed. 2.00 (ISBN 0-914720-05-8). Pale Horse.

Review Tests for Nursing Competence. Ed. by Martha Valesco-Whetsell. 302p. (Orig.). 1986. pap. 12.95 (ISBN 0-935236-50-3). Genl Med Pub.

Review Text in American History. Irving L. Gordon. (Illus., Orig.). (gr. 10-12). 1968. pap. text ed. 11.67 (ISBN 0-87720-606-6). AMSCO Sch.

Review Text in Biology. Mark A. Hall & Milton S. Lesser. (Illus., Orig.). (gr. 10-12). 1966. pap. text ed. 9.67 (ISBN 0-87720-051-3). AMSCO Sch.

Review Text in Chemistry. Maxwell Gelender. (Illus., Orig.). (gr. 10-12). 1964. pap. text ed. 10.17 (ISBN 0-87720-104-8). AMSCO Sch.

Review Text in Earth Science, Intermediate Level. Constantine Constant. (Orig.). (gr. 7-9). 1971. pap. text ed. 10.58 (ISBN 0-87720-152-8). AMSCO Sch.

Review Text in French First Year. Eli Blume. 1984. pap. 9.08 (ISBN 0-87720-474-8, 240P). Amsco Sch.

Review Text in French Three Years. Blume. 1980. pap. text ed. 10.33 (ISBN 0-87720-471-3). AMSCO Sch.

Review Text in French Two Years. Eli Blume. 1982. pap. 9.67 (ISBN 0-87720-456-X, 214P). AMSCO Sch.

Review Text in General Science. 2nd ed. J. Albert Mould & Saul L. Geffner. (gr. 10-12). 1974. pap. text ed. 9.92 (ISBN 0-87720-001-7). AMSCO Sch.

Review Text in German: First Year. Harry Reinert. (Orig.). (gr. 10-12). 1971. pap. text ed. 9.33 (ISBN 0-87720-581-7). AMSCO Sch.

Review Text in Health. Bro. Patricius Dougherty & Sr. Carmel Leifer. (gr. 7-12). 1962. pap. text ed. 9.58 (ISBN 0-87720-161-7). AMSCO Sch.

Review Text in Latin First Year. 2nd ed. Charles I. Freundlich. (Illus., Orig.). (gr. 7-12). 1966. pap. text ed. 9.42 (ISBN 0-87720-551-5). AMSCO Sch.

Review Text in Latin Second Year. Charles I. Freundlich. (gr. 7-12). 1966. pap. text ed. 9.83 (ISBN 0-87720-555-8). AMSCO Sch.

Review Text in Latin Third & Fourth Years. Charles I. Freundlich. (Orig.). (gr. 7-12). 1967. pap. text ed. 10.50 (ISBN 0-87720-558-2). AMSCO Sch.

Review Text in Physical Science: Intermediate Level. Jules Weisler. (gr. 7-10). 1970. pap. text ed. 10.17 (ISBN 0-87720-007-6). AMSCO Sch.

Review Text in Physics. Walter L. Ahner & Harold G. Kastan. (Illus., Orig.). (gr. 10-12). 1966. pap. text ed. 9.67 (ISBN 0-87720-171-4). AMSCO Sch.

Review Text in Preliminary Mathematics. Isidore Dressler. (Illus.). (gr. 7-9). 1962. text ed. 15.75 (ISBN 0-87720-203-6); pap. text ed. 11.42 (ISBN 0-87720-202-8). AMSCO Sch.

Review Text in Spanish First Year. 2nd ed. Robert J. Nassi & Bernard Bernstein. (Illus., Orig.). (gr. 7-12). 1972. pap. text ed. 9.33 (ISBN 0-87720-500-0). AMSCO Sch.

Review Text in Spanish Three Years. Robert J. Nassi et al. (Illus., Orig.). (gr. 7-12). 1965. pap. text ed. 9.33 (ISBN 0-87720-508-6). AMSCO Sch.

Review Text in Spanish Two Years. 2nd ed. Robert J. Nassi & Bernard Bernstein. (Illus., Orig.). (gr. 7-12). 1969. pap. text ed. 9.33 (ISBN 0-87720-505-1). AMSCO Sch.

Review Text in United States History. rev. ed. Paul M. Roberts. (Illus., Orig.). (gr. 7-9). 1967. pap. text ed. 10.83 (ISBN 0-87720-601-5). AMSCO Sch.

Review Text in World History. Irving L. Gordon. (Illus., Orig.). (gr. 10-12). 1968. pap. text ed. 10.83 (ISBN 0-87720-604-X). AMSCO Sch.

Review, Vol. 8. Ed. by James O. Hoge & James L. West, III. 300p. 1987. 30.00x (ISBN 0-8139-1113-3). U Pr of VA.

Review Workbook for Adult Education in Mathematics & English. Leonard S. Bennett et al. pap. 7.50 (ISBN 0-87738-001-5). Youth Ed.

Review Workbook for High School Entrance Plus Scholarship Examination. Leonard S. Bennett. pap. 8.95. Youth Ed.

Review X-Ray. Siemens. 1979. 22.00 (ISBN 0-85501-246-3). Wiley.

Review, 1987, Vol. 9. Ed. by James O. Hoge & James L. West, III. 356p. 1988. text ed. 30.00x (ISBN 0-8139-1160-5). U Pr of VA.

Reviewed Contents of Major Diabetes Congresses. F. Belfiore. (Frontiers in Diabetes Ser.: Vol. 1). xii, 162p. 1981. 59.50 (ISBN 3-8055-3414-0). S Karger.

Reviewer's A B C see Collected Criticism.

Reviewers Guide, Vol. 1. National Association of Review Appraisers. LC 80-53456. (Illus.). 214p. 1981. 28.50 (ISBN 0-935988-20-3). Todd Pub.

Reviewing. Virginia Woolf. 65p. 1984. Repr. of 1939 ed. lib. bdg. 15.00 (ISBN 0-89987-879-2). Darby Bks.

Reviewing Academic Performance Approaches to the Evaluation of Departments & Individuals. Ernest Roe et al. LC 85-21016. (Scholars' Library). (Illus.). 341p. 1987. text ed. 42.50x (ISBN 0-7022-1967-3). U of Queensland Pr.

Reviewing Apartment Leasing Techniques to Improve Profits. (Journal Reprint Ser.). 8.75 (ISBN 0-686-46404-4, 892). Inst Real Estate.

Reviewing Basic EMT Skills: A Guide for Self-Evaluation. Bertram M. Siegel. 1981. 15.50 (ISBN 0-940432-00-5, Pub. by Emergency Training) (ISBN 0-686-96964-2). Educ Direction.

Reviewing Basic Grammar. 2nd ed. Robert E. Yarber. 1986. pap. text ed. write for info. (ISBN 0-673-16662-7); instr's. manual, test items & answer key avail. Scott F.

Reviewing Before the Edinburgh, 1788-1802. Derek Roper. LC 77-2446. (Illus.). 1978. 27.50 (ISBN 0-87413-128-6). U Delaware Pr.

Reviewing Biology. Carl M. Raab. (YA) (gr. 10). 1987. pap. 5.42 (ISBN 0-87720-050-5). AMSCO Sch.

Reviewing Condominium Projects. National Association of Review Appraisers. LC 80-53455. (Illus.). 156p. 1981. 22.50 (ISBN 0-935988-21-1). Todd Pub.

Reviewing for the Spacecraft Landing on Earth 2001 A. D. Ruth Norman. (Illus.). 139p. 1987. 7.50 (ISBN 0-935097-06-6). Unarius Pubns.

Reviewing German Grammar: A Self-Instructional Reference Book for Elementary German Grammar. Janet D. Rodewald. LC 84-21884. 364p. (Orig.). 1985. pap. text ed. 20.75 (ISBN 0-8191-4366-9). U Pr of Amer.

Reviewing German Grammar & Building Vocabulary. Roselinde Konrad. LC 80-6238. 415p. (Ger.). 1981. pap. text ed. 22.00 (ISBN 0-8191-1605-X). U Pr of Amer.

Reviewing Histories: Selections from New Latin American Cinema. Glauber Rocha et al. Ed. by Coco Fusco. Tr. by Jon Davis et al. (Illus.). 224p. (Orig.). Date not set. pap. 10.00 (ISBN 0-936739-06-1). Hallwalls Inc.

Reviewing Public Administration: A Study Guide. David Swain. LC 87-13288. 238p. (Orig.). 1987. lib. bdg. 24.50 (ISBN 0-8191-6472-0); pap. text ed. 12.75 (ISBN 0-8191-6473-9). U Pr of Amer.

Reviewing Sequential Mathematics Course I. Marilyn Occhiogrosso. (gr. 9). 1985. pap. text ed. 7.92 (ISBN 0-87720-255-9). AMSCO Sch.

Reviewing Sequential Mathematics Course II. Marilyn Occhiogrosso. (gr. 10). 1986. pap. text ed. 7.92 (ISBN 0-87720-258-3). AMSCO SCh.

Reviewing the German-American Relationship. Ed. by Gale A. Mattox & John Vaughan. 150p. 1989. 35.00 (ISBN 0-8133-0769-4). Westview.

Reviewing the Operation of Small Computer Systems. Chantico-QED Staff. LC 85-60180. (Chantico Technical Management Ser.). (Illus.). 166p. (Orig.). 1985. pap. 34.95 (ISBN 0-89435-153-2, CP 1532). QED Info Sci.

Reviewing Your Data Transmission Network. P. R. Scott. 160p. 1982. pap. 54.65 (ISBN 0-471-89424-9). Wiley.

Reviewing Your Writing Skills. Ledford. 192p. 1985. pap. text ed. 14.95 (ISBN 0-8403-3842-2). Kendall-Hunt.

Reviews & Critical Essays. Charles H. Pearson. 1973. Repr. of 1896 ed. 30.00 (ISBN 0-8274-1232-0). R West.

Reviews & Critical Papers. facs. ed. Lionel P. Johnson. LC 67-22099. (Essay Index Reprint Ser). 1921. 12.00 (ISBN 0-8369-0574-1). Ayer Co Pubs.

Reviews & Essays. William Permewan & Phillippa Permewan. 1973. Repr. of 1929 ed. 20.00 (ISBN 0-8274-1225-8). R West.

Reviews & Essays in English Literature. Duncan C. Tovey. LC 70-105842. 1970. Repr. of 1897 ed. 21.50x (ISBN 0-8046-0984-5, Pub. by Kennikat). Assoc Faculty Pr.

Reviews & Essays in English Literature. Duncan C. Tovey. 1973. Repr. of 1897 ed. 25.00 (ISBN 0-8274-0607-X). R West.

Reviews & Reviewing: A Guide. A. J. Walford. 208p. 1986. 38.50 (ISBN 0-89774-390-3). Oryx Pr.

Reviews in Biochemical Toxicology, Vol. 1. Ed. by E. Hodgson et al. 328p. 1979. 62.25 (ISBN 0-444-00317-7, Biomedical Pr). Elsevier.

Reviews in Biochemical Toxicology, Vol. 2. Ed. by E. Hodgson & J. R. Bend. 300p. 1980. 66.00 (ISBN 0-444-00386-X, Biomedical Pr). Elsevier.

Reviews in Biochemical Toxicology, Vol. 3. Ed. by E. Hodgson et al. 1981. 82.25 (ISBN 0-444-00436-X, Biomedcial Pr). Elsevier.

Reviews in Biochemical Toxicology, No. 4. Ed. by E. Hodgson et al. 288p. 1982. 57.00 (ISBN 0-444-00685-0, Biomedical Pr). Elsevier.

Reviews in Biochemical Toxicology, Vol. 5. Ed. by E. Hodgson. 416p. 1983. 83.25 (ISBN 0-444-00808-X, Biomedical Pr). Elsevier.

Reviews in Biochemical Toxicology, Vol. 7. Ed. by E. Hodgson et al. 320p. 1985. 57.50 (ISBN 0-444-00828-4). Elsevier.

Reviews in Biochemical Toxicology, Vol. 7. Ed. by E. Hodgson et al. 320p. 1985. 52.75 (Biomedical Pr). Elsevier.

Reviews in Biochemical Toxicology, Vol. 8. Ed. by E. Hodgson et al. 315p. 1986. 69.00 (ISBN 0-444-01169-2). Elsevier.

Reviews in Biochemical Toxicology, Vol. 9. Ed. by E. Hodgson et al. 366p. 1988. 75.00 (ISBN 0-444-01321-0). Elsevier.

Reviews in Cancer Epidemiology, Vol. 1. A. M. Lilienfeld. 338p. 1980. 83.25 (ISBN 0-444-00382-7, Biomedical Pr). Elsevier.

Reviews in Cancer Epidemiology, Vol. 2. A. M. Lilienfeld. 456p. 1983. 68.00 (ISBN 0-444-00742-3, Biomedical Pr). Elsevier.

Reviews in Environmental Toxicology, Vol. 1. E. Hodgson. 1984. 126.50 (ISBN 0-444-80562-1, I-252-84). Elsevier.

Reviews in Environmental Toxicology, Vol. 2. Ed. by E. Hodgson. 354p. 1986. 138.50 (ISBN 0-444-80767-5). Elsevier.

Reviews in Environmental Toxicology, Vol. 3. Ed. by E. Hodgson. 282p. 1987. 115.25 (ISBN 0-444-80902-3). Elsevier.

Reviews in Global Analysis, 1980-1986. (REVGLO Ser.: Vol. 86, Section 58). 3968p. 1988. pap. text ed. 295.00 (ISBN 0-8218-0104-X, REVGLO-86). Am Math.

Reviews in Graph Theory, 4 vols. Ed. by William G. Brown. LC 80-17817. 1980. Set. 333.00 (ISBN 0-8218-0214-3); Vol. 1. 111.00 (ISBN 0-8218-0210-0); Vol. 2. 111.00 (ISBN 0-8218-0211-9); Vol. 3. 111.00 (ISBN 0-8218-0212-7); Vol. 4. 67.00 (ISBN 0-8218-0213-5). Am Math.

Reviews in Number Theory. Ed. by William J. LeVeque. LC 74-11335. 1974. Set. pap. 443.00 (REVNUM); pap. 100.00 ea. Vol. 1 (ISBN 0-8218-0203-8, REVNUM-1). Vol. 2 (ISBN 0-8218-0204-6, REVNUM-2). Vol. 3 (ISBN 0-8218-0205-4, REVNUM-3). Vol. 4 (ISBN 0-8218-0206-2, REVNUM-4). Vol. 5 (ISBN 0-8218-0207-0, REVNUM-5). Vol. 6 (ISBN 0-8218-0208-9, REVNUM-6). Am Math.

Reviews in Number Theory II: Revnum II. Ed. by Richard K. Guy. 3573p. pap. 581.00 set (ISBN 0-8218-0218-6); pap. 144.00 Vol. 1 (ISBN 0-8218-0219-4); Vol. 2 144.00 (ISBN 0-8218-0220-8); pap. 144.00 Vol. 3 (ISBN 0-8218-0221-6); pap. 144.00 Vol. 4 (ISBN 0-8218-0222-4); pap. 144.00 Vol. 5 (ISBN 0-8218-0223-2); pap. 144.00 Vol. 6 (ISBN 0-8218-0224-0). Am Math.

Reviews in Numerical Analysis, 1980-1986, Section 65. (REVNAM Ser.: Vol. 86). 3608p. 1988. 250.00 (ISBN 0-8218-0102-3, REVNAM-86). Am Math.

Reviews in Partial Differential Equations, 1980-1986, Section 35. (REVPDE Ser.: Vol. 86). 4040p. 1988. 295.00 (ISBN 0-8218-0103-1, REVPDE-86). Am Math.

Reviews in Pediatric Hem-Oncology VI. Ed. by Carl Pochedly. LC 85-9547. 222p. 1985. 44.95 (ISBN 0-275-91306-6, C1306). Praeger.

Reviews in Perinatal Medicine, Vol. 2. Ed. by Emile M. Scarpelli & Ermelando V. Cosmi. LC 77-74616. 405p. 1978. 62.50 (ISBN 0-89004-195-4). Raven.

Reviews in Perinatal Medicine, Vol. 3. Ed. by Emile M. Scarpelli & Ermelando V. Cosmi. LC 77-74616. 493p. 1979. text ed. 82.50 (ISBN 0-89004-249-7). Raven.

Reviews in Perinatal Medicine, Vol. 4. Ed. by Emile M. Scarpelli & Ermelando V. Cosmi. 544p. 1981. 99.50 (ISBN 0-89004-364-7). Raven.

Reviews in Perinatal Medicine, Vol. 5. Emile M. Scarpelli & Ermelando V. Cosmi. 214p. 1984. 47.00 (ISBN 0-8451-0400-4). A R Liss.

Reviews in Ring Theory. Lance W. Small. LC 81-10770. 277.00 (ISBN 0-8218-0215-1, REVRING). Am Math.

Reviews in Ring Theory, 1980-1984. Small. LC 86-10907. (Reviews in Ring Theory Ser.: Vol. 84). 685p. 1986. 88.00 (ISBN 0-8218-0097-3). Am Math.

Reviews in Weed Science, Vol. 1. Ed. & intro. by J. S. Bannon. 74p. 1985. text ed. 9.00. Weed Sci Soc.

Reviews in Weed Science, Vol. 2. Ed. & intro. by C. L. Foy. 90p. 1986. text ed. 12.00 (ISBN 0-911733-06-X). Weed Sci Soc.

Reviews of Clinical Infectious Diseases. Ed. by Robert Fekety. 1983. 47.50 (ISBN 0-8089-1606-8, 791233). Grune.

Reviews of Clinical Infectious Diseases, 1984. Ed. by Robert Fekety. 528p. 1984. 47.50 (ISBN 0-8089-1684-X, 791234). Grune.

Reviews of Clinical Infectious Diseases, 1985. Ed. by Robert Fekety et al. LC 79-1232. 1985. 47.50 (ISBN 0-8089-1748-X, 791232). Grune.

Reviews of English Language Proficiency Tests. Ed. by J. Charles Alderson et al. 88p. 1987. 16.50 (ISBN 0-939791-31-5). Tchrs Eng Spkrs.

Reviews of Environmental Contamination & Toxicology, Vol. 100. Ed. by G. W. Ware. (Illus.). 170p. 1987. 41.00 (ISBN 0-387-96583-1). Springer-Verlag.

Reviews of Environmental Contamination & Toxicology. Ed. by G. W. Ware. (Vol. 101). 200p. 1987. 43.00 (ISBN 0-387-96593-9). Springer-Verlag.

Reviews of Environmental Contamination & Toxicology. Ed. by G. W. Ware. (Vol. 102). (Illus.). 195p. 1988. 38.00 (ISBN 0-387-96647-1). Springer-Verlag.

Reviews of Environmental Contamination & Toxicology, Vol. 103. Ed. by G. W. Ware. (Illus.). 180p. 1988. 38.00 (ISBN 0-387-96693-5). Springer-Verlag.

Reviews of Environmental Contamination & Toxicology, Vol. 104. 210p. 1988. 38.00 (ISBN 0-387-96725-7). Springer-Verlag.

Reviews of Environmental Contamination & Toxicology, Vol. 105. 185p. 1988. 37.00 (ISBN 0-387-96723-0). Springer-Verlag.

Reviews of Environmental Contamination & Toxicology, Vol. 98. Ed. by G. W. Ware. (Illus.). 185p. 1986. 39.00 (ISBN 0-387-96448-7). Springer-Verlag.

Reviews of Environmental Contamination & Toxicology, Vol. 99. Ed. by G. W. Ware. (Illus.). 185p. 1987. 41.00 (ISBN 0-387-96498-3). Springer-Verlag.

Reviews of George Gissing. Desmond MacCarthy. LC 74-20618. 1974. Repr. of 1938 ed. lib. bdg. 17.50 (ISBN 0-8414-5916-9). Folcroft.

Reviews of Immunoassay, 2 vols. Ed. by S. B. Pal. 1988. lib. bdg. 89.95 ea. (Pub. by Chapman & Hall England). Vol. 1, 200p (ISBN 0-412-01841-1, Pub. by Chapman & Hall England). Vol. 2, 208p (ISBN 0-412-01851-9, Pub. by Chapman & Hall England). Routledge Chapman & Hall.

Reviews of Infrared & Millimeter Waves, Vol. 1. Ed. by Kenneth J. Button. 366p. 1983. 65.00x (ISBN 0-306-41260-8, Plenum Pr). Plenum Pub.

Reviews of Infrared & Millimeter Waves, Vol. 2: Optically Pumped Far-Infrared Lasers. Ed. by Kenneth J. Buttton et al. 492p. 1984. 79.50x (ISBN 0-306-41487-2, Plenum Pr). Plenum Pub.

Reviews of Lunar Sciences. Ed. by Joseph Chamberlain. (Illus.). 540p. 1977. pap. 5.00 (ISBN 0-87590-220-0). Am Geophysical.

Reviews of National Policies for Education: Spain. OECD. 108p. (Orig.). 1987. pap. 18.00x (ISBN 92-64-12902-2). OECD.

Reviews of National Policies for Education: Educational Reforms in Italy. OECD. 112p. (Orig.). 1985. pap. 15.00x (ISBN 92-64-12702-X). OECD.

Reviews of National Policies for Education: New Zealand. OECD Staff. 140p. 1983. pap. 13.00x (ISBN 92-64-12477-2). OECD.

Reviews of National Policies for Education: Portugal. OECD. 110p. (Orig.). 1984. pap. 12.00x (ISBN 0-318-01270-7). OECD.

Reviews of National Policy for Education: Yugoslavia. 152p. (Orig.). 1982. pap. 9.50x (ISBN 92-64-12270-2). OECD.

Reviews of National Science & Technology Policy: Australia. OECD Staff. 120p. (Orig.). 1986. pap. 15.00x (ISBN 92-64-12851-4). OECD.

Reviews of National Science & Technology Policy: Denmark. OECD. 120p. (Orig.). 1988. pap. 19.80x (ISBN 92-64-13058-6). OECD.

Reviews of National Science & Technology Policy: Finland. OECD. 154p. (Orig.). 1987. pap. 19.00x (ISBN 92-64-12928-6). OECD.

Reviews of National Science & Technology Policy: Netherlands. OECD. 141p. (Orig.). 1987. pap. 20.00x (ISBN 92-64-12955-3, ECD134). OECD.

Reviews of National Science & Technology Policy: Portugal. OECD Staff. 136p. (Orig.). 1986. pap. 16.00x (ISBN 9-2641-2840-9). OECD.

Reviews of National Science & Technology Policy: Sweden. OECD. 112p. (Orig.). 1987. pap. 13.00x (ISBN 92-64-12958-8). OECD.

Reviews of National Science Policy: Greece. OECD. 120p. (Orig.). 1984. pap. 11.00x (ISBN 92-64-12645-7). OECD.

Reviews of National Science Policy: Iceland. OECD Staff. 130p. pap. 10.00 (ISBN 92-64-12506-X). OECD.

Reviews of National Science Policy: Norway. OECD. 108p. (Orig.). 1985. pap. 11.00x (ISBN 92-64-12701-1). OECD.

Reviews of National Science Policy: United States. OECD. Ed. by I. Bernard Cohen. LC 79-7979. (Three Centuries of Science in America Ser.). 1980. Repr. of 1968 ed. lib. bdg. 50.50x (ISBN 0-405-12561-5). Ayer Co Pubs.

Reviews of Neuroscience, Vol. 3. Ed. by Seymour Ehrenpreis & Irwin J. Kopin. LC 74-80538. 238p. 1978. 44.00 (ISBN 0-89004-168-7). Raven.

Reviews of Papers in Algebraic & Differential Topology, Topological Groups, & Homological Algebra. Ed. by Norman E. Steenrod. LC 68-58968. 1448p. 1969. pap. 77.00 (ISBN 0-8218-0046-9, REVTOP). Am Math.

Reviews of Physiology & Biochemistry. Ed. by L. Brown et al. Incl. Vol. 57. 1966. 64.90 (ISBN 0-387-03499-4); Vol. 59. 1967. 73.80 (ISBN 0-387-03783-7); Vol. 60. 1968. 79.70 (ISBN 0-387-04103-6); Vol. 61. 1969; Vol. 62. 1970. o.p. (ISBN 0-387-04811-1); Vol. 63. 1971; Vol. 64. 1972. o.p.; Vol. 65. 1972; Vol. 66. 1972; Vol. 67. 1972; Vol. 68. 1973. Springer-Verlag.

Reviews of Physiology, Biochemistry & Pharmacology, Vol. 100. (Illus.). 250p. 1984. 49.00 (ISBN 0-387-13327-5). Springer-Verlag.

Reviews of Physiology, Biochemistry & Pharmacology, Vol. 101. M. Hulliger et al. (Illus.). 255p. 1984. 53.00 (ISBN 0-387-13679-7). Springer-Verlag.

Reviews of Physiology, Biochemistry & Pharmacology, Vol. 102. (Illus.). 265p. 1985. 56.00 (ISBN 0-387-15300-4). Springer-Verlag.

Reviews of Physiology, Biochemistry & Pharmacology, Vol. 103. (Illus.). 240p. 1985. 44.50 (ISBN 0-387-15333-0). Springer-Verlag.

Reviews of Physiology, Biochemistry & Pharmacology, Vol. 104. (Illus.). 250p. 1985. 65.00 (ISBN 0-387-15940-1). Springer-Verlag.

Reviews of Physiology, Biochemistry & Pharmacology, Vol. 105. (Illus.). 280p. 1986. 70.40 (ISBN 0-387-16874-5). Springer-Verlag.

Reviews of Physiology, Biochemistry & Pharmacology, Vol. 106. (Illus.). 190p. 1987. 59.50 (ISBN 0-387-17608-X). Springer-Verlag.

Reviews of Physiology, Biochemistry & Pharmacology, Vol. 107. (Illus.). 230p. 1987. 77.50 (ISBN 0-387-17609-8). Springer-Verlag.

Reviews of Physiology, Biochemistry & Pharmacolgy, Vol. 109. (Illus.). 200p. 1987. 70.50 (ISBN 0-387-18108-3). Springer-Verlag.

Reviews of Physiology, Biochemistry, & Pharmacology, Vol. 110. (Illus.). v, 292p. 1988. 89.50 (ISBN 0-387-18736-7). Springer-Verlag.

Reviews of Physiology, Biochemistry & Pharmacology, Vol. 70. Ed. by R. H. Adrian et al. (Illus.). 260p. 1974. 52.00 (ISBN 0-387-06716-7). Springer-Verlag.

Reviews of Physiology, Biochemistry & Pharmacology, Vol. 71. Ed. by R. H. Adrian et al. (Illus.). vi, 175p. 1974. 57.00 (ISBN 0-387-06939-9). Springer-Verlag.

Reviews of Physiology, Biochemistry & Pharmacology, Vol. 72. I. A. Shapovalou et al. LC 74-3674. (Illus.). 200p. 1975. 68.00 (ISBN 0-387-07077-X). Springer-Verlag.

Reviews of Physiology, Biochemistry & Pharmacology, Vol. 73. Ed. by R. H. Adrian. LC 74-3674. (Illus.). 190p. 1975. 57.00 (ISBN 0-387-07357-4). Springer-Verlag.

Reviews of Physiology, Biochemistry & Pharmacology, Vol. 74. LC 74-3674. (Illus.). 270p. 1975. 59.00 (ISBN 0-387-07483-X). Springer-Verlag.

Reviews of Physiology, Biochemistry & Pharmacology, Vol. 75. E. Hofmann. LC 74-3674. 1976. 71.00 (ISBN 0-387-07639-5). Springer-Verlag.

Reviews of Physiology, Biochemistry & Pharmacology, Vol. 76. Ed. by R. H. Adrian et al. LC 74-3674. (Illus.). 1976. 71.00 (ISBN 0-387-07757-X). Springer-Verlag.

Reviews of Physiology, Biochemistry & Pharmacology, Vol. 77. Ed. by R. H. Adrian et al. LC 74-3674. (Illus.). 1977. 74.00 (ISBN 0-387-07963-7). Springer-Verlag.

Reviews of Physiology, Biochemistry & Pharmacology, Vol. 78. Ed. by R. H. Adrian et al. LC 74-3674. 1977. 61.00 (ISBN 0-387-07975-0). Springer-Verlag.

Reviews of Physiology, Biochemistry & Pharmacology, Vol. 79. Ed. by R. H. Adrian. LC 74-3674. 1977. 64.00 (ISBN 0-387-08326-X). Springer-Verlag.

Reviews of Physiology, Biochemistry & Pharmacology, Vol. 80. Ed. by R. H. Adrian et al. LC 74-3674. (Illus.). 1977. 56.00 (ISBN 0-387-08466-5). Springer-Verlag.

Reviews of Physiology, Biochemistry & Pharmacology, Vol. 81. Ed. by R. H. Adrian et al. LC 74-3674. (Illus.). 1978. 56.00 (ISBN 0-387-08554-8). Springer-Verlag.

Reviews of Physiology, Biochemistry & Pharmacology, Vol. 82. Ed. by R. H. Adrian et al. (Illus.). 1978. 52.00 (ISBN 0-387-08748-6). Springer-Verlag.

Reviews of Physiology, Biochemistry & Pharmacology, Vol. 83. Ed. by R. H. Adrian et al. LC 74-3674. (Illus.). 1978. 51.00 (ISBN 0-387-08907-1). Springer-Verlag.

Reviews of Physiology, Biochemistry & Pharmacology, Vol. 84. (Illus.). 1978. 51.00 (ISBN 0-387-08984-5). Springer-Verlag.

Reviews of Physiology, Biochemistry & Pharmacology, Vol. 85. Ed. by R. H. Adrian et al. (Illus.). 1979. 51.00 (ISBN 0-387-09225-0). Springer-Verlag.

Reviews of Physiology, Biochemistry & Pharmacology, Vol. 86. (Illus.). 1979. 57.00 (ISBN 0-387-09488-1). Springer-Verlag.

Reviews of Physiology Biochemistry & Pharmacology, Vol. 87. (Illus.). 250p. 1980. 58.00 (ISBN 0-387-09944-1). Springer-Verlag.

Reviews of Physiology, Biochemistry, & Pharmacology, Vol. 88. R. H. Adrian. (Illus.). 264p. 1981. 54.00 (ISBN 0-387-10408-9). Springer-Verlag.

Reviews of Physiology, Biochemistry & Pharmacology, Vol. 89. Ed. by R. H. Adrian. (Illus.). 260p. 1981. 56.00 (ISBN 0-387-10495-X). Springer-Verlag.

Reviews of Physiology, Biochemistry & Pharmacology, Vol. 90. Ed. by R. H. Adrain et al. (Illus.). 300p. 1981. 52.00 (ISBN 0-387-10657-X). Springer-Verlag.

Reviews of Physiology, Biochemistry & Pharmacology, Vol. 91. Ed. by R. H. Adrian et al. (Illus.). 240p. 1981. 44.00 (ISBN 0-387-10961-7). Springer-Verlag.

Reviews of Physiology, Biochemistry, & Pharmacology, Vol. 92. Ed. by R. H. Adrian et al. (Illus.). 220p. 1982. 44.00 (ISBN 0-387-11105-0). Springer-Verlag.

Reviews of Physiology, Biochemistry, & Pharmacology, Vol. 93. Ed. by R. H. Adrian. (Illus.). 220p. 1982. 45.00 (ISBN 0-387-11297-9). Springer-Verlag.

Reviews of Physiology, Biochemistry & Pharmacology, Vol. 94. Ed. by R. H. Adrian et al. (Illus.). 225p. 1982. 49.00 (ISBN 0-387-11701-6). Springer-Verlag.

Reviews of Physiology, Biochemistry, & Pharmacology, Vol. 95. Ed. by R. H. Adrian. (Illus.). 235p. 1983. 49.00 (ISBN 0-387-11736-9). Springer-Verlag.

Reviews of Physiology, Biochemistry & Pharmacology, Vol. 96. Ed. by R. H. Adrian et al. (Illus.). 194p. 1983. 47.00 (ISBN 0-387-11849-7). Springer-Verlag.

Reviews of Physiology, Biochemistry, & Pharmacology, Vol. 97. Ed. by R. H. Adrian et al. (Illus.). 176p. 1983. 44.00 (ISBN 0-387-12135-8). Springer-Verlag.

Reviews of Physiology, Biochemistry & Pharmacology, Vol. 98. H. Blashko et al. (Illus.). 260p. 1983. 56.00 (ISBN 0-387-12817-4). Springer-Verlag.

Reviews of Physiology, Biochemistry & Pharmacology, Vol. 99. (Illus.). 240p. 1984. 49.00 (ISBN 0-387-12989-8). Springer-Verlag.

Reviews of Plasma Physics. Ed. by M. A. Leontovich. LC 64-23244. Vol. 1, 1965, 326p. 59.50x (ISBN 0-306-17061-2, Consultants); Vol. 2, 1966, 298p. 59.50x (ISBN 0-306-17062-0); Vol. 3, 1967, 326p. 59.50x (ISBN 0-306-17063-9); Vol. 4, 1966, 242p. 55.00x (ISBN 0-306-17064-7); Vol. 5, 1970, 526p. 85.00x (ISBN 0-306-17065-5); Vol. 6, 1975, 332p. 59.50x (ISBN 0-306-17066-3). Plenum Pub.

Reviews of Plasma Physics, Vol. 8. Ed. by M. A. Leontovich. LC 64-23244. 472p. 1980. 79.50x (ISBN 0-306-17068-X, Consultants). Plenum Pub.

Reviews of Plasma Physics, No. 9. Ed. by M. A. Leontovich. Tr. by A. B. Mikhailovskii et al from Rus. 342p. 1986. 69.50x (ISBN 0-306-10999-9, Consultants). Plenum Pub.

Reviews of Plasma Physics, No. 10. Ed. by M. A. Leontovich. Tr. by Oleg Glebov from Rus. 526p. 1986. 89.50x (ISBN 0-306-11000-8, Consultants). Plenum Pub.

Reviews of Plasma Physics, No. 11. Ed. by M. A. Leontovich. Tr. by J. Hugill from Rus. 308p. 1986. 75.00x (ISBN 0-306-11001-6, Consultants). Plenum Pub.

Reviews of Plasma Physics, Vol. 12. Ed. by M. A. Leontovich et al. (Illus.). 388p. 1987. 79.50x (ISBN 0-306-11002-4, Consultants). Plenum Pub.

Reviews of Plasma Physics, Vol. 13. Ed. by B. B. Kadomtsev. Tr. by J. G. Adashko from Rus. (Illus.). 388p. 1987. 89.50x (ISBN 0-306-11003-2, Consultants). Plenum Pub.

Reviews of Plasma Physics, Vol. 7. Ed. by M. A. Leontovich. LC 64-23244. (Illus.). 390p. 1979. 69.50x (ISBN 0-306-17067-1, Consultants). Plenum Pub.

Reviews of Renewable Energy Resources, Vol. 3. Ed. by M. S. Sodha et al. (Renewable Energy Ser.). 426p. 1986. 49.95 (ISBN 0-470-20695-0). Wiley.

Reviews of the World Situation: 1949-50. Ed. by Richard D. Challener. (Legislative Origins of American Foreign Policy Ser.: Vol. 8). 1979. lib. bdg. 67.00 (ISBN 0-8240-3037-0). Garland Pub.

Reviews of Weed Science, Vol. 3. Ed. by Chester L. Foy. 204p. 1987. text ed. 19.50 (ISBN 0-911733-07-8). Weed Sci Soc.

Reviling of the Great. Arnold Petersen. 112p. 1949. 1.50 (ISBN 0-935534-24-5); pap. 0.75 (ISBN 0-935534-25-3). NY Labor News.

Revised Code of Canon Law: A Missed Opportunity, Vol. 147. Ed. by Peter Huizing & Knut Walf. (Concilium 1981). 128p. (Orig.). 1981. pap. 6.95 (ISBN 0-8164-2347-4, HarpR). Har-Row.

Revised Code of Washington Annotated. write for info. West Pub.

Revised Compleat Sinatra. new, rev. ed. Albert I. Lonstein & Vito Marino. LC 79-88307. (Illus.). 702p. 1980. 49.95 (ISBN 0-87990-000-8). Lonstein Pubns.

Revised Financial Reporting Model for Municipalities, No. 6-7. John C. Burton. (Government Auditing Ser.). 1980. pap. 6.00 (ISBN 0-686-70150-X). Nat Civic League.

Revised Good Housekeeping Illustrated Cookbook. rev. ed. 1988. 24.95 (Pub. by Hearst Bks). Morrow.

Revised Handbook on Prepaid Legal Services. 400p. 1972. spiral 7.50 (ISBN 0-686-48105-4). Amer Bar Assn.

Revised Key to the Adults of the British Species of Ephemeroptera. 2nd ed. D. E. Kimmins. 1972. 20.00x (ISBN 0-900386-17-7, Pub. by Freshwater Bio). State Mutual Bk.

Revised Key to the British Water Bugs (Hempitera-Heteroptera) 2nd ed. T. T. Macan. 1976. 20.00x (ISBN 0-900386-07-X, Pub. by Freshwater Bio). State Mutual Bk.

Revised List of Hawaiian Pteridophyta. C. Christensen. (BMB Ser.). pap. 10.00 (ISBN 0-527-02128-8). Kraus Repr.

Revised MDC Behavior Identification Form. rev. ed. Karl F. Botterbusch. 126p. (Orig.). 1985. pap. 12.50 (ISBN 0-916671-49-6). Material Dev.

Revised Medieval Latin Word-List from British & Irish Sources. Ed. by Ronald E. Latham. (British Academy Ser.). 1965. 42.00x (ISBN 0-19-725891-3). Oxford U Pr.

Revised Minimum Standards & Other Changes under the Tax Reform Act. Goodman. 32p. (Orig.). 1987. pap. 2.00 (5281). Commerce.

Revised Model Business Corporation Act: Adopted by Committee on Corporate Laws of the Section of Corporation, Banking & Business Law of the American Bar Association Spring 1984: Offical Text with Offical Comments & Statutory Cross References. American Bar Association Committee on Corporate Laws. LC 85-5238. write for info. Amer Bar Assn.

Revised Model Business Corporation Act (1984) 480p. 1985. 55.00 (ISBN 0-317-29376-1, #H43880). HarBraceJ.

Revised Model Non Profit Corporation Act. American Bar Association, Committee on Nonprofit Organizations. LC 86-172281. Date not set. 15.00. Amer Bar Assn.

Revised Model Nonprofit Corporation Act: Exposure Draft. 1986. pap. 15.00 (507-0068-01). Amer Bar Assn.

Revised New General Catalogue of Nonstellar Astronomical Objects. Jack W. Sulentic & William G. Tifft. LC 73-83378. 384p. 1973. 35.00x (ISBN 0-8165-0421-0). U of Ariz Pr.

Revised Nomenclature for Museum Cataloging. 2nd, rev. ed. James R. Blackbaby & Patricia Greeno. 528p. 1988. 62.00 (ISBN 0-910050-93-7). AAslh Pr.

Revised OECD Model Double Taxation Convention on Income & Capital. Ed. by International Fiscal Association. (Congress Seminar Series of the Inter-National Fiscal Association: No. 2). 1979. pap. 12.50 (ISBN 90-200-0536-7, Pub. by Kluwer Law Netherlands). Kluwer Academic.

Revised RECON. Date not set. pap. 14.95 (ISBN 0-916211-19-3, 610). Palladium Bks.

Revised Retailer's Handbook of Federal Credit Regulations. James M. Goldberg. LC 82-82384. 80p. (Orig.). 1982. pap. 7.50 (ISBN 0-9603074-2-7). J M Goldberg.

Revised Seafood Secrets: A Nutritional Guide to Seafood. rev. ed. R. Marilyn Schmidt. (Orig.). 1986. pap. 9.95 (ISBN 0-937996-07-6). Barnegat.

Revised Shapley-Ames Catalog of Bright Galaxies. 2nd ed. Allan Sandage & G. A. Tammann. LC 80-68146. 1987. 29.00 (ISBN 0-87279-652-3, 635). Carnegie Inst.

Revised Standards & Guidelines of Service for the Library of Congress Network of Libraries for the Blind & Physically Handicapped, 1984. Ed. by Association of Specialized & Cooperative Library Agencies Headquarters Staff. LC 84-6356. 55p. 1984. pap. 6.50x (ISBN 0-8389-3306-8). ALA.

Revised Taxonomic Account of Gymnosporangium. Frank D. Kern. LC 79-165358. (Illus.). 136p. 1973. 17.95x (ISBN 0-271-01105-X). Pa St U Pr.

Revised Technique of Ballroom Dancing. Alex Moore. (Ballroom Dancing Ser.). 1984. lib. bdg. 79.95 (ISBN 0-87700-498-6). Revisionist Pr.

Revised Technique of Ballroom Dancing. Alex Moore. (Ballroom Dance Ser.). 1986. lib. bdg. 79.95 (ISBN 0-8490-3311-X). Gordon Pr.

Revised Technique of Latin American Dancing. Imperial Society of Teachers of Dancing Staff. (Ballroom Dancing Ser.). 1984. lib. bdg. 79.95 (ISBN 0-87700-502-8). Revisionist Pr.

Revised Uniform Single Audit Program. 1983. pap. 12.50 (ISBN 0-945359-68-3). Mortgage Bankers.

Revised Yale Isochrones & Luminosity Functions. E. M. Green et al. 365p. 1987. pap. 30.00 (ISBN 0-317-61465-7). Yale U Observ.

Revising Business Prose. 2nd ed. Richard A. Lanham. 138p. 1987. pap. write for info. (ISBN 0-02-367430-X). Macmillan.

Revising Business Prose Self-Teaching Exercise Book. Richard A. Lanham. 96p. 1987. pap. write for info. (ISBN 0-02-367480-6). Macmillan.

Revising Fiction: A Handbook for Writers. David Madden. 320p. 1988. pap. 8.95 (ISBN 0-452-26088-4, Plume). NAL.

Revising Metropolitan Concentration as an Economic Issue. Charles L. Leven. (Regional Population Studies: RPS 2). 1982. pap. 2.00. Inst for Urban & Regional.

Revising Mythologies: The Composition of Thoreau's Major Works. Stephen Adams & Donald Ross, Jr. LC 88-801. 325p. 1988. text ed. 27.50 (ISBN 0-8139-1185-0). U Pr of VA.

Revising Prose. 2nd ed. Richard A. Lanham. 116p. 1987. pap. write for info. (ISBN 0-02-367440-7). Macmillan.

Revising Prose Self-Teaching Exercise Book. Richard A. Lanham. 96p. 1987. pap. write for info. (ISBN 0-02-367490-3). Macmillan.

Revising State Theory: Essays in Politics & Postindustrialization. Fred Block. 256p. 1987. 34.95 (ISBN 0-87722-465-X). Temple U Pr.

Revising State Theory: Essays in Politics & Postindustrialism. Fred Block. 256p. 1988. pap. 16.95 (ISBN 0-87722-524-9). Temple U Pr.

Revising U. S. Military Strategy: Tailoring Means to Ends. Jeffrey Record. LC 84-9228. 128p. 1984. 18.95 (ISBN 0-08-031619-0); pap. 10.95 (ISBN 0-08-031618-2). Pergamon.

Revising Your Resume. Nancy Schuman & William Lewis. LC 85-32320. 156p. 1987. pap. 12.95 (ISBN 0-471-84523-X); 19.95 (ISBN 0-471-62485-3). Wiley.

Revisio Physolychnidum: Silene Subg. Physolychnis. Gilbert Bocquet. (Phanero Gamarum Monographiae: Vol. 1). (Illus.). 1969. 90.00x (ISBN 3-7682-0624-6). Lubrecht & Cramer.

Revision & Amendment of State Constitutions. W. F. Dodd. LC 73-120854. (American Constitutional & Legal History Ser.). 1970. Repr. of 1910 ed. lib. bdg. 42.50 (ISBN 0-306-71959-2). Da Capo.

Revision & Amendment of State Constitutions. Walter F. Dodd. LC 78-64273. (Johns Hopkins University. Studies in the Social Sciences. Extra Volumes-New Ser.: 1). Repr. of 1910 ed. 19.00 (ISBN 0-404-61374-8). AMS Pr.

Revision del Genero Bistropogon L'Hrt. (Lamiaceae-Stachyoideae) Endemismo de la Region Macaronesica. Irene E. LaSerna Ramos. (Phanerogamarum Monographiae Ser.: Vol. 18). (Illus.). 380p. (Span.). 1984. lib. bdg. 90.00x (ISBN 3-7682-1399-4). Lubrecht & Cramer.

Revision der Gattung Pediastrum Meyen (Chlorophyta) Parra O. Barrientos. (Bibliotheca Phycologica: No. 48). (Illus.). 1979. 36.00x (ISBN 3-7682-1254-8). Lubrecht & Cramer.

Revision der Gattung Pulicaria (Compositae Inuleae) fuer Afrika, Makaronesien und Arabian. E. Gamal-Eldin. (Phanerogamarum Monographiae: No. 14). (Illus.). 406p. (Ger.). 1981. text ed. 60.00x (ISBN 3-7682-1294-7). Lubrecht & Cramer.

Revision der Laubmoosgattung Mitthyridium (Mitten) Robinson Fuer Oreanien (Calymperaceae) H. Nowak. (Bryophytorum Bibliotheca: No. 20). (Illus., Ger.). 1981. lib. bdg. 36.00x (ISBN 3-7682-1236-X). Lubrecht & Cramer.

Revision der Niederlaendishen Heterobasidiomycetae und Homobasidiomycetae-Aphyllophoraceae, 2 parts in 1 vol. M. A. Donk. (Illus.). 1969. Repr. of 1933 ed. 44.00x (ISBN 3-7682-0621-1). Lubrecht & Cramer.

Revision der Sektion Alopecuroideae DC. der Gattung Astragalus L. R. Becht. (Phanerogamarum Monographiae Ser: No. 10). (Illus.). 1979. lib. bdg. 36.00x (ISBN 3-7682-1188-6). Lubrecht & Cramer.

Revision der Sektion Chronopus Bge. der Gattung Astragalus. L. E. Ott. (Phanerogamarum Monographiae Ser.: No. 9). (Illus.). 1979. lib. bdg. 30.00x (ISBN 3-7682-1187-8). Lubrecht & Cramer.

Revision Des Noostocacees Heterocystees: Contocacees Dans les Principaux Herbiers De France, Vol. 1. E. Bornet & C. Flahault. 1969. 30.00x (ISBN 3-7682-0002-7). Lubrecht & Cramer.

Revision Einiger Calciphiler Formenkreise der Flechtengattung Lecidea. Hannes Hertel. (Illus.). 1967. pap. 36.00x (ISBN 3-7682-5424-0). Lubrecht & Cramer.

Revision Gesteinsbewohnender Sippen der Flechtengattung Catillaria Mass in Europa(Lecanorales, Lecideaceae) H. Kilias. (Illus.). 240p. (Ger.). 1981. pap. text ed. 18.00x (ISBN 3-7682-1318-8). Lubrecht & Cramer.

Revision in Chemistry, No. I. D. P. Goel & S. P. Mittal. (Illus.). vi, 91p. (Orig.). 1983. pap. text ed. 5.95x (ISBN 0-86131-378-X, Pub. by Orient Longman Ltd India). Apt Bks.

Revision in Physics, No. I. A. K. Bhargava. (Illus.). vi, 158p. (Orig.). 1983. pap. text ed. 7.95x (ISBN 0-686-44137-0, Pub. by Orient Longman Ltd India). Apt Bks.

Revision in Strafsachen. 5th ed. Werner Sarstedt & Rainer Hamm. xl, 420p. 1983. 44.00x (ISBN 3-11-009712-5). De Gruyter.

Revision of African Species of Labeo: Pieces, Cyprinidae & a Redefinition of the Genus. G. Mcg. Reid. (THeses Zoologicae Ser.: No. 6). (Illus.). 322p. 1985. lib. bdg. 95.00x (ISBN 3-7682-1413-3). Lubrecht & Cramer.

Revision of B. E. Dahlgren's Index of American Palms. S. F. Glassmann. (Phaneroga Marum Mongraphiae: No. 6). 1972. 74.00x (ISBN 3-7682-0765-X). Lubrecht & Cramer.

Revision of Beaumontia Wallich, Kibatalia G. Don & Vallariopsis Woodson (Apocynaceae) rev. ed. Rudjiman. (Agricultural University Wageningen: No. 86-5). (Illus.). 99p. (Orig.). 1987. pap. text ed. 20.00 (ISBN 90-6754-099-4, PDC378, Pub. by PUDOC). UNIPUB.

Revision of Colubrid Snakes of the Subfamily Homalopsinae. Ko Ko Gyi. (Museum Ser.: Vol. 20, No. 2). 177p. 1970. pap. 9.00 (ISBN 0-686-80361-2). U of KS Mus Nat Hist.

Revision of Cuphea Section Heterodon - Lythraceae. Shirley A. Graham. Ed. by Christiane Anderson. (Systematic Botany Monographs: Vol. 20). (Illus.). 168p. 1988. lib. bdg. 20.00 (ISBN 0-912861-20-7). Am Soc Plant.

Revision of Demand Theory. J. R. Hicks. (Illus.). 196p. 1986. 42.00x (ISBN 0-19-828110-2); pap. 13.95x (ISBN 0-19-828550-7). Oxford U Pr.

Revision of Forms for Use in Cases of Children in Need of Supervision (CHINS) in Massachusetts District Court. National Center for State Courts Staff. 50p. 1975. manuscript 3.00 (MAB-107). Natl Ctr St Courts.

Revision of Haplostachys, Phyllostegia, & Stenogyne. E. E. Sherff. (BMB). pap. 13.00 (ISBN 0-527-02242-X). Kraus Repr.

Revision of Melanconis, Pseudovalva, Prostecium & Titania. L. E. Wehmeyer. (Univ. of Michigan Studies: No. 14). (Illus.). 1941. Repr. 30.00x (ISBN 3-7682-0929-6). Lubrecht & Cramer.

Revision of Neotropical Menispermaceae Tribe Tinosporeae see Memoirs of the New York Botanical Garden.

Revision of North American Liris Fabricius (Hymeno ptera) Sphecoides, Larridae. Karl V. Krombein. LC 84-600998. (Smithsonian Contributions to Zoology: No. 404). pap. 25.00 (ISBN 0-317-30394-5, 2024751). Bks Demand UMI.

Revision of North American Trichodes (Herbst) (Coleoptera: Cleridae) David E. Foster. (Special Publications: No. 11). (Illus.). 86p. 1976. pap. 4.00 (ISBN 0-89672-037-3). Tex Tech Univ Pr.

Revision of Nostocaceae with Cylindrical Trichomes. new ed. Francis Drouet. (Illus.). 256p. 1973. 18.95x (ISBN 0-02-844060-9). Hafner.

Revision of R. P. Whitfield's Types of Rugose & Tabulate Corals in the Museum of Paleontology, University of California, & in the United States National Museum see Bulletins of American Paleontology.

Revision of Spathiphyllum (Araceae) G. S. Bunting. (Memoirs of the New York Botanical Garden Ser.: Vol. 10 (3)). 54p. 1960. 8.00x (ISBN 0-89327-037-7). NY Botanical.

Revision of Tetramolopium, Lipochaeta, Dubautia, & Railliardia. E. E. Sherff. (BMB). Repr. of 1935 ed. 12.00 (ISBN 0-527-02241-1). Kraus Repr.

Revision of the Adult & Larval Mosquitoes of Japan & Korea. Kazuo Tanaka et al. (Contributions Ser.: Vol. 16). (Illus.). 987p. 1979. 60.00x (ISBN 0-686-40429-7). AM Entom Inst.

Revision of the American Species of Eriosema (Leguminosae-Lotoideae) J. W. Grear. (Memoirs of the New York Botanical Garden Ser.: Vol. 20 (3)). 98p. 1970. 10.00x (ISBN 0-89327-069-5). NY Botanical.

Revision of the American Species of Epilobium Occurring North of Mexico. W. Trelease. 1977. Repr. of 1891 ed. 18.00x (ISBN 3-7682-0600-9). Lubrecht & Cramer.

Revision of the American Species of Rourea Subgenus Rourea (Connaraceae) see Memoirs of the New York Botanical Garden.

TITLE INDEX REVITALIZING U. S. LEADERSHIP

Revision of the Atlantic Brisingida (Echinodermata: Asteroidea), with Description of a New Genus & Family. Maureen E. Downey. LC 86-6579. (Smithsonian Contributions to Zoology Ser.: No. 435). pap. 20.00 (ISBN 0-317-55530-8, 2029553). Bks Demand UMI.

Revision of the Cardinalfish Subgenera Pristiapogon & Zoramia (Genus Apogon) of the Indo-Pacific Region (Teleostei: Apogonidae) Thomas H. Fraser & Ernest A. Lachner. LC 84-600287. (Smithsonian Contributions to Zoology Ser.: No. 412). pap. 20.00 (ISBN 0-317-30175-6, 2025357). Bks Demand UMI.

Revision of the Cestode Family, Proteocephalidae. George R. LaRue. (University of Illinois Biological Monographs: Vol. 1, No. 12). Repr. of 1914 ed. 30.00 (ISBN 0-384-31420-1). Johnson Repr.

Revision of the Classification of the Calcarous Sponges: With a Catalogue of the Specimens in the British Museum (Natural History) Maurice Burton. (Illus.). 693p. 1963. 75.00x (ISBN 0-565-00698-3, Pub. by Brit Mus Nat Hist England). Sabbot-Natural Hist Bks.

Revision of the Classification of the Oscillatoriaceae. Francis Drouet. (Monograph: No. 15). (Illus.). 370p. 1968. lib. bdg. 18.00 (ISBN 0-910006-23-7). Acad Nat Sci Phila.

Revision of the Convention Concerning Statistics of Wages & Hours of Work, 1938, No. 63: International Labor Conference, 71st Session 1985, 2, Report V. 107p. 1985. pap. 12.25 (ISBN 92-2-103731-2). Intl Labour Office.

Revision of the Convention Concerning Statistics of Wages & Hours of Work, 1938: Report VI (2, No. 63. 106p. (Orig.). 1984. pap. text ed. 12.25 (ISBN 92-2-103447-X, ILO289, ILO). UNIPUB.

Revision of the Corixidae of India & Adjacent Regions. G. Evelyn Hutchinson. (CT Academy of Arts & Science Transactions Ser.: Vol. 33). 1940. pap. 75.00x (ISBN 0-686-51302-9). Elliots Bks.

Revision of the Dryinidoe Hymenopters, 2 Vols. M. Olmi. (Memoir Ser.: No. 37). (Illus.). 1938p. 1984. 118.00 (ISBN 0-318-19084-2). Am Entom Inst.

Revision of the Ektopodontidae (Mammalia, Marsupialia, Phalangeroidea) of the Australian Neogene. Ed. by Michael O. Woodburne & William A. Clemens. (UC Publications in Geological Sciences: Vol. 131). 1986. pap. 15.95x (ISBN 0-520-09961-3). U of Cal Pr.

Revision of the European Species of Cladophora. C. Van den Hoek. (Illus.). 1976. Repr. of 1963 ed. lib. bdg. 75.50x (ISBN 3-87429-112-X). Lubrecht & Cramer.

Revision of the Family Seraphsidae (Gastropoda: Strombacea) see Palaeontographica Americana.

Revision of the Fungi Described As Gloesporium. J. A. Von Arx. 1970. 48.00x (ISBN 3-7682-0667-X). Lubrecht & Cramer.

Revision of the Fungi Formerly Classified As Nectria Subgenus Hyphonectria. Gary J. Samuels. LC 66-6394. (Memoirs of the New York Botanical Garden Ser.: Vol. 26, No. 3). 1976. pap. 12.00x (ISBN 0-89327-008-3). NY Botanical.

Revision of the Genus Brachyotum (Tibouchineae-Melastomataceae) see Memoirs of the New York Botanical Garden.

Revision of the Genus Declieuxia (Rubiaceae) Joseph H. Kirkbride, Jr. LC 66-6394. (Memoirs of the New York Botanical Garden Ser.: Vol. 28, No. 4). 1976. pap. 10.95x (ISBN 0-89327-010-5). NY Botanical.

Revision of the Genus Enallagma of the United States West of the Rocky Mountains & Identification of Certain Larvae by Discriminant Analysis. Rosser W. Garrison. (UC Publications in Entomology: Vol. 105). 1985. pap. 15.00x (ISBN 0-520-09954-0). U of Cal Pr.

Revision of the Genus Hackelia (Boraginaceae) in North America, North of Mexico see Memoirs of the New York Botanical Garden.

Revision of the Genus Hypochrysops C. & R. Felder (Lepidoptera: Lycaenidae) D. P. Sands. (Entomonography Ser.: No. 7). (Illus.). 116p. 1986. 38.25 (ISBN 90-04-08089-9, Pub. by E J Brill). Heinman.

Revision of the Genus Lespedeza Section Macrolespedeza: (Leguminosae) Shinobu Akiyama. (Illus.). 142p. 1988. 79.50x (ISBN 0-86008-429-9, Pub. by U of Tokyo Japan). Columbia U Pr.

Revision of the Genus Orthotricham in North America, North of Mexico. Dale H. Vitt. (Bryophytorum Bibliotheca: No. 1). (Illus.). 36.00x (ISBN 3-7682-0825-7). Lubrecht & Cramer.

Revision of the Genus Rhodocybe Maire (Agaricales) rev. ed. T. J. Baroni. (Nova Hedwigia Beiheft). (Illus.). 300p. 1981. text ed. 74.00x (ISBN 3-7682-5467-4). Lubrecht & Cramer.

Revision of the Genus Rhodocybe Maire: Agaricales. T. J. Baroni. (Nova Hedwigia Beiheft: No. 67). (Illus.). 300p. 1981. lib. bdg. 74.00x (ISBN 3-7682-5467-4). Lubrecht & Cramer.

Revision of the Genus Sagittaria (Alismataceae) see Memoirs of the New York Botanical Garden.

Revision of the Genus Stigeoclonium. A. K. Islam. (Illus.). 1963. pap. 36.00x (ISBN 3-7682-5410-0). Lubrecht & Cramer.

Revision of the Genus Synchiropus (Teleostei: Callionymidae) Ronald Fricke. (Theses Zoologicae: Vol. 1). (Illus.). 194p. 1981. text ed. 30.00x (ISBN 3-7682-1306-4). Lubrecht & Cramer.

Revision of the Hawaiian Species of Peperomia. T. G. Yuncker. (BMB). Repr. of 1933 ed. 20.00 (ISBN 0-527-02218-7). Kraus Repr.

Revision of the Jumping Spider Genus Habronattus F.O.P.-Cambridge (Arancae, Salticidera), with Phenetic & Cladistic Analysis. Charles E. Griswold. (UC Publications in Entomolgy: Vol. 107). 1987. pap. 34.00x (ISBN 0-520-09696-7). U of Cal Pr.

Revision of the Marine Nematodes of the Superfamily Draconematoidea Filipjev, 1918 (Nematoda: Draconematina) M. W. Allen & Ella M. Noffsinger. (U C Publications in Zoology: Vol. 109). 1978. 17.50x (ISBN 0-520-09583-9). U of Cal Pr.

Revision of the Mexican-Central American Species of Cavendishia (Vacciniaceae) James L. Luteyn. LC 66-6394. (Memoirs of the New York Botanical Garden Ser.: Vol. 28, No. 3). 1976. pap. 19.00x (ISBN 0-89327-011-3). NY Botanical.

Revision of the Modern: The German Architecture Museum in Frankfurt. Ed. by Heinrich Klotz. (Academy Architecture Ser.). (Illus.). 88p. 1986. pap. 14.95 (ISBN 0-312-67938-6). St Martin.

Revision of the New World Species of Rhynchosia (Leguminosae-Faboideae) John W. Grear. LC 78-17663. (Memoirs Ser.: Vol. 31, No. 1). 1978. pap. 15.00x (ISBN 0-89327-208-6). NY Botanical.

Revision of the North American & West Indian Species of Cuscuta. Truman G. Yuncker. (Illinois Biological Monographs: Vol. 6, Nos. 2 & 3). 12.00 (ISBN 0-384-70540-5). Johnson Repr.

Revision of the North American Genus Argoporis: Coleoptera Tenebrionidae Cevenopini. Richard L. Berry. 1980. 10.00 (ISBN 0-86727-089-6). Ohio Bio Survey.

Revision of the North American Species of Lathyrus. C. Leo Hitchcock. LC 53-9615. (Publications in Biology Ser.: No. 15). (Illus.). 104p. 1952. pap. 10.00x (ISBN 0-295-73913-4). U of Wash Pr.

Revision of the North Central Tremellales. G. W. Martin. 1969. Repr. of 1952 ed. 24.00x (ISBN 3-7682-0636-X). Lubrecht & Cramer.

Revision of the Nostocaceae with Constricted Trichomes. F. Drouet. (Beihefte zur Nova Hedwigia: No. 57). (Illus.). 1978. text ed. 60.00x (ISBN 3-7682-5457-7). Lubrecht & Cramer.

Revision of the Old World Genus Zamarada: (Lepidoptera: Geometridae) D. S. Fletcher. (Bulletin of the British Museum Natural History Ser.: Supplement No. 2). (Illus.). 1974. pap. text ed. 93.00x (ISBN 0-565-00906-0, Pub. by Brit Mus Nat Hist). Sabbot-Natural Hist Bks.

Revision of the Order Phalangida of Ohio. Mary E. Walker. 1928. 1.00 (ISBN 0-86727-018-7). Ohio Bio Survey.

Revision of the Palm Genus Syragus. Sidney F. Glassman. LC 86-11380. (Illinois Biological Monograph: No. 56). (Illus.). 248p. 1987. 19.95 (ISBN 0-252-01366-2). U of Ill Pr.

Revision of the Plantations Convention (No. 110) & Recommendation (No. 110), 1958, Repot VIII(2) International Labour Conference, 68th Session, 1982. 31p. (Orig.). 1982. pap. 8.75 (ISBN 92-2-102800-3). Intl Labour Office.

Revision of the Polynesian Species of Peperomia. T. G. Yuncker. (BMB). Repr. of 1937 ed. 12.00 (ISBN 0-527-02251-9). Kraus Repr.

Revision of the Pteridophyta of Samoa. C. Christensen. (BMB Ser.). Repr. of 1943 ed. 21.00 (ISBN 0-527-02285-3). Kraus Repr.

Revision of the Sawfly Family: Orussidae for North & Central America (Hymenoptera: Symphyta, Orussidae) Woodrow M. Middlekauff. LC 83-1397. (U C Publications in Entomology: Vol. 101). 1984. pap. text ed. 9.75x (ISBN 0-520-09683-5). U of Cal Pr.

Revision of the Serphidae (Hymenoptera) Henry Townes & Marjorie Townes. (Memoir Ser.: No. 32). (Illus.). 541p. 48.00x (ISBN 0-686-30277-X). Am Entom Inst.

Revision of the South American Genus Otachyrium (Poaceae: Panicoideae) Tatiana Sendulsky. LC 84-600087. (Smithsonian Contributions to Botany Ser.: No. 57). pap. 20.00 (ISBN 0-317-20823-3, 2024794). Bks Demand UMI.

Revision of the South American Nematognathi or Catfishes. Carl H. Eignmann. pap. 55.00 (ISBN 0-384-14040-8). Johnson Repr.

Revision of the South American Species of Trachysphyrus -(Hymenoptera, Ichneumonidae) Charles Porter. (Memoirs Ser: No. 10). (Illus.). 387p. 1967. 25.00x (ISBN 0-686-17146-2). Am Entom Inst.

Revision of the Stigonematacaea: With a Summary of the Classification of Blue-Green Algae. F. Drouet. (Nova Hedwigia Beiheft: No. 66). (Illus.). 300p. 1981. lib. bdg. 60.00x (ISBN 3-7682-5466-6). Lubrecht & Cramer.

Revision of the Symplocaceae of the Old World. H. P. Nooteboom. (Leiden Botanical Ser: No. 1). 1975. lib. bdg. 53.00 (ISBN 90-6021-242-8, Pub. by Leiden Univ Holland). Kluwer Academic.

Revision of the Treaty. facsimile ed. John M. Keynes. LC 73-37888. (Select Bibliographies Reprint Ser). Repr. of 1922 ed. 16.00 (ISBN 0-8369-6725-9). Ayer Co Pubs.

Revision of the Treaty see Collected Writings.

Revision of the Tribe Antirrhineae, (Scrophulariaceae) David A. Sutton. (Illus.). 548p. 1988. 150.00 (ISBN 0-19-858520-9). Oxford U Pr.

Revision of the World Species of Synophoras Foerster (Ichneumanidae) M. Sanborne. (Memoir Ser.: No. 38). (Illus.). 403p. 1984. 31.50 (ISBN 0-318-19086-9). Am Entom Inst.

Revision of Tornatellinidae & Achatinellidae. C. M. Cooke, Jr. & Y. Kondo. (BMB Ser.: No. 221). Repr. of 1960 ed. 36.00 (ISBN 0-527-02329-9). Kraus Repr.

Revision of Tristerix Loranthaceae. Job Kuijt. Ed. by Christiane Anderson. (Systematic Botany Monographs: Vol. 19). (Illus., Orig.). 1988. lib. bdg. 8.00 (ISBN 0-912861-19-3). Am Soc Plant.

Revision Success: The Sixth Illinois Constitutional Convention. Samuel K. Gove & Thomas R Kitsos. 185p. 1974. 1.00 (ISBN 0-318-15814-0). Citizens Forum Gov.

Revision Taxonomique et possibilites d'Hybridation de Nematanthus Schrader (Gesneriaceae), genre endemique de la Foret cotiere Bresilienne: Dissertations Botanicae Ser. Alain Chautems. (Vol. 112). (Illus.). 230p. (Fr.). 1988. pap. 58.50x (ISBN 3-443-64024-9). Lubrecht & Cramer.

Revision: The Rhythm of Meaning. Marian M. Mohr. 256p. (Orig.). 1984. pap. text ed. 13.50x (ISBN 0-86709-087-1). Boynton Cook Pubs.

Revision Total Hip Arthoplasty. Ed. by Roderick Turner & Arnold Scheller. 412p. 1982. 84.50 (ISBN 0-8089-1466-9, 794652). Grune.

Revisional Study of the Masarid Wasps (Hymenoptera, Vespoidea) O. W. Richards. (Illus.). 294p. 1962. 33.50x (ISBN 0-565-00697-5, Pub. by Brit Mus Nat Hist England). Sabbot-Natural Hist Bks.

Revisionary Study of Leaf-Mining Flies: Agromyzidae of California. LC 81-70585. 1981. pap. text ed. 20.00x (ISBN 0-931876-53-2, 3273). ANR Pubns CA.

Revisioning the Church: Ecclesial Freedom in the New Paradigm. Peter C. Hodgson. LC 87-45894. 128p. 1988. pap. 8.95 (ISBN 0-8006-2072-0). Fortress.

Revisionism: A Key to Peace. Harry E. Barnes. 59.95 (ISBN 0-87700-192-8). Revisionist Pr.

Revisionism & Brainwashing. Harry E. Barnes. 59.95 (ISBN 0-685-26298-7). Revisionist Pr.

Revisionism & Empire: Socialist Imperialism in Germany 1897-1914. Roger Fletcher. (Illus.). 224p. 1984. text ed. 34.95 (ISBN 0-04-943031-9). Unwin Hyman.

Revisionism & the Origins of Pearl Harbor. Frank P. Mintz. 156p. (Orig.). 1985. lib. bdg. 24.50 (ISBN 0-8191-4796-6); pap. text ed. 11.50 (ISBN 0-8191-4797-4). U Pr of Amer.

Revisionism & the Promotion of Peace. Harry E. Barnes. 59.95 (ISBN 0-87700-284-3). Revisionist Pr.

Revisionism: Essays on the History of Marxist Ideas. Ed. by Leopold Labedz. (Essay Index Reprint Ser.). Repr. of 1962 ed. 24.25 (ISBN 0-518-10166-5). Ayer Co Pubs.

Revisionist Bibliography. Keith Stimely. 1981. lib. bdg. 59.95 (ISBN 0-686-73186-7). Revisionist Pr.

Revisionist Historians & German War Guilt. Warren B. Morris. 1976. lib. bdg. 69.95 (ISBN 0-87700-257-6). Revisionist Pr.

Revisionist Hungary. S. Fenyes. 250p. 1988. price not set (ISBN 0-937019-10-0); pap. 20.00 (ISBN 0-937019-11-9). Romanian Hist.

Revisionist Plays. John Harms. 69.95 (ISBN 0-685-26304-5). Revisionist Pr.

Revisionist Viewpoints: Essays in a Dissident Historical Tradition. James J. Martin. LC 75-187779. 1971. pap. 2.50 (ISBN 0-87926-008-4). R Myles.

Revisions: Changing Perspectives in Moral Philosophy. Ed. by Stanley Hauerwas & Alasdair MacIntyre. (Revisions Ser.). 320p. 1983. text ed. 24.95 (ISBN 0-268-01614-3); pap. text ed. 9.95 (ISBN 0-268-01617-8). U of Notre Dame Pr.

Revisions of the Miocene Suidae & Tayassuidae (Artiodactyla, Mammalia) Martin Pickford. (Tertiary Research Special Paper: No. 7). (Illus.). 83p. 1986. 23.75 (ISBN 90-04-07573-9, Pub. by E J Brill). Heinman.

Revisions of the Repatriation of Seament Convention 1926 (No. 23), & of the Reaptiration (Ship Masters & Apprentices) Recommendation, 1926, Report V, No. 27. 47p. 1987. pap. text ed. 10.50 (ISBN 92-2-105792-5, ILO632, ILO). UNIPUB.

Revisiting Blassingame's "The Slave Community" The Scholar's Respond. Ed. by Al-Tony Gilmore. LC 77-84765. (Contributions in Afro-American & African Studies: No. 37). 1978. lib. bdg. 35.00 (ISBN 0-8371-9879-8, GJB/). Greenwood.

Revisiting My Pygmy Hosts. Paul Schebesta. Tr. by Gerald Griffin from Ger. LC 74-15087. (Illus.). Repr. of 1936 ed. 15.00 (ISBN 0-404-12137-3). AMS Pr.

Revisiting the Default Debtor: A Study of the Role of the Civil Court in Consumer Credit Disputes. Francis G. Caro & Suzanne Weiss. LC 84-167374. 1983. 4.00 (ISBN 0-88156-009-X). Comm Serv Soc NY.

Revisiting Wertheimer's Seminars, 2 vols. Abraham S. Luchins & Edith H. Luchins. Incl. Vol. 1. Value, Social Influence, & Power (ISBN 0-8387-1227-4); Vol. 2. Problems in Social Psychology (ISBN 0-8387-1570-2). LC 72-3525. 1046p. 1978. 60.00 ea. (ISBN 0-686-96685-6). Bucknell U Pr.

Revista. Nancy Levy-Konesky & Karen Daggert. Ed. by Marilyn Perez-Abreu et al. 323p. (Orig.). 1988. pap. text ed. 14.00 (ISBN 0-03-014214-8). HR&W.

Revista a los Examenes De Cosmetologia Que Hace la Junta Estatal (State Board Review Examinations in Cosmetology) Anthony B. Colletti. 1976. pap. 6.00 (ISBN 0-912126-12-4, 1271-00). Keystone Pubns.

Revista Interamericana De Bibliografia, Vol. XXX, No. 4, 1980. OAS General Secretariat. 150p. (Span. & Port.). 1980. pap. 2.00 (ISBN 0-686-74520-5). OAS.

Revista Interamericana De Bibliografia, Vol. 31, No. 1. OAS General Secretariat. 196p. (Fr., Span. & Port.). 1981. pap. 3.00 (ISBN 0-686-75080-2). OAS.

Revista Interamericana De Bibliografia: (Inter-American Review of Bibliography) OAS General Secretariat. (Vol. XXX, No. 3). 116p. (Eng. & Span.). 1980. pap. text ed. 2.00 (ISBN 0-686-69868-1). OAS.

Revistas: An Annotated Bibliography of Spanish Language Periodicals for Public Libraries. Periodical Committee of Bibliotecas Para La Gente. (Chicano Studies Library Publications: No. 9). 31p. (Orig.). 1983. pap. 6.00x (ISBN 0-918520-07-X). UC Chicano Lib.

Revitalising Urban Economies. OECD. 102p. (Orig.). 1987. pap. 13.00x (ISBN 92-64-12979-0). OECD.

Revitalization of Basic Business Education at All Instructional Levels. 160p. 1982. 12.00 (ISBN 0-933964-22-6). Natl Busn Ed Assoc.

Revitalize Your Body with Nature's Secrets. Edwin Flatto. 1981. pap. 3.95 (ISBN 0-935540-14-8). Plymouth Pr.

Revitalizing American Industry: Lessons from Our Competitors. Milton Hochmuth & William Davidson. LC 84-18471. 440p. 1985. 39.95x (ISBN 0-88730-019-7). Ballinger Pub.

Revitalizing America's Cities: Neighborhood Reinvestment & Displacement. Ed. by Michael H. Schill & Richard P. Nathan. LC 83-396. (Urban Public Policy Ser.). 184p. 1984. 52.50 (ISBN 0-87395-742-3); pap. 17.95 (ISBN 0-87395-743-1). State U NY Pr.

Revitalizing Cities. H. Briavel Holcomb & Robert A. Beauregard. Ed. by C. Gregory Knight. LC 81-69237. (Resource Publications in Geography Ser.). (Orig.). 1982. pap. 6.00 (ISBN 0-89291-148-4). Assn Am Geographers.

Revitalizing Development, Growth & International Trade: Assessment & Policy Options. 256p. 1987. pap. 30.00 (ISBN 92-1-112236-8, E.87.II.D.9). UN.

Revitalizing Educational Psychology: Readings in Method & Substance. Ed. by William E. Roweton. LC 76-20603. 400p. 1976. 26.95x (ISBN 0-88229-195-5). Nelson-Hall.

Revitalizing International Law. Richard A. Falk. (Illus.). 248p. 1988. text ed. 24.95xt (ISBN 0-8138-1532-0). Iowa St U Pr.

Revitalizing Neighborhoods & Downtowns: A Selective, Annotated Bibliography on Urban Ecology. Susan C. Marcavage et al. (Public Administration Series: Bibliography: No. P 1767). 47p. 1985. pap. 6.75 (ISBN 0-89028-567-5). Vance Biblios.

Revitalizing New York City's Economy: The Role of Public Pension Funds. Ruth Messinger. 55p. 1980. 5.95 (ISBN 0-89788-040-4). NCPA Washington.

Revitalizing Remediation in the Middle Grades: An Invitational Approach. D. B. Strahan & J. D. Strahan. 22p. (Orig.). 1988. 2.00 (ISBN 0-88210-208-7). Natl Assn Principals.

Revitalizing Residential Settings: Problems & Potential in Education, Health, Rehabilitation, & Social Service. Martin Wolins & Yochanan Wozner. LC 81-20804. (Social & Behavioral Science Ser.). 1982. text ed. 39.95x (ISBN 0-87589-517-4). Jossey-Bass.

Revitalizing the American Economy. F. Stevens Redburn et al. LC 83-22370. (National University Publications. Policy Studies Organization). 215p. 1986. text ed. 30.00x (ISBN 0-8046-9333-1, 9333, Natl U). Assoc Faculty Pr.

Revitalizing the Church. Bill Hull. 1986. pap. cancelled (ISBN 0-89109-539-X). NavPress.

Revitalizing the Older Suburb. David Listokin & W. Patrick Beaton. 243p. 1983. pap. text ed. 12.95x (ISBN 0-88285-094-6). Ctr Urban Pol Res.

Revitalizing the Twentieth Century Church. Lloyd M. Perry & Norman Shawchuck. LC 81-16974. 1986. pap. 7.95 (ISBN 0-8024-7318-0). Moody.

Revitalizing the U. S. Economy. Ed. by F. Steven Redburn et al. LC 85-30166. 242p. 1986. lib. bdg. 36.95 (ISBN 0-275-92101-8, C2101). Praeger.

Revitalizing the Waterfront: International Dimensions of Dockland Redevelopment. B. S. Hoyle et al. (Belhaven Press Bk.). (Illus.). 256p. 1988. 49.00x (ISBN 1-85293-047-0, Pub. by Pinter Pubs UK). Columbia U Pr.

Revitalizing U. S. Leadership in the Middle East. Robert G. Neumann et al. (CSIS Significant Issues Ser.). 1988. write for info. CSI Studies.

Revitalizing Western Economies: A New Agenda for Business & Government. Russell L. Ackoff et al. LC 84-47977. (Management Ser.). 1984. 27.95x (ISBN 0-87589-609-X). Jossey-Bass.

Revitalizing Your Business: Five Steps to Successfully Turning Around Your Company. Edmond Freiermuth. 192p. 1985. 19.95 (ISBN 0-917253-05-1). Probus Pub Co.

Revival. D. Martyn Lloyd-Jones. LC 86-72057. 320p. (Orig.). 1987. pap. 9.95 (ISBN 0-89107-415-5, Crossway Bks). Good News.

Revival! Richard O. Roberts. 186p. 1982. pap. 6.95 (ISBN 0-8423-5575-8). Tyndale.

Revival! Ed. by Wayne E. Warner. (Illus.). 163p. (Orig.). 1978. pap. 4.95 (ISBN 0-89274-303-4). Harrison Hse.

Revival Addresses. R. A. Torrey. 282p. 1974. Repr. of 1903 ed. 12.95 (ISBN 0-227-67808-7). Attic Pr.

Revival & Its Fruit. Emyr Roberts & R. Geraint Gruffydd. 1981. pap. 2.25 (ISBN 0-317-65600-7). CHR Lit.

Revival & Reaction: The Right in Contemporary America. Gillian Peele. 280p. 1986. pap. 14.95x (ISBN 0-19-821132-5). Oxford U Pr.

Revival & Rebellion in Colonial Central Africa. Karen E. Fields. LC 84-42884. (Illus.). 324p. 1985. text ed. 38.50x (ISBN 0-691-09409-8). Princeton U Pr.

Revival Architecture in Hungary: Classicism & Romanticism. Anna Zabor. 28p. 1985. 130.00x (ISBN 0-317-42871-3, Pub by Collets (UK)). State Mutual Bk.

Revival Comes to Wales. Eifion Evans. pap. 5.95 (ISBN 0-317-65611-2). ChR Lit.

Revival in the Rust Belt: Tracking the Evolution of an Urban Industrial Region. Daniel R. Denison & Stuart L. Hart. LC 87-26264. 224p. (Orig.). 1987. pap. text ed. 15.00x (ISBN 0-87944-322-7). Inst Soc Res.

Revival in Tin Town. Effie M. Williams. 84p. pap. 0.75 (ISBN 0-686-29164-6). Faith Pub Hse.

Revival Lectures. Charles G. Finney. 544p. 15.95 (ISBN 0-8007-0272-7). Revell.

Revival Literature: An Annotated Bibliography with Biographical & Historical Notices. Richard O. Roberts. 607p. 1987. lib. bdg. 50.00x (ISBN 0-940033-27-5). R O Roberts.

Revival of a Classical Tongue: Elizer Ben Yehuda & the Modern Hebrew Language. Jack Fellman. (Contributions to the Sociology of Language: No. 6). 1973. pap. text ed. 15.60x (ISBN 90-2792-495-3). Mouton.

Revival of American Socialism: Selected Papers of the Socialist Scholars Conference. Ed. by George Fischer. (Orig.). 1971. pap. 5.95 (ISBN 0-19-501413-8). Oxford U Pr.

Revival of Aristocracy. Oscar Levy. 59.95 (ISBN 0-8490-0952-9). Gordon Pr.

Revival of Civic Learning: A Rationale for Citizenship Education in American Schools. R. Freeman Butts. LC 80-81870. (Foundation Monograph Ser.). 170p. (Orig.). 1980. pap. 6.00 (ISBN 0-87367-423-5). Phi Delta Kappa.

Revival of Constitutionalism. James W. Muller. LC 87-30177. xiv, 262p. 1988. 29.95x (ISBN 0-8032-3127-X). U of Nebr Pr.

Revival of Ideology: The Afro-American Society Movement. Ione D. Vargus. LC 77-75756. 1977. 13.95 (ISBN 0-88247-466-9). R & E Pubs.

Revival of Injured Microbes. Malcolm H. Andrew & A. Denver Russell. (Society for Applied Bacteria Symposium Ser.). 1984. 57.00 (ISBN 0-12-058520-0). Acad Pr.

Revival of Interest in the Dream. Robert Fliess. 164p. 1953. text ed. 22.50x (ISBN 0-8236-5820-1). Intl Univs Pr.

Revival of Metaphysical Poetry. Joseph E. Duncan. LC 79-75991. 1969. Repr. of 1959 ed. lib. bdg. 19.00x (ISBN 0-374-92394-9, Octagon). Hippocrene Bks.

Revival of Natural Law Concepts: A Study of the Establishment & of the... Charles G. Haines. LC 30-16115. (Harvard Studies in Jurisprudence: Vol. 4). xii, 388p. 1979. Repr. of 1930 ed. lib. bdg. 40.00 (ISBN 0-89941-139-8). W S Hein.

Revival of Pascal: A Study of His Relation to Modern French Thought. Dorothy M. Eastwood. LC 37-2631. (Oxford Studies in Modern Languages & Literature). pap. 56.00 (ISBN 0-317-08091-1, 2051242). Bks Demand UMI.

Revival of Phrenology: Mental Functions of the Brain. Bernard Hollander. LC 78-72801. Repr. of 1901 ed. 40.00 (ISBN 0-404-60865-5). AMS Pr.

Revival of Religion. Burns et al. 449p. 1984. Repr. of 1840 ed. 18.95 (ISBN 0-85151-435-9). Banner of Truth.

Revival of Scholastic Philosophy in the Nineteenth Century. Joseph L. Perrier. LC 9-10966. Repr. of 1909 ed. 17.50 (ISBN 0-404-04994-X). AMS Pr.

Revival of the Tamima: Mandala in Medieval Japan. Elizabeth Ten Grotenhuis. Ed. by S. J. Freedberg. (Outstanding Dissertations in Fine Arts Ser.). (Illus.). 610p. 1985. Repr. of 1980 ed. 75.00 (ISBN 0-8240-6869-6). Garland Pub.

Revival of Values Education in Asia & the West. Ed. by W. K. Cummings & Y. Tomoda. (Comparative & International Education Ser.: No. 7). (Illus.). 225p. (Orig.). 1988. text ed. 37.01 (ISBN 0-08-035854-3); pap. text ed. 18.51 (ISBN 0-08-035853-5). Pergamon.

Revival or Ruin: God's Plan for Restoration. Glenn Foster. 1986. pap. 6.95 (ISBN 0-910311-46-3). Huntington Hse Inc.

Revival Praying. Leonard Ravenhill. 176p. 1962. pap. 4.95 (ISBN 0-87123-482-3, 210482). Bethany Hse.

Revival: Principles to Change the World. Winkie Pratney. 320p. (Orig.). 1983. pap. 3.95 (ISBN 0-88368-124-2). Whitaker Hse.

Revival Sermon Outlines. Ed. by Charles R. Wood. 64p. 1975. pap. 2.95 (ISBN 0-8254-4005-X). Kregel.

Revival Sermons. William C. Burns. 205p. 1981. pap. 5.95 (ISBN 0-85151-316-6). Banner of Truth.

Revival: Southern Writers in the Modern City. Ted R. Spivey. LC 85-29507. 224p. 1986. pap. 20.00 (ISBN 0-8130-0741-0). U Presses Fla.

Revivalism & Social Reform: American Protestantism on the Eve of the Civil War. Timothy Smith. LC 80-8114. 272p. 1980. pap. text ed. 10.95x (ISBN 0-8018-2477-X). Johns Hopkins.

Revivalism & Social Reform: American Protestantism on the Eve of the Civil War. Timothy L. Smith. 11.25 (ISBN 0-8446-2960-X). Peter Smith.

Revivalism in America. William W. Sweet. 1944. 12.75 (ISBN 0-8446-1430-0). Peter Smith.

Revivalism, Social Conscience, & Community in the Burned-Over District: The Trial of Rhoda Bement. Glenn C. Altschuler & Jan M. Saltzgaber. (Paperback Ser.). (Illus.). 184p. 1983. 27.95x (ISBN 0-8014-1541-1); pap. 8.95x (ISBN 0-8014-9246-7). Cornell U Pr.

Revivals. Eifion Evans. pap. 2.25. Chr Lit.

Revivals & Importations of French Comedies in England, 1749-1800. Willard A. Kinne. LC 40-3880. Repr. of 1939 ed. 24.50 (ISBN 0-404-03705-4). AMS Pr.

Revivals, Awakening, & Reform: An Essay on Religion & Social Change in America, 1607 to 1977. William G. McLoughlin. LC 77-27830. xvi, 240p. 1980. pap. 9.00x (ISBN 0-226-56092-9, P891, Phoen). U of Chicago Pr.

Revivals of the Eighteenth Century. Duncan MacFarlan. 312p. 1980. Repr. 12.95 (ISBN 0-939464-32-2). Labyrinth Pr.

Revivals of the Eighteenth Century, Particulary at Cambuslang: With Three Sermons by the Rev. George Whitefield. Duncan Macfarlan. (Revival Library). (Illus.). 263p. 1980. Repr. of 1847 ed. lib. bdg. 12.95 (ISBN 0-940033-14-3). R O Roberts.

Revived Life. Lewis A. Drummond. LC 82-71217. 1982. pap. 6.95 (ISBN 0-8054-5205-2). Broadman.

Reviving Cities with Tax Abatement. Daniel R. Mandelker et al. LC 79-92785. 160p. (Orig.). 1980. pap. text ed. 12.95 (ISBN 0-88285-065-2). Ctr Urban Pol Res.

Reviving Cities with Tax Abatement. Daniel R. Mandleker et al. 176p. 1979. 12.95. Transaction Bks.

Reviving Industry in America: Japanese Influences on Manufacturing & the Service Sector. Harris J. Shapiro & Teresa Cosenza. LC 87-17585. 224p. 1987. 32.00x (ISBN 0-88730-118-5). Ballinger Pub.

Reviving Main Street. Ed. by Deryck Holdsworth. 256p. 1985. 25.00x (ISBN 0-8020-2542-0); pap. 13.95 (ISBN 0-8020-6556-2). U of Toronto Pr.

Reviving the Death Penalty. Ed. by Gary E. McCuen & R. A. Baumgart. (Ideas in Conflict Ser.). (Illus.). 134p. 1985. lib. bdg. 11.95 (ISBN 0-86596-052-6). G E McCuen Pubns.

Reviving the English Revolution Reflections & Elaborations on the Work of Christopher Hill. Ed. by Geoff Eley & William Hunt. 368p. 1988. text ed. 42.50 (ISBN 0-86091-194-2, Pub. by Verso). Routledge Chapman & Hall.

Reviving the Industrial City: The Politics of Urban Renewal in Lyon & Birmingham. Jerry A. Webman. 208p. 1982. 29.00 (ISBN 0-8135-0947-5). Rutgers U Pr.

Reviving the World Court. Richard Falk. LC 85-31451. (Procedural Aspects of International Law Ser.: No. 18). xx, 197p. 1986. text ed. 25.00x (ISBN 0-8139-1084-6). U Pr of Va.

Reviving Tired Faith. Terry Bell. 128p. 1988. pap. 4.95 (ISBN 0-89225-309-6). Gospel Advocate.

Revizor. N. V Gogol. Ed. by W Harrison. (Library of Russian Classics). 215p. pap. text ed. 9.95x (ISBN 0-631-13864-1). Basil Blackwell.

Revnitel' Blagotchestija 19-go vjeka, Episkop Theofan Zatvornik. Priest Nikolai Deputatov. 71p. 1971. pap. 3.00 (ISBN 0-317-29261-7). Holy Trinity.

Revocable Trust. rev. ed. A. James Casner. 67p. 1977. pap. 3.50 (ISBN 0-317-32256-7, B318). Am Law Inst.

Revocable Trusts. George M. Turner. 488p. 1984. text ed. 90.00 (ISBN 0-07-009642-2). Shepards-McGraw.

Revocation of Professional Licenses by Governmental Agencies. William O. Morris. 304p. 1984. 30.00x (ISBN 0-87215-829-2, 64868). Michie Co.

Revolt Against Chivalry: Jessie Daniel Ames & the Women's Campaign Against Lynching. Jacquelyn D. Hall. LC 78-11815. 373p. 1979. 35.00x (ISBN 0-231-04040-7); pap. 15.00 (ISBN 0-231-04041-5). Columbia U Pr.

Revolt Against Civilization, the Menace of the Under-Man. Lothrop Stoddard. Ed. by Charles Rosenberg. LC 83-48558. (History of the Hereditarian Thought Ser.). 225p. 1985. Repr. of 1923 ed. lib. bdg. 32.00 (ISBN 0-8240-5828-3). Garland Pub.

Revolt Against Dualism. 2nd ed. Arthur O. Lovejoy. (Paul Carus Lecture Ser.). 420p. 1960. pap. 6.95 (ISBN 0-87548-107-8). Open Court.

Revolt Against Hitler. Fabian Von Schlabrendorff. LC 78-63714. (Studies in Fascism: Ideology & Practice). (Illus.). 184p. Repr. of 1948 ed. 24.00 (ISBN 0-404-16985-6). AMS Pr.

Revolt Against Mechanism. Lawrence P. Jacks. LC 77-27140. (Hibbert Lectures: 1933). Repr. of 1934 ed. 12.50 (ISBN 0-404-60429-3). AMS Pr.

Revolt Against Reason. Arnold H. Lunn. LC 72-108396. xiv, 273p. 1971. Repr. of 1951 ed. lib. bdg. 35.00x (ISBN 0-8371-3819-1, LURA). Greenwood.

Revolt Against Regulation: The Rise & Pause of the Consumer Movement. Michael Pertschuk. LC 82-40108. 192p. 1982. 22.50x (ISBN 0-520-04824-5); pap. 8.95x (ISBN 0-520-05074-6). U of Cal Pr.

Revolt Against Romanticism in American Literature As Evidenced in the Work of S. L. Clemens. S. B. Liljegren. 59p. 1983. pap. 12.50. Saifer.

Revolt Against Romanticism in American Literature As Evidenced in the Works of S. L. Clemens. S. B. Liljegren. (Essays & Studies on American Language & Literature: Vol. 1). pap. 15.00 (ISBN 0-8115-0183-3). Kraus Repr.

Revolt Against Romanticism in American Literature: As Evidenced in the Works of S. L. Clemens. Sten Liljegren. LC 65-15896. (Studies in Fiction: No. 34). 1969. Repr. of 1945 ed. lib. bdg. 29.95x (ISBN 0-8383-0583-0). Haskell.

Revolt Against the Dead: The Modernization of a Mayan Community in the Highlands of Guatemala. D. E. Brintnall. (Library of Anthropology). 224p. 1979. 32.00x (ISBN 0-677-05170-0). Gordon & Breach.

Revolt Among the Sharecroppers. Howard Kester. LC 69-18576. (American Negro: His History & Literature Ser., No. 2). 1969. Repr. of 1936 ed. 10.00 (ISBN 0-405-01876-2). Ayer Co Pubs.

Revolt & Revolution in Early Modern Europe: An Essay on the History of Political Violence. Yves-Marie Berce. Tr. by Joseph Bergin. LC 87-4863. 256p. 1987. 37.50 (ISBN 0-312-00919-4); pap. 14.95 (ISBN 0-312-00946-1). St Martin.

Revolt at Sea: A Narration of Many Mutinies. Irvin Anthony. Repr. of 1937 ed. 25.00 (ISBN 0-686-19878-6). Ridgeway Bks.

Revolt from the Centre. Niels I. Meyer et al. Tr. by Christine Hauch. LC 79-56838. (Open Forum Ser.). 224p. 1981. 14.00 (ISBN 0-7145-2701-7, Dist by Scribner); pap. 7.95 (ISBN 0-7145-2702-5). M Boyars Pubs.

Revolt in Aspromonte. Corrado Alvaro. Tr. by Frances Frenaye from Ital. LC 62-12393. 128p. 1962. pap. 1.35 (ISBN 0-8112-0002-7, NDP119). New Directions.

Revolt in Athens: The Greek Communist "Second Round", 1944-1945. John O. Iatrides. LC 76-39052. 352p. 1972. 37.00x (ISBN 0-691-05203-4). Princeton U Pr.

Revolt in Louisiana: The Spanish Occupation, 1766-1770. John P. Moore. LC 75-5349. (Illus.). xiv, 246p. 1976. text ed. 30.00 (ISBN 0-8071-0180-X). La State U Pr.

Revolt in Palestine the Eighteenth Century. Ahmad H. Joudah. LC 86-83198. (Leaders, Politics & Social Change in the Middle East Ser.: Vol. 6). 150p. 1987. 25.00 (ISBN 0-940670-11-9). Kingston Pr.

Revolt in Socialist Yugoslavia. F. Perlman. 1969. 1.50x (ISBN 0-934868-16-6). Black & Red.

Revolt in Southern Rhodesia 1896-7. T. O. Ranger. (Illus.). 416p. (Orig.). 1978. pap. text ed. 17.50x (ISBN 0-435-94799-0). Heinemann Ed.

Revolt in the Desert. T. E. Lawrence. 288p. 1987. pap. 13.95 (ISBN 0-7126-1281-5, Pub. by Century Hutchinson). David & Charles.

Revolt in the Netherlands: Brussels-Eighteen Thirty. John W. Rooney, Jr. 250p. 1982. pap. text ed. 12.50x (ISBN 0-87291-156-X). Coronado Pr.

Revolt in Twenty-One Hundred. Robert A. Heinlein. 1986. 3.50 (ISBN 0-671-65589-2). Baen Bks.

Revolt in Two Thousand One-Hundred. Robert A. Heinlein. pap. 2.50 (ISBN 0-451-11148-6, AE1148, Sig). NAL.

Revolt of Mamie Stover. William B. Huie. 16.95 (ISBN 0-89190-321-6, Pub. by Am Repr). Amereon Ltd.

Revolt of Modern Youth. Ben B. Lindsey & Wainwright Evans. LC 73-8818. (Americana Library Ser.: No. 28). 388p. 1973. Repr. of 1925 ed. 17.50x (ISBN 0-295-95298-9). U of Wash Pr.

Revolt of Mother. Mary W. Freeman. (Perfect Presents Story-Gifts Ser.). (Illus.). 32p. 1987. pap. 4.95 (ISBN 0-317-56383-1). Redpath Pr.

Revolt of Nineteen Hundred & Five in Bengal. Benoy J. Ghosh. 1987. 25.00x (ISBN 0-8364-2126-4, Pub. by KL Mukhopadhyay). South Asia Bks.

Revolt of Nineteen-Sixteen in Russian Central Asia. Edward D. Sokol. LC 78-64219. (Johns Hopkins University. Studies in the Social Sciences. Seventy-First Ser. 1953: 1). Repr. of 1954 ed. 18.50 (ISBN 0-404-61323-3). AMS Pr.

Revolt of Silken Thomas: A Challenge to Henry VIII. Laurence McCorristine. (Topics in Irish History Ser.). (Illus.). 176p. 1987. 29.95 (ISBN 0-86327-120-0, Pub. by Wolfhound Pr Ireland); pap. 17.95 (ISBN 0-86327-126-X). Irish Bks Media.

Revolt of the Black Athlete. Harry Edwards. LC 70-85475. 1970. pap. 14.95 (ISBN 0-02-909030-X). Free Pr.

Revolt of the Catalans: A Study in the Decline of Spain 1598-1640. J. H. Elliott. LC 83-20929. 641p. 1984. pap. 24.95 (ISBN 0-521-27890-2). Cambridge U Pr.

Revolt of the Comuneros, 1721-1735: A Study in the Colonial History of Paraguay. Adalberto Lopez. 212p. 1976. 14.95x (ISBN 0-87073-124-6). Schenkman Bks Inc.

Revolt of the Conservation Democrats: An Essay on American Political Culture & Political Development, 1837-1844. Jean E. Friedman. LC 78-27449. (Studies in American History & Culture: No. 9). pap. 41.40 (2070119). Bks Demand UMI.

Revolt of the Conservatives. George Wolfskill. LC 73-17626. (Illus.). 303p. 1974. Repr. of 1962 ed. lib. bdg. 35.00 (ISBN 0-8371-7251-9, WORC). Greenwood.

Revolt of the Eighth Grade. Kate Kenyon. (Junior High Ser.: No. 12). 176p. (gr. 5-9). 1988. pap. 2.50 (ISBN 0-590-41788-6). Scholastic Inc.

Revolt of the Engineers: Social Responsibility & the American Engineering Profession. Edwin T. Layton, Jr. LC 85-23981. 312p. (Orig.). 1986. text ed. 32.50x (ISBN 0-8018-3286-1); pap. text ed. 12.95x (ISBN 0-8018-3287-X). Johns Hopkins.

Revolt of the Hereros. Jon M. Bridgman. LC 80-13965. (Perspectives on Southern Africa: No. 30). 200p. 1981. 25.00x (ISBN 0-520-04113-5). U of Cal Pr.

Revolt of the Idiots. Burton Blatt. 1976. 10.95 (ISBN 0-686-84868-3). Exceptional Pr Inc.

Revolt of the Judges: The Parlement of Paris & the Fronde, 1643-1652. A. Lloyd Moote. LC 78-155003. 1972. 47.00x (ISBN 0-691-05191-7). Princeton U Pr.

Revolt of the Masses. Jose Ortega Y Gasset. 1932. (NortonC); pap. 3.95x 1964 (ISBN 0-393-09637-8). Norton.

Revolt of the Masses. Jose Ortega y Gasset. Ed. by Kenneth Moore. Tr. by Anthony Kerrigan. LC 81-40457. 240p. 1985. 21.95 (ISBN 0-268-01609-7). U of Notre Dame Pr.

Revolt of the Middle-Aged Man. Edmund Bergler. LC 84-22396. xxi, 312p. 1985. text ed. 30.00x (ISBN 0-8236-5830-9, 05830). Intl Univs Pr.

Revolt of the Mind. Tamas Aczel & Tibor Meray. LC 74-20275. 449p. 1975. Repr. of 1960 ed. lib. bdg. 35.00x (ISBN 0-8371-7851-7, ACRM). Greenwood.

Revolt of the Netherlands Fifteen Fifty-Five to Sixteen Hundred & Nine. 2nd ed. Pieter Geyl. LC 79-53235. (Illus.). 1980. text ed. 26.50x (ISBN 0-06-492382-7); pap. text ed. 9.95x (ISBN 0-06-492383-5). B&N Imports.

Revolt of the Perverts (Gay Short Stories) Daniel Curzon. LC 77-83394. (Orig.). 1978. pap. 4.95 (ISBN 0-930650-01-8). D Brown Bks.

Revolt of the Teddy Bears: A May Gray Mystery. James Duffy. LC 84-15522. (Illus.). 80p. (gr. 5 up). 1985. 7.95 (ISBN 0-517-55533-6). Crown.

Revolt of the Tenantry: The Transformation of Local Government in Ireland, 1875-1895. William L. Feingold. LC 84-4080. (Illus.). 318p. 1984. text ed. 24.95x (ISBN 0-930350-55-3). NE U Pr.

Revolt of the Widows: The Social World of the Apocryphal Acts. Stevan L. Davies. LC 80-11331. 150p. 1980. 13.95x (ISBN 0-8093-0958-0). S Ill U Pr.

Revolt on the Campus. James Wechsler. LC 73-8748. (Americana Library Ser.: No. 26). 258p. 1973. Repr. of 1935 ed. 16.50x (ISBN 0-295-95296-2). U of Wash Pr.

Revolt, U. S. A. facs. ed. Lamar Middleton. LC 68-29232. (Essay Index Reprint Ser). (Illus.). 1968. Repr. of 1938 ed. 17.50 (ISBN 0-8369-0708-6). Ayer Co Pubs.

Revolte des Anges. Anatole France. (Coll. Bleue). pap. 14.50 (ISBN 0-685-34120-8). French & Eur.

Revolte des Anges. Anatole France. 320p. 1972. 9.95 (ISBN 0-686-55875-8). French & Eur.

Revolte Du Conte De Warwick Contre le Roi Edward 4e. Ed. by John A. Giles. (Fr). 1849. 24.00 (ISBN 0-8337-1347-7). B Franklin.

Revoltee. Guy Des Cars. 314p. 1968. 15.95 (ISBN 0-686-55655-0); pap. 4.50 (ISBN 0-686-55656-9). French & Eur.

Revoltes de la Bounty. Jules Verne. 192p. 1976. 8.95 (ISBN 0-686-55945-2). French & Eur.

Revolting Development. Lora R. Smith. LC 87-72895. 175p. (Orig.). 1988. pap. 8.95 (ISBN 0-9602676-6-2). Perseverance Pr.

Revolting Development. Lora R. Smith. 180p. 1988. Repr. lib. bdg. 19.95x (ISBN 0-8095-4200-5). Borgo Pr.

Revoltosos: Mexico's Rebels in the United States, 1903-1923. W. Dirk Raat. LC 80-6109. (Illus.). 368p. 1981. 22.50 (ISBN 0-89096-114-X). Tex A&M Univ Pr.

Revolucija I Sloboda. Hrvoje Lun. 1978. pap. 16.00 (ISBN 0-9602138-1-3). Plamen Pub.

Revolucion Cubana 25 Anos Despues. Hugh S. Thomas et al. Tr. by Andres Hernandez from Eng. (Biblioteca Cubana Contemporanea Ser.). 155p. (Span.). 1985. pap. 7.95 (ISBN 84-359-0427-X). Ediciones.

Revolution in Consciousness. Frederic Lionel. 144p. (Orig.). 1984. pap. 8.95 (ISBN 0-7102-0066-8). Routledge Chapman & Hall.
Revolution in Corporate Finance. Joel M. Stern & Donald H. Chew, Jr. 450p. 1986. text ed. 49.95 (ISBN 0-631-15114-1); pap. text ed. 19.95x (ISBN 0-631-15203-2). Basil Blackwell.
Revolution in Education. Mortimer J. Adler & Milton Mayer. LC 58-5534. viii, 224p. 1958. 15.00x (ISBN 0-226-00765-0). U of Chicago Pr.
Revolution in El Salvador: Origins & Evolution. 2nd, rev. & updated ed. Tommie Montgomery. 320p. Date not set. 35.00x (ISBN 0-8133-0070-3); pap. text ed. 17.95x (ISBN 0-8133-0071-1). Westview.
Revolution in El Salvador: Origins & Evolution. Tommie S. Montgomery. (Illus.). 255p. 1982. lib. bdg. 42.50x (ISBN 0-86531-049-1); pap. text ed. 15.95x (ISBN 0-86531-386-5). Westview.
Revolution in European Poetry, 1660-1900. Emery Neff. LC 73-19762. 279p. 1974. Repr. lib. bdg. 20.00x (ISBN 0-374-96040-2, Octagon). Hippocrene Bks.
Revolution in Financial Services. Harold W. Gourgues, Jr. & Jeffrey R. Lauterbach. 264p. 1987. text ed. 29.50 (ISBN 0-87179-561-2, 0561). BNA.
Revolution in Glassmaking: Entrepreneurship & Technological Change in the American Industry, 1880-1920. Warren C. Scoville. LC 76-38264. (Evolution of Capitalism Ser.). 440p. 1972. Repr. of 1948 ed. 30.00 (ISBN 0-405-04144-6). Ayer Co Pubs.
Revolution in Guinea: Selected Texts. Amilcar Cabral. LC 73-124084. pap. 45.80 (2030758). Bks Demand UMI.
Revolution in History. Ed. by Roy Porter & Mikulas Teich. 339p. 1986. 39.50 (ISBN 0-521-25978-9); pap. 12.95 (ISBN 0-521-27784-1). Cambridge U Pr.
Revolution in History: The Jihad of Usman Dan Fodio. Ibraheem Sulaiman. 189p. 1986. 53.00x (ISBN 0-7201-1815-8). Mansell.
Revolution in Hungary. Paul E. Zinner. LC 74-39215. (Select Bibliographies Reprint Ser). Repr. of 1962 ed. 21.00 (ISBN 0-8369-6817-4). Ayer Co Pubs.
Revolution in Hungary & the Dissolution of the Multinational State 1918. Andras Siklos. (Studia Historica). 172p. 1988. text ed. 25.00 (ISBN 963-05-4466-0, Pub. by Akademiai Kiado). Humanities.
Revolution in International Finance. Ed. by Joel M. Stern & Donald H. Chew, Jr. 228p. text ed. 44.95 (ISBN 0-631-15115-X); pap. text ed. 24.95 (ISBN 0-631-15204-0). Basil Blackwell.
Revolution in Iran. Leonard Binder. 62p. 4.95 (ISBN 0-317-31966-3). AAAPME.
Revolution in Iran. A. Husain. (Flashpoints Ser.). (Illus.). 80p. (gr. 7 up). Date not set. PLB 15.93 (ISBN 0-86592-038-9). Rourke Corp.
Revolution in Iran: A Reappraisal. Ed. by Enver M. Koury & Charles G. MacDonald. LC 81-85470. 109p. 1982. pap. 7.00 (ISBN 0-934484-16-3). Inst Mid East & North Africa.
Revolution in Iran: The Politics of Countermobilization. Jerold Green. LC 82-11295. 218p. 1982. 35.00 (ISBN 0-275-90809-7, C0809). Praeger.
Revolution in Judaea: Jesus & the Jewish Resistance. Hyam Maccoby. LC 80-16752. 256p. 1980. 9.95 (ISBN 0-8008-6784-X). Taplinger.
Revolution in Land. Charles Abrams. Ed. by Stuart Bruchey. LC 78-56679. (Management of Public Lands in the U. S. Ser.). (Illus.). 1979. Repr. of 1939 ed. lib. bdg. 25.50x (ISBN 0-405-11316-1). Ayer Co Pubs.
Revolution in Laos. K. Phomvihane. 255p. 1981. 5.00 (ISBN 0-8285-2017-8, Pub. by Progress Pubs USSR). Imported Pubns.
Revolution in Manufacturing: The SMED System. Shigeo Shingo. Tr. by Andrew P. Dillon from Japanese. LC 84-61450. (Illus.). 383p. 1985. 65.00 (ISBN 0-915299-03-8). Prod Press.
Revolution in Merchant Shipping. Ewan Corlett. (Ship Ser.). (Illus.). 60p. 1981. 10.95 (ISBN 0-11-290320-7). Sheridan.
Revolution in Mexico: Years of Upheaval, 1910-1940. Ed. by James W. Wilkie & Albert L. Michaels. LC 84-8813. 299p. 1984. pap. 8.95x (ISBN 0-8165-0887-9). U of Ariz Pr.
Revolution in Miniature: The History & Impact of Semiconductor Electronics Re-Explored. 2nd ed. Ernest Braun & Stuart Macdonald. LC 82-1117. (Illus.). 250p. 1982. 32.50 (ISBN 0-521-24701-2); pap. 10.95 (ISBN 0-521-28903-3). Cambridge U Pr.
Revolution in Perception: The Ecological Psychology of James J. Gibson. Edward S. Reed. 1988. 32.50 (ISBN 0-300-04289-2). Yale U Pr.
Revolution in Perspective: Essays on the Hungarian Soviet Republic. Ed. by Andrew C. Janos & William B. Slottman. LC 74-138510. 1971. 32.00x (ISBN 0-520-01920-2). U of Cal Pr.
Revolution in Peru: Mariategui & the Myth. John M. Baines. LC 72-148690. 216p. 1972. 14.00 (ISBN 0-8173-4721-6). U of Ala Pr.
Revolution in Physics: A Non-Mathematical Survey of Quanta. Louis De Broglie. Tr. by Ralph W. Niemeyer. LC 76-95113. Repr. of 1953 ed. lib. bdg. 35.00x (ISBN 0-8371-2582-0, BRRP). Greenwood.
Revolution in Poetic Language. Julia Kristeva. Tr. by Margaret Waller. LC 84-12181. (European Perspectives Ser.). 256p. 1984. 27.50x (ISBN 0-231-05642-7); pap. 15.00x (ISBN 0-231-05643-5). Columbia U Pr.
Revolution in Psychiatry. Ernest Becker. 17.75 (ISBN 0-8446-6276-3). Peter Smith.
Revolution in Psychiatry: The New Understanding of Man. Ernest Becker. LC 64-11213. 1974. pap. 10.95x (ISBN 0-02-902510-9). Free Pr.
Revolution in Real Estate: Extraordinary Listing & Selling Techniques That Dramatically Boost Income. Paul Christian. 1982. 100.00 (ISBN 0-13-780619-1). Exec Reports.
Revolution in Real Estate Finance. Anthony Downs. LC 85-14941. 345p. 1985. 32.95 (ISBN 0-8157-1918-3); pap. 12.95 (ISBN 0-8157-1917-5). Brookings.
Revolution in Science. I. Bernard Cohen. (Illus.). 704p. 1985. 29.95 (ISBN 0-674-76777-2, Belknap Pr). Harvard U Pr.
Revolution in Science. I. Bernard Cohen. LC 84-12916. (Illus.). 736p. 1987. pap. 14.95 (ISBN 0-674-76778-0, Belknap Pr). Harvard U Pr.
Revolution in Science. Time-Life Books Editors. (Understanding Computers Ser.). 1987. write for info. (ISBN 0-8094-5687-7); lib. bdg. write for info. (ISBN 0-8094-5688-5). Time-Life.
Revolution in Science Fifteen Hundred to Seventeen Fifty. A. Rupert Hall. LC 82-8978. 1983. text ed. 19.95x (ISBN 0-582-49133-9). Longman.
Revolution in Seattle: A Memoir by Harvey O' Connor. Harvey O'Connor. LC 81-80332. (Illus.). 300p. (Orig.). 1981. pap. 7.50 (ISBN 0-939306-01-8). Left Bank.
Revolution in Spain: A Greenwood Archival Edition. Karl Marx & Frederick Engels. LC 74-27667. 255p. 1975. Repr. of 1939 ed. lib. bdg. 48.50x (ISBN 0-8371-7909-2, MARS). Greenwood.
Revolution in Statecraft: Intervention in an Age of Interdependence. Rev. ed. Andrew M. Scott. LC 82-9768. (Duke Press Policy Studies). xvii, 214p. 1982. pap. text ed. 10.95 (ISBN 0-8223-0494-5). Duke.
Revolution in Tanner's Lane. Mark Rutherford. 1974. Repr. of 1923 ed. lib. bdg. 37.00 (ISBN 0-8414-7496-6). Folcroft.
Revolution in Tanner's Lane. Mark Rutherford. 288p. (Orig.). 1984. pap. 7.95 (ISBN 0-7012-1901-7). Salem Hse Pubs.
Revolution in Tanner's Lane, 1887. William H. White. Ed. by Robert L. Wolff. Bd. with Miriam's Schooling, Eighteen Ninety. LC 75-1515. (Victorian Fiction Ser.). 1975. lib. bdg. 73.00 (ISBN 0-8240-1588-6). Garland Pub.
Revolution in the Affluent Society. Erik Dammann. 206p. 1982. pap. 8.95 (ISBN 0-946097-06-2, Pub. by GMP England). Alyson Pubns.
Revolution in the Americas: Proceedings. Ed. by Lewis A. Tambs. (PCCLAS Ser.: Vol. 6). 280p. 1979. pap. 10.00 (ISBN 0-916304-43-4). SDSU Press.
Revolution in the Courts: Computers in the Housing Court of New York City. National Center for State Courts Staff. (Paul Reardon Ser.). 10p. 1983. manuscript 0.60 (PRS-041). Natl Ctr St Courts.
Revolution in the Development of Capitalism. Mark Gould. LC 86-11310. 520p. 1987. 48.00x (ISBN 0-317-65325-3); pap. 14.95x (ISBN 0-520-06101-2). U of Cal Pr.
Revolution in the Earth Sciences: Advances in the Past Half-Century. Shelby J. Boardman. 400p. 1983. pap. text ed. 23.95 (ISBN 0-8403-3147-9). Kendall-Hunt.
Revolution in the Earth Sciences: From Continental Drift to Plate Tectonics. A. Hallam. (Illus.). 1973. pap. text ed. 9.95x (ISBN 0-19-858145-9). Oxford U Pr.
Revolution in the Hudson Highlands. Thomas A. Ware. 1965. pap. 1.50 (ISBN 0-910746-11-7). Hope Farm.
Revolution in the Mind & Practice of the Human Race. Robert Owen. LC 74-183620. 1973. Repr. of 1849 ed. 39.50x (ISBN 0-678-00892-2). Kelley.
Revolution in the New York Party System: 1840-1860. Mark L. Berger. LC 72-89990. 184p. 1973. 18.95x (ISBN 0-8046-9030-8, Pub. by kennikat). Assoc Faculty Pr.
Revolution in the North: Soviet Ethnography & National Policy. Kerstin E. Kuoljok. 196p. (Orig.). 1986. pap. text ed. 24.00x (ISBN 91-554-1794-9, Pub. by Almqvist & Wiksell). Coronet Bks.
Revolution in the Phillipines: The U. S. in Hall of Cracked Mirrors. Fred Poole & Max Vanzi. 368p. 1984. text ed. 18.85 (ISBN 0-07-050438-5). McGraw.
Revolution in the Revolution? Armed Struggle & Political Struggle in Latin America. Regis Debray. Tr. by Bobbye Ortiz from Fr., Span. LC 80-19409. 126p. 1980. Repr. of 1967 ed. lib. bdg. 35.00 (ISBN 0-313-22669-5, DERE). Greenwood.
Revolution in the Revolution? Armed Struggle & Political Struggle in Latin America. Regis Debray. LC 80-19409. pap. 32.80 (2030760). Bks Demand UMI.
Revolution in the Theatre: French Romantic Theories of Drama. Barry V. Daniels. LC 83-1705. (Contributions in Drama & Theatre Studies: No. 7). xii, 249p. 1983. lib. bdg. 35.00 (ISBN 0-313-22476-5, DRT/). Greenwood.
Revolution in the Third World. Gerard Chaliand. 1978. pap. 6.95 (ISBN 0-14-004796-4). Penguin.
Revolution in the Wasteland. Ronald Cass. LC 81-10283. viii, 238p. 1981. 14.95x (ISBN 0-8139-0900-7). U Pr of Va.
Revolution in the World Petroleum Market. Mary A. Tetreault. LC 84-24931. (Illus.). xviii, 271p. 1985. lib. bdg. 46.95 (ISBN 0-89930-012-X, TWP/, Quorum). Greenwood.
Revolution in Time: Clocks & the Making of the Modern World. David S. Landes. LC 83-8489. (Illus.). 428p. 1983. 25.00 (ISBN 0-674-76800-0, Belknap). Harvard U Pr.
Revolution in Time: Clocks & the Making of the Modern World. David S. Landes. (Illus.). 544p. 1985. pap. 8.95 (ISBN 0-674-76802-7, Belknap Pr). Harvard U Pr.
Revolution in Toulouse: An Essay on Provincial Terrorism. Martyn Lyons. 210p. 1978. 26.55 (ISBN 3-261-03119-0). P Lang Pubs.
Revolution in Virginia. Hamilton J. Eckenrode. LC 64-7769. 311p. 1964. Repr. of 1916 ed. 29.50 (ISBN 0-208-00525-0, Archon). Shoe String.
Revolution in Virginia, Seventeen Seventy-Five to Seventeen Eighty-Three. John E. Selby. (Illus.). 450p. 1988. lib. bdg. 24.95x (ISBN 0-87935-075-X). Williamsburg.
Revolution in Warfare. Basil H. Liddell Hart. LC 79-22632. 1980. Repr. of 1947 ed. lib. bdg. 35.00x (ISBN 0-313-22173-1, LHRW). Greenwood.
Revolution in Writing. Cecil Day-Lewis. LC 74-14996. 1974. Repr. of 1935 ed. lib. bdg. 27.00 (ISBN 0-8414-3797-1). Folcroft.
Revolution in Writing. C. Day Lewis. LC 75-37952. (Studies in English Literature, No. 33). 1976. lib. bdg. 75.00x (ISBN 0-8383-2115-1). Haskell.
Revolution in Writing. C. Day Lewis. 1979. 42.50 (ISBN 0-685-94343-7). Bern Porter.
Revolution Machine. rev. ed. Donna M. Swajeski. (gr. 3-12). 1985. pap. text ed. 6.00 (ISBN 0-88734-511-5). Players Pr.
Revolution Myth. Gene Fisher & Glen Chambers. (Illus.). 161p. (Orig.). 1981. pap. 6.28 (ISBN 0-89084-152-7). Bob Jones Univ Pr.
Revolution oder Reform see Revolution or Reform: A Confrontation.
Revolution of America. Guillaume T. Raynal. Ed. by George Billias. LC 72-10134. (American Revolutionary Ser.). 1979. Repr. of 1783 ed. lib. bdg. 39.50 (ISBN 0-8398-1774-6). Irvington.
Revolution of Being: A Latin American View of the Future. Gustavo Lagos & Horacio H. Godoy. LC 77-3848. (Preferred Worlds for the 1990's). 1977. 19.95 (ISBN 0-02-917840-1). Free Pr.
Revolution of Cola di Rienzo. 2nd, rev. ed. Francesco Petrarch. Ed. by Roanld G. Musto. LC 86-80577. Orig. Title: Francesco Petrarca & the Revolution of Cola di Rienzo. 277p. 1986. pap. 12.50 (ISBN 0-934977-00-3). Italica Pr.
Revolution of Color. Thomas P. Melady. LC 75-41507. 208p. 1976. Repr. of 1966 ed. lib. bdg. 35.00x (ISBN 0-8371-8701-X, MERC). Greenwood.
Revolution of Everyday Life. Raoul Vaneigem. Tr. by Donald Nicholson-Smith from Fr. Orig. Title: Traite de Savior-Vivre a l'usage des Jeunes Generationse. 300p. (Orig.). 1983. pap. 8.50 (ISBN 0-939306-06-9). Left Bank.
Revolution of Fifteen Twenty-Five: The German Peasants' War from a New Perspective. Peter Blickle. Tr. by H. C. Erik Midelfort & Thomas A. Brady, Jr. LC 81-47603. (Illus.). 272p. 1982. text ed. 28.50x (ISBN 0-8018-2472-9). Johns Hopkins.
Revolution of Fifteen Twenty-Five: The German Peasants' War from a New Perspective. Peter Blickle. Tr. by Thomas A. Brady, Jr. & H. C. Midelfort. LC 81-47603. 272p. 1985. pap. text ed. 10.95x (ISBN 0-8018-3162-8). Johns Hopkins.
Revolution of Mary Leary. Susan Shreve. LC 82-185. 192p. (gr. 5-9). 1982. 9.95 (ISBN 0-394-84776-8). Knopf.
Revolution of Mary Leary. Susan Shreve. 192p. (YA) (gr. 7 up). 1984. pap. 2.25 (ISBN 0-380-68494-2, 68494-2, Flare). Avon.
Revolution of Moral Consciousness: Nietzsche in Russian Literature, 1890-1914. Edith W. Clowes. 326p. 1988. text ed. 27.50 (ISBN 0-87580-139-0). N Ill U Pr.
Revolution of Nihilism: Warning to the West. Hermann Rauschning. Tr. by E. W. Dickes. LC 72-180666. Repr. of 1939 ed. 28.50 (ISBN 0-404-56402-X). AMS Pr.
Revolution of Nihilism: Warning to the West. Hermann Rauschning. LC 72-4291. (World Affairs Ser.: National & International Viewpoints). 318p. 1972. Repr. of 1939 ed. 20.00 (ISBN 0-405-04583-2). Ayer Co Pubs.
Revolution of Rising Frustrations. D. R. Mankekar. (Illus.). 1975. 10.50 (ISBN 0-7069-0348-X). Intl Bk Dist.
Revolution of Sixteen Eighty-Eight & the Birth of the English Political Nation: Whig Triumph or Palace Revolution. 2nd ed. Ed. by Gerald M. Straka. (Problems in European Civilization Ser.). 1973. pap. text ed. 7.50 (ISBN 0-669-82032-6). Heath.
Revolution of Sixteen Eighty-Eight in England. J. R. Jones. (Revolutions in the Modern World Ser.). 1973. pap. text ed. 9.95x (ISBN 0-393-09998-9). Norton.
Revolution of the Dons: Cambridge & Society in Victorian England. Sheldon Rothblatt. LC 80-41865. 325p. pap. 84.50 (2030618). Bks Demand UMI.
Revolution of the Heart: Essays on the Catholic Worker. Ed. by Patrick G. Coy. (Illus.). 408p. 1988. 34.95 (ISBN 0-87722-531-1). Temple U Pr.
Revolution of the Latin American Church. Hugo Latorre Cabal. Tr. by Frances K. Hendricks & Beatrice Berler. LC 77-9117. 1978. 14.95x (ISBN 0-8061-1449-5). U of Okla Pr.
Revolution of the Saints: A Study in the Origins of Radical Politics. Michael Walzer. LC 65-22048. 352p. 1982. pap. text ed. 9.95x (ISBN 0-674-76786-1). Harvard U Pr.
Revolution of Things. Miron Bialoszewski. Tr. by Bogdan Czaykowski & Andrzej Busza. LC 74-81212. 1974. 7.50 (ISBN 0-910350-01-9). Charioteer.
Revolution of 1905: Russia in Disarray. Abraham Ascher. LC 87-26657. (Illus.). 420p. 1988. text ed. 39.50x (ISBN 0-8047-1436-3). Stanford U Pr.
Revolution on Balance. Hugh Thomas. 1983. 2.00. Cuban Amer Natl Fndtn.
Revolution on the Border: The United States & Mexico, 1910-1920. Linda B. Hall & Don M. Coerver. (Illus.). 216p. Date not set. 27.50x (ISBN 0-8263-1099-0). U of NM Pr.
Revolution on the Upper Ohio, 1775-1777. Ed. by Reuben G. Thwaites & Louise P. Kellogg. LC 76-120895. (American Bicentennial Ser). 1970. Repr. of 1908 ed. 26.00x (ISBN 0-8046-1288-9, Pub. by kennikat). Assoc Faculty Pr.
Revolution on the Volga: 1917 in Saratov. Donald J. Raleigh. LC 85-12792. (Studies in Soviet History & Society). (Illus.). 376p. 1986. 34.50x (ISBN 0-8014-1790-2). Cornell U Pr.
Revolution or Reform: A Confrontation. Herbert Marcuse & Karl Popper. LC 75-12192. (Studies in Ethics & Society Ser.: Vol. 2). Orig. Title: Revolution oder Reform. 120p. 1976. 14.95 (ISBN 0-89044-020-4). New Univ Pr.
Revolution Postponed: Women in Contemporary China. Margery Wolf. LC 83-40696. xii, 285p. 1986. 29.50x (ISBN 0-8047-1243-3); pap. 8.95 (ISBN 0-8047-1348-0, SP 187). Stanford U Pr.
Revolution, Reaction, & the Triumph of Conservatism: English History, 1558-1700. Michael A. Graves & Robin H. Silcock. 524p. 1984. pap. text ed. 12.95 (ISBN 0-582-68394-7). Longman.
Revolution Reassessed: Revisions in the History of Tudor Government & Administration. Ed. by Christopher Coleman & David Starkey. 228p. 1986. 55.00x (ISBN 0-19-873064-0); pap. 16.95x (ISBN 0-19-873063-2). Oxford U Pr.
Revolution Reform & Social Justice: Studies in the Theory & Practice of Marxism. Sidney Hook. LC 74-21610. 307p. 1975. uKE 25.00x (ISBN 0-8147-3368-9). NYU Pr.
Revolution, Reform, & the Politics of American Taxation, 1763-1783. Robert A. Becker. LC 79-19729. viii, 312p. 1980. 35.00 (ISBN 0-8071-0654-2). La State U Pr.
Revolution Remembered: Eyewitness Accounts of the War for Independence. John C. Dann. LC 79-19254. 1980. 20.00x (ISBN 0-226-13622-1). U of Chicago Pr.
Revolution Remembered: Eyewitness Accounts of the War for Independence. Ed. by John D. Dann. LC 79-19254. (Clements Library Bicentennial Studies). (Illus.). xxvi, 446p. 1983. pap. 15.95 (ISBN 0-226-13624-8, Phoen). U of Chicago Pr.
Revolution Sans Modele. Francois Chatelet et al. (Archontes Ser: No. 6). 188p. (Fr.). 1975. pap. text ed. 25.00x (ISBN 90-2797-615-5). Mouton.
Revolution: Stories & Essays. Jack London. 160p. (Orig.). 1985. pap. 4.50 (ISBN 0-904526-29-1, Pub. by Journeyman Pr. England). Riverrun NY.
Revolution Surrealiste. No. One - Twelve. Ed. by Pierre Naville et al. LC 68-28660. (Contemporary Art Ser.). (Illus., Fr.). 1968. Repr. of 1929 ed. 132.00 (ISBN 0-405-00706-X). Ayer Co Pubs.
Revolution That Wasn't: A Contemporary Assessment of 1776. Ed. by Richard M. Fulton. (National University Publication, American Studies). 1981. 24.95x (ISBN 0-8046-9259-9, Pub. by Kennikat). Assoc Faculty Pr.
Revolution, the Constitution & America's Third Century, 2 vols. American Academy of Political & Social Science Staff. 1980. 62.95x (ISBN 0-8122-7763-5); manual 4.95x (ISBN 0-686-77594-5). U of Pa Pr.
Revolution: The History of the Idea. Ed. by David Close & Carl Bridge. LC 84-28372. 240p. 1985. 23.50x (ISBN 0-389-20560-5). B&N Imports.
Revolution, the Story of the Early Church, Vol 1. Gene Edwards. 1974. pap. text ed. 6.95 (ISBN 0-940232-02-2). Christian Bks.
Revolution: Theoretical, Comparative, & Historical Studies. Jack A. Goldstone. 343p. 1986. pap. text ed. 13.00 net (ISBN 0-15-576710-0, HC). HarBraceJ.
Revolution Through Reform: A Comparison of Sarvodaya & Conscientization. Matthew Zachariah. Ed. by Philip G. Altbach. LC 85-17023. (Praeger Special Studies Series in Comparative Education). 160p. 1985. 35.00 (ISBN 0-275-90240-4, C0240). Praeger.

Revolution von Rechts. Hans Freyer. LC 78-63670. (Studies in Fascism: Ideology & Practice). Repr. of 1931 ed. 16.50 (ISBN 0-404-16527-3). AMS Pr.

Revolution Was. Garet Garrett. 23p. Date not set. pap. 2.00 (ISBN 0-317-53216-2). Noontide.

Revolution Within the Revolution: Workers' Control in Rural Portugal. Nancy Bermeo. LC 85-42675. (Illus.). 264p. 1986. 31.50x (ISBN 0-691-07688-X). Princeton U Pr.

Revolutionaire Kriegswissenschaft. John Most. Bd. with Beast of Property. (History of Political Violence Ser.). 1985. Repr. of 1885 ed. lib. bdg. 23.00 (ISBN 0-527-41194-9). Kraus Repr.

Revolutionaries. Eric J. Hobsbawn. 1975. pap. 3.95 (ISBN 0-452-00425-X, F425, Mer). NAL.

Revolutionaries & Functionaries. Richard Falk. 144p. 1988. 17.95 (ISBN 0-525-24604-5). Dutton.

Revolutionaries for the Gospel: Testimonies of Fifteen Christians in the Nicaraguan Government. Teofilo Cabestrero. Tr. by Phillip Berryman from Span. LC 85-25865. 176p. (Orig.). 1986. pap. 9.95 (ISBN 0-88344-406-2). Orbis Bks.

Revolutionaries in Modern Britain. Peter Shipley. 256p. 1976. 16.95 (ISBN 0-370-11311-X). Transatl Arts.

Revolutionaries in the Theater: Meyerhold, Brecht, & Witkiewicz. Christine Kiebuzinska. Ed. by Oscar Brockett. LC 87-25516. (Theater & Dramatic Studies: No. 49). 192p. 1987. 44.95 (ISBN 0-8357-1850-6). UMI Res Pr.

Revolutionaries of India in Soviet Russia. M. A. Persits. 260p. 1986. 8.50x (ISBN 0-8364-1817-4, Pub. by Somaiya). South Asia Bks.

Revolutionaries, Traditionalists & Dictators in Latin America. Harold E. Davis. LC 72-77988. 1973. lib. bdg. 20.00x (ISBN 0-8154-0420-4). Cooper Sq.

Revolutionary Adventurism. Vladimir I. Lenin. 40p. 1975. pap. 0.75 (ISBN 0-8285-0166-1, Pub. by Progress Pubs USSR). Imported Pubns.

Revolutionary Afghanistan. Beverly Male. 1982. 27.50x (ISBN 0-312-67997-1). St Martin.

Revolutionary Age, Vols. 1-2, No. 7. Communist Labor Party of America Staff. 1969. Repr. of 1918 ed. Vol. 1. lib. bdg. 97.00 (ISBN 0-313-21936-2, RA21); Vols. 2 & 3. lib. bdg. 97.00 (ISBN 0-313-21937-0, RA22). Greenwood.

Revolutionary Age of Andrew Jackson. Robert V. Remini. LC 74-2623. (YA) (gr. 7 up). 1976. PLB 13.89 (ISBN 0-06-024857-2). HarpJ.

Revolutionary Age of Andrew Jackson. Robert V. Remini. LC 85-42588. (Illus.). 224p. 1985. pap. 5.95 (ISBN 0-06-091290-1, PL 1290, PL). Har-Row.

Revolutionary America: An Interpretive Overview. Robert M. Calhoun. (History of the United States Ser.). (Illus.). 212p. (Orig.). 1976. pap. text ed. 12.00 net (ISBN 0-15-576712-7, HC). HarBraceJ.

Revolutionary America, Seventeen Sixty-Three to Seventeen Eighty-Nine, 2 vols. Ed. by Ronald M. Gephart. LC 80-606802. 1984. 2 vol. set 38.00. Vol. 1, xl, pgs.1-780 (ISBN 0-8444-0359-8). Vol. 2,xl, pgs. 781-1672 (ISBN 0-8444-0379-2). Lib Congress.

Revolutionary America, 1763-1789: A Bibliography. Ed. by Ronald E. Gephart. LC 80-606802. (Illus.). 1752p. 1984. text ed. 38.00 (S/N 030-000-00125-7). USGPO.

Revolutionary & Dissident Movements: An International Guide. 2nd ed. Ed. by Henry W. Degenhardt. 600p. 1988. 140.00x (Pub. by Longman). Gale.

Revolutionary Approach to Successful Fly Fishing: Swimming Flies. Georges Odier. LC 83-51086. (Illus.). 222p. 1984. 19.95 (ISBN 0-913276-48-0). Stone Wall Pr.

Revolutionary Armies: The Historical Development of the Soviet & the Chinese People's Liberation Armies. Jonathan R. Adelman. LC 79-7728. (Contributions in Political Science Ser.: No. 38). (Illus.). 1980. lib. bdg. 35.00 (ISBN 0-313-22026-3, ADR/). Greenwood.

Revolutionary Army. Tsou Jung. 152p. 1968. pap. 75.00x (Pub. by Han-Shan Tang Ltd). State Mutual Bk.

Revolutionary Bishop Who Saw God at Work in Africa: An Autobiography. Ralph E. Dodge. LC 85-29092. (Illus.). 211p. (Orig.). 1986. pap. 7.95 (ISBN 0-87808-203-4, WCL203-4). William Carey Lib.

Revolutionary Botany: "Thalassiophyta" & Other Essays of A. H. Church. A. H. Church. Ed. by D. J. Mabberly. (Illus.). 1981. 49.95x (ISBN 0-19-854548-7). Oxford U Pr.

Revolutionary Breakthroughs & National Development: The Case of Romania, 1944-1965. Kenneth Jowitt. LC 71-123625. 1971. 45.00x (ISBN 0-520-01762-5). U of Cal Pr.

Revolutionary Career of Maximilien Robespierre. David P. Jordan. 308p. 1985. 24.95 (ISBN 0-02-916530-X). Free Pr.

Revolutionary Census of New Jersey: An Index, Based on Rateables, of the Inhabitants of New Jersey During the Period of the American Revolution. rev. ed. Kenn Stryer-Rodda. 413p. 1986. Repr. of 1972 ed. lib. bdg. 23.00 (ISBN 0-912606-27-4). Hunterdon Hse.

Revolutionary Change. 2nd ed. Chalmers Johnson. LC 81-85448. 232p. 1982. 20.00x (ISBN 0-8047-1144-5); pap. 7.95 (ISBN 0-8047-1145-3, SP 47). Stanford U Pr.

Revolutionary Change in Cuba. Ed. by Carmelo Mesa-Lago. LC 73-158190. (Pitt Latin American Ser). 1971. 54.95x (ISBN 0-8229-3232-6). U of Pittsburgh Pr.

Revolutionary Clergy: The Filipino Clergy & the Nationalist Movement, 1850-1903. John N. Schumacher. 306p. 1982. (Pub. by Ateneo De Manila U Pr Philippines); pap. 17.50. Cellar.

Revolutionary Conservative: James Duane of New York. Edward P. Alexander. LC 78-38479. Repr. of 1938 ed. 15.00 (ISBN 0-404-00321-4). AMS Pr.

Revolutionary Continuity: Birth of the Communist Movement, 1918-1922, Vol. 2. Farrell Dobbs. Ed. by Jack Barnes. LC 80-84850. 1983. lib. bdg. 22.00 (ISBN 0-913460-92-3); pap. 8.95 (ISBN 0-913460-93-1). Anchor Found.

Revolutionary Continuity: Marxist Leadership in the U. S., 1848-1917. 1981. 22.00 (ISBN 0-913460-85-0); pap. 8.95 (ISBN 0-913460-84-2). Anchor Found.

Revolutionary Cuba: A Bibliographical Guide 1968. Ed. by Fermin Peraza. LC 68-21369. 1970. 5.95x (ISBN 0-87024-153-2). U of Miami Pr.

Revolutionary Cuba: A Bibliographical Guide 1967. Ed. by Fermin Peraza. LC 75-92596. 1969. 5.95x (ISBN 0-87024-136-2). U of Miami Pr.

Revolutionary Cuba: A Bibliographical Guide, 1966. Ed. by Fermin Peraza. LC 68-21369. 1967. 5.95 (ISBN 0-87024-075-7). U of Miami Pr.

Revolutionary Cuba in the World Arena. Ed. by Martin Weinstein. LC 79-10313. 176p. 1979. text ed. 15.00x (ISBN 0-915980-73-8). ISHI PA.

Revolutionary Cuba: The Challenge: Economic Growth, with Equity. Claes Brundenius. (WVSS on Latin America & the Caribbean). 160p. 1984. lib. bdg. 31.50x (ISBN 0-86531-355-5). Westview.

Revolutionary Days: Recollections of Romanoffs & Bolsheviki 1914-1917. Princess Cantacuzene. LC 76-115515. (Russia Observed, Ser.1). 1970. Repr. of 1919 ed. 21.00 (ISBN 0-405-03012-6). Ayer Co Pubs.

Revolutionary Democracy: Challenge & Testing in Japan. E. Wight Bakke. LC 68-25173. x, 343p. 1968. 30.00 (ISBN 0-208-00627-3, Archon). Shoe String.

Revolutionary Democracy in Africa. N. Kosukhin. 167p. 1985. pap. 3.95 (ISBN 0-8285-3039-4, Pub. by Progress Pubs USSR). Imported Pubns.

Revolutionary Diplomacy: Chinese Foreign Policy & the United Front Doctrine. J. D. Armstrong. LC 76-14315. 259p. 1977. 39.50x (ISBN 0-520-03251-9); pap. 8.95x (ISBN 0-520-04273-5). U of Cal Pr.

Revolutionary Dreams: Utopian Vision & Experimental Life in the Russian Revolution. Richard Stites. (Illus.). 352p. 1989. 32.50 (ISBN 0-19-505536-5). Oxford U Pr.

Revolutionary Dynamics of Women's Liberation. George Novack. 1970. pap. 0.25 (ISBN 0-87348-120-8). Path Pr NY.

Revolutionary Education in China: Documents & Commentary. Peter J. Seybolt. LC 72-77204. pap. 115.00 (ISBN 0-317-29623-X, 2021860). Bks Demand UMI.

Revolutionary Emperor: Joseph the Second, 1741-1790. S. K. Padover. 414p. 1984. Repr. of 1934 ed. lib. bdg. 65.00 (ISBN 0-8495-4449-1). Arden lib.

Revolutionary Ethiopia: From Empire to People's Republic. Edmond J. Keller. LC 87-46090. 320p. 1989. 35.00 (ISBN 0-253-35014-X). Ind U Pr.

Revolutionary Europe Seventeen Eighty-Nine to Eighteen Fifteen. Stephens H. Morse. 423p. 1985. Repr. of 1904 ed. lib. bdg. 85.00 (ISBN 0-8492-8211-X). R West.

Revolutionary Exiles: The Russians in the First International & the Paris Commune. Woodford McClellan. (Illus.). 266p. 1979. 29.50x (ISBN 0-7146-3115-9, F Cass Co). Biblio Dist.

Revolutionary for Our Times: Rosa Luxemburg. Stephen E. Bronner. 128p. 1981. pap. 5.95 (ISBN 0-86104-348-0, Pub by Pluto Pr). Longwood Pub Group.

Revolutionary Forgiveness: Feminist Reflections on Nicaragua. Frwd. by Dorothee Solle. LC 86-5434. 192p. (Orig.). 1987. pap. 9.95 (ISBN 0-88344-264-7). Orbis Bks.

Revolutionary Grenada: A Study in Political Economy. Frederic L. Pryor. LC 86-8109. 415p. 1986. lib. bdg. 46.95 (ISBN 0-275-92155-7, C2155). Praeger.

Revolutionary Guerrilla Warfare. Sarkesian. 1975. text ed. 12.95 (ISBN 0-07-054745-9). McGraw.

Revolutionary Guerrilla Warfare. Ed. by Sam C. Sarkesian. LC 74-12995. (Illus.). 623p. 1975. 19.95. Precedent Pub.

Revolutionary Guerrilla Warfare. Ed. by Sam C. Sarkesian. 644p. 1975. 39.95. Transaction Bks.

Revolutionary Hamburg: Labor Politics in the Early Weimar Republic. Richard A. Comfort. 1966. 22.50x (ISBN 0-8047-0284-5). Stanford U Pr.

Revolutionary Histories: Contemporary Narratives of the American Revolution. Lester H. Cohen. LC 80-11243. 286p. 1980. 32.50x (ISBN 0-8014-1277-3). Cornell U Pr.

Revolutionary Humanism & Historicism in Modern Italy. Edmund D. Jacobitti. LC 80-23619. 240p. 1981. text ed. 27.50x (ISBN 0-300-02479-7). Yale U Pr.

Revolutionary Hungary: 1918-1921. Sander Szilassy. (Behind the Iron Curtain Ser.: No. 9). 1971. pap. 4.00 (ISBN 0-87934-005-3). Danubian.

Revolutionary Idea in France, 1789-1871. Godfrey Elton. 1969. 17.50x (ISBN 0-86527-170-4). Fertig.

Revolutionary Idea in France, 1789-1871. 2nd ed. Godfrey E. Elton. LC 74-147116. Repr. of 1931 ed. 25.00 (ISBN 0-404-02325-8). AMS Pr.

Revolutionary Imagination: The Poetry & Politics of John Wheelwright & Sherry Mangan. Alan M. Wald. LC 82-8498. xix, 288p. 1983. 30.00x (ISBN 0-8078-1535-7). U of NC Pr.

Revolutionary Internationals, 1864-1943. Ed. by Milorad M. Drachkovitch. 1966. 25.00x (ISBN 0-8047-0293-4). Stanford U Pr.

Revolutionary Iran: Challenge & Response in the Middle East. R. K. Ramazani. LC 86-45440. 304p. 1987. text ed. 27.50 (ISBN 0-8018-3377-9). Johns Hopkins.

Revolutionary Iran: Challenge & Response in the Middle East. R. K. Ramazani. LC 86-45440. 352p. 1988. pap. text ed. 10.95 (ISBN 0-8018-3610-7). Johns Hopkins.

Revolutionary Journal of Colonel Jeduthan Baldwin, 1775-1778. Jeduthan Baldwin. Ed. by Thomas W. Baldwin. LC 73-140853. (Eyewitness Accounts of the American Revolution Ser., No. 3). (Illus.). 1970. Repr. of 1906 ed. 14.00 (ISBN 0-405-01223-3). Ayer Co Pubs.

Revolutionary Justice: The Social & Political Theory of P.-J. Proudhon. Robert L. Hoffman. LC 76-180482. (Illus.). 446p. 1972. 34.95 (ISBN 0-252-00240-7). U of Ill Pr.

Revolutionary Law & Order: Politics & Social Change in the U. S. S. R. Peter H. Juviler. LC 76-12832. 1976. 19.95 (ISBN 0-02-916800-7). Free Pr.

Revolutionary Leaders of Modern China. Ed. by Chun-Tu Hsueh. (Orig.). 1971. pap. text ed. 8.95x (ISBN 0-19-501274-7). Oxford U Pr.

Revolutionary Leadership. G. Terry Madonna. Ed. by Joseph E. Walker. LC 76-8955. (Lancaster County During the American Revolution Ser). (Illus.). 56p. 1976. pap. 2.00 (ISBN 0-915010-07-0). Sutter House.

Revolutionary Left in Spain: 1914-1923. Gerald H. Meaker. LC 73-80622. xii, 564p. 1974. 45.00x (ISBN 0-8047-0845-2). Stanford U Pr.

Revolutionary Letters. Diane Di Prima. LC 78-134224. (Pocket Poets Ser.: No. 27). 1971. pap. 3.50 (ISBN 0-87286-059-0). City Lights.

Revolutionary Literature in China: An Anthology. John Berninghausen & Ted Huters. LC 76-51581. Repr. of 1976 ed. text ed. 27.30 (ISBN 0-317-30479-8, 2024814). Bks Demand UMI.

Revolutionary Love. Festo Kivengere. 1983. pap. 2.95 (ISBN 0-87508-298-X). Chr Lit.

Revolutionary Medicine, Seventeen Hundred to Eighteen Hundred. C. Keith Wilbur. LC 80-82790. (Illus.). 88p. (Orig.). 1980. pap. 9.95 (ISBN 0-87106-041-8). Globe Pequot.

Revolutionary Mexico: The Coming & Process of the Revolution. John M. Hart. LC 87-5399. 478p. 1988. text ed. 37.50 (ISBN 0-520-05995-6). U of Cal Pr.

Revolutionary Mission of Modern Art: Or Crud & Other Essays on Art. Margaret E. Stucki. 215p. 1973. pap. 20.00 (ISBN 0-686-14979-3). Birds' Meadow Pub.

Revolutionary Movement in France: Eighteen Fifteen to Eighteen Seventy-One. John P. Plamenatz. LC 78-14135. 1986. Repr. of 1952 ed. 19.25 (ISBN 0-88355-809-2). Hyperion Conn.

Revolutionary Movement of Eighteen Forty-Eight to Forty-Nine in Italy, Austria-Hungary, & Germany. C. E. Maurice. LC 68-25250. (World History Ser., No. 48). (Illus.). 1969. Repr. of 1887 ed. lib. bdg. 49.95x (ISBN 0-8383-0215-7). Haskell.

Revolutionary Movement of 1848-49 in Italy, Austria, Hungary, & Germany. Charles E. Maurice. LC 3-13471. 1968. Repr. of 1887 ed. 14.00x (ISBN 0-403-00075-0). Scholarly.

Revolutionary Mystery. Spiros Zodhiates. (I Corinthians). (Illus.). 1974. pap. 6.95 (ISBN 0-89957-507-2). AMG Pubs.

Revolutionary New England, Sixteen Ninety One to Seventeen Seventy Six. James T. Adams. LC 68-19139. 1968. Repr. of 1923 ed. 27.50x (ISBN 0-8154-0002-0). Cooper Sq.

Revolutionary New Hampshire. Richard F. Upton. LC 70-120896. (American Bicentennial Ser). 1970. Repr. of 1936 ed. 24.95x (ISBN 0-8046-1289-7, Pub. by Kennikat). Assoc Faculty Pr.

Revolutionary New Hampshire. Richard F. Upton. LC 74-148460. 1970. Repr. lib. bdg. 20.50x (ISBN 0-374-98061-6, Octagon). Hippocrene Bks.

Revolutionary Origins of Modern Japan. Thomas M. Huber. LC 79-64214. 272p. 1981. 25.00x (ISBN 0-8047-1048-1). Stanford U Pr.

Revolutionary Pamphlets. Peter Kropotkin. Ed. by Roger N. Baldwin. LC 68-56519. 1968. Repr. of 1927 ed. 14.00 (ISBN 0-405-08720-9, Blom Pubns). Ayer Co Pubs.

Revolutionary Party: Essays in the Sociology of Politics. Feliks Gross. LC 72-806. (Contributions in Sociology Ser.: No. 12). 1974. lib. bdg. 36.95 (ISBN 0-8371-6376-5, GRV/). Greenwood.

Revolutionary Party: Its Role in the Struggle. James P. Cannon. pap. 0.50 (ISBN 0-87348-346-4). Path Pr NY.

Revolutionary Patience. Dorothee Solle. Tr. by Rita Kimber & Robert Kimber. LC 77-24313. Orig. Title: Meditationen und Gebrauchstexte; Die Revolutionare Geduld. 82p. (Orig.). 1977. pap. 5.95 (ISBN 0-88344-439-9). Orbis Bks.

Revolutionary People at War: The Continental Army & American Character, 1775-1783. Charles Royster. (Illus.). 512p. 1982. pap. text ed. 10.95x (ISBN 0-393-95173-1). Norton.

Revolutionary People at War: The Continental Army & American Character, 1775-1783. Charles Royster. LC 79-10152. (Institute of Early American History Culture Ser.). (Illus.). 1980. 29.95x (ISBN 0-8078-1385-0). U of NC Pr.

Revolutionary Petunias & Other Poems. Alice Walker. LC 72-88796. 70p. 1973. pap. 4.95 (ISBN 0-15-676620-5, Harv). HarBraceJ.

Revolutionary Phrase. Vladimir I. Lenin. 171p. 1972. pap. 1.45 (ISBN 0-8285-0167-X, Pub. by Progress Pubs USSR). Imported Pubns.

Revolutionary Poet in the United States: The Poetry of Thomas McGrath. Ed. by Frederick C. Stern. LC 88-4846. 208p. 1988. text ed. 24.00 (ISBN 0-8262-0682-4). U of Mo Pr.

Revolutionary Politics & Locke's "Two Treatises of Government". Richard Ashcraft. LC 85-43269. 624p. 1986. text ed. 65.00x (ISBN 0-691-07703-7); pap. 16.95x (ISBN 0-691-10205-8). Princeton U Pr.

Revolutionary Politics in Massachusetts: The Boston Committee of Correspondence & the Towns, 1772-1774. Richard D. Brown. LC 71-119072. (Illus.). 1970. 20.00x (ISBN 0-674-76781-0). Harvard U Pr.

Revolutionary Politics in Massachusetts: The Boston Committee of Correspondence & the Towns, 1772-1774. Richard D. Brown. (Illus.). 304p. 1976. pap. 4.95x (ISBN 0-393-00810-X, Norton Lib). Norton.

Revolutionary Politics in the Long Parliament. John R. MacCormack. LC 72-93952. 352p. 1973. text ed. 24.50x (ISBN 0-674-76775-6). Harvard U Pr.

Revolutionary Portugal. Vincente Braganca-Cunha. 1976. lib. bdg. 59.95 (ISBN 0-8490-2521-4). Gordon Pr.

Revolutionary Potential of the Working Class. George Novack & Ernest Mandel. LC 74-75357. (Illus.). 80p. 1974. 12.00 (ISBN 0-87348-363-4); pap. 3.95 (ISBN 0-87348-364-2). Path Pr NY.

Revolutionary Pressures in Africa. Claude Ake. 112p. 1978. 17.00x (ISBN 0-905762-14-2, Pub. by Zed Pr); pap. 7.95x (ISBN 0-905762-15-0, Pub by Zed Pr). Humanities.

Revolutionary Process in the East: Past & Present. R. A. Ulyanovsky et al. 315p. 1985. 8.95 (ISBN 0-8285-3101-3, Pub. by Progress Pubs USSR). Imported Pubns.

Revolutionary Prose of the English Civil War. Ed. by Howard Erskine-Hill & Graham Storey. LC 82-12904. (Cambridge English Prose Texts). (Illus.). 280p. 1983. 42.50 (ISBN 0-521-24404-8); pap. 15.95 (ISBN 0-521-28670-0). Cambridge U Pr.

Revolutionary Radicalism, 4 vols. in 5. New York State Legislature Joint Committee Investigating Seditious Activities. LC 78-12114. (Civil Liberties in American History Ser.). 1971. Repr. of 1920 ed. Set. lib. bdg. 295.00 (ISBN 0-306-71974-6). Da Capo.

Revolutionary Radicalism: Its History, Purpose & Tactics, 6 vols. Ed. by New York State Legislature, Joint Committee Investigating Seditious Activities. 1980. Set. lib. bdg. 500.00 (ISBN 0-8490-3152-4). Gordon Pr.

Revolutionary Records of the State of Georgia, 1769-1784, 3 vols. Georgia General Assembly Staff. Ed. by Allen D. Candler. LC 72-965. Repr. of 1908 ed. Set. 225.00 (ISBN 0-404-07300-X); 75.00 ea. Vol. 1 (ISBN 0-404-07301-8). Vol. 2 (ISBN 0-404-07302-6). Vol. 3 (ISBN 0-404-07303-4). AMS Pr.

Revolutionary Religion: Christianity, Fascism, & Communism. Roger B. Lloyd. LC 78-63686. (Studies in Fascism: Ideology & Practice). Repr. of 1938 ed. 24.50 (ISBN 0-404-16903-1). AMS Pr.

Revolutionary Rexroth: Poet of East-West Wisdom. Morgan Gibson. LC 86-7948. ix, 153p. 1986. 22.50 (ISBN 0-208-02121-3, Archon Bks). Shoe String.

Revolutionary Road. Richard Yates. LC 70-163123. 1971. Repr. of 1961 ed. lib. bdg. 35.00 (ISBN 0-8371-6221-1, YARR). Greenwood.

Revolutionary Road. Richard Yates. 1983. pap. 7.95 (ISBN 0-385-29203-1, Delta). Dell.

Revolutionary Russia: 1917. John M. Thompson. (Illus.). 206p. 1981. (ScribT); pap. text ed. 8.95 (ISBN 0-684-17277-1). Scribner.

Revolutionary Russia, 1917. John M. Thompson. 206p. 1981. pap. text ed. write for info. (ISBN 0-02-420700-4, Pub. by Scribner). Macmillan.

Revolutionary Sarvodaya. Vinoba Bhave. Ed. & tr. by Vasant Nargolkar. 64p. (Orig.). 1980. pap. 1.25 (ISBN 0-934676-23-2). Greenlf Bks.

Revolutionary Services & Civil Life of General William Hull. Ed. by Maria Campbell. 1972. Repr. of 1848 ed. lib. bdg. 29.50 (ISBN 0-8422-8022-7). Irvington.

Revolutionary Social Democracy: The Chilean Socialist Party. Benny Pollack & Herman Roencranz. LC 86-15507. 200p. 1986. 29.95 (ISBN 0-312-68031-7). St Martin.

Revolutionary Socialism in the Work of Ernst Toller. Richard Dove. Ed. by Gerhard P. Knapp & Luis Lorenzo-Rivero. (Utah Studies in Literature & Linguistics: Vol. 26). 509p. 1987. lib. bdg. 49.50 (ISBN 0-8204-0382-2). P Lang Pubs.

Revolutionary Socialist Development in the Third World. Ed. by Gordon White et al. LC 82-23705. 288p. 1983. 13.00 (ISBN 0-8131-1485-3). U Pr of Ky.

Revolutionary Soldiers Buried in Indiana, with Supplement, 2 Vols in 1. Margaret R. Waters. LC 72-107084. 207p. 1970. Repr. of 1954 ed. 18.50 (ISBN 0-8063-0385-9). Genealog Pub.

Revolutionary Soldiers in Alabama. Thomas M. Owen. LC 67-28598. 131p. 1975. Repr. of 1911 ed. 12.00 (ISBN 0-8063-0269-0). Genealog Pub.

Revolutionary Soldiers in Kentucky. Anderson C. Quisenberry. LC 68-22328. 206p. 1982. Repr. of 1896 ed. 15.00 (ISBN 0-8063-0283-6). Genealog Pub.

Revolutionary Soldiers of Kentucky. Anderson C. Quisenberry. xix, 206p. 1985. Repr. of 1895 ed. lib. bdg. 39.00 (Pub. by Am Repr Serv). Am Biog Serv.

Revolutionary Soviet Film Posters. Mildred Constantine & Alan Fern. LC 74-6817. (Illus.). 112p. 1974. pap. 9.95 (ISBN 0-8018-1760-9). Johns Hopkins.

Revolutionary Spirit in France & America. Bernard Fay. Tr. by Ramon Guthrie. LC 66-26824. Repr. of 1927 ed. 28.50x (ISBN 0-8154-0067-5). Cooper Sq.

Revolutionary Spirit in Modern Literature & Drama. C. H. Norman. LC 74-95335. 1971. Repr. of 1937 ed. 16.50x (ISBN 0-8046-1346-X, Pub. by Kennikat). Assoc Faculty Pr.

Revolutionary Spirit in Modern Literature & Drama & the Class War in Europe: 1918-36. C. H. Norman. 1937. lib. bdg. 27.50 (ISBN 0-8414-6659-9). Folcroft.

Revolutionary Statesman: Charles Carroll & the War. Thomas O. Hanley. 1983. 15.95 (ISBN 0-8294-0407-4). Loyola.

Revolutionary Struggle in Manchuria: Chinese Communism & Soviet Interest, 1922-1945. Chong-Sik Lee. LC 82-7083. (Illus.). 366p. 1983. text ed. 45.00x (ISBN 0-520-04375-8). U of Cal Pr.

Revolutionary Student Movement: Theory & Practice. Ernest Mandel et al. pap. 0.85 (ISBN 0-87348-088-0). Path Pr NY.

Revolutionary Textile Design: Russia in the 1920's & 1930's. I. Yasinskaya. 1984. 30.00 (ISBN 0-670-59712-0); pap. 15.95 (ISBN 0-670-59713-9). Viking.

Revolutionary Theories of Louis-Auguste Blanqui. Alan B. Spitzer. LC 70-120198. (Columbia University Social Science Studies Ser.: No. 594). Repr. of 1957 ed. 12.50 (ISBN 0-404-51594-0). AMS Pr.

Revolutionary Theory. William H. Friedland et al. LC 80-70921. 264p. 1982. text ed. 26.50x (ISBN 0-86598-074-8, Pub. by Allanheld); pap. 9.50x (ISBN 0-86598-075-6). Rowman.

Revolutionary Theory & Political Reality. N. K. O'Sullivan. LC 82-16878. 260p. 1983. 26.50x (ISBN 0-312-68033-3). St Martin.

Revolutionary Thought from Marx to Mao, 10 vols. 1977. Set. pap. 14.95 (ISBN 0-8351-0310-2). China Bks.

Revolutionary Thought in the Twentieth Century. Ben Turok. 360p. (Orig.). 1980. 29.50x (ISBN 0-905762-42-8, Pub. by Zed Pr England); pap. 10.75 (ISBN 0-905762-43-6, Pub. by Zed Pr England). Humanities.

Revolutionary Town. Louise K. Brown. LC 74-30897. (Illus.). 336p. 1975. 15.00 (ISBN 0-914016-14-8). Phoenix Pub.

Revolutionary Tracings. James Jackson. LC 74-23242. 273p. 1974. 9.50 (ISBN 0-7178-0451-8); pap. 3.50 (ISBN 0-7178-0452-6). Intl Pubs Co.

Revolutionary Vanguard: The Early Years of the Communist Youth International, 1914-1924. Richard Cornell. 368p. 1982. 35.00x (ISBN 0-8020-5559-1). U of Toronto Pr.

Revolutionary Virginia: The Road to Independence, Vol. 1: Forming Thunderclouds & the First Convention, 1763-1774: A Documentary Record. Ed. by Robert L. Scribner. LC 72-96023. 308p. 1973. 37.50x (ISBN 0-8139-0500-1). U Pr of Va.

Revolutionary Virginia: The Road to Independence, Vol. 2: The Committees & the Second Convention, 1773-75. A Documentary Record. Ed. by Robert L. Scribner. LC 72-96023. (Illus.). 418p. 1975. 37.50x (ISBN 0-8139-0601-6). U Pr of Va.

Revolutionary Virginia, the Road to Independence, Vol, 3: Breaking Storm & the Third Convention, 1775 - a Documentary Record. Ed. by Robert L. Scribner & Brent Tarter. LC 72-96023. 548p. 1977. 37.50x (ISBN 0-8139-0685-7). U Pr of Va.

Revolutionary Virginia, the Road to Independence, Vol. 4: The Committee of Safety & the Balance of Forces, 1775 a Documentary Record. Compiled by Robert L. Scribner & Brent Tarter. LC 72-96023. 543p. 1978. 37.50x (ISBN 0-8139-0748-9). U Pr of Va.

Revolutionary Virginia: The Road to Independence, Vol. 5, Clash of Arms & the Fourth Convention, 1775-1776, a Documentary Record. Compiled by Robert L. Scribner & Brent Tarter. LC 72-96023. 471p. 1979. 37.50x (ISBN 0-8139-0806-X). U Pr of Va.

Revolutionary Virginia, The Road to Independence, Vol. 6: The Time for Decision, 1776: A Documentary Record. Ed. by Robert L. Scribner & Brent Tarter. LC 72-96023. 594p. 1981. 37.50x (ISBN 0-8139-0880-9). U Pr of Va.

Revolutionary Virginia, The Road to Independence, Vol. 7: Independence & the Fifth Convention, 1776, A Documentary Record, Vol. 7. Ed. by Robert L. Scribner & Brent Tarter. LC 72-96023. 1983. 50.00x (ISBN 0-8139-0968-6). U Pr of Va.

Revolutionary War: America's Fight for Freedom. 4th ed. Bart McDowell. LC 67-25820. (Special Publications Series 2: No. 3). (Illus.). 1980. avail. only from Natl. Geog. 7.95 (ISBN 0-87044-047-0). Natl Geog.

Revolutionary War: An Outline & Calendar. Arthur A. Merrill. (Illus.). (YA) (gr. 7 up). 1976. pap. 2.00 (ISBN 0-911894-35-7). Analysis.

Revolutionary War & Issachar Bates. John S. Williams. 14p. 1960. 0.50 (ISBN 0-937942-02-2). Shaker Mus.

Revolutionary War Bounty Land Grants in South Carolina. Tony Draine & John Skinner. 1987. pap. text ed. 10.00 (ISBN 0-938599-03-8). Congaree Pubns.

Revolutionary War for Independence & the Russian Question - Czechoslovak Army in Russia, 1914-1918. Victor M. Fic. 1977. 15.00x (ISBN 0-88386-968-3). South Asia Bks.

Revolutionary War Genealogy. 104p. 1987. pap. 7.00 (ISBN 0-913857-04-1). Genealog Sources.

Revolutionary War in the Hackensack Valley: The Jersey Dutch & Neutral Ground, 1775 - 1783. Adrian C. Leiby. 329p. 1980. pap. 9.95 (ISBN 0-8135-0898-3). Rutgers U Pr.

Revolutionary War Journals of Henry Dearborn, 1775-1783. Ed. by Lloyd A. Brown & Howard H. Peckham. LC 74-146143. (Era of the American Revolution Ser). 1971. Repr. of 1939 ed. lib. bdg. 37.50 (ISBN 0-306-70107-3). Da Capo.

Revolutionary War Journals, 1775-1783. facsimile ed. Henry Dearborn. Ed. by Lloyd A. Brown & Howard H. Peckham. LC 74-102233. (Select Bibliographies Reprint Ser). 1939. 29.00 (ISBN 0-8369-5118-2). Ayer Co Pubs.

Revolutionary War Memoir & Selected Correspondence of Philip Van Cortlandt. Philip Van Cortlandt. Ed. by Jacob Judd. LC 75-43654. (Van Cortlandt Family Papers: Vol. 1). (Illus.). 208p. 1976. 12.00 (ISBN 0-912882-27-1). Sleepy Hollow.

Revolutionary War Records: Mecklenburg County, Virginia. (Katherine B. Elliott Books on Southern Virginia). 230p. 1964. 30.00 (ISBN 0-89308-422-0, VA 62); pap. 25.00 (ISBN 0-89308-381-X, VA 61). Southern Hist Pr.

Revolutionary War Sermons. Ed. by David R. Williams. LC 84-14188. 1985. Repr. of 1777 ed. 75.00x (ISBN 0-8201-1400-6). Schol Facsimiles.

Revolutionary War Sketches of William R. Davie. Blackwell P. Robinson. (Illus.). xi, 67p. 1976. pap. 3.00 (ISBN 0-86526-113-X). NC Archives.

Revolutionary War Soldiers of Western North Carolina: Burke County, Vol. 1. Emmett R. White. 330p. 1984. 30.00 (ISBN 0-89308-536-7). Southern Hist Pr.

Revolutionary War Veterans of Madison County, New York. Ed. by Isabel Bracy. 130p. (Orig.). 1987. pap. 10.00 (ISBN 0-932334-96-2). Heart of the Lakes.

Revolutionary War Veterans Who Settled in Butler County, Pennsylvania. Paul W. Myers. 30p. 1987. pap. text ed. 5.00 perfect bdg. (ISBN 0-933227-69-8). Closson Pr.

Revolutionary War: Western Response. Ed. by David S. Sullivan & Martin J. Sattler. LC 73-171976. 145p. 1971. 35.00x (ISBN 0-231-03564-0). Columbia U Pr.

Revolutionary War Years. 2nd ed. W. Edmunds Claussen. (Illus.). 182p. 1974. 5.00 (ISBN 0-9616068-2-7). Boyertown Hist.

Revolutionary Woman. Sheila Fugard. 160p. 1985. 14.95 (ISBN 0-8076-1127-1). Braziller.

Revolutionary Women: Gender & the Socialist Revolutionary Role. Maria M. Mullaney. LC 82-22437. 414p. 1983. 38.95 (ISBN 0-275-91049-0, C1049); pap. 14.95 (ISBN 0-275-91776-2, B1776). Praeger.

Revolutionary Work in a Non-Revolutionary Situation: Report to the Second Plenary Session of the First Central Committee of the Revolutionary Communist Party, U. S. A. (1976) 70p. 1978. 1.00 (ISBN 0-89851-013-9). RCP Pubns.

Revolutionary Writers: Literature & Authority in the New Republic, 1725-1810. Emory Elliott. 1982. 24.95x (ISBN 0-19-502999-2). Oxford U Pr.

Revolutionary Writers: Literature & Authority in the New Republic, 1725-1810. Emory Elliott. 336p. 1986. pap. 9.95x (ISBN 0-19-503995-5). Oxford U Pr.

Revolutionary Years: West Africa Since Eighteen Hundred. J. B. Webster & A. A. Boahen. (Growth of African Civilization Ser.). (Illus.). 1981. pap. text ed. 12.95x (ISBN 0-582-60332-3). Longman.

Revolutionary's Quest. Ed. by Bimal Prasad. 406p. 1980. 29.95. Asia Bk Corp.

Revolutionist. Robert Littell. 1988. 18.95 (ISBN 0-553-05260-8). Bantam.

Revolutionizing Reform. Jerome Shuchter. 160p. 1987. 10.95 (ISBN 0-317-53946-9). Dorrance.

Revolutions & Dictatorships. facs. ed. Hans Kohn. LC 75-80388. (Essay Index Reprint Ser). 1939. 25.50 (ISBN 0-8369-1145-8). Ayer Co Pubs.

Revolutions & Interventions in Hungary & Its Neighbor States, 1918-1919. Ed. by Peter Pastor. 320p. 1988. 35.00 (ISBN 0-88033-137-2). East Eur Quarterly.

Revolutions & Military Rule in the Middle East: Egypt, Sudan, Yemen, Vol. 3. George M. Haddad. 14.95 (ISBN 0-8315-0061-1). Speller.

Revolutions & Military Rule in the Middle East: The Arab States, Vol. 2. George M. Haddad. 14.95 (ISBN 0-8315-0060-3). Speller.

Revolutions & Military Rule in the Middle East: The Northern Tier, Vol. 1. George M. Haddad. 12.95 (ISBN 0-8315-0059-X). Speller.

Revolutions & Rebellions in Afghanistan: Anthropological Perspectives. Ed. by M. Nazif Shahrani & Robert L. Canfield. LC 84-15713. (Research Ser.: No. 57). (Illus.). xiv, 394p. 1984. pap. 14.95x (ISBN 0-87725-157-6). U of Cal Intl St.

Revolutions & Revolutionaries: Four Theories. B. Salert. 1976. 29.95 (ISBN 0-444-99021-6, SRV/, Pub. by Elsevier). Greenwood.

Revolutions & Revolutionists: A Comprehensive Guide to the Literature. Robert Blackey. LC 82-6653. (War-Peace Bibliography Ser.: No. 17). 488p. 1982. lib. bdg. 58.00 (ISBN 0-87436-330-6). ABC-Clio.

Revolution's Godchild: The Birth, Death & Regeneration of the Society of the Cincinnati in North Carolina. Curtis C. Davis. LC 76-7967. (Illus.). xviii, 301p. 1976. 27.50x (ISBN 0-8078-1280-3). U of NC Pr.

Revolutions in American's Lives: A Demographic Perspective on the History of Americans, Their Families, & Their Society. Robert V. Wells. LC 81-6949. (Contributions in Family Studies: No. 6). (Illus.). xvi, 311p. 1982. lib. bdg. 35.00 (ISBN 0-313-23019-6, WRA/). Greenwood.

Revolutions in Knowledge: Feminism in the Social Sciences. Ed. by Sue R. Zalk & Janice Gordon-Kelter. 224p. 1989. 35.00 (ISBN 0-8133-0584-5). Westview.

Revolutions in Physics. Barry M. Casper & Richard J. Noer. (Illus.). 1972. text ed. 21.95x (ISBN 0-393-09992-X); instr's. guide avail. (ISBN 0-393-09405-7). Norton.

Revolutions of Civilization. W. M. Petrie. LC 73-158202. (World History Ser., No. 48). 1972. Repr. of 1911 ed. lib. bdg. 36.95x (ISBN 0-8383-1268-3). Haskell.

Revolutions of the Night. Alan Burns. 176p. 1986. 13.95 (ISBN 0-85031-734-7, Pub. by Allison & Busby England). Schocken.

Revolutions of Wisdom: Studies in the Claims & Practice of Ancients Greek Science. G. E. Lloyd. (Sather Classical Lectures: Vol. 52). 336p. 1987. 45.00x (ISBN 0-317-60055-9). U of Cal Pr.

Revolutions of 1848. Roger Price. (Studies in European History). 1988p. 1988. price not set (Co-Pub. by Macmillan Pubs UK). Humanities.

Revolutions of 1848: A Social History. Priscilla Robertson. 1952. 44.00x (ISBN 0-691-05147-X); pap. 11.50x (ISBN 0-691-00756-X). Princeton U Pr.

Revolver De Maigret. Georges Simenon. pap. 3.95 (ISBN 0-685-11528-3). French & Eur.

Revolver Guide. George C. Nonte, Jr. (Illus.). 288p. pap. 10.95 (ISBN 0-88317-094-9). Stoeger Pub Co.

Revolver Rifles. Edsall James. 2.50 (ISBN 0-913150-30-4). Pioneer Pr.

Revolvers. Ian V. Hogg. (Illus.). 1984. 14.95 (ISBN 0-85368-674-2, Arms & Armour Pr). Sterling.

Revolvers & Pistols. A. B. Zhuk. 304p. 1983. 40.00x (ISBN 0-317-61365-0, Pub. by Collets (UK)). State Mutual Bk.

Revolving Door Identification Model. Joseph S. Renzulli et al. 1981. pap. 19.95 (ISBN 0-936386-16-9). Creative Learning.

Revolving Doors: Sex Segregation & Women's Careers. Jerry A. Jacobs. 208p. 1988. 25.00x (ISBN 0-8047-1489-4). Stanford U Pr.

Revolving Pictures. Ernest Nister & Clifton Bingham. LC 79-12438. (Illus.). (ps-4). 1981. 10.95 (ISBN 0-399-20802-X, Philomel). Putnam Pub Group.

Revue. Robert Baral. LC 62-7579. (Illus.). 1970. 18.95 (ISBN 0-8303-0091-0). Fleet.

Revue Belge d'Archeologie et d'Histoire de l'Art: Vols. 1-44, Brussels, 1931-1975. write for info. Kraus Repr.

Revue de la Musique Dramatique en France. Felix Crozet. Bd. with Supplement a la Revue de la Musique Dramatique en France. LC 80-2270. Repr. of 1866 ed. 48.50 (ISBN 0-404-18833-8). AMS Pr.

Revue de l'Histoire Juive en Egypte. Ed. & intro. by Rene C. Bey. (Illus.). viii, 178p. 1987. pap. 35.00 (ISBN 0-9613805-2-7). Halgo Inc.

Revue de Mai a Octobre (1850) see Cahiers de l'Institut de Science Economique Appliquee.

Revue Du Cinema Anthology. Ed. by R. Gordon. 1976. lib. bdg. 75.00 (ISBN 0-8490-2522-2). Gordon Pr.

Revue Sommaire Le Doctrines Economiques. Augustin Cournot. LC 68-22372. (Fr). 1968. Repr. of 1877 ed. 39.50x (ISBN 0-678-00377-7). Kelley.

Revues Surrealistes Francaises Autour d'Andre Breton, 1948-1972. Marguerite Bonnet & Jacqueline Chenieux-Gendron. LC 82-14045. 294p. (Orig.). 1982. lib. bdg. 40.00 (ISBN 0-527-09750-0). Kraus Intl.

Reward. Max Brand. 1979. pap. 1.75 (ISBN 0-671-82892-4). PB.

Reward & Punishment-Love & Grace. David Cox. 1986. 10.00x (ISBN 0-317-62135-1, Guild of Pastoral Psych). State Mutual Bk.

Reward Systems & Power Distribution: Searching for Solutions. Ed. by Tove H. Hammer & Samuel B. Bacharach. (Pierce Ser.: No. 5). 124p. 1977. pap. 4.75 (ISBN 0-87546-223-5); pap. 8.75 special bdg. (ISBN 0-87546-290-1). ILR Pr.

Rewarding Management, 1983: The Annual Guide to Remuneration, Benefits & Conditions for Directors & Executives. Tony Vernon-Harcourt. (Annual Guide Ser.). 144p. (Orig.). 1982. pap. text ed. 38.00x (ISBN 0-566-02399-7). Gower Pub Co.

Rewards & Fairies. Rudyard Kipling. Ed. by Roger Lewis. 304p. 1988. pap. 3.95 (ISBN 0-14-043315-5). Penguin.

Rewards & Punishments in the Arthurian Romances & Lyric Poetry of Medieval France: Essays Presented to Benneth Varty on the Occasion of His Sixtieth Birthday. Ed. by Peter Davies & Angus J. Kennedy. 1987. 63.00 (ISBN 0-85991-250-7, Pub. by Boydell & Brewer). Longwood Pub Group.

Reweave It Yourself. 4th ed. Virginia Saunders & Elsie Cronk. LC 58-13832. 118p. 1981. Repr. of 1958 ed. 11.95 (ISBN 0-686-34357-3). Shepard J.

Reweaving the Web of Life: Feminism & Nonviolence. Ed. by Pam McAlister. LC 82-81879. 456p. 1982. 19.95 (ISBN 0-86571-017-1); pap. 12.95 (ISBN 0-86571-016-3). New Soc Pubs.

Rewind to Yesterday. Susan B. Pfeffer. (Illus.). (gr. 4-7). 1988. 13.95 (ISBN 0-440-50048-6). Delacorte.

Rewiring of America: The Fiber Optics Revolution. G. David Chaffee. 256p. 1987. 24.95 (ISBN 0-12-166360-4). Acad Pr.

Rewrite Man. Brian Forbes. 320p. 1985. 16.95 (ISBN 0-671-50610-2). S&S.

Rewrite Man. Bryan Forbes. 1988. 8.95 (ISBN 0-671-66193-0, Fireside). S&S.

Rewrite Right! Jan Venolia. 128p. 1987. pap. 6.95 (ISBN 0-89815-202-X). Ten Speed Pr.

ReWriter, Bk. I. Larry Berliner & Susan Berliner. (Illus.). 38p. (Orig.). (gr. 5 up). 1985. pap. text ed. 17.95 ea. Bk. I, gr. 5-8 & high school sp. needs (ISBN 0-913935-28-X). Bk. II, gr. 6-9 & high school sp. needs (ISBN 0-913935-29-8). ERA-CCR.

Rewriting English: The Politics of Gender & Class. Janet Batsleer et al. (New Accents Ser.). 160p. 1986. text ed. 25.00 (ISBN 0-416-38930-9, 9473); pap. text ed. 11.95 (ISBN 0-416-38940-6, 9474). Routledge Chapman & Hall.

Rewriting History: The Original & Revised World War II Diaries of Curt Prufer, Nazi Diplomat. Ed. by Donald M. McKale. Tr. by Judith M. Melton. LC 88-12034. 350p. 1988. 24.00x (ISBN 0-87338-364-8). Kent St U Pr.

Rewriting Nursing History. Ed. by Celia Davies. 226p. 1980. 28.50x (ISBN 0-389-20153-7). B&N Imports.

Rewriting Techniques & Applications. J. P. Jouannaud. (Lecture Notes in Computer Science: Vol. 202). vi, 441p. 1985. pap. 25.00 (ISBN 0-387-15976-2). Springer-Verlag.

Rewriting Techniques & Applications. Ed. by Jean-Pierre Jouannaud. 216p. 1988. pap. 25.00 (ISBN 0-12-390960-0). Acad Pr.

Rewriting Techniques & Applications. Ed. by P. Lescanne. (Lecture Notes in Computer Science Ser.: Vol. 256). vi, 285p. 1987. pap. 23.10 (ISBN 0-387-17220-3). Springer-Verlag.

Rewriting the Book. H. R. Coursen. Ed. by Napoleon St. Cyr. 48p. (Orig.). 1987. pap. 4.50 (ISBN 0-910380-06-6). Cider Mill.

Rewriting the Renaissance: The Discourses of Sexual Difference in Early Modern Europe. Ed. by Margaret W. Ferguson et al. LC 85-28829. (Illus.). 464p. 1986. 50.00x (ISBN 0-226-24313-3); pap. 15.95 (ISBN 0-226-24314-1). U of Chicago Pr.

Rewriting Writing: A Rhetoric. Jo Ray McCuen & Anthony C. Winkler. 438p. 1987. text ed. 13.00 (ISBN 0-15-576716-X); instr's. manual 2.00 (ISBN 0-15-576717-8). HarBraceJ.

Rewriting Writing: A Rhetoric & Handbook. Jo R. McCuen & Anthony C. Winkler. 531p. 1987. text ed. 14.00 net (ISBN 0-15-576718-6, HC). HarBraceJ.

Rewyll of Seynt Sauiore & Other Middle English Brigittine Legislative Texts, Vol. 2. James Hogg. 176p. (Orig.). 1978. pap. 16.00 (ISBN 3-7052-0256-1, Pub. by Salzburg Studies). Longwood Pub Group.

Rhetoric in Classical Historiography. A. J. Woodman. 224p. 1988. lib. bdg. 37.50 (ISBN 0-7099-5256-2, Pub. by Croom Helm UK). Routledge Chapman & Hall.
Rhetoric in Classical Historiography: Four Studies. A. J. Woodman. 236p. 1988. text ed. 37.95x (ISBN 0-918400-07-4). Areopagitica.
Rhetoric in Greco-Roman Education. Donald L. Clark. LC 77-21723. 1977. Repr. of 1957 ed. lib. bdg. 59.50x (ISBN 0-8371-9790-2, CLRH). Greenwood.
Rhetoric in Spenser's Poetry. Herbert D. Rix. 1978. Repr. of 1940 ed. lib. bdg. 19.50 (ISBN 0-8495-4523-4). Arden Lib.
Rhetoric in Spenser's Poetry. Herbert D. Rix. 88p. 1980. Repr. of 1940 ed. lib. bdg. 15.00 (ISBN 0-89987-712-5). Darby Bks.
Rhetoric in Spenser's Poetry. Herbert D. Rix. LC 73-7577. 1940. lib. bdg. 17.00 (ISBN 0-8414-2572-8). Folcroft.
Rhetoric in the Classical Tradition. Winifred B. Horner. LC 87-60578. 512p. 1988. text ed. write for info. (ISBN 0-312-00252-1); write for info. instr's. manual (ISBN 0-312-00253-X). St Martin.
Rhetoric in the Middle Ages: A History of Phetorical Theory from Saint Augustine to the Renaissance. James J. Murphy. 1974. pap. 12.95x (ISBN 0-520-04406-1). U of Cal Pr.
Rhetoric in the Plays of Thomas Dekker. Suzanne Blow. Ed. by James Hogg. (Jacobean Drama Studies). 138p. (Orig.). 1972. pap. 15.00 (ISBN 3-7052-0302-9, Pub. by Salzburg Studies). Longwood Pub Group.
Rhetoric in Transition: Studies in the Nature & Uses of Rhetoric. Ed. by Eugene E. White. LC 79-15061. 1980. text ed. 24.50x (ISBN 0-271-00223-9). Pa St U Pr.
Rhetoric, Literature, & Interpretation. Ed. by Harry Garvin. LC 83-2553. (Bucknell Review Ser.: Vol. 28, No. 2). (Illus.). 184p. 1983. 16.50 (ISBN 0-8387-5057-5). Bucknell U Pr.
Rhetoric Made Plain. 5th ed. Anthony C. Winkler & JoRay McCuen. 555p. 1988. text ed. 17.00 (ISBN 0-15-577081-0, HC); instr's. manual 1.50 (ISBN 0-15-577082-9). HarBraceJ.
Rhetoric of Agitation & Control. John W. Bowers & Donovan J. Ochs. 152p. 1971. pap. text ed. 8.00 (ISBN 0-394-34965-2, RanC). Random.
Rhetoric of American Politics: A Study of Documents. William R. Smith. 1970. lib. bdg. 56.95x (ISBN 0-8371-1495-0, SMA/). Greenwood.
Rhetoric of American Romance: Dialectic & Identity in Emerson, Dickinson, Poe, & Hawthorne. Evan Carton. LC 84-27770. 304p. 1985. text ed. 32.50x (ISBN 0-8018-2544-X). Johns Hopkins.
Rhetoric of Aristotle, 2 vols. in 1. Aristotle. Ed. by John E. Sandys. LC 72-9304. (Philosophy of Plato & Aristotle Ser.). (Gr. & Eng.). Repr. of 1877 ed. 55.00 (ISBN 0-405-04858-0). Ayer Co Pubs.
Rhetoric of Aristotle. Tr. by Lane Cooper. (Orig.). 1960. pap. text ed. write for info. (ISBN 0-13-780692-2). P-H.
Rhetoric of Aristotle with a Commentary, 3 vols. E. M. Cope. Ed. by J. E. Sandys. (Classical Studies Ser.). (Gr. & Eng.). Repr. of 1877 ed. Set. lib. bdg. 177.00 (ISBN 0-89197-922-0); Vol. 1. lib. bdg. 59.00 (ISBN 0-697-00033-8); Vol. 2. lib. bdg. 59.00 (ISBN 0-697-00034-6); Vol. 3. lib. bdg. 59.00 (ISBN 0-697-00035-4). Irvington.
Rhetoric of Black Power. Compiled by Robert L. Scott & Wayne Brockriede. LC 78-31755. 1979. Repr. of 1969 ed. lib. bdg. 35.00x (ISBN 0-313-20973-1, SCRB). Greenwood.
Rhetoric of Chin p'ing mei. Katherine Carlitz. LC 85-45576. (Studies in Chinese Literature & Society). 256p. 1986. 20.00x (ISBN 0-253-35009-3). Ind U Pr.
Rhetoric of Christian Socialism. Paul H. Boase. 9.00 (ISBN 0-8446-0501-8). Peter Smith.
Rhetoric of Confession. Edward Fowler. 1988. 32.50 (ISBN 0-520-06064-4). U of Cal Pr.
Rhetoric of Conservatism: The Virginia Convention of 1829-30 & the Conservative Tradition in the South. Dickson D. Bruce, Jr. LC 82-9224. 218p. 1982. 22.95 (ISBN 0-87328-121-7). Huntington Lib.
Rhetoric of Cultural Pluralism vs. the Drive Toward Total Assimilation: The Mexican American Cultural Component of Federally Funded Bilingual Projects. Worth L. Nicholl. LC 78-64358. 1978. soft cover 12.95 (ISBN 0-88247-545-2). R & E Pubs.
Rhetoric of Doubtful Authority: Deconstructive Readings of Self-Questioning Narratives, St. Augustine to Faulkner. Ralph Flores. LC 83-15297. 176p. 1984. 22.50x (ISBN 0-8014-1625-6). Cornell U Pr.
Rhetoric of Dreams. Bert O. States. LC 88-47766. (Illus.). 240p. 1988. 22.50x (ISBN 0-8014-2198-5). Cornell U Pr.
Rhetoric of Economics. Donald N. McCloskey. LC 85-40373. (Rhetoric of the Human Sciences Ser.). 209p. 1985. text ed. 21.50x (ISBN 0-299-10380-3). U of Wis Pr.
Rhetoric of Economics. Donald N. McCloskey. LC 85-40373. (Rhetoric of the Human Sciences Ser.). 232p. 1987. pap. text ed. 12.95x (ISBN 0-299-10384-6). U of Wis Pr.
Rhetoric of Everyday English Texts. Michael P. Jordan. (Illus.). 192p. 1984. text ed. 34.95x (ISBN 0-04-420047-1); pap. text ed. 11.95x (ISBN 0-04-420048-X). Unwin Hyman.
Rhetoric of Fiction. 2nd ed. Wayne C. Booth. LC 82-13592. 1983. pap. 30.00x (ISBN 0-226-06556-1, Phoen). U of Chicago Pr.
Rhetoric of Fiction. 2nd ed. Wayne C. Booth. 576p. 1983. pap. 12.95x (ISBN 0-226-06558-8). U of Chicago Pr.
Rhetoric of History. Savoie Lottinville. LC 75-19418. 272p. 1976. 15.95x (ISBN 0-8061-1330-8). U of Okla Pr.
Rhetoric of Humanism: Spanish Culture After Ortega y Gasset. Thomas Mermall. LC 76-45293. 1976. lib. bdg. 15.00x (ISBN 0-916950-02-6); pap. 10.00x (ISBN 0-916950-16-6). Biling Rev-Pr.
Rhetoric of Imitation: Genre & Poetic Memory in Virgil & Other Latin Poets. Gian B. Conte. Ed. & tr. by Charles Segal. LC 85-24316. (Studies in Classical Philology). 224p. 1986. 24.95x (ISBN 0-8014-1733-3). Cornell U Pr.
Rhetoric of Interpersonal Communication. Marcus L. Ambrester & Glynis Holm Strause. 336p. (Orig.). 1984. pap. text ed. 14.95x (ISBN 0-88133-036-1). Waveland Pr.
Rhetoric of Irony. Wayne C. Booth. LC 73-87298. xviii, 292p. 1975. 20.00x (ISBN 0-226-06552-9); pap. 12.95x (ISBN 0-226-06553-7, P641). U of Chicago Pr.
Rhetoric of John Donne's Verse. W. F. Melton. 59.95 (ISBN 0-8490-0953-7). Gordon Pr.
Rhetoric of Joseph Conrad. James L. Guetti, Jr. LC 76-18209. Repr. of 1860 ed. lib. bdg. 17.00 (ISBN 0-8414-4542-7). Folcroft.
Rhetoric of Leviathan: Thomas Hobbes & the Politics of Cultural Transformation. David Johnston. (Studies in Moral, Political, & Legal Philosophy). 256p. 1986. text ed. 25.00x (ISBN 0-691-07717-7). Princeton U Pr.
Rhetoric of Literary Character: Some Women of Henry James. Mary D. Springer. LC 78-6699. 1978. lib. bdg. 21.00x (ISBN 0-226-76983-6). U of Chicago Pr.
Rhetoric of Love: Das Menschenbild und die Form des Romans bei Iris Murdoch. Wolfram Volker. (Bochum Studies in English: No. 6). vi, 168p. (Orig.). 1978. pap. 25.00x (ISBN 90-6032-099-9, Pub by B R Gruener Amsterdam). Benjamins North Am.
Rhetoric of Love in Lyly's 'Euphues & His England' & Sydney's Arcadia' 1590. James Eugene O'Hara. Ed. by James Hogg. (Elizabethan & Renaissance Studies). 159p. (Orig.). 1978. pap. 15.00 (ISBN 3-7052-0720-2, Pub. by Salzburg Studies). Longwood Pub Group.
Rhetoric of Menachem Begin: The Myth of Redemption Through Return. Robert C. Rowland. 330p. (Orig.). 1985. lib. bdg. 31.00 (ISBN 0-8191-4735-4); pap. text ed. 15.50 (ISBN 0-8191-4736-2). U Pr of Amer.
Rhetoric of Motives. Kenneth Burke. LC 69-16742. 1969. pap. 10.95x (ISBN 0-520-01546-0). U of Cal Pr.
Rhetoric of Oratory. Edwin D. Shurter. 1978. Repr. of 1909 ed. lib. bdg. 35.00 (ISBN 0-8495-4860-8). Arden Lib.
Rhetoric of Poetry in the Renaissance & Seventeenth Century. John P. Houston. LC 82-17227. 344p. 1983. text ed. 37.50 (ISBN 0-8071-1066-3). La State U Pr.
Rhetoric of Protest & Reform, 1878-1898. Ed. by Paul H. Boase. LC 80-11631. viii, 354p. 1980. 18.00x (ISBN 0-8214-0421-0). Ohio U Pr.
Rhetoric of Religion: Studies in Logology. Kenneth Burke. 1970. pap. 11.95x (ISBN 0-520-01610-6). U of Cal Pr.
Rhetoric of Renaissance Poetry from Wyatt to Milton. Ed. by Thomas O. Sloan & Raymond B. Waddington. LC 73-80824. 1974. 32.50x (ISBN 0-520-02501-6). U of Cal Pr.
Rhetoric of Romanticism. Paul DeMan. LC 84-3213. 300p. 1984. 30.00x (ISBN 0-231-05526-9). Columbia U Pr.
Rhetoric of Romanticism. Paul De Man. LC 84-3213. 327p. 1986. pap. 14.50 (ISBN 0-231-05527-7). Columbia U Pr.
Rhetoric of Space: Literary & Artistic Representations of Landscape in Republican & Augustan Rome. Eleanor Leach. (Illus.). 552p. 1988. 75.00 (ISBN 0-691-04237-3). Princeton U Pr.
Rhetoric of the Arts 1550-1650, Vol. 3. Gerard G. Lecoat. (European Universtiy Studies: Series 18, Comparative Literature Vol. 6). 208p. 1975. pap. 26.75 (ISBN 3-261-01689-2). P Lang Pubs.
Rhetoric of the Contemporary Lyric. Jonathan Holden. LC 79-3383. 160p. 1980. 15.00x (ISBN 0-253-15667-X). Ind U Pr.
Rhetoric of the Human Sciences: Language & Argument in Scholarship & Public Affairs. John Nelson et al. LC 86-34030. (Rhetoric of the Human Sciences Ser.). (Illus.). 408p. 1987. text ed. 24.00x (ISBN 0-299-11020-6). U of Wis Pr.
Rhetoric of the Unreal: Studies in Narrative & Structure, Especially of the Fantastic. Christine Brooke-Rose. LC 80-41720. 380p. 1981. 62.50 (ISBN 0-521-22561-2). Cambridge U Pr.
Rhetoric of the Unreal: Studies in Narrative & Structure, Especially of the Fantastic. Christine Brooke-Rose. LC 80-41720. 446p. 1983. pap. 18.95 (ISBN 0-521-27656-X). Cambridge U Pr.
Rhetoric of Valery's Prose Aubades. Ursula Franklin. LC 78-13044. pap. 42.00 (ISBN 0-317-55687-8, 2029330). Bks Demand UMI.
Rhetoric of Western Thought. 3rd ed. James L. Golden et al. 1982. pap. text ed. 18.95 (ISBN 0-8403-2916-4, 40291601). Kendall Hunt.
Rhetoric, Philosophy, & Literature: An Exploration. Ed. by Don M. Burks. LC 77-92712. 128p. 1978. 7.50 (ISBN 0-911198-52-0). Purdue U Pr.
Rhetoric, Prudence, & Skepticism in the Renaissance. Victoria Kahn. LC 84-21362. 248p. 1985. 27.50x (ISBN 0-8014-1736-8). Cornell U Pr.
Rhetoric Revalued: Papers from the International Society for the History of Rhetoric. Ed. by Brian Vickers. LC 82-12447. (Medieval & Renaissance Texts & Studies: Vol. 19). 288p. 1982. 16.00 (ISBN 0-86698-020-2). Medieval & Renaissance NY.
Rhetoric, Romance & Technology: Studies in the Interaction of Expression & Culture. Walter J. Ong. LC 74-153722. 358p. 1971. 37.50x (ISBN 0-8014-0645-5). Cornell U Pr.
Rhetoric Three: The Rhetoric Section from Rhetoric in a Modern Mode. 3rd ed. James K. Bell & Adrian Cohn. 1976. pap. text ed. write for info. (ISBN 0-02-470620-5). Macmillan.
Rhetorica, 2 vols. Cicero. Ed. by A. S. Wilkins. Incl. Vol. 1. Libros De Oratore Tres. 1903. 18.95x (ISBN 0-19-814615-9); Vol. 2. Brutus, Orator, De Optimo Genere Oratorum, Partitiones Oratoriae, Topica. 1935. 18.95x (ISBN 0-19-814616-7). (Oxford Classical Texts Ser). Oxford U Pr.
Rhetorica ad Alexandrum see Problems, Bks 22-38.
Rhetorical Act. Karlyn K. Campbell. 310p. 1982. text ed. write for info. (ISBN 0-534-01008-3). Wadsworth Pub.
Rhetorical Analysis. John F. Genung. 1897. 10.00 (ISBN 0-8274-3277-1). R West.
Rhetorical Analysis of under the Volcano: Malcolm Lowry's Design Governing Postures. Dana Grove. (Studies in British Literature: Vol. 2). 170p. 1988. lib. bdg. 39.95 (ISBN 0-88946-929-6). E Mellen.
Rhetorical Approach to College Reading & Study Skills. Joan Kimmelman et al. 256p. 1984. pap. text ed. write for info. (ISBN 0-02-364070-7). Macmillan.
Rhetorical Considerations. 4th ed. Harry Brent & William Lutz. 1983. write for info. (ISBN 0-673-39198-1). Scott F.
Rhetorical Criticism: A Study in Method. Edwin Black. LC 77-91050. 1978. pap. text ed. 11.95x (ISBN 0-299-07554-0). U of Wis Pr.
Rhetorical Criticism: Essays in Honor of James Muilenburg. Ed. by Jared J. Jackson & Martin Kessler. LC 74-22493. (Pittsburgh Theological Monographs: No. 1). 1974. pap. 9.50 (ISBN 0-915138-00-X). Pickwick.
Rhetorical Dimensions in Criticism. Donald C. Bryant. LC 72-94149. x, 146p. 1973. 17.50x (ISBN 0-8071-0214-8). La State U Pr.
Rhetorical Dimensions in Media: A Critical Casebook. Martin J. Medhurst & Thomas W. Benson. 496p. 1984. 32.95 (ISBN 0-8403-4067-2). Kendall Hunt.
Rhetorical Elements in the Tragedies of Seneca. Howard V. Canter. Repr. of 1925 ed. 15.00 (ISBN 0-384-07325-5). Johnson Repr.
Rhetorical Form of Carlyle's Sartor Resartus. Gerry H. Brookes. LC 71-185974. 208p. 1972. 35.00x (ISBN 0-520-02213-0). U of Cal Pr.
Rhetorical Models for Effective Writing. 3rd ed. J. Karl Nicholas & James R. Nicholl. 1985. pap. text ed. write for info. (ISBN 0-673-39230-9). Scott F.
Rhetorical Patterns: An Anthology of Contemporary Essays. John P. Ferre & Steven E. Pauley. (Illus.). 208p. 1981. pap. text ed. 13.95 (ISBN 0-675-08023-1). Merrill.
Rhetorical Poetics: Theory & Practice of Figural & Symbolic Reading in Modern French Literature. Donald Rice & Peter Schofer. LC 83-47768. 256p. 1983. text ed. 22.50x (ISBN 0-299-09440-5). U of Wis Pr.
Rhetorical Presidency. Jeffrey K. Tulis. 208p. 1987. text ed. 19.95 (ISBN 0-691-07751-7); pap. 9.95 (ISBN 0-691-02295-X). Princeton U Pr.
Rhetorical Reader for ESL Students. Caroline B. Raphael. 384p. 1983. text ed. write for info. (ISBN 0-02-398300-0). Macmillan.
Rhetorical Stance in Modern Literature: Allegories of Love & Death. Lynette Hunter. LC 83-40546. 140p. 1984. 19.95 (ISBN 0-312-68087-2). St Martin.
Rhetorical Studies Honoring James L. Golden. Lawrence W. Hugenberg. 224p. 1986. pap. text ed. 22.95 (ISBN 0-8403-4142-3). Kendall Hunt.
Rhetorical Town. Sebastian Barry. 1985. pap. 10.95 (ISBN 0-85105-426-9, Pub. by Colin Smythe Ltd Britain). Dufour.
Rhetorical Tradition & Modern Writing. James J. Murphy et al. LC 82-2103. 141p. 1982. 20.00 (ISBN 0-87352-097-1); pap. 16.50 (ISBN 0-87352-098-X). Modern Lang.
Rhetorical Traditions & the Teaching of Writing. C. H. Knoblauch & Lil Brannon. 192p. (Orig.). 1984. pap. text ed. 12.50x (ISBN 0-86709-105-3). Boynton Cook Pubs.
Rhetorical World of Augustan Humanism: Ethics & Imagery from Swift to Burke. Paul Fussell. LC 66-1724. pap. 82.50 (ISBN 0-317-29155-6, 2055599). Bks Demand UMI.
Rhetorics of Popular Culture: Advertising, Advocacy & Entertainment. Robert L. Root, Jr. LC 86-14974. (Contributions to the Study of Popular Culture Ser.: No. 16). 192p. 1987. lib. bdg. 29.95 (ISBN 0-313-24403-0). Greenwood.
Rhetorics of Reason & Desire: Vergil, Augustine, & the Troubadours. Sarah Spence. LC 87-47953. (Illus.). 192p. 1988. 22.50x (ISBN 0-8014-2129-2). Cornell U Pr.
Rhetorics of Thomas Hobbes & Bernard Lamy. John T. Harwood. (Landmarks in Rhetoric & Public Address Ser.). 320p. (Orig.). 1986. text ed. 19.95x (ISBN 0-8093-1301-4); pap. text ed. 10.95x (ISBN 0-8093-1302-2). S Ill U Pr.
Rheumatic & Metabolic Bone Diseases in the Elderly. David F. Giansiracusa & Fred G. Kantrowitz. LC 79-57515. (Illus.). 240p. 1981. 25.95 (ISBN 0-669-03630-7, Collamore). Heath.
Rheumatic & Skin Disease. Wyrnn Smith. (Profile of Health & Disease in America Ser.). (Illus.). 142p. 1988. 35.00x (ISBN 0-8160-1456-6). Facts on File.
Rheumatic Disease. H. Capell et al. (Treatment in Clinical Medicine Ser.). (Illus.). 210p. 1983. pap. 19.00 (ISBN 0-387-12622-8). Springer-Verlag.
Rheumatic Disease. M. H. Weisman. text ed. cancelled (ISBN 0-443-08100-X). Churchill.
Rheumatic Diseases. Terry Gibson. (Illus.). 216p. 1986. pap. text ed. 18.95 (ISBN 0-407-00315-0). Butterworth.
Rheumatic Diseases. M. E. Shipley. (Pocket Picture Guides to Clincial Medicine Ser.). 100p. 1984. text ed. 9.95 (ISBN 0-683-07699-X). Williams & Wilkins.
Rheumatic Diseases. M. E. Shipley. (Pocket Picture Guides for Nurses Ser.). 100p. 1984. text ed. 9.95 (ISBN 0-683-07700-7). Williams & Wilkins.
Rheumatic Diseases: Rehabilitation & Management. Ed. by Gail K. Riggs & Eric P. Gall. (Illus.). 480p. 1984. text ed. 39.95 (ISBN 0-409-95051-3). Butterworth.
Rheumatic Disorders in Children. Barbara M. Ansell. LC 80-40275. (Postgraduate Paediatrics Ser.). (Illus.). 344p. 1980. text ed. 90.00 (ISBN 0-407-00186-7). Butterworth.
Rheumatic Fever. 2nd ed. Milton Markowitz & Leon Gordis. LC 72-82808. (Major Problems in Clinical Pediatrics: Vol. 2). pap. 81.80 (ISBN 0-317-26114-2, 2024997). Bks Demand UMI.
Rheumatic Fever: A Guide to Its Recognition, Prevention & Cure. A. Taranta & M. Markowitz. 1981. pap. 15.00 (ISBN 0-85200-431-1, Pub by MTP Pr England). Kluwer Academic.
Rheumatic Fever: A Symposium Held At the Univesity of Minnesota on November 29, 30, & December 1, 1951. Minnesota Heart Association. Ed. by Lewis Thomas. LC 52-11108. pap. 89.80 (ISBN 0-317-29474-1, 2055922). Bks Demand UMI.
Rheumatic Therapeutics. Ed. by S. H. Roth et al. (Illus.). 550p. 1985. text ed. 45.00 (ISBN 0-07-054010-1). McGraw.
Rheumatoid Arthritis. 2nd ed. D. Gordon. (Contemporary Patient Management Ser.: Vol. 10). 1985. 31.25 (ISBN 0-87488-380-6). Med Exam.
Rheumatoid Arthritis. Ed. by Morris Ziff et al. (Advances in Inflammation Research Ser.: Vol. 3). 365p. 1982. text ed. 80.00 (ISBN 0-89004-657-3). Raven.
Rheumatoid Arthritis - The Treatment Controversy: Proceedings of the Meeting Held at Stratford-on-Avon, March 9-10, 1984. Ed. by David Goddard & Robin Butler. 166p. 1986. pap. text ed. 23.50x (ISBN 0-333-41920-0, Pub. by Macmillan Educ Ltd UK). Sheridan Med Bks.
Rheumatoid Arthritis: An Illustrated Guide to Pathogenesis, Diagnosis & Management. Ralph Schumacher & Eric Gall. LC 65-40264. (Illus.). 260p. 1988. 65.00 (ISBN 0-397-44653-5, Lippincott Medical). Lippincott.
Rheumatoid Arthritis: Diagnosis & Comprehensive Management. Norman O. Rothermich & Ronald L. Whisler. (Manuals of Clinical Medicine Ser.). 288p. 1985. 26.50 (ISBN 0-8089-1716-1, 793665). Grune.
Rheumatoid Arthritis: Etiology, Diagnosis, Management. Peter D. Utsinger et al. LC 65-7503. 960p. 1985. text ed. 79.00 (ISBN 0-397-50588-4, Lippincott Medical). Lippincott.
Rheumatoid Arthritis: Its Cause & Its Treatment. Thomas M. Brown & Henry Scammell. 256p. 1988. 16.95 (ISBN 0-87131-543-2). M Evans.
Rheumatoid Arthritis of the Hand & Wrist. Strickland. (Illus.). 480p. 1990. 150.00 (ISBN 0-8016-4282-5). Mosby.
Rheumatoid Arthritis Surgery of the Complex Hand & Foot. Ed. by F. W. Hagena. (Rheumatology Ser.: Vol. 11). (Illus.). xiv, 190p. 1987. 118.00 (ISBN 3-8055-4408-1). S Karger.
Rheumatoid Arthritis Surgery of the Shoulder. Ed. by A. W. Lattin & C. Peterson. (Rheumatology. the Interdisciplinary Concept Ser.: Vol. 12). (Illus.). x, 200p. 1988. 120.00 (ISBN 3-8055-4804-4). S Karger.

Rheumatoid Diseases Cured at Last. 3rd ed. Anthony Di Fabio. LC 82-72042. (Illus.). 136p. (Orig.). 1984. pap. 15.00 (ISBN 0-931150-12-4). Rheumatoid.

Rheumatological Medicine. Paul A. Dieppe et al. LC 84-17070. (Illus.). 522p. 1985. text ed. 101.75 (ISBN 0-443-02524-X). Churchill.

Rheumatological Physical Examination. Hugh Little. 160p. 1986. 42.50 (ISBN 0-8089-1824-9, 792577). Grune.

Rheumatologie fuer die Praxis. H. J. Albrecht. (Unveraenderte Auflage: Vol. 2). (Illus.). 1979. pap. 27.50 (ISBN 3-8055-3047-1). S Karger.

Rheumatology. H. Berry & Asm Jawad. 1985. lib. bdg. 20.75 (ISBN 0-85200-900-3, Pub. by MTP Pr England). Kluwer Academic.

Rheumatology. David M. Grennan. (Illus.). 255p. 1984. pap. write for info. (ISBN 0-7216-0962-7, Bailliere-Tindall). Saunders.

Rheumatology. Ed. by H. Hall. (New Medicine Ser.). 1986. lib. bdg. 21.25 (ISBN 0-85200-400-1, Pub. by MTP Pr England). Kluwer Academic.

Rheumatology. J. M. Moll. (Colour Aids Ser.). (Illus.). 106p. (Orig.). 1984. pap. text ed. 12.00 (ISBN 0-443-02882-6). Churchill.

Rheumatology & Immunology. 2nd ed. Alan S. Cohen. 544p. 1986. 79.50 (ISBN 0-8089-1809-5, 790874). Grune.

Rheumatology & Rehabilitation: Diagnosis & Management. Ed. by Hedley Berry et al. (Illus.). 266p. 1983. text ed. 35.00x (ISBN 0-7099-0678-1, Pub. by Croom Helm England); pap. text ed. 19.95x (ISBN 0-7099-3204-9). Sheridan.

Rheumatology Disease Process - Focus on Piroxicam. Ed. by R. G. Richardson. (International Congress & Symposium Ser.: No. 67). 104p. 1985. pap. 15.00 (ISBN 1-85315-033-9, Pub. by Royal Society of Medicine Services Ltd). Longwood Pub Group.

Rheumatology Disorders. Lawrence F. Layfer et al. (Illus.). 208p. 1988. 29.50 (ISBN 0-7216-2385-9). Saunders.

Rheumatology for GPs. H. L. Curry & Sally Hull. (Oxford General Practice Ser.: No. 11). (Illus.). 272p. 1987. pap. 33.95 (ISBN 0-19-261657-9). Oxford U Pr.

Rheumatology Nursing: A Problem-Oriented Approach. Janice S. Pigg et al. LC 84-19551. 462p. 1985. 26.95 (ISBN 0-471-05301-5, Pub. by Wiley Med). Wiley.

Rheumatology-85. Ed. by P. M. Brooks & J. R. York. 486p. 1986. 152.00 (ISBN 0-444-80734-9, Excerpta Medica). Elsevier.

Rhialto the Marvelous. Jack Vance. 224p. 1984. 12.95 (ISBN 0-671-55911-7, Baen Enterprises). S&S.

Rhiannon. Roberta Gellis. (Roselynde Chronicles Ser.). 1984. lib. bdg. 13.95 (ISBN 0-8398-2864-0, Gregg). G K Hall.

Rhind Mathematical Papyrus. LC 78-23203. (Classics in Mathematics Education Ser.: Vol. 8). (Illus.). 160p. 1979. Repr. 17.00 (ISBN 0-87353-133-7). NCTM.

Rhine. C. A. R. Hills. LC 78-62989. (Rivers of the World Ser.). (Illus.). 68p. 1978. PLB 14.96 (ISBN 0-382-06202-7). Silver.

Rhine. Karl-Wilhelm Koch & Gustav Rohr. (Illus.). 200p. (Ger. & Eng.). 1987. 45.00 (ISBN 3-88490-162-1, Pub. by Rohr-Vlg BRD). Seven Hills Bks.

Rhine. (Panorama Bks.). (Illus., Fr.). 3.95 (ISBN 0-685-11529-1). French & Eur.

Rhine Flows into the Tiber: A History of Vatican II. Ralph M. Wiltgen. LC 82-50583. 304p. pap. 8.00 (ISBN 0-89555-186-1). Tan Bks Pubs.

Rhine Journey. Ann Schlee. 1983. pap. 3.95 (ISBN 0-14-006215-7). Penguin.

Rhine, Mosel & Eifel. (New Visitor's Guides). 240p. 1988. 9.95 (ISBN 1-55650-075-0). Hunter Pub NY.

Rhine Pollution: Legal, Economic & Technical Aspects, La Pollution Du Rhin, Aspects Juridiques, Economiques et Techniques. R. Hueting & C. Van Der Veen. 136p. 1978. pap. 16.00 (ISBN 90-27-1146-92, Pub. by Kluwer Law Netherlands). Kluwer Academic.

Rhine Valley Travel Guide. (Berlitz Travel Guides). (Illus.). 1982. pap. 4.95 (ISBN 0-02-969450-7, Berlitz). Macmillan.

Rhinegold. Richard Wagner. Ed. by Nicholas John. Tr. by Andrew Porter from Ger. LC 85-52161. (English National Opera - the Royal Opera House Opera Guide Ser.: No. 35, Libretto, Articles). (Illus.). 96p. (Orig.). 1986. pap. 5.95 (ISBN 0-7145-4078-1). Riverrun NY.

Rhinelander Center. Barbara Harrison. 464p. (Orig.). 1981. pap. 2.75 (ISBN 0-89083-704-X). Zebra.

Rhinelander Pavilion. Barbara Harrison. (Orig.). 1980. pap. 2.50 (ISBN 0-89083-572-1). Zebra.

Rhinemann Exchange. Robert Ludlum. 448p. 1975. pap. 4.95 (ISBN 0-440-15079-5). Dell.

Rhinestone Sharecropping. Bill Gunn. LC 81-52032. 194p. (Orig.). 1981. pap. 5.95 (ISBN 0-918408-19-9). Reed & Cannon.

Rhinitis. Ed. by Guy A. Settipane. (Illus.). 170p. 1984. text ed. 48.00 (ISBN 0-936587-00-8). New Eng & Reg All.

Rhino Ritz: An American Mystery. Keith Abbott. LC 78-23542. 1979. 19.95 (ISBN 0-912652-42-X, Dynamite Bks); pap. 9.95 (ISBN 0-912652-43-8); signed ed. 29.95x (ISBN 0-912652-44-6). Blue Wind.

Rhinoceros. Eugene Ionesco. (Folio Ser.: No. 816). 1959. pap. 6.95 (ISBN 0-685-11530-5). Schoenhof.

Rhinoceros. Eugene Ionesco. 1959. write for info. French & Eur.

Rhinoceros. L. Martin. (Wildlife in Danger Ser.). (Illus.). 24p. (gr. k-5). Date not set. PLB 11.33 (ISBN 0-86592-997-1). Rourke Corp.

Rhinoceros see Theatre.

Rhinoceros & Other Plays. Eugene Ionesco. Tr. by Derek Prouse. 15.75 (ISBN 0-8446-2293-1). Peter Smith.

Rhinoceros & Other Plays: The Leader, The Future Is in Eggs. Eugene Ionesco. Tr. by Derek Prouse from Fr. 1960. pap. 6.95 (ISBN 0-394-17226-4, E259, Ever). Grove.

Rhinoceros & Other Plays: The Leader, The Future Is in Eggs, It Takes All Kinds to Make a World. Eugene Ionesco. Tr. by Derek Prouse. 142p. (Orig.). Date not set. pap. 7.95 (ISBN 0-8021-3098-4). Grove.

Rhinoceros Bound: Cluny in the Tenth Century. Barbara H. Rosenwein. LC 81-43525. (Middle Ages Ser.). 192p. 1982. 27.95x (ISBN 0-8122-7830-5). U of Pa Pr.

Rhinoceros from Durer to Stubbs: An Aspect of the Exotic. T. H. Clark. LC 86-50086. (Illus.). 216p. 1988. 29.95 (ISBN 0-85667-322-6, Pub. by P Wilson Pubs). Sotheby Pubns.

Rhinoceros Horn & Other Early Buddhist Poems (Sutta-Nipata) The Group of Discourses, Vol. I. Tr. by K. R. Norman et al. (Pali Text Translation Ser.). 384p. 1986. pap. text ed. 9.95 (ISBN 0-86013-154-8). Routledge Chapman & Hall.

Rhinoceros in the Classroom. R. Murray Schafer. 1975. pap. 12.00 (ISBN 0-900938-44-7, UE26922). Eur-Am Music.

Rhinoceros Success. 25th ed. Scott Alexander. LC 80-51648. (Illus.). 123p. (Orig.). (gr. 1 up). 1985. pap. 5.95 (ISBN 0-937382-00-0). Rhinos Pr.

Rhinoceros Wakes Me up in the Morning. Peter Goodspeed. (Picture Puffin Ser.). (Illus.). 32p. (ps-k). 1984. pap. 3.95 (ISBN 0-14-050455-9, Puffin). Penguin.

Rhinocerotic Relativity. 5th ed. Scott R. Alexander. LC 83-60933. (Illus.). 120p. (Orig.). 1985. pap. 5.95 (ISBN 0-937382-02-7). Rhinos Pr.

Rhinoplasty - Emphasizing the External Approach. Jack R. Anderson. Ed. by Russel Ries. (American Academy of Facial Plastic & Reconstructive Surgery Monograph: Vol. 3). (Illus.). 177p. 1986. text ed. 55.00 (ISBN 0-86577-238-X). Thieme Med Pubs.

Rhinoplasty & Other Nasal Surgery. Berman. (Illus.). 400p. 1988. text ed. 99.95 (ISBN 0-8016-0623-3). Mosby.

Rhinoplasty Problems & Controversies: A Discussion with the Experts. Rees & Baker. 1986. 80.00 (ISBN 0-8016-4111-X). Mosby.

Rhinos. Wildlife Education Staff et al. (Zoobooks Ser.). (Illus.). 20p. (Orig.). (gr. 1-8). 1985. pap. 1.95 (ISBN 0-937934-29-1). Wildlife Educ.

Rhinos: An Endangered Species. Malcolm Penny. LC 87-22360. (Illus.). 128p. 1988. 19.95 (ISBN 0-8160-1882-0); LTD. Ed. 1500.00. Facts on File.

Rhinos Don't Climb! Ruth Rosner. LC 83-47708. (Illus.). 32p. (ps-3). 1984. 12.70i (ISBN 0-06-025068-2); PLB 11.89g (ISBN 0-06-025069-0). HarpJ.

Rhinoviruses see Simian Viruses.

Rhizoctonia Solani: Biology & Pathology. Ed. by J. R. Parmeter. LC 69-16510. (Illus.). 1970. 46.50x (ISBN 0-520-01497-9). U of Cal Pr.

Rhizome & the Flower: The Perennial Philosophy--Yeats & Jung. James Olney. 1980. 42.00x (ISBN 0-520-03748-0). U of Cal Pr.

Rhizosphere. E. A. Curl & B. Truelove. (Agricultural Sciences Advanced Ser.: Vol. 15). (Illus.). 328p. 1985. 83.00 (ISBN 0-387-15803-0). Springer-Verlag.

Rhizosphere. Lynch. 1990. price not set (ISBN 0-471-61016-X). Wiley.

RHM; Robert Hunter Middleton: The Man & His Letters; Essays on His Life & Career. Ed. by Bruce Young & Bruce Beck. (Illus.). 1985. 25.00 (ISBN 0-940550-08-3). Caxton Club.

Rhoda, Straight & True. Roni Schotter. LC 86-107. 192p. (gr. 6 up). 1986. 10.25 (ISBN 0-688-06157-5). Lothrop.

Rhode Island. Allan Carpenter. LC 78-16446. (New Enchantment of America State Bks). (Illus.). 96p. (gr. 4 up). 1979. PLB 15.93 (ISBN 0-516-04139-8). Childrens.

Rhode Island. 1986. pap. 7.95 (ISBN 0-393-30271-7). Norton.

Rhode Island. Turner Programs Services, Inc. Staff et al. (Portrait of America Library). 48p. (gr. 4 up). 1986. PLB 15.33 (ISBN 0-86514-457-5); pap. text ed. 9.27 (ISBN 0-86514-532-6); Beta Video 113.33 (ISBN 0-86514-082-0); VHS Video 113.33 (ISBN 0-86514-157-6); 3-4" Video 136.00 (ISBN 0-86514-232-7); tchr. study guide 13.27 (ISBN 0-86514-307-2); student activity bk. 6.60 (ISBN 0-86514-382-X); Index 13.27. Raintree Pubs.

Rhode Island: A Bibliography of Its History. Ed. by Roger Parks. LC 83-50139. (Bibliographies of New England History Ser.: No. 5). 262p. 1983. 30.00x (ISBN 0-87451-284-0). U Pr of New Eng.

Rhode Island: A Guide to the Smallest State. Federal Writers' Project Staff. (American Guidebook Ser.). 500p. 1937. Repr. 69.00x (ISBN 0-403-02188-X). Somerset Pub.

Rhode Island: A History. William G. McLoughlin. (States and the Nation Ser.). (Illus.). 1978. 14.95 (ISBN 0-393-05675-9). Norton.

Rhode Island: A Scenic Discovery. Steve Dunwell. Ed. by James B. Patrick. (Scenic Discovery Ser.). 120p. 1983. Repr. of 1976 ed. 25.00 (ISBN 0-940078-03-1). Foremost Pubs.

Rhode Island: A Study in Separatism. Irving B. Richman. LC 72-3749. (American Commonwealths: No. 17). Repr. of 1905 ed. 35.00 (ISBN 0-404-57217-0). AMS Pr.

Rhode Island: Agency. suppl. 6.50 (ISBN 0-686-90882-1). Am Law Inst.

Rhode Island & the Formation of the Union. Frank G. Bates. LC 68-1297. (Columbia University Studies in the Social Sciences: No. 27). Repr. of 1898 ed. 16.50 (ISBN 0-404-51027-2). AMS Pr.

Rhode Island & the Union, 1774-1795. Irwin H. Polishook. LC 69-18021. (Studies in History Ser.: No. 5). pap. 70.00 (ISBN 0-8357-9469-5, 2013681). Bks Demand UMI.

Rhode Island Appellate Practice. Weisberger. 1980. 65.00 (ISBN 0-88063-068-X). Butterworth Legal Pubs.

Rhode Island Architecture. 2nd ed. Henry-Russell Hitchcock. LC 68-27725. (Architecture & Decorative Art Ser.: Vol. 19). (Illus.). 1968. Repr. of 1939 ed. lib. bdg. 42.50 (ISBN 0-306-71037-4). Da Capo.

Rhode Island Arms Makers & Gunsmiths: 1643-1883. William O. Achtermier. LC 80-84583. (Illus.). 108p. 1980. 16.50 (ISBN 0-917218-15-9). Mowbray.

Rhode Island Atlas. Marion I. Wright & Robert J. Sullivan. LC 80-52911. (Illus.). 239p. (Orig., Contains considerable text). 1983. 22.50 (ISBN 0-917012-52-6); pap. 12.95 (ISBN 0-917012-19-4). RI Pubns Soc.

Rhode Island Campaign of 1778: Inauspicious Dawn of Alliance. Paul F. Dearden. LC 78-68920. (Illus.). 169p. 1980. 6.95 (ISBN 0-917012-17-8). RI Pubns Soc.

Rhode Island Catholicism: A Historical Guide. Patrick T. Conley. 24p. (Orig.). 1984. pap. 2.95 (ISBN 0-917012-56-9). RI Pubns Soc.

Rhode Island Census Index 1790. Ronald V. Jackson. (Illus.). lib. bdg. 20.00 (ISBN 0-317-17066-X). Accelerated Index.

Rhode Island Census Index 1800. Ronald V. Jackson. LC 77-86085. (Illus.). lib. bdg. 26.00 (ISBN 0-89593-127-3). Accelerated Index.

Rhode Island Census Index: 1810. Ronald V. Jackson. LC 77-86092. (Illus.). lib. bdg. 23.00 (ISBN 0-89593-122-2). Accelerated Index.

Rhode Island Census Index 1820. Ronald V. Jackson. LC 77-86091. (Illus.). lib. bdg. 24.00 (ISBN 0-89593-123-0). Accelerated Index.

Rhode Island Census Index 1830. Ronald V. Jackson. LC 77-86092. (Illus.). lib. bdg. 26.00 (ISBN 0-89593-124-9). Accelerated Index.

Rhode Island Census Index 1840. Ronald V. Jackson. LC 77-86093. (Illus.). lib. bdg. 29.00 (ISBN 0-89593-125-7). Accelerated Index.

Rhode Island Census Index 1850. Ronald V. Jackson. LC 77-86084. (Illus.). lib. bdg. 42.00 (ISBN 0-89593-126-5). Accelerated Index.

Rhode Island Census Index, 1860: Heads of Households & Other Surnames in Households Index. Bryan L. Dilts. LC 84-10880. xxiv, 251p. 1985. 91.00 (ISBN 0-914311-22-0); microfiche 56.00x. Index Pub.

Rhode Island Census Index, 1870: Heads of Households & Other Surnames in Households Index. Bryan L. Dilts. LC 85-11828. xxiv, 272p. 1985. 91.00x (ISBN 0-914311-44-1); 56.00x (ISBN 0-914311-45-X). Index Pub.

Rhode Island Census Index 1890: Union Veterans. Ronald V. Jackson. (Illus.). lib. bdg. 25.00 (ISBN 0-317-16989-0). Accelerated Index.

Rhode Island Chaplain in the Revolution. Ebenezer David. Ed. by Jeannette D. Black & W. Greene Roelker. LC 73-159068. 1971. Repr. of 1949 ed. 21.50x (ISBN 0-8046-1662-0, Pub. by Kennikat). Assoc Faculty Pr.

Rhode Island Chronology & Factbook, Vol. 39. Robert I. Vexler. LC 78-26348. (Chronologies & Documentary Handbook of the States). 150p. 1978. 8.50 (ISBN 0-379-16164-8). Oceana.

Rhode Island: Conflict of Laws. suppl. 6.00 (ISBN 0-686-90884-8). Am Law Inst.

Rhode Island Constitutional Development, 1636-1775: A Survey. Patrick T. Conley. 35p. 1968. pap. 2.75 (ISBN 0-917012-42-9). RI Pubns Soc.

Rhode Island: Contracts. 9.50 (ISBN 0-686-90885-6); suppl. 7.00 (ISBN 0-686-90886-4). Am Law Inst.

Rhode Island Criminal Procedure. McFadyen & Hurst. 1986. write for info. legal looseleaf (ISBN 0-88063-075-2). Butterworth Legal Pubs.

Rhode Island Directory of Manufacturers, 1986. 268p. 1986. pap. 18.00 (ISBN 0-318-02868-9). Manufacturers.

Rhode Island District Court Operations Manual. National Center for State Courts Staff. 365p. 1977. manuscript 21.90 (NERO-047). Natl Ctr St Courts.

Rhode Island: Eight Poems. Michael S. Harper. 17p. 1981. pap. 3.00 (ISBN 0-913219-26-6); signed 10.00 (ISBN 0-913219-27-4). Pym-Rand Pr.

Rhode Island Family Court Benchbook: Adult Criminal, Jury & Miscellaneous Matters, Vol. III. 276p. 1984. manuscript 17.00 (NERO-153). Natl Ctr St Courts.

Rhode Island Family Court Benchbook: Domestic Relations Matters, Vol.I. National Center for State Courts Staff. 237p. 1984. manuscript 14.00 (NERO-151). Natl Ctr St Courts.

Rhode Island Family Court Benchbook: Juvenile Matters, Vol. II. National Center for State Courts Staff. 206p. 1984. manuscript 13.00 (NERO-152). Natl Ctr St Courts.

Rhode Island: Forgotten Leader of the Revolutionary Era. John F. Millar. (Illus.). 64p. (Orig.). 1987. pap. 5.00 (ISBN 0-934943-26-5). Thirteen Colonies Pr.

Rhode Island Freemen, 1747-1755: A Census of Registered Voters. Bruce C. MacGunnigle. LC 76-55839. 49p. 1982. pap. 5.00. Genealog Pub.

Rhode Island General Laws Annotated. write for info (ISBN 0-672-83449-9, Bobbs-Merrill Law). Michie Co.

Rhode Island Historical & Biographical Index, Vol. 1. Ronald Vern Jackson. LC 78-53715. (Illus.). 1984. lib. bdg. 30.00 (ISBN 0-89593-198-2). Accelerated Index.

Rhode Island Historical Development: An Interpretative Essay. Patrick T. Conley & Paul R. Campbell. 64p. 1985. pap. cancelled (ISBN 0-917012-69-0). RI Pubns Soc.

Rhode Island in the Continental Congress, 1765-1790. W. R. Staples. LC 71-153373. (Era of the American Revolution Ser.). 726p. 1971. Repr. of 1870 ed. lib. bdg. 75.00 (ISBN 0-306-70203-7). Da Capo.

Rhode Island: In Words & Pictures. Dennis Fradin. LC 80-22497. (Young People's Stories of Our States Ser.). (Illus.). 48p. (gr. 2-5). 1981. PLB 13.27 (ISBN 0-516-03939-3). Childrens.

Rhode Island: Judgements. 8.50 (ISBN 0-686-90889-9); suppl. 6.00 (ISBN 0-686-90890-2). Am Law Inst.

Rhode Island Land Evidences, Vol. 1: 1648-1696. Rhode Island Historical Society. LC 79-77882. (Illus.). 246p. 1970. Repr. of 1921 ed. 17.50 (ISBN 0-8063-0391-3). Genealog Pub.

Rhode Island Music & Musicians, 1733-1850. Joyce E. Mangler. (Detroit Studies in Music Bibliography Ser.: No. 7). 1965. pap. 6.00 (ISBN 0-911772-27-8). Harmonie Pk Pr.

Rhode Island Politics & the American Revolution, 1760-1776. David S. Lovejoy. LC 58-10478. (Brown University Studies: Vol. 23). 266p. pap. 69.20 (2030025). Bks Demand UMI.

Rhode Island Profile. Patrick T. Conley. LC 82-62009. (Illus.). 60p. (Orig.). 1983. pap. 3.95 (ISBN 0-917012-40-2). RI Pubns Soc.

Rhode Island: Restitution. 8.50 (ISBN 0-686-90891-0); suppl. 6.00 (ISBN 0-686-90892-9). Am Law Inst.

Rhode Island Scene. Ed. by Peter C. Crolius. (Illus.). 160p. (Orig.). 1986. pap. 10.95 (ISBN 0-934881-01-4). Dutch Island.

Rhode Island: Security. 8.50 (ISBN 0-686-90893-7); suppl. 6.00 (ISBN 0-686-90894-5). Am Law Inst.

Rhode Island Seventeen Eighty Two Census. Jay M. Holbrook. LC 78-78163. 241p. 1979. lib. bdg. 30.00 (ISBN 0-931248-00-0). Holbrook Res.

Rhode Island Study Manual for Life & Accident & Health Insurance. 1986. pap. 5.95 (ISBN 0-88462-645-8, 5310-25, Longman Fin Serv Pub). Longman Finan.

Rhode Island Superior Court Operations Manual. National Center for State Courts Staff. 294p. 1978. manuscript 17.64 (NERO-004). Natl Ctr St Courts.

Rhode Island Supreme Court & the Law of Crimes. Pollack. 1980. 25.00 (ISBN 0-88063-092-2); Supplement, 1986. 10.00 (ISBN 0-88063-087-6). Butterworth Legal Pubs.

Rhode Island Towns & Counties. Michael J. Denis. (New England Towns & Counties Ser.). 8p. (Orig.). 1983. pap. 2.00 (ISBN 0-935207-05-8). Danbury Hse Bks.

Rhode Island Transit Album. D. Scott Molloy. (Illus.). 64p. (Orig.). 1978. pap. 4.95 (ISBN 0-686-32864-7). Boston St Rwy.

Rhode Island 1777 Military Census. Mildred M. Chamberlain. LC 84-82485. 181p. 1985. 20.00 (ISBN 0-8063-1107-X). Genealog Pub.

Rhode Islanders Record the Revolution: The Journals of William Humphrey & Zuriel Waterman. Nathaniel N. Shipton & David Swain. LC 78-68840. (Rhode Island Revolutionary Heritage Ser.: Vol. 4). (Illus.). 131p. 1984. 8.95 (ISBN 0-917012-03-8). RI Pubns Soc.

Rhode Island's Ocean Sands: Management Guidelines for Sand & Gravel Extraction in State Waters. M. J. Grant. 51p. 1973. free (P310). Sea Grant Pubns.

Rhode Island's Road to Liberty. Patrick T. Conley & Albert T. Klyberg. (Illus.). 24p. (Orig.). 1987. pap. 3.50 (ISBN 0-917012-85-2). Ri Pubns Soc.

Rhodes. Brian Dicks. (Islands Ser.). 1974. 19.95 (ISBN 0-7153-6571-1). David & Charles.

Rhodes & Rhodesia: The White Conquest of Zimbabwe, 1884-1902. Arthur Keppel-Jones. (Illus.). 674p. 1983. text ed. 70.00x (ISBN 0-7735-0534-2). McGill-Queens U Pr.

Rhodes & the Dodecanese Islands. Geoffrey O'Connell. (Greek Islands: GROC's Candid Guides Ser.). 225p. (Orig.). 1985. pap. 4.95 (ISBN 0-9509104-6-5, Pub. by Willowbridge Bucks UK). Bradt Ent.

Rhodes & the Dodecanese Islands. Trevor Webster. (Where to Go in Greece Ser.). (Illus.). 130p. (Orig.). 1987. pap. 9.95 (ISBN 0-87052-358-9). Hippocrene Bks.

Rhodes in the Bronze Age. C. B. Mee. 160p. 1982. pap. text ed. 60.00x (ISBN 0-85668-143-1, Pub. by Aris & Phillips UK). Humanities.

Rhodes in the Hellenistic Age. Richard M. Berthold. LC 83-23127. (Illus.). 243p. 1984. 29.95x (ISBN 0-8014-1640-X). Cornell U Pr.

Rhodes, the Tswana, & the British: Colonialism, Collaboration, & Conflict in the Bechuanaland Protectorate, 1885-1899. Paul Maylam. LC 79-8582. (Contributions in Comparative Colonial Studies: No. 4). (Illus.). x, 245p. 1980. lib. bdg. 67.95 (ISBN 0-313-20885-9, MTB/). Greenwood.

Rhodes Travel Guide. Berlitz Editors. (Travel Guides for English Speakers Ser.). 1976. pap. 4.95 (ISBN 0-02-969460-4, Berlitz). Macmillan.

Rhodes Travel Guide--Florida. William W. Rhodes. Ed. by Anthony Lualdi. LC 79-63598. (Illus.). 1979. 9.95 (ISBN 0-933768-00-1); pap. 6.95 (ISBN 0-933768-01-X). Rhodes Geo Lib.

Rhodesia Today: A Description of the Prospects of Matabeleland & Mashonaland. Edward F. Knight. LC 75-100266. Repr. of 1895 ed. cancelled (ISBN 0-8371-2853-6). Greenwood.

Rhodesia-Zimbabwe. Oliver Pollak & Karen Pollak. (World Bibliographical Ser.: No. 4). 195p. 1979. 25.25 (ISBN 0-903450-14-3). ABC-Clio.

Rhodesia-Zimbabwe: A Bibliographic Guide to the Nationalist Period. Marion E. Doro. 1984. lib. bdg. 55.00 (ISBN 0-8161-8275-2, Hall Reference). G K Hall.

Rhodesian Light Infantry Commando Combat Manual. Cranbourne Barracks Staff. (Illus.). 111p. 1986. wkbk. 10.95x (ISBN 0-940005-04-2). Crocker Edwards Pub.

Rhodesian Man & Associated Remains. British Museum Staff et al. LC 77-86422. (Illus.). Repr. of 1928 ed. 17.00 (ISBN 0-404-16624-5). AMS Pr.

Rhodesian Paratrooper Combat Training Manual. Parachute Training Wing Staff. (Illus.). 279p. 1986. pap. 14.95 (ISBN 0-940005-03-4). Crocker Edwards Pub.

Rhodesian Ridgeback Champions, 1955-1980. Jan L. Pata. (Illus.). 97p. 1981. pap. 29.95 (ISBN 0-940808-04-8). Camino E E & B.

Rhodesian Ridgeback Champions, 1981-1986. Camino, E. E. & B., Co. Staff. (Illus.). 132p. 1988. pap. 24.95 (ISBN 0-940808-65-X). Camino E E & B.

Rhodesian S. A. S. Combat Manual, Counter Guerilla Tactics in Africa. 1986. lib. bdg. 79.95 (ISBN 0-8490-3833-2). Gordon Pr.

Rhodesian Sellout. Robert Skimin. LC 77-79579. 1978. 6.95 (ISBN 0-87212-089-9). Libra.

Rhodian Funerary Monuments. P. M. Fraser. (Illus.). 1978. text ed. 76.00x (ISBN 0-19-813192-5). Oxford U Pr.

Rhododendron Hybrids. Harold Greer & Homer Salley. (Illus.). 484p. 1986. 55.00 (ISBN 0-88192-061-4). Timber.

Rhododendron Ponticum As a Forest Weed. P. M. Tobbush. (Forestry Commission Bulletin: No. 73). 7p. (Orig.). 1987. pap. text ed. 5.00 (ISBN 0-11-710254-7, HM1447, Pub. by Her Maj Station Ofc). UNIPUB.

Rhododendron Species: The Lepidotes, Vol. I. H. H. Davidian. LC 81-23232. (Illus.). 470p. 1982. cloth 59.95 (ISBN 0-917304-71-3). Timber.

Rhododendrons. John Street. LC 87-32549. (Classic Garden Plants Ser.). (Illus.). 114p. 1988. casebound 18.95 (ISBN 0-87106-742-0). Globe Pequot.

Rhododendrons & Their Relatives. 3.95 (ISBN 0-686-21158-8). Bklyn Botanic.

Rhododendrons in America. 2nd ed. Ted Van Veen. LC 77-104390. (Illus.). 192p. 1986. 39.95 (ISBN 0-8323-0450-6); pap. 25.00 (ISBN 0-8323-0374-7). Binford-Metropolitan.

Rhododendrons of China. Tr. by Judy Young & Lu-Sheng Chong. LC 80-68082. 1980. 18.00 (ISBN 0-8323-0373-9). Binford-Metropolitan.

Rhododendrons of the World. David G. Leach. (Illus.). 1961. 70.00 (ISBN 0-684-10351-6, ScribT). Scribner.

Rhodomelaceen Des Golfes Von Neapel und der Angrenzenden Meenesabschnitte. P. Falkenberg. (Fauna & Flor d. Golfes v. Neapel). (Illus., Ger.). 1979. Repr. of 1901 ed. lib. bdg. 195.00x (ISBN 3-87429-143-X). Lubrecht & Cramer.

Rhodophylles des Forets Cotieres du Gabon et de la Cote d'Ivoire. H. Romagnesi & G. Gilles. (Nova Hedwigia Beiheft: No. 59). (Illus.). lib. bdg. 150.00x (ISBN 3-7682-5459-3). Lubrecht & Cramer.

Rhombus: The Cajun Unicorn. Timothy J. Edler. (Tim Edler's Tales from the Atchafalaya Ser.). (Illus.). 40p. (gr. k up). 1984. pap. 10.00 (ISBN 0-931108-10-1). Little Cajun Bks.

Rhomeo & Julietta see Romeus & Iuliet.

Rhone: River of Contrasts. Frances Von Maltitz. (Rivers of the World Ser.). (Illus.). 96p. (gr. 4-7). 1965. PLB 3.98 (ISBN 0-8116-6364-7). Garrard.

RHS Encyclopedia of House Plants: Including Greenhouse Plants. Kenneth A. Beckett. (Illus.). 1987. 34.95 (ISBN 0-317-66284-8). Salem Hse Pubs.

Rhubarb. Stephen Cosgrove. (Serendipity Bks.). (Illus.). 32p. (gr. k-4). 1988. pap. 2.50 (ISBN 0-8431-2300-1). Price Stern.

Rhubarb & Covertside Courtship, 2 vol. set. J. Stanley Reeve & Katherine Roosevelt Reeve. (Illus.). 1988. Repr. 125.00x (ISBN 0-944766-02-1). Bright Bks PA.

Rhubarb Cookbook. Pamela G. Wubben. LC 79-66754. (Illus.). 65p. 1979. 5.95 (ISBN 0-935442-00-6). One Percent.

Rhubarb Renaissance: A Cookbook. 3rd ed. Ann Saling. LC 77-29214. (Illus.). 159p. 1978. pap. 4.95 (ISBN 0-914718-31-2). ANSAL Pr.

Rhubarb: The Diary of a Gentleman's Hunter. J. Stanley Reeve. (Illus.). 1987. Repr. write for info. (ISBN 0-944766-03-X). Bright Bks PA.

Rhum: The Natural History of an Island. Tim Clutton-Brock & Martim Ball. 160p. 1987. 25.00x (ISBN 0-85224-513-0, Pub. by Edinburgh U Pr Scotland). Columbia U Pr.

Rhumb Line of Symbolism: French Poets from Sainte-Beuve to Valery, Presentation & Selected Texts. Laurent Le Sage. LC 77-8020. 1978. text ed. 24.50x (ISBN 0-271-00513-0). Pa St U Pr.

Rhumbs. Ian Reid. Ed. by Peter Kaplan. LC 75-10586. 1975. 1.50x (ISBN 0-915176-07-6). Pourboire.

Rhyme & Meaning in Crashaw. Mary E. Rickey. LC 72-5491. (Studies in Poetry, No. 38). 1972. Repr. of 1957 ed. lib. bdg. 35.95x (ISBN 0-8383-1603-4). Haskell.

Rhyme & Meaning in the Poetry of Yeats. Marjorie Perloff. LC 78-102959. (De Proprietatibus Litterarum, Ser. Practica). (Illus.). 1970. pap. text ed. 28.00x (ISBN 0-686-22420-5). Mouton.

Rhyme & Meter. James W. Pool. 1987. 6.95 (ISBN 0-533-07508-4). Vantage.

Rhyme & Punishment: Random & Not So Academic Graffiti. S. Santhi. (Indian Poetry Ser.). 80p. 1975. 6.00 (ISBN 0-89253-015-4). Ind-US Inc.

Rhyme & Reason. Ed. by Bob Jones. (Illus.). 222p. (Orig.). 1981. pap. 10.95 (ISBN 0-89084-142-X). Bob Jones Univ Pr.

Rhyme & Reason. Nancy Lamb & Muff Singer. (Illus.). 48p. (ps-3). 1988. pap. 2.95 (ISBN 0-8431-2227-7). Price Stern.

Rhyme & Reason in Reading & Spelling. Lynette Bradley & Peter Bryant. (Int'l Academy for Research in Learning Disabilities Ser.). 112p. 1985. pap. text ed. 7.95x (ISBN 0-472-08055-5). U of Mich Pr.

Rhyme & Reason of Curt Sytsma. Curt Sytsma. LC 81-67557. (Illus.). 224p. 1982. 14.95 (ISBN 0-942170-05-9). CSS Pubns.

Rhyme & Reason: St. Thomas & Modes of Discourse. Ralph McInerny. LC 81-80234. (Aquinas Lecture Ser.). 84p. 1981. 7.95 (ISBN 0-87462-148-8). Marquette.

Rhyme & Revolution in Germany. J. E. Legge. 59.95 (ISBN 0-8490-0954-5). Gordon Pr.

Rhyme & Revolution in Germany: A Study in German History, Life, Literature & Character. James G. Legge. LC 72-126646. Repr. of 1918 ed. 33.45 (ISBN 0-404-03947-2). AMS Pr.

Rhyme Chronicle of Livonia (Livonische Reimchronik) Ausma Jaunzemis. LC 78-68148. 1978. 20.00 (ISBN 0-912852-21-6). Echo Pubs.

Rhyme Lines. 416p. (Orig.). 1986. pap. 15.95 (ISBN 0-948552-00-X, Pub. by Pendragon Pub UK). H Leonard Pub Corp.

Rhyme of the Flying Bomb. Mervyn Peake. (Illus.). 43p. 1973. 9.95 (ISBN 0-317-61324-3, Pub. by Colin Smythe Ltd Britain). Dufour.

Rhyme or Reason: A Limerick History of Philosophy. Richard E. Aquila. LC 81-40013. 126p. (Orig.). 1981. lib. bdg. 16.50 (ISBN 0-8191-1562-2); pap. text ed. 6.25 (ISBN 0-8191-1563-0). U Pr of Amer.

Rhyme Readers, 6 vols, Vol. 9-14. Illus. by Caroline Sharpe. (Illus.). 12p. (ps-1). 1987. Teacher's Notes incl. pap. 14.80 (ISBN 1-55624-125-9, WG1259). Wright Group.

Rhyme Readers One to Eight, 8 bks. Illus. by Caroline Sharpe et al. (Illus.). (ps-1). 1986. Set. pap. text ed. 16.60 (ISBN 1-55624-001-5). Wright Group.

Rhyme Tyme. rev. ed. William-Alan Landes. (Wondrawhopper Ser.). (gr. 3-12). 1985. pap. text ed. 6.00 (ISBN 0-88734-108-X). Players Pr.

Rhyme Tyme. William-Alan Landes. LC 87-62593. (Wondrawhopper Ser.). (Orig.). 1988. pap. 26.00 tchr's ed. (ISBN 0-88734-009-1). Players Pr.

Rhyme Tyme: Music & Lyrics. rev. ed. William-Alan Landes & Jeff Rizzo. (Wondrawhopper Ser.). (gr. 3-12). 1985. pap. text ed. 12.00 (ISBN 0-88734-008-3). Players Pr.

Rhyme with Reason. Lucille King. 32p. 1982. 5.95 (ISBN 0-89962-243-7). Todd & Honeywell.

Rhymers' Lexicon. 2nd. ed. Andrew Loring. LC 78-156926. 928p. 1971. Repr. of 1905 ed. 51.00x (ISBN 0-8103-3341-4). Gale.

Rhymes. Graham D. McKie. 1986. 7.95 (ISBN 0-533-06694-8). Vantage.

Rhymes. (Preschool Puppet Board Bks.). (Illus.). 7p. (ps-1). 1976. 2.50 (ISBN 0-448-09743-5, G&D). Putnam Pub Group.

Rhymes & Ballads of London. Carole Tate. LC 72-90691. (Illus.). 32p. (gr. k-4). 1973. 6.95 (ISBN 0-87592-042-X). Scroll Pr.

Rhymes & Verses: Collected Poems for Young People. Walter De La Mare. 368p. (gr. 2-4). 1988. pap. 7.95 (ISBN 0-8050-0848-9). H Holt & Co.

Rhymes & Verses: Collected Poems for Young People. Walter De la Mare. (Illus.). 368p. (gr. 2-4). 1988. 15.95 (ISBN 0-8050-0847-0). H Holt & Co.

Rhymes Around the Day. Pat Thomson. LC 82-24001. (Illus.). 32p. (ps-1). 1983. 10.25 (ISBN 0-688-02073-9); lib. bdg. 10.88 (ISBN 0-688-02074-7). Lothrop.

Rhymes for Learning Times. Louise B. Scott. LC 82-73392. 145p. (Orig.). (ps). 1984. pap. 14.95 (ISBN 0-513-01763-1). Denison.

Rhymes for Talking Time. Lois B. Lee. 1973. text ed. 2.50 (ISBN 0-686-09389-5). Expression.

Rhymes from Ring O'Rose. L. Leslie Brooke. (ps-3). 1987. 4.95 (ISBN 0-7232-3529-5). Warne.

Rhymes of a Bluejacket: Verses of a World War II Navy Vet. Robin R. Leatherman. LC 86-82065. (Illus.). 112p. (Orig.). 1986. pap. 6.95 (ISBN 0-939127-00-8). Gulf Coast Pub.

Rhymes of a Jerk. Larry Fagin. 7.00 (ISBN 0-686-09760-2); pap. 3.50 (ISBN 0-686-09761-0). Kulchur Foun.

Rhymes of Boys & Girls. Illus. by Blanche F. Wright. (Real Mother Goose Mini Boxed Set Ser.). (Illus.). (ps-1). 1987. pap. 6.95 (ISBN 0-02-689015-1, Checkerboard Pr). Macmillan.

Rhymes of Childhood. Edgar Guest. 190p. 1981. Repr. lib. bdg. 14.95 (ISBN 0-89968-220-0). Lightyear.

Rhymes of the Orbiters, Pioneers in Space. James A. Coffeen. (Illus.). 98p. (Orig.). 1984. pap. 9.95 (ISBN 0-930271-00-9). Grounder Pub.

Rhymes of the Ranges: A New Collection of the Poems of Bruce Kiskaddon. Bruce Kiskaddon. Intro. by Hal Cannon. (Illus.). 144p. 1987. 14.95 (ISBN 0-87905-264-3). Gibbs Smith Pub.

Rhyme's Reason. enl. ed. John Hollander. 1989. price not set (ISBN 0-300-04306-6); pap. price not set (ISBN 0-300-04307-4). Yale U Pr.

Rhyme's Reason: A Guide to English Verse. John Hollander. LC 81-51342. (Illus.). 64p. 1981. text ed. 18.50x (ISBN 0-300-02735-4); pap. 6.95 (ISBN 0-300-02740-0, Y-407). Yale U Pr.

Rhymes to Predict the Weather. Don Haggerty. LC 84-52672. (Illus.). 132p. (Orig.). 1985. pap. 8.00 (ISBN 0-9614703-0-5). Springmeadow Pub.

Rhyming at the Kitchen Sink. Hazel H. O'Quinn. LC 77-175113. (Illus.). 151p. 5.95 (ISBN 0-8363-0085-8). Jenkins.

Rhyming: Cut & Paste & More. (Let's Learn Ser.). (Illus.). 32p. (gr. 1). 1983. pap. 1.98 (ISBN 0-88724-011-9, CD-7012). Carson-Dellos.

Rhyming Dictionary. Rosalind Ferguson. 1986. pap. 6.95 (ISBN 0-14-051136-9). Penguin.

Rhyming Families. Barbara Gregorich. Ed. by Joan Hoffman. (I Know It! Bks.). (Illus.). 32p. (gr. 1-3). 1981. wkbk. 1.95 (ISBN 0-938256-38-6). Sch Zone Pub Co.

Rhyming in the Rigging: Poems of the Sea. Ed. by Lahaina Harry. LC 77-80048. 174p. 1978. 14.00 (ISBN 0-918024-04-8); pap. 6.95 (ISBN 0-918024-05-6). Ox Bow.

Rhyming Pattern, Bk. 1. Alpha Pyramis Research Division Staff. 8p. 1984. pap. text ed. 7.95 (ISBN 0-913597-46-5, Pub. by Alpha Pyramis). Prosperity & Profits.

Rhyming Pictures. Barbara Gregorich. Ed. by Joan Hoffman. (Get Ready! Bks.). (Illus.). 32p. (ps). 1983. wkbk. 1.95 (ISBN 0-938256-53-X). Sch Zone Pub Co.

Rhyming Recipe & Cookbook, Vol. 1. Alpha Pyramis Research Division Staff. 21p. 1984. pap. text ed. 5.95 (ISBN 0-913597-50-3, Pub. by Alpha Pyramis). Prosperity & Profits.

Rhyming Words for Insects, Animals & Birds. Francis M. Daves. (Illus.). 78p. (gr. 3-7). 1975. pap. 2.95 (ISBN 0-89783-027-X). Larlin Corp.

Rhynchonellidae of the British Chalk, 2 Pts. N. E. Pettit. Repr. of 1950 ed. Set. 18.00 (ISBN 0-384-46080-1). Johnson Repr.

Rhynchota: Heteroptera, Vol. 1. W. L. Distant. (Fauna of British India Ser.). xxxviii, 438p. 1977. Repr. of 1902 ed. 25.00 (ISBN 0-88065-048-6, Pub. by Messers Today & Tomorrows Printers & Publishers India). Scholarly Pubns.

Rhynchota: Heteroptera, Vol. 2. W. L. Distant. (Fauna of British India Ser.). xviii, 504p. 1977. Repr. of 1902 ed. 25.00 (ISBN 0-88065-049-4, Pub. by Messers Today & Tomorrows Printers & Publishers India). Scholarly Pubns.

Rhynchota: Heteroptera - Appendix, Vol. 5. W. L. Distant. (Fauna of British India Ser.). xii, 362p. 1977. Repr. of 1910 ed. 20.00 (ISBN 0-88065-077-X, Pub. by Messers Today & Tomorrows Printers & Publishers India). Scholarly Pubns.

Rhynchota: Heteroptera-Homoptera, Vol. 3. W. L. Distant. (Fauna of British India Ser.). iiv, 504p. 1977. Repr. of 1906 ed. 25.00 (ISBN 0-88065-075-3, Pub. by Messers Today & Tomorrows Printers & Publishers India). Scholarly Pubns.

Rhynchota: Homoptera - Appendix, Vol. 4. W. L. Distant. (Fauna of British India Ser.). xiv, 502p. 1977. Repr. of 1908 ed. 25.00 (ISBN 0-88065-076-1, Pub. by Messers Today & Tomorrows Printers & Publishers India). Scholarly Pubns.

Rhynchota: Homoptera - Appendix, Vol. 6. W. L. Distant. (Fauna of British India Ser.). viii, 250p. 1977. Repr. of 1916 ed. 15.00 (ISBN 0-88065-078-8, Pub. by Messers Today & Tomorrows Printers & Publishers India). Scholarly Pubns.

Rhynchota: Homoptera - Appendix, Heteroptera - Addenda, Vol. 7. W. L. Distant. (Fauna of British India Ser.). viii, 212p. 1977. Repr. of 1918 ed. 15.00 (ISBN 0-88065-079-6, Pub. by Messers Today & Tomorrows Printers & Publishers India). Scholarly Pubns.

Rhyolite-Death Valley's Ghost City of Golden Dreams. 11th ed. Harold O. Weight & Lucile Weight. 1988. pap. 1.95 (ISBN 0-912714-04-2). Calico Pr.

Rhys Davies: A Critical Sketch. R. L. Megroz. 1973. Repr. of 1932 ed. 20.00 (ISBN 0-8274-0775-0). R West.

Rhythm-A-Ning: Jazz Tradition & Innovation in the '80s. Gary Giddins. 1985. 24.95 (ISBN 0-19-503558-5). Oxford U Pr.

Rhythm-a-Ning: Jazz Tradition & Innovation in the '80s. Gary Giddins. 320p. 1986. pap. 8.95 (ISBN 0-19-504214-X). Oxford U Pr.

Rhythm: An Annotated Bibliography. Steven D. Winick. LC 74-14582. 1974. 17.50 (ISBN 0-8108-0767-X). Scarecrow.

Rhythm & Blues. Lynn E. McCutcheon. (Illus.). 1971. 10.95 (ISBN 0-87948-028-9); pap. 7.95 (ISBN 0-686-96672-4). Beatty.

Rhythm & Blues in New Orleans. John Broven. LC 77-13351. Orig. Title: Walking To New Orleans. (Illus.). 250p. 1983. pap. 9.95 (ISBN 0-88289-433-1). Pelican.

Rhythm & Blues Story. Gene Busnar. LC 85-13691. (Illus.). 224p. (gr. 7 up). 1985. 9.79 (ISBN 0-671-42145-X). Messner.

Rhythm & Dues. 2nd ed. Linda M. Baron. 32p. 1981. 6.00. Harlin Jacque.

Rhythm & Intent: Ritual Studies from South India. Fred W. Clothey. 1984. 15.00x (ISBN 0-8364-1219-2, Pub. by Blackie & Sons). South Asia Bks.

Rhythm & Meter. Ed. by Paul Kiparsky & Gilbert Youmans. (Phonetics & Phonology Ser.: Vol. 1). 660p. 1988. price not set (ISBN 0-12-409340-X). Acad Pr.

Rhythm & Metre: Towards a Systematic Description of Greek Stichic Verse. M. Van Raalte. (Studies in Greek & Latin Linguistics: No. 3). 480p. 1986. pap. 35.00 (ISBN 90-232-2229-6, Pub. by Van Gorcum Holland). Longwood Pub Group.

Rhythm & Movement: Applications of Dalcroze Eurhythmics. Elsa Findlay. LC 71-169706. 96p. 1971. pap. 12.95 (ISBN 0-87487-078-X). Birch Tree Gr.

Rhythm & Writing. Robert S. Ochsner. LC 87-50836. 150p. 1988. price not setx (ISBN 0-87875-347-8). Whitston Pub.

Rhythm, Content & Flavor: New & Selected Poems. Victor H. Cruz. Date not set. 8.00 (ISBN 0-934770-93-X). Arte Publico.

Rhythm Factor in Human Behavior. Salvatore J. Garzino. LC 81-81611. 1982. 8.95 (ISBN 0-87212-151-8). Libra.

Rhythm Games: For Perception & Cognition. 36p. 1973. pap. 4.50 (ISBN 0-913650-08-0). Columbia Pictures.

Rhythm Guitar. Harvey Vinson. (Orig.). 1969. pap. 9.95 (Consolidated). Music Sales.

Rhythm in Drama. Kathleen George. LC 79-24432. 1980. 19.95x (ISBN 0-8229-3416-7); pap. 6.95x (ISBN 0-8229-5316-1). U of Pittsburgh Pr.

Rhythm in English Poetry. Stanley Leathes. 1973. lib. bdg. 20.00 (ISBN 0-8414-5782-4). Folcroft.

Rhythm in Prose Illustrated from Authors of the 19th Century. Olive M. Savage. LC 73-13853. 1974. Repr. of 1917 ed. lib. bdg. 20.00 (ISBN 0-8414-7635-7). Folcroft.

Rhythm in Psychological, Linguistic & Musical Processes. Ed. by James R. Evans & Manfred Clynes. (Illus.). 302p. 1986. 38.25x (ISBN 0-398-05235-2). C C Thomas.

Rhythm in the Novel. E. K. Brown. LC 77-14165. xvi, 118p. 1978. 11.95x (ISBN 0-8032-1150-3); pap. 3.25x (ISBN 0-8032-6050-4, BB 667, Bison). U of Nebr Pr.

Rhythm, Music, & Education. rev. ed. Emile J. Dalcroze. Tr. by Harold F. Rubenstein. 200p. (Orig.). pap. text ed. 12.95 (ISBN 0-916622-47-9). Princeton Bk Co.

Rhythm, Music & Education. Emile Jaques-Dalcroze. LC 77-187829. (Illus.). Repr. of 1921 ed. 20.00 (ISBN 0-405-08666-0, Blom Pubns). Ayer Co Pubs.

Rhythm of Being: A Study of Temporality. Howard Trivers. LC 84-20680. 346p. 1985. 22.50 (ISBN 0-8022-2466-0). Philos Lib.

Rhythm of English Prose. Andre Classe. 1978. Repr. of 1939 ed. lib. bdg. 27.00 (ISBN 0-8495-0900-9). Arden Lib.

Rhythm of English Prose. Andre Classe. LC 73-12136. 1939. lib. bdg. 29.00 (ISBN 0-8414-3416-6). Folcroft.

Rice Marketing. J. C. Abbott et al. (Marketing Guides: No. 6). (Illus.). 189p. (Orig.). 1972. pap. 15.00 (ISBN 92-5-101540-6, F411, FAO). UNIPUB.

Rice Marketing System & Compulsory Levies in Andhra Pradesh: A Study of Public Intervention in Food Grain Marketing, India. K. Subbarao. 1979. 12.00x (ISBN 0-8364-0365-7). South Asia Bks.

Rice Milling Equipment Operation & Maintenance. F. Garibaldi. (Agricultural Services Bulletins: No. 22). 101p. (2nd Printing 1981). 1974. pap. 7.50 (ISBN 92-5-101095-1, F1972, FAO). UNIPUB.

Rice Paddy Grunt: Unfading Memories of the Vietnam Generation. John M. Brown. (Illus.). 356p. 1986. 18.95 (ISBN 0-89526-589-3). Regnery Gateway.

Rice Parboiling. F. Garibaldi. (Agricultural Services Bulletins: No. 56). (Illus.). 73p. 1985. pap. 7.50 (ISBN 92-5-101400-0, F2671, FAO). UNIPUB.

Rice Planters Recipes. David L. Gilbert, Jr. Tr. & intro. by Dorothy M. Gilbert. (Illus.). 103p. (Orig.). 1984. pap. 4.00 (ISBN 0-9615765-0-2). Cane Patch.

Rice Postproduction Technology in the Tropics. Merle L. Esmay et al. LC 79-15428. (An East-West Center Book). (Illus.). 146p. (Orig.). 1979. pap. text ed. 8.00x (ISBN 0-8248-0638-7). UH Pr.

Rice Powder. Sergio Galindo. Ed. by Bert Patrick & Lura L. Patrick. LC 78-51332. (Perivale Translation Ser: No. 5). Orig. Title: Polvos De Arroz. 43p. 1978. pap. 6.00 (ISBN 0-912288-12-4). Perivale Pr.

Rice Powder, Peanut Powder & Soybean Powder Suggestion Rhymes with Recipes. Cookbook Consortium Staff. 1984. pap. text ed. 1.50 (ISBN 0-318-01294-4, Pub. by Cookbk Consort). Prosperity & Profits.

Rice Processing in Peninsula Malaysia. Lee Fredericks & R. G. Wells. (Illus.). 1983. 25.95x (ISBN 0-19-582522-5). Oxford U Pr.

Rice Production Potential & Constraints. G. S. Kainth & P. L. Mehra. (Illus.). xv, 144p. 1985. text ed. 40.00x (ISBN 0-86590-601-7, Pub. by B R Pub Corp Delhi). Apt Bks.

Rice, Rivalry & Politics: Managing Cambodian Relief. Linda Mason & Roger Brown. 240p. 1983. text ed. 22.95 (ISBN 0-268-01615-1); pap. text ed. 9.95 (ISBN 0-268-01616-X). U of Notre Dame Pr.

Rice Societies: Asian Problems & Prospects. Ed. by Irene Norlund et al. (Studies on Asian Topics (Scandinavian Institute of Asian Studies): No. 10). 322p. 1986. pap. 25.00 (ISBN 0-913215-17-1). Riverdale Co.

Rice Storage & Insect Pest Management. A. Prakash et al. (Illus.). xi, 337p. 1987. text ed. 50.00x (ISBN 81-7018-397-9, Pub. by B R Pub Corp Delhi). Apt Bks.

Rice Testing - Methods & Equipment. F. Garibaldi. (Agricultural Services Bulletins: No. 18). 55p. (3rd Printing 1979). 1973. pap. 7.50 (ISBN 92-5-100739-X, F1897, FAO). UNIPUB.

Rice University: A Seventy-Fifth Anniversary Portrait. Geoff Winningham. LC 87-60696. (Illus.). 160p. 1987. 34.95 (ISBN 0-89263-265-8). Rice Univ.

Rice Wine. Barry Came. LC 87-21057. 320p. 1988. 17.95 (ISBN 1-55584-036-1). Weidenfeld.

Rice Without Rain. Minfong Ho. LC 86-33745. 176p. (gr. 6 up). 1988. 12.00 (ISBN 0-688-06355-1). Lothrop.

Ricerche sul Pitagorismo: I: Biografia di Pitagora. Rita C. Melloni. (Studi Pubblicati Dall'Istituto di Filologia Classica (Universita di Bolonga): No. XXV). 232p. (Ital.). 1969. pap. text ed. 20.00 (ISBN 0-905205-57-X, Pub. by F Cairns). Longwood Pub Group.

Riceyman Steps. Arnold Bennett. 393p. pap. 8.95 (ISBN 0-89733-093-5). Academy Chi Pubs.

Rich! Churches Alive, Inc. Staff. (God in You Bible Ser.). (Illus.). 1986. 3.95 (ISBN 0-89109-094-0). Churches Alive.

Rich Against Poor: The Reality of Aid. C. R. Hensman. 308p. 1971. text ed. 18.95x (ISBN 0-87073-294-3). Schenkman Bks Inc.

Rich & Famous. John Guare. 1977. pap. 3.50x (ISBN 0-685-81648-6). Dramatists Play.

Rich & Famous Like My Mom. Hila Colman. LC 87-27448. 144p. (gr. 4-7). 1988. 12.95 (ISBN 0-517-56836-5). Crown.

Rich & Poor. Photos by Jim Goldberg. 1985. pap. 15.95 (ISBN 0-394-74156-0). Random.

Rich & Poor Countries. 4th ed. Hans W. Singer & Javed A. Ansari. (Studies in Economics). 330p. 1988. pap. text ed. 16.95 (ISBN 0-04-445044-3). Unwin Hyman.

Rich & Poor Countries. Hans Wolfgang Singer & Javed A. Ansari. LC 76-49137. (Studies in Economics: No. 12). pap. 57.00 (ISBN 0-317-42344-4, 2025872). Bks Demand UMI.

Rich & Poor Countries: A Study in the Problems of Comparison of Real Incomes. Don Usher. (Institute of Economic Affairs, Eaton Papers Ser.: No. 9). (Orig.). pap. 2.50 technical (ISBN 0-255-69540-3). Transatl Arts.

Rich & Poor in Grenoble: 1600-1814. Kathryn Norberg. LC 84-16262. 1985. 40.00x (ISBN 0-520-05260-9). U of Cal Pr.

Rich & Poor in the Shepherd of Hermas: An Exegetical-Social Investigation. Carolyn Osiek. Ed. by Bruce Vawter. LC 83-7385. (Catholic Biblical Quarterly Monographs: No. 15). xi, 184p. (Orig.). 1983. pap. 6.00x (ISBN 0-915170-14-0). Catholic Biblical.

Rich & Reckless. Barney Leason. 400p. (Orig.). 1988. pap. 4.50 (ISBN 0-553-27328-0). Bantam.

Rich & Super-Rich. Ferdinand Lundberg. 820p. (YA) pap. 14.95 (ISBN 0-8184-0486-8). Lyle Stuart.

Rich & the Mighty. Vera Cowie. 1986. pap. 3.95 (ISBN 0-380-69971-0). Avon.

Rich & the Poor. Carl Kreider. LC 86-33614. 168p. (Orig.). 1987. pap. 8.95 (ISBN 0-8361-3433-8). Herald Pr.

Rich & the Poor. Henry Parker. LC 77-7419. (English Experience Ser.: No. 882). 1977. Repr. of 1493 ed. lib. bdg. 69.00 (ISBN 90-221-0882-1). Walter J Johnson.

Rich & the Poor in Supreme Court History. Russell Galloway. Ed. by Hal Aigner. LC 82-62643. 200p. 1983. pap. 7.95 (ISBN 0-937572-01-2). Paradigm Pr.

Rich & the Righteous. Helen Van Slyke. 352p. 1986. pap. 4.50 (ISBN 0-446-31298-3). Warner Bks.

Rich & the Super-Rich. Ferdinand Lundberg. Ed. by Eileen Brand. LC 67-10015. 1968. 15.00 (ISBN 0-8184-0069-2). Lyle Stuart.

Rich Are Different. Susan Howatch. 704p. 1985. pap. 4.95 (ISBN 0-449-20770-6, Crest). Fawcett.

Rich Cabinet Furnished with Varietie of Excellent Descriptions. Thomas Gainsford. LC 77-38417. (English Experience Ser.: No. 458). 368p. 1972. Repr. of 1616 ed. 45.00 (ISBN 90-221-0458-3). Walter J Johnson.

Rich Cat. Judy Sutcliffe. (Illus.). 1985. 2.50 (ISBN 0-943164-07-9). Geronima.

Rich Christian in the Church of the Early Empire: Contradictions & Accomodations. L. William Countryman. LC 80-81884. (Texts & Studies in Religion: Vol. 7). viii, 248p. 1980. lib. bdg. 49.95x (ISBN 0-88946-970-9). E Mellen.

Rich Christians in an Age of Hunger: A Biblical Study. 2nd, rev. ed. Ronald J. Sider. LC 84-4549. (Illus.). 257p. 1984. pap. 8.95 (ISBN 0-87784-977-3). Inter-Varsity.

Rich Church, Poor Church: The Catholic Church & Its Money. Malachi Martin. LC 84-1939. 256p. 1984. 16.95 (ISBN 0-399-12906-5, Putnam). Putnam Pub Group.

Rich Countries & Poor Countries: Reflections from the Past, Lessons for the Future. W. W. Rostow. 224p. 1987. 34.50 (ISBN 0-8133-0497-0). Westview.

Rich Country Interests & Third World Development. Ed. by Robert Cassen & Richard Jolly. LC 82-42561. 1982. 35.00 (ISBN 0-312-68101-1). St Martin.

Rich Dreams. Ben Barzman & Norma Barzman. 528p. 1982. pap. 3.50 (ISBN 0-446-90034-6). Warner Bks.

Rich Friends. Jacqueline Briskin. 468p. 1976. 8.95 (ISBN 0-440-07367-7). Delacorte.

Rich Friends. Jacqueline Briskin. 1977. pap. 4.50 (ISBN 0-685-75577-0). Dell.

Rich Get Richer & the Poor Get Prison: Ideology, Class, & Criminal Justice. 2nd ed. Jeffrey H. Reiman. LC 83-12551. (Deviance & Criminology Ser.). 199p. 1984. pap. text ed. write for info. (ISBN 0-02-399240-9). Macmillan.

Rich Get Richer & the Poor Write Proposals. Nancy Mitiguy. LC 79-624731. (Illus., Orig.). 1978. pap. 7.00 (ISBN 0-934210-02-0). Devlp Commy.

Rich Get Richer & the Poor Write Proposals. Nancy Mitiguy. 147p. (Citizen Involvement Training Project). 1978. pap. 6.85 (ISBN 0-318-17147-3, C24). VTNC Arlington.

Rich Hall's Vanishing America. Rich Hall. (Illus.). 112p. 1986. pap. 9.95 (ISBN 0-02-547480-4, Collier). Macmillan.

Rich Have Secrets. Unity Hall. (Orig.). 1982. pap. 3.25 (ISBN 0-440-16786-8). Dell.

Rich Heritage of Quakerism. 2nd ed. Walter R. Williams, Jr. et al. LC 87-71513. (Illus.). 326p. pap. 13.95 (ISBN 0-913342-60-2). Barclay Pr.

Rich in Love. Josephine Humphreys. LC 86-40611. 304p. 1987. 16.95 (ISBN 0-670-81810-0). Viking.

Rich in Love. Josephine Humphreys. 262p. 1988. pap. 7.95 (ISBN 0-14-010283-3). Penguin.

Rich in Mercy. Pope John Paul II. 61p. 1980. pap. 3.95 (ISBN 1-55586-734-0). US Catholic.

Rich Is Best. Julie Ellis. 720p. 1986. pap. 4.50 (ISBN 0-8217-1924-6). Zebra.

Rich Kid. Bill Gillham. LC 85-71252. (Illus.). 112p. (gr. 3-7). 1985. 9.95 (ISBN 0-233-97684-1). Andre Deutsch.

Rich Land, Poor Land. Stuart Chase. LC 70-92612. (Illus.). Repr. of 1936 ed. 26.50 (ISBN 0-404-01478-X). AMS Pr.

Rich Like Us. Nayantara Sahgal. 236p. 1986. 14.95 (ISBN 0-393-02309-5). Norton.

Rich Like Us. Nayantara Sahgal. LC 88-5306. 240p. 1988. pap. 8.95 (ISBN 0-8112-1078-2, NDP665). New Directions.

Rich Man & Lazarus. Brownlow North. 1979. pap. 3.95 (ISBN 0-85151-121-X). Banner of Truth.

Rich Man & the Diseased Poor in Early Victorian Literature. A. Susan Williams. LC 86-21029. 144p. 1987. 25.00 (ISBN 0-391-03498-7). Humanities.

Rich Man & the Shoe-Maker. Brian Wildsmith & Jean de LaFontaine. (Illus.). (ps-3). 1965. pap. 6.95 (ISBN 0-19-272104-6). Oxford U Pr.

Rich Man, Poor Man. John Hilton. (English Workers & the Coming of the Welfare State Ser., 1918-1945). 174p. 1985. lib. bdg. 25.00 (ISBN 0-8240-7614-1). Garland Pub.

Rich Man, Poor Man. Irwin Shaw. 1971. pap. 4.25 (ISBN 0-440-17424-4). Dell.

Rich Man, Poor Man see Heinemann Guided Readers.

Rich Man, Poor Man, Beggarman, Theif: Folk Tales from Around the World. Marcus Crouch. (Illus.). 188p. (ps up). 1987. 13.95 (ISBN 0-19-278111-1). Oxford U Pr.

Rich Man's, Poor Man's, & Every Man's Goods: Aspects of Industrialization. Seev Hirsch. 1977. lib. bdg. 32.00 (Pub. by J C B Mohr BRD). Coronet Bks.

Rich Men, Single Women. Pamela Beck & Patti Massman. 384p. 1988. pap. 18.95 (ISBN 0-385-29667-3). Delacorte.

Rich Men, Single Women. Pamela Beck & Patti Massman. 1989. pap. price not set. Dell.

Rich Mitch. Marjorie W. Sharmat. LC 83-5398. (Illus.). 144p. (gr. 3-7). 1983. 10.25 (ISBN 0-688-02407-6). Morrow.

Rich Mitch. Marjorie W. Sharmat. (Illus.). 144p. (gr. 4-6). 1985. pap. 2.50 (ISBN 0-590-40576-4, Apple Paperbacks). Scholastic Inc.

Rich Mrs. Robinson. Winifred Beechey. (Illus.). 1984. pap. 12.95 (ISBN 0-19-211783-1). Oxford U pr.

Rich Nations & the Poor Nations. Barbara Ward. 1962. pap. 5.95 (ISBN 0-393-00746-4, Norton Lib). Norton.

Rich Noble, Poor Noble. M. L. Bush. 240p. 1988. 55.00 (ISBN 0-7190-2381-5, Pub. by Manchester Univ Pr). St Martin.

Rich on Any Allowance. James P. Christensen & Clint Combs. LC 86-72093. (gr. 4-12). 1986. pap. 8.95 (ISBN 0-87579-065-8, Pub. by Shadow Mount). Deseret Bk.

Rich on Any Income: The Easy Budgeting System That Fits in Your Checkbook. James P. Christensen et al. LC 85-22222. (Illus.). 102p. 1985. pap. 8.95 (ISBN 0-87579-009-7, Pub. by Shadow Mountain). Deseret Bk.

Rich Papers: Letters from Bermuda 1615-1646. Ed. by Vernon A. Ives. (Illus.). 448p. 1984. 75.00x (ISBN 0-8020-3405-5). U of Toronto Pr.

Rich Pay Late. Simon Raven. 1987. 15.95 (ISBN 0-8253-0415-6). Beaufort Bks NY.

Rich-Poor Man's Guide to Pittsburgh. 6th ed. Dorothy A. Miller. 1988. pap. 7.95 (ISBN 0-944101-00-3). New Pittsburgh.

Rich Radiant Love. Valerie Sherwood. 576p. 1983. pap. 4.95 (ISBN 0-446-30555-3). Warner Bks.

Rich, Radiant Slaughter. Orania Papazoglou. (Crime Club Ser.). 1989. 12.95 (ISBN 0-385-24612-9). Doubleday.

Rich, Rare & Red. Ben Howkins. 172p. 1987. pap. 9.95 (ISBN 0-932664-54-7). Wine Appreciation.

Rich Rewards. Alice Adams. LC 80-10214. 224p. 1980. 9.95 (ISBN 0-394-51101-8). Knopf.

Rich Rewards. Alice Adams. (Contemporary American Fiction Ser.). 205p. 1981. pap. 7.95 (ISBN 0-14-005918-0). Penguin.

Rich Schools, Poor Schools: The Promise of Equal Educational Opportunity. Arthur E. Wise. LC 66-84485. 1969. 19.00x (ISBN 0-226-90299-4). U of Chicago Pr.

Rich Schools, Poor Schools: The Promise of Equal Educational Opportunity. Arthur E. Wise. LC 68-54485. 288p. 1972. pap. 2.25X (ISBN 0-226-90300-1, P484, Phoen). U of Chicago Pr.

Rich, the Poor & the Bible. rev. ed. Conrad Boerma. Tr. by John Bowden from Dutch. LC 80-15337. 120p. 1980. pap. 5.95 (ISBN 0-664-24349-5). Westminster John Knox.

Rich, the Poor, & the Taxes They Pay. Joseph A. Pechman. 317p. 1986. 44.00 (ISBN 0-8133-0376-1). Westview.

Rich, the Well Born, & the Powerful: Elites & Upper Classes in History. Federic C. Jaher. LC 72-89605. 379p. 1974. 29.95 (ISBN 0-252-00319-5). U of Ill Pr.

Rich, the Wellborn, & the Powerful. Frederic C. Jaher. 384p. 1975. pap. 5.95 (ISBN 0-8065-0505-2, Pub. by Citadel Pr). Lyle Stuart.

Rich Wife. Barbara Wyden. 368p. 1986. pap. 3.95 (ISBN 0-446-30105-1). Warner Bks.

Rich World, Poor World. Geoffrey Lean. 1979. pap. 13.50 (ISBN 0-04-309012-5). Unwin Hyman.

Richard Aldington. Thomas McGreevey. LC 74-1231. (English Biography Ser., No. 31). 1974. lib. bdg. 43.95x (ISBN 0-8383-1785-5). Haskell.

Richard Aldington. Thomas McGreevey. LC 74-1231. (Twayne's English Authors Ser.). 1974. lib. bdg. 17.95 (ISBN 0-8290-2404-2). Irvington.

Richard Aldington. Thomas McGreevy. Repr. lib. bdg. 17.00 (ISBN 0-8414-6431-6). Folcroft.

Richard Aldington: Selected Critical Writing, 1928-1960. Richard Aldington. Ed. by Alister Kershaw. LC 78-86189. (Crosscurrents-Modern Critique Ser.). 158p. 1970. 6.95 (ISBN 0-8093-0451-1). S Ill U Pr.

Richard Allen. Mel Williamson. (Black Americans of Achievement Ser.). (Illus.). 112p. (gr. 5 up). Date not set. lib. bdg. 16.95x (ISBN 1-55546-570-6). Chelsea Hse.

Richard Allen: The First Exemplar of African American Education. E. Curtis Alexander. LC 83-85051. (African American Educator Ser.: Vol. III). (Illus.). 174p. (Orig.). 1985. pap. 8.95 (ISBN 0-938818-06-6). ECA Assoc.

Richard Alsop "A Hartford Wit". Karl P. Harrington. LC 69-17788. 1969. 15.00x (ISBN 0-8195-4000-5). Wesleyan U Pr.

Richard & the Vratch. Beatrice Gormley. 144p. 1987. pap. 2.75 (ISBN 0-380-75207-7, Camelot). Avon.

Richard Anuszkiewicz. Richard Armstrong. (Illus.). 40p. 1976. 10.00 (ISBN 0-686-99811-1). La Jolla Mus Contemp Art.

Richard Armour's Punctured Poems: Famous First & Infamous Second Lines. Richard Armour & Eric Gurney. LC 82-10989, (Illus.). 96p. 1982. pap. 3.95 (ISBN 0-912800-55-0). Woodbridge Pr.

Richard Artschwager. 1988. 40.00 (ISBN 0-393-02596-9); pap. 25.00 (ISBN 0-393-30551-1). Norton.

Richard Artschwager, Chuck Close, Joe Zucker. Catherine Kord. (Illus.). 28p. 1976. 3.00x (ISBN 0-686-99810-3). La Jolla Mus Contemp Art.

Richard Attenborough's a Chorus Line. Diana Carter. (Illus.). 1985. pap. 9.95 (ISBN 0-452-25799-9, Plume). NAL.

Richard B. Moore, Caribbean Militant in Harlem: Collected Writings, 1920-1972. Ed. by W. Burghardt Turner & Joyce M. Turner. LC 87-37382. (Blacks in the Diaspora Ser.). 352p. 1988. 57.50. Ind U Pr.

Richard Barnfield Colin's Child. Harry Morris. LC 63-63443. (FSU Studies: No. 38). 1963. 10.00x (ISBN 0-8130-0477-2). U Presses Fla.

Richard Barrett's Journal New York & Canada 1816: Critique of the Young Nation by an Englishman Abroad. Ed. by Thomas Brott & Philip Kelley. LC 83-50936. (Illus.). 144p. (Orig.). 1983. pap. 18.50x (ISBN 0-911459-07-3). Wedgestone Pr.

Richard Baxter: Puritan Man of Letters. N. H. Keeble. 1982. 45.00x (ISBN 0-19-811716-7). Oxford U Pr.

Richard Beer-Hofmann: His Life & Work. Esther N. Elstun. LC 82-14990. (Penn State Studies in German Literature). 225p. 1983. 24.95x (ISBN 0-271-00335-9). Pa St U Pr.

Richard Bentley: A Descriptive, Annotated Bibiography. Robert E. Bourdette. LC 84-45392. 275p. 1985. lib. bdg. 37.00 (ISBN 0-8240-8849-2). Garland Pub.

Richard Boleslavsky: His Life & Work in the Theatre. J. W. Roberts. LC 81-16411. (Theater & Dramatic Studies: No. 7). (Illus.). pap. 77.50 (ISBN 0-8357-1250-8, 2070279). Bks Demand UMI.

Richard Brathwaits's Comments in 1665 upon Chaucer's Tales of the Miller & His Wife of Bath. Intro. by C. F. Spurgeon. (Chaucer Society Second Ser.: No. 33). 124p. Repr. of 1901 ed. 10.95x. Ibis Pub VA.

Richard Brauer: Collected Papers, 3 vols. Richard Brauer. Ed. by Warren J. Wong & Paul Fong. 1980. Vol. 1. 80.00x (ISBN 0-262-02135-8); Vol. 2. 80.00x (ISBN 0-262-02148-X). MIT Pr.

Richard Brautigan. Jay Boyer. LC 87-70030. (Western Writers Ser.: 79). (Illus.). 52p. (Orig.). 1987. pap. 2.95x (ISBN 0-88430-078-1). Boise St Univ.

Richard Brautigan. Marc Chenetier. LC 82-20880. (Contemporary Writers Ser.). 96p. 1983. pap. 4.75 (ISBN 0-416-32960-8, NO. 3751). Routledge Chapman & Hall.

Richard Brinsley Sheridan: A Reference Guide. Jack D. Durant. 1981. lib. bdg. 36.50 (ISBN 0-8161-8146-2, Hall Reference). G K Hall.

Richard Brome: A Study of His Life & Works. Clarence E. Andrews. LC 72-6665. (Yales Studies in English Ser.: No. 46). vi, 140p. 1972. Repr. of 1913 ed. 19.50 (ISBN 0-208-01122-6, Archon). Shoe String.

Richard Buckminster Fuller: Journal Articles Published 1970-1986. Mary Vance. (Architecture Ser.: A 1831). 9p. 1987. 3.00 (ISBN 1-55590-341-X). Vance Biblios.

Richard Burton, My Brother. Graham Jenkins. 1988. 17.95 (ISBN 0-06-015952-9). Har-Row.

Richard C. Young's Financial Armadillo Strategy. Richard C. Young & David Franke. LC 86-16446. (Illus.). 224p. 1987. 17.95 (ISBN 0-688-05830-2). Morrow.

Richard Carew of Antony: The Survey of Cornwall & C. F. E. Halliday. 1953. lib. bdg. 30.00 (ISBN 0-8414-9148-8). Folcroft.

Richard Carvel. Winston Churchill. 1899. lib. bdg. 49.00 (ISBN 0-8414-3036-5). Folcroft.

Richard Chamberlain: An Unauthorized Biography. Jeffrey Ryder. (Orig.). 1988. pap. 3.50 (ISBN 0-440-20048-2). Dell.

Richard Clague: 1821-1873. LC 74-25157. (Illus.). 128p. 1974. pap. 5.00x (ISBN 0-913060-23-2, New Orleans Museum of Art). Norton Art.

Richard Cobden. Wendy Hinde. LC 86-26661. 376p. 1987. text ed. 30.00 (ISBN 0-300-03880-1). Yale U Pr.

Richard Cobden: Independent Radical. Nicholas C. Edsall. (Illus.). 416p. 1986. text ed. 31.95x (ISBN 0-674-76879-5). Harvard U Pr.

Richard Crashaw. Thomas F. Healy. (Medieval & Renaissance Authors Ser.: Vol. 8). x, 162p. 1986. 31.75 (ISBN 90-04-07864-9, Pub. by E J Brill). Heinman.

Richard Crashaw. Basil Willey. LC 76-26647. 1949. lib. bdg. 17.00 (ISBN 0-8414-9386-3). Folcroft.

Richard Crashaw: An Annotated Bibliography of Criticism, 1632-1980. John R. Roberts. LC 84-52264. 488p. 1985. text ed. 39.00x (ISBN 0-8262-0468-6). U of Mo Pr.

Richard Crashaw & the Spanish Golden Age. R. V. Young. LC 82-1850. (Studies in English Ser.: No. 191). 240p. 1982. text ed. 25.50t (ISBN 0-300-02766-4). Yale U Pr.

Richard Crashaw Poet & Saint. Thomas Foy. LC 74-9797. 1933. lib. bdg. 16.00 (ISBN 0-8414-4204-5). Folcroft.

Richard Cumberland's - The Wheel of Fortune: A Critical Edition. Ed. by Stephen Orgel. (Satire & Sense Ser.). 296p. 1987. lib. bdg. 45.00 (ISBN 0-8240-6016-4). Garland Pub.

Richard D. Irwin Presents Basic Building Blocks. Meca. 1986. Apple. pap. 17.95x (ISBN 0-256-03607-1); IBM. pap. 17.95x (ISBN 0-256-03608-X). Irwin.

Richard D. Irwin Presents P C CALC Version 2.0. Jim Button. 1987. 13.95x (ISBN 0-256-05618-8); disk 18.95x (ISBN 0-256-05619-6). Irwin.

Richard D. Irwin Presents PC-File III & PC CALC. Jim Button. 1985. pap. 15.95x (ISBN 0-256-03507-5). Irwin.

Richard D. Irwin Presents PC File-r. Jim Button. 1987. 18.95x (ISBN 0-256-05622-6). Irwin.

Richard D. Irwin Presents PC-Write 2.6. Bob Wallace. 1987. pap. 16.95x (ISBN 0-256-05659-5); manual with disk 19.95 (ISBN 0-256-05660-9). Irwin.

Richard Daley: The Strong Willed Mayor of Chicago. Gerald Kurland. Ed. by D. Steve Rahmas. LC 70-190236. (Outstanding Personalities Ser.: No. 18). 32p. (Orig.). (gr. 7-12). lib. bdg. 3.75 incl. catalog cards (ISBN 0-87157-518-3); pap. 2.50 vinyl laminated covers (ISBN 0-87157-018-1). SamHar Pr.

Richard Deacon. John Caldwell et al. (Illus.). 96p. (Orig.). 1988. pap. 11.95 (ISBN 0-88039-018-2). Mus Art Carnegie.

Richard Deacon's Microwave Cookery. Richard Deacon. LC 73-93782. (Illus.). 160p. 1977. pap. 8.95 (ISBN 0-912656-73-5). Price Stern.

Richard Dehmels Gesammelte Werke, 10 Vols. in 3. Richard Dehmel. LC 76-163694. (BCL Ser. I). Repr. of 1913 ed. Set. 110.00 (ISBN 0-404-02070-4). AMS Pr.

Richard Diebenkorn. Gerald Nordland. LC 87-42688. (Illus.). 224p. 1987. 65.00 (ISBN 0-8478-0870-X). Rizzoli Intl.

Richard Diebenkorn: Small Paintings from Ocean Park. Dore Ashton. LC 85-60997. 48p. 1986. 18.00 (ISBN 0-939931-00-1). Houston Fine Art Pr.

Richard Diebenkorn: Works on Paper. Ed. & intro. by Richard Newlin. LC 86-82665. 293p. 1987. 65.00 (ISBN 0-940619-00-8). Houston Fine Art Pr.

Richard Doddridge Blackmore: His Life & Novels. Quincy G. Burris. LC 70-136909. 219p. Repr. of 1930 ed. lib. bdg. 35.00x (ISBN 0-8371-5356-5, BURB). Greenwood.

Richard Doyle. Rodney Engen. (Artist & the Critic Ser.). (Illus.). 216p. cancelled (ISBN 0-904995-05-4). Parkwest Pubns.

Richard Doyle & His Family. Lionel Lambourne. (Illus.). 96p. (Orig.). 1984. pap. 9.95 (ISBN 0-905209-58-3, Pub. by Victoria & Albert Mus UK). Faber & Faber.

Richard, Duke of York, 1411-1460. P. A. Johnson. (Oxford Historical Monographs). 330p. 1988. 65.00 (ISBN 0-19-822946-1). Oxford U Pr.

Richard Eberhart. Ralph J. Mills, Jr. (Pamphlets on American Writers Ser: No. 55). (Orig.). 1966. pap. 1.25x (ISBN 0-8166-0385-5, MPAW55). U of Minn Pr.

Richard Eberhart: A Celebration. Ed. by Sydney Lea & Jay Parini. 76p. (Orig.). 1980. pap. 6.00 (ISBN 0-917241-00-2). Kenyon Hill.

Richard Eberhart: Poet of Life in Death. Wade Van Dore. 12p. (Orig.). 1982. pap. 1.50 (ISBN 0-934996-17-2). American Studies Pr.

Richard Erdoes Illustrated Treasury of Classic Unlaundered Limericks. Illus. by Richard Erdoes. LC 84-11014. (Illus.). 160p. 1984. pap. 6.95 (ISBN 0-917439-01-5). Balsam Pr.

Richard Estes: The Complete Paintings 1966-1985. Louis K. Meisel. (Illus.). 144p. 1986. 39.95 (ISBN 0-8109-0881-6). Abrams.

Richard Estes: The Urban Landscape. John Canaday. LC 78-59702. (Illus., Catalogue & Interview by John Arthur). 1979. pap. 16.95 (ISBN 0-87846-126-4, 760668, A Boston Museum of Fine Arts Books). NYGS.

Richard F. Burton. Glenn S. Burne. (Twayne English Author Ser.: No. 412). 192p. 1985. lib. bdg. 23.95 (ISBN 0-8057-6903-X, Twayne). G K Hall.

Richard Furman: Life & Legacy. James A. Rogers. LC 84-27248. (Illus.). xxxii, 336p. 1985. 24.95 (ISBN 0-86554-151-5, MUP/H142). Mercer Univ Pr.

Richard Goldschmidt: Controversial Geneticist & Creative Biologist. Ed. by L. K. Pitternick. (Experientia Supplementa: No. 35). 154p. 1980. 16.95x (ISBN 0-8176-1093-6). Birkhauser.

Richard Guindon Nineteen Eighty-One to Nineteen Eighty-Four. Christopher R. Young. (Illus.). 24p. 1985. pap. 3.50 (ISBN 0-317-26892-9). Flint Inst Arts.

Richard Hakluyt & His Successors. Ed. by Edward Lynam. (Hakluyt Society Works Ser.: No. 2, Vol. 93). Repr. of 1946 ed. 21.00 (ISBN 0-8115-0389-5). Kraus Repr.

Richard Harding Davis & His Day. Fairfax Downey. 1933. 25.00 (ISBN 0-8274-3279-8). R West.

Richard Harrington's Antarctic. Richard Harrington. LC 75-43581. (Illus.). 1976. Album Style. pap. 8.95 (ISBN 0-88240-054-1). Alaska Northwest.

Richard Henry Dana, 2 Vols. Charles F. Adams. LC 67-23883. 838p. 1968. Repr. of 1890 ed. 43.00x (ISBN 0-8103-3038-5). Gale.

Richard Henry Dana, Jr. Samuel Shapiro. xv, 245p. 1961. 5.00 (ISBN 0-87013-062-5). Mich St U Pr.

Richard Henry Lee: Statesman of the Revolution. Oliver P. Chitwood. (Illus.). 1967. 7.00 (ISBN 0-685-30817-0). McClain.

Richard Henry Lee, Statesman of the Revolution. Oliver P. Chitwood. LC 67-31697. 310p. 1967. 3.50. West VA U Pr.

Richard Henry of Resolution Island. Suzanne Hill & John Hill. (Illus.). 1987. 44.95 (ISBN 0-86868-094-X, Pub. by J McIndoe Ltd New Zealand). Intl Spec Bk.

Richard Hildreth. Donald E. Emerson. LC 78-64201. (Johns Hopkins University. Studies in the Social Sciences. Sixty-Fourth Ser. 1946: 2). Repr. of 1946 ed. 18.50 (ISBN 0-404-61307-1). AMS Pr.

Richard Hittleman's Introduction to Yoga. Richard Hittleman. (Orig.). 1969. pap. 4.50 (ISBN 0-553-24787-5). Bantam.

Richard Holt Hutton of "The Spectator". Richard H. Hutton. 1973. Repr. of 1899 ed. 25.00 (ISBN 0-8274-0356-9). R West.

Richard Hooker: A Descriptive Bibliography of the Early Editions, 1593-1724. Ed. by W. Speed Hill. LC 72-147090. 153p. 1970. pap. 10.00 (ISBN 0-8295-0211-4). UPB.

Richard Hooker: A Selected Bibliography. Egil Grislis & W. Speed Hill. LC 79-32321. 1981. 5.50 (ISBN 0-931222-03-6). Pitts Theolog.

Richard Hooker & Contemporary Political Ideas. John Shirley. LC 78-20491. 1980. Repr. of 1949 ed. 25.00 (ISBN 0-88355-868-8). Hyperion Conn.

Richard Hooker & the Politics of a Christian England. Robert K. Faulkner. LC 79-65776. 195p. 1981. 35.00x (ISBN 0-520-03993-9). U of Cal Pr.

Richard Hughes: Novelist. Richard Poole. LC 86-63545. 253p. 1987. 30.00 (ISBN 0-907476-52-X, Pub. by Poetry Wales Pr UK). Dufour.

Richard Hugo. Donna Gerstenberger. LC 82-74093. (Western Writers Ser.: No. 59). (Illus., Orig.). 1983. pap. 2.95x (ISBN 0-88430-033-1). Boise St Univ.

Richard Hurdis: Tale of Alabama. rev. ed. W. Gilmore Simms. LC 70-176021. Repr. of 1890 ed. 10.00 (ISBN 0-404-06035-8). AMS Pr.

Richard Hurd's Letters on Chivalry & Romance. Audley L. Smith. 1939. lib. bdg. 19.00 (ISBN 0-8414-7540-7). Folcroft.

Richard I in England, Eleven Eighty Nine & Eleven Ninety Four: Medieval People, Vol. 1. Harry S. Howser. (Illus.). 115p. (Orig.). 1986. pap. 9.95 (ISBN 0-934667-04-7). Tangelwuld.

Richard II. Jeanne T. Newlin. LC 83-48290. (Shakespearean Criticism Ser.). 302p. 1984. lib. bdg. 35.00 (ISBN 0-8240-9238-4). Garland Pub.

Richard II. Malcolm Page. LC 86-18640. (Text & Performance Ser.). (Illus.). 88p. 1987. pap. text ed. 7.95 (ISBN 0-391-03466-9). Humanities.

Richard II. William Shakespeare. LC 78-24130. (Shakespeare Plays Ser.). (Illus.). 1979. pap. 2.95 (ISBN 0-8317-7396-0, Mayflower Bks). Smith Pubs.

Richard II. William Shakespeare. (Classics Ser.). 1988. pap. 2.50 (ISBN 0-553-21303-2, Bantam Classics). Bantam.

Richard II in the Early Chronicles. L. D. Duls. LC 73-80355. (Studies in English Literature: No. 79). 274p. 1975. pap. text ed. 24.00x (ISBN 90-2793-326-X). Mouton.

Richard III. Charles Ross. LC 81-43381. (English Monarchs Ser.: No. 6). (Illus.). 263p. 1982. 27.95x (ISBN 0-520-04589-0); pap. 9.95 (ISBN 0-520-05075-4). U of Cal Pr.

Richard III. William Shakespeare. Ed. by Mark Eccles. pap. 2.75 (ISBN 0-451-51936-1, CE1833, Sig Classics). NAL.

Richard III. William Shakespeare. (Book Notes Ser.). 1985. pap. 2.50 (ISBN 0-8120-3537-2). Barron.

Richard III. William Shakespeare. (Classics Ser.). 1988. pap. 2.75 (ISBN 0-553-21304-0, Bantam Classics). Bantam.

Richard III: England's Black Legend. Desmond Seward. LC 83-50348. (Illus.). 220p. 1984. 18.95 (ISBN 0-531-09817-6). Watts.

Richard Irvine Manning & the Progressive Movement in South Carolina. Robert M. Burts. LC 73-19814. xii, 262p. 1974. lib. bdg. 24.95x (ISBN 0-87249-292-3). U of SC Pr.

Richard Jefferies. Reginald Arkell. 294p. 1983. Repr. of 1933 ed. text ed. 45.00 (ISBN 0-89984-020-5). Century Bookbindery.

Richard Jefferies: A Study. H. S. Salt. 1977. Repr. of 1894 ed. lib. bdg. 20.50 (ISBN 0-8495-4817-9). Arden Lib.

Richard Jefferies: A Study. H. S. Salt. 1978. Repr. of 1894 ed. lib. bdg. 20.00 (ISBN 0-8414-7873-2). Folcroft.

Richard Jefferies: A Study. H. S. Salt. 128p. 1982. Repr. of 1894 ed. lib. bdg. 25.00 (ISBN 0-89984-610-6). Century Bookbindery.

Richard Jefferies: A Tribute by Various Writers. Ed. by Samuel J. Looker. 1978. Repr. of 1946 ed. lib. bdg. 32.00 (ISBN 0-8414-5273-3). Folcroft.

Richard Jefferies Centenary 1948. Samuel J. Looker. 1978. Repr. of 1948 ed. lib. bdg. 30.00 (ISBN 0-8414-5884-7). Folcroft.

Richard Jefferies: His Life & His Ideals. Henry S. Salt. 1978. Repr. of 1905 ed. lib. bdg. 27.00 (ISBN 0-8414-8168-7). Folcroft.

Richard Jefferies: His Life & His Ideals. Henry S. Salt. LC 77-113320. 1970. Repr. of 1905 ed. 18.00x (ISBN 0-8046-1033-9, Pub. by Kennikat). Assoc Faculty Pr.

Richard Jefferies: His Life & His Ideals. Henry S. Salt. 1973. Repr. of 1905 ed. 20.00 (ISBN 0-8274-1344-0). R West.

Richard Jefferies: His Life & Work. Edward Thomas. 1973. lib. bdg. 20.50 (ISBN 0-8414-8043-5). Folcroft.

Richard Jefferies: His Life & Work. Edward Thomas. LC 78-160785. 1971. Repr. of 1909 ed. 26.50x (ISBN 0-8046-1617-5, Pub. by Kennikat). Assoc Faculty Pr.

Richard Joseph Neutra: Update to A 288. Sara Richardson. (Architecture Ser.: A 1704). 10p. 1986. 3.00 (ISBN 1-55590-074-7). Vance Biblios.

Richard Kennedy: Collected Stories. Richard Kennedy. LC 86-45495. (Illus.). 288p. (gr. 1-6). 1987. 14.95i (ISBN 0-06-023255-2); PLB 14.89 (ISBN 0-06-023256-0). HarpJ.

Richard Kennedy: Collected Stories. Richard Kennedy. (Illus.). 270p. (gr. 1-6). Date not set. 14.95 (ISBN 0-317-67705-5). Har-Row.

Richard Kern: Expeditionary Artist in the Far Southwest, 1848-1853. David J. Weber. LC 84-19497. (Illus.). 369p. 1985. 45.00 (ISBN 0-8263-0770-1). U of NM Pr.

Richard Knight's Treasure! The True Story of His Extraordinary Quest for Captain Kidd's Cache. Glenys Roberts. 1987. 17.95 (ISBN 0-670-80761-3). Viking.

Richard Kostelanetz. Richard Kostelanetz. 1980. 25.00 (ISBN 0-686-47151-2). RK Edns.

Richard Lamb. Richard S. Wheeler. 1987. 16.95 (ISBN 0-8027-4076-6). Walker & Co.

Richard Lester: A Guide to References & Resources. Diane Rosenfeldt. 1978. lib. bdg. 21.50 (ISBN 0-8161-8185-3, Hall Reference). G K Hall.

Richard Lionheart: The Crusader King. John Matthews. (Heroes & Warriors Ser.). (Illus.). 52p. (Orig.). 1988. pap. 7.95 (ISBN 1-85314-007-4, Pub. by Firebird Bks UK). Sterling.

Richard Long: Works to Date. R. H. Fuchs. (Illus.). 244p. 1986. 45.00 (ISBN 0-500-23467-1). Thames Hudson.

Richard Lovelace & the Uses of Obscurity. Gerald Hammond. 1985. pap. 5.50 (ISBN 0-85672-541-2, Pub. by British Acad). Longwood Pub Group.

Richard M. Nixon. Ed. by Carol B. Fitzgerald. (Meckler's Bibliographies of the Presidents of the United States, 1789-1989 Ser.: No. 36). (Illus.). 1988. lib. bdg. 45.00x (ISBN 0-88736-148-X). Meckler Corp.

Richard M. Nixon: A Biographic Exploration. Dale E. Casper. (Reference Library of Social Science). 232p. 1988. lib. bdg. 30.00 (ISBN 0-8240-8478-0). Garland Pub.

Richard M. Nixon: Chronology; Documents; Bibliographical Aids. Ed. by H. F. Bremer. LC 75-23324. (Presidential Chronology Ser.). 250p. 1975. 15.00 (ISBN 0-379-12083-6). Oceana.

Richard M. Nixon: The Thirty-Seventh President. Jim Hargrove. LC 84-27416. (People of Distinction Ser.). (Illus.). 128p. (gr. 4 up). 1985. lib. bdg. 14.60 (ISBN 0-516-03212-7). Childrens.

Richard Mansfield, the Man & the Actor. facsimile ed. Paul Wilstach. LC 79-107836. (Select Bibliographies Reprint Ser). 1908. 27.50 (ISBN 0-8369-5201-4). Ayer Co Pubs.

Richard Mather of Dorchester. B. R. Burg. LC 75-41987. 224p. 1976. 21.00x (ISBN 0-8131-1343-1). U Pr of Ky.

Richard Maurice Bucke, Medical Mystic: Letters of Dr. Bucke to Walt Whitman & His Friends. Richard M. Bucke. Ed. by Artem Lozynsky. LC 77-6818. 172p. 1977. 19.95x (ISBN 0-8143-1576-3). Wayne St U Pr.

Richard Meier, Architect. Compiled by Rykwert. LC 83-42911. (Illus.). 416p. 1984. 60.00 (ISBN 0-8478-0496-8); pap. 40.00 (ISBN 0-8478-0497-6). Rizzoli Intl.

Richard Meier, Architect: A Selected Bibliography. Jamie W. Coniglio. (Architecture Ser.: A 1462). 6p. 1985. 2.00 (ISBN 0-89028-552-7). Vance Biblios.

Richard Meltzer's Guide to the Ugliest Buildings of Los Angeles. Richard Meltzer. 40p. (Orig.). 1984. pap. 4.95 (ISBN 0-89807-116-X). Illuminati.

Richard Middleton, the Man & His Work. Henry Savage. 210p. 1981. Repr. of 1922 ed. lib. bdg. 35.00 (ISBN 0-89984-600-9). Century Bookbindery.

Richard Middleton: The Man & His Work. Henry Savage. 1973. lib. bdg. 27.50 (ISBN 0-8414-8163-6). Folcroft.

Richard Middleton: The Man & His Work. Henry Savage. LC 70-160780. 1971. Repr. of 1922 ed. 28.50x (ISBN 0-8046-1612-4, Pub. by Kennikat). Assoc Faculty Pr.

Richard Middleton's Letters to Henry Savage. Richard Middleton. 1929. 52.50 (ISBN 0-8274-3280-1). R West.

Richard Morris Hunt. Paul R. Baker. 125p. 1980. pap. 17.50 (ISBN 0-262-52109-1). MIT Pr.

Richard Morris, Kenneth Brewer, Ronald Anthony Punnet, Halvard Johnson, Peter Wild, David Tammer. Carlos Reyes. 16p. (Orig.). 1968. pap. 2.00 (ISBN 0-685-59507-2). Trask Hse Bks.

Richard Navin: The Mycenae Circle. Richard Navin. LC 80-1216. (Illus.). 20p. 1981. soft cover museum catalogue 5.00 (ISBN 0-89207-028-5). S R Guggenheim.

Richard Nelson's American Cooking. Richard Nelson. 1983. 17.95 (ISBN 0-453-00442-3). NAL.

Richard Neutra & the Search for Modern Architecture: A Biography & History. Thomas S. Hines. LC 81-22530. (Illus.). 1982. 65.00x (ISBN 0-19-503028-1); pap. 29.95x (ISBN 0-19-503029-X). Oxford U Pr.

Richard Neutra: Promise & Fulfillment, 1919-1932: Selections from the Letters & Diaries of Richard & Dione Neutra. Compiled by & tr. by Dione Neutra. 264p. 1986. 24.95 (ISBN 0-8093-1228-X). S Ill U Pr.

Richard Nixon: The Man Behind the Mask. Gary Allen. 434p. pap. 4.95 (ISBN 0-686-31149-3). Concord Pr.

Richard Nixon: The Man Behind the Mask. Gary Allen. LC 73-31048. 433p. 1971. 8.00 (ISBN 0-88279-222-9). Western Islands.

Richard Nixon: The Shaping of His Character. Fawn M. Brodie. (Illus.). 1981. 18.95 (ISBN 0-393-01467-3). Norton.

Richard Nixon: The Shaping of His Character. Fawn M. Brodie. 576p. 1983. pap. 10.95 (ISBN 0-674-76880-9). Harvard U Pr.

Richard Norman Shaw. Andrew Saint. LC 75-43333. (Studies in British Art Ser.). 1976. 77.00x (ISBN 0-300-01955-6); pap. 18.95 (ISBN 0-300-02174-7). Yale U Pr.

Richard Oastler: King of Factory Children, 1835-61. LC 72-2541. (British Labour Struggles Before 1850 Ser). 1972. 23.50 (ISBN 0-405-04433-X). Ayer Co Pubs.

Richard of Devizes: Chronicon Ricardi Divisiensis de Rebus Gestis Ricardi I Regis Angliae. Ed. by J. Stevenson. (English History Society Publications Ser.: Vol. 11). Repr. of 1838 ed. 25.00 (ISBN 0-8115-1536-2). Kraus Repr.

Richard of St. Victor: The Twelve Patriarchs, the Mystical Ark Book, Three of the Trinity. Ed. by Grover A. Zinn. LC 79-83834. (Classics of Western Spirituality Ser.). 448p. 1979. 13.95 (ISBN 0-8091-0241-2); pap. 9.95 (ISBN 0-8091-2122-0). Paulist Pr.

Richard of Wallingford: An Edition of His Writings with Introduction, English Translation & Commentary, 3 vols. Ed. by J. D. North. (Illus.). 1976. 275.00x (ISBN 0-19-858139-4). Oxford U Pr.

Richard Olney & His Public Service. Henry James. LC 70-87445. (American Scene Ser). (Illus.). 1971. Repr. of 1923 ed. lib. bdg. 39.50 (ISBN 0-306-71516-3). Da Capo.

Richard Olney: Evolution of a Statesman. Gerald G. Eggert. LC 73-6878. (Illus.). 432p. 1974. 29.50x (ISBN 0-271-01162-9). Pa St U Pr.

Richard Parkes Bonington. Carlos Peacock. LC 79-63955. (Illus.). 1980. 25.00 (ISBN 0-8008-6793-9). Taplinger.

Richard Parkes Bonington. Carlos Peacock. (Illus.). 110p. 25.00 (ISBN 0-317-54916-2). Apollo.

Richard Paul Lohse: Drawings 1935-1985. Hans P. Riese et al. LC 86-42750. (Illus.). 144p. 1986. 35.00 (ISBN 0-8478-0758-4). Rizzoli Intl.

Richard Payne Knight: The Twilight of Virtuosity. Frank J. Messman. 1974. text ed. 31.25x (ISBN 0-686-22564-3). Mouton.

Richard Peters: Champion of the New South. Royce Shingleton. LC 84-22701. xiv, 258p. 1985. 21.95 (ISBN 0-86554-126-4, MUP/H117). Mercer Univ Pr.

Richard Porson: A Biographical Essay. M. L. Clarke. 1978. Repr. of 1937 ed. lib. bdg. 27.50 (ISBN 0-8495-0828-2). Arden Lib.

Richard Porson, Seventeen Fifty-Nine to Eighteen Hundred Eight. D. L. Page. 1959. pap. 5.50 (ISBN 0-85672-632-X, Pub. by British Acad). Longwood Pub Group.

Richard Price & the Ethical Foundations of the American Revolution. Ed. by W. Bernard Peach. LC 77-91081. 1979. 35.00 (ISBN 0-8223-0400-7). Duke.

Richard Pryor. Joseph Nazel. (Orig.). 1980. pap. 2.25 (ISBN 0-87067-013-1, BH013). Holloway.

Richard R. Niebuhr on Christ & Religion: The Four-Stage Development of His Theology. Patrick Primeaux. LC 81-38369. (Toronto Studies in Theology: Vol. 4). (Illus.). xiv, 288p. 1981. lib. bdg. 49.95x (ISBN 0-88946-973-3). E Mellen.

Richard Redgrave. Susan P. Casteras & Ronald Parkinson. LC 87-51378. 224p. 1988. text ed. 40.00 (ISBN 0-300-04221-3). Yale U Pr.

Richard Robertovich. Mark Frankland. 1987. 16.95 (ISBN 0-8253-0442-3). Beaufort Bks NY.

Richard Rodgers: A Check List of His Published Songs. Compiled by Steven Suskin. (Illus.). 25p. (Orig.). 1988. pap. 10.00 (ISBN 0-87104-404-8). NY Pub Lib.

Richard Rogers: A Biography. Bryan Appleyard. (Orig.). 1986. pap. 22.95 (ISBN 0-571-13756-3). Faber & Faber.

Richard Rogers & Partners: An Architectural Monograph. Contrib. by Peter Cook. (Academy Architecture Ser.). (Illus.). 160p. 1985. 35.00 (ISBN 0-312-68208-5); pap. 24.95 (ISBN 0-312-68207-7). St Martin.

Richard Rogers: RIBA Gold Medallist, 1985. Valerie J. Nurcombe. (Architecture Ser.: A 1496). 24p. 1985. 3.75 (ISBN 0-89028-626-4). Vance Biblios.

Richard Rolle. Ed. by Rosamund S. Allen. (Classics of Western Spirituality Ser.). 1988. 16.95; pap. 12.95. Paulist Pr.

Richard Rolle & de Holy Boke Gratia Dei: An Edition with Commentary. Mary Luke Arntz. Ed. by James Hogg. (Elizabethan & Renaissance Studies). 207p. (Orig.). 1981. pap. 15.00 (ISBN 3-7052-0743-1, Pub. by Salzburg Studies). Longwood Pub Group.

Richard Rolle: Prose & Verse Edited from MS Longleat 29 & Related Manuscripts. Ed. by Sarah Ogilvie-Thomson. (Early English Text Society-Original Ser.: No. 293). (Illus.). 372p. 1989. 45.00 (ISBN 0-19-722295-1). Oxford U Pr.

Richard Rolle's Expositio Super Novem Lectiones Mortuorum. Malcolm Moyes. Ed. by James Hogg. (Elizabethan & Renaissance Studies). (Orig.). 1984. pap. 15.00 (ISBN 3-7052-0753-9, Pub. by Salzburg Studies). Longwood Pub Group.

Richard Rufus of Cornwall & the Tradition of Oxford Theology. Peter Raedts. (Oxford Historical Monographs). 1987. 53.00 (ISBN 0-19-822941-0). Oxford U Pr.

Richard S. Hill: Tributes from Friends. Compiled by Carol J. Bradley & James B. Coover. (Detroit Studies in Music Bibliography: No. 58). xv, 397p. 1987. 45.00 (ISBN 0-89990-035-6). Harmonie Pk Pr.

Richard Sans Peur. Ed. by Denis J. Conlon. (Studies in the Romance Languages & Literatures: No.192). 120p. (Orig.). 1978. pap. 10.00x (ISBN 0-8078-9192-4). U of NC Pr.

Richard Savage: A Mystery in Biography. Stanley V. Makower. LC 72-160770. 1971. Repr. of 1909 ed. 24.50 (ISBN 0-8046-1597-7, Pub. by Kennikat). Assoc Faculty Pr.

Richard Savage: A Mystery in Biography. Stanley V. Makower. 1973. Repr. of 1900 ed. 14.50 (ISBN 0-8274-1567-2). R West.

Richard Scarry Huckle's Book. Richard Scarry. (Cloth Bks). (Illus.). (ps). 1979. 2.95 (ISBN 0-394-84130-1, BYR). Random.

Richard Scarry's ABC Word Book. Richard Scarry. (Illus.). (ps-2). 1971. 8.95 (ISBN 0-394-82339-7, BYR); lib. bdg. 5.99 (ISBN 0-394-92339-1). Random.

Richard Scarry's Animal Nursery Tales. Richard Scarry. (Illus.). (ps-1). 1975. 7.95 (ISBN 0-307-16810-7, Golden Bks). Western Pub.

Richard Scarry's Best Christmas Book Ever. Richard Scarry. LC 80-5172. (Illus.). 48p. (ps-2). 1981. 8.95 (ISBN 0-394-84936-1); lib. bdg. 5.99 (ISBN 0-394-94936-6). Random.

Richard Scarry's Best Coloring Activity Book Ever. Richard Scarry. LC 74-6872. (Illus.). 176p. (ps-4). 1974. 6.95 (ISBN 0-394-83018-0, BYR). Random.

Richard Scarry's Best Counting Book Ever. Richard Scarry. LC 74-2544. (Illus.). 48p. (ps-2). 1975. 8.95 (ISBN 0-394-82924-7, BYR); lib. bdg. 9.99 (ISBN 0-394-92924-1). Random.

Richard Scarry's Best First Book Ever. Richard Scarry. LC 79-3900. (Illus.). (ps-1). 1979. 7.95 (ISBN 0-394-84250-2, BYR); lib. bdg. 8.99 (ISBN 0-394-94250-7). Random.

Richard Scarry's Best Make-It Book Ever. Richard Scarry. (Illus.). (gr. k-3). 1977. pap. 8.95 (ISBN 0-394-83492-5, BYR). Random.

Richard Scarry's Best Mother Goose Ever. Illus. by Richard Scarry. (Illus.). (ps-1). 1970. 7.95 (ISBN 0-307-15578-1, Golden Bks). Western Pub.

Richard Scarry's Best Story Book Ever. Richard Scarry. (Illus.). (gr. 1-5). 1968. 8.95 (ISBN 0-307-16548-5, Golden Bks). Western Pub.

Richard Scarry's Best Times Ever: A Book about Seasons & Holidays. Richard Scarry. LC 87-81758. (Golden Look-Look Books). (Illus.). 24p. (ps-3). 1988. pap. 1.60 (ISBN 0-307-11913-0, Pub. by Golden Bks). Western Pub.

Richard Scarry's Best Word Book Ever. Richard Scarry. (Illus.). (ps-3). 1963. 7.95 (ISBN 0-307-15510-2, Golden Bks). Western Pub.

Richard Scarry's Biggest Word Book Ever! Richard Scarry. (Illus.). 12p. (ps-1). 1985. bds. 29.95 (ISBN 0-394-87374-2, BYR). Random.

Richard Scarry's Busiest People Ever. Richard Scarry. LC 76-8123. (Illus.). (ps-2). 1976. lib. bdg. 9.99 (ISBN 0-394-93293-5, BYR); PLB 7.95 (ISBN 0-394-83293-0). Random.

Richard Scarry's Busy Busy World. Richard Scarry. (Illus.). (gr. k-5). 8.95 (ISBN 0-307-15511-0, Golden Bks). Western Pub.

Richard Scarry's Busy Houses. Richard Scarry. LC 81-50713. (Shape Bks.). (Illus.). 24p. (ps-k). 1981. spiral plastic bdg. 2.95 (ISBN 0-394-84937-X). Random.

Richard Scarry's Cars & Trucks & Things That Go. Richard Scarry. (ps-2). 1974. 7.95 (ISBN 0-307-15785-7, Golden Bks). Western Pub.

Richard Scarry's Color Book. Richard Scarry. LC 75-36465. (Illus.). 14p. (ps-1). 1976. 3.95 (ISBN 0-394-83237-X, BYR). Random.

Richard Scarry's Find Your ABC's. Richard Scarry. (Pictureback Bks.). (Illus.). (ps-1). 1973. pap. 1.95 (ISBN 0-394-82683-3). Random.

Richard Scarry's Find Your ABC's see Big Blue Box of Books: Five Picture-Book Favorites.

Richard Scarry's Great Big Air Book. Richard Scarry. LC 79-146649. (Illus.). (gr. k-3). 1971. 8.95 (ISBN 0-394-82167-X, BYR); lib. bdg. 11.99 (ISBN 0-394-92167-4). Random.

Richard Scarry's Great Big Schoolhouse. Richard Scarry. (Illus.). (ps-2). 1969. 8.95 (ISBN 0-394-80874-6, BYR). Random.

Richard Scarry's Great Steamboat Mystery. Richard Scarry. LC 75-6237. (Picturebacks Ser). (Illus.). 32p. (ps-1). 1975. pap. 1.95 (ISBN 0-394-83124-1, BYR). Random.

Richard Scarry's Little Miss Muffet & Other Rhymes. Illus. by Richard Scarry. LC 88-80232. (Golden Little Board Bks.). (Illus.). 12p. (ps). 1988. 1.69 (ISBN 0-307-06101-9). Western Pub.

Richard Scarry's Lowly Worm Bath Book. Richard Scarry. (Bathtime Bks). (Illus.). 10p. (ps). 1984. 2.95 (ISBN 0-394-86838-2, BYR). Random.

Richard Scarry's Lowly Worm Car & Truck Book. Richard Scarry. LC 82-61012. (Illus.). 16p. (ps-2). 1983. pap. 2.95 (ISBN 0-394-85760-7). Random.

Richard Scarry's Lowly Worm Word Book. Richard Scarry. LC 80-53103. (Chunky Bks.). (Illus.). 28p. (ps). 1981. pap. 2.95 board (ISBN 0-394-84728-8). Random.

Richard Scarry's Lowly Worm's Schoolbag, 4 bks. Richard Scarry. (Illus.). 18p. (Early learning concepts). (ps-k). 1987. boxed set 6.95 (ISBN 0-394-87871-X, BYR). Lowly Learns about Colors. Lowly Learns His ABC's. Lowly Learns to Count. Lowly Learns Words. Random.

Richard Scarry's Mother Goose. Illus. by Richard Scarry. (Big Golden Storybooks). (Illus.). 24p. (ps-1). 1983. 2.95 (ISBN 0-307-10383-8, 10383, Golden Bks). Western Pub.

Richard Scarry's Peasant Pig & the Terrible Dragon. Richard Scarry. LC 80-5086. (Illus.). 48p. (ps-3). 1980. bds. 4.95 (ISBN 0-394-84567-6); lib. bdg. 5.99 (ISBN 0-394-94567-0). Random.

Richard Scarry's Please & Thank You Book. Richard Scarry. LC 73-2441. (Pictureback Library Editions). (ps-2). 1978. 1.95 (ISBN 0-394-82681-7, BYR); lib. bdg. 5.99 (ISBN 0-394-92681-1). Random.

Richard Scarry's Postman Pig & His Busy Neighbors. Richard Scarry. LC 77-91646. (Picturebacks Ser.). (Illus.). (ps-2). 1978. lib. bdg. 5.99 (ISBN 0-394-93898-4, BYR). Random.

Richard Scarry's Simple Simon & Other Rhymes. Illus. by Richard Scarry. LC 88-80233. (Golden Little Board Bks.). (Illus.). 12p. (ps). 1988. 1.69 (ISBN 0-307-06102-7). Western Pub.

Richard Scarry's Splish-Splash Sounds. (Illus.). (gr. k-9). 1988. pap. 1.50. Scholastic Inc.

Richard Scarry's Splish-Splash Sounds. Richard Scarry. (Golden Story Book 'n' Tape Ser.). (Illus.). 24p. (Orig.). (ps-3). 1988. pap. 5.45 (ISBN 0-307-13964-6). Western Pub.

Richard Scarry's Stories to Color: With Lowly Worm & Mr. Paint Pig. Richard Scarry. (Illus.). (ps-3). 1978. pap. 2.95 (ISBN 0-394-83961-7, BYR). Random.

Richard Scarry's Storybook Dictionary. Richard Scarry. LC 99-901821. (Illus.). (gr. k-2). 1966. 9.95 (ISBN 0-307-15548-X, Golden Bks). Western Pub.

Richard Scarry's Take-Along Library. (Illus.). 32p. (gr. 3-6). 1986. pap. 9.95 boxed set (ISBN 0-394-88238-5, BYR). Random.

Richard Scarry's Toy Book. Richard Scarry. (Illus.). (ps-3). 1978. pap. 2.95 (ISBN 0-394-83962-5, BYR). Random.

Richard Scarry's What Do People Do All Day? Richard Scarry. (Illus.). (ps-3). 1968. 9.95 (ISBN 0-394-81823-7); lib. bdg. 7.99 (ISBN 0-394-91823-1). Random.

Richard Second see also King Richard Second.

Richard Second see also Tragedy of King Richard Second.

Richard Second. William Shakespeare. (Airmont Shakespeare Ser.). (gr. 9 up). pap. 0.60 (ISBN 0-8049-1014-6, S14). Airmont.

Richard Second. William Shakespeare. Ed. by Arthur Quiller-Couch et al. (New Shakespeare Ser). pap. 5.95x (ISBN 0-521-09495-X). Cambridge U Pr.

Richard Second. William Shakespeare. Ed. by Kenneth Muir. pap. 2.50 (ISBN 0-451-51921-3, CJ1518, Sig Classics). NAL.

Richard Second. William Shakespeare. Ed. by Stanley Wells. 1981. pap. 3.75 (ISBN 0-14-070719-0). Penguin.

Richard Second. William Shakespeare. Ed. by Matthew W. Black. (Shakespeare Ser.). (YA) (gr. 9 up). 1957. pap. 2.95 (ISBN 0-14-071406-5, Pelican). Penguin.

Richard Second Notes. Denis Calandra. (Orig.). 1982. pap. 3.25 (ISBN 0-8220-0068-7). Cliffs.

Richard Serra. Ernst-Gerhard Guse et al. LC 87-63251. (Illus.). 400p. 1988. 65.00 (ISBN 0-317-66842-0). Rizzoli Intl.

Richard Serra - Sculpture. Rosalind E. Krauss et al. Ed. & intro. by Laura Rosenstock. LC 85-62476. (Illus.). 184p. 1986. pap. 27.50 (ISBN 0-87070-590-3). Museum Mod Art.

Richard Shirley Smith. Henry Ford & Brian L. North. (Illus.). 55p. 1985. pap. 14.95 (ISBN 0-946676-06-2, Pub. by Ashmolean Mus). Longwood Pub Group.

Richard Simmons' Better Body Book. Richard Simmons. LC 83-42690. (Illus.). 240p. (Orig.). 1983. 16.50 (ISBN 0-446-51263-X). Warner Bks.

Richard Simmons' Never-Say-Diet Book. Richard Simmons. (Illus., Orig.). 1980. 14.95 (ISBN 0-446-51209-5); pap. 7.95 (ISBN 0-446-97041-7). Warner Bks.

Richard Simmons Never-Say-Diet Cookbook. Richard Simmons. LC 81-19640. (Illus.). 224p. (Orig.). 1982. 15.95 (ISBN 0-446-51243-5); pap. 7.95 (ISBN 0-446-37078-9). Warner Bks.

Richard Simmons' Reach for Fitness: A Special Book of Exercise for the Physically Challenged. Richard Simmons. LC 85-43168. 1986. 17.95 (ISBN 0-446-51302-4). Warner Bks.

Richard Smith: Recent Work, 1972-1977 - Paintings, Drawings, Graphics. Richard Smith. Ed. by Marjory Supovitz. (Illus.). 1978. pap. 6.00x (ISBN 0-262-69061-6). MIT Pr.

Richard Stanihurst the Dubliner, 1547-1618: A Biography with a Stanihurst Text on Ireland's Past. Colm Lennon. (Illus.). 186p. 1981. 30.00x (ISBN 0-7165-0069-8, BBA 03643, Pub. by Irish Academic Pr Ireland). Biblio Dist.

Richard Steele. Austin Dobson. 1973. 15.00 (ISBN 0-8274-0064-0). R West.

Richard Steele. Austin Dobson. Ed. by Andrew Long. LC 72-108475. 1970. Repr. of 1888 ed. 39.00x (ISBN 0-403-00229-X). Scholarly.

Richard Steele. Richard Steele. Ed. by George A. Aitken. LC 68-9714. 1971. Repr. of 1894 ed. lib. bdg. 35.00x (ISBN 0-8371-4461-2, STRS). Greenwood.

Richard Steele & the Sentimental Comedy. M. E. Hare. (Studies in Drama, No. 39). 1970. pap. 39.95x (ISBN 0-8383-0041-3). Haskell.

Richard Steere: Colonial Merchant Poet. Donald P. Wharton. LC 78-68169. (Penn State Studies: No. 44). 1979. pap. text ed. 4.95x (ISBN 0-271-00207-7). Pa St U Pr.

Richard Sterba: The Collected Papers. Ed. by Herman Daldin. LC 87-11129. 320p. 1987. 37.50 (ISBN 0-88427-071-8). North River.

Richard Strauss. Henry T. Finck. 59.95 (ISBN 0-8490-0955-3). Gordon Pr.

Richard Strauss. Michael Kennedy. (Illus.). 286p. 1983. pap. 7.95 (ISBN 0-8226-0386-1, Helix). Rowman.

Richard Strauss. Ernest Newman. LC 79-94279. (Select Bibliographies Reprint Ser). 1908. 19.00 (ISBN 0-8369-5053-4). Ayer Co Pubs.

Richard Strauss. Ernest Newman. 1970. Repr. of 1908 ed. lib. bdg. 35.00x (ISBN 0-8371-4297-0, NERS). Greenwood.

Richard Strauss: A Chronicle of the Early Years 1864-1898. Willi Schuh. Tr. by Mary Whittall. LC 81-12200. (Illus.). 576p. 1982. 82.50 (ISBN 0-521-24104-9). Cambridge U Pr.

Richard Strauss: A Critical Commentary on His Life & Works. Norman Del Mar. LC 85-19033. (Paperback Ser.). (Illus.). 1986. Vol. I, 464p. 34.95x (ISBN 0-8014-1780-5); Vol. II, 480p. 34.95x (ISBN 0-8014-1781-3); Vol. III, 584p. 34.95x (ISBN 0-8014-1782-1); Vol I. pap. 12.95 (ISBN 0-8014-9317-X); Vol. II. pap. 12.95 (ISBN 0-8014-9318-8); Vol. III. pap. 12.95 (ISBN 0-8014-9319-6). Cornell U Pr.

Richard Strauss: Complete Catalog. Ernst Roth & Willi Schuh. LC 64-6063. 1964. pap. 7.50 (ISBN 0-913932-31-0). Boosey & Hawkes.

Richard Strauss: Der Rosenkavalier. Ed. by Alan Jefferson. (Cambridge Opera Handbooks). (Illus.). 178p. 1986. 34.50 (ISBN 0-521-26036-1); pap. 11.95 (ISBN 0-521-27811-2). Cambridge U Pr.

Richard Strauss et Romain Rolland. Romain Rolland & Richard Strauss. (Illus.). 1951. 6.95 (ISBN 0-686-55269-5). French & Eur.

Richard Strauss: The Staging of His Operas & Ballets. Rudolf Hartmann. (Illus.). 1981. 75.00 (ISBN 0-19-520251-1). Oxford U Pr.

Richard T. Greener & Grant's Tomb. Ruth A. Stewart. Repr. cancelled (ISBN 0-915992-08-6). Eastern Acorn.

Richard Tauber. Diana Naper Tauber. LC 80-17085. (Music Ser.). 1980. Repr. of 1949 ed. 32.50 (ISBN 0-306-76049-5). Da Capo.

Richard Taylor's U. S. Revenue Cutter Virginia, 1791-1797. Florence Kern. 1977. 3.95 (ISBN 0-913377-06-6). Alised.

Richard the Liar-Hearted. Ron Dalrymple. 40p. (Orig.). 1979. pap. 1.95 (ISBN 0-935882-01-4). Celestial Gifts.

Richard the Lion Heart. Kate Norgate. LC 69-17841. 1969. Repr. of 1924 ed. 12.00x (ISBN 0-8462-1326-5). Russell.

Richard the Lion-Hearted in England. Harry S. Howser. (Illus.). 1984. lib. bdg. cancelled (ISBN 0-86663-100-3); pap. text ed. cancelled (ISBN 0-86663-101-1). Ide Hse.

Richard the Lionheart. John Gillingham. LC 78-63599. (Illus.). 1979. write for info. (ISBN 0-8129-0802-3). Times Bks.

Richard the Lionheart & the Crusades. Christopher Gibb. (Life & Times Ser.). (Illus.). 64p. (gr. 7-9). 1985. s&l 12.40 (ISBN 0-531-18011-5, Pub. by Bookwright Pr). Watts.

Richard the Second. William Shakespeare. Ed. by Theodore Spencer. LC 49-8074. (Crofts Classics Ser.). 1949. pap. text ed. 0.85x (ISBN 0-88295-080-0). Harlan Davidson.

Richard the Second. William Shakespeare. Ed. by Louis B. Wright & Virginia LaMar. (Folger Edition). 288p. (gr. 9 up). pap. 3.50. WSP.

Richard the Third. Paul M. Kendall. 602p. 1975. pap. 12.95 (ISBN 0-393-00785-5, N785, Norton Lib). Norton.

Richard the Third. William Shakespeare. LC 79-133735. (Tudor Facsimile Texts. Old English Plays: No. 79). Repr. of 1913 ed. 49.50 (ISBN 0-404-53379-5). AMS Pr.

Richard the Third. William Shakespeare. Ed. by Louis B. Wright & Virginia A. LaMar. (Folger Library). 368p. (gr. 11-12). pap. text ed. 3.50 (ISBN 0-671-00642-8). WSP.

Richard the Third up to Shakespeare. George B. Churchill. 55.00 (ISBN 0-384-09040-0); pap. 50.00 (ISBN 0-685-02232-3). Johnson Repr.

Richard Third see also King Richard Third.

Richard Third see also Tragedy of King Richard Third.

Richard Third. Jon Nichol. (Resource Units: Middle Ages, 1066-1485 Ser.). (Illus.). 24p. 1974. pap. text ed. 12.95 10 copies & tchr's guide (ISBN 0-582-39391-4). Longman.

Richard Third. William Shakespeare. (Airmont Shakespeare Ser.). (gr. 9 up). pap. 0.60 (ISBN 0-8049-1015-4, S15). Airmont.

Richard Third. William Shakespeare. Ed. by Arthur Quiller-Couch et al. LC 68-133495. (New Shakespeare Ser). 1968. pap. 5.95x (ISBN 0-521-09496-8). Cambridge U Pr.

Richard Third. William Shakespeare. Ed. by E. A. Honigmann. 1981. pap. 3.75 (ISBN 0-14-070712-3). Penguin.

Richard Third. William Shakespeare. Ed. by G. Evans. (Shakespeare Ser.). 1959. pap. 3.50 (ISBN 0-14-071416-2, Pelican). Penguin.

Richard Third & His Early Historians 1483-1535. Alison Hanham. 1975. 47.00x (ISBN 0-19-822434-6). Oxford U Pr.

Richard Third Notes. James K. Lowers. (Orig.). 1966. pap. 3.50 (ISBN 0-8220-0071-7). Cliffs.

Richard Upjohn, Architect & Churchman. Everard M. Upjohn. LC 68-26119. (Architecture & Decorative Art Ser). (Illus.). 1968. Repr. of 1939 ed. lib. bdg. 45.00 (ISBN 0-306-71043-9). Da Capo.

Richard Vaughan. Tony Bianchi. (Writers of Wales Ser.). 96p. 1984. pap. text ed. 12.50x (ISBN 0-7083-0848-1, Pub. by U of Wales). Humanities.

Richard Wagner. William H. Hadow. LC 74-24097. Repr. of 1934 ed. 15.00 (ISBN 0-404-12942-0). AMS Pr.

Richard Wagner. (Richard Wagner's Prose Works Ser.: Vol. 8). 1967. Repr. of 1897 ed. 22.50x. Broude.

Richard Wagner: A Biography. D. Watson. 384p. 1983. pap. text ed. 8.95 (ISBN 0-07-068479-0). McGraw.

Richard Wagner: A Biography. Derek Watson. LC 81-1161. (Illus.). 384p. 1981. 19.95 (ISBN 0-02-872700-2). Schirmer Bks.

Richard Wagner & the English. Anne D. Sessa. LC 76-50287. 191p. 1979. 20.00 (ISBN 0-8386-2055-8). Fairleigh Dickinson.

Richard Wagner & the Modern British Novel. John L. DiGaetani. 179p. 1978. 18.50 (ISBN 0-8386-1955-X). Fairleigh Dickinson.

Richard Wagner & the Music of the Future. facsimile ed. Franz Hueffer. LC 70-37122. (Essay Index Reprint Ser). Repr. of 1874 ed. 19.50 (ISBN 0-8369-2508-4). Ayer Co Pubs.

Richard Wagner & the Synthesis of the Arts. Jack M. Stein. LC 73-1840. (Illus.). 229p. 1973. Repr. of 1960 ed. lib. bdg. 41.50x (ISBN 0-8371-6806-6, STRX). Greenwood.

Richard Wagner: His Life & His Dramas. rev. 2nd ed. William J. Henderson. LC 70-137240. Repr. of 1923 ed. 29.50 (ISBN 0-404-03239-7). AMS Pr.

Richard Wagner: His Life & Works. Adolphe Jullien. Tr. by Florence P. Hall from Fr. (Illus.). 432p. 1981. Repr. of 1892 ed. 19.95 (ISBN 0-87666-579-2, Z-48). Paganiniana Pubns.

Richard Wagner: His Life, Art & Thought. Ronald Taylor. LC 78-63053. 1979. 14.95 (ISBN 0-8008-4792-X, Crescendo). Taplinger.

Richard Wagner, His Life, Art & Thought. Ronald Taylor. 480p. pap. 8.95 (ISBN 0-586-06061-8, Pub. by Granada England). Academy Chi Pubs.

Richard Wagner: His Life in His Work. facsimile ed. Paul Bekker. Tr. by M. M. Bozman. LC 70-107792. (Select Bibliographies Reprint Ser). 1931. 32.00 (ISBN 0-8369-5176-X). Ayer Co Pubs.

Richard Wagner: His Life in His Work. Paul Bekker. Tr. by M. M. Bozman. LC 74-106713. Repr. of 1931 ed. lib. bdg. 22.50x (ISBN 0-8371-3443-9, BERW). Greenwood.

Richard Wagner in Bayreuth: Unzeitgemaesse Betrachtungen, Nummer 4; Nachgelassene Fragmente, Anfang 1875 bis Fruehjahr, 1876 see Nietzsche Werke.

Richmond Surrey As It Was: Fifth Impression. Hendon Publishing Co., Ltd. Staff. 1986. 21.00x (ISBN 0-317-54159-5, Pub. by Hendon Pub UK). State Mutual Bk.
Richmond Theater Fire, 1862. J. Wayne Beachy. (Illus.). 24p. (Orig.). (gr. 5 up). 1987. pap. 3.00 (ISBN 0-9608084-3-4). B Hawkins Studio.
Richmond, Vol. 1: The Flame. Elizabeth Fritch. 480p. (Orig.). 1980. pap. 2.75 (ISBN 0-89083-654-X). Zebra.
Richmond Vol. 2: The Fire. Elizabeth Fritch. 1980. pap. 2.75 (ISBN 0-89083-679-5). Zebra.
Richmond Vol. 3: The Embers. Elizabeth Fritch. 1981. pap. 2.75 (ISBN 0-89083-716-3). Zebra.
Richmond, Vol. 5: The Blaze. (Orig.). 1982. pap. 3.50 (ISBN 0-8217-1054-0). Zebra.
Richmond Volunteers: The Volunteer Companies of the City of Richmond & Henrico County, Virginia, 1861-1865. Louis H. Manarin & Lee A. Wallace, Jr. LC 72-100103. pap. 78.00 (ISBN 0-8357-9815-1, 2014632). Bks Demand UMI.
Richmond's Jewry, Seventeen Sixty-Nine to Nineteen Seventy-Six. Myron Berman. LC 78-6377. 438p. 1979. 20.00x (ISBN 0-8139-0743-8). U Pr of Va.
Richmondtown Recipes - Three Centuries of Staten Island Cookery. Dorothy Fingado & Loretta McMillen. (Illus.). 1976. spiral bdg. 5.00 (ISBN 0-686-20333-X). Staten Island.
Rich's Apolonius & Silla, an Original of Shakespeare's Twelfth Night. Morton Luce. LC 77-11067. 1977. Repr. lib. bdg. 17.00 (ISBN 0-8414-5819-7). Folcroft.
Rich's Business Guide to Silicon Valley & No. CA: 1987-1988. (Illus.). 400p. 1987. 109.50 (ISBN 0-914189-05-0). Busn Direct CA.
Rich's Everyday Sales Prospecting Directory: Alameda County, 1988. 425p. 1988. 3-ring binder 149.00 (ISBN 0-914189-06-9). Busn Direct CA.
Rich's Everyday Sales Prospecting Directory: Contra Costa County, 1988. 300p. 1988. 3-ring binder 119.00 (ISBN 0-914189-07-7). Busn Direct CA.
Richt Vay to the Kingdome of Heuine. John Gau. Ed. by A. F. Mitchell. Repr. of 1888 ed. 24.00 (ISBN 0-384-17750-6). Johnson Repr.
Richter und Duerer: Studien zur Rezeption des Altdeutschen Stils im 19. Jahrhundert. Karl-Heinz Weidner. (European university Studies: No. 28, Vol. 26). 230p. (Ger.). 1983. 35.80 (ISBN 3-8204-7779-9). P Lang Pubs.
Richter und Sein Henker. Friedrich Durrenmatt. Ed. by William Gillis & J. J. Neumaier. 1964. pap. text ed. 16.76 (ISBN 0-395-04499-5). HM.
Richtiges Deutsch. Fluckiger & Gallmann. 17.50 (ISBN 0-317-66685-1). Langenscheidt.
Richtlijnen Voor Herwaarderings Counseling Gemeen Chappen: 1981 Guidelines. (Dutch.). 1981. pap. 0.50 (ISBN 0-911214-90-9). Rational Isl.
Richtlinien fur die Verwaltung und wissenschaftliche Erschliebung von Nachlassen in Literaturarchiven. Christoph Konig. 144p. (Ger.). 1988. lib. bdg. 24.00 (ISBN 3-598-10741-2). K G Saur.
Richtlinien zur Infusiontherapie mit Aminosaeuren. Ed. by P. Schoelmerich & H. Schoenborn. (Beitraege zu Infusionstherapie und Klinische Ernaehrung: Band 4). (Illus.). 1979. pap. 11.50 (ISBN 3-8055-3058-7). S Karger.
Rick & Po, Special Agents. Dorothy B. Artes. 1988. write for info. (ISBN 0-932433-39-1). Windswept Hse.
Rick & Po: Village Detectives, Bk. 1. Dorothy B. Artes. (Illus.). 98p. (Orig.). (gr. 4-8). 1987. pap. 5.95 (ISBN 0-932433-28-6). Windswept Hse.
Rick Elstein's Tennis Kinetics with Martina Navratilova. Mary Carillo. 1985. 17.95 (ISBN 0-671-55540-5). S&S.
Rick Hansen: Man in Motion. Rick Hansen & Jim Taylor. 1988. 19.95. P Bedrick Bks.
Rick Shannon & the Case of the Missing Pilot. Allan Stewart. (Fingerprint Mystery Ser.). 144p. (gr. 8-12). 1984. pap. 2.95 (ISBN 0-8423-0212-3). Tyndale.
Rick Shannon & the Secret of the Blue Dragon. Allan Stewart. (Finger Print Mystery Bks.). 160p. (gr. 6-8). 1985. pap. 3.50 (ISBN 0-8423-5857-9). Tyndale.
Rick Springfield. Simone Gillianti. 1984. pap. 2.95 (ISBN 0-671-53104-2). Wanderer Bks.
Rick Tees Off. David Walker. Ed. by Malcolm Wright. (Illus.). 112p. (Orig.). (gr. 4-9). 1985. pap. text ed. 3.95 (ISBN 0-9614856-0-4). Pro Golfers.
Rickenbacker. Edward V. Rickenbacker. (Airlines History Project Ser.). (Illus.). Date not set. Repr. of 1967 ed. 57.50 (ISBN 0-404-19332-3). AMS Pr.
Rickenbacker Guitar: The History. Richard Smith. LC 87-71571. 256p. 1987. pap. text ed. 29.95 (ISBN 0-931759-15-3). Centerstream Pub.
Rickettsiae & Rickettsial Diseases. Willy Burgdorfer & Robert Anacker. 1981. 83.00 (ISBN 0-12-143150-9). Acad Pr.
Rickety Witch. Maggie S. Davis. LC 84-498. (Illus.). 32p. (ps-3). 1984. reinforced bdg. 10.95 (ISBN 0-8234-0521-4). Holiday.
Rickover: Controversy & Genius. Norman Polmar & Thomas P. Allen. LC 81-14327. (Illus.). 745p. 1982. pap. 15.95. Nautical & Aviation.
Rickover: Controversy & Genius - A Biography. Norman Polmar & Thomas B. Allen. 784p. 1984. pap. 12.95 (ISBN 0-671-52815-7, Touchstone Bks). S&S.
Rickshaw. Lao She. Tr. by Jean M. James from Chinese. LC 79-10658. Orig. Title: Lo-to Hsiang Tzu. 1979. text ed. 12.00x (ISBN 0-8248-0616-6); pap. text ed. 5.95x (ISBN 0-8248-0655-7). UH Pr.
Rickshaw to Horror. Robert Quackenbush. LC 83-19083. (Miss Mallard Mystery Ser.). (Illus.). 48p. 1984. 11.95 (ISBN 0-13-781014-8). P-H.
Rickshaw Towers. Samuel Beckoff. 256p. (Orig.). 1988. pap. 9.95 (ISBN 0-936784-62-8, Fithian Pr). J Daniel.
Ricky & Rodney in Welcome to the Neighborhood. Jim Glaser. (Illus.). 32p. (Orig.). (gr. k-4). 1988. pap. text ed. 0.65 (ISBN 0-941197-01-8). Fat Cat Ent.
Ricky, Rocky & Ringo Count on Pizza. Mauri Kunnas. (Illus.). (ps-2). 1986. 4.95 (ISBN 0-517-56089-5). Crown.
Ricky, Rocky & Ringo Go to the Moon. Mauri Kunnas. (Illus.). (ps-2). 1986. 4.95 (ISBN 0-517-56232-4). Crown.
Ricky, Rocky & Ringo on TV. Mauri Kunnas. (Illus.). (ps-2). 1986. 4.95 (ISBN 0-517-56414-9). Crown.
Ricky, Rocky & Ringo's Colorful Day. Mauri Kunnas. (Illus.). (ps-2). 1986. 4.95 (ISBN 0-517-56125-5). Crown.
Ricky the Raccoon. (Frog Pond Ser.). (Illus.). (ps-1). 2.98 (ISBN 0-517-46985-5). Outlet Bk Co.
Ricky's Last Chance. James L. Jordon. (Illus.). 48p. 1989. 6.95 (ISBN 0-89962-776-5). Todd & Honeywell.
RICO: Expanding Uses in Civil Litigation. Law & Business Inc. Staff & Arthur F. Mathews. LC 84-149429. v, 649p. Date not set. price not set (Law & Business). HarBraceJ.
RICO (Racketeer Influenced & the Corrupt Organizations) Business Disputes & the "Racketeering" Laws-Federal & State. 224p. 1984. pap. 20.00 (ISBN 0-317-19245-0, 4831). Commerce.
Ricochet. Stuart Blazer. 51p. (Orig.). 1983. pap. 4.50 (ISBN 0-914278-39-8). Copper Beech.
Ricochet. Ovid Demaris. 224p. 1988. 17.95 (ISBN 0-684-19009-5). Scribner.
Ricochets: Miniature Tales of Human Life. facsimile ed. Andre Maurois. Tr. by Hamish Miles from Fr. LC 73-150551. (Short Story Index Reprint Ser.). Repr. of 1935 ed. 13.00 (ISBN 0-8369-3848-8). Ayer Co Pubs.
Ricordi: Italian Text with English Translation. Franceso Guicciardini. Tr. by Ninian H. Thomson. 1949. 12.95x (ISBN 0-913298-41-7). S F Vanni.
Riddell Diaries: 1908-1923. Ed. by John M. McEwen. 320p. 1986. 50.00 (ISBN 0-485-11300-7, Pub. by Athlone Pr). Humanities.
Riddick's Rules of Procedure. Floyd M. Riddick & Miriam Butcher. 224p. 1985. 19.95 (ISBN 0-684-18427-3, ScribT). Scribner.
Riddle. Tom Hillstrom. 352p. 1987. pap. 3.95 (ISBN 0-515-08949-4). Jove Pubns.
Riddle Ages. Ann Bishop. Ed. by Caroline Rubin. LC 77-12828. (Riddle Bks.). (Illus.). (gr. 1-4). 1977. PLB 7.75 (ISBN 0-8075-6965-8). A Whitman.
Riddle & Incest. Lawrence W. Markert. (New Poets Ser.: Vol. 3). 1974. pap. 1.95 (ISBN 0-685-52489-2). New Poets.
Riddle & the Rune. Grace Chetwin. LC 87-10284. (Tales of Gom Ser.). 256p. (gr. 5 up). 1987. 13.95 (ISBN 0-02-718312-2). Bradbury Pr.
Riddle Book. Mik Brown. Ed. by Warwick Press. (Illus.). 32p. (gr. k-6). 1988. 8.90 (ISBN 0-531-19036-6, Warwick). Watts.
Riddle Book. Roy McKie. LC 77-85237. (Picturebacks Ser.). (ps-2). 1978. lib. bdg. 5.99 (ISBN 0-394-93732-5, BYR); pap. 1.95 (ISBN 0-394-83732-0). Random.
Riddle-De-Dee. Ed. by Bennett Cerf. 1962. 10.45 (ISBN 0-394-44304-7, BYR). Random.
Riddle Fun with the Scrabble People. Katherine Ross. (Illus.). 32p. (ps-2). 1985. pap. 1.95 (ISBN 0-394-87172-3, BYR). Random.
Riddle-Master of Hed. Patricia A. McKillip. LC 76-5492. 240p. (gr. 6-12). 1976. 14.95 (ISBN 0-689-30545-1, Atheneum Childrens Bks). Macmillan.
Riddle-Master of Hed. Patricia A. McKillip. (Del Rey Bk.). 1978. pap. 2.95. Ballantine.
Riddle Me a Murder. Duane Crowley. Ed. by Ken Hatfield. LC 86-71586. 234p. (Orig.). 1987. pap. 7.95x (ISBN 0-9617182-0-X). Blue Boar Pr.
Riddle Monster. Lisl Weil. LC 81-1030. (Illus.). 32p. (ps-3). 1981. 7.95 (ISBN 0-395-31019-9, Clarion). HM.
Riddle of Cancer. Charles Oberling. 1944. 49.50x (ISBN 0-685-89779-6). Elliots Bks.
Riddle of Cruelty. G. Rothman. 1971. 8.95 (ISBN 0-8022-2345-1). Philos Lib.
Riddle of Existence: An Essay in Idealistic Metaphysics. Nicholas Rescher. (Nicholas Rescher Ser.). 112p. (Orig.). 1985. 23.00 (ISBN 0-8191-4127-5); pap. text ed. 9.25 (ISBN 0-8191-4128-3). U Pr of Amer.
Riddle of Freud: Jewish Influences on His Theory of Female Sexuality. Estelle Roith. 250p. 1987. lib. bdg. 49.95x (ISBN 0-422-61380-0, Pub. by Tavistock England); pap. 15.95 (ISBN 0-422-61760-1, Pub. by Tavistock England). Routledge Chapman & Hall.
Riddle of Genesis. R. Koch. pap. 0.75 (ISBN 0-8199-0395-7). Franciscan Herald.
Riddle of Goethe's Faust. Arnold Freeman. LC 76-46931. 1976. Repr. of 1954 ed. lib. bdg. 20.50 (ISBN 0-8414-4151-0). Folcroft.
Riddle of Gravitation. rev. ed. Peter G. Bergman. 272p. 1987. 18.95 (ISBN 0-684-18460-5). Scribner.
Riddle of Gravitation. Peter G. Bergmann. LC 68-11537. 1968. lib. bdg. 25.00 (ISBN 0-684-15378-5, ScribT). Scribner.
Riddle of Justice: A Monograph Together with Suggestions for Much-Needed New Laws. James Mulligan. xvi, 155p. 1983. Repr. of 1925 ed. lib. bdg. 20.00x (ISBN 0-8377-0849-4). Rothman.
Riddle of Liberty: Emerson on Alienation, Freedom & Obedience. Lou A. Lange. LC 86-6605. (Scholar Press Studies in the Humanities). 1986. 26.95 (ISBN 1-55540-019-1, 00-01-11). Scholars Pr GA.
Riddle of Life. Beasant. 4.50 (ISBN 0-8356-0231-1). Theos Pub Hse.
Riddle of Migration. William Rowan. 1977. lib. bdg. 59.95 (ISBN 0-8490-2523-0). Gordon Pr.
Riddle of Pyramids. Kurt Mendelssohn. (Illus.). 1986. 24.95f (ISBN 0-500-05015-5); pap. 12.95f (ISBN 0-500-27388-X). Thames Hudson.
Riddle of Raven Hollow. Mary F. Shura. (Cat's Eye Mysteries Ser.). 126p. (gr. 3-6). 1983. pap. 1.95 (ISBN 0-590-32784-4). Scholastic Inc.
Riddle of Shakespeare's Sonnets. Edward Hubbler et al. LC 81-22340. 346p. 1982. Repr. of 1962 ed. lib. bdg. 31.50 (ISBN 0-374-94014-2, Octagon). Hippocrene Bks.
Riddle of the Dinosaur. John N. Wilford. LC 85-40015. (Illus.). 320p. 1985. 22.95 (ISBN 0-394-52763-1). Knopf.
Riddle of the Dinosaur. John N. Wilford. 1987. pap. 8.95 (ISBN 0-394-74392-X, Vin). Random.
Riddle of the Double Ring. Margaret Sutton. Incl. Judy Bolton Mysteries. 16.95 (ISBN 0-88411-717-0, Pub. by Aeonian Pr). Amereon Ltd.
Riddle of the Early Academy. Harold Cherniss. LC 78-66594. (Ancient Philosophy Ser.). 111p. 1982. lib. bdg. 18.00 (ISBN 0-8240-9604-5). Garland Pub.
Riddle of the Fly & Other Stories. facsimile ed. Elizabeth Enright. LC 70-121538. (Short Story Index Reprint Ser.). Repr. of 1959 ed. 17.00 (ISBN 0-8369-3494-6). Ayer Co Pubs.
Riddle of the Frozen Fountain. Carolyn Keene. (Dana Girls Ser.: Vol. 2). (Illus.). 192p. (gr. 4-7). 1972. 2.95 (ISBN 0-448-09082-1, G&D). Putnam Pub Group.
Riddle of the Future: A Modern Study of Precognition. Andrew MacKenzie. LC 75-8199. 176p. 1975. 8.50 (ISBN 0-8008-6795-5). Taplinger.
Riddle of the Griffon. Laura Hickman. LC 84-91361. (Crimson Crystal Adventures Ser.). (Illus.). 160p. (gr. 4-6). 1985. pap. 2.95 (ISBN 0-394-73979-5). Random.
Riddle of the Irish. Chartres J. Molony. LC 74-102619. (Irish Culture & History Ser). 1970. Repr. of 1927 ed. 22.50x (ISBN 0-8046-0796-6, Pub. by Kennikat). Assoc Faculty Pr.
Riddle of the Outlaw Bear & Other Faith-Building Stories. John H. Leeper. (Illus.). (gr. 1-6). 1984. pap. 4.95 (ISBN 0-8024-7352-0). Moody.
Riddle of the Pacific. John M. Brown. LC 75-35177. Repr. of 1924 ed. 38.00 (ISBN 0-404-14205-2). AMS Pr.
Riddle of the Pianist's Fingers: & Its Relationship to a Touch-Scheme. Arnold Schultz. 317p. 1949. pap. 14.95 (ISBN 0-8258-0009-9, 03645). Fischer Inc NY.
Riddle of the Realms. Lyndon Hardy. 416p. 1988. pap. 3.95 (ISBN 0-345-32820-5, Del Rey). Ballantine.
Riddle of the Red Purse. Patricia R. Giff. (Polka Dot Detective Ser.: No. 2). (Orig.). (gr. k-6). 1987. pap. 2.50 (ISBN 0-440-47534-1, YB). Dell.
Riddle of the Runaway. Heather Fisher. (Starlight Adventure Ser.). (Illus.). 300p. (gr. 7 up). 1985. pap. 2.95 (ISBN 0-14-031841-0, Puffin). Penguin.
Riddle of the Runes. Arthur G. Brodeur. 1932. lib. bdg. 16.00 (ISBN 0-8414-3210-4). Folcroft.
Riddle of the Sands. Erskine Childers. 1976. Repr. of 1913 ed. lib. bdg. 18.95 (ISBN 0-89190-240-6, Pub. by River City Pr). Amereon Ltd.
Riddle of the Sands. Erskine Childers. 352p. 1976. pap. 4.95 (ISBN 0-486-23280-8). Dover.
Riddle of the Sands. Erskine Childers. (Crime Ser.). 1978. pap. 5.95 (ISBN 0-14-000905-1). Penguin.
Riddle of the Sands. Erskine Childers. (Illus.). 280p. 1986. pap. 12.95 (ISBN 0-246-13039-3). Sheridan.
Riddle of the Seven Realms. Lyndon Hardy. 1988. pap. 3.95 (Del Rey). Ballantine.
Riddle of the Sphinx. N. B. Ashby. LC 75-300. (Radical Tradition in America Ser.). 474p. 1975. Repr. of 1890 ed. 31.25 (ISBN 0-88355-205-1). Hyperion Conn.
Riddle of the Sphinx, or Human Origins. Geza Roheim. Tr. by R. Money-Kryle. 10.75 (ISBN 0-8446-5238-5). Peter Smith.
Riddle of the Tariff. Arthur C. Pigou. LC 74-1328. 1977. Repr. of 1904 ed. 15.00x (ISBN 0-678-01227-X). Kelley.
Riddle of the Third Mile. 224p. 1988. pap. 3.50 (ISBN 0-553-27363-9). Bantam.
Riddle of the Universe at the Close of the 19th Century. Ernst Haeckel. LC 6403. 1900. 18.00x (ISBN 0-403-00117-X). Scholarly.
Riddle of the Voucher. Arthur Seldon. (Hobart Paperback Ser.: No. 21). 100p. (Orig.). 1986. pap. text ed. 12.50x (ISBN 0-255-36184-X, Pub. by Inst Econ Affairs UK). Transatl Arts.
Riddle of This World. Sri Aurobindo. 98p. 1984. pap. 1.50. (ISBN 0-89071-306-5, Pub. by Sri Aurobindo Ashram India). Aurobindo Assn.
Riddle Rhyme Book. 1981. pap. 2.95 (ISBN 0-87306-259-0). Feldheim.
Riddle Romp. Giulio Maestro. LC 83-2067. (Illus.). 64p. (gr. k-3). 1983. 10.95 (ISBN 0-89919-180-0, Pub. by Clarion); pap. 3.95 (ISBN 0-89919-207-6). Ticknor & Fields.
Riddle Soup. Valiska Gregory. LC 87-190. (Mr. Poggle & Scamp Bk.). (Illus.). 24p. (ps-k). 1987. PLB 8.95 (ISBN 0-02-738090-4, Four Winds). Macmillan.
Riddle Walk. Lilian Moore. LC 76-157849. (Garrard Venture Ser.). (Illus.). 40p. (gr. 1). 1971. PLB 6.69 (ISBN 0-8116-6715-4); pap. 1.19 (9023). Garrard.
Riddle Whiz Quiz. Louis Phillips & Karen Markoe. (Magic Answer Bks.). (Illus.). 64p. (gr. 3-7). 1984. pap. 2.95 (ISBN 0-671-44920-6). Wanderer Bks.
Riddle Zoo. Andrea G. Zimmerman. 64p. (gr. 3-7). 1981. 9.25 (ISBN 0-525-38300-X). Dutton.
Riddled with Puzzles. Helene Hovanec. 64p. (Orig.). (gr. k-3). 1986. pap. 1.95 (ISBN 0-590-33823-4). Scholastic Inc.
Riddlemaster of Hed, No. 1. Patricia McKillip. pap. 2.95 (ISBN 0-345-33104-4). Ballantine.
Riddler's Riddle Book. 128p. 1988. pap. 1.95 (ISBN 0-8125-7626-8). Tor Bks.
Riddles: Ancient & Modern. Mark Bryant. LC 83-73464. 208p. 1984. P Bedrick Bks.
Riddles & More Riddles. J. Michael Shannon. LC 82-19765. (Laughing Matters Ser.). (Illus.). 48p. (gr. 1-5). 1983. PLB 10.60 (ISBN 0-516-01873-6). Childrens.
Riddles & Rhymes & Rigmaroles. John Cunliffe. (Illus.). 80p. (gr. 1-5). 1982. 10.95 (ISBN 0-233-96306-5). Andre Deutsch.
Riddles in Filipino Folklore: An Anthropological Analysis. Donn V. Hart. LC 64-23338. 1964. 24.95x (ISBN 0-8156-2069-1). Syracuse U Pr.
Riddles in Mathematics: A Book of Paradoxes. Eugene P. Northrop. LC 74-32267. 270p. 1975. pap. 17.50 (ISBN 0-88275-273-1). Krieger.
Riddles in Rhyme. Le Baron R. Briggs. 59.95 (ISBN 0-8490-0957-X). Gordon Pr.
Riddles of Aldhelm. James H. Pitman. LC 75-91189. (Yale Studies in English Ser.: No. 67). vii, 79p. 1970. Repr. of 1925 ed. 18.50 (ISBN 0-208-00910-8, Archon). Shoe String.
Riddles of Finnegans Wake. Patrick A. McCarthy. LC 79-24075. 184p. 1980. 20.00 (ISBN 0-8386-3005-7). Fairleigh Dickinson.
Riddles of Hamlet & the Newest Answers. Simon A. Blackmore. LC 73-4188. 1973. lib. bdg. 49.00 (ISBN 0-8414-1762-8). Folcroft.
Riddles of Jesus & Answers of Science: Modern Verification of His Wisdom & How It Can Help You. Osborn Segerberg, Jr. Ed. by Marcia Drennen. 272p. (Orig.). 1987. 21.95 (ISBN 0-9618626-0-2); pap. 14.95 (ISBN 0-9618626-1-0). Reges Bks.
Riddles of Love. Judy Baer. (Sweet Dreams Ser.: No. 148). 176p. (Orig.). 1988. pap. 2.50 (ISBN 0-553-27275-6). Bantam.
Riddles of Science. facsimile ed. John A. Thomson. LC 77-152218. (Essay Index Reprint Ser). Repr. of 1932 ed. 21.50 (ISBN 0-8369-2257-3). Ayer Co Pubs.
Riddles of the Russian People: A Collection of Riddles, Questions, Parables & Puzzles. Compiled by D. N. Sadovnikov. Tr. by Ann C. Bigelow from Rus. 566p. 1986. 37.50 (ISBN 0-88233-987-7). Ardis Pubs.
Riddles of the Sphinx. facs. ed. Ferdinand C. Schiller. LC 70-126254. (Select Bibliographies Reprint Ser). 1910. 24.50 (ISBN 0-8369-5481-5). Ayer Co Pubs.
Riddles of the Sphinx & Other Mathematical Puzzle Tales. Martin Gardner. LC 87-62657. (MAA Spectrum Ser.). (Illus., Orig.). 1987. pap. 14.50 (ISBN 0-88385-632-8); 16.95 (ISBN 0-88385-633-6). Math Assn.
Riddles of Three Oceans. A. Kondratov. 267p. 1974. 4.45 (ISBN 0-8285-0833-X, Pub. by Progress Pubs USSR). Imported Pubns.
Riddles That Rhyme for Halloween Time. Leonard Kessler. LC 77-13140. (Imagination Ser.). (Illus.). (gr. k-4). 1978. PLB 6.69 (ISBN 0-8116-4409-X). Garrard.
Riddles to Take on Vacation. Joanne Bernstein & Paul Cohen. Ed. by Ann Fay. LC 87-2071. (Illus.). (gr. 1-5). 1987. PLB 7.95 (ISBN 0-8075-6999-2). A Whitman.
Riddley Walker. Russell Hoban. 240p. 1982. pap. 6.95 (ISBN 0-671-52694-4). WSP.
Riddley Walker. Russell Hoban. Date not set. pap. 2.95 (ISBN 0-671-60777-4). PB.
Ride a Blue Horse. Aurand Harris. 44p. (Orig.). (gr. k-3). 1986. pap. 3.50 playscript (ISBN 0-87602-264-6). Anchorage.
Ride a Cock Horse. Elma Williams. 1972. 8.95 (ISBN 0-7181-0930-9). Transatl Arts.
Ride a Cock-Horse. Ed. by Sarah Williams. (Illus.). 48p. (ps up). 1988. pap. 4.95 (ISBN 0-19-272152-6); Cassette. 6.95 (ISBN 0-19-279867-7); Counterpk. 49.50 (ISBN 0-19-272189-5). Oxford U Pr.

Riding Machines for Kids. Ed Baldwin & Stevie Baldwin. LC 83-43300. 156p. 1984. pap. 10.95 (ISBN 0-8019-7506-9). Chilton.

Riding Old Trails. rev. ed. James Curtis. (Illus.). 330p. 1983. 13.95 (ISBN 0-914459-00-7). Rocky Mount CO.

Riding on a Blue Note: Jazz & American Pop. Gary Giddins. 1981. 21.95x (ISBN 0-19-502835-X); pap. 9.95 (ISBN 0-19-503213-6). Oxford U Pr.

Riding out the Tropical Depression. Ellen Gilchrist. (Illus.). 35p. 1986. signed, ltd. ed. 50.00 (ISBN 0-917905-03-2); deluxe ed. 125.00 (ISBN 0-317-46894-4). Faust Pub Co.

Riding Rhymes for Young Riders. Harry Disston. (Illus.). (gr. 1-6). 1951. pap. 1.95 (ISBN 0-87027-100-8). Cumberland Pr.

Riding Shotgun. John Benteen. (Sundance Ser.: No. 20). 160p. 1981. pap. 1.75 (ISBN 0-8439-1051-8, Leisure Bks). Leisure NY.

Riding That Strawberry Roan. Marcia Sewall. LC 84-21904. (Illus.). 32p. (ps-2). 1985. 9.95 (ISBN 0-670-80623-4). Viking.

Riding the Boom Extension. John McPhee. (Metacom Limited Editions Ser.: No. 9). 32p. 1983. pap. 32.50 ltd. (ISBN 0-911381-08-2). Metacom Pr.

Riding the Dirt. Bob Sanford. (Illus.). 1973. 10.95 (ISBN 0-393-60018-1). Norton.

Riding the Dolphin. Amanda Thomas. (Peter Weed Bks.). 320p. 1987. 17.95 (ISBN 0-8253-0427-X). Beaufort Bks NY.

Riding the Good Earth: Poems 1980-86. Joseph Richey. (Collected Poems Ser.). 64p. 1986. pap. 8.95 (ISBN 0-915032-89-9). Natl Poet Foun.

Riding the Gymkana Winner see Farnam Horse Library Series.

Riding the High Country. Patrick T. Tucker. LC 87-27562. (Western Writers Ser.: No. 1). 165p. 1987. lib. bdg. 17.95 (ISBN 0-940242-33-8); pap. 8.95 (ISBN 0-940242-32-X). Fjord PR.

Riding the Iron Rooster by Train Through China. Paul Theroux. 480p. 1988. 21.95 (ISBN 0-399-13309-7). Putnam Pub Group.

Riding the Mast Where It Swings. 2nd ed. Anne Paolucci. 1981. pap. 10.95 (ISBN 0-918680-10-7). Griffon Hse.

Riding the Midnight River: Selected Poems of Pritish Nandy. Pritish Nandy. (Indian Poetry Ser.). 144p. 1975. 9.00 (ISBN 0-89253-013-8). Ind-US Inc.

Riding the One-Eyed Ford. 2nd ed. Diane Burns. (Poetry Ser.). (Illus.). 50p. (Orig.). 1984. pap. 3.50 (ISBN 0-936556-05-6). Contact Two.

Riding the Ox Home: A History of Meditation from Shamanism to Science. Willard Johnson. LC 86-47752. (Illus.). 262p. 1987. pap. 9.95 (ISBN 0-8070-1305-6, BP-735). Beacon Pr.

Riding the Recession. John Morine. 184p. 1981. pap. text ed. 8.50x (ISBN 0-09-141580-2, Pub. by Busn Bks England). Brookfield Pub Co.

Riding the Show Ring Hunter see Farnam Horse Library Series.

Riding the Torch. Norman Spinrad. LC 84-12307. 166p. (Orig.). 1984. pap. 6.95 (ISBN 0-317-58848-6). Ultramarine Pub.

Riding the Twister. Dorothy Jo Schaper. (Illus.). 36p. 1985. pap. 2.00 (ISBN 0-317-39899-7). Samisdat.

Riding the Waves of Change: Developing Managerial Competencies for a Turbulent World. Gareth Morgan. LC 87-46337. (Management Ser.). 1988. 19.95x (ISBN 1-55542-093-1). Jossey-Bass.

Riding the Wind. Everett L. Fullam. 182p. (Orig.). 1987. pap. 7.95 (ISBN 0-88419-196-6, Creation Hse). Strang Comms Co.

Riding to Greylock. Stephen Sandy. LC 82-48741. (Poetry Ser.). 115p. 1983. pap. 6.95 (ISBN 0-394-71314-1). Knopf.

Riding to Music: Music for the Individual Kur, Pax de Deux & the Classical Quadrille. Werner Storl. Tr. by Sandra L. Newkirk from Gr. Orig. Title: Musik Zum Reiten. (Illus.). 96p. (Orig.). 1987. pap. 9.95 (ISBN 0-914327-17-8). Breakthrough.

Riding Tough. Jim Busbee. 1981. pap. 1.95 (ISBN 0-8439-0912-9, Leisure Bks). Leisure NY.

Riding with the Fireworks. Ann Darr. LC 80-70830. 72p. 1981. pap. 7.95 (ISBN 0-914086-33-2). Alicejamesbooks.

RIE Abstracts, 1986. 1987. Pt. 1. write for info. (ISBN 0-89774-237-0); Pt. 2. write for info. (ISBN 0-89774-238-9). Oryx Pr.

Rie Munoz, Alaskan Artist: An Illustrated Selection of Her Work. (Illus.). 80p. 1984. 19.95 (ISBN 0-88240-257-9). Alaska Northwest.

Riege Master: Roxanna & the Quest for Time Bird Ser. Regis Loisel. Ed. by Serge Letendre. Tr. by Erick Gilbert from Fr. (Illus.). 64p. (Orig.). 1988. pap. 8.95x (ISBN 0-918348-47-1). NBM.

Riegel's Handbook of Industrial Chemistry. 8th ed. Ed. by James A. Kent. 1008p. 1983. 69.95 (ISBN 0-442-20164-8). Van Nos Reinhold.

Riel Rebellions: A Cartographic History. Ed. by William A. Oppen. LC 79-94166. (Illus.). 1980. pap. 15.00 (ISBN 0-8020-6427-2). U of Toronto Pr.

Riel's People: How the Metis Lived. Maria Campbell. (Illus.). (YA) (gr. 5 up). pap. 6.95 (ISBN 0-317-62416-4, Pub. by Douglas & McIntyre-Grounwood). Salem Hse Pubs.

Riemann Boundary Problem on Riemann Surfaces. Y. L. Rodin. 1988. lib. bdg. 64.00 (ISBN 90-277-2653-1, Pub. by Reidel Holland). Kluwer Academic.

Riemann Hypothesis & Hilberts Tenth Problem. S. Chowla. (Mathematics & Its Applications Ser.). 134p. 1965. 54.00 (ISBN 0-677-00140-1). Gordon & Breach.

Riemann Musiklexikon. W. Gurlitt & H. Eggebrecht. 108p. (Ger.). 1967. 350.00 (ISBN 3-7957-0031-0, M-7602, Pub. by Schatt's Soehne). French & Eur.

Riemann Problem: Complete Integrability & Arithmetic Applications Proceedings. D. V. Chudnovsky & G. V. Chudnovsky. (Lecture Notes In Mathematics: Vol. 925). 373p. 1982. pap. 22.00 (ISBN 0-387-11483-1). Springer-Verlag.

Riemann-Roch Algebra. W. Fulton & S. Lang. LC 84-26842. (Grundlehren der Mathematischen Wissenschaften: Vol. 277). x, 208p. 1985. 53.00 (ISBN 0-387-96086-4). Springer-Verlag.

Riemann Surfaces & Generalized Theta Functions. R. C. Gunning. (Illus.). 1976. 31.00 (ISBN 0-387-07744-8). Springer-Verlag.

Riemann Surfaces & Related Topics: Proceedings of the 1978 Stony Brook Conference. Ed. by I. Kra & B. Maskit. LC 79-27923. (Annals of Mathematics Studies: No.97). 400p. 1981. 41.00x (ISBN 0-691-08264-2); pap. 18.50x (ISBN 0-691-08267-7). Princeton U Pr.

Riemann Surfaces, Theta Functions, & Abelian Automorphisms Groups. R. D. Accola. LC 75-25928. (Lecture Notes in Mathematics: Vol. 483). iii, 105p. 1975. pap. text ed. 13.00 (ISBN 0-387-07398-1). Springer-Verlag.

Riemann, Topology & Physics. Michael Monastyrsky. 1987. 39.50 (ISBN 0-8176-3262-X). Birkhauser.

Riemann-Type Integral that Includes Lebesgue-Stieltjes, Bochner & Stochastic Integrals. E. J. McShane. LC 52-42839. (Memoirs: No. 88). 54p. 1983. pap. 12.00 (ISBN 0-8218-1288-2, MEMO-88). Am Math.

Riemann Zeta-Function: The Theory of the Riemann Zeta-Function with Applications. Aleksandar Ivic. LC 84-26940. (Pure & Applied Mathematics Ser.). 517p. 1985. 54.95 (ISBN 0-471-80634-X). Wiley.

Riemannian Foliations. Pierre Molino. (Progress in Mathematics Ser.: No. 73). 360p. 1987. 44.00 (ISBN 0-8176-3370-7). Birkhauser.

Riemannian Geometry. rev. ed. Luther P. Eisenhart. 1950. 35.50x (ISBN 0-691-08026-7). Princeton U Pr.

Riemannian Geometry. Wilhelm Klingenberg. LC 82-9772. (De Gruyter Studies in Mathematics). x, 396p. 1982. 59.95 (ISBN 3-11-008673-5). De Gruyter.

Riemannian Geometry. J. Lafontaine et al. (Universitext Ser.). x, 248p. 1987. pap. 29.00 (ISBN 0-387-17923-2). Springer-Verlag.

Riemannian Geometry, Fibre Bundles, Kaluza-Klein Theories & All That. R. Coquereaux & A. Jadczyk. 360p. 1987. 67.00 (ISBN 9971-50-426-X); pap. 39.00 (ISBN 9971-50-427-8). World Scientific Pub.

Riemannian Symmetric Spaces of Rank One. Isaac Chavel. LC 72-76060. (Lecture Notes in Pure & Applied Mathematics Ser.: Vol. 5). pap. 23.30 (2027114). Bks Demand UMI.

Riemann's Zeta Function. Harold M. Edwards. (Pure & Applied Mathematics: A Series of Monographs & Textbooks, Vol. 59). 1974. 59.50 (ISBN 0-12-232750-0). Acad Pr.

Rienzi: The Last of the Roman Tribune. Edward Bulwer-Lytton. LC 70-145150. 1971. Repr. of 1885 ed. 69.00x (ISBN 0-403-01079-9). Scholarly.

Rienzo: The Rise & Fall of a Dictator. Victor Fleischer. LC 76-112801. 1970. Repr. of 1948 ed. 15.50x (ISBN 0-8046-1067-3, Pub. by Kennikat). Assoc Faculty Pr.

Riera: Stone Age Hunter-Gatherers in Northern Spain. Ed. by Lawrence Straus & Geoffrey Clark. LC 86-71561. (Arizona State University Anthropological Research Papers: No. 36). (Illus.). 515p. (Orig.). 1987. pap. 28.50 (ISBN 0-9611932-4-7). AZ Univ ARP.

Riesco Collection of Old Chinese Pottery & Porcelain. Edgar E. Bluett. 38p. 1951. 75.00x (ISBN 0-317-43949-9, Pub. by Han-Shan Tang Ltd). State Mutual Bk.

Riesz & Fredholm Theory in Banach Algebras. B. A. Barnes. 132p. 1982. pap. 21.95 (ISBN 0-470-20414-1, Co-Pub. with Longman). Wiley.

Riesz Spaces. W. A. Luxemburg & A. C. Zaanen. (Mathematical Library: Vol. 1). 514p. 1972. 116.00 (ISBN 0-444-10129-2, North-Holland). Elsevier.

Riesz Spaces, II. A. C. Zaanen. (North-Holland Mathematical Library: Vol. 30). 720p. 1983. 94.75 (ISBN 0-444-86626-4, North Holland). Elsevier.

Rietveld Schroder House. Paul Overy et al. (Illus.). 108p. 1988. 25.00 (ISBN 0-262-15033-6). MIT Pr.

RIF Survival Handbook: How to Manage Your Money if You're Unemployed. John May. LC 82-80357. 132p. (Orig.). 1982. pap. 4.95 (ISBN 0-9605750-2-2). Tilden Pr.

Rifampicin in Extra-Pulmonary Tuberculosis. Ed. by A. D. Caldwell. (International Congress & Symposium Ser.: No. 11). 64p. 1979. pap. 12.00 (ISBN 1-85315-050-9, Pub. by Royal Society of Medicine Services Ltd). Longwood Pub Group.

Rife Volunteers, Eighteen Fifty-Nine to Nineteen Eight. Ray Westlake. 173p. 1987. 70.00x (ISBN 0-902633-79-1, Pub. by Picton UK). State Mutual Bk.

Rifle, Blanket & Kettle: Selected Indian Treaties & Laws. Frederick E. Hosen. LC 84-43208. 191p. 1985. lib. bdg. 24.95x (ISBN 0-89950-153-2). McFarland & Co.

Rifle Book. 3rd, Rev. ed. Jack O'Connor. (Illus.). 1978. o. p. 13.95 (ISBN 0-394-41314-8); pap. 13.95 (ISBN 0-394-73458-0). Knopf.

Rifle Guide. R. A. Steindler. (Illus.). 304p. pap. 9.95 (ISBN 0-88317-092-2). Stoeger Pub Co.

Rifle in America. Philip Sharpe. (Library Classics Ser.). (Illus.). 726p. 1987. Repr. of 1938 ed. 59.00 (ISBN 0-935632-49-2). Wolfe Pub Co.

Rifle River. Roy LeBeau. (Buckskin Ser.: No. 1). 240p. 1984. pap. 2.50 (ISBN 0-8439-2066-1, Leisure Bks). Leisure NY.

Rifle Shooting As a Sport. Ed. by Bernd Klinger. (Illus.). 186p. 1981. 15.00 (ISBN 0-498-02581-0). A S Barnes.

Rifled Sanctuaries: Some Views of the Pacific Islands in Literature to 1900. Bill Pearson. 1984. pap. 13.95x (ISBN 0-19-648029-9). Oxford U Pr.

Rifleman of Ohio. Joseph Alsheler. 432p. 1981. Repr. lib. bdg. 20.95x (ISBN 0-89968-226-X). Lightyear.

Rifleman of the Ohio. Joseph Altsheler. (Young Trailer Ser.). 319p. 1984. Repr. lib. bdg. 20.95 (ISBN 0-89966-483-0). Buccaneer Bks.

Rifleman Went to War. Herbert W. McBride. 425p. 1987. Repr. of 1935 ed. 19.95 (ISBN 0-935856-01-3). Lancer.

Rifleman's Bible. Sam Fadala. LC 87-431. (Illus.). 208p. 1987. pap. 7.95 (ISBN 0-385-23747-2, Pub. by Outdoor Bible). Doubleday.

Riflemen Form: Study of the Rifle Volunteer Movement, 1859-1908. Jan Beckett. 368p. 1986. 53.00x (ISBN 0-85936-271-X, Pub. by Spellmount Ltd Pubs). State Mutual Bk.

Riflemen Form: The War Scare of 1859-60 in England. Michael J. Salevouris. Ed. by Peter Stansky & Leslie Hume. LC 81-48367. (Modern British History Ser.). 326p. 1982. lib. bdg. 48.00 (ISBN 0-8240-5163-7). Garland Pub.

Rifles & Romance. Clint Berryhill. 200p. 1983. pap. 5.00 (ISBN 0-942698-09-6). Trends & Events.

Rifles for Watie. Harold Keith. LC 57-10280. (YA) (gr. 7 up). 1957. 13.95i (ISBN 0-690-70181-0, Crowell Jr Bks). HarpJ.

Rifles for Watie. Harold Keith. LC 57-10280. 352p. (YA) (gr. 7 up). 1987. pap. 2.95 (ISBN 0-694-05613-8, Harper Keypoint). HarpJ.

Rifles of Colonial America, 2 vols. George Shumway. Incl. Vol. 1. 352p (ISBN 0-87387-079-4); Vol. 2. 318p (ISBN 0-87387-082-4). (Congrifle Ser.). (Illus.). 1980. casebound ea. 49.50 (ISBN 0-686-65023-9). Shumway.

Rifles of Revenge. Lewis B. Patten. 1979. pap. 1.95 (ISBN 0-89083-568-3). Zebra.

Rifles on the Range. Lee Floren. 1978. pap. 1.25 (ISBN 0-8439-0531-X, Leisure Bks). Leisure NY.

Rift: A Novel of Suspense. Liza Cody. 224p. 1988. 15.95 (ISBN 0-684-18959-3). Scribner.

Rift & Revolution: The Central American Imbroglio. Ed. by Howard J. Wiarda. 392p. 1984. 25.00 (ISBN 0-8447-3539-6); pap. 13.50 (ISBN 0-8447-3538-8). Am Enterprise.

Rift Valley Fever. Ed. by N. Goldblum et al. (Contributions to Epidemiology & Biostatistics Ser.: Vol. 3). (Illus.). xii, 196p. 1981. pap. 55.50 (ISBN 3-8055-1770-X). S Karger.

Rift Valleys & Geology of East Africa. John W. Gregory. LC 76-44726. Repr. of 1921 ed. 47.50 (ISBN 0-404-15863-3). AMS Pr.

Rift Zones of the World Ocean. Ed. by A. P. Vinogradov & G. B. Udintsev. Tr. by N. Kaner. LC 75-16178. 503p. 1975. 63.25 (ISBN 0-470-90838-6, JW). Krieger.

Rifts in the Universe: A Study of the Historic Dichotomies & Modalities of Being. Jared S. Moore. 1927. 39.50x (ISBN 0-686-51303-7). Elliots Bks.

Rig. Ronald Wilcox. 256p. 1986. pap. 2.95 (ISBN 0-8439-2313-X, Leisure Bks). Leisure NY.

Rig Equipment. Philip F. Lynch. LC 80-24533. (Primer in Drilling & Production Equipment Ser.: Vol. 2). (Illus.). 134p. (Orig.). 1981. pap. 21.00x (ISBN 0-87201-199-2). Gulf Pub.

Rig Veda. Wendy O'Flaherty. (Pengiun Classic Ser.). 1982. pap. 6.95 (ISBN 0-14-044402-5). Penguin.

Rig Veda, 4 pts. Vedas. Ed. by Daniel H. Ingalls. LC 54-10046. (Oriental Ser: No. 33-35). Pts. 1-3. 1952 65.00x (ISBN 0-674-76965-1); Pt. 4. 1957 16.50x (ISBN 0-674-76967-8). Harvard U Pr.

Rig Veda Americanus. Ed. by Daniel G. Brinton. LC 73-83463. (Library of Aboriginal American Literature Ser.: No. 8). Repr. of 1890 ed. 30.00 (ISBN 0-404-52188-6). AMS Pr.

Rig Veda Americanus: Sacred Songs of the Ancient Mexicans. D. Brinton. 1976. lib. bdg. 59.95 (ISBN 0-8490-2524-9). Gordon Pr.

Rig-Veda-Samhita: The Sacred Hymns of the Brahmans, 4 vols. 2nd ed. Friedrich M. Mueller. LC 73-18831. 1892. Set. 176.00 (ISBN 0-404-11461-X); Vol. 1. (ISBN 0-404-11462-8); Vol. 2. (ISBN 0-404-11463-6); Vol. 3. (ISBN 0-404-11464-4); Vol. 4. (ISBN 0-404-11465-2). AMS Pr.

Rig-Veda Sanhita, 7 vols. H. H. Wilson. Incl. Vol. I. 348p. Repr. of 1850 ed (ISBN 0-89684-125-1); Vol. II. 346p. Repr. of 1854 ed (ISBN 0-89684-126-X); Vol. III. 249p. Repr. of 1857 ed (ISBN 0-89684-127-8); Vol. IV. 179p. Repr. of 1857 ed (ISBN 0-89684-128-6); Vol. V. 314p. Repr. of 1866 ed (ISBN 0-89684-129-4); Vol VI. 443p. Repr. of 1888 ed (ISBN 0-89684-130-8); Vol. VII. 436p. Repr. of 1888 ed (ISBN 0-89684-131-6). 1977. 120.00 set (ISBN 0-686-77518-X, Pub. by Cosmo Pubns India). Orient Bk Dist.

Rig-Veda-Sanhita, Liber Primus, Sanskrit & Latine. Vedas. Ed. by F. Rosen. (Oriental Translation Fund Ser: No. 48). (Sanskrit & Lat). Repr. of 1838 ed. 28.00 (ISBN 0-384-64125-3). Johnson Repr.

Rig-Veda (Summary) Date not set. 5.00 (ISBN 0-938924-29-X). Sri Shirdi Sai.

Rig Warrior. William W. Johnstone. 288p. 1987. pap. 3.50 (ISBN 0-8217-2066-X). Zebra.

Rig Warrior, No. 3: Eighteen-Wheel Avenger. William W. Johnstone. 256p. 1988. pap. 2.95 (ISBN 0-8217-2433-9). Zebra.

Rigadoon. Louis-Ferdinand Celine. Tr. by Ralph Manheim from Fr. 304p. 1975. pap. 4.95 (ISBN 0-14-004083-8). Penguin.

Rigger's Apprentice. Brion Toss. LC 84-47755. (Illus.). 208p. 1985. 27.50 (ISBN 0-87742-165-X). Intl Marine.

Riggers Bible Handbook of Heavy Rigging. Robert P. Leach, Jr. 1983. Repr. of 1965 ed. 13.50 (ISBN 0-9600992-1-2). Riggers Bible.

Rigger's Notebook. Brion Toss. 208p. (Orig.). 1989. pap. 24.95. Intl Marine.

Rigging. Enrico Sala. (Illus.). 1988. 22.00 (ISBN 0-393-03324-4). Norton.

Rigging Equipment & Outfit of Seagoing Ships, Pt. 1. J. P. De Haan. 464p. 1957. 200.00x (ISBN 0-85950-070-5, Pub. by Stam Pr England). State Mutual Bk.

Rigging of Ships: In the Days of the Spritsail Topmast, 1600-1720. R. C. Anderson. LC 82-71502. (Illus.). 320p. 1982. Repr. 25.00 (ISBN 0-87033-294-5). Cornell Maritime.

Rigging Sail. Percy W. Blandford. (Illus.). 272p. (Orig.). 1983. pap. 15.50 (ISBN 0-8306-1634-9, 1634P). TAB Bks.

Rigging Small Sailboats. Ken Hankinson. LC 72-97327. (Illus.). pap. 7.50 (ISBN 0-939070-04-9). Glen-L Marine.

Right Actions in Sport: Ethics for Contestants. Warren P. Fraleigh. LC 83-83165. 208p. 1984. text ed. 26.00x (ISBN 0-931250-55-2, BFRA0055). Human Kinetics.

Right & Left Hemispheres of the Animal Brain: Cerebral Lateralization of Function. V. L. Bianki. (Monographs in Neuroscience Ser.: Vol. 3). 430p. Date not set. text ed. 84.00 (ISBN 2-88124-197-2). Gordon & Breach.

Right & the Good. W. D. Ross. LC 88-11019. 184p. 1988. lib. bdg. 27.50 (ISBN 0-87220-059-0); pap. 14.50 (ISBN 0-87220-058-2). Hackett Pub.

Right & the Power: The Prosecution of Watergate. Leon Jaworski. LC 76-22594. 316p. 1976. 15.00x (ISBN 0-87201-792-3). Gulf Pub.

Right & Wrong. Charles Fried. 1979. 20.00x (ISBN 0-674-76905-8); pap. 6.95x (ISBN 0-674-76975-9). Harvard U Pr.

Right & Wrong: A Brief Guide to Understanding Ethics. Thomas I. White. 128p. 1988. pap. text ed. price not set (ISBN 0-13-781170-5). P-H.

Right & Wrong: A Philosophical Dialogue Between Father & Son. Paul Weiss & Jonathan Weiss. LC 73-12702. (Arcturus Books Paperbacks). 222p. 1974. pap. 5.95x (ISBN 0-8093-0658-1). S Ill U Pr.

Right & Wrong: Basic Readings in Ethics. Hoff Sommers. 192p. 1986. pap. text ed. 12.00 net (ISBN 0-15-577110-8, Pub. by HC). HarBraceJ.

Right & Wrong of Compulsion by the State, & Other Essays. Auberon Herbert. LC 78-4879. 1978. 9.00 (ISBN 0-913966-41-X, Liberty Clas); pap. 3.50 (ISBN 0-913966-42-8). Liberty Fund.

Right & Wrong Thinking. 2nd ed. Kenneth E. Hagin. 1966. pap. 1.00 (ISBN 0-89276-004-4). Hagin Ministries.

Right Angle Triangle: The Prince & the Singer. Ferdinand Voteur. 13.50 (ISBN 0-8369-9180-X, 9053). Ayer Co Pubs.

Right Before Your Eyes. Grady Clay. LC 87-70550. 250p. (Orig.). 1987. lib. bdg. 45.95 (ISBN 0-918286-47-6); pap. 24.95. Planners Pr.

Right Behind the Rain. Joyce Sweeney. LC 86-19953. 160p. (YA) (gr. 7 up). 1987. pap. 14.95 (ISBN 0-385-29551-0). Delacorte.

Right Brain. Thomas R. Blakeslee. LC 82-60690. 288p. 1984. pap. 3.95 (ISBN 0-425-09163-5). Berkley Pub.

Right Brain Book: How to Unleash Your Child's Genius for Self-Esteem & Success. Barbara Caldirola & Marcia C. Tobin. Ed. by Arline Broy & Janice Kennedy. (Illus.). 1987. wkbk. 14.95 (ISBN 0-945399-00-6). Floyd-Mantz.

Right Brain Experience: An Intimate Program to Free the Powers of Your Imagination. Marilee Zdenek. 384p. 1983. text ed. 15.95 (ISBN 0-07-072737-6). McGraw.

Right Brain Experience: An Intimate Program to Free the Powers of Your Imagination. Marilee Zdenek. 1985. pap. text ed. 6.95 (ISBN 0-07-072744-9). McGraw.

Right to Communicate: Collected Papers. Ed. by L. S. Harms et al. LC 77-71944. 149p. 1977. pap. text ed. 7.00x (ISBN 0-8248-0567-4). UH Pr.
Right to Counsel in American Courts. William M. Beaney. LC 72-5275. (University of Michigan Publications History & Political Science Ser.: Vol. 19). 268p. 1972. Repr. of 1955 ed. lib. bdg. 35.00x (ISBN 0-8371-5725-0, BERC). Greenwood.
Right to Development at the International Level. R. J. Dupuy. 458p. 1981. 40.00 (ISBN 90-286-0990-3, Pub. by Sijthoff & Noordhoff). Kluwer Academic.
Right to Die. Meisel. (Medico-Legal Library). 1988. write for info. (ISBN 0-471-84687-2). Wiley.
Right to Die: Decision & Decision Makers. Group for the Advancement of Psychiatry Staff. LC 84-45126. 96p. 1983. 15.00x (ISBN 0-87668-721-4). Aronson.
Right to Die: Decision & Decision Makers, Vol. 8. GAP Committee on Aging. LC 64-138. (Symposium No. 12). 1973. pap. 5.00 (ISBN 0-87318-123-9, Pub. by GAP). Brunner-Mazel.
Right to Die: Legal & Ethical Problems. Irving J. Sloan. (Legal Almanac Ser.: No. 90). 160p. 1988. lib. bdg. 10.00 (ISBN 0-379-11167-5). Oceana.
Right to Die or Right to Live: Legal Aspects of Dying & Death. Peter J. Riga. 228p. 1981. 28.50x (ISBN 0-86733-993-4, 5993). Assoc Faculty Pr.
Right to Die: Understanding Euthanasia. Derek Humphrey & Ann Wickett. LC 85-45737. 256p. 1986. 18.45i (ISBN 0-06-015578-7, HARPT); 18.45i. Har-Row.
Right to Die: Understanding Euthanasia. Derek Humphry & Ann Wickett. LC 85-45737. 372p. 1987. pap. 9.95 (ISBN 0-06-091411-4, PL 1411, PL). Har-Row.
Right to Education: Anatomy of the Pennsylvania Case & Its Implications for Exceptional Children. Leopold D. Lippman & I. Ignacy Goldberg. LC 73-78038. (Teachers College Series in Special Education). 153p. pap. 39.80 (2030172). Bks Demand UMI.
Right-to-Education Child: A Curriculum for the Severely & Profoundly Mentally Retarded. Donald G. Myers et al. (Illus.). 248p. 1978. 27.25 (ISBN 0-398-02923-7). C C Thomas.
Right to Education: From Proclamation to Achievement, 1948-1968. Louis Francois. 1968. pap. 7.50 (ISBN 92-3-100700-9, U558, UNESCO). UNIPUB.
Right to Education: What Kind of Management? Daniel Haag. (IBE Studies & Surveys in Comparative Education). (Illus.). 175p. 1982. pap. 6.50 (ISBN 92-3-101930-9, U1213, UNESCO). UNIPUB.
Right to Feel Bad. Lesley Hazelton. 1985. pap. 3.50 (ISBN 0-345-32401-3). Ballantine.
Right to Fly. I. Egorov. 240p. 1983. pap. 3.95 (ISBN 0-8285-2469-6, Pub. by Progress Pubs USSR). Imported Pubns.
Right to Food. Philip Alston & Katarina Tomasevski. 1984. text ed. 36.50 (ISBN 90-247-3087-2, Pub. by Martinus Nijhoff Netherlands). Kluwer Academic.
Right to Food. A. H. Boerma. 177p. 1976. pap. 11.25 (ISBN 92-5-101642-9, F1146, FAO). UNIPUB.
Right to Grow Up: An Introduction to Adults with Developmental Disabilities. Jean Ann Summers. LC 85-15000. 352p. (Orig.). 1986. pap. text ed. 21.95 (ISBN 0-933716-47-8, 478). P H Brookes.
Right to Health As a Human Right: Colloquim 1978 of the Hague Academy of International Law. Ed. by R. J. Dupuy. 513p. 1980. 40.00x (ISBN 90-286-1028-6, Pub. by Sijthoff & Noordhoff). Kluwer Academic.
Right to Health Care: An Advocate's Guide to the Hill-Burton Uncompensated Care & Community Services Requirements. Armin Freifeld. 326p. (Orig.). 1986. pap. 15.00 (ISBN 0-941077-16-0, 41,900). NCLS Inc.
Right to Hope: Crisis & Community. Melvin Rader. LC 81-51284. 148p. 1981. 16.50x (ISBN 0-295-95836-7). U of Wash Pr.
Right to Information: Legal Questions & Policy Issues. Ed. by Jana Varlejs. LC 83-26750. 96p. 1984. pap. 9.95x (ISBN 0-89950-097-8). McFarland & Co.
Right to Keep & Bear Arms. 185p. 1982. 5.00 (ISBN 0-318-23088-7, 052-070-05686-0). USGPO.
Right to Keep & Bear Arms: A Continuing American Dilemma. Earl R. Kruschke. 208p. 1985. 27.00x (ISBN 0-398-05141-0). C C Thomas.
Right to Keep & Bear Arms: A Presentation of Both Sides. 1986. lib. bdg. 79.95 (ISBN 0-8490-3538-4). Gordon Pr.
Right to Kill. Scott Jansen. 192p. (Orig.). 1982. pap. 2.25 (ISBN 0-8439-1112-3, Leisure Bks). Leisure NY.
Right to Know: A Guide to Federal & State Requirements. 2nd ed. Interface Associates Staff. LC 86-21128. 270p. 1986. 3-ring looseleaf binder 65.00 (ISBN 0-938135-07-4). Interface Assocs.
Right to Know Compliance Guide. rev. ed. Ed. by N. Randall Phillips. 65p. 1988. pap. 49.95 (ISBN 0-87425-078-1). Human Res Dev Pr.
Right to Know Employee Self-Study Booklet. rev. ed. Sharon Fisher. 100p. 1988. pap. 3.95 (ISBN 0-87425-090-0). Human Res Dev Pr.
Right-to-Know: For Workers & Community--OSHA, EPA & the States. George G. Lowry & Robert C. Lowry. (Illus.). 350p. 1988. 45.95 (ISBN 0-87371-112-2). Lewis Pubs Inc.
Right to Know One's Human Rights: A Road Toward Marriage & Family. Vratislav Pechota. LC 83-72868. 52p. 1983. pap. 2.50 (ISBN 0-87495-056-2). Am Jewish Comm.
Right-to-Know Planning Guide. 1987. looseleaf 396.00. BNA.
Right to Know: The Inside Story of the Belgrano Affair. Clive Ponting. 1985. 20.00x (ISBN 0-317-54919-7, Pub. by NCCL UK). State Mutual Bk.
Right to Learn: The Struggle for Education in South Africa. Pamela Christie. 256p. 1986. pap. 9.95 (ISBN 0-86975-286-3, Pub. by Ravan Pr). Ohio U Pr.
Right to Leave & Return in International Law & Practice. Hurst Hannum. LC 86-23905. 1987. 57.50 (ISBN 9-02-473445-2, Pub. by Kluwer-Nijhoff (Netherlands)). Kluwer Academic.
Right to Life. A. Delafield Smith. 1955. 12.95x; pap. 8.95x. New Coll U Pr.
Right to Life in International Law. Ed. by B. G. Ramchran. 1985. lib. bdg. 57.50 (ISBN 90-247-3074-0, Pub. by Martinus Nijhoff Netherlands). Kluwer Academic.
Right to Life Movement & Third Party Politics. Robert J. Spitzer. LC 86-14209. (Contributions in Political Science Ser.: No. 160). 167p. 1987. lib. bdg. 29.95 (ISBN 0-313-25390-0, SRT/). Greenwood.
Right to Lifers: Who They Are, How They Operate, Where They Get Their Money. Connie Paige. LC 83-4795. 1983. 14.95 (ISBN 0-671-43180-3). Summit Bks.
Right to Live: Essays. Max Plowman. 1979. Repr. of 1942 ed. lib. bdg. 22.50 (ISBN 0-8492-2155-2). R West.
Right to Live: The Right to Die. C. Everett Koop. 1980. pap. 3.95 (ISBN 0-8423-5594-4). Tyndale.
Right to Love. Jennifer A. Lawson. 64p. 1980. 5.00 (ISBN 0-682-49651-0). Exposition-Phoenix.
Right to Manage: A Study of Leadership & Reform in Employee Relations. W. W. Daniel & Neil McIntosh. 192p. 1972. 15.95x (ISBN 0-8464-0798-1). Beekman Pubs.
Right to Manage: Industrial Relations Policies of American Business in the 1940s. Howell J. Harris. LC 81-69820. 312p. 1982. text ed. 25.00x (ISBN 0-299-08640-2). U of Wis Pr.
Right to Membership of a Trade Union. R. W. Rideout. LC 75-17201. (Univ. of London Legal Ser.: No. 5). 243p. 1975. Repr. of 1963 ed. lib. bdg. 35.00x (ISBN 0-8371-8295-6, RIMTU). Greenwood.
Right to Organize. Jay A. Erstling. 82p. 1977. 17.50 (ISBN 92-2-101790-7). Intl Labour Office.
Right to Organize. Jay A. Erstling. vi, 82p. 1977. pap. 10.50 (ISBN 92-2-101790-7, ILO1107, ILO). UNIPUB.
Right to Participate: The Law & Individuals with Handicapping Conditions in Physical Education & Sports. Herb Appenzeller. 421p. 1983. 25.00x (ISBN 0-87215-620-6). Michie Co.
Right to Picket & the Freedom of Public Discourse. John W. Whitehead. LC 84-72425. (Rutherford Institute Report Ser.: Vol. 3). 176p. (Orig.). 1984. pap. 6.95 (ISBN 0-89107-344-2). Good News.
Right to Privacy. Adam C. Breckenridge. LC 73-88084. viii, 155p. 1970. 16.50x (ISBN 0-8032-0702-6). U of Nebr Pr.
Right to Private Property. Jeremy Waldron. (Illus.). 496p. 1988. 85.00 (ISBN 0-19-824959-4). Oxford U Pr.
Right to Property. A. L. Gandhi. 308p. 1985. 75.00x (ISBN 81-85046-22-0, Pub. by Scientific). State Mutual Bk.
Right to Refuse Antipsychotic Medication. Bruce J. Winnick et al. LC 86-219899. 112p. 1986. pap. 9.95. Amer Bar Assn.
Right to Remain Silent. Charles Brandt. 304p. 1988. 17.95x (ISBN 0-312-01372-8). St Martin.
Right to Remain Silent. Milton Meltzer. LC 72-76366. (Illus.). 128p. (gr. 7 up). 1972. 5.95 (ISBN 0-15-266990-6, HJ). HarBraceJ.
Right to Silence: Privileged Clergy Communication & the Law. William H. Tiemann & John C. Bush. 256p. (Orig.). 1983. pap. 11.95 (ISBN 0-687-36315-2). Abingdon.
Right to Sing the Blues. John Lutz. 256p. 1985. 14.95 (ISBN 0-312-68235-2). St Martin.
Right to Sing the Blues. John Lutz. 256p. 1988. pap. 2.95 (ISBN 0-8125-0646-4). Tor Bks.
Right to Song: The Life of John Clare. Edward Storey. (Illus.). 330p. 1982. 38.00 (ISBN 0-413-39940-0, NO. 3825). Heinemann Ed.
Right to Strike in Community Law: The Incorporation of Fundamental Rights in the Legal Order of the European Communities. L. Betten. 326p. 1985. 84.25 (ISBN 0-444-87845-9, North Holland). Elsevier.
Right to Survive: Subsistence Marketing in a Lowland Philippine Town. Maria C. Szanton. LC 72-157769. (Illus.). 161p. 1973. 20.00x (ISBN 0-271-00555-6). Pa St U Pr.
Right to the Land: Essays on the Freedmen's Community. Edward Magdol. LC 76-39707. (Contributions in American History: No. 61). (Illus.). 1977. lib. bdg. 35.00 (ISBN 0-8371-9409-1, MFC/). Greenwood.
Right to the Whole Produce of Labour. Anton Menger. LC 68-54737. 1970. Repr. of 1899 ed. lib. bdg. 39.50x (ISBN 0-678-00714-4). Kelley.
Right to Travel under the Constitution. B. Errabi. 1986. 50.00. State Mutual Bk.
Right to Treatment for Mental Patients. Ed. by Stuart Golann & William J. Fremouw. (Illus.). 320p. 1976. 29.95x (ISBN 0-8290-0863-2). Irvington.
Right to Treatment in Mental Health Law. 97p. 1976. 4.00 (ISBN 0-318-15226-6). Natl Attys General.
Right to Treatment in Mental Health Law. W. Schmidt. 1976. write for info. FSU CSP.
Right to Treatment Under Civil Commitment. Elizabeth W. Browne. 160p. 1975. 8.50 (ISBN 0-318-15773-X, T350). Natl Juv & Family Ct Judges.
Right to Treatment under Civil Commitment. Elizabeth W. Browne. 160p. 1977. 8.50. Natl Juv & Family Ct Judges.
Right to Useful Work. Ken Coates. 287p. 50.00x (ISBN 0-85124-219-7, Pub. by Bertrand Russell Hse). State Mutual Bk.
Right to Vote. Carole L. Corbin. LC 84-26979. (Issues in American History Ser.). (Illus.). 112p. (YA) (gr. 7 up). 1985. lib. bdg. 12.90 (ISBN 0-531-04932-9). Watts.
Right to Vote: Politics & the Passage of the Fifteenth Amendment. William Gillette. LC 74-94492. (Studies in Historical & Political Science: Eighty-Third Series (1965)). 192p. 1965. pap. 7.95x (ISBN 0-8018-1090-6). Johns Hopkins.
Right to Vote: Politics & the Passage of the 15th Amendment. William Gillette. LC 78-64243. (Johns Hopkins University. Studies in the Social Sciences. Eighty-Third Ser. 1965: 1). Repr. of 1965 ed. 18.50 (ISBN 0-404-61348-9). AMS Pr.
Right to Welfare. T. H. Marshall. 192p. 1981. text ed. 15.00 (ISBN 0-02-920200-0). Free Pr.
Right-to-Work Laws: A Study in Conflict. Paul Sultan. pap. 5.00 looseleaf. U Cal LA Indus Rel.
Right Toys: A Guide to Selecting the Best Toys for Children. Helen Boehm. LC 86-47577. 176p. 1986. pap. 8.95 (ISBN 0-553-34304-1). Bantam.
Right Turn: The Decline of the Democrats & the Future of American Politics. Thomas Ferguson & Joel Rogers. 160p. 1986. 19.95 (ISBN 0-8090-8191-1). Hill & Wang.
Right Turn: The Decline of the Democrats & the Future of American Politics. Thomas Ferguson & Joel Rogers. (American Century Ser.). 288p. 1987. pap. 8.95 (ISBN 0-8090-0170-5). Hill & Wang.
Right Usefulness. Thomas Hora. 35p. 1987. pap. 4.00 (ISBN 0-913105-12-0). PAGL Pr.
Right Ventricle. Ed. by Marvin A. Konstam & Jeffrey M. Isner. 1988. lib. bdg. 125.00 (ISBN 0-89838-987-9, Pub. by M Nijhoff Boston MA). Kluwer Academic.
Right Versus Privilege: The Open Admissions Experiment at the City University of New York. David E. Lavin et al. LC 80-69571. (Illus.). 1981. 24.95 (ISBN 0-02-918080-5). Free Pr.
Right Way the Safe Way Proved by Emancipation in the British West Indies, & Elsewhere. Lydia M. Child. LC 76-82184. (Anti-Slavery Crusade in America Ser.). 1969. Repr. of 1860 ed. 9.50 (ISBN 0-405-00623-3). Ayer Co Pubs.
Right Way to a Good Job. F. J. Taylor. 174p. 1979. pap. 9.75x (ISBN 0-220-66364-5, Pub. by Busn Bks England). Brookfield Pub Co.
Right Way to do Wrong. Harry Houdini. 17.95 (ISBN 0-89190-259-7, Pub. by Am Repr). Amereon Ltd.
Right Way to Eat Spaghetti. Bob Donahue & Marilyn Donahue. (Help Yourself Ser.: No. 5). (Illus.). 128p. (Orig.). (YA) (gr. 9-12). 1988. pap. 4.95 (ISBN 0-8423-5597-9). Tyndale.
Right Way to Play Chess. D. Brine Pritchard. (Illus.). 1977. 11.95 (ISBN 0-87523-087-3). Emerson.
Right Way to Start Horse Riding. Kurt Hoffmann. (Illus.). 128p. 1986. Repr. of 1984 ed. 4.95 (ISBN 0-86622-176-X, PS836). TFH Pubns.
Right Where You Live. Constance Brady. (Illus.). 188p. (Orig.). 1982. pap. 9.95 (ISBN 0-686-35975-5). Conarc.
Right Wing in France: From 1815 to De Gaulle. rev. ed. Rene Remond. Tr. by James M. Laux. LC 72-87940. 1969. 18.95x (ISBN 0-8122-7490-3). U of Pa Pr.
Right Wing Individualist Tradition in America, 38 bks. Ed. by Murray N. Rothbard & Jerome Tuccille. 1972. Set. 812.00 (ISBN 0-405-00410-9). Ayer Co Pubs.
Right-Wing Press in France, 1792-1800. Jeremy D. Popkin. LC 79-14067. (Illus.). xix, 234p. 1980. 27.50x (ISBN 0-8078-1393-1). U of NC Pr.
Right-Wing Press in the French Revolution: 1789-1792, No. 44. William J. Murray. (Royal Historical Society Ser.). 349p. 1986. 54.00 (ISBN 0-86193-201-3, Pub. by Boydell & Brewer). Longwood Pub Group.
Right-Wing Radicalism & Political Intolerance: A Study of Support for McCarthy in a New England Town. Martin A. Trow. Ed. by Harriet Zuckerman & Robert K. Merton. LC 79-9035. (Dissertations on Sociology Ser.). 1980. lib. bdg. 32.50x (ISBN 0-405-13002-3). Ayer Co Pubs.
Right-Wing Women: The Politics of Domesticated Females. Andrea Dworkin. 256p. 1983. pap. 8.95 (ISBN 0-399-50671-3, Perigee). Putnam Pub Group.
Right with God. John Blanchard. LC 78-6809. 1978. pap. 3.95 (ISBN 0-8024-7357-1). Moody.
Right with God. rev. ed. John Blanchard. 126p. 1985. pap. 3.95 (ISBN 0-85151-045-0). Banner of Truth.
Right Word. Rev. ed. Ed. by Houghton Mifflin Company Staff. LC 83-8502. (Word Desk Set II Ser.). 288p. 1983. text ed. 3.95 (ISBN 0-395-34808-0). HM.
Right Word: A Concise Thesauras. LC 78-3461. (gr. 9 up). 1978. 3.95 (ISBN 0-395-26672-6). HM.
Right Word in Chinese. Date not set. 9.95 (RIWOIN). China Bks.
Right Words in Right Places: A Workbook in Diction & Sentence Style. Milton Chaikin. 1979. pap. text ed. 12.95 (ISBN 0-8403-2080-9). Kendall-Hunt.
Right Work: Finding it & Making it Right. John Caple. 224p. 1987. 17.95 (ISBN 0-396-09064-8, Gamut Bk); pap. 9.95 (ISBN 0-396-09195-4, Gamut Bk). Dodd.
Right You Are, Mr. Moto. John P. Marquand. 1986. pap. 4.95 (ISBN 0-316-54706-9). Little.
Righte Merrie Christmasse. John Ashton. LC 68-56543. (Illus.). 1968. Repr. of 1894 ed. 15.00 (ISBN 0-405-08225-8, Pub. by Blom). Ayer Co Pubs.
Righteous Cause: The Life of William Jennings Bryan. Robert W. Cherny. (Library of American Biography). 1984. 15.95 (ISBN 0-316-13854-1); pap. text ed. write for info. (ISBN 0-673-39328-3). Scott F.
Righteous Gentile: The Story of Raoul Wallenberg, Missing Hero of the Holocaust. John Bierman. LC 80-52465. (Illus.). 256p. 1981. 12.95 (ISBN 0-670-74924-9). Viking.
Righteous Gentile: The Story of Raoul Wallenberg, Missing Hero of the Holocaust. John Bierman. 210p. Repr. 12.95 (ISBN 0-686-95084-4). ADL.
Righteous Rakehell. Gayle Buck. 1988. pap. 2.95 (ISBN 0-451-15668-4, Sig). NAL.
Righteous Rama: The Evolution of an Epic. J. L. Brockington. 1984. 36.00x (ISBN 0-19-561710-X). Oxford U Pr.
Righteous Remnant: The House of David. Robert S. Fogarty. LC 80-84666. (Illus.). 208p. 1981. 17.50 (ISBN 0-87338-251-X). Kent St U Pr.
Righteous Rhymes, Vol. 1. Jamie S. Lash. (Illus.). 24p. (gr. 2-7). 1983. pap. 2.95 (ISBN 0-915775-00-X, Dist. by Stardust). Love Song Mess Assn.
Righteous Struggle. Mahadev Desai. 105p. 1983. pap. 1.25 (ISBN 0-934676-34-8). Greenlf Bks.
Righteousness. Ronald D. Tucker. (Illus.). 48p. (Orig.). 1983. pap. 2.00 (ISBN 0-933643-09-8). Grace World Outreach.
Righteousness in Matthew & His World of Thought. Benno Przybylski. LC 79-41371. (Society for New Testament Studies Monographs: No. 41). 240p. 1981. 32.50 (ISBN 0-521-22566-3). Cambridge U Pr.
Righteousness in the New Testament: Justification in Lutheran-Catholic Dialogue. John Reumann. LC 81-43086. 320p. 1982. pap. 13.95 (ISBN 0-8006-1616-2, 1-1616). Fortress.
Righteousness in the New Testament: Justification in Lutheran-Catholic Dialogue. John Reumann. LC 81-85385. 320p. (Orig.). 1982. pap. 13.95 (ISBN 0-8091-2436-X). Paulist Pr.
Righteousness in the Septuagint of Isaiah: A Contextual Study. John W. Olley. LC 78-3425. (Society of Biblical Literature, Septuagint & Cognate Studies: No. 8). 1979. pap. 9.95 (ISBN 0-89130-226-3, 06-04-08). Scholars Pr GA.
Righteousness Inside-Out. Mike Cope. 1988. pap. 5.95 (ISBN 0-89225-333-9). Gospel Advocate.
Righteousness Which Is of Faith. Charles Capps. (Orig.). 1986. mini bk. 0.75 (ISBN 0-89274-411-1). Harrison Hse.
Rightfully Mine: One Woman's Pursuit of Love & Justice in the Time of Moses. Aggie Villanueva. LC 86-747. 176p. 1986. pap. 6.95 (ISBN 0-8407-3050-0). Nelson.
Righthandedness & Lefthandedness: With Chapters Treating of the Writing Posture, the Rule of the Road, Etc. George M. Gould. LC 78-72794. Repr. of 1908 ed. 26.50 (ISBN 0-404-60859-0). AMS Pr.
Righting. Ernest Joselovitz. 1977. pap. 1.95 (ISBN 0-685-81649-4). Dramatists Play.
Rightly Dividing. Truman H. Etheridge. 1955. 6.00 (ISBN 0-88027-017-9). Firm Foun Pub.
Rightly Dividing the Word of Truth. C. I. Scofield. pap. 1.50 (ISBN 0-87213-770-8). Loizeaux.
Rightly Dividing the Word of Truth see Traza Bien la Palabra de Verdad.
Rights. Theodore M. Benditt. LC 81-23448. (Philosophy & Society Ser.). 158p. 1982. text ed. 27.50x (ISBN 0-8476-6754-5). Rowman.
Rights. Alan R. White. 1984. 22.00x. Oxford U Pr.
Rights. Alan R. White. 608p. 1986. pap. 13.95x (ISBN 0-19-824923-3). Oxford U Pr.
Rights & Goods: Justifying Social Action. Virginia Held. 384p. 1984. 22.95x (ISBN 0-02-914710-7). Free Pr.
Rights & Liabilities of Public School Boards under Capital Outlay Contracts. Frank E. Henzlik. LC 76-176859. (Columbia University. Teachers College. Contributions to Education: No. 153). Repr. of 1924 ed. 22.50 (ISBN 0-404-55153-X). AMS Pr.
Rights & Liabilities of Publishers, Broadcasters & Reporters. Slade R. Metcalf & Robin Bierstedt. LC 82-16839. (Individual Rights Ser.). 1982. text ed. 90.00 (ISBN 0-07-041685-0). Shepards-McGraw.

Riksdag: A History of the Swedish Parliament. Ed. by Michael Metcalf. 220p. 1987. 29.95 (ISBN 0-312-00784-1). St Martin.

Riley Child-Rhymes. facs. ed. James W. Riley. LC 74-121933. (Granger Index Reprint Ser). 1898. 15.00 (ISBN 0-8369-6174-9). Ayer Co Pubs.

Riley's Flute Melodies, 2vols. in 1. Edward Riley. Ed. & intro. by H. Wiley Hitchcock. LC 72-14213. (Earlier American Music Ser.: Vol. 18). 200p. 1973. Repr. of 1816 ed. lib. bdg. 27.50 (ISBN 0-306-70565-6). Da Capo.

Riley's Last Hunt. Frank Calkins. LC 86-24086. 360p. 1987. 16.95 (ISBN 0-385-23981-5, GC Large Print). Doubleday.

Riley's Last Hunt. Frank Calkins. 1987. pap. 2.50 (ISBN 0-345-34465-0). Ballantine.

Rilke. Art Beck. LC 82-84119. 70p. (Orig.). pap. 3.95 (ISBN 0-941692-06-X). Elysian Pr.

Rilke. Lou A. Salome. Tr. & ed. by A. Von der Lippe. (Austrian-German Culture Ser.). 120p. 1986. 20.00 (ISBN 0-933806-30-2). Black Swan CT.

Rilke: A Biography. Ralph Freedman. LC 87-42657. (Illus.). 1988. 24.45 (ISBN 0-394-52269-9). Random.

Rilke: A Life. Wolfgang Leppmann. Tr. by Russell Stockman from Ger. LC 84-6062. (Illus.). 438p. 1984. 22.50 (ISBN 0-88064-014-6); pap. 12.95 (ISBN 0-88064-015-4). Fromm Intl Pub.

Rilke & Benvenuta: An Intimate Correspondence. Ed. by Magda von Hattingberg. Tr. by Joel Agee from Ger. 160p. 1987. 16.95 (ISBN 0-88064-072-3). Fromm Intl Pub.

Rilke & the Visual Arts. Jennifer Liebnitz & Joan E. Holmes. Ed. by Frank Baron. (Illus.). 150p. 1982. 12.50x (ISBN 0-87291-153-5). Coronado Pr.

Rilke: Between Roots Selected Poems Rendered from German By Rika Lesser. Rainer M. Rilke. Tr. by Rika Lesser from Ger. LC 85-43204. (Lockert Library of Poetry in Translation). 75p. 1986. text ed. 21.00x (ISBN 0-691-06668-X); pap. 9.95 (ISBN 0-691-01429-9). Princeton U Pr.

Rilke, Europe, & the English-speaking World. Eudo C. Mason. LC 61-16153. pap. 69.30 (ISBN 0-317-20596-X, 2024492). Bks Demand UMI.

Rilke in Transition: An Exploration of His Earliest Poetry. James Rolleston. LC 73-99839. (Yale Germanic Studies: 4). pap. 64.00 (ISBN 0-317-29716-3, 2022035). Bks Demand UMI.

Rilke: Kommentar Zu Den "Aufzeichnungen des Malte Laurids Brigge". William Small. (Studies in the Germanic Languages & Literatures Ser.: No. 101). ix, 175p. 1983. 20.00x (ISBN 0-8078-8101-5). U of NC Pr.

Rilke on Love & other Difficulties: Translations & Considerations of Rainer Maria Rilke. Rainer M. Rilke. Ed. by John Mood. 121p. 1975. pap. 5.95 (ISBN 0-393-04404-1). Norton.

Rilke: The Alchemy of Alienation. Ed. by Frank Baron et al. LC 79-19759. xvi, 268p. 1980. 29.95x (ISBN 0-7006-0198-8). U Pr of KS.

Rilla of Ingleside. L. M. Montgomery. 1986. 24.75X (ISBN 0-245-52799-0, Pub. by Harrap Ltd England). State Mutual Bk.

Rilla of Ingleside, No. 8. L. M. Montgomery. (Anne of Green Gables Ser.). 288p. 1985. pap. 2.95 (ISBN 0-553-25241-0, Starfire). Bantam.

RIM: Growing up. Business Communications Staff. 186p. 1987. pap. 1950.00 (ISBN 0-89336-535-1, P-054N). BCC.

Rim of Christendom: A Biography of Eusebio Francisco Kino, Pacific Coast Pioneer. Herbert E. Bolton. LC 84-8814. 644p. 1984. Repr. of 1960 ed. 40.00x (ISBN 0-8165-0863-1). U of Ariz Pr.

Rim of the Desert. Ernest Haycox. 305p. 1975. Repr. of 1941 ed. lib. bdg. 9.95 (ISBN 0-89190-974-5, Pub. by River City Pr). Amereon Ltd.

Rim of the Desert. Ernest Haycox. 224p. 1988. pap. 2.95 (ISBN 1-55817-126-6). Windsor NY.

Rim of the Pit. Hake Talbot. 278p. 1985. pap. 4.95 (ISBN 0-930330-30-7). Intl Polygonics.

Rim of the Prairie. Bess S. Aldrich. 296p. Repr. of 1925 ed. lib. bdg. 18.95x (ISBN 0-88411-259-4, Pub. by Aeonian Pr). Amereon Ltd.

Rim of the Prairie. Bess S. Aldrich. LC 25-19624. xii, 352p. 1966. pap. 9.95 (ISBN 0-8032-5002-9, Bison). U of Nebr Pr.

Rim of the Range. Al Cody. 1980. pap. 1.75 (ISBN 0-8439-0822-X, Leisure Bks). Leisure NY.

Rim of the Sea. William H. Loke. 96p. 1984. 12.00 (ISBN 0-918999-00-6). Wagapaw Pr.

Rima, the Monkey Child. Harry L. Little. xvi, 123p. 1983. 14.95x (ISBN 0-88864-040-4, Pub. by Univ of Alta Pr Canada). U of Nebr Pr.

Rimac: River of Peru. Alexander L. Crosby. LC 67-10021. (Illus.). 96p. (gr. 4-7). 1965. PLB 3.98 (ISBN 0-8116-6366-3). Garrard.

Rimas. Archer M. Huntington. 1936. 4.00 (ISBN 0-87535-037-2). Hispanic Soc.

Rimas del Pesebre. Luis Salem. LC 77-82265. 86p. (Orig., Span.). (gr. 4 up). 1978. pap. 3.75 (ISBN 0-89922-118-1). Edit Caribe.

Rimas of Gustavo Becquer. Gustavo Becquer. Tr. by Jules Renard. 1976. lib. bdg. 59.95 (ISBN 0-8490-2525-7). Gordon Pr.

Rimbaud. C. Chadwick. (French Poets Ser.). 152p. 1979. 32.50 (ISBN 0-485-14610-X, Pub. by Athlone Pr UK); pap. 14.95 (ISBN 0-485-12210-3, Pub. by Athlone Pr Uk). Humanities.

Rimbaud. Wallace Fowlie. LC 65-20963. pap. 72.00 (2027211). Bks Demand UMI.

Rimbaud. Pierre Petitfils. Tr. by Alan Sheridan from Fr. LC 87-6109. (Illus.). 400p. 1988. 34.95 (ISBN 0-8139-1142-7). U Pr of VA.

Rimbaud: A Critical Introduction. C. A. Hackett. LC 80-40455. (Major European Authors Ser.). 250p. 1981. 42.50 (ISBN 0-521-22976-6); pap. 14.95 (ISBN 0-521-29756-7). Cambridge U Pr.

Rimbaud: Collected Poems. Arthur Rimbaud. Tr. by Oliver Bernard. 384p. 1987. pap. 6.95 (ISBN 0-14-042064-9). Penguin.

Rimbaud et le probleme des Illuminations. Henry D. Bouillane De Lacoste. LC 77-10253. Repr. of 1949 ed. 23.50 (ISBN 0-404-16308-4). AMS Pr.

Rimbaud: Illuminations. Roger Little. (Critical Guides to French Texts Ser.: No. 29). 81p. 1983. pap. 4.50 (ISBN 0-7293-0167-2, Pub. by Grant & Cutler). Longwood Pub Group.

Rimbaud tel que je l'ai connu. Georges Izambard. LC 77-10271. Repr. of 1946 ed. 19.50 (ISBN 0-404-16323-8). AMS Pr.

Rimbaud: The Boy & the Poet. Edgell Rickword. LC 72-163208. (Studies in French Literature, No. 45). 1971. Repr. of 1924 ed. lib. bdg. 49.95x (ISBN 0-8383-1309-4). Haskell.

Rimbaud under the Steel Helmet. Helmut M. Soik. Tr. by George M. Gugelberger & Lydia Perera. 1976. pap. 4.00 (ISBN 0-88031-025-1). Invisible-Red Hill.

Rimbaud: Visions & Habitations. Edward J. Ahearn. LC 82-2776. 383p. 1983. text ed. 40.00x (ISBN 0-520-04591-2). U of Cal Pr.

Rimbaud's Illuminations: A Study in Angelism. Jean N. Rimbaud. Ed. by Wallace Fowlie. Repr. of 1953 ed. lib. bdg. 35.00x (ISBN 0-8371-2240-6, RIIL). Greenwood.

Rime-Index to Chaucer's Troilus & Criseyde. Walter W. Skeat. LC 77-94621. 1978. Repr. of 1892 ed. lib. bdg. 15.00 (ISBN 0-89341-190-6). Longwood Pub Group.

Rime Isle. Fritz Leiber. (Illus.). 1977. 10.00 (ISBN 0-918372-01-1). Whispers.

Rime of the Ancient Mariner. Samuel Taylor Coleridge. Ed. by Gustave Dorbe. 16.95 (ISBN 0-405-11896-1). Ayer Co Pubs.

Rime of the Ancient Mariner. T. Coleridge & L. Clarke. 1986. 34.75X (ISBN 0-317-52512-3, Pub. by Harrap Ltd England). State Mutual Bk.

Rime of the Ancient Mariner. Gustave Dore. (Illus.). 1970. pap. 4.95 (ISBN 0-486-22305-1). Dover.

Rimers of Eldritch & Other Plays. Lanford Wilson. Incl. The Rimers of Eldritch; This Is the Rill Speaking; Wandering; Days Ahead; The Madness of Lady Bright. (Mermaid Dramabook Ser.). 122p. (Orig.). 1967. pap. 5.95 (ISBN 0-8090-1214-6). Hill & Wang.

Rimmonim Bells: Ten Generations of the Behrman, Drucker, Hahn, Stockler & Sztynberg Families Plus Ten Related Lines. Richard J. Alperin. LC 80-65119. (Illus.). 249p. 1980. 39.95x (ISBN 0-9603932-0-X). Junius Inc.

Rimrock. Don P. Jenison. (Orig.). 1980. pap. 1.95 (ISBN 0-89083-576-4). Zebra.

Rimrock. Dennis Maloney. 1978. 1.50 (ISBN 0-934834-12-1). White Pine.

Rimrock Renegade. Lee Floren. 1978. pap. 1.25 (ISBN 0-505-51247-5, Pub. by Tower Bks). Leisure NY.

Rimrock Vengeance. Al Cody. 1981. pap. 1.75 (ISBN 0-8439-0879-3, Leisure Bks). Leisure NY.

RIMS Symposia on Software Science & Engineering II. Ed. by K. Araki. (Lecture Notes In Computer Science Ser.: Vol. 220). xi, 323p. 1986. pap. 20.50 (ISBN 0-387-16470-7). Springer-Verlag.

RIMS Symposia on Software Science & Engineering: Proceedings, Kyoto, Japan, 1982. Ed. by E. Goto et al. (Lecture Notes in Computer Science Ser.: Vol. 147). 232p. 1983. pap. 13.50 (ISBN 0-387-11980-9). Springer-Verlag.

Rimshot. Ted Perry. (Illus.). 140p. 1982. 9.95 (ISBN 0-87754-357-7). Chelsea Hse.

Rimskie Elegii. Joseph Brodsky. LC 82-60519. 20p. (Rus.). 1982. pap. 5.00 (ISBN 0-89830-062-2). Russica Pubs.

Rimsky-Korsakov. Gerald E. Abraham. LC 75-41002. (BCL Ser.: No. II). Repr. of 1945 ed. 15.00 (ISBN 0-404-14500-0). AMS Pr.

Rimsky-Korsakov. Montagu Montagu-Nathan. LC 74-24158. Repr. of 1917 ed. 14.00 (ISBN 0-404-13051-8). AMS Pr.

Rina Peleg: Ceramic Structures. Rina Peleg & John Perreault. Ed. by Thomas Piche, Jr. LC 85-80584. (Illus.). 20p. 1985. pap. 5.00 (ISBN 0-914407-04-X). Everson Mus.

Rincon Hill & South Park: San Francisco's Fashionable Neighborhood 1853-1873. Albert Shumate. Ed. by Wayne Bonnett. (Illus.). 120p. 1988. 24.95 (ISBN 0-915269-08-2). Windgate Pr.

Rinconete & Cortadillo. Miguel de Cervantes. pap. 2.50 (ISBN 0-8283-1453-5, IPL). Branden Pub Co.

Rinderpest Virus see Cytomegloviruses.

Rinds & Peels: A Recycling Cookbook. Date not set. pap. text ed. 3.95 (ISBN 0-318-01302-9, Pub. by Cookbk Consort). Prosperity & Profits.

Rinehart Guide to Grammar & Usage. Bonnie Carter & Craig Skates. 720p. Date not set. text ed. price not set (ISBN 0-03-013619-9). HR&W.

Rinehart Handbook for Writers. Bonnie Carter & Craig Skates. 832p. 1987. text ed. 12.95 (ISBN 0-03-071167-3); Ditto Masters Tests 19.95 (ISBN 0-03-071172-X). HR&W.

Rinehart Lifts. R. R. Knudson. 88p. (gr. 4-7). 1982. pap. 1.95 (ISBN 0-380-57059-9, 57059-9, Camelot). Avon.

Rinehart Lifts. R. R. Knudson. LC 80-66825. 192p. (gr. 4 up). 1980. 9.95 (ISBN 0-374-36294-7). FS&G.

Rinehart Shouts. R. R. Knudson. LC 86-29540. 115p. (gr. 4 up). 1987. 10.95 (ISBN 0-374-36296-3). FS&G.

Ring. Piers Anthony & Robert E. Margroff. 295p. 1986. pap. 2.95 (ISBN 0-8125-3118-3, Dist. by Warner Publisher Services & St. Martin's Press). Tor Bks.

Ring. Daniel K. Moran. 1988. 19.95 (ISBN 0-385-24816-4, Foundation Bks). Doubleday.

Ring. Danielle Steel. 1980. 19.95. Delacorte.

Ring. Danielle Steel. 480p. 1983. pap. 4.95 (ISBN 0-440-17392-2). Dell.

Ring: A Biography of Ring Lardner. Jonathan Yardley. LC 84-45028. (Illus.). 448p. 1984. pap. 13.95 (ISBN 0-689-70681-2, 321). Atheneum.

Ring: Anatomy of an Opera. Stephen Fay. (Illus.). 218p. 1985. 25.00 (ISBN 0-89341-532-4). Longwood Pub Group.

Ring & the Book. Robert Browning. Ed. by Richard D. Altick. LC 80-53977. 707p. 1981. text ed. 47.50 (ISBN 0-300-02677-3); pap. 13.95x (ISBN 0-300-02685-4, YEP-3). Yale U Pr.

Ring Around a Rosy: Action Rhymes. Illus. by Jenny Williams. (Mother Goose Play Rhymes Ser.). (Illus.). 24p. (ps-1). 1987. 3.95 (ISBN 0-8037-0391-0, 0383-120). Dial Bks Young.

Ring Around Duffy. Emily Hearn. LC 74-8102. (Garrard Venture Ser.). (Illus.). 64p. (gr. 1-3). 1974. PLB 6.89 (ISBN 0-8116-6976-9). Garrard.

Ring Around Max: The Correspondence of Ring Lardner & Maxwell Perkins. Ed. & intro. by Clifford M. Caruthers. LC 72-6919. (Illus.). 192p. 1973. 12.50 (ISBN 0-87580-041-6); pap. 6.50 (ISBN 0-87580-512-4). N Ill U Pr.

Ring Around the Moon: Two Hundred Songs, Tongue Twisters, Riddles & Rhymes for Children. Edith Fowke. (Illus.). 160p. (gr. k-5). 1987. pap. 12.95 (Pub. by NC Press Ltd). U of Toronto Pr.

Ring, Bluebell, Ring! J. Donald Walters. (Illus.). 130p. (ps-12). 1988. pap. 7.95 (ISBN 0-916124-33-9, CCP4). Crystal Clarity.

Ring-Chain Tautomerism. Raimonds E. Valters & Wilhelm Flitsch. 270p. 1985. 45.00x (ISBN 0-306-41870-3, Plenum Pr). Plenum Pub.

Ring Complex Granites & Anorogenic Magmatism. Bernard Bonin. 196p. 1986. 47.75 (ISBN 0-444-01075-0). Elsevier.

Ring Cycle. Melvin Gorham. LC 79-64509. (Orig.). 1979. 8.95 (ISBN 0-914752-11-1); pap. 5.00 (ISBN 0-914752-10-3). Sovereign Pr.

Ring: Four Plays for Children. Adapted by Philip Caggiano. 96p. 1982. pap. 2.50 (ISBN 0-380-79434-9, 79434-9, Bard). Avon.

Ring in Meiji. William Butler. 464p. 1965. 16.95 (ISBN 0-7206-7450-6, Pub. by P Owen Ltd). Dufour.

Ring in the Jubilee: The Story of America's Liberty Bell. Charles M. Boland. LC 72-80407. (Illus.). 96p. (gr. 6 up). 1973. pap. 5.95 (ISBN 0-85699-055-8). Chatham Pr.

Ring Lardner. Elizabeth Evans. LC 79-4829. (Literature and Life Ser.). 160p. 1980. 16.95x (ISBN 0-8044-2185-4). Ungar.

Ring Lardner. Otto Friedrich. LC 65-64769. (University of Minnesota Pamphlets on American Writers Ser.: No. 49). pap. 20.00 (ISBN 0-317-29459-8, 2055932). Bks Demand UMI.

Ring Lardner. Walton R. Patrick. (Twayne's United States Authors Ser). 1963. pap. 8.95x (ISBN 0-8084-0261-7, T32, Twayne). New Coll U Pr.

Ring Lardner. Walton R. Patrick. (United States Authors Ser.: No. 32). 1970. lib. bdg. 14.95 (ISBN 0-8057-0440-X, Twayne). G K Hall.

Ring Lardner Reader. Ring Lardner. Ed. by Maxwell Geismar. 1963. 40.00x (ISBN 0-684-15365-3, ScribT). Scribner.

Ring Lardner's "You Know Me Al" The Comic Strip Adventures of Jack Keefe. Ring Lardner. LC 78-20641. 160p. (Orig.). 1979. pap. 6.95 (ISBN 0-15-676696-5, Harv). HarBraceJ.

Ring Master. David Gurr. LC 87-10860. 752p. 1987. 25.00 (ISBN 0-689-11935-6). Atheneum.

Ring O' Roses. Ronald Ridout. (Match Them Ser.). 24p. (ps-k). 1988. pap. 2.95 (ISBN 0-8249-8232-0). Ideals.

Ring of Allaire. Susan Dexter. 224p. 1986. pap. 2.75 (ISBN 0-345-31121-3, Del Rey). Ballantine.

Ring of Alta Napa. Carl T. Endemann. 35p. pap. 1.75 (ISBN 0-931926-01-7). Gondwana Bks.

Ring of Bone: Collected Poems 1950-1971. rev. ed. Lew Welch. Ed. by Donald Allen. LC 72-85644. (Illus.). 244p. (Orig.). 1979. pap. 6.00 (ISBN 0-912516-03-8). Grey Fox.

Ring of Bright Water. Gavin Maxwell. 236p. 1987. pap. 6.95 (ISBN 0-14-003923-6). Penguin.

Ring of Claddagh. Annabel Murray. (Romances Ser.: No. 2843). 192p. Date not set. pap. 1.95 (ISBN 0-317-63900-5). Harlequin Bks.

Ring of Dancers: Images of Faroese Culture. Jonathan Wylie & David Margolin. (Symbol & Culture Ser.). 1981. text ed. 29.95x (ISBN 0-8122-7783-X). U of Pa Pr.

Ring of Earth: A Child's Book of Seasons. Jane Yolen. LC 86-4800. (Illus.). 32p. (ps-3). 1986. 14.95 (ISBN 0-15-267140-4, HJ). HarBraceJ.

Ring of Endless Light. Madeleine L'Engle. 336p. (YA) (gr. 9 up). 1981. pap. 3.25 (ISBN 0-440-97232-9, LE). Dell.

Ring of Endless Light. Madeleine L'Engle. LC 79-27679. 356p. (gr. 7 up). 1980. 13.95 (ISBN 0-374-36299-8). FS&G.

Ring of Fire. Lawrence Blair & Lorne Blair. 224p. 1988. 24.95 (ISBN 0-553-05232-2). Bantam.

Ring of Fire. Shirley R. Murphy. 226p. 1979. pap. 1.75 (ISBN 0-380-47191-4, 47191-4, Flare). Avon.

Ring of Fire: And the Hawaiian Islands & Iceland. Alice Gilbreath. LC 85-6971. (Ocean World Library). (Illus.). 96p. (gr. 4 up). 1986. PLB 11.95 (ISBN 0-87518-302-6). Dillon.

Ring of Ikribu. David C. Smith & Richard L. Tierney. (Red Sonja Ser.: No. 1). 224p. (Orig.). 1985. pap. 2.95 (ISBN 0-441-71167-7). Ace Bks.

Ring of Jingles. Mitchell B. Carroll. (Illus.). 64p. 1979. 4.00 (ISBN 0-682-49282-5). Exposition-Phoenix.

Ring of Keys. Jack Lovejoy. Ed. by Helen Graves. LC 88-50115. 71p. 1988. 6.95 (ISBN 1-55523-145-4). Winston-Derek.

Ring of Power: The White House Staff & It's Expanding Role in Government. Bradley H. Patterson, Jr. LC 88-47670. 320p. 1988. 19.95 (ISBN 0-465-07025-6). Basic.

Ring of Return. Eva Martin. 306p. 1981. pap. 18.00 (ISBN 0-89540-109-6, SB-109). Sun Pub.

Ring of the Dove: A Treatise on the Art & Practice of Arab Love. Ali ibn Ahmad Ibn-Hazm. Tr. by A. J. Arberry. LC 78-63500. 288p. Repr. of 1953 ed. 34.50 (ISBN 0-404-17148-6). AMS Pr.

Ring of the Nibelung. Alice L. Cleather. LC 77-18100. 1977. Repr. of 1924 ed. lib. bdg. 30.00 (ISBN 0-8414-1844-6). Folcroft.

Ring of the Nibelung. Richard Wagner. Tr. by Andrew Porter from Ger. (Illus.). standard 1977 17.50 (ISBN 0-393-02200-5); pap. 8.95 (ISBN 0-393-00867-3). Norton.

Ring of the Way. Taisen Deshimaru. (Illus.). 128p. 1987. pap. 8.95 (ISBN 0-525-48293-8). Dutton.

Ring of Truth. Vernon Scannel. 342p. (Orig.). 1988. pap. 8.95 (ISBN 0-86051-416-1, Pub. by Robson UK). Parkwest Pubns.

Ring of Truth. Vernon Scannell. LC 85-16734. 342p. 1985. 16.95 (ISBN 0-88186-350-5). Parkwest Pubns.

Ring of Truth: A Translator's Testimony. J. B. Phillips. LC 77-80627. 124p. 1977. pap. 6.95 (ISBN 0-87788-724-1). Shaw Pubs.

Ring of Truth: An Inquiry into How We Know What We Know. Philip Morrison & Phyllis Morrison. LC 87-42646. (Illus.). 320p. 1987. 24.95 (ISBN 0-394-55663-1). Random.

Ring of Words: An Anthology of Song Texts. Ed. by Philip Miller. 544p. 1973. pap. 10.95 (ISBN 0-393-00677-8). Norton.

Ring-Opening Polymerization, Vols. 1-3. K. J. Ivin. 1984. Set. 331.25 (ISBN 0-85334-211-3, I-220-84). Elsevier.

Ring-Opening Polymerization, Vols. 1-3. Ed. by K. J. Ivin & T. Saegusa. 1260p. 1984. Set. 331.75 (ISBN 0-85334-237-7, Pub. by Elsevier Applied Sci England). Vol. 1 (ISBN 0-85334-208-3). Vol. 2 (ISBN 0-85334-209-1). Vol. 3. Elsevier.

Ring Resounding. John Culshaw. LC 87-2592. (Illus.). 276p. 1987. pap. 13.95 (ISBN 0-87910-101-6). Limelight Edns.

Ring-Tailed Panther: A Biographical Novel. F. B. Von Rosenberg. 1987. 13.95 (ISBN 0-533-07203-4). Vantage.

Ring-Tailed, Red-Eyed Sons o' Trouble. Damon Runyon. 19.95 (ISBN 0-8488-0144-X, Pub Amereon Hse). Amereon Ltd.

Ring the Doorbell with Your Elbow: A Cookbook of "Portables". rev. ed. Wilma M. McCartney. LC 80-84349. (Illus.). 136p. 1981. pap. 8.95 (ISBN 0-933050-07-0). New Eng Pr VT.

Ring, the Witch, & the Crystal. Cathy East-Dubowski. Ed. by Stephanie Spinner. LC 85-25700. (Ewok Adventure). (Illus.). 32p. (ps-3). 1986. pap. 1.95 (ISBN 0-394-88057-9). Random.

Ring Theory. Ernst-August Behrens. (Pure & Applied Mathematics Ser.: Vol. 44). 1972. 78.00 (ISBN 0-12-085250-0). Acad Pr.

Ring Theory. Ed. by F. M. Oystaeyen. (Lecture Notes in Mathematics: Vol. 1197). v, 231p. 1986. pap. 19.10 (ISBN 0-387-16496-0). Springer-Verlag.

Ring Theory. F. Van Oystaeyen. (Lecture Notes in Pure & Applied Mathematics Ser.: Vol. 40). 1978. 45.00 (ISBN 0-8247-6814-0). Dekker.

Ring Theory. F. Van Oystaeyen. (Lecture Notes in Pure & Applied Ser.: Vol. 51). 1979. 99.75 (ISBN 0-8247-6854-X). Dekker.

Ring Theory, Vol. 1. Louis H. Rowen. (Pure & Applied Mathematics Ser.). 538p. 1988. 89.50 (ISBN 0-12-599841-4). Acad Pr.

Ring Theory, Vol. 2. Louis H. Rowen. (Pure & Applied Mathematics Ser.). 462p. 1988. 84.00 (ISBN 0-12-599842-2). Acad Pr.

Ring Theory, Vol. 25. Ed. by S. R. Jain. (Lecture Notes in Pure & Applied Mathematics). 1977. 49.75 (ISBN 0-8247-6577-X). Dekker.

Ring Theory & Algebra Three. Ed. by Bernard McDonald. (Pure & Applied Mathematics Ser.: Vol. 55). (Illus.). 448p. 1980. 75.00 (ISBN 0-8247-1158-0). Dekker.

Ring Theory, Antwerp Nineteen-Eighty: Prooceedings. Ed. by F. Van Oystaeyen. (Lecture Notes in Mathematics Ser.: Vol. 825). 209p. 1980. pap. 17.00 (ISBN 0-387-10246-9). Springer-Verlag.

Ring Theory II: Proceedings of the Second Oklahoma Conference. Ring Theory Conference, 2d: 1975: University of Oklahoma. Ed. by Bernard R. McDonald & Robert A. Morris. LC 76-55134. (Lecture Notes in Pure & Applied Mathematics: Vol. 26). pap. 78.80 (ISBN 0-317-08349-X, 2017693). Bks Demand UMI.

Ring Theory: Nonsingular Rings & Modules. Kenneth R. Goodearl. (Lecture Notes in Pure & Applied Mathematics: Vol.33). 224p. 1976. 55.00 (ISBN 0-8247-6354-8). Dekker.

Ring Theory: Proceedings of the Oklahoma Conference. Ed. by Bernard R. McDonald et al. (Lecture Notes in Pure & Applied Mathematics Ser: Vol. 7). 264p. 1974. 49.75 (ISBN 0-8247-6162-6). Dekker.

Ring Transformation of Heterocycles, 2 vols. H. C. Van Der Plas. 1973. Vol. 2. 101.50 (ISBN 0-12-711702-4). Acad Pr.

Ring up the Curtain. facsimile ed. Ernest H. Short & Arthur Compton-Rickett. LC 78-114895. (Select Bibliographies Reprint Ser). 1938. 22.00 (ISBN 0-8369-5299-5). Ayer Co Pubs.

Ring W. Lardner: A Descriptive Bibliography. Matthew J. Bruccoli & Richard Layman. LC 75-9126. (Pittsburgh Ser. in Bibliography). 1976. 90.00x (ISBN 0-8229-3306-3). U of Pittsburgh Pr.

Ringan Gilhaize; or the Covenanters, 3 vols. in 2. John Galt. LC 79-8266. Repr. of 1823 ed. Set. 84.50 (ISBN 0-404-61855-3). Vol. 1 (ISBN 0-404-61856-1). Vol. 2 (ISBN 0-404-61857-X). AMS Pr.

Ringarra. Coral Lansbury. LC 85-45206. 224p. 1986. 15.45i (ISBN 0-06-015516-7, HarpT). Har-Row.

Ringarra. Coral Lansbury. 224p. 1987. pap. 3.95 (ISBN 0-8041-0119-1, Pub. by Ivy). Ballantine.

Ringdoves: From the Fables of Bidpai. Gloria Kamen. LC 87-17404. (Illus.). 32p. (gr. k-3). 1988. 13.95 (ISBN 0-689-31312-8, Atheneum Childrens Bks). Macmillan.

Ringed Castle. Dorothy Dunnett. 425p. 1983. Repr. lib. bdg. 22.95x (ISBN 0-89966-322-2). Buccaneer Bks.

Ringed Castle. Dorothy Dunnett. 640p. 1984. pap. 4.95 (ISBN 0-446-31296-7). Warner Bks.

Ringed in Steel. Michael D. Mahler. 1987. pap. 3.50 (ISBN 0-515-09074-3). Jove Pubns.

Ringed in Steel: Armored Cavalry, Vietnam 1967-68. Michael D. Mahler. (Illus.). 224p. 1986. 16.95 (ISBN 0-89141-264-6). Presidio Pr.

Ringed Seal, Phoga Hispida of the Canadian Western Artic. Thomas G. Smith. (Canadian Bulletin of Fisheries & Equatic Science Ser.: No. 216). 81p. Date not set. pap. text ed. 10.00 (ISBN 0-660-12463-7, SSC249, SSC). UNIPUB.

Ringer. Marshall Terry. LC 87-70379. 239p. 1987. 16.95 (ISBN 0-931722-61-6). Corona Pub.

Ringer. James S. Thayer. 1988. 18.95 (ISBN 0-517-56970-1). Crown.

Ringer the Kitten Learns to Read. Jewell S. Auvinen. (Illus.). 22p. (ps-3). 1982. pap. 2.95 (ISBN 0-9610158-0-2). J A McDermott.

Ringers in the Tower. Harold Bloom. LC 73-149595. xii, 352p. 1973. pap. 3.45x (ISBN 0-226-06049-7, P536, Phoen). U of Chicago Pr.

Ringgold Cavalry: The Rest of the Story. Ralph Haas. 277p. 1988. text ed. 24.95 (ISBN 0-933227-55-8). Closson Pr.

Ringing Changes. R. A. Lafferty. 288p. 1984. pap. 2.95 (ISBN 0-441-72607-0). Ace Bks.

Ringing Ears: An Original Tinnitus Guide. John Griggs. 53p. 1982. pap. text ed. 3.95x (ISBN 0-8134-2531-X). Inter Print Pubs.

Ringing Ears: An Original Tinnitus Guide. John D. Griggs. Ed. by Cynthia M. Buddy et al. (Illus.). 60p. (Orig.). 1982. pap. 10.00x (ISBN 0-9612648-1-0). Natl Tinn Fund.

Ringing Glass: The Life of Rainer Maria Rilke. Donald Prater. LC 85-7830. (Illus.). 488p. 1986. 29.50 (ISBN 0-19-815755-X). Oxford U Pr.

Ringing in Hertfordshire. L. Goodman. 1986. 35.00x (ISBN 0-317-54314-8, Pub. by J Richardson UK). State Mutual Bk.

Ringing the Children In: Texas Country Schools. Thad Sitton & Milam C. Rowold. LC 86-14444. (Illus.). 256p. 1987. 16.95 (ISBN 0-89096-290-1). Tex A&M Univ Pr.

Ringling Museum of Art Journal. Ed. by William H. Wilson. (Illus.). 272p. 1983. write for info. (ISBN 0-916758-12-5); pap. 2.00. Ringling Mus Art.

Ringmacher Thematic Catalogue (1773) Ed. by Barry S. Brook. (Thematic Catalogue Ser.: No. 14). (Illus.). 150p. 1988. lib. bdg. 54.00 (ISBN 0-918728-91-6). Pendragon NY.

Ringmakers of Saturn. Norman R. Bergrun. Ed. by Meg Ross. LC 86-81530. (Illus.). 128p. 1986. 42.50 (ISBN 0-946270-33-3, Pub. by Pentland Pr UK). Bergrun Res.

Ringmakers of Saturn. Norman R. Bergrun. 1986. 80.00x (Pub. by Pentland Pr UK). State Mutual Bk.

Ringmaster. Lee Dunne. 256p. (Orig.). 1986. pap. 5.95 (ISBN 0-86327-166-9, Pub. by Wolfhound Pr Ireland). Irish Bks Media.

Ringmaster's Secret. rev. ed. Carolyn Keene. LC 74-3867. (Nancy Drew Ser.: Vol. 31). (Illus.). 196p. (gr. 4-7). 1974. Repr. of 1954 ed. 4.50 (ISBN 0-448-09531-9, G&D). Putnam Pub Group.

Ringneck! Pheasants & Pheasant Hunting. E. C. Janes. (Sportsmen's Classics Ser.). (Illus.). 215p. 1975. 8.95 (ISBN 0-517-52321-3). Crown.

Ringold Formation of Pleistocene Age in Type Locality, The White Bluffs, Washington. R. C. Newcomb. (Reprint Ser.: No. 1). (Illus.). 13p. 1958. 0.25 (ISBN 0-686-36909-2). WA Div Geol.

Ringo's Tombstone. William R. Garwood. LC 81-67729. 215p. 1981. 11.95 (ISBN 0-937618-01-2). Bath St Pr.

Rings. Shirley Bury. (V & A Introductions to the Decorative Arts Ser.). (Illus.). 48p. 1985. 9.95 (ISBN 0-88045-040-1). Stemmer Hse.

Rings & Factorization. LC 86-33365. (Illus.). 120p. 1987. 34.50 (ISBN 0-521-33072-6); pap. 14.95 (ISBN 0-521-33718-6). Cambridge U Pr.

Rings & Geometry. Ed. by Rustem Kaya et al. 1985. lib. bdg. 69.50 (ISBN 90-277-2112-2, Pub. by Reidel Holland). Kluwer Academic.

Rings & Ideals. N. H. McCoy. (Carus Monograph: No. 8). 216p. 1948. 21.00 (ISBN 0-88385-008-7). Math Assn.

Rings Around Your Mind: How to Program Your Mind to Control Stress, Fear, & Self-Destructive Behavior Patterns. Michael C. Giammatteo. (Illus.). 1976. pap. text ed. 6.00 (ISBN 0-918428-08-4). Sylvan Inst.

Rings, Clusters, & Polymers of the Main Group Elements. Ed. by Alan H. Cowley. LC 83-15462. (ACS Symposium Ser.: No. 232). 182p. 1983. lib. bdg. 32.95x (ISBN 0-8412-0801-8). Am Chemical.

Rings: Discoveries from Galileo to Voyager. James Elliot & Richard Kerr. (Illus.). 224p. 1987. pap. text ed. 8.95 (ISBN 0-262-55013-X). MIT Pr.

Rings for the Finger. George F. Kunz. LC 78-172181. (Illus.). 512p. 1973. pap. 7.95 (ISBN 0-486-22226-8). Dover.

Rings in a Tree Trunk. S. Ramnath. (Writers Workshop Redbird Ser.). 46p. 1976. 8.00 (ISBN 0-86578-271-7); flexible cloth 4.00 (ISBN 0-86578-272-5). Ind-US Inc.

Rings in Your Fingers. Dariel Fitzkee. 1977. 10.00 (ISBN 0-87505-253-3). Borden.

Rings in Your Fingers. 1981. 10.00 (ISBN 0-915926-49-0). Magic Ltd.

Rings, Modules & Linear Algebra. B. Hartley & T. Hawkes. (Mathematics Ser.). 1970. pap. 15.95x (ISBN 0-412-09810-5, NO. 6144, Pub. by Chapman & Hall). Routledge Chapman & Hall.

Rings of Burnished Brass. Yusuf Idris. Tr. by Catherine Cobham from Arabic. LC 85-50528. (Arab Authors Ser.: No. 21). 142p. 1984. pap. 7.00 (ISBN 0-89410-469-1). Three Continents.

Rings of Continuous Function. Aull. (Lecture Notes in Pure & Applied Mathematics Ser.: Vol. 95). 336p. 1985. 69.75 (ISBN 0-8247-7144-3). Dekker.

Rings of Continuous Functions. M. Jerison & L. Gillman. Ed. by F. W. Gehring & C. C. Moore. LC 76-20442. (Graduate Texts in Mathematics: Vol. 43). xi, 300p. 1960. 34.00 (ISBN 0-387-90198-1). Springer-Verlag.

Rings of Differential Operators. J. E. Bjork. (Mathematical Library: Vol. 21). 360p. 1979. 94.75 (ISBN 0-444-85292-1, North Holland). Elsevier.

Rings of Dimension II. Ed. by Wolmer V. Vasconcelos. (Lecture Notes in Pure & Applied Mathematics Ser.: Vol. 22). 1976. 35.00 (ISBN 0-8247-6447-1). Dekker.

Rings of Faith. Mary M. Wrede. LC 85-91315. (Illus.). 160p. 1986. 9.95 (ISBN 0-9615969-0-2). M M Wrede.

Rings of Grass. Nancy Hedberg. (Living Bks.). 240p. 1985. pap. 3.50 (ISBN 0-8423-5605-3). Tyndale.

Rings of Green. Ann Peters. 84p. 1982. 16.95 (ISBN 0-86140-124-7); pap. 7.95 (ISBN 0-86140-129-8). Dufour.

Rings of Ice. Piers Anthony. 192p. 1982. pap. 3.50 (ISBN 0-380-00036-9). Avon.

Rings of Kether. Steve Jackson & Ian Livingstone. (Fighting Fantasy Gamebooks: No. 15). (Orig.). (gr. 6-12). 1986. pap. 2.50 (ISBN 0-440-97407-0, LFL). Dell.

Rings of Quotients: An Introduction to Methods of Ring Theory. B. Stenstroem. LC 75-1003. (Grundlehren der Mathematischen Wissenschaften Ser.: Vol. 217). 315p. 1975. text ed. 56.00 (ISBN 0-387-07117-2). Springer-Verlag.

Rings of Saturn. Arthur B. Cover. (Time Machine Ser.: No. 6). 144p. (gr. 5 up). 1985. pap. 2.25 (ISBN 0-553-25797-8). Bantam.

Rings of Saturn. Diane Wakoski. LC 86-9539. 126p. (Orig.). 1986. 17.50 (ISBN 0-87685-675-X); pap. 9.00 (ISBN 0-87685-674-1); signed ltd. o.p. 25.00 (ISBN 0-87685-676-8). Black Sparrow.

Rings of the Master, Bk. 2. Jack L. Chalker. (Orig.). 1987. pap. 3.50 (ISBN 0-345-32561-3, Del Rey). Ballantine.

Rings on Woot-Kew's Tail: Indian Legends of the Origin of the Sun, Moon & Stars. Will Gerber et al. (Indian Culture Ser.). (gr. 3-9). 1973. 1.95 (ISBN 0-89992-059-4). Coun India Ed.

Rings, Swings & Climbing Things: Enhancing Your Child's Development with Easy-to-Make Play Equipment. 1985. 10.95 (ISBN 0-8092-5264-3). Contemp Bks.

Rings That Are Nearly Associative. K. A. Zhevlakov et al. (Pure & Applied Mathematics Ser.). 1982. 69.50 (ISBN 0-12-779850-1). Acad Pr.

Rings with Involution. I. N. Herstein. LC 76-27861. (Chicago Lectures in Mathematics). 1976. pap. text ed. 8.00x (ISBN 0-226-32806-6). U of Chicago Pr.

Rings with Polynomial Identities. Claudio Procesi. (Pure & Applied Mathematics Ser: Vol. 17). 202p. 1973. 49.75 (ISBN 0-8247-6015-8). Dekker.

Ringside Seats. facsimile ed. Katharine F. Gerould. LC 71-156647. (Essay Index Reprint Ser). Repr. of 1937 ed. 18.00 (ISBN 0-8369-2318-9). Ayer Co Pubs.

Ringstones & Other Curious Tales. John W. Wall. 21.00 (ISBN 0-405-08174-X, 18500). Ayer Co Pubs.

Ringtail. Patricia Sillers. (Illus.). 32p. (ps up). 1988. bds. 8.95 (ISBN 0-19-540585-4). Oxford U Pr.

Ringtime. Thomas M. Disch. LC 82-19279. (Singularities Ser.). (Illus.). 48p. (Orig.). 1983. (Pub. by Toothpaste); pap. 10.00 (ISBN 0-915124-71-8). Coffee Hse.

Ringworld. Larry Niven. 352p. (Orig.). 1981. pap. 4.50 (ISBN 0-345-33392-6, Del Rey). Ballantine.

Ringworld Engineers. Larry Niven. 368p. 1981. pap. 3.95 (ISBN 0-345-33430-2, Del Rey). Ballantine.

Rinky-Dink Cafe. Maggie S. Davis. (Illus.). 32p. (ps-3). 1988. PLB 12.95 (ISBN 0-671-66408-5). S&S.

Rinnovare la Nostra Vita Salesiana see Renewal of Our Salesian Life.

Rinorea & Rinoreocarpus (Violaceae) W. H. Hekking. (Flora Neotropica Monograph Ser.: No. 46). 1988. pap. text ed. 40.50 (ISBN 0-89327-316-3). NY Botanical.

Rio. Doug Wildey. (Illus.). 64p. 1987. ltd. signed ed. (No. 6) 34.95 (ISBN 0-936211-04-0); pap. 6.95 (ISBN 0-317-57743-3). Graphitti Designs.

Rio. Doug Wildey. (Illus.). 64p. (gr. 6 up). 1987. pap. 8.95 (ISBN 0-938965-04-2). Comico Comic Co.

Rio see Joy of Rio.

Rio Alive. 4th ed. Arnold Greenberg & Harriet Greenberg. (Alive Travel Ser.). (Illus.). 1980. pap. 4.95 (ISBN 0-935572-00-7). Alive Pubns.

Rio Alive. 5th ed. Arnold Greenberg & Harriet Greenberg. (Alive Travel Ser.). 300p. 1987. pap. 9.95 (ISBN 0-935572-12-0). Alive Pubns.

Rio Alive. Harriet Greenberg. (Alive Guides Ser.). (Illus.). 256p. (Orig.). 1988. pap. 10.95 (ISBN 1-55650-098-X). Hunter Pub NY.

Rio Alive. rev. ed. Harriet Greenberg & Arnold Greenberg. 1977. pap. 2.95 (ISBN 0-686-23067-1). Alive Pubns.

Rio Arriba. Elihu Blotnick. (Illus.). 342p. (Orig.). Date not set. pap. 17.95 (ISBN 0-915090-24-4). Calif Street.

Rio Casino Intrigue. F. Van Wyck Mason. Repr. lib. bdg. 15.95 (ISBN 0-89190-356-9, Pub. by River City Pr). Amereon Ltd.

Rio Claro: A Brazilian Plantation System, 1820-1920. Warren Dean. 234p. 1976. 22.50x (ISBN 0-8047-0902-5). Stanford U Pr.

Rio de Janeiro. (Frommer's City Guides Ser.). (Illus.). 224p. 1988. pap. 5.95 (ISBN 0-13-332065-0). Prentice Hall Pr.

Rio De Janeiro Travel Guide. (Berlitz Travel Guides). (Illus.). 1982. pap. 6.95 (ISBN 0-02-969830-8, Berlitz). Macmillan.

Rio Desperado. Gordon D. Shirreffs. 128p. 1988. pap. 2.50 (ISBN 0-380-70637-7). Avon.

Rio Grande. Raymond Strauss. LC 80-53849. (Rivers of the World Ser.). 68p. (gr. 4 up). PLB 14.96 (ISBN 0-382-06521-2). Silver.

Rio Grande--Ruler of the Rockies. R. C. Farewell & Bill Bradley. (Illus.). 176p. 1987. 34.95 (ISBN 0-87046-080-3). Interurban.

Rio Grande Death Ride. Terrell L. Bowers. (YA) (gr. 7 up). 1980. 9.95 (ISBN 0-686-73924-8, Avalon). Bouregy.

Rio Grande Diesels Pictorial, Vol. 1. Joseph A. Strapac. (Illus.). 1982. pap. 17.95 (ISBN 0-930742-07-9). Shade Tree.

Rio Grande Diesels Pictorial, Vol. 2. Joseph A. Strapac. (Illus.). 1984. pap. 17.95 (ISBN 0-930742-09-5). Shade Tree.

Rio Grande Do Norte: The Story of Maine's Partner State in Brazil. Neil Rolde. LC 84-81146. (Illus.). 78p. (Orig.). 1984. pap. 4.00 (ISBN 0-88448-027-5). Harpswell Pr.

Rio Grande Do Sul & Brazilian Regionalism: 1882-1930. Joseph L. Love. LC 71-130829. (Illus.). 1971. 29.50x (ISBN 0-8047-0759-6). Stanford U Pr.

Rio Grande: Mountains to the Sea. Jim Bones. Ed. by Suzanne Winkler. (Illus.). 224p. 1985. 39.95 (ISBN 0-87719-008-9). Texas Month Pr.

Rio Grande Narrow Gauge. John B. Norwood. Ed. by Donald J. Heimburger & Marilyn M. Heimburger. LC 82-84384. (Illus.). 312p. 1983. 39.95 (ISBN 0-911581-00-6). Heimburger Hse Pub.

Rio Grande Narrow Gauge Recollections. John B. Norwood. Ed. by Donald J. Heimburger & Marilyn M. Heimburger. LC 86-81505. (Illus.). 272p. 1986. 38.95 (ISBN 0-911581-07-3). Heimburger Hse Pub.

Rio Grande Pictorial. Dell McCoy & Russell Collman. (Illus.). 216p. 32.00x (ISBN 0-913582-02-6). Sundance.

Rio Grande Rift: Tectonics & Magmatism. Ed. by R. E. Riecker. (Special Publication Ser.). (Illus.). 438p. 1979. 25.00 (ISBN 0-87590-214-6). Am Geophysical.

Rio Grande Ski Train. Steve Patterson & Kenton Forrest. (Illus.). 64p. 1984. pap. 9.95 (ISBN 0-932497-00-4). Tramway Pr.

Rio Grande... to the Pacific! Robert A. LeMassena. (Illus.). 416p. 1974. 40.00x (ISBN 0-913582-10-7). Sundance.

Rio Grande West, a Contemporary Glimpse. Ronald C. Hill. (Illus.). 80p. 1982. pap. 9.95 (ISBN 0-918654-33-5). CO RR Mus.

Rio Hondo. Matt Braun. (Brannocks Ser.: No. 3). 320p. 1987. pap. 3.50 (ISBN 0-451-14955-6, Sig). NAL.

Rio in the Time of the Viceroys. Luiz E. Costa. 1976. lib. bdg. 59.95 (ISBN 0-8490-2526-5). Gordon Pr.

Rio in the Time of the Viceroys. facsimile ed. Luiz Edmundo. LC 71-165628. (Select Bibliographies Reprint Ser). Repr. of 1936 ed. 30.00 (ISBN 0-8369-5935-3). Ayer Co Pubs.

Rio Loja Ringmaster. Lamar Herrin. 304p. 1983. pap. 3.50 (ISBN 0-380-55673-1, 55673, Bard). Avon.

Rio Renegade. Leslie Erenwein. 1975. pap. 0.95 (ISBN 0-685-54125-8, LB296NK, Leisure Bks). Leisure NY.

Rio Seco. Louis Fury. Tr. by Eugene Denes. 1988. 14.95 (ISBN 0-533-07421-5). Vantage.

Rio Tigre & Beyond: The Amazon Jungle Medicine of Manuel Cordova. F. Bruce Lamb. (Illus.). 256p. (Orig.). 1985. 25.00 (ISBN 0-938190-60-1); pap. 12.95 (ISBN 0-938190-59-8). North Atlantic.

Rio Volcado. Evaristo Ribera Chevremont. 4.35_o.p (ISBN 0-8477-3214-2); pap. 3.10 (ISBN 0-8477-3215-0). U of PR Pr.

Rios de Agua Viva. Ruth Paxson. 96p. 1983. pap. 1.95 (ISBN 0-311-46065-8). Casa Bautista.

Rios de Tinta: Historia y Ministerio De la Casa Bautista De Publicaciones. Tomas Hill. Tr. by Josie Smith from Eng. Orig. Title: Rivers of Ink. 64p. 1980. pap. 1.95 (ISBN 0-311-29009-4). Casa Bautista.

Rios Profundos. Jose M. Arguedas. (Ayacucho Library Collection Ser.: Vol. 38). (Span.). 1978. 29.95 (ISBN 0-317-56395-5, Pub. by Biblioteca Ayacucho); pap. 15.00 (ISBN 0-317-56396-3, Pub. by Biblioteca Ayacucho). Humanities.

Rios Redimidos. Jorge L. Morales. (Illus.). 2.15 (ISBN 0-8477-3209-6). U of PR Pr.

Rios y Lagos Internacionales-Utilizacion Para Fines Agricolas E Industriales: Documento De Antecedentes. 4th rev. ed. (Serie De Derecho y Relaciones Internacionales). (Span.). 1971. 3.00 (ISBN 0-8270-5210-3). OAS.

Rios y Palmas: Poesias. Oscar P. Moro. LC 85-80622. (Coleccion Espejo de Paciencia Ser.). 127p. (Orig., Span.). 1985. pap. 8.95 (ISBN 0-89729-377-0). Ediciones.

Riot Act: A Version of Sophocles' Antigone. Tom Paulin. LC 85-10140. 64p. (Orig.). 1985. pap. 8.95 (ISBN 0-571-13613-3). Faber & Faber.

Riot Control: Materiel & Techniques. 4th rev. ed. Rex Applegate. (Illus.). 300p. 1981. 19.95 (ISBN 0-87364-208-2). Paladin Pr.

Riot in the Cities. Journal Of Urban Law Editors. Ed. by Michael C. Moran & Richard A. Chikota. LC 74-76132. 411p. 1970. 28.50 (ISBN 0-8386-7443-7). Fairleigh Dickinson.

Riot, Rout, & Tumult: Readings in American Social & Political Violence. Ed. by Roger Lane & John J. Turner, Jr. LC 77-84752. (Contributions in American History: No. 69). 1978. lib. bdg. 36.95 (ISBN 0-8371-9845-3, LRR/). Greenwood.

Riot, Rout, & Tumult: Readings in American Social & Political Violence. Ed. by Roger Lane & John J. Turner, Jr. LC 82-42513. 416p. 1984. pap. text ed. 16.50 (ISBN 0-8191-2666-7). U Pr of Amer.

Riot War. Buster R. Cluff. LC 76-13240. 1977. 12.95 (ISBN 0-87949-073-X). Ashley Bks.

Riotous Assembly. Tom Sharpe. 224p. 1972. 25.95 (ISBN 0-436-45800-4, Pub. by Secker & Warburg UK). David & Charles.

Riotous Assembly. Tom Sharpe. LC 86-28702. 256p. 1987. pap. 6.95 (ISBN 0-87113-143-9). Atlantic Monthly.

Riotous Victorians. Donald C. Richter. LC 80-15055. (Illus.). xii, 185p. 1981. text ed. 16.95x (ISBN 0-8214-0571-3); pap. 7.95x (ISBN 0-8214-0618-3). Ohio U Pr.

Riots. Alan Dures & Katherine Dures. (History in Focus Ser.). (Illus.). 72p. (gr. 7-12). 1985. 17.95 (ISBN 0-7134-4350-2, Pub. by Batsford England). David & Charles.

Riots & Community Politics in England & Wales, 1790-1810. John Bohstedt. (Illus.). 336p. 1983. text ed. 32.00x (ISBN 0-674-77120-6). Harvard U Pr.

Riots & Disturbances in Correctional Institutions. rev. ed. 56p. 1982. pap. 10.00 (ISBN 0-942974-07-7). Am Correctional.

Riots in Jerusalem-San Remo Conference, April 1920. Ed. by Isaiah Friedman & Howard M. Sachar. (Rise of Israel Ser.). 370p. 1987. lib. bdg. 80.00 (ISBN 0-8240-4911-X). Garland Pub.

Riots, U. S. A. rev. ed. Willard A. Heaps. LC 69-13444. (gr. 6 up). 1970. 6.95 (ISBN 0-395-28907-6, Clarion). HM.

RIP: Five Stories of the Supernatural. original anthology ed. Ed. by R. Reginald & Douglas Menville. LC 75-1539. (Supernatural & Occult Fiction Ser.). (Illus.). 1976. lib. bdg. 24.50x (ISBN 0-405-08425-0). Ayer Co Pubs.

Rip Ford's Texas. John S. Ford. Ed. by Stephen B. Oates. (Personal Narratives of the West Ser.). 573p. 1987. 27.50x (ISBN 0-292-77033-2); pap. 12.95 (ISBN 0-292-77034-0). U of Tex Pr.

Rip-Off. Carter Brown. 1979. pap. 1.50 (ISBN 0-505-51425-7, Pub. by Tower Bks). Leisure NY.

Rip-Off. Pat R. Mauser. LC 85-7958. 156p. (gr. 5-9). 1985. 11.95 (ISBN 0-689-31134-6, Atheneum Childrens Bks). Macmillan.

Rip-Off, Vol. II. Victor Santoro. LC 84-81631. 173p. (Orig.). 1986. pap. 10.95 (ISBN 0-915179-47-4). Loompanics.

Rip-Off Book. Victor Santoro. LC 84-81631. 200p. (Orig.). 1984. pap. 10.95 (ISBN 0-915179-18-0). Loompanics.

Rip-Off U: The Annual Theft & Exploitation of Major College Revenue Producing Student-Athletes. Dick DeVenzio. 256p. 1986. 15.95 (ISBN 0-910305-01-3). Fool Court.

Rip-Roaring Races & Rallies. Elwood D. Baumann. (Illus.). 128p. (gr. 7 up). 1981. lib. bdg. 8.90 (ISBN 0-531-04344-4). Watts.

Rip-Roaring Russell. Johanna Hurwitz. LC 83-1019. (Illus.). 96p. (ps-1). 1983. 10.25 (ISBN 0-688-02347-9); lib. bdg. 10.88 (ISBN 0-688-02348-7). Morrow.

Rip, Strip & Row: A Builder's Guide to the Cosine Wherry. Brown et al. LC 85-51141. 1985. pap. 19.95 (ISBN 0-917436-02-4). Tamal Vista.

Rip Up! Get Rock Hard & Supercut Now! Robert Kennedy. (Illus.). 128p. (Orig.). 1988. pap. 7.95 (ISBN 0-8069-6423-5). Sterling.

Rip Van Winkle. George Bristow. (Earlier American Music Ser.: No. 25). 297p. 1986. 39.50 (ISBN 0-306-76124-6). Da Capo.

Rip Van Winkle. Charlotte B. Chorpenning. (Children's Theatre Playscript Ser.). (gr. k-12). 1954. pap. 2.25x (ISBN 0-88020-050-2). Coach Hse.

Rip Van Winkle. Morrell Gipson. LC 83-20624. (Illus.). 32p. (ps-3). 1984. pap. 11.95 (ISBN 0-385-18757-2); pap. 11.95 (ISBN 0-385-18758-0). Doubleday.

Rip Van Winkle. Morrell Gipson. LC 83-20624. (Illus.). 32p. (gr. k-3). 1987. pap. 4.95 (ISBN 0-385-23965-3, Pub. by Zephyr-BFYR). Doubleday.

Rip Van Winkle. Washington Irving. (Illus.). 1982. 18.95 (ISBN 0-434-95859-X, Pub. by W. Heinemann Ltd). David & Charles.

Rip Van Winkle. Washington Irving. 73p. 1983. Repr. lib. bdg. 16.95x (ISBN 0-89966-411-3). Buccaneer Bks.

Rip Van Winkle. Washington Irving. (Puffin Classics Ser.). 1987. pap. 2.25 (ISBN 0-14-035051-9, Puffin Bks). Penguin.

Rip Van Winkle. Washington Irving. LC 87-60720. (Illus.). 110p. (ps up). 1987. 15.00 (ISBN 0-688-07459-6, Morrow Junior Books). Morrow.

Rip Van Winkle. Washington Irving. Ed. by Sandra Saunders. (Illus.). 80p. (gr. 4-7). pap. 1.95 (ISBN 0-590-40110-6). Scholastic Inc.

Rip Van Winkle. Washington Irving. Retold by & illus. by John Howe. (Illus.). (ps-3). 1988. 14.95 (ISBN 0-316-37578-0). Little.

Rip Van Winkle. Adapted by & illus. by Thomas Locker. LC 87-24448. (Illus.). 32p. (ps up). 1988. 15.95 (ISBN 0-8037-0520-4, 01549-460); PLB 15.89 (ISBN 0-8037-0521-2). Dial Bks Young.

Rip Van Winkle. (Derrydale Fairytale Library). (Illus.). (ps-3). 1985. 1.98 (ISBN 0-517-28806-0). Outlet Bk Co.

Rip Van Winkle. Retold by Catherine Storr. LC 83-26996. (Stories Clippers Ser.). (Illus.). 32p. (gr. k-4). 1984. PLB 15.33 (ISBN 0-8172-2108-5); pap. 9.27 (ISBN 0-8172-2252-9); PLB 27.99 incl. cassette (ISBN 0-8172-2236-7); pap. 23.95 incl. cassette (ISBN 0-8172-2267-7); cassette only 14.00. Raintree Pubs.

Rip Van Winkle. new ed. Ed. by Carol B. York. Irving Washington. LC 79-66314. (Illus.). 48p. (gr. 3-6). 1980. lib. bdg. 9.59 (ISBN 0-89375-300-9); pap. 1.95 (ISBN 0-89375-299-1). Troll Assocs.

Rip Van Winkle & the Legend of Sleepy Hollow. 2nd ed. Washington Irving. (Illus.). 152p. (gr. 4-12). 1980. 13.95 (ISBN 0-912882-42-5). Sleepy Hollow.

Rip Van Winkle & The Legend of Sleepy Hollow see **New Method Supplementary Readers.**

Rip Van Winkle, As Played by Joseph Jefferson. Joseph Jefferson. LC 79-95154. (Illus.). Repr. of 1895 ed. 18.45 (ISBN 0-404-03557-4). AMS Pr.

Rip Van Winkle Goes to the Play. Brander Matthews. LC 67-27625. 1967. Repr. of 1926 ed. 23.00x (ISBN 0-8046-0303-0, Pub. by Kennikat). Assoc Faculty Pr.

Rip Van Winkle Railroads. W. F. Helmer. LC 77-116732. (Railroadiana). (Illus.). 1970. 19.95 (ISBN 0-8310-7079-X). Howell-North.

Rip Van Winkle: Renascent. Roger Hill. 72p. 1984. pap. write for info. (ISBN 0-9613799-0-1). Hort Gettys Hill Mem.

Riparian Forests in California. Ed. by Anne Sands. LC 80-53162. (Illus.). 121p. 1980. pap. 4.00x (ISBN 0-931876-41-9, 4101). ANR Pubns CA.

Ripcord. Shirley Aycock. 24p. 1978. stapled chapbook 2.25 (ISBN 0-942432-00-2). M O P Pr.

Ripe for Resolution: Conflict & Intervention in Africa. I. William Zartman. (Illus.). 1985. 28.00x (ISBN 0-19-503578-X). Oxford U Pr.

Ripe Harvest: Educating Migrant Children. Ed. by Arnold B. Cheyney. LC 73-158927. 256p. 1972. 12.95x (ISBN 0-87024-206-7). U of Miami Pr.

Ripen Our Darkness & the Devil's Door. Sara Daniels. (Theatrescripts Ser.). 88p. 1986. pap. 7.95 (ISBN 0-413-41140-0, 9926). Heinemann Ed.

Ripened Fields: 15 Sonnets of a Marriage. Peggy P. Church. 1978. pap. 3.95 (ISBN 0-89016-043-0). Lightning Tree.

Ripeness is All. Eric Linklater. 1983. 30.00x (ISBN 0-86334-038-5, Pub. by Macdonald Pub UK). State Mutual Bk.

Ripening. Edouard Glissant. Tr. by Michael Dash from Fr. (Caribbean Writers Ser.: No. 34). 204p. (Orig.). 1984. pap. text ed. 7.50 (ISBN 0-435-98222-2). Heinemann Ed.

Ripening. Richard Hague. LC 83-19414. 102p. 1984. 12.50 (ISBN 0-8142-0354-X). Ohio St U Pr.

Ripening Seed. Colette. Tr. by Roger Senhouse from Fr. 186p. 1975. 7.95 (ISBN 0-374-25069-3); pap. 6.25 (ISBN 0-374-51264-7). FS&G.

Ripening: Selected Work, 1927-1980. 2nd ed. Meridel Le Seuer. Ed. by Elaine Hedges. (Illus.). 306p. Date not set. pap. 9.95 (ISBN 0-935312-41-2). Feminist Pr.

Ripley's Believe It or Not, No. 13. 1st ed. 1978. pap. 1.50 (ISBN 0-671-81933-X). PB.

Ripley's Believe It or Not, No. 15. (Ripley Ser.). 1978. pap. 1.50 (ISBN 0-671-80473-1). PB.

Ripley's Believe It or Not, No. 18. 1978. pap. 1.50 (ISBN 0-671-82277-2). PB.

Ripley's Believe It or Not, No. 30. 1982. pap. 2.25 (ISBN 0-671-46217-2). PB.

Ripley's Giant Book of "Believe It or Not". Robert L. Ripley. (Illus.). 256p. (Orig.). 1976. pap. 9.95 (ISBN 0-446-37891-7). Warner Bks.

Ripoff: A Report on Moral Collapse & Corruption in America. Steve Allen. 1979. 9.95 (ISBN 0-8184-0249-0). Lyle Stuart.

Ripon Minister: The Beginning of the Gothic Style in Northern England. M. F. Hearn. LC 83-71300. (Transactions Ser.: Vol. 73, Pt. 6). 1983. 18.00 (ISBN 0-87169-736-X). Am Philos.

Ripped: The Sensible Way to Achieve Ultimate Muscularity. Clarence Bass. LC 80-81446. (Illus.). 104p. 1980. pap. 10.95 (ISBN 0-9609714-0-8). Clarence Bass.

Ripped Three: The Recipes, the Routines & the Reasons. Clarence Bass. LC 80-81446. (Illus.). 195p. 1986. pap. 13.95 (ISBN 0-9609714-3-2). Clarence Bass.

Ripped Two. Clarence Bass. LC 80-81446. (Illus.). 179p. 1982. pap. 13.95 (ISBN 0-9609714-1-6). Clarence Bass.

Ripper! Gardner Dozois. 488p. 1988. pap. 3.95 (ISBN 0-8125-1700-8). Tor Bks.

Ripping & Running: A Formal Ethnograph of Urban Heroin Addicts. Michael Agar. (Language, Thought & Culture: Advances in the Study of Cognition Ser.). 1973. 19.95 (ISBN 0-12-785020-1). Acad Pr.

Ripple. Mary Sloan. (Orig.). 1986. pap. 5.00 (ISBN 0-912449-22-5). Floating Island.

Ripple: A Novel about Sexual Invasion. William Zinn. 1987. 16.95 (ISBN 0-88191-056-2). Freundlich.

Ripple from the Storm: A Complete Novel from Doris Lessing's Masterwork, Children of Violence. Doris Lessing. 1970. pap. 6.95 (ISBN 0-452-25632-1, Plume). NAL.

Ripple in Entropy. Paul J. Payack. 80p. 1973. pap. 2.50 (ISBN 0-686-15402-9). Chthon Pr.

Ripple on the Seas. Achilles N. Sakell. LC 84-91267. 301p. 1986. 15.50 (ISBN 0-533-06348-5). Vantage.

Ripples in the Chichimec Sea: New Considerations of Southwestern-Meso-American Interactions. Ed. by Frances J. Mathien & Randall H. McGuire. (Publications in Archaeology Ser.). 420p. 1986. text ed. 34.95x (ISBN 0-8093-1247-6). S Ill U Pr.

Ripples in the Pool. Rebeka Njau. (African Writers Ser.). 1978. pap. text ed. 6.50 (ISBN 0-435-90203-2). Heinemann Ed.

Ripples of Intuition. Merlo J. Pusey. 134p. 1986. 5.00 (ISBN 0-941214-29-X, Eden Hill Pub). Signature Bks.

Ripples of Stillness. Ralph Wright. 1978. 5.95 (ISBN 0-8198-0365-0). Dghtrs St Paul.

Rippling Rhymes & Fairy Tales. Robert S. Cunningham. (Poetry for Today Ser.: Vol. 3). x, 52p. 1975. 5.50 (ISBN 0-87881-030-7). Mojave Bks.

Rippon Rides Double. Max Brand. 176p. 1975. pap. 2.25 (ISBN 0-671-47983-0). PB.

Riprap & Cold Mountain Poems. Gary Snyder. LC 66-3169. (Illus.). 72p. 1965. pap. 3.95 (ISBN 0-912516-47-X). Grey Fox.

Riptide. Ella T. Ellis. (Illus.). (gr. 7 up). 1973. pap. 0.95 (ISBN 0-689-70361-9, Aladdin). Macmillan.

Rires et Pleurs; Poesies, 2 pts. Oswald Durand. (Fr.). 1896. 50.00 (ISBN 0-8115-2954-1). Pt. 1, Poemes, Eclairs, Satires, Odelettes. Pt. 2, Fleurs des Mornes, Refrains, Nos Payses, Contes Creoles. Kraus Repr.

RIS A Bhruthaich: Somhairle MacGill-eain, the Criticism & Prose Writing of Sorley Maclean. Ed. by Acair Ltd. Staff. 1985. 90.00x (ISBN 0-86152-041-6, Pub. by Acair Ltd Scotland). State Mutual Bk.

Risa Sheppard's Fitness Formula for a Firm & Flat Stomach. Risa Sheppard & Diane Foglesong-Bos. (Illus.). 24p. (Orig.). 1987. pap. 3.95 (ISBN 0-939939-00-2). Multi Fit Pubns.

Risalat at-Tawabic Wa Z-Zawabi (the Treatise of Familiar Spirits - Demons) by Abu a Mir Ibn Shuhaid Al-Ashja I, Al-Andalusi. Ed. & tr. by James T. Monroe. (U C Publications in Near Eastern Studies: Vol. 15). 1971. pap. 15.50x (ISBN 0-520-09382-8). U of Cal Pr.

Risale-I Mi Mariyye: An Early Seventeenth-Century Ottoman Treatise on Architeture. H. Crane. (Illus.). 152p. 1987. 54.50 (ISBN 90-04-07826-6, Pub. by E J Brill). Heinman.

Rise & Awakening of Depressed Classes in India. J. R. Kamble. 327p. 1979. 25.95. Asia Bk Corp.

Rise & Decline of a Dialect: A Study in the Revival of Modern Hebrew. Aaron Bar-Adon. LC 74-80121. (Janua Linguarum, Ser. Practica: No. 197). 116p. (Orig.). 1975. pap. text ed. 19.20x (ISBN 90-2793-206-9). Mouton.

Rise & Decline of Fianna Fail. Kevin Boland. 150p. 1982. pap. 6.50 (ISBN 0-85342-683-X, Pub. by Mercier Pr Ireland). Irish Bks Media.

Rise & Decline of Jacksonian Democracy. Glyndon Van Deusen. LC 78-11435. (Anvil Ser.). 270p. 1979. pap. 10.50 (ISBN 0-88275-784-9). Krieger.

Rise & Decline of Nations: Economic Growth, Stagflation, & Social Rigidities. Mancur Olson. LC 82-40163. 287p. 1982. 27.50x (ISBN 0-300-02307-3). Yale U Pr.

Rise & Decline of Nations: Economic Growth, Stagflation, & Social Rigidities. Mancur Olson. LC 82-40163. 287p. 1984. pap. 10.95x (ISBN 0-300-03079-7, Y-487). Yale U Pr.

Rise & Decline of the American Cut Nail Industry: A Study of the Interrelationships of Technology, Business Organization, & Management Techniques. Amos J. Loveday, Jr. LC 83-5542. (Contributions in Economics & Economic History Ser.: No. 53). (Illus.). xx, 160p. 1983. lib. bdg. 36.95 (ISBN 0-313-23918-5, LAC/). Greenwood.

Rise & Decline of the Great Atlantic & Pacific Tea Company. William I. Walsh. (Illus.). 256p. 1986. 17.95 (ISBN 0-8184-0382-9). Lyle Stuart.

Rise & Decline of the Medici Bank: 1397-1494. Raymond A. De Roover. LC 63-11417. (Studies in Business History: No. 21). (Illus.). 1963. 30.00x (ISBN 0-674-77145-1). Harvard U Pr.

Rise & Decline of the Program for Black Education in the United Presbyterian Church, U. S. A. 1865-1970. Inez M. Parker. LC 76-49248. (Presbyterian Historical Ser.). 320p. 1977. 10.00 (ISBN 0-911536-66-3). Trinity U Pr.

Rise & Decline of the Wheat Growing Industry in Wisconsin. John G. Thompson. LC 72-2868. (Use & Abuse of America's Natural Resources Ser). 254p. 1972. Repr. of 1909 ed. 19.00 (ISBN 0-405-04536-0). Ayer Co Pubs.

Rise & Decline of the Zairian State. Crawford Young & Thomas Turner. LC 84-40204. (Illus.). 472p. 1985. text ed. 37.50x (ISBN 0-299-10110-X). U of Wis Pr.

Rise & Decline of Western Liberalism. Anthony Arblaster. 450p. 1984. 34.95x (ISBN 0-85520-765-5). Basil Blackwell.

Rise & Decline of Western Liberalism. Anthony Arblaster. 400p. 1986. pap. text ed. 14.95 (ISBN 0-631-14618-0). Basil Blackwell.

Rise & Demise of Democratic Kampuchea. Craig Etcheson. (Illus.). 300p. 1984. 38.50x (ISBN 0-86531-650-3). Westview.

Rise & Destiny of the German Jew. rev. ed. Jacob R. Marcus. 1971. 15.00x (ISBN 0-87068-148-6). Ktav.

Rise & Development of Military Music. Henry G. Farmer. LC 79-107801. (Select Bibliographies Reprint Ser). 1912. 16.00 (ISBN 0-8369-5204-9). Ayer Co Pubs.

Rise & Development of the Bicameral System in America. T. F. Moran. 1973. pap. 9.00 (ISBN 0-384-40025-6). Johnson Repr.

Rise & Development of the Bicameral System in America. Thomas F. Moran. LC 78-63839. (Johns Hopkins University. Studies in the Social Sciences. Thirteenth Ser. 1895: 5). Repr. of 1895 ed. 11.50 (ISBN 0-404-61097-8). AMS Pr.

Rise & Development of the Gerrymander. Elmer C. Griffith. LC 73-19149. (Politics & People Ser.). 124p. 1974. Repr. 11.00x (ISBN 0-405-05872-1). Ayer Co Pubs.

Rise & Development of Western Civilization, 3 vols. 2nd ed. John L. Stipp & C. Warren Hollister. LC 76-171915. Vol. 1. pap. 160.00 (ISBN 0-317-10555-8, 2013057); Vol. 2. pap. 128.80 (ISBN 0-317-10556-6); Vol. 3. pap. 159.00 (ISBN 0-317-10557-4). Bks Demand UMI.

Rise & Expansion of the British Dominion in India. Alfred Lyall. LC 67-24585. 1968. Repr. of 1894 ed. 40.00x (ISBN 0-86527-172-0). Fertig.

Rise & Expansion of the British Dominion in India. 5th ed. Alfred C. Lyall. (Illus.). Repr. of 1920 ed. text ed. 28.50x. Coronet Bks.

Rise & Extension of Submarine Telegraphy. Willouby Smith. LC 74-4695. (Telecommunications Ser). (Illus.). 410p. 1974. Repr. of 1891 ed. 32.00x (ISBN 0-405-06058-0). Ayer Co Pubs.

Rise & Fall. Milovan Djilas. Tr. by John Loud. LC 84-12972. 352p. 1985. 24.95 (ISBN 0-15-177572-9). HarBraceJ.

Rise & Fall. Milovan Djilas. LC 84-12972. 432p. 1986. pap. 8.95 (ISBN 0-15-676708-2, Harv). HarBraceJ.

Rise & Fall in Shakespeare's Dramatic Art. Roman Dyboski. LC 73-13527. 1923. lib. bdg. 15.00 (ISBN 0-8414-3679-7). Folcroft.

Rise & Fall of a Teen Age Wacko. Mary Anderson. 1982. pap. 2.25 (ISBN 0-553-24027-7). Bantam.

Rise & Fall of Adolf Hitler. William L. Shirer. (World Landmark Ser). (gr. 7-11). 1963. lib. bdg. 6.99 (ISBN 0-394-90547-4). Random.

Rise & Fall of Adolf Hitler. William L. Shirer. LC 61-7317. (Landmark Paperbacks Ser.: No. 13). (Illus.). 192p. (gr. 5-9). 1984. pap. 2.95 (ISBN 0-394-86270-8, BYR). Random.

Rise & Fall of American Communism. Philip J. Jaffe. 240p. 1975. pap. 5.95 (ISBN 0-8180-0817-2). Horizon.

Rise & Fall of American Humor. Jesse Bier. xii, 544p. 1980. Repr. of 1968 ed. lib. bdg. 40.00x (ISBN 0-374-90632-7, Octagon). Hippocrene Bks.

Rise & Fall of an American Army. Shelby L. Stanton. (U. S. Ground Forces in Vietnam, 1965-1973 Ser.). 1988. pap. 4.95 (ISBN 0-440-17444-9). Dell.

Rise & Fall of an American Army: U. S. Ground Forces in Vietnam, Nineteen Sixty-Five to Nineteen Seventy-Three. Shelby L. Stanton. (Illus.). 429p. 1985. 22.50 (ISBN 0-89141-232-8). Presidio Pr.

Rise & Fall of Anarchy in America. George N. McLean. LC 72-885. (American History & Americana Ser., No. 47). 1973. Repr. of 1888 ed. lib. bdg. 49.95x (ISBN 0-8383-1426-0). Haskell.

Rise & Fall of Athens: Nine Greek Lives. Plutarch. Tr. by Ian Scott-Kilvert. (Classics Ser.). 320p. 1960. pap. 5.95 (ISBN 0-14-044102-6). Penguin.

Rise & Fall of Black Slavery. C. Duncan Rice. LC 72-9149. (Louisiana Paperbacks Ser.). (Illus.). xiv, 429p. 1976. pap. 10.95 (ISBN 0-8071-0257-1). La State U Pr.

Rise & Fall of British Documentary: The Story of the Film Movement Founded by John Grierson. Elizabeth Sussex. LC 74-16719. (Illus.). 1976. 32.50x (ISBN 0-520-02869-4). U of Cal Pr.

Rise & Fall of British India: Imperialism as Inequality. K. de Schweintz, Jr. 1983. 32.00x (ISBN 0-416-33530-6, NO. 3784); pap. 13.95x (ISBN 0-416-33540-3, NO. 3496). Routledge Chapman & Hall.

Rise & Fall of British Naval Mastery. Paul M. Kennedy. (Illus.). 436p. 1986. pap. text ed. 17.50x (ISBN 0-948660-01-5, Pub. by Ashfield Pr UK). Humanities.

Rise & Fall of Cesar Birotteau. Honore De Balzac. Tr. by Francis T. Furey. (Illus.). 449p. 1989. pap. 8.95 (ISBN 0-88184-448-9). Carroll & Graf.

Rise & Fall of Childhood. John Sommerville. (Sage Library of Social Research: Vol. 140). (Illus.). 256p. 1982. 29.95 (ISBN 0-8039-1823-2); pap. 14.95 (ISBN 0-8039-1824-0). Sage.

Rise & Fall of Chilean Christian Democracy. Michael Fleet. LC 84-42885. 292p. 1985. text ed. 39.00x (ISBN 0-691-07684-7); pap. 15.95x (ISBN 0-691-02217-8). Princeton U Pr.

Rise & Fall of Civilization: An Inquiry into the Relationship Between Economic Development & Civilization. Shepard B. Clough. LC 77-25973. (Illus.). 1978. Repr. of 1951 ed. lib. bdg. 35.00x (ISBN 0-313-20092-0, CLRI). Greenwood.

Rise & Fall of Detente: Relaxations of Tension in U. S.-Soviet Relations, 1953-1984. Richard W. Stevenson. LC 84-23965. 256p. 1985. 22.50 (ISBN 0-252-01215-1). U of Ill Pr.

Rise & Fall of Disease. Alfred J. Bollet. 225p. text ed. cancelled (ISBN 0-88167-221-1). Raven.

Rise & Fall of Economic Growth: A Study in Contemporary Thought. H. W. Arndt. LC 83-24185. vi, 162p. 1984. pap. 6.95x (ISBN 0-226-02717-1). U of Chicago Pr.

Rise & Fall of Economic Justice & Other Essays. C. B. Macpherson. 176p. 1987. pap. 9.95 (ISBN 0-19-285186-1). Oxford U Pr.

Rise & Fall of Economic Justice & Other Papers. C. B. Macpherson. 1985. 19.95x (ISBN 0-19-215360-9). Oxford U Pr.

Rise & Fall of Freedom of Contract. Patrick S. Atiyah. LC 85-10515. 1979. 79.00x (ISBN 0-19-825342-7); pap. 29.95x (ISBN 0-19-825527-6). Oxford U Pr.

Rise & Fall of Italian Terrorism. Leonard Weinberg & William L. Eubank. (New Directions in Comparative & International Politics Ser.). 160p. 1987. 25.00 (ISBN 0-8133-0541-1). Westview.

Rise & Fall of Keynesian Economics: An Investigation of Its Contribution to Capitalist Development. Michael Bleaney. LC 84-17746. 256p. 1985. 29.95 (ISBN 0-312-68267-0). St Martin.

Rise & Fall of King Cotton. Anthony Burton. (Illus.). 240p. 1985. 25.95 (ISBN 0-233-97148-3, Pub. by A Deutsch England). David & Charles.

Rise of Formal Satire in England under Classical Influence. Raymond M. Alden. LC 73-1450. Repr. of 1899 ed. lib. bdg. 19.50 (ISBN 0-8414-1706-7). Folcroft.

Rise of French Liberal Thought: A Study of Political Ideas from Bayle to Condorcet. 2nd ed. Kingsley Martin. Ed. by J. P. Mayer. LC 80-11662. xviii, 316p. 1980. Repr. of 1954 ed. lib. bdg. 35.00x (ISBN 0-313-22368-8, MARF). Greenwood.

Rise of Gawain, Nephew of Arthur: De Ortu Waluuanii Nepotis Arturi. Mildred L. Day. Ed. by James J. Wilhem & Lowry Nelson. LC 83-48237. (Library of Medieval Literature). 150p. 1984. lib. bdg. 30.00 (ISBN 0-8240-9423-9). Garland Pub.

Rise of German Industrial Power, 1834-1914. W. O. Henderson. LC 75-17293. 1976. 45.00x (ISBN 0-520-03073-7). U of Cal Pr.

Rise of Ghingis Khan & His Conquest of North China. Henry D. Martin. LC 70-120647. 1970. Repr. lib. bdg. 27.50x (ISBN 0-374-95287-6, Octagon). Hippocrene Bks.

Rise of Gladstone to the Leadership of the Liberal Party, 1859-1868. W. E. Williams. LC 73-17482. 189p. 1973. Repr. of 1934 ed. lib. bdg. 16.50x (ISBN 0-374-98614-2, Octagon). Hippocrene Bks.

Rise of Grammatical Categories: Cognition & Language Change in Africa. Bernd Heine. (Hans Wolff Memorial Lecture). 22p. 1986. pap. text ed. 5.00 (ISBN 0-941934-49-7). Indiana Africa.

Rise of Great Britain & Russia, 1688-1725 see Cambridge New Modern History.

Rise of Guardian Democracy: The Supreme Court's Role in Voting Rights Disputes, 1845-1969. Ward E. Elliott. LC 73-90611. (Political Studies). 368p. 1974. text ed. 27.00x (ISBN 0-674-77156-7). Harvard U Pr.

Rise of Historical Critisism. Oscar Wilde. LC 72-194458. 1905. lib. bdg. 25.50 (ISBN 0-8414-9732-X). Folcroft.

Rise of Historical Writing among the Arabs. A. A. Duri. Ed. & tr. by Lawrence I. Conrad. LC 82-24028. (Modern Classics in Near Eastern Studies). 192p. 1984. 26.50x (ISBN 0-691-05388-X). Princeton U Pr.

Rise of Hitler: Revolution & Counter-Revolution in Germany, 1918-1933. Simon Taylor. LC 83-4903. (Illus.). 131p. (Orig.). 1983. pap. 9.95x (ISBN 0-87663-591-5). Universe.

Rise of Independent Study: The Politics & the Philosophy of an Educational Innovation, 1970-1987. Derek Robbins. 160p. 1988. 52.00x (ISBN 0-335-15848-X, Open Univ Pr). Taylor & Francis.

Rise of Industrial America. Page Smith. 965p. 1984. text ed. 29.95 (ISBN 0-07-058572-5). McGraw.

Rise of Instrumental Music & Concert Series in Paris, 1828-1871. Jeffrey H. Cooper. Ed. by George Buelow. LC 83-1062. (Studies in Musicology: No. 65). 402p. 1983. 54.95 (ISBN 0-8357-1403-9). UMI Res Pr.

Rise of Integral Nationalism in France with Special Reference to the Ideas & Activities of Charles Maurras. W. C. Buthman. LC 78-120239. 1970. Repr. lib. bdg. 27.50x (ISBN 0-374-91128-2, Octagon). Hippocrene Bks.

Rise of International Organization. David Armstrong. LC 82-16767. (Making of the 20th Century Ser.). 180p. 1983. 23.95 (ISBN 0-312-68427-4). St Martin.

Rise of Islam. Mokhtar Moktefi. Tr. by Nan Buranelli from Fr. LC 86-11859. (Picture Histories Ser.). (Illus.). 64p. (gr. 5 up). PLB 14.96 (ISBN 0-382-09275-9). Silver.

Rise of Italian Fascism, 1918-1922. A. Rossi. 75.00 (ISBN 0-87968-435-6). Gordon Pr.

Rise of Labour: The British Labour Party 1890-1979. Keith Laybourn. (Illus.). 192p. 1988. text ed. 34.95 (ISBN 0-7131-6600-2, Pub. by E Arnold UK); pap. text ed. 14.95 (ISBN 0-7131-6524-3, Pub. by E Arnold UK). Routledge Chapman & Hall.

Rise of Large American Corporations, 1889-1919. David Bunting. Ed. by Stuart Bruchey. (American Business History Ser.). 350p. 1987. lib. bdg. 45.00 (ISBN 0-8240-8353-9). Garland Pub.

Rise of Life: The First 3.5 Billion Years. John Reader. LC 86-7316. 208p. 1986. pap. 15.95 (ISBN 0-394-74051-3). Knopf.

Rise of Literacy & the Common School in the United States: A Socioeconomic Analysis to 1870. Lee Soltow & Edward Stevens. LC 81-7464. (Chicago Originals Ser.). 1982. 20.00x (ISBN 0-226-76812-0). U of Chicago Pr.

Rise of Local School Supervision in Massachusetts. Henry Suzzallo. LC 70-89241. (American Education: Its Men, Institutions & Ideas, Ser. 1). 1969. Repr. of 1906 ed. 12.50 (ISBN 0-405-01478-3). Ayer Co Pubs.

Rise of Local School Supervision in Massachusetts (the School Committee, 1635-1827) Henry Suzzallo. LC 70-177735. (Columbia University. Teachers College. Contributions to Education: No. 3). Repr. of 1906 ed. 22.50 (ISBN 0-404-55003-7). AMS Pr.

Rise of Major Religions. Georgia Makhlouf. Tr. by Walter O. Moeller from Fr. (Human Story Ser.). Orig. Title: Grandes Religions. (Illus.). 80p. (YA) (gr. 6-12). 1988. 14.96 (ISBN 0-382-09482-4). Silver.

Rise of Mammals. Ray A. Gallent. LC 86-11161. (First Bks.). (Illus.). 72p. (gr. 4-9). 1986. PLB 10.40 (ISBN 0-531-10206-8). Watts.

Rise of Managerial Computing: The Best of the Center for Information Systems Research. John F. Rockart & Christine V. Bullen. 350p. 1986. 35.00 (ISBN 0-87094-757-5). Dow Jones-Irwin.

Rise of Market Culture: The Textile Trade & French Society, 1750-1900. William M. Reddy. (Illus.). 352p. 1984. 49.50 (ISBN 0-521-25653-4). Cambridge U Pr.

Rise of Market Culture: The Textile Trade & French Society, 1750-1900. William M. Reddy. (Illus.). 400p. 1987. 14.95 (ISBN 0-521-34779-3). Cambridge U Pr.

Rise of Merchant Banking. Stanley Chapman. (Illus.). 240p. 1984. text ed 39.95x (ISBN 0-04-332094-5). Unwin Hyman.

Rise of Modern Business in Great Britain, the United States & Japan. Mansel G. Blackford. LC 87-10022. (Illus.). xiv, 176p. 1988. 19.95x (ISBN 0-8078-1760-0); pap. 8.95x (ISBN 0-8078-4202-8). U of NC Pr.

Rise of Modern China. 3rd ed. Immanuel C. Hsu. LC 81-22409. (Illus.). 1983. 29.95x (ISBN 0-19-503218-7). Oxford U Pr.

Rise of Modern Industry. J. L. Hammond & Barbara Hammond. LC 74-30150. (World History Ser., No. 48). 1974. lib. bdg. 75.00x (ISBN 0-8383-1795-2). Haskell.

Rise of Modern Japan. Peter Duus. LC 75-33416. (Illus.). 304p. 1976. text ed. 31.56 (ISBN 0-395-20665-0). HM.

Rise of Modern Judaism: An Intellectual History of German Jewry 1650-1942. Heinz M. Graupe. LC 77-9059. 344p. 1979. lib. bdg. 24.00 (ISBN 0-88275-395-9); pap. text ed. 12.50 (ISBN 0-89874-562-4). Krieger.

Rise of Modern Judicial Review: From Constitutional Interpretation to Judge-Made Law. Christopher Wolfe. LC 85-47569. 393p. 1986. 24.95 (ISBN 0-465-07033-7). Basic.

Rise of Modern Judicial Review: From Constitutional Interpretation to Judge-Made Law. Christopher Wolfe. LC 85-47564. 416p. 1988. pap. 12.95 (ISBN 0-465-07034-5, PL 5204). Basic.

Rise of Modern Mythology, Sixteen Hundred Eighty to Eighteen Hundred Sixty. Burton Feldman & Robert D. Richardson. LC 71-135005. pap. 147.80 (2056249). Bks Demand UMI.

Rise of Modern Society: Aspects of the Social & Political Development of the West. Krishan Kumar. 288p. 1989. text ed. 55.00x (ISBN 0-631-16007-8). Basil Blackwell.

Rise of Modern Urban Planning Eighteen Hundred to Nineteen Fourteen. Ed. by Anthony Sutcliffe. 1980. 30.00 (ISBN 0-312-68430-4). St Martin.

Rise of Moralism. C. FitzSimons Allison. LC 84-61194. 262p. (Orig.). pap. 9.95 (ISBN 0-8192-1353-5). Morehouse.

Rise of Nationalism in Central Africa: The Making of Malawi & Zambia, 1873-1964. Robert I. Rotberg. LC 65-19829. (Center for International Affairs Ser). (Illus.). 1965. 22.50x (ISBN 0-674-77190-7); pap. 7.95x (ISBN 0-674-77191-5, HP39). Harvard U Pr.

Rise of Nationalism in the Balkans, 1800-1930. Wesley M. Gewehr. LC 67-22304. xi, 137p. 1967. Repr. of 1931 ed. 19.50 (ISBN 0-208-00507-2, Archon). Shoe String.

Rise of Nationalism in Vietnam: 1900-1941. William J. Duiker. LC 75-18723. (Illus.). 320p. 1976. 28.50x (ISBN 0-8014-0951-9). Cornell U Pr.

Rise of Nationality in Eastern Europe. Emil Niederhauser. 340p. 1982. 29.00x (ISBN 0-317-54550-7, Pub. by Collets (UK)). State Mutual Bk.

Rise of Nationality in Eastern Europe. Emil Niederhauser. 339p. 1981. 12.95x (ISBN 963-13-1199-6, Pub. by Corvina Kiado Hungary). Intl Spec Bk.

Rise of Neo-Confucianism in Korea. Ed. by William T. De Bary & Jahyun K. Haboush. 512p. 1985. 45.00x (ISBN 0-231-06052-1). Columbia U Pr.

Rise of New York Port, Eighteen Fifteen to Eighteen Sixty. Robert G. Albion. LC 83-27190. 499p. 1984. text ed. 29.95x (ISBN 0-930350-58-8); pap. 9.95x (ISBN 0-930350-59-6). NE U Pr.

Rise of Opera. Robert Donington. (Illus.). 362p. 1981. 45.00 (ISBN 0-684-17165-1, ScribT). Scribner.

Rise of Our East African Empire: Early Efforts in Nyasaland Uganda, 2 vols Frederick J. Lugard. (Illus.). 1968. Repr. of 1893 ed. 95.00x set (ISBN 0-7146-1691-5, F Cass Co). Biblio Dist.

Rise of Pennsylvania Protectionism. Malcolm R. Eiselen. LC 73-18438. (Perspectives in American History Ser.: No. 8). 287p. 1974. Repr. of 1932 ed. lib. bdg. 35.00x (ISBN 0-87991-342-8). Porcupine Pr.

Rise of Photography, Eighteen Fifty to Eighteen Eighty: The Age of Collodion. Helmut Gernsheim. LC 87-51303. (Illus.). 250p. 1988. 65.00 (ISBN 0-500-97349-0). Thames Hudson.

Rise of Political Anti-Semitism in Germany & Austria. rev. ed. Peter Pulzer. 384p. 1988. pap. text ed. 14.50 (ISBN 0-674-77166-4). Harvard U Pr.

Rise of Political Consultants: New Ways of Winning Elections. Larry J. Sabato. LC 81-66104. 376p. 1983. pap. 11.95x (ISBN 0-465-07039-6, TB-5114). Basic.

Rise of Popular Antimodernism in Germany: The Urban Master Artisans, 1873-1896. Shulamit Volkov. LC 77-85571. 1978. 49.50x (ISBN 0-691-05264-6). Princeton U Pr.

Rise of Portuguese Power in India 1497-1550. Richard S. Whiteway. LC 76-407549. 1967. Repr. of 1899 ed. 37.50x (ISBN 0-678-07258-2). Kelley.

Rise of Pragmatic Thought in the Nineteenth & Twentieth Century, Vol. II. (Pragmatics: Handbook of Pragmatic Thought Ser.). 484p. 1987. 79.95 (ISBN 3-7873-0644-7). Transaction Bks.

Rise of Professionalism: A Sociological Analysis. Magali S. Larson. LC 74-30533. 1977. pap. 11.95x (ISBN 0-520-03950-5). U of Cal Pr.

Rise of Puritanism. William Haller. LC 57-10117. 479p. 1972. pap. 16.95x (ISBN 0-8122-1048-4, Pa Paperbks). U of Pa Pr.

Rise of Reform Judaism: A Sourcebook of Its European Origins. W. Gunther Plaut. Incl. Growth of Reform Judaism: American & European Sources to 1948. 1965. 1963. 10.00 (ISBN 0-8074-0089-0, 382770, Pub. by World Union). UAHC.

Rise of Religious Liberty in America. Sanford H. Cobb. 1978. pap. write for info. (ISBN 0-89102-115-9, Artemis). B Franklin.

Rise of Religious Liberty in America: A History. Sanford H. Cobb. LC 68-27517. 541p. 1968. Repr. of 1902 ed. 32.50x (ISBN 0-8154-0051-9). Cooper Sq.

Rise of Religious Liberty in America: A History. Sanford H. Cobb. (American Studies). 1970. Repr. of 1902 ed. 30.00 (ISBN 0-384-09445-7). Johnson Repr.

Rise of Respectable Society: A Social History of Victorian Britain, 1830-1900. F. M. Thompson. 384p. 1988. text ed. 30.00 (ISBN 0-674-77285-7). Harvard U Pr.

Rise of Robert Millikan: Portrait of a Life in American Science. Robert H. Kargon. (Illus.). 206p. 1982. 28.95x (ISBN 0-8014-1459-8). Cornell U Pr.

Rise of Romance. Eugene Vinaver. LC 84-284. (Illus.). 172p. 1984. Repr. of 1971 ed. 28.50x (ISBN 0-389-20449-8, 08030). B&N Imports.

Rise of Romance. Eugene Vinaver. (Illus.). 190p. 1984. 33.00 (ISBN 0-85991-158-6, Pub. by Boydell & Brewer). Longwood Pub Group.

Rise of Romantic Hellenism in English Literature, 1732-1786. Bernard H. Stern. LC 72-86288. 1969. Repr. of 1940 ed. lib. bdg. 18.50x (ISBN 0-374-97619-8, Octagon). Hippocrene Bks.

Rise of Romanticism: Essential Texts. Ed. by Brian Hepworth. 366p. 22.50 (ISBN 0-85635-112-1). Carcanet.

Rise of Rome. Jacques Heurgon. LC 70-126762. 1973. 36.00x (ISBN 0-520-01795-1). U of Cal Pr.

Rise of Scientific Philosophy. Hans Reichenbach. 1951. pap. 9.95 (ISBN 0-520-01055-8). U of Cal Pr.

Rise of Sentimental Comedy. James E. Cox. 1979. Repr. of 1926 ed. lib. bdg. 29.00 (ISBN 0-8495-0945-9). Arden Lib.

Rise of Sentimental Comedy. James E. Cox. LC 74-9974. 1926. lib. bdg. 25.00 (ISBN 0-8414-3360-7). Folcroft.

Rise of Settler Power in Southern Rhodesia (Zimbabwe) 1898-1923. James A. Mutambirwa. LC 78-75181. 248p. 1980. 24.50 (ISBN 0-8386-2267-4). Fairleigh Dickinson.

Rise of Silas Lapham. Howells. (American Classics Ser.). (gr. 9-12). 1977. pap. text ed. 5.16 (ISBN 0-88343-412-1); tchrs'. manual o.p. 1.89 (ISBN 0-88343-414-8); cassettes 57.00 (ISBN 0-88343-425-3). McDougal-Littell.

Rise of Silas Lapham. William Howells. 1977. Repr. of 1885 ed. lib. bdg. 19.95x (ISBN 0-89244-043-0). Queens Hse-Focus Serv.

Rise of Silas Lapham. William D. Howells. (Airmont Classics Ser.). (gr. 11 up). pap. 1.95 (ISBN 0-8049-0165-1, CL-165). Airmont.

Rise of Silas Lapham. William D. Howells. Repr. lib. bdg. 21.95 (ISBN 0-89190-456-5, Pub. by River City Pr). Amereon Ltd.

Rise of Silas Lapham. William D. Howells. (Literature Ser.). (gr. 10-12). 1970. pap. text ed. 7.17 (ISBN 0-87720-737-2). AMSCO Sch.

Rise of Silas Lapham. William D. Howells. Ed. by E. H. Cady. LC 57-14612. (YA) (gr. 9 up). 1957. pap. 6.50 (ISBN 0-395-05126-6, RivEd). HM.

Rise of Silas Lapham. William D. Howells. LC 70-92321. (Selected Edition of W.D. Howells: Center for Editions of American Authors: Vol. 12). 434p. 1971. 25.00x (ISBN 0-253-35016-6). Ind U Pr.

Rise of Silas Lapham. William D. Howells. (YA) (RL 9). pap. 2.95 (ISBN 0-451-51850-0, CE1850, Sig Classics). NAL.

Rise of Silas Lapham. William D. Howells. Ed. by Don L. Cook. (Norton Critical Edition Ser.). 1982. 24.95 (ISBN 0-393-04433-5); pap. text ed. 10.95x (ISBN 0-393-09165-1). Norton.

Rise of Silas Lapham. rev. ed. William D. Howells. Ed. by Robert J. Dixson. (American Classics Ser.: No. 8). 1974. pap. text ed. 4.25 (ISBN 0-13-024589-5, 18127); cassettes 55.00 (ISBN 0-13-024761-8, 58231). Prentice ESL.

Rise of Silas Lapham. William D. Howells. (Penguin American Library). 352p. 1983. pap. 4.95 (ISBN 0-14-039030-8). Penguin.

Rise of Silas Lapham see Novels Eighteen Seventy-Five to Eighteen Eighty-Six.

Rise of Silas Lapham Notes. Patrick Keating. (Orig.). 1964. pap. 3.75 (ISBN 0-8220-1147-6). Cliffs.

Rise of Socialist Fiction 1880-1914. Gustav H Klaus. LC 87-9483. 272p. 1987. 35.00 (ISBN 0-312-00949-6). St Martin.

Rise of Solidarity. (Flashpoints Ser.). (Illus.). (YA) (gr. 7 up). Date not set. write for info. Rourke Corp.

Rise of Statistical Thinking, 1820-1900. Theodore Porter. LC 85-43306. 350p. 1986. text ed. 42.50x (ISBN 0-691-08416-5). Princeton U Pr.

Rise of Statistical Thinking, 1820-1900. Theodore M. Porter. 352p. 1988. pap. text ed. 12.50 (ISBN 0-691-02409-X). Princeton U Pr.

Rise of Suburbia. Ed. by F. M. Thompson. LC 81-21304. (Themes in Urban History Ser.). 300p. 1982. 40.00x (ISBN 0-312-68433-9). St Martin.

Rise of Surgery: From Empiric Craft to Scientific Discipline. Owen H. Wangensteen & Sarah D. Wangensteen. LC 77-87933. (Illus.). 1979. 45.00x (ISBN 0-8166-0829-6). U of Minn Pr.

Rise of Systems Theory. Robert Lilienfeld. LC 85-5531. 302p. 1987. Repr. of 1978 ed. text ed. 42.50 (ISBN 0-89874-857-7). Krieger.

Rise of Teamster Power in the West. Donald Garnel. 1971. 40.00x (ISBN 0-520-01733-1). U of Cal Pr.

Rise of the Accounting Profession, 2 vols. John L. Carey. LC 75-7181. Repr. of 1969 ed. Vol. 1. 101.30 (2027591); Vol. 2. 140.30. Bks Demand UMI.

Rise of the American Electrochemicals Industry, 1880-1910: Studies in the American Technological Environment. Martha M. Trescott. LC 80-23469. (Contributions in Economics & Economic History Ser.: No. 38). (Illus.). 424p. 1981. lib. bdg. 46.95 (ISBN 0-313-20766-6, TRI/). Greenwood.

Rise of the Anglo-German Antagonism: 1860-1914. Paul M. Kennedy. 624p. 1987. text ed. 22.50 (ISBN 0-948660-06-6, Pub. by Ashfield Pr UK). Humanities.

Rise of the Anti-Mission Baptists: Sources & Leaders, 1800-1840. Byron C. Lambert. Ed. by Edwin S. Gaustad. LC 79-52573. (Baptist Tradition Ser.). 1980. lib. bdg. 39.00x (ISBN 0-405-12441-4). Ayer Co Pubs.

Rise of the Antichrist. Gordon Lindsay. (Revelation Ser.). 1.25 (ISBN 0-89985-042-1). Christ Nations.

Rise of the Asian Superpowers. Negel De Lee. (Conflict in the 20th Century Ser.). (Illus.). 64p. (gr. 4 up). 1987. PLB 12.90 (ISBN 0-531-10407-9). Watts.

Rise of the Atlantic Economies. Ralph Davis. Ed. by Charles Wilson. (Paperback Ser.). 340p. 1973. pap. 12.50x (ISBN 0-8014-9143-6). Cornell U Pr.

Rise of the Authoritarian State in Peripheral Societies. Clive Y. Thomas. LC 84-16490. 288p. 1984. 27.00 (ISBN 0-85345-657-7); pap. 11.00 (ISBN 0-85345-658-5). Monthly Rev.

Rise of the Baltic Question. Walther Kirchner. Repr. of 1954 ed. lib. bdg. 35.00x (ISBN 0-8371-3009-3, KIBQ). Greenwood.

Rise of the Barristers: A Social History of the English Bar, 1590-1640. Wilfrid R. Prest. (Oxford Studies in Social History). 440p. 1987. 62.00x (ISBN 0-19-821764-1). Oxford U Pr.

Rise of the Black Magus in Western Art. Paul H. Kaplan. Ed. by Linda Seidel. LC 85-8461. (Studies in the Fine Arts: Iconography: No. 10). 344p. 1985. 49.95 (ISBN 0-8357-1667-8). UMI Res Pr.

Rise of the British Coal Industry, 2 vols. facsimile ed. John U. Nef. LC 71-37902. (Select Bibliographies Reprint Ser). Repr. of 1932 ed. Set. 81.50 (ISBN 0-8369-6740-2). Ayer Co Pubs.

Rise of the British Coal Industry, 2 vols. John U. Nef. (Illus.). 1966. Repr. of 1932 ed. 85.00x set (ISBN 0-7146-1346-0, BHA-01346, F Cass Co). Biblio Dist.

Rise of the British Treasury: Colonial Administration in the 18th Century. Dora M. Clark. LC 69-16613. x, 249p. 1969. Repr. of 1960 ed. 26.00 (ISBN 0-208-00788-1, Archon). Shoe String.

Rise of the Carolingians & the Liber Historiae Francorum. Richard A. Gerbering. (Oxford Historical Monographs). (Illus.). 224p. 1987. 49.95 (ISBN 0-19-822940-2). Oxford U Pr.

Rise of the Celts. Henri H. Hubert. LC 66-23521. (Illus.). 1934. 18.00 (ISBN 0-8196-0183-7). Biblo.

Rise of the Chinese Communist Party, 1928-1938: Volume Two of the Autobiography of Chang Kuo-t'ao. Chang Kuo-t'ao. LC 76-141997. viii, 628p. 1972. 35.00x (ISBN 0-7006-0088-4). U Pr of KS.

Rise of the Chinese Republic: From the Last Emperor to Deng Xiaoping. Edwin P. Hoyt. (Illus.). 1988. 19.95 (ISBN 0-07-030619-2). McGraw.

Rise of the Cinema in Great Britain. John Barnes. 272p. 1985. 95.00x (ISBN 0-900873-51-5, Pub. by Bishopsgate Pr. Ltd.). State Mutual Bk.

Rise of the Cinema in Great Britain. John Barnes. 272p. 1987. 24.95 (ISBN 0-317-64181-6, Pub. by Bishopsgate Pr London). Intl Spec Bk.

Rise of the Common Player. Muriel C. Bradbrook. LC 79-2314. (History of Elizabethan Drama Ser.: Vol. 3). (Illus.). 1979. pap. 12.95 (ISBN 0-521-29527-0). Cambridge U Pr.

Rise of the Community Builders: The American Real Estate Industry & Urban Land Planning. Marc A. Weiss. (Columbia History of Urban Life Ser.). 240p. 1987. 27.50 (ISBN 0-231-06504-3). Columbia U Pr.

TITLE INDEX RISING ABOVE COLOR.

Rise of the Computer State. David Burnham. LC 82-42808. 1983. 17.45 (ISBN 0-394-51437-8). Random.
Rise of the Computer State. David Burnham. Date not set. pap. 6.95 (ISBN 0-394-72375-9, Vin). Random.
Rise of the Corporate Commonwealth: U. S. Business & Public Policy in the Twentieth Century. Louis Galambos & Joseph Pratt. LC 87-47784. (Illus.). 288p. 1988. 19.95 (ISBN 0-465-07029-9). Basic.
Rise of the Corporate Commonwealth: United States Business & Public Policy in the 20th Century. Louis Galambos & Joseph Pratt. LC 87-47784. 304p. 1989. pap. 9.95 (ISBN 0-465-07028-0, PL 5230). Basic.
Rise of the Corporate Economy. Leslie Hannah. 288p. 1983. 24.00 (ISBN 0-416-34850-5, NO. 4046); pap. 10.95 (ISBN 0-416-34860-2, NO. 4045). Routledge Chapman & Hall.
Rise of the Corporate Economy: The British Experience. Leslie Hannah. LC 76-17228. pap. 63.80 (ISBN 0-317-42336-3, 2025816). Bks Demand UMI.
Rise of the Counter-Establishment: From Conservative Ideology to Political Power. Sidney Blumenthal. 1986. 19.95 (ISBN 0-8129-1205-5). Times Bks.
Rise of the Counter-Establishment: From Conservative Ideology to Political Power. Sidney Blumenthal. LC 88-45014. 384p. 1988. pap. 9.95 (ISBN 0-06-097140-1, PL 7140, PL). Har-Row.
Rise of the Dictators, Nineteen Twenty to Nineteen Thirty-Nine. Peter Banyard. LC 86-50274. (Conflict in the 20th Century Ser.). (Illus.). 64p. (gr. 4-12). 1986. PLB 12.90 (ISBN 0-531-10233-5). Watts.
Rise of the Dutch Republic see Writings of John Lothrop Motley.
Rise of the English Prep School. Donald Leinster-Mackay. (Illus.). 280p. 1984. 44.00x (ISBN 0-905273-74-5, Falmer Pr). Taylor & Francis.
Rise of the Entrepreneurial State: State & Local Economic Development Policy in the United States. Peter K. Eisinger. LC 88-40184. 337p. 1988. text ed. 40.00x (ISBN 0-299-11870-3); pap. text ed. 17.50x (ISBN 0-299-11874-6). U of Wis Pr.
Rise of the European Economy: An Economic History of Continental Europe from Fifteenth Hundred to Seventeen Fifty. Hermann Kellenbenz. LC 76-7487. 350p. 1976. 34.50 (ISBN 0-8419-0273-9). Holmes & Meier.
Rise of the Expert Company: How Visionary Companies Are Using Computers to Make Huge Profits. Edward Feigenbaum et al. 256p. 1988. 19.95 (ISBN 0-8129-1731-6). Times Bks.
Rise of the Feudal Monarchies. Sidney Painter. (Development of Western Civilization Ser.). (Illus.). 147p. 1951. pap. 7.95x (ISBN 0-8014-9851-1). Cornell U Pr.
Rise of the Fighter Aircraft: Nineteen Fourteen to Nineteen Eighteen. Richard P. Hallion. LC 83-26947. (Illus.). 196p. 1988. Repr. of 1984 ed. 22.95 (ISBN 0-933852-42-8). Nautical & Aviation.
Rise of the French Communist Party. Edward Mortimer. 431p. 1984. 65.00 (ISBN 0-571-09754-5). Faber & Faber.
Rise of the French Novel. Martin Turnell. LC 77-26792. 1978. pap. 8.95 (ISBN 0-8112-0716-1, NDP474). New Directions.
Rise of the Gothic. William Anderson. (Illus.). 208p. 1985. 29.95 (ISBN 0-88162-109-9). Salem Hse Pubs.
Rise of the Great Powers: The Great Powers & European States Systems, 1648-1815. Derek Mckay & H. M. Scott. LC 82-159. 1983. text ed. pap. text ed. 16.95 (ISBN 0-582-48554-1). Longman.
Rise of the Greek Socialist Party. Michalis Spourdalakis. 352p. 1988. lib. bdg. 57.50 (ISBN 0-415-00499-3). Routledge Chapman & Hall.
Rise of the Greeks. Michael Grant. (Illus.). 416p. 1988. 27.50 (ISBN 0-684-18536-9). Scribner.
Rise of the Habsburg Empire: 1526-1815. Victor S. Mamatey. LC 77-15525. (Berkshire Studies). 192p. 1978. pap. text ed. 6.50 (ISBN 0-88275-639-7). Krieger.
Rise of the High School in Massachusetts. A. J. Inglis. LC 70-176895. (Columbia University. Teachers College. Contributions to Education: No. 45). Repr. of 1911 ed. 22.50 (ISBN 0-404-55045-2). AMS Pr.
Rise of the House of Rothschild. E. Corti. 75.00 (ISBN 0-87968-170-5). Gordon Pr.
Rise of the House of Rothschild. Egon C. Corti. 430p. 1972. pap. 4.95 (ISBN 0-88279-112-5). Western Islands.
Rise of the Imams of Sanaa. Arthur S. Tritton. LC 79-2887. 144p. 1981. Repr. of 1925 ed. 15.00 (ISBN 0-8305-0053-7). Hyperion Conn.
Rise of the Indian Novel in English. K. S. Ramamurti. 305p. 1987. text ed. 35.00x (ISBN 81-207-0642-0, Pub. by Sterling Pubs India). Apt Bks.
Rise of the Irish Trade Unions. rev. ed. Andrew Boyd. 160p. 1985. pap. 9.95 (ISBN 0-900068-21-3, Pub. by Anvil Pr Ireland). Irish Bks Media.
Rise of the Ironclads. George F. Amadon. LC 88-60845. (Illus.). 80p. 1988. pap. 9.95 (ISBN 0-933126-90-5). Pictorial Hist.
Rise of the Jew in the Western World. Uriah Z. Engelman. LC 73-2194. (Jewish People: History, Religion, Literature Ser.). Repr. of 1944 ed. 22.00 (ISBN 0-405-05260-X). Ayer Co Pubs.
Rise of the Labor Movement in Ceylon. Visakha Jayawardena. LC 77-185465. pap. 99.50 (ISBN 0-317-42174-3, 2026205). Bks Demand UMI.
Rise of the Labour Movement. Geoffrey Morris. 128p. 1986. 30.00x (Pub. by S P A Bks Ltd). State Mutual Bk.
Rise of the Latin American Labor Movement. Ben G. Burnett & Moises P. Troncoso. 1960. 12.95x; pap. 8.95x (ISBN 0-8084-0406-7). New Coll U Pr.
Rise of the London Money Market: Sixteen Forty to Eighteen Twenty Six. W. R. Bisschop. LC 68-56765. (Research & Source Works Ser: No. 250). 1968. Repr. of 1910 ed. 20.50 (ISBN 0-8337-0297-1). B Franklin.
Rise of the London Money Market: 1640-1826. W. R. Bisschop. 256p. 1968. Repr. of 1826 ed. 30.00x (ISBN 0-7146-1206-5, F Cass Co). Biblio Dist.
Rise of the Medici: Faction in Florence 1420-1434. Dale Kent. 1978. 65.00x (ISBN 0-19-822520-2). Oxford U Pr.
Rise of the Medieval Church & Its Influence on the Civilization of Western Europe from the 1st to the 13th Century. Alexander C. Flick. 636p. 1973. Repr. of 1909 ed. lib. bdg. 33.50 (ISBN 0-8337-1159-8). B Franklin.
Rise of the Merchant Class in Tokugawa Japan, 1600-1868: An Introductory Survey. Charles D. Sheldon. LC 72-97536. xiv, 220p. (With a new introduction & appendix). 1973. Repr. of 1958 ed. 18.00x (ISBN 0-8462-1725-2). Russell.
Rise of the Midland Railway 1844-1874. E. G. Barnes. LC 76-83157. (Illus.). 1969. 27.95x (ISBN 0-678-06000-2). Kelley.
Rise of the Midwestern Meat Packing Industry. Margaret Walsh. LC 82-40184. 192p. 1982. 15.00 (ISBN 0-8131-1473-X). U Pr of Ky.
Rise of the Missionary Spirit in America 1790-1815. Oliver W. Elsbree. LC 79-13028. (Perspectives in American History Ser.: No. 55). 187p. 1980. Repr. of 1928 ed. 27.50x (ISBN 0-87991-376-2). Porcupine Pr.
Rise of the Modern Educational System: Structural Change & Social Reproduction, 1870-1920. Ed. by Detlef Muller et al. 280p. 1987. 49.50 (ISBN 0-521-33001-7). Cambridge U Pr.
Rise of the Modern German Novel: Crisis & Charisma. Russell A. Berman. LC 85-24770. (Central Asian Studies). 184p. 1986. text ed. 31.50x (ISBN 0-674-77250-4). Harvard U Pr.
Rise of the Modern State. Ed. by James Anderson. LC 85-27104. 274p. 1986. text ed. 39.95x (ISBN 0-391-03387-5). Humanities.
Rise of the Modern Woman. Ed. by Peter N. Stearns. LC 78-56350. (Problems in Civilization Ser). (Orig.). 1978. pap. text ed. 6.95x (ISBN 0-88273-404-0). Forum Pr IL.
Rise of the Monophysite Movement: Chapters in the History of the Church in the Fifth & Sixth Centuries. W. H. Frend. LC 72-75302. (Illus.). 400p. 1972. 77.50 (ISBN 0-521-08130-0). Cambridge U Pr.
Rise of the National Trade Union: The Development & Significance of Its Structure, Governing Institutions, & Economic Policies. 2nd ed. Lloyd Ulman. LC 66-5206. (Wertheim Publications in Industrial Relations Ser). (Illus.). 1955. 37.50x (ISBN 0-674-77280-6). Harvard U Pr.
Rise of the Nazi Regime: Historical Reassessments. Charles S. Maier & Stanley Hoffman. (Westview Special Study). 160p. 1985. pap. 22.00x (ISBN 0-8133-0192-0). Westview.
Rise of the New Model Army. Mark A. Kishlansky. LC 79-4285. 1979. 32.50 (ISBN 0-521-22751-8). Cambridge U Pr.
Rise of the New Model Army. Mark A. Kishlansky. LC 79-4285. (Cambridge Paperback Library). 337p. 1983. pap. 15.95 (ISBN 0-521-27377-3). Cambridge U Pr.
Rise of the New Physics. 2nd ed. A. Abro. (Illus.). 994p. 1951. pap. 7.95 ea.; Vol. 1. pap. (ISBN 0-486-20003-5); Vol. 2. pap. (ISBN 0-486-20004-3). Dover.
Rise of the New Physics: Its Mathematical & Physical Theories, 2 vols. A. D'Abro. Orig. Title: Decline of Mechanism. 14.50 ea (ISBN 0-8446-0569-7); Set. 29.00. Peter Smith.
Rise of the New York Intellectuals: Partisan Review & Its Circle. Terry A. Cooney. LC 86-40049. (History of American Thought & Culture). 352p. 1986. 25.00x (ISBN 0-299-10710-8). U of Wis Pr.
Rise of the Novel: Studies in Defoe, Richardson & Fielding. Ian Watt. 1957. 26.95x (ISBN 0-520-04656-0); pap. 8.95x (ISBN 0-520-01318-2). U of Cal Pr.
Rise of the Ottoman Empire. Paul Wittek. LC 70-153023. (Research & Source Works Ser.: No. 769). 1971. Repr. of 1938 ed. lib. bdg. 10.50 (ISBN 0-8337-3855-0). B Franklin.
Rise of the Peking Opera 1770-1870: Social Aspects of the Theatre in Manchu China. Colin P. Mackerras. (Illus.). 1972. 39.95x (ISBN 0-19-815137-3). Oxford U Pr.
Rise of the Phoenix: The United States in a Restructured World Economy. Jack N. Behrman. (Studies in American Business & the International Economy). 128p. 1987. pap. 12.85 (ISBN 0-8133-7511-8). Westview.
Rise of the Phoenix: Universal Government by Nature's Laws. new ed. Christopher Hills. Ed. by Ann Ray & Deborah Rozman. LC 76-53176. (Illus.). 1024p. (Orig.). 1979. 24.95 (ISBN 0-916438-04-X). Univ of Trees.
Rise of the Public Library in California. Ray E. Held. LC 73-12719. pap. 54.30 (ISBN 0-317-27845-2, 2024218). Bks Demand UMI.
Rise of the Revolutionary Party in the English House of Commons, 1603-1629. Williams M. Mitchell. LC 75-31471. 209p. 1976. Repr. of 1957 ed. lib. bdg. 25.00x (ISBN 0-8371-8535-1, MIRR). Greenwood.
Rise of the Roman Empire. Polybius. Tr. by Ian Scott-Kilvert. 1980. pap. 8.95 (ISBN 0-14-044362-2). Penguin.
Rise of the Roman Jurists: Studies in Cicero's pro Caecina. Bruce W. Frier. LC 84-42886. (Illus.). 312p. 1985. text ed. 40.00x (ISBN 0-691-03578-4). Princeton U Pr.
Rise of the Russian Consumer. Margaret Miller. (gr. 10 up). pap. 2.50 technical (ISBN 0-255-69564-0). Transatl Arts.
Rise of the Saracens & the Foundation of the Western Empire see Cambridge Medieval History.
Rise of the Social Gospel in American Protestantism, 1865-1895. Charles H. Hopkins. LC 75-41141. (BCL Ser.: Vol. II). 368p. Repr. of 1940 ed. 30.00 (ISBN 0-404-14771-2). AMS Pr.
Rise of the Spanish American Republics As Told in the Lives of Their Liberators. William S. Robertson. 1976. lib. bdg. 59.95 (ISBN 0-8490-2527-3). Gordon Pr.
Rise of the Spanish Inquisition. Jean Plaidy. (Illus.). 192p. 1959. text ed. 24.95x (ISBN 0-7091-5080-6, Pub. by Robert Hale). Trans-Atl-Phila.
Rise of the Student Estate in Britain. Eric Ashby & Mary Anderson. 196p. 1970. 15.00x (ISBN 0-674-77290-3). Harvard U Pr.
Rise of the Sunbelt Cities. Ed. by David C. Perry & Alfred J. Watkins. LC 77-93698. (Urban Affairs Annual Reviews: No. 14). 309p. 1978. 35.00 (ISBN 0-8039-1029-0); pap. 16.95 (ISBN 0-8039-1030-4). Sage.
Rise of the Swiss Republic. 2nd ed. William D. McCracken. LC 75-130235. Repr. of 1901 ed. 29.45 (ISBN 0-404-04109-4). AMS Pr.
Rise of the Trading State: Commerce & Conquest in the Modern World. Richard Rosecrance. LC 85-47558. 273p. 1986. 19.95 (ISBN 0-465-07035-3). Basic.
Rise of the Trading State: Commerce & Conquest in the Modern World. Richard Rosecrance. LC 85-47558. 288p. 1987. pap. 9.95 (ISBN 0-465-07036-1, PL 5183). Basic.
Rise of the United Association: National Unionism in the Pipe Trades 1884-1924. Martin Segal. LC 79-101012. (Wertheim Publications in Industrial Relations Ser). 258p. 1969. text ed. 16.50x (ISBN 0-674-77300-4). Harvard U Pr.
Rise of the Urban South. Lawrence H. Larsen. LC 84-25596. 232p. 1985. 22.00 (ISBN 0-8131-1538-8, Dist. by Har-Row). U Pr of Ky.
Rise of the Welsh Republic. Derrick Hearne. 20.00X (ISBN 0-317-52163-2, Pub. by Y Lolfa Wales). State Mutual Bk.
Rise of the West: A History of the Human Community. William H. McNeill. LC 63-13067. 1970. pap. 14.95 (ISBN 0-226-56144-5, P385, Phoen). U of Chicago Pr.
Rise of the West, 1754-1830. Francis S. Philbrick. LC 65-21377. (New American Nation Ser.). 1965. 20.00xi (ISBN 0-06-013330-9, HarpT). Har-Row.
Rise of the Western World: A New Economic History. D. C. North & R. P. Thomas. LC 73-77258. (Illus.). 192p. 1973. 32.50 (ISBN 0-521-20171-3); pap. 9.95 (ISBN 0-521-29099-6). Cambridge U Pr.
Rise of the Wheat State: A History of Kansas Agriculture, 1861-1986. Ed. by George Ham & Robin Higham. 1987. 25.00 (ISBN 0-89745-082-5); pap. 12.00 (ISBN 0-89745-083-3). Sunflower U Pr.
Rise of the Woman Novelist: From Aphra Behn to Jane Austen. Jane Spencer. 256p. 1986. 50.00 (ISBN 0-631-13915-X); pap. 14.95 (ISBN 0-631-13916-8). Basil Blackwell.
Rise of Theodore Roosevelt. Edmund Morris. 1980. pap. 10.95 (ISBN 0-345-33902-9). Ballantine.
Rise of Theodore Roosevelt. Edmund Morris. LC 78-23789. (Illus.). 1979. 24.95 (ISBN 0-698-10783-7, Coward). Putnam Pub Group.
Rise of Turkish Nationalism 1876-1908. David Kushner. 126p. 1977. 29.50x (ISBN 0-7146-3075-6, F Cass Co). Biblio Dist.
Rise of U. S. Grant. facs. ed. Arthur L. Conger. LC 74-137371. (Select Bibliographies Reprint Ser). (Illus.). 1931. 23.50 (ISBN 0-8369-5572-2). Ayer Co Pubs.
Rise of Universities. C. H. Haskins. 69.95 (ISBN 0-87968-379-1). Gordon Pr.
Rise of Universities. Charles H. Haskins. (Paperback Ser.). 118p. (YA) (gr. 9-12). 1957. pap. 4.50x (ISBN 0-8014-9015-4). Cornell U Pr.
Rise of Urban America, 57 vols. Ed. by Richard C. Wade. 1970. Repr. 1539.50 (ISBN 0-405-02430-4). Ayer Co Pubs.
Rise of Urbanization & the Decline of Citizenship. Murray Bookchin. LC 86-22083. 356p. 1987. 22.95 (ISBN 0-87156-706-7). Sierra.
Rise of Warren Gamaliel Harding, 1865-1920. Randolph C. Downes. LC 68-31421. (Illus.). 744p. 1970. 17.50 (ISBN 0-8142-0140-7). Ohio St U Pr.
Rise of Western Rationalism: Max Weber's Developmental History. Wolfgang Schluchter. Tr. by Guenther Roth from Ger. LC 81-2763. 300p. 1981. pap. 10.95x (ISBN 0-520-05464-4). U of Cal Pr.
Rise of World Lutheranism: An American Perspective. E. Clifford Nelson. LC 80-2376. pap. 111.30 (ISBN 0-317-55549-9, 2029618). Bks Demand UMI.
Rise to Be a People: A Biography of Paul Cuffe. Lamont D. Thomas. LC 85-16335. (Blacks in the New World Ser.). 208p. 1986. 21.95 (ISBN 0-252-01212-7). U of Ill Pr.
Rise to Follow. Albert Spalding. 1988. Repr. lib. bdg. 75.00x. Am Biog Serv.
Rise to Follow: An Autobiography. Albert Spalding. LC 77-5563. (Music Reprint Ser.). 1977. Repr. of 1943 ed. lib. bdg. 39.50 (ISBN 0-306-77421-6). Da Capo.
Rise to Globalism. 4th ed. Stephen Ambrose. 368p. (Orig.). 1985. pap. 7.95 (ISBN 0-14-022622-2). Penguin.
Rise to Globalism: American Foreign Policy Since 1938. 5th, rev. ed. Stephen E. Ambrose. 416p. pap. 8.95 (ISBN 0-14-022826-8). Penguin.
Rise to World Power: Selected Letters of Whitelaw Reid, 1895-1912. David R. Contosta & Jessica Hawthorne. LC 84-45907. (Transaction Ser.: Vol. 76, Pt. 2). 200p. 1986. 18.00 (ISBN 0-87169-762-9). Am Philos.
Rise up & Call Her Blessed. Marilyn Kiteley. 96p. (Orig.). 1987. pap. 4.95 (ISBN 0-914903-19-5). Destiny Image.
Rise up in Anger: Latin America Today. Robert A. Karlowich. LC 82-22646. (Illus.). 160p. (gr. 7 up). 1985. 9.29 (ISBN 0-671-46525-2). Messner.
Rise up Singing. Ed. by Peter Blood-Patterson. 256p. 1988. 29.95 (ISBN 0-86571-136-4); pap. 12.95 (ISBN 0-86571-138-0); spiral bdg. 14.95 (ISBN 0-86571-137-2). New Soc Pubs.
Rise up So Early: A History of Florence County, South Carolina. G. Wayne King. LC 81-17778. (Illus.). 424p. 1981. 20.00 (ISBN 0-87152-355-8). Reprint.
Risen & with You Always: Daily Meditations for the Easter Season Masses. Emeric Lawrence. 140p. 1986. pap. 5.95 (ISBN 0-8146-1448-5). Liturgical Pr.
Risen from the Ashes: A Story of the Jewish Displaced Persons in the Aftermath of World War II, Being a Sequel to Survivors. Jacob Biber. LC 87-851. (Studies in Judaica & the Holocaust: No. 5). 160p. 1988. lib. bdg. 19.95x (ISBN 0-89370-372-9); pap. 9.95x (ISBN 0-89370-472-5). Borgo Pr.
Risen Indeed: Lessons of Faith from the U. S. S. R. Michael Boudeaux. 113p. (Orig.). 1983. pap. text ed. 6.95 (ISBN 0-88141-021-7). St Vladimirs.
Risen Jesus. rev. ed. Alban Goodier. 4.00 (ISBN 0-8198-6411-0); 3.00 (ISBN 0-8198-6412-9). Dghtrs St Paul.
Risen Lord. (Baker Flip & Find Bks.). (Illus.). (ps-2). 1986. pap. 2.95 (ISBN 0-8010-3532-5). Baker Bk.
Risen Sons: Flannery O'Connor's Vision of History. John F. Desmond. LC 86-30828. (Illus.). 152p. 1987. 18.00x (ISBN 0-8203-0945-1). U of Ga Pr.
Risen Today. Thorogood. Date not set. 7.50 (Pub. by SCM Pr England). Fortress.
Risen with Christ: Celebrating the Paschal Mystery with the Parish Family. Gretchen W. Pritchard. (Illus.). 118p. (Orig.). 1988. pap. 15.00 (ISBN 0-9614022-3-7). Sunday Paper.
Risers, Arctic Design Criteria, Equipment Reliability in Hydrocarbon Processing: A Workbook for Engineers, Presented at 37th Petroleum Mechanical Engineering Workshop & Conference, September 13-15, 1981, Dallas, Texas. American Society of Mechanical Engineers Staff. Ed. by Thomas J. Kozik. LC 81-186405. pap. 62.50 (ISBN 0-317-29899-2, 2019351). Bks Demand UMI.
Rishi. Leo Giroux, Jr. 1987. pap. 4.50 (ISBN 0-317-56185-5). Ivy Books.
Rishi: A Novel. Leo Giroux, Jr. LC 85-10314. 372p. 1985. 16.95 (ISBN 0-87131-463-0). M Evans.
Rishonim: Biographical Sketches of the Prominent Early Rabbinic Sages & Leaders from the Tenth-Fifteenth Centuries. Shmuel Teich. Ed. & intro. by Hersh Goldwurm. (ArtScroll History Ser.). (Illus.). 224p. (YA) (gr. 7-8). 1982. 13.95 (ISBN 0-89906-452-3); pap. 10.95 (ISBN 0-89906-453-1). Mesorah Pubns.
Risho's Registry. Ray Risho. 130p. (Orig.). 1985. pap. 5.00 (ISBN 0-939872-03-X). MRP.
Rising. Alison Smith. 256p. 1987. 16.95 (ISBN 0-312-00675-6, J Kahn). St Martin.
Rising above Color. facsimile ed. Ed. by Philip H. Lotz. LC 78-152190. (Essay Index Reprints - Creative Personalities Ser.: Vol. 5). Repr. of 1943 ed. 12.00 (ISBN 0-8369-2605-6). Ayer Co Pubs.

Rising above Decline. Betsy Wachtel & Brian Powers. 198p. (Orig.). 1979. pap. 4.50 (ISBN 0-917754-14-X). Inst Responsive.

Rising above Strife. Ed. by Nancy I. Witte. pap. 4.95 (ISBN 0-89137-424-8). Quality Pubns.

Rising above the Crowd. Brian L. Harbour. LC 87-17361. (Orig.). 1988. 8.95 (ISBN 0-8054-5730-5). Broadman.

Rising American Empire. Richard W. Van Alstyne. 240p. 1974. pap. 6.95x (ISBN 0-393-00750-2). Norton.

Rising & Falling. Margot Farrington. 94p. 1985. pap. 5.00 (ISBN 0-942292-09-X). Warthog Pr.

Rising Cost of Hospital Care. Martin S. Feldstein. LC 72-171922. (Illus.). viii, 88p. 1971. pap. 9.00 (ISBN 0-87815-004-8). Info Resources.

Rising Damp: Sydney 1870-90. Shirley Fitzgerald. (Illus.). 280p. 1987. 45.00 (ISBN 0-19-554750-0). Oxford U Pr.

Rising Fawn & the Fire Mystery. Marilou Awiakta. Ed. by Roger R. Easson. LC 83-13824. (Child's Christmas in Memphis Ser.: Vol. 1). (Illus.). 48p. (Orig.). (gr. 5 up). 1984. lib. bdg. 9.95 (ISBN 0-918518-35-0, St Luke TN); pap. 6.95 (ISBN 0-918518-29-6). Peachtree Pubs.

Rising from History: U. S. Catholic Theology Looks to the future. Ed. by Robert J. Daly. LC 87-2011. (Annual Publication of the College Theology Society, 1984: Vol. 30). 234p. (Orig.). 1987. lib. bdg. 24.50 (ISBN 0-8191-6155-1, Pub. by College Theology Society); pap. text ed. 12.75 (ISBN 0-8191-6156-X, Pub. by College Theology Society). U Pr of Amer.

Rising from the Plains. John McPhee. 224p. 1987. 15.95 (ISBN 0-374-25082-0). FS&G.

Rising from the Plains. John McPhee. 224p. 1987. pap. 7.95 (ISBN 0-374-52065-8). FS&G.

Rising Generation. LC 87-70805. 1987. pap. 5.95 (ISBN 0-87579-088-7). Deseret Bk.

Rising Germanophobia: The Chief Obstacle to Current World War II Revisionism. Michael F. Conners. (Studies in Revisionist Historiography). 1980. lib. bdg. 59.95 (ISBN 0-686-59416-9). Revisionist Pr.

Rising Gorge. S. J. Perelman. 288p. 1987. pap. 6.95 (ISBN 0-14-008041-4). Penguin.

Rising in Love. Alan Cohen. 150p. (Orig.). 1982. pap. 5.95 (ISBN 0-910367-31-0). A Cohen.

Rising in Western Upper Canada, 1837-38: The Duncombe Revolt & After. Colin Read. 320p. 1982. 40.00x (ISBN 0-8020-5498-6). U of Toronto Pr.

Rising of a New Moon: A Century of Tabwa Art. Evan M. Maurer & Allen F. Roberts. (Illus.). 288p. (Orig.). 1986. pap. 39.95 (ISBN 0-912303-32-8). Michigan Mus.

Rising of a New Moon: A Century of Tabwa Art. Ed. by Allen F. Roberts & Evan M. Maurer. (Illus.). 304p. 1985. pap. 39.95 (ISBN 0-295-96447-2, Pub. by U MI Mus Art). U of Wash Pr.

Rising of Agricultural Laborers: 1830-(1831?) LC 72-2542. (British Labour Struggles Before 1850 Ser). 1972. 24.50 (ISBN 0-405-04434-8). Ayer Co Pubs.

Rising of al-Husayn: Its Impact on the Consciousness of Muslim Society. Shaykh M. Al-Din. Tr. by I. K. Howard. 1987. pap. 15.95 (ISBN 0-7103-0191-X, Kegan Paul). Routledge Chapman & Hall.

Rising of the Flesh. Karla Andersdatter. 96p. (Orig.). 1983. pap. 5.95 (ISBN 0-911051-00-7). Plain View.

Rising of the Moon. Peter B. Ellis. 640p. 1987. 19.95 (ISBN 0-312-00676-4). St Martin.

Rising of the Moon. William Martin. 480p. 1987. 18.95 (ISBN 0-517-56315-0). Crown.

Rising of the Moon. William Martin. 480p. 1988. pap. 4.95 (Pub. by Ivy). Ballantine.

Rising of the Moon. Gladys Mitchell. 1986. 13.95 (ISBN 0-317-53148-4, Large Print Bks). G K Hall.

Rising of the Red Shawls: A Revolt in Madagascar 1895-1899. Stephen Ellis. (African Studies: No. 43). 230p. 1985. 47.50 (ISBN 0-521-26287-9). Cambridge U Pr.

Rising of the Wind: Adventures along the Beaufort Scale. Jacques Yvart. Tr. by Jean Lazorthes from Fr. LC 83-83203. (Illus.). 48p. (Orig.). (YA) (gr. 7 up). 1984. 15.95 (ISBN 0-88138-031-8). Green Tiger Pr.

Rising of the Women. Meredith Tax. LC 80-8087. 332p. 1981. pap. 8.50 (ISBN 0-85345-549-X). Monthly Rev.

Rising: Pygmies & Pyramids, Vol. 1. Edgar White. 224p. 1988. 18.95 (ISBN 0-7145-2878-1, Dist. by Kampmann & Co). M Boyars Pubs.

Rising Sign: Your Astrological Mask. Jeanne Avery. LC 77-16894. (Illus.). 480p. 1982. pap. 9.95 (ISBN 0-385-13278-6, Dolp). Doubleday.

Rising Signs. Carolyn R. Dodson. LC 82-71708. 120p. 1979. 8.00 (ISBN 0-86690-034-9, 2405-01). Am Fed Astrologers.

Rising Son: The Antecedents & Advancement of the Colored Race. facs. ed. William W. Brown. LC 79-79008. (Black Heritage Library Collection Ser). 1874. 22.50 (ISBN 0-8369-8519-2). Ayer Co Pubs.

Rising Star: Kelly Blake, Teen Model, No. 2. Yvonne Green. 176p. (YA) (gr. 7-12). 1986. pap. 2.50 (ISBN 0-553-25639-4). Bantam.

Rising Storm. Anne Sadowski. LC 87-17275. 80p. (Orig.). 1988. pap. 2.95 (ISBN 0-7178-0664-2). Intl Pubs Co.

Rising Storm: An Analysis of the Growing Conflict Over the Political Dilemma of Roman Catholics in America. Hiram W. Evans. Ed. by Gerald Grob. LC 76-46075. (Anti-Movements in America). 1977. lib. bdg. 27.50x (ISBN 0-405-09948-7). Ayer Co Pubs.

Rising Sun. John Toland. (Illus.). 1982. pap. 6.95 (ISBN 0-553-26435-4). Bantam.

Rising Sun. Ed. by Arthor Zich. (World War II Ser.). 1977. 14.95 (ISBN 0-8094-2462-2). Time-Life.

Rising Sun: A History of the All People's Congress Party of Sierra Leone. Intro. by Siaka P. Stevens. 512p. 1986. 59.80x (ISBN 0-946041-21-0, Pub. by Kensal Pr UK). State Mutual Bk.

Rising Sun or the Antecedents & Advancement of the Colored Race. William W. Brown. (Basic Afro-American Reprint Library). 1970. Repr. of 1874 ed. lib. bdg. 26.00 (ISBN 0-384-05995-3). Johnson Repr.

Rising Sun: The Decline & Fall of the Japanese Empire: 1936-1945. John Toland. 1970. 25.00 (ISBN 0-394-44311-X). Random.

Rising Tide. M. J. Farrell, pseud. (Virago Modern Classics Ser.). 336p. 1985. pap. 7.95 (ISBN 0-14-016100-7). Penguin.

Rising Tide. Richard F. Pourade. LC 67-11865. (Illus.). 280p. 1967. 14.50 (ISBN 0-913938-06-8). Copley Bks.

Rising Tide of Change. Michael Burghley & Nancy Burghley. (Illus.). 69p. (Orig.). 1986. pap. 5.95 (ISBN 0-935427-12-0). Foundation Hse.

Rising Tide of Color. Lothrop Stoddard. 1984. lib. bdg. 79.95 (ISBN 0-87700-598-2). Revisionist Pr.

Rising Tide of Color. T. Lothrop Stoddard. 320p. 1986. pap. 7.50 (ISBN 0-317-53267-7). Noontide.

Rising Tide of Suicide: A Guide to Prevention, Intervention & Postvention. Louis R. Batzler. 200p. (Orig.). 1988. pap. 10.00 (ISBN 0-935710-08-6). Hid Valley MD.

Rising Tide of Truth see Nation of Crusaders: The General Plan for the Second American Revolution.

Rising to Life: Aids to Reflection & Prayer for the Easter Triduum & Easter Season. Gregory Manly & Anneliese Reinhard. 160p. (Orig.). 1987. pap. 8.95 (ISBN 0-86786-115-0, Pub. by Spectrum Pub). ANZ Religious Pubns.

Rising Wind. Walter F. White. LC 78-138684. Repr. of 1945 ed. 35.00x (ISBN 0-8371-5520-7, WRW&). Greenwood.

Rising Yen. Richard S. Thorn. 121p. 1987. text ed. 18.00 (ISBN 9971-988-74-7, Pub. by Inst Southeast Asian Stud). Gower Pub Co.

Risis in Ancient India. Chandra B. Pandey. 265p. 1987. 26.00x (ISBN 0-8364-2022-5, Pub. by Sundeep). South Asia Bks.

Risk! Steve Boga. (Illus.). 224p. (Orig.). 1988. pap. 9.95 (ISBN 1-55643-042-6). North Atlantic.

Risk. Dick Francis. 1984. pap. 3.50 (ISBN 0-671-50755-9). PB.

Risk: A Philosophical Introduction to the Theory of Risk Evaluation & Management. Nicholas Rescher. LC 82-21970. (Nicholas Rescher Ser.). 218p. (Orig.). 1983. lib. bdg. 31.25 (ISBN 0-8191-2269-6); pap. text ed. 13.00 (ISBN 0-8191-2270-X). U Pr of Amer.

Risk Acceptability According to the Social Sciences. Mary Douglas. LC 85-60758. (Social Research Perspectives: Occasional Reports on Current Topics Ser.). 160p. (Orig.). 1986. pap. text ed. 6.95x (ISBN 0-87154-211-0). Russell Sage.

Risk Analysis & Decision Processes. H. C. Kunreuther et al. (Illus.). 290p. 1983. 29.00 (ISBN 0-387-12804-2). Springer-Verlag.

Risk Analysis & Its Applications. David B. Hertz & Howard Thomas. 323p. 1983. 49.95 (ISBN 0-471-10145-1, Pub. by Wiley-Interscience). Wiley.

Risk Analysis & Risk Management: A Selected Bibliography. Susan Rafter. (Public Administration Ser.: P 2218). 9p. 1987. 3.00 (ISBN 1-55590-438-6). Vance Biblios.

Risk Analysis & the Security Survey. James F. Broder. 320p. 1984. text ed. 26.95 (ISBN 0-409-95085-8). Butterworth.

Risk Analysis Controversy-An Institutional Perspective, Laxenburg, Austria: Proceedings, 1981. Ed. by H. Kuhnreuther & E. V. Ley. (Illus.). 236p. 1982. 34.00 (ISBN 0-387-12012-2). Springer-Verlag.

Risk Analysis for Offshore Structures & Equipment. Ed. by Asteo. 1987. lib. bdg. 87.00 (ISBN 0-86010-894-5, Pub. by Graham & Trotman UK). Kluwer Academic.

Risk Analysis Guide to Insurance & Employee Benefits. A. E. Pfaffle & Sal Nicosia. LC 77-10973. pap. 20.00 (ISBN 0-317-26314-5, 2055752). Bks Demand UMI.

Risk Analysis Guide to Insurance & Employee Benefits. A. E. Pfaffle & Sal Nicosia. (AMA Management Briefings). 108p. 1986. 10.00 (ISBN 0-8144-2323-X). AMACOM.

Risk Analysis: How to Reduce Insurance Costs. Gary Robinson. (Successful Business Library). 300p. 1986. 3-ring binder 33.95 (ISBN 0-916378-85-3, Oasis); pap. 18.95 (ISBN 0-916378-84-5, Oasis). PSI Res.

Risk Analysis in Project Appraisal. Louis Y. Pouliquen. LC 70-120739. (World Bank Staff Occasional Papers Ser: No. 11). (Illus.). 79p. (Orig.). 1970. pap. 7.95x (ISBN 0-8018-1155-4). Johns Hopkins.

Risk Analysis in Some Production & Refining Systems in the Petroleum Industry. R. De Malherbe & M. C. De Malherbe. 1981. 45.00 (ISBN 3-18-141216-3, Pub. by VDI W Germany). IPS.

Risk Analysis in the Chemical Industry. Chemical Manufacturers Association Staff. 278p. 1985. pap. 46.00 (ISBN 0-86587-044-6). Gov Insts.

Risk Analysis in the Private Sector. Ed. by Chris Whipple & Vincent Covello. (Advances in Risk Analysis Ser.: Vol. 3). 516p. 1985. 85.00x (ISBN 0-306-41924-6, Plenum Pr). Plenum Pub.

Risk Analysis in Transportation Systems. R. De Malherbe & M. C. De Malherbe. 1981. 45.00 (ISBN 3-18-141813-7, Pub. by VDI W Germany). IPS.

Risk Analysis, Institutions & Public Policy. Ed. by Stuart S. Nagel & Susan G. Hadden. LC 83-15792. (Policy Studies Organization). 180p. 1984. 24.95x (ISBN 0-8046-9332-3, 9332, Natl U). Assoc Faculty Pr.

Risk Analysis of Spent Fuel Transportation. Barbara Foster. 50p. (Orig.). 1986. pap. text ed. 8.00 (ISBN 1-55516-478-1). Natl Conf State Legis.

Risk & Aging. Paul C. Brearley & M. R. P. Hall. (Hazards & Helping). 250p. (Orig.). 1982. pap. 9.95x (ISBN 0-7100-9080-3). Routledge Chapman & Hall.

Risk & Capital Adequacy in Commercial Banks. Ed. by Sherman J. Maisel. LC 81-3324. (National Bureau of Economic Research Monograph). x, 436p. 1986. pap. 35.00 (ISBN 0-226-50282-1, Midway Reprint). U of Chicago Pr.

Risk & Capital: Proceedings of the 2nd Summer Workshop on Risk & Capital Held at the University of Ulm, West Germany, June 20-24, 1983. Ed. by G. Bamberg & A. Spremann. (Lecture Notes in Economics & Mathematical Systems Ser.: Vol. 227). 320p. 1984. pap. 25.00 (ISBN 0-387-12923-5). Springer Verlag.

Risk & Decision Analysis for Hazardous Waste Disposal. LC 81-84397. 216p. 1981. 30.00 (ISBN 0-686-39192-6). Hazardous Mat Control.

Risk & Failure in English Business 1700-1800. Julian Hoppit. 232p. 1987. 39.50 (ISBN 0-521-32624-9). Cambridge U Pr.

Risk & Human Rationality. Richard Jeffrey. (Working Papers on Risk & Rationality). Date not set. 2.50 (RR7). IPPP.

Risk & Insurance. 5th ed. James L. Athearn & S. Travis Pritchett. (Illus.). 608p. 1984. text ed. 40.00 (ISBN 0-314-77828-4); instrs.' manual avail. (ISBN 0-314-77833-0). West Pub.

Risk & Insurance. 7th ed. Mark R. Greene & James S. Trieschmann. 768p. 1988. text ed. write for info. (ISBN 0-538-06550-8, F55). SW Pub.

Risk & Insurance Management Guide for Financial Institutions. 1976. 25.00 (ISBN 0-89982-060-3, 212000); non-members 45.00. Am Bankers.

Risk & Its Treatment: Changing Societal Consequences. Ed. by George E. Rejda & Ralph B. Ginsberg. LC 78-72994. (Annals: No. 443). 1979. 15.00 (ISBN 0-87761-238-2); pap. 7.95 (ISBN 0-87761-239-0). Am Acad Pol Soc Sci.

Risk & Other Four-Letter Words. Walter Wriston. LC 85-45245. 256p. 1987. pap. 8.95 (ISBN 0-06-091389-4, PL 1389, PL). Har-Row.

Risk & Other Four-Letter Words. Walter B. Wriston. LC 85-45245. 224p. 1986. 19.45i (ISBN 0-06-015544-2, HarpT). Har-Row.

Risk & Outcome in Anesthesia. Brown. LC 65-9590. 1988. text ed. 49.50 (ISBN 0-397-50794-1, Lippincott Nursing). Lippincott.

Risk & Prevention of Arterial Lipidoses. P. Schwandt. 300p. 1988. 22.50 (ISBN 0-87527-232-0). Green.

Risk & Reason: Risk Assessment in Relation to Environmental Mutagens & Carcinogens. Ed. by Per Oftedal & Anton Brogger. LC 85-23784. (PCBR Ser.: Vol. 208). 206p. 1986. 38.00 (ISBN 0-8451-5058-8, 5058). A R Liss.

Risk & Return; or, How to Live with Wall Street. Sharp & Matlock. 5.00 (ISBN 0-87505-528-1). Borden.

Risk & Reward: How Investors Helped Create America's Industries & What You Should Know About Venture Capital Today. Thomas Doerflinger & Jack L. Rivkin. LC 86-10107. 288p. Date not set. 19.95 (ISBN 0-394-54929-5). Random.

Risk & Rhetoric in Religion: Whitehead's Theory of language & the Discourse of Faith. Lyman T. Lundeen. LC 71-171501. pap. 72.00 (2026868). Bks Demand UMI.

Risk & Society: Studies of Risk Generation & Reactions to Risks. Lennart Sjoberg. (Risks & Hazzards Ser.: No. 3). 320p. 1987. text ed. 27.95x (ISBN 0-04-604001-3). Unwin Hyman.

Risk & Survival: Mineral & Petroleum Exploration in Australia. 67p. 1987. text ed. 30.00x (ISBN 0-949106-13-5, Pub. by Australasian Inst M&M). Brookfield Pub Co.

Risk & Technological Innovation: American Manufacturing Methods During the Nineteenth Century. Wolfgang P. Strassmann. LC 81-4252. x, 249p. 1981. Repr. lib. bdg. 35.00x (ISBN 0-313-23083-8, STRIT). Greenwood.

Risk & Technology Choice in Developing Countries: The Case of Philippine Sugar Factories. Fred S. Avestruz. (Illus.). 192p. (Orig.). 1985. lib. bdg. 23.25 (ISBN 0-8191-4774-5); pap. text ed. 11.50 (ISBN 0-8191-4775-3). U Pr of Amer.

Risk & the Control Technology: Public Policies for Road-Traffic Safety in Britain & the United States. Alan Irwin. LC 84-17153. 224p. 1988. pap. 17.50 (ISBN 0-7190-1829-3, Pub. by Manchester Univ Pr). St Martin.

Risk & the Political Economy of Resource Development. David W. Pearce et al. LC 83-13726. 450p. 1984. 39.95 (ISBN 0-312-68447-9). St Martin.

Risk & Uncertainty. Ed. by C. Borch & Jan Mossiv. LC 68-29940. (International Economic Assn. Ser). (Illus.). 1969. 35.00 (ISBN 0-312-68460-6). St Martin.

Risk & Uncertainty: Non-Deterministic Decision Making in Engineering Economy. Ed. by G. A. Fleischer. 1985. pap. 19.00 (ISBN 0-89806-018-4, NO. 105). Inst Indus Eng.

Risk Approach in Health Care with Special Reference to Maternal & Child Health, including Family Planning. E. M. Backett et al. (Public Health Papers: No. 76). 121p. 1984. pap. 6.60 (ISBN 92-4-130076-0); slides & presentation notes 19.20 (ISBN 0-318-22001-6). World Health.

Risk Assessment & Decision Making Using Test Results: The Carcinogenicity Predicition & Battery Selection Approach. J. Pet-Edwards et al. (Illus.). 240p. Date not set. price not set (ISBN 0-306-43067-3, Plenum Pr). Plenum Pub.

Risk Assessment & Management. Ed. by L. B. Lave. LC 87-21288. (Advances in Risk Analysis Ser.: Vol. 5). (Illus.). 752p. 1987. 125.00x (ISBN 0-306-42683-8, Plenum Pr). Plenum Pub.

Risk Assessment & Risk Control. Conservation Foundation Staff. LC 85-5743. 69p. 1985. pap. 7.50 (ISBN 0-89164-091-6). Conservation Foun.

Risk Assessment & Risk Management of Industrial & Envrionmental Chemicals. Ed. by William L. Marcus et al. (Advances in Modern Envrionmental Toxicology Ser.). (Illus.). 275p. 1988. 58.00 (ISBN 0-911131-16-7). Princeton Sci Pubs.

Risk Assessment at Hazardous Waste Sites. Ed. by F. A. Long & Glenn E. Schweitzer. LC 82-16376. (Symposium Ser.: No. 204). 128p. 1982. lib. bdg. 34.95 (ISBN 0-8412-0747-X). Am Chemical.

Risk Assessment for Deliberate Releases. W. Klingmuller. (Illus.). 215p. 1988. 47.90 (ISBN 0-387-18930-0). Springer-Verlag.

Risk Assessment for Hazardous Installations. Ed. by J. C. Chicken. 350p. 1986. 58.00 (ISBN 0-08-033457-1, A110, K111, Pub. by PPL). Pergamon.

Risk Assessment in Financial Institutions: A Systematic Approach. Bank Administration Institute. 96p. 1983. 60.00 (205). Bank Admin Inst.

Risk Assessment in the Federal Government: Managing the Process. National Research Council. 191p. 1983. pap. text ed. 11.75 (ISBN 0-309-03349-7). Natl Acad Pr.

Risk Assessment of Environmental Hazards. Ed. by Dennis J. Paustenbach. LC 87-35056. 1600p. 1988. price not set (ISBN 0-471-84998-7). Wiley.

Risk Assessment of N-Nitroso Compounds for Human Health. Dietrich Schmaehl. (Journal: Oncology: Vol. 37, No. 4). (Illus.). 120p. 1980. pap. 40.75 (ISBN 3-8055-1137-X). S Karger.

Risk Assessment of Radioactive Waste Management: A Bibliography. Frederick Frankena. (Public Administration Ser.: P 2073). 13p. 1986. 3.75 (ISBN 1-55590-133-6). Vance Biblios.

Risk Assessment of Wastewater Disinfection. David Hulby et al. 175p. 1985. pap. 35.00 (ISBN 0-87762-517-4). Technomic.

Risk at Delivery. Ed. by G. P. Mandruzzato. (Contributions to Gynecology & Obstetrics Ser.: Vol. 3). (Illus.). 1977. 32.75 (ISBN 3-8055-2421-8). S Karger.

Risk Aversion, Insurance, & the Future. Mark R. Greene. LC 70-633854. (Sequeinnial Insurance Ser.: No. 2). 1971. 7.50 (ISBN 0-685-00048-6). Ind U Busn Res.

Risk-Based Decision Making in Water Resources. Ed. by Yacov Y. Haimes & Eugene Z. Stakhiv. LC 86-25942. 340p. 1986. pap. 32.00x (ISBN 0-87262-575-3). Am Soc Civil Eng.

Risk-Benefit Analysis. Richard Wilson & Edmond Crouch. LC 81-22832. 240p. 1982. prof. ref. 32.00x (ISBN 0-88410-667-5). Ballinger Pub.

Risk-Benefit Analysis in Decisions Concerning Public Safety & Health. ITT(Sagoff) 48p. 1985. Saddle-Stitch 4.95 (ISBN 0-8403-3600-4). Kendall-Hunt.

Risk Benefit Analysis in Water Resources Planning & Management. Ed. by Yacov Y. Haimes. LC 81-17824. 302p. 1981. 59.50x (ISBN 0-306-40884-8, Plenum Pr). Plenum Pub.

Risk Benefit Analysis: The Microwave Case. Ed. by N. H. Steneck. (Illus.). 1982. 15.00 (ISBN 0-911302-44-1). San Francisco Pr.

Risk Business. Michael Blakstad. 144p. 1979. pap. 11.95x (ISBN 0-85072-098-2, Pub. by Design Council England). Intl Spec Bk.

Risk by Choice: Regulating Health & Safety in the Workplace. W. Kip Viscusi. (Illus.). 216p. 1983. text ed. 20.00x (ISBN 0-674-77302-0). Harvard U Pr.

RISS: A Relational Data Base Management System for Minicomputers. Monte Meldman et al. LC 81-8256. 122p. 1981. Repr. of 1978 ed. lib. bdg. 16.50 (ISBN 0-89874-373-7). Krieger.

Rissa & Tregare. F. M. Busby. 272p. 1984. pap. 2.95 (ISBN 0-425-10140-1). Berkley Pub.

RIST Dialogues. (Project on Goals, Processes & Indicators of Development). 44p. 1981. pap. 5.00 (ISBN 92-808-0328-X, TUNU164, UNU). UNIPUB.

Rita & Frits Markus Collection of European Ceramics & Enamels. Christina S. Corsiglia et al. Ed. by D. Margaret Jupe. LC 83-63520. (Illus.). 288p. 1984. pap. 17.50 (ISBN 0-87846-238-4). Mus Fine Arts Boston.

Rita & Tim Hildebrandt Fantasy Cookbook. Rita Hildebrandt & Timothy Hildebrandt. LC 82-17798. (Illus.). 208p. 1983. 14.95 (ISBN 0-672-52703-0). Bobbs.

Rita Hayworth: Her Story. Barbara Leaming. Date not set. price not set. Viking.

Rita Hayworth: The Time, the Place & the Woman. John Kobal. 320p. 1983. pap. 3.50 (ISBN 0-425-07170-7). Berkley Pub.

Rita Reif's the New York Times World Guide to Antiques Shopping. Rita Reif. LC 87-40193. 448p. 1987. pap. 14.95 (ISBN 0-8129-1251-9). Times Bks.

Rita, Sue & Bob Too. Andrea Dunbar. (Methuen New Theatrescript Ser.). 160p. 1988. pap. 8.95 (ISBN 0-413-18340-8). Heinemann Ed.

Rita Wolff Paintings. Ed. by Academy Editions. (Illus.). 96p. 1986. 29.95 (ISBN 0-312-68463-0); pap. 24.95. St Martin.

Ritchie Valens, The First Latino Rocker. Beverly Mendheim. LC 87-71700. 176p. 1987. pap. 10.00 (ISBN 0-916950-79-4). Biling Rev-Pr.

Rite. Gregory Douglas. (Orig.). 1979. pap. 2.50 (ISBN 0-89083-529-2). Zebra.

Rite & Man: Natural Sacredness & Christian Liturgy. Louis Bouyer. Tr. by Joseph Costelloe. 224p. 1985. pap. text ed. 13.00 (ISBN 0-8191-4340-5). U Pr of Amer.

Rite, Drama, Festival, Spectacle: Rehearsals Toward a Theory of Cultural Performance. Ed. by John J. MacAloon. LC 83-8516. 300p. 1984. text ed. 32.50 (ISBN 0-89727-045-2). ISHI PA.

Rite for the Beautification of All Beings. John Brandi. LC 83-4774. (Illus.). 24p. 1983. (Pub. by Toothpaste); pap. 7.50 (ISBN 0-915124-65-3). Coffee Hse.

Rite of Anointing & Pastoral Care of the Sick. pocket ed. 6.95 (ISBN 0-89942-156-3, 156/04). Catholic Bk Pub.

Rite of Baptism for Children. green cloth 8.50 (ISBN 0-89942-136-9, 136/22). Catholic Bk Pub.

Rite of Funerals. Tr. by International Committee on English in the Liturgy. blue cloth 8.50 (ISBN 0-89942-350-7, 350/22). Catholic Bk Pub.

Rite of Love. Lucy Lee. (Superromances Ser.). 384p. 1982. pap. 2.50 (ISBN 0-373-70044-X, Pub. by Worldwide). Harlequin Bks.

Rite of Marriage. (Large Type, Two Colors, Homiletic Notes). red cloth 8.50 (ISBN 0-89942-238-1, 238/22). Catholic Bk Pub.

Rite of Passage. Alexei Panstin. 1982. pap. 2.50 (ISBN 0-671-44068-3, Timescape). PB.

Rite of Penance. pocket ed. 3.95 (ISBN 0-89942-128-8, 128/04). Catholic Bk Pub.

Rite of Penance. large ed. 160p. (Large, Two-Color Type). 8.50 (ISBN 0-89942-528-3, 528/22). Catholic Bk Pub.

Rite of Spring. Andrew M. Greeley. 1988. 18.95 (ISBN 0-446-51295-8). Warner Bks.

Rite of Spring. Andrew M. Greeley. 416p. 1988. pap. 4.95 (ISBN 0-446-34341-2). Warner Bks.

Rite of Spring: Sketches, 1911-1913. LC 79-6004. (Illus.). 139p. 1969. 125.00 (ISBN 0-913932-10-8). Boosey & Hawkes.

Rite of Survivorship. Bart McGullion. (Illus.). 62p. (Orig.). 1984. pap. 3.00 (ISBN 0-88680-221-0); write for info. royalty. I E Clark.

Rite of War. S. Windass. 128p. 1986. pap. 7.00 (ISBN 0-08-033605-1, Pub. by BDP). Pergamon.

Rites. George McKenna. 240p. 1981. pap. 2.25 (ISBN 0-8439-0979-X, Leisure Bks). Leisure NY.

Rites: A Guatemalan Boyhood. Victor Perera. 192p. 1986. 15.95 (ISBN 0-15-177678-4). HarBraceJ.

Rites & Ceremonies of the Greek Church in Russia. John G. King. LC 73-126673. Repr. of 1772 ed. 34.50 (ISBN 0-404-03692-9). AMS Pr.

Rites & Meditations. Paul Murray. 1981. pap. 6.95 (ISBN 0-85105-393-9, Pub. by Colin Smythe Ltd Britain). Dufour.

Rites & Passages. James B. Hall. LC 77-80023. (Illus.). 144p. 1981. 30.00 (ISBN 0-89381-022-3); pap. 15.00 (ISBN 0-89381-069-X). Aperture.

Rites & Rhythms: Hemingway, a Genuine Character. Anders Naessil. 1988. 10.95 (ISBN 0-533-07245-X). Vantage.

Rites & Rituals for Women's Programs. Date not set. price not set. Hot Flash Pr.

Rites & Symbols of Initiation: The Mysteries of Birth & Rebirth. Mircea Eliade. Orig. Title: Birth & Rebirth. pap. 6.95x (ISBN 0-06-131236-3, TB1236, Torch). Har-Row.

Rites & Witnesses. Rolando Hinojosa. LC 82-71655. 120p. (Orig.). 1982. pap. 7.50 (ISBN 0-934770-19-0). Arte Publico.

Rites for a Plebian Statue. Pritish Nandy. flexible cloth 4.80 (ISBN 0-89253-655-1). Ind-US Inc.

Rites of Autumn. Cliff Schimmels. 180p. 1985. pap. 4.95 (ISBN 0-89693-334-2). Victor Bks.

Rites of Autumn: A Falconer's Journey Across the American West. Dan O'Brien. Ed. by Majorie Braman & Carl Navarre. (Illus.). 1988. 17.95 (ISBN 0-87113-245-1). Atlantic Monthly.

Rites of Birth, Marriage, Death, & Kindred Occasions among the Semites. Julian Morgenstern. 1966. 20.00x (ISBN 0-87068-230-X). Ktav.

Rites of Christian Initiation. Michel Dujarier. 244p. 1982. pap. 5.95 (ISBN 0-8215-9328-5). Sadlier.

Rites of Death & Dying: Three Papers Given at the 1987 National Meeting of the Federation of Diocesan Liturgical Commissions. Lawrence Boadt et al. (Illus.). 108p. 1988. pap. 4.95 (ISBN 0-8146-1597-X). Liturgical Pr.

Rites of Eastern Christendom, 2 Vols. Archdale A. King. LC 70-142246. Repr. of 1948 ed. Set. 125.00 (ISBN 0-404-03677-5). Vol. 1 (ISBN 0-404-03678-3). Vol. 2 (ISBN 0-404-03679-1). AMS Pr.

Rites of Execution: Capital Punishment & the Transformation of America Culture, 1776-1865. Louis P. Masur. 224p. 1988. 27.95 (ISBN 0-19-504899-7). Oxford U Pr.

Rites of Fall: High School Football in Texas. Geoff Winningham & Al Reinert. (Illus.). 176p. 1979. 24.95 (ISBN 0-292-77020-0); pap. 14.95 (ISBN 0-292-77021-9). U of Tex Pr.

Rites of Modernization: Symbolic & Social Aspects of Indonesian Proletarian Drama. James L. Peacock. LC 68-15931. (Symbolic Anthropology Ser: Vol. 1). (Illus.). 1968. 26.00x (ISBN 0-226-65130-4). U of Chicago Pr.

Rites of Modernization: Symbols & Social Aspects of Indonesian Proletarian Drama. James Peacock. LC 68-15931. (Symbolic Anthropology Ser.). (Illus.). xxvi, 318p. 1987. pap. 15.95 (ISBN 0-226-65131-2). U of Chicago Pr.

Rites of Passage. Ed. by John Duckworth et al. (Pacesetter Ser.). 64p. 1987. tchr's. ed. 7.95 (ISBN 1-55513-789-X). Cook.

Rites of Passage. William Golding. 278p. 1980. 14.95 (ISBN 0-374-25086-3). FS&G.

Rites of Passage. Joanne Greenberg. LC 84-19250. 1985. pap. 6.95 (ISBN 0-03-003677-1, Owl Bks). H Holt & Co.

Rites of Passage. Ed. by Garrett Solyom & Bronwen Solyom. LC 79-84170. (Illus.). 48p. 1979. 6.00 (ISBN 0-317-68013-7). Mingei Intl Mus.

Rites of Passage. Arnold Van Gennep. Tr. by Monika B. Vizedon & Gabrielle L. Caffee. LC 59-14321. 1961. pap. 6.95x (ISBN 0-226-84849-3, P64, Phoen). U of Chicago Pr.

Rites of Passage at One-Hundred-Thousand Dollars Plus: The Insider's Guide to Absolutely Everything about Executive Job-Changing. John Lucht. LC 87-50459. 560p. 1988. 24.95 (ISBN 0-942785-07-X). Viceroy Pr.

Rites of Passage at One Hundred Thousand Dollars Plus: The Insider's Guide to Absolutely Everything about Executive Job-Changing. John Lucht. 1988. 24.95 (ISBN 0-317-70080-4). H Holt & Co.

Rites of Passage: Emigrant Voyages to Australia in the Nineteenth Century. Helen R. Woolcock. 350p. 1986. 49.95 (ISBN 0-422-60240-X, 1041, Pub. by Tavistock England). Routledge Chapman & Hall.

Rites of Passage in a Student Culture. Thomas A. Leemon. LC 72-81190. 1972. pap. text ed. 9.95x (ISBN 0-8077-1673-1). Tchrs Coll.

Rites of Passage: Selected Translations. Edwin Morgan. 190p. 1976. 21.00 (ISBN 0-85635-164-4); pap. 9.50 (ISBN 0-317-46528-7). Carcanet.

Rites of Power: Symbolism, Ritual & Politics since the Middle Ages. Ed. by Sean Wilentz. LC 84-20937. (Shelby Cullom Davis Center Ser.). (Illus.). 320p. 1985. text ed. 39.95 (ISBN 0-8122-7948-4). U of Pa Pr.

Rites of Rulers: Ritual in Industrial Society-the Soviet Case. Christel Lane. LC 80-41747. (Illus.). 338p. 1981. 57.50 (ISBN 0-521-22608-2). Cambridge U Pr.

Rites of Sodom: Professor Spender's Strange Adventures in the Mid East. 1988. pap. 4.50 (ISBN 0-8216-5026-2). Blue Moon Bks.

Rites of Spring. Bree Saunders. (American Romance Ser.). 256p. 1983. pap. 2.25 (ISBN 0-373-16043-7). Harlequin Bks.

Rites of Spring: The Great War of the Twentieth Century. Modris Eksteins. 1989. 21.95 (ISBN 0-395-49856-2). HM.

Rites of Strangers. Phyllis Janowitz. Ed. by Walton Beacham. LC 78-16729. (Associated Writing Programs Series for Contemporary Poetry). 68p. 1978. 10.95x (ISBN 0-8139-0797-7). U Pr of Va.

Rites of the Catholic Church, Vol. III. International Commission on English in the Liturgy Staff et al. 600p. (Orig.). 1989. pap. 15.00 (ISBN 0-916134-96-2). Pueblo Pub Co.

Rites of the Catholic Church, Vol. 1. rev. ed. Sacred Congregation for Divine Worship. Tr. by International Committee on English in the Liturgy. 1983. 14.50 (ISBN 0-916134-15-6). Pueblo Pub Co.

Rites of the Catholic Church, Vol. 2. Sacred Congregation for Divine Worship. Tr. by International Commission on English in the Liturgy. 1980. pap. 11.50 (ISBN 0-916134-37-7). Pueblo Pub Co.

Rites of the Catholic Church, Vol. IA: Initiation. International Commission on English in the Liturgy Staff et al. 550p. (Orig.). 1988. pap. 13.50 (ISBN 0-916134-94-6). Pueblo Pub Co.

Rites of the Catholic Church, Vol. IB: Community. International Commission on English in the Liturgy Staff et al. 600p. (Orig.). 1988. pap. 14.00 (ISBN 0-916134-95-4). Pueblo Pub Co.

Rites of the Gods. Aubrey Burl. (Illus.). 272p. 1981. text ed. 26.50x (ISBN 0-460-04313-7, BKA 04660, Pub. by J M Dent England). Biblio Dist.

Ritmos y Melodias. Eliseo Colon. (Lecturas Faciles). 67p. (Span.). 1983. pap. 3.75 (ISBN 0-88345-529-3, 21294). Prentice ESL.

Ritorno Di Columella Da Padova Ossia Il Pazzo Per Amore. Vincenzo Fioravanti. Ed. by Philip Gosset. (Italian Opera Ser., 1810-1840). 85.00 (ISBN 0-8240-6556-5). Garland Pub.

Ritos de Iniciacion: Tres Nouvelas Cortas de Hispanoamerica. Grinor Rojo & Cynthia Steele. LC 85-80939. 224p. (Span.). 1986. pap. text ed. 16.76 (ISBN 0-395-38125-8). HM.

Ritratto Dell'Italia. 2nd ed. Aldo S. Bernardo & Rigo Mignani. 1978. pap. text ed. 23.50 (ISBN 0-669-01157-6). Heath.

Ritsos in Parentheses. Yannis Ritsos. Tr. by Edmund Keeley from Gr. LC 78-70317. (Lockert Library of Poetry in Translation). 1979. 28.50x (ISBN 0-691-06397-4); pap. 9.50 (ISBN 0-691-01358-6). Princeton U Pr.

Rittenhouse Square. Arthur R. Solmssen. LC 68-17265. 313p. 1968. 20.00 (ISBN 0-940846-03-9). Hastings Bks.

Ritter Galmy see Saemtliche Werke.

Ritter, Harlekin und Henker. Juergen Voigt. (European University Studies: No. 1, Vol. 454). 486p. (Ger.). 1982. 31.60 (ISBN 3-8204-5952-9). P Lang Pubs.

Ritter Von Schulthess-Rechberg'sche Munz-U. Medaillen Sammlung. Julius Erbstein & Albert Erbstein. LC 73-92777. 1120p. 1974. Repr. 50.00x (ISBN 0-88000-029-5). Quarterman.

Ritual. Theodore Reik. pap. text ed. 19.95 (ISBN 0-8236-8269-2, 025840). Intl Univs Pr.

Ritual. J. N. Williamson. 320p. 1987. 3.75 (ISBN 0-8439-2539-6). Leisure NY.

Ritual & Belief among the Sa'dan Toraja. Roxana Waterson. (No. 2). i, 73p. (Orig.). 1984. pap. 4.50x (ISBN 0-318-18413-3, Ctr SE Asian Stud). Cellar.

Ritual & Drama: The Medieval Theatre. Francis Edwards. 128p. pap. 17.00 (ISBN 0-7188-2180-7, Pub. by Lutterwrth). Attic Pr.

Ritual & Knowledge among the Baktaman of New Guinea. Fredrik Barth. LC 74-19572. (Illus.). pap. 74.00 (ISBN 0-317-11336-4, 2021979). Bks Demand UMI.

Ritual & Pastoral Care. Elaine Ramshaw. LC 85-45487. (Theology and Pastoral Care Ser.). 128p. 1987. pap. 7.95 (ISBN 0-8006-1738-X). Fortress.

Ritual & Pathos: The Theater of O'Neill. Leonard Chabrowe. (Illus.). 226p. 1976. 20.00 (ISBN 0-8387-1575-3). Bucknell U Pr.

Ritual & Reality. Robert E. Birdsong. (Aquarian Academy Monograph, Series F: Lecture No. 1). 1975. pap. 1.25 (ISBN 0-917108-05-1). Sirius Bks.

Ritual & Reality: Prints of the Nabis. Jeanne Stump et al. LC 79-84066. (Illus.). 1979. pap. 3.00 (ISBN 0-913689-19-X). Spencer Muse Art.

Ritual & Religion among Muslims in India. Ed. by Imtiaz Ahmad. 1982. 20.00x (ISBN 0-8364-0852-7, Pub. by Manohar India). South Asia Bks.

Ritual & Rhetoric. Norman T. Simms. LC 75-35853. 1975. lib. bdg. 50.00 (ISBN 0-8414-7648-9). Folcroft.

Ritual & Symbol: Essays on Lamaism & Chinese Symbolism. Ferdinand D. Lessing. (Asian Folklore & Social Life Monographs: No. 91). (Ger. & Eng.). 1976. 20.00x (ISBN 0-89986-305-1). Oriental Bk Store.

Ritual & Symbol: In Transitional Zaramo Society. Marja-Liisa Swantz. 452p. 1988. pap. 60.00 (ISBN 0-8419-9792-6). Holmes & Meier.

Ritual & Symbol in Transitional Zaramo Society with Special Reference to Women. Marja-Liisa Swantz. (Scandinavian Institute of African Studies). (Illus.). 452p. (Orig.). 1970. pap. text ed. 42.50x (ISBN 91-7106-253-X, Pub. by Nordiska Afrikainstitutet (Uppsala Sweden)). Coronet Bks.

Ritual Art of India. Ajit Mookerjee. (Illus.). 1986. 39.95f (ISBN 0-500-23423-X). Thames Hudson.

Ritual Bath. Faye Kellerman. 1986. 15.95 (ISBN 0-87795-771-1). Morrow.

Ritual Bath. Faye Kellerman. 288p. 1987. pap. 3.95 (ISBN 0-317-58579-7, Crest). Fawcett.

Ritual Book of Magic. Compiled by Clifford Bias. 160p. 1981. pap. 6.95 (ISBN 0-87728-532-2). Weiser.

Ritual Bronzes of Ancient China. Phyllis Ackerman. 114p. 1945. 245.00x (ISBN 0-317-68564-3, Pub. by Han-Shan Tang Ltd). State Mutual Bk.

Ritual Brotherhood in Renaissance Florence. Ronald F. Weissman. LC 81-17536. (Population & Social Structure Advances in Historical Demography Ser.). 1981. 24.95 (ISBN 0-12-744480-7). Acad Pr.

Ritual Conflict at Farlington & Wymering. Nigel Yates. 1978. 42.00x (ISBN 0-317-43733-X, Pub. by City of Portsmouth). State Mutual Bk.

Ritual Cosmos: The Sanctification of Life in African Religions. Evan Zuesse. LC 79-13454. 256p. 1985. pap. 12.95x (ISBN 0-8214-0814-3). Ohio U Pr.

Ritual Dinners in Early Historic Sardis. Crawford H. Greenewalt. LC 76-24474. (University of California Publications: Classical Studies: No. 17). (Illus.). 144p. pap. 37.50 (2029873). Bks Demand UMI.

Ritual Healing in Suburban America. Meredith B. Mcguire & Debra Kantor. 328p. 1988. text ed. 39.00 (ISBN 0-8135-1312-X); pap. text ed. 13.00 (ISBN 0-8135-1313-8). Rutgers U Pr.

Ritual Human Sacrifice in Mesoamerica: A Conference at Dumbarton Oaks, October 13 & 14, 1979. Ed. by Elizabeth H. Boone. LC 83-14059. (Illus.). 256p. 1984. 18.50x (ISBN 0-88402-120-3). Dumbarton Oaks.

Ritual Humor in Highland Chiapas. Victoria R. Bricker. LC 73-6501. (Texas Pan American Ser. & Texas Press Sourcebooks: No. 12). (Illus.). 293p. 1973. 20.00x (ISBN 0-292-77004-9). U of Tex Pr.

Ritual Humor in Highland Chiapas. Victoria R. Bricker. (Texas Pan American Series & Texas Press Sourcebooks in Anthropology: No. 12). (Illus.). 278p. 1983. pap. 8.95 (ISBN 0-292-77029-4). U of Tex Pr.

Ritual in Pueblo Art: Hopi Life in Hopi Painting. Byron Harvey. LC 67-30973. (Illus.). 1970. soft cover 10.00 (ISBN 0-934490-15-5). Mus Am Ind.

Ritual in the Dark. Colin Wilson. 416p. 1982. pap. 5.95 (ISBN 0-586-04391-8). Academy Chi Pubs.

Ritual in the United States: Acts & Representations, SEASA 85 Proceedings, Biennial Convention. Southeastern American Studies Association. Ed. by Don Harkness. LC 85-71824. (Illus.). 60p. (Orig.). 1985. pap. 5.00 (ISBN 0-934996-34-2). American Studies Pr.

Ritual Irony: Poetry & Sacrifice in Euripides. Helene P. Foley. LC 84-17470. 288p. 1985. 29.95x (ISBN 0-8014-1692-2). Cornell U Pr.

Ritual Kinship: Ideological & Structural Integration of the Compadrazgo System in Rural Tlaxcala, Vol. 2. Hugo G. Nutini. LC 79-3225. 520p. 1984. 61.00x (ISBN 0-691-07649-9); pap. 24.50x (ISBN 0-691-10144-2). Princeton U Pr.

Ritual Kinship: The Structure & Historical Development of the Compadrazgo System in Rural Tlaxcala. H. G. Nutini & B. Bell. 444p. 1980. 47.00x (ISBN 0-691-09382-2); pap. 19.50x LPE (ISBN 0-691-10093-4). Princeton U Pr.

Ritual Magic. E. M. Butler. LC 78-73949. 1979. 42.50 (ISBN 0-521-22563-9); pap. 15.95 (ISBN 0-521-29553-X). Cambridge U Pr.

Ritual Magic Workbook. Dolores Ashcroft-Nowicki. 224p. Date not set. pap. 15.50 (ISBN 0-85030-467-9, Pub. by Thorsons UK). Weiser.

Ritual, Myth & Magic in Early Modern Europe. William Monter. LC 83-43136. (Illus.). viii, 184p. 1984. cloth 24.95x (ISBN 0-8214-0762-7). Ohio U Pr.

Ritual of Interpretation: The Fine Arts As Literature in Ruskin, Rossetti, & Pater. Richard L. Stein. LC 74-34540. (Illus.). 384p. 1975. text ed. 27.00x (ISBN 0-674-77313-6). Harvard U Pr.

Ritual of Music. Ed. by Doris H. Cooley. 12p. 1968. pap. text ed. 1.00 (ISBN 0-88053-318-8, S-79). Macoy Pub.

Ritual of Royalty: The Ceremony & Pageantry of Britain's Monarchy. Michele Brown. (Illus.). 178p. 1983. 19.95 (ISBN 0-13-781047-4). P-H.

Ritual of the Mystery of the Judgement of the Soul: From an Ancient Egyptian Papyrus. Ed. & tr. by M. W. Blackden. 1986. pap. 5.95 (ISBN 0-916411-58-3, Pub. by Alexandrian Pr). Holmes Pub.

Ritual of Wind: North American Indian Ceremonies, Music, & Dance. rev. ed. Jamake Highwater. LC 83-80563. (Illus.). 196p. 1983. pap. 14.95 (ISBN 0-912383-02-X). Van der Marck.

Ritual, Politics, & Power. David I. Kertzer. LC 87-16122. 1988. 22.50 (ISBN 0-300-04007-5). Yale U Pr.

Ritual Process: Structure & Anti-Structure. Victor Turner. LC 75-56627. (Paperback Ser.). 224p. 1977. pap. 8.95x (ISBN 0-8014-9163-0). Cornell U Pr.

Ritual Process: Structure & Anti-Structure. Victor W. Turner. LC 67-17612. (Illus.). 1969. lib. bdg. 29.95x (ISBN 0-202-01043-0). Aldine de Gruyter.

Ritual, Religion, & the Sacred. Ed. by Robert Forster & Orest A. Ranum. Tr. by Elborg Forster & Patricia Ranum. LC 81-48184. (Selections from the Annales: No. 7). (Illus.). 256p. 1982. text ed. 27.50x (ISBN 0-8018-2776-0); pap. text ed. 9.95x (ISBN 0-8018-2778-7). Johns Hopkins.

Ritual Songs. James Cody. (Illus., Orig.). 1982. pap. 2.00 (ISBN 0-916908-41-0). Place Herons.

Ritual Structure & Language Structure of the Todas. Murray B. Emeneau. LC 74-84603. (Transactions Ser.: Vol. 64, Pt. 6). 1974. pap. 10.00 (ISBN 0-87169-646-0). Am Philos.

Ritual Vessels of Bronze Age China. Max Loehr. 183p. 1968. 245.00x (ISBN 0-317-69002-7, Pub. by Han-Shan Tang Ltd). State Mutual Bk.

Ritualised Friendship & the Greek State. Gabriel Herman. LC 86-4211. (Illus.). 200p. 1987. 44.50 (ISBN 0-521-32541-2). Cambridge U Pr.

River Mist & Other Stories. Kunikida Doppo. Tr. by David G. Chibbett from Japanese. LC 82-84515. 182p. 1983. 14.95 (ISBN 0-87011-591-X). Kodansha.

River Mist & Other Stories. Kunikida Doppo. Tr. by David Chibbett. 176p. 1985. 49.00x (ISBN 0-904404-40-4, Pub. by Norbury Pubns Ltd). State Mutual Bk.

River Morphology. Stanley A. Schumm. 1982. pap. 45.95 (ISBN 0-87933-001-5). Van Nos Reinhold.

River Navigation in England: 1600-1750. 2nd ed. T. S. Willan. 163p. 1964. 29.50x (ISBN 0-7146-1383-5, F Cass Co). Biblio Dist.

River Networks. R. Jarvis & M. Woldenberg. 1983. 62.95 (ISBN 0-87933-106-2). Van Nos Reinhold.

River Niger. Joseph A. Walker. (Mermaid Dramabook Ser.). 177p. 1973. 7.95 (ISBN 0-8090-8239-X); pap. 5.50 (ISBN 0-8090-1231-6). Hill & Wang.

River, No More: The Colorado River & the West. Philip L. Fradkin. LC 80-2713. (Illus.). 384p. 1981. 15.95 (ISBN 0-394-41579-5). Knopf.

River No More: The Colorado River & the West. Philip L. Fradkin. LC 83-18053. (Illus.). 360p. 1984. pap. 10.95 (ISBN 0-8165-0823-2). U of Ariz Pr.

River Notes. 160p. flexible plastic binding 3.95 (ISBN 0-89886-059-8). Mountaineers.

River Notes: The Dance of the Herons. Barry H. Lopez. LC 79-17192. 1979. 6.95 (ISBN 0-8362-6106-2). Andrews & McMeel.

River Notes: The Dance of the Herons. Barry H. Lopez. 96p. 1980. pap. 3.95 (ISBN 0-380-52514-3, Bard). Avon.

River of Blood. John Mackie. 208p. 1983. pap. 2.50 (ISBN 0-515-07111-0). Jove Pubns.

River of Blood: A Novel. Indira Parthasarthy. 1980. text ed. 10.50x (ISBN 0-7069-0715-9, Pub. by Vikas India). Advent NY.

River of Compassion. Bede Griffiths. (Wellspring Bk.). 224p. (Orig.). pap. 11.95 (ISBN 0-916349-08-X). Amity Hse Inc.

River of Dancing Gods. Jack L. Chalker. 1985. pap. 3.50 (ISBN 0-345-34501-0, Del Rey). Ballantine.

River of Death. Alistair MacLean. 224p. 1984. pap. 4.95 (ISBN 0-449-20684-X, Crest). Fawcett.

River of Death-Song Vam Sat. James Butler. 1979. pap. 1.95 (ISBN 0-87881-089-7). Mojave Bks.

River of Desire. Abra Taylor. (Super Romance Ser.). 1982. pap. 2.50 (ISBN 0-373-70021-0). Harlequin Bks.

River of Dreams. Gay Courter. LC 83-22747. (Illus.). 544p. 1984. 16.95 (ISBN 0-395-35301-7). HM.

River of Dreams. Gay Courter. 592p. 1987. pap. 4.50 (ISBN 0-451-13510-5, Sig). NAL.

River of Earth. James Still. LC 77-92928. 256p. 1978. pap. 7.00 (ISBN 0-8131-1372-5). U Pr of Ky.

River of Eternity. Philip Jose Farmer. 1983. 17.00 (ISBN 0-932096-28-X). Phantasia Pr.

River of Flesh. (S.O.B. Ser.: No. 7). Date not set. pap. 2.50 (Pub. by Worldwide). Harlequin Bks.

River of Fortune: The Passion. Arthur Moore. (Orig.). 1979. pap. 2.50 (ISBN 0-89083-561-6). Zebra.

River of Glass. Wilfred Martens. LC 79-23122. 232p. 1980. pap. 6.95 (ISBN 0-8361-1913-4). Herald Pr.

River of Gold. Date not set. pap. 2.25 (ISBN 0-317-63934-X, Pub. by Worldwide). Harlequin Bks.

River of Golden Sand. William Gill. 1074p. Repr. of 1880 ed. text ed. 165.60x (ISBN 0-576-79201-2, Pub. by Gregg Intl Pubs England). Gregg Intl.

River of Heaven. Garrett Hongo. LC 87-40485. 88p. 1988. 16.95 (ISBN 0-394-56843-5); pap. 8.95 (ISBN 0-394-75785-8). Knopf.

River of Joy. Jack Metzler. (Serenade Super Saga Ser.: No. 4). 288p. (Orig.). 1987. pap. 6.95 (ISBN 0-310-47881-2, 15674P). Zondervan.

River of Life. Subramuniya. pap. 1.00 (ISBN 0-87516-360-2). DeVorss.

River of Life, & Other Stories. facs. ed. Alexander Kuprin. LC 75-75781. (Short Story Index Reprint Ser.). 1916. 18.00 (ISBN 0-8369-3006-1). Ayer Co Pubs.

River of Light. Brenda Peterson. 303p. 1986. pap. 8.00 (ISBN 0-915308-89-4). Graywolf.

River of Light: Monet's Impressions of the Seine. Douglas Skeggs. LC 87-4015. 160p. 1987. 25.00 (ISBN 0-394-56131-7). Knopf.

River of Light: Spirituality, Judaism, & the Evolution of Consciousness. Lawrence Kushner. LC 80-7738. 192p. (Orig.). 1981. pap. 7.95 (ISBN 0-06-064902-X, RD 370, HarpR). Har-Row.

River of Light: Spirituality, Judaism, & the Evolution of Consciousness. Lawrence Kushner. LC 80-7738. 192p. 1981. 12.95 (ISBN 0-940646-00-5). Rossel Bks.

River of Lost Dreams: Navigation on the Rio Grande. Pat Kelley. LC 86-4340. (Illus.). xii, 149p. 1986. 19.95x (ISBN 0-8032-2712-4). U of Nebr Pr.

River of Miracles. G. R. Schoepfer. Ed. by Virginia B. Schoepfer. (Illus.). (gr. 1-11). 1978. pap. text ed. 2.75x (ISBN 0-931436-01-X, Children's Books). G R Schoepfer.

River of Mystery. Jeff Zucker. 120p. (Orig.). 1985. pap. 2.95 (ISBN 0-88120-732-2). SRA.

River of No Return. Cort Conley & John Carrey. LC 78-52373. 1978. pap. 10.95 (ISBN 0-9603566-2-2). Backeddy Bks.

River of Red Wine. Jack Micheline. 60p. 1986. Signed, limited ed. 25.00 (ISBN 0-934953-05-8); pap. 6.95 (ISBN 0-934953-04-X). Water Row Pr.

River of Sorrows: Life History of the Maidu-Nisenan Indians. Richard Burrill. (Illus.). 192p. (Orig.). 1988. 14.95 (ISBN 0-87961-186-3); pap. 8.95 (ISBN 0-87961-187-1). Naturegraph.

River of Swans. Don Coldsmith. (Spanish Bit Saga Ser.: Bk. 10). (Orig.). 1989. pap. 2.95 (ISBN 0-553-27708-1). Bantam.

River of Tears. Charles W. Clark. 64p. 1986. 6.95 (ISBN 0-8062-2964-0). Carlton.

River of the Carolinas: The Santee. Henry Savage, Jr. LC 56-6469. (Illus.). x, 435p. 1968. Repr. of 1956 ed. 16.95 (ISBN 0-8078-1059-2). U of NC Pr.

River of the Long Water. Alma Hetherington. LC 79-92112. (Illus.). 1980. 17.95 (ISBN 0-913122-09-2). Mickler Hse.

River of the West: The Adventures of Joe Meek, Vol. I: The Mountain Years. Frances F. Victor. Ed. by Winfred Blevins. LC 83-11399. (Classics of the Fur Trade Ser.). (Illus.). 288p. 1983. 24.95 (ISBN 0-87842-164-5); pap. 9.95 (ISBN 0-87842-165-3). Mountain Pr.

River of the West: The Adventures of Joe Meek, Vol. II: The Oregon Years. Frances F. Victor. Ed. by Lee Nash. LC 83-11399. (Classics of the Fur Trade Ser.). (Illus.). 382p. 1985. 24.95 (ISBN 0-87842-178-5); pap. 9.95 (ISBN 0-87842-179-3). Mountain Pr.

River of the Wind. Kenn Smith. (Orig.). 1980. pap. text ed. 2.25 (ISBN 0-505-51534-2, Pub. by Tower Bks). Leisure NY.

River of Time. David Brin. (Illus.). 375p. 1986. 18.00 (ISBN 0-913165-11-5). Dark Harvest.

River of Time. David Brin. 304p. (Orig.). 1987. pap. 3.50 (ISBN 0-553-26281-5, Spectra). Bantam.

River of Time see Creation Trilogy.

River of Tomorrow. Dorothy Garlock. 1988. pap. 4.50 (Pub. by Popular Lib). Warner Bks.

River of Wealth, River of Sorrow: The Central Zaire Basin in the Era of the Slave & Ivory Trade, 1500 to 1891. Robert W. Harms. LC 81-1702. (Illus.). 275p. 1981. 32.00x (ISBN 0-300-02616-1). Yale U Pr.

River Painter. Emily Grosholz. LC 83-4875. 96p. 1984. pap. 8.95 (ISBN 0-252-01098-1). U of Ill Pr.

River People: Adventuring with Otters. Philip Wayre. LC 75-33551. (Illus.). 215p. 1976. 9.95 (ISBN 0-8008-6797-1). Taplinger.

River Phoenix: Hero & Heartthrob. Grace Catalano. (YA) (gr. 7 up). 1988. pap. 2.75 (ISBN 0-553-27728-6, Starfire). Bantam.

River Piking. John Sidley. 1987. 24.00 (ISBN 0-85115-466-2, Pub. by Boydell & Brewer). Longwood Pub Group.

River Place. Doug Baker. LC 79-27119. 176p. 1980. pap. 7.95 (ISBN 0-917304-57-8). Timber.

River Plants. S. M. Haslam. LC 76-46857. (Illus.). 1978. 99.00 (ISBN 0-521-21493-9); pap. 29.95x o. p. (ISBN 0-521-29172-0). Cambridge U Pr.

River Plants of Western Europe: The Macrophytic Vegetation of Watercourses of the European Economic Community. S. M. Haslam. 650p. 1987. 125.00 (ISBN 0-521-26427-8). Cambridge U Pr.

River Pollution Control. Ed. by M. J. Stiff. LC 80-49989. 423p. 1980. 129.95x (ISBN 0-470-27004-7). Halsted Pr.

River Pollution Studies. G. A. Best & S. L. Ross. (Illus.). 102p. 1977. pap. text ed. 9.95x (ISBN 0-85323-363-2, Pub. by Liverpool U Pr). Humanities.

River-Quality Assessments: Proceedings of a Symposium Held in Tucson, Arizona, November 2-3, 1977. Ed. by Phillip E. Greeson. LC 79-87721. pap. 49.80 (ISBN 0-317-11245-7, 2017814). Bks Demand UMI.

River Quality in Northern Ireland. 20p. (Orig.). 1987. pap. text ed. 20.00 (ISBN 0-337-08208-1, HBL45, Pub. by Her Maj Station Ofc). UNIPUB.

River Rafting. Cecil Kuhne. LC 78-64389. (Illus.). 144p. 1979. pap. 5.95 (ISBN 0-89037-154-7). Anderson World.

River Rafting in Canada. Richard Harrington. LC 87-1053. (Illus.). 110p. (Orig.). 1987. pap. 14.95 (ISBN 0-88240-323-0). Alaska Northwest.

River Rapture. Kay McMahon. 496p. 1986. pap. 3.95 (ISBN 0-8217-1942-4). Zebra.

River Rat. Hollis C. Powell. 224p. 1982. 10.50 (ISBN 0-682-49891-2, Banner). Exposition-Phoenix.

River Reflections: A Collection of River Writings. Ed. by Verne Huser. (Illus.). 272p. 1988. pap. 12.95 (ISBN 0-87106-673-4). Globe Pequot.

River Reflections: An Anthology. Verne Huser. LC 84-48040. 272p. 1984. 14.95 (ISBN 0-88742-014-1). Globe Pequot.

River Remembers. S. L. Shneiderman. LC 77-93935. (Illus.). 1978. 8.95 (ISBN 0-8180-0821-0). Horizon.

River Rescue. Les Bechdel & Slim Ray. (Illus.). 220p. (Orig.). 1985. pap. 9.95 (ISBN 0-910146-55-1). Appalach Mtn.

River River. Arthur Sze. LC 87-17384. (Lost Roads Ser.: No. 31). 64p. (Orig.). 1987. pap. 7.95 (ISBN 0-918786-35-5). Lost Roads.

River Road. C. F. Borgman. 1988. 18.95 (ISBN 0-453-00612-4). NAL.

River Road. Robert Ferguson. 64p. 1978. 4.00 (ISBN 0-317-14570-3). Truck Pr.

River Road Recipes. Ed. by Junior League of Baton Rouge, Inc. (Illus.). 262p. (Orig.). 1959. pap. 10.95 spiral back (ISBN 0-9613026-0-7); Large Print Edition. 1985 14.00 (ISBN 0-9613026-2-3). Jr League Baton Rouge Inc.

River Road Recipes II: A Second Helping. Ed. by Junior League of Baton Rouge, Inc. (Illus.). 256p. (Orig.). 1976. pap. 10.95 spiral back (ISBN 0-9613026-1-5). Jr League Baton Rouge Inc.

River Roads to Freedom: Fugitive Slave Notices & Sheriff Notices Found in Illinois Sources. Helen C. Tregillis. (Illus.). vi, 122p. (Orig.). 1988. pap. 10.00 (ISBN 1-55613-120-8). Heritage Bk.

River Root: A Suzygy for the Bicentennial of These States. William Everson. 1976. signed ltd. ed. 50.00 (ISBN 0-685-79268-4); pap. 2.50 (ISBN 0-685-79269-2). Oyez.

River Runaways. David Roth. (gr. 5-9). 1981. 7.95 (ISBN 0-395-31678-2). HM.

River Runner's Guide to the History of the Grand Canyon. Kim Crumbo. (Illus.). 96p. (Orig.). 1981. pap. 5.95 (ISBN 0-933472-61-7). Johnson Bks.

River Runners' Guide to Utah & Adjacent Areas. Gary C. Nichols. LC 86-1688. (Bonneville book). (Illus.). 130p. (Orig.). 1986. pap. 14.95 (ISBN 0-87480-254-7). U of Utah Pr.

River Runners of the Grand Canyon. LC 85-70524. (Illus.). 147p. 1985. 12.95 (ISBN 0-938216-23-6). GCNHA.

River Runner's Recipes. Patricia Chambers. LC 83-19644. (Illus.). 132p. 1984. pap. 6.95 (ISBN 0-914718-85-1). Pacific Search.

River Runoff Regulation & Water Management Calculations. P. A Lyapichev. 304p. 1975. text ed. 60.00x (ISBN 0-317-46431-0, Pub. by Keter Pub Jerusalem). Coronet Bks.

River Runs Through It. Norman Maclean. LC 82-23759. (Illus.). 128p. 1983. gift ed. 25.00 (ISBN 0-226-50058-6); deluxe ed. 50.00 o.s.i (ISBN 0-226-50059-4). U of Chicago Pr.

River Runs Through It & Other Stories. Norman Maclean. LC 75-20895. 232p. 1976. 15.00 (ISBN 0-226-50055-1); pap. 7.95 (ISBN 0-226-50057-8, P821, Phoen). U of Chicago Pr.

River Salmon Fishing. Bill Stinson. (Illus.). 147p. 1986. pap. 8.95 (ISBN 0-936608-46-3). F Amato Pubns.

River Sedimentation: Proceedings of the Second International Symposium, 11-16 October, 1983, Nanjing, China, 2 vols. Organizing Committee of the Symposium. 1658p. 1985. Vol. 1. 97.50x (ISBN 0-8133-0253-6); Vol. 2. 97.50x (ISBN 0-8133-0275-7); Set. 140.00x. Westview.

River Syndicate & Other Stories. facsimile ed. Charles E. Carryl. LC 70-106258. (Short Story Index Reprint Ser.). 1899. 18.00 (ISBN 0-8369-3295-1). Ayer Co Pubs.

River Temptress. Myra Rowe. 512p. 1987. pap. 3.95 (ISBN 0-8217-2227-1). Zebra.

River That Flows Uphill: A Journey from the Big Bang to the Big Brain. William H. Calvin. LC 87-381. (Illus.). 544p. 1987. pap. 12.95 (ISBN 0-87156-719-9). Sierra.

River That Gave Gifts. Rev. ed. Margo Humphrey. LC 78-61980. (Fifth World Tales Ser.). (Illus.). (gr. 2-9). 1987. pap. 12.95 (ISBN 0-89239-027-1). Children's Book Pr.

River, the Kettle, & the Bird: A Torah Guide to a Successful Marriage. Aharon Felsman. 1987. 10.95 (ISBN 0-87306-440-2). Feldheim.

River Thrill Sports. Andrew David & Tom Moran. LC 82-24966. (Superwheels & Thrill Sports Bks.). (Illus.). 48p. (gr. 4-9). 1983. PLB 8.95 (ISBN 0-8225-0506-1). Lerner Pubns.

River Through Rivertown. Merrill Gilfillan. 1982. 4.00 (ISBN 0-935724-08-7). Figures.

River Through Time: The Course of Western Civilization. Charles W. Hollister. LC 74-14972. pap. 143.50 (ISBN 0-317-28075-9, 2055765). Bks Demand UMI.

River to River: A Poetric Trilogy, 3 vols. Douglas Messer. Bd. with Dinner on the Lawn; River to River: A Manifesto; Some Distance. 1984. Boxed Set 9.95 (ISBN 0-940650-28-2). Sun & Moon CA.

River Towns of Connecticut: A Study of Wethersfield, Hartford & Windsor. C. M. Andrews. Repr. of 1889 ed. 14.00 (ISBN 0-384-01454-2). Johnson Repr.

River Towns of Connecticut: A Study of Wethersfield, Hartford & Windsor. Charles M. Andrews. LC 78-63790. (Johns Hopkins University. Studies in the Social Sciences. Seventh Ser. 1889: 7-9). Repr. of 1889 ed. 11.50 (ISBN 0-404-61055-2). AMS Pr.

River View & Other Hudson Valley Essays. John Burroughs. LC 81-16945. (Illus.). 224p. 1981. 11.95 (ISBN 0-88427-049-1). North River.

River Volga & Its Life. Ed. by D. Mordukhai-Boltovskoi. (Monographiae Biologicae: No. 33). 1979. lib. bdg. 74.00 (ISBN 90-6193-084-7, Pub. by Junk Pubs Netherlands). Kluwer Academic.

River Wall. Randall Garrett & Vicki A. Heydron. 288p. (Orig.). 1986. pap. 3.50 (ISBN 0-553-25565-7, Spectra). Bantam.

River Water Quality Assessment. (AWWA Handbooks - Proceedings). (Illus.). 112p. 1976. pap. text ed. 7.20 (ISBN 0-89867-048-9). Am Water Wks Assn.

River Water Quality Monitoring. L. W. Canter. LC 84-29702. (Illus.). 230p. 1985. 30.00 (ISBN 0-87371-011-8). Lewis Pubs Inc.

River Why. Duncan. 1985. pap. 7.95 (ISBN 0-553-34486-2, Windstone). Bantam.

River Why. David J. Duncan. LC 82-5508. 320p. (Orig.). 1983. 12.95 (ISBN 0-87156-321-5). Sierra.

River Why. David J. Duncan. 352p. 1984. pap. 7.95 (ISBN 0-553-34192-8). Bantam.

River Winding. new ed. Charlotte Zolotow. LC 77-27670. (Illus.). (gr. 3 up). 1978. 11.70i (ISBN 0-690-03866-6, Crowell Jr Bks); PLB 11.89 (ISBN 0-690-03867-4). HarpJ.

River Witches. Ben Shecter. LC 75-25397. (Illus.). 192p. (gr. 5 up). 1979. PLB 7.89 (ISBN 0-06-025608-7). HarpJ.

River Woman. Mel Donalson. 320p. (Orig.). 1988. pap. 9.95 (ISBN 0-936784-41-5). J Daniel.

River World. Berton Roueche. 246p. 11.95 (ISBN 0-317-27106-7). Yankee Peddler.

River Writing: An Eno Journal. James Applewhite. (Princeton Series of Contemporary Poets). 60p. 1988. text ed. 17.50 (ISBN 0-691-06726-0); pap. text ed. 8.95 (ISBN 0-691-01442-6). Princeton U Pr.

Riverbed. David Wagoner. LC 74-166118. (Poetry Ser.). 80p. 1972. 4.95x (ISBN 0-253-17475-9). Ind U Pr.

Riverbend. V. May. 105p. 1984. 4.25 (ISBN 0-89697-131-7). Intl Univ Pr.

Riverboat Gang. J. R. Roberts. (Gunsmith Ser.: No. 23). 192p. 1985. pap. 2.50 (ISBN 0-441-30881-3). Ace Bks.

Riverboat Queen. Warren T. Longtree. (Ruff Justice Ser.: No. 18). 1985. pap. 2.50 (ISBN 0-451-13412-5, Sig). NAL.

Riverboating in Lower Carolina. F. Roy Johnson. (Illus.). 1977. 9.50 (ISBN 0-930230-32-9). Johnson NC.

Riverdale School Eighteen Eighty-Eight to Nineteen Eighty-Eight. Helen W. Bledsoe. LC 88-70297. (Illus.). 176p. 1988. pap. 17.00 (ISBN 0-8323-0462-X). Binford Metropolitan.

Rivergods: Exploring the World's Great Wild Rivers. Richard Bangs & Christian Kallen. LC 85-2147. (Illus.). 224p. 1985. pap. 18.95 (ISBN 0-87156-773-3). Sierra.

Riverhouse Stories: How Pubah S. Queen & Lazy LaRue Save the World. Andrea Carlisle. LC 86-20783. (Illus.). 125p. (Orig.). 1986. 15.95 (ISBN 0-934971-08-0); pap. 7.95 (ISBN 0-934971-01-3). Calyx Bks.

Riverine: The Brown Water Navy in Vietnam. (Vietnam Studies Group). (Illus.). 64p. 1986. pap. 8.95 (ISBN 0-89747-163-6, 6041). Squad Sig Pubns.

Riverlisp. Frederick Ward. LC 73-76299. 160p. 1974. 12.95 (ISBN 0-88776-024-4). Tundra Bks.

Rivermen. Paul O'Neil. LC 75-7193. (Old West Ser.). (Illus.). (gr. 7 up). 1975. 19.94 (ISBN 0-8094-1498-8, Pub. by Time-Life). Silver.

Rivers. Norman Carlisle & Madelyn Carlisle. LC 81-38448. (New True Bks.). (Illus.). 48p. (gr. k-4). 1982. PLB 12.60 (ISBN 0-516-01645-8). Childrens.

Rivers. Saw Hunter. (Modern Painters Ser). (Illus.). pap. 3.95 (ISBN 0-452-00357-1, #FM, Mer). NAL.

Rivers. Marie Morisawa. (Illus.). pap. text ed. 27.95x (ISBN 0-582-48982-2). Wiley.

Rivers. Geoffrey E. Petts. (Sources & Methods in Geography Ser.). (Illus.). 216p. (Orig.). 1983. pap. text ed. 19.95 (ISBN 0-408-11070-8). Butterworth.

Rivers. Laurence Santrey. LC 84-8818. (Illus.). 32p. (gr. 3-6). 1985. lib. bdg. 8.45 (ISBN 0-8167-0210-1); pap. text ed. 1.95 (ISBN 0-8167-0211-X). Troll Assocs.

Rivers Amazon. Alex Shoumatoff. LC 78-8585. (Club Paperback Library). 256p. 1986. pap. 8.95 (ISBN 0-87156-771-7). Sierra.

Rivers & Lakes. Ronald Bailey. (Planet Earth Ser.). (Illus.). 176p. (YA) (gr. 7 up). 1984. 18.60 (ISBN 0-8094-4508-5); lib. bdg. 22.60. Time-Life.

Rivers & Lakes. Martyn Bromwell. (Earth Science Library). (Illus.). 32p. (gr. 4-8). 1987. lib. bdg. 11.40 (ISBN 0-531-10262-9). Watts.

Rivers & Lakes. Jenny Mulherin. LC 84-51228. (Picture Atlas Ser.). (Illus.). 38p. (gr. 4-6). 1984. PLB 12.40 (ISBN 0-531-04836-5). Watts.

Rivers & Lakes. LC 84-24463. (Planet Earth Ser.). (gr. 7 up). 1985. lib. bdg. 19.94 (ISBN 0-8094-4509-3, Pub. by Time-Life). Silver.

Rivers & Lakes. Theodore Rowland-Entwistle. (Our World Ser.). (Illus.). 48p. (gr. 5-8). 1987. PLB 12.96 (ISBN 0-382-09499-9). Silver.

Rivers & Lakes. Imelda Updegraff & Robert Updegraff. (Turning Points Ser.). (Illus.). (gr. 4 up). PLB 9.95. Creative Ed.

Rivers & Lakes of the North Island: New Zealand Trout Fisherman's Guide. George Ferris. (Illus.). 54p. 1983. pap. 2.95x (ISBN 0-89955-371-0, Pub. by Heinemann Pub New Zealand). Intl Spec Bk.

Rivers & Lakes of the South Island: New Zealand Trout Fisherman's Guide. George Ferris. (Illus.). 46p. 1983. pap. 2.95x (ISBN 0-908592-04-3, Pub. by Heinemann Pub New Zealand). Intl Spec Bk.

Rivers & Mountains. John Ashbery. LC 76-46176. (American Poetry Ser: Vol. 12). 1977. pap. 4.95 (ISBN 0-912946-38-5). Ecco Pr.

Rivers & People. Tom Browne. LC 82-50394. (Nature's Landscape Ser.). 91p. PLB 15.96 (ISBN 0-382-06671-5). Silver.

Road Haulage Licensing & EC Transport Policy. Kenneth Button. LC 84-6112. 127p. 1984. text ed. 32.95x (ISBN 0-566-00702-9). Gower Pub Co.
Road Hogs (for TMNT) Erik Wujcik. Ed. by Alex Marciniszyn. 1986. pap. 6.95 (ISBN 0-916211-20-7, 505). Palladium Bks.
Road Home. Christine Rimmer. (Temptation Ser.: No. 154). 224p. Date not set. pap. 2.25 (ISBN 0-317-63843-2). Harlequin Bks.
Road I Came: Some Recollections & Reflections Concerning Changes in American Life & Manner Since 1890. Paul J. Smith. LC 60-11328. pap. 119.00 (2027150). Bks Demand UMI.
Road I Travel. Susan J. Gordon. 1964. 4.95 (ISBN 0-911566-02-3). Ventnor.
Road in the Dark. Mary Griffith. LC 85-875. 1986. pap. 11.95 (ISBN 0-87949-257-0). Ashley Bks.
Road in Tuscany: A Commentary, 2 vols. Maurice Hewlett. (Illus.). 1985. Repr. of 1904 ed. Set. lib. bdg. 65.00 (ISBN 0-89984-924-5). Century Bookbindery.
Road: Indian Tribes & Political Liberty. Russel L. Barsh & James Y. Henderson. LC 77-91777. 1979. pap. 9.95x (ISBN 0-520-04636-6). U of Cal Pr.
Road Is Everywhere or Stop This Body. Rosmarie Waldrop. LC 77-91130. (Open Places Poets Ser.: No. 5). 1978. pap. 3.00x (ISBN 0-913398-04-7). Open Places.
Road Is For Walking. John R. Terry. 120p. 1988. pap. 4.95 (ISBN 0-933704-40-2). Dawn Pr.
Road Kill: Goremet Cooking. Richard Marcou. (Illus.). 96p. 1987. pap. 7.95 (ISBN 0-9692624-0-X, Prographics Publishing). Publishers Group.
Road Kills. Christopher C. Gilmore. 224p. (Orig.). 1986. pap. 3.50 (ISBN 0-446-34031-6). Warner Bks.
Road Less Traveled. M. Scott Peck. 1980. pap. 9.95 (ISBN 0-671-25067-1, Touchstone Bks). S&S.
Road Less Traveled. Gift ed. M. Scott Peck. 1985. 17.95 (ISBN 0-671-60559-3). S&S.
Road Less Traveled. M. Scott Peck. 320p. 1988. pap. 12.95 flexibind edition (ISBN 0-671-67300-9, Touchstone Bks). S&S.
Road Lighting. W. J. Van Bommel & J. B. DeBoer. (Philips Technical Library). (Illus.). 363p. 1980. text ed. 85.00x (ISBN 0-333-30679-1, Pub. by Macmillan England). Scholium Intl.
Road Maintenance Problem & International Assistance. 71p. (Eng. , Fr. & Span.). 1981. Eng. Ed. 5.00 (ISBN 0-686-36216-0, BK9075); Fr. Ed. avail.; Span. Ed. avail. World Bank.
Road Noise & Sentiments. Moustache Pete. (Illus.). 65p. (Orig.). 1987. pap. 6.95 (ISBN 0-939303-03-5). Educ Lrn Syst.
Road Not Taken. Robert Frost. 16.95 (ISBN 0-8050-0529-3); pap. 9.95 (ISBN 0-8050-0528-5). H Holt & Co.
Road Not Taken: A Selection of Robert Frost's Poems. Ed. by Louis Untermeyer. pap. 8.95 (ISBN 0-03-000073-4). H Holt & Co.
Road Not Taken: The Editorial Opinions of Frederick C. Thorne. Ed. by T. S. Krawiec. 1981. pap. 11.95 (ISBN 0-88422-013-3). Clinical Psych.
Road of Ages. Robert Nathan. 232p. 1986. Repr. of 1935 ed. lib. bdg. 25.00 (ISBN 0-89987-613-7). Darby Bks.
Road of Azrael. Robert E. Howard. 20.00 (ISBN 0-937986-23-2); deluxe ed. 35.00 (ISBN 0-937986-24-0). D M Grant.
Road of Destiny: Darjeeling Letters 1839. Fred Pinn. (Illus.). 310p. 1987. 29.95 (ISBN 0-19-561930-7). Oxford U Pr.
Road of Inquiry: Charles Pierce's Pragmatic Realism. Peter Skagestad. LC 80-25278. 261p. 1981. 35.00x (ISBN 0-231-05004-6). Columbia U Pr.
Road of Life. Ed. by Blaire Meyer et al. (Illus.). 70p. (Orig.). 1987. pap. 5.00 (ISBN 0-9615214-1-4). Barton Cty Comm.
Road of Science & the Ways to God. Stanley L. Jaki. LC 77-21667. viii, 478p. 1980. pap. 17.00x (ISBN 0-226-39145-0, P897). U of Chicago Pr.
Road of Science & the Ways to God. Stanley L. Jaki. LC 77-21667. 1978. lib. bdg. 17.00x. U of Chicago Pr.
Road of the Dashing Commuter. A. J. McNulty. 1980. 6.00 (ISBN 0-682-49564-6). Exposition-Phoenix.
Road of the Sea Horse. Poul Anderson. (Last Viking Ser.: No. 2). 400p. (Orig.). 1980. pap. 2.50 (ISBN 0-89083-610-8). Zebra.
Road of the Sun. Emilie. 32p. 1987. 20.00x (ISBN 0-7223-2143-0, Pub. by A H Stockwell). State Mutual Bk.
Road of the Sun: Travels of the Zodiac King in Near Eastern & European Myth. D. August Hunt. LC 86-80967. (Illus.). 102p. (Orig.). 1988. pap. 15.00X (ISBN 0-911437-40-1). Labyrinthos.
Road Passenger Transport & Road Goods Transport. Denys Munby & A. H. Watson. Ed. by W. F. Manunder. LC 77-30558. 1978. 57.00 (ISBN 0-08-022449-0). Pergamon.
Road Past His Door: Gasquet. Don Chase. (Illus.). 1973. velo-bind 2.50 (ISBN 0-918634-30-X); pap. 2.25 (ISBN 0-918634-37-7). D M Chase.
Road Pricing & Transit Improvement Program in Berkeley, California: A Preliminary Analysis. Melvyn Cheslow. 73p. 1978. pap. 6.00x (ISBN 0-87766-233-9, 22300). Urban Inst.
Road Project Appraisal for Developing Countries. John W. Dickey & Leon H. Miller. LC 83-10270. 279p. 1984. 51.95x (ISBN 0-471-90239-X, Pub. by Wiley-Interscience). Wiley.
Road Racing. Nicole Puleo. LC 72-5417. (Superwheels & Thrill Sports Bks.). (Illus.). 48p. (gr. 4-9). 1973. PLB 8.95 (ISBN 0-8225-0404-9). Lerner Pubns.
Road Racing Technique & Training. Bernard Hinault & Claude Genzling. Ed. by Barbara George. Tr. by Veronica Brelsford & Georges Herzog. 224p. 1988. 16.95 (ISBN 0-941950-13-1). Velo-News.
Road Reports, 1989. Daniel Heraud. (Illus.). 240p. (Orig.). 1988. pap. 12.95 (ISBN 0-8092-4448-9). Contemp Bks.
Road Research: Traffic Measurement Methods for Urban and Suburban Areas. 1979. 8.25 (ISBN 92-64-11939-6). OECD.
Road Retaken: Women Reenter the Academy. Ed. by Irene Thompson & Audrey Roberts. 152p. 1985. 32.00 (ISBN 0-87352-347-0); pap. 17.50x. Modern Lang.
Road Runner: A Source Book. Samuel A. Shields, Jr. (Illus.). 144p. (Orig.). 1983. pap. 12.95 (ISBN 0-934780-20-X). Bookman Pub.
Road Safety at Night. (Road Research Ser.). 112p. 1980. 10.00x (ISBN 92-64-12069-6). OECD.
Road Safety: Research & Practice. Ed. by Hugh Foot et al. LC 81-191962. 244p. 1981. 42.95 (ISBN 0-275-90625-6, C0625). Praeger.
Road Show. William Marshall. 1988. pap. 3.95 (ISBN 0-317-65553-1). Mysterious Pr.
Road Show. Murray Schisgal. 55p. 1987. pap. 3.75. Dramatists Play.
Road Show: A Handbook for Successful Booking & Touring in the Performing Arts. Rena Shagan. LC 84-20491. (Illus.). 288p. (Orig.). 1985. pap. 14.95 (ISBN 0-915400-48-0). Am Council Arts.
Road Surface Characteristics: Their Interaction & Their Optimisation. OECD Staff. (Road Transport Research Ser.). 206p. 1984. pap. 19.00 (ISBN 92-64-12563-9). OECD.
Road Tank Vehicle Workshop Code. Institute of Petroleum. 1980. pap. 21.95x (ISBN 0-471-25799-0, Wiley Heyden). Wiley.
Road Tank Wagon Design Notes. Institute of Petroleum. 1980. 21.95x (ISBN 0-471-25798-2, Wiley Heyden). Wiley.
Road That Bends. Ruby M. Ayres. 1975. lib. bdg. 15.80x (ISBN 0-89966-004-5). Buccaneer Bks.
Road Through Kurdistan. Archibald M. Hamilton. LC 70-180345. Repr. of 1937 ed. 26.00 (ISBN 0-404-56275-2). AMS Pr.
Road Through the Isles. John Sharkey & Keith Payne. 256p. 1986. text ed. 29.95 (ISBN 0-7045-0498-7, Pub. by Gower Pub England). Gower Pub Co.
Road to Appomattox. Bell I. Wiley. LC 68-9470. (Illus.). 1968. pap. text ed. 5.95x (ISBN 0-689-70210-8, 136). Atheneum.
Road to Armageddon: The Martial Spirit in English Popular Literature, 1870-1914. Cecil B. Eby. ix, 280p. 1988. lib. bdg. 27.50 (ISBN 0-8223-0775-8). Duke.
Road to Avalon. Joan Wolf. LC 88-1773. 400p. 1988. 18.95 (ISBN 0-453-00607-8). NAL.
Road to Balumnia. James P. Blaylock. (Orig.). Date not set. pap. price not set (ISBN 0-345-32888-4, Del Ray). Ballantine.
Road to Bellapais: The Turkish Cypriot Exodus to Northern Cyprus. Pierre Oberling. (Brooklyn College Studies on Society in Change). 256p. 1982. 28.00x (ISBN 0-88033-000-7). East Eur Quarterly.
Road to Berlin: Continuing the History of Stalin's War with Germany. John Erickson. (Illus.). 700p. 1983. 59.00x (ISBN 0-89158-795-0). Westview.
Road to Bethlehem: An Ethiopian Nativity. Adapted by Elizabeth Laird. LC 87-45112. (Illus.). 32p. (gr. 1-5). 1987. 12.95 (ISBN 0-8050-0539-0). H Holt & Co.
Road to Birth Game. Julie Burns & Frank Bialosiewicz. (Technical Note Ser.: No. 24). (Illus.). 33p. (Orig.). 1983. pap. text ed. 2.00 (ISBN 0-932288-71-5). Ctr Intl Ed U of Ma.
Road to Black Mountain. Joseph Bruchac. LC 76-28248. (Orig.). 1976. pap. 4.00x (ISBN 0-914476-45-9). Thorp Springs.
Road to Bloody Sunday. Raymond McClean. (Illus.). 189p. 1983. pap. 8.95 (ISBN 0-907085-63-6, Pub. by Ward River Pr Ireland). Irish Bks Media.
Road to Bloody Sunday: Father Gapon & the Petersburg Massacre of 1905. Walter Sablinsky. LC 75-30206. (Studies of the Russian Institute, Columbia). 1976. 50.00x (ISBN 0-691-05233-6); 16.50x (ISBN 0-691-10204-X). Princeton U Pr.
Road to Botany Bay: An Exploration of Landscape & History. Paul Carter. LC 87-46076. 1988. 22.95 (ISBN 0-394-57035-9). Knopf.
Road to Bristoe Station Campaigning with Lee & Meade, August 1-October 20, 1863. William D. Henderson. (Illus.). 259p. 1987. 16.95 (ISBN 0-930919-45-9). H E Howard.
Road to Buenos Aires. Albert Londres. 260p. 1974. lib. bdg. 59.95 (ISBN 0-8490-0959-6). Gordon Pr.
Road to Camlann: The Death of King Arthur. Rosemary Sutcliff. (Illus.). 144p. (gr. 4-7). 1982. 14.95 (ISBN 0-525-44018-6). Dutton.
Road to Canaan. Pernet Patterson. 14.00 (ISBN 0-8369-9193-1, 9062). Ayer Co Pubs.
Road to Cibola. Carl O. Sauer. LC 76-43819. (Ibero-Americana Ser.: 3). Repr. of 1932 ed. 14.50 (ISBN 0-404-15669-X). AMS Pr.
Road to Confederation: The Emergence of Canada, 1863-1867. Donald G. Creighton. LC 75-27652. (Illus.). 1976. Repr. of 1965 ed. lib. bdg. 29.75x (ISBN 0-8371-8435-5, CRRC). Greenwood.
Road to Confrontation: American Policy Toward China & Korea, 1947 - 1950. William W. Stueck, Jr. LC 80-11818. (Illus.). ix, 326p. 1981. 25.00x (ISBN 0-8078-1445-8); pap. 10.95x (ISBN 0-8078-4080-7). U of NC Pr.
Road to Corinth. Alan L. Steinberg. (Orig.). 1984. pap. 5.00 (ISBN 0-88734-211-6). Players Pr.
Road to Corlay. Richard Cowper. 1986. pap. 2.95 (ISBN 0-671-61213-1, Timescape). PB.
Road to Crisis: An Analysis of Water Problems & Institutional Responses, 2 pts. Incl. Pt. I-Water Policy Search; Pt. II-Water Paper. 1983. Set 9.00 (ISBN 0-317-03318-2). Tech Info Proj.
Road to Damascus. Ralph Carnes & Valerie Carnes. 336p. 1986. 16.95 (ISBN 0-312-68517-3, Thomas Dunne Bks). St Martin.
Road to Damascus. Wyatt T. Walker. 163p. 1985. 10.00 (ISBN 0-937644-03-X). M L King Pr.
Road to Damietta. Scott O'Dell. 256p. (gr. 6 up). 1985. 14.95 (ISBN 0-395-38923-2). HM.
Road to Damietta. Scott O'Dell. 240p. 1987. pap. 2.50 (ISBN 0-449-70233-2, Juniper). Fawcett.
Road to Daulis: Psychoanalysis, Psychology & Classical Mythology. Robert Eisner. 284p. 1987. 32.50 (ISBN 0-8156-0210-3). Syracuse U Pr.
Road to Daybreak: A Spiritual Journey. Henri J. Nouwen. 1988. 15.95 (ISBN 0-385-24553-X). Doubleday.
Road to Deadman Cove Selected Poems. George Anthony. LC 77-91127. (Open Places Poets Ser.: No. 4). 1978. 7.00x (ISBN 0-913398-03-9). Open Places.
Road to Dictatorship: Germany Nineteen Eighteen - Nineteen Thirty-Three. Theodor Eschenburg et al. Tr. by Lawrence Wilson from Ger. 174p. (Orig.). 1964. pap. 10.95 (ISBN 0-85496-117-8, Pub. by Berg Pubs). St Martin.
Road to Disappearance: A History of the Creek Indians. Angie Debo. (CAI Ser.). (Orig.). 1984. pap. 12.95 (ISBN 0-8061-1532-7). U of Okla Pr.
Road to Disunity. Howard J. Schwach. (Foundations in History: Bk. 2). (gr. 7-12). 1979. pap. text ed. 4.95 (ISBN 0-86703-007-0); 7.35 (ISBN 0-86703-006-2). Opportunities Learn.
Road to Ein Harod. Amos Kenan. Tr. by Anselm Hollo. 112p. 1988. 15.95 (ISBN 0-8021-1083-5). Grove.
Road to El-Aguzein. M. V. Seton-Williams. (Illus.). 220p. 1988. text ed. 29.95 (ISBN 0-7103-0286-X). Routledge Chapman & Hall.
Road to Europe. Ferdinand Oyono. Tr. by Richard Bjornson from Fr. LC 86-51301. 120p. (Orig.). 1988. 24.00 (ISBN 0-89410-590-6); pap. 10.00 (ISBN 0-89410-591-4). Three Continents.
Road to Extinction: Problems of Categorizing the Status of Taxa Threatened with Extinction - Proceedings of a Symposium Held by the Species Survival Commission of IUCN in Madrid, November, 1984. Richard Fitter & Maisie Fitter. (International Union for the Conservation of Nature & Natural Resources: A Belhaven Press Bk.). (Illus.). 132p. 1987. pap. 12.50x (ISBN 2-88032-929-9, Pub. by Pinter Pubs UK). Columbia U Pr.
Road to France: The Transportation of Troops & Military Supplies, 1917-1918, 2 vols. in one. Benedict Crowell & Robert F. Wilson. LC 74-75238. (United States in World War 1 Ser). (Illus.). xv, 675p. 1974. Repr. of 1921 ed. lib. bdg. 46.95x (ISBN 0-89198-100-4). Ozer.
Road to Freedom. Geo Milev. Tr. by Ewald Osers from Bulgarian. (Illus.). 96p. 1988. pap. 14.00 (Pub. by Forest Bks London). Three Continents.
Road to Freedom. Lev S. Pinsker. LC 70-162734. 142p. 1975. Repr. of 1944 ed. lib. bdg. 35.00x (ISBN 0-8371-6195-9, PIRF). Greenwood.
Road to Freedom, Vols. 1-8, No. 10. Repr. of 1924 ed. Vol. 1, No. 1-4. lib. bdg. 92.00 (ISBN 0-8371-3673-3, RF01); Vol. 2, No. 5-8. lib. bdg. 92.00 (ISBN 0-8371-3674-1, RF02). Greenwood.
Road to Freedom: Revealing Sidelights. Ram Chandra. 362p. 1980. 29.95x; lib. bdg. 29.95x (ISBN 0-686-92327-8). Asia Bk Corp.
Road to Freedom: 1815-1900. James McCague. LC 72-75074. (Toward Freedom Ser.). (gr. 5-9). 1972. PLB 3.98 (ISBN 0-8116-4803-6). Garrard.
Road to Full Employment. Sean Glynn & Alan Booth. 220p. 1987. text ed. 34.95x (ISBN 0-04-330360-9); pap. text ed. 14.95x (ISBN 0-04-330361-7). Unwin Hyman.
Road to Full Employment. Dewey B. Larson. LC 75-44558. 1976. 8.50 (ISBN 0-913138-06-1). North Pacific.
Road to Full Employment: An Essay on Regulation, Deregulation, Enterprise Zones & the Productibility of Jobs. Anton J. Butter. 108p. (Orig.). 1982. pap. 13.00x (ISBN 90-6032-239-8, Pub. by B R Gruner Netherlands). Benjamins North Am.
Road to Galveston. Beatrice S. Smith. LC 72-7657. (Books for Adults & Young Adults). (Illus.). (gr. 4 up). 1973. PLB 6.95 (ISBN 0-8225-0755-2). Lerner Pubns.
Road to Gandolfo. Robert Ludlum. 1982. pap. 4.95 (ISBN 0-553-26081-2). Bantam.
Road to Great Victory. V. Sipols. 324p. 1985. 8.95 (ISBN 0-8285-3033-5, Pub. by Progress Pubs USSR). Imported Pubns.
Road to Haworth. John Cannon. 1981. 11.95 (ISBN 0-670-60079-2). Brown Bk.
Road to Hell. Larry Incollingo. 175p. 1987. pap. 8.95 (ISBN 0-9619795-0-X). Incollingo.
Road to Hillsborough: The Shaping of the Anglo-Irish Agreement. A. Kenny. LC 86-21259. 152p. 1986. (PBL); pap. text ed. 12.75 (ISBN 0-08-034248-5, PBL). Pergamon.
Road to India: Guide to the Overland Routes to India. John Prendergast. (Illus.). 1978. 19.50 (ISBN 0-7195-3396-1). Transatl Arts.
Road to Infinity. Isaac Asimov. 256p. 1981. pap. 2.75 (ISBN 0-380-54155-6, 54155-6, Discus). Avon.
Road to Intervention: March - November 1918. Michael Kettle. 512p. 1988. lib. bdg. 49.95 (ISBN 0-415-00371-7). Routledge Chapman & Hall.
Road to Jaramillo: Critical Years of the Revolution in Earth Science. William Glen. LC 80-51647. (Illus.). xvi, 459p. 1982. 40.00x (ISBN 0-8047-1119-4). Stanford U Pr.
Road to Justice. Alfred Denning. (Legal Reprint Ser.). viii, 118p. 1988. Repr. of 1955 ed. lib. bdg. 22.50x (ISBN 0-8377-2034-6). Rothman.
Road to Kabul: The Second Afghan War, 1878-1881. Brian Robson. (Illus.). 320p. 1987. 39.95 (ISBN 0-85368-719-6, Pub. by Arms & Armour). Sterling.
Road to Kadesh: A Historical Interpretation of the Battle Reliefs of King Sety I at Karnak. William J. Murnane. LC 84-62072. (Studies in Ancient Oriental Civilization: No. 42). (Illus.). 1985. pap. 20.00 (ISBN 0-918986-43-5). Oriental Inst.
Road to Khartoum: Life of General Charles Gordon. Charles C. Trench. 289p. 1988. 18.95 (ISBN 0-88029-152-4). Dorset Pr.
Road to Kitty Hawk. Valerie Moolman. LC 79-21943. (Epic of Flight Ser.). (gr. 7 up). lib. bdg. 21.27 (ISBN 0-8094-3259-5, Pub. by Time-Life). Silver.
Road to Kitty Hawk. Valerie Moolman. Ed. by Time-Life Books. (Epic of Flight Ser.). (Illus.). 176p. 1980. 14.95 (ISBN 0-8094-3258-7). Time-Life.
Road to Komatsubara: A Classical Reading of the Renga Hyakuin. Steven D. Carter. LC 87-15713. (Harvard East Asian Monographs: No. 124). 311p. 1986. text ed. 21.00x (ISBN 0-674-77385-3). Harvard U Pr.
Road to Kona Never Ends: The Endurance Athlete-Deeper Dimensions. Patrick W. McCary. Ed. by Libby James & Diane McCary. 224p. (Orig.). 1986. pap. 8.95 (ISBN 0-9616954-0-4). Sports Psych Pubns.
Road to Lagoa Santa. Henrik Stangerup. Tr. by Barbara Bluestone from Danish. 288p. 1984. 14.95 (ISBN 0-7145-2797-1, Dist. by Kampmann & Co.). M Boyars Pubs.
Road to Life, 2 vols. A. S. Makarenko. 828p. 1973. 8.95 (ISBN 0-8285-0427-X, Pub. by Progress Pubs USSR). Imported Pubns.
Road to Los Angeles. John Fante. LC 85-15098. 167p. (Orig.). 1985. 17.50 (ISBN 0-87685-650-4); pap. 10.00 (ISBN 0-87685-649-0). Black Sparrow.
Road to Manhood: The Male Adolescent's Guide to Survival in a Disorderly & Dangerous Age. Ralph Costello. LC 83-91230. 60p. 1983. pap. 4.95 (ISBN 0-9612900-0-5). R H Costello.
Road to Mawab & Other Stories. Leoncio P. Deriada. 160p. (Orig.). 1984. pap. 8.75x (ISBN 971-10-0084-9, Pub. by New Day Philippines). Cellar.
Road to Mecca. Muhammad Asad. 380p. (Orig.). 1981. 14.95 (ISBN 0-317-52460-7, Pub. by Dar Al Andalus). New Era Pubns MI.
Road to Mecca. Athol Fugard. LC 88-2110. 88p. 1988. 14.95 (ISBN 0-930452-78-X); pap. 6.95 (ISBN 0-930452-79-8). Theatre Comm.
Road to Miklagard. Henry Treece. LC 57-12280. (Illus.). (gr. 6-10). 1957. 14.95 (ISBN 0-87599-118-1). S G Phillips.
Road to Mingulay. Derek Cooper. (Illus.). 224p. 1985. 25.00 (ISBN 0-317-30921-8). Routledge Chapman & Hall.
Road to Mobocracy: Popular Disorder in New York City, 1763-1834. Paul A. Gilje. LC 86-30852. (Illus.). xviii, 316p. 1987. 32.50x (ISBN 0-8078-1743-0, Published for the Institute of Early American History & Culture, Williamsburg, VA); pap. 9.95x (ISBN 0-8078-4198-6). U of NC Pr.
Road to Modern Music. Paul Emerich. 1960. pap. 4.00 (ISBN 0-318-19426-0, 61037-940). Peer-Southern.
Road to Music. Nicolas Slonimsky. LC 79-14882. (Music Reprint Ser.). 1979. Repr. of 1966 ed. lib. bdg. 27.50 (ISBN 0-306-79566-3). Da Capo.
Road to Nazareth: Through Palestine Today. John Gibbons. LC 77-180339. Repr. of 1936 ed. 26.00 (ISBN 0-404-56264-7). AMS Pr.
Road to New York: The Emigration of Berlin Journalists 1933-1945. 2nd ed. Michael Gorth. x, 384p. 1988. 60.00 (ISBN 3-598-10782-X). K G Saur.
Road to Nineteen Eighty-Four. Willis Hall. Date not set. write for info. S&S.
Road to Normalcy: The Presidential Campaign & Election of 1920. Wesley M. Bagby. LC 78-64237. (Johns Hopkins University. Studies in the Social Sciences. Eightieth Ser. 1962: 1). Repr. of 1962 ed. 11.50 (ISBN 0-404-61342-X). AMS Pr.

Road to Normalcy: The Presidential Campaign & the Election of 1920. Wesley M. Bagby. (Johns Hopkins University, Studies in Historical & Political Science: Ser. 80, No. 1). pap. 52.00 (ISBN 0-317-39641-2, 2023108). Bks Demand UMI.

Road to Now. John Moffitt. LC 82-4650. 176p. 1982. pap. 7.95 (ISBN 0-8245-0514-X). Crossroad NY.

Road to Nowhere see Heinemann Guided Readers.

Road to Nunavut: The Progress of the Eastern Arctic Inuit since the Second World War. R. Quinn Duffy. 376p. 1987. 35.00x (ISBN 0-7735-0619-5). McGill-Queens U Pr.

Road to Olmutz: The Political Career of Joseph Maria Von Radowitz. Warren B. Morris. 1975. lib. bdg. 69.95 (ISBN 0-87700-230-4). Revisionist Pr.

Road to OPEC: United States Relations with Venezuela, 1919-1976. Stephen G. Rabe. (Texas Pan American Ser.). 272p. 1982. text ed. 27.50x (ISBN 0-292-76020-5). U of Tex Pr.

Road to Oregon. William J. Ghent. LC 77-111787. (BCL Ser.: I). (Illus.). Repr. of 1929 ed. 22.00 (ISBN 0-404-02717-2). AMS Pr.

Road to Oregon: A Chronicle of the Great Emigrant Trail. William J. Ghent. (Illus.). 1971. Repr. of 1929 ed. 19.00x (ISBN 0-403-00987-1). Scholarly.

Road to Oregon: A Chronicle of the Great Emigrant Trail. William J. Ghent. 1988. Repr. of 1929 ed. lib. bdg. 49.00x. Am Biog Serv.

Road to Osambre. John Ridgway. Date not set. pap. price not set (ISBN 0-14-010039-3). Penguin.

Road to Osambre. John Ridgway. 237p. 1987. 18.95 (ISBN 0-670-81650-7). Viking.

Road to Oxiana. Robert Byron. (Illus.). 1982. pap. 8.95 (ISBN 0-19-503067-2). Oxford U Pr.

Road to Oz. L. Frank Baum. LC 79-88480. 1984. pap. 2.95. Ballantine.

Road to Oz. L. Frank Baum. 272p. 1986. pap. 4.95 (ISBN 0-486-25208-6). Dover.

Road to Oz. L. Frank Baum. 15.00 (ISBN 0-8446-6250-X). Peter Smith.

Road to Paradise Island. Victoria Holt. 1986. pap. 4.50 (ISBN 0-449-20888-5, Pub. by Crest). Fawcett.

Road to Paradise Island. Victoria Holt. (General Ser.). 648p. 1986. lib. bdg. 19.95 (ISBN 0-8161-4054-5, Large Print Bks). G K Hall.

Road to Peace. facsimile ed. James J. Daly. LC 78-107691. (Essay Index Reprint Ser.). 1936. 17.00 (ISBN 0-8369-1495-3). Ayer Co Pubs.

Road to Pearl Harbor. Herbert Feis. 1950. pap. 14.95 (ISBN 0-691-01061-7). Princeton U Pr.

Road to Readability: Basics of Writing & Editing. Digby Whitman. 72p. (Orig.). 1984. pap. text ed. 11.95 (ISBN 0-931368-17-0). Ragan Comm.

Road to Realism: The Early Years 1837-1886 of William Dean Howells. Edwin H. Cady. LC 86-4633. 293p. 1986. Repr. of 1956 ed. lib. bdg. 52.50x (ISBN 0-313-25206-8, CARO). Greenwood.

Road to Reality: The Spiritual Path for Everyone. Ed. by Iris M. Turner. 124p. 1986. 29.00x (ISBN 0-7212-0732-4, Pub. by Regency Pr). State Mutual Bk.

Road to Rebellion: Class Formation & Kansas Populism 1865-1900. Scott G. McNall. (Illus.). xviii, 354p. 1988. 49.95x (ISBN 0-226-56126-7); pap. 19.95x (ISBN 0-226-56127-5). U of Chicago Pr.

Road to Redemption: Southern Politics, 1869-1879. Michael Perman. LC 83-12498. (Fred W. Morrison Series in Southern Studies). xiv, 353p. 1985. 32.50x (ISBN 0-8078-1526-8); pap. 8.95x (ISBN 0-8078-4141-2). U of NC Pr.

Road to Reno: A History of Divorce in the United States. Nelson M. Blake. 1977. Repr. of 1962 ed. lib. bdg. 66.50x (ISBN 0-8371-9797-X, BLRR). Greenwood.

Road to Respectability: James A. Garfield & His World, 1844-1852. Booraem V. Hendrik. LC 86-50895. (Illus.). 304p. 1988. 37.50x (ISBN 0-8387-5135-0). Bucknell U Pr.

Road to Revolution. Avrahm Yarmolinsky. (Illus.). 400p. 1986. text ed. 42.00x (ISBN 0-691-05478-9); pap. text ed. 9.95x (ISBN 0-691-00809-4). Princeton U Pr.

Road to Revolution: Benjamin Franklin in England 1765-1775. Cecil B. Currey. (Illus.). 13.25 (ISBN 0-8446-1931-0). Peter Smith.

Road to Revolution, German Marxism & World War 1. John W. Mishark. 15.00 (ISBN 0-685-16805-0). Moira.

Road to Revolution in Spain: The Coal Miners of Asturias, 1860-1934. Adrian Shubert. LC 86-24998. (Working Class in European History Ser.). (Illus.). 205p. 1988. 22.95 (ISBN 0-252-01368-9). U of Ill Pr.

Road to Revolution: Scotland under Charles I, 1625-37. Maurice Lee, Jr. LC 84-8750. 276p. 1985. 21.95 (ISBN 0-252-01136-8). U of Ill Pr.

Road to Romance. Hope Jordan. (YA) (gr. 7 up). 1982. 9.95 (ISBN 0-686-84749-0, Avalon). Bouregy.

Road to Rome. Conrad R. Stein. LC 82-17853. (World at War Ser.). (Illus.). 48p. (gr. 4-7). 1984. pap. 7.45 (ISBN 0-516-04772-8). Childrens.

Road to Ruin. Thomas Holcroft. Ed. by Ruth I. Aldrich. LC 68-18245. xx, 136p. 1968. 13.95x (ISBN 0-8032-0074-9). U of Nebr Pr.

Road to Rydal Mount: A Survey of William Wordsworth's Reading. Ronald B. Hearn. Ed. by James Hogg. (Romantic Reassessment Ser.). 300p. (Orig.). 1973. pap. 15.00 (ISBN 0-317-40090-8, Pub. by Salzburg Studies). Longwood Pub Group.

Road to Salem. Ed. by Adelaide L. Fries. LC 44-2329. x, 316p. 1988. pap. 14.95 (ISBN 0-8078-4213-3). U of NC Pr.

Road to Salvation. A. A. Maududi. pap. 1.00 (ISBN 0-686-18583-8). Kazi Pubns.

Road to Sampo & Other Korean Short Stories. Hwang Sok-yong et al. Ed. by The Korean National Commission for UNESCO. Tr. by B. McHale et al from Korean. (Modern Korean Short Stories Ser.: No. 9). viii, 237p. 1983. 20.00 (ISBN 0-89209-210-6). Pace Intl Res.

Road to San Jacinto. L. L. Foreman. 1977. pap. 1.25 (ISBN 0-505-51117-7, Pub. by Tower Bks). Leisure NY.

Road to San Luis Rey. Thelma H. Jones. LC 73-87882. (Illus.). (gr. 7-12). 1974. text ed. 5.00 (ISBN 0-912472-18-9). Miller Bks.

Road to Science Fiction, No. 3. Ed. by James Gunn. (Orig.). 1979. pap. 4.95 (ISBN 0-451-62427-0, ME1910, Ment). NAL.

Road to Sedan: The French Army 1866-1870, No. 41. Richard Holmes. (Royal Historical Society Ser.). 272p. 1984. 38.00 (ISBN 0-901050-95-4, Pub. by Boydell & Brewer). Longwood Pub Group.

Road to Self Knowledge. Rudolf Steiner. 1975. 10.95 (ISBN 0-85440-290-X, Pub by Steinerbooks); pap. 6.95 o. p. (ISBN 0-85440-291-8). Anthroposophic.

Road to Self-Rule: A Study in Colonial Evolution. facsimile ed. William M. Macmillan. LC 77-140365. (Select Bibliographies Repirnt Ser). Repr. of 1959 ed. 19.00 (ISBN 0-8369-5608-7). Ayer Co Pubs.

Road to Serfdom. Friedrich A. Hayek. 1944. 12.50x (ISBN 0-226-32077-4). U of Chicago Pr.

Road to Serfdom. Friedrich A. Hayek. 1956. pap. 8.95 (ISBN 0-226-32078-2, P4, Phoen). U of Chicago Pr.

Road to Shiloh. David Miller. (Civil War Ser.). (Illus.). 176p. 1983. 14.95 (ISBN 0-8094-4712-6). Time Life.

Road to Shiloh. D. Nevin. LC 83-4692. (Civil War Ser.). (gr. 7 up). 1983. lib. bdg. 19.94 (ISBN 0-8094-4717-7, Pub. by Time Life). Silver.

Road to Solvency. Rudiges Dornbusch. (Report of the Twentieth Century Fund Task Force on International Debt Ser.). (Orig.). 1988. text ed. 18.95x (ISBN 0-87078-228-2); pap. 9.95 (ISBN 0-87078-227-4). Priority Pr Pubns.

Road to Solvency: Report of the Twentieth Century Fund Task Force on International Debt. Rudiger Dornbusch. (Orig.). 1988. pap. text ed. 18.95x; pap. 9.95. Priority PR Pubns.

Road to Spindletop: Economic Change in Texas, 1875-1901. John S. Spratt. LC 55-8782. (Texas History Ser.). 367p. 1983. pap. 9.95 (ISBN 0-292-70030-X). U Of Tex Pr.

Road to Stalingrad. John Erickson. 604p. 1983. 55.00x (ISBN 0-86531-744-5). Westview.

Road to Stratford. Michael O'Donovan. Repr. of 1948 ed. 29.00x (ISBN 0-403-04239-9). Somerset Pub.

Road to Stratford. Michael O'Donovan. 1988. Repr. of 1948 ed. lib. bdg. 39.00x. Am Biog Serv.

Road to Syndication. W. H. Thomas. pap. 5.00 (ISBN 0-8303-0066-X). Fleet.

Road to Tamazunchale. Ron Arias. LC 86-70700. (United States Hispanic Creative Literature Ser.). (Illus.). 134p. 1987. pap. 9.00X (ISBN 0-916950-70-0). Biling Rev-Pr.

Road to the Isles. Ed. by L. M. Smith. 1983. 59.00x (ISBN 0-86334-002-4, Pub. by Macdonald Pub UK). State Mutual Bk.

Road to the Land of R. 2nd ed. Cameron Garbut. 48p. 1988. 2.95x (ISBN 0-8134-2808-4). Inter Print Pubs.

Road to the Land of S. Cameron W. Garbutt. (Illus.). 1969. pap. text ed. 2.95x (ISBN 0-8134-1116-5, 1116). Inter Print Pubs.

Road to the Land of TH. Cameron W. Garbutt. (Illus.). 48p. 1971. pap. text ed. 2.95x (ISBN 0-8134-1324-9, 1324). Inter Print Pubs.

Road to the Law. Dudley C. Lunt. 1962. pap. 1.65x (ISBN 0-393-00183-0, Norton Lib). Norton.

Road to the Military Courthouse. 2nd ed. 19p. 1981. pap. 1.50 (ISBN 0-686-48176-3). Amer Bar Assn.

Road to the Road to the Isles. Picton Publishing Staff. 1987. 7.00x (Pub. by Picton UK). State Mutual Bk.

Road to the Somme: Men of the Ulster Division Tell Their Story. Phillip Orr. 256p. 1987. pap. 22.95 (ISBN 0-85640-390-3, Pub. by Blackstaff Ireland). Irish Bks Media.

Road to the Stars. Robert E. Vardeman. LC 87-45307. 224p. (YA) (gr. 7 up). 1988. 13.70i (ISBN 0-06-026288-5); PLB 13.89 (ISBN 0-06-026289-3). HarpJ.

Road to the White House: The Politics of Presidential Elections. 3rd ed. Stephen J. Wayne. LC 87-60555. 336p. 1987. pap. text ed. write for info. (ISBN 0-312-00319-6). St Martin.

Road to Tokyo. Keith Wheeler. LC 79-810. (World War II Ser.). lib. bdg. 22.60 (ISBN 0-8094-2539-4, Pub. by Time-Life). Silver.

Road to Tokyo. Keith Wheeler. Ed. by Time-Life Books. (World War Two Ser.). 1980. 14.95 (ISBN 0-8094-2538-6). Time-Life.

Road to Total Freedom. Roy Wallis. LC 76-27273. 1977. 35.00x (ISBN 0-231-04200-0). Columbia U Pr.

Road to Trillion Dollar Energy Savings: A Safe Energy Platform. Intro. by Michael Totten. (Illus.). 84p. 1984. 25.00 (ISBN 0-937188-15-8); pap. 5.00 saddle stitched (ISBN 0-317-11381-X). Pub Citizen Inc.

Road to Trinity. K. D. Nichols. LC 87-1718. (Illus.). 384p. 1987. 19.95 (ISBN 0-688-06910-X). Morrow.

Road to Tryermaine: A Study of the History, Background & Purposes of Coleridge's "Christabel". Arthur H. Nethercot. LC 77-13736. 1978. Repr. of 1962 ed. lib. bdg. 35.00x (ISBN 0-313-20001-7, NERT). Greenwood.

Road to Understanding. Eleanor H. Porter. 1976. lib. bdg. 16.75x (ISBN 0-89968-108-5). Lightyear.

Road to Vichy, 1918-1938. rev. ed. Yves R. Simon. Tr. by James A. Corbett & George J. McMorrow. 246p. 1988. pap. text ed. 12.75 (ISBN 0-8191-6796-7). U Pr of Amer.

Road to Wholeness. Laura Mathis. 240p. 1986. pap. 6.95 (ISBN 0-8423-5674-6). Tyndale.

Road to Wigan Pier. George Orwell. LC 58-10888. 232p. 1972. pap. 4.95 (ISBN 0-15-676750-3, Harv). HarBraceJ.

Road to World War II: A Documentary History. Ed. by Keith Eubank. LC 74-179768. 1973. pap. 12.95x (ISBN 0-88295-734-1). Harlan Davidson.

Road to Xanadu: A Study in the Ways of the Imagination. John L. Lowes. 639p. 1985. Repr. of 1977 ed. lib. bdg. 65.00 (ISBN 0-89987-530-0). Darby Bks.

Road to Xanadu: A Study in the Ways of the Imagination. John L. Lowes. LC 85-42661. 656p. 1986. 55.50x (ISBN 0-691-06645-0); pap. 14.95x (ISBN 0-691-01421-3). Princeton U Pr.

Road Traffic Control. Ed. by Hiroshi Inose & Takashi Hamada. Tr. by Edward C. Posner. 331p. 1975. 25.00x (ISBN 0-86008-153-2, Pub. by U of Tokyo Japan). Columbia U Pr.

Road Traffic Control. (IEE Conference Publication Ser.: No. 260). 205p. 1986. pap. 57.00 (ISBN 0-85296-326-2, IC260). Inst Elect Eng.

Road Traffic Data Collection. (IEE Conference Publication: No. 242). 128p. 1984. pap. 62.00 (IC242). Inst Elect Eng.

Road Traffic Noise. A. Alexandre et al. 1975. 63.00 (ISBN 0-85334-628-3, Pub. by Elsevier Applied Sci England). Elsevier.

Road Traffic Noise see Progress in Planning.

Road Traffic Offenders & Crime Policy. Laszlo Viski. 206p. 1982. 67.50x (ISBN 0-317-53861-6, Pub. by Collets (UK)). State Mutual Bk.

Road Transport Industry's Guide to Software. Martin Avery. Ed. by Peter Rodwell. (Microcomputing for the Professions Ser.). 163p. 1985. 17.50 (ISBN 0-86187-520-6, Pub. by Frances Pinter). Longwood Pub Group.

Road Transport of Fish & Fishery Products. G. C. Eddie. (Fisheries Technical Paper Ser.: No. 232). 54p. (Orig.). 1984. pap. 7.50 (ISBN 92-5-101362-4, F2570, FAO). UNIPUB.

Road Transport Taxation in Developing Countries: The Design of User Charges & Taxes for Tunisia. David M. Newbery et al. (Discussion Paper Ser.: No. 26). 106p. 1988. 6.50 (ISBN 0-8213-1045-3, DP0026). World Bank.

Road Trip: An Interpersonal Adventure. Rebecca B. Rubin & Randi J. Nevins. 164p. 1988. pap. text ed. 7.95x (ISBN 0-88133-328-X). Waveland Pr.

Road Unseen. Peter Jenkins & Barbara Jenkins. LC 85-25952. 224p. 1985. 12.95 (ISBN 0-8407-5961-4). Nelson.

Road Unseen. Peter Jenkins & Barbara Jenkins. (General Ser.). 406p. 1986. lib. bdg. 18.95 (ISBN 0-317-46368-3, Large Print Bks). G K Hall.

Road Unseen. Peter Jenkins & Barbara Jenkins. 256p. 1987. pap. 3.95 (ISBN 0-449-21212-2, Crest). Fawcett.

Road up to the Rim: The Hard Way up. A. Bertram Chandler. 352p. 1981. pap. 2.75 (ISBN 0-441-73102-3). Ace Bks.

Road User Charges in Central America. Anthony Churchill et al. LC 70-187219. (World Bank Staff Occasional Papers Ser.: No. 15). 192p. 1972. pap. 6.00x (ISBN 0-8018-1334-4). Johns Hopkins.

Road User Information Needs, Pedestrian Movement, & Bicycle Travel Patterns. (Transportation Research Record Ser.). 53p. 1978. 3.40 (ISBN 0-309-02828-0). Transport Res Bd.

Road Users & the Police. M. C. Dix & A. D. Layzell. (Illus.). 152p. 1983. 27.00 (ISBN 0-7099-2059-8, Pub. by Croom Helm Ltd); pap. 13.00 (ISBN 0-7099-2060-1). Routledge Chapman & Hall.

Road Users & Traffic Safety. J. A. Rothengatter & R. A. De Bruin. 190p. 1987. 37.50 (ISBN 90-232-2316-0, Pub. by Van Gorcum Holland). Longwood Pub Group.

Road Vehicle Aerodynamics. 2nd ed. A. J. Scibor-Rylski. LC 84-13196. 244p. 1984. text ed. 43.95x (ISBN 0-470-20097-9). Wiley.

Road Vehicle Performance. G. G. Lucas. (Transportation Studies: Vol. 7). 218p. 1986. text ed. 50.00 (ISBN 0-677-21400-6). Gordon & Breach.

Road Warriors. Zadra. (All Star Wrestling Ser.). (Illus.). (gr. 4 up). PLB 8.95 (ISBN 0-88682-088-X). Creative Ed.

Road Wet, the Wind Close: Celtic Ireland. James C. Roy. LC 85-31100. (Illus.). 219p. 1988. pap. 15.95 (ISBN 0-8023-1283-7). Dufour.

Roadbook Europe. Rune Lagerqvist. (Illus.). 480p. 1985. 29.95 (ISBN 0-86145-169-4, Pub. by Automobile Assn Brit). Salem Hse Pubs.

Roadfood & Goodfood: A Restaurant Guidebook. Jane Stern & Michael Stern. 1986. pap. 12.95 (ISBN 0-394-74396-2). Knopf.

Roadkill. Linda Hasselstrom. (Orig.). 1987. pap. 5.95 (ISBN 0-944024-02-5). Spoon Riv Poetry.

Roadmap: Anthology of Durham Authors. Ed. by Judy Hogan. (Illus.). 150p. 1984. pap. 7.00 (ISBN 0-932112-17-X). Carolina Wren.

Roadmarks. Roger Zelazny. 192p. 1980. pap. 2.95 (ISBN 0-345-34515-0, Del Rey). Ballantine.

Roadmarks. Roger Zelazny. LC 79-2280. 185p. 1979. 15.00 (ISBN 0-345-28530-1). Ultramarine Pub.

RoadRace & More for the Commodore 64. Tom Rugg. 1.95 (ISBN 0-88056-231-5). Weber Systems.

Roadrunner (& His Cuckoo Cousin) Virginia Douglas. 48p. 1984. 10.95 (ISBN 0-87961-146-4); pap. 4.95 (ISBN 0-87961-147-2). Naturegraph.

Roadrunner-GTX Databook & Price Guide: 1965-1980. R. Perry Zavitz. (Data Bks.). (Illus.). 128p. 1986. pap. 9.95 (ISBN 0-934780-86-2). Bookman Pub.

Roads. Cass R. Sandak. (Easy-Read Modern Wonders Ser.). (Illus.). 32p. (gr. k-4). 1984. lib. bdg. 9.90 (ISBN 0-531-04710-5). Watts.

Roads & Canals in the Eighteenth Century. Marjorie Greenwood. Ed. by Marjorie Reeves. (Then & There Ser.). (Illus.). 92p. (Orig.). (gr. 7-12). 1977. pap. text ed. 4.95 (ISBN 0-582-20383-X). Longman.

Roads & Resources: Appropriate Technology in Road Construction in Developing Countries. Ed. by G. A. Edmonds & J. D. Howe. (Illus.). 200p. (Orig.). 1980. pap. 13.50x (ISBN 0-903031-69-8, Pub. by Intermediate Tech England). Intermediate Tech.

Roads & Traffic in Urban Areas. 456p. (Orig.). 1987. pap. 56.00 (ISBN 0-11-550818-X, HM1718, Pub. by Her Maj Station Ofc). UNIPUB.

Roads in the Sand. Adriana M. Gibbs. (Illus.). 240p. 18.00 (ISBN 0-317-54816-6); text ed. 18.00 (ISBN 0-317-54817-4); pap. text ed. 17.00 (ISBN 0-317-54818-2). Lorrah & Hitchcock.

Roads of Adventure: Stephen Crane. Ralph D. Paine. 452p. 1983. Repr. of 1922 ed. lib. bdg. 55.00 (ISBN 0-89984-832-X). Century Bookbindery.

Roads of Fife. Owen Silver. 1987. pap. text ed. 29.95 (ISBN 0-85976-160-6, Pub. by John Donald UK). Humanities.

Roads of Home: Lanes & Legends of New Jersey. Henry C. Beck. 301p. 1983. pap. 9.95 (ISBN 0-8135-1018-X). Rutgers U Pr.

Roads of Melody. Carrie Jacobs-Bond. Ed. by Annette K. Baxter. LC 79-8776. (Signal Lives Ser.). (Illus.). 1980. Repr. of 1927 ed. lib. bdg. 27.50x (ISBN 0-405-12825-8). Ayer Co Pubs.

Roads of Texas. Ed. by Christopher Mueller-Wille. 160p. 1988. pap. 12.95 (ISBN 0-940672-45-6). Shearer Pub.

Roads, Rails & Waterways: The Army Engineers & Early Transportation. Forest G. Hill. LC 77-14558. 1977. Repr. of 1957 ed. lib. bdg. 35.00x (ISBN 0-8371-9839-9, HIRW). Greenwood.

Roads Taken: A Country Lawyer Looks Back. Kermit R. Mason. Ed. & intro. by Carl B. Taylor. 152p. 1986. 12.95 (ISBN 0-9605948-2-5). C B Taylor.

Roads They Made, Women in Illinois History. Adade M. Wheeler & Marlene S. Wortman. LC 76-42591. (Illus.). 1977. lib. bdg. 22.95 (ISBN 0-88286-020-8); pap. 6.95 (ISBN 0-88286-019-4). C H Kerr.

Roads Through the Summer. Brian H. Johnson. Ed. by Malcolm Johnson. LC 84-81933. 100p. (Orig.). 1985. pap. 7.95x (ISBN 0-930639-00-6). Harker Van Pelt.

Roads to a New America. facsimile ed. David C. Coyle. LC 77-103649. (Select Bibliographies Reprint Ser). 1938. 29.00 (ISBN 0-8369-5149-2). Ayer Co Pubs.

Roads to Castles see California.

Roads to Dawn Lake. John O. Simon. 1968. pap. 2.00 (ISBN 0-685-29877-9). Oyez.

Roads to Extinction: Essays on the Holocaust. Philip Friedman. Ed. by Ada J. Friedman. LC 79-89818. 616p. 1980. 27.50 (ISBN 0-8276-0170-0, 446). JPS Phila.

Roads to Freedom: Socialism, Anarchism & Syndication. Bertrand Russell. (Unwin Paperbacks). 1966. text ed. 9.50x o. p. (ISBN 0-04-335019-4); pap. 7.95 (ISBN 0-04-335033-X). Unwin Hyman.

Roads to Gettysburg. John W. Schildt. 1978. 18.00 (ISBN 0-87012-295-9). McClain.

Roads to Glory. facs. ed. Richard Aldington. (Short Story Index Reprint Ser). 1931. 18.00 (ISBN 0-8369-3666-3). Ayer Co Pubs.

Roads to Nowhere: A Child of Lebanon. Mansour Labaky. Tr. by Allen Annelyse. 1988. pap. 5.95 (ISBN 0-932506-61-5). St Bedes Pubns.

Roads to Paradise: Reading the Lives of the Early Saints. Alison G. Elliott. LC 86-40384. (Illus.). 260p. 1987. 25.00x (ISBN 0-87451-389-8). U Pr of New Eng.

Roads to Radiology: An Imaging Guide to Medicine & Surgery. T. Sherwood et al. (Illus.). 96p. 1983. pap. 21.00 (ISBN 0-387-11801-2). Springer-Verlag.

Roads to Reading. Ralph C. Staiger. (Books About Books). 141p. (2nd. Printing 1982). 1979. pap. 5.25 (ISBN 92-3-101642-3, U922, UNESCO). UNIPUB.

Roads to Reason: Transportation, Administration, & Rationality in Colombia. Richard E. Hartwig. LC 83-3676. (Illus.). 295p. 1983. 30.95x (ISBN 0-8229-3806-5). U of Pittsburgh Pr.

Roads to Recovery: A National Directory of Alcohol & Drug Addiction Treatment Centers. Ed. by Jean Moore. LC 85-19538. 480p. 1986. pap. 17.95 (ISBN 0-02-059470-4, Collier). Macmillan.

Roads to Ride: A Bicyclist's Topographic Guide to Alameda, Contra Costa, & Marin Counties. Grant Petersen. 144p. 1984. pap. 6.95 (ISBN 0-930588-07-X). Heyday Bks.

Roads to Ride, South: A Bicyclist's Topographic Guide to San Mateo, Santa Clara, & Santa Cruz Counties. Grant Petersen. (Illus.). 160p. 1985. pap. 7.95 (ISBN 0-930588-17-7). Heyday Bks.

Roads to Sata. Alan Booth. 288p. 1987. pap. 6.95 (ISBN 0-14-009566-7). Penguin.

Roads to Sata: A Two Thousand-Mile Walk Through Japan. Alan Booth. LC 86-50050. 292p. 1986. 16.95 (ISBN 0-670-80776-1). Viking.

Roads to Social Peace. Edward A. Ross. LC 79-117830. (Essay Index Reprint Ser.). 1924. 14.00 (ISBN 0-8369-1679-4). Ayer Co Pubs.

Roads to the Isles: A Guidebook to Scotland's Far West: Morar, Moidart, Morvern Ardnamurchan. Tom Atkinson. 120p. 1986. pap. 12.00x (ISBN 0-946487-01-4, Pub. by Luath Pr UK). State Mutual Bk.

Roads to Today's Portugal. Ed. by Nelson H. Vieira. LC 83-83071. (Illus.). 157p. (Orig.). 1983. pap. 8.00 (ISBN 0-943722-11-X). Gavea Brown.

Roadshow. William Marshall. 1988. pap. 3.95 (ISBN 0-317-67174-X). Mysterious Pr.

Roadside America. Jack Berth et al. 1986. pap. 9.95 (ISBN 0-671-60688-3, Fireside). S&S.

Roadside Bicycle Repairs: The Simple Guide to Fixing Your Bike. Rob Van der Plas. LC 87-70731. (Illus.). 112p. (Orig.). 1987. pap. 3.95 (ISBN 0-933201-16-8). Bicycle Books.

Roadside Development Evaluation of Research. (National Cooperative Highway Research Program Report). 78p. 1972. 4.20 (ISBN 0-309-02022-0). Transport Res Bd.

Roadside Drainage. (Publications for Developing Countries: Compendium 5). 196p. 1979. 9.00 (ISBN 0-309-02820-5). Transport Res Bd.

Roadside Empires: How the Chains Franchised America. Stan Luxenberg. LC 83-40231. 324p. 1985. 17.95 (ISBN 0-670-32658-5). Viking.

Roadside Empires: How the Chains Franchised America. Stan Luxenberg. 1986. pap. 7.95 (ISBN 0-14-007734-0). Penguin.

Roadside Flowers of Oklahoma, Vol. 1. Doyle McCoy. (Illus.). 116p. 1976. pap. 10.00 (ISBN 0-9619985-2-0). McCoy Pub Co.

Roadside Flowers of Oklahoma, Vol. 2. Doyle McCoy. (Illus.). 60p. 1978. pap. 5.00 (ISBN 0-9619985-3-9). McCoy Pub Co.

Roadside Flowers of Texas. Mary M. Wills & Howard S. Irwin. (Elma Dill Russell Spencer Foundation Ser.: No. 1). (Illus.). 309p. 1961. pap. 12.95 (ISBN 0-292-77009-X). U of Tex Pr.

Roadside Food: Good Home-Style Cooking Across America. LeRoy Woodson, Jr. LC 85-30254. (Illus.). 160p. (Orig.). 1986. pap. 14.95 (ISBN 0-941434-68-0). Stewart Tabori & Chang.

Roadside Geology of Alaska. Cathy Conner & Daniel O'Haire. (Roadside Geology Ser.). (Illus.). 256p. 1988. pap. 12.95 (ISBN 0-87842-213-7). Mountain Pr.

Roadside Geology of Arizona. Halka Chronic. LC 83-2233. 320p. 1983. pap. 9.95 (ISBN 0-87842-147-5). Mountain Pr.

Roadside Geology of Colorado: Roadside Geology Ser. Halka Chronic. LC 79-11148. (Illus.). 322p. 1980. pap. 9.95 (ISBN 0-87842-105-X). Mountain Pr.

Roadside Geology of Idaho. David Alt & Donald Hyndman. (Roadside Geology Ser.). (Illus.). 224p. 1988. pap. 9.95 (ISBN 0-87842-219-6). Mountain Pr.

Roadside Geology of Montana. David Alt & Donald Hyndman. LC 86-17954. (Roadside Geology Ser.). (Illus.). 432p. 1986. pap. 12.95 (ISBN 0-87842-202-1). Mountain Pr.

Roadside Geology of New Mexico. Halka Chronic. Ed. by David Alt & Donald Hyndman. (Roadside Geology Ser.). (Illus., Orig.). 1987. pap. 9.95 (ISBN 0-87842-209-9). Mountain Pr.

Roadside Geology of New York. Van Diver. 1985. pap. 12.95 (ISBN 0-87892-190-7). North Country.

Roadside Geology of New York. Bradford B. Van Diver. LC 85-13871. (Roadside Geology Ser.). (Illus.). 400p. 1985. pap. 12.95 (ISBN 0-87842-180-7). Mountain Pr.

Roadside Geology of Northern California. David Alt & Donald Hyndman. LC 74-81834. (Roadside Geology Ser.). (Illus.). 244p. 1975. pap. 9.95 (ISBN 0-87842-055-X). Mountain Pr.

Roadside Geology of Oregon. David Alt & Donald Hyndman. LC 77-25841. (Roadside Geology Ser.). (Illus.). 268p. 1978. pap. 9.95 (ISBN 0-87842-063-0). Mountain Pr.

Roadside Geology of the Yellowstone Country. William J. Fritz. LC 85-4934. (Roadside Geology Ser.). (Illus., Orig.). 1985. pap. 8.95 (ISBN 0-87842-170-X). Mountain Pr.

Roadside Geology of U. S. Interstate 80 Between Salt Lake City & San Francisco. W. Kenneth Hamblin et al. 53p. 1975. pap. 3.00 (ISBN 0-913312-43-6). Am Geol.

Roadside Geology of Vermont-New Hampshire. Bradford B. Van Diver. Ed. by David Alt & Donald Hyndman. LC 87-3897. (Roadside Geology Ser.). (Illus., Orig.). 1987. pap. 9.95 (ISBN 0-87842-203-X). Mountain Pr.

Roadside Geology of Virginia. Keith Frye. Ed. by David Alt & Donald Hyndman. LC 86-8755. (Roadside Geology Ser.). (Illus.). 256p. (Orig.). (gr. 5 up). 1986. pap. 9.95 (ISBN 0-87842-199-8). Mountain Pr.

Roadside Geology of Washington. David Alt & Donald Hyndman. LC 84-8409. (Roadside Geology Ser.). (Illus.). 320p. (Orig.). 1984. pap. 9.95 (ISBN 0-87842-160-2). Mountain Pr.

Roadside Geology of Wyoming. David R. Lageson & Darwin R. Spearing. Ed. by David Alt & Donald Hyndman. (Roadside Geology Ser.). (Illus.). 272p. (Orig.). 1988. pap. 9.95 (ISBN 0-87842-216-1). Mountain Pr.

Roadside Guide to Bike Repair. Dennis L. Coello. 112p. (Orig.). Date not set. pap. 3.95 (ISBN 0-446-34820-1). Warner Bks.

Roadside Guide to the Geology of the Great Smoky Mountains National Park. Harry L. Moore. LC 87-18796. (Illus.). 192p. 1988. lib. bdg. 17.95x (ISBN 0-87049-557-7); pap. 8.95 (ISBN 0-87049-558-5). U of Tenn Pr.

Roadside Hazards & Safety Improvements: Four Reports. (Transportation Research Record Ser.). 52p. 1975. 2.40 (ISBN 0-309-02396-3). Transport Res Bd.

Roadside History of Arizona. Marshall Trimble. LC 85-28521. (Roadside History Ser.). (Illus.). 480p. (Orig.). 1987. 24.95 (ISBN 0-87842-197-1); pap. 14.95 (ISBN 0-87842-198-X). Mountain Pr.

Roadside History of Colorado. James McTighe. LC 84-80537. (Illus.). 362p. (Orig.). 1984. pap. 9.95 (ISBN 0-933472-83-8). Johnson Bks.

Roadside Kansas: A Traveler's Guide to Its Geology & Landmarks. Rex Buchanan & James R. McCauley. (Illus.). 368p. 1987. 25.00x (ISBN 0-7006-0323-9); pap. 9.95 (ISBN 0-7006-0322-0). U Pr of KS.

Roadside Meetings. Hamlin Garland. 474p. Repr. of 1930 ed. lib. bdg. 57.00 (ISBN 0-8414-4331-9). Folcroft.

Roadside Meetings. Hamlin Garland. (Collected Works of Hamlin Garland). 1988. Repr. of 1930 ed. lib. bdg. 59.00x. Am Biog Serv.

Roadside Meetings see Collected Works.

Roadside New England, 1900-1955. R. Brewster Harding. 80p. pap. 9.95 (ISBN 0-89272-158-8). Down East.

Roadside Plants & Flowers: A Traveler's Guide to the Midwest & Great Lakes Area. Marian S. Edsall. LC 84-40148. (Illus.). 144p. 1985. 17.50t (ISBN 0-299-09700-5); pap. 12.95x (ISBN 0-299-09704-8). U of Wis Pr.

Roadside Plants of Northern New Mexico. Gail D. Tierney & Phyllis Hughes. LC 80-82718. (Illus.). 175p. 1983. 22.50 (ISBN 0-89016-067-8); pap. 9.95 (ISBN 0-89016-061-9). Lightning Tree.

Roadside Plants of Southern California. Thomas J. Belzer. LC 83-8082. (Illus.). 172p. 1984. pap. 8.95 (ISBN 0-87842-158-0). Mountain Pr.

Roadside Safety Improvement Programs on Freeways: A Cost-Effectiveness Priority Approach. (National Cooperative Highway Research Program Report). 64p. 1974. 4.00 (ISBN 0-309-02208-8). Transport Res Bd.

Roadside Sobriety Tests: A Police Officer's Guide to Making Drunk Driving Arrests Stand up in Court. James Whitmore. LC 87-17890. (Illus.). 86p. (Orig.). 1987. pap. 9.95 (ISBN 0-8366-0001-0). Callaghan.

Roadside Trees & Shrubs of Oklahoma. Doyle McCoy. LC 80-5944. (Illus.). 180p. (Orig.). 1981. pap. 10.95 (ISBN 0-8061-1556-4). U of Okla Pr.

Roadside Valentine. C. S. Adler. LC 83-9394. 280p. (gr. 7 up). 1983. 9.95 (ISBN 0-02-700350-7). Macmillan.

Roadside Valentine. C. S. Adler. 1984. pap. 2.25 (ISBN 0-399-21146-2). Putnam Pub Group.

Roadside Wild Fruits of Oklahoma. Doyle McCoy. LC 79-6705. (Illus.). 96p. (Orig.). 1980. pap. 10.95 (ISBN 0-8061-1626-9). U of Okla Pr.

Roadsigns. Gary Hines. 16p. 1978. 7.00 (ISBN 0-913719-28-5); pap. 2.00. High-Coo Pr.

Roadsigns: Spirituality & Homily Ideas for the Weekdays of Lent. Jay Cormier. LC 87-62534. 82p. (Orig.). 1988. pap. 6.95 (ISBN 0-89390-107-5). Resource Pubns.

Roadstriker: The Transformable Vehicle Supplement for Mekton. Michael Pondsmith & Derek Quintanar. (Illus.). 36p. (Orig.). (YA) (gr. 5-12). 1986. wkbk. 8.00 (ISBN 0-937279-01-3, MK 1101). R Talsorian.

Roadway Delineation Systems. (National Cooperative Highway Research Program Report). 349p. 1972. 14.00 (ISBN 0-309-02011-5). Transport Res Bd.

Roadway Design in Seasonal Frost Areas. (National Cooperative Highway Research Program Synthesis of Highway Practice). 104p. 1975. 6.00 (ISBN 0-309-02307-6). Transport Res Bd.

Roadway Drivage Techniques in the Coal Mines of the European Community. Commission of the European Communities Staff. 392p. 1984. 59.00 (ISBN 0-86010-575-X). Graham & Trotman.

Roadway Maintenance. Business Communications Staff. 269p. 1983. 1000.00 (ISBN 0-89336-223-9, E-027). BCC.

Roadway Signs & Markings. Transportation Engineers Institute. (Illus.). 608p. 1984. text ed. 74.67 (ISBN 0-13-781428-3). P-H.

Roadways & Airport Pavements. American Concrete Institute Staff. LC 75-10374. (American Concrete Institute Publications: SP-51). (Illus.). pap. 72.80 (ISBN 0-317-10031-9, 2017593). Bks Demand UMI.

Roadways: The History of Swindon's Street Names. Peter Sheldon & Richard Tomkins. 112p. 1987. 39.00x (Pub. by Picton UK); pap. 21.00x (ISBN 0-902633-62-7, Pub. by Picton UK). State Mutual Bk.

Roadwork. Robert Bell. 1979. pap. 2.25 (ISBN 0-8439-0697-9, Leisure Bks). Leisure NY.

Roald Dahl. Alan Warren. (Starmont Contemporary Writers: No. 1). 112p. 1988. lib. bdg. 16.95x (ISBN 0-8095-5200-0). Borgo Pr.

Roald Dahl. Alan Warren. (Starmont Contemporary Writers Ser.: Vol. 1). 1988. 17.95x (ISBN 1-55742-013-0); pap. 8.95x (ISBN 1-55742-012-2). Starmont Hse.

Roald Dahl Omnibus. Roald Dahl. 1987. 22.50 (ISBN 0-88029-123-0, Pub. by Dorset Pr). Hippocrene Bks.

Roald Dahl's Book of Ghost Stories. Ed. by Roald Dahl. 235p. (gr. 5 up). 1984. 12.95 (ISBN 0-374-25131-2); pap. 4.95 (ISBN 0-374-51868-8). FS&G.

Roald Dahl's Charlie & the Chocolate Factory, 4 vols. Boxed Set. pap. 8.70 (ISBN 0-553-30173-X). Bantam.

Roald Dahl's Tales of the Unexpected. Roald Dahl. pap. 2.95 (ISBN 0-394-74081-5, V-81, Vin). Random.

Roaming the Back Roads: Twenty-eight Delightful Drives Through the Most Beautiful Countryside in Northern California. rev. ed. Peter Browning & Carol Holleuffer. LC 78-27569. (Illus.). 176p. (Orig.). 1981. pap. 8.95 (ISBN 0-87701-235-0). Chronicle Bks.

Roanoke County Marriages, Eighteen Thirty-Eight to Eighteen Fifty. John Vogt & T. William Kethley, Jr. (Virginia Historic Marriage Register Ser.). (Illus.). viii, 54p. (Orig.). 1984. pap. 3.50 (ISBN 0-935931-15-5). Iberian Pub.

Roanoke County Marriages, Eighteen Thirty-Eight to Eighteen Fifty. John Vogt & T. William Kethley, Jr. (Virginia Historic Marriage Register Ser.). 54p. 1988. Repr. lib. bdg. 15.95x (ISBN 0-8095-8229-5). Borgo Pr.

Roanoke Hundred. Inglis Fletcher. (Albemarle Ser.). 501p. 1976. Repr. of 1948 ed. lib. bdg. 25.95x (ISBN 0-89244-007-4, Pub. by Queens Hse). Amereon Ltd.

Roanoke Island: The Beginnings of English America. David Stick. LC 83-7014. (Illus.). xiii, 266p. 1983. 14.95 (ISBN 0-8078-1554-3); pap. 5.95 (ISBN 0-8078-4110-2). U of NC Pr.

Roanoke; Story of County & City. Writers Program, Virginia. LC 73-3658. (American Guide Ser.). 1942. Repr. 18.50 (ISBN 0-404-57958-2). AMS Pr.

Roanoke: The Abandoned Colony. Karen O. Kupperman. LC 83-24419. 200p. 1984. 27.50x (ISBN 0-8476-7127-5, Rowman & Allanheld); pap. 12.50x (ISBN 0-8476-7339-1). Rowman.

Roanoke Voyages, Fifteen Eighty-Four to Fifteen Ninety, 2 vols. in 1. Ed. by David B. Quinn. (Hakluyt Society Works Ser.: No. 2, Vols. 104-105). (Illus.). Repr. of 1952 ed. 102.00 (ISBN 0-8115-0397-6). Kraus Repr.

Roar Lion Roar. Irvin Faust. 1966. pap. 1.45 (ISBN 0-380-01532-3, 15396, Bard). Avon.

Roar of the Crowd. James J. Corbett. LC 76-6330. (Irish American Ser.). 1976. Repr. of 1925 ed. 26.50 (ISBN 0-405-09326-8). Ayer Co Pubs.

Roar of the Robin. Elgar Houghton. 1978. 6.95 (ISBN 0-87881-067-6). Mojave Bks.

Roar of Thunder. Wilbur Smith. 1977. pap. 1.95 (ISBN 0-440-18146-1). Dell.

Roar of Thunder, Whisper of Wind. Edna A. Elfont. LC 83-620006. 128p. 1984. 24.95. Mich Nat Res.

Roar of Thunder, Whisper of Wind: A Portrait of Michigan Waterfalls. Edna Elfont. Ed. by Richard Morscheck. (Michigan Heritage Bks.: Vol. 5). (Illus.). 128p. 1984. 24.95 (ISBN 0-941912-06-X). TwoPeninsula Pr.

Roarin' Twenties: A History of the 312th Bombardment Group- U. S. Army Air Force World War II. Russell L. Sturzebecker. LC 76-6652. (Illus.). 301p. 1986. 15.00 (ISBN 0-9600466-1-5). Sturzebecker.

Roaring Eighties. Adam Smith. 224p. 1988. 18.95 (ISBN 0-671-44788-2). Summit Bks.

Roaring Fork Valley: An Illustrated Chronicle. 3rd ed. Len Shoemaker. Ed. by Russ Collman. (Illus.). 216p. 1979. 32.00 (ISBN 0-913582-06-9). Sundance.

Roaring Girl. Thomas Middleton. Ed. by Thomas Dekker & A. H. Gomme. (New Mermaid Ser.). 1976. pap. 3.95x (ISBN 0-393-90024-X). Norton.

Roaring Girl. Thomas Middleton & Thomas Dekker. LC 71-133654. (Tudor Facsimile Texts. Old English Plays: No. 130). Repr. of 1914 ed. 49.50 (ISBN 0-404-53430-9). AMS Pr.

Roaring Lion of the East. Marvin Yakos. Ed. by David Bernard. LC 87-26001. (Illus.). 264p. (Orig.). 1988. pap. 7.95 (ISBN 0-932581-25-0). Word Aflame.

Roaring Queen. Wyndham Lewis. 1973. 10.00 (ISBN 0-87140-576-8). Liveright.

Roaring Redhead: Larry MacPhail - Baseball's Great Innovator. Don Warfield. LC 86-13437. (Illus.). 266p. 1987. 16.95 (ISBN 0-912083-18-2). Diamond Communications.

Roaring River Mystery. Franklin W. Dixon. Ed. by Betty Schwartz. (Hardy Boys Ser.: No. 80). (Illus.). 192p. (Orig.). (gr. 3-7). 1984. 9.95 (ISBN 0-671-49722-7); pap. 3.50 (ISBN 0-671-49721-9). Wanderer Bks.

Roaring Twenties & the Depression. (C. C. Publications Social Studies Ser.). (Illus.). 64p. pkg of 5 wkbk 21.25 (ISBN 0-574-51771-5); includes text, tchr's guide, tests & ans. key 19.85. SRA.

Roaring Twenties & the Great Depression, 1920-1940. Naunerle Farr. Ed. by D'Ann Calhoun & Lawrence W. Bloch. (Basic Illustrated History of America). (Illus.). (gr. 4-12). 1977. text ed. 7.50 (ISBN 0-88301-257-X). Pendulum Pr.

Roaring Twenties & the Great Depression: 1920-1940. Naunerle Farr & Dennis Dostert. Ed. by Lawrence W. Bloch. (Basic Illustrated History of America Ser.). (Illus., Orig.). (gr. 4-12). 1976. pap. text ed. 2.95 (ISBN 0-88301-232-4); 1.25 (ISBN 0-88301-244-8). Pendulum Pr.

Roaring Twenties Pop-Up. 12p. (Orig.). 1984. 9.95 (ISBN 0-8431-1171-2). Price Stern.

Roaring U 50's...Union Pacific's Twin Diesels. Harold Keekley. LC 78-51508. (Great Railroading Ser.). 1978. pap. 10.95 (ISBN 0-916160-06-8). G R Cockle.

Roark's Formulas for Stress & Strain. 6th ed. Warren C. Young. 800p. 1988. text ed. 62.50 (ISBN 0-07-072541-1). McGraw.

Roast Beef, Medium: The Business Adventures of Emma McChesney. facsimile ed. Edna Ferber. LC 70-169550. (Short Story Index Reprint Ser.). (Illus.). Repr. of 1913 ed. 18.00 (ISBN 0-8369-4012-1). Ayer Co Pubs.

Roast Leviathan. facsimile ed. Louis Untermeyer. LC 74-29528. (Modern Jewish Experience Ser.). 1975. Repr. of 1923 ed. 19.00x (ISBN 0-405-06752-6). Ayer Co Pubs.

Roast of the Town. Joey Adams. (Illus.). 288p. 1986. 15.95 (ISBN 0-13-781436-4). P-H.

Roasted Chestnuts. Michael Dudley. 24p. 1979. 10.00 (ISBN 0-913719-11-0); pap. 3.50 (ISBN 0-913719-10-2). High-Coo Pr.

Roatry Basic Library. David H. Bailey & Louise Gottlieb. Ed. by Willmon L. White & Mark Perlberg. (Illus.). 506p. (Japanese.). 1982. 16.75 (ISBN 0-915062-13-5). Rotary Intl.

Rob & Smith's Operative Surgery: Neurosurgery. 4th ed. Symon et al. 1986. 99.95 (ISBN 0-8016-4418-6). Mosby.

Rob & Smith's Operative Surgery: Paediatric Surgery. 4th ed. Spitz & Nixon. 1986. 99.95 (ISBN 0-8016-4417-8). Mosby.

Rob Krier on Architecture. Rob Krier. (Academy Architecture Ser.). (Illus.). 96p. 1982. 25.00 (ISBN 0-312-68541-6); pap. 19.95 (ISBN 0-312-68542-4). St Martin.

Rob Nixon, the Old White Trapper. W. H. Kingston. Ed. by Dick Harrison. xxvi, 92p. 1983. pap. 6.95x (ISBN 0-88864-080-3, Pub. by Univ of Alta Pr Canada). U of Nebr Pr.

Rob of the Bowl. John P. Kennedy. Ed. by William S. Osborne. (Masterworks of Literature Ser.). 1965. 12.95x (ISBN 0-8084-0263-3); pap. 8.95x (ISBN 0-8084-0264-1). New Coll U Pr.

Rob Roy. Walter Scott. 1982. (Evman); pap. 7.95x (ISBN 0-460-01142-1, Evans). Biblio Dist.

Rob Stene's Dream, a Poem. LC 70-173003. (Maitland Club. Glasgow. Publications: No. 52). Repr. of 1836 ed. 12.50 (ISBN 0-404-53033-8). AMS Pr.

Robak's Fire. Joe L. Hensley. LC 86-31903. (Crime Club Ser.). 312p. 1987. 16.95 (ISBN 0-385-23986-6, GC Large Print). Doubleday.

Robak's Fire. Joe L. Hensley. Ed. by Jim Connor. 192p. 1988. pap. 3.50 (ISBN 0-7701-1004-5). PaperJacks US.

Robak's Firm. Joe L. Hensley. LC 86-23929. (Crime Club Ser.). 1987. 12.95 (ISBN 0-385-23829-0). Doubleday.

Robbe-Grillet: Les Gommes & le Voyeur. B. G. Garnham. (Critical Guides to French Texts Ser.: No. 19). 79p. 1982. pap. 3.95 (ISBN 0-7293-0142-7, Pub. by Grant & Cutler). Longwood Pub Group.

Robben Island. D. M. Zwelonke. (African Writers Ser.). 1973. pap. 7.00 (ISBN 0-435-90128-1). Heinemann Ed.

Robben Island, Hell-Hole: Reminiscences of a Political Prisoner in South Africa. Moses Dlamini. LC 84-72593. 202p. 1985. text ed. 25.95 (ISBN 0-86543-008-X); pap. 8.95 (ISBN 0-86543-009-8). Africa World.

Robert Browning: The Poet & the Man. F. Sim. LC 72-3196. (Studies in Browning, No. 4). 1972. Repr. of 1923 ed. lib. bdg. 49.95x (ISBN 0-8383-1538-0). Haskell.

Robert Browning's Poetry. Robert Browning. Ed. by James M. Loucks. (Critical Editions). 1979. pap. 12.95x (ISBN 0-393-09092-2). Norton.

Robert Browning's: Sordello: a Marginally Amended Edition. Ed. by Morse Peckham. LC 76-58619. 468p. 1977. 15.00x (ISBN 0-87875-114-9). Whitston Pub.

Robert Browning's Theory of the Poet, 1833-1841. Charles L. Rivers. Ed. by James Hogg. (Romantic Reassessment Ser.). 224p. (Orig.). 1976. pap. 15.00 (ISBN 3-7052-0513-7, Pub. by Salzburg Studies). Longwood Pub Group.

Robert Bruce & the Community of the Realm of Scotland. rev. ed. Geoffrey W. Barrow. (Illus.). 450p. 1987. 35.00 (ISBN 0-85224-539-4, Pub. by Edinburgh U Pr Scotland). Columbia U Pr.

Robert Bruce, King of Scots. facsimile ed. Agnes M. Mackenzie. LC 78-128880. (Select Bibliographies Reprint Ser). Repr. of 1934 ed. 22.00 (ISBN 0-8369-5500-5). Ayer Co Pubs.

Robert Buchanan. Harriett Jay. LC 72-130237. Repr. of 1903 ed. 13.00 (ISBN 0-404-03555-8). AMS Pr.

Robert Buchanan: A Critical Appreciation & Other Essays. Henry Murray. 1973. Repr. of 1901 ed. 30.00 (ISBN 0-8274-1172-3). R West.

Robert Buchanan: The Poet of Modern Revolt: An Introduction to His Poetry. Archibald Stodart-Walker. 1978. Repr. of 1901 ed. lib. bdg. 30.00 (ISBN 0-8495-4948-5). Arden Lib.

Robert Buchanan: The Poet of Modern Revolt. Archibald Stodart-Walker. 1973. Repr. of 1901 ed. 25.00 (ISBN 0-8274-0861-7). R West.

Robert Buhler. Colin Hayes. (Royal Academy Painters & Sculptors Ser.). (Illus.). 73p. 1987. 16.95 (ISBN 0-89733-240-7). Academy Chi Pubs.

Robert Burns. Catherine Carswell. 1973. Repr. of 1933 ed. 10.00 (ISBN 0-8274-1505-2). R West.

Robert Burns. John Drinkwater. 1973. Repr. of 1925 ed. 10.00 (ISBN 0-8274-1648-2). R West.

Robert Burns. T. F. Henderson. 1904. 17.50 (ISBN 0-8274-3289-5). R West.

Robert Burns. Thomas F. Henderson. LC 73-144556. (Illus.). Repr. of 1904 ed. 18.00 (ISBN 0-404-08514-8). AMS Pr.

Robert Burns. Donald A. Low. Ed. by David Daiches. (Scottish Writers Ser.: Vol. 8). 144p. 1986. pap. 7.00 (ISBN 0-7073-0368-0, Pub. by Scot Acad Pr). Longwood Pub Group.

Robert Burns. William A. Neilson. 1917. 25.00 (ISBN 0-8274-3290-9). R West.

Robert Burns. facsimile ed. Picton Publishing Staff. 240p. 1987. 28.00x (Pub. by Picton UK); deluxe ed. 333.00 ltd. ed. (Pub. by Picton UK). State Mutual Bk.

Robert Burns. (English Author Ser.). 160p. 1987. lib. bdg. 19.95x (ISBN 0-8057-6952-8, Twayne). G K Hall.

Robert Burns. Gabriel Setoun. 1973. Repr. of 1896 ed. lib. bdg. 20.00 (ISBN 0-8414-8122-9). Folcroft.

Robert Burns. John C. Shairp. Ed. by John Morley. (English Men of Letters). Repr. of 1887 ed. lib. bdg. 12.50 (ISBN 0-404-51727-7). AMS Pr.

Robert Burns. Principal Shairp. 1979. Repr. of 1879 ed. lib. bdg. 19.50 (ISBN 0-8495-4901-9). Arden Lib.

Robert Burns: A Summary of His Career & Genius. John Nichol. 1973. Repr. of 1882 ed. 35.00 (ISBN 0-8274-0298-8). R West.

Robert Burns: An Inquiry into Certain Aspects of His Life & Character & the Moral Influence of His Poetry. (Written by a scotchwoman). 1887. 20.00 (ISBN 0-8274-3288-7). R West.

Robert Burns & His Masonic Circle. Dudley Wright. LC 72-10784. 1978. Repr. lib. bdg. 35.00. Folcroft.

Robert Burns & His Rhyming Friends. John D. Ross. LC 77-144478. Repr. of 1928 ed. 14.00 (ISBN 0-404-08538-5). AMS Pr.

Robert Burns & His Rhyming Friends. John D. Ross. 1928. 25.00 (ISBN 0-8274-3292-5). R West.

Robert Burns & the Common People. William Stewart. LC 74-169187. (English Literature Ser., No. 33). 1971. Repr. of 1925 ed. lib. bdg. 39.95x (ISBN 0-8383-1333-7). Haskell.

Robert Burns & the Medical Profession. W. Findlay. 59.95 (ISBN 0-8490-0961-8). Gordon Pr.

Robert Burns & the Peasantry, Seventeen Eighty-Five. J. Kinsley. (Warton Lectures on English Poetry). 1974. pap. 5.50 (ISBN 0-85672-107-7, Pub. by British Acad). Longwood Pub Group.

Robert Burns & the Riddell Family. J. Maxwell Wood. LC 73-21743. (English Biography Ser., No. 31). 1974. lib. bdg. 52.95x (ISBN 0-8383-1802-9). Haskell.

Robert Burns & the Riddell Family. John M. Wood. LC 74-11156. 1922. 20.50 (ISBN 0-8414-9535-1). Folcroft.

Robert Burns & the Sentimental Era. Carol McGuirk. LC 84-12378. 224p. 1985. 25.00x (ISBN 0-8203-0739-4). U of Ga Pr.

Robert Burns: His Life & Genius. Andrew Dakers. LC 72-3378. (English Literature Ser., No. 33). 1972. Repr. of 1923 ed. lib. bdg. 39.95x (ISBN 0-8383-1507-0). Haskell.

Robert Burns: Poet-Laureate. Wallace Bruce. LC 73-18124. 1893. lib. bdg. 15.00 (ISBN 0-8414-9895-4). Folcroft.

Robert Burns: Poet-Laureate of Lodge Canongate Kilwinning. Wallace Bruce. 1978. Repr. of 1893 ed. lib. bdg. 17.50 (ISBN 0-8495-0436-8). Arden Lib.

Robert Burns: Selected Poems & Songs. Ed. by David Daiches et al. (Illus.). 196p. 1987. pap. 6.95 (ISBN 0-7073-0527-6, Pub. by Scot Acad Pr). Longwood Pub Group.

Robert Burns: The Critical Heritage. Ed. by Donald Low. (The Critical Heritage Ser.). 1984. pap. 15.00 (ISBN 0-7102-0395-0). Routledge Chapman & Hall.

Robert Burns: The Critical Heritage. Ed. by Donald A. Low. (Critical Heritage Ser.). 1974. 38.00x (ISBN 0-7100-7797-1). Routledge Chapman & Hall.

Robert Burns: The Man & His Work. Hans Hecht. 316p. 1985. 30.00x (ISBN 0-907526-04-7, Pub. by Alloway Pub). State Mutual Bk.

Robert Burton. Michael O'Connell. (Twayne English Authors Ser.: No. 426). 152p. 1986. lib. bdg. 18.95x (ISBN 0-8057-6919-6, Twayne). G K Hall.

Robert Burton & the Anatomy of Melancholy. William Osler et al. Ed. by F. Madan. (Oxford Bibliography Society Ser.: Vol. 1, Pt. 3). pap. 13.00 (ISBN 0-8115-1227-4). Kraus Repr.

Robert Burton's Philosophaster. Robert Burton. Tr. by Paul Jordan-Smith. 1977. Repr. of 1931 ed. lib. bdg. 21.50x (ISBN 0-374-91125-8, Octagon). Hippocrene Bks.

Robert Cantwell. Merrill Lewis. LC 85-70130. (Western Writers Ser.: No. 70). (Illus.). 54p. (Orig.). 1985. pap. 2.95x (ISBN 0-88430-044-7). Boise St Univ.

Robert Capa: A Biography. Richard Whelan. LC 85-40126. (Illus.). 342p. 1985. 19.45 (ISBN 0-394-52488-8). Knopf.

Robert Capa: A Biography. Richard Whelan. xvi, 448p. 1986. pap. 5.95 (ISBN 0-345-33449-3). Ballantine.

Robert Carter of Nomini Hall: A Virginia Tobacco Planter of the 18th Century. Louis Morton. LC 83-45824. 1983. Repr. of 1941 ed. 31.00 (ISBN 0-404-20187-3). AMS Pr.

Robert Challe: Intimations of the Enlightenment. Lawrence J. Forno. LC 77-139993. 199p. 1972. 18.50 (ISBN 0-8386-7846-7). Fairleigh Dickinson.

Robert Chester's "Love's Martyr, Or Rosalins Complaint" 1601 & Its Supplement "Diverse Poeticall Essaies" on the Turtle & Phoenix by Shakespeare, Ben Jonson, George Chapman, John Marston, Etc... see Letter on Shakespeare's Authorship of the Two Noble Kinsmen.

Robert Clive & Imperialism: Mini-Play & Activities. Lawrence Stevens. (World History Ser.). (gr. 7 up). 1981. 7.50 (ISBN 0-89550-343-3). Stevens & Shea.

Robert Cochran's U. S. Revenue Cutter South Carolina, 1793-1798. Florence Kern. 1979. 3.95 (ISBN 0-913377-08-2). Alised.

Robert Colescott: Another Judgment. Kenneth Baker. Ed. by Henry Barendse. (Illus.). 34p. 1985. 7.50 (ISBN 0-915427-04-4). Knight Gallery-Spirit.

Robert Coover: The Universal Fictionmaking Process. Lois Gordon. LC 82-10337. (Crosscurrents-Modern Critiques-New Ser.). 192p. 1983. 16.95x (ISBN 0-8093-1092-9). S Ill U Pr.

Robert Coover's Fictions. Jackson I. Cope. LC 86-45445. 168p. 1986. text ed. 18.95x (ISBN 0-8018-3365-5). JOhns Hopkins.

Robert Cottingham: A Print Retrospective 1972-1986. John Arthur. LC 86-61945. (Illus.). 72p. (Orig.). 1986. pap. text ed. 21.95 (ISBN 0-934306-07-9). Springfield.

Robert Cottingham: A Print Retrospective, 1972-1986. William C. Landwehr. (Illus.). 72p. 1988. pap. 21.95 (ISBN 0-295-96565-7). U of Wash Pr.

Robert Creeley: An Inventory. Mary Novik. LC 72-96943. (Serif Ser.: No. 28). 227p. 1973. 12.00x (ISBN 0-87338-139-4). Kent St U Pr.

Robert Creeley: An Inventory, 1945-1970. Mary Novik. LC 74-156902. pap. 57.00 (ISBN 0-317-26061-8, 2023844). Bks Demand UMI.

Robert Creeley: The Poet's Workshop. Ed. by Carroll F. Terrell. LC 83-61521. (Poet's Workshop Ser.). 384p. 1984. 25.00x (ISBN 0-915032-75-9); pap. 15.95 (ISBN 0-915032-76-7). Natl Poet Foun.

Robert Creeley's Life & Work: A Sense of Increment. Ed. by John Wilson. 1987. 25.00 (ISBN 0-472-09374-6); pap. 11.95 (ISBN 0-472-06374-X). U of Mich Pr.

Robert Crowther's Most Amazing Pop-Up Book of Machines. Robert Crowther. (ps-3). 1988. 14.95 (ISBN 0-670-82339-2, Viking Kestrel). Viking.

Robert Curthose, Duke of Normandy. Charles W. David. LC 78-63356. (Crusades & Military Orders: Second Ser.). (Illus.). 296p. Repr. of 1920 ed. 32.50 (ISBN 0-404-17007-2). AMS Pr.

Robert Curzon: The Heir of Parham. Ian Fraser. (Illus.). 248p. 1986. 35.00. Archival Facsimiles.

Robert D. FitzGerald. Robert D. FitzGerald. Ed. by Julian Croft. LC 85-32300. (UQP Australian Authors Ser.). 239p. (Orig.). 1987. pap. text ed. 12.50x (ISBN 0-7022-1917-7). U of Queensland Pr.

Robert Dale Owen. Richard W. Leopold. LC 71-96184. 1969. Repr. of 1940 ed. lib. bdg. 31.50x (ISBN 0-374-94940-9, Octagon). Hippocrene Bks.

Robert Davidson: Haida Printmaker. Hilary Stewart. LC 79-4915. (Illus.). 120p. 1980. 27.50 (ISBN 0-295-95690-9). U of Wash Pr.

Robert De Blois's Floris et Lyriope. Paul Barrette. LC 68-66610. 152p. 1983. Repr. of 1968 ed. lib. bdg. 19.95x (ISBN 0-89370-767-8). Borgo Pr.

Robert De Handlo. Ed. by Luther Dittmer. (Musical Theorists in Translation Ser.: Vol. 2). 1961. pap. 14.00 (ISBN 0-912024-22-4). Inst Mediaeval Mus.

Robert de Navarre: The Last of the Bourbons. Olive C. Lauther. (Illus., Eng. & Fr.). 1970. 7.95 (ISBN 0-87482-082-0). Wake-Brook.

Robert De Niro. Keith McKay. 1988. pap. 3.95 (ISBN 0-312-90475-4). St Martin.

Robert De Niro: The Hero Behind the Mask. Keith McKay. (Illus.). 224p. 1986. 14.95 (ISBN 0-312-68706-0). St Martin.

Robert Delaunay: The Eiffel Tower: An Art Play Book. Text by Milos Cvach. (Illus.). 32p. (gr. 2 up). 1988. 17.95 (ISBN 0-8109-1141-8). Abrams.

Robert Dinwiddie: His Career in American Colonial Government & Westward Expansion. facsimile ed. Louis K. Koontz. LC 76-140362. (Select Bibliographies Reprint Ser). Repr. of 1941 ed. 22.00 (ISBN 0-8369-5605-2). Ayer Co Pubs.

Robert Dinwiddie: Servant of the Crown. John R. Alden. LC 72-86731. (Williamsburg in America Ser.). 1973. 6.95x (ISBN 0-8139-0440-4). U Pr of Va.

Robert Dodsley: Poet, Publisher, Playwright. Ralph Straus. LC 68-57919. (Research & Source Works Ser.: No. 305). 1968. Repr. of 1910 ed. 25.50 (ISBN 0-8337-3430-X). B Franklin.

Robert Dolsneau: Photographs. Gordon Fraser. (Photographic Monographs: No. 9). 144p. 1981. 120.00x (ISBN 0-86092-050-X, Pub. by Gordon Fraser). State Mutual Bk.

Robert Duncan. Mark A. Johnson. (United States Authors Ser.). (Illus.). 144p. 1988. 21.95 (ISBN 0-8057-7511-0, Twayne). G K Hall.

Robert Duncan: A Descriptive Bibliography. Robert Bertholf. LC 84-16740. (Illus.). 492p. 1986. 65.00 (ISBN 0-87685-620-2); signed ed. 90.00 (ISBN 0-87685-621-0). Black Sparrow.

Robert Duncan: Scales of the Marvelous. Ed. by Robert J. Bertholf & Ian W. Reid. LC 79-19861. (New Directions Insights III). 1979. pap. 5.95 (ISBN 0-8112-0735-8, NDP487). New Directions.

Robert Duvall. Judith Slawson. 1988. pap. 3.95 (ISBN 0-312-90422-3). St Martin.

Robert Duvall: Hollywood Maverick. Judith Slawson. (Illus.). 176p. 1985. 13.95 (ISBN 0-312-68708-7). St Martin.

Robert E. Howard. Marc A. Cerasini & Charles Hoffman. LC 87-32652. (Starmont Reader's Guide Ser.: No. 35). 156p. 1987. Repr. lib. bdg. 17.95x (ISBN 0-89370-962-X). Borgo Pr.

Robert E. Howard. Marc A. Cerasini & Charles E. Hoffman. (Reader's Guides to Contemporary Science Fiction & Fantasy Authors Ser.: Vol. 35). (Illus., Orig.). 1987. 17.95x (ISBN 0-930261-28-3); pap. 9.95x (ISBN 0-930261-27-5). Starmont Hse.

Robert E. Lee. Keith Brandt. LC 84-2687. (Illus.). 32p. (gr. 3-6). 1985. PLB 8.45 (ISBN 0-8167-0278-0); pap. text ed. 1.95 (ISBN 0-8167-0279-9). Troll Assocs.

Robert E. Lee. Jefferson Davis & Alexander Stephens. Ed. by Harold B. Simpson. 1983. 10.00 (ISBN 0-912172-28-2). Hill Coll Pr.

Robert E. Lee. Douglas S. Freeman. (Hudson River Edition Ser.). 1977. Vol. 1. 45.00 (ISBN 0-684-15482-X); Vol. 2. 45.00 (ISBN 0-684-15483-8); Vol. 3. 40.00 (ISBN 0-684-15484-6); Vol. 4. 45.00 (ISBN 0-684-15485-4). Scribner.

Robert E. Lee. William P. Trent. 34.95 (ISBN 0-8490-0962-6). Gordon Pr.

Robert E. Lee. Manfred Weidhorn. LC 87-14500. (Illus.). 160p. (gr. 5 up). 1988. 13.95 (ISBN 0-689-31340-3, Atheneum Childrens Bks). Macmillan.

Robert E. Lee & the Southern Confederacy. Henry White. LC 68-25004. (American Biography Ser., No. 32). 1969. Repr. of 1902 ed. lib. bdg. 59.95x (ISBN 0-8383-0259-9). Haskell.

Robert E. Lee, Brave Leader. Rae Bains. LC 85-1092. (Illus.). 48p. (gr. 4-6). 1985. lib. bdg. 9.79 (ISBN 0-8167-0545-3); pap. text ed. 1.95 (ISBN 0-8167-0546-1). Troll Assocs.

Robert E. Lee: Confederate General. Ed. by Arthur M. Schlesinger. (World Leaders - Past & Present Ser.). (Illus.). (gr. 5-12). 1989. 16.95 (ISBN 1-55546-814-4). Chelsea Hse.

Robert E. Lee: The Soldier. facsimile ed. Frederick Maurice. LC 70-37898. (Select Bibliographies Reprint Ser). Repr. of 1925 ed. 32.00 (ISBN 0-8369-6736-4). Ayer Co Pubs.

Robert E. Lee: Young Confederate. new ed. Helen A. Monsell. LC 82-17848. (Bobbs Merrill Childhood of Famous Americans Ser.). (Illus.). 196p. (Orig.). (gr. 2 up). 1983. pap. 3.95 (ISBN 0-672-52750-2). Bobbs.

Robert E. Lee: Young Confederate. Helen A. Monsell. LC 86-10736. (Macmillan Childhood of Famous Americans Ser.). (Illus.). 192p. (gr. 2-6). 1986. pap. 3.95 (ISBN 0-02-042020-X, Aladdin Bks). Macmillan.

Robert E. Park: Biography of a Sociologist. Winifred Raushenbush. LC 77-88063. pap. 55.00 (ISBN 0-317-55491-3, 2052212). Bks Demand UMI.

Robert E. Sherwood. R. Baird Shuman. (Twayne's United States Authors Ser.). 1964. pap. 8.95x (ISBN 0-8084-0265-X, T58, Twayne). New Coll U Pr.

Robert E. Sherwood: Film Critic. Robert E. Sherwood. (Illus.). 359p. 1973. 95.00 (ISBN 0-685-32337-4). Revisionist Pr.

Robert Elsmere. Mrs. Humphrey Ward. Ed. by Clyde L. Ryals. 9.00 (ISBN 0-8446-3135-3). Peter Smith.

Robert Elsmere. Mrs. Humphrey Ward. Ed. by Clyde De L. Ryals. LC 67-12116. xlvi, 636p. 1967. pap. 9.95x (ISBN 0-8032-5210-2, BB 348, Bison). U of Nebr Pr.

Robert Elsmere. Humphry Ward. Ed. by Rosemary Ashton. (World's Classics Ser.). 624p. 1987. pap. 8.95 (ISBN 0-19-281752-3). Oxford U Pr.

Robert et Elizabeth Browning. Andre Maurois. pap. 17.50 (ISBN 0-685-36958-7). French & Eur.

Robert Experiences Distilled. Robert D. Wuraftic. LC 86-90133. (Illus.). 86p. (Orig.). 1986. pap. 5.95 (ISBN 0-9616959-0-0). R D Wuraftic.

Robert Eyres Landor: A Biographical & Critical Sketch, 2 vols. in one. Eric Partridge. Bd. with Selections from Robert Landor. Ed. by Eric Partridge. LC 78-117909. (Select Bibliographies Reprint Ser). Repr. of 1927 ed. 24.50 (ISBN 0-8369-5362-2). Ayer Co Pubs.

Robert Eyres Landor: A Biographical Sketch. Eric Partridge. 1973. lib. bdg. 17.50 (ISBN 0-8414-9247-6). Folcroft.

Robert F. Kennedy: Man Who Dared to Dream. Charles P. Graves. LC 76-101302. (Americans All Ser.). (Illus.). 96p. (gr. 3-6). 1970. PLB 7.12 (ISBN 0-8116-4557-6). Garrard.

Robert Feke, Colonial Portrait Painter. Henry W. Foote. LC 72-75357. (Library of American Art Ser). 1969. Repr. of 1950 ed. lib. bdg. 37.50 (ISBN 0-306-71319-5). Da Capo.

Robert Ferguson & the Poetry of Compromise: A Study of Eighteenth Century Scottish Humanism. F. W. Freeman. 249p. 1983. 25.00x (ISBN 0-85224-474-6, Pub. by Edinburgh U Pr Scotland). Columbia U Pr.

Robert Fergusson. David Daiches. (Scottish Writers Ser.). 127p. (Orig.). 1983. pap. 6.50x (ISBN 0-7073-0313-3, Pub. by Scot Acad Pr). Longwood Pub Group.

Robert Fergusson. Allan H. MacLaine. LC 65-18225. (Twayne's English Authors Ser.). 178p. 1965. lib. bdg. 17.95 (ISBN 0-8057-1192-9). Irvington.

Robert Fergusson: Scots Poems. Ed. by Alexander Law. 70p. 1986. 20.00x (ISBN 0-85411-022-4, Pub. by Saltire Soc). State Mutual Bk.

Robert Finigan's Essentials of Wine. 1987. 19.95 (ISBN 0-394-51591-9). Knopf.

Robert Flaherty & Hans Richter. Herman G. Weinberg. (Film Ser.). 1979. lib. bdg. 59.95 (ISBN 0-8490-3001-3). Gordon Pr.

Robert Florey: The French Expressionist. Brian Taves. LC 86-17919. (Filmmakers Ser.: No. 14). (Illus.). 438p. 1987. 39.50 (ISBN 0-8108-1929-5). Scarecrow.

Robert Fludd & His Philosophicall Key. Robert Fludd. (Illus.). 156p. 1979. 45.00 (ISBN 0-88202-037-4). Watson Pub Intl.

Robert Francis: Collected Poems, 1936-1976. Robert Francis. LC 76-8753. 304p. 1986. pap. 11.95 (ISBN 0-87023-510-9). U of Mass Pr.

Robert Francis Kennedy: The Biography of a Compulsive Politician. Allen Roberts. 1984. 15.90 (ISBN 0-8283-1890-5). Branden Pub Co.

Robert Francis Weatherbee. Munro Leaf. LC 87-26046. (Illus.). 75p. (ps-3). 1988. Repr. of 1935 ed. PLB 14.50 (ISBN 0-208-02211-2, Linnet). Shoe String.

Robert Frank. Pantheon Photo Library. 144p. 1985. pap. 7.95 (ISBN 0-394-74085-8). Pantheon.

Robert Frank: New York to Nova Scotia. Ed. by Anne Tucker & Philip Brookman. 1986. 35.00 (ISBN 0-8212-1623-6, Pub. by National Gallery of Art). NYGS.

Robert Frank: Photographs. LC 85-43182. 192p. 1986. 24.50 (ISBN 0-394-55143-5). Pantheon.

Robert Frost. Elaine Barry. LC 72-79942. (Literature and Life Ser.). 1973. 16.95x (ISBN 0-8044-2016-5). Ungar.

Robert Frost. Intro. by Harold Bloom. (Modern Critical Views Ser.). 183p. 1986. 24.50 (ISBN 0-87754-626-6). Chelsea Hse.

Robert Frost. Philip L. Gerber. (Twayne's United States Authors Ser). 1966. pap. 8.95x (ISBN 0-8084-0266-8, T107, Twayne). New Coll U Pr.

Robert Frost. rev. ed. Philip L. Gerber. (United States Authors Ser.). 1982. lib. bdg. 16.95 (ISBN 0-8057-7348-7, Twayne). G K Hall.

Robert Frost. Richard Poirier. LC 76-57259. (The Work of Knowing). 1977. 24.95x (ISBN 0-19-502216-5). Oxford U Pr.

Robert Frost. Intro. by Peter Porter. (Great Poets Ser.). (Illus.). 1986. 6.95 (ISBN 0-517-56289-8, C N Potter Bks). Crown.

Robert Frost. Lawrance R. Thompson. LC 59-63268. (University of Minnesota Pamphlets on American Writers Ser.: No. 2). pap. 20.00 (ISBN 0-317-29464-4, 2055927). Bks Demand UMI.

Robert Frost: A Biography. Lawrence Thompson & R. H. Winnick. Ed. by Edward C. Lathem. LC 80-28337. (Illus.). 592p. 1981. 25.00 (ISBN 0-03-050921-1). H Holt & Co.

Robert Frost: A Chronological Survey. Lawrence Thompson. LC 74-9991. 1973. lib. bdg. 27.00 (ISBN 0-8414-8583-6). Folcroft.

Robert Frost: A Collection of Critical Essays. Ed. by James M. Cox. 1962. 12.95 (ISBN 0-13-331512-6, Spec). P-H.

Robert Frost: A Descriptive Catalog of Books & Manuscripts in the Clifton Waller Barrett Library, University of Virginia. Compiled by Joan St. C. Crane. LC 73-89904. (Illus.). xxvi, 280p. 1974. 20.00x (ISBN 0-8139-0509-5). U Pr of Va.

Robert Frost: A Friend to a Younger Poet. Henry Dierkes. 80p. 1984. 12.00x (ISBN 0-915739-03-8). Armstrong Pr.

Robert Frost: A Living Voice. Reginald L. Cook. LC 74-78982. (New England Writers Ser.). 360p. 1974. 25.00x (ISBN 0-87023-165-0). U of Mass Pr.

Robert Frost: A Study in Sensibility & Good Sense. Gorham B. Munson. LC 72-10857. (Studies in Poetry, No. 38). 1969. Repr. of 1927 ed. lib. bdg. 75.00x (ISBN 0-8383-0788-4). Haskell.

Robert Frost: A Tribute to the Source. Dewitt Jones & David Bradley. LC 78-10444. (Illus.). 176p. 1979. 22.95 (ISBN 0-03-046326-2). H Holt & Co.

Robert Frost & His Printers. Joseph Blumenthal. 85.00x. W T Taylor.

Robert Frost & His Reputation. Douglas Grant. LC 77-7604. 1977. Repr. of 1965 ed. lib. bdg. 17.00 (ISBN 0-8414-4595-8). Folcroft.

Robert Frost & New England: The Poet As Regionalist. John C. Kemp. LC 78-70301. 1979. 30.50x (ISBN 0-691-06393-1). Princeton U Pr.

Robert Frost & Sidney Cox: Forty Years of Friendship. William R. Evans. LC 80-54464. 315p. 1981. 30.00x (ISBN 0-87451-195-X). U Pr of New Eng.

Robert Frost & the New England Renaissance. George Monteiro. LC 88-5479. 192p. 1988. 17.00 (ISBN 0-8131-1649-X). U Pr of Ky.

Robert Frost & the Opposing Lights of the Hour. Richard Wakefield. LC 84-47877. (American University Studies IV (English Language & Literature): Vol. 16). 238p. (Orig.). 1984. text ed. 27.70 (ISBN 0-8204-0152-8). P Lang Pubs.

Robert Frost & Wade Van Dore: The Life of the Hired Man. Wade Van Dore. (Illus.). 291p. 1987. pap. 19.95 (ISBN 0-932429-01-7). Univ Monographs.

Robert Frost: Contours of Belief. Dorothy J. Hall. LC 83-4247. 148p. 1986. 23.95x (ISBN 0-8214-0672-8); pap. text ed. 10.95x (ISBN 0-8214-0841-0). Ohio U Pr.

Robert Frost, Farm Poultryman--The Story of Robert Frost's Career As a Breeder & Fancier of Hens. Robert Frost. Ed. by Edward C. Lathem & Lawrance Thompson. LC 64-638. 116p. 1963. 10.00x (ISBN 0-87451-032-5). U Pr of New Eng.

Robert Frost Handbook. James L. Potter. LC 79-9145. 1980. text ed. 22.50x (ISBN 0-271-00230-1). Pa St U Pr.

Robert Frost Himself. Stanley Burnshaw. (Illus.). 328p. 1986. 19.95 (ISBN 0-8076-1164-6). Braziller.

Robert Frost: Modern Poetics & the Landscapes of Self. Frank Lentricchia. LC 74-83787. 1975. 19.95 (ISBN 0-8223-0329-9). Duke.

Robert Frost One Hundred. Edward Lathem. LC 74-15258. 1974. 10.00 (ISBN 0-87923-111-4). Godine.

Robert Frost Poetry & Prose. Lathem. pap. 9.95 (ISBN 0-8050-0245-6). H Holt & Co.

Robert Frost: Poetry & Prose. Ed. by Lawrence Thompson & Edward C. Latham. LC 74-188990. 496p. 1973. pap. 13.95 (ISBN 0-03-000206-0). H Holt & Co.

Robert Frost: Poetry & Prose. Ed. by Lawrence Thompson & Edward C. Latham. LC 74-188990. 496p. 1984. pap. 9.95 (ISBN 0-03-000074-2, Owl Bks). H Holt & Co.

Robert Frost Speaks. Daniel Smyth. 158p. 29.95x (ISBN 0-8290-0203-0). Irvington.

Robert Frost: Studies of the Poetry. Kathryn G. Harris. 1980. lib. bdg. 28.00 (ISBN 0-8161-8397-X, Hall Reference). G K Hall.

Robert Frost: The Critical Reception. Ed. by Linda Wagner. 1977. 21.50 (ISBN 0-89102-096-9); pap. 8.95 (ISBN 0-685-81130-1). B Franklin.

Robert Frost: The Work of Knowing. Richard Poirier. 1977. pap. 8.95 (ISBN 0-19-502615-2). Oxford U Pr.

Robert Frost: Twentieth Century Modern American Poet Laureate. Lucas Longo. Ed. by D. Steve Rahmas. LC 70-190239. (Outstanding Personalities Ser.: No. 21). 32p. (Orig.). (gr. 7-12). 1972. lib. bdg. 3.75 incl. catalog cards (ISBN 0-87157-521-3); pap. 2.50 vinyl laminated covers (ISBN 0-87157-021-1). SamHar Pr.

Robert Frost's Emergent Design: The Truth of the Self In-Between Belief & Unbelief. Ed. by Johannes Kjorven. LC 86-7271. 208p. 1987. text ed. 39.95 (ISBN 0-391-03441-3, Pub. by Humanities Press & Solum Forlag). Humanities.

Robert Frost's Imagery & the Poetic Consciousness. Dennis Vail. (Graduate Studies: No. 12). 83p. (Orig.). 1976. pap. 8.00 (ISBN 0-89672-022-5). Tex Tech Univ Pr.

Robert Frost's Poems. enl. ed. Robert Frost. Ed. by Louis Untermeyer. 280p. 1982. pap. 3.50. WSP.

Robert Frost's Poems. Ed. by Louis Untermeyer. pap. 4.95 (ISBN 0-671-49617-4). WSP.

Robert Fulton: A Biography. Cynthia O. Philip. (Illus.). 384p. 1985. 18.95 (ISBN 0-531-09756-0). Watts.

Robert Fulton & the Submarine. W. Barclay Parsons. LC 23-5456. Repr. of 1922 ed. 16.00 (ISBN 0-404-04888-9). AMS Pr.

Robert Fulton, Engineer & Artist. facsimile ed. Henry W. Dickinson. LC 77-148879. (Select Bibliographies Reprint Ser). Repr. of 1913 ed. 26.50 (ISBN 0-8369-5649-4). Ayer Co Pubs.

Robert Fulton: Pioneer of Undersea Warfare. Wallace S. Hutcheon, Jr. LC 80-81094. (Illus.). 191p. 1981. 18.95 (ISBN 0-87021-547-7); bulk rates avail. Naval Inst Pr.

Robert Fulton: Steamboat Builder. Joanne L. Henry. LC 74-18326. (Garrard Discovery Ser.). (Illus.). 80p. (gr. 2-5). 1975. PLB 6.69 (ISBN 0-8116-6317-5). Garrard.

Robert G. Ingersoll: A Checklist. Gordon Stein. LC 78-626234. (Serif Ser.: No. 9). 158p. 1969. 10.00x (ISBN 0-87338-047-9). Kent St U Pr.

Robert Garnier & the Themes of Political Tragedy. Gillian Jondorf. LC 69-11027. 1969. Cambridge U Pr.

Robert Gerberg's Job Changing System. Robert Gerberg. 236p. 1986. pap. 8.95 (ISBN 0-8362-7932-8). Andrews & McMeel.

Robert Glenn Ketchum. Cathy Colman. 32p. (Orig.). 1983. art catalogue 10.00 (ISBN 0-9610972-0-5). PWBBA Prod.

Robert Goodnough. Martin Bush. LC 81-68051. 260p. 1982. 85.00 (ISBN 0-89659-260-X). Abbeville Pr.

Robert Gordy - Robert Warrens: Painted Faces - Painted Fantasies. Ed. by Audrey Hammill. (Illus.). 40p. (Orig.). 1988. pap. write for info. (ISBN 0-944564-01-1). Alex Mus.

Robert Gordy: Paintings & Drawings. Gene Baro. LC 81-81139. (Illus.). 112p. 1981. pap. 10.95 (ISBN 0-89494-011-2). New Orleans Mus Art.

Robert Gover: A Descriptive Bibliography. Michael Hargraves. 1988. lib. bdg. 29.50x (ISBN 0-88736-165-X). Meckler Corp.

Robert Graves. Ed. & intro. by Harold Bloom. (Modern Critical Views Ser.). 197p. 1987. lib. bdg. 24.50x (ISBN 0-87754-644-4). Chelsea Hse.

Robert Graves. Katherine Snipes. LC 78-20943. (Literature & Life Ser.). 1979. 16.95x (ISBN 0-8044-2825-5). Ungar.

Robert Graves. George Stade. LC 67-16890. (Columbia Essays on Modern Writers Ser.: No. 25). (Orig.). 1967. pap. 5.00 (ISBN 0-231-02907-1). Columbia U Pr.

Robert Graves: An Annotated Bibliography. Hallman B. Bryant. LC 86-7669. (Reference Library of the Humanities: Vol. 671). 240p. 1986. lib. bdg. 38.00 (ISBN 0-8240-8556-6). Garland Pub.

Robert Graves & the Decline of Modernism. D. J. Enright. LC 74-12209. 1960. lib. bdg. 12.50 (ISBN 0-8414-3960-5). Folcroft.

Robert Graves & the White Goddess. John B. Vickery. LC 70-183363. Repr. of 1972 ed. 29.50 (ISBN 0-8357-9713-9, 2011899). Bks Demand UMI.

Robert Graves: His Life & Work. Martin Seymour-Smith. (Illus.). 624p. 1983. 22.50 (ISBN 0-03-022171-4). H Holt & Co.

Robert Graves: His Life & Works. Martin Seymour-Smith. LC 87-9409. (Illus.). 609p. 1988. pap. 10.95 (ISBN 0-913729-18-3). Paragon Hse.

Robert Graves Manuscripts & Letters at Southern Illinois University: An Inventory. John W. Presley. LC 75-8383. vii, 261p. 1976. 18.00x (ISBN 0-87875-075-4). Whitston Pub.

Robert Graves: Peace-Weaver. James S Mehoke. (Studies in English Literature: No. 63). 168p. 1975. pap. text ed. 20.00x (ISBN 90-2793-194-1). Mouton.

Robert Greene. Charles Crupi. (Twayne's English Author Ser.: 416). 200p. 1986. lib. bdg. 21.95 (ISBN 0-8057-6905-6, Twayne). G K Hall.

Robert Greene. John C. Jordan. 1965. lib. bdg. 18.50x (ISBN 0-374-94408-3, Octagon). Hippocrene Bks.

Robert Greene: A Reference Guide. James S. Dean. (Reference Guides to Literature Ser.). 1984. lib. bdg. 61.00 (ISBN 0-8161-7854-2, Hall Reference). G K Hall.

Robert Greene Criticism: A Comprehensive Bibliography. Tetsumaro Hayashi. LC 79-142235. (Author Bibliographies Ser.: No. 6). 146p. 1971. 17.50 (ISBN 0-8108-0340-2). Scarecrow.

Robert Greene's 'The Scotish History of James IV: A Critical, Old-Spelling Edition. Charles H. Stein. Ed. by James Hogg. (Elizabethan & Renaissance Studies). 144p. (Orig.). 1977. pap. 15.00 (ISBN 3-7052-0703-2, Pub. by Salzburg Studies). Longwood Pub Group.

Robert Gregory: 1881-1918. Ed. by Colin Smythe. (Illus.). 40p. 1981. pap. 7.00 (ISBN 0-86140-108-5). Dufour.

Robert Grillery: A Retrospective. Howard D. Spencer. LC 87-50792. (Illus.). 28p. 1987. pap. 7.00 (ISBN 0-317-70029-4). Wichita Art Mus.

Robert Grilley: A Retrospective. Howard DaLee Spencer. LC 87-50792. (Illus.). 28p. 1987. pap. 7.00 (ISBN 0-939324-30-X). Wichita Art Mus.

Robert Grosseteste, Bishop of Lincoln: A Contribution to the Religious, Political & Intellectual History of the Thirteenth Century. F. S. Stevenson. (Medieval Studies Ser.). Repr. of 1899 ed. lib. bdg. 39.50 (ISBN 0-697-00018-4). Irvington.

Robert Grosseteste: The Growth of an English Mind in Medieval Europe. Richard Southern. 300p. 1986. 58.00x (ISBN 0-19-826450-X). Oxford U Pr.

Robert Grosseteste: The Growth of an English Mind in Medieval Europe. Richard W. Southern. 352p. 1988. pap. 19.95 (ISBN 0-19-826455-0). Oxford U Pr.

Robert H. Goddard: Pioneer of Space Research. Milton Lehman. (Quality Paperbacks Ser.). (Illus.). 488p. 1988. pap. 12.95 (ISBN 0-306-80331-3). Da Capo.

Robert H. Lowie, Ethnologist: A Personal Record. Robert H. Lowie. LC 59-8762. (Illus.). 226p. pap. 58.80 (2029955). Bks Demand UMI.

Robert H. Montgomery: A Pioneer Leader of American Accounting. Alfred R. Roberts. LC 75-31805. (Research Monograph: No. 63). 1975. spiral bdg. 35.00 (ISBN 0-88406-095-0). Ga St U Busn Pub.

Robert H. Schuller Tells You How to Be an Extraordinary Person in an Ordinary World. Robert H. Schuller. 192p. 1986. pap. 3.50 (ISBN 0-515-08577-4). Jove Pubns.

Robert H. Schuller Tells You How to Be an Extraordinary Person in an Ordinary World. Robert H. Schuller. Ed. by Robert A. Schuller. 1987. 16.95 (ISBN 0-8161-4159-2, Large Print Bks). G K Hall.

Robert Half on Hiring. Robert Half. LC 84-16957. 256p. 1985. 15.95 (ISBN 0-517-55436-4). Crown.

Robert Half on Hiring. Robert Half. LC 85-29771. 256p. 1986. pap. 8.95 (ISBN 0-452-25811-1, Plume). NAL.

Robert Half Way to Get Hired in Today's Job Market. 1983. pap. 4.50 (ISBN 0-553-27048-6). Bantam.

Robert Half's Success Guide for Accountants. R. Half. 1984. 20.00 (ISBN 0-07-025569-5). McGraw.

Robert Harley & the Press. J. A. Downie. LC 78-67810. 1979. 42.50 (ISBN 0-521-22187-0). Cambridge U Pr.

Robert Harley: Speaker, Secretary of State & Premier Minister. Brian Hill. LC 87-37186. 1988. text ed. 35.00 (ISBN 0-300-04284-1). Yale U Pr.

Robert Hayden: A Critical Analysis of His Poetry. Pontheolla T. Williams. LC 86-6932. 264p. 1987. 21.95 (ISBN 0-252-01289-5). U of Ill Pr.

Robert Henri & Five of His Pupils: Loan Exhibition of Paintings, April 5, to June 1, 1946. Century Association, New York Staff. LC 74-160918. (Biography Index Reprint Ser). Repr. of 1946 ed. 16.00 (ISBN 0-8369-8081-6). Ayer Co Pubs.

Robert Henri & His Circle. William I. Homer. LC 87-81951. (Illus.). 308p. 1988. Repr. of 1969 ed. lib. bdg. 50.00 (ISBN 0-87817-326-9). Hacker.

Robert Henri: His Life & Art. Bennard B. Perlman. (Illus.). 352p. 1984. 45.00 (ISBN 0-8180-0136-4). Horizon.

Robert Henryson. Matthew P. McDiarmid. Ed. by David Daiches. (Scottish Writers Ser.). 125p. (Orig.). 1983. pap. 6.50x (ISBN 0-7073-0306-0, Pub. by Scot Acad Pr). Longwood Pub Group.

Robert Henryson. Marshall W. Stearns. LC 73-182718. Repr. of 1949 ed. 16.50 (ISBN 0-404-06225-3). AMS Pr.

Robert Henryson: Selected Poems. Ed. by David Murison. 58p. 1986. 20.00x (ISBN 0-85411-010-0, Pub. by Saltire Soc). State Mutual Bk.

Robert Herrick. A. Fowler. (Warton Lectures on English Poetry). 1980. pap. 5.80 (ISBN 0-85672-240-5, Pub. by British Acad). Longwood Pub Group.

Robert Herrick: The Hesperides & Noble Numbers, 2 vols. 1979. Repr. of 1891 ed. Set. lib. bdg. 50.00 (ISBN 0-8495-4359-2). Arden Lib.

Robert Herrick's Hesperides & the Epigram Book Tradition. Ann B. Coiro. LC 87-22827. 280p. 1988. text ed. 28.50x (ISBN 0-8018-3571-2). Johns Hopkins.

Robert Hudson. Fuller G. Gallery. (Illus.). 12p. 1985. pap. 5.00 (ISBN 0-9607452-4-6). Fuller Golden Gal.

Robert Hudson: A Survey. Graham Beal et al. LC 85-8239. (Illus.). 80p. 1985. pap. 14.95 (ISBN 0-918471-02-8). San Fran MOMA.

Robert Hudson Tannahill Bequest to the Detroit Institute of Arts: A Catalogue Issued on the Occasion of the Exhibition. Detroit Institute Of Arts. LC 71-122774. (Illus.). 209p. 1970. 19.95x (ISBN 0-8143-1445-7). Wayne St U Pr.

Robert Hudson: 1983. Ed. by Fuller Golden Gallery Staff. LC 83-80400. (Illus.). 1983. pap. 8.00x (ISBN 0-9607452-2-X). Fuller Golden Gal.

Robert Hunter, Sixteen Sixty-Six to Seventeen Thirty-Four: New York's Augustan Statesman. Mary L. Lustig. LC 83-4750. (New York State Ser.). (Illus.). 312p. 1983. text ed. 32.00X (ISBN 0-8156-2296-1). Syracuse U Pr.

Robert Ingersoll. David D. Anderson. LC 71-183736. (Twayne's United States Authors Ser.). 137p. 1972. lib. bdg. 17.95 (ISBN 0-8290-1703-8). Irvington.

Robert J. Flaherty: A Biography. Paul Rotha. Ed. by Jay Ruby. LC 83-6986. (Illus.). 448p. 1984. 30.95 (ISBN 0-8122-7887-9). U of Pa Pr.

Robert K. Merton: An Intellectual Profile. Piotr Sztompka. LC 85-22273. (Theoretical Traditions in the Social Sciences Ser.). 256p. 1986. 29.95 (ISBN 0-312-68741-9); pap. 11.95 (ISBN 0-312-68739-7). St Martin.

Robert Kennedy. Daniel J. Petrillo. (World Leaders Past & Present Ser.). (Illus.). 112p. (gr. 5 up). 1989. 16.95x (ISBN 1-55546-840-3). Chelsea Hse.

Robert Kennedy. C. Peter Ripley. (World Leaders Ser.). (Illus.). 112p. (Orig.). 1989. pap. 9.95 (ISBN 0-7910-0581-X). Chelsea Hse.

Robert Kennedy: A Memoir. Jack Newfield. LC 87-30685. 320p. 1988. pap. 7.95 (ISBN 0-452-26064-7, Plume). NAL.

Robert Kennedy & His Times. Arthur M. Schlesinger, Jr. (Illus.). 1985. pap. 4.95 (ISBN 0-345-32547-8). Ballantine.

Robert Kennedy & His Times. Arthur M. Schlesinger, Jr. 1978. 19.95 (ISBN 0-395-24897-3). HM.

Robert Kennedy: In His Own Words: The Unpublished Recollections of the Kennedy Years. Ed. by Edwin O. Guthman & Jeffrey Shulman. LC 88-47680. 1988. 22.50 (ISBN 0-553-05316-7). Bantam.

Robert Keyser. Frank Zadlo. (Illus., Orig.). 1987. pap. 7.00 (ISBN 0-939351-02-1). Temple Univ Gallery.

Robert Kilwardby: De Otru Scientiarum. Ed. by Albert Judy. (Auctores Britannici Mediiaevi: Vol. IV). 280p. 1976. 40.00 (ISBN 0-85672-126-3, Pub. by British Acad). Longwood Pub Group.

Robert Kilwardby O. P., on Time & Imagination: De Tempore, De Spiritu Fantastico. Ed. by Osmund Lewry. (Auctores Britannici Medii Aevi IX). 224p. 1987. 120.00 (ISBN 0-19-726054-3). Oxford U Pr.

Robert Koch: A Life in Medicine & Bacteriology Scientific Revolutionaries. Ed. by Thomas D. Brock. (Biographical Ser.). (Illus.). 368p. 1988. 35.00 (ISBN 0-910239-19-3). Sci Tech Pubs.

Robert Koch: His Life & His Work. Thomas D. Bochalli. 1987. cancelled (ISBN 0-910239-05-3). Sci Tech Pubs.

Robert Kroetsch. Robert Lecker. (Twayne's World Author Series-Canada). 189p. 1986. lib. bdg. 19.95 (ISBN 0-8057-6619-7, Twayne). G K Hall.

Robert Kushner. Janet Kardon & Donald Kuspit. 64p. (Orig.). Date not set. pap. 18.00 (ISBN 0-88454-043-X). U of Pa Contemp Art.

Robert L. Robb's Bible Heritage Cookbook: A Gourmet Guide to Cooking with the Bible. Robert L. Robb. LC 78-59914. (Illus.). 14.95 (ISBN 0-917182-08-1). Triumph Pub.

Robert L. Vann of the Pittsburgh Courier: Politics & Black Journalism. Andrew Buni. LC 73-7700. 1974. 26.95x (ISBN 0-8229-3274-1). U of Pittsburgh Pr.

Robert Laneham's Letters see **Rogues & Vagabonds of Shakespeare's Youth, Described by John Awdeley in His Fraternitye Vacabondes 1561-1573; Thomas Harman in His Caveat for Common Cursetors, 1567-1573; & in the Groundworke of Conny-Catching, 1552.**

Robert Lansing: An Interpretive Biography. Thomas H. Hartig. 50.00 (ISBN 0-405-14085-1). Ayer Co Pubs.

Robert Lansing & American Neutrality, 1914-1917. Daniel M. Smith. LC 79-126610. (American Scene: Comments & Commentators Ser.). (Illus.). 254p. 1972. Repr. of 1958 ed. lib. bdg. 29.50 (ISBN 0-306-70057-3). Da Capo.

Robert Lawson: A Minister's Fortunes, a Story of New England. Horatio Alger, Jr. (Gold Signature Ser.). (Illus.). 120p. 1987. 20.00 (ISBN 0-317-59461-3). G K Westgard.

Robert le Diable, 2 vols. Giacomo Meyerbeer. Ed. by Phillip Gossett & Charles Rosen. LC 76-49194. (Early Romantic Opera Ser.: No. 19). 1980. Set. lib. bdg. 198.00 (ISBN 0-8240-2918-6). Garland Pub.

Robert le Diable: Roman D'Aventures. Robert Le Diable. pap. 28.00 (ISBN 0-384-51430-8). Johnson Repr.

Robert Lehman Collection at the Metropolitan Museum of Art: Italian Painting, Fourteenth Through Eighteenth Centuries, Vol. I. John Pope-Hennessy & Laurence B. Kanter. LC 86-43127. (Illus.). 352p. 1988. 90.00 (ISBN 0-691-04045-1). Princeton U Pr.

Robert Lehman Collection at the Metropolitan Museum of Art: Italian Eighteenth-Century Drawings, Vol. VI. James B. Shaw & George Knox. LC 86-43127. (Illus.). 272p. 1988. 65.00 (ISBN 0-691-04046-X). Princeton U Pr.

Robert Levy's Magic Book. Robert Levy & Joan Joseph. LC 76-16016. (Illus.). 216p. (gr. 5 up). 1976. 5.95 (ISBN 0-87131-219-0). M Evans.

Robert Ley: Hitler's Labor Leader. Ronald Smelser. (Illus.). 300p. 1988. 35.00 (ISBN 0-85496-161-5, Pub. by Berg Pubs). St Martin.

Robert Longo. Carter Ratcliff. (Illus.). 120p. pap. 25.00 (ISBN 0-8478-0602-2). Rizzoli Intl.

Robert Louis Stevenson. Margaret M. Black. LC 73-12450. 1978. Repr. of 1898 ed. lib. bdg. 20.00 (ISBN 0-8414-3233-3). Folcroft.

Robert Louis Stevenson. G. K. Chesterton. 1978. Repr. of 1928 ed. lib. bdg. 30.00 (ISBN 0-8414-0077-6). Folcroft.

Robert Louis Stevenson. Lettice Cooper. LC 73-12552. 1947. lib. bdg. 15.00 (ISBN 0-8414-3443-3). Folcroft.

Robert Louis Stevenson. Lettice Cooper. (English Novelists Ser.). 1948. 4.95x (ISBN 0-317-39777-X). Brown Bk.

Robert Louis Stevenson. L. Cope Cornford. 1979. Repr. of 1899 ed. lib. bdg. 20.00 (ISBN 0-8495-0783-9). Arden Lib.

Robert Louis Stevenson. Amy Cruse. LC 73-12592. 1915. lib. bdg. 20.50 (ISBN 0-8414-3447-6). Folcroft.

Robert Louis Stevenson. Sidney Dark. LC 76-173849. (English Literature Ser., No. 33). 1971. Repr. of 1924 ed. lib. bdg. 49.95x (ISBN 0-8383-1343-4). Haskell.
Robert Louis Stevenson. Stephen Gwynn. 1939. Repr. lib. bdg. 30.00 (ISBN 0-8414-4412-9). Folcroft.
Robert Louis Stevenson. Alexander H. Japp. 1973. Repr. of 1905 ed. 25.00 (ISBN 0-8274-0018-7). R West.
Robert Louis Stevenson. Rosaline Masson. LC 73-12875. 1914. Repr. lib. bdg. 15.50 (ISBN 0-8414-6004-3). Folcroft.
Robert Louis Stevenson. Rosaline Masson. LC 77-103204. 1970. Repr. of 1914 ed. 16.50x (ISBN 0-8046-0841-5, Pub.by Kennikat). Assoc Faculty Pr.
Robert Louis Stevenson. W. Robertson Nicoll. LC 72-13050. 1973. lib. bdg. 17.50 (ISBN 0-8414-1140-9). Folcroft.
Robert Louis Stevenson. Ed. by Andrew Noble. LC 82-24465. (Critical Studies). 232p. 1983. text ed. 28.50x (ISBN 0-389-20369-6, 07234). B&N Imports.
Robert Louis Stevenson. Walter Raleigh. 1979. Repr. of 1919 ed. lib. bdg. 17.50 (ISBN 0-8495-4612-5). Arden Lib.
Robert Louis Stevenson. Walter Raleigh. 1978. Repr. of 1895 ed. lib. bdg. 17.00 (ISBN 0-8414-7401-X). Folcroft.
Robert Louis Stevenson. Irving S. Saposnik. (English Authors Ser.: No. 167). 168p. 1974. lib. bdg. 14.95 (ISBN 0-8057-1517-7, Twayne). G K Hall.
Robert Louis Stevenson. E. Blantyre Simpson. 1973. Repr. of 1906 ed. 15.00 (ISBN 0-8274-0455-7). R West.
Robert Louis Stevenson. Evelyn B. Simpson. LC 77-10079. 1977. Repr. of 1906 ed. lib. bdg. 17.50 (ISBN 0-8414-7875-9). Folcroft.
Robert Louis Stevenson: A Critical Celebration. Ed. by Jenni Calder. (Illus.). 104p. 1980. 24.50x (ISBN 0-389-20145-6, 06916). B&N Imports.
Robert Louis Stevenson: A Life Study. Jenni Calder. (Illus.). 1980. 27.50x (ISBN 0-19-520210-4). Oxford U Pr.
Robert Louis Stevenson: A Teller of Tales. Eulalie O. Grover. LC 71-164308. (Illus.). x, 282p. (YA) (gr. 9-12). 1975. Repr. of 1940 ed. 40.00x (ISBN 0-8103-4080-1). Gale.
Robert Louis Stevenson: An Appreciation. Benjamin A. Barber. LC 74-17085. Repr. of 1910 ed. lib. bdg. 8.50 (ISBN 0-8414-3114-0). Folcroft.
Robert Louis Stevenson, an Essay. Leslie Stephen. 1979. lib. bdg. 17.00 (ISBN 0-8414-8005-2). Folcroft.
Robert Louis Stevenson & France. Charles Sarolea. LC 76-55792. 1976. Repr. of 1923 ed. lib. bdg. 25.00 (ISBN 0-8414-7708-6). Folcroft.
Robert Louis Stevenson & 'The Beach of Falesa' A Study in Victorian Publishing with the Original Text. Barry Menikoff. LC 82-61072. (Illus.). 216p. 1984. 27.50x (ISBN 0-8047-1162-3). Stanford U Pr.
Robert Louis Stevenson & the Scottish Highlanders. David B. Morris. 158p. 1982. Repr. of 1929 ed. lib. bdg. 40.00 (ISBN 0-89984-800-1). Century Bookbindery.
Robert Louis Stevenson, As a Dramatist. Arthur W. Pinero. LC 76-18307. Repr. of 1914 ed. lib. bdg. 16.00 (ISBN 0-8414-6741-2). Folcroft.
Robert Louis Stevenson: Catalogue of Collections in the Department of Rare Books. Compiled by A. D. Wainwright. LC 75-163868. (Illus.). 142p. 1971. 12.50 (ISBN 0-87811-017-8). Princeton Lib.
Robert Louis Stevenson: His Life & His Personality. St. John Adcock. 1924. Repr. 25.00 (ISBN 0-8274-3294-1). R West.
Robert Louis Stevenson in California. Katherine D. Osborne. 1973. Repr. of 1911 ed. 35.00 (ISBN 0-8274-1010-7). R West.
Robert Louis Stevenson in California: A Remarkable Courtship. Roy Nickerson. LC 82-9643. (Illus.). 128p. (Orig.). 1982. pap. 5.95 (ISBN 0-87701-246-6). Chronicle Bks.
Robert Louis Stevenson in the South Seas: An Intimate Photographic Record. Robert Louis Stevenson. Ed. by Alanna Knight. LC 86-25171. (Illus.). 192p. 1986. 18.95 (ISBN 0-913729-32-9). Paragon Hse.
Robert Louis Stevenson: Man & Writer. J. A. Steuart. 1973. Repr. of 1924 ed. 30.00 (ISBN 0-8274-0466-2). R West.
Robert Louis Stevenson Originals. E. Blantyre Simpson. 1973. Repr. of 1912 ed. 17.50 (ISBN 0-8274-0456-5). R West.
Robert Louis Stevenson: Some Recollections. Lord Guthrie. 1978. Repr. of 1924 ed. lib. bdg. 25.00 (ISBN 0-8414-5885-5). Folcroft.
Robert Louis Stevenson: The Critical Heritage. Paul Maixner. (Critical Heritage Ser.). 556p. 1981. 48.00x (ISBN 0-7100-0505-9). Routledge Chapman & Hall.
Robert Louis Stevenson: The Frail Warrior. facsimile ed. Jean M. Carre. Tr. by Eleanor Hard from Fr. LC 78-165619. (Select Bibliographies Reprint Ser). Repr. of 1930 ed. 18.00 (ISBN 0-8369-5926-4). Ayer Co Pubs.
Robert Louis Stevenson Treasury. Ed. by Alanna Knight. LC 85-2150. 384p. 1986. 32.50 (ISBN 0-312-68742-7). St Martin.
Robert Louis Stevenson's Attitude to Life. John F. Genung. 59.95 (ISBN 0-8490-0963-4). Gordon Pr.
Robert Louis Stevenson's Edinburgh Days. E. Blantyre Simpson. 1973. Repr. of 1898 ed. 20.00 (ISBN 0-8274-0457-3). R West.
Robert Louis Stevenson's Selected Essays. Ed. by George Scott-Moncrieff. 246p. 1987. pap. 7.95 (ISBN 0-89526-781-0). Regnery Gateway.
Robert Lowe & Education. David W. Sylvester. LC 73-82446. (Cambridge Texts & Studies in the History of Education). pap. 62.50 (ISBN 0-317-20811-X, 2024535). Bks Demand UMI.
Robert Lowell. Intro. by Harold Bloom. (Modern Critical Views Ser.). 181p. 1987. 19.95 (ISBN 0-87754-629-0). Chelsea Hse.
Robert Lowell. Jay Martin. (Pamphlets on American Writers Ser: No. 92). (Orig.). 1970. pap. 1.25x (ISBN 0-8166-0564-5, MPAW92). U of Minn Pr.
Robert Lowell. Burton Raffel. LC 81-40470. (Literature & Life Ser.). 160p. 1982. 16.95x (ISBN 0-8044-2707-0). Ungar.
Robert Lowell: A Biography. Ian Hamilton. LC 82-40121. 576p. 1983. 19.45 (ISBN 0-394-50965-X, Vin); pap. 8.95 (ISBN 0-394-71646-9). Random.
Robert Lowell: A Descriptive Bibliography. Steven G. Axelrod & Renee Kilmer. 300p. 1989. lib. bdg. 47.50x (ISBN 0-88736-227-3). Meckler Corp.
Robert Lowell: A Reference Guide. Steven G. Axelrod & Helen Deese. 460p. 1982. lib. bdg. 40.50 (ISBN 0-8161-7814-3, Pub by Hall Reference). G K Hall.
Robert Lowell: An Introduction to the Poetry. Mark Rudman. LC 83-2091. 224p. 1983. 24.00 (ISBN 0-231-04672-3). Columbia U Pr.
Robert Lowell: Essays on the Poetry. Ed. by Steven Axelrod & Helen Deese. (Illus.). 320p. 1987. 29.95 (ISBN 0-521-30872-0). Cambridge U Pr.
Robert Lowell: Interviews & Memoirs. Ed. by Jeffrey Meyers. 300p. 1988. 22.00 (ISBN 0-472-10089-0). U of Mich Pr.
Robert Lowell: Life of Art. Steven G. Axelrod. LC 78-51155. (Illus.). 1978. text ed. 39.00x (ISBN 0-691-06363-X); pap. 13.95x (ISBN 0-691-01364-0). Princeton U Pr.
Robert Lowell: Nihilist as Hero. Vereen M. Bell. 272p. 1983. text ed. 21.95x (ISBN 0-674-77585-6). Harvard U Pr.
Robert Lowell, the Poet & His Critics. Norma Procopiow. LC 84-467. (Poet & His Critics Ser.). pap. 88.00 (2027726). Bks Demand UMI.
Robert Lowell's Language of the Self. Katharine Wallingford. LC 87-37210. 180p. 1988. 24.95x (ISBN 0-8078-1799-6). U of NC Pr.
Robert Lowell's Poems: A Selection. Ed. by Jonathan Raban. Robert Lowell. 192p. 1974. pap. 5.95 (ISBN 0-571-10182-8). Faber & Faber.
Robert Ludlum. Robert Ludlum. (Classics Ser.). 832p. 1986. deluxe ed. write for info. (ISBN 1-55580-012-2). Octopus Bks.
Robert Ludlum, 4 vols. Boxed Set. pap. 15.80 (ISBN 0-553-30203-5). Bantam.
Robert M. La Follette & the Insurgent Spirit. David P. Thelen. LC 85-40844. 224p. 1986. pap. text ed. 9.95 (ISBN 0-299-10644-6). U of Wis Pr.
Robert M. LaFollette, Jr. & the Decline of the Progressive Party in Wisconsin. Roger T. Johnson. LC 70-113017. ix, 195p. 1970. Repr. of 1964 ed. 23.00 (ISBN 0-208-00847-0, Archon). Shoe String.
Robert M. MacIver on Community, Society, & Power. Robert MacIver. Ed. by Leon Bramson. LC 70-123374. (Heritage of Sociology Ser.). 1971. pap. 3.45x (ISBN 0-226-50048-9, P375, Phoen). U of Chicago Pr.
Robert M. MacIver on Community, Society & Power. Robert MacIver. Ed. by Leon Bramson. LC 70-123374. (Heritage of Sociology Ser). 1970. text ed. 20.00x (ISBN 0-226-50047-0). U of Chicago Pr.
Robert M. Trueblood, CPA: The Consummate Professional. R. Eugene Bryson, Jr. LC 76-48284. (Research Monograph: No. 75). 302p. 1977. spiral bdg. 35.00 (ISBN 0-88406-112-4). Ga St U Busn Pub.
Robert M. Utley: Bibliographic Checklist. Intro. by Lawrence Frost. 1985. pap. 6.95 (ISBN 0-8488-0004-4, Pub. by J M C & Co). Amereon Ltd.
Robert Mackintosh: Theologian of Integrity. Alan P. Sell. (European University Studies: Ser. 23, Vol. 95). 107p. 1977. pap. 16.95 (ISBN 3-261-03008-9). P Lang Pubs.
Robert McLean's Bulletin & a Look at Our Free Press in 1987. Robert E. Taylor. (Illus.). 372p. 1988. pap. 14.95 (ISBN 0-8059-3102-3). Dorrance.
Robert McNamara: Soldier of the American Century. Deborah Shapley. (Illus.). 480p. 1988. 20.95 (ISBN 0-688-03971-5). Morrow.
Robert Maillart's Bridges: The Art of Engineering. David P. Billington. LC 78-70279. (Illus.). 1979. 38.50x (ISBN 0-691-08203-0). Princeton U Pr.
Robert Malthey Dedication. Ed. by Martine Jotterand-Bellomo & H. P. Klinger. (Cytogenetics & Cell Genetics: Vol. 34, Nos. 1-2). (Illus.). vi, 192p. 1982. pap. 106.75 (ISBN 3-8055-3650-X). S Karger.
Robert Mangurian: Studio Works. Sara A. Richardson. (Architecture Ser.: A 1805). 5p. 1987. 3.00 (ISBN 1-55590-275-8). Vance Biblios.
Robert Mapplethorpe. Ed. by Dimitri Levas. 96p. 1988. 36.95 (ISBN 4-89194-149-9). Bks Nippan.
Robert Mapplethorpe. Richard Marshall & Robert Mapplethorpe. (Illus.). 1988. 50.00 (ISBN 0-8212-1728-3). NYGS.
Robert Mapplethorpe: Portraits. Photos by Robert Mapplethorpe. (Illus.). 132p. 1985. 50.00x. Twelvetrees Pr.
Robert Mills: Architect of the Washington Monument, 1781-1855. Helen M. Gallagher. LC 74-168092. Repr. of 1935 ed. 21.00 (ISBN 0-404-02668-0). AMS Pr.
Robert Mills's Courthouses & Jails. Gene Wadell & Rhodri W. Liscombe. (Illus.). 143p. 1982. 30.00 (ISBN 0-89308-249-X). Southern Hist Pr.
Robert Mitchum. George Eells. 336p. 1985. pap. 3.95 (ISBN 0-515-08213-9). Jove Pubns.
Robert Mitchum. Derek Malcolm. Ed. by John L. Smith. (Film & Theatre Stars Ser.). (Illus.). 96p. 1984. 6.95 (ISBN 0-88254-942-1). Hippocrene Bks.
Robert Mondavi of the Napa Valley. Cyril Ray. 192p. 1986. pap. 12.95 (ISBN 0-446-38322-8). Warner Bks.
Robert Montgomery Bird. Curtis Dahl. (Twayne's United States Authors Ser.). 1963. pap. 8.95x (ISBN 0-8084-0267-6, T31, Twayne). New Coll U Pr.
Robert Montgomery Bird. Curtis Dahl. (Twayne's U. S. Authors Ser.). 1963. lib. bdg. 17.95 (ISBN 0-317-38184-9). Irvington.
Robert Morris: Land Speculator 1790-1801. Barbara A. Chernow. LC 77-14762. (Dissertations in American Economic History Ser.). 1978. 27.50 (ISBN 0-405-11029-4). Ayer Co Pubs.
Robert Morris: Patriot & Financier. Ellis P. Oberholtzer. LC 68-57120. (Research & Source Works Ser: No. 317). (Illus.). 1969. Repr. of 1903 ed. 29.00 (ISBN 0-8337-2598-X). B Franklin.
Robert Morris: Revolutionary Financier. Clarence L. Ver Steeg. LC 71-120674. 276p. 1970. Repr. of 1954 ed. lib. bdg. 20.00x (ISBN 0-374-98078-0, Octagon). Hippocrene Bks.
Robert Morrison: The Scholar & the Man. Lindsay Ride. 48p. 1957. 40.00x (ISBN 0-317-68618-6, Pub. by Han-Shan Tang Ltd). State Mutual Bk.
Robert Morton: The Collected Works. Robert Morton. Ed. by Allan Atlas. (Masters & Monuments of the Renaissance: Vol. 2). xxxvi, 105p. 1981. 30.00x (ISBN 0-8450-7302-8). Broude.
Robert Moskowitz - Recent Paintings & Pastels, Judith Shea - Recent Sculpture. Katy Kline. (Illus.). 44p. (Orig.). 1985. pap. 4.00 (ISBN 0-938437-11-9). MIT List Visual Arts.
Robert Motherwell. Dore Ashton & Jack Flam. LC 83-3859. (Illus.). 156p. 1983. 35.00 (ISBN 0-89659-387-8); pap. 24.95 (ISBN 0-89659-388-6). Abbeville Pr.
Robert Motherwell & Black. Stephanie Terenzio. LC 79-66305. (Illus.). 156p. (Orig.). 1982. pap. 30.00 (ISBN 0-918386-28-4). Petersburg Pr.
Robert Motherwell: New & Revised. H. H. Arnason & Barbaralee Diamonstein. (Illus.). 252p. 1982. 75.00 (ISBN 0-8109-1333-X). Abrams.
Robert Motherwell: The Dedalus Sketchbooks. Ed. by Constance Glenn & Jack Glenn. 1988. slipcased 300.00 (ISBN 0-8109-4990-3); pap. 24.95 (ISBN 0-8109-2395-5). Abrams.
Robert Motherwell: The Formative Years. Robert S. Mattison. Ed. by Stephen C. Foster. LC 87-10742. (Studies in the Fine Arts: The Avant-Garde: No. 56). (Illus.). 256p. 1987. 44.95 (ISBN 0-8357-1810-7). UMI Res Pr.
Robert Mugabe. Lorraine Eide. (World Leaders - Past & Present Ser.). (Illus.). 112p. (YA) (gr. 7-12). 1989. 16.95 (ISBN 1-55546-845-4). Chelsea Hse.
Robert Murray McCheyne: A Biography. A. A. Bonar. 224p. 1983. pap. 4.95 (ISBN 0-310-44701-1, 12374P). Zondervan.
Robert Musil. Lowell Bangerter. (Literature & Life Ser.). 176p. 1988. 19.95x (ISBN 0-8044-2054-8). Ungar.
Robert Musil & the Crisis of European Culture, 1880-1942. David S. Luft. LC 78-66008. 336p. 1980. 33.00x (ISBN 0-520-03852-5); pap. 11.95 (ISBN 0-520-05328-1). U of Cal Pr.
Robert Musil, Master of the Hovering Life: A Study of the Major Fiction. Frederick G. Peters. LC 78-5158. 286p. 1978. 35.00x (ISBN 0-231-04476-3). Columbia U Pr.
Robert Musil's "Nachlass zu Lebzeiten". Gudrun Brokoph-Mauch. (New Yorker Studien zur Neueren Deutschen Literaturgeschichte: Band 4). 228p. (Orig.). 1984. pap. text ed. 24.35 (ISBN 0-8204-0174-9). P Lang Pubs.
Robert Musil's The Man Without Qualities: A Critical Study. Philip Payne. (Cambridge Studies in German). (Illus.). 272p. Date not set. 49.50 (ISBN 0-521-34032-2). Cambridge U Pr.
Robert Nadeau's Guide to Boston Restaurants: Not Including Locke-Ober, Cafe Budapest or The Ritz. Mark Zanger. LC 78-50749. 1978. pap. 3.95 (ISBN 0-930922-00-X). World Food.
Robert Needham Cust, 1821-1909: A Personal Biography. Peter Penner. LC 86-23821. (Studies in British History: Vol. 5). (Illus.). 360p. 1987. lib. bdg. 59.95x (ISBN 0-88946-456-1). E Mellen.
Robert O. Anderson Building. Earl A. Powell, III et al. (Illus.). 96p. (Orig.). 1986. pap. 14.95 (ISBN 0-87587-132-1). LA Co Art Mus.
Robert O. Anderson: Oil Man-Environmentalist & His Leading Role in the International Environmentalist Movement. Jack Raymond. 64p. (Orig.). 1988. pap. text ed. 6.50 (ISBN 0-8191-7043-7, Pub. by Aspen Inst for Humanities Studies). U Pr of Amer.
Robert of Brunne's Handlyng Synne, Pts. 1-2. Robert Mannyng. Ed. by Frederic J. Furnivall. (EETS, OS Ser.: No. 119, 123). Repr. of 1903 ed. 52.00 (ISBN 0-527-00117-1). Kraus Repr.
Robert Oliver & Mercantile Bookkeeping in the Early Nineteenth Century. Stuart W. Bruchey. LC 75-18460. (History of Accounting Ser.). 1976. 14.00x (ISBN 0-405-07544-8). Ayer Co Pubs.
Robert Oliver: Merchant of Baltimore, 1783-1819. Stuart W. Bruchey. LC 78-64225. (Johns Hopkins University. Studies in the Social Sciences. Seventy-Fourth Ser. 1956: 1). Repr. of 1956 ed. 31.00 (ISBN 0-404-61327-6). AMS Pr.
Robert Oliver, Merchant of Baltimore, 1783-1819. Stuart W. Bruchey. Ed. by Vincent P. Carosso. LC 78-18954. (Small Business Enterprise in America Ser.). 1979. Repr. of 1956 ed. lib. bdg. 32.50x (ISBN 0-405-11458-3). Ayer Co Pubs.
Robert Oppenheimer: Letters & Recollections. Robert Oppenheimer. Ed. by Alice K. Smith & Charles Weiner. LC 80-10106. (Harvard Paperbacks Ser.). 408p. 1981. 27.00x (ISBN 0-674-77605-4); pap. 8.95 (ISBN 0-674-77606-2). Harvard U Pr.
Robert Oppenheimer: Letters & Recollections. Ed. by Alice K. Smith & Charles Weiner. LC 80-10106. 1980. 20.00x. Harvard U Pr.
Robert Owen. Frank Podmore. LC 78-156295. (World History Ser., No. 48). 1971. lib. bdg. 79.95x (ISBN 0-8383-1265-9). Haskell.
Robert Owen, 2 Vols. in One. Frank Podmore. LC 68-9762. 1968. Repr. of 1906 ed. 49.50x (ISBN 0-678-00417-X). Kelley.
Robert Owen: A Chronology. V. Munoz. Tr. by W. Scott Johnson. (Libertarian & Anarchist Chronology Ser.). 1979. lib. bdg. 59.95 (ISBN 0-8490-3054-4). Gordon Pr.
Robert Owen & His Social Philosophy. William L. Sargant. LC 78-134409. Repr. of 1860 ed. 31.50 (ISBN 0-404-08455-9). AMS Pr.
Robert Owen at New Lanark: 1824-1838. LC 72-2543. (British Labour Struggles Before 1850 Ser). 1972. 18.00 (ISBN 0-405-04435-6). Ayer Co Pubs.
Robert Owen of New Lanark. Margaret I. Cole. LC 75-77254. 1969. Repr. of 1953 ed. 27.50x (ISBN 0-678-00565-6). Kelley.
Robert Owen: Prophet of the Poor. Ed. by Sidney Pollard & John Salt. LC 70-156269. 318p. 1971. 27.50 (ISBN 0-8387-7952-2). Bucknell U Pr.
Robert Owen, Social Idealist. R. H. Harvey. (California Univ. Publ. in History Mono.). Repr. of 1949 ed. 24.00 (ISBN 0-527-00976-8). Kraus Repr.
Robert Owen's Millennial Gazette. Robert Owen. LC 74-134408. Repr. of 1858 ed. 49.50 (ISBN 0-404-08454-0). AMS Pr.
Robert Owen's Millennial Gazette, Nos. 1-16. Repr. of 1858 ed. Set. 49.50 (ISBN 0-404-19546-6). AMS Pr.
Robert Owen's New Harmony Addresses. Robert Owen. LC 76-57445. 1977. 3.50x (ISBN 0-686-00153-2). Scholars Portable.
Robert Parker. Marilyn Kurata. (Mystery & Detective Ser.: No. 5). Date not set. 17.95; pap. 9.95. Starmont Hse.
Robert Peel's Irish Policy: 1812-1846. Robert C. Shipkey. Ed. by William H. McNeill & Peter Stansky. (Modern European History Ser.). 400p. 1987. lib. bdg. 60.00 (ISBN 0-8240-7831-4). Garland Pub.
Robert Penn Warren. Intro. by Harold Bloom. (Modern Critical Views Ser.). 261p. 1986. 27.50 (ISBN 0-87754-662-2). Chelsea Hse.
Robert Penn Warren. rev. ed. Charles Bohner. (United States Authors Ser.). 1981. lib. bdg. 16.95 (ISBN 0-8057-7345-2, Twayne). G K Hall.
Robert Penn Warren. Charles H. Bohner. (Twayne's United States Authors Ser.). 1964. pap. 8.95x (ISBN 0-8084-0268-4, T69, Twayne). New Coll U Pr.
Robert Penn Warren. Katherine Snipes. LC 82-40265. (Literature & Life Ser.). 170p. 1984. 16.95x (ISBN 0-8044-2828-X). Ungar.
Robert Penn Warren. Paul West. (Pamphlets on American Writers Ser: No. 44). (Orig.). 1964. pap. 1.25x (ISBN 0-8166-0336-7, MPAW44). U of Minn Pr.
Robert Penn Warren: A Collection of Critical Essays. Ed. by John L. Longley. LC 78-25757. 1979. Repr. of 1965 ed. lib. bdg. 35.00x (ISBN 0-313-20807-7, LORW). Greenwood.
Robert Penn Warren: A Descriptive Bibliography, 1922-1979. James A. Grimshaw, Jr. LC 81-3003. (Illus.). 494p. 1982. 35.00x (ISBN 0-8139-0891-4). U Pr of Va.
Robert Penn Warren: A Reference Guide. Ed. by Neil Nakadate. 1977. lib. bdg. 36.50 (ISBN 0-8161-7820-8, Hall Reference). G K Hall.
Robert Penn Warren: A Vision Earned. Marshall Walker. LC 78-31126. 279p. 1979. text ed. 28.50x (ISBN 0-06-497368-9). B&N Imports.
Robert Penn Warren & American Idealism. John Burt. LC 87-14742. 256p. 1988. text ed. 22.50 (ISBN 0-300-04067-9). Yale U Pr.

Robin Hood. Retold by Catherine Storr. LC 83-24417. (Stories Clippers Ser.). (Illus.). 32p. (gr. k-4). 1984. PLB 15.33 (ISBN 0-8172-2109-3); PLB 27.99 incl. cassette (ISBN 0-8172-2235-9); pap. 9.27g (ISBN 0-8172-2253-7); pap. text ed. 23.95 incl. cassette (ISBN 0-8172-2268-5); cassette 14.00. Raintree Pubs.

Robin Hood see New Method Supplementary Readers.

Robin Hood see New Method Supplementary Readers: Bestseller Pack.

Robin Hood: A Collection of All the Ancient Poems, Songs & Ballads, 2 vols. 200.00 (ISBN 0-8490-0965-0). Gordon Pr.

Robin Hood: A High-Spirited Tale of Adventure, Starring Jim Henson's Muppets. Jocelyn Stevenson. LC 80-5083. (Illus.). 48p. (gr. 2-6). 1980. bds. o.p. 4.95 (ISBN 0-394-84568-4). Random.

Robin Hood: An Historical Enquiry. J. G. Bellamy. LC 84-48552. 160p. 1985. 19.50x (ISBN 0-253-35015-8). Ind U Pr.

Robin Hood: His Life & Legend. Bernard Miles. LC 79-64615. (Illus.). 128p. (gr. 4 up). 11.95 (ISBN 0-528-82340-X, Checkerboard Pr). Macmillan.

Robin Hood of Sherwood Forest. Ann McGovern. (Illus.). (gr. 4-6). 1970. pap. 2.50. Scholastic Inc.

Robin Hood of Sherwood Forest. Ann McGovern. (Illus.). 128p. (gr. 4-6). 1987. pap. 2.50 (ISBN 0-590-40842-9, Pub. by Apple Classics). Scholastic Inc.

Robin Hood Stories. Edward W. Dolch & M. P. Dolch. (Dolch Pleasure Reading Ser.). 176p. (gr. 3 up). 1957. PLB 6.57 (ISBN 0-8116-2604-0). Garrard.

Robin Hood Stories. Ed. by William A. Kottmeyer et al. (Everyreader Ser.). 1962. pap. 7.96 (ISBN 0-07-033731-4). McGraw.

Robin Hood Tradition in the English Renaissance. Malcolm A. Nelson. Ed. by James Hogg. (Elizabethan & Renaissance Studies). 269p. (Orig.). 1973. pap. 15.00 (ISBN 3-7052-0663-X, Pub. by Salzburg Studies). Longwood Pub Group.

Robin Hood's Bay As It Was: Second Impression. Hendon Publishing Co., Ltd. Staff. 1986. 21.00x (ISBN 0-317-54160-9, Pub. by Hendon Pub UK). State Mutual Bk.

Robin Hyde Selected Poems. Robin Hyde. Ed. by Linda Wevers. 1985. 14.95x (ISBN 0-19-558114-8). Oxford U Pr.

Robin Hyman's Dictionary of Quotations. 516p. Date not set. 19.95 (ISBN 0-8442-5449-5, Passport Bks); pap. 14.95 (ISBN 0-8442-5448-7, Passport Bks). Natl Textbk.

Robin MacNaughton's Sun Sign Personality Guide. Robin MacNaughton. 1978. pap. 4.50 (ISBN 0-553-25747-1). Bantam.

Robin of Bray. Jean Marzollo & Claudio Marzollo. (Easy-to-Read Bks.). (Illus.). 56p. (ps-3). 1982. PLB 8.89 (ISBN 0-8037-7332-3); pap. 3.75 (ISBN 0-8037-7329-3). Dial Bks Young.

Robin of Sherwood. Richard Carpenter. (Puffin Novels Ser.). 160p. (Orig.). (gr. 5-9). 1986. pap. 2.95 (ISBN 0-14-031690-6, Puffin). Penguin.

Robin of Sherwood & the Hounds of Lucifer. Richard Carpenter & Robin May. (Puffin Novels Ser.). 176p. (Orig.). (gr. 5-9). 1986. pap. 2.95 (ISBN 0-14-031869-0, Puffin). Penguin.

Robin Sees a Song. James Pahz & Cheryl Pahz. 1977. pap. 3.75 (ISBN 0-913072-27-3). Natl Assn Deaf.

Robin Tanner. Francis Greenacre & Katherine Eustace. 56p. 1981. 30.00x (ISBN 0-317-20345-2, Pub. by Ashmolean Museum). State Mutual Bk.

Robin Who Was Afraid to Fly. Elaine Weingarten. (SIRS Stories in Rhyme Ser.). (Illus.). 50p. (ps-3). 1988. lib. bdg. 13.50 (ISBN 0-89777-701-8, 97002). Soc Issues.

Robin Winters Think Tank. Wim Bereem et al. 60p. 1986. pap. 15.00 (ISBN 0-910663-45-9). ICA Inc.

Robin Yount. Libman. (Sports Superstars Ser.). (Illus.). 32p. (gr. 4 up). 1985. PLB 8.95 (ISBN 0-317-31204-9). Creative Ed.

Robin's Play & Learn Book: Creative Activities for Preschoolers. Patricia C. Gallagher. (Illus.). 100p. (Orig.). 1987. pap. 8.95 (ISBN 0-943135-10-9). Gallagher Jordon.

Robin's Red Breast. Retold by Ellen M. Dolan & Janet L. Bolinske. (Children's Classics Ser.). (Illus.). 30p. (Orig.). (gr. 1-3). 1987. text ed. 9.95 (ISBN 0-88335-568-X); pap. text ed. 4.95 (ISBN 0-88335-588-4). Milliken Pub Co.

Robin's Return & Ray. Dorothy W. Davis. LC 85-91396. 170p. 1986. 10.95 (ISBN 0-533-06906-8). Vantage.

Robin's Story: Physical Abuse & Seeing the Doctor. Deborah Anderson & Martha Finne. LC 85-25383. (Child Abuse Bks.). (Illus.). 48p. (gr. 1-4). 1986. lib. bdg. 9.95 (ISBN 0-87518-321-2). Dillon.

Robinsheugh. Eileen Dunlop. 100p. 1987. pap. 2.95 (ISBN 0-441-73201-1). Ace Bks.

Robinson. Muriel Spark. 1978. pap. 1.25 (ISBN 0-380-01388-6, 10736, Bard). Avon.

Robinson. Jules Supervielle. 192p. 1948. 3.95 (ISBN 0-686-55103-6). French & Eur.

Robinson Crusoe see also Adventures of Robinson Crusoe.

Robinson Crusoe see also Life & Adventures of Robinson Crusoe.

Robinson Crusoe. Daniel Defoe. (Airmont Classics Ser.). (gr. 6 up). 1964. pap. 2.95 (ISBN 0-8049-0022-1, CL-22). Airmont.

Robinson Crusoe. Daniel Defoe. (Literature Ser.). (gr. 7-12). 1970. pap. text ed. 7.08 (ISBN 0-87720-736-4). AMSCO Sch.

Robinson Crusoe. Daniel Defoe. 288p. (gr. 7-12). 1982. pap. 1.95 (ISBN 0-553-21105-6, Bantam Classics). Bantam.

Robinson Crusoe. Daniel Defoe. 1977. 14.95x (ISBN 0-460-00059-4, Evman); pap. 2.50x (ISBN 0-460-01059-X, Evman). Biblio Dist.

Robinson Crusoe. Daniel Defoe. (Span.). 9.95 (ISBN 84-241-5636-6). E Torres & Sons.

Robinson Crusoe. Daniel Defoe. (Illus.). (gr. 4-6). 1952-63. il. jr. lib. o.p. 5.95 (ISBN 0-448-05821-9, G&D); Companion Lib. Ed. o.p. 2.95 (ISBN 0-448-05467-1); deluxe ed. 12.95 (ISBN 0-448-06021-3); PLB 3.79 (ISBN 0-448-03260-0). Putnam Pub Group.

Robinson Crusoe. Daniel Defoe. 320p. (RL 6). pap. 2.25 (ISBN 0-451-51606-0, CJ1606, Sig Classics). NAL.

Robinson Crusoe. Daniel Defoe. Ed. by Michael Shinagel. (Critical Editions Ser.). 399p. 1975. pap. text ed. 7.95x (ISBN 0-393-09231-3). Norton.

Robinson Crusoe. Daniel Defoe. Ed. by John N. Fago. (Now Age Illustrated IV Ser.). (Illus.). (gr. 4-12). 1978. text ed. 7.50 (ISBN 0-88301-332-0); pap. text ed. 2.95 (ISBN 0-88301-320-7); activity bk. 1.25 (ISBN 0-88301-344-4). Pendulum Pr.

Robinson Crusoe. Daniel Defoe. Ed. by Angus Ross. (English Library Ser.). (YA) (gr. 9 up). 1966. pap. 2.25 (ISBN 0-14-043007-5). Penguin.

Robinson Crusoe. Daniel Defoe. (Regents Illustrated Classics Ser.). 62p. (gr. 7-12). 1982. pap. text ed. 3.50 (ISBN 0-13-795410-7, 20418). Prentice ESL.

Robinson Crusoe. Daniel Defoe. Ed. by Edward W. Dolch et al. (gr. k-3). 1973. pap. 2.50 (ISBN 0-590-41841-6). Scholastic Inc.

Robinson Crusoe. Daniel Defoe. (Bambi Classics Ser.). (Illus.). 384p. (Orig.). (YA) (gr. 9-12). 1981. pap. 3.95 (ISBN 0-89531-067-8, 0221-48). Sharon Pubns.

Robinson Crusoe. Daniel Defoe. 1982. Repr. lib. bdg. 19.95x (ISBN 0-89966-403-2). Buccaneer Bks.

Robinson Crusoe. Daniel Defoe. (Children's Classics Ser.). (gr. 3-6). 1981. 6.95 (ISBN 0-86020-554-1, Usborne-Hayes); PLB 11.96 (ISBN 0-88110-062-5); pap. 2.95 (ISBN 0-86020-553-3). EDC.

Robinson Crusoe. Daniel Defoe. (Illus.). 368p. 1983. 22.50 (ISBN 0-684-17946-6, Pub. by Scribner); Deluxe, numbered, boxed ed. o.p. 75.00 (ISBN 0-684-17947-4). Macmillan.

Robinson Crusoe. Daniel Defoe. LC 84-50438. (Silver Burdett Classics for Kids Ser.). (Illus.). 32p. (gr. 2 up). 1984. 5.96 (ISBN 0-382-06815-7). Silver.

Robinson Crusoe. Daniel Defoe. LC 84-504380. (Silver Burdett Classics for Kids Ser.). 32p. (gr. 2 up). 1985. pap. 3.60 (ISBN 0-382-06958-7). Silver.

Robinson Crusoe. Daniel Defoe. 21.95 (ISBN 0-88411-594-1, Pub. by Aeonian Pr). Amereon Ltd.

Robinson Crusoe. Daniel Defoe. LC 84-52575. (Silver Burdett Classics for Kids Ser.). (Illus.). 32p. (Span.). (gr. 3 up). 1985. pap. 3.60 (ISBN 0-382-09024-1). Silver.

Robinson Crusoe. Daniel Defoe. (Puffin Classics Ser.). 1987. pap. 2.25 (ISBN 0-14-035072-1, Puffin). Penguin.

Robinson Crusoe. Edward W. Dolch & M. P. Dolch. (Dolch Pleasure Reading Ser.). 176p. (gr. 3 up). 1958. PLB 6.57 (ISBN 0-8116-2610-5). Garrard.

Robinson Crusoe. (Guild Books Classics Illustrated Ser.). (Illus.). pap. 0.59 (ISBN 0-685-74081-1, 10). Guild Bks.

Robinson Crusoe. (gr. k-2). pap. 1.95 (ISBN 0-87497-110-1, 18155). Merrimack.

Robinson Crusoe. (Classics Ser.). (gr. 4 up). 1988. pap. 3.95 (ISBN 0-582-54156-5). Longman.

Robinson Crusoe see New Method Supplementary Readers.

Robinson Crusoe: A New Fiction. Barbara Einzig. 62p. (Orig.). 1984. pap. 2.00 (ISBN 0-87924-048-2). Membrane Pr.

Robinson Crusoe: An Annotated Checklist of English Editions, 1719-1985. Robert W. Lovett. 1988. lib. bdg. 39.50x (ISBN 0-88736-058-0). Meckler Corp.

Robinson Crusoe & Its Printing, 1719-1731. Henry C. Hutchins. LC 25-11861. Repr. of 1925 ed. 16.50 (ISBN 0-404-03463-2). AMS Pr.

Robinson Crusoe & Other Writings. Daniel Defoe. Ed. by James Sutherland. LC 77-77300. (Gotham Library). 416p. 1977. pap. 12.50x (ISBN 0-8147-7785-6). NYU Pr.

Robinson Crusoe: Examin'd & Criticis'd on A New Edition of Charles Gildon's Famous Pamphlet. Paul Dottin. LC 74-5071. 1923. lib. bdg. 25.00 (ISBN 0-8414-3754-8). Folcroft.

Robinson Crusoe Notes. Cynthia McGowan. (Orig.). 1976. pap. text ed. 3.50 (ISBN 0-8220-1150-6). Cliffs.

Robinson Crusoe's Return. Eric Odell. Ed. by R. Reginald & Douglas Menville. LC 75-46298. (Supernatural & Occult Fiction Ser.). 1976. Repr. of 1907 ed. lib. bdg. 14.00x (ISBN 0-405-08158-8). Ayer Co Pubs.

Robinson Jeffers. Robert J. Brophy. LC 75-29982. (Western Writers Ser.: No. 19). (Illus., Orig.). 1975. pap. 2.95x (ISBN 0-88430-018-8). Boise St Univ.

Robinson Jeffers. Frederic I. Carpenter. (Twayne's United States Authors Ser.). 1962. pap. 8.95x (ISBN 0-8084-0269-2, T22, Twayne). New Coll U Pr.

Robinson Jeffers: A Portrait. Louis Adamic. 1978. Repr. of 1929 ed. lib. bdg. 27.50 (ISBN 0-8495-0048-6). Arden Lib.

Robinson Jeffers: A Portrait. Louis Adamic. LC 73-11375. 1929. lib. bdg. 16.50 (ISBN 0-8414-2881-6). Folcroft.

Robinson Jeffers & the Critics, 1912-1983: A Bibliography of Secondary Sources with Selective Annotations. Jeanetta Boswell. LC 86-17862. (Scarecrow Author Bibliographics Ser.). 184p. 1986. 18.50 (ISBN 0-8108-1914-7). Scarecrow.

Robinson Jeffers & the Sea. Melba B. Bennett. LC 73-9. 1971. Repr. of 1936 ed. lib. bdg. 20.00 (ISBN 0-8414-3154-X). Folcroft.

Robinson Jeffers: Fragments of an Older Fury. Bro. Antoninus. 1970. 7.50 (ISBN 0-685-04672-9). Oyez.

Robinson Jeffers: Myth, Ritual & Symbol in His Narrative Poems. Robert J. Brophy. LC 75-38928. (Illus.). xxii, 323p. 1976. Repr. of 1973 ed. 29.50 (ISBN 0-208-01574-4, Archon). Shoe String.

Robinson Jeffers: Poet of California. James Karman. LC 87-6396. (Literary West Ser.). (Illus.). 160p. (Orig.). 1987. pap. 6.95 (ISBN 0-87701-359-4). Chronicle Bks.

Robinson Jeffers: Poet of Inhumanism. Arthur B. Coffin. LC 74-121767. 324p. 1971. 32.50x (ISBN 0-299-05840-9). U of Wis Pr.

Robinson Jeffers: The Man & His Work. Clark Powell. 222p. 1983. lib. bdg. 50.00 (ISBN 0-89984-834-6). Century Bookbindery.

Robinson Jeffers: The Man & His Work. Lawrence C. Powell. 1973. lib. bdg. 59.95 (ISBN 0-8490-0966-9). Gordon Pr.

Robinson Jeffers: The Man & His Work. Lawrence C. Powell. LC 68-54176. (American Biography Ser., No. 32). (Illus.). 1969. Repr. of 1934 ed. lib. bdg. 49.95x (ISBN 0-8383-0675-6). Haskell.

Robinson-Patman Act. Richard Posner. 1976. pap. 7.00 (ISBN 0-8447-3228-1). Am Enterprise.

Robinson-Patman Act & Effective Competition. John S. McGee. Ed. by Stuart Bruchey & Vincent P. Carosso. LC 78-18968. (Small Business Enterprise in America Ser.). (Illus.). 1979. lib. bdg. 51.50x (ISBN 0-405-11472-9). Ayer Co Pubs.

Robinson-Patman Act: Policy & Law, 2 vols. Incl. Vol. 1. 178p. 1980 (ISBN 0-89707-025-9); Vol. 2. 1983. 10.00 ea. Amer Bar Assn.

Robinson-Patman Primer: A Businessman's Guide to the Law Against Price Discrimination. 2nd ed. Earl W. Kintner. (Illus.). 1979. write for info. (ISBN 0-02-364370-6). Macmillan.

Robinson's Lake (11-Ms-582) Site: Emergent Mississippian Occupation. George R. Milner. LC 84-24107. (American Bottom Archaeology: Selected FAI-270 Site Reports Ser.: Vol. 10). (Illus.). 240p. 1985. pap. 14.95 (ISBN 0-252-01072-8). U of Ill Pr.

Robitnychyj Strayku v Polyshi. Ed. by Myroslav Prokop. 193p. (Ukrainian.). 1981. write for info. Ukrainian Pol.

Robland. Michael Randolph. 1985. 7.95 (ISBN 0-533-05284-X). Vantage.

Robo Force & the Giant Robot. Seth McEvoy. LC 84-62029. (Illus.). 32p. (ps-2). 1985. pap. 1.95 (ISBN 0-394-87271-1, BYR). Random.

Robo Force & the Mountain of Burning Ice. Seth McEvoy. LC 84-62028. (Illus.). 32p. (ps-2). 1985. pap. 1.95 (ISBN 0-394-87170-7, BYR). Random.

Robocop. Ed Naha. (Orig.). 1987. pap. 3.50 (ISBN 0-440-17479-1). Dell.

Robojox. Robert Thurston. 1988. pap. 3.50 (ISBN 0-380-75444-4). Avon.

Robomatix Reporter Annual Index, 1983. Ed. by Janice K. Mandell. 80p. write for info. (ISBN 0-89947-033-5, EIC Intell). Bowker.

Robomatix Reporter Annual Index, 1984. 131p. write for info. (ISBN 0-89947-039-4, EIC Intell). Bowker.

Robomatix Reporter Annual Index, 1985. Ed. by Barry Lenson & Carol Wierzbicki. 113p. 1986. pap. write for info. (ISBN 0-89947-041-6, EIC Intell). Bowker.

Robomatix Reporter Annual Index, 1986. write for info. (ISBN 0-89947-056-4, EIC Intell). Bowker.

Robomatix Reporter Annual Index, 1987. Ed. by Glenn Schaefer. 1988. pap. text ed. 155.00 (ISBN 0-89947-057-2, EIC Intell). Bowker.

Robot. Jan Pienkowski. (Illus.). 12p. (gr. 1 up). 1981. 9.95 (ISBN 0-440-07459-2). Delacorte.

Robot Adept. Piers Anthony. LC 87-19148. (Apprentice Adept Ser.: Bk. 5). 288p. 1988. 16.95 (ISBN 0-399-13359-3). Putnam Pub Group.

Robot Adept. Piers Anthony. Date not set. price not set. Ace Bks.

Robot Age. Graham Storrs. LC 85-70451. (Tomorrow's World Ser.). (gr. 4-6). 1986. lib. bdg. 12.40 (ISBN 0-531-18020-4, Pub. by Bookwright Pr). Watts.

Robot Analysis & Control. Jean-Jacques E. Slotine & Haruhiko Asada. LC 85-1579. 266p. 1986. 37.95 (ISBN 0-471-83029-1). Wiley.

Robot & Rebecca the Missing Owser. Jane Yolen. LC 81-4870. (Capers Bks.). (Illus.). 96p. (gr. 3-6). 1981. lib. bdg. 4.99 (ISBN 0-394-94832-7); pap. 1.95 (ISBN 0-394-84832-2). Knopf.

Robot & Rebecca: The Mystery of the Code-Carrying Kids. Jane Yolen. LC 79-27391. (Capers Ser.). (Illus.). 96p. (gr. 3-6). 1980. lib. bdg. 4.99 (ISBN 0-394-94488-7); pap. 1.95 (ISBN 0-394-84488-2). Knopf.

Robot Applications. Karl Wojcikiewicz & Ron Johnson. LC 84-12757. (Illus.). 600p. 1984. 99.95 (ISBN 0-87119-055-9); pap. text ed. 19.95 (ISBN 0-317-14618-1); tchr's. ed. 9.95 (ISBN 0-87119-108-3); 10.95 (ISBN 0-87119-056-7). Heathkit-Zenith Ed.

Robot Birthday. Eve Bunting. LC 79-19185. (Smart Cat Bks.). (Illus.). 80p. (gr. 1-3). 1980. 7.95 (ISBN 0-525-38542-8). Dutton.

Robot Book. Phyllis Hoffman. (Colorforms Board Bks.). (Illus.). 14p. (ps-1). 1986. bds. 5.95 (ISBN 0-590-40106-8). Scholastic Inc.

Robot-Bot-Bot. Fernando Krahn. LC 78-21959. (ps-1). 1979. 6.95 (ISBN 0-525-38545-2). Dutton.

Robot Changer: Master of Doom. (Illus.). (gr. k-9). 1988. pap. 1.95. Scholastic Inc.

Robot Changer: Quest for Power. (Illus.). (gr. k-9). 1988. pap. 1.95. Scholastic Inc.

Robot Control (SYROCO 1985) Proceedings of the IFAC Symposium, Barcelona, Spain, 18-20 November 1985. Ed. by L. Basanez et al. (IFAC Proceedings Ser.: Vol. 9). 500p. 1987. 180.00 (ISBN 0-08-033446-6, Pub. by PPL). Pergamon.

Robot Design Handbook. Ed. by Gerry B. Andeen & SRI International Staff. (Illus.). 384p. 1988. 42.50. McGraw.

Robot Dreams. Isaac Asimov. Ed. by Bryon Preiss. (Masterworks of Science Fiction & Fantasy: No. 5). 336p. 1987. ltd. ed. 50.00 (ISBN 0-425-09346-8, Berkley Trade Pbks); pap. 8.95 (ISBN 0-425-09345-X). Berkley Pub.

Robot Dynamics Algorithms. Roy Featherstone. 1987. lib. bdg. 42.50 (ISBN 0-89838-230-0). Kluwer Academic.

Robot Dynamics & Control. Spong. 1988. write for info. (ISBN 0-471-61243-X). Wiley.

Robot Engineering Textbook. Mo Shahinpoor. 450p. text ed. 43.95t scp (ISBN 0-06-045931-X, HarpC). Har-Row.

Robot Exhibit: History, Fantasy & Reality. American Craft Council. (Illus.). 64p. 1984. 10.00 (ISBN 0-88321-052-5). AM Craft.

Robot Grippers. Ed. by D. T. Pham & W. B. Heginbotham. (International Trends in Manufacturing Technology Ser.). 360p. 1986. 70.00 (ISBN 0-387-16004-3). Springer-Verlag.

Robot Grippers. Ed. by D. T. Pham & W. B. Heginbotham. 450p. 1986. 80.00x (ISBN 0-948507-03-9, Pub. by IFS Pubns UK). Air Sci Co.

Robot Hands & the Mechanics of Manipulation. Matthew T. Mason & J. Kenneth Salisbury. (Artificial Intelligence Ser.). (Illus.). 275p. 1985. text ed. 32.50x (ISBN 0-262-13205-2). MIT Pr.

Robot in Every Home: An Introduction to Personal Robots & Brand-Name Buyer's Guide. Mike Higgins. LC 84-28915. (Illus.). 192p. 1985. o. p. 24.95 (ISBN 0-931445-15-9); pap. 14.95 (ISBN 0-931445-16-7). Kensington Pub.

Robot in Every Home: An Introduction to Personal Robots & Brand-Name Buyer's Guide. Mike Higgins. 192p. (Orig.). 1985. pap. 16.95 (ISBN 0-317-39392-8). Robot Inst Am.

Robot Intelligence... with Experiments. David L. Heiserman. LC 80-21440. (Illus.). 322p. 1981. pap. 10.95 (ISBN 0-8306-1191-6, 1191P). TAB Bks.

Robot Manipulators: Mathematics, Programming, & Control. Richard P. Paul. (MIT Press Artificial Intelligence Ser.). (Illus.). 279p. 1981. text ed. 37.50x (ISBN 0-262-16082-X). MIT Pr.

Robot Math. Patricia Rex. (ps-k). 1989. pap. 6.95 (ISBN 0-8224-5841-1). D S Lake Pubs.

Robot Modelling. P. G. Ra'nky & C. Y. Ho. 380p. 1985. 49.50 (ISBN 0-387-15373-X). Springer-Verlag.

Robot Modelling: Control & Applications with Software. P. Ranky & C. Y. Ho. 380p. 1985. 59.00x (ISBN 0-903608-72-3, Pub. by IFS Pubns UK). Air Sci Co.

Robot Motion: Planning & Control. Michael Brady et al. (Artificial Intelligence Ser.). (Illus.). 585p. 1982. 42.50x (ISBN 0-262-02182-X). MIT Pr.

Robot Novels. Isaac Asimov. 656p. 1988. pap. 14.95 (ISBN 0-345-33119-2, Del Rey). Ballantine.

Robot Odyssey I: Escape from Robotropolis. Fred D'Ignazio. 288p. 1988. 18.95 (ISBN 0-312-93081-X). Tor Bks.

Robot on Vacation. Marie Tenaille. Tr. by Didi Charney from Fr. LC 88-16743. (Aladdin Storybooks Ser.). (Illus.). 36p. (Orig.). (gr. 1-3). Date not set. pap. 2.95 (ISBN 0-689-71280-4, Aladdin Bks). Macmillan.

Robot Ping-Pong Player: Experiment in Real-Time Intelligent Control. Russell L. Anderson. (Artificial Intelligence Ser.). 312p. 1988. text ed. 35.00x (ISBN 0-262-01101-8). MIT Pr.

Robot Psychiatrist. Joseph L. Palotta. 603p. 1981. pap. 29.95 (ISBN 0-9604852-0-1). Revelation Hse.

Robot Race. David A. Kraft. (Micro Adventure Ser.: No. 6). 128p. (Orig.). (gr. 6 up). 1984. pap. 1.95 (ISBN 0-590-33170-1). Scholastic Inc.

Robot Raiders. Ellen Leroe. LC 86-45782. 192p. (gr. 6-9). 1987. 11.70i (ISBN 0-06-023835-6); PLB 11.89 (ISBN 0-06-023836-4). HarpJ.

Robot Readiness. Patricia Rex. (ps-k). 1989. pap. 6.95 (ISBN 0-8224-5842-X). D S Lake Pubs.

Robots, 2 Vols. David M. Osborne. Incl. Bk. 1. Robots, An Introduction to Basic Concepts & Applications; Bk. 2. The Application of Robots to Practical Work. 1984. Bk. 1. 29.95 (ISBN 0-910853-00-2); Bk. 2. 27.50 (ISBN 0-910853-02-9); softcover 19.95 ea. (ISBN 0-910853-03-7). Midwest Sci-Tech.

Robots. Kate Petty. (First Library). (Illus.). 32p. (gr. k-3). 1985. lib. bdg. 10.90 (ISBN 0-531-04900-0). Watts.

Robots. Price, Stern & Sloan Staff. (How & Why Wonder Bks.). (Illus.). 32p. (YA) (gr. 7-12). 1987. pap. 1.95 (ISBN 0-8431-4290-1). Price Stern.

Robots. Graham Richard. (Topics Ser.). (Illus.). 32p. (gr. 1-6). 1986. PLB 11.90 (ISBN 0-531-18061-1, Pub. by Bookwright). Watts.

Robots. LC 80-11681. (Look Inside Ser.). (Illus.). 48p. (gr. 4-12). 1985. pap. 9.27 (ISBN 0-8172-1433-X). Raintree Pubs.

Robots, Bk. 8. Joe D. Fugate, Sr. & Gary Thomas. (Traveller Ser.). (Illus.). 49p. (Orig.). 1986. pap. 6.00 (ISBN 0-943580-10-2). Game Designers.

Robots: A Gentle Introduction. Bettie C. Hall & Ernest Hall. Date not set. price not set. P-H.

Robots A Two Z. Thomas H. Metos. LC 80-21004. (Illus.). 80p. (gr. 4 up). 1980. PLB 9.29 (ISBN 0-671-34027-1). Messner.

Robots & Automated Manufacture. Ed. by J. Billingsley et al. (Control Ser.). 248p. 1985. casebound 43.00 (ISBN 0-86341-053-7, CE028). Inst Elect Eng.

Robots & Computers. Nigel Hawkes. LC 84-50614. (Electronic Revolution Bk.). (Illus.). 29p. (gr. 4-7). 1984. PLB 11.90 (ISBN 0-531-04816-0). Watts.

Robots & Empire. Isaac Asimov. 1986. pap. 4.50 (ISBN 0-345-32894-9, Del Rey). Ballantine.

Robots & Gardens: Science Fantasy Poems. Al Montes. 48p. 1985. 4.00 (ISBN 0-918476-14-3). Cornerstone Pr.

Robots & Manipulator Systems: Papers, 2 pts. Conference on Remotely Manned Systems, 2nd, June 1975. Ed. by E. Heer. LC 77-73105. 336p. 1977. pap. text ed. 32.00 ea. o.p. Pergamon.

Robots & Manufacturing Automation. C. Ray Asfahl. LC 84-23706. 490p. 1985. write for info. (ISBN 0-471-80212-3). Wiley.

Robots & Robotics. Margaret Baldwin & Gary Peck. (Computer Awareness Bk.). 72p. (gr. 5 up). 1984. lib. bdg. 9.90 (ISBN 0-531-04705-9). Watts.

Robots & the Intelligent Computer. David Darling. LC 85-25369. (World of Computers Ser.). (Illus.). 80p. (gr. 5 up). 1986. lib. bdg. 11.95 (ISBN 0-87518-315-8). Dillon.

Robots, Androids, & Mechanical Oddities: The Science Fiction of Philip K. Dick. Philip K. Dick. Ed. by Patricia S. Warrick & Martin H. Greenberg. (Alternatives Ser.). 248p. (Orig.). 1986. 19.95; pap. 10.95. S Ill U Pr.

Robots, Androids & Mechanical Oddities: The Science Fiction of Philip K. Dick. Ed. by Patricia S. Warrick & Martin H. Greenberg. LC 83-19627. 248p. 1984. 19.95 (ISBN 0-8093-1159-3); pap. 10.95. S Ill U Pr.

Robots Are Here. Alvin Silverstein & Virginia B. Silverstein. LC 83-9555. (Illus.). 128p. (gr. 5-9). 1983. 12.95 (ISBN 0-13-782185-9). P-H.

Robots Are Here. Alvin Silverstein & Virginia Silverstein. 128p. (Orig.). (gr. 3-7). 1986. pap. 7.95 (ISBN 0-13-782111-5). P-H.

Robots at Work. John Hartley. 192p. 1983. 39.00 (ISBN 0-444-86638-8, North-Holland). Elsevier.

Robot's Dilemma: The Frame Problem in Artificial Intelligence. Ed. by Zenon Pylyshyn. LC 86-10801. (Theoretical Issues in Cognitive Science: Vol. 4). 168p. 1987. text ed. 34.50 (ISBN 0-89391-371-5). Ablex Pub.

Robots East Seminar: Proceedings. Robotic Industries Association Staff. 200p. 1985. pap. 42.00 (ISBN 0-317-39390-1). Robot Inst Am.

Robots Eight Conference Proceedings, 2 Vols. Robots Eight, Detroit, Mich., June 1984. Incl. Vol. I. Applications for Today; Vol. II. Future Considerations. 1800p. 1984. Set. 113.00 (ISBN 0-318-01664-8); 67.00 ea. Robot Inst Am.

Robots: Facts Behind the Fiction. Michael Chester. LC 83-61237. (Illus.). 96p. (gr. 5-9). 1983. 9.95 (ISBN 0-02-718220-7). Macmillan.

Robots in Assembly. A. H. Redford & E. K. Lo. LC 86-7603. (Open University Press Robotics Ser.). 176p. 1986. 46.95 (ISBN 0-470-20326-9). Wiley.

Robots in Automobile Industy: Proceedings of the Second International Conference. 1985. 75.00x (ISBN 0-903608-89-8, Pub by IFS Pubns UK). Air Sci Co.

Robots in Industry: Applications for Assembly. 2nd ed. Richard K. Miller. (Illus.). 210p. 1984. pap. text ed. 125.00 (ISBN 0-89671-054-8). SEAI Tech Pubns.

Robots in Industry: Applications for Foundries. 2nd ed. Richard K. Miller. (Illus.). 190p. 1984. pap. text ed. 125.00 (ISBN 0-89671-055-6). SEAI Tech Pubns.

Robots in Industry: Applications for Metal Fabrication. 2nd ed. Richard R. Miller. (Illus.). 226p. 1984. pap. text ed. 125.00 (ISBN 0-89671-057-2). SEAI Tech Pubns.

Robots in Industry: Applications for the Electronics Industry. Richard K. Miller. (Illus.). 190p. 1984. pap. text ed. 125.00 (ISBN 0-89671-049-1). SEAI Tech Pubns.

Robots in Industry: Applications for the Plastics Industry. 2nd ed. Richard K. Miller. 180p. 1984. pap. text ed. 125.00 (ISBN 0-89671-053-X). SEAI Tech Pubns.

Robots in Industry: General Applications. 2nd ed. Richard K. Miller. (Illus.). 219p. 1984. pap. text ed. 125.00 (ISBN 0-89671-056-4). SEAI Tech Pubns.

Robots in Inspection. Ed. by J. Lee. 170p. 1987. 23.00 (ISBN 0-87263-286-5). SME.

Robots in Manufacturing: Key to International Competitiveness. Jack Baranson. LC 83-81240. 168p. 1983. 32.50 (ISBN 0-912338-39-3); microfiche 16.50 (ISBN 0-912338-40-7). Lomond.

Robots in the Automotive Industry: Proceedings. International Conference, 1st, Birmingham, UK, April 1982. 218p. 1982. text ed. 62.00x (ISBN 0-903608-22-7, Pub. by IFSPUBS). Scholium Intl.

Robots in the Automotive Industry 1985: Proceedings of the Second International Conference, Birmingham, U. K. 14-17 May, 1985. Ed. by T. Husband. 300p. 1985. 105.25 (ISBN 0-444-87769-X, North-Holland). Elsevier.

Robots in the Japanese Economy. Kuni Sadamoto. (Illus.). 280p. 1981. 30.00 (ISBN 0-89955-344-3, Pub. by Survey Japan). Intl Spec BK.

Robots: Japanese Tin Toys from the Late 1940's to the 1970's. Teruhisa Kitahara. LC 84-23313. (Illus.). 112p. (Orig.). 1985. pap. 9.95 (ISBN 0-87701-355-1). Chronicle Bks.

Robots: Machines in Man's Image. Isaac Asimov & Karen A. Frenkel. LC 84-22758. 246p. 19.95 (ISBN 0-517-55110-1, Harmony). Crown.

Robots: Machines in Man's Image. Isaac Asimov & Karen A. Frenkel. (Illus.). 160p. 1985. 21.95 (ISBN 0-317-39396-0). Robot Inst Am.

Robots Nine Conference Proceedings, 2 vols. 2000p. (Orig.). 1985. Vol. 1 Advancing Applications. pap. 67.00 ea.; Vol. 2 Current Issues, Future Concerns. pap. 113.00 set (ISBN 0-317-39397-9). Robot Inst Am.

Robots of Dawn, Vol. 3. Isaac Asimov. 416p. 1984. pap. 3.95 (ISBN 0-345-31571-5, Del Rey). Ballantine.

Robots or Men: French Workman's Experience in American Industry. Hyacinth Dubreuil. Ed. by Leon Stein. LC 77-70491. (Work Ser.). 1977. Repr. of 1930 ed. lib. bdg. 24.50x (ISBN 0-405-10163-5). Ayer Co Pubs.

Robots Out of Wonderland: How to Use Robots in the Age of CIM. Tony Owen. (Illus.). 80p. 1987. 50.00 (ISBN 0-947767-59-2). Manufacturing Techn.

Robots: Proceedings, 2 vols, No. 8. Society of Manufacturing Engineers. 1984. Set. 110.00 (ISBN 0-87263-147-8). SME.

Robots: Proceedings, 2 vols, No. 9. Society of Manufacturing Engineers. 1985. Set. 110.00 (ISBN 0-87263-189-3). SME.

Robots Three-D Coloring Book. Illus. by Steve Pileggi. (Illus., Orig.). (gr. k-5). Date not set. Incl. crayons. pap. 2.99 (ISBN 0-86679-070-5). Oak Tree Pubns.

Rob's Place. John R. Townsend. LC 86-27373. (gr. 4-9). 1988. PLB 11.95 (ISBN 0-688-07258-5). Lothrop.

Robsart Affair. Jeannette Letton. 268p. 1976. Repr. of 1956 ed. lib. bdg. 17.95x (ISBN 0-89244-015-5, Pub. by Queens Ltd). Amereon Ltd.

Robsart Affair. Jennette Letton & Francis Letton. Repr. lib. bdg. 17.95 (ISBN 0-89190-237-6, Pub. by River City Pr). Amereon Ltd.

Robson Guide - Stillwater Trout Flies: An Alphabetical Survey in Colour. Kenneth Robson. 1985. 90.00x (ISBN 0-317-39170-4, Pub. by BeeKay Pubs Ltd); pap. 40.00 (ISBN 0-317-39171-2, Pub. by BeeKay Pubs Ltd). State Mutual Bk.

Robson's Guide: Stillwater Trout Flies, An Alphabetical Survey in Colour. Kenneth Robson. 302p. 1985. 36.95 (ISBN 0-947674-02-0). Greycliff Pub.

Robur le Conquerant. Jules Verne. (Illus.). 185p. 1977. 10.95 (ISBN 0-686-55946-0); pap. 3.95 (ISBN 0-686-55947-9). French & Eur.

Robust & Insensitive Design of Multivariable Feedback Systems: Multimodel Design. I. Hartmann et al. (Advances in Control Systems & Signal Processing Ser.: Vol. 6). (Illus.). 166p. 1986. pap. text ed. 26.00 (ISBN 3-528-08960-1, Pub. by Vieweg & Sohn). IPS.

Robust & Nonlinear Time Series Analysis. 2nd ed. Ed. by J. Franke et al. (Lecture Notes in Statistics Ser.: Vol. 26). ix, 286p. 1984. pap. 19.50 (ISBN 0-387-96102-X). Springer-Verlag.

Robust Control. Peter Dorato. LC 87-12448. 528p. 1987. 62.95 (ISBN 0-87942-233-5, PCO2204). Inst Electrical.

Robust Estimates of Location: Survey & Advances. D. F. Andrews et al. LC 72-39019. 376p. 1972. pap. 12.50 (ISBN 0-691-08116-6). Princeton U Pr.

Robust Estimation. Staudte. (Probability & Mathematical Statistics Ser.). 1988. price not set (ISBN 0-471-85547-2). Wiley.

Robust Inferences. Tiku et al. (Lecture Notes in Pure & Applied Mathematics). 320p. 1986. 59.75 (ISBN 0-8247-7532-5). Dekker.

Robust Methods & Asymptotic Theory in Nonlinear Econometrics. H. J. Bierens. (Lecture Notes in Economics & Mathematical Systems Ser.: Vol. 192). (Illus.). 198p. 1981. pap. 20.00 (ISBN 0-387-10838-6). Springer-Verlag.

Robust Regression & Outlier Detection. Peter J. Rousseeuw & Annick M. Leroy. LC 87-8234. (Probability & Mathematical Statistics Ser.). 329p. 1987. 36.95 (ISBN 0-471-85233-3). Wiley.

Robust Stabilization Against Structured Perurbations. S. P. Bhattacharyya. (Lecture Notes in Control & Information Science Ser.: Vol. 99). ix, 172p. 1987. pap. 25.10 (ISBN 0-387-18056-7). Springer-Verlag.

Robust Statistical Procedures. Peter J. Huber. (CBMS-NSF Regional Conference Ser.: No. 27). v, 56p. (Orig.). 1977. pap. text ed. 12.00 (ISBN 0-89871-024-3). Soc Indus-Appl Math.

Robust Statistical Procedures: Asymptotics & Inter-Relations. Jureckova. 1988. write for info. (ISBN 0-471-82221-3). Wiley.

Robust Statistics. Peter J. Huber. LC 80-18627. (Probability & Mathematical Statistics Ser.). 308p. 1981. 43.95x (ISBN 0-471-41805-6, Pub. by Wiley-Interscience). Wiley.

Robust Statistics: Approach Based on Influence Functions. Hampel et al. (Probability & Mathematical Statistics Ser.). 1987. pap. 29.95 (ISBN 0-471-63238-4). Wiley.

Robust Statistics: The Approach Based on Influence Functions. Frank R. Hampel et al. LC 85-9428. (Probability & Mathematical Statistics Ser.). 502p. 1986. 41.95 (ISBN 0-471-82921-8). Wiley.

Robustness in Statistics. Ed. by Robert L. Launer & Graham N. Wilkinson. LC 79-13893. 1979. 41.50 (ISBN 0-12-438150-2). Acad Pr.

Robustness of Bayesian Anaysis. J. B. Kadane. (Studies in Bayesian Economics: Vol. 4). 462p. 1984. 92.00 (ISBN 0-444-86209-9, North-Holland). Elsevier.

Robustness of Statistical Methods & Nonparametric Statistics. Ed. by Dieter Rasch & Moti L. Tiku. 1985. lib. bdg. 54.00 (ISBN 90-277-2076-2, Pub. by Reidel Holland). Kluwer Academic.

Robustness of Statistical Tests. Takeaki Kariya & Bimal K. Sinha. 251p. 1988. price not set (ISBN 0-12-398230-8). Acad Pr.

Robyna Neilson Ketchum Collection of Bells. Richard Rephann & Nicholas Renouf. (Illus.). 28p. (Orig.). 1975. pap. 3.00 (ISBN 0-929530-00-4). Yale U Coll Musical Instruments.

Robyn's Book: A True Diary. Robyn Miller. 179p. (Orig.). (gr. 7 up). 1986. pap. 2.25 (ISBN 0-590-41331-7, Point). Scholastic Inc.

Rocannon's World. Ursula K. LeGuin. Ed. by Lester Del Rey. LC 75-419. (Library of Science Fiction). 1975. lib. bdg. 21.00 (ISBN 0-8240-1424-3). Garland Pub.

Rocannon's World. Ursula K. Le Guin. LC 76-47250. 136p. 1977. 15.50 (ISBN 0-06-012568-3). Ultramarine Pub.

Rocannon's World. Ursula K. LeGunn. 144p. (Orig.). 1983. pap. 2.50 (ISBN 0-441-73296-8). Ace Bks.

Rochdale: The Runaway College. David Sharpe. (Illus.). 297p. 1987. pap. 14.95 (ISBN 0-88784-155-4, Pub. by Hse Anansi Pr). U of Toronto Pr.

Roche Collection. Francis Roche. 1983. pap. 12.95 (ISBN 0-8256-0292-0, Oak). Music Sales.

Rochefoucauld: The Art of Abstraction. Philip E. Lewis. LC 76-28016. 208p. 1977. 24.95x (ISBN 0-8014-0848-2). Cornell U Pr.

Rochelle & the Atlantic Economy During the Eighteenth Century. John G. Clark. LC 80-29275. (Illus.). 304p. 1981. text ed. 32.50x (ISBN 0-8018-2529-6). Johns Hopkins.

Rocher des Adieux. Pamela Kent. (Harlequin Romantique Ser.). 192p. 1983. pap. 1.95 (ISBN 0-373-41221-5). Harlequin Bks.

Rochester. David Farley-Hills. (Critical Heritage Ser.). 288p. 1985. pap. 15.00 (ISBN 0-7102-0594-5). Routledge Chapman & Hall.

Rochester. Charles W. Williams. LC 76-28065. 1973. lib. bdg. 39.00 (ISBN 0-8414-9476-2). Folcroft.

Rochester: A Brief History. Blake McKelvey. 110p. 1984. lib. bdg. 19.95x (ISBN 0-88946-026-4). E Mellen.

Rochester: A Conversation Between Sir George Etherege & Mister Fitzjames. Bonamy Dobree. LC 73-13531. 1926. lib. bdg. 12.00 (ISBN 0-8414-3672-X). Folcroft.

Rochester Applications Conference, 1983: Proceedings. Ed. by Diane D. Ranocchia. 300p. 1983. pap. 25.00 (ISBN 0-914593-00-5). Inst Appl Forth.

Rochester Carburetors. rev. ed. Doug Roe. LC 86-81204. 176p. 1986. 12.95 (ISBN 0-89586-301-4). Price Stern.

Rochester Conference on Data Bases & Process Control, 1982: Proceedings. Ed. by Thea Martin. 321p. 1982. pap. 25.00 (ISBN 0-914593-03-X). Inst Appl Forth.

Rochester Diet. Paul Cherkasky. LC 82-83773. 288p. 1983. 14.95 (ISBN 0-8119-0488-1). Fell.

Rochester Forth Applications Conference, 1984: Proceedings. Ed. by Diane D. Ranocchia. 1984. pap. 25.00 (ISBN 0-914593-05-6). Inst Appl Forth.

Rochester Institute of Technology: Industrial Development & Educational Innovation in a American City. Dane R. Gordon. LC 82-6389. (Illus.). 450p. 1982. fine binding 89.95x (ISBN 0-88946-150-3). E Mellen.

Rochester: Portrait of a Restoration Poet. facsimile ed. Vivian De Sola Pinto. LC 73-175707. (Select Bibliographies Reprint Ser). Repr. of 1935 ed. 21.00 (ISBN 0-8369-6622-8). Ayer Co Pubs.

Rochester Sketchbook. Arch Merrill. LC 86-25741. (Arch Merrill's New York Ser.: Vol. 5). (Illus.). 192p. 1986. pap. 7.95 (ISBN 0-932334-84-9, Empire State Bks). Heart of the Lakes.

Rochester Standards Conference, 1981: Proceedings. Ed. by Thea Martin. 374p. 1981. pap. 25.00 (ISBN 0-914593-04-8). Inst Appl Forth.

Rochester Studies, Nineteen Twenty-Five to Nineteen Eighty-Two: An Annotated Bibliography. David M. Vieth. (Reference Library of the Humanities). 1984. lib. bdg. 36.00 (ISBN 0-8240-9022-5). Garland Pub.

Rochester: The Critical Heritage. Ed. by David Farley-Hills. 1978. 34.00x (ISBN 0-7100-7157-4). Routledge Chapman & Hall.

Rochester's Wife. D. E. Stevenson. 335p. 1976. lib. bdg. 19.95x (ISBN 0-89966-164-5). Buccaneer Bks.

Rochestrivia: An Illuminating Look at Rochester. Peter Dobrovitz. (Illus.). 226p. (Orig.). 1984. pap. 9.95 (ISBN 0-930249-00-3). Big Kids Pub.

Rock. new ed. Arlo Blocher. LC 75-39819. (Illus.). 32p. (gr. 5-10). 1976. PLB 9.79 (ISBN 0-89375-015-8); pap. 2.50 (ISBN 0-89375-031-X). Troll Assocs.

Rock-a-Bye Baby. Illus. by Eloise Wilkin. LC 84-60029. (Music Box Ser.). (Illus.). (ps up). 1984. 5.95 (ISBN 0-394-86798-X, Pub. by BYR). Random.

Rock-a-Bye, Baby: Nursery Songs & Cradle Games. Illus. by Eloise Wilkin. LC 80-54774. (Rocking Bks.). (Illus.). 24p. (ps). 1981. 2.95 (ISBN 0-394-84824-1). Random.

Rock-a-Bye Snoopy. Lee Mendelson. (World of Snoopy Ser.). (Illus.). 26p. (ps up). 1986. 12.95 (ISBN 1-55578-011-3). Worlds Wonder.

Rock-a-Bye Whale. Florence Strange. LC 77-83196. (Illus.). (gr. k-4). 1977. 11.95 (ISBN 0-931644-00-3). Manzanita Pr.

Rock-a-Doodle-Doo. David B. Zaslow & Lawson F. Inada. (Shakin' Loose with Mother Goose Ser.: No. 2). (Illus.). 32p. (Orig.). (ps-8). 1986. pap. 7.95 (ISBN 0-89411-005-5). Kids Matter.

Rock: A History of Alcatraz, the Fort - The Prison. Pierre Odier. (Illus.). 260p. 1982. 17.00 (ISBN 0-9611632-0-8). Odier CA.

Rock Album Art. Gary Herman. (Octopus Bk.). (Illus.). 1979. pap. 3.98 (ISBN 0-7064-0915-9, Mayflower Bks). Smith Pubs.

Rock Alteration as a Guide to Ore East Tintic District, Utah. Thomas S. Lovering & W. M. Stoll. LC 50-6493. (Economic Geology, Monograph Ser.: No. 1). pap. 25.50 (ISBN 0-317-27607-7, 2014764). Bks Demand UMI.

Rock: An Illustrated History. Stephen Barnard. (Illus.). 256p. (YA) (gr. 7 up). 1987. 50.00 (ISBN 0-02-870251-4). Schirmer Bks.

Rock & A Fortress. Robert H. Arnold. LC 78-75365. 1979. 6.95 (ISBN 0-686-25996-3). Blue Horizon.

Rock & A Hard Place. David Sherman. 304p. 1988. pap. 3.95 (ISBN 0-8041-0191-4, Pub. by Ivy). Ballantine.

Rock & Hawk: A Selection of Shorter Poems by Robinson Jeffers. Robinson Jeffers. Ed. by Robert Hass. LC 87-9612. 336p. 1987. 19.95 (ISBN 0-394-55769-7). Random.

Rock & Hawk: Robinson Jeffers & the Romantic Agony. William H. Nolte. LC 77-22982. 224p. 1978. 22.00x (ISBN 0-8203-0432-8). U of Ga Pr.

Rock & Mineral Magnetism. W. O'Reilly. LC 83-20012. 224p. 1984. 45.00x (ISBN 0-412-00401-1, NO. 5049). Routledge Chapman & Hall.

Rock & Roll. J. Brent Bill. 160p. (Orig.). 1984. pap. 4.95 (ISBN 0-8007-5156-6, Power Bks). Revell.

Rock & Roll Babylon. John Pidgeon. 1981. 8.95 (ISBN 0-686-30381-4, Pub. by Mayflower Bks). Smith Pubs.

Rock & Roll Mystery, No. 69. Wallace. (CYOA Ser.). 1987. pap. 2.25 (ISBN 0-553-26653-5). Bantam.

Rock & Roll Story. Charles T. Brown. (Illus.). 128p. 1984. pap. 12.95 (ISBN 0-13-782227-8). P-H.

Rock & Roll to Paradise: The History of the Mumbles Railway. Rob Gittins. 170p. 1982. 35.70x (ISBN 0-85088-638-4, Pub. by Gomer Pr). State Mutual Bk.

Rock & Roll Waltz. (Ballroom Dance Ser.). 1985. lib. bdg. 60.00 (ISBN 0-87700-782-9). Revisionist Pr.

Rock & Roll Waltz. (Ballroom Dance Ser.). 1986. lib. bdg. 59.95 (ISBN 0-8490-3290-3). Gordon Pr.

Rock & Roll, 1955-1970. Richard Carlin. (World of Music Ser.). (Illus.). 128p. 1988. 14.95x (ISBN 0-8160-1383-7). Facts on File.

Rock & Soil Mechanics. Derski. (Developments in Geotechnical Engineering Ser.: Vol. 48). 1987. 166.00 (ISBN 0-444-98950-1). Elsevier.

Rock & Wall Paintings of Sri Lanka. Senake Bandaranayake. 1986. 145.00x (ISBN 0-8364-2281-3, Pub. by Navrang). South Asia Bks.

Rock Anisotropy & the Theory of Stress Measurements. B. Amadei. (Lecture Notes in Engineering Ser.: Vol. 2). 478p. 1983. pap. 32.50 (ISBN 0-387-12388-1). Springer-Verlag.

Rock Archives: A Photographic Journey Through the First Two Decades of Rock & Roll. Michael Ochs. LC 84-4063. (Illus.). 416p. 1984. pap. 17.95 (ISBN 0-385-19434-X). Doubleday.

Rock-Ola Jukebox Installation, Instruction Manual, Parts List & Brochure for Model 1436A of 1953 (Fireball-120) 54p. 1983. Repr. of 1952 ed. 10 mil. laminated spiral bdg. 27.50 (ISBN 0-913698-65-2, R-215). AMR Pub Co.

Rock-Ola Jukebox Installation, Instruction Manuals, Schematic & Parts List for Model 1448 (120 Selection Hi-Fidelity) of 1955. 66p. 1982. Repr. of 1955 ed. lam. covers, spiral bound 29.50 (ISBN 0-913698-67-9, R-171). AMR Pub Co.

Rock-Ola Jukebox Installation Manual & Operating Instructions for Models 1478 & 1485: Instruction Manual for Models 1478 & 1485, Parts List for Model 1478 (Tempo II) & Schematic for Model 1478 All of 1960. 116p. 1983. Repr. of 1960 ed. lam. covers, spiral bound 29.50 (ISBN 0-913698-69-5, R-176). AMR Pub Co.

Rock-Ola Jukebox Installation Manual for Rock-Ola Tone Columns & 1941 Remote Control Systems: Spectrvox & Glamour Tone Columns with 1937 Through 1940 Models. 44p. 1982. Repr. of 1941 ed. spiral bdg. 9.50 (ISBN 0-913698-58-X, R-94). AMR Pub Co.

Rock-Ola Jukebox Installation Manual Service Manual & Parts List for Model 1438 (Comet-Fireball-120 of 1954) 66p. 1983. Repr. of 1954 ed. 10 mil. laminated spiral bdg. 29.50 (ISBN 0-913698-66-0, R-169). AMR Pub Co.

Rock-Ola Jukebox Instruction Manual & Parts List & Schematic for Model 1475 (Tempo 1) of 1959: Part Nos. 33129 & 33138: 72p. 1983. Repr. of 1959 ed. 10 mil. laminated spiral bdg. 29.50 (ISBN 0-913698-68-7, R-174). AMR Pub Co.

Rock-Ola Jukebox Instruction Manual, Parts List & Schematic for Model 1465 Hi-Fidelity 200 Selection of 1958. 74p. 1983. Repr. of 1958 ed. 10 mil. laminated spiral bdg. 27.50 (ISBN 0-913698-70-9, R-172). AMR Pub Co.

Rock-Ola Jukebox Instruction Manual Parts Manual & Brochure for Model 1436 (Fireball-120) of 1952. 58p. 1983. Repr. of 1952 ed. 10 mil. laminated spiral bdg. 29.50 (ISBN 0-913698-64-4, R-194). AMR Pub Co.

Rock-Ola Jukebox Model 1452 (50 Selection) Installation Manual, Service, Parts Manual & Schematic of 1955. Rock-Ola Mfg. Corp. Ed. by Frank Adams. 56p. 1984. Repr. of 1955 ed. 10 mil laminated spiral bdg. 29.50 (ISBN 0-913599-39-5, R-279). AMR Pub Co.

Rock-Ola Jukebox Model 426 "Grand Prix" II of 1965: Service, Parts Manual. Rock-Ola Mfg. Corporation. Ed. by Frank Adams. 112p. 1984. Repr. 10 mil laminated covers, spiral bound 32.50 (ISBN 0-913599-30-1, R282). AMR Pub Co.

Rock-Ola Jukebox Model 429 "Starlet" Service Manuals of 1965-1966 (100 Selections) Rock-Ola Mfg. Corp. Ed. by Frank Adams. 76p. 1984. Repr. 10 mil laminated cover, spiral bound 29.50 (ISBN 0-913599-38-7, R-283). AMR Pub Co.

Rock-Ola Jukebox Models Super, Master, Junior, "Luxury LIghtup" Service Manual of 1940. 40p. 1983. Repr. of 1940 ed. spiral bound. incl. a 78 rpm strobe disc 15.00 (R-146). AMR Pub Co.

Rock-Ola Jukebox Models 1455-D & 1455-S: Installation, Operation, Service Manual & Schematic of 1957. Rock-Ola Manufacturing Corporation. 60p. 1983. Repr. of 1957 ed. spiral bound, laminated covers 32.50 (ISBN 0-913599-28-X, R-241). AMR Pub Co.

Rock-Ola Jukebox, Models 1488 & 1495: Regis Service, Parts Manual, Installation Instructions & fold-out Schematics. One for Each Model of 1961. Rock-Ola Company Staff. 106p. 1984. Repr. 10 mil laminated covers & sectiondividers spiral bdg. 32.50 (ISBN 0-913599-05-0, R-248). AMR Pub Co.

Rock-Ola Jukebox Service & Part Manual for the Models 1422, 1424, 1426 & 1428. 50p. 1983. Repr. of 1948 ed. 10 mil. lam. covers, spiral bound 19.50 (ISBN 0-913698-63-6, R-229). AMR Pub Co.

Rock-Ola Jukebox Service Manual for 12, 16, & 20 Record Models 1936-1942. 36p. 1983. Repr. of 1939 ed. 10 mil. lam. covers, spiral bound. incl. 78 rpm strobe disc 12.50 (ISBN 0-913698-60-1, R-210). AMR Pub Co.

Rock-Ola Jukebox Service Specialist's Handbook for the Models 1422, 1424, 1426 & 1428. (Trouble Shooting Guide Ser.). 46p. 1983. Repr. of 1947 ed. 10 mil. lam. covers, spiral bound 19.50 (ISBN 0-913698-62-8, R-214). AMR Pub Co.

Rock-Ola Jukeboxes. Frank Adams. 140p. (Orig.). 1987. 24.50 (ISBN 0-939971-17-8, R-450). AMR Pub Co.

Rock-Ola Model 1493 "Princess" Service Manual, Parts List & Schematic for the 100 Selection Model "Princess" Jukebox of 1962. Rock-Ola Manufacturing Corporation. 106p. 1984. Repr. of 1962 ed. spiral bound, laminated covers 32.50 (ISBN 0-913599-29-8, R-269). AMR Pub Co.

Rock-Ola Models 1544 & 1546 3 Wire 120 Selection Wall Box Service Manual, Installation Instructions & Parts List: Designed to Operate with Models 1436, 1436-A, 1438 & 1446 Jukeboxes. Rock-Ola Mfg. Co. 26p. 1984. Repr. of 1954 ed. 10 mil laminated spiral bound cover 16.50 (ISBN 0-913599-32-8, R-272). AMR Pub Co.

Rock on the Hudson. John Van de Water. 128p. 1984. 13.95 (ISBN 0-912526-37-8). Lib Res.

Rock On: The Illustrated Encyclopedia of Rock n' Roll, Vol. I. Norm N. Nite. LC 81-48240. (Illus.). 736p. 1982. 27.00 (ISBN 0-06-181642-6, HarpT). Har-Row.

Rock On: The Illustrated Encyclopedia of Rock 'n Roll: the Solid Gold Years, Updated. Norm N. Nite. LC 74-12247. (Illus.). 448p. 1978. 24.50 (ISBN 0-690-00583-0). T Y Crowell.

Rock On: The Illustrated Encyclopedia of Rock 'n Roll: The Years of Change 1964-1978, Vol. II. Norm N. Nite. LC 83-48371. (Illus.). 608p. 1984. 27.00i (HarpT). Har-Row.

Rock On: The Illustrated Encyclopedia of Rock N' Roll, Vol. III. Norm N. Nite. LC 85-42723. (Illus.). 416p. 1985. 27.00i (ISBN 0-06-181644-2, HarpT). Har-Row.

Rock On: The Illustrated Encyclopedia of Rock'n Roll: the Modern Years 1964 to the Present, Vol. 2. rev. ed. Norm N. Nite. LC 78-3312. (Illus.). 1984. 24.50. T Y Crowell.

Rock One Hundred. 3rd ed. Jim Quinn & Barry Cohen. (Illus.). 1981. Set. pap. text ed. 6.00 (ISBN 0-917190-09-2). Suppl., 1982 (ISBN 0-917190-10-6). Chartmasters.

Rock Paintings of Southern Andalusia: A Description of a Neolithic & Copper Age Art Group. Henri Breuil & M. C. Burkitt. LC 76-44695. Repr. of 1929 ed. 30.00 (ISBN 0-404-15935-4). AMS Pr.

Rock Pictures of Europe. Herbert Kuhn. (Illus.). 5.95 (ISBN 0-8079-0113-X); pap. 2.95 (ISBN 0-8079-0114-8). October.

Rock Pool. Cyril Connolly. 190p. 1982. cancelled (ISBN 0-89255-073-2); pap. 5.95 (ISBN 0-89255-059-7). Persea Bks.

Rock Quarry Book. Michael Kehoe. LC 80-28165. (Carolrhoda Photo Bks.). (Illus.). 32p. (gr. k-4). 1981. PLB 9.95 (ISBN 0-87614-142-4, AACR1). Carolrhoda Bks.

Rock Quiz. Joshua Feigenbaum & David Schulps. (Illus.). 160p. 1983. pap. 5.95 (ISBN 0-399-50734-5, Perigee). Putnam Pub Group.

Rock Record. 3rd ed. Terry Hounsome. 752p. 24.95 (ISBN 0-8160-1754-9); pap. 14.95 (ISBN 0-8160-1755-7). Facts on File.

Rock Rhythms for the Young. Joe Ambrosio. 24p. 1984. pap. 5.95 (ISBN 0-938170-06-6). Wimbledon Music.

Rock Sculpture for Beginners: The Joy of Carving from Stone. Violet Stage. (Illus.). 48p. 1987. 11.95 (ISBN 0-87961-166-9); pap. 5.95 (ISBN 0-87961-167-7). Naturegraph.

Rock Shelters of the Perigord: Geological Stratigraphy & Archaeological Succession. Henri Laville et al. LC 80-511. (Studies in Archaeology). 1980. 29.95 (ISBN 0-12-438750-0). Acad Pr.

Rock Shots. (Illus.). 32p. (gr. 4-12). 1985. pap. 3.95 (ISBN 0-88188-351-4, Robus Books). H Leonard Pub Corp.

Rock Slope Engineering. 3rd ed. E. Hoek & J. W. Bray. 360p. 1981. pap. text ed. 43.25x (ISBN 0-900488-57-3). IMM North Am.

Rock Springs. Richard Ford. 1988. pap. 6.95 (ISBN 0-394-75700-9, Vin). Random.

Rock Springs. Richard C. Ford. Ed. by Gary Fisketjon. (Fiction Ser.). 256p. 1987. 17.95 (ISBN 0-87113-159-5). Atlantic Monthly.

Rock Star. Jackie Collins. 544p. 1988. 19.95 (ISBN 0-671-61881-4). S&S.

Rock Star. Jackie Collins. 1989. pap. price not set. PB.

Rock Stars. Alan C. McLean. (American Structural Readers Ser.: Stage 2). (Illus.). 27p. (Orig.). 1982. pap. 3.95 (ISBN 0-582-79817-5). Longman.

Rock Stars. Timothy White. LC 84-2531. (Illus.). 288p. 1984. 35.00 (ISBN 0-941434-50-8). Stewart Tabori & Chang.

Rock Synthesizer Manual. Geary Yelton. LC 83-62290. (Illus.). 124p. (Orig.). 1983. pap. 15.00 (ISBN 0-914283-01-4). Rock Tech Pubns.

Rock Synthesizer Manual. rev., 2nd ed. Geary Yelton. LC 86-4918. (Illus.). 128p. 1986. pap. 11.95 (ISBN 0-914283-25-1). Rock Tech Pubns.

Rock Tombs of El Amarna, Pt. VI. N. De G. Davies. 1975. 99.00x (ISBN 0-85698-050-1, Pub. by Egypt Exploration). State Mutual Bk.

Rock Tombs of El-Hawaish, Vol. 6: The Cemetery of Akhmim. Ed. by Naguib Kanawati. (Ancient History Documentary Research Centre Ser.). (Illus.). 100p. 1986. pap. text ed. 60.00 (ISBN 0-85837-547-8, Pub. by Aris & Phillips UK). Humanities.

Rock Tombs of El-Hawawish: The Cemetery of Akhmim, Vol. 2. N. Kanawati. (Illus.). 51p. 1982. pap. text ed. 60.00 (ISBN 0-908299-04-4, Pub. by Aris & Phillips UK). Humanities.

Rock Tombs of El-Hawawish, Vol. 1: The Cemetery of Akhmim. N. Kanawti. (Illus.). 44p. 1980. 55.00x (ISBN 0-908299-01-X, Pub. by Aris & Phillips UK). Humanities.

Rock Toons: A Cartoon History of the First 30 Years of Rock 'N' Roll. Dominique Farran & Mike Sadler. (Illus.). 96p. 1986. pap. 7.95 (ISBN 0-517-56325-8, Harmony). Crown.

Rock Video Book. Paulette Weiss. 1985. pap. 9.95 (ISBN 0-671-55339-9). PB.

Rock Video Strikes Again. Barbara Adams. (Kid TV Ser.: No. 3). (Orig.). (gr. 2-6). 1986. pap. 2.50 (ISBN 0-440-47170-2, YB). Dell.

Rock Video Superstars. Daniel Cohen & Susan Cohen. (Illus.). (gr. 4 up). pap. 2.50 (ISBN 0-317-62751-1). Archway.

Rock Video Superstars II. Daniel Cohen & Susan Cohen. (Illus.). (gr. 4 up). pap. 2.50 (ISBN 0-671-63397-X). Archway.

Rock Video Trivia Book. Paulette Weiss. (Illus.). 128p. (gr. 5 up). 1985. 9.79 (ISBN 0-671-55340-2). Messner.

Rock Voices. Matt Damsker. 160p. 1980. pap. 5.95 (ISBN 0-312-68791-5). St Martin.

Rock Weathering. Dorothy Carroll. LC 77-107534. 204p. 1970. 45.00x (ISBN 0-306-30434-1, Plenum Pr). Plenum Pub.

Rock Who's Who: A Biographical Dictionary & a Critical Discography. Brock Helander. LC 82-80804. 684p. 1982. 25.00; pap. 16.95. Schirmer Bks.

Rock Who's Who: A Complete Guide to the Great Artists & Albumns of 30 Years - From Rockabilly to New Wave. Brock Helander. (Schirmer Book). 600p. 1982. 25.00; pap. 16.95. Macmillan.

Rock Witch. Jim Dierbeck. (YA) (gr. 5-9). 1988. pap. text ed. 8.00 (ISBN 0-910303-10-X). Writers Pub Serv.

Rock Wives: The Hard Lives & Good Times of the Wives, Girlfriends, & Groupies of Rock 'n' Roll. Victoria Balfour. LC 85-13525. (Illus.). 256p. (Orig.). 1987. pap. 5.95 (ISBN 0-688-06966-5, Quill). Morrow.

Rock Yearbook 1981. Michael Gross & Maxim Jakubowski. 1981. pap. 11.95 (ISBN 0-394-17794-0, E774, Ever). Grove.

Rock Yearbook 1985. Ed. by Al Clark. (Illus.). 224p. 1985. 24.95 (ISBN 0-312-68788-5); pap. 13.95 (ISBN 0-312-68787-7). St Martin.

Rock Yearbook 1987. Ed. by Tom Hibbert. (Illus.). 224p. 1986. pap. 14.95 (ISBN 0-312-68794-X). St Martin.

Rock Yearbook, 1988. Ed. by Ian Cranna. (Illus.). 208p. 1987. pap. 15.95 (ISBN 0-312-01082-6). St Martin.

Rock Yearbook, 1989. Ed. by Lloyd Bradley. (Illus.). 208p. 1988. pap. 15.95 (ISBN 0-312-02134-8). St Martin.

Rockaby & Other Works. Samuel Beckett. LC 80-8916. 128p. 1981. 12.50 (ISBN 0-394-51953-1, GP844). Grove.

Rockaby & Other Works. Samuel Beckett. 128p. 1981. pap. 3.95 (ISBN 0-394-17924-2, E777, Ever). Grove.

Rockabye. Laird Koenig. 235p. 1981. 11.95 (ISBN 0-312-68793-1). St Martin.

Rockabye Baby. Stephen Gresham. 1984. pap. 3.50 (ISBN 0-8217-1470-8). Zebra.

Rockabye Baby: Lullabies from Many Nations & Peoples. Compiled by Carl Miller. (gr. k-8). 1975. pap. 2.50 (ISBN 0-935738-04-5, 5035). US Comm Unicef.

Rockabye Crocodile. Jose Aruego & Ariane Dewey. LC 87-463. (Illus.). 32p. (ps-3). 1988. 11.95 (ISBN 0-688-06738-7); lib. bdg. 11.88 (ISBN 0-688-06739-5). Greenwillow.

Rockbound. Frank P. Day. LC 73-81763. (Literature of Canada, Poetry & Prose in Reprint). pap. 81.00 (ISBN 0-317-26917-8, 2023609). Bks Demand UMI.

Rockbound. Red Robinson & Peggy Hodgins. 232p. 1983. 19.95 (ISBN 0-88839-162-5). Hancock House.

Rockbridge County Marriages, Seventeen Seventy-Eight to Eighteen Fifty. Dorthie Kirkpatrick & Edwin C. Kirkpatrick. (Virginia Historic Marriage Register Ser.). 443p. 1988. Repr. lib. bdg. 29.95x (ISBN 0-8095-8230-9). Borgo Pr.

Rockbridge County Marriages, 1778-1850. Dorthie Kirkpatrick & Edwin C. Kirkpatrick. (Virginia Historic Marriage Register Ser.). (Illus.). ix, 443p. (Orig.). 1985. pap. 15.00 (ISBN 0-935931-16-3). Iberian Pub.

Rockbridge County, Virginia: Notebook. 235p. 1982. 27.75 (ISBN 0-686-35848-1); pap. 22.75 (ISBN 0-686-37183-6). A M Coppage.

Rockburg Railroad Murder. Constantine. 1982. pap. 3.95 (ISBN 0-87923-662-0, Nonpareil Bks). Godine.

Rockbursts: Prediction & Control (Papers Presented at a Symposium, London, October 20, 1983) Institution of Mining & Metallurgy & Institute of Mining Engineers, London. 173p. (Orig.). 1984. pap. text ed. 26.95x (ISBN 0-900488-67-0). IMM North Am.

Rockdale: The Growth of an American Village in the Early Industrial Revolution. Anthony F. Wallace. (Illus.). 576p. 1980. pap. 10.95 (ISBN 0-393-00991-2). Norton.

Rockefeller & His Times. Clemente Cimmora. 1974. lib. bdg. 59.95 (ISBN 0-8490-0967-7). Gordon Pr.

Rockefeller Center. Carol H. Krinsky. (Illus.). 1978. pap. 10.95 (ISBN 0-19-502404-4). Oxford U Pr.

Rockefeller Century: Three Generations of America's Greatest Family - John D. Rockefeller, John D. Rockefeller, Jr., John D. Rockefeller III. John E. Harr & Peter J. Johnson. (Illus.). 604p. 1988. 29.95 (ISBN 0-684-18936-4). Scribner.

Rockefeller Encyclopedia: 100 Years of Marriages & Births in the Eight Branches of the John & William Rockefeller Clans. Dick Frost. (Illus.). 250p. (Orig.). 1987. pap. 50.00 (ISBN 0-933883-05-6). Aquarius Rising Pr.

Rockefeller File. Gary Allen. 200p. pap. 2.00 (ISBN 0-686-31144-2). Concord Pr.

Rockefeller File. Gary Allen. LC 75-39136. (Orig.). 1976. pap. 7.00. Concord Bks.

Rockefeller Internationalist. Emanuel Josephson. 1979. write for info. (ISBN 0-685-96465-5). Revisionist Pr.

Rockefeller "Internationalist" The Man Who Misrules the World. Emanuel M. Josephson. 100.00 (ISBN 0-685-56223-9). Chedney.

Rockefeller of New York: Executive Power in the Statehouse. Robert H. Connery & Gerald Benjamin. LC 78-23947. (Illus.). 480p. 1979. 37.50x (ISBN 0-8014-1188-2). Cornell U Pr.

Rockefeller, Old Money, New Politics. Richard Grimes. (Illus.). 250p. 1984. 9.95 (ISBN 0-934750-31-9). Jalamap.

Rockefeller Papiere. Orig. Title: Rockerfeller File. 256p. pap. 5.00 (ISBN 0-686-31150-7). Concord Pr.

Rockefeller Public Number One. Emanuel M. Josephson. 1979. write for info. (ISBN 0-685-96466-3). Revisionist Pr.

Rockefeller Sheet Seminar, 4th: Proceedings. (Illus.). 441p. 1975. pap. 23.25 (ISBN 0-685-54192-4, F1073, FAO). UNIPUB.

Rockefeller Syndrome. Ferdinand Lundberg. LC 75-23031. 1975. 12.50 (ISBN 0-8184-0215-6). Lyle Stuart.

Rockefellers: An American Dynasty. Peter Collier & David Horowitz. (Illus.). 1977. pap. 4.95 (ISBN 0-451-13455-9, Sig). NAL.

Rockefellers: An American Dynasty. Peter Collier & David Horowitz. 1989. 8.95. Summit Bks.

Rockerfeller File see Rockefeller Papiere.

Rocket Book. Peter Newell. LC 69-12080. (Illus.). 52p. (gr. k-4). 1969. Repr. of 1912 ed. 8.95 (ISBN 0-8048-0505-9). C E Tuttle.

Rocket Book: A Guide to Building & Launching Model Rockets for Teachers & Students Of the Space Age. Robert L. Cannon & Michael A. Banks. (Illus.). 240p. 1985. 22.95 (ISBN 0-13-782251-0); pap. 12.95 (ISBN 0-13-782244-8). P-H.

Rocket Drive for Long Range Bombers. E. Sanger & J. Bredt. Tr. by M. Hamermesh. 1944. pap. 3.95 (ISBN 0-910266-21-2). Bk Page.

Rocket Fighter. Mano Ziegler. 208p. 1989. pap. 2.95 (ISBN 0-553-27348-5). Bantam.

Rocket in My Pocket: The Rhymes & Chants of Young Americans. Carl Withers. (Illus.). 224p. (gr. 1-6). 1988. 14.95 (ISBN 0-8050-0821-7); pap. 7.95 (ISBN 0-8050-0804-7). H Holt & Co.

Rocket Island. Theodore Taylor. 144p. 1985. pap. 2.50 (ISBN 0-380-89674-5, Flare). Avon.

Rocket Jockey. Lester Del Rey. 1982. pap. 1.95 (ISBN 0-345-30655-4, Del Rey). Ballantine.

Rocket Mail: Flights of the World. Max Kronstein. 191p. 20.00 (ISBN 0-317-60407-4). Am Air Mail.

Rocket Man: The Roger Clemens Story. Roger Clemens & Peter Gammons. 1987. 15.95 (ISBN 0-8289-0629-7). Greene.

Rocket Man: The Roger Clemens Story. Roger Clemens & Peter Gammons. 224p. 1988. pap. 3.95 (ISBN 0-14-010949-8). Penguin.

Rocket-Powered Cars. Paul Estrem. Ed. by Howard Schroeder. LC 87-22374. (Super-Charged Ser.). (Illus.). 48p. (gr. 5-6). 1987. PLB 10.95 (ISBN 0-89686-352-2). Crestwood Hse.

Rocket Propulsion Elements: An Introduction to the Engineering of Rockets. 4th ed. George A. Sutton & Donald M. Ross. LC 75-29197. 557p. 1976. 52.95x (ISBN 0-471-83836-5, Pub. by Wiley-Interscience). Wiley.

Rocket Propulsion Elements: An Introduction to the Engineering of Rockets. 5th ed. George P. Sutton. LC 85-20398. 342p. 1986. 47.95 (ISBN 0-471-80027-9). Wiley.

Rocket Ship Galileo. Robert A. Heinlein. 1985. pap. 2.95 (ISBN 0-345-33660-7). Ballantine.

Rocket Ship Galileo. Robert A. Heinlein. (Hudson River Editions). (gr. 5-11). 1977. lib. rep. ed. 15.00x (ISBN 0-684-15595-8, ScribJ). Scribner.

Rocket Team. Frederick I. Ordway, III & Mitchell R. Sharpe. (Illus.). 496p. 1982. pap. 11.95x (ISBN 0-262-65013-4). MIT Pr.

Rocket to Limbo. Alan E. Nourse. 192p. 1987. pap. 2.95 (ISBN 0-441-73339-5, Pub. by Charter Bks.). Ace Bks.

Rocket to the Moon. Brooks Frederick, pseud. (Redbird Ser). 118p. 1975. 15.00 (ISBN 0-88253-616-8); pap. text ed. 4.80 (ISBN 0-88253-615-X). Ind-US Inc.

Rocket to the Moon. Von Harbou. LC 77-5956. 187p. 1977. Repr. of 1930 ed. 15.00 (ISBN 0-8398-2378-9). Ultramarine Pub.

Rocket to the Morgue. Anthony Boucher. 176p. 1988. pap. 4.95 (ISBN 0-930330-82-X). Intl Polygonics.

Rocketeer. Dave Stevens. 72p. (Orig.). 1985. pap. 7.95 (ISBN 0-913035-06-8). Eclipse Bks.

Rocketry: From Goddard to Space Travel. Christopher Lampton. Ed. by M. Kline. (First Bk.). (Illus.). 96p. (YA) (gr. 7-9). 1988. 9.90 (ISBN 0-531-10483-4). Watts.

Rockets: An Educational Coloring Book. Spizzirri Publishing Co. Staff. Ed. by Linda Spizzirri. (Illus.). 32p. (gr. 1-8). 1986. pap. 1.49 (ISBN 0-86545-072-2). Spizzirri.

Rocky Mountain National Park Hiking Trails. 7th ed. Kent Dannen & Donna Dannen. (Illus.). 1989. pap. price not set (ISBN 0-87106-604-1). Globe Pequot.
Rocky Mountain National Park Trail Guide. Erik Nilsson. LC 78-362. (Illus.). 187p. 1978. pap. 4.95 (ISBN 0-89037-098-2). Anderson World.
Rocky Mountain Railroads of Colorado. William M. Thayer. Ed. by William R. Jones. (Illus.). 1977. pap. 3.95 (ISBN 0-89646-020-7). Outbooks.
Rocky Mountain Rendezvous. Fred Gowans. LC 84-27586. (Illus.). 256p. 1985. pap. 9.95 (ISBN 0-87905-193-0). Gibbs Smith Pub.
Rocky Mountain Section Field Guide. Ed. by S. S. Beus. (DNAG Centennial Field Guides Ser.: No. 2). (Illus.). 1987. 43.50 (ISBN 0-8137-5402-X). Geol Soc.
Rocky Mountain Sketches. Marj Dunmire. (Illus.). 24p. (Orig.). 1978. pap. 4.95 (ISBN 0-942559-00-2). Pegasus Graphics.
Rocky Mountain States. L. B. Taylor, Jr. & C. Taylor. (First Book Ser.). (gr. 4 up). lib. bdg. 10.40 (ISBN 0-531-04735-0). Watts.
Rocky Mountain: The Story Behind the Scenery. Michael Smithson. LC 86-80495. (Illus.). 48p. (Orig.). 1986. pap. 4.50 (ISBN 0-88714-007-6). KC Pubns.
Rocky Mountain Tree Finder: A Manual for Identifying Rocky Mountain Trees. Tom Watts. 58p. 1972. pap. 1.50 (ISBN 0-912550-05-8). Nature Study.
Rocky Mountain Trees: A Handbook of the Native Species, with Plates & Distribution Maps. 3rd rev. ed. Richard J. Preston, Jr. (Illus.). 13.50 (ISBN 0-8446-2758-5). Peter Smith.
Rocky Mountain Urban Politics. Ed. by Jedon A. Emenhiser. 166p. (Orig.). 1971. pap. 6.95 (ISBN 0-87421-041-0). Utah St U Pr.
Rocky Mountain Vamp. Dirk Fletcher. (Spur Ser.: No. 4). 224p. (Orig.). 1982. pap. 2.50 (ISBN 0-8439-1180-8, Leisure Bks). Leisure NY.
Rocky Mountain West in 1867. Louis L. Simonin. Tr. by Wilson O. Clough. LC 66-16514. (Illus.). xiv, 170p. 1966. 16.95x (ISBN 0-8032-0175-3). U of Nebr Pr.
Rocky Mountain Wildflowers. Kent Dannen & Donna Dannen. LC 81-7439. (Illus.). 64p. (Orig.). 1981. pap. 3.95 (ISBN 0-9606768-0-5). Tundra Pubns.
Rocky Mountain Wildflowers. A. E. Porsild. (Illus.). viii, 454p. 1986. pap. 9.95 (56495-9, Pub. by Natl Gallery Canada). U of Chicago Pr.
Rocky Mountain Wildflowers. 2nd ed. Ronald Taylor & Bob Spring. (Illus.). 96p. 1986. pap. 5.95 (ISBN 0-89886-131-4). Mountaineers.
Rocky Mountain Wildflowers. Ronald J. Taylor. 1983. 14.50 (ISBN 0-8446-6050-7). Peter Smith.
Rocky Mountains. Insight Guides Staff. (Illus.). 384p. 1985. pap. 15.95 (ISBN 0-13-782277-4). P-H.
Rocky Mountains. J. A. Kraulis & John Gault. (Illus.). 200p. Date not set. 19.95 (ISBN 0-919493-95-5, Pub. by Key Porter Canada). U of Toronto Pr.
Rocky Mountains. Photos by David Muench. LC 74-33864. (Belding Imprint Ser.). (Illus.). 192p. (Text by David Sumner). 1975. 29.50 (ISBN 0-912856-16-5). Gr Arts Ctr Pub.
Rocky Mountains: A Vision for Artists in the Nineteenth Century. Patricia Trenton & Peter H. Hassrick. LC 82-21879. (Illus.). 440p. 1983. 65.00 (ISBN 0-8061-1808-3). U of Okla Pr.
Rocky Mountains: Crest of a Continent. J. A. Kraulis & John Gault. (Illus.). 200p. 35.00 (ISBN 0-8160-1604-6). Facts on File.
Rocky Mountains: Der Geologische Aufbau Des Kanadischen Felsengebirges. Dietrich H. Roeder. (Illus.). 1967. 75.95x (ISBN 3-443-11005-3). Lubrecht & Cramer.
Rocky Mountains Receipts Remedies. Rev. ed. Ed. by Jack Benham & Sarah Benham. (Illus.). 60p. (Orig.). 1966. pap. text ed. 2.50 (ISBN 0-941026-08-6). Bear Creek Pub.
Rocky Road: The Pilgrimage of the Grape. 2nd ed. Charles W. Bonner. 172p. 1984. 11.95 (ISBN 0-914330-61-6). Panorama West.
Rocky Road to Dublin. Seumas MacManus. 9.95 (ISBN 0-8159-6712-8). Devin.
Rocky Romance, No. 137. Sharon D. Wyeth. (Sweet Dreams Ser.). 192p. (Orig.). (YA) (gr. 7-12). 1988. pap. 2.50 (ISBN 0-553-26948-8, Sweet Dreams). Bantam.
Rocky Shore. John M. Kingsbury. LC 71-122758. (Illus.). 1970. pap. 6.95 (ISBN 0-85699-015-9). Chatham Pr.
Rocky the Cat. A. R. Swinnerton. LC 84-46024. (Illus.). 1981. 11.70i (ISBN 0-201-07606-3, Crowell Jr Bks). HarpJ.
Rocky's Boxing Book. Rocky Graziano & Howard Liss. (Illus.). 96p. 1980. PLB 6.95 (ISBN 0-686-63048-3); pap. 8.95 (ISBN 0-87460-377-3). Lion Bks.
Rococo Age: French Masterpieces of the Eighteenth Century. Eric M. Zafran & Jean-Luc Bordeaux. LC 83-81104. (Illus.). 168p. 1983. pap. 24.95 (ISBN 0-939802-19-8). High Mus Art.
Rococo & Eighteenth-Century French Literature: A Study Through Marivaux's Theater. George Poe. (American University Studies II- Romance Languages & Literature: Vol. 30). 347p. 1987. text ed. 45.00 (ISBN 0-8204-0234-6). P Lang Pubs.
Rococo Silks. (Victoria & Albert Colour Bks). (Illus.). 64p. 1986. 10.95 (ISBN 0-8109-1716-5). Abrams.
Rococo to Revolution. Michael Levey. (World of Art Ser.). (Illus.). 252p. 1985. pap. 11.95 (ISBN 0-500-20050-5). Thames Hudson.
Rococo to Romanticism: Art & Architecture 1700-1850. LC 76-14072. (Garland Library of the History of Art). 1976. lib. bdg. 61.00 (ISBN 0-8240-2420-6). Garland Pub.
Rod & Bar Production in the 1980's. 188p. 1982. text ed. 60.00x (ISBN 0-904357-40-6, Pub. by Inst Metals). Brookfield Pub Co.
Rod & Lightning. Carroll F. Terrell. (Collected Poetry Ser.). 130p. (Orig.). 1985. 8.95x (ISBN 0-915032-49-X); pap. 5.00 (ISBN 0-915032-37-6). Natl Poet Foun.
Rod Campbell's Noisy Book. Rod Campbell. (Board Book Ser.). (Illus.). 16p. (ps). 1987. 7.95 (ISBN 0-87226-146-8). P Bedrick Bks.
Rod Carew's Art & Science of Hitting. Rod Carew et al. 192p. 1986. pap. 7.95 (ISBN 0-14-008516-5). Penguin.
Rod Carew's Art & Science of Hitting. Rod Carew et al. LC 85-40799. (Illus.). 192p. 1986. 17.95 (ISBN 0-670-80905-5). Viking.
Rod in India: Being Hints How to Obtain Sport. Henry S. Thomas. write for info. (Pub. by Han-Shan Tang Ltd). State Mutual Bk.
Rod of Iron: French Counterinsurgency Policy in Aragon During the Peninsular War. Don W. Alexander. LC 84-5561. 260p. 1985. 35.00 (ISBN 0-8420-2218-X). Scholarly Res Inc.
Rod of Light. Barrington J. Bayley. 192p. 1987. 15.95 (ISBN 0-87795-935-8, Arbor Hse). Morrow.
Rod Serling's Night Gallery Reader. Ed. by Carol Serling et al. LC 87-14360. 1987. 15.95 (ISBN 0-934878-93-5). Dembner Bks.
Rod, the Root & the Flower. facs. ed. Coventry K. Patmore. Ed. by Derek Patmore. LC 68-16966. (Essay Index Reprint Ser). 1950. 17.00 (ISBN 0-8369-0775-2). Ayer Co Pubs.
Rod, Write On: Pts. I-VIII, 1970-80. Rod Law. (Orig.). text ed. 19.95 (ISBN 0-9601730-2-1); pap. text ed. 12.50 (ISBN 0-9601730-3-X). Rod Law.
Rodale Book of Pregnancy & Birth. Nicola McLure & Jovanka Bach. Ed. by Bill Hylton. (Illus.). 224p. 1985. pap. text ed. 14.95 (ISBN 0-87857-590-1). Rodale Pr Inc.
Rodale Guide to Composting. Organic Gardening & Jerry Minnich. (Illus.). 1979. 14.95 (ISBN 0-87857-212-0). Rodale Pr Inc.
Rodale's Basic Natural Foods Cookbook. Ed. by Charles Gerras. 1989. 15.95 (ISBN 0-671-67338-6, Fireside). S&S.
Rodale's Basic Natural Foods Cookbook. Ed. by Rodale Press Staff & Charles Gerras. (Illus.). 912p. 1983. 21.95 (ISBN 0-87857-469-7). Rodale Pr Inc.
Rodale's Best Recipes 1988. Rodale Press Editors. 224p. 1988. 14.95 (ISBN 0-87857-739-4). Rodale Pr Inc.
Rodale's Book of Hints, Tips & Everyday Wisdom. Ed. by Carol Hupping et al. (Illus.). 400p. 1985. 21.95 (ISBN 0-87857-578-2). Rodale Pr Inc.
Rodale's Book of Shortcuts. Ed. by Cheryl W. Tetreau & Carol Hupping. 384p. 1988. 21.95 (ISBN 0-87857-720-3). Rodale Pr Inc.
Rodale's Color Handbook of Garden Insects. Anna Carr. (Illus.). 256p. 1983. pap. 12.95 (ISBN 0-87857-460-3). Rodale Pr Inc.
Rodale's Complete Book of Home Freezing. Marilyn Hodges & Rodale Test Kitchen Staff. Ed. by Anne Halpin. (Illus.). 384p. 1984. 18.95 (ISBN 0-87857-514-6); pap. 12.95 (ISBN 0-87857-525-1). Rodale Pr Inc.
Rodale's Complete Home Products Manual. 1989. 19.95 (ISBN 0-87857-797-1); pap. 14.95 (ISBN 0-87857-798-X). Rodale Pr Inc.
Rodale's Encyclopedia of Natural Home Remedies. Mark Bricklin. (Illus.). 528p. 1982. 21.95 (ISBN 0-87857-396-8). Rodale Pr Inc.
Rodale's Garden Insect, Disease & Weed Identification Guide. Miranda Smith & Ana Carr. (Illus.). 352p. 1988. 21.95 (ISBN 0-87857-758-0); pap. 15.95 (ISBN 0-87857-759-9). Rodale Pr Inc.
Rodale's Garden Problem Solver: Vegetables, Fruits & Herbs. Jeff Ball. (Illus.). 448p. 1988. 24.95 (ISBN 0-87857-762-9). Rodale Pr Inc.
Rodale's Illustrated Encyclopedia of Herbs. Ed. by Rodale Books editors & William H. Hylton. (Illus.). 552p. 1987. 24.95 (ISBN 0-87857-699-1). Rodale Pr Inc.
Rodale's Naturally Delicious Desserts & Snacks. LC 78-9145. 1978. 19.95 (ISBN 0-87857-211-2). Rodale Pr Inc.
Rodale's Sensational Desserts. Joan Bingham & Delores Riccio. Ed. by Charles Gerras. (Illus.). 320p. 1985. 21.95 (ISBN 0-87857-542-1); pap. 12.95 (ISBN 0-87857-585-5). Rodale Pr Inc.
Rodchenko: Centre National de la Photographie. Pantheon Photo Library. LC 87-42620. (Illus.). 144p. 1987. 7.95 (ISBN 0-394-75624-X). Pantheon.
Rodchenko: The Complete Work. Selim O. Khan-Magomedov. (Illus.). 275p. 1986. 50.00 (ISBN 0-262-11116-0). MIT Pr.
Rodd's Chemistry of Carbon Compounds, 2 pts. in 1, Suppl. Vol. 1 C & D. Ed. by M. F. Ansell. (Pt. A: Monocarbonyl Derivatives, Pt. 2: Dihydric Alcohols). 1973. 155.25 (ISBN 0-444-41072-4). Elsevier.
Rodd's Chemistry of Carbon Compounds, 2 pts. in 1, Suppl. Vol. 1 A & B. Ed. by M. F. Ansell. (Pt. A: Hydrocarbons, Pt. B: Monohydric Alcohols). 1975. 116.00 (ISBN 0-444-40972-6). Elsevier.
Rodd's Chemistry of Carbon Compounds, Vols. 1-3 in 20 pts. 2nd. ed. E. H. Rodd. Ed. by S. Coffey. Incl. Vol. 1, Pt. A. Hydrocarbon-Halogen Derivatives. S. Coffey. 569p. 1964. 176.00 (ISBN 0-444-40131-8); Vol. 1, Pt. B. Monohydric Alcohols, Their Ethers & Esters. S. Coffey. 373p. 1965. 134.25 (ISBN 0-444-40132-6); Vol. 1, Pt. C. Monocarbonyl Derivatives of Aliphatic Hydrocarbons, Analogues & Derivatives. S. Coffey. 432p. 1965. 150.00 (ISBN 0-444-40133-4); Vol. 1, Pt. D. Dihydric Alcohols, Their Oxidation Products & Derivatives. S. Coffey. 418p. 1965. 150.00 (ISBN 0-444-40134-2); Vol. 1, Pt. E. Tri & Tetra-hydric Alcohols, Their Oxidation Products & Derivatives. S. Coffey. 488p. 1976. 166.00 (ISBN 0-444-40680-8); Vol. 1, Pt. F. Carbohydrate Chemistry. S. Coffey. 780p. 1968. 234.25 (ISBN 0-444-40135-0); Vol. 1, Pt. G. Enzymes, Macromolecules: Cumulative Index to Vol. 1. S. Coffey. 344p. 1976. 150.00 (ISBN 0-444-41447-9); Vol. 2, Pt. A. Monocarbocyclic Compounds to & Including Five Ring Atoms. S. Coffey. 228p. 1968. 134.25 (ISBN 0-444-40136-9); Vol. 2, Pt. B. Six & Higher-Membered Monocarbocyclic Compounds. S. Coffey. 463p. 1968. 150.00 (ISBN 0-444-40137-7); Vol. 2, Pt. C. Polycyclic Compounds Excluding Steroids. S. Coffey. 521p. 1969. 176.50 (ISBN 0-444-40681-6); Vol. 2, Pt. D. Steroids. S. Coffey. 500p. 1970. 176.50 (ISBN 0-444-40774-X); Vol. 2, Pt. E. Steroids. S. Coffey. 289p. 1971. 144.75 (ISBN 0-444-40775-8); Vol. 3, Pt. A. Mononucleic Hydrocarbons & Their Halogen Derivatives. 559p. 1971. 194.75 (ISBN 0-444-40878-9); Vol. 3, Pt. B. Benzoquinones & Related Compounds. S. Coffey. 559p. 1974. 194.75 (ISBN 0-444-40971-8); Vol. 3, Pt. C. Nuclear Sub-Benzene Hydrocarbons. S. Coffey. 334p. 1973. 150.00 (ISBN 0-444-41092-9); Vol. 3, Pt. D. Aralkyl Compounds: Their Derivatives & Oxidation Products. S. Coffey. 322p. 150.00 (ISBN 0-444-41209-3); Vol. 3, Pt. E. Monobenzine Hydrocarbons Derivatives with Functional Groups. 314p. 150.00 (ISBN 0-444-41210-7); Vol. 3, Pt. F. Polybenzine Hydrocarbons & their Derivatives. S. Coffey. 416p. 163.25 (ISBN 0-444-41211-5); Vol. 3, Pts. G & H. Aromatic Compounds with Fused Carbocyclic Ring Systems, 2 Pts. Ed. by S. Coffey. 1979. Pt. G. 221.00 (ISBN 0-444-41573-4); Pt. H. 159.75 (ISBN 0-444-41645-5). Elsevier.
Rodd's Chemistry of Carbon Compounds, 3 pts. in 1, Suppl. Vol. 2, Pts. C-E. Ed. by M. F. Ansell. 1974. 123.75 (ISBN 0-444-41135-6). Elsevier.
Rodd's Chemistry of Carbon Compounds, 2 pts. in 1, Suppl. Vol. 2 A & B. Ed. by M. F. Ansell. 1974. 155.25 (ISBN 0-444-41133-X). Elsevier.
Rodd's Chemistry of Carbon Compounds, Suppl. Vol 3F, (Partial) G. 2nd ed. M. F. Ansell. 1984. 123.75 (ISBN 0-444-42269-2, I-479-83). Elsevier.
Rodd's Chemistry of Carbon Compounds, Suppl. Vols. 3 B & C. Ed. by M. F. Ansell. 1981. 155.25 (ISBN 0-444-42017-7). Elsevier.
Rodd's Chemistry of Carbon Compounds, Suppl. Vols. 3, Pts. D-F. Ed. by M. F. Ansell. 1983. 155.25 (ISBN 0-444-42088-6). Elsevier.
Rodd's Chemistry of Carbon Compounds: Aromatic Compounds, Part A, Vol. 3, Pt. A. 2nd ed. Ed. by M. F. Ansell. 1983. 155.25 (ISBN 0-444-42150-5). Elsevier.
Rodd's Chemistry of Carbon Compounds-Heterocyclic Compounds: Part A-3, 4, 5 Membered Compounds. M. F. Ansell. 1984. Vol. 4A, Supplement. 210.75 (ISBN 0-444-42397-4). Elsevier.
Rodd's Chemistry of Carbon Compounds: Heterocyclic Compounds, Part D: Five Membered Heterocyclic Compunds with more than two Hetero-Atoms in the Ring. Ed. by S. Coffey & M. Ansell. 274p. 1986. 152.75 (ISBN 0-444-42556-X). Elsevier.
Rodd's Chemistry of Carbon Compounds, Vol. IV--Heterocyclic Compounds, Part C: Five-Membered Heterocyclic Compounds with Two Hetero-Atoms in the Ring from Groups V & VI of the Periodic Table. 2nd ed. Ed. by S. Coffey & M. Ansell. 594p. 1986. 305.25 (ISBN 0-444-42555-1). Elsevier.
Rodd's Chemistry of Carbon Compounds, Vol. 4, Pt. A: Three, Four & Five Membered Heterocyclic Compounds. S. Coffey. 1973. 221.00 (ISBN 0-444-41093-7). Elsevier.
Rodd's Chemistry of Carbon Compounds, Vol. 4, Pts. B & F. 2nd ed. Ed. by S. Coffey. Incl. Pt. B. Five-Membered Heterocyclic Compounds, Alkaloids, Dyes & Pigments. Ed. by S. Coffey. 1977. 176.00 (ISBN 0-444-41504-1); Pt. F. Six Membered Heterocyclic Compounds with a Single Atom in the Rind, Pyridine, Polymethyl-Epyridines, Quinoline, Isoquinoline & Their Derivatives. S. Coffey. 1977. 176.50 (ISBN 0-444-41503-3). LC 64-4605. Elsevier.
Rodd's Chemistry of Carbon Compounds, Vol. 4, Pt. E: Heterocyclic Compounds; Six-Membered Monoeterocyclic Compounds. S. Coffey. 522p. 1978. 194.75 (ISBN 0-444-41363-4). Elsevier.
Rodd's Chemistry of Carbon Compounds, Vol. 4, Pt. G: Heterocyclic Compounds - 6 Membered Heterocyclic Compounds with a Single Nitrogen Atom from Group V of the Periodic Table. Ed. by Coffey. 1977. 194.75 (ISBN 0-444-41644-7). Elsevier.
Rodd's Chemistry of Carbon Compounds, Vol. 4, Pt. H: Heterocyclic Compounds. 2nd ed. Ed. by S. Coffey. 1978. 194.75 (ISBN 0-444-41575-0). Elsevier.
Rodd's Chemistry of Carbon Compounds, Vol. 4, Pt. J: Proteins. S. Coffey. Date not set. price not set (ISBN 0-685-84873-6). Elsevier.
Rodd's Chemistry of Carbon Compounds, Vol. 4, Pt. K: Six Membered Heterocyclic Compounds with Two or More Hetero-Atoms. S. Coffey. 552p. 1979. 194.75 (ISBN 0-444-41647-1). Elsevier.
Rodd's Chemistry of Carbon Compounds, Vol. 4, Pt. L: Heterocyclic Compounds, Fused-Ring Heterocycles with Three or More N Atoms. Ed. by S. Coffey. 506p. 1980. 194.75 (ISBN 0-444-40664-6). Elsevier.
Rodeada Esta de Ensueno see Aguilas.
Rodent Control in Agriculture: A Handbook on the Biology & Control of Commensal Rodents as Agricultural Pests. J. H. Greaves. (Plant Production & Protection Papers: No. 40). 95p. 1982. pap. text ed. 7.50 (ISBN 92-5-101295-4, F2407, FAO). UNIPUB.
Rodent Malaria. Ed. by R. Killick-Kendrick & W. Peters. 1978. 96.00 (ISBN 0-12-407150-3). Acad Pr.
Rodent Pest Management, 2 vols. Ed. by Ishwar Prakash. 1988. 195.00. Vol. I, 240 pgs (6726). Vol. II, 224 pgs. cancelled (ISBN 0-8493-6727-1, 6727). CRC Pr.
Rodent Tumor Models in Experimental Cancer Therapy. Ed. by Robert F. Kallman. 432p. 1987. 55.00 (ISBN 0-08-033145-9, H220, H230, PBI). Pergamon.
Rodenticides: Analyses, Specifications, Formulations. (Plant Production & Protection Papers: No. 16). 81p. 1979. pap. 7.50 (ISBN 92-5-100798-5, F1867, FAO). UNIPUB.
Rodents of Uganda. M. J. Delany. (Illus.). xii, 159p. 1975. pap. text ed. 20.00x (ISBN 0-565-00764-5, Pub. by Brit Mus Nat Hist England). Sabbot-Natural Hist Bks.
Rodents of West Africa. D. R. Rosevear. (Illus.). 1969. text ed. 75.50x (ISBN 0-565-00677-0, Pub. by Brit Mus Nat Hist). Sabbot-Natural Hist Bks.
Rodeo. Cheryl W. Bellville. LC 84-14981. (Carolrhoda Photo Bks.). (Illus.). 32p. (gr. 1-5). 1985. PLB 12.95 (ISBN 0-87614-272-2). Carolrhoda Bks.
Rodeo, America's Number One Sport. 2nd ed. Thomas A. Bryant. (Illus.). 64p. (gr. 3-5). 1986. pap. 3.00 (ISBN 0-941875-00-8, WB1). Wolverine Gallery.
Rodeo: An Anthropologist Looks at the Wild & the Tame. Elizabeth A. Lawrence. LC 81-3330. (Illus.). 304p. 1982. 29.95x (ISBN 0-87049-328-0). U of Tenn Pr.
Rodeo: An Anthropologist Looks at the Wild & the Tame. Elizabeth A. Lawrence. LC 83-18176. (Illus.). xvi, 288p. 1984. pap. text ed. 11.95x (ISBN 0-226-46955-7). U of Chicago Pr.
Rodeo Champions: Eight Memorable Moments in Riding, Wrestling, & Roping. Larry Pointer. LC 84-20826. (Illus.). 152p. 1985. pap. 9.95 (ISBN 0-8263-0798-1). U of NM Pr.
Rodeo Cowboy. Chuck Martin. 1979. pap. 1.75 (ISBN 0-8439-0696-0, Leisure Bks). Leisure NY.
Rodeo Days. Carol McGinnis. 256p. (Orig.). 1987. pap. 2.95 (ISBN 0-345-33904-5). Ballantine.
Rodeo Drive. Barney Leason. 416p. 1988. pap. 3.95 (ISBN 1-55817-093-6). Windsor NY.
Rodeo Horses. Candace T. Philp. Ed. by Howard Schroeder. LC 83-11732. (Horses (Pasture to Paddock) Ser.). (Illus.). 48p. (gr. 4 up). 1983. PLB 9.95 (ISBN 0-89686-230-5). Crestwood Hse.
Rodeo Love. Fern Brown. 128p. (YA) (gr. 7 up). 1988. pap. 2.75 (ISBN 0-449-70249-9, Juniper). Fawcett.
Rodeo of John A. Stryker. Ron Tyler. (Illus.). 1978. 15.00 (ISBN 0-88426-050-X). Encino Pr.
Rodeo: Photographs. Photos by Norman Mauskoff. (Illus.). 96p. 1985. 30.00 (ISBN 0-942642-20-1). Twelvetrees Pr.
Rodeo Summer. Judie Gulley. LC 84-9129. 192p. (gr. 5-9). 1984. 11.95 (ISBN 0-395-36174-5). HM.
Rodeo: The Great American Sport. Murray Tinkelman. LC 81-6359. (Illus.). 64p. (gr. 3 up). 1982. pap. 7.50 (ISBN 0-688-01194-2). Greenwillow.
Rodeos. James W. Fain. LC 82-23460. (New True Bks.). (Illus.). 48p. (gr. k-4). 1983. PLB 12.60 (ISBN 0-516-01685-7); pap. 3.95 (ISBN 0-516-41685-5). Childrens.
Rodeos. James W. Fain. LC 82-23460. (Spanish - New True Bks.). 48p. (Span.). (gr. k-4). 1987. PLB 13.00 (ISBN 0-516-31685-0). Childrens.
Roderick. John Sladek. 210p. 1987. pap. 3.95 (ISBN 0-88184-325-3). Carroll & Graf.
Roderick at Random. John Sladek. 316p. 1988. pap. 3.95 (ISBN 0-88184-341-5). Carroll & Graf.
Roderick D. McKenzie on Human Ecology. Roderick D. McKenzie. Ed. by Amos H. Hawley. LC 68-9728. (Heritage of Sociology Ser.). 1969. pap. 3.45x (ISBN 0-226-31982-2, P326, Phoen). U of Chicago Pr.

Roger Zelazny. 2nd ed. Carl B. Yoke. (Starmont Reader's Guide Ser.: No. 2). 128p. Date not set. Repr. lib. bdg. 15.95x (ISBN 0-89370-769-4). Borgo Pr.

Roger Zelazny: A Primary & Secondary Bibliography. Joseph L. Sanders. 1980. lib. bdg. 19.00 (ISBN 0-8161-8081-4, Hall Reference). G K Hall.

Rogers & Hart: A Musical Anthology. Richard Rodgers & Lorenz Hart. (Illus.). 288p. 1984. perfect bd. 12.95 (ISBN 0-88188-337-9). H Leonard Pub Corp.

Roger's BS. Roger Olson. 120p. 1985. pap. 7.95 (ISBN 0-8059-2977-0). Dorrance.

Rogers Crossing: A Novella of California. Carl Patton, Jr. 1983. pap. 5.95 (ISBN 0-911003-00-2). Patton Creative.

Roger's Recovery from AIDS. Bob Owen. 210p. 1987. 19.95 (ISBN 0-937831-01-8). Davar Pub.

Rogers' Reminiscences of the French War & Memoir of General Stark. Robert Rogers. Intro. by Nelson Works. LC 88-80441. (Illus.). 343p. (Orig.). 1988. pap. 20.00 (ISBN 0-9620261-3-1). Freedom Historical.

Rogers' Rules for Businesswomen: How to Start a Career & Move up the Ladder. Henry C. Rogers. 224p. 1988. 16.95 (ISBN 0-312-01081-8). St Martin.

Rogers' Rules for Success: Tips That Will Take You to the Top by One of America's Foremost Public Relations Experts. Henry C. Rogers. 256p. 1984. 13.95 (ISBN 0-312-68829-6, Pub. by Marek). St Martin.

Rogers' Rules for Success: Tips That Will Take You to the Top by One of America's Foremost Public Relations Expert. Henry C. Rogers. 304p. 1986. pap. 7.95 (ISBN 0-312-68830-X). St Martin.

Roger's Rules of Public Relations. William R. Davis & Judy G. Davis. (Illus.). 100p. (Orig.). 1984. pap. 8.95 (ISBN 0-915113-01-5). Bizarre Butterfly.

Roger's Umbrella. Daniel Pinkwater. LC 81-2294. (Illus.). 32p. (gr. 1-3). 1982. 8.95 (ISBN 0-525-38555-X). Dutton.

Roger's Umbrella. Daniel Pinkwater. LC 81-2294. (Unicorn Paperback Ser.). (Illus.). 32p. (gr. 1-3). 1985. pap. 3.95 (ISBN 0-525-44223-5). Dutton.

Roger's Version. John Updike. 1986. 17.45 (ISBN 0-394-55435-3). Knopf.

Roger's Version. John Updike. 368p. 1987. pap. 4.95 (ISBN 0-449-21288-2, Crest). Fawcett.

Roget's II: The New Thesaurus. 1980. Plain-edged. 10.95 (ISBN 0-395-29604-8); Thumb-indexed. 12.95 (ISBN 0-395-29605-6); deluxe ed. 12.95. HM.

Roget's II the New Thesaurus see American Heritage Dictionary.

Roget's International Thesaurus. 4th ed. Peter M. Chapman. LC 62-12806. 1977. 13.95 (ISBN 0-690-00010-3); 14.95 (ISBN 0-690-00011-1). T y Crowell.

Roget's International Thesaurus. 4th ed. Robert L. Chapman. LC 84-47562. 1318p. (Orig.). 1984. pap. 9.95 (ISBN 0-06-091169-7, CN 1169, PL). Har-Row.

Roget's Pocket Thesaurus. Ed. by Mawson. pap. 3.95 (ISBN 0-317-56742-X). PB.

Roget's: The New Thesaurus, No. II. 528p. 1987. pap. 3.95 (ISBN 0-425-09974-1). Berkley Pub.

Roget's Thesaurus. 1981. pap. 3.95 (ISBN 0-671-53090-9). PB.

Roget's Thesaurus of English Words & Phrases. Peter M. Roget. Ed. by Robert A. Dutch. 1978. 12.50 (ISBN 0-312-68880-6); thumb indexed 13.95 (ISBN 0-312-68845-8). St Martin.

Roget's Thesaurus of Synonyms & Antonyms. 1972. pap. 4.25 (ISBN 0-87505-254-1). Borden.

Roget's Thesaurus of Synonyms & Antonyms. pap. 3.35 (ISBN 0-686-17306-6). Dennison.

Roget's Thesaurus of Words & Phrases. Peter M. Roget. 774p. 1960. 8.95 (ISBN 0-399-12943-X, G&D). Putnam Pub Group.

Roget's Thesaurus: Vest-Pocket Edition. LC 87-3799. 272p. 1987. pap. 2.25 (ISBN 0-395-44296-6). HM.

Roget's Two: The New Thesaurus. American Heritage Dictionary Editors. 1152p. 1988. 12.95 (ISBN 0-395-48317-4); deluxe ed. 14.95 (ISBN 0-395-48318-2). HM.

Roget's University Thesaurus. Peter M. Roget. Ed. by C. Sylvester Mawson. LC 81-47081. 768p. 1981. pap. 8.95 (ISBN 0-06-463537-6, EH 537, B&N Bks). Har-Row.

Rogue. Janet Dailey. Date not set. pap. 4.50 (ISBN 0-671-49982-3). PB.

Rogue: A River to Run. Florence Arman & Glen Wooldridge. LC 81-52732. (Illus.). 1982. pap. 11.95 (ISBN 0-9607260-0-4). Wildwood Pr.

Rogue & a Pirate. Carole Mortimer. (Harlequin Presents Ser.: No. 1005). 192p. Date not set. pap. 1.95 (ISBN 0-317-63751-7). Harlequin Bks.

Rogue Bear. Donald Seaman. 224p. 1988. 19.95 (ISBN 0-241-12363-1, Pub. by Hamish Hamilton). David & Charles.

Rogue Black. Raymond Giles. 208p. 1980. pap. 2.25 (ISBN 0-449-13809-7, GM). Fawcett.

Rogue Bolo. Keith Laumer. 256p. 1988. pap. 2.95 (ISBN 0-671-65545-0). Baen Bks.

Rogue Bull: The Story of Lang Hancock King of the Pilbara. Robert Duffield. 231p. 1982. 20.95x (ISBN 0-00-216423-X, Pub. by W. Collins Australia); pap. 8.95x (ISBN 0-00-634515-8). Intl Spec Bk.

Rogue Cop. William P. McGivern. 1987. pap. 2.95 (ISBN 0-425-10342-0). Berkley Pub.

Rogue Emperor, a Novel of the Chronoplane Wars. Crawford Kilian. 1988. pap. 3.95 (Del Rey). Ballantine.

Rogue Force. (SuperBolan Ser.: No. 8). 384p. 1987. pap. 3.95 (ISBN 0-373-61408-X, Pub. by Gold Eagle). Harlequin Bks.

Rogue in Space. Frederick Brown. 1976. Repr. of 1957 ed. lib. bdg. 8.95 (ISBN 0-88411-891-6, Pub. by Aeonian Pr). Amereon Ltd.

Rogue Justice. Geoffrey Household. 224p. 1984. pap. 3.95 (ISBN 0-14-006853-8). Penguin.

Rogue! Life & High Times of Stephen W. Dorsey. Thomas J. Caperton. 1978. pap. 4.95 (ISBN 0-89013-114-7). Museum NM Pr.

Rogue Male. Geoffrey Household. 1977. pap. 3.95 (ISBN 0-14-000695-8). Penguin.

Rogue Male. Geoffrey Household. 15.95 (ISBN 0-89190-435-2, Pub. by Am Repr). Amereon Ltd.

Rogue Moon. Algis Budrys. 1981. pap. 2.45 (ISBN 0-380-00100-4, 38950-9, Equinox). Avon.

Rogue Moon. Algis Budrys. 224p. 1986. pap. 3.50 (ISBN 0-445-20318-8, Pub. by Popular Lib). Warner Bks.

Rogue Mustang. Max Brand. 176p. 1985. pap. 2.50 (ISBN 0-446-32686-0). Warner Bks.

Rogue of Falconhurst. Ashley Carter. 384p. 1983. pap. 3.50 (ISBN 0-449-12514-9, GM). Fawcett.

Rogue of Gor, No. 15. John Norman. (Science Fiction Ser.). 1986. pap. 3.50 (ISBN 0-87997-892-9). DAW Bks.

Rogue of Publishers' Row. 9th ed. Edward Uhlan. 1956. 10.00 (ISBN 0-682-40103-X, Banner); pap. 10.00 (ISBN 0-682-40104-8). Exposition-Phoenix.

Rogue: Or the Life of Guzman De Alfarache, 4 vols. James Nabbe. 1979. Repr. of 1924 ed. Set. lib. bdg. 200.00 (ISBN 0-8495-3777-0). Arden Lib.

Rogue or the Life or Guzman De Alfarache, 4 Vols. Matheo Aleman. Tr. by James Mabbe. (Tudor Translations, Second Series: No. 2-5). Repr. of 1924 ed. Set. 180.00 (ISBN 0-404-51970-9); 45.00 ea. Vol. 1 (ISBN 0-404-51971-7). Vol. 2 (ISBN 0-404-51972-5). Vol. 3 (ISBN 0-404-51973-3). Vol. 4 (ISBN 0-404-51974-1). AMS Pr.

Rogue Pirate. John G. Betancourt. LC 86-51268. (Windwalker Bks.). 224p. (Orig.). 1987. pap. 2.95. TSR Inc.

Rogue Powers. Roger M. Allen. 1986. 3.50 (ISBN 0-671-65584-1). Baen Bks.

Rogue Queen. L. Sprague De Camp. (Illus.). 176p. pap. text ed. 7.95 (ISBN 0-312-94396-2). Bluejay Bks.

Rogue Rancher. Will Travers. (Orig.). 1980. pap. 1.75 (ISBN 0-505-51602-0, Pub. by Tower Bks). Leisure NY.

Rogue Rancher. Will Travers. (Lythway Ser.). 176p. 1988. lib. bdg. 17.50 (ISBN 0-7451-0672-2, Pub. by Chivers Pr UK). G K HAll.

Rogue River. James Reno. (Anthem Family Ser.: No. 4). 224p. 1988. pap. 2.95 (ISBN 0-451-15129-1, Sig). NAL.

Rogue Sergeant. Lawrence Cortesi. 224p. 1982. pap. 2.50 (ISBN 0-505-51854-6, Pub. by Tower Bks). Leisure NY.

Rogue Sergeant. Lawrence Cortesi. 224p. 1983. pap. 2.50 (ISBN 0-8439-2016-5, Leisure Bks). Leisure NY.

Rogue Sword. Poul Anderson. 256p. (Orig.). 1980. pap. 2.25 (ISBN 0-89083-638-8). Zebra.

Rogue Waves: Tales under Sail from Well-Known Personalities. Ed. by Nicole Swengley. (Illus.). 160p. 1985. 14.95 (ISBN 0-229-11751-1, Pub. by Adlard Coles). Sheridan.

Rogues. Peter Whalley. 1988. 16.95 (ISBN 0-8027-0988-5). Walker & Co.

Rogues & Heroes from Iowa's Amazing Past. George Mills. (Iowa Heritage Collection Ser.). (Illus.). 252p. 1986. pap. 4.95 (ISBN 0-8138-1446-4). Iowa St U Pr.

Rogues & Running Dogs. rev. ed. D. Brian Plummer. (Illus.). 1984. 18.00 (ISBN 0-85115-166-3, Pub. by Boydell & Brewer). Longwood Pub Group.

Rogues & Vagabonds of Shakespeare's Youth, Described by John Awdeley in His Fraternitye Vacabondes 1561-1573; Thomas Harman in His Caveat for Common Cursetors, 1567-1573; & in the Groundworke of Conny-Catching, 1552. Ed. by Edward Viles & F. J. Furnivall. Bd. with Robert Laneham's Letters. (New Shakespeare Society London Series 6: Nos. 7 & 14). pap. 37.00 (ISBN 0-8115-0246-5). Kraus Repr.

Rogues & Vagabonds: The Vagrant Underworld in Britain 1815-1985. Lionel Rose. 272p. 1988. lib. bdg. 65.00 (ISBN 0-415-00275-3). Routledge Chapman & Hall.

Rogue's Bride. Paula Roland. 304p. 1987. pap. 2.95 (ISBN 0-8217-1976-9). Zebra.

Rogues in the House. Robert E. Howard. 15.00 (ISBN 0-937986-25-9). D M Grant.

Rogue's Lady. Robyn Carr. 480p. 1988. pap. 3.95 (ISBN 1-55817-078-2). Windsor NY.

Rogue's Lady. Victoria Thompson. 352p. (Orig.). 1988. pap. 3.95 (ISBN 0-380-75526-2). Avon.

Rogue's Life. Wilkie Collins. 144p. 1985. pap. 4.95 (ISBN 0-86299-183-8, Pub. by A Sutton Pub England). Academy Chi Pubs.

Rogue's Life: From His Birth to His Marriage. Wilkie Collins. 192p. 1985. pap. 4.95 (ISBN 0-486-24947-6). Dover.

Rogue's Mistress. Constance Gluyas. (Orig.). 1977. pap. 2.95 (ISBN 0-451-11099-4, AE1099, Sig). NAL.

Rogues of the South Seas. A. Grove Day. Orig. Title: Adventures of the South Pacific. 292p. 1986. pap. 3.95 (ISBN 0-935180-24-9). Mutual Pub HI.

Rogues, Rebels, & Reformers. Ted R. Gurr. LC 76-17370. pap. 25.50 (ISBN 0-317-09470-X, 2021909). Bks Demand UMI.

Rogues River. Frank Martin. 1985. 25.00x (ISBN 0-86025-874-2, Pub. by Ian Henry Pubns England). State Mutual Bk.

Rogues' River. Frank Martin. 1988. 30.00x (Pub. by Ian Henry Pubns England). State Mutual Bk.

Rohan Master. Intro. by Millard Meiss. LC 73-77880. (Illus.). 248p. 1973. slipcase 80.00 (ISBN 0-8076-0690-1). Braziller.

Rohanta & Nandriya. Krishna Chaitanya. (Nehru Library for Children). (Illus.). (gr. 1-9). 1979. pap. 2.00 (ISBN 0-89744-179-6). Auromere.

Rohault's System of Natural Philosophy. Jacques Rohault. Ed. by Willis Doney. Tr. by John Clarke. (Philosophy of Descartes Ser.). (Illus.). 670p. 1987. lib. bdg. 120.00 (ISBN 0-8240-4668-4). Garland Pub.

Rohm & Haas: History of a Chemical Company. Sheldon Hochheiser. (Illus.). 300p. 1985. text ed. 22.95 (ISBN 0-8122-7940-9). U of Pa Pr.

Rohrbach Genealogy, Vol. III: The Rorabaugh, Rohrbaugh, Rohrbaugh, Rohrabaugh, Rohrabaugh, Rorabaugh & Rhorabaugh Families of America Who Are Descendants of Johann Reinhart Rohrbach Who Emigrated from Germany to America in 1749. Lewis B. Rohrbach. LC 71-118879. 376p. 1982. 40.00. Picton Pr.

Rohstoffe Des Pflanzenreichs, 7 pts. 5th ed. J. Von Wiesner & C. Von Regel. Incl. Pt. 1. Tanning Materials (Gerbstoffe) H. Endres et al. (Eng. & Ger.). 1962. 44.00x (ISBN 3-7682-0111-2); Pt. 2. Antibiotiques (Antibiotica) G. Hagemann. (Fr.). 1964. 59.00x (ISBN 3-7682-0170-8); Pt. 3. Organic Acids. G. C. Whitting. 1964. 33.50x (ISBN 3-7682-0244-5); Pt. 4. Insecticides. A. J. Fuell. 1965. 48.00x (ISBN 3-7682-0259-3); Pt. 5. Glykoside. L. Zechner. 1966. 45.00x (ISBN 3-7682-0298-4); Pt. 6. Staerke. E. Samecl & M. Bling. (Illus.). 1966. 49.50x (ISBN 3-7682-0186-4); Pt. 7. Aetherische Oele. K. Bournot & M. Weber. (Illus.). 1968. 49.50x (ISBN 3-7682-0562-2). Lubrecht & Cramer.

Roi Babar. Laurent De Brunhoff. (Fr.). (gr. 4-6). 1975. 15.95 (ISBN 0-685-11533-X). French & Eur.

Roi Basics for Nonfinancial Executives. Allen Sweeny. 1980. 11.95 (ISBN 0-8144-5553-0). AMACOM.

Roi Candaule see Theatre.

Roi Pecheur. Julien Gracq. 156p. 1955. 25.00 (ISBN 0-686-54027-1). French & Eur.

ROI: Practical Theory & Innovative Application. rev. & enl. ed. Robert A. Peters. 1979. 23.95 (ISBN 0-8144-5496-8). AMACOM.

Roi Qui Aimait Trop les Fleurs. Francoise Mallet-Joris. 64p. 1971. 8.95 (ISBN 0-686-56314-X). French & Eur.

Roi sans Divertissement. Jean Giono. (Folio Ser.: No. 220). 256p. 1972. 6.95 (ISBN 0-686-53987-7). Schoenhof.

Roi se Meurt. Eugene Ionesco. (Folio Ser.: No. 361). pap. 5.95 (ISBN 0-685-34258-1). Schoenhof.

Roi se Meurt see Theatre.

Roi Vert see Green King.

Rois En Exil. Alphonse Daudet. 1940. 8.95 (ISBN 0-686-55596-1). French & Eur.

Rois et Serfs: Un Chapitre D'Histoire Capetienne. Marc Bloch. 224p. (Fr.). Repr. of 1920 ed. lib. bdg. 52.50x. Coronet Bks.

Roister Doister. Nicholas Udall. LC 82-45679. (Malone Society Reprints Ser.: No. 76). Repr. of 1934 ed. 40.00 (ISBN 0-404-63076-6). AMS Pr.

Roister Doister: From Eton Copyright Edited by G. Scheurweghs. Nicholas Udall. (Materials for the Study of the Old English Drama Series 2: Vol. 16). pap. 21.00 (ISBN 0-8115-0309-7). Kraus Repr.

Roister Doister: Written before 1553. Nicholas Udall. Ed. by Edward Arber. pap. 12.50 (ISBN 0-87556-340-6). Saifer.

Rokudan: A Tale of Love in Six Movements. Pat Burch. LC 80-29375. 192p. 1981. 9.95 (ISBN 0-8008-6818-8). Taplinger.

Rokyo No Bijutsu. Osaka Municipal Museum Staff. 300p. 1976. 1050.00x (ISBN 0-317-68491-4, Pub. by Han-Shan Tang Ltd). State Mutual Bk.

Rol' Pravoslavnoi Tserkvi V Istorii Rosii: The Role of the Orthodox Church in Russian History. Sergei Pushkarev. Pref. by Protoierei. LC 85-80831. 125p. (Rus.). 1985. 9.50 (ISBN 0-911971-13-0). Effect Pub.

Roland. Niccolo Piccinni. Ed. by Gustave Lefevre. (Chefs-d'oeuvre classiques de l'opera francais Ser.: Vol. 29). (Illus.). 390p. (Fr.). 1972. pap. 32.50x. Broude.

Roland Barthes. Roland Barthes. Tr. by Richard Howard from Fr. (Illus.). 188p. 1977. 8.95 (ISBN 0-8090-8245-4); pap. 7.25 (ISBN 0-8090-1385-1). Hill & Wang.

Roland Barthes. Jonathan Culler. 1983. 21.95x (ISBN 0-19-520420-4); pap. 6.95 (ISBN 0-19-520421-2). Oxford U Pr.

Roland Barthes: A Bibliographical Reader's Guide. Sanford Freedman & Carole A. Taylor. LC 81-43338. (Modern Critics & Critical Schools Ser.). 445p. 1982. lib. bdg. 55.00 (ISBN 0-8240-9292-9). Garland Pub.

Roland Barthes: A Conservative Estimate. Philip Thody. LC 83-5112. 208p. 1984. pap. 7.95x (ISBN 0-226-79513-6). U of Chicago Pr.

Roland Barthes: Structuralism & After. Annette Lavers. LC 81-13447. 320p. 1982. text ed. 29.50x (ISBN 0-674-77721-2). Harvard U Pr.

Roland Barthes: The Professor of Desire. Steven Ungar. LC 83-6836. xx, 206p. 1984. 19.50x (ISBN 0-8032-4551-3). U of Nebr Pr.

Roland Batchelor: Water-Color & Drawings. Patricia Jarrett. (Illus.). 1983. 30.00 (ISBN 0-8390-0319-6). Abner Schram Ltd.

Roland H. Bainton: An Examination of His Reformation Historiography. Steven Simpler. LC 85-21567. (Texts & Studies in Religion: Vol. 24). 266p. 1985. lib. bdg. 49.95x (ISBN 0-88946-812-5). E Mellen.

Roland Harvey's Incredible Book of Almost Everything. Roland Harvey. (Illus.). 160p. (Orig.). (gr. 1-9). 1985. pap. 9.95 (ISBN 0-86788-024-4, Pub. by Five Mile Pr Australia). Sterling.

Roland LaVoie's Model Railroading with Lionel Trains. Roland LaVoie. 96p. (Orig.). (YA) (gr. 9-12). 1988. pap. 14.95 (ISBN 0-89778-054-X, 10-6745). Greenberg Pub Co.

Roland Martin's One Hundred One Bass-Catching Secrets. Roland Martin. Ed. by Tim Tucker. 1988. 18.95 (ISBN 0-8329-0457-0, Pub. by Winchester Pr). New Century.

Roland-Michel Barrin de la Galissoni Ere, 1693-1756. Lionel A. Groulx. LC 74-22181. (Canadian Biographical Studies: No. 2). pap. 26.00 (ISBN 0-317-27037-0, 2023627). Bks Demand UMI.

Roland the Minstrel Pig. William Steig. (Illus.). (gr. k-3). 1968. 11.25i (ISBN 0-06-025761-X); PLB 11.89 (ISBN 0-06-025762-8). HarpJ.

Roland the Minstrel Pig. William Steig. (Illus.). 32p. (ps-3). 1988. pap. 5.95 (ISBN 0-671-66841-2). S&S.

Rolando Hinojosa Reader. Ed. by Jose D. Saldivar. LC 83-72578. 190p. (Orig.). 1985. 10.00 (ISBN 0-934770-30-1). Arte Publico.

Role & Career Problems of the Chicago Public School Teacher. Howard S. Becker. Ed. by Harriet Zuckerman & Robert K. Merton. LC 79-8974. (Dissertations on Sociology Ser.). 1980. lib. bdg. 28.50x (ISBN 0-405-12951-3). Ayer Co Pubs.

Role & Character of the Civil Service. W. Armstrong. (Thank-Offering to Britain Fund Lectures). 1970. pap. 5.50 (ISBN 0-85672-343-6, Pub. by British Acad). Longwood Pub Group.

Role & Function of Government Laboratories & the Transfer of Technology to the Manufacturing Sector. Ed. by Arthur J. Cordell & James Gilmour. (Science Council of Canada Background Studies: No. 35). 1976. pap. 12.00 (SSC72, SSC). UNIPUB.

Role & Functions of Lower Order Centres in Rural Development. (Working Papers Ser.: No. 79-7). 35p. 1979. pap. 6.00 (ISBN 0-686-78252-6, CRD033, UNCRD). UNIPUB.

Role & Impact of Local Co-Operative Support Organizations. Chris Cornforth & Jenny Lewis. 1985. 27.15x (ISBN 0-317-54797-6, Pub. by Plunkett Foundation). State Mutual Bk.

Role & Limits of Government: Essays in Political Economy. Ed. by Samuel Brittan. 288p. 1984. 37.50x (ISBN 0-8166-1278-1); pap. 14.95 (ISBN 0-8166-1276-5). U of Minn Pr.

Role & Record of the U. N. High Commissioner for Refugees. Nagendra Singh. 1985. 14.00x (ISBN 0-8364-1379-2, Pub. by Macmillan India). South Asia Bks.

Role & Responsibility of the Moral Philosopher: Proceedings, Vol. 56. Ed. by John T. Noonan, Jr. et al. LC 81-69068. 214p. 1982. pap. 15.00 (ISBN 0-918090-16-4). Am Cath Philo.

Role & Status of Women in India. R. Ray et al. 167p. 1978. 11.95. Asia Bk Corp.

Role & Status of Women in India. 1978. 11.00x (ISBN 0-8364-0180-8). South Asia Bks.

Role & Status of Women in the Soviet Union. Ed. by Donald R. Brown. LC 68-27326. pap. 37.80 (ISBN 0-317-42025-9, 2025995). Bks Demand UMI.

Role Conception & Vocational Success & Satisfaction: A Study of Student & Professional Nurses. Marvin J. Taves et al. (Illus.). 125p. 1963. pap. 4.00x (ISBN 0-87776-112-4, R-112). Ohio St U Admin Sci.

Role Conflict among the Working Women. Puspa Sinha. 1987. 17.50 (ISBN 0-8364-2257-0, Pub. by Anmol Delhi). South Asia Bks.

Role Conflict among the Working Women. Pusps Sinha. 1987. 24.95. Asia Bk Corp.

Role De Dupont De Nemours En Matiere Fiscale a l'Assemblee Constituante. L. Cuny. LC 74-132533. (Research & Source Works Ser.: No. 823). (Fr). 1971. Repr. of 1909 ed. lib. bdg. 22.50 (ISBN 0-8337-0741-8). B Franklin.

Role de l'ecrivain dans le monde d'aujourd'hui see Soixante Ans de Ma Vie Litteraire.

TITLE INDEX ROLE OF HONOR.

Role des Groupements dans la Politique des Salaires en Israel see Cahiers de l'Institut de Science Economique Appliquee.

Role du Langage dans les Processus Perceptuals. Alfred Korzybski. 93p. (Fr.). 1951. pap. 4.75x (ISBN 0-937298-03-4). Inst Gen Seman.

Role et Signification Des Conseils Ouvriers D'Apres Max Adler see Cahiers de l'Institut de Science Economique Appliquee.

Role for Marketing in College Admissions. 128p. 1976. pap. 5.00 (ISBN 0-87447-078-1, 200685). College Bd.

Role for Private Citizens in Historic Preservation. Ann Swanson. (Local History Technical Leaflets Ser.). (Illus.). 14p. (Orig.). 1985. pap. 1.50 (ISBN 0-931406-10-2). Idaho State Soc.

Role Model Blacks: Known but Little Known Role Models of Successful Blacks. Carroll L. Miller. LC 82-70535. 328p. 1982. pap. text ed. 12.95 (ISBN 0-915202-30-1). Accel Devel.

Role of a Consultant in a Superintendency Search. 31p. (Orig.). 1983. pap. 3.50 (ISBN 0-87652-079-4, 021-00822). Am Assn Sch Admin.

Role of Accounting in the Stock Market Crash of 1929. Gadis J. Dillon. 200p. 1984. Spiral. 35.00 (ISBN 0-88406-170-1). Ga St U BUsn Pub.

Role of Accreditation in Directly Improving Educational Quality. Steven M. Jung. 30p. 1986. 8.00 (ISBN 0-318-20486-X). Coun Postsecondary Accredit.

Role of Acetaldehyde in the Actions of Ethanol: Satellite Symposium to the Sixth International Congress of Pharmacology. Ed. by K. O. Lindros & C. J. Eriksson. (Finnish Foundation for Alcohol Studies: Vol. 23). (Illus.). 1975. pap. 8.00 (ISBN 951-9191-23-2). Rutgers Ctr Alcohol.

Role of Adenosine in Cerebral Metabolism & Blood Flow. Ed. by V. Stefanovich & I. Okyayuz-Baklouti. 141p. 1987. lib. bdg. 83.50x (ISBN 90-6764-098-0). Coronet Bks.

Role of Advertising in Worldwide Media Development. IAA Global Media Commission. 30p. 1986. 5.00 (ISBN 0-318-22254-X). Intl Advertising Assn.

Role of Affect in Consumer Behavior: Emerging Theories & Applications. Ed. by Robert A. Peterson et al. LC 85-45039. (Illus.). 208p. 1985. 33.00x (ISBN 0-669-12874-0). Lexington Bks.

Role of Aggression in Human Pathology. Ed. by H. Musaph & P. J. Mettrop. (Psychotherapy & Psychosomatics: Vol. 20, No. 5). (Illus.). 1972. pap. 12.00 (ISBN 3-8055-1562-6). S Karger.

Role of Agriculture in Economic Development. Ed. by Erik Thorbecke. (Universities-National Bureau Conference Ser.: No. 21). 490p. 1970. 29.00 (ISBN 0-87014-203-8, Dist by Columbia U Pr). Natl Bur Econ Res.

Role of Air-Sea Exchange in Geochemical Cycling. Ed. by Patrick Buat-Menard. 1986. lib. bdg. 98.00 (ISBN 90-277-2318-4, Pub. by Reidel Holland). Kluwer Academic.

Role of Animals in Biomedical Research. Ed. by Jeri A. Sechzer. 1983. 40.00x (ISBN 0-89766-204-0); pap. 40.00x (ISBN 0-89766-205-9, VOL. 406). NY Acad Sci.

Role of Anxiety in English Tragedy 1580-1642. Charlotte N. Clay. Ed. by James Hogg. (Jacobean Drama Studies). 251p. (Orig.). 1974. pap. 15.00 (ISBN 3-7052-0321-5, Pub. by Salzburg Studies). Longwood Pub Group.

Role of Arab Development Funds in the World Economy. Ed. by Michele Achilli & Mohamed Khaldi. LC 84-15907. 320p. 1984. 32.50 (ISBN 0-312-68921-7). St Martin.

Role of Architects & Planners in Post-Earthquake Studies: Proceedings of a Colloquium Held February 23-24, 1982 in Berkeley, CA. 24p. 1982. 10.00. Earthquake Eng.

Role of Arthropods in Forest Ecosystems: Proceedings in Life Sciences. Ed. by W. J. Mattson. (Illus.). 1977. 37.00 (ISBN 0-387-08296-4). Springer-Verlag.

Role of Ascorbic Acid in Growth, Differentiation & Metabolism of Plants. Ed. by N. J. Chinoy. (Advances in Agricultural Biotechnology Ser.). 1984. lib. bdg. 46.50 (ISBN 90-247-2908-4, Pub. by Martinus Nijhoff Netherlands). Kluwer-Academic.

Role of Asia in the Historical Growth of the World, 2 vols. A. T. Mahan. (Illus.). 266p. 1988. Set. 227.55 (ISBN 0-86722-187-9). Inst Econ Pol.

Role of Bacteria in the Corrosion of Oil Field Equipment (TPC-3) (Illus.). 84p. 20.00 (ISBN 0-915567-76-8). Natl Corrosion Eng.

Role of Banks in Economic Development: The Economics of Industrial Resurgence. George T. Edwards. 220p. 1987. 59.00x (ISBN 0-333-41302-4, Pub. by Macmillan Pr Ltd). Intl Spec Bk.

Role of Behavior in Evolution. Ed. by Henry C. Plotkin. 240p. 1988. text ed. 27.50x (ISBN 0-262-16107-9). MIT Pr.

Role of Business in Society. John Diebold. LC 82-71322. pap. 36.00 (ISBN 0-317-26958-5, 2023576). Bks Demand UMI.

Role of Calcium in Biological Systems, Vol. I. Ed. by Leopold J. Anghileri & Anne M. Tuffet-Anghileri. 288p. 1982. 95.00 (ISBN 0-8493-6280-6). CRC Pr.

Role of Calcium in Biological Systems, Vol. II. Ed. by Leopold J. Anghileri & Ann M. Tuffet-Anghileri. 240p. 1982. 79.00 (ISBN 0-8493-6281-4). CRC Pr.

Role of Calcium in Biological Systems, Vol. III. Ed. by Leopold J. Anghileri & Ann M. Tuffet-Anghileri. 272p. 1982. 89.00 (ISBN 0-8493-6282-2). CRC Pr.

Role of Calcium Ions in Drug Action. M. Denborough. (International Encyclopedia of Pharmacology & Therapeutics Ser.: No. 124). (Illus.). 200p. 1987. 99.00 (ISBN 0-08-034193-4, PBL). Pergamon.

Role of Capital: Improving Innovations in American Manufacturing During the 1920's. John H. Lorant. LC 75-2588. (Dissertations in American Economic History). (Illus.). 1975. 31.00x (ISBN 0-405-07207-4). Ayer Co Pubs.

Role of Cell Interactions in Early Neurogenesis. Ed. by A. M. Duprat et al. (NATO ASI Series A, Life Sciences: Vol. 77). 344p. 1984. 65.00x (ISBN 0-306-41716-2, Plenum Pr). Plenum Pub.

Role of Chemical Engineering in Utilizing the Nation's Forest Resources. LC 79-27547. 120p. 1980. pap. 22.00 (ISBN 0-8169-0124-4, S-195). Am Inst Chem Eng.

Role of Chemical Mediators in the Pathophysiology of Acute Illness & Injury. Ed. by Rita McConn. 408p. 1982. text ed. 94.00 (ISBN 0-89004-682-4). Raven.

Role of Chemicals & Radiation in the Etiology of Cancer. Ed. by Eliezer Huberman & Susan H. Barr. (Carcinogenesis: A Comprehensive Survey Ser.: Vol. 10). 560p. 1985. text ed. 86.00 (ISBN 0-88167-130-4). Raven.

Role of Chromosomes in Cancer Biology. P. C. Koller. LC 72-77247. (Recent Results in Cancer Research: Vol. 38). (Illus.). 150p. 1972. 35.00 (ISBN 0-387-05812-5). Springer-Verlag.

Role of Cities in Attaining a Desirable Population Distribution in the Context of Rapid Urbanization; Japan Study, Pt. II: Nationwide Review of Urban Employment & Case Studies of Tsu & Hamamatsu. 129p. pap. 6.00 (CRD057, UNCRD). UNIPUB.

Role of Citrus in Health & Disease. Willard A Krehl. LC 76-4502. 1976. 10.50x (ISBN 0-8130-0532-9). U Presses Fla.

Role of Coherent Structures in Modelling Turbulence & Mixing: Proceedings. Ed. by J. Jimenez. (Lecture Notes in Physics Ser.: Vol. 136). 393p. 1981. pap. 30.00 (ISBN 0-387-10289-2). Springer-Verlag.

Role of Computers in Manufacturing Processes. Gideon Halevi. LC 80-11378. 502p. 1980. 69.50x (ISBN 0-471-04383-4, Pub. by Wiley-Interscience). Wiley.

Role of Computers in Radiotherapy. (Panel Proceedings Ser.), (Illus.). 211p. 1968. pap. 13.00 (ISBN 92-0-111668-3, ISP203, IAEA). UNIPUB.

Role of Computers in Religious Education. Kenneth Bedell. 144p. 1986. pap. 7.95 (ISBN 0-687-36540-6). Abingdon.

Role of Computers in Sci-Tech Libraries. Ed. by Ellis Mount. LC 86-7619. (Science & Technology Libraries: Vol. 6(4)). 145p. 1986. 24.95 (ISBN 0-86656-577-9). Haworth Pr.

Role of Computing in Developing Countries. Bogod. 1979. pap. 14.95 (ISBN 0-471-25599-8, Wiley Heyden). Wiley.

Role of Crack Growth in Metal Fatigue. P. L. Pook. 157p. (Orig.). 1983. pap. text ed. 30.00x (ISBN 0-904357-63-5, Pub. by Inst Metals). Brookfield Pub Co.

Role of Culture in Developmental Disorder. Ed. by Charles M. Super. 254p. 1987. 45.00 (ISBN 0-12-676840-4). Acad Pr.

Role of Cyclic AMP in Cell Function. Ed. by P. Greengard & E. Costa. LC 73-84113. (Advances in Biochemical Psychopharmacology Ser.: Vol. 3). 386p. 1970. 45.00 (ISBN 0-911216-15-4). Raven.

Role of Cyclic Nucleic Acid Adducts in Carcinogenesis & Mutagenesis. Ed. by B. Singer & H. Bartsch. (IARC Scientific Publications: No. 70). (Illus.). 500p. 1986. 80.00 (ISBN 9-28-321170-7). Oxford U Pr.

Role of Dampers in a Total Fire Protection System. Kenneth J. Schwartz. 1986. pap. 7.50 (ISBN 0-318-22361-9, TR 86-2). Society Fire Protect.

Role of Data in Judicial Planning. National Center for State Courts Staff. 101p. 1977. manuscript 6.06 (DC-005). Natl Ctr St Courts.

Role of Demand & Supply in the Generation & Diffusion of Technical Change. Colin G. Thritle & Vernon W. Ruttan. (Fundamentals of Pure & Applied Economics Ser: Vol. 21). 166p. 1987. pap. text ed. 34.00 (ISBN 3-7186-0384-5). Harwood Academic.

Role of Design in International Competitiveness. M. J. Baker & D. O. Ughanwa. 448p. 1988. lib. bdg. 87.50 (ISBN 0-415-00013-0). Routledge Chapman & Hall.

Role of Design in the Profitable Architectural Office. American Institute of Architects Committee on Design. 1985. 11.25 (ISBN 0-317-40651-5, R318). Am Inst Arch.

Role of Development Banks in a Planned Economy. P. N. Singh. 1974. 8.25x (ISBN 0-686-20301-1). Intl Bk Dist.

Role of Diffusion in Catalysis. Charles N. Satterfield & Thomas K. Sherwood. LC 63-16570. (Addison Wesley Series in Chemical Engineering). pap. 31.30 (ISBN 0-317-10680-5, 2055595). Bks Demand UMI.

Role of Direct & Indirect Taxes in the Federal Reserve System, A Conference. National Bureau of Economic Research. (Special Conference Series by the Universities). 1964. 32.00x (ISBN 0-691-04173-3). Princeton U Pr.

Role of Domestic Courts in International Legal Order, Vol. 3. Richard A. Falk. (Procedural Aspects of International Law Ser.). 1964. 20.00x (ISBN 0-8139-0836-1). U Pr of Va.

Role of Dominant Caste in Indian Politics. P. Ranjani Reddy. 218p. 1987. text ed. 27.50x (ISBN 81-85024-18-9, Pub. by Uppal Hse). Advent NY.

Role of Drug Treatments for Eating Disorders. Ed. by Paul E. Garfinkel & David M. Garner. LC 86-33367. (Eating Disorders Monograph Ser.). 208p. 1987. 22.50 (ISBN 0-87630-460-9). Brunner-Mazel.

Role of Drugs & Electrolytes in Hormonogenesis. Ed. by K. Fotherby & S. B. Pal. LC 84-7611. (Illus.). xii, 360p. 1984. 95.00x (ISBN 3-11-008463-5). De Gruyter.

Role of Drugs in Community Psychiatry. Ed. by Charles Shagass. (Modern Problems of Pharmacopsychiatry Ser.: Vol. 6). 1971. 23.50 (ISBN 3-8055-1200-7). S Karger.

Role of Dust in Dense Regions of Interstellar Matter. Ed. by Thomas Henning. 1987. lib. bdg. 79.00 (ISBN 90-277-2421-0, Pub. by Reidel Holland). Kluwer Academic.

Role of Economic Advisors in Developing Countries. Lauchlin Currie. LC 81-6623. (Contributions in Economics & Economic History Ser.: No. 44). (Illus.). 288p. 1981. 35.00 (ISBN 0-313-23064-1, CUE/). Greenwood.

Role of Education in National Defense. Alvin Tucker. 15p. 1982. 2.25 (ISBN 0-318-22194-2, OC86). Natl Ctr Res Voc Ed.

Role of Embassies in Promoting Business: A Symposium. Ed. by Martin F. Herz. LC 81-6427. 75p. (Orig.). 1981. pap. 5.50 (ISBN 0-934742-13-8, Inst Study Diplomacy). Geo U Sch For Serv.

Role of Embassies in Promoting Business: A Symposium. Ed. by Martin F. Herz. 80p. 1985. pap. text ed. 5.25 (ISBN 0-8191-5053-3, Inst for Study Diplomacy). U Pr of Amer.

Role of Employer's Organisations in Asian Countries. (Labour-Management Relations Ser.: No. 39). iii, 344p. 1971. 11.20 (ISBN 92-2-100133-4). Intl Labour Office.

Role of Employers' Organizations in English-Speaking African Countries. (Labour-Management Relations Ser.: No. 42). iv, 151p. 1973. 8.75 (ISBN 92-2-100961-0). Intl Labour Office.

Role of Employment & Earnings in Analyzing Levels of Living: A General Methodology with Applications to Malaysia & Thailand. Christiaan Grootaert. (LSMS Working Paper: No. 27). 80p. 1986. 5.00 (ISBN 0-317-59153-3, BK 0826). World Bank.

Role of Endorphins & Neuropsychiatry. Ed. by H. M. Emrich. (Modern Problems in Pharmacopsychiatry Ser.: Vol. 17). (Illus.). viii, 292p. 1981. 88.75 (ISBN 3-8055-2918-X). S Karger.

Role of Equalization in Federal Grants. U.S Advisory Commission on Intergovernmental Relations. LC 77-74926. (American Federalism-the Urban Dimension). (Illus.). 1978. Repr. of 1964 ed. lib. bdg. 20.00x (ISBN 0-405-10475-8). Ayer Co Pubs.

Role of Evaluators in Curriculum Development. Ed. by Pinchas Tamir. LC 84-17610. 232p. 1984. 29.95 (ISBN 0-7099-2470-4, Pub. by Croom Helm Ltd). Routledge Chapman & Hall.

Role of Exercise in Internal Medicine. Ed. by E. Jokl & D. Brunner. (Medicine & Sport Ser.: No. 10). 160p. 1976. 65.50 (ISBN 3-8055-2362-9). S Karger.

Role of Experts in Business Litigation. 45p. 1979. pap. 5.00 (ISBN 0-317-63788-6, 531-0019-01). Amer Bar Assn.

Role of Extracellular Matrix in Development. Robert L. Trelstad. LC 84-5689. (Symposium of the Society for Developmental Biology Ser.: No. 42). 662p. 1984. 84.00 (ISBN 0-8451-1503-0). A R Liss.

Role of Faith in the Process of Healing. Edgar N. Jackson. 216p. 1982. pap. 9.95 (ISBN 0-86683-679-9, HarpR). Har-Row.

Role of FAO in the Development of Inland Fishery Resources. (Fisheries Technical Papers: No. 81). 73p. 1969. pap. 7.50 (ISBN 0-686-92749-4, F1739, FAO). UNIPUB.

Role of Fats in Food & Nutrition. Ed. by M. I. Gurr. 176p. 1984. 54.00 (ISBN 0-85334-298-9, Pub. by Elsevier Applied Sci England). Elsevier.

Role of Fats in Human Nutrition. F. B. Padley & J. Podmore. 210p. 1985. lib. bdg. 44.00 (ISBN 0-89573-398-6). VCH Pubs.

Role of Feelings in Morals. William Neblett. LC 81-40105. 114p. (Orig.). 1981. lib. bdg. 26.00 (ISBN 0-8191-1752-8); pap. text ed. 10.25 (ISBN 0-8191-1753-6). U Pr of Amer.

Role of Finance in the Transition to Socialism. Stephany Griffith-Jones. LC 81-12844. 208p. 1981. text ed. 29.95x (ISBN 0-86598-069-1, Pub. by Allanheld). Rowman.

Role of Fine-Scale Magnetic Fields on the Structure of the Solar Atmosphere. Ed. by Egon-Horst Schroter et al. (Illus.). 430p. 1988. 59.50 (ISBN 0-521-34281-3). Cambridge U Pr.

Role of Fire in Northern Circumpolar Ecosystems. Ed. by Ross W. Wein & David A. MacLean. LC 82-2036. (Scientific Committee on Problems of the Enviroment Ser.: No. 18). 322p. 1983. 94.95x (ISBN 0-471-10222-9, Pub. by Wiley-Interscience). Wiley.

Role of Fishery Technology in the Management & Development of Freshwater Fisheries in Africa. (Commission for Inland Fisheries of Africa (CIFA): Technical Papers: No. 6). 71p. (Eng. & Fr.). 1979. pap. 7.50 (ISBN 92-5-100831-0, F1888, FAO). UNIPUB.

Role of Flight Simulation: To Train or Assess? Ed. by Network Staff. 1982. 95.00x (ISBN 0-904999-47-5, Pub. by Network Events Ltd). State Mutual Bk.

Role of Fluoride in Bone Structure. I. Gedalia et al. LC 72-87824. 48p. 1973. 5.00 (ISBN 0-87527-103-0). Green.

Role of Foreign Investments in the United States & the Inevitable Economic & Financial Collapse of the World Order. Antonino Villafranca. (Illus.). 161p. 1986. 243.50 (ISBN 0-86722-138-0). Inst Econ Pol.

Role of Foreign Languages in American Life see Culture, Literature, & Articulation.

Role of Foreign Languages in American Life see Foreign Language Teachers & Tests.

Role of Foreign Trade in Indian Economy. Ed. by Malcom S. Adisheshiah. 216p. 1986. 24.50x (ISBN 81-7062-001-5, Pub. by Lancer India). South ASia Bks.

Role of Fouche During the Hundred Days. Ray E. Cubberly. LC 78-626285. 1969. 3.50 (ISBN 0-87020-136-0, Logmark Eds). State Hist Soc Wis.

Role of Fracture Mechanics in Modern Technology: Proceedings of the Internat. Conf. Fukuoka, Japan, 2-6 June, 1986. Ed. by G. C. Sih et al. 916p. 1987. 117.00 (ISBN 0-444-70240-7, North Holland). Elsevier.

Role of Freshwater Outflow in Coastal Marine Ecosystems. Ed. by S. Skreslet. (NATO ASI Series G: Ecological Sciences: No. 7). xi, 453p. 1986. 104.00 (ISBN 0-387-16089-2). Springer-Verlag.

Role of Gender in Precolumbian Art & Architecture. Virginia E. Miller. LC 88-17316. (Illus.). 222p. (Orig.). 1988. lib. bdg. 29.50 (ISBN 0-8191-7066-6); pap. text ed. 16.75 (ISBN 0-8191-7067-4). U Pr of Amer.

Role of General Trading Firms in Trade & Industry: Some Experiences. Ed. by Terutomo Ozawa. 165p. 1987. 20.50 (ISBN 0-317-59540-7, U-APO204, Pub. by APO); pap. 15.00 (ISBN 0-317-59541-5, U-APO205, Pub. by APO). UNIPUB-Kraus Intl.

Role of Government in a Free Society: A Collection of Speeches & Articles. Phil Gramm. LC 82-70597. 150p. 1982. pap. text ed. 7.95 (ISBN 0-933028-20-2). Fisher Inst.

Role of Government in a Market Economy. Ed. by Lowell D. Hill. (Illus.). 1982. 16.95x (ISBN 0-8138-1576-2). Iowa St U Pr.

Role of Government in Mineral Resources Development. Ed. by M. J. Jones. 1985. text ed. 73.00 (ISBN 0-900488-72-7). Brookfield Pub Co.

Role of Government in the Industrialization of Iraq. F. Jalal. 160p. 1972. 28.50x (ISBN 0-7146-2586-8, F Cass Co). Biblio Dist.

Role of Government in the United States-Practice & Theory: A Report of a Conference at the College of Public & International Affairs of the American University, Washington, D. C., March 2-3. 1984. Ed. by Robert E. Cleary. 250p. (Orig.). 1985. lib. bdg. 26.75 (ISBN 0-8191-4798-2); pap. text ed. 12.50 (ISBN 0-8191-4799-0). U Pr of Amer.

Role of Governments in the Regional Development Process. 89p. 1977. pap. 7.25 (ISBN 0-686-75157-4, CRD003, UNCRD). UNIPUB.

Role of Gut Flora in Toxicity & Cancer. Ed. by I. Rowland. 250p. 1988. 110.00 (ISBN 0-12-599920-8). Acad Pr.

Role of Health Behaviour in Health Promotion. Robert Anderson et al. (Illus.). 288p. 1988. 70.00 (ISBN 0-19-261600-5). Oxford U Pr.

Role of Health Insurance in the Health Services Sector. Ed. by Richard N. Rosett. LC 76-8856. (Universities-National Bureau Conference Ser.: No. 27). 1976. 20.00 (ISBN 0-87014-272-0). Watson Pub Intl.

Role of Health Insurance in the Health Services Sector: A Conference of the Universities-National Bureau Committee for Economic Research. Ed. by Richard N. Rosett. LC 76-8856. (Universities-National Bureau Conference Ser.: 27). pap. 140.50 (ISBN 0-317-42091-7, 2052158). Bks Demand UMI.

Role of Heat in the Development of Energy & Mineral Resources in the Northern Basin & Range Province. Ed. by Gordon Eaton. (Special Report Ser.: No. 13). 500p. 1983. 40.00 (ISBN 0-934412-13-8). Geothermal.

Role of History As a Social Force. A. E. Afigbo. LC 79-88988. Date not set. price not set (ISBN 0-88357-013-0); pap. price not set (ISBN 0-88357-052-1). NOK Pubs.

Role of Honor. John Gardner. (James Bond Ser.). 304p. 1984. 11.95 (ISBN 0-399-12912-X, Putnam). Putnam Pub Group.

Role of Honor. John Gardner. 1987. pap. 3.95 (ISBN 0-441-73437-5, Charter Pub). Berkley Pub.

Role of Hospitals in Geriatric Care. Ed. by Carl Eisdorfer & George L. Maddox. 160p. 1988. 25.95 (ISBN 0-8261-5310-0). Springer Pub.

Role of Human Love. Dietrich Von Hildebrand. 1978. 0.75 (ISBN 0-8199-0719-7). Franciscan Herald.

Role of Hyperparasitism in Biological Control: A Symposium. David Rosen. LC 81-65779. (Illus.). 55p. 1981. pap. 3.00 (ISBN 0-931876-47-8, 4103). ANR Pubns CA.

Role of Ideology in Church Participation. Phillip E. Hammond. Ed. by Harriet Zuckerman & Robert K. Merton. LC 79-9003. (Dissertations on Sociology Ser.). 1980. lib. bdg. 27.50x (ISBN 0-405-12972-6). Ayer Co Pubs.

Role of Ideology in the American Revolution. Ed. by John R. Howe, Jr. LC 76-3777. (American Problem Studies). 132p. 1976. pap. 6.50 (ISBN 0-88275-406-8). Krieger.

Role of Immunization in Communicable Disease Control. R. Cruickshank et al. (Public Health Papers Ser: No. 8). 118p. (Eng., Fr., Rus. & Span.). 1961. pap. 2.00 (ISBN 92-4-130008-6). World Health.

Role of Immunological Factors in Infectious, Allergic, & Autoimmune Processes. Ed. by Roland F. Beers, Jr. & Edward G. Bassett. LC 75-25109. (Miles International Symposium Ser: No. 8). 556p. 1976. 73.50 (ISBN 0-89004-073-7). Raven.

Role of India in the Emergence of Bangladesh. Sucheta Ghosh. 1984. 18.50x (ISBN 0-8364-0780-6). South Asia Bks.

Role of Industrial Incentives in Regional Development. (Document Ser.). 94p. 1980. 5.50x (ISBN 92-64-12003-3). OECD.

Role of Industrial Property in the Protection of Consumers. 69p. 1983. pap. text ed. 12.75 (ISBN 92-805-0105-4, WIPO76, WIPO). UNIPUB.

Role of Informatics in Health Data Coding & Classification Systems: Proceedings of the IFIP-IMIA International Working Conference on the Role of Informatics in Health Data Decoding & Classification Systems, Ottawa, Canada, 26-28 September, 1984. Ed. by R. A. Cote et al. 394p. 1985. 84.25 (ISBN 0-444-87682-0, North-Holland). Elsevier.

Role of Insectivorous Birds in Forest Ecosystems. Ed. by James G. Dickson et al. LC 79-12111. 1979. 72.50 (ISBN 0-12-215350-2). Acad Pr.

Role of Institutional Finance in Agriculture. J. P. Singh. 378p. 1986. 36.00X (ISBN 81-7024-029-8, Pub. by Ashish). South Asia Bks.

Role of Integrated Rural Development Projects in Developing Local Institutional Capacity. Ed. by Diana Conyers et al. (Studies in Technology & Social Change: No. 2). 50p. (Orig.). 1988. pap. text ed. 6.00 (ISBN 0-945271-02-6). ISU-TSCP.

Role of Interest Groups in the European Community. Emil Kirchner & Konrad Schwaiger. 192p. 1981. text ed. 34.25x (ISBN 0-566-00257-4). Gower Pub Co.

Role of International Companies in Latin American Integration: Autos & Petrochemicals. Jack N. Behrman. LC 79-183711. 185p. 1972. pap. 4.50 (ISBN 0-87186-235-2). Comm Econ Dev.

Role of International Nongovernmental Organizations in World Politics. Werner J. Feld & Roger A. Coate. (CISE Learning Package Ser.: No. 17). (Illus.). 56p. (Orig.). 1976. pap. text ed. 3.00x (ISBN 0-936876-30-1). LRIS.

Role of Intonation in Spoken English. Maria Schubiger. 1973. text ed. 1.00 (ISBN 0-686-09402-6). Expression.

Role of Intravenous Miconazole in the Treatment of Systemic Mycoses. Ed. by G. Towse. (International Congress & Symposium Ser.: No. 45). 52p. 1981. pap. 15.00 (ISBN 1-85315-022-3, Pub. by Royal Society of Medicine Services Ltd). Longwood Pub Group.

Role of Joseph McGarrity in the Struggle for Irish Independence. Marie V. Tarpey. LC 76-6368. (Irish Americans Ser). 1976. 30.00 (ISBN 0-405-09360-8). Ayer Co Pubs.

Role of Judicial Decisions & Doctrine in Civil Law & in Mixed Jurisdictions. Joseph Dainow. LC 73-90871. xviii, 350p. 1974. 37.50x (ISBN 0-8071-0080-3). La State U Pr.

Role of Knowledge in the World System. B. Landheer. 128p. (Orig.). 1974. pap. text ed. 17.50x (ISBN 90-232-1189-8, Pub. by Van Gorcum Holland). Coronet Bks.

Role of Knowledge in Western Religion. John H. Randall, Jr. 160p. 1986. pap. text ed. 11.50 (ISBN 0-8191-5167-X). U Pr of Amer.

Role of Labor & the Policy of High Wages in the Growth of Modern Capitalism. John A. Hobson. 149p. 1985. 147.75. Inst Econ Finan.

Role of Labor in African Nation-Building. Ed. by Willard A. Beling. 15.00 (ISBN 0-685-37307-X). Univ Place.

Role of Laboratory Teaching in University Courses. Ed. by A. R. Cole et al. 1979. 22.00 (ISBN 0-08-023914-5). Pergamon.

Role of Language in Problem Solving One: Proceedings of the Symposium, the Johns Hopkins University Applied Physics Laboratory, Laurel, MD, 29-31 Oct., 1984. Ed. by R. Jernigan et al. 406p. 1985. 79.00 (ISBN 0-444-87764-9, North Holland). Elsevier.

Role of Language in Problem Solving 2: Proceedings of the Johns Hopkins University Applied Physics Laboratory Symposium on the Role of Language in Problem Solving, Laurel, Maryland, April 2-4, 1986. Johns Hopkins University Applied Physics Laboratory Symposium on the Role of Language in Problem Solving Staff. Ed. by J. C. Boudreaux et al. 480p. 1986. 92.00 (ISBN 0-444-70114-1, North Holland). Elsevier.

Role of Law in Population Planning: Working Paper & Proceedings of the Sixteenth Hammarskjold Forum. D. H. Berman. LC 72-2061. (Hammarskjold Forum Ser.: No. 16). 90p. 1972. 10.00 (ISBN 0-379-11816-5). Oceana.

Role of Legislation in Land Use Planning for Developing Countries. Gregory K. Wilkinson. (Legislative Study Ser.: No. 31). 160p. (Orig.). 1986. pap. text ed. 11.25 (ISBN 0-317-53467-X, F2857, FAO). UNIPUB.

Role of Legumes in Conservation Tillage Systems. Ed. & intro. by J. F. Power. 153p. (Orig.). 1987. pap. text ed. 12.00 (ISBN 0-935734-15-5). Soil & Water Conserv.

Role of Libraries in the Growth of Knowledge: Proceedings of the 40th Conference of the Graduate Library School, May 18-19, 1978. Chicago University, Graduate Library School Staff. Ed. by Don R. Swanson. LC 79-5467. (University of Chicago Studies in Library Science). pap. 35.50 (2026746). Bks Demand UMI.

Role of Literature in Language Teaching see Culture, Literature, & Articulation.

Role of Low-Cost Power in Economic Development: A Case Study; Alaska. Gunter Schramm. Ed. by Stuart Bruchey. LC 78-22707. (Energy in the American Economy Ser.). (Illus.). 1979. lib. bdg. 25.50x (ISBN 0-405-12009-5). Ayer Co Pubs.

Role of Magnetic Fields in Physics & Astrophysics, Vol. 257. Ed. by V. Canuto. (Annals of the New York Academy of Sciences). 226p. 1975. 38.00x (ISBN 0-89072-012-6). NY Acad Sci.

Role of Man in the Historical Revolution of the Universe, 2 vols. Georg Wilhelm Hegel. (Illus.). 287p. 1984. Set 187.55 (ISBN 0-89266-493-2). Am Classical Coll Pr.

Role of Maps in Sci-Tech Libraries. Ed. by Ellis Mount. LC 84-27919. (Science & Technology Libraries: Vol. 5, No. 3). 122p. 1985. text ed. 22.95 (ISBN 0-86656-395-4). Haworth Pr.

Role of Markets in the World Food Economy. D. Gale Johnson & George E. Schuh. LC 83-6518. (Special Studies in Agriculture Science & Policy). 336p. 1983. 35.50x (ISBN 0-86531-620-1). Westview.

Role of Mathematics in Science. M. M. Shiffer & Leon Bowden. (New Mathematical Library: No. 30). 220p. 1984. pap. 16.00 (ISBN 0-88385-630-1). Math Assn.

Role of Medical Inspection of Labour. 111p. 1968. 5.60 (ISBN 92-2-100004-4). Intl Labour Office.

Role of Medicine. Thomas McKeown. LC 79-84025. 180p. 1980. 25.00x (ISBN 0-691-08235-9); pap. 9.50x (ISBN 0-691-02362-X). Princeton U Pr.

Role of Medroxyprogesterone in Endocrine-Related Tumors, Vol. 2. Ed. by L. Campio et al. 230p. 1983. text ed. 40.00 (ISBN 0-89004-865-7). Raven.

Role of Medroxyprogesterone in Endocrine-Related Tumors, Vol. 3. Ed. by A. Pellegrini et al. 192p. 1984. text ed. 49.00 (ISBN 0-88167-032-4). Raven.

Role of Mental Imagery in Text Comprehension: Preliminary Studies. Alan M. Lesgold et al. 67p. 1974. 1.50 (ISBN 0-318-14735-1, ED 094 317). Learn Res Dev.

Role of Mind in Hugo, Faulkner, Beckett & Grass. Martha O'Nan. LC 78-86505. 1969. 5.95 (ISBN 0-8022-2296-X). Philos Lib.

Role of Minorities in Freedom Struggle. Asghar A. Engineer. 195p. 1986. 18.00 (ISBN 81-202-0164-7, Pub. by Ajanta). South Asia Bks.

Role of Money: What It Should Be, Contrasted to What It Has Become. Frederick Soddy. 1976. lib. bdg. 59.95 (ISBN 0-8490-2530-3). Gordon Pr.

Role of Movement Patterns in Development, 2 vols, Vol. I. Judith Kestenberg. (Illus.). 1977. pap. text ed. 17.95 ea. (ISBN 0-932582-05-2) (ISBN 0-932582-01-X). Dance Notation.

Role of Multilateral Food Aid Programs. J. Dessau. (World Food Programme Studies: No. 5). (Orig.). 1965. pap. 5.75 (ISBN 0-685-09405-7, F415, FAO). UNIPUB.

Role of Multinationals in India's Foreign Trade. Usha Saxena. 1987. 34.00x (ISBN 81-7024-081-6, Pub. by Ashish India). South Asia Bks.

Role of Music in Art. Ennis L. May. (Human Development Library Bk.). (Illus.). 151p. Repr. of 1903 ed. 115.00 (ISBN 0-89901-075-X). Found Class Reprints.

Role of Music in the New Roman Liturgy. William Herring. LC 75-14548. 1971. pap. 0.50 (ISBN 0-915866-01-3). Am Cath Pr.

Role of Muslims in Indian Politics, 1857-1947. Kamalesh Sharma. 295p. 1986. text ed. 45.00x (ISBN 81-210-0028-9, Pub. by Inter India Pubns N Delhi). Apt Bks.

Role of Muslims in the National Movement. Muhammad M. Imam. 306p. 1987. 27.50x (ISBN 81-7099-033-5, Pub. by Mittal). South Asia Bks.

Role of National Libraries in Developing Countries with Special Reference to Saudi Arabia. Abdulaziz M. Al-Nahari. 174p. 1984. 27.00x (ISBN 0-7201-1696-1). Mansell.

Role of Neurotransmitter Systems in Anxiety Modulation. (Journal: Psychopathology: Vol. 17, Suppl. 3, 1984). (Illus.). iv, 84p. 1984. pap. 18.75 (ISBN 3-8055-3983-5). S Karger.

Role of New Testament Examples As Related to Biblical Authority. M. R. Hadwin. 1974. pap. 2.75 (ISBN 0-88027-038-1). Firm Foun Pub.

Role of Non-Cash Assistance in Corporate Philanthropy. Alex J. Plinio & Joanne B. Scanlon. 56p. 1986. pap. 10.00 (6745). Ind Sector.

Role of Non-Governmental Organisations in Development Co-Operation. OECD Staff. (Liaison Bulletin: No. 10). 84p. (Orig.). 1983. pap. 10.00x (ISBN 92-64-12463-2). OECD.

Role of Nucleation in Boiling & Cavitation: Symposium Presented at Joint Fluids Engineering, Heat Transfer & Lubrication Conference, Detroit, Michigan, May 26-27, 1970. American Society of Mechanical Engineers Staff. pap. 20.00 (ISBN 0-317-09023-2, 2016877). Bks Demand UMI.

Role of Occupational Therapy with the Elderly (ROTE) Linda J. Davis. Ed. by Martha Kirkland. 436p. 1986. 3-ring binder 29.50 (ISBN 0-910317-19-4). Am Occup Therapy.

Role of Organic Matter in Modern Agriculture. Ed. by Y. Chen & Y. Avnimelech. (Developments in Plant & Soil Sciences Ser.). 1986. lib. bdg. 74.95 (ISBN 90-247-3360-X, Pub. by Martinus Nijhoff Netherlands). Kluwer Academic.

Role of OSHA in Safety & Health. Center for Occupational Research & Development Staff. (Job Safety & Health Instructional Materials Ser.). (Illus.). 47p. 1981. pap. text ed. 3.50 (ISBN 1-55502-080-1). Ctr Res & Dev.

Role of Outside Powers. Ed. by Shahram Chubin. LC 80-28314. (Security in the Persian Gulf Ser.: Vol. 4). 180p. 1982. pap. 12.50x (ISBN 0-86598-047-0, Pub. by Allanheld). Rowman.

Role of Oxygen in Chemistry & Biochemistry: Proceedings of an International Symposium, Tsukuba, Japan, 12-16 July, 1987. Ed. by W. Ando & Y. Moro-oka. (Studies in Organic Chemistry: Vol. 33). 634p. 1988. 223.75 (ISBN 0-444-42937-9). Elsevier.

Role of Patent Information in Research & Development: WIPO Moscow Symposium, 1974. 1975. pap. 27.50 (ISBN 0-686-53031-4, WIPO45, WIPO). UNIPUB.

Role of Patents in Sci-Tech Libraries. Ed. by Ellis Mount. LC 82-2885. (Science & Technology Libraries Ser.: Vol. 2, No. 2). 97p. 1982. 25.00 (ISBN 0-86656-114-5, B114). Haworth Pr.

Role of Peptides & Amino Acids As Neurotransmitters. Barry J. Lombardini & Alexander D. Kenny. LC 81-8335. (Progress in Clinical & Biological Research Ser.: Vol. 68). 248p. 1981. 44.00 (ISBN 0-8451-0068-8). A R Liss.

Role of Peptides & Proteins in the Control of Reproduction. McCann & Dhindsa. 370p. 1983. 95.75 (ISBN 0-444-00737-7, Biomedical Pr). Elsevier.

Role of Peptides in Neuronal Function. Ed. by J. Barker & T. Smith. 1980. 110.00 (ISBN 0-8247-6926-0). Dekker.

Role of Pharmacology in Pediatric Oncology. Ed. by D. G. Poplack et al. (Developments in Oncology Ser.). 1986. lib. bdg. 92.50 (ISBN 0-89838-795-7, Pub. by Martinus Nijhoff Netherlands). Kluwer Academic.

Role of Phoenicians in the Interaction of Mediterranean Civilizations. Ed. by William A. Ward. 1968. 22.95x (ISBN 0-8156-6011-1, Am U Beirut). Syracuse U Pr.

Role of Phosphonates in Living Systems. Ed. by Richard L. Hilderbrand. 216p. 1983. 75.00 (ISBN 0-8493-5724-1). CRC Pr.

Role of Phosphorous in Agriculture. Ed. by F. E. Khasawneh et al. (Illus.). 1980. 25.00 (ISBN 0-89118-062-1). Am Soc Agron.

Role of Place in Literature. Leonard Lutwack. LC 83-24264. 304p. 1984. 24.95 (ISBN 0-8156-2305-4). Syracuse U Pr.

Role of Platelet-Activating Factor in Immune Disorders, Part 2. Ed. by P. Braquet. (New Trends in Lipid Mediators Research Ser.: Vol. 2). (Illus.). viii, 214p. 1988. 132.00 (ISBN 3-8055-4744-7). S Karger.

Role of Politics in Social Change. Charles E. Merriam. LC 83-1490. 149p. 1983. Repr. of 1936 ed. lib. bdg. 35.00x (ISBN 0-313-23852-9, MERO). Greenwood.

Role of Potassium in Agriculture. Ed. by V. J. Kilmer et al. (Illus.). 1968. 7.50 (ISBN 0-89118-003-6). Am Soc Agron.

Role of Prescriptivism in American Linguistics 1820-1970. Glendon F. Drake. x, 130p. 1977. 24.00x (ISBN 90-272-0954-5, SIHOL 13). Benjamins North Am.

Role of Private Pensions in Maintaining Living Standards in Retirement. Robert Clark. LC 77-87188. 64p. 1977. 3.50 (ISBN 0-89068-041-8). Natl Planning.

Role of Probability & Statistics in the Structural Analysis of Pavements: Five Reports. (Transportation Research Record Ser.). 73p. 1976. 3.20 (ISBN 0-309-02489-7). Transport Res Bd.

Role of Programming in Teaching Informatics: Proceedings of the IFIP TC3 Working Conference on Teaching Programming, Paris, France, 7-9 May, 1984. Ed. by M. Griffiths & E. D. Tagg. 212p. 1985. 52.75 (ISBN 0-444-87664-2, North-Holland). Elsevier.

Role of Prolactin in Human Reproduction. Ed. by M. Mizuno et al. (Illus.). x, 314p. 1988. 172.75 (ISBN 3-8055-4786-2). S Karger.

Role of Prostaglandins in Labour. Ed. by Clive Wood. (International Congress & Symposium Ser.: No. 92). 100p. 1985. pap. 15.00 (ISBN 1-85315-059-2, Pub. by Royal Society of Medicine Services Ltd). Longwood Pub Group.

Role of Providence in the Social Order: An Essay in Intellectual History. Jacob Viner. 1976. pap. 8.95x (ISBN 0-691-01990-8). Princeton U Pr.

Role of Providence in the Social Order: An Essay in Intellectual History. Jacob Viner. LC 72-184168. (American Philosophical Society Memoirs Ser.: Vol. 90). pap. 30.80 (ISBN 0-317-29441-5, 2024290). Bks Demand UMI.

Role of Psychiatric Reports in the Crown Court Trial Process. Ronald D. Mckay. 21p. 1986. pap. 5.00 (ISBN 0-948997-30-3, Pub. by Leicester Poly Law Schl). Pickering Pubns.

Role of Psychiatry in Medical Education: An Appraisal & a Forecast. Sidney L. Werkman. LC 66-10810. (Commonwealth Fund Publications Ser). (Illus.). 1966. 16.00x (ISBN 0-674-77730-1). Harvard U Pr.

Role of Psychoanalysis in Psychiatric Education: Past, Present, & Future. Ed. by Sidney H. Weismann & Robert Thurnblad. (Emotions & Behavior - Monograph: No. 7). 1987. text ed. 30.00x (ISBN 0-8236-5850-3). Intl Univs Pr.

Role of Psychosocial Factors in the Pathogenesis of Coronary Heart Disease, 1980. Ed. by A. Appels & P. Falger. (Journal: Psychotherapy & Psychosomatics: Vol. 34, No. 2-3). (Illus.). iv, 160p. 1981. pap. 27.50 (ISBN 3-8055-2286-X). S Karger.

Role of Public Enterprises in National Development. Pavle Sicheri. (ICPE Monographs: No. 14). 64p. 1983. pap. 10.00x (ISBN 92-9038-913-3). Kumarian Pr.

Role of Public Enterprises in the Advancement of Women in Mexico. Alberto M. Alvarez. (ICPE Monograph: No. 10). 87p. 1983. pap. 10.00x (ISBN 92-9038-909-5). Kumarian Pr.

Role of Public Enterprises in the Advancement of Women in Yugoslavia. Dimitar Mircev et al. (ICPE Monograph: No. 11). 95p. 1983. pap. 10.00x (ISBN 92-9038-910-9). Kumarian Pr.

Role of Public Libraries in the Provision of Educational Guidance for Adults. Linda Butler. (Library Information Report: No. 22). (Orig.). 1985. pap. 17.25 (ISBN 0-7123-3032-1, Pub. by British Lib). Longwood Pub Group.

Role of Receptors in Biology & Medicine: Proceedings of the Ninth Argenteuil Symposium Held Under the Auspices of the Fondation Princesse Liliane in Brussels, Belgium. Ed. by Antonio M. Gotto, Jr. & Bert W. O'Malley. (Illus.). 234p. 1986. text ed. 48.50 (ISBN 0-88167-161-4). Raven.

Role of Religion in American Life: An Interpretive Historical Anthology. Ed. by Robert R. Mathisen. LC 80-6246. 420p. (Orig.). 1982. pap. text ed. 15.50 (ISBN 0-8191-2514-8). U Pr of Amer.

Role of Religion in Ethnic Self-Identity: A Vietnamese Community. Paul Rutledge. (Illus.). 140p. (Orig.). 1985. lib. bdg. 22.75 (ISBN 0-8191-4505-X); pap. text ed. 10.00 (ISBN 0-8191-4506-8). U Pr of Amer.

Role of Research in Educational Change. Ed. by Alfred Yates. LC 75-134226. (International Studies in Education, No. 20). (Illus.). 1971. 14.95x (ISBN 0-87015-187-8). Pacific Bks.

Role of RNA & DNA in Brain Function. Ed. by Antonia Giuditta et al. 1986. lib. bdg. 55.00 (ISBN 0-89838-814-7, Pub. by Martinus Nijhoff Netherlands). Kluwer Academic.

Role of Rules in the International Monetary System. Kenneth W. Dam. LC 76-47303. 1976. pap. 1.50 (ISBN 0-916770-03-6). Law & Econ U Miami.

Role of Rural Women in Development. Ed. by V. Mazumdar. 373p. 1979. 9.95. Asia Bk Corp.

Role of Salt in Cardiovascular Hypertension. Melvin Fregly & Morley Kare. (Nutrition Foundation Ser.). 473p. 1982. 65.00 (ISBN 0-12-267280-1). Acad Pr.

Role of Science & Technology in Rural & Economic Development in India. Ed. by B. N. Pandey. 1983. text ed. 26.50x. Coronet Bks.

Role of Science & Technology in Rural & Economic Development of India. B. N. Pandey. 220p. 1983. 27.95. Asia Bk Corp.

Role of Science in Civilization. Robert B. Lindsay. LC 73-3234. (Illus.). 318p. 1973. Repr. of 1963 ed. lib. bdg. 22.50x (ISBN 0-8371-6837-6, LIRS). Greenwood.

Role of the State in the Socio-Economic Structure of India. V. Malyaro. 473p. 1983. text ed. 45.00x (ISBN 0-7069-1372-8, Pub. by Vikas India). Advent NY.
Role of the State Legislatures in the Confederacy. May S. Ringold. LC 66-27607. pap. 38.80 (2031051). Bks Demand UMI.
Role of the Supreme Court in American Government & Politics 1835-1864. Charles G. Haines. LC 73-604. (American Constitutional & Legal History Ser.). 544p. 1973. Repr. of 1957 ed. lib. bdg. 59.50 (ISBN 0-306-70566-4). Da Capo.
Role of the Supreme Court in American Government & Politics 1795-1835. Charles G. Haines. LC 73-604. (American Constitutional & Legal History Ser.). 698p. 1973. Repr. of 1944 ed. lib. bdg. 79.50 (ISBN 0-306-70571-0). Da Capo.
Role of the Supreme Court in American Government. x1976 ed. Archibald Cox. LC 75-29958. 1977. pap. 6.95 (ISBN 0-19-519909-X). Oxford U Pr.
Role of the Supreme Court: Policymaker or Adjudicator. Sam J. Ervin, Jr. & Ramsey Clark. 85p. 1970. 14.00 (ISBN 0-8447-2018-6). Am Enterprise.
Role of the Symbol in French Romantic Poetry. Marion E. Carter. LC 77-94178. (Catholic University of America. Studies in Romance Languages & Literatures: No. 32). Repr. of 1946 ed. 19.00 (ISBN 0-404-50332-2). AMS Pr.
Role of the Theologian in Today's Church. Monika K. Hellwig. 52p. (Orig.). 1987. pap. 2.95 (ISBN 1-55612-105-9). Sheed & Ward MO.
Role of the Trial in the School Prose of the Weimar Republic. Roy L. Ackermann. (European University Studies: No. 1, Vol. 488). 138p. 1983. 16.20 (ISBN 3-261-04980-4). P Lang Pubs.
Role of the Trypanosomiases in African Ecology: A Study of the Tsetse Fly Problem. John Ford. LC 76-23168. pap. 145.50 (ISBN 0-317-29955-7, 2051719). Bks Demand UMI.
Role of the Unconscious in Poetic Experience. D. N. Sharma. 1974. Repr. of 1953 ed. lib. bdg. 20.00 (ISBN 0-8414-8111-3). Folcroft.
Role of the United Nations in the Indo-Pakistan Conflict, 1971. R. P. Misra. 1973. 9.00 (ISBN 0-686-20302-X). Intl Bk Dist.
Role of the United States in International Legislation. H. Bokor-Szego. 192p. 1979. 58.00 (ISBN 0-444-85041-4, North Holland). Elsevier.
Role of the University in Extension Education. Ed. by Munir Bashshur. (Middle East Bks.). 176p. 1982. text ed. 24.95x (ISBN 0-8156-6062-6, Pub. by Am U Beirut). Syracuse U Pr.
Role of the University in National Development: Four Asian Case Studies. Y. Kim et al. 328p. 1980. text ed. 30.00x (ISBN 0-7069-0969-0, Pub. by Vikas India). Advent NY.
Role of the University Teaching Hospital: An International Perspective: Report of a Conference. Ed. by Elizabeth F. Purcell. LC 82-83988. pap. 66.50 (2026696). Bks Demand UMI.
Role of the USDA, Land-Grant Universities & Other Agencies in Assisting Rural America: Research, Education & Technology Transfer. LC 84-80803. pap. 15.00 (ISBN 0-942875-02-8). Tuskegee U Human Resc Dev Ctr.
Role of the Volunteer Director in the Care of the Terminal Patient & the Family. Harriet H. Naylor. 17.00 (ISBN 0-405-13092-9). Ayer Co Pubs.
Role of the Volunteer in the Care of the Terminal Patient & the Family. Harriet H. Naylor. 15.50 (ISBN 0-405-13091-0). Ayer Co Pubs.
Role of Theory in Linguistic Analysis: The Spanish Pronoun System. E. Garcia. (N-H Linguistic Ser.: Vol. 19). 522p. 1975. pap. 42.75 (ISBN 0-444-10940-4, North-Holland). Elsevier.
Role of Top Management in the Control of Inventory. George W. Plossl & W. Evert Welch. (Illus.). 1978. 35.00 (ISBN 0-8359-6697-6, Reston). P-H.
Role of Trade Associations & Professional Business Societies in America. Joseph F. Bradley. LC 64-8082. 1965. 19.95x (ISBN 0-271-73097-8). Pa St U Pr.
Role of Traditional Rulers in Elective Politics in Nigeria. William C. Reed. (Graduate Student Term Paper Ser.: No. 5). 1982. pap. text ed. 2.00 (ISBN 0-686-46780-9). Indiana Africa.
Role of Traditional Water Management in Modern Paddy Cultivation in Sri Lanka. (Project on the Sharing of Traditional Technology). 78p. 1981. pap. 5.00 (ISBN 92-808-0248-8, TUNU153, UNU). UNIPUB.
Role of Translations in Sci-Tech Libraries. Ed. by Ellis Mount. LC 82-23353. (Science & Technology Libraries: Vol. 3, No. 2). 94p. 1983. 24.95 (ISBN 0-86656-217-6, B217). Haworth Pr.
Role of Trazodone in Antidepressant Therapy: Safety & Clinical Efficacy. Ed. by B. Silvestrini et al. (Journal - Psychopathology: Vol. 17, Supp. 2). (Illus.). iv, 104p. 1984. pap. 38.75 (ISBN 3-8055-3884-7). S Karger.
Role of U. S. Agriculture on Foreign Policy. Ed. by Richard Fraenkel et al. LC 78-19761. 270p. 1979. 40.95 (ISBN 0-275-90353-2, C0353). Praeger.
Role of U. S. Government in Aquaculture: Nonfederal Perspectives. Ed. by R. L. Kendall. 39p. 1985. pap. 5.00 (ISBN 0-913235-36-9). Am Fisheries Soc.
Role of Universities in Workers' Education. 216p. 1974. 10.50 (ISBN 92-2-101096-1). Intl Labour Office.
Role of Utility Companies in Solar Energy Executive Conference, November 1977. (Solar Energy). 176p. 25.00 (ISBN 0-910091-41-2). Inst Gas Tech.
Role of Vincent Van Gogh's Copies in the Development of His Art. Charles Chetham. LC 75-23788. (Outstanding Dissertations in the Fine Arts - 19th Century). (Illus.). 1976. lib. bdg. 50.00 (ISBN 0-8240-1984-9). Garland Pub.
Role of Viruses in Human Cancer. Ed. by G. Giraldo & E. Beth. 292p. 1980. 60.00 (ISBN 0-444-00440-8, Biomedical Pr). Elsevier.
Role of Viruses in Human Cancer, Vol. 2. G. Giraldo & E. Beth. 1984. 118.50 (ISBN 0-444-80584-2, I-201-84). Elsevier.
Role of Volcanism in Climate & Evolution. Daniel I. Axelrod. LC 81-80345. (Special Paper: No. 185). (Illus.). 1981. pap. 5.60 (ISBN 0-8137-2185-7). Geol Soc.
Role of Voluntary Organizations in Social Welfare. Hugh W. Mellor. LC 85-6626. 216p. 1985. 26.00 (ISBN 0-7099-3581-1, Pub. by Croom Helm Ltd); pap. 12.00 (ISBN 0-7099-3586-2). Routledge Chapman & Hall.
Role of Water in Socio-Economic Development. Ed. by W. E. Cox. 91p. (Orig.). 1987. pap. text ed. 12.00 (ISBN 92-3-102534-1, U1646, UNESCO). UNIPUB.
Role of Water in Urban Ecology. Ed. by H. Hengeveld & C. De Vocht. (Developments in Landscape Management & Urban Planning Ser.: Vol. 5). 362p. 1982. 110.75 (ISBN 0-444-42078-9). Elsevier.
Role of Woman in the Middle Ages. Ed. by Rosemarie T. Morewedge. 212p. 10.00 (Pub. by SUNY Pr). Medieval & Renaissance NY.
Role of Woman in the Middle Ages. Ed. by Rosmarie T. Morewedge. LC 74-23227. (Illus.). 195p. 1975. 39.50x (ISBN 0-87395-274-X). State U NY Pr.
Role of Women in Developing Countries: A Study. (ICPE Books). 122p. 1986. pap. 10.00x (ISBN 92-9038-115-9). Kumarian Pr.
Role of Women in Early Christianity. Jean LaPorte. LC 82-8281. (Studies in Women & Religion: Vol. 7). 196p. 1982. lib. bdg. 39.95x (ISBN 0-88946-545-2). E Mellen.
Role of Women in Engineering: Report of Working Party. 12p. 1971. pap. 2.25 (ISBN 0-317-59720-5, Pub. by T Telford UK). Am Soc Civil Eng.
Role of Women in Korean Society with Emphasis on the Economic System. Moon J. Madrigal. LC 78-68450. 1979. perfect bdg. 10.95 (ISBN 0-88247-568-1). R & E Pubs.
Role of Women in Librarianship, 1876-1976: The Entry, Advancement & Struggle for Equalization in One Profession. Kathleen Weibel & Kathleen M. Heim. (Neal-Schuman Professional Bks.). 552p. 1979. lib. bdg. 36.00x (ISBN 0-912700-01-7). Oryx Pr.
Role of Women in Rural Development. S. P. Jain & Reddy Jain. 94p. 1979. 7.95. Asia Bk Corp.
Role of Women in the Church. Charles C. Ryrie. LC 58-8329. 1979. pap. 6.95 (ISBN 0-8024-7371-7). Moody.
Role of Women in the History of Science, Technology & Medicine in the 19th & 20th Centuries, 2 vols. Ed. by Collet's Holdings, Ltd. Staff. Vol. 1, 186p. 88.00x (ISBN 0-317-46712-3, Pub. by Collets (UK)). Vol.2, 116p. State Mutual Bk.
Role of Women: New Testament Perspectives. Neil R. Lightfoot. 1988. pap. 4.95. Student Assn.
Role of Women's Organizations in Eradicating Illiteracy in Jordan. Kamal K. Nimer. LC 85-48189. 150p. 1986. 34.50 (ISBN 0-88164-512-5); pap. 26.50 (ISBN 0-88164-513-3). ABBE Pubs Assn.
Role-Play: A Practical Guide. Ed. by E. Milroy. (Illus.). 150p. 1982. text ed. 19.75 (ISBN 0-08-025744-5, R130); pap. text ed. 13.00 (ISBN 0-08-025745-3, R132). Pergamon.
Role Play & Simulation Games: Uses in Social Work Education. Nano McCaughan & Tony Scott. 1979. 25.00x (ISBN 0-317-05760-X, Pub. by Natl Soc Work). State Mutual Bk.
Role Play in Language Learning. Carol Livingstone. Ed. by Donn Byrne. (Handbooks for Language Teachers Ser.). 94p. (Orig.). 1983. pap. 13.50 (ISBN 0-582-74611-6). Longman.
Role-Play Technique: A Handbook for Management & Leadership Practice. Norman R. F. Maier et al. LC 74-30943. 290p. 1975. pap. 9.95 (ISBN 0-88390-104-8). Univ Assocs.
Role Played by the American Political Scientists in the Supreme Command for the Allied Powers: The Purge Program. Joseph D. Lowe. (Illus.). xii, 201p. 1982. pap. 30.00 (ISBN 0-9605506-3-1). Lowe Pub.
Role Played by the Ch'in Army: With Emphasis on Politica & Legal Aspects. Joseph D. Lowe. (Illus.). iii, 24p. pap. 6.00 (ISBN 0-9605506-7-4). Lowe Pub.
Role Playing. Wallace Wohlking & Patricia J. Gill. Ed. by Danny G. Langdon. LC 79-23435. (Instructional Design Library). 136p. 1980. 23.95 (ISBN 0-87778-152-4). Educ Tech Pubns.
Role Playing: A Real Estate Training Tool. Alice McIntyre. Ed. by Dawn M. Gerth. LC 82-83133. (Illus.). 151p. (Orig.). 1982. pap. text ed. 14.95 (ISBN 0-913652-43-1, 152). Realtors Natl.
Role Playing & Identity: The Limits of Theatre As Metaphor. Bruce Wilshire. LC 81-47779. (Studies in Phenomenology & Existential Philosophy). 320p. 1982. 24.95x (ISBN 0-253-35025-5). Ind U Pr.
Role Playing for Managers. J. Towers. 1974. 45.00 (ISBN 0-08-017827-8). Pergamon.
Role Playing in the Curriculum. 2nd ed. George Shaftel & Fannie R. Shaftel. 464p. 1982. write for info. (ISBN 0-13-782482-3). P-H.
Role-Playing Mastery. Gary Gygax. 160p. 1987. 7.95 (ISBN 0-399-51293-4, Perigee). Putnam Pub Group.
Role Portrayal & Stereotyping on Television: An Annotated Bibliography of Studies Relating to Women, Minorities, Aging, Sexual Behavior, Health & Handicaps. Compiled by Nancy Signorielli. LC 85-9823. (Bibliographies & Indexes in Sociology Ser.: No. 5). xix, 214p. 1985. lib. bdg. 40.95 (ISBN 0-313-24855-9, SRP/). Greenwood.
Role Relationship of Men & Women. George W. Knight, III. 1985. pap. 5.95 (ISBN 0-8024-7369-5). Moody.
Role-Sharing Marriage. Audrey D. Smith & William J. Reid. LC 85-9650. 224p. 1985. 25.00x (ISBN 0-231-06110-2). Columbia U Pr.
Role Theory. R. C. Hesterman. 320p. 1981. 10.00 (ISBN 0-682-49812-2). Exposition-Phoenix.
Role Theory & Foreign Policy Analysis. Stephen J. Walker. LC 86-29162. xvi, 304p. 1987. text ed. 49.95x (ISBN 0-8223-0714-6). Duke.
Role Theory & Illness. Gerald Gordon. 11.95x (ISBN 0-8084-0270-6); pap. 7.95x (ISBN 0-8084-0271-4). New Coll U Pr.
Role Theory: Concepts & Research. Ed. by B. J Biddle & E. J. Thomas. LC 78-25644. 468p. 1979. Repr. of 1966 ed. lib. bdg. 32.50 (ISBN 0-88275-817-9). Krieger.
Role Theory: Expectations, Identities & Behaviors. Bruce J. Biddle. 1979. 30.00 (ISBN 0-12-095950-X). Acad Pr.
Role Theory: Perspectives for Health Professionals. Ed. by Margaret E. Hardy & Mary Conway. (Illus.). 354p. 1978. 27.50 (ISBN 0-8385-8471-3). Appleton & Lange.
Role Theory: Perspectives for Health Professionals. 2nd ed. Ed. by Margaret E. Hardy & Mary E. Conway. 384p. 1988. 29.95 (ISBN 0-8385-8472-1). Appleton & Lange.
Role Transitions. Ed. by Vernon L. Allen & Evert Van de Vliert. (NATO Conference Series III, Human Factors: Vol. 23). 384p. 1984. 65.00x (ISBN 0-306-41506-2, Plenum Pr). Plenum Pub.
Rolemaps. Diane Dormant. Ed. by Danny G. Langdon. LC 79-23398. (Instructional Design Library). 128p. 1980. 23.95 (ISBN 0-87778-153-2). Educ Tech Pubns.
Rolemaster. S. C. Charlton et al. (Illus.). 288p. 1982. 34.00 (ISBN 0-915795-04-3). Iron Crown Ent Inc.
Rolemaster Combat Screen. S. Coleman Charlton. 16p. (YA) (gr. 10-12). 1987. pap. 6.00 (ISBN 0-915795-13-2). Iron Crown Ent Inc.
Rolemaster Companion. Mark Colborn. Ed. by S. C. Charlton. 96p. (YA) (gr. 10-12). 1986. pap. 12.00 (ISBN 0-915795-12-4). Iron Crown Ent Inc.
RoleMaster Companion II. Khanna & Ridley. 112p. (Orig.). (YA) (gr. 10-12). 1987. pap. 12.00 (ISBN 0-915795-97-3). Iron Crown Ent Inc.
Roleplaying in Psychotherapy: A Manual. Raymond J. Corsini & Samuel Cardone. LC 65-22488. 1966. lib. bdg. 24.95x (ISBN 0-202-26007-0). Aldine de Gruyter.
Roles. Brunetta R. Wolfman. LC 83-12441. (Choices: Guides for Today's Woman: Vol. 3). 118p. (Orig.). 1983. pap. 6.95 (ISBN 0-664-24542-0). Westminster John Knox.
Roles & Functions of the Prosecutor, 6 vols. Ed. by John J. Douglass. Incl. Prosecutor in America. 4.25 (ISBN 0-318-18681-0); Discretionary Authority of the Prosecutor. 4.25 (ISBN 0-318-18682-9); Ethical Considerations in Prosecution. 5.25 (ISBN 0-318-18683-7); Special Problems in Prosecution. 4.25 (ISBN 0-318-18684-5); Prosecutorial Relationships in Criminal Justice. 4.25 (ISBN 0-318-18685-3); Pretrial Problems of the Prosecutor. 4.25 (ISBN 0-318-18686-1). Date not set. Set. 26.50 (ISBN 0-318-18680-2). Natl Coll DA.
Roles & Paradigms in Psychotherapy. Ed. by Marie C. Nelson et al. LC 67-28011. (Illus.). 384p. 1968. 75.00 (ISBN 0-8089-0344-6, 793095). Grune.
Roles & Relationships in Otto Ludwig's Narrative Fiction. David Turner. (Occasional Papers in Modern Languages: No. 10). 72p. 1975. pap. text ed. 6.95x (ISBN 0-900480-97-1, Pub. by U Hull UK). Humanities.
Roles & Relationships: School Boards & Superintendents. American Association of School Administrators & National School Boards Association. 3.50 (ISBN 0-318-01720-2, 021-00204). Am Assn Sch Admin.
Roles & Responsibilities in Geoscience Information: Proceedings, Geoscience Information Society Meeting, Indianapolis, 1983. Ed. by U. H. Rowell. (Proceedings, Vol. 14). 1984. 20.00 (ISBN 0-934485-11-9). Geosci Info.
Roles & Values. R. S. Downie. 1979. pap. 10.95x (ISBN 0-416-14920-0, NO. 2167). Routledge Chapman & Hall.
Roles for Government in Public & Private Retirement Programs. Charles I. Schottland. 52p. 5.00 (ISBN 0-317-35047-1, 5817). Natl Conf Soc Welfare.
Roles for Sociologists in Service Organizations. James E. Trela & Richard O'Toole. LC 74-81674. pap. 22.80 (2027308). Bks Demand UMI.
Roles for Writers & Readers: Rhetorical Anthology. Jack Dodds. 488p. 1989. price not set (ISBN 0-02-330720-X). Macmillan.
Roles in Interpretation. Judy E. Yordon. 352p. 1982. pap. text ed. write for info. (ISBN 0-697-04199-9); instructor's manual avail. (ISBN 0-697-04212-X). Wm C Brown.
Roles in Literacy Learning. Ed. by Duane R. Tovey & James E. Kerber. 188p. 1986. 10.50 (ISBN 0-87207-962-7). Intl Reading.
Roles in the Liturgical Assembly. Von Allmen et al. Tr. by Matthew J. O'Connell from Fr. (Orig.). 1981. pap. 17.50 (ISBN 0-916134-44-X). Pueblo Pub Co.
Roles of Magistrates: Nine Case Studies. Federal Judicial Center Staff & Carroll Seron. LC 85-602312. (Illus.). xiii, 149p. Date not set. price not set. Fed Judicial Ctr.
Roles of Men & Women in Eskimo Culture. Naomi M. Giffen. LC 74-5837. Repr. of 1930 ed. 14.00 (ISBN 0-404-11642-6). AMS Pr.
Roles of Occupational Therapists in Continuity of Care. Ed. by Florence S. Cromwell. LC 85-899. (Occupational Therapy in Health Care Ser.: Vol. 2, No. 1). 159p. 1985. text ed. 28.95 (ISBN 0-86656-392-X); pap. text ed. 19.95 (ISBN 0-86656-393-8). Haworth Pr.
Roles of Organic Matter in Sediment Diagenesis. Ed. by Donald L. Gautier. (Special Publications Ser.: No. 38). 203p. 1986. 37.00 (ISBN 0-918985-59-5). SEPM.
Roles of the Labor Leader. Duane Beeler & Harry Krushenbaum. 131p. (Orig.). 1969. pap. 3.95 (ISBN 0-317-12249-5). Union Rep.
Roles of the Professional & Paraprofessional in Team Teaching see Team Teaching Modules.
Rolfing: The Integration of Human Structures. Ida P. Rolf. (Illus.). 304p. 1978. pap. 13.95 (ISBN 0-06-465096-0, PBN 5096, B&N Bks). Har-Row.
Rolfing: The Integration of Human Structures. Ida P. Rolf. LC 76-52192. (Illus.). 1977. 27.50 (ISBN 0-930422-10-4). Dennis-Landman.
Rolf's "Per Stirpes". L. H. Angles. 1987. 8.95 (ISBN 0-533-07431-2). Vantage.
Roll Around a Point: Aerobatics. Duane Cole. pap. 8.95x (ISBN 0-911721-28-2, Pub. by Cole). Aviation.
Roll Away Saloon: Cowboy Tales of the Arizona Strip. Rowland Rider & Deirdre Paulsen. (Western Experience Ser.). 114p. 1985. pap. 9.95 (ISBN 0-87421-124-7). Utah St U Pr.
Roll Basket. Sue A. Gross. 1975. 2.95 (ISBN 0-917234-06-5). Kitchen Harvest.
Roll-Call. Arnold Bennett. LC 74-17047. (Collected Works of Arnold Bennett: Vol. 71). 1976. Repr. of 1918 ed. 24.25 (ISBN 0-518-19152-4). Ayer Co Pubs.
Roll Call at Oeyama. Frank Evans. 1985. 33.00x (ISBN 0-317-54067-X, Pub. by Gomer Pr). State Mutual Bk.
Roll Call at the Alamo. Bill Groneman & Phil Rosenthal. (Source Texana Ser.: No. 1). (Illus.). 1985. 37.50 (ISBN 0-88342-065-1). Old Army.
Roll Call of Death. P. J. Kumar. 1971. 6.95 (ISBN 0-87141-033-8). Manyland.
Roll Call of Mirrors: Selected Poems of Ivan V. Lalic. Ivan V. Lalic. Tr. by Charles Simic from Serbo-Croatian. LC 87-21185. vi, 74p. 1988. 18.50x (ISBN 0-8195-2151-5); pap. 10.95 (ISBN 0-8195-1152-8). Wesleyan U Pr.
Roll Call of the Blessed Ones. Janos Starker. (Illus.). 132p. 1985. 11.95 (ISBN 0-911050-60-4). Occidental.
Roll Call of the Iroquois Chiefs: A Study of a Mnemonic Cane from the Six Nations Reserve. William N. Fenton. LC 76-43704. (Smithsonian Miscellaneous Collections Ser.: Vol. 3, No. 15). Repr. of 1950 ed. 20.00 (ISBN 0-404-15536-7). AMS Pr.
Roll Call! Patterns of Voting in the Sixth Illinois Constitutional Convention. David Kenney et al. LC 74-32337. (Studies in Illinois Constitution Making Ser). 95p. 1975. pap. 10.00 (ISBN 0-252-00524-4). U of Ill Pr.
Roll Call Voting Behavior in the South Dakota Legislature. Alan L. Clem. 1966. 1.00 (ISBN 1-55614-110-6). U of SD Gov Res Bur.
Roll-Call Voting Handbook, 1986. Thomas Basil. 200p. 1986. pap. 59.00 (ISBN 0-938585-03-7). Legislative Track.
Roll Call, 1986. Congressional Quarterly Staff. 243p. 1987. pap. 15.95 (ISBN 0-87187-414-8). Congr Quarterly.
Roll, Jordan, Roll: The World the Slaves Made. Eugene D. Genovese. 1976. pap. 14.95 (ISBN 0-394-71652-3, Vin). Random.
Roll of Graduates of the University of Aberdeen, 1956-1970: With Supplement 1860-1955. Compiled by L. Donald & W. S. MacDonald. 1982. 58.00 (ISBN 0-08-028469-8). Pergamon.

Roman Army: Papers, Nineteen Twenty-Nine to Nineteen Eighty-Six. Eric Birley. (Mavor's Roman Army Researches Ser.: Vol. IV). 460p. 1988. 102.00x (ISBN 90-5063-002-2, Pub. by Gieben Amsterdam). Benjamins North Am.

Roman Army Studies, Vol. I. M. P. Speidel. 448p. 1984. 85.00x (ISBN 90-70265-75-3, Pub. by Gieben Amsterdam). Benjamins North Am.

Roman Art. Donald Strong. (Pelican History of Art Ser.). (Illus.). 1981. pap. 18.95x (ISBN 0-14-056139-0, Pelican Bks). Penguin.

Roman Art. rev. ed. Donald Strong & Roger Ling. 360p. 1988. pap. 18.95 (ISBN 0-317-66049-7, Pelican Bks). Penguin.

Roman Art: A Modern Survey of the Art of Ancient Rome. George M. Hanfmann. (Illus.). 250p. 1975. pap. text ed. 13.95x (ISBN 0-393-09222-4). Norton.

Roman Art & Architecture. Mortimer Wheeler. (World of Art Ser.). (Illus.). 252p. 1985. pap. 11.95 (ISBN 0-500-20021-1). Thames Hudson.

Roman Art & Imperial Policy. Niels Hannestad. (Jutland Archaeological Society Publications: Vol. XIX). 486p. (Orig.). 1988. pap. 72.50x (ISBN 87-7288-166-6). Coronet Bks.

Roman Art of War under the Republic. rev ed. Frank E. Adcock. (Martin Classical Lectures: Vol. 8). 140p. 1970. Repr. of 1960 ed. 14.95x (ISBN 0-06-490017-7, 06306). B&N Imports.

Roman Augury & Etruscan Divination. W. R. Connor. LC 75-10649. (Ancient Religion & Mythology Ser.). 1976. 14.00x (ISBN 0-405-07273-2). Ayer Co Pubs.

Roman Bath. Barry W. Cunliffe. LC 72-856399. (Society of Antiquaries of London, Research Committee, Reports: No. 24). pap. 91.00 (ISBN 0-317-28840-7, 2020785). Bks Demand UMI.

Roman Bath Discovered. rev. ed. Barry Cunliffe. 256p. 1984. 30.00x (ISBN 0-7102-0196-6). Routledge Chapman & Hall.

Roman Black-&-White Figural Mosaics. John R. Clarke. LC 78-68553. (College Art Association Monograph Ser.: Vol. 35). (Illus.). 172p. 1985. Repr. of 1979 ed. 30.00x (ISBN 0-271-00401-0). PA St U Pr.

Roman Brick Stamps in the Kelsey Museum. John Bodel. (Kelsey Museum Ser.). (Illus.). 1983. pap. text ed. 24.95x (ISBN 0-472-08039-3). U of Mich Pr.

Roman Bridal Drama. Alan Little. 1978. 6.50 (ISBN 0-89679-009-6). Moretus Pr.

Roman Britain. Aileen Fox. LC 68-23081. (Illus.). (gr. 7 up). 1968. 13.95 (ISBN 0-8023-1143-1). Dufour.

Roman Britain. T. W. Potter. (Illus.). 72p. 1983. pap. 6.95 (ISBN 0-674-77766-2). Harvard U Pr.

Roman Britain. I. A. Richmond. 1978. pap. 5.95 (ISBN 0-14-020315-X, Pelican). Penguin.

Roman Britain. Peter Salway. (Oxford History of England Ser.). (Illus.). 1981. 49.95x (ISBN 0-19-821717-X); pap. 14.95x (ISBN 0-19-285143-8). Oxford U Pr.

Roman Britain. John Wacher. (Illus.). 288p. 1986. pap. 8.95 (ISBN 0-460-02432-9, Pub. by J M Dent England). Biblio Dist.

Roman Britain: A Sourcebook. S. Ireland. LC 86-1764. 224p. 1986. 27.50 (ISBN 0-312-68964-0). St Martin.

Roman Britain & Early England 55 B. C. to A. D. 871. Peter H. Blair. (Library History of England). (Illus.). 1966. pap. 8.95 (ISBN 0-393-00361-2, Norton Lib). Norton.

Roman Britain from the Air. S. S. Frere & J. K. St. Joseph. LC 82-9746. (Cambridge Air Surveys Ser.). (Illus.). 240p. 1983. 42.50 (ISBN 0-521-25088-9). Cambridge U Pr.

Roman Britain: History & Sites. Plantagenet S. Fry. LC 83-21412. (Illus.). 560p. 1984. 37.50x (ISBN 0-389-20439-0, 08001). B&N Imports.

Roman Britain: Outpost of the Empire. H. H. Scullard. (Illus.). 1979. 17.95 (ISBN 0-500-45019-6). Thames Hudson.

Roman Britain: Outpost of the Empire. H. H. Scullard. LC 78-63042. (Illus.). 192p. 1986. pap. 10.95 (ISBN 0-500-27405-3). Thames Hudson.

Roman Britain to Saxon England. C. J. Arnold. LC 84-47813. (Illus.). 192p. 1984. 22.50x (ISBN 0-253-35017-4). Ind U Pr.

Roman Buildings of the Republic: An Attempt to Date Them from Their Materials. Tenney Frank. LC 25-7064. (American Academy in Rome. Papers & Monographs: Vol. 3). pap. 40.80 (2026718). Bks Demand UMI.

Roman by Polanski. Roman Polanski. 448p. 1985. pap. 4.95 (ISBN 0-345-30512-4). Ballantine.

Roman-Byzantine Burial Cave in Northern Palestine. O. R. Sellers & D. C. Baramki. (American Schools of Oriental Research, Supplementary Ser.: Vols. 15-16). 55p. 1953. pap. text ed. 7.50x (ISBN 0-89757-315-3, Am Sch Orient Res). Eisenbrauns.

Roman Cambridgeshire. David M. Browne. (Cambridge Town, Gown & County Ser.: Vol. 13). (Illus.). 1977. pap. 4.50 (ISBN 0-900891-09-2). Oleander Pr.

Roman Candle. Glen Chase. (Cherry Delight Ser.). (Orig.). 1975. pap. 1.25 (ISBN 0-685-54127-4, LB2932K, Leisure Bks). Leisure NY.

Roman Canon Law in the Church of England. Frederic W. Maitland. 1969. Repr. of 1898 ed. 21.00 (ISBN 0-8337-2186-0). B Franklin.

Roman Catholic - Pentecostal Dialogue (1977-1982) A Study in Developing Ecumenism. Jerry L. Sandidge. (Studies in the Intercultural History of Christianity: Vol. 44). 1048p. 1987. pap. 92.20 (ISBN 3-8204-9877-X). P Lang Pubs.

Roman Catholic Church & the Creation of the Modern Irish State, 1878-1886. Emmet J. Larkin. LC 75-7169. (American Philosophical Society Memoirs Ser.: Vol. 108). pap. 109.00 (ISBN 0-317-29437-7, 2024293). Bks Demand UMI.

Roman Catholic Church & the North-West School Question: A Study in Church-State Relations in Western Canada, 1875-1905. M. R. Lupul. LC 73-89844. 1974. 27.50x (ISBN 0-8020-5301-7). U of Toronto Pr.

Roman Catholic Church in England 1780-1850: A Study in Internal Politics. Joan Connell. 215p. 1984. 14.00 (ISBN 0-87169-158-2). Am Philos.

Roman Catholic Church in Ireland & the Fall of Parnell, 1888-1891. Emmet Larkin. LC 78-22056. xxi, 316p. 1979. 34.95x (ISBN 0-8078-1352-4). U of NC Pr.

Roman Catholic Church Index of Prohibited Books As Issued by Pope Leo XIII. 201p. 1985. Repr. of 1907 ed. 127.55 (ISBN 0-89901-199-3). Found Class Reprints.

Roman Catholic Hierarchy. Thomas E. Watson. (Studies in Populism). 1980. lib. bdg. 69.95 (ISBN 0-686-68883-X). Revisionist Pr.

Roman Catholic Modernism. Ed. by Bernard M. Reardon. 1970. 25.00x (ISBN 0-8047-0750-2). Stanford U Pr.

Roman Catholic Theology of Pastoral Care. Regis A. Duffy. LC 83-48006. (Theology & Pastoral Care Ser.). 128p. 1983. pap. 2.50 (ISBN 0-8006-1727-4, 1-1727). Fortress.

Roman Catholicism. Loraine Boettner. 10.95 (ISBN 0-8010-0685-6). Baker Bk.

Roman Catholicism. Loraine Boettner. LC 61-11748. 1962. 10.95 (ISBN 0-87552-130-4). Presby & Reformed.

Roman Catholicism. Peter Kelly. 1985. 13.00x (ISBN 0-7062-3601-7, Pub. by Ward Lock Educ Co Ltd). State Mutual Bk.

Roman Catholicism: A Contemporary Evangelical Perspective. Ed. by Paul G. Schrotenboer. 96p. 1989. pap. 5.95. Baker Bk.

Roman Catholicism & Freemasonry. Dudley Wright. 1977. lib. bdg. 69.95 (ISBN 0-8490-2531-1). Gordon Pr.

Roman Catholicism & the American Way of Life. Ed. by Thomas T. McAvoy. LC 72-13177. (Essay Index Reprint Ser.). Repr. of 1960 ed. 14.75 (ISBN 0-8369-8167-7). Ayer Co Pubs.

Roman Catholicism & the Right to Work. Edward B. McLean. 186p. (Orig.). 1986. lib. bdg. 27.00 (ISBN 0-8191-5009-6); pap. text ed. 12.00 (ISBN 0-8191-5010-X). U Pr of Amer.

Roman Catholicism in England from the Elizabethan Settlement to the Second Vatican Council. Edward Norman. (OPUS). 160p. 1985. 18.95x (ISBN 0-19-219181-0); pap. 9.95 (ISBN 0-19-281935-6). Oxford U Pr.

Roman Catholicism: The Search for Relevance. William McSweeney. 1980. 25.00 (ISBN 0-312-68969-1). St Martin.

Roman Catholicism: Yesterday & Today. Robert Burns. 1988. text ed. 21.95x (ISBN 0-268-01638-0). U of Notre Dame Pr.

Roman Catholics in England: Studies in Social Structure Since the Second World War. Michael P. Hornsby-Smith. (Illus.). 288p. 1987. 29.50 (ISBN 0-521-30313-3). Cambridge U Pr.

Roman Centurion. (How They Lived Ser.). (Illus.). (gr. 3-8). Date not set. write for info. Rourke Corp.

Roman Chancery Tradition. G Viden. (Studia Graeca et Latina Gothoburgensia: Vol. xlvi). 168p. 1984. pap. 19.95x (ISBN 91-7346-153-9, Pub. by Acta-Universitat Sweden). Humanities.

Roman Chester. Hendon Publishing Co., Ltd. Staff. 1986. 12.60x (ISBN 0-317-54161-7, Pub. by Hendon Pub UK). State Mutual Bk.

Roman Cinerary Urns in Stockholm Collections. Charlotte Scheffer. (Illus.). 96p. (Orig.). 1987. pap. 62.50x (ISBN 91-7192-676-3). Coronet Bks.

Roman Circuses: Arenas for Chariot Racing. John Humphrey. LC 82-40413. 1985. 65.00x (ISBN 0-520-04921-7). U of Cal Pr.

Roman Cities: 'Les villes romaines". Pierre Grimal. Ed. & tr. by Michael Woloch. LC 81-69831. (Illus.). 349p. 1984. pap. 12.50x. (ISBN 0-299-08934-7). U of Wis Pr.

Roman Citizenship. 2nd ed. A. N. Sherwin-White. 1980. pap. 29.95x (ISBN 0-19-814847-X). Oxford U Pr.

Roman Citizenship & the Athenian Elite: AD 96-161. M. Woloch. xviii, 315p. 1988. pap. text ed. 57.50x (ISBN 90-256-0939-2, Pub. by A M Hakkert). Coronet Bks.

Roman Civilization: Sourcebook 1-The Republic, Sourcebook 2-The Empire. Ed. by Naphtali Lewis & Meyer Reinhold. Bk. 1. pap. 9.95x (ISBN 0-06-131231-2, TB1231, Torch); Bk. 2. pap. 9.95x (ISBN 0-06-131232-0, TB1232, Torch). Har-Row.

Roman Classics Notes. Mary E. Snodgrass. 376p. 1988. pap. 5.95 (ISBN 0-8220-1152-2). Cliffs.

Roman Coins & Their Values. 4th ed. David R. Sear. 1988. 49.95 (ISBN 0-900652-98-5). Numismatic Fine Arts.

Roman Coins & Values. D. Sear. 1979. lib. bdg. 35.00 (Pub. by B A Seaby England). S J Durst.

Roman Coins from Lincoln: 1970-1979. J. E. Mann & R. Reece. (Archaeology of Lincoln Ser.: Vol. VI-2). 72p. 1983. pap. text ed. 10.50x (Pub. by Council British Archaeology). Humanities.

Roman Colonate: The Theories of Its Origin. Roth Clausing. LC 70-78011. (Columbia University Studies in the Social Sciences: No. 260). 1969. Repr. of 1925 ed. 27.50 (ISBN 0-404-51260-7). AMS Pr.

Roman Colosseum, 2 vols. Justus Lipsius. (Printed Sources of Western Art Ser.). (Illus., Lat.). 1981. pap. 40.00 (ISBN 0-915346-58-3). A Wofsy Fine Arts.

Roman Comedy. David Konstan. LC 82-22112. 184p. 1983. 27.50x (ISBN 0-8014-1531-4). Cornell U Pr.

Roman Comedy. David Konstan. LC 82-22112. (Paperback Ser.). 184p. 1986. pap. 7.95x (ISBN 0-8014-9398-6). Cornell U Pr.

Roman Comedy. K. McLeish. 80p. 1986. Repr. 11.00 (ISBN 0-86292-186-4, Pub. by Bristol Classical UK). Focus Info Gr.

Roman Commonwealth. Ralph W. Moore. LC 72-101048. 1969. Repr. of 1942 ed. 25.00x (ISBN 0-8046-0713-3, Pub. by Kennikat). Assoc Faculty Pr.

Roman Conquests. Phil Andros. LC 83-5486. (Perineum Press Bk.). 164p. 1983. pap. 7.95 (ISBN 0-912516-76-3). Grey Fox.

Roman Construction in Italy from Nerva Through the Antonines. Marion E. Blake & Doris T. Bishop. LC 72-83463. (Memoirs Ser.: Vol. 96). (Illus.). 1973. 30.00 (ISBN 0-87169-096-9). Am Philos.

Roman Converts. Arnold Lunn. (Essay Index Reprint Ser.). 275p. 1982. Repr. of 1924 ed. lib. bdg. 17.00 (ISBN 0-8290-0482-3). Irvington.

Roman Converts. facs. ed. Arnold H. Lunn. LC 67-22102. (Essay Index Reprint Ser). 1923. 18.00 (ISBN 0-8369-0636-5). Ayer Co Pubs.

Roman Cookery of Apicius: A Treasury of Gourmet Recipes & Herbal Cookery. John Edwards. LC 84-19348. (Illus.). 322p. 1984. 19.95 (ISBN 0-88179-008-7). Hartley & Marks.

Roman Copies of Greek Sculpture: The Problem of the Originals. Brunilde S. Ridgway. (Jerome Lectures, Fifteenth Ser.). 304p. 1983. text ed. 30.00x (ISBN 0-472-10038-6). U of Mich Pr.

Roman Cordoba. Robert Knapp. LC 83-1195. (UC Publications in Classical Studies: Vol. 30). 1983. pap. text ed. 20.00x (ISBN 0-520-09676-2). U of Cal Pr.

Roman Craftsmen & Tradesmen of the Early Empire. Ethel H. Brewster. LC 72-81956. 101p. 1972. Repr. of 1917 ed. lib. bdg. 20.00 (ISBN 0-8337-4822-X). B Franklin.

Roman Crete: An Archaeological Survey & Gazetteer of Late Hellenistic, Roman & Early Byzantine Crete. I. F. Sanders. (Illus.). 208p. 1982. 65.00x (ISBN 0-85668-150-4, Pub. by Aris & Phillips UK). Humanities.

Roman Cursive Writing. Henry B. Van Hoesen. LC 34-20123. pap. 83.00 (ISBN 0-317-10623-6, 2050380). Bks Demand UMI.

Roman d'Alexandre, Vols. 1-7. Alexander The Great. (Elliott Monographs: Nos. 36-42). Repr. of 1955 ed. 184.00. Vol. 36 (ISBN 0-527-02639-5). Vol. 37 (ISBN 0-527-02640-9). Vol. 38 (ISBN 0-527-02641-7). Vol. 39 (ISBN 0-527-02642-5). Vol. 40 (ISBN 0-527-02643-3). Vol. 40 (ISBN 0-527-02644-1). Vol. 41 (ISBN 0-527-02645-X). Kraus Repr.

Roman de Fauvel. Fauvel. 1914-19. pap. 28.00 (ISBN 0-384-15210-4). Johnson Repr.

Roman De Jehan de Paris. Jean de Paris. 1923. pap. 19.00 (ISBN 0-384-27020-4). Johnson Repr.

Roman De La Manekine Par Philippe de Reimes. Philippe De Remi. LC 74-174193. (Bannatyne Club, Edinburgh. Publications: No. 68). Repr. of 1840 ed. 37.50 (ISBN 0-404-52788-4). AMS Pr.

Roman de la Momie. Theophile Gautier. Ed. by Boschot. (Class. Garnier). pap. 24.95 (ISBN 0-685-34912-8). French & Eur.

Roman de la Momie. Theophile Gautier & G. Van Den Bogaert. 186p. 1966. 9.95 (ISBN 0-686-55911-8). French & Eur.

Roman de la Monie. Theophile Gautier. Ed. by Boschot. (Coll. Prestige). 49.95 (ISBN 0-685-34913-6). French & Eur.

Roman de la Rose. Guillaume De Lorris. Ed. by Stephen G. Nichols, Jr. LC 67-25114. (Medieval French Literature Ser). (Orig., Fr.). 1967. pap. text ed. 6.95x (ISBN 0-89197-496-2). Irvington.

Roman De La Rose, 5 Vols. Guillaume De Lorris & Jean De Meun. Ed. by E. Langlois. 1914-24. Set. pap. 160.00 (ISBN 0-384-51883-4). Johnson Repr.

Roman de la Rose, 5 tomes. Guillaume De Lorris & Jean De Meur. Ed. by Langlois. Set. 199.00 (ISBN 0-685-34019-8). French & Eur.

Roman de la Rose see Romance of the Rose.

Roman de la Rose Ou de Guillaume de Dole. Guillaume De Dole. Ed. by G. Servois. pap. 31.00 (ISBN 0-384-20310-8). Johnson Repr.

Roman de Renart, 3 vols. Ed. by Ernest Martin. 1476p. 1973. Repr. of 1891 ed. 190.00 (ISBN 3-11-003337-2). De Gruyter.

Roman de Renart, 6 tomes. Ed. by Roques. Set. 75.00 (ISBN 0-685-34018-X). French & Eur.

Roman de Thebes, 2 Vols. 1890. pap. 74.00 (ISBN 0-384-60006-9). Johnson Repr.

Roman de Tristan & un Anonyme Poeme du 12th Siecle. Beroul. Ed. by E. Muret. pap. 32.00 (ISBN 0-685-13586-1). Johnson Repr.

Roman De Tristan En Prose, Vol. II. Renee L. Curtis. (Arthurian Studies: No. XIII). 320p. (Fr.). 1985. 36.50 (ISBN 0-85991-182-9, Pub. by Boydell & Brewer). Longwood Pub Group.

Roman De Tristan En Prose, Vol. I. rev. ed. Renee L. Curtis. (Arthurian Studies: No. XII). 260p. (Fr.). 1985. 36.50 (ISBN 0-85991-181-0, Pub. by Boydell & Brewer). Longwood Pub Group.

Roman De Tristan En Prose, Vol. III. Ed. by Renee L. Curtis. LC 84-24337. (Arthurian Studies: No. XIV). 294p. (Fr.). 1985. 45.00 (ISBN 0-85991-183-7, Pub. by Boydell & Brewer). Longwood Pub Group.

Roman de Troie, 6 Vols. Benoit de Saint-More. Set. 215.00 (ISBN 0-384-03915-4); Set. pap. 167.00 (ISBN 0-384-03916-2). Johnson Repr.

Roman Declamation. Michael Winterbottom. 120p. 12.25 (ISBN 0-906515-10-6, Pub. by Bristol Classical Pr). Focus Info Gr.

Roman des Eles. Raoul de Hodenc. (Utrecht Publications in Comparative Literature: Vol. 17). x, 175p. 1983. 36.00x (ISBN 90-272-2192-8); pap. 24.00x (ISBN 90-272-2202-9). Benjamins North Am.

Roman des Romans. Ed. by I. C. LeCompte. (Elliott Monographs: Vol. 14). Repr. of 1923 ed. 11.00 (ISBN 0-527-02617-4). Kraus Repr.

Roman Dmowski: Party, Tactics, Ideology, Eighteen Ninety-Five to Nineteen Seven. Alvin M. Fountain, 2nd. (East European Monographs: No. 60). 240p. 1980. 24.00x (ISBN 0-914710-53-2). East Eur Quarterly.

Roman Documents from the Greek East: Senatus Consulta & Epistulae to the Age of Augustus. Robert K. Sherk. LC 68-19442. pap. 77.60 (ISBN 0-317-29909-3, 2017565). Bks Demand UMI.

Roman Dogma vs. Bible Doctrine. E. Harold Henderson. 152p. 1964. pap. 1.00 (ISBN 0-89114-066-2). Baptist Pub Hse.

Roman Drama: Nine Plays of Terence, Plautus & Seneca. Tr. by Frank O. Copley. LC 64-66074. (YA) (gr. 11 up). 1965. pap. 11.49 scp (ISBN 0-672-60455-8, LLA209). Bobbs.

Roman Drawings from the Musee de Louvre, Paris. (Illus.). 168p. 1979. 12.50 (02806-2, Pub. by Art Institute of Chicago). U of Chicago Pr.

Roman Drawings of the Sixteenth Century from the Musee du Louvre, Paris. Catherine M. Goguel & Fransoise Viatte. Tr. by Anselmo Carini & Suzanne Folds McCullagh. LC 79-90234. (Illus.). 166p. (Orig.). 1979. pap. 5.95 (ISBN 0-86559-036-2). Art Inst Chi.

Roman Economic Policy in the Erythra Thalassa. Steven E. Sidebotham. (Mnemosyne Supplements Ser.: No. 91). (Illus.). xiv, 226p. 1986. pap. 38.75 (ISBN 90-04-07644-1, Pub. by E J Brill). Heinman.

Roman Elegies. bilingual ed. Joseph Brodsky. 32p. pap. cancelled (ISBN 0-374-25149-5). FS&G.

Roman Elegies & Other Poems. Johann Wolfgang von Goethe. Tr. by Michael Hamburger. (Austrian-German Culture Ser.). 220p. 1983. 20.00 (ISBN 0-933806-18-3). Black Swan CT.

Roman Elegists' Attitude Towards Women. Saara Lilja. Ed. by Steele Commager. LC 77-70836. (Latin Poetry Ser.: Vol. 25). 1979. Repr. of 1965 ed. lib. bdg. 37.00 (ISBN 0-8240-2974-7). Garland Pub.

Roman Emperors: A Biographical Guide to the Rulers of Imperial Rome: 31 B.C.-476 A.D. Michael Grant. LC 85-8391. (Illus.). 416p. 1985. 25.00 (ISBN 0-684-18388-9, ScribT). Scribner.

Roman Empire. Martin P. Charlesworth. LC 86-29443. (Oxford Paperbacks University Ser.). (Illus.). 155p. 1987. Repr. of 1968 ed. lib. bdg. 35.00x (ISBN 0-313-25669-1, CHAR). Greenwood.

Roman Empire. Colin Wells. LC 83-40699. (Illus.). 368p. 1984. 37.50x (ISBN 0-8047-1237-9); pap. 10.95x (ISBN 0-8047-1238-7). Stanford U Pr.

Roman Empire & Its Neighbours. Ed. by Fergus Millar. 1967. pap. 9.95 (ISBN 0-440-01769-6). Delacorte.

Roman Empire & Its Neighbours. 2nd ed. Ed. by Fergus Millar. LC 81-326. 376p. 1981. 49.50 (ISBN 0-8419-0711-0). Holmes & Meier.

Roman Empire & the Dark Ages. Giovanni Caselli. LC 84-6480. (History of Everyday Things Ser.). (Illus.). 48p. (YA) (gr. 6-8). 1985. 14.95 (ISBN 0-911745-58-0). P Bedrick Bks.

Roman Empire: Augustus to Hadrian. Ed. & tr. by Robert K. Sherk. (Translated Documents of Greece & Rome Ser.: No. 6). 304p. 1988. 54.50 (ISBN 0-521-33025-4); pap. 16.95 (ISBN 0-521-33887-5). Cambridge U Pr.

Roman Empire: Economy, Society & Culture. Peter Garnsey & Richard Saller. LC 86-25029. 232p. 1987. 35.00x (ISBN 0-520-06066-0); pap. 12.95x (ISBN 0-520-06067-9). U of Cal Pr.

Roman Empire, Twenty-Seven B.C. Four Hundred Seventy-Six A.D. A Study in Survival. Chester G. Starr. LC 81-22310. (Illus.). 1982. 29.95x (ISBN 0-19-503129-6); pap. 10.95x (ISBN 0-19-503130-X). Oxford U Pr.

Roman Policy in Epirus & Acarnania in the Age of the Roman Conquest of Greece. Stewart I. Oost. LC 75-7333. (Roman History Ser.). 1975. Repr. 10.00 (ISBN 0-405-07050-0). Ayer Co Pubs.

Roman Political Ideas & Practice. Frank E. Adcock. (Jerome Lecture Ser). 1959. pap. 6.95x (ISBN 0-472-06088-0, 88, AA). U of Mich Pr.

Roman Political Life 90 BC-69 AD. Ed. by T. Wiseman. (Exeter Studies in History: No. 7). 96p. 1985. pap. text ed. 7.95 (ISBN 0-85989-225-5, Pub. by U of Exeter UK). Humanities.

Roman Politics. Frank F. Abbott. LC 63-10295. (Our Debt to Greece & Rome Ser). Repr. of 1930 ed. 15.00 (ISBN 0-8154-0000-4). Cooper Sq.

Roman Politics Two Hundred Twenty to One Hundred Fifty B.C. Howard H. Scullard. LC 81-13434. (Illus.). xvi, 325p. 1982. Repr. of 1973 ed. lib. bdg. 38.50x (ISBN 0-313-23296-2, SCRP). Greenwood.

Roman Port & Fishery of Cosa: A Center of Ancient Trade. Anna M. McCann et al. LC 85-42693. (Illus.). 750p. 1985. text ed. 150.00x (ISBN 0-691-03581-4). Princeton U Pr.

Roman Portrait Sculpture 217-260 A.D. The Transformation of an Artistic Tradition. B. Wood. (Columbia Studies in the Classical Tradition: No. 12). (Illus.). xiv, 150p. 1986. 37.25 (ISBN 90-04-07282-9, Pub. by E J Brill). Heinman.

Roman Portraits. Andrea Fulvio. (Printed Sources of Western Art Ser.). (Illus.). 236p. (Lat.). 1981. pap. 30.00 slipcase (ISBN 0-915346-57-5). A Wofsy Fine Arts.

Roman Portraits. Ludwig Goldscheider. LC 76-42709. Repr. of 1940 ed. 28.50 (ISBN 0-404-15363-1). AMS Pr.

Roman Portraits in the Getty Museum. Jiri Frel. LC 81-50775. (Illus.). 137p. 1981. pap. 17.00 (ISBN 0-86659-004-8). Philbrook Mus Art.

Roman Portraits in the J. Paul Getty Museum. rev. ed. Jiri Frel. (Illus.). 137p. 1981. pap. 16.95 (ISBN 0-89236-100-X). J P Getty Mus.

Roman Portraits: The Flavian-Trajanic Period. William C. McDermott & Anne E. Orentzel. LC 79-1559. 176p. 1979. text ed. 19.00x (ISBN 0-8262-0275-6). U of Mo Pr.

Roman Pottery from the Colonia: Skeldergate & Bishophill. J. R. Perrin. (Archaeology of York Ser.: Vol. 16, Fasc. 2). 68p. 1981. pap. text ed. 15.00x (ISBN 0-900312-71-8, Pub. by Council British Archaeology). Humanities.

Roman Pottery from the Upper Defences. M. Darling et al. (Archaeology of Lincoln: Vol. XVI-2). 57p. 1984. pap. text ed. 17.50x (ISBN 0-906780-38-1, Pub. by Coun Brit Archaeology England). Humanities.

Roman Private Law in the Times of Cicero & of the Antonines, 2 vols. Henry J. Roby. 1977. lib. bdg. 195.00 (ISBN 0-8490-2533-8). Gordon Pr.

Roman Provincial Administration. W. T. Arnold. 298p. 1974. 15.00 (ISBN 0-89005-027-9). Ares.

Roman Provincial Administration. J. Richardson. 88p. 1984. Repr. of 1976 ed. 11.00 (ISBN 0-86292-128-7, Pub. by Bristol Classical UK). Focus Info Gr.

Roman, Provincial & Islamic Law: The Origins of the Islamic Patronate. Patricia Crone. (Cambridge Studies in Islamic Civilization). 200p. 1987. 39.50 (ISBN 0-521-32253-7). Cambridge U Pr.

Roman Quarry & Other Sequences. David Jones. LC 81-52307. 300p. 1982. pap. 14.95 (ISBN 0-935296-24-7). Sheep Meadow.

Roman Question. Noel Blakiston. LC 79-91770. 360p. 1980. 35.00 (ISBN 0-89453-150-6). M Glazier.

Roman Questions of Plutarch. facsimile ed. Plutarch. Ed. by Herbert J. Rose. LC 75-14267. (Ancient Religion & Mythology Ser.). 1976. Repr. of 1924 ed. 17.00x (ISBN 0-405-07272-4). Ayer Co Pubs.

Roman Questions of Plutarchus. Plutarchus. Tr. by H. J. Rose. 1924. 15.00 (ISBN 0-8196-0284-1). Biblo.

Roman Realities. Finley Hooper. LC 78-15237. (Illus.). 584p. 1978. pap. 9.50x (ISBN 0-8143-1594-1). Wayne St U Pr.

Roman Reformer & Inventor: Being a New Text of the Treatise De rebus bellicis. E. A. Thompson. Ed. by Moses Finley. LC 79-5008. (Ancient Economic History Ser.). (Illus.). 1980. Repr. of 1952 ed. lib. bdg. 14.00x (ISBN 0-405-12396-5). Ayer Co Pubs.

Roman Religion. Michael Massey. Ed. by Peter Hodge. (Aspects of Roman Life Ser.). 48p. (Orig.). (gr. 7-12). 1979. pap. text ed. 4.75 (ISBN 0-582-21573-0). Longman.

Roman Religion & Roman Empire: Five Essays. Robert E. Palmer. LC 73-89289. (Haney Foundation Ser.: No. 15). Repr. of 1974 ed. 36.40 (2055281). Bks Demand UMI.

Roman Replies & CLSA Advisory Opinions, 1984. Ed. by William A. Schumacher. vii, 63p. (Orig.). 1984. pap. 5.50 (ISBN 0-943616-26-3). Canon Law Soc.

Roman Replies & CLSA Advisory Opinions, 1985. Ed. by William A. Schumacher & J. James Cuneo. 68p. (Orig.). 1985. pap. 5.50 (ISBN 0-943616-30-1). Canon Law Soc.

Roman Replies, 1981. Ed. by William A. Schumacher. 46p. (Orig.). 1981. pap. 3.00 (ISBN 0-943616-09-3). Canon Law Soc.

Roman Replies, 1982. William A. Schumacher. 42p. (Orig.). 1982. pap. 3.00 (ISBN 0-943616-13-1). Canon Law Soc.

Roman Replies, 1983. William A. Schumacher. 24p. (Orig.). 1983. pap. 3.00 (ISBN 0-943616-21-2). Canon Law Soc.

Roman Republic. Henry C. Boren. (Anvil Ser.). 192p. (Orig.). 1965. pap. 7.50 (ISBN 0-686-47408-2, Pub. by Van Nostrand). Krieger.

Roman Republic. Michael Crawford. LC 81-20047. (Illus.). 224p. 1982. pap. text ed. 7.95x (ISBN 0-674-77931-2). Harvard U Pr.

Roman Republic. Erich S. Gruen. LC 72-94085. (AHA Pamphlets: No. 312). 1972. pap. text ed. 1.50 (ISBN 0-87229-009-3). Am Hist Assn.

Roman Republic, 3 vols. William E. Heitland. 1970. Repr. of 1923 ed. Vol. 2. lib. bdg. 22.70 (ISBN 0-8371-2078-0, HERB); Vol. 3. lib. bdg. 22.70 (HERC). Greenwood.

Roman Republic, One Hundred Thirty-Three to Forty-Four B.C. see Cambridge Ancient History Series.

Roman Republican Coinage. Michael Crawford. LC 77-164450. (Illus.). 750p. 1975. 290.00 (ISBN 0-521-07492-4). Cambridge U Pr.

Roman Revolution. Ronald Syme. (Oxford Paperbacks Ser). 1939. pap. 10.95x (ISBN 0-19-881001-6). Oxford U Pr.

Roman Rhetorical Schools As Preparation for the Courts Under the Early Empire. Edilbert P. Parks. LC 78-64198. (Johns Hopkins University. Studies in the Social Sciences. Sixty-Third Ser. 1945: 2). Repr. of 1945 ed. 16.00 (ISBN 0-404-61304-7). AMS Pr.

Roman Rite in Orthodoxy, Part I: Additional Testimonies, Pt. II. Chrysostomos H. Stratman & Apostolos Makrakis. 62p. 1957. pap. 1.00x (ISBN 0-938366-38-6). Orthodox Chr.

Roman Road. facsimile ed. Gwendoline Keats. LC 71-157782. (Short Story Index Reprint Ser.). Repr. of 1903 ed. 17.00 (ISBN 0-8369-3894-1). Ayer Co Pubs.

Roman Roads. Raymond Chevallier. LC 74-82845. 1975. 55.00x (ISBN 0-520-02834-1). U of Cal Pr.

Roman Rococo Architecture from Clement XI to Benedict XIV (1700-1758) Nina A. Mallory. LC 76-23640. (Outstanding Dissertations in the Fine Arts Ser.). 1977. lib. bdg. 55.00x (ISBN 0-8240-2710-8). Garland Pub.

Roman Rolland: The Man & His World. Stefan Zweig. 1921. Repr. 30.00 (ISBN 0-8274-3297-6). R West.

Roman Rule in Asia Minor to the End of the Third Century After Christ, 2 vols. David Magie. LC 75-7328. (Roman History Ser.). 1975. Repr. Set. 110.00x (ISBN 0-405-07098-5); 55.00x ea. Vol. 1 (ISBN 0-405-07099-3). Vol. 2 (ISBN 0-405-07100-0). Ayer Co Pubs.

Roman Rulers & Rebels. Gordon P. Stillman. (gr. 8-11). 1972. pap. text ed. 6.25x (ISBN 0-88334-048-8). Ind Sch Pr.

Roman Sarcophagi in The Metropolitan Museum of Art. Anna M. McCann. LC 77-28089. (Illus.). 152p. 1978. 25.00 (ISBN 0-87099-173-6). Metro Mus Art.

Roman Satire. Michael Coffey. LC 76-28824. 1976. 16.95x (ISBN 0-416-85120-7, NO. 2146); pap. 16.95x (ISBN 0-416-85130-4, NO. 2147). Routledge Chapman & Hall.

Roman Satirical Poems & Their Translation. Carlo A. Salustri. Tr. by Grant Showerman from Ital. LC 78-21559. 1979. Repr. of 1945 ed. lib. bdg. cancelled (ISBN 0-313-20745-3, SARS). Greenwood.

Roman Satirists & Their Satire: The Fine Art of Criticism in Ancient Rome. E. S. Ramage et al. LC 74-81538. 212p. 1974. 12.50 (ISBN 0-8155-5028-6, NP). Noyes.

Roman Satirists in Seventeenth Century England. William Kupersmith. LC 85-1103. xii, 193p. 1985. 19.95x (ISBN 0-8032-2710-8). U of Nebr Pr.

Roman Science: Origins, Development, & Influence to the Later Middle Ages. William H. Stahl. LC 78-5597. 1978. Repr. of 1962 ed. lib. bdg. 52.50 (ISBN 0-313-20473-X, STRO). Greenwood.

Roman Sculpture from Augustus to Constantine. Eugene S. Strong. LC 79-88825. (Art Histories Collection Ser). Repr. of 1907 ed. 33.00 (ISBN 0-405-02230-1). Ayer Co Pubs.

Roman Sculpture from Augustus to Constantine. Eugenie Strong. LC 76-116362. (Illus.). 1971. lib. bdg. 30.00 (ISBN 0-87817-053-7). Hacker.

Roman Seaborne Commerce: Archaeology & Economic History. (Memoirs: No. 36). (Illus.). 300p. 1980. 45.00 (ISBN 0-318-12331-2). Am Acad Rome.

Roman Silver Coins. Incl. Vol. I. The Republic. lib. bdg. 30.00 (ISBN 0-686-45272-0); Vol. II. Tiberius to Commodus. lib. bdg. 30.00 (ISBN 0-686-45273-9). Pub. by B A Seaby England). S J Durst.

Roman Silver Coins: Carausius to Romulus Augustus, Vol. V. C. E. King & D. R. Sear. (Illus.). 225p. 1987. 30.00 (ISBN 0-900652-80-2, Pub. by Seaby UK). Numismatic Fine Arts.

Roman Silver Coins: Gordian III to Postumus, Vol. IV. 2nd ed. B. A. Seaby. (Illus.). 136p. 1982. 30.00 (ISBN 0-900652-62-4, Pub. by Seaby UK). Numismatic Fine Arts.

Roman Silver Coins: Pertinax, to Balbinus & Pupienus, Vol. III. 2nd ed. B. A. Seaby. (Illus.). 161p. 1982. 30.00 (ISBN 0-900652-61-6, Pub. by Seaby UK). Numismatic Fine Arts.

Roman Silver Coins: The Republic to Augustus, Vol. 1. 3rd ed. H. A. Seaby. (Illus.). 166p. 1978. 30.00 (ISBN 0-900652-44-6, Pub. by Seaby UK). Numismatic Fine Arts.

Roman Silver Coins: Tiberius to Commodus, Vol. 2. 3rd, rev. ed. H. A. Seaby. (Illus.). 255p. 1979. 30.00 (ISBN 0-900652-48-9, Pub. by Seaby UK). Numismatic Fine Arts.

Roman Slave Law. Alan Watson. LC 86-21351. 1987. 19.50x (ISBN 0-8018-3439-2). Johns Hopkins.

Roman Social En Angleterre, 1830-1850: Dickens, Disraeli, Mrs. Gaskell, Kingsley, 2 Vols. in One. rev. ed. Louis F. Cazamian. LC 66-27050. (Fr). 1967. Repr. of 1934 ed. 13.50x (ISBN 0-8462-0986-1). Russell.

Roman Social Relations, 50 B. C to A. D. 284. Ramsay MacMullen. LC 73-86909. 317p. 1981. pap. 10.95x (ISBN 0-300-02702-8, Y-392). Yale U Pr.

Roman Society. Henry Boren. (Civilization & Society Ser.). 1977. pap. text ed. 10.50x (ISBN 0-669-84681-3). Heath.

Roman Society from Nero to Marcus Aurelius. S. Dill. 75.00 (ISBN 0-87968-059-8). Gordon Pr.

Roman Society in the Last Century of the Western Empire. Samuel Dill. 1979. Repr. of 1898 ed. lib. bdg. 50.00 (ISBN 0-8492-4201-0). R West.

Roman Society in the Last Century of the Western Empire. S. Dill. 75.00 (ISBN 0-87968-060-1). Gordon Pr.

Roman Soldier. Giovanni Caselli. LC 86-4366. (Everyday Life of Ser.). (Illus.). 30p. (gr. 4-6). 1986. 9.95 (ISBN 0-87226-106-9). P Bedrick Bks.

Roman Soldier. G. R. Watson. LC 69-11153. (Aspects of Greek & Roman Life Ser.). (Illus.). 256p. 1985. 34.50x (ISBN 0-8014-0519-X); pap. 10.95x (ISBN 0-8014-9312-9). Cornell U Pr.

Roman Solution. Wallace Henley. (Living Bks.). 128p. 1986. pap. 4.95 (ISBN 0-8423-5660-6). Tyndale.

Roman Sonnets. G. G. Belli. Tr. by Harold Norse. LC 60-9955. 1960. pap. 4.00 (ISBN 0-317-02755-7, Dist. by Inland Bk). Jargon Soc.

Roman Sonnets of Giuseppe Gioacchino Belli. Giuseppe G. Belli. Tr. & intro. by Harold Norse. LC 73-79284. (Perivale Translation Ser.: No. 1). 54p. 1974. pap. 7.95 (ISBN 0-912288-06-X). Perivale Pr.

Roman Sources of Christian Art. Emerson H. Swift. (Illus.). 1970. Repr. of 1951 ed. lib. bdg. 35.00x (ISBN 0-8371-3430-7, SWCA). Greenwood.

Roman Spain. S. J. Keay. (Exploring the Roman World: Vol. 2). (Illus.). 240p. 1988. 27.50 (ISBN 0-520-06188-8). U of Cal Pr.

Roman Sport & Entertainment. David Buchanan. Ed. by Peter Hodge. (Aspects of Roman Life Ser.). (Illus.). 64p. (Orig.). (gr. 7-12). 1976. pap. text ed. 4.75 (ISBN 0-582-31415-1). Longman.

Roman Spring of Alice Toklas: 44 Letters by Alice Toklas in a Reminiscence. limited ed. Donald Windham. (Illus.). 1987. 35.00x (ISBN 0-917366-08-5). S Campbell.

Roman Spring of Mrs. Stone. Tennessee Williams. 128p. 1985. pap. 3.50 (ISBN 0-345-32690-3). Ballantine.

Roman Stamp: Frame & Facade in Some Forms of Neo-Classicism. Robert M. Adams. LC 72-50241. (Illus.). 1974. pap. 8.95x (ISBN 0-520-03715-4). U of Cal Pr.

Roman Stoicism. facsimile ed. Edward V. Arnold. LC 76-169750. (Select Bibliographies Reprint Ser). Repr. of 1911 ed. 27.50 (ISBN 0-8369-5970-1). Ayer Co Pubs.

Roman Stoicism. Edward V. Arnold. LC 76-169750. 468p. Repr. of 1911 ed. 26.50 (ISBN 0-8290-0494-7). Irvington.

Roman Stoicism: Being Lectures. E. Vernon Arnold. Repr. of 1911 ed. 35.00 (ISBN 0-8274-4331-5). R West.

Roman Stopa: Die Schnalze Ihre Natur Entwicklung und Ursprung. (Bibliotheca Nostratica Ser.: Vol. 7). 213p. 1986. 26.00 (ISBN 0-931922-25-9). Eurolingua.

Roman Studies: Literary & Historical. T. P. Wiseman. (Collected Classical Papers). 1987. 45.00 (ISBN 0-905205-62-6, Pub. by F Cairns). Longwood Pub Group.

Roman Summer. Jane Arbor. (Nightingale Paperbacks). 1985. pap. 9.95 (ISBN 0-8161-3872-9, Large Print Bks). G K Hall.

Roman System of Provincial Adminstration: To the Accession of Constantine the Great. facsimile & 3rd ed. William T. Arnold. Ed. by E. S. Bouchier. LC 79-179501. (Select Bibliographies Reprint Ser). Repr. of 1914 ed. 23.50 (ISBN 0-8369-6630-9). Ayer Co Pubs.

Roman Tale. Caroll Baker. 1987. pap. 3.95 (ISBN 0-451-14772-3, Sig). NAL.

Roman Tale. Carroll Baker. LC 85-81166. 316p. 1986. 17.95 (ISBN 0-917657-53-5). D I Fine.

Roman Technology & Crafts. Miranda Green. Ed. by Peter Hodge. (Aspects of Roman Life Ser.). 48p. (Orig.). (gr. 7-12). 1979. pap. text ed. 4.75 (ISBN 0-582-20162-4). Longman.

Roman Thin Walled Pottery from Cosa, from 1948-1954. M. T. Moevs. 324p. 1973. 56.00x (ISBN 0-271-00454-1). Pa St U Pr.

Roman Thin Walled Pottery from Cosa: 1948-1954. M. T. Moevs. (Memoirs: No. 32). (Illus.). 324p. 1973. 49.00 (ISBN 0-318-12332-0). Am Acad Rome.

Roman Towns. Peter Hodge. (Aspects of Roman Life Ser.). (Illus.). 48p. (Orig.). (gr. 7-12). 1977. pap. text ed. 4.75 (ISBN 0-582-20301-5). Longman.

Roman Urban Defences in the West. J. Maloney & B. Hobley. (CBA Research Reports Ser.: No. 51). 154p. 1983. pap. text ed. 32.50x (ISBN 0-906780-23-3, Pub. by Council British Archaeology). Humanities.

Roman Urban Topography in Britain & the Western Empire. Ed. by F. Grew & B. Hobley. (CBA Research Reports: No. 59). (Illus.). 136p. 1985. pap. text ed. 32.50x (ISBN 0-906780-47-0, Pub. by Coun Brit Archaeology). Humanities.

Roman Villa: A Historical Introduction. John Percival. LC 76-7766. 1976. 48.00x (ISBN 0-520-03233-0). U of Cal Pr.

Roman Water Law. Translated from the Pandects of Justinian. Eugene F. Ware. 160p. 1985. Repr. of 1905 ed. lib. bdg. 22.50x (ISBN 0-8377-1336-6). Rothman.

Roman Way. Edith Hamilton. 1981. pap. 2.95 (ISBN 0-380-01533-1, 51391-9, Discus). Avon.

Roman Way. Edith Hamilton. 224p. 1984. pap. 4.95 (ISBN 0-393-00232-2). Norton.

Roman West & the Byzantine East. Bishop Chrysostomos & Hieromonk Auxentios. 57p. (Orig.). 1988. pap. 5.00 (ISBN 0-911165-12-6). Ctr Trad Orthodox.

Roman West & the Parthian East. J. B. Ward-Perkins. 1965. pap. 5.50 (ISBN 0-85672-657-5, Pub. by British Acad). Longwood Pub Group.

Roman Women. J. P. Balsdon. LC 82-48825. (Illus.). 354p. 1983. pap. 7.95 (ISBN 0-06-464062-0, BN 4062, B&N Bks). Har-Row.

Roman Women, Their History & Habits. John Balsdon. LC 75-8718. (Illus.). 351p. 1975. Repr. of 1962 ed. lib. bdg. 48.50x (ISBN 0-8371-8040-6, BAROW). Greenwood.

Roman World. Mike Corbishley. LC 85-52280. (Illus.). 96p. (gr. 4-12). 1986. PLB 13.90 (ISBN 0-531-19018-8, Pub. by Warwick). Watts.

Roman World, 2 vols. Ed. by John Wacher. LC 85-24476. 872p. 1987. Set. 225.00 (ISBN 0-7100-9975-4, Pub. by Routledge UK). Routledge Chapman & Hall.

Roman World of Dio Chrysostom. C. P. Jones. LC 78-5869. (Loeb Classical Monograph). 1978. 27.00x (ISBN 0-674-77915-0). Harvard U Pr.

Romance. Gillian Beer. (Critical Idiom Ser.: Vol. 10). 1970. pap. 5.50x (ISBN 0-416-17260-1, NO. 2081). Routledge Chapman & Hall.

Romance. Rosetta Brooks et al. Ed. by Henry Barendse et al. LC 87-81971. 35p. (Orig.). 1987. 7.50 (ISBN 0-915427-07-9). Knight Gallery-Spirit.

Romance. Joseph Conrad & Ford Madox Ford. 558p. 1985. pap. 8.95 (ISBN 0-88184-166-8). Carroll & Graf.

Romance. Gwen Davis. 288p. 1984. pap. 3.50 (ISBN 0-8217-1406-6). Zebra.

Romance. William P. Ker. 1909. lib. bdg. 17.00 (ISBN 0-8414-5566-X). Folcroft.

Romance. John Reason. 1982. 15.00x (ISBN 0-906660-41-6, Pub. by New Playwrights Network). State Mutual Bk.

Romance. Robert Waller. (Illus.). 1985. 2.50 (ISBN 0-943164-09-5). Geronima.

Romance. Bruce Weigl. LC 78-23603. (Pitt Poetry Ser.). 1979. 16.95x (ISBN 0-8229-3393-4); pap. 8.95 (ISBN 0-8229-5303-X). U of Pittsburgh Pr.

Romance al Divin Martir, Juda Creyente Don Lope de Vera y Alarcon Martirizado en Valladolid por la Inquisicion. Antonio E. Gomez. Ed. & tr. by Timothy Oelman. LC 83-49348. (Illus.). 216p. 1986. 33.50x (ISBN 0-8386-3219-X). Fairleigh Dickinson.

Romance & Capitalism at the Movies. Joan J. Hall. LC 84-72767. 1985. 14.95 (ISBN 0-914086-54-5); pap. 7.95 (ISBN 0-914086-55-3). Alicejamesbooks.

Romance & Humanity of Charles Dickens. J. B. Simons. LC 77-4684. Repr. of 1956 ed. lib. bdg. 20.00 (ISBN 0-8414-7653-5). Folcroft.

Romance & Legend of Chivalry. Ascott R. Hope-Moncrieff. LC 77-91529. 1977. Repr. of 1913 ed. lib. bdg. 50.00 (ISBN 0-89341-318-6). Longwood Pub Group.

Romance & Legend of Chivalry see Romance of Chivalry.

Romance & Legends of Chivalry. A. R. Hope-Moncrieff. 1979. Repr. lib. bdg. 35.00 (ISBN 0-8495-2343-5). Arden Lib.

Romance & Love Divination-Business & Financial Divination. D. A. Shanelec. (Illus.). 130p. 1987. 9.95 (ISBN 0-914833-02-2). Kapala Pr.

Romance & Psychological Realism in William Godwin's Novels. Dean T. Hughes. Ed. by Devendra P. Varma. LC 79-8459. (Gothic Studies & Dissertations Ser.). 1980. lib. bdg. 20.00x (ISBN 0-405-12673-5). Ayer Co Pubs.

Romance & Realism: A Study in English Bourgeois Literature. Christopher Caudwell & C. St. John Sprigg. LC 78-120752. 1970. 22.00x (ISBN 0-691-06195-5). Princeton U Pr.

Romance & Rise of the American Tropics. Samuel Crowther. Ed. by Stuart Bruchey & Eleanor Bruchey. LC 76-4999. (American Business Abroad Ser.). (Illus.). 1976. Repr. of 1929 ed. lib. bdg. 43.00 (ISBN 0-405-09268-7). Ayer Co Pubs.

Romance & the Erotics of Property: Mass Market Fiction for Women. Jan Cohn. LC 87-27401. vii, 181p. 1988. lib. bdg. 27.95 (ISBN 0-8223-0799-5). Duke.

Romance & Tragedy: A Study of the Classic & Romantic Elements in the Great Tragedies of European Literature. Prosser H. Frye. LC 61-10518. (Landmark Ed.). xiv, 372p. 1980. 28.95x (ISBN 0-8032-1955-5). U of Nebr Pr.

Romance & Tragedy of Banking: Problems & Incidents of Government Supervision of National Banks. Thomas P. Kane. Ed. by Stuart Bruchey. Vincent Corosso. LC 80-1153. (Rise of Commercial Banking Ser.). (Illus.). 1981. Repr. of 1923 ed. lib. bdg. 50.00x (ISBN 0-405-13659-5). Ayer Co Pubs.

Romance at Redhaven. Kathleen Yapp. (Chime Romance Ser.: No. 101). 1980. pap. 2.50 (ISBN 0-89191-292-4). Cook.

Romance! Can You Survive It? A Guide to Sticky Dating Situations. Meg Schneider. 160p. (Orig.). (gr. 7-12). 1984. pap. 2.25 (ISBN 0-440-97478-X, LFL). Dell.

Romance Comparative & Historical Linguistics. Ed. by Rebecca Posner. John N. Green. (Trends in Linguistics Studies & Monographs: No. 12). 386p. 1980. 59.20 (ISBN 90-279-7886-7). Mouton.

Romance Cycle of Charlemagne & His Peers. Jessie L. Weston. LC 77-139173. (Popular Studies in Mythology, Romance & Folklore: No. 10). Repr. of 1905 ed. 5.50 (ISBN 0-404-53510-0). AMS Pr.

Romance Cycle of Charlemagne & His Peers. Jessie L. Weston. 1977. lib. bdg. 59.95 (ISBN 0-8490-2534-6). Gordon Pr.

Romance d'Automne. Jocelyn Haley. (Harlequin Seduction Ser.). 332p. 1983. pap. 3.25 (ISBN 0-373-45025-7). Harlequin Bks.

Romance De Carnaval. Maria J. Santiago. (Romance Real Ser.). 192p. 1981. pap. 1.50 (ISBN 0-88025-000-3). Roca Pub.

Romance de la Guardia Civil Espanola (Ballad of the Spanish Civil Guard) Federico Garcia Lorca. Tr. by A. L. Lloyd. (Illus., Span. & Eng.). 1962. 35.00 (ISBN 0-317-61299-9). Dufour.

Romance Emporium: Hundreds of Things to Buy & Do to Help Keep Love Alive. Judy Kennedy & Judy Babcock. 336p. (Orig.). 1986. pap. 8.95 (ISBN 0-8362-2903-7). Andrews & McMeel.

Romance Epic: Essays on a Medieval Literary Genre. Ed. by Hans-Erich Keller. (Studies in Medieval Culture: No. 24). 1987. price not set (ISBN 0-918720-85-0); pap. price not set (ISBN 0-918720-86-9). Medieval Inst.

Romance Factor. Alan L. McGinnis. LC 81-47839. 224p. 1982. 11.45 (ISBN 0-06-065360-4, HarpR). Har-Row.

Romance Factor. Alan L. McGinnis. LC 81-47838. 224p. 1983. pap. 7.95 (ISBN 0-06-065361-2, CN 4077, HarpR). Har-Row.

Romance: Generic Transformation from Chretien de Troyes to Cervantes. Ed. by Kevin Brownlee & Marina S. Brownlee. LC 84-40581. 303p. 1985. 35.00x (ISBN 0-87451-338-3). U Pr of New Eng.

Romance in G Minor. Bess S. Aldrich. 20.95 (ISBN 0-8488-0066-4, Pub. by Amereon Hse). Amereon Ltd.

Romance in Poetry. John M. Switzer. 48p. 1988. 6.95 (ISBN 0-8062-3223-4). Carlton.

Romance in the Making: Chretien de Troyes & the Earliest French. Foster E. Guyer. 1954. 7.00x (ISBN 0-913298-35-2). S F Vanni.

Romance in the Roaring Forties & Other Stories. Damon Runyon. LC 85-15788. 324p. (Orig.). 1986. 19.95 (ISBN 0-688-05421-8, Pub. by Beech Tree Bks). Morrow.

Romance in the Roaring Forties & Other Stories. Damon Runyon. LC 85-15788. 324p. (Orig.). 1986. pap. 9.95 (ISBN 0-688-06148-6, Quill). Morrow.

Romance Is a Riot. Joan Winslow. LC 83-47993. (Lippincott Page-Turner Ser.). 160p. (YA) (gr. 7 up). 1983. 11.25i (ISBN 0-397-32063-9, Lipp Jr Bks); PLB 11.89 (ISBN 0-397-32064-7). HarpJ.

Romance Is a Wonderful Thing. Ellen E. White. 208p. 1983. pap. 2.50 (ISBN 0-380-83907-5, Flare). Avon.

Romance Kharjas in Andalusian Arabic Muwassah Poetry: A Palaeographic Analysis. Alan Jones. (Oxford Oriental Monographs: No. 9). 180p. 1988. text ed. 39.95 (ISBN 0-86372-085-4, Pub. by Ithaca Pr). Humanities.

Romance, Language & Education in Jane Austen's Novels. Laura G. Mooneyham. LC 87-16126. 216p. 1987. 35.00 (ISBN 0-312-01191-1). St Martin.

Romance Languages. Ed. by Martin Harris & Nigel Vincent. (Illus.). 512p. 1988. 59.00 (ISBN 0-19-520628-2). Oxford U Pr.

Romance Languages: A Linguistic Introduction. R. Posner. 15.25 (ISBN 0-8446-0853-X). Peter Smith.

Romance Linguistics & the Romance Languages: A Bibliography of Bibliographies. Kathryn F. Bach & Glanville Price. (Research Bibliographies & Checklists Ser.: No. 22). 194p. (Orig.). 1977. pap. 14.95 (ISBN 0-7293-0055-2, Pub. by Grant & Cutler). Longwood Pub Group.

Romance Literatures, 2 Vols. Ed. by George B. Parks & Ruth Z. Temple. LC 70-98341. (Literatures of the World in English Translation: Vol. 3). 1970. Set. 110.00x (ISBN 0-8044-3239-2). Ungar.

Romance of a Great Singer: Memoir of Mario. Cecilia M. Pearse & Frank Hird. Ed. by Andrew Farkas. LC 76-29961. (Opera Biographies). (Illus.). 1977. Repr. of 1910 ed. lib. bdg. 25.50x (ISBN 0-405-09701-8). Ayer Co Pubs.

Romance of Alexander the Great. Tr. by Albert M. Wolohojian from Armenian. LC 74-84593. (Records of Civilization Ser: No. 82). 1969. 28.00x (ISBN 0-231-03297-8). Columbia U Pr.

Romance of an Eastern Capital. Birt Bradley. (Illus.). 360p. 1986. Repr. 26.00X (ISBN 0-8364-1751-8, Pub. by Chanakya India). South Asia Bks.

Romance of an Empress: Catherine Second of Russia. K. Waliszewski. viii, 458p. 1969. Repr. of 1894 ed. 40.00 (ISBN 0-208-00395-9, Archon). Shoe String.

Romance of Arthur: An Anthology. Ed. by James J. Wilhelm & Laila Z. Gross. LC 83-48252. 322p. 1983. lib. bdg. 43.00 (ISBN 0-8240-9098-5); pap. 15.00 (ISBN 0-8240-9099-3). Garland Pub.

Romance of Arthur II. James J. Wilhelm. LC 86-19486. (Reference Library of the Humanities: Vol.696). 278p. 1986. 15.00 (ISBN 0-8240-8516-7); lib. bdg. 45.00 (ISBN 0-8240-8936-7). Garland Pub.

Romance of Astoria - Extracts. facs. ed. T. T. Geer. (Shorey Historical Ser.). 8p. pap. 1.95 (ISBN 0-8466-0169-9, S169). Shorey.

Romance of Astronomy: The Music of the Spheres. Florence A. Grondal. 1937. 25.00 (ISBN 0-686-17424-0). Ridgeway Bks.

Romance of Atlantis. Taylor Caldwell & Jess Stearn. 272p. 1980. pap. 2.95 (ISBN 0-449-23787-7, Crest). Fawcett.

Romance of Balboa Park. 4th ed. Florence Christman. (Illus.). 136p. 1985. pap. 9.50 (ISBN 0-918740-03-7). San Diego Hist.

Romance of Blonde of Oxford & Jehan of Dammartin. Philippe De Remi. Ed. by M. Le-Roux De Lincy. (Camden Society, London. Publications, First Ser.: No. 72). Repr. of 1858 ed. 28.00 (ISBN 0-404-50172-9). AMS Pr.

Romance of Blonde of Oxford & Jehan of Danmartin. Philippe De Remi & De Beaumanoir. Repr. of 1858 ed. 28.00 (ISBN 0-384-46270-7). Johnson Repr.

Romance of Book Collecting. J. Slater. 1976. lib. bdg. 59.95 (ISBN 0-8490-2535-4). Gordon Pr.

Romance of Caerbhall & Fearbhlaidh. James E. Doan. 1984. 16.95 (Pub. by Colin Smythe Ltd Britain). Dufour.

Romance of Chivalry. A. R. Moncrieff. LC 80-23872. (Newcastle Mythology Library: Vol. 2). 439p. 1980. Repr. of 1976 ed. lib. bdg. 19.95x (ISBN 0-89370-638-8). Borgo Pr.

Romance of Chivalry. A. R. Moncrieff. (Newcastle Mythology Library: Vol. 2). Orig. Title: Romance & Legend of Chivalry. (Illus.). 439p. 1976. pap. 5.95 (ISBN 0-87877-038-0, M-38). Newcastle Pub.

Romance of Commerce & Culture: Capitalism, Modernism & the Chicago-Aspen Crusade for Cultural Reform. James S. Allen. LC 83-4816. xvi, 336p. 1986. lib. bdg. 27.50x (ISBN 0-226-01458-4); pap. 13.95 (ISBN 0-226-01459-2). U of Chicago Pr.

Romance of Dollard. facs. ed. Mary Catherwood. LC 75-137725. (American Fiction Reprint Ser). 1889. 18.00 (ISBN 0-8369-7024-1). Ayer Co Pubs.

Romance of Education. Robert Welch. LC 73-162083. (Americanist Classics Ser). 1973. 7.00 (ISBN 0-88279-225-3). Western Islands.

Romance of Emare. Ed. by Edith Rickert. (EETS ES Ser.: Vol. 99). Repr. of 1906 ed. 32.00 (ISBN 0-8115-3407-3). Kraus Repr.

Romance of Essex Inns. Glyn Morgan. 1985. 25.00x (ISBN 0-86025-872-6, Pub. by Ian Henry Pubns Englan d). State Mutual Bk.

Romance of Essex Inns. Glyn Morgan. 1988. 30.00x (Pub. by Ian Henry Pubns England). State Mutual Bk.

Romance of Failure: The First-Person Fictions of Poe, Hawthorne, & James. Jonathan Auerbach. 224p. 1988. 29.95 (ISBN 0-19-505721-X). Oxford U Pr.

Romance of Fire. Paul Hutchens. 1969. 2.95 (ISBN 0-87148-734-9). Pathway Pr.

Romance of Forgotten Men. facs. ed. John T. Faris. LC 68-58787. (Essay Index Reprint Ser). 1928. 23.75 (ISBN 0-8369-1033-8). Ayer Co Pubs.

Romance of Golden Star. George Griffith. Ed. by R. Reginald & Douglas Melville. LC 77-84234. (Lost Race & Adult Fantasy Ser.). (Illus.). 1978. Repr. of 1897 ed. lib. bdg. 24.50x (ISBN 0-405-10982-2). Ayer Co Pubs.

Romance of Greeting Cards: An Historical Account of the Origin, Evolution, & Development. Ernest D. Chase. LC 76-159914. (Tower Bks.). (Illus.). 278p. 1971. Repr. of 1926 ed. 54.00x (ISBN 0-8103-3903-X). Gale.

Romance of His Life, & Other Romances. facsimile ed. Mary Cholmondeley. LC 70-37540. (Short Story Index Reprint Ser.). Repr. of 1921 ed. 17.00 (ISBN 0-8369-4099-7). Ayer Co Pubs.

Romance of History. Herbert G. Smith. LC 72-5733. (Essay Index Reprint Ser.). Repr. of 1891 ed. 21.00 (ISBN 0-8369-7285-6). Ayer Co Pubs.

Romance of History: Spain. Don T. De Trueba. 1979. Repr. lib. bdg. 30.00 (ISBN 0-8495-1049-X). Arden Lib.

Romance of Indian Life. facsimile ed. Mary Eastman. LC 77-104445. (Illus.). 298p. Repr. of 1852 ed. lib. bdg. 29.00 (ISBN 0-8398-0451-2). Irvington.

Romance of Indian Life. Mary Eastman. (Illus.). 298p. 1986. pap. text ed. 8.95x (ISBN 0-8290-1927-8). Irvington.

Romance of Interpretation: Visionary Criticism from Pater to de Man. Daniel T. O'Hara. LC 85-477. 256p. 1985. 27.50x (ISBN 0-231-06068-8). Columbia U Pr.

Romance of Isabel Lady Burton: The Story of Her Life, 2 vols. W. H. Wilkins. 1979. Repr. of 1897 ed. Set. lib. bdg. 100.00 (ISBN 0-8492-2961-8). R West.

Romance of Language. A. Chaplin. 1920. 12.50 (ISBN 0-8274-3302-6). R West.

Romance of Life in the Ancient World. F. A. Wright. 35.00 (ISBN 0-8274-3990-3). R West.

Romance of London. John Timbs. LC 68-22058. 1004p. 1968. Repr. of 1865 ed. 70.00x (ISBN 0-8103-3498-4). Gale.

Romance of London: Historic Sketches, Remarkable Duels, Notorious Highwaymen, Rogueries, Crimes, & Punishments, & Love & Marriage. John Timbs. 509p. 1982. Repr. lib. bdg. 50.00 (ISBN 0-89984-469-3). Century Bookbindery.

Romance of London's Underground. W. J. Passingham. LC 72-80705. (Illus.). Repr. of 1932 ed. 33.00 (ISBN 0-405-08839-6). Ayer Co Pubs.

Romance of Lust, Bk. 1. 1988. pap. 3.95 (ISBN 0-8216-5006-8). Blue Moon Bks.

Romance of Lust, Bk. 2. 1988. pap. 3.95 (ISBN 0-8216-5014-9). Blue Moon Bks.

Romance of Lust, or Early Experiences. LC 78-73427. 1979. pap. 4.95 (ISBN 0-394-17540-9, B424, BC). Grove.

Romance of Mary W. Shelley, John Howard Payne & Washington Irving. Howard Harper. LC 72-7323. 1973. lib. bdg. 30.00 (ISBN 0-8414-0324-4). Folcroft.

Romance of Money. Duane R. Pappas. (Library of Business Psychology). (Illus.). 119p. 1983. 57.15x (ISBN 0-86722-024-4). Inst Econ Pol.

Romance of Mount Desert. A. A. Hayes. 306p. 1985. pap. 8.95 (ISBN 0-934745-01-3). Acadia Pub Co.

Romance of Navigation. W. B. Whall. LC 72-83272. (Illus.). Repr. of 1930 ed. 22.00 (ISBN 0-405-09061-7). Ayer Co Pubs.

Romance of Perfume. F. S. Clifford. 1977. lib. bdg. 59.95 (ISBN 0-8490-2536-2). Gordon Pr.

Romance of Proctology. Charles E. Blanchard. LC 75-23684. Repr. of 1938 ed. 29.50 (ISBN 0-404-13237-5). AMS Pr.

Romance of Publishing: An Agent Recalls Thirty-Three Years with Authors & Editors. Alex Jackinson. LC 85-41059. 232p. 1987. 16.95 (ISBN 0-8453-4797-7, Cornwall Bks). Assoc Univ Prs.

Romance of Sorcery. Sax Rohmer. 1976. Repr. of 1914 ed. lib. bdg. 19.95 (ISBN 0-89190-808-0, Pub. by River City Pr). Amereon Ltd.

Romance of Steel: Story of a Thousand Millionaires. facsimile ed. Herbert N. Casson. LC 72-179510. (Select Bibliographies Reprint Ser). Repr. of 1907 ed. 37.50 (ISBN 0-8369-6639-2). Ayer Co Pubs.

Romance of Symbolism & Its Relation to Church Ornament & Architecture. Sidney Heath. LC 70-174054. (Illus.). 282p. 1976. Repr. of 1909 ed. 40.00x (ISBN 0-8103-4302-9). Gale.

Romance of the American Theatre. Mary C. Crawford. LC 70-144957. 1971. Repr. of 1940 ed. 59.00x (ISBN 0-403-00909-X). Scholarly.

Romance of the Buyer. Paul Breslow. 180p. Date not set. 11.95 (ISBN 0-8180-0637-4). Horizon.

Romance of the Castle. Raoul J. Fajardo. 156p. (Orig.). 1986. pap. 15.00 (ISBN 0-940774-02-X). Pulsante Assn News.

Romance of the Chevelere Assigne. Beatrix Chanson Degeste. Ed. by Lord Aldenham. (EETS, ES Ser.: No. 6). pap. 20.00 (ISBN 0-527-00221-6). Kraus Repr.

Romance of the Commonplace. facs. ed. Gelett Burgess. LC 68-57308. (Essay Index Reprint Ser). 1916. 19.00 (ISBN 0-8369-0103-7). Ayer Co Pubs.

Romance of the English Bible. Laura H. Wild. 1929. 25.00 (ISBN 0-8274-3303-4). R West.

Romance of the English Stage, 2 vols. Percy Fitzgerald. LC 72-6956. (Essay Index Reprint Ser). 1972. Repr. of 1874 ed. 36.00 (ISBN 0-8369-7256-2). Ayer Co Pubs.

Romance of the Episcopal Church in West Tennessee. Ellen Davies-Rodgers. 12.00 (ISBN 0-685-84991-0). Plantation.

Romance of the Floridas. Michael Kenny. LC 70-120573. (Illus.). Repr. of 1934 ed. 15.00 (ISBN 0-404-03656-2). AMS Pr.

Romance of the Floridas: The Finding & the Founding. Michael Kenny. 1971. Repr. of 1934 ed. 13.00x (ISBN 0-403-00767-4). Scholarly.

Romance of the Forest. Ann Radcliffe. Ed. & intro. by Chloe Chard. (World's Classics Ser.). 427p. 1986. pap. 6.95 (ISBN 0-19-281712-4). Oxford U Pr.

Romance of the Forest, 3 Vols. 4th ed. Ann W. Radcliffe. LC 76-135896. 1971. Repr. of 1794 ed. Set. 90.00 (ISBN 0-384-49430-7). Johnson Repr.

Romance of the Forest: Interspersed with Some Pieces of Poetry, 3 vols, Vol. 2. Ann Radcliffe. LC 73-22770. 794p. 1974. Repr. of 1791 ed. Set. 86.00x (ISBN 0-405-06020-3). Ayer Co Pubs.

Romance of the Fungus World. R. T. Rolfe & F. W. Rolfe. (Illus.). Repr. of 1925 ed. 25.00 (ISBN 0-384-51830-3). Johnson Repr.

Romance of the Fungus World: An Account of Fungus Life in Its Numerous Guises, Both Real & Legendary. R. T. Rolfe & F. W. Rolfe. LC 74-81401. (Illus.). 352p. 1974. pap. 6.95 (ISBN 0-486-23105-4). Dover.

Romance of the Hebrew Language. William H. Saulez. 1979. Repr. of 1913 ed. lib. bdg. 35.50 (ISBN 0-8414-8013-3). Folcroft.

Romance of the Lace Pillow. Thomas Wright. 1984. 21.95 (ISBN 0-903585-12-X). Robin & Russ.

Romance of the Law Merchant: Being an Introduction to the Study of International & Commercial Law with Some Account of the Commerce & Fairs of the Middle Ages. Wyndham A. Bewes. (Legal Reprint Ser.). ix, 148p. 1986. Repr. of 1923 ed. lib. bdg. 22.50x (ISBN 0-8377-1940-2). Rothman.

Romance of the Milky Way & Other Studies & Stories. facs. ed. Lafcadio Hearn. LC 77-75779. (Short Story Index Reprint Ser.). 1905. 12.00 (ISBN 0-8369-3004-5). Ayer Co Pubs.

Romance of the Milky Way & Other Studies & Stories. Lafcadio Hearn. LC 73-184818. 1972. pap. 4.95 (ISBN 0-8048-1040-0). C E Tuttle.

Romance of the National Parks. Harlean James. LC 72-2847. (Use & Abuse of America's Natural Resources Ser). (Illus.). 258p. 1972. Repr. of 1939 ed. 24.50 (ISBN 0-405-04513-1). Ayer Co Pubs.

Romance of the Piano. Eric Blom. LC 69-15608. (Music Ser). (Illus.). 1969. Repr. of 1928 ed. 32.50 (ISBN 0-306-71060-9). Da Capo.

Romance of the Portuguese in Abyssinia. Charles F. Rey. LC 77-98729. Repr. of 1929 ed. cancelled (ISBN 0-8371-2787-4). Greenwood.

Romance of the Rails, 2 vols. facsimile ed. Agnes C. Laut. LC 75-37891. (Select Bibliographies Reprint Ser). Repr. of 1929 ed. Set. 44.00 (ISBN 0-8369-6728-3). Ayer Co Pubs.

Romance of the Republic. facs. ed. Lydia M. Child. LC 76-83926. (Black Heritage Library Collection Ser). 1867. 18.00 (ISBN 0-8369-8540-0). Ayer Co Pubs.

Romance of the River Plate, 2 vols. W. H. Koebel. (Latin America Ser.). 1979. Set. lib. bdg. 200.00 (ISBN 0-8490-3002-1). Gordon Pr.

Romance of the Rose. Heather Arden. (World Authors Ser.). 144p. 1987. 21.95 (ISBN 0-8057-6645-6, Twayne). G K Hall.

Romance of the Rose. Guillaume De Lorris & Jean De Meun. Tr. by Harry W. Robbins. 1962. pap. 13.95 (ISBN 0-525-48395-0). Dutton.

Romance of the Rose. Guillaume De Lorris & Jean De Meun. Tr. by Charles Dahlberg from Fr. LC 83-40017. Orig. Title: Roman de la Rose. (Illus.). 468p. 1983. pap. 16.00x (ISBN 0-87451-267-0). U Pr of New Eng.

Romance of the Rose, 3 Vols. Guillaume de Lorris & J. Clopinel. Tr. by Frederick S. Ellis. LC 74-154119. Repr. of 1928 ed. Set. 75.00 (ISBN 0-404-09640-9). AMS Pr.

Romance of the Rothschilds. Ignatius Balla. 1981. lib. bdg. 75.00 (ISBN 0-87700-280-0). Revisionist Pr.

Romance of the Three Kingdoms, 2 Vols. Kuan-Chung Lo. Tr. by C. H. Brewitt-Taylor. LC 59-10407. 1969. Set. boxed 37.50 (ISBN 0-8048-0726-4). C E Tuttle.

Romance of the Three Kingdoms, 2 vols. 2nd ed. Luo Guan Zhong. Tr. by C. H. Brewitt-Taylor from Chinese. 623p. 1985. Repr. of 1925 ed. 25.00 (ISBN 9971-947-95-1, Pub. by Graham Brash Singapore); 40.00 set (ISBN 0-317-52352-X). Three Continents.

Romance of the Western Frontier. Fletcher M. Green. LC 77-16305. 1977. Repr. of 1932 ed. lib. bdg. 17.00 (ISBN 0-8414-4609-1). Folcroft.

Romance of Trade: A Commercial & Economic Survey. A. W. Kirkaldy. 1977. 59.95 (ISBN 0-8490-2537-0). Gordon Pr.

Romance of Tristan. Beroul. Tr. by Alan S. Fredrik. (Classics Ser.). 1978. pap. 4.95 (ISBN 0-14-044230-8). Penguin.

Romance of Tristan & Iseult. Joseph Bedier. 1965. pap. 2.95 (ISBN 0-394-70271-9, Vin, V271). Random.

Romance of Tristan & Isolt. Tr. by Norman B. Spector. (Medieval French Texts Ser.). 91p. 1973. text ed. 19.95 (ISBN 0-8101-0405-9). Northwestern U Pr.

Romance of Tristan & Isolt. Tr. by Norman B. Spector from Fr. 91p. 1987. pap. 9.95 (ISBN 0-8101-0767-8). Northwestern U Pr.

Romance of Tristram & Ysolt. Thomas of Britain. Tr. by Roger S. Loomis. LC 81-19029. xxxiii, 293p. 1982. Repr. of 1951 ed. lib. bdg. 29.00 (ISBN 0-374-95097-0, Octagon). Hippocrene Bks.

Romance of Tristram & Ysolt. Thomas of Britain. Tr. by Roger S. Loomis. 294p. 1983. Repr. of 1923 ed. lib. bdg. 50.00 (ISBN 0-8495-3413-5). Arden Lib.

Romance of Two Worlds. Marie Corelli. (Illus.). pap. 5.95 (ISBN 0-910122-03-2). Amherst Pr.

Romance of Two Worlds. Marie Corelli. Ed. by Robert L. Wolff. LC 75-484. (Victorian Fiction Ser.). 1975. Repr. of 1886 ed. lib. bdg. 73.00 (ISBN 0-8240-1561-4). Garland Pub.

Romance of Two Worlds. 3rd ed. Marie Corelli. LC 85-80918. (Spiritual Fiction Ser.). 320p. 1986. pap. 12.00 (ISBN 0-8334-0018-5, Freedeeds Bks). Garber Comm.

Romance of Two Worlds. Marie Corelli. 15.95 (ISBN 0-87505-333-5). Borden.

Romance of Victorian Natural History. Lynn L. Merrill. (Illus.). 320p. 1988. 29.95 (ISBN 0-19-505203-X). Oxford U Pr.

Romance of War; or the Highlanders in Spain, 4 vols. in 2. James Grant. LC 79-8276. Repr. Set. 84.50 (ISBN 0-404-61887-1). AMS Pr.

Romance of William Morris. Carole Silver. LC 82-2278. xviii, 233p. 1983. text ed. 22.95x; 12.95 (ISBN 0-8214-0706-6). Ohio U Pr.

Romance of William of Palerne. Guillaume De Palerne. Ed. by W. W. Skeat. (EETS, ES Ser.: No. 1). Repr. of 1867 ed. 35.00 (ISBN 0-527-00211-9). Kraus Repr.

Romance of Wisconsin Place. rev. ed. Robert Gard & L. G. Sorden. LC 68-29817. 201p. 1979. pap. 4.95 (ISBN 0-686-28112-8). Milwaukee Sentinel.

Romance of Woman's Influence: (Dorothy Wordsworth) Alice Corkran. 377p. 1981. Repr. of 1906 ed. lib. bdg. 50.00. Darby Bks.

Romance of World Trade. Alfred P. Dennis. 1977. lib. bdg. 59.95 (ISBN 0-8490-2538-9). Gordon Pr.

Romance of Yder. Ed. & tr. by Alison Adams. (Arthurian Studies: No. VIII). 259p. 1983. 45.00 (ISBN 0-85991-133-0, Pub. by Boydell & Brewer). Longwood Pub Group.

Romance on Trial. Betty Cavanna. LC 84-10415. 96p. (gr. 6-9). 1984. 10.95 (ISBN 0-664-32715-X). Westminster John Knox.

Romance Rekindled: The Art of Loving Your Spouse. Rick Bundschuh & Dave Gilbert. LC 87-82790. 160p. (Orig.). 1988. pap. 4.95 (ISBN 0-89081-650-6). Harvest Hse.

Romance Revolution: Erotic Novels for Women & the Quest for a New Sexual Identity. Carol Thurston. LC 86-30759. (Illus.). 272p. 1987. 27.95 (ISBN 0-252-01247-X); pap. 9.95 (ISBN 0-252-01442-1). U of Ill Pr.

Romance, Romance & the Bride. Rarrukh Dhondy. 90p. (Orig.). 1985. pap. 8.95 (ISBN 0-571-13548-X). Faber & Faber.

Romance Thing. Anne Waldman. LC 86-73203. 80p. (Orig.). 1987. Signed Ltd. ed. pap. 25.00x (ISBN 0-917453-12-3); pap. 8.50 (ISBN 0-917453-11-5). Bamberger.

Romance Treasury, 3 bks, Vol. 140. Date not set. Set. pap. 7.95 (ISBN 0-317-63793-2). The Sleeping Fire by Daphne Clair. Tiger Sky by Rose Elver. Shadow of an Eagle by Sue Peters. Harlequin Bks.

Romance Treasury, 3 bks, Vol. 141. Date not set. Set. pap. 7.95 (ISBN 0-317-63794-0). Island of Escape by Dorothy Cork. Stormy Affair by Margaret Mayo. Hostile Engagement by Jessica Steele. Harlequin Bks.

Romance Treasury, 3 bks, Vol. 142. Date not set. Set. pap. 7.95 (ISBN 0-317-63795-9). Sea Lightning by Linda Harrel. White Hibiscus by Rosemary Pollock. Liberated Lady by Sally Wentworth. Harlequin Bks.

Romance Treasury, 3 bks, Vol. 143. Date not set. Set. pap. 7.95 (ISBN 0-317-63797-5). The Spanish Uncle by Jane Corrie. Sweet Not Always by Karen Van der Zee. Wife to Charles by Sophie Weston. Harlequin Bks.

Romance Treasury, 3 bks, Vol. 144. Date not set. Set. pap. 7.95 (ISBN 0-317-63800-9). Heart of the Scorpion by Janice Gray. The Winds of Heaven by Margaret Way. Sweet Compulsion by Victoria Woolf. Harlequin Bks.

Romance Treasury, 3 bks, Vol. 145. Date not set. Set. pap. 7.95 (ISBN 0-317-63802-5). Yours with Love by Mary Burchell. Man in the Shadows by Rosemary Carter. The Everywhere Man by Victoria Gordon. Harlequin Bks.

Romance Treasury, 3 bks, Vol. 146. Date not set. Set. pap. 7.95 (ISBN 0-317-63805-X). Night of No Moon by Margaret Chapman. The Black Hunter by Jane Donnelly. Return to Silver Creek by Elizabeth Graham. Harlequin Bks.

Romance Writer's Phrase Book. Jean Kent et al. LC 83-22947. 156p. 1984. pap. 7.95 (ISBN 0-399-51002-8, Perigee); pap. 69.50 sets of 10 (ISBN 0-399-51047-8). Putnam Pub Group.

Romanceiro: choix de vieux chants portugais. T. J. Boudet De Puymaigre. LC 78-20109. (Collection de contes et de chansons populaires: No. 2). Repr. of 1881 ed. 21.50 (ISBN 0-404-60352-1). AMS Pr.

Romancero de la Conquista. Ester M. Feliciano. (Coleccion Ninos y Letras). (Illus.). 1986. 8.00 (ISBN 0-8477-3533-8). U of PR Pr.

Romancero General. (Span). 1904. 48.00 (ISBN 0-527-76500-7). Kraus Repr.

Romancero Gitano. Federico Garcia Lorca. Intro. by & notes by H. Ramsden. LC 87-38262. (Spanish Texts Ser.). 160p. 1988. 11.00 (ISBN 0-7190-1724-6, Pub. by Manchester Univ Pr). St Martin.

Romancero scandinave. L. Pineau. LC 78-20140. (Collection de contes et de chansons populaires: Vol. 30). Repr. of 1905 ed. 21.50 (ISBN 0-404-60380-7). AMS Pr.

Romances & Ballads of Ireland. Hercules Ellis. 1980. lib. bdg. 79.95 (ISBN 0-8490-3172-9). Gordon Pr.

Romances & Epics of the Northern Ancestors: Norse, Celt & Teuton. W. Wagner. 1977. lib. bdg. 59.95 (ISBN 0-8490-2539-7). Gordon Pr.

Romances & Narratives, 16 Vols. Daniel Defoe. Ed. by George Aitken. (Illus.). Repr. of 1895 ed. Set. 520.00 (ISBN 0-404-07910-5); 32.50 ea. AMS Pr.

Romances of Blanche La Mare. LC 85-80714. (Classics of the Victorian Imagination Ser.). 180p. 1985. pap. 6.95 (ISBN 0-394-62093-3, Ever). Grove.

Romances of Chivalry Told & Illustrated in Facsimile. John Ashton. LC 78-63486. Repr. of 1887 ed. AMS Pr.

Romances of Chretien de Troyes: A Symposium. Ed. by Douglas Kelly. LC 85-70103. (Edward C. Armstrong Monographs on Medieval Literature: No. 3). 353p. (Orig.). 1985. pap. 24.95x (ISBN 0-917058-59-3). French Forum.

Romances of Colonial Days. Geraldine Brooks. 1978. Repr. of 1903 ed. lib. bdg. 25.00 (ISBN 0-8495-0336-1). Arden Lib.

Romances of John Fowles. Simon Loveday. LC 84-13396. 174p. 1985. 25.00 (ISBN 0-312-69107-6). St Martin.

Romances of Old France. facs. ed. Richard Le Gallienne. LC 75-81271. (Short Story Index Reprint Ser.). 1905. 18.00 (ISBN 0-8369-3023-1). Ayer Co Pubs.

Romances of Roguery: An Episode in the History of the Novel. Frank W. Chandler. 1961. Repr. of 1899 ed. 29.00 (ISBN 0-8337-0527-X). B Franklin.

Romances of Roguery: The Picaresque Novel in Spain. F. W. Chandler. 1977. lib. bdg. 59.95 (ISBN 0-8490-2540-0). Gordon Pr.

Romances of the East. Conte D. Gobineau. LC 73-6282. (Middle East Ser.). Repr. of 1878 ed. 24.50 (ISBN 0-405-05340-1). Ayer Co Pubs.

Romances of William Morris. Amanda Hodgson. 221p. 1987. 29.95 (ISBN 0-521-32075-5). Cambridge U Pr.

Romances sans Paroles. Paul Verlaine. Ed. by D. Hillery. (French Poets Ser.). 106p. (Fr.). 1976. 14.95 (ISBN 0-485-14712-2, Pub. by Athlone Pr UK). Humanities.

Romances Tradicionales de Castilla y Leon. Joaquin Diaz & Luis D. Viana. (Spanish Ser: No. 7). 162p. 1981. 12.50x (ISBN 0-942260-22-8). Hispanic Seminary.

Romancier et Ses Personnages. Francois Mauriac. Bd. with Education des Filles. 6.50 (ISBN 0-685-34303-0). French & Eur.

Romanciers & Conteurs Du 19e Siecle. new ed. Ed. by Jean Sareil & Jacqueline Sareil. 429p. (gr. 12 up). 1974. pap. text ed. 6.75 (ISBN 0-88345-207-3, 18134). Prentice ESL.

Romanciers Du XVII Siecle: Sorel Scarron, Furetiere, Mme. de La Fayette. (Pleiade Ser.). 1512p. 39.95 (ISBN 0-686-56555-X). Schoenhof.

Romanciers Du XVIII Siecle: Les Egarements du Coeur et de l'Esprit, Les Amours du Chevalier de Faublas, etc, Vol. 2. (Pleiade Ser.). 2048p. 45.95 (ISBN 0-686-56557-6). Schoenhof.

Romanciers Du XVIII Siecle: Memoires du Comte de Gramont, Gil Blas de Santillane, Manon Lescaut, Etc, Vol. 1. (Pleiade Ser.). 1572p. 40.95 (ISBN 0-686-56556-8). Schoenhof.

Romancing Your Marriage. H. Norman Wright. 1987. pap. 7.95 (ISBN 0-8307-1212-7, 5419168). Regal.

Romane der Konservativen Revolution in der Nachfolge von Nietzsche und Spengler: 1918-1941. Hans-Georg Meier. (European University Studies: No. 1, Vol. 656). 309p. (Ger.). 1983. 41.05 (ISBN 3-8204-7670-9). P Lang Pubs.

Romanesque & Gothic: Essays for George Zarnecki. Ed. by Neil Stratford. 1987. 135.00 set (ISBN 0-85115-472-7, Pub. by Boydell & Brewer). Longwood Pub Group.

Romanesque Architecture. rev. ed. Hans E. Kubach. LC 87-43256. (History of World Architecture Ser.). (Illus.). 224p. 1988. pap. 25.00 (ISBN 0-8478-0920-X). Rizzoli Intl.

Romanesque Architecture of the Order of Cluny. Joan Evans. LC 75-136385. (Illus.). Repr. of 1938 ed. 46.00 (ISBN 0-404-02358-4). AMS Pr.

Romanesque Art in Poland. Zygmunt Swiechowski. 1983. 135.00x (ISBN 0-317-57340-3, Pub. by Collets UK). State Mutual Bk.

Romanesque Art: Selected Papers, Vol. 1. Meyer Schapiro. LC 76-11842. (Illus.). 448p. 1977. 30.00 (ISBN 0-8076-0853-X). Braziller.

Romanesque Bible Illumination. Walter Cahn. LC 82-71593. (Illus.). 308p. 1982. 95.00x (ISBN 0-8014-1446-6). Cornell U Pr.

Romanesque Church Facade in Britain. J. Phillip McAleer. LC 83-48699. (Theses from the Courtauld Institute of Art Ser.). (Illus.). 785p. 1984. lib. bdg. 80.00 (ISBN 0-8240-5979-4). Garland Pub.

Romanesque Illuminated Manuscripts in the British Museum, rev. ed. D. H. Turner. (Illus.). 48p. 1972. pap. 2.95 (ISBN 0-7141-0449-3, Pub. by British Lib). Longwood Pub Group.

Romanesque Sculpture from the Cathedral of Saint-Etienne, Toulouse. Linda Seidel. LC 76-23646. (Outstanding Dissertations in the Fine Arts). (Illus.). 1977. Repr. of 1965 ed. lib. bdg. 63.00 (ISBN 0-8240-2729-9). Garland Pub.

Romanesque Sculpture in American Collections, Vol. 1. Cahn. (Illus.). 1979. lib. bdg. 38.50x (ISBN 0-89102-131-0). B Franklin.

Romanesque Sculpture in Saintonge. Elizabeth L. Mendell. (Illus.). 1940. 100.00x (ISBN 0-685-89780-X). Elliots Bks.

Romanesque Sculpture: The Revival of Monumental Stone Sculpture in the Eleventh & Twelfth Centuries. M. F. Hearn. LC 80-14383. (Paperback Ser.). (Illus.). 240p. 1985. pap. 19.50x (ISBN 0-8014-9304-8). Cornell U Pr.

Romanesque Signs: Early Medieval Narrative & Iconography. Stephan G. Nichols, Jr. LC 82-7028. (Illus.). 264p. 1983. text ed. 32.00x (ISBN 0-300-02833-4); pap. 12.95x (ISBN 0-300-03677-9, Y-572). Yale U Pr.

Romanesque Wooden Doors of Auvergne. Walter Cahn. LC 74-15391. (College Art Association Monograph Ser.: Vol. 30). (Illus.). 225p. 1985. Repr. of 1974 ed. 30.00x (ISBN 0-271-00400-2). Pa St U Pr.

Romanesques. Edmond Rostand. 3.95 (ISBN 0-686-55337-3). French & Eur.

Romani Sociolinguistics. Ed. by Ian F. Hancock. (International Journal of the Sociology of Language Ser.: No. 19). 1979. pap. text ed. 19.00x (ISBN 90-279-7817-4). Mouton.

Romania. Andrea Deletant & Dennis Deletant. (World Bibliographical Ser.: No. 59). 236p. 1985. 38.00 (ISBN 1-85109-002-9, Pub. by Clio Pr England Ltd). ABC-Clio.

Romania. (Let's Visit Places & Peoples - - Nations, Dependencies, & Sovereignties of the World Ser.). (Illus.). (gr. 5 up). 1988. 12.95 (ISBN 0-222-01023-1). Chelsea Hse.

Romania see Business Opportunity Report Series.

Romania Between East & West. Ed. by Stephen Fischer-Galati & Radu R. Florescu. (East European Monographs: No. 103). 414p. 1982. 35.00x (ISBN 0-914710-97-4). East Eur Quarterly.

Romania: Forty Years: 1944-1984. Ed. by Vlad Georgescu. (The Washington Papers: Vol. XXIII, No. 115). 112p. 1985. 35.00 (ISBN 0-275-90213-7, C0213); pap. 9.95 (ISBN 0-275-91644-8, B1644). Praeger.

Romania Germanica: Sprach-und Siedlungsgeschichte der Germanen auf dem Boden des alten Roemerreiches. Ernst Gamillscheg. Incl. Vol. 1. Zu den aeltesten Beruehrungen zwischen Roemern und Germanen: Die Franken. rev. 2nd ed. (Illus.). xvi, 474p. 1970. 70.00x (ISBN 3-11-002680-5). (Ger.). De Gruyter.

Romania Historica et Romania Hodierna. Peter Wunderli & Wulf Muller. (Studia Romanica et Linguistica: Vol. 15). xi, 431p. (Ger.). 1982. 42.10 (ISBN 3-8204-5791-7). P Lang Pubs.

Romania: Politics, Economics & Society. Michael Shafir. Ed. by Bogdan Szajkowski. LC 84-62183. (Marxist Regimes Ser.). (Illus.). 232p. 1985. lib. bdg. 30.00x (ISBN 0-931477-02-6); pap. text ed. 11.95x (ISBN 0-931477-03-4). Lynne Rienner.

Romania si Romanii: Romania & the Romanians. Octavian Barlea. Tr. by George C. Muresan & Enea Motiu. (American Romanian Academy Ser.: Vol. I). (Illus.). 1977. 7.00 (ISBN 0-686-23262-3). Am Romanian.

Romania: The Industrialization of an Agrarian Economy under Socialist Planning. Andreas C. Tsantis & Roy Pepper. LC 79-84315. (World Bank Ser.). 744p. 1979. pap. 17.00x (ISBN 0-8018-2262-9). Johns Hopkins.

Romania: The Jewries of the Levant After the Fourth Crusade. Joshua Starr. 1943. 10.00x (ISBN 0-87068-108-7). Ktav.

Romania: The Penal Code of the Romanian Socialist Republic. Tr. by Simone-Marie Kleckner from Romanian. (American Series of Foreign Penal Codes: Vol. 20). xvi, 143p. 1976. text ed. 17.50x (ISBN 0-8377-0040-X). Rothman.

Romanian Americans. Arthur Diamond. (The Peoples of North America Ser.). (Illus.). 112p. (gr. 5 up). 1988. lib. bdg. 16.95 (ISBN 0-87754-898-6). Chelsea Hse.

Romanian Artist in the West, Vol. V. Ed. by Ionel Jianou. (Illus.). 184p. 1986. 48.00x (ISBN 0-317-56044-1). Am Romanian.

Romanian Continuity in Roman Dacia: Linguistic Evidence. Virgiliu Stefanescu-Draganesti. 90p. 1986. write for info. (ISBN 0-937019-04-6); pap. 15.00 (ISBN 0-937019-05-4). Romanian Hist.

Romanian Economy in the Twentieth Century. David Turnock. 320p. 1986. 35.00 (ISBN 0-312-69164-5). St Martin.

Romanian-English & English-Romanian Dictionary. Irina Panovf. 828p. (Romanian & Eng.). 1982. 50.00x (ISBN 0-317-59444-3, Pub. by Collets (UK)). State Mutual Bk.

Romanian-English Dictionary & Grammar for the Mathematical Sciences. Ed. by S. H. Gould & P. E. Obreanu. 51p. (Eng. & Romanian.): 1979. pap. 14.00 (ISBN 0-8218-0038-8, ROMA). Am Math.

Romanian-English, English-Romanian (Pocket) Dictionary. 3rd ed. Irene Parovf. 500p. 1986. 19.95 (ISBN 0-87052-129-2). Hippocrene Bks.

Romanian-English Metallurgical Dictionary. M. L. Breaban & L. Ionescu. 358p. (Romanian & Eng.). 1982. 50.00x (ISBN 0-317-59445-1, Pub. by Collets (UK)). State Mutual BK.

Romanian-English Phraseological Dictionary. L. Levitchi. 654p. (Romanian & Eng.). 1981. 50.00x (ISBN 0-317-59447-8, Pub. by Collets (UK)). State Mutual Bk.

Romanian-Finnish Seminar on Complex Analysis. Ed. by C. A. Cazacu et al. (Lecture Notes in Mathematics: Vol. 743). 713p. 1979. pap. 40.00 (ISBN 0-387-09550-0). Springer-Verlag.

Romanian Folk Music Texts. Bartok. (Rumanian Folk Music Ser: Vol. 3). lib. bdg. 53.00 (ISBN 90-247-0625-4, Pub. by Martinus Nijhoff Netherlands). Kluwer Academic.

Romanian Foreign Policy & the United Nations. Robert Weiner. LC 84-2149. 208p. 1984. 35.00 (ISBN 0-275-91290-6, C1290). Praeger.

Romanian Foreign Policy since 1965: The Political & Military Limits of Autonomy. Aurel Braun. LC 78-9516. (Praeger Special Studies). 1978. 44.95 (ISBN 0-275-90287-0, C0287). Praeger.

Romanian History Eighteen Forty-Eight to Nineteen Eighteen: Essays from the First Dutch-Romanian Colloquium of Historians Utrecht 1977. Ed. by A. P. Van Goudoever. (Historische Studies: No. XXXVI). 159p. (Orig.). 1979. pap. 23.00x (ISBN 90-01-39022-6, Pub. by Boumas Boekhuis Netherlands). Benjamins North AM.

Romanian Icons on Glass. Juliana Dancu & Dumitru Dancu. LC 82-10846. (Illus.). 176p. 1983. 22.50x (ISBN 0-8143-1711-1). Wayne St U Pr.

Romanian Icons Painted on Glass. Cornel Irimie & Marcela Focsa. (Illus.). 1971. 75.00 (ISBN 0-393-04309-6). Norton.

Romanian Military Doctrine. Constantin Olteanu. 288p. 1986. cancelled (ISBN 0-88033-098-8). East Eur Quarterly.

Romanian Military Doctrine: Past & Present. Ilie Ceausescu. 256p. Date not set. 30.00. East Eur Quarterly.

Romanian Nationalism: The Legionary Movement. Alexander. Ronnett. Tr. by Uasile C. Barsan from Romanian. LC 74-3350. pap. 17.70 (ISBN 0-8357-9431-8, 2015062). Bks Demand UMI.

Romanian Painting. Vasile Florea. LC 82-23740. (Illus.). 154p. 1984. 22.50x (ISBN 0-8143-1731-6). Wayne St U Pr.

Romanian Public Law. H. B. Jacobini. 256p. 1987. 25.00 (ISBN 0-88033-119-4, 223). East Eur Quarterly.

Romanians in America & Canada: A Guide to Information Sources. Ed. by Vladimir Wertsman. LC 80-191. (Gale Information Guide Library, Ethnic Information Guide Ser.: Vol. 5). 184p. 1980. 68.00x (ISBN 0-8103-1417-7). Gale.

Romanians in America Seventeen Forty-Eight to Nineteen Seventy-Four: A Chronology & Fact Book. Vladimir Wertsman. LC 75-11506. (Ethnic Chronology Ser.: No. 19). 118p. 1975. text ed. 8.50 (ISBN 0-379-00518-2). Oceana.

Romaniote Penitential Poetry. Ed. by Leon J. Weinberger. 192p. (Hebrew.). 1980. pap. 19.50 (ISBN 0-8173-0047-3, Pub. by Am Aced Jewish). U of Ala Pr.

Romanischen Wandmalereien von San Silvestro in Tivoli: Ein Roemisches Apsisprogramm der Zeit Innozenz III. Hanspeter Lanz. (European University Studies: No. 28, Vol. 22). 139p. (Ger.). 1983. 15.60 (ISBN 3-261-05080-2). P Lang Pubs.

Romanisches Etymologisches Woerterbuch. 5th ed. Wilhelm Meyer-Luebke. (Ital. & Ger.). 1972. 295.00 (ISBN 3-533-01394-4, M-7604, Pub. by Carl Winter). French & Eur.

Romanism & Truth. G. G. Coulton. 1977. lib. bdg. 59.95 (ISBN 0-8490-2541-9). Gordon Pr.

Romanism in Russia, 2 Vols. Dimitrii A. Tolstoi. LC 76-131026. Repr. of 1874 ed. Set. 75.00 (ISBN 0-404-06494-9). AMS Pr.

Romanist: 1980-81, No. 4-5. Ed. by John C. Moran et al. 1982. 10.00 (ISBN 0-318-20641-2). F M Crawford.

Romanist: 1982-84, No. 6-8. Ed. by John C. Moran et al. 1986. 10.00 (ISBN 0-318-20642-0). F M Crawford.

Romanitas: Studies in Romance Linguistics, Vol. 4. William Ashby et al. Ed. by Ernst Pulgram. (Michigan Romance Studies). 272p. (Orig.). 1984. pap. 8.00 (ISBN 0-939730-03-0). Mich Romance.

Romanization of Africa Proconsularis. Thomas R. Broughton. LC 78-64276. (Johns Hopkins University. Studies in the Social Sciences. Extra Volumes-New Ser.: 5). Repr. of 1929 ed. 11.50 (ISBN 0-404-61377-2). AMS Pr.

Romanization of Africa Proconsularis. Thomas R. Broughton. LC 68-23279. 1968. Repr. of 1929 ed. lib. bdg. 35.00x (ISBN 0-8371-0030-5, BRAP). Greenwood.

Romanization of Roman Britain. Francis J. Haverfield. LC 78-12798. (Illus.). 1979. Repr. of 1923 ed. lib. bdg. 35.00x (ISBN 0-313-21148-5, HARM). Greenwood.

Romano-British Bibliography: 55B.C.-449A.D, Vol. 1 & 2. Wilfrid Bonser. 1964. Set. 75.00x (ISBN 0-631-18980-7). Vol. 1 (ISBN 0-631-08370-7). Vol. 2 (ISBN 0-631-08380-4). Basil Blackwell.

Romano-British Coarse Pottery: A Student's Guide. 3rd ed. Graham Webster. (CBA Research Report Ser.: No. 6). 37p. 1976. pap. text ed. 6.95x (ISBN 0-900312-38-6, Pub. by Coun Brit Archaeology). Humanities.

Romanoff. Sobolev Leonid. Tr. by Alfred Freemantle from Rus. LC 74-10091. (Soviet Literature in English Translation Ser). 311p. 1975. Repr. of 1935 ed. 21.45 (ISBN 0-88355-177-2). Hyperion Conn.

Romanos: Versiculo por Versiculo. William R. Newell. Orig. Title: Romans: Verse by Verse. 464p. (Span.). 1984. pap. 9.75 (ISBN 0-8254-1507-1). Kregel.

Romantic Ballet As Seen by Theophile Gautier. Theophile Gautier. LC 79-7764. (Dance Ser.). (Illus.). 1980. Repr. of 1932 ed. lib. bdg. 14.00x (ISBN 0-8369-9292-X). Ayer Co Pubs.
Romantic Ballet in Paris. Ivor Guest. (Illus.). xix, 314p. 1980. 39.95 (ISBN 0-903102-45-5, Pub. by Dance Bks. England). Princeton Bk Co.
Romantic Bards & British Reviewers: A Selected Edition of Contemporary Reviews of the Works of Wordsworth, Coleridge, Byron, Keats & Shelley. Ed. by John O. Hayden. LC 71-125670. (Landmark Ed.). xx, 433p. 1971. 32.50x (ISBN 0-8032-0773-5). U of Nebr Pr.
Romantic Biography of the Age of Elizabeth: Or, Sketches of Life from the Bye-Ways of History, 2vols. Ed. by William C. Taylor. LC 72-14121. (Essay Index Reprint Ser.). Repr. of 1842 ed. 46.50 (ISBN 0-518-10027-8). Ayer Co Pubs.
Romantic Body: Love & Sexuality in Keats, Wordsworth, & Blake. Jean H. Hagstrum. LC 85-7485. (Hodges Lectures Ser.). (Illus.). 196p. 1986. text ed. 14.95x (ISBN 0-87049-482-1). U of Tenn Pr.
Romantic Child: From Runge to Sendak. Robert Rosenblum. (Illus.). 1989. 12.95 (ISBN 0-500-55020-4). Thames Hudson.
Romantic China. Herbert C. White & J. Henry. 260.00x (ISBN 0-317-69003-5, Pub. by Han-Shan Tang Ltd). State Mutual Bk.
Romantic Chivalrous Epic As a Phenomenon of the German Rococo. Richard M. Ilgner. (European University Studies: Series 1, German Language & Literature: Vol. 275). 148p. 1979. pap. 15.85 (ISBN 3-261-04604-X). P Lang Pubs.
Romantic Colonial Homesteads & Their Stories of Strange Intrigue. Marion Harland. (American Culture Library Bk.). (Illus.). 128p. 1983. Repr. of 1897 ed. 127.75 (ISBN 0-89901-096-2). Found Class Reprints.
Romantic Comedians. Ellen Glasgow. 346p. Repr. of 1926 ed. lib. bdg. 49.50 (ISBN 0-918377-33-1). Russell Pr.
Romantic Comedians. Ellen Anderson Gholson Glasgow. Ed. by Elizabeth Hardwick. LC 76-51668. (Rediscovered Fiction by American Women). 1977. Repr. of 1926 ed. lib. bdg. 30.00 (ISBN 0-405-10047-7). Ayer Co Pubs.
Romantic Comedy. David G. James. LC 80-18323. Repr. of 1948 ed. 14.50 (ISBN 0-404-14011-4). AMS Pr.
Romantic Comedy: In Hollywood from Lubitsch to Sturges. James Harvey. LC 87-45127. (Illus.). 688p. 1987. 35.00 (ISBN 0-394-50339-2). Knopf.
Romantic Composers. Daniel G. Mason. LC 73-119654. Repr. of 1906 ed. 14.00 (ISBN 0-404-04223-6). AMS Pr.
Romantic Composers. Daniel G. Mason. 1970. Repr. of 1906 ed. lib. bdg. 35.00x (ISBN 0-8371-4096-X, MARC). Greenwood.
Romantic Contraries: Freedom vs. Destiny. Peter I. Thorslev, Jr. LC 83-17114. 256p. 1984. 27.00x (ISBN 0-300-03047-9). Yale U Pr.
Romantic Critical Essays. Ed. by David Bromwich. (Cambridge English Prose Texts Ser.). 350p. 1988. 34.50 (ISBN 0-521-24411-0); pap. 12.95 (ISBN 0-521-28672-7). Cambridge U Pr.
Romantic Criticism of Shakespearian Drama. John Crawford. Ed. by James Hogg. (Romantic Reassessment Ser.). 202p. (Orig.). 1978. pap. 15.00 (ISBN 3-7052-0536-6, Pub. by Salzburg Studies). Longwood Pub Group.
Romantic Criticism: 1800-1850. Ed. by R. A. Foakes. LC 76-116476. (English Library). 224p. 1970. pap. text ed. 5.95x (ISBN 0-87249-165-X). U of SC Pr.
Romantic Cruxes: The English Essayists & the Spirit of the Age. Thomas McFarland. 150p. 1988. 32.50 (ISBN 0-19-812895-9). Oxford U Pr.
Romantic Days in Old Boston. Mary C. Crawford. 1973. Repr. of 1910 ed. 30.00 (ISBN 0-8274-1518-4). R West.
Romantic Decatur. facsimile ed. Charles L. Lewis. LC 79-164614. (Select Bibliographies Reprint Ser). Repr. of 1937 ed. 21.00 (ISBN 0-8369-5898-5). Ayer Co Pubs.
Romantic Dialogue: Communication in Dating & marriage. Michael J. Beatty. 160p. 1986. pap. text ed. 10.95x (ISBN 0-89582-146-X). Morton Pub.
Romantic Dramas Garcia Gutierrez. Nicholson B. Adams. 149p. 1.00 (ISBN 0-318-14303-8). Hispanic Inst.
Romantic Dramas of Garcia Gutierrez. Nicholson B. Adams. 1976. lib. bdg. 59.95 (ISBN 0-8490-2542-7). Gordon Pr.
Romantic Education. Patricia Hampl. 320p. 1981. 11.95 (ISBN 0-395-29697-8); pap. 7.95 (ISBN 0-395-34638-X). HM.
Romantic Enlightenment. Geoffrey Clive. LC 72-8238. 219p. 1973. Repr. of 1960 ed. lib. bdg. 35.00x (ISBN 0-8371-6544-X, CLRE). Greenwood.
Romantic Ethic & the Spirit of Modern Consumerism. Colin Campbell. 320p. Date not set. 24.95 (ISBN 0-631-15539-2). Basil Blackwell.
Romantic Exiles. Edward H. Carr. 391p. 1975. Repr. of 1933 ed. lib. bdg. 27.50x (ISBN 0-374-91297-1, Octagon). Hippocrene Bks.
Romantic Exiles: A Nineteenth-Century Portrait Gallery. Edward Hallet Carr. 392p. 1981. pap. 9.95x (ISBN 0-262-53040-6). MIT Pr.
Romantic Fairy Tale: Seeds of Surrealism. Marianne Thalmann. Tr. by Mary B. Corcoran. LC 64-17439. pap. 35.80 (ISBN 0-317-26227-0, 2055656). Bks Demand UMI.
Romantic Faith: 1780-1830 see Religious Trends in English Poetry.
Romantic Fallacies. Richard Hoffpauir. (American University Studies IV - English Language & Literature: Vol. 31). 338p. 1985. text ed. 30.50 (ISBN 0-8204-0257-5). P Lang Pubs.
Romantic Fantastic. Tobin Siebers. LC 83-20999. 195p. 1984. 22.50x (ISBN 0-8014-1671-X). Cornell U Pr.
Romantic Fantasy & Science Fiction. Karl Kroeber. LC 88-2046. 1988. text ed. 20.00t (ISBN 0-300-04241-8). Yale U Pr.
Romantic Foundations of the American Renaissance. Leon Chai. LC 87-5428. 448p. 1987. 29.95x (ISBN 0-8014-1929-8). Cornell U Pr.
Romantic Fragment Poem: A Critique of a Form. Marjorie Levinson. LC 85-28927. x, 268p. 1986. 29.00x (ISBN 0-8078-1684-1). U of NC Pr.
Romantic Garden. Graham Rose. LC 87-40316. (Illus.). 1988. 27.50 (ISBN 0-670-82068-7). Viking.
Romantic Garden: A Practical Guide to Creating a Beautiful Garden That Appeals to the Emotions As Well As the Senses. Graham Rose. (Illus.). 168p. 1988. pap. 14.95 (ISBN 0-14-046828-5). Penguin.
Romantic Genesis of the Modern Novel. Charles Schug. LC 78-26484. (Critical Essays in Modern Literature Ser.). 1979. 26.95x (ISBN 0-8229-3397-7). U of Pittsburgh Pr.
Romantic German Literature. Glyn T. Hughes. LC 79-12994. 183p. 1979. 34.50 (ISBN 0-8419-0521-5). Holmes & Meier.
Romantic Germany. (Panorama Bks.). (Illus., Eng. & Fr.). 3.95 (ISBN 0-685-11540-2). French & Eur.
Romantic Ghost of Greenwich Village: Guido Bruno in His Garret. Arnold I. Kisch. (Illus.). 154p. 1976. pap. 19.60 (ISBN 3-261-01727-9). P Lang Pubs.
Romantic Heritage of Marxism: A Study of East German Love Poetry. Boria Sax. (Studies in Modern German Literature: Vol. 15). 199p. 1987. text ed. 34.00 (ISBN 0-8204-0487-X). P Lang Pubs.
Romantic Hero & His Biblical Sources. Wolf Z. Hirst. Ed. by James Hogg. (Romantic Reassessment ser.). (Orig.). 1985. pap. 15.00 (ISBN 3-7052-0573-0, Pub. by Salzburg Studies). Longwood Pub Group.
Romantic Hero & His Heirs in French Literature. Lloyd Bishop. LC 83-49351. (American University Studies II Romance Languages & Literature: Vol. 10). 295p. 1984. text ed. 32.50 (ISBN 0-8204-0096-3). P Lang Pubs.
Romantic Heroes of Fiction Paper Dolls. John Axe. 32p. 1988. write for info. Hobby Hse.
Romantic Heroic Ideal. James D. Wilson. LC 82-58. xii, 223p. 1982. text ed. 27.50 (ISBN 0-8071-1030-2). La State U Pr.
Romantic History of the Successes & Failures of Humanity's Primitive Spirit, 2 vols. L. T. Haines. (Illus.). 437p. 1987. Repr. of 1882 ed. 237.75 (ISBN 0-89901-348-1). Found Class Reprints.
Romantic Horizons: Aspects of the Sublime in English Poetry & Painting, 1770-1850. James B. Twitchell. LC 83-3679. (Illus.). 248p. 1983. text ed. 27.00x (ISBN 0-8262-0411-2). U of Mo Pr.
Romantic Ideal. Christopher A. Anderson. LC 87-71911. (Illus.). 103p. (Orig.). 1987. pap. text ed. 9.00 (ISBN 0-931353-12-2). Andersons Pubns.
Romantic Idealism & Roman Catholicism: Schelling & the Theologians. Thomas F. O'Meara. LC 81-40449. 240p. 1982. 25.00 (ISBN 0-268-01610-0). U of Notre Dame Pr.
Romantic Ideology: A Critical Investigation. Jerome J. McGann. LC 82-17494. 184p. 1983. lib. bdg. 15.00x (ISBN 0-226-55849-5). U of Chicago Pr.
Romantic Ideology: A Critical Investigation. Jerome J. McGann. LC 82-17494. x, 172p. 1985. pap. text ed. 6.50x (ISBN 0-226-55850-9). U of Chicago Pr.
Romantic Image. Frank Kermode. 192p. (Orig.). 1986. pap. 5.95 (ISBN 0-7448-0037-4, Ark Paperbks). Routledge Chapman & Hall.
Romantic Imagery in the Novels of Charlotte Bronte. Cynthia A. Linder. LC 78-2903. 138p. 1978. text ed. 26.50x (ISBN 0-06-494280-5). B&N Imports.
Romantic Imagination. C. Maurice Bowra. (Oxford Paperbook Bks). 1961. pap. 9.95x (ISBN 0-19-281006-5). Oxford U Pr.
Romantic Imprisonment: Women & Other Glorified Outcasts. Nina Auerbach. LC 85-11005. 328p. 1985. 27.50x (ISBN 0-231-06004-1). Columbia U Pr.
Romantic Imprisonment: Women & Other Glorified Outcasts. Nina Auerbach. LC 85-11005. (Gender & Culture Ser.). (Illus.). 315p. 1987. pap. text ed. 13.00 (ISBN 0-231-06005-X). Columbia U Pr.
Romantic Impulse in Victorian Fiction. Donald D. Stone. LC 79-27736. 404p. 1980. 29.50x (ISBN 0-674-77932-0). Harvard U Pr.
Romantic Indian: Sentimental Views from Nineteenth-Century American Literature, 4 vols. LC 80-19248. 1981. Set. 200.00x (ISBN 0-8201-1356-5). Schol Facsimilies.
Romantic Interludes: A Sensuous Lovers Guide. 2nd ed. Kenneth R. Stubbs. (Illus.). 112p. 1988. pap. 12.95 (ISBN 0-939263-01-7). Secret Garden.
Romantic Ironists & Goethe. Kathleen Wheeler. (German Aesthetics & Literary Criticism Ser.). 330p. 1984. 52.50 (ISBN 0-521-23631-2); pap. 16.95 (ISBN 0-521-28087-7). Cambridge U Pr.
Romantic Irony of Semiotics: Friedrich Schiegel & the Crisis of Representation. Marike Finlay. (Approaches to Semiotics Ser.). 293p. 1988. text ed. 95.50x (ISBN 0-89925-330-X). Mouton.
Romantic Italian Cooking. Mary Cadogan. LC 85-81328. (Creative Cuisine Ser.). 80p. pap. 4.95 (ISBN 0-89586-395-2). Price Stern.
Romantic Lace Designs. Ondori Publishing Company Staff. (Illus.). 92p. (Orig.). 1984. pap. 6.50 (ISBN 0-87040-586-1). Japan Pubns USA.
Romantic Lady. Sylvia Thorpe. 224p. 1980. pap. 1.75 (ISBN 0-449-50057-8, Coventry). Fawcett.
Romantic Landscape Vision: Constable & Wordsworth. Karl Kroeber. LC 74-5905. (Illus.). 156p. 1975. 27.50x (ISBN 0-299-06710-6). U of Wis Pr.
Romantic Legend of Sakya Buddha. Samuel Beal. xii, 395p. 1986. Repr. 17.50x (ISBN 0-89581-820-5, Pub. by Motilal Banaisidass). South Asia Bks.
Romantic Legends of Spain. facsimile ed. Gustavo A. Becquer. Tr. by Cornelia F. Bates & Katharine L. Bates. LC 78-169539. (Short Story Index Reprint Ser.). Repr. of 1909 ed. 19.50 (ISBN 0-8369-4000-8). Ayer Co Pubs.
Romantic Life of Shelley & the Sequel. Francis Gribble. LC 72-3624. (Studies in Shelley, No. 25). 1972. Repr. of 1911 ed. lib. bdg. 58.95x (ISBN 0-8383-1566-6). Haskell.
Romantic Life of Shelley & the Sequel. Francis Gribble. 1977. Repr. lib. bdg. 35.00 (ISBN 0-8492-1018-6). R West.
Romantic Love: A Philosophical Inquiry. Dwight Van de Vate, Jr. LC 81-47171. 176p. 1981. 22.50x (ISBN 0-271-00288-3). Pa St U Pr.
Romantic Love Question & Answer Book. Nathaniel Branden & E. Devers Branden. 304p. 1987. pap. 3.95 (ISBN 0-553-23059-X). Bantam.
Romantic Lovers. David Hocking. pap. 6.95 (ISBN 0-89081-522-4). Harvest Hse.
Romantic Manifesto. Ayn Rand. 1971. pap. 3.95 (ISBN 0-451-14916-5, AE2374, Sig). NAL.
Romantic Meals for Lovers. Gabrielle Kirschbaum. 144p. 1987. pap. 15.95 (ISBN 1-55013-057-9, Pub. by Key Porter Canada). U of Toronto Pr.
Romantic Meals for Lovers: Recipes for 50 Intimate Occasions. Gabrielle Kirschbaum. Orig. Title: Picnics for Lovers. (Illus.). 144p. 1987. pap. 11.95 (ISBN 0-914629-38-7, Dist. by St. Martin's). Prima Pub Comm.
Romantic Memory Pieces. Dorothy Radcliffe & Carolyn Cook. (Illus.). 32p. 1987. pap. 4.95 (ISBN 0-87588-303-6). Hobby Hse.
Romantic Mother: Narcissistic Patterns in Romantic Poetry. Barbara A. Schapiro. LC 82-14023. 160p. 1983. text ed. 18.50x (ISBN 0-8018-2896-1). Johns Hopkins.
Romantic Movement. David Erdman et al. Incl. A Selective & Critical Bibliography for 1982. LC 83-16354. 550p. lib. bdg. 74.00 (ISBN 0-8240-9507-3); A Selective & Critical Bibliography for 1984. LC 84-48854. 484p. 1986. lib. bdg. 67.00 (ISBN 0-8240-9505-7). 1985. Garland Pub.
Romantic Movement. Alan Menhennet. (Literary History of Germany Ser.: Vol. 6). 276p. 1981. 28.50x (ISBN 0-389-20104-9). B&N Imports.
Romantic Movement: A Selective & Critical Bibliography for Nineteen Seventy-Nine. Compiled by David V. Erdman et al. LC 80-8494. 350p. 1980. lib. bdg. 43.00 (ISBN 0-8240-9512-X). Garland Pub.
Romantic Movement: A Selective & Critical Bibliography for 1981. David V. Erdman. LC 82-48435. (Romantic Movement Bibliographies Ser.). 417p. 1982. lib. bdg. 55.00 (ISBN 0-8240-9508-1). Garland Pub.
Romantic Movement: A Selective & Critical Bibliography for 1980. David V. Erdman. LC 81-43336. (Romantic Movement Bibliographies Ser.). 411p. 1981. lib. bdg. 48.00 (ISBN 0-8240-9509-X). Garland Pub.
Romantic Movement: A Selective & Critical Bibliography for 1983. David V. Erdman. (Reference Library of the Humanities). 1984. lib. bdg. 67.00 (ISBN 0-8240-9506-5). Garland Pub.
Romantic Movement: A Selective & Critical Bibliography for 1985. David V. Erdman. (Reference Library of Humanities Romantic Movement Bibliographies Ser.). 1986. lib. bdg. 65.00 (ISBN 0-8240-9515-4). Garland Pub.
Romantic Movement & Methodism: A Study of English Romanticism & the Evangelical Revival. Frederick C. Gill. 1978. Repr. of 1937 ed. lib. bdg. 25.00 (ISBN 0-8492-4910-4). R West.
Romantic Movement Bibliography, 1936-1970: A Master Cumulation from ELH, Philological Quarterly & English Language Notes, 7 Vols. Ed. by A. C. Elkins & Lorne Forstner. LC 77-172773. (Cumulated Bibliography Ser.: No. 3). 1973. Set. 290.00 (ISBN 0-87650-025-4). Pierian.
Romantic Movement in English Poetry. Arthur Symons. LC 76-22792. Repr. of 1909 ed. lib. bdg. 45.00 (ISBN 0-8414-7676-4). Folcroft.
Romantic Movement in English Poetry. Arthur Symons, LC 74-90371. 356p. 1969. Repr. of 1909 ed. 40.00x (ISBN 0-87753-038-6). Phaeton.
Romantic Movement in English Poetry. Arthur Symons. 1979. Repr. of 1909 ed. lib. bdg. 35.00 (ISBN 0-8492-8240-3). R West.
Romantic Movement in Spain - a Short History. E. Peers. (Liverpool Studies in Spanish Literature Ser.). 240p. 1968. Repr. of 1949 ed. text ed. 12.50x (ISBN 0-85323-280-6, Pub. by Liverpool U Pr). Humanities.
Romantic Muse. Jay C. Livingston. LC 78-71646. (Illus.). 1978. pap. 3.50 (ISBN 0-931412-10-2). Metatron Pr.
Romantic Music. Leon Plantinga. LC 83-42653. (Introduction to Music History Ser.). (Illus.). 1985. 22.95x (ISBN 0-393-95196-0). Norton.
Romantic Music: A Concise History from Schubert to Sibelius. Arnold Whittall. LC 86-71617. (World of Art Ser.). (Illus.). 1987. pap. 11.95 (ISBN 0-500-20215-X). Thames Hudson.
Romantic Narrative Art. Karl Kroeber. (Illus.). 238p. 1966. pap. 10.95x (ISBN 0-299-02244-7). U of Wis Pr.
Romantic Nationalism & Liberalism: Joachim Lelewel & the Polish National Idea. Joan S. Skurnowicz. (East European Monographs: No. 83). 202p. 1981. 20.00x (ISBN 0-914710-77-X). East Eur Quarterly.
Romantic New Orleans. Deirdre Stanforth. (Illus.). 136p. 1986. pap. 9.95 (ISBN 0-88289-496-X). Pelican.
Romantic Nineties. Richard Le Gallienne. 1926. Repr. lib. bdg. 35.00 (ISBN 0-8414-5797-2). Folcroft.
Romantic Novel in England. Robert Kiely. LC 79-186677. 288p. 1972. 20.00x (ISBN 0-674-77935-5). Harvard U Pr.
Romantic Novellas. Heinrich Von Kleist & Jean Paul. Ed. by Frank G. Ryder & Robert M. Browning. (German Library: Vol. 34). 320p. 1985. 27.50x (ISBN 0-8264-0294-1); pap. 10.50 (ISBN 0-8264-0295-X). Continuum.
Romantic Obsessions & Humiliations of Annie Sehlmeier. Louise Plummer. LC 86-32795. 192p. (YA) (gr. 7 up). 1987. pap. 14.95 (ISBN 0-385-29574-X). Delacorte.
Romantic Opera & Literary Form. Peter Conrad. (Quantum Books: No. 9). (Illus.). 185p. 1977. 25.00x (ISBN 0-520-03258-6); pap. 9.95x (ISBN 0-520-04508-4). U of Cal Pr.
Romantic Paintings in America. James T. Soby & Dorothy C. Miller. LC 73-86430. (Museum of Modern Art Publications in Reprint Ser). (Illus.). 1970. Repr. of 1943 ed. 22.00 (ISBN 0-405-01550-X). Ayer Co Pubs.
Romantic Paradox: An Essay on the Poetry of Wordsworth. Colin C. Clarke. LC 78-10859. 1979. Repr. of 1963 ed. lib. bdg. 25.00x (ISBN 0-313-20758-5, CLPA). Greenwood.
Romantic Period: Excluding the Novel, 1 of 7 vols. Intro. by Kenneth Muir. (Great Writers Library). 113p. pap. 7.95 (ISBN 0-312-34705-7). Academy Chi Pubs.
Romantic Perspectives. Ed. by Patricia Hodgart & Theodore Redpath. Repr. of 1964 ed. 25.00 (ISBN 0-8492-9967-5). R West.
Romantic Perspectives: The Work of Crabbe, Blake, Wordsworth, & Coleridge As Seen by Their Contemporaries & by Themselves. Ed. by Patricia Hodgart & Theodore Redpath. 1979. Repr. of 1964 ed. lib. bdg. 30.00 (ISBN 0-8495-2345-1). Arden Lib.
Romantic Poetry & Prose. Ed. by Harold Bloom & Lionel Trilling. (Anthology of English Literature Ser.). (Illus.). 1973. pap. 18.95x (ISBN 0-19-501615-7). Oxford U Pr.
Romantic Poetry on the European Continent: An English Language Anthology, Vol. I. Ed. by Miroslav J. Hanak. LC 83-1169. 624p. (Orig.). 1983. pap. text ed. 22.00 (ISBN 0-8191-3059-1). U Pr of Amer.
Romantic Poets & Prose Writers. Compiled by Richard H. Fogle. LC 66-29743. (Goldentree Bibliographies in Language & Literature Ser.). (Orig.). 1967. pap. 13.95x (ISBN 0-88295-513-6). Harlan Davidson.
Romantic Predicament. Geoffrey Thurley. LC 83-15995. 240p. 1984. 22.50 (ISBN 0-312-69182-3). St Martin.
Romantic Prison: The French Tradition. Victor Brombert. LC 77-85532. 1978. 30.50x (ISBN 0-691-06352-4). Princeton U Pr.
Romantic Professions. W. P. James. 1973. Repr. of 1894 ed. 30.00 (ISBN 0-8274-0256-2). R West.
Romantic Professions & Other Papers. W. P. James. 225p. 1980. Repr. of 1894 ed. lib. bdg. 25.00 (ISBN 0-89984-257-7). Century Bookbindery.
Romantic Prose of the Early Nineteenth Century. Ed. by Carl H. Grabo. 1978. Repr. of 1927 ed. lib. bdg. 29.00 (ISBN 0-8495-1915-2). Arden Lib.
Romantic Rascals. Charles J. Finger. LC 71-90637. (Essay Index Reprint Ser.). 1927. 20.00 (ISBN 0-8369-1259-4). Ayer Co Pubs.
Romantic Re-Vision: Culture & Consciousness in Nineteenth Century American Painting & Literature. Bryan J. Wolf. LC 82-2741. (Illus.). 320p. 1983. lib. bdg. 30.00x (ISBN 0-226-90501-2). U of Chicago Pr.
Romantic Re-Vision: Culture & Consciousness in Nineteenth Century American Painting & Literature. Bryan J. Wolf. LC 82-2741. (Illus.). xx, 272p. 1987. pap. 15.95 (ISBN 0-226-90502-0). U of Chicago Pr.

Romantic Rebellion. Kenneth Clark. 366p. 1987. pap. 22.95i (ISBN 0-06-430167-2, Icon Edns). Har-Row.

Romantic Rebels: Essays on Shelley & His Circle. Ed. by Kenneth N. Cameron. LC 72-97087. (Carl H. Pforzheimer Library). 1973. 25.00x (ISBN 0-674-77937-1). Harvard U Pr.

Romantic Recollections. Lydia Kyasht. Ed. by Erica Beale. LC 77-27057. (Series in Dance). (Illus.). 1978. Repr. of 1929 ed. lib. bdg. 29.50 (ISBN 0-306-77572-7). Da Capo.

Romantic Reviewers, 1802-1824. John O. Hayden. LC 68-16694. pap. 85.00 (ISBN 0-317-26507-5, 2024045). Bks Demand UMI.

Romantic Revival-Setting the Record Straight. Frank Cooper & Jesse F. Knight. Ed. by Robert Villegas. LC 79-50797. (gr. 7 up). 1980. pap. 2.95 (ISBN 0-930962-02-8). Lion Ent.

Romantic Revolt. Charles E. Vaughan. 507p. 1980. Repr. of 1907 ed. lib. bdg. 59.50 (ISBN 0-8495-5527-2). Arden Lib.

Romantic Revolt. Charles E. Vaughan. LC 72-191239. 1907. lib. bdg. 49.00 (ISBN 0-8414-0841-6). Folcroft.

Romantic Revolution in America: 1800-1860 see Main Currents in American Thought.

Romantic Rooms. Robert Harling. (Illus.). 256p. 1985. 29.95 (ISBN 0-88162-097-1). Salem Hse Pubs.

Romantic School & Other Essays, Vol. 33. Heinrich Heine. Ed. by Volkmar Sander. (German Library). 320p. 1985. 27.50x (ISBN 0-8264-0290-9); pap. 10.95 (ISBN 0-8264-0291-7). Continuum.

Romantic Scottish Ballads. Robert Chambers. LC 76-58428. 1977. Repr. of 1849 ed. lib. bdg. 22.50 (ISBN 0-8414-3430-1). Folcroft.

Romantic Scottish Ballads & the Lady Wardlaw Heresy. Norval Clyne. LC 77-27936. 1859. 20.00 (ISBN 0-8414-0567-0). Folcroft.

Romantic Spirit. Mary J. Kay. (Romance Bibliography Ser.). (Orig.). 1982. pap. 8.95 (ISBN 0-9610996-0-7). MJK Ent.

Romantic Spirit: German Drawings, 1780-1850, from the German Democratic Republic. P. Betthausen et al. 1988. 55.00 (ISBN 0-19-520715-7). Oxford U Pr.

Romantic Spirit: 1983-1984 Update. Mary J. Kay. (Orig.). 1984. pap. 5.95 (ISBN 0-9610996-1-5). MJK Ent.

Romantic Sublime: Studies in the Structure & Psychology of Transcendence. Thomas Weiskel. LC 75-36932. (Illus.). Repr. of 1976 ed. 44.90 (ISBN 0-8357-9283-8, 2019109). Bks Demand UMI.

Romantic Sublime: Studies in the Structure & Psychology of Transcendence. Thomas Weiskel. LC 75-36932. 240p. 1986. pap. text ed. 8.95x (ISBN 0-8018-3347-7). Johns Hopkins.

Romantic Syndrome Toward a New Method in Cultural Anthropology & History of Ideas. W. T. Jones. 255p. 1983. Repr. of 1961 ed. lib. bdg. 65.00 (ISBN 0-89984-928-8). Century Bookbindery.

Romantic Texts & Contexts. Donald H. Reiman. 408p. 1988. text ed. 32.00 (ISBN 0-8262-0649-2). U of Mo Pr.

Romantic Theatre: An International Symposium. Ed. by Richard A. Cave. LC 86-26492. 144p. 1987. 24.50 (ISBN 0-389-20697-0). B&N Imports.

Romantic Theories of Architecture of the 19th Century, in Germany, England & France. Ronald Bradbury. LC 75-28994. Repr. of 1934 ed. 20.00 (ISBN 0-404-14005-X). AMS Pr.

Romantic Theory of Poetry: An Examination in the Light of Croce's Aesthetic. Annie E. Dodds. LC 75-28996. Repr. of 1926 ed. 28.00 (ISBN 0-404-14007-6). AMS Pr.

Romantic Times. 24p. 1.25 (ISBN 0-940338-00-9). Romantic Times.

Romantic to Modern Literature: Essays & Ideas of Culture 1750-1900. John Lucas. LC 82-6842. 240p. 1982. text ed. 27.50x (ISBN 0-389-20311-4). B&N Imports.

Romantic Tradition in American Literature, 33 bks. Ed. by Harold Bloom. 1972. Repr. Set. 891.00 (ISBN 0-405-04620-0). Ayer Co Pubs.

Romantic Tradition in British Political Thought. Jonathan Mendilow. LC 85-22871. 272p. 1985. 31.50x (ISBN 0-389-20595-8). B&N Imports.

Romantic Tradition in Modern English Poetry: Rhetoric & Experience. Geoffrey Harvey. LC 85-24988. 112p. 1985. 25.00x (ISBN 0-312-69188-2). St Martin.

Romantic Triumph. Thomas S. Omond. LC 74-38364. (Select Bibliographies Reprint Ser.). Repr. of 1900 ed. 23.50 (ISBN 0-8369-6781-X). Ayer Co Pubs.

Romantic Vegetarian: A Seasonal Cookbook. Judith Sharlin. (Illus.). 204p. 1984. pap. 9.95 (ISBN 0-914091-50-6). Chicago Review.

Romantic View of Poetry. Joseph W. Beach. Repr. of 1944 ed. 29.00x (ISBN 0-403-03886-3). Somerset Pub.

Romantic View of Poetry. Joseph W. Beach. 11.25 (ISBN 0-8446-1061-5). Peter Smith.

Romantic View of Poetry. Joseph W. Beach. 1988. Repr. of 1944 ed. lib. bdg. 29.00x. Am Biog Serv.

Romantic Vision & the Novel. Jay Clayton. LC 86-12918. 264p. 1987. 34.50 (ISBN 0-521-32776-8). Cambridge U Pr.

Romantic Vision, Ethical Context: Novalis & Aritistic Autonomy. Geza Von Molnar. LC 86-11229. (Theory & History of Literature Ser.: Vol. 32). 275p. (Orig.). 1987. 35.00x (ISBN 0-8166-1496-2); pap. 14.95 (ISBN 0-8166-1497-0). U of Minn Pr.

Romantic Weather: The Climates of Coleridge & Baudelaire. Arden Reed. LC 83-40014. 366p. 1983. 35.00x (ISBN 0-87451-277-8). U Pr of New Eng.

Romantic World of Music. facs. ed. William Armstrong. LC 71-90602. (Essay Index Reprint Ser). 1922. 19.00 (ISBN 0-8369-1271-3). Ayer Co Pubs.

Romanticism. Jean Clay. Tr. by Dan Wheeler from Fr. (Illus.). 320p. 1981. 60.00 (ISBN 0-86565-012-8). Vendome.

Romanticism. 2nd ed. Lilian R. Furst. (Critical Idiom Ser.). 1976. pap. 5.50x (ISBN 0-416-83920-7, NO. 2209). Routledge Chapman & Hall.

Romanticism. Hugh Honour. LC 78-2146. (Icon Editions). (Illus.). 1979. (HarpT); pap. 12.95 (ISBN 0-06-430089-7, IN-89, HarpT). Har-Row.

Romanticism. Ernest A. Seilliere. LC 72-194775. 1929. lib. bdg. 17.50 (ISBN 0-8414-8135-0). Folcroft.

Romanticism: A Structural Analysis. David Morse. 316p. 1982. 28.50x (ISBN 0-389-20165-0). B&N Imports.

Romanticism & Consciousness. Ed. by Harold Bloom. (Orig.). 1970. pap. text ed. 10.95x (ISBN 0-393-09954-7, NortonC). Norton.

Romanticism & Contemporary Criticism. Ed. by Morris Eaves & Michael Fischer. LC 85-19472. (Paperback Ser.). (Illus.). 256p. 1986. 29.95x (ISBN 0-8014-1795-3); pap. 8.95x (ISBN 0-8014-9352-8). Cornell U Pr.

Romanticism & Culture: A Festschrift for Morse Peckham. Ed. by H. W. Matalene. LC 83-72541. (Studies in English & American Literature, Linguistics, & Culture, Vol. 1). (Illus.). 180p. 1984. 25.50x (ISBN 0-938100-27-0). Camden Hse.

Romanticism & Evolution: The Nineteenth Century, an Anthology. Ed. by Bruce Wilshire. 320p. (Orig.). 1985. pap. text ed. 12.50 (ISBN 0-8191-4383-9). U Pr of Amer.

Romanticism & Feminism. Ed. by Anne K. Mellor. LC 87-45406. 256p. 1988. 37.50x (ISBN 0-253-35083-2); pap. 12.95x (ISBN 0-253-20462-3). Ind U Pr.

Romanticism & Ideology. David Aers et al. 240p. (Orig.). 1981. pap. 12.95X (ISBN 0-7100-0781-7). Routledge Chapman & Hall.

Romanticism & Ideology. Morse Peckham. 400p. 1985. lib. bdg. 32.50x (ISBN 0-913283-05-3). Penkevill.

Romanticism & Language. Ed. by Arden Reed. LC 84-45146. 320p. 1984. pap. 12.95x (ISBN 0-8014-9891-0). Cornell U Pr.

Romanticism & Marxism: The Philosophical Development of Literary Theory & Literary History in Walter Benjamin & Frederick Schlegel. Marcus P. Bullock. (American University Studies I - Germanic Languages & Literature: Vol. 51). 276p. 1987. 32.90 (ISBN 0-8204-0317-2). P Lang Pubs.

Romanticism & Realism: The Mythology of Nineteenth-Century Art. Charles Rosen & Henri Zerner. LC 83-47921. (Illus.). 244p. 1984. 22.50 (ISBN 0-670-54817-0). Viking.

Romanticism & Realism: The Mythology of Nineteenth-Century Art. Charles Rosen & Henri Zerner. (Illus.). 1985. pap. 8.95 (ISBN 0-393-30196-6). Norton.

Romanticism & Religion. Stephen Prickett. LC 75-2254. 320p. 1976. 49.50 (ISBN 0-521-21072-0). Cambridge U Pr.

Romanticism & Revolt. J. R. Talmon. (Library of World Civilization). (Illus.). 1979. pap. text ed. 7.95x (ISBN 0-393-95081-6). Norton.

Romanticism & the Forms of Ruin: Wordsworth, Coleridge & Modalities of Fragmentation. Thomas McFarland. LC 80-7546. 432p. 1981. 50.00x (ISBN 0-691-06437-7). Princeton U Pr.

Romanticism & the Gothic Revival. Agnes Addison. 204p. 1967. Repr. of 1938 ed. 25.00x (ISBN 0-87752-000-3). Gordian.

Romanticism & the Romantic School in Germany. Robert M. Wernaer. LC 68-681. (Studies in German Literature, No. 13). 1969. Repr. of 1910 ed. lib. bdg. 51.95x (ISBN 0-8383-0685-3). Haskell.

Romanticism Comes of Age. Owen Barfield. 254p. 1986. pap. 12.95 (ISBN 0-8195-6152-5). Wesleyan U Pr.

Romanticism: Critical Essays in American Literature. 352p. 1986. 17.50 (ISBN 0-8240-9348-8); pap. 8.95 (ISBN 0-8240-9349-6). Garland Pub.

Romanticism in France. Nemours H. Clement. (MLA Rev. Fund Ser.). 1938. 45.00 (ISBN 0-527-17800-4). Kraus Repr.

Romanticism in National Context. Ed. by Roy Porter & Mikulas Teich. 382p. 1988. 54.50 (ISBN 0-521-32605-2); pap. 17.95 (ISBN 0-521-33913-8). Cambridge U Pr.

Romanticism in Puerto Rican Literature. Cesario Rosa-Nieves. (Puerto Rico Ser.). 1979. lib. bdg. 59.95 (ISBN 0-8490-3003-X). Gordon Pr.

Romanticism in Shakespearian Comedy. H. B. Charlton. 1930. lib. bdg. 15.00 (ISBN 0-8414-3566-9). Folcroft.

Romanticism in Shakespearian Comedy. Henry B. Charlton. 1978. lib. bdg. 16.50 (ISBN 0-8495-0955-6). Arden Lib.

Romanticism, Modernism, Postmodernism. Ed. by Harry Garvin. LC 79-50103. (Bucknell Review Ser.: Vol.25, No. 2). 192p. 1980. 16.50 (ISBN 0-8387-5004-4). Bucknell U Pr.

Romanticism: Points of View. 2nd ed. Ed. by Robert Gleckner & Gerald Enscoe. LC 75-4682. (Waynebks Ser: No. 40). 352p. 1975. pap. text ed. 8.95x (ISBN 0-8143-1543-7). Wayne St U Pr.

Romanticism Reconsidered. Ed. by Northrop Frye. LC 63-18020. (Essays of the English Institute). 144p. 1963. 25.00x (ISBN 0-231-02671-4). Columbia U Pr.

Romanticism Reconsidered see English Institute Essays.

Romanticism Reconsidered: Selected Papers from the English Institute. Ed. by Northrop Frye. LC 63-18020. pap. 35.30 (2026709). Bks Demand UMI.

Romanticism Revisited. (YFS Ser.: No. 13). 1964. pap. 16.00 (ISBN 0-527-01721-3). Kraus Repr.

Romantics. Nazim Hikmet. 224p. 1988. 15.95 (ISBN 0-916650-36-7). Banner Pr.

Romantics. Ed. by Stephen Prickett. (Context of English Literature Ser.). 270p. 1981. 37.50 (ISBN 0-8419-0723-4); pap. 19.50 (ISBN 0-8419-0724-2). Holmes & Meier.

Romantics at School. Morris Marples. 206p. 1982. Repr. of 1967 ed. lib. bdg. 30.00 (ISBN 0-8495-3934-X). Arden Lib.

Romantic's Guide to Country Inns. Stuart Woods. (Illus.). 1979. 17.95 (ISBN 0-393-01240-9). Norton.

Romantics, Rebels, & Reactionaries: English Literature & Its Background, 1760 to 1830. Marilyn Butler. (OPUS). 1982. 22.95x (ISBN 0-19-520384-4); pap. 8.95x (ISBN 0-19-289132-4). Oxford U Pr.

Romantics Reviewed: A Collection in Depth of Periodical Reviews (1793-1830, 11 vols. Ed. & intro. by Donald H. Reiman. Incl. Vols. I & II. Pt. A. lib. bdg. 226.00each (ISBN 0-8240-0509-0); Vols. I To V. Pt. B. lib. bdg. 563.00 5 vol. set (ISBN 0-8240-0510-4); Vols. I & II. Pt. C. lib. bdg. 226.00 2 vol. set (ISBN 0-8240-0511-2); Vols. I & II. Bibliography of Literary Reviews in British Periodicals 1798-1820. Ed. by William S. Ward. Garland Pub.

Romantics to Rodin. H. W. Janson & Peter Fusco. LC 79-27101. (Illus.). 368p. 1980. pap. 11.95 (ISBN 0-8076-0953-6). Braziller.

Romantik Hotels & Restaurants: Charming Historic Hotels in Europe & the United States. Ed. by The Romantik Hotel & Restaurants Association Staff. (Illus.). 287p. pap. 6.95 (ISBN 0-916782-91-3, Dist. by Kampmann). Harvard Common Pr.

Romantiques Allemands: Brentano, von Arnim, Grimm, Chamisso, Morike, Buchner, etc, Vol. 2. 1792p. 48.95 (ISBN 0-686-56561-4). French & Eur.

Romantiques Allemands: Jean-Paul, Novalis, E. T. A. Hoffman, H. von Kleist, etc, Vol. 1. 1648p. 42.95 (ISBN 0-686-56560-6). French & Eur.

Romantische Poesie. Raimund Belgardt. (Ger). 1970. text ed. 37.20x (ISBN 90-2791-248-3). Mouton.

Romantische Schule. Rudolf Haym. LC 72-168953. Repr. of 1870 ed. 42.50 (ISBN 0-404-03166-8). AMS Pr.

Romantisme En France Au Dix-Huitieme Siecle. Daniel Mornet. LC 76-159705. (Research & Source Works Ser: No. 853). 1971. Repr. of 1912 ed. lib. bdg. 21.50 (ISBN 0-8337-4294-9). B Franklin.

Romantist: 1977, No. 1. Ed. by John C. Morgan & Don Herron. 1977. 10.00. F M Crawford.

Romantist: 1985-86, No. 9-10. Ed. by John C. Moran et al. 1988. 10.00. F M Crawford.

Romany Herbal Remedies. Gipsy Petulengro. LC 80-20035. 106p. 1980. Repr. of 1972 ed. lib. bdg. 19.95x (ISBN 0-89370-616-7). Borgo Pr.

Romany Herbal Remedies. Gipsy Petulengro. 1972. pap. 5.95 (ISBN 0-87877-016-X, H-16). Newcastle Pub.

Romany Life: Experienced & Observed During Many Years of Friendly Intercourse with the Gypsies. Frank Cuttriss. LC 75-3453. (Illus.). Repr. of 1915 ed. 34.50 (ISBN 0-404-16887-6). AMS Pr.

Romany of the Snows. facsimile ed. Gilbert Parker. LC 79-94741. (Short Story Index Reprint Ser.). 1896. 17.00 (ISBN 0-8369-3121-1). Ayer Co Pubs.

Romany Rye. George Borrow. 1984. pap. 8.95x (ISBN 0-19-281406-0). Oxford U Pr.

Romany Summer. Ellen Fitzgerald. 224p. 1987. pap. 2.50 (ISBN 0-451-15008-2, Sig). NAL.

Romany Wood. Beshlie. (Illus.). 1977. 9.95 (ISBN 0-8464-0800-7). Beekman Pubs.

Romanza: The California Architecture of Frank Lloyd Wright. David Gebhard. (Illus.). 1988. 25.00 (ISBN 0-87701-379-9). Chronicle Bks.

Rombo y Otros Momentos. Sarah Baquedano. LC 83-82850. (Coleccion Caniqui Ser.). 309p. (Span.). 1984. pap. 9.95 (ISBN 0-89729-345-2). Ediciones.

Rome. G. W. Edwards. 59.95 (ISBN 0-8490-0969-3). Gordon Pr.

Rome. Simon James. (Great Civilizations Ser.). (Illus.). 32p. (gr. 4-6). 1987. PLB 10.90 (ISBN 0-531-10399-4). Watts.

Rome. (Panorama Bks.). (Illus., Fr.). 3.95 (ISBN 0-685-11541-0). French & Eur.

Rome. (Baedeker's City Guides Ser.). 1986. pap. 10.95 (ISBN 0-13-058074-0). P-H.

Rome. (Berlitz Deluxe Guides). (Illus.). 1988. pap. 10.95 (ISBN 2-831-50366-3, Berlitz). Macmillan.

Rome. (Berlitz Travel Guides). (Illus.). 1988. pap. 6.95 (ISBN 2-831-50259-4, Berlitz). Macmillan.

Rome. (Berlitz Deluxe Guides). (Illus.). 336p. 1988. 10.95 (ISBN 0-02-968250-9, Berlitz). Macmillan.

Rome. (Berlitz Deluxe Guide). (Illus.). 336p. 1988. 10.95 (ISBN 2-8315-0366-3, Berlitz). Macmillan.

Rome. Mikhail I. Rostovtzeff. Ed. by Elias J. Bickerman. Tr. by J. D. Duff. 1960. pap. 10.95x (ISBN 0-19-500224-5). Oxford U Pr.

Rome. Emile Zola. 710p. 1955. 8.95 (ISBN 0-686-55802-2). French & Eur.

Rome see Trois Villes.

Rome Access. (Access Ser.). 1986. pap. 10.95. P-H.

Rome Access. Richard S. Wurman. (Access Guidebooks). (Illus.). 136p. (Orig.). 1986. pap. 14.95 (ISBN 0-671-62578-0). Access Pr.

Rome & a Villa. enl. ed. Eleanor Clark. LC 74-5979. (Illus.). 384p. 1982. pap. 8.95 (ISBN 0-689-70630-8, 1). Atheneum.

Rome & Byzantium. Clive Foss & Paul Magdalino. 1981. 30.00x (ISBN 0-7290-0012-5, Pub. by Phaidon Pr). State Mutual Bk.

Rome & China: A Study of Correlations in Historical Events. Frederick J. Teggart. LC 83-8511. (Illus.). xvii, 283p. 1983. Repr. of 1969 ed. lib. bdg. 38.50x (ISBN 0-313-24061-2, TERC). Greenwood.

Rome & Constantinople: Essays in the Dialogue of Love. Ed. by Robert Barringer. 86p. (Orig.). 1985. pap. 4.95. Holy Cross Orthodox.

Rome & Environs. Alta Macadam. (Blue Guide Ser.). (Illus.). 1982. 24.95 (ISBN 0-393-01550-5). Norton.

Rome & Environs. 3rd ed. Alta Macadam. (Blue Guides Ser.). (Illus.). 1985. cancelled (ISBN 0-393-01667-6); pap. 19.70 (ISBN 0-393-30074-9). Norton.

Rome & Her Kings: Extracts from Livy I. Ed. by W. D. Lowe & C. E. Freeman. (Bolchazy-Carduci Textbooks). 110p. 1981. pap. text ed. 9.00 (ISBN 0-86516-000-7). Bolchazy-Carducci.

Rome & Italy. Titus Livy. 1982. pap. 5.95 (ISBN 0-14-044388-6). Penguin.

Rome & Its Story. St. Clair Baddeley & L. D. Gordon. 1977. lib. bdg. 59.95 (ISBN 0-8490-2543-5). Gordon Pr.

Rome & Latium Phaidon Cultural Guide. (Phaidon Cultural Guides Ser.). (Illus.). 1987. 17.95 (ISBN 0-13-782855-1). P-H.

Rome & Medieval Culture. Ferdinand Gregorovius. Ed. by K. F. Morrison. Tr. by Mrs. Gustavus Hamilton from Ger. LC 72-142683. (Classic European Historians Ser). xxviii, 466p. 1973. pap. 4.75x (ISBN 0-226-30750-6, P427, Phoen). U of Chicago Pr.

Rome & Pompeii: Archaeological Rambles. Gaston Boissier. Tr. by D. Havelock Fisher. LC 77-39193. (Select Bibliographies Reprint Ser.). (Illus.). 435p. Repr. of 1896 ed. lib. bdg. 28.00 (ISBN 0-8290-0505-6). Irvington.

Rome & Pompeii: Archeological Rambles. Gaston Boissier. Tr. by D. Havelock Fisher. LC 77-39193. (Select Bibliographies Reprint Ser.). (Illus.). 1896. 29.00 (ISBN 0-8369-6795-X). Ayer Co Pubs.

Rome & Reform, 2 vols. Thomas L. Kington-Oliphant. LC 76-118541. Repr. of 1902 ed. Set. lib. bdg. 66.00 (ISBN 0-8290-1928-6). Irvington.

Rome & Reform, 2 Vols. Thomas L. Kington-Oliphant. LC 76-118541. 1971. Repr. of 1902 ed. Set. 47.50x (ISBN 0-8046-1165-3, Pub. by Kennikat). Assoc Faculty Pr.

Rome & Romans. Amery & Vanage. (Time Travelers Bks.). (gr. 4-9). 1976. 7.95 (ISBN 0-86020-069-8, Usborne-Hayes); PLB 12.96 (ISBN 0-88110-101-X); pap. 5.95 (ISBN 0-86020-070-1). EDC.

Rome & Romans According to Shakespeare. rev. ed. Michael Platt. LC 83-19855. 338p. (Orig.). 1984. pap. text ed. 14.50 (ISBN 0-8191-3625-5). U Pr of Amer.

Rome & Romans According to Shakespeare. Michael Platt. Ed. by JAmes Hogg. (JAcobean Drama Studies). 295p. (Orig.). 1976. pap. 15.00 (ISBN 3-7052-0346-0, Salzburg Studies). Longwood Pub Group.

Rome & Surroundings. Mill House Staff. (Illus.). 416p. 1989. pap. 12.95 (ISBN 0-02-035123-2, Collier). Macmillan.

Rome & the Anglicans: Historical & Doctrinal Aspects of Anglican-Roman Catholic Relations. J. C. Aveling et al. Ed. by Wolfgang Haase. 301p. 1982. 89.25 (ISBN 3-11-008267-5). De Gruyter.

Rome & the Arabs: A Prolegomenon to the Study of Byzantium & the Arabs. Irfan Shahid. LC 83-8930. (Illus.). 228p. 1984. 12.50x (ISBN 0-88402-115-7). Dumbarton Oaks.

Rome & the Friendly King: The Character of Client Kingship. David Braund. LC 83-40184. 224p. 1984. 22.95 (ISBN 0-312-69210-2). St Martin.

Rome & the Greek East to the Death of Augustine. Robert K. Sherk. LC 83-1833. (Translated Documents of Greece & Rome Ser.: No. 4). 224p. 1984. 47.50 (ISBN 0-521-24995-3); pap. 14.95 (ISBN 0-521-27123-1). Cambridge U Pr.

Rome & the Mediterranean. Livy. Tr. by Henry Bettenson. (Classics Ser.). 1976. pap. 6.95 (ISBN 0-14-044318-5). Penguin.

Rome & the Mediterranean, Two Hundred Eighteen to One Hundred Thirty-Three B.C. see Cambridge Ancient History Series.

Rome & the Neapolitan Revolution of 1820-1821. Joseph H. Brady. 1971. lib. bdg. 20.50x (ISBN 0-374-90933-4, Octagon). Hippocrene Bks.

Rome & the Romans As the Greeks Saw Them. B. Forte. (Papers & Monographs: No. 24). 730p. 1972. 24.50 (ISBN 0-318-12333-9). Am Acad Rome.

Rome & the Romans as the Greeks Saw Them. B. Forte. 730p. 1972. 42.00x (ISBN 0-271-00472-X). Pa St U Pr.

Rome & the Unification of Italy. A. Keaveney. 226p. 1987. lib. bdg. 37.50 (ISBN 0-7099-3121-2, Pub. by Croom Helm UK). Routledge Chapman & Hall.

Rome & the Unification of Italy. Arthur Keaveny. LC 87-1221. 256p. 1987. text ed. 28.50 (ISBN 0-389-20737-3). B&N Imports.

Rome Beyond the Southern Egyptian Frontier. L. P. Kirwan. (Mortimer Wheeler Archaeological Lectures). 1977. pap. 5.50 (ISBN 0-85672-152-2, Pub. by British Acad). Longwood Pub Group.

Rome, Conservatoria di Musica Santa Cecilia MS A-400. Ed. by Alexander Silbiger. (Seventeenth-Century Keyboard Music Ser.). 175p. 1988. lib. bdg. 60.00 (ISBN 0-8240-8012-2). Garland Pub.

Rome Convention for the Protection of Performers, Producers of Phonograms & Broadcasting Organizations. 15p. 1976. pap. 7.50 (ISBN 0-686-53032-2, WIPO38, WIPO). UNIPUB.

Rome, England, the United States & the Forces for the Decline & the Death of the Empires. Peter H. Wright. 155p. 1983. 145.50 (ISBN 0-86722-042-2). Inst Econ Pol.

Rome Express. Arthur Griffiths. LC 75-35443. (Literature of Mystery & Detection). 1976. Repr. of 1907 ed. 19.00x (ISBN 0-405-07874-9). Ayer Co Pubs.

Rome: French Edition-Country & City. (Michelin Green Guides). pap. 12.95 (ISBN 0-686-56410-3). French & Eur.

Rome: Frommer's City Guides Ser. rev. ed. (Illus.). 224p. 1988. pap. 5.95 (ISBN 0-13-047564-5). Prentice Hall Pr.

Rome Haul. Walter D. Edmonds. (York State Ser.). 347p. 1987. pap. text ed. 12.95x (ISBN 0-8156-0213-8). Syracuse U Pr.

Rome in Color see Travel Guides in Color.

Rome in Rome. Bill Knott. LC 75-44678. 1976. pap. 2.50 (ISBN 0-913722-07-3, Pub. by Release). Small Pr Dist.

Rome in the Age of Bernini: From the Election of Innocent X to the Death of Innocent XI. Torgil Magnuson. Tr. by Nancy Adler from Swedish. (Illus.). 420p. 1986. 39.95 (ISBN 0-391-03448-0, Pub. by Humanities Press & Almgvist & Wiksell). Humanities.

Rome in the Augustan Age. Henry T. Rowell. (Centers of Civilization Ser: Vol. 5). 258p. 1985. pap. 6.95x (ISBN 0-8061-0956-4). U of Okla Pr.

Rome in the High Renaissance: The Age of Leo X. Bonner Mitchell. LC 72-9277. (Centers of Civilization Ser.: Vol. 33). 1973. 11.95x (ISBN 0-8061-1052-X). U of Okla Pr.

Rome in the Late Republic. Mary Beard & Michael Crawford. LC 85-480. 106p. 1985. 22.50x (ISBN 0-8014-1824-0). Cornell U Pr.

Rome in the Late Republic. Mary Beard & Michael Crawford. LC 85-480. 106p. 1986. pap. 7.95x (ISBN 0-8014-9333-1). Cornell U Pr.

Rome in the Renaissance: The City & the Myth. Ed. by P. A. Ramsey. LC 83-14273. (Medieval & Renaissance Texts & Studies: Vol. 18). (Illus.). 464p. 1982. 22.00 (ISBN 0-86698-057-1). Medieval & Renaissance NY.

Rome in Your Pocket. Barbara Hults. 224p. 1988. pap. 3.95 (ISBN 0-8120-4030-9). Barron.

Rome, Judea & Christianity: The Crucifixion. James P. Jacobs. 300p. 1987. pap. 7.95 (ISBN 0-9617280-0-0). James Pr Inc.

Rome, Kiev et Byzance a la Fin du Onzieme Siecle. Bernard Leib. (Research & Source Works Ser.: No. 166). 1968. 26.00 (ISBN 0-8337-2060-0). B Franklin.

Rome: Mirror of the Centuries. Dominique Fernandez. Tr. by Peter Lauritzen. LC 84-7337. (Illus.). 252p. 1984. 50.00 (ISBN 0-86565-049-7). Vendome.

Rome, Naples et Florence. Stendhal, pseud. (Folio Ser.: No. 1845). 10.95 (ISBN 0-685-35020-7). Schoenhof.

Rome, Naples et Florence, 3 vols. facsimile ed. Stendhal. Set. 100.00 (ISBN 0-686-55081-1). French & Eur.

Rome, Naples et Florence. Stendhal. write for info. French & Eur.

Rome of Alexander VII, 1655-1667. Richard Krautheimer. LC 84-26553. (Illus.). 214p. 1987. 34.50 (ISBN 0-691-04032-X); pap. 12.95 (ISBN 0-691-00277-0). Princeton U Pr.

Rome on the Euphrates. Freya Stark. 1975. 28.50 (ISBN 0-7195-1335-9). Transatl Arts.

Rome or Brussels. W. R. Lewis. (Institute of Economic Affairs Hobart Paperbacks: No. 3). 1972. pap. 4.25 technical (ISBN 0-255-36024-X). Transatl Arts.

Rome Plenary Meeting of the Trilateral Commission. write for info. Trilateral Comm.

Rome: Profile of a City, 312-1308. Richard Krautheimer. LC 78-70304. (Illus.). 1980. 102.00x (ISBN 0-691-03947-X); pap. 29.95x (ISBN 0-691-00319-X). Princeton U Pr.

Rome, Seventeen Forty-Eight: The Pianta Grande Di Roma GiamBattista Nolli in Facsimile. (Illus.). 1984. deluxe ed. 315.00 (ISBN 0-9613348-1-9); pap. 96.00 (ISBN 0-9613348-2-7). J H Aronson.

Rome: The Augustan Age: A Source Book. Kitty Chisolm & John Ferguson. (Illus.). 1981. text ed. 62.00x (ISBN 0-19-872108-0); pap. text ed. 29.95x (ISBN 0-19-872109-9). Oxford U Pr.

Rome: The Biography of a City. Christopher Hibbert. LC 84-22684. (Illus.). 1985. 25.00 (ISBN 0-393-01984-5). Norton.

Rome: The Biography of a City. Christopher Hibbert. (Penguin Nonfiction Ser.). 400p. 1988. pap. 14.95 (ISBN 0-14-007078-8). Penguin.

Rome-the Biography of Its Architecture from Bernini to Thorvaldsen. Christian Elling. (Illus.). 1976. Repr. of 1975 ed. 100.00x (ISBN 87-002-7821-1, D-752). Vanous.

Rome, the Law-Giver. Joseph Declareuil. Tr. by Edward A. Parker. LC 73-98752. xvi, 400p. Repr. of 1927 ed. lib. bdg. 35.00x (ISBN 0-8371-2796-3, DERL). Greenwood.

Rome, the Sweet Tempestuous Life. Paul Hoffman. 224p. 1982. 14.95. St Martin.

Rome Was My Beat. Reynolds Packard. LC 74-31665. 1975. 8.95 (ISBN 0-8184-0216-4). Lyle Stuart.

Rome 1987-1988. (Frommer's City Guides). 224p. 5.95 (ISBN 0-671-62362-1). Prentice Hall Pr.

Romeo & Juliet see also Tragedy of Romeo & Juliet.

Romeo & Juliet. Center for Learning Staff. (YA) (gr. 9-12). 1988. pap. text ed. 14.95 (ISBN 0-697-02616-7). Wm C Brown.

Romeo & Juliet. Jill L. Levenson. (Shakespeare in Performance Ser.). 260p. 1987. 30.00 (ISBN 0-7190-2218-5, Pub. by Manchester Univ Pr); pap. 11.00 (ISBN 0-7190-2353-X, Pub. by Manchester Univ Pr). St Martin.

Romeo & Juliet. Maurer. 1986. lib. bdg. 54.00 (ISBN 0-8240-8837-9). Garland Pub.

Romeo & Juliet. Date not set. pap. price not set (Camelot). Avon.

Romeo & Juliet. Ed. by A. L. Rowse. LC 84-5086. (Contemporary Shakespeare Ser.: Vol. I). 140p. (Orig.). 1984. pap. text ed. 3.45 (ISBN 0-8191-3903-3). U Pr of Amer.

Romeo & Juliet. William Shakespeare. (Airmont Shakespeare Ser.). (gr. 8 up). pap. 1.75 (ISBN 0-8049-1009-X, S9). Airmont.

Romeo & Juliet. William Shakespeare. 1980. 37.00x (ISBN 0-416-17850-2, NO. 2872); pap. 7.95 (ISBN 0-416-17860-X, NO. 2873). Routledge Chapman & Hall.

Romeo & Juliet. William Shakespeare. Ed. by Joseph Bryant. pap. 2.75 (ISBN 0-451-52060-2, Sig Classics, L1040). NAL.

Romeo & Juliet. William Shakespeare. Ed. by R. E. Houghton. (New Clarendon Shakespeare Ser.). (Illus.). 1947. 5.95x (ISBN 0-19-831923-1). Oxford U Pr.

Romeo & Juliet. William Shakespeare. Ed. by Louis B. Wright & Virginia A. LaMar. (Folger Library). (Illus.). (gr. 9 up). 1960. pap. text ed. 2.95 (ISBN 0-671-00643-6). PB.

Romeo & Juliet. William Shakespeare. Ed. by T. J. Spencer. 1981. pap. 3.75 (ISBN 0-14-070701-8). Penguin.

Romeo & Juliet. William Shakespeare. Ed. by John E. Hankins. (Shakespeare Ser.). 1960. pap. 2.95 (ISBN 0-14-071419-7, Pelican). Penguin.

Romeo & Juliet. William Shakespeare. LC 79-24465. (Short Classics Ser.). (Illus.). 48p. (gr. 4 up). 1980. PLB 15.99 (ISBN 0-8172-1653-7). Raintree Pubs.

Romeo & Juliet. William Shakespeare. (Illus.). (gr. 7 up). 1970. pap. 1.95 (ISBN 0-590-02921-5, Schol Pap). Scholastic Inc.

Romeo & Juliet. William Shakespeare. LC 78-24129. (Shakespeare Plays Ser.). (Illus.). 296p. 1979. pap. 2.95 (ISBN 0-8317-7469-X, Mayflower Bks). Smith Pubs.

Romeo & Juliet. William Shakespeare. Adapted by Diana Stewart. LC 79-24465. (Short Classics Ser.). (Illus.). 48p. (gr. 4-12). 1983. pap. 9.27 (ISBN 0-8172-2020-8). Raintree Pubs.

Romeo & Juliet. William Shakespeare. Ed. by Maynard Mack & Robert W. Boynton. 1984. pap. 3.96 (ISBN 0-676-39637-2, Pub. by Boynton Cook). Random.

Romeo & Juliet. William Shakespeare. (Shakespeare Made Easy Ser.). 288p. (gr. 9-12). 1985. pap. 4.95 (ISBN 0-8120-3572-0). Barron.

Romeo & Juliet. William Shakespeare. (Classics Ser.). 1988. pap. 2.75 (ISBN 0-553-21305-9, Bantam Classics). Bantam.

Romeo & Juliet. rev. ed. William Shakespeare. Ed. by Joseph Bryant. 248p. 1987. pap. 2.75 (ISBN 0-451-52136-6, Sig Classics). NAL.

Romeo & Juliet. William Shakespeare. Ed. by Richard Adams. (Study Texts). 1988. pap. 4.75 (ISBN 0-582-33192-7). Longman.

Romeo & Juliet. William Shakespeare. Ed. by G. Blakemore Evans. (New Cambridge Shakespeare Ser.). (Illus.). 263p. 1984. 29.95 (ISBN 0-521-22223-0); pap. 6.95 (ISBN 0-521-29405-3). Cambridge U Pr.

Romeo & Juliet. William Shakespeare & Diane Davidson. LC 83-12309. (Shakespeare on Stage Ser.: Vol. 3). (YA) (gr. 8-12). 1983. casebound 7.95 (ISBN 0-934048-07-X); pap. 3.95 (ISBN 0-934048-06-1). Swan Books.

Romeo & Juliet - Together (and Alive) at Last. Avi. 128p. 1988. pap. 2.50 (ISBN 0-380-70525-7, Camelot). Avon.

Romeo & Juliet: A Study Text. Ed. by John S. Nickelsen. 128p. 1969. pap. text ed. write for info. (ISBN 0-02-387390-6, Pub. by Scribner). Macmillan.

Romeo & Juliet: American Style. Budd Robinson. (Illus.). 72p. (Orig.). 1985. pap. 3.00 (ISBN 0-88680-234-2). I E Clark.

Romeo & Juliet & West Side Story. Ed. by Norris Houghton. 256p. (YA) (gr. 7 up). 1965. pap. 3.25 (ISBN 0-440-97483-6, LFL). Dell.

Romeo & Juliet As an Experimental Tragedy. H. B. Charlton. 1939. lib. bdg. 15.00 (ISBN 0-685-10560-1). Folcroft.

Romeo & Juliet: Complete Study Edition. William Shakespeare. Ed. by Sidney Lamb. (Illus., Orig.). 1968. pap. 3.95 (ISBN 0-8220-1437-8). Cliffs.

Romeo & Juliet for Young People. William Shakespeare. Ed. by Diane Davidson. LC 86-5958. (Shakespeare for Young People Ser.: Vol. 2). 64p. (YA) (gr. 5-8). 1986. pap. 2.95 (ISBN 0-934048-19-3). Swan Books.

Romeo & Juliet Notes. Gary K. Carey. (Orig.). 1979. pap. 3.25 (ISBN 0-8220-0074-1). Cliffs.

Romeo & Juliet of Another Century. Michael Bertone. LC 78-50635. 1979. 12.95 (ISBN 0-87949-118-3). Ashley Bks.

Romeo & Juliet: Parallel Texts of the First 2 Quartos; Quarto 1, 1597 & Quarto 2, 1599. Ed. by P. A. Daniel. Incl. Romeo & Juliet: Reprint of Quarto 1, 1597. Repr. of 1874 ed; Romeo & Juliet: Reprint of Q. 2, 1599. Repr. of 1874 ed; Romeo & Juliet: Revised Edition Quarto 2, 1599. Repr. of 1875 ed. (New Shakespeare Society, London, Ser. 2: Nos. 1-4). pap. 47.00 (ISBN 0-8115-0233-3). Kraus Repr.

Romeo & Juliet: Plainspoken. Greta B. Lipson & Susan Solomon. (Illus.). 247p. (gr. 7-12). 1985. 13.95 (ISBN 0-86653-283-8). Good Apple.

Romeo & Juliet: Reprint of Q. 2, 1599 see Romeo & Juliet: Parallel Texts of the First 2 Quartos; Quarto 1, 1597 & Quarto 2, 1599.

Romeo & Juliet: Reprint of Quarto 1, 1597 see Romeo & Juliet: Parallel Texts of the First 2 Quartos; Quarto 1, 1597 & Quarto 2, 1599.

Romeo & Juliet: Revised Edition Quarto 2, 1599 see Romeo & Juliet: Parallel Texts of the First 2 Quartos; Quarto 1, 1597 & Quarto 2, 1599.

Romeo & Juliet (Shakespeare) Linnea. (Book Notes Ser.). 1984. pap. 2.50 (ISBN 0-8120-3440-6). Barron.

Romeo & Juliet: The Play of Opposites & the Law of Polarity. Theodore Heline. pap. 1.00 (ISBN 0-87613-042-2). New Age.

Romeo & Juliet-Together (& Alive!) at Last. Avi. LC 87-7680. 128p. (gr. 6-8). 1987. 11.95 (ISBN 0-531-05721-6); PLB 11.99 (ISBN 0-531-08321-7). Orchard Bks Watts.

Romeo & Juliet, with Reader's Guide. William Shakespeare. (Orig.). (gr. 10-12). 1974. text ed. 12.83 (ISBN 0-87720-828-X); pap. text ed. 8.58 (ISBN 0-87720-821-2); tchr's. ed. 8.91 (ISBN 0-87720-921-9). AMSCO Sch.

Romeo & Smurfette & Twelve Other Smurfy Stories. Delporte, pseud. LC 82-60258. (Smurf Adventures Ser.). (Illus.). 48p. (gr. 4-7). 1983. 2.95 (ISBN 0-394-85618-X). Random.

Romeo et Juliette see Eurydice.

Romeo et Juliette see Nouvelles Pieces Noires.

Romeo und Julie see German Opera.

Romeo und Julie: Gotha, Seventeen Seventy-Six. Georg A. Benda. Ed. by Thomas Bauman. Bd. with Alchymist: Dresden, Seventeen Seventy-Eight. Joseph Schuster. (German Opera Ser., 1770-1800). 280p. 1986. lib. bdg. 65.00 (ISBN 0-8240-8854-9). Garland Pub.

Romeow & Mewliet: (The Melancholy Ballad of) The Immortal Bard. Ed. by I. M. Bratt. (Illus., Orig.). 1981. pap. 1.50 (ISBN 0-934646-04-X). TX S & S Pr.

Romero: El Salvador's Martyr: A Study of the Tragedy of El Salvador. Dermot Keogh. 160p. 1981. 20.00x (ISBN 0-686-78988-1, Pub. by Dominican Ireland). State Mutual Bk.

Romerzimmer. Winnig. (EMC Easy Readers: Series A). (YA) (gr. 7-12). pap. 3.95 (ISBN 0-88436-041-5, 45261). EMC.

Rome's Northwest Frontier: The Antonine Wall. W. Hanson & G. Maxwell. (Illus.). 265p. 1987. pap. 15.00 (ISBN 0-317-61519-X, Pub. by Edinburgh U Pr Scotland). Columbia U Pr.

Romeus & Iuliet. Arthur Brooke. Ed. by P. A. Daniel. Bd. with Rhomeo & Julietta. William Painter. (New Shakespeare Society London Ser.: Ser. 3, No. 1). pap. 23.00 (ISBN 0-8115-0237-6). Kraus Repr.

Romewalks. Shetterly. pap. 9.95 (ISBN 0-8050-0553-6). H Holt & Co.

Romewalks. Anya Shetterly. 1984. 9.95 (ISBN 0-03-061913-0). H Holt & Co.

Romeyn De Hooghe, the Etcher: Contemporary Portrayal of Europe 1662-1707. John Landwehr. LC 72-92918. (Illus.). 406p. 1973. lib. bdg. 75.00x (ISBN 0-379-00011-3). Oceana.

Romische Agrargeschichte. Max Weber. Ed. by Moses Finley. LC 79-5013. (Ancient Economic History Ser.). (Ger.). 1980. Repr. of 1891 ed. lib. bdg. 23.00x (ISBN 0-405-12405-8). Ayer Co Pubs.

Romische Heeresgeschichte: Beitrage 1962-1985. Geza Alfoldy. (Mavors Roman Army Researches Ser.: Vol. III). 587p. (Ger.). 1987. 102.00x (ISBN 90-70265-48-6, Pub. by Gieben Amsterdam). Benjamins North Am.

Romische Militargeschichte Von Gallienus Bis Zum Beginn der Byzantinischen Themenverfassung. Robert Grosse. LC 75-7319. (Roman History Ser.). (Ger.). 1975. Repr. 26.50x (ISBN 0-405-07083-7). Ayer Co Pubs.

Romische Mythologie: Roman Mythology. Ludwig Preller. Ed. by Kees W. Bolle. LC 77-79154. (Mythology Ser.). (Ger.). 1978. Repr. of 1865 ed. lib. bdg. 53.00x (ISBN 0-405-10563-0). Ayer Co Pubs.

Romische Namengebung: Ein Historischer Versuch. Bruno Doer. LC 75-7317. (Roman History Ser.). (Ger.). 1975. Repr. 18.00x (ISBN 0-405-07081-0). Ayer Co Pubs.

Romische Staatsverwaltung, 3 vols. Joachim Marquardt. LC 75-7329. (Roman History Ser.). 1975. Repr. Set. 132.00x (ISBN 0-405-07101-9); 44.00x ea. Vol. 1 (ISBN 0-405-07102-7). Vol. 2 (ISBN 0-405-07103-5). Vol. 3 (ISBN 0-405-07104-3). Ayer Co Pubs.

Romischen Grabaltare der Kaiserzeit. facsimile ed. Walter Altmann. LC 75-10626. (Ancient Religion & Mythology Ser.). (Illus., Ger.). 1975. Repr. of 1905 ed. 26.50x (ISBN 0-405-07002-0). Ayer Co Pubs.

Rommel: As Military Commander. Ronald Lewin. pap. 2.50 (ISBN 0-345-28797-5). Ballantine.

Rommel: Battles & Campaigns. Kenneth Macksey. LC 78-31786. (Illus.). 1979. 14.95 (ISBN 0-8317-7477-0, Mayflower Bks). Smith Pubs.

Rommel Papers. Intro. by B. H. Liddell-Hart. (Quality Paperbacks Ser.). (Illus.). xxx, 544p. 1982. pap. 9.95 (ISBN 0-306-80157-4). Da Capo.

Rommel: The Desert Fox. Desmond Young. (Illus.). 264p. 1987. pap. 9.95 (ISBN 0-688-06771-9, Quill). Morrow.

Rommel the Desert Warrior: The Afrika Korps in World War II. Richard L. Blanco. LC 82-2293. 192p. (gr. 7 up). 1982. PLB 9.79 (ISBN 0-671-42245-6); pap. 4.95 (ISBN 0-671-49582-8). Messner.

Rommel's Last Stand. Lawrence Cortesi. 320p. 1984. pap. 3.25 (ISBN 0-8217-1415-5). Zebra.

Romola. George Eliot. Ed. by Andrew Sanders. (English Library). 1980. pap. 5.95 (ISBN 0-14-043139-X). Penguin.

Romontsch: Language & Literature: Sursilvan Rhaeto Romance of Switzerland. Douglas B. Gregor. (Oleander Language & Literature Ser.: Vol. 11). viii, 388p. 1982. pap. 35.00 (ISBN 0-900891-39-4). Oleander Pr.

Romp Through the Bible. William R. Phillippe. 192p. (Orig.). 1987. 20.00 (ISBN 0-940473-01-1); pap. 9.95 (ISBN 0-940473-02-X). Wm Caxton.

Romualdo Pacheco: Governor of California. Anthony Ramirez, Jr. (Illus.). 1974. 5.00 (ISBN 0-911302-26-3). San Francisco Pr.

Romulan Ship Recognition Manual. Forest G. Brown. (Star Trek Ser.). (Illus.). 48p. (Orig.). 1987. pap. 8.00 (ISBN 0-931787-43-2). FASA Corp.

Romulans, 2 bks. Fantasimulations Association Staff. (Star Trek Ser.). 80p. (Orig.). 1984. Set. pap. 12.00 (ISBN 0-931787-05-X). FASA Corp.

Romulo Betancourt & the Transformation of Venezuela. Robert J. Alexander. LC 81-14684. 600p. 1982. 39.95 (ISBN 0-87855-450-5). Transaction Bks.

Romulo Gallegos: An Oklahoma Encounter & the Writing of the Last Novel. Lowell Dunham. LC 73-19391. (Illus.). 100p. (Orig.). 1974. pap. 5.95x (ISBN 0-8061-1188-7). U of Okla Pr.

Ron Cooper. Jay Belloli. (Illus.). 38p. 1973. 6.00x (ISBN 0-686-99822-7). La Jolla Mus Contemp Art.

Ron Goularts's Great History of Comicbooks. Ron Goulart. (Illus.). 256p. (Orig.). 1986. pap. 14.95 (ISBN 0-8092-5045-4). Contemp Bks.

Ron Rood's Vermont: A Nature Guide. Ronald Rood. LC 88-9856. (Illus.). 224p. (Orig.). 1988. pap. 10.95 (ISBN 0-933050-56-9). New Eng Pr VT.

Ron Schara's Minnesota Fishing Guide. Ron Schara. (Illus.). 274p. (Orig.). 1978. pap. 9.95 (ISBN 0-931674-01-8). Waldman Hse Pr.

Ron Schara's Twin Cities Fishing Guide. Ron Schara. LC 81-22555. (Illus.). 120p. 1982. pap. 6.95 (ISBN 0-932272-08-8). Minneapolis Tribune.

Ron Van Clief Green & Purple Belt Guide Book. Ron Van Clief. LC 84-1926. (Illus.). 160p. 1985. pap. 9.95 (ISBN 0-517-55183-7). Crown.

Ron Van Clief White Belt Guide Book. Ron Van Clief. (Illus.). 1985. pap. 9.95 (ISBN 0-517-55181-0). Crown.

Ron Wood. Ron Wood. LC 86-45164. (Illus.). 160p. (Orig.). Numbered, signed, boxed ed. 50.00 (ISBN 0-06-055100-3). Har-Row.

Room in Chelsea Square. Michael Nelson. (Gay Modern Classics Ser.). 188p. 1986. pap. 7.50 (ISBN 0-85449-020-5, Pub. by GMP England). Alyson Pubns.

Room in the City. Ed. by Raymond Beeler. (Illus.). 64p. (Orig.). 1987. pap. 5.00 (ISBN 0-910413-38-X). Princeton Arch.

Room Made of Windows. Eleanor Cameron. (gr. 7 up). 1971. 14.95 (ISBN 0-316-12523-7, Joy St Bks). Little.

Room of Doom. Molly Albright. LC 88-15912. (Two of a Kind Ser.). (Illus.). 96p. (gr. 3-6). 1988. PLB 8.95 (ISBN 0-8167-1482-7); pap. text ed. 2.95 (ISBN 0-8167-1483-5). Troll Assocs.

Room of One's Own. Virginia Woolf. LC 29-27524. 118p. 1963. pap. 2.95 (ISBN 0-15-678732-6, Harv). HarBraceJ.

Room of One's Own Revisited. Teresa Susskind. 1977. pap. 3.50 (ISBN 0-911302-30-1). San Francisco Pr.

Room Service. Frank Moorhouse. 176p. 1987. pap. 5.95 (ISBN 0-14-010198-5). Penguin.

Room Temperature Phosphorimetry for Chemical Analysis. Tuan Vo-Dinh. (Chemical Analysis Monographs on Analytical Chemistry & it Applications: 1-075). 304p. 1984. 63.00 (ISBN 0-471-87884-7, Pub. by Wiley-Interscience). Wiley.

Room to Breathe. David Clewell. LC 76-42865. 1976. pap. 7.50 (ISBN 0-915316-29-3); signed ltd. ed. o.p. 15.00x (ISBN 0-915316-30-7). Pentagram.

Room to Breathe. Joann B. Guernsey. LC 86-2688. 192p. (gr. 7 up). 1986. 12.95 (ISBN 0-89919-465-6, Pub. by Clarion). Ticknor & Fields.

Room to Breathe. Jenny James. LC 83-62656. 340p. 1984. pap. 6.75 (ISBN 0-904573-77-X, Pub. by Caliban Bks). Longwood Pub Group.

Room to Move: An Anthology of Australian Women Writers. Ed. by Suzanne Falkiner. 1986. 15.95 (ISBN 0-531-15019-4). Watts.

Room Upstairs. Norma Levinson. LC 84-5606. 756p. 1984. 15.95 (ISBN 0-671-52377-5). S&S.

Room Where Summer Ends. Peter Cooley. LC 79-51605. (Poetry Ser.). 1979. 8.95 (ISBN 0-915604-27-2); pap. 4.50 (ISBN 0-915604-28-0). Carnegie-Mellon.

Room with a View. E. M. Forster. LC 85-40672. 248p. 1961. pap. 3.95 (ISBN 0-394-74318-0, V187, Vin). Random.

Room with a View. E. M. Forster. 1988. pap. 3.95 (ISBN 0-553-21323-7, Bantam Classics). Bantam.

Room with Walls: Selected Poems. Bo Carpelan. Tr. by Anne Born from Finland-Swedish. LC 87-80139. 1987. pap. 10.00. McGraw.

Room Without Walls: Selected Poems. Bo Carpelan. Tr. by Anne Borne from Swedish. (Illus.). 144p. 1987. pap. 12.00 (ISBN 0-948259-08-6, Pub. by Forest Bks London). Three Continents.

Room Without Walls: Selected Poems. Ernst Meister. Ed. by Georg M. Gugelberger. Orig. Title: Wandloser Raum. 64p. 1981. pap. 4.00 (ISBN 0-88031-057-X). Invisible-Red Hill.

Roomers: A One-Act Comedy. Jerome McDonough. 36p. 1983. pap. 2.00x (ISBN 0-88680-165-6). I E Clark.

Roomful of Hovings & Other Profiles. John McPhee. LC 68-23746. 250p. 1969. 14.95 (ISBN 0-374-25208-4); pap. 8.95 (ISBN 0-374-51501-8). FS&G.

Rooming-House Roomies: A Kaleidoscope of Life. Nancy S. Rizzo. 1988. 8.95 (ISBN 0-533-07543-2). Vantage.

Roominghouse Madrigals: Early Selected Poems 1946-1966. Charles Bukowski. LC 88-10426. 260p. 1988. 20.00 (ISBN 0-87685-733-0); pap. 12.50 (ISBN 0-87685-732-2). Black Sparrow.

Roommate & the Cowboy. Emily Chase. (Girls of Canby Hall Ser.: No. 27). 160p. (YA) (gr. 6-10). 1988. pap. 2.50 (ISBN 0-590-41390-2). Scholastic Inc.

Roommate Returns. Emily Chase. (Girls of Canby Hall Ser.: No. 29). 176p. (gr. 5-9). 1988. pap. 2.50 (ISBN 0-590-41671-5). Scholastic Inc.

Roommates. Emily Chase. (Girls of Canby Hall Ser.: No. 1). 224p. (Orig.). (gr. 7 up). 1986. pap. 2.50 (ISBN 0-590-41212-4). Scholastic Inc.

Roomrimes. Sylvia Cassedy. LC 86-4583. (Illus.). 80p. (gr. k-3). 1987. 12.95i (ISBN 0-690-04466-6, Crowell Jr Bks); PLB 12.89 (ISBN 0-690-04467-4). HarpJ.

Rooms. John Stefanidis & Mary Henderson. (Illus.). 160p. 1988. 45.00 (ISBN 0-8478-0962-5). Rizzoli Intl.

Room's Classical Dictionary. Adrian Room. 320p. 1983. 19.95 (ISBN 0-7100-9262-8). Routledge Chapman & Hall.

Room's Dictionary of Confusibles. Adrian Room. 1979. 16.00 (ISBN 0-7100-0120-7). Routledge Chapman & Hall.

Room's Dictionary of Confusing Words & Meanings. Adrian Room. 304p. 1985. 22.50 (ISBN 0-7102-0661-5). Routledge Chapman & Hall.

Room's Dictionary of Distinguishables. Adrian Room. 220p. 1981. 13.95 (ISBN 0-7100-0775-2). Routledge Chapman & Hall.

Room's Dictionary of Distinguishables & Confusibles, 2 vols. Adrian Room. 1981. 23.95 (ISBN 0-7100-9472-8). Routledge Chapman & Hall.

Rooms in the Darwin Hotel: Studies in English Literary Criticism & Ideas 1880-1920. Tom Gibbons. LC 73-83715. 174p. 1973. 15.00x (ISBN 0-85564-072-3, Pub. by U of W Austral Pr). Intl Spec Bk.

Rooms of the Soul: A Novel Told in Hasidic Tales. Howard Schwartz. (Illus.). 208p. 1984. pap. 7.95 (ISBN 0-940646-11-0). Rossel Bks.

Rooms of Their Own. Compiled by Jennifer Ellison. 256p. 1987. pap. 7.95 (ISBN 0-14-009218-8). Penguin.

Rooms Overhead. Betsy Sholl. LC 86-70727. 72p. 1986. 14.95 (ISBN 0-914086-66-9); pap. 7.95 (ISBN 0-914086-67-7). Alicejamesbooks.

Rooms to Grow up In. Rosie Fisher. (Illus.). 128p. 1985. 16.95 (ISBN 0-88162-084-X). Salem Hse Pubs.

Rooney Crooney's Second Chance. E. Lorraine Miller. LC 77-88334. (Miller Enterprises Self-Help Bks.). (Illus.). (ps-4). 1978. perfect bdg. 6.50x (ISBN 0-89566-351-1). Miller Ent.

Rooney's Guide to the Dissection of the Horse. W. O. Sack & R. E. Habel. LC 76-56521. (Illus.). 1982. with 10 microfiches 23.50x (ISBN 0-9601152-1-8). Veterinary Textbks.

Roosevelt. Edmund O'Connor. Ed. by Malcolm Yapp & Margaret Killingray. (World History Ser.). (Illus.). 32p. (gr. 6-11). 1980. lib. bdg. 6.95 (ISBN 0-89908-125-8); pap. text ed. 2.45 (ISBN 0-89908-100-2). Greenhaven.

Roosevelt - & Then? facsimile ed. Stanley High. LC 78-165643. (Select Bibliographies Reprint Ser). Repr. of 1937 ed. 21.00 (ISBN 0-8369-5952-3). Ayer Co Pubs.

Roosevelt after Inauguration. William S. Burroughs. LC 79-21111. 1979. pap. 3.00 (ISBN 0-87286-115-5). City Lights.

Roosevelt & De Gaulle: Allies in Conflict: A Personal Memoir. Raoul Aglion. (Illus.). 400p. 1988. 22.50 (ISBN 0-02-901540-5). Free Pr.

Roosevelt & Garrett. Jack DeMattos. 151p. 1986. 15.95 (ISBN 0-932702-42-2). Creative Texas.

Roosevelt & His America. Bernard Fay. 59.95 (ISBN 0-8490-0970-7). Gordon Pr.

Roosevelt & Romanism: Catholics & American Diplomacy, 1937-1945. George Q. Flynn. LC 75-35343. (Contributions in American History: No. 47). 272p. 1976. lib. bdg. 35.00 (ISBN 0-8371-8581-5, FRR/). Greenwood.

Roosevelt & Stalin: The Failed Courtship. Robert Nisbet. 160p. 1988. 14.95 (ISBN 0-89526-558-3). Regnery Gateway.

Roosevelt & the Hundred Days: Struggle for the Early New Deal. James Sargent. Ed. by Frank Freidel. LC 80-8465. (Modern American Hsitory Ser.). 367p. 1982. lib. bdg. 55.00 (ISBN 0-8240-4866-0). Garland Pub.

Roosevelt & the Isolationists, 1932-1945. Wayne S. Cole. LC 82-8624. xii, 698p. 1983. 34.00x (ISBN 0-8032-1410-3). U of Nebr Pr.

Roosevelt & the Russians: The Yalta Conference. Edward R. Stettinius. Ed. by Walter Johnson. (Illus.). Repr. of 1949 ed. lib. bdg. 35.00x (ISBN 0-8371-2976-1, STRR). Greenwood.

Roosevelt & the Russo-Japanese War. Tyler Dennett. 1958. 11.75 (ISBN 0-8446-1150-6). Peter Smith.

Roosevelt & World War Two. Robert A. Divine. LC 69-13655. (Albert Shaw Lectures on Diplomatic History Ser). (Illus.). 117p. 1969. 17.00x (ISBN 0-8018-1079-5). Johns Hopkins.

Roosevelt & World War Two. Robert A. Divine. 1970. pap. 5.95 (ISBN 0-14-021191-8, Pelican). Penguin.

Roosevelt Bears Go to Washington. Seymour Eaton. (Illus.). 192p. (gr. 6 up). 1981. pap. 4.50 (ISBN 0-486-24163-7). Dover.

Roosevelt Bears: Their Travels & Adventures. Seymour Eaton. (Illus.). 192p. (gr. 1 up). 1979. pap. 4.50 (ISBN 0-486-23819-9). Dover.

Roosevelt Confronts Hitler: America's Entry into World War II. Patrick J. Hearden. LC 86-23688. 1987. 27.00 (ISBN 0-87580-124-2). N Ill U Pr.

Roosevelt Confronts Hitler: America's Entry into World War II. 2nd ed. Patrick J. Hearden. 1987. pap. 9.00 (ISBN 0-87580-538-8). N Ill U Pr.

Roosevelt, de Gaulle & the Posts: Franco-American War Relations Viewed Through Their Effects on the French Postal System, 1942-1944. D. M. Giangreco. LC 86-72122. (Illus.). 192p. (Orig.). 1986. pap. 9.95 (ISBN 0-9616684-0-7). J V Bush.

Roosevelt Diplomacy & World War II. Ed. by Robert Dallek. LC 78-8325. (American Problem Studies). 126p. 1979. pap. text ed. 6.95 (ISBN 0-88275-687-7). Krieger.

Roosevelt File. Michael Rawcliffe. (Illus.). 96p. (YA) (gr. 9-12). 1980. 17.95 (ISBN 0-7134-1921-0, Pub. by Batsford England). David & Charles.

Roosevelt Foreign-Policy Establishment & the "Good Neighbor" The United States & Argentina, 1941-1945. Randall B. Woods. LC 78-10435. xiv, 278p. 1979. 27.50x (ISBN 0-7006-0188-0). U Pr of KS.

Roosevelt: From Munich to Pearl Harbor. Basil Rauch. LC 74-34446. (FDR & the Era of the New Deal Ser). 527p. 1975. Repr. of 1967 ed. lib. bdg. 45.00 (ISBN 0-306-70739-X). Da Capo.

Roosevelt Leadership Nineteen Thirty-three to Nineteen Fourty-Five. E. E. Robinson. LC 75-146154. (American Scene Ser.). 1972. Repr. of 1955 ed. lib. bdg. 49.50 (ISBN 0-306-70202-9). Da Capo.

Roosevelt Legacy & the Kent Case. Tyler Kent. 1983. lib. bdg. 79.95 (ISBN 0-87700-467-6). Revisionist Pr.

Roosevelt-Litvinov Agreements: The American View. Donald G. Bishop. LC 65-15852. 1965. 29.95x (ISBN 0-8156-2077-2). Syracuse U Pr.

Roosevelt Myth: A Critical Account of the New Deal & Its Creator. John T. Flynn & Murray Rothbard. 454p. 1985. pap. cancelled (ISBN 0-8159-6713-6). Devin.

Roosevelt New Deal: A Program Assessment Fifty Years After. (Symposia Ser.). 357p. 1986. 10.50 (ISBN 0-89940-416-2). LBJ Sch Pub Aff.

Roosevelt Policy: Speeches, Letters, & State Papers Relating to Corporate Wealth & Closely Allied Topics, 3 Vols. in 1. Theodore Roosevelt. Ed. by W. Griffith. Repr. of 1919 ed. 51.00 (ISBN 0-527-76768-9). Kraus Repr.

Roosevelt Presidency: Four Intimate Perspectives of FDR. Ed. by Kenneth W. Thompson. LC 82-17479. (Portraits of American Presidents Ser.: Vol. I). 100p. 1983. lib. bdg. 24.75 (ISBN 0-8191-2827-9); pap. text ed. 8.25 (ISBN 0-8191-2828-7). U Pr of Amer.

Roosevelt Red Background & Its Background. Elizabeth Dilling. 439p. 1986. 25.00 (ISBN 0-317-52985-4). Noontide.

Roosevelt Red Record & Its Background. Elizabeth Dilling. 1985. lib. bdg. 79.95 (ISBN 0-87700-654-7). Revisionist Pr.

Roosevelt Revolution, First Phase. Ernest K. Lindley. LC 74-637. (FDR & the Era of the New Deal Ser.). 328p. 1974. Repr. of 1933 ed. lib. bdg. 39.50 (ISBN 0-306-70651-2). Da Capo.

Roosevelt: The Story of a Friendship, 1880-1919. Owen Wister. 1978. Repr. of 1930 ed. lib. bdg. 25.00 (ISBN 0-8492-2954-5). R West.

Roosevelt to Reagan: A Reporter's Encounters with Nine Presidents. Hedley Donovan. LC 84-48592. 352p. 1987. pap. 8.95 (ISBN 0-06-039067-0, PL 1397, PL). Har-Row.

Roosevelt's Communist Manifesto. Emanuel M. Josephson. Repr. of 1841 ed. 75.00 (ISBN 0-685-37104-2). Chedney.

Roosevelt's Communist Manifesto. Emanuel M. Josephson. 1979. write for info. (ISBN 0-685-96467-1). Revisionist Pr.

Roosevelt's Communist Manifesto: Incorporating a Reprint of the Science of Goverment Founded on Natural Law by Clinton Roosevelt. Emanuel M. Josephson. (Illus.). 1976. Repr. of 1841 ed. 75.00 (ISBN 0-685-66410-4). Chedney.

Roosevelt's Farmer: Claude R. Wickard in the New Deal. Dean Albertson. LC 74-23430. (F. D. R. & the Era of the New Deal Ser.). 1975. Repr. of 1961 ed. lib. bdg. 49.50 (ISBN 0-306-70702-0). Da Capo.

Roosevelts Forest Army: A History of the Civilian Conservation Corps, 1933-42. Perry H. Merrill. (Illus.). ix, 224p. 1984. pap. 8.95x (ISBN 0-9605806-0-3). P H Merrill.

Roosevelt's Image Brokers: Poets, Playwrights & the Use of the Lincoln Symbol. Alfred H. Jones. LC 74-77651. 129p. 1974. 18.95x (ISBN 0-8046-9079-0, Pub. by Kennikat). Assoc Faculty Pr.

Roosevelt's Road to Russia. George N. Crocker. LC 74-26540. (FDR & the Era of the New Deal Ser.). (Illus.). xvii, 312p. 1975. Repr. of 1959 ed. lib. bdg. 39.50 (ISBN 0-306-70714-4). Da Capo.

Roosevelt's Road to Russia. George N. Crocker. 320p. 1986. Repr. of 1959 ed. 18.95 (ISBN 0-89526-587-7). Regnery Gateway.

Rooster & the Weather Vane. Sharon Peters. LC 86-30838. (Illus.). 32p. (gr. k-2). 1987. PLB 5.41 (ISBN 0-8167-0980-7); pap. text ed. 1.50 (ISBN 0-8167-0981-5). Troll Assocs.

Rooster Bingo & Other Mostly True Stories. Jerry Thompson. 204p. 1987. pap. 12.95 (ISBN 0-934395-69-1). Rutledge Hill Pr.

Rooster Crows. Maud Petersham & Miska Petersham. LC 46-446. (Illus.). 64p. (ps-2). 1969. 13.95 (ISBN 0-02-773100-6). Macmillan.

Rooster Crows: A Book of American Rhymes & Jingles. Maud Petersham & Miska Petersham. LC 87-1138. (Illus.). 64p. (ps-3). 1987. pap. 4.95 (ISBN 0-689-71153-0, Aladdin Bks). Macmillan.

Rooster Reminds Peter. (Magic Picture Bks.). (ps-2). 1988. pap. 0.59 (ISBN 1-55513-920-5, Chariot Bks). Cook.

Rooster Strut on the Suwannee & Two Short Stories. Grace E. Moses. LC 87-3458. 149p. 1988. 13.75 (ISBN 0-930950-15-1); pap. 7.75 (ISBN 0-930950-16-X). Nopoly Pr.

Rooster Who Refused to Crow. Thomas Crawford. (Illus.). (gr. 3-4). 1972. pap. 1.50 (ISBN 0-89375-050-6). Troll Assocs.

Rooster's off to See the World. Eric Carle. LC 86-25509. (Illus.). 28p. (ps up). 1987. 14.95 (ISBN 0-88708-042-1). Picture Bk Studio.

Roosters, Rhymes, & Railroad Tracks. George D. Hendricks. LC 80-26473. 200p. 1980. pap. 6.95 (ISBN 0-87074-177-2). SMU Press.

Root Activity Patterns of Some Tree Crops. (Technical Reports Ser.: No. 170). (Illus.). 154p. 1976. pap. 18.50 (ISBN 92-0-115175-6, IDC170, IAEA). UNIPUB.

Root Anatomy & Morphology: A Guide to the Literature. Robert H. Miller. LC 74-8606. viii, 271p. 1974. 27.50 (ISBN 0-208-01452-7, Archon). Shoe String.

Root & Its Modification in Primitive Indo-European. Benjamin Schwartz. (LD). 1947. pap. 16.00 (ISBN 0-527-00786-2). Kraus Repr.

Root & Sky: Poetry from the Plays of Christopher Fry. Ed. by Charles E. Wadsworth & Jean G. Wadsworth. (Illus., Ltd. ed. 220 copies, original intaglio prints by C. E. Wadsworth). slipcased 250.00 (ISBN 0-930954-17-3); 27 copies avail. Tidal Pr.

Root & the Branch: Judaism & the Free Society. Robert Gordis. LC 62-17133. 1962. 20.00x (ISBN 0-226-30411-6). U of Chicago Pr.

Root & the Flower. L. H. Myers. (Twentieth-Century Classics Ser.). 583p. 1986. pap. 7.95 (ISBN 0-19-281911-9). Oxford U Pr.

Root-Bound & Other Sketches. facsimile ed. Rose Cooke. LC 68-23719. (Americans in Fiction Ser.). (Illus.). 264p. lib. bdg. 24.00 (ISBN 0-8398-0275-7); pap. text ed. 6.95x (ISBN 0-89197-924-7). Irvington.

Root Cellar. Janet Lunn. LC 83-3246. 240p. (gr. 5-8). 1983. 12.95 (ISBN 0-684-17855-9, Pub. by Scribner). Macmillan.

Root Cellar. Janet Lunn. 230p. (gr. 7 up). 1985. pap. 3.95 (ISBN 0-14-031835-6, Puffin). Penguin.

Root Cellaring: The Simple No-Processing Way to Store Fruits & Vegetables. Mike Bubel & Nancy Bubel. (Illus.). 320p. 1979. 12.95 (ISBN 0-87857-277-5). Rodale Pr Inc.

Root-Determinatives in Semitic Speech. Solomon T. Hurwitz. LC 14-7725. (Columbia University. Contributions to Oriental History & Philology: No. 6). Repr. of 1913 ed. 15.25 (ISBN 0-404-50536-8). AMS Pr.

Root Development & Function: Effects of the Physical Environment. Ed. by P. J. Gregory et al. (Society for Experimental Biology Seminar Ser.: No. 30). (Illus.). 224p. 1987. 34.50 (ISBN 0-521-32931-0). Cambridge U Pr.

Root Diseases & Soil-Borne Pathogens. Ed. by T. A. Toussoun et al. LC 73-84531. (Illus.). 1970. 60.00x (ISBN 0-520-01582-7). U of Cal Pr.

Root Growth: Proceedings. Easter School in Agricultural Science (15th 1968, University of Nottingham) Ed. by W. J. Whittington. pap. 115.50 (ISBN 0-317-42111-5, 2025755). Bks Demand UMI.

Root-Knot Nematodes: Meloidogyne Species: Systematics, Biology & Control. Ed. by F. Lamberti & C. E. Taylor. 1979. 76.00 (ISBN 0-12-434850-5). Acad Pr.

Root Metaphor-the Live Thought of Stephen C. Pepper. Ed. by Arthur Efron & John Herold. LC 79-92716. (Paunch Ser.: Nos. 53-54). 224p. 1980. pap. 10.00 (ISBN 0-9602478-4-X). Paunch.

Root Nudules of Legumes: Structure & Functions. F. J. Bergersen. LC 83-185046. (Botanical Research Studies Press). 164p. 1982. 51.95x (ISBN 0-471-10456-6, Pub. by Res Stud Pr). Wiley.

Root of All Evil. E. X. Ferrars. (Large Print Books). 1985. lib. bdg. 14.95 (ISBN 0-8161-3879-6). G K Hall.

Root of All Evil. Dell Shannon. 288p. 1986. pap. 3.95 (ISBN 0-445-40259-8). Mysterious Pr.

Root of All Evil: The Thematic Unity of William Styron's Fiction. John K. Crane. 250p. 1985. 21.95x (ISBN 0-87249-447-0). U of SC Pr.

Root of Bitterness: Documents of the Social History of American Women. Ed. & frwd. by Nancy F. Cott. 385p. 1986. text ed. 30.00x (ISBN 1-55553-002-8); pap. text ed. 9.95x (ISBN 0-930350-95-2). NE U Pr.

Root of His Evil. James M. Cain. LC 87-72703. 192p. 1988. pap. 4.95 (ISBN 0-88739-087-0, Pub. by Black Lizard Bks). Creative Arts Bk.

Root of the Matter. facs. ed. Ed. by Hugh R. Sheppard. LC 67-26784. (Essay Index Reprint Ser). 1937. 18.00 (ISBN 0-8369-0874-0). Ayer Co Pubs.

Root of the Righteous. Aiden W. Tozer. 160p. pap. 5.95 (ISBN 0-87509-375-2). Chr Pubns.

Root of the World. Roger Bacon. pap. 2.95 (ISBN 0-916411-42-7, Pub. by Alchemical Pr). Holmes Pub.

Root Out of Dry Ground. Gilbert Morris. LC 81-65365. (Illus.). 100p. 1981. 4.95 (ISBN 0-935304-25-8); pap. 2.95 (ISBN 0-935304-26-6). August Hse.

Root Planing & Scaling. Wasserman. (Illus.). 160p. 1986. text ed. 84.00 (ISBN 0-86715-177-3, 1773). Quint Pub Co.

Root Planning see D.A.E Project: Instructional Materials for Dental Health Professions.

Root River Run. David Kherdian. LC 84-14244. (Illus.). 160p. (gr. 7 up). 1984. 10.95 (ISBN 0-87614-274-9). Carolrhoda Bks.

Root, Route & Range. Edward Mycue. 24p. 1977. pap. 3.00 (ISBN 0-914974-16-5). Holmgangers.

Root Song. Cid Corman. 96p. (Orig.). 1986. pap. 7.50 (ISBN 0-937013-15-3). Potes Poets.

Root: The Marines in Beirut, August 1982 - February 1984. Eric Hammel. LC 85-805. (Illus.). 320p. 1985. 19.95 (ISBN 0-15-179006-X). HarBraceJ.

Rootabaga Stories. Carl Sandburg. LC 36-27138. (Illus.). (gr. 4-6). 15.95 (ISBN 0-15-269057-3, HJ). HarBraceJ.

Rootabaga Stories, Pt. 1. Carl Sandburg. LC 73-13875. (Illus.). 230p. (gr. 4-6). 1974. pap. 5.95 (ISBN 0-15-678900-0, VoyB). HarBraceJ.

Rootabaga Stories, Pt. 1. Carl Sandburg. (Illus.). 192p. (gr. 1 up). 1988. 19.95 (ISBN 0-15-269061-1). HarBraceJ.

Roots of Pendle Hill. Carol R. Murphy. LC 78-1768. (Orig.). pap. 2.50x (ISBN 0-87574-223-8). Pendle Hill.

Roots of Perception: Individual Differences in Information Processing Within & Beyond Awareness. Ed. by U. Hentschel et al. (Advances in Psychology Ser.: No. 38). 476p. 1986. 105.25 (ISBN 0-444-70075-7, North-Holland). Elsevier.

Roots of Perinatal Medicine. Gosta Rooth. (Illus.). 148p. 1985. pap. 39.95 (ISBN 0-86577-173-1). Thieme Med Pubs.

Roots of Phonics: A Historical Introduction. Miriam Balmuth. 272p. 1986. Repr. of 1982 ed. text ed. 15.95x (ISBN 0-8077-2836-5). Tchrs Coll.

Roots of Political Philosophy: Ten Forgotten Socratic Dialogues. Ed. by Thomas L. Pangle. LC 87-47550. (Paperback Ser.). 424p. 1987. 44.50x (ISBN 0-8014-1986-7); pap. 12.95x (ISBN 0-8014-9465-6). Cornell U Pr.

Roots of Power: One Hundred Fifty Years of British Trade Union - a Personal View. Mark Stephens. 260p. 1986. 65.00x (ISBN 0-907590-06-3, Pub. by S P A Bks Ltd). State Mutual Bk.

Roots of Psychotherapy. Carl A. Whitaker & Thomas P. Malone. LC 80-24437. (Brunner Mazel Classics in Psychoanalysis & Psychotherapy: No. 9). 272p. 1981. Repr. 27.50 (ISBN 0-87630-265-7). Brunner-Mazel.

Roots of Psychotherapy. Carl A. Whitaker & Thomas P. Malone. LC 80-24437. (Classics in Psychoanalysis & Psychotherapy Ser: No.9). 272p. 1987. pap. 20.00 (ISBN 0-87630-498-6). Brunner-Mazel.

Roots of Radicalism: Jews, Christians & the New Left. Stanley Rothman & Robert S. Licther. (Illus.). 1982. 32.95x (ISBN 0-19-503125-3). Oxford U Pr.

Roots of Rastafari. Virginia L. Jacobs. LC 85-51342. 144p. (Orig.). 1985. pap. 9.95 (ISBN 0-932238-25-4, Pub. by Avant Bks). Slawson Comm.

Roots of Rebellion. Clarence A. Weber. LC 79-111802. 142p. 1971. 9.00 (ISBN 0-87527-085-9). Green.

Roots of Rebellion: Land & Hunger in Central America. Tom Barry. 250p. (Orig.). 1987. 25.00 (ISBN 0-89608-288-1); pap. 9.00 (ISBN 0-89608-287-3). South End Pr.

Roots of Rebellion: Workers' Politics & Organizations in St. Petersburg & Moscow, 1900-1914. Victoria E. Bonnell. LC 83-1084. 528p. 1983. text ed. 42.00x (ISBN 0-520-04740-0); pap. 11.95x (ISBN 0-520-05114-9). U of Cal Pr.

Roots of Reference. Willard van Orman Quine. LC 73-86488. (Carus Lecture Ser.: Vol. 14). 163p. 1973. 15.95 (ISBN 0-87548-123-X). Open Court.

Roots of Renewal in Myth & Madness: The Meaning of Psychotic Episodes. John W. Perry. LC 76-19500. (Jossey-Bass Behavioral Science Ser.). pap. 67.00 (ISBN 0-317-42373-8, 2052164). Bks Demand UMI.

Roots of Resistance: The Nonviolent Ethic of Martin Luther King Jr. William D. Watley. 160p. 1985. 12.95 (ISBN 0-8170-1092-0). Judson.

Roots of Revolution: A History of the Populist & Socialist Movements in Nineteenth-Century Russia. Franco Venturi. Tr. by Francis Haskell. xxxviii, 850p. 1960. pap. 20.00x (ISBN 0-226-85270-9). U of Chicago Pr.

Roots of Revolution: An Interpretive History of Modern Iran. Nikki R. Keddie & Yann Richard. LC 81-40438. (Illus.). 316p. 1981. text ed. 36.00 (ISBN 0-300-02606-4); pap. 10.95x (ISBN 0-300-02611-0, YF-24). Yale U Pr.

Roots of Revolution: Radical Thought in Cuba. Sheldon B. Liss. LC 86-7109. xxvi, 269p. 1987. 21.95x (ISBN 0-8032-2873-2); pap. 9.95x (ISBN 0-8032-7920-5). U of Nebr Pr.

Roots of Rock. Robert Palmer. Date not set. price not set (ISBN 0-670-60810-6). Viking.

Roots of Rural Poverty in Central & Southern Africa. Ed. by Robin Palmer & Neil Parsons. LC 76-24600. (Perspectives on Southern Africa: No. 25). 1978. 40.00x (ISBN 0-520-03318-3); pap. 11.95x (ISBN 0-520-03505-4). U of Cal Pr.

Roots of Russian Communism: A Social & Historical Study of Russian Social Democracy 1898-1907. David Lane. LC 74-15196. 1975. pap. text ed. 12.75x (ISBN 0-271-01178-5). Pa St U Pr.

Roots of Russian Through Chekhov: A Study in Word-Formation. Margaret I. Gibson. LC 81-43705. 236p. (Orig.). 1982. lib. bdg. 30.00 (ISBN 0-8191-2681-0); pap. text ed. 13.25 (ISBN 0-8191-2682-9). U Pr of Amer.

Roots of St. Francis. Raphael Brown. 9.50 (ISBN 0-8199-0824-X). Franciscan Herald.

Roots of Sorrow: Reflections on Depression & Hope. Richard Winter. LC 85-72916. 1986. pap. 7.95 (ISBN 0-89107-383-3, Crossway Bks). Good News.

Roots of Southern Distinctiveness: Tobacco & Society in Danville, Virginia, 1790-1865. Frederick F. Siegel. LC 86-19356. xvi, 206p. 1987. 22.00x (ISBN 0-8078-1727-9). U of NC Pr.

Roots of Southern Populism: Yeoman Farmers & the Transformation of the Georgia Upcountry, 1850-1890. Steven Hahn. 320p. 1983. 32.00x (ISBN 0-19-503249-7); pap. 9.95x (ISBN 0-19-503508-9). Oxford U Pr.

Roots of Southern Writing: Essays on the Literature of the American South. Clarence H. Holman. LC 74-184774. pap. 65.00 (2031175). Bks Demand UMI.

Roots of Soviet Power: Domestic Determinants of Foreign & Defense Policy. Ed. by Roman Kolkowicz. 288p. 1988. 38.50 (ISBN 0-8133-0543-8). Westview.

Roots of Special Interests in American Higher Education: A Social Psychological Historical Perspective. E. C. Wallenfeldt. LC 86-9234. 232p. (Orig.). 1986. lib. bdg. 22.75 (ISBN 0-8191-5415-6); pap. text ed. 13.00 (ISBN 0-8191-5416-4). U Pr of Amer.

Roots of State Intervention in the Brazilian Economy. Gustavo M. Gomes. LC 85-31174. 394p. 1986. lib. bdg. 44.95 (ISBN 0-275-92144-1, C2144). Praeger.

Roots of Strategy: A Collection of Classics. Raphael T. Phillips. LC 82-11890. 448p. 1982. Repr. of 1940 ed. lib. bdg. 45.50x (ISBN 0-313-23657-7, PHRS). Greenwood.

Roots of Strategy Book Two. (Illus.). 560p. (Orig.). 1987. pap. 12.95 (ISBN 0-8117-2260-0). Stackpole.

Roots of Strategy: The Five Greatest Military Classics of All Time-Complete in One Volume. Ed. by Thomas R. Phillips. 448p. 1985. pap. 10.95 (ISBN 0-8117-2194-9). Stackpole.

Roots of Success: Why Children Follow in Their Parents' Career Footsteps. David N. Laband & Bernard F. Lentz. LC 84-26309. 192p. 1985. 35.00 (ISBN 0-275-90132-7, C0132). Praeger.

Roots of Survival: Policy & Perspectives on Western Agriculture. Ed. by John Thorson. (Current Issues in the American West Ser.: Vol. III). (Illus.). 200p. (Orig.). pap. cancelled (ISBN 0-935704-23-X). Howe Brothers.

Roots of the American Working Class: The Industrialization of Crafts in Newark, 1800-1860. Susan E. Hirsch. LC 78-51784. (Illus.). 1978. 26.95x (ISBN 0-8122-7747-3). U of Pa Pr.

Roots of the Bill of Rights: An Illustrated Source Book of American Freedom, 5 vols. Bernard Schwartz. LC 80-22931. (Illus.). 1500p. 1981. Set. pap. 85.00 (ISBN 0-87754-207-4). Chelsea Hse.

Roots of the Blues. Charters. 15.00 (ISBN 0-7145-2705-X, Dist. by Kampmann & Co). M Boyars Pubs.

Roots of the Catholic Tradition. Thomas P. Rausch. (Theology & Life Ser.: Vol. 16). 1986. pap. 9.95 (ISBN 0-89453-538-2). M Glazier.

Roots of the Earthman. Dan Smith. (Illus.). 67p. 1981. pap. 4.95 (ISBN 0-932642-63-2). Unarius Pubns.

Roots of the Modern Christian Tradition. Ed. by E. R. Elder. 1984. 24.95; pap. 10.00. Cistercian Pubns.

Roots of the Mountains. William Morris. (Forgotten Fantasy Library: Vol. 19). 1979. pap. 6.95 (ISBN 0-87877-118-2). Newcastle Pub.

Roots of the Mountains: Wherein Is Told Somewhat of the Lives of the Men of Burgdale, Their Friends, Their Neighbours, Their Foeman & Their Fellows in Arms. William Morris. Ed. by R. Reginald & Douglas Menville. LC 80-19676. (Newcastle Forgotten Fantasy Library Ser.: Vol. 19). 424p. 1980. Repr. of 1979 ed. lib. bdg. 19.95x (ISBN 0-89370-518-7). Borgo Pr.

Roots of the Radical Theology. John C. Cooper. 174p. 1988. pap. text ed. 14.50 (ISBN 0-8191-7115-8). U Pr of Amer.

Roots of the Reorganization: French Polynesia. F. Edward Butterworth. LC 77-944. (Illus.). 1977. pap. 8.00 (ISBN 0-8309-0176-0). Herald Hse.

Roots of the Synoptic Gospels. Bo Reicke. LC 85-45485. 224p. 1986. 22.95 (ISBN 0-8006-0766-X, 1-766). Fortress.

Roots of the Western Tradition: A Short History of the Ancient World. 4th ed. C. Warren Hollister. (Illus.). 244p. 1982. pap. text ed. write for info (ISBN 0-394-34190-2, RanC). Random.

Roots of Ticasuk: An Eskimo Woman's Family Story. Emily I. Brown. LC 81-3458. (Illus.). 120p. (Orig.). 1981. pap. 4.95 (ISBN 0-88240-117-3). Alaska Northwest.

Roots of Tragedy: The United States & the Struggle for Asia, 1945-1953. Lisle A. Rose. LC 75-35354. (Contributions in American History: No. 48). 352p. 1976. lib. bdg. 35.00 (ISBN 0-8371-8592-0, RRT/). Greenwood.

Roots of Treason: Ezra Pound & the Secret of St. Elizabeths. E. Fuller Torrey. LC 84-10727. (Illus.). 368p. 1984. pap. 9.95 (ISBN 0-15-679015-7, Harv). HarBraceJ.

Roots of Two Black Marine Sergeant Majors: Sargent Major Edgar R. Huff & Gilbert H. "Hashmark" Johnson. Jesse J. Johnson. LC 78-55171. (Illus.). 1978. 10.00 (ISBN 0-915044-13-7); pap. 2.25 (ISBN 0-915044-14-5). Carver Pub.

Roots of Unbelief: In Defense of Everything. William J. O'Malley. LC 75-34840. 96p. 1976. pap. 2.95 (ISBN 0-8091-1915-3). Paulist Pr.

Roots of U. S. History. Blaine Coleman. 379p. (Orig.). 1987. pap. 24.00 (ISBN 0-318-22773-8). Philis Pub.

Roots of Urban Unrest. Ed. by John Benyon & John Solomos. 200p. 1987. text ed. 44.00 (ISBN 0-08-035840-3); pap. text ed. 14.50 (ISBN 0-08-035839-X). Pergamon.

Roots of Violence. Vincent Miceli. 19.95 (ISBN 0-8158-0449-0). Chris Mass.

Roots of Violence in Black Philadelphia, 1860-1900. Roger Lane. (Illus.). 224p. 1986. text ed. 27.00x (ISBN 0-674-77990-8). Harvard U Pr.

Roots of War. Richard Barnet. 1973. pap. 7.95 (ISBN 0-14-021698-7, Pelican). Penguin.

Roots of Western Civilization, 2 vols. Wesley D. Camp. Incl. Vol. 1. From Ancient Times to 1715 (ISBN 0-394-34167-8); Vol. 2. From the Enlightenment to the 1980's (ISBN 0-394-34168-6). (Illus.). 1983. pap. text ed. write for info (RanC). Random.

Roots of Western Culture: Pagan, Secular & Christian Options. Herman Dooyeweerd. 1979. 12.95x (ISBN 0-88906-104-1). Radix Bks.

Roots of Whitman's Grass. T. R. Rajasekharaiah. LC 76-85762. 522p. 1970. 32.50 (ISBN 0-8386-7493-3). Fairleigh Dickinson.

Roots of William Powell Lear. Institute of Family Research Staff. (Illus.). pap. 21.80 (ISBN 0-317-09100-X, 2051627). Bks Demand UMI.

Roots of Wisdom. Hung Ying-Ming. Tr. by William S. Wilson. LC 84-48125. (Illus.). 136p. (Japanese.). 1985. 17.95 (ISBN 0-87011-701-7). Kodansha.

Roots of Witchcraft. Michael Harrison. 280p. 1974. 7.95 (ISBN 0-8065-0444-7, Pub. by Citadel Pr). Lyle Stuart.

Roots out of Dry Ground. Reuben J. Swanson. 1979. 8.50 (ISBN 0-915948-06-0); pap. 6.50 (ISBN 0-686-57420-6). Bks Distinction.

Roots, Radicals & Quadratic Equations. rev. ed. Mervin Keedy & Marvin Bittinger. (Algebra, a Modern Introduction Ser.). (gr. 7-9). 1981. pap. text ed. write for info. (ISBN 0-201-03988-5). Addison-Wesley.

Roots, Renewal & the Brethren. 2nd ed. Nathan D. Smith. 152p. (Orig.). 1986. text ed. 12.95 (ISBN 0-932727-09-3, 86-76136); pap. 6.95 (ISBN 0-932727-08-5). Hope Pub Hse.

Roots-Routes. Richard Burns. (Illus.). 44p. (Orig.). 1982. pap. 8.00 (ISBN 0-914946-32-3). Cleveland St Univ Poetry Ctr.

Roots to Power: A Manual for Grassroots Organizing. Lee Staples. LC 84-3405. 176p. 1984. 35.00 (ISBN 0-275-91275-2, C1275); pap. 12.95 (ISBN 0-275-91800-9, B1800). Praeger.

Roots, Verb Forms & Primary Derivatives of the Sanskrit Language. W. D. Whitney. (Sanskrit.). 1976. 12.50 (ISBN 0-89684-308-4); pap. 9.95 (ISBN 0-89684-309-2). Orient Bk Dist.

Roots, Verb Forms & Primary Derivatives of the Sanskrit Language. William D. Whitney. (American Oriental Ser.: Vol. 30). 1945. 9.00x (ISBN 0-940490-30-7). Am Orient Soc.

Rootstocks for Fruit Crops. Ed. by Roy C. Rom & Robert F. Carlson. LC 86-15730. 480p. 1987. 54.95 (ISBN 0-471-80551-3). Wiley.

Rootstocks for Grape-Vines. D. P. Pongracz. LC 85-1420. (Illus.). 158p. 1983. 16.95x (ISBN 0-389-20567-2). B&N Imports.

Rootwork & Voodoo in Mental Health. Faheem C. Ashanti. LC 87-71941. 280p. 1987. lib. bdg. 43.50 (ISBN 0-911325-04-2). Tone Bks Inc.

Rootworker. Glenda Dumas. (Orig.). 1983. pap. 1.95 (ISBN 0-87067-711-X, BH711). Holloway.

Rooty Tooty Snooty. Stephen Cosgrove. (Snuffin Chronicles Ser.). (Illus.). 32p. (Orig.). (ps-3). 1988. pap. 3.95 (ISBN 0-8249-8209-6). Ideals.

Rope see Little Carthaginian.

Rope & Faggot: Biography of Judge Lynch. Walter F. White. LC 69-18545. (American Negro: His History & Literature Ser. No. 2). 1969. Repr. of 1929 ed. 17.00 (ISBN 0-405-01907-6). Ayer Co Pubs.

Rope & Other Plays. Plautus. Tr. by E. F. Watling. Incl. Ghost; Three-Dollar Day; Amphitryon. (Classics Ser.). 1964. pap. 4.95 (ISBN 0-14-044136-0). Penguin.

Rope Dancer. Roberta Gellis. 432p. 1987. pap. 3.95 (ISBN 0-515-08977-X). Jove Pubns.

Rope Dancer. Roberta Gellis. 1987. pap. 6.95 (ISBN 0-515-08593-6). Jove Pubns.

Rope-Dancer: Short Stories. M. J. Fitzgerald. LC 86-26159. 158p. 1987. 15.45 (ISBN 0-394-55921-5). Random.

Rope Dances. David Porush. LC 78-68135. 127p. 1979. 10.95 (ISBN 0-914590-50-2); pap. 5.95 (ISBN 0-914590-51-0). Fiction Coll.

Rope Drawings by Patrick Ireland: An Exhibition. Edit Deak. (Illus.). 32p. 1977. pap. 3.00x (ISBN 0-934418-04-7). La Jolla Mus Contemp Art.

Rope for Dr. Webster. James Gould Cozzens. 1976. ltd. ed. boxed 45.00 (ISBN 0-89723-010-8). Bruccoli.

Rope of God. James T. Siegel. LC 69-15942. (Center for South & Southeast Asia Studies, UC Berkeley: No. 29). 1978. Repr. of 1969 ed. 35.00x (ISBN 0-520-03714-6). U of Cal Pr.

Rope of Gold. Josephine Herbst. (Novels of the Thirties Ser.). 465p. 1984. pap. 9.95 (ISBN 0-935312-33-1). Feminist Pr.

Rope of Gold. Josephine Herbst. 416p. (Orig.). 1986. pap. 3.95 (ISBN 0-446-32871-5). Warner Bks.

Rope of Matuska. Giovanni Presutti. 1988. 14.95 (ISBN 0-533-07786-9). Vantage.

Rope of Moka. Andrew Strathern. Cambridge U Pr.

Rope of Sand: The AFL-CIO Committee on Political Education, 1955-1967. Alan Draper. 1988. price not set (ISBN 0-275-93045-9, C3045). Praeger.

Rope of Sand: The Colonial Agents, British Politics, & the American Revolution. Michael G. Kammen. LC 68-16383. (Illus.). 367p. 1968. 29.95x (ISBN 0-8014-0222-0). Cornell U Pr.

Rope Skipping for Fun & Fitness. Bob Melson & Vicki Worrell. LC 86-50270. (Illus.). 116p. (Orig.). 1986. pap. text ed. 6.95 (ISBN 0-914111-06-X). Woodlawn Pubs.

Ropeless Jumping: The Conversion of a Jogger. Bruce McBogg. (Illus.). 71p. 1981. 3.45 (ISBN 0-686-32863-9). B McBogg.

Ropemakers of Plymouth: A History of the Plymouth Cordage Company, 1824-1949. Samuel E. Morison. LC 75-41772. (Companies & Men: Business Enterprises in America). (Illus.). 1976. Repr. of 1950 ed. 21.00x (ISBN 0-405-08086-7). Ayer Co Pubs.

Ropes, Knots & Slings for Climbers. rev. ed. Walt Wheelock. (Illus.). 1985. wrappers 2.50 (ISBN 0-910856-00-1). La Siesta.

Ropes to Skip & the Ropes to Know: Studies in Organizational Behavior. 2nd ed. R. Richard Ritti & G. Ray Funkhouser. LC 81-6714. (Management Ser.). 200p. 1984. pap. text ed. write for info. (ISBN 0-471-84193-5). Wiley.

Ropes to Skip & the Ropes to Know: Studies in Organizational Behavior. 3rd ed. R. Richard Ritti & G. Ray Funkhouser. LC 86-13330. 271p. 1987. 17.95 (ISBN 0-471-85093-4); pap. write for info. (ISBN 0-471-81789-9). Wiley.

Ropespinner Conspiracy. Michael M. Thomas. 448p. 1987. 18.95 (ISBN 0-446-51290-7). Warner Bks.

Ropespinner Conspiracy. Michael M. Thomas. 432p. 1987. pap. 4.95 (ISBN 0-446-34676-4). Warner Bks.

Roping: Trick & Fancy Rope Spinning. Chester Byers. 96p. 1986. pap. 7.95 (ISBN 0-918222-95-8). Applewood.

Roquefort Gang. Sandy Clifford. (Illus.). (gr. 2-6). 1981. 7.95 (ISBN 0-395-29521-1). HM.

Rororo Musikhandbuch, 2 vols. H. Lindlar. (Ger.). 1976. pap. 35.00 (ISBN 3-499-16167-2, M-7605, Pub. by Rowohlt). French & Eur.

Rorschach: A Comprehensive System, Assessment of Children & Adolescents, Vol. 3. John E. Exner & Irving B. Weiner. LC 74-8888. (Personality Processes Ser.). 449p. 1982. Vol. 1. 58.95 (ISBN 0-471-24964-5); Vol. 2. 57.50 (ISBN 0-471-09364-5). Wiley.

Rorschach: A Comprehensive System: Assessment of Personality & Psychopathology, Vol. 2. 2nd ed. Exner. (Personality Processes Ser.). 1988. write for info. (ISBN 0-471-85080-2). Wiley.

Rorschach: A Comprehensive System, Basic Foundation, Vol. 1. 2nd ed. John E. Exner. LC 85-17870. (Personality Processes Ser.). 522p. 1986. 58.95 (ISBN 0-471-80704-4). Wiley.

Rorschach: A Comprehensive System, Current Research & Advanced Interpretatiom, Vol. 2. John E. Exner. LC 74-8888. (Personality Processes Ser.). 448p. 1978. 58.95 (ISBN 0-471-04166-1, Pub. by Wiley-Interscience). Wiley.

Rorschach Content Interpretation. Edward Aronow & Marvin Reznikoff. LC 76-25544. 384p. 1976. 56.50 (ISBN 0-8089-0961-4, 790200). Grune.

Rorschach Interpretation: Advanced Technique. Leslie Phillips & Joseph G. Smith. LC 53-9833. (Illus.). 400p. 1953. 35.50 (ISBN 0-8089-0361-6, 793287). Grune.

Rorschach Introduction: Content & Perceptual Approaches. Ed. by Edward Aronow & Marvin Reznikoff. 160p. 1982. 21.50 (ISBN 0-8089-1516-9, 790201). Grune.

Rorschach Location & Scoring Manual. Leonard Small. LC 55-10398. (Illus.). 224p. 1956. 49.50 (ISBN 0-8089-0432-9, 794140). Grune.

Rorschach Psychology. 2nd ed. M. Rickers-Ovsiankina. LC 74-266. 672p. 1977. 46.50 (ISBN 0-88275-168-9). Krieger.

Rorschach Scoring. Ed. by Clifford M. DeCato et al. (Illus.). 222p. 1987. pap. text ed. 25.00 (ISBN 0-8058-0119-7). L Erlbaum Assocs.

Rorschach Scoring: A Workbook for the Perceptanalytic System. Clifford M. Decato et al. LC 84-9566. 224p. 1984. spiral bdg. 32.50 (ISBN 0-87630-364-5). Brunner-Mazel.

Rorschach Study of Child Development. Nettie H. Ledwith. LC 75-26632. 336p. 1975. Repr. of 1960 ed. lib. bdg. 35.00x (ISBN 0-8371-8365-0, LERS). Greenwood.

Rorschach Systems. John F. Exner. LC 68-31431. 392p. 1969. 49.50 (ISBN 0-8089-0128-1, 791180). Grune.

Rorschach Technique: An Introductory Manual. Bruno Klopfer & Helen H. Davidson. (Ilius.). 245p. 1962. text ed. 27.00 net (ISBN 0-15-577873-0, HC). HarBraceJ.

Rorschach Technique with Children & Adolescents: Application & Norms. Eugene E. Levitt & Aare Truumaa. LC 72-7362. 160p. 1972. 42.50 (ISBN 0-8089-0785-9, 792520). Grune.

Rorschach Workbook. rev. ed. Lucille H. Blum et al. LC 74-10227. 193p. (Orig.). 1975. spiral bdg. 22.50x (ISBN 0-8236-5901-1). Intl Univs Pr.

Rose Rent. Ellis Peters. 1988. pap. 3.95 (ISBN 0-449-21495-8, Crest). Fawcett.
Rose Royce in Floral Delivery Manuals. Freddie L. Wade. (Illus.). 32p. (Orig.). (YA) 1988. pap. 12.95 (ISBN 0-9620447-0-9). Wade-Inn-Sonn.
Rose Tatoo see Theatre of Tennessee Williams.
Rose, the Book, & the Puppy. Dick Dilley. (People Patch Ser.). (Illus.). 48p. (gr. 1-5). 1986. PLB 9.95 (ISBN 0-936535-01-6). People Patch.
Rose Theatre. Gilbert Sorrentino. 160p. 1987. 20.00 (ISBN 0-916583-23-6). Dalkey Arch.
Rose Township Eighteen Thirty-Seven - Nineteen Eighty-Seven. Rose Township Historical Society. Ed. by Betty Trimmer. LC 86-63912. (Illus.). 141p. 1987. 18.50 (ISBN 0-9617648-0-5). Rose Twsp Hist Soc.
Rose Tree. John Broderick. (Fiction Ser.). 192p. 1985. 14.95 (ISBN 0-7145-2824-2, Dist. by Kampmann & Co). M Boyars Pubs.
Rose Tree. Date not set. price not set. Viking.
Rose, Where Did You Get That Red: Teaching Great Poetry to Children. Kenneth Koch. LC 73-17480. 1974. pap. 5.95 (ISBN 0-394-71885-2, Vin). Random.
Rose, Where Do You Get That Red? Kenneth Koch. 1973. 7.95 (ISBN 0-394-48320-0). Random.
Rose White, Rose Red. Daisy Vivian. 192p. 1983. 12.95 (ISBN 0-8027-0750-5). Walker & Co.
Rose Window. Bridget Wood. 1985. 24.95x (ISBN 0-7090-2190-9, Pub. by R Hale Ltd UK). State Mutual Bk.
Roseanna. Maj Sjowall & Per Wahloo. 1976. pap. 4.95 (ISBN 0-394-71779-1, Vin). Random.
Roseanne Roseannadanna's "Hey, Get Back to Work!" Book. Roseanne Roseannadanna & Alan Zweibel. (Long Shadows Bks.). (Orig.). 1983. pap. 4.95 (ISBN 0-671-47394-8). PB.
Roseate Spoonbill. Robert P. Allen. (Illus.). 7.00 (ISBN 0-8446-1528-5). Peter Smith.
Rosebud. Gerard Malanga. (Illus.). 40p. 1975. signed ed. 15.00x (ISBN 0-915778-15-7); pap. 5.00 (ISBN 0-915778-40-8). Penmaen Pr.
Rosebud Bursts. Randy Brooks. 40p. 1979. 10.00 (ISBN 0-913719-68-4); pap. 3.50 (ISBN 0-913719-67-6). High-Coo Pr.
Rosebud, with Fangs. Beverly Keller. 128p. (gr. 4-6). 1985. 10.25 (ISBN 0-688-03747-X). Lothrop.
Rosebud, with Fangs. Beverly Keller. LC 87-46443. 160p. (gr. 3-7). 1988. pap. 3.50 (ISBN 0-06-440245-2, Trophy). HarpJ.
Rosebuds: A Collection of Poems & Songs. Rose B. Isaacs. 1977. Repr. of 1976 ed. 6.95 (ISBN 0-87012-263-0). McClain.
Rosecran's Campaigns. LC 76-42129. (Civil War Monographs). 1977. lib. bdg. 16.00 (ISBN 0-527-17564-1); pap. 10.00 (ISBN 0-527-17565-X). Kraus Repr.
Rosedale Hoax. Rachel Wyatt. (Anansi Fiction Ser.: No. 37). 136p. (Orig.). 1977. pap. 8.95 (ISBN 0-88784-061-2, Pub. by Hse Anansi Pr Canada). U of Toronto Pr.
Rosegarden & Labyrinth: A Study in Art Education. Seonaid M. Robertson. xxix, 216p. (Orig.). 1982. pap. 13.50 (ISBN 0-88214-319-0). Spring Pubns.
Rosegger's Religion. Henry C. Sorg. LC 78-140029. (Catholic University Studies in German Ser.: No. 11). 1970. Repr. of 1938 ed. 24.00 (ISBN 0-404-50231-8). AMS Pr.
Roseland Peabody. (Ballroom Dance Ser.). 1985. lib. bdg. 66.00 (ISBN 0-87700-771-3). Revisionist Pr.
Roseland Peabody. (Ballroom Dance Ser.). Date not set. lib. bdg. 79.95 (ISBN 0-8490-3418-3). Gordon Pr.
Rosella & the Butterfly. Rose Selarose. Adapted by Jennifer Magnani. (Rosella Ser.). (ps-3). 1987. 5.95 (ISBN 0-671-64347-9, Little Simon). S&S.
Rosella & the Star. Rose Selarose. Adapted by Jennifer Magnani. (Rosella Ser.). (ps-3). 1987. 5.95 (ISBN 0-671-64346-0, Little Simon). S&S.
Roselynde. Roberta Gellis. (Roselynde Chronicles Ser.). 1984. lib. bdg. 13.95 (ISBN 0-8398-2860-8, Gregg). G K Hall.
Rosemaling ABC. 6th ed. E. Sjovaag. 1982. pap. 11.00x (ISBN 8-2531-9190-1, N519). Vanous.
Rosemaling Designs (Eight) Telmark O. Floors. 10.00x (ISBN 0-89918-421-9, N-421). Vanous.
Rosemaling Designs (8) Nordmore. O. Floors. pap. 10.00x (ISBN 0-89918-422-7, N422). Vanous.
Rosemaling Designs (8) Sunnmore. O. Floors. pap. 10.00x (ISBN 0-89918-423-5, N423). Vanous.
Rosemaling, the Beautiful Norwegian Art. (Illus.). 1974. spiral bdg. 8.00 (ISBN 0-9603700-0-5). H E Blanck.
Rosemary for Remembrance. June Thomson. LC 87-28742. (Crime Club Ser.). 192p. 1988. 12.95 (ISBN 0-385-24328-6). Doubleday.
Rosemary for Remembrance: A Keepsake Book. Tasha Tudor. (Illus.). 32p. 1981. 10.95 (ISBN 0-399-20812-7, Pub. by Philomel). Putnam Pub Group.
Rosemary Tree. Elizabeth Goudge. 381p. 1979. Repr. lib. bdg. 16.95x (ISBN 0-89966-107-6). Buccaneer Bks.
Rosemary's Baby. Ira Levin. 1979. pap. 2.25 (ISBN 0-440-17541-0). Dell.
Rosemary's Baby. Ira Levin. 1967. 10.95 (ISBN 0-394-44308-X). Random.
Rosemary's Letter Book: The Record of a Year Edgar A. Poe, Milton, Barrie, Swinburne, Kipling, Fitzgerald, Galsworthy, George Meredith. W. L. Courtney. 1973. Repr. of 1909 ed. 25.00 (ISBN 0-8274-1524-9). R West.
Rosemonde E. & Emile Kuntz Collection: A Catalogue of the Manuscripts & Printed Ephemera. Ed. by Guillermo Nanez-Falcon. LC 81-13168. 1981. pap. 20.00 (ISBN 0-9603212-3-3). Tulane Univ.
Rosen by Any Other Name. Israel Horovitz. 73p. 1987. pap. 3.50 (ISBN 0-317-60251-9). Dramatists Play.
Rosen Photo Guide to a Career in Animal Care. Susan Jeffers. (Careers Ser.). (Illus.). (YA) (gr. 7-12). 1988. lib. bdg. 10.95 (ISBN 0-8239-0818-6). Rosen Group.
Rosen Photo Guide to a Career in Health & Fitness. Arnold Hammer. (Careers Ser.). (Illus.). (YA) (gr. 7-12). 1988. lib. bdg. 10.95 (ISBN 0-8239-0820-8). Rosen Group.
Rosen Photo Guide to a Career in Magic. Randall Williams. (Careers Ser.). (Illus.). (YA) (gr. 7-12). 1988. lib. bdg. 10.95 (ISBN 0-8239-0817-8). Rosen Group.
Rosen Photo Guide to a Career in the Circus. Cynthia Laslo. (Illus.). (YA) (gr. 7-12). 1988. lib. bdg. 10.95 (ISBN 0-8239-0819-4). Rosen Group.
Rosen, Rosen, Rosen see Complete Book of Roses.
Rosenbaums of Zell. Strauss. cancelled (ISBN 0-685-48598-6). Feldheim.
Rosenberg-Barthes-Hassan: The Postmodern Habit of Thought. Jerome Klinkowitz. LC 87-22195. (Illus.). 232p. 1988. 26.00x (ISBN 0-8203-0997-4). U of GA Pr.
Rosenberg Dictionary Library. Rosenberg. 1986. 92.52 (ISBN 0-471-85137-X). Wiley.
Rosenberg File: A Search for the Truth. Ronald Radosh & Joyce Milton. LC 84-40019. 640p. 1984. pap. 8.95 (ISBN 0-394-72594-8, Vin). Random.
Rosenbergs: Collected Visions of Artists & Writers. Ed. by Robert A. Okun. (Illus.). 160p. (Orig.). 1988. pap. 24.95 (ISBN 0-87663-543-5). Universe.
Rosencrantz & Guildenstern Are Dead. Tom Stoppard. 1967. 10.00 (ISBN 0-394-50380-5, GP817). Grove.
Rosencrantz & Guildenstern Are Dead. Tom Stoppard. (Orig.). 1967. pap. 4.95 (ISBN 0-394-17260-4, B319, BC). Grove.
Rosencrantz & Guildenstern Are Dead. Tom Stoppard. 126p. (Orig.). Date not set. pap. 4.95 (ISBN 0-8021-3033-X). Grove.
Rosenkavalier. Richard Strauss. Ed. by Nicholas John. Tr. by Alfred Kalisch from Ger. (English National Opera Guide Ser.: No. 8, Libretto, Articles). (Illus., Orig.). 1982. pap. 4.95 (ISBN 0-7145-3851-5). Riverrun NY.
Rosenthal Story. 1985. write for info. Lloylds Pub.
Rosenthal's Computer Glossary. Steven Rosenthal. 350p. 1984. 17.95 (ISBN 0-13-783192-7). P-H.
Rosenthal's Dictionary of the Automated Office. Steven Rosenthal. 350p. 1984. 19.95 (ISBN 0-13-783218-4); pap. 12.95 (ISBN 0-13-783200-1). P-H.
Rosenwald & Rosenbach, Two Philadelphia Bookmen: Catalogue of an Exhibition at the Rosenbach Museum & Library from the Lessing J. Rosenwald Collection at the Library of Congress, April 30 to July 31, 1983. Rosenwald & Rosenbach. (Illus.). 40p. 1983. pap. 10.00x (ISBN 0-939084-15-5, Rosenbach Museum & Library). U Pr of Va.
Rosenzweig Picture-Frustration (P-F) Study--Basic Manual. Saul Rosenzweig. LC 77-95428. 1978. 9.00 (ISBN 0-930172-02-7). Rana Hse.
Rosepath Motif: An Approach to Weaving Design. Margaret B. Windeknecht. (Illus.). 64p. (Orig.). 1987. pap. text ed. 8.50 (ISBN 0-9618797-0-X). T G Windeknecht.
Roses. Barbara Cohen. LC 83-23881. (Illus.). 224p. (gr. 6 up). 1984. 11.75 (ISBN 0-688-02166-2). Lothrop.
Roses. Barbara Cohen. 222p. (gr. 7 up). 1985. pap. 2.25 (ISBN 0-590-33602-9, Point). Scholastic Inc.
Roses. rev. ed. Gertrude Jekyll & Edward Mawley. LC 82-16337. (Jekyll Garden Bks.). Orig. Title: Roses for English Gardens. (Illus.). 301p. 1984. 23.50 (ISBN 0-88143-001-3); pap. 10.95 (ISBN 0-88143-057-9). Ayer Co Pubs.
Roses. Roger Phillips & Martyn Rix. LC 87-43216. (Illus.). 224p. 1988. pap. 19.95 (ISBN 0-394-75867-6). Random.
Roses. Ellis Rawnsley. (Illus.). 48p. 1984. 18.00 (ISBN 0-88014-070-4). Mosaic Pr OH.
Roses. rev. ed. Richard Ray & Michael MacCaskey. LC 80-82532. (Gardening Ser.). (Illus., Orig.). 1984. pap. 9.95 (ISBN 0-89586-079-1). Price Stern.
Roses. 3.95 (ISBN 0-686-21143-X). Bklyn Botanic.
Roses. 4th ed. Sunset Editors. LC 79-90334. (Illus.). 96p. 1980. pap. 6.95 (ISBN 0-376-03656-7, Sunset Bks). Sunset-Lane.
Roses. Time-Life Books Editors. (Gardener's Guide Ser.). 144p. 1989. 17.27 (ISBN 0-8094-6628-7); lib. bdg. 21.27 (ISBN 0-8094-6629-5). Time-Life.
Roses. Diane Wakoski. (Illus.). 22p. 1987. ltd. ed. 40.00 (ISBN 0-936897-08-2). Caliban.
Roses: A Celebration. Rosamond Richardson. (Illus.). 96p. 1985. 9.95. Salem Hse Pubs.
Roses & Champagne. Betty Neels. (Harlequin Romances Ser.). 192p. 1984. pap. 1.75 (ISBN 0-373-02597-1). Harlequin Bks.
Roses & Flowering Branches in Counted Cross-Stitch. Gerda Bengtsson. (Illus.). 64p. 1986. pap. 14.95 (ISBN 0-13-783291-5). P-H.
Roses & Rainbows. Florence M. McDowell. (Illus.). 234p. 1983. pap. 5.95 (ISBN 0-85640-009-2, Pub. by Blackstaff Pr). Longwood Pub Group.
Roses & Thorns. Beatrice Woods. 1982. write for info. (ISBN 0-87012-455-2). McClain.
Roses & Thorns: The Second Blooming of the Hundred Flowers in Chinese Fiction, 1979-80. Perry Link. LC 83-9147. (Illus.). 300p. 1984. lib. bdg. 35.00x (ISBN 0-520-04979-9); pap. 10.95x (ISBN 0-520-04980-2). U of Cal Pr.
Roses Are Dead. Loren D. Estleman. 240p. 1985. 15.95 (ISBN 0-89296-136-8). Mysterious Pr.
Roses Are Dead. Loren D. Estleman. 240p. 1987. pap. 3.95 (ISBN 0-445-40574-0). Mysterious Pr.
Roses Are for the Rich. Jonell Lawson. 1987. pap. 3.95 (ISBN 0-451-15087-2, Sig). NAL.
Roses Are Red Violets Are Blue I Don't Know What to Say to You. 2nd ed. Eileen A. Loos et al. (Illus.). 130p. Date not set. pap. 4.95 (ISBN 0-9616160-3-2). Bench Pr NY.
Rose's Bath. Marie Wabbes. (ps). 1988. 6.95 (ISBN 0-671-66612-6). Messner.
Roses Charted Designs. Ed. by Lindberg Press Staff. (Illus.). 32p. (Orig.). 1987. pap. 2.95 (ISBN 0-486-25523-9). Dover.
Roses de Septembre. Andre Maurois. 123.50 (ISBN 0-685-36968-4). French & Eur.
Roses for English Gardens. G. Jekyll. (Illus.). 389p. 29.50 (ISBN 0-686-47030-3). Apollo.
Roses for English Gardens. Gertrude Jekyll. (Illus.). 392p. 1982. 29.50 (ISBN 0-907462-24-3). Antique Collect.
Roses for English Gardens see Roses.
Rose's for You: Inspirational. Earlene Rose. 1982. 4.95 (ISBN 0-916620-66-2). Portals Pr.
Roses; Four One-Act Plays. Hermann Sudermann. Tr. by Grace Frank. LC 79-50031. (One-Act Plays in Reprint Ser.). (Ger.). Repr. of 1909 ed. 17.75x (ISBN 0-8486-2055-0). Roth Pub Inc.
Roses from Heaven, 2 vols. Ed. by Ella A. McBride. Incl. Vol. 1, 594 pgs. 19.50 (ISBN 0-933731-00-0). Vol. 2, 484 pgs (ISBN 0-933731-01-9); Vol. 1, 594 pgs. pap. 13.50 (ISBN 0-933731-03-5). Vol. 2, 484 pgs (ISBN 0-933731-04-3). (Orig.). 1984. Set. 33.00 (ISBN 0-933731-02-7); Set. pap. 27.00 (ISBN 0-933731-05-1). Children of Mary.
Roses in December. Esther S. Myers. (Illus.). 164p. 1979. 13.00 (ISBN 0-931068-01-0). Purcells.
Roses in December: An Anthology. Ed. by Doras Benbow. 1986. 5.00 (ISBN 0-931611-09-1). D R Benbow.
Roses in December: Finding Strength Within Grief. Marilyn W. Heavilin. 1987. pap. 6.95 (ISBN 0-317-57145-1). Heres Life.
Roses in Gardens. Alan Toogood. (Gardening by Design Ser.). (Illus.). 80p. 1987. 14.95 (ISBN 0-88162-244-3). Salem Hse Pubs.
Roses in Porcelain by Jean du Tilleux. Norton (R. W.) Art Gallery. LC 73-81397. (Illus.). 16p. 1973. pap. 3.50x (ISBN 0-913060-02-X). Norton Art.
Rose's Last Summer. Margaret Millar. 223p. 1985. pap. 4.95 (ISBN 0-930330-26-9). Intl Polygonics.
Roses Love Garlic: Secrets of Companion Planting with Flowers. Louise Riotte. LC 83-1464. (Illus.). 236p. (Orig.). 1983. pap. 6.95 (ISBN 0-88266-331-3, Garden Way Pub). Storey Comm Inc.
Roses of Glory. Mary Pershall. 1987. pap. 3.95 (ISBN 0-425-10006-5). Berkley Pub.
Roses of Remembrance. Lillian S. Lewis. 64p. 1988. 7.95 (ISBN 0-8062-3209-9). Carlton.
Roses of Yesterday & Today. Will Tillotson. Ed. by Dorothy Stemler. (Illus.). 88p. 1980. pap. 5.00 (ISBN 0-936736-03-8). Sweetbrier.
Roses Open. Adele Kenny. (Illus.). 12p. 1984. pap. 4.00 Haiku Booklet (ISBN 0-916133-01-X). Jade Mtn.
Rose's Picture. Marie Wabbes. (ps). 1988. 6.95 (ISBN 0-671-66613-4). Messner.
Roses, Rhodedendron. Alice Adams. (Perfect Presents Story-Gifts Ser.). (Illus.). 32p. pap. 4.95 (ISBN 1-55628-020-3). Redpath Pr.
Roses: Uses for Rose. Recycling Consortium Staff. 1984. pap. text ed. 1.95 (Pub. by Recycling Concept). Prosperity & Profits.
Roseto Story: An Anatomy of Health. John G. Bruhn & Stewart Wolf. LC 78-21364. (Illus.). 1979. 14.95x (ISBN 0-8061-1491-6). U of Okla Pr.
Rosetsu. Robert Moes. (Illus.). 256p. (Orig.). 1973. pap. 10.00 (ISBN 0-914738-18-6). Denver Art Mus.
Rosetta Stone. Wallis Budge. 32p. 1986. pap. 3.00 (ISBN 0-89005-331-6). Ares.
Rosetta Stone see Decrees of Memphis & Canopus.
Rosetta Stone in the British Museum. Ernest A. Budge. LC 73-16549. (Illus.). Repr. of 1929 ed. 18.50 (ISBN 0-404-11362-1). AMS Pr.
Rosetti Family, Eighteen Twenty-Four to Eighteen Fifty-Four. R. D. Waller. LC 73-15815. 1932. lib. bdg. 47.00 (ISBN 0-8414-9477-0). Folcroft.
Rosewell, Garland of Virginia. Claude Lanciano. (Illus.). 1978. 12.50 (ISBN 0-9603558-3-9). Lands End Bks.
Rosey: The Gentle Giant. Rosey Grier. 1986. 17.95 (ISBN 0-89274-406-5). Harrison Hse.
Rosh Hashana - Ashkenaz: Zichron Reuven see Machzor.
Rosh Hashanah, 1 vol. (Hebrew & Eng.). 15.00 (ISBN 0-910218-56-0). Bennet Pub.
Rosh Hashanah. Norma Simon. (Festival Series of Picture Storybooks). (Illus.). (ps-k). 1961. plastic cover 4.50 (ISBN 0-8381-0700-1). United Syn Bk.
Rosh Hashanah: A Holiday Funtext. Judy Bin-Nun & Franne Einhorn. (Illus.). (gr. 1-3). 1978. pap. 5.00 (ISBN 0-8074-0010-6, 101300). UAHC.
Rosh Hashanah Anthology. Ed. by Philip Goodman. LC 74-105069. (Illus.). 379p. 1970. 10.95 (ISBN 0-8276-0023-2, 246). JPS Phila.
Rosh Hashanah: Its Significance, Laws, & Prayers. Hersh Goldwurm & Avie Gold. (ArtScroll Mesorah Ser.). 128p. 1983. 11.95 (ISBN 0-89906-195-8); pap. 8.95 (ISBN 0-89906-196-6). Mesorah Pubns.
Rosh Hashanah Sefard: Zichron Moshe see Machzor.
Rosh Hashanah Walk. Carol Levin. LC 87-3106. (Illus.). (ps-3). 1987. 3.95 (ISBN 0-930494-70-9). Kar Ben.
Rosh Yeshiva: The Story of Rav Chaim Shmulevitz, the "Stutchiner". Reaven Grossman. Tr. by Yaakov M. Rapoport from Hebrew. (Illus.). 240p. 1988. 14.95 (ISBN 0-944070-03-5); pap. 11.95 (ISBN 0-944070-05-1). Targum Pr.
Rosicrucian Enlightenment. Frances A. Yates. (Illus.). 320p. 1986. pap. 7.95 (ISBN 0-7448-0051-X, 0051W, Ark Paperbks). Routledge Chapman & Hall.
Rosicrucian Esotericism. Rudolf Steiner. Tr. by Dorothy S. Osmond from Ger. 122p. 1978. 14.00 (ISBN 0-910142-78-5). Anthroposophic.
Rosicrucian Fraternity in America, 2 vols. R. Swinborne Clymer. 1935. 75.00 (ISBN 0-686-10446-3). Philos Pub.
Rosicrucian Manual. 28th ed. H. Spencer Lewis. LC 78-104932. (Illus.). 214p. Date not set. 8.95 (ISBN 0-912057-39-4, G-508). AMORC.
Rosicrucian Principles for the Home & Business. H. Spencer Lewis. LC 54-21694. 241p. 1981. pap. 9.95 (ISBN 0-912057-54-8, G-676). AMORC.
Rosicrucian Questions & Answers with Complete History. 16th ed. H. Spencer Lewis. LC 65-14964. 358p. 1969. 12.50 (ISBN 0-912057-37-8, G-501). AMORC.
Rosicrucian Seer. John Hamill. 176p. 1986. pap. 13.95 (ISBN 0-85030-289-7, Pub. by Thorsons UK). Weiser.
Rosicrucian Symbols. Franz Hartman. 1983. 2.95 (ISBN 0-916411-15-X). Sure Fire.
Rosicrucian Thoughts on the Ever-Burning Lamps of the Ancients. W. W. Westcott. 1986. pap. 2.95 (ISBN 0-916411-56-7). Sure Fire.
Rosicrucianism & Modern Initiation: Mystery Centres of the Middle Ages. 3rd. ed. Rudolf Steiner. Tr. by Mary Adams. 98p. 1982. pap. 11.95 (ISBN 0-85440-381-7, Pub by Steinerbooks). Anthroposophic.
Rosicrucians & Magister Christoph Schlegel. Manly P. Hall. 15.00 (ISBN 0-89314-422-3). Philos Res.
Rosicrucians: Their Rites & Mysteries. 4th ed. Hargrave Jennings. LC 75-36845. (Occult Ser.). (Illus.). 1976. Repr. of 1907 ed. 36.50x (ISBN 0-405-07957-5). Ayer Co Pubs.
Rosie & Michael. Judith Viorst. LC 74-75571. (Illus.). 40p. (gr. 1-4). 1974. 13.95 (ISBN 0-689-30439-0, Atheneum Childrens Bks). Macmillan.
Rosie & Michael. Judith Viorst. (Illus.). (gr. 1-4). 1979. pap. 3.95 (ISBN 0-689-70466-6, Aladdin). Macmillan.
Rosie & Michael. 2nd ed. Judith Viorst. LC 86-13969. (Illus.). 40p. (gr. 1-4). Date not set. pap. 3.95 (ISBN 0-689-71272-3, Aladdin Bks). Macmillan.
Rosie Cross Uncovered. John Heydon & J. D. Holmes. 1988. pap. 7.95 (ISBN 0-916411-62-1). Sure Fire.
Rosie Crucian Secrets. John Dee. 288p. Date not set. pap. 15.50 (ISBN 0-85030-441-5, Pub. by Thorsons UK). Weiser.
Rosie Posie Has a Bath. Joan Haines. (Illus.). 16p. (ps-1). 1985. pap. 2.65 (ISBN 0-936652-02-0, Pub. by Ed Concern Pubns). Two Ems.
Rosie Posie Makes Friends. Joan Haines. (Illus.). 16p. (Orig.). (ps-1). 1985. pap. 2.65 (ISBN 0-936652-01-2, Pub. by Ed Concern Pubns). Two Ems.
Rosie: The Oldest Horse in St. Augustine. Miriam Gilbert. LC 67-30409. (Illus., Eng., Fr. & Span.). (gr. k-6). 1974. pap. 3.95 (ISBN 0-87208-007-2). Island Pr Pubs.
Rosie the Riveter Revisited: Women, the War & Social Change. Sherna B. Gluck. 1987. lib. bdg. 19.95x (ISBN 0-8057-9022-5, Twayne). G K Hall.
Rosie the Riveter Revisited: Women, the War, & Social Change. Sherna B. Gluck. LC 87-30685. (Illus.). 304p. 1988. pap. 8.95 (ISBN 0-452-00911-1, Mer). NAL.
Rosie, the Rosedown Rabbit: A Storybook to Color. Poppy Sundeen. Ed. & illus. by Joanne West. (Illus.). 26p. (Orig.). 1988. pap. text ed. 5.95 (ISBN 0-929317-00-9). Rosedown Plantation.
Rosiebelle Lee Wildcat Tennessee. Raymond Andrews. LC 87-21160. (Illus.). 290p. 1988. pap. 9.95 (ISBN 0-8203-0994-X). U of Ga Pr.
Rosier de Madame Husson. Guy De Maupassant & Pierre Cogny. 1976. 9.95 (ISBN 0-686-54793-4). French & Eur.

Rosie's Double Dare. Robie Harris. LC 79-26907. (Capers Ser.). (Illus.). 128p. (gr. 3-6). 1980. lib. bdg. 5.99 (ISBN 0-394-94459-3); pap. 1.95 (ISBN 0-394-84459-9). Knopf.

Rosie's Razzle Dazzle Deal. Robie H. Harris. LC 81-2627. (Capers Bks.). (Illus.). 128p. (gr. 3-6). 1982. pap. 1.95 (ISBN 0-394-84975-2). Knopf.

Rosie's Walk. Pat Hutchins. LC 68-12090. (Illus.). 32p. (ps-1). 1968. 12.95 (ISBN 0-02-745850-4). Macmillan.

Rosie's Walk. Pat Hutchins. LC 87-17550. (Illus.). (ps-1). 1971. pap. 4.95 (ISBN 0-02-043750-1, Aladdin Bks). Macmillan.

Rosita y Su Alhmohada. Galina Lebedeva. (Illus.). 11p. (Span.). 1975. pap. 1.49 (ISBN 0-8285-1302-3, Pub. by Progress Pubs USSR). Imported Pubns.

Rosita's Christian Wish. Mary-Ann S. Bruni. (Illus.). 48p. (gr. k-8). 1985. 12.95 (ISBN 0-317-62764-3). Texart.

Rosita's Christmas Wish. Mary A. Bruni. LC 85-52040. (Texas Ser.). (Illus.). 48p. (gr. k-8). 1985. 13.95 (ISBN 0-935857-00-1); ltd. ed. 125.00 (ISBN 0-935857-03-6); write for info. (ISBN 0-935857-09-5); pap. write for info. (ISBN 0-935857-01-X); pap. write for info. (ISBN 0-935857-10-9). Texart.

Rosmersholm see Ibsen Plays.

Rosmini, Priest & Philosopher. Claude Leetham. LC 81-85754. 508p. 1982. Repr. of 1957 ed. 22.50 (ISBN 0-911782-39-7). New City.

Ross & Wilson Anatomy & Physiology in Health & Illness. 6th ed. Kathleen J. Wilson. LC 86-23268. (Illus.). 354p. (Orig.). 1987. pap. text ed. 22.00 (ISBN 0-443-03530-X). Churchill.

Ross Hannas: Living, Laughing, Loving. Wayne Grinstead. LC 86-6807. (Meet the Missionary Ser.). (gr. 4-6). 1986. 5.95 (ISBN 0-8054-4325-8). Broadman.

Ross Ice Shelf: Glaciology & Geophysics. Ed. by C. R. Bentley & D. E. Hayes. (Geophysical Monograph: Vol. 42). Papers 1-2, 1984, 56p. 14.50 (ISBN 0-87590-195-6). Am Geophysical.

Ross Information Processing Assessment. Deborah G. Ross. 44p. 1986. spiral bdg. 49.00x (ISBN 0-88120-379-3, 2102). Pro Ed.

Ross MacDonald. Matthew J. Bruccoli. LC 83-293. 176p. 1984. pap. 7.95 (ISBN 0-15-679082-3, Harv). HarBraceJ.

Ross MacDonald. Jerry Speir. LC 78-4297. (Recognitions Ser.). 1978. 16.95x (ISBN 0-8044-2824-7). Ungar.

Ross MacDonald-Kenneth Millar: A Descriptive Bibliography. Matthew J. Bruccoli. LC 83-1398. (Pittsburgh Ser. in Bibliography). (Illus.). 278p. 1983. 70.00x (ISBN 0-8229-3482-5). U of Pittsburgh Pr.

Rossel Island: An Ethnological Study. Wallace E. Armstrong. LC 75-32798. Repr. of 1928 ed. 34.00 (ISBN 0-404-14101-3). AMS Pr.

Rossetti. Arthur C. Benson. 1973. Repr. of 1906 ed. 15.00 (ISBN 0-8274-1669-5). R West.

Rossetti. H. C. Marillier. LC 73-15949. 1906. Repr. lib. bdg. 32.00 (ISBN 0-8414-6066-3). Folcroft.

Rossetti: A Critical Essay on His Art. Ford Madox Ford. LC 76-40417. 1976. Repr. of 1914 ed. lib. bdg. 35.00 (ISBN 0-8414-4939-2). Folcroft.

Rossetti & His Circle. M. Beerbohm. 59.95 (ISBN 0-8490-0974-X). Gordon Pr.

Rossetti & His Circle. Max Beerbohm. LC 87-10539. (Illus.). 128p. 1987. 19.95x (ISBN 0-300-03986-7). Yale U Pr.

Rossetti & His Poetry. F. S. Boas. 1982. 42.50 (ISBN 0-685-94344-5). Bern Porter.

Rossetti & His Poetry. Frederick S. Boas. LC 75-22072. (English Literature Ser., No. 33). 1975. lib. bdg. 39.95x (ISBN 0-8383-2074-0). Haskell.

Rossetti & His Poetry. Mrs. Frederick S. Boas. LC 72-191813. 1918. lib. bdg. 17.50 (ISBN 0-8414-2531-0). Folcroft.

Rossetti & His Poetry. Henrietta O. Boas. LC 74-120979. (Poetry & Life Ser.). Repr. of 1914 ed. 7.25 (ISBN 0-404-52504-0). AMS Pr.

Rossetti, Dante & Ourselves. Nicolette Gray. LC 74-11358. 1974. Repr. of 1947 ed. lib. bdg. 17.00 (ISBN 0-8414-4531-1). Folcroft.

Rossetti, Dante & Ourselves. Nicolette Gray. LC 74-6406. (Studies in Italian Literature, No. 46). 1974. lib. bdg. 47.95x (ISBN 0-8383-1917-3). Haskell.

Rossetti Family, 1824-1854. R. D. Waller. LC 73-145352. 324p. 1972. Repr. of 1932 ed. 39.00x (ISBN 0-403-01261-9). Scholarly.

Rossetti: His Life & Works. Evelyn Waugh. LC 72-6678. 1928. lib. bdg. 45.00 (ISBN 0-8414-0141-1). Folcroft.

Rossetti Papers, 1862-1870. William M. Rossetti. LC 76-130238. Repr. of 1903 ed. 17.50 (ISBN 0-404-05438-2). AMS Pr.

Rossettiana. S. N. Ray. iv, 202p. 1981. text ed. 17.95x (ISBN 0-86590-015-9, Pub. by Atma Ram India). Apt Bks.

Rossettis. Elizabeth L. Cary. LC 74-30190. (Studies in the Rossettis, No. 81). 1974. lib. bdg. 57.95x (ISBN 0-8383-1943-2). Haskell.

Rossetti's Sister Helen. Ed. by Janet C. Troxell. LC 72-85328. (Illus.). 128p. 1973. Repr. of 1939 ed. 23.95 (ISBN 0-8046-1769-4, Pub. by Kennikat). Assoc Faculty Pr.

Rossignol. Joseph L. Baird & John R. Kane. LC 78-38. 93p. 1978. 13.00x (ISBN 0-87338-211-0). Kent St U Pr.

Rossignol de l'Empereur de Chine. Jean Cocteau & J. Trinka. 9.95 (ISBN 0-686-54559-1). French & Eur.

Rossii Pervaia Liubov' Ed. by Collet's Holdings, Ltd. Staff. 240p. 1983. 39.00x (ISBN 0-317-40745-7, Pub. by Collets UK). State Mutual Bk.

Rossiia I Evropa. Nikolai I. Danilevskii. 1966. Repr. of 1895 ed. 33.00 (ISBN 0-384-10785-0). Johnson Repr.

Rossiia V Pis'menakh: Tom 1. Aleksei Remizov. LC 79-91965. (Illus.). 232p. (Rus.). 1982. pap. 7.95 (ISBN 0-89830-013-4). Russica Pubs.

Rossiiskoe Zakonodatel'Stvo x-xx Vekov: V9 Tomakh. Ed. by Collet's Holdings, Ltd. Staff. 430p. (Rus.). 1984. 49.00x (ISBN 0-317-42736-9, Pub by Collets (UK)). State Mutual Bk.

Rossini. Richard Osborne. (Illus.). 346p. 1986. 29.95x (ISBN 0-460-03179-1, Pub. by J M Dent England). Biblio Dist.

Rossini. (Portraits of Greatness Ser.: No. II). (Eng. & Ital.). 1987. pap. 12.50 (ISBN 0-918367-11-5). Elite.

Rossini: A Biography. Herbert Weinstock. LC 87-2588. (Illus.). 640p. 1987. 32.50 (ISBN 0-87910-071-0); pap. 19.95 (ISBN 0-87910-102-4). Limelight Edns.

Rossini: A Study in Tragi-Comedy. Francis Toye. LC 77-181281. 269p. 1954. Repr. 39.00x (ISBN 0-403-01704-1). Scholarly.

Rossini: A Study in Tragi-Comedy. Francis Toye. 1988. Repr. of 1954 ed. lib. bdg. 49.00x. Am Biog Serv.

Rossini: The Man & His Music. Francis Toye. 288p. 1987. pap. 6.95 (ISBN 0-486-25396-1). Dover.

Rossmore Appliances. Ruth Patmore & Elizabeth Ross. 50p. 1972. 5.50 (ISBN 0-686-66706-9). Macmillan.

Ross's Adventures of the First Settlers on the Oregon or Columbia River, 1810-13 see Early Western Travels, 1748-1846.

Rossya: A Journey Through Siberia. Michael Pennington. (Oleander Travel Bks.: Vol. 9). (Illus.). 96p. (Orig.). 1982. 12.50 (ISBN 0-906672-10-4). Oleander Pr.

Roster of all Regimental Surgeons & Assistant Surgeons in the Late War, with Their Service, & Last-Known Post-Office Address. United States Pension Office Staff. LC 88-60668. (American Civil War Surgery Ser.). 313p. 1988. price not set (ISBN 0-930405-10-2). Norman SF.

Roster of Blacks in the U. S. House & Senate: 1869 to 1981. Richard A. Hudlin & Brimah K. Farouk. 1981. 1.00 (ISBN 0-686-38014-2). Voter Ed Proj.

Roster of Civilizations & Culture. A. L. Kroeber. LC 85-747. 96p. 1985. Repr. of 1962 ed. lib. bdg. 35.00x (ISBN 0-313-24838-9, KRCI). Greenwood.

Roster of General Officers of the Confederate Service During the Civil War. John M. Carroll. 24.95 (ISBN 0-8488-0009-5, Pub. by J M C & Co); 14.95 (ISBN 0-8488-0043-5). Amereon Ltd.

Roster of Non-Commissioned Officers of the Tenth U. S. Cavalry. 1897. pap. 7.95 (ISBN 0-8488-0002-8, Pub. by J M C & Co). Amereon Ltd.

Roster of Officers & Similar Assigned Persons, Listed by Ranks, in the Hungarian Armed Forces, 3 vols. LC 76-17260. Orig. Title: A M. Kir. honvedseg Csendorseg Tisztjeinek Es Hasonlo Allasuaknak Rangsorolasa. 1340p. 1976. Set (ISBN 0-935484-01-9). Vols. 1 & 2. 20.00 ea.; Vol. 3. 50.00 (ISBN 0-686-61485-2). Universe Pub Co.

Roster of Revolutionary Soldiers & Patriots in Alabama. Louise Julich. (Alabama Society Daughters of the American Revolution). 1979. 25.00 (ISBN 0-88428-045-4). Parchment Pr.

Roster of Revolutionary Soldiers in Georgia, Vol. 3. Mrs. Howard H. McCall. LC 68-9361. 463p. 1969. 21.50 (ISBN 0-8063-0221-6). Genealog Pub.

Roster of Soldiers from North Carolina in the American Revolution: With an Appendix Containing a Collection of Miscellaneous Records. Ed. by N.C.D.A.R. Staff. 709p. 1988. Repr. of 1932 ed. 35.00 (4150). Genealog Pub.

Roster of Soldiers from North Carolina in the American Revolution. North Carolina Daughters of the American Revolution. LC 67-28097. 709p. 1984. Repr. of 1932 ed. 30.00 (ISBN 0-8063-0091-4). Genealog Pub.

Roster of South Carolina Patriots in the American Revolution. Bobby G. Moss. LC 82-83584. (Illus.). 1023p. 1985. Repr. of 1983 ed. 45.00 (ISBN 0-8063-1005-7). Genealog Pub.

Roster of Spanish American War Soldiers from Georgia. Intro. by Carlton J. Thaxton et al. 139p. 1987. Repr. of 1984 ed. 48.00x (ISBN 0-931739-01-2). Thaxton Co.

Roster of Texas Daughters Revolutionary Ancestors, 3 vols. Texas Society NSDAR. 1976. 37.50 ea. Vol. 1, A-C, 568 Pp (ISBN 0-89308-234-1). Vol. 2, D-H, 589pp (ISBN 0-89308-235-X). Vol. 3, I-O, 630 Pp (ISBN 0-89308-236-8). Vol. 4, r-Z, 621pp (ISBN 0-89308-237-6). 150.00 set (ISBN 0-89308-238-4). Southern Hist Pr.

Roster of the Confederate Soldiers of Georgia, 1861-1865: Index. Juanita S. Brightwell & Eunice S. Lee. 520p. 1982. 32.50 (ISBN 0-87152-360-4). Reprint.

Roster Officers of the New Jersey Continental Line in the Revolutionary War Were Eligible to Membership in the Society of the Cincinnati. James W. Campbell. 55p. 1987. pap. 7.00 (ISBN 1-55613-033-3). Heritage Bk.

Roster '87. write for info. County Super Assn CA.

Rostislav Zakharov. V. Ivashev & K Il'ina. 240p. (Rus.). 1982. 35.00x (ISBN 0-317-40797-X, Pub. by Collets (UK)). State Mutual Bk.

Rostro Cercano: (Antologia Poetica) Maricel Mayor Marsan. LC 86-82717. 62p. (Span.). 1986. pap. 8.00 (ISBN 0-935318-12-7). Edins Hispamerica.

Roswell: A Pictorial History. Ed. by Darlene M. Walsh. LC 85-51805. (Illus.). 256p. 1985. lib. bdg. 49.95 (ISBN 0-9615854-2-0). Roswell Hist.

Roswell Garst: A Biography. Harold Lee. LC 83-26452. (Illus.). 310p. 1984. 12.95 (ISBN 0-8138-0796-4). Iowa St U Pr.

Roswell Legacy. Frances P. Statham. 384p. 1988. pap. 7.95 (ISBN 0-449-90250-1, Columbine). Fawcett.

Roswell Women. Frances P. Statham. 384p. (Orig.). 1987. pap. 7.95 (ISBN 0-449-90182-3, Columbine). Fawcett.

Rosy Cole's Great American Guilt Club. Sheila Greenwald. LC 85-47876. (Illus.). 96p. (gr. 3-7). 1985. 12.95 (ISBN 0-316-32709-3, Joy St Bks). Little.

Rosy Cole's Great American Guilt Club. Sheila Greenwald. (gr. 3-7). 1987. pap. 2.50 (ISBN 0-671-63794-0, Minstrel Bks). S&S.

Rosy Cross: Its Teachings. R. Swinburne Clymer. 287p. 1965. 7.95 (ISBN 0-932785-43-3). Philos Pub.

Rosy Crucifixion. Henry Miller. Incl. Sexus; Plexus; Nexus. LC 80-8064. 1600p. 1980. pap. 12.85 box set (ISBN 0-394-17774-6, B 449, BC). Grove.

Rosy Glasses. Ed. by Paul Norbury. 1985. 35.00x (ISBN 0-317-39107-0, Pub. by Norbury Pubns Ltd). State Mutual Bk.

Rota Veneris. Boncompagno da Signa. Ed. by Josef Purkart. LC 74-18250. 128p. 1975. Repr. of 1474 ed. lib. bdg. 25.00x (ISBN 0-8201-1137-6). Schol Facsimiles.

Rotan Mosle Guide, 1985-86. Texas & Oklahoma Corporations. Ed. by Jessica Spring. LC 86-645349. (Corporate Guides Ser.). 350p. 1985. pap. 23.50 (ISBN 0-912519-03-7). Scholl.

Rotan Mosle Guide 1986-87: Texas & Oklahoma Corporations. Ed. by Jessica Spring. LC 86-645349. (Corporate Guides Ser.). 360p. 1986. pap. 24.95 (ISBN 0-912519-04-5). Scholl.

Rotan Mosle Guide 1987-88: Texas & Oklahoma Corporations. Ed. by Dave Scholl. LC 86-645349. (Scholl Corporate Guides Ser.). 360p. 1987. pap. 24.95 (ISBN 0-912519-06-1). Scholl.

Rotary Basic Library, 7 vols. David H. Bailey & Louise Gottlieb. Ed. by Willmon L. White & Mark Perlberg. (Illus.). 506p. 1987. 16.75 (ISBN 0-915062-08-9). Rotary Intl.

Rotary Cement Kiln. 2nd, rev. & enl. ed. K. Peray. (Illus.). 1986. 55.00 (ISBN 0-8206-0314-7). Chem Pub.

Rotary Drilling Rig & Camp: Physical Conditions for Inspections. 1981. pap. 2.00 (ISBN 0-88061-043-3). Institute Pr.

Rotary in Baton Rouge 1918-1970. M. E. Blankenstein. 10.00x (ISBN 0-685-00412-0). Claitors.

Rotary, Kelly, & Swivel. Ed. by Fernando Albornoz. Tr. by Roberto Quiroga. (Rotary Drilling Ser.: Unit I, Lesson 4). (Illus.). 69p. (Orig., Span.). 1982. pap. text ed. 6.95 (ISBN 0-88698-032-1, 2.10422). PETEX.

Rotary, Kelly, & Swivel. 2nd ed. Ed. by Jodie Leecraft. (Rotary Drilling Ser.: Unit I, Lesson 4). (Illus.). 68p. 1981. pap. text ed. 6.95 (ISBN 0-88698-008-9, 2.10420). PETEX.

Rotary, Kelly & Swivel: Canadian Metric Edition. 2nd ed. Ed. by Jodie Leecraft. (Rotary Drilling Ser.: Unit I, Lesson 4). (Illus.). 1981. pap. text ed. 6.95 (ISBN 0-88698-020-8, 2.10421). PETEX.

Rotary Metalworking Processes: Proceedings of the 3rd International Conference, Kyoto, Japan, 8-10 September 1984. Ed. by M. Kobayashi. 522p. 1984. 131.75 (ISBN 0-444-87622-7, North-Holland). Elsevier.

Rotary Positive Displacement Pumps (Newtonian Liquids) 27p. 1968. pap. 9.00 (ISBN 0-8169-0028-0, E-14). Am Inst Chem Eng.

Rotary Rig & Its Components. Ed. by Fernando Albornoz. Tr. by Vivian Carmona-Agosto. (Rotary Drilling Ser.: Unit I, Lesson 1). (Illus.). 47p. (Orig., Span.). 1980. pap. 6.95 (ISBN 0-88698-029-1, 2.10132). PETEX.

Rotary Rig & Its Components. 3rd ed. Ed. by Mildred Gerding. (Rotary Drilling Ser.: Unit I, Lesson 1). (Illus.). 1980. pap. text ed. 6.95 (ISBN 0-88698-005-4, 2.10130). PETEX.

Rotary Rig & Its Components: Canadian Metric Edition. 3rd ed. Ed. by Mildred Gerding. (Rotary Drilling Ser.: Unit I, Lesson 1). (Illus.). 1979. pap. text ed. 6.95 (ISBN 0-88698-017-8, 2.10131). PETEX.

Rotary Tiller Service Manual. 2nd ed. Intertec Publishing Corp. Staff. (Illus.). 160p. 1985. pap. 8.95 (ISBN 0-87288-198-9, RTS-2). Intertec Pub.

Rotary-Wing Aerodynamics. W. Z. Stepniewski & C. N. Keys. (Engineering Ser.). 640p. 1984. pap. 14.50 (ISBN 0-486-64647-5). Dover.

Rotary Wing Flight. 1988. 14.95 (ASA-RW4). Av Suppl & Acad.

Rotary Wing Flight. U. S. Army. Ed. by Nicholas Ean. 124p. 1987. pap. 14.95 (ISBN 0-940732-38-6, Pub. by ASA). Aviation.

Rotaryn Peruskirjaston, 7 Vols. David H. Bailey & Louise Gottlieb. Ed. by Willmon L. White & Mark Perlberg. (Illus.). 506p. (Finnish.). 1982. 16.75 (ISBN 0-915062-09-7). Rotary Intl.

Rotarys Handbibliotek. David H. Bailey & Louise Gottlieb. Ed. by Willmon L. White & Mark Perlberg. (Illus.). 506p. (Swedish.). 1982. 16.75 (ISBN 0-915062-16-X). Rotary Intl.

Rotating Electric Machinery & Transformer Technology. 3rd ed. Donald V. Richardson & Arthur J. Caisse, Jr. (Illus.). 672p. 1987. text ed. 42.00 (ISBN 0-8359-6747-6). P-H.

Rotating Electrical Equipment Testing, 2 vols. Ed. by R. L. Caton et al. (Engineering Craftsmen: No. G22). (Illus.). 1969. Set. spiral bdg. 69.95x (ISBN 0-85083-072-9). Trans-Atl Phila.

Rotating Electrical Equipment Winding & Building, 2 vols. Ed. by R. T. Anderson et al. (Engineering Craftsmen: No. G2). (Illus.). 1969. Set. spiral bdg. 79.95x (ISBN 0-85083-030-3). Trans-Atl Phila.

Rotating Electrical Machinery & Power Systems. Stephen W. Fardo & Dale R. Patrick. (Illus.). 304p. 1985. text ed. 41.00 (ISBN 0-13-783309-1). P-H.

Rotating Fields in General Relativity. J. N. Islam. 136p. 1985. 39.50 (ISBN 0-521-26082-5). Cambridge U Pr.

Rotating Fluids in Geophysics. Ed. by P. H. Roberts & A. M. Soward. 1979. 76.00 (ISBN 0-12-589650-6). Acad Pr.

Rotating Machinery Equipment Design: Apple II Plus, IIe, IIc. L. Fielding. 176p. 1985. 750.00 (ISBN 0-07-079368-9). McGraw.

Rotating Machinery Explained: DC Motors. Richard Hunter. LC 80-730089. (Orig.). 1980. wkbk. 6.00 (ISBN 0-8064-0315-2, 810); audio visual pkg. 299.00 (ISBN 0-8064-0316-0). Bergwall.

Rotating Machinery Explained: Single Phase AC Motors. Richard Hunter. LC 82-730333. (Orig.). 1982. wkbk. 7.00 (ISBN 0-8064-0317-9, 812); audio visual pkg. 269.00 (ISBN 0-8064-0318-7). Bergwall.

Rotating Machinery Explained: Three Phase AC Motors. Richard Hunter. (Orig.). 1982. wkbk. 7.00 (ISBN 0-8064-0319-5, 813); audio visual pkg. 269.00 (ISBN 0-8064-0320-9). Bergwall.

Rotation Diet. Martin Katahn. 272p. 1987. pap. 4.95 (ISBN 0-553-26395-1). Bantam.

Rotation Diet. Martin Katahn. 1986. 15.95 (ISBN 0-317-64887-X). Norton.

Rotation Diet Cookbook: A Lifetime of Good Eating & Staying Slim. Martin Katahn & Terri Katahn. (Illus.). 1987. 18.95 (ISBN 0-393-02457-1). Norton.

Rotation in the Solar System: Proceedings of a Royal Society Discussion Meeting Held March 8-9, 1984. Ed. by R. Hide et al. (Illus.). 191p. 1985. lib. bdg. 58.00x (ISBN 0-85403-236-3, Pub. by Royal Soc England). Scholium Intl.

Rotation of the Earth: Proceedings. International Astronomical Union, 48th Symposium, Morioka, Japan, 1971. Ed. by P. Melchior & S. Yumi. LC 70-188004. 244p. 1972. lib. bdg. 34.00 (ISBN 90-277-0242-X, Pub. by Reidel Holland). Kluwer Academic.

Rotation Theory of Stock Market Trading & Its Major Anticipatory Value in Technical Analysis. Alden G. Somerville. (Illus.). 113p. 1983. 117.75 (ISBN 0-86654-086-5). Inst Econ Finan.

Rotation-Vibration of Polyatomic Molecules: Higher Order Energies & Frequencies of Spectral Transitions. Gilbert Amat et al. LC 71-152569. pap. 111.80 (2027115). Bks Demand UMI.

Rotational Brownian Motion & Dielectric Theory. James McConnell. 1980. 78.50 (ISBN 0-12-481850-1). Acad Pr.

Rotational Dynamics of Small & Macromolecules. Ed. by T. Dorfmueller & R. Pecora. (Lecture Notes in Physics Ser.: Vol. 293). 250p. 24.20 (ISBN 0-387-18688-3). Springer-Verlag.

Rotational Physics: The Principles of Energy. Myrna M. Milani & Brian R. Smith. LC 85-16305. (Rotational Physics Ser.). (Illus., Orig.). 1986. pap. 12.00 (ISBN 0-943290-03-1). Fainshaw Pr.

Rotational Spectra & Molecular Structure. James E. Wollrab. (Physical Chemistry Ser.; Vol. 13). 1967. 88.50 (ISBN 0-12-762150-4). Acad Pr.

Rotations, Quaternions, & Double Groups. Simon L. Altmann. (Illus.). 300p. 1986. 69.00 (ISBN 0-19-855372-2). Oxford U Pr.

Rotatoria. Ed. by H. J. Dumont & J. Green. (Developments in Hydrobiology Ser.: No. 1). 268p. 1980. lib. bdg. 79.00 (ISBN 90-6193-754-X, Pub. Junk Pubs Netherlands). Kluwer Academic.

Rotatoria. Die Raedertiere Mitteleuropas. Monogonta, 2 vols. 2nd, rev. ed. Max Voigt. (Illus.). 673p. (Ger.). 1978. lib. bdg. 150.00x. Lubrecht & Cramer.

ROTC College Handbook. Ed. by College Research Group of Concord, Massachusetts Staff. (ARCO Education & Guidance Ser.). 1988. pap. 14.95 (ISBN 0-13-044835-4). S&S.

Rote Kapelle. CIA Staff. Ed. by Paul Kesaris. LC 79-51270. 404p. 1979. 29.50 (ISBN 0-89093-203-4). U Pubns Amer.

Rote Walker. Mark Jarman. (Poetry Ser.). 14.95 (ISBN 0-915604-58-2); pap. 6.95 (ISBN 0-915604-59-0). Carnegie-Mellon.

Rotha on the Film. Paul Rotha. Ed. by Bruce S. Kupelnick. LC 76-52126. (Classics of Film Literature Ser.). 1978. lib. bdg. 23.00 (ISBN 0-8240-2892-9). Garland Pub.

Rothenberg Lease-Option Strategy. Ed Rothenberg. (Orig.). 1986. pap. 7.95 (ISBN 0-9613865-1-7). E Rothenberg.

Roth's Index to Literary Criticism. Ed. by Roth Publishing, Inc. Editorial Board. (Reference & Research Guides). 400p. 1988. pap. text ed. 49.95x (ISBN 0-89609-279-8). Roth Pub Inc.

Roth's Index to Short Stories. Ed. by Roth Publishing, Inc. Editorial Board. (Reference & Research Guides). 300p. 1988. pap. text ed. 49.95x (ISBN 0-89609-280-1). Roth Pub Inc.

Roth's Reference & Research Guide to the World at War. Ed. by Roth Publishing, Inc. Editorial Board. (Reference & Research Guides). 150p. 1988. pap. text ed. 19.95x (ISBN 0-89609-281-X). Roth Pub Inc.

Rothschild. Derek Wilson. 352p. 1988. 22.50 (ISBN 0-684-19018-4). Scribner.

Rothschild Mahzor. Schmelzer et al. Date not set. pap. 25.00. Ktav.

Rothschild Money Trust. George W. Armstrong. lib. bdg. 75.00 (ISBN 0-87700-370-X). Revisionist Pr.

Rothschild on Antiques & Collectibles: A Practical Guide to Collecting. Sigmund Rothschild & Reni L. Witt. (Illus.). 192p. 1986. 17.95 (ISBN 0-345-33410-8). Pharos Bks NY.

Rothschild Rhododendrons: A Record of the Gardens at Exbury. C. E. Phillips & Peter N. Barber. (Illus.). 1980. 65.00 (ISBN 0-02-597440-8). Macmillan.

Rothschilds: A Family Portrait. Frederic Morton. LC 83-6328. (Illus.). 352p. 1983. pap. 9.95 (ISBN 0-689-70657-X, 301). Atheneum.

Rothschilds Battle Rockefellers: The Bankers World Power Struggle. C Baker. 1982. lib. bdg. 69.00 (ISBN 0-87700-435-8). Revisionist Pr.

Rothschild's Fiddle, & Other Stories. Anton P. Chekhov. LC 72-121528. (Short Story Index Reprint Ser). 1917. 16.00 (ISBN 0-8369-3484-9). Ayer Co Pubs.

Rothschilds: Financial Rulers of Nations. John Reeves. 75.00 (ISBN 0-87968-193-4). Gordon Pr.

Rothschilds: Five Men of Frankfurt. M. E. Ravage. 1973. Repr. of 1930 ed. lib. bdg. 75.00 (ISBN 0-8490-0975-8). Gordon Pr.

Rotifer Fauna of Wisconsin. H. K. Harring & F. J. Myers. (Illus.). 1973. Repr. of 1927 ed. 88.00x (ISBN 3-7682-0820-6). Lubrecht & Cramer.

Rotifer Symposium, No. IV. Ed. by L. May et al. 1987. lib. bdg. 140.00 (ISBN 90-6193-645-4, Pub. by Junk Pubs Netherlands). Kluwer Academic.

Rotisserie de la reine Pedauque. Anatole France. LC 75-41103. Repr. of 1899 ed. 17.50 (ISBN 0-404-14788-7). AMS Pr.

Rotisserie De la Reine Pedauque. Anatole France. (Coll. Bleue). 1959. pap. 18.50 (ISBN 0-685-11542-9). French & Eur.

Rotisserie de la Reine Pedauque. Anatole France. 256p. 1959. 9.95 (ISBN 0-686-55876-6). French & Eur.

Rotisserie League Baseball, 1987: The Official Rulebook & How-to-Play Guide. Ed. by Glen Waggoner & Robert Sklar. LC 86-47880. 215p. 1987. pap. 8.95 (ISBN 0-553-34393-9). Bantam.

Rotor Dynamics. J. S. Rao. 244p. 1983. 31.95x (ISBN 0-470-27448-4). Halsted Pr.

Rotor Forgings for Turbines & Generators: Proceedings of an International Workshop by Electric Power Research Institute, Palo Alto, California, U. S. A., September 14-17, 1980. Ed. by R. I. Jaffee. LC 82-5358. (Illus.). 932p. 1982. 230.00 (ISBN 0-08-029373-5, A115). Pergamon.

Rotordynamics of Turbomachinery. John M. Vance. LC 87-34055. 448p. 1988. 59.95 (ISBN 0-471-80258-1). Wiley.

Rotten Book. Mary Rodgers. LC 75-85029. (Trophy Picture Bks.). (Illus.). 32p. (ps-3). 1985. pap. 3.95 (ISBN 0-06-443081-2, Trophy). HarpJ.

Rotten Chicken: A Modern Fable. L. Ursa Solomon. (Illus.). 24p. (gr. 1 up). 1985. spiral bdg. 6.95 (ISBN 0-9615756-0-3). Henchanted Bks.

Rotten Island. William Steig. LC 70-86945. (Illus.). 32p. 1985. 12.95 (ISBN 0-87923-526-8). Godine.

Rotten Ralph. Jack Gantos. LC 75-34101. (Illus.). 48p. (gr. k-3). 1976. PLB 12.95 (ISBN 0-395-24276-2); pap. 4.50. HM.

Rotten Ralph. Jack Gantos. (Illus.). (gr. k-3). 1980. Repr. 4.95 (ISBN 0-395-29202-6, Sandpiper). HM.

Rotten Ralph. Jack Gantos. (Houghton Mifflin Book & Cassette Favorites Ser.). (Illus.). Date not set. incl. cass. 6.95 (ISBN 0-395-48873-7). HM.

Rotten Ralph's Rotten Christmas. Jack Gantos. LC 84-644. (Illus.). 32p. (ps-3). 1984. PLB 12.95 (ISBN 0-395-35380-7). HM.

Rotten Ralph's Rotten Christmas. Jack Gantos. LC 84-664. (Illus.). 32p. (ps-3). 1987. pap. 3.95 (ISBN 0-395-45346-1); incl. bk. & doll 17.95 (ISBN 0-317-60450-3). HM.

Rotten Ralph's Show & Tell. Jack Gantos. (Illus.). Date not set. price not set. HM.

Rotten Ralph's Trick or Treat. Jack Gantos. LC 86-7276. (Illus.). 32p. (gr. k-3). 1986. 12.95 (ISBN 0-395-38943-7). HM.

Rotten Ralph's Trick or Treat. Jack Gantos. (Illus.). 32p. (gr. k-3). 1988. pap. 4.95 (ISBN 0-395-48655-6, Sandpiper). HM.

Rotten Reviews: A Literary Companion. Ed. by Bill Henderson. 112p. 1986. 12.50 (ISBN 0-916366-40-5). Pushcart Pr.

Rotten Reviews: A Literary Companion. Ed. by Bill Henderson. 96p. 1987. pap. 4.95 (ISBN 0-14-010195-0). Penguin.

Rotten Reviews II: A Literary Companion. Ed. by Bill Henderson. (Illus.). 1987. 12.95 (ISBN 0-916366-46-4). Pushcart Pr.

Rotten Reviews II: A Literary Companion. Ed. by Bill Henderson. 96p. 1988. pap. 4.95 (ISBN 0-14-011248-0). Penguin.

Rotten Rhymes & Other Crimes. Nick Meglin & Al Jaffee. (Illus.). 1978. pap. 1.25 (ISBN 0-451-07891-8, Y7891, Sig). NAL.

Rotterdam in Drawings - Rotterdam Getekend. P. Ratsma. (Illus.). 1979. 30.00 (ISBN 90-247-2261-6). Heinman.

Rotting Hill. Wyndham Lewis. Ed. by Paul Edwards. LC 85-22834. 355p. (Orig.). 1986. 20.00 (ISBN 0-87685-647-4); deluxe ed. 30.00 (ISBN 0-87685-648-2); pap. 12.50 (ISBN 0-87685-646-6). Black Sparrow.

Rottkapchen see Little Red Cap.

Rottweiler. Judy Elsden & Lary Elsden. (Illus.). 200p. 1988. 29.95 (ISBN 0-09-171400-1, Pub. by Century Hutchinson). David & Charles.

Rottweiler. Richard F. Stratton. (Illus.). 224p. 1985. 16.95 (ISBN 0-86622-153-0, PS-820). TFH Pubns.

Rottweiler: An International Study of the Breed. Dagmar Hodinar. (Illus.). 347p. (Orig.). 1986. pap. 25.95 (ISBN 0-932375-00-6). Von Palisaden Pubns.

Rottweiler Champions, 1948-1981. Jan L. Freund. (Illus.). 118p. 1983. 29.95 (ISBN 0-940808-24-2). Camino E E & B.

Rottweiler Champions: 1982-1986. Camino E. E. & B. Co. Staff. (Illus.). 128p. 1987. pap. 24.95 (ISBN 0-940808-53-6). Camino E E & B.

Rottweilers. Joan R. Klem & Susan C. Rademacher. (Illus.). 125p. 1981. 9.95 (ISBN 0-87666-747-7, KW-116). TFH Pubns.

Rottweilers. Herbert Richards. (Illus.). 80p. 1984. pap. text ed. 5.95 (ISBN 0-86622-206-5, PB-132). TFH Pubns.

Rotuli de Dominabus et Pueris et Puellis de XII Comitatibus: 1185. Ed. by John H. Round. (Pipe Roll Society, London, Ser.: No. 1, Vol. 35). Repr. of 1913 ed. 25.00 (ISBN 0-8115-0598-7). Kraus Repr.

Rotuman Grammar & Dictionary. Clerk M. Churchward. LC 75-32808. Repr. of 1940 ed. 37.50 (ISBN 0-404-14112-9). AMS Pr.

Rotunda, a Selection from the Works of Aldous Huxley. Aldous Huxley. 1081p. Repr. of 1932 ed. lib. bdg. 50.00 (ISBN 0-8495-2405-9). Arden Lib.

Rotweiler. Jim Pettengell. LC 88-679. (Illus.). 248p. 1988. 19.95 (ISBN 0-87605-272-3). Howell Bk.

Rouault. Pierre Courthion. (Library of Great Painters). (Illus.). 1977. 45.00 (ISBN 0-8109-0459-4). Abrams.

Rouault's Complete Graphic Work, 2 Vols. Francois Chapon & Isabelle Rouault. (Illus.). 714p. 1978. Vol. 1, 340p. 325.00 (ISBN 0-915346-86-9). Vol. 2, 374p. A Wofsy Fine Arts.

Rouault's Complete Paintings, 2 vols. Isabelle Rouault. (Illus.). 672p. 1988. 795.00 (ISBN 1-55660-031-3). A Wofsy Fine Arts.

Roubles in Words, Kopeks in Figures & Other Stories. V. Shukshin. Tr. by Ward & Tliffe. 207p. 1985. 49.00x (ISBN 0-317-40709-0, Pub. by Collets UK). State Mutual Bk.

Roubles in Words, Kopeks in Figures & Other Stories. Vasily Shuksin. Tr. by Natasha Ward & David Iliffe. 224p. 1985. 14.95 (ISBN 0-7145-2813-7, Dist. by Kampmann & Co). M Boyars Pubs.

Rouen During the Wars of Religion. Philip Benedict. LC 79-50883. (Cambridge Studies in Early Modern History). (Illus.). 324p. 1981. 54.50 (ISBN 0-521-22818-2). Cambridge U Pr.

Rouge. Janet Dailey. pap. 4.50 (ISBN 0-671-63038-5). PB.

Rouge et le Noir, 2 tomes. Stendhal, pseud. Set. deluxe ed. 150.00 (ISBN 0-685-35027-4). French & Eur.

Rouge et le Noir. Stendhal. Ed. by Martineau. 1958. pap. 9.95 (ISBN 0-685-11543-7). French & Eur.

Rouge et le Noir. Stendhal, pseud. Ed. by Martineau. (Coll. Prestige). 27.95 (ISBN 0-685-35021-5). French & Eur.

Rouge et le Noir, 2 vols. Stendhal & Beatrice Didier. pap. 4.50 ea. French & Eur.

Rough & Rowdy Ways: The Life & Hard Times of Edward Anderson. Patrick Bennett. LC 88-1151. (Tarleton State University Southwestern Studies in the Humanities: No. 4). (Illus.). 200p. 1988. 16.95 (ISBN 0-89096-352-5). Tex A&M Univ Pr.

Rough & the Righteous. (Illus.). 1979. limited ed. 700 copies 14.00 (ISBN 0-686-73992-2). Acoma Bks.

Rough & the Righteous. Ardis Walker. (Illus.). 1971. 14.00 (ISBN 0-685-59752-0). Acoma Bks.

Rough Cider. Peter Lovesey. 224p. 1987. 15.95 (ISBN 0-89296-194-5). Mysterious Pr.

Rough Cider. Peter Lovesey. 1988. pap. 3.95 (ISBN 0-317-67173-1). Mysterious Pr.

Rough Country. Lee Floren. 1976. pap. 0.95 (ISBN 0-685-69149-7, LB362NK, Leisure Bks). Leisure NY.

Rough Crossing. Tom Stoppard. LC 85-4423. 96p. 1985. 16.95 (ISBN 0-571-13594-3); pap. 5.95 (ISBN 0-571-13595-1). Faber & Faber.

Rough Cut. Edward Gorman. 160p. 1986. pap. 2.95 (ISBN 0-345-33379-9). Ballantine.

Rough Edges of the Christian Life. Inter-Varsity Staff. pap. 2.95 (ISBN 0-87784-442-9). Inter-Varsity.

Rough Field. rev. ed. John Montague. 83p. 1979. pap. 4.95 (ISBN 0-916390-10-1). Wake Forest.

Rough Guide to Amsterdam. Martin Dunford & Jack Holland. (Rough Guide). 1988. pap. 11.95 (ISBN 0-7102-1191-0, Pub. by Routledge UK). Routledge Chapman & Hall.

Rough Guide to Amsterdam & Holland. Martin Dunford & Jack Holland. (Routledge Rough Guides Ser.). 192p. (Orig.). 1984. pap. 8.95 (ISBN 0-7102-0158-3). Routledge Chapman & Hall.

Rough Guide to Brittany & Normandy. Greg Ward. (Rough Guide). 1988. pap. 11.95 (ISBN 0-7102-1119-8, Pub. by Routledge UK). Routledge Chapman & Hall.

Rough Guide to China. Rhonda Evans et al. (Illus.). 500p. 1987. pap. 12.95 (ISBN 0-7102-0423-X). Routledge Chapman & Hall.

Rough Guide to France. Kate Baillie et al. 475p. 1986. pap. 11.95 (ISBN 0-7102-0438-8). Routledge Chapman & Hall.

Rough Guide to Greece. rev. ed. Mark Ellingham et al. (Routledge Rough Guides Ser.). 320p. 1984. pap. 7.95 (ISBN 0-7102-0311-X). Routledge Chapman & Hall.

Rough Guide to Greece. Mark Ellingham et al. (Rough Guide). 1987. pap. 10.95 (ISBN 0-7102-1189-9, Pub. by Routledge UK). Routledge Chapman & Hall.

Rough Guide to Kenya. Richard Trillo. (Illus.). 300p. 1987. pap. 12.95 (ISBN 0-7102-0616-X). Routledge Chapman & Hall.

Rough Guide to Mexico. Jack Fisher. (Routledge Rough Guides Ser.). 232p. (Orig.). 1985. pap. 9.95 (ISBN 0-7102-0059-5). Routledge Chapman & Hall.

Rough Guide to Morocco. Mark Ellington & Shaun McViegh. (Routledge Rough Guides Ser.). 232p. (Orig.). 1985. pap. 11.95 (ISBN 0-7102-0153-2). Routledge Chapman & Hall.

Rough Guide to New York. Jack Holland & Martin Dunford. (Illus.). 240p. 1987. pap. 9.95 (ISBN 0-317-56855-8). Routledge Chapman & Hall.

Rough Guide to Paris. Kate Baillie & Tim Salmon. (Illus.). 240p. 1987. pap. 11.95 (ISBN 0-7102-0712-3). Routledge Chapman & Hall.

Rough Guide to Peru. Dilwyn Jenkins & Clare Jenkins. (Routledge Rough Guides Ser.). 264p. (Orig.). 1985. pap. 9.95 (ISBN 0-7102-0058-7). Routledge Chapman & Hall.

Rough Guide to Portugal. rev. ed. Mark Ellingham et al. (Routledge Rough Guides Ser.). 224p. 1984. pap. 7.95 (ISBN 0-7102-0345-4). Routledge Chapman & Hall.

Rough Guide to Spain. rev. ed. Mark Ellingham & John Fisher. (Routledge Rough Guide Ser.). (Illus.). 250p. (Orig.). 1985. pap. 9.95 (ISBN 0-7102-0344-6). Routledge Chapman & Hall.

Rough Guide to Tunisia. Peter Morris. (Routledge Rough Guides Ser.). 192p. (Orig.). 1985. pap. 7.95 (ISBN 0-7102-0148-6). Routledge Chapman & Hall.

Rough Guide to Yugoslavia. John McGhie et al. (Routledge Rough Guides Ser.). 224p. (Orig.). 1985. pap. 9.95 (ISBN 0-7102-0159-1). Routledge Chapman & Hall.

Rough in Brutal Print: The Legal Sources of Browning's "Red Cotton Night-Cap Country". Mark Siegchrist. LC 81-3993. 197p. 1981. 20.00x (ISBN 0-8142-0327-2). Ohio St U Pr.

Rough Justice. LC 79-50482. (Mary Elizabeth Braddon Ser.: Vol. 12). 1980. Repr. of 1898 ed. lib. bdg. 46.00 (ISBN 0-8240-4361-8). Garland Pub.

Rough Notes from Buck Creek I. rev. ed. Harvey Jackins et al. LC 78-68934. 1979. pap. 15.00 (ISBN 0-911214-52-6). Rational Isl.

Rough Notes from Calvinwood I. 2nd ed. Harvey Jackins et al. 135p. 1983. pap. 10.00 (ISBN 0-911214-85-2). Rational Isl.

Rough Notes from La Scherpa I. Harvey Jackins et al. 1977. pap. 50.00 (ISBN 0-911214-50-X). Rational Isl.

Rough Notes from Liberation I & II. Harvey Jackins et al. LC 76-9553. 260p. 1976. 15.00 (ISBN 0-911214-46-1); pap. 10.00 (ISBN 0-911214-42-9). Rational Isl.

Rough Passage. R. D. Graham. 256p. (Orig.). 1984. pap. 12.95 (ISBN 0-246-12311-7, Pub. by Granada England). Sheridan.

Rough Passage. R. D. Graham. 256p. 1985. pap. 7.95 (Pub. by Granada England). Academy Chi Pubs.

Rough Pulpwood Operating in Northwest Maine, 1935-1940. Max Hilton. 1942. pap. 6.95 (ISBN 0-89101-000-9). U Maine Orono.

Rough Rider. C. J. Naden. LC 79-52177. (Illus.). 32p. (gr. 4-9). 1980. PLB 9.79 (ISBN 0-89375-250-9); pap. 2.50 (ISBN 0-89375-251-7). Troll Assocs.

Rough Riders. Theodore Roosevelt. (Illus.). 384p. 1971. Repr. of 1899 ed. 21.00 (ISBN 0-87928-018-2). Corner Hse.

Rough Riding. Dick Cepek & Walt Wheelock. (Illus.). 1969. wrappers 1.00 (ISBN 0-910856-29-X). La Siesta.

Rough Road Home. Melissa Mather. LC 58-9537. 256p. (YA) 1988. pap. 9.95 (ISBN 0-8397-7237-8). Eriksson.

Rough Road Home: A True & Moving Story of One Woman's Courage under Adversity. Melissa Mather. LC 86-19774. 256p. 1986. 14.95 (ISBN 0-8397-7236-X); pap. 9.95. Eriksson.

Rough Road in the Rockies. Hermina G. Kilgore. LC 61-16173. (Illus.). 135p. 1961. 6.50 (ISBN 0-9609280-0-6); pap. 9.75 (ISBN 0-9609280-1-4). Kilgore.

Rough Side of War: The Civil War Journal of Chesley A. Mosman, 1st Lieutenant, Company D, 59th Illinois Volunteer Infantry Regiment, 1862-1866. Chesley A. Mosman. Intro. by Arnold Gates. (Illus.). 448p. 1987. 25.00 (ISBN 0-940591-06-5). Basin Pub.

Rough Strife. Lynne S. Schwartz. LC 79-2740. 224p. 1985. pap. 7.95 (ISBN 0-06-091282-0, PL 1282, PL). Har-Row.

Rough Surfaces. D. R. Thomas. 310p. 1982. 55.00 (ISBN 0-470-20601-2, Co-Pub. with Longman). Wiley.

Rough Surfaces. R. R. Thomas. (Illus.). 310p. 1982. text ed. 55.00x (ISBN 0-582-46816-7). Wiley.

Rough Trade. Cole Riley. (Orig.). 1988. pap. 3.50. Holloway.

Rough Translations. Molly Giles. LC 84-16363. (Flannery O'Connor Award for Short Fiction Ser.). 144p. 1985. 13.95 (ISBN 0-8203-0744-0). U of Ga Pr.

Rough Weather Makes Good Timber: Carolinians Recall. Patsy M. Ginns. LC 76-20765. (Illus.). xiv, 189p. 1980. 14.95 (ISBN 0-8078-1288-9); pap. 8.95 (ISBN 0-8078-4071-8). U of NC Pr.

Rough-Winged Swallow Stelgidopteryx Ruficollis (Viellot) A Study Based on Its Breeding Biology in Michigan. William A. Lunk. (Illus.). 155p. 1962. 6.00 (ISBN 0-686-35790-6). Nuttall Ornith.

Roughdrafts: The Process of Writing. Alice Calderonello & Bruce Edwards, Jr. LC 85-80767. 576p. 1986. pap. text ed. 22.36 (ISBN 0-395-35501-X); instr's. manual 2.76 (ISBN 0-395-35502-8). HM.

Roughened Roundnesses. Barriss Mills. 1976. 10.00 (ISBN 0-685-79208-0); pap. 5.00 (ISBN 0-685-79209-9). Elizabeth Pr.

Roughing It, 2 vols. Samuel L. Clemens. (Works of Mark Twain). 1988. Repr. of 1900 ed. Set. lib. bdg. 99.00x. Am Biog Serv.

Roughing It. Mark Twain. (Airmont Classics Ser.). (Illus.). (gr. 8 up). pap. 2.95 (ISBN 0-8049-0134-1, CL-134). Airmont.

Roughing It. Mark Twain. (YA) (RL 10). pap. 3.50 (ISBN 0-451-52046-7, CE1829, Sig Classics). NAL.

Roughing It. Mark Twain. Ed. by Hamlin Hill. (Penguin American Library). 1981. pap. 4.95 (ISBN 0-14-039010-3). Penguin.

Roughing It. Mark Twain. Intro. by Franklin R. Rogers. (Iowa-California Edition of the Works of Mark Twain: Vol. 2). 1972. 35.00x (ISBN 0-520-02018-9); pap. 9.95 (ISBN 0-520-02478-8). U of Cal Pr.

Roughing It. Mark Twain. 448p. 1986. Repr. lib. bdg. 25.95x (ISBN 0-89966-524-1). Buccaneer Bks.

Roughing It. Mark Twain. (Illus.). 592p. 1988. 19.95 (ISBN 0-87052-707-X); pap. 9.95 (ISBN 0-87052-708-8). Hippocrene Bks.

Roughing It Easy. Dian Thomas. (Illus.). 248p. 1976. pap. 3.95 (ISBN 0-446-32489-2). Warner Bks.

Roughing It Easy: A Unique Ideabook for Camping & Cooking. Dian Thomas. LC 73-22348. (Illus.). 200p. 1974. pap. 6.95 (ISBN 0-8425-0892-9). Brigham.

Roughing It Easy, Two. Dian Thomas. (Illus.). 224p. (Orig.). 1978. pap. 3.95 (ISBN 0-446-32668-2). Warner Bks.

Roughing It Elegantly: A Practical Guide to Canoe Camping. Patricia J. Bell. LC 87-7138. (Illus.). 175p. (Orig.). 1987. pap. 9.95 (ISBN 0-9618227-1-6). Cats-Paw MN.

Roughing It in the Bush. Susanna Moodie. LC 86-47871. (Virago Beacon Traveler Ser.). 520p. 1987. pap. 10.95 (ISBN 0-8070-7023-8, BP 748). Beacon Pr.

Roughing It, Pts. 1 & 2 see Writings of Mark Twain.

Roughing It with Charlie, "C" Co., 2nd. Ranger Btn. 2nd ed. Edwin M. Sorvisto. LC 78-71271. (Illus.). 1978. pap. 5.95x (ISBN 0-932572-02-2). Phillips Pubns.

Roughneck. Jim Thompson. 1988. pap. 3.95. Mysterious Pr.

Roughnecks, Drillers, & Tool Pushers: Thirty-three Years in the Oil Fields. Gerald Lynch. (Personal Narratives of the West Ser.). (Illus.). 278p. 1987. 16.95 (ISBN 0-292-71553-6). U of Tex Pr.

Roughnecks: Oilpatch U. S. A. Kit Kittle. LC 85-25016. (Illus.). 192p. 1985. 29.95 (ISBN 0-87833-466-1). Taylor Pub.

Rougon-Macquart, 5 tomes. Emile Zola. Ed. by Lanoux & Mitterand. (Pleiade Ser.). 1960-68. Vol. 1. 45.95 (ISBN 0-685-11544-5); Vol. 2. 44.95 (ISBN 0-685-11545-3); Vol. 3. 46.95 (ISBN 0-685-11546-1); Vol. 4. 45.95 (ISBN 0-685-11547-X); Vol. 5. 49.95 (ISBN 0-685-11548-8). Schoenhof.

Rouleaux Des Morts Du IXe Au XVe Siecle. Ed. by Leopold V. Delisle. 1866. 43.00 (ISBN 0-384-11361-3); pap. 37.00 (ISBN 0-384-11360-5). Johnson Repr.

Rousseau's "Social Contract" A Conceptual Analysis. John B. Noone, Jr. LC 79-28560. 232p. 1980. 20.00x (ISBN 0-8203-0511-1). U of Ga Pr.

Rousseau's Social Contract: The Design of the Argument. Hilail Gildin. LC 82-20148. 240p. 1983. lib. bdg. 22.50x (ISBN 0-226-29368-8); pap. 7.95 (ISBN 0-226-29369-6). U of Chicago Pr.

Rousseau's State of Nature: An Interpretation of the "Discourse on Inequality". Marc F. Plattner. LC 78-60453. 1979. 9.50 (ISBN 0-87580-074-2). N Ill U Pr.

Rousseau's Theory of Literature: The Poetics of Art & Nature. James F. Hamilton. 219p. 1979. 16.95 (ISBN 0-917786-09-2). Summa Pubns.

Route Across the Rocky Mountains. Overton Johnson. Ed. by William H. Winter. LC 77-87648. (American Scene Ser.). (Illus.). 200p. 1972. Repr. of 1932 ed. lib. bdg. 29.50 (ISBN 0-306-71780-8). Da Capo.

Route Across the Rocky Mountains. Overton Johnson & William H. Winter. 166p. 1982. pap. 12.95 (ISBN 0-87770-269-1). Ye Galleon.

Route de la Soie: Les Arts de l'Asie Centrale Ancienne. 116p. 1976. 48.00x (ISBN 0-317-69446-4, Pub. by Han-Shan Tang Ltd). State Mutual Bk.

Route des Flandres see Flanders Road.

Route Guidance & In-Car Communications Systems. OECD Staff. (Road Transport Research Ser.). 104p. (Orig.). 1988. pap. 16.50x (ISBN 92-64-13046-2). OECD.

Route Location & Design. 5th ed. Thomas F. Hickerson. (Illus.). 1967. text ed. 50.95 (ISBN 0-07-028680-9). McGraw.

Route of the Electroliners: Bulletin No. 107. (Illus.). 188p. 1975. 15.00 (ISBN 0-915348-07-1). Central Electric.

Route of the Erie Limited. Dirkes & Krause. 1986. pap. 8.95 (ISBN 0-911868-57-7, C57). Carstens Pubns.

Route of the Orange Limited. William R. Gordon. LC 86-12042. (Illus.). 100p. 1986. pap. 5.95 (ISBN 0-932334-80-6). Heart of the Lakes.

Route of the Warbonnets. Joe McMillan. LC 77-81470. (Illus.). 1977. 27.95 (ISBN 0-934228-01-9). McMillan Pubns.

Route Sixty-Six Revisited, a Wanderer's Guide to New Mexico: Albuquerque to the Arizona Border. K. Hilleson. (Wanderer's Guide Ser.: Vol. 2). (Illus.). 127p. (Orig.). 1988. pap. 9.95 (ISBN 0-9615195-4-1). Nakii Ent.

Route Sixty-Six: The Highway & Its People. Photos by Quinta Scott. LC 88-40208. (Illus.). 224p. 1988. 24.95 (ISBN 0-8061-2133-5). U of Okla Pr.

Route Step March: Edwin M Stanton's Special Military Units & the Prosecution of the War, 1862-1865. Robert G. Mangrum. 237p. 1980. 25.00x (ISBN 0-89126-091-9). MA-AH Pub.

Route Surveying & Design. 5th ed. Carl F. Meyer & David W. Gibson. (Illus.). 1980. text ed. 40.50 scp (ISBN 0-7002-2524-2, HarpC). Har-Row.

Route to Food Self-Sufficiency in Mexico: Interactions with the U. S. Food System. Cassio L. Fernandez. Tr. by Sandra Del Castillo from Span. (Monograph: No. 17). viii, 64p. (Orig.). 1985. pap. 8.50 (ISBN 0-935391-68-1). Ctr Mex Studies.

Router. Bruce Hunter. LC 81-730633. (Orig.). 1982. wkbk. 5.00 (ISBN 0-8064-0269-5, 706); audio visual pkg. 199.00 (ISBN 0-8064-0270-9). Bergwall.

Router Handbook. Patrick Spielman. LC 83-14566. (Illus.). 192p. (Orig.). 1983. pap. 10.95 (ISBN 0-8069-7776-0). Sterling.

Router Jigs & Techniques. Patrick Spielman. LC 87-33674. (Illus.). 352p. (Orig.). 1988. pap. 14.95 (ISBN 0-8069-6694-7). Sterling.

Routes & Results. A. Ryrie. (SCRE Publications Ser.: No. 75). 135p. 1981. text ed. 19.95x (ISBN 0-901116-76-9, Pub. by Scot Council Research); pap. text ed. 10.50x (ISBN 0-901116-77-7, Pub. by Scot Council Research). Humanities.

Routes & Roads. T. Mavrina. 180p. 1980. 39.00x (ISBN 0-317-14287-9, Pub. by Collets (UK)). State Mutual Bk.

Routes De France: Etude Bibliographique sur les Cartes Routiers. Suivie D'un catalogue des Intineraires et Guides Routiers (1552-1850) George Fordham. 106p. (Fr.). Repr. of 1929 ed. lib. bdg. 35.00x. Coronet Bks.

Routes of the Valkyries. John Pickering. 94p. 1987. 49.00x (ISBN 0-902633-43-0, Pub. by Picton UK). State Mutual Bk.

Routes to the Executive Suite. Eugene E. Jennings. LC 70-134596. (McGraw-Hill Paperbacks). 1976. pap. text ed. 5.95 (ISBN 0-07-032444-1). McGraw.

Routine Circumcision: The Tragic Myth. N Carter. 1982. lib. bdg. 59.75 (ISBN 0-87700-398-X). Revisionist Pr.

Routine Circumcision: The Tragic Myth. Nicholas Carter. 1979. pap. 4.00 (ISBN 0-911038-26-4). Noontide.

Routine Complications: Troubles with Talk Between Doctors & Patients. Candace West. LC 83-48733. (Illus.). 216p. 1984. 27.50x (ISBN 0-253-35030-1). Ind U Pr.

Routine Cytological Staining Techniques: Theoretical Background & Practice. M. E. Boon & J. S. Drijver. 250p. 1986. 33.25 (ISBN 0-444-01055-6). Elsevier.

Routine Justice: Processing Cases in Women's Court. Marcia J. Lipetz. (New Observations Ser.). 128p. 1983. 24.95 (ISBN 0-87855-483-1). Transaction Bks.

Routine Surveillance for Radionuclides in Air & Water. (Illus.). 64p. 1968. pap. 3.60 (ISBN 92-4-156005-3, 595). World Health.

Routines. Lawrence Ferlinghetti. LC 64-23652. (Orig.). 1964. pap. 1.00 (ISBN 0-8112-0044-2, NDP187). New Directions.

Routines in Neonatal Care. Cooke. 1986. 35.00 (ISBN 0-8016-1121-0). Mosby.

Routlage-French-English & English-French Dictionary of Commercial & Financial Terms. Phrases & Practice. 2nd ed. J. O. Kettridge. (Fr. & Eng.). 1969. Repr. of 1968 ed. 30.00 (ISBN 0-7100-1671-9). Routledge Chapman & Hall.

Routledge French Dictionary. Compiled by J. O. Kettridge & A. J. Strahan. 600p. 1985. pap. 9.95 (ISBN 0-317-30925-0). Routledge Chapman & Hall.

Routledge Rides Alone. Will L. Comfort. 1976. Repr. of 1910 ed. lib. bdg. 19.95 (ISBN 0-89190-852-8, Pub. by River City Pr). Amereon Ltd.

Roux Brothers on Patisserie: Pastries & Desserts from Three-Star Master Chefs. Michel Roux & Albert Roux. (Illus.). 256p. 1986. 24.95 (ISBN 0-13-783382-2). P-H.

Rover. Aphra Behn. Ed. by Frederick M. Link. LC 66-20828. (Regents Restoration Drama Ser). xvi, 144p. 1967. pap. 4.50x (ISBN 0-8032-5350-8, Bison). U of Nebr Pr.

Rover. Margo Mason. (Illus.). 32p. (ps-1). Date not set. price not set. Bantam.

Rover: A Comedy. Aphra Behn. (Swan Theatre Plays). 72p. 1987. pap. 8.95 (ISBN 0-413-40550-8, 1033). Heinemann Ed.

Rover & Coo Coo. John Hay. (Illus.). 32p. (gr. 3-6). 1986. 12.95 (ISBN 0-88138-078-4). Green Tiger Pr.

Rover Boys at College. Arthur Winfield. 191p. 1981. Repr. PLB 12.95x (ISBN 0-89966-330-3). Buccaneer Bks.

Rover Boys at College. Arthur Winfield. 312p. 1980. Repr. PLB 12.95x (ISBN 0-89967-008-3). Harmony Raine.

Rover Boys at School. Arthur Winfield. 302p. 1980. Repr. PLB 12.95x (ISBN 0-89967-009-1). Harmony Raine.

Rover's Riddles. Illus. by Jean Rudegeair. (Illus.). 24p. (gr. 1-5). 1983. pap. 1.95 (ISBN 0-89954-209-3). Antioch Pub Co.

Rovin' the Years with Our Man Gwin. Adrian Gwin. LC 82-83701. (Illus.). 188p. (Orig.). 1982. pap. 5.95 (ISBN 0-934750-33-5). Jalamap.

Roving Across Fields: A Conversation with William Stafford. William Stafford. Ed. & intro. by Thom Tammaro. LC 82-73446. 48p. (Orig.). 1983. pap. 6.95 (ISBN 0-935306-15-3). Barnwood Pr.

Roving Critic. Carl C. Van Doren. LC 66-21390. Repr. of 1923 ed. 21.50x (ISBN 0-8046-0472-X, Pub. by Kennikat). Assoc Faculty Pr.

Roving Mind. Isaac Asimov. LC 83-60203. 350p. 1983. 19.95 (ISBN 0-87975-201-7); pap. 13.95 (ISBN 0-87975-315-3). Prometheus Bks.

Roving Naturalist: Travel Letters of Theodosius Dobzhansky. Ed. by H. Bentley Glass. LC 79-55229. (Memoirs Ser.: Vol. 139). 1980. pap. 10.00 (ISBN 0-87169-139-6). Am Philos.

Rovings in the Pacific, from 1837 to 1849, 2 vols. in 1. Edward Lucatt. LC 75-35203. Repr. of 1851 ed. 72.50 (ISBN 0-404-14280-X). AMS Pr.

Rovinsky & Guttmacher's Medical Surgical & Gynecologic Complications of Pregnancy. 3rd ed. Sheldon H. Cherry. 1056p. 1985. 99.50 (ISBN 0-683-01670-9). Williams & Wilkins.

Row AMI MM3 "Music Miracle" & MM4 "Trimount" Combined Service Manual of 1969-70. rev. ed. Ami Rowe. Ed. by Frank Adams. 200p. 1986. Repr. of 1969 ed. 39.50 (ISBN 0-939971-12-7, R-370). AMR Pub Co.

Row by Row: A Crop of Thoughts from a New Hampshire Farm. Jane W. Lauber. LC 88-80079. (Illus.). 80p. Date not set. 8.50x (ISBN 0-8233-0445-0). Golden Quill.

Row for Your Life: A Complete Program of Aerobic & Strength Endurance. Reed W. Hoyt et al. 1985. 7.95 (ISBN 0-671-55447-6). S&S.

Row Houses: A Bibliography. Mary Vance. (Architecture Ser.: A 1972). 13p. 1988. 3.75 (ISBN 1-55590-622-2). Vance Biblios.

Row This Boat Ashore. Nancy Rue. LC 86-70282. 256p. (Orig.). (YA) (gr. 9-12). 1986. pap. 6.95 (ISBN 0-89107-393-0, Crossway Bks). Good News.

Row upon Row: Sea Grass Baskets of the South Carolina Lowcountry. Dale Rosengarten. (Illus.). 64p. (Orig.). 1986. pap. 10.00 (ISBN 0-938983-02-4). McKissick.

Rowallan. Lord Rowallan. (Illus.). 1977. 19.95x (ISBN 0-8464-0802-3). Beekman Pubs.

Rowan County, N. C., Abstracts of Deeds, 1753-1785. LC 83-81914. (Illus.). 270p. 1983. 30.00 (ISBN 0-918470-16-1). J W Linn.

Rowan County, N. C., Tax List 1815. Jo W. Linn. LC 87-92111. (Illus.). 1987. pap. 12.00 (ISBN 0-918470-18-8). J W Linn.

Rowan Head. Elizabeth Ogilvie. 1976. Repr. of 1949 ed. lib. bdg. 19.95x (ISBN 0-88411-181-4, Pub. by Aeonian Pr). Amereon Ltd.

Rowboat Book. 1986. cancelled (ISBN 0-442-25866-6). Van Nos Reinhold.

Rowboat to Prague see So Many Heroes.

Rowdy & Laughing. B. L. Holmes. LC 87-90460. 88p. (Orig.). 1987. pap. 4.95 (ISBN 0-941300-06-4). Mother Courage.

Rowdy Richard: A Firsthand Account of the National League Baseball Wars of the 1930's & the Men Who Fought Them. Dick Bartell & Norman Macht. (Illus.). 388p. 1987. 18.95 (ISBN 0-938190-97-0). North Atlantic.

Rowdy Tales from Early Alabama: The Humor of John Gorman Barr. Ed. by G. Ward Hubbs. LC 80-19299. (Illus.). xii, 217p. 1981. 15.95 (ISBN 0-8173-0057-0). U of Ala Pr.

Rowe AMI Continental II Parts Catalog of 1962. Rowe Ami. Ed. by Frank Adams. 102p. 1986. Repr. of 1962 ed. 32.50 (ISBN 0-939971-15-1, R-373). AMR Pub Co.

Rowe AMI MM3 & MM4 Parts Catalog of 1969-70. rev. ed. Ami Rowe. Ed. by Frank Adams. 140p. 1986. Repr. of 1969 ed. 32.50 (ISBN 0-939971-13-5, R-371). AMR Pub Co.

Rowe AMI MM6 "Super Star" Service & Parts Manual Supplement of 1971-72. rev. ed. Rowe Ami. Ed. by Frank Adams. 88p. 1986. 27.50 (ISBN 0-939971-14-3, R-372). AMR Pub Co.

Rowing. Michael T. Cannell & Judith Zimmer. Ed. by Susan Wallach. LC 84-40601. (At Home Gym Ser.). 64p. 1985. pap. 2.95 (ISBN 0-394-72971-4, Pub. by Villard Bks). Random.

Rowing. (Illus.). 48p. (gr. 6-12). 1964. pap. 1.25x. (ISBN 0-8395-3392-6, 3392). BSA.

Rowing Across the Dark. Franz Douskey. LC 81-1936. (Contemporary Poetry Ser.). 96p. 1981. 9.95x (ISBN 0-8203-0574-X); pap. 5.95 (ISBN 0-8203-0578-2). U of Ga Pr.

Rowing for the Hell of It: A Manual for Recreational Rowers. Peter Raymond. (Illus.). 154p. 1982. 11.95 (ISBN 0-89182-048-5). Charles River Bks.

Rowing: Power & Endurance. Susan Lezotte. (Sportsperformance Ser.). (Illus.). 144p. 1987. pap. 6.95 (ISBN 0-8092-4729-1). Contemp Bks.

Rowing the Experience. Bob Stewart. 128p. 1988. 35.00 (ISBN 0-944738-00-1). Boathouse Row.

Rowland & Magee's Accounting. Magee. 1977. pap. 27.95 (ISBN 0-85258-158-0). Van Nos Reinhold.

Rowland Hilder: Painter of the English Landscape. John Lewis. (Illus.). 176p. 1987. 49.50 (ISBN 1-85149-050-7). Antique Collect.

Rowley Poems. Thomas Chatterton. 17.50 (ISBN 0-8369-7105-1, 7939). Ayer Co Pubs.

Rowlf-Underground Three. Richard Corben. (Illus.). 80p. 1987. pap. 10.95 (ISBN 0-87416-031-6). Catalan Communs.

Rows of Corn: A True Account of a Parris Island Recruit. Herbert L. Moore, Jr. LC 83-3229. (Illus.). 232p. 1983. 13.95 (ISBN 0-87844-048-8). Sandlapper Pub Co.

Roxana. Daniel Defoe. Ed. by David Blewett. 1982. pap. 4.95 (ISBN 0-14-043149-7). Penguin.

Roxana. Daniel Defoe. Ed. by Jane Jack. (World's Classics Paper Ser.). 1981. pap. 4.95 (ISBN 0-19-281563-6). Oxford U Pr.

Roxana: The Fortunate Mistress. Daniel Defoe. 1979. pap. 2.25 (ISBN 0-451-51190-5, CE1190, Sig Classics). NAL.

Roxane, the Blue Dane. Alice Kingham-LaChevre. (Illus.). 156p. (Orig.). 1988. pap. 12.00 (ISBN 0-917665-22-8). Bookmakers Guild.

Roxanna Mennella, in Search of a Song, Vol. 6. Roxanna Mennella. Ed. by Barbara Fisher & Richard Spiegel. 40p. (Orig.). (gr. 4-7). 1984. pap. 2.00 (ISBN 0-934830-32-0). Ten Penny.

Roxanna Mennella, in Search of a Song: Inner Clockwork, Vol. 8. Roxanna Mennella. Ed. by Barbara Fisher. (Illus.). 10p. (Orig.). (gr. 5-9). 1985. pap. 2.00 (ISBN 0-934830-36-3). Ten Penny.

Roxanne, Vol. 15. Jane C. Miner. 368p. (Orig.). (YA) (gr. 11 up). 1985. pap. 2.95 (ISBN 0-590-33686-X, Sunfire). Scholastic Inc.

Roxanne Bookman: Live at Five! Cathy Warren. LC 88-964. 112p. (gr. 3-7). 1988. 11.95 (ISBN 0-02-792492-0). Bradbury Pr.

Roxanne, Does Your Husband Travel? The Corporate Wife: for Bitters or Wurst. Georgina R. Doyle. 196p. 1985. pap. write for info. (ISBN 0-931515-07-6). Triumph Pr.

Roxburghe Ballads, 8 Vols. Ed. by W. Chappell & J. W. Ebsworth. Repr. of 1899 ed. Set. 570.00 (ISBN 0-404-50840-5); 71.25 ea. AMS Pr.

Roxy. facsimile ed. Edward Eggleston. LC 68-20010. (Americans in Fiction Ser.). (Illus.). 432p. lib. bdg. 32.00 (ISBN 0-8398-0455-5); pap. text ed. 6.95x (ISBN 0-89197-926-3). Irvington.

Roxy. Edward Eggleston. (Collected Works of Edward Eggleston). 1988. Repr. of 1878 ed. lib. bdg. 59.00x. Am Biog Serv.

Roxy see Collected Works.

Roxy the Robin: Sequence Relationships for Children. Marjorie E. Olson. (Illus.). 48p. (gr. k-1). 1974. pap. text ed. 3.00 (ISBN 0-89039-126-2). Ann Arbor FL.

Roy Acuff: The Smoky Mountain Boy. Elizabeth Schlappi. Ed. by James Calhoun. LC 77-11649. (Illus.). 289p. 1978. 13.95 (ISBN 0-88289-144-8). Pelican.

Roy Bean: Law West of the Pecos. C. L. Sonnichsen. (Illus.). Devin.

Roy Bean: Law West of the Pecos. C. L. Sonnichsen. LC 85-16519. (Illus.). 219p. 1986. pap. 9.95 (ISBN 0-8263-0846-5). U of NM Pr.

Roy Blakely on the Mohawk Trail. Percy K. Fitzhugh. LC 74-15738. (Popular Culture in America Ser.). 222p. 1975. Repr. of 1925 ed. 20.00x (ISBN 0-405-06373-3). Ayer Co Pubs.

Roy Campbell. John Povey. LC 77-1358. (Twayne's World Authors Ser.). 233p. 1977. lib. bdg. 17.95 (ISBN 0-8057-6277-9). Irvington.

Roy Campbell: A Biography. Peter Alexander. (Illus.). 34.00x (ISBN 0-19-211750-5). Oxford U Pr.

Roy Campbell: A Descriptive & Annotated Bibliography. D. S. Parsons. LC 79-7930. (Illus.). 306p. 1980. lib. bdg. 43.00 (ISBN 0-8240-9526-X). Garland Pub.

Roy Castle on Tap: His Unique Tap Dancing Course. Roy Castle. (Illus.). 144p. 1987. 19.95 (ISBN 0-7153-8869-X). David & Charles.

Roy DeCarava: Photographs. Roy DeCarava. Ed. by James Alinder. LC 81-68286. (Illus.). 192p. 1982. 40.00 (ISBN 0-933286-26-0). Friends Photography.

Roy Harris: An American Musical Pioneer. Dan Stehman. (Twayne Music Ser.). 1984. lib. bdg. 32.95 (ISBN 0-8057-9461-1, Twayne). G K Hall.

Roy Jenkins: A Biography. John Campbell. LC 83-10927. (Illus.). 280p. 1983. 22.50 (ISBN 0-312-69460-1). St Martin.

Roy Lichtenstein. Lawrence Alloway. LC 83-2788. (Modern Masters Ser.). (Illus.). 128p. 1983. 29.95 (ISBN 0-89659-330-4); pap. 19.95 (ISBN 0-89659-331-2). Abbeville Pr.

Roy Lichtenstein Ceramic Sculpture. Constance W. Glenn. (Illus.). 64p. (Orig.). 1977. pap. 35.00 (ISBN 0-936270-05-5). CA St U LB Art.

Roy Lichtenstein: Landscape Sketches 1984-1985. Ed. by Constance Glenn & Jack Glenn. (Abrams Facsimile Reproduction Sketchbook Ser.). (Illus.). 1986. 75.00 (ISBN 0-8109-1264-3). Abrams.

Roy Lichtenstein: Mural with Blue Brushstroke. Ed. by Calvin Tomkins. (Illus.). 128p. 1988. pap. 19.95 (ISBN 0-8109-2356-4). Abrams.

Roy Lichtenstein: The Modren Work, 1965 - 1970. Elisabeth Sussman. (Illus.). 1978. 4.00 (ISBN 0-910663-16-5). ICA Inc.

Roy Rogers Book: A Reference-Trivia-Scrapbook. David Rothel. 224p. 1987. 25.00 (ISBN 0-944019-00-5); pap. 20.00 (ISBN 0-944019-01-3). Empire NC.

Roy Rogers-Dale Evans: Happy Trails. Roy Rogers et al. 1979. 2.50 (ISBN 0-8499-0086-7); 13.95. Word Bks.

Roy Stryker Papers Nineteen Hundred Twelve to Nineteen Seventy-Two: A Guide to the Microfilm Edition. Ed. by David G. Horvath. 142p. 1982. pap. 75.00 (ISBN 0-667-00697-4). Chadwyck-Healey.

Roy Stryker: U. S. A., 1943-1950, The Standard Oil (New Jersey) Photography Project. Steven W. Plattner. (Illus.). 144p. 1983. 25.00 (ISBN 0-292-77028-6). U of Tex Pr.

Royal Abbey of Saint-Denis from Its Beginnings to the Death of Suger 475-1151. Sumner M. Crosby. LC 85-26464. 570p. 1987. text ed. 55.00 (ISBN 0-300-03143-2). Yale U Pr.

Royal Academy Exhibitors, 1905-1970, Vol. V: Sherras-Z. 356p. 1982. 110.00x (ISBN 0-85409-984-0, Pub. by EP Pub England). State Mutual Bk.

Royal Academy of Arts, a Complete Dictionary of Contributors & Their Work from Its Foundation in 1769 to 1904, Compiled with the Sanction of the President & Council of the Royal Academy, 8 vols. in 4. Algernon Graves. LC 76-118750. 1972. Repr. of 1905 ed. Set. lib. bdg. 181.00 (ISBN 0-8337-1425-2). B Franklin.

Royal Academy of Arts: A Complete Dictionary of Contributors & Their Work from Its Foundation in 1769-1904, 8 vols. Algernon Graves. 1986. Repr. of 1905 ed. Set. lib. bdg. 200.00 (ISBN 0-89984-196-1). Century Bookbindery.

Royal Academy of Arts Year Book 1981. Intro. by Hugh Casson. (Illus.). 1981. 35.00 (ISBN 0-8390-0281-5). Abner Schram Ltd.

Royal African Company. Kenneth G. Davies. 390p. 1975. Repr. of 1957 ed. lib. bdg. 23.00x (ISBN 0-374-92074-5, Octagon). Hippocrene Bks.

Royal Air Force Between the Wars. Raymond L. Rimell. (Vintage Warbirds Ser.: No. 3). (Illus.). 64p. (Orig.). 1985. pap. 9.95 (ISBN 0-85368-703-X, Pub. by Arms & Armour). Sterling.

Royal Album. Patrick Lichfield. (Illus.). 151p. 1985. pap. 19.95 (ISBN 0-241-11335-0, Pub. by Hamish Hamilton England). David & Charles.

Royal & Ancient. F. Ward-Thomas. (Illus.). 200p. 1980. 14.95x (ISBN 0-7073-0260-9, Pub. by Scot Acad Pr). Longwood Pub Group.

Royal & Other Historical Letters Illustrative of the Reign of Henry III, from the Originals in the Public Record Office, 2 vols. Ed. by Walter W. Shirley. Incl. Vol. 1. Twelve Sixteen to Twelve Thirty-Five (ISBN 0-8115-1045-X); Vol. 2. Twelve Thirty-Six to Twelve Seventy-One (ISBN 0-8115-1046-8). (Rolls Ser.: No. 27). Repr. of 1866 ed. Set. 88.00. Kraus Repr.

Royal & Republican Rome. Tyler Whittle. (History in Pictures Ser.: Bk. 3). (Illus.). 60p. 1972. 7.95 (ISBN 0-8464-1185-7). Beekman Pubs.

Royal Aquarium: Failure of a Victorian Compromise. John M. Munro. 1971. 10.00x (ISBN 0-8156-6033-2, Am U Beirut). Syracuse U Pr.

Royal Arch: Its Hidden Meaning. George H. Steinmetz. (Illus.). 145p. 1987. Repr. of 1946 ed. softcover 9.50 (M-302). Macoy Pub.

Royal Australian Navy see Official History of Australia in the War of 1914-1918.

Royal Baby: The Private Life of His Royal Highness Prince William. Clarissa Harlowe & Cathy Camhy. (Illus., Orig.). 1983. pap. 4.95x (ISBN 0-671-49892-4). PB.

Royal Ballet. Katherine S. Walker & Sarah Woodcock. (Quality Paperbacks Ser.). (Illus.). 144p. 1982. pap. 10.95 (ISBN 0-306-80176-0). Da Capo.

Royal Ballet: The First 50 Years. A. Bland. 1986. 89.75X (ISBN 0-901366-11-0, Pub. by Harrap Ltd England). State Mutual Bk.

Royal Bastards of Medieval England. C. Given-Wilson & A. Curteis. (Illus.). 200p. 1984. 25.00x (ISBN 0-7102-0025-0). Routledge Chapman & Hall.

Royal Bastards of Medieval England. Chris Given-Wilson & Alice Curteis. 195p. 1988. pap. text ed. 12.95. Routledge Chapman & Hall.

Royal Bavarian Castles. J. H. Spronge. 1976. lib. bdg. 75.00 (ISBN 0-8490-2545-1). Gordon Pr.

Royal Beasts & Other Works. William Empson. LC 87-51312. 201p. 1988. text ed. 20.00x (ISBN 0-87745-195-8); pap. 7.95 (ISBN 0-87745-196-6). U of Iowa Pr.

Royal Benin Art: Selections from the National Museum of African Art. Bryna M. Freyer. LC 87-42637. (Illus.). 64p. (Orig.). 1987. pap. 14.95 (ISBN 0-87474-445-8). Smithsonian.

Royal Bloodline: Ellery Queen, Author & Detective. Francis M. Nevins, Jr. 1973. 9.95 (ISBN 0-87972-066-2); pap. 5.95 (ISBN 0-87972-067-0). Bowling Green Univ.

Royal Book of Ballet. Shirley Goulden. LC 64-16319. (Illus.). (gr. 5 up). 1964. 10.74 (ISBN 0-8136-6021-1, Dist. by Caroline Hse). Modern Curr.

Royal Botanic Gardens, Sydney: A History, 1816-1985. Lionel Gilbert. (Illus.). 224p. 1988. 45.00x (ISBN 0-19-554719-5). Oxford U Pr.

Royal Bounty. F. R. Havergal. pap. 2.95 (ISBN 0-685-88391-4). Reiner.

Royal Canadian Academy of Arts: Exhibitions & Members, 1880-1979. Ed. by Evelyn McMann. 464p. 1981. 80.00x (ISBN 0-8020-2366-5). U of Toronto Pr.

Royal Canadian Air Force Exercise Plans for Physical Fitness. Date not set. pap. 3.50 (ISBN 0-671-54341-5). PB.

Royal Canon of Turin. Alan Gardiner. (Illus.). 400p. 1987. pap. text ed. 35.00 (ISBN 0-900416-48-3, Pub. by Aris & Phillips UK). Humanities.

Royal Captive. Jennifer O'Green. (Orig.). 1987. pap. 3.95 (ISBN 0-440-14125-7). Dell.

Royal Charles: Charles II & the Restoration. Antonia Fraser. LC 79-2208. (Illus.). 1979. 19.45 (ISBN 0-394-49721-X). Knopf.

Royal Charlie. Robert Steelman. 256p. 1983. pap. 2.95 (ISBN 0-441-73609-2). Ace Bks.

Royal Chef's Notebook. Ronald Aubery. 160p. 1980. 29.00x (ISBN 0-905418-28-X, Pub. by Gresham England). State Mutual Bk.

Royal Childhoods. Charles Carlton. (Illus.). 192p. 1986. 29.95 (ISBN 0-7102-0185-0). Routledge Chapman & Hall.

Royal City. Les Savage, Jr. Ed. by Richard C. Weaver. (Orig.). 1988. pap. 0.40 (ISBN 0-941108-01-5). Friends Palace Pr.

Royal Clocks: British Monarchy & Its Timekeepers 1300-1900. Cedric Jagger. (Illus.). 340p. 1983. deluxe ed. 100.00x (ISBN 0-7091-9562-1, Pub. by Robert Hale); pap. 42.50x. Trans-Atl-Phila.

Royal College of Art: One Hundred & Fifty Years of Art & Design. Christopher Frayling. (Illus.). 208p. 1988. pap. 29.95 (ISBN 0-7126-1820-1, Pub. by Century Hutchinson). David & Charles.

Royal College of General Practitioners: The First 25 Years. John Fry & Hunt. (Illus.). 350p. 1982. text ed. 29.00 (ISBN 0-85200-360-9, Pub. by MTP Pr England). Kluwer Academic.

Royal College of Physicians & Surgeons of Glasgow. Tom Gibson. 1983. 90.00x (ISBN 0-86334-013-X, Pub. by Macdonald Pub UK). State Mutual Bk.

Royal College of Physicians of London, Portrait Catalogue II. Ed. by Gordon Wolstenholme & John F. Kerslake. 240p. 1977. 43.25 (ISBN 0-444-15265-2, Excerpta Medica). Elsevier.

Royal College of San Carlos: Surgery & Spanish Medical Reform in the Late Eighteenth Century. Michael E. Burke. LC 76-50237. xv, 215p. 1977. 21.75 (ISBN 0-8223-0382-5). Duke.

Royal Commandments. F. R. Havergal. pap. 3.95 (ISBN 0-686-64393-3). Reiner.

Royal Commentaries of the Incas, 2 vols. Garcilaso De La Vega. Ed. & tr. by Clements R. Markham. (Hakluyt Society, First Ser.: Nos. 41 & 45). Repr. of 1869 ed. 63.00 (ISBN 0-8337-2233-6). B Franklin.

Royal Commentaries of the Incas & General History of Peru, Pt. I. Garcilaso De la Vega. Tr. by Harold V. Livermore. (Texas Pan American Ser.). (Illus.). 740p. 1987. pap. 14.95 (ISBN 0-292-77038-3). U of Tex Pr.

Royal Commentaries of the Incas, & General History of Peru. Garcilaso de la Vega. Tr. by Harold V. Livermore. LC 65-13518. (The Texas Pan-American Ser.). Pts. 1 & 2. pap. 160.00 ea. (2025129). Bks Demand UMI.

Royal Commission on the Losses & Services of American Loyalists, 1783-85. Daniel P. Coke. Ed. by Hugh E. Egerton. LC 79-131450. (Research & Source Works Ser.: No. 756). 1971. Repr. of 1915 ed. lib. bdg. 29.00 (ISBN 0-8337-0995-X). B Franklin.

Royal Commission on the Losses & Services of the American Loyalists 1783 - 1785. Daniel P. Coke. Ed. by Hugh E. Egerton. LC 79-90166. (Mass Violence in America Ser). Repr. of 1915 ed. 25.00 (ISBN 0-405-01308-6). Ayer Co Pubs.

Royal Commission on the Ocean Ranger Marine Disaster: Report One: The Loss of the Semisubmersible Drill Rig & Its Crew. Canadian Government Publishing Centre Staff. 400p. 1985. pap. 55.25 (ISBN 0-660-11682-0, SSC191, SSC). UNIPUB.

Royal Commission Report, 1937. Ed. by Aaron Klieman & Howard M. Sachar. (Rise of Israel Ser.). 430p. 1987. lib. bdg. 85.00 (ISBN 0-8240-4922-5). Garland Pub.

Royal Commissions of Inquiry: The Significance of Investigation in British Politics. Hugh M. Clokie & J. William Robinson. LC 70-86274. 1969. Repr. of 1937 ed. lib. bdg. 17.00x (ISBN 0-374-91710-8, Octagon). Hippocrene Bks.

Royal Company of Printers & Booksellers of Madrid: 1763-1794. Diana M. Thomas. LC 82-50405. 100p. 1982. 18.50 (ISBN 0-87875-237-4). Whitston Pub.

Royal Cookery Book. Jules Gouffe. (Illus.). 1977. Repr. of 1869 ed. 21.00x (ISBN 0-85409-809-7). Charles River Bks.

Royal Copenhagen. H. V. F. Winstone. (Illus.). 160p. 1984. 50.00 (ISBN 0-905743-37-7, Pub. by Stacey Intl UK). Humanities.

Royal Correspondence in the Hellenistic Period. H. B. Welles. (Illus.). 510p. 1974. 25.00 (ISBN 0-89005-019-8). Ares.

Royal Correspondence of the Assyrian Empire, 4 vols in 3 vols. Ed. by Leroy Waterman. Vols. 17, 18. 31.00 ea. (ISBN 0-384-38817-5); vols. 19 & 20 bound in 1 vol 74.00 (ISBN 0-384-38819-1). Johnson Repr.

Royal County of Berkshire: Official Guide. 104p. 1987. pap. 30.00x (ISBN 0-317-61995-0, Countryside Bks). State Mutual BK.

Royal Crescent in Bath: A Fragment of English Life. William Lowndes. 96p. 40.00x (ISBN 0-905459-34-2, Pub. by Redcliffe Pr Ltd). State Mutual Bk.

Royal Cricket of Japan: An Original Fantasy. James Lash. Ed. by Christian Moe & Darwin R. Payne. 44p. 1971. pap. 1.00 (ISBN 0-8093-0554-2). S Ill U Pr.

Royal Crown Derby. 3rd ed. John Twitchett & Betty Bailey. (Illus.). 260p. 1988. 69.50 (ISBN 1-85149-057-4). Antique Collect.

Royal Deeside Line. Grahame Farr. LC 68-23820. (Illus.). 1968. 19.95x (ISBN 0-678-05596-3). Kelley.

Royal Demesne in English Constitutional History, 1066-1272. Robert S. Hoyt. LC 68-23299. xii, 253p. 1968. Repr. of 1950 ed. lib. bdg. 35.00x (ISBN 0-8371-0109-3, HORD). Greenwood.

Royal Designers on Design. The Design Council. 200p. 1987. 59.00x (ISBN 0-85072-167-9, Design Council Bks). State Mutual Bk.

Royal Disclosure Problematics of Representation in French Classical Tragedy. Harriet Stone. LC 87-62170. 176p. 1988. lib. bdg. 23.95 (ISBN 0-917786-57-2). Summa Pubns.

Royal Doulton Bunnykins Collectors Book. Louise Irvine. (Illus.). 48p. pap. 12.00 (ISBN 0-317-55041-1). Apollo.

Royal Doulton Figures Supplement 1: 1979-1982. Louise Irvine & Richard Dennis. (Illus.). 48p. pap. 12.95 (ISBN 0-317-55038-1). Apollo.

Royal Doulton Limited Edition Loving-Cups & Jugs. (Illus.). 32p. pap. 10.95 (ISBN 0-317-55040-3). Apollo.

Royal Doulton Series Ware, Vol. 1. Louise Irvine. (Illus.). 112p. 12.95 (ISBN 0-317-55036-5). Apollo.

Royal Doulton Series Ware, Vol. 2. Louise Irvine. (Illus.). 144p. 17.50 (ISBN 0-317-55037-3). Apollo.

Royal Dragoons Immortal Love. Marian Helm-Pirgo. 314p. 1976. 10.00 (ISBN 0-686-30919-7). Polish Inst Arts.

Royal Dynasties in Ancient Israel. Tomoo Ishida. 1977. 45.25 (ISBN 3-1100-6519-3). De Gruyter.

Royal Elizabeths: The Romance of Five Princesses, 1464-1840. facs. ed. Elsie Thornton-Cook. LC 67-23274. (Essay Index Reprint Ser). 1967. Repr. of 1929 ed. 13.00 (ISBN 0-8369-0938-0). Ayer Co Pubs.

Royal Escape. Georgette Heyer. 1985. pap. 2.95 (ISBN 0-451-13332-3, Sig). NAL.

Royal Faces: Nine Hundred Years of British Monarchy. Hugh Clayton. LC 82-80980. (Illus.). 1982. 14.95 (ISBN 0-500-01287-3). Thames Hudson.

Royal Facts of Life: Biology & Politics in Sixteenth-Century Europe. Mark Hansen. LC 80-12557. 354p. 1980. lib. bdg. 22.50 (ISBN 0-8108-1297-5). Scarecrow.

Royal Family. Theo Aronson. (Illus.). 272p. 1986. pap. 12.95 (ISBN 0-88162-251-6). Salem Hse Pubs.

Royal Family Album. (Illus.). 1978. 25.00 (ISBN 0-8317-7520-3, Mayflower Bks). Smith Pubs.

Royal Family of the Columbia. Alberta B. Fogdall. (Illus.). 330p. 1978. 14.95 (ISBN 0-87770-168-7). Ye Galleon.

Royal Family of the Columbia: Dr. John McLoughlin & His Family. 2nd ed. Alberta B. Fogdall. LC 78-17170. (Illus.). 1982. 16.95 (ISBN 0-8323-0413-1). Binford-Metropolitan.

Royal Family Pop-Up. L. Leete-Hodge. 12p. 1984. 9.98 (ISBN 0-517-44650-2, Bounty). Outlet Bk Co.

Royal Family Quiz & Fact Book. Timothy B. Benford. LC 86-46044. (Illus.). 256p. 1987. pap. 8.95 (ISBN 0-06-096182-1, PL 6182, PL). Har-Row.

Royal Feud. Michael Thornton. 1986. pap. 4.95 (ISBN 0-345-33682-8). Ballantine.

Royal Feud: The Dark Side of the Love Story of the Century. Michael Thornton. 1985. 17.45 (ISBN 0-671-60298-5). S&S.

Royal Flash. George M. Fraser. 1985. pap. 6.95 (ISBN 0-452-25676-3, Plume). NAL.

Royal Flying Corps in World War I. Raymond L. Rimell. (Vintage Warbirds Ser.: No. 1). (Illus.). 64p. (Orig.). 1985. pap. 9.95 (ISBN 0-85368-693-9, Pub. by Arms & Armour). Sterling.

Royal Flying Corps: (Military Wing) 256p. 1987. 105.00x (ISBN 0-948251-29-8, Pub. by Picton UK). State Mutual Bk.

Royal Follies: A Chronicle of Royal Misbehavior. David Randall. (Illus.). 272p. 1988. 17.95 (ISBN 0-8069-6734-X). Sterling.

Royal French Patronage of Art in the Fourteenth Century: An Annotated Bibliography. Carla Lord. (Reference Publications in Art History). 1985. lib. bdg. 55.00 (ISBN 0-8161-8509-3). G K Hall.

Royal Funding of the Parisian Academie Royale des Sciences During the 1690s. Alice Stroup. LC 86-71785. (Transactions Ser.: Vol. 77, Pt. 4). 167p. (Orig.). 1987. pap. 15.00 (ISBN 0-87169-774-2). Am Philos.

Royal Game: Chess for Young People. Edith Weart & B. Brussel-Smith. (Illus.). (gr. 6 up). 9.95 (ISBN 0-8149-0436-X). Vanguard.

Royal Gentleman. facsimile ed. Albion W. Tourgee. LC 67-29281. (Illus.). 467p. lib. bdg. 49.50 (ISBN 0-8398-1970-6). Irvington.

Royal Government in Colonial Brazil: With Special Reference to the Administration of the Marquis of Lavradio, Viceroy, 1769-1779. Dauril Alden. LC 68-26064. (Illus.). 583p. pap. 151.60 (2029942). Bks Demand UMI.

Royal Government in Virginia, 1624-1775. Percy S. Flippin. LC 76-168047. (Columbia University. Studies in the Social Sciences: No. 194). Repr. of 1919 ed. 27.50 (ISBN 0-404-51194-5). AMS Pr.

Royal Governors of Georgia, 1754-1775. W. W. Abbot. LC 59-9568. (Institute of Early American History & Culture Ser.). x, 198p. 1959. 20.00x (ISBN 0-8078-0758-3). U of NC Pr.

Royal Guest & Other Classical Danish Narratives. Ed. by P. M. Mitchell & Kenneth H. Ober. LC 77-78070. (Phoenix Ser.). vi, 242p. 1982. pap. 6.95 (ISBN 0-226-53214-3). U of Chicago Pr.

Royal Guest & Other Classical Danish Narrative. Tr. by P. M. Mitchell & Kenneth H. Ober. LC 77-78070. 1977. lib. bdg. 15.00x (ISBN 0-226-53213-5). U of Chicago Pr.

Royal Handbook. Alan Hamilton. (Illus.). 176p. 1986. 12.95 (ISBN 0-13-783358-X). P-h.

Royal Highness. Thomas Mann. LC 83-5921. 368p. 1983. pap. 7.95 (ISBN 0-394-71739-2, Vin). Random.

Royal Historical Society Annual Bibliography of British & Irish History Publications of 1984. Ed. by Geoffrey R. Elton. LC 81-641280. 192p. 1986. 25.00 (ISBN 0-312-69474-1). St Martin.

Royal Historical Society Annual Bibliography of British & Irish History: Publications of 1983. Ed. by Geoffrey R. Elton. LC 81-641280. 208p. 1984. 29.95 (ISBN 0-312-69472-5). St Martin.

Royal Historical Society Annual Bibliography of British & Irish History: Publications of 1985. Ed. by David M. Palliser. 184p. 1986. 29.95 (ISBN 0-312-00228-9). St Martin.

Royal Historical Society Annual Bibliography of British & Irish History: Pulications of 1986. Ed. by David M. Palliser. LC 81-641280. 175p. 1987. 29.95 (ISBN 0-312-01587-9). St Martin.

Royal Historie of the Excellent Knight Generides. Generides. Ed. by Frederick J. Furnivall. LC 70-147837. (Research & Source Works Ser.: No. 727). 1971. Repr. 25.50 (ISBN 0-8337-1252-7). B Franklin.

Royal Honiton Lace. Elise Luxton & Yusai Fukuyama. (Illus.). 94p. 1989. 39.95 (ISBN 0-7134-5764-3, Pub. by Batsford England). David & Charles.

Royal Horticulture Society's Gardener's Calendar: A Guide to Gardening Through the Year. Ed. by John Main. (Illus.). 376p. Date not set. price not set (ISBN 0-356-12302-2). Trans-Atl Phila.

Royal House of Portugal. Francis Gribble. LC 73-110904. 1970. Repr. of 1915 ed. 28.50x (ISBN 0-8046-0887-3, Pub. by Kennikat). Assoc Faculty Pr.

Royal House of Windsor. Elizabeth Longford. (Illus.). 304p. 1984. 16.95 (ISBN 0-517-55586-7). Crown.

Royal Household & the King's Affinity: Service, Politics, & Finance in England. Chris Given-Wilson. LC 85-52145. 384p. 1986. 35.00 (ISBN 0-300-03570-5). Yale U Pr.

Royal Houses of Europe. Ed. by Marlene A. Eilers & G. Nicholas Tantzos. (Illus.). 500p. 1988. 65.00 (ISBN 0-938311-05-0). Atlantic Intl Pubns.

Royal Hunt. D. R. Popescu. Tr. by J. E. Cottrell & M. Bogdan. LC 85-4985. Orig. Title: Vinatoarea Regala. 187p. 1985. 14.95 (ISBN 0-8142-0386-8). Ohio St U Pr.

Royal Hunter: Art of the Sasanian Empire. Prudence O. Harper. LC 77-13082. (Illus.). 1978. 19.95 (ISBN 0-87848-050-1). Asia Soc.

Royal Hymns of Shulgi, King of Ur: Man's Quest for Immortal Fame. Jacob Klein. LC 81-65929. (Transactions Ser.: Vol. 71, Pt. 7.). 1981. 10.00 (ISBN 0-87169-717-3). Am Philos.

Royal India. facs. ed. Katherine H. Diver. LC 76-142620. (Essay Index Reprint Ser). 1942. 22.00 (ISBN 0-8369-2152-6). Ayer Co Pubs.

Royal India. facsimile ed. Maud Diver. (Essay Index Reprint Ser.). (Illus.). 288p. Repr. of 1942 ed. lib. bdg. 21.00 (ISBN 0-8290-0780-6). Irvington.

Royal Indian Cookery: A Taste of Palace Life. Manju S. Singh. (Illus.). 192p. 1988. text ed. 18.95 (ISBN 0-07-057534-7). McGraw.

Royal Indian Hospital of Mexico City. David Howard. LC 80-11131. (Special Studies: No. 20). 99p. 1980. pap. text ed. 5.95x (ISBN 0-87918-045-5). ASU Lat Am St.

Royal Indian Navy, 1612-1950. D. J. Hastings. LC 87-42510. 383p. 1988. lib. bdg. 39.95x (ISBN 0-89950-276-8). McFarland & Co.

Royal Inscriptions on Clay Cones from Ashur Now in Istanbul. Veysel Donbaz & A. Kirk Grayson. 144p. 1984. 37.50x (ISBN 0-8020-5650-4). U of Toronto Pr.

Royal Institute of British Architects: A Guide to Its Archive & History. Angela Mace. 378p. 1986. 65.00x (ISBN 0-7201-1773-9). Mansell.

Royal Institute of International Affairs. LC 76-29396. Repr. of 1937 ed. 32.00 (ISBN 0-404-15350-X). AMS Pr.

Royal Institute of International Affairs: Problem of International Investment. 371p. 1965. 35.00x (ISBN 0-7146-1247-2, F Cass Co). Biblio Dist.

Royal Institute of International Affairs: Review of the Foreign Press, 1939 to 1945, Individual Series Avail. (Individual Vols. avail. Write for info.). Set. lib. bdg. write for info. Kraus Intl.

Royal Institution: Its Founder & First Professors. Bence Jones. LC 74-26270. (History, Philosophy & Sociology of Science Ser). 1975. Repr. 34.50x (ISBN 0-405-06598-1). Ayer Co Pubs.

Royal Interiors of Regency England. David Watkin. (Illus.). 128p. 29.95 (ISBN 0-317-54972-3). Apollo.

Royal Interiors of Regency England: From Watercolors First Published by W. H. Pyne, 1817-1820. David Watkin. LC 84-7349. (Illus.). 128p. 1985. 29.95 (ISBN 0-86565-048-9). Vendome.

Royal Intrigue: Crisis at the Court of Charles VI, 1392-1420. R. C. Famiglietti. LC 85-48004. (Studies in the Middle Ages: No. 9). 1986. 39.50 (ISBN 0-404-61439-6). AMS Pr.

Royal Journey to London. Emily V. Warinner. LC 75-28654. 1975. pap. 1.95 (ISBN 0-914916-11-4). Topgallant.

Royal Kingdom of Egypt Military Decorations & Medals: Pre-1952 (French Version) David V. Olson. 75p. 1987. pap. 10.00. WW Milit Exch.

Royal Knits. Nicolette McGuire. 80p. 1987. 39.00x (ISBN 0-7063-6593-3, Pub. by Ward Lock Educ Co Ltd). State Mutual Bk.

Royal Letters, Charters, & Tracts. Bannatyne Club Staff. LC 78-174971. (Bannatyne Club, Edinburgh. Publications: No. 119). Repr. of 1867 ed. 31.00 (ISBN 0-404-52878-3). AMS Pr.

Royal Letters, Charters, & Tracts. Ed. by David Laing. LC 70-171639. (Bannatyne Club, Edinburgh. Publications: No. 114). Repr. of 1867 ed. 42.50 (ISBN 0-404-52869-4). AMS Pr.

Royal Line of France: The Story of the Kings & Queens of France. facs. ed. Elsie Thornton-Cook. LC 67-26789. (Essay Index Reprint Ser). 1934. 19.50 (ISBN 0-8369-0939-9). Ayer Co Pubs.

Royal London Guide & Streetfinder. (Nicholson Guides). (Illus.). 96p. 1988. pap. 6.95 (ISBN 0-948576-10-3, Pub. by British Tour). Salem Hse Pubs.

Royal Mail Case: Rex V. Lord Kylsant, & Another. Ed. by Collin Brooks & Richard P. Brief. LC 80-1475. (Dimensions of Accounting Theory & Practice Ser.). 1981. Repr. of 1933 ed. lib. bdg. write for info. Ayer Co Pubs.

Royal Mail Case: Rex vs. Lord Kylsant, & Another. Owen C. Kylsant et al. 32.50 (ISBN 0-405-13505-X). Ayer Co Pubs.

Royal Mail: The Post Office since 1840. M. J. Daunton. (Illus.). 388p. 1985. 36.50 (ISBN 0-485-11280-9, Pub. by Athlone Pr UK). Humanities.

Royal Marines Commandos Fitness & Survival Skills. John Watney. (Illus.). 176p. 1988. 17.95 (ISBN 0-7153-8716-2). David & Charles.

Royal Marys, Princess Mary & Her Predecessors. facs. ed. Elsie Thornton-Cook. LC 67-23275. (Essay Index Reprint Ser). 1930. 17.00 (ISBN 0-8369-0940-2). Ayer Co Pubs.

Royal Masonic Cyclopaedia. Kenneth MacKinzie. (Illus.). 800p. (Orig.). 1987. pap. 19.95 (ISBN 0-85030-521-7, Pub. by Aquarian Pr). Sterling.

Royal Matron's Treasury of Addresses & Ceremonies, No. 2. Geraldine Boldt Maxwell. 1975. pap. 2.00 29 selections (ISBN 0-88053-320-X, S-423). Macoy Pub.
Royal Navy: A History from the Earliest Times, 7 vols. Ed. by William L. Clowes. Repr. of 1903 ed. Set. 290.00 (ISBN 0-404-01640-5); 41.50 ea. AMS Pr.
Royal Navy & North America: The Warren Papers, 1736-1752. Ed. by Julian Gwyn. 69.00x (ISBN 0-317-44224-4, Pub. by Navy Rec Soc). State Mutual Bk.
Royal Navy & the Falklands War. David Brown. (Illus.). 374p. 1988. 29.95 (ISBN 0-87021-572-8). Naval Inst Pr.
Royal Navy & the Siege of Bilbao. Sir James Cable. LC 78-73238. (Illus.). 1980. Cambridge U Pr.
Royal Navy & the Slave Trade. Raymond Howell. LC 87-9608. 224p. 1987. 35.00 (ISBN 0-312-00854-6). St Martin.
Royal Navy Day by Day. R. E. Schrubb. 432p. 1981. 95.00x (ISBN 0-900000-91-0, Pub. by Centaur Bks). State Mutual Bk.
Royal Navy in the Mediterranean 1915-1918. Paul G. Halpern. 580p. 1987. text ed. 60.00x (ISBN 0-566-05488-4, Pub. by Gower Pub England). Gower Pub Co.
Royal Navy on the Danube. Charles Fryer. (East European Monographs: No. 232). 240p. 1988. text ed. 25.00 (ISBN 0-88033-129-1). East Eur Quarterly.
Royal Navy Today & Tomorrow. J. R. Hill. LC 82-60915. (Illus.). 144p. 1982. 22.95 (ISBN 0-7110-1168-0). Naval Inst Pr.
Royal Office of Master of the Horse. M. M. Reese. 1986. 99.75X (ISBN 0-901366-90-0, Pub. by Harrap Ltd England). State Mutual Bk.
Royal One Hundred. Alan Hamilton. 144p. 1986. 12.95 (ISBN 0-670-81460-1). Viking.
Royal Opera House Covent Garden: A History From 1732. Ellenor Handley & Martin Kinna. LC 83-18938. (Music Reprint Ser.). 64p. 1987. Repr. of 1978 ed. lib. bdg. 18.50 (ISBN 0-306-76231-5). Da Capo.
Royal Pain. Ellen Conford. 176p. (gr. 7 up). 1986. 11.95 (ISBN 0-590-33269-4, Scholastic Hardcover). Scholastic Inc.
Royal Pain. Ellen Conford. 176p. (Orig.). (gr. 7 up). 1987. pap. 2.50 (ISBN 0-590-40548-9, Point). Scholastic Inc.
Royal Palaces of Europe. Hugh Montgomery-Massingberd. LC 83-5882. (Illus.). 208p. 1983. 40.00 (ISBN 0-86565-033-0). Vendome.
Royal Palaces of France. Ian Dunlop. (Illus.). 282p. 1985. 35.00 (ISBN 0-393-02222-6). Norton.
Royal Pardon. John Arden & Margaretta D'Arcy. 109p. 1967. pap. 6.95 (ISBN 0-413-33410-4, NO. 2980). Heinemann Ed.
Royal Parks of London. Guy Williams. (Illus.). 234p. 1985. pap. 8.95 (ISBN 0-89733-145-1). Academy Chi Pubs.
Royal Passion. Jennifer Blake. 384p. (Orig.). 1986. pap. 7.95 (ISBN 0-449-90101-7, Columbine). Fawcett.
Royal Patronage of Buddhism in Ancient India. Hazra Kanai Lal. 1984. text ed. 55.00x (ISBN 0-86590-167-8). Apt Bks.
Royal Patronage of Indian Music. Gowri Kuppuswamy & M. Hariharan. 1985. 36.00x (ISBN 0-8364-1488-8, Pub. by Sundeep Prakashan India). South Asia Bks.
Royal Pavilion, Brighton. John Dinkle. LC 83-14676. (Illus.). 144p. 1983. 19.95 (ISBN 0-86565-035-7). Vendome.
Royal Pines: An On-Line Case Study in Business Systems Design. Alan L. Eliason. 144p. (Orig.). 1984. pap. text ed. write for info (ISBN 0-574-21700-2, 13-4700); solns. manual avail. (ISBN 0-317-03528-2, 13-4701). SRA.
Royal Play of Macbeth. Henry N. Paul. LC 75-154016. 1971. Repr. of 1950 ed. lib. bdg. 26.00x (ISBN 0-374-96319-3, Octagon). Hippocrene Bks.
Royal Poinciana. Thea C. Douglass. LC 87-81426. 448p. 1988. 18.95 (ISBN 1-55611-048-0). D I Fine.
Royal Postcards. Jack H. Smith. LC 87-50014. (Illus.). 168p. (Orig.). 1987. pap. 12.95 (ISBN 0-87069-495-2). Wallace-Homestead.
Royal Priesthood. Nolan P. Howington. LC 85-22376. 1986. pap. 4.95 (ISBN 0-8054-1622-6). Broadman.
Royal Priesthood. Basilea Schlink. 1971. pap. 0.95 (ISBN 3-87209-654-0). Evang Sisterhood Mary.
Royal Protomedicato: The Regulation of the Medical Profession in the Spanish Empire. John T. Lanning. Ed. by John J. TePaske. LC 85-4611. v, 485p. 1985. 40.00 (ISBN 0-8223-0651-4). Duke.
Royal Quest. Mary Lide. 384p. 1987. 5.95 (ISBN 0-446-34672-1). Warner Bks.
Royal Quest. Mary Lide. Date not set. pap. 12.95 (ISBN 0-446-38791-6). Warner Bks.
Royal Quest. Mary Lide. 1988. 15.95 (ISBN 0-446-51362-8). Warner Bks.
Royal Reach. Lamm. 11.95 (ISBN 0-87306-133-0). Feldheim.
Royal Rebel: A Psychological Portrait of Crown Prince Rudolf of Austria-Hungary. John T. Salvendy. LC 87-25317. (Illus.). 278p. (Orig.). 1988. lib. bdg. 26.75 (ISBN 0-8191-6675-8); pap. text ed. 14.25 (ISBN 0-8191-6676-6). U Pr of Amer.
Royal Recipes from the Cajun Country. John Uhler & Glenna Uhler. 1969. pap. 4.95 (ISBN 0-87511-125-4). Claitors.
Royal Republicans: The French Naval Dynasties Between the World Wars. Chalmers Hood, 3rd. LC 84-21331. (Illus.). 221p. (Orig.). 1985. text ed. 27.50 (ISBN 0-8071-1211-9). La State U Pr.
Royal Residences. John M. Robinson. 320p. 1982. 55.00x (Pub. by MacDonald & Co Pubs England). State Mutual Bk.
Royal Resident. Marcus Lehmann. 1981. 7.95 (ISBN 0-686-76251-7). Feldheim.
Royal River Highway. Frank L. Dix. (Illus.). 336p. 1985. 49.95 (ISBN 0-7153-8005-2). David & Charles.
Royal River: The Thames from Source to Sea. 1984. 75.00x (Pub. by Gresham England). State Mutual Bk.
Royal Road. Stephan H. Hoeller. LC 75-4244. (Illus.). 119p. (Orig.). 1975. pap. 4.75 (ISBN 0-8356-0465-9, Quest). Theos Pub Hse.
Royal Road to Card Magic. Jean Hugard & Frederick Braue. 304p. 1949. 12.95 (ISBN 0-571-06389-6); pap. 7.95 (ISBN 0-571-11399-0). Faber & Faber.
Royal Romance Paper Dolls. Peggy DeRosemond. (gr. 8-12). 1984. pap. 4.00 (ISBN 0-914510-14-2). Evergreen.
Royal Saints of Anglo-Saxon England: A Study of West Saxon & East Anglian Cults. Susan J. Ridyard. (Cambridge Studies in Medieval Life & Thought, Fourth Ser.: No. 9). 376p. Date not set. price not set (ISBN 0-521-30772-4). Cambridge U Pr.
Royal Scotland. Roddy Martine. (Illus.). 160p. (Orig.). 1985. pap. 10.95 (ISBN 0-86228-045-1, Paul Harris, England). Riverrun NY.
Royal Secrets: The View from Downstairs. Stephen P. Barry. Ed. by Diane Reverand. LC 84-40604. 256p. 1985. 16.45 (ISBN 0-394-54403-X, Pub. by Villard Bks). Random.
Royal Seduction. Jennifer Blake. 416p. 1985. pap. 3.95 (ISBN 0-449-12979-9, GM). Fawcett.
Royal Service. Stephen P. Barry. 288p. 1984. pap. 3.95 (ISBN 0-380-67397-5). Avon.
Royal Shakespeare Company: A History of Ten Decades. Sally Beauman. 1982. 29.95x (ISBN 0-19-212209-6). Oxford U Pr.
Royal Shakespeare Company's Centenary Production of Henry V. Sally Beauman. 1976. 11.00 (ISBN 0-08-020874-6). Pergamon.
Royal Singles. Christopher Egerton-Thomas. (Illus.). 176p. (Orig.). 1985. pap. 9.95 (ISBN 0-671-49634-4, Fireside). S&S.
Royal Slave. Julia Fitzgerald. 400p. (Orig.). 1988. pap. 4.50 (ISBN 1-55785-063-1). Bart Books.
Royal Snuff Box. Barbara Hazard. 1987. pap. 2.50 (ISBN 0-451-14746-4, Sig). NAL.
Royal Society Catalogue of Portraits. (Illus.). 170p. 1980. lib. bdg. 90.00x (ISBN 0-85403-136-7, Pub. by Royal Soc London). Scholium Intl.
Royal Society of British Artists: 1824-1893. Antique Collector's Club Staff. 620p. 1975. 89.50 (ISBN 0-902028-35-9). Antique Collect.
Royal Society of Literature & the Patronage of George IV. David G. Williams. Ed. by Stephen Orgel. (Harvard Dissertations in American & English Literature Ser.). 843p. 1987. lib. bdg. 125.00 (ISBN 0-8240-0084-6). Garland Pub.
Royal Society, Sixteen Sixty to Nineteen Forty: A History of Its Administration under Its Charters. Henry G. Lyons. LC 69-10124. (Illus.). 1968. Repr. of 1944 ed. lib. bdg. 35.00x (ISBN 0-8371-0155-7, LYRS). Greenwood.
Royal South Carolina, 1719-1763. Bradley D. Bargar. LC 77-133843. (Tricentennial Booklet: No. 7). viii, 76p. 1970. pap. 4.95 (ISBN 0-87249-206-0). U of SC Pr.
Royal Stars of the States: Fifty Fabulous Quilts with Complete Instructions. Ed. by Sandra Hatch. (Illus.). 184p. Date not set. price not set (ISBN 0-929138-00-7). Hse White Birches.
Royal Street, a Novel of Old New Orleans. Walter A. Roberts. LC 73-18605. Repr. of 1944 ed. 24.50 (ISBN 0-404-11415-6). AMS Pr.
Royal Style: An Intimate Look Inside the Palaces & Royal Houses of Britain's Royal Family. Ingrid Seward. (Illus.). 208p. 1988. 16.95 (ISBN 0-312-02274-3). St Martin.
Royal Succession in Capetian France: Studies on Familial Order & the State. Andrew W. Lewis. LC 81-6360. (Harvard Historical Studies: No. 100). (Illus.). 376p. 1982. text ed. 37.00x (ISBN 0-674-77985-1). Harvard U Pr.
Royal Tapestry. Christopher Howkins. 96p. 1987. 50.00x (ISBN 0-9509105-1-1, Countryside Bks). State Mutual Bk.
Royal Tastes: Erotic Writings of Paul Verlaine. Tr. by Alan Stone. 1984. 12.95 (ISBN 0-517-55495-X, Harmony). Crown.
Royal Taxation in Fourteenth Century France: The Captivity & Ransom of John II, 1356-1370. John B. Henneman. LC 76-8595. (Memoirs Ser.: Vol. 116). 1976. 15.00 (ISBN 0-87169-116-7). Am Philos.
Royal Taxation in Fourteenth Century France: The Development of War Financing. John B. Henneman. LC 78-147945. 1971. 44.50x (ISBN 0-691-05188-7). Princeton U Pr.
Royal Tour of France by Charles IX & Catherine de' Medici: Festivals & Entries, 1564-6. Ed. by Victor E. Graham & W. McAllister Johnson. LC 78-4841. pap. 120.50 (2056124). Bks Demand UMI.
Royal Tours of the British Empire: 1860-1927. John Fabb. (Illus.). 128p. 1989. 29.95 (ISBN 0-7134-5191-2, Pub. by Batsford England). David & Charles.
Royal Tradition: The Queen & Her Family in Scotland. Roddy Martine. 160p. 1987. 25.00x (ISBN 1-85158-018-2, Pub. by Mainstream Scotland). State Mutual Bk.
Royal Trains: From Queen Victoria to the Present. Patrick Kingston & Geoffrey Kichenside. (Illus.). 192p. 1986. 39.95 (ISBN 0-7153-8594-1). David & Charles.
Royal Treasuries of the Spanish Empire in America, 3 vols. John J. TePaske & Herbert S. Klein. LC 82-2457. 1982. Set. 125.00 (ISBN 0-8223-0486-4); Vol. I: Peru, 563 p. 55.00 (ISBN 0-8223-0530-5); Vol. II: Peru (Bolivia), 422 p. 45.00 (ISBN 0-8223-0531-3); Vol. III: Chile & the Rio de la Plata, 406 p. 45.00 (ISBN 0-8223-0532-1). Duke.
Royal Way of the Cross. Archbishop Fenelon. Ed. by Hal M. Helms. LC 80-67874. (Living Library Ser.). 166p. 1982. 7.95 (ISBN 0-941478-00-9). Paraclete Pr.
Royal Weddings. Dulcie M. Ashdown. (Illus.). 208p. 1981. 32.00x (ISBN 0-7091-9383-1, Pub. by Robert Hale). Trans-Atl-Phila.
Royal Worcester Porcelain: From 1862 to the Present Day. Henry Sandon. (Illus.). 279p. 1989. 55.00 (Pub. by Century Hutchinson). David & Charles.
Royal Yankee. Victor Suthren. 192p. 1987. 13.95 (ISBN 0-312-01084-2). St Martin.
Royal Year. Tim Graham. 1983. pap. 7.95 (ISBN 0-03-064168-3). H Holt & Co.
Royal Year. Ed. by Lynn Picknett & Shona Grimbly. (Illus.). 160p. 1985. 14.95 (ISBN 0-318-11699-5). Salem Hse Pubs.
Royal Year, 1988. Tim Graham. 1989. 15.95 (ISBN 0-671-67363-7). Summit Bks.
Royalist Officers in England & Wales, 1642 to 1660: A Biographical Dictionary. P. R. Newman. LC 80-8594. 1981. lib. bdg. 109.00 (ISBN 0-8240-9503-0). Garland Pub.
Royalist War Effort, 1642-1646. Ronald Hutton. (Illus.). 288p. 1984. pap. text ed. 14.95 (ISBN 0-582-49411-7). Longman.
Royalist's Notebook: The Commonplace Book of Sir John Oglander. John Oglander. Ed. by Francis Bamford. LC 72-174427. (Illus.). Repr. of 1936 ed. 17.00 (ISBN 0-405-08827-2). Ayer Co Pubs.
Royall Tyler. George T. Tanselle. LC 67-12103. (Illus.). 1967. 19.50x (ISBN 0-674-78000-0). Harvard U Pr.
Royals: An Intimate Look at the Lives & Lifestyles of Britain's Royal Family. Jeannie Sakol & Caroline Latham. (Illus.). 1988. 19.95 (ISBN 0-86553-194-3). Congdon & Weed.
Royalty for Commoners: The Complete Known Ancestry of John of Gaunt, Son of Edward III, King of England, & Queen Phillippa. Roderick W. Stuart. xi, 292p. 1988. 21.50 (ISBN 1-55613-097-X). Heritage Bk.
Royalty of the Pulpit. Edgar D. Jones. LC 79-134105. (Essay Index Reprint Ser.). 1951. 27.50 (ISBN 0-8369-1979-3). Ayer Co Pubs.
Royaume Latin de Jerusalem. Jean Richard. LC 78-63359. (Crusades & Military Orders: Second Ser.). Repr. of 1953 ed. 28.50 (ISBN 0-404-17029-3). AMS Pr.
Royaume Secret. Pat Robertson. Ed. by Annie L. Cosson. Tr. by Anne Gimenez. 261p. (Fr.). 1985. pap. 2.75 (ISBN 0-8297-1277-1). Life Pubs Intl.
Royaume Thai ou Siam. Jean B. Pallegoix. 917p. (Fr.). Repr. of 1854 ed. text ed. 165.60x (ISBN 0-576-03971-3, Pub. by Gregg Intl Pubs England). Gregg Intl.
Royce & Hocking - American Idealists. Daniel S. Robinson. 1968. 6.95 (ISBN 0-8158-0178-5). Chris Mass.
Royce's Logical Essays. Daniel S. Robinson. 1971. 10.00 (ISBN 0-8158-0261-7). Chris Mass.
Royce's Mature Philosophy of Religion. Frank M. Oppenheim. LC 87-12458. 432p. 1987. text ed. 32.95x (ISBN 0-268-01633-X). U of Notre Dame Pr.
Royce's Metaphysics. Gabriel Marcel. Tr. by Virginia Ringer & Gordon Ringer. LC 74-33746. 180p. 1975. Repr. of 1956 ed. lib. bdg. 35.00x (ISBN 0-8371-7978-5, MARO). Greenwood.
Royce's Metaphysics. Gabriel Marcel. LC 56-11854. pap. 45.00 (ISBN 0-317-08060-1, 2055292). Bks Demand UMI.
Royce's Social Infinite: The Community of Interpretation. John E. Smith. LC 69-13630. xvii, 176p. 1969. Repr. of 1950 ed. 23.50 (ISBN 0-208-00729-6, Archon). Shoe String.
Royce's Voyage Down Under: A Journey of the Mind. Frank M. Oppenheim. LC 79-4007. 136p. 1980. 12.00 (ISBN 0-8131-1394-6). U Pr of Ky.
Roycroft Furniture. Ed. by Stephen Gray. (Mission Furniture Catalogues: No. 3). 52p. 1981. pap. 4.95 (ISBN 0-940326-03-5). Turn of Cent.
Roycroft Furniture: 1906 Catalog. (Illus.). 52p. 1985. pap. 4.95 (ISBN 0-87905-413-1). Gibbs Smith Pub.
Royer-Collard. Gabriel Remond. Ed. by J. P. Mayer. LC 78-67377. (European Political Thought Ser.). (Fr.). 1979. Repr. of 1933 ed. lib. bdg. 14.00x (ISBN 0-405-11727-2). Ayer Co Pubs.
Roy's Rot: Rules of Thumb to Wit & Wisdom. Roy T. Maloney. LC 85-7015. (Illus.). 1985. pap. 12.95 (ISBN 0-913257-01-X). Dropzone Pr.
Royster Memorial Studies. Ed. by Louis B. Wright et al. LC 74-12493. 1974. Repr. of 1931 ed. lib. bdg. 47.50 (ISBN 0-8414-9541-6). Folcroft.
Royston. Helen Bryant. 1986. 13.95 (ISBN 0-533-06742-1). Vantage.
Royte Pomerantsen or How to Laugh in Yiddish. Ed. by Immanuel Olsvanger. 1979. pap. 7.95 (ISBN 0-8052-0099-1). Schocken.
Rozhdestvo Khristovo. M. Skaballanovitch. 195p. pap. 7.00 (ISBN 0-317-29162-9). Holy Trinity.
Rozhdestvo Presvjatia Bogoroditsi. M. Skaballanovitch. 134p. pap. 5.00 (ISBN 0-317-29149-1). Holy Trinity.
RP Processing. Business Communications Staff. 1988. 2650.00 (ISBN 0-89336-684-6, P-114). BCC.
RPG & RPG II Programming: Applied Fundamentals. William E. Bux & Edward G. Cunningham. (Illus.). 1979. pap. text ed. write for info (ISBN 0-13-783423-3). P-H.
RPG II & RPG III Programming. Nancy Stern et al. LC 83-12536. 680p. 1984. pap. text ed. 40.25 (ISBN 0-471-87625-9). Wiley.
RPG II & RPG III Programming. Dennie Van Tassell. (Illus.). 397p. (Orig.). 1986. pap. text ed. 27.95 (ISBN 0-938188-26-7); tchr's. ed. avail. (ISBN 0-938188-33-X). Mitchell Pub.
RPG II & RPG III with Business Applications. Stanley E. Myers. 1983. text ed. write for info. (ISBN 0-8359-6753-0, Reston). P-H.
RPG-II Programming. Edward Essick. 354p. 1981. pap. text ed. write for info. (ISBN 0-574-21315-5, 13-4315); instr's. guide avail. (ISBN 0-574-21316-3, 13-4316). SRA.
RPG II Programming. Carl Feingold. 720p. 1982. pap. text ed. write for info. (ISBN 0-697-08150-8); instrs.' manual avail. (ISBN 0-697-08152-4). Wm C Brown.
RPG II Programming. 2nd ed. Douglas D. Minkema & Gerald L. Carter. (RPG II Programming-Advanced Topics Ser.). 1977. pap. text ed. 17.50 (ISBN 0-9610582-2-6). Apollo Com.
RPG II Programming Advanced Topics. Douglas D. Minkema & Mark T. Pasquini. (RPG II Programming-Advanced Topics Ser.). 187p. 1977. pap. text ed. 14.50 (ISBN 0-9610582-3-4). Apollo Com.
RPG II Programming-Advanced Topics Teacher's Guide. Douglas D. Minkema & Mark T. Pasquini. 210p. (gr. 9-12). text ed. 55.00 (ISBN 0-9610582-6-9). Apollo Com.
RPG II Programming Teacher's Guide. Douglas D. Minkema & Gerald L. Carter. 175p. text ed. 55.00 (ISBN 0-9610582-5-0). Apollo Com.
RPG II with Business Applications. Stanley E. Myers. (Illus.). 1979. text ed. write for info. (ISBN 0-8359-6303-9, Reston); instr's. manual avail. (ISBN 0-8359-6304-7). P-H.
RPL Dosimetry: Radiophotoluminscence in Health Physics. Ed. by J. A. Perry & R. F. Mould. (Medical Science Ser.). 192p. 1987. 75.00x (ISBN 0-85274-272-X, Pub. by A Hilger UK). Taylor & Francis.
RPM Unlimited: A Business Machines Practice Set. 2nd ed. Dorothy L. Albertson. (Illus.). (gr. 9-12). 1980. 13.92 (ISBN 0-07-000955-4). McGraw.
R.P.O. Routes of Nebraska. William F. Rapp. (Postal History Monograph Ser.). (Illus.). 1978. lib. bdg. cancelled (ISBN 0-916170-04-7). J-B Pub.
RPV. Louis Gerken. 300p. Date not set. 29.95 (ISBN 0-317-61594-7). Amer Scientific.
RR & Bentley Collector Guide, Vol. 1. Graham Robson. (Collector Guide Ser.). (Illus.). 144p. 1984. 29.95 (ISBN 0-900549-86-6, Pub. by Motor Racing England). Motorbooks Intl.
RR Lyrae Stars. V. P. Tsesevich. 368p. 1969. text ed. 73.00x (ISBN 0-7065-0707-X, Pub. by Keter Pub Jerusalem). Coronet Bks.
R.S. Ninoy Aquino: A Portrait. (Human Rights Ser.). 1986. write for info. Grunwald & Radcliff.
RS Opiuchi (1985) & the Recurrent Nova Phenomenon. Ed. by M. F. Bode. 270p. 1986. lib. bdg. 85.00x (ISBN 90-6764-074-3). Coronet Bks.
RS-232 & Parallel Connections Made Easy: A Step-by-Step Approach to Connecting Computers, Printers, Terminals, & Modems. Martin D. Seyer. (Illus.). 246p. 1987. pap. 27.95 (ISBN 0-13-783515-9). P-H.
RS-232-C & Modem's. Alan Murtha. Ed. by W. M. Farber. (Illus.). 75p. (Orig.). 1982. pap. text ed. 14.95 (ISBN 0-943600-00-6). Trade House.
RS-232 Solution. Joe Campbell. LC 83-51568. 194p. (Orig.). 1984. pap. 18.95 (ISBN 0-89588-140-3). SYBEX.
RS-232C Made Easy: Connecting Computers, Printers, Terminals & Modems. Martin D. Seyer. LC 83-13939. 214p. 1983. text ed. 38.00 (ISBN 0-13-783480-2); pap. text ed. 25.95 (ISBN 0-13-783472-1). P-H.

Rubik's Cubic Compendium. Erno Rubik et al. (Recreations in Mathematics Ser.). 200p. 1988. 14.95 (ISBN 0-19-853202-4). Oxford U Pr.
Rubinstein Variation: Nimzo-Indian Defense. Tim Taylor. (Illus.). 76p. (Orig.). 1984. pap. 5.00 (ISBN 0-931462-30-4). Chess Ent Inc.
Rubinstein's Chess Masterpieces. Akiba Rubinstein. Ed. by Hans Kmoch. Tr. by Barnie F. Winkelman. 1941. pap. 4.95 (ISBN 0-486-20617-3). Dover.
Rubinstejn & the Philosophical Foundations of Soviet Psychology. T. R. Payne. (Sovietica Ser.: No. 30). 184p. 1968. lib. bdg. 29.00 (ISBN 90-277-0062-1, Pub. by Reidel Holland). Kluwer Academic.
Rubout at the Onyx. H. Paul Jeffers. 1987. pap. 2.95 (ISBN 0-345-34676-9). Ballantine.
Rubricae Cartusiae Gosnayensis: (MS. Grande Chartreuse 1 Stat 33) James Hogg. (Analecta Carusiana Ser.: No. 23). 146p. (Orig., Lat. & Eng.). 1974. pap. 25.00 (ISBN 3-7052-0023-2, Pub by Salzburg Studies). Longwood Pub Group.
Rubs of the Green: Golf's Triumphs & Tragedies. Webster Evans. (Illus.). 1970. 8.95 (ISBN 0-7207-0251-8). Transatl Arts.
Ruby. Helen Ashfield. 1988. pap. 2.95 (ISBN 0-312-90318-9). St Martin.
Ruby. Susie Jenkin-Pearce. (Illus.). 24p. (ps-6). 1987. 7.95 (ISBN 0-19-278209-6). Oxford U pr.
Ruby. Alison Lester. LC 87-16997. (Illus.). 32p. (ps-3). 1988. 13.95 (ISBN 0-395-46477-3). HM.
Ruby Cover Up. Seth Kantor. 1980. pap. 2.95 (ISBN 0-89083-680-9). Zebra.
Ruby for Grief. Michael Burkard. LC 81-40484. (Pitt Poetry Ser.). 77p. 1981. 16.95x (ISBN 0-8229-3450-7); pap. 8.95 (ISBN 0-8229-5333-1). U of Pittsburgh Pr.
Ruby in the Rough. Robert Ruby. LC 76-40031. 1976. 8.95 (ISBN 0-88289-099-9). Pelican.
Ruby in the Smoke. Philip Pullman. Ed. by Frances Foster. LC 86-20983. 208p. (YA) (gr. 7 up). 1987. 11.95 (ISBN 0-394-88826-X); lib. bdg. 11.99 (ISBN 0-394-98826-4). Knopf.
Ruby in the Smoke. Philip Pullman. LC 86-20983. 240p. (gr. 7 up). 1988. pap. 2.95 (ISBN 0-394-89589-4). Knopf.
Ruby Slippers. Carol F. Laque. 308p. (Orig.). Date not set. pap. 8.50 (ISBN 0-9619532-0-9). Circumference Pr.
Ruby-Stained Glass from A to Z see Encyclopedia of Victorian Colored Pattern Glass.
Ruby Sweetwater & the Ringo Kid. Sheldon Bart. LC 80-14683. 384p. 1981. text ed. 11.95 (ISBN 0-07-003872-4). McGraw.
Ruby, the Red Knight. Amy Aitken. LC 82-9590. (Illus.). 32p. (ps-2). 1983. 12.95 (ISBN 0-02-700340-X). Bradbury Pr.
Rubyfruit Jungle. Rita Mae Brown. 1977. pap. 4.50 (ISBN 0-553-23813-2). Bantam.
Rubyfruit Jungle. Rita Mae Brown. LC 88-47535. 224p. 1988. 18.95 (ISBN 0-553-05284-5). Bantam.
Rucker's Personal Guide to Successful Money Making Opportunities & Credit Information. Edward W. Rucker. LC 86-90451. 245p. 1987. pap. 21.95 (ISBN 0-9614352-1-6). Edw Rucker Ent.
Rudder & the Rock. Charles W. Conn. 1976. pap. 4.25 (ISBN 0-87148-733-0). Pathway Pr.
Rudder: Divine Canons of the Seven Decumenical & of Local Synods. Agapius et al. Ed. by Orthodox Christian Educational Society Staff & Apostolos Makrakis. Tr. by Denver Cummings from Hellenic. Orig. Title: Pedalion. 1097p. 1957. 26.00x (ISBN 0-938366-00-9). Orthodox Chr.
Rudder Grangers Abroad, & Other Stories. facs. ed. Frank R. Stockton. LC 79-90592. (Short Story Index Reprint Ser.). 1891. 15.00 (ISBN 0-8369-3075-4). Ayer Co Pubs.
Rudder's Rangers. Ronald L. Lane. LC 79-65328. (Illus.). 198p. 1979. 12.95 (ISBN 0-934588-00-7). Ranger Assocs.
Rude & Barbarous Kingdom: Russia in the Accounts of Sixteenth-Century English Voyagers. Ed. by Lloyd E. Berry & Robert O. Crummey. LC 68-16059. pap. 77.00 (ISBN 0-317-27784-7, 2015353). Bks Demand UMI.
Rude Assignment. Wyndham Lewis. Ed. by Toby Foshay. LC 84-16837. (Illus.). 315p. 1984. 20.00 (ISBN 0-87685-604-0); pap. 12.50 (ISBN 0-87685-603-2); deluxe cloth ed. 30.00 (ISBN 0-87685-605-9). Black Sparrow.
Rude Awakenings. Bob Rosenthal. LC 81-21943. 1981. pap. 3.50 (ISBN 0-916328-16-3). Yellow Pr.
Rude Food. Pierre Le Postre. (Illus.). 48p. 1983. pap. 9.95 (ISBN 0-345-31234-1). Ballantine.
Rude Hiver. Raymond Queneau. (Poesie Ser.). 174p. 1977. 4.95 (ISBN 0-686-54684-9). Schoenhof.
Rude Mechanicals: An Account of Tank Maturity During World War II. A. J. Smithers. (Illus.). 152p. 1988. 39.95 (ISBN 0-87052-499-2). Hippocrene Bks.
Rudelstein Affair. Michael Marsh. LC 80-29323. 205p. 1981. 9.95 (ISBN 0-918056-02-0). Ariadne Pr.
Rudens. Plautus. Ed. & intro. by H. C. Fay. (College Classical Ser.). v, 221p. 1984. pap. text ed. 17.50x (ISBN 0-89241-386-7). Caratzas.
Rudens, Curculio, Casina. Plautus. Tr. by Christopher Stace. LC 81-6086. (Translations from Greek & Roman Authors Ser.). (Illus.). 160p. 1982. pap. 6.95 (ISBN 0-521-28046-X). Cambridge U Pr.
Rudimental Divine Science & No & Yes. Mary Baker Eddy. Danish 12.50 (ISBN 0-87952-105-8); German 12.50 (ISBN 0-87952-158-9); Italian 12.50 (ISBN 0-87952-183-X); Portugese 12.50 (ISBN 0-87952-208-9); Swedish 12.50 (ISBN 0-87952-253-4); Spanish 12.50 (ISBN 0-87952-232-1). First Church.
Rudimental Divine Science: No & Yes. Mary Baker Eddy. 1976. lib. bdg. 69.95 (ISBN 0-8490-2546-X). Gordon Pr.
Rudimentary Society among Boys. J. H. Johnson. 1973. pap. 9.00. Johnson Repr.
Rudimentary Society among Boys. J. Helmsley Johnson. LC 78-63750. (Johns Hopkins University. Studies in the Social Sciences. Second Ser. 1884: 11). Repr. of 1884 ed. 11.50 (ISBN 0-404-61019-6). AMS Pr.
Rudimentary Treatise on Well-Digging, Boring & Pumpwork, Eighteen Forty-Nine. John G. Swindell. (Illus.). 88p. pap. 17.50. Saifer.
Rudiments of Architecture: 1814 see Works of Asher Benjamin: Boston, 1806-1843.
Rudiments of Ballroom Dancing. V. Barton. (Ballroom Dance Ser.). 1986. lib. bdg. 79.95 (ISBN 0-8490-3261-X). Gordon Pr.
Rudiments of Ballroom Dancing. V. Varton. (Ballroom Dance Ser.). 1985. lib. bdg. 76.00 (ISBN 0-87700-853-1). Revisionist Pr.
Rudiments of Criticism. E. A. Lamborn. 191p. 1980. Repr. of 1925 ed. lib. bdg. 35.50 (ISBN 0-8495-3252-3). Arden Lib.
Rudiments of Criticism. E. A. Lamborn. LC 73-14520. 1973. lib. bdg. 25.50 (ISBN 0-8414-5675-5). Folcroft.
Rudiments of Logic. George Myro & Mark Bedau. 336p. 1987. text ed. write for info. (ISBN 0-13-783648-1). P-H.
Rudiments of Militarie Dicipline. LC 70-25967. (English Experience Ser.: No. 105). 14p. 1969. Repr. of 1638 ed. 20.00 (ISBN 90-221-0105-3). Walter J Johnson.
Rudiments of Mining Practice. C. E. Gregory. LC 83-80651. 128p. 1983. 24.00x (ISBN 0-87201-783-4). Gulf Pub.
Rudiments of Mining Practice. C. E. Gregory. (Mining Engineering Ser.: Vol. 3). 143p. 1983. 24.00x (ISBN 0-87849-042-6, Trans Tech Germany). Trans Tech.
Rudiments of Music. Ed. by Ernest J. Bontrager & Ida Bontrager. 1968. pap. 1.00x (ISBN 0-87813-102-7). Park View.
Rudiments of Music. John Castellini. (Illus.). 1962. 15.95x (ISBN 0-393-09573-8, NortonC). Norton.
Rudiments of Music. 2nd ed. Robert W. Ottman & Frank D. Mainous. (Illus.). 320p. 1987. write for info. P-H.
Rudiments of Music: A Detailed Study in Music Essentials. Jeannette Cass. (Illus., Orig.). 1956. pap. text ed. write for info. (ISBN 0-13-783654-6). P-H.
Rudiments of Plane Affine Geometry. Peter Scherk & R. Lingenberg. LC 75-11705. (Mathematical Expositions: No. 20). pap. 30.50 (2056135). Bks Demand UMI.
Rudiments of Ramsey Theory. Ronald L. Graham. LC 80-29667. (CBMS Ser.: No. 45). 1983. pap. 10.00 (ISBN 0-8218-1696-9). Am Math.
Rudin. Ivan S. Turgenev. Ed. by Galina Stilman. LC 54-5784. (Slavic Studies). (Rus). (gr. 9 up). 1962. pap. 13.00x (ISBN 0-231-01965-3). Columbia U Pr.
Rudin. Ivan S. Turgenev. Tr. by Richard Freeborn from Rus. (Classics Ser.). (Orig.). 1975. pap. 5.95 (ISBN 0-14-044304-5). Penguin.
Rudin. Ivan S. Turgenev. Ed. by Patrick Waddington. 300p. pap. 9.95x (ISBN 0-900186-19-4). Basil Blackwell.
Rudin: A Nest of the Gentry. Ivan S. Turgenev. 319p. 1985. 9.95 (Pub. by Raduga Pubs USSR). Imported Pubns.
Rudists of Jamaica see Palaeontographica Americana.
Rudo Ensayo: A Description of Sonora & Arizona in 1764. Juan Nentvig. Tr. by Alberto F. Pradeau & Robert R. Rasmussen. LC 79-20420. 160p. 1980. 16.95x (ISBN 0-8165-0696-5); pap. 7.95 (ISBN 0-8165-0624-8). U of Ariz Pr.
Rudolf Bahro: Critical Responses. Ed. by Ulf Wolter. Tr. by Michel Vale from Ger., Fr. & Ital. LC 80-5453. 250p. 1980. 37.50 (ISBN 0-87332-159-6). M E Sharpe.
Rudolf Baranik: Words from Twenty-Five Years. Jonathan Green. (Illus.). 56p. 1987. pap. 9.95 (ISBN 0-87663-514-1). Universe.
Rudolf Borchardt & the Middle Ages: Translation, Anthology & Nationalism. Fred Wagner. (Mikrokosmos: Vol. 6). 181p. 1980. pap. 23.00 (ISBN 3-8204-6407-7). P Lang Pubs.
Rudolf Bultmann: Interpreting Faith for the Modern Era. Ed. by Roger Johnson. (Making of Modern Theology Ser.). 256p. 1987. 19.95 (ISBN 0-00-599061-0, Pub. by Collins Liturgical). Har Row.
Rudolf Flesch on Business Communications: How to Say What You Mean in Plain English. Rudolf Flesch. pap. 6.95 (ISBN 0-06-463393-4, EH 393, B&N Bks). Har-Row.
Rudolf Hess: Prisoner of Peace. Ilse Hess & Rudolf Hess. Ed. by George Pile. Tr. by Meyrick Booth. LC 82-83959. (Illus.). 151p. 1982. pap. 6.00 (ISBN 0-939484-02-1). Inst Hist Rev.
Rudolf Hess: Prisoner of Peace. 1984. lib. bdg. 79.95 (ISBN 0-87700-611-3). Revisionist Pr.
Rudolf Hess: The Last Nazi. Wulf Schwarzwaller. Ed. by S. C. Sattler. (Illus.). 312p. 1988. 17.95 (ISBN 0-915765-52-7, Pub. by Zenith Edit). Natl Pr Inc.
Rudolf II & His World: A Study in Intellectual History 1576-1612. R. J. Evans. (Illus.). 1984. 19.95x (ISBN 0-19-821961-X). Oxford U Pr.
Rudolf Otto: An Introduction to His Philosophical Theology. Philip C. Almond. LC 83-19865. (Studies in Religion). x, 172p. 1984. 25.00x (ISBN 0-8078-1589-6). U of NC Pr.
Rudolf Schwarz: Bibliography & Building List. Edward H. Teague. (Architecture Ser.: A 1451). 9p. 1985. 2.00 (ISBN 0-89028-541-1). Vance Biblios.
Rudolf Steiner: A Documentary Biography. Johannes Hemleben. Tr. by Leo Twyman. (Illus.). cancelled (ISBN 0-904822-02-8, Pub by Henry Goulden, Ltd); pap. 15.50 (ISBN 0-904822-03-6). St George Bk Serv.
Rudolf Steiner: An Autobiography, Vol. 1. 2nd ed. Rudolf Steiner. LC 72-95242. (Spiritual Science Library). (Illus.). 560p. 1980. lib. bdg. 30.00 (ISBN 0-89345-031-6); pap. 20.00 (ISBN 0-89345-210-6). Garber Comm.
Rudolf Steiner & Holistic Medicine. Francis X. King. LC 87-12290. 224p. (Orig.). 1987. pap. 9.95 (ISBN 0-89254-015-X). Nicolas-Hays.
Rudolf Steiner Education & the Developing Child. Willi Aeppli. Tr. by Angelika V. Ritscher from Ger. 200p. 1987. pap. 10.95 (ISBN 0-88010-164-4). Anthroposophic.
Rudolf Steiner Education: The Waldorf Schools. 2nd ed. Francis Edmonds. 139p. 1982. pap. 9.50 (ISBN 0-85440-344-2, Pub. by Steinerbooks). Anthroposophic.
Rudolf Steiner: Herald of a New Epoch. Stewart C. Easton. LC 80-67026. (Illus.). 1980. pap. 10.95 (ISBN 0-910142-93-9). Anthroposophic.
Rudolf Steiner on His Book, The Philosophy of Freedom. Otto Palmer. Tr. by Marjorie Spock from Ger. 1975. 4.50 (ISBN 0-910142-68-8). Anthroposophic.
Rudolf Steiner: Scientist of the Invisible. A. P. Shepherd. 224p. 1987. pap. 9.95 (ISBN 0-89281-174-9). Inner Tradit.
Rudolf Steiner: The Man & His Vision. Colin Wilson. 176p. 1985. pap. 11.50 (ISBN 0-85030-398-2, Pub. by Thorsons UK). Weiser.
Rudolf Steiner's New Approach to Color on the Ceiling of the First Goetheanum. D. J. Van Bemmelen. (Illus.). 1980. pap. 15.95 (ISBN 0-916786-44-7). St George Bk Serv.
Rudolf Steiner's Sculpture in Dornach. Ake Fant & Arne Klingborg. Tr. by Erik Westerberg. (Illus.). 85p. (Ger.). 1975. 22.50 (ISBN 0-85440-301-9, Pub. by Steinerbooks). Anthroposophic.
Rudolph J. Nunnemacher Collection of Projectile Arms, 2 pts, Vol. 9. Milwaukee Public Museum. Ed. by John Metschl. Bd. with Pt. 1. Long Arms; Pt. 2. Short Arms. (Illus.). 1970. Repr. of 1928 ed. Vol. 1. lib. bdg. 32.50 (ISBN 0-8371-4627-5, MPMO); Vol. 2. lib. bdg. 37.50 (ISBN 0-8371-4628-3, MPMP). Greenwood.
Rudolph Shines Again. Robert L. May. (Illus.). 48p. (gr. 3-5). 1981. 7.95 (ISBN 0-8136-6023-8, Dist. by Caroline Hse). Modern Curr.
Rudolph the Red-Nosed Reindeer. Eileeni Daly. (Super Shape Bks.). (Illus.). 24p. (gr. 2-5). 1972. pap. write for info. (ISBN 0-307-10045-6, Pub. by Golden Bks). Western Pub.
Rudolph the Red-Nosed Reindeer. Barbara S. Hazen. (Big Golden Storybooks Bks.). (Illus.). 24p. (ps-1). 1985. Repr. of 1958 ed. 2.95 (ISBN 0-307-10203-3, Pub. by Golden Bks). Western Pub.
Rudolph the Red-Nosed Reindeer. Johnny Marks. LC 85-60077. (Music Box Bks.). (Illus.). 16p. (ps). 1985. bds. 6.95 (ISBN 0-394-87446-3, BYR). Random.
Rudolph the Red-Nosed Reindeer. Illus. by Christopher Santoro. LC 86-62550. (Night Light Bks.). (Illus.). 14p. (ps-1). 1987. 4.95 (ISBN 0-394-88923-1, BYR). Random.
Rudolph Virchow: Doctor, Statesman, Anthropologist & Virchow-Bibliographie 1843-1901. Erwin H. Ackerknecht. Ed. by J. Schwalbe & I. Bernard Cohen. LC 80-2112. (Development of Science Ser.). (Illus.). 1981. Repr. of 1901 ed. lib. bdg. 45.00 two vols.in one (ISBN 0-405-13832-6). Ayer Co Pubs.
Rudolph's Pediatrics: A Study Guide. Ed. by Robert Pantell. 256p. 1987. pap. 29.95 (ISBN 0-317-62382-6, A8487-9). Appleton & Lange.
Rudy, Fred & Linda. Randy L. Leggett. 32p. 6.00 (ISBN 0-8062-2852-0). Carlton.
Rudy Vallee Discography, No. 15. Compiled by Larry F. Kiner. LC 84-22491. (Discographies Ser.). xxi, 190p. 1985. lib. bdg. 36.95 (ISBN 0-313-24512-6, KIR/). Greenwood.
Rudyard Kipling. Kingsley Amis. LC 85-51357. (Literary Lives Ser.). (Illus.). 128p. 1986. pap. 9.95 (ISBN 0-500-26019-2). Thames Hudson.
Rudyard Kipling. Lord Birkenhead. 1978. 15.00 (ISBN 0-394-50315-5). Random.
Rudyard Kipling. Intro. by Harold Bloom. (Modern Critical Views Ser.). 154p. 1987. 19.95 (ISBN 0-87754-646-0). Chelsea Hse.
Rudyard Kipling. Hilton Brown. LC 74-7017. (English Literature Ser., No. 33). 1974. lib. bdg. 49.95x (ISBN 0-8383-1853-3). Haskell.
Rudyard Kipling. Hilton Brown. 237p. Repr. of 1945 ed. lib. bdg. 45.00. Century Bookbindery.
Rudyard Kipling. Rupert Croft-Cooke. LC 74-7100. (English Biography Ser., No. 31). 1974. lib. bdg. 31.95x (ISBN 0-8383-1856-8). Haskell.
Rudyard Kipling. James Harrison. (English Authors Ser.). 1982. lib. bdg. 16.95 (ISBN 0-8057-6825-4, Twayne). G K Hall.
Rudyard Kipling. Richard LeGallienne. LC 73-21739. (English Literature Ser, No. 33). 1974. lib. bdg. 49.95x (ISBN 0-8383-1838-X). Haskell.
Rudyard Kipling. J. Palmer. LC 73-21706. (English Literature Ser., No. 33). 1974. lib. bdg. 49.95x (ISBN 0-8383-1830-4). Haskell.
Rudyard Kipling. John Palmer. LC 73-13777. 1973. Repr. of 1915 ed. lib. bdg. 20.00 (ISBN 0-8414-6717-X). Folcroft.
Rudyard Kipling. 128p. 1980. Repr. of 1915 ed. lib. bdg. 17.50 (ISBN 0-8492-2168-4). R West.
Rudyard Kipling. (Illus.). 700p. 8.98 (ISBN 0-517-34798-9). Outlet Bk Co.
Rudyard Kipling: A Bibliographical Catalogue. James M. Stewart. Ed. by A. W. Yeats. LC 60-339. pap. 160.00 (2626548). Bks Demand UMI.
Rudyard Kipling: A Character Study. Thurston Hopkins. 1915. Repr. 30.00 (ISBN 0-8274-3911-3). R West.
Rudyard Kipling: A Critical Study. Cyril Falls. LC 72-13996. 1915. lib. bdg. 32.00 (ISBN 0-8414-1312-6). Folcroft.
Rudyard Kipling: A Critical Study. Cyril B. Falls. 208p. 1980. Repr. of 1915 ed. lib. bdg. 29.00 (ISBN 0-8495-1710-9). Arden Lib.
Rudyard Kipling: A Literary Appreciation. R. Thurston Hopkins. LC 78-13606. 1978. Repr. of 1916 ed. lib. bdg. 39.00 (ISBN 0-8414-4871-X). Folcroft.
Rudyard Kipling: A Study in Literature & Political Ideas. Edward Shanks. LC 71-126931. (Illus.). 1971. Repr. of 1940 ed. 22.50x (ISBN 0-8154-0344-5). Cooper Sq.
Rudyard Kipling: A Study in Literature & Political Ideas. Edward Shanks. 270p. 1985. Repr. of 1941 ed. lib. bdg. 30.00 (ISBN 0-89984-639-4). Century Bookbindery.
Rudyard Kipling: Activist & Artist. Vasant A. Shahane. LC 73-9536. (Crosscurrents-Modern Critiques Ser.). 172p. 1973. 6.95x (ISBN 0-8093-0622-0). S Ill U Pr.
Rudyard Kipling: An Attempt at Appreciation. G. F. Monkshood. 1899. Repr. 30.00 (ISBN 0-8274-3310-7). R West.
Rudyard Kipling & the Fiction of Adolescence. Robert F. Moss. LC 81-14561. 256p. 1982. 23.95x (ISBN 0-312-69549-7). St Martin.
Rudyard Kipling: Craftsman. George F. MacMunn. LC 74-14563. 1974. Repr. of 1937 ed. lib. bdg. 17.50 (ISBN 0-8414-6102-3). Folcroft.
Rudyard Kipling, His Life & Works. Cecil Charles. 1978. Repr. of 1911 ed. lib. bdg. 29.50 (ISBN 0-8495-0838-X). Arden Lib.
Rudyard Kipling: His Life & Works. Cecil Charles. 1973. lib. bdg. 12.00 (ISBN 0-8414-0903-X). Folcroft.
Rudyard Kipling in New England. Howard C. Rice. LC 72-6747. (English Biography Ser., No. 31). 39p. 1972. Repr. of 1936 ed. lib. bdg. 40.95x (ISBN 0-8383-1635-2). Haskell.
Rudyard Kipling: The Story of a Genius. Robert T. Hopkins. LC 77-10659. 1977. lib. bdg. 37.00 (ISBN 0-8414-4956-2). Folcroft.
Rudyard Kipling to Rider Haggard. Morton Cohen. LC 68-22229. 196p. 1968. 18.00 (ISBN 0-8386-6881-X). Fairleigh Dickinson.
Rudyard Kipling's India. K. Bhaskara Rao. LC 67-10208. 1967. pap. 7.95x (ISBN 0-8061-1243-3). U of Okla Pr.
Rudyard Kipling's Kim. Intro. by Harold Bloom. (Modern Critical Interpretations Ser.). 136p. 1987. 19.95 (ISBN 1-55546-022-4). Chelsea Hse.
Rudyard Kipling's Vermont Feud. F. F. Van De Water. LC 74-1100. (English Literature Ser., No. 33). 1974. lib. bdg. 49.95x (ISBN 0-8383-2024-4). Haskell.
Rudyard Kipling's Vermont Feud. Fredric Van de Water. LC 81-69854. (Illus.). 112p. pap. 5.95 (ISBN 0-914960-37-7). Academy Bks.
Rudyard Kipling's Verse. Rudyard Kipling. LC 40-29931. 1940. 22.95 (ISBN 0-385-04407-0). Doubleday.
Rudyard Kipling's World. R. Thurston Hopkins. 1977. Repr. of 1925 ed. lib. bdg. 30.50 (ISBN 0-8495-2224-2). Arden Lib.
Rudyard Kipling's World. Thurston Hopkins. 1925. Repr. 30.00 (ISBN 0-8274-3910-5). R West.
Rudy's Red Wagon: Communication Strategies in Contemporary Society. Irving J. Rein. 1972. pap. write for info. (ISBN 0-673-07623-7). Scott F.
Rue Aux Trois Poussins - Le Mari de Melie. Georges Simenon. (French Easy Readers, A Ser.). 48p. (Fr.). 1986. pap. text ed. 4.95 (ISBN 0-88436-985-4, 40301). EMC.
Rue Cases-Negres. Joseph Zobel. (Fr.). 1955. 18.00 (ISBN 0-8115-2969-X). Kraus Repr.
Rue Cases-Negres see Black Shack Alley.
Rue sans Nom. Marcel Ayme. (Imaginaire Ser.). 1930. pap. 5.95 (ISBN 0-686-50128-4). Schoenhof.

Rule Interaction & the Organization of a Grammar. Geoffrey K. Pullum. Ed. by Jorge Hankamer. LC 78-64618. (Outstanding Dissertations in Linguistics Ser.). 1985. lib. bdg. 56.00 (ISBN 0-8240-9668-1). Garland Pub.

Rule Nine: Politics, Administration & Civil Rights. Norman C. Thomas. 7.00 (ISBN 0-8446-3063-2). Peter Smith.

Rule of Darkness: British Literature & Imperialism, 1830-1914. Patrick Brantlinger. (Illus.). 1988. 29.95x (ISBN 0-8014-2090-3). Cornell U Pr.

Rule of Experts: Occupational Licensing in America. S. David Young. 100p. 1987. 15.95 (ISBN 0-932790-61-5); pap. 7.95 (ISBN 0-932790-62-3). Cato Inst.

Rule of Force: Readings on the Totalitarian Challenge to Democracy. Ed. by Erwin R. Steinberg. 7.00 (ISBN 0-8446-3004-7). Peter Smith.

Rule of Gold. Norma M. Bracy. (Illus.). 20p. (gr. k-12). 1983. pap. text ed. 2.00g (ISBN 0-915783-00-2). Book Binder.

Rule of Iosif of Volokolamsk. D. Goldfrank. (Cistercian Studies: No. 36). pap. 14.95 (ISBN 0-87907-836-7). Cistercian Pubns.

Rule of Law. Ed. by A. Hutchinson & P. Monahan. 224p. 1987. 35.00 (Pub. by Carswell-Canada). Transnatl Pubs.

Rule of Law As a Channel of Right or Power? Vigdor Schreibman. LC 87-6206. (Essays on the Impact of the Constitution & Legal System on American Life & Government Ser.: 1st). (Illus.). 138p. (Orig.). 1987. pap. 19.90 (ISBN 0-942539-00-1). Amicas Pubns.

Rule of Law As a Channel of Right or Power? Vigdor Schreibman. LC 87-6206. (Essays on the Impact of the Constitution & Legal System on American Life & Government Ser.: No. 1). (Illus.). 138p. (Orig.). 1988. pap. 17.90 (ISBN 0-942539-06-0). Amicas Pubns.

Rule of Law in the United States, Pt. 1. 108p. 1958. pap. 2.50 (ISBN 0-89192-121-4, Pub. by Intl Commission of Jurists). Interbk Inc.

Rule of Law: Political Theory & the Legal System in Modern Society. Franz L. Neumann. LC 85-3958. 416p. 1986. 42.50 (ISBN 0-907582-36-2, Pub. by Berg Pubs). St Martin.

Rule of Metaphor: Multi-Disciplinary Studies of the Creation of Meaning in Language. Paul Ricoeur. Tr. by Robert Czerny. 1977. pap. 16.95c (ISBN 0-8020-6447-7). U of Toronto Pr.

Rule of Property for Bengal: An Essay on the Idea of Permanent Settlement. 2nd ed. Ranajit Guha. 22p. 1982. text ed. 17.95x (ISBN 0-86131-289-9, Pub. by orient Longman Ltd India). Apt Bks.

Rule of Reason. Thomas Wilson. LC 75-25441. (English Experience Ser.: No. 261). 320p. 1970. Repr. of 1551 ed. 25.00 (ISBN 90-221-0261-0). Walter J Johnson.

Rule of Reason: A New Approach to Corporate Litigation. Milton R. Wessel. LC 83-18719. 1983. 40.00 (ISBN 0-15-004362-7, Law & Business). HarBraceJ.

Rule of Saint Augustine. St. Augustine. Tr. by Raymond Canning. LC 85-20760. 128p. 1986. pap. 3.95 (ISBN 0-385-23241-1, Im). Doubleday.

Rule of St. Benedict. Tr. by Anthony C. Meisel & M. L. Del Mastro. LC 74-33611. 120p. 1975. pap. 4.95 (ISBN 0-385-00948-8, Im). Doubleday.

Rule of St. Benedict see Early English Manuscripts in Facsimile.

Rule of Saint Benedict: A Doctrinal & Spiritual Commentary. Adalbert De Vogue. Tr. by John B. Hasbrouck from Fr. (Cistercian Studies: No. 54). 1983. pap. 25.95 (ISBN 0-87907-845-6). Cistercian Pubns.

Rule of St. Benedict in English. Ed. by Timothy Fry & Imogene Baker. 96p. (Orig.). 1982. pap. 2.25 (ISBN 0-8146-1272-5). Liturgical Pr.

Rule of St. Cormac: Irish Monastic Rules. St. Cormac, Bishop of Munster. (Vol. III). pap. 1.50 (ISBN 0-317-11386-0). Eastern Orthodox.

Rule of St. Pachomius. Saint Pachomius. Tr. by E. A. Budge from Coptic. 1975. pap. 1.95 (ISBN 0-686-10939-2). Eastern Orthodox.

Rule of Taste. John Steegman. (Century English Tradition Ser.). 170p. 1986. pap. 13.95 (ISBN 0-7126-9463-3, Pub. by Century Hutchinson). David & Charles.

Rule of Taste from George First to George Fourth. John Steegman. LC 68-20986. (Illus., With a new intro. by James Laver). 1968. Repr. of 1936 ed. 8.50x (ISBN 0-8462-1136-X). Russell.

Rule of the Chalukya-Cholas in Andhradesa. Krishna Kumari. (Illus.). 276p. 1986. text ed. 40.00x (ISBN 0-86590-798-6, Pub. by B R Pub Corp Delhi). Apt Bks.

Rule of the Master: Regula Magistri. Tr. & Luke Eberle. LC 77-3986. (Cistercian Studies Ser.: No. 6). 1977. 12.95 (ISBN 0-87907-806-5). Cistercian Pubns.

Rule of the Road: An International Guide to History & Practice. Peter Kincaid. LC 86-354. 249p. 1986. lib. bdg. 36.95 (ISBN 0-313-25249-1, KRU/). Greenwood.

Rule of the Secular Franciscan Order: With a Catechism & Instructions. 350p. 1980. pap. 7.50 (ISBN 0-8199-0810-X). Franciscan Herald.

Rule of the Taewon'gun, 1864-1873: Restoration in Yi Korea. Choe Ching Young. LC 73-183975. (East Asian Monographs Ser: No. 45). 1972. pap. 11.00x (ISBN 0-674-78030-2). Harvard U Pr.

Rule-of-Thumb Cost Estimating for Building Mechanical Systems: Accurate Estimating & Budgeting Using Unit Assembly Costs. J. H. Konkel. 288p. 1987. text ed. 40.00 (ISBN 0-07-044957-0). McGraw.

Rule of Two. Ann Woodin. (Illus.). 136p. 1985. 27.95. Vanguard.

Rule of Two: Observations on Close Relationship. Ann Woodin. LC 84-60490. (Illus.). 136p. 1984. 22.50 (ISBN 0-917041-01-1). Oracle Pr AZ.

Rule of Walter De Wenlok, Abbot of Westminster. Ed. by Camden Society, Royal Historical Society Staff. (Camden Fourth Ser.: No. 2). 1970. 27.00 (ISBN 0-901050-63-6, Pub. by Boydell & Brewer). Longwood Pub Group.

Rule Statutes & Customs of the Hospitallers, 1099-1310. Knights of Malta. LC 78-63347. (Crusades & Military Orders: Second Ser.). 272p. Repr. of 1934 ed. 29.00 (ISBN 0-404-16246-0). AMS Pr.

Rulebook for Arguments. Anthony Weston. 112p. 1986. lib. bdg. 18.50 (ISBN 0-87220-030-2); pap. text ed. 3.45 (ISBN 0-87220-029-9). Hackett Pub.

Rulemakers of the House. Spark M. Matsunaga & Ping Chen. LC 76-18985. 224p. 1976. 22.95 (ISBN 0-252-00626-7). U of Ill Pr.

Ruler of the Kings on the Earth: A Clear Look at Amillennialism for the Lay Person. R. G. Currell & E. P. Hurlbut. 126p. 1983. pap. 4.95 (ISBN 0-87552-211-4). Presby & Reformed.

Ruler of the Nations: Biblical Blueprints on Government. Gary DeMar. write for info. Am Bur Eco Res.

Ruler of the Nativity. Alexander Volguine. LC 74-90427. (French Astrology Ser.). 1973. 6.95 (ISBN 0-88231-076-3). ASI Pubs Inc.

Rulers & the Ruled. rev. ed. Robert E. Agger & Bert Swanson. (Illus.). 1984. text ed. cancelled (ISBN 0-8290-0104-2); pap. text ed. cancelled (ISBN 0-8290-0105-0). Irvington.

Ruler's Imperative: Strategies for Political Survival in Asia & Africa. W. Howard Wriggins. LC 73-90431. (Southern Asian Institute Publications Ser.). 1969. 30.00x (ISBN 0-231-03314-1). Columbia U Pr.

Rulers of Belgian Africa: 1884-1914. Lewis H. Gann & Peter J. Duignan. LC 79-83989. 1979. 38.00x (ISBN 0-691-05277-8). Princeton U Pr.

Rulers of British Africa, 1870-1914. L. H. Gann & Peter Duignan. LC 77-92945. (Illus.). 1978. 35.00x (ISBN 0-8047-0981-5). Stanford U Pr.

Rulers of Empire: The French Colonial Service in Africa. William B. Cohen. LC 76-137405. (Publications Ser.: No. 95). 1971. 11.95x (ISBN 0-8179-1951-1). Hoover Inst Pr.

Rulers of German Africa, 1884-1914. L. H. Gann & Peter Duignan. LC 76-54100. (Illus.). 1977. 27.50x (ISBN 0-8047-0938-6). Stanford U Pr.

Rulers of Mecca. Gerald De Gaury. LC 78-63458. (Pilgrimages Ser.). (Illus.). 1982. Repr. of 1954 ed. 34.50 (ISBN 0-404-16517-6). AMS Pr.

Rulers of Russia. Denis Fahey. 1986. pap. 5.50 (ISBN 0-317-52999-4). Noontide.

Rulers of Russia: Jewish Bolshevism & Jewish Influence in the Soviet Government. Dennis Fahey. 1980. lib. bdg. 59.95 (ISBN 0-8490-3098-6). Gordon Pr.

Rulers of the Indian Ocean. G. A. Ballard. 336p. 1983. Repr. text ed. 50.00x (ISBN 0-86590-204-6). Apt Bks.

Rulers of the Mediterranean. facsimile ed. Richard H. Davis. LC 76-38788. (Essay Index Reprint Ser). Repr. of 1893 ed. 21.00 (ISBN 0-8369-2645-5). Ayer Co Pubs.

Rulers of the Mind. Alden B. Starr. LC 74-92088. 108p. 1970. 5.95 (ISBN 0-8022-2333-8). Philos Lib.

Rulers of the South, 2 vols. Francis M. Crawford. Set. 250.00 (ISBN 0-8490-0979-0). Gordon Pr.

Rulers, Townsmen & Bazaars: North Indian Society in the Age of British Expansion, 1770-1870. O. A. Bayly. (Cambridge South Asian Studies: No. 28). (Illus.). 502p. 1988. pap. 22.95 (ISBN 0-521-31054-7). Cambridge U Pr.

Rulership Book: A Directory of Astrological Correspondences. 4th ed. Rex E. Bills. 438p. 1984. Repr. of 1979 ed. clothbound 15.00 (ISBN 0-88053-759-0, A-310). Macoy Pub.

Rulership of Heaven. Wim Malgo. 9.95 (ISBN 0-937422-28-2); pap. 6.95 (ISBN 0-937422-27-4). Midnight Call.

Rules. Ed. by Marc G. Perlin. 1985. 35.00 (ISBN 0-318-18709-4). Lawyers Weekly.

Rules: A Systematic Study. Joan S. Ganz. (Janua Linguarum, Ser. Minor: No. 96). (Illus.). 144p. (Orig.). 1972. pap. text ed. 13.20x (ISBN 90-2791-853-8). Mouton.

Rules Against Discrimination. Leo Brown & Jeffrey D. Mamorsky. (Requirements for Qualification of Plans Ser.). 17p. 1983. pap. 2.00 (ISBN 0-317-31140-9, B445). Am Law Inst.

Rules & Examples of Prespective. Andrea Pozzo. LC 69-13450. (Illus.). Repr. of 1707 ed. 35.00 (ISBN 0-405-08861-2, Pub. by Blom). Ayer Co Pubs.

Rules & Mysteries of Brother Solomon. Sandol Stoddard. 48p. (Orig.). 1987. pap. 2.95 (ISBN 0-8091-6560-0). Paulist Pr.

Rules & Precepts of the Jesuit Missions of Northwestern New Spain. Charles Polzer. LC 75-8456. 141p. 1976. pap. 4.50 (ISBN 0-8165-0488-1). U of Ariz Pr.

Rules & Processes: The Cultural Logic of Dispute in An African Context. John L. Comaroff & Simon Roberts. LC 80-26640. (Illus.). 304p. 1986. lib. bdg. 27.50x (ISBN 0-226-11424-4); pap. 12.50x (ISBN 0-226-11425-2). U of Chicago Pr.

Rules & Racial Equality. Edwin Dorn. LC 79-64228. 1979. 26.50x (ISBN 0-300-02362-6). Yale U Pr.

Rules & Regulations for the Field Exercise & Manoeuvres of the French Infantry: Issued August 1, 1791, 2 vols. 2nd ed. France, Ministere de la Guerre Staff. Tr. by John MacDonald from Fr. LC 68-54795. (Illus.). Repr. of 1806 ed. cancelled (ISBN 0-8371-2336-4). Greenwood.

Rules & Representations. Noam Chomsky. LC 79-26145. (Woodbridge Lectures Ser.: No. 11). 1980. 30.00x (ISBN 0-231-04826-2); pap. 16.00x (ISBN 0-231-04827-0). Columbia U Pr.

Rules & Resolutions, Nineteen Eighty. Ed. by Paul A. Wellington. LC 74-84765. 1980. 10.00 (ISBN 0-8309-0136-1). Includes Supplements 1982, 1984 & 1986. Herald Hse.

Rules & Statute: Supplement to Evidence, 1984. Weinstein et al. 8.75 (ISBN 0-317-06406-1, 9833). Foundation Pr.

Rules & the Emergence of Society. Meyer Fortes. (Occasional Papers: No. 39). 52p. 1983. pap. text ed. 7.50x (ISBN 0-900633-39-5, Pub. by Royal Anthropological Institute UK). Humanities.

Rules Are No Game: The Strategy of Communication. Anthony Wilden. (Illus.). 368p. 1987. 29.95 (ISBN 0-7100-9868-5, 98685, Pub. by Routledge UK). Routledge Chapman & Hall.

Rules Book 1977-1980. Eric Twiname. (Illus.). 156p. 1977. 8.95x (ISBN 0-8464-1130-X). Beekman Pubs.

Rules, Exceptions, & Social Order. Robert B. Edgerton. LC 84-28134. 1985. 32.50x (ISBN 0-520-05481-4). U of Cal Pr.

Rules for Admission to the Bar in the United States & Territories: 1982 Edition. Ed. by William H. Morris. 95p. 1982. pap. text ed. write for info. (ISBN 0-314-66184-0). West Pub.

Rules for Determining Income & Expenses As Domestic or Foreign, Vol. LXVb. 690p. pap. 42.00 (ISBN 0-686-41005-X). Kluwer Academic.

Rules for Leadership: Improving Unit Performance. John W. Blades. LC 85-28556. (Illus.). 139p. (Orig.). 1986. pap. 4.00 (ISBN 0-318-20386-3, S/N 008-020-01054-5). USGPO.

Rules for Radicals. Saul D. Alinsky. 224p. 1972. pap. 3.95 (ISBN 0-394-71736-8, V736, Vin). Random.

Rules for Raising Kids. Robert I. Lesowitz. (Illus.). 200p. 1974. pap. 23.00x spiral (ISBN 0-398-03146-0). C C Thomas.

Rules for Regulating Intervention under a Managed Float. Marsha R. Shelburn. LC 84-25287. (Princeton Studies in International Finance: No. 55). 1984. pap. text ed. 6.50x (ISBN 0-88165-227-X). Princeton U Int Finan Econ.

Rules for Sports Played in the U. S. Army. Intro. by Tom Heski. (Guidon Monograph Ser.). 1891. 7.00 (Pub. by J M C & Co). Amereon Ltd.

Rules for the Traditional Family. Nicholas Puiia. (Illus.). 114p. (Orig.). 1988. pap. 6.95 (ISBN 0-912769-19-X). L Tapley.

Rules for Writers. 2nd ed. Diana Hacker. 500p. 1988. pap. text ed. write for info. (ISBN 0-312-00357-9); write for info. (ISBN 0-312-01366-3); write for info. study guide (ISBN 0-312-01326-4). St Martin.

Rules for Writers: A Brief Handbook. Diana Hacker. LC 84-51141. 500p. 1985. pap. 11.00 (ISBN 0-312-69585-3, Pub. by Bedford Bks); instr's. manual avail. St Martin.

Rules Governing the Courts of Ohio, 1987-88. Anderson Publishing Co. Staff. 1986. 30.00 (ISBN 0-317-57021-8). Anderson Pub Co.

Rules I Follow in Stock Market Trading & Future Forecasting. Richard Wyckoff De Mille. (Illus.). 211p. 1987. 145.75 (ISBN 0-86654-209-4). Inst Econ Finan.

Rules in Practice. Bryan Willis. (Sail to Win Ser.). (Illus.). 64p. 1987. pap. 9.95 (ISBN 0-87742-231-1). Intl Marine.

Rules in the Making: A Statistical Analysis. Wesley A. Magat et al. 194p. 1986. text ed. 22.50 (ISBN 0-915707-24-1). Resources Future.

Rules Mean Happiness. Bonita Kraemer. (Come Unto Me Ser.). (ps). 1979. pap. 1.95 (ISBN 0-8127-0254-9). Review & Herald.

Rules of Attraction. Bret E. Ellis. 256p. 1987. 17.95 (ISBN 0-671-62234-X). S&S.

Rules of Attraction. Bret Easton Ellis. 288p. pap. 6.95 (ISBN 0-14-011228-6). Penguin.

Rules of Civil Procedure for the United States District Courts, with Forms, Aug. 1, 1987. 134p. 1987. pap. 3.75 (ISBN 0-318-23521-8, S/N 052-070-06358-1). USGPO.

Rules of Civil Procedure: Proceedings of the Federal Bar Association, Conference, December 1980. Federal Bar Association Staff. 93p. 15.00 (ISBN 0-318-14093-4). Federal Bar.

Rules of Compensability & Valuation Evidence in Highway Land Acquisition. (National Cooperative Highway Research Program Report). 77p. 1970. 4.40 (ISBN 0-309-01892-7). Transport Res Bd.

Rules of Criminal Procedure, 4 vols. Robert M. Cipes et al. Ed. by Marvin Waxner & Michael Eisenstein. 1965. looseleaf 360.00 (201); Updates 1985. 270.00; Supplement 1986. 350.00. Bender.

Rules of Criminal Procedure for the United States District Courts, Aug. 1, 1987. 70p. 1987. pap. 2.25 (ISBN 0-318-23522-6, S/N 052-070-06357-2). USGPO.

Rules of Decoration see Decoration.

Rules of Descent: Studies in the Sociology of Parentage. Guy E. Swanson. (Anthropological Papers: No. 39). 1969. pap. 2.00x (ISBN 0-932206-37-9). U Mich Mus Anthro.

Rules of Golf. Illus. by Tom Watson & Frank Hannigan. (Illus.). 192p. 1988. pap. 14.95 (ISBN 0-8129-1729-4); pap. 9.95 (ISBN 0-8129-1728-6). Times Bks.

Rules of Golf Explained & Illustrated. Thom Watson & Frank Hannigan. LC 79-4758. (Illus.). 1984. 14.95; pap. 7.95 (ISBN 0-394-72181-0). Random.

Rules of Golf Illustrated & Explained. Tom Watson & Frank Hannigan. 14.95 (ISBN 0-686-30836-0); pap. 7.95 (ISBN 0-686-30837-9). US Golf Assn.

Rules of HAJJ. Ayatullah Al-Khu'i. Tr. by Shaikh Muhammad Sarwar from Arabic. 50p. 1981. pap. 3.00 (ISBN 0-941724-02-6). Islamic Seminary.

Rules of Law on Technical Data. 1971. 7.00 (ISBN 0-686-27831-3). M & A Products.

Rules of Life. Fay Weldon. LC 86-46107. (Short Novel Ser.). 80p. 1987. 10.95i (ISBN 0-06-015759-3, HarpT). Har-Row.

Rules of Life. Fay Weldon. LC 86-46107. (Harper Short Novel Ser.). (Illus.). 80p. 1988. pap. 5.95 (ISBN 0-06-091499-8, PL 1499, PL). Har-Row.

Rules of Marriage. Sheila Bishop. (Regency Romance Ser.). 1986. pap. 2.50 (ISBN 0-449-21234-3, Crest). Fawcett.

Rules of Procedure of the Committee on the Elimination of Racial Discrimination. 15.50 (ISBN 92-1-054001-8, 85.XIV.11). UN.

Rules of Procedure of the Economic & Social Council. 31p. 1983. pap. text ed. 4.00 (ISBN 92-1-100086-6, E.83.I.9). UN.

Rules of Procedure of the Trade & Development Board. United Nations Conference on Trade & Development, Trade & Development Board. LC 84-104968. 1980. 3.50 (ISBN 92-1-112111-6, E.80.II.D.7). UN.

Rules of Riot: Internal Conflict & the Law of War. James E. Bond. LC 72-5390. 240p. 1974. 33.50x (ISBN 0-691-05651-X). Princeton U Pr.

Rules of Sleep. Howard Moss. LC 83-45123. 64p. 1984. 12.95 (ISBN 0-689-11422-2); pap. 6.95 (ISBN 0-689-11423-0). Atheneum.

Rules of Soccer: Simplified. Larry Maisner & Bill Mason. (Illus.). 16p. 1978. pap. 1.95 (ISBN 0-9611406-0-7). Maisner & Mason.

Rules of Soccer: Simplified. Larry Maisner & Bill Mason. Tr. by Dio Cordero. (Illus.). 18p. (Span.). 1986. pap. cancelled (ISBN 0-9611406-1-5, Dist. by MFB Enterprises, Inc.). Maisner & Mason.

Rules of Sociological Method. 8th ed. Emile Durkheim. 1950. 12.95 (ISBN 0-02-908490-3); pap. text ed. 13.95 (ISBN 0-02-908500-4). Free Pr.

Rules of Sociological Method. Emile Durkheim. 1982. pap. 10.95 (ISBN 0-02-907940-3). Free Pr.

Rules of Sociological Method & Selected Texts on Sociology & Its Method. Emile Durkheim. Ed. by Steven Lukes. Tr. by W. D. Halls. 1982. pap. text ed. 8.95 (ISBN 0-02-907930-6). Free Pr.

Rules of Tennis Cases & Decisions. 1988. pap. 0.75 (ISBN 0-938822-78-0). USTA CERT.

Rules of the Aztec Language: Classical Nahuatl Grammar. Arthur J. Anderson. LC 72-88553. 1973. pap. text ed. 10.00x (ISBN 0-87480-023-4). U of Utah Pr.

Rules of the Communist Party of the Soviet Union. CPSU Central Committee. 30p. 1986. pap. 0.95 (ISBN 0-8285-3180-3, Pub. by Novosti Pr USSR). Imported Pubns.

Rules of the Communist Party of the Soviet Union. Ed. by Graeme Gill. LC 87-4815. 250p. 1988. 39.95 (ISBN 0-87332-434-X). M E Sharpe.

Rules of the District & Municipal Courts in Washington: State - Local. Butterworths Staff. LC 87-22429. 440p. 1987. looseleaf 65.00 (ISBN 0-409-20550-8). Butterworth WA.

Rules of the Game. Georges Simenon. Tr. by Howard Curtis. (Helen & Kurt Wolff Bk.). 160p. 1988. 18.95 (ISBN 0-15-169475-3). HarBraceJ.

Rules of the Game: Constraints & Opportunities for the Central America Movement. Joshua Cohen & Joel Rogers. (PACCA Domestic Roots Ser.: No. 2). 64p. (Orig.). 1986. pap. 4.75 (ISBN 0-89608-326-8). South End Pr.

Rules of the Game: Culture Defining Gender. Judith Barter & Anne Mochon. (Illus.). 32p. (Orig.). 1986. pap. text ed. 1.00 (ISBN 0-914337-08-4). Mead Art Mus.

Rules of the Game in Paris. Nathan C. Leites. Tr. by Derek Coltman. LC 69-19276. pap. 91.30 (ISBN 0-317-26519-9, 2024055). Bks Demand UMI.

Rules of the Game: Reform & Evolution in the International Monetary System. Kenneth W. Dam. LC 81-10416. 1982. pap. 12.50x (ISBN 0-226-13500-4). U of Chicago Pr.

Rules of the Game: Reform & Evolution in the International Monetary System. Kenneth W. Dam. 408p. 1988. pap. 16.95x (ISBN 0-226-13501-2, Midway Reprint). U of Chicago Pr.

TITLE INDEX RUMPTY-DUDGET'S TOWER.

Rules of the Game: The Logical Structure of Economic Theories. Johannes J. Klant. Tr. by Iva Swart. LC 83-23941. 220p. 1984. 44.50 (ISBN 0-521-23502-2). Cambridge U Pr.

Rules of the Heart. Charlotte Tranbarger. (YA) (gr. 7 up). 1982. 9.95 (ISBN 0-686-84743-1, Avalon). Bouregy.

Rules of the Heart, No. 429. Samantha Quin. 192p. 1987. pap. 2.50 (ISBN 0-317-63163-2). Berkley Pub.

Rules of the Italian Political Game. Franco D. Marengo. 144p. 1981. text ed. 35.50x (ISBN 0-566-00301-5). Gower Pub Co.

Rules of the Knife Fight. Walter Walker. LC 86-45160. 352p. 1986. 17.45i (ISBN 0-06-015646-5, HarpT). Har-Row.

Rules of the Knife Fight. Walter Walker. 480p. 1987. pap. 4.50 (ISBN 0-14-010327-9). Penguin.

Rules of the Road. Lucien K. Truscott, IV. Date not set. 18.95 (ISBN 0-88184-428-4). Carroll & Graf.

Rules of the U. S. Courts in New York. 2nd ed. Ed. by A. Daniel Fusaro. LC 65-16452. 1978. 75.00 (ISBN 0-87632-070-1). Clark Boardman.

Rules of Thumb. Tom Parker. 1983. pap. text ed. 6.95 (ISBN 0-395-34642-8). HM.

Rules of Thumb. Faye H. Winters. Incl. Presents of Mind. 150p (ISBN 0-935011-02-1). (Illus.). 178p. (gr. 1-5). 1985. pap. 29.95 (ISBN 0-935011-01-3) (ISBN 0-935011-03-X). Winters Pubns.

Rules of Thumb, Vol. 2. Tom Parker. 160p. 1987. pap. 6.95 (ISBN 0-395-42955-2). HM.

Rules of Thumb for the Physical Scientist. D. J. Fisher. 320p. 1987. text ed. 46.00x (ISBN 0-87849-524-X). Trans Tech.

Rules, Perception & Intelligibility. F. A. Hayek. 1962. pap. 5.50 (ISBN 0-85672-671-0, Pub. by British Acad). Longwood Pub Group.

Rules That Babies Look by: The Organization of Newborn Visual Activity. Marshall M. Haith. LC 80-10601. (Child Psychology Ser.). (Illus.). 159p. 1980. text ed. 19.95x (ISBN 0-89859-033-7). L Erlbaum Assocs.

Rules Updates. Ed. by Marc G. Perlin. Date not set. 23.80 (ISBN 0-318-18710-8). Lawyers Weekly.

Rulfo: El llano en llamas. William Rowe. (Critical Guides to Spanish Literature). 1987. pap. 8.95 (ISBN 0-7293-0267-9, Pub. by Grant & Cutler). Longwood Pub Group.

Ruling Class. Gaetano Mosca. Ed. by Arthur Livingston. Tr. by Hannah D. Kahn from Ital. LC 80-17230. xli, 514p. 1980. Repr. of 1939 ed. lib. bdg. 45.50x (ISBN 0-313-22617-2, MORU). Greenwood.

Ruling Class: A Baroque Comedy. Peter Barnes. 1969. pap. text ed. 7.00x (ISBN 0-435-20965-5). Heinemann Ed.

Ruling Class: A Study of British Finance Capital. Sam Aaronovitch. LC 78-23485. 1979. Repr. of 1961 ed. lib. bdg. 35.00x (ISBN 0-313-20764-X, AARC). Greenwood.

Ruling Class in Italy Before 1900. Vilfredo Pareto. LC 73-20130. 143p. 1975. Repr. of 1950 ed. 23.50x (ISBN 0-86527-176-3). Fertig.

Ruling Class of Judaea: The Origins of the Jewish Revolt Against Rome AD 66-70. Martin Goodman. 272p. 1987. 39.50 (ISBN 0-521-33401-2). Cambridge U Pr.

Ruling Class, Ruling Culture. R. W. Connell. LC 76-22981. (Illus.). 1977. 39.50 (ISBN 0-521-21392-4); pap. 12.95 (ISBN 0-521-29133-X). Cambridge U Pr.

Ruling Communist Parties & Their Status under Law. Ed. by D. A. Loeber. 1987. lib. bdg. 135.00 (ISBN 90-247-3209-3, Pub. by Martinus Nijhoff Netherlands). Kluwer Academic.

Ruling from Horseback: Manchu Politics in the Oboi Regency, 1661-1669. Robert B. Oxnam. LC 74-10343. xii, 250p. 1975. 20.00x (ISBN 0-226-64244-5). U of Chicago Pr.

Ruling Ideas of the Present Age. Washington Gladden. 1971. Repr. of 1895 ed. 23.00 (ISBN 0-384-18865-6). Johnson Repr.

Ruling Lines. 44p. 1985. 16.00 (ISBN 0-88362-059-6, 0241); instr's guide 3.00 (0240). Graphic Arts Tech Found.

Ruling Passion. Reginald Hill. 1982. pap. 3.25 (ISBN 0-440-16889-9). Dell.

Ruling Passion: Tales of Nature & Human Nature. facsimile ed. Henry Van Dyke. LC 71-38725. (Short Story Index Reprint Ser.). (Illus.). Repr. of 1901 ed. 21.00 (ISBN 0-8369-4138-1). Ayer Co Pubs.

Ruling Performance: British Governments from Attlee to Thatcher. Ed. by Peter Hennessy & Anthony Seldon. Date not set. text ed. 34.95 (ISBN 0-631-15645-3). Basil Blackwell.

Ruling Power: A Study of the Roman Empire in the Second Century After Christ Through the Roman Oration of Aelius Aristides. James H. Oliver. LC 53-10559. (Transactions Ser.: Vol. 43, Pt. 4). 1980. pap. 12.00 (ISBN 0-87169-434-4). Am Philos.

Ruling Race: A History of American Slaveholders. James Oakes. LC 81-48124. 352p. 1982. 16.45 (ISBN 0-394-52163-3). Knopf.

Ruling Race: A History of American Slaveholders. James Oakes. LC 83-3472. 336p. 1983. pap. 6.36 (ISBN 0-394-71639-6, Vin). Random.

Ruling Russia. John LeDonne. LC 84-2168. (Illus.). 368p. 1984. text ed. 44.50x (ISBN 0-691-05425-8). Princeton U Pr.

Ruling the Waves: The Political Economy of International Shipping. Alan W. Cafruny. LC 86-30889. (Studies in International Political Economy: Vol. 17). 356p. 1987. 40.00 (ISBN 0-520-05968-9). U of Cal Pr.

Ruling Trinity: A Community Study of Chruch, State & Business in Ireland. Chris Eipper. 1986. text ed. 42.00 (ISBN 0-566-05173-7, Pub. by Gower Pub England). Gower Pub Co.

Rum & Coca-Cola. Ralph De Boissiere. 352p. 1984. 16.95 (ISBN 0-8052-8195-9, Pub. by Allison & Busby England). Schocken.

Rum & Reggae: What's Hot & What's Not in the Caribbean. Jonathan Runge. LC 87-29938. (Illus.). 224p. 1988. pap. 9.95x (ISBN 0-312-01509-7). St Martin.

Rum Island. Simon Vestkijk. (Orig.). 1986. pap. 5.95 (ISBN 0-7145-0509-9). Riverrun NY.

Rum Rebellion: A Study of the Overthrow of Governor Bligh by John Macarthur & the New South Wales Corps, Including the John Murtagh Macrossan Memorial Lectures Delivered at the University of Queensland, June, 1937. Herbert V. Evatt. 17.00 (ISBN 0-8369-7109-4, 7943). Ayer Co Pubs.

Rum Road to Spokane: A Story of Prohibition. Edmund B. Fahey. (Illus.). 150p. 1975. 6.95 (ISBN 0-686-15663-3). U of MT Pubns Hist.

Rum-Tum-Tum: Mississippi Recipes for a Festive Southern Christmas. Joy Price. (Illus.). 48p. (Orig.). 1985. pap. 5.00 (ISBN 0-945301-01-4). Druid Pr.

Rumania. Romulus Seisanu. 116p. 1987. write for info. (ISBN 0-937019-06-2); pap. 15.00 (ISBN 0-937019-07-0). Romanian Hist.

Rumania: A Bibliographic Guide. Stephen A. Fischer-Galati. LC 63-60076. (Bibliographic Guides Ser). 1969. Repr. of 1963 ed. 10.00 (ISBN 0-405-00057-X). Ayer Co Pubs.

Rumania: Painted Churches of Moldavia. (Art Slides: No. 21, UNESCO). UNIPUB.

Rumania: Political Problems of an Agrarian State. Henry L. Roberts. LC 69-13629. (Illus.). xiv, 414p. 1969. Repr. of 1951 ed. 39.50 (ISBN 0-208-00651-6, Archon). Shoe String.

Rumanian. Graham Mallinson. (Descriptive Grammars Ser.). 384p. 1986. 60.00 (ISBN 0-7099-3537-4, Pub. by Croom Helm Ltd). Routledge Chapman & Hall.

Rumanian-English Conversation Book. Mihai Miroiu. LC 77-160435. 168p. 20.00x (ISBN 0-8044-0379-1). Ungar.

Rumanian-English Dictionary. Serban Andronescu. 32.50 (ISBN 0-87557-063-1). Saphrograph.

Rumanian-English, English-Rumanian Dictionary, with Supplement. Ed. by M. Schonkron. (Romanian & Eng.). 49.50x (ISBN 0-8044-0546-8). Ungar.

Rumanian National Movement in Transylvania, 1780-1849. Keith Hitchins. LC 69-12724. (Historical Monographs Ser: No. 61). 1969. text ed. 20.00x (ISBN 0-674-78035-3). Harvard U Pr.

Rumanian Prose & Verse. E. D. Tappe. (London East European Ser.). 195p. 1956. 32.50 (ISBN 0-485-17503-7, Pub. by Athlone Pr UK). Humanities.

Rumanian Verb System. Alphonse Juilland & P. M. Edwards. LC 66-15853. (Janua Linguarum, Ser. Practica: No. 28). (Orig.). 1971. pap. text ed. 43.00x (ISBN 90-2791-605-5). Mouton.

Rumba. Earl Atkinson. (Ballroom Dance Ser.). 1986. lib. bdg. 79.95 (ISBN 0-8490-3631-3). Gordon Pr.

Rumba Combinations. Earl Atkinson. (Ballroom Dancing Ser.). 1983. lib. bdg. 79.95 (ISBN 0-87700-477-3). Revisionist Pr.

Rumba Is My Life. X. Cugat. (Ballroom Dance Ser.). 1985. lib. bdg. 79.95 (ISBN 0-87700-848-5). Revisionist Pr.

Rumba Is My Life. X. Cugat. (Ballroom Dance Ser.). 1986. lib. bdg. 69.95 (ISBN 0-8490-3262-8). Gordon Pr.

Rumba Made Easy. (Ballroom Dance Ser.). 1985. lib. bdg. 77.95 (ISBN 0-87700-670-9). Revisionist Pr.

Rumbeard. Sandra Valerius. LC 84-90154. 76p. (gr. 3-5). 1985. 6.45 (ISBN 0-533-06211-X). Vantage.

Rumble Fish. S. E. Hinton. LC 75-8004. 112p. (gr. 7 up). 1975. pap. 13.95 (ISBN 0-385-28675-9). Delacorte.

Rumble Fish. S. E. Hinton. 112p. (gr. 7 up). 1976. pap. 2.95 (ISBN 0-440-97534-4, LFL). Dell.

Rumblings. Peter Gibbs. (Theatrescripts Ser.). 48p. 1985. pap. 4.95 (ISBN 0-413-59650-8, 9682). Heinemann Ed.

Rumbo. Joaquin Delgado-Sanchez. LC 85-81208. (Coleccion Caniqui Ser.). 118p. (Orig., Span.). 1986. pap. 9.95 (ISBN 0-89729-381-9). Ediciones.

Rumbo Al Punto Cierto. Rosario Rexach. 1979. pap. 7.50 (ISBN 0-686-80420-1). Edit Mensaje.

Rumbuli. Frida Michelson. Tr. by Wolf Goodman from Rus. 224p. 1983. 10.95 (ISBN 0-686-95085-2); pap. 5.95 (ISBN 0-686-99459-0). ADL.

Rumen & Its Microbes. Robert E. Hungate. 1966. 90.50 (ISBN 0-12-361650-6). Acad Pr.

Rumery Family. G. T. Ridlon. LC 78-138073. (Saco Valley Settlements Ser). 1970. pap. 2.50 (ISBN 0-8048-0830-9). C E Tuttle.

Rumi & Sufism. Eva De Vitray-Meyerovitch. Tr. by Simone Fattal. (World of Islam Ser.). (Illus., Orig., Fr.). 1987. pap. 12.95 (ISBN 0-942996-08-9). Post Apollo Pr.

Rumi the Persian Mystic. 1970. 15.00 (ISBN 0-87902-185-3). Orientalia.

Rumi the Persian: Rebirth in Creativity & Love. A. R. Arasteh. 1970. 6.50x (ISBN 0-87902-043-1). Orientalia.

Ruminant Animal: Digestive Physiology & Nutrition. 2nd ed. David C. Church. (Illus.). 576p. 1987. text ed. 50.00 (ISBN 0-13-783754-2). P-H.

Ruminant Immune System. Ed. by John E. Butler. LC 80-29702. (Advances In Experimental Medicine & Biology Ser.: Vol. 137). 916p. 1981. 125.00x (ISBN 0-306-40641-1, Plenum Pr). Plenum Pub.

Ruminant Immune System in Health & Disease. Ed. by W. Ivan Morrison. 650p. 1987. 89.50 (ISBN 0-521-32443-2). Cambridge U Pr.

Ruminant Nitrogen Usage. National Research Council. 138p. 1985. pap. text ed. 14.95x (ISBN 0-309-03597-X). Natl Acad Pr.

Ruminant Nutrition: Selected Articles from the World Animal Review. (Animal Production & Health Papers: No. 12). 165p. 1978. pap. 11.25 (ISBN 92-5-100650-4, F1889, FAO). UNIPUB.

Ruminant Urogenital Surgery. C. F. B. Hofmeyr. 174p. 1987. text ed. 36.95x (ISBN 0-8138-1591-6). Iowa St U Pr.

Ruminations. facs. ed. Arthur S. McDowall. LC 68-22925. (Essay Index Reprint Ser). 1925. 14.25 (ISBN 0-8369-0646-2). Ayer Co Pubs.

Ruminations. William Steig. LC 84-45423. (Illus.). 160p. 1984. 20.00 (ISBN 0-374-25283-1); pap. 9.95 (ISBN 0-374-51875-0). FS&G.

Ruminator. Humphrey B. Neil. 124p. Date not set. pap. 3.00 (ISBN 0-317-53236-7). Noontide.

Rummage Sale. 2nd ed. Donald R. Marshall. (Illus.). 164p. 1985. 8.95 (ISBN 0-87747-695-0). Deseret Bk.

Rummage Sale & Mr. & Mrs. Bumba. Pearl A. Harwood. LC 70-156361. (Mr. & Mrs. Bumba Bks.). (Illus.). (gr. k-3). 1971. PLB 3.95 (ISBN 0-8225-0122-8). Lerner Pubns.

Rumor! Hal Morgan & Kerry Tucker. (Illus.). 160p. 1987. pap. 3.50 (ISBN 0-14-010029-6). Penguin.

Rumor & Gossip. R. L. Rosnow & G. A. Fine. 166p. 1976. pap. 21.50 (ISBN 0-444-99035-6). Elsevier.

Rumor & Gossip: The Social Psychology of Hearsay. R. L. Rosnow & G. A. Fine. 27.95 (ISBN 0-444-99031-3, RRG/, Pub. by Elsevier). Greenwood.

Rumor & Other Stories. James Robison. 151p. 1985. 14.95 (ISBN 0-671-52722-3). Summit Bks.

Rumor & Other Stories. James Robison. 170p. 1986. pap. 6.95 (ISBN 0-14-009332-X). Penguin.

Rumor in the Marketplace: The Social Psychology of Commercial Hearsay. Frederick W. Koenig. LC 84-12379. 224p. 1985. 26.00 (ISBN 0-86569-117-7). Auburn Hse.

Rumor of an Elephant. Alain Gerber. Tr. by Jeremy Leggatt. LC 86-23700. 325p. 1987. 17.95 (ISBN 0-916515-19-2). Mercury Hse Inc.

Rumor of Angels. Peter L. Berger. LC 68-27103. 1970. pap. 3.95 (ISBN 0-385-06630-9, Anch). Doubleday.

Rumor of Otters. Deborah Savage. (gr. 6 up). 1986. 12.95 (ISBN 0-395-41186-6). HM.

Rumor of Pavel & Paali: A Ukranian Folktale. Adapted by Carole Kismaric. LC 87-19958. (Illus.). 32p. (gr. 1-3). 1988. 13.95i (ISBN 0-06-023277-3); PLB 13.89 (ISBN 0-06-023278-1). HarpJ.

Rumor of Revolt: The "Great Negro Plot" in Colonial New York. Thomas J. Davis. LC 82-48427. 336p. 1985. 21.95 (ISBN 0-02-907740-0). Free Pr.

Rumor of Trumpets: The Return of God to Secular Society. Jerry D. Cardwell. 118p. (Orig.). 1985. lib. bdg. 23.25 (ISBN 0-8191-4791-5); pap. text ed. 9.25 (ISBN 0-8191-4792-3). U Pr of Amer.

Rumor of War. Philip Caputo. 1988. pap. 4.95 (ISBN 0-345-33122-2). Ballantine.

Rumor of War. Philip Caputo. LC 76-29900. 1977. 10.00 (ISBN 0-03-017631-X). H Holt & Co.

Rumor Transmissable Ad Infinitum in Either Direction. Raymond Federman. (Illus.). 1976. pap. 5.00 (ISBN 0-685-53325-5). Assembling Pr.

Rumor Verified: Poems, 1979-1980. Robert Penn Warren. 91p. 1981. 9.95 (ISBN 0-394-52136-6); pap. 5.95 (ISBN 0-394-74960-X). Random.

Rumors. Caroline B. Cooney. (Cheerleaders Ser.: No. 3). 208p. (Orig.). (gr. 7 up). 1985. pap. 2.25 (ISBN 0-590-33404-2). Scholastic Inc.

Rumors. Catherine Mann. 1988. 18.95. Delacorte.

Rumors. Francine Pascal. (Sweet Valley High Ser.: No. 37). 1987. pap. 2.75 (ISBN 0-553-26530-X). Bantam.

Rumors see Cheerleaders Boxed Set.

Rumors of Ecstasy... Rumors of Death. Grace Butcher. 62p. 1971. pap. 2.50 (ISBN 0-912592-06-0). Ashland Poetry.

Rumors of Ecstasy, Rumors of Death. Grace Butcher. 64p. (Orig.). 1981. pap. 6.95 (ISBN 0-935306-13-7). Barnwood Pr.

Rumors of No Law: Poems from Berkeley 1968-1977. Peter D. Scott. LC 80-17862. (Orig.). 1981. pap. 4.50x (ISBN 0-914476-88-2). Thorp Springs.

Rumors of Peace. Ella Leffland. LC 78-20209. 400p. 1985. pap. 8.95 (ISBN 0-06-091301-0, PL 1301, PL). Har-Row.

Rumors of Rain. Andre Brink. 448p. 1984. pap. 6.95 (ISBN 0-14-006891-0). Penguin.

Rumors of Spring. Richard Grant. LC 86-22359. 448p. 1987. 18.95 (ISBN 0-553-05190-3, Spectra). Bantam.

Rumors of Spring. Richard Grant. 448p. 1987. pap. 9.95 (ISBN 0-553-34369-6, Spectra). Bantam.

Rumors of War: A Moral & Theological Perspective on the Arms Race. Ed. by Charles A. Cesaretti & Joseph T. Vitale. 128p. (Orig.). 1982. pap. 6.95 (ISBN 0-8164-2365-2, HarpR). Har-Row.

Rumors, Race, & Riots. Terry A. Knopf. LC 73-85098. (Social Policy Ser.). 390p. 1975. text ed. 34.95 (ISBN 0-87855-063-1). Transaction Bks.

Rumour of Angels. M. Bradley Kellogg. 277p. 1983. pap. 2.75 (ISBN 0-451-13223-8, Sig). NAL.

Rumour of Heaven. Beatrix Lehmann. 304p. 1987. pap. 6.95 (ISBN 0-14-016166-X). Penguin.

Rumour of the Flesh & Soul. Modhusudan Sanyal. (Writers Workshop Redbird Ser.). 1975. 8.00 (ISBN 0-88253-620-6); pap. text ed. 4.00 (ISBN 0-88253-619-2). Ind-US Inc.

Rumoured City. Ed. by Douglas Dunn. 1982. pap. 8.95 (ISBN 0-906427-41-X, Pub. by Bloodaxe Bks). Dufour.

Rumours of Spring. Richard Grant. (Spectra Ser.). 448p. (Orig.). 1988. pap. 4.50 (ISBN 0-553-26648-9). Bantam.

Rump Songs see Bibliography of John Bale.

Rumpelstiltskin. Patricia Daniels. LC 79-27140. (Fairy Tales Ser.). (Illus.). 24p. (gr. k-3). 1980. PLB 13.31 (ISBN 0-8393-0252-5). Raintree Pubs.

Rumpelstiltskin. Patricia Daniels. LC 79-27140. (Fairy Tale Clippers Ser.). (Illus.). 24p. (gr. k-3). 1981. PLB 27.99 incl. cassette (ISBN 0-8172-1831-9); cassette 14.00. Raintree Pubs.

Rumpelstiltskin. Margery Evernden. (Children's Theatre Playscript Ser.). (gr. k-12). 1955. pap. 2.25x (ISBN 0-88020-051-0). Coach Hse.

Rumpelstiltskin. Paul Galdone. LC 84-12741. (Illus.). 32p. (ps-3). 1985. pap. 13.95 (ISBN 0-89919-266-1, Clarion). HM.

Rumpelstiltskin. Jacob Grimm & Wilhelm K. Grimm. LC 78-18079. (Illus.). 32p. (gr. k-3). 1979. PLB 9.79 (ISBN 0-89375-140-5); pap. 1.95 (ISBN 0-89375-118-9). Troll Assocs.

Rumpelstiltskin. Jacob Grimm & Wilhelm K. Grimm. LC 83-90. (Illus.). 32p. (gr. k-3). 1983. reinforced bdg. 10.95 (ISBN 0-8234-0488-9). Holiday.

Rumpelstiltskin. Jacob Grimm & Wilhelm K. Grimm. Retold by & illus. by Paul O. Zelinsky. LC 86-4482. (gr. k up). 1986. 13.95 (ISBN 0-525-44265-0). Dutton.

Rumpelstiltskin. Wilhelm K. Grimm & Jacob Grimm. (Tell Me a Story Ser.). (Illus.). 26p. 1988. incl. cassette 9.95 (ISBN 1-55578-910-2). Worlds Wonder.

Rumpelstiltskin. Adapted by Margaret A. Hughes et al. (Talking Mother Goose Ser.). (Illus.). 26p. (ps). 1986. packaged with preprogrammed audio cassette tapes 9.95 (ISBN 0-934323-32-1). Alchemy Comms.

Rumpelstiltskin. R. Eugene Jackson. 52p. 1978. pap. 2.25 (ISBN 0-88680-166-4); royalty 35.25 (ISBN 0-317-03617-3). I E Clark.

Rumpelstiltskin. rev. ed. William-Alan Landes. (Wondrawhopper Ser.). 52p. (gr. 3-12). 1985. pap. text ed. 6.00 (ISBN 0-88734-104-7); tchr's ed 26.00 (ISBN 0-88734-005-9). Players Pr.

Rumpelstiltskin. Ed McBain. 240p. 1982. pap. 2.95 (ISBN 0-345-33149-4). Ballantine.

Rumpelstiltskin. (Ladybird Stories Ser.). (Illus., Arabic.). (gr. 4-6). 3.50x (ISBN 0-86685-265-4). Intl Bk Ctr.

Rumpelstiltskin. Retold by Edith Tarcov. 48p. (gr. k-3). 1973. pap. 2.50 (ISBN 0-590-42130-1). Scholastic Inc.

Rumpelstiltskin. John Wallner. LC 83-19100. (Illus.). 32p. 1984. 10.95 (ISBN 0-13-783747-X). P-H.

Rumpelstiltskin: A Participation Play. Moses Goldberg. (gr. k-3). 1987. pap. 3.00 playscript (ISBN 0-87602-269-7). Anchorage.

Rumpelstiltskin: Music & Lyrics. rev. ed. William-Alan Landes & Jeff Rizzo. (Wondrawhopper Ser.). (gr. 3-12). 1985. pap. text ed. 12.00 (ISBN 0-88734-004-0). Players Pr.

Rumpf und Extremitaeten see Atlas der Plastischen Chirurgie.

Rumpole & the Golden Thread. John Mortimer. (Crime). 256p. 1984. pap. 3.95 (ISBN 0-14-006331-5). Penguin.

Rumpole for the Defence. John Mortimer. (Crime Monthly Ser.). 192p. 1984. pap. 3.95 (ISBN 0-14-006060-X). Penguin.

Rumpole of the Bailey. John Mortimer. 1980. pap. 3.95 (ISBN 0-14-004670-4). Penguin.

Rumpole of the Bailey. John Mortimer. 12.95 (ISBN 0-89190-275-9, Pub. by Am Repr). Amereon Ltd.

Rumpoles & the Barleys. Karen Mezek. LC 88-80376. (Illus.). 40p. (Orig.). (ps-2). 1988. 8.95 (ISBN 0-89081-657-3). Harvest Hse.

Rumpole's Last Case. John Mortimer. 288p. 1988. pap. 3.95 (ISBN 0-14-010447-X). Penguin.

Rumpole's Return. John Mortimer. 160p. 1982. pap. 3.95 (ISBN 0-14-005571-1). Penguin.

Rumpole's Return. John Mortimer. 13.95 (ISBN 0-89190-277-5, Pub. by Am Repr). Amereon Ltd.

Rumprump. Ivan Gantschev. LC 83-25006. (Illus.). 32p. (ps up). 1984. 13.95 (ISBN 0-907234-53-4). Picture Bk Studio.

Rumpty-Dudget's Tower. Julian Hawthorne. (Illus.). 48p. (gr. 1-4). 1987. Repr. of 1879 ed. 11.95 (ISBN 0-394-87862-0); lib. bdg. 12.99 (ISBN 0-394-97862-5). Knopf.

Rumptydoolers. Ester Wier. LC 64-16260. (Illus.). (gr. 4-7). 6.95 (ISBN 0-8149-0439-4). Vanguard.
Rumpus in Regalia. Geoffrey Thornber. 1982. 15.00x (ISBN 0-903653-41-9, Pub. by New Playwrights Network). State Mutual Bk.
Rumrunners. Eldon W. Eberhard. 1982. 8.50 (ISBN 0-682-49822-X). Exposition-Phoenix.
Run. John Hay. (Illus.). 1979. 9.95 (ISBN 0-393-01269-7); pap. 3.95 (ISBN 0-393-00946-7). Norton.
Run. William Sleator. 140p. (gr. 7 up). 1981. pap. 1.95 (ISBN 0-590-31767-9). Scholastic Inc.
Run-&-Shoot Football: The Now Attack. Glenn Ellison. 194p. 1984. 19.95 (ISBN 0-13-783879-4, Parker). P-H.
Run Away Home. Marianne Shock. (Silhouette Special Edition). pap. 2.75 (ISBN 0-317-65568-X). Harlequin Bks.
Run Baby Run. Nicky Cruz & Jamie Buckingham. (gr. 9-12). 1984. pap. 3.50 (ISBN 0-515-09105-7). Jove Pubns.
Run Baby Run: The Story of a Gang-Lord Turned Crusader. Nicky Cruz & Jamie Buckingham. LC 68-23446. 239p. 1968. pap. 3.95 (ISBN 0-88270-630-6). Bridge Pub.
Run Before Midnight. Anne Maguire. (YA) (gr. 7 up). 1981. 9.95 (ISBN 0-686-84705-9, Avalon). Bouregy.
Run Before the Wind. Mary Moore. (Harlequin Romances Ser.). 192p. 1982. pap. 1.50 (ISBN 0-373-02512-2). Harlequin Bks.
Run Before the Wind. Stuart Woods. 320p. Date not set. pap. 3.95 (ISBN 0-380-70507-9). Avon.
Run, Billy, Run. Matt Christopher. (gr. 3-6). 1988. pap. 3.95 (ISBN 0-316-13993-9). Little.
Run: Computer Education. 2nd ed. Dennis O. Harper & James H. Stewart. LC 85-15182. (Computer Science Ser.). 250p. 1985. pap. text ed. 16.50 pub net (ISBN 0-534-05406-4). Brooks-Cole.
Run, Computer, Run: The Mythology of Educational Innovation-An Essay. Anthony G. Oettinger & Sema Marks. LC 71-78522. (Studies in Technology & Society). 1969. 24.50x (ISBN 0-674-78041-8). Harvard U Pr.
Run Devil Run. Hugh Van Eaton. (Illus.). 1975. pap. 4.95 (ISBN 0-89957-513-7). AMG Pubs.
Run, Don't Walk. Harriet M. Savitz. 132p. 1980. pap. 2.25 (ISBN 0-451-14627-1, AE1488, Sig). NAL.
Run, Ellen, Run. Elaine F. Wells. (YA) (gr. 7 up). 1978. 9.95 (ISBN 0-685-87348-X, Avalon). Bouregy.
Run Far, Run Fast. Walt Morey. 174p. (gr. 10 up). 1984. pap. 1.50 (ISBN 0-380-43356-7, 43356-7, Camelot). Avon.
Run Farther, Run Faster. Joe Henderson. LC 78-64507. (Illus.). 225p. 1979. pap. 6.95 (ISBN 0-89037-162-8). Anderson World.
Run Farther, Run Faster. Joe Henderson. 256p. 1985. pap. 6.95 (ISBN 0-02-028240-0, Collier). Macmillan.
Run for Cover. John Benteen. (Sundance Ser.: No. 16). 176p. 1983. pap. 2.25 (ISBN 0-8439-1172-7, Leisure Bks). Leisure NY.
Run for the Elbertas. James Still. LC 80-51019. 160p. 1980. 14.00 (ISBN 0-8131-1414-4); pap. 6.00 (ISBN 0-8131-0151-4). U Pr of Ky.
Run for the Sun. Barry Sadler. 256p. (Orig.). 1986. pap. 3.50 (ISBN 0-8125-8829-0, Dist. by Warner Pub Services & St. Martin's Press). Tor Bks.
Run for Your Life. Phil Arnot & Elvira Monroe. 1977. pap. 3.95 (ISBN 0-933174-01-2). Wide World-Tetra.
Run for Your Life. Kin Platt. 96p. (YA) (gr. 7 up). 1979. pap. 1.95 (ISBN 0-440-97557-3, LFL). Dell.
Run for Your Life & Other Stories. Jane Anderson et al. (Follett Adult Basic Reading Comprehension Program Ser.). 64p. pap. 2.95 (ISBN 0-8428-2257-7). Cambridge Bk.
Run for Your Sweet Life. Rex Benedict. LC 86-45507. (Illus.). 128p. (gr. 5 up). 1986. 11.95 (ISBN 0-374-36359-5). FS&G.
Run Gently, Run Long. Joe Henderson. LC 74-83665. (Illus.). 96p. 1978. pap. 5.95 (ISBN 0-89037-040-0). Anderson World.
Run Man Run. Chester Himes. 192p. 1975. Repr. of 1966 ed. 8.50x (ISBN 0-911860-56-8). Chatham Bkseller.
Run of the Brush. William M. Raine. 1976. Repr. of 1936 ed. lib. bdg. 18.95x (ISBN 0-88411-554-2, Pub. by Aeonian Pr). Amereon Ltd.
Run of the Brush. William M. Raine. 1986. pap. 2.95 (ISBN 0-445-20326-9, Pub. by Popular Lib). Warner Bks.
Run-On. Bernard H. Porter. (Illus.). 1975. 42.50 (0-911156-14-9). Bern Porter.
Run out of Time. Matthew Carney. LC 81-68605. 334p. 1982. 14.95 (ISBN 0-937444-02-2); pap. 9.95 (ISBN 0-937444-03-0). Caislan Pr.
Run Patty, Run. Sheila Cragg. LC 78-20583. (Illus.). 192p. 1980. 12.00 (ISBN 0-06-250160-7, HarpR). Har-Row.
Run Rabbit, Run! A Pop-Up Book. Rodney Peppe. LC 82-70307. (Illus.). 12p. (ps-3). 1982. pap. 8.95 (ISBN 0-385-28851-4). Delacorte.
Run, Rainey, Run see Top Dogs.
Run River. Joan Didion. 1961. 18.95 (ISBN 0-8392-1094-9). Astor-Honor.
Run River. Joan Didion. 256p. 1978. pap. 3.95 (ISBN 0-671-60315-9). WSP.
Run, River, Run: A Naturalist's Journey down One of the Great Rivers of the West. Ann Zwinger. LC 84-8640. (Illus.). 317p. 1984. pap. 10.95 (ISBN 0-8165-0885-2). U of Ariz Pr.
Run Roadrunner. Bevan Clair. LC 80-82912. (ps-6). 1980. pap. 1.50 (ISBN 0-686-30719-4). B A Scott.
Run! Run! Harriet Ziefert. LC 85-45328. (Illus.). 26p. (ps). 1986. 3.95 (ISBN 0-694-00097-3). HarpJ.
Run, Run, As Fast As You Can. Mary P. Osborne. LC 81-68781. 160p. (gr. 5 up). 1982. 12.95 (ISBN 0-8037-7535-0, 01258-370); PLB 12.89 (ISBN 0-8037-7561-X). Dial Bks Young.
Run, Run, As Fast As You Can. Mary P. Osborne. 128p. (gr. 7 up). 1983. pap. 1.95 (ISBN 0-590-32576-0, Vagabond). Scholastic Inc.
Run, Run Fast. George Sullivan. LC 78-22502. (Illus.). 64p. (gr. 4 up). 1980. 11.89 (ISBN 0-690-03969-7, Crowell Jr Bks); PLB 10.89 (ISBN 0-690-03970-0). HarpJ.
Run, Sara, Run. Anne Worboys. 240p. 1982. pap. 2.75 (ISBN 0-441-73705-6). Ace Bks.
Run Scared. Mignon G. Eberhart. 176p. (Orig.). 1987. pap. 3.50 (ISBN 0-446-34745-0). Warner Bks.
Run School Run. Roland S. Barth. LC 79-25686. (Illus.). 1980. text ed. 21.95x (ISBN 0-674-78036-1). Harvard U Pr.
Run School Run. Roland S. Barth. 304p. 1985. pap. text ed. 8.95x (ISBN 0-674-78037-X). Harvard U Pr.
Run, Shelley, Run! Gertrude Samuels. LC 73-12310. 192p. (YA) (gr. 7 up). 1974. 12.70i (ISBN 0-690-00295-5, Crowell Jr Bks). HarpJ.
Run, Shelley, Run. Gertrude Samuels. (YA) (RL 7). 1975. pap. 2.50 (ISBN 0-451-13987-9, AE2746, Sig). NAL.
Run Silent, Run Deep. Edward L. Beach. (Classics of Naval Literature Ser.). 304p. 1986. Repr. 21.95 (ISBN 0-87021-557-4). Naval Inst Pr.
Run Silent, Run Deep. Edward L. Beach. 432p. 1988. pap. 3.95 (ISBN 0-8217-2408-8). Zebra.
Run So As to Win: A Leader's Guide. George Simons & Marietta Starrie. 1985. 14.95 (ISBN 0-932895-01-8). Intl Prtn Pr.
Run Swift, Run Free. Tom McCaughran. (Illus.). 192p. 1987. pap. text ed. 3.95 (ISBN 0-86327-106-5, Pub. by Wolfhound Pr Ireland). Irish Bks Media.
Run Swift, Run Free. Tom McCaughren. (Illus.). 160p. (gr. 4-8). 1986. 13.95 (ISBN 0-86327-111-1, Pub. by Wolfhound Pr Ireland); pap. 8.95. Irish Bks Media.
Run-Through. John Houseman. 544p. 1984. pap. 9.95 (ISBN 0-671-41390-2, Touchstone Bks). S&S.
Run to Earth. Tom McCaughren. (Illus.). 144p. (gr. 4-8). 1985. 10.95 (ISBN 0-86327-060-3, Pub. by Wolfhound Pr Ireland); pap. 8.95 (ISBN 0-86327-116-2, Pub. by Wolfhound Pr Ireland). Irish Bks Media.
Run to Ground. (Executioner Ser.: No. 106). Date not set. pap. 2.25 (ISBN 0-317-63974-9, Pub. by Worldwide). Harlequin Bks.
Run to the Lee. Kenneth F. Brooks, Jr. LC 87-46314. (Maryland Paperback Bookshelf Ser.). 192p. 1988. pap. 7.95 (ISBN 0-8018-3677-8). Johns Hopkins.
Run to the Rainbow. Margaret Hillert. (Just-Beginning-to-Read Ser.). (Illus.). 32p. (ps-k). 1980. PLB 4.39 (Dist. by Caroline Hse); pap. 1.95. Modern Curr.
Run to the Roar. Jim Bakker & Tammy Bakker. LC 80-80656. 142p. 1982. pap. 2.95 (ISBN 0-89221-104-0). New Leaf.
Run to the Roar. Tammy Bakker & Cliff Dudley. LC 80-80656. 142p. 1980. 7.95 (ISBN 0-89221-073-7). New Leaf.
Run to the Roar. Tammy Bakker & Cliff Dudley. 1985. pap. 4.95 (ISBN 0-89221-140-7). New Leaf.
Run to the Stars. Mike S. Rohan. 256p. 1986. pap. 2.95 (ISBN 0-441-73663-7, Pub. by Ace Science Fiction). Ace Bks.
Run to the Sun: Bike Week - Daytona. Bob Jones, Jr. Ed. by Mark Smith. 96p. 1988. 19.95 (ISBN 0-9620663-0-3). Puttin Group.
Run to Win: Training for the Overcoming Life. Glenyce Coffin. (Cornerstone Ser.). 40p. 1984. pap. 2.50 (ISBN 0-930756-87-8, 533010). Aglow Pubns.
Run Today's Race. Oswald Chambers. 1968. pap. 3.95 (ISBN 0-87508-125-8). Chr Lit.
Run Toward the Nightland: Magic of the Oklahoma Cherokees. Jack F. Kilpatrick & Anna G. Kilpatrick. LC 67-19814. (Illus.). 212p. 1967. pap. 9.95 (ISBN 0-87074-084-9). SMU Press.
Run Wild, Run Free. Richard Haydn. 192p. 1985. 24.95x (ISBN 0-7090-2091-0, Pub. by R Hale Ltd UK). State Mutual Bk.
Run Wild, Run Free. Nancy Morse. (Intimate Moments Ser.). pap. 2.75 (ISBN 0-373-07210-4). Harlequin Bks.
Run with the Horseman. Ferrol Sams. (Contemporary American Fiction Ser.). 432p. 1984. pap. 7.95 (ISBN 0-14-007274-8). Penguin.
Run with the Horsemen. Ferrol Sams. LC 81-22671. 422p. 1982. 14.95 (ISBN 0-931948-32-0). Peachtree Pubs.
Run with the Horses. Eugene Peterson. LC 83-13005. 216p. (Orig.). 1983. pap. 7.95 (ISBN 0-87784-905-6). Inter-Varsity.
Run with the Wind. Tom McCaughren. (Illus.). 160p. 1984. 10.95 (ISBN 0-86327-010-7, Pub. by Wolfhound Pr Ireland). Irish Bks Media.
Run with the Wind. Tom McCaughren. (Illus.). 160p. (Orig.). (YA) (gr. 7 up). 1985. pap. 7.95 (Pub. by Wolfhound Pr Ireland). Irish Bks Media.
Run with the Winners. Warren W. Wiersbe. Ed. by Wightman Weese. 160p. (Orig.). 1985. pap. 5.95 (ISBN 0-8423-5798-X); study guide 2.95 (ISBN 0-8423-5799-8). Tyndale.
Run with Your Dreams. Maureen A. Burns. (Illus.). 60p. 1982. pap. 5.00 (ISBN 0-9613084-0-0). Empey Ent.
Run Your Car on Sunshine: Using Solar Energy for a Solar Powered Car. James N. Blake. LC 80-82734. (Illus.). 64p. 1981. lib. bdg. 12.95 (ISBN 0-915216-64-7); pap. 4.95 (ISBN 0-915216-65-5). Marathon Intl Pub Co.
Run Your Own Retail Store: From Raising the Money to Counting the Profits. Irving Burstinger. (Illus.). 304p. 1981. (Spec); pap. 14.95 (ISBN 0-13-784009-8). P-H.
Runagate Courage. H. J. Von Grimmelshausen. Tr. by Robert L. Hiller & John C. Osborne. LC 64-19584. (Illus.). xiv, 200p. 1965. 17.95x (ISBN 0-8032-0061-7). U of Nebr Pr.
Runaway. Stephen Gresham. 448p. 1988. pap. 3.95 (ISBN 0-8217-2482-7). Zebra.
Runaway. Lucy Irvine. LC 86-20198. 272p. (YA) 1987. 18.95 (ISBN 0-394-54510-9). Random.
Runaway. Paul Kropp. LC 81-5356. (Encounters Ser.). (Illus.). 96p. (gr. 7-12). 1982. pap. 3.95 (ISBN 0-88436-822-X, 35273); wkbk. 1.20 (ISBN 0-88436-931-5, 35686). EMC.
Runaway. Gilbert Morris. (Living Bks.). 400p. (Orig.). 1987. 4.50 (ISBN 0-8423-5797-1). Tyndale.
Runaway. Francine Pascal. (Sweet Valley High Ser.: No. 21). 176p. (Orig.). (gr. 5 up). 1985. pap. 2.75 (ISBN 0-553-26682-9). Bantam.
Runaway. 1982. 15.00x (ISBN 0-906660-05-X, Pub. by New Playwrights Network). State Mutual Bk.
Runaway. Patricia St. John. 1985. pap. 3.95 (ISBN 0-8024-9159-6). Moody.
Runaway. Clarissa Watson. LC 84-45633. 250p. 1985. 12.95 (ISBN 0-689-11521-0). Atheneum.
Runaway. Clarissa Watson. 208p. 1986. pap. 2.95 (ISBN 0-345-33114-1). Ballantine.
Runaway Ants. Gerald D. O'Nan & Lawrence W. O'Nan. (Adventures of Andy Ant Ser.: Vol. 4). (Illus.). 32p. (gr. 3 up). 1988. 6.95 (ISBN 0-8423-0315-4). Tyndale.
Runaway Ball. Bobbi Katz. (Pop-up Storybooks). (Illus.). 14p. (ps-3). 1986. 5.95 (ISBN 0-394-87429-3). Random.
Runaway Boy in the Correctional School. Zena C. O'Connor. LC 74-177128. (Columbia University. Teachers College. Contributions to Education: No. 742). Repr. of 1938 ed. 22.50 (ISBN 0-404-55742-2). AMS Pr.
Runaway Bride. Rosalyn Alsobrook. 512p. 1987. pap. 3.95 (ISBN 0-8217-2226-3). Zebra.
Runaway Bride. Rachelle Edwards. 149p. 1988. pap. 2.50 (ISBN 0-449-21364-1, Crest). Fawcett.
Runaway Bunny. Margaret W. Brown. LC 71-183168. (Illus.). 40p. (ps-2). 1972. 9.70i (ISBN 0-06-020765-5); PLB 11.89 (ISBN 0-06-020766-3). HarpJ.
Runaway Bunny. Margaret W. Brown. LC 71-183168. (Trophy Picture Bks.). (Illus.). 40p. (ps-2). 1977. pap. 3.50 (ISBN 0-06-443018-9, Trophy). HarpJ.
Runaway Bunny. Margaret W. Brown. (Illus.). (ps-k-3). 1985. incl. cassette 19.95 (ISBN 0-941078-78-7); pap. 12.95 incl. cassette (ISBN 0-941078-76-0); cassette, 4 paperbacks & guide 27.95 (ISBN 0-941078-77-9). Live Oak Media.
Runaway Chick. Robin Ravilious. (Illus.). 32p. (gr. k-3). 1987. 12.95 (ISBN 0-02-775640-8). Macmillan.
Runaway Christmas Toy: (Just Right for 3's & 4's) Linda Hayward. LC 88-4522. (Just Right Bks.). (Illus.). 32p. (ps). 1988. 4.95 (ISBN 0-394-89693-9, BYR); PLB 5.95 (ISBN 0-394-99693-3, BYR). Random.
Runaway Convention or Proving a Preposterous Negative. Aaron Wildavsky. (Orig.). 1983. pap. 2.50. Natl Taxpayers Found.
Runaway Coordinator. (Career Examination Ser.: C-3467). Date not set. pap. 16.00 (ISBN 0-8373-3467-5). Natl Learning.
Runaway Duck. David Lyon. LC 84-5677. (Illus.). 32p. (ps-1). 1985. PLB 11.95 (ISBN 0-688-04003-9); 11.88 (ISBN 0-688-04002-0). Lothrop.
Runaway Duck. David Lyon. (ps-1). 1987. pap. 3.95 (ISBN 0-688-07334-4, Mulberry). Morrow.
Runaway Elephant Calf. E. R. Davidar & Jagadish Joshi. (Illus.). 24p. (Orig.). (gr. k-3). 1980. pap. 2.75 (ISBN 0-89744-216-4, Pub. by Children's Bk Trust India). Auromere.
Runaway Father: One Family's Seventeen-Year Search. Richard Rashke. 304p. 1988. 17.95 (ISBN 0-15-179040-X). HarBraceJ.
Runaway Heart. Norma E. Koenig. (Orig.). (gr. 4-6). 1981. pap. 4.95 (ISBN 0-377-00112-0). Friendship Pr.
Runaway Homeless Youth: FY 1985 Annual Report to the Congress. U. S. Dept. of Health & Human Services Editorial Staff. 60p. 1986. write for info. US HHS.
Runaway Horse. Martin Walser. pap. 6.95 (ISBN 0-317-58523-1). H Holt & Co.
Runaway Horses. Yukio Mishima. 1973. 13.45 (ISBN 0-394-46618-7). Knopf.
Runaway Horses. Yukio Mishima. (Sea of Fertility Tetralogy Ser.). 432p. 1975. pap. 5.95 (ISBN 0-671-43495-0). WSP.
Runaway Housekeeper. Vivian Liverman. 9p. (Orig.). pap. 5.00x saddle stitched (ISBN 0-9611952-2-3). Viv-Poo.
Runaway Magic. Elaine Pageler. Ed. by Betty L. Kratoville. (Meridian Bks.). (Illus.). 64p. (gr. 3-9). 1989. lib. bdg. 4.95 (ISBN 0-87879-652-5, High Noon Books). Acad Therapy.
Runaway Mittens. Jean Rogers. LC 87-12024. (Illus.). 24p. (ps-3). 1988. 11.95 (ISBN 0-688-07053-1); lib. bdg. 11.88 (ISBN 0-688-07054-X). Greenwillow.
Runaway Molly Midnight, the Artist's Cat. Nadja Maril. LC 80-17097. (Illus.). 40p. (gr. k up). 1980. 9.95 (ISBN 0-916144-62-3). Stemmer Hse.
Runaway Presents. Judith Martin & Donald Ashwander. 16p. (Orig.). (ps up). 1977. playscript 2.00 (ISBN 0-87602-197-6). Anchorage.
Runaway Princess. Caroline Brooks. 1987. pap. 2.50 (ISBN 0-451-14780-4, Sig). NAL.
Runaway Ralph. Beverly Cleary. 176p. (gr. k-6). 1981. pap. 3.25 (ISBN 0-440-47519-8, YB). Dell.
Runaway Ralph. Beverly Cleary. (Illus.). (gr. 3-7). 1970. 13.00 (ISBN 0-688-21701-X); PLB 12.88 (ISBN 0-688-31701-4). Morrow.
Runaway Rancher, No. 58. J. D. Hardin. 192p. 1986. pap. 2.50 (ISBN 0-425-08665-8). Berkley Pub.
Runaway Randy. Bruce Sigmon. (gr. 5 up). 1988. 5.95 (ISBN 0-533-07854-7). Vantage.
Runaway Rapture. Wanza J. Campbell. 1983. pap. 3.75 (ISBN 0-8217-1231-4). Zebra.
Runaway Slave Advertisements: A Documentary History from the 1730s to 1790, 4 vols. Lathan A. Windley. LC 83-1486. (Documentary Reference Collection Ser.). 1983. Vol. 3. lib. bdg. 75.00 (ISBN 0-313-23945-2, WRS/03); Vol. 4. lib. bdg. 39.95 (ISBN 0-313-23946-0, WRS/04); Vol. 1. lib. bdg. 50.00 (ISBN 0-313-23911-8, WRS/01); Vol. 2. lib. bdg. 50.00 (ISBN 0-313-23912-6, WRS/02). Greenwood.
Runaway Sleigh Ride. Astrid Lindren. LC 83-23347. (Illus.). 32p. (ps-3). 1984. 11.95 (ISBN 0-670-40454-3, Viking Kestrel). Viking.
Runaway Soup & Other Stories. Michaela Muntean. LC 86-82360. (Sesame Street Silly Stories Ser.). (Illus.). 32p. (gr. 2-5). 1987. 3.95 (ISBN 0-307-12811-3, Pub. by Golden Bks). Western Pub.
Runaway Spaceship. Susan Saunders. (Skylark Choose Your Own Adventure Ser.: No. 30). 64p. 1985. pap. 2.25 (ISBN 0-553-15463-X). Bantam.
Runaway Sugar: About Diabetes. Alvin Silverstein & Virginia B. Silverstein. LC 80-8727. (Illus.). 48p. (gr. 3-5). 1981. 11.70i (ISBN 0-397-31928-2, Lipp Jr Bks). HarpJ.
Runaway Teddy Bear. Ginnie Hofman. LC 84-23740. (Picturebacks Ser.). (Illus.). 32p. (ps-3). 1986. lib. bdg. 5.99 (ISBN 0-394-96286-9, BYR); pap. 1.95 (ISBN 0-394-86286-4). Random.
Runaway Teens: An American Tragedy. Arnold Madison. LC 79-11683. 1979. 10.95 (ISBN 0-525-66636-2). Lodestar Bks.
Runaway to Freedom. Barbara Smucker. LC 77-11834. (Trophy I Can Read Bks.). (Illus.). 110p. (gr. 4-8). 1979. pap. 2.95 (ISBN 0-06-440106-5, Trophy). HarpJ.
Runaways. Beverley Ashwill. LC 87-72441. (Illus.). 48p. (gr. 4-8). 1988. 12.95 (ISBN 0-941381-02-1); pap. 5.95 (ISBN 0-941381-01-3). BJO Enterprises.
Runaways. Lyle M. Crist. (Illus.). 1976. pap. text ed. 3.00 (ISBN 0-914720-06-6). Pale Horse.
Runaways & Non-Runaways in American Suburbs. Albert R. Roberts. 117p. 1981. pap. 12.00x (ISBN 0-256-05650-1). Dorsey.
Runaway's Diary. Marilyn Harris. (gr. 7-10). 1983. pap. 2.25 (ISBN 0-671-49751-0). Archway.
Runaways, Illegal Aliens in Their Own Land: Implications for Service. Dorothy Miller. LC 79-11682. (Praeger Special Studies Ser.). 224p. 1980. 38.95 (ISBN 0-275-90525-X, C0525). Praeger.
Runaways in Texas: A Statistical Estimate, 1985. (Special Project Report Ser.). 33p. 1985. 5.00 (ISBN 0-89940-852-4). LBJ Sch Pub Aff.
Rundbauten im Kerameikos, Vol. 12. Wolf Koenigs et al. (Illus.). 1979. 48.00 (ISBN 3-11007-210-6). De Gruyter.
Rundfunk gegen das Dritte Reich: Deutschprachige Rundfunkaktivitaten im Exil 1933-45: Ein Hanbuch. Conrad Putter. (Runfunkstudien Ser.: Vol. 3). 388p. (Ger.). 1986. lib. bdg. 50.00 (ISBN 3-598-10470-7). K G Saur.
Rundfunkwissenschaft im Dritten Reich. Arnulf Kutsch. (Rundfunkstudien Ser.: Vol. 2). 600p. (Ger.). 1985. lib. bdg. 32.00 (ISBN 3-598-21572-X). K G Saur.
Rune. Karl Kempton. (Illus.). 100p. 1981. 75.00 (ISBN 0-686-69461-9). Bern Porter.
Rune Games. Marijane Osborn & Stella Longland. (Illus.). 200p. (Orig.). 1982. pap. 11.95 (ISBN 0-7100-9303-9). Routledge Chapman & Hall.
Rune Magic. Donald Tyson. Ed. by Phyllis Galde. LC 87-45741. (Practical Magick Ser.). (Illus., Orig.). 1988. pap. 9.95 (ISBN 0-87542-826-6). Llewellyn Pubns.
Rune Magic: A Celtic Tradition. Deon Dolphin. 160p. (Orig.). 1987. pap. 9.95 (ISBN 0-87877-127-1). Newcastle Pub.

Running in Place: Inside the Senate. James A. Miller. 208p. 1987. pap. 7.95 (ISBN 0-671-63604-9, Touchstone Bks). S&S.
Running in Salt Lake City. Ken Rudolph. LC 86-1498. (Bonneville Book). (Illus.). 72p. (Orig.). 1986. pap. 4.95 (ISBN 0-87480-252-0). U of Utah Pr.
Running in the Family. Michael Ondaatje. 212p. 1982. 12.95 (ISBN 0-393-01637-4). Norton.
Running in the Family. Michael Ondaatje. 208p. 1984. pap. 6.95 (ISBN 0-14-006966-6). Penguin.
Running in the Red: The Political Dynamics of Urban Fiscal Stress. Irene Rubin. LC 81-9329. 184p. 1983. 59.50 (ISBN 0-87395-564-1); pap. 19.95 (ISBN 0-87395-565-X). State U NY Pr.
Running Indians. Mary A. Lutz & Dick L. Lutz. (Illus.). 128p. 1989. pap. price not set (ISBN 0-931625-19-X). Dimi Pr.
Running Is for Me. Fred Neff. LC 79-16789. (Sports for Me Bks.). (Illus.). (gr. 2-5). 1980. PLB 7.95 (ISBN 0-8225-1093-6). Lerner Pubns.
Running Lights. Henry Carlile. LC 80-67971. 66p. 1981. 9.00 (ISBN 0-937872-00-8); pap. 5.00 (ISBN 0-937872-01-6). Dragon Gate.
Running Loose. Chris Crutcher. LC 82-20935. 160p. (YA) (gr. 10 up). 1983. reinforced bdg. 10.25 (ISBN 0-688-02002-X). Greenwillow.
Running Loose. Chris Crutcher. (YA) (gr. 7 up). 1986. pap. 2.95 (ISBN 0-440-97570-0, LFL). Dell.
Running Lucky. R. P. Dickey. LC 71-84954. (New Poetry Ser.: No. 39). 80p. 1969. 6.95 (ISBN 0-8040-0265-7, Pub. by Swallow). Ohio U Pr.
Running Man. Richard Bachman, pseud. 1987. pap. 3.95 (ISBN 0-451-15122-4, Sig). NAL.
Running Microsoft Excel. Douglas Cobb & Judy Mynhier. 736p. 1988. softcover 24.95 (ISBN 1-55615-108-X). Microsoft.
Running Mind. Jim Lilliefors. LC 78-58053. (Illus.). 182p. 1979. pap. 4.95 (ISBN 0-89037-144-X). Anderson World.
Running MS-DOS. 3rd ed. Van Wolverton. 496p. 1988. 35.00 (ISBN 1-55615-116-0); pap. 22.95 (ISBN 1-55615-115-2). Microsoft.
Running Octopus. 2nd ed. Ruth Hayes. (Illus.). 48p. 1985. pap. 3.95 (ISBN 0-933457-04-9). Random Motion.
Running of Beasts. Bill Pronzini & Barry Malzberg. LC 86-72530. 320p. 1988. pap. 4.95 (ISBN 0-88739-076-5, Pub. by Black Lizard Bks). Creative Arts Bk.
Running on Empty: The Future of the Automobile in An Oil-Short World. Lester Brown et al. 1979. 9.95 (ISBN 0-393-01334-0). Norton.
Running OS-2. Michael Hyman. 256p. 1988. pap. 19.95 (ISBN 0-553-34566-4). Bantam.
Running Out of Magic with Houdini. Elizabeth Levy. LC 80-28427. (Illus.). 128p. (gr. 3-6). 1981. lib. bdg. 4.99 (ISBN 0-394-94685-5); pap. 1.95 (ISBN 0-394-84685-0). Knopf.
Running Out of Space: What Are the Alternatives? American Library Association, Library Administration Division, Buildings & Equipment Section, Buildings for College & University Libraries Committee. LC 78-1796. 172p. 1978. pap. 15.00x. ALA.
Running Out of Space: What Are the Alternatives? 172p. 1978. pap. 15.00 (ISBN 0-8389-3215-0). Library Admin.
Running Out of Time. Elizabeth Levy. LC 79-28064. (Capers Ser.). (Illus.). 128p. (gr. 3-6). 1980. lib. bdg. 4.99 (ISBN 0-394-94422-4); pap. 1.95 (ISBN 0-394-84422-X). Knopf.
Running Owl the Hunter. Nathaniel Benchley. LC 78-22156. (Harper I Can Read Bks.). (Illus.). 64p. (gr. k-3). 1979. PLB 10.89 (ISBN 0-06-020454-0). HarpJ.
Running Patterns. Randall R. Freisinger. LC 85-25273. 1985. pap. 4.00 (ISBN 0-9613984-1-8). Flume Pr.
Running: Psychological & Performance Aspects with Subject Analyses & Bibliography. Walt E. Weldome. LC 83-45290. 160p. 1984. 34.50 (ISBN 0-88164-070-0); pap. 26.50 (ISBN 0-88164-071-9). ABBE Pubs Assn.
Running R: Base for DOS. Alan Shilepsky & Thomas Goodell. 450p. (Orig.). 1988. pap. 21.95. MIS Press.
Running Register: Recording the State of the English Colledges in All Forraine Parts. Lewis Owen. LC 68-54654. (English Experience Ser.: No. 19). 118p. 1968. Repr. of 1626 ed. 13.00 (ISBN 90-221-0019-7). Walter J Johnson.
Running Repairs. Norman Dugdale. 64p. (Orig.). 1983. pap. 5.95 (ISBN 0-85640-283-4, Pub. by Blackstaff Pr). Longwood Pub Group.
Running Scared. Gregory McDonald. 1964. 12.95 (ISBN 0-8392-1095-7). Astor-Honor.
Running Scared. Gregory McDonald. 208p. pap. 3.95 (ISBN 0-446-32676-3). Warner Bks.
Running Scared. Jean Thesman. 176p. (Orig.). 1987. pap. 2.50 (ISBN 0-380-75230-1, Flare). Avon.
Running Scared: Silver in Mississippi. James W. Silver. LC 83-21668. (Illus.). 268p. 1984. 14.95 (ISBN 0-87805-209-7). U Pr of Miss.
Running Shoe Book. Peter Cavanagh. LC 80-20365. (Illus.). 400p. 1980. pap. 11.95 (ISBN 0-89037-182-2). Anderson World.
Running the American Corporation. Ed. by William R. Dill. LC 78-16922. 1978. 10.95 (ISBN 0-13-783894-8, Spec); pap. 4.95 (ISBN 0-13-783886-7). Am Assembly.
Running the Blockade: A Personal Narrative of Adventures, Risks, & Escapes During the American Civil War. facsimile ed. Thomas E. Taylor. LC 79-154163. (Select Bibliographies Reprint Ser.). Repr. of 1896 ed. 19.00 (ISBN 0-8369-5779-2). Ayer Co Pubs.
Running: The Consequences. Richard C. Crandall. LC 85-43574. 300p. 1986. lib. bdg. 24.95x (ISBN 0-89950-201-6). McFarland & Co.
Running the Gauntlet: Cultural Sources of Violence Against the I. W. W. John C. Townsend. Ed. by Harold Hyman & Stuart Bruchey. (American Legal & Constitutional History Ser.). 400p. 1986. lib. bdg. 50.00 (ISBN 0-8240-8298-2). Garland Pub.
Running the Lydiard Way. Arthur Lydiard & Garth Gilmour. LC 78-360. (Illus.). 241p. 1978. 12.95 (ISBN 0-89037-096-6). Anderson World.
Running the Race. Judson Edwards. LC 85-4700. 1985. pap. 5.95 (ISBN 0-8054-5711-9). Broadman.
Running the Race: Keeping the Faith. Sandy Larsen. (Young Fisherman Bible Studyguide Ser.). 64p. (Orig.). (gr. 6-12). 1986. pap. 2.95 (ISBN 0-87788-740-3); tchr's. ed. 4.95 (ISBN 0-87788-741-1). Shaw Pubs.
Running the Red Lights. Charles Mylander. LC 86-444. 250p. (Orig.). 1986. pap. 7.95 (ISBN 0-8307-1103-1, 5418666). Regal.
Running: The Women's Handbook. Liz Sloan & Ann Kramer. (Illus.). 138p. (Orig.). 1985. pap. 6.95 (ISBN 0-86358-043-2, Pandora Pr). Routledge Chapman & Hall.
Running Things: The Art of Making Things Happen. Philip Crosby. 254p. 1986. text ed. 19.95 (ISBN 0-07-014513-X). McGraw.
Running Things: The Art of Making Things Happen. Philip B. Crosby. LC 86-28508. 272p. 1987. pap. 9.95 (ISBN 0-452-25915-0, Plume). NAL.
Running Tide. Joan Benoit & Sally Baker. LC 86-46318. (Illus.). 224p. 1987. 16.95 (ISBN 0-394-55457-4). Knopf.
Running to Keep Fit. Brian Mitchell. 96p. 1980. pap. 2.95 (ISBN 0-679-12428-4). McKay.
Running to the Shrouds. Konstantin Stanyukovich. Tr. by Neil Parsons from Rus. LC 86-81346. 100p. (Orig.). 1986. pap. 10.00 (ISBN 0-317-63871-8, Pub. by Forest Bks London). Three Continents.
Running to the Top. Derek Clayton. LC 79-64297. (Illus.). 160p. 1980. pap. 5.95 (ISBN 0-89037-212-8). Anderson World.
Running to Win. Martha Josey & Linda Clack. Ed. by Josey Enterprises Staff. (Illus., Orig.). 1985. pap. 29.95 (ISBN 0-934499-00-4). Josey Enter Inc.
Running Together: The Family Book of Jogging. Jed Cantlay & Robert Hoffman. LC 79-92135. (Illus.). 112p. 1981. pap. 8.95 (ISBN 0-918438-18-7, PCAN0018). Leisure Pr.
Running Toward a New Life. Marcus Cumberlege. 1972. 5.95 (ISBN 0-685-27677-5, Pub. by Anvil Pr); signed ltd. ed. 15.00 (ISBN 0-685-27678-3). Small Pr Dist.
Running, Walking & Jumping: The Science of Locomotion. A. J. Dagg. 143p. 1977. pap. 18.00x (ISBN 0-85109-530-5). Taylor & Francis.
Running Wild. Helen Griffiths. LC 77-3814. (Illus.). 160p. (gr. 5 up). 1977. 6.95 (ISBN 0-8234-0309-2). Holiday.
Running Wild. Shirley Powell. 192p. 1984. pap. 2.25 (ISBN 0-380-78170-0, 78170, Flare). Avon.
Running Wild: A Photographic Tribute to the NFL's Greatest Runners. Beau Riffenburgh & David Ross. 1987. pap. 14.95 (ISBN 0-452-26022-1, Pub. by Plume). NAL.
Running Windows: The Microsoft Guide to Windows 2.0 & Windows 2.0 & Windows 386. Nancy Andrews & Craig Stinson. 368p. 1988. softcover 19.95 (ISBN 1-55615-047-4). Microsoft.
Running with Man's Best Friend. Davia A. Gallup. (Illus.). 128p. (Orig.). 1986. pap. 7.98 (ISBN 0-931866-25-1). Alpine Pubns.
Running with the Fox. David MacDonald. (Illus.). 228p. 1988. 23.95 (ISBN 0-8160-1886-3). Facts on File.
Running with the Whole Body: A Thirty-Day Program to Running Faster with Less Effort. Jack Heggie. 192p. 1986. pap. 10.95 (ISBN 0-87857-635-5). Rodale Pr Inc.
Running with Your Dog. John A. Sanford. Ed. by William W. Denlinger & R. Annabel Rathman. LC 87-534. (Other Dog Bks.). (Illus.). 96p. 1987. pap. 9.95 (ISBN 0-87714-125-8). Denlingers.
Running Without Fear. Kenneth H. Cooper. 192p. 1986. pap. 3.95 (ISBN 0-553-25546-0). Bantam.
Running Workshops: A Guide for Trainers in the Helping Professions. The Coping with Crisis Research & Training Group, the Open University Staff. 176p. 1986. 22.95 (ISBN 0-7099-4809-3, Pub. by Croom Helm UK). Routledge Chapman & Hall.
Running Your Best: The Committed Runner's Guide to Training & Racing. Ron Daws. LC 85-7614. (Illus.). 1985. pap. 8.95 (ISBN 0-8289-0559-2). Greene.
Running Your Business with Excel. Amanda C. Hixson. (Illus.). 250p. (Orig.). 1986. pap. text ed. 16.95 (ISBN 0-07-881206-2). Osborne-McGraw.
Running Your Own Business. rev. ed. Howard H. Stern. 224p. 1985. pap. 7.95 (ISBN 0-517-55820-3). Crown.
Running Your Own Co-Operative: A Guide to the Setting up of Worker & Community Owned Enterprises. John Pearce. 174p. 1984. 29.75x (ISBN 0-317-54693-7, Pub. by Plunkett Foundation). State Mutual Bk.
Running Your Own Restaurant. 2nd ed. R. H. Johnson. 185p. (Orig.). 1982. pap. text ed. 14.50x (ISBN 0-09-149231-9, Hutchinson & Co). Brookfield Pub Co.
Running Your Own Show: Mastering the Basics of Small Business. Richard Curtin. 1983. pap. 4.50 (ISBN 0-451-62400-9, Ment). NAL.
Running 4Word. Kay Nelson. (Illus.). 350p. (Orig.). 1987. pap. text ed. 19.95 (ISBN 0-07-881258-5). Osborne-McGraw.
Runs Far, Son of the Chichimecs. Alice M. Wesche. (gr. 3-7). 1982. pap. 6.95 (ISBN 0-89013-133-3). Museum NM Pr.
Runs, Hits & Errors: A Treasury of Cub History & Humor. Jim Langford. LC 87-27272. 1987. 14.95 (ISBN 0-912083-22-0). Diamond Communications.
Runt. Elizabeth Levy. (Fat Albert Ser.). (Orig.). (gr. k-6). 1986. pap. 2.95 (ISBN 0-440-47538-4, YB). Dell.
Runway at Eland Springs. Rebecca Beguin. LC 87-60528. 240p. (Orig.). 1987. pap. 7.95 (ISBN 0-934678-10-3). New Victoria Pubs.
Runway Towards Orion: The True Adventures of a Red Cross Girl on a B-29 Air Base in World War II India. Mary T. Sargent. (Illus.). 240p. (Orig.). 1984. pap. 10.95 (ISBN 0-931515-01-7). Triumph Pr.
Runway U. S. A. A Pilot's Guide to Destination Cities in Flight Simulator. Charles Gulick. (Flight Simulator Co-Pilot Ser.). 232p. (Orig.). 1987. pap. 9.95 (ISBN 1-55615-002-4). Microsoft.
Ruodlieb. Ed. & intro. by C. W. Grocock. (BC-AP Classical Ser.). 240p. (Orig., Eng & Lat.). 1986. 49.00x (ISBN 0-86516-098-8); pap. 16.50x (ISBN 0-86516-073-2). Bolchazy Carducci.
Ruodlieb. Ed. by C. W. Grocock. (Classical Texts - Medieval Latin Texts Ser.). 240p. (Eng. & Lat.). 1985. text ed. 49.95 (ISBN 0-85668-292-6, Pub. by Aris & Phillips UK); pap. text ed. 16.50 (ISBN 0-85668-293-4, Pub. by Aris & Phillips UK). Humanities.
Ruodlieb: The Earliest Courtly Novel after 1050. Ed. & tr. by Edwin H. Zeydel. LC 59-63490. (North Carolina University. Studies in the Germanic Languages & Literatures: NO. 23). 1959. 27.00 (ISBN 0-404-50923-1). AMS Pr.
Ruodlieb: The First Medieval Epic of Chivalry from 11th Century Germany. Tr. by Gordon B. Ford, Jr. from Lat. 1965. pap. cancelled (ISBN 0-685-05284-2). Adlers Foreign Bks.
Rupam' An Illustrated Quarterly Journal of Oriental Art Chiefly Indian, 11 vols. Ed. by Ordhendra C. Ganaoly. (Illus.). 1986. text ed. 2000.00x (ISBN 81-7018-303-0, Pub. by B R Pub Corp Delhi). Apt Bks.
Rupert & Monck Letterbook, 1666. J. R. Powell & E. K. Timings. 1985. 69.00x (ISBN 0-317-44226-0, Pub. by Navy Rec Soc). State Mutual Bk.
Rupert Annual. Alfred Bestall. (Rupert Daily Express Annual Ser.). (Illus.). (gr. 4-6). 1975. 6.50x (ISBN 0-685-56545-9). Scholium Intl.
Rupert Brooke. Rupert Brooke. (Pocket Poet Ser.). 1968. pap. 3.50 (ISBN 0-8023-9042-0). Dufour.
Rupert Brooke: A Biography. Christopher Hassall. 1972. pap. 5.95 (ISBN 0-571-10196-8). Faber & Faber.
Rupert Brooke: A Memoir. Edward Marsh. 1918. 20.00 (ISBN 0-8274-3314-X). R West.
Rupert Brooke & the Intellectual Imagination. W. De La Mare. LC 72-3166. (English Literature Ser., No. 33). 1972. Repr. of 1919 ed. lib. bdg. 29.95x (ISBN 0-8383-1515-1). Haskell.
Rupert of Deutz. John Van Engen. LC 82-40089. (Center for Medieval & Renaissance Studies, UCLA: Publication: No. 18). 1983. text ed. 42.00x (ISBN 0-520-04577-7). U of Cal Pr.
Rupert of Hentzau. Anthony Hope. (Puffin Classics Ser.). 256p. (gr. 4-6). 1984. pap. 2.25 (ISBN 0-14-035033-0, Puffin). Penguin.
Rupert of Hentzau (Sequel to Prisoner of Zenda) Anthony Hope. lib. bdg. 17.95x (ISBN 0-89966-227-7). Buccaneer Bks.
Rupert Penguin. Amye Rosenberg. LC 85-81132. (Golden Sturdy Shape Bks.). (Illus.). 14p. (ps). 1986. 2.95 (ISBN 0-307-12309-X, Pub. by Golden Bks). Western Pub.
Rupert, Polly & Daisy. Jody Silver. LC 83-24979. (Illus.). 48p. (ps-3). 1984. 5.95 (ISBN 0-8193-1124-3). Parents.
Rupert Weddington & His Small Dogs. Ed Bluestone. (Storybook Special Ser.). (Illus.). 48p. (gr. k-3). 1987. 7.95 (ISBN 0-8431-1945-4). Price Stern.
Ruptured Diamond: The Politics of the Decentralization of the District of Columbia Public Schools. Barbara A. Sizemore. LC 80-5698. (Illus.). 569p. (Orig.). 1981. lib. bdg. 22.00 (ISBN 0-8191-1618-1). U Pr of Amer.
Rural Access Road Program: Appropriate Technology in Kenya. (WEP Study Ser.). 167p. 1981. pap. 11.50 (ILO165, ILO). UNIPUB.
Rural Access Roads Programme: Apropriate Technology in Kenya. J. J. De Veen. (Illus.). 175p. (Orig.). 1984. pap. 17.50 (ISBN 92-2-102204-8). Intl Labour Office.
Rural Africa. A. T. Grove & F. Klein. LC 77-82496. (Topics in Geography Ser.). (Illus.). 1979. pap. 9.95 (ISBN 0-521-29282-4). Cambridge U Pr.
Rural Aint Necessarily Country. Jack M. Holland. (Illus.). 208p. (Orig.). 1985. pap. 5.95 (ISBN 0-935777-03-2). Country Pub.
Rural America. Ed. by Morrow Wilson & Suzanne Fremon. (Reference Shelf Ser.). 1976. 10.00 (ISBN 0-8242-0597-9). Wilson.
Rural America a Century Ago. 160p. 11.95 (ISBN 0-916150-06-2, HO776). Am Soc Ag Eng.
Rural America Chart Book. 1983. 1.95 (ISBN 0-318-01719-9). Rural America.
Rural America, Why Bother? Richard Margolis. 1980. 1.25 (ISBN 0-318-01735-0). Rural America.
Rural & Small Town Planning. Ed. by Judith Getzels & Charles Thurow. 359p. 1980. 4.95 (ISBN 0-318-13075-0). Am Plan Assn.
Rural & Urban Income Inequalities in Indonesia, Mexico, Pakistan, Tanzania & Tunisia. Wouter Van Ginneken. (WEP Study Ser.). viii, 67p. 1976. pap. 10.50 (ISBN 92-2-101538-6, ILO1120, ILO). UNIPUB.
Rural & Urban Islam in West Africa. Ed. by Nehemia Levtzion & Humphrey J. Fisher. LC 87-4712. 192p. 1987. lib. bdg. 23.50x (ISBN 0-317-56323-8). Lynne Rienner.
Rural & Urban Vocational Training, Report 2: Tenth Asian Regional Conference. 108p. (Orig.). 1985. pap. text ed. 12.25 (ISBN 92-2-105262-1). Intl Labour Office.
Rural & Urban Vocational Training: 10th Asian Regional Conference, Report No. II. 108p. (Orig.). 1987. pap. text ed. 12.25 (ISBN 0-317-68053-6, ILO621, ILO). UNIPUB.
Rural Architecture in Hong Kong. Hong Kong Government Information Service. 120p. 1979. 72.00x (ISBN 0-317-68619-4, Pub. by Han-Shan Tang Ltd). State Mutual Bk.
Rural Architecture in the Chinese Taste. William Halfpenny & John Halfpenny. LC 68-58993. (Illus.). 1968. Repr. of 1755 ed. 17.00 (ISBN 0-405-08591-5, Blom Pubns). Ayer Co Pubs.
Rural Area Development: Perspectives & Approaches. K. V. Sundaram. 1979. 17.50 (ISBN 0-89684-534-6). Orient Bk Dist.
Rural Aristocracy in Northern Ireland. Amouda Shanks. 207p. 1988. text ed. 43.40x (ISBN 0-566-05237-7, Pub. by Gower Pub England). Gower Pub Co.
Rural Australia & New Zealand: Some Observations of Current Trends. Edmund D. Brunner. LC 75-30123. (Institute of Pacific Relations). Repr. of 1938 ed. 20.00 (ISBN 0-404-59513-8). AMS Pr.
Rural Bangladesh: Competition for Scarce Resources. Eirik G. Jansen. (Norwegian University Press Publication Ser.). (Illus.). 240p. 1987. 48.00 (ISBN 8-20-007617-2). Oxford U Pr.
Rural Banks for Rural Development. Charan D. Wadhva. 1980. 16.00x (ISBN 0-8364-0642-7, Pub. by Macmillan India). South Asia Bks.
Rural Black Heritage Between Chicago & Detroit, 1850-1929: A Photograph Album & Random Thoughts. Benjamin C. Wilson. 1985. pap. 8.95 (ISBN 0-932826-19-9). New Issues MI.
Rural Britain: A Social Geography. David Phillips & Allan Williams. 288p. 1984. 45.00x (ISBN 0-631-13238-4); pap. 12.95x (ISBN 0-631-13237-6). Basil Blackwell.
Rural Canada: Structure & Change. Satadal Dasgupta. LC 87-21644. (Canadian Studies: Vol. 3). 1987. lib. bdg. 49.95x (ISBN 0-88946-196-1). E Mellen.
Rural Carrier (U.S.P.S.) Jack Rudman. (Career Examination Ser.: C-678). (Cloth bdg. avail. on request). pap. 10.00 (ISBN 0-8373-0678-7). Natl Learning.
Rural Catalonia under the Franco Regime. E. C. Hansen. LC 76-9177. 1977. 32.50 (ISBN 0-521-21457-2). Cambridge U Pr.
Rural Challenge: Proceedings of the 17th International Conference of Agricultural Economists, Vol. II. Ed. by Margot A. Bellamy & Bruce L. Greenshields. 346p. 1981. text ed. 30.00x (ISBN 0-566-00472-0). Gower Pub Co.
Rural Change & Public Policy: Eastern Europe, Latin America & Australia. Ed. by William P. Avery et al. (Pergamon Policy Studies). 1980. 60.00 (ISBN 0-08-023109-8). Pergamon.
Rural Change & Royal Finances in Spain at the End of the Old Regime. Richard Herr. 1988. 75.00x (ISBN 0-520-05948-4). U of Cal Pr.
Rural China Today. F. Leeming. 232p. 1986. pap. 24.95 (ISBN 0-470-20528-8, Co-Pub. with Longman). Wiley.
Rural China Today. Frank Leeming. (Illus.). 1984. pap. text ed. 22.95 (ISBN 0-582-30144-0). Wiley.
Rural Church. Edward W. Hassinger et al. Ed. by Lyle E. Schaller. (Creative Leadership Ser.). 1988. pap. 9.95 (ISBN 0-687-36587-2). Abingdon.
Rural Communities in Advanced Industrial Society: Development & Developers. Ted K. Bradshaw & Edward J. Blakely. LC 78-19736. 202p. 1979. 38.95 (ISBN 0-275-90333-8, C0333). Praeger.
Rural Communities of Hong Kong: Studies & Themes. James Hayes. (EASSM Ser.). (Illus.). 1983. 29.95x (ISBN 0-19-581504-1). Oxford U Pr.

Rural Health. N. D. Kamble. 1985. 19.00x (ISBN 0-8364-1327-X, Pub. by Ashish India). South Asia Bks.

Rural Health & Health Communications. Ed. by S. N. Barton. (Biosciences Communications Ser.: Vol. 4, No. 1). (Illus.). 1977. 17.50 (ISBN 3-8055-2838-8). S Karger.

Rural Health Care. Roger A. Rosenblatt & Ira S. Moscovice. LC 82-4892. (Health Services Ser.). 301p. 1982. 30.00 (ISBN 0-471-05419-4). Wiley.

Rural Health Development in Tanzania: A Case-Study of Medical Sociology in a Developing Country. G. M. Van Etten. (Studies of Developing Countries). 194p. 1976. pap. text ed. 15.00 (ISBN 90-232-1378-5, Pub. by Van Gorcum Holland). Longwood Pub Group.

Rural Health Organization: Social Networks & Regionalization. Edward W. Hassinger. 194p. 1982. pap. text ed. 12.95x (ISBN 0-8138-1589-4). Iowa St U Pr.

Rural Health Services: Organization, Delivery, & Use. North Central Regional Center for Rural Development. Ed. by Larry Whiting & E. Hassinger. 308p. 1976. text ed. 10.50x (ISBN 0-8138-1465-0). Iowa St U Pr.

Rural Home Techniques - Labour-Saving Ideas: Food, Water, Transport. (Economic & Social Development Papers: No. 5-4). (Folder - 20 loose sheets). 1977. pap. 9.50 (F230, FAO). UNIPUB.

Rural Home Techniques - Labour-Saving Ideas: Sanitation, Food, Water. (Economic & Social Development Papers: No. 5-6). (Folder - 20 loose sheets). 1977. pap. 9.50 (ISBN 92-5-000267-X, F1402, FAO). UNIPUB.

Rural Home Techniques: Furnishing & Equipment, Series 1 - Seating & Sleeping, Tables & Surfaces, Modular Furniture. (Economic & Social Development Papers: No. 5-7). 20p. 1978. pap. 9.50 (ISBN 92-5-000332-3, F1445, FAO). UNIPUB.

Rural Hospital: Its Structure & Organization. R. F. Bridgman. (Monograph Ser: No. 21). (Illus.). 162p. (Eng. & Fr.). 1970. 8.00 (ISBN 92-4-140021-8). World Health.

Rural Household Studies in Asia. Ed. by Hans P. Binswanger et al. 1981. pap. 14.00x (ISBN 9971-69-002-0, Pub. by Singapore U Pr). Ohio U Pr.

Rural Housing & the Public Sector. David R. Phillips & Allan M. Williams. 184p. 1982. text ed. 35.00 (ISBN 0-566-00456-9). Gower Pub Co.

Rural Housing: Recent Research & Policy Issues. Mark Shucksmith et al. (Illus.). 224p. 1987. pap. text ed. 17.90 (ISBN 0-08-034529-8, AUP). Pergamon.

Rural Hunterdon: An Agricultural History. Hubert G. Schmidt. LC 77-139149. (Illus.). 331p. 1972. Repr. of 1945 ed. lib. bdg. 35.00x (ISBN 0-8371-5765-X, SCRH). Greenwood.

Rural Income Distribution (An Analytical Study of Punjab) Inder P. Singh. xvi, 123p. 1986. text ed. 25.00x (ISBN 81-7018-299-9, Pub. by B R Pub Corp Delhi). Apt Bks.

Rural Industialization in China. Jon Sigurdson. (East Asian Monographs: No. 73). 1977. 22.50x (ISBN 0-674-78072-8). Harvard U Pr.

Rural Industrialisation & Regional Development. Mohan Lal. 168p. 1987. 21.00x (ISBN 0-8364-2031-4, Pub. by Deep). South Asia Bks.

Rural Industrialisation in India. R. V. Rao. 1987. Repr. of 1978 ed. 10.50 (ISBN 0-8364-2258-9, Pub. by Concept). South Asia Bks.

Rural Industrialization in India. Bepin Behari. 1976. 13.50 (ISBN 0-7069-0448-6). Intl Bk Dist.

Rural Industrialization in India. S. Y. Thakur. 156p. 1985. text ed. 25.00x (ISBN 0-86590-727-7, Pub. by Sterling Pubs India). APT Bks.

Rural Industrialization in Israel. Ed. by Raphael Bar-El & A. Nesher. (Special Studies in Industrial Policy & Development). 180p. 1987. pap. 25.00 (ISBN 0-8133-7393-X). Westview.

Rural Industrialization in Third World Countries. R. P. Misra. 332p. 1986. text ed. 37.50x (ISBN 0-86590-795-1, Pub. by Sterling Pubs India). Apt Bks.

Rural Industrialization: Problems & Potentials. North Central Regional Center for Rural Development Staff. LC 73-20027. pap. 40.80 (ISBN 0-317-55353-4, 2029164). Bks Demand UMI.

Rural Industry in the Port Phillip Region: 1835-1880. Lynnette J. Peel. (Illus.). xiv, 196p. 1974. 30.00x (ISBN 0-522-84064-7, Pub by Melbourne U Pr). Intl Spec Bk.

Rural Influence Districts in the 97th Congress. George Rucker. 1983. 2.95 (ISBN 0-318-01726-1). Rural America.

Rural Innovations in Agriculture. Mohammad Salim. 1986. 38.50 (ISBN 81-85076-09-X, Pub. by Chugh Pubns India). South Asia Bks.

Rural Institutions 1945-1966. pap. 8.50 (F941, FAO). UNIPUB.

Rural Journalism in Africa. Paul Ansah. (Reports & Papers on Mass Communication: No. 88). 35p. 1981. pap. 5.00 (ISBN 92-3-101752-7, U1098, UNESCO). UNIPUB.

Rural Land Tenure in the United States: A Socioeconomic Approach to Problems, Programs, & Trends. Ed. by Alvin L. Bertrand & Floyd L. Corty. LC 62-16212. (Illus.). xii, 314p. 1962. 37.50 (ISBN 0-8071-0325-X). La State U Pr.

Rural Land Uses & Planning: A Comparative Study of the Netherlands & the United States. R. B. Held & D. W. Visser. (Developments in Landscape Management & Urban Planning Ser.: No. 6A). 360p. 1984. 121.00 (ISBN 0-444-42284-6). Elsevier.

Rural Landscape: Abstracts of Papers Presented at the Annual Meeting of CELA, October 23-27, 1982. Council of Educators in Landscape Architecture Staff. pap. 31.80 (ISBN 0-317-29834-8, 2019634). Bks Demand UMI.

Rural Landscape & Communities. Ed. by Colin Thomas. 200p. 1986. 45.00x (ISBN 0-7165-2375-2, Pub. by Irish Academic Pr Ireland). Biblio Dist.

Rural Leadership among Scheduled Castes. D. R. Singh. 238p. 1986. 30.00x (ISBN 0-8364-1643-0, Pub. by Chugh Pubns India). South Asia Bks.

Rural Leadership & Population Control in Bangladesh. M. Rashiduzzaman. LC 82-40245. 110p. (Orig.). 1982. lib. bdg. 26.00 (ISBN 0-8191-2637-3); pap. text ed. 10.00 (ISBN 0-8191-2638-1). U Pr of Amer.

Rural Leadership in the Context of India's Modernization. Parmatma Saran. 1978. 10.00x (ISBN 0-8364-0207-3). South Asia Bks.

Rural Legal Services from the Pit to the Pendulum. Jim Massey & Ron Byers. 193p. 1981. 15.75. NCLS Inc.

Rural Legislators in an Indian State. H. D. Lakshminarayana. (Illus.). 75p. 1986. text ed. 25.00x (ISBN 81-210-0030-0, Pub. by Inter India Pubns N Delhi). Apt Bks.

Rural Life in England in the First World War. Pamela Horn. LC 84-17885. 320p. 1985. 30.00 (ISBN 0-312-69604-3). St Martin.

Rural Life in Northern Ireland: Five Regional Studies Made for the Northern Ireland Council of Social Service, Inc. John M. Mogey. LC 77-87692. Repr. of 1947 ed. 38.00 (ISBN 0-404-16488-9). AMS Pr.

Rural Life of England. William Howitt. (Development of Industrial Society Ser.). 416p. 1971. Repr. of 1844 ed. 37.50x (ISBN 0-7165-1582-2, BBA 03062, Pub. by Irish Academic Pr). Biblio Dist.

Rural Life of Shakespeare. C. Roach Smith. 1874. lib. bdg. 27.50 (ISBN 0-8414-1578-1). Folcroft.

Rural Local Government & Rural Development in Malaysia. Stephen Chee. (Special Series on Rural Local Government: No. 9). 112p. (Orig.). 1974. pap. text ed. 3.50 (ISBN 0-86731-095-2). Cornell CIS RDC.

Rural Local Government in India. S. Bhatnagar. 278p. 1978. 16.95. Asia Bk Corp.

Rural Malay Women in Tradition & Transition. Heather Strange. LC 81-5140. 288p. 1981. 36.95 (ISBN 0-275-90724-4, C0724). Praeger.

Rural Markets & Trade in East Africa. Charles M. Good. LC 72-128466. (Research Papers Ser.: No. 128). 252p. 1970. pap. 12.00 (ISBN 0-89065-035-7). U Chicago Comm Geo.

Rural Middlemen: Network of Patronage. H. C. Srivastava & M. K. Chaturvedi. 1986. 19.00X (ISBN 81-7024-042-5, Pub. by Ashish India). South Asia Bks.

Rural Migrants in An Urban Setting. P. S. Majumdar & Ila Majumdar. 176p. 1978. text ed. 29.95 (ISBN 0-87855-330-4). Transaction Bks.

Rural Migration in Developing Nations: Comparative Studies of Korea, Sri Lanka, & Mali. Calvin Goldsheider. (Replica Edition Ser.). 275p. 1984. 33.00x (ISBN 0-86531-832-8). Westview.

Rural Migration in the United States. C. E. Lively & Conrad Taeuber. LC 71-165601. (Research Monograph Ser.: Vol. 19). 1971. Repr. of 1939 ed. 25.00 (ISBN 0-306-70351-3). Da Capo.

Rural New York. Elmer O. Fippin. LC 79-137943. (Economic Thought, History & Challenge Ser). 1971. Repr. of 1921 ed. 36.00x (ISBN 0-8046-1446-6, Pub. by Kennikat). Assoc Faculty Pr.

Rural North Korea under Communism: A Study of Sociocultural Change. Mun Woong Lee. LC 76-1745. (Rice University Studies: Vol. 62, No. 1). (Illus.). 176p. (Orig.). 1976. pap. 10.00x (ISBN 0-89263-227-5). Rice Univ.

Rural Oasis: History of Windham, New Hampshire, 1883-1975 see History of Windham in New Hampshire, 1719-1883.

Rural One-Room Schools of Mid-America. Leslie C. Swanson. (Illus.). 1976. 3.00 (ISBN 0-911466-23-1). Swanson.

Rural Organization in Bukoba District, Tanzania. Jorgen Rald & Karen Rald. 123p. 1976. 15.50 (ISBN 0-8419-9718-7, Africana). Holmes & Meier.

Rural People's Responses to Change, Dumaguete Trade Area. Agaton P. Pal & Robert A. Polson. 1973. wrps. 4.75x (ISBN 0-686-18705-9, Pub. by New Day Pub.). Cellar.

Rural Police & Rural Youth. Michael P. Roche. LC 84-13156. (Virginia Legal Ser.). 217p. 1985. 25.00x (ISBN 0-8139-1035-8). U Pr of Va.

Rural Policy. Ed. by William Browne & Don Hadwiger. (Orig.). 1982. pap. 8.00 (ISBN 0-918592-55-0). Policy Studies.

Rural Policy for the EEC? H. Clout. (EEC Ser.). 227p. 1984. text ed. 27.00 (ISBN 0-416-34540-9, 9104); pap. text ed. 12.95 (ISBN 0-416-34550-6, 9105). Routledge Chapman & Hall.

Rural Policy Research Alternatives. Ed. by Larry Whiting & David Rogers. (Illus.). 1978. pap. text ed. 9.50x (ISBN 0-8138-1875-3). Iowa St U Pr.

Rural Politics & Social Change in the Middle East. LC 77-180485. (Studies in Development: No. 5). pap. 128.00 (ISBN 0-317-10061-0, 2050046). Bks Demand UMI.

Rural Politics & the Collapse of Pennsylvania Federalism. Kenneth Keller. (Transactions Ser.: Vol. 72, Pt. 6). 1982. 9.00 (ISBN 0-87169-726-2). Am Philos.

Rural Poor in the Great Depression: Three Studies. LC 70-137177. (Poverty U. S. A. Historical Record Ser.). 1971. Repr. of 1938 ed. 32.00 (ISBN 0-405-03133-5). Ayer Co Pubs.

Rural Population Growth in New England. A. E. Luloff & Thomas E. Steahr. 92p. 1987. pap. 5.00 (ISBN 0-9609010-2-7). NE Regional Ctr.

Rural Population in Indian Urban Setting. Jakka Parthasarathy. (Illus.). xv, 272p. 1984. text ed. 60.00x (ISBN 0-86590-329-8, Pub. by B R Publishing Corp). Apt Bks.

Rural Poverty & Agrarian Reform. Steve Jones et al. 390p. 1986. 32.50X (ISBN 0-907108-45-8, Pub. by Allied India). South Asia Bks.

Rural Poverty & Public Policy in the United States. Ed. by Aruna N. Michie. (Orig.). 1986. pap. 8.00 (ISBN 0-918592-93-3). Policy Studies.

Rural Poverty & the Policy Crisis. Ed. by Robert O. Coppedge & Carlton G. Davis. 1977. text ed. 12.50x (ISBN 0-8138-1220-8). Iowa St U Pr.

Rural Poverty & the Urban Crisis: A Strategy for Regional Development. Niles M. Hansen. LC 78-10260. (Illus.). 1979. Repr. of 1970 ed. lib. bdg. 35.00x (ISBN 0-313-21079-9, HARP). Greenwood.

Rural Poverty in South Asia. Ed. by T. N. Srinivasan & Pranab K. Bardhan. (Illus.). 608p. 1988. 50.00 (ISBN 0-231-06224-9). Columbia U Pr.

Rural Poverty Unperceived: Problems & Remedies. Robert Chambers. (Working Paper: No. 400). 51p. 1980. 5.00 (ISBN 0-686-36076-1, WP-0400). World Bank.

Rural Problems in the Alpine Region: An International Study. M. Cepede & E. S. Abensour. 201p. (Orig.). 1961. pap. 9.50 (ISBN 92-5-101667-4, F416, FAO). UNIPUB.

Rural Profile: Halting Change in Mode of Production (A Study of the Comprehensive Area Development Strategy) Asok Kumar Maiti. 249p. 1988. text ed. 40.00x (ISBN 81-210-0189-7, Pub. by Inter India Pubns N Delhi). Apt Bks.

Rural Property in Transition. (Monographs). 1985. 6.00 (ISBN 0-911780-82-3). Am Inst Real Estate Appraisers.

Rural Psychology. Ed. by Alan W. Childs & Gary B. Melton. 458p. 1983. 55.00x (ISBN 0-306-41045-1, Plenum Pr). Plenum Pub.

Rural Public Administration: Problems & Prospects. Jim Seroka. LC 85-27253. (Contributions in Political Science Ser.). 217p. 1986. 38.95 (ISBN 0-313-25246-7, SRL/). Greenwood.

Rural Public Management. OECD. 86p. (Orig.). 1986. pap. 10.00 (ISBN 92-64-12858-1). OECD.

Rural Public Transportation. (Transportation Research Record Ser.). 88p. 1978. 5.00 (ISBN 0-309-02835-3). Transport Res Bd.

Rural Public Welfare: Selected Records. Grace Browning. LC 75-17209. (Social Problems & Social Policy Ser.). 1976. Repr. of 1941 ed. 43.00x (ISBN 0-405-07481-6). Ayer Co Pubs.

Rural Radio: Programme Format. Kiranmani A. Dikshit et al. (Monographs on Communication Technology & Utilization: No. 5). 94p. 1979. pap. 5.00 (ISBN 92-3-101616-4, U893, UNESCO). UNIPUB.

Rural Railroads-Prelude: Trails to Rails. Carlton J. Corliss. 76p. 1976. Repr. 6.00 (ISBN 0-686-27589-6). E S Cunningham.

Rural Rebels: A Study of Two Protest Movements in Kenya. Audrey Wipper. (Illus.). 1977. 24.95x (ISBN 0-19-572430-5). Oxford U Pr.

Rural Reconstruction & Development: A Manual for Field Workers. Y. C. Yen et al. 456p. 1969. Repr. of 1967 ed. 15.00 (ISBN 0-942717-14-7). Intl Inst Rural.

Rural Reconstruction in Ireland. Lionel Smith-Gordon. 1919. 75.00x (ISBN 0-685-69866-1). Elliots Bks.

Rural Residences. Alexander J. Davis. (Architecture & Decorative Art Ser.). 1980. Repr. of 1838 ed. 110.00 (ISBN 0-306-71165-6). Da Capo.

Rural Resource Development. 2nd ed. M. C. Whitby et al. (Illus.). 240p. 1978. pap. 12.95x (ISBN 0-416-70720-3, NO. 2582). Routledge Chapman & Hall.

Rural Resource Management. Paul J. Cloke & Chris C. Park. LC 84-22858. 496p. 1985. 40.00 (ISBN 0-312-69602-7). St Martin.

Rural Responses to Industrialization: A Study of Village Zambia. Robert H. Bates. LC 75-43301. 1976. 42.00 (ISBN 0-300-01920-3). Yale U Pr.

Rural Revolution in an English Village. Roy Sturgess. (Cambridge Introduction to World History Topic Bks.). (Illus.). 48p. (YA) (gr. 7 up). 1982. pap. 4.95 (ISBN 0-521-22800-X). Cambridge U Pr.

Rural Revolution in France: The Peasantry in the Twentieth Century. Gordon Wright. (Illus.). 1964. 27.50x (ISBN 0-8047-0190-3). Stanford U Pr.

Rural Revolution in South China: Peasants & the Making of History in Haifeng County, 1570-1930. Robert B. Marks. LC 83-16980. (Illus.). 368p. 1984. 32.50x (ISBN 0-299-09530-4). U of Wis Pr.

Rural Rides. William Cobbett. 1973. Repr. of 1912 ed. 11.95x (ISBN 0-460-00638-X, Evman). Biblio Dist.

Rural Rides. William Cobbett. Ed. by George Woodcock. (English Library Ser.). 554p. 1963. pap. 5.95 (ISBN 0-14-043023-7). Penguin.

Rural Rides of the Bristol Churchgoer. Ed. by Joseph Leech & Alan Sutton. 352p. 1987. 29.95 (ISBN 0-312-01214-4). St Martin.

Rural Roads & Poverty Alleviation. Ed. by John Howe & Peter Richards. (Illus.). 191p. 1984. 19.50x (ISBN 0-946688-05-2, Pub. by Intermediate Tech England). Intermediate Tech.

Rural Roots: Getting to Know Grandma. Ed. by Eleanor Jacobs. LC 86-62272. 64p. 1986. pap. 8.95 (ISBN 0-89821-077-1). Reiman Assocs.

Rural Roots: Getting to Know Grandpa. Ed. by Eleanor Jacobs. LC 86-62273. 64p. 1986. pap. 8.95 (ISBN 0-89821-078-X). Reiman Assocs.

Rural Route. R. T. Smith. 96p. 1981. pap. 6.00 (ISBN 0-918092-25-6); pap. 10.00 signed ed. (ISBN 0-918092-24-8). Tamarack Edns.

Rural-Rural Migrations in Africa see Cahiers de l'Institut de Science Economique Appliquee.

Rural Russia under the New Regime. Viktor Danilov. Tr. & intro. by Orlando Figes. LC 88-2778. (Second World Ser.). 352p. 1988. 45.00 (ISBN 0-253-35075-1). Ind U Pr.

Rural Russia under the Old Regime: A History of the Landlord-Peasant World & a Prologue to the Peasant Revolution of 1917. Geroid T. Robinson. 1967. pap. 11.95x (ISBN 0-520-01075-2). U of Cal Pr.

Rural Sanitation in the Tropics. M. Watson. 1976. lib. bdg. 69.95 (ISBN 0-8490-2548-6). Gordon Pr.

Rural Sanitation: Planning & Appraisal. Compiled by Arnold Pacey. (Illus.). 68p. (Orig.). 1980. pap. 8.95x (ISBN 0-903031-72-8, Pub. by Intermediate Tech England). Intermediate Tech.

Rural Schools in Canada. James C. Miller. LC 74-177073. (Columbia University. Teachers College. Contributions to Education: No. 61). Repr. of 1913 ed. 22.50 (ISBN 0-404-55061-4). AMS Pr.

Rural Scotland During the War. David T. Jones et al. (Economic & Social History of the World War, British Ser.). 1926. 95.00x (ISBN 0-317-27576-3). Elliots Bks.

Rural Settlement in an Urban World. Michael Bunce. LC 81-52986. 1981. 25.00x (ISBN 0-312-69605-1). St Martin.

Rural Settlement in Britain. Brian K. Roberts. LC 76-30000. (Studies in Historical Geography Ser.). (Illus.). 221p. 1977. 24.50 (ISBN 0-208-01621-X, Archon). Shoe String.

Rural Settlements: A Cultural-Geographical Analysis (A Case Study of Northern Haryana) Neelam Grover. (Illus.). xxiii, 316p. 1986. text ed. 75.00x (ISBN 81-210-0031-9, Pub. by Inter India Pubns N Delhi). Apt Bks.

Rural Shelter in Southern Africa: A Survey of the Architecture, House Forms & Construction Methods of the Black Rural Peoples of Southern Africa. Franco Frescura. (Illus.). 208p. 1981. pap. 16.95 (ISBN 0-86975-205-7, Pub. by Ravan Pr). Ohio U Pr.

Rural Small-Scale Industries & Employment in Africa & Asia: A Review of Programmes & Policies. Ed. by E. Chuta & S. V. Sethuraman. x, 159p. (Orig.). 1983. pap. 17.50 (ISBN 92-2-103513-1). Intl Labour Office.

Rural Small-Scale Industries & Employment in Africa & Asia: A Review of Programmes & Policies. Ed. by Enyinna Chuta & S. V. Sethuraman. 159p. 1984. pap. text ed. 19.95 (ILO274, ILO). UNIPUB.

Rural Small-Scale Industry in the People's Republic of China. Ed. by Dwight Perkins. LC 76-20015. 1977. 40.00x (ISBN 0-520-03284-5); pap. 9.95x (ISBN 0-520-04401-0). U of Cal Pr.

Rural Social & Community Work in the U. S. & U. K. A Cross-Cultural Perspective. Emilia E. Martinez-Brawley. 304p. 1982. 36.95 (ISBN 0-275-90855-0, C0855). Praeger.

Rural Social Organization in a Spanish-American Culture Area. Sigurd Johansen. LC 48-45369. 146p. 1982. lib. bdg. 29.95x (ISBN 0-89370-730-9). Borgo Pr.

Rural Social Systems & Adult Education. Charles P. Loomis. (Illus.). viii, 392p. 1957. 5.00 (ISBN 0-87013-023-4). Mich St U Pr.

Rural Social Trends. Edmund Brunner & John H. Kolb. LC 70-98825. Repr. of 1933 ed. lib. bdg. 35.00x (ISBN 0-8371-2889-7, BRRS). Greenwood.

Rural Social Welfare: An Annotated Bibliography for Educators & Practitioners. Dennis L. Poole. LC 80-28691. 334p. 1981. 40.95 (ISBN 0-275-90704-X, C0704). Praeger.

Rural Social Work Practice. O. William Farley. 256p. 1982. text ed. 24.95 (ISBN 0-02-910480-7). Free Pr.

Rural Society. Irwin T. Sanders. (Illus.). 192p. 1977. pap. text ed. 12.95 (ISBN 0-13-784439-5). P-H.

Rural Society & Environment in America. Carlson & William R. Lassey. (Agricultural Science Ser.). (Illus.). 448p. 1981. text ed. 33.95 (ISBN 0-07-009959-6). McGraw.

Rural Society & French Politics. Michael Burns. LC 84-3253. (Illus.). 264p. 1984. text ed. 29.00x (ISBN 0-691-05423-1). Princeton U Pr.

Ruskin Spear. Mervyn Levy. (Royal Academy Painters & Sculptors Ser.). 73p. 1986. 16.95 (ISBN 0-89733-183-4). Academy Chi Pubs.
Ruskin: The Critical Heritage. J. L. Bradley. LC 83-11102. (Critical Heritage Ser.). 436p. 1984. 29.95x (ISBN 0-7100-9286-5). Routledge Chapman & Hall.
Ruskin the Prophet & Other Centenary Studies. John H. Whitehouse. LC 73-11306. 1920. lib. bdg. 30.00 (ISBN 0-8414-9368-5). Folcroft.
Ruskinian Gothic: The Architecture of Deane & Woodward, 1845-1861. Eve Blau. LC 81-7302. (Illus.). 350p. 1982. cloth 54.00x (ISBN 0-691-03984-4); pap. 22.50x LPE (ISBN 0-691-10127-2). Princeton U Pr.
Ruskin's Influence Today. John Howard Whitehouse. LC 72-13681. 1974. Repr. of 1945 ed. lib. bdg. 30.00 (ISBN 0-8414-1281-2). Folcroft.
Ruskin's Landscape of Beatitude. David A. Downes. LC 83-48767. (American University Studies IV (English Language & Literature): Vol. 4). 247p. 1984. pap. text ed. 24.75 (ISBN 0-8204-0049-1). P Lang Pubs.
Ruskin's Letters from Venice Eighteen Forty-One to Eighteen Fifty-Two. John Ruskin. Ed. by John L. Bradley. LC 78-6260. (Yale Studies in English Ser.: Vol. 129). 1978. Repr. of 1955 ed. lib. bdg. 35.00x (ISBN 0-313-20456-X, RULE). Greenwood.
Ruskin's Maze: Mastery & Madness in His Art. Jay Fellows. LC 81-47131. 375p. 1981. 38.00x (ISBN 0-691-06479-2). Princeton U Pr.
Ruskin's Myths. Dinah Birch. (Oxford English Monographs). 224p. 1988. 54.00 (ISBN 0-19-812872-X). Oxford U Pr.
Ruskin's Poetic Argument: The Design of the Major Works. Paul L. Sawyer. LC 84-45801. 320p. 1985. 29.95x (ISBN 0-8014-1739-2). Cornell U Pr.
Ruskin's Politics. George Bernard Shaw. LC 76-28956. 1921. lib. bdg. 19.50 (ISBN 0-8414-7725-6). Folcroft.
Ruslan & Ludmila. A. Pushkin. 94p. 1987. 6.95 (ISBN 0-8285-3752-6, Pub. by Raduga Pubs USSR). Imported Pubns.
Ruslan I. Liudmila. Aleksandr Pushkin. 134p. 1985. 95.00x (ISBN 0-317-61367-7, Pub. by Collets (UK)). State Mutual Bk.
Russe Sans Peine. Albert O. Cherel. 24.95 (ISBN 0-685-11550-X); Three cassettes. 125.00. French & Eur.
Russell. C. W. Kilmister. LC 84-18050. 1984. 27.50 (ISBN 0-312-69613-2). St Martin.
Russell. C. W. Kilmister. LC 84-18050. 262p. pap. cancelled (ISBN 0-312-69617-5). St Martin.
Russell. Mark Sainsbury. (Arguments of the Philosophers Ser.). 1979. 36.00x (ISBN 0-7100-0155-X); pap. 14.95 (ISBN 0-7102-0536-8). Routledge Chapman & Hall.
Russell, Alexandra, & John. Ed. by Joseph R. Simonetta. LC 81-90481. (Illus.). 144p. (Orig.). 1981. pap. 7.95 (ISBN 0-941594-00-9). Simonetta Pr.
Russell & Moore: The Analytical Heritage. Alfred J. Ayer. LC 77-133216. (William James Lectures Ser: 1970). 1971. 17.50x (ISBN 0-674-78103-1). Harvard U Pr.
Russell Baker, Erma Bombeck, & Me. Margery Eliscu. (Illus.). 175p. (Orig.). 1987. pap. 8.95 (ISBN 0-912769-27-0). L Tapley.
Russell Chatham. Etel Adnan et al. (Illus.). 61p. 1984. signed limited ed. 175.00 (ISBN 0-916947-01-7); pap. 14.95 (ISBN 0-916947-00-9). Winn Bks.
Russell Chatham. rev. ed. Etel Adnan et al. (Illus.). 72p. 1987. pap. 14.95 (ISBN 0-944439-00-4). Clark City Pr.
Russell County. Theodosia Barrett. LC 81-69331. 148p. 1981. 10.95 (ISBN 0-89227-047-0). Commonwealth Pr.
Russell Grimwade. J. R. Poynter. 1967. 20.00x (ISBN 0-522-83827-8, Pub. by Melbourne U Pr). Intl Spec Bk.
Russell Jennings Manufacturing Company Trade Catalog, 1899. Ed. by Kenneth D. Roberts. (Illus.). 32p. 1981. pap. 4.00 (ISBN 0-913602-48-5). K Roberts.
Russell Kelso Carter on "Faith Healing" The Atonement for Sin & Sickness, "Faith Healing" Reviewed after Twenty Years. Russell K. Carter. Ed. by Donald W. Dayton. (Higher Christian Life Ser.). 411p. 1985. 50.00 (ISBN 0-8240-6409-7). Garland Pub.
Russell Kirk: A Bibliography. Ed. by Charles Brown. LC 82-182871. (Illus.). 172p. 1981. 7.50 (ISBN 0-916699-05-6). CMU Clarke Hist Lib.
Russell Lee: Farm Security Administration Photographs, 1936-1942, 2 vols. 1983. cancelled. Text-Fiche.
Russell Lee's FSA Photographs of Chamisal & Penasco, New Mexico. Ed. by William Wroth. LC 85-71305. (Illus.). 152p. (Orig.). 1985. 24.95 (ISBN 0-941270-24-6); pap. 11.95 (ISBN 0-941270-23-8). Ancient City Pr.
Russell Register, 8 vols. Ed. by Frances Nelson. LC 83-10269. 1986. lib. bdg. 19.95x ea. Vol. 1 (ISBN 0-8095-6928-0). Vol. 2 (ISBN 0-8095-6929-9). Vol. 3 (ISBN 0-8095-6930-2). Vol. 4 (ISBN 0-8095-6931-0). Vol. 5 (ISBN 0-8095-6932-9). Vol. 6 (ISBN 0-8095-6933-7). Vol. 7 (ISBN 0-8095-6934-5). Vol. 8 (ISBN 0-8095-6945-0). Borgo Pr.
Russell Register. Ed. by Frances Nelson. lib. bdg. 19.95x ea. Vol. 9 (ISBN 0-8095-6956-6). Vol. 10 (ISBN 0-8095-6957-4). Borgo Pr.
Russell Rides Again. Johanna Hurwitz. LC 85-7287. (Illus.). 64p. (ps-2). 1985. 10.25 (ISBN 0-688-04628-2, Morrow Junior Books); lib. bdg. 10.88 (ISBN 0-688-04629-0). Morrow.
Russell Sage. Paul Sarnoff. (Illus.). 1965. 17.95 (ISBN 0-8392-1142-2). Astor-Honor.
Russell Sprouts. Johanna Hurwitz. LC 87-5494. (Illus.). 80p. (ps-2). 1987. 10.25 (ISBN 0-688-07165-1, Morrow Junior Books); lib. bdg. 10.88 (ISBN 0-688-07166-X, Morrow Junior Books). Morrow.
Russell Sturgis: Eighteen Thirty-Six to Nineteen Nine. Lamia Doumato. (Architecture Ser.: Bibliography A 1339). 1985. pap. 2.00 (ISBN 0-89028-309-5). Vance Biblios.
Russell W. Porter, Arctic Explorer, Artist, Telescope Maker. Berton C. Willard. LC 76-8090. (Illus.). 1976. 12.50 (ISBN 0-87027-168-7). Cumberland Pr.
Russell Wright: American Designer. William Hennessey. (Illus.). 96p. (Orig.). 1983. pap. 15.00 (ISBN 0-262-58066-7). MIT Pr.
Russell Wright Dinnerware. Ann Kerr. (Illus.). 160p. 1985. pap. 9.95 (ISBN 0-89145-292-3). Collector Bks.
Russellism Unveiled. O. C. Lambert. 1940. pap. 3.50 (ISBN 0-88027-090-X). Firm Foun Pub.
Russell's Civil War Photographs. Andrew J. Russell. 1983. 15.25 (ISBN 0-8446-5939-8). Peter Smith.
Russell's Civil War Photographs: 115 Historic Prints. Andrew J. Russell. (Illus.). 128p. 1982. pap. 7.95 (ISBN 0-486-24283-8). Dover.
Russell's Magazine, Vol. 1-6. Repr. of 1860 ed. Set. lib. bdg. 405.00 (ISBN 0-404-19547-4); lib. bdg. 34.50 ea. AMS Pr.
Russell's Soil Conditions & Plant Growth. 11th ed. Alan Wild. 1216p. 1987. 95.00 (ISBN 0-470-20796-5, Co-Pub. with Longman). Halsted Pr.
Russet Coat: A Study of Robert Burns Poetry. Christina Keith. LC 70-130263. (Studies in Poetry, No. 38). 1970. Repr. of 1952 ed. lib. bdg. 51.95x (ISBN 0-8383-1170-9). Haskell.
Russia. Edward Acton. (Present & the Past Ser.). 352p. 1986. 32.95 (ISBN 0-582-49322-6); pap. text ed. 16.95 (ISBN 0-582-49323-4). Longman.
Russia. Theophile Gautier. LC 77-115550. (Russia Observed, Series I). 1970. Repr. of 1905 ed. 51.00 (ISBN 0-405-03028-2). Ayer Co Pubs.
Russia. Robert G. Kaiser. (gr. 10 up). 1984. pap. 5.95 (ISBN 0-671-50324-3). PB.
Russia. Robert G. Kaiser. 576p. 1984. pap. 5.95. WSP.
Russia. (Let's Visit Places & Peoples - - Nations, Dependencies, & Sovereignties of the World Ser.). (Illus.). (gr. 5 up). 1989. 12.95 (ISBN 0-7910-0174-1). Chelsea Hse.
Russia. Donald Wallace. LC 73-112349. Repr. of 1877 ed. 27.50 (ISBN 0-404-06809-X). AMS Pr.
Russia: A History of the Soviet Period. Woodford McClellan. (Illus.). 416p. 1986. pap. text ed. write for info. (ISBN 0-13-784455-7). P-H.
Russia: A History to 1917. Abraham Resnick. LC 83-7369. (Enchantment of the World Ser.). (Illus.). 128p. (gr. 5-8). 1983. PLB 22.60 (ISBN 0-516-02785-9). Childrens.
Russia: A Social History. D. Mirsky. Ed. by C. G. Seligman. LC 83-26517. (Illus.). 312p. 1983. lib. bdg. 41.55 (ISBN 0-313-24296-8, MRUS). Greenwood.
Russia Against Japan, Nineteen Hundred Four to Nineteen Hundred Five: A New Look at the Russo-Japanese War. J. N. Westwood. LC 85-22112. 183p. 1986. 34.50x (ISBN 0-88706-191-5). State U NY Pr.
Russia, America, the Bomb & the Fall of Western Europe. Brian May. 260p. 1984. 19.95x (ISBN 0-7100-9757-3). Routledge Chapman & Hall.
Russia: An Architecture for World Revolution. El Lissitzky. Tr. by Eric Dluhosch from Rus. (Illus.). 240p. 1970. pap. 7.95 (ISBN 0-262-62047-2). MIT Pr.
Russia & America: A Philosophical Comparison. new ed. William J. Gavin & Thomas J. Blakeley. (Sovietica Ser: No. 38). 1976. lib. bdg. 24.00 (ISBN 90-277-0749-9, Pub. by Reidel Holland). Kluwer Academic.
Russia & America: The Roots of Economic Divergence. Colin White. 272p. 1987. lib. bdg. 39.95x (ISBN 0-7099-5246-5, Pub. by Croom Helm UK). Routledge Chapman & Hall.
Russia & Arabia: Soviet Foreign Policy Toward the Arabian Peninsula. Mark N. Katz. LC 85-45046. 296p. 1986. text ed. 32.50x (ISBN 0-8018-2897-X). Johns Hopkins.
Russia & Asia. Andrei A. Lobanov-Rostovsky. 1951. 10.00x (ISBN 0-685-21802-3). Wahr.
Russia & Black Africa Before World War II. Edward Wilson. LC 73-84939. 300p. 1974. 42.50 (ISBN 0-8419-0109-0). Holmes & Meier.
Russia & China: Their Diplomatic Relations to 1728. Mark Mancall. LC 74-85077. (Harvard East Asian Ser.: No. 61). 412p. pap. 107.20 (2029993). Bks Demand UMI.
Russia & Europe Eighteen Twenty-Five to Eighteen Seventy-Eight. Andrei A. Lobanov-Rostovsky. 1954. 10.00x (ISBN 0-685-21803-1). Wahr.
Russia & Iran, Seventeen Eighty to Eighteen Twenty-Eight. Muriel Atkin. LC 80-10391. (Illus.). 1980. 20.00x (ISBN 0-8166-0924-1). U of Minn Pr.
Russia & Nationalism in Central Asia: The Case of Tadzhikistan. Published in Cooperation with the Institute for Sino-Soviet Studies, the George Washington University. Teresa Rakowska-Harmstone. LC 69-13722. pap. 85.50 (ISBN 0-317-41760-6, 2025866). Bks Demand UMI.
Russia & Postwar Europe. David J. Dallin. 1943. 39.50x (ISBN 0-685-69808-4). Elliots Bks.
Russia & Reform. Bernard Pares. LC 73-849. (Russian Studies: Perspectives on the Revolution Ser.). 576p. 1973. Repr. of 1907 ed. 41.25 (ISBN 0-88355-046-6). Hyperion Conn.
Russia & the American Revolution. Nikolai Bolkhovitinov. Tr. by C. Jay Smith from Rus. LC 74-42220. 277p. 1976. 29.70 (ISBN 0-910512-20-5). Diplomatic IN.
Russia & the Austrian State Treaty: A Case Study of Soviet Policy in Europe. Sven Allard. LC 68-8176. 1970. 24.50x (ISBN 0-271-00083-X). Pa St U Pr.
Russia & the Balkan Alliance of Nineteen Twelve. Edward C. Thaden. LC 64-8086. 1965. 22.50x (ISBN 0-271-73099-4). Pa St U Pr.
Russia & the Balkans: Inter-Balkan Rivalries & Russian Foreign Policy, 1908 -1914. Andrew Rossos. LC 81-142342. pap. 81.80 (2026405). Bks Demand UMI.
Russia & the Cholera, Eighteen Twenty-Three to Eighteen Thirty-Two. Roderick E. McGrew. (Illus.). 240p. 1965. 27.50x (ISBN 0-299-03710-X). U of Wis Pr.
Russia & the First Serbian Revolution, 1804-1813. Lawerence P. Meriage. Ed. by William H. McNeill & Barbara Jelavich. (Modern European History Ser.). 300p. 1987. lib. bdg. 45.00 (ISBN 0-8240-8058-0). Garland Pub.
Russia & the Formation of the Romanian Empire: 1821 to 1878. Barbara Jelavich. LC 82-23578. (Illus.). 360p. 1984. 52.50 (ISBN 0-521-25318-7). Cambridge U Pr.
Russia & the Golden Horde: The Mongol Impact on Medieval Russian History. Charles J. Halperin. LC 84-48254. (Illus.). 192p. 1985. 22.50x (ISBN 0-253-35033-6); pap. 7.95x (ISBN 0-253-20445-3, MB-445). Ind U Pr.
Russia & the Khanates of Central Asia to 1865. John L. Evans. LC 81-68026. 148p. (Orig.). 1982. pap. text ed. 15.00x (ISBN 0-86733-014-7). Assoc Faculty Pr.
Russia & the Mediterranean 1797-1807. Norman E. Saul. LC 72-96755. 1970. 22.00x (ISBN 0-226-73540-0). U of Chicago Pr.
Russia & the Negro: Blacks in Russian History & Thought. Allison Blakely. LC 85-5251. (Illus.). 224p. 1987. 17.95 (ISBN 0-88258-146-5). Howard U Pr.
Russia & the Origins of the First World War. D. C. Lieven. LC 82-24095. (The Making of the Twentieth Century Ser.). 225p. 1984. 27.50 (ISBN 0-312-69608-6); pap. 10.50 (ISBN 0-312-69611-6). St Martin.
Russia & the Road to Appeasement: Cycles of East-West Conflict in War & Peace. George Liska. LC 81-48188. 288p. 1982. text ed. 32.50x (ISBN 0-8018-2763-9). Johns Hopkins.
Russia & the Roots of the Chinese Revolution, 1896-1911. Don C. Price. LC 74-80443. (East Asian Monographs: No. 79). 256p. 1974. text ed. 21.00x (ISBN 0-674-78320-4). Harvard U Pr.
Russia & the Rumanian National Cause, 1858-1859. Barbara Jelavich. xv, 169p. 1974. Repr. of 1959 ed. 20.00 (ISBN 0-208-01430-6, Archon). Shoe String.
Russia & the Russians: Inside the Closed Society. Kevin Klose. 352p. 1986. pap. 9.95 (ISBN 0-393-30312-8). Norton.
Russia & the Soviet Union. John M. Thompson. 437p. 1985. text ed. write for info. (ISBN 0-02-420720-9). Macmillan.
Russia & the Soviet Union: A Bibliographic Guide to Western-Language Publications. Ed. by Paul L. Horecky. LC 65-12041. 1965. 35.00x (ISBN 0-226-35186-6). U of Chicago Pr.
Russia & the Soviet Union in the Far East. Victor A. Yakhontov. LC 73-861. (Russian Studies: Perspectives on the Revolution Ser.). (Illus.). 454p. 1973. Repr. of 1931 ed. 32.45 (ISBN 0-88355-057-1). Hyperion Conn.
Russia & the United States. Nikolai V. Sivachev & Nikolai N. Yakovlev. Tr. by Olga A. Titelbaum. LC 78-10554. (U. S. in the World: Foreign World Perspectives Ser). 1979. 20.00x (ISBN 0-226-76149-5); pap. 11.00x (ISBN 0-226-76150-9, P902, Phoen). U of Chicago Pr.
Russia & the United States: An Analytical Survey of Archival Documents & Historical Studies. N. N. Bolkhovitinov. Ed. & tr. by J. Dane Hartgrove. (Illus.). 112p. (Orig.). pap. 16.95 (ISBN 0-87332-414-5). M E Sharpe.
Russia & the West: Gorbachev & the Politics of Reform. Jerry F. Hough. 272p. 1988. 19.95 (ISBN 0-671-61839-3). S&S.
Russia & the West in Iran, 1918-1948: A Study in Big Power Rivalry. George Lenczowski. LC 68-23307. (Illus.). 1968. Repr. of 1949 ed. lib. bdg. 41.50x (ISBN 0-8371-0144-1, LERW). Greenwood.
Russia & the West in the Eighteenth Century. Ed. by A. G. Cross. (Illus.). 371p. 1983. 36.00. Orient Res Partners.
Russia & the West in the Teaching of the Slavophiles. Nicholas Riasanovsky. 11.75 (ISBN 0-8446-1383-5). Peter Smith.
Russia & the West under Lenin & Stalin. George F. Kennan. pap. 4.95 (ISBN 0-451-62460-2, ME2326, Ment). NAL.
Russia & the World of the Eighteenth Century. Ed. by R. P. Bartlett et al. (Illus.). viii, 684p. 1988. 34.95 (ISBN 0-89357-186-5). Slavica.
Russia & World Order: Strategic Choices & the Laws of Power in History. George Liska. LC 79-22872. 1980. 14.50x (ISBN 0-8018-2314-5). Johns Hopkins.
Russia & World Order: Strategic Choices & the Laws of Power in History. George Liska. LC 79-22872. pap. 52.00 (ISBN 0-317-20468-8, 2023001). Bks Demand UMI.
Russia As State-Capitalist Society: The Original Historical Analysis. Raya Dunayevskaya. 27p. (Orig.). 1973. pap. 1.00x (ISBN 0-914441-23-X). News & Letters.
Russia at the Close of the Sixteenth Century. Giles Fletcher. Ed. by Augustus Bond. (Hakluyt Soc., First Ser Publ.: Vol. 20). 32.00 (ISBN 0-8337-0334-X). B Franklin.
Russia at the Crossroads: The Twenty-Sixth Congress of the CPSU. Ed. by Seweryn Bialer & Thane Gustafson. 256p. 1982. text ed. 34.95x (ISBN 0-04-329039-6). Unwin Hyman.
Russia at War. Alexander Werth. 1136p. 1984. pap. 15.95 (ISBN 0-88184-084-X). Carroll & Graf.
Russia at War: Nineteen Forty-One to Nineteen Forty-Five. Vladimir Karpov. (Illus.). 256p. 1987. 30.00 (ISBN 0-317-66280-5). Vendome.
Russia Besieged. Nicholas Bethell & Time-Life Books Editors. (World War II Ser.). 1977. 14.95 (ISBN 0-8094-2470-3). Time-Life.
Russia: Broken Idols, Solemn Dreams. David K. Shipler. LC 83-45042. 404p. 1983. 17.95 (ISBN 0-8129-1080-X). Times Bks.
Russia: Broken Idols, Solemn Dreams. David K. Shipler. (Penguin Nonfiction Ser.). 416p. 1984. pap. 7.95 (ISBN 0-14-007408-2). Penguin.
Russia: By a Recent Traveler. Charles H. Pearson. (Russia Through European Eyes Ser). 1971. Repr. of 1859 ed. lib. bdg. 39.50 (ISBN 0-306-77030-X). Da Capo.
Russia Complex: The British Labour Party & the Soviet Union. Bill Jones. 229p. 1977. 24.50x (ISBN 0-8476-6082-6). Rowman.
Russia from the American Embassy April, 1916 - November, 1918. David R. Francis. LC 78-115537. (Russia Observed, Series I). 1970. Repr. of 1921 ed. 24.50 (ISBN 0-405-03026-6). Ayer Co Pubs.
Russia Gathers Her Jews: The Origins of the "Jewish Question" in Russia, 1772-1825. John Klier. LC 86-2473. 1986. 28.00 (ISBN 0-87580-117-X). N Ill U Pr.
Russia in Asia: 1558-1899. Alexis Krausse. LC 76-27537. (Illus.). 1976. Repr. of 1899 ed. lib. bdg. 40.00 (ISBN 0-89341-045-4). Longwood Pub Group.
Russia in Central Asia in 1889 & the Anglo-Russian Question. new ed. George N. Curzon. (Illus.). 477p. 1967. 39.50x (ISBN 0-7146-1465-3, F Cass Co). Biblio Dist.
Russia in Flux. John Maynard. Ed. by S. Haden Guest. LC 83-45812. Repr. of 1948 ed. 48.50 (ISBN 0-404-20173-3). AMS Pr.
Russia in the Age of Catherine the Great. Isabel De Madariaga. LC 80-21993. 710p. 1982. 55.00x (ISBN 0-300-02515-7, Y-419); pap. 17.95x (ISBN 0-300-02843-1). Yale U Pr.
Russia in the Age of Enlightenment. Erich Donnert. (Illus.). 288p. 1987. 25.00 (ISBN 0-87052-393-7). Hippocrene Bks.
Russia in the Age of Modernisation & Revolution: 1881-1917. Hans Rogger. LC 83-714. (History of Russia Ser.). 323p. (Orig.). 1983. pap. 16.95 (ISBN 0-582-48912-1). Longman.
Russia in the Economic War (Economic & Social History of the World War) Boris E. Nolde. 1928. 85.00x (ISBN 0-686-51304-5). Elliots Bks.
Russia in the Far East. Leo Pasvolsky. LC 79-2918. 181p. 1981. Repr. of 1922 ed. 19.25 (ISBN 0-8305-0087-1). Hyperion Conn.
Russia in the Reign of Aleksej Mixajlovic: Text & Commentary. Grigorij Kotosixin. Ed. by A. E. Pennington. (Illus.). 1980. 145.00x (ISBN 0-19-815639-1). Oxford U Pr.
Russia in the Shadows. H. G. Wells. LC 73-858. (Russian Studies: Perspectives on the Revolution Ser.). (Illus.). 179p. 1973. Repr. of 1921 ed. 18.35 (ISBN 0-88355-055-5). Hyperion Conn.
Russia in the Twentieth Century: The Catalog of the Bakhmeteff Archive of Russian & East European History & Culture, the Rare Book & Manuscript Library, Columbia University. (Library Catalogs). 200p. 1987. lib. bdg. 100.00 (ISBN 0-8161-0462-X, Hall Library). G K Hall.
Russia in the Works of Rainer Maria Rilke. Patricia P. Brodsky. LC 84-75570. 264p. 1984. 29.95x (ISBN 0-8143-1757-X). Wayne St U Pr.

Russian Church under the Soviet Regime. Dimitry Pospielovsky. 533p. Set. 19.95 (ISBN 0-88141-033-0); Vol. I, 248 pgs. 10.95 (ISBN 0-88141-015-2); Vol. II, 285 pgs. 10.95 (ISBN 0-88141-016-0). St Vladimirs.

Russian Civil War. Evan Mawdsley. (Illus.). 320p. 1987. text ed. 14.95x (ISBN 0-04-947024-8); pap. text ed. 45.00x (ISBN 0-04-947025-6). Unwin Hyman.

Russian Civil War Diary: Alexis V. Babine in Saratov, 1917-1922. Ed. by Donald J. Raleigh. LC 88-3967. (Illus.). 264p. 1988. lib. bdg. 29.95 (ISBN 0-8223-0835-5). Duke.

Russian Civilization. David A. Law. (Illus.). 490p. 1975. 39.50x (ISBN 0-8422-5232-0); pap. text ed. 12.50x (ISBN 0-8422-0529-2). Irvington.

Russian Civilization & the Life of the Russian Common People. Marco Vovchock. 171p. 1984. 88.45x (ISBN 0-86722-091-0). Inst Econ Pol.

Russian Clergy. Jean X. Gagarin. LC 70-131035. Repr. of 1872 ed. 21.00 (ISBN 0-404-02666-4). AMS Pr.

Russian Colonial Expansion to 1917. Ed. by Michael Rywkin. LC 84-71094. (Issue Studies (U. S. S. R. & East Europe): No. 4). 250p. 1987. 25.00 (ISBN 0-910895-01-5). Assn Study Nat.

Russian Colonization of Kazakhstan, 1896-1916. George J. Demko. LC 67-66166. (Uralic & Altaic Ser.: No. 99). 271p. (Orig.). 1969. pap. text ed. 10.50x (ISBN 0-87750-082-7). Res Ctr Lang Semiotic.

Russian Comedy of Errors: With Other Stories & Sketches of Russian Life. George Kennan. LC 72-11847. (Short Story Index Reprint Ser). 1973. Repr. of 1915 ed. 23.50 (ISBN 0-8369-4238-8). Ayer Co Pubs.

Russian Comic Fiction. Guy Daniels. LC 85-22208. 208p. 1986. pap. 7.50 (ISBN 0-8052-0815-1). Schocken.

Russian Communism. William H. Wilbur. LC 64-17829. 1964. 5.95 (ISBN 0-87004-173-8). Caxton.

Russian Communist Party & the Sovietization of Ukraine: A Study in the Communist Doctrine of the Self-Determination of Nations. Jurij Borys. LC 79-2895. 374p. 1983. Repr. of 1960 ed. 56.50 (ISBN 0-8305-0063-4). Hyperion Conn.

Russian Community Reference Guide. 48p. 1980. pap. write for info (ISBN 0-935090-04-5). Almanac Pr.

Russian Community Reference Guide. 78p. 1984. pap. write for info (ISBN 0-935090-12-6). Almanac Pr.

Russian Community Reference Guide. 96p. 1985. pap. write for info (ISBN 0-935090-15-0). Almanac Pr.

Russian Composers & Musicians: A Biographical Dictionary. Ed. by Alexandria Vodorsky-Shiraeff. LC 71-76422. (Music Ser.). 1969. Repr. of 1940 ed. lib. bdg. 25.00 (ISBN 0-306-71321-7). Da Capo.

Russian Conquest of the Caucasus. John F. Baddeley. LC 78-75459. (Illus.). 518p. 1969. Repr. of 1908 ed. 17.50x (ISBN 0-8462-1331-1). Russell.

Russian Constitution of April 23, 1906: Political Institutions of the Duma Monarchy. Marc Szeftel. 517p. 1982. 39.45. P Lang Pubs.

Russian Constitutional Experiment: Government & Duma, 1907-1914. Geoffrey A. Hosking. LC 72-87181. (Soviet & East European Studies). pap. 72.80 (ISBN 0-317-28403-7, 2022456). Bks Demand UMI.

Russian Constructivism. Christina Lodder. LC 83-40002. (Illus.). 328p. 1985. pap. text ed. 17.95x (ISBN 0-300-03406-7, Y-516). Yale U Pr.

Russian Consular Records Index & Catalog. Sallyann A. Sack. LC 86-31981. (Garland Reference Library of Social Science Ser.). 1987. lib. bdg. 121.00 (ISBN 0-8240-8467-5). Garland Pub.

Russian Convoys 1941-1945. (Warships Illustrated Ser.: No. 9). (Illus.). 64p. (Orig.). 1987. pap. 9.95 (ISBN 0-85368-773-0, Pub. by Arms & Armour). Sterling.

Russian Cooking. Miyo Nagaya. (Golden Cooking Card Bk.). (Illus.). 42p. (Orig.). 1973. pap. 3.95 (ISBN 4-07-973642-8, Pub. by Shufunmoto Co Ltd Japan). C E Tuttle.

Russian Course: Teacher's Manual. Steven J. Molinsky. (Illus.). 222p. (Orig.). 1981. pap. 9.95 (ISBN 0-89357-083-4). Slavica.

Russian Course: 1981 Edition, Pt. 1. Alexander Lipson. (Illus.). ix, 338p. (Orig.). 1981. pap. text ed. 12.95 (ISBN 0-89357-080-X). Slavica.

Russian Course: 1981 Edition, Pt. 2. Alexander Lipson. (Illus.). 343p. (Orig.). 1981. pap. text ed. 12.95 (ISBN 0-89357-081-8). Slavica.

Russian Course: 1981 Edition, Pt. 3. Alexander Lipson. (Illus.). iv, 105p. (Orig.). 1981. pap. text ed. 9.95 (ISBN 0-89357-082-6). Slavica.

Russian Crucifix. Richard Freeborn. 258p. 1987. 16.95 (ISBN 0-312-01156-3, Pub. by Thomas Dunne Bks). St Martin.

Russian Cubo-Futurism, 1910-1930: A Study in Avant-Gardism. Vahan D. Barooshian. LC 73-81271. (De Proprietatibus Litterarum, Ser. Major: No. 24). 176p. 1974. text ed. 19.20x (ISBN 90-2792-659-X). Mouton.

Russian Cultural Revival: A Critical Anthology of Russian Emigre Literature Before Nineteen Thirty-Nine. Temira Pachmuss. LC 80-20670. 476p. 1981. 38.95x (ISBN 0-87049-296-9); pap. 18.95x (ISBN 0-87049-306-X). U of Tenn Pr.

Russian Culture in the 1980's. Maurice Friedberg. (Significant Issues Ser.: Vol. VII, No. 6). 87p. 1985. pap. 8.95 (ISBN 0-89206-083-2). CSI Studies.

Russian Culture in the 1980s. Maurice Friedberg. (Significant Issues Ser.: Vol. VII, No. 6). 96p. (Orig.). 1985. pap. text ed. 6.95 (ISBN 0-8191-5938-7, Pub. by CSIS). U Pr of Amer.

Russian-Czechoslovakian Dictionary. Vlchek. 896p. (Rus. & Czech.). 1974. 29.95 (ISBN 0-686-92111-9, M-9116). French & Eur.

Russian-Czechoslovakian Polytechnical Dictionary. V. S. Petrov & S. A. Tulin. 639p. (Rus. & Czech.). 1962. leatherette 49.95 (ISBN 0-686-92116-X, M-9074). French & Eur.

Russian Debts & Russian Reconstruction: A Study of the Relation of Russia's Foreign Debts to Her Economic Recovery. Leo Pasvolsky & Harold G. Moulton. LC 24-12018. 1971. Repr. of 1924 ed. 24.00 (ISBN 0-384-45070-9). Johnson Repr.

Russian Declension & Conjugation: A Structural Sketch with Exercises. Maurice I. Levin. x, 159p. 1978. softcover 10.95 (ISBN 0-89357-048-6). Slavica.

Russian Decorative & Applied Art in the Collection of the Pavlovsk Palace Museum. 380p. 1981. 115.00x (ISBN 0-317-14291-7, Pub. by Collets (UK)). State Mutual Bk.

Russian Democracy's Fatal Blunder: The Summer Offensive of 1917. Louise E. Heenan. LC 87-12505. 224p. 1987. lib. bdg. 37.95 (ISBN 0-275-92829-2, C2829). Praeger.

Russian Desubstantival Derivation: A Paradigmatic View. Richard D. Schupbach. (Studia Linguistica et Philologica: No. 2). 1977. pap. 29.50 (ISBN 0-915838-41-9). Anma Libri.

Russian Dilemma. 2nd, rev. ed. Robert Wesson. LC 85-16742. 206p. 1985. 35.00 (ISBN 0-275-90234-X, C0234); pap. 13.95 (ISBN 0-275-91677-4, B1677). Praeger.

Russian Diplomatic & Consular Officials in East Asia. Ed. by George A. Lensen. LC 68-26393. (Monumenta Nipponica Monograph Ser). 294p. 1968. 15.00 (ISBN 0-910512-06-X). Diplomatic IN.

Russian Discovery of Hawaii. Glynn Barratt. (Illus.). 259p. 1987. 27.50 (ISBN 0-915013-08-8). Editions Ltd.

Russian Dissenters. Frederick C. Conybeare. LC 79-2897. 370p. 1980. Repr. of 1921 ed. 29.25 (ISBN 0-8305-0068-5). Hyperion Conn.

Russian Doctor: A Surgeon's Life in Contemporary Russia & Why He Chose to Leave. Vladimir Golyakhovsky. (Illus.). 384p. 1983. 17.95 (ISBN 0-312-69609-4, Pub. by Marek). St Martin.

Russian Drama from Its Beginnings to the Age of Pushkin. Simon Karlinsky. LC 84-8442. 1985. 42.50x (ISBN 0-520-05237-4); pap. 12.95x (ISBN 0-520-05882-8). U of Cal Pr.

Russian Drama of the Revolutionary Period. Robert Russell. 192p. 1987. 28.50 (ISBN 0-389-20757-8). B&N Imports.

Russian Dramatic Theory from Pushkin to the Symbolists: An Anthology. Ed. & tr. by Laurence Senelick. (University of Texas Press Slavic Ser.: No. 5). 393p. 1981. text ed. 37.50x (ISBN 0-292-77025-1). U of Tex Pr.

Russian Drawings in the Ashmolean Museum. Larrissa Salmina-Haskell. 60p. 1984. 6.00x (ISBN 0-907849-08-3, Pub. by Ashmolean Museum). State Mutual Bk.

Russian Drawings of the Eighteenth Century: Russkii Risunok XVIII Veka. E. I. Gavrilova. 202p. 1983. 89.00x (ISBN 0-317-57444-2, Pub. by Collets UK). State Mutual Bk.

Russian Drinking: Use & Abuse of Alcohol in Pre-Revolutionary Russia. Boris M. Segal. LC 86-620003. (Monographs of the Rutgers Center of Alcohol Studies: No. 15). xx, 383p. 1987. 29.95x (ISBN 0-911290-18-4); pap. 19.95x (ISBN 0-911290-19-2). Rutgers Ctr Alcohol.

Russian Eagle: A History of Russia from Its Origins to the End of the Romanoff Dynasty. Louise C. Samoiloff. LC 85-18432. 1987. lib. bdg. 79.95 (ISBN 0-87700-866-3). Revisionist Pr.

Russian Ecclestastical Mission in Peking During the Eighteenth Century. Eric Widmer. (East Asian Monographs: No. 69). 1976. 21.00x (ISBN 0-674-78129-5). Harvard U Pr.

Russian Economic Development Since the Revolution. Maurice Dobb. (Business Enterprises Reprint Ser.). xii, 415p. 1986. Repr. of 1928 ed. lib. bdg. 38.00 (ISBN 0-89941-502-4). W S Hein.

Russian Economic History: A Guide to Information Sources. Ed. by Daniel R. Kazmer & Vera Kazmer. LC 73-17588. (Economics Information Guide Ser.: Vol. 4). 536p. 1977. 68.00x (ISBN 0-8103-1304-9). Gale.

Russian Elementary, Vol. 2. N. F. Potapova. pap. 22.50 (ISBN 0-317-02504-X, 070-4X). Saphrograph.

Russian Elementary Course, 2 Vols. 3rd ed. Nina Potapova. 1969. Vol. 1, 366p. 79.00 (ISBN 0-677-20890-1); Vol. 2, 488p. 90.00 (ISBN 0-677-20900-2). Gordon & Breach.

Russian Embroidery & Lace. L. Yefimova & R. Belogorskaya. LC 85-51460. (Illus.). 272p. 1987. 35.00f (ISBN 0-500-01358-6). Thames Hudson.

Russian Empire & Grand Duchy of Muscovy: A Seventeenth-Century French Account. Jacques Margeret. Ed. & tr. by Chester S. Dunning. LC 82-20126. (Illus.). 252p. 1983. 24.95x (ISBN 0-8229-3805-7). U of Pittsburgh Pr.

Russian Empire, Eighteen Hundred One to Nineteen Seventeen. Hugh Seton-Watson. (History of Modern Europe Ser.). (Illus.). 840p. 1988. pap. 29.95 (ISBN 0-19-822152-5). Oxford U Pr.

Russian Empire: Its People, Institutions & Resources, 2 vols. Baron Von Haxthausen. (Russia Through European Eyes Ser.). 1968. Repr. of 1856 ed. Set. lib. bdg. 125.00 (ISBN 0-306-77024-5). Da Capo.

Russian Empire, Its People, Institutions, & Resources. Franz A. Von Haxthausen. LC 78-115545. (Russia Observed, Series I). 1970. Repr. of 1856 ed. 42.00 (ISBN 0-405-03033-9). Ayer Co Pubs.

Russian Empire, 1801-1917. Hugh Seton-Watson. (Oxford History of Modern Europe Ser). 1967. 59.00x (ISBN 0-19-822103-7). Oxford U Pr.

Russian-English & English-Russian Dictionary. O. P. Benyuch & G. V. Chernov. (Concise Dictionaries Ser.). 640p. 1987. pap. 9.95 (ISBN 0-87052-336-8). Hippocrene Bks.

Russian-English & English-Russian Dictionary. W. Harrison & Svetlana LeFlemming. (Routledge Pocket Dictionaries Ser.). 580p. (Orig.). 1981. pap. 8.95 (ISBN 0-7100-0800-7). Routledge Chapman & Hall.

Russian-English Atomic Dictionary: Physics, Mathematics, Nucleonics. rev. ed. 2nd ed. Eugene A. Carpovich. LC 57-8256. (Rus. & Eng.). 1959. 15.00 (ISBN 0-911484-00-0). Tech Dict.

Russian-English Biological & Medical Dictionary. 2nd ed. Eugene A. Carpovich. LC 58-7915. (Rus. & Eng.). 1960. 25.00 (ISBN 0-911484-01-9). Tech Dict.

Russian-English Botanical Dictionary. Paul Macura. 678p. (Rus. & Eng.). 1982. 49.95 (ISBN 0-89357-092-3). Slavica.

Russian English Chemical & Polytechnical Dictionary. 4th ed. Callaham. 1990. price not set (ISBN 0-471-61139-5). Wiley.

Russian-English Chemical & Polytechnical Dictionary. 3rd ed. Ludmilla I. Callaham. LC 75-5982. 852p. (Rus. & Eng.). 1975. 69.95x (ISBN 0-471-12998-4, Pub. by Wiley-Interscience). Wiley.

Russian-English Chemical Dictionary. 2nd ed. Eugene A. Carpovich. LC 61-11700. (Rus. & Eng.). 1963. 25.00 (ISBN 0-911484-03-5). Tech Dict.

Russian-English Dictionaries with Aids for Translators: A Selected Bibliography. Wojciech Zalewski. LC 81-50870. (Bibliography Ser.: No. 1). 101p. (Orig.). 1981. pap. 7.50 (ISBN 0-89830-041-X). Russica Pubs.

Russian-English Dictionary. O. S. Akhmanova & E. Wilson. 416p. (Rus. & Eng.). 1985. 39.00x (ISBN 0-317-59424-9, Pub. by Collets (UK)). State Mutual Bk.

Russian-English Dictionary. O. S. Akmanova & E. A. Wilson. 521p. (Rus. & Eng.). 1974. 4.45 (ISBN 0-8285-0607-8, Pub. by Rus Lang Pubs USSR). Imported Pubns.

Russian-English Dictionary. A. S. Romanov. pap. 4.95 (ISBN 0-317-56743-8). PB.

Russian-English Dictionary. A. I. Smirnitskii. 766p. (Rus. & Eng.). 1978. 70.00x (ISBN 0-317-59423-0, Pub. by Collets (UK)). State Mutual Bk.

Russian-English Dictionary. T. Smirnitskii. 766p. (Rus. & Eng.). 1980. 60.00x (ISBN 0-569-00006-8, Pub. by Collets (UK)). State Mutual Bk.

Russian-English Dictionary. 3rd ed. A. I. Smirnitsky. large ed. 35.00 (ISBN 0-87557-066-6, 066-6). Saphrograph.

Russian-English Dictionary. A. I. Smirnitsky. 766p. (Eng. & Rus.). 1987. 19.95 (ISBN 0-8285-0608-6, Pub. by Rus Lang Pubs USSR). Imported Pubns.

Russian-English Dictionary. A. M. Taube. 832p. (Rus. & Eng.). 1980. vinyl bds. 39.00x (ISBN 0-569-06453-8, Pub. by Collets (UK)). State Mutual Bk.

Russian-English Dictionary. A. M. Taube. 832p. (Rus. & Eng.). 1982. 70.00x (ISBN 0-317-59421-4, Pub. by Collets (UK)). State Mutual Bk.

Russian-English Dictionary. A. M. Taube et al. Ed. by R. C. Daglish. 831p. (Rus. & Eng.). 1978. leatherette 24.95 (ISBN 0-686-92120-8, M-9108). French & Eur.

Russian-English Dictionary. A. M. Taube et al. 831p. (Rus. & Eng.). 1978. 14.50 (ISBN 0-8285-0609-4, Pub. by Rus Lang Pubs USSR). Imported Pubns.

Russian-English Dictionary of Electrotechnology & Applied Sciences. Paul Macura. LC 85-8653. 840p. 1986. Repr. of 1971 ed. lib. bdg. 65.00 (ISBN 0-89874-869-0). Krieger.

Russian-English Dictionary of Modern Terms in Aeronautics & Rocketry. M. M. Konarski. (Rus. & Eng.). 1962. 130.00 (ISBN 0-08-009658-1). Pergamon.

Russian-English Dictionary of Prestressed Concrete & Concrete Construction. Ed. by Ben C. Gerwick, Jr. & V. P. Peters. 120p. (Rus. & Eng.). 1966. 55.00 (ISBN 0-677-00260-2). Gordon & Breach.

Russian-English Dictionary of Scientific & Technical Usage. B. V. Kuznetsov. 500p. 1987. 110.00 (ISBN 0-08-032551-3, PBL). Pergamon.

Russian-English Dictionary of Sports Terms & Phrases. A. V. Gavrilovets. (Rus. & Eng.). 40.00x (ISBN 0-569-08607-8, Pub. by Collets (UK)). State Mutual Bk.

Russian-English Dictionary of Sports Terms & Phrases. Y. G. Nevsky & A. V. Gorovoy. 224p. 1983. 30.00x (ISBN 0-317-39527-0, Pub. by Collets (UK)). State Mutual Bk.

Russian-English Dictionary of Sports Terms & Phrases. Russkii Yazyk. 352p. (Rus. & Eng.). 1980. pap. 26.00x (ISBN 0-686-72092-X, Pub. by Collets (UK)). State Mutual Bk.

Russian-English Dictionary of the Mathematical Sciences. A. J. Lohwater. LC 61-15685. 267p. (Eng. & Rus.). 1982. pap. 20.00 (ISBN 0-8218-0036-1, RED). Am Math.

Russian-English English-Russian Dictionary. S. G. Zaimovsky. 12.50 (ISBN 0-87557-069-0). Saphrograph.

Russian-English Geological Dictionary. 559p. 1983. 18.95 (ISBN 0-317-02600-3). Am Geol.

Russian-English Mathematical Dictionary: Words & Phrases in Pure & Applied Mathematics with Roots & Accents, Arranged for Easy Reference. Louis M. Milne-Thomson. LC 62-7217. (Mathematics Research Center, United States Army, University of Wisconsin Publication: No. 7). pap. 51.30 (ISBN 0-317-28131-3, 2055742). Bks Demand UMI.

Russian-English Metals & Machines Dictionary. Eugene A. Carpovich. LC 60-12013. (Rus. & Eng.). 1960. 15.00x (ISBN 0-911484-02-7). Tech Dict.

Russian-English Oil-Field Dictionary. Ed. by D. E. Stoliarov. 432p. (Rus. & Eng.). 1983. 36.00 (ISBN 0-08-028169-9). Pergamon.

Russian-English Phrase-Book for Physicists. L. A. Smirnova. 336p. 1968. 19.95leatherette (ISBN 0-686-92126-7, M-9109). French & Eur.

Russian-English Plastics Dictionary: Reversed From an English-Russian Dictionary by Computer Processing. Ed. by Harry H. Josselson. LC 76-99790. (Autolex Series of Scientific & Technical Dictionaries: No. 1). Repr. of 1970 ed. 79.00 (2027607). Bks Demand UMI.

Russian-English Pocket Dictionary. O. P. Beniukh & G. V. Chernov. 286p. (Rus. & Eng.). 1984. 40.00x (ISBN 0-317-59425-7, Pub. by Collets (UK)). State Mutual Bk.

Russian-English Polytechnical Dictionary. Ed. by B. Kuznetsov. LC 80-41193. 900p. (Rus. & Eng.). 1981. 145.00 (ISBN 0-08-023609-X). Pergamon.

Russian-English Polytechnical Dictionary. B. V. Kuznetzov. 723p. (Rus. & Eng.). 1981. 30.00 (ISBN 0-8285-1851-3, Pub. by Rus Lang Pubs USSR). Imported Pubns.

Russian-English Scientific & Technical Dictionary, 2 vols. M. H. Alford & V. L. Alford. LC 73-88348. (Rus. & Eng.). 1970. Set. 99.50 (ISBN 0-08-012227-2). Pergamon.

Russian-English Scientific & Technical Dictionary of Useful Combinations & Expressions. M. G. Zimmerman. (Rus. & Eng.). 27.50 (ISBN 0-87559-119-1); thumb indexed 32.50 (ISBN 0-87559-140-X). Shalom.

Russian-English Space Technology Dictionary. M. M. Konarski. LC 72-99990. (Rus. & Eng.). 1970. 110.00 (ISBN 0-08-015617-7). Pergamon.

Russian-English Technical Dictionary of Defects & Breakdowns. N. N. Levinskii & G. A. Mkrtchian. 334p. 1985. 59.00x (ISBN 0-317-42707-5, Pub. by Collets (UK)). State Mutual Bk.

Russian-English Translators Dictionary: A Guide to Scientific & Technical Usage. 2nd ed. Mikhail Zimmerman. LC 83-10229. 544p. 1984. 87.95 (ISBN 0-471-90218-7, Pub. by Wiley-Interscience). Wiley.

Russian-English Translators Dictionary: A Guide to Scientific & Technical Usage. Mikhail G. Zimmerman. LC 67-19391. pap. 73.30 (ISBN 0-317-27885-1, 2055793). Bks Demand UMI.

Russian-English Vocabulary with Grammatical Sketch. Ed. by Gabrielle Rainich & A. H. Kuipers. 66p. (Rus. & Eng.). 1980. pap. 12.00 (ISBN 0-8218-0037-X, REV). Am Math.

Russian Engravings of the Late Seventeenth & Eighteenth Centuries. M. I. Flekel. 1983. 347.00x (ISBN 0-317-61371-5, Pub. by Collets (UK)). State Mutual Bk.

Russian Engravings of the Late Seventeenth & Eighteenth Centuries: Russkaia Graviur Kontsa XVIII Veka. 1983. 297.00x (ISBN 0-317-57445-0, Pub. by Collets UK). State Mutual Bk.

Russian Enigma. Ante Ciliga. Tr. by Fernand G. Fernier et al from Fr. Orig. Title: Au pays du grand mensonge, Siberie, terre de l'exil et du grand mensonge. 573p. 1979. 22.95 (Pub. by Ink Links Ltd); pap. 11.95 (Pub. by Ink Links Ltd). Longwood Pub Group.

Russian Enigma. Anton Ciliga. Tr. by Fernand G. Renier & Anne Cliff. LC 73-836. (Russian Studies: Perspectives on the Revolution Ser.). xi, 304p. 1973. Repr. of 1940 ed. 25.85 (ISBN 0-88355-032-6). Hyperion Conn.

Russian Epic Studies. Roman Jakobson & Ernest J. Simmons. LC 50-5215. (American Folklore Society Memoirs). Repr. of 1949 ed. 23.00 (ISBN 0-527-01094-4). Kraus Repr.

Russian European: Paul Miliukov in Russian Politics. Thomas Riha. LC 68-27582. pap. 97.80 (ISBN 0-317-55789-0, 2029312). Bks Demand UMI.

Russian Literature & Modern English Fiction: A Collection of Critical Essays. Ed. by Donald Davie. LC 65-18337. (Patterns of Literary Criticism Ser.). pap. 62.50 (ISBN 0-317-09846-2, 2020052). Bks Demand UMI.

Russian Literature from Pushkin to the Present Day. facs. ed. Richard Hare. LC 76-126237. (Select Bibliographies Reprint Ser). 1947. 16.00 (ISBN 0-8369-5463-7). Ayer Co Pubs.

Russian Literature in the Baltic Between the World Wars. Temira Pachmuss. 448p. 1988. 24.95 (ISBN 0-89357-181-4). Slavica.

Russian Literature of the Twenties: An Anthology. Ed. by Carl R. Proffer et al. 1987. 39.50 (ISBN 0-317-66502-2); pap. 18.00 (ISBN 0-317-66503-0). Ardis Pubs.

Russian Literature Since the Revolution. Rev. & Enl. ed. Edward J. Brown. (Illus.). 400p. 1982. text ed. 32.00x (ISBN 0-674-78203-8); pap. text ed. 10.95x (ISBN 0-674-78204-6). Harvard U Pr.

Russian Local Government During the War & the Union of Zemstvos. Tikhon J. Polner et al. (Economic & Social History of the World War, Russian Ser.). 1930. 100.00x (ISBN 0-317-27559-3). Elliots Bks.

Russian Looks at America: The Journey of Aleksandr Borisovich Lakier in 1857. Aleksandr B. Lakier. Ed. by Arnold Schrier & Joyce Story. LC 79-11205. 1979. 15.95x (ISBN 0-226-46795-3). U of Chicago Pr.

Russian Martyr. Ivan V. Moiseyev. 0.95 (ISBN 0-89985-107-X). Christ Nations.

Russian Marxists & the Origins of Bolshevism. Leopold H. Haimson. LC 55-10972. (Russian Research Center Studies: No. 19). pap. 49.40 (ISBN 0-317-09492-0, 2003777). Bks Demand UMI.

Russian Master & Other Stories. Anton Chekhov. Tr. by Ronald Hingley from Rus. (World's Classics Ser.). 1984. pap. 3.95 (ISBN 0-19-281680-2). Oxford U Pr.

Russian Medicine. William A. Gantt. LC 75-23669. (Clio Medica: 20). (Illus.). 1978. Repr. of 1937 ed. 28.50 (ISBN 0-404-58920-0). AMS Pr.

Russian Memoirs of John Quincy Adams: His Diary from 1809 to 1814. Ed. by Charles F. Adams. LC 74-115501. (Russia Observed, Series 1). 1970. Repr. of 1874 ed. 26.50 (ISBN 0-405-03001-0). Ayer Co Pubs.

Russian Metaphysical Romanticism: The Poetry of Tiutchev & Boratynskii. Sarah Pratt. LC 82-42863. 272p. 1984. 35.00x (ISBN 0-8047-1188-7). Stanford U Pr.

Russian Military History. Jones. 1985. lib. bdg. 40.00 (ISBN 0-8240-8924-3). Garland Pub.

Russian Miniature Portraits, 18th-Early 20th Century from the Hermitage Collection. Ed. by G. N. Komelova. 336p. 1986. 25.00 (ISBN 0-8285-3572-8, Pub. by Khudozhnik Pubs USSR). Imported Pubns.

Russian Minstrels: A History of the Skomorokhi. Russell Zguta. LC 78-53331. (Illus.). 1979. 23.95x (ISBN 0-8122-7753-8). U of Pa Pr.

Russian Missions in China & Japan. Charles Hale. 1974. pap. 1.50 (ISBN 0-686-10198-7). Eastern Orthodox.

Russian Museum: A Guide. A. Gubarev. 175p. 1981. 5.95 (ISBN 0-8285-2298-7, Pub. by Progress Pubs USSR). Imported Pubns.

Russian Museum, Leningrad. N. Novouspensky. 193p. 1975. 29.00x (ISBN 0-317-14293-3, Pub. by Collets (UK)). State Mutual Bk.

Russian Museum, Leningrad: Paintings of the Twelfth to Early Twentieth Centuries. Izobrazitel'noe Iskusstvo. 132.00x (ISBN 0-317-14295-X, Pub. By Collets UK). State Mutual Bk.

Russian Mystics. Sergius Bolshakoff. (Cistercian Studies: No. 26). Orig. Title: I Mistici Russi. 303p. 1981. pap. 6.95 (ISBN 0-87907-926-6). Cistercian Pubns.

Russian Names for Russian Dogs. Irene H. Zerebko. LC 84-14238. (Other Dog Bks.). (Illus.). 1985. 12.95 (ISBN 0-87714-113-4). Denlingers.

Russian National Income, Eighteen Eighty-Five to Nineteen Thirteen. Paul R. Gregory. (Illus.). 350p. 1983. Repr. 34.50 (ISBN 0-521-24382-3). Cambridge U Pr.

Russian Nationalism & Soviet Politics. Darrell P. Hammer. 200p. 1988. 26.50 (ISBN 0-8133-0440-7). Westview.

Russian New Right: Right-Wing Ideologies in the Contemporary U. S. S. R. Alexander Yanov. Tr. by Stephen P. Dunn from Rus. LC 78-620020. (Research Ser: No. 35). 1978. pap. 5.95x (ISBN 0-87725-135-5). U of Cal Intl St.

Russian Nineteenth Century Verse. Ed. by Collet's Holdings, Ltd. Staff. 368p. 1983. 49.00x (ISBN 0-317-39528-9, Pub. by Collets (UK)). State Mutual Bk.

Russian Nineteenth Century Verse. Ed. by I. Zheleznova. 368p. 1983. 9.95 (ISBN 0-8285-2576-5, Pub. by Raduga Pubs USSR). Imported Pubns.

Russian Noble Family: Structure & Change. Jessica Tovrov. Ed. by William H. McNeill & Barbara Jelavich. (Modern European History Ser.). 400p. 1987. lib. bdg. 60.00 (ISBN 0-8240-8064-5). Garland Pub.

Russian Nonconformity: The Story of Unofficial Religion in Russia. Serge Bolshakoff. Repr. of 1950 ed. 10.00 (ISBN 0-404-00933-6). AMS Pr.

Russian Normative Stress Notation. John G. Nicholson. 176p. 1968. 29.95x (ISBN 0-7735-0020-0). McGill-Queens U Pr.

Russian Novel. Eugene M. Vogue. 59.95 (ISBN 0-8490-0982-0). Gordon Pr.

Russian Novel from Pushkin to Pasternak. Ed. by John Garrard. LC 83-1070. 320p. 1983. 35.00x (ISBN 0-300-02935-7). Yale U Pr.

Russian Novel in English Fiction. Gilbert Phelps. LC 79-158907. 1971. Repr. of 1956 ed. 39.00x (ISBN 0-403-01301-1). Scholarly.

Russian Novelists. E. M. De Vogue. LC 74-28331. (Studies in Russian Literature & Life, No. 100). 1974. lib. bdg. 49.95x (ISBN 0-8383-1949-1). Haskell.

Russian Novelists. Eugene N. De Vogue. Tr. by Jane L. Edmands. LC 72-1328. (Essay Index Reprint Ser.). Repr. of 1887 ed. 16.00 (ISBN 0-8369-2870-9). Ayer Co Pubs.

Russian Opera. Martin Cooper. LC 77-181127. 65p. 1951. Repr. 29.00x (ISBN 0-403-01528-6). Scholarly.

Russian Opera. Martin Cooper. 1988. Repr. of 1951 ed. lib. bdg. 49.00x. Am Biog Serv.

Russian Opera. Rosa Newmarch. LC 72-109807. (Illus.). 403p. 1972. Repr. of 1914 ed. lib. bdg. 48.50x (ISBN 0-8371-4298-9, NERO). Greenwood.

Russian Orders, Decorations & Medals Including a Historical Resume & Notes under the Monarchy. C. Hurley. 90p. 1987. 84.00x (Pub. by Picton UK). State Mutual Bk.

Russian Orders, Decorations & Medals Including Those of Imperial Russia, the Provisional Government, the Civil War & the Soviet Union. Robert Werlich. (Illus.). 1981. lib. bdg. 50.00x (ISBN 0-911200-03-7). Quaker.

Russian Orders, Decorations & Medals. 2nd ed. Robert Werlich. LC 81-171055. (Illus.). 1981. 50.00 (ISBN 0-685-90818-6). Quaker.

Russian Orthodox Church: A Contemporary History. Jane Ellis. LC 85-45884. 700p. 1986. 39.95x (ISBN 0-253-35029-8). Ind U Pr.

Russian Orthodox Missions. Eugene Smirnoff. pap. 8.95 (ISBN 0-686-01299-2). Eastern Orthodox.

Russian Orthodoxy under the Old Regime. Ed. by Robert L. Nichols & Theofanis G. Stavrou. LC 78-3196. 1978. pap. text ed. 8.95x (ISBN 0-8166-0847-4). U of Minn Pr.

Russian Painting of the Mid 19th Century. M. N. Shumova. 238p. (Rus.). 1984. 50.00x (ISBN 0-317-57342-X, Pub. by Collets UK). State Mutual Bk.

Russian Painting of the 17th Century. V. G. Briusova. (Illus.). 338p. (Rus.). 1984. 277.00x (ISBN 0-317-57433-7, Pub. by Collets UK). State Mutual Bk.

Russian Peasant. Howard P. Kennard. LC 77-87519. (Anthro. Ser.). (Illus.). Repr. of 1908 ed. 28.50 (ISBN 0-404-16607-5). AMS Pr.

Russian Peasant Design Motifs for Needleworkers & Craftsmen. V. Stasov. (Pictorial Archives Ser.). (Illus.). 32p. (Orig.). 1976. pap. 2.75 (ISBN 0-486-23235-2). Dover.

Russian Peasant Schools: Officialdom, Village Culture & Popular Pedagaogy, 1861-1914. Ben Eklof. 592p. 1987. text ed. 55.00x (ISBN 0-520-05171-8). U of Cal Pr.

Russian Peasant, 1920 & 1984. Ed. by Robert E. Smith. (Library of Peasant Studies: No. 4). 120p. 1977. 28.50x (ISBN 0-7146-3078-0, F Cass Co). Biblio Dist.

Russian Peasantry: Their Agrarian Condition, Social Life, & Religion. Sergiel M. Kravchinskii. LC 75-39055. (Russian Studies: Perspectives on the Revolution Ser). vi, 401p. 1977. Repr. of 1888 ed. 32.45 (ISBN 0-88355-435-6). Hyperion Conn.

Russian Peasants & Soviet Power: A Study of Collectivization. Moshe Lewin. 544p. 1975. pap. 11.95x (ISBN 0-393-00752-9). Norton.

Russian Penetration of the North Pacific Ocean, 1700-1799: A Documentary Record. Ed. by Basil Dmytryshyn et al. Orig. Title: To Siberia & Russian America: Three Centuries of Russian Eastward Expansion, Vol. 2. 640p. 1988. 30.00x (ISBN 0-87595-149-X). Oregon Hist.

Russian People: A Reader on their History & their Culture. 3rd ed. Ed. by V. Tschebotarioff Bill. LC 74-17005. pap. 47.80 (ISBN 0-317-42257-X, 2025784). Bks Demand UMI.

Russian Philosophe, Alexander Radischev, Seventeen Forty-Nine to Eighteen Hundred Two. Allen McConnell. LC 79-2911. 228p. 1981. Repr. of 1964 ed. 23.00 (ISBN 0-8305-0080-4). Hyperion Conn.

Russian Philosophical Terminology. K. G. Ballestrem. (Sovietica Ser: No. 19). 117p. (Eng., Fr., Ger. & Rus.). 1964. lib. bdg. 18.50 (ISBN 90-277-0036-2, Pub. by Reidel Holland). Kluwer Academic.

Russian Philosophy, 3 vols. James M. Edie et al. LC 64-10928. 1976. Vol. 1. pap. 9.95x (ISBN 0-87049-200-4); Vol. 2. pap. 8.95x (ISBN 0-686-91542-9); Vol. 3. pap. 10.95x (ISBN 0-686-77174-5). U of Tenn Pr.

Russian Phonetic Variants & Phonostylistics. Michael Shapiro. LC 68-63839. 55p. 1983. Repr. of 1968 ed. lib. bdg. 19.95x (ISBN 0-89370-759-7). Borgo Pr.

Russian Physicians in An Era of Reform & Revolution, 1856-1905. Nancy M. Frieden. LC 81-47128. (Illus.). 432p. 1981. 39.00x (ISBN 0-691-05335-9). Princeton U Pr.

Russian Piety. Nicholas Arseniev. 143p. 1964. pap. 5.95 (ISBN 0-913836-21-4). St Vladimirs.

Russian Pillow Lace. V. A. Faleeya. 326p. 1983. 95.00x (ISBN 0-317-39529-7, Pub. by Collets (UK)). State Mutual Bk.

Russian Plays for Young Audiences. Ed. by Miriam Morton. 401p. 1977. 11.95 (ISBN 0-932720-62-5); pap. 7.50 (ISBN 0-932720-61-7). New Plays Bks.

Russian Poetics Proceedings of the International Colloquium at UCLA, September 22-26. Ed. by Thomas Eekman & Dean S. Worth. (UCLA Slavic Studies: Vol. 4). 544p. 1983. 29.95 (ISBN 0-89357-101-6). Slavica.

Russian Poetry: A Personal Anthology. Ed. & tr. by R. A. Ford. (Orig.). 1985. (Pub. by Mosaic Pr Canada); pap. 9.95 (ISBN 0-88962-267-1). Riverrun NY.

Russian Poetry for Children. Elena Sokol. LC 83-6703. (Illus.). 258p. 1984. text ed. 24.95x (ISBN 0-87049-406-6). U of Tenn Pr.

Russian Poetry for Intermediates. Ed. by Eleanor Aitken. 150p. pap. 9.95x (ISBN 0-900186-36-4). Basil Blackwell.

Russian Poetry: Meter, Rhythm & Rhyme. Barry P. Scherr. LC 84-28045. 475p. 1986. 48.50x (ISBN 0-520-05299-4). U of Cal Pr.

Russian Poetry: Reader--I. Ed. by S. Knovalov et al. 153p. pap. text ed. 25.00x (ISBN 0-8236-5940-2). Intl Univs Pr.

Russian Poetry: The Modern Period. Ed. by John Glad & Daniel Weissbort. LC 78-8650. (Iowa Translations Ser.). 424p. 1978. pap. 12.50 (ISBN 0-87745-084-6). U of Iowa Pr.

Russian-Polish Political Dictionary. B. Dudawaki et al. 726p. (Rus. & Pol.). 1955. leatherette 29.95 (ISBN 0-686-92134-8, M-9114). French & Eur.

Russian Porcelain Private Factories. V. Popov. 314p. 1980. 95.00x (ISBN 0-317-14296-8, Pub. by Collets (UK)). State Mutual Bk.

Russian Portrait in Watercolours & Pencil. S. M. Gorbacheva & S. V. Iamshchikov. 1983. 150.00x (ISBN 0-317-61384-7, Pub. by Collets (UK)). State Mutual Bk.

Russian Portrait of the Late Nineteenth-Early Twentieth Centuries. I. Pruzham & V. Kniazeva. 294p. 1980. 90.00x (ISBN 0-686-97600-2, Pub. by Collets (UK)). State Mutual Bk.

Russian Primary Chronicle: Laurentian Text. Ed. by Samuel H. Cross. Tr. by O. P. Sherbowitz-Wetzor. LC 53-10264. 1968. Repr. of 1953 ed. 10.00x (ISBN 0-910956-34-0). Medieval Acad.

Russian Primer. Agnes Jacques. 1959. pap. 5.45 (ISBN 0-87532-159-3). Hendricks House.

Russian Printed Shawls. G. A. Makarovskaia. 182p. 1986. 88.00x (ISBN 0-317-61387-1, Pub. by Collets (UK)). State Mutual Bk.

Russian Printed Shawls. G. A. Makarovskaya. 183p. 1986. 35.00 (ISBN 0-8285-3573-6, Pub. by Sovietskaya Rossia Pubs USSR). Imported Pubns.

Russian Proprietor & Other Stories. Tolstoy Leo. Tr. by Nathan H. Dole. LC 77-110219. (Short Story Index Reprint Ser.). 1887. 21.00 (ISBN 0-8369-3371-0). Ayer Co Pubs.

Russian Prose. Boris Eikhenbaum. Tr. by Ray Parrott from Rus. 250p. 1985. 22.50 (ISBN 0-88233-892-7). Ardis Pubs.

Russian Prose Composition: Annotated Passages for Translation into Russian. F. M. Borras & R. F. Christian. 1964. pap. 12.95x (ISBN 0-19-815646-4). Oxford U Pr.

Russian Prose: Reader--I. S. Knovalov et al. 1545p. 1945. text ed. 25.00X (ISBN 0-8236-5960-7). Intl Univs Pr.

Russian Protestants: Evangelicals in the Soviet Union. Steve Durasoff. LC 72-76843. (Illus.). 312p. 1969. 27.50 (ISBN 0-8386-7465-8). Fairleigh Dickinson.

Russian Provisional Government, 1917: Documents, 3 Vols. Ed. by Robert P. Browder & Alexander F. Kerensky. 1961. 125.00x set (ISBN 0-8047-0023-0). Stanford U Pr.

Russian Punch Needle Embroidery. Gail Bird. 1981. pap. 3.50 (ISBN 0-486-24146-7). Dover.

Russian Rambles. Isabel Hapgood. 1973. Repr. of 1895 ed. 20.00 (ISBN 0-8274-1574-5). R West.

Russian Rambles. Isabel F. Hapgood. LC 77-115542. (Russia Observed, Series I). 1970. Repr. of 1895 ed. 19.00 (ISBN 0-405-03031-2). Ayer Co Pubs.

Russian Reactions to German Air Power in World War II. Klaus Uebe. LC 68-22556. (German Air Force in World War 2 Series). (Illus.). 1968. 15.00 (ISBN 0-405-00049-9). Ayer Co Pubs.

Russian Readings & Grammatical Terminology. Susan Wobst. 88p. 1978. pap. 3.95 (ISBN 0-89357-049-4). Slavica.

Russian Rebels, 1600-1800. Paul Avrich. (Illus.). 1976. pap. 7.95 (ISBN 0-393-00836-3, Norton Lib). Norton.

Russian Religious Philosophy: Selected Aspects. Frederick C. Copleston. 1988. text ed. 24.95x (ISBN 0-268-01635-6). U of Notre Dame Pr.

Russian Review Grammar. Marianna Bogojavlensky. xviii, 450p. (Orig.). 1982. pap. text ed. 17.95 (ISBN 0-89357-096-6). Slavica.

Russian Revolution. Ed. by Daniel Brower. LC 78-67917. (Problems in Civilization Ser.). (Orig.). 1979. pap. text ed. 6.95x (ISBN 0-88273-406-7). Forum Pr IL.

Russian Revolution. E. H. Carr. LC 79-2295. (Illus.). 1979. 16.95 (ISBN 0-02-905140-1). Free Pr.

Russian Revolution. Sheila Fitzpatrick. 1984. 21.95x (ISBN 0-19-219162-4); pap. 7.95 (ISBN 0-19-289148-0). Oxford U Pr.

Russian Revolution. David Killingray. Ed. by Malcolm Yapp et al. (World History Ser.). (Illus.). (gr. 6-11). 1980. lib. bdg. 6.95 (ISBN 0-89908-138-X); pap. text ed. 2.45 (ISBN 0-89908-113-4). Greenhaven.

Russian Revolution. Ed. by V. D Medlin. LC 79-4332. (European Problem Ser.). 218p. 1979. pap. 6.50 (ISBN 0-88275-937-X). Krieger.

Russian Revolution. Alan Moorehead. (Illus.). 301p. 1987. pap. 10.95 (ISBN 0-88184-331-8). Carroll & Graf.

Russian Revolution. Beryl Williams. (Historical Studies Association). 96p. 1987. pap. text ed. 7.95 (ISBN 0-631-15083-8). Basil Blackwell.

Russian Revolution: A Study in Mass Mobilization. John Keep. (Revolutions in the Modern World Ser.). 1977. 19.50x (ISBN 0-393-05616-3). Norton.

Russian Revolution & Bolshevik Victory: Causes & Processes. 2nd ed. Ed. by Arthur E. Adams. (Problems in European Civilization Ser.). (Orig.). 1972. pap. text ed. 8.00 (ISBN 0-669-81745-7). Heath.

Russian Revolution, & Leninism or Marxism? Rosa Luxemburg. LC 80-24374. (Ann Arbor Ser. for the Study of Communism & Marxism). 109p. 1981. Repr. of 1961 ed. lib. bdg. 35.00x (ISBN 0-313-22429-3, LURR). Greenwood.

Russian Revolution & Leninism or Marxism? Rosa Luxemburg. 1961. pap. 6.95 (ISBN 0-472-06057-0, 57, AA). U of Mich Pr.

Russian Revolution & the Peasant. E. H. Carr. (Raleigh Lectures on History). 1963. pap. 5.50 (ISBN 0-85672-315-0, Pub. by British Acad). Longwood Pub Group.

Russian Revolution: Historical Problems & Perspectives. Dietrich Geyer. Tr. by Bruce Little. 172p. 1987. 31.50 (ISBN 0-85496-513-0, Pub. by Berg Pubs); pap. 11.95 (ISBN 0-85496-518-1, Pub. by Berg Pubs). St Martin.

Russian Revolution in Switzerland, 1914-1917. Alfred E. Senn. LC 76-143766. 266p. 1971. 30.00x (ISBN 0-299-05941-3). U of Wis Pr.

Russian Revolution, Nineteen Seventeen, & Indian Nationalism: Studies of Lajpat Rai, Subhas Chandra Bose, & Rammonohar Lohia. Karuna Kaushik. 1985. 20.00x (ISBN 0-8364-1314-8, Pub. by Chanakya India). South Asia Bks.

Russian Revolution, Nineteen Seventeen. N. N. Sukhanov. Ed. by Joel Carmichael. LC 83-43102. (Illus.). 744p. 1984. 64.50x (ISBN 0-691-05406-1); pap. 17.50x (ISBN 0-691-00799-3). Princeton U Pr.

Russian Revolution, Nineteen Seventeen to Nineteen Twenty-One, Vol. 1: 1917-1918: From the Overthrow of the Tsar to the Assumption of Power by the Bolsheviks. William H. Chamberlin. Ed. by Diane Koenker. 536p. 1987. 50.00 (ISBN 0-691-05492-4); pap. 12.50 (ISBN 0-691-00814-0). Princeton U Pr.

Russian Revolution, Nineteen Seventeen to Nineteen Twenty-One, Vol. II: 1918-1921: From the Civil War to the Consolidation of Power. William H. Chamberlin. Ed. by Diane Koenker. 612p. 1987. 52.00 (ISBN 0-691-05493-2); pap. 14.50 (ISBN 0-691-00815-9). Princeton U Pr.

Russian Revolution of 1917: Contemporary Accounts. Ed. by Dimitri Von Mohrenschildt. 1971. 22.50x (ISBN 0-19-501420-0). Oxford U Pr.

Russian Revolution: The Overthrow of Tzarism & the Triumph of the Soviets. abr. ed. Leon Trotsky. LC 59-6990. 1959. pap. 9.95 (ISBN 0-385-09398-5, A170, Anch). Doubleday.

Russian Revolution: What Actually Happened. Y. Dobrovolskaya & Y. Makarov. 161p. 1985. pap. 4.95 (ISBN 0-8285-3156-0, Pub. by Progress Pubs USSR). Imported Pubns.

Russian Revolution 1900-1927. Robert Service. LC 86-213. (Studies in European History). (Illus.). 96p. 1986. pap. text ed. 8.50x (ISBN 0-391-03405-7). Humanities.

Russian Revolution, 1978-1984, Vols. 1, 2 & 3. rev. ed. Paul N. Miliukov. Set. 75.00. Academic Intl.

Russian Revolutionary Emigres, Eighteen Twenty-Five to Eighteen Seventy. Martin A. Miller. LC 86-2715. (Studies in Historical & Political Science: 104th Ser., No. 2). 320p. 1986. text ed. 34.50x (ISBN 0-8018-3303-5). Johns Hopkins.

Russian Revolutionary Intelligentsia. Philip Pomper. LC 75-107303. (Europe Since 1500 Ser.). 1970. pap. 9.95x (ISBN 0-88295-749-X). Harlan Davidson.

Russian Revolutionary Movement in the 1880s. Derek Offord. (Illus.). 230p. 1986. 39.50 (ISBN 0-521-32723-7). Cambridge U Pr.

Russian Revolutionary Novel. Richard Freeborn. 302p. 1985. pap. 18.95 (ISBN 0-521-31737-1). Cambridge U Pr.

Russian Revolutions of 1917. John S. Curtiss. LC 82-15180. (Anvil Ser.). 192p. 1982. pap. 7.50 (ISBN 0-89874-499-7). Krieger.

Russian Revolutions of 1917: The Origins of Modern Communism. Leonard Schapiro. LC 83-45262. (Illus.). 253p. 1986. pap. 10.95x (ISBN 0-465-07156-2, TB-5132). Basic.

Russia's Second Revolution: The February 1917 Uprising in Petrograd. E. N. Burdzhalov. Ed. by Donald J. Raleigh. LC 86-45955. (Indiana-Michigan Series in Russian & East European Studies). (Illus.). 448p. 35.00 (ISBN 0-253-35037-9); pap. 14.50 (ISBN 0-253-20440-2). Ind U Pr.

Russia's Underground Press: The Chronicle of Current Events. Mark Hopkins. 208p. 1983. 35.00 (ISBN 0-275-91008-3, C1008). Praeger.

Russia's Western Borderlands, 1710-1870. Edward C. Thaden & Marian F. Thaden. LC 84-13300. (Illus.). 275p. 1985. text ed. 33.50x (ISBN 0-691-05420-7). Princeton U Pr.

Russia's Women. Nina N. Selivanova. LC 75-7715. (Pioneers of the Woman's Movement: an International Perspective Ser.). 223p. 1976. Repr. of 1923 ed. 19.80 (ISBN 0-88355-352-X). Hyperion Conn.

Russica Eighty-One: Literaturnyi sbornik. Ed. by Alexander Sumerkin. LC 82-80731. (Illus.). 420p. (Rus.). 1982. 25.00 (ISBN 0-89830-047-9); pap. 20.00 (ISBN 0-89830-048-7). Russica Pubs.

Russie Epique: Etude Sur les Chansons Heroiques De la Russie, Traduites Du Analysees Pour la Premier Fois. Alfred N. Rambaud. LC 73-131411. (Research & Source Works Ser: No. 564). (Fr). 1970. Repr. of 1876 ed. lib. bdg. 32.50 (ISBN 0-8337-2899-7). B Franklin.

Russification in the Baltic Provinces & Finland, 1855-1914. Ed. by E. C. Thaden. LC 80-7557. 1980. 64.50x (ISBN 0-691-05314-6); pap. 24.50x (ISBN 0-691-10103-5). Princeton U Pr.

Russisch-Deutsches Woerterbuch. 7th ed. Edmund Daum & W. Schenk. (Rus. & Ger.). 1976. 45.00 (ISBN 3-19-006219-6, M-7606, Pub. by Max Hueber). French & Eur.

Russisch-Deutsches Woerterbuch Fuer Naturwissenschaftler und Ingenieure. S. Halbauer. 170p. (Ger. & Rus.). 1971. 24.95 (ISBN 0-686-56466-9, M-7607, Pub. by M. Hueber). French & Eur.

Russisch-Deutsches Worterbuch der Funkechnik. P. K. Gorochow. 390p. (Rus. & Ger.). 1961. leatherette 6.95 (ISBN 0-686-92169-0). French & Eur.

Russisch Elymologisches Woerterbuch, Vol. 1. Max Vasmer. (Rus. & Ger.). 1953. 175.00 (ISBN 3-533-00665-4, M-7608, Pub. by Carl Winter). French & Eur.

Russisch Etymologisches Woerterbuch, Vol. 2. Max Vasmer. (Rus. & Ger.). 1955. 175.00 (ISBN 3-533-00666-2, M-7609, Pub. by Carl Winter). French & Eur.

Russisch Etymologisches Woerterbuch, Vol. 3. Max Vasmer. (Rus. & Ger.). 1958. 175.00 (ISBN 3-533-00667-0, M-7610, Pub. by Carl Winter). French & Eur.

Russkaia Armiia Na Chuzhbine: The Russian Army in Exile (1920-1923) V. Davats & N. Lvov. LC 85-62402. 124p. (Rus.). 1985. 9.50 (ISBN 0-911971-18-1). Effect Pub.

Russkaia Kriticheskaia Literatura o Proizvedeniiakh N. V. Gogolia. Ed. by V. Zelinskii. 776p. 1984. Repr. of 1910 ed. cancelled 75.00 (ISBN 0-88233-959-1). Ardis Pubs.

Russkaia Leksika. K. A. Timofeev. 112p. (Rus.). 1985. 29.00x (ISBN 0-317-42779-2, Pub by Collets (UK)). State Mutual Bk.

Russkaia Literaturnaia Parodiia. (Rus.). 1981. pap. 6.50 (ISBN 0-88233-604-5); write for info. Ardis Pubs.

Russkaia Poeziia XiX Veka. V. J. Korovin. 126p. 1983. pap. 25.00 (ISBN 0-317-40702-3, Pub. by Collets UK). State Mutual Bk.

Russkaja Pravoslavnaja Tserkov' v Severnoj Ameriki. N. D. Talberg. 224p. 1955. pap. 8.00 (ISBN 0-317-30366-X). Holy Trinity.

Russkaya Amerika V. Neopubkikovannykh Zapiskakh K. T. Khlebnikova. Ed. by R. G. Lyapunova & S. G. Fedorova. 280p. (Rus.). 1979. 39.00x (ISBN 0-317-40842-9, Pub. by Collets (UK)). State Mutual Bk.

Russkie Dobrovoltsy Vispanii Nineteen Thirty-Six to Nineteen Thirty-Nine: Russian Volunteers in Spain. A. P. Yaremchuk et al. Ed. by U. N. Azar. (Illus.). 330p. (Orig., Rus.). 1983. pap. 16.00 (ISBN 0-88669-056-0). Globus Pubs.

Russkie Knigi Za Rubezhom: 1980-1985. David Arans. (Russica Bibliography Ser.: No. 7). 130p. (Rus.). Date not set. pap. 13.50 (ISBN 0-89830-106-8). Russica Pubs.

Russkie Narodnye Ballady. Ed. by Collet's Holdings, Ltd. Staff. 310p. (Rus.). 1983. 59.00x (ISBN 0-317-40861-5, Pub. by Collets (UK)). State Mutual Bk.

Russkie Perezvony: An Album of Soviet Russian Recordings. Alexander Blum. LC 71-136569. 155p. 1972. 34.00 (ISBN 0-08-006878-2). Pergamon.

Russkie Pis'Mennye J Ustnye Traditsii J Dukhovnaia Kul'Tura. Ed. by Collet's Holdings, Ltd. Staff. 318p. (Rus.). 1982. 39.00x (ISBN 0-317-40866-6, Pub. by Collets (UK)). State Mutual Bk.

Russkii Arkhierei iz Vizantii i Pravo Ego Naznacheniia do Nachala XV Veka. P. Sokolov. 582p. 1913. text ed. 74.52x (ISBN 0-576-99187-2, Pub. by Gregg Intl Pubs England). Gregg Intl.

Russkii Iazyk: Grammaticheskoe Uchenie O Slove. V. V. Vinogradov. (Russian Ser.: Vol. 19). 1947. 30.00 (ISBN 0-87569-021-1). Academic Intl.

Russkii Narodnye Skazkii: (Russian Fairy Tales) A. Kurkin. 72p. 1987. 10.95 (ISBN 0-8285-3748-8, Pub. by Aurora Pubs USSR). Imported Pubns.

Russkii Padezhii: (Russian Cases) G. G. Malshev. 48p. (Rus.). 1987. Incl. wall charts. pap. 13.95 (ISBN 0-8285-3732-1, Pub. by Rus Lang Pubns USSR). Imported Pubns.

Russkii romantizm, Sbornik statei. A. I. Beletskii. 152p. Repr. of 1927 ed. cancelled (ISBN 0-88233-963-X). Ardis Pubs.

Russkii Skazkii: (Russian Fairy Tales) Ed. by N. N. Kovacheva. 158p. (Rus.). 1987. 7.95 (ISBN 0-8285-3736-4, Pub. by Rus Lang Pubns USSR). Imported Pubns.

Russkije Podvizhniki Blagotchestija 19-20 vekev. E. Poseljanin. 908p. Repr. of 1966 ed. 35.00 (ISBN 0-317-29250-1). Holy Trinity.

Russko-Transkaia Torgovlia. N. G. Kukanova. 294p. (Rus.). 1984. 39.00x (ISBN 0-317-40851-8, Pub. by Collets (UK)). State Mutual Bk.

Russko-Ukrainsko-Latinskii Zoologicheskii Slovar. A. P. Markevich & K. I. Iatarko. 412p. 1983. 50.00x (ISBN 0-317-59452-4, Pub. by Collets (UK)). State Mutual Bk.

Russkoya-Celo: The Ethnography of a Russian-American Community. Stanford N. Gerber. LC 83-45354. (Immigrant Communities & Ethnic Minorities in the United States & Canada Ser.: No. 11). 135p. 1985. 37.50 (ISBN 0-404-19407-9). AMS Pr.

Russo-American Relations, 1815-1867. Benjamin P. Thomas. LC 78-64136. (Johns Hopkins University. Studies in the Social Sciences. Forty-Eighth Ser. 1930: 2). Repr. of 1930 ed. 16.50 (ISBN 0-404-61248-2). AMS Pr.

Russo-American Relations, 1815-1867. Benjamin P. Thomas. LC 70-87709. (American History, Politics & Law Ser). 1970. Repr. of 1930 ed. lib. bdg. 25.00 (ISBN 0-306-71681-X). Da Capo.

Russo-Chinese Diplomacy. Ken S. Weigh. LC 79-2845. 382p. 1981. Repr. of 1928 ed. 32.40 (ISBN 0-8305-0021-9). Hyperion Conn.

Russo-Chinese Empire. Alexander Ular. LC 75-32325. (Studies in Chinese History & Civilization). 334p. 1977. Repr. of 1904 ed. 24.00 (ISBN 0-89093-086-4). U Pubns Amer.

Russo-Finnish War. Alan L. Paley. Ed. by D. Steve Rahmas. LC 72-89216. (Events of Our Times Ser.: No. 5). 32p. 1973. lib. bdg. 3.75 incl. catalog cards (ISBN 0-87157-705-4); pap. 2.50 vinyl laminated covers (ISBN 0-87157-205-2). SamHar Pr.

Russo-German War: Autumn 1944 to January 25 1945. Ed. by W. Victor Madeja. (Battle Situation - East Front Ser.). (Illus.). 78p. (Orig., Ger.). 1987. pap. text ed. 9.95 (ISBN 0-941052-89-3, 34). Valor Pub.

Russo-German War: Defense Against Russian Breakthroughs. Ed. by W. Victor Madej. (Illus.). 184p. 1984. cancelled (ISBN 0-317-19791-6); pap. cancelled (ISBN 0-317-19792-4). Valor Pub.

Russo-German War: January 25 Through Spring 1945: The Last 100 Days. Ed. by W. Victor Madej. (No. 35). 80p. (Ger.). 1987. pap. text ed. 12.95 (ISBN 0-317-56100-6). Valor Pub.

Russo-German War July 1943-May 1945: Defense Against Russian Breakthroughs. Ed. by W. Victor Madej. 192p. 1986. 13.95 (ISBN 0-941052-65-6); pap. 9.95 (ISBN 0-941052-35-4). Valor Pub.

Russo-German War, June 1941 - May 1945: Small Unit Actions, Improvisations, Partisan Warfare. Ed. by W. Victor Madej. 194p. 1986. 13.95 (ISBN 0-941052-74-5); pap. 9.95. Valor Pub.

Russo-German War: June 1941-June 1943. LC 83-81814. 204p. 1983. 13.95; pap. 9.95 (ISBN 0-941052-13-3). Valor Pub.

Russo-German War: Summer-Autumn 1942. Ed. by W. Victor Madej. (Ost-Lage Ser.: No. 29). 72p. (Ger.). 1988. pap. text ed. 12.95 (ISBN 0-941052-84-2). Valor Pub.

Russo-German War: Summer-Autumn 1943. Ed. by W. Victor Madeja. (Battle Situation - East Front Ser.). (Illus.). 100p. (Orig.). 1987. pap. text ed. 12.95 (ISBN 0-941052-86-9, 31). Valor Pub.

Russo-German War: Summer 1941. Ed. by W. Victor Madeja. (Battle Situation - East Front Ser.). (Illus.). 80p. (Orig., Ger.). 1988. pap. text ed. 12.95 (ISBN 0-941052-81-8, 26). Valor Pub.

Russo-German War: Summer 1944. Ed. by W. Victor Madeja. (Battle Situation - East Front Ser.). (Illus.). 80p. (Orig., Ger.). 1987. pap. text ed. 9.95 (ISBN 0-941052-88-5, 33). Valor Pub.

Russo-German War: Winter-Spring 1942. Ed. by W. Victor Madeja. (Battle Situation - East Front Ser.). (Illus.). 80p. (Orig., Ger.). 1988. pap. text ed. 12.95 (ISBN 0-941052-83-4, 28). Valor Pub.

Russo-German War: Winter-Spring 1943. Ed. by W. Victor Madeja. (Battle Situation - East Front Ser.). (Illus.). 80p. (Orig.). 1987. pap. text ed. 9.95 (ISBN 0-941052-85-0, 30). Valor Pub.

Russo-German War: Winter-Spring 1944. Ed. by W. Victor Madeja. (Battle Situation - East Front Ser.). (Illus.). 80p. (Orig., Ger.). 1988. pap. text ed. 12.95 (ISBN 0-941052-87-7, 32). Valor Pub.

Russo-Japanese Conflict: Its Causes & Issues. K. Asakawa. (Illus.). 399p. 1972. Repr. of 1904 ed. 37.50x (ISBN 0-7165-2048-6, BBA 02211, Pub. by Irish Academic Pr Ireland). Biblio Dist.

Russo-Japanese Treaties of 1907-1916. Ernest B. Price. LC 76-101274. Repr. of 1933 ed. 17.50 (ISBN 0-404-05135-9). AMS Pr.

Russo-Japanese War: A Complete Photographic Record. 1986. lib. bdg. 90.00 (ISBN 0-8490-3842-1). Gordon Pr.

Russo-Persian Commercial Relations, 1828-1914. Marvin L. Entner. LC 65-64001. (University of Florida Social Sciences Monographs: No. 28). 1965. pap. 6.00x (ISBN 0-8130-0073-4). U Presses Fla.

Russules d'Europe et d'Afrique du Nord: With English Translation of the Keys by R. W. G. Dennis. Henri Romagnesi. (Illus.). 1030p. Repr. of 1967 ed. lib. bdg. 150.00x (ISBN 3-7682-1316-1). Lubrecht & Cramer.

Rust. Michael Hogan. 1977. 15.00 (ISBN 0-918824-01-X); pap. 3.50 (ISBN 0-918824-00-1). Turkey Pr.

Rust Fungi. Ed. by K. J. Scott & A. K. Chakravorty. 1982. 76.00 (ISBN 0-12-633520-6). Acad Pr.

Rust Fungi on Legumes & Composites in North America. George B. Cummins. LC 78-60541. 424p. 1978. pap. 14.95x (ISBN 0-8165-0653-1). U of Ariz Pr.

Rust on My Soul. Neil V. Wyrick. LC 85-70874. 126p. 1985. pap. 3.95 (ISBN 0-88270-589-X). Bridge Pub.

Rusted Dreams. David Bensman & Roberta Lynch. 1987. 17.95 (ISBN 0-317-56501-X). McGraw.

Rusted Dreams: Hard Times in a Steel Community. David Bensman & Roberta Lynch. 1988. pap. 8.95 (ISBN 0-520-06302-3). U of Cal Pr.

Rusted Laughter. Vijay N. Shankar. (Writers Workshop Redbird Ser.). 1975. 6.75 (ISBN 0-88253-622-2); pap. text ed. 4.00 (ISBN 0-88253-621-4). Ind-US Inc.

Rustic Artistry of Clarence O. Nichols. Ed. by Craig Gilborn. (Illus.). 1987. 11.25 (ISBN 0-910020-39-6). Adirondack Mus.

Rustic Moralist. William R. Inge. text ed. 16.25 (ISBN 0-8369-8161-8, 8301). Ayer Co Pubs.

Rustic Sounds & Other Studies in Literature & Natural History. facs. ed. Francis Darwin. LC 69-17572. (Essay Index Reprint Ser). 1917. 17.00 (ISBN 0-8369-0069-3). Ayer Co Pubs.

Rustic Speech & Folklore. Elizabeth M. Wright. LC 68-18011. 368p. 1968. Repr. of 1913 ed. 40.00x (ISBN 0-8103-3294-9). Gale.

Rustic Vignettes. W. H. Pyne. LC 77-80117. (Orig.). 1977. pap. 6.95 (ISBN 0-486-23547-5). Dover.

Rustication of Urban Youth in China: A Social Experiment. Ed. by Peter J. Seybolt. LC 76-17395. 232p. 1977. 37.50 (ISBN 0-87332-082-4). M E Sharpe.

Rustico di Filippo & the Florentine Lyric Tradition. Joan H. Levin. (American University Studies II - Romance Languages & Literature: Vol. 16). 197p. 1985. text ed. 29.50 (ISBN 0-8204-0150-1). P Lang Pubs.

Rustle in the Grass. Robin Hawdon. LC 84-13780. 248p. 1985. 13.95 (ISBN 0-396-08522-9). Dodd.

Rustle in the Grass. Robin Hawdon. 224p. 1989. pap. 2.95. Tor Bks.

Rustle of Language. Roland Barthes. Tr. by Richard Howard from Fr. 374p. 1986. 25.00 (ISBN 0-8090-8344-2). Hill & Wang.

Rustle of Language. Roland Barthes. Tr. by Richard Howard. 384p. 1987. pap. 9.95 (ISBN 0-8090-1527-7). Hill & Wang.

Rustler on the Beach. Frank Mulville. 160p. 1982. 12.95 (ISBN 0-89182-047-7). Charles River Bks.

Rustler's Blood. David Everitt. 208p. 1985. pap. 2.25 (ISBN 0-8439-2254-0, Leisure Bks). Leisure NY.

Rustlers of Pecos County. Zane Grey. 256p. 1982. pap. 2.50 (ISBN 0-505-51831-7, Pub. by Tower Bks). Leisure NY.

Rustlers of Pecos County. Zane Grey. 240p. 1987. pap. 2.95 (ISBN 0-8439-2498-5, Leisure Bks). Leisure NY.

Rustlers of Silver River. Zane Grey. 226p. Repr. of 1920 ed. lib. bdg. 16.95 (ISBN 0-89190-765-3, Pub. by River City Pr). Amereon Ltd.

Rustler's Trail. Doyle Trent. 240p. 1988. pap. 2.95 (ISBN 0-8217-2263-8). Zebra.

Rustlers Valley. Clarence Mulford. 333p. 1974. Repr. of 1923 ed. lib. bdg. 20.95x (ISBN 0-88411-211-X, Pub. by Aeonian Pr). Amereon Ltd.

Rustler's Valley. large type ed. Clarence E. Mulford. Repr. lib. bdg. 20.95x (ISBN 0-88411-239-X, Pub. by Aeonian Pr). Amereon Ltd.

Rustling Grass. Joanne E. De Jonge. LC 85-7762. (My Father's World Ser.). (Illus.). 144p. 1985. pap. 4.25 (ISBN 0-930265-10-6). CRC Pubns.

Rustling of Many Winds. 10.95 (ISBN 0-318-00147-0). R Basu.

Rustlings above Saururus Hollow. John Caldwell. Ed. by Genevieve A. Brune. LC 85-60024. (Illus.). 90p. 1985. 8.00 (ISBN 0-932777-00-7). Caldwell Pubns.

Rusty & Kristy Visit Aunt Lois. (Michaels Twins Ser.: Bk. 1). (Orig.). (gr. 4-6). 1986. pap. text ed. write for info. (ISBN 0-9616264-1-0). F Evans Kimbrell.

Rusty & Mitzi. (ps). 1976. 2.50 (ISBN 0-904494-28-4, Brimax Bks). Borden.

Rusty at the Circus. (Magiscope Bks). (Illus.). 24p. (ps-3). 1988. 7.95 (ISBN 0-02-688545-X, Checkerboard Pr). Macmillan.

Rusty Charm. James H. Goodman. Ed. by Fred Zuber. 272p. 1986. pap. 9.95 (ISBN 0-89896-270-6). Larksdale.

Rusty Fertlanger, Lady's Man. Christi Killien. LC 87-31001. 144p. (gr. 5-9). 1988. 12.95 (ISBN 0-395-46762-4). HM.

Rusty Goes to the Park. (Magiscope Bks). (Illus.). 24p. (ps-3). 1988. 7.95 (ISBN 0-02-688546-8, Checkerboard Pr). Macmillan.

Rusty Irons. Dan Cushman. LC 83-40428. 224p. 1984. 12.95 (ISBN 0-8027-4031-6). Walker & Co.

Rusty Irons. Dan Cushman. 1985. pap. 2.50 (ISBN 0-345-32697-0). Ballantine.

Rusty Lizard: A Population Study. W. Frank Blair. LC 59-8122. pap. 47.80 (ISBN 0-317-29262-5, 2055521). Bks Demand UMI.

Rusty Person Is Worse than Rusty Iron: Adult Education & the Development of Africa. L. Brown. (Tolley Medal Ser). 1975. pap. text ed. 1.50 (ISBN 0-685-76692-6, WPT 6). Syracuse U Cont Ed.

Rusty the Irish Setter. Cynthia Overbeck. Tr. by Dyan Hammarberg from Fr. LC 76-29463. (Animal Friends Books). (Illus.). (gr. k-4). 1977. PLB 5.95 (ISBN 0-87614-080-0). Carolrhoda Bks.

Rusty Timmons' First Million. Joan Carris. LC 85-40096. (Illus.). 192p. (gr. 5-9). 1985. 11.25i (ISBN 0-397-32154-6, Lipp Jr Bks); PLB 10.89g (ISBN 0-397-32155-4). HarpJ.

Rusty Timmons' First Million. Joan Carris. LC 85-40096. (Trophy Bks.). (Illus.). 192p. (gr. 5-8). 1987. pap. 2.95 (ISBN 0-06-440197-9, Trophy). HarpJ.

Rusty's Story. Carol Gino. 352p. 1986. pap. 3.95 (ISBN 0-553-25351-4). Bantam.

Rusum Dar Al-Khila Fah (Rules & Regulations of Abbasid Court) Hilal Al-Sabi. Ed. by Elie A. Salem. 1977. 19.95x (ISBN 0-8156-6046-4, Am U Beirut). Syracuse U Pr.

Rut. Gordon Stowell. Tr. by S. D. de Lerin from Eng. (Libros Pescaditos Sobre Personajes Biblicos). Orig. Title: Ruth - the Little Fish Book Series. (Illus.). 24p. (gr. 1). 1981. pap. 0.60 (ISBN 0-311-38513-3, Edit Mundo). Casa Bautista.

Ruta de Don Quijote. Azorin, pseud. Intro. by H. Ramsden. (Spanish Texts Ser.). 220p. (Orig., Span.). 1966. pap. 11.00 (ISBN 0-7190-0204-4, Pub. by Manchester Univ Pr). St Martin.

Ruta de Escape. Don Wilkerson & David Manuel. Tr. by Juan S. Araujo from Eng. 224p. (Span.). 1986. pap. 4.75 (ISBN 0-88113-266-7). Edit Betania.

Rutaceae of the Guyana Highland see Memoirs of the New York Botanical Garden.

Rutan Voyager. I. Goold. (Great Adventure Ser.). (Illus.). 32p. (gr. 4 up). Date not set. PLB 13.27 (ISBN 0-86592-869-X). Rourke Corp.

Rutgers & the Water-Snouts. Barbara Dana. (Illus.). 160p. (gr. 3-6). 1983. pap. 1.25 (ISBN 0-380-01536-6, 24067, Camelot). Avon.

Rutgers Guide to Lowering Your Cholestrol: A Common Sense Approach. Hans Fisher & Eugene Boe. 224p. 1986. pap. 3.95 (ISBN 0-446-32657-7). Warner Bks.

Rutgers Guide to Lowering Your Cholesterol: A Common Sense Approach. Hans Fisher & Eugene Boe. 220p. 1985. 16.95 (ISBN 0-8135-1135-6). Rutgers U Pr.

Rutgers Law Journal: 1969-1985, 16 vols. Bound set. 565.50x (ISBN 0-686-90036-7). microfilm avail. Rothman.

Rutgers Law Review: 1947-1985, 37 vols. Bound set. 1235.00x (ISBN 0-686-90037-5). Rothman.

Rutgers Picture Book: An Illustrated History of Student Life in the Changing College & University. Michael Moffatt. (Illus.). 250p. 1985. text ed. 25.00 (ISBN 0-8135-1091-0); deluxe ed. 75.00 (ISBN 0-8135-1092-9). Rutgers U Pr.

Ruth. Marlee Alex. (Women of the Bible Ser.). (Illus.). 32p. (gr. 3-6). 1987. 7.95 (ISBN 0-8028-5017-0). Eerdmans.

Ruth. Ethel Barrett. LC 80-52961. (Bible Biography Ser.). 128p. (gr. 3-9). 1980. pap. 2.95 (ISBN 0-8307-0764-6, 5810418). Regal.

Ruth. Edward F. Campbell. LC 74-18785. (Anchor Bible Ser.: Vol. 7). (Illus.). 216p. 1975. pap. 14.00 (ISBN 0-385-05316-9). Doubleday.

Ruth. Elizabeth Gaskell. 1982. pap. 4.50x (ISBN 0-460-01673-3, Evman). Biblio Dist.

Ruth. Elizabeth Gaskell. Ed. by Alan Shelston. (World's Classics Ser.). 1985. pap. 4.95 (ISBN 0-19-281669-1). Oxford U Pr.

Ruth. R. H. Munce. 117p. 1971. spral bdg 3.95x (ISBN 0-914674-00-5). Freelandia.

Ruth. Robert E. Tourville. 60p. (Orig.). 1984. pap. 3.00 (ISBN 0-912981-12-1). Hse Bon Giovanni.

Ruth. Ellen G. Traylor. (Living Books Ser.). 224p. (Orig.). 1986. 3.95 (ISBN 0-8423-5809-9). Tyndale.

Ruth: A Bible Study Commentary. Paul P. Enns. 96p. (Orig.). 1982. pap. 4.95 (ISBN 0-310-44061-0, 11832P). Zondervan.

Ruth: A Novel. Lois T. Henderson. LC 81-65722. 256p. 1981. 7.95 (ISBN 0-915684-91-8, RD/429, HarpR). Har-Row.

Ruth: A Woman of Worth. Joyce M. Smith. 1979. pap. 2.50 (ISBN 0-8423-5810-2). Tyndale.

Ruth Abrams: Paintings, 1940-1985. Thomas Livesay. LC 86-80994. (Illus.). 94p. (Orig.). 1986. pap. 12.00 (ISBN 0-934349-03-7). Grey Art Gallery Study Ctr.

Ruth & Daniel: God's People in an Alien Society. Penelope Stokes. (Fisherman Bible Studyguide Ser.). 64p. (Orig.). 1986. pap. 2.95 (ISBN 0-87788-735-7). Shaw Pubs.

Ruth & Esther: Women of Faith. J. Vernon McGee. 1988. pap. 9.95 (ISBN 0-8407-3119-1). Nelson.

Ruth & Jonah: People in Process. Bob & Win Couchman. (Carpenter Studyguide). 80p. 1983. saddle-stiched member's handbk. 1.95 (ISBN 0-87788-736-5); leader's handbook 2.95 (ISBN 0-87788-737-3). Shaw Pubs.

Ruth & Naomi. (Arch Book Ser.: No. 21). 1984. pap. 1.29 (ISBN 0-570-06188-1, 59-1289). Concordia.

Ruth Benedict. Margaret Mead. LC 74-6400. (Leaders in Modern Anthropology Ser.). (Illus.). 1974. 27.50x (ISBN 0-231-03519-5); pap. 14.00x (ISBN 0-231-03520-9). Columbia U Pr.

Ruth Benedict: Patterns of a Life. Judith Modell. LC 82-21989. (Illus.). 400p. 1983. 35.95x (ISBN 0-8122-7874-7). U of Pa Pr.

Ruth Benedict: Patterns of a Life. Judith S. Modell. LC 82-21989. (Illus.). 400p. (Orig.). 1984. 33.95; pap. 14.95 (ISBN 0-8122-1175-8). U of Pa Pr.

Ruth Benedict: Stranger in This Land. Margaret M. Caffrey. (Illus.). 464p. 1989. 24.95 (ISBN 0-292-74655-5). U of Tex Pr.

Ruth Bernhard: The Eternal Body. Margaretta Mitchell. Ed. by David Featherstone. LC 86-18723. (Illus.). 70p. 1986. 50.00 (ISBN 0-9616515-1-2). Photog West Graphics.

Ruth Buxton Sayre: First Lady of the Farm. new ed. Julie McDonald. 206p. 1980. 12.95 (ISBN 0-8138-0420-5). Iowa St U Pr.

Ruth Crawford Seeger: Memoirs, Memories, Music. Matilda Gaume. LC 86-15632. (Composers of North America Ser.: No. 3). (Illus.). 288p. 1986. 27.50 (ISBN 0-8108-1917-1). Scarecrow.

Ruth, Esther, Jonah. Johanna W. Bos. LC 85-45793. (Preaching Guides Ser.). 108p. 1986. pap. 4.95 (ISBN 0-8042-3227-X, John Knox). Westminster John Knox.

Ruth Fane. (Cost Containment Learning Modules Ser.: No. 2). (Orig.). 1985. pap. text ed. 47.50 (ISBN 0-931369-04-5). Southern IL Univ Sch.

Ruth Hall & Other Writing. Fanny Fern. Ed. by Joyce W. Warren. (American Women Writers Ser.). 400p. 1986. text ed. 30.00 (ISBN 0-8135-1167-4); pap. text ed. 9.95 (ISBN 0-8135-1168-2). Rutgers U Pr.

Ruth Heller's World of Nature. (Postcard Bks.). (Illus.). (ps up). 1988. 3.95 (ISBN 0-448-09826-1, G&D). Putnam Pub Group.

Ruth Marini: Dodger Ace. Mel Cebulash. LC 82-20383. (Ruth Marini on the Mound Ser.). 144p. (gr. 4up). 1983. PLB 8.95 (ISBN 0-8225-0726-9). Lerner Pubns.

Ruth Marini of the Dodgers. Mel Cebulash. LC 82-20403. (Ruth Marini on the Mound Ser.). 144p. (gr. 4up). 1983. PLB 8.95 (ISBN 0-8225-0725-0). Lerner Pubns.

Ruth Marini: World Series Star. Mel Cebulash. (Ruth Marini on the Mound Ser.). 144p. (gr. 4 up). 1985. 8.95 (ISBN 0-8225-0727-7). Lerner Pubns.

Ruth Montgomery: Herald of the New Age. Ruth Montgomery & Joanne Garland. 288p. 1987. pap. 3.50 (ISBN 0-449-21252-1, Crest). Fawcett.

Ruth Page's Gardening Journal. Ruth Page. 1989. pap. 7.95 (ISBN 0-395-50091-5). HM.

Ruth Prawer Jhabvala. 2nd, rev. ed. Vasant A. Shahane. (Indian Writers Ser.: Vol. XI). 206p. 1983. lib. bdg. 12.00 (ISBN 0-89253-074-X). Ind-US Inc.

Ruth St. Denis: An Unfinished Life. Ruth St. Denis. LC 80-2893. (BCL Ser.: No. II). Repr. of 1939 ed. 42.50 (ISBN 0-404-18075-2). AMS Pr.

Ruth Stout No-Work Garden Book. Ruth Stout & Richard Clemence. LC 70-152102. (Illus.). 1971. 9.95 (ISBN 0-87857-000-4). Rodale Pr Inc.

Ruth Suckow. Abigail A. Hamblen. LC 78-52563. (Western Writers Ser.: No. 34). 1978. pap. 2.95x (ISBN 0-88430-058-7). Boise St Univ.

Ruth Suckow. Leedice M. Kissane. LC 68-24300. (Twayne's United States Authors Ser.). 1969. lib. bdg. 17.95 (ISBN 0-8057-0712-3). Irvington.

Ruth Suckow: A Critical Study of Her Fiction. Margaret Omrcanin. LC 70-184135. 1972. 5.95 (ISBN 0-8059-1658-X). Dorrance.

Ruth, The Gleaner, & the Boy Samuel. Gordon Lindsay. (Old Testament Ser.). 1.25 (ISBN 0-89985-137-1). Christ Nations.

Ruth - the Little Fish Book Series see Rut.

Ruth V. Hemenway, M.D. A Memoir of Revolutionary China, 1924-1941. Ruth V. Hemenway. Ed. by Fred W. Drake. LC 76-45245. (Illus.). 232p. 1977. 17.50 (ISBN 0-87023-230-4). U of Mass Pr.

Ruth Weiberg: A Circle of Life. Ann S. Harris & Selma Holo. 48p. (Orig.). 1986. pap. write for info. (ISBN 0-9602974-3-X). USC Fisher Gallery.

Ruth Weisberg: Paintings, Drawings, Prints, 1968-1988. Ed. by Marion E. Jackson. (Illus.). 64p. (Orig.). 1988. pap. 15.00 (ISBN 0-935312-96-X, Co-pub. by University of Michigan School of Art). Feminist Pr.

Ruth: Woman of Courage. Paula Parris. (BibLearn Ser.). (Illus.). (gr. 1-6). 1977. bds. 5.95 (ISBN 0-8054-4229-4, 4242-29). Broadman.

Ruthenium. T. D. Adtokratova. (Analytical Chemistry of the Elements Ser.). 260p. 1970. text ed. 53.00x (ISBN 0-7065-0745-2, Pub. by Keter Pub Jerusalem). Coronet Bks.

Rutherford & Boltwood: Letters on Radioactivity. Ernest Rutherford & Bertram B. Boltwood. Ed. by Lawrence Badash. LC 78-81411. (Yale Studies in the History of Science & Medicine Ser.: No. 4). (Illus.). pap. 100.50 (ISBN 0-8357-9490-3, 2016787). Bks Demand UMI.

Rutherford & Physics at the Turn of the Century. Ed. by William R. Shea & M. A. Bunge. 1979. 20.00x (ISBN 0-88202-184-2). Watson Pub Intl.

Rutherford & the Nature of the Atom. E. N. Andrade. (Illus.). 11.25 (ISBN 0-8446-2053-X). Peter Smith.

Rutherford B. Hayes. Ed. by Carol B. Fitzgerald. (Meckle's Bibliographies of the Presidents of the United States, 1789-1989 Ser.: No. 19). (Illus.). 1989. lib. bdg. 45.00x (ISBN 0-88736-133-1). Meckler Corp.

Rutherford B. Hayes Show. Ron Wertheimer. 224p. 1986. 11.95 (ISBN 0-8184-0391-8). Lyle Stuart.

Rutherford B. Hayes, 1822-1893: Chronology, Documents, Bibliographical Aids. Ed. by A. Bishop. LC 69-15394. (Presidential Chronology Ser.: No. 12). 96p. 1969. 8.00 (ISBN 0-379-12062-3). Oceana.

Rutherford County. Mabel Pittard. Ed. by Robert E. Corlew, III. (Tennessee County History Ser.: No. 75). (Illus.). 1985. 12.50x (ISBN 0-87870-182-6). Memphis St Univ.

Rutherford County, North Carolina, Wills & Miscellaneous Records, 1783-1868. James E. Wooley & Vivian Wooley. 184p. 1984. pap. 22.50 (ISBN 0-89308-413-1). Southern Hist Pr.

Rutherford Mound, Hardin County, Illinois. facsimile ed. Melvin L. Fowler. (Scientific Papers Ser.: Vol. VII, No. 1). (Illus.). 44p. 1974. pap. 2.00x (ISBN 0-89792-015-5). Ill St Museum.

Rutherford: Simple Genius. David Wilson. (Illus.). 625p. 1983. 32.50x (ISBN 0-262-23115-8). MIT Pr.

Ruthie Greene Show. Nancy S. Levinson. 128p. (YA) (gr. 7 up). 1985. 11.95 (ISBN 0-525-67172-2, 01160-350). Lodestar Bks.

Ruthie: My Life with Ruthie. Eric M. Stewart, Jr. 1987. 8.95 (ISBN 0-533-07288-3). Vantage.

Ruthie's Rude Friends. Jean Marzollo & Claudio Marzollo. LC 84-1707. (Easy-to-Read Bks.). (Illus.). (ps-3). 1984. 8.95 (ISBN 0-8037-0115-2, 0869-260); PLB 8.89 (ISBN 0-8037-0116-0). Dial Bks Young.

Ruthie's Rude Friends. Jean Marzollo & Claudio Marzollo. LC 84-1707. (Easy-to-Read Paperback Ser.). (Illus.). 48p. (ps-3). 1987. pap. 4.95 (ISBN 0-8037-0378-3, 0481-140). Dial Bks Young.

Ruthless Gun. Ted Lewellen. 160p. 1981. pap. 1.75 (ISBN 0-449-12796-6, GM). Fawcett.

Ruthless Lord Rule. Michelle Casey. 224p. 1987. pap 2.50 (ISBN 0-451-15007-4, Sig). NAL.

Ruthless Range. Lewis B. Patten. 160p. 1987. pap. 2.50 (ISBN 0-441-74181-9, Pub. by Charter Bks). Ace Bks.

Ruth's Adventures in Israel. Harriett Ottow. LC 87-51493. 44p. (gr. k-2). 1988. 5.95 (ISBN 1-55523-133-0). Winston-Derek.

Ruth's Loose Tooth. Price, Stern & Sloan Staff. (Suprise Bks.). (Illus.). 22p. (gr. 3-6). 1986. 5.95 (ISBN 0-8431-1823-7). Price Stern.

Ruth's Story. Catherine Storr. (People of the Bible Ser.). (Illus.). 24p. (Orig.). (gr. k-4). 1988. pap. 7.95 (ISBN 0-8249-7257-0). Ideals.

Ruth's Story. As told by Catherine Storr. (People of the Bible Ser.). (Illus.). 32p. (gr. k-4). 1985. PLB 11.33 (ISBN 0-8172-2043-7). Raintree Pubs.

Rutiodon. D. White. (Dinosaur Library). (Illus.). 24p. (gr. 3 up). Date not set. PLB 13.27 (ISBN 0-86592-522-4). Rourke Corp.

Rutland in Retrospect. Ed. by Robert E. West. LC 78-56622. (Illus.). 176p. 1978. pap. 17.00 (ISBN 0-914960-11-3). Academy Bks.

Rutland Papers. John H. Rutland. Repr. of 1842 ed. 19.00 (ISBN 0-384-52640-3). Johnson Repr.

Rutland Papers Original Documents Illustrative of the Courts & Times of Henry Seven & Henry Eight. John H. Rutland. Ed. by William Jerden. LC 17-1204. (Camden Society, London. Publications. First Ser.: No. 21). Repr. of 1842 ed. 19.00 (ISBN 0-404-50121-4). AMS Pr.

Rutland Road. rev. ed. Jim Shaugnessy. LC 80-19534. (Illus.). 370p. 1980. 30.00 (ISBN 0-8310-7128-1). Howell-North.

Rutland Street: The Story of an Educational Experiment for Disadvantaged Children in Dublin. Seamas Holland. (Illus.). 1979. 27.00 (ISBN 0-08-024264-2). Pergamon.

Rutland Water: A Decade of Change. Ed. by D. M. Harper & J. A. Bullock. 1982. lib. bdg. 54.50 (ISBN 90-6193-759-0, Pub. by Junk Pubs Netherlands). Kluwer Academic.

Rutland Words. C. Wordsworth. (English Dialect Society Publications Ser.: No. 64). pap. 15.00 (ISBN 0-8115-0484-0). Kraus Repr.

Rutta. Barbara Bentley. 1988. 12.95 (ISBN 0-533-07507-6). Vantage.

Rutters of the Sea: The Sailing Directions of Pierre Garcie. Pierre Garcie. LC 67-17722. (Illus.). pap. 125.30 (ISBN 0-317-08232-9, 2022051). Bks Demand UMI.

Ruxton of the Rockies. George F. Ruxton. Ed. by LeRoy R. Hafen. (AET Ser.: Vol. 13). (Illus.). 1982. 22.95 (ISBN 0-8061-1591-2). U of Okla Pr.

Ruxton of the Rockies. George F. Ruxton. Ed. by LeRoy R. Hafen. LC 50-9832. (American Exploration & Travel Ser.: Vol. 13). (Illus.). 344p. (Orig.). 1984. pap. 9.95 (ISBN 0-8061-1603-X). U of Okla Pr.

Ruy Blas. Victor Hugo. (Univers des Lettres Bordas). pap. 5.95 (ISBN 0-685-34921-7). French & Eur.

Ruy Blas, 2 vols. Victor Hugo. 1971. Vol. 1. 30.00 (ISBN 0-686-54039-5); Vol. 2. 22.50 (ISBN 0-686-54040-9). French & Eur.

Ruy Blas. Victor Hugo. 192p. 1970. pap. 2.95 (ISBN 0-686-54041-7). French & Eur.

Ruy Lopez Arkhangelsk System. Jerzy Konikowski. Tr. by Paul Janicki. 89p. (Orig.). 1987. pap. 6.00 (ISBN 0-317-65605-8). Chess Ent Inc.

Ruy Lopez: Breyer System. L. S. Blackstock. (Illus.). 112p. 1976. pap. 18.95 (ISBN 0-7134-3142-3, Pub. by Batsford England). David & Charles.

Ruy Lopez: Winning Chess with 1P-K4. L. W. Barden. 185p. 1963. 14.50 (ISBN 0-08-013006-2); pap. 7.75 (ISBN 0-08-009997-1). Pergamon.

RV & the Haunted Garage. Mel Gilden. (Zoomers of Motor City Ser.). (Illus.). (gr. k-3). Date not set. pap. 2.25 (ISBN 0-317-62493-8). Wanderer Bks.

RV Owner' Manual. 2nd ed. Intertec Publishing Corp. (Illus.). 160p. pap. 5.95 (ISBN 0-87288-197-0, RVO-2). Intertec Pub.

RV Park & Campground Directory: United States, Canada, Mexico. 976p. 1989. pap. 13.95 (ISBN 0-13-650268-7). Prentice Hall Pr.

RV Park & Campground Directory, 1989: Eastern U.S. & Canada. 582p. 1989. pap. 9.95 (ISBN 0-13-650227-X). Prentice Hall Pr.

RV Repair & Maintenance Manual. 288p. 1980. 12.98 (ISBN 0-318-17003-5). RV Indus Assn.

RVers Guide to Solar Battery Charging. Noel Kirkby. (Illus.). 176p. 1987. pap. 12.95x (ISBN 0-937948-08-X). AATEC Pubns.

RVing with Dolly. Virgil Gorans. 131p. (Orig.). 1988. pap. 6.95 (ISBN 0-9620138-0-3). M-V Charters.

Rwala Bedouin Today. William Lancaster. (Changing Cultures Ser.). (Illus.). 192p. 1981. 44.50 (ISBN 0-521-23877-3); pap. 16.95 (ISBN 0-521-28275-6). Cambridge U Pr.

Rwanda. Ed. by J. K. Pomeray. (Places & Peoples of the World Ser.). (Illus.). 96p. (gr. 5 up). 1988. lib. bdg. 12.95x (ISBN 1-55546-783-0). Chelsea Hse.

Rx - Spiritist As Needed: A Study of a Puerto Rican Community Mental Health Resource. Alan Harwood. LC 87-47599. (Anthropology of Contemporary Issues Ser.). 288p. 1987. pap. 12.95x (ISBN 0-8014-9470-2). Cornell U Pr.

RX & OTC Cough & Cold Products. Ed. by Peter Allen. 206p. 1985. pap. text ed. 2955.00 (ISBN 0-931634-51-2). FIND SVP.

RX: Applause-Biography of a Blind Performer. Mason Turner. 1983. pap. 5.95 (ISBN 0-8283-1879-4). Branden Pub Co.

Rx DOS. Bill J. Frye. 80p. (Orig.). 1986. pap. 9.95 (ISBN 0-940017-04-0). Info Tec OH.

RX Executive Diet. Virginia Aronson & Fredrick Stare. 1985. 9.75 (ISBN 0-8158-0424-5). Chris Mass.

Rx: For a Liberated Childbirth. Bev Smucha & Alice Unger. Ed. by Evie Heilbrun. LC 77-80302. 1979. 14.95 (ISBN 0-87949-098-5). Ashley Bks.

Rx for DSO. William H. Bryan. (New Horizons Ser.: No. 2). 1975. pap. 3.25 (ISBN 0-934914-25-7). NACM.

Rx for Hilarity. Abraham Unger. 1980. pap. 1.50 (ISBN 0-505-51468-0, Pub. by Tower Bks). Leisure NY.

Rx for Learning Disability. Emmett C. Velten, Jr. & Carlene Sampson. LC 77-8595. 174p. 1978. 18.95x (ISBN 0-88229-330-3). Nelson-Hall.

Rx for Living: Take as Needed. Max L. Foreman. 1982. 20.00x (ISBN 0-8197-0490-3). Bloch.

RX for Premedical Minority Students. Date not set. price not set (ISBN 0-933483-01-5). Kwibidi Pub.

Rx for Recovery: The Medical Health Guide for Families of Recovering Alcoholics & Addicts. Jeffrey Weisberg & Gene Hawes. 512p. 1988. 19.95. Watts.

RX for RV Performance & Mileage: How to Diagnose Your RVs Mechanical Problems & Make Your Engine More Powerful. Bill Estes & John Geraghty. 360p. 1983. 14.95 (ISBN 0-934798-06-0). TL Enterprises.

Rx for Small Business Success: Accounting, Planning, & Recordkeeping Techniques for a Healthy Bottom Line. Jeffrey Slater. (Illus.). 256p. 1981. 18.95 (Spec). P-H.

Rx for Stress: A Nurse's Guide. Jenny Steinmetz & Stewart Proctor. 176p. (Orig.). 1984. leader manual 3.95 (ISBN 0-915950-65-0); student manual 9.95 (ISBN 0-915950-63-4). Bull Pub.

Rx for Success. R. L. Bladwin et al. (Illus.). 318p. 1983. 48.00 (ISBN 0-912063-00-9). Vision Pubns.

Rx for the Classroom Blahs. Lynn Embry. (Illus.). 64p. (gr. 4-8). 1983. wkbk. 6.95 (ISBN 0-86653-104-1, GA 462). Good Apple.

Rx for Vegetable Gardens. Duane Newcomb. LC 81-50328. (Illus.). 256p. (Orig.). 1982. pap. 8.95 (ISBN 0-87477-185-4). J P Tarcher.

Rx: Handwriting; An Individualized, Prescriptive System for Painless Managing Handwriting Instruction. Jane E. Bluestein. (Illus.). 48p. 1983. pap. 5.95 (ISBN 0-915817-01-2). ISS Pubns.

RX Shikse: A Transplacental Romance. 1st ed. J R Ephraim. LC 88-81437. 1988. pap. 9.95 (ISBN 0-941404-75-7). Falcon Pr Az.

RX Television: Enhancing the Preventive Impact of TV. Ed. by Joyce Sprafkin et al. LC 82-15778. (Prevention in Human Services Ser.: Vol. 2, Nos. 1-2). 139p. 1983. text ed. 29.95 (ISBN 0-86656-168-4, B168); pap. text ed. 12.95 (ISBN 0-86656-219-2). Haworth Pr.

Rx to Help You Get Well. (Illus.). 1971. pap. 1.50 (ISBN 0-87067-903-1, BH903, Melrose Sq). Holloway.

RX to OTC Market Approach. 338p. 1985. 1625.00 (ISBN 0-86621-347-3, A1431). Frost & Sullivan.

RX-7 & Mazda Rotary Engine Sportscars. Jack K. Yamaguchi. (Illus.). 280p. 1986. 19.95 (ISBN 0-312-69456-3). St Martin.

Ryan & the Circus Wheels. Joni E. Tada. LC 87-26912. 1988. 6.95 (ISBN 1-55513-154-9, Chariot Bks). Cook.

Ryan Rides Back. Bill Grider. 192p. 1988. 14.95 (ISBN 0-87131-542-4). M Evans.

Ryan's Gold. Cordia Byers. 324p. 1988. pap. 3.95 (ISBN 0-449-13144-0, GM). Fawcett.

Ryan's Master: The Story of John Whitaker. Jane Fuller. (Illus.). 144p. 1986. 24.95 (ISBN 0-09-162360-X, Pub. by Century Hutchinson). David & Charles.

Ryan's Return. Lynsey Stevens. (Harlequin Presents Ser.). 192p. 1982. pap. 1.75 (ISBN 0-373-10497-9). Harlequin Bks.

Rydberg Series in Atoms & Molecules. A. B. Duncan. (Physical Chemistry Ser, Vol. 23). 1971. 59.00 (ISBN 0-12-223950-4). Acad Pr.

Rydberg States of Atoms & Molecules. Ed. by R. F. Stebbings & F. B. Dunning. LC 82-1181. (Illus.). 500p. 1983. 95.00 (ISBN 0-521-24823-X). Cambridge U Pr.

Ryde to Ventnor. Vic Mitchell & Keith Smith. 1986. 34.75x (ISBN 0-906520-19-3, Pub. by Middleton Pr UK). State Mutual Bk.

Ryder's Army. Cole Weston. (Ryder Ser.). 224p. 1987. pap. 2.95 (ISBN 0-8041-0023-3, Pub. by Ivy). Ballantine.

Ryder's Standard Geographic Reference: The United States of America. Nicholas G. Ryder. LC 81-90461. (Satellite Photo Maps of the World Ser.). (Illus.). 223p. 1981. 85.00 (ISBN 0-941784-00-2). Ryder Geo.

Rye in the Twenties. Colin Dunne. 12.00 (ISBN 0-405-09141-9, 19506). Ayer Co Pubs.

Rye: Production, Chemistry, & Technology. W. Bushuk. LC 76-29382. 181p. 1976. text ed. 34.00x (ISBN 0-913250-11-2). Am Assn Cereal Chem.

Ryerson Genealogy: Genealogy & History of the Knickerbocker Families of Ryerson, Ryerse, Ryerss, Also Adriane & Martense Families All Descendants of Martin & Adriane Reyersz (Reyerszen) of Amsterdam, Holland. Albert W. Ryerson. Ed. by Alfred L. Holman. 150.00x (ISBN 0-685-88555-0). Elliots Bks.

Rylands Haggadah: A Medieval Sephardi Masterpiece in Facsimile. Raphael Loewe. 1988. 95.00 (ISBN 0-8109-1568-5). Abrams.

Ryme & Thought. Mary A. Bailes. 48p. (Orig.). 1981. pap. 2.95 (ISBN 0-938468-00-6). Marcella.

Ryme Index to the Manuscript Texts of Chaucer's Minor Poems. Walter W. Skeat. 1887. 40.00 (ISBN 0-8274-3318-2). R West.

Rymes of Robyn Hood: An Introduction to the English Outlaw. R. B. Dobson & J. Taylor. LC 75-31564. (Illus.). 1976. 35.95x (ISBN 0-8229-1126-4). U of Pittsburgh Pr.

Ryne Sandberg: The Triple Threat. Hal Lundgren. LC 85-29895. (Sports Stars Ser.). (Illus.). 48p. (gr. 2-8). 1986. PLB 11.27 (ISBN 0-516-04357-9); pap. 2.95 (ISBN 0-516-44357-7). Childrens.

Ryno! Ryne Sandberg & Fred Mitchell. (Illus.). 96p. (Orig.). 1985. pap. 5.95 (ISBN 0-8092-5147-7). Contemp Bks.

Ryodai Toji Ceramics of the Liao Period. Nora National Museum Staff. 18p. 1954. 20.00x (ISBN 0-317-44947-8, Pub. by Han-Shan Tang Ltd). State Mutual Bk.

Rypins' Medical Licensure Examinations: Topical Summaries & Questions. 14th ed. Edward D. Frohlich et al. LC 65-8402. (Illus.). 1094p. 1987. text ed. 49.00 (ISBN 0-397-50674-0, Lippincott Medical). Lippincott.

Rypins' Questions & Answers for Boards Review: Basic Sciences. Ed. by Edward D. Frolich. LC 65-9889. 1987. pap. text ed. 16.95 (ISBN 0-397-50823-9, Lippincott Medical). Lippincott.

Rystari Dukha. M. S. Cherepakhov. 78p. 1983. 25.00x (Pub. by Collets UK). State Mutual Bk.

Ryukyuan Culture & Society. Pacific Science Congress, 10th, Honolulu, 1961. LC 63-19525. pap. 30.30 (ISBN 0-317-08484-4, 2000073). Bks Demand UMI.

Ryusei-Ha. Kasen Yoshimura. (Ikebana Card Bks.). (Illus., Eng. & Japanese.). 1970. pap. 5.95 ea (Pub. by Shufunmoto Co Ltd Japan). Motifs Base on Materials, 42pgs (ISBN 4-07-973346-1). Motifs Based on Containers, 42pgs (ISBN 4-07-973352-6). Natural & Abstract, 42pgs (ISBN 4-07-973369-0). C E Tuttle.

Ryzhii D'Iavol. Mikhail Dyomin. LC 87-60055. 300p. (Orig.). 1987. pap. 18.00 (ISBN 0-89830-110-6). Russica Pubs.

S

S. Cid Corman. 1976. boards 16.00 (ISBN 0-686-63994-4); pap. 8.00 (ISBN 0-686-63995-2). Elizabeth Pr.

S. Christopher Franke. 1977. chapbook 0.71 (ISBN 0-9601640-0-6). Deciduous.

S. John Updike. LC 87-40496. 288p. 1988. 17.95 (ISBN 0-394-56835-4). Knopf.

S. A. Rachinskij i jego Shkola. 84p. 1956. pap. 2.00 (ISBN 0-317-30334-1). Holy Trinity.

S. A. Review: Two. Ed. by South African Research Service. 340p. 1984. pap. text ed. 16.95x (ISBN 0-86975-238-3, Pub. by Ravan Pr). Ohio U Pr.

S & M: Studies in Sadomasochism. Ed. by Thomas Weinberg & G. Levi W. Kamel. LC 83-61030. 211p. 1983. 20.95 (ISBN 0-87975-218-1); pap. text ed. 13.95 (ISBN 0-87975-230-0). Prometheus Bks.

S & Z Correction Contracts. Marilyn Cilick & Jerrie Ueberle. 30p. pap. text ed. 6.95x (ISBN 0-8134-2625-1). Inter Print Pubs.

S. Andrea in Mantua: The Building. Eugene J. Johnson. LC 74-30085. (Illus.). 220p. 1975. 42.50x (ISBN 0-271-01186-6). Pa St U Pr.

S. Aureli Augustini: De Beata Vita: A Translation with an Introduction & Commentary, Vol. 72. Ruth A. Brown. (Patristic Studies). 211p. 1984. Repr. of 1944 ed. 30.00x (ISBN 0-939738-30-9). Zubal Inc.

S. B. C.: House on the Sand? David O. Beale. 246p. (Orig.). 1985. pap. 5.95 (ISBN 0-89084-281-7). Bob Jones Univ Pr.

S-B Stock Market Ratio: Profiting from Legal Insider Trading. Edwin A. Buck. 1988. 14.95 (ISBN 0-13-785643-1). Prentice Hall Pr.

S Corporation Desk Book. Michael Schlesinger. 336p. 1988. 49.95 (ISBN 0-13-785635-0, Busn). P-H.

S Corporation Handbook. Peter M. Fass & Barbara S. Gerrard. 1987. pap. 75.00 (ISBN 0-87632-570-3, SS). Clark Boardman.

"S" Corporation Handbook. Ted Nicholas. 1988. looseleaf 69.95 (ISBN 0-942103-01-7). Enterprise Del.

S Corporation Manual: A Special Tax Break for Small Business Corporations. Peter L. Faber & Martin E. Holbrook. LC 86-194493. 250p. 1988. looseleaf 306.00 (ISBN 0-13-785528-1); pap. 41.50 (ISBN 0-13-785544-3); looseleaf 282.00; write for info. P-H.

S Corporation: Planning & Operation. Irving Schreiber et al. 500p. 1983. 125.00 (ISBN 0-916592-45-6). Panel Pubs.

S Corporations Tax & Business Manual. Strobel. (Tax & Business Guides for Professionals Ser.). 1988. price not set (ISBN 0-471-62566-3). Wiley.

S Corporations: Tax Choices for Business Planning. Ed. by Prentice Hall Inc. Editorial Staff. 1984. write for info. P-H.

S-Curve. Richard Foster. Date not set. write for info. S&S.

S. E. Britaines Busse: Or Herring-Fishing Ship, with the States Proclamation Annexed Unto the Same, As Concerning Herring-Fishing. LC 74-80211. (English Experience Ser.: No. 690). 1974. Repr. of 1615 ed. 5.00 (ISBN 90-221-0690-X). Walter J Johnson.

S. E. M. Atlas of Cells & Tissues. Tsuneo Fujita et al. LC 80-85298. (Illus.). 338p. 1981. 90.00 (ISBN 0-89640-051-4). Igaku-Shoin.

S. E. S. Study Series. Sensa Educational Systems, Inc. (S. E. S. Ser.). (gr. 4). 1986. pap. text ed. 8.95 student text (ISBN 0-941535-54-1); tchr's. manual 45.00 (ISBN 0-317-56091-3). Sensa Educ Syst.

S. E S Study Series. Sensa Educational Systems, Inc. (gr. 5). 1987. pap. text ed. 8.95 student text (ISBN 0-941535-55-X). Sensa Educ Syst.

S. E S Study Series. Sensa Educational Systems, Inc. (S. E. S. Study Ser.). (gr. 6). 1986. pap. text ed. 8.95 student text (ISBN 0-941535-56-8). Sensa Educ Syst.

S. E. S. Study Series. Sensa Educational Systems, Inc. (S. E. S. Study Ser.). (gr. 7). 1986. pap. text ed. 8.95 student text (ISBN 0-941535-57-6). Sensa Educ Syst.

S. E. S. Study Series. Sensa Educational Systems, Inc. (S. E. S. Study Ser.). (gr. 8). 1986. pap. text ed. 8.95 student text (ISBN 0-941535-58-4). Sensa Educ Syst.

S. E. S. Study Series. Sensa Educational Systems, Inc. (S. E. S. Study Ser.). (gr. 9). 1986. pap. text ed. 8.95 (ISBN 0-941535-59-2). Sensa Educ Syst.

S. E. S. Study Series. Sensa Educational Systems, Inc. (S. E. S. Study Ser.). (gr. 10). pap. text ed. 8.95 student text (ISBN 0-941535-60-6). Sensa Educ Syst.

S. E. S. Study Series. Sensa Educational Systems, Inc. (S. E. S. Study Ser.). (gr. 11). 1986. pap. text ed. 8.95 student text (ISBN 0-941535-61-4). Sensa Educ Syst.

S. E. S. Study Series. Sensa Educational Systems, Inc. (S. E. S. Study Ser.). (gr. 12). 1986. pap. text ed. 8.95 (ISBN 0-941535-62-2). Sensa Educ Syst.

S. E. S. Study Series. rev ed. Sensa Educational Systems, Inc. (S. E. S. Study Ser.). (gr. 4-5). 1987. tchr's. manual 45.00 (ISBN 0-941535-63-0). Sensa Educ Syst.

S. E. S. Study Series. Sensa Educational Systems, Inc. (S. E. S. Study Ser.). (gr. 6-8). 1987. tchr's. ed. 45.00 (ISBN 0-941535-64-9). Sensa Educ Syst.

S. E. S. Study Series. Sensa Educational Systems, Inc. (S. E. S. Study Ser.). (gr. 9-10). tchr's. manual 45.00 (ISBN 0-941535-65-7). Sensa Educ Syst.

S. E. S. Study Series. rev. ed. Sensa Educational Systems, Inc. (S. E. S. Study Ser.). 1987. tchr's. manual 45.00 (ISBN 0-941535-66-5). Sensa Educ Syst.

S. E. S. Study Series. rev. ed. Sensa Educational Systems, Inc. (S. E. S. Study Ser.). (gr. 4). 1987. pap. text ed. 8.95 student text (ISBN 0-941535-67-3). Sensa Educ Syst.

S. E. S. Study Series. Sensa Educational Systems, Inc. (S. E. S. Study Ser.). (gr. 5). 1987. pap. text ed. 8.95 student text (ISBN 0-941535-68-1). Sensa Educ Syst.

S. E. S. Study Series. Sensa Educational Systems, Inc. (S. E. S. Study Ser.). (gr. 6). 1987. pap. text ed. 8.95 student text (ISBN 0-941535-69-X). Sensa Educ Syst.

S. E. S. Study Series. Sensa Educational Systems, Inc. (gr. 7). 1987. pap. text ed. 8.95 (ISBN 0-941535-70-3). Sensa Educ Syst.

S. E. S. Study Series. Sensa Educational Systems, Inc. (S. E. S. Study Ser.). (gr. 8). pap. text ed. 8.95 student text (ISBN 0-941535-71-1). Sensa Educ Syst.

S. E. S. Study Series. Sensa Educational Systems, Inc. (gr. 9). 1987. pap. text ed. 8.95 student text (ISBN 0-941535-72-X). Sensa Educ Syst.

S. E. S. Study Series. Sensa Educational Systems, Inc. (gr. 10). 1987. pap. text ed. 8.95 student text (ISBN 0-941535-73-8). Sensa Educ Syst.

S. E. S. Study Series. Sensa Educational Systems, Inc. (gr. 11). 1987. pap. text ed. 8.95 student text (ISBN 0-941535-74-6). Sensa Educ Syst.

S. E. S. Study Series. Sensa Educational Systems, Inc. (gr. 12). 1987. pap. text ed. 8.95 student text (ISBN 0-941535-75-4). Sensa Educ Syst.

S. E. S. Study Series. Sensa Educational Systems, Inc. (S. E. S. Study Ser.). (gr. 4-5). 1986. tchr's. manual 45.00 (ISBN 0-941535-50-9). Sensa Educ Syst.

S. E. S. Study Series. Sensa Educational Systems, Inc. (S. E. S. Study Ser.). (gr. 6-8). 1986. tchr's manual 45.00 (ISBN 0-941535-51-7). Sensa Educ Syst.

S. E. S. Study Series. Sensa Educational Systems, Inc. (S. E. S. Study Ser.). (gr. 9-10). 1986. 45.00 (ISBN 0-941535-52-5). Sensa Educ Syst.

S. E. X. Blackjack System. Alan Mandel. LC 86-70882. (Illus.). 224p. (Orig.). 1987. pap. 12.95 (ISBN 0-9616765-0-7). Bronx Bks.

S. Ephraim's Quotations from the Gospel. F. C. Burkitt. (Texts & Studies Ser.: No. 1, Vol. 7, Pt. 2). pap. 13.00 (ISBN 0-8115-1704-7). Kraus Repr.

S-F Two: A Pictorial History of Science Fiction Films from Rollerball to Return of the Jedi. Richard Meyers. (Illus.). 256p. 1984. 19.95 (Pub. by Citadel Pr). Lyle Stuart.

S-F 2: A Pictorial History of Science Fiction Films from Roller Ball to Return of the Jedi. Richard Meyers. LC 83-20964. (Illus.). 1984. 19.95 (ISBN 0-8065-0875-2, Pub. by Citadel Pr). Lyle Stuart.

S. Gernsback's Nineteen Twenty-Seven Radio Encyclopedia. Sidney Gersback. (Illus.). 172p. pap. 11.95 (ISBN 0-914126-07-5). Vintage Radio.

S Gsllinh Dyst. Betty Leslie-Melville. (Illus.). 320p. 1988. pap. 4.50 (ISBN 0-671-64254-5). PB.

S-He. Randy W. Rader. 20p. 1983. 7.00 (ISBN 0-913719-66-8); pap. 2.00 (ISBN 0-913719-65-X). High-Coo Pr.

S I Units: A Source Book. G. S. Ramaswamy & V. V. Rao. 1973. text ed. 15.00 (ISBN 0-07-096575-7). McGraw.

S Is for Sun Shimmers. Ellyn Mosbarger. (Illus.). 8p. (Orig.). 1983. pap. 5.95 (ISBN 0-943134-04-8). Ojai.

S. J. Perelman: A Critical Study. Steven H. Gale. LC 86-12106. (Contributions to the Study of Popular Culture Ser.: No. 15). 251p. 1987. 29.95 (ISBN 0-313-25003-0, GSJ/). Greenwood.

S. J. Perelman: A Life. Dorothy Hermann. 1987. pap. 8.95 (ISBN 0-671-64199-9, Fireside). S&S.

S. J. Perelman: A Life. Dorothy Herrmann. 1986. 18.95 (ISBN 0-399-13154-X). Putnam Pub Group.

S. J. Perelman: An Annotated Bibliography. Steven H. Gale. LC 84-45389. (Reference Library of the Humanities). 150p. 1985. lib. bdg. 26.00 (ISBN 0-8240-8845-X). Garland Pub.

S. Klein Directory of Computer Graphics Suppliers. 200p. 1987. 77.50. B Klein Pubns.

S Klein Directory of Computer Graphics Suppliers: Hardware, Software Systems, Services & Supplies. 5th ed. 224p. 1987. 73.00 (ISBN 0-317-65576-0). TBC Inc.

S. Klein Directory of Computer Suppliers: Hardware, Software, Systems & Services. Ed. by Malcolm Stiefel. 224p. 1987. 73.00 (ISBN 0-317-20391-6). TBC Inc.

S. L. A. Conference Proceedings 1985. Alan F. Taylor. 1987. 32.00x (ISBN 0-900649-58-5, Pub. by Scottish Libr Assn). State Mutual Bk.

S L R Nineteen Eighty-Three: Sign Language Research. Ed. by William Stokoe & Virginia Volterra. LC 84-52800. 1985. pap. text ed. 17.50x (ISBN 0-932130-08-9). Linstok Pr.

S. M. Eisenstein: Selected Works: Vol. I: Writings, 1922-34. S. M. Eisenstein. Ed. by Richard Taylor. LC 86-45516. write for info (ISBN 0-253-35042-5). Ind U Pr.

S. M. Eisenstein: Selected Works, Vol. 2: Towards a Theory of Montage, 1937-40. Ed. & tr. by Michael Glenny. LC 86-45516. 300p. 1988. 40.00 (ISBN 0-253-35043-3). Ind U Pr.

S-M: The Last Taboo. Gerald Greene & Caroline Greene. LC 74-7680. 1974. pap. 2.95 (ISBN 0-394-17832-7, B376, BC). Grove.

S-Matrix. D. Iagolnitzer. 1978. 42.00 (ISBN 0-444-85060-0, North-Holland). Elsevier.

S. O. Davies: A Socialist Faith. Robert Griffiths. 312p. 1983. 58.50x (ISBN 0-85088-887-5, Pub. by Gomer Pr). State Mutual Bk.

S. O. R. Losers. Avi. 96p. (gr. 3-7). 1986. pap. 2.50 (ISBN 0-380-69993-1, Camelot). Avon.

S O S. Eleanor I. Jackson. (Destiny Ser.). 90p. (Orig.). 1987. pap. 6.95 (ISBN 0-8163-0673-7). Pacific Pr Pub Assn.

S. O. S. Kit for Directors. Early Childhood Directors Association. Ed. by Jill Hix. (Illus.). 160p. (Orig.). 1987. pap. text ed. 9.95 (ISBN 0-317-67888-4). Toys 'n Things.

S. O. S. Rhino. C. A. W. Guggisberg. (Illus.). 1967. 12.50 (ISBN 0-8079-0116-4). October.

S. O. S. Save on Shopping Directory. Iris Ellis. Ed. by Marc Jaffe. LC 81-64190. 768p. 1985. pap. 10.95 (ISBN 0-394-73805-5, Pub. by Villard Bks). Random.

S. O. S: The Meaning of Our Crisis. P. A. Sorokin. Repr. of 1951 ed. 16.00 (ISBN 0-527-84832-8). Kraus Repr.

S. P. Eagle: A Biography of Sam Spiegel. Andrew Sinclair. 256p. 1988. 17.95 (ISBN 0-316-79236-5). Little.

S-Potential. Ed. by Boris D. Drujan & Miguel Laufer. LC 82-20394. (Progress in Clinical & Biological Research Ser.: Vol. 113). 364p. 1982. 66.00 (ISBN 0-8451-0113-7). A R Liss.

S. S. Consultation Handbook. Joanne S. Hayden. 1988. pap. price not set (ISBN 0-9619427-2-X). J S Hayden.

S. S. Great Britain: The Model Ship. William Mowll. LC 82-60766. (Illus.). 175p. 1983. 22.95 (ISBN 0-87021-866-2). Naval Inst Pr.

S. S. Norway the World's Largest Ship. 176p. 1985. 27.50x (N555). Vanous.

S-S Prodigal. David C. Wood. LC 86-90170. (Illus.). 204p. (Orig.). 1987. pap. 9.95 (ISBN 0-9616862-0-0). XyloPub Ltd.

S. S. San Pedro. James G. Cozzens. LC 67-19206. 85p. 1968. pap. 1.15 (ISBN 0-15-684830-9, Harv). HarBraceJ.

S. S. Stewart's Extra Fine Banjos. S. S. Stewart Banjo Company. Repr. of 1896 ed. 6.00 (ISBN 0-686-21421-8). Mih.

S. S. Valentine. Terry W. Phelan. LC 79-10037. (Illus.). 48p. (gr. 2-6). 1979. 6.95 (ISBN 0-02-774570-8, Four Winds). Macmillan.

S. T. Coleridge: Little Journeys to the Homes of English Authors. Elbert Hubbard. 1900. 15.00 (ISBN 0-8274-3505-3). R West.

S. T. Coleridge's Treatise on Method As Published in the Encyclopedia Metropolitan. Alice D. Snyder. 1974. Repr. of 1934 ed. lib. bdg. 32.00 (ISBN 0-8414-2679-1). Folcroft.

S. Thomas of Canterbury. W. H. Hutton. 59.95 (ISBN 0-8490-0983-9). Gordon Pr.

S-Ticulation. Mary Zellmer. (Illus.). 1987. 12.00 (ISBN 0-930599-24-1). Thinking Pubns.

S-V Forty Viruses. Keerti V. Shah et al. (Illus.). 220p. 1973. text ed. 27.50x (ISBN 0-8422-7064-7). Irvington.

S. W. A. K. Sealed with a Kiss. Judith Enderele. 100p. 1987. pap. 2.50 (ISBN 0-425-09570-3, Pub. by Berkley-Pacer). Berkley Pub.

S. W. A. T. Team Manual. Robert P. Cappel. (Illus.). 150p. 1979. pap. 12.00 (ISBN 0-87364-169-8). Paladin Pr.

S. Weir Mitchell. Joseph P. Lovering. LC 76-125256. (Twayne's United States Authors Ser.). 1971. lib. bdg. 17.95 (ISBN 0-89197-984-0); pap. text ed. 9.95x (ISBN 0-8290-0002-X). Irvington.

S. Weir Mitchell As a Psychiatric Novelist. David M. Rein. 207p. 1986. Repr. of 1952 ed. lib. bdg. 45.00 (ISBN 0-89984-649-1). Century Bookbindery.

S. Y. Agnon. Harold Fisch. LC 74-76126. (Literature and Life Ser.). 124p. 1975. 14.95 (ISBN 0-8044-2197-8). Ungar.

S-Z. Roland Barthes. 280p. 1970. 29.95 (ISBN 0-686-53944-3); pap. 9.95 (ISBN 0-686-53945-1). French & Eur.

S-Z. Roland Barthes. Tr. by Richard Miller from Fr. pap. 8.95 (ISBN 0-8090-1377-0). Hill & Wang.

SA: A Historical Perspective. Jill Halcomb. (Illus.). 277p. pap. 29.95 Dust jacket (ISBN 0-317-55236-8). Johnson Ref Bks.

Saad Ahaah Sinil: Dual Language. Martha Austin & Regina Lynch. 42p. 1983. 6.00 (ISBN 0-936008-18-0). Navajo Curr.

Saadia Anniversary Volume. Ed. by Boaz Cohen & Steven Katz. LC 79-7168. (Jewish Philosophy, Mysticism & History of Ideas Ser.). 1980. Repr. of 1943 ed. lib. bdg. 28.50x (ISBN 0-405-12244-6). Ayer Co Pubs.

Saadia Gaon Book of Beliefs & Opinions. Tr. by Samuel Rosenblatt. (Judaica Ser.: No. 1). 1948. 55.00t (ISBN 0-300-00865-1). Yale U Pr.

Saadiah Gaon: Selected Essays: An Original Anthology. Ed. by Steven Katz. LC 79-7171. (Jewish Philosophy, Mysticism & History of Ideas Ser.). 1980. lib. bdg. 34.50x (ISBN 0-405-12230-6). Ayer Co Pubs.

Saadiah Weissman. Benzion Firer. 140p. (gr. 5-12). 1982. 9.95 (ISBN 0-87306-294-9); pap. 5.95. Feldheim.

Saadya Studies: In Commemoration of the One Thousandth Anniversary of the Death of R. Saadya Gaon. Ed. by Erwin I. Rosenthal & Steven Katz. LC 79-7170. (Jewish Philosophy, Mysticism & History of Ideas Ser.). 1980. Repr. of 1943 ed. lib. bdg. 25.50x (ISBN 0-405-12284-5). Ayer Co Pubs.

Saal-Buch Des Benedictiner-Stiftes Gottweig (Benedictine Abbey) Repr. of 1855 ed. 23.00 (ISBN 0-384-19080-4). Johnson Repr.

Saama-Veda (Summary) Date not set. 5.00 (ISBN 0-938924-31-1). Sri Shirdi Sai.

Saar Controversy. W. R. Bisschop. (Grotius Society Publication: No. 2). 186p. 1961. 22.00 (ISBN 0-379-00399-6). Oceana.

Saba Saba Forever. Lucien E. Palmieri. LC 86-90285. 370p. 1987. 14.95 (ISBN 0-533-07218-2). Vantage.

Saba Silhouettes: Life Stories from a Caribbean Island. Julia G. Crane. 1987. 20.00 (ISBN 0-533-06831-2). Vantage.

Sabaean Inscriptions from Mahram Bilgis (Marib) Jamme Albert. LC 62-10311. (American Foundation for the Study of Man Publications: Vol. 3). pap. 139.30 (ISBN 0-317-09904-3, 2005199). Bks Demand UMI.

Sabana see Abahn.

Sabanu: Studies of a Sub-Visayan Mountain Folk of Mindanao. John P. Finley. 1913. 24.00 (ISBN 0-384-15700-9). Johnson Repr.

Sabate: Guerilla Extraordinary. Antonio Tellez. Tr. by Stuart Christie from Span. (Anarchist Pocketbooks: No. 1). 208p. 1985. pap. 7.00 (ISBN 0-317-67951-1). Left Bank.

Sabbaath in England. Max Levy. Repr. of 1933 ed. 24.00 (ISBN 0-384-32425-8). Johnson Repr.

Sabbatai Sevi: The Mystical Messiah. Gershom Scholem. Tr. by R. Zwi Werblowski from Hebrew. LC 75-166389. (Bollingen Series, Vol. 93). (Illus.). 1040p. 1973. 79.00x (ISBN 0-691-09916-2); pap. 22.50x (ISBN 0-691-01809-X). Princeton U Pr.

Sabbatai Zevi. Shalom Asch. Tr. by Florence Whyte & George R. Noyes. LC 74-3622. (Illus.). 131p. 1974. Repr. of 1930 ed. lib. bdg. 48.50x (ISBN 0-8371-7449-X, ASSZ). Greenwood.

Sabbath. Samuel H. Dresner. 1970. pap. 2.95 (ISBN 0-8381-2114-4). United Syn Bk.

Sabbath. Abraham J. Heschel. 118p. 1975. pap. 5.95 (ISBN 0-374-51267-1). FS&G.

Sabbath: A Guide to Its Understanding & Observance. I. Grunfeld. 6.95; pap. 4.95 (ISBN 0-87306-099-7). Feldheim.

Sabbath & Festival Praybook. 9.85 (ISBN 0-686-96035-1). United Syn Bk.

Sabbath & Holidays Prayer Book. S. Singer. 330p. 1925. 8.00 (ISBN 0-88482-003-3). Hebrew Pub.

Sabbath & Sectarianism in Seventeenth-Century England. David S. Katz. Ed. by A. J. Vanderjagt. LC 88-2849. (Studies in Intellectual History: Vol. 10). xiv, 224p. 1988. 60.00 (ISBN 90-04-08754-0, Pub. by E J Brill). Heinman.

Sabbath & the Lord's Day. H. M. Riggle. 160p. pap. 1.50 (ISBN 0-686-29165-4). Faith Pub Hse.

Sabbath at Sea. Michael L. Roland. (Destiny II Ser.). 108p. 1984. pap. 6.95 (ISBN 0-8163-0547-1). Pacific Pr Pub Assn.

Sabbath Bread: For Personal Sacred-Searching & Group Faith-Sharing. Georgene Wilson. LC 87-62530. 145p. (Orig.). 1987. pap. 9.95 (ISBN 0-89390-101-6). Resource Pubns.

Sabbath Breaking & the Death Penalty: A Theological Investigation. James B. Jordan. LC 86-80679. 109p. (Orig.). 1986. pap. 9.95 (ISBN 0-939404-13-3). Geneva Ministr.

Sabbath in Puritan New England. Alice M. Earle. 335p. 1969. Repr. of 1891 ed. 20.00 (ISBN 0-87928-005-0). Corner Hse.

Sabbath in the Classical Kabbalah. Elliot K. Ginsburg. (Judaica: Hermeneutics, Mysticism & Religion Ser.). 384p. 1988. 44.50x (ISBN 0-88706-778-6); pap. 14.95x (ISBN 0-88706-779-4). State U NY Pr.

Sabbath-Law of R. Meir. Robert Goldenberg. LC 78-14370. (Brown University. Brown Judaic Studies: No. 6). 1978. pap. 9.00 (ISBN 0-89130-249-2, 140006). Scholars Pr GA.

Sabbath Prayerbook. Ed. by Mordecai M. Kaplan & Eugene Kohn. LC 57-9678. 573p. 1979. 11.50 (ISBN 0-935457-32-1). Reconstructionist Pr.

Sabbath School Manual. rev. ed. General Conference, Sabbath School Department Staff. 1982. pap. 5.95 (ISBN 0-8127-0228-X). Review & Herald.

Sabbath Service: Shaharit L'Shabbat. Abraham Shumsky. Date not set. pap. 3.95x (ISBN 0-940646-35-8). Rossel Bks.

Sacramento: Excursions into Its History & Natural World. William M. Holden. (Illus.). 496p. (Orig.). 1988. pap. 11.95 (ISBN 0-9619561-0-0). Two Rivers Pub CA.

Sacramento-Napa Counties Street Atlas 1985. Thomas Bros. Maps. (Illus.). 324p. pap. cancelled (ISBN 0-88130-123-X). Thomas Bros Maps.

Sacramento, River of Gold. Julian Dana. Ed. by Constance L. Skinner. LC 72-144963. (Illus.). 1971. Repr. of 1939 ed. 29.00x (ISBN 0-403-00932-4). Scholarly.

Sacramento-Solano Counties Street Atlas & Directory, 1980. rev. ed. Thomas Bros. Maps Staff. (Illus.). 1988. pap. 18.95. Thomas Bros Maps.

Sacramento-Solano Counties Street Guide & Directory, 1988. Thomas Bros. Maps Staff. (Illus.). 242p. (Orig.). 1988. pap. 18.95 (ISBN 0-88130-271-6). Thomas Bros Maps.

Sacraments. Maureen Curley. (Children of the Kingdom Activities Ser.). (gr. 4-7). 1975. 9.95 (ISBN 0-89837-019-1, Pub. by Pflaum Pr). Pflaum Pr.

Sacraments. Peter A. Judd. LC 78-12776. 1978. pap. 7.00 (ISBN 0-8309-0225-2). Herald Hse.

Sacraments see Studies in Dogmatics: Theology.

Sacraments & Liturgy. Louis Weil. 116p. 1984. 29.95 (ISBN 0-631-13192-2); pap. 7.95 (ISBN 0-631-13229-5). Basil Blackwell.

Sacraments & Sacramentality. Bernard Cooke. LC 82-38794. 240p. 1983. pap. 7.95 (ISBN 0-89622-161-X). Twenty-Third.

Sacraments & Their Celebration. Nicholas Halligan. LC 85-23031. 284p. (Orig.). 1986. pap. 14.95 (ISBN 0-8189-0489-5). Alba.

Sacraments & You. Daughters of St. Paul. 2.50 (ISBN 0-8198-6866-3). Dghtrs St Paul.

Sacraments & You: Living Encounters with Christ. Michael Pennock. LC 81-65227. (High School Religion Text Program Ser.). (Illus.). (gr. 10-12). 1981. pap. text ed. 5.50 student text, 272p (ISBN 0-87793-221-2); tchr's. manual, 96p 2.95 (ISBN 0-87793-222-0). Ave Maria.

Sacraments As Encasement: Jesus Is with Us. Michael J. Taylor. 80p. 1986. pap. 4.95 (ISBN 0-8146-1469-8). Liturgical Pr.

Sacraments: Celebrations of Conversion. Partick J. Brennan. (Illus.). 30p. (Orig.). 1986. pap. 2.00 (ISBN 1-55612-046-X). Sheed & Ward MO.

Sacraments: Encountering the Risen Lord. Paul A. Feider. LC 85-73569. 128p. (Orig.). 1986. pap. 4.95 (ISBN 0-87793-327-8). Ave Maria.

Sacraments in Religious Education & Liturgy: An Ecumenical Model. Robert L. Browning & Roy A. Reed. LC 84-27536. 313p. (Orig.). 1985. pap. 14.95 (ISBN 0-89135-044-6). Religious Educ.

Sacraments in Theology & Canon Law. Ed. by Neophytos Edelby et al. LC 68-58308. (Concilium Ser.: Vol. 38). 191p. 1968. 7.95 (ISBN 0-8091-0132-7). Paulist Pr.

Sacraments, Liturgy & Prayer. Megan McKenna & Darryl Ducote. LC 78-71531. (Followers of the Way Ser.: Vol. 5). 221p. (gr. 9-12). 1979. 22.50 (ISBN 0-8091-9546-1). Paulist Pr.

Sacraments of Life, Life of the Sacraments. Leonardo Boff. 88p. 1987. pap. 7.95 (ISBN 0-912405-38-4). Pastoral Pr.

Sacraments of Simple Folk. Robert R. Marett. LC 77-27192. (Gifford Lectures: 1932-33). Repr. of 1933 ed. 28.00 (ISBN 0-404-60488-9). AMS Pr.

Sacraments: Readings in Contemporary Theology. Ed. by Michael J. Taylor. LC 80-9534. 274p. (Orig.). 1981. pap. 8.95 (ISBN 0-8189-0406-2). Alba.

Sacraments: The Symbols of Our Faith. Garabed Kochakian. (Illus.). 99p. (Orig.). 1983. pap. 5.00 (ISBN 0-934728-07-0). D O A C.

Sacre du Printemps: Seven Productions from Nijinsky to Martha Graham. Shelley C. Berg. Ed. by Oscan Brockett. LC 87-29421. (Theater & Dramatic Studies: No. 48). 118p. 1988. 44.95 (ISBN 0-8357-1842-5). UMI Res Pr.

Sacred Adventure. El Morya. LC 81-85464. 130p. 1981. 7.95 (ISBN 0-916766-53-5). Summit Univ.

Sacred Affair. 1982. 2.98. Cherubim.

Sacred & Civil Calendar of the Athenian Year. Jon D. Mikalson. 200p. 1975. 29.50x (ISBN 0-691-03545-8). Princeton U Pr.

Sacred & Legendary Art. Anna Jameson. Ed. by Estelle M. Hurll. LC 72-145108. (Illus.). 800p. 1972. Repr. of 1895 ed. 17.50x (ISBN 0-403-01045-4). Scholarly.

Sacred & Legendary Art, 2 Vols. Anna B. Jameson. LC 71-124594. Repr. of 1896 ed. 18.50 (ISBN 0-404-03551-5). AMS Pr.

Sacred & Legendary Art, 2 vols. Anna B. Jameson. 1973. lib. bdg. 55.00 (ISBN 0-8414-5371-3). Folcroft.

Sacred & Profane. Faye Kellerman. 320p. 1987. 16.95 (ISBN 0-87795-887-4). Morrow.

Sacred & Profane. Faye Kellerman. 1988. pap. 3.95 (ISBN 0-449-21502-4). Fawcett.

Sacred & Profane. Margaret Maitland. 1978. pap. 1.75 (ISBN 0-505-51241-6, Pub. by Tower Bks). Leisure NY.

Sacred & Profane Love Machine. Iris Murdoch. 1974. 12.95 (ISBN 0-670-61433-5). Viking.

Sacred & Profane Love Machine. Iris Murdoch. 368p. 1984. pap. 5.95 (ISBN 0-14-004111-7). Penguin.

Sacred & Profane Memories. facsimile ed. Carl Van Vechten. LC 75-156727. (Essay Index Reprint Ser). Repr. of 1932 ed. 20.00 (ISBN 0-8369-2337-5). Ayer Co Pubs.

Sacred & Profane Memories. Carl Van Vechten. LC 78-27584. 1979. Repr. of 1932 ed. lib. bdg. 35.00x (ISBN 0-313-20835-2, VVSP). Greenwood.

Sacred & Shakespearean Affinities. Charles Swinburne. LC 76-159973. (Studies in Shakespeare, No. 24). 1971. Repr. of 1890 ed. lib. bdg. 52.95x (ISBN 0-8383-1263-2). Haskell.

Sacred & the Feminine: Toward a Theology of Housework. Kathryn A. Rabuzzi. 224p. 1982. 15.95 (ISBN 0-8164-0509-3, HarpR). Har-Row.

Sacred & the Profane: The Nature of Religion. Mircea Eliade. Tr. by Willard Trask. LC 58-10904. 1968. pap. 4.95 (ISBN 0-15-679201-X, Harv). HarBraceJ.

Sacred & the Profane: The Nature of Religion. Mircea Eliade. 1983. 15.25 (ISBN 0-8446-6080-9). Peter Smith.

Sacred & the Psychic: Parapsychology & Christian Theology. John J. Heaney. LC 83-82015. (Orig.). 1984. pap. 9.95 (ISBN 0-8091-2594-3). Paulist Pr.

Sacred & the Secular in India's Performing Arts. Ed. by V. Subramaniam. 1983. 21.50x (ISBN 0-8364-0974-4, Pub. by Ashish India). South Asia Bks.

Sacred & the Subversive: Political Witch-Hunts as National Rituals. Albert Bergessen. LC 84-61370. (Society for Scientific Study of Religion Monograph: No. 4). 1984. pap. 5.50 (ISBN 0-932566-03-0). Soc Sci Stud Rel.

Sacred Art of Dying: How the World Religions Understand Death. Kenneth P. Kramer. 1988. pap. 11.95 (ISBN 0-8091-2942-6). Paulist Pr.

Sacred Art of Tibet. 2nd ed. Tarthang Tulku. LC 72-96555. (Illus.). 1972. pap. 9.95. Dharma Pub.

Sacred Art of Tibet. Tulku Tarthang. 98p. 1974. pap. 100.00x (Pub. by Han-Shan Tang Ltd). State Mutual Bk.

Sacred Art Tibetan Thanka Portfolios, 8 portfolios of 15 prints each. (Illus.). 1974. casebound 35.00 ea. No. 1: Lineage of Rainbow Light (ISBN 0-89800-170-6). No. 2: Heart of Compassion (ISBN 0-89800-171-4). No. 3: The Great Siddhas I (ISBN 0-89800-172-2). No. 4: The Great Siddhas II (ISBN 0-89800-173-0). No. 5: The Buddha's Previous Lives (ISBN 0-89800-174-9). No. 6: Path of Liberation (ISBN 0-89800-175-7). No. 7: Knowledge, Elixir of Immortality (ISBN 0-89800-176-5). No. 8: Enlightened Masters (ISBN 0-89800-177-3). Dharma Pub.

Sacred Bee in Ancient Times & Folklore. Hilda M. Ransome. 1976. lib. bdg. 100.00 (ISBN 0-8490-2552-4). Gordon Pr.

Sacred Beetle & Other Essays in Science. Ed. by Martin Gardner. 1986. pap. 10.95 (ISBN 0-452-00804-2, Mer). NAL.

Sacred Beetle & Other Great Essays in Science. Ed. by Martin Gardner. LC 84-42795. 427p. 1984. 24.95 (ISBN 0-87975-257-2). Prometheus Bks.

Sacred Biography: Saints & Their Biographers in the Middle Ages. Thomas J. Heffernan. 256p. 1988. 29.95 (ISBN 0-19-505225-0). Oxford U Pr.

Sacred Bond: The Legacy of Baby M. Phyllis Chesler. 256p. 1988. 16.95 (ISBN 0-8129-1745-6). Times Bks.

Sacred Book of the East: Vedic Hymns, 2 vols. Ed. by Max Muller. 250.00 (ISBN 0-8490-3963-0). Krishna Pr.

Sacred Books of China, 6 vols. James Legge. 600.00. Krishna Pr.

Sacred Books of China: Text of Taoism, 2 vols. Ed. by Max Muller. lib. bdg. 250.00 (ISBN 0-87968-298-1). Krishna Pr.

Sacred Books of the East, 50 vols. Ed. by Max Muller. 1977-1980. Repr. of 1975 ed. Set. 630.00; 15.50 ea. (ISBN 0-89684-310-6). Orient Bk Dist.

Sacred Books of the East. 457p. 1986. Repr. of 1900 ed. lib. bdg. 150.00 (ISBN 0-8495-5928-6). Arden Lib.

Sacred Books of the East. Epiphanius Wilson. 472p. 1981. pap. 15.00 (ISBN 0-89540-099-5, SB-099). Sun Pub.

Sacred Books of the East. Epiphanius Wilson. 464p. 1986. Repr. 25.00X (ISBN 0-8364-1764-X, Pub. by Usha). South Asia Bks.

Sacred Books of the East, including Selections from Vedic Hymns, The Zend Avesta, The Dhammapada, The Upanishads, The Koran & The Life of Budha. Epiphanius Wilson. 457p. 1987. Repr. of 1900 ed. 21.00x (ISBN 0-8364-2192-2, Pub. by Usha). South Asia Bks.

Sacred Books of the Hindus, 47 vols. Ed. by Baman Das Basu. Repr. of 1937 ed. 1575.50 (ISBN 0-404-19548-2). AMS Pr.

Sacred Books of the Jainas (Bibliotheca Jainica, 11 vols. Ed. by Sarat C. Ghoshal. Repr. of 1940 ed. 324.00 (ISBN 0-404-19549-0). AMS Pr.

Sacred Books of the Past, 50 vols. Ed. by Max Muller. 1983-87. Set. 630.00x (ISBN 81-208-0289-6, Pub. by Motilal Banarsidass India). Orient Bk Dist.

Sacred Bridge. Eric Werner. LC 79-18082. (Music Reprint Ser.). 1979. Repr. of 1959 ed. lib. bdg. 65.00 (ISBN 0-306-79581-7). Da Capo.

Sacred Bridge. Eric Werner. 640p. 1981. 60.00x (ISBN 0-234-77352-9, Pub. by Dobson Bks England). State Mutual Bk.

Sacred Bridge, Vol. 2. Eric Werner. 1985. 39.50 (ISBN 0-88125-052-X). Ktav.

Sacred Bridge: Supplementary Volume. Ed. by Dobson Books, Ltd. Staff. 256p. 1981. 75.00x (ISBN 0-234-77038-4, Pub. by Dobson Bks England). State Mutual Bk.

Sacred Bullock & Other Stories. facsimile ed. Mazo De La Roche. LC 76-101798. (Short Story Index Reprint Ser.). 1939. 14.00 (ISBN 0-8369-3186-6). Ayer Co Pubs.

Sacred Bundles of the Sac & Fox Indians. Mark R. Harrington. LC 76-43732. (Univevisty of Pennsylvania Museum Anthropological Publications: Vol. 4, No. 1). (Illus.). 192p. Repr. of 1914 ed. 30.00 (ISBN 0-404-15573-1). AMS Pr.

Sacred Calligraphy of the East. rev. ed. John Stevens. Ed. by Kendra Crossen. LC 80-53446. (Illus.). 224p. 1988. pap. 18.95 (ISBN 0-87773-458-5). Shambhala Pubns.

Sacred Canopy: Elements of a Sociological Theory of Religion. Peter L. Berger. LC 67-19805. 1969. pap. 5.95 (ISBN 0-385-07305-4, Anch). Doubleday.

Sacred Cause of Liberty: Republican Thought & the Millenium in Revolutionary New England. Nathan O. Hatch. LC 77-76299. 1977. 25.00x (ISBN 0-300-02092-9). Yale U Pr.

Sacred Ceremonies. Ed. by Rabia Clark & Alima McMillan. (Illus.). 115p. (Orig.). 1988. pap. 9.95 (ISBN 0-945324-00-6). Ziraat.

Sacred Charity: Confraternities & Social Welfare in Spain, 1400-1700. Maureen Flynn. LC 88-47727. 256p. 1988. 32.50x (ISBN 0-8014-2227-2). Cornell U Pr.

Sacred Choral Music in Print, 2 vols. 2nd ed. Ed. by Gary S. Eslinger & F. Mark Daugherty. LC 85-15368. (Music in Print Ser.: Vol. 1). 1312p. 1985. lib. bdg. 195.00 (ISBN 0-88478-017-1). Musicdata.

Sacred Choral Music in Print: Arranger Index. 2nd ed. LC 87-5337. (Music-in-Print Ser.: Vol. 1C). 137p. 1987. lib. bdg. 35.00 (ISBN 0-88478-019-8). Musicdata.

Sacred Chow. Adell Harvey & Mari Gonzalez. 176p. 1987. pap. 9.95 (ISBN 0-687-36713-1). Abingdon.

Sacred Circle: The Dilemma of the Intellectual in the Old South, 1840-1860. Drew G. Faust. LC 77-4547. 208p. 1978. text ed. 18.50x (ISBN 0-8018-1967-9). Johns Hopkins.

Sacred Circle: The Dilemma of the Intellectual in the Old South, 1840-1860. Drew G. Faust. LC 86-7014. 208p. (Orig.). pap. text ed. 13.95 (ISBN 0-8122-1229-0). U of Pa Pr.

Sacred Circles: Two Thousand Years of North American Indian Art. Ralph T. Coe. LC 77-153583. (Illus.). 260p. 1977. pap. 15.00 (ISBN 0-295-95584-8). U of Wash Pr.

Sacred Circles: Two Thousand Years of North American Indian Art. Ralph T. Coe. Ed. by Irena Hoare. (Illus.). 252p. 1977. pap. 12.95 (ISBN 0-942614-05-4). Nelson Atkins.

Sacred City of Anuradhapura. Chandra B. Charish. (Illus.). 132p. 1986. Repr. 26.00X (ISBN 0-8364-1746-1, Pub. by Abhinav India). South Asia Bks.

Sacred Complex of Kashi: A Microcosm of Indian Civilization. L. P. Vidyarthi et al. 1979. 20.00x (ISBN 0-8364-0335-5). South Asia Bks.

Sacred Complex: On the Psychogenesis of Paradise Lost. William Kerrigan. 368p. 1983. text ed. 27.00x (ISBN 0-674-78500-2). Harvard U Pr.

Sacred Cow & the Abominable Pig: Riddles of Food & Culture. Marvin Harris. 288p. 1987. pap. 7.95 (ISBN 0-671-63308-2, Touchstone Bks). S&S.

Sacred Cows at the Public Trough. Nancy Ferguson & Denzel Ferguson. (Illus.). 260p. 1983. pap. 8.95 (ISBN 0-89288-091-0). Maverick.

Sacred Cows in Education. Ed. by Frank Coffield & Richard Goodings. 214p. 1984. pap. 16.00x (ISBN 0-85224-484-3, Pub. by Edinburgh U Pr Scotland). Columbia U Pr.

Sacred Cows, Sacred Places: Origins & Survivals of Animal Homes in India. Deryck O. Lodrick. (Illus.). 350p. 1981. 37.50x (ISBN 0-520-04109-7). U of Cal Pr.

Sacred Cows...& Other Edibles. Nikki Giovanni. LC 87-22045. 192p. 1988. 12.95 (ISBN 0-688-04333-X). Morrow.

Sacred Dance. Maria-Gabriele Wosien. LC 85-52298. (Art & Imagination Ser.). (Illus.). 128p. 1986. pap. 11.95 (ISBN 0-500-81006-0). Thames Hudson.

Sacred Dance of India. Mrinalini Sarabhai. 43p. 1979. 6.95. Asia Bk Corp.

Sacred Dance with Physically & Mentally Handicapped. Ann M. Blessin. Ed. by Doug Adams. 1982. pap. 3.00 (ISBN 0-941500-28-4). Sharing Co.

Sacred Dance with Senior Citizens in Churches, Convalescent Homes, & Retirement Homes. Doug Adams. 1982. pap. 3.00 (ISBN 0-941500-27-6). Sharing Co.

Sacred Dimensions of Women's Experience. Ed. by Elizabeth D. Gray. (Illus.). 256p. (Orig.). 1988. pap. price not set (ISBN 0-934512-05-1). Roundtable Pr.

Sacred Dramas Sensibility. Hannah More. (Children's Books from the Past: Vol. 5). 290p. 1973. Repr. of 1782 ed. 42.40 (ISBN 3-261-01007-X). P Lang Pubs.

Sacred Earth, Metaphysical Poetry & the Advance of Science. A. J. Smith. 1985. pap. 5.50 (ISBN 0-85672-543-9, Pub. by British Acad). Longwood Pub Group.

Sacred Edict of K'ang Hsi. F. W. Baller. LC 79-89636. 18.00x (ISBN 0-915032-25-2); pap. 12.95x (ISBN 0-915032-28-7). Natl Poet Foun.

Sacred Executioner: Human Sacrifice & the Legacy of Guilt. Hyam Maccoby. LC 82-80492. (Illus.). 208p. 1983. 19.95 (ISBN 0-500-01281-4). Thames Hudson.

Sacred Farce from Medieval Bohemia Mastickar. Jarmila F. Veltrusky. (Michigan Studies in Humanties: No. 6). 1985. 25.00 (ISBN 0-936534-05-2). Mich Slavic Pubns.

Sacred Feathers: The Reverend Peter Jones (Kahkewaquonaby) & the Mississauga Indians. Donald B. Smith. LC 86-24914. (American Indian Lives Ser.). (Illus.). xx, 390p. 1988. 22.95x (ISBN 0-8032-4173-9). U of Nebr Pr.

Sacred Fire. B. Z. Goldberg. 285p. 1974. pap. 3.95 (ISBN 0-8065-0456-0, Pub. by Citadel Pr). Lyle Stuart.

Sacred Fire. B. Z. Goldberg. (Illus.). 1958. 7.50 (ISBN 0-8216-0146-6, Pub. by Univ Bks). Lyle Stuart.

Sacred Fire. Larry M. Laraby. (Illus.). 16p. 1983. pap. 5.00 (ISBN 0-910871-04-3). Spirit Mount Pr.

Sacred Fire Christian Marriage Through the Ages. David Mace & Vera Mace. 1986. 16.95 (ISBN 0-687-36712-3). Abingdon.

Sacred Flame: A Play in Three Acts. W. Somerset Maugham. LC 75-25390. (Works of W. Somerset Maugham Ser.). 1977. Repr. of 1928 ed. 20.00x (ISBN 0-405-07847-1). Ayer Co Pubs.

Sacred Fortress: Byzantine Art & Statecraft in Ravenna. Otto G. Von Simson. (Illus.). 168p. 1986. text ed. 34.50 (ISBN 0-691-04038-9); pap. 12.50x (ISBN 0-691-00276-2). Princeton U Pr.

Sacred Game: Provincialism & Frontier Consciousness in American Literature, 1630-1860. Albert Von Frank. (Cambridge Studies in American Literature & Culture). 192p. 1985. 24.95 (ISBN 0-521-30159-9). Cambridge U Pr.

Sacred Ground. Victor Briggs. 416p. 1982. pap. 2.95 (ISBN 0-441-74601-2). Ace Bks.

Sacred Grove: Essays on Museums. S. Dillon Ripley. LC 78-10785. 1979. pap. 6.95 (ISBN 0-87474-809-7, RISGP). Smithsonian.

Sacred Groves & Ravaged Gardens: The Fiction of Eudora Welty, Carson McCullers, & Flannery O'Conner. Louise Westling. LC 84-16434. 232p. 1985. 22.50x (ISBN 0-8203-0746-7); pap. 9.95 (ISBN 0-8203-0831-5). U of GA Pr.

Sacred Harp. Benjamin F. White. 432p. Repr. of 1968 ed. lib. bdg. 59.00 (Pub. by Am Repr Serv). Am Biog Serv.

Sacred Harp: A Tradition & Its Music. Buell E. Cobb, Jr. LC 76-12680. 256p. 1978. 15.00x (ISBN 0-8203-0426-3). U of Ga Pr.

Sacred Harp: A Tradition & Its Music. Buell E. Cobb, Jr. LC 77-6323. 265p. 1988. pap. 12.95 (ISBN 0-8203-1022-0). U of Ga Pr.

Sacred Heart & the Priesthood. Louise M. De La Touche. LC 79-90487. 1979. pap. 6.00 (ISBN 0-89555-128-4). TAN Bks Pubs.

Sacred Heart of Christmas. 2nd ed. Flower A. Newhouse. Ed. by Athene Bengtson. LC 78-74956. (Illus.). 1978. pap. 7.00 (ISBN 0-910378-14-2). Christward.

Sacred Hearts. Phebe Hanson. LC 85-61269. (Thistle Ser.). (Illus.). 48p. 1985. pap. 5.00 (ISBN 0-915943-08-5). Milkweed Ed.

Sacred Hoop: Recovering the Feminine in American Indian Traditions. Paula G. Allen. LC 85-47950. 288p. 1986. 24.95 (ISBN 0-8070-4600-0). Beacon Pr.

Sacred Hoop: Recovering the Feminine in American Indian Traditions. Paula G. Allen. LC 85-47950. 328p. 1987. pap. 10.95 (ISBN 0-8070-4601-9, BP 758). Beacon Pr.

Sacred Hour of Song. Ed. by Mack Harrell. 67p. 1939. pap. 9.95 (ISBN 0-8258-0153-2, 02933). Fischer Inc NY.

Sacred in a Secular Age: Toward Revision in the Scientific Study of Religion. Philip E. Hammond. LC 84-16470. 380p. 1985. 37.50x (ISBN 0-520-05342-7); pap. 10.95x (ISBN 0-520-05343-5). U of Cal Pr.

Sacred in All Its Forms. Pope John Paul II. 482p. 1984. 7.50 (ISBN 0-8198-6845-0); pap. 6.50 (ISBN 0-8198-6846-9). Dghtrs St Paul.

Sacred in Nature. Rosemary C. Wilkinson. 54p. (Orig.). 1988. pap. text ed. 5.00 (ISBN 0-931471-15-X). Pul-Star Pub.

Sacred Journey. Frederick Buechner. LC 81-47843. 128p. 1982. 13.95 (ISBN 0-06-061158-8, HarpR). Har-Row.

Sacred Journey. Frederick Buechner. 224p. 1984. pap. 8.95 large print ed. (ISBN 0-8027-2479-5). Walker & Co.

Sacred Journeys: Conversion & Commitment to Divine Light Mission. James V. Downton, Jr. LC 79-546. (Illus.). 1979. 29.00x (ISBN 0-231-04198-5). Columbia U Pr.

Sacred Keeper: A Biography of Patrick Kavonagh. Peter Kavanagh. LC 84-61576. (Irish Art Ser.). 403p. (Orig.). 1986. 25.00x (ISBN 0-915032-31-7); pap. 15.95 (ISBN 0-915032-32-5). Natl Poet Foun.

Sacred Knowledge: The Altaf Al-Quds of Shah Waliullah. Shah Waliullah. Tr. by G. N. Jalbani & D. L. Pendlebury. 1982. 18.95 (ISBN 0-900860-93-6, Pub. by Octagon Pr England). Ins Study Human.

Sacred Kural. 2nd. ed. Ed. & tr. by H. A. Popley. Orig. Title: Tamil Veda of Tiruvalluvar. 159p. pap. 2.80 (ISBN 0-88253-386-X). Ind-US Inc.

Sacred Kurral of Tiruvalluva Nayanar. G. U. Pope. 448p. 1986. Repr. of 1886 ed. 22.00X (ISBN 0-8364-1681-3, Pub. by Abhinav India). South Asia Bks.

Sacred Land, Sacred Sex: Rapture of the Deep. Dolores LaChapelle. (Illus., Orig.). 1988. pap. 22.00 (ISBN 0-917270-05-3). Finn Hill.

Sacred Landscape. Frederic Lehrman. 1988. 34.95. Celestial Arts.

Sacred Language: The Nature of Supernatural Discourse in Lakota. William Powers. LC 86-40079. (Civilization of the American Indians Ser.: Vol. 179). (Illus.). 320p. 1986. 24.95x (ISBN 0-8061-2009-6). U of Okla Pr.

Sacred Literature. George Hurst. LC 74-3454. Repr. lib. bdg. 30.00 (ISBN 0-8414-4813-2). Folcroft.

Sacred Lyre. D. Blagoy. 422p. 1982. 11.95 (ISBN 0-8285-2344-4, Pub. by Progress Pubs USSR). Imported Pubns.

Sacred Magic. William A. Oribello. (Orig.). 1984. pap. 10.00 (ISBN 0-910433-01-1). Mystic Soc.

Sacred Magic of Abra Melin. S. L. Mathers. 19.95x (ISBN 0-685-22092-3). Wehman.

Sacred Marriage: Psychic Integration in the Faerie Queene. Benjamin G. Lockerd, Jr. LC 85-48293. (Illus.). 216p. 1987. 29.50x (ISBN 0-8387-5106-7). Bucknell U Pr.

Sacred Meadows: A Structural Analysis of Religious Symbolism in an East African Town. Abdul H. El-Zein. LC 73-91310. (Studies in African Religion). 368p. 1974. text ed. 26.95 (ISBN 0-8101-0443-1). Northwestern U Pr.

Sacred Memory of Mary. Walter T. Brennan. 1988. pap. 5.95. Paulist Pr.

Sacred Mirror: A Spiritual Diary. Margery Eyre. 94p. 9.95 (ISBN 0-86140-068-2). Dufour.

Sacred Moon Tree. Laura J. Shore. LC 85-17487. 224p. (gr. 6-8). 1986. 13.95 (ISBN 0-02-782790-9). Bradbury Pr.

Sacred Mysteries among the Mayas & the Quiches. Augustus Le Plongeon. LC 73-76094. (Secret Doctrine Reference Ser). (Illus.). 200p. 1985. Repr. of 1886 ed. 12.00 (ISBN 0-913510-02-5). Wizards.

Sacred Narrative: Reading in the Theory of Myth. Ed. by Alan Dundes. LC 83-17921. (Illus.). ix, 352p. 1984. 45.00x (ISBN 0-520-05156-4); pap. 12.95x (ISBN 0-520-05192-0). U of Cal Pr.

Sacred Ninety Minutes: Popular History of the Service Club Movement. Oren Arnold. LC 75-15283. (Illus.). 1975. 10.00 (ISBN 0-916620-00-X). Portals Pr.

Sacred Oasis. Irene V. Vincent. 114p. 1953. 180.00x (ISBN 0-317-68438-8, Pub. by Han-Shan Tang Ltd). State Mutual Bk.

Sacred Officials of the Eleusinian Mysteries. Kevin Clinton. LC 73-79573. (Transaction Ser.: Vol. 64, Pt. 3). (Illus.). 1974. pap. 16.00 (ISBN 0-87169-643-6). Am Philos.

Sacred Path: Spells, Prayers & Power Songs of the American Indians. Ed. by John Bierhorst. LC 82-14118. (Illus.). 191p. (gr. 5 up). 1983. PLB 10.25 (ISBN 0-688-01699-5, Guill); pap. 7.95. Morrow.

Sacred Path: Spells, Prayers, & Power Songs of the American Indians. Ed. by John Bierhorst. LC 83-19460. (Illus.). 192p. 1984. pap. 7.95 (ISBN 0-688-02647-8, Quill). Morrow.

Sacred Paw: The Bear in Nature, Myth & Literature. Paul Shepard & Barry Sanders. (Nonfiction Ser.). 272p. 1985. 17.95 (ISBN 0-670-15133-5). Viking.

Sacred Pipe: Black Elk's Account of the Seven Rites of Oglala Sioux. Ed. by Joseph E. Brown. LC 53-8810. (Civilization of the American Indian Ser.: No. 36). (Illus.). 1981. 18.95 (ISBN 0-8061-0272-1). U of Okla Pr.

Sacred Pipe: Black Elk's Account of the Seven Rites of the Oglala Sioux. Ed. by Joseph E. Brown. Black Elk. (Metaphysical Library Ser.). 1971. pap. 4.95 (ISBN 0-14-003346-7). Penguin.

Sacred Places: Religious Architecture of the 18th & 19th Centuries in British Columbia. Barry Downs. LC 81-670050. (Illus.). 160p. 1980. 29.95 (ISBN 0-295-95774-3, Pub. by Douglas & McIntyre Canada). U of Wash Pr.

Sacred Play of Children. Ed. by Diane Apostolos-Cappadona. 160p. 1983. pap. 9.95 (ISBN 0-8164-2427-6, HarpR). Har-Row.

Sacred Poetry of the Seventeenth Century: Including the Whole of Giles Fletcher's Christ's Victory & Triumph, 2 vols. Ed. by Richard Cattermole. (Research & Source Works Ser.: No. 346). 1969. Repr. of 1835 ed. Set. 44.50 (ISBN 0-8337-0499-0). B Franklin.

Sacred Pony. Ray Fox. LC 87-18977. (Contemporary Poets Ser.: No. 2). 36p. (Orig.). 1987. pap. 7.95 (ISBN 0-916843-02-5, 106, Pub. by Writers Hse Pr). Inst Human Soc.

Sacred Portal: A Primary Symbol in Ancient Judaic Art. Bernard Goldman. LC 86-10983. (Brown Classics in Judaica Ser.). (Illus.). 260p. 1986. pap. text ed. 16.75 (ISBN 0-8191-5269-2). U Pr of Amer.

Sacred Rage: The Crusade of Modern Islam. Robin Wright. 1985. 17.95 (ISBN 0-671-60113-X, Linden Pr.). S&S.

Sacred Rage: The Wrath of Militant Islam. Robin Wright. 336p. 1986. pap. 8.95 (ISBN 0-671-62811-9, Touchstone Bks). S&S.

Sacred Readings: The Gathas. Inayat Khan. (Sufi Message of Hazrat Inayat Khan Ser.: Vol. 13). 304p. 1982. 14.95 (ISBN 90-6325-021-5, Pub. by Servire BV Netherlands). Hunter Hse.

Sacred Refuge. Ralph Romig. LC 80-14984. 1987. pap. 11.95 (ISBN 0-87949-189-2). Ashley Bks.

Sacred Remains: Myth, History, & Polity in Belau. Richard J. Parmentier. LC 87-6051. (Illus.). 368p. (Orig.). 1987. 49.95x (ISBN 0-226-64695-5); pap. 15.95 (ISBN 0-226-64696-3). U of Chicago Pr.

Sacred Rhetoric: The Christian Grand Style in the English Renaissance. Debora K. Shuger. 336p. 1988. text ed. 32.50 (ISBN 0-691-06736-8). Princeton U Pr.

Sacred River. Leonard A. Strong. LC 74-7049. (Studies in Joyce, No. 96). 1974. lib. bdg. 49.95x (ISBN 0-8383-1951-3). Haskell.

Sacred Rose Tarot. Johanna Sherman. 56p. 1982. pap. 12.00 incl. card deck (ISBN 0-88079-012-1). US Games Syst.

Sacred Round. Thelma Palmer. LC 85-18006. (Illus.). 68p. (Orig.). 1985. pap. 7.95 (ISBN 0-9615580-0-8). Island Pubs Wa.

Sacred Round. 2nd ed. Thelma Palmer. (Illus.). 68p. 1988. pap. 7.95 (ISBN 0-9615580-3-2). Island Pubs WA.

Sacred Sands: The Struggle for Community in the Indiana Dunes. J. Ronald Engel. (Illus.). 288p. 1982. 27.50x (ISBN 0-8195-5073-6). Wesleyan U Pr.

Sacred Sands: The Struggle for Community in the Indiana Dunes. J. Ronald Engel. (Illus.). xxii, 354p. 1986. pap. 14.95 (ISBN 0-8195-6129-0). Wesleyan U Pr.

Sacred Science of Numbers. Corinne Heline. 140p. 1981. pap. 4.00 (ISBN 0-87516-442-0). DeVorss.

Sacred Science of Numbers. Corinne Heline. 33p. pap. 4.00 (ISBN 0-87613-027-9). New Age.

Sacred Science: The King of Pharaonic Theocracy. R. A. Schwaller De Lubicz. Tr. by A. Vandenbroeck & G. Vandenbroeck. LC 81-344. (Illus.). 310p. 1982. pap. 12.95 (ISBN 0-89281-222-2). Inner Tradit.

Sacred Scrolls of the Southern Ojibway. Selwyn Dewdney. LC 73-90150. 1974. 27.50x (ISBN 0-8020-3321-0). U of Toronto Pr.

Sacred Seasons: Poems. Carl Bode. LC 75-179807. (New Poetry Ser.). Repr. of 1953 ed. 16.00 (ISBN 0-404-56007-5). AMS Pr.

Sacred Sex. Twenty-Four Magazine Editors & John Burns. Ed. by Thomas R. White. LC 74-84538. (Illus.). 150p. (Orig.). 1975. pap. 1.95 (ISBN 0-914896-01-6, Strength). East Ridge Pr.

Sacred Sins. Nora Roberts. 304p. (Orig.). 1987. pap. 3.95 (ISBN 0-553-26574-1). Bantam.

Sacred Sites: A Guidebook for the New Age Traveler. Natasha Peterson. (Illus.). 192p. (Orig.). (YA) 1989. pap. 9.95 (ISBN 0-8092-4517-5). Contemp Bks.

Sacred Sound: Music in Religious Thought & Practice. Ed. by Joyce Irwin. LC 83-15390. (AAR Thematic Studies). 180p. 1984. 22.50 (ISBN 0-89130-655-2, 01 25 01). Scholars Pr GA.

Sacred Space: An Aesthetic for the Liturgical Environment. Dennis McNally. 215p. (Orig.). 1985. pap. 9.95x (ISBN 0-932269-45-1). Wyndham Hall.

Sacred Spaces. Domingue Nahas & David L. Miller. LC 87-81634. (Illus.). 40p. (Orig.). 1987. pap. text ed. write for info. (ISBN 0-914407-09-0). Everson Mus.

Sacred Stories from Byzantium. Eva C. Topping. LC 77-16696. (Illus.). 79p. 1977. 5.95 (ISBN 0-916586-15-4); pap. 3.95 (ISBN 0-916586-16-2). Holy Cross Orthodox.

Sacred Stories of the Sweet Grass Cree. Leonard Bloomfield. LC 74-7933. Repr. of 1930 ed. 34.50 (ISBN 0-404-11821-6). AMS Pr.

Sacred Survival: The Civil Religion of American Jews. Jonathan S. Woocher. LC 85-45790. (Jewish Political & Social Studies). (Illus.). 224p. 1986. 25.00x (ISBN 0-253-35041-7). Ind U Pr.

Sacred Symbols of Mu. (Illus.). 296p. Date not set. pap. 12.95 (ISBN 0-914732-24-2). Bro Life Inc.

Sacred Symbols of the Ancients. Edith Randall & Florence Campbell. (Illus.). 200p. 1982. Repr. of 1947 ed. spiral bdg. 12.50 (ISBN 0-87516-487-0). DeVorss.

Sacred Symbols of the Ancients. Edith L. Randall & Florence Campbell. (Illus.). 1970. pap. 11.95 (ISBN 0-912504-00-5). Sym & Sign.

Sacred Symbols That Speak, Vol. I. A. Coniaris. 1986. pap. 7.95 (ISBN 0-937032-39-5). Light&Life Pub Co MN.

Sacred Symbols That Speak, Vol. 2. Anthony Coniaris. 1987. pap. 7.95 (ISBN 0-937032-49-2). Light&Life Pub Co MN.

Sacred Symphony: The Chanted Sermon of the Black Preacher. Jon M. Spencer. LC 87-29547. (Contributions in Afro-American & African Studies: No. 111). 160p. 1987. lib. bdg. 29.95 (ISBN 0-313-25999-2, SSX/). Greenwood.

Sacred Tarot: Course VI, Lessons 48, 22-33. (Illus.). 1976. pap. 13.25 (ISBN 0-87887-329-5). Church of Light.

Sacred Tears: Sentimentality in Victorian Literature. Fred Kaplan. 176p. 1987. 19.50 (ISBN 0-691-06700-7). Princeton U Pr.

Sacred Texts of the World. Ninian Smart & Richard Hecht. 496p. 1984. pap. 16.95 (ISBN 0-8245-0639-1). Crossroad NY.

Sacred Texts of the World: A Universal Anthology. Ed. by Ninian Smart & Richard Hecht. LC 82-7375. 1982. 27.50x (ISBN 0-8245-0483-6). Crossroad NY.

Sacred Texts of the World: A Universal Anthology. Ed. by Ninian Smart & Richard B. Hecht. (Illus.). 496p. 1987. pap. 22.00 (ISBN 0-8334-1001-6, Freedeeds Bks). Garber Comm.

Sacred Theory of the Earth. Thomas Burnet. LC 65-10027. (Centaur Classics Ser.). (Illus.). 414p. 1965. 22.50x (ISBN 0-8093-0186-5). S Ill U Pr.

Sacred Theory of the Earth. Thomas Burnet. 1985. 90.00x (ISBN 0-900000-31-7, Pub. by Centaur Bks). State Mutual Bk.

Sacred Theory of the Earth. Ed. by Thomas Frick. 256p. 1985. IO Ser., #36. 25.00 (ISBN 0-938190-63-6); pap. 12.95 (ISBN 0-938190-62-8). North Atlantic.

Sacred Thread: Hinduism in Continuity & Diversity. J. L. Brockington. 222p. 1981. pap. 10.50x (ISBN 0-85224-393-6, Pub. by Edinburgh U Pr Scotland). Columbia U Pr.

Sacred Threshold: A Life of Rainer Maria Rilke. J. F. Hendry. 184p. 1985. 18.50 (ISBN 0-85635-369-8); pap. 9.50 (ISBN 0-85635-601-8). Carcanet.

Sacred Times, Timeless Seasons. Gary J. Boelhower. LC 86-82885. (Illus.). 76p. 1986. pap. 6.95 (ISBN 0-937997-05-6). Hi-Time Pub.

Sacred Tradition in the Orthodox Church. Lazarus Moore. 1984. pap. 2.95 (ISBN 0-937032-34-4). Light&Life Pub Co MN.

Sacred Tree: The Tree in Religion & Myth. J. H. Philpot. 1977. lib. bdg. 69.95 (ISBN 0-8490-2553-2). Gordon Pr.

Sacred Trust: Brian Mulroney & the Conservative Party in Power. David Bercuson. LC 86-29204. 256p. 1987. 22.95 (ISBN 0-385-25060-6). Doubleday.

Sacred Trusts. Barbara Atlee & Bryn Chandler. 448p. 1987. pap. 3.95 (ISBN 0-671-61170-4). PB.

Sacred: Ways of Knowledge, Sources of Life. Peggy V. Beck & Anna L. Walters. (Illus.). 384p. 1977. 16.00x (ISBN 0-912586-24-9). Navajo Coll Pr.

Sacred Wood. 7th ed. T. S. Eliot. 171p. 1960. pap. 12.95x (ISBN 0-416-67610-3, NO. 2185). Routledge Chapman & Hall.

Sacred Word & Sacred Text: Scripture in World Religions. Compiled by Harold Coward. 209p. (Orig.). 1988. 21.95; pap. 10.95. Orbis Bks.

Sacred Words: A Study of Navajo Religion & Prayer. Sam D. Gill. LC 80-659. (Contributions in Intercultural & Comparative Studies: No. 4). (Illus.). xxvi, 257p. 1981. lib. bdg. 35.00 (ISBN 0-313-22165-0, GSW/). Greenwood.

Sacred Wrath: The Selected Poems of Vahan Tekeyan. Tr. by Diana Der Hovanessian & Marzbed Margossian. LC 81-20559. 176p. 1982. 12.50 (ISBN 0-935102-08-6); pap. 7.50 (ISBN 0-935102-09-4). Ashod Pr.

Sacred Writings of the Worlds Great Religions. Ed. by S. E. Frost, Jr. 416p. 1972. pap. text ed. 7.95 (ISBN 0-07-022520-6). McGraw.

Sacred Yes. Bhagwan Shree Rajneesh. Ed. by Ma Prem Maneesha. LC 83-17665. (Initiation Talks Ser.). 448p. (Orig.). 1983. pap. 4.95 (ISBN 0-88050-624-5). Chidvilas Inc.

Sacri Musicali Affetti, Op. 5. Barbara Strozzi. (Women Composers Ser.). 1989. 25.00 (ISBN 0-306-76195-5). Da Capo.

Sacrifice. Frank Bidart. LC 83-47794. 96p. 1983. (Vin); pap. 5.95 (ISBN 0-394-71638-8). Random.

Sacrifice. Graham Masterton. 384p. (Orig.). 1986. pap. 3.95 (ISBN 0-8125-2197-8, Dist. by Warner Pub Services & St. Martin's Press). Tor Bks.

Sacrifice. Marvin Moore. LC 78-21712. (Flame Ser.). 1979. pap. 1.25 (ISBN 0-8127-0214-X). Review & Herald.

Sacrifice. Lucien Palmieri. 1986. 10.95 (ISBN 0-533-06657-3). Vantage.

Sacrifice. Rabindranath Tagore. 256p. Date not set. 5.95. Asia Bk Corp.

Sacrifice & Death of Christ. Date not set. 8.95 (Pub. by SCM Pr England). Fortress.

Sacrifice & Sharing in the Philippine Highlands: Religion & Society among the Buid of Mindoro. Thomas Gibson. LC 85-15771. (London School of Economics Monographs on Social Anthropology: No. 57). (Illus.). 1986. 49.95 (ISBN 0-485-19559-3, Pub. by Athlone Pr). Humanities.

Sacrifice Consenting. W. Dickey. 60p. 1982. casebound 17.00 (ISBN 0-931757-09-6); text ed. 100.00 handbound (ISBN 0-931757-10-X). Pterodactyl Pr.

Sacrifice in Africa: A Structuralist Approach. Luc de Heusch. Tr. by Linda O'Brien & Alice Morton. LC 84-48487. (African Systems of Thought Ser.). 240p. 1985. 22.50x (ISBN 0-253-35038-7). Ind U Pr.

Sacrifice: Its Nature & Function. Henri Hubert & Marcel Mauss. Tr. by W. D. Halls. LC 64-12260. 1964. pap. 11.00x (ISBN 0-226-35679-5). U of Chicago Pr.

Sacrifice of Isabel. A Poem see Consolation; a Poem Addressed to Lady Brydges.

Sacrifice of the Lilies. ltd. ed. Virginia Walker. (Illus.). 48p. (Orig.). 1985. pap. 4.95 (ISBN 0-9615628-0-3). Tree Hse Pr.

Sacrifice Play. John Ballem. 256p. 1981. pap. 2.25 (ISBN 0-449-14381-3, GM). Fawcett.

Sacrifice to Attis: A Study of Sex & Civilization. W. A. Brend. 59.95 (ISBN 0-8490-0985-5). Gordon Pr.

Sacrifice We Offer: Tridentine Dogma & Its Reinterpretation. David N. Power. 240p. 1987. 16.95 (ISBN 0-8245-0743-6). Crossroad NY.

Sacrifices. M. F. C. Bourdillon & M. Fortes. 1980. 54.50 (ISBN 0-12-119040-4). Acad Pr.

Sacrifices & Offerings in Ancient Israel. Gary Anderson. LC 87-20498. (Harvard Semitic Museum-Monographs). 174p. 1988. 14.95 (ISBN 1-55540-169-4, 04-00-41). Scholars Pr GA.

Sacrificial Bone Inscriptions. Haven O'More. 60p. 1987. 45.00 (ISBN 0-942065-00-X). Aperture.

Sacrificial Ground. Thomas H. Cook. 288p. 1988. 16.95 (ISBN 0-399-13339-9). Putnam Pub Group.

Sacrificial Ground. Thomas H. Cook. 486p. 1988. Repr. of 1988 ed. lib. bdg. 18.95 (ISBN 0-89621-183-5). Thorndike Pr.

Sacrificial Ideas in Greek Christian Writers. Frances M. Young. LC 78-61400. (Patristic Monograph: No. 5). 1979. pap. 10.00 (ISBN 0-915646-04-8). N Amer Patristic Soc.

Sacrificial Interpretation of Jesus' Achievement in the New Testament. Tibor Horvath. 1980. 9.95 (ISBN 0-8022-2240-4). Philos Lib.

Sacrificial Worship of the Old Testament. J. H. Kurtz. Tr. by James Martin. (Twin Brooks Ser.). 454p. 1980. pap. 8.95 (ISBN 0-8010-5419-2). Baker Bk.

Sacrificio de la Misa, La Vida de Sante Oria Y el Martirio de San Lorenzo: Estudio Y Edicion Critica por Brian Dutton (Vol. 5 of the Obras Completas) Gonzalo De Berceo. Ed. by Brian Dutton. (Serie A: Monagrafías, LXXX). 208p. (Orig., Span.). 1981. pap. 18.00 (ISBN 0-7293-0099-4, Pub. by Tamesis Bks Ltd). Longwood Pub Group.

Sacris Erudiri, Vol. XXV. 1982. pap. text ed. 28.00 (ISBN 90-247-2841-X, Pub. by Martinus Nijhoff Netherlands). Kluwer Academic.

Sacris Erudiri. Ed. by St. Pietersabdij van Steenbrugge. 1988. pap. 52.00 (ISBN 90-247-3672-2, Pub. by Martinus Nijhoff Netherlands). Kluwer Academic.

Sacrorum Emblematum Centuria Una. Andrew Willet. LC 84-5360. 1984. Repr. of 1592 ed. 35.00x (ISBN 0-8201-1395-6). Schol Facsimiles.

Sacrosomataceae (Pezizales Sarcosyphgineae) Joseph Paden. (Flora Neotropica Monograph Ser.: No. 37). (Orig.). 1983. pap. 5.50x (ISBN 0-89327-250-7). NY Botanical.

Sad. Sylvia R. Tester. LC 79-26252. (What Does It Mean? Ser.). (Illus.). (ps-2). 1980. 10.33 (ISBN 0-516-06448-7). Childrens.

Sad. Sylvia R. Tester. LC 79-26252. (What Does It Mean? Ser.). (Illus.). (ps-2). 1980. PLB 6.75 (ISBN 0-89565-112-2). Childs World.

Sad Abodes. Bryn Thomas. (Illus.). 1983. pap. 10.95 (ISBN 0-686-39884-X). Working Dir PA Artists.

Sad, but O.K. - My Daddy Died Today: A Child's View of Death. Barbara F. Juneau & Paul M. Clemens. (Illus.). 112p. (Orig.). (gr. 5 up). 1988. pap. 9.95 (ISBN 0-931892-19-8). B Dolphin Pub.

Sad, But O.K...My Daddy Died Today. Barbara Juneau. Ed. by Paul M. Clemens. (Illus.). 112p. (Orig.). 1988. pap. 9.95. B Dolphin Pub.

Sad Carnival: 1982. Clark W. Holtzman. 1983. pap. 2.00t (ISBN 0-918476-04-6). Cornerstone Pr.

Sad Clowns & Pale Pierrots: Literature & the Popular Comic Arts in 19th Century France. Louisa E. Jones. LC 83-81596. (French Forum Monographs: 48). 296p. (Orig.). 1984. pap. 17.95x (ISBN 0-917058-48-8). French Forum.

Sad Cypress. Agatha Christie. 224p. 1970. pap. 2.50 (ISBN 0-440-17552-6). Dell.

Sad Cypress. Agatha Christie. 240p. 1986. pap. 3.50 (ISBN 0-425-09853-2). Berkley Pub.

Sad-Darsana Samuccaya (A Compendium of 6 Philosophies) Haribhadra. Tr. by Satchidananda Murty. 128p. 1986. Repr. 9.95 (ISBN 0-317-69969-5). Orient Bk Dist.

Sad Days of Light. Peter Balakian. LC 82-10823. 72p. 1983. 13.95 (ISBN 0-935296-33-6); pap. 7.95 (ISBN 0-935296-34-4). Sheep Meadow.

Sad Dust Glories: Poems Work Summer in Woods 1974. 2nd ed. Allen Ginsberg. 1975. saddlestitched in wrappers 2.50 (ISBN 0-935388-01-X). Workingmans Pr.

Sad Eyes A-Lookin' Timothy M. Herken. 26p. 1986. 5.95 (ISBN 0-533-06453-8). Vantage.

Sad-Faced Men. William Logan. LC 80-83947. (Poetry Chapbook, Fourth Ser.). 40p. 1981. 8.95 (ISBN 0-87923-365-6). Godine.

Sad Geraniums. Wolfgang Borchert. LC 73-11251. 1973. cancelled (ISBN 0-912946-10-5). Ecco Pr.

Sad Movies. Mark Lindquist. Ed. by Gary Fisketjon. (Fiction Ser.). 208p. 1987. pap. 6.95 (ISBN 0-87113-173-0). Atlantic Monthly.

Sad Sack. George Baker. LC 83-46010. (Classics of Modern American Humor Ser.). Date not set. Repr. of 1944 ed. 30.00 (ISBN 0-404-19926-7). AMS Pr.

Sad Shepherd. Ben Jonson. Ed. by W. W. Greg. Bd. with Waldron's Continuation. (Material for the Study of the Old English Drama Ser.: No. 1, Vol. 11). pap. 14.00 (ISBN 0-8115-0260-0). Kraus Repr.

Sad Song Singing. Thomas B. Dewey. Ed. by J. Barzun & W. h. Taylor. LC 81-47377. (Crime Fiction 1950-1975 Ser.). 159p. 1982. lib. bdg. 18.00 (ISBN 0-8240-4980-2). Garland Pub.
Sad Song Singing. Thomas B. Dewey. 192p. 1984. pap. 3.50 (ISBN 0-88184-067-X). Carroll & Graf.
Sad Sontag Plays His Hunch. Wilbur C. Tuttle. 1976. lib. bdg. 10.95x (ISBN 0-89968-129-8). Lightyear.
Sad Story of Mary Wanna: On, How Marijuana Harms You. Peggy Mann. 40p. (gr. 1-4). pap. cancelled (ISBN 0-317-61868-7). Woodmere Press.
Sadako & the Thousand Paper Cranes. Eleanor Coerr. (Illus.). 64p. (gr. 2-5). 1979. pap. 2.50 (ISBN 0-440-47465-5, YB). Dell.
Sadako & the Thousand Paper Cranes. Eleanor B. Coerr. LC 76-9872. (Illus.). (gr. 3-5). 1977. 9.95 (ISBN 0-399-20520-9, Putnam). Putnam Pub Group.
Sadar-I-Riyasat: An Autobiography, Vol. 2: 1953-1967. Karan Singh. (Illus.). 1985. 16.95x (ISBN 0-19-561723-1). Oxford U Pr.
Sadas Statistical & Data Analysis System. Edgeman. 1988. pap. write for info. (ISBN 0-471-83064-X). Wiley.
Sadat. David Hirst & Irene Beeson. 384p. 1982. 19.95 (ISBN 0-571-11690-6). Faber & Faber.
Sadat & Begin: The Domestic Politics of Peacemaking. Melvin A. Friedlander. LC 82-21826. 338p. 1983. pap. 33.00x (ISBN 0-86531-949-9). Westview.
Sadat & His Statecraft. Felipe Fernandez-Armesto. 186p. 1986. 42.00x (ISBN 0-946041-14-8, Pub. by Kensal Pr UK). State Mutual Bk.
Sadat: The Man Who Changed Mid-East History. George Sullivan. LC 81-50739. (Illus.). 99p. (gr. 6 up). 1981. reinforced bdg 9.85 (ISBN 0-8027-6435-5). Walker & Co.
Sadat's Journey. Louise Neaderland. (Illus.). 1981. 5.00 (ISBN 0-942561-14-7). Bone Hollow.
SADCC Country Studies, Part 1: Energy & Development in Southern Africa. (Energy, Environment, & Development in Africa Ser.: Vol. 3). 201p. 24.50 (ISBN 0-8419-9771-3, Africana). Holmes & Meier.
SADCC Country Studies, Part 2: Energy & Development in Southern Africa. (Energy, Environment & Development in Africa Ser.: Vol. 4). 289p. 24.50 (ISBN 0-8419-9772-1, Africana). Holmes & Meier.
SADCC: Energy & Development to the Year 2000. Ed. by J. T. Simoes. (Energy, Environment & Development in Africa Ser.: Vol. 2). 197p. 24.50 (ISBN 0-8419-9770-5, Africana). Holmes & Meier.
SADCC: Problems & Prospects for Disengagement & Development in South Africa. Ed. by Samir Amin et al. 304p. 1987. text ed. 49.95 (ISBN 0-86232-748-2, Pub. by Zed Pr UK); pap. text ed. 15.95 (ISBN 0-86232-749-0, Pub. by Zed Pr). Humanities.
Saddam Hussein on Current Events in Iraq. Saddam Hussein. Tr. by Khalid Kishtainy. LC 78-323367. 103p. pap. 26.80 (2030347). Bks Demand UMI.
Saddam's Iraq-Revolution or Reaction? Ed. by Cardri. 272p. 1986. 35.00 (ISBN 0-86232-333-9, Pub. by Zed Pr); pap. 12.50 (ISBN 0-86232-334-7, Pub. by Zed Pr). Humanities.
Saddest Story: A Biography of Ford Madox Ford. Arthur Mizener. (Illus.). 616p. 1985. pap. 12.95 (ISBN 0-88184-187-0). Carroll & Graf.
Saddest Time. Norma Simon. (Albert Whitman Concept Bks.). (Illus.). 40p. (gr. 1-4). 1986. 10.50 (ISBN 0-8075-7203-9). A Whitman.
Saddharma-Pundarika: Lotus of True Law. Tr. by H. Kern. lib. bdg. 79.95 (ISBN 0-87968-530-1). Krishna Pr.
Saddle & Ride. Ernest Haycox. 256p. 1988. pap. 2.95 (ISBN 1-55817-085-5). Windsor NY.
Saddle Bag Yarns. Byron Grosfield. 171p. (Orig.). Date not set. pap. price not set (ISBN 0-9613875-0-5). Wild Horse Pubns.
Saddle Bow Slim. Nelson Nye. 1979. pap. 1.25 (ISBN 0-505-51378-1, Pub. by Tower Bks). Leisure NY.
Saddle Club, Bk. 2. B. B. Hiller. (Skylark Ser.). 144p. (Orig.). 1988. pap. 2.75 (ISBN 0-553-15611-X, Skylark). Bantam.
Saddle Club, No. 4. B. B. Hiller. 144p. (Orig.). Date not set. pap. 2.95 (ISBN 0-553-15637-3). Bantam.
Saddle Marks. Carter White. Ed. by Sybil White & Cynthia Thurman. (Illus.). 182p. 1983. 22.40 (ISBN 0-9613384-1-5). C White.
Saddle Seat Equitation. rev. ed. Helen K. Crabtree. LC 81-43770. (Illus.). 384p. 1982. pap. 24.95 (ISBN 0-385-17217-6). Doubleday.
Saddle Shoe Blues. Carroll H. Morris. LC 87-595. 168p. 1987. 9.95 (ISBN 0-87579-077-1). Deseret Bk.
Saddle Up: The Farm Journal Book of Western Horsemanship. Charles E. Ball. LC 71-11065. (Illus.). 1973. pap. 10.95 (ISBN 0-397-00990-9, LP-083). Har-Row.
Saddlebottom. Dick King-Smith. (Lythway Ser.). (gr. 2-5). 1987. lib. bdg. 12.95x (ISBN 0-7451-0629-3, Pub. by Chivers Pr UK). G K Hall.
Saddlebrook Papers: A Reader on Growth Management. 177p. 1985. 10.00. FLA Atlantic.
Saddlemakers of Sheridan County, Wyoming. Ann L. Gorzalka. LC 82-23043. 1984. 14.95 (ISBN 0-87108-634-4). Pruett.
Saddlery. British Horse Society Staff. (British Horse Society Manual of Stable Management Ser.: Bk. 4). (Illus.). 128p. 1988. pap. 11.95 (ISBN 0-939481-12-X). Half Halt Pr.
Saddlery. E. H. Edwards. (Illus.). 9.95 (ISBN 0-85131-151-2, BL2405, Pub. by J A Allen U K). S R Smith Sporting Bks.
Saddlery & Harness Making. Paul N. Hasluck. (Illus.). 9.95 (ISBN 0-85131-148-2, BL6610, Pub. by J A Allen U K). S R Smith Sporting Bks.
Saddlery & Horse Equipment. Jennifer Baker. LC 82-11468. (Illus.). 96p. 1985. 9.95 (ISBN 0-668-05633-9, 5633). Arco.
Saddles. Russel H. Beatie. LC 79-6708. (Illus.). 408p. 1981. 45.00 (ISBN 0-8061-1584-X). U of Okla Pr.
Saddles. Russell Beattie. (Illus.). 800p. 55.00 (ISBN 0-87556-611-1). Saifer.
Saddles & Sabers: Black Men of the Old West. LaVere Anderson. LC 74-18122. (Toward Freedom Ser.). (Illus.). (gr. 5-9). 1975. PLB 3.98 (ISBN 0-8116-4805-2). Garrard.
Saddles & Spurs: The Pony Express Saga. Raymond W. Settle & Mary L. Settle. LC 55-10776. x, 217p. 1972. pap. 8.95 (ISBN 0-8032-5765-1, BB 556, Bison). U of Nebr Pr.
Sade, Fourier, Loyola. Roland Barthes. 1971. 24.95 (ISBN 0-686-53941-9). French & Eur.
Sade-Fourier-Loyola. Roland Barthes. Tr. by Richard Miller from Fr. 184p. 1976. pap. 8.25 (ISBN 0-8090-1381-9). Hill & Wang.
Sade: Leser und Autor, Vol. 11. Hans-Ulrich Seifert. (Studien und Dokumente zur Geschichte Romanischen Literaturen). 457p. (Ger.). 1983. 43.70 (ISBN 3-8204-7295-9). P Lang Pubs.
Sadeian Woman: And the Ideology of Pornography. Angela Carter. LC 78-20412. 160p. 1988. pap. 7.95 (ISBN 0-394-75893-5). Pantheon.
Sadeq Chubak: An Anthology. Sadeq Chubak. Ed. by F. R. Bagley. LC 81-17970. (Modern Persian Literature Ser.). 1983. 35.00x (ISBN 0-88206-048-1). Caravan Bks.
Sadeq Hedayat: An Anthology. Sadiq Hidayat. LC 79-5100. 176p. 1983. 20.00x (ISBN 0-89158-387-4). Caravan Bks.
Sadguru Speaks. Satguru S. Keshavadas. (Illus.). 96p. (Orig.). 1975. pap. 3.50 (ISBN 0-942508-06-8). Vishwa.
Sadhak's Companion. Svami Kripalvananda. Ed. by Darshana Shakti Ma. Tr. by Gauri Modi from Gujarati. Orig. Title: Guru Vachanamrit. (Illus., Orig.). 1977. pap. text ed. 2.95 (ISBN 0-933116-04-7). Sanatana.
Sadhana. Swami Sivananda. 1978. 17.95 (ISBN 0-89684-311-4). Orient Bk Dist.
Sadhana: A Way to God. Anthony DeMello. LC 84-6735. 144p. 1984. pap. 6.95 (ISBN 0-385-19614-8, Im). Doubleday.
Sadhana: A Way to God, Christian Exercises in Eastern Form. Anthony De Mello. LC 78-70521. (Study Aids on Jesuit Topics: No. 9). 146p. 1978. pap. 6.50 (ISBN 0-912422-46-7). Inst Jesuit.
Sadhana Guidelines. (Illus.). 122p. 9.95 (ISBN 0-89509-004-X). Arcline Pubns.
Sadhana in Our Daily Lives: A Handbook for the Awakening of the Spiritual Self. John Ernst. LC 81-51360. 320p. (Orig.). 1981. pap. 9.95 (ISBN 0-9606482-0-8). Valley Lights.
Sadhu: A Study in Mysticism & Practical Religion. rev. ed. B. H. Streeter & A. J. Appasamy. 264p. 1987. 17.50x (ISBN 0-8364-2097-7, Pub. by Mittal). South Asia Bks.
Sadhus of India. M. M. Pickthal. 258p. 19.95. Asia Bk Corp.
Sadi: The Rose Garden. Edward Eastwick. 1979. 19.95. Ins Study Human.
Sadie & the Snowman. Allen Morgan. (Illus.). 32p. (ps-2). 1987. pap. 2.25 (ISBN 0-590-40632-9). Scholastic Inc.
Sadie Shapiro in Miami. Robert K. Smith. 1978. pap. 1.95 (ISBN 0-449-23764-8, Crest). Fawcett.
Sadie Shapiro, Matchmaker. Robert K. Smith. 192p. 1981. pap. 2.50 (ISBN 0-449-24406-7, Crest). Fawcett.
Sadie When She Died. Ed McBain. 1982. pap. 2.50 (ISBN 0-451-11975-4, Sig). NAL.
Sadie When She Died. Ed McBain. 1988. pap. 3.50 (ISBN 0-451-15366-9, Sig). NAL.
Sadisfactions. Paul Nagy. 1977. pap. 5.00 (ISBN 0-918406-08-0). Future Pr.
Sadism & Masochism, 2 Vols. rev. ed. Wilhelm Stekel. 1953. 15.95x (ISBN 0-87140-838-4). Liveright.
Sadistic Statistics: An Introduction to Statistics for the Social & Behavioral Sciences. 2nd ed. Gideon Horowitz. (Illus.). 170p. 1981. pap. text ed. 11.95 (ISBN 0-89529-135-5). Avery Pub.
Sadler's Wells Ballet: A History & an Appreciation. Mary Clarke. LC 77-563. (Series in Dance). 1977. Repr. of 1955 ed. lib. bdg. 37.50 (ISBN 0-306-70863-9). Da Capo.
Sadler's Wells Royal Ballet "Swan Lake". Barbara Newman & Leslie E. Spatt. (Illus.). 143p. 1983. 29.95 (ISBN 0-903102-72-2, Pub. by Dance Bks England). Princeton Bk Co.
Sadness. Donald Barthelme. 1980. pap. 2.95 (ISBN 0-671-83204-2). PB.
Sadness & Happiness: Poems. Robert Pinsky. LC 75-3486. (Princeton Ser. of Contemporary Poets). 740p. 1975. pap. 8.50 (ISBN 0-691-01322-5, 358). Princeton U Pr.
Sadness at Leaving: A Novel of Espionage. Erje Ayden. 110p. (Orig.). 1972. pap. 9.00 (ISBN 0-89366-005-1). Ultramarine Pub.
Sadness at the Private University. Ralph Adamo. LC 77-79216. (Lost Roads Poetry Ser.: No. 3). 1978. 6.00 (ISBN 0-918786-04-5); pap. 3.00 (ISBN 0-918786-05-3). Lost Roads.
Sadness Because the Video Rental Store Was Closed & Other Stories. Mark Kostabi. (Illus.). 176p. 1988. 19.95 (ISBN 0-89659-800-4). Abbeville Pr.
Sadomasochism: Etiology & Treatment. Suzanne P. Schad-Somers. LC 81-6460. 300p. 1982. 34.95 (ISBN 0-89885-059-2). Human Sci Pr.
Sadopaideia. (Victorian Library). 256p. 1984. 14.95 (ISBN 0-394-54265-7, GP952). Grove.
Sadopaideia. 256p. 1984. pap. 5.95 (ISBN 0-394-62341-X, E-971, Ever). Grove.
Sadtler Guide to Carbon-13 NMR Spectra. 1982. 195.00 (ISBN 0-8456-0087-7). Sadtler Res.
Sadtler Guide to NMR Spectra. W. W. Simons & M. Zanger. 1972. 150.00 (ISBN 0-8456-0001-X). Sadtler Res.
Sadtler Guide to the NMR Spectra of Polymers. W. W. Simons & M. Zanger. 1973. 125.00 (ISBN 0-8456-0002-8). Sadtler Res.
Sadtler Handbooks. Sadtler Research Laboratories, Inc. Incl. Sadtler Handbook of Proton NMR Spectra. 295.00; Sadtler Handbook of Ultraviolet Spectra. 295.00 (ISBN 0-8456-0035-4); Sadtler Handbook of Infrared Spectra. 295.00 (ISBN 0-8456-0033-8). 1978. Set. 690.00 (ISBN 0-685-51844-2). Sadtler Res.
Sadtler Spectra Handbooks of Esters: IR, NMR. 195.00 ea.; Set. 295.00. Sadtler Res.
Sadtler's Spectra Handbook of Esters Ir. 1982. 195.00 (ISBN 0-8456-0078-8). Sadtler Res.
Saducismus Triumphatus: Or, Full & Plain Evidence Concerning Witches & Apparitions. Joseph Glanvill. LC 66-60009. 1966. Repr. of 1689 ed. 75.00x (ISBN 0-8201-1021-3). Schol Facsimiles.
SAE Handbook Nineteen Eighty-Eight: Engines, Emissions, Noise, Fuels, & Lubricants, Vol. 3. 1988. 45.00 (ISBN 0-89883-884-3, 88HB3). Soc Auto Engineers.
SAE Handbook Nineteen Eighty-Eight: Materials, Vol. 1. 1988. 45.00 (ISBN 0-89883-882-7, 88HB1). Soc Auto Engineers.
SAE Handbook Nineteen Eighty-Eight: On Highway Vehicles & Off-Highway Machinery, Vol. 4. 1988. 45.00 (ISBN 0-89883-885-1, 88HB4). Soc Auto Engineers.
SAE Handbook Nineteen Eighty-Eight: Parts & Components, Vol. 2. 1988. 45.00 (ISBN 0-89883-883-5, 88HB2). Soc Auto Engineers.
SAE Handbook: 1986. 140.00 (86 HBST). Soc Auto Engineers.
SAE Handbook, 1987. 1987. 140.00 (ISBN 0-89883-875-4, 87HBST). Soc Auto Engineers.
SAE Handbook: 1988, 4 vols. 1988. Set. 140.00 (ISBN 0-89883-881-9, 88HBST). Soc Auto Engineers.
SAE Motor Vehicle, Safety & Environmental Terminology. 179p. pap. 20.00 (ISBN 0-89883-370-1, HS-215). Soc Auto Engineers.
Saeculum: History & Society in the Theology of St. Augustine. Robert A. Markus. LC 71-87136. pap. 68.70 (2031687). Bks Demand UMI.
Saecvli noni avctoris in Boetii Consolationem Philosophiae Commentarivs. Ed. by Edmund T. Silk. LC 36-7788. (American Academy in Rome. Papers & Monographs: Vol. 9). pap. 102.80 (2026725). Bks Demand UMI.
Saemaul Undong: The Korean Way of Rural Transformation. Fu-Chen & Song Byung-Nak. (Working Papers Ser.: No. 79-9). 23p. 1979. pap. 6.00 (ISBN 0-686-78258-5, CRD036, UNCRD). UNIPUB.
Saemmtliche Werke, 8 vols. Johann G. Fichte. 1965-66. Repr. of 1846 ed. 216.00x (ISBN 3-11-005147-8). De Gruyter.
Saemtliche Briefe: Kritische Studienausgabe in 8 Baenden. Friedrich Nietzsche. Ed. by Giorgio Colli & Mazzino Montinari. 3630p. 1986. pap. 95.75x (ISBN 3-11-010963-8). De Gruyter.
Saemtliche Dramen, 2 vols. Jos Murer. Ed. by Hans-Joachim Adomatis et al. LC 73-78235. (Ausgaben Deutscher Literatur des 15. bis 18. Jahrhunderts, Reihe Dramen 4). 1974. 192.00x (ISBN 3-11-003865-X). De Gruyter.
Saemtliche Dramen, Vol. 2. Sixt Birck. Ed. by M. Brauneck. (Ausgaben Deutscher Literatur Des 15-18 Jahrhunderts Ser.). 1976. 128.00x (ISBN 3-11-006758-7). De Gruyter.
Saemtliche Schriften, 4 vols. Alexander Seitz. Ed. by Peter Ukena. Incl. Vol. 1. Medizinische Schriften. iv, 299p. 1970. 61.00x (ISBN 3-11-000362-7); Vol. 2. Politische und theologische schriften, monucleus aureus. iv, 481p. 1975. 100.00 (ISBN 3-11-005715-8); Vol. 3. Tragedi vom Grossen Abentmal. iv, 132p. 1969. 19.20 (ISBN 3-11-000356-2). (Ausgaben Deutscher Literatur des Fuenfzehnten bis Achtzehnten Jahrhunderts). (Ger.). De Gruyter.
Saemtliche Werke, 26 Vols. Georg W. Hegel. Ed. by H. Glockner. Set. 2614.00x (ISBN 3-7728-0171-4). Adlers Foreign Bks.
Saemtliche Werke. Johann Rist. Ed. by Eberhard Mannack. Incl. Vol. 1. Dramatische Dichtungen: Irenaromachia, Perseus. (Illus.). iv, 289p. 1967. 39.20x (ISBN 3-11-000346-5); Vol. 2. Dramatische Dichtungen. 1972. 76.00x (ISBN 3-11-004125-1); Vol. 4. Epische Dichtungen. 1972. 64.00x (ISBN 3-11-004124-3); Vol. 5. Epische Dichtungen. Die Alleredelste Torheit. Die Alleredelste Belustigugh. 1974. 84.00xx (ISBN 3-11-004591-5); Vol. 6. Epische Dichtungen: Die alleredelste Erfindung, Die alleredelste Zeitverkuerzung. 1976. 92.80 (ISBN 3-11-006817-6); Vol. 7. Philosophischer Phoenix, Rettung des Phoenix, Teutsche Hauptsprache, Adelicher Hausvatter. 1982. 100.00 (ISBN 3-11-008659-X). (Ausgaben Deutscher Literatur des Fuenfzehnten bis Achtzehnten Jahrhunderts). (Ger.). De Gruyter.
Saemtliche Werke, 5 Vols. Arthur Schopenhauer. 1960-65. Set. 205.95x (ISBN 3-458-09581-0). Adlers Foreign Bks.
Saemtliche Werke, 14 vols. Georg Wickram. Ed. by Hans-Gert Roloff. Incl. Vol. 1. Ritter Galmy. (Illus.). vi, 338p. 1967. 48.00x (ISBN 3-11-000347-3); Vol. 2. Gabriotto und Reinhart. vi, 297p. 1967. 39.20x (ISBN 3-11-000348-1); Vol. 3. Knaben Spiegel: Dialog vom ungeratnen Sohn. (Illus.). iv, 208p. 1968. 28.80x (ISBN 3-11-000354-6); Vol. 4. Von Guten und Boesen Nachbaurn. (Illus.). iv, 207p. 1969. 28.80x (ISBN 3-11-000358-9); Vol. 5. Goldtfaden. viii, 294p. 1968. 39.20x (ISBN 3-11-000352-X); Vol. 6. irr reitende Pilger. 1972. 39.20x (ISBN 3-11-003923-0); Vol. 7. Rollwagenbuechlein. 1973. 67.20x (ISBN 3-11-004126-X); Vol. 8. Sieben Hauptlaster. 1972. 39.20x (ISBN 3-11-004002-6); Vol. 11. Verlorene Sohn. (Tobias). 1971. 60.80x (ISBN 3-11-003736-X); Vol. 12. Apostelspiel: Knaben Spiegel. (Illus.). vi, 281p. 1968. 37.60x (ISBN 3-11-000349-X). (Ausgaben Deutscher Literatur des Fuenfzehnten bis Achtzehnten Jahrhunderts). (Ger.). De Gruyter.
Saemtliche Werke: Ausgaben Deutscher Literatur des 15 bis 18 Jahrhunderts. Phiiipp Von Zesen. Ed. by Ferdinand Van Inger et al. Incl. Vol. 6. Afrikanische Sofonisbe. 1972. 108.00x (ISBN 3-11-003918-4); Vol. 8. Simson. 1970. 80.00x (ISBN 3-11-006364-6); Vol. 9. Deutscher Helicon. 1971. 92.00x (ISBN 3-11-003598-7); Vol. 11. Sprach-Vebung, Rosen-Mand, Helikonische Hechell, Sendeschreiben a Den Kreutztragenden. 1973. 96.00x (ISBN 3-11-004525-7). De Gruyter.
Saemtliche Werke: Ibrahim. Philipp Von Zesen. Ed. by Ferdinand Von Inger & Volker Ulrich Mache. Incl. Vol. 5, Pt. 1. In. 128.00x (ISBN 3-11-007081-2); Vol. 5, Pt. 2. 144.00x (ISBN 3-11-007082-0). (Ausgaben Deutscher Literatur). 1977. De Gruyter.
Saemtliche Werke: Kritische Studierausgabe, 15 vols. Friedrich Nietzsche. 8800p. (Ger.). 1980. 149.95 (ISBN 3-11-008117-2). De Gruyter.
Saemtliche Werke: Salomon, Vol. 2. Wolfhart Spangenberg. Ed. by M. Bircher-Glueckswechsel & A. Vizkelety. 420p. (Ger.). 1975. 120.00 (ISBN 3-11-005883-9). De Gruyter.
Saemtliche Werke, Vol. I: Historische Dramen 1. Christian Weise. iv, 629p. 1971. 80.00x (ISBN 3-11-001891-8). De Gruyter.
Saemtliche Werke, Vol. III: Historische Dramen 3. Christian Weise. iv, 433p. 1971. 58.00x (ISBN 3-11-003592-8). De Gruyter.
Saemtliche Werke, Vol. IV: Biblische Dramen I. Christian Weise. LC 71-860995. (Ausgaben Deutscher Literatur des XV. bis XVIII. Jahrhunderts). iv, 440p. 1973. 71.20x (ISBN 3-11-004246-0). De Gruyter.
Saemtliche Werke, Vol. V. Biblische Dramen II. Christian Weise. LC 71-860995. (Ausgaben Deutscher Literatur des XV. bis XVIII. Jahrhunderts). 1973. 78.40x (ISBN 3-11-003969-9). De Gruyter.
Saemtliche Werke, Vol. 1: Trauerspiele 1; Theodoricus Veronensis, Mariamne. Johann C. Hallmann. Ed. by Gerhard Spellerberg. (Ausgaben Deutscher Literatur des 15. Bis 18. Jahrhunderts). 1975. 74.40x (ISBN 3-11-004065-4). De Gruyter.
Saemtliche Werke, Vol. 1: Von der Musica. Singschul. Wolfhart Spangenberg. Ed. by A. Vizkelety. 173p. 1971. 38.95x (ISBN 3-11-001846-2). De Gruyter.
Saemtliche Werke, Vol. 21: Gedichte II. Christian Weise. Ed. by John D. Lindberg. (Ausgaben Deutscher Literatur des XV bis XVII Jahrhunderts). (Illus.). 1978. 144.00x (ISBN 3-11-006745-5). De Gruyter.
Saemund Sigfusson & the Oddaverjar. Halldor Hermannsson. LC 33-5652. (Islandica Ser.: Vol. 22). 1932. pap. 16.00 (ISBN 0-527-00352-2). Kraus Repr.
Saenredam: The Art of Perspective. Rob Ruurs. (Illus.). 228p. 1987. 50.00 (ISBN 1-55619-015-8). Benjamins North Am.
Saeta Voladora. F. Sanchez. 58p. 0.90 (ISBN 0-318-14305-4). Hispanic Inst.
SAF Forest Policies & Positions, 1985. Society of Americam Foresters. 68p. 1985. pap. 6.00 (ISBN 0-939970-30-9). Soc Am Foresters.
SAF Forest Policies & Positions, 1988. Society of American Foresters Staff. 80p. (Orig.). 1988. pap. 10.00 (ISBN 0-939970-36-8). Soc Am Foresters.
Safari. Bartle Bull. 1988. 40.00 (ISBN 0-670-81880-1). Viking.

Safari! LC 80-8799. (Books for World Explorers Series 3: No. 3). (Illus.). 104p. (gr. 3-8). 1982. 6.95 (ISBN 0-87044-385-2); lib. bdg. 8.50 (ISBN 0-87044-390-9). Natl Geog.

Safari. Caren B. Stelson. (Photo Bks.). 40p. (gr. k-4). 1988. PLB 12.95 (ISBN 0-87614-324-9). Carolrhoda Bks.

Safari. Roger Young & Rosemary Caggiano. 48p. (gr. k-8). 1979. pap. 8.95 (ISBN 0-86704-006-8). Clarus Music.

Safari: A Saga of the African Blue. Martin Johnson. LC 72-170251. (Tower Bks). (Illus.). x, 310p. 1972. Repr. of 1928 ed. 40.00x (ISBN 0-8103-3934-X). Gale.

Safari of African Cooking. Bill Odarty. 1971. pap. 5.00 (ISBN 0-910296-63-4). Broadside Pr.

Safari South America: The Saki Monkeys of Guyana & Other Wildlife. Christina Wood. LC 73-1764. (Illus.). 224p. 1973. 7.95 (ISBN 0-8008-6945-1). Taplinger.

Safari: The African Diaries of a Wildlife Photographer. Gunter Ziesler & Angelika Hofer. (Illus.). 192p. 1984. 24.95 (ISBN 0-87196-847-9). Facts on File.

Safari-The Last Adventure: How You Can Share in It. Peter H. Capstick. (Illus.). 352p. 1984. 15.95 (ISBN 0-312-69657-4). St Martin.

Safari Ya Imani Ya Kanisa la Mennonite Tanzania 1934-1983. Mahlon M. Hess. (Illus.). 120p. (Orig.). 1984. pap. 5.00 (ISBN 0-9613368-0-3). E Mennonite Bd.

Safarikleid. Lore Frobenius. 1968. pap. text ed. 3.50x (ISBN 0-435-38321-3). Heinemann Ed.

Safarnama & Zafarnama. I. S. Nara. 327p. 1986. 25.00x (ISBN 0-8364-1793-3, Pub. by Minerva India). South Asia Bks.

Safe. Dennis Cooper. LC 83-51376. 110p. (Orig.). 1984. pap. 5.95 (ISBN 0-933322-16-X). Sea Horse.

Safe Alternatives in Childbirth. 3rd ed. David Stewart & Lee Stewart. LC 76-19336. 1978. pap. 5.95 (ISBN 0-917314-06-9). NAPSAC.

Safe Alternatives in Childbirth. 4th ed. David Stewart & Lee Stewart. LC 76-19336. 200p. (YA) (gr. 7 up). pap. 5.95 (ISBN 0-934426-17-1). NAPSAC Reprods.

Safe & Sane: The Sensible Way to Protect Yourself, Your Loved Ones, Your Property & Possessions. Joseph D. McNamara. LC 83-22087. 224p. 1984. pap. 7.95 (ISBN 0-399-50859-7, G&D). Putnam Pub Group.

Safe & Simple Book of Electricity see Safe & Simple Electrical Experiments.

Safe & Simple Electrical Experiments. Rudolf F. Graf. Orig. Title: Safe & Simple Book of Electricity. 1973. pap. 4.50 (ISBN 0-486-22950-5). Dover.

Safe & Simple Electrical Experiments. Rudolf F. Graf. (Illus.). 14.25 (ISBN 0-8446-4747-0). Peter Smith.

Safe & Sound. Lucia Berlin. 64p. 1987. price not set (ISBN 0-918395-05-4). Poltroon Pr.

Safe & Sound. Ed. by Sanger. pap. 7.95 (ISBN 0-86232-122-0, Pub. by Zed Pr England). Humanities.

Safe & Sound: A Parent's Guide to Child Protection. Roderick Townley. 233p. 1985. 16.95 (ISBN 0-671-54420-9). S&S.

Safe & Sound: A Parent's Guide to Child Protection. Roderick Townley. 256p. 1986. pap. 7.95 (ISBN 0-671-62804-6, Fireside). S&S.

Safe & Sound: A Parent's Guide to the Care of Children at Home Alone. Trudy K. Dana. 240p. 1988. text ed. 17.95 (ISBN 0-07-015283-7). McGraw.

Safe & Sound: How to Prevent & Treat the Most Common Childhood Emergencies. Elena Bosque & Sheila Watson. (Illus.). 128p. 1988. pap. 8.95 (ISBN 0-312-02276-X). St Martin.

Safe at Home. Myers. 1982. pap. 3.95 (ISBN 0-915936-10-0). Armstrong Pub.

Safe at Home, Safe Alone. Educational Challenges Staff. (Illus.). 64p. (Orig.). (gr. 3-5). 1985. pap. 4.95 (ISBN 0-917917-01-4). Miles River.

Safe at Home with Teddy Ruxpin. Michelle Baron. (Teddy Ruxpin Safe 'N' Sound Ser.). (Illus.). 34p. (ps). Date not set. price not set incl. audio tapes (ISBN 0-934323-70-4). Alchemy Comms.

Safe at Last. Barbara Cartland. (Camfield Ser.: No. 31). 176p. 1986. pap. 2.75 (ISBN 0-515-08493-X). Jove Pubns.

Safe at Last in the Middle Years: The Invention of Midlife Progress Novel - Saul Belloe, Margaret Drabble, Anne Tyler, John Updike. Margaret M. Gullette. 300p. 1988. 19.95 (ISBN 0-520-06282-5). U of Cal Pr.

Safe Banks. Warren Weagant. 128p. 1988. pap. 19.95. Command Prods.

Safe Chain Saw Design. Thomas et al. (Illus.). 1983. 39.95 (ISBN 0-938830-02-3). Inst Product.

Safe Change of Pace for the Beginning Jogger. Myron W. Davis & Carol Van Woerkom. (Illus.). 64p. 1981. 5.95 (ISBN 0-8403-2576-2). Kendall-Hunt.

Safe Child Book. Sherryll K. Kraizer. (Illus.). 82p. 1985. 10.95 (ISBN 0-385-29403-4); pap. 6.95. Delacorte.

Safe Cigarette. Ed. by Gio B. Gori & Fred G. Bock. LC 79-47999. (Banbury Report Ser.: Vol. 3). (Illus.). 364p. 1980. 52.00x (ISBN 0-87969-202-2). Cold Spring Harbor.

Safe Conduct. Boris Pasternak. LC 58-12799. 1958. pap. 6.25 (ISBN 0-8112-0135-X, NDP77). New Directions.

Safe Construction for the Future: Conference Proceedings. 120p. 1980. 25.00 (ISBN 0-7277-0105-3, Pub. by T Telford UK). Am Soc Civil Eng.

Safe Delivery: Protect Your Baby During High Risk Pregnancy. R. Freeman & S. Pescar. 320p. 1983. pap. text ed. 7.95 (ISBN 0-07-022048-4). McGraw.

Safe Design & Use of Chain Saws: An ILO Code of Practice. 72p. 1978. pap. 10.50 (ISBN 92-2-101927-6, ILO90, ILO). UNIPUB.

Safe Drinkers Guide to Cocktail Construction. Rob Haiber. Ed. by W. Haiber. (Illus.). 64p. (Orig.). Date not set. pap. text ed. 9.95 (ISBN 0-944089-03-8). Info Devels.

Safe Drinking Water Act Self-Study Training Course. 154p. 1978. pap. 6.00 (ISBN 0-89867-034-9, 1620). Am Water Wks Assn.

Safe Drinking Water; Current & Future Problems: Proceedings of a Natonal Conference in Washngton D. C. Ed. by Clifford S. Russell. LC 78-19840. (Resources for the Future Research Paper Ser.). 1978. pap. 30.00x. Johns Hopkins.

Safe Drinking Water: The Impact of Chemicals on a Limited Resource. Ed. by Rip G. Rice. LC 84-25105. (Illus.). 280p. 1985. 34.95 (ISBN 0-9614032-0-9). Lewis Pubs Inc.

Safe Drinking Water: The Impact of Chemicals on a Limited Resource. Ed. by Rip G. Rice. 275p. 1985. 34.95; 29.95 (ISBN 0-318-17815-X). Intl Bottled Water.

Safe Encounters: How Women Can Say "Yes" to Pleasure & "No" to Unsafe Sex. Beverly Whipple & Gina Ogden. (Illus.). 256p. 1988. 16.95 (ISBN 0-07-069519-9). McGraw.

Safe for Democracy: The Anglo-American Response to Revolution, 1913-1923. Lloyd C. Gardner. 1984. 29.95x (ISBN 0-19-503429-5). Oxford U Pr.

Safe Handling & Use of Flammable & Combustible Materials. Center for Occupational Research & Development Staff. (Job Safety & Health Instructional Materials Ser.). (Illus.). 40p. 1981. pap. text ed. 3.00 (ISBN 1-55502-132-8). Ctr Res & Dev.

Safe Handling of Plutonium. (Safety Ser.: No. 39). (Illus.). 135p. (Orig.). 1974. pap. 15.00 (ISBN 92-0-123473-2, ISP358, IAEA). UNIPUB.

Safe Handling of Radioactive Materials. LC 63-60093. (NCRP Reports Ser.: No. 30). 1964. 8.00 (ISBN 0-913392-12-X). NCRP Pubns.

Safe Handling of Radionuclides. (Safety Ser.: No. 1). 94p. (Orig.). 1973. pap. 10.00 (ISBN 92-0-123073-7, ISP319, IAEA). UNIPUB.

Safe Houses. Lynne Alexander. LC 85-47594. 272p. 1985. 13.95 (ISBN 0-689-11606-3). Atheneum.

Safe Houses. Lynne Alexander. 1987. pap. 4.50 (ISBN 0-440-17640-9). Dell.

Safe in His Care. Lily A. Bear. 1984. 7.95 (ISBN 0-318-03659-2). Rod & Staff.

Safe in the Streets: Don't Be a Victim. Sandra Merwin. 112p. (Orig.). 1985. Repr. of 1982 ed. 5.95 (ISBN 0-916773-03-5). Book Peddlers.

Safe Medicine Book: The Informed Person's Guide to Prescription & Over-the-Counter Medications. Kathryn Watterson. 1987. text ed. 16.95 (ISBN 0-345-32907-4). Ballantine.

Safe Motherhood Initiative: Proposals for Action. Barbara Herz & Anthony R. Measham. (Discussion Paper: No. 9). 62p. 1987. 6.50 (ISBN 0-8213-0907-2, DP0009). World Bank.

Safe Navigation Symposium Papers Washington, D. C. OCIMF. 1978. 198.00x (ISBN 0-317-61463-0, Pub. by Witherby & Co England). State Mutual Bk.

Safe Not Sorry. Phyllis Schlafly. 1967. 1.00 (ISBN 0-934640-06-8). Pere Marquette.

Safe Operation of Agricultural Equipment. Thomas A. Silletto & Dale O. Hull. (Illus.). 1988. pap. text ed. 4.00x (10076); instr's. bk. 4.00 (ISBN 0-913163-21-X, 10176). Hobar Pubns.

Safe Operation of Auxiliaries. (Safety Digest of Lessons Learned: Sec. 3). 59p. 1980. 8.00 (ISBN 0-317-33098-5, 82275803). Am Petroleum.

Safe Operation of Commercial Vehicles. Center for Occupational Research & Development Staff. (Job Safety & Health Instructional Materials Ser.). (Illus.). 36p. 1981. pap. text ed. 3.00 (ISBN 1-55502-096-8). Ctr Res & Dev.

Safe Operation of Nuclear Power Plants. (Safety Ser.: No. 31). (Illus.). 125p. (Orig.). 1969. pap. 12.50 (ISBN 92-0-123169-5, ISP222, IAEA). UNIPUB.

Safe Operation of Research Reactors & Critical Assemblies 1984: Code of Practice & Annexes. (Safety Ser.: No. 35). 216p. 1985. pap. 36.00 (ISBN 92-0-123784-7, ISP667, IAEA). UNIPUB.

Safe Passage. Ellyn Bache. 1988. 16.95 (ISBN 0-517-56807-1). Crown.

Safe Passage. James Magorian. LC 77-87243. (Stone Country Poetry Ser.: No. 4). (Illus.). 1977. pap. text ed. 3.00 (ISBN 0-930020-03-0). Stone Country.

Safe Passages: A Guide for Teaching Children Personal Safety. Karla Hull. 154p. 1987. pap. 9.95 (ISBN 0-915035-26-X). Dawn Sign.

Safe Paving with Sulfur. (Information Ser.: No. 81). 1981. 10.00 (ISBN 0-317-58395-6). Natl Asphalt Pavement.

Safe Place to Live: A Management Manual to Help Communities Plan Crime Prevention Programs. Georgette Bennet. 136p. (Orig.). 1982. pap. 4.95 (ISBN 0-932387-07-1). Insur Info.

Safe Place to Work. D. James. (Illus.). 128p. 1983. text ed. 24.95 (ISBN 0-408-01304-4). Butterworth.

Safe Places to Winter. (Illus.). 192p. 1987. pap. 9.95 (ISBN 0-934523-77-0). Middle Coast Pub.

Safe Practices Guide for Air Separation Plants. 2nd ed. 64p. 1976-1981. 18.00 (ISBN 0-318-17555-X, CGA P-8). Compress Gas.

Safe Pregnancy Book. Carol A. Rinzler. LC 84-20571. 224p. 1985. pap. 6.95 (ISBN 0-452-25610-0, Plume). NAL.

Safe Pregnancy Book. Carol A. Rinzler. 240p. 1987. pap. 4.50 (ISBN 0-451-14888-6, Sig). NAL.

Safe Racing. Illus. by Mones. (Fast Rolling Race Cars Ser.). (Illus.). (ps-2). 1987. 3.95 (ISBN 0-448-09885-7, G&D). Putnam Pub Group.

Safe Return Doubtful: The Heroic Age of Polar Exploration. John Maxtone-Graham. (Illus.). 512p. 1989. 27.50 (ISBN 0-684-18987-9). Scribner.

Safe Sally Seat Belt & the Magic Click. Phyllis Gobbell & Jim Laster. (Illus.). 48p. (gr. k-5). 1986. 3.95 (ISBN 0-8249-8122-7). Ideals.

SAFE: Security Audit & Field Evaluation for Computer Facilities & Information Systems. Leonard I. Krauss. 336p. 1981. 29.95 (ISBN 0-8144-5526-3). AMACOM.

SAFE: Security Audit & Field Evaluation for Computer Facilities & Information Systems. Rev. ed. Leonard I. Krauss. LC 80-67963. pap. 80.00 (ISBN 0-317-27189-X, 2023923). Bks Demand UMI.

Safe Sex. Harvey Fierstein. LC 87-11507. 96p. 1987. 15.95 (ISBN 0-689-11953-4). Atheneum.

Safe Sex. Harvey Fierstein. 96p. 1988. pap. 8.95 (ISBN 0-689-70802-5). Atheneum.

Safe Sex. Alan E. Nourse. Ed. by M. Kline. (Teen Guide Ser.). (Illus.). 64p. (YA) (gr. 6-12). 1988. price not set (ISBN 0-531-10592-X). Watts.

Safe Sex: How Safe is Safe. 1987. pap. 0.25 (ISBN 0-89230-221-6). Do It Now.

Safe Sex in a Dangerous World. Art Ulene. LC 87-40122. 100p. (Orig.). 1987. pap. 3.95 (ISBN 0-394-75625-8, Vin). Random.

Safe Sex in the Age of AIDS. Ed. by Ted McIlvenna. 96p. 1986. pap. 3.95 (ISBN 0-8065-0996-1, Pub. by Citadel Pr). Lyle Stuart.

Safe Sex: The Pleasures Without the Pitfalls. Elliot Phillipp. 1987. 25.00x (ISBN 0-86287-352-5, Pub. by Harrap Ltd England). State Mutual Bk.

Safe Sex: The Ultimate Erotic Guide. Glen Swann & John Preston. 224p. 1987. pap. 8.95 (ISBN 0-452-25896-0, Plume). NAL.

Safe Sex: What Everyone Should Know about Sexually Transmitted Diseases. Angelo T. Scotti. 208p. (Orig.). 1987. pap. 3.95 (ISBN 0-7701-0641-2). PaperJacks US.

Safe Sex Workbook. John Preston. (Illus.). 64p. (Orig.). 1988. pap. 10.00 (ISBN 1-55583-131-1). Alyson Pubns.

Safe Ship - Safe Cargo, Vol. II. Ed. by Cargo Systems Staff. 1987. 195.00x (ISBN 0-907499-56-2, Pub. by Cargo Systs UK). State Mutual Bk.

Safe Storage of Laboratory Chemicals. David A. Pipitone. LC 83-21641. 280p. 1984. 68.00 (ISBN 0-471-89610-1, Pub. by Wiley-Interscience). Wiley.

Safe Storage of Pyroxylin Plastics. National Fire Protection Association Staff. 1986. 10.50 (ISBN 0-317-63073-3, 40E-86). Natl Fire Prot.

Safe, Strong & Streetwise: The Teenager's Guide to Preventing Sexual Assault. Helen Benedict. (Joy Street Bks.). (Illus.). 192p. (YA) (gr. 7 up). 1986. 14.95 (ISBN 0-316-08899-4, 088994); pap. 5.95 (ISBN 0-87113-100-5, 089001). Little.

Safe Studies. Lionel Tollemache. 1973. Repr. of 1884 ed. 40.00 (ISBN 0-8274-0828-5). R West.

Safe Therapeutic Exercise for the Frail Elderly: An Introduction. Olga Hurley. (Illus.). 1988. pap. 14.95x (ISBN 0-937829-02-1). Ctr Study Aging.

Safe Tractor Operation & Daily Care. Rev. ed. (Illus.). 120p. 1981. pap. 11.00 (ISBN 0-89606-056-X, 103). Am Assn Voc Materials.

Safe Travel Book. Peter V. Savage. (Issues in Low-Intensity Conflict Ser.). 128p. 1988. 21.95 (ISBN 0-669-17380-0); pap. 9.95 (ISBN 0-669-17381-9). Lexington Bks.

Safe Use of Pesticides. (Technical Report Ser.: No. 720). 60p. 1985. pap. 3.60 (ISBN 92-4-120720-5). World Health.

Safe Use of Pesticides: Report. WHO Expert Committee on Insecticides. Geneva, 1972, 20th. (Technical Report Ser.: No. 513). (Also avail. in French & Spanish). 1973. pap. 2.40 (ISBN 92-4-120513-X). World Health.

Safe Use of Powered Industrial Trucks. Center for Occupational Research & Development Staff. (Job Safety & Health Instructional Materials Ser.). (Illus.). 36p. 1981. pap. text ed. 3.00 (ISBN 1-55502-143-3). Ctr Res & Dev.

Safe Use of Radioactive Tracers in Industrial Processes. (Safety Ser.: No. 40). 54p. (Orig.). 1974. pap. 7.00 (ISBN 92-0-123074-5, ISP369, IAEA). UNIPUB.

Safe Use of Solvents. A. J. Collings & S. G. Luxon. 1982. 60.00 (ISBN 0-12-181250-2). Acad Pr.

Safe Use of Vitamin A. J. C. Bauernfeind. Ed. by G. Arroyave et al. (Illus.). 44p. (Orig.). 1980. pap. text ed. 3.50. Nutrition Found.

Safe Uses of Cortisone. William M. Jefferies. (Illus.). 214p. 1981. 30.25x (ISBN 0-398-04531-3). C C Thomas.

Safe Water: A Factbook on the SDWA for Noncommunity Water Systems. American Water Works Association Staff. (Illus.). 52p. 1980. pap. 1.80 (ISBN 0-89867-224-4). Am Water Wks Assn.

Safe Within Yourself: A Woman's Guide to Rape Prevention & Self-Defense. Doris Kaufman et al. LC 79-566334. (Illus.). 1980. pap. 15.00 (ISBN 0-916818-05-5). Victimology.

Safecracking the Mortgage Secrets: The Complete Guide to Home Loans. Janet T. Freidman. Ed. by Marie-Louise Crozat. (Illus.). 192p. (Orig.). 1987. pap. 24.95 (ISBN 0-318-22506-9). Win Pubs.

Safed Spirituality: Rules of Mystical Piety, the Beginning of Wisdom. Safed. Tr. by Lawrence Fine. (Classics of Western Spirituality Ser.). 1984. 12.95 (ISBN 0-8091-0349-4); pap. 9.95 (ISBN 0-8091-2612-5). Paulist Pr.

Safeguard of Sailors, or Great Rutter. Tr. by Robert Norman. LC 76-57412. (English Experience Ser.: No. 827). 1977. Repr. of 1584 ed. lib. bdg. 30.00 (ISBN 90-221-0827-9). Walter J Johnson.

Safeguard Techniques & Equipment: IAEA Safeguards. (Safeguards Information Ser.: No. 5). (Illus.). 35p. 1985. pap. 7.50 (ISBN 92-0-179084-8, ISGINF5, IAEA). UNIPUB.

Safeguarding Building Construction & Demolition Operations. National Fire Protection Association Staff. 1986. 10.50 (ISBN 0-317-63358-9, 241-86). Natl Fire Prot.

Safeguarding Building Construction & Demolition Operations. (Two Hundred Ser). 1973. pap. 2.00 (ISBN 0-685-58173-X, 241). Natl Fire Prot.

Safeguarding Civil Liberty Today. Carl L. Becker. 1949. 11.25 (ISBN 0-8446-1064-X). Peter Smith.

Safeguarding Concepts Illustrated. LC 86-61185. (Professionals Library). (Illus.). 96p. (Orig.). 1987. pap. 24.75 (ISBN 0-87912-134-3, 13003). Natl Safety Coun.

Safeguarding Motherhood. 7th ed. DeLee. LC 65-1126. (Illus.). 188p. 1976. pap. text ed. 5.50 (ISBN 0-397-50365-2, 65-01126, Lippincott Medical). Lippincott.

Safeguarding Nuclear Materials, Vol. 1: Proceedings, 2 Vols. (Proceedings Ser.). (Illus.). 1976. pap. 75.00 (ISBN 92-0-070076-4, ISP408-1, IAEA); pap. 75.25 (ISBN 92-0-070176-0, ISP408-2). UNIPUB.

Safeguarding School Funds. Henry H. Linn. LC 76-176997. (Columbia University. Teachers College. Contributions to Education: No. 387). Repr. of 1929 ed. 22.50 (ISBN 0-404-55387-7). AMS Pr.

Safeguarding the Atom: A Critical Appraisal. David Fischer & Paul Szasz. Ed. by Jozef Goldblat. 250p. 1985. 29.00x (ISBN 0-85066-306-7). Taylor & Francis.

Safeguarding the Hospital's Assets. 2nd ed. LC 78-67106. (Illus.). 1978. 11.80 (ISBN 0-930228-09-X). Healthcare Fin Man Assn.

Safeguarding the Public Health. Stuart Galishoff. LC 75-66. (Illus.). 191p. 1975. lib. bdg. 46.95 (ISBN 0-8371-7956-4, GPH/). Greenwood.

Safeguarding the Public: Historical Aspects of Medicinal Drug Control. Conference on the History of Medicinal Drug Control (1968: National Library of Medicine) Ed. by John B. Blake. LC 76-84651. pap. 53.30 (ISBN 0-317-19888-2, 2023084). Bks Demand UMI.

Safeguarding the School Board's Purchase of Architects' Working Drawings. Arthur M. Proctor. LC 73-177168. (Columbia University. Teachers College. Contributions to Education: No. 474). Repr. of 1931 ed. 22.50 (ISBN 0-404-55474-1). AMS Pr.

Safeguarding Your Love Affair with the Bottle: A Tongue-in-Cheek Approach to Getting Sober. Jerry Fite. 160p. (Orig.). 1988. pap. 6.95. CompCare.

Safeguards: Proceedings, American Nuclear Society Executive Conference, Cape Cod MA, 16-19 October 1977. 360p. softcover 34.00 (ISBN 0-317-33077-2, 650005). Am Nuclear Soc.

Safeguards Systems Analysis: With Applications to Nuclear Material Safeguards & Other Inspection Problems. Rudolf Avenhaus. 380p. 1986. 59.50x (ISBN 0-306-42169-0, Plenum Pr). Plenum Pub.

Safeguards Techniques, 2 Vols. (Illus.). 1116p. (Orig.). 1970. Vol. 1. pap. 48.50 (ISBN 92-0-070270-8, ISP260-1, IAEA); Vol. 2. pap. 39.50 (ISBN 92-0-070370-4, ISP260-2). UNIPUB.

Safekeeping. Gregory McDonald. LC 85-16708. 1985. 15.95 (ISBN 0-89296-139-2, Penzler Bks); ltd. ed. 45.00 (ISBN 0-89296-140-6). Mysterious Pr.

Safekeeping. Gregory McDonald. 1987. pap. 7.95 (ISBN 0-440-57599-0, LE). Dell.

Safely to the Grave. Margaret Yorke. 240p. 1986. 14.95 (ISBN 0-312-69666-3). St Martin.

Safer Cancer Chemotherapy. Leonard Price & Margaret Ghilchik. (Illus.). 128p. 1981. text ed. 27.95 (ISBN 0-7216-0755-1, Bailliere-Tindall). Saunders.

Safer Death: Multidisciplinary Aspects of Terminal Care. Ed. by A. Gilmore & S. Gilmore. LC 88-12414. (Illus.). 228p. 1988. 49.50x (ISBN 0-306-42912-8, Plenum Pr). Plenum Pub.

Safer Lifting for Patient Care. 2nd ed. Margaret Hollis. (Illus.). 160p. 1985. pap. text ed. 7.95 (ISBN 0-632-01392-3, B-2259-X). Mosby.

Safer Pest Control for Australian Homes & Gardens. Paul Rogers. 160p. 1987. pap. 9.95 (ISBN 0-86417-104-8, Pub. by Kangaroo Pr). Intl Spec Bk.

Safer Than a Known Way. Pamela R. Moore. 224p. 1988. 10.95 (ISBN 0-8007-9137-1). Revell.

Safer Than Love. Margery Allingham. 12.95 (ISBN 0-89190-166-3, Pub. by Am Repr). Amereon Ltd.

Safestud: The Safesex Chronicles of Max Exander. Max Exander. 130p. (Orig.). 1985. pap. 6.95 (ISBN 0-932870-88-0). Alyson Pubns.

Safety. (Illus.). 48p. (gr. 6-12). 1986. pap. 1.25x (ISBN 0-8395-3347-0, 3347). BSA.

Safety. Laurence Santrey. LC 84-2700. (Illus.). 32p. (gr. 3-6). 1985. PLB 8.45 (ISBN 0-8167-0230-6); pap. text ed. 1.95 (ISBN 0-8167-0231-4). Troll Assocs.

Safety. 2nd ed. Alton L. Thygerson. (Illus.). 400p. 1986. text ed. 31.00 (ISBN 0-13-785726-8). P H.

Safety: A Personal Focus. Bever. (Illus.). 432p. 1987. text ed. 30.95 (ISBN 0-8016-0675-6). Mosby.

Safety Against Strangers. Kathi Thaxton. (Stick out Your Neck Ser.). (Illus.). 32p. 1985. pap. write for info. (ISBN 0-88724-168-9, CD-8060). Carson-Dellos.

Safety Analysis Methodologies for Radioactive Waste Repositories in Shallow Ground: Procedures & Data. (Safety Ser.: No. 64). 53p. (Orig.). 1984. pap. 11.75 (ISBN 92-0-123484-8, ISP656, IAEA). UNIPUB.

Safety & Accident Prevention in Chemical Operations. 2nd ed. Ed. by Howard H. Fawcett & William S. Wood. LC 82-2623. 910p. 1982. 96.00 (ISBN 0-471-02435-X). Wiley.

Safety & Clinical Efficacy of Implanted Neuroaugmentive Devices. Ed. by P. L. Gildenberg. (Applied Neurophysiology: Vol. 40, Nos. 2-4). (Illus.). 1978. pap. 38.75 (ISBN 3-8055-2925-2). S Karger.

Safety & Cost Containment in Anesthesia. J. S. Gravenstein & J. F. Holzer. 1988. text ed. 22.95 (ISBN 0-409-90141-5). Butterworth.

Safety & Efficacy of Radiopharmaceuticals. Ed. by K. Kristensen & E. Norbygaard. (Developments in Nuclear Medicine Ser.). 1984. text ed. 54.00 (ISBN 0-89838-609-8, Pub. by Martinus Nijhoff Netherlands). Kluwer Academic.

Safety & Efficacy of Radiopharmacueticals 1987. Ed. by Knud Kristensen & Elisabeth Norbygaard. (Developments in Nuclear Medicine Ser.). 1988. lib. bdg. 100.00 (ISBN 0-89838-986-0, Pub. by Martinus Nijhoff Netherlands). Kluwer Academic.

Safety & Fire Protection. (Principles of Steam Generation Ser.: Module 1). 80p. 1982. spiral bdg. 17.50x (ISBN 0-87683-251-6). GP Pub.

Safety & Health - A Guide to Law. 1980. 2.00. Natl Lawyers Guild.

Safety & Health Abroad: How to Pack Peace of Mind into Your Next Trip. John A. Giordano & Mary S. Shea. 107p. (Orig.). 1985. pap. 4.95 (ISBN 0-935169-00-8). Venture Abroad.

Safety & Health & the Working Environment: International Labour Conference, 1981, 67th Session. 68p. (Orig.). 1980. pap. 10.50 (ISBN 92-2-102407-5). Intl Labour Office.

Safety & Health & the Working Environment, Report VI, Pt. 2. International Labour Conference, 67th Session, 1981. 79p. (Orig.). 1981. pap. 10.50 (ISBN 92-2-102408-3). Intl Labour Office.

Safety & Health Aspects of Organic Solvents. Ed. by Vesa Riihimaaki & Ulf Ulfvarson. LC 86-20137. (Progress in Clinical & Biological Research Ser.: Vol. 220). 348p. 1986. 64.00 (ISBN 0-8451-5070-7, 5070). A R Liss.

Safety & Health Core Chapters. Center for Occupational Research & Development Staff. (Job Safety & Health Instructional Materials Ser.). (Illus.). 130p. 1981. pap. text ed. 28.00 (ISBN 1-55502-032-1). Ctr Res & Dev.

Safety & Health in Agricultural Work: An ILO Code of Practice. 4th ed. 1983. 12.25. Intl Labour Office.

Safety & Health in Building & Civil Engineering Work: An ILO Code of Practice. 3rd ed. 1985. 28.00. Intl Labour Office.

Safety & Health in Coal Mines: An ILO Code of Practice. v, 176p. 1986. pap. 14.00 (ISBN 92-2-105339-3). Intl Labour Office.

Safety & Health in Construction. 83p. (Orig.). 1987. pap. text ed. 12.25 (ISBN 92-2-106018-7, ILO1274, ILO). UNIPUB.

Safety & Health in Construction, Report V (1) Fifth Item on the Agenda (International Labour Conference, 73rd Session, 1987. 90p. (Orig.). 1986. pap. text ed. 12.25 (ISBN 92-2-105576-0, ILO566, ILO). UNIPUB.

Safety & Health in Dock Work: An ILO Code of Practice. 1984. 19.25 (ISBN 92-2-101593-9). Intl Labour Office.

Safety & Health in Purchasing: Procurement Materials Management. J. B. Mackie & R. L. Kuhlman. LC 81-82010. (Illus.). 364p. 1981. text ed. 32.00 (ISBN 0-88061-003-4). Institute Pr.

Safety & Health in Shipbuilding & Ship Repairing: An ILO Code of Practice. 3rd ed. viii, 260p. 1984. 19.25. Intl Labour Office.

Safety & Health in the Construction of Fixed Offshore Installations in the Petroleum Industry: An ILO Code of Practice. xi, 135p. (Orig.). 1982. pap. 14.00 (ISBN 92-2-102900-X). Intl Labour Office.

Safety & Health in the Oil & Gas Extractive Industries. Commission of the European Communities Staff. 442p. 1983. 70.00 (ISBN 0-86010-452-4). Graham & Trotman.

Safety & Health in Vocational Education. Center for Occupational Research & Development Staff. (Job Safety & Health Instructional Materials Ser.). (Illus.). 32p. 1981. pap. text ed. 2.50 (ISBN 1-55502-146-8). Ctr Res & Dev.

Safety & Health in Wastewater Systems. (Manual of Practice: 1). 106p. 1983. pap. 35.00 (ISBN 0-943244-41-2, MOOO1). Water Pollution.

Safety & Health Inspector. Jack Rudman. (Career Examination Ser.: C-3143). (Cloth bdg. avail. on request). 1988. pap. 14.00 (ISBN 0-8373-3143-9). Natl Learning.

Safety & Health of Migrant Workers: International Symposium. (Occupational Safety & Health Ser.: No. 41). 337p. 1982. 21.00 (ISBN 92-2-001906-X). Intl Labour Office.

Safety & Health Practices of Multinational Enterprises. 2nd ed. 1986. pap. 12.25. Intl Labour Office.

Safety & Health Requirements Manual. (Engineers Manual: No. 385-1). (Illus.). 445p. 1987. pap. 9.00 (ISBN 0-318-23841-1, S/N 008-022-00243-0). USGPO.

Safety & Health Training Manual. (Health & Safety Ser.: No. 3-3A). 1980. instr's. manual 60.00 (ISBN 0-317-58397-2); student manual 40.00 (ISBN 0-317-58398-0). Natl Asphalt Pavement.

Safety & Quality in Food. (Developments in Animal & Veterinary Sciences Ser.: Vol. 17). 1984. 68.50 (ISBN 0-444-42409-1). Elsevier.

Safety & Reliability of Existing Structures. J. T. Yao. 144p. 1985. 37.00 (ISBN 0-470-20620-9, Co-Pub. with Longman). Wiley.

Safety & Reliability of Metal Structures: Specialty Conference, Pittsburgh, PA, Nov. 2-3, 1972. Specialty Conference on Safety & Reliability of Metal Structures. LC 78-322838. (Illus.). pap. 114.30 (ISBN 0-317-08324-4, 2019538). Bks Demand UMI.

Safety & Reliability of Programmable Electronic Systems: Proceedings of the Programmable Electronic Systems Safety Symposium, Beau Sejour Center, Gvernsey, Channel Islands, U. K., 28-30 May 1986. Ed. by B. K. Daniels. 288p. 1986. 48.00 (ISBN 0-317-47139-2). Elsevier.

Safety & Seamanship. John Chamier. (Illus.). 1979. encore ed. 3.75 (ISBN 0-229-11501-2, ScribT). Scribner.

Safety & Security Handbook: A Modern Investigative Approach. N. R. Brooks & W. A. Frost. 100p. 1985. pap. 19.95. Creative Alter Pr.

Safety & Security in Building Design. Ralph Sinnott. (Illus.). 258p. 1985. 33.95 (ISBN 0-442-28212-5). Van Nos Reinhold.

Safety & Survival Education see Individualized Health Incentive Program Modules For Physically Disabled Students.

Safety & Systems Assurance. C. Whetton. write for info. (ISBN 0-442-29270-8). Van Nos Reinhold.

Safety & Techniques in Perfusion. Charles C. Reed et al. LC 88-61551. (Illus.). 250p. 1988. 60.00x. Quali-Med.

Safety & the Work Force: Incentives & Disincentives in Worker's Compensation. Ed. by John D. Worrall. 200p. 1983. 26.00 (ISBN 0-87546-101-8, 83-12706). ILR Pr.

Safety Aspects of Core Management & Fuel Handling for Nuclear Power Plants: A Safety Guide. (Safety Ser.: No. 50-SG-010). 40p. 1985. pap. 10.00 (ISBN 92-0-123085-0, ISP685, IAEA). UNIPUB.

Safety Aspects of Fuel Behavior in Off-Normal & Accident Conditions. OECD. 658p. (Orig.). 1981. pap. text ed. 28.00x (ISBN 92-64-02234-1). OECD.

Safety Aspects of the Aging & Maintenance of Nuclear Power Plants. (Proceedings Ser.). 449p. (Orig.). 1988. pap. 91.00 (ISBN 92-0-020088-5, ISP759, IAEA). UNIPUB.

Safety Assessment for the Underground Disposal of Radioactive Wastes. (Safety Ser.: No. 56). 46p. 1982. pap. 9.00 (ISBN 92-0-623181-2, ISP590, IAEA). UNIPUB.

Safety at Narrow Bridge Sites. (National Cooperative Highway Research Program Report). 63p. 1979. 6.00 (ISBN 0-309-02909-0). Transport Res Bd.

Safety at Work. 2nd ed. John R. Ridley. 704p. 1986. text ed. 110.00 (ISBN 0-408-00840-7). Butterworth.

Safety at Work & the Unions. P. B. Beaumont. (Illus.). 192p. 1983. 25.25 (ISBN 0-7099-0097-X, Pub. by Croom Helm Ltd). Routledge Chapman & Hall.

Safety at Work: The Limits of Self-Regulation. Sandra Dawson et al. (Cambridge Studies in Management: No. 12). 400p. Date not set. price not set (ISBN 0-521-35497-8). Cambridge U Pr.

Safety by Objectives. Dan Peterson. LC 78-12057. 1978. 28.50x (ISBN 0-913690-07-4). Aloray.

Safety Can Be Fun. rev. ed. Munro Leaf. LC 61-14579. (Illus.). (gr. k-3). 1961. PLB 12.89 (ISBN 0-397-31593-7, Lipp Jr Bks). HarpJ.

Safety Can Be Fun. 2nd rev. ed. Munro Leaf. LC 86-45499. (Trophy Picture Book). (Illus.). 48p. (ps-2). 1988. pap. 3.95 (ISBN 0-06-443111-8, Trophy). HarpJ.

Safety Catch. Jaron Summers. 400p. (Orig.). 1985. pap. 3.95 (ISBN 0-8439-2301-6, Leisure Bks). Leisure NY.

Safety Checklists for Health Care Facilities, Vol. 1. 78p. 1983. pap. 10.00 (ISBN 0-87912-126-2, 129.52). Natl Safety Coun.

Safety Checklists for Health Care Facilities, Vol. 2. 50p. 1983. pap. 10.00 (ISBN 0-87912-127-0). Natl Safety Coun.

Safety Code for Elevators & Escalators: ANS u-c17.1, 1987. (No. AX9687). 1987. 85.00 (ISBN 0-685-37579-X). ASME.

Safety Code for Elevators & Escalators: Handbook on A17.1. Ed. by E. A. Donoghue. 372p. 1987. 95.00 (A00112). ASME.

Safety Code for Mechanical Refrigeration, 1978. (ASHRAE Standards Ser.: No. 15). 30.00 (ISBN 0-317-58656-4). Am Heat Ref & Air Eng.

Safety Considerations in the Use of Ports & Approaches by Nuclear Merchant Ships. (Safety Ser.: No. 27). 20p. 1968. pap. 6.25 (ISBN 92-0-123168-7, ISP206, IAEA). UNIPUB.

Safety Considerations of Energy Saving Materials & Devices. Steve Mazzoni. 3.25 (ISBN 0-686-12080-9, TR 78-6). Society Fire Protect.

Safety Consultant. Jack Rudman. (Career Examination Ser.: C-2640). (Cloth bdg. avail. on request). pap. 16.00 (ISBN 0-8373-2640-0). Natl Learning.

Safety Coordinator. Jack Rudman. (Career Examination Ser.: C-1921). (Cloth bdg. avail. on request). pap. 16.00 (ISBN 0-8373-1921-8). Natl Learning.

Safety: Directions Toward an Improved Lifestyle. Dean F. Miller. (Illus.). 450p. 1982. write for info. ref. ed. (ISBN 0-13-785782-9). P-H.

Safety Education. 4th, rev. ed. A. E. Florio & Alles. (Illus.). 1979. text ed. 38.95 (ISBN 0-07-021371-2). McGraw.

Safety Education in the Elementary School. Joseph Wayne. LC 81-86314. (Fastback Ser.: No. 170). 50p. (Orig.). 1982. pap. 0.90 (ISBN 0-87367-170-8). Phi Delta Kappa.

Safety Education: Man, His Machines & His Environment. W. Wayne Worick. (Illus.). 320p. 1975. 29.00 (ISBN 0-13-785683-0). P-H.

Safety Engineer. Jack Rudman. (Career Examination Ser.: C-797). (Cloth bdg. avail. on request). pap. 16.00 (ISBN 0-8373-0797-X). Natl Learning.

Safety Evaluation & Regulation of Chemicals, No. 1. Ed. by F. Homburger. (Illus.). xiv, 294p. 1983. 132.00 (ISBN 3-8055-3578-3). S Karger.

Safety Evaluation & Regulation of Chemicals, No. 2. Ed. by F. Homburger. (Illus.). xvi, 326p. 1985. 145.50 (ISBN 3-8055-3942-8). S Karger.

Safety Evaluation & Regulation of Chemicals, No. 3. Ed. by F. Homburger. (Illus.). xiv, 242p. 1985. 112.75 (ISBN 3-8055-4017-5). S Karger.

Safety Evaluation of Chemicals in Food: Toxicological Data Profiles for Pesticides, Pt. 1: Carbamate & Organophosphorus Insecticides Used in Agriculture & Public Health. (Progress in Standardization: No. 3). (WHO bulletin vol. 52, supp. no. 2). 1975. pap. 4.00 (ISBN 92-4-068522-7). World Health.

Safety Evaluation of Drugs & Chemicals. Ed. by W. Eugene Lloyd. LC 84-12912. (Illus.). 487p. 1985. text ed. 69.95 (ISBN 0-89116-352-2). Hemisphere Pub.

Safety Evaluation: Toxicology, Methods, Concepts & Risk Assessment. Ed. by M. A. Mehlman. (Illus.). 278p. 1987. 58.00 (ISBN 0-911131-13-2). Princeton Sci Pubs.

Safety Features for Floor & Wall Openings & Stairways. Center for Occupational Research & Development Staff. (Job Safety & Health Instructional Materials Ser.). (Illus.). 18p. 1981. pap. text ed. 2.00 (ISBN 1-55502-138-7). Ctr Res & Dev.

Safety Features of Material & Personnel Movement Devices. Center for Occupational Research & Development Staff. (Job Safety & Health Instructional Materials Ser.). (Illus.). 32p. 1981. pap. text ed. 2.50 (ISBN 1-55502-127-1). Ctr Res & Dev.

Safety First - Bicycle. Cynthia F. Klingel. LC 86-72590. (Safety First Ser.). (ps up). 1987. lib. bdg. 9.95 (ISBN 0-88682-085-5). Creative Ed.

Safety First - Home. Cynthia F. Klingel. LC 86-72591. (Safety First Ser.). (ps up). 1986. lib. bdg. 9.95 (ISBN 0-88682-081-2). Creative Ed.

Safety First - Outdoors. Cynthia F Klingel. LC 86-72592. (Safety First Ser.). (ps up). 1986. lib. bdg. 9.95 (ISBN 0-88682-082-0). Creative Ed.

Safety First - School. Cynthia F. Klingel. LC 86-72593. (Safety First Ser.). (ps up). 1986. lib. bdg. 9.95 (ISBN 0-88682-084-7). Creative Ed.

Safety First - Water. Cynthia F. Klingel. LC 86-72673. (Safety First Ser.). (ps up). lib. bdg. 9.95 (ISBN 0-88682-083-9). Creative Ed.

Safety First: Fire. Cynthia Klingel. LC 86-72672. (ps up). 1986. PLB 9.95 (ISBN 0-88682-080-4). Creative Ed.

Safety First Manual. Mark Winnitz. Ed. by Ed Sawicki. (Illus.). 154p. (Orig.). 1985. pap. 23.00 (ISBN 0-9613880-2-1); pap. text ed. 23.00 (ISBN 0-317-43289-3). Semiconductor.

Safety for Carpenters & Woodworkers. Gaspar Lewis. LC 80-66859. (Carpentry-Cabinetmaking Ser.). 1981. pap. text ed. 10.95 (ISBN 0-8273-1869-3); instr's. guide 3.50 (ISBN 0-8273-1870-7). Delmar.

Safety for Compressed Gas & Air Equipment. Center for Occupational Research & Development Staff. (Job Safety & Health Instructional Materials Ser.). (Illus.). 36p. 1981. pap. text ed. 3.00 (ISBN 1-55502-128-X). Ctr Res & Dev.

Safety for Masons. Richard T. Kreh, Sr. LC 78-53663. 1979. pap. text ed. 8.95 (ISBN 0-8273-1668-2); instr's. guide 4.50 (ISBN 0-8273-1669-0). Delmar.

Safety for People & for Chemicals. Eugene N. Garcia & Wanda Spencer. LC 79-90457. (Illus.). 80p. (Orig.). (gr. 10-12). 1979. pap. 4.50x (ISBN 0-87881-096-X); incl. 2 tests. Mojave Bks.

Safety for Welders. Larry Jeffus. LC 78-73579. (Metalworking Ser.). (gr. 8). 1980. pap. text ed. 8.50 (ISBN 0-8273-1684-4); instr's. guide 4.50 (ISBN 0-8273-1685-2). Delmar.

Safety Functions & Component Classification from BWR, PWR & PTR: A Safety Guide. (Safety Ser.: No. 50-SG-D1). 68p. 1980. pap. 11.75 (ISBN 92-0-123979-3, ISP542, IAEA). UNIPUB.

Safety Guards for Machinery. Center for Occupational Research & Development Staff. (Job Safety & Health Instructional Materials Ser.). (Illus.). 26p. 1981. pap. text ed. 2.00 (ISBN 1-55502-136-0). Ctr Res & Dev.

Safety Guide for Health Care Institutions. 3rd ed. American Hospital Association & National Safety Council Staff. LC 83-12265. (Illus.). 160p. 1983. pap. 35.00 (ISBN 0-939450-85-2, 181136). AHPI.

Safety Guide for Terminals: Handling Ships Carrying Liquefield Gases in Bulk. OCIMF. 1982. 135.00x (ISBN 0-317-61466-5, Pub. by Witherby & Co England). State Mutual Bk.

Safety, Health & Welfare in the Printing Industry. M. C. Fairley. 1968. pap. 7.75 (ISBN 0-08-013033-X). Pergamon.

Safety, Health & Working Conditions in the Transfer of Technology to Developing Countries. (ILO Code of Practice Ser.). v, 81p. (Orig.). 1988. pap. 10.50 (ISBN 92-2-106122-1). Intl Labour Office.

Safety in Ammonia Nitrate Plants. 16p. 1966. pap. 12.00 (ISBN 0-8169-0333-6, T-20). Am Inst Chem Eng.

Safety in Biological Laboratories. Ed. by C. H. Collins. LC 85-16908. 1985. 12.00 (ISBN 0-471-90833-9). Wiley.

Safety in Chemical Tankers. ICS Staff. 1977. 36.00x (ISBN 0-317-61468-1, Pub. by Witherby & Co England). State Mutual Bk.

Safety in Construction & Maintenance Work Zones & Transportation of Hazardous Materials. (Transportation Research Record Ser.). 51p. 1978. 3.00 (ISBN 0-309-02839-6). Transport Res Bd.

Safety in Decommissioning of Research Reactors. (Safety Series, IAEA Safety Guides: No. 74). 44p. 1986. pap. text ed. 15.50 (ISBN 92-0-123086-9, ISP713, IAEA). UNIPUB.

Safety in Elevators & Grain Handling Facilities. (Job Safety & Health Instructional Materials Ser.). (Illus.). 43p. 1981. pap. text ed. 3.50 (ISBN 1-55502-129-8). Ctr Res & Dev.

Safety in Everyday Living. Joseph H. Mroz. 400p. 1978. pap. text ed. write for info. (ISBN 0-697-07371-8). Wm C Brown.

Safety in Gymnastics. Gerald A. Carr. (Illus.). 248p. pap. 9.95 (ISBN 0-88839-054-8). Hancock House.

Safety in Liquefied Gas Tankers. ICS Staff. 1980. 36.00x (ISBN 0-317-61469-X, Pub. by Witherby & Co England). State Mutual Bk.

Safety in Manned Diving. Erik Jacobsen et al. 90p. 1984. pap. 16.00x (ISBN 82-00-06369-0). Oxford U Pr.

Safety in Mines Research: Proceedings of the 22nd International Conference on Safety in Mines Research Institutes 1987. Ed. by Dai Guoquan. 1220p. 1988. pap. write for info. (ISBN 7-5020-0041-0, Pub. by A A Balkema). Brookfield Pub Co.

Safety in Mines Research: 21st International Conference of Safety in Mines Research Institutes, 21-25 Oct. 1985. A. R. Green. 798p. 1985. text ed. 122.50 (ISBN 90-6191-610-0, Pub. by A A Balkema). Brookfield Pub Co.

Safety in Museums & Galleries. Frank Howie. (Conservation & Museology Bks.). (Illus.). 192p. 1988. pap. text ed. 33.00 (ISBN 0-408-02362-7). Butterworth.

Safety in Nuclear Power Plant Operation, Including Commissioning & Decommissioning: A Code of Practice. (Safety Ser.: No. 50-C-O). 36p. 1979. pap. 9.25 (ISBN 92-0-123578-X, ISP503, IAEA). UNIPUB.

Safety in Nuclear Power Plant Operation, Including Commissioning & Decommissioning: A Code of Practice. (Safety Ser.: No. 50-C-O). 40p. (Fr., Eng., Rus. & Span.). 1979. pap. (ISP503, IAEA). UNIPUB.

Safety in Nuclear Power Plant Siting. (Safety Ser.: No. 50-C-S). 38p. 1979. pap. 9.25 (ISBN 92-0-123378-7, ISP510, IAEA). UNIPUB.

Safety in Oil Tankers. 2nd ed. ICS Staff. (gr. 5 up). 1978. 36.00x (ISBN 0-317-61470-3, Pub. by Witherby & Co England). State Mutual Bk.

Saga of an Ego Trip. Jeannette V. Durlach. 48p. 1976. pap. 1.00 (ISBN 0-87844-038-0). Sandlapper Pub Co.
Saga of an Irish Immigrant Family: The Descendants of John Mullanphy. Alice L. Cochran. LC 76-6328. (Irish Americans Ser.). 1976. 23.50 (ISBN 0-405-09325-X). Ayer Co Pubs.
Saga of an Ordinary Man. Goldie Down. (Dest Two Ser.). 1984. pap. 6.95 (ISBN 0-8163-0554-4). Pacific Pr Pub Assn.
Saga of Belle Lea Acres: Any Fool Can Do It. Jay Gould. (Orig.). pap. write for info. J Gould.
Saga of Billy the Kid. Walter N. Burns. Repr. of 1926 ed. 47.00 (ISBN 0-686-19886-7). Ridgeway Bks.
Saga of Billy the Kid. Walter N. Burns. 322p. 1984. Repr. of 1925 ed. lib. bdg. 47.50 (ISBN 0-918377-03-X). Russell Pr.
Saga of Cape Ann. Melvin T. Copeland & Elliot C. Rogers. 1984. 14.75 (ISBN 0-8446-6067-1). Peter Smith.
Saga of Chief Joseph. Helen Addison Howard. LC 78-16138. (Illus.). 421p. 1978. pap. 7.95 (ISBN 0-8032-7202-2, BB 699, Bison). U of Nebr Pr.
Saga of Cimba. Richard Maury. (Illus.). 1973. 7.50 (ISBN 0-8286-0063-5). J De Graff.
Saga of Coe Ridge: A Study in Oral History. William L. Montell. LC 74-77846. (Illus.). 1970. 19.95x (ISBN 0-87049-096-6); pap. 9.95x (ISBN 0-87049-315-9). U of Tenn Pr.
Saga of Dazai Osamu: A Critical Study with Translations. Phyllis I. Lyons. LC 83-42542. (Illus.). 432p. 1985. 38.50x (ISBN 0-8047-1197-6). Stanford U Pr.
Saga of Denny McCune. Burt Arthur & Budd Arthur. 1979. pap. 1.25 (ISBN 0-505-51397-8, Pub. by Tower Bks). Leisure NY.
Saga of Erik the Viking. Terry Jones. (Puffin Storybooks Ser.). (Illus.). 144p. (ps up). 1986. pap. 7.95 (ISBN 0-14-031713-9, Puffin). Penguin.
Saga of Felix Senac: Being the Legend & Biography of a Confederate Agent in Europe. Regina Rapier. (Illus.). 216p. 1972. 20.00 (ISBN 0-9600584-1-9). R C Rapier.
Saga of Felix Senac: Supplement. Regina C. Rapier. (Illus.). 1982. 2.00x (ISBN 0-9600584-3-5). R C Rapier.
Saga of Filster Stein. Gary Lovisi. (Illus.). 60p. (Orig.). 1988. saddle stitched 4.00 (ISBN 0-936071-07-9). Gryphon Pubns.
Saga of Gisli the Outlaw. Tr. by George Johnston. LC 67-207. (Illus.). 1963. pap. 9.95c (ISBN 0-8020-6219-9). U of Toronto Pr.
Saga of Grettir the Strong. Tr. by G. A. Hight. 1978. 12.95x (ISBN 0-460-00699-1, Evman); pap. 6.95x (ISBN 0-460-01699-7). Biblio Dist.
Saga of Halfaday Creek. James B. Hendryx. 1976. Repr. of 1947 ed. lib. bdg. 15.95x (ISBN 0-88411-837-1, Pub. by Aeonian Pr). Amereon Ltd.
Saga of Hog Island & Other Essays in Inconvenient History. James J. Martin. LC 76-52654. 1977. pap. 3.95 (ISBN 0-87926-021-1). R Myles.
Saga of Hrafn Sveinbjarnarson. Hrafn Sveinbjarnarson. Tr. by Anne Tjomsland. (Islandica Ser.: Vol. 35). 1951. 13.00 (ISBN 0-527-00365-4). Kraus Repr.
Saga of Hugh Glass: Pirate, Pawnee, & Mountain Man. John M. Myers. LC 75-38613. viii, 237p. 1976. pap. 6.95 (ISBN 0-8032-5834-8, BB 614, Bison). U of Nebr Pr.
Saga of Iron Mining in Michigan's Upper Peninsula. Burton H. Boyum. 1977. pap. 5.95 (ISBN 0-938746-03-0). Marquette Cnty.
Saga of Kettle Falls. Orville Dutro. (Illus.). 44p. (Orig.). Date not set. pap. 4.95 (ISBN 0-940151-06-5). Statesman Exam.
Saga of Kosovo: Focus on Serbian-Albanian Relationships. Alex N. Dragnich & Slavko Todorovich. (East European Monographs). 1985. 22.50 (ISBN 0-317-18452-0). Brooklyn Coll Pr.
Saga of Old City. Gary Gygax. Ed. by Kim Mohan. LC 85-51041. (Greyhawk Adventures Ser.). (Illus.). 352p. (Orig.). 1985. pap. 3.95 (ISBN 0-88038-257-0). TSR Inc.
Saga of Prayer: The Poetry of Dylan Thomas. Robert K. Burdette. LC 68-23203. (Studies in English Literature: No. 67). 160p. 1973. text ed. 18.40x (ISBN 90-2792-072-9). Mouton.
Saga of Ranch El Tejon. Frank F. Latta. (Illus.). 1979. 18.75 (ISBN 0-686-26702-8). Bear State.
Saga of Saga Hill. Theodore C. Blegen. (Illus.). 85p. 1971. Repr. of 1970 ed. 6.95 (ISBN 0-87351-068-2). Minn Hist.
Saga of Sagebrush Sal. I. E. Clark. (Illus.). 20p. 1972. pap. 1.75 (ISBN 0-88680-167-2); royalty 25.00 (ISBN 0-317-03597-5). I E Clark.
Saga of Sagebrush Sal. I. E. Clark. (Illus.). 38p. (Director's Production Script). 1972. pap. 6.50 (ISBN 0-88680-168-0). I E Clark.
Saga of Saints. facs. ed. Sigrid Undset. Tr. by E. C. Ramsden. LC 68-22952. (Essay Index Reprint Ser). 1968. Repr. of 1934 ed. 20.00 (ISBN 0-8369-0959-3). Ayer Co Pubs.
Saga of Sammy-Cat. Ethel Mannin. (gr. 1-3). 1969. Repr. of 1969 ed. 2.59 (ISBN 0-08-013397-5). Pergamon.
Saga of Silent Sue. Leigh Williams. LC 85-25721. (Chumble Chums Ser.). (Illus.). 32p. (ps-3). 1987. 5.95 (ISBN 0-394-87849-3, BYR). Random.
Saga of Simon Fry. Roe Richmond. 160p. 1986. pap. 2.75 (ISBN 0-553-25905-9). Bantam.
Saga of Sitting Bull's Bones: The Unusual Story Behind Sculptor Korczak Ziolkowski's Memorial to Chief Sitting Bull. Robb DeWall. LC 84-48122. (Illus.). 320p. 15.95 (ISBN 0-318-18779-5). Crazy Horse.
Saga of Smokey Stover. Clark G. Reynolds. LC 78-64485. 1978. 6.00 (ISBN 0-937684-06-6). Tradd St Pr.
Saga of Swamp Thing. Alan Moore. 184p. (Orig.). 1987. pap. 10.95 (ISBN 0-446-38690-1). Warner Bks.
Saga of Sydney A. Moore: A History of a Maryland Farming Family, 1820 to the Present. Robert E. Greene. LC 85-81232. (Illus.). 138p. 1985. pap. 9.95 (ISBN 0-9603320-6-5). R E Greene.
Saga of Texas Cookery. Sarah Morgan. 1981. 10.95 (ISBN 0-88426-032-1). Texian.
Saga of the Air Mail. Carroll V. Glines, Jr. Ed. by James Gilbert. LC 79-2192. (Flight: Its First Seventy-Five Years Ser.). (Illus.). 1979. Repr. of 1968 ed. lib. bdg. 19.00x (ISBN 0-405-12213-6). Ayer Co Pubs.
Saga of the American Soul. Richard E. Wentz. LC 80-5598. 163p. 1980. pap. text ed. 10.00 (ISBN 0-8191-1150-3). U Pr of Amer.
Saga of the Bluebird. Katherine M. Braun. (Illus.). 62p. 1982. pap. 7.00 (ISBN 0-682-49913-7). Exposition-Phoenix.
Saga of the Chouteaus of Oklahoma: French Footprints in the Valley Grand. Shelby Fly. Ed. by Molly L. Griffins. LC 87-83112. (Land We Belong to Is Grand Ser.: Bk. 4). (Illus.). 70p. 1988. pap. 5.00 (ISBN 0-9618634-4-7). Levite Apache.
Saga of the Coeur D'Alene Indian Nation. Joseph Seltice. Intro. by Edward J. Kowrach. Date not set. write for info. Ye Galleon.
Saga of the Cotton Exchange. Madhav Pavaskar. 1985. 18.00x (ISBN 0-8364-1405-5, Pub. by Popular Prakashan). South Asia Bks.
Saga of the Grey Seal. Ronald M. Lockley. 8.50 (ISBN 0-8159-6801-9). Devin.
Saga of the Jomsvikings. facsimile ed. Ed. by Lee M. Hollander. LC 76-157341. (Select Bibliographies Reprint Ser). (Illus.). Repr. of 1955 ed. 12.00 (ISBN 0-8369-5801-2). Ayer Co Pubs.
Saga of the Norse Kings: Illustrated Tales from Prehistoric Times to Vikings. Snorri. (Illus.). 390p. 1984. 57.50x (ISBN 8-2091-0173-0, N393). Vanous.
Saga of the Pliocene Exile. Julian May. 1984. boxed set 85.00 (ISBN 0-395-36515-5). HM.
Saga of the Ridge. J. H. Pratt. 224p. 1983. pap. 9.50 (ISBN 1-55787-023-3). Heart of the Lakes.
Saga of the Sea. facsimile ed. Frederick B. Austin. LC 76-116930. (Short Story Index Reprint Ser.). Repr. of 1929 ed. 19.00 (ISBN 0-8369-3432-6). Ayer Co Pubs.
Saga of the South. Edward P. Lawton. LC 65-19041. (Illus.). 1974. deluxe ed. 12.00 (ISBN 0-87208-005-6). Island Pr Pubs.
Saga of the Spirit. Morris A. Inch. pap. 12.95 (ISBN 0-8010-5037-5). Baker Bk.
Saga of the Sword. facsimile ed. Frederick B. Austin. LC 75-106243. (Short Story Index Reprint Ser.). 1929. 19.00 (ISBN 0-8369-3279-X). Ayer Co Pubs.
Saga of the Sword That Sings & Other Realities. Stephanie Stearns. (Illus.). 111p. (Orig.). 1988. pap. text ed. 7.98. Dubless Pubns.
Saga of the Volsungs. Tr. by George K. Anderson. LC 80-65685. 272p. 1982. 29.50 (ISBN 0-87413-172-3). U Delaware Pr.
Saga of the Volsungs, the Saga of Ragnar Lodbrook, Together with the Lay of Kraka. Tr. by Margaret Schlauch. LC 75-41284. Repr. of 1930 ed. 21.50 (ISBN 0-404-14704-6). AMS Pr.
Saga of the 320th: A B-26 Marauder Group in WW II. Victor C. Tannehill. (Illus.). 80p. 1984. pap. text ed. 9.95 (ISBN 0-9605900-2-1). Boomerang.
Saga of Thorgils & Haflidi. Halldor Hermannsson. LC 35-15601. (Islandica Ser.: Vol. 31). 1945. pap. 16.00 (ISBN 0-527-00362-X). Kraus Repr.
Saga of Tom Horn: The Story of a Cattlemen's War. Dean F. Krakel. LC 87-33019. (Illus.). xii, 274p. 1988. 22.95x (ISBN 0-8032-2719-1); pap. 8.95 (Bison). U of Nebr Pr.
Saga of Tristram & Isond. Tr. by Paul Schach from Old Norse. LC 73-76351. (Illus.). xxiv, 148p. 1973. 15.95x (ISBN 0-8032-0832-4); pap. 3.95x (ISBN 0-8032-5847-X, BB 608, Bison). U of Nebr Pr.
Saga of Walther of Aquitaine. Ed. by Marion D. Learned. 1970. Repr. of 1892 ed. lib. bdg. 35.00x (ISBN 0-8371-3903-1, LEWA). Greenwood.
Saga of Wealth: An Anecdotal History of the Texas Oilman. 2nd ed. James Presley. Ed. by Barbara Reavis. 468p. 1983. pap. 9.95 (ISBN 0-932012-61-2). Texas Month Pr.
Saga of '54: And More. Charles A. Hair. LC 87-50301. (Illus.). xiv, 210p. 1987. 37.50 (ISBN 0-918837-07-3); deluxe ed. 49.50 (ISBN 0-918837-08-1). Robinson Typos.
Saga School. Saga Ikebana Academy Staff. (Ikebana Card Bks.). (Illus., Eng. & Japanese.). 1970. pap. 5.95 ea (Pub. by Shufunmoto Co Ltd Japan). Principal Styles, 42pgs (ISBN 4-07-973205-8). Shogonka Style, 42pgs (ISBN 4-07-973211-2). Seika Style, 42pgs (ISBN 4-07-973228-7). Moribana Style, 42pgs (ISBN 4-07-973234-1). Heika Style, 42pgs (ISBN 4-07-973240-6). Ikebana in Living, 42pgs. 5.95 (ISBN 4-07-973257-0). C E Tuttle.
Sagacity. Janet Hamilton. (Anansi Fiction Ser.: No. 44). 135p. (Orig.). 1981. pap. 7.95 (ISBN 0-88784-087-6, Pub. by Hse Anansi Pr Canada). U of Toronto Pr.
Sagadahoc Colony: Comprising the Relation of a Voyage into New England. Henry Thayer. LC 76-173865. (Illus.). Repr. of 1892 ed. 24.50 (ISBN 0-405-09026-9). Ayer Co Pubs.
Sagas & Songs of Norseman. Albany F. Major. LC 73-15520. 1904. Repr. lib. bdg. 30.00 (ISBN 0-8414-6046-9). Folcroft.
Sagas from the Far East. Rachel H. Busk. LC 78-67693. (Folktale). Repr. of 1873 ed. 33.00 (ISBN 0-404-16064-6). AMS Pr.
Sagas of Icelanders. Halldor Hermannsson. (Islandica Ser.: Vol. 24). 1935. 18.00 (ISBN 0-527-00354-9). Kraus Repr.
Sagas of Old Western Travel & Transport. H. Wilbur Hoffman. (Illus.). 300p. 1980. 25.00 (ISBN 0-8310-7123-0). Howell-North.
Sagas of the Kings & the Mythical-Heroic Sagas. Halldor Hermannsson. LC 38-32451. (Islandica Ser.: Vol. 26). 1937. pap. 16.00 (ISBN 0-527-00356-5). Kraus Repr.
Sagasha: Mysterious Dust from Space. Elgar Brom. (Illus.). 72p. 1981. pap. 9.95 (ISBN 0-938294-00-8). Global Comm.
Sage & Society: The Life & Thought of Ho Hsin-yin. Ronald G. Dimberg. (Society for Asian & Comparative Philosophy Monographs: No. 1). 190p. (Orig.). 1974. pap. text ed. 8.00x (ISBN 0-8248-0347-7). UH Pr.
Sage & the Way: Spinoza's Ethics of Freedom. Jon Wetlesen. (Philosophia Spinozae Perennis Ser.: No. 4). 474p. 1979. text ed. 50.00 (ISBN 90-232-1596-6, Pub. by Van Gorcum Holland). Longwood Pub Group.
Sage from Concord. Compiled by Virginia Hanson & Clarence Pedersen. LC 84-40510. 160p. (Orig.). 1985. pap. 4.25 (ISBN 0-8356-0593-0). Theos Pub Hse.
Sage in Harlem: H. L. Mencken & the Black Writers of the 1920s. Charles Scruggs. LC 83-6246. 213p. 1983. text ed. 25.00x (ISBN 0-8018-3000-1). Johns Hopkins.
Sage Lake Road. Ron Rau. 126p. 1983. 15.00 (ISBN 0-932558-17-8). Willow Creek Pr.
Sage Ninomiya's Evening Talks. Sontoku Ninomiya. Tr. by Isoh Yamagata. Repr. of 1953 ed. lib. bdg. 35.00x (ISBN 0-8371-3134-0, NIEV). Greenwood.
Sage of Kanchi. Ed. by T. M. Mahadevan. 93p. 1975. lib. bdg. cancelled (ISBN 0-89253-018-9). Ind-US Inc.
SAGE (Self-Awareness Growth Experiences) V. Alex Kahayan. Ed. by Janet Lovelady. LC 83-60150. (Creative Teaching Ser.). 160p. (Orig.). (gr. 7-12). 1983. pap. text ed. 14.95 (ISBN 0-935266-08-9, SC-18). Jalmar Pr.
Sagebrush Bandit. Bliss Lomax. 224p. 1986. pap. 2.95 (ISBN 0-445-20223-8, Pub. by Popular Bks). Warner Bks.
Sagebrush, Buttes & Buffalo: North Dakota Centennial Ser. Nancy E. Hanson. (Vol. IV). (Illus.). 128p. (Orig.). 1987. pap. 15.95 (ISBN 0-911007-08-3). Prairie Hse.
Sagebrush Girl. Margaret F. Garrison. 96p. 1981. 8.75 (ISBN 0-930142-05-5). Merlin Pr.
Sagebrush, Gunnysacks & Bailing Wire. Grace C. Gregory. Ed. by Sharyn G. Guthridge. (Illus.). 1982. pap. 8.00 (ISBN 0-936204-36-2). Jelm Mtn.
Sagebrush Seed. Don I. Smith. (Illus.). 112p. 1987. pap. 5.95 (ISBN 0-932773-02-8). High Country Bks.
Sagebrush Showdown. Tom West. (Orig.). 1979. pap. 1.95 (ISBN 0-89083-520-9). Zebra.
Sagebrush Soldiers. Philip D. Smith, Jr. Ed. by Mrs. Andy Weliver. (Illus.). 87p. (Orig.). 1981. pap. 4.00 (ISBN 0-9616643-0-4). P D Smith.
Sagebrush to Shakespeare. Carrol B. Howe. (Illus.). 214p. 1984. 16.00 (ISBN 0-939860-06-6). Tremaine Graph & Pub.
Sagebrush Wildflowers. J. E. Underhill. 64p. pap. 4.95 (ISBN 0-88839-171-4). Hancock House.
Sages & Heroes of the American Revolution. L. Carroll Judson. LC 74-120881. (American Bicentennial Ser). 1970. Repr. of 1851 ed. 39.50x (ISBN 0-8046-1274-9, Pub.by Kennikat). Assoc Faculty Pr.
Sages & Saints. Leo Jung. (Jewish Library: Vol. X). 1987. pap. 20.00 (ISBN 0-88125-103-8). Ktav.
Sages & Schoolmen. Arland Ussher. LC 66-29650. 1967. 10.95 (ISBN 0-8023-1139-3). Dufour.
Sages & Seers. Manly P. Hall. pap. 7.95 (ISBN 0-89314-393-6). Philos Res.
Sages of China. Manly P. Hall. (Adepts Ser). pap. 3.95 (ISBN 0-89314-531-9). Philos Res.
Sages of Sport. Jerome Romanowski. (Illus.). 44p. 1984. pap. 4.95 (ISBN 0-940056-10-0). Chapter & Cask.
Sages: Their Concepts & Beliefs. Ephraim E. Urbach. LC 87-8415. 1120p. 1987. pap. 18.95 (ISBN 0-674-78523-1). Harvard U Pr.
Sagesse. Paul Verlaine. (Illus.). deluxe ed. 110.00 (ISBN 0-685-37129-8). French & Eur.
Sagesse: Avec: Parallelement, Les Memoirs d'un Veuf. Paul Verlaine & Jean Gaudon. 247p. 1977. 3.95 (ISBN 0-686-55155-9). French & Eur.
Sagesse ou La Parabole du Festin. Paul Claudel. 1939. 8.95 (ISBN 0-686-54432-3). French & Eur.
Sagesses. Paul Verlaine. Ed. by C. Chadwick. (French Poets Ser.). 103p. (Fr.). 1973. 32.50 (ISBN 0-485-14704-1, Pub. by Athlone Pr UK); pap. 14.95 (ISBN 0-485-12704-0, Pub. by Athlone Pr UK). Humanities.
Saggi Pliniani. Seato Prete. (Studi Pubblicati Dall'Istituto di Filologia Classica (Universita di Bologna): No. 3). 105p. (Ital.). 1948. pap. text ed. 6.75 (ISBN 0-905205-40-5, Pub. by F Cairns). Longwood Pub Group.
Saggio di Bibliografia Veneziana, 2 vols. Emmanuele A. Cicogna. Bd. with Bibliografia Veneziana, 2 vols in 1. Girolamo Sorarzo. Repr. of 1885 ed. 58.50 (ISBN 0-685-23105-4). 1965. Repr. of 1847 ed. Set. 105.50 (ISBN 0-8337-0574-1). B Franklin.
Saggio Sopra la pittura. Francesco Algarotti. (Documents of Art & Architectural History, Series 2: Vol. 6). (Ital.). 1981. Repr. of 1763 ed. 27.50 (ISBN 0-686-90615-2). Broude Intl Edns.
Saginaw Circuit Court Management Study Report, 2 vols. National Center for State Courts Staff. 1982. Vol. I, 83p. manuscript 4.98 (NCRO-064); Vol. II: Data Processing, 114 pgs. manuscript 6.84 (NCRO-065). Natl Ctr St Courts.
Saginaw District Court Implementation Project: Final Report. National Center for State Courts Staff. 26p. 1981. manuscript 1.56 (NCRO-059). Natl Ctr St Courts.
Saginaw Paul Bunyan. James Stevens. LC 87-24395. (Great Lakes Bks.). 264p. 1987. 25.00x (ISBN 0-8143-1929-7); pap. 12.95x (ISBN 0-8143-1930-0). Wayne St U Pr.
Sagittal Section: Poems by Miroslav Holub. Miroslav Holub. Tr. by Dana Habova & Stuart Friebert. (Field Translation Ser.: No. 3). (Orig.). 1980. 9.95 (ISBN 0-932440-04-5). Oberlin Coll Pr.
Sagittarius. (Day by Day Horoscopes 1988 Ser.). 192p. 1987. pap. 2.95 (ISBN 0-425-10126-6). Berkley Pub.
Sagittarius. (Super Horoscopes Ser.). 256p. 1985. pap. 3.95 (ISBN 0-441-79338-X). Ace Bks.
Sagittarius. (Total Horoscopes 1986 Ser.). 256p. 1985. pap. 2.95 (ISBN 0-441-82038-7). Ace Bks.
Sagittarius. (Super Horoscope 1987 Ser.). 1987. pap. 3.95 (ISBN 0-441-79320-7, Pub. by Charter Bks). Ace Bks.
Sagittarius. (Astroanalysis Ser.). 1987. pap. 8.95 (ISBN 0-317-63345-7, Charter Pub). Berkley Pub.
Sagittarius. 1987. pap. 3.95 (Pub. by Charter Bks). Ace Bks.
Sagittarius. 1987. pap. 3.50 (ISBN 0-515-09129-4). Jove Pubns.
Sagittarius. 1988. pap. 8.95 (ISBN 0-425-11214-4). Berkley Pub.
Sagittarius see Astroanalysis.
Sagittarius: Astro-Numerology. Michael J. Kurban. (Illus.). 50p. (Orig.). 1986. pap. 8.00 (ISBN 0-938863-17-7). Libra Press Chi.
Sagittarius Serving. Joanna Kroll. (Zodiac Club Ser.: No. 6). (gr. 7 up). 1985. pap. 1.95 (ISBN 0-399-21188-8). Putnam Pub Group.
Sagittarius: Through the Numbers. Paul Rice & Valeta Rice. 40p. 1983. pap. 2.50 (ISBN 0-87728-573-X). Weiser.
Sagittarius 1987. Sydney Omarr. 1987. pap. 8.95 (ISBN 0-451-14411-2, Sig). NAL.
Sago Palm. (Plant Production & Protection Paper: No. 47). 85p. 1984. pap. text ed. 7.50 (ISBN 92-5-101425-6, F2539, FAO). UNIPUB.
SAGO: The Equatorial Swamp As a Natural Resource. Ed. by W. R. Stanton & M. Flach. 258p. 1981. 44.50 (ISBN 90-247-2470-8, Pub. by Martinus Nijhoff Netherlands). Kluwer Academic.
Sagomi Gambit. Jonathan Evans. 416p. (Orig.). 1983. pap. 3.95 (ISBN 0-523-48064-4, Dist. by Warner Pub Services & Saint Martin's Press). Tor Bks.
Sagomi Gambit. Jonathan Evans. 384p. 1988. pap. 3.95 (ISBN 0-8125-8248-9). Tor Bks.
Sagouin. Francois Mauriac. 1963. pap. 11.50 (ISBN 0-685-11551-8). French & Eur.
Sagouin. Francois Mauriac. 9.95 (ISBN 0-686-55477-9). French & Eur.
Sag's Auf Deutsch: A First Book for German Conversation. C. R. Goedsche. (Illus., Ger.). (gr. 10 up). 1979. pap. text ed. 6.95x (ISBN 0-8290-0026-7). Irvington.
Saguaro: A Naturalist Looks at Saguaro National Monument & the Tucson Basin. Gary P. Nabhan. Ed. by T. J. Priehs & Carolyn Dodson. LC 86-61422. (Orig.). 1986. pap. 6.95 (ISBN 0-911408-69-X). SW Pks Mnmts.
Saguaro: The Desert Flower Book. new ed. Millie Miller. (Pocket Nature Guides Ser.). (Illus., Orig.). 1982. pap. 4.95 (ISBN 0-933472-69-2). Johnson Bks.
Sahaidak: Virshi, 1922-1924. Iurii Darahan. LC 75-546612. (Ukrainian.). 1965. pap. 5.00 (ISBN 0-918884-16-0). Slavia Lib.
Sahajayoga & Other Meditations. C. S. Pillai. 1987. 8.95. Asia Bk Corp.

Sailing to Corinth. Irene Wanner. 1988. 15.95 (ISBN 0-937669-29-6, Dist. by Kampmann). Owl Creek Pr.

Sailing to Cythera. Nancy Willard. LC 74-5602. (Anatole Trilogy Ser.: Bk. 1). (Illus.). 72p. (gr. 3-7). 1985. pap. 5.95 (ISBN 0-15-269961-9, VoyB). HarBraceJ.

Sailing with Ham Radio. Ian Keith & Derek Van Loan. (Illus.). 132p. (Orig.). (YA) (gr. 5-9). 1987. pap. 9.95 (ISBN 0-939837-17-X). Paradise Cay Pubns.

Sailing with Mr. Belloc. Dermod MacCarthy. (Illus.). 176p. 1987. pap. 12.95 (ISBN 0-246-13244-2, Pub. by Collins England). Sheridan.

Sailing with Paul. H. A. Ironside. pap. 1.35 (ISBN 0-87213-387-7). Loizeaux.

Sailing with the Wind. Thomas Locker. LC 85-23381. (Illus.). 32p. (ps up). 1986. 15.00 (ISBN 0-8037-0311-2, 01456-440); PLB 14.89 (ISBN 0-8037-0312-0). Dial Bks Young.

Sailing Yacht Design: An Appreciation of a Fine Art. Robert G. Henry & Richareds T. Miller. LC 65-18207. (Illus.). pap. 38.30 (ISBN 0-317-08203-5, 2022554). Bks Demand UMI.

Sailing Years: An Autobiography. K. Adlard Coles. LC 80-1216. 1981. 4.95 (ISBN 0-8286-0100-3). J De Graff.

Sailmaker. Alan Spence. 28p. 1983. pap. 5.95 (ISBN 0-907540-19-8, NO.3987). Routledge Chapman & Hall.

Sailor - The Bitter Years. Dragutin Domac. 1987. 12.95 (ISBN 0-940168-10-3). Boxwood.

Sailor Beware. John A. North, Jr. (Illus.). 48p. 1984. 7.95 (ISBN 0-89962-370-0). Todd & Honeywell.

Sailor Chanties & Cowboy Songs. Charles J. Finger. LC 77-27604. 32.00 (ISBN 0-8414-4353-X). Folcroft.

Sailor-Diplomat: A Biography of Commodore James Biddle, 1783-1848. David F. Long. LC 82-22236. (Illus.). 328p. 1983. 22.95x (ISBN 0-930350-39-1). NE U Pr.

Sailor Dog. Margaret W. Brown. (Illus.). 24p. (ps-2). 1988. 3.95 (ISBN 0-307-16533-7). Western Pub.

Sailor from Gibraltar. Marguerite Duras. Tr. by Barbara Bray. 1986. pap. 8.95 (ISBN 0-394-74451-9). Pantheon.

Sailor Historian: The Best of Samuel Eliot Morison. Ed. by Emily M. Beck. 1977. 15.00 (ISBN 0-395-25444-2). HM.

Sailor Historian: The Best of Samuel Eliot Morison. 1989. pap. 9.95 (ISBN 0-395-50074-5). HM.

Sailor in English Fiction & Drama: 1550-1800. Harold F. Watson. LC 31-32461. Repr. of 1931 ed. 16.00 (ISBN 0-404-06873-1). AMS Pr.

Sailor on the Sea of Fate. Michael Moorcock. 160p. 1984. pap. 2.95 (ISBN 0-425-10329-3). Berkley Pub.

Sailor Remembers. R. D. Kataria. 1983. text ed. 18.95x (ISBN 0-7069-2064-3, Pub. by Vikas India). Advent NY.

Sailor-Scholar: Admiral Sir Herbert Richmond, 1871-1946. Barry D. Hunt. 285p. 1982. text ed. 22.95x (ISBN 0-88920-104-8, Pub. by Wilfrid Laurier Canada). Humanities.

Sailor Who Fell from Grace with the Sea. Yukio Mishima. Tr. by John Nathan. (The Perigee Japanese Library). 192p. 1981. pap. 6.95 (ISBN 0-399-50489-3, Perigee). Putnam Pub Group.

Sailor 1930-1945: The Image of an American Demigod. Thomas W. Sokolowski. LC 82-84472. (Illus.). 116p. (Orig.). 1982. pap. 12.50 (ISBN 0-940744-41-4). Chrysler Museum.

Sailor's Calendar. Ian H. Finlay. (Illus.). 1971. Ultramarine Pub.

Sailor's Garland. John Masefield. LC 77-19059. 1908. 47.50 (ISBN 0-8414-2301-6). Folcroft.

Sailor's Garland. Ed. by John Masefield. LC 70-80376. (Granger Index Reprint Ser). 1924. 23.50 (ISBN 0-8369-6108-0). Ayer Co Pubs.

Sailor's Guide to Production Sailboats. Roger Marshall & Paul Larsen. LC 86-224. (Illus.). 304p. (Orig.). 1986. pap. 17.95 (ISBN 0-688-05842-6, Pub. by Hearst Marine Bks). Morrow.

Sailor's Handbook. Ed. by Halsey C. Herreshoff. LC 82-83810. (Illus.). 224p. 1983. 14.95 (ISBN 0-316-54693-3). Little.

Sailor's Home, & Other Stories. Clotilde I. Graves. LC 77-122711. (Short Story Index Reprint Ser). 1919. 18.00 (ISBN 0-8369-3544-6). Ayer Co Pubs.

Sailors in Revolt: The Russian Baltic Fleet in 1917. Norman E. Saul. LC 77-24915. (Illus.). xiv, 314p. 1978. 29.95x (ISBN 0-7006-0166-X). U Pr of KS.

Sailors' Narratives of Voyages along the New England Coast, 1524-1624. Ed. by George P. Winship. (Research & Source Works Ser.: No. 188). (Maps). 1968. Repr. of 1905 ed. 23.50 (ISBN 0-8337-3819-4). B Franklin.

Sailor's Poem Book of God, Places, War, & Romance. Lee Holland. (Illus.). 1988. 6.95 (ISBN 0-533-06944-0). Vantage.

Sailor's Sketchbook. Bruce Bingham. LC 83-531. (Illus.). 144p. 1983. pap. 10.50 (ISBN 0-915160-55-2). Seven Seas.

Sailors Snug Harbor Eighteen Hundred One to Nineteen Seventy-Six. Barnett Shepard. LC 79-16979. (Illus.). 105p. (Orig.). 1979. pap. 7.95x (ISBN 0-9604254-0-3). Snug Harbor NY.

Sailors' Snug Harbor: Eighteen Hundred One to Nineteen Seventy-Six. Barnett Shepherd. (Illus.). 105p. (Orig.). 1979. pap. 15.00 (ISBN 0-89062-202-7). Snug Harbor NY.

Sailor's Songbag: An American Rebel in an English Prison,1777-1779. Ed. by George G. Carey. LC 75-32483. (Illus.). 176p. 1976. lib. bdg. 16.00x (ISBN 0-87023-200-2). U of Mass Pr.

Sailor's Tales. Bill Robinson. (Illus.). 1978. 14.95 (ISBN 0-393-03211-6). Norton.

Sailors' Union of the Pacific. Paul S. Taylor. LC 70-156427. (American Labor Ser., No. 2). 1971. Repr. of 1923 ed. 16.00 (ISBN 0-405-02946-2). Ayer Co Pubs.

Sailor's Weather Guide. Jeff Markell. (Illus.). 1988. 27.50 (ISBN 0-393-03320-1). Norton.

Sailor's Word Book: An Alphabetical Digest of Nautical Terms & an Authoritative Encyclopedia of Naval Science & Nomenclature. W. H. Smyth. 1977. pap. 75.00 (ISBN 0-8490-2555-9). Gordon Pr.

Sails. 5th ed. Jeremy Howard-Williams. LC 68-19075. (Illus.). 1983. 22.50 (ISBN 0-8286-0093-7). J De Graff.

Sailsbury: The Man & His Policies. Ed. by Lord Blake & Hugh Cecil. LC 87-4752. 280p. 1987. 29.95 (ISBN 0-312-69748-1). St Martin.

Sailsports: Complete Practice Set. Patricia Bille & Suzanne M. Williamson. 1985. pap. text ed. 16.76 (ISBN 0-395-39042-7); solutions manual 1.56 (ISBN 0-395-39043-5). HM.

Saino Kaihatsu Wa Zero-Sai Kara see Ability Development from Age Zero.

Saint. Christine Bell. LC 85-12256. 236p. 1985. 14.95 (ISBN 0-910923-21-3). Pineapple Pr.

Saint. Christine Bell. 272p. 1987. pap. 6.95 (ISBN 0-671-63847-5). WSP.

Saint. Conrad F. Meyer. Tr. by E. F. Hauch from Ger. 1976. Repr. of 1930 ed. 25.00x (ISBN 0-86527-298-0). Fertig.

St.-Gilles-du-Gard: The West Facade Figured Frieze - Irregularities & Relative Chronology, Vol. 1. Judy F. Scott. (Sanctuaries of the Gallic-Frankish Church). 161p. 1981. pap. 25.60 (ISBN 3-8204-6437-9). P Lang Pubs.

Saint: A Fictional Biography of Thomas Becket. Conrad F. Meyer. Tr. by W. F. Twaddell from Ger. LC 77-7038. 137p. pap. 35.70 (2030027). Bks Demand UMI.

Saint-Adventurers of the Virginia Frontier. Klaus Wust. LC 76-48566. (Illus.). 1977. 8.50 (ISBN 0-917968-29-8). Shenandoah Hist.

St. Agnes. M. R. Berardi. (gr. 1 up). 1988. plastic bdg. 2.00 (ISBN 0-317-67481-1, CH0490); pap. 1.25 (ISBN 0-317-67482-X). Dghtrs St Paul.

St. Agnes-Portrait of a Cornish Village. 1985. 9.00x (ISBN 1-85022-006-9, Pub. by Dyllansow & Truran). State Mutual Bk.

St. Alban's Abbey, a Metrical Tale, with Some Poetical Pieces see Gaston de Blondeville, or, the Court of Henry III.

St. Alban's College, Valladolid: Four Centuries of English Catholic Presence in Spain. Michael C. Williams. LC 86-17787. 278p. 1987. 35.00 (ISBN 0-312-69736-8). St Martin.

St. Alexander Nevsky. pap. 0.50 (ISBN 0-686-05660-4). Eastern Orthodox.

Saint Alphonsus Liguori: Bishop, Confessor, Founder of the Redemptorist & Doctor of the Church. D. F. Miller & L. X. Aubin. Orig. Title: Saint Alphonsus Mary de' Liquori - Founder, Bishop, & Doctor (1696-1780) 388p. 1987. pap. 12.50 (ISBN 0-89555-329-5). TAN Bks Pubs.

Saint Alphonsus Mary de' Liquori - Founder, Bishop, & Doctor (1696-1780) see Saint Alphonsus Liguori: Bishop, Confessor, Founder of the Redemptorist & Doctor of the Church.

Saint Ambrose: His Life & Times. Angela Paredi. LC 63-19325. pap. 123.80 (ISBN 0-317-26143-6, 2024372). Bks Demand UMI.

Saint & a Half. Denis Meadows. 220p. 1963. 10.00 (ISBN 0-8159-6803-5). Devin.

Saint & His Savior. C. H. Spurgeon. Date not set. pap. write for info. Pilgrim Pubns.

Saint & Singer: Edward Taylor's Typology & the Poetics of Meditation. Karen E. Rowe. (Cambridge Studies in American Literature & Culture). 320p. 1986. 34.50 (ISBN 0-521-30865-8). Cambridge U Pr.

Saint & Sufi in Modern Egypt: An Essay in the Sociology of Religion. Michael Gilsenan. (Monographs in Social Anthropology). (Illus.). 1973. 42.00x (ISBN 0-19-823181-4). Oxford U Pr.

Saint & Symbol: Images of Saint Jerome in Early Italian Art. Bernhard Ridderbos. (Illus.). xv, 126p. 1984. pap. 23.00x (ISBN 90-6088-087-0, Pub. by Boumas Boekhuis Netherlands). Benjamins North AM.

Saint & the Skeptics: Joan of Arc in the World of Mark Twain, Anatole France, & Bernard Shaw. William Searle. LC 75-26709. 178p. 1976. text ed. 22.50x (ISBN 0-8143-1541-0). Wayne St U Pr.

Saint & the Templar Treasure. Leslie Charteris. 15.95 (ISBN 0-88411-266-7, Pub. by Aeonian Pr). Amereon Ltd.

Saint & Thought for Every Day. James Alberione. 1976. 4.50 (ISBN 0-8198-0471-1); pap. 3.50 (ISBN 0-8198-6800-0). Dghtrs St Paul.

St. Andrews, Home of Golf. J. K. Robertson & Tom Jarrett. 1983. 35.00x (ISBN 0-86334-044-X, Pub. by Macdonald Pub UK). State Mutual Bk.

St. Andrews Seven. Scotish Missions Promotion. (Orig.). 1985. pap. 7.95 (ISBN 0-85151-428-6). Banner of Truth.

St. Andrews the Home of Golf: The Course, the History, the Players. Louis T. Stanley. (Illus.). 216p. 29.95 (ISBN 0-88162-235-4). Salem Hse Pubs.

Saint Anselm & His Biographer: A Study of Monastic Life & Thought, 1059c-1130. Richard W. Southern. (Birkbeck Lectures: 1959). pap. 101.30 (ISBN 0-317-09510-2, 2022473). Bks Demand UMI.

St. Anselm, Archbishop of Canterbury: A Concordance to the Works of St. Anselm, 4 vols. Ed. by Gillian Evans. LC 82-48973. (Orig.). 1985. Set. lib. bdg. 400.00 (ISBN 0-527-03661-7). Kraus Intl.

Saint Anselm: Basic Writings. 2nd ed. St. Anselm. Tr. by Sidney M. Deane. Incl. Proslogium; Monologium; Gaunilo's "In Behalf of the Fool"; Cur Deus Homo. LC 74-3309. 371p. 1974. o. p. 19.95 (ISBN 0-87548-108-6); pap. 7.95 (ISBN 0-87548-109-4). Open Court.

St. Anselm's Proslogion. Tr. by M. J. Charlesworth. LC 78-63300. 1979. text ed. 17.95x (ISBN 0-268-01696-8); pap. text ed. 7.95x (ISBN 0-268-01697-6). U of Notre Dame Pr.

St. Antholin's; or, Old Churches & New: A Tale for the Times, 1841. Francis E. Paget. Ed. by Robert L. Wolff. Bd. with Milford Malvoisin; or, Pews & Pew-Holders, 1842. LC 75-469. (Victorian Fiction Ser.). 1975. lib. bdg. 73.00 (ISBN 0-8240-1547-9). Garland Pub.

Saint Anthony & Other Stories. facsimile ed. Guy De Maupassant. Tr. by Lafcadio Hearn from Fr. LC 79-150479. (Short Story Index Reprint Ser.). Repr. of 1924 ed. 16.00 (ISBN 0-8369-3820-8). Ayer Co Pubs.

St. Anthony & the Temptations of the Flesh. Gustave Flaubert. (Illus.). 240p. 1988. 163.75 (ISBN 0-89901-365-1). Found Class Reprints.

St. Anthony: Doctor of the Church. Sophronius Clausen. Tr. by Ignatius Brady from Ger. LC 61-11200. Orig. Title: Antonius. 140p. pap. 2.50 (ISBN 0-8199-0458-9). Franciscan Herald.

St. Anthony of Padua. Isidore O'Brien. 1976. 5.00 (ISBN 0-8198-0472-X); pap. 4.00 (ISBN 0-8198-0473-8). Dghtrs St Paul.

St. Anthony, the Wonder-Worker of Padua. 2nd ed. Charles W. Stoddard. 1971. pap. 2.50 (ISBN 0-89555-039-3). TAN Bks Pubs.

St. Athanasius on the Incarnation. St. Anthanasius. 120p. 1977. pap. 5.95 (ISBN 0-913836-40-0). St Vladimirs.

St. Athanasius: The Life of St. Antony. Ed. by W. J. Burghardt et al. LC 78-62454. (ACW Ser.: No. 10). 155p. 1950. 12.95 (ISBN 0-8091-0250-1). Paulist Pr.

Saint Augustine. Adolphe Hatzfeld. LC 71-168252. 155p. 1975. Repr. of 1903 ed. 16.00 (ISBN 0-404-03155-2). AMS Pr.

St. Augustine. Rebecca West. 174p. 1979. Repr. of 1938 ed. lib. bdg. 22.50 (ISBN 0-89987-853-9). Darby Bks.

St. Augustine, Against the Academics. Ed. by W. J. Burghardt et al. LC 78-62461. (ACW Ser.: No. 12). 220p. 1950. 10.95 (ISBN 0-8091-0252-8). Paulist Pr.

St. Augustine & St. Johns County: A Pictoral History. Karen G. Harvey. LC 79-19039. (Illus.). 1980. pap. 14.95 (ISBN 0-89865-011-9). Donning Co.

Saint Augustine & the Donatist Controversy. Geoffrey G. Willis. LC 82-45826. (Orthodoxies & Heresies in the Early Church Ser.). Date not set. Repr. of 1950 ed. 26.50 (ISBN 0-404-62397-2). AMS Pr.

St. Augustine: Aspects of His Life & Thought. W. Montgomery. 1977. lib. bdg. 34.95 (ISBN 0-8490-2556-7). Gordon Pr.

St. Augustine: Being & Nothingness in the Dialogs & Confessions. Emilie Z. Brunn. LC 86-22642. 129p. 1987. 21.95 (ISBN 0-913729-17-5). Paragon Hse.

St. Augustine, Faith, Hope & Charity. Ed. by J. Kuasten & J. Plumpe. Tr. by Louis A. Arand. LC 78-62450. (Ancient Christian Writers Ser.: No. 3). 165p. 1947. 10.95 (ISBN 0-8091-0045-2). Paulist Pr.

Saint Augustine: Man, Pastor, Mystic. Augustine Trape. (Orig.). 1985. pap. 6.95 (ISBN 0-89942-172-5, 172/02). Catholic BK Pub.

St. Augustine of Hippo: Life & Controversies. Gerald I. Bonner. LC 82-45807. (Orthodoxies & Heresies in the Early Church Ser.). 1985. Repr. of 1963 ed. 42.50 (ISBN 0-404-62376-X). AMS Pr.

St. Augustine: On Faith & Works, Vol. No. 48. Gregory J. Lombardo. (Ancient Christian Writers Ser.). 1988. 14.95 (ISBN 0-8091-0406-7). Paulist Pr.

St. Augustine on Nature, Sex & Marriage. John Hugo. 249p. 1969. pap. 8.95 (ISBN 0-933932-23-5). Scepter Pubs.

Saint Augustine on the End of the World. Ed. by George N. Thompson. 55p. (Orig.). pap. text ed. 5.95 (ISBN 0-940564-15-7). Directions Pr.

St. Augustine on the Psalms, Vol. 1. St. Augustine. Ed. by J. Quasten & W. J. Burghardt. Tr. by Scholastica Hebgin & Felicitas Corrigan. LC 60-10722. (Ancient Christian Writers Ser.: No. 29). 360p. 1960. 12.95 (ISBN 0-8091-0104-1). Paulist Pr.

St. Augustine on the Psalms: Vol. 2. St. Augustine. Ed. by J. Quasten & W. J. Burghardt. Tr. by D. Scholastica Hebgin & D. Felicitas Corrigan. LC 60-10722. (Ancient Christian Writers Ser.: No. 30). 425p. 1961. 14.95 (ISBN 0-8091-0105-X). Paulist Pr.

St. Augustine, Sermons for Christmas & Epiphany. St. Augustine. Ed. by J. Quasten & J. Plumpe. Tr. by Thomas Lawler. LC 78-62464. (Ancient Christian Writers Ser.: No. 15). 250p. 1952. 10.95 (ISBN 0-8091-0137-8). Paulist Pr.

St. Augustine, the First Catechetical Instruction. St. Augustine. Ed. by J. Quasten & J. Plumpe. Tr. by Joseph P. Christopher. LC 78-62449. (Ancient Christian Writers Ser.: No. 2). 170p. 1946. 10.95 (ISBN 0-8091-0047-9). Paulist Pr.

St. Augustine: The Greatness of the Soul. St. Augustine. Ed. by J. Quasten & J. Plumpe. Tr. by Joseph M. Colleran. LC 78-62455. (Ancient Christian Writers Ser.: No. 9). 255p. 1950. 14.95 (ISBN 0-8091-0060-6). Paulist Pr.

St. Augustine: The Literal Meaning of Genesis, Vol. 1. Tr. & annotations by John H. Taylor. (Ancient Christian Writers Ser.: Vol. 41). 292p. 1983. 19.95 (ISBN 0-8091-0326-5). Paulist Pr.

St. Augustine: The Literal Meaning of Genesis, Vol. 2. Tr. & annotations by John H. Taylor. (Ancient Christian Writers Ser.: Vol. 42). 358p. 1983. 22.95 (ISBN 0-8091-0327-3). Paulist Pr.

St. Augustine, the Lord's Sermon on the Mount. Ed. by W. J. Burghardt et al. LC 78-62451. (ACW Ser.: No. 5). 227p. 1948. 13.95 (ISBN 0-8091-0246-3). Paulist Pr.

St. Augustine, the Problem of Free Choice. Ed. by W. J. Burghardt et al. LC 78-62469. (ACW Ser.: No. 22). 298p. 1955. 11.95 (ISBN 0-8091-0259-5). Paulist Pr.

St. Augustine Today. Ed. & intro. by M. E. Morrow. (Illus.). 1985. write for info. (ISBN 0-933959-01-X). Merton Pr.

St. Augustine's Comments on Imago Dei. Joseph Heijke. 3.00 (ISBN 0-686-23375-1). Classical Folia.

St. Augustine's De Musica: A Synopsis. William F. Knight. LC 78-13795. (Encore Music Editions Ser.). 1986. Repr. of 1949 ed. 18.75 (ISBN 0-88355-737-1). Hyperion Conn.

Saint Augustine's Early Theory of Man, A. D. 386-391. Robert J. O'Connell. LC 68-21981. 1968. text ed. 22.00x (ISBN 0-674-78520-7, Belknap Pr). Harvard U Pr.

Saint Augustine's Meter & George Herbert's Will. William H. Pahlka. LC 87-4252. 232p. 1987. 26.00x (ISBN 0-87338-339-7). Kent St U Pr.

Saint Augustine's Pigeon: The Selected Stories. Evan S. Connell. Ed. by Gus Blaisdell. LC 81-83972. 304p. 1980. pap. 10.00 (ISBN 0-86547-014-6). N Point Pr.

St. Augustine's Theory of Knowledge: A Contemporary Analysis. Bruce Bubacz. LC 81-18754. (Texts & Studies in Religion: Vol. 11). 248p. 1982. lib. bdg. 39.95x (ISBN 0-88946-959-8). E Mellen.

St. Bartholomew's Church in the City of New York. Christine Smith. (Illus.). 288p. 1988. 45.00 (ISBN 0-19-505406-7). Oxford U Pr.

Saint Basil & Monasticism. Sr. M. Gertrude Murphy. LC 70-144661. Repr. of 1930 ed. 14.75 (ISBN 0-404-04543-X). AMS Pr.

Saint Basil on the Value of Greek Literature. Ed. by N. G. Wilson. 1975. 23.95x (ISBN 0-685-88342-6); pap. 14.95x (ISBN 0-7156-0872-X). Trans-Atl Phila.

St. Basil the Great & Apollinaris of Laodicea. George L. Prestige. LC 82-45832. (Othodoxies & Heresies in the Early Church Ser.). Date not set. Repr. of 1956 ed. 17.50 (ISBN 0-404-62399-9). AMS Pr.

St. Basil the Great on The Forty Martyrs of Sebaste, Paradise, & the Catholic Faith. Saint Basil. 1979. pap. 3.95 (ISBN 0-686-25227-6). Eastern Orthodox.

St. Bede: A Tribute. Jean Leclercq et al. LC 85-8214. (Word & Spirit Ser.: Vol. VII). 1985. pap. 7.00. St Bedes Pubns.

Saint Benedict & the Sixth Century. John Chapman. LC 79-109719. 239p. 1971. Repr. of 1929 ed. lib. bdg. 35.00x (ISBN 0-8371-4209-1, CHSB). Greenwood.

Saint Bernadette. Leon Cristiani. LC 65-15727. (Illus.). 181p. 1981. pap. 3.95 (ISBN 0-8189-0421-6). Alba.

Saint Bernadette Soubirous. Francois Trochu. LC 84-51819. 432p. 1985. pap. 15.00 (ISBN 0-89555-253-1). Tan Bks Pubs.

Saint Bernard Classic. De La Rie. Ed. by Richard L. Steinberger. LC 74-80478. 1974. 6.75 (ISBN 0-915754-01-0). Briarcliff.

St. Bernard of Clairvaux. Leon Cristiani. 1977. 3.95 (ISBN 0-8198-0463-0); pap. 2.95 (ISBN 0-8198-0464-9). Dghtrs St Paul.

St. Issacs Cathedral - Leningrad. Georgy Butikov. 164p. 1980. 86.00x (ISBN 0-317-61398-7, Pub. by Collets (UK)). State Mutual Bk.

St. Ives. Robert Louis Stevenson. 1958. 8.95x (ISBN 0-460-00904-4, Evman). Biblio Dist.

St. Ives Mining District, Vol. 1. Cyril Noall. 1985. 25.00x (ISBN 0-907566-33-2, Pub. by Dyllansow & Truran). State Mutual Bk.

St. Ives: Nineteen Thirty-Six to Nineteen Sixty-Four. Intro. by Alan Bowness. (Illus.). 248p. 1985. pap. 14.95 (ISBN 0-946590-20-6). Salem Hse Pubs.

Saint Jack. Paul Theroux. 1973. 14.95 (ISBN 0-395-17118-0). HM.

Saint Jack. Paul Theroux. 1984. pap. 3.95 (ISBN 0-671-49822-3). WSP.

St. James: Critical & Exegetical Commentary. James H. Ropes. LC 16-6543. (International Critical Commentary Ser.). 336p. 1916. 29.95 (ISBN 0-567-05035-1, Pub. by T & T Clark Ltd UK). Fortress.

St. James Reference Guide to American Literature. 2nd ed. Ed. by D. L. Kirkpatrick. 1987. 85.00 (ISBN 0-912289-61-9); Standing Order. 76.50. St James Pr.

St. James Reference Guide to English Literature, 8 Vols. Ed. by James Vinson. Incl. Vol. 1. Beginnings & the Renaissance. 1985. 25.00 (ISBN 0-912289-18-X); Vol. 2. Restoration & Eighteenth Century. 1985. 25.00 (ISBN 0-912289-20-1); Vol. 3. Romantic & Victorian Periods. 1985. 25.00 (ISBN 0-912289-23-6); Vol. 5. Twentieth Century Poetry. 1985. 30.00 (ISBN 0-912289-21-X); Vol. 4. Novel to 1900. 1985. 25.00 (ISBN 0-912289-22-8); Vol. 6. Twentieth Century Fiction. 1985. 35.00 (ISBN 0-912289-19-8); Vol. 7. Twentieth Century Drama. 1985. 25.00 (ISBN 0-912289-25-2); Vol. 8. Commonwealth Literature. 1985. 25.00 (ISBN 0-912289-24-4). Set. 172.00. St James Pr.

St. James, Westminster: Pt. II, North of Piccadilly, 2 vols. Ed. by F. H. Sheppard. (Survey of London Ser.: XXXI, XXXII). 150.00 (ISBN 0-485-48231-2, Pub. by Athlone Pr UK). Humanities.

St. James's Catapult: The Life & Times of Diego Gelmirez of Santiago de Compostela. R. A. Fletcher. (Illus.). 341p. 1984. 59.00x (ISBN 0-19-822581-4). Oxford U Pr.

St. James's Square: People, Houses, Happenings. Denys Forrest. 160p. 1986. 19.95 (ISBN 0-907621-74-0, Pub. by Quiller Pr). Intl Spec Bk.

Saint Jean De Crevecoeur. Julia P. Mitchell. LC 71-181959. Repr. of 1916 ed. 20.00 (ISBN 0-404-04347-X). AMS Pr.

St. Jeremies Fifteen Tokens Before Doomsday see Adam Davy's Five Dreams about Edward 2nd.

Saint Jerome in the Renaissance. Eugene F. Rice, Jr. LC 84-21321. (Symposia in Comparative History Ser.: No. 13). (Illus.). 272p. 1985. text ed. 32.50x (ISBN 0-8018-2381-1). Johns Hopkins.

Saint Jerome in the Renaissance. Eugene F. Rice, Jr. LC 84-21324. (Symposia in Comparative History Ser.: No. 13). (Illus.). 304p. 1988. pap. text ed. 12.95x (ISBN 0-8018-3747-2). Johns Hopkins.

Saint Joan. George Bernard Shaw. (Penguin Plays Ser.). (YA) (gr. 9 up). 1950. pap. 2.95 (ISBN 0-14-048005-6). Penguin.

Saint Joan, a Screenplay. George Bernard Shaw. Ed. by Bernard F. Dukore. LC 68-11039. (Illus.). 224p. 1968. 15.00x (ISBN 0-295-97885-6); pap. 5.95x (ISBN 0-295-95072-2, WP56). U of Wash Pr.

Saint Joan, Major Barbara, Androcles. George Bernard Shaw. Bd. with Major Barbara; Androcles & the Lion. LC 56-5413. 6.95 (ISBN 0-394-60480-6). Modern Lib.

St. Joan of Arc. John Beevers. 1974. pap. 7.00 (ISBN 0-89555-043-1). TAN Bks Pubs.

Saint Joan of Arc. Vita Sackville-West. LC 84-9125. 416p. 1984. pap. 7.95 (ISBN 0-8398-2856-X, Gregg). G K Hall.

St. Joan of Arc, Virgin-Soldier. Leon Cristiani. 1977. 3.95 (ISBN 0-8198-0465-7); pap. 2.95 (ISBN 0-8198-0466-5). Dghtrs St Paul.

Saint Joan of the Stockyards. Bertolt Brecht. Tr. by Frank Jones. LC 69-16006. (Midland Bks.: No. 127). 128p. 1970. 15.00x (ISBN 0-253-17671-9); pap. 3.95x (ISBN 0-253-20127-6). Ind U Pr.

St. John. Richardson. Date not set. 8.95 (Pub. by SCM Pr England). Fortress.

St. John, 2 vols, Vol. I & 2. George Reith. Ed. by A. Whyte & J. Moffatt. (Handbooks for Bible Classes & Private Students Ser.). 1889. 11.95 ea. (Pub. by T & T Clark Ltd UK). Vol. 1, 200 pgs (ISBN 0-567-08114-1). Vol. 2, 180 pgs (ISBN 0-567-08115-X). Fortress.

St. John see Expository Thoughts on the Gospels.

St. John Backtime. Ed. by Ruth H. Low & Lito Valls. LC 80-68089. (Illus.). 96p. (Orig.). 1985. pap. 14.95 (ISBN 0-9614355-0-X). Eden Hill Pr.

Saint John Bosco. Augustine Auffray. 393p. 1930. pap. 12.95 (ISBN 0-89944-060-6). Don Bosco Multimedia.

Saint John Chrysostom: A Scripture Index. R. A. Krupp. LC 84-21028. 270p. 1985. lib. bdg. 29.00 (ISBN 0-8191-4380-4). U Pr of Amer.

St. John Chrysostom, Apologist. LC 84-21416. (Fathers of the Church Ser.: Vol. 73). 350p. 1985. 29.95 (ISBN 0-8132-0073-3). Cath U Pr.

St. John Chrysostom, Baptismal Instructions. Ed. by W. J. Burghardt et al. LC 62-21489. (Ancient Christian Writers Ser.: No. 31). 381p. 1963. 14.95 (ISBN 0-8091-0262-5). Paulist Pr.

St. John Chrysostom on the Priesthood. John Chrysostom. 160p. 1977. pap. 5.95 (ISBN 0-913836-38-9). St Vladimirs.

Saint John Damascene: De Fide Orthodoxa, Versions of Burgundio & Cerbanus. Ed. by Eligius M. Buytaert. (Text Ser.). 1955. 23.00 (ISBN 0-686-11554-6). Franciscan Inst.

Saint John Damascene: Dialectica, Version of Robert Grosseteste. Ed. by Owen A. Colligan. (Text Ser.). 1953. 3.50 (ISBN 0-686-11552-X). Franciscan Inst.

St. John Hankin: Edwardian Mephistopheles. William H. Phillips. LC 77-89783. 150p. 1979. 15.00 (ISBN 0-8386-2155-4). Fairleigh Dickinson.

St. John of Patmos & the Seven Churches of the Apocalypse. Otto F. Meinardus. LC 78-51245. (In the Footsteps of the Saints Ser.). (Illus.). 160p. 1979. 17.50 (ISBN 0-89241-070-1); pap. 6.95 (ISBN 0-89241-043-4). Caratzas.

St. John of the Cross & Dr. C. G. Jung: Christian Mysticism in the Light of Jungian Psychology. James Arraj. LC 86-11315. 200p. (Orig.). 1986. pap. 11.95 (ISBN 0-914073-02-8). Inner Growth Bks.

Saint John of the Cross & Modern Psychology. Dom O. Sumner. 1985. 10.00x (ISBN 0-317-62181-5, Guild of Pastoral Psych). State Mutual Bk.

St. John of the Cross & Other Lectures & Addresses. E. Allison Peers. 1977. lib. bdg. 59.95 (ISBN 0-8490-2558-3). Gordon Pr.

St. John of the Cross, & Other Lectures & Addresses, 1920-1945. facs. ed. Edgar A. Peers. LC 70-136650. (Biography Index Reprint Ser.). 1946. 16.00 (ISBN 0-8369-8045-X). Ayer Co Pubs.

Saint John of the Cross: Doctor of Divine Love, an Introduction to His Philosophy, Theology & Spirituality. Bede Frost. 1977. lib. bdg. 59.95 (ISBN 0-8490-2559-1). Gordon Pr.

St. John of the Cross: His Life & Poetry. Gerald Brenan. LC 72-83577. pap. 61.30 (ISBN 0-317-26068-5, 2024428). Bks Demand UMI.

St. John Ogilvie S.J., 1579-1615. 68p. 1979. 30.00x (Pub. by Third Eye Centre). State Mutual Bk.

Saint-John Perse. Roger Little. (French Poets Ser.). 139p. 1973. 32.50 (ISBN 0-485-14602-9, Pub. by Athlone Pr UK); pap. 14.95 (ISBN 0-485-12202-2, Pub. by Athlone Pr UK). Humanities.

Saint-John Perse: A Bibliography for Students of His Poetry. Roger Little. (Research Bibliographies & Checklists Ser.: No. 1). 76p. (Orig.). 1971. pap. 7.25 (ISBN 0-900411-32-5, Pub. by Grant & Cutler). Longwood Pub Group.

Saint-John Perse: A Bibliography for Students of His Poetry, Supplement No. 1. Roger Little. (Research Bibliographies & Checklists Ser.: No. 1a). 88p. (Orig.). 1976. pap. 7.25 (ISBN 0-7293-0026-9, Pub. by Grant & Cutler). Longwood Pub Group.

Saint-John Perse: A Bibliography for Sudents of His Poetry, Supplement No. 2. Roger Little. (Research Bibliographies & Checklists Ser.: No. 1b). 58p. (Orig.). 1982. pap. 8.95 (ISBN 0-7293-0131-1, Pub. by Grant & Cutler). Longwood Pub Group.

St. John Perse: Collected Poems, Complete Bilingual Edition. rev. ed. Tr. by W. H. Auden et al. LC 82-47633. (Bollingen Ser.: No. 87). 1982. 70.00x (ISBN 0-691-09949-9). Princeton U Pr.

St. John Perse: Letters. John Perse. Ed. by Arthur J. Knodel. LC 79-9080. (Bollingen Ser.: LXXXVII: 2). (Illus.). 712p. 1979. 47.00x (ISBN 0-691-09868-9); pap. 16.50x (ISBN 0-691-01836-7). Princeton U Pr.

Saint John the Evangelist Church, Indianapolis, Indiana: A Photographic Essay of the Oldest Catholic Church in Indianapolis & Marion County. William F. Stineman & Jack W. Porter. LC 85-63564. (Illus.). 80p. 1986. 29.95 (ISBN 0-9616134-0-8). ST John Evang.

Saint John: The Making of a Colonial Urban Community. T. W. Acheson. 310p. 1985. 29.95x (ISBN 0-8020-2586-2). U of Toronto Pr.

St. John the Pursuer: Vampire in Moscow. Richard Henrick. LC 87-51449. 352p. (Orig.). 1988. pap. 3.95. TSR Inc.

St. John, Vols. 1 & 2: Critical & Exegetical Commentary. J. H. Bernard. Ed. by Samuel R. Driver & Alfred Plummer. (International Critical Commentary Ser.). 29.95 ea. (Pub. by T & T ClarK Ltd UK). Vol. I, 480p (ISBN 0-567-05024-6). Vol. II, 456p (ISBN 0-567-05025-4). Fortress.

St. John's Baptism. William Babula. 256p. 1988. 14.95 (ISBN 0-8184-0461-2). Lyle Stuart.

St. John's Eve & Other Stories. facsimile ed. Nikolai V. Gogol. Tr. by Isabelf. Hapgood from Rus. LC 70-152941. (Short Story Index Reprint Ser.). (From Evenings at the Farm - St. Petersburg Stories). Repr. of 1886 ed. 17.00 (ISBN 0-8369-3800-3). Ayer Co Pubs.

Saint John's Tower & Health Care Facility: An Architectural Evaluation. William F. Gartz et al. Ed. by Gary T. Moore. (Publications in Archtecture & Urban Planning Ser.: R81-7). (Illus.). iv, 135p. 1981. 7.50 (ISBN 0-938744-20-8). U of Wis Ctr Arch-Urban.

St. Joseph Cafasso: Priest of the Gallows. Saint John Bosco. LC 82-50979. Orig. Title: Saint Speaks for Another Saint. 80p. 1983. pap. 2.00 (ISBN 0-89555-194-2). TAN Bks Pubs.

Saint Joseph Circuit Court: Final Report. National Center for State Courts Staff. 110p. 1981. manuscript 6.60 (NCRO-048). Natl Ctr St Courts.

Saint Joseph Commentary on the Sunday Readings, 3 vols. Achille Degeest. 3.95 ea. Year A (ISBN 0-89942-341-8, 341/04). Year B (ISBN 0-89942-342-6, 342/04). Year C (ISBN 0-89942-343-4, 343/04). Catholic Bk Pub.

Saint Joseph Concise Bible History. (Capsule Comments, Catechetical Aids). flexible bdg. 2.25 (ISBN 0-89942-770-7, 77004). Catholic Bk Pub.

Saint Joseph County Circuit & Superior Court. National Center for State Courts Staff. 17p. 1982. manuscript 1.02 (NCRO-054). Natl Ctr St Courts.

St. Joseph: His Life As He Might Tell It. Robert J. Fox. 1983. pap. 1.00 (ISBN 0-911988-55-6). AMI Pr.

Saint Joseph New American Catechism. Lawrence Lovasik. (Illus.). flexible bdg. 3.00 (ISBN 0-89942-253-5, 253/05). Catholic Bk Pub.

Saint Joseph of Copertino. Angelo Pastrovicchi. LC 79-91298. 135p. 1980. pap. 4.00 (ISBN 0-89555-135-7). TAN Bks Pubs.

Saint Joseph Polish Cemetary: Inscriptions from the "Old Section". Genevieve S. Szymarek. v, 148p. (Orig.). 1987. pap. 10.00 (ISBN 1-55613-076-7). Heritage Bk.

Saint Judas. James Wright. LC 59-12481. (Wesleyan Poetry Program: Vol. 4). 56p. 1982. pap. 8.95 (ISBN 0-8195-1110-2). Wesleyan U Pr.

St. Jude & "His People". Antoinette Ancona. LC 85-90095. 124p. 1985. 10.95 (ISBN 0-533-06604-2). Vantage.

St. Julian. Richard A. Hawley. 72p. (Orig.). 1987. pap. 8.95 (ISBN 0-933248-08-3). Bits Pr.

Saint-Just: Apostle of the Terror. Geoffrey Bruun. LC 66-16083. viii, 168p. 1966. Repr. of 1932 ed. 24.00 (ISBN 0-208-00531-5, Archon). Shoe String.

Saint-Just, Colleague of Robespierre. Eugene W. Curtis. LC 73-14540. xi, 402p. 1973. Repr. of 1935 ed. lib. bdg. 31.50x (ISBN 0-374-92010-9, Octagon). Hippocrene Bks.

St. Kilda & Other Hebridean Outliners. rev. ed. Francis Thompson. (Island Ser.). (Illus.). 220p. 1988. 29.95 (ISBN 0-7153-9214-X). David & Charles.

St. Kitts Vervet. Ed. by M. T. McGuire. (Contributions to Primatology Ser.: Vol. 1). 202p. 1974. 37.50 (ISBN 3-8055-1692-4). S Karger.

St. Lawrence. Trudy J. Hanmer. (First Bks.). (Illus.). 72p. 1984. lib. bdg. 10.40 (ISBN 0-531-04831-4). Watts.

St. Lawrence. Honor L. Winks & Robin W. Winks. LC 80-50937. (Rivers of the World Ser.). (Illus.). 68p. (gr. 4 up). PLB 14.96 (ISBN 0-382-06368-6). Silver.

St. Lawrence Blues. Marie-Claire Blais. Tr. by Ralph Manheim from Fr. 229p. 1974. 7.95 (ISBN 0-374-25350-1). FS&G.

St. Lawrence Islands National Park. Don Ress. (Illus.). 136p. 1985. pap. 7.95 (ISBN 0-88894-379-2, Pub. by Douglas & McIntyre-Grounwood). Salem Hse Pubs.

St. Lawrence Seaway. Gennifer Sussman. LC 78-71332. (Canadian-U. S. Prospect Ser.). 90p. 1978. 5.00 (ISBN 0-88806-041-6). Natl Planning.

St. Lawrence: Seaway of North America. Anne T. White. LC 61-11147. (Rivers of the World Ser.). (Illus.). 96p. (gr. 4-7). 1961. PLB 3.98 (ISBN 0-8116-6352-3). Garrard.

St. Leon: A Tale of the Sixteenth Century. William Godwin. LC 74-162884. (Illus.). Repr. of 1835 ed. 32.50 (ISBN 0-404-54405-3). AMS Pr.

St. Leon: A Tale of the Sixteenth Century. William Godwin. LC 70-131318. (Gothic Novels Ser). 1971. Repr. of 1831 ed. 46.50 (ISBN 0-405-00802-3). Ayer Co Pubs.

St. Leon: A Tale of the Sixteenth Century, 4 vols. William Godwin. (Feminist Controversy in England, 1788-1810 Ser.). 1974. Set. lib. bdg. 242.00 (ISBN 0-8240-0862-6). Garland Pub.

St. Lo. Ed. by Historical Section European Theater of Operations Staff. (Combat Arms Ser.: No. 10). (Illus.). 128p. 1984. Repr. 25.00x (ISBN 0-89839-080-X). Battery Pr.

St. Louis. (Documentary History of American Cities Ser.). 220p. pap. 6.95 (ISBN 0-8160-1503-1). Facts on File.

St. Louis. Ed. by Selwyn K. Troen et al. LC 77-5907. (Documentary History of American Cities Ser.). 220p. 1977. pap. text ed. 6.95x (ISBN 0-531-05603-1). Wiener Pub Inc.

St. Louis: A Chronological & Documentary History 1762-1970. Robert I. Vexler. LC 74-5179. (American Cities Chronology Ser). 153p. 1974. PLB 8.50 (ISBN 0-379-00607-3). Oceana.

St. Louis: And the Court Style in Gothic Architecture. Robert Branner. Ed. by John Harris & Alastair Laing. (Studies in Architecture: No. VII). (Illus.). 157p. 1986. pap. 39.95 (ISBN 0-302-02753-X, Pub. by Zwemmer Bks UK). Sotheby Pubns.

St. Louis at War. Betty Burnett. (Illus.). 175p. 1987. 14.95 (ISBN 0-935284-52-4). Patrice Pr.

St. Louis Car Company Album. Andrew D. Young. Ed. by Mac Sebree. (Interurbans Special Ser.: No. 91). (Illus.). 160p. 1984. 29.95 (ISBN 0-916374-62-9). Interurban.

St. Louis Cardinals. rev. ed. Martin. (Baseball Today Ser.). 48p. (gr. 4 up). 1982. PLB 11.45 (ISBN 0-87191-875-7). Creative Ed.

Saint Louis Cardinals. James R. Rothaus. (NFL Today Ser.). 48p. (gr. 4 up). 1986. PLB 10.45 (ISBN 0-88682-046-4). Creative Ed.

St. Louis Cardinals. James R. Rothaus. (Baseball: The Great American Game Ser.). 48p. (gr. 4-10). 1987. PLB 14.89 (ISBN 0-88682-148-7). Creative Ed.

St. Louis Church Survey: A Religious Investigation with a Social Background. Harlan P. Douglass. LC 77-112540. (Rise of Urban America). (Illus.). 1970. Repr. of 1924 ed. 21.00 (ISBN 0-405-02449-5). Ayer Co Pubs.

St. Louis Clock Company 1904. 1983. pap. 7.95 (ISBN 0-915706-08-3). Am Reprints.

St. Louis Conundrum: The Effective Treatment of Antisocial Youth. Ronald A. Feldman & Timothy E. Caplinger. (Illus.). 320p. 1983. text ed. write for info. (ISBN 0-13-786202-4). P-H.

St. Louis Encephalitis. Ed. by Thomas P. Monath. LC 79-53721. (Illus.). 680p. 1980. text ed. 50.00x (ISBN 0-87553-090-7, 046). Am Pub Health.

St. Louis Epicure. J. Arthur Baer & Terence Baer. Ed. by Gretchen Weidenbach. (American Epicure Ser.). 160p. 1986. pap. 7.95 (ISBN 0-89716-155-6). Peanut Butter.

St. Louis Fed's Monetarist Model: Whence It Came; How It Thrived, 1970-1982. Donald Elliott. Ed. by Stuart Bruchey. LC 84-45425. (American Economic History Ser.). 180p. 1985. lib. bdg. 30.00 (ISBN 0-8240-6668-5). Garland Pub.

St. Louis Germans, 1850-1920: The Nature of an Immigrant Community & Its Relation to the Assimilation Process. Audrey L. Olson. Ed. by Fransecso Cordasco. LC 80-886. (American Ethnic Groups Ser.). 1981. lib. bdg. 38.50x (ISBN 0-405-13447-9). Ayer Co Pubs.

Saint Louis in 1884. William H. Bishop. Ed. by William R. Jones. (Illus.). 24p. 1977. pap. 2.95 (ISBN 0-89646-024-X). Outbooks.

St. Louis Jezebel. Dirk Fletcher. (Spur Ser.: No. 3). 208p. (Orig.). 1983. pap. 2.50 (ISBN 0-8439-1157-3, Leisure Bks). Leisure NY.

Saint Louis: Louis IX of France, the Most Christian King. Frederick Perry. LC 73-14462. Repr. of 1901 ed. 30.00 (ISBN 0-404-58280-X). AMS Pr.

St. Louis Marie Grignon de Montfort: His Life As He Might Tell It. Robert J. Fox. 20p. 1983. 1.00 (ISBN 0-911988-62-9). Ami Pr.

St. Louis Movement in Philosophy: Some Source Material. Ed. by Charles M. Perry. LC 31-8773. (Illus.). pap. 37.50 (ISBN 0-317-09234-0, 2016248). Bks Demand UMI.

St. Louis Streetcar Story. Andrew D. Young. Ed. by Mac Sebree. (Interurbans Special Ser.: No. 108). (Illus.). 232p. 1988. 39.95 (ISBN 0-916374-79-3). Interurban.

Saint Louis Treasures. Elinor M. Coyle. Tr. by Missouri Historical Society. (Saint Louis Photo History Ser.). (Illus.). 176p. 1986. text ed. 24.95 (ISBN 0-910600-87-2). Folkestone.

St. Louis Union Station & Its Railroads. rev. ed. Norbury L. Wayman. LC 86-217654. (Illus.). 176p. 1988. 11.95 (ISBN 0-9616356-1-4). E E Newman.

St. Louis Woman. Helen Traubel & Richard G. Hubler. Ed. by Andrew Farkas. LC 76-29974. (Opera Biographies). (Illus.). 1977. Repr. of 1959 ed. lib. bdg. 25.50x (ISBN 0-405-09712-3). Ayer Co Pubs.

St. Louise de Marillac: Servant of the Poor. Sr. Vincent Regnault. LC 83-50058. 136p. 1984. pap. 3.50 (ISBN 0-89555-215-9). TAN Bks Pubs.

Saint Lucia. Kevin Law. (Places & Peoples of the World Ser.). (Illus.). 104p. (gr. 5 up). 1988. lib. bdg. 12.95x (ISBN 1-55546-198-0). Chelsea Hse.

St. Lucia. (Let's Visit Places & Peoples - - Nations, Dependencies, & Sovereignties of the World Ser.). (Illus.). (gr. 5 up). 1988. 12.95. Chelsea Hse.

St. Lucia see Statements of the Laws of the OAS Member States in Matters Affecting Business.

Saint Lucia: Consolidated Index & Statutes of Subsidiary Legislation. Ed. by C. J. Hammett. (West Indian Legislation Indexing Project Ser.). v, 113p. (Orig.). 1987. pap. text ed. 20.00 (ISBN 0-317-60545-3, Pub. by UWI Fac Law). W W Gaunt.

Saint Lucia Diary. Hazel Eggleston. 1977. pap. 10.00 (ISBN 0-8159-6839-6). Devin.

St. Lucia: Economic Performance & Prospects. 114p. 1985. 5.00 (ISBN 0-8213-0624-3, BK 0624). World Bank.

St. Luke. Browning. Date not set. 6.95 (Pub. by SCM Pr England). Fortress.

St. Luke see Expository Thoughts on the Gospels.

St. Luke: Critical & Exegetical Commentary. Alfred Plummer. Ed. by Samuel R. Driver & Alfred Plummer. (International Critical Commentary Ser.). 688p. 1901. 34.95 (ISBN 0-567-05023-8, Pub. by T & T Clark Ltd UK). Fortress.

Saint Luke's Life of Christ. W. M. Wightman. pap. 1.00x (ISBN 0-685-02586-1). Outlook.

St. Lydwine of Schiedam. J. K. Huysmans. Tr. by Agnes Hastings from Fr. LC 79-87551. 1979. pap. 6.00 (ISBN 0-89555-087-3). TAN Bks Pubs.

St. Margaret Mary Alacoque. Leon Cristiani. 1976. 5.00 (ISBN 0-8198-0456-8); pap. 4.00 (ISBN 0-8198-0457-6). Dghtrs St Paul.

St. Margaret's Cave: Or, the Nun's Story, 4 vols. Elizabeth Helme. Ed. by Devendra P. Varma. LC 77-2040. (Gothic Novels Ser. III). 1977. Set. lib. bdg. 92.50x (ISBN 0-405-10139-2). Ayer Co Pubs.

St. Seraphim of Sarov. Valentine Zander. LC 75-24136. Orig. Title: Seraphim of Sarov. 150p. 1975. pap. 8.95 (ISBN 0-913836-28-1). St Vladimirs.

St. Sergius & Russian Spirituality. Pierre Kovalevsky. LC 76-13018. (Illus.). 190p. 1976. 8.95 (ISBN 0-913836-24-9). St Vladimirs.

St. Sharbel, Mystic of the East. Clare M. Benedict. 1977. 6.95 (ISBN 0-911218-11-4); pap. 3.45 (ISBN 0-911218-12-2). Ravengate Pr.

St. Simeon's Shrine in Zadar. Ivo Petricioli. 108p. 1983. 182.00x (ISBN 0-317-61400-2, Pub. by Collets (UK)). State Mutual Bk.

Saint Simon. Clifton W. Collins. 216p. 1980. Repr. lib. bdg. 25.00 (ISBN 0-8492-3874-9). R West.

Saint-Simon et le Systeme Industriel. Emmanuel de Witt. LC 75-153149. 189p. (Fr.). 1973. Repr. of 1902 ed. lib. bdg. 18.50 (ISBN 0-8337-3854-2). B Franklin.

Saint-Simon Memorialist. Ed. by Herbert De Ley. LC 75-4491. 153p. 1975. pap. 9.95 (ISBN 0-252-00556-2). U of Ill Pr.

Saint-Simonian Religion in Germany. E. M. Butler. 1968. Repr. of 1926 ed. 45.00x (ISBN 0-86527-177-1). Fertig.

Saint-Simonism et Pensee Contemporaine see Saint-Simonisme et Pari pour l'Industrie, XIXe et XXe Siecles.

Saint-Simonism in the Radicalism of Thomas Carlyle. David B. Cofer. (English Literature Ser., No. 33). 1970. pap. 39.95x (ISBN 0-8383-0017-0). Haskell.

Saint-Simonisme et Pari pour l'Industrie, XIXe et XXe Siecles, 4 tomes. Ed. by Schuhl & Perroux. Incl. Tome I. Theorie et Politique; Tome II. Saint-Simonism et Pensee Contemporaine; Tome III. Influence a l'Etranger; Tome IV. Economie Politique. (Cahiers de l'ISEA). 8.95 ea. French & Eur.

St. Simons: Enchanted Island. Barbara S. Hull. LC 80-80048. (Illus.). 152p. 1980. bds. 8.50 (ISBN 0-87797-049-1). Cherokee.

Saint Simons Island. 2nd ed. R. Edwin Greene. (Illus.). 90p. (Orig.). 1983. pap. 10.95 (ISBN 0-914124-10-2). Arner Pubns.

St. Simons Memoir. Eugenia Price. 1987. pap. 3.95 (ISBN 0-515-09264-9). Jove Pubns.

St. Simons-Sea Island Report: Living, Vacationing, Investing, Retiring. Jeanne Harmann & Harry E. Harmann, III. 96p. 1982. pap. 4.95 (ISBN 0-686-39842-4). Natl Res Group.

Saint Speaks for Another Saint see St. Joseph Cafasso: Priest of the Gallows.

St. Stephen's Green: Generous Lovers. William Philips. 1980. 19.95 (ISBN 0-85105-367-X, Pub. by Colin Smythe Ltd Britain). Dufour.

St. Stephen's Handbook for Alter Servers. Edward Matthews. (Illus.). 64p. (Orig.). 1986. pap. 2.25 (ISBN 0-00-599955-3, Collins Liturgical). HarpR.

Saint Steps In. Leslie Charteris. 1976. Repr. of 1943 ed. lib. bdg. 16.95 (ISBN 0-89190-385-2, Pub. by River City Pr). Amereon Ltd.

Saint Susanna. J. A. Fastre. pap. 1.95 (ISBN 0-317-60814-2). Eastern Orthodox.

St. Symeon, the New Theologian: Theological & Practical Discourses & Three Theological Discourses. St. Symeon. Ed. by David N. Bell. Tr. by Paul McGuckin from Gr. (Cistercian Studies: No. 41). 1982. write for info. (ISBN 0-87907-841-3); pap. 8.00 (ISBN 0-87907-941-X). Cistercian Pubns.

St. Tammany Parish: L'autre Cote du lac. Frederick S. Ellis. LC 80-63. (Illus.). 304p. 1982. 25.00 (ISBN 0-88289-252-5). Pelican.

St. Tarcisius. Mary Berardi. (gr. 4-8). plastic bdg. 2.00 (ISBN 0-8198-0222-0); pap. 1.25 (ISBN 0-8198-0223-9). Dghtrs St Paul.

St. Teresa of Avila. Marcelle Auclair. Tr. by Kathleen Pond from Fr. LC 53-6126. (Illus.). 458p. 1988. pap. write for info. (ISBN 0-932506-67-4). St Bedes Pubns.

St. Teresa of Avila. Stephen Clissold. 288p. (Orig.). 1982. pap. 8.95 (ISBN 0-8164-2621-X, HarpR). Har-Row.

St. Teresa of Avila. Giorgio Papasogil. Tr. by Gloria I. Anzilotti from Ital. LC 58-12223. 1988. price not set (ISBN 0-8198-6879-5); pap. write for info. (ISBN 0-8198-6880-9). Dghtrs St Paul.

St. Teresa of Avila. Giorgio Papasogli. LC 58-12223. 1973. Repr. 5.00 (ISBN 0-8198-0511-4). Dghtrs St Paul.

St. Teresa of Avila: A Biography. William T. Walsh. LC 87-50928. 592p. 1987. pap. 16.50 (ISBN 0-89555-325-2). TAN Bks Pubs.

St. Theodore the Studite on the Holy Icons. Tr. by Catherine Roth. LC 81-18319. 115p. (Orig.). pap. 5.95 (ISBN 0-913836-76-1). St Vladimirs.

Saint Theresa, the Little Flower. Sr. Gesualda Of The Holy Spirit. (Illus.). 1960. 4.95 (ISBN 0-8198-0142-9); pap. 3.95. Dghtrs St Paul.

Saint Therese of Lisieux General Correspondence: Vol. I, 1877-1890. Tr. by John Clarke. LC 81-6474. 700p. (Orig.). 1982. pap. 9.95x (ISBN 0-9600876-9-9). ICS Pubns.

St. Therese of Lisieux: Her Last Conversations. Tr. by John Clarke from Fr. LC 76-27207. (Illus.). 1977. pap. 6.95x (ISBN 0-9600876-3-X). ICS Pubns.

St. Therese of Lisieux: Her Life As She Might Tell It. Robert J. Fox. 20p. 1982. pap. 1.00 (ISBN 0-911988-54-8). AMI Pr.

Saint Therese, the Little Flower: The Making of a Saint. John Beevers. LC 73-80147. (Orig.). 1976. pap. 3.50 (ISBN 0-89555-035-0). TAN Bks Pubs.

Saint Thomas & Analogy. Gerald B. Phelan. (Aquinas Lecture). 1941. 7.95 (ISBN 0-87462-105-4). Marquette.

Saint Thomas & Epistemology. Louis-Marie Regis. (Aquinas Lecture Ser.). 1946. 7.95 (ISBN 0-87462-110-0). Marquette.

St. Thomas & Historicity. Armand A. Maurer. LC 79-84278. (Aquinas Lecture Ser.). 1979. 7.95 (ISBN 0-87462-144-5). Marquette.

Saint Thomas & Philosophy. Anton C. Pegis. (Aquinas Lecture). 1964. 7.95 (ISBN 0-87462-129-1). Marquette.

Saint Thomas & the Future of Metaphysics. Joseph C. Owens. (Aquinas Lecture). 1957. 7.95 (ISBN 0-87462-122-4). Marquette.

Saint Thomas & the Gentiles. Mortimer J. Adler. (Aquinas Lecture). 1938. 7.95 (ISBN 0-87462-102-X). Marquette.

Saint Thomas & the Greek Moralists. Vernon J. Bourke. (Aquinas Lecture). 1947. 7.95 (ISBN 0-87462-111-9). Marquette.

Saint Thomas & the Greeks. Anton C. Pegis. (Aquinas Lecture). 1939. 7.95 (ISBN 0-87462-103-8). Marquette.

Saint Thomas & the Life of Learning. John F. McCormick. (Aquinas Lecture). 1937. 7.95 (ISBN 0-87462-101-1). Marquette.

Saint Thomas & the Object of Geometry. Tr. by Vincent E. Smith. (Aquinas Lecture). 1953. 7.95 (ISBN 0-87462-118-6). Marquette.

Saint Thomas & the Problem of Evil. Jacques Maritain. (Aquinas Lecture). 1942. 7.95 (ISBN 0-87462-106-2). Marquette.

Saint Thomas & the World State. Robert M. Hutchins. (Aquinas Lecture). 1949. 7.95 (ISBN 0-87462-114-3). Marquette.

Saint Thomas Aquinas. G. K. Chesterton. 200p. 1974. pap. 3.95 (ISBN 0-385-09002-1, Im). Doubleday.

St. Thomas Aquinas. Ralph McInerny. LC 81-16293. 197p. 1982. pap. text ed. 5.95 (ISBN 0-268-01707-7). U of Notre Dame Pr.

St. Thomas Aquinas & Karl Marx (Archbishop Helder Camara, Brazil) CIIR Staff. 1982. 15.00x (ISBN 0-904393-70-4, Pub. by CIIR). State Mutual Bk.

St. Thomas Aquinas on Analogy: A Textual Analysis & Systematic Synthesis. George P. Klubertanz. LC 60-9602. (Jesuit Studies). pap. 81.80 (ISBN 0-317-09004-6, 2000813). Bks Demand UMI.

Saint Thomas Aquinas: On Charity. St. Thomas Aquinas. Tr. by Lotti H. Kendzierski. (Medieval Philosophical Texts in Translation: No. 10). 1960. pap. 7.95 (ISBN 0-87462-210-7). Marquette.

St. Thomas Aquinas on Politics & Ethics. St. Thomas Aquinas. Ed. by Paul E. Sigmund. (Critical Editions Ser.). 1987. text ed. 17.95x (ISBN 0-393-02534-9); pap. 7.95 (ISBN 0-393-95243-6). Norton.

Saint Thomas Aquinas: On Spiritual Creatures. St. Thomas Aquinas. Tr. by Mary C. Fitzpatrick. (Medieval Philosophical Texts in Translation: No. 5). 1949. pap. 7.95 (ISBN 0-87462-205-0). Marquette.

St. Thomas Aquinas on the Existence of God: Collected Papers of Joseph Owens. Joseph Owens. Ed. by John R. Catan. LC 79-13885. 291p. 1980. 49.50 (ISBN 0-87395-401-7); pap. 16.95x (ISBN 0-87395-446-7). State U NY Pr.

Saint Thomas Aquinas: On the Unity of the Intellect Against the Averroists. Ed. by Beatrice H. Zedler. (Medieval Philosophical Texts in Translation: No. 19). 1968. pap. 7.95 (ISBN 0-87462-219-0). Marquette.

St. Thomas Aquinas: Philosophical Texts. St. Thomas Aquinas. Ed. by Thomas Gilby. xxiv, 430p. 1982. pap. 14.95x (ISBN 0-939464-06-3). Labyrinth Pr.

Saint Thomas Aquinas: Questions on the Soul. James H. Robb. (Medieval Philosophical Texts in Translation: NO. 27). 1984. 24.95 (ISBN 0-87462-226-3). Marquette.

St. Thomas Aquinas: Scriptum Super Sententiis - An Index of Authorities Cited. Charles H. Lohr. viii, 391p. 1980. 50.00x (ISBN 0-8232-0103-1). Fordham.

St. Thomas Aquinas: Theological Texts. St. Thomas Aquinas. Ed. by Thomas Gilby. 444p. 1982. pap. 14.95x (ISBN 0-939464-01-2). Labyrinth Pr.

Saint Thomas et le Pseudo-Denis. J. Durantel. (Medieval Studies Ser.). (Fr.). Repr. of 1919 ed. lib. bdg. 45.00x (ISBN 0-697-00036-2). Irvington.

St. Thomas More: Vol. 3, Pt. 2-Latin Poems. St. Thomas More. Ed. by Clarence H. Miller et al. LC 63-7949. (Yale Edition of the Complete Works of St. Thomas More). 800p. 1984. text ed. 65.00t (ISBN 0-300-02591-2). Yale U Pr.

St. Thomas of Canterbury: His Death & Miracles, 2 vols. in 1. Edwin A. Abbott. LC 80-18216. (Crusades & Military Orders: Second Ser.). Repr. of 1898 ed. 55.00 (ISBN 0-404-16366-1). AMS Pr.

Saint Thomas: Poems. Tram Combs. LC 65-14050. (Wesleyan Poetry Program: Vol. 25). (Orig.). 1965. 17.00x (ISBN 0-8195-2025-X); pap. 8.95 (ISBN 0-8195-1025-4). Wesleyan U Pr.

Saint Thomas, Sieger De Brabant, St. Bonaventure: On the Eternity of the World. Tr. by Cyril Vollert et al. (Medieval Philosophical Texts in Translation: No. 16). 1965. pap. 7.95 (ISBN 0-87462-216-6). Marquette.

Saint Tikhon of Zadonsk: Inspirer of Dostoevsky. Nadejda Gorodetzky. LC 76-49919. 320p. 1977. pap. 9.95 (ISBN 0-913836-32-X). St Vladimirs.

Saint Valentine's Day. Clyde R. Bulla. LC 65-11643. (Harper Holiday Ser.). (Illus.). (gr. 1-3). 1965. PLB 12.89 (ISBN 0-690-71744-X, Crowell Jr Bks). HarpJ.

Saint-Venant's Problem. D. Iesan. (Lecture Notes in Mathematics Ser.: Vol. 1279). viii, 162p. Date not set. pap. 16.30 (ISBN 0-387-18361-2). Springer-Verlag.

St. Veronica Gig Stories. Jack Pulaski. LC 86-50657. 178p. (Orig.). 1986. 15.95 (ISBN 0-939010-10-0); pap. 8.95 (ISBN 0-939010-09-7); signed ed. 25.00. Zephyr Pr.

St. Vincent & the Grenadines. (Let's Visit Places & Peoples - - Nations, Dependencies, & Sovereignties of the World Ser.). (Illus.). (gr. 5 up). 1988. 12.95 (ISBN 0-7910-0153-9). Chelsea Hse.

St. Vincent & the Grenadines: A Plural Country. Jill Bobrow & Dana Jinkins. (Illus.). 1985. 29.95 (ISBN 0-393-03309-0). Norton.

Saint Vincent & the Grenadines: Consolidated Index of Statutes & Subsidiary Legislation. Ed. by C. J. Hammett. (West Indian Legislation Indexing Project Ser.). x, 107p. (Orig.). 1988. pap. text ed. 20.00 (ISBN 0-317-60547-X, Pub. by UWI Fac Law). W W Gaunt.

St. Vincent & the Grenadines: Economic Situation & Selected Development Issues. 122p. 1985. 5.00 (ISBN 0-8213-0625-1, BK 0625). World Bank.

St. Vith: Lion in the Way: The 106th Infantry Division in World War II. R. Ernest Dupuy. (Divisional Ser.: 30th). (Illus.). 284p. 1986. Repr. of 1949 ed. 27.50 (ISBN 0-89839-092-3). Battery Pr.

Saint Voyage De Jherusalem Du Seigneur D'Anglure. Ogier D' Anglure. Ed. by F. Bonnardot & A. Longnon. 1878. pap. 22.00 (ISBN 0-384-53018-4). Johnson Repr.

Saint vs. Scotland Yard. Leslie Charteris. 1975. Repr. of 1932 ed. lib. bdg. 16.95x (ISBN 0-89190-390-9, Pub. by River City Pr). Amereon Ltd.

Saint Watching. Phyllis McGinley. (Crossroad Paperback Ser.). 256p. 1982. pap. 11.95 (ISBN 0-8245-0450-X). Crossroad NY.

Saint with a Gun: The Unlawful American Private Eye. William Ruehlman. 172p. 1985. pap. 11.50x (ISBN 0-8147-7393-1). NYU Pr.

Sainte Agnes et Poemes Inedits. Paul Claudel. (Illus.). 60.00 (ISBN 0-686-54433-1). French & Eur.

Sainte-Beuve. Harold Nicolson. 274p. Repr. of 1957 ed. lib. bdg. 45.00 (ISBN 0-89984-853-2). Century Bookbindery.

Sainte-Beuve. Harold G. Nicolson. LC 77-20072. (Illus.). 1978. Repr. of 1957 ed. lib. bdg. 35.00x (ISBN 0-313-20013-0, NISB). Greenwood.

Sainte-Beuve a l'Academie de Lausanne: Chronique du Cours sur Port-Royal (1837-1838) Bray. 9.95 (ISBN 0-685-34976-4). French & Eur.

Sainte-Beuve: A Literary Portrait. William F. Giese. LC 76-137054. (University of Wisconsin Studies, Language & Literature: No. 31). 368p. 1974. Repr. of 1931 ed. lib. bdg. 35.00x (ISBN 0-8371-5515-0, GISB). Greenwood.

Sainte-Beuve & the French Romantics. N. Scarlyn Wilson. 1973. Repr. of 1931 ed. 25.00 (ISBN 0-8274-0557-X). R West.

Sainte-Beuve: Selected Essays. Ed. by Francis Steegmuller & Norbert Guterman. 320p. Repr. of 1965 ed. lib. bdg. 45.00 (ISBN 0-89984-636-X). Century Bookbindery.

Sainte Genevieve. Charles Peguy. pap. 4.50 (ISBN 0-685-37038-0). French & Eur.

Sainte Marguerite de Cortone. Francois Mauriac. pap. 9.95 (ISBN 0-685-34304-9). French & Eur.

Saints. Orson S. Card. 720p. 1988. pap. 4.95 (ISBN 0-8125-8140-7, Dist. by St Martin's Pr & Warner Pub Servs). Tor Bks.

Saints. Jean Pedrick. (Chapbook Ser.: No. 1). 40p. (Orig.). 1980. pap. 4.95 (ISBN 0-937672-00-9). Rowan Tree.

Saints! A Complete Record of Southampton Football Club, 1885-1987. Gary Chalk & Duncan Holly. 320p. 1987. 60.00x (ISBN 0-907969-22-4, Pub. by Breedon Bks Pub UK). State Mutual Bk.

Saints Alive. facsimile ed. James R. Adair. LC 76-117319. (Biography Index Reprint Ser). 1951. 18.00 (ISBN 0-8369-8011-5). Ayer Co Pubs.

Saints Alive! Judith Bisignano & Corine Sanders. LC 86-63988. 64p. (Orig.). (gr. 5-7). 1987. pap. 6.95 (ISBN 1-55612-038-9). Sheed & Ward MO.

Saints Alive! the Book. Ed. by Hal M. Helms. 416p. (Orig.). 1985. pap. 12.95 (ISBN 0-941478-44-0). Paraclete Pr.

Saints Always Belong to the Present. John Wright. Pref. by Stephen Almagno. LC 84-80016. 221p. 1984. pap. 8.95 (ISBN 0-89870-047-7). Ignatius Pr.

Saints & Feasts. Torkom Koushagian. Ed. by Elise Antreassian. Tr. by Haigazoun Melkonian from Armenian. LC 88-18447. (Illus., Orig.). 1988. pap. text ed. write for info. (ISBN 0-934728-18-6). D O A C.

Saints & Festivals of the Christian Church. Harold P. Brewster. LC 73-159869. (Illus.). xiv, 576p. 1975. Repr. of 1904 ed. 48.00x (ISBN 0-8103-3992-7). Gale.

Saints & Heroes Since the Middle Ages. George Hodges. LC 75-107713. (Essay Index Reprint Ser.). 1912. 21.50 (ISBN 0-8369-1515-1). Ayer Co Pubs.

Saints & Heroes Speak. Robert J. Fox. 512p. 1983. 7.95 (ISBN 0-911988-43-2). Ami Pr.

Saints & Heroes to the End of the Middle Ages. facs. ed. George Hodges. LC 67-26749. (Essay Index Reprint Ser). 1911. 20.00 (ISBN 0-8369-0544-X). Ayer Co Pubs.

Saints & Heroes to the End of the Middle Ages. facsimile ed. George Hodges. LC 67-26749. (Essay Index Reprint Ser.). (Illus.). 268p. 1982. Repr. of 1911 ed. lib. bdg. 19.00 (ISBN 0-8290-0526-9). Irvington.

Saints & Innocents. Barbara Rex. 1972. 6.95 (ISBN 0-393-08664-X). Norton.

Saints & Martyrs of Ireland: Feast Days Calendar. H. Patrick Montague. (Illus.). 138p. 1987. 15.95 (ISBN 0-86140-106-9); pap. 5.95 (ISBN 0-86140-107-7). Dufour.

Saints & Non-Saints: Some Saintly & Not so Saintly Figures from Church History. Christa G. Habegger. 205p. (Orig.). 1987. pap. 7.95 (ISBN 0-89084-388-0). Bob Jones Univ Pr.

Saints & Politicians: Essays in the Organisation of a Senegalese Peasant Society. Donal B. Cruise O'Brien. LC 74-82221. (African Studies Ser.: No. 15). 221p. pap. 57.50 (2030612). Bks Demand UMI.

Saints & Rebels. facsimile ed. Eloise Lownsbery. LC 72-156682. (Essay Index Reprint Ser). Repr. of 1937 ed. 22.00 (ISBN 0-8369-2322-7). Ayer Co Pubs.

Saints & Rebels: Seven Nonconformists in Stuart England. Richard L. Greaves. LC 84-22799. xiv, 224p. 1985. 18.95 (ISBN 0-86554-136-1, MUP-H127). Mercer Univ Pr.

Saints & Revolutionaries: Essays on Early American History. Ed. by David Hall et al. LC 83-42667. 1984. 27.50 (ISBN 0-393-01751-6). Norton.

Saints & Revolutionaries: Essays on Early American History. Ed. by David D. Hall et al. 416p. 1986. pap. text ed. 8.95x (ISBN 0-393-95522-2). Norton.

Saints & Sandinistas. Bradstock. Date not set. 8.95 (Pub. by SCM Pr England). Fortress.

Saints & Scamps: Ethics in Academia. Steven M. Cahn. 128p. 1986. 16.95 (ISBN 0-8476-7517-3); pap. 7.95x (ISBN 0-8476-7518-1). Rowman.

Saints & Scholars. Terry Eagleton. LC 87-14991. 160p. 1987. 14.95 (ISBN 0-86091-180-2, AO800, Pub. by Verso). Routledge Chapman & Hall.

Saints & Scholars: Twenty-five Medieval Portraits. David Knowles. LC 87-29456. (Illus.). 232p. 1988. Repr. of 1962 ed. lib. bdg. 45.00x (ISBN 0-313-26219-5, KNSS). Greenwood.

Saints & She-Devils: Images of Women in the 15th & 16th Centuries. Ed. by Lene Dresen-Coenders. (Illus.). 159p. 1987. pap. 19.95 (ISBN 0-948695-06-4, Rubicon Pr England). Intl Spec Bk.

Saints & Shrews: Women & Aging in American Popular Film. Karen M. Stoddard. LC 82-15821. (Contributions in Women's Studies: No. 39). x, 174p. 1983. lib. bdg. 35.00 (ISBN 0-313-23391-8, STS/). Greenwood.

Saints & Sinners in the Early Church: Differing & Conflicting Traditions in the First Six Centuries. W. H. Frend. LC 84-48454. (Theology & Life Ser.: Vol. 11). 1985. pap. 8.95 (ISBN 0-89453-451-3). M Glazier.

Saints & Sinners Punchbook. Bill J. Cook. 64p. 1981. pap. 3.95 (ISBN 0-938400-05-3). Donahoe Pubs.

Saints & Sinners: The Planting of New England Congregationalism in Portland, Oregon, 1851-1876. Egbert S. Oliver. Ed. by Joe E. Pierce. (Illus.). 250p. 1987. pap. 9.95 (ISBN 0-913244-66-X). Hapi Pr.

Saints & Society: The Two Worlds of Western Christendom, 1000 to 1700. Donald Weinstein & Rudolph M. Bell. LC 82-7972. (Illus.). xii, 314p. 1986. 25.00x (ISBN 0-226-89055-4); pap. 13.95 (ISBN 0-226-89056-2). U of Chicago Pr.

Saints & Strangers. Angela Carter. 128p. 1986. 13.95 (ISBN 0-670-81139-4). Viking.

Saints & Strangers. Angela Carter. 128p. 1987. pap. 5.95 (ISBN 0-14-008973-X). Penguin.

Saints & Strangers. Andrew Hudgins. (New Poetry Ser.). (Illus.). 82p. 1985. 13.95 (ISBN 0-395-39384-1); pap. 6.95 (ISBN 0-395-39383-3). HM.

Saints & Strangers. George F. Willison. 520p. 1983. pap. 9.95 (ISBN 0-940160-19-6). Parnassus Imprints.

Saints & the Union: Utah Territory During the Civil War. E. B. Long. LC 80-16775. (Illus.). 326p. 1981. 22.50 (ISBN 0-252-00821-9). U of Ill Pr.

Saints & Their Cults: Studies in Religious Sociology, Folklore & History. Ed. by Stephen Wilson. 447p. 1986. pap. 21.95 (ISBN 0-521-31181-0). Cambridge U Pr.

Saints & Their Emblems. Maurice Drake. (Illus.). 1971. Repr. of 1916 ed. lib. bdg. 24.50 (ISBN 0-8337-0902-X). B Franklin.

Saints & Their Stories. Mary Montgomery. LC 86-43013. 96p. 1987. pap. 13.95 (ISBN 0-06-065912-2, HarpR). Har-Row.

Saints & Vertues. Ed. by John S. Hawley. LC 86-24993. (Comparative Studies in Religion & Society: Vol. 2). 352p. 1988. 48.00x (ISBN 0-520-05984-0); pap. 12.95x (ISBN 0-520-06163-2). U of Cal Pr.

Saints Are People: Church History Through the Saints. Alfred McBride. 144p. (Orig.). 1981. pap. 4.50 (ISBN 0-697-01785-0). Wm C Brown.

Saints Beyond the White Cliffs: Stories of English Saints. facs. ed. Margaret Gibbs. LC 75-148211. (Biography Index Reprint Ser.). (Illus.). 1947. 20.00 (ISBN 0-8369-8058-1). Ayer Co Pubs.

Saints Book: Stories for Children. Kate Dooley. LC 80-82814. 48p. (Orig.). (gr. k-3). 1981. pap. 3.95 (ISBN 0-8091-6547-3). Paulist Pr.

Saints Daily Exercise. John Preston. LC 76-57409. (English Experience Ser.: No. 824). 1977. Repr. of 1629 ed. lib. bdg. 53.00 (ISBN 90-221-0824-4). Walter J Johnson.

Saints de France. Charles Peguy. pap. 1.95 (ISBN 0-685-37039-9). French & Eur.

Saints de Notre Calendrier. Jules Romains. 256p. 1952. 4.95 (ISBN 0-686-55290-3). French & Eur.

Saints' Everlasting Rest. Richard Baxter. 1978. pap. 7.95 (ISBN 0-87552-986-0, Evangel Pr UK). Presby & Reformed.

Saints for All Seasons. Ed. by John J. Delaney. LC 77-81438. 1979. pap. 3.50 (ISBN 0-385-12909-2, Im). Doubleday.

Saints for Contemporary Women. Mary H. Valentine. 1988. pap. 9.95 (ISBN 0-88347-235-X). Thomas More.

Saints for Kids by Kids. Robert Charlebois et al. 80p. 1984. pap. 2.95 (ISBN 0-89243-223-3). Liguori Pubns.

Saints for Sinners. Alban Goodier. LC 70-99637. (Essay Index Reprint Ser.). 1930. 18.00 (ISBN 0-8369-1504-6). Ayer Co Pubs.

Saints for This Age. A. J. Muste. LC 62-21962. (Orig.). 1962. pap. 2.50x (ISBN 0-87574-124-X, 124). Pendle Hill.

Saints for Young People for Every Day, Vol. 1, Jan.-june, Vol. 2, July-dec. Daughters Of St. Paul. (Illus.). (gr. 4-8). 6.00 ea. (ISBN 0-8198-0143-7); pap. 4.50 ea. (ISBN 0-8198-0144-5). Dghtrs St Paul.

Saints for Young People for Every Day of the Year, Vol. 2. Daughters of St Paul. (Illus.). (gr. 4 up). 6.00 (ISBN 0-8198-0647-1); pap. 4.50 (ISBN 0-8198-0648-X). Dghtrs St Paul.

Saints Francis of Assisi. Dorothy Smith. 1988. pap. 2.95. Paulist Pr.

Saints Galore. David L. Veal. 160p. (Orig.). 1972. pap. 1.85 (ISBN 0-88028-009-3, 405). Forward Movement.

Saints Go Marching In. rev. ed. Robert F. Holtzclaw. LC 84-52751. (Illus.). 194p. (Orig.). 1984. write for info.; pap. 10.00 (ISBN 0-933144-00-8). Keeble Pr.

Saints in Action. facs. ed. Dumas Malone. LC 70-142664. (Essay Index Reprint Ser). 1939. 15.00 (ISBN 0-8369-2062-7). Ayer Co Pubs.

Saints in Arms. Leo F. Solt. LC 74-153355. (Stanford University. Stanford Studies in History, Economics & Political Science: No. 18). Repr. of 1959 ed. 19.00 (ISBN 0-404-50976-2). AMS Pr.

Saints in Art. Clara E. Clement. LC 77-89303. 240p. 1976. Repr. of 1899 ed. 46.00x (ISBN 0-8103-3030-X). Gale.

Saints in Art. M. Tabor. 59.95 (ISBN 0-8490-0986-3). Gordon Pr.

Saints in Due Season. Thomas P. McDonnell. LC 83-60742. 196p. (Orig.). 1983. pap. 2.95 (ISBN 0-87973-623-2, 623). Our Sunday Visitor.

Saints Joke Book. John Deaux. (Illus.). 48p. (Orig.). (gr. 6 up). 1981. pap. 2.95 (ISBN 0-937552-08-9). Quail Ridge.

Saints, Knights & Llannau. T. Thornley Jones. 79p. 1985. 19.50x (ISBN 0-85088-325-3, Pub. by Gomer Pr). State Mutual Bk.

Saints Knowledge of Christ's Love. John Bunyan. pap. 1.50 (ISBN 0-685-19843-X). Reiner.

Saints' Legends. G. H. Gerould. 59.95 (ISBN 0-8490-0987-1). Gordon Pr.

Saints' Legends. Gordon H. Gerould. 1980. Repr. of 1916 ed. lib. bdg. 39.00 (ISBN 0-8414-4627-X). Folcroft.

Saints of African Descent. Jacob A. Welbourne. 72p. 1987. cancelled (ISBN 0-8062-2839-3). Carlton.

Saints of Chaos. facs. ed. Peter Oliver. LC 67-23255. (Essay Index Reprint Ser). 1934. 17.00 (ISBN 0-8369-0752-3). Ayer Co Pubs.

Saints of Cornwall. Catherine R. John. 1985. 60.00x (ISBN 0-907566-13-8, Pub. by Dyllansow & Truran); linen bdg. 39.00x (ISBN 0-907566-14-6, Pub. by Dyllansow & Truran). State Mutual Bk.

Saints of Gwynedd. Molly Miller. (Studies in Celtic History: No. I). (Illus.). 148p. 1979. 45.00 (ISBN 0-85115-114-0, Pub. by Boydell & Brewer). Longwood Pub Group.

Saints of India. Satguru S. Keshavadas. 100p. (Orig.). 1975. pap. 3.50 (ISBN 0-942508-05-X). Vishwa.

Saints of India. Anna A. Subramanian. (Illus.). 1978. pap. 3.25 (ISBN 0-87481-479-0). Vedanta Pr.

Saints of Ireland. Mary R. D'Arcy. 241p. 1985. pap. 9.95 (ISBN 0-9614900-0-4). Irish Am Cult.

Saints of Qumran: Stories & Essays on Jewish Themes. Rudolf Kayser. Ed. by Harry Zohn. LC 76-20273. 188p. 1977. 18.00 (ISBN 0-8386-2024-8). Fairleigh Dickinson.

Saints of Sage & Saddle: Folklore Among the Mormons. Austin Fife & Alta Fife. 375p. 1980. pap. 14.95 (ISBN 0-87480-180-X). U of Utah Pr.

Saints on the Seas: A Maritime History of Morman Migration, 1830-1890. Conway B. Sonne. LC 83-3604. (University of Utah Publications in the American-West: No. 17). pap. 59.80 (ISBN 0-317-58119-8, 2029672). Bks Demand UMI.

Saints: Poems. Reginald Gibbons. (National Poetry Series 1985). 96p. 1986. 14.95 (ISBN 0-89255-106-2); pap. 8.95 (ISBN 0-89255-107-0). Persea Bks.

Saint's Revelation. LC 84-90117. 51p. 1985. 6.95 (ISBN 0-533-06193-8). Vantage.

Saints, Scholars & Schizophrenics: Mental Illness in Rural Ireland. Nancy Scheper-Hughes. 259p. 1979. 30.00x (ISBN 0-520-03444-9); pap. 11.95x (ISBN 0-520-04786-9). U of Cal Pr.

Saints, Seaways & Settlements in the Celtic Lands. 2nd ed. E. G. Bowen. 277p. 1983. pap. text ed. 12.50x (ISBN 0-7083-0650-0, Pub. by U of Wales). Humanities.

Saints, Signs & Symbols. W. Ellwood Post. (Illus.). 96p. 1974. pap. 6.50 (ISBN 0-8192-1171-0). Morehouse.

Saints, Sinners & Beechers. Lyman B. Stowe. LC 71-117847. (Essay Index Reprint Ser). 1934. 31.00 (ISBN 0-8369-1720-0). Ayer Co Pubs.

Saints, Sinners & Comedians. Roger Sharrock. LC 81-40457. 304p. 1984. text ed. 10.95 (ISBN 0-268-01713-1); pap. text ed. 10.95. U of Notre Dame Pr.

Saints, Slaves, & Blacks: The Changing Place of Black People Within Mormonism. Newell G. Bringhurst. LC 81-1093. (Contributions to the Study of Religion Ser.: No. 4). (Illus.). 256p. 1981. lib. bdg. 35.00 (ISBN 0-313-22752-7, BSB/). Greenwood.

Saint's Sporting Chance. Leslie Charteris. 17.95 (ISBN 0-89190-344-5, Pub. by Am Repr). Amereon Ltd.

Saints That Moved the World: Anthony, Augustine, Francis, Ignatius, Theresa. Rene Fulop-Miller. LC 72-13293. (Essay Index Reprint Ser.). Repr. of 1945 ed. 32.00 (ISBN 0-8369-8159-6). Ayer Co Pubs.

Saints, the Churches & the Holy Places of England: The West Country. John R. Popp. (Illus.). 175p. (Orig.). 1988. pap. 12.95 (ISBN 0-945565-01-1). Shiro Pubs.

Saints: Visible, Orderly & Catholic: The Congregational Idea of the Church. Alan P. Sell. LC 86-9457. (Princeton Theological Monograph Ser.: No. 7). (Orig.). 1986. pap. 15.00 (ISBN 0-915138-89-1). Pickwick.

Saints Who Shaped the Church. Jerry Schmalenberger. Ed. by Michael L. Sherer. LC 86-28395. (Orig.). 1987. pap. 6.50 (ISBN 0-89536-856-0, 7815). CSS of Ohio.

Saints Without Halos: The Human Side of Mormon History. Leonard J. Arrington & Davis Bitton. 168p. 1981. 10.95 (ISBN 0-941214-01-X). Signature Bks.

Saintspeak: The Mormon Dictionary. Orson S. Card. 60p. (Orig.). 1981. pap. 2.95 (ISBN 0-941214-00-1). Signature Bks.

Saipan: The War Diary of John Ciardi. John Ciardi. LC 87-25564. 138p. 1988. 15.00 (ISBN 1-55728-017-7); pap. 9.00 (ISBN 1-55728-018-5). U of Ark Pr.

Saison au Congo. Aime Cesaire. 1975. pap. 8.95 (ISBN 0-686-51958-2). French & Eur.

Saison en Enfer see Illuminations.

Saisons. Pascal Collasse. Ed. by Louis Soumis. (Chefs-d'oeuvre classiques de l'opera francais Ser.: Vol. 8). (Illus.). 226p. (Fr.). 1972. pap. 25.00x. Broude.

Saisons Pascal Collasse see Chefs-D'oeuvres Classiques De L'opera Francais Ser.

Saite & Persian Demotic Cattle Documents: A Study in Legal Forms & Principles in Ancient Egypt. Eugene Cruz-Uribe. (ASP Monographs). 1985. 23.95 (ISBN 0-89130-854-7, 31-00-26). Scholars Pr GA.

Saiva Art & Architecture in South India. C. Krishna Murthy. 1985. 48.00x (ISBN 0-8364-1417-9, Pub. by Sundeep). South Asia Bks.

Saiva Siddhanta Theology. R. A. Dunuwila. 320p. 1985. 20.00 (ISBN 0-89581-675-X, Pub. by Motilal Banarsidass). South Asia Bks.

Saivism: A Perspective of Grace. S. Arulsamy. 252p. 1988. text ed. 35.00x (ISBN 81-207-0757-5, Pub. by Sterling Pubs India). Apt Bks.

Saivism in Philosophical Perspective. K. Sivaraman. 1973. 28.00 (ISBN 0-8426-0538-X). Orient Bk Dist.

Saiyid Ahmad Shahid. M. Ahmad. pap. 19.00 (ISBN 0-686-18311-8). Kazi Pubns.

Sajo & Her Beaver People. Grey Owl. 225p. 1988. 39.00x (ISBN 1-85219-035-3, Pub. by Bishopgate Pr Ltd). State Mutual Bk.

Sakada: Filipino Adaptation in Hawaii. Ruben R. Alcantara. LC 80-5858. 202p. (Orig.). 1981. pap. text ed. 12.00 (ISBN 0-8191-1579-7). U Pr of Amer.

Sakahlin Breakout. (S.O.B. Ser.: No. 18). Date not set. pap. 2.50 (Pub. by Worldwide). Harlequin Bks.

Sakaki Hyakusen & Early Nanga Painting. James Cahill. LC 82-84050. (Japan Research Monograph: No. 3). (Illus.). 145p. (Orig.). 1983. pap. 5.00x (ISBN 0-912966-58-0). IEAS.

Sakamoto Ryoma & the Meiji Restoration. Marius B. Jansen. LC 77-153818. 1961. pap. 20.00x (ISBN 0-8047-0784-7). Stanford U Pr.

Sake. Hiroshi Kondo. LC 83-48880. (Illus.). 160p. 1984. 18.95 (ISBN 0-87011-653-3). Kodansha.

Sakharov File. Suzanne LeVert. LC 85-26037. (Illus.). 128p. (YA) (gr. 7 up). 1986. 9.79 (ISBN 0-671-60070-2). Messner.

Sakharov-Solzhenitsyn Fraud: What's Behind the Hue & Cry for Intellectual Freedom. Gus Hall. 32p. 1973. pap. 0.40 (ISBN 0-87898-102-0). New Outlook.

Sakharov Speaks. Andrei D. Sakharou. Intro. by Harrison E. Salisbury. 1974. pap. 1.65 (ISBN 0-394-71302-8, Vin). Random.

Saki: Short Stories. Saki. 250p. 1982. pap. text ed. 3.95x (ISBN 0-460-11105-1, Pub. by Evman England). Biblio Dist.

Saki: Short Stories, Vol. 2. Ed. by Peter Haining. 240p. 1983. pap. 3.95x (ISBN 0-460-01354-8, Pub. by Evman England). Biblio Dist.

Sakkara. Noel Barber. 1985. pap. 3.95 (ISBN 0-380-70091-3). Avon.

Sakshi Gopal: A Witness for the Wedding. Illus. by Tom Foley. (Illus.). 16p. (gr. 1-4). 1981. pap. 2.00 (ISBN 0-89647-036-9). Bala Bks.

Sakta Upanisads. A. Krishna Warrier. 3.50 (ISBN 0-8356-7318-9). Theos Pub Hse.

Sakti & Sakta. John Woodroffe. 28.50 (ISBN 0-89744-116-8, Pub. by Ganesh & Co. India). Auromere.

Sakya of Buddhist Origins. Rhys Davids. lib. bdg. 79.95 (ISBN 0-87968-512-3). Krishna Pr.

Sakya or Buddhist Origins. Caroline A. Davids. 444p. 1931. Repr. text ed. 32.50x. Coronet Bks.

Sakyamuni Worship & Seiryo-Ji Temple. Kyoto National Museum Staff. (Illus.). 146p. 1982. 200.00x (Pub. by Han-Shan Tang Ltd). State Mutual Bk.

Sala Family Archives: A Handlist of Medieval & Early Modern Catalonian Charters. Joseph J. Gwara, Jr. 152p. (Orig.). 1984. pap. 6.95 (ISBN 0-87840-090-7). Georgetown U Pr.

Salad a Day. Ruth Moorman & Lalla Williams. (Cookbook Ser.: No. 3). (Illus.). 80p. 1980. pap. 5.95 (ISBN 0-937552-02-X). Quail Ridge.

Salad: An All-Color Portfolio of Innovative Salad A Feast for Palate & Eye. Amy Nathan. LC 84-28519. (Illus.). 120p. (Orig.). 1985. pap. 14.95 (ISBN 0-87701-348-9). Chronicle Bks.

Salad & Soup Book: More Than Two Hundred & Fifty Delectable Recipes from Annie's Kitchen. Annie Lerman. LC 83-9178. (Illus.). 144p. (Orig.). 1983. lib. bdg. 15.90 (ISBN 0-89471-236-5); pap. 6.95 (ISBN 0-89471-235-7). Running Pr.

Salad Crops All Year Round. H. Witham Fogg. (Illus.). 200p. 1983. 19.95 (ISBN 0-7153-8411-2). David & Charles.

Salad Days. Douglas Fairbanks, Jr. LC 87-15621. (Illus.). 504p. 1988. 19.95 (ISBN 0-385-17404-7). Doubleday.

Salad Days. Christopher Idone. LC 86-29750. (Illus.). 192p. 1988. 19.95 (ISBN 0-394-56584-3). Random.

Salad Days in Baghdad. Clementina Owles. 130p. 1986. 39.00x (ISBN 0-7212-0712-X, Pub. by Regency Pr). State Mutual Bk.

Salad Dressing, Sauces, & Condiments. 210p. 1985. 595.00 (ISBN 0-686-38414-8, 155). Busn Trend.

Salad Dressings! Jane C. Dieckmann. 1987. 19.95 (ISBN 0-89594-224-0); pap. 7.95 (ISBN 0-89594-223-2). Crossing Pr.

Salad Garden. Elisabeth Arter. 190p. 15.00 (ISBN 0-7099-0530-0, Pub. by Croom Helm Ltd). Routledge Chapman & Hall.

Salad Garden: Salads from Seed to Table; A Complete, Illustrated, Year-Round Guide. Joy Larkcom. LC 83-40382. (Viking Home Gardening Book Shelf Ser.). (Illus.). 168p. 1984. 27.50 (ISBN 0-670-61572-2); pap. 12.95 (ISBN 0-670-61573-0). Viking.

Salad Menus. LC 85-2773. (Great Meals in Minutes Ser.). 1985. lib. bdg. 18.60 (ISBN 0-86706-261-4, Pub. by Time-Life). Silver.

Saladin. S. Lane-Poole. 528p. 1985. 300.00x (ISBN 1-85077-068-9, Pub. by Darf). State Mutual Bk.

Saladin & the Fall of Jerusalem. Geoffrey Regan. 192p. 1988. lib. bdg. 50.00x (ISBN 0-7099-4208-7, Pub. by Croom Helm UK). Routledge Chapman & Hall.

Saladin & the Fall of the Kingdom of Jerusalem. S. Lane-Poole. 528p. 1985. 59.00x (ISBN 0-317-39203-4, Pub. by Luzac & Co Ltd). State Mutual Bk.

Saladin & the Fall of the Kingdom of Jerusalem. Stanley Lane-Poole. LC 73-14453. (Heroes of the Nation Ser.). Repr. of 1926 ed. 37.50 (ISBN 0-404-58270-2). AMS Pr.

Saladin & the Fall of the Kingdom of Jerusalem. 35.50 (ISBN 0-686-18313-4). Kazi Pubns.

Saladin in His Time. P. H. Newby. LC 83-20831. 224p. 1984. 23.95 (ISBN 0-571-13044-5). Faber & Faber.

Saladin: The Politics of the Holy War. Malcolm C. Lyons & David E. Jackson. (Oriental Publications Ser.: No. 30). (Illus.). 468p. 1985. pap. 15.95 (ISBN 0-521-31739-8). Cambridge U Pr.

Saladin: The Politics of the Holy War. Malcom C. Lyons & D. E. Jackson. LC 79-13078. (Cambridge University Oriental Publications Ser.: No. 30). (Illus.). 400p. 1982. 49.50 (ISBN 0-521-22358-X). Cambridge U Pr.

Saladmaker. rev. ed. David McFadden. 1977. pap. 2.00 (ISBN 0-916696-03-0). Cross Country.

Salads. Better Homes & Gardens Editors. (Great Cooking Made Easy Ser.). 1986. 9.95 (ISBN 0-696-02197-8). BH&G.

Salads. Cherie Lambourne. Ed. by Martina Bourdreaux. 64p. 1988. pap. 2.95 (ISBN 0-942320-08-5). Am Cooking.

Salads. LC 79-27419. (Good Cook Ser.). (gr. 7 up). 22.60 (Pub. by Time-Life). Silver.

Salads. Cynthia Scheer. Ed. by Jill Fox. LC 85-72804. (California Culinary Academy Ser.). (Illus.). 128p. (Orig.). 1986. pap. 7.95 (ISBN 0-89721-050-6). Ortho.

Salads. Time-Life Books Editors. (Good Cook Ser.). (Illus.). 176p. 1980. 14.95 (ISBN 0-8094-2879-2). Time-Life.

Salads & Summer Dishes. Maren Lopategui. (Step-by-Step Cooking Ser.). 160p. 1986. 10.95 (ISBN 0-8120-5683-3). Barron.

Salads for All the Year Round. Mary Woodman. 1974. lib. bdg. 69.95 (ISBN 0-685-51353-X). Revisionist Pr.

Salads for Foodservice Menu Planning. Blair. 1987. 29.95 (ISBN 0-442-21186-4). Van Nos Reinhold.

Salads: Fresh Ways With. Sunset Editors. LC 86-82778. (Illus.). 96p. 1987. 6.95 (ISBN 0-376-02608-1). Sunset-Lane.

Salads: From Amish & Mennonite Kitchens. Ed. by Phyllis P. Good & Rachel T. Pellman. (Pennsylvania Dutch Cookbooks Ser.). (Illus., Orig.). 1983. pap. 2.50 (ISBN 0-934672-10-5). Good Bks PA.

Salads from Beginning to Endive. Kraft Kitchens. LC 79-54947. (Orig.). pap. 5.95 (ISBN 0-87502-073-9). Benjamin Co.

Salads of India. Varsha Dandekar. LC 83-1776. 94p. 1983. 18.95 (ISBN 0-89594-075-2); pap. 6.95 (ISBN 0-89594-074-4). Crossing Pr.

Salads, Sandwiches & Chafing Dish Recipes. Marion H. Neil. 1974. 69.95 (ISBN 0-685-51384-X). Revisionist Pr.

Sala'ilua: A Samoan Mystery. Bradd Shore. (Illus.). 338p. 1982. pap. 20.00x (ISBN 0-231-05383-5). Columbia U Pr.

Salamander. facsimile ed. Ed. by Keith Bullen & John Cromer. LC 79-103084. (Granger Index Reprint Ser). 1947. 17.00 (ISBN 0-8369-6099-8). Ayer Co Pubs.

Salamander & Other Stories. Masuji Ibuse. Tr. by John Bester. LC 80-84421. 134p. 1981. pap. 4.95 (ISBN 0-87011-458-1). Kodansha.

Salamander & the Fire. Dan Davin. (New Zealand Classics Ser.). 240p. 1987. pap. 8.95 (ISBN 0-19-558147-4). Oxford U Pr.

Salamander Migration & Other Poems. Cary Waterman. LC 79-24291. (Pitt Poetry Ser.). 1980. 16.95x (ISBN 0-8229-3415-9); pap. 8.95 (ISBN 0-8229-5315-3). U of Pittsburgh Pr.

Salamander: Selected Poems of Robert Marteau. Robert Marteau. Tr. by A. Winters. LC 78-70307. (Lockert Library of Poetry in Translation). 1979. 19.50x (ISBN 0-691-06396-6); pap. 7.50 (ISBN 0-691-01357-8). Princeton U Pr.

Salamander: The Story of the Mormon Forgery Murders. Linda Sillitoe & Allen D. Roberts. (Illus.). 592p. 1988. 17.95 (ISBN 0-941214-65-6). Signature Bks.

Salamanders & Newts. Byron Bjorn. (Illus.). 91p. (Orig.). 1987. pap. 5.95 (ISBN 0-86622-389-4, CO-0435). TFH Pubns.

Salamanders of Ohio. Ed. by Ralph Pfingsten & Floyd L. Downs. LC 85-60845. (Bulletin New Ser.: Vol. 7, No. 2). (Illus.). 300p. (Orig.). 1986. pap. text ed. 20.00 (ISBN 0-86727-099-3). Ohio Bio Survey.

Salammbo. Gustave Flaubert. (Coll. GF). 1961. pap. 8.95 (ISBN 0-685-11553-4, 2794). French & Eur.

Salammbo. Gustave Flaubert. Ed. by Maynial. (Class. Garnier). (Fr.). pap. 29.95 (ISBN 0-685-34901-2). French & Eur.

Salammbo. Gustave Flaubert. Ed. by Maynial. (Coll. Prestige). (Fr.). 49.95 (ISBN 0-685-34902-0). French & Eur.

Salammbo. Gustave Flaubert. Tr. by A. J. Krailsheimer. (Classics Ser.). 1977. pap. 5.95 (ISBN 0-14-044328-2). Penguin.

Salar the Salmon. Henry Williamson. (Illus.). 210p. (Orig.). 1973. pap. 6.95 (ISBN 0-571-04811-0). Faber & Faber.

Salaries & Attitudes: A Profile of the Internal Auditing Profession. S. L. Newman. Ed. by Richard Holman. 80p. 1984. pap. text ed. 27.00 (ISBN 0-89413-126-5, 411). Inst Inter Aud.

Salaries & Bonuses in Personnel-Industrial Relations Functions (1986-87) Ed. by Steven Langer. 672p. 1986. pap. 250.00 (ISBN 0-916506-31-2). Abbott Langer Assocs.

Salaries & Bonuses in the Service Department - 1986. Ed. by Steven Langer. 115p. 1986. pap. 150.00 (ISBN 0-317-55974-5). Abbott Langer Assocs.

Salaries & Fringe Benefits in Virginia's Cities, Counties & Selected Towns. Ed. by Mary Jo Fields. (Salary Surveys Ser.). 87p. 1985. pap. 15.00 (ISBN 0-932993-00-1). VA Muni League.

Salaries & Fringe Benefits in Virginia's Small Towns. Ed. by Mary Jo Fields. (Salary Surveys Ser.). 1986. pap. 15.00 (ISBN 0-932993-01-X). VA Muni League.

Salaries & Wages in California Public Schools, 1986-87. Educational Research Service. 134p. 1987. pap. text ed. 20.00 (ISBN 0-943397-00-6). Assn Calif Sch Admin.

Salaries & Wages in California Public Schools: 1987-88. Educational Research Service Staff. 134p. 1988. pap. text ed. 20.00 (ISBN 0-943397-07-3). Assn Calif Sch Admin.

Salaries & Wages in Michigan Municipalities over 1,000. Michigan Municipal League. (Information Bulletin Ser.: No. 109). 1987. 40.00 (ISBN 0-318-19474-0). MI Municipal.

Salaries in Virginia's Small Towns, 1987. Ed. by Mary Jo Fields. (Salary Survey Ser.). 24p. 1988. pap. 10.00 (ISBN 0-932993-03-6). VA Muni League.

Salaries of Engineers in Education 1986. Engineering Manpower Commission & R. A. Ellis. (Orig.). 1987. pap. 80.00 (ISBN 0-87615-156-X). AAES.

Salaries of Scientists, Engineers & Technicians: A Summary of Salary Surveys. 196p. 1987. pap. 45.00. Comm Prof Sci & Tech.

Salaries Paid Professional Personnel in Public Schools, 1987-88. 127p. 1988. 36.00. Ed Research.

Salario, Precio y Ganancia. Karl Marx. 62p. (Span.). 1979. pap. 0.95 (ISBN 0-8285-1356-2, Pub. by Progress Pubs USSR). Imported Pubns.

Salary Administration for Community Banks. 1977. 9.00 (ISBN 0-89982-131-6, 282300); non-members 30.00. Am Bankers.

Salary & Fringe Benefit Study. 60p. 125.00 (ISBN 0-318-15775-6). Natl Kitchen Cabinet.

Salary Compensation Systems for Librarians. 24p. 1981. 15.00 (ISBN 0-318-18568-7). OMS.

Salary Management for the Nonspecialist. Stanley B. Henrici. 256p. 1980. 15.95 (ISBN 0-8144-5565-4). AMACOM.

Salary Management for the Nonspecialist. Stanley B. Henrici. LC 80-65877. pap. 63.30 (ISBN 0-317-27190-3, 2023924). Bks Demand UMI.

Salary Reduction Arrangements. Isidore Goodman. (Pension & ERISA Ser.). 24p. 1985. 2.00 (ISBN 0-317-47597-5, 5467). Commerce.

Salary Study. 1985. text ed. 10.00 (ISBN 0-87868-244-9, 2449). Child Welfare.

Salary Survey. Ed. by Earl J. Gerson. 100p. 1986. 70.00 (ISBN 0-915274-34-5). Am Assn Clinical Chem.

Salary Survey Report: 1987. 64p. Date not set. write for info. Nat Assn Expo Mgrs.

Salary Systems in Public Higher Education: A Microeconomic Analysis. Marion S. Beaumont. 240p. 1985. 38.95 (ISBN 0-275-90059-2, C0059). Praeger.

Salaryman in Japan. Ed. by Japan Travel Bureau. (JTB's Illustrated Japan in Your Pocket Ser.: No. 8). (Illus.). 192p. 1986. pap. 9.95 (ISBN 4-53300-66-55, Japan Trvl Bur). Bks Nippan.

Salat Iz Bulavok. Arkadii Averchenko. LC 82-60958. 230p. 1982. pap. 9.95 (ISBN 0-89830-064-9). Russica Pubs.

Salata Kalman: Dokumentumdrama. Istvan Csicsery-Ronay. LC 84-60250. 91p. (Hungarian.). 1984. 8.00 (ISBN 0-911050-55-8); pap. 6.00 (ISBN 0-911050-54-X). Occidental.

Salavin. Georges Duhamel. 144p. 1972. 9.95 (ISBN 0-686-55195-8). French & Eur.

Salazar. F. C. Egerton. 59.95 (ISBN 0-8490-0988-X). Gordon Pr.

Salazar Blinks. David Slavitt. 176p. 1988. 16.95 (ISBN 0-689-12030-3). Atheneum.

Sale & Distribution of Books from Seventeen Hundred. Ed. by Robin Myers & Michael Harris. (Publishing Pathways Ser.). (Illus.). 130p. 1986. pap. 10.00 (ISBN 0-317-47132-5). Chadwyck-Healey.

Sale & Purchase of Restaurants. John Stefanelli. LC 84-10468. (Tourism-Hospitality Ser.). 237p. 1985. 27.95 (Pub. by Grid); text ed. 29.95x (ISBN 0-471-84230-3). Wiley.

Sale of a Small Business. William H. Dunn. (Orig.). 1982. 1984 supplement 65.00 (ISBN 0-933808-02-X). Busn Sale Inst.

Sale of Books Through Non-Bookstore Retailers. Coopers & Lybrand Strategic Management Services Staff. (Illus.). 110p. 1988. pap. 650.00. Bk Indus Study.

Sale of Corporate Control. Andrew N. Grass. (Corporate Practice Ser.: No. 19). 1980. 92.00 (ISBN 0-317-55347-X). BNA.

Sale of Goods & Hire-Purchase. Avtar Singh. 189p. 1985. 60.00x (ISBN 0-317-57660-7, Pub. by Eastern Bk India). State Mutual Bk.

Sale of Liquor in the South. Leonard S. Blakey. LC 74-94922. (Columbia University Studies in the Social Sciences: No. 127). Repr. of 1912 ed. 15.00 (ISBN 0-404-51127-9). AMS Pr.

Salekov Kill. Guy Richards. 256p. (Orig.). 1981. pap. 2.50 (ISBN 0-449-14405-4, GM). Fawcett.

Salem & Marblehead. Peter E. Randall. (Illus.). 88p. 1983. pap. 8.95 (ISBN 0-89272-163-4). Down East.

Salem Area Community Corrections: State Clients, Local Services, & Policy Choices, Vol. 2. (Research Monographs). 64p. 1987. pap. 12.00. U OR BGR.

Salem Area Institutions: Correctional & Mental Health Institutions & the Ex-Institutional Population, Vol. 1. (Research Monographs). 123p. 1987. pap. 15.00. U OR BGR.

Salem Chapel. Margaret Oliphant. 378p. 1986. pap. 6.95 (ISBN 0-14-016152-X). Penguin.

Salem Chapel. Margaret W. Oliphant. Ed. by Robert L. Wolff. LC 75-1508. (Victorian Fiction Ser.). 1975. Repr. of 1863 ed. lib. bdg. 66.00 (ISBN 0-8240-1582-7). Garland Pub.

Salem Church Embattled. Ralph Happel. (Illus.). 62p. 1980. pap. 1.50 (ISBN 0-915992-15-9). Eastern Acorn.

Salem Days, Life in a Colonial Seaport. James E. Knight. LC 81-23076. (Illus.). 32p. (gr. 5-9). 1982. PLB 9.79 (ISBN 0-89375-732-2); pap. text ed. 1.95 (ISBN 0-89375-733-0). Troll Assocs.

Salem in the Eighteenth Century. James D. Phillips. LC 37-36381. (Illus.). 533p. 1969. Repr. of 1937 ed. 25.00 (ISBN 0-88389-017-8). Essex Inst.

Salem Kirban Reference Bible. (Illus.). 1979. skivertex flexible bdg. 49.95 (ISBN 0-912582-31-6); leather ed. 69.95 (ISBN 0-686-52197-8). Kirban.

Salem Kittredge, & Other Stories. facs. ed. Bliss Perry. LC 71-133165. (Short Story Index Reprint Ser). 1894. 17.00 (ISBN 0-8369-3689-2). Ayer Co Pubs.

Salem Light Guard. Lester L. Kempfer. LC 73-76068. (Illus.). 128p. 1973. 5.95 (ISBN 0-686-04916-0); pap. 3.95 (ISBN 0-686-04917-9). L Kempfer.

Salem: Maritime Salem in the Age of Sail. LC 85-21545. (National Park Service Handbook: No. 126). (Illus.). 159p. 1987. pap. 5.00 (ISBN 0-912627-30-1, S/N 024-005-01014-9). USGPO.

Salem, Massachusetts, 1626-1683: A Covenant Community. Richard P. Gildrie. LC 74-20841. pap. 51.80 (ISBN 0-317-58137-6, 2029686). Bks Demand UMI.

Salem-Peoria, Eighteen Eighty-Three to Nineteen Eighty-Two. David R. Pichaske. (Illus.). 256p. (Orig.). 1982. pap. 6.95 (ISBN 0-933180-40-3). Ellis Pr.

Salem Possessed: The Social Origins of Witchcraft. Paul Boyer & Stephen Nissenbaum. LC 73-84399. 320p. 1974. pap. 7.95x (ISBN 0-674-78526-6). Harvard U Pr.

Salem, Transcendentalism, & Hawthorne. Alfred Rosa. LC 77-89784. 108p. 1980. 19.50 (ISBN 0-8386-2159-7). Fairleigh Dickinson.

Salem Vessels & Their Voyages, 2 vols. George G. Putnam. Incl. A History of the Pepper Trade with the Island of Sumatra. Vol. 1 (ISBN 0-88389-105-0); A History of the "George", "Glide", "Taria Topan" & "St Paul", in Trade with Calcutta, East Coast of Africa, Madagascar, & the Philippine Islands. Vol. 2 (ISBN 0-88389-106-9); History of the 'Astrea', 'Mindoro', 'Sooloo', 'Panay', 'Dragon', 'Highlander', 'Shirley', & 'Formosa', with Some Account of Their Masters, & Other Reminiscences of Salem Shipmasters. Vol. 3 (ISBN 0-88389-107-7); A History of the European, African, Australian, & South Pacific Islands Trade As Carried on by Salem Merchants, Particularly the Firm of N. L. Rogers & Brothers. LC 30-1353. (Illus.). 680p. 1924-25. 15.00 ea. Essex Inst.

Salem Village Greens. Harry A. Grace. LC 87-90050. 216p. (Orig.). 1987. write for info. (ISBN 0-9618083-0-6); pap. write for info. (ISBN 0-9618083-1-4). Vyoupoint.

Salem Witchcraft, 2 vols. C. Upham. 1022p. 1971. Repr. of 1867 ed. Set. 60.00 (ISBN 0-87928-024-7). Corner Hse.

Salem Witchcraft, 2 Vols. Charles W. Upham. LC 59-10887. (American Classics Ser.). (Illus.). 1959. 40.00x (ISBN 0-8044-1947-7). Ungar.

Salem Witchcraft Papers: Verbatim Transcripts, 3 vols. Ed. by Paul Boyer & Stephen Nissenbaum. (Civil Liberties in American History Ser.). 1977. Set. lib. bdg. 145.00 (ISBN 0-306-70655-5). Da Capo.

Salem's Child. Robert Walker. 400p. (Orig.). 1987. pap. 3.95 (ISBN 0-8439-2445-4, Leisure Bks). Leisure NY.

Salem's Children. Mary Leader. 368p. 1981. pap. 2.75 (ISBN 0-8439-0982-X, Leisure Bks). Leisure NY.

Salem's Lot. Stephen King. LC 73-22804. 1975. 18.95 (ISBN 0-385-00751-5). Doubleday.

Salem's Lot. Stephen King. (Illus.). 427p. (RL 10). 1983. pap. 4.50 (ISBN 0-451-15065-1, Sig). NAL.

Saleratus & Sagebrush: The Oregon Trail Through Wyoming. 2nd ed. Robert L. Munkres. (Illus.). 156p. pap. 3.50 (ISBN 0-943398-02-9). Wyoming State Press.

Salerno Ivories: Ars Sacra from Medieval Amalfi. Robert P. Bergman. LC 79-22616. (Illus.). 268p. 1981. 40.00x (ISBN 0-674-78528-2). Harvard U Pr.

Sales. 3rd ed. William Hawkland. (Sum & Substance Ser.). 1985. 13.95. Herbert Legal Ser.

Sales. 3rd ed. (Sum & Substance Ser.). 1985. write for info. (ISBN 0-940366-11-8). Herbert Legal Ser.

Sales Analysis from the Management Standpoint. D. R. Cowan. LC 67-24325. 210p. 1967. 15.00 (ISBN 0-379-00072-5). Oceana.

Sales & Bulk Sales. 3rd ed. William D. Hawkland. 232p. 1976. pap. 12.00 (ISBN 0-317-30893-9, B377). Am Law Inst.

Sales & Bulk Transfers under the Uniform Commercial Code, 2 vols. Richard W. Dusenberg & Lawrence P. King. (Bender's Uniform Commercial Code Service: Volumes 3 & 3A). 1966. Set, updates avail. looseleaf 165.00 (612); Updates 1985. 91.50; Supplement 1986. 710.00. Bender.

Sales & Credit Transactions Handbook. T. Le & Edward J. Murphy. 784p. 1986. text ed. 90.00 (ISBN 0-07-044069-7). Shepards McGraw.

Sales & Distribution Guide to Malaysia. Tim Allen et al. (SABG Ser.: No. 1). 192p. 1988. text ed. 49.00 (ISBN 0-08-034987-0); pap. text ed. 25.00 (ISBN 0-08-034986-2). Pergamon.

Sales & Distribution Guide to Thailand. P. Renard et al. (SABG Ser.: No. 2). 144p. 1988. text ed. 39.00 (ISBN 0-08-035838-1); pap. text ed. 19.75 (ISBN 0-08-035837-3). Pergamon.

Sales & Marketing Casebook 1986. Hobsons, Ltd. Staff. 52p. 1986. pap. 35.00x (ISBN 0-317-54246-X, Pub. by Hobsons Ltd UK). State Mutual Bk.

Sales & Marketing for Travel & Tourism. Philip G. Davidoff & Doris S. Davidoff. (Illus.). 296p. 1983. pap. text ed. 19.75x (ISBN 0-935920-09-9). Natl Pub Black Hills.

Sales & Sales Financing. Richard E. Speidel. LC 84-13095. (Black Letter Ser.). 363p. 1984. pap. text ed. 14.95 (ISBN 0-314-82587-8). West Pub.

Sales & Sales Financing, Cases & Materials: Manual for Teachers to Accompany Fifth Edition. John Honnold. (University Casebook Ser.). 79p. 1985. pap. text ed. write for info. (ISBN 0-88277-258-9). Foundation Pr.

Sales & Sales Financing Law: Cases & Materials. 5th ed. John Honnold. LC 84-13778. (University Casebook Ser.). 856p. 1984. text ed. write for info. (ISBN 0-88277-189-2). Foundation Pr.

Sales & Sales Management. 2nd ed. P. Allen. (Illus.). 288p. 1979. pap. 15.95x (ISBN 0-7121-1962-0, Pub. by Macdonald & Evans England). Trans-Atl Phila.

Sales & Use Tax Rules. write for info. AL Revenue.

Sales & Use Taxes in State. LC 86-165881. 1987. 30.00. Natl Busn Inst.

Sales Artillery: How to Arm the Sales Force for Successful Selling. Gene Plotnik. 240p. 1988. pap. 9.95 (ISBN 0-13-786575-9, Busn). P-H.

Sales Budgeting. (PRIME-PRIME 100 Ser). 1969. 35.00 (ISBN 0-8144-1106-1). AMACOM.

Sales, Cases & Materials on. 2nd ed. Marion W. Benfield, Jr. & William D. Hawkland. LC 86-2019. (University Casebook Ser.). 575p. 1986. text ed. 22.00 (ISBN 0-88277-324-0). Foundation Pr.

Sales Catalogues of British Government Publications, 1836-1921, 4 vols. Her Majesty's Stationery Office Staff. LC 75-6964. 1977. lib. bdg. 85.00 ea (ISBN 0-379-00550-6); lib. bdg. 340.00 set. Oceana.

Sales Closing Book. Gerhard Gschwandtner. LC 88-90648. (Illus.). 145p. 1988. text ed. 99.00 (ISBN 0-939613-02-6). Personal Selling.

Sales Closing Power. J. Douglas Edwards. LC 87-81171. 240p. 1987. pap. 19.95 (ISBN 0-942645-02-2); 6 audio cassette album 99.95, (ISBN 0-942645-03-0). Hampton Hse Pub.

Sales Cybernetics: New Scientific Techniques in Motivational Selling. Brian Adams. 1985. pap. 7.00 (ISBN 0-87980-412-2). Wilshire.

Sales Engineering: An Emerging Profession. 2nd ed. George Black. LC 79-17716. 228p. 1979. 19.00x (ISBN 0-87201-799-0). Gulf Pub.

Sales Force Compensation: Dartnell's 24th Biennial Survey. William A. O'Connell. 353p. 1988. 124.50 (ISBN 0-85013-160-X). Dartnell Corp.

Sales Force Management. Kenneth Davis & Frederick E. Webster. LC 68-20549. pap. 160.00 (ISBN 0-317-28587-4, 2055189). Bks Demand UMI.

Sales Force Management. Joe L. Welch & Charles Lapp. 1983. text ed. write for info. (ISBN 0-538-19530-4, S53). SW Pub.

Sales Force Management: Planning, Implementation & Control. 2nd ed. Gilbert A. Churchill, Jr. et al. 1985. 36.95x (ISBN 0-256-03184-3). Irwin.

Sales Force Management: Text & Cases. Derek Newton. 1982. text ed. 37.95 (ISBN 0-256-02755-2). Business Pubns.

Sales Force Performance. Neil M. Ford et al. LC 84-17166. 480p. 1984. 42.00x (ISBN 0-669-09376-9). Lexington Bks.

Sales Forecasting. David L. Hurwood et al. LC 78-67315. (Report Ser.: No. 730). (Illus.). 226p. 1978. pap. 100.00 (ISBN 0-8237-0164-6). Conference Bd.

Sales Forecasting for the Field Sales Manager. (PRIME-PRIME 100 Ser). 1973. 35.00 (ISBN 0-8144-1110-X). AMACOM.

Sales Forecasting: How to Prepare & Use Market Data & Sales Forecasts in Profit Planning. T. F. Dodd. 220p. 1974. text ed. 44.50x (ISBN 0-7161-0233-1). Gower Pub Co.

Sales Forecasting Models: A Diagnostic Approach. Lester C. Sartorius & N. Carroll Mohn. LC 76-9812. (Research Monograph: No. 69). 1976. pap. 34.95 (ISBN 0-88406-105-1). Ga St U Busn Pub.

Sales Forecasting Systems. Eugene A. Imhoff, Jr. 104p. Date not set. 16.95 (ISBN 0-318-22908-0, 85169). Natl Assn Accts.

Sales Forecasting: Timesaving & Profit-Making Strategies That Work. Sales Executives Club of New York. 192p. 1984. 24.95 (ISBN 0-673-15948-5). Scott F.

Sales Ideas from the All Stars. 64p. 4.00 (ISBN 0-686-31044-6, 29413). Rough Notes.

Sales in a Nutshell. 2nd ed. John M. Stockton. LC 80-25579. (Nutshell Ser.). 370p. 1981. pap. text ed. 9.95 (ISBN 0-8299-2116-8). West Pub.

Sales-in-Sight. 29.95 (ISBN 0-318-02583-3). Print Indus Am.

Sales Law & the Contracting Process. Alan Schwartz & Robert E. Scott. LC 82-82575. (University Casebook Ser.). 512p. 1982. text ed. 14.50 (ISBN 0-88277-077-2). Foundation Pr.

Sales Laws (N. Y.) 1976 ed. Paul Zola. 100p. 1975. 5.00 (ISBN 0-87526-210-4). Gould.

Sales Lead-Getting Model Letter Book. Luther A. Brock. LC 85-43236. 261p. 1986. 27.95 (ISBN 0-13-787599-1, Busn). P-H.

Sales Leadership Techniques. George McArdle. 1982. 14.00 (ISBN 0-942326-45-8, 29201). Rough Notes.

Sales Letters That Sell. 1987. lib. bdg. 79.25 (ISBN 0-8490-3891-X). Gordon Pr.

Sales Magic. Rick Maltin. Date not set. 99.95 (ISBN 0-87280-526-3). Asher-Gallant.

Sales Management. Rolph Anderson & Joseph Hair. Ed. by Paul Donnelly. LC 82-23014. (Random House Business Division Ser.). 576p. 1983. text ed. write for info (ISBN 0-394-32293-2, RanC). Random.

Sales Management. Chonko & Enis. 1989. price not set (ISBN 0-256-05965-9). Business Pubns.

Sales Management. 2nd, rev. ed. Charles Futrell. (Illus.). 832p. 1988. text ed. price not set (ISBN 0-03-010963-9). Dryden Pr.

Sales Management. Charles M. Futrell. LC 80-65796. 528p. 1981. text ed. 32.95x (ISBN 0-03-049276-9); instr's. manual 10.00 (ISBN 0-03-052201-3). Dryden Pr.

Sales Management. Robert Hartley. 608p. 1988. 35.95 (ISBN 0-675-20747-9). Merrill.

Sales Management. Robert F. Hartley. LC 78-69614. (Illus.). 1979. text ed. 34.50 (ISBN 0-395-26511-8); test bank 1.50. HM.

Sales Management. E. M. Johnson et al. (Marketing Ser.). 608p. 1986. text ed. 37.95 (ISBN 0-07-032637-1). McGraw.

Sales Management. 2nd ed. Dan H. Robertson et al. 480p. 1985. text ed. write for info. (ISBN 0-02-402210-1). Macmillan.

Sales Management. Thomas Wotruba. 1980. text ed. write for info. (ISBN 0-673-16142-0). Scott F.

Sales Management: A Practitioner's Guide to Sales Force Development. Roger F. Smith. (Illus.). 288p. 1987. text ed. 31.00 (ISBN 0-13-786534-1). P-H.

Sales Management: A Review of the Current Literature, Danny N. Bellenger & Robert L. Berl. LC 81-6559. (Research Monograph: No. 89). 1981. spiral bdg. 16.50 (ISBN 0-88406-147-7). GA St U Busn Pub.

Sales Management & Motivation. Joseph A. Callan & Porler Henry. Ed. by William Newton. 224p. 1987. 24.95 (ISBN 0-531-15516-1). Watts.

Sales Management by Objectives. George S. Odiorne. 1982. 61.95 (ISBN 0-85013-139-1). Dartnell Corp.

Sales Management: Concepts & Cases. 3rd ed. Douglas J. Dalrymple. LC 87-23749. 681p. 1988. write for info. (ISBN 0-471-62495-0). Wiley.

Sales Management: Decisions, Strategies & Cases. 4th ed. R. R. Still et al. (Illus.). 656p. 1981. text ed. write for info. (ISBN 0-13-788059-6). P-H.

Sales Management: Decisions, Strategies, & Cases. 5th ed. Richard Still et al. (Illus.). 656p. 1988. text ed. write for info. (ISBN 0-13-786542-2). P-H.

Sales Management for Hotels. Derek Taylor. Ed. by J. Mall. (Professional Book Ser.). (Illus.). 241p. 1986. 25.95 (ISBN 0-442-28317-2). Van Nos Reinhold.

Sales Management Handbook. Patrick Forsyth. LC 87-8619. 500p. 1988. text ed. 75.00 (ISBN 0-566-02585-X). Gower Pub Co.

Sales Management Simulation. Paul D. Cretien. 64p. 1988. pap. 16.95 (ISBN 0-675-21012-7). Merrill.

Sales Management Simulation: Participants Manual. 2nd ed. Day. 1988. pap. write for info. (ISBN 0-471-63750-5). Wiley.

Sales Management Simulation: Participant's Manual. Ralph L. Day & Douglas J. Dalrymple. 1985. pap. 16.95 (ISBN 0-471-82361-9). Wiley.

Sales Management: Text, Readings, & Cases. Joseph P. Vaccaro. (Illus.). 352p. 1987. pap. text ed. write for info. (ISBN 0-13-787870-2). P-H.

Sales Management: The Complete Marketeer's Guide. Chris Noonan. 1986. text ed. 39.95x (ISBN 0-04-658254-1). Unwin Hyman.

Sales Management with dBASE III. Timothy Berry. 150p. 1986. documentation manual 49.95 (ISBN 0-934375-15-1). M & T Pub Inc.

Sales Manager's Desk Book. Gene Garofalo. 384p. 1988. 59.95 (ISBN 0-13-786583-X). P-H.

Sales Manager's Guide to the U. S. School Market: 1986. 1986. 65.00 (ISBN 0-89770-391-X). Market Data Ret.

Sales Manager's Handbook. Ed. by Edwin E. Bobrow & Larry Wizenberg. LC 82-71068. 576p. 1983. 55.00 (ISBN 0-87094-240-9). Dow Jones-Irwin.

Sales Manager's Model Letter Desk Book. Hal Fahner. 1977. 32.95 (ISBN 0-13-787663-7, Parker). P-H.

Sales Manager's Model Letter Desk Book. 2nd ed. Hal Fahner & Morris E. Miller. 240p. 1988. 39.95 (ISBN 0-13-787789-7, Busn). P-H.

Sally Wister's Journal. Sarah Wister. 96p. 1988. pap. 7.95 (ISBN 1-55709-114-5). Applewood.
Sally Wister's Journal: A True Narrative Being a Quaker Maiden's Account of Her Experiences with Officers of the Continental Army, 1777-1778. Sally Wister. Ed. by Albert C. Myers. LC 73-78039. (Eyewitness Accounts of the American Revolution Ser., No. 2). 1969. Repr. of 1902 ed. 16.00 (ISBN 0-405-01169-5). Ayer Co Pubs.
Sally's Calendar Book. Gloria G. Morrell. (gr. 1-3). 1986. pap. 3.95 (ISBN 0-8054-4337-1). Broadman.
Sally's Secret. Shirley Hughes. (Illus.). 32p. (ps-1). 1988. pap. 3.50 (ISBN 0-14-050160-6, Puffin Bks). Penguin.
Salmagundi. Joy Cowley. (Illus.). 36p. (ps-3). 1988. 12.95 (ISBN 0-19-558117-2). Oxford U Pr.
Salmagundi. Launcelott Langstaff. 1972. Repr. of 1819 ed. lib. bdg. 39.50 (ISBN 0-8422-8162-2). Irvington.
Salmagundi see History, Tales & Sketches.
Salmagundi: Second Series, 2 Vols. in 1. James K. Paulding. LC 70-144669. Repr. of 1835 ed. 49.50 (ISBN 0-404-04944-3). AMS Pr.
Salman el-Farsi. Sayed A. Razwy. 1985. pap. 3.95 (ISBN 0-933543-02-6). Aza Khana.
Salmon. Paula Hogan. LC 78-21178. (Life Cycle's Clippers Ser.). (Illus.). 32p. (gr. k-3). 1984. PLB 27.99 incl. cassette (ISBN 0-8172-2232-4); cassette 14.00. Raintree Pubs.
Salmon. Paula Z. Hogan. LC 78-21178. (Life Cycles Bks.). (Illus.). 32p. (gr. k-3). 1979. PLB 14.65 (ISBN 0-8172-1255-8). Raintree Pubs.
Salmon & Sea Trout Fishing: A Practical Guide. Charles Bingham. (Illus.). 224p. 1989. 34.95 (ISBN 0-7134-5639-6, Pub. by Batsford England). David & Charles.
Salmon & Trout Farming. Laird. (Aquaculture & Fisheries Support Ser.). 272p. 1988. 59.95 (ISBN 0-470-21087-7). Wiley.
Salmon & Trout Farming in Norway. David J. Edwards. 1978. 50.00x (ISBN 0-685-63450-7). State Mutual Bk.
Salmon & Trout Farming in Norway. David J. Edwards. (Illus.). 208p. 1978. 26.50 (ISBN 0-85238-093-3, FN75, FNB). UNIPUB.
Salmon & Trout Feeds & Feeding. (European Inland Fisheries Advisory Commision (EIFAC): Technical Papers: No. 12). 33p. (Eng. & Fr.). 1971. pap. 7.50 (ISBN 92-5-100823-X, F1862, FAO). UNIPUB.
Salmon Cookbook. 2nd ed. Jerry Dannon. Ed. by Deborah Easter. LC 87-8864. (Illus.). 128p. 1987. pap. 7.95 (ISBN 0-931397-19-7). Globe Pequot.
Salmon Country. Jack Byrne. (Illus.). 224p. 1982. 15.95 (ISBN 0-00-216975-4, Pub. by W Collins New Zealand). Intl Spec Bk.
Salmon: Economics & Marketing. Susan A. Shaw & James F. Muir. 270p. 1987. text ed. 34.95x (ISBN 0-88192-077-0). Timber.
Salmon Fisheries of Scotland. Association of Scottish District Salmon Fishery Boards. (Illus.). 80p. 1978. pap. 11.00 (ISBN 0-85238-091-7, FN67, FNB). UNIPUB.
Salmon Fishers of the Columbia. Courtland L. Smith. (Illus.). 128p. 1979. 15.95 (ISBN 0-87071-313-2). Oreg St U Pr.
Salmon Fishing: A Practical Guide. Hugh Falkus. (Illus.). 448p. 1984. 43.95 (ISBN 0-85493-144-9). Greycliff Pub.
Salmon Flies: Their Character, Style, & Dressings. Poul Jorgensen. LC 78-17941. (Illus.). 192p. 1978. 29.95 (ISBN 0-8117-1426-8). Stackpole.
Salmon for Simon. Betty Waterton. (Illus.). 28p. (Orig.). (ps-4). 1987. pap. 3.95 (ISBN 0-88894-533-7, Pub. by Douglas & McIntyre-Grounwood). Salem Hse Pubs.
Salmon Handbook. Stephen D. Sedgwick. (Illus.). 1982. 26.50 (ISBN 0-233-97331-1, Pub. by A Deutsch England). Scholium Intl.
Salmon: International Chef's Recipes. Willy Wyssenbach. (Illus.). 128p. 1987. 19.95 (ISBN 0-312-01047-8). St Martin.
Salmon P. Chase. Albert B. Hart. LC 80-21705. (American Statesmen Ser.). 470p. 1981. pap. 6.95 (ISBN 0-87754-191-4). Chelsea Hse.
Salmon P. Chase: A Life in Politics. Frederick J. Blue. LC 86-27664. (Illus.). 408p. 1987. 28.00x (ISBN 0-87338-340-0). Kent St U Pr.
Salmon Portland Chase. Albert Hart. LC 68-24981. (American Biography Ser., No. 32). 1969. Repr. of 1899 ed. lib. bdg. 59.95x (ISBN 0-8383-0952-6). Haskell.
Salmon Portland Chase. Albert B. Hart. Ed. by John T. Morse, Jr. LC 74-108489. 1970. Repr. of 1899 ed. 20.00x (ISBN 0-403-00216-8). Scholarly.
Salmon Portland Chase. Ed. by Albert B. Hart. LC 79-128954. (American Statesmen: No. 28). Repr. of 1899 ed. 18.00 (ISBN 0-404-50878-2). AMS Pr.
Salmon Production, Management, & Allocation: Biological, Economic, & Policy Issues. Ed. by William J. McNeil. LC 87-22135. (Illus.). 208p. 1988. 29.95x (ISBN 0-87071-354-X). Oreg St U Pr.
Salmon Ranching. Ed. by John Thorpe. 1981. 94.50 (ISBN 0-12-690660-2). Acad Pr.
Salmon River, Digby County, Nova Scotia: Vital Records 1849-1907. Ed. by Leonard H. Smith, Jr. LC 77-79479. 22.50 (ISBN 0-932022-10-3). L H Smith.
Salmon River Saga. Kenneth B. Platt. (Illus.). 1978. 17.95 (ISBN 0-87770-210-1). Ye Galleon.
Salmon Rivers of Scotland. Derek Mills & Neil Graesser. (Illus.). 352p. 1985. 24.95 (ISBN 0-913276-49-9). Stone Wall Pr.
Salmonia. Humphry Davy. (Illus.). 273p. 1970. boxed 10.75 (ISBN 0-88395-004-9). Freshet Pr.
Salmonid Ecosystems of the North Pacific. Ed. by William J. McNeil & Daniel C. Himsworth. LC 80-17800. (Illus.). 348p. 1980. pap. 21.95x (ISBN 0-87071-335-3). Oreg St U Pr.
Salmonid Reproduction: Review Papers from an International Symposium. Ed. by Robert N. Iwamoto & Stacia Sower. LC 85-13764. (Illus.). viii, 167p. (Orig.). 1985. pap. text ed. 10.00 (ISBN 0-934539-00-6, WSG-WO85-2). Wash Sea Grant.
Salmos. Mary J. Tully. Tr. by Angelina Marquez. 1986. pap. 3.95 (ISBN 0-697-02202-1). Wm C Brown.
Salmos: Cantos de Vida. Fred M. Wood. Tr. by Edna L. De Gutierrez from Span. 160p. 1984. pap. 3.25 (ISBN 0-311-04032-2). Casa Bautista.
Salo Wittmayer Baron Jubilee Volume: On the Occasion of His Eightieth Birthday, 3 vols. new ed. Ed. by Saul Lieberman & Arthur Hyman. LC 74-82633. 1533p. 1975. 119.00x set (ISBN 0-685-51945-7); Vol. 1. (ISBN 0-231-03911-5); Vol. 2. (ISBN 0-231-03912-3); Vol. 3. (ISBN 0-231-03913-1). Columbia U Pr.
Salome. Oscar Wilde. (Illus.). 96p. 1987. pap. 9.95 (ISBN 0-7043-0026-5, Pub. by Quartet Bks). Salem Hse Pubs.
Salome. Oscar Wilde. Ed. by Aubrey Beardsley. LC 64-21052. (Illus.). 64p. 1988. pap. 3.95 (ISBN 0-8283-1467-5, Pub. by Intl Pocket Lib). Branden Pub Co.
Salome: A Tragedy in One Act. Aubrey Beardsley & Oscar Wilde. Tr. by Alfred Douglas. pap. 4.95 (ISBN 0-486-21830-9). Dover.
Salome & Judas in the Cave of Sex. Ewa Kuryluk. (Illus.). 385p. 1987. 48.95x (ISBN 0-8101-0739-2); pap. 26.95x (ISBN 0-8101-0740-6). Northwestern U Pr.
Salome & the Dance of Writing: Portraits of Mimesis in Literature. Francoise Meltzer. LC 86-24983. (Illus.). xii, 226p. 1987. lib. bdg. 24.95x (ISBN 0-226-51971-6). U of Chicago Pr.
Salome: Her Life & Work. Angela Livingstone. (Illus.). 529p. 1985. 18.95 (ISBN 0-918825-04-0, Dist. by Kampmann & Co.); pap. 9.95. Moyer Bell Limited.
Salome: Her Life & Work. Ed. by Angela Livingstone. (Illus.). 255p. 1987. pap. 18.95 (ISBN 0-918825-61-X, Dist. by Kampmann & Co.). Moyer Bell Limited.
Salomo Gabirol und seine Dichtungen. Abraham Geiger. Ed. by Steven Katz. LC 79-7130. (Jewish Philosophy, Mysticism & History of Ideas Ser.). 1980. Repr. of 1867 ed. lib. bdg. 14.00x (ISBN 0-405-12254-3). Ayer Co Pubs.
Salomon de Brosse & the Development of the Classical Style in French Architecture from 1565 to 1630. Rosalys Coope. LC 70-127381. (Illus.). 295p. 1972. 60.00x (ISBN 0-271-00140-2). Pa St U Pr.
Salomon de Brosse: And the Development of the Classical Style in French Architecture from 1565 to 1630. Rosalys Coope. Ed. by John Harris & Alastair Laing. (Studies in Architecture: No. XI). (Illus.). 295p. 1986. 75.00 (ISBN 0-302-02195-7, Pub. by Zwemmer Bks UK). Sotheby Pubns.
Salon & English Letters. Chauncey B. Tinker. LC 67-21716. 300p. 1967. Repr. of 1915 ed. 35.00x (ISBN 0-87752-113-1). Gordian.
Salon & Picturesque Photography in Cuba, 1860-1920. Gary R. Libby. Ed. by Sandra L. Miller. (Illus.). 50p. 1988. pap. 5.00 (ISBN 0-933053-02-9). Museum Art Sciences.
Salon de Madame Helvetius: Cabanis et les Ideologues. Antoine Guillois. LC 74-159698. (Research & Source Works Ser: No. 892). 250p. (Selected essays in History, Economics, & Social Science, No. 323). 1972. Repr. of 1894 ed. lib. bdg. 23.50 (ISBN 0-8337-4145-4). B Franklin.
Salon Management. Susan Green & Peter Green. (Illus.). 160p. 1984. text ed. 27.00 (ISBN 0-13-788217-3). P-H.
Salon Management: For Hairdressers & Beauty Therapists. T. W. Masters. 250p. 1987. text ed. 21.90x (ISBN 0-291-39709-3, Pub. by Gower Pub England). Gower Pub Co.
Salon Psychology: How to Succeed with People & Be a Positive Person. Lewis E. Losoncy. LC 87-63500. (Illus.). 242p. (Orig.). 1988. pap. text ed. 19.95 (ISBN 0-9619951-0-6). Matrix Univ Pr.
Salonica Travel Guide. Berlitz Editors. (Travel Guides Ser.). 1980. pap. 4.95 (ISBN 0-317-12280-0, Berlitz). Macmillan.
Salonika. Louise Page. (New Theatrescripts Ser.). 76p. 1983. pap. 4.95 (ISBN 0-413-52180-X, NO. 3823). Heinemann Ed.
Salons, 4 vols. Diderot. Ed. by Jean Seznec & Jean Adhemar. Incl. Vol. 1. 1759, 1761, 1763. 2nd ed. 1975. 56.00x (ISBN 0-19-817181-1); Vol. 2. 1765. 2nd ed. 1979. 74.00x (ISBN 0-19-817354-7); Vol. 3. 1767. 2nd ed. 1983. 159.00x (ISBN 0-19-817372-5); Vol. 4. 1769, 1771, 1775, 1781. 1967. 85.00x (ISBN 0-19-817155-2). Oxford U Pr.
Salons. 2nd ed. Denis Diderot & R. Desne. 9.95 (ISBN 0-686-56029-9). French & Eur.
Salons: Colonial & Republican. Anne H. Wharton. LC 75-172550. (Illus.). Repr. of 1900 ed. 22.00 (ISBN 0-405-09063-3). Ayer Co Pubs.
Salons of the "Independants", 1884 to 1891. Ed. by Theodore Reff. (Modern Art in Paris 1855 to 1900 Ser.). 253p. 1981. lib. bdg. 53.00 (ISBN 0-8240-4709-5). Garland Pub.
Salons of the "Independants", 1892 to 1895. Ed. by Theodore Reff. (Modern Art in Paris 1855 to 1900 Ser.). 320p. 1981. lib. bdg. 53.00 (ISBN 0-8240-4710-9). Garland Pub.
Salons of the "Independants", 1896 to 1900. Ed. by Theodore Reff. (Modern Art in Paris 1855 to 1900 Ser.). 280p. 1981. lib. bdg. 53.00 (ISBN 0-8240-4711-7). Garland Pub.
Salons of the "Nationale", 1890. Ed. by Theodore Reff. (Modern Art in Paris 1855 to 1900 Ser.). (Illus.). 256p. 1981. lib. bdg. 53.00 (ISBN 0-8240-4712-5). Garland Pub.
Salons of the "Nationale", 1891. Ed. by Theodore Reff. (Modern Art in Paris 1855 to 1900 Ser.). (Illus.). 302p. 1981. lib. bdg. 53.00 (ISBN 0-8240-4713-3). Garland Pub.
Salons of the "Nationale", 1892. Ed. by Theodore Reff. (Modern Art in Paris 1855 to 1900 Ser.). (Illus.). 294p. 1981. lib. bdg. 53.00 (ISBN 0-8240-4714-1). Garland Pub.
Salons of the "Nationale", 1893. Ed. by Theodore Reff. (Modern Art in Paris 1855 to 1900 Ser.). (Illus.). 275p. 1981. lib. bdg. 53.00 (ISBN 0-8240-4715-X). Garland Pub.
Salons of the "Nationale", 1894. Ed. by Theodore Reff. (Modern Art in Paris 1855 to 1900 Ser.). (Illus.). 254p. 1981. lib. bdg. 53.00 (ISBN 0-8240-4716-8). Garland Pub.
Salons of the "Nationale", 1895. Ed. by Theodore Reff. (Modern Art in Paris 1855 to 1900 Ser.). (Illus.). 288p. 1981. lib. bdg. 53.00 (ISBN 0-8240-4717-6). Garland Pub.
Salons of the "Nationale", 1896. Ed. by Theodore Reff. (Modern Art in Paris 1855 to 1900 Ser.). (Illus.). 263p. 1981. lib. bdg. 53.00 (ISBN 0-8240-4718-4). Garland Pub.
Salons of the "Nationale", 1897. Ed. by Theodore Reff. (Modern Art in Paris 1855 to 1900 Ser.). (Illus.). 291p. 1981. lib. bdg. 53.00 (ISBN 0-8240-4719-2). Garland Pub.
Salons of the "Nationale", 1898. Ed. by Theodore Reff. (Modern Art in Paris 1855 to 1900 Ser.). (Illus.). 259p. 1981. lib. bdg. 53.00 (ISBN 0-8240-4720-6). Garland Pub.
Salons of the "Nationale", 1899. Ed. by Theodore Reff. (Modern Art in Paris 1855 to 1900 Ser.). (Illus.). 256p. 1981. lib. bdg. 53.00 (ISBN 0-8240-4721-4). Garland Pub.
Salons of the "Refuses". Ed. by Theodore Reff. (Modern Art in Paris 1855 to 1900 Ser.). 133p. 1981. lib. bdg. 53.00 (ISBN 0-8240-4722-2). Garland Pub.
Salons Success Society. Karl H. Flugel. LC 78-73478. 330p. 1981. lib. bdg. 50.00 (ISBN 0-933136-00-5). Academie Pr.
Salons Victoriens aux Cabanes D'Emigrants: Il y a Cent Ans Erckman-Chatrian. Stephen J. Foster. (American University Studies II-Romance Languages & Literature: Vol. 38). 259p. 1986. text ed. 39.45 (ISBN 0-8204-0281-8). P Lang Pubs.
Saloon Girl. Dirk Fletcher. (Spur Ser.: No. 17). 208p. (Orig.). 1986. pap. 2.50 (ISBN 0-8439-2383-0, Leisure). Leisure NY.
Saloon Keeper's Daughter Saved. Bertha Mackey. 15p. 1982. pap. 0.15 (ISBN 0-686-36264-0); pap. 0.25 2 copies (ISBN 0-686-37285-9). Faith Pub HSe.
Saloon on the Rocky Mountain Mining Frontier. Elliott West. LC 78-24090. (Illus.). xx, 197p. 1979. 17.95x (ISBN 0-8032-4704-4). U of Nebr Pr.
Saloon Problem & Social Reform. John M. Barker. LC 76-112521. (Rise of Urban America Ser.). 1970. Repr. of 1905 ed. 23.50 (ISBN 0-405-02434-7). Ayer Co Pubs.
Saloon: Public Drinking in Chicago & Boston, 1880-1920. Perry Duis. LC 83-6971. (Illus.). 392p. 1983. 34.95 (ISBN 0-252-01010-8). U of Ill Pr.
Saloon Survival. Andy Kane. LC 83-6414. (Illus.). 112p. 1983. pap. 6.00 (ISBN 0-87364-267-8). Paladin Pr.
Saloon Tokens of the United States. Joseph Schmidt & Rich Hartzog. 400p. 1988. write for info. (ISBN 0-912317-06-X). World Exo.
Saloons of the American West: An Illustrated Chronicle. Robert L. Brown & Ed Collman. (Illus.). 144p. 1978. 16.50x (ISBN 0-913582-24-7). Sundance.
Saloons of the Old West. Richard Erdoes. LC 79-2220. (Illus.). 1979. 13.95 (ISBN 0-394-49824-0). Knopf.
Saloons of the Old West. Richard Erdoes. LC 84-22537. (Illus.). 288p. 1985. pap. 12.50 (ISBN 0-935704-25-6). Howe Brothers.
Sal's Book. Sal Liquori. (PSI Patrol Ser.). 160p. (Orig.). (gr. 7 up). 1985. 2.25 (ISBN 0-590-33201-5, Point). Scholastic Inc.
Salsa. Earl Atkinson. (Ballroom Dance Ser.). 1986. lib. bdg. 79.95 (ISBN 0-8490-3639-9). Gordon Pr.
Salsa. Ed. by Raoul Gordon. 1976. lib. bdg. 59.95 (ISBN 0-8490-0989-8). Gordon Pr.
Salsa. (Ballroom Dance Ser.). 1985. lib. bdg. 64.00 (ISBN 0-87700-791-8). Revisionist Pr.
Salsa. (Ballroom Dance Ser.). 1986. lib. bdg. 64.95 (ISBN 0-8490-3282-2). Gordon Pr.
Salsa Book. Jacqueline H. McMahan. LC 85-63671. 160p. 1986. 12.95 (ISBN 0-9612150-2-X); pap. 9.95 perfect bdg. (ISBN 0-9612150-3-8). Olive Pr.
Salsa! The Rhythm of Latin Music. Charley Gerard & Marty Sheller. Ed. by Larry W. Smith. (Performance in World Music Ser.: No. 3). 160p. 1988. 24.95 (ISBN 0-941677-11-7); pap. 14.95 (ISBN 0-941677-09-5). White Cliffs Media.
Salsas! Andrea Chesman. LC 85-17114. (Specialty Cookbook Ser.). (Illus.). 144p. (Orig.). 1985. 19.95 (ISBN 0-89594-179-1); pap. 7.95 (ISBN 0-89594-178-3). Crossing Pr.
Salsbury Story: A Medical Missionary's Lifetime of Public Service. Clarence G. Salsbury. LC 72-101100. (Illus.). pap. 74.10 (ISBN 0-317-58773-0, 2029657). Bks Demand UMI.
Salt. Norma M. Bracy. (Illus.). 32p. (gr. k-12). 1986. pap. text ed. 2.00 (ISBN 0-915783-03-7). Book Binder.
SALT. Duncan Bush. LC 86-70095. 70p. 1986. pap. 9.95 (ISBN 0-907476-55-4, Pub. by Poetry Wales Pr UK). Dufour.
Salt. Harve Zemach & Margot Zemach. LC 65-12312. (Illus.). 32p. (ps-3). 1977. 10.95 (ISBN 0-374-36385-4). FS&G.
Salt Air. Sharon Bryan. (New Poets Ser.). 64p. 1983. 15.00x (ISBN 0-8195-2112-4); pap. 8.95 (ISBN 0-8195-1112-9). Wesleyan U Pr.
Salt & Hypertension: Proceedings of the Lewis K. Dahl Symposium. Ed. by Junichi Iwai. LC 82-1090. (Illus.). 320p. 1982. monograph 32.50 (ISBN 0-89640-072-7). Igaku-Shoin.
Salt & Light. Matthew De Brincat. 56p. (gr. 6up). 1983. pap. 3.00 (ISBN 0-911423-00-1). Bible-Speak.
Salt & Light: Talks & Writings on the Sermon on the Mount. rev. ed. Eberhard Arnold. Ed. & tr. by Hutterian Brethren. 338p. 1986. pap. 6.00 (ISBN 0-87486-174-8). Plough.
Salt & Pepper Shakers. Helene Guarnaccia. (Illus.). 176p. 1985. pap. 9.95 (ISBN 0-89145-295-8). Collector Bks.
Salt-Cellars. C. H. Spurgeon. 1976. pap. 7.75 (ISBN 0-686-16837-2). Pilgrim Pubns.
Salt Dome Utilization & Environmental Considerations: Proceedings of a Symposium. Ed. by Joseph D. Martinez. x, 424p. 1977. pap. 25.00 (ISBN 0-8071-0380-2). La State U Pr.
Salt Domes, Gulf Region, United States & Mexico. 2nd ed. Michel T. Halbouty. LC 79-16044. 584p. 1979. 85.00x (ISBN 0-87201-803-2). Gulf Pub.
Salt Eaters. Toni C. Bambara. LC 81-51023. 304p. 1981. pap. 5.95 (ISBN 0-394-75050-0, Vin). Random.
Salt Ecstasies. James L. White. LC 81-82140. 53p. 1981. 10.00 (ISBN 0-915308-31-2); pap. 5.00 (ISBN 0-915308-32-0). Graywolf.
Salt, Evaporites & Brines: An Annotated Bibliography. Vivian S. Hall & Mary R. Spencer. LC 83-42609. 224p. 1984. lib. bdg. 87.50x (ISBN 0-89774-042-4). Oryx Pr.
Salt for Society. Phillip Keller. 1986. 5.95 (ISBN 0-8499-3059-6). Word Bks.
Salt for Society. W. Phillip Keller. 160p. 1981. 8.95 (ISBN 0-8499-0290-8). Word Bks.
Salt-Free Baking at Home. Prudence H. Ahrens. 1985. pap. 10.95 (ISBN 0-911506-19-5). Thueson.
Salt-Free Cooking with Herbs & Spices. June Roth. LC 77-81178. 204p. 1977. pap. 9.95 (ISBN 0-8092-7722-0). Contemp Bks.
Salt-Free Diet Book: An Appetizing Way to Help Reduce High Blood Pressure. Graham MacGregor. (Illus.). 128p. 1985. 12.95 (ISBN 0-668-05966-4); pap. 7.95 (ISBN 0-668-05972-9). Arco.
Salt-Free Diet Cook Book. Emil G. Conason & Ella Metz. pap. 4.95 (ISBN 0-399-51052-4, G&D). Putnam Pub Group.
Salt Free Health Sauerkraut Cook Book. 8th ed. Paul C. Bragg & Patricia Bragg. (Illus.). pap. 3.95 (ISBN 0-87790-025-6). Health Sci.
Salt-Free Herb Cookery. Edith Stovel. (Illus.). 32p. 1986. pap. 1.95 (ISBN 0-88266-342-9, Garden Way Pub). Storey Comm Inc.
Salt Glands in Birds & Reptiles. M. Peaker & J. L. Linzell. LC 75-314900. (Monographs of the Physiological Society: No. 32). pap. 79.50 (ISBN 0-317-28146-1, 2022465). Bks Demand UMI.
SALT Handbook. Michael B. Donley. 1979. pap. text ed. 3.75 (ISBN 0-686-50012-1). Heritage Found.
SALT Handbook: Key Documents & Issues, 1972-1979. Ed. by Roger Labrie. 1979. pap. 17.00 (ISBN 0-8447-3316-4). Am Enterprise.
Salt II & American Security. Gordon T. Humphrey et al. LC 80-82366. (Special Report Ser.). 65p. 1980. write for info. Inst Foreign Policy Anal.
Salt II: Illusion & Reality. Robert Johanson. (Working Papers: No.9). 1978. pap. 2.00 (ISBN 0-911646-16-7). World Policy.
Salt in My Kitchen. Jeanette W. Lockerbie. (Quiet Time Books). 1967. pap. 3.50 (ISBN 0-8024-7500-0). Moody.
Salt Industry of Bengal Seventeen Fifty-Seven to Eighteen Hundred. Balai Barui. 1985. 17.50x (ISBN 0-8364-1478-0, Pub. by KP Bagchi India). South Asia Bks.

Salt Is Leaving. J. B. Priestley. Ed. by J. Barzun & W. H. Taylor. LC 81-47381. (Crime Fiction 1950-1975 Ser.). 247p. 1983. lib. bdg. 18.00 (ISBN 0-8240-4988-8). Garland Pub.

Salt Is Leaving. J. B. Priestley. 224p. 1986. pap. 3.50 (ISBN 0-88184-227-3). Carroll & Graf.

Salt Lake City: The Center of Scenic America. Ed. by Charles Tomas. (Colourpicture Travel Ser.). 32p. pap. write for info. (ISBN 0-938440-49-7). Colourpicture.

Salt Lake Guide, 1988. Ed. by Marrian Montgomery et al. (Illus.). 256p. 1987. pap. text ed. 6.95 (ISBN 0-318-23177-8). Martam Pubns.

Salt Lake Temple: A Monument to a People. Ed. by Charles M. Hamilton & C. Nina Cutrubus. (Illus.). 208p. 1983. write for info. (ISBN 0-913535-01-X); pap. write for info. (ISBN 0-913535-02-8); Ltd. Ed. 250.00 (ISBN 0-913535-00-1). Univ Servs Inc.

Salt Lakes. W. D. Williams. (Developments in Hydrobiology Ser.: No. 5). 458p. 1982. 95.00 (ISBN 90-6193-756-6, Pub. by Junk Pubs Netherlands). Kluwer Academic.

Salt Line. Elizabeth Spencer. (Penguin Fiction Ser.). 312p. 1985. pap. 6.95 (ISBN 0-14-007665-4). Penguin.

Salt Maker of Maloon. Gillian Soudah. 1988. 30.00x (ISBN 0-86025-414-3, Pub. by Ian Henry Pubns England). State Mutual Bk.

Salt Marshes & Salt Deserts of the World. 2nd ed. V. J. Chapman. 1974. 90.00x (ISBN 3-7682-0927-X). Lubrecht & Cramer.

Salt of Pleasure: Twentieth Century Finnish Poetry. Tr. by Aili Jarvenpa. Date not set. pap. 7.50 (ISBN 0-89823-048-9). New Rivers Pr.

Salt of the Desert Sun: A History of Salt Production & Trade in the Central Sudan. Paul E. Lovejoy. (African Studies Ser.: No. 46). (Illus.). 352p. 1986. 47.50 (ISBN 0-521-30182-3). Cambridge U Pr.

Salt of the Earth. Bernadette Pruitt. LC 87-83381. 90p. 1988. 14.95 (ISBN 0-934188-27-0). Evans Pubns.

Salt of the Earth. Clarence M. Wagner. Ed. by Tru-Faith Pub. 80p. (Orig.). 1981. pap. 3.50x (ISBN 0-937498-01-7). Tru-Faith.

Salt of the Earth. Michael Wilson. (Illus.). 208p. 1978. pap. 10.95 (ISBN 0-912670-45-2). Feminist Pr.

Salt of the Earth: A Narrative on the Life of Abba Isidore of Gethsemane Skete. Paul Florensky. Ed. by Abbot Herman. Tr. by Richard Betts & Abbott Herman. LC 88-60563. (Illus.). 150p. (Orig.). 1988. pap. 5.00 (ISBN 0-938635-25-5). St Herman AK.

Salt of the Earth: The History of the Catholic Diocese of Salt Lake City 1776-1987. Bernice M. Mooney. Ed. by Jerome C. Stoffel. LC 87-72756. (Illus.). 546p. 1987. 25.00 (ISBN 0-9619627-0-4). Catholic Diocese SLC.

Salt of the Earth: The Story of a Film. Herbert Biberman. Ed. by Carlos E. Cortes. LC 76-1248. (Chicano Heritage Ser.). (Illus.). 1976. Repr. of 1965 ed. 14.00x (ISBN 0-405-09486-8). Ayer Co Pubs.

Salt of the Earth: The Story of a Film. Herbert Biberman. 373p. 1987. 5.95 (ISBN 0-918432-83-9, Beacon Press). NY Zoetrope.

Salt One: The Limitations of Arms Negotiations. Jonathan Haslam & Theresa Osborne. 56p. (Orig.). 1987. pap. text ed. 7.00 (ISBN 0-941700-09-7). JH FPI SAIS.

Salt: Or, the Education of Griffith Adams. A Novel. Charles G. Norris. LC 80-25152. (Lost American Fiction Ser.). 394p. 1981. Repr. of 1918 ed. 19.95x (ISBN 0-8093-1011-2). S Ill U Pr.

Salt River Project: A Case Study in Cultural Adaptation to an Urbanizing Community. Courtland Smith. LC 76-187826. 151p. 1972. pap. 3.75x (ISBN 0-8165-0336-2). U of Ariz Pr.

Salt Satyagraha in Coastal Andhra. C. M. Naidu. 238p. 1986. 13.50x (ISBN 0-8364-2033-0, Pub. by Mittal). South Asia Bks.

Salt-Sea Mastodon: A Reading of Moby-Dick. Robert Zoellner. 1973. 30.00x (ISBN 0-520-02339-0). U of Cal Pr.

Salt Stone: Selected Poems. John Woods. LC 83-20747. 224p. 1985. 16.00 (ISBN 0-937872-18-0); pap. 8.00 (ISBN 0-937872-19-9). Dragon Gate.

Salt Tectonics. M. K. Jenyon. 196p. 1986. 92.50 (ISBN 1-85166-015-1, Pub. by Elsevier Applied Sci England). Elsevier.

Salt: The Brand Name Guide to Sodium Content. Bonnie F. Liebman et al. 1985. pap. 4.50 (ISBN 0-446-32847-2). Warner Bks.

Salt: The Complete Brand Name Guide to Sodium Content. Michael M. Jacobson et al. LC 82-40505. 320p. 1983. pap. 5.95 (ISBN 0-89480-361-1, 361). Workman Pub.

SALT: The Primary Cause of Disease? James H. Johnson. pap. 3.00 (ISBN 0-317-55120-5). Truth Seeker.

SALT Twelve. Francis A. Porter. 288p. (Orig.). 1988. pap. 9.95 (ISBN 0-936784-58-X, Fithian Pr). J Daniel.

Salt-Water Aquarium in the Home. Robert P. Straughan. (Illus.). 384p. 1959. 19.95 (ISBN 0-498-01531-9). A S Barnes.

Salt Water Fishing. Mark Sosin & George Poveromo. (Illus.). 88p. (Orig.). 1988. pap. 12.95 (ISBN 0-945443-00-5). M Sosin Comns.

Salt Water Fishing for Fun & Food. M. John Powell. (Illus.). 1982. pap. 8.95 (ISBN 0-941238-03-2). Penobscot Bay.

Salt-Water Purification. 2nd ed. K. S. Spiegler. LC 77-21330. (Illus.). 190p. 1977. 45.00x (ISBN 0-306-31030-9, Plenum Pr). Plenum Pub.

Saltair. Nancy D. McCormick & John S. McCormick. (Bonneville Bks.). (Illus.). 136p. (Orig.). 1985. 30.00 (ISBN 0-87480-244-X); pap. 9.95 (ISBN 0-87480-133-8). U of Utah Pr.

Saltair na Rann. Oengus the Culdee. Tr. by B. MacCarthy from Irish. 1987. pap. 9.95 (ISBN 0-89979-036-4). British Am Bks.

Saltair Na Rann. Ed. by William H. Stokes. (Anecdota Oxoniensia Ser.: No. 3). 1988. Repr. of 1883 ed. 35.00 (ISBN 0-404-63953-4). AMS Pr.

Saltatoria (Bush-Crickets, Crickets & Grasshoppers) of Northern Europe. Knud T. Holst. (Fauna Entomologica Scandinavica: No. 16). (Illus.). 127p. 1986. 21.75 (ISBN 90-04-07860-6, Pub. by E J Brill). Heinman.

Saltbound: A Winter on Block Island. Chip Williamson. LC 79-26330. (Illus.). 1980. 10.95 (ISBN 0-416-00501-2, 0166). Routledge Chapman & Hall.

Salted Lemons. Doris B. Smith. LC 80-66250. 240p. (gr. 3-7). 1980. 9.95 (ISBN 0-02-778060-0, Four Winds). Macmillan.

Salterton Trilogy. Robertson Davies. 1986. pap. 9.95 (ISBN 0-14-008446-0). Penguin.

Salterton Trilogy. Date not set. 9.95 (ISBN 0-317-53372-X, Harv). HarBraceJ.

Saltmaker. Bob Reiss. 1988. 17.95 (ISBN 0-317-66851-X). Viking.

Saltmaker. Robert Reiss. LC 87-40447. 368p. 1988. 17.95 (ISBN 0-670-80247-6). Viking.

Saltmarsh Ecology. S. P. Long & C. F. Mason. (Tertiary Level Biology Ser.). 1983. 35.00 (ISBN 0-412-00301-5, NO. 5034, Pub. by Chapman & Hall); pap. 16.95 (ISBN 0-412-00311-2, NO. 5035). Routledge Chapman & Hall.

Saltmarsh Murders. Gladys Mitchell. (Portway Ser.). 328p. 1987. lib. bdg. 17.50 (ISBN 0-7451-7079-X, Pub. by Chivers Pr UK). G K Hall.

Saltonstall Papers, 1607-1815, 2 vols. Ed. by Robert E. Moody. (Collections of the Massachusetts Historical Society: Vols. 80-81). (Illus.). 1972-74. 40.00 (ISBN 0-934909-24-5). Vol. 1 1972, 574 pps (ISBN 0-934909-25-3). Vol. 2 1974, 655 pps. Mass Hist Soc.

Saltonstalls of New England: 350 Years in Public Life. Ed. by Robert E. Moody. (Massachusetts Historical Society Picture Book Ser.). 1978. pap. 2.50 (ISBN 0-934909-14-8). Mass Hist Soc.

Saltwater Aquarium Fishes. Herbert R. Axelrod & Warren Burgess. 16.95 (ISBN 0-87666-138-X, H-914). TFH Pubns.

Saltwater Fisherman's Bible. rev. ed. Erwin A. Bauer. LC 82-2388. (Illus.). 208p. 1983. pap. 7.95 (ISBN 0-385-17220-6, Pub. by Outdoor Bible). Doubleday.

Saltwater Fishing in Washington. 2nd ed. Frank Haw & Raymond M. Buckley. Ed. by Stan Jones. (Illus.). 200p. (Orig.). 1988. pap. 8.95 (ISBN 0-939936-00-3). Jones Pub.

Saltwater Flats: A Silent Film. Elihu Blotnick. LC 74-18166. (Illus.). 64p. 1975. pap. 12.95 (ISBN 0-915090-00-7). Calif Street.

Saltwater Intrusion. Sam F. Atkinson et al. (Illus.). 433p. 1986. 49.95 (ISBN 0-87371-054-1). Lewis Pubs Inc.

Salty Colorado. Taylor O. Miller et al. (Illus.). 103p. (Orig.). 1986. pap. 9.50 (ISBN 0-89164-093-2). Conservation Foun.

Salty Dog Talk: The Nautical Origins of Everyday Expressions. Bill Beavis & Richard G. McCloskey. (Illus.). 96p. 1983. pap. 5.95 (ISBN 0-229-11705-8, Pub. by Adlard Coles). Sheridan.

Salty Stories of Cape Cod. Noel W. Beyle. (No. 23). (Illus.). 48p. (Orig., Recipes by Lee Baldwin). 1984. pap. 0.95 (ISBN 0-912609-06-0). First Encounter.

Saltykov & the Russian Squire. Nikander Strelsky. Repr. of 1940 ed. 17.50 (ISBN 0-404-06298-9). AMS Pr.

Salud, Amor y Pesetas! Basic Communication in Spanish. Frederick Suarez-Richard. 169p. 1980. pap. text ed. 9.00 net (ISBN 0-15-578050-6, HC). HarBraceJ.

Salud Mental: Un Enfoque Cristiano. Mark Cosgrove & James Mallory, Jr. Tr. by Wesley Vargas from Eng. (Curriculo de la Universidad Cristiana Libre Ser.). 88p. 1982. pap. text ed. 3.75 (ISBN 0-89922-195-5). Edit Caribe.

Saluda County, South Carolina, Epitaphs: Still Villages. June A. Seay. LC 86-90675. (Registry of Tombstone Epitaphs Ser.: Vol. I). (Illus.). 227p. (Orig.). 1987. pap. 32.50 (ISBN 0-9617786-0-1) (ISBN 0-9617786-1-X). June A Seay.

Salus: Low-Cost Rural Health Care & Health Manpower Training, Vol. 10. Ed. by Rosanna M. Bechtel. 148p. 1984. pap. text ed. 10.00 (ISBN 0-88936-388-9, IDRC216, IDRC). UNIPUB.

Salus: Low-Cost Rural Health Care & Health Manpower Training: A Cumulative Index of Volumes One Through Ten. Ed. by Rosanna M. Bechtel. 150p. 1984. pap. text ed. 10.00 (ISBN 0-88936-389-7, IDRC217, IDRC). UNIPUB.

SALUS: Low-Cost Rural Health Care & Health Manpower Training: A Cumulative Index to Volumes 11-15. Ed. by Rosanna M. Bechtel. 97p. 1985. pap. 10.00 (ISBN 0-88936-428-1, IDRC232 5071, IDRC). UNIPUB.

Salus: Low-Cost Rural Health Care & Health Manpower Training: An Annotated Bibliography with Special Emphasis on Developing Countries, Vol. 5. Ed. by Rosanna M. Bechtel. 94p. 1980. pap. 10.00 (ISBN 0-88936-233-5, IDRC144, IDRC). UNIPUB.

Salus: Low Cost Rural Health Care & Health Manpower Training: An Annotated Bibliography with Special Emphasis on Developing Countries, Vol. 6. 157p. 1981. pap. 10.00 (ISBN 0-88936-249-1, IDRC153, IDRC). UNIPUB.

Salus: Low-Cost Rural Health Care & Health Manpower Training: An Annotated Bibliography with Special Emphasis on Developing Countries, Vol. 7. Ed. by R. M. Bechtel. 144p. 1981. pap. 10.00 (ISBN 0-88936-287-4, IDRC165, IDRC). UNIPUB.

SALUS: Low-Cost Rural Health Care & Health Manpower Training: An Annotated Bibliography with Special Emphasis on Developing Countries, Vol. 8. 1981. pap. 10.00 (ISBN 0-88936-301-3, IDRC173, IDRC). UNIPUB.

Salus: Low-Cost Rural Health Care & Health Manpower Training: An Annotated Bibliography with Special Emphasis on Developing Countries, Vol. 9. Ed. by Rosanna M. Bechtel. 149p. 1983. pap. 10.00 (ISBN 0-88936-322-6, IDRC187, IDRC). UNIPUB.

SALUS: Low-Cost Rural Health Care & Health Manpower Training: An Annotated Bibliography with Special Emphasis on Developing Countries, Vols. 12-14. Ed. by Rosanna M. Bechtel. 1984. Vol. 12, 137p. pap. 10.00 (ISBN 0-88936-417-6, IDRC225, IDRC); Vol. 13, 140p. pap. 10.00 (ISBN 0-88936-420-6, IDRC227); Vol. 14, 143p. pap. 10.00 (ISBN 0-88936-421-4, IDRC228). UNIPUB.

SALUS: Low-Cost Rural Health Care & Health Manpower Training: An Annotated Bibliography with Special Emphasis on Developing Countries, Vol. 15. Ed. by Rosanna M. Bechtel. 145p. 1985. pap. 10.00 (ISBN 0-88936-425-7, IDRC230, IDRC). UNIPUB.

Salut et Fraternite: Avec: Alain et R. Rolland. Romain Rolland. 184p. 1969. 7.95 (ISBN 0-686-55272-5). French & Eur.

Salut (1944-1946; see Memoires de Guerre.

Salutary Neglect: Colonial Administration Under the Duke of Newcastle. James A. Henretta. LC 70-166377. 388p. 1972. 46.00x (ISBN 0-691-05196-8). Princeton U Pr.

Salutation to Five: Mrs. Fitzherbert, Edmund Warre, Sir William Butler, Leo Tolstoy, Sir Mark Sykes. facs. ed. Shane Leslie, 3rd. LC 75-126231. (Biography Index Reprint Ser.). 1951. 17.00 (ISBN 0-8369-8027-1). Ayer Co Pubs.

Salutations see Hunger & Thirst & Other Plays.

Salute America. Arno Breker. (Illus.). 6p. 1985. portfolio 90.00 (ISBN 0-914301-02-0). West Art.

Salute to Bazarada & Other Stories. Sax Rohmer. 311p. 1972. 10.00 (ISBN 0-685-26828-4). Bookfinger.

Salute to Black Civil Rights Leaders. Ed. by Richard L. Green et al. (Black History Publications Ser.). (Illus., Orig.). pap. text ed. 1.00 (ISBN 0-9616156-3-X). Empak Pub.

Salute to Hill County (TX) Its History & Its People. Jack W. Smith & Judith Swearingen. (Illus.). 100p. 1987. write for info. (ISBN 0-912172-32-0). Hill Coll Pr.

Salute to Roy Campbell. Alister Kershaw et al. (Illus.). 128p. 1984. 75.00x (ISBN 0-930126-14-9). Typographeum.

Salute to Spring. Meridel Le Sueur. LC 75-38588. 192p. (Orig.). 1983. pap. 2.75 (ISBN 0-7178-0463-1). Intl Pubs Co.

Salute to Truro. Kenneth Pelmear. 1985. 6.00x (ISBN 0-907566-31-6, Pub. by Dyllansow & Truran). State Mutual Bk.

Salute to Valor: Heroes of the United Nations. Linton Wells. LC 73-167435. (Essay Index Reprint Ser.). Repr. of 1942 ed. 20.00 (ISBN 0-8369-2729-X). Ayer Co Pubs.

Salute Your Shorts: Life at Summer Camp. Thomas Hill & Steve Slavkin. LC 84-40677. (Illus.). 160p. 1986. pap. 5.95 (ISBN 0-89480-034-5). Workman Pub.

Salutes & Censures. Dennis Brutus. LC 85-71383. 224p. 1988. 29.95 (ISBN 0-86543-011-X); pap. 9.95 (ISBN 0-86543-012-8). Africa World.

Salvacion: Obra de Dios. Bert Dominy. Tr. by Ruben Zorzoli & Alicia Zorzoli. (Biblioteca de Doctrina Cristiana). 156p. (Orig., Span.). 1988. pap. 5.25 (ISBN 0-311-09118-0). Casa Bautista.

Salvacion: Su Seguridad, Creteza y Gozo. 2nd ed. Jorge Cutting. Ed. by Roger P. Daniel. Tr. by Sara Bautista from Eng. (Serie Diamante). (Illus.). 48p. (Span.). 1982. pap. 0.85 (ISBN 0-942504-05-4). Overcomer Pr.

Salvacion y las Dudas de Algunas Personas. 2nd ed. Alejandro Marshall & Gordon H. Bennett. Tr. by Sara Bautista from Span. (Serie Diamante). (Illus.). 36p. (Eng.). 1982. pap. 0.85 (ISBN 0-942504-01-1). Overcomer Pr.

Salvado Margen. Jorge L. Morales. (Coleccion Algas: No. 1). 184p. 1983. 12.00. Edit Asol.

Salvador. Joan Didion. 1983. pap. 5.95 (ISBN 0-671-50174-7). WSP.

Salvador Allende. Hedda Garza. (World Leaders - Past & Present Ser.). (Illus.). 112p. (YA) (gr. 7-12). 1989. 16.95 (ISBN 1-55546-824-1). Chelsea Hse.

Salvador Dali. Meryle Secrest. (Illus.). 320p. 1986. 22.50 (ISBN 0-525-24459-X). Dutton.

Salvador Dali. Meryle Secrest. (Illus.). 320p. 1987. pap. 9.95 (ISBN 0-525-48334-9, Obelisk). Dutton.

Salvador Dali. James T. Soby. LC 68-8368. (Museum of Modern Art Publications in Reprint Ser). (Illus.). 1970. Repr. of 1946 ed. 19.00 (ISBN 0-405-01522-4). Ayer Co Pubs.

Salvador Dali: Master of Surrealism & Modern Art. G. A. Cevasco. Ed. by D. Steve Rahmas. LC 79-185661. (Outstanding Personalities Ser.: No. 5). 32p. 1972. lib. bdg. 3.75 incl. catalog cards (ISBN 0-87157-505-1); pap. 2.50 vinyl laminated covers (ISBN 0-87157-005-X). SamHar Pr.

Salvador Dali: The Surrealist Angel. rev. ed. Rudolf Rom. LC 85-71012. (Illus.). 181p. 1985. 65.00 (ISBN 0-933709-00-5). DeLorenzo DiSalvo.

Salvador Land Reform: Nineteen Eighty to Nineteen Eighty-One. Laurence R. Simon. Ed. by James C. Stephens, Jr. (Impact Audit Ser.: No. 2). 55p. (Orig.). 1981. pap. 5.00 (ISBN 0-910281-01-7). Oxfam Am.

Salvador of the Twentieth Century. Percy F. Martin. 1977. lib. bdg. 59.95 (ISBN 0-8490-2562-1). Gordon Pr.

Salvador Witness: The Life & Calling of Jean Donovan. Ana Carrigan. 320p. 1984. 16.95 (ISBN 0-671-47992-X). S&S.

Salvador Witness: The Life & Calling of Jean Donvan. Ana Carrigan. 320p. 1986. pap. 3.95 (ISBN 0-345-32984-8). Ballantine.

Salvadoran Asylum Documentation Materials - Supplement II. 40.00. Natl Lawyers Guild.

Salvadoran Asylum Documentation Materials - Supplement III. 45.00. Natl Lawyers Guild.

Salvadoran Asylum Documentation Materials. 100.00. Natl Lawyers Guild.

Salvadoran Asylum Documentation Materials: Supplement I. 35.00. Natl Lawyers Guild.

Salvadorans in the United States: The Case for Extended Voluntary Departure. (Public Policy Report Ser.: No. 1). 1984. 2.00 (ISBN 0-86566-034-4). ACLU DC.

Salvados por Su Vida. Harold J. Brokke. 224p. 1978. 2.50 (ISBN 0-88113-317-5). Edit Betania.

Salvage & Destroy. Edward Llewellyn. 256p. 1986. pap. 2.95 (ISBN 0-88677-009-2). DAW Bks.

Salvage & Overhaul. 7th ed. International Fire Services Training Association Committee. Ed. by Gene P. Carlson & David England. LC 85-70110. (Illus.). 248p. 1985. pap. text ed. 13.00 (ISBN 0-87939-058-1). Fire Protect Pubns.

Salvage Archaeology at a Mississippian Burial Ground, Jefferson County, Missouri. Harold M. Ross. Ed. by Carl H. Chapman. (Research Ser.: No. 4). (Illus.). 27p. (Orig.). 1966. pap. 3.00 (ISBN 0-943414-04-0). MO Arch Soc.

Salvage Archaeology in Painted Rocks Reservoir, Western Arizona. William W. Wasley & Alfred E. Johnson. LC 64-63815. (Anthropological Papers: No. 9). 123p. 1965. pap. 10.95x (ISBN 0-8165-0273-0). U of Ariz Pr.

Salvage Archaeology in the Cow Springs Area, 1960. J. Richard Ambler & Alan P. Olson. (Technical Ser.). 57p. 1977. pap. 7.95 (TS-15). Mus Northern Ariz.

Salvage: Japanese-American Evacuation & Resettlement. Dorothy S. Thomas et al. 1975. Repr. of 1952 ed. 42.50x (ISBN 0-520-02915-1). U of Cal Pr.

Salvage of the Cynthia. Jules Verne. 4.95 (ISBN 0-685-06593-6). Assoc Bk.

Salvage of Water Damaged Books, Documents, Micrographic & Magnetic Media. Eric G. Lundquist. 144p. (Orig.). 1986. pap. 12.95 (ISBN 0-9616850-0-X). Doc Reprocessors.

Salvaged Sites in Greene County, Missouri. Richard A. Marshall. Ed. by Richard Keslin. (Missouri Archaeologist Ser.: Vol. 17, No. 4). (Illus.). 40p. (Orig.). 1955. pap. 2.00 (ISBN 0-943414-35-0). MO Arch Soc.

Salvagers. Hervey Beham. 211p. 1980. 30.00x (ISBN 0-686-78989-X, Pub. by Essex County England). State Mutual Bk.

Salvagers. Harvey Benham. (Illus.). 212p. 1980. 14.00 (ISBN 0-9505944-2-3, Pub. by Boydell & Brewer). Longwood Pub Group.

Salvaging Damaged dBASE Files. Paul W. Heiser. 200p. 1987. pap. 19.95 (ISBN 0-9616370-0-5). Comtech Pub.

Salvaging Democracy: Human Rights in the Philippines. 1985. 10.00 (ISBN 0-934143-01-3). Lawyers Comm Intl.

Salvaging Operations. (Six Hundred Ser). 1964. pap. 2.00 (ISBN 0-685-58209-4, 604). Natl Fire Prot.

Salvat Medicina, Enciclopedia de Conocimientos Basicos, 10 vols. 3000p. (Span.). 1974. Set. 320.00 (ISBN 84-7137-380-7, S-50559). French & Eur.

Salvation. Perry A. Gaspard. 1983. pap. 1.50 (ISBN 0-931867-00-2). Abundant Life Pubns.

Salvation. Ed. by John E. Hartley & R. L. Shelton. (Wesleyan Theological Perspectives Ser.: Vol. I). 1981. 14.95 (ISBN 0-87162-240-8, D4850). Warner Pr.

Salvation. Robert Hicks & Richard Bewes. (Understanding Bible Truth Ser.). (Orig.). 1981. pap. 0.95 (ISBN 0-89840-019-8). Heres Life.

Salvation. Ernest F. Kevan. 1973. pap. 4.50 (ISBN 0-87552-923-2, Evangel Pr Uk). Presby & Reformed.

Salvation see Summa Contra Gentiles.

Salvation & Atonement in the Qumran Scrolls. Paul Garnett. 160p. 1977. pap. 24.00x (Pub. by J C B Mohr BRD). Coronet Bks.

Salvation & Behavior. W. Graham Scroggie. LC 80-8075. (W. Graham Scroggie Library). 104p. 1981. pap. 4.50 (ISBN 0-8254-3735-0). Kregel.

Salvation & Liberation: In Search of a Balance Between Faith & Politics. Clodovis Boff & Leonardo Boff. Tr. by Robert R. Barr from Port. LC 84-7220. 128p. (Orig.). 1984. pap. 6.95 (ISBN 0-88344-451-8). Orbis Bks.

Salvation & Nurture of the Child of God. G. Temp Sparkman. 1983. 9.95 (ISBN 0-8170-0985-X). Judson.

Salvation & Protest: Studies of Social & Religious Movements. Roy Wallis. 1979. 26.00x (ISBN 0-312-69834-8). St Martin.

Salvation & Sanctification. John A. Hardon. 156p. 1988. write for info. (SP0680); pap. 2.50 (ISBN 0-317-67464-1). Dghtrs St Paul.

Salvation & Suicide: An Interpretation of Jim Jones, the Peoples Temple, & Jonestown. David Chidester. LC 87-45015. (Illus.). 208p. 1988. 18.95 (ISBN 0-253-35056-5). Ind U Pr.

Salvation & the Church. ARCIC II Staff. (Lambeth Study Papers). 32p. 1987. pap. 1.40 (ISBN 0-88028-063-8). Forward Movement.

Salvation & the Perfect Society: The Eternal Quest. Alfred Braunthal. LC 79-4705. 448p. 1979. lib. bdg. 25.00x (ISBN 0-87023-273-8). U of Mass Pr.

Salvation & the Savage: An Analysis of Protestant Missions & American Indian Response, 1787-1862. Robert F. Berkhofer. LC 77-22857. 1977. Repr. of 1965 ed. lib. bdg. 35.00x (ISBN 0-8371-9745-7, BESSA). Greenwood.

Salvation & the Savage: An Analysis of Protestant Missions & American Indian Response, 1787-1862. Robert F. Berkhofer, Jr. LC 65-11826. 1972. pap. text ed. 4.95x (ISBN 0-689-70290-6, 184). Atheneum.

Salvation Army & the Children. John D. Waldron. 135p. (Orig.). 1985. pap. 3.00 (ISBN 0-89216-060-8). Salvation Army.

Salvation Army & the Churches. John D. Waldron. 142p. (Orig.). 1986. pap. 3.95 (ISBN 0-89216-064-0). Salvation Army.

Salvation Army Farm Colonies. Clark C. Spence. LC 85-8763. 151p. 1985. 19.95x (ISBN 0-8165-0897-6). U of Ariz Pr.

Salvation Army in America: Selected Reports, 1899-1903. Frederick Booth-Tucker. LC 79-38439. (Religion in America, Ser. 2). 212p. 1972. Repr. of 1972 ed. 19.00 (ISBN 0-405-04060-1). Ayer Co Pubs.

Salvation Army Word Search Puzzles. David Cedervall. 75p. (Orig.). 1985. pap. 1.65 (ISBN 0-89216-061-6). Salvation Army.

Salvation Behind Bars. Roger Elwood. 1977. pap. 1.50 (ISBN 0-505-51142-8, Pub. by Tower Bks). Leisure NY.

Salvation by Faith & Your Will. Morris L. Venden. LC 78-7597. (Horizon Ser.). 1978. pap. 6.50 (ISBN 0-8127-0190-9). Review & Herald.

Salvation by Grace Through Faith in Contrast to the Restorationist Doctrine. Bob L. Ross. 1979. pap. 1.50 (ISBN 0-686-35836-8). Pilgrim Pubns.

Salvation Comes from the Lord. Arnold V. Wallenkampf. Ed. by Gerald Wheeler. LC 83-3297. 128p. (Orig.). 1983. pap. 5.95 (ISBN 0-8280-0210-X). Review & Herald.

Salvation, Entire Sanctification. Jernigan. pap. 1.95 (ISBN 0-686-12907-5). Schmul Pub Co.

Salvation for a Doomed Zoomie. Ed. by John Galvin & Frank Allnutt. LC 83-70694. 272p. 1983. 9.95 (ISBN 0-934374-01-5). Allnutt Pub.

Salvation for Sale: An Insider's View of Pat Robertson. Gerard T. Straub. 400p. 1988. 14.95 (ISBN 0-87975-436-2). Prometheus Bks.

Salvation for Sale: An Insider's View of Pat Robertson's Ministry. Gerald T. Straub. LC 86-17000. (Illus.). 323p. 1986. 19.95 (ISBN 0-87975-357-9). Prometheus Bks.

Salvation from Sin. John H. Noyes. 59.95 (ISBN 0-8490-0990-1). Gordon Pr.

Salvation from Sin, the End of Christian Faith see Male Continence.

Salvation: Growing Strong on the Bread of Life. Dusty Kemp. (Foundations for a Balaced Christian Life Ser.). 40p. 1987. pap. 1.00 (ISBN 0-944970-00-1). Kemp Ministries.

Salvation, Health & Prosperity. Paul Y. Cho. 176p. 1987. 12.95 (ISBN 0-88419-201-6, Creation Hse). Strang Comms Co.

Salvation in the Book of Acts. Fred Kinzie. Ed. by David Bernard. 224p. (Orig.). 1988. pap. 6.95 (ISBN 0-932581-40-4). Word Aflame.

Salvation in the Secular: The Moral Law in Thomas Mann's "Joseph und seine Brueder". Elaine Murdaugh. (Stanford German Studies: Vol. 10). 117p. 1976. pap. 19.60 (ISBN 3-261-01914-X). P Lang Pubs.

Salvation Is a Necessary Evil. Joseph S. Russo. Bd. with Science of Human Existence. LC 74-17615. LC 74-11822. 1981. pap. 5.95 (ISBN 0-932742-01-7). World Action.

Salvation, Learning about God's Plan. (BMC Teaching Bks.). (Illus.). 19p. (Orig.). (gr. 1-8). 1974. pap. text ed. 3.50 (ISBN 0-86508-151-4). BCM Pubn.

Salvation of the Soul. Watchman Nee. Tr. by Stephen Kaung. 1978. pap. 2.75 (ISBN 0-935008-31-4). Christian Fellow Pubs.

Salvation of the Soul & Islamic Devotion. M. A. Quasem. 200p. (Orig.). 1984. pap. 12.95 (ISBN 0-7103-0033-6, Kegan Paul). Routledge Chapman & Hall.

Salvation of the Soul & Islamic Devotion. Muhammad A. Quasem. 1981. 19.95 (ISBN 0-318-00411-9). Quasem.

Salvation on the Installment Plan. Anthony S. Magistrale. (Lamont Hall Chapbook Series for Poetry). 20p. 1982. 1.75 (ISBN 0-9603840-3-0). Andrew Mtn Pr.

Salvation Peddler. Jerry Marcus. LC 87-71614. 235p. 1988. 15.95 (ISBN 0-941394-01-8). Brittany Pubns.

Salvation, Present, Perfect, Now or Never. D. S. Warner. 63p. pap. 0.40 (ISBN 0-686-29138-7); pap. 1.00 3 copies (ISBN 0-686-29139-5). Faith Pub Hse.

Salvation: The Way Made Plain. James H. Brookes. pap. 4.95 (ISBN 0-685-61831-5). Reiner.

Salvation, Then What. Marjorie Soderholm. 1968. pap. 2.95 (ISBN 0-911802-14-2). Free Church Pubns.

Salvation Through the Gutters: Deviance & Transcendance. S. Giora Shoham. LC 78-24376. (Illus.). 274p. 1979. pap. text ed. 16.50 (ISBN 0-89116-144-9). Hemisphere Pub.

Salvationist & the Scriptures. John D. Waldron. 176p. (Orig.). 1988. pap. 3.95 (ISBN 0-89216-080-2). Salvation Army.

Salvator, 4 vols. Alexandre Dumas. 1976. pap. 9.95 ea. French & Eur.

Salvator Mundi of Leonardo da Vinci. Joanne Snow-Smith. LC 82-21190. (Illus.). 96p. (Orig.). 1982. pap. 29.95 (ISBN 0-935558-11-X). Henry Art.

Salvator Mundi of Leonardo Da Vinci. Joanne Snow-Smith. LC 82-21190. (Illus.). 96p. 1982. pap. 12.95 (ISBN 0-295-96414-6). U of Wash Pr.

Salvatore: Bull of Salvation. Eduard Pesek-Marous. Ed. by Tau Editors. LC 76-49340. (Illus.). 111p. 1976. pap. 4.95 (ISBN 0-916453-00-6). TAU Pr.

Salvatore Di Giacomo & Neapolitan Dialectal Literature. Ferdinando D. Maurino. 1951. 6.50x (ISBN 0-913298-30-1). S F Vanni.

Salve America! LC 86-80886. (Coleccion Espejo de Paciencia Ser.). 61p. (Orig.). 1986. pap. 5.95 (ISBN 0-89729-400-9). Ediciones.

Salvesen of Leith. Wray Vamplen. 320p. 1974. 17.50x (ISBN 0-7073-0152-1, Pub. by Scot Acad Pr). Longwood Pub Group.

Salz und Licht. Ed. & tr. by Hutterian Society of Brothers Staff. 186p. (Ger.). 1982. pap. 4.95 (ISBN 3-87067-166-1, Pub. by Brendow-Verlag, West Germany). Plough.

Salzburg, Pt. 2. Ed. by M. Michaela Schneider-Cuvay & Werner Rainer. (Symphony 1720-1840 Series B: Vol. 8). lib. bdg. 90.00 (ISBN 0-8240-3818-5). Garland Pub.

Salzburg Connection. Helen MacInnes. 384p. 1985. pap. 3.95 (ISBN 0-449-20895-8, Crest). Fawcett.

Salzburg Dance of Death see Jewish Wife & Other Short Plays.

Salzburg One Hundred One Zeichnungen. Marie Z. Greene-Mercier. 112p. 1969. pap. 3.50x (ISBN 0-910790-16-7). Intl Bk Co IL.

Salzburg Peter Russell Seminar 1981-1982. James Hogg. Ed. by James Hogg. (Poetic Drama & Poetic Theory Ser.). 143p. (Orig.). 1982. pap. 15.00 (ISBN 3-7052-0905-1, Pub. by Salzburg Studies). Longwood Pub Group.

Salzburg Seminar: The First Forty Years. Thomas H. Eliot & Lois J. Eliot. (Illus.). 168p. 1987. 15.95 (ISBN 0-938864-10-6). Ipswich Pr.

Salzburg Studies in English Literature & the Critics. James Hogg. (Romantic Reassessment Ser.). 94p. (Orig.). 1974. pap. 15.00 (ISBN 0-317-40091-6, Pub. by Salzburg Studies). Longwood Pub Group.

Salzburger Saga: Religious Exiles & Other Germans along the Savannah. George F. Jones. LC 83-10384. (Illus.). 221p. 1984. 18.00 (ISBN 0-8203-0689-4). U of Ga Pr.

Salzburgers & Their Descendants: Being the History of a Colony of German, Lutheran, Protestants Who Migrated to Georgia in 1734. P. A. Strobel. 320p. 1980. Repr. of 1855 ed. 15.00 (ISBN 0-89308-248-1). Southern Hist Pr.

Sam. Ann H. Scott. (Illus.). (ps-3). 1967. text ed. 14.95 (ISBN 0-07-055803-5). McGraw.

Sam. Jack Weyland. LC 81-682. 158p. 1981. 9.95 (ISBN 0-87747-854-6). Deseret Bk.

Sam, a Goat. Bayard Dominick. (Illus.). (gr. 3-5). 1968. 9.95 (ISBN 0-8392-3062-1). Astor-Honor.

Sam, a Special Puppy. Rebekah Stion. (Happy Day Bks.). (Illus.). 24p. (ps-2). 1985. 1.59 (ISBN 0-87239-879-X, 3679). Standard Pub.

Sam Adams: Pioneer in Propaganda. John C. Miller. (Illus.). 1936. 30.00x (ISBN 0-8047-0024-9); pap. 9.95x (ISBN 0-8047-0025-7). Stanford U Pr.

Sam & the Big Machines. Kathy Henderson. (Illus.). (ps-1). 1987. 10.95 (ISBN 0-233-97802-X). Andre Deutsch.

Sam & the Firefly. Philip D. Eastman. LC 58-11966. (Illus.). 72p. (gr. 1-2). 1958. 5.95 (ISBN 0-394-80006-0); lib. bdg. 6.99 (ISBN 0-394-90006-5). Beginner.

Sam & the Golden People. Marjorie Vandervelde. (Indian Culture Ser.). (gr. 4-9). 1972. 1.95 (ISBN 0-89992-027-6). Coun India Ed.

Sam & Violet Are Twins. Nicole Rubel. (Illus.). 32p. (gr. 1-3). 1981. pap. 1.95 (ISBN 0-380-76919-0, 76919-0, Camelot). Avon.

Sam & Violet Go Camping. Nicole Rubel. (Illus.). 32p. (gr. 1-3). 1981. pap. 1.95 (ISBN 0-380-76927-1, 76927-1, Camelot). Avon.

Sam & Violet's Bedtime Mystery. Nicole Rubel. (gr. k-3). 1985. pap. 2.50 (ISBN 0-380-89820-9, Camelot). Avon.

Sam & Violet's Birthday Book. Nicole Rubel. (Snuggle & Read Story Bks.). (Illus.). 32p. (Orig.). (ps-3). 1982. pap. 1.95 (ISBN 0-380-79095-5, 79095-5, Camelot). Avon.

Sam & Violet's Christmas Story. Nicole Rubel. (Illus.). 32p. (Orig.). (ps-3). 1981. pap. 1.95 (ISBN 0-380-78063-1, 78063, Camelot). Avon.

Sam & Violet's Get Well Book. Nicole Robel. 1985. pap. 2.50 (ISBN 0-380-89821-7, Camelot). Avon.

Sam at the Sea. Heinz Kurth. (Illus.). 32p. (gr. k-2). 1986. 12.95 (ISBN 0-437-53623-8, Pub. by W Heinemann Ltd). David & Charles.

Sam at the Seaside. Keith Faulkner. (Illus.). 14p. (ps-1). 1988. bds. 4.95 (ISBN 0-689-71183-2, Aladdin Bks). Macmillan.

Sam, Bangs & Moonshine. Evaline Ness. LC 66-10113. (Illus.). 48p. (ps-2). 1966. 11.95 (ISBN 0-8050-0314-2); pap. 3.95 (ISBN 0-8050-0315-0). H Holt & Co.

Sam Bass: A Novel. Bryan Woolley. LC 83-70812. 214p. 1983. 12.95 (ISBN 0-931722-25-X). Corona Pub.

Sam Cat: A Book about Weather. Gillinan Humphries & Francis Thatcher. LC 84-26297. (Stories to Learn By Ser.). (Illus.). 32p. (ps-3). 1984. lib. bdg. 12.33 (ISBN 0-516-08944-7); pap. 2.95 (ISBN 0-516-48944-5). Childrens.

Sam Chance. Benjamin Capps. 272p. 1986. pap. 2.50 (ISBN 0-441-74920-8, Pub. by Charter Bks). Ace Bks.

Sam Chance. Benjamin Capps. LC 87-9757. (Southwest Life & Letters Ser.). 281p. 1987. 22.50x (ISBN 0-87074-250-7); pap. 10.95 (ISBN 0-87074-251-5). SMU Press.

Sam Clemens of Hannibal. Dixon Wecter. LC 76-6595. Repr. of 1952 ed. 36.00 (ISBN 0-404-15328-3). AMS Pr.

Sam Crockers Boats: A Design Catalog. Sturgis Crocker. LC 84-48687. (Illus.). 320p. 1985. 18.95 (ISBN 0-87742-195-1). Intl Marine.

Sam Curd's Diary: The Diary of a True Woman. Ed. by Susan S. Arpad. LC 83-22082. viii, 172p. 1984. 24.95x (ISBN 0-8214-0730-9). Ohio U Pr.

Sam Diego, a Coloring Adventure in San Diego, California. Barbara Plunkett. (Illus.). (ps). 1977. pap. 1.25 (ISBN 0-914488-14-7). Rand-Tofua.

Sam Ellis's Island. Beatrice Siegel. LC 85-42799. (Illus.). 128p. (gr. 4-7). 1985. PLB 11.95 (ISBN 0-02-782720-8, Four Winds). Macmillan.

Sam Et Violet Sont Jumeaux. Nicole Rubel. (Illus.). 32p. (Fr.). (ps-3). 1982. pap. 1.95 (ISBN 0-380-81281-9, 81281, Camelot). Avon.

Sam Fadala's Muzzleloading Notebook. Sam Fadala. LC 85-22601. 256p. 1985. 17.95 (ISBN 0-8329-0406-6, Pub. by Winchester Pr). New Century.

Sam Fow: The San Joaquin Chinese Legacy. Sun Sylvia Minnick & Thomas W. Chinn. (Illus.). 320p. 1988. 25.00 (ISBN 0-944194-09-5); pap. 14.95 (ISBN 0-944194-10-9). Panorama West.

Sam Francis. rev. ed. Peter Selz. Ed. by Susan Einstein & Jan Butterfiled. 1985. write for info. (ISBN 0-8109-0928-6); limited edition 150.00 (ISBN 0-8109-0931-6). Abrams.

Sam Francis: Works On Paper. 1979. 3.00 (ISBN 0-910663-20-3). ICA Inc.

Sam Goldwyn. M. Freedland. 1986. 49.75X (ISBN 0-245-54262-0, Pub. by Harrap Ltd England). State Mutual Bk.

Sam H. Moore's Lost Mineral Spring. Michael P. Jones et al. (Illus.). 1984. pap. text ed. write for info. (ISBN 0-89904-073-X). Crumb Elbow Pub.

Sam Helps Out. Keith Faulkner. (Illus.). 14p. (ps-1). 1988. bds. 4.95 (ISBN 0-689-71182-4, Aladdin Bks). Macmillan.

Sam Higginbottom of Allahabad. Gary R. Hess. LC 67-17631. Repr. of 1967 ed. 37.70 (ISBN 0-8357-9816-X, 2015747). Bks Demand UMI.

Sam Hill: The Prince of Castle Nowhere. John Tuhy. (Illus.). 360p. 1983. pap. 9.95 (ISBN 0-917304-77-2). Timber.

Sam Holman. James T. Farrell. LC 83-60204. 276p. 1983. 20.95 (ISBN 0-87975-202-5). Prometheus Bks.

Sam Hook. Richard S. Wheeler. 192p. 1986. 14.95 (ISBN 0-8027-4064-2). Walker & Co.

Sam Hook. Richard S. Wheeler. 208p. 1987. pap. 2.50 (ISBN 0-345-34058-2). Ballantine.

Sam Houston. Jan Gleiter & Kathleen Thompson. LC 87-24161. (Raintree Stories Ser.). (Illus.). 32p. (Orig.). (gr. 2-3). 1987. PLB 15.33 (ISBN 0-8172-2660-5); pap. text ed. 9.26 (ISBN 0-8172-2664-8). Raintree Pubs.

Sam Houston. Herman Toepperwein. pap. 1.75 (ISBN 0-910722-09-9). Highland Pr.

Sam Houston: American Hero. Ann F. Crawford. Ed. by Melissa Roberts. (Illus.). 48p. (gr. 2-3). 1988. 10.95 (ISBN 0-89015-644-1). Eakin Pr.

Sam Houston & the Senate. John F. Kennedy. Ed. by Larry Smitherman. LC 79-14422. (Illus.). 12.50 (ISBN 0-8363-0087-4). Jenkins.

Sam Houston: Hero at San Jacinto. Catherine T. Gonzalez. (Illus.). 88p. (gr. 4-7). 6.95 (ISBN 0-89015-382-5). Eakin Pr.

Sam Houston: Hero of Texas. Jean L. Latham. LC 65-10101. (Garrard Discovery Ser.). (Illus.). (gr. 2-5). 1965. pap. 1.19 (9055). Garrard.

Sam Houston: Man of Destiny. Clifford Hopewell. 400p. 1987. 19.95 (ISBN 0-89015-572-0). Eakin Pr.

Sam Houston: The Great Designer. Llerena Friend. LC 54-13252. (Illus.). 408p. 1954. pap. 9.95 (ISBN 0-292-78422-8). U of Tex Pr.

Sam Houston...Champion of America. Allan Carpenter. (Mighty Warriors Ser.). (Illus.). 112p. (gr. 4-8). 1987. PLB 66.64 4 bk. set (ISBN 0-317-60484-8); PLB 16.06 (ISBN 0-86625-327-0). Rourke Corp.

Sam Houston's Texas. Sue Flanagan. LC 64-22338. (Illus.). 231p. 1973. Repr. of 1964 ed. 27.50 (ISBN 0-292-73363-1). U of Tex Pr.

Sam Huff: Tough Stuff. 1988. price not set. St Martin.

Sam Hughes: The Public Career of a Controversial Canadian, 1885-1916. Ronald G. Haycock. 504p. 1986. 45.00 (ISBN 0-88920-177-3, Pub. by Wilfrid Laurier Canada). Humanities.

Sam Johnson & the Blue Ribbon Quilt. Lisa C. Ernst. LC 82-9980. (Illus.). 32p. (gr. k-3). 1983. 11.75 (ISBN 0-688-01516-6); lib. bdg. 11.88 (ISBN 0-688-01517-4). Lothrop.

Sam Lawson's Oldstown Fireside Stories. facsimile ed. Harriet Beecher Stowe. LC 67-29279. (Americans in Fiction Ser.). (Illus.). 287p. lib. bdg. 27.50 (ISBN 0-8398-1874-2); pap. text ed. 12.95x (ISBN 0-89197-928-X). Irvington.

Sam Lovel's Boy, with Forest & Stream Fables. facsimile ed. Rowland E. Robinson. Ed. by Llewellyn R. Perkins. LC 70-160949. (Short Story Index Reprint Ser.). Repr. of 1901 ed. 18.00 (ISBN 0-8369-3928-X). Ayer Co Pubs.

Sam Lovel's Camps: & Other Stories, Including 'In the Green Wood' facsimile ed. Rowland E. Robinson. Ed. by Llewellyn R. Perkins. LC 77-37558. (Short Story Index Reprint Ser.). Repr. of 1934 ed. 19.00 (ISBN 0-8369-4117-9). Ayer Co Pubs.

Sam Maloof, Woodworker. Sam Maloof. LC 83-47622. (Illus.). 264p. 1983. 65.00 (ISBN 0-87011-596-0). Kodansha.

Sam Myers (Eighteen Five to Eighteen Eighty-Three) & Lydia Horner (Eighteen Thirty-Three to Nineteen Seven) Their Ancestors & Descendants. Forrest D. Myers. LC 78-71401. (Illus., Orig.). 1979. 15.00x (ISBN 0-9602156-0-3). A E Myers.

Sam Nunn on Arms Control. Ed. by Kenneth W. Thompson. LC 87-25351. (W. Alton Jones Foundation Series on Arms Control: Vol. V). 334p. (Orig.). 1988. lib. bdg. 29.75 (ISBN 0-8191-6615-4, Co-pub. by White Miller Center); pap. text ed. 16.50 (ISBN 0-317-64812-8). U Pr of Amer.

Sam Patch: Ballad of a Jumping Man. William Getz. 384p. 1986. 17.95 (ISBN 0-531-15026-7). Watts.

Sam Patch, the Big Time Jumper. new ed. Carol B. York. LC 79-66318. (Illus.). 48p. (gr. 3-6). 1980. lib. bdg. 9.59 (ISBN 0-89375-306-8); pap. 1.95 (ISBN 0-89375-305-X); cassette avail. Troll Assocs.

Sam Pezzo, P. I, Bk. 1. Vittorio Giardino. Ed. by Bernd Metz. Tr. by Tom Leighton from Fr. (Illus.). 48p. 1988. pap. 8.95 (ISBN 0-87416-057-X). Catalan Communs.

Sam Pollard of Yunnan. pap. 3.95 (ISBN 0-686-23584-3). Schmul Pub Co.

Sam Rayburn: A Bio-Bibliography. Anthony Champagne. (Bio-Bibliographies in Law & Political Science Ser.: No. 4). 1988. 35.95 (ISBN 0-313-25864-3, CSR/). Greenwood.

Sam Shepard. Ellen Oumano. 1988. pap. 3.50 (ISBN 0-312-90687-0). St Martin.

Sam Shepard. Vivian M. Patraka & Mark Siegel. LC 85-70129. (Western Writers Ser.: No. 69). (Illus.). 49p. (Orig.). 1985. pap. 2.95x (ISBN 0-88430-043-9). Boise St Univ.

Sam Shepard: Seven Plays. Sam Shepard. 288p. (Orig.). 1981. pap. 7.95 (ISBN 0-553-34330-0). Bantam.

Sam Shepard: The Life & Work of an American Dreamer. Ellen Oumano. 192p. 1986. 12.95 (ISBN 0-312-69839-9). St Martin.

Sam Shepard's Dog. Dina VonZweck. 32p. (Orig.). 1984. pap. 4.00 (ISBN 0-931567-00-9). White Deer Bks.

Sam Shepard's Metaphorical Stages. Lynda Hart. LC 86-4616. (Contributions in Drama & Theatre Studies: No. 22). 166p. 1987. 29.95 (ISBN 0-313-25373-0, HSS/). Greenwood.

Sam Shue & the Seven Satchels. LC 76-1480. (Illus.). 64p. (ps-4). 1977. 4.95 (ISBN 0-915998-02-5). Lime Rock Pr.

Sam Slick. Thomas C. Haliburton. Ed. by Ray P. Baker. 420p. 1981. Repr. of 1923 ed. lib. bdg. 45.00 (ISBN 0-8495-2373-7). Arden Lib.

Sam Szafran: Recent Works. James Lord. (Illus.). 10.00 (ISBN 0-936827-05-X). C Bernard Gallery Ltd.

Sam the Allergen. Charlotte L. Casterline. (Illus.). 26p. (Orig.). (ps-6). 1985. pap. 4.95 (ISBN 0-9617218-1-2). Info All Bk.

Sam, the Ceiling Needs Painting. Mel Poretz et al. 1977. pap. 1.75 (ISBN 0-8431-0418-X). Price Stern.

Sam the Detective & the Alef Bet Mystery. Amye Rosenberg & Patrice G. Mason. Ed. by Seymour Rossel. (Illus.). 64p. (Orig.). (gr. 1-3). 1980. pap. text ed. 3.95x (ISBN 0-87441-328-1). Behrman.

Sam the Detective's Reading Readiness Book. Amye Rosenberg. (Illus.). 63p. (ps). 1982. pap. text ed. 3.95x (ISBN 0-87441-361-3). Behrman.

Sam the Lamb & Miss Perky Pig. Davene Handershot. (Illus.). 32p. (gr. 1-3). 1986. 5.95 (ISBN 0-89962-570-3). Todd & Honeywell.

Sam the Minuteman. Nathaniel Benchley. LC 68-10211. (I Can Read History Bks.). (Illus.). 64p. (gr. k-3). 1969. 9.70i (ISBN 0-06-020479-6); PLB 10.89 (ISBN 0-06-020480-X). HarpJ.

Sam the Minuteman. Nathaniel Benchley. LC 68-10211. (Trophy I Can Read Bks.). (Illus.). 64p. (gr. k-3). 1987. pap. 3.50 (ISBN 0-06-444107-5, Trophy). HarpJ.

Sam the Scarecrow. Sharon Gordon. (Illus.). 32p. (gr. k-2). 1980. PLB 5.41 (ISBN 0-89375-387-4); pap. 1.50 (ISBN 0-89375-287-8). Troll Assocs.

Sam Thompson & Modern Drama in Ulster. Hagal Mengel. (Bremer Beitrage zur Literatur-und Ideologiegeschichte Ser.: Bd. 3). xxiv, 603p. 1986. pap. 48.55 (ISBN 3-8204-9370-0). P Lang Pubs.

Sam Tuttle's Picture Book of Old Connecticut. Sam Tuttle. LC 78-73606. (Illus., Orig.). 1979. pap. 7.95 (ISBN 0-914166-20-4). Americana Rev.

Sam-Veda Sanhita. Tr. by Ralph T. Griffith from Sanskrit. 338p. 1978. Repr. of 1907 ed. 22.00 (ISBN 0-89684-160-X). Orient Bk Dist.

Sam White's Paris: Collected Dispatches of a Newspaper Legend. Sam White. 336p. 1984. 22.95 (ISBN 0-450-06015-2, New Eng Lib). David & Charles.

Sam Who Never Forgets. Eve Rice. LC 76-30370. 32p. (ps-3). 1977. PLB 11.88 (ISBN 0-688-84088-4). Greenwillow.

Sam Who Never Forgets. Eve Rice. (Illus.). (gr. 3-5). 1980. pap. 3.95 (ISBN 0-14-050348-X, Puffin). Penguin.

Sam Who Never Forgets. Eve Rice. (ps-3). 1987. pap. 3.95 (ISBN 0-688-07335-2, Mulberry). Morrow.

Sam Williams. facsimile ed. W. S. Harrison. LC 70-39088. (Black Heritage Library Collection). Repr. of 1892 ed. 19.75 (ISBN 0-8369-9026-9). Ayer Co Pubs.

Sam, You're a Hero! Rebekah Stion. (Happy Day Bks.). (Illus.). 32p. (gr. k-2). 1987. 1.59 (ISBN 0-87403-280-6, 3780). Standard Pub.

Samadhi & Beyond. Sri S. Chakravarti. LC 74-79444. 1974. pap. 3.50 (ISBN 0-87707-135-7). Ranney Pubns.

Samadhi: Self Development in Zen, Swordsmanship, & Psychotherapy. Mike Sayama. LC 85-9894. (Transpersonal & Humanistic Psychology). 160p. 1985. 34.50x (ISBN 0-88706-146-X); pap. 10.95 (ISBN 0-88706-147-8). State U NY Pr.

Samadhi: The Superconsciousness of the Future. Mouni Sadha. (Unwin Paperbacks). 1977. pap. 8.95 (ISBN 0-04-149039-8). Unwin Hyman.

Samantha among the Brethren, by Josiah Allen's Wife. Marietta Holley. Ed. by Carolyn Gifford & Donald Dayton. (Women in American Protestan Religion 1800-1930 Ser.). 437p. 1987. lib. bdg. 60.00 (ISBN 0-8240-0664-X). Garland Pub.

Samantha Learns a Lesson, A School Story. Susan S. Adler. LC 86-60624. (American Girls Collection Ser.). (Illus.). 61p. (Orig.). (gr. 2-5). 1986. 12.95 (ISBN 0-937295-12-4); pap. 5.95 (ISBN 0-937295-13-2); audio cassette tape 8.95 (ISBN 0-937295-14-0). Pleasant Co.

Samantha on the Race Problem. Marietta Holley. LC 71-91082. (American Humorists Ser.). (Illus.). 387p. Repr. of 1892 ed. lib. bdg. 39.50 (ISBN 0-8398-0786-4). Irvington.

Samantha Rastles the Woman Question. Marietta Holley. Ed. by Jane Curry. LC 82-13482. (Illus.). 256p. 1983. 21.95 (ISBN 0-252-01020-5); cassette 8.95 (ISBN 0-252-01062-0); bk. & cassette 27.95 (ISBN 0-252-01103-1). U of Ill Pr.

Samantha Rastles the Woman Question. Marietta Holley. Ed. by Jane Curry. (Illus.). 256p. 1983. pap. 10.95 (ISBN 0-252-01306-9). U of Ill Pr.

Samantha-Rey. Sandy E. Marinacci. 112p. 1986. 7.95 (ISBN 0-8059-3022-1). Dorrance.

Samantha Saves the Day: A Summer Story. Valerie Tripp. (American Girls Collection Ser.). (Illus.). 65p. (Orig.). (gr. 2-5). 1988. 12.95 (ISBN 0-937295-40-X); pap. 5.95 (ISBN 0-937295-41-8). Pleasant Co.

Samantha Seagull's Sandals. Gordon Winch. Ed. by Rhoda Sherwood. LC 88-42923. (Partly True Tales Ser.). (Illus.). 32p. 1988. PLB 11.25 (ISBN 1-55532-909-8). Stevens Inc.

Samantha Smith: A Journey for Peace. Anne Galicich. LC 87-13614. (Taking Part Ser.). (Illus.). 64p. (gr. 3 up). 1987. PLB 9.95 (ISBN 0-87518-367-0). Dillon.

Samantha Smith: Little Ambassador. Patricia S. Martin. (Reaching Your Goal Bks.). (Illus.). 24p. (gr. 1-4). 1987. PLB 10.60 (ISBN 0-86592-173-3); PLB 84.80 set (ISBN 0-317-60376-0). Rourke Corp.

Samantha the Heroine. Muriel Miller. LC 84-81278. (Woodlander Ser.: No. 6). (Illus.). 32p. (gr. 1-4). Date not set. pap. 7.95 (ISBN 0-915677-19-9). Roundtable Pub.

Samantha the Hungry Squirrel. Muriel Miller. LC 84-81273. (Woodlander Ser.: No. 1). (Illus.). 32p. (gr. 1-4). Date not set. pap. 7.95 (ISBN 0-915677-14-8). Roundtable Pub.

Samantha's Keepsake Edition, 6 bks. Susan S. Adler et al. (American Girls Collection). (Illus.). 432p. (gr. 2-5). 1988. Boxed Set. 84.95 (ISBN 0-937295-52-3); Boxed Set. pap. 44.95 (ISBN 0-937295-53-1). Pleasant Co.

Samantha's Surprise, A Christmas Story. Maxine R. Schur. LC 86-60625. (American Girls Collection Ser.). (Illus.). 67p. (Orig.). (gr. 2-5). 1986. 12.95 (ISBN 0-937295-21-3); pap. 5.95 (ISBN 0-937295-22-1); audio cassette tape 8.95 (ISBN 0-937295-23-X). Pleasant Co.

Samaras: Photographs, 1969-1986. Lucas Samaras. Ed. by Ben Lifson. (Illus.). 176p. 1988. 50.00 (ISBN 0-89381-241-2). Aperture.

Samaritaine. Edmond Rostand. 158p. 1953. 6.95 (ISBN 0-686-55338-1). French & Eur.

Samaritan. Chaz Brenchley. 256p. 1988. 16.95 (ISBN 0-312-01813-4). St Martin.

Samaritan Chronicle No. 2 (or, Sepher Ha-Yamim) from Joshua to Nebuchadnezzar. John Macdonald. (Beiheft 107 zur Zeitschrift fuer die alttestamentliche Wissenschaft). 1969. 34.80 (ISBN 3-11-002582-5). De Gruyter.

Samaritan Liturgy, 2 vols. Ed. by Arthur E. Cowley. LC 77-87608. Repr. of 1909 ed. Set. 65.00 (ISBN 0-404-16430-7). AMS Pr.

Samaritan Oral Law & Ancient Traditions. Moses Gaster. LC 77-87609. Repr. of 1932 ed. 22.00 (ISBN 0-404-16433-1). AMS Pr.

Samaritan Problem: Studies in the Relationship of Samaritanism, Judaism, & Early Christianity. John Bowman. Tr. by Alfred M. Johnson, Jr. from Ger. LC 75-20042. (Pittsburgh Theological Monographs: No. 4). 1975. pap. 8.75 (ISBN 0-915138-04-2). Pickwick.

Samaritan Scheme. David Christopher. (Orig.). 1978. pap. 2.25 (ISBN 0-89083-413-X). Zebra.

Samaritan Strategy: A New Agenda for Christian Activism. V. Doner. 13.95 (ISBN 0-943497-29-9); pap. 13.95 (ISBN 0-943497-23-X). Wolgemuth & Hyatt.

Samaritans. Reinhard Pummer. (Iconography of Religions Ser.: Vol. XXIII-5). (Illus.). xiv, 46p. 1987. pap. 32.75 (ISBN 90-04-07891-6, Pub. by E J Brill). Heinman.

Samaritans Documents Relating to Their History, Religion & Life. Ed. & tr. by John Bowman. LC 77-4949. (Pittsburgh Original Texts & Translations Ser.: No. 2). 1977. pap. 11.50 (ISBN 0-915138-27-1). Pickwick.

Samaritans: History, Doctrine & Literature. M. Gaster. 1976. lib. bdg. 134.95 (ISBN 0-8490-2563-X). Gordon Pr.

Samaritans of Molokai. facsimile ed. Charles J. Dutton. (Select Bibliographies Reprint Ser). Repr. of 1932 ed. 23.50 (ISBN 0-8369-5733-4). Ayer Co Pubs.

Samaritans: Their History, Doctrines & Literature. M. Gaster. (British Academy, London, Schweich Lectures on Biblical Archaeology Series, 1923). 1980. pap. 28.00 (ISBN 0-8115-1265-7). Kraus Repr.

Samaritans: Their Testimony to the Religion of Israel. J. Thomson. 1976. lib. bdg. 59.95 (ISBN 0-8490-2564-8). Gordon Pr.

Samarkand Dimension. David Wise. LC 86-19945. 312p. 1987. 16.95 (ISBN 0-385-19755-1). Doubleday.

Samarkand Dimension. David Wise. 272p. 1988. pap. 3.95 (ISBN 0-380-70518-4). Avon.

Samas Religious Texts Classified in the British Museum Catalogue As Hymns, Prayers, & Incantations. Ed. by Clifton D. Gray. LC 78-72728. (Ancient Mesopotamian Texts & Studies). Repr. of 1901 ed. 17.50 (ISBN 0-404-18176-7). AMS Pr.

Samavedic Chant. Wayne Howard. LC 76-49854. (Illus.). 1977. 52.00x (ISBN 0-300-01956-4). Yale U Pr.

Samayasara (the Soul Essence) Kundakunda Acharya. Tr. & commentaries by Rai B. Jaini. LC 73-3843. (Sacred Books of the Jainas: No. 8). Repr. of 1930 ed. 25.00 (ISBN 0-404-57708-3). AMS Pr.

Samba. Michael Abbensetts. 1981. pap. 4.95 (ISBN 0-413-48140-9, NO. 2569). Heinemann Ed.

Samba. Earl Atkinson. (Ballroom Dancing Ser.). 1983. lib. bdg. 79.95 (ISBN 0-87700-473-0). Revisionist Pr.

Samba. Earl Atkinson. (Ballroom Dance Ser.). 1986. lib. bdg. 79.95 (ISBN 0-8490-3632-1). Gordon Pr.

Samba Made Easy. (Ballroom Dance Ser.). 1985. lib. bdg. 74.95 (ISBN 0-87700-672-5). Revisionist Pr.

Samba Spying Case. B. M. Sinha. 200p. 1981. text ed. 17.95x (ISBN 0-7069-1392-2, Pub. by Vikas India). Advent NY.

Sambaqui: A Novel of Prehistory. Stella C. Ribeiro. Tr. by Claudia Van der Heuvel. 144p. (Port.). 1987. pap. 3.95 (ISBN 0-380-89624-9). Avon.

Sambas & Bossas: The Popular Music of Brazil. Claus Schreiner. 1988. 35.00; pap. 19.95. Chicago Review.

Sambia: Ritual & Gender in New Guinea. Gilbert Herdt. 200p. 1987. pap. text ed. write for info. (ISBN 0-03-068907-4). HR&W.

Sambo Sahib: "The Story of Little Black Sambo" & Helen Bannerman. Elizabeth Hay. (Illus.). 206p. 1981. 24.50x (ISBN 0-389-20151-0). B&N Imports.

Sambo: The Rise & Demise of an American Jester. Joseph Boskin. LC 86-8451. (Illus.). 304p. 1986. 22.95 (ISBN 0-19-504074-0). Oxford U Pr.

Sambo: The Rise & Demise of an American Jester. Joseph Boskin. 272p. 1988. pap. 8.95 (ISBN 0-19-505658-2). Oxford U Pr.

Same & Different. Illus. by Pam Adams. (Motivation Ser.). (Illus.). 16p. (Orig.). (ps-2). 1975. pap. 2.00 (ISBN 0-85953-043-4, Pub. by Child's Play England). Playspaces.

Same Blood. Mermer Blakeslee. 1989. 16.95 (ISBN 0-395-48601-7). HM.

Same Both Sides. Date not set. 4.00 (ISBN 0-87505-255-X). Borden.

Same-Day Diagnosis of Human Virus Infections. Donald M. McLean & Kathleen K. Wong. 144p. 1984. 55.00 (ISBN 0-8493-6590-2). CRC Pr.

Same-Day Surgical & Medical Care. Earleen H. Cook & Joseph L. Cook. (Public Administration Ser.: P 1738). 18p. 1985. 3.00 (ISBN 0-89028-518-7). Vance Biblios.

Same-Different. Ed. by Sharon Wheeler. (Preschool Express Ser.). (Illus.). (ps). 1984. wkbk 1.95 (ISBN 0-916119-07-6). Creat Teach Pr.

Same Door. John Updike. 1959. 11.95 (ISBN 0-394-44361-6). Knopf.

Same Door: Short Stories. John Updike. LC 81-40079. 256p. 1981. pap. 4.95 (ISBN 0-394-74763-1, Vin). Random.

Same Ghost. Jack Ridl. LC 84-73042. 68p. (Orig.). 1984. pap. 5.00 (ISBN 0-936014-13-X). Dawn Valley.

Same Jesus. Clarence M. Wagner. Ed. by Tru-Faith Publishers. 72p. (Orig.). 1981. pap. 3.50x (ISBN 0-937498-00-9). Tru-Faith.

Same Jesus: A Contemporary Christology. Ed. by Daniel A. Helminiak. 368p. 1986. 15.95 (ISBN 0-8294-0521-6). Loyola.

Same Last Name. Kathleen G. Seidel. (American Romance Ser.). 192p. 1983. pap. 2.25 (ISBN 0-373-16002-X). Harlequin Bks.

Same or Different. Barbara Gregorich. Ed. by Joan Hoffman. (Get Ready! Bks.). (Illus.). 32p. (ps). 1983. wkbk. 1.95 (ISBN 0-938256-52-1). Sch Zone Pub Co.

Same Sea in Us All. Jaan Kaplinski. Tr. by Sam Hamill from Estonian. LC 85-3743. 110p. 1985. 14.95 (ISBN 0-932576-29-X); pap. 8.95 (ISBN 0-932576-30-3). Breitenbush Bks.

Same Sex: An Appraisal of Homosexuality. Ed. by Ralph Weltge. LC 71-88184. 1969. pap. 3.95 (ISBN 0-8298-0118-9). Pilgrim NY.

Same Song--Separate Voices. The Lennon Sisters. 368p. 1987. pap. 3.95 (ISBN 0-7701-0625-0). PaperJacks US.

Same Song-Separate Voices: The Collective Memoirs of the Lennon Sisters. Dianne Lennon et al. LC 84-60761. (Illus.). 352p. 1985. 17.95 (ISBN 0-915677-10-5). Roundtable Pub.

Same Task: Different Mask Fundraising Cookbook. Cookbook Consortium Staff. 1985. pap. 1.95 (ISBN 0-318-04323-8, Pub. by Cookbk Consorts). Prosperity & Profits.

Same Thing Happened Over & Over see Novella Box.

Samed. Raja Shehaden. 172p. 1984. pap. 9.95 (ISBN 0-531-09839-7). Watts.

Samed: Journal of a West Bank Palestinian. Raja Shehadeh. LC 83-25647. 144p. 1984. pap. 9.95 (ISBN 0-915361-02-7, Dist. by Watts). Adama Pubs Inc.

Sameness & Substance. David Wiggins. 256p. 1980. 27.00x (ISBN 0-674-78595-9). Harvard U Pr.

Samenhangrelaties in de Lge-eeuwse Zinsgrammatica in Nederland. J. A. Le Loux-Schuringa. (Geschiedenis van de Taalkunde Ser.). viii, 135p. 1985. pap. write for info. (ISBN 90-6765-101-X). Foris Pubns.

Samgharakkita's Vuttodaya. 2nd ed. R. Siddharatha. 54p. 1981. Repr. of 1929 ed. 9.50 (ISBN 81-7030-083-5, Pub. by Motilal Banarsidass India). Orient Bk Dist.

Samgraha-Cudamani of Govinda. S. Subrahmanya Sastri. 4.75 (ISBN 0-8356-7354-5). Theos Pub Hse.

Samit & the Dragon. (Wellinworld Tapes & Books for Children: 2-9). 36p. (ps-4). 1985. 8.95 (ISBN 0-88684-177-1); cassette tape avail. Listen USA.

Samizdat Press in China's Provinces 1979-1981: An Annotated Guide. Claude Widor. (Bibliographical Ser.: No. 70). 157p. 1988. pap. text ed. 11.95 (ISBN 0-8179-2702-6). Hoover Inst Pr.

Samizdat Register. Ed. by Roy A. Medvedev. 1977. pap. 10.95x (ISBN 0-393-05652-X); pap. write for info. (ISBN 0-393-09081-7). Norton.

Samizdat Register Two. Ed. by Roy A. Medvedev. 1981. 24.95 (ISBN 0-393-01419-3). Norton.

Samizdat: Voices of the Soviet Opposition. Ed. by George Saunders. Tr. by Marilyn Vogt from Rus. & Ukrainian. LC 75-186692. 464p. 1974. 33.00 (ISBN 0-913460-27-3, Dist. by Path Pr NY); pap. 12.95 (ISBN 0-913460-28-1). Anchor Found.

Samkara & Bradley. S. N. Shrivastava. 1968. 18.50 (ISBN 0-89684-312-2). Orient Bk Dist.

Samkara's Universal Philosophy of Religion. Y. Masih. 163p. 1986. 22.00 (ISBN 0-317-69970-9). Orient Bk Dist.

Samkhya: A Dualist Tradition in Indian Philosophy. Ed. by Gerald J. Larson & Ram Shankar Bhattacharya. LC 85-43199. (Encyclopedia of Indian Philosophies: Vol. 4). 800p. 1987. 75.00x (ISBN 0-691-07301-5). Princeton U Pr.

Samkhya Philosophy. Kapila. Tr. by Nandalal Sinha. LC 73-3799. (Sacred Books of the Hindus: No. 11). Repr. of 1915 ed. 74.50 (ISBN 0-404-57811-X). AMS Pr.

Samkhya-Pravacana-Bhasya, or Commentary on the Exposition of the Sankhya Philosophy. Vijnanabhiksu. Ed. by Richard Garbe. Tr. by Edward Shils. LC 5-36539. (Oriental Ser.: No. 2). 1895. 14.00x (ISBN 0-674-78630-0). Harvard U Pr.

Samkhya-Sutras of Pancasikha & the Samkhyatattvalcka. Hariharananda Aranya. 1977. 12.50 (ISBN 0-89684-313-0, Pub. by Motilal Banarsidass India). Orient Bk Dist.

Samkhya System, a History of the Samkhya Philosophy. Arthur B. Keith. LC 78-72452. Repr. of 1918 ed. 24.00 (ISBN 0-404-17319-5). AMS Pr.

Samkyha-Yoga: Proceedings of the IASWR Conference, 1981. Ed. by Christopher Chapple. 181p. 1983. pap. text ed. 10.00 (ISBN 0-915078-04-X). Inst Adv Stud Wld.

SAMLA Studies in Milton: Essays on John Milton & His Works. Ed. by J. Max Patrick. LC 53-12340. 1953. pap. 8.00x (ISBN 0-8130-0183-8). U Presses Fla.

Sammelbuch griechischer Urkunden aus Aegypten, 3 vols. Friedrich Preisigke. 1530p. 1974. Repr. of 1927 ed. 194.00x (ISBN 3-11-004756-X). De Gruyter.

Sammlung Hobrecker der Universitatsbibliothek Braunschweig. Ed. by Universitatsbibliothek der Technischen Universitat Braunschweig. 1157p. 1985. lib. bdg. 165.00 (ISBN 3-598-10559-2). K G Saur.

Sammlung und Auszuge Des Sammtlichen Streitschriften Wegen der Wolffischen Philosophie, 2 vols. Carl G. Ludovici. Repr. of 1737 ed. Set. 85.00 (ISBN 0-384-34111-X). Johnson Repr.

Sammy & Rosie Get Laid. Hanif Kureishi. 1988. pap. 6.95 (ISBN 0-14-011262-6). Penguin.

Sammy Miller on Trials. Sammy Miller. (Illus.). 1971. 5.95 (ISBN 0-393-60015-7). Norton.

Sammy Morris: Believing in God's Power. Fern N. Stocker. (Guessing Bks.). (Orig.). (gr. 1-6). 1986. pap. 4.50 (ISBN 0-8024-5443-7). Moody.

Sammy Robin Learns to Fly. Ruth Boldan. 1984. 5.95 (ISBN 0-934860-38-6). Adventure Pubns.

Sammy Seal. (Derrydale Bath Bks.). (Illus.). (ps). 1.79 (ISBN 0-517-46416-0). Outlet Bk Co.

Sammy Skunk. Ron Reese. Ed. by Alton Jordan. (I Can Read Underwater Bks.). (Illus.). (gr. k-3). 1974. PLB 3.95 (ISBN 0-89868-009-3, Read Res); pap. text ed. 1.75 (ISBN 0-89868-042-5). ARO Pub.

Sammy Skunk Plays the Clown. LaRue Selman. Ed. by Alton Jordan. (Buppet Ser.). (Illus.). (gr. k-3). 1981. PLB 5.95 (ISBN 0-89868-097-2, Read Res); pap. text ed. 1.95 (ISBN 0-89868-108-1). ARO Pub.

Sammy Streetsinger. Charles Keeping. (Illus.). 36p. (ps up). 1987. 11.95 (ISBN 0-19-279782-4). Oxford U Pr.

Sammy the Elephant & Mr. Camel: A Story to Help Children Overcome Enuresis While Discovering Self Appreciation. Joyce Mills & Richard J. Crowley. 14.95; pap. 5.95. Brunner-Mazel.

Sammy the Elephant & Mr. Camel: A Story to Help Children Overcome Enuresis While Discovering Self-Appreciation. Joyce C. Mills & Richard J. Crowley. (Illus.). 48p. (ps-6). 1988. PLB 15.95 (ISBN 0-945354-09-6); pap. 6.95 (ISBN 0-945354-08-8). Magination Pr.

Sammy the Seal. Syd Hoff. LC 59-5316. (Harper I Can Read Bks.). (Illus.). 64p. (gr. k-3). 1959. PLB 10.89 (ISBN 0-06-022526-2). HarpJ.

Sammy the Seal. Syd Hoff. LC 59-5316. (Trophy I Can Read Bks.). (Illus.). 64p. (gr. k-3). 1980. pap. 3.50 (ISBN 0-06-444028-1, Trophy). HarpJ.

Sammy the Sloth. Alice L. Mason. (Illus.). 16p. (gr. k-6). 1984. pap. 1.50 (ISBN 0-8249-8064-6). Ideals.

Sammy the Squirrel. (Frog Pond Ser.). (Illus.). (ps-1). 2.98 (ISBN 0-517-46987-1). Outlet Bk Co.

Sammy Younge, Jr. The First Black College Student to Die in the Black Liberation Movement. James Forman. 285p. 1986. 16.95 (ISBN 0-940880-12-1); pap. 7.95 (ISBN 0-940880-13-X). Open Hand.

Sammy's Missing Blanket. Roxanne D. Cote. 32p. 1986. 6.75 (ISBN 0-8062-2923-3). Carlton.

Samna: Luxury Word Processing. Rabin Rabinovitz. (Illus.). 288p. 1986. 24.95 (ISBN 0-8306-0634-3); pap. 16.95 (ISBN 0-8306-2734-0, NO. 2734). TAB Bks.

Samoa, a Hundred Years Ago & Long Before. George Turner. LC 75-35213. 1976. Repr. of 1884 ed. 41.50 (ISBN 0-404-14236-2). AMS Pr.
Samoa: A Photographic Essay. Frederick Sutter. (Illus.). 104p. 1971. 25.00 (ISBN 0-87022-778-5). UH Pr.
Samoa under the Sailing Gods. Newton A. Rowe. LC 75-35209. Repr. of 1930 ed. 28.00 (ISBN 0-404-14232-X). AMS Pr.
Samoa: Yesterday, Today & Tommorow. Napoleone A. Tuiteleleapaga. 160p. 1980. 9.95 (ISBN 0-89962-018-3). Todd & Honeywell.
Samoan Dance of Life: An Anthropological Narrative. John D. Copp & Faafouina I. Pula. LC 83-26370. xvi, 176p. 1984. Repr. of 1950 ed. lib. bdg. 35.00x (ISBN 0-313-24244-5, COSD). Greenwood.
Samoan Housebuilding, Cooking & Tattooing. E. S. Handy & Willowdean C. Handy. (BMB). pap. 10.00 (ISBN 0-527-02118-0). Kraus Repr.
Samoan Islands Bibliography. Ed. by Lowell D. Holmes. LC 83-62482. 335p. 1984. 85.00 (ISBN 0-915203-00-6). Poly Concepts.
Samoan Material Culture. Peter H. Buck. (BMB). Repr. of 1930 ed. 100.00 (ISBN 0-527-02181-4). Kraus Repr.
Samoan Tangle: A Study in Anglo-German-American Relations 1878-1900. Paul M. Kennedy. 342p. 1972. 35.00x (ISBN 0-7165-2150-4, BBA 03053, Pub. by Irish Academic Pr). Biblio Dist.
Samoans! June Behrens. LC 85-32529. (Illus.). 31p. (gr. 2-4). 1986. PLB 12.60 (ISBN 0-516-02388-8). Childrens.
Samoans: A Selected Bibliography. Ramsay L. Shu. LC 81-22315. (Bibliography Ser.: No. 2). iii, 33p. (Orig.). 1982. pap. 2.00 (ISBN 0-934584-15-X). Pacific-Asian.
Samoe Glavnoe. Nikolai Evreinov. (Rus.). 1980. 13.00 (ISBN 0-88233-700-9); pap. 4.50 (ISBN 0-88233-701-7). Ardis Pubs.
Samora Machel: An African Revolutionary, Selected Speeches & Writings. Samora Machel. Ed. by Barry Munslow. 240p. 1985. 26.25x (ISBN 0-86232-339-8, Pub. by Zed Pr England); pap. 9.95 (ISBN 0-86232-340-1, Pub. by Zed Pr England). Humanities.
Samos & Samian Coins. Percy Gardner. 1985. Repr. of 1878 ed. lib. bdg. 20.00 (ISBN 0-915262-61-4). S J Durst.
Samothrace, a Guide to the Excavation & the Museum. 5th ed. Karl Lehman. LC 55-8563. pap. 8.50 (ISBN 0-685-73230-4). J J Augustin.
Samothrace Excavations: Conducted by the Institute of Fine Arts of New York University, 5 vols. Ed. by Karl Lehmann & P. W. Lehmann. Incl. Vol. 1. Ancient Literary Sources. Ed. & tr. by Naphtali Lewis. 1958; Vol. 2, Pt. 1. Inscriptions on Stone. P. M. Fraser. 1960. 47.00x (ISBN 0-691-09821-2); Vol. 2, Pt. 2. Inscriptions on Ceramics & Minor Objects. Karl Lehmann. 1960. 47.00x (ISBN 0-691-09822-0); Vol. 3. Hieron. P. Lehmann. 1969. 3 vols. boxed set 115.00x (ISBN 0-691-09823-9); Vol. 4, Pt. 1. Hall of Votive Gifts. Karl Lehmann. 1962. 50.00x (ISBN 0-691-09824-7); Vol. 4, Pt. 2. Altar Court. Karl Lehmann & Denys Spittle. 1964. 58.50x (ISBN 0-691-09825-5). (Bollingen Ser.: Vol. 60). Princeton U Pr.
Samothracian Reflections: Aspects of the Revival of the Antique. Phyllis Lehmann & Karl Lehman. LC 71-163867. (Bollingen Ser.: No. 92). 216p. 1973. 64.50x (ISBN 0-691-09909-X). Princeton U Pr.
Samovnushenie I Ego Vliianie Na Organizm Cheloveka see Self-Suggestion & Its Influence on the Human Organism.
Samoyed Champions, Nineteen Fifty-Two to Nineteen Eighty-Seven. Camino E. E. & B. Co. Staff. (Illus.). 200p. (YA) 1988. pap. 29.95 (ISBN 0-940808-85-4). Camino E E & B.
Samoyeds. Joyce Reynaud. (Illus.). 128p. 1980. 9.95 (ISBN 0-87666-680-2, KW-072). TFH Pubns.
Sampatti Antaran Adhiniyam, Eighteen Eighty-Two. G. K. Khanna. 209p. (Hindi.). pap. 15.00x (ISBN 0-317-54620-1, Pub. by Eastern Bk India). State Mutual Bk.
Sampedrana: Entrepreneurial Women in a Guatemala Town. Tracy B. Ehlers. (Special Study on Latin America & the Caribbean: No. 16). 200p. 1988. 22.00 (ISBN 0-8133-7581-9). Westview.
Sample Analysis of a Piping System: Class One Nuclear. 1972. pap. text ed. 4.50 (ISBN 0-685-30778-6, E00063). ASME.
Sample Application: FHA Section Five Hundred Fifteen Loan. 152p. 1978. 5.00 (ISBN 0-318-16419-1). Rural America.
Sample Application for Farmers Home Administration Self-Help Technical Assistance Grants. 161p. 1980. 10.95 (ISBN 0-318-16420-5). Rural America.
Sample By-laws for Community Schools of the Arts. 1986. 4.00 (ISBN 0-318-21713-9). NGCSA.
Sample Cataloguing Forms: Illustrations of Solutions to Problems of Description (with Particular Reference to Chapters 1-13 of the Anglo-American Cataloguing Rules, Second Edition) 3rd ed. Robert B. Slocum. LC 80-21507. (Illus.). 121p. 1980. 19.50 (ISBN 0-8108-1364-5). Scarecrow.
Sample Contracts for Physical Plant Services. Date not set. price not set. Assn Phys Plant Admin.
Sample Design in Business Research. W. Edward Deming. LC 60-6451. (Probability & Mathematical Statistics Ser.). 517p. 1960. 61.50x (ISBN 0-471-20724-1). Wiley.
Sample Design, Sampling Variance, & Estimation Procedure for the National Ambulatory Medical Care Survey. Earl Bryant et al. Ed. by Klaudia Cox. LC 88-1382. (Series 2: No. 108). Date not set. pap. 2.00 (ISBN 0-8406-0394-0). Natl Ctr Health Stats.
Sample Faculty Manuals & Personnel Policy Documents. 1986. 6.00 (ISBN 0-318-21714-7). NGCSA.
Sample Incorporating Indenture. American Bar Foundation Staff. Bd. with Model Debenture Indenture Provisions, 1965. 18p. 1965. pap. 1.00 (ISBN 0-910058-27-X). Am Bar Foun.
Sample Incorporating Indenture: All Registered Issues 1967. American Bar Foundation Staff. 22p. 1967. pap. 1.00 (ISBN 0-317-63191-8, 765-0042-01). Amer Bar Assn.
Sample Incorporating Indenture & Model Debenture Indenture Provisions: All Registered Issues 1967. 128p. 1967. 5.00 (ISBN 0-910058-28-8). Amer Bar Assn.
Sample Incorporating Indenture (Demonstrating a Method of Incorporating by Reference Model Debenture Indenture Provisions) & Model Debenture Indenture Provisions, 1965. American Bar Foundation Staff. 120p. 1965. 5.00 (ISBN 0-910058-25-3, 765-0032-01). Amer Bar Assn.
Sample Incorporating Indenture 1965. American Bar Foundation Staff. 18p. pap. 1.00 (ISBN 0-317-63188-8, 765-0041-01). Amer Bar Assn.
Sample Indicators for Evaluating Quality in Ambulatory Health Care. William F. Card et al. Ed. by Maureen Duffy & Karen L. Hill. 20p. 1987. pap. 12.50 (ISBN 0-86688-139-5). Joint Comm Hlthcare.
Sample Jury Instruction in Criminal Antitrust Cases. 196p. 1984. pap. 35.00 (ISBN 0-89707-144-1). Amer Bar Assn.
Sample Jury Instructions in Civil Antitrust Cases. American Bar Association, Antitrust Law Staff. LC 87-70624. 500p. 1987. losseleaf 75.00. Amer Bar Assn.
Sample Lexicon of Pan-Arabic. Ernest T. Abdel-Massih. LC 75-18985. (Arabic.). 1975. pap. text ed. 10.00x (ISBN 0-932098-10-X). UM Ctr NENAS.
Sample Nursing Procedures Manual for Correctional Health Services. 320p. Date not set. 6.00. NCCHC.
Sample Office Building Lease Form. National Association of Home Builders. 21p. 1987. pap. 10.50 (ISBN 0-86718-310-1). Nat Assn H Build.
Sample Pleadings for Use in Juvenile Deliquency Proceedings. American Bar Association, Criminal Justice Staff. 55p. 1986. pap. 7.50. Amer Bar Assn.
Sample Policy Manual for Correctional Health Care. 134p. Date not set. 8.00. NCCHC.
Sample Preparation for Chromatographic Analysis. Rogers. 1988. price not set (ISBN 0-471-09600-8). Wiley.
Sample Pretreatment & Separation. Richard Anderson. LC 87-10655. (Analytical Chemistry by Open Learning Ser.). 632p. 1987. pap. 37.95 (ISBN 0-471-91361-8). Wiley.
Sample Problem Book for Standards of the Tubular Exchanger Manufacturers Association. 67p. 1980. 25.00 (ISBN 0-318-16765-4). Tubular Exch.
Sample Quality Control Documents for Local CPA Firms. 1981. pap. 7.00 (ISBN 0-686-84314-2). Am Inst CPA.
Sample Sales Letter Portfolio: How You Can Write Winning Sales Letters. Galen Stilson. 24p. pap. 4.95 (ISBN 0-915665-14-X). Premier Publishers.
Sample Searchers, 2 vols. Sheila Hardy. 1987. Vol. 1. lib. bdg. 19.95x (ISBN 0-8095-6952-3); Vol. 2. lib. bdg. 19.95x (ISBN 0-8095-6953-1). Borgo Pr.
Sample Selection, Aging & Reactivity of Coals. Ralph Klein & Robert Wellek. 416p. 1988. 49.95 (ISBN 0-471-87555-4). Wiley.
Sample Shopping Center Lease Form. National Association of Home Builders. 36p. 1987. pap. 12.00 (ISBN 0-86718-311-X). Nat Assn H Build.
Sample Size Choice. Odeh & Fox. (Illus.). 200p. 27.50 (ISBN 0-318-13244-3, P170). Am Soc QC.
Sample Survey Methods & Theory, 2 Vols. Morris H. Hansen et al. LC 53-8112. (Probability & Mathematical Statistics Ser.). 1953. Vol. 1: Methods & Applications 638pp. 55.50x (ISBN 0-471-34914-3); Vol. 2: Theory. 53.95x (ISBN 0-471-34947-X, Pub. by Wiley-Interscience). Wiley.
Sample Survey Methods & Theory, Vol. 1: Methods & Applications. Morris H. Hansen et al. LC 53-8112. pap. 160.00 (2056296). Bks Demand UMI.
Sample Survey: Theory & Practice. Donald P. Warwick & Charles A. Lininger. (Illus.). 384p. 1975. pap. text ed. 24.95 (ISBN 0-07-068395-6). McGraw.
Sample Surveys of Current Interest: Fourteenth Report. (Statistical Papers Ser.: No. 15). pap. 26.00 (ISBN 92-1-161149-0, E.82.XVII.9). UN.
Sample West Kentucky. Ed. by Paula Cunningham. LC 85-60764. (Illus.). 112p. 1985. pap. 7.95 (ISBN 0-913383-03-1). McClanahan Pub.
Sampled-Data Control Systems. J. Ackermann. LC 85-10012. (Communications & Control Engineering Ser.). (Illus.). 620p. 1985. 65.00 (ISBN 0-387-15610-0). Springer-Verlag.
Sampled-Data Control Systems. Eliahu I. Jury. LC 76-57949. 476p. 1977. Repr. of 1958 ed. 29.50 (ISBN 0-88275-529-3). Krieger.
Sampler. Robert H. Morrison. 100p. 1986. 20.00 (ISBN 0-9614906-1-6). Comp Info Ltd.
Sampler Book: Old Samplers from Museums & Private Collections. Irmgard Gierl. LC 86-82530. (Illus.). 86p. 1987. 16.95 (ISBN 0-937274-32-1, Dist. by Sterling Publishing Co.). Lark Bks.
Sampler of Alphabets. LC 86-63821. (Lark Ser.). (Illus.). 124p. 1987. pap. 9.95 (ISBN 0-8069-6506-1). Sterling.
Sampler of Forms for Special Libraries. Joan Bow & Olivia Kredel. LC 81-8747. (Illus.). 212p. 1982. spiral bdg. 26.00 (ISBN 0-87111-262-0). SLA.
Sampler of New England Land Use. Aubrey W. Birkelbach. 1975. pap. 2.00 (ISBN 0-686-17294-9). Lincoln Inst Land.
Sampler of the Month. Ed. by Burda Staff. (Burda Bks.). Date not set. 5.95x (ISBN 0-686-64664-9, B805). Toggitt.
Sampler of Wayside Herbs: Rediscovering Old Uses for Familiar Wild Plants. Barbara Pond. LC 73-89773. (Illus.). 1974. 24.95 (ISBN 0-85699-096-5). Chatham Pr.
Sampler of Women. Ginny Knight et al. LC 83-82097. 60p. (Orig.). (YA) (gr. 9-12). 1984. pap. text ed. 6.50 (ISBN 0-940248-18-2). Guild Pr.
Sampler on Sampling. Bill Williams. LC 77-23839. (Probability & Mathematical Statistics Ser.). 254p. 1978. 30.95x (ISBN 0-471-03036-8, Pub. by Wiley-Interscience). Wiley.
Sampler: Patterns for Composition. 2nd ed. Rance G. Baker & Billie R. Phillips. LC 85-80169. 203p. 1986. pap. text ed. 11.00 (ISBN 0-669-07684-8). Heath.
Sampler Quilt. 9th ed. Diana Leone. (Illus.). 68p. 1985. pap. text ed. 11.95 (ISBN 0-942786-01-7). Leone Pubns.
Sampler Supreme. 2nd ed. Anthony Lehman. (Illus.). 1985. 11.95 (ISBN 0-942786-18-1). Leone Pubns.
Samplers & Stitches. Grace Christie. (Illus.). 192p. 1985. pap. 16.95 (ISBN 0-7134-4796-6, Pub. by Batsford England). David & Charles.
Samplers & Tapestry Embroideries. Marcus Huish. LC 78-107667. (Illus.). 1970. pap. 6.95 (ISBN 0-486-22070-2). Dover.
Samplers & Tapestry Embroideries. 2nd ed. Marcus B. Huish. (Illus.). 10.00 (ISBN 0-8446-0149-7). Peter Smith.
Samplers: Four Centuries of a Gentle Craft. Anne Sebba. (Illus.). 1979. 12.98 (ISBN 0-500-23300-4). Thames Hudson.
Samplers You Can Use: A Handweavers Guide to Creative Exploration. Penelope B. Drooker. LC 84-80008. (Illus.). 104p. 1986. spiral bdg. 12.00 (ISBN 0-934026-13-0). Interweave.
Samples & Standards. Brian W. Woodget & Derek Cooper. Ed. by Norman B. Chapman. (Analytical Chemistry by Open Learning Ser.). 200p. 1986. pap. 19.95 (ISBN 0-471-91290-5). Wiley.
Samples from the Love of King David & Fair Bethsabe: With Reference Portions of the Bible. George Peele. Ed. by G. K. Dreher. LC 79-56834. 71p. (Orig.). 1980. pap. 4.95 (ISBN 0-9601000-2-4). Longshanks Bk.
Sampling. Juanita Casey. (Chapbook Ser.). 1981. pap. 2.95x (ISBN 0-912262-72-9). Proscenium.
Sampling. Ed. by P. R. Krishaiah & C. R. Rao. (Hanbook of Statistics Ser.: Vol. 6). 594p. 1988. 125.00 (ISBN 0-444-70289-X, North Holland). Elsevier.
Sampling & Analysis for the Minerals Industry: Symposium held in London, November 1982. 119p. (Orig.). 1982. pap. text ed. 31.50x (ISBN 0-900488-64-6). IMM North Am.
Sampling & Analysis of Copper Cathodes - STP 831. Ed. by W. M. Tuddenham & R. J. Hibbeln. LC 83-72052. 179p. 1984. text ed. 29.00 (ISBN 0-8031-0217-8, 04-831000-03). ASTM.
Sampling & Analysis of Rain - STP 823. Ed. by S. Campbell. 96p. 1984. pap. 18.00 (ISBN 0-8031-0266-6, 04-823000-17). ASTM.
Sampling & Analysis of Toxic Organics in the Atmosphere -STP 721. Ed. by S. Verner. 192p. 1981. 19.75 (ISBN 0-8031-0604-1, 04-721000-19). ASTM.
Sampling & Calibration for Atmospheric Measurements. Ed. by John K. Taylor. LC 87-12439. (Special Technical Publications: No. 957). (Illus.). viii, 225p. 1987. text ed. 39.00 (ISBN 0-8031-0955-5, 04-957000-17). ASTM.
Sampling & Identifying Allergenic Pollens & Molds: An Illustrated Manual for Physicians & Lab Technicians. E. Grant Smith. LC 84-72281. (Illus.). 100p. (Orig.). 1984. pap. text ed. 41.50x (ISBN 0-930961-00-5). Blewstone Pr.
Sampling & Identifying Allergenic Pollens & Molds: An Illustrated Identification Manual for Air Samplers, Vol. 2. E. Grant Smith. LC 86-70134. (Illus.). 104p. (Orig.). 1986. pap. text ed. 62.50x (ISBN 0-930961-01-3). Blewstone Pr.
Sampling & Modeling Biological Populations & Population Dynamics see Statistical Ecology.
Sampling & Statistics Handbook for Research. Chester H. McCall, Jr. (Illus.). 340p. 1982. pap. text ed. 19.95x (ISBN 0-8138-1628-9). Iowa St U Pr.
Sampling & Statistics Handbook for Research in Education. Chester H. McCall, Jr. 368p. 1980. 15.00 (ISBN 0-8106-3089-3). NEA.
Sampling & Testing Aggregates. (Training Aids Ser.: No. 6). 1974. Package: instr's. manual, student wkbk., slides, tape. 400.00 (ISBN 0-317-58403-0); Instr's. manual, 55 pg. 12.00 (ISBN 0-317-58404-9); Student wkbk., 47 pg. 8.00 (ISBN 0-317-58405-7). Natl Asphalt Pavement.
Sampling & Testing of Residual Soils: A Review of International Practices. Ed. by E. W. Brand & H. B. Phillipson. 194p. 1985. text ed. 1.00 (ISBN 90-6191-640-2, Pub. by A A Balkema). Brookfield Pub Co.
Sampling & Weighing of Bulk Solids. J. W. Merks. LC 85-70381. (Illus.). 224p. 1985. 49.00x (ISBN 0-87201-860-1). Gulf Pub.
Sampling & Weighting of Bulk Solids. J. W. Merks. (Bulk Material Handling Ser.: Vol. 4). 1985. 45.00x (ISBN 0-87849-053-1, Trans Tech Germany). Trans Tech.
Sampling Asia. Eva L. Hall. 163p. 1974. 5.95 (ISBN 0-686-10563-X). E L Hall.
Sampling Biological Populations. Ed. by R. M. Cormack et al. (Statistical Ecology Ser.: Vol. 5). 1979. 45.00 (ISBN 0-89974-002-2). Intl Co-Op.
Sampling Book. Joe Scacciaferro & Steve DeFuria. (Ferro Technlogies Ser.). (Illus.). 144p. (Orig.). 1988. pap. 17.95 (ISBN 0-88188-966-0). H Leonard Pub Corp.
Sampling Design & Statistical Methods for Environmental Biologists. Roger H. Green. LC 78-24422. 257p. 1979. 36.00x (ISBN 0-471-03901-2). Wiley.
Sampling for Health Officials. Levy & Lemeshow. 34.95 (ISBN 0-317-64269-3). Van Nos Reinhold.
Sampling for Health Professionals. Paul S. Levy & Stanley Lemeshow. LC 80-14733. 320p. 1980. pap. 31.50 (ISBN 0-534-97986-6, Lifetime Learn); solutions manual 4.95 (ISBN 0-534-97971-8). Van Nos Reinhold.
Sampling for Modern Auditors: A Personal Study Course. (Assignments Ser.: No. 11). 1977. 3 ring bdg. 80.00 (ISBN 0-89413-057-9). Inst Inter Aud.
Sampling for Monitoring & Evaluation. Chris Scott et al. LC 85-12019. 1985. 5.00 (ISBN 0-8213-0535-2). World Bank.
Sampling for Social Research Surveys, 1947-1980. Irene Hess. LC 84-26193. 304p. (Orig.). 1985. pap. text ed. 20.00x (ISBN 0-87944-299-9). Inst Soc Res.
Sampling from a Finite Population. Hajek. (Statistics: Textbooks & Monographs: Vol. 35). 264p. 1981. 49.75 (ISBN 0-8247-1291-9). Dekker.
Sampling Health professioanls Solution Manual. Levy. pap. 6.95 (ISBN 0-317-64270-7). Van Nos Reinhold.
Sampling in Archaeology. Ed. by James W. Mueller. LC 74-26372. 300p. 1975. pap. 8.50x (ISBN 0-8165-0482-2). U of Ariz Pr.
Sampling in Auditing: A Simplified Guide & Statistical Tables. Henry P. Hill et al. LC 79-23351. 180p. 1979. Repr. of 1962 ed. lib. bdg. 13.50 (ISBN 0-89874-102-5). Krieger.
Sampling Inspection & Quality Control. 2nd ed. G. Barrie Wetherill. 1977. pap. 13.95 (ISBN 0-412-14960-5, NO. 6316, Pub. by Chapman & Hall). Routledge Chapman & Hall.
Sampling Inspection in Statistical Quality Control. William C. Guenther. (Charles Griffin Series Griffins Statistical Monographs: No. 37). (Illus.). 213p. 1987. pap. 19.95 (ISBN 0-19-520568-5). Oxford U Pr.
Sampling Inspection Tables: Single & Double Sampling. 2nd ed. Dodge. 224p. 40.95 (ISBN 0-318-13245-1, P46). Am Soc QC.
Sampling Inspection Tables: Single & Double Sampling. 2nd ed. Harold F. Dodge & Harry G. Romig. LC 59-6763. (Probability & Mathematical Statistics Ser.). (Illus.). 224p. 1959. 52.95 (ISBN 0-471-21747-6, Pub. by Wiley-Interscience). Wiley.
Sampling Methods. Kish. (Probability & Mathematical Statistics Ser.). 1988. write for info. (ISBN 0-471-08360-7). Wiley.
Sampling Methods for Censuses & Surveys. 4th ed. F. Yates. (Charles Griffin Bk.). (Illus.). 474p. 1987. 57.50 (ISBN 0-19-520591-X). Oxford U Pr.
Sampling Methods for the Auditor: An Advanced Treatment. Herbert Arkin. LC 81-2735. (Illus.). 288p. 1982. text ed. 40.00 (ISBN 0-07-002194-5). McGraw.
Sampling Methods in Soybean Entomology. Ed. by M. Kogan & D. C. Herzog. (Springer Series in Experimental Entomology). (Illus.). 550p. 1980. 71.40 (ISBN 3-540-90446-8). Springer-Verlag.
Sampling: Microbiological Monitoring of Environments. Ed. by R. G. Board & D. W. Lovelock. (Society for Applied Bacteriology Technical Ser.: No. 7). 1973. 62.50 (ISBN 0-12-108250-4). Acad Pr.
Sampling of Particulate Materials. 2nd ed. P. M. Gy. LC 79-16075. (Developments in Geomathematics Ser.: Vol. 4). 432p. 1982. 84.25 (ISBN 0-444-42079-7). Elsevier.

Samuel F. B. Morse: His Letters & Journals, 2 Vols. in 1. Samuel F. Morse. Ed. by Edward L. Morse. (Illus.). Repr. of 1914 ed. 63.00 (ISBN 0-527-65250-4). Kraus Repr.

Samuel F.B. Morse: His Letters & Journals, 2 vols. Ed. by Edward L. Morse. 440p. 1980. Repr. of 1914 ed. lib. bdg. 65.00 (ISBN 0-89984-331-X). Century Bookbindery.

Samuel Foote: A Biography. Percy Fitzgerald. LC 72-84512. 1910. 18.00 (ISBN 0-405-08519-2, Blom Pubns). Ayer Co Pubs.

Samuel Gompers: A Selected List of References about the Man & His Times. David R. Myers. LC 86-600163. (Illus.). 63p. 1986. pap. 2.00 (ISBN 0-8444-0539-6, S/N 030-000-00177-0). USGPO.

Samuel Gompers, American Statesman. Florence C. Thorne. Repr. of 1957 ed. lib. bdg. 35.00x (ISBN 0-8371-2293-7, THSG). Greenwood.

Samuel Gompers & Organized Labor in America. Harold Livesay. (Library of American Biography). 1978. pap. text ed. write for info. (ISBN 0-673-39345-3). Scott F.

Samuel Gompers & the Origins of the American Federation of Labor, 1848-1896. Stuart B. Kaufman. LC 76-176430. (Contributions in Economics and Economic History: No. 8). 1973. lib. bdg. 35.00 (ISBN 0-8371-6277-7, KAP/). Greenwood.

Samuel Gompers: Champion of the Toiling Masses. Rowland H. Harvey. 1973. lib. bdg. 25.50x (ISBN 0-374-93730-3, Octagon). Hippocrene Bks.

Samuel Gompers: Founder of the American Labor Movement. Gerald Kurland. Ed. by D. Steve Rahmas. LC 72-190242. (Outstanding Personalities Ser.: No. 24). 32p. (Orig.). (gr. 7-12). 1972. lib. bdg. 3.75 incl. catalog cards (ISBN 0-87157-524-8); pap. 2.50 vinyl laminated covers (ISBN 0-87157-024-6). SamHar Pr.

Samuel Gompers Papers: The Early Years of the American Federation of Labor, 1887-90, Vol. 2. Ed. by Stuart B. Kaufman et al. LC 84-2469. (Illus.). 536p. 1987. 39.95 (ISBN 0-252-01350-6). U of Ill Pr.

Samuel Gompers Papers, Vol. 1: The Making of a Union Leader, 1850-86. Ed. by Stuart B. Kaufman et al. LC 84-2469. (Illus.). 568p. 1986. 39.95 (ISBN 0-252-01137-6). U of Ill Pr.

Samuel Gridley Howe: Social Reformer, 1801-1876. Harold Schwartz. LC 56-11286. (Historical Studies: No. 67). 1956. 20.00x (ISBN 0-674-78721-8). Harvard U Pr.

Samuel Griswold Goodrich, Creator of Peter Parley. Daniel Roselle. LC 68-19534. 1968. 44.50x (ISBN 0-87395-033-X). State U Ny Pr.

Samuel H. Walker's Account of the Mier Expedition. Samuel H. Walker. Ed. by Marilyn M. Sibley. LC 78-63306. (Illus.). 1978. 12.95; special collector's edition 40.00. Tex St Hist Assn.

Samuel Hopkins & the New Divinity Movement: Calvinism, the Congregational Ministry, & Reform in New England Between the Great Awakenings. Joseph A. Conforti. LC 80-28268. pap. 62.30 (ISBN 0-317-08398-8, 2020840). Bks Demand UMI.

Samuel Hopkins Works, 3 vols. Bruce Kuklick. (American Religious Thought of the 18th & 19th Centuries Ser.). 1838p. 1987. Set. lib. bdg. 240.00 (ISBN 0-8240-6951-X). Garland Pub.

Samuel I & II: A Commentary. Robert P. Gordon. 372p. 1988. text ed. 17.95 (ISBN 0-310-41200-5, 12864). Zondervan.

Samuel I & II: Critical & Exegetical Commentary. Henry P. Smith. Ed. by Samuel R. Driver et al. LC 99-1607. (International Critical Commentary Ser.). 462p. 1898. 29.95 (ISBN 0-567-05005-X, Pub. by T & T Clark Ltd UK). Fortress.

Samuel II. Ed. by P. Kyle McCarter, Jr. LC 81-43919. (Anchor Bible Ser.: No. 9). (Illus.). 576p. 1984. pap. 20.00 (ISBN 0-385-06808-5, Anchor Pr). Doubleday.

Samuel Johnson. W. Jackson Bate. LC 77-73044. (Illus.). 646p. 1977. 19.95 (ISBN 0-15-179260-7). HarBraceJ.

Samuel Johnson. W. Jackson Bate. LC 79-10586. (Illus.). 1979. pap. 7.95 (ISBN 0-15-679259-1, Harv). HarBraceJ.

Samuel Johnson. Ed. by Donald Greene. (Oxford Author Ser.). (Illus.). 1984. pap. 11.95x (ISBN 0-19-281340-4). Oxford U Pr.

Samuel Johnson. Samuel Johnson. Ed. by Alice Meynell & G. K. Chesterton. LC 76-10963. 1976. Repr. of 1911 ed. lib. bdg. 30.00 (ISBN 0-8414-6143-0). Folcroft.

Samuel Johnson. Hugh Kingsmill. LC 75-42205. (English Literature Ser., No. 33). 1974. lib. bdg. 49.95x (ISBN 0-8383-2018-X). Haskell.

Samuel Johnson. Alice Meynell & G. K. Chesterton. Repr. 27.50 (ISBN 0-8274-3320-4). R West.

Samuel Johnson. Walter Raleigh. LC 74-14565. 1907. lib. bdg. 15.00 (ISBN 0-8414-7352-8). Folcroft.

Samuel Johnson. Walter A. Raleigh. 1978. Repr. of 1907 ed. lib. bdg. 15.50 (ISBN 0-8495-4525-0). Arden Lib.

Samuel Johnson. Leslie Stephen. Ed. by John Morley. LC 68-58398. (English Men of Letters Ser). Repr. of 1887 ed. lib. bdg. 12.50 (ISBN 0-404-51729-3). AMS Pr.

Samuel Johnson. Leslie Stephen. 1979. Repr. of 1878 ed. lib. bdg. 12.50 (ISBN 0-8492-8241-1). R West.

Samuel Johnson. Leslie Stephen. Ed. by John Morley. 195p. 1984. Repr. of 1900 ed. lib. bdg. 20.00 (ISBN 0-918377-04-8). Russell Pr.

Samuel Johnson. Leslie Stephen. 195p. 1985. Repr. of 1882 ed. lib. bdg. 25.00 (ISBN 0-8414-8191-1). Folcroft.

Samuel Johnson. Leslie Stephen. Ed. by John Morley. 195p. Repr. of 1878 ed. lib. bdg. 25.00 (ISBN 0-918377-97-8). Russell Pr.

Samuel Johnson: A Layman's Religion. Maurice J. Quinlan. (Illus.). 256p. 1963. 20.00x (ISBN 0-299-03030-X). U of Wis Pr.

Samuel Johnson Als Kritiker Im Lichte Von Pseudoklassizismus und Romantik. Sigyn Christiani. 1931. 12.00 (ISBN 0-384-08955-0). Johnson Repr.

Samuel Johnson: An Analysis. Charles H. Hinnant. 280p. 1987. 32.50 (ISBN 0-312-01346-9). St Martin.

Samuel Johnson & Eighteenth Century Thought. Nicholas Hudson. (English Monographs). (Illus.). 288p. 1988. 45.00 (ISBN 0-19-812899-1). Oxford U Pr.

Samuel Johnson & Neoclassical Dramatic Theory: The Intellectual Context of the "Preface to Shakespeare". R. D. Stock. LC 72-77194. xxiv, 226p. 1973. 22.00x (ISBN 0-8032-0819-7). U of Nebr Pr.

Samuel Johnson & Poetic Style. William Edinger. LC 77-5137. 1977. 20.00x (ISBN 0-226-18446-3). U of Chicago Pr.

Samuel Johnson & the Life of Writing. Paul Fussell. 320p. 1986. pap. 6.95 (ISBN 0-393-30258-X). Norton.

Samuel Johnson & the New Science. Richard B. Schwartz. 198p. 1971. 30.00x (ISBN 0-299-06010-1). U of Wis Pr.

Samuel Johnson & the Problem of Evil. Richard B. Schwartz. LC 74-27314. 128p. 1975. 27.50x (ISBN 0-299-06790-4). U of Wis Pr.

Samuel Johnson & the Scale of Greatness. Isobel Grundy. LC 86-4288. 260p. 1986. 30.00x (ISBN 0-8203-0867-6). U of GA Pr.

Samuel Johnson & the Sense of History. John A. Vance. LC 83-18190. 224p. 1984. 22.50x (ISBN 0-8203-0712-2). U of Ga Pr.

Samuel Johnson & the Theme of Hope. T. F. Wharton. LC 83-2859. 192p. 1984. 21.95 (ISBN 0-312-69861-5). St Martin.

Samuel Johnson & the Tragic Sense. Leopold Damrosch, Jr. LC 72-38514. 284p. 1972. 32.00x (ISBN 0-691-06233-1). Princeton U Pr.

Samuel Johnson & Three Infidels: Rousseau, Voltaire, Diderot. Mark Temmer. LC 87-5930. 224p. 1988. 25.00x (ISBN 0-8203-0962-1). U of Ga Pr.

Samuel Johnson: His Words & His Ways. Edward T. Mason. LC 72-2104. (Studies in Samuel Johnson, No. 97). 1972. Repr. of 1879 ed. lib. bdg. 49.95x (ISBN 0-8383-1491-0). Haskell.

Samuel Johnson: New Critical Essays. Ed. by Isobel Grundy. LC 84-18401. (Critical Studies). 208p. 1984. 27.50x (ISBN 0-389-20534-6, BNB-08096). B&N Imports.

Samuel Johnson on Literature. Samuel Johnson. Ed. by Marlies K. Danziger. LC 78-20936. (Milestones of Thought Ser.). 1979. pap. text ed. 5.95x (ISBN 0-8044-6097-3). Ungar.

Samuel Johnson on Shakespeare. Karl Young. LC 75-37625. (Studies in Shakespeare, No. 24). 1976. lib. bdg. 49.95x (ISBN 0-8383-2109-7). Haskell.

Samuel Johnson on Shakespeare: One Aspect. Karl Young. LC 77-4953. 1923. lib. bdg. 17.50 (ISBN 0-8414-9759-1). Folcroft.

Samuel Johnson, President of King's College: His Career & Writings, 4 Vols. Samuel Johnson. Ed. by Herbert Schneider & Carol Schneider. LC 72-153333. Repr. of 1929 ed. Set. 150.00 (ISBN 0-404-03600-7); 37.50 ea. AMS Pr.

Samuel Johnson: Selected Poetry & Prose. Ed. by Frank Brady & William K. Wimsatt. 1978. 45.00x (ISBN 0-520-02929-1); pap. 10.95x (ISBN 0-520-03552-6). U of Cal Pr.

Samuel Johnson: The Complete English Poems. Samuel Johnson. Ed. by J. D. Fleeman. LC 81-16065. (English Poets Ser.: No. 11). 256p. 1982. pap. 9.95x (ISBN 0-300-02826-1, YEP-11). Yale U Pr.

Samuel Johnson the Moralist. Robert B. Voitle, Jr. LC 61-8842. 1961. 15.00x (ISBN 0-674-78766-8). Harvard U Pr.

Samuel Johnson: Writer. S. C. Roberts. 1926. Repr. 17.50 (ISBN 0-8274-3321-2). R West.

Samuel Johnson's Early Biographers. Robert E. Kelley & O. M. Brack, Jr. LC 74-151649. pap. 43.80 (ISBN 0-317-42128-X, 2025941). Bks Demand UMI.

Samuel Johnson's Literary Criticism. Jean H. Hagstrum. LC 52-12060. 1967. pap. 1.95x (ISBN 0-226-31292-5, P268, Phoen). U of Chicago Pr.

Samuel Johnson's Literary Criticism. Samuel Johnson. Ed. by R. D. Stock. LC 73-91398. (Regents Critics Ser). xvi, 286p. 1974. 25.00x (ISBN 0-8032-0469-8). U of Nebr Pr.

Samuel Johnson's Prefaces & Dedications. Allen T. Hazen. LC 72-86538. 228p. 1973. Repr. of 1937 ed. 27.00x (ISBN 0-8046-1749-X, Pub. by Kennikat). Assoc Faculty Pr.

Samuel K. Mirsky Memorial Volume. Gersion Appel. 1970. 25.00x (ISBN 0-87068-084-6). Ktav.

Samuel Kelso (Kelsey) Seventeen Twenty to Seventeen Ninety-Six: Scotch-Irish Immigrant & Revolutionary Patriot of Chester County South Carolina. Mr. & Mrs. Mavis P. Kelsey, Sr. LC 84-80307. 1984. 75.00 (ISBN 0-9613308-0-5). M P Kelsey.

Samuel Kirk & Son: American Silver Craftsmen since Eighteen Fifteen. Norton (R. W.) Art Gallery. (Illus.). 32p. 1971. pap. 1.00x (ISBN 0-913060-17-8). Norton Art.

Samuel L. Clemens: First Editions & Values. John K. Potter. 1973. Repr. of 1932 ed. 25.00 (ISBN 0-8274-1794-2). R West.

Samuel L. Southard: Jeffersonian Whig. Michael J. Birkner. LC 82-48517. 32.50 (ISBN 0-8386-3160-6). Fairleigh Dickinson.

Samuel Langhorne Clemens: A Mysterious Stranger: Tubingen Essays in Celebration of the Mark Twain - Year 1985. Ed. by Hans Borchers & Daniel E. Williams. (Studien und Texte zur Amerikanistik: Vol. 11). 232p. 1986. pap. 31.25 (ISBN 3-8204-9531-2). P Lang Pubs.

Samuel Lived Here. (Building Books Ser.). (ps-1). 1988. 3.95 (ISBN 0-8024-0841-9). Moody.

Samuel Logan Brengle: Portrait of a Prophet. Clarence W. Hall. 1978. Repr. of 1933 ed. 3.95 (ISBN 0-86544-006-9). Salv Army Suppl South.

Samuel Longfellow: Memoir & Letters. Joseph May. 1894. Repr. 30.00 (ISBN 0-8274-3322-0). R West.

Samuel Longfellow Memoir & Letters. Joseph May. Repr. of 1894 ed. 20.00 (ISBN 0-686-19898-0). Ridgeway Bks.

Samuel Lorenzo Knapp & Early American Biography: Proceedings of the American Antiquarian Society. Ben H. McClary. 30p. 1985. pap. 4.50 (ISBN 0-912296-80-1, Dist. by U Pr of Va). Am Antiquarian.

Samuel Lover: A Biographical Sketch with Selections from His Writings & Correspondence. Andrew J. Symington. 1973. Repr. of 1880 ed. 17.50 (ISBN 0-8274-0845-5). R West.

Samuel Lyle Criminologist. Arthur Crabb. LC 74-121531. (Short Story Index Reprint Ser). (Illus.). 1920. 21.00 (ISBN 0-8369-3487-3). Ayer Co Pubs.

Samuel McIntire of Salem. Lamia Doumato. (Architecture Ser.: A 1643). 10p. 1986. 3.00 (ISBN 0-89028-953-0). Vance Biblios.

Samuel Mareschal: Melodiae Suaves. J. M. Bonhote. (Wissenschaftliche Abhandlungen-Musicological Studies: Vol. 25). 36p. (Fr.). 1976. pap. 6.00 (ISBN 0-912024-77-1). Inst Mediaeval Mus.

Samuel Marsden: The Great Survivor. A. T. Yarwood. 1977. 28.50x (ISBN 0-522-84120-1, Pub. by Melbourne U Pr). Intl Spec Bk.

Samuel May Williams: Early Texas Entrepreneur. Margaret S. Henson. LC 75-40894. 222p. 1976. 14.50x (ISBN 0-89096-009-7); pap. 6.95 (ISBN 0-89096-192-1). Tex A&M Univ Pr.

Samuel Milton Jones Papers: An Inventory to the Microfilm Edition. Morgan J. Barclay & Jean W. Strong. 95p. 1978. 5.95 (ISBN 0-318-03217-1). Ohio Hist Soc.

Samuel Morris. Lindley Baldwin. 74p. 1980. 1.50 (ISBN 0-88113-319-1). Edit Betania.

Samuel Morris. Lindley Baldwin. 96p. 1987. pap. 3.50 (ISBN 0-87123-950-7). Bethany Hse.

Samuel Oldknow & the Arkwrights. George Unwin. LC 68-5554. (Illus.). 1968. Repr. of 1924 ed. 35.00x (ISBN 0-678-06767-8). Kelley.

Samuel One & Two. James D. Nawsome. Ed. by James D. Hayes. (Knox Preaching Guide Ser.). 1983. pap. 5.95 (ISBN 0-8042-3211-3, John Knox). Westminster John Knox.

Samuel One: Volume Eight, a New Translation with Introduction & Commentary. P. Kyle McCarter, Jr. LC 79-7201. (Anchor Bible Ser.). 1980. 20.00 (ISBN 0-385-06760-7). Doubleday.

Samuel Palmer: A Vision Recaptured. Ed. by Ashmolean Museum. 88p. 1978. 14.50x (ISBN 0-317-20346-0, Pub. by Ashmolean Museum). State Mutual Bk.

Samuel Palmer: A Vision Recaptured. Raymond Lister & Graham Reynolds. (Illus.). 102p. (Orig.). 1978. pap. 20.75 (ISBN 0-907849-36-9, Pub. by Ashmolean Mus). Longwood Pub Group.

Samuel Palmer & 'The Ancients' Raymond Lister. (Illus.). 116p. 1984. 49.50 (ISBN 0-521-26126-0); pap. 17.95 (ISBN 0-521-27847-3). Cambridge U Pr.

Samuel Palmer: Catalogue Raisonne of the Paintings, Drawings, & a Selection of the Prints in the Ashmolean Museum, Oxford. D. B. Brown. (Illus.). 74p. (Orig.). 1983. pap. 10.50x (ISBN 0-900090-95-2, Pub. by Ashmolean Museum). State Mutual Bk.

Samuel Palmer: Catalogue Raisonne of the Paintings, Drawings & a Selection of the Prints in the Ashmolean Museum, Oxford. D. B. Brown. (Illus.). 74p. (Orig.). 1983. pap. 14.75 (ISBN 0-317-58652-1, Pub. by Ashmolean Mus). Longwood Pub Group.

Samuel Palmer: His Life & Art. Raymond Lister. (Illus.). 296p. 1987. 49.50 (ISBN 0-521-32850-0). Cambridge U Pr.

Samuel Papys's Naval Minutes. J. R. Tanner. 1985. 69.00x (ISBN 0-317-44228-7, Pub. by Navy Rec Soc). State Mutual Bk.

Samuel Pepys. G. Bradford. LC 75-42291. (English Biography Ser., No. 31). 1974. lib. bdg. 52.95x (ISBN 0-8383-2061-9). Haskell.

Samuel Pepys. Gamaliel Bradford. 1924. Repr. 15.00 (ISBN 0-8274-3323-9). R West.

Samuel Pepys. Percy Lubbock. LC 74-9975. 1909. 27.20 (ISBN 0-8414-5751-X). Folcroft.

Samuel Pepys. E. Hallam Moorhouse. LC 74-30375. (English Biography Ser., No. 31). 1974. lib. bdg. 52.95x (ISBN 0-8383-1908-4). Haskell.

Samuel Pepys. facsimile ed. Arthur Ponsonby. LC 71-160987. (Select Bibliographies Reprint Ser). Repr. of 1928 ed. 22.00 (ISBN 0-8369-5855-1). Ayer Co Pubs.

Samuel Pepys. Arthur Ponsonby. LC 72-153238. 1971. Repr. of 1928 ed. 23.00x (ISBN 0-8046-1548-9, Pub. by Kennikat). Assoc Faculty Pr.

Samuel Pepys. Arthur Ponsonby. 160p. 1982. Repr. of 1928 ed. lib. bdg. 27.00 (ISBN 0-8495-4410-6). Arden Lib.

Samuel Pepys: A Portrait in Miniature. J. Lucas Dubreton. Tr. by H. F. Stenning. 280p. 1980. Repr. lib. bdg. 25.00 (ISBN 0-89984-150-3). Century Bookbindery.

Samuel Pepys: A Portrait in Miniature. J. Lucas-Dubreton. Tr. by H. J. Stenning. 1978. Repr. lib. bdg. 25.00 (ISBN 0-8492-1600-1). R West.

Samuel Pepys: Administrator, Observer, Goddip. Hallam Moorhouse. 1973. Repr. of 1909 ed. 35.00 (ISBN 0-8274-0129-9). R West.

Samuel Pepys & the Minxes. R. M. Freeman. 1973. 20.00 (ISBN 0-8274-0538-3). R West.

Samuel Pepys & the Royal Navy. J. R. Tanner. LC 73-13909. 1974. Repr. of 1920 ed. lib. bdg. 20.50 (ISBN 0-8414-8532-1). Folcroft.

Samuel Pepys & the Royal Navy. Joseph R. Tanner. LC 79-163207. (English Literature Ser., No. 33). 1971. Repr. of 1920 ed. lib. bdg. 44.95x (ISBN 0-8383-1314-0). Haskell.

Samuel Pepys & the World He Lived In. Henry B. Wheatley. 1973. Repr. of 1963 ed. 45.00 (ISBN 0-8274-0575-8). R West.

Samuel Pepys & the World He Lived In. P. Wheatley. LC 75-34323. (English Literature, No. 30). 1977. lib. bdg. 55.95x (ISBN 0-8383-1895-9). Haskell.

Samuel Pepys Esq. Richard Barber. LC 70-123622. (Illus.). 1970. 18.95x (ISBN 0-520-01763-3). U of Cal Pr.

Samuel Pepys in the Diary. Percival Hunt. LC 78-2747. 1978. Repr. of 1958 ed. lib. bdg. 35.00x (ISBN 0-313-20363-6, HUSD). Greenwood.

Samuel Pepys, Listener. R. M. Freeman. 1973. Repr. of 1931 ed. 20.00 (ISBN 0-8274-0537-5). R West.

Samuel Pepys' Penny Merriments. Roger Thompson. LC 76-50544. 1977. 35.00x (ISBN 0-231-04280-9); pap. 14.50x (ISBN 0-231-04281-7). Columbia U Pr.

Samuel Pepys's Spanish Plays. Edward M. Wilson & Don W. Cruickshank. 1980. 74.00x (ISBN 0-19-721793-1). Oxford U Pr.

Samuel Peter Heintzelman & the Sonora Exploring & Mining Company. Diane M. North. LC 79-15307. 248p. 1980. 12.50x (ISBN 0-8165-0679-5); pap. 7.95 (ISBN 0-8165-0574-8). U of Ariz Pr.

Samuel: Prophet & Judge. Richie Whaley. (BibLearn Ser.). (Illus.). (gr. 1-6). 1979. 5.95 (ISBN 0-8054-4242-1, 4242-42). Broadman.

Samuel Prout. Richard Lockett. (British Watercolour Ser.). (Illus.). 200p. 1985. 35.95 (ISBN 0-7134-3490-2, Pub. by Batsford England); pap. 22.95 (ISBN 0-7134-3491-0, Pub. by Batsford England). David & Charles.

Samuel R. B. Morse. William Kloss. (Library of American Art). 1988. 35.00 (ISBN 0-8109-1531-6). Abrams.

Samuel R. Delany. Seth McEvoy. (Recognitions Ser.). 170p. (Orig.). 1985. 16.95x (ISBN 0-8044-2669-4). Ungar.

Samuel R. Delany. Jane B. Weedman. LC 81-21673. (Starmont Reader's Guide Ser.: No. 10). 79p. 1982. Repr. lib. bdg. 16.95x (ISBN 0-89370-040-1). Borgo Pr.

Samuel R. Delany: A Primary & Secondary Bibliography, 1962-1979. Michael W. Peplow & Robert S. Bravard. 1980. lib. bdg. 30.50 (ISBN 0-8161-8054-7, Hall Reference). G K Hall.

Samuel Richardson. Ed. & intro. by Harold Bloom. (Modern Critical Views Ser.). 184p. 1987. lib. bdg. 19.95x (ISBN 1-55546-286-3). Chelsea Hse.

Samuel Richardson. Elizabeth B. Brophy. (English Author Ser.). 152p. 1987. lib. bdg. 18.95x (ISBN 0-8057-6951-X, Twayne). G K Hall.

Samuel Richardson. Austin Dobson. LC 67-23877. 224p. 1968. Repr. of 1902 ed. 35.00x (ISBN 0-8103-3055-5). Gale.

Samuel Richardson. Austin Dobson. 1902. 7.00 (ISBN 0-403-00018-1). Scholarly.

Samuel Richardson. Jocelyn Harris. (British & Irish Authors Ser.). 192p. 1987. 39.50 (ISBN 0-521-30501-2); pap. 11.95 (ISBN 0-521-31542-5). Cambridge U Pr.

Samuel Richardson. Francis Jeffrey. 1853. lib. bdg. 25.00 (ISBN 0-8414-5377-2). Folcroft.

Samuel Richardson: A Biographical & Critical Study. Clara L. Thomson. 1978. Repr. of 1900 ed. lib. bdg. 35.00 (ISBN 0-8495-5109-9). Arden Lib.

Samuel Richardson: A Biographical & Critical Study. Clara L. Thomson. LC 72-192842. 1900. lib. bdg. 25.50 (ISBN 0-8414-8045-1). Folcroft.

San Diego Street Guide & Directory Including Imperial County, 1988: Census Tract Edition. Thomas Bros. Maps Staff. (Illus.). 218p. 1988. pap. 25.95. Thomas Bros Maps.
San Diego Where California Began. rev., 5th ed. James R. Mills. (Illus.). 84p. 1985. pap. 4.95 (ISBN 0-918740-04-5). San Diego Hist.
San Diego: Where Tomorrow Begins. Dan Berger et al. LC 87-10638. 224p. 1987. 29.95 (ISBN 0-89781-212-3). Windsor Pubns Inc.
San Diego Women's Haggadah. rev. ed. Ed. by Jane S. Zones. LC 85-51376. (Illus.). 80p. 1986. pap. 7.50 (ISBN 0-9608054-5-1). Womans Inst-Cont Jewish Ed.
San Diego Workshop on the Interaction Between Man-Made Noise & Vibration & Artic Marine Wildlife, 25-29 February 1980. 84p. 1980. pap. 8.00. Acoustical Soc Am.
San Diego's Scenic Drive. Leslie Bergstrom. (Illus.). 68p. Date not set. pap. 4.50 (ISBN 0-9612668-3-X). Talk Town.
San Diego's South Bay Interurban. Ralph Forty. Ed. by Paul Hammond. (Interurbans Special 106 Ser.). (Illus.). 96p. 1986. pap. 14.95 (ISBN 0-916374-76-9). Interurban.
San Domingo: The Medicine Hat Stallion. Marguerite Henry. LC 72-7416. (Illus.). 224p. (gr. 2-9). 1972. 8.95 (ISBN 0-528-82443-0, Checkerboard Pr). Macmillan.
San Elizario. Eugene Porter. (Illus.). 14.95 (ISBN 0-8363-0117-X); special ed 125.00 (ISBN 0-685-83963-X). Jenkins.
San Fernando Valley: Past & Present. Lawrence C. Jorgensen et al. LC 81-83166. (Illus.). 264p. 1982. 9.95 (ISBN 0-941014-00-2). Pacific Rim Res.
San Fin la Fete see Endless Party.
San Franciciana Photographs of the Cliff House. LC 85-90624. 1985. 10.00 (ISBN 0-934715-00-9). San Francisciana.
San Francisco. Photos by Morton Beebe. (Illus.). 208p. (Text by Herb Caen, Tom Cole, Barnaby Gold, Kevin Starr). 1985. 49.50 (ISBN 0-8109-1608-8). Abrams.
San Francisco. Robert W. Cherny & William Issel. Ed. by Norris Hundley, Jr. & John A. Schutz. LC 81-67253. (Golden State Ser.). (Illus.). 120p. 1981. pap. text ed. 6.95x (ISBN 0-87835-120-5). Boyd & Fraser.
San Francisco. Robert W. Cherny & William Issel. Ed. by Norris Hundley, Jr. & John A. Schutz. (Golden State Ser.). (Illus.). 136p. 1981. pap. 7.50. MTL.
San Francisco. Federal Writers' Project Staff. (American Guidebook Ser.). 538p. 1940. Repr. 11.00 (ISBN 0-403-02205-3). Somerset Pub.
San Francisco. Patricia Haddock. (Downtown America Bks.). (Illus.). 60p. (gr. 3 up). 1988. PLB 12.95 (ISBN 0-87518-383-2). Dillon.
San Francisco. Hans W. Hannau. (Panorama Bks.). (Illus., Fr.). 1966. 3.95 (ISBN 0-685-11554-2). French & Eur.
San Francisco. Greg Lawson. (Illus.). 72p. Date not set. pap. 9.95 (ISBN 0-9606704-8-3). First Choice.
San Francisco. Larry Lee et al. (Illus.). 1985. 16.95 (ISBN 0-19-540626-5). Skyline Press.
San Francisco. (L-38 Travel Ser.). (Illus.). 72p. (Orig.). 1981. pap. 6.95 (ISBN 0-938440-03-9). Colourpicture.
San Francisco. 1988. 12.95 (ISBN 0-933692-31-5). A R Collings.
San Francisco. (Baedeker's City Guides Ser.). 1987. pap. 10.95 (ISBN 0-13-058082-1). P-H.
San Francisco. (In Your Pocket Ser.). 112p. 1987. pap. 3.95 (ISBN 0-8120-3758-8). Barron.
San Francisco. rev. ed. (Frommer's City Guides Ser.). (Illus.). 224p. 1988. pap. 5.95 (ISBN 0-13-047508-4). Prentice Hall Pr.
San Francisco. 2nd ed. Sunset Books & Sunset Magazine Editors. 1987. pap. text ed. 17.95 (ISBN 0-376-05672-X). Sunset-Lane.
San Francisco. Sunset Editors. LC 86-82231. (Illus.). 256p. 1986. pap. 12.95 (ISBN 0-376-05666-5, Sunset Bks.). Sunset-Lane.
San Francisco, No. 1. Paul Block. 352p. (Orig.). 1988. pap. 4.95 (ISBN 1-55802-187-6). Lynx Bks.
San Francisco - Access. (Access Guides Ser.). pap. 9.95 (ISBN 0-671-60336-1). S&S.
San Francisco - Marin Counties Street Guide & Directory Census Tract Edition 1988. Thomas Bros. Maps Staff. (Illus.). 172p. 1988. pap. 39.95 (ISBN 0-88130-278-3). Thomas Bros Maps.
San Francisco--I Love It! Pace International Research, Inc. Staff. (AAA Video Ser.). (Illus.). 144p. 1984. text ed. 8.95 (ISBN 0-89209-047-2); pap. text ed. 4.25 (ISBN 0-89209-076-6); audiocassette 3.25 (ISBN 0-89209-077-4); videocassette 125.00 (ISBN 0-89209-044-8). Pace Intl Res.
San Francisco: A Chronological & Documentary History 1542-1970. Compiled by Robert Mayer. LC 74-8846. (American Cities Chronology Ser.). 152p. 1974. lib. bdg. 8.50 (ISBN 0-379-00614-6). Oceana.
San Francisco a la Carte see Encore.
San Francisco a la Carte: A Cookbook. Junior League of San Francisco. LC 78-14702. 1979. pap. 22.50 (ISBN 0-385-13545-9). Doubleday.
San Francisco: A Portrait. Photos by Roger C. Miller. Date not set. 34.50 (ISBN 0-911897-11-9). Image Ltd.
San Francisco Access. rev. ed. Richard S. Wurman. (Access Guidebooks). (Illus.). 144p. 1985. pap. 9.95 (ISBN 0-915461-09-9). Access Pr.
San Francisco Access. rev. ed. Richard S. Wurman. (Access Series). (Illus.). 135p. 1987. pap. 12.95 (ISBN 0-13-001836-8). P-H.
San Francisco: Adventurers & Visionaries. new ed. Richard H. Dillon. Ed. by Sharon Mason. LC 83-70414. (American Portrait Ser.). (Illus.). 240p. 1983. 29.95 (ISBN 0-932986-35-8). Continent Herit.
San Francisco Adventures. Charles C. Dobie. LC 70-101800. (Short Story Index Reprint Ser.). 1937. 17.00 (ISBN 0-8369-3188-2). Ayer Co Pubs.
San Francisco AM-PM. 1985. 5.00 (ISBN 0-933875-02-9). AM-PM Pub Co.
San Francisco AM-PM, 1984-1985. 1984. 5.00 (ISBN 0-933875-00-2). AM-PM Pub Co.
San Francisco at Your Feet: The Great Walks in a Walker's Town. rev. ed. Margot P. Doss. LC 79-6170. (Illus.). 204p. 1980. pap. 5.95 (ISBN 0-394-17863-7, E639, Ever). Grove.
San Francisco Bar Book. Ed. by William Ristow. LC 81-66873. (Illus.). 128p. 1981. pap. 3.95 (ISBN 0-913192-03-1, Co-Pub. by Downwind). SF Bay Guardian.
San Francisco Bay Area. 3rd ed. (Job Bank Ser.). 204p. 1987. pap. 9.95 (ISBN 0-937860-55-7). Adams Inc MA.
San Francisco Bay Area: A Metropolis in Perspective. 2nd ed. Mel Scott. LC 84-24152. 340p. 1985. text ed. 48.50x (ISBN 0-520-05510-1); pap. text ed. 16.95x (ISBN 0-520-05512-8). U of Cal Pr.
San Francisco Bay Area Annual Air Quality Report for 1983. 64p. 1985. 10.00 (ISBN 0-318-22701-0). Assn Bay Area.
San Francisco Bay Area Environmental Management Plan: Appendix J. 511p. 1981. 30.00 (ISBN 0-318-22704-5). Assn Bay Area.
San Francisco Bay Area Environmental Management Plan: Appendix O, 2 vols, Vols. I & II. 260p. 1983. Set. 30.00 (ISBN 0-318-22706-1); Vol. I: Regional Wetlands Plan for Urban Runoff Treatment. avail.; Vol. II: A Compendium of Eight Technical Memoranda on Wetlands Treatment Mechanisms, Case Studies, Inventory of Sites & Institutional Financial Mechanisms & Sources. avail. Assn Bay Area.
San Francisco Bay Area: Its Problems & Future. new ed. Ed. by Stanley Scott. LC 66-7975. (Franklin K. Lane Monographs: Vol. 3). (Illus.). 499p. 1972. 11.00x (ISBN 0-87772-151-3); pap. 8.00x (ISBN 0-686-66682-8). UCB IGS.
San Francisco Bay Area Landmarks: Reflections of Four Centuries. Charles Kennard. LC 87-14647. (Illus.). 160p. 1987. 35.00 (ISBN 0-935382-63-1). Tioga Pub Co.
San Francisco Bay Region Architecture: An Introductory Bibliography. Kenneth Caldwell. (Architecture Ser.: A 1780). 11p. 1987. 3.75 (ISBN 1-55590-230-8). Vance Biblios.
San Francisco Bay: Use & Protection. W. J. Kockelman & A. E. Leviton. LC 82-71291. 310p. (Orig.). 1982. 17.95 (ISBN 0-934394-04-0). AAASPD.
San Francisco Begins, Seventeen Seventy-Six. Parker L. Johnstone. (Illus.). 174p. 7.95 (ISBN 0-917802-17-9). Theoscience Found.
San Francisco by Cable Car. George Young & Bill Henkin. (Illus.). 196p. (Orig.). 1983. pap. 7.95 (ISBN 0-914728-46-6). Wingbow Pr.
San Francisco Calamity by Earthquake & Fire. facsimile ed. Charles Morris. (Illus.). 224p. 1986. pap. 9.95 (ISBN 0-8065-0984-8, Pub. by Citadel Pr). Lyle Stuart.
San Francisco Celebrity Chef. Sam Bronfman. Ed. by Sheila Hosner. (Celebrity Chef Ser.). 240p. (Orig.). 1987. pap. 9.95 (ISBN 0-89716-164-5). Peanut Butter.
San Francisco Chronicles 1982: A Collection of Professional Papers. 500p. 1982. 60.00 (ISBN 0-317-31117-4). Amer Bar Assn.
San Francisco Clearing House Certificates: Last of California's Private Money. Robert J. Chandler. 32p. (Orig.). 1986. pap. text ed. 3.95 (ISBN 0-932151-01-9). McDonald Pub.
San Francisco County Street Guide & Directory 1988. Thomas Bros. Maps Staff. (Illus.). 98p. 1988. pap. 10.95 (ISBN 0-88130-277-5). Thomas Bros Maps.
San Francisco Dinner Party Cookbook. rev. ed. Judith Ets-Hokin. LC 81-68589. 256p. 1982. pap. 9.95 (ISBN 0-89087-338-0). Celestial Arts.
San Francisco Dinner Party Cookbook. Judith Ets-Hokin. 260p. 1987. comb-bound 9.95 (ISBN 0-89087-349-6). Celestial Arts.
San Francisco Earthquake. John Dudman. Ed. by Janet Caulkins. (Great Disasters Ser.). (Illus.). 32p. (gr. 1-6). 1988. 10.90 (ISBN 0-531-18163-4, Pub. by Bookwright Pr). Watts.
San Francisco Encore: A Cookbook. Junior League of San Francisco. LC 85-31107. (Illus.). 464p. 1986. pap. 22.50 (ISBN 0-385-19237-1). Doubleday.
San Francisco Epicure. Maria T. Caen. Ed. by Gretchen Weidenbach. (American Epicure Ser.). 160p. 1986. pap. 7.95 (ISBN 0-89716-154-8). Peanut Butter.
San Francisco Experience. Bd. with Orange Telephone. Salvatore Farinella (ISBN 0-915480-04-2); Nuestra Senora De los Dolores. Charley Shively (ISBN 0-915480-03-4). 1975. 10.00 (ISBN 0-686-20500-6). Good Gay.
San Francisco Fatty Arbuckle Past &-Virginia Present. Penny Skillman. 1979. 3.45 (ISBN 0-317-15620-9). P Skillman.
San Francisco Forty Nine'ers. James R. Rothaus. (NFL Today Ser.). (gr. 4 up). 1986. PLB 10.45 (ISBN 0-88682-048-0). Creative Ed.
San Francisco Forty Niners. Julian May. (NFL Today Ser.). (Illus.). (gr. 3-6). 1977. PLB 10.45 (ISBN 0-87191-599-5). Creative Ed.
San Francisco Free & Easy. rev. ed. Ed. by William Ristow. LC 80-66932. (Illus.). 352p. 1980. pap. 5.95 (ISBN 0-913192-02-3, Co-Pub by Downwind). SF Bay Guardian.
San Francisco Giants. rev. ed. Brannon. LC 82-16177. (Baseball Today Ser.). 48p. (gr. 4 up). 1982. PLB 11.45 (ISBN 0-87191-873-0). Creative Ed.
San Francisco Giants. James R. Rothaus. (Baseball: The Great American Game Ser.). 48p. (gr. 4-10). 1987. PLB 14.89 (ISBN 0-88682-150-9). Creative Ed.
San Francisco Giants Almanac: Thirty Years of Baseball by the Bay. Nick Peters. (Illus.). 200p. (Orig.). 1988. 20.00 (ISBN 1-55643-041-8); pap. 8.95 (ISBN 1-55643-040-X). North Atlantic.
San Francisco in Color. T. H. Watkins. LC 68-16004. (Profiles of America Ser). (Illus.). 1968. 9.95 (ISBN 0-8038-6645-3). Hastings.
San Francisco in the 1850's. G. R. Fardon. (Illus.). 11.25 (ISBN 0-8446-5574-0). Peter Smith.
San Francisco in the 1850's: 32 Photographic Views by G. R. Fardon. G. R. Fardon. (Illus.). 1977. pap. 4.50 (ISBN 0-486-23459-2). Dover.
San Francisco Insider's Guide: A Unique Guide to Bay Area Restaurants, Bars, Best Bets, Bargains, the Outdoors & More... 2nd, rev. ed. John K. Bailey. LC 84-60548. 160p. 1984. pap. 4.95 (ISBN 0-936816-04-X). Non Stop Bks.
San Francisco Irish, 1884-1880. R. A. Burchell. LC 79-65764. 1980. 27.00x (ISBN 0-520-04003-1). U of Cal Pr.
San Francisco Job Bank. 4th ed. 276p. 1988. 12.95 (ISBN 1-55850-958-5). Adams Inc MA.
San Francisco Little Restaurant Guide. Camaro Editors. (Illus.). 1985. pap. 4.95 (ISBN 0-913290-86-6). Camaro Pub.
San Francisco: Marin Counties Street Guide & Directory Census Tract Edition, 1987. Thomas Bros. Maps Staff. (Illus.). 174p. 1987. pap. 39.95 (ISBN 0-88130-241-4). Thomas Bros Maps.
San Francisco Mime Troupe: The First Ten Years. R. G. Davis. LC 74-19943. (Illus.). 220p. 1975. 14.00 (ISBN 0-87867-058-0); pap. 5.95 (ISBN 0-87867-059-9). Ramparts.
San Francisco: Mission to Metropolis. 2nd ed. Oscar Lewis. LC 66-23944. (Illus.). 1980. 12.95 (ISBN 0-8310-7129-X). Howell-North.
San Francisco Museum of Modern Art: The Painting & Sculpture Collection. Diana DuPont et al. LC 84-11844. (Illus.). 404p. 1985. 75.00 (ISBN 0-933920-59-8, Dist. by Rizzoli); pap. 32.50 museum distribution only (ISBN 0-933920-60-1). Hudson Hills.
San Francisco Nights. Eudora Carroll. (Orig.). 1983. pap. 1.95 (BH169). Holloway.
San Francisco Nights: The Psychedelic Music Trip, 1965-1968. Gene Sculatti & Davin Seay. (Illus.). 191p. 1985. pap. 12.95 (ISBN 0-312-69903-4). St Martin.
San Francisco-Oakland Metropolitan Area, Strukturwandlungen Eines U. S. Amerikanischen Grossstadtkomplexes. Fritz Bartz. Repr. of 1954 ed. 20.00 (ISBN 0-384-03495-0). Johnson Repr.
San Francisco Observed: A Photographic Portfolio from 1850 to the Present. Compiled by Ruth Silverman. LC 86-14708. (Illus.). 120p. (Orig.). 1986. pap. 14.95 (ISBN 0-87701-388-8). Chronicle Bks.
San Francisco on a Shoestring: The Intelligent Traveller's (& Natives) Guide to Budget Living in San Francisco. 4th ed. Louis E. Madison. (Illus.). 160p. 1987. pap. 5.95 (ISBN 0-912125-02-0). A M Zimmermann.
San Francisco Peaks: A Guidebook to the Geology. 2nd ed. Troy L. Pewe & Randall G. Updike. 84p. 1976. pap. 2.50 (ISBN 0-89734-010-8). Mus Northern Ariz.
San Francisco Peninsula Birdwatching. Sequoia Audubon Society. Ed. by Anne Scanlan-Rohrer. (Illus., Orig.). 1985. pap. 8.95 (ISBN 0-9614301-0-9). Sequoia Aud Soc.
San Francisco Poems. Victor di Suvero. 64p. 1987. pap. 5.95 (ISBN 0-938631-00-4). Pennywhistle Pr.
San Francisco Restaurant Survey Update, 1988. rev. ed. Eugene H. Zagat, Jr. Ed. by Anthony D. Blue & Edwin J. Schwartz. 112p. (Orig.). 1987. pap. 8.95 (ISBN 0-943421-06-3). Zagat.
San Francisco Review of Books, Vol. XII, No. 1. (Illus.). 48p. 1987. 3.00 (ISBN 1-55660-017-8). A Wofsy Fine Arts.
San Francisco Review of Books, Vol. XII, No. 2. (Illus.). 48p. 1988. 3.00 (ISBN 1-55660-018-6). A Wofsy Fine Arts.
San Francisco Review of Books, Vol. XII, No. 3. (Illus.). 48p. 1988. 3.00 (ISBN 1-55660-019-4). A Wofsy Fine Arts.
San Francisco Review of Books, Vol. XII, No. 4. (Illus.). 48p. 1988. 3.00 (ISBN 1-55660-020-8). A Wofsy Fine Arts.
San Francisco Scavengers: Dirty Work & the Pride of Ownership. Stewart E. Perry. LC 77-78382. 1978. 25.00x (ISBN 0-520-03518-6). U of Cal Pr.
San Francisco Scenes. Greg Frazier. (City Scenes Ser.). (Illus.). 32p. 1972. pap. 3.95 (ISBN 0-912300-29-9, 29-9). Troubador Pr.
San Francisco Ship Passenger Lists, Vol. I. Louis J. Rasmussen. LC 78-60799. (Illus.). 273p. 1978. Repr. of 1965 ed. 17.50 (ISBN 0-8063-0823-0). Genealog Pub.
San Francisco Ship Passenger Lists, 5 vols. Louis J. Rasmussen. Incl. Vol. 1 o.p. 1965; Vol. 2. April 6, 1850 to November 4, 1851. 1966. 9.75 (ISBN 0-911792-01-5); Vol. 3. November 7, 1851 to June 17, 1852; Vol. 4. June 17, 1852 to 1853. 1970. 9.75 (ISBN 0-911792-03-1); Vol. 5. 1973. LC 65-13821. (Ship, Rail & Wagon Train Series). SF Hist Records.
San Francisco Stage: A History. Edmond M. Gagey. 1970. Repr. of 1950 ed. lib. bdg. 35.00x (ISBN 0-8371-3927-9, GAFS). Greenwood.
San Francisco Stages: A Concise History, 1849-1986. Dean Goodman. LC 86-62236. (Illus.). 222p. 1986. pap. 10.95 (ISBN 0-939477-01-7). Micro Pro Litera Pr.
San Francisco Statistical Abstract, 1986. Virgil L. Elliott. 75p. (Orig.). 1986. pap. 12.75 (ISBN 0-9610700-3-X). Statistical Pr.
San Francisco Symphony: Music, Maestros & Musicians. rev. ed. David Schneider. (Illus.). 336p. 1987. pap. 11.95 (ISBN 0-89141-296-4). Presidio Pr.
San Francisco: The Way It Was Then & Now. Phyllis Zauner & Lou Zauner. 1982. 4.95 (ISBN 0-936914-10-6). Zanel Pubns.
San Francisco, the Way It Was Then & Now. Phyllis Zauner & Lou Zauner. (Western Mini-Histories Ser.). (Illus.). 64p. (Orig.). 1980. pap. 4.50 (ISBN 0-936914-04-1). Zanel Pubns.
San Francisco Trivia. Karen Warner & Bill Dolon. LC 85-15383. (Illus.). 240p. (Orig.). 1985. pap. 7.95 (ISBN 0-89286-255-6, F869S345SD65). One Hund One Prods.
San Francisco Underground Gourmet. 4th ed. R. B. Read. 1977. pap. 6.95 (ISBN 0-671-22770-X, Fireside). S&S.
San Francisco, 1846-1856: From Hamlet to City. Roger W. Lotchin. LC 78-27192. (Illus.). xxvi, 406p. 1979. pap. 8.95 (ISBN 0-8032-7904-3, BB 701, Bison). U of Nebr Pr.
San Francisco, 1865-1932: Politics, Power, & Urban Development. William Issel & Robert W. Cherny. (Illus.). 352p. 1986. 40.00x (ISBN 0-520-05263-3); pap. 14.95x (ISBN 0-520-06033-4). U of Cal Pr.
San Francisco's Burning. Helen Adam. 1985. 25.00 (ISBN 0-914610-43-0); pap. 15.00 (ISBN 0-914610-33-3). Hanging Loose.
San Francisco's Chinatown: How Chinese a Town? Christopher L. Salter. LC 77-91458. 1978. soft cover 9.95 (ISBN 0-88247-500-2). R & E Pubs.
San Francisco's Literary Frontier. Franklin Walker. LC 74-8955. (Americana Library Ser.: No. 10). (Illus.). 480p. 1969. 20.00x (ISBN 0-295-95025-0, AL10). U of Wash Pr.
San Francisco's Ultimate Dining Guide: A Survey of over 300 Bay Area Restaurants by the REAL Experts; Chefs, Concierges, Cafe Critics & Community Leaders. Don W. Martin & Betty W. Martin. (Illus.). 224p. (Orig.). 1988. pap. 9.95 (ISBN 0-942053-03-6). Pine Cone Pr CA.
San Franciso Rock: The Illustrated History of San Fransisco Rock Music. Jack McDonough. LC 85-12768. (Illus.). 236p. 1985. pap. 16.95 (ISBN 0-87701-286-5). Chronicle Bks.
San Gabriel Mountains. Roy Murphy & Julia Murphy. (Illus.). 88p. 1985. 25.00 (ISBN 0-9615421-0-1). Big Santa Hist.
San Gabriels: Southern California Mountain Country. John Robinson. LC 77-24507. (Illus.). 200p. 1977. 28.95 (ISBN 0-87095-061-4). Gldn West Bks.
San, Hunter-Gatherers of the Kalahari: A Study in Ecological Anthropology. Jiro Tanaka. 199p. 1980. 22.50 (ISBN 0-86008-276-8, Pub. by U of Tokyo Japan). Columbia U Pr.
San Jacinto College: South Campus Library Handbook. Mary L. Barham. 96p. 1981. pap. text ed. 4.95 (ISBN 0-8403-2553-3). Kendall-Hunt.
San Joaquin Vignettes: The Reminiscences of Captain John Barker. William H. Boyd & Glendon J. Rodgers. (Illus.). 121p. 1955. 3.50 (ISBN 0-943500-08-7). Kern Historical.
San Jose Bride Book. Deborah Wood. 240p. 1987. pap. 16.95 (ISBN 0-937533-04-1). TEC Pubns.
San Jose de Gracia: Mexican Village in Transition. Luis Gonzalez. Tr. by John Upton from Span. LC 73-11495. (Texas Pan American Ser.). (Illus.). 406p. 1974. pap. 12.95x (ISBN 0-292-77571-7). U of Tex Pr.
San Jose Reflections. Edith Brackway. 1977. 13.00 (ISBN 0-912314-18-4); pap. 4.90 (ISBN 0-912314-17-6). Academy Santa Clara.
San Juan Bautista: Gateway to Spanish Texas. Robert S. Weddle. (Illus.). 485p. 1968. 27.50x (ISBN 0-292-73306-2). U of Tex Pr.
San Juan Country. Thomas M. Griffiths. LC 82-16544. (Illus.). 1984. 19.95 (ISBN 0-87108-753-7). Pruett.

Sandalwood Tree. Margaret Chatterjee. 4.80 (ISBN 0-89253-457-5); flexible cloth 4.00 (ISBN 0-89253-458-3). Ind-US Inc.

Sandarbh-MulAK Shabd-Kosh: Hindi-English-Hindi Dictionary of Phrase & Fable Including Symbolic & Idiomatic Expressions. Om P. Gauba. viii, 258p. 1986. text ed. 35.00x (ISBN 81-7018-363-4, Pub. by B. R. Pub Corp Delhi). Apt Bks.

Sandbar Sinister. Phoebe A. Taylor. (Asey Mayo Cape Cod Adventure Ser.). 296p. 1986. pap. 5.95 (ISBN 0-88150-063-1, Foul Play). Countryman.

Sandblaster. Jack Rudman. (Career Examination Ser.: C-1461). (Cloth bdg. avail. on request). pap. 10.00 (ISBN 0-8373-1461-5). Natl Learning.

Sandbox. Edward Albee. Bd. with Death of Bessie Smith. 1964. pap. 2.95 (ISBN 0-451-12819-2, AE2819, Sig). NAL.

Sandbox: A Study in the Optimal Lifestyle. Conrad Manning. 175p. (Orig.). Date not set. pap. 14.95 (ISBN 0-9618479-0-5). Sandbox Inc.

Sandbox & the Death of Bessie Smith. Edward Albee. 1988. pap. 6.95 (ISBN 0-452-26083-3, Plume). NAL.

Sandbox Betty. Catherine Petrie. LC 81-15547. (Rookie Readers Ser.). (Illus.). 32p. (ps-2). 1982. PLB 9.93 (ISBN 0-516-03578-9); pap. 2.50 (ISBN 0-516-43578-7). Childrens.

Sandbox Society: Early Education in Black & White America - An Ethnographic Comparison. Sally Lubeck. LC 85-10422. 160p. 1985. 31.00x (ISBN 1-85000-051-4, Falmer Pr); pap. 14.00x (ISBN 1-85000-050-6, Falmer Pr). Taylor & Francis.

Sandburg Treasury: Prose & Poetry for Young People. Carl Sandburg. LC 79-120818. (Illus.). (gr. 7 up). 1970. 19.95 (ISBN 0-15-270180-X, HJ). HarBraceJ.

Sandburrs. facs. ed. Alfred H. Lewis. LC 72-90585. (Short Story Index Reprint Ser.). (Illus.). 1900. 19.00 (ISBN 0-8369-3068-1). Ayer Co Pubs.

Sandburrs. facsimile ed. Alfred H. Lewis. LC 72-104512. (Illus.). 318p. Repr. of 1900 ed. lib. bdg. 18.00 (ISBN 0-8398-1158-6). Irvington.

Sandburrs. Alfred H. Lewis. 318p. 1986. pap. text ed. 7.95x (ISBN 0-8290-2029-2). Irvington.

Sandcast. Wayne Turiansky. 36p. 1975. pap. 2.00 (ISBN 0-913028-35-5). North Atlantic.

Sandcastle. Iris Murdoch. 1978. pap. 6.95 (ISBN 0-14-001474-8). Penguin.

Sandcastle Murder. Elizabeth St. Clair. (Mystery Puzzler: No. 24). (Illus., Orig.). 1979. pap. 1.95 (ISBN 0-89083-478-4). Zebra.

Sandcastle Seahorses. Nikia C. Leopold. 1988. cancelled (ISBN 0-913123-16-1); pap. 10.95 (ISBN 0-913123-17-X). Galileo.

Sandcastles. Lynn Sebastian. 189p. 1984. 7.48 (ISBN 0-89697-204-6). Intl Univ Pr.

Sandcastles & Cucumber Ships Last Forever. LC 78-74555. 48p. (Orig.). (gr. 3-8). 2.95 (ISBN 0-916872-06-8). Delafield Pr.

Sandeagozu. Jahann V. Jenner. LC 86-45119. 448p. 1986. 18.95i (ISBN 0-06-015633-3, HarpT). Har-Row.

Sandenny. Maryhelen Clague. 336p. (Orig.). 1986. pap. 3.95 (ISBN 0-441-75348-5, Pub. by Charter Bks). Ace Bks.

Sandford Ballard Dole: Hawaii's Only President, 1844-1926. Helena G. Allen. LC 87-72591. (Illus.). 304p. 1988. 19.95 (ISBN 0-87062-184-X). A H Clark.

Sandglass. Danilo Kis. Tr. by Ammiel Alcalay & Klara Alcalay. 304p. Date not set. 18.95 (ISBN 0-374-25386-2). FS&G.

Sandgrains on a Tray: Poems. Alan Brownjohn. LC 69-19125. 1969. 10.95 (ISBN 0-8023-1212-8). Dufour.

Sandgropers. Dorothy Hewett. 1973. 19.95 (ISBN 0-85564-070-7, Pub. by U of W Austral Pr). Intl Spec Bk.

Sandhi Phenomena in the Languages of Europe. Ed. by Henning Andersen. (Trends in Linguistics, Studies & Monographs: No. 33). (Illus.). xii, 616p. 1986. lib. bdg. 152.00x (ISBN 3-11-009882-2). Mouton.

Sandhi: The Theoretical, Phonetic, & Historical Bases of Word-Junction in Sanskrit. W. Sidney Allen. (Janua Linguarum Ser. Minor: No. 17). 1972. pap. text ed. 12.80x (ISBN 90-2792-360-4). Mouton.

Sandhill Century, Eighteen Eighty-Three to Nineteen Eighty-Three, 2 vols. set. Ed. by Marianne Beel. LC 85-70605. (Illus.). 1986. Set. 61.00 (ISBN 0-9614508-2-7); Book I: The Land 400pp. 0.00 (ISBN 0-9614508-0-0); Book II: The People 562pp. 0.00 (ISBN 0-9614508-1-9). Cherry County Cent.

Sandhill Sundays & Other Recollections. Mari Sandoz. LC 78-82707. x, 167p. 1984. pap. 5.95 (ISBN 0-8032-9148-5, BB 901, Bison). U of Nebr Pr.

Sandhills Beckon. Maxine B. Isackson. 1977. 13.00 (ISBN 0-931068-08-8). Purcells.

Sandhurst: A Documentary. Michael Yardley. 1987. 60.00x (ISBN 0-245-54492-5, Pub. by Harrap Ltd England). State Mutual Bk.

Sandi Patti: A Biography. Don Cusic. LC 87-27444. 168p. 1988. pap. 8.95 (ISBN 0-385-24353-7, Dolp). Doubleday.

Sandi Patti: The Book of Words. (Illus.). 80p. (Orig.). 1986. pap. 9.95 (ISBN 0-88188-463-4, HL00183671). H Leonard Pub Corp.

Sandia Mountain Sequence. Carl Mayfield. 20p. 1982. 7.00 (ISBN 0-913719-58-7); pap. 2.00 (ISBN 0-913719-57-9). High-Coo Pr.

Sandinista. Marie Jakober. 237p. (Orig.). 1985. pap. 8.95 (ISBN 0-919573-43-6, Pub. by New Star Bks BC). Left Bank.

Sandinista Constitution. (State Department Publications). 58p. 1987. pap. 3.00 (ISBN 0-318-23759-8, 044-000-02190-1). USGPO.

Sandinista Nicaragua: Pragmatism in a Political Economy in Formation & Reform with Repression: The Land Reform in El Salvador. Harold Sims & Edward F. Lehoucq. LC 80-20048. (ISHI Occasional Papers in Social Change Ser.: Nos. 5 & 6). 48p. 1982. pap. text ed. 6.95 (ISBN 0-89727-027-4). ISHI PA.

Sandinista Revolution: National Liberation & Social Transformation in Central America. Carlos Vilas. Tr. by Judy Butler from Span. 384p. 1986. 27.50 (ISBN 0-85345-679-8); pap. 12.00 (ISBN 0-85345-680-1). Monthly Rev.

Sandinistas Speak: Speeches & Writings of Nicaragua's Leaders. Tomas Borge et al. Tr. by Taber & Reissner. 250p. 1982. PLB 15.00 (ISBN 0-87348-618-8); pap. 5.95 (ISBN 0-87348-619-6). Path Pr NY.

Sandinistas: The Party & the Revolution. Dennis Gilbert. 244p. Date not set. 24.95 (ISBN 1-55786-006-8). Basil Blackwell.

Sandino. Gregorio Selser. Tr. by Cedric Belfrage. LC 80-8086. 256p. 1982. pap. 8.00 (ISBN 0-85345-559-7). Monthly Rev.

Sandino Affair. Neill Macaulay. LC 85-20430. (Illus.). 320p. 1985. pap. 12.50 (ISBN 0-8223-0696-4). Duke.

Sandino's Daughters. Margaret Randall. Ed. & illus. by Linda Yanz. (Illus.). 220p. 1981. lib. bdg. 15.95 (ISBN 0-317-65204-4); pap. 7.95 (ISBN 0-919888-33-X). Left Bank.

Sandition see Northanger Abbey.

Sanditon: A Facsimile of the Manuscript. Jane Austen. 1975. 39.95x (ISBN 0-19-812556-9). Oxford U Pr.

Sanditon, the Watsons, Lady Susan, & Other Miscellanea. Jane Austen. 1978. Repr. of 1934 ed. 11.95x (ISBN 0-460-00004-7, Evman). Biblio Dist.

Sandkings. George R. Martin. (Orig.). 1986. pap. 2.95 (ISBN 0-671-42663-X, Timescape). PB.

Sandlapper Cookbook. Compiled by Catha W. Reid & Joseph T. Bruce, Jr. LC 73-88594. (Illus.). 241p. 1982. pap. 6.95 (ISBN 0-87844-020-8). Sandlapper Pub Co.

Sandlot Seasons: Sport in Black Pittsburgh. Rob Ruck. LC 86-4272. (Sport & Society Ser.). (Illus.). 258p. 1987. 21.95 (ISBN 0-252-01322-0). U of Ill Pr.

Sandlot Summit. Richard A. Fishman. LC 85-63032. (Illus.). 197p. (Orig.). (gr. 4-9). 1985. pap. 3.95 (ISBN 0-9615884-0-3). Sunlakes Pub.

Sandman. Miles Gibson. 192p. 1985. 12.95 (ISBN 0-312-69912-3, Pub. by Marek). St Martin.

Sandman. Miles Gibson. 192p. 1987. pap. 3.50 (ISBN 0-345-34217-8). Ballantine.

Sandman. William W. Johnstone. 432p. 1988. pap. 3.95 (ISBN 0-8217-2376-6). Zebra.

Sandman. Bob Shepperson. (Illus.). 32p. (ps up). Date not set. 12.95 (ISBN 0-374-36405-2). FS&G.

Sandman's Eyes. Patricia Windsor. (gr. k-12). 1987. pap. 2.95 (ISBN 0-440-97585-9, LFL). Dell.

Sandmouth. Ronald Frame. LC 87-45232. 476p. 1987. 19.95 (ISBN 0-394-56357-3). Knopf.

Sandon Guide to Royal Worcester Figures, 1900-1970. Henry Sandon & John Sandon. (Illus.). 224p. 1988. 65.00 (ISBN 0-946619-18-2, Pub. by Alderman Pr London). Seven Hills Bks.

Sandpainting. Gray Jacobik. LC 80-50065. (Ser. Five). 50p. 1980. pap. 2.50 (ISBN 0-931846-15-3). Wash Writers Pub.

Sandpainting. Michael Rothberg. 16p. 1980. pap. 2.50 (ISBN 0-938370-01-4). Wildflower.

Sandpiper: The Life & Letters of Celia Thaxter. Rosamond Thaxter. LC 82-16531. (Illus.). 354p. pap. 8.50 (ISBN 0-914339-01-X). P E Randall Pub.

Sandpipers: Selected Poems, 1965-1975. David Posner. LC 76-13586. (University of Central Florida Contemporary Poetry Ser.). 1976. 8.95 (ISBN 0-8130-0549-3); deluxe ed. 20.00 (ISBN 0-8130-0573-6). U Presses Fla.

Sandplay: A Psychotherapeutic Approach to the Psyche. rev. ed. Dora M. Kalff. Tr. by Hilde Kirsch & Wendayne Ackerman. LC 80-27195. (Illus.). 166p. 1981. pap. 12.95 (ISBN 0-938434-00-4). Sigo Pr.

Sandra & Syd. Sandra Paxford & Madeleine Parker. 32p. (YA) (gr. 7-10). 1986. pap. 12.00x (ISBN 0-7223-2067-1, Pub. by A H Stockwell England). State Mutual Bk.

Sandra Day O'Connor: First Woman on the Supreme Court. Carol Greene. LC 81-18038. (Picture Story Ser.). (Illus.). 32p. (gr. 1-4). 1982. PLB 11.93 (ISBN 0-516-03618-1). Childrens.

Sandra Mendelsohn Rubin: Paintings & Drawings, March 4-April 4, 1987. LC 87-70243. (Illus.). 36p. (Orig.). 1987. pap. 10.00 (ISBN 0-936827-04-1). C Bernard Gallery Ltd.

Sandritter's Color Atlas & Textbook of Histopathology. 7th ed. Thomas. 1984. 34.95 (ISBN 0-8151-8794-7). Year Bk Med.

Sandritter's Color Atlas & Textbook of Macropathology. 4th ed. Thomas. 1985. 34.95 (ISBN 0-8151-8789-0). Year Bk Med.

Sandro of Chegem. Fazil Iskander. Tr. by Susan Brownsberger from Rus. LC 82-13219. 369p. (Orig.). 1983. pap. 9.95 (ISBN 0-394-71516-0, Vin). Random.

S&S Book of Cryptic Crossword Puzzles, No. 1. Eugene T. Maleska. 1980. 3.95 (ISBN 0-671-25307-7, 25307, Fireside). S&S.

S&S Crossword Series, No. 147. Ed. by Eugene T. Maleska & John M. Sampson. 1989. 5.95 (ISBN 0-671-67593-1, Fireside). S&S.

S&S Crosswords from the Times, No. 38. Margaret P. Farrar. 1980. 3.95 (ISBN 0-686-62843-8, 25503, Fireside). S&S.

S&S Crostics, No. 83. Thomas H. Middleton. 1980. 3.95 (ISBN 0-686-61340-6, 25464). S&S.

Sands Family. LC 71-138074. (Saco Valley Settlements Ser). 1970. pap. 2.50 (ISBN 0-8048-0831-7). C E Tuttle.

S&S Guide to Birds of the World. John Bull. 1981. (Fireside); pap. 12.95 (ISBN 0-671-42235-9). S&S.

S&S Guide to Insects. R. Arnett & R. Jacques, Jr. 1981. pap. 12.95 (ISBN 0-671-25014-0). S&S.

S&S Guide to Mushrooms. Gary Lincoff. 1982. pap. 11.95 (ISBN 0-671-42849-7). S&S.

Sands of Mars. Arthur C. Clarke. (RL 7). pap. 2.50 (ISBN 0-451-12312-3, AE2312, Sig). NAL.

Sands of Sorrow: Israel's Journey from Independence to Uncertainty. Milton Viorst. LC 86-45705. 256p. 1987. 19.95i (ISBN 0-06-015707-0, HarpT). Har-Row.

Sands of the Kalahari. William Mulvihill. 15.95 (ISBN 0-89190-869-2, Pub. by Am Repr). Amereon Ltd.

Sands of Time. Sidney Sheldon. 320p. 1988. 19.95 (ISBN 0-688-06571-6). Morrow.

Sands of Time, Vol. 1. Carolyn E. Cardwell. (Illus.). 225p. (Orig.). 1986. pap. 10.95 (ISBN 0-916395-21-9, ST-1). Hieroglyphics.

Sands of Time, Vol. 2. Carolyn E. Cardwell. (Illus.). 225p. (Orig.). 1986. pap. 10.95 (ISBN 0-916395-23-5, ST-2). Hieroglyphics.

Sands of Time Recollections & Reflections: Edmund Burke, Carlyle, Disraeli, W. H. Mallock, Ruskin, Sheridan, Swinburne, Tennyson, Wilde. Walter Sichel. 1923. Repr. 25.00 (ISBN 0-8492-9975-6). R West.

Sands of Valor. Geoffrey Wagner. 1979. pap. 2.25 (ISBN 0-8439-0667-7, Leisure Bks). Leisure NY.

Sands of Valor. Geoffrey Wagner. 1985. pap. 3.95 (ISBN 0-8217-1633-6). Zebra.

Sands of Valour. Geoffrey Wagner. (Echoes of War Ser.). 1987. 12.95 (ISBN 0-907675-51-4, Pub. by Buchan & Enright England). Seven Hills Bks.

Sands of Windee. Arthur Upfield. (Napoleon Bonaparte Mystery Ser.). 16.95 (ISBN 0-89190-570-7, Pub. by Am Repr). Amereon Ltd.

Sands of Windee. Arthur W. Upfield. 224p. 1985. pap. 3.95 rack size (ISBN 0-684-18502-4, ScribT). Scribner.

Sandscripts, Vol. I: Word Pictures of Life. W. L. Lambert. Ed. & illus. by Mary H. Lambert. LC 88-91181. (Illus.). 102p. (Orig.). 1988. pap. 7.00 (ISBN 0-929357-00-0). Sandscript Creations.

Sandstone Depositional Models for Exploration for Fossil Fuels. 3rd ed. George Klein. LC 84-29735. (Illus.). 218p. 1985. text ed. 48.00 (ISBN 0-934634-82-3). Intl Human Res.

Sandstone Papers: On the Crisis of Contemporary Life. Martin Glass. LC 86-50781. 192p. (Orig.). 1986. pap. 9.00 (ISBN 0-939660-18-0). Threshold VT.

Sandtiquity. Connie Simo et al. LC 78-20696. (Illus.). 1980. pap. 10.95 (ISBN 0-8008-6989-3). Taplinger.

Sandusky Tool Co. Illustrated List of Planes, Etc. 1978. Repr. of 1877 ed. 5.00 (ISBN 0-913602-24-8). K Roberts.

Sandwich Book: A Complete Guide to America's Favorite Food, from Child-Pleasers to Classics to Calzones & Other Dagwood Dreams. Judy Gethers. LC 87-45929. (Illus.). 256p. (Orig.). 1988. pap. 8.95 (ISBN 0-394-75497-2, Vin). Random.

Sandwich Glass. Ruth W. Lee. (Illus.). 620p. 1966. 35.00 (ISBN 0-8048-7009-8). C E Tuttle.

Sandwich Glass Handbook. Ruth W. Lee. 238p. 1985. pap. 13.25 (ISBN 0-8048-7010-1). C E Tuttle.

Sandwich Glass: The History of the Boston & Sandwich Glass Company. Ruth W. Lee. (Illus.). 590p. 35.00 (ISBN 0-317-55000-4). Apollo.

Sandwich Maker. Bob Altshuler. LC 84-730283. (Series 927). (Orig.). 1985. pap. 7.00 wkbk. (ISBN 0-8064-0405-1); audio-visual pkg. 239.00 (ISBN 0-8064-0406-X). Bergwall.

Sandwich Mas Grande, Jamas. Rita G. Gelman. Tr. by Otto R. Vasquez. (Illus.). 48p. (Span.). (gr. k-3). 1987. pap. 2.95 (ISBN 0-590-40884-4). Scholastic Inc.

Sandwich Preparation. 1974. pap. 8.95 (ISBN 0-317-55379-8). Van Nos Reinhold.

Sandwich: The Town That Glass Built. Harriet B. Barbour. LC 72-153125. (Illus.). 318p. 1972. Repr. of 1948 ed. lib. bdg. 35.00x (ISBN 0-678-03564-4). Kelley.

Sandwriter. Monica Hughes. LC 87-21198. 159p. (gr. 5 up). 1988. 12.95 (ISBN 0-8050-0617-6). H Holt & Co.

Sandy. Lois A. Eggers et al. Ed. by Gerald Wheeler. (Banner Ser.). 96p. (Orig.). 1985. pap. 6.95 (ISBN 0-8280-0235-5). Review & Herald.

Sandy. Helen B. King. (Illus.). 18p. (ps-3). 1985. pap. 4.95 (ISBN 0-9615366-4-0). King ME.

Sandy. Rachel Segall. 1988. 5.95 (ISBN 0-533-07621-8). Vantage.

Sandy: A Heart for God. Leighton Ford. LC 85-52. 192p. (Orig.). 1985. 9.95 (ISBN 0-87784-824-6); pap. 5.95 (ISBN 0-8308-1709-3). Inter-Varsity.

Sandy, a Snake with Destiny. Wayne Shaw. 1984. 4.95 (ISBN 0-533-06001-X). Vantage.

Sandy & the Rock Star. Walt Morey. LC 78-12375. (gr. 4-7). 1979. 13.95 (ISBN 0-525-38785-4). Dutton.

Sandy Hook--In 1879. George Houghton. Ed. by William R. Jones. (Illus.). 16p. 1978. pap. 2.50 (ISBN 0-89646-047-9). Outbooks.

Sandy Shore. John Hay. LC 68-18991. (Illus.). 1968. 8.95 (ISBN 0-85699-006-X). Chatham Pr.

Sandy Soils: Report of the FAO-UNDP Seminar on Reclamation & Management of Sandy Soils in the Near East & North Africa, Nicosia, 3-8 Dec. 1973. (Soils Bulletins: No. 25). (Illus.). 251p. 1975. pap. 18.75 (ISBN 92-5-100613-X, F1167, FAO). UNIPUB.

Sandy: The Girl Who Was Rescued. Douglas Blackwood. (Children Around the World Ser.). 1988. 7.95 (ISBN 0-8028-5026-X). Eerdmans.

Sandy's Casuals. Jerry A. Funk & Warern A. Smith. 56p. 1985. pap. text ed. 11.95 (ISBN 0-03-000319-9). Dryden Pr.

Sandyvale Cemetery, Johnstown, PA: A Recreation of Burials, 1850-1906. Phyllis Oyler. 363p. Date not set. pap. text ed. 30.00 (ISBN 0-933227-72-8). Closson Pr.

Sane Alternative: A Choice of Futures. 3rd ed. James Robertson. 152p. (Orig.). 1983. pap. 4.95 (ISBN 0-936106-00-X). River Basin.

Sane Occultism & Practical Occultism in Daily Life. Dion Fortune. 256p. (Orig.). 1987. pap. 11.95 (ISBN 0-85030-663-9, Pub. by Thorsons UK). Weiser.

Sane Sex Life. H. W. Long. 7.95x (ISBN 0-685-22094-X). Wehman.

Sane Society. Erich Fromm. 1955. pap. 5.95 (ISBN 0-03-025540-6). H Holt & Co.

Sane Society Ideal in Modern Utopianism: A Study in Ideology. Kerry S. Walters. LC 87-28126. (Problems in Contemporary Philosophy Ser.: Vol. 7). 344p. 1988. lib. bdg. 59.95 (ISBN 0-88946-331-X). E Mellen.

Sanford Hirsch: Painted Sculptures. Alain Joyaux & Richard Wattenmaker. (Illus.). 16p. (Orig.). 1985. pap. 2.00 (ISBN 0-915511-04-5). Ball State Art.

Sanford Meisner on Acting. Sanford Meisner & Dennis Longwell. LC 86-46187. 1987. pap. 8.95 (ISBN 0-394-75059-4, Vin). Random.

Sang d'Afrique. Guy Des Cars. 408p. 1963. 14.95 (ISBN 0-686-55657-7). French & Eur.

Sang d'Afrique: L'Africain, Vol. 1. Guy Des Cars. 1971. 9.95 (ISBN 0-686-55658-5). French & Eur.

Sang d'Afrique: L'Amoureuse, Vol. 2. Guy Des Cars. 1971. 9.95 (ISBN 0-686-55659-3). French & Eur.

Sang Des Autres. Simone de Beauvoir. (Folio Ser.: No. 363). 320p. 1973. 7.95 (ISBN 0-686-54093-X). Schoenhof.

Sang Dore des Borgia. Francoise Sagan & Jacques Quoirez. 216p. 1978. 12.95 (ISBN 0-686-55398-5). French & Eur.

Sang Thong: A Dance-Drama from Thailand. King Rama, 2nd. Tr. by Fern S. Ingersoll. LC 72-88097. (Illus.). 1972. 6.00 (ISBN 0-8048-1002-8). C E Tuttle.

Sangam City: Delhi. Intro. by Khushwant Singh. (Illus.). 152p. (Orig.). 1983. pap. text ed. 5.00x (ISBN 0-86131-373-9, Pub. by Orient Longman Ltd India). Apt Bks.

Sangamon. Edgar L. Masters. (Prairie State Bks.). (Illus.). 296p. 1988. pap. 8.95 (ISBN 0-252-06038-5). U of Ill Pr.

Sangaree. Frank G. Slaughter. 290p. 1975. lib. bdg. 19.95x (ISBN 0-89190-283-X, Pub. by River City Pr). Amereon Ltd.

Sangeeth Bhashya: Terminology of Musical Terms (In Hindi) S. Bandyopadhyaya. (Illus.). 479p. 1986. text ed. 60.00x (ISBN 81-7018-285-9, Pub. by B R Pub Corp Delhi). Apt Bks.

Sangha & State in Burma: A Study of Monastic Sectarianism & Leadership. E. Michael Mendelson. Ed. by John P. Ferguson. LC 75-13398. (Illus.). 416p. 1975. 45.00x (ISBN 0-8014-0875-X). Cornell U Pr.

Sangha, State, & Society: Thai Buddhism in History. Yoneo Ishii. Tr. by Peter Hawkes from Japanese. (Monographs, Center for Southeast Asian Studies, Kyoto University). 224p. 1986. text ed. 25.00x (ISBN 0-8248-0993-9); pap. text ed. 16.00x (ISBN 0-8248-0994-7). UH Pr.

Sangita Ratnakara of Sarngadeva, Vol. 1. Sarangadeva. Tr. by R. K. Shringy from Sanskrit. 1978. 35.00 (ISBN 0-89684-009-3, Pub. by Motilal Banarsidass India). Orient Bk Dist.

Sangre Bajo Las Banderas (de Rusia Vino el Martillo - y la Hoz de Mi Garganta) Joaquin E. Piedra. LC 85-81209. (Espejo de Paciencia Ser.). 101p. (Orig., Span.). 1986. pap. 9.95 (ISBN 0-89729-382-7). Ediciones.

Sangreal Ceremonies & Rituals. William G. Gray. LC 85-51169. (Sangreal Sodality Ser.: Vol. 4). 1986. pap. 12.95 (ISBN 0-87728-583-7). Weiser.

Sangreal Sacrament. William G. Gray. LC 82-62847. (Sangreal Sodality Ser.: Vol. 2). 224p. 1983. pap. 8.95 (ISBN 0-87728-562-4). Weiser.
Sangreal Tarot. William G. Gray. (Illus.). 256p. (Orig.). 1988. pap. 12.95 (ISBN 0-87728-665-5). Weiser.
Sanguinet's Crown. Patricia Veryan. 368p. 1985. 15.95 (ISBN 0-312-69922-0). St Martin.
Sanguinet's Crown. Patricia Veryan. (General Ser.). 517p. 1986. lib. bdg. 15.95x (ISBN 0-8161-4028-6, Large Print Bks). G K Hall.
Sanhedrin, 2 vols. (Hebrew & Eng.). 30.00 (ISBN 0-910218-74-9). Bennet Pub.
Sanibel Shell Guide. Margaret Greenberg & Nancy J. Olds. LC 82-71090. (Illus.). 117p. (Orig.). 1982. pap. 5.95 (ISBN 0-89305-041-5). Anna Pub.
Sanilac Petroglyphs. rev. ed. Robert T. Hatt et al. (Cranbrook Institute of Science Bulletin Ser.: No.36). (Illus.). 48p. 1987. pap. write for info. (ISBN 0-87737-038-9). Cranbrook.
Sanitarian. Jack Rudman. (Career Examination Ser.: C-1462). (Cloth bdg. avail. on request). pap. 14.00 (ISBN 0-8373-1462-3). Natl Learning.
Sanitarian Trainee. Jack Rudman. (Career Examination Ser.: C-1463). (Cloth bdg. avail. on request). pap. 12.00 (ISBN 0-8373-1463-1). Natl Learning.
Sanitarian's Handbook: Theory & Administrative Practice for Environmental Health. Ben Freedman. 1977. 69.50 (ISBN 0-930234-02-2). Peerless.
Sanitary Centennial & Selected Short Stories. Fernando Sorrentino. Tr. by Thomas C. Meehan from Span. (Texas Pan American Ser.). 216p. 1988. 19.95 (ISBN 0-292-77608-X). U of Tex Pr.
Sanitary Chemist. Jack Rudman. (Career Examination Ser.: C-3266). (Cloth bdg. avail. on request). 1988. pap. 18.00 (ISBN 0-8373-3266-4). Natl Learning.
Sanitary Commission of the U. S. Army, a Succinct Narrative of Its Works & Purposes. U. S. Sanitary Commission. LC 78-180567. (Medicine & Society in America Ser). 326p. 1972. Repr. of 1864 ed. 20.00 (ISBN 0-405-03978-6). Ayer Co Pubs.
Sanitary Condition of Boston: The Report of a Medical Commission. Boston Medical Commission. Ed. by Barbara G. Rosenkrantz. LC 76-25655. (Public Health in America Ser.). 1977. Repr. of 1875 ed. lib. bdg. 17.00x (ISBN 0-405-09808-1). Ayer Co Pubs.
Sanitary Condition of the Laboring Population of New York, with Suggestions for Its Improvement. John H. Griscom. LC 75-125742. (American Environmental Studies). Repr. of 1845 ed. 12.00x (ISBN 0-405-02667-6). Ayer Co Pubs.
Sanitary Construction Inspector. Jack Rudman. (Career Examination Ser.: C-3195). 1988. pap. 18.00 (ISBN 0-8373-3195-1). Natl Learning.
Sanitary Engineer. Jack Rudman. (Career Examination Ser.: C-798). (Cloth bdg. avail. on request). pap. 14.00 (ISBN 0-8373-0798-8). Natl Learning.
Sanitary Engineer II. Jack Rudman. (Career Examination Ser.: C-2945). (Cloth bdg. avail. on request). pap. 14.00 (ISBN 0-8373-2945-0). Natl Learning.
Sanitary Engineer III. Jack Rudman. (Career Examination Ser.: C-2946). (Cloth bdg. avail. on request). pap. 16.00 (ISBN 0-8373-2946-9). Natl Learning.
Sanitary Engineer IV. Jack Rudman. (Career Examination Ser.: C-2947). (Cloth bdg. avail. on request). pap. 16.00 (ISBN 0-8373-2947-7). Natl Learning.
Sanitary Engineering: Problems & Calculations for the Professional Engineer. Harry Harbold. LC 79-88898. (Illus.). 1980. 32.95 (ISBN 0-250-40319-6). Butterworth.
Sanitary Evolution of London. Henry Jephson. LC 70-173152. Repr. of 1909 ed. 33.00 (ISBN 0-405-08671-7, Blom Pubns). Ayer Co Pubs.
Sanitary Improvement District As a Mechanism for Urban Development. Center for Applied Urban Research Staff. 126p. 1975. pap. 9.00 (ISBN 1-55719-027-5). U NE Ctr Applied Urban Rsch.
Sanitary Laboratory Technician. Jack Rudman. (Career Examination Ser.: C-1037). 1988. pap. 16.00 (ISBN 0-8373-1037-7). Natl Learning.
Sanitary Landfill. (ASCE Manual & Report on Engineering Practice Ser.: No. 39). 105p. 1976. 27.00x (ISBN 0-87262-215-0). Am Soc Civil Eng.
Sanitary Lessons of the War & Other Papers. George M. Sternberg. Ed. by Barbara G. Rosenkrantz. LC 76-40647. (Public Health in America Ser.). 1977. Repr. of 1912 ed. lib. bdg. 17.00x (ISBN 0-405-09832-4). Ayer Co Pubs.
Sanitary Ramblings: Sketches & Illustrations of Bethal Green. Hector Gavin. (Illus.). 132p. 1971. Repr. of 1848 ed. 27.50x (ISBN 0-7146-2417-9, F Cass & Co). Biblio Dist.
Sanitary Regulations for Molluscs. R. Coppini. (GFCM Studies & Reviews: No. 29). 19p. (Eng. & Fr.). 1965. pap. 7.50 (ISBN 92-5-101947-9, F1790, FAO). UNIPUB.
Sanitary Techniques in Food Service. 2nd ed. Karla Longree. LC 81-3047. 271p. 1982. pap. write for info. (ISBN 0-02-371550-2). Macmillan.
Sanitation & Disease: Health Aspects of Excreta & Wastewater Management. Richard G. Feachem et al. (World Bank Studies in Water Supply & Sanitation). 501p. 1983. 107.00x (ISBN 0-471-90094-X). Wiley.
Sanitation & Parking Violation Inspector. Jack Rudman. (Career Examination Ser.: C-1873). (Cloth bdg. avail. on request). pap. 14.00 (ISBN 0-8373-1873-4). Natl Learning.
Sanitation Aspects of Food Service Facility Plan Preparation & Review: Reference Guide. 100p. 2.00 (ISBN 0-317-35247-4). Natl Sanit Foun.
Sanitation Dispatcher. Jack Rudman. (Career Examination Ser.: C-2881). (Cloth bdg. avail. on request). pap. 14.00 (ISBN 0-8373-2881-0). Natl Learning.
Sanitation Enforcement Agent. Jack Rudman. (Career Examination Ser.: C-3177). (Cloth bdg. avail. on request). 1988. pap. 14.00 (ISBN 0-8373-3177-3). Natl Learning.
Sanitation for Food Service Workers. 3rd ed. Treva Richardson & Wade Nicodemus. 368p. 1983. 23.95 (ISBN 0-8436-2205-9). Van Nos Reinhold.
Sanitation, Hydrology, Hydraulics. 20.00. Am Consul Eng.
Sanitation in Developing Countries: Proceedings of a Workshop on Training Held in Labaste, Botswana, 14-20 Aug. 1980. 172p. 1981. pap. 9.00 (ISBN 0-88936-293-9, IDRC168, IDRC). UNIPUB.
Sanitation in Food Processing. Ed. by John A. Troller. LC 82-16291. (Food Science & Technology Ser.). 1983. 36.50 (ISBN 0-12-700660-5). Acad Pr.
Sanitation Inspector. Jack Rudman. (Career Examination Ser.: C-2152). (Cloth bdg. avail. on request). 1988. pap. 14.00 (ISBN 0-8373-2152-2). Natl Learning.
Sanitation Inspector Trainee. Jack Rudman. (Career Examination Ser.: C-2029). (Cloth bdg. avail. on request). pap. 12.00 (ISBN 0-8373-2029-1). Natl Learning.
Sanitation Man. Jack Rudman. (Career Examination Ser.: C-700). (Cloth bdg. avail. on request). pap. 12.00 (ISBN 0-8373-0700-7). Natl Learning.
Sanitation Management: Strategies for Success. Ronald F. Cichy. Ed. by Margo Bogart. LC 84-4092. (Illus.). 481p. 1984. 36.95 (ISBN 0-86612-018-1). Educ Inst Am Hotel.
Sanitation Management: Strategies for Success. 2nd ed. Ronald F. Cichy. (Illus.). 500p. Date not set. text ed. 36.95 (ISBN 0-86612-054-8). Educ Inst Am Hotel.
Sanitation Operations Manual. rev. ed. 390p. 1984. 3-ring binder 24.95 (ISBN 0-317-57918-5, MG857). Natl Restaurant Assn.
Sanitation, Safety & Environmental Standards. Lewis J. Minor. (L. J. Minor Foodservice Statndard Ser.: Vol. 2). (Illus.). 1983. text ed. 23.95 (ISBN 0-87055-428-X). AVI.
Sanitation Self-Inspection Program for Foodservice Operators. rev. ed. 32p. 1983. 5.00 (ISBN 0-317-57920-7, MG869). Natl Restaurant Assn.
Sanitation Strategy for a Lakefront Metropolis: The Case of Chicago. Louis P. Cain. LC 76-14711. 173p. 1978. 15.00 (ISBN 0-87580-064-5). N Ill U Pr.
Sanitation Supervisor. Jack Rudman. (Career Examination Ser.: C-2151). (Cloth bdg. avail. on request). 1988. pap. 14.00 (ISBN 0-8373-2151-4). Natl Learning.
Sanitation Worker. 6th ed. Hy Hammer. LC 82-11440. 192p. (Orig.). 1983. pap. 8.00 (ISBN 0-668-05491-3). Arco.
Sanitation Worker. Susan C. Poskanzer. LC 88-10044. (What's It Like to Be a... Ser.). (Illus.). 32p. (gr. k-2). 1988. PLB 9.89 (ISBN 0-8167-1436-3); pap. text ed. 1.95 (ISBN 0-8167-1437-1). Troll Assocs.
Sanity & Survival in the Nuclear Age. Jerome D. Frank. LC 82-9872. 1982. pap. text ed. write for info (ISBN 0-394-33229-6, RanC). Random.
Sanity & Survival in the Nuclear Age: Psychological Aspects of War & Peace. Jerome D. Frank. 346p. Date not set. pap. 12.75 (ISBN 0-8191-6744-4). U Pr of Amer.
Sanity in Bedlam: A Study of Robert Burton's "Anatomy of Melancholy". Lawrence Babb. LC 77-13309. 1977. lib. bdg. 25.00x (ISBN 0-8371-9856-9, BBSB). Greenwood.
Sanity in the Summertime: Creative Ideas & Plans for the 90 Days When School Is Out. Linda Dillow & Claudia Arp. LC 80-27279. 224p. 1981. pap. 5.95 (ISBN 0-8407-5754-9). Nelson.
Sanity, Madness & the Family. R. D. Laing & A. Esterson. 1970. pap. 6.95 (ISBN 0-14-021157-8, Pelican). Penguin.
Sanity Matinee. Michael Zagst. LC 87-81419. 352p. 1987. 18.95 (ISBN 1-55611-059-6). D I Fine.
Sanity of Mysticism. Geraldine E. Hodgson. LC 76-11826. 1976. Repr. of 1926 ed. lib. bdg. 29.00 (ISBN 0-8414-4845-0). Folcroft.
Sanity of William Blake. Greville MacDonald. LC 75-22387. 1975. Repr. of 1920 ed. lib. bdg. 20.00 (ISBN 0-8414-6156-2). Folcroft.
Sanity of William Blake. Greville Macdonald. (Studies in Blake, No. 3). 1970. pap. 24.95x (ISBN 0-8383-0097-9). Haskell.
Sanity Plea: Schizophrenia in the Novels of Kurt Vonnegut. Lawrence Broer. Ed. by Robert Scholes. (Studies in Speculative Fiction: No. 18). 1988. price not set (ISBN 0-8357-1885-9). UMI Res Pr.
Sanjay Story. Vinod Mehta. 192p. 1978. 9.95. Asia Bk Corp.
Sanjo. Evelyn W. Mayerson. 320p. (gr. 10 up). 1981. pap. 2.75 (ISBN 0-671-83397-9). PB.
Sankar Company Limited: A Novel. Moni S. Mukherjee. Tr. by Achala Moulik from Bengali. 162p. 1977. pap. text ed. 5.95x (ISBN 0-86125-336-1, Pub. by Orient Longman Ltd.). Apt Bks.
Sankara-Dig-Vijaya: The Traditional Life of Sri Sankaracharya. Madhava-Vidyaranya. Tr. by Swami Tapasyananda. 1979. pap. 3.95 (ISBN 0-87481-484-7). Vedanta Pr.
Sankara on the Yoga-Sutras: The Vivarana Sub-Commentary to Vyasa-Bhasya on the Yoga-Sultras of Pantanjali. Trevor Leggett. 600p. 1988. text ed. 75.00 (ISBN 0-7103-0277-0, Kegan Paul). Routledge Chapman & Hall.
Sankara on the Yoga-Sutras: The Vivarana Sub-Commentary to Vyasa-Bhasya. Tr. by Trevor Leggett. 220p. 1983. 24.95 (ISBN 0-7100-9539-2). Routledge Chapman & Hall.
Sankaracharya. T. M. Mahadevan. 119p. 1968. 3.95. Asia Bk Corp.
Sanmau, the Second Grader. Jenny Li. (Illus., Orig., Chinese). (gr. 6-10). 1968. pap. text ed. 2.75 (ISBN 0-910286-00-0). Boxwood.
Sanpoil & Nespelem: Salishan Peoples of Northeastern Washington. Verne F. Ray. LC 76-43809. (Univ. of Washington Publications in Anthropology: Vol. 5). Repr. of 1933 ed. 24.50 (ISBN 0-404-15663-0). AMS Pr.
Sans Attendre. Elizabeth Graham. (Harlequin Romantique Ser.). 192p. 1984. pap. 1.95 (ISBN 0-373-41233-9). Harlequin Bks.
Sans-Culottes: The Popular Movement & Revolutionary Government, 1793-1794. A. Soboul. 1981. pap. 11.50x (ISBN 0-691-00782-9). Princeton U Pr.
Sans Dessus-Dessous. Jules Verne. 1978. 8.95 (ISBN 0-686-55948-7). French & Eur.
Sans Serif Display Alphabets: 100 Complete Fonts. Ed. by Dan X. Solo. LC 78-74144. (Illus.). 1979. pap. 4.95 (ISBN 0-486-23785-0). Dover.
Sanshiro. Natsume Soseki. Tr. by Jay Rubin from Japanese. (Perigee Japanese Library). 248p. 1982. pap. 5.95 (ISBN 0-399-50613-6, Perigee). Putnam Pub Group.
Sanskrit & Indian Studies: Essays in Honour of Daniel H. H. Ingalls. Ed. by Masatoshi Nagatomi et al. (Studies in Classical India: No. 2). 1980. lib. bdg. 39.50 (ISBN 90-277-0991-2, Pud. by Reidel Holland). Kluwer Academic.
Sanskrit & Indological Studies. V. Raghavan. Ed. by Danekar & Sharma. 1975. 19.50 (ISBN 0-8426-0821-4). Orient Bk Dist.
Sanskrit & Its Kindred Literatures. Laura E. Poor. LC 76-27525. 1976. Repr. of 1880 ed. lib. bdg. 35.00 (ISBN 0-89341-038-1). Longwood Pub Group.
Sanskrit Buddhism in Burma. Nihar-Ranjan Ray. LC 78-70112. Repr. of 1936 ed. 22.00 (ISBN 0-404-17367-5). AMS Pr.
Sanskrit Drama in Performance. Rachel Baumer & James R. Brandon. LC 80-26900. (Illus.). 334p. 1981. text ed. 27.50x (ISBN 0-8248-0688-3). UH Pr.
Sanskrit Drama: Its Origins & Decline. Indu Sekhar. (Illus.). 1977. 22.00x. Coronet Bks.
Sanskrit Drama, Problems & Prospects. G. K. Bhat. 1986. 37.50x (ISBN 0-8364-1531-0, Pub. by Ajanta). South Asia Bks.
Sanskrit Dramas. S. Subramnia Iyer. 326p. 38.00 (ISBN 0-89684-360-2, Pub. by Sundeep Prakashan). Orient Bk Dist.
Sanskrit-English Dictionary. rev. ed. Monier Monier-Williams et al. (Sanskrit & Eng.). 1899. 110.00x (ISBN 0-19-864308-X). Oxford U Pr.
Sanskrit-English Dictionary. 4th ed. Monier M. Williams. 1333p. 1985. Repr. of 1899 ed. 36.00x (ISBN 81-208-0065-6, Pub. by Motilal Banarsidass India); lib. bdg. 54.00x deluxe (ISBN 81-208-0069-9). South Asia Bks.
Sanskrit-English, English-Sanskrit Student's Dictionary, 2 vols. V. S. Apte. (Sanskrit & Eng.). 35.00; Sanskrit-English. 17.50; English-Sanskrit. 17.50. Heinman.
Sanskrit Grammar. W. D. Whitney. 1977. Repr. 18.50 (ISBN 0-8426-0624-6). Orient Bk Dist.
Sanskrit Grammar. 2nd ed. William D. Whitney. 1880. 34.50x (ISBN 0-674-78810-9). Harvard U Pr.
Sanskrit Grammar (Ashtadhyayj) in Sanskirt & English, 2 vols. Panini. Repr. of 1968 ed. 65.00x (ISBN 0-87902-123-3). Orientalia.
Sanskrit Grammar for Students. A. A. Macdonell. 1974. Repr. 8.00 (ISBN 0-89684-315-7). Orient Bk Dist.
Sanskrit Grammar for Students. 3rd ed. Arthur A. Macdonell. 284p. 1986. pap. 18.95 (ISBN 0-19-815466-6). Oxford U Pr.
Sanskrit Grammar for Students. Arthur A. MacDonnel. xviii, 264p. 1986. Repr. 9.00x (ISBN 0-89581-198-7, Pub. by Motilal Banarsidass). South Asia Bks.
Sanskrit Grammar, with Comparative Indo-European Explanations. Manfred Mayrhofer. Tr. by Gordon Ford, Jr. from Ger. LC 68-13738. (Alabama Linguistic & Philological Ser: Vol. 20). 115p. 1972. 10.75 (ISBN 0-8173-0353-7). U of Ala Pr.
Sanskrit Indeclinables of the Hindu Grammarians & Lexicographers. I. Dyen. (Language Dissertations: No. 31). 1939. pap. 16.00 (ISBN 0-527-00777-3). Kraus Repr.
Sanskrit Keys to the Wisdom-Religion. Judith M. Tyberg. 180p. 1976. pap. 5.00 (ISBN 0-913004-29-4). Point Loma Pub.
Sanskrit Love Lyrics. Tr. by P. Lal from Sanskrit. 31p. 1973. 6.75 (ISBN 0-88253-265-0); flexible bdg. 4.80 (ISBN 0-89253-525-3). Ind-US Inc.
Sanskrit Mantras. 1977. 10.00x (ISBN 0-930736-03-6); cassett tape recording incl. (ISBN 0-685-32618-7). E W Cultural Ctr.
Sanskrit Manual. 3rd ed. Monier Williams. 1977. 10.50x (ISBN 0-686-22671-2). Intl Bk Dist.
Sanskrit Poems of Mayura. Mayura. Tr. by George P. Quackenbos. LC 77-181072. (Columbia University. Indo-Iranian Ser.: No. 9). Repr. of 1917 ed. 28.50 (ISBN 0-404-50479-5). AMS Pr.
Sanskrit Poetry from Vidyakara's Treasury. Vidvakara. Tr. by Daniel H. Ingalls. LC 67-29627. 1968. 40.00x (ISBN 0-674-78855-9, Belknap Pr). Harvard U Pr.
Sanskrit Primer. 2nd ed. Edvard D. Perry. 230p. (Orig.). 1986. 12.50 (ISBN 81-208-0206-3, Pub. by Motilal Banarsidass India); pap. 9.00 (ISBN 81-208-0207-1). Orient Bk Dist.
Sanskrit Primer. 4th ed. Edward D. Perry. LC 36-19814. 230p. 1959. 24.00x (ISBN 0-231-00858-9). Columbia U Pr.
Sanskrit Reader: Text & Vocabulary & Notes. Charles R. Lanman. LC 11-24320. 1883. 29.50x (ISBN 0-674-78900-8). Harvard U Pr.
Sanskrit Reader with Vocabulary & Notes. Charles R. Laxmann. 405p. 1987. Repr. of 1906 ed. 19.95 (ISBN 81-7030-058-4, Pub. by SRI SATGURU Pubns India). Orient Bk Dist.
Sanskrit Speech: Habits & Panini. Vasant V. Bhandare. 387p. 1986. 16.00X (ISBN 0-8364-1674-0, Pub. by Ajanta). South Asia Bks.
Sanskrit Studies of M. B. Emeneau: Selected Papers. M. B. Emeneau. Pref. by B. A. Van Nooten. LC 87-72589. (Occasional Papers Ser.). (Illus.). 224p. (Orig.). 1988. pap. write for info. (ISBN 0-944613-02-0). UC Berkeley Ctr SE Asia.
Sanskrit-Woerterbuch. 2nd, rev. ed. Carl Capeller. (Ger). 1966. 28.80x (ISBN 3-11-000191-8). De Gruyter.
Sansoni Harrap English-Italian Dictionary, Vol. 3, A-L. Ed. by Harrap Limited Staff. 1986. 175.00x (ISBN 0-245-59635-6, Pub. by Harrap Ltd English). State Mutual Bk.
Sansoni Harrap English-Italian Dictionary, Vol. 4, M-Z. Ed. by Harrap Limited Staff. 1986. 175.00x (ISBN 0-245-59636-4, Pub. by Harrap Ltd England). State Mutual Bk.
Sansoni Harrap Italian-English Dictionary, Vol. 1, A-L. Ed. by Harrap Limited Staff. 1986. 175.00x (ISBN 0-245-59633-X, Pub. by Harrap Ltd England). State Mutual Bk.
Sansoni Harrap Italian-English Dictionary, Vol. 2, M-Z. Ed. by Harrap Limited Staff. 1986. 175.00x (ISBN 0-245-59634-8, Pub. by Harrap Ltd England). State Mutual Bk.
Santa Ana Wind. Helen Van Slyke. 256p. 1982. pap. 3.95 (ISBN 0-446-31284-3). Warner Bks.
Santa Anna: Prisoner of War in Texas. Ken Durham. Ed. by Skipper Steely. (Illus.). 125p. 1986. 13.95 (ISBN 0-915263-09-2); pap. 9.95 (ISBN 0-915263-10-6). Wright Pr.
Santa Anna: The Story of an Enigma Who Once Was Mexico. Wilfrid H. Callcott. LC 36-37514. pap. 101.30 (ISBN 0-317-28705-2, 2055509). Bks Demand UMI.
Santa Anna's Campaign Against Texas, 1835-1836. Richard G. Santos. 1982. 24.95 (ISBN 0-89712-107-4). Documentary Pubns.
Santa Apolonia (Patrona Dental) Cesar A. Mena. LC 86-80092. (Illus.). 79p. (Orig., Span.). 1985. pap. 10.00 (ISBN 0-89729-388-6). Ediciones.
Santa, Are You for Real? Harold Myra. LC 77-23023. (Illus.). 6.95 (ISBN 0-8407-5122-2). Nelson.
Santa Barbara. David Temple. (Illus.). 1984. 15.00 (ISBN 0-19-540614-1). Skyline Press.
Santa Barbara: A Guide to El Pueblo Viejo. Rebecca Conard & Christopher H. Nelson. Ed. by Mary L. Days. LC 84-72199. (Illus.). 160p. (Orig.). 1986. pap. 9.95 (ISBN 0-88496-226-1). Capra Pr.
Santa Barbara: A Guide to the Channel City & Its Environs. Federal Writers' Project Staff. LC 73-4574. (American Guidebook Ser.). 1980. Repr. of 1941 ed. lib. bdg. 59.00x (ISBN 0-403-02216-9). Somerset Pub.
Santa Barbara Architecture: From Spanish Colonial to Modern. Noel Young & Herb Andree. (Illus.). 300p. 1980. 70.00 (ISBN 0-88496-053-6). Capra Pr.
Santa Barbara by the Sea. Ed. by Rochelle Bookspan. (Illus.). 236p. pap. 10.00 (ISBN 0-87461-036-2). McNally & Loftin.
Santa Barbara Collects. Santa Barbara Museum of Art Staff. LC 84-27608. (Illus.). 84p. (Orig.). 1984. pap. 12.00 (ISBN 0-89951-057-4). Santa Barb Mus Art.

Santa Barbara County, Including Portions of San Luis Obispo County Thomas Guide 1988. Thomas Bros. Maps Staff. (Illus.). 214p. 1988. pap. 12.95 (ISBN 0-88130-272-4). Thomas Bros Maps.

Santa Barbara County, Including Portions of San Luis Obispo County & Ventura County Thomas Guide 1988. Thomas Bros. Maps Staff. (Illus.). 311p. 1988. pap. 19.95 (ISBN 0-88130-273-2). Thomas Bros Maps.

Santa Barbara: El Pueblo Viejo: A Walking Guide to the Historic Districts of Santa Barbara. Rebecca Conard & Christopher H. Nelson. 160p. 1988. Repr. lib. bdg. 24.95x (ISBN 0-8095-4021-5). Borgo Pr.

Santa Barbara History Makers. Walker Tomkins. 423p. 1983. pap. 15.00 (ISBN 0-87461-059-1). McNally & Loftin.

Santa Barbara History Makers. Walker A. Tompkins. Ed. by Barbara H. Tompkins. LC 83-17591. (Illus.). 440p. 25.00 (ISBN 0-87461-053-2). McNally & Loftin.

Santa Barbara: How to Discover America's Eden. Pauline J. Thompson. LC 84-11276. (Illus., Orig.). 1984. pap. 5.95 (ISBN 0-918785-00-6). Kricket.

Santa Biblia Dios Habla Hoy. 1504p. 1980. pap. 15.95 (ISBN 0-311-48716-5, Edit Mundo). Casa Bautista.

Santa Biblia: Edicion Bilingue Espanol-Ingles. 1812p. 1986. bonded leather 39.95 (ISBN 0-311-48748-3). Casa Bautista.

Santa Carving. Ron Ransom. (Illus.). 48p. 1987. pap. 8.95 (ISBN 0-88740-107-4). Schiffer.

Santa Casa di Loreto: Problems in Cinquecento Sculpture, 2 Vols. Kathleen W. Garris. LC 76-23653. (Outstanding Dissertations in the Fine Arts Ser.). 1977. lib. bdg. 161.00 (ISBN 0-8240-2735-3). Garland Pub.

Santa Catalina: An Island Adventure. Terrence D. Martin. LC 83-83007. (Illus.). 48p. (Orig.). 1984. pap. 4.50 (ISBN 0-916122-97-2). KC Pubns.

Santa Catalina Cookbook, Vol. I. 2nd rev. ed. Ed. by Terri C. Brazinsky & Kathi Bowden. Tr. by Santa Catalina Students & Faculty. (Illus.). 293p. 1983. 15.50 (ISBN 0-9612300-0-2). Santa Catalina.

Santa Catalina Cookbook, Vol. 2. Ed. by Terri C. Brazinsky & Kathi Bowden. (Illus.). 400p. 1983. 17.50 (ISBN 0-9612300-1-0). Santa Catalina.

Santa Clara - San Mateo Counties Street Guide & Directory 1988. Thomas Bros. Maps Staff. (Illus.). 218p. 1988. pap. 18.95 (ISBN 0-88130-280-5). Thomas Bros Maps.

Santa Clara Country '88: McCormack's Guides. Don McCormack. Ed. by Allen Kanda. 128p. 1987. pap. 3.95 (ISBN 0-931299-09-8). Donnan Pubns.

Santa Clara County: Harvest of Change, An Illustrated History. Stephen M. Payne. Ed. by Michelle Hudun. LC 87-8195. 264p. 1987. 27.95 (ISBN 0-89781-185-2). Windsor Pubns Inc.

Santa Clara County Street Guide & Directory 1988. Thomas Bros. Maps Staff. (Illus.). 144p. 1988. pap. 10.95 (ISBN 0-88130-279-1). Thomas Bros Maps.

Santa Clara Pottery Today. Betty LeFree. LC 73-92996. (School of American Research Monograph: No. 29). (Illus.). 125p. 1975. pap. 9.95 (ISBN 0-8263-0322-6). U of NM Pr.

Santa Clara Valley-California: An Artist's View Today & Yesterday Painting & Sketching the Valley I Love. Anthony Quartuccio. LC 85-90472. (Illus.). 128p. (Orig.). 1986. pap. 12.00 (ISBN 0-9606934-2-4). A Quartuccio.

Santa Clara Valley Corridor Evaluation: Summary. 21p. 1979. 2.00 (ISBN 0-318-22733-9). Assn Bay Area.

Santa Clara Valley Memoirs: My Life As a California Reporter from Prohibition to Pearl Harbor. John V. Young. LC 80-81419. (Illus.). 176p. 1980. 9.95 (ISBN 0-934136-05-X). Western Tanager.

Santa Claus & His Elves. Mauri Kunnas. Tr. by Maria R. Robbins from Finnish. LC 82-6053. (Illus.). 48p. (ps up). 1985. bds. 7.95 (ISBN 0-517-54781-3); pap. 4.95 (ISBN 0-517-55818-1). Crown.

Santa Claus & His Works. George P. Webster & Thomas Nast. (Illus.). 12p. (gr. 1-8). 1972. pap. 3.25 (ISBN 0-914510-03-7). Evergreen.

Santa Claus Around the World. Lisl Weil. LC 87-45334. (Illus.). 32p. (gr. k-3). 1987. PLB 11.95 (ISBN 0-8234-0665-2). Holiday.

Santa Claus Bank Robbery. A. C. Greene. LC 86-5976. 270p. 1986. pap. 9.95 (ISBN 0-87719-055-0). Texas Month Pr.

Santa Claus Bank Robbery. A. C. Greene. 1988. pap. 4.95. St Martin.

Santa Claus Bank Robbery. A. C. Greene. 1988. pap. 4.95 (ISBN 0-944276-25-3). Tudor Pub NYC.

Santa Claus Book. Eileen Daly. (Super Shape Bks.). (Illus.). 24p. (gr. 2-5). 1972. pap. write for info. (ISBN 0-307-10046-4, Pub. by Golden Bks). Western Pub.

Santa Claus Book. Alden Perkes. 144p. 1982. 19.95 (ISBN 0-8184-0327-6). Lyle Stuart.

Santa Claus Book. Alden Perkes. (Illus.). 144p. 1985. pap. 12.95 (ISBN 0-8184-0381-0). Lyle Stuart.

Santa Claus Forever! Carolyn Haywood. LC 83-1017. (Illus.). 32p. (gr. k-3). 1983. 10.25 (ISBN 0-688-02344-4); lib. bdg. 10.88 (ISBN 0-688-02345-2). Morrow.

Santa Claus: Forty Antique Post Cards. Jill Bossert. (Illus.). 24p. (Orig.). 1986. pap. 8.95 (ISBN 0-942604-15-6). Madison Square.

Santa Claus in My Kitchen. Candy Coleman. Ed. by Candy Coleman. (Illus.). 48p. (Orig.). 1979. pap. text ed. 3.00 (ISBN 0-943768-01-2). C Coleman.

Santa Claus Is Coming! Illus. by Francesca Crespi. (Illus.). 8p. (ps-k). 1987. 3.95 (ISBN 0-8050-0472-6). H Holt & Co.

Santa Claus Picture Book: An Appraisal Guide. Maggie Rogers. (Illus.). 96p. 1984. 29.95 (ISBN 0-525-24282-1); pap. 18.95 (ISBN 0-525-48148-6). Dutton.

Santa Claus' Snack. Robert L. Merriam. (Illus.). 14p. (ps-6). pap. 2.00x (ISBN 0-686-32491-9). R L Merriam.

Santa Claus Stories: Broadcast on 1927 from Palais Royal Department Store, Washington DC. 1988. write for info. Interspace Bks.

Santa Claus Storybook: Santa Claus the Movie. Joan D. Vinge. (Illus.). 64p. (gr. 3 up). 1985. 6.95 (ISBN 0-448-10281-1, G&D). Putnam Pub Group.

Santa Claus: The Movie. Joan D. Vinge. 256p. 1985. pap. 3.50 (ISBN 0-425-08385-3). Berkley Pub.

Santa Claus the Movie: Patch & the Evil Toymaker. Daisy Miller. (Illus.). 24p. (ps-1). 1985. pap. 1.95 (ISBN 0-448-10278-1, G&D). Putnam Pub Group.

Santa Claus the Movie: Pop-up Panorama Book. Daniel Kirk. (Illus.). 12p. (ps-3). 1985. 7.95 (ISBN 0-448-10276-5, G&D). Putnam Pub Group.

Santa Claus the Movie: Santa's Sleigh. DeWitt Conyers. (Fast Rolling Bks.). (Illus.). 12p. (ps). 1985. 5.95 (ISBN 0-448-10282-X, G&D). Putnam Pub Group.

Santa Claus the Movie: The Boy Who Didn't Believe in Christmas. Michael Teitelbaum. (Illus.). 24p. (ps-1). 1985. pap. 1.95 (ISBN 0-448-10277-3, G&D). Putnam Pub Group.

Santa Claus the Movie: The Elves at the Top of the World. Meg Waters. (Illus.). 24p. (ps-1). 1985. pap. 1.95 (ISBN 0-448-10279-X, Pub. by G&D). Putnam Pub Group.

Santa Claus the Movie: The Legend of Santa Claus. Mary Oliver. (Illus.). 24p. (ps-1). 1985. pap. 1.95 (ISBN 0-448-10280-3, G&D). Putnam Pub Group.

Santa Claus: The Tooth Fairy & Other Stories - A Child's Introduction to Religion. Ronald Gestwicki. Ed. by Sylvia Ashton. LC 77-80276. 1977. 15.95 (ISBN 0-87949-108-6). Ashley Bks.

Santa Claus Visits the Thinggumajigs. Dick Keller & Irene Keller. (Illus.). 48p. (gr. k-6). 1982. 2.95 (ISBN 0-8249-8045-X). Ideals.

Santa Clauses. Achim Broger. LC 86-2147. (Illus.). 28p. (ps-3). 1986. 11.95 (ISBN 0-8037-0266-3, 01160-350). Dial Bks Young.

Santa Clauses. Retold by Achim Broger. LC 86-2147. (Pied Piper Paperback Ser.). (Illus.). 28p. (ps-3). 1988. pap. 3.95 (ISBN 0-8037-0557-3, 0383-120). Dial Bks Young.

Santa Clawfish. Charles A. Lemoine. (Christmas Story & Coloring Book Ser.). (Illus.). 32p. (Orig.). 1986. pap. 3.20 (ISBN 0-941327-00-0). Charles A Lemoine.

Santa Cruz County: Parade of the Past. Margaret Koch. LC 73-89823. (Illus.). 254p. 1973. 19.95 (ISBN 0-913548-16-2, Valley Calif). Western Tanager.

Santa Cruz County Place Names: A Geographical Dictionary. Donald T. Clark. LC 86-24840. (Illus.). 624p. 1986. 33.95 (ISBN 0-940283-00-X); pap. 23.95 (ISBN 0-940283-01-8). Santa Cruz Hist.

Santa Cruz Mountains Trail Book. 5th, rev. ed. Tom Taber. (Illus.). 144p. 1988. pap. 7.95 (ISBN 0-9609170-3-9). Oak Valley.

Santa Cruz: The Early Years. Leon Rowland. Ed. by Michael S. Gant. LC 80-81418. (Illus.). 273p. 1980. pap. 7.95 (ISBN 0-934136-04-1). Western Tanager.

Santa Eucarista y Otros Servicios. 44p. (Span.). 1983. pap. 1.50 (ISBN 0-935461-05-1). St Alban Pr CA.

Santa Fe. Lisl Dennis & Landt. 1987. 35.00 (ISBN 0-317-62594-2). Herring Pr.

Santa Fe. Melinda Snodgrass. 1988. pap. 4.50 (ISBN 0-451-15709-5, Sig). NAL.

Santa Fe: A Pictorial History. John Sherman. LC 80-39666. 1984. pap. 19.95 (ISBN 0-88307-665-9). Gannon.

Santa Fe: An Intimate View. Bill Jamison. LC 82-81390. (Illus., Orig.). 1982. pap. 7.95 (ISBN 0-9608504-0-6). Milagro Pr Inc.

Santa Fe & Taos. (Frommer's City Guides Ser.). (Illus.). 224p. 1988. pap. 5.95 (ISBN 0-13-791096-7). Prentice Hall Pr.

Santa Fe & Taos Colonies: Age of the Muses, 1900-1942. Arrell M. Gibson. LC 82-40452. (Illus.). 328p. 1983. 24.95 (ISBN 0-8061-1835-0). U of Okla Pr.

Santa Fe & Taos Colonies: Age of the Muses, 1900-1942. Arrell M. Gibson. LC 82-40452. (Illus.). 320p. 1988. pap. 12.95 (ISBN 0-8061-2116-5). U of Okla Pr.

Santa Fe & Taos, Eighteen Ninety-Eight to Nineteen Forty-Two: An American Cultural Center. Kay A. Reeve. (Southwestern Studies: No. 67). (Illus.). 72p. 1982. 10.00 (ISBN 0-87404-126-0); pap. 5.00. Tex Western.

Santa Fe & Taos: The Writer's Era, 1916-1941. Marta Weigle & Kyle Fiore. LC 81-71485. (Illus.). 239p. 1982. 16.95 (ISBN 0-941270-08-4). Ancient City Pr.

Santa Fe Art Colony, Nineteen Hundred to Nineteen Forty-Two. Sharyn Udall. Ed. by Nancy Pierson. LC 87-80960. 92p. 1987. softcover 25.00 (ISBN 0-935037-15-2). Peters Corp NM.

Santa Fe Dream. David Norman. (Frontier Rakers Ser.: No. 6). 1983. pap. 3.50 (ISBN 0-8217-1260-8). Zebra.

Santa Fe Guide. 4th ed. Waite Thompson & Richard M. Gottlieb. LC 86-5769. (Illus.). 64p. 1988. pap. 5.95 (ISBN 0-86534-087-0). Sunstone Pr.

Santa Fe in Topeka. Ed. by John W. Ripley & Robert W. Richmond. (Illus.). 1979. pap. 6.95 (ISBN 0-685-96284-9). Shawnee County Hist.

Santa Fe Meeting: Proceedings of 1984 Division of Particicles & Fields, American Physical Society. Ed. by T. Goldman & M. M. Neito. 600p. 1985. 74.00 (ISBN 9971-978-46-6); pap. 41.00 (ISBN 9971-978-82-2). World Scientific Pub.

Santa Fe Motive Power. Joe McMillan. LC 85-72215. (Illus.). 1985. 39.95 (ISBN 0-934228-08-6). McMillan Pubns.

Santa Fe, Ole! A Foreign City in the U. S. of A. Ed. by Pancho Epstein. (Illus.). 112p. (Orig.). 1988. pap. 6.95 (ISBN 0-945650-00-0). Southern Rockies Pub.

Santa Fe on Foot: Walking, Running & Bicycling Routes in the City Different. Elaine Pinkerton. (Cota Editions Ser.: No. 1). (Illus.). 120p. 1986. pap. 7.50 (ISBN 0-943734-05-3). Ocean Tree Bks.

Santa Fe Public Library Select Southwest Bibliography. Laurie Macrae. 48p. (Orig.). Date not set. pap. price not set (ISBN 0-86534-126-5). Sunstone Pr.

Santa Fe Route to the Pacific. Phil Serpico. LC 87-46360. (Illus.). 150p. (YA) (gr. 6 up). 1988. 25.00 (ISBN 0-88418-000-X). Omni Hawthorne.

Santa Fe Slaughter. Jon Sharpe. (Trailsman Ser.: No. 73). 176p. 1988. pap. 2.75 (ISBN 0-451-15139-9, Sig). NAL.

Santa Fe Steam Finale in Kansas: 1952-1955. Lloyd E. Stagner. Ed. by James J. Reisdorff. (Illus.). 48p. (Orig.). 1988. pap. 11.95 (ISBN 0-942035-07-0). South Platte.

Santa Fe: Steel Rails Through California. Donald Duke & Stan Kistler. LC 63-23869. (Illus.). 184p. 1963. 22.95 (ISBN 0-87095-009-6). Gldn West Bks.

Santa Fe Streamliners. Karl Zimmermann. 1987. pap. 14.95 (ISBN 0-915276-41-0). Quadrant Pr.

Santa Fe Style. Christine Mather & Sharon Woods. LC 86-42715. (Illus.). 256p. 1986. 35.00 (ISBN 0-8478-0734-7). Rizzoli Intl.

Santa Fe: The Autobiography of a Southwestern Town. Oliver LaFarge & Arthur N. Morgan. LC 59-7958. 436p. 1985. pap. 14.95 (ISBN 0-8061-1696-X). U of Okla Pr.

Santa Fe-the City in Photographs. Ed. by Karen Evans. (Illus.). 80p. (Orig.). 1984. pap. 14.95 (ISBN 0-916795-01-2). Gannon.

Santa Fe: The Railroad That Built an Empire. James L. Marshall. LC 83-45453. Repr. of 1945 ed. 45.00 (ISBN 0-404-20168-7). AMS Pr.

Santa Fe Then & Now. Sheila Morand. LC 84-2503. (Illus.). 96p. (Orig.). 1984. pap. 14.95 (ISBN 0-86534-046-3). Sunstone Pr.

Santa Fe Trail. R. L. Duffus. (Illus.). 1971. Repr. of 1930 ed. 39.00x (ISBN 0-403-00918-9). Scholarly.

Santa Fe Trail; The National Park Service 1963 Historic Sites Survey. William E. Brown. (Illus.). 219p. Date not set. 17.95 (ISBN 0-935284-64-8). Patrice Pr.

Santa Fe Trail to California Eighteen Forty-Nine to Eighteen Fifty Two. Ed. by Douglas S. Watson. (Illus.). 1985. 295.00 (ISBN 0-317-28320-0, Pub. by J M C & Co). Amereon Ltd.

Santa Fe Trail to California, 1849-1852. H. M. Powell. Ed. by Douglas S. Watson. LC 79-174284. (Illus.). Repr. of 1931 ed. lib. bdg. 125.00 (ISBN 0-404-05099-9). AMS Pr.

Santa Grows up in Mother Goose Land. Ruth Waldrop. (Illus.). 34p. (ps-3). 1986. pap. 4.95 (ISBN 0-9616894-0-4); cassette incl. RuSk Inc.

Santa Is Coming. (Christmas Ser.). (ps). 2.95 (ISBN 0-86112-229-1, Pub. by Brimax Bks). Borden.

Santa Is Coming. Illus. by Noel Tennyson. LC 80-54768. (Shape Bks.). (Illus.). 24p. (ps-k). 1981. spiral plastic bdg. 3.95 (ISBN 0-394-84797-0). Random.

Santa Maria de Guadalupe. Jose Chavez. (Span.). 1963. pap. 2.00 (ISBN 0-8198-6825-6). Dghtrs St Paul.

Santa Maria del Fiore, Florence (The Duomo) A Bibliography of Recent Scholarship. Carole Cable. (Architecture Ser.: A 1552). 7p. 1986. 3.00 (ISBN 0-89028-742-2). Vance Biblios.

Santa Maria del Monte: The Presence of the Past in a Spanish Village. Ruth Behar. LC 85-43270. (Illus.). 409p. 1986. text ed. 33.50x (ISBN 0-691-09419-5). Princeton U Pr.

Santa Monica Poems. Steve Richmond. (Illus.). 48p. 1987. pap. 7.00 (ISBN 0-941543-00-5). Sun Dog Pr.

Santa Mouse. Michael Brown. (Illus.). (gr. k-3). 1966. 4.95 (ISBN 0-448-04213-4, G&D); PLB 3.09 (ISBN 0-448-13914-6). Putnam Pub Group.

Santa Mouse. Michael Brown. (Pudgy Pals Ser.). (Illus.). 16p. (ps). 1984. 3.95 (ISBN 0-448-10215-3, G&D). Putnam Pub Group.

Santa Mouse Meets Marmaduke. Michael Brown. LC 74-92384. (Elephant Books Ser.). (Illus.). (gr. k-7). 1978. pap. 2.50 (ISBN 0-448-14749-1, G&D). Putnam Pub Group.

Santa Mouse Pencil, Puzzle & Fun Book. Illus. by Nina Barbaresi. (Illus.). 48p. (ps-3). 1984. pap. 1.50 (ISBN 0-448-07327-7, G&D). Putnam Pub Group.

Santa Mouse, Where Are You? Michael Brown. (All Aboard Bks.). (Illus.). 32p. (ps-2). 1988. pap. 1.95 (ISBN 0-448-19109-1). Platt.

Santa Rita. Martin W. Schwettmann. 1958. 9.50 (ISBN 0-87611-018-9). Tex St Hist Assn.

Santa Will Love My Tree (Play Format) Humberto Almaraz. 12p. (Orig.). (ps-3). 1982. pap. 5.00 incl. 45 rpm record (ISBN 0-9616528-1-0). Alpha-Beto Music.

Santa Will Love My Tree (Story Format) Humberto Almaraz. 12p. (Orig.). (ps-2). 1982. pap. 5.00 incl. 45 rpm record (ISBN 0-9616528-0-2). Alpha-Beto Music.

Santabear's High Flying Adventure. Lenore Kletter. (Illus.). 32p. (gr. 1-3). 1987. 12.99 (ISBN 0-9619204-0-8). Santabear Bks.

Santaberry & the Snard. Joel Schick & Alice Schick. (gr. 4). 1976. 6.95 (ISBN 0-912846-23-2). Bookstore Pr.

Santaberry & the Snard. Joel Schick & Alice Schick. LC 78-23796. (I-Like-to-Read Books). (Illus.). (gr. k-2). 1979. 7.95i (ISBN 0-397-31824-3, Harper Medical). Lippincott.

Santal: A Tribe in Search of a Great Tradition. Martin Orans. LC 65-12595. Repr. of 1965 ed. 42.00 (2027605). Bks Demand UMI.

Santal Folk Tales, 3 vols. Paul O. Bodding. LC 78-67688. (Folktale). Repr. of 1923 ed. AMS Pr.

Santal Folk Tales. A. Campbell. LC 78-67700. (Folktale). Repr. of 1891 ed. 17.00 (ISBN 0-404-16066-2). AMS Pr.

Santal Music: A Study in Pattern & Process of Cultural Persistence. Onkar Prasad. (Illus.). 133p. 1986. text ed. 30.00x (ISBN 81-210-0032-7, Pub. by Inter India Pubns N Delhi). Apt Bks.

Santal Parganas. L. S. O'Malley. x, 298p. 1984. Repr. of 1910 ed. text ed. 45.00x (ISBN 0-86590-343-3, Pub. by B R Pub Corp Delhi). Apt Bks.

Santals: A Classified & Annotated Bibliography. J. Troisi. LC 76-901556. 1976. 14.50x (ISBN 0-88386-816-4). South Asia Bks.

Santals, Religion & Rituals. A. B. Chaudhri. 1987. 26.50x (ISBN 81-7024-085-9, Pub. by Ashish India). South Asia Bks.

Santan Dharma Ka Mahatva: (Uttarpara Speech) Sri Aurobindo. 14p. 3.00 (ISBN 0-317-17480-0). Auromere.

Santana Enslaved. John Cleve. LC 81-85828. (Spaceways Ser.: No. 4). 224p. (Orig.). 1982. pap. 2.50 (ISBN 0-86721-111-3). Playboy Pbks.

Santander. E. Allison Peers. 1977. Repr. of 1927 ed. lib. bdg. 25.00 (ISBN 0-8495-4309-6). Arden Lib.

Santander Regime in Gran Colombia. David Bushnell. LC 78-100248. Repr. of 1954 ed. lib. bdg. 35.00x (ISBN 0-8371-2981-8, BUSR). Greenwood.

Santaroga Barrier. Frank Herbert. 256p. 1985. pap. 2.95 (ISBN 0-425-08987-8). Berkley Pub.

Santa's Beard Is Soft & Warm. Bob Ottum & JoAnne Wood. (Golden Touch & Feel Bk). (Illus.). (ps). 1974. 4.95 (ISBN 0-307-12148-8, Golden Bks). Western Pub.

Santa's Cajun Christmas Adventure. Timothy J. Edler. (Tim Edler's Tales from the Atchafalaya Ser.). (Illus.). 48p. (gr. k-8). 1981. pap. 6.00 (ISBN 0-931108-07-1). Little Cajun Bks.

Santa's Christmas Journey. Roger Brooke. LC 84-9796. (Stories Clippers Ser.). (Illus.). 32p. (gr. k-4). 1984. PLB 15.33 (ISBN 0-8172-2116-6); pap. 9.27 (ISBN 0-8172-2259-6); incl. cassette 27.99 (ISBN 0-8172-2244-8); incl. cassette 23.95 (ISBN 0-8172-2269-3); cassette 14.00. Raintree Pubs.

Santa's Christmas Journey. Roger Brooke. LC 85-61188. (Illus.). 32p. (ps-3). 1985. 5.95 (ISBN 0-528-82688-3, Checkerboard Pr). Macmillan.

Santa's Christmas Surprise. Edith Adams. LC 85-60216. (Illus.). 14p. (gr. 2-6). 1985. bds. 3.95 (ISBN 0-394-87538-9, BYR). Random.

Santa's Cookie Surprise. Janet Craig. LC 88-19997. (First-Start Easy Readers Ser.). (Illus.). 32p. (gr. k-2). 1988. lib. bdg. 5.41 (ISBN 0-8167-1538-6); pap. text ed. 1.50 (ISBN 0-8167-1539-4). Troll Assocs.

Santa's Crash-Bang Christmas. Steven Kroll. LC 77-3025. (Illus.). 32p. (gr. k-3). 1977. reinforcedbdg. 12.95 (ISBN 0-8234-0302-5); pap. 5.95 (ISBN 0-8234-0621-0). Holiday.

Santa's Favorite Story. Hisako Aoki & Ivan Gantschev. LC 82-60895. (Illus.). 28p. (ps up). 1982. 13.95 (ISBN 0-907234-16-X). Picture Bk Studio.

Santa's First Helper. Gerald M. Hoppe & Anne M. Hickman. 18p. 1987. 5.95 (ISBN 0-533-07493-2). Vantage.

Santa's Gift to the Littlest Penguin **see Rocky Duck.**

Santa's Hat. Claire Schumacher. (ps-3). Date not set. 10.95 (ISBN 0-317-62030-4). P-H.

Santa's Hawaiian Party. Carol Roes. (gr. 1-8). 1966. pap. 5.50 (ISBN 0-930932-19-6); record incl. M Loke.

Santa's Helper. Sherry Miller. LC 83-72493. (Molly Character - Color Me Ser.: No. 1). (Illus.). 32p. (Orig.). (gr. k-5). 1983. pap. 1.95 saddle-stitched (ISBN 0-913379-00-X). Double M Pub.

Saracens. E. Gibbon & S. Ockley. 450p. 1985. 250.00x (ISBN 1-85077-048-4, Pub. by Darf). State Mutual Bk.

Saracen's Country: Some Southeast Arkansas History. James W. Leslie. (Illus.). 216p. 1974. 19.95 (ISBN 0-914546-03-1). J W Bell.

Sarada Devi, Sri: The Great Wonder. 508p. 1985. pap. 8.50 (ISBN 0-87481-569-X, Pub. by Ramakrishna Mission India). Vedanta Pr.

Sarada Devi, Sri the Holy Mother, 2 bks. rev. ed. Incl. Bk. 1. Life. Swami Tapasyananda. pap. 4.95 (ISBN 0-87481-485-5); Bk. 2. Conversations. Tr. by Swami Nikhilananda from Bengali. pap. 3.95 (ISBN 0-87481-486-3). 1978. pap. Vedanta Pr.

Sarada Devi, the Holy Mother: Her Life & Conversations. Swami Tapasyananda & Swami Nikhilananda. (Illus.). 6.50 (ISBN 0-87481-435-9). Vedanta Pr.

Saragarhi Battalion - Ashes to Glory: History of the Fourth Battalion, The Sikh Regiment XXXVI. Kanwaljit Singh. 300p. 1987. 32.50x (ISBN 81-7062-022-8, Pub. by Lancer India). South Asia Bks.

Saragosa: The Town Killed by a Tornado. Derwood Lane. (Illus.). 288p. Date not set. 17.95 (ISBN 0-89015-677-8); pap. 12.95 (ISBN 0-89015-672-7). Eakin Pr.

Sarah. Marlee Alex. (Women of the Bible Ser.). 32p. (gr. 3-6). 1987. 7.95 (ISBN 0-8028-5015-4). Eerdmans.

Sarah. Joel Gross. LC 87-7785. 384p. 1987. 18.95 (ISBN 0-688-06703-4). Morrow.

Sarah. Diane Pearson. 304p. 1986. pap. 3.50 (ISBN 0-449-20984-9, Crest). Fawcett.

Sarah. Maura Seger. 400p. (Orig.). 1987. pap. 3.95 (ISBN 0-373-97041-2, Pub. by Worldwide). Harlequin Bks.

Sarah: A Novel of Sarah Bernhardt. Joel Gross. 352p. 1988. pap. 4.50 (ISBN 0-380-70277-0). Avon.

Sarah: A Sexual Biography. Paul R. Abramson. LC 83-17983. (Sexual Behavior Ser.). 142p. 1984. pap. 14.95 (ISBN 0-87395-863-2). State U NY Pr.

Sarah & the Dragon. Bruce Coville. LC 83-48447. (Illus.). 48p. (gr. k-3). 1984. 9.70i (ISBN 0-397-32069-8, Lipp Jr Bks); PLB 11.89 (ISBN 0-397-32070-1). HarpJ.

Sarah & the Persian Shepherd. Margaret Epp & Ruth Wiens. 123p. (Orig.). (gr. 3-6). 1982. pap. 3.95 (ISBN 0-919797-06-7). Kindred Pr.

Sarah Bernhardt. Maurice Baring. LC 78-91893. 1933. 18.00 (ISBN 0-405-08237-1, Blom Pubns). Ayer Co Pubs.

Sarah Bernhardt. Maurice Baring. LC 70-98809. Repr. of 1934 ed. lib. bdg. 35.00x (ISBN 0-8371-3018-2, BASB). Greenwood.

Sarah Bernhardt, My Grandmother. Lysiane S. Bernhardt. Tr. by Vyvyan Holland. LC 79-8054. Repr. of 1949 ed. 26.50 (ISBN 0-404-18365-4). AMS Pr.

Sarah Bernhardt: The Art Within the Legend. Gerda Taranow. LC 70-90962. (Illus.). 1972. 38.00x (ISBN 0-691-06181-5). Princeton U Pr.

Sarah Bernhardt's Leg. David Kirby. (CSU Poetry Ser.: No. XI). 56p. (Orig.). 1983. pap. 5.00 (ISBN 0-914946-36-6). Cleveland St Univ Poetry Ctr.

Sarah Bishop. Scott O'Dell. (gr. 7 up). 1980. 10.95 (ISBN 0-395-29185-2). HM.

Sarah Bishop. Scott O'Dell. 240p. (gr. 7up). 1988. pap. 2.75 (ISBN 0-590-42298-7). Scholastic Inc.

Sarah Elizabeth: A Tale of Old Colorado. J. G. Masters. 208p. 1985. 13.95 (ISBN 0-940672-29-4). Shearer Pub.

Sarah Faulkner's Planning a Home: A Projects Manual. Karen G. Bromberg. LC 78-22021. 1980. projects manual 12.95 (ISBN 0-03-045476-X). HR&W.

Sarah Ferguson: The Royal Redhead. David Banks. LC 87-15567. (Taking Part Ser.). (Illus.). 64p. (gr. 3 up). 1987. PLB 9.95 (ISBN 0-87518-369-7). Dillon.

Sarah Josepha Hale, a New England Pioneer, 1788-1879. Sherbrooke Rogers. LC 84-20520. (Illus.). 135p. (Orig.). 1985. pap. 7.95 (ISBN 0-936988-10-X, Dist. by Shoe String Press). Tompson Rutter Inc.

Sarah M. Peale: America's First Woman Artist. Joan King. (Illus.). 1987. 18.95 (ISBN 0-8283-1999-5). Branden Pub Co.

Sarah, or the Exemplary Wife. Susanna Rowson. LC 78-64090. Repr. of 1813 ed. 37.50 (ISBN 0-404-17165-6). AMS Pr.

Sarah Orne Jewett. Richard Cary. (Twayne's United States Authors Ser). 1962. pap. 8.95x (ISBN 0-8084-0272-2, T19, Twayne). New Coll U Pr.

Sarah Orne Jewett. Josephine L. Donovan. LC 80-5334. (Literature and Life Ser.). 175p. 1980. 16.95x (ISBN 0-8044-2137-4). Ungar.

Sarah Orne Jewett. Francis O. Matthiessen. 1929. 11.25 (ISBN 0-8446-1305-3). Peter Smith.

Sarah Orne Jewett. Margaret F. Thorp. (Pamphlets on American Writers Ser: No. 61). (Orig.). 1966. pap. 1.25x (ISBN 0-8166-0406-1, MPAW61). U of Minn Pr.

Sarah Pardee Winchester: A Driven Woman - Her Compelling Story. Genevieve Woelfl. Ed. by Sean McGuire. (Illus.). 32p. (Orig.). 1986. pap. 4.95 (ISBN 0-917928-02-4). Redwood.

Sarah Phillips. Andrea Lee. LC 83-43182. 224p. 1984. 12.45 (ISBN 0-394-53547-2). Random.

Sarah Phillips. Andrea Lee. (Contemporary American Fiction Ser.). 128p. 1985. pap. 5.95 (ISBN 0-14-008469-X). Penguin.

Sarah, Plain & Tall. Patricia MacLachlan. LC 83-49481. (Charlotte Zolotow Bks.). 64p. (gr. 3-5). 1985. 9.95i (ISBN 0-06-024101-2); PLB 9.89g (ISBN 0-06-024102-0). HarpJ.

Sarah, Plain & Tall. Patricia MacLachlan. LC 83-49481. (Trophy Bks.). 64p. (gr. 3 up). 1987. pap. 2.50 (ISBN 0-06-440205-3, Trophy). HarpJ.

Sarah, Queen of Mongolia. Manny S. Fredkin. 369p. 1986. 13.95 (ISBN 0-9617790-0-4). M S Fredkin.

Sarah Sells Soccer. H. R. Sheffer. Ed. by Howard Schroeder. LC 80-28622. (Teamates Ser.). (Illus.). 48p. (gr. 3 up). 1981. PLB 7.95 (ISBN 0-89686-100-7). Crestwood Hse.

Sarah T. Portrait of a Teenage Alcoholic. Robert Wagnen. (Orig.). 1984. pap. 2.50 (ISBN 0-345-34242-9). Ballantine.

Sarah the Dragon Lady. Martha B. Stiles. LC 86-8411. 96p. (gr. 3-7). 1986. 10.95 (ISBN 0-02-788400-7). Macmillan.

Sarah the Dragon Lady. Martha B. Stiles. 96p. (gr. 3-7). 1988. pap. 2.50 (ISBN 0-380-70471-4, Camelot). Avon.

Sarah the Priestess: The First Matriarch of Genesis. Savina J. Teubal. LC 84-96. xx, 201p. 1984. 16.95 (ISBN 0-8040-0843-4, Swallow); pap. 8.95 (ISBN 0-8040-0844-2, Swallow). Ohio U Pr.

Sarah Tyson Rorer: The Nation's Instructress in Dietetics & Cookery. Emma S. Weigley. LC 77-2115. (Memoirs Ser.: Vol.119). (Illus.). 1977. 10.00 (ISBN 0-87169-119-1). Am Philos.

Sarah Wilkins, in Search of a Song, Vol. 7. Sarah Wilkins. Ed. by Barbara Fisher. 22p. (Orig.). (gr. 5-8). 1984. pap. 2.00 (ISBN 0-934830-35-5). Ten Penny.

Sarah Winnemucca of the Northern Paiutes. Gae W. Canfield. LC 82-40448. (Illus.). 336p. 1983. 19.95 (ISBN 0-8061-1814-8). U of Okla Pr.

Sarah Winnemucca of the Northern Paiutes. Gae W. Canfield. LC 82-40448. (Illus.). 320p. (Orig.). 1988. pap. 9.95 (ISBN 0-8061-2090-8). U of Okla Pr.

Sarah's Awakening. Susan V. Billings. (Orig.). 1979. pap. 2.50 (ISBN 0-89083-536-5). Zebra.

Sarah's Bear. Marta Koci. LC 86-30241. (Illus.). 28p. (ps). 1987. 13.95 (ISBN 0-88708-038-3). Picture Bk Studio.

Sarah's Book. Anne Rothman et al. (Illus.). 48p. 5.95 (ISBN 0-88693-090-1). Putnam Pub Group.

Sarah's Great Idea. Elizabeth Van Steenwyk. (Treetop Tales Ser.). (Illus.). 96p. (Orig.). (gr. 3-5). 1987. pap. 2.25 (ISBN 0-87406-275-6). Willowisp Pr.

Sarah's Questions. Harriet Ziefert. LC 85-10947. (Illus.). 32p. (ps-1). 1986. 11.75 (ISBN 0-688-05614-8); PLB 11.88 (ISBN 0-688-05615-6). Lothrop.

Sarah's Room. Doris Orgel. LC 63-13675. (Illus.). (gr. k-3). 1963. 8.70 (ISBN 0-06-024605-7). HarpJ.

Sarah's Story. Lillian Cantleberry. (Continued Applied Christianity Ser.). 1983. pap. 4.95 (ISBN 0-570-03898-7, 12-2980). Concordia.

Sarah's Story. Ed. by Bobbie C. Jobe. 1987. pap. 2.70 (ISBN 0-89137-442-6). Quality Pubns.

Sarah's Unicorn. Bruce Coville & Katherine Coville. LC 79-2408. (Lippincott I-Like-to-Read Bks.). (Illus.). (ps-2). 1979. (Lipp Jr Bks); PLB 11.89 (ISBN 0-397-31873-1). HarpJ.

Sarah's Unicorn. Bruce Coville & Katherine Coville. LC 85-42749. (Trophy Picture Bks.). (Illus.). 48p. (ps-3). 1985. pap. 3.50 (ISBN 0-06-443084-7, Trophy). HarpJ.

Sarajevo. Ahmed Ceric. 130p. 1983. 193.00x (ISBN 0-317-61388-X, Pub. by Collets (UK)). State Mutual Bk.

Sarajevo: A Study in the Origins of the Great War. R. W. Seton-Watson. 303p. 1988. Repr. of 1926 ed. lib. bdg. 35.00 (ISBN 0-86527-357-X). Fertig.

Sarajevo Haggadah. Intro. by C. Roth. 50.00 (ISBN 0-87068-761-1). Ktav.

Sarajevo Haggadah. Eugen Werber. 1985. 147.00x (ISBN 0-317-61390-1, Pub. by Collets (UK)). State Mutual Bk.

Sarajevo Shots: Studies in the Immediate Origin of World War I. C. Patrick Joyce. (Studies in Revisionist Historiography). 1979. lib. bdg. 69.95 (ISBN 0-87700-263-0). Revisionist Pr.

Sarajevo Trial, 2 vols. W. A. Dolph Owings. Ed. by E. Pribic & N. Pribic. 1984. 59.95x (ISBN 0-89712-122-8). Documentary Pubns.

Saranac: America's Magic Mountain. Robert Taylor. LC 85-24911. (Illus.). 308p. 1986. 17.95 (ISBN 0-395-37905-9). HM.

Saranac: America's Magic Mountain. Robert Taylor. LC 87-29104. (Illus.). 309p. 1988. pap. 9.95 (ISBN 1-55778-069-2). Paragon Hse.

Sarapis & Isis: Collected Essays. Thomas A. Brady. Ed. by Fordyce Mitchel. 129p. 1978. 25.00 (ISBN 0-89005-253-0). Ares.

Sara's Ghost. Patricia Welles. Orig. Title: The Ghost of S. W. I. 320p. 1987. pap. 3.50 (ISBN 0-7701-0663-3). Paperjacks US.

Sara's Trek. Florence E. Schloneger. (Illus.). 100p. (YA) (gr. 7 up). 1982. pap. 4.95 (ISBN 0-87303-071-0). Faith & Life.

Saraswattee: A Novel of India. Kit P. Singh. LC 82-7175. 304p. 1982. 14.95 (ISBN 0-914842-88-9). Madrona Pubs.

Sarat Chandra Chatterji. V. S. Naravane. 1976. 11.00x (ISBN 0-8364-0465-3). South Asia Bks.

Saratoga: A Season of Elegance. Photos by William Strode. LC 85-52217. (Illus.). 104p. 1986. 24.95 (ISBN 0-934738-19-X). Thomasson-Grant.

Saratoga Bestiary. Stephen Dobyns. 1988. 16.95 (ISBN 0-670-82024-5). Viking.

Saratoga Diary: 1912. Anne D. Shepherd. 176p. 1987. 10.95 (ISBN 0-8062-3164-5). Carlton.

Saratoga Headhunter. Stephen Dobyns. 201p. 1985. 13.95 (ISBN 0-670-80488-6). Viking.

Saratoga Headhunter. Stephen Dobyns. 208p. 1986. pap. 3.50 (ISBN 0-14-007772-3). Penguin.

Saratoga Longshot. Stephen Dobyns. 256p. 1987. pap. 3.95 (ISBN 0-14-009627-2). Penguin.

Saratoga Snapper. Stephen Dobyns. 288p. 1986. 15.95 (ISBN 0-670-81059-2). Viking.

Saratoga Snapper. Stephen Dobyns. 272p. 1987. pap. 3.95 (ISBN 0-14-008812-1). Penguin.

Saratoga Snapper. Stephen Dobyns. (Large Print Bks.). 329p. 1988. lib. bdg. 17.95x (ISBN 0-8161-4348-X, Large Print Bks). G K Hall.

Saratoga Swimmer. Stephen Dobyns. 224p. 1983. pap. 3.95 (ISBN 0-14-006357-9). Penguin.

Saratoga: The Place & Its People. Ed. by Peter Andrews et al. (Illus.). 208p. 1988. 45.00 (ISBN 0-8109-1518-9). Abrams.

Saratoga Trunk. Edna Ferber. 1980. pap. 1.95 (ISBN 0-449-24115-7, Crest). Fawcett.

Saratoga Trunk. Edna Ferber. 17.95 (ISBN 0-89190-323-2, Pub. by Am Repr). Amereon Ltd.

Saratoga Yearling. Kevin J. Reed. Ed. by Meri G. Herold. (Illus.). 110p. (Orig.). (gr. 5-9). 1985. pap. 3.95 (ISBN 0-9614546-0-1). Chowder Pr.

Sarawak Chinese. John M. Chin. (Illus.). 1981. 24.95x (ISBN 0-19-580470-8). Oxford U Pr.

Sarawak: Its Inhabitants & Productions. Hugh Low. (Illus.). 416p. 1968. Repr. of 1848 ed. 35.00x (ISBN 0-7146-2017-3, F Cass Co). Biblio Dist.

Sarayacu Quichua Pottery. Carolyn Orr & Patricia Kelley. (Museum of Anthropology Publications: No. 1). 37p. 1976. 3.00x (ISBN 0-88312-150-6); microfiche 2.00 (ISBN 0-88312-240-5). Summer Inst Ling.

Sarca Ainda Arde. Lloyd J. Ogilvie. Orig. Title: Bush Is Still Burning. (Port.). 1986. write for info. (ISBN 0-8297-1093-0). Life Pubs Intl.

Sarcoidosis. Ed. by Jack Lieberman. (Illus.). 224p. 1985. 43.00 (ISBN 0-8089-1728-5, 792539). Grune.

Sarcoidosis. Ed. by Riichiro Mikami & Yutaka Hosoda. 413p. 1981. 57.50 (ISBN 0-86008-295-4, Pub. by U of Tokyo Japan). Columbia U Pr.

Sarcoidosis. 2nd ed. J. G. Scadding & D. N. Mitchell. (Illus.). 720p. 1985. text ed. 110.00x (ISBN 0-412-21760-0, Pub. by Chapman & Hall UK). Sheridan Med Bks.

Sarcoidosis & Other Granulomatous Disorders: International Conference, 9th, Paris, 31 August - 4 September 1981. Ed. by J. Chretien & J. Marsac. (Illus.). 950p. 1983. 145.00 (ISBN 0-08-027088-3). Pergamon.

Sarcoidosis & Other Granulomatous Disorders. D. Geraint James & W. Jones Williams. (Problems in Internal Medicine Ser.: Vol. 24). (Illus.). 256p. 1985. 58.00 (ISBN 0-7216-1044-7). Saunders.

Sarcoidosis: Clinical Management. Om P. Sharma. (Illus.). 216p. 1984. text ed. 90.00 (ISBN 0-407-00326-6). Butterworth.

Sarcolemmal Biochemistry, 2 vols. Ed. by Abdul M. Kidwai. 1987. Vol. I. 195.00 set (ISBN 0-8493-5908-2). Vol. II, 384 pgs. CRC Pr.

Sarcophagi from Jewish Catacombs of Ancient Rome. Adia Konikoff. (Illus.). 65p. 1986. text ed. 42.00x (ISBN 3-515-04464-7, Pub by Franz Steiner). Coronet Bks.

Sarcophagus: A Tragedy. Vladimir Gubaryev. Tr. by Michael Glenny. LC 87-40112. 96p. 1987. pap. 6.95 (ISBN 0-394-75590-1, Vin). Random.

Sarcoplasmic Reticulum in Muscle Physiology. Ed. by Mark L. Entman & W. Barry Van Winkle. 1986. Vol. I, 184p. 89.00 (ISBN 0-8493-6180-X); Vol. II, 184p. 95.00. CRC Pr.

Sarcoplasmic Reticulum: Transport & Energy Transduction. Leopoldo DeMeis. LC 81-2325. 182p. 1981. 52.50 (ISBN 0-471-05025-3, Pub. by John Wiley). Krieger.

Sardine Anchovy Complex. Murphy. 1990. price not set (ISBN 0-471-61411-4). Wiley.

Sardine Deception. Leif Davidsen. Tr. by Tiina Nunnally & Steve Murray. LC 86-2094. 199p. (Orig.). 1986. pap. 15.95 (ISBN 0-940242-39-7). Fjord Pr.

Sardines. Nuruddin Farah. 256p. 1982. 13.95 (ISBN 0-8052-8126-6, Pub. by Allison & Busby England). Schocken.

Sardi's Bar Guide. Vincent Sardi, Jr. Date not set. pap. 3.50. Ballantine.

Sardis from Prehistoric to Roman Times: Results of the Archaeological Exploration of Sardis, 1958-1975. George M. Hanfmann & William E. Mierse. (Illus.). 528p. 1983. text ed. 47.00x (ISBN 0-674-78925-3). Harvard U Pr.

Sardis in the Age of Croesus. John G. Pedley. LC 67-64447. (Centers of Civilization Ser.). pap. 38.80 (ISBN 0-317-28329-4, 2016247). Bks Demand UMI.

Sardis: Twenty-Seven Years of Discovery. Ed. by Eleanor Guralnick. 1988. write for info. (ISBN 0-9609042-1-2). Archaeol Chi.

Sardonic Humor of Ambrose Bierce. Ambrose Bierce. Ed. by George Barkin. 232p. (Orig.). 1963. pap. 4.50 (ISBN 0-486-20768-4). Dover.

Sardonic Tales (Contes Cruels) Jean M. Villiers De l'Isle-Adam. Tr. by Hamish Miles. LC 77-11497. Repr. of 1927 ed. 22.00 (ISBN 0-404-16356-4). AMS Pr.

Sardonyx Net. Elizabeth A. Lynn. 432p. (Orig.). 1985. pap. 3.50 (ISBN 0-425-08635-6). Berkley Pub.

Sarepta: A Preliminary Report on the Iron Age. James B. Pritchard et al. (University Museum Monographs: No. 35). (Illus.). ix, 114p. 1975. pap. 30.00 (ISBN 0-934718-24-5). Univ Mus of U Pa.

Sarepta Three: The Imported Bronze & Iron Age Wares from Area II,X. Robert B. Koehl. (Publications de l'Universite Libanaise Section des Etudes Archaeologiques: No. II). (Illus.). 210p. 1985. pap. text ed. 35.00x (Pub. by Librairie Orientale). Univ Mus of U PA.

Sargam: An Introduction to Indian Music. Vishnudas Shirali. 1978. 37.00x (ISBN 0-88386-830-X). South Asia Bks.

Sargasso. Edwin Corley. 1978. pap. 2.50 (ISBN 0-440-17575-5). Dell.

Sargasso Sea. William McPherson. 1988. 7.95. PB.

Sargent at Broadway: The Impressionist Years, 1883-1889. Richard L. Ormond et al. LC 85-24595. (Illus.). 112p. 1986. 19.95 (ISBN 0-87663-492-7). Universe.

Sargent Portrait Drawings: 42 Works. John S. Sargent. (Dover Art Library). (Illus.). 48p. (Orig.). 1983. pap. 3.50 (ISBN 0-486-24524-1). Dover.

Sargent Watercolors. Donelson F. Hoopes. (Illus.). 88p. 1984. pap. 16.95 (ISBN 0-8230-4641-9). Watson-Guptill.

Sargonic Texts from Telloh in the Istanbul Archaeological Museums. Benjamin R. Foster & Veysel Donbaz. (Occasional Publications of the Babylonian Fund: No. 5 OPBF 5). (Illus.). xi, 17p. 1982. 20.00x (ISBN 0-934718-44-X). Univ Mus of U PA.

Sargonic Texts in the Ashmolean Museum, Oxford. Ignace J. Gelb. LC 79-111601. (Materials for the Assyrian Dictionary Ser: No. 5). 1970. pap. 12.50x (ISBN 0-226-62309-2). U of Chicago Pr.

Sargonic Texts in the Louvre. Ignace J. Gelb. LC 79-111600. (Materials for the Assyrian Dictionary Ser: No. 4). 1970. pap. 11.00x (ISBN 0-226-62308-4). U of Chicago Pr.

Sari-Sarna: Santhal Religion. P. C. Hembram. 129p. 1988. 19.00x (ISBN 81-7099-044-0, Pub. by Mittal). South Asia Bks.

Sarim. limited ed. Don Herrin. (Illus.). 17.50 (ISBN 0-8363-0088-2). Jenkins.

Sarkhan see Deceptive American.

Sarmiento Anthology. Domingo F. Sarmiento et al. Ed. by Allison Bunkley. Tr. by Stuart E. Grummon. LC 73-159104. 1971. Repr. of 1948 ed. 25.50x (ISBN 0-8046-1647-7, Pub. by Kennikat). Assoc Faculty Pr.

Sarmiento: Facundo. C. A. Jones. (Critical Guides to Spanish Texts Ser.: No. 10). 87p. (Orig.). 1974. pap. 4.95 (ISBN 0-900411-76-7, Pub. by Grant & Cutler). Longwood Pub Group.

Sarmiento's Travels in the U. S. in 1847. Tr. by M. A. Rockland. 1970. 41.00x (ISBN 0-691-04602-6). Princeton U Pr.

Sarna Deep Sky Atlas. Thomas Sarna. pap. 29.95x (ISBN 0-943396-06-9). Willmann Bell.

Sarngadhara Samhita: A Trestise on Ayurveda. Sarngadhara. Tr. by Srikanata K. Murthy from Sanskrit. 335p. 1984. text ed. 65.00 (ISBN 0-89744-056-0). Auromere.

Sarnia: Gateway to Bluewater Land. Edward Phelps. Ed. by Marilyn Horn. (Illus.). 128p. 1987. 24.95 (ISBN 0-89781-222-0). Windsor Pubns Inc.

Sarojini Naidu: An Introduction to Her Life, Work & Poetry. V. S. Naravane. 160p. 1980. 20.00x (ISBN 0-86131-253-8, Pub. by Orient Longman Ltd India). Apt Bks.

Saroyan: A Biography. Lawrence Lee & Barry Gifford. LC 83-48794. 320p. 1984. 18.45i (ISBN 0-06-015141-2, HarpT). Har-Row.

Saroyan: A Biography. Lawrence Lee & Barry Gifford. LC 87-9025. (Illus.). 338p. 1987. pap. 9.95 (ISBN 0-913729-96-5). Paragon Hse.

Saroyan Special. facs. ed. William Saroyan. LC 70-134979. (Short Story Index Reprint Ser). (Illus.). 1948. 24.00 (ISBN 0-8369-3709-0). Ayer Co Pubs.

Sarraute: Le Planetarium. Roger McLure. (Critical Guides to French Texts). 1987. pap. 4.50 (ISBN 0-7293-0274-1, Pub. by Grant & Cutler). Longwood Pub Group.

Sarsfield; or Wanderings of Youth: An Irish Tale, 3 vols. in 2. John Gamble. LC 79-8268. Repr. of 1814 ed. Set. 84.50 (ISBN 0-404-61859-6). Vol. 1 (ISBN 0-404-61860-X). Vol. 2 (ISBN 0-404-61861-8). AMS Pr.

Sarsiellidae of the Western Atlantic & Northern Gulf of Mexico & Revision of the Sarsiellinae (Ostracoda: Myodocopina) LC 85-600238. (Smithsonian Contributions to Zoology Ser.: No. 415). pap. 55.30 (2027313). Bks Demand UMI.

Sarten Por el Mango: Encuentro de Escritoras Latinoamericanas. Ed. by Patricia E. Gonzalez & Eliana Ortega. LC 83-83056. (Nave & el Puerto). 173p. (Span.). 1985. pap. 5.95 (ISBN 0-940238-72-1). Ediciones Huracan.

Sassafras. Stephen Cosgrove. (Serendipity Bks.). (Illus.). 32p. (gr. k-4). 1988. pap. 2.50 (ISBN 0-8431-2302-8). Price Stern.

Sassafras. Jack Matthews. 288p. 1983. 14.95 (ISBN 0-395-34640-1). HM.

Sassafras, Cypress & Indigo. Ntozake Shange. 224p. 1983. pap. 6.95 (ISBN 0-312-69972-7). St Martin.

Sassafras! The Ozarks Cookbook. Junior League of Springfield, Missouri, Inc. LC 84-81440. (Illus.). 408p. 1985. 14.95 (ISBN 0-9613307-1-6). Jr League MO.

Sassone. Donelson F. Hoopes. Ed. by Douglas Reeve. LC 79-90217. 304p. 1979. 80.00 (ISBN 0-935194-00-2). Arti Grafiche.

Sassone Serigraphs: Catalogue Raisonne. Phyllis S. Barton. LC 84-71654. 90p. (Orig.). 1984. pap. 25.00 (ISBN 0-935194-01-0). Arti Grafiche.

Sassoon Dynasty. Cecil Roth. Ed. by Mira Wilkins. LC 76-29982. (European Business Ser.). (Illus.). 1977. Repr. of 1941 ed. lib. bdg. 23.50x (ISBN 0-405-09747-6). Ayer Co Pubs.

Sassoon's Sketches. Elias Sassoon. LC 86-72870. 168p. (Orig.). 1987. pap. 8.00 (ISBN 0-916383-20-2). Aegina Pr.

Sassy Sayin's & Mountain Badmouth. Jesse Masters & Don Johnston. (Illus.). 80p. (Orig.). 1985. pap. 3.95 (ISBN 0-9615347-0-2). Sassy Sayings.

Sat at a Glance. Ronald G. Vlk. Date not set. write for info. S&S.

SAT (Scholastic Aptitude Test) Preparation Guide. Jerry Bobrow & William A. Covino. (Cliffs Test Preparation Ser.). (Illus.). (gr. 11-12). 1982. pap. 4.95 wkbk. (ISBN 0-8220-2000-9). Cliffs.

SAT Success: Peterson's Study Guide to English & Math Skills for College Entrance Examinations: SAT, ACT and PSAT. Joan D. Carris & Michael R. Crystal. LC 82-16165. 386p. (Orig.). 1982. pap. 9.95 (ISBN 0-87866-208-1). Petersons Guides.

SAT Success: Peterson's Study Guide to English & Math Skills for College Entrance Examinations. rev. ed. Joan D. Carris et al. LC 87-12163. 523p. (Orig.). 1987. pap. 9.95 (ISBN 0-87866-580-3). Petersons Guides.

Satan. C. H. Spurgeon. 1978. pap. 1.95 (ISBN 0-686-23026-4). Pilgrim Pubns.

Satan: A Defeated Foe. Charles H. Usher. 1964. pap. 1.95 (ISBN 0-87508-546-6). Chr Lit.

Satan, A Portrait: A Study of the Character of Satan Through All the Ages. Edward Langton. LC 74-2434. 1973. lib. bdg. 40.00 (ISBN 0-8414-5716-6). Folcroft.

Satan, a Portrait: A Study of the Character of Satan Through All the Ages. Edward Langton. 1976. lib. bdg. 59.95 (ISBN 0-8490-2568-0). Gordon Pr.

Satan & Israel. Date not set. pap. 0.95 (ISBN 0-937408-13-1). GMI Pubns Inc.

Satan Bug. Alistair MacLean. 224p. 1983. pap. 2.95 (ISBN 0-449-20394-8, GM). Fawcett.

Satan Exposed. B. D. Voarhis. 1975. pap. 2.25 (ISBN 0-87148-785-3). Pathway Pr.

Satan, Fallen Angels & Demons. Gordon Lindsay. (Satan Ser.: Vol. 2). pap. 1.25 (ISBN 0-89985-954-2). Christ Nations.

Satan: His Psychotherapy & Cure by the Unfortunate Dr. Kassler. Jeremy Leven. LC 81-48107. 352p. 1982. 13.45 (ISBN 0-394-52370-9). Knopf.

Satan: His Psychotherapy & Cure by the Unfortunate Dr. Kassler, J.S.P.S. Jeremy Leven. 512p. 1983. pap. 3.95 (ISBN 0-345-30265-6). Ballantine.

Satan Hunter. Thomas W. Wedge & Robert L. Powers. LC 87-20219. (Illus.). 256p. (Orig.). 1988. pap. 7.95 (ISBN 0-938936-73-5). Daring Bks.

Satan in Goray. Isaac Bashevis Singer. 1978. pap. 1.65 (ISBN 0-380-01538-2, 23200, Bard). Avon.

Satan in Goray. Isaac Bashevis Singer. 224p. 1980. pap. 2.50 (ISBN 0-449-24326-5, Crest). Fawcett.

Satan in Goray. Isaac Bashevis Singer. Tr. by Jacob Sloan from Yiddish. 239p. 1955. 8.95 (ISBN 0-374-25404-4); pap. 4.95 (ISBN 0-374-50082-7). FS&G.

Satan in St. Mary's. P. C. Doherty. 176p. 1987. 12.95 (ISBN 0-312-00059-6). St Martin.

Satan in Society. Nicholas F. Cooke. LC 73-20617. (Sex, Marriage & Society Ser.). 412p. 1974. Repr. of 1876 ed. 31.00x (ISBN 0-405-05796-2). Ayer Co Pubs.

Satan in the Sanctuary see Anticristo y el Santuario.

Satan in the Woods. Moses J. Steiner. LC 78-54567. 1978. 10.95 (ISBN 0-88400-057-5). Shengold.

Satan Is Alive & Well on Planet Earth. Hal Lindsey. 256p. 1985. pap. 3.95 (ISBN 0-553-24406-X). Bantam.

Satan Is Alive & Well on Planet Earth. Hal Lindsey & C. C. Carlson. 224p. 1972. pap. 6.95 (ISBN 0-310-27791-4, 18189P). Zondervan.

Satan Is No Myth. J. Oswald Sanders. LC 74-15358. 1983. pap. 6.95 (ISBN 0-8024-7525-6). Moody.

Satan Is Now a Light Bearer. Ruth Norman. 24p. (Orig.). 1984. pap. 1.00 (ISBN 0-932642-88-8). Unarius Pubns.

Satan Is Subtle. Larry Clapp. 96p. 1988. 8.95 (ISBN 0-8062-3214-5). Carlton.

Satan Loves Tired People. Barbara H. Seguin. 46p. 1987. pap. 2.75 (ISBN 0-88144-110-4). Christian Pub.

Satan of Milton. R. H. Anstice. LC 72-191957. 1910. lib. bdg. 17.00 (ISBN 0-8414-0289-2). Folcroft.

Satan, Rebellion & Fall, 3 vols. Gordon Lindsay. (Sorcery & Spirit World Ser.: Vol. 3). 1.25 ea. (ISBN 0-89985-953-4). Christ Nations.

Satan Revisted: The Old New England Blue s. Richard E. Petitti. (Illus.). 150p. 1985. pap. 20.00 (ISBN 0-938582-02-X). Sensitive Man.

Satan Says. Sharon Olds. LC 79-24300. (Pitt Poetry Ser.). 1980. 16.95x (ISBN 0-8229-3413-2); pap. 8.95 (ISBN 0-8229-5314-5). U of Pittsburgh Pr.

Satan-Seller. Mike Warnke et al. LC 79-94042. 214p. 1972. pap. 3.95 (ISBN 0-88270-096-0). Bridge Pub.

Satan Sleuth. Michael Avallone. (Popular Fiction Ser.: No. 4). Date not set. cancelled; pap. 9.95. Starmont Hse.

Satan Strike see Atague Diabolico.

Satan: The Early Christian Tradition. Jeffrey B. Russell. LC 81-66649. (Illus.). 258p. 1981. 32.50x (ISBN 0-8014-1267-6). Cornell U Pr.

Satan: The Early Christian Tradition. Jeffrey B. Russell. LC 81-66649. (Paperback Ser.). (Illus.). 258p. 1987. pap. 10.95 (ISBN 0-8014-9413-3). Cornell U Pr.

Satan Unmasked. Earl Paulk. 344p. (Orig.). 1984. pap. 7.95 (ISBN 0-917595-03-3). K-Dimension.

Satan Unmasked: Principles & Practice of Christian Exorcism. G. M. Farley & Robert W. Pelton. LC 78-70632. (Illus.). 1979. 7.50 (ISBN 0-916620-24-7). Portals Pr.

Satan Wants You: The Cult of Devil Worship in America. Arthur Lyons. LC 87-40387. (Illus.). 192p. 1988. 15.95 (ISBN 0-89296-217-8). Mysterious Pr.

Satan Whispers. W. E. Ross. 1981. pap. 2.50 (ISBN 0-8439-0913-7, Leisure Bks). Leisure NY.

Satanic Bible. Anton S. La Vey. 1969. pap. 4.50 (ISBN 0-380-01539-0, 60096-X). Avon.

Satanic Mass. H. T. Rhodes. 256p. 1974. 7.95 (ISBN 0-8065-0405-6, Pub. by Citadel Pr). Lyle Stuart.

Satanic Mass. H. T. Rhodes. 254p. 1975. pap. 3.95 (ISBN 0-8065-0484-6, Pub. by Citadel Pr). Lyle Stuart.

Satanic Mill. Otfried Preussler. (gr. 5-9). 15.75 (ISBN 0-8446-6196-1). Peter Smith.

Satanic Rituals. Anton S. LaVey. 1972. pap. 4.50 (ISBN 0-380-01392-4). Avon.

Satanic Troika. Therese M. La Bouche. 224p. 1985. 12.50 (ISBN 0-89962-407-3). Todd & Honeywell.

Satanic Verses. Salman Rushdie. 1989. 19.95 (ISBN 0-670-82537-9). Viking.

Satanism. Ted Schwarz & Duane Empey. 256p. 1988. pap. 8.95 (ISBN 0-310-45041-1, Pub. by Zondervan Bks). Zondervan.

Satanism & Witchcraft. Jules Michelet. 352p. 1983. pap. 6.95 (ISBN 0-8065-0059-X, 89, Pub. by Citadel Pr). Lyle Stuart.

Satanism in French Romanticism. M. Rudwin. 59.59 (ISBN 0-8490-0993-6). Gordon Pr.

Satanist: Anniversary Edition. 75th ed. Hugh Fraser & J. I. Stahlmann. Ed. by John C. Moran. (Worthies Library: No. 4). 480p. 1987. 10.00 (ISBN 0-318-22842-4). F M Crawford.

Satan's Angels Exposed. Salem Kirban. 1980. pap. 5.95 (ISBN 0-912582-32-4). Kirban.

Satan's Cage. John Mackie. (Rat Bastards Ser.: No. 15). 208p. 1985. pap. 2.75 (ISBN 0-515-08394-1). Jove Pubns.

Satan's Child. Angela Kirsten. 1985. 24.95x (ISBN 0-7090-2116-X, Pub. by R Hale Ltd UK). State Mutual Bk.

Satan's Demon Manifestations & Delusions. Gordon Lindsay. (Satan Ser.: Vol. 3). pap. 1.25 (ISBN 0-89985-955-0). Christ Nations.

Satan's Devices see Occult ABC.

Satan's Fat Attack!!! Carrier M. Meeks. Ed. by Martha Williams. (Illus.). 168p. (Orig.). 1986. pap. 9.95 (ISBN 0-941513-00-9). C & M Pubs & Distributors.

Satan's Folly. Patricia A. Holland. 48p. 1988. 6.95 (ISBN 0-8062-3358-3). Carlton.

Satan's Invisible World Discovered. George Sinclair. LC 68-17017. 1969. Repr. of 1685 ed. 45.00x (ISBN 0-8201-1068-X). Schol Facsimiles.

Satan's Invisible World Displayed: A Study of Greater New York. William T. Stead. LC 73-19180. (Politics & People Ser.). (Illus.). 222p. 1974. Repr. 18.00x (ISBN 0-405-05901-9). Ayer Co Pubs.

Satan's Manor. Mark Andrews. 288p. 1983. pap. 2.95 (ISBN 0-8439-2014-9, Leisure Bks). Leisure NY.

Satan's Mark. C. C. Risenhoover. Ed. by Shirley D. Ratisseau. 340p. 1987. 14.95 (ISBN 0-918865-12-3). McLennan Hse.

Satan's Mark Exposed. Salem Kirban. 1981. pap. 5.95 (ISBN 0-912582-36-7). Kirban.

Satan's Master. Joseph Nazel. (Orig.). 1983. pap. 2.50 (ISBN 0-87067-259-2, BH259). Holloway.

Satan's Music Exposed. Salem Kirban. 1980. pap. 5.95 (ISBN 0-912582-35-9). Kirban.

Satan's Power: A Deviant Psychotherapy Cult. William S. Bainbridge. LC 77-80466. 1978. 36.00x (ISBN 0-520-03546-1). U of Cal Pr.

Satan's Secret Revealed: From the Files of a Christian Exorcist. Frank M. Brim. 176p. 1983. pap. 5.00 (ISBN 0-9612676-0-7). World Wide Mini.

Satan's Spawn. Richard J. Silverthorn. 256p. (Orig.). 1988. pap. 3.95 (ISBN 0-380-75316-2). Avon.

Satans Suckhole. Willard Gellis. 1988. pap. 8.00 (ISBN 0-917455-05-3). Big Foot NY.

Satan's Ten Most Believable Lies. 2nd ed. David Breese. 1987. pap. 6.95 (ISBN 0-8024-7675-9). Moody.

Satan's Underground. Lauren Stratford. LC 87-81660. 224p. (Orig.). 1988. pap. 6.95 (ISBN 0-89081-630-1). Harvest Hse.

Satanstoe. James Fenimore Cooper. LC 62-9515. (Bison Book: BB138). pap. 110.50 (ISBN 0-317-29729-5, 2022205). Bks Demand UMI.

Satanstoe or the Littlepage Manuscripts. James Fenimore Cooper. (Writings of James Fenimore Cooper). (Orig.). (YA) (gr. 9-12). 1989. text ed. 44.50x (ISBN 0-88706-903-7); pap. 14.95x (ISBN 0-88706-904-5). State U NY Pr.

Satanta, the Great Chief of the Kiowas & His People. Clarence R. Wharton. LC 76-43889. Repr. of 1935 ed. 29.50 (ISBN 0-404-15748-3). AMS Pr.

Satapancasatka of Matrceta: Sanskirt Text, Tibetan Translation & Commentary, & Chinese Translation. Ed. by Bailey Shackleton. LC 61-28529. pap. 62.30 (ISBN 0-317-10105-6, 2051469). Bks Demand UMI.

Satapatha Brahmana, 5 vols. Ed. by Julius Eggeling. 1974. lib. bdg. 500.00 (ISBN 0-8490-0994-4). Gordon Pr.

Satch & Motormouth. Karen Sommer. (Satch Ser.). (gr. 3-7). 1987. pap. 3.95 (ISBN 1-55513-063-1, Chariot Bks). Cook.

Satch & the New Kid. Karen Sommer. LC 86-24323. (Satch Ser.). (gr. 3-7). 1987. pap. 3.95 (ISBN 0-317-56110-3, Chariot Bks). Cook.

Satchel Paige. Kathryn L. Humohrey. Ed. by Frank Sloan. (Impact Biography Ser.). (Illus.). 128p. (YA) (gr. 7-12). 1988. 11.90 (ISBN 0-531-10513-X). Watts.

Satchelmouse & the Dinosaurs. Antonia Barber. (gr. 2 up). 1988. 9.95 (ISBN 0-8120-5872-0). Barron.

Satchelmouse & the Doll's House. Antonia Barber. LC 87-14340. (Illus.). (ps-3). 1988. 9.95 (ISBN 0-8120-5873-9). Barron.

Satchmo. Gary Giddins. (Illus.). 1988. pap. 24.95 (ISBN 0-385-24428-2, Dolph). Doubleday.

Satchmo: My Life in New Orleans. Louis Armstrong. 220p. 1986. 9.95 (ISBN 0-306-80276-7). Da Capo.

Satchmo My Life in New Orleans: My Life in New Orleans. Louis Armstrong. 240p. Repr. of 1954 ed. lib. bdg. 39.00 (Pub. by Am Repr Serv). Am Biog Serv.

Satellite & Cable TV: Scrambling & Descrambling. Frank Baylin & Brent Gale. 272p. (Orig.). 1986. pap. text ed. 19.95 (ISBN 0-917893-07-7, Baylin Gale). Consol.

Satellite & Computer Communications. Ed. by J. L. Grange. 380p. 1984. 63.25 (ISBN 0-444-86730-9, North Holland). Elsevier.

Satellite-Based Educational Infrastructure in Alaska - The Educational Satellite Communications Demonstration: A Selective, Annotated Bibliography. James J. Sanchez. (Public Administration Ser.: P 2267). 8p. 1987. 3.00 (ISBN 1-55590-527-7). Vance Biblios.

Satellite Broadcasting. P. Rainger et al. LC 85-9366. 326p. 1985. 47.95 (ISBN 0-471-90421-X). Wiley.

Satellite Broadcasting Systems Planning. L. A. Trinogga & J. Slater. LC 85-14031. 168p. 1985. 31.95 (ISBN 0-470-20217-3). Halsted Pr.

Satellite Broadcasting: The Politics & Implications of the New Media. Ed. by Ralph M. Negrine. 320p. 1988. lib. bdg. 65.00 (ISBN 0-415-00109-9). Routledge Chapman & Hall.

Satellite Business Networks & Systems. Ed. by Ivan Kadar & Reuben E. Eaves. (AIAA Selected Reprint Ser.: Vol. XX). (Illus.). 270p. (Orig.). 1985. pap. 27.50 (ISBN 0-915928-96-5). AIAA.

Satellite Cells of the Sensory Canglia. E. Pannese. (Advances in Antomy, Embryology & Cell Biology Ser.: Vol. 65). (Illus.). 98p. 1981. pap. 28.00 (ISBN 0-387-10219-1). Springer-Verlag.

Satellite Cities: A Study of Industrial Suburbs. Graham R. Taylor. LC 70-112576. (Rise of Urban America). (Illus.). 1970. Repr. of 1915 ed. 22.00 (ISBN 0-405-02478-9). Ayer Co Pubs.

Satellite Communication Antenna Technology. Ed. by R. Mittra et al. 600p. 1984. 105.25 (ISBN 0-444-86733-3, North-Holland). Elsevier.

Satellite Communication Broadcasting. Ed. by L. Ya Kantor. Tr. by Donald M. Jansky. 350p. 1987. text ed. 79.00. Artech Hse.

Satellite Communications. Gagliardi. 43.95 (ISBN 0-317-64271-5). Van Nos Reinhold.

Satellite Communications. Timothy Pratt & Charles W. Postian. 472p. 1986. write for info. (ISBN 0-471-87837-5). Wiley.

Satellite Communications. Stan Prentiss. (Illus.). 288p. 1983. pap. 12.95 (ISBN 0-8306-1632-2, 1632). TAB Bks.

Satellite Communications. 2nd ed. Stan Prentiss. (Illus.). 152p. (Orig.). 1987. 21.95 (ISBN 0-8306-0192-9); pap. 16.95 (ISBN 0-8306-2792-8). TAB Bks.

Satellite Communications. Ed. by H. L. Van Trees. LC 78-65704. 676p. 1979. 65.95 (ISBN 0-87942-121-5, PC01222). Inst Electrical.

Satellite Communications: A Practical Guide. D. I. Dalgleish & E. C. Johnson. Date not set. price not set. Inst Elect Eng.

Satellite Communications: Advanced Technologies, PAAS55. Ed. by David Jarett. LC 77-8524. (Illus.). 489p. 1977. 59.50 (ISBN 0-915928-19-1). AIAA.

Satellite Communications-An Introduction. Robert M. Gagliardi. (Engineering Ser.). (Illus.). 475p. 1984. 41.95 (ISBN 0-534-02976-0, Lifetime Learn). Van Nos Reinhold.

Satellite Communications: Dictionary of Technical Vocabulary & Terminology English-Spanish - Spanish-English. Ismael S. Dieguez. Ed. by Teresa Plata. LC 81-68868. 235p. (Span. & Eng.). 1982. 25.00 (ISBN 0-9620427-0-6). Duplicata Pr.

Satellite Communications in the Next Decade: Proceedings of the 14th Goddard Memorial Symposium. Ed. by Leonard Jaffe. (Science & Technology: Vol. 44). (Illus.). 1977. 20.00x (ISBN 0-87703-088-X, Pub. by Am Astronaut). Univelt Inc.

Satellite Communications Market. Frost & Sullivan, Inc. Staff. 330p. 1986. 2450.00 (ISBN 0-86621-750-9, E820). Frost & Sullivan.

Satellite Communications: Proceedings of the Canadian Domestic & International Conference, 1st, June 15-17, Ottawa, Canada. Ed. by K. Feher. 670p. 1983. 121.00 (ISBN 0-444-86690-6, North-Holland). Elsevier.

Satellite Communications Services & Equipment Markets, U. S. 269p. 1987. 2300.00x (ISBN 0-317-66665-7). Intl Res Dev.

Satellite Communications Systems. G. Maral & M. Bousquet. LC 84-24433. 401p. 1986. 49.95 (ISBN 0-471-90220-9). Wiley.

Satellite Communications Technology. Robert L. Douglas. (Illus.). 160p. 1988. pap. 20.00 (ISBN 0-13-791286-2). P-H.

Satellite Communications 87: Proceedings of the European Satellite Communications Conference Held in London, December 1987. 180p. 1987. pap. text ed. 130.00 (ISBN 0-86353-094-X, Online Pubns). Online.

Satellite Directory. 700p. 1986. 200.00 (ISBN 0-317-55717-3). B Klein Pubns.

Satellite DNA. T. Beridze. (Illus.). 150p. 1986. 70.00 (ISBN 0-387-15876-6). Springer-Verlag.

Satellite Doppler Tracking & Its Geodetic Applications. A. R. Robbins et al. (Royal Society Ser.). (Illus.). 196p. 1980. Repr. of 1980 ed. text ed. 54.00x (ISBN 0-85403-128-6, Pub. by Royal Soc London). Scholium Intl.

Satellite Dynamics: Proceedings of the COSPAR-IAU-IUTAM Symposium, Sao Paulo, Brazil, June 19-21, 1974. COSPAR-IAU-IUTAM Symposium Staff. Ed. by G. E. Giacaglia & A. C. Stickland. (Illus.). 390p. 1975. 37.80 (ISBN 0-387-07087-7). Springer-Verlag.

Satellite Environment Handbook. 2nd ed. Ed. by Francis S. Johnson. LC 64-8894. pap. 30.00 (2026811). Bks Demand UMI.

Satellite Experimenter's Handbook. Martin Davidoff. LC 83-71699. 10.00 (ISBN 0-87259-004-6). Am Radio.

Satellite Information Systems. Edward S. Binkowski. (Professional Librarian Ser.). 237p. 1988. lib. bdg. 38.50x (ISBN 0-8161-1856-6); pap. 29.95x (ISBN 0-8161-1880-9). G K Hall.

Satellite Master Antenna TV Market Opportunities. 179p. 1983. 985.00x (ISBN 0-88694-545-3). Intl Res Dev.

Satellite Microwave Remote Sensing. Thomas D. Allan. (Marine Science Ser.). 526p. 1983. 116.95x (ISBN 0-470-27397-6). Halsted Pr.

Satellite Monitoring of the Earth. Karl-Heinz Szekielda. (Remote Sensing & Image Processing Ser.). 1988. price not set (ISBN 0-471-61330-4). Wiley.

Satellite Oceanography: An Introduction for Oceanographers & Remote-Sensing Scientist. I. Robinson. LC 84-25142. (Marine Science Ser.). 455p. 1985. 65.95 (ISBN 0-470-20148-7). Halsted Pr.

Satellite Program Services. 23p. 1987. 5.00 (ISBN 0-317-40072-X). Cable TV Info Ctr.

Satellite Reconnaissance: The Role of Informal Bargaining. Gerald M. Steinberg. LC 82-19020. 208p. 1983. 35.00 (ISBN 0-275-91085-7, C1085). Praeger.

Satellite Regulatory Compendium. Christine A. Meagher. LC 85-206066. 1985. 197.00 (ISBN 0-934960-26-7). Phillips Pub Inc.

Satellite Remote Sensing: An Introduction. Ray Harris. LC 87-4927. 256p. 1987. text ed. 60.00x (ISBN 0-7102-0305-5, Pub. by Routledge UK); pap. text ed. 25.00x (ISBN 0-7102-1312-3, Pub. by Routledge UK). Routledge Chapman & Hall.

Satellite Remote Sensing for Resources Development. United Nations & German Foundation for International Development. (Illus.). 160p. 1985. pap. 70.00 (ISBN 0-86010-805-8). Graham & Trotman.

Satellite Sensing of a Cloudy Atmosphere: Observing the Third Planet. Ed. by A. Sellers Henderson. (Illus.). 336p. 1984. 55.00x (ISBN 0-85066-254-0). Taylor & Francis.

Satellite Services Sourcebook. Samuel L. Hoard & Beach Associates Consultants. LC 82-72850. 1982. 75.00 (ISBN 0-910339-00-7). Drake's Ptg & Pub.

Satellite Surveying. Leick. 1986. write for info. (ISBN 0-471-81990-5). Wiley.

Satellite Systems for Mobile Communications & Navigation: Related Conference Proceedings. Ed. by J. E. Flood & C. J. Hughes. (IEE Conference Publication: No. 222). 224p. 1983. pap. 72.00 (ISBN 0-85296-273-8, IC222). Inst Elect Eng.

Satellite Systems of the U. S. Domestic Communications Carriers. 275.00 (ISBN 0-686-32999-6). Info Gatekeepers.

Satellite Tech Talk. Ruth Radlauer et al. LC 83-21059. (Tech Talk Bks.). (Illus.). 64p. (gr. 4 up). 1984. lib. bdg. 14.60 (ISBN 0-516-08253-1). Childrens.

Satellite Technology & Its Applications. P. R. Chetty. 352p. 1988. 39.95. TAB BKS.

Satellite Television & Your Backyard Dish. Steve Crowe. Ed. by Robin Krieger. LC 81-90593. (Illus.). 200p. (Orig.). 1982. 20.00 (ISBN 0-910419-00-0); pap. 15.00 (ISBN 0-910419-01-9); trade special 15.00 (ISBN 0-910419-02-7). Satellite.

Satellite Television in Indonesia. Ed. by Alfian Chu. Godwin C. Chu. vi, 211p. (Orig.). 1981. pap. 6.00 (ISBN 0-86638-002-7). EW Ctr HI.

Satellite Television Reception: A Personal User's Guide. Joel Goldberg. (Illus.). 128p. 1984. pap. 23.25 (ISBN 0-13-791251-X). P-H.

Satellite Transmission. Business Communications Staff. 268p. 1987. pap. 1750.00 (ISBN 0-89336-518-1, G-094). BCC.

Satellite Warfare a Challenge for the International Community. 42p. 1988. pap. 19.00 (ISBN 92-9045-018-5, GV.E.87.0.1). UN.

Satellites. N. S. Barrett. LC 84-52002. (Picture Library). (Illus.). 32p. (gr. 2-4). 1985. PLB 10.90 (ISBN 0-531-04948-5). Watts.

Satellites. Ed. by Joseph A. Burns & Mildred S. Matthews. LC 86-19145. (Space Science Ser.). (Illus.). 1021p. 1986. 55.00x (ISBN 0-8165-0983-2). U of Ariz Pr.

Satellites. David Jefferis. (Easy-Read Fact Bks.). (Illus.). 32p. (gr. k-3). 1987. PLB 9.90 (ISBN 0-531-10348-X). Watts.

Satellites. Lenrie Peters. (African Writers Ser.). 1967. pap. text ed. 7.00 (ISBN 0-435-90037-4). Heinemann Ed.

Satellites. Kate Petty. LC 84-50605. (First Library Ser.). (Illus.). 30p. (gr. k-4). 1984. PLB 10.90 (ISBN 0-531-04809-8). Watts.

Satellites. Gregory B. Richards. LC 83-7434. (New True Bks.). (Illus.). 48p. (gr. k-4). 1983. lib. bdg. 12.60 (ISBN 0-516-01708-X). Childrens.

Satellites: An Educational Coloring Book. Spizzirri Publishing Co. Staff. Ed. by Linda Spizzirri. (Illus.). 32p. (gr. 1-8). 1986. pap. 1.49 (ISBN 0-86545-074-9). Spizzirri.

Satellites & Computers. Mat Irvine. LC 84-50615. (Electronic Revolution Bk.). (gr. 4-7). 1984. PLB 11.90 (ISBN 0-531-04817-9). Watts.

Satellites & Forecasting of Solar Radiation. E. A. Aronson et al. Ed. by Raymond E. Bahm. LC 80-70943. (International Solar Energy Society, American Section, Workshop Ser.). 1982. pap. text ed. 32.50x (ISBN 0-89553-026-0). Am Solar Energy.

Satellites & Space Stations: What They Can Do & How They Work. (New Technology Ser.). 48p. (gr. 6 up). 1986. PLB 12.96 (ISBN 0-88110-223-7); pap. 5.95 (ISBN 0-86020-937-7). EDC.

Satellites for Arms Control & Crisis Monitoring. Ed. by Bhupendra Jasani. LC 86-21864. (SIPRI Ser.). 200p. 1987. 37.00 (ISBN 0-19-829101-9). Oxford U Pr.

Satellites in Eastern Europe. Ed. by Henry L. Roberts. LC 74-10705. (American Academy of Political & Social Science). 170p. 1974. Repr. of 1958 ed. lib. bdg. 35.00x (ISBN 0-8371-7646-8, ROSE). Greenwood.

Satellites International. Joseph Pelton. Ed. by John Howkins. LC 87-6507. 352p. 1988. 190.00x (ISBN 0-935859-07-1, Stockton Pr). Groves Dict Music.

Satellites of Jupiter. Ed. by David Morrison. LC 81-13050. 972p. 1982. 49.50x (ISBN 0-8165-0762-7). U of Ariz Pr.

Satellites, Packet Switching & Distributed Telecommunications. Rosner. 44.95 (ISBN 0-317-64272-3). Van Nos Reinhold.

Satellites, Packets & Distributed Telecommunications: A Compendium of Source Materials. Ed. by Roy D. Rosner. (Illus.). 628p. 1984. 39.50 (ISBN 0-534-97924-6, Lifetime Learn). Van Nos Reinhold.

Satellites Today. Baylin & Gale. 175p. 1986. pap. 12.95 (ISBN 0-672-22492-5, 22492). Sams.

Satellites Today: The Complete Guide to Satellite Television. Frank Baylin & Amy Toner. (Illus.). 163p. (Orig.). 1985. pap. 11.95 (ISBN 0-917893-01-8). ConSol.

Sati Widow Burning in India. V. W. Datta. LC 87-63322. (Illus.). 279p. 1988. 29.00 (ISBN 0-913215-31-7). Riverdale Co.

Satie: His World Through His Letters. Satie. Ed. by Ornella Volta. Tr. by Michael Bullock. (Illus.). 220p. 1989. 30.00 (ISBN 0-7145-2811-0, Dist. by Kampmann & Co). M Boyars Pubs.

Satie, Ravel, Poulenc. Manuel Rosenthal. 86p. (Orig.). 1987. pap. 4.00 (ISBN 0-937815-09-8). Hanuman Bks.

Satin & Steel. Catherine Hart. 480p. (Orig.). 1986. pap. 3.95 (ISBN 0-8439-2349-0, Pub. by Leisure Bks Ct). Leisure NY.

Satin Doll. Maggie Davis. 352p. (Orig.). 1987. pap. 3.95 (ISBN 0-425-09773-0). Berkley Pub.

Satin Dolls. Elsa Cook. 1987. pap. 4.50 (ISBN 0-671-62327-3). PB.

Satin Fires. Rebecca Flanders. 496p. 1986. pap. 3.95 (ISBN 0-8217-1840-1). Zebra.

Satin Palms. Elizabeth Inness-Brown. LC 81-71001. 119p. (Orig.). 1981. pap. 6.95 (ISBN 0-931362-04-0). Fiction Intl.

Satin Slippers: Temptations. Elizabeth Bernard. (Girls Only Ser.: No. 7). (YA) (gr. 6 up). 1988. pap. 2.95 (ISBN 0-449-14543-3). Fawcett.

Satin Surrender. Carol Finch. 1986. pap. 3.95 (ISBN 0-8217-1861-4). Zebra.

Satin Tunnels. Beth Brown. LC 87-46317. 127p. 1988. lib. bdg. 8.50 perfect bdg. (ISBN 0-916418-69-3). Lotus.

Satir Step by Step. Virginia Satir & Michelle Baldwin. 1984. 14.95 (ISBN 0-8314-0068-4). Sci & Behavior.

Satire. Gilbert Cannan. lib. bdg. 20.00 (ISBN 0-8414-3535-9). Folcroft.

Satire. Arthur Pollard. (Critical Idiom Ser.: Vol. 7). 1970. pap. 5.50x (ISBN 0-416-17240-7, NO. 2379). Routledge Chapman & Hall.

Satire: An Anthology. Ed. by Ashley Brown & John L. Kimmey. 1978. pap. text ed. 13.95 scp (ISBN 0-690-01524-0, HarpC). Har-Row.

Satire & Allegory in "Wynnere & Wastoure". Thomas H. Bestul. LC 73-77750. xiv, 121p. 1974. 12.50x (ISBN 0-8032-0829-4). U of Nebr Pr.

Satire & Fiction. Wyndham Lewis. 63p. 1980. Repr. of 1927 ed. lib. bdg. 20.50 (ISBN 0-8495-3328-7). Arden Lib.

Satire & Fiction. Wyndham Lewis. LC 74-34424. 1927. lib. bdg. 20.00 (ISBN 0-8414-5713-1). Folcroft.

Satire & Irony: A Jr. High-Intermediate Language Arts Unit. Frances Corvasse. 1984. text ed. 4.00 (ISBN 0-89824-103-0); tchr's. manual 5.00 (ISBN 0-89824-102-2). Trillium Pr.

Satire & Politischer Roman: Untersuchungen Zum Romanwerk Benjamin Disrealis. Ulrich C. Janiesch. (Bochum Studies in English Ser.: No. 1). vi, 300p. (Orig.). 1975. pap. 32.00x (ISBN 90-6032-055-7). Benjamins North Am.

Satire & Satirists. James Hannay. LC 76-2325. 1854. lib. bdg. 32.00 (ISBN 0-8414-4835-3). Folcroft.

Satire & Society in Wilhelmine Germany: Kladderadatsch & Simplicissimus 1890-1914. Ann T. Allen. LC 84-5114. (Illus.). 280p. 1984. 25.00x (ISBN 0-8131-1512-4). U Pr of KY.

Satire & the Correspondence of Swift. Craig H. Ulman. LC 72-95457. (LeBaron Russell Briggs Prize Honors Essays in English Ser: 1972). 1973. pap. 2.50x (ISBN 0-674-78976-8). Harvard U Pr.

Satire & the Transformation of Genre. Leon Guilhamet. 208p. 1987. text ed. 31.95x (ISBN 0-8122-8053-9). U of Pa Pr.

Satire Anthology. facs. ed. Ed. by Carolyn Wells. LC 70-128161. (Granger Index Reprint Ser). 1905. 19.00 (ISBN 0-8369-6190-0). Ayer Co Pubs.

Satire Anthology. Ed. by Carolyn Wells. LC 70-128161. (Granger Index Reprint Ser.). 369p. Repr. of 1905 ed. lib. bdg. 18.00 (ISBN 0-8290-0511-0). Irvington.

Satire, Burlesque, Protest & Ridicule 1. Ed. by Walter H. Rubsamen. (Ballad Opera Ser.). 1975. lib. bdg. 61.00 (ISBN 0-8240-0904-5). Garland Pub.

Satire, Burlesque, Protest, & Ridicule 2. Ed. by Walter H. Rubsamen. (Ballad Opera Ser.). 1974. lib. bdg. 61.00 (ISBN 0-8240-0905-3). Garland Pub.

Satire Caricature & Perspectivism in the Works of Georg Buchner. Henry J. Schmidt. 1970. text ed. 8.40x (ISBN 0-686-22398-5). Mouton.

Satire En France, Ou la Litterature Militante Au Seizieme Siecle, 2 vols. 3rd rev. ed. Charles F. Lenient. 1966. Repr. of 1886 ed. 36.50 (ISBN 0-8337-2067-8). B Franklin.

Satire: From Aesop to Buchwald. Frederick Kiley. 496p. 1971. pap. text ed. write for info. (ISBN 0-02-363590-8). Macmillan.

Satire: From Aesop to Buchwald. Ed. by Frederick T. Kiley & Jack M. Shuttleworth. LC 70-134892. 1971. pap. 10.83 scp (ISBN 0-672-63110-5). Odyssey Pr.

Satire in Joacobean Tragedy. Joseph H. Stodder. Ed. by James Hogg. (Jacobean Drama Studies). 186p. (Orig.). 1974. pap. 15.00 (ISBN 0-317-40092-4, Pub. by Salzburg Studies). Longwood Pub Group.

Satire in Persian Literature. Hasan Javadi. LC 84-46118. (Illus.). 336p. 1988. 39.50x (ISBN 0-8386-3260-2). Fairleigh Dickinson.

Satire in the Comedies of Congreve, Sheridan, Wilde & Coward. Rose Snider. 1937. lib. bdg. 30.00 (ISBN 0-8414-7878-3). Folcroft.

Satire in the Comedies of Congreve, Sheridan, Wilde & Coward. Rose Snider. LC 79-159119. 145p. 1971. Repr. of 1937 ed. text ed. 20.00x (ISBN 0-87753-055-6). Phaeton.

Satire in the Early English Drama. Eva M. Campbell. 1914. lib. bdg. 27.00 (ISBN 0-8414-3550-2). Folcroft.

Satire in the Early English Drama. Eva M. Campell. 1978. Repr. of 1914 ed. lib. bdg. 29.00 (ISBN 0-8495-0813-4). Arden Lib.

Satire in the Eighteenth Century. John D. Browning. LC 82-49148. (McMaster Studies in the 18th Century). 231p. 1983. lib. bdg. 36.00 (ISBN 0-8240-4009-0). Garland Pub.

Satire in the Struggle for Peace. Ed. by Collet's Holdings, Ltd. Staff. 110p. 1979. 25.00x (ISBN 0-317-39531-9, Pub. by Collets (UK)). State Mutual Bk.

Satire of John Marston. Morse S. Allen. LC 65-26460. (Studies in Drama, No. 39). 1969. Repr. of 1920 ed. lib. bdg. 45.95x (ISBN 0-8383-0500-8). Haskell.

Satire on Stone: The Political Cartoons of Joseph Keppler. Richard S. West. LC 87-19212. 488p. 1988. 39.95 (ISBN 0-252-01497-9). U of Ill Pr.

Satire, Parodie, Calembour: Esquisse d'une Theorie des Devalues. Lionel Duisit. (Stanford French & Italian Studies: No. 11). vi, 164p. (Fr.). 1978. pap. 29.50 (ISBN 0-915838-26-5). Anma Libri.

Satires. Juvenal & Persius. (Loeb Classical Library: No. 91). 13.95x (ISBN 0-674-99102-8). Harvard U Pr.

Satires. Persius. Ed. by J. R. Jenkinson. 49.00 (ISBN 0-86516-109-7); pap. 16.50 (ISBN 0-86516-110-0). Bolchazy Carducci.

Satires. Mac Wellman. Date not set. pap. 8.00 (ISBN 0-89823-063-2). New Rivers Pr.

Satires Against Man: The Poems of Rochester. Dustin H. Griffin. LC 72-95304. 1974. 32.50x (ISBN 0-520-02394-3). U of Cal Pr.

Satires & Epistles. Horace. Tr. by Smith P. Bovie. LC 59-16413. 1959. pap. 10.00 (ISBN 0-226-06777-7, P39, Phoen). U of Chicago Pr.

Satires & Miscellaneous Poetry & Prose. Samuel Butler. Ed. by Rene Lamar. LC 76-29457. (BCL Ser. II). Repr. of 1928 ed. 33.50 (ISBN 0-404-15301-1). AMS Pr.

Satires & Personal Writings. Jonathan Swift. Ed. by W. A. Eddy. (Oxford Standard Authors Ser). 1932. 35.00 (ISBN 0-19-254147-1). Oxford U Pr.

Satires, Epigrams & Verse Letters. John Donne. Ed. by W. Milgate. (Oxford English Texts Series). (Illus.). 1967. 64.00x (ISBN 0-19-811842-2). Oxford U Pr.

Satires, Epistles & Ars Poetica. Horace. (Loeb Classical Library: No. 194). 13.95x (ISBN 0-674-99214-8). Harvard U Pr.

Satires, Le Lutrin see Oeuvres.

Satires of Decimus Junius Juvenalis. Juvenal. Tr. by John Dryden. LC 70-161788. Repr. of 1735 ed. 37.50 (ISBN 0-404-54124-0). AMS Pr.

Satires of Horace. Niall Rudd. 318p. 1982. pap. 12.95x (ISBN 0-520-04718-4). U of Cal Pr.

Satires of Horace: A Study. Niall Rudd. LC 66-11031. pap. 82.50 (ISBN 0-317-26383-8, 2024525). Bks Demand UMI.

Satires of Horace & Persius. Tr. by Niall Rudd. (Classics Ser.). 186p. 1974. pap. 6.95 (ISBN 0-14-044279-0). Penguin.

Satires of Juvenal. Juvenal. Tr. by William Gifford. LC 72-964. (Temple Greek & Latin Classics: No. 1). Repr. of 1906 ed. 27.00 (ISBN 0-404-07901-6). AMS Pr.

Satires of Juvenal. Juvenal. Tr. by Rolfe Humphries. LC 58-12213. (Midland Bks: Indiana University Greek & Latin Classics: No. 20). 192p. 1958. pap. 5.95x (ISBN 0-253-20020-2). Ind U Pr.

Satires of Juvenal, 2 vols. Decimus J. Juvenalis. (Illus.). 278p. 1985. Repr. of 1911 ed. 237.45 (ISBN 0-89901-195-0). Found Class Reprints.

Satires of Juvenal Translated. Juvenal. Tr. by Thomas Sheridan. LC 72-179336. Repr. of 1739 ed. 40.00 (ISBN 0-404-54125-9). AMS Pr.

Satires of Persius. Persius. Tr. by W. S. Merwin. LC 72-85278. 120p. 1973. Repr. of 1961 ed. 24.00x (ISBN 0-8046-1708-2, Pub. by Kennikat). Assoc Faculty Pr.

Satires of Persius. Persius. Ed. by W. S. Merwin. (Poetry in Translation Ser.). 112p. (Orig.). 1981. pap. 8.95 (ISBN 0-85646-019-2, Pub. by Anvil Pr Poetry). Longwood Pub Group.

Satires of Persius Flaccus. Persius. Ed. by W. R. Connor & Basil L. Gildersleeve. LC 78-67138. (Latin Texts & Commentaries Ser.). (Lat. & Eng.). 1979. Repr. of 1903 ed. lib. bdg. 17.00x (ISBN 0-405-11605-5). Ayer Co Pubs.

Satires of Persius: The Latin Text with a Verse Translation. Guy Lee. (Latin & Greek Texts Ser.). 1987. 27.75 (ISBN 0-905205-37-5, Pub. by F Cairns); pap. text ed. 9.00 (ISBN 0-905205-65-0). Longwood Pub Group.

Satire's Persuasive Voice. Edward A. Bloom & Lillian D. Bloom. LC 78-11668. 305p. 1979. 32.50x (ISBN 0-8014-0839-3). Cornell U Pr.

Satires: With the Satires of Persius. Juvenal. Tr. by William Gifford, Jr. 1954. 11.95x (ISBN 0-460-00997-4, Evman). Biblio Dist.

Satiric Allegory: Mirror of Man. Ellen D. Leyburn. LC 78-5886. (Yale Studies in English: Vol. 130). 1978. Repr. of 1956 ed. lib. bdg. 35.00 (ISBN 0-313-20457-8, LESM). Greenwood.

Satiric Catharsis in Shakespeare: A Theory of Dramatic Structure. Alice L. Birney. LC 79-185976. 1973. 33.00x (ISBN 0-520-02214-9). U of Cal Pr.

Satiric Inheritance, Rabelais to Sterne. Michael Seidel. LC 79-84016. 1979. 32.00x (ISBN 0-691-06408-3). Princeton U Pr.

Satiric Perspective: A Structural Analysis of Late Medieval, Early Renaissance Satiric Treatises. Suzanne D. Valle-Killeen. LC 79-92419. (Senda de Estudios y Ensayos). 204p. (Orig.). 1980. pap. 12.95 (ISBN 0-918454-18-2). Senda Nueva.

Satiric Poems of John Trumbull: "The Progress of Dulness" & "M'Fingal". Ed. by Edwin T. Bowden. LC 61-15829. (Illus.). 230p. 1971. Repr. of 1962 ed. 14.50x (ISBN 0-292-73366-6). U of Tex Pr.

Satiric Treatise in Eighteenth Century Germany. Peter E. Carels. (Germanic Studies in America: Vol. 24). 170p. 1977. 22.20 (ISBN 3-261-01931-X). P Lang Pubs.

Satiric Vision of Blas de Otero. Geoffrey R. Barrow. LC 88-4877. 224p. 1988. text ed. 26.00 (ISBN 0-8262-0687-5). U of Mo Pr.

Satirical Element in the American Novel. Ernest J. Hall. 59.95 (ISBN 0-87968-033-4). Gordon Pr.

Satirical Element in the American Novel. Ernest J. Hall. LC 76-98994. (American Literature Ser., No. 49). 1970. pap. 39.95x (ISBN 0-8383-0036-7). Haskell.

Satirical Etchings of James Gillray. James Gillray. Ed. by Draper Hill. (Illus.). 144p. (Orig.). 1976. pap. 8.95 (ISBN 0-486-23340-5). Dover.

Satirical Poems of the Time of the Reformation, 2 Vols. James Cranstoun. LC 71-144550. Repr. of 1893 ed. Set. 74.50 (ISBN 0-404-08629-2). AMS Pr.

Satirical Rogue on Poetry. Robert Francis. LC 68-13940. 136p. 1968. 10.00x (ISBN 0-87023-034-4). U of Mass Pr.

Satiricon. 2nd rev. & expanded ed. Petronius. Ed. by Evan T. Sage & Brady B. Gilleland. LC 72-87112. (Lat.). 1969. pap. text ed. 12.95x (ISBN 0-89197-338-9). Irvington.

Satirische Kurzprosa Heinrich Bolls. Erhard Friedrichsmeyer. (Studies in the Germanic Languages & Literatures: No. 97). xiv, 223p. 1981. 22.50x (ISBN 0-8078-8097-3). U of NC Pr.

Satirist Looks at the World. Richard Armour. (William K. McInally Memorial Lecture Ser.: 2nd). 1967. pap. 1.00 (ISBN 0-87712-146-X). UMI Div Res GSBA.

Satiro, Ninfas, y Cia. Leon Calvino. (Pimienta Collection Ser). 160p. (Span.). 1974. pap. 1.00 (ISBN 0-88473-211-8). Fiesta Pub.

Satisfaction. Rae Lawrence. 448p. 1987. 18.95 (ISBN 0-671-60760-X, Poseidon Pr). PB.

Satisfaction. Rae Lawrence. 480p. 1988. pap. 4.95 (ISBN 0-671-66492-1). PB.

Satisfaction Guaranteed: Simply Sumptuous Mail Order Foods with Recipes & Menus for Fast & Fabulous Meals. Linda W. Eckhardt. 272p. 1986. pap. 12.95 (ISBN 0-87477-387-3). J P Tarcher.

Satisfaction Guaranteed: The Ultimate Guide to Consumer Self-Defense. Ralph Charell. 1985. 14.95 (ISBN 0-671-49804-5, Linden Pr). S&S.

Satisfaction of Food Requirements in Mali to 2000 A. D. J. Mondot-Bernard & M. Labonne. 214p. (Orig.). 1982. pap. 15.00x (ISBN 92-64-12300-8). OECD.

Satisfaction of Interest & the Concept of Morality. Steven A. Smith. LC 73-8305. 165p. 1975. 18.00 (ISBN 0-8387-1383-1). Bucknell U Pr.

Satisfactions in White-Collar Job. Nancy C. Morse. Ed. by Leon Stein. LC 77-70518. (Work Ser.). (Illus.). 1977. Repr. of 1953 ed. lib. bdg. 21.00x (ISBN 0-405-10187-2). Ayer Co Pubs.

Satisfactions in Work Design: Ergonomics & Other Approaches. Ed. by R. G. Sell & Patricia Shipley. LC 79-311845. 220p. 1979. 33.00x (ISBN 0-85066-180-3). Taylor & Francis.

Satisfied...A Promise of Peace in a Troubled World. Rexella Van Impe. 142p. 1984. pap. 4.95 (ISBN 0-934803-15-3). J Van Impe.

Satisfying Africa's Food Needs: Food Production & Commercialization in African Agriculture. Ed. by Ronald Cohen. LC 88-3164. (Carter Studies on Africa). 210p. 1987. lib. bdg. 25.00x (ISBN 0-317-60675-1). Lynne Rienner.

Satori. Dennis Schmidt. 304p. (Orig.). 1986. pap. 2.95 (ISBN 0-441-75059-1, Pub. by Ace Science Fiction). Ace Bks.

Satori in Paris. Jack Kerouac. 1966. pap. 2.25 (ISBN 0-394-17437-2, B135, BC). Grove.

Satori in Paris & Pic. Jack Kerouac. LC 85-81781. 1986. pap. 4.95 (ISBN 0-394-62173-5, BC). Grove.

Satori in Paris & PIC. Jack Kerouac. 1988. 7.95 (ISBN 0-8021-3061-5). Grove.

Satori West. Thomas Krampf. Ed. by Edith Schrot. (Illus.). 78p. (Orig.). 1987. pap. 6.00 (ISBN 0-9616797-0-0). Ischua Bks.

Satrianum: The Archaeological Investigations Conducted by Brown University in 1966 & 1967. R. Ross Holloway. LC 76-91654. (Illus.). 170p. 1970. 35.00x (ISBN 0-87057-118-4). U Pr of New Eng.

Satsang. M. P. Pandit. Ed. by Vasanti R. Golikhere. (Vol. I). 298p. (Orig.). 1979. pap. 11.00 (ISBN 0-941524-10-8). Lotus Light.

Satsang Notes of Swami Amar Jyoti. Kessler Frey. LC 77-89524. (Illus.). 1977. 4.95 (ISBN 0-933572-01-8); pap. 2.95 (ISBN 0-933572-02-6). Truth Consciousness.

Satsang with Baba. Swami Muktananda. LC 76-1384. Vol. 1 1974, 348p. pap. 6.50 (ISBN 0-914602-30-6); Vol. 2 1976, 382p. pap. 6.50 (ISBN 0-914602-31-4); Vol. 3, 1977, LC #76-670008. pap. 6.50 (ISBN 0-914602-38-1); Vol. 4, 1978. pap. 6.50 (ISBN 0-914602-32-2); Vol. 5, 1978. pap. 6.50 (ISBN 0-914602-33-0); Set of 5 vols. write for info. (ISBN 0-914602-40-3). SYDA Found.

Satsuma Rebellion: An Episode of Modern Japanese History. Augustus H. Mounsey. LC 79-65367. (Studies in Japanese History & Civilization). 294p. Repr. of 1879 ed. 24.00 (ISBN 0-89093-259-X). U Pubns Amer.

Satterwhite on Color & Design. Joy Satterwhite & Al Satterwhite. (Illus.). 144p. 1986. 27.50 (ISBN 0-8174-5804-2, Amphoto); pap. 18.95 (ISBN 0-8174-5805-0, Amphoto). Watson-Guptill.

Sattigung: Moralische & Psychologische Grenzen des Wachstums. Josef Falkinger. 228p. (Orig., Ger.). 1986. pap. text ed. 57.50x (ISBN 3-16-945008-5, Pub. by J C B Mohr BRD). Coronet Bks.

Sattukku dans l'Esumesa durant la periode d'Isin et Larsa. Rene M. Sigrist. LC 79-65002. (Bibliotheca Mesopotamica Ser.: Vol. 11). 166p. (Fr.). 1984. 33.00x (ISBN 0-89003-047-2); pap. 24.50x (ISBN 0-89003-048-0). Undena Pubns.

Saturae with Juvenal's Saturae. Persius & Juvenal. Ed. by W. V. Clausen. (Oxford Classical Texts Ser). 1959. 14.95x (ISBN 0-19-814640-X). Oxford U Pr.

Saturated Heterocyclic Chemistry, Vols. 2-5. M. F. Ansell & G. Pattenden. LC 72-83454. Vol. 2 1974. 47.00 (ISBN 0-85186-532-1); Vol. 3 1975. 1973 literature 43.00 (ISBN 0-85186-562-3); Vol. 4 1977. 1974 literature 77.00 (ISBN 0-85186-592-5); Vol. 5 1978. 66.00 (ISBN 0-85186-622-0). Am Chemical.

Saturation & Material Balances. LC 80-25594. (AIChEMI Modular Instruction F Ser.: Vol. 2: Material & Energy Balances). 79p. 1981. pap. 30.00 (ISBN 0-8169-0181-3, J-12). Am Inst Chem Eng.

Saturday. Denys Cazet. LC 84-24306. (Illus.). 64p. (ps-2). 1985. 10.95 (ISBN 0-02-717800-5). Bradbury Pr.

Saturday. Denys Cazet. LC 87-2388. (Illus.). 64p. (gr. 1-4). 1988. pap. 3.95 (ISBN 0-689-71065-8, Aladdin Bks). Macmillan.

Saturday Academy Concept. Ed. by Nellouise D. Watkins & William B. DeLauder. (Illus.). 250p. 1987. write for info. (ISBN 0-940823-24-1). Bennett Coll.

Saturday Afternoon: College Football & the Men Who Made the Day. Richard Whittingham. LC 85-40522. (Illus.). 320p. (Orig.). 1985. pap. 11.95 (ISBN 0-89480-933-4). Workman Pub.

Saturday Always Comes: The Relaxed Way to Sales Success. Irwin B. Meisel. 180p. 1984. pap. 9.95 (ISBN 0-87863-222-0, Farnsworth Pub Co). Longman Finan.

Saturday & Sunday. facs. ed. Edmund K. Broadus. LC 67-23186. (Essay Index Reprint Ser). 1935. 17.00 (ISBN 0-8369-0255-6). Ayer Co Pubs.

Saturday Belongs to Sara. Cathy Warren. LC 87-11783. (Illus.). 48p. (gr. 1-5). 1988. 12.95 (ISBN 0-02-792491-2). Bradbury Pr.

Saturday Bloody Saturday. V. Rockliff. 1987. 39.00x (ISBN 0-7223-2097-3, Pub. by A H Stockwell England). State Mutual Bk.

Saturday Night. Caroline B. Cooney. 240p. (Orig.). (YA) (gr. 7 up). 1986. pap. 2.50 (ISBN 0-590-40156-4, Point). Scholastic Inc.

Saturday Night. Marjorie Holmes. 224p. (YA) (gr. 7 up). 1982. pap. 1.95 (ISBN 0-440-97645-6, LFL). Dell.

Saturday Night: A Backstage History of "Saturday Night Live". Doug Hill & Jeff Weingrad. LC 86-46180. 560p. 1987. pap. 8.95 (ISBN 0-394-75053-5, Vin). Random.

Saturday Night: A Backstage History of Saturday Night Live. Jeff Weingrad & Doug Hill. LC 85-19991. (Illus.). 608p. 1986. 17.95 (ISBN 0-688-05099-9, Pub. by Beech Tree Bks). Morrow.

Saturday Night & Sunday Morning. Alan Sillitoe. 1959. 16.45 (ISBN 0-394-44377-2). Knopf.

Saturday Night & Sunday Morning. Alan Sillitoe. 192p. 1973. pap. 3.50 (ISBN 0-451-13590-3, AE2162, Sig). NAL.

Saturday Night at Moody's Diner Other Stories. Tim Sample. (Illus.). 96p. (Orig.). 1985. pap. 7.95 (ISBN 0-88448-036-4). Harpswell Pr.

Saturday Night at San Marcos. William Packard. 200p. 1985. 14.95 (ISBN 0-938410-25-3). Thunder's Mouth.

Saturday Night at San Marcos. William Packard. LC 86-80909. 240p. 1987. pap. 7.95 (ISBN 0-394-62273-1). Grove.

Saturday Night Date. Maud Johnson. 160p. (Orig.). (gr. 7 up). 1982. pap. 1.95 (ISBN 0-590-31963-9, Wildfire). Scholastic Inc.

Saturday Night Dead. Richard Rosen. LC 87-40449. 1988. 16.95 (ISBN 0-670-81977-8). Viking.

Saturday Night in the Prime of Life. Dodici Azpadu. 1983. pap. 5.95 (ISBN 0-918040-04-3). Spinsters Aunt Lute.

Saturday Night, Sunday Morning: Singles & the Church. Nicholas B. Christoff. LC 77-7841. 160p. 1980. pap. 4.95 (ISBN 0-06-061381-5, RD 341, HarpR). Har-Row.

Saturday Night Women. Michael Judge. (Contemporary Drama Ser.). 1977. pap. 2.50x (ISBN 0-912262-42-7). Proscenium.

Saturday Nite-Mambo-Cha. (Ballroom Dance Ser.). 1986. lib. bdg. 79.95 (ISBN 0-8490-3409-4). Gordon Pr.

Saturday Notebook: A Diary for Children & Adults to Use Together. Thomas Moore & Norris Frederick. (Illus.). 112p. (ps up). 1983. concealed wire binding 8.95 (ISBN 0-914788-72-8). Globe Pequot.

Saturday Papers, Essays on Literature from the Literary Review. Henry S. Canby et al. 1969. Repr. of 1921 ed. 15.00 (ISBN 0-384-07310-7). Johnson Repr.

Saturday Parent: A Book for Separated Families. Peter Rowlands. 144p. 1982. pap. 5.95 (ISBN 0-8264-0205-4). Continuum.

Saturday Review, Eighteen Fifty-Five to Eighteen Sixty-Eight: Representative Educated Opinion in Victorian England. Merle M. Bevington. LC 41-25970. Repr. of 1941 ed. 17.50 (ISBN 0-404-00795-3). AMS Pr.

Saturday School: A Success Story. 1978. 2.50 (ISBN 0-939418-27-4). Ferguson-Florissant.

Saturday, Sunday & Salvation. Dwight Herbert. (Stories That Win Ser.). 1980. pap. 1.25 (ISBN 0-8163-0355-X). Pacific Pr Pub Assn.

Saturday, Sunday, Monday. Eduardo De Filippo. Tr. by Keith Waterhouse & Willis Hall. (YA) (gr. 7 up). 1974. pap. text ed. 6.50x (ISBN 0-435-23201-0). Heinemann Ed.

Saturday-Sunday Shuffle. Russell Holt. (Discovery Ser.). 29p. 1987. pap. 0.75 (ISBN 0-8163-0758-X). Pacific Pr Pub Assn.

Saturday the Rabbi Went Hungry. Harry Kemelman. 224p. 1987. pap. 3.50 (ISBN 0-449-21392-7, Crest). Fawcett.

Saturday, the Twelfth of October. Norma F. Mazer. 256p. (gr. 7 up). 1989. pap. price not set (ISBN 0-440-99592-2, LFL). Dell.

Saturday Town. Thomas Thornburg. LC 76-15749. (Living Poets' Library Ser.). 1976. pap. 3.50 (ISBN 0-686-17004-0). Dragons Teeth.

Saturdays. Elizabeth Enright. (Illus.). (gr. k-6). 1987. pap. 2.95 (ISBN 0-440-47615-1, YB). Dell.

Saturdays. Elizabeth Enright. 184p. (gr. 2-6). 1987. 12.95 (ISBN 0-8050-0291-X). H Holt & Co.

Saturday's Child. Suzanne Seed. LC 72-12599. (Illus.). (gr. 6-12). 1973. PLB 8.95 (ISBN 0-87955-803-2); pap. 6.95 (ISBN 0-87955-203-4). O'Hara.

Saturday's Children: Poems of Work. Ed. by Helen Plotz. LC 82-3087. 160p. (gr. 7 up). 1982. Greenwillow.

Saturdays Forever. Harold Smith. 138p. 1985. 9.95 (ISBN 0-89826-016-7). Natl Paperback.

Saturdays in the City. Ann S. Bond. (gr. 3-6). 1979. 8.95 (ISBN 0-395-28376-0). HM.

Saturday's Women. Ed. by Charlotte Mandel et al. LC 82-10278. (Eileen W. Barnes Award Anthology). 102p. (Orig.). 1982. pap. 6.50 (ISBN 0-938158-02-3). Saturday Pr.

Saturdee. Norman Lindsay. LC 75-41175. (Illus.). Repr. of 1939 ed. 18.45 (ISBN 0-404-14716-X). AMS Pr.

Saturn. Franklyn M. Branley. LC 81-43890. (Illus.). 64p. (gr. 3-6). 1983. 12.70i (ISBN 0-690-04213-2, Crowell Jr Bks); PLB 12.89g (ISBN 0-690-04214-0). HarpJ.

Saturn. Ed. by Tom Gehrels & Mildred S. Matthews. LC 84-2517. 968p. 1984. 37.50x (ISBN 0-8165-0829-1). U of Ariz Pr.

Saturn. Seymour Simon. LC 85-2995. (Illus.). 32p. (ps-3). 1985. 13.00 (ISBN 0-688-05798-5, Morrow Junior Books); lib. bdg. 12.88 (ISBN 0-688-05799-3). Morrow.

Saturn. Seymour Simon. (Illus.). Date not set. pap. 4.95 (ISBN 0-688-08404-4). Morrow.

Saturn: A New Look at an Old Devil. Liz Greene. 1976. pap. 6.95 (ISBN 0-87728-306-0). Weiser.

Saturn Return. Ehresman & Albaugh. LC 83-71150. 104p. 1984. 9.00 (ISBN 0-86690-240-6, 2298-01). Am Fed Astrologers.

Saturn: The Reaper. Alan Leo. LC 75-16450. 1975. pap. 3.95 (ISBN 0-87728-019-3). Weiser.

Saturn: The Ringed Beauty. Isaac Asimov. LC 88-17563. (Isaac Asimov's Library of the Universe). (Illus.). 32p. (gr. 3-4). 1988. PLB 10.95 (ISBN 1-55532-364-2). Stevens Inc.

Saturn: The Spectacular Planet. Franklyn M. Branley. LC 81-43890. (Trophy Nonfiction Bks.). (Illus.). 64p. (gr. 4-7). 1987. pap. 4.95 (ISBN 0-06-446056-8, Trophy). HarpJ.

Saturnalia. Carole Marsh. (Carol Marsh Short Story Ser.). (Illus.). 48p. (Orig.). (gr. 4-12). 1988. pap. 7.95 (ISBN 1-55609-238-5). Gallopade Pub Group.

Satvotpatti Vinischaya & Nirvana Vibhaga: An Enquiry into the Origin of Beings & Discussions about Nirvana. Tr. by Henry M. Gunasekera. Compiled by M. Dharmaratna. LC 78-72424. Repr. of 1902 ed. 17.50 (ISBN 0-404-17285-7). AMS Pr.

Satvrae. Decimus J. Juvenalis. Ed. by A. E. Housman. Repr. of 1931 ed. lib. bdg. 35.00x (ISBN 0-8371-2749-1, JUSA). Greenwood.

Satya Sai Avtar: Glimpses of Divinity. R. Mohan Rai. 132p. 1988. text ed. 25.00x (ISBN 81-207-0707-9, Pub. by Sterling Pubs India). Apt Bks.

Satyagraha in South Africa. M. K. Gandhi. Tr. by V. G. Desai. 1980. 10.00 (ISBN 0-934676-15-1). Greenlf Bks.

Satyagraha in South Africa. M. K. Gandhi. Tr. by V. G. Desai from Gujarati. 1979. pap. 5.00 (ISBN 0-934676-03-8). Greenlf Bks.

Satyagraha: M. K. Gandhi in South Africa, 1893-1914. Constance DeJong & Philip Glass. (Illus.). 80p. (Orig.). 1983. 12.95 (ISBN 0-934378-43-6); pap. 5.95 (ISBN 0-934378-44-4). Tanam Pr.

Satyagraha: The Gandhian Approach to Non-Violent Social Change. Timmon M. Wallis. 82p. (Orig.). Date not set. pap. 3.95 (ISBN 0-938875-05-1). Pittenbruach Pr.

Satyagrahas in Bengal, Nineteen Twenty-One to Nineteen Thirty-Nine. Buddhadeva Bhattacharyya. 1977. 15.00x (ISBN 0-88386-901-2). South Asia Bks.

Satyajit Ray: A Study of His Films. Ben Nyce. LC 88-6620. 240p. 1988. lib. bdg. 37.95 (ISBN 0-275-92666-4, C2666). Praeger.

Satyendra Nath Bose. Santimay Chatterjee & Enakshi Chatterjee. (National Biography Ser.). 1979. pap. 4.25 (ISBN 0-89744-196-6). Auromere.

Satyr. Susan Hartman. Ed. by Stanley H. Barkan. (Cross-Cultural Review Chapbook 7: American Poetry 4). (Illus.). 16p. 1980. pap. 2.00 (ISBN 0-89304-806-2). Cross Cult.

Satyr. Hugh Knox. (Orig.). 1970. pap. 1.25 (ISBN 0-87067-305-X, BH305). Holloway.

Satyr Candidate. Richard M. Rose. 1979. 7.50 (ISBN 0-682-49383-X). Exposition-Phoenix.

Satyr Candidate. Richard M. Rose. (Private Library Collection). 283p. 1986. mini-bound 6.95 (ISBN 0-938422-30-8). SOS Pubns CA.

Satyr Ring. Alison Quinn. (Harlequin Category Romances Ser.). 224p. 1983. pap. 2.25 (ISBN 0-373-32001-9). Harlequin Bks.

Satyrday. Steven Bauer. 224p. 1985. pap. 2.75 (ISBN 0-425-07964-3). Berkley Pub.

Satyre of the Thrie Estaits. Lindsay, David, 1490-1555. LC 75-26333. (English Experience Ser.: No. 137). 156p. 1969. Repr. of 1602 ed. 45.00 (ISBN 90-221-0137-1). Walter J Johnson.

Satyricon. Petronius. Bd. with Apocolocyntosis. Seneca. (Loeb Classical Library: No. 15). 13.95x (ISBN 0-674-99016-1). Harvard U Pr.

Satyricon. Petronius. Tr. by William Arrowsmith. 1983. pap. 2.95 (ISBN 0-452-00653-8, Mer). NAL.

Satyricon. rev. ed. Petronius & Lucius Annaeus Seneca. Tr. by J. P. Sullivan. Bd. with Apocolocyntosis. 240p. 1986. pap. 4.95 (ISBN 0-14-044489-0). Penguin.

Satz-Lexikon des Englischen Geschaeftsbriefes. Burfeindt-Moral & H. H. Zacher. 400p. (Ger.). 1972. 20.95 (ISBN 3-468-39120-X). Langenscheidt.

Satzbau in der Prosa des Jungen Goethe. Hans G. Heun. 1930. 18.00 (ISBN 0-384-22781-3); pap. 13.00 (ISBN 0-384-22780-5). Johnson Repr.

Satzlexicon der Handelskorrespondenz. Dusan Zavada. 388p. (Ger. & Ital.). 1972. 55.00 (ISBN 0-686-56467-7, M-7618, Pub. by Brandstetter). French & Eur.

Satzlexikon der Handelskorrespondenz. Dusan Zavada. (Span. & Ger.). 1973. 55.00 (ISBN 3-87097-057-X, M-7612, Pub. by Brandstetter). French & Eur.

Satzlexikon der Handelskorrespondenz. Dusan Zavada. (Fr. & Ger.). 1971. 55.00 (ISBN 3-87097-050-2, M-7613, Pub. by Brandstetter). French & Eur.

Satzlexikon der Handelskorrespondenz. Dusan Zavada. (Eng. & Ger., Lexikon of Commercial Correspondance). 1969. 55.00 (ISBN 3-87097-048-0, M-7615, Pub. by Brandstetter). French & Eur.

Satzmelodie und Sprachwahrnehmung: Psycholinguistische Untersuchungen zur Grundfrequenz. Hede Helfrich. (Grundlagen der Kommunikation-Bibliotheksausgabe Ser.). xviii, 400p. (Ger.). 1985. 67.20x (ISBN 3-11-009918-7). De Gruyter.

Satzstellung des Finiten Verbs im Tocharischen. Stefan Zimmer. (Janua Linguarum, Ser. Practica: No. 238). 108p. 1976. pap. text ed. 16.80x (ISBN 90-279-3461-4). Mouton.

Sauce for the Goose. Peter De Vries. 1982. pap. 4.95 (ISBN 0-14-006281-5). Penguin.

Saucerama. 5th ed. Frank E. Stranges. (Illus.). pap. 4.50 (ISBN 0-686-20563-4). Intl Evang.

Sauces. LC 82-19701. (Good Cook Ser.). (gr. 7 up). 1983. lib. bdg. 22.60 (ISBN 0-8094-2972-1, Pub. by Time-Life). Silver.

Sauces. (Good Cook Ser.). (Illus.). 176p. 1983. 16.95 (ISBN 0-8094-2971-3). Time Life.

Sauces & Gravies Market. Ed. by Peter Allen. 200p. 1988. 995.00 (ISBN 0-941285-19-7). FIND-SVP.

Sauces, French & Famous. Louis Diat. 1978. pap. 3.95 (ISBN 0-486-23663-3). Dover.

Sauces: French & Famous. Louis Diat. 12.50 (ISBN 0-8446-5677-1). Peter Smith.

Saucier's Apprentice: A Modern Guide to Classic French Sauces for the Home. Raymond Sokolov. (Illus.). 1976. 18.95 (ISBN 0-394-48920-9). Knopf.

Saucing the Fish: A Chef's Collection of Recipes for Stylish Fish Dishes. Shirley King. 300p. 1986. 16.95 (ISBN 0-671-54076-9). S&S.

Saucy Sailor & Other Dramatized Ballads. Compiled by Alice M. White & Janet E. Tobitt. LC 70-80381. (Granger Index Reprint Ser.). 1940. 15.00 (ISBN 0-8369-6066-1). Ayer Co Pubs.

Saudaryalahari or, Flood of Beauty. Sankaracarya. Ed. by William N. Brown. LC 57-9072. (Oriental Ser: No. 43). (Illus.). 1958. 16.50x (ISBN 0-674-78990-3). Harvard U Pr.

Saudi. Laurie Devine. 520p. 1985. 17.95 (ISBN 0-671-47453-7). S&S.

Saudi Arabia. rev., 2nd ed. Frank A. Clements. (World Bibliographical Ser.: No. 5). 310p. 1988. 50.00 (ISBN 1-85109-067-3). ABC-Clio.

Saudi Arabia. George A. Lipsky et al. LC 59-8227. (Area & Country Surveys Ser.). 381p. 1959. 18.00x (ISBN 0-87536-907-3). HRAFP.

Saudi Arabia. 2nd ed. Middle East Economic Digest Staff. Ed. by Trevor Mostyn. (MEED Practical Guides Ser.). (Illus.). 350p. (Orig.). 1985. pap. 16.95x (ISBN 0-946510-00-8). Lynne Rienner.

Saudi Arabia. E. Eugene Oliver. LC 87-1204. (World Education Ser.). (Illus.). 132p. (Orig.). 1987. pap. 8.00 (ISBN 0-910054-88-6). Am Assn Coll Registrars.

Sa'udi Arabia. Harry Philby. LC 72-4289. (World Affairs Ser.: National & International Viewpoints). (Illus.). 422p. 1972. Repr. of 1955 ed. 24.00 (ISBN 0-405-04581-6). Ayer Co Pubs.

Saudi Arabia. (Let's Visit Places & Peoples - - Nations, Dependencies, & Sovereignties of the World Ser.). (Illus.). (gr. 5 up). 1988. 12.95 (ISBN 1-55546-179-4). Chelsea Hse.

Saudi Arabia see Business Opportunity Report Series.

Saudi Arabia: A Case Study in Development. Fouad Al-Farsey. 20.00x (ISBN 0-905743-20-2). Intl Bk Ctr.

Saudi Arabia: A Case Study in Development. Fouad Al-Farsy. 224p. (Orig.). 1982. pap. 17.50x (ISBN 0-7103-0005-0). Routledge Chapman & Hall.

Saudi Arabia: A Case Study in Development. Fouad Al-Farsy. 300p. 1986. 55.00 (ISBN 0-7103-0128-6, 01286). Routledge Chapman & Hall.

Saudi Arabia: A Country Study. 4th ed. Richard F. Nyrop. LC 84-28460. (Area Handbook Ser.: DA Pam 550-51). (Illus.). 444p. 1984. 15.00 (ISBN 0-318-21898-4, S/N 008-020-01020-1). USGPO.

Saudi Arabia: A Desert Kingdom. Kevin McCarthy. LC 85-6941. (Discovering Our Heritage Ser.). (Illus.). 128p. (gr. 5 up). 1986. PLB 12.95 (ISBN 0-87518-295-X). Dillon.

Saudi Arabia: An Artist's View of the Past. Safeya Binzagr. (Illus.). 1979. 60.00 (ISBN 2-88001-076-4). Three Continents.

Saudi Arabia & Its Place in the World. (Illus.). cased 45.00 (ISBN 0-686-70494-0). Three Continents.

Saudi Arabia & Its Royal Family. William Powell. 384p. 1982. 14.95 (ISBN 0-8184-0326-8). Lyle Stuart.

Saudi Arabia & the Economic & Political Control of the World. Harry M. Hallam. (Illus.). 149p. 1983. 89.75x (ISBN 0-86722-045-7). Inst Econ Pol.

Saudi Arabia & the Explosion of Terrorism in the Middle East. Emil Doumergu. (Great Currents of History Library Book). (Illus.). 137p. 1983. 87.85x (ISBN 0-86722-016-3). Inst Econ Pol.

Saudi Arabia & the World's Oil Political Strategy. Kenneth K. Regensberg. (Illus.). 147p. 1982. 89.75x (ISBN 0-86722-007-4). Inst Econ Pol.

Saudi Arabia: Bibliography on Politics, Society & Economics from the 18th Century to the Present. Hans-Jurgen Philipp. 405p. 1984. lib. bdg. 41.00 (ISBN 3-598-21134-1). K G Saur.

Saudi Arabia Business Outlook. 1983. 50.00 (ISBN 0-916400-15-8). Inter Crescent.

Saudi Arabia: Energy, Developmental Planning, & Industrialization. Ed. by Ragael E. El Mallakh & Dorothea H. El Mallakh. LC 81-47746. 224p. 1982. 26.50x (ISBN 0-669-04801-1). Lexington Bks.

Saudi Arabia: Forces of Modernization. Bob Abdrabboh. 125p. (Orig.). 1985. pap. 9.95 (ISBN 0-915597-19-5). Amana Bks.

Saudi Arabia in the Nineteenth Century. R. Bayly Winder. LC 80-13191. xiv, 312p. 1980. Repr. of 1965 ed. lib. bdg. 23.00x (ISBN 0-374-98676-2, Octagon). Hippocrene Bks.

Saudi Arabia in the Oil Era: Regime & Elites-- Conflict & Collaboration. Mordechai Abir. 400p. 1988. 38.50 (ISBN 0-8133-0643-4). Westview.

Saudi Arabia in the 1980's: Foreign Policy, Security, & Oil. William B. Quandt. LC 82-18086. 190p. 1981. 26.95 (ISBN 0-8157-7286-6). Brookings.

Saudi Arabia: Past & Present. Shirley Kay. 12.95 (ISBN 0-7043-2223-4, Pub. by Quartet England). Charles River Bks.

Saudi Arabia: Rush to Development. Ragaei El Mallakh. LC 81-48189. 480p. 1982. text ed. 47.50x (ISBN 0-8018-2783-3). Johns Hopkins.

Saudi Arabia Sociological Research Project. Center for Applied Urban Research Staff. 52p. (Orig.). 1977. pap. 3.50 (ISBN 1-55719-070-4). U NE Ctr Applied Urban Rsch.

Saudi Arabia: The Ceaseless Quest for Security. Nadav Safran. (Illus.). 592p. 1985. 25.00 (ISBN 0-674-78985-7, Belknap). Harvard U Pr.

Saudi Arabia: The Ceaseless Quest for Security. Nadav Safran. (Paperback Ser.). 1988. pap. 15.95 (ISBN 0-8014-9484-2). Cornell U Pr.

Saudi Arabia, the West & the Security of the Arab Gulf. Mazher Hameed. 192p. 1986. 37.50 (ISBN 0-7099-4663-5, Pub. by Croom Helm UK). Routledge Chapman & Hall.

Saudi Arabia: Through the Eyes of an Artist. Malin Basil. 84p. 1984. 100.00x (ISBN 0-907151-17-5, Pub. by IMMEL UK). State Mutual Bk.

Savage Stronghold. Craig Sargent. 224p. (Orig.). 1986. pap. 2.95 (ISBN 0-445-20237-8, Pub. by Popular Lib). Warner Bks.

Savage Summer. Constance O'Banyon. 448p. 1986. pap. 3.95 (ISBN 0-8217-1922-X). Zebra.

Savage Sundown. Elizabeth Forbush. 243p. 1987. pap. text ed. 6.95x (ISBN 0-942809-00-9). Summit Pr Va.

Savage Surrender. Cassie Edwards. 1987. pap. 3.95 (ISBN 0-441-05384-X, Charter Pub). Berkley Pub.

Savage Trail. James Persak. 1985. pap. 2.25 (ISBN 0-8217-1594-1). Zebra.

Savage War of Peace: Algeria, Nineteen Fifty-Four to Nineteen Sixty-Two. Alistair Horne. (Illus.). 592p. 1979. pap. 7.95 (ISBN 0-14-005137-6). Penguin.

Savage War of Peace: Algeria 1954-1962. Alistair Horne. 608p. 1987. pap. 8.95 (ISBN 0-14-010191-8). Penguin.

Savage Wars. Lawrence James. (Illus.). 272p. 1986. 19.95 (ISBN 0-312-69987-5). St Martin.

Savage Winter. Constance O'Banyon. 1985. pap. 3.75 (ISBN 0-8217-1584-4). Zebra.

Savage Women. Mike Curtis. 1976. pap. 1.50 (ISBN 0-685-72353-4, LB379DK, Leisure Bks). Leisure NY.

Savages. Shirley Conran. (Illus.). 560p. 1987. 19.95 (ISBN 0-317-60403-1). S&S.

Savages. Shirley Conran. 1988. pap. 4.95 (ISBN 0-671-66320-8). PB.

Savages. James Douglas. (Irish Play Ser.). 1979. 6.95x (ISBN 0-912262-60-5); pap. 2.95x (ISBN 0-912262-61-3). Proscenium.

Savages. Christopher Hampton. 86p. 1974. pap. 6.95 (ISBN 0-571-10348-0). Faber & Faber.

Savages & Naturals: Black Portraits by White Writers in Modern American Literature. John Cooley. 208p. 1982. 21.50 (ISBN 0-87413-167-7). U Delaware Pr.

Savages & Scientists: The Smithsonian Institution & the Development of American Anthropology 1846-1910. Curtis M. Hinsley, Jr. LC 80-20193. (Illus.). 320p. 1981. text ed. 24.95x (ISBN 0-87474-518-7, HISS). Smithsonian.

Savages & Shakespeare Wallah. James Ivory. 1973. pap. 3.95 (ISBN 0-394-17799-1, E604, Ever). Grove.

Savages & Shakespeare Wallah: Two Films. James Ivory. (Illus.). 152p. (Orig.). 1986. pap. 7.95 (ISBN 0-936839-54-6). Applause Theatre Bk Pubs.

Savages of Gor, No. 17. John Norman. 1986. pap. 3.95 (ISBN 0-88677-191-9). DAW Bks.

Savage's Romance: The Poetry of Marianne Moore. John M. Slatin. LC 85-43250. 276p. 1986. 24.50x (ISBN 0-271-00425-8). Pa St U Pr.

Savagism & Civility. Bernard Sheehan. LC 79-18189. 1980. pap. 11.95 (ISBN 0-521-29723-0). Cambridge U Pr.

Savagism & Civilization: A Study of Indians & the American Mind. Roy H. Pearce. 1988. pap. 9.95x (ISBN 0-520-06227-2). U of Cal Pr.

Savagism & Civilization: A Study of the Indian & the American Mind. Ed. by Roy Harvey Pearce & J. Hillis Miller. LC 53-6486. 272p. 1967. pap. 9.95x (ISBN 0-8018-0525-2). Johns Hopkins.

Savannah. Federal Writer's Project, Georgia. LC 73-3608. (American Guide Ser.). Repr. of 1937 ed. 12.50 (ISBN 0-404-57912-4). AMS Pr.

Savannah. John T. Foster. (Orig.). 1982. pap. 3.50 (ISBN 0-89083-953-0). Zebra.

Savannah. Eugenia Price. LC 82-45572. 608p. 1983. 18.95 (ISBN 0-385-15274-4). Doubleday.

Savannah. Eugenia Price. 608p. 1986. pap. 4.95 (ISBN 0-425-10004-9). Berkley Pub.

Savannah. Thomas L. Stokes. LC 82-2665. (Brown Thrasher Bks). (Illus.). 416p. 1982. pap. 8.95 (ISBN 0-8203-0621-5). U of Ga Pr.

Savannah Collection: Favorite Recipes from Savannah Cooks. Martha G. Nesbit. (Illus.). 250p. 1986. pap. 10.95 Cardboard back (ISBN 0-9617126-0-0). M Nesbit.

Savannah: Proud As A Peacock. The Savannah Junior Auxiliary. Ed. by Carol Barker & Lynn Patrick. 320p. 1982. pap. 9.95 (ISBN 0-939114-45-3). Savannah Jr Aux.

Savannah Purchase. Jane A. Hodge. 1979. pap. 1.95 (ISBN 0-449-24097-5, Crest). Fawcett.

Savannah River Plantations. M. Granger. LC 71-187384. (Illus.). 532p. 1972. Repr. of 1947 ed. 32.50 (ISBN 0-87152-079-6). Reprint.

Savannah River Plantations. Writers Program, Georgia. LC 73-3610. (American Guide Ser.). Repr. of 1947 ed. 27.50 (ISBN 0-404-57913-2). AMS Pr.

Savannah Sampler Cookbook. Margaret W. DeBolt & Emma Law. LC 78-1078. (Illus.). 298p. 1978. pap. 8.95 (ISBN 0-915442-49-3). Donning Co.

Savannah Score. Lew Dykes. 1987. pap. 3.50 (ISBN 0-425-10411-7). Berkley Pub.

Savannah Spectres. Margaret W. DeBolt. Ed. by Robert Friedman. LC 82-23455. (Illus., Orig.). 1984. pap. 7.95 (ISBN 0-89865-201-4). Donning Co.

Savannah Swing Saw. (Executioner Ser.: No. 74). Date not set. pap. 2.25 (ISBN 0-317-63943-9, Pub. by Worldwide). Harlequin Bks.

Savannah's Old Jewish Community Cemeteries. B. H. Levy. LC 83-1045. vii, 118p. 1983. 10.95 (ISBN 0-86554-076-4, H68). Mercer Univ Pr.

Savannas: Biogeography & Geobotany. Monica Cole. 1986. 79.50 (ISBN 0-12-179520-9). Acad Pr.

Savantasse of Montparnasse. Allen Mandelbaum. (Illus.). 206p. 1988. 19.95 (ISBN 0-935296-70-0); pap. text ed. 12.95 (ISBN 0-935296-71-9). Sheep Meadow.

Savaric De Mavleon. H. J. Chaytor. 1939. 29.50 (ISBN 0-8274-3326-3). R West.

Savate. 3rd rev. ed. Bruce Tegner. (Illus.). 109p. 1983. pap. 5.95 (ISBN 0-87407-042-2, T-2). Thor.

Savate: Martial Art of France. rev. ed. Philip Reed & Richard Muggeridge. (Illus.). 72p. 1986. pap. text ed. 12.00 (ISBN 0-87364-379-8). Paladin Pr.

Save a Fortune: A Common Sense Guide to Building Wealth. Phillip Godwin. 209p. 1988. 12.95 (ISBN 0-945332-05-X). Agora Inc MD.

Save Hundreds-Thousands Buying Your New Car. Dick Krol. LC 86-91246. (Illus.). 288p. (Orig.). 1986. pap. 19.95 (ISBN 0-938879-00-6). RMK Pub.

Save Me a Seat. Rhea Kohan. 320p. 1980. pap. 2.25 (ISBN 0-449-24281-1, Crest). Fawcett.

Save Money & Grow Rich. John King. 1968. 4.95 (ISBN 0-8184-0070-6). Lyle Stuart.

Save Our Shop: The Fall & Rise of the Small Co-Operative Store. Johnston Birchall. 109p. 1987. 70.00 (ISBN 0-317-68766-2, Pub. by Plunkett Foundation). State Mutual Bk.

Save Queen of Sheba. Louise Moeri. 112p. 1982. pap. 2.75 (ISBN 0-380-58529-4, Flare). Avon.

Save Queen of Sheba. Louise Moeri. LC 80-23019. (gr. 4-7). 1981. 13.95 (ISBN 0-525-33202-2). Dutton.

Save Room for Dessert! Sensational Sweets: A Serious Cookbook. Selene Ganek. (Illus.). 178p. 1986. Repr. of 1985 ed. 11.95 (ISBN 0-9616186-0-4). S Ganek.

Save Save Save Save. Nichola Manning. 1986. Signed & Lettered. 20.00 (ISBN 0-930090-25-X); pap. 5.95 (ISBN 0-930090-26-8). Applezaba.

Save Save Save Save. Nichola Manning. 65p. 1986. 14.95 (ISBN 0-930090-27-6). Applezaba.

Save That House. A. J. Hupp. LC 83-72006. (Illus.). 88p. (Orig.). 1984. pap. 6.95 (ISBN 0-9611744-0-4). D J Pub.

Save the Children. (Executioner Ser.: No. 94). Date not set. pap. 2.25 (ISBN 0-317-63962-5, Pub. by Worldwide). Harlequin Bks.

Save the Dolphins. Horace Dobbs. 128p. 1981. 14.95 (ISBN 0-285-62437-7, Pub. by Souvenir Pr). Intl Spec Bk.

Save the Earth! An Ecology Handbook for Kids. Betty Miles. LC 73-15116. (Illus.). 96p. (gr. 2 up). 1974. Knopf.

Save the Inch! Aron Breslow. Date not set. 2.00 (ISBN 0-918430-02-X). Happy History.

Save the Last Dance for Me. Judi Miller. 1984. pap. 2.75 (ISBN 0-671-83650-1). PB.

Save the Loonies. Joyce Milton. 160p. (gr. 4-6). 1985. pap. 2.25 (ISBN 0-590-32859-X, Apple Paperbacks). Scholastic Inc.

Save the Three Pigs. Kevin Scally. (Magic Road Bks.). (Illus.). 32p. (ps-3). 1984. 3.95 (ISBN 0-448-11127-6, G&D). Putnam Pub Group.

Save the Wetlands. Luke Fontana. (Illus.). 1982. 14.00 (ISBN 0-942494-20-2). Coleman Pub.

Save Thirty Percent on Your Casualty Insurance: Yet Improve Coverage. Robert A. Wilson. Ed. by Irving L. Blackman. (Special Report Ser.: No. 130). 52p. 1985. pap. 21.00 (ISBN 0-916181-22-7). Blackman Kallick Bartelstein.

Save Thousands of Dollars for Sale by Owner. L. J. Lejon & Associates Staff. (Illus.). 64p. 1983. pap. 4.95 (ISBN 0-9612812-0-0). L J Lejon & Assocs.

Save Thousands When You Buy or Sell Your Home. new ed. John D. Bowers. 132p. (Orig.). 1974. pap. 3.95. J D Bowers.

Save Tomorrow for the Children. E. Paul Torrance et al. 234p. (Orig.). 1987. pap. 12.95 (ISBN 0-943456-22-3). Bearly Ltd.

Save Your Arteries--Save Your Life. Charles Klieman. 208p. (Orig.). 1987. pap. 4.50 (ISBN 0-446-34583-0). Warner Bks.

Save Your Child's Life. David Hendin. (Illus.). 96p. 1986. pap. 4.95 (ISBN 0-345-33718-2). Pharos Bks NY.

Save Your Hide! Tools for Self-Defense. John Watson. (Illus.). 64p. (Orig.). 1987. pap. text ed. 7.00 (ISBN 0-87364-417-4). Paladin Pr.

Save Your Home: Avoid Foreclosure & Make a Fat Profit. Steven L. Porter. LC 87-3916. (Orig.). 1987. pap. 12.00 (ISBN 0-941599-02-7). Java Pub Co.

Save Your Horse Handbook: Care & Treatment of Sick Horses see Farnam Horse Library Series.

Save Your Knees. James Fox & Rick Mcguire. (Orig.). 1988. pap. 6.95 (ISBN 0-440-50011-7, Dell Trade Books). Dell.

Save Your License: A Driver's Survival Guide. Gene Mason. LC 78-2218. (Illus.). 150p. 1978. 14.95 (ISBN 0-87364-103-5). Paladin Pr.

Save-Your-Life Defense Handbook. Matthew Braun. (Illus.). 1977. pap. 9.95 (ISBN 0-8159-5712-2). Devin.

Save Your Life Diet. David Reuben. 192p. 1988. pap. 3.50 (ISBN 0-345-34330-1). Ballantine.

Save-Your-Life-Diet High Fiber Cookbook. David Reuben & Barbara Reuben. 1977. pap. 3.50. Ballantine.

Save Your Marriage. Barry R. Berkey. LC 75-45338. 313p. 1976. 20.95x (ISBN 0-88229-235-8). Nelson-Hall.

Save Your Money, Save Your Face: What Every Cosmetics Buyer Needs to Know. Elaine Brumberg. 368p. 1986. 17.95 (ISBN 0-8160-1080-3). Facts on File.

Save Your Money, Save Your Face: What Every Cosmetics Buyer Needs to Know. Elaine Brumberg. LC 86-46048. 368p. 1987. pap. 8.95 (ISBN 0-06-097097-9, PL 7097, PL). Har-Row.

Saved. Edward Bond. (Metheun Modern Plays Ser.). 123p. 1984. pap. 6.95 (ISBN 0-413-31360-3, NO. 9049). Heinemann Ed.

Saved & Certain. Thomas G. Davis. (Orig.). 1955. pap. 4.95 (ISBN 0-8054-1611-0). Broadman.

Saved & Kept. F. B. Meyer. 1970. pap. 4.50 (ISBN 0-87508-350-1). Chr Lit.

Saved by a Broken Pole & Other Stories. Compiled by Joyce K. Ellis. 75p. (Orig.). (gr. 2-6). 1980. pap. 1.75 (ISBN 0-89323-007-3, 096). Bible Memory.

Saved by a Ghost. Charles W. Leadbeater. LC 79-9981. 1979. pap. 5.50 (ISBN 0-8356-0526-4, Quest). Theos Pub Hse.

Saved by Grace. John Bunyan. pap. 2.95 (ISBN 0-685-88393-0). Reiner.

Saved by Grace...for Service. Robert L. Sumner. 1979. 8.95 (ISBN 0-87398-797-7). Sword of Lord.

Saved by Hope: Essays in Honor of Richard C. Oudersluys. Ed. by James I. Cook. LC 78-5416. Repr. of 1978 ed. 49.50 (ISBN 0-8357-9132-7, 2016060). Bks Demand UMI.

Saved by the Slime Box. Barbara Aiello. (Kids on the Block Ser.). Date not set. price not set. Twenty First Bks.

Saved in Eternity: The Assurance of Our Salvation. Martyn Lloyd-Jones. LC 87-70457. 192p. (Orig.). 1988. pap. 12.95 (ISBN 0-89107-448-1, Crossway Bks). Good News.

Saved on Monday. Vivian D. Gunderson. (gr. k-8). 1964. pap. 1.95 (ISBN 0-915374-14-5, 14-5). Rapids Christian.

Saved? What Do You Mean Saved? A Journalist's Report on Salvation. Joe Ortiz. Ed. by Mark D. Feldstein. (Illus.). 95p. (Orig.). 1983. pap. 4.95 (ISBN 0-912695-00-5). GBM Bks.

Saved! Where Do We Go from Here? Clayton Watkins. 147p. (Orig.). 1987. pap. 5.95 (ISBN 0-914903-39-X). Destiny Image.

Saver's Guide to Sound Investments. David M. Brownstone. 208p. 1985. 15.95 (ISBN 0-531-09589-4). Watts.

Savidge Brothers, Sandhills Aviators. Duane Hutchinson. (Illus.). 332p. 1982. 19.95 (ISBN 0-934988-06-4). Foun Bks.

Savile Correspondence. Henry Savile. LC 17-3795. (Camden Society, London, Publicatons, First Ser.: No. 71). Repr. of 1858 ed. 37.00 (ISBN 0-404-50171-0). AMS Pr.

Savile Correspondence. Henry Savile. Repr. of 1858 ed. 37.00 (ISBN 0-384-53280-2). Johnson Repr.

Saving a Generation. Blanche Bernstein. (Twentieth Century Fund Paper). 63p. (Orig.). 1986. pap. text ed. 7.50x (ISBN 0-87078-206-1). Priority Pr Pubns.

Saving America's Birds. Paula Hendrich. LC 81-15624. (Illus.). 160p. (gr. 6 up). 1982. 11.75 (ISBN 0-688-00417-2). Lothrop.

Saving America's Cities. Ed. by Evelyn Geller. (Reference Shelf Ser.). 1979. 10.00 (ISBN 0-8242-0631-2). Wilson.

Saving America's Wildlife. Thomas R. Dunlap. 264p. 1988. text ed. 24.95 (ISBN 0-691-04750-2). Princeton U Pr.

Saving & Economic Growth: Is the United States Really Falling Behind? Robert E. Lipsey & Irving B. Kravis. (Report Ser.: No. 901). (Illus.). x, 86p. (Orig.). 1987. pap. text ed. 35.00 (ISBN 0-8237-0344-4). Conference Bd.

Saving & Investing. rev. ed. Changing Times Education Service Editors. LC 81-7860. (Illus.). 112p. 1982. pap. text ed. 4.95 (ISBN 0-88436-807-6, 30266). EMC.

Saving & Investment in the U. K. & West Germany. J. M. Samuels & P. C. McMahon. 144p. 1978. text ed. 49.95x (ISBN 0-566-00302-0). Gower Pub Co.

Saving & Spending. Jeffrey Mark. 1980. lib. bdg. 59.95 (ISBN 0-8490-3083-8). Gordon Pr.

Saving & Spending: The Working-Class Economy in Britain, 1870-1939. Paul Johnson. (Historical Monographs). (Illus.). 320p. 1985. 39.95x (ISBN 0-19-822933-X). Oxford U Pr.

Saving Babies: Children's Bureau Studies of Infant Mortality, 1913-1917. Ed. by David J. Rothman & Sheila M. Rothman. (Women & Children First Ser.). 360p. 1986. lib. bdg. 45.00 (ISBN 0-8240-7693-1). Garland Pub.

Saving Belief: A Critique of Physicalism. Lynne R. Baker. 192p. 1988. text ed. 19.95 (ISBN 0-691-07320-1). Princeton U Pr.

Saving Capitalism: The Reconstruction Finance Corporation & the New Deal, 1933-1940. James S. Olson. 315p. 1988. text ed. 31.50 (ISBN 0-691-04749-9). Princeton U Pr.

Saving Challenge of Religion. Budhananda. 272p. (Orig.). 1982. pap. 7.95 (ISBN 0-87481-567-3). Vedanta Pr.

Saving China. Alvyn Austin. 395p. 1959. 80.00x (ISBN 0-317-69447-2, Pub. by Han-Shan Tang Ltd). State Mutual Bk.

Saving China: Canadian Missionaries in the Middle Kingdom, 1888-1959. Alvyn J. Austin. (Illus.). 416p. 1987. 27.50 (ISBN 0-8020-5687-3). U of Toronto Pr.

Saving Civilization: Yeats, Eliot, & Auden Between the Wars. Lucy McDiarmid. 190p. 1984. pap. 10.95 (ISBN 0-521-26930-X). Cambridge U Pr.

Saving Energy. (Wonders of Learning Kit Ser.). (gr. 3-6). 1981. incl. cass. & tchr's. guide 28.95 (ISBN 0-686-73893-4, 04917). Natl Geog.

Saving Face. Nancy Lane. write for info. World Pr Ltd.

Saving Face: A Dermatologist's Guide to Maintaining a Healthier & Younger Looking Face. Nelson L. Novick. 288p. 1986. 16.95 (ISBN 0-531-15022-4). Watts.

Saving Face: A Dermatologist's Guide to Maintaining a Healthier & Younger Looking Face. Nelson L. Novick. Ed. by Samuel Mitnick. LC 87-24241. (Illus.). 272p. (Orig.). 1987. pap. 7.95 (ISBN 0-89586-653-6, Body Press). Price Stern.

Saving Face Through Surrender & Grace: A First Step Guide for Codependents. Evelyn Leite. 24p. 1988. pap. 2.95 (ISBN 0-945485-03-4). Comm Intervention.

Saving Farmland. John Kolesar & Jaye Scholl. 1975. 4.25 (ISBN 0-943136-17-2). Ctr Analysis Public Issues.

Saving for Development: Report of the International Symposium on the Mobilization of Personal Savings in Developing Countries, 3rd. 114p. 1986. pap. 14.50 (ISBN 92-1-104172-4, E.85II.A.17). UN.

Saving Free Trade: A Pragmatic Approach. Robert Z. Lawrence & Robert E. Litan. LC 86-14705. 132p. 1986. 22.95 (ISBN 0-8157-5178-8); pap. 8.95t (ISBN 0-8157-5177-X). Brookings.

Saving Fuel with Furnaces. Elmer S. Monroe, Jr. Ed. by Elias P. Gyftopoulos & Karen C. Cohen. (Industrial Energy-Conservation Manuals: No. 6). 56p. 1982. loose-leaf 20.00x (ISBN 0-262-13171-4). MIT Pr.

Saving Grace. Celia Gittelson. LC 81-47520. 224p. 1981. 10.95 (ISBN 0-394-51776-8). Knopf.

Saving Grace. Celia Gittleson. (Fiction Ser.). 256p. 1986. pap. 4.95 (ISBN 0-14-007789-8). Penguin.

Saving Grace. Ken Hartnett. 1984. 15.95 (ISBN 0-395-36298-9). HM.

Saving Grace. R. W. Jones. 240p. 1986. 14.95 (ISBN 0-312-69986-7). St Martin.

Saving Homes for the Poor: Low Income Tenants Can Own Their Apartments (with Case Summaries) Alfred Drummond & Yvette Shiffman. 21p. (Orig.). 1984. pap. 2.25 (ISBN 0-88156-017-0). Comm Serv Soc NY.

Saving in a Free Society. 2nd ed. Enoch J. Powell. (gr. 10-12). 1966. technical 4.25 (ISBN 0-685-29099-9). Transatl Arts.

Saving in Postwar Japan. Tuvia Blumenthal. LC 78-119071. (East Asian Monographs Ser.: No. 35). 1970. pap. 11.00x (ISBN 0-674-78997-0). Harvard U Pr.

Saving Lake Superior. Wendy W. Adamson. LC 74-17351. (Story of Environmental Action Ser.). (Illus.). (gr. 7 up). 1974. PLB 8.95 (ISBN 0-87518-083-3). Dillon.

Saving Life of Christ. W. Ian Thomas. 1961. pap. 4.95 (ISBN 0-310-33262-1, 10908S). Zondervan.

Saving Lost Positions: Intermediate Level. Leonid Shamkovich & Eric Schiller. (Chess Library). (Illus.). 128p. 1987. pap. 8.95 (ISBN 0-02-053770-0, Collier). Macmillan.

Saving of America. Clifford Goldstein. (Anchors Ser.). 96p. 1988. pap. 6.95. Pacific Pr Pub Assn.

Saving Oiled Seabirds. Rev. ed. Anne S. Williams. Ed. by Meryl L. Kane. LC 87-70495. (Illus.). 50p. 1987. pap. 8.00 (ISBN 0-89364-057-3, 841-44470). Am Petroleum.

Saving Our Animal Friends see Books for Young Explorers.

Saving Quetico-Superior: A Land Set Apart. rev. ed. R. Newell Searle. LC 77-21883. (Illus.). 275p. 1979. 11.50 (ISBN 0-87351-116-6); pap. 7.95 (ISBN 0-87351-140-9). Minn Hist.

Saving Rain. Elsie Webber. 1988. 15.95 (ISBN 0-8283-1911-1). Branden Pub co.

Saving Social Security. Ed. by Jason Berger. (Reference Shelf Ser.: Vol. 54, No. 4). 158p. pap. text ed. 10.00 (ISBN 0-8242-0668-1). Wilson.

Saving the Appearances: A Study in Idolatry. Owen Barfield. LC 65-23538. 190p. 1965. pap. 4.95 (ISBN 0-15-679490-X, Harv). HarBraceJ.

Saving the Appearances: A Study in Idolatry. 2nd, rev. ed. Owen Barfield. 190p. 1988. 35.00x (ISBN 0-8195-5199-6); pap. 10.95 (ISBN 0-8195-6205-X). Wesleyan U Pr.

Saving the Big-Deal Baby. Louise Armstrong. LC 79-22838. (Skinny Bks.). (Illus.). (gr. 7 up). 1980. 7.95 (ISBN 0-525-38805-2). Dutton.

Saving the Canadian City, the First Phase 1880-1920: An Anthology of Articles on Urban Reform. Ed. by Paul Rutherford. LC 73-91560. (Social History of Canada Ser.). 1974. pap. 9.50 (ISBN 0-8020-6247-4). U of Toronto Pr.

Saving the Fragments: From Auschwitz to New York. Isabella Leitner & Irving Leitner. LC 84-8815. 128p. 1986. 12.95 (ISBN 0-453-00502-0). NAL.

Saving the Great Swamp: The People, the Power Brokers & an Urban Wilderness. Cam Cavanaugh. LC 78-8132. (Illus.). 1978. 11.95 (ISBN 0-914366-11-4). Columbia Pub.
Saving the Jewish Family: Myths & Realities in the Diaspora Strategies for the Future (An Analysis & Cumulative Bibliography 1970-1982) Gerald B. Bubis. 216p. (Orig.). 1987. lib. bdg. 27.75 (ISBN 0-8191-6574-3, Co-Pub. by Ctr Jewish Comm Studies); pap. text ed. 14.50 (ISBN 0-8191-6575-1, Co-Pub. by Ctr Jewish Comm Studies). U Pr of Amer.
Saving the Peregrine Falcon. Caroline Arnold. LC 84-15576. (Carolrhoda Nature Watch Bks.). (Illus.). 48p. (gr. 2-5). 1985. PLB 12.95 (ISBN 0-87614-225-0). Carolrhoda Bks.
Saving the Planet: The Politics of Hope. Norman Walbek. 180p. (Orig.). 1988. pap. 7.95 (ISBN 0-929021-01-0). Northland MN.
Saving the Plenty: Pickling & Preserving. Richard Humphrey. LC 85-51151. (Antique Eating Ser.: Vol. 14). 126p. (Orig.). 1986. pap. 4.95 (ISBN 0-9610602-3-9). Teaparty Bks.
Saving the Prairies: The Life Cycle of the Founding School of American Plant Ecology, 1895-1955. Ronald C. Tobey. LC 80-28200. (Illus.). 310p. 1981. 35.00x (ISBN 0-520-04352-9). U of Cal Pr.
Saving the President. Barbara Brenner. LC 87-7790. (Illus.). 128p. (gr. 5 up). 1988. 9.29 (ISBN 0-671-62023-1); pap. 4.95 (ISBN 0-671-64954-X). Messner.
Saving the Queen. William F. Buckley, Jr. 288p. 1981. pap. 3.95 (ISBN 0-380-55111-X). Avon.
Saving the Queen. William F. Buckley, Jr. LC 75-17405. 1976. 7.95 (ISBN 0-385-03800-3). Doubleday.
Saving the Revolution: The Federalist Papers & the American Founding. Charles Kesler. LC 87-7412. 1987. 29.95 (ISBN 0-317-58127-9). Free Pr.
Saving the River: The St. Croix River Association. James T. Dunn. (Illus.). 56p. (Orig.). 1986. pap. 7.50 (ISBN 0-9617292-0-1). St Croix River Assn.
Saving the Text: Literature-Derrida-Philosophy. Geoffrey H. Hartman. LC 80-21748. (Illus.). 190p. (Orig.). 1982. text ed. 24.50x (ISBN 0-8018-2452-4); pap. 7.95x (ISBN 0-8018-2453-2). Johns Hopkins.
Saving the Tropical Forests. Judith Gradwohl & Russell Greenberg. (Illus.). 207p. 1988. Repr. of 1988 ed. 24.95x (ISBN 0-933280-81-5). Island CA.
Saving the Tropical Rain Forests. Judith Gradwohl & Russell Greenberg. (Illus.). 224p. (Orig.). 1988. pap. 12.75 (ISBN 1-85383-014-3, Pub. by Earthscan Pubns London). Longwood Pub Group.
Saving the Waifs: Reformers & Dependent Children, 1890-1917. LeRoy Ashby. (American Civilization Ser.). 336p. 1984. 37.95 (ISBN 0-87722-337-8). Temple U Pr.
Saving the Whale. Michael Bright. (Survival Ser.). (Illus.). 32p. (gr. 4-9). 1987. lib. bdg. 10.90 (ISBN 0-531-17061-6, Gloucester Pr). Watts.
Saving the World from Your Home: What One Person Can Do. P. H. Raynis. LC 86-64001. 168p. (Orig.). 1987. pap. 5.95 (ISBN 0-87973-489-2, 489). Our Sunday Visitor.
Saving the Young Men of Vienna. David Kirby. LC 87-40148. (Brittingham Prize in Poetry 1987 Ser.). 1987. 12.50 (ISBN 0-299-11220-9); pap. 7.95 (ISBN 0-299-11224-1). U of Wis Pr.
Saving Time & Taxes in Planning & Preparing Estate, Gift, & Fiduciary Returns. George M. Schain. LC 84-28702. 1985. 75.00 (ISBN 0-8240-7292-8). Garland Pub.
Saving Water from the Ground up: A Pilot Study of Irrigation Scheduling on Four California Farms. Gail Richardson & Peter Mueller-Beilschmidt. LC 85-60576. (Illus.). 72p. (Orig.). 1985. pap. 1.50x (ISBN 0-918780-31-4). INFORM.
Saving Water in a Desert City. William E. Martin et al. xiii, 111p. 1984. pap. 10.00 (ISBN 0-915707-04-7). Resources Future.
Saving Word, Years A, B & C. W. Harrington et al. LC 80-68395. 370p. 1982. pap. 12.00 ea. (ISBN 0-89453-266-9); Set. pap. 30.00. M Glazier.
Saving Your Child's Mind. Vincent R. Ruggiero. (Illus.). 210p. 1988. text ed. 27.50x (ISBN 0-398-05506-8). C C Thomas.
Savings. Linda Hogan. 1988. pap. 7.95 (ISBN 0-918273-41-2). Coffee Hse.
Savings Accounts see Getting Ready for Pay Day.
Savings & Capital Formation: The Policy Options. F. Gerard Adams & Susan Wachter. LC 85-40328. (Illus.). 224p. 33.00x (ISBN 0-669-11017-5). Lexington Bks.
Savings & Loan Associations. (American Institute of CPAs Audit Guides Ser.). 1987. pap. 11.50 (ISBN 0-87051-025-8). Am Inst CPA.
Savings & Loan Associations: Ohio Laws & Regulations. 587p. 1985. 40.00; Suppl. 1984. 25.00. Anderson Pub Co.
Savings & Loan Holding Companies & Alternative Thrift Financing Devices. 35.00 (ISBN 0-317-29531-4, #CO3085, Law & Business). HarBraceJ.
Savings & Loan Industry: Current Problems & Possible Solutions. Walter J. Woerheide. LC 83-13686. (Illus.). xviii, 216p. 1984. lib. bdg. 36.95 (ISBN 0-89930-038-3, WOL/, Quorum). Greenwood.
Savings & Loan Proxy Contests. 35.00 (ISBN 0-317-29532-2, #CO3344, Law & Business). HarBraceJ.
Savings & Time Deposit Banking. 1982. 12.00 (ISBN 0-89982-157-X, 053200); members 8.00. Am Bankers.
Savings & Withdrawal Tables for Retirement Accounts. Financial Publishing Co. Staff. 130p. 1982. pap. 13.25 (ISBN 0-87600-148-7). Finan Pub.
Savings Bank of Baltimore, 1818-1866: A Historical & Analytical Study. Peter L. Payne & Lance E. Davis. LC 75-41778. (Companies & Men: Business Enterprises in America). (Illus.). 1976. Repr. of 1956 ed. 20.00x (ISBN 0-405-08093-X). Ayer Co Pubs.
Savings Banking: An Industry in Change. Franklin Ornstein. 1984. text ed. 44.00 (ISBN 0-8359-6883-9, Reston). P-H.
Savings Banking: An Industry in Change. 350p. 1985. 36.00 (ISBN 0-318-04773-X, 116). Bank Admin Inst.
Savings Banking Today. 156p. 1980. 16.25 (ISBN 0-317-32413-6, 051700); members 13.00 (ISBN 0-317-32414-4); leader's guide 10.00 (ISBN 0-317-32415-2, 251700); members 8.00 (ISBN 0-317-32416-0). Am Bankers.
Savings Behavior & Its Implications for Domestic Resource Mobilization: The Case of the Republic of Korea. Shahid Yusuf & R. Kyle Peters. (World Bank Staff Working Papers: No. 628). 62p. 1985. 3.50 (ISBN 0-8213-0304-X, WP0628). World Bank.
Savings Factor Tables for Monthly, Quarterly, Semiannual & Annual Compounding. Financial Publishing Co. Staff. 334p. 1982. pap. 29.95 (ISBN 0-87600-532-6). Finan PUb.
Savings for Development: Report of the Second International Symposium on the Mobilization of Personal Savings in Developing Countries. LC 84-46787. 185p. 19.00 (ISBN 92-1-104150-3, E.84.II.A.1). UN.
Savings in Bank Postal Operations. 1978. 18.75 (ISBN 0-89982-059-X, 060100); members 17.50. Am Bankers.
Savings Institution Operations: A Functional Approach. 3rd ed. 352p. 1985. pap. 22.95 (ISBN 0-912857-29-3). Inst Finan Educ.
Savings Institutions Today. 440p. 1985. 24.95 (ISBN 0-912857-28-5). Inst Finan Educ.
Savings Mobilization Through Social Security: The Case of Chile, 1916-1977. Christine Wallich. (Staff Working Paper: No. 553). 109p. 1983. 5.00 (ISBN 0-8213-0123-3, WP 0553). World Bank.
Savings Plants & Jobs: Union-Management Negotiations in the Context of Threatened Plant Closings. Paul F. Gerhart. 107p. 1987. pap. text ed. 9.95 (ISBN 0-88099-046-5). W E Upjohn.
Savio: A Study Guide. Joseph Aubry. Tr. by Joe Boenzi from Ital. LC 79-50460. 73p. (Orig.). 1979. pap. 2.75 (ISBN 0-89944-038-X). Don Bosco Multimedia.
Savior. Marvin Werlin & Mark Werlin. 480p. (YA) (gr. 9 up). 1979. pap. 2.75 (ISBN 0-440-17748-0, LFL). Dell.
Savior for All Seasons. William P. Barker. 192p. 1986. 10.95 (ISBN 0-8007-1485-7). Revell.
Savior of Science. Stanley L. Jaki. 200p. (Orig.). 1988. pap. 10.95 (ISBN 0-89526-767-5). Regnery Gateway.
Savior Partage: Semiotique et Theorie de la Connaissance Chez Marcel Proust. Jacques Fontanille. LC 87-30929. (Actes Semiotiques: 4). 227p. (Orig., Fr.). 1987. pap. 33.00x (ISBN 90-272-2265-7, Hades-Benjamins). Benjamins North Am.
Saviors. Helen Yglesias. 1987. 17.95 (ISBN 0-395-35419-6). HM.
Saviors of God. Nikos Kazantzakis. Tr. by Kimor Friar. 1969. pap. 7.95 (ISBN 0-671-20232-4, Touchstone Bks). S&S.
Saviors of Islamic Spirit, 4 Vols. Nadvi. 60.00 set (ISBN 0-686-18312-6); 20.00 ea. Kazi Pubns.
Saviors of Mankind. William R. Van Buskirk. LC 71-86790. (Essay Index Reprint Ser.). 1929. 32.00 (ISBN 0-8369-1432-5). Ayer Co Pubs.
Saviour God: Comparative Studies in the Concept of Salvation Presented to Edwin Oliver James. Ed. by Samuel G. Brandon. LC 80-14924. xxii, 242p. 1980. Repr. of 1963 ed. lib. bdg. 35.00x (ISBN 0-313-22416-1, BRSG). Greenwood.
Savitri: A Legend & a Symbol. Sri Aurobindo. 1984. 16.00 (ISBN 0-89071-266-2). Aurobindo Assn.
Savitri: A Legend & a Symbol. Sri Aurobindo. (Life Companion Ser.). 1978. 24.00 (ISBN 0-89744-933-9). Two-vol. Set. lib. bdg. 40.00 (ISBN 0-89744-953-3); pap. 20.00 (ISBN 0-89744-934-7). Auromere.
Savitri: A Legend & a Symbol. Sri Aurobindo. 1984. pap. 12.00 (ISBN 0-89071-250-6). Aurobindo Assn.
Savitri & Satyavan. Savitri. (Illus.). (gr. 1-9). 1979. pap. 2.75 (ISBN 0-89744-160-5). Auromere.
Savitri Unveiled. Mehdi Imam. 1981. 10.00x (ISBN 0-8364-0768-7, Pub. by Motilal Banarsidass). South Asia Bks.
Savitri Unveiled: A Selection. Syed Mehdi Imam. 144p. 1980. text ed. 9.00 (ISBN 0-89684-269-X, Pub. by Motilal Banarsidass India). Orient Bk Dist.
Savoia Marchetti SM.79 in Action. (Illus.). 50p. 1987. pap. 5.95 (ISBN 0-89747-173-3). Squad Sig Pubns.
Savoie, Nice et le Rhin see Cahiers de l'Institut de Science Economique Appliquee.
Savoir Partage: Semiotique it Theorie de la Connaissance Dans l'Oeuvre de Marcel Proust. Jacques Fontanille. LC 87-30929. (Actes Semiotiques Ser.: Vol. 4). 227p. (Orig.). 1987. pap. 33.00x (Hades-Benjamins). Benjamins North Am.
Savoir Rire: The Humorists' Guide to France. Intro. by Robert Wechsler. (Illus.). 272p. (Orig.). 1988. pap. 9.95 (ISBN 0-945774-00-1). Catbird Pr.
Savoir Vivre En Francais: Culture et Communication. Howard L. Nostrand et al. 412p. 1988. pap. write for info. (ISBN 0-471-82724-X); wkbk. avail. (ISBN 0-471-82725-8). Wiley.
Savon. Francis Ponge. 136p. 1966. 10.95 (ISBN 0-686-54895-7). French & Eur.
Savonarola & Florence: Prophecy & Patriotism in the Renaissance. Donald Weinstein. LC 76-113013. Repr. of 1970 ed. 102.80 (ISBN 0-8357-9511-X, 2015484). Bks Demand UMI.
Savonarola, His Life & Times. William R. Clark. LC 83-45654. Date not set. Repr. of 1890 ed. 34.50 (ISBN 0-404-19804-X). AMS Pr.
Savonarola, Protestantism & the Church of Rome, 2 vols. Peter Miscitelli. (Illus.). 247p. 1985. Set. 187.50 (ISBN 0-89901-230-2). Found Class Reprints.
Savonius Rotor Construction. Josef A. Kozlowski. (Illus.). 1977. English, 54pp. write for info (ISBN 0-86619-062-7). French, 54pp (ISBN 0-86619-063-5). Vols Tech Asst.
Savonnerie. Pierre Verlet. (Waddesdon Catalogues Ser.). (Illus.). 528p. 1985. text ed. 160.00 (ISBN 0-7078-0082-X, Pub. by P Wilson Pubs). Sotheby Pubns.
Savor the Huckleberry. Dolores Nicolai. (Orig.). 1979. pap. 3.50 (ISBN 0-933992-05-X). Coffee Break.
Savoring Mexico: Ninety-six Classic Recipes of Traditional Cuisine from All Regions of Mexico. Sharon Cadwallader. (Illus.). 210p. (Orig.). 1987. pap. 7.95 (ISBN 0-87701-427-2). Chronicle Bks.
Savoring the Past: The French Kitchen & Table from 1300 to 1789. Barbara K. Wheaton. LC 82-40486. (Illus.). 352p. (Orig.). 1983. pap. 21.95 (ISBN 0-8122-1146-4). U of Pa Pr.
Savoring the Sabbath. Janet Watkins. LC 80-83865. 80p. (Orig.). 1980. pap. 4.95 (ISBN 0-88290-165-6, 1058). Horizon Utah.
Savoring the Southwest. Roswell Symphony Guild-Board of Directors. LC 83-62041. (Illus.). 332p. 1983. 15.95 (ISBN 0-9612466-0-X). Roswell Symphony Guild.
Savory Sandwiches. Better Homes & Gardens Editors. 1988. pap. 2.95 (ISBN 0-696-01718-0). BH&G.
Savory Sausage: A Culinary Tour Around the World. Linda Merinoff. 368p. 1987. 18.95 (ISBN 0-671-62727-9, Poseidon Pr). PB.
Savory Shellfish of North America. Sandra Romashko. LC 77-74610. (Illus.). 1977. pap. 3.50 (ISBN 0-89317-015-1). Windward Pub.
Savory Suppers & Fashionable Feasts: Dining in Victorian America. Susan Williams. (Illus.). 335p. (Orig.). 1985. 17.95 (ISBN 0-318-23129-8). Strong Mus.
Savour of Life. Arnold Bennett. LC 74-17048. (Collected Works of Arnold Bennett: Vol. 72). 1976. Repr. of 1928 ed. 24.25 (ISBN 0-518-19153-2). Ayer Co Pubs.
Savoury Coatings. D. B. Fuller & R. T. Parry. 1987. 47.00 (ISBN 1-85166-140-9). Elsevier.
Savoy, 5 vols. Ed. by Arthur Symonds. 1967. Repr. of 1896 ed. 265.00x set (ISBN 0-7146-2115-3, F Cass Co). Biblio Dist.
Savoy Food & Drink Book. Ed. by Alison Leach. (Illus.). 224p. 1988. 29.95 (ISBN 0-88162-374-1). Salem Hse Pubs.
Savoy: Nineties Experiment. Ed. by Stanley Weintraub. LC 65-26099. (Illus.). 1966. 29.75x (ISBN 0-271-73100-1). Pa St U Pr.
Savoy Operas: A Guide to Gilbert & Sullivan. Geoffrey Smith. LC 84-8907. (Illus.). 236p. 1985. 15.00x (ISBN 0-87663-455-2). Universe.
Savrola. Winston S. Churchill. 241p. 1976. Repr. of 1900 ed. lib. bdg. 17.95x (ISBN 0-88411-074-5, Pub. by Queens Hse). Amereon Ltd.
Savta Simcha & the Incredible Shabbes Bag: Jewish Mary Poppins. Illus. by Bina Gewirth. (Illus.). (gr. 1-5). 1980. 9.95 (ISBN 0-87306-187-X). Feldheim.
Savta Simcha & the Seven Splendid Gifts. Yaffa Gauz. (Illus.). (gr. 4-7). 1987. 11.95 (ISBN 0-87306-437-2). Feldheim.
Savvy Sayin's: Lean & Meaty One-Liners. Ken Alstad. (Illus.). 192p. (Orig.). 1986. pap. 5.95 (ISBN 0-9616985-0-0). K Alstad.
Savvy Secs: Street Wise & Book Smart. Lynda R. Abegg & Peggy J. Grillot. Ed. by Millicent Treloar. LC 84-91839. 140p. (Orig.). 1985. pap. 9.95 (ISBN 0-9614131-0-7). Abegg Grillot Ent.
Saw. Steve Katz. LC 74-178961. 1972. bound in boards 3.50 (ISBN 0-394-47930-0). Small Pr Dist.
Saw the House in Half: A Novel. Oliver Jackman. LC 73-88971. 337p. 1974. 9.95 (ISBN 0-88258-010-8). Howard U Pr.
Sawanih: Inspiration from the World of Pure Spirits. Ahmad Ghazzali. Tr. by Nasrollah Pourjavady. (Ancient Persian Treatise on Love Ser.). 132p. 1985. 29.95 (ISBN 0-7103-0091-3, Kegan Paul). Routledge Chapman & Hall.
Sawdoctoring Manual. (Forestry Papers: No. 58). 227p. 1986. pap. 17.50 (ISBN 92-5-102264-X, F2811, FAO). UNIPUB.
Sawdust & Six Guns. Evan Evans, pseud. 256p. 1986. pap. 2.50 (ISBN 0-515-08529-4). Jove Pubns.
Sawdust & Sixguns. Evan Evans, pseud. 246p. 1976. Repr. of 1950 ed. lib. bdg. 17.95x (ISBN 0-89190-208-2, Pub. by River City Pr). Amereon Ltd.
Sawdust Ceaser: The Untold Story of Mussolini & Fascism. George H. Seldes. LC 70-180277. Repr. of 1935 ed. 37.50 (ISBN 0-404-56197-7). AMS Pr.
Sawdust Empire: The Texas Lumber Industry, 1830-1940. Robert S. Maxwell & Robert D. Baker. LC 82-40442. (Illus.). 256p. 1983. 24.95 (ISBN 0-89096-148-4). Tex A&M Univ Pr.
Sawdust in Your Eyes. W. E. Blackhurst. 1963. 10.00 (ISBN 0-87012-006-9). McClain.
Sawdust Pulping. (Bibliographic Ser.: No. S65). 59p. 1975. 10.00 (ISBN 0-317-34443-9). Inst Paper Chem.
Sawdust Trail Preacher: Billy Sunday. Betty S. Everett & Billy Sunday. (Faith & Fame Ser.). pap. 3.50 (ISBN 0-87508-499-0). ChR Lit.
Sawhorse Layout with the Framing Square. rev. ed. W. Forrest Bear & Thomas A. Hoerner. (Illus.). 8p. 1971. pap. text ed. 1.40x (ISBN 0-913163-01-5, 165). Hobar Pubns.
Sawing Technology: The Key to Improved Profits. 108p. (Orig.). 1986. pap. 18.00 (ISBN 0-935018-23-9). Forest Prod.
Sawmill. Kenneth L. Smith. LC 86-1453. 256p. 1986. 28.00x (ISBN 0-938626-68-X); pap. 15.00 (ISBN 0-938626-69-8). U of Ark Pr.
Saws: Design, Selection, Operation, Maintenance. Ed M. Williston. LC 77-93351. (Forest Industries Book). (Illus.). 288p. 1978. pap. 32.50 (ISBN 0-87930-073-6). Miller Freeman.
Sawtooth National Recreation Area. 2nd ed. Luther Linkhart. LC 87-40156. (Illus.). 224p. (Orig.). 1988. pap. 14.95. Wilderness Pr.
Sawtooth Tales. Dick D'Easum. LC 76-24379. (Illus.). 1977. pap. 7.95 (ISBN 0-87004-259-9). Caxton.
Sawyer Family. G. T. Ridlon. LC 75-138075. (Saco Valley Settlements Ser). 1970. pap. 3.00 (ISBN 0-8048-0832-5). C E Tuttle.
Sawyer on Audit Supervision: Student Workbook. Lawrence B. Sawyer. 1987. pap. text ed. 20.00 (ISBN 0-89413-169-9). Inst Inter Aud.
Sawyer on Audit Supervision: Videotapes (4) & Discussion Leader's Guide. Lawrence B. Sawyer. 1987. pap. text ed. 795.00 (ISBN 0-89413-170-2). Inst Inter Aud.
Sawyer on Internal Auditing: Student Workbook. Lawrence B. Sawyer. 1986. pap. text ed. 35.00 (ISBN 0-89413-154-0). Inst Inter Aud.
Sawyer on Internal Auditing: Videotapes (5) & Instructor's Guide. Lawrence B. Sawyer. 1986. pap. text ed. 905.00 (ISBN 0-89413-155-9). Inst Inter Aud.
Sawyer's Gas Turbine Engineering Handbooks, 3 Vols. 3rd ed. Ed. by John W. Sawyer & David Japikse. Set. 248.50 (ISBN 0-937506-13-3); Vol. 1: Theory & Design. 89.50 (ISBN 0-937506-14-1); Vol. 2: Selection & Application. 79.50 (ISBN 0-937506-15-X); Vol. 3: Accessories & Support. 79.50 (ISBN 0-937506-16-8). Turbo Intl Pubn.
Sawyer's Internal Auditing: The Practice of Modern Internal Auditing. rev. & enl. ed. Lawrence B. Sawyer & Glenn E. Sumners. 1300p. 1988. pap. text ed. 92.50 (ISBN 0-89413-178-8); instr's. guide avail. Inst Inter Aud.
Sawyer's Turbomachinery Maintenance Handbooks, 3 vols. Ed. by John W. Sawyer & Kurt Hallberg. LC 80-53539. (Illus.). 1060p. 1981. Set. 180.00x (ISBN 0-937506-03-6). Turbo Intl Pubn.
Sawyer's Turbomachinery Maintenance Handbook, Vol. I: Gas Turbines-Turbocompressors. Ed. by John W. Sawyer & Kurt Hallberg. (Illus.). 375p. 1980. 60.00x (ISBN 0-937506-01-X). Turbo Intl Pubn.
Sawyer's Turbomachinery Maintenance Handbook, Vol. III: Support Services & Equipment. Ed. by John W. Sawyer & Kurt Hallberg. (Illus.). 340p. 1981. 60.00x (ISBN 0-937506-02-8). Turbo Intl Pubn.
Sawyer's Turbomachinery Maintenance Handbook, Vol. II: Steam Turbines-Power Recovery Turbines. Ed. by John W. Sawyer & Kurt Hallberg. (Illus.). 350p. 1981. 60.00x (ISBN 0-937506-00-1). Turbo Intl Pubn.
Sax Company. Arthur Francia & Robert Strawser. 1988. pap. 5.95 (ISBN 0-256-06494-6). Irwin.
Saxa Loquuntur. J. J. Hondius. 169p. 1976. Repr. of 1938 ed. 15.00 (ISBN 0-89005-116-X). Ares.
Saxe Gallante; or, the Amorous Adventures & Intrigues of Frederick-Augustus 2. Karl L. Pollnitz. LC 78-170589. (Foundations of the Novel Ser.: Vol. 59). lib. bdg. 61.00 (ISBN 0-8240-0571-6). Garland Pub.
Saxe Holm's Stories, 2 vols. Helen H. Jackson. (Reprint of 1874 & 1878 eds.). 1972. Vol. 1 (First Ser.) lib. bdg. 16.00 (ISBN 0-8290-0660-5); Vol. 2 (Second Ser.) lib. bdg. 16.00 (ISBN 0-8290-0670-2). Irvington.
Saxe Holm's Stories, Vol. 1. Helen H. Jackson. (First Ser.). 1988. pap. text ed. 5.95x (ISBN 0-8290-2251-1). Irvington.
Saxe Holm's Stories, Vol. 2 (Second Ser.) Helen H. Jackson. 1986. pap. text ed. 5.95x (ISBN 0-8290-1946-4). Irvington.
Saxe Holm's Stories, First Series. Helen M. Jackson. LC 74-110225. (Short Story Index Reprint Ser.). 1873. 19.00 (ISBN 0-8369-3375-3). Ayer Co Pubs.

Saxe Holm's Stories, Second Series. facsimile ed. Helen H. Jackson. LC 74-110225. (Short Story Index Reprint Ser.). Repr. of 1878 ed. 18.00 (ISBN 0-8369-3817-8). Ayer Co Pubs.

Saxicolen Arten der Flechtengattung Rinodina in Europa. '. Mayrhofer & J. Poelt. (Bibliotheca Lichenologica: No. 12). (Illus., Ger.). 1979. lib. bdg. 36.00x (ISBN 3-7682-1237-8). Lubrecht & Cramer.

Saxifrages & Related Genera. Fritz Kohlein. (Illus.). 289p. 1985. 34.95 (ISBN 0-88192-008-8). Timber.

Saxo Grammaticus & the Life of Hamlet: A Translation, History, & Commentary. William F. Hansen. LC 82-2671. xvi, 206p. 1982. 18.95x (ISBN 0-8032-2318-8). U of Nebr Pr.

Saxo Grammaticus: I, Translation: The History of the Danes. Hilda E. Davidson & Peter Fisher. 303p. 1979. 51.00 (ISBN 0-85991-043-1, Pub. by Boydell & Brewer). Longwood Pub Group.

Saxo Grammaticus: II, Introduction & Commentary: The History of the Danes. Hilda E. Davidson & Peter Fisher. (Illus.). 225p. 1979. 51.00 (ISBN 0-85991-062-8, Pub. by Boydell & Brewer). Longwood Pub Group.

Saxo Grammaticus or First Aid for the Best Seller. Ernest Weekly. 1973. Repr. of 1930 ed. lib. bdg. 17.50 (ISBN 0-8414-9663-3). Folcroft.

Saxo: The First Nine Book of the Danish History of Saxo-Grammaticus. Tr. by Oliver Elton. (Folk-Lore Society, London, Monographs: Vol. 33). pap. 47.00 (ISBN 0-8115-0515-4). Kraus Repr.

Saxon England. John Hamilton & Alan Sorrell. LC 68-25985. (Illus.). (gr. 6-9). 1968. 13.95 (ISBN 0-8023-1149-0). Dufour.

Saxon House. George E. Burcaw. LC 79-65600. (GEM Books Ser.). (Illus.). 122p. (Orig.). 1980. pap. 5.95 (ISBN 0-89301-065-0). U of Idaho Pr.

Saxon Inheritance. Lillian Cheatham. 1988. pap. 2.95 (ISBN 0-449-44508-9, Crest). Fawcett.

Saxon Kings. Richard Humble. (Kings & Queens of England Ser.). (Illus.). 224p. 1980. 17.50x (ISBN 0-297-77784-X, GWN 03577, Pub. by Weidenfeld & Nicolson England). Biblio Dist.

Saxon Shore. David Rudkin. 1987. pap. 8.95 (ISBN 0-413-14100-4, 1046). Heinemann Ed.

Saxon Tithing-Men in America. Herbert B. Adams. LC 78-63734. (Johns Hopkins University. Studies in the Social Sciences. First Ser. 1882-1883: 4). Repr. of 1883 ed. 11.50 (ISBN 0-404-61004-8). AMS Pr.

Saxon Tithing-Men in America. Herbert B. Adams. pap. 9.00 (ISBN 0-384-00332-X). Johnson Repr.

Saxons. Tony D. Triggs. LC 79-93056. (Peoples of the Past Ser.). (Illus.). 61p. (gr. 4 up). 1985. PLB 13.96 (ISBN 0-317-31389-4). Silver.

Saxons in England, 2 Vols. rev. ed. John Kemble. Ed. by Walter D. Birch. LC 72-151600. Repr. of 1876 ed. 80.00 (ISBN 0-404-03647-3). AMS Pr.

Saxophone Soloists & Their Music, 1844-1985: An Annotated Bibliography. Harry R. Gee. LC 85-45537. 304p. 1986. 22.50x (ISBN 0-253-35091-3). Ind U Pr.

Sax's Songs. James Connolly. (Illus.). 1975. pap. 4.00 (ISBN 0-916906-05-1). Konglomerati.

SAY! Lyn Mandelbaum. (Illus.). 1982. soft cover, signed, & numbered 10.00 (ISBN 0-935694-02-1). St Edns.

Say a Fast Goodbye to Fat Forever! Mary E. McNeil. (Illus.). 272p. (Orig.). 1987. pap. 9.95 (ISBN 0-915451-08-5). New Start Pubns.

Say a Prayer for Me. Larry Craig. LC 87-71468. pap. 1.25 (ISBN 0-914904-30-4). ACTA Pubns.

Say Another One about How I Feel. Kathleen Pendergast. LC 81-90678. (Illus.). 54p. (Orig.). (gr. k-6). 1982. pap. 6.95 (ISBN 0-942178-00-9). Madison Park Pr.

Say Another One about My Family. Kathleen Pendergast. LC 82-61139. (Say Another One Ser.). (Illus.). 54p. (gr. k-6). 1982. pap. 6.95 (ISBN 0-942178-01-7). Madison Park Pr.

Say Another One about Playing. Kathleen Pendergast. LC 83-62129. (Say Another One Ser.). (Illus.). 54p. (gr. k-6). 1983. pap. 6.95 (ISBN 0-942178-02-5). Madison Park Pr.

Say Cheese. Betty Bates. LC 84-47837. (Illus.). 112p. (gr. 3-6). 1984. 12.95 (ISBN 0-8234-0540-0). Holiday.

Say Cheese! Carolyn Dinan. LC 85-40591. (Viking Kestrel Picture Bks.). (Illus.). 32p. (ps-3). 1986. 9.95 (ISBN 0-670-80954-3, Viking Kestrel). Viking.

Say "Cheese". Patricia R. Giff. (Kids of the Polk Street School Ser.). (Illus.). (ps-2). 1986. pap. 8.95 (ISBN 0-385-29501-4). Delacorte.

Say "Cheese", No. 10. Patricia R. Giff. (Kids of the Polk Street School Ser.). (Illus.). (gr. 6-9). 1985. pap. 2.50 (ISBN 0-440-47639-9, YB). Dell.

Say Cheese & Milk Please. Marjorie A. Fontana & Jean L. Larson. LC 78-67289. (Illus.). 62p. (Orig.). 1978. 7.95 (ISBN 0-9603596-0-5); pap. 5.95 (ISBN 0-9603596-1-3). Fontastic.

Say Cheesecake & Smile. 2nd rev. ed. Elvira Monroe. LC 80-54453. (Illus.). 176p. 1983. pap. 6.95 (ISBN 0-933174-17-9). Wide World-Tetra.

Say Good-Bye to PMS: The Step-by-Step Guide That Lets You Help Yourself. Barbara Kass-Annese & Hal Danzer. 128p. 1987. pap. 3.95 (ISBN 0-446-30281-3). Warner Bks.

Say Good Night. Barbara Gregorich. Ed. by Joan Hoffman. (Start to Read! Ser.). (Illus.). 16p. (Orig.). (gr. k-2). 1984. pap. 1.95 (ISBN 0-88743-010-4, 06010). Sch Zone Pub Co.

Say Good Night! Harriet Ziefert. (Hello Reading Ser.). (Illus.). 32p. 1987. 7.95 (ISBN 0-670-81722-8); pap. 2.95 (ISBN 0-14-050747-7). Viking.

Say Goodbye. Created by Francine Pascal. (Sweet Valley High Ser.: No. 23). 160p. (Orig.). 1985. pap. 2.75 (ISBN 0-553-26689-6). Bantam.

Say Goodbye to Sam. Michael J. Arlen. LC 84-48378. 231p. 1984. 12.95 (ISBN 0-374-25409-5). FS&G.

Say Goodbye to Sam. Michael J. Arlen. (Contemporary American Fiction Ser.). 246p. 1985. pap. 6.95 (ISBN 0-14-008224-7). Penguin.

Say Goodnight. Helen Oxenbury. (Macmillan Big Board Bks.). 10p. (ps). 1987. bds. 4.95 (ISBN 0-02-769010-5, Aladdin Bks). Macmillan.

Say Goodnight! Harriet Ziefert. (Hello Reading Ser.). (Illus.). (ps-3). Date not set. 7.95 (ISBN 0-317-62548-9, Viking Kestrel); pap. 2.95 (ISBN 0-317-62549-7). Viking.

Say Goodnight, Gracie. Julie R. Deaver. LC 87-45278. (Charlotte Zolotow Book). 224p. (YA) (gr. 7 up). 1988. 12.95i (ISBN 0-06-021418-X); PLB 12.89 (ISBN 0-06-021419-8). HarpJ.

Say Hello to the Care Bear Cousins. David Polter. (Illus.). 64p. (ps-3). 1985. pap. 2.95 (ISBN 0-394-87114-6, BYR). Random.

Say Hello to the Hit Man. Jay Bennett. 144p. (gr. 7 up). 1981. pap. 1.95 (ISBN 0-440-97618-9, LFL). Dell.

Say Hello, Vanessa. Majorie W. Sharmat. LC 79-1511. (Illus.). 32p. (gr. k-3). 1979. reinforced bdg. 7.95 (ISBN 0-8234-0354-8). Holiday.

Say Hey: The Autobiography of Willie Mays. Willie Mays & Lou Sahadi. 1988. 17.95 (ISBN 0-671-63292-2). S&S.

Say, Is This the U. S. A. M. Bourke-White & E. Caldwell. LC 77-9598. (Photography Ser.). (Illus.). 1977. lib. bdg. 35.00 (ISBN 0-306-77434-8); pap. 8.95 (ISBN 0-306-80071-3). Da Capo.

Say It. Roland Flint. LC 78-5149. 1979. pap. 5.95 (ISBN 0-931848-21-0). Dryad Pr.

Say It! Charlotte Zolotow. LC 79-25115. (Illus.). 24p. (gr. k-3). 1980. 11.75 (ISBN 0-688-80276-1); PLB 11.88 (ISBN 0-688-84276-3). Greenwillow.

Say It Ain't So Joe! The True Story of Shoeless Joe Jackson & the 1919 World Series. Donald Gropman. (Illus.). 1988. pap. 3.95 (ISBN 1-55802-392-5). Lynx Bks.

Say it Clearly: Exercises & Activities for Oral Communication. Susan L. English. 319p. 1988. pap. write for info. Macmillan.

Say-It-Faith. Elmer L. Towns. 1983. pap. 5.95 (ISBN 0-8423-5825-0). Tyndale.

Say It Graciously. Marion Boyd. 40p. 1984. pap. 3.00 s.p. (ISBN 0-88053-321-8, S-296). Macoy Pub.

Say It in Another Language: Phrases in Spanish, French, Japanese, Swahili, & German. Lore S. Bonar et al. 16p. (YA) (gr. 7 up). 1976. pap. text ed. 3.75 pkg. of 20 (ISBN 0-88441-414-0, 26-814). Girl Scouts USA.

Say It in Arabic. Farouk El-Baz. pap. 3.00 (ISBN 0-486-22026-5). Dover.

Say It in Chinese. Nancy D. Lay. (Say It Ser.). (Orig.). 1980. pap. 3.50 (ISBN 0-486-23325-1). Dover.

Say It in Czech. Milan Fryscak. LC 76-173447. (Orig.). 1973. pap. text ed. 3.50 (ISBN 0-486-21538-5). Dover.

Say It in Danish. Gerda M. Andersen. (Orig.). pap. 2.50 (ISBN 0-486-20818-4). Dover.

Say It in Dutch. Anna M. Hunningher. (Orig.). pap. 2.95 (ISBN 0-486-20817-6). Dover.

Say It in Finnish. Aili Flint. (Language & Linguistics Ser.). 192p. (Orig.). 1984. pap. 3.50 (ISBN 0-486-24591-8). Dover.

Say It in French. Leon J. Cohen. (Orig.). pap. 2.50 (ISBN 0-486-20803-6). Dover.

Say It in French. Leon J. Cohen. LC 55-13819. 1962. lib. bdg. 8.50x (ISBN 0-88307-555-5). Gannon.

Say It in German. Gustave Mathieu & Guy Stern. (Orig.). 1957. pap. 2.95 (ISBN 0-486-20804-4). Dover.

Say It in Hindi. Veena T. Oldenburg. (Say It Ser.). 192p. (Orig.). 1981. pap. 3.50 (ISBN 0-486-23959-4). Dover.

Say It in Hungarian. Juliette Victor-Rood. (Say It In Ser.). (Illus.). 224p. (Orig.). 1983. pap. 3.50 (ISBN 0-486-24423-7). Dover.

Say It in Indonesian: Malay. John U. Wolff. (Language & Linguistics Ser.). 192p. (Orig.). 1983. pap. 3.50 (ISBN 0-486-24424-5). Dover.

Say It in Italian. Olga Ragusa. pap. 2.50 (ISBN 0-486-20806-0). Dover.

Say It in Japanese. Miwa Kai. (Say It Ser.). 220p. (Orig.). 1984. pap. 3.00 (ISBN 0-486-20807-9). Dover.

Say It in Modern Greek. George Pappageotes. 1956. pap. 2.75 (ISBN 0-486-20813-3). Dover.

Say It in Modern Greek. George Pappageotes. LC 57-804. 1956. lib. bdg. 8.50x (ISBN 0-88307-559-8). Gannon.

Say It in Modern Hebrew. Aleeza Cerf. (Orig.). pap. 2.95 (ISBN 0-486-20805-2). Dover.

Say It in Norwegian. Samuel Abrahamsen. (Orig.). 1957. pap. 2.50 (ISBN 0-486-20814-1). Dover.

Say It in Polish. Victor Raysman. (Orig.). 1954. pap. 2.75 (ISBN 0-486-20808-7). Dover.

Say It in Portuguese. M. M. Mickle & Francisco Da Costa. (Orig.). 1954. pap. 2.50 (ISBN 0-486-20809-5). Dover.

Say It in Portuguese (Continental Usage) Alexander R. Prista. LC 77-73311. 1979. pap. 2.95 (ISBN 0-486-23676-5). Dover.

Say It in Russian. N. C. Stepanoff & Michael S. Flier. (Say It In...Ser.). 256p. (gr. 6 up). pap. 2.95 (ISBN 0-486-20810-9). Dover.

Say It in Serbo-Croatian. Produced by Vasa D. Mihailovich. (Say It Ser.). 160p. 1987. pap. 3.50 (ISBN 0-486-25261-2). Dover.

Say It in Sign: A Workbook of Sign Language Exercises. Carol B. Carpenter & Sue F. Rakow. (Illus.). 266p. 1983. pap. 24.00x spiral (ISBN 0-398-04779-0). C C Thomas.

Say It in Spanish. Leon J. Cohen & A. C. Rogers. (Orig.). 1951. pap. 2.50 (ISBN 0-486-20811-7). Dover.

Say It in Swahili. Sharifa M. Zawawi. (Say It Language Ser.). 205p. (Orig.). 1972. pap. 2.95 (ISBN 0-486-22792-8). Dover.

Say It in Swedish. Kerstin Norris. LC 72-94755. 1979. pap. 2.95 (ISBN 0-486-20812-5). Dover.

Say It in Turkish. Jeanne M. Blackburn & Refah Seniz. (Orig.). pap. 2.50 (ISBN 0-486-20821-4). Dover.

Say It in Yiddish. Uriel Weinreich & Beatrice Weinreich. (Orig.). pap. 2.95 (ISBN 0-486-20815-X). Dover.

Say It Naturally. Allie P. Wall. 288p. 1987. pap. text ed. write for info. (ISBN 0-03-002873-6). HR&W.

Say it, Spirit. Geraldine B. Sheard. 128p. 1987. 8.95 (ISBN 0-8062-2917-9). Carlton.

Say It with Charts: The Executive's Guide to Successful Presentations. Gene Zelazny. LC 83-73367. 150p. 1985. 22.50 (ISBN 0-87094-533-5). Dow Jones-Irwin.

Say It with Figures. rev. ed. Hans Zeisel. LC 84-48207. (Illus.). 256p. 1985. 14.00i (ISBN 0-06-181982-4, HarpT). Har-Row.

Say It with Figures. 6th ed. Hans Zeisel. LC 84-48207. (Illus.). 256p. 1985. pap. 7.95x (ISBN 0-06-131994-5, TB1994, TORCH). Har-Row.

Say It with Flowers. Beverly Parkin. 48p. 5.95 (ISBN 0-85648-496-2). Lion USA.

Say It with Hands. Louie J. Fant, Jr. (Illus.). 1964. 8.50 (ISBN 0-913072-02-8). Natl Assn Deaf.

Say It with Love. Howard G. Hendricks. LC 72-77011. 143p. 1972. pap. 5.95 (ISBN 0-88207-050-9). Victor Bks.

Say It with Sign: Silent Network. 208p. 1982. pap. text ed. 19.95 (ISBN 0-8403-2863-X). Kendall-Hunt.

Say It with Words. Charles W. Ferguson. LC 59-8085. x, 219p. 1969. pap. 4.95x (ISBN 0-8032-5058-4, BB 395, Bison). U of Nebr Pr.

Say Jesus & Come to Me. Ann Shockley. 288p. 1985. pap. 2.95 (ISBN 0-380-79657-0, 79657-0, Bard). Avon.

Say Jesus & Come to Me. Ann A. Shockley. 288p. 1987. pap. 8.95 (ISBN 0-930044-98-3). Naiad Pr.

Say Kids! What Time Is It? Notes from the Peanut Gallery. Stephen Davis. (Illus.). 240p. 1987. 16.45 (ISBN 0-316-17662-1). Little.

Say No to Cancer. Barbara Waters. LC 83-90862. (Illus.). 453p. (Orig.). 1984. pap. 12.00 (ISBN 0-930107-01-2). Waters Pub.

Say No to Murder. Nancy Pickard. 1988. pap. 3.50 (ISBN 0-671-66396-8). PB.

Say "No!" to Violence. Mary Maracek. (Illus.). 50p. Date not set. 4.50. Morning Glory.

Say That the River Turns: The Impact of Gwendolyn Brooks. Ed. by Haki R. Madhubuti. (Orig.). 1987. pap. 8.95 (ISBN 0-88378-117-4). Third World.

Say the Right Thing! C. Meloni & S. Thompson. 1982. text ed. write for info. (ISBN 0-201-10205-6, World Lanuage Div). Addison-Wesley.

Say These Names (Remember Them) Betty S. Cummings. LC 84-11422. 300p. 1984. 14.95 (ISBN 0-910923-15-9). Pineapple Pr.

Say Uncle. Dick Jewett. (Quest Ser.). 32p. 1982. pap. 1.25 (ISBN 0-8163-0489-0). Pacific Pr Pub Assn.

Say What You Mean: The Sentence, Bk 1. John Gehlmann & Philip Eisman. LC 66-19065. 1967. scp 7.64 (ISBN 0-672-73232-7). Odyssey Pr.

Say When. Felix Pollak. (Juniper Bk.: No. 2). 1969. pap. 5.00 (ISBN 1-55780-001-4). Juniper Pr WI.

Say Yes to Life: Daily Meditations for Recovery. Leo Booth. 1987. pap. 6.95 (ISBN 0-932194-46-X). Health Comm.

Say "Yes" to Success: The Wellness Way to Living. Candace I. Jennings. LC 83-51482. 160p. 1983. pap. 15.95 spiral bd. (ISBN 0-934104-05-0). Woodland.

Say Yes to Your Potential. Skip Ross & Carole C. Carlson. 166p. 1985. pap. 6.95 (ISBN 0-8499-3014-6, 3014-6). Word Bks.

Say You Love Satan. David St. Clair. (Orig.). 1987. pap. 3.95 (ISBN 0-440-17574-7). Dell.

Say You Want Me. Richard Cohen. LC 88-4492. 268p. 1988. 17.95 (ISBN 0-939149-12-5). Soho Press.

Sayahane Urupani dar Iran see European Travelers to Iran: From the Earliest Times to the 17th Century.

Saybrook at the Mouth of the Connecticut River: The First One Hundred Years. Gilman C. Gates. 1935. 59.50x (ISBN 0-685-89040-6). Elliots Bks.

Sayeh yi Omr. Rahi Mo'ayeri. 246p. (Orig., Persian.). 1986. pap. 10.00x. Iran Bks.

Sayeh yi Omr: (Shadow of Life) Rahi Moayeri. (Illus.). 246p. (Orig., Persian, Old.). 1988. pap. 10.00. Iran Bks.

Sayer & Bennett's Catalogue of Prints for 1775. (Illus.). xvi, 216p. 1970. Repr. of 1770 ed. 20.00 (ISBN 0-686-30085-8). Oak Knoll.

Saying & Meaning in Puerto Rico: Some Problems in the Ethnography of Discourse. Marshall Morris. (Language & Communication Library: Vol. 1). 186p. 1981. text ed. 26.00 (ISBN 0-08-025822-0). Pergamon.

Saying Good-Bye: A Manager's Guide to Employee Dismissal. Paula Michal-Johnson. 144p. 1985. pap. 7.95 (ISBN 0-673-15843-8). Scott F.

Saying Good-bye to Grandma. Jane R. Thomas. LC 87-20826. (Illus.). 48p. (gr. 1-4). 1988. 13.95 (ISBN 0-89919-645-4, Pub. by Clarion). Ticknor & Fields.

Saying Goodbye. Darlene Ellison. (Illus.). 138p. (Orig.). 1981. pap. 6.95 (ISBN 0-9604344-6-1). Sunrise Pub OR.

Saying Goodbye: Ending a Group Experience. Lois B. Hart. LC 83-82678. 100p. (Orig.). 1983. spiral bdg. 16.95 (ISBN 0-911777-02-4). Leadership Dyn.

Saying Goodbye to Loneliness & Finding Intimacy. Craig W. Ellison. LC 82-48927. Orig. Title: Loneliness. 240p. (Orig.). 1983. pap. 7.95 (ISBN 0-06-062242-3, RD/456, HarpR). Har-Row.

Saying Hello: Getting your Group Started. Lois B. Hart. LC 82-91013. (Illus.). 153p. 1983. spiral bdg. 16.95 (ISBN 0-911777-00-8). Leadership Dyn.

Saying I'm Sorry. Laura Alden. LC 82-19945. (What's in a Word Ser.). (Illus.). 32p. (gr. 1-2). 1983. PLB 7.95 (ISBN 0-89565-247-1). Childs World.

Saying I'm Sorry. Laura Alden. LC 82-19945. (What's In a Word Ser.). (Illus.). 32p. (ps-2). 1983. 11.93 (ISBN 0-516-06324-3). Childrens.

Saying Is Believing: Developing Credential Speeches. James E. Jones. 272p. 1979. pap. text ed. 16.95 (ISBN 0-8403-3341-2, 40334102). Kendall-Hunt.

Saying It Aint So: American Values As Revealed in Children's Baseball Stories 1880-1950. Debra A. Dagavarian. (American University Studies: Series XI: Anthropology & Sociology, Vol. 16). 223p. 1988. text ed. 32.50 (ISBN 0-8204-0583-3). P Lang Pubs.

Saying It Straight: Writing by Ordinary People. Ed. by Clark Sturges. LC 83-73469. 155p. (Orig.). 1984. pap. 8.95 (ISBN 0-915685-01-9). Devil Mountain Bks.

Saying My Name Out Loud. Arthur Dobrin. (Illus.). 1978. pap. 2.50 (ISBN 0-918870-05-4); signed & numbered ed. 3.50 (ISBN 0-918870-06-2). Pleasure Dome.

Saying No. Sally Jordan. (Weathering Storms Ser.). (Illus.). 32p. (gr. 5-9). 1986. saddle stitch 0.79 (ISBN 0-87403-040-4, 3538). Standard Pub.

Saying No. Ann E. Steinke. (Cheerleaders Ser.: No. 33). 176p. (Orig.). (gr. 7 up). 1987. pap. 2.50 (ISBN 0-590-41010-5). Scholastic Inc.

Saying "No" Its Meaning in Child Development, Psychoanalysis, Linguistics & Hegel. Wilfried Ver Eecke. LC 84-1617. 224p. 1984. text ed. 23.00x (ISBN 0-8207-0169-6); pap. text ed. 15.00x (ISBN 0-8207-0171-8). Duquesne.

Saying No to Alcohol. Nancy Abbey & Ellen Wagman. Ed. by Mary Nelson. (Illus.). 72p. 1987. tchrs. ed. 11.95 (ISBN 0-941816-37-0). Network Pubns.

Saying No to Marijuana. Nancy Abbey & Ellen Wagman. Ed. by Mary Nelson. (Illus.). 72p. 1987. tchrs. ed. 11.95 (ISBN 0-941816-39-7). Network Pubns.

Saying No to Tobacco. Nancy Abbey & Ellen Wagman. Ed. by Mary Nelson. (Illus.). 72p. 1987. tchrs. ed. 11.95 (ISBN 0-941816-38-9). Network Pubns.

Saying No When You'd Rather Say Yes. Gene A. Getz. LC 87-4961. (Measure of...Ser.). 200p. 1983. pap. 6.95 (ISBN 0-8307-1205-4, 5419099). Regal.

Saying Please. Jane B. Moncure. LC 82-19927. (What's in a Word Ser.). (Illus.). 32p. (ps-2). 1983. PLB 7.95 (ISBN 0-89565-248-X). Childs World.

Saying Please. Jane B. Moncure. LC 82-19927. (What's In a Word? Ser.). (Illus.). 32p. (ps-2). 1983. 11.93 (ISBN 0-516-06325-1). Childrens.

Saying Rhymes. (Tiny Tots Rhymes Ser.). (ps). 1982. 2.95 (ISBN 0-86112-087-6). Borden.

Saying Thank You. Colleen L. Reece. LC 82-21992. (What's in a Word Ser.). (Illus.). 32p. (gr. 1-2). 1983. PLB 7.95 (ISBN 0-89565-249-8). Childs World.

Saying Thank You. Colleen L. Reece. LC 82-21992. (What's In a Word Ser.). (Illus.). 32p. (ps-2). 1983. 11.93 (ISBN 0-516-06326-X). Childrens.

Saying Thank You Makes Me Happy. Wanda Hayes. (Happy Day Bks.). (Illus.). 24p. (gr. k-3). 1979. 1.59 (ISBN 0-87239-353-4, 3623). Standard Pub.

Saying What You Mean: A Common Sense Guide to American Usage. Robert Claiborne. 272p. 1987. pap. 3.95 (ISBN 0-345-34705-6). Ballantine.

Saying What You Mean: A Commonsense Guide to American Usage. Robert Claiborne. 1986. 16.95 (ISBN 0-393-02312-5). Norton.

Saying Yes. Caroline B. Cooney. (Cheerleaders Ser.: No. 30). 176p. (Orig.). (YA) (gr. 10 up). 1987. pap. 2.50 (ISBN 0-590-40635-3). Scholastic Inc.

Saying Yes & Saying No: On Rendering to God & Caesar. Robert M. Brown. LC 85-29575. 144p. (Orig.). 1986. pap. 7.95 (ISBN 0-664-24695-8). Westminster John Knox.

Saying Yes, Saying No: You & Drugs--A Positive Approach to Staying Drug Free. Community Intervention, Inc. Staff. 24p. (Orig.). (YA) (gr. 8-12). 1986. pap. 2.95 (ISBN 0-9613416-4-5). Comm Intervention.

Sayings & Doings. Wendell Berry. LC 75-39229. 1975. 5.00 (ISBN 0-917788-03-6). Gnomon Pr.

Sayings & Doings of Pai-Chang. Tr. by Thomas Cleary. LC 78-21228. (Zen Writings Ser.: Vol. 6). 1979. pap. 5.95 (ISBN 0-916820-10-6). Center Pubns.

Sayings & Riddles in New Mexico. Arthur L. Campa. LC 37-28299. 67p. 1982. lib. bdg. 22.95x (ISBN 0-89370-731-7). Borgo Pr.

Sayings & Stories. Marcia Cebulska. (Literacy Volunteers of America Readers Ser.). 32p. (Orig.). 1983. pap. 1.95 (ISBN 0-8428-9622-8). Cambridge Bk.

Sayings from Old Smoky. Joseph S. Hall. (Illus.). 1972. pap. 4.50 (ISBN 0-9600168-1-3). Hall J.

Sayings of Buddha. K. R. Moore. 159p. 1982. 15.95x. Coronet Bks.

Sayings of Buddha: The Iti-Vuttaka. Itivuttaka. LC 9-4569. (Columbia University. Indo-Iranian Ser.: No. 5). Repr. of 1908 ed. 16.50 (ISBN 0-404-50475-2). AMS Pr.

Sayings of Chairman Lee. Bill Adler. 142p. 1987. cancelled (ISBN 0-88184-302-4). Carroll & Graf.

Sayings of Confucius. Confucius. Tr. by James R. Ware. (Orig.). pap. 2.95 (ISBN 0-451-62168-9, Ment). NAL.

Sayings of Jesus. Edward Dumbauld. (Illus.). 196p. 1988. pap. text ed. 10.75 (ISBN 0-8191-6753-3). U Pr of Amer.

Sayings of Jesus in the Pseudo-Clementine Homilies. Leslie L. Kline. LC 75-1645. (Society of Biblical Literature. Dissertation Ser.: No. 14). Repr. of 1975 ed. 52.00 (ISBN 0-8357-9579-9, 2017517). Bks Demand UMI.

Sayings of K'ung the Master. Allen Upward. LC 78-64056. (Des Imagistes: Literature of the Imagist Movement). Repr. of 1904 ed. 11.00 (ISBN 0-404-17110-9). AMS Pr.

Sayings of Mahatma Gandhi. Mahatma Gandhi. Ed. by Peter H. Burgess. (Illus.). 99p. 1984. pap. 8.00 (ISBN 9971-947-65-X, Pub. by Graham Brash Singapore). Three Continents.

Sayings of Muhammad. G. Ahmad. 8.25 (ISBN 0-87902-036-9). Orientalia.

Sayings of Muhammad. Ghazi Ahmad. pap. 2.00 (ISBN 0-686-18342-8). Kazi Pubns.

Sayings of Muhammad. Allama Sir Abdullah al-Mamun alsuhrawardy. LC 79-52559. (Islam Ser.). 1980. Repr. of 1941 ed. lib. bdg. 12.00x (ISBN 0-8369-9266-0). Ayer Co Pubs.

Sayings of Muhammad, the Last Prophet. S. A. Hussain. pap. 1.25 (ISBN 0-686-18340-1). Kazi Pubns.

Sayings of Paramahansa Yogananda. Paramahansa Yogananda & Self-Realization Fellowship Editorial Staff. LC 79-66287. (Illus.). 136p. 1980. 4.95 (ISBN 0-87612-115-6); Italian ed. 4.00x (ISBN 0-87612-113-X); German ed. 7.50x (ISBN 0-87612-114-8); Spanish ed. 2.25x (ISBN 0-87612-111-3); Icelandic ed. 9.00x (ISBN 0-87612-112-1). Self Realization.

Sayings of Poor Richard: The Prefaces, Proverbs & Poems of Benjamin Franklin. Benjamin Franklin. Compiled by Paul Leicester. LC 74-23378. 1975. Repr. of 1890 ed. 24.50 (ISBN 0-8337-1198-9). B Franklin.

Sayings of Shigeo Shingo: Key Strategies for Plant Improvement. Shigeo Shingo. Tr. by Andrew P. Dillon from Japanese. (Japanese Management Ser.). (Illus.). 295p. 1987. 36.95 (ISBN 0-915299-15-1). Prod Press.

Sayings of Sri Ramakrishna. Sri Ramakrishna. 3.95 (ISBN 0-87481-431-6). Vedanta Pr.

Sayings of the Ancient One. Patrick G. Bowen. lib. bdg. 79.95 (ISBN 0-87968-490-9). Krishna Pr.

Sayings of the Desert Fathers. (Cistercian Studies: No. 59). pap. 7.95 (ISBN 0-87907-859-6). Cistercian Pubns.

Sayings of the Fathers. E. A. Budge. 1975. pap. 5.95 (ISBN 0-686-10941-4). Eastern Orthodox.

Sayings of the Hour. Salvatore Cipparone. 4.95 (ISBN 0-686-20575-8). Ivory Scroll.

Sayings of the Jewish Fathers, 2 Vols. in 1. rev. ed. Charles Taylor. (Library of Jewish Classics). 1969. 35.00x (ISBN 0-87068-114-1). Ktav.

Sayings of the Jewish Fathers. Charles W. Taylor. 59.95 (ISBN 0-8490-0995-2). Gordon Pr.

Sayings of the Prophet Muhammad: English-Arabic. (Hadith Qudsi). 1982. 8.50x (ISBN 0-86685-285-9). Intl Bk Ctr.

Sayings Traditions in the Apocryphon of James. Ron Cameron. LC 84-45189. (Harvard Theological Studies). 160p. 1984. pap. 12.95 (ISBN 0-8006-7015-9). Fortress.

Sayonara. James A. Michener. 1983. pap. 2.95 (ISBN 0-449-20414-6, Crest). Fawcett.

Sayonara. James A. Michener. 1954. 19.45 (ISBN 0-394-44385-3). Random.

Sayonara, Sweet Amaryllis. James Melville. 160p. 1985. 10.95 (ISBN 0-312-69995-6). St Martin.

Sayonara, Sweet Amaryllis. James Melville. 208p. 1987. pap. 2.95 (ISBN 0-449-20825-7, Crest). Fawcett.

Says I, Says He. Ron Hutchinson. (Phoenix Theatre Ser.). 1980. pap. 6.95x (ISBN 0-912262-69-9). Proscenium.

Say's Law: An Historical Analysis. Thomas Sowell. LC 78-38515. 248p. 1972. 31.00x (ISBN 0-691-04166-0). Princeton U Pr.

Sayula Popoluca Verb Derivation. Lawrence Clark. (Language Data, Amerindian Ser.: No. 8). 80p. (Orig.). 1983. pap. 8.50x (ISBN 0-88312-616-8); microfiche 2.00 (ISBN 0-88312-508-0). Summer Inst Ling.

Sayyid Jamal Ad-Din "Al-Afghani" A Political Biography. Nikki R. Keddie. LC 74-159671. (Near Eastern Center, UCLA: No. 10). 520p. 1972. 44.50x (ISBN 0-520-01986-5). U of Cal Pr.

SBBA Stud Book. Spanish Barb Breeders Association. 72p. 1983. 25.00 (ISBN 0-318-16921-5); pap. 12.50 (ISBN 0-318-16922-3). Sp Barb Breeders.

SBC's One Hundred & One Laws--& Perhaps More. Austin M. Elliott. 109p. 1984. 101.00 (ISBN 0-914285-00-9). Sm Busn Clinic.

SBD Dauntless in Action. Robert Stern. Ed. by Jerry Campbell. (Aircraft in Action Ser.). (Illus.). 50p. (Orig.). 1984. pap. 4.95 (ISBN 0-89747-153-9). Squad Sig Pubns.

Sbornik Detskij, Tysacha Let (988-1988) Sophie Koulomzin. (Rus.). (gr. 2-4). 1985. write for info. RBR.

Sbornik P'es Dlia Zhizni Solo: Stikhi. Aleksei Tsvetkov. 1978. 18.50 (ISBN 0-88233-347-X); pap. 4.00 (ISBN 0-88233-348-8). Ardis Pubs.

Sbornik Statei. V. Mire Leskova. 368p. 1983. 39.00x (Pub. by Collets UK). State Mutual Bk.

Sborniki Dukhovno-Muzikal'nikh Proizvjedenij Borisa Mikhajlovicha Ledkovskago, 3 Vols. 1972. Vol. 1, 47p. 5.00 (ISBN 0-317-30399-6); Vol. 2, 88p. 8.00 (ISBN 0-317-30400-3); Vol. 3, 185p. 15.00 (ISBN 0-317-30401-1). Holy Trinity.

SB2C Helldiver in Action. Rob Stern. (Aircraft in Action Ser.). (Illus.). 50p. 1982. saddlestitch 4.95 (ISBN 0-89747-128-8, 1054). Squad Sig Pubns.

Scab. Jack London. (Illus.). 55p. 1984. pap. 1.95 (ISBN 0-932458-23-8). Star Rover.

Scabbardless Sword: Criminal Justice & the Quality of Mercy. Harold A. Buetow. LC 82-71695. (New Studies on Law & Society). 390p. (Orig.). 1982. 37.50x (ISBN 0-86733-022-8); pap. 17.50x (ISBN 0-86733-048-1). Assoc Faculty Pr.

Scabies. K. Mellanby. 87p. 1972. 20.00x (ISBN 0-317-07173-4, Pub. by FW Classey UK). State Mutual Bk.

Scaffold. Chingiz Aitmatov. Tr. by Natasha Ward from Rus. 352p. 1989. 18.95 (ISBN 0-8021-1000-2). Grove.

Scaffold. Edward Lurie. 304p. 1986. 19.95x (ISBN 0-86232-600-1, Pub. by Zed Pr England); pap. 7.95 (ISBN 0-86232-601-X, Pub. by Zed Pr England). Humanities.

Scaffold Falsework Design to BS 5975. Murray Grant. (Viewpoint Publication Ser.). (Illus.). 1982. pap. text ed. 17.95x (ISBN 0-86310-005-8, Pub. by Palladian). Scholium Intl.

Scaffolding: New & Selected Poems. Jane Cooper. 144p. (Orig.). 1985. pap. 8.95 (ISBN 0-85646-106-7, Pub. by Anvil Pr Poetry). Longwood Pub Group.

Scagel: The Man & his Knives. Harry McEvoy. (Illus.). 28p. 1985. 3.00 (ISBN 0-940362-09-0). Knife World.

Scalable Choice Models. Tony E. Smith. (Discussion Paper Ser.: No. 84). 1975. pap. 5.50 (ISBN 0-686-32250-9). Regional Sci Res Inst.

Scalacronica: A Chronicle of England & Scotland from A.D. 1066 to A. D. 1362. Thomas Gray. Ed. by Joseph Stevenson. LC 70-168186. (Maitland Club. Glasgow. Publications: No. 40). Repr. of 1836 ed. 47.50 (ISBN 0-404-53015-X). AMS Pr.

Scalded to Death by the Steam. Katie L. Lyle. LC 88-830. (Illus.). 214p. 1988. pap. 9.95 (ISBN 0-945575-01-7). Algonquin Bks.

Scalded to Death by the Steam: Authentic Stories of Railroad Disasters & the Ballads That Were Written about Them. Katie Lyle. (Illus.). 212p. 1983. 22.50 (ISBN 0-912697-01-6). Algonquin Bks.

Scale Aircraft Drawings, Vol. 1, WW I. Model Airplane News Staff. 154p. 1986. pap. 12.95 (ISBN 0-911295-02-X). Air Age.

Scale & Arpeggio Studies. Gaylord Yost. 3.50 (ISBN 0-913650-52-8). Columbia Pictures.

Scale & Conformal Symmetry in Hadron Physics. Ed. by R. Gatto. LC 73-4324. pap. 60.00 (ISBN 0-317-09058-5, 2011957). Bks Demand UMI.

Scale Effects in Animal Locomotion. Ed. by T. J. Pedley. 1977. 118.50 (ISBN 0-12-549650-8). Acad Pr.

Scale for Measuring the Antero-Posterior Posture of Ninth Grade Boys. C. L. Brownell. LC 74-176601. (Columbia University. Teachers College. Contributions to Education: No. 325). Repr. of 1928 ed. 22.50 (ISBN 0-404-55325-7). AMS Pr.

Scale in Architecture. Frank Orr. (Illus., Orig.). 1985. pap. 24.95 (ISBN 0-442-27245-6). Van Nos Reinhold.

Scale in Production Systems: Based on an IIASA Workshop June 26-29, 1979. Ed. by J. A. Buzacott et al. (IIASA Proceedings: Vol. 15). (Illus.). 256p. 1982. 73.00 (ISBN 0-08-028725-5). Pergamon.

Scale Insects of Central Europe. M. Kosztarab & F. Kozar. (Entomologica Ser.). 1987. lib. bdg. 112.00 (ISBN 90-6193-623-3, Pub. by Junk Pubs Netherlands). Kluwer Academic.

Scale Model Aircraft from Vac-Form Kits. Hugh Markham. 1980. 25.00x (ISBN 0-905418-34-4, Pub. by Gresham England). State Mutual Bk.

Scale Model Aircraft in Wood. V. J. Woodason. 64p. 1980. 25.00x (ISBN 0-905418-27-1, Pub. by Gresham England). State Mutual Bk.

Scale-Model Airplanes. Don Berliner. LC 81-17120. (Superwheels & Thrill Sports Bks.). (Illus.). (gr. 4-9). 1982. PLB 8.95 (ISBN 0-8225-0446-4). Lerner Pubns.

Scale Model Electric Tramways & How to Model Them. E. Jackson Stevens. (Illus.). 196p. 1986. 24.95 (ISBN 0-7153-8632-8). David & Charles.

Scale Model of Human Surface Anatomy & Musculature. Leon Schlossberg. 1979. 39.50 (ISBN 0-8018-2165-7). Johns Hopkins.

Scale Model Sailing Ships. Ed. by John Bowen. (Illus.). 1978. 12.95 (ISBN 0-8317-7700-1, Mayflower Bks). Smith Pubs.

Scale Model Warships. Ed. by John Bowen. LC 78-25641. (Illus.). 1979. 12.95 (ISBN 0-8317-7702-8, Mayflower Bks). Smith Pubs.

Scale Models in Engineering: Fundamentals & Applications. 2nd ed. Dieterich J. Schuring. 1977. pap. text ed. 25.00 (ISBN 0-08-020860-6). Pergamon.

Scale of Perfection & the English Mystical Tradition. Joseph E. Milosh. LC 66-22857. pap. 56.50 (ISBN 0-317-07863-1, 2010975). Bks Demand UMI.

Scale of Performance Tests. Rudolf Pintner & Donald G. Paterson. 1978. Repr. of 1925 ed. lib. bdg. 30.00 (ISBN 0-8492-2154-4). R West.

Scale Operator. Jack Rudman. (Career Examination Ser.: C-3008). (Cloth bdg. avail. on request). 1988. pap. 14.00 (ISBN 0-8373-3008-4). Natl Learning.

Scale Problems in Hydrology. Ed. by V. K. Gupta et al. 1986. lib. bdg. 39.50 (ISBN 90-277-2258-7, Pub. by Reidel Holland). Kluwer Academic.

Scale Removal. Wire Association International. 15.00 (ISBN 0-318-03183-3, 7514). Wire Assn Intl.

Scale Studies for Violin. J. Hrimaly. (Carl Fischer Music Library: No. 114). 1900. pap. 4.50 (ISBN 0-8258-0020-X, L114). Fischer Inc NY.

Scale Studies for Violin. Henry Schradieck. Ed. by Saenger. (Carl Fischer Music Library: No. 641). pap. 6.00 (ISBN 0-8258-0085-4, L641). Fischer Inc NY.

Scale Studies for Violin: Appendix to H. Schradieck's Scales. H. Sitt. (Carl Fischer Music Library: No. 346). 1903. pap. 4.95 (ISBN 0-8258-0043-9, L346). Fischer Inc NY.

Scale System. Carl Flesch. 112p. 1942. pap. 15.00 (ISBN 0-8258-0231-8, 02921). Fischer Inc NY.

Scale-up in Biotechnology. Business Communications Staff. 240p. 1987. pap. 1950.00 (ISBN 0-89336-504-1, C-061). BCC.

Scalehunter's Beautiful Daughter. Lucius Shepard. LC 87-5193. 160p. 1988. 16.95 (ISBN 0-9612970-8-5); 35.00 (ISBN 0-9612970-9-3). Mark Ziesing.

Scales & Arpeggios for Five String Banjo. 2nd ed. Peter W. Pardee. (Illus.). 180p. (Orig.). 1985. pap. 25.00 (ISBN 0-933611-00-5). Harbinger Pubns.

Scales & Chords for Piano. F. A. Schultz. (Carl Fischer Music Library: No. 176). 1900. pap. 3.00 (ISBN 0-8258-0097-8, L176). Fischer Inc NY.

Scales, Arpeggios, & Exercises for the Recorder. Margaret Donington & Robert Donington. (YA) (gr. 9 up). 1961. 8.50 (ISBN 0-19-322160-8). Oxford U Pr.

Scales for Rating Behavioral Characteristics of Superior Students. Joseph S. Renzulli et al. 1977. pap. 8.95 (ISBN 0-936386-00-2). Creative Learning.

Scales, Intervals, Keys, Triads, Rhythm & Meter. rev. ed. John Clough & Joyce Conley. 1983. 14.95x (ISBN 0-393-95189-8). Norton.

Scales Made Easy. 2nd ed. Virginia Taylor & Eva T. Kozak. 48p. 1984. pap. 5.95 (ISBN 0-938170-04-X). Wimbledon Music.

Scales, Norms, & Equivalent Scores. William H. Angoff. 1988. 6.00 (ISBN 0-317-67895-7). Educ Testing Serv.

Scales of Justice. Ngaio Marsh. 1976. Repr. of 1955 ed. lib. bdg. 19.95x (ISBN 0-88411-493-7, Pub. by Aeonian Pr). Amereon Ltd.

Scaleup in the Chemical Process Industries: Conversion from Laboratory Scale Tests to Successful Commercial Size Design. Attilio Bisio & Robert L. Kabel. LC 84-25767. 699p. 1985. 75.00 (ISBN 0-471-05747-9). Wiley.

Scaling Concepts in Polymer Physics. Pierre-Gilles De Gennes. LC 78-21314. 319p. 1979. 59.50x (ISBN 0-8014-1203-X). Cornell U Pr.

Scaling Copy. 1985. 16.00 (ISBN 0-88362-065-0, 0231); instr's guide 3.00 (0230). Graphic Arts Tech Found.

Scaling Methods. Peter Dunn-Rankin. (Illus.). 448p. 1983. text ed. 45.00x (ISBN 0-89859-203-8). L Erlbaum Assocs.

Scaling Phenomena in Disordered Systems. Ed. by Roger Pynn & Arne Skjeltorp. (NATO ASI Series B, Physics: Vol. 133). 592p. 1986. 92.50x (ISBN 0-306-42112-7, Plenum Pr). Plenum Pub.

Scaling the Ivory Tower: Merit & Its Limits in Academic Careers. Lionel S. Lewis. LC 75-11358. (Illus.). 256p. 1975. 27.50x (ISBN 0-8018-1734-X). Johns Hopkins.

Scaling the Ivy Wall: Twelve Winning Steps for College Admission. Howard Greene & Robert Minton. 1987. pap. 12.50 (ISBN 0-316-32683-6). Little.

Scaling the Secular City: A Defense of Christianity. J. P. Moreland. 256p. (Orig.). 1987. pap. 12.95 (ISBN 0-8010-6222-5). Baker Bk.

Scaling the Walls: Poems Nineteen Sixty-Seven to Nineteen Seventy-Four. Jonathan Greene. LC 74-18770. 1975. limited ed. 25.00x (ISBN 0-917788-06-0); pap. 5.00 (ISBN 0-917788-05-2). Gnomon Pr.

Scaling: Why Is Animal Size So Important? Knut Schmidt-Nielsen. LC 84-5841. (Illus.). 240p. 1984. 37.50 (ISBN 0-521-26657-2); pap. 11.95 (ISBN 0-521-31987-0). Cambridge U Pr.

Scallion Stone. Basil A. Smith. (Illus.). 1980. 12.00 (ISBN 0-918372-07-0); signed slipcased ed. 25.00x (ISBN 0-918372-06-2). Whispers.

Scallop & Queen Fisheries in the British Isles. 141p. 1983. pap. text ed. 16.95 (ISBN 0-85238-128-X, FN104, FNB). UNIPUB.

Scallops & the Diver-Fisherman. Ed. by Fishing News Books Ltd. Staff. 144p. 1981. 40.00x (Pub. by Fishing News England). State Mutual Bk.

Scallops & the Diver-Fisherman. David Hardy. (Illus.). 144p. 1981. pap. 22.00 (ISBN 0-85238-114-X, FN90, FNB). UNIPUB.

Scalp Ceremonial of Zuni. Elsie C. Parsons. LC 25-1663. (American Anthro. Association Memoirs). 1924. pap. 15.00 (ISBN 0-527-00530-4). Kraus Repr.

Scalp, Skull & Meninges see Neuroradiology Workshop.

Scalpel. Ira Corn, Jr. 1984. pap. 3.50 (ISBN 0-8217-1371-X). Zebra.

Scalpel & the Sword. Dell Shannon. LC 86-31218. 416p. 1987. 18.95 (ISBN 0-688-07216-X). Morrow.

Scalpel & the Sword: The Story of Doctor Norman Bethune. rev. ed. Ted Allan & Sydney Gordon. LC 73-8059. 336p. 1974. pap. 5.95 (ISBN 0-85345-302-0). Monthly Rev.

Scalpels & Sabers: Nineteenth Century Medicine in Texas. Sylvia Van Voast Ferris. Ed. by Eleanor S. Hoppe. (Illus.). 280p. 1985. 16.95 (ISBN 0-89015-514-3). Eakin Pr.

Scalpers Trail. Will C. Knott. (Golden Hawk Ser.: No. 6). 176p. 1987. pap. 2.75 (ISBN 0-451-15108-9, Sig). NAL.

Scalphunters. Ed Friend. 128p. 1981. pap. 1.75 (ISBN 0-449-12351-0, GM). Fawcett.

Scalping in America. Tr. by Georg Friederici from Ger. Repr. of 1907 ed. 9.95 (ISBN 0-8488-0034-6, Pub. by J M C & Co). Amereon Ltd.

Scaly Babies: Reptiles Growing Up. Ginny Johnston & Judy Cutchins. LC 87-18599. 48p. (gr. 2-5). 1988. 12.95 (ISBN 0-688-07305-0); PLB 12.88 (ISBN 0-688-07306-9). Morrow.

Scam. Nina Vida. 288p. 1984. 15.95 (ISBN 0-02-622010-5). Macmillan.

Scamp & the Blizzard Boys. Dorothy Hamilton. LC 79-23670. (Illus.). 80p. (gr. 5-9). 1980. o. p. 4.95 (ISBN 0-8361-1918-5); pap. 3.95 (ISBN 0-8361-1919-3). Herald Pr.

Scamper: Games for Imagination Development. Robert F. Eberle. (Illus.). 64p. (Orig.). 1971. tchrs' ed. 3.95 (ISBN 0-914634-04-6). DOK Pubs.

Scamper On. Bob Eberle. (Illus.). 64p. (Orig.). (gr. k-12). 1984. 5.95 (ISBN 0-88047-047-X, 8413). DOK Pubs.

Scampers. Betty Bailey. LC 85-90772. 1985. 15.00 (ISBN 0-682-40208-7). Exposition-Phoenix.

Scandal. Shusaku Endo. Tr. by Van C. Gessel from Japanese. 272p. 1988. 18.95 (ISBN 0-396-09320-5). Dodd.

Scandal. A. N. Wilson. (Fiction Ser.). 240p. 1985. pap. 4.95 (ISBN 0-14-006997-6). Penguin.

Scandal & Reform: Controlling Police Corruption. Lawrence W. Sherman. LC 77-79236. 1978. 37.50x (ISBN 0-520-03523-2). U of Cal Pr.

Scandal & the Star. W. Robert McClelland. Ed. by Herbert Lambert. 128p. (Orig.). 1988. pap. 8.95 (ISBN 0-8272-3430-9). CBP.

Scandal Annual. Paragon Project Staff. 224p. (Orig.). 1986. pap. 3.50 (ISBN 0-7701-0548-3). Paperjacks US.

Scandal Annual. Paragon Project Staff. Ed. by Jim Connor. 224p. (Orig.). 1988. pap. 3.95 (ISBN 0-7701-0762-1). Paperjacks US.

Scandal at High Chimneys. John D. Carr. 192p. 1988. pap. 3.95 (ISBN 0-88184-394-6). Carroll & Graf.

Scandal Bound. Anita Mills. 1987. pap. 2.50 (ISBN 0-451-14853-3, Sig). NAL.

Scandal Broth. Marion Devon. 192p. (Orig.). 1987. pap. 2.50 (ISBN 0-449-21039-1, Crest). Fawcett.

Scandal in Bath. Samantha Holder. (Regency Romance Ser.). 224p. (Orig.). Date not set. pap. 2.95 (ISBN 0-446-34770-1). Warner Bks.

Scandal of Falconhurst. Ashley Carter. (Orig.). 1983. pap. 2.50 (ISBN 0-449-12601-3, GM). Fawcett.

Scandal of Father Brown. G. K. Chesterton. (Crime Monthly Ser.). 176p. 1988. pap. 4.95 (ISBN 0-14-008256-5). Penguin.

Scandal of Father Brown. G. K. Chesterton. 1986. pap. 10.95 (ISBN 0-8161-3930-X, Large Prints Bks). G K Hall.

Scandal of the Fabliaux. R. Howard Bloch. LC 85-16428. 1986. 22.50x (ISBN 0-226-05975-8); pap. text ed. 8.95 (ISBN 0-226-05976-6). U of Chicago Pr.

Scandal: Or Priscilla's Kindness. A. N. Wilson. LC 83-40663. 240p. 1984. 15.95 (ISBN 0-670-62007-6). Viking.

Scandalabra. limited ed. Zelda Fitzgerald. 1980. 40.00x (ISBN 0-89723-022-1). Bruccoli.

Scandale de la Verite see Essais et Ecrits de Combat.

Scandalize My Name: Black Imagery in American Popular Music, Vol. 13. Sam Dennison. (Critical Studies on Black Life & Culture). 1981. lib. bdg. 73.00 (ISBN 0-8240-9309-7). Garland Pub.

Scandalous Affair. Clarissa Ross. 1977. pap. 1.50 (ISBN 0-505-51213-0, Pub. by Tower Bks). Leisure NY.

Scandalous Bequest. April Kihlstrom. 224p. 1987. pap. 2.75 (ISBN 0-451-15211-5, Sig). NAL.

Scandalous Desires. Diana Stainforth. (Orig.). (YA) (gr. 9-12). 1989. pap. 3.95 (ISBN 0-440-20269-8). Dell.

Scandalous Grace. Jeris E. Bragan. Ed. by Gerald Wheeler. (Banner Ser.). 128p. (Orig.). 1987. pap. 6.95 (ISBN 0-8280-0357-2). Review & Herald.

Scandalous Life of Cesar Moro in His Own Words: Peruvian Surrealist Poetry. Cesar Moro. Tr. by Philip Ward. (Oleander Modern Poets Ser.: Vol. 6). 1976. pap. 3.25 (ISBN 0-902675-73-7). Oleander Pr.

Scandalous Spirits. Erin Yorke. 464p. Date not set. pap. 4.50 (ISBN 0-373-97054-4, Pub. by Worldwide). Harlequin Bks.

Scandalous Widow. Monette Cummings. 192p. (Orig.). 1982. pap. 2.25 (ISBN 0-8439-1102-6, Leisure Bks). Leisure NY.

Scandals. Una-Mary Parker. 1988. pap. 4.50 (ISBN 0-451-40102-6, Onyx). NAL.

Scanderberg, His Life, Correspondence, Vicotries. Nelo Drizari. 102p. 1968. 17.50 (ISBN 0-318-23351-7). Szwede Slavic.

Scandinavia. LC 85-629040. (Library of Nations Ser.). 1986. lib. bdg. 18.60 (ISBN 0-8094-5310-X, Pub. by Time-Life). Silver.

Scandinavia. (Library of Nations). 1987. 14.95 (ISBN 0-8094-5177-8). Time Life.

Scandinavia. rev. ed. Franklin D. Scott. LC 75-2818. (American Foreign Policy Library). 416p. 1975. text ed. 27.50x (ISBN 0-674-79000-6). Harvard U Pr.

Scandinavia. Marion Sichel. (National Costume Reference Ser.). (Illus.). 80p. 1987. lib. bdg. 12.95x (ISBN 1-55546-739-3). Chelsea Hse.

Scandinavia. Time-Life Books Editors. (Library of Nations). (Illus.). 160p. (YA) (gr. 7 up). 1986. lib. bdg. 23.93. Time-Life.

Scandinavia-A Hugo Phrase Book. (Hugo's Language Courses Ser.: No. 566). 1970. pap. 3.25 (ISBN 0-8226-0566-X). Littlefield.

Scandinavia: A New Geography. Brian John. (Illus.). 352p. 1984. pap. text ed. 29.95 (ISBN 0-582-48950-4). Wiley.

Scandinavia at the Polls. Ed. by Karl Cerny. 1977. pap. 13.75 (ISBN 0-8447-3240-0). Am Enterprise.

Scandinavia: Between East & West. Ed. by Henning K. Friis. LC 78-21137. 1979. Repr. of 1950 ed. lib. bdg. 29.75x (ISBN 0-313-20864-6, FRSB). Greenwood.

Scandinavia, Denmark, Norway, Sweden 1319-1974: A Chronology & Fact Book. Robert I. Vexler. LC 76-37538. (World Chronology Ser.). 185p. 1977. 8.50x (ISBN 0-379-16314-4). Oceana.

Scandinavia, Design, Annual. Bjerregaard. 144p. 1983. pap. 15.00x (D754). Vanous.

Scandinavia During the Second World War. Ed. by Henrik S. Nissen. Tr. by Thomas Munch-Petersen from Scandinavian. LC 82-2779. (Nordic Ser.: Vol. 9). (Illus.). x, 398p. 1983. 39.50x (ISBN 0-8166-1110-6). U of Minn Pr.

Scandinavia in the Revolutionary Era, 1760-1815. H. Arnold Barton. LC 84-26972. 455p. 1986. 39.50x (ISBN 0-8166-1392-3); pap. 16.95 (ISBN 0-8166-1393-1). U of Minn Pr.

Scandinavia: Living Design. Elizabeth Gaynor. LC 87-9966. (Illus.). 256p. 1987. 40.00 (ISBN 1-55670-009-1). Stewart Tabori & Chang.

Scandinavia on Thirty-Five Dollars a Day. Darwin Porter. 480p. 1985. pap. 9.95 (ISBN 0-671-52437-2). Prentice Hall Pr.

Scandinavian-American. Alfred O. Fonkalsrud. 13.95 (ISBN 0-88247-026-4). R & E Pubs.

Scandinavian-American Heritage. LC 88-45086. (Ethnic Heritage of America Ser.). 160p. (gr. 5-9). 1988. 16.95 (ISBN 0-8160-1626-7). Facts On File.

Scandinavian Americans see How & Where to Research Your Ethnic-American Cultural Heritage.

Scandinavian Archaeology. Haakon Shetelig. Tr. by E. V. Gordon. LC 75-41251. Repr. of 1937 ed. 32.00 (ISBN 0-404-14600-7). AMS Pr.

Scandinavian Archaeology. Hakon Shetelig & Hjalmar Falk. LC 75-44911. (Illus.). 1978. Repr. of 1937 ed. lib. bdg. 40.00 (ISBN 0-87817-193-2). Hacker.

Scandinavian Art. Carl Laurin et al. LC 69-13242. (Illus.). Repr. of 1922 ed. 55.00 (ISBN 0-405-08735-7). Ayer Co Pubs.

Scandinavian Caledonides. Trygve Strand & O. Kulling. LC 77-78474. (Regional Geology Ser.). pap. 80.80 (ISBN 0-317-29870-4, 2016158). Bks Demand UMI.

Scandinavian Charted Designs. Lindberg Press. (Illus.). 1979. pap. 2.50 (ISBN 0-486-23787-7). Dover.

Scandinavian Christmas Charted Designs. Jana Hauschild. 48p. (Orig.). 1985. pap. 2.95 (ISBN 0-486-24914-X). Dover.

Scandinavian Christmas Recipes & Traditions. Ed. by Sue Roemig. (Illus.). 40p. 1985. pap. 3.95 (ISBN 0-941016-28-5). Penfield.

Scandinavian Cooking. Beatrice Ojakangas. LC 83-80804. (Illus.). 160p. 1983. pap. 12.95 (ISBN 0-89586-230-1). Price Stern.

Scandinavian Countries, Seventeen Twenty to Eighteen Sixty-Five, 2 Vols. B. J. Hovde. LC 75-159055. 1971. Repr. of 1948 ed. Set. 65.00x (ISBN 0-8046-1678-7, Pub. by Kennikat). Assoc Faculty Pr.

Scandinavian Country Inns & Manors. Karen Brown. 1988. pap. 12.95 (ISBN 0-446-38810-6). Warner Bks.

Scandinavian Country Inns & Manors. Karen Brown & Clare Brown. LC 87-50254. (Karen Brown's: European Country Inn Ser.). (Illus.). 280p. (Orig.). 1987. pap. 10.95 (ISBN 0-930328-21-3). Travel Pr.

Scandinavian Design: Objects of a Life Style. Eileene H. Beer. LC 75-25732. (Illus.). 214p. 1975. 35.00 (ISBN 0-89067-055-2). Am Scandinavian.

Scandinavian Development Agreements with African Countries. Carl Widstrand & Zdenek Cervenka. (Scandinavian Institute of African Studies). 74p. 1971. pap. 5.50 (ISBN 0-8419-9712-8, Africana). Holmes & Meier.

Scandinavian Element in the United States. Kendric C. Babcock. LC 69-18757. (American Immigration Collection Ser., No. 1). 1969. Repr. of 1914 ed. 10.00 (ISBN 0-405-00505-9). Ayer Co Pubs.

Scandinavian Element in the United States. Kendric C. Babcock. 15.00 (ISBN 0-384-02915-9). Johnson Repr.

Scandinavian Embroidery: Past & Present. Edith Nielsen. LC 77-7185. (Illus.). 1978. (ScribT). Scribner.

Scandinavian England: Collected Papers. Frederick T. Wainwright. Ed. by H. P. Finberg. 387p. 1975. 28.50x (ISBN 0-87471-783-3). Rowman.

Scandinavian Exodus: Demographic & Social Development in 19th Century Rural Communities. Briant L. Lowell. LC 87-50656. (Brown University Studies in Population & Development). 262p. 1987. pap. 27.50 (ISBN 0-8133-7327-1). Westview.

Scandinavian Film. Forsyth Hardy. Ed. by Roger Manvell. LC 79-169330. (National Cinema Series). (Illus.). 108p. 1972. Repr. of 1952 ed. 18.00 (ISBN 0-405-03895-X). Ayer Co Pubs.

Scandinavian Folk & Fairy Tales. Ed. by Claire Booss. 666p. 1984. 7.98 (ISBN 0-517-43620-5). Outlet Bk Co.

Scandinavian Folk Belief & Legend, Vol. 15. Ed. by Reimund Kvideland & Henning K. Sehmsdorf. LC 86-25049. (Nordic Ser.). (Illus.). 1988. 29.50 (ISBN 0-8166-1503-9). U of Minn Pr.

Scandinavian Folk Designs. Lis Bartholm. (Design Library). (Illus.). 48p. (Orig.). 1988. pap. 3.50 (ISBN 0-486-25578-6). Dover.

Scandinavian Folk Patterns for Counted Thread Embroidery. Claudia R. Finseth. Ed. by Margaret Foster-Finan. LC 87-9111. (Illus.). 200p. (Orig.). 1987. casebound 24.95 (ISBN 0-931397-21-9); pap. 16.95 (ISBN 0-931397-20-0). Globe Pequot.

Scandinavian Folklore. W. A. Craigie. 59.95 (ISBN 0-8490-0996-0). Gordon Pr.

Scandinavian Guide. Ed. by Peter Cowie. 288p. 1988. pap. 13.95 (ISBN 0-317-66245-7, Pub. by Tantivy). NY Zoetrope.

Scandinavian Guide 1986. Ed. by Peter Cowie. (Illus.). 288p. 1986. pap. 11.95 (ISBN 0-900730-23-4, Pub. by Tantivy). NY Zoetrope.

Scandinavian Guide, 1987. Ed. by Peter Cowie. 288p. 1987. pap. 12.95 (ISBN 0-900730-39-0, Pub. by Tantivy). NY Zoetrope.

Scandinavian Heritage. Arland O. Fiske. (Illus.). 248p. (Orig.). 1987. pap. 9.95 (ISBN 0-942323-00-9). N Amer Heritage Pr.

Scandinavian Humour & Other Myths. John L. Anderson. 218p. 1987. pap. 9.95 (ISBN 0-9616967-0-2). Nordbook.

Scandinavian Hymnody from the Reformation to the Present. Howard C. Smith. LC 87-1001. (ATLA Monograph Ser.). (Illus.). 343p. 1987. 37.50 (ISBN 0-8108-1938-4). Scarecrow.

Scandinavian Immigrant Literature. Christer L. Mossberg. (Western Writers Ser.: No. 47). (Illus., Orig.). 1981. pap. 2.95x (ISBN 0-88430-071-4). Boise St Univ.

Scandinavian Immigrants in New York, 1630-1674. John O. Evjen. LC 76-39383. (Illus.). xxiv, 438p. 1972. Repr. of 1916 ed. 22.50 (ISBN 0-8063-0501-0). Genealog Pub.

Scandinavian Influence on Southern Lowland Scotch. George T. Flom. LC 70-168048. (Columbia University. Germanic Studies, Old Ser.: No. 1). Repr. of 1900 ed. 14.00 (ISBN 0-404-50401-9). AMS Pr.

Scandinavian Influences in the English-Romantic Movement. Frank Farley. lib. bdg. 59.95 (ISBN 0-8490-0997-9). Gordon Pr.

Scandinavian Joint Expedition to Sudanese Nubia, Vol.5: Pharaonic New Kingdom Sites-The Pottery. Ed. by Torgny Save-Soderbergh. 264p. 65.00x (ISBN 0-8419-8804-8, Africana). Holmes & Meier.

Scandinavian Joint Expedition to Sudanese Nubia, Vol. 1: The Rock Drawings, 2 pts. Ed. by Torgny Save-Soderbergh. (Illus.). 497p. Set. 145.00 (ISBN 0-8419-8800-5, Africana). Holmes & Meier.

Scandinavian Joint Expedition to Sudanese Nubia, Vol. 2: Preceramic Sites. Ed. by Torgny Save-Soderbergh. 89p. 35.00 (ISBN 0-8419-8801-3, Africana). Holmes & Meier.

Scandinavian Joint Expedition to Sudanese Nubia, Vol. 3: Neolithic & A-Group Sites, 2 pts. Ed. by Torgny Save-Soderbergh. 420p. 1973. 75.00 set (ISBN 0-8419-8802-1, Africana). Holmes & Meier.

Scandinavian Joint Expedition to Sudanese Nubia, Vol. 4: C-Group, Pangrave & Kerma Sites. Ed. by Torgny Save-Soderbergh. 1984. write for info. (ISBN 0-8419-8803-X, Africana). Holmes & Meier.

Scandinavian Joint Expedition to Sudanese Nubia, Vol. 6: Late Nubian Cemeteries. Ed. by Torgny Save-Soderbergh. 307p. 1983. 85.00 (ISBN 0-8419-8805-6, Africana). Holmes & Meier.

Scandinavian Joint Expedition to Sudanese Nubia, Vol. 7: Late Nubian Sites, Churches & Settlementsq. C. J. Gardberg & Torgny Save-Soderbergh. (Illus.). 1970. text ed. 45.00 (ISBN 0-8419-8806-4, Africana). Holmes & Meier.

Scandinavian Joint Expedition to Sudanese Nubia, Vol. 8: Late Nubian Textiles. Ed. by Torgny Save-Soderbergh. 161p. 45.00 (ISBN 0-8419-8807-2, Africana). Holmes & Meier.

Scandinavian Joint Expedition to Sudanese Nubia. Vol. 9: Human Remains. Ed. by Torgny Save-Soderbergh. 155p. 1970. 55.00 (ISBN 0-8419-8808-0, Africana). Holmes & Meier.

Scandinavian Kings in the British Isles, 850-880. Alfred P. Smyth. (Oxford Historical Monographs). 1977. 45.00x (ISBN 0-19-821865-6). Oxford U Pr.

Scandinavian Knitting Designs. Pauline Chatterton. LC 76-27879. (Encore Edition). (Illus.). 272p. 1977. 5.95 (ISBN 0-684-16538-4, ScribT). Scribner.

Scandinavian Language Contacts. P. Sture Ureland & Iain Clarkson. (Illus.). 350p. 1984. 59.50 (ISBN 0-521-25685-2). Cambridge U Pr.

Scandinavian Language Structures: A Comparative Historical Analysis. Einar Haugen. 240p. 1982. 29.50x (ISBN 0-8166-1106-8); pap. 12.95x (ISBN 0-8166-1107-6). U of Minn Pr.

Scandinavian Languages. E. Haugen. 507p. 1976. text ed. 35.00 (ISBN 0-571-10423-1, Pub. by Faber & Faber UK). Humanities.

Scandinavian Languages: An Introduction to Their History. Einar Haugen. LC 74-81625. 1976. text ed. 30.00x (ISBN 0-674-79002-2). Harvard U Pr.

Scandinavian Languages: Fifty Years of Linguistic Research (1918-1968) Hinar G. Haugen. (Janus Linguarum, Series Practica). 1972. pap. text ed. 32.75x (ISBN 90-2792-358-2). Mouton.

Scandinavian Legends & Folk-Tales. Gwyn Jones. (Oxford Myths & Legends Ser.). (Illus.). (gr. 4 up). 1956. 14.95 (ISBN 0-19-274124-1). Oxford U Pr.

Scandinavian Loan-Words in Middle English. E. Bjorkman. LC 68-24897. (Studies in Language, No. 41). 1969. Repr. of 1902 ed. lib. bdg. 54.95x (ISBN 0-8383-0913-5). Haskell.

Scandinavian Loan-Words in Middle English. Erik Bjorkman. LC 75-107161. 360p. 1972. Repr. of 1900 ed. 14.00 (ISBN 0-403-00450-0). Scholarly.

Scandinavian Model: Welfare States & Welfare Research. Robert Erikson et al. LC 85-10912. 250p. 1986. 35.00 (ISBN 0-87332-348-3). M E Sharpe.

Scandinavian Music: A Short History. John Horton. LC 73-7673. (Illus.). 180p. 1975. Repr. of 1963 ed. lib. bdg. 35.00x (ISBN 0-8371-6944-5, HOSM). Greenwood.

Scandinavian Music: Finland & Sweden. Antony Hodgson. LC 84-47547. 224p. 1984. 26.50 (ISBN 0-8386-2346-8). Fairleigh Dickinson.

Scandinavian Mythology. H. R. Davidson. LC 85-22895. (Library of the World's Myths & Legends). (Illus.). 144p. 1986. 18.95 (ISBN 0-87226-041-0). P Bedrick Bks.

Scandinavian Mythology: An Annotated Bibliography. John Lindow. LC 82-49170. (Folklore Ser.). 200p. 1986. lib. bdg. 25.00 (ISBN 0-8240-9173-6). Garland Pub.

Scandinavian Mythology: An Annotated Bilbliography. John Lindow. (Reference Library of the Humanities). 610p. 1988. lib. bdg. 43.00. Garland Pub.

Scandinavian Northlands. W. R. Mead. (Problem Regions of Europe Ser.). (Illus.). 1974. pap. text ed. 6.95x (ISBN 0-19-913107-4). Oxford U Pr.

Scandinavian Plays of the Twentieth Century, 2 Vols. Repr. of 1944 ed. Set. 39.00 (ISBN 0-527-79200-4). Kraus Repr.

Scandinavian Proverbs. Ed. by Julie J. McDonald. 32p. 1985. 18.50 (ISBN 0-941016-27-7); pap. 6.50 (ISBN 0-941016-11-0). Penfield.

Scandinavian Races: The Northmen; the Sea-Kings & Vikings. Paul C. Sinding. LC 78-31800. 1979. Repr. of 1876 ed. lib. bdg. 50.00 (ISBN 0-89341-324-0). Longwood Pub Group.

Scandinavian, Russian & Eastern European Paintings: 1820-1920. (Illus.). 1985. pap. write for info. W Whitney.

Scandinavian Smorgasbord, Soups, Savouries & Sweets. M. Savonius. pap. 3.95 (107-7). Saphrograph.

Scandinavian States & the League of Nations. Samuel S. Jones. LC 39-8287. pap. 77.80 (ISBN 0-317-26669-1, 2055992). Bks Demand UMI.

Scandinavian Studies. Ed. by Carl F. Bayerschmidt & Erik Friis. LC 65-22388. 1965. 10.95x (ISBN 0-89067-043-9). Am Scandinavian.

Scandinavian Studies: Essays Presented to Dr. Henry Goddard Leach. Ed. by Carl F. Bayerschmidt & Erik J. Friis. LC 65-22388. (American-Scandinavian Foundation Scandinavian Studies). (Illus.). 472p. 1965. 20.00x (ISBN 0-295-73924-X). U of Wash Pr.

Scandinavian Treasury: Cookery & Culture of Scandinavia. 5.95 (ISBN 0-87741-010-0). Makepeace Colony.

Scandinavian Yearbook of Folklore 1984. Ed. by Bengt R. Jonsson. 164p. 1986. text ed. 32.00x (ISBN 0-317-54535-3, Pub. by Almqvist & Wiksell). Coronet Bks.

Scandinavian Yearbook of Folklore, 1985. Ed. by Bengt R. Jonsson. 144p. (Orig.). 1987. pap. 37.50x (ISBN 91-22-00887-X, Pub. by Almqvist & Wiksell). Coronet Bks.

Scandinavians & America. Ed. by H. Arnold Barton. 1974. pap. 1.50 (ISBN 0-318-03682-7). Swedish Am.

Scandinavians in America, Nine Hundred Eighty-Six to Nineteen Seventy: A Chronology & Fact Book. Ed. & compiled by Howard B. Furer. LC 72-10257. (Ethnic Chronology Ser.: No. 6). 152p. 1972. 8.50 (ISBN 0-379-00505-0). Oceana.

Scandinavians in America Series, 36 bks. Ed. by Franklyn D. Scott. (Illus.). 1979. Set. lib. bdg. 920.00 (ISBN 0-405-11628-4). Ayer Co Pubs.

Scandinavians in History. facsimile ed. S. M. Toyne. LC 79-114898. (Select Bibliographies Reprint Ser). 1948. 29.00 (ISBN 0-8369-5302-9). Ayer Co Pubs.

Scandinavians in History. facsimile ed. S. M. Toyne. 352p. 1982. Repr. of 1948 ed. lib. bdg. 21.50 (ISBN 0-8290-0833-0). Irvington.

Scandinavians in History. Stanley M. Toyne. LC 75-110926. 1970. Repr. of 1948 ed. 25.50x (ISBN 0-8046-0908-X, Pub. by Kennikat). Assoc Faculty Pr.

Scandium: Its Geochemistry & Mineralogy. Leonid F. Borisenko. LC 62-15551. pap. 20.50 (ISBN 0-317-10633-3, 2003358). Bks Demand UMI.

Scandium: Its Occurence, Chemistry, Physics, Metallurgy, Biology & Technology. C. T. Horovitz et al. 1975. 132.00 (ISBN 0-12-355850-6). Acad Pr.

Scandium, Yttrium, Lanthanum & Lanthanide Halides in Nonaqueous Solvents. Ed. by T. Mioduski & M. Salomon. (Illus.). 418p. 1985. 110.00 (ISBN 0-08-030709-4, Pub. by PPL). Pergamon.

Scandium, Yttrium, Lanthanum & Lanthanide Nitrates. Ed. by S. Siekierski & M. Salomon. LC 83-8145. (Solubility Data Ser.: Vol. 13). 514p. 1983. 110.00 (ISBN 0-08-026192-2). Pergamon.

Scanlon Plan: A Frontier in Labor-Management Cooperation. Ed. by Frederick G. Lesieur. 1958. pap. 11.95x (ISBN 0-262-62008-1). MIT Pr.

Scanlon Plan for Organization Development: Identity, Participation & Equity. Carl Frost et al. 197p. 1974. 15.00x (ISBN 0-87013-184-2). Mich St U Pr.

Scanlon Way to Improved Productivity: A Practical Guide. Brian E. Moore & Timothy L. Ross. LC 77-14396. 228p. 1978. 42.50x (ISBN 0-471-03269-7, Pub. by Wiley-Interscience). Wiley.

Scanned Image Microscopy. Ed. by Eric Ash. LC 80-41580. 1981. 69.00 (ISBN 0-12-065180-7). Acad Pr.

Scanner Darkly. Philip Dick. LC 73-11630. 220p. 1977. 20.00. Ultramarine Pub.

Scanner Darkly. Philip K. Dick. 224p. 1984. pap. 2.50 (ISBN 0-87997-923-2). DAW Bks.

Scanner Master Connecticut & Rhode Island Guide. 2nd ed. Ed. by Richard Barnett & Keith Victor. (Frequency Guide Ser.: No. 3). 300p. 1988. 19.95 (ISBN 0-939430-15-0). Scanner Master.

Scanner Master Connecticut & Rhode Island Guide: Frequency Manual. Ed. by Richard Barnett. (Scanner Master Frequency Guides Ser.: No. 2). (Illus.). 96p. 1983. 9.95 (ISBN 0-939430-01-0). Scanner Master.

Scanner Master Greater Philadelphia-South Jersey Guide. 3rd ed. Ed. by Chuck Gysi. (Scanner Master Frequency Guides Ser.: No. 5). (Illus.). 200p. 1986. 24.95 (ISBN 0-939430-04-5). Scanner Master.

Scanner Master Greater Philadelphia-South Jersey Pocket Guide. Ed. by Chuck Gysi. (Frequency Guide Ser.: No. 5A). 112p. 1987. 12.95. Scanner Master.

Scanner Master Maine Guide. Ed. by Edward Soomre & Richard Barnett. (Frequency Guide Ser.: No. 12). 280p. 1987. 17.95 (ISBN 0-939430-13-4). Scanner Master.

Scanner Master Massachusetts Guide. 3rd ed. Ed. by Richard Barnett. (Frequency Guides Ser.: No. 10). (Illus.). 300p. 1987. write for info. (ISBN 0-939430-09-6). Scanner Master.

Scanner Master Massachusetts Pocket Guide. Ed. by Richard Barnett. (Frequency Guide Ser.: No. 1A). 108p. 1986. 12.95 (ISBN 0-939430-10-X). Scanner Master.

Scanner Master Metro D. C.-Baltimore Guide. 2nd ed. Ed. by Michael Ericson. (Scanner Master Frequency Guides Ser.: No. 6). (Illus.). 128p. 1986. 16.95 (ISBN 0-939430-11-8). Scanner Master.

Scanner Master Metropolitan New York Guide. Ed. by Warren Silverman. (Frequency Guides Ser.: No. 11). (Illus.). 470p. 1988. 24.95 (ISBN 0-939430-16-9). Scanner Master.

Scanner Master New Hampshire & Vermont Guide. Ed. by Edward Soomre & Richard Barnett. (Frequency Guide Ser.: No. 13). 330p. 1987. 17.95 (ISBN 0-939430-12-6). Scanner Master.

Scanner: Read Fast, Read Smart, Boost Your Grades. (Illus.). 24p. (gr. 4 up). Date not set. price not set (ISBN 0-930251-01-6). Bluechip Pubs.

Scanners. Leon Whiteson. (Orig.). 1981. pap. 2.25 (ISBN 0-505-51675-6, Pub. by Tower Bks). Leisure NY.

Scanning: Digitizing. Association for Information & Image Management Staff. (Special Interest Package Ser.). (Illus.). 113p. 1987. pap. 25.00 (ISBN 0-317-65901-4, P028). Assn Inform & Image Mgmt.

Scanning Electron Microscope: Atlas of Periodontal Biology & Pathology. Carranza et al. (Illus.). 250p. 1989. 42.50. Ishiyaku Euro.

Scanning Electron Microscope Atlas of the Honey Bee. Eric H. Erickson, Jr. et al. 292p. 1986. text ed. 51.95x (ISBN 0-8138-0546-5). Iowa St U Pr.

Scanning Electron Microscope Studies of the Brain Ventricular Surfaces. Ed. by Om Johari. (Illus.). 1978. pap. text ed. 14.95 (ISBN 0-931288-03-7). Scanning Microscopy.

Scanning Electron Microscope Survey of the Epidermis of East African Grasses, Pt. 3. Patricia G. Palmer et al. LC 80-19201. (Smithsonian Contributions to Botany: No. 55). pap. 35.50 (ISBN 0-317-42001-1, 2025684). Bks Demand UMI.

Scanning Electron Microscope Survey of the Epidermis of East African Grasses, Vol. 4. Patricia G. Palmer & Susan Gerbeth-Jones. LC 80-19201. (Smithsonian Contributions to Botany Ser.: No. 62). pap. 31.00 (ISBN 0-317-55524-3, 2029551). Bks Demand UMI.

Scanning Electron Microscopy. L. Reimer. (Series in Optical Sciences: Vol. 45). (Illus.). 480p. 1985. 39.00 (ISBN 0-387-13530-8). Springer-Verlag.

Scanning Electron Microscopy & X-Ray Microanalysis. Lawes. (Analytical Chemistry by Open Learning Ser.). 1987. pap. write for info. (ISBN 0-471-91391-X). Wiley.

Scanning Electron Microscopy & X-Ray Microanalysis: A Text for Biologists, Materials Scientists & Geologists. Joseph I. Goldstein et al. 688p. 1981. 37.50x (ISBN 0-306-40768-X, Plenum Pr). Plenum Pub.

Scanning Electron Microscopy of Cells in Culture. Ed. by Paul B. Bell, Jr. (Illus.). vi, 314p. 1984. pap. 29.00 (ISBN 0-931288-31-2). Scanning Microscopy.

Scanning Electron Microscopy of Normal & Abnormal Human Skin. (Illus.). 221p. 1985. pap. 32.00 (ISBN 0-9612934-1-1). Electron Optics Pub Grp.

Scanning Electron Microscopy of Normal & Abnormal Human Skin. W. H. Wilborn et al. LC 84-82408. (Illus.). 221p. 1986. text ed. 53.00 (ISBN 0-89573-277-7). VCH Pubs.

Scanning Electron Microscopy of the Eye. Serge Liotet & Gerard Clergue. (Illus.). 128p. 1985. text ed. 75.00 (ISBN 0-86577-185-5). Thieme Med Pubs.

Scanning Electron Microscopy: Systems & Applications 1973. (Institute of Physics Conference Ser.: No. 18). 1973. cancelled 49.00 (ISBN 0-85498-108-X, Pub. by Inst Physics England). IPS.

Scanning Electron Microscopy 1978: International Review of Advances in Techniques & Applications of the Scanning Electron Microscope, 1978, 2 pts. Ed. by Om Johari & Robert P. Becker. LC 72-626068. (Illus.). 1978. Set. text ed. 65.00 (ISBN 0-931288-00-2); Pt. I. text ed. 37.00 (ISBN 0-931288-01-0); Pt. II. text ed. 37.00 (ISBN 0-931288-02-9). Scanning Microscopy.

Scanning Electron Microscopy 1979: International Review of Advances in Techniques & Applications of the Scanning Electron Microscope, 1979, 3 pts. Ed. by Om Johari & Robert P. Becker. LC 72-626068. (Illus.). 1979. Pts. I & II. text ed. 65.00 (ISBN 0-931288-08-8); Pt. I. text ed. 37.00 (ISBN 0-931288-04-5); Pt. III. Scanning Microscopy.

Scanning Electron Microscopy 1980, Pt. II. R. P. Becker & O. Johari. LC 72-626068. (Illus.). xiv, 658p. 52.00 (ISBN 0-931288-12-6). Scanning Microscopy.

Scanning Electron Microscopy 1980, Pt. I. Om Johari. LC 72-626068. (Illus.). xvi, 608p. 1980. 52.00 (ISBN 0-931288-11-8). Scanning Microscopy.

Scanning Electron Microscopy 1980, Pt. III. Ed. by Om Johari & R. P. Becker. LC 72-62608. (Illus.). xx, 670p. 52.00 (ISBN 0-931288-13-4). Scanning Microscopy.

Scanning Electron Microscopy 1980, Pt. IV. Ed. by Om Johari & R. P. Becker. (Scanning Electron Microscopy Ser.). (Illus.). iv, 220p. 1981. 52.00 (ISBN 0-931288-14-2). Scanning Microscopy.

Scanning Electron Microscopy, 1981, Pt. III. Ed. by O. Johari et al. (Illus.). xvi, 624p. 1981. 52.00 (ISBN 0-931288-19-3); of 4 pts. 109.00 set (ISBN 0-931288-21-5). Scanning Microscopy.

Scanning Electron Microscopy 1981, Pt. IV. Ed. by Om Johari & R. M Albrecht. LC 72-626068. viii, 312p. 1982. 52.00 (ISBN 0-931288-20-7). Scanning Microscopy.

Scanning Electron Microscopy, 1982, Pt. I. Ed. by Om Johari & R. M. Albrecht. LC 72-626068. (Illus.). xvi, 464p. 1983. 52.00 (ISBN 0-931288-23-1); Set of 4 pts. 109.00 (ISBN 0-931288-27-4). Scanning Microscopy.

Scanning Electron Microscopy 1982, Part II. Ed. by Om Johari & R. M. Albrecht. LC 72-626068. (Illus.). xvi, 432p. 1983. 52.00 (ISBN 0-931288-24-X); Set of 4 parts. 109.00. Scanning Microscopy.

Scanning Electron Microscopy 1982, Pt. IV. Ed. by Om Johari & R. M. Albrecht. LC 72-626068. (Scanning Electron Microscopy Ser.). (Illus.). xxii, 458p. 1983. 52.00 (ISBN 0-931288-26-6); Set of 4 parts. 109.00. Scanning Microscopy.

Scanning Electron Microscopy, 1982, Pt. III. Ed. by Om Johari & R. A. Sharma. LC 72-626068. (Scanning Electron Microscopy Ser.). (Illus.). xviii, 462p. 1983. 52.00 (ISBN 0-931288-25-8); of 4 parts 109.00 set. Scanning Microscopy.

Scanning Imaging Technology. Ed. by Wilson & Balk. 182p. 1987. 43.00 (ISBN 0-89252-844-3, 809). SPIE.

Scanning Microscopy Technologies & Applications. Ed. by Teague. 1988. 43.00 (ISBN 0-89252-932-6, 897). SPIE.

Scanning Nature. D. Claugher. LC 83-5155. 116p. 1983. pap. 11.95 (ISBN 0-521-27664-0). Cambridge U Pr.

Scanning Patterns of Human Infants: Implications for Visual Learning. Gordon Bronson. LC 81-20543. (Monographs on Infancy: Vol. 2). 1982. 34.50 (ISBN 0-89391-114-3). Ablex Pub.

Scanning the Land, Poems in North Dakota. Richard Lyons. LC 80-149876. (Illus.). 157p. 1980. 11.75 (ISBN 0-911042-23-7). N Dak Inst.

Scannning Electron Microscopy in Cell Biology & Medicine. K. Tanaka & T. Fujita. (International Congress Ser.: Vol. 545). 500p. 1981. 101.25 (ISBN 0-444-90191-4, Excerpta Medica). Elsevier.

SCANS: Key to Bird Watching. Virginia Holmgren. LC 82-25597. (Illus.). 176p. (Orig.). 1983. pap. 12.95 (ISBN 0-917304-48-9). Timber.

Scanty Plot of Ground: Studies in the Victorian Sonney. William T. Going. (Studies in English Literature: No. 106). 1976. text ed. 17.60x (ISBN 90-2793-015-5). Mouton.

Scapegoat. Daphne Du Maurier. 1977. Repr. of 1957 ed. lib. bdg. 18.95x (ISBN 0-89190-154-X, Pub. by Queens Hse). Amereon Ltd.

Scapegoat. Daphne DuMaurier. 21.95x (ISBN 0-89233-037-6). Queens Hse-Focus Serv.

Scapegoat. Daphne Du Maurier. 348p. 1988. pap. 4.50 (ISBN 0-88184-409-8). Carroll & Graf.

Scapegoat. Rene Girard. Tr. by Yvonne Freccero. 224p. 1986. text ed. 27.50x (ISBN 0-8018-3315-9). Johns Hopkins.

Scapegoat. Mary L. Settle. 288p. 1982. pap. 3.95 (ISBN 0-345-29802-0). Ballantine.

Scapegoat. Mary L. Settle. 350p. 1980. 11.95 (ISBN 0-394-50477-1). Random.

Scapegoat. Mary L. Settle. (Beulah Quintet - Signature Edition Ser.). 288p. 1988. pap. 9.95 (ISBN 0-684-18848-1). Scribner.

Scapegoat: A Romance, 2 vols. in 1. Hall Caine. LC 79-8244. Repr. of 1891 ed. 44.50 (ISBN 0-404-61802-2). AMS Pr.

Scapegoat General: The Story of General Benjamin Huger C. S. A. Jeffrey L. Rhoades. LC 85-18530. (Illus.). xi, 164p. 1986. 21.50 (ISBN 0-208-02069-1, Archon). Shoe String.

Scapegoat: The Impact of Death-Fear on an American Family. Eric Bermann. LC 73-80573. (Illus.). 370p. 1973. 10.00 (ISBN 0-472-14300-X). U of Mich Pr.

Scapegoat: The Persecuted Jew. Wesley Shaw. Ed. by David Bernard. (Illus.). 128p. (Orig.). 1988. pap. 5.95 (ISBN 0-932581-38-2). Word Aflame.

Scapegoats: The Exodus of the Remnants of Polish Jewry. Josef Banas. Tr. by Tadeusz Szafar. 221p. 1979. 34.50 (ISBN 0-8419-6303-7). Holmes & Meier.

Scapegrace. Sylvia Thorpe. 1978. pap. 1.50 (ISBN 0-449-23478-9, Crest). Fawcett.

Scapes. Phyllis Plous. LC 85-62051. (Illus.). 64p. 1986. pap. 15.00 (ISBN 0-295-96331-X). U of Wash Pr.

Scapescope. John E. Stith. 224p. 1984. pap. 2.75 (ISBN 0-441-75391-4, Pub. by Ace Science Fiction). Ace Bks.

Scapin & Don Juan. Moliere. Adapted by & tr. by Albert Bermel. (Actor's Moliere Series: Vol. 3). 1987. pap. 5.95. Applause Theatre Bk Pubs.

Scapular of Carmel. rev. 2nd ed. Kilian Lynch. 48p. 1973. 1.00 (ISBN 0-911988-11-4). AMI Pr.

Scar Across the Heart. Bob Prouty. (Destiny Ser.). 107p. 1986. pap. 6.95 (ISBN 0-8163-0629-X). Pacific Pr Pub Assn.

Scar Mirror. Derek Pell. (Illus.). 1979. signed ed. cancelled (ISBN 0-916866-06-8); pap. 2.50 (ISBN 0-916866-05-X). Cats Pajamas.

Scar of Montaigne: An Essay in Personal Philosophy. Philip P. Hallie. LC 66-23925. 1966. 16.00x (ISBN 0-8195-3068-9). Wesleyan U Pr.

Scar-Strangled Banner. Ralph Steadman. (Illus.). 224p. 1988. 29.95 (ISBN 0-88162-314-8). Salem Hse Pubs.

Scar Tissue. Leonard Randolph. (Hollow Spring Poetry Ser.). (Illus.). 64p. 1984. pap. text ed. 5.00 (ISBN 0-318-00815-7). Hollow Spring Pr.

Scar Tissue & Other Stories. Gary Indiana. LC 86-873140. 150p. (Orig.). 1987. pap. 6.95 (ISBN 0-930762-09-6). Calamus Bks.

Scarab Murder Case. S. S. Van Dine. (Philo Vance Mystery Ser.). 1984. pap. 4.50 (ISBN 0-684-18159-2). Scribner.

Scarabs & Cylinders with Names. W. M. Petrie. 47p. 1978. Repr. of 1917 ed. text ed. 50.00x (ISBN 0-85668-010-9, Pub. by Aris & Phillips UK). Humanities.

Scarabs, Cylinders & Other Ancient Egyptian Seals: A Checklist of Publications. Geoffrey T. Martin. (Egyptology Ser.). 1985. text ed. 22.50 (ISBN 0-86516-076-7). Bolchazy-Carducci.

Scarabs, Cylinders & Other Ancient Egyptian Seals: A Checklist of Publications. Geoffrey T. Martin. 72p. 1985. pap. 18.50 (ISBN 0-85668-317-5, Pub. by Aris & Phillips UK). Humanities.

Scaramouche. Raphael Sabatini. 1976. Repr. of 1931 ed. lib. bdg. 23.95 (ISBN 0-89190-744-0, Pub. by River City Pr). Amereon Ltd.

Scarboro, Maine, Marriages of the Second Congregational Church. Michael J. Denis. 21p. 1983. pap. 3.25 (ISBN 0-935207-12-0). Danbury Hse Bks.

Scarborough & Whitby Railway: A Centenary Volume. Hendon Publishing Co., Ltd. Staff. 1986. 23.80x (ISBN 0-317-54174-9, Pub. by Hendon Pub UK). State Mutual Bk.

Scarborough & Whitby Railway: Fifth Impression. Hendon Publishing Co., Ltd. Staff. 1986. 21.00x (ISBN 0-317-54175-7, Pub. by Hendon Pub UK). State Mutual Bk.

Scarborough (Maine) Town Records-Births. 62p. 1986. pap. 7.25 (ISBN 0-935207-45-7). DanBury Hse Bks.

Scarborough Revisited Through Photographs. Hendon Publishing Co., Ltd. Staff. 1986. 12.60x (ISBN 0-317-54176-5, Pub. by Hendon Pub UK). State Mutual Bk.

Scarce Medical Resources & Justice. Pope John XXIII Medical-Moral Research & Education Center Staff. Ed. by Donald G. McCarthy. 297p. (Orig.). 1987. pap. 17.95 (ISBN 0-935372-21-0). Pope John Ctr.

Scarce Natural Resources: The Challenge to Public Policymaking. Ed. by Susan Welch & Robert Miewald. (Sage Yearbooks in Politics & Public Policy: Vol. 11). 288p. 1983. 35.00 (ISBN 0-8039-1981-6); pap. 16.95 (ISBN 0-8039-1982-4). Sage.

Scarce Water & Institutional Change. Kenneth D. Frederick. LC 85-20999. 210p. 1986. text ed. 22.50 (ISBN 0-915707-21-7). Resources Future.

Scarcity & Choice in History. William H. Court. LC 74-113460. 1970. lib. bdg. 35.00x (ISBN 0-678-08017-8). Kelley.

Scarcity & Growth Reconsidered. Ed. by V. Kerry Smith. xvi, 298p. 1979. 22.50 (ISBN 0-8018-2232-7); pap. 9.95 (ISBN 0-8018-2233-5). Resources Future.

Scarcity & Growth: The Economics of Natural Resource Availability. Harold J Barnett & Chandler Morse. 304p. 1963. 25.00 (ISBN 0-8018-0056-0); 9.95. Resources Future.

Scarcity & Opportunity in an Indian Village. James M. Freeman. (Illus.). 177p. 1985. pap. text ed. 8.50x (ISBN 0-88133-165-1). Waveland Pr.

Scarcity & Survival: A Study in Culture Ecology. G. Prakash Reddy. (Illus.). 186p. 1983. text ed. 27.50x (ISBN 0-86590-127-9). Apt Bks.

Scarcity & Survival in Central America: Ecological Origins of the Soccer War. William H. Durham. LC 78-55318. (Illus.). xx, 209p. 1979. 22.50x (ISBN 0-8047-1000-7); pap. 6.95 (ISBN 0-8047-1154-2, SP5). Stanford U Pr.

Scarcity, Choice, & Public Policy in Middle Africa. Donald Rothchild & Robert L. Curry, Jr. LC 76-50255. 1978. 36.50x (ISBN 0-520-03378-7); pap. 11.95x (ISBN 0-520-03534-8). U of Cal Pr.

Scarcity, Exploitation, & Poverty: Malthus & Marx in Mexico. Luis A. Serron. LC 79-4735. (Illus.). 1980. 24.95x (ISBN 0-8061-1460-6). U of Okla Pr.

Scare a Ghost, Tame a Monster. Jeanne Bendick. LC 82-23696. (Illus.). 120p. (gr. 3-6). 1983. 11.95 (ISBN 0-664-32701-X). Westminster John Knox.

Scare Tactics. John Farris. 288p. 1988. 17.95 (ISBN 0-312-93085-2). Tor Bks.

Scare Yourself to Sleep see Creepies.

Scarebird. Sid Fleischman. LC 87-4099. 32p. (gr. k-3). 1988. 11.95 (ISBN 0-688-07317-4); lib. bdg. 11.88 (ISBN 0-688-07318-2). Greenwillow.

Scarecrows. George D. Gribble. (Illus.). 32p. 1985. 25.00x (ISBN 0-930126-16-5). Typographeum.

Scarecrows. Robert Westall. LC 81-2052. 192p. (gr. 7 up). 1981. reinforced bdg. 11.75 (ISBN 0-688-00612-4). Greenwillow.

Scarecrows & Their Child. Mary Stolz. LC 87-115. (Illus.). 80p. (gr. 3-6). 1987. 10.95i (ISBN 0-06-026007-6); PLB 10.89 (ISBN 0-06-026008-4). HarpJ.

Scared, but Not Too Scared. Dave Jackson. (Storybooks for Caring Parents). (Illus.). 1985. pap. 3.95 (ISBN 0-89191-962-7, 59626). Cook.

Scared of the Dark. Liza Alexander. (Sesame Street Growing-Up Bks.). (Illus.). 32p. (ps-k). 1986. 2.95 (ISBN 0-307-12020-1, Pub by Golden Bks). Western Pub.

Scared of the Dark. Liza Alexander. (Golden Story Book 'n' Tapes). (Illus.). 24p. (ps-3). 1987. pap. write for info incl. cassette (ISBN 0-307-13948-4, Pub. by Golden Bks). Western Pub.

Scared Silly. Eth Clifford. LC 87-30694. (Illus.). 128p. (gr. 3-7). 1988. 13.95 (ISBN 0-395-46845-0). HM.

Scared Silly. Mike Thaler. (Illus.). (gr. 3-7). 1982. pap. 1.95 (ISBN 0-380-80291-0, 80291-0, Camelot). Avon.

Scared Stiff: Seven Tales of Seduction & Terror. Ramsey Campbell. 192p. Date not set. pap. 8.95 (ISBN 0-446-38783-5). Warner Bks.

Scared Stiff: Tales of Sex & Death. Ramsey Campbell. 1987. 25.00 (ISBN 0-910489-17-3). Scream Pr.

Scared Straight: & the Panacea Phenomenon. James O. Finckenauer. (Prentice Hall Criminal Justice Ser.). (Illus.). 288p. 1982. pap. 32.00 (ISBN 0-13-791558-6). P-H.

Scared Woman: True Expose, Vol. I. Beulah S. Kershaw. (Illus.). 44p. (Orig.). 1981. pap. 3.00x (ISBN 0-911870-03-2). Beulah.

Scaredy Cat. Virginia Vail. (Animal Inn Ser.: No. 4). (Illus.). 128p. (gr. 4-6). 1987. pap. 2.50 (ISBN 0-590-40184-X, Apple Paperbacks). Scholastic Inc.

Scaredy Cats. Audrey Woods. (Illus.). 32p. (ps-2). 1981. 5.50 (ISBN 0-85953-110-4, Pub. by Child's Play England). Playspaces.

Scaremongers: The Advocacy of War & Rearmament 1896-1914. A. J. Morris. 400p. 1984. 49.95x (ISBN 0-7102-0162-1). Routledge Chapman & Hall.

Scarf Tying Magic. Bobbie J. Thompson. (Illus.). 96p. 1988. pap. 6.95 (ISBN 0-87491-892-8). Acropolis.

Scarface. Paul Monette. 320p. (Orig.). 1983. pap. 3.50 (ISBN 0-425-06424-7). Berkley Pub.

Scarfe by Scarfe: An Autobiography in Pictures. Gerald Scarfe. (Illus.). 192p. 1988. 34.95 (ISBN 0-241-11959-6, Pub. by Hamish Hamilton). David & Charles.

Scarifications. Jayne Cortez. 1973. 4.00 (ISBN 0-9608062-2-9). Bola Pr.

Scarista Style: A Free Range & Humane Approach to Cooking & Eating. Alison Johnson. (Illus.). 224p. 1988. 24.95 (ISBN 0-575-03907-8, Pub. by Gollancz England). David & Charles.

Scarlatti Inheritance. Robert Ludlum. 1982. pap. 4.95 (ISBN 0-553-25856-7). Bantam.

Scarlatti: Solo Piano Literature-A Comprehensive Guide Annotated & Evaluated with Thematics. Ed. by Carolyn Maxwell. (Maxwell Music Evaluation Bks.). (Illus.). 412p. (Orig.). 1985. pap. 13.95 (ISBN 0-912531-02-9). Maxwell Mus Eval.

Scarlet. Ellin Hall. 304p. Date not set. pap. 4.50 (ISBN 0-553-27542-9). Bantam.

Scarlet & Black. Stendhal. Tr. by M. R. Shaw. (Classics Ser.). (Orig.). 1953. pap. 3.95 (ISBN 0-14-044030-5). Penguin.

Scarlet & Gold. Ellen T. Marsh. 480p. 1985. pap. 6.95 (ISBN 0-425-08395-0). Berkley Pub.

Scarlet & Gold. Ellen T. Marsh. 400p. 1986. pap. 3.95 (ISBN 0-515-08792-0). Jove Pubns.

Scarlet Arena 30303. Silas Moore. Ed. by Genevieve Oddo. LC 74-190272. (Illus.). 196p. (gr. 8-12). 1972. PLB 3.95 (ISBN 0-87783-063-0). Oddo.

Scarlet Domino. Sylvia Thorpe. 224p. 1978. pap. 1.50 (ISBN 0-449-23220-4, Crest). Fawcett.

Scarlet Empire. David M. Parry. LC 77-154456. (Utopian Literature Ser). (Illus.). 1971. Repr. of 1906 ed. 30.00 (ISBN 0-405-03538-1). Ayer Co Pubs.

Scarlet Feather. Joan Grant. 290p. 1989. pap. 7.95 (ISBN 0-89804-148-1). Ariel OH.

Scarlet Feather. Joan M. Grant. 23.00 (ISBN 0-405-11789-2). Ayer Co Pubs.

Scarlet Fish & Other Stories. Joan M. Grant. 14.00 (ISBN 0-405-11790-6). Ayer Co Pubs.

Scarlet Flower. 6.00 (ISBN 0-686-23329-8). Rochester Folk Art.

Scarlet Hourglass. Del J. Ventruella. 148p. 1984. 6.95 (ISBN 0-89697-160-0). Intl Univ Pr.

Scarlet Ibis: A Classic Story of Brotherhood. James Hurst. (Creative's Classic Short Stories Ser.). (Illus.). (gr. 4 up). 1987. PLB 8.95 (ISBN 0-88682-000-6). Creative Ed.

Scarlet Letter. Nathaniel Hawthorne. (Airmont Classics Ser.). (gr. 9 up). 1964. pap. 1.95 (ISBN 0-8049-0007-8, CL-7). Airmont.

Scarlet Letter. Nathaniel Hawthorne. (Literature Ser). (gr. 9-12). 1969. pap. text ed. 7.17 (ISBN 0-87720-714-3). AMSCO Sch.

Scarlet Letter. Nathaniel Hawthorne. Ed. by Robert D. Spector. 256p. (Orig.). 1981. pap. 1.50 (ISBN 0-553-21009-2, Bantam Classics). Bantam.

Scarlet Letter. Nathaniel Hawthorne. LC 69-13317. (Merrill Standard Ser). 1975. 6.00 (ISBN 0-910294-31-3); pap. 4.00 (ISBN 0-910294-32-1). Brown Bk.

Scarlet Letter. Nathaniel Hawthorne. Ed. by Harry Levin. LC 60-2662. (YA) (gr. 9 up). 1960. pap. 5.95 (ISBN 0-395-05142-8, RivEd). HM.

Scarlet Letter. Nathaniel Hawthorne. 256p. (YA) (RL 10). 1986. pap. 1.50 (ISBN 0-451-51652-4, CW1652, Sig Classics). NAL.

Scarlet Letter. Nathaniel Hawthorne. Bd. with House of the Seven Gables. 544p. 1981. pap. 4.95 (ISBN 0-451-51908-6, Sig Classics). NAL.

Scarlet Letter. 2nd ed. Nathaniel Hawthorne. Ed. by Sculley Bradley et al. (Norton Critical Edition Ser.). 1977. 12.95 (ISBN 0-393-04495-5); pap. 7.95x (ISBN 0-393-09073-6). Norton.

Scarlet Letter. Nathaniel Hawthorne. Ed. by William Charvat et al. (Centenary Edition of the Works of Nathaniel Hawthorne: Vol. 1). (Illus.). 359p. 1963. 25.00x (ISBN 0-8142-0059-1). Ohio St U Pr.

Scarlet Letter. new ed. Nathaniel Hawthorne. Ed. by Naunerle Farr. (Now Age Illustrated Ser.). (Illus.). 64p. (gr. 5-10). 1974. 7.50 (ISBN 0-88301-215-4); pap. text ed. 2.95 (ISBN 0-88301-141-7). Pendulum Pr.

Scarlet Letter. Nathaniel Hawthorne. (gr. 7 up). 1972. pap. 2.25 (ISBN 0-590-09075-5). Scholastic Inc.

Scarlet Letter. Nathaniel Hawthorne. (Enriched Classics Ser.). 336p. (gr. 9 up). 1972. pap. 2.95 (ISBN 0-671-55441-7, RE). WSP.

Scarlet Letter. Nathaniel Hawthorne. Notes by Thomas E. Connolly. (Penguin American Library). 256p. 1983. pap. 2.25 (ISBN 0-14-039019-7). Penguin.

Scarlet Letter. Nathaniel Hawthorne. (Illus.). 1984. 11.95 (ISBN 0-396-08262-9). Dodd.

Scarlet Letter. Nathaniel Hawthorne. 523p. 1984. Repr. lib. bdg. 18.95x (ISBN 0-89966-494-6). Buccaneer Bks.

Scarlet Letter. Nathaniel Hawthorne. 220p. 1984. lib. bdg. 18.95x (ISBN 0-89968-258-8). Lightyear.

Scarlet Letter. Nathaniel Hawthorne. LC 81-83603. (Silver Burdett Classics for Kids Ser.). 288p. (gr. 6 up). 1985. pap. 3.67 (ISBN 0-382-09991-5). Silver.

Scarlet Letter. Nathaniel Hawthorne. LC 86-45559. (Running Press Classics Ser.). 192p. 1986. lib. bdg. 12.90 (ISBN 0-89471-475-9); pap. 3.95 (ISBN 0-89471-474-0). Running Pr.

Scarlet Letter. Nathaniel Hawthorne. (Illus.). 256p. 1986. 22.95 (ISBN 0-15-179568-1). HarBraceJ.

Scarlet Letter. Nathaniel Hawthorne. pap. 3.50 (ISBN 0-671-63751-7). WSP.

Scarlet Letter. 3rd ed. Nathaniel Hawthorne. Ed. by Seymour Gross et al. (Critical Editions Ser.). 480p. 1988. pap. text ed. 7.95x (ISBN 0-393-95653-9). Norton.

Scarlet Letter see Best Known Works.

Scarlet Letter see Four Classic American Novels.

Scarlet Letter see Novels.

Scarlet Letter: A Reading. Nina Baym. 152p. 1986. 17.95 (ISBN 0-317-67677-6, Twayne); pap. 6.95 (ISBN 0-8057-8001-7). G K Hall.

Scarlet Letter: A Romance. Nathaniel Hawthorne. Ed. by Larzer Ziff. LC 62-21260. 1963. pap. 6.65 scp (ISBN 0-672-60966-5, LL1). Bobbs.

Scarlet Letter & Other Tales of the Puritans. Nathaniel Hawthorne. Ed. by Harry Levin. LC 61-2662. pap. 6.50 (ISBN 0-395-05153-3, RivEd). HM.

Scarlet Letter & Selected Writings. Nathaniel Hawthorne. Ed. by Stephen Nissenbaum. (Modern Library College Edition). 400p. 1983. pap. text ed. write for info (ISBN 0-394-33269-5, RanC). Random.

Scarlet Letter Guides. Abram Wessels. Ed. by Diane Zimmerman. (LifeView: a Christian Approach to Literature Studies). (gr. 10-12). 1977. pap. 0.85 student guide (ISBN 0-915134-31-4); tchrs. ed. 1.50 (ISBN 0-915134-35-7). Mott Media.

Scarlet Letter Notes. Paul Stewart. (Orig.). 1960. pap. 3.50 (ISBN 0-8220-1165-4). Cliffs.

Scarlet Letter: Student Activity Book. Marcia Sohl & Gerald Dackerman. (Now Age Illustrated). (Illus.). (gr. 4-10). 1976. wkbk 1.25 (ISBN 0-88301-194-8). Pendulum Pr.

Scarlet Letter with Reader's Guide. Nathaniel Hawthorne. (AMSCO Literature Program). (gr. 10-12). 1970. text ed. 11.83 (ISBN 0-87720-836-0); pap. text ed. 8.08 (ISBN 0-87720-808-5); tchr's. ed. 8.41 (ISBN 0-87720-908-1). AMSCO Sch.

Scarlet Letters. Ellery Queen. Bd. with Glass Village. 1984. pap. 3.50 (ISBN 0-451-12887-7, E9675, Sig). NAL.

Scarlet Lies. Jo Goodman. 480p. 1988. pap. 3.95 (ISBN 0-8217-2503-3). Zebra.

Scarlet Mansion. Allan W. Eckert. 496p. 1986. pap. 4.95 (ISBN 0-553-25925-3). Bantam.

Scarlet Monster Lives Here. Reissue. ed. Marjorie W. Sharmat. LC 78-19484. (Harper I Can Read Bks.). (Illus.). 64p. (gr. k-3). 1988. 9.70i (ISBN 0-06-025526-9); PLB 10.89 (ISBN 0-06-025527-7). HarpJ.

Scarlet Monster Lives Here. Marjorie W. Sharmat. LC 78-19484. (Trophy I Can Read Bks.). (Illus.). 64p. (gr. k-3). 1986. pap. 3.50 (ISBN 0-06-444098-2, Trophy). HarpJ.

Scarlet Patch. Bruce Lancaster. 1976. Repr. of 1947 ed. lib. bdg. 25.15x (ISBN 0-88411-682-4, Pub. by Aeonian Pr). Amereon Ltd.

Scarlet Pimpernel. Baroness Orczy. Ed. by Naunerle Farr. (Now Age Illustrated IV Ser.). (Illus.). (gr. 4-12). 1978. text ed. 7.50 (ISBN 0-88301-333-9); pap. text ed. 2.95 (ISBN 0-88301-321-5); activity bk. 1.25 (ISBN 0-88301-345-2). Pendulum Pr.

Scarlet Pimpernel. Baroness Orczy. 256p. 1984. Repr. lib. bdg. 16.95x (ISBN 0-89966-508-X). Buccaneer Bks.

Scarlet Pimpernel. Emma Orczy. (Illus.). 304p. 1985. 11.95 (ISBN 0-396-08690-X). Dodd.

Scarlet Pimpernel. Emmuska Orczy. (Airmont Classics Ser.). (gr. 7 up). 1964. pap. 1.95 (ISBN 0-8049-0028-0, CL-28). Airmont.

Scarlet Pimpernel. Emmuska Orczy. 1976. lib. bdg. 16.95x (ISBN 0-89968-072-0). Lightyear.

Scarlet Pimpernel. Emmuska Orczy. 256p. (RL 7). 1974. pap. 2.50 (ISBN 0-451-51762-8, CE1762, Sig Classics). NAL.

Scarlet Plague. Jack London. LC 74-16506. (Science Fiction Ser). (Illus.). 181p. 1975. Repr. 18.00x (ISBN 0-405-06304-0). Ayer Co Pubs.

Scarlet Plume. Frederick Manfred. LC 83-5788. xviii, 365p. 1983. pap. 8.95 (ISBN 0-8032-8120-X, BB 839, Bison). U of Nebr Pr.

Scarlet Poppies. Janet L. Roberts. 480p. 1983. pap. 3.50 (ISBN 0-446-30211-2). Warner Bks.

Scarlet Poppy & Other Stories. Harriet P. Spofford. 1972. Repr. of 1894 ed. lib. bdg. 24.00 (ISBN 0-8422-8111-8). Irvington.

Scarlet Poppy & Other Stories. Harriet P. Spofford. 1986. pap. text ed. 7.95x (ISBN 0-8290-2017-9). Irvington.

Scarlet Princess. Christopher Nicole. 1984. pap. 3.95 (ISBN 0-451-13269-6, Sig). NAL.

Scarlet Rebel. Jean Saunders. 352p. (Orig.). 1985. pap. 3.50 (ISBN 0-345-31497-2). Ballantine.

Scarlet Ribbons: American Indian Technique for Today's Quilters. Helen Kelley. (Illus.). 120p. 1987. pap. 15.95 (ISBN 0-89145-924-3, 1819). Collector Bks.

Scarlet Riders, No. 3: Beyond the Stone Heaps. Ian Anderson. 240p. 1986. pap. 2.50 (ISBN 0-8217-1884-3). Zebra.

Scarlet Riders, No. 4: Sergeant O'Reilly. Ian Anderson. 288p. 1987. pap. 2.50 (ISBN 0-8217-1977-7). Zebra.

Scarlet Riders, No. 6: The Flying Patrol. Ian Anderson. 240p. 1988. pap. 2.50 (ISBN 0-8217-2437-1). Zebra.

Scarlet Scourge. Johnston McCully. Repr. lib. bdg. 17.95 (ISBN 0-89190-998-2, Pub. by River City Pr). Amereon Ltd.

Scarlet Shadows. Emma Drummond. 1978. pap. 2.25 (ISBN 0-440-17812-6). Dell.

Scarlet Slipper Mystery. rev. ed. Carolyn Keene. LC 74-3869. (Nancy Drew Ser.: Vol. 32). (Illus.). 196p. (gr. 4-7). 1955. 4.50 (ISBN 0-448-09532-7, G&D); PLB 3.29 (ISBN 0-448-19532-1). Putnam Pub Group.

Scarlet Sorcerer. Joe Dever. Ed. by Hillary Cige. (Combat Heroes Ser.). 352p. 1988. pap. 3.95 (ISBN 0-425-10754-X, Pub. by Berkley-Pacer). Berkley Pub.

Scarlet Spinster. Cleo Chadwick. 384p. 1988. pap. 3.95 (ISBN 0-8217-2381-2). Zebra.

Scarlet Storm. Marquerite DeMoss. 272p. 1986. pap. 2.95 (ISBN 0-8439-2397-0, Leisure Bks). Leisure NY.

Scarlet Sunrise. Leigh Bristol. 384p. 1987. pap. 3.95 (ISBN 0-446-34241-6). Warner Bks.

Scarlet Surrender. Sandra DuBay. 480p. (Orig.). 1987. pap. 3.95 (ISBN 0-8439-2555-8). Leisure NY.

Scarlet Town. Maryhelen Clague. (Orig.). 1986. pap. 2.95 (GM). Fawcett.

Scarlet Tree. Osbert Sitwell. 4.95 (ISBN 0-7043-3157-8, Pub. by Quartet England). Charles River Bks.

Scarlet Woman. Julia Fitzgerald. 352p. 1981. pap. 2.75 (ISBN 0-8439-0967-6, Leisure Bks). Leisure NY.

Scarlet Woman of Wall Street: Jay Gould, Jim Fisk, Cornelius Vanderbilt, the Erie Railway Wars & the Birth of Wall Street. John S. Gordon. LC 88-230. (Illus.). 512p. 1988. 22.95 (ISBN 1-55584-212-7). Weidenfeld.

Scarlet Wreath: The Murder of Jeanne Anderson. Philip J. Carraher. Ed. by Ann M. Carraher. LC 85-80039. (Orig.). 1985. 11.50 (ISBN 0-9615097-0-8); pap. 5.50 (ISBN 0-9615097-1-6). Phian Bks.

Scarlett Greene. Barbara Ucko. 352p. 1986. 18.95 (ISBN 0-312-00184-3). St Martin.

Scarlett Letter. Nathaniel Hawthorne. (Book Notes). 1984. pap. 2.50 (ISBN 0-8120-3442-2). Barron.

Scarlett Letters. Glenna Luschei. Hand-marbled paper with mixed media interior. 125.00 (ISBN 0-318-23706-7). Solo Pr.

Scarlett Letters. Glenna Luschei & William K. Murphy. 1987. Handoriented artist bk. 50.00 (ISBN 0-318-22924-2). Solo Pr.

Scarlett O'Hara's Younger Sister: My Lively Life in & Out of Hollywood. Evelyn Keyes. 1977. 10.00 (ISBN 0-8184-0243-1). Lyle Stuart.

Scarman & After: Essays Reflecting on Lord Scarman's Report, the Riots & Their Aftermath. Ed. by J. Benyon. 270p. 1984. text ed. 38.00 (ISBN 0-08-030217-3); pap. text ed. 16.25 (ISBN 0-08-030218-1). Pergamon.

Scarne on Card Tricks. John Scarne. 352p. 1974. pap. 4.95 (ISBN 0-451-14949-1, Sig). NAL.

Scarne's Complete Guide to Gambling. John Scarne. (Illus.). 900p. 1974. 24.00 (ISBN 0-671-21734-8). S&S.

Scarne's Encyclopedia of Games. John Scarne. LC 83-47571. 448p. 1983. pap. 12.95 (ISBN 0-06-091052-6, CN1052, PL). Har-Row.

Scarne's Guide to Modern Poker. John Scarne. 1980. 11.95 (ISBN 0-671-24796-4). S&S.

Scarne's Guide to Modern Poker. John Scarne. 320p. 1984. pap. 9.95 (ISBN 0-671-53076-3, Fireside). S&S.

Scarne's Magic Tricks. John Scarne. 256p. (RL 7). 1987. pap. 3.50 (ISBN 0-451-14708-1, AE1162, Sig). NAL.

Scarne's Magic Tricks: Two Hundred Best Tricks That Anyone Can Do. John Scarne. (Illus.). 1951. 6.95 (ISBN 0-517-54311-7). Crown.

Scarne's New Complete Guide to Gambling. John Scarne. (Illus.). 900p. 1986. pap. 14.95 (ISBN 0-671-63063-6, Fireside). S&S.

Scarpa, Planet of the Mindless Ones. Ruth Norman. 700p. 1988. text ed. 17.95 (ISBN 0-932642-91-8). Unarius Pubns.

Scarperer. Brendan Behan. Repr. lib. bdg. 13.95x (ISBN 0-89190-573-1, Pub. by River City Pr). Amereon Ltd.

Scarron's Roman Comique: A Comedy of the Novel-A Novel of Comedy, French Language & Literature, Vol. 46. Joan E. DeJean. (European University Studies: Ser. 13). 110p. 1977. pap. 19.60 (ISBN 3-261-02943-9). P Lang Pubs.

Scars. Anne Bailey. 160p. (YA) (gr. 7 up). 1987. 10.95 (ISBN 0-571-14806-9). Faber & Faber.

Scars & Other Distinguishing Marks. Christian Matheson. 288p. 1988. pap. 3.95 (ISBN 0-8125-2254-0, Dist. by St Martin's Pr & Warner Pub Servs). Tor Bks.

Scars of the Soul. Mary A. Woodward. LC 85-70207. 200p. 1985. 12.95 (ISBN 0-89804-902-4, Pub. by Brindabella Bks); pap. 6.95 (ISBN 0-89804-903-2, Pub.by Brindabella Bks). Ariel OH.

Scarsdale Murder. Jay David. 1981. pap. 2.50 (ISBN 0-8439-0866-1, Leisure Bks). Leisure NY.

Scarsdale Nutritionist's Weight-Loss Program for Teenagers. Judith R. Corlin & Mary S. Miller. 208p. 1983. 8.95 (ISBN 0-671-46262-8, Fireside). S&S.

Scarsdale; or, Life on the Lancashire & Yorkshire Border, 3 vols. in 2. Kay-Shuttleworth. LC 79-8146. Repr. of 1860 ed. Set. 84.50 (ISBN 0-404-61956-8). AMS Pr.

Scary Basketball Player. Jerry Jenkins. (Dallas O'Neil & the Baker Street Sports Club Ser.). (Orig.). (YA) (gr. 9-12). 1986. pap. text ed. 3.95 (ISBN 0-8024-8233-3). Moody.

Scary Book. Sheila Front. (Illus.). 32p. (gr. k-3). 1986. 10.95 (ISBN 0-233-97751-1). Andre Deutsch.

Scary Day. Doreen Rappaport. (ps-1). 1988. pap. 1.95 (ISBN 0-87386-052-7). Jan Prods.

Scary Halloween Costume Book. Carol Barkin & Elizabeth James. LC 81-14249. (Illus.). (gr. 3-6). 1983. 10.25 (ISBN 0-688-00956-5); PLB 10.88 (ISBN 0-688-00957-3). Lothrop.

Scary Kisses. Brad Gooch. 272p. 1988. 17.95 (ISBN 0-399-13410-7, Putnam). Putnam Pub Group.

Scary Larry Meets Big Willie. Bob Reese. LC 83-7553. (Critterland Readers). (Illus.). 32p. (ps-2). 1983. PLB 10.60 (ISBN 0-516-02323-3); pap. 2.95 (ISBN 0-516-42323-1). Childrens.

Scary Larry the Very Very Hairy Tarantula. Bob Reese. LC 81-3871. (Critterland Desert Adventures Ser.). (Illus.). 24p. (ps-2). 1981. 9.27 (ISBN 0-516-02306-3); pap. 1.95 (ISBN 0-516-42306-1). Childrens.

Scary, Scary Halloween. Eve Bunting. LC 86-2642. (Illus.). 32p. (ps-3). 1986. 12.95 (ISBN 0-89919-414-1, Pub. by Clarion). Ticknor & Fields.

Scary, Scary Halloween. Eve Bunting. LC 86-2642. (Illus.). 32p. (ps-k). 1988. pap. 4.95 (ISBN 0-89919-799-X, Pub. by Clarion). Ticknor & Fields.

Scary! Spooky! 32p. 1989. pap. 1.95. Tor Bks.

Scary Stories to Tell in the Dark. Alvin Schwartz. LC 80-8728. (Illus.). 128p. (gr. 5 up). 1981. 11.25i (ISBN 0-397-31926-6, Lipp Jr Bks); PLB 12.89g (ISBN 0-397-31927-4); pap. 4.95i (ISBN 0-397-31970-3). HarpJ.

Scat, Scat! (Platt & Munk Cricket Bks.). (Illus.). 24p. (ps-3). 1978. 2.50 (ISBN 0-448-46521-3, G&D); PLB 3.59 (ISBN 0-448-13056-4). Putnam Pub Group.

Scat: The Movie Cat. Justin F. Denzel. LC 77-23300. (Famous Animal Stories Ser.). (Illus.). (gr. 2-5). 1977. PLB 6.89 (ISBN 0-8116-4861-3). Garrard.

Scatology in Modern Drama. Sidney Shrager. 128p. 1981. 24.50 (ISBN 0-8290-0261-8). Irvington.

Scatology in Modern Drama. Sidney Shrager. 128p. 1986. pap. text ed. 9.95x (ISBN 0-8290-2015-2). Irvington.

Scatter Diagrams: Leader Manual & Instructional Guide. Donald L. Dewar. (Advance Quality Circle Ser.). (Illus.). 58p. 1982. pap. 12.00 (ISBN 0-937670-22-7). Quality Circle.

Scatter Diagrams: Member Manual. Donald L. Dewar. (Advance Quality Circle Ser.). (Illus.). 58p. 1982. pap. 8.00 (ISBN 0-937670-27-8). Quality Circle.

Scatter of Memories. Margaret Gardiner. 192p. Date not set. 45.00 (ISBN 1-853430-43-9, Pub. by Free Association Bks). Columbia U Pr.

Scatter the Tempest. Joyce McLean. 368p. (Orig.). 1988. pap. 3.95 (ISBN 0-8439-2568-X). Leisure NY.

Scattered Light. Doraine Poretz. 32p. (Orig.). 1987. pap. 3.95 (ISBN 0-941017-09-5). Bombshelter Pr.

Scattered People: An American Family Moves West. Gerald McFarland. 288p. 1987. pap. 8.95 (ISBN 0-14-009366-4). Penguin.

Scattered Poems. Jack Kerouac. (Pocket Poets Ser.: No. 28). 1971. pap. 3.50 (ISBN 0-87286-064-7). City Lights.

Scattered Portions. Rodney Baine. (Illus.). 304p. 1985. 24.95 (ISBN 0-935265-10-4). Agee Pub.

Scattered-Site Housing. 62p. 1982. 9.00 (ISBN 0-318-17322-0, IB/82-900). Pub Tech Inc.

Scattered Sunbeams. Mildred J. Vail. LC 84-90361. 1984. 6.50 (ISBN 0-8233-0384-5). Golden Quill.

Scattered to All the Winds (Sixteen Eighty-Five to Seventeen Twenty): Migrations of the Dauphine French Huguenots into Italy, Switzerland, & Germany. rev. ed. Eugen Bellon. Ed. by Willis Schalliol. Tr. by Erika Gautschi from Ger. LC 83-70252. Orig. Title: Zerstreut in alle Winde. (Illus.). 284p. (Orig.). 1983. pap. 8.00x (ISBN 0-9605732-1-6). Belle Pubns.

Scattergun. Kit Dalton. (Buckskin Ser.: No. 15). 208p. (Orig.). 1987. pap. 2.50 (ISBN 0-8439-2439-X, Leisure Bks). Leisure NY.

Scattering & Diffraction of Waves. LC 59-11511. (Harvard Monographs in Applied Science: No. 7). (Illus.). pap. 59.00 (ISBN 0-317-09160-3, 2002784). Bks Demand UMI.

Scattering & Oneing: A Study of Conflict in the Works of the Author of the Cloud of Unknowing. Robert W. Englert. Ed. by James Hogg. (Analecta Cartusiana Ser.: No. 105). 184p. (Orig.). 1983. pap. 25.00 (ISBN 0-317-42594-3, Pub. by Salzburg Studies). Longwood Pub Group.

Scattering Branches: Tributes to the Memory of W. B. Yeats. Ed. by Stephen Gwynn. 229p. 1981. Repr. of 1940 ed. lib. bdg. 35.00 (ISBN 0-89987-901-2). Darby Bks.

Scattering by Obstacles. A. G. Ramm. 1986. lib. bdg. 89.00 (ISBN 90-277-2103-3, Pub. by Reidel Holland). Kluwer-Academic.

Scattering by Spheres. Nussenzveig. 1986. write for info. (ISBN 0-471-08318-6). Wiley.

Scattering, Deformation & Fracture in Polymers: Proceedings of Symposium Held at Mrs Fall Meeting, Boston, MA, Dec. 1-6, 1986. Ed. by G. D. Wignall et al. (MRS Symposia Proceedings Ser.: Vol. 79). 1987. text ed. 38.00 (ISBN 0-931837-44-8). Materials Res.

Scattering from Black Holes. J. Futterman et al. (Cambridge Monographs on Mathmatical Physics). (Illus.). 230p. 1988. 44.50 (ISBN 0-521-32986-8). Cambridge U Pr.

Scattering of Electromagnetic Waves from Rough Surfaces. Petr Beckmann & Andre Spizzichino. 1987. text ed. 66.00 (ISBN 0-89006-238-2). Artech Hse.

Scattering of Light & Other Electromagnetic Radiation. Milton Kerker. (Physical Chemistry Ser.: Vol. 16). 1969. 112.00 (ISBN 0-12-404550-2). Acad Pr.

Scattering of Light by Crystals. William Hayes & Rodney Loudon. LC 78-9008. 360p. 1978. 56.95 (ISBN 0-471-03191-7, Pub. by Wiley-Interscience). Wiley.

Scattering of Mrs. Blake & Related Matters. Terry Prone. 112p. 1986. 13.95 (ISBN 0-7145-2838-2, Dist. by Kampmann & Co). M Boyars Pubs.

Scattering Techniques Applied to Supramolecular & Non-Equilibrium Systems. Ed. by Sow-Hsin Chen et al. LC 81-13767. (NATO ASI Series B, Physics: Vol. 73). 942p. 1981. 135.00x (ISBN 0-306-40828-7, Plenum Pr). Plenum Pub.

Scattering Theory. Peter D. Lax & Ralph S. Phillips. (Pure & Applied Mathematics Ser.,: Vol. 26). 1967. 78.00 (ISBN 0-12-440050-7). Acad Pr.

Scattering Theory: Aspects of Scattering Processes in Atomic, Nuclear, & Particle Physics. Ed. by Asim O. Barut. 440p. 1969. 152.00 (ISBN 0-677-12730-8). Gordon & Breach.

Scattering Theory by the Enss Method. P. Perry. (Mathematical Reports: Vol. 1, No. 1). 347p. 1984. 90.00 (ISBN 3-7186-0093-5). Harwood Academic.

Scattering Theory for Automorphic Functions. Peter D. Lax & Ralph S. Phillips. LC 76-3028. (Annals of Mathematics Studies: No. 87). 260p. 1976. 38.50x (ISBN 0-691-08179-4); pap. 17.95x (ISBN 0-691-08184-0). Princeton U Pr.

Scattering Theory for Diffraction Gratings. C. H. Wilcox. (Applied Mathematical Sciences: Vol. 46). (Illus.). 170p. 1984. pap. 23.00 (ISBN 0-387-90924-9). Springer-Verlag.

Scattering Theory for Many-Body Quantum Mechanical Systems. I. M. Sigal. (Lecture Notes in Mathematics: Vol. 1011). 132p. 1983. pap. 10.00 (ISBN 0-387-12672-4). Springer-Verlag.

Scattering Theory for the d'Alembert Wave Equation in Exterior Domains. C. H. Wilcox. (Lecture Notes in Mathematics Ser.: Vol. 442). iii, 184p. 1975. pap. 14.00 (ISBN 0-387-07144-X). Springer-Verlag.

Scattering Theory in Mathematical Physics: Proceedings of the NATO Advanced Study Institute, Denver, Colorado, June, 1973. NATO Advanced Study Institute Staff. Ed. by J. A. LaVita & J. P. Marchand. LC 73-91205. 1974. lib. bdg. 47.50 (ISBN 90-277-0414-7, Pub. by Reidel Holland). Kluwer Academic.

Scattering Theory of Waves & Particles. 2nd ed. R. G. Newton. (Texts & Monographs in Physics). 800p. 1982. 56.00 (ISBN 0-387-10950-1). Springer-Verlag.

Scattering Theory: The Quantum Theory of Nonrelativitistic Collisions. John R. Taylor. LC 83-1. 496p. 1983. Repr. of 1972 ed. text ed. 34.95 (ISBN 0-89874-607-8). Krieger.

Scatterings (Based upon a True Story) A. D. Printup, II. LC 85-71343. 192p. 1986. pap. 6.95 (TS-027). DeWitt & Sheppard.

Scattershot. Bill Pronzini. (Nameless Detective Ser.). 176p. 1987. pap. 3.50 (ISBN 0-7701-0601-3). PaperJacks US.

Scavengers. Yvonne Montgomery. 240p. 1987. 16.95 (ISBN 0-87795-897-1). Morrow.

Scavengers & Decomposers: Nature's Clean-Up Crew. Pat Hughey. LC 83-17474. (Illus.). 64p. (gr. 3-7). 1984. 13.95 (ISBN 0-689-31032-3, Atheneum Childrens Bks). Macmillan.

Scavenger's Hunt. Arthur Bicknell. (Twilight Ser.: No. 26). (Orig.). (gr. k-12). 1987. pap. 2.95 (ISBN 0-440-97672-3, LFL). Dell.

Scavenger's Son. Thakazhi S. Pillai. Tr. by R. E. Asher from Malayalam. 143p. 1975. pap. 2.50 (ISBN 0-89253-025-1). Ind-US Inc.

Scavullo Women. Francesco Scavullo. LC 81-48326. (Illus.). 192p. 1982. 24.45i (ISBN 0-06-014838-1, HarpT). Har-Row.

Scavullo Women. Francesco Scavullo. LC 81-48326. (Illus.). 224p. 1985. pap. 14.95 (ISBN 0-06-091298-7, PL 1298, PL). Har-Row.

SCBA: A Fire Service Guide to the Selection, Use, Care, & Maintenance of Self-Contained Breathing Apparatus. National Fire Protection Association Staff. 228p. 1987. 22.50 (ISBN 0-317-63604-9, FSP-57). Natl Fire Prot.

SCCS Reference Card. Anatole Olczak. 6p. (Orig.). pap. 3.00 (ISBN 0-935739-04-1). A System Pubns.

Sceince of Bharata Natyam. S. Vaidyanathan. (Illus.). 80p. 1984. 34.95. Asia Bk Corp.

Scenario. Jean Anouilh. (Folio Ser.: No. 1610). 1976. 6.95 (ISBN 0-686-51892-6). Schoenhof.

Scenario, 3 Vols. Elaine Kirn. 1984. Vol. 1, 217 pp. pap. text ed. 11.95 (ISBN 0-03-063218-8); Vol. 2, 237 pp. pap. text ed. 11.95 (ISBN 0-03-063222-6); Vol. 3, 211 pp. pap. text ed. 11.95 (ISBN 0-03-063223-4). HR&W.

Scenario see Pieces Secretes.

Scenarios. Ed. by Richard Kostelanetz. LC 80-68155. (Illus.). 1981. pap. 16.00 (ISBN 0-686-69411-2). Assembling Pr.

Scenarios & Strategic Management: A Handbook on Concepts, Tools & Applications. Michel Godet. (Illus.). 290p. 1987. 65.00 (ISBN 0-408-02890-4). Butterworth.

Scenarios for a Mixed Landscape. John Allman. LC 86-2421. 80p. (Orig.). 1986. pap. 7.95 (ISBN 0-8112-0989-X, NDP619). New Directions.

Scenarios of Modernist Disintegration: Tryggve Andersen's Prose Fiction. Timothy Schiff. LC 85-12493. (Contributions to the Study of World Literature: No. 11). xiii, 147p. 1985. lib. bdg. 35.00 (ISBN 0-313-24818-4, SFM/). Greenwood.

Scenarios of the Imaginary: Theorizing the French Englightenment. Josue V. Harari. LC 86-24247. 240p. 1987. 24.95x (ISBN 0-8014-1842-9). Cornell U Pr.

Scene. Edward G. Craig. LC 65-20498. (Illus.). 1968. Repr. of 1923 ed. 18.00 (ISBN 0-405-08381-5, Blom Pubns). Ayer Co Pubs.

Scene a Quatre see Theatre.

Scene de Ballet Fantasia for Violin & Piano Op.100 Beriot. Ed. by Jules Centano. (Carl Fischer Music Library: No. 64). 1912. pap. 6.00 (ISBN 0-8258-0012-9, L64). Fischer Inc NY.

Scene Design: A Guide to the Stage. Henning Nelms. LC 74-25249. (Illus.). 96p. 1975. pap. 4.95 (ISBN 0-486-23153-4). Dover.

Scene Design: A Guide to the Stage. Henning Nelms. (Illus.). 13.00 (ISBN 0-8446-5507-4). Peter Smith.

Scene Design & Stage Lighting. 5th ed. Oren Parker et al. 596p. 1985. text ed. 33.95 (ISBN 0-03-064248-5, HoltC). HR&W.

Scene Design, Stage Lighting, Sound, Costume, & Makeup: A Scenographic Approach. Willard F. Bellman. 474p. 1983. text ed. 38.95 scp (ISBN 0-06-040612-7, HarpC). Har-Row.

Scene-Four. Ed. by Stanley Nelson. LC 77-70415. (Illus.). 272p. 1977. pap. 5.00 (ISBN 0-912292-42-3). The Smith.

Scene of Linguistic Action & Its Perspectivization by SPEAK, TALK, SAY & TELL. Rene Dirven et al. (Pragmatics & Beyond: III-6). vi, 186p. (Orig.). 1983. pap. 36.00 (ISBN 90-272-2528-1). Benjamins North Am.

Scene Painting: Tools & Techniques. Daniel Veaner. LC 83-27028. (Illus.). 208p. 1984. 22.95 (ISBN 0-13-791658-2); pap. 14.95 (ISBN 0-13-791641-8). P-H.

Scene Seventy: Recent Non Fiction see Houghton Books in Literature.

Scene Technology. Richard L. Arnold. (Illus.). 352p. 1985. text ed. 29.95 (ISBN 0-13-791765-1). P-H.

Scene-Three. Ed. by Stanley Nelson. LC 72-89382. 196p. 1975. pap. 5.00 (ISBN 0-912292-38-5). The Smith.

Scene-Two. annual LC 70-94633. 192p. 1974. pap. 5.00 (ISBN 0-912292-34-2). The Smith.

Scenebook for Student Actors. Ruth Lane. 264p. 1973. Spiralbound. text ed. write for info. (ISBN 0-8221-0099-1). Wadsworth Pub.

Scenery for a Play & Other Poems. Ettore Rella. LC 81-12207. 64p. (Orig.). 1981. pap. 4.95 (ISBN 0-8076-1020-8). Braziller.

Scenery for Model Railroads. Bill McClanahan. LC 67-14545. (Illus.). 104p. (Orig.). 1967. pap. 6.25 (ISBN 0-89024-508-8). Kalmbach.

Scenery for the Theatre. 2nd, rev. ed. Harold Burris-Meyer & Edward C. Cole. (Illus.). 1972. 65.00 (ISBN 0-316-11754-4). Little.

Scenery in Shakespeare's Plays & Other Studies. David W. Rannie. LC 70-153346. Repr. of 1926 ed. 32.00 (ISBN 0-404-05225-8). AMS Pr.

Scenery of the Plains, Mountains & Mines. Franklin Langworthy. LC 76-87645. (American Scene Ser). (Illus.). 292p. 1972. Repr. of 1932 ed. lib. bdg. 39.50 (ISBN 0-306-71785-9). Da Capo.

Scenery of the White Mountains. William Oakes. LC 77-135880. (Illus.). 1970. Repr. of 1848 ed. 45.00x (ISBN 0-912274-05-0). NH Pub Co.

Scenes. John Irwin. LC 77-528. (City & Society Ser.: Vol. 1). pap. 59.00 (ISBN 0-317-09003-8, 2021914). Bks Demand UMI.

Scenes along the Road. Allen Ginsberg. Compiled by Ann Charters. (Illus.). 56p. (Orig.). 1985. pap. 7.95 (ISBN 0-87286-168-6). City Lights.

Scenes & Actions: Unpublished Manuscripts. Christopher Caudwell et al. (Illus.). 224p. 1986. 45.00 (ISBN 0-7102-0374-8, 03748); pap. 19.95 (ISBN 0-7102-0985-1, 09851). Routledge Chapman & Hall.

Scenes & Adventures in the Army; or Romance of Military Life. Philip St. George Cooke. LC 72-9436. (Far Western Frontier Ser.). 436p. 1973. Repr. of 1857 ed. 26.50 (ISBN 0-405-04966-8). Ayer Co Pubs.

Scenes & Characters of the Middle Ages. Edward L. Cutts. LC 67-27866. (Social History Reference Ser.). (Illus.). 560p. 1968. Repr. of 1872 ed. 40.00x (ISBN 0-8103-3257-4). Gale.

Scenes & Characters of the Middle Ages. Edward L. Cutts. 1977. lib. bdg. 59.95 (ISBN 0-8490-2569-9). Gordon Pr.

Scenes & Characters of the Middle Ages. Edward L. Cutts. LC 77-23575. 1977. Repr. of 1922 ed. lib. bdg. 45.00 (ISBN 0-89341-160-4). Longwood Pub Group.

Scenes & Legends of the North of Scotland: Traditional History of Cromarty. 2nd rev. ed. Hugh Miller. Ed. by Richard M. Dorson. (International Folklore Ser.). 1977. Repr. of 1869 ed. lib. bdg. 37.50x (ISBN 0-405-10110-4). Ayer Co Pubs.

Scenes & Monologues from the New American Theater. Frank Pike & Thomas G. Dunn. 304p. 1988. pap. 4.95 (ISBN 0-451-62547-1, Ment). NAL.

Scenes & Motifs. (Album of Cross-Stitch Designs Library: Bk. 6). (Illus.). 32p. 1985. pap. 3.95 (ISBN 0-668-06363-7). Arco.

Scenes & Silhouettes. D. L. Murray. 1926. 30.00 (ISBN 0-8274-3331-X). R West.

Scenes & Silhouettes. facs. ed. David L. Murray. LC 68-16959. (Essay Index Reprint Ser). 1968. Repr. of 1926 ed. 17.50 (ISBN 0-8369-0727-2). Ayer Co Pubs.

Scenes Beyond the Grave. Gordon Lindsay. (Sorcery & Spirit World Ser.). 2.95 (ISBN 0-89985-091-X). Christ Nations.

Scenes Choisies. Andre Malraux. 8.50 (ISBN 0-685-34268-9). French & Eur.

Scenes de la Vie Francaise. Mauger. 6.95 (ISBN 0-685-36697-9). French & Eur.

Scenes de la Vie Parisienne. Guy De Maupassant. 192p. 1968. 9.95 (ISBN 0-686-54794-2). French & Eur.

Scenes for a Raja: Study of an Indian Kalamkari Found in Indonesia. Nina W. Gwatkin. (Monograph Ser.: No. 27). (Illus.). 24p. (Orig.). 1986. pap. text ed. 9.00 (ISBN 0-930741-06-4). UCLA Mus Cultural Hist.

Scenes for Student Actors, 6 Vols. Frances Cosgrove. 5.00 ea.; Vol. 1. (ISBN 0-573-69025-1); Vol. 2. (ISBN 0-573-69026-X); Vol. 3. (ISBN 0-573-69027-8); Vol. 4. (ISBN 0-573-69028-6); Vol. 5. (ISBN 0-573-69029-4); Vol. 6. (ISBN 0-573-69030-8). French.

Scenes for Teenagers. Roger Karshner. 48p. (Orig.). 1986. pap. 4.95 (ISBN 0-9611792-9-5). Dramaline Pubns.

Scenes for the Actor. Robert Westrom. 76p. (Orig.). 1979. pap. 2.95 (ISBN 0-938230-03-4, TX356-231). Westrom.

Scenes for Young Actors. Lorraine Cohen. (gr. 6 up). 1973. pap. 4.95 (ISBN 0-380-00997-8, Discus). Avon.

Scenes from a Divorce: A Book for Friends & Relatives of a Divorcing Family. Neil Paylor & Barry Head. 120p. 1983. pap. 6.95 (ISBN 0-86683-635-7, HarpR). Har-Row.

Scenes from a Marriage. David Barker. 40p. 1979. pap. 3.00 (ISBN 0-935390-04-9). Wormwood Rev.

Scenes from a Receding Past. Aidan Higgins. 1979. 9.95 (ISBN 0-7145-3556-7). Riverrun NY.

Scenes from a Second Adolescence, & Other Poems. Gerald Locklin. 1979. pap. 4.95 (ISBN 0-930090-08-X). Applezaba.

Scenes from a Silent World, or Prisons & Their Inmates: London 1889. Francis Scougal, pseud. LC 83-49254. (Crime & Punishment in England, 1850-1922 Ser.). 252p. 1984. lib. bdg. 30.00 (ISBN 0-8240-6217-5). Garland Pub.

Scenes from Another Life. J. D. McClatchy. LC 80-24741. (Poetry Ser.). 63p. 1981. 4.95 (ISBN 0-8076-1000-3). Braziller.

Scenes from Corporate Life: The Politics of Middle Management. Earl Shorris. 400p. 1984. pap. 7.95 (ISBN 0-14-007277-2). Penguin.

Scenes from Dickens. Guy Portwee. 25.00 (ISBN 0-8274-3330-1). R West.

Scenes from Greek Drama. Bruno Snell. (Sather Classical Lectures: No. 34). 1964. 33.00x (ISBN 0-520-01191-0). U of Cal Pr.

Scenes from Indian Mythology. 2nd ed. S. M. Imam. 1975. pap. 1.50 (ISBN 0-89684-347-5). Orient Bk Dist.

Scenes from Married Life & Scenes from Later Life. William Cooper. 528p. 1985. pap. 5.95 (ISBN 0-380-69896-X, Bard). Avon.

Scenes from Provincial Life & Scenes from Metropolitan Life. William Cooper. 432p. 1984. pap. 4.95 (ISBN 0-380-69302-X, Bard). Avon.

Scenes from Provincial Life: Knightly Families in Sussex, 1280-1400. Nigel Saul. (Illus.). 204p. 1987. 45.00 (ISBN 0-19-820077-3). Oxford U Pr.

Scenes from Shakespeare: A Workbook for Actors. Robin J. Holt. LC 87-46388. 220p. 1988. lib. bdg. 19.95x (ISBN 0-89950-310-1). McFarland & Co.

Scenes from Some Theban Tombs. Nina Davies. (Private Tombs at Thebes Ser.: Vol. IV). 22p. 1963. text ed. 26.00x (ISBN 0-900416-17-3, Pub. by Aris & Philips UK). Humanities.

Scenes From Surgical Life. David LeVay. 200p. 1976. 17.96 (ISBN 0-8464-0813-9). Beekman Pubs.

Scenes from the Anti-Nazi War. Basil Davidson. LC 81-81696. 288p. 1981. pap. 6.50 (ISBN 0-85345-588-0). Monthly Rev.

Scenes from the Anti-Nazi War. Basil Davidson. 288p. 1980. pap. 6.50 (ISBN 0-317-61680-3). Monthly Rev.

Scenes from the Bathhouse: And Other Stories of Communist Russia. Mikhail Zoshchenko. Tr. by Sidney Monas. 1961. pap. 8.95 (ISBN 0-472-06070-8, 70, AA). U of Mich Pr.

Scenes from the Classics. Ed. by Edith B. Maag. 1987. pap. 4.95 (ISBN 0-9611792-5-2). Dramaline Pubns.

Scenes from the Drama of European Literature: Six Essays. Erich Auerbach. 11.50 (ISBN 0-8446-5834-0). Peter Smith.

Scenes from the Drama of European Literature. Erich Auerbach. LC 83-12549. (Theory & History of Literature Ser.: Vol. 9). 272p. 1984. 25.00x (ISBN 0-8166-1242-0); pap. 10.95 (ISBN 0-8166-1243-9). U of Minn Pr.

Scenes from the Fashionable World. Kennedy Fraser. 1987. 17.95 (ISBN 0-394-55483-3). Knopf.

Scenes from the "George Eliot" Country. S. Parkinson. LC 77-9386. 1977. lib. bdg. 30.00 (ISBN 0-8414-6833-8). Folcroft.

Scenes from the Homefront. Sara Vogan. LC 87-4996. (Illinois Short Fiction Ser.). 144p. 1987. 11.95 (ISBN 0-252-01430-8). U of Ill Pr.

Scenes from the Life of a Faun. Arno Schmidt. Tr. by John Woods. LC 82-12901. 160p. 1983. 13.95 (ISBN 0-7145-2762-9, Dist. by Kampmann & Co). M Boyars Pubs.

Scenes from the Life of a Faun. Arno Schmidt. Tr. by John E. Woods from Ger. 160p. 1987. pap. 8.95 (ISBN 0-7145-2763-7, Dist. by Kampmann & Co). M Boyars Pubs.

Scenes from the Life of an Actor. George H. Hill. LC 75-81204. 1853. lib. bdg. 22.00x (ISBN 0-405-08617-2, Blom Pubns). Ayer Co Pubs.

Scenes from the Mesozoic & Other Drawings. Clarence Day. 1935. 29.50x (ISBN 0-686-51306-1). Elliots Bks.

Scenes from the Music of Charles Ives: L-N Score. Sokolow & Fox. (EPC Ser.). 154p. 1985. pap. write for info. (ISBN 0-932582-44-3). Dance Notation.

Scenes from the Nineteenth-Century Stage in Advertising Woodcuts. Ed. by Stanley Appelbaum. (Pictorial Archive Ser.). (Illus.). 176p. 1977. pap. 8.95 (ISBN 0-486-23434-7). Dover.

Scenes from the Nineteenth-Century Stage in Advertising Woodcuts. Ed. by Stanley Appelbaum. 13.25 (ISBN 0-8446-5552-X). Peter Smith.

Scenes from the Past of Nevada, Missouri. Betty Sterett. Ed. by Donna Logan. (Illus.). 288p. (Orig.). 1985. 15.00 (ISBN 0-9614944-0-9); pap. 10.00 (ISBN 0-9614944-1-7). DGL InFoWrite.

Scenes in America, for the Amusement & Instruction of Little Tarry-At-Home Travellers. Isaac Taylor. Repr. of 1821 ed. 17.00 (ISBN 0-384-59610-X). Johnson Repr.

Scenes in Black & White. James Penzi. (Contact II Chapbook). (Illus.). 32p. (Orig.). 1982. pap. 3.00 (ISBN 0-936556-06-4). Contact Two.

Scenes in Nineteenth Century English Fiction. R. N. Sarkar. 216p. 1988. text ed. 30.00x (ISBN 81-7045-036-5, Pub. by Associated Pub House). Advent NY.

Scenes in the Life of Harriet Tubman. facs. ed. Sarah H. Bradford. LC 70-154071. (Black Heritage Library Collection). 1869. 19.00 (ISBN 0-8369-8782-9). Ayer Co Pubs.

Scenes in The South, & Other Miscellaneous Pieces. James R. Creecy. 18.00 (ISBN 0-8369-9186-9, 9055). Ayer Co Pubs.

Scenes of American Life. 2nd ed. Martha E. Kendall. 124p. 1987. wkbk. 12.95 (ISBN 0-945783-00-0). Highland Pub Group.

Scenes of Childhood, Op. 15. Robert Schumann. Ed. by Maxwell Eckstein. (Carl Fischer Music Library: No. 256). 1949. pap. 3.95 (ISBN 0-8258-0100-1, L256). Fischer Inc NY.

Scenes of Clerical Life. George Eliot. 1976. 14.95x (ISBN 0-460-00468-9, Evman); pap. 2.95x (ISBN 0-460-01468-4, Evman). Biblio Dist.

Scenes of Clerical Life. George Eliot. Ed. by Robert L. Wolff. LC 75-491. (Victorian Fiction Ser.). 1975. Repr. of 1858 ed. lib. bdg. 73.00 (ISBN 0-8240-1567-3). Garland Pub.

Scenes of Clerical Life. George Eliot. Ed. by David Lodge. (English Library). (Orig.). 1973. pap. 4.95 (ISBN 0-14-043087-3). Penguin.

Scenes of Clerical Life. George Eliot. Ed. by Thomas A. Noble. (Clarendon Edition of the Novels of George Eliot Ser.). 334p. 1985. 49.95x (ISBN 0-19-812559-3). Oxford U Pr.

Scenes of Clerical Life. George Eliot. Intro. by Thomas A. Noble. (World's Classics Ser.). 352p. 1989. pap. 4.95 (ISBN 0-19-281786-8). Oxford U Pr.

Scenes of Life at the Capital. Philip Whalen. LC 72-163756. 84p. (Orig.). 1971. 5.00 (ISBN 0-912516-10-0); pap. 2.50 (ISBN 0-912516-00-3). Grey Fox.

Scenes of Nature, Signs of Man: Essays in 19th & 20th Century American Literature. Tony Tanner. (Cambridge Studies in American Literature & Culture). 288p. 1987. 29.95 (ISBN 0-521-32318-5). Cambridge U Pr.

Scenes of Southern Arizona: What to See & Where to Go. Jim Klar & Joyce Ryan. (Illus.). 96p. (Orig.). 1986. pap. 6.00 (ISBN 0-939077-00-0). Butterfly Bks.

Scenes of Wonder & Curiosity. Ed. by R. R. Olmsted. LC 62-20618. (Illus.). 1962. 9.95 (ISBN 0-8310-7032-3). Howell-North.

Scenes of Wonder & Curiosity. Ted Orland. (Illus.). 1988. 40.00. Godine.

Scenes They Haven't Seen. Roger Karshner. 53p. (Orig.). 1983. pap. 4.95 (ISBN 0-9611792-1-X). Dramaline Pubns.

Scenic America. K. Westcott-Jones. (Illus.). 224p. Date not set. 12.98 (777044). Smith Pubs.

Scenic & Costume Design for the Ballets Russes. Robert C. Hansen. Ed. by Oscar Brockett. LC 85-14029. (Theater & Dramatic Studies: No. 30). 231p. 1985. 49.95 (ISBN 0-8357-1681-3). UMI Res Pr.

Scenic Form in Shakespeare. Emrys Jones. 1971. pap. 13.95x (ISBN 0-19-812325-6). Oxford U Pr.

Scenic Great Smoky Mountains National Park Address Book. (Illus.). 2.50 (ISBN 0-936672-64-1). Aerial Photo.

Scenic Highway One: Monterey to Morro Bay. rev., 1985 ed. Vicki Leon. (Illus.). 64p. (Orig.). 1984. pap. 6.95 (ISBN 0-918303-02-8). Blake Print Pub.

Scenic Mountains see West on Wood: Antique Wood Engravings of the Old West.

Scenic North Carolina Address Book: From Mountains to the Sea. (Illus.). 4.50 (ISBN 0-936672-63-3). Aerial Photo.

Scenic Rail Guide to Central & Atlantic Canada. Bill Coo. (Illus.). 160p. 1983. pap. 9.95 (ISBN 0-919872-76-X). NY Zoetrope.

Scenic Rail Guide to Western Canada. rev. ed. Bill Coo. (Illus.). 192p. 1986. pap. 9.95 (ISBN 0-920775-14-4, Pub. by Grey de Pencer Bks). NY Zoetrope.

Scenic Route. Bruce Francis. 100p. 1987. 15.00 (ISBN 0-935716-45-9). Lord John.

Scenic South Carolina. 2nd, rev. ed. Eugene B. Sloan. LC 79-183143. (Illus.). 1971. text ed. 12.95 (ISBN 0-915114-00-3). Lewis-Sloan.

Scenic Southwest see West on Wood: Antique Wood Engravings of the Old West.

Scenic Tunnels. Louise Neaderland. (Illus.). 16p. (Orig.). 1983. pap. 12.00 (ISBN 0-942561-03-1). Bone Hollow.

Scenic Utah. Colourpicture Publishing Co. Staff. (Travel Ser.: No. L-23). (Illus.). 32p. 1981. pap. text ed. 2.50 (ISBN 0-938440-48-9). Colourpicture.

Scenic Wonders of America: An Illustrated Guide to Our Natural Splendors. Reader's Digest Editors. LC 72-91832. (Illus.). 575p. 1973. 21.99 (ISBN 0-89577-009-1). RD Assn.

Sceno Graphic Techniques. W. Oren Parker. 92p. 1969. spiral bdg. 7.95x (ISBN 0-685-83021-7). Scenographic.

Sceno-Graphic Techniques. 3rd ed. W. Oren Parker. (Illus.). 112p. 1987. pap. 14.95x (ISBN 0-8093-1350-2). S Ill U Pr.

Scenographic Imagination. 2nd, rev. ed. Darwin R. Payne. (Illus.). 316p. 1986. pap. text ed. 19.95x. S Ill U Pr.

Scenography of Josef Svoboda. Jarka Burian. LC 77-152101. (Illus.). 197p. 1971. pap. 12.95 (ISBN 0-8195-6032-4). Wesleyan U Pr.

Scent & the Scenting Dog. 3rd ed. William G. Sjrotuck. LC 72-94862. (Illus.). 102p. 1972. pap. 7.95 (ISBN 0-914124-03-X). Arner Pubns.

Scent of Apples: A Collection of Stories. Bienvenido N. Santos. LC 79-4857. 250p. 1979. pap. 8.95 (ISBN 0-295-95695-X). U of Wash Pr.

Scent of Cloves. Norah Lofts. Repr. lib. bdg. 19.95 (ISBN 0-89190-228-7, Pub. by River City Pr). Amereon Ltd.

Scent of Gold. Hilary London. (Harlequin American Romance Ser.). 256p. 1983. pap. 2.25 (ISBN 0-373-16027-5). Harlequin Bks.

Scent of Murder. Elizabeth Howard. LC 87-4583. (My Name Is Paris Ser.: Bk. III). (Illus.). 144p. (gr. 5 up). 1987. pap. 5.99 (ISBN 0-394-97548-0, BYR); PLB 3.95 (ISBN 0-394-87548-6, BYR). Random.

Scent of Nutmeg. Colleen Cairns. 288p. 1985. pap. 3.25 (ISBN 0-8439-2202-8, Leisure Bks). Leisure NY.

Scent of Water. Vera J. Nelson. (Western Americana Book). 104p. (Orig.). 1973. pap. 3.00x (ISBN 0-913626-19-8). S S S Pub Co.

Scent Smile & Sorrow: Selected Verse 1891-1957 & Jottings from Notebooks. Avedick Issahakian. Ed. & tr. by E. B. Chrakian. LC 75-12440. (Illus.). 1984. pap. 5.75 (ISBN 0-910154-02-3). Library of Armenian.

Scent: Training to Track, Search, & Rescue. Milo D. Pearsall & Hugo Verbruggen. (Illus.). 224p. 1982. 14.98 (ISBN 0-931866-11-1). Alpine Pubns.

Scented Garden. Eleanour S. Rohde. LC 70-175781. 330p. 1974. Repr. of 1931 ed. 46.00x (ISBN 0-8103-3874-2). Gale.

Scented Gardens for the Blind. Janet Frame. LC 64-10786. 1980. pap. 4.95 (ISBN 0-8076-0985-4). Braziller.

Scented Room: Cherchez's Book of Dried Flowers, Fragrance, & Potpourri. Barbara M. Ohrbach. 1986. 17.95 (ISBN 0-517-56081-X, C N Potter Bks). Crown.

Scenter Pieces of Fragrance: Creative Recipe Pages. Bibliotheca Press Staff. 17p. 1987. pap. text ed. 3.95 (ISBN 0-939476-88-6, Pub. by Biblio Pr GA). Prosperity & Profits.

Scentouri Guide to Wild Fragrances for Potpourri, Etc. Scentouri Staff. 1985. pap. 4.95 (ISBN 0-318-03762-9, Pub. by Scentouri). Prosperity & Profits.

Scentouri Potpourri Recipe Book. Frieda Carrol. 15p. 1983. pap. 3.95 (ISBN 0-939476-94-0, Pub. by Biblio Pr GA). Prosperity & Profits.

Scents. Johanna Kingsley. 448p. 1985. pap. 4.50 (ISBN 0-553-26583-0). Bantam.

Scents of Place: Season of the St. Croix Valley. Cynthia B. Gustavson. (Illus., Orig.). (YA) (gr. 9-12). 1987. pap. 8.95. Country Messenger Inc.

Scents-Sational Smelly Sticker Kit. Chip Lovitt. 16p. (ps-3). 1988. pap. 3.95 (ISBN 0-590-40538-1). Scholastic Inc.

Scentual Touch: A Personal Guide to Aromatherapy. Judith Jackson. 1987. pap. 9.95 (ISBN 0-449-90245-5, Columbine). Fawcett.

Scentuous Cookery: Or How to Make It in the Kitchen. Jane Johnston & Phyllis Jedlicka. LC 76-174740. (Illus.). 1971. 15.00 (ISBN 0-87832-004-0). Piper.

Scepsis Scientifics: Or Confest Ignorance, the Way to Science, 2 vols. in 1. Joseph Glanvill. Ed. by Rene Wellek. LC 75-11222. (British Philosophers & Theologians of the 17th & 18th Centuries Ser.). 330p. 1978. lib. bdg. 51.00 (ISBN 0-8240-1776-5). Garland Pub.

Scepter of Egypt: A Background for the Study of Egyptian Antiquities in the Metropolitan Museum of Art. William C. Hayes. Incl. Vol. 1. From the Earliest Times to the End of the Middle Kingdom; Vol. 2. Hyksos Period & the New Kingdom (1675-1080 B.C.. LC 52-7286. (Illus.). 1959. Metro Mus Art.

Sceptical Anthropologist? Social Anthropology & Marxist Views on Society. R. Firth. (Radcilffe-Brown Lectures in Social Anthropology). 1976. pap. 2.50 (ISBN 0-85672-064-X, Pub. by British Acad). Longwood Pub Group.

Sceptical Dialogue on Induction. A. Naess. (Methodology & Science: Vol. 3). 76p. 1984. pap. text ed. 14.00x (ISBN 90-232-2047-1, Pub. by Van Gorcum Holland). Humanities.

Sceptical Essays. Bertrand Russell. (Unwin Paperbacks). 1960. pap. 7.95 (ISBN 0-04-104003-1). Unwin Hyman.

Sceptical Feminist: A Philosophical Enquiry. Janet R. Richards. 320p. 1980. 26.95x (ISBN 0-7100-0673-X); pap. 9.95 (ISBN 0-7100-9217-2). Routledge Chapman & Hall.

Sceptical Realism of David Hume. John P. Wright. ix, 250p. 1983. 29.50x (ISBN 0-8166-1223-4); pap. 13.95 (ISBN 0-8166-1224-2). U of Minn Pr.

Sceptical Sociology. John Carroll. 256p. 1980. 26.00x (ISBN 0-7100-0587-3). Routledge Chapman & Hall.

Scepticism. Kai E. Nielsen. LC 72-77776. (New Studies in the Philosophy of Religion Ser.). 96p. 1973. 18.95 (ISBN 0-312-70070-9). St Martin.

Scepticism: A Critical Reappraisal. Nicholas Rescher. LC 79-22990. 265p. 1980. 30.00x (ISBN 0-8476-6240-3). Rowman.

Scepticism & Animal Faith. George Santayana. 14.75 (ISBN 0-8446-2863-8). Peter Smith.

Scepticism & Animal Faith: Introduction to a System of Philosophy. George Santayana. 1955. pap. text ed. 6.00 (ISBN 0-486-20236-4). Dover.

Scepticism & Animal Faith of Wallace Stevens. Richard N. Sawaya. Ed. by Stephen Orgel. (Harvard Dissertations in American & English Literature Ser.). 357p. 1987. lib. bdg. 55.00 (ISBN 0-8240-0075-7). Garland Pub.

Scepticism & Belief in Hume's Dialogues Concerning Natural Religion. Stanley Tweyman. 1986. lib. bdg. 45.00 (ISBN 90-247-3090-2, Pub. by Martinus Nijhoff Netherlands). Kluwer Academic.

Scepticism, Man & God: Selections from the Major Writings Of Sextus Empiricus. Sextus Empiricus. Ed. by Philip P. Hallie. Tr. by Sanford G. Etheridge. LC 64-22377. pap. 62.00 (ISBN 0-317-08988-9, 2001959). Bks Demand UMI.

Scepticism or Platonism: The Philosophy of the Fourth Academy. Harold Tarrant. (Cambridge Classical Studies). 192p. 1985. 44.50 (ISBN 0-521-30191-2). Cambridge U Pr.

Scepticism, Rules & Language. G. P Baker & P. M. Hacker. 160p. 1986. pap. text ed. 19.95 (ISBN 0-631-14703-9). Basil Blackwell.

Scepticism, Society & the Eighteenth-Century Novel. Eve Tavor. LC 86-6595. 192p. 1987. 29.95 (ISBN 0-312-70071-7). St Martin.

Scepticisms, Notes on Contemporary Poetry. Conrad P. Aiken. Repr. of 1919 ed. 18.00 (ISBN 0-384-00525-X). Johnson Repr.

Scepticisms: Notes on Contemporary Poetry. facs. ed. Conrad P. Aiken. LC 67-30170. (Essay Index Reprint Ser). 1919. 16.00 (ISBN 0-8369-0140-1). Ayer Co Pubs.

Sceptics of the Old Testament. Emile J. Dillon. LC 73-16064. (Studies in Comparative Literature, No. 35). 1974. Repr. of 1895 ed. lib. bdg. 51.95x (ISBN 0-8383-1723-5). Haskell.

Sceptre D'ottokar. Herge. (Illus., Fr.). (gr. 7-9). looseleaf bdg. 15.95 (ISBN 0-685-28411-5). French & Eur.

Scettro di Ottokar. Herge. (Illus.). 62p. (Ital.). pap. 15.95 (ISBN 0-686-54353-X). French & Eur.

Schaffer's Diseases of the Newborn. 5th ed. Mary E. Avery & H. William Taeusch, Jr. (Illus.). 1040p. 1984. 99.00 (ISBN 0-7216-1458-2). Saunders.

Schaldach. Etchings. The Sporting Art of William J. Schaldach. Ed. by Edward Gray & DeCourcy Taylor. LC 87-82427. (Illus.). 160p. 1988. limited ed. 45.00 (ISBN 0-9609842-9-1). GSJ Press.

Schalliol Is Our Family Name: Its History from 1323 to 1985. Trilingual ed. Willis L. Schalliol. Tr. by Paul Challiol & Helga C. Gay. (Illus.). 502p. (Orig., Fr., Ger. & Eng.). 1985. lib. bdg. 28.00x (ISBN 0-9605732-4-0); pap. 20.00x (ISBN 0-9605732-3-2). Belle Pubns.

Schalm's Veterinary Hematology. 4th ed. Nemi C. Jain. LC 84-27811. (Illus.). 1221p. 1986. text ed. 125.00 (ISBN 0-8121-0942-2). Lea & Febiger.

Schambach-Kaston Collection of Musical Instruments. Richard T. Rephann. (Illus.). 88p. (Orig.). 1988. pap. write for info. (ISBN 0-929530-05-5). Yale U Coll Musical Instruments.

Schantung Und Deutsch-China. Ernst Von Hesse-Warteg. 294p. 1898. 1050.00x (ISBN 0-317-69006-X, Pub. by Han-Shan Tang Ltd). State Mutual Bk.

Schapiro, Leonard Bertram, Nineteen Eight to Nineteen Eighty-Three. Peter Reddaway. (Memoirs of the Fellows of the British Academy Ser.). (Illus.). 1986. pap. 5.50 (ISBN 0-85672-510-2, Pub. by British Acad). Longwood Pub Group.

Scharansky: Hero of our Time. Martin Gilbert. 512p. 1986. 24.95 (ISBN 0-317-46605-4). Viking.

Schat-Chen: History, Traditions & Narratives of the Queres Indians of Laguna & Acoma. John M. Gunn. LC 76-43720. Repr. of 1917 ed. 22.00 (ISBN 0-404-15553-7). AMS Pr.

Schattenwirtschaft: Eine Moeglichkeit zur Einschraenkung der Oeffentlichen Verwaltung? Hannelore Weck. (Finanzwissenschaftliche Schriften: Vol. 22). 160p. (Ger.). 1983. 17.90 (ISBN 3-8204-7590-7). P Lang Pubs.

Schatz Rackhams des Roten. Herge. (Illus.). 62p. (Ger.). pap. 15.95 (ISBN 0-686-54315-7). French & Eur.

Schatzbehalter. Michael Wolgemut & Stephan Fridolin. (Illus.). 708p. (Ger.). 1981. pap. 75.00 slipcase (ISBN 0-915346-69-9). A Wofsy Fine Arts.

Schauder Bases: Behavior & Stability. Kamthan et al. (Pure & Applied Mathematics Ser.). 456p. 1988. 79.00 (ISBN 0-470-21029-X). Wiley.

Schauder Bases in Banach Spaces of Continuous Functions. Z. Semadeni. (Lecture Notes in Mathematics Ser.: Vol. 918). 136p. 1982. pap. 12.00 (ISBN 0-387-11481-5). Springer-Verlag.

Schaum's Outline for Physical Chemistry. Clyde Metz. 448p. 1988. 10.95 (ISBN 0-07-041715-6). McGraw.

Schaum's Outline of Accounting I. 3rd ed. James A. Cashin & Joel J. Lerner. 304p. 1987. pap. text ed. 8.95 (ISBN 0-07-010353-4). McGraw.

Schaum's Outline of Accounting II. 2nd ed. James A. Cashin & Joel J. Lerner. (Schaum's Outline Ser.). 288p. 1981. pap. text ed. 8.95 (ISBN 0-07-010252-X). McGraw.

Schaum's Outline of Accounting II. 3rd ed. James A. Cashin & Joel J. Lerner. (Outline Ser.). 320p. 1989. 9.95 (ISBN 0-07-010271-6). McGraw.

Schaum's Outline of Advanced Accounting. J. A. Wiseman & James A. Cashin. 1982. pap. text ed. 9.95 (ISBN 0-07-071138-0). McGraw.

Schaum's Outline of Advanced COBOL with COBOL File Processing. L. Newcomer. 384p. 1986. pap. text ed. 10.95 (ISBN 0-07-037999-8). McGraw.

Schaum's Outline of Advanced Cost Accounting see Schaum's Outline of Cost Accounting II.

Schaum's Outline of Analytical Chemistry. A. A. Gordus. 256p. 1985. pap. text ed. 8.95 (ISBN 0-07-023795-6). McGraw.

Schaum's Outline of Applied Physics. 2nd ed. Arthur Beiser. (Schaum Outline Ser.). 352p. 1988. pap. text ed. 10.50 (ISBN 0-07-004379-5). McGraw.

Schaum's Outline of Basic Circuit Analysis. John O'Malley. (Schaum's Outline Ser.). 400p. 1982. pap. text ed. 9.95 (ISBN 0-07-047820-1). McGraw.

Schaum's Outline of Basic Electrical Engineering. J. J. Cathey & Syed A. Nasar. 1983. pap. text ed. 9.95 (ISBN 0-07-010234-1). McGraw.

Schaum's Outline of Basic Electricity. W. Gussow. (Schaum Outline Ser.). 448p. 1983. pap. text ed. 10.95 (ISBN 0-07-025240-8). McGraw.

Schaum's Outline of Basic Mathematics for Electricity & Electronics. Arthur Beiser. (Schaum's Outline Ser.). (Illus.). 208p. 1981. pap. text ed. 7.95 (ISBN 0-07-004378-7). McGraw.

Schaum's Outline of Beginning Calculus. Elliot Mendelson. (Schaum's Outline Ser.). 384p. 1985. pap. text ed. 9.95 (ISBN 0-07-041465-3). McGraw.

Schaum's Outline of Business Law. Donald A. Wiesner & Nicholas A. Glaskowsky. (Schaum's Outline Ser.). 416p. 1985. pap. text ed. 10.95 (ISBN 0-07-069062-6). McGraw.

Schaum's Outline of Business Statistics. 2nd ed. Leonard J. Kazmier. 424p. 1988. 10.95 (ISBN 0-07-033533-8). McGraw.

Schaum's Outline of Child Psychology. Terry Faw. (Illus., Orig.). 1980. pap. text ed. 7.95 (ISBN 0-07-020110-2). McGraw.

Schaum's Outline of College Business Law. R. Robert Rosenberg. LC 77-940. (Schaum's Outline Ser.). 1977. pap. text ed. 8.95 (ISBN 0-07-053805-0). McGraw.

Schaum's Outline of College Chemistry. 6th ed. Jerome L. Rosenberg. (Schaum's Outline Ser.). (Illus.). 1980. pap. text ed. 8.95 (ISBN 0-07-053706-2). McGraw.

Schaum's Outline of College Physics. 8th ed. Frederick Bueche. 432p. 1988. pap. price not set. McGraw.

Schaum's Outline of College Physics. 7th ed. Frederick J. Bueche. (Schaum's Outline Ser.). (Illus.). 1979. pap. text ed. 8.95 (ISBN 0-07-008857-8). McGraw.

Schaum's Outline of Computer Graphics. R. A. Plastock & G. Kalley. (Schaum's Outline Ser.). 352p. 1986. pap. text ed. 9.95 (ISBN 0-07-050326-5). McGraw.

Schaum's Outline of Computers & Business. Lawrence S. Orilia. 304p. 1984. pap. text ed. 8.95 (ISBN 0-07-047834-1). McGraw.

Schaum's Outline of Computers & Programming. Francis Scheid. (Schaum's Outline Ser.). 320p. 1982. pap. text ed. 10.95 (ISBN 0-07-055196-0). McGraw.

Schaum's Outline of Contemporary Mathematics of Finance. R. G. Brown. (Schaum Outline Ser.). 192p. 1983. pap. text ed. 8.95 (ISBN 0-07-008146-8). McGraw.

Schaum's Outline of Cost Accounting I. 2nd ed. Ralph S. Polimeni & James A. Cashin. 272p. 1984. pap. text ed. 8.95 (ISBN 0-07-010273-2). McGraw.

Schaum's Outline of Cost Accounting II. James A. Cashin et al. (Schaum's Outline Ser.). Orig. Title: Schaum's Outline of Advanced Cost Accounting. 240p. 1982. pap. text ed. 8.95 (ISBN 0-07-010207-4). McGraw.

Schaum's Outline of Data Processing. Martin Lipschutz & Seymour Lipschutz. (Schaum's Outline Ser.). (Illus.). 224p. (Orig.). 1981. pap. text ed. 8.95 (ISBN 0-07-037983-1). McGraw.

Schaum's Outline of Data Structure. Seymour Lipschutz. (Schaum Outline Ser.). 320p. 1986. pap. text ed. 9.95 (ISBN 0-07-038001-5). McGraw.

Schaum's Outline of Development Economics. Dominick Salvatore & Edward T. Dowling. (Schaum's Outline Ser.). 1977. pap. text ed. 9.95 (ISBN 0-07-054494-8). McGraw.

Schaum's Outline of Digital Principles. Roger L. Tokheim. (Illus., Orig.). 1980. pap. text ed. 9.95 (ISBN 0-07-064928-6). McGraw.

Schaum's Outline of Digital Principles. 2nd ed. Roger L. Tokheim. (Schaum's Outline Ser.). 336p. 1988. pap. text ed. 8.95 (ISBN 0-07-065012-8). McGraw.

Schaum's Outline of Dynamic Structural Analysis. Jan J. Tuma & F. Y. Cheng. (Schaum's Outline Ser.). 240p. 1983. pap. text ed. 12.95 (ISBN 0-07-065437-9). McGraw.

Schaum's Outline of Electric Circuits. 2nd ed. Joseph Edminister. (Schaum's Outline Ser.). 304p. 1983. pap. text ed. 8.95 (ISBN 0-07-018984-6). McGraw.

Schaum's Outline of Electric Machines & Electromechanics. Syed A. Nasar. (Schaum's Outline Ser.). (Illus.). 208p. 1981. pap. text ed. 8.95 (ISBN 0-07-045886-3). McGraw.

Schaum's Outline of Electromagnetics. Joseph A. Edminister. (Schaum's Outline Ser). (Illus.). 1979. pap. text ed. 8.95 (ISBN 0-07-018990-0). McGraw.

Schaum's Outline of Electronic Communication. Lloyd Temes. (Schaum Outline Ser.). (Illus.). 1979. pap. text ed. 8.95 (ISBN 0-07-063495-5). McGraw.

Schaum's Outline of Electronic Devices & Circuits. J. J. Cathey. 352p. 1988. pap. 8.95 (ISBN 0-07-010274-0). McGraw.

Schaum's Outline of Electronics Technology, Including 240 Solved Problems. J. A. Wilson & Milton Kaufman. (Schaum's Outline Ser.). 1982. pap. text ed. 9.95 (ISBN 0-07-070690-5). McGraw.

Schaum's Outline of Engineering Mechanics. 3rd ed. William G. McLean & E. W. Nelson. (Schaum's Outline Ser.). 1978. pap. text ed. 10.95 (ISBN 0-07-044816-7). McGraw.

Schaum's Outline of Engineering Mechanics. 4th ed. William G. McLean & E. W. Nelson. (Schaum's Outline Ser.). 448p. 1988. pap. text ed. 9.95 (ISBN 0-07-044822-1). McGraw.

Schaum's Outline of Essential Computer Mathematics. Seymour Lipschutz. 256p. 1982. pap. text ed. 9.95 (ISBN 0-07-037990-4). McGraw.

Schaum's Outline of Financial Accounting. Joel G. Siegel & Jae K. Shim. (Schaum's Outline Ser.). 272p. 1983. pap. text ed. 8.95 (ISBN 0-07-057304-2). McGraw.

Schaum's Outline of French Grammar. Mary E. Coffman. (Schaum's Outline Ser.). 288p. 1981. pap. text ed. 7.95 (ISBN 0-07-011553-2). McGraw.

Schaum's Outline of French Vocabulary. Mary E. Coffman. (Schaum's Outline Ser.). 256p. 1985. pap. text ed. 8.95 (ISBN 0-07-011561-3). McGraw.

Schaum's Outline of Genetics. 2nd ed. William D. Stansfield. 416p. 1983. pap. text ed. 9.95 (ISBN 0-07-060845-8). McGraw.

Schaum's Outline of German Grammar. 2nd ed. E. Gschossmann-Hendershot. (Schaum's Outline Ser.). 272p. 1983. pap. text ed. 7.95 (ISBN 0-07-025097-9). McGraw.

Schaum's Outline of Human Anatomy & Physiology: Including 1450 Problems & Questions. Kent Van De Graaf & R. Ward Rhees. (Schaum's Outline Ser.). 368p. 1987. text ed. 10.95 (ISBN 0-07-066884-1). McGraw.

Schaum's Outline of International Economics. 2nd ed. Dominick Salvatore. 1984. pap. text ed. 8.95 (ISBN 0-07-054503-0). McGraw.

Schaum's Outline of Introduction to Business Organizations & Management. Joel J. Lerner. (Schaum's Outline Ser.). 304p. 1982. pap. text ed. 7.95 (ISBN 0-07-037214-4). McGraw.

Schaum's Outline of Introduction to Psychology. Arno F. Wittig. (Schaum's Outling Ser.). 1977. pap. text ed. 8.95 (ISBN 0-07-071194-1). McGraw.

Schaum's Outline of Introductory Surveying. R. Wirshing & J. Wirshing. 368p. 1985. pap. text ed. 9.95 (ISBN 0-07-071124-0). McGraw.

Schaum's Outline of Italian Grammar. 2nd ed. Joseph Germano & Conrad J. Schmitt. (Schaum's Outline Ser.). 288p. 1982. pap. text ed. 8.95x (ISBN 0-07-023031-5). McGraw.

Schaum's Outline of Italian Vocabulary. F. C. Clark & Conrad J. Schmitt. (Schaum Outline Ser.). 256p. 1987. pap. text ed. 8.95 (ISBN 0-07-023032-3). McGraw.

Schaum's Outline of Logic. John Nolt & Dennis Rohatyn. 288p. 1988. pap. 9.95 (ISBN 0-07-053628-7). McGraw.

Schaum's Outline of Managerial Finance. Jae K. Shim & Joel G. Siegel. 432p. 1986. pap. text ed. 9.95 (ISBN 0-07-057306-9). McGraw.

Schaum's Outline of Marketing. Herbert F. Holtje. (Schaum's Outline Ser.). (Illus.). 176p. 1981. pap. text ed. 6.95 (ISBN 0-07-029661-8). McGraw.

Schaum's Outline of Mathematics for Economists. Seward T. Dowling. (Illus., Orig.). 1980. pap. text ed. 11.95 (ISBN 0-07-017760-0). McGraw.

Schaum's Outline of Mathematics for Nurses. E. Nishiura. 208p. 1986. pap. text ed. 7.95 (ISBN 0-07-046100-7). McGraw.

Schaum's Outline of Matrix Operations. (Schaum's Outline Ser.). 288p. 1988. pap. 8.95 (ISBN 0-07-007978-1). McGraw.

Schaum's Outline of Microeconomic Theory. 2nd ed. Dominick Salvatore. (Schaum's Outline Ser.). 336p. 1983. pap. text ed. 8.95 (ISBN 0-07-054514-6). McGraw.

Schaum's Outline of Microprocessor Fundamentals. Roger L. Tokheim. (Schaum's Outline Ser.). 384p. 1983. pap. text ed. 8.95 (ISBN 0-07-064958-8). Mcgraw.

Schaum's Outline of Modern Physics. Ronald Gautreau & William Savin. (Schaum's Outline Ser.). (Illus.). 1978. pap. text ed. 9.95 (ISBN 0-07-023062-5). McGraw.

Schaum's Outline of Money & Banking: Including 900 Solved Problems. Eugene Diulio. (Schaum's Outline Ser.). 268p. 1987. pap. text ed. 8.95 (ISBN 0-07-017050-9). McGraw.

Schaum's Outline of Numerical Analysis. 2nd ed. Francis Scheid. (Outline Ser.). 352p. 1988. 10.95 (ISBN 0-07-055221-5). McGraw.

Schaum's Outline of Operations Research. R. Bronson. (Schaum Paperback Ser.). 1982. pap. text ed. 10.95 (ISBN 0-07-007977-3). McGraw.

Schaum's Outline of Organic Chemistry. Herbert Meislich et al. 1977. pap. text ed. 12.95 (ISBN 0-07-041457-2). McGraw.

Schistosoma Mansoni: The Parasite Surface in Relation to Host Immunity, Vol. 1. Diane J. McLaren. LC 80-40955. (Tropical Medicine Research Studies). 229p. 1980. 91.95x (ISBN 0-471-27869-6, Pub. by Res Stud Pr). Wiley.

Schistosomiasis Control: Report. WHO Expert Committee. Geneva, 1972. (Technical Report Ser.: No. 515). (Also avail. in French & Spanish). 1973. pap. 1.60 (ISBN 92-4-120515-6). World Health.

Schistosomiasis in Egypt. Ed. by M. F. Abdel-Wahab. 256p. 1982. 84.00 (ISBN 0-8493-6220-2). CRC Pr.

Schistosomiasis in Twentieth Century Africa: Historical Studies on West Africa & Sudan. K. David Patterson & Gerald Hartwig. 1984. pap. 15.00 (ISBN 0-918456-54-1). African Studies Assn.

Schistosomiasis IV: Condensations of the Selected Literature 1963-1975, 2 vols. Ed. by Donald B. Hoffman, Jr. & Kenneth S. Warren. LC 77-11864. (Illus.). 538p. 1978. Set. text ed. 119.00 (ISBN 0-89116-164-3). Hemisphere Pub.

Schistosomiasis: The Evolution of a Medical Literature 1852-1972. Kenneth S. Warren. 1200p. 1974. 85.00x (ISBN 0-262-23057-7). MIT Pr.

Schistosomiasis: The St. Lucia Project. Peter Jordan. (Illus.). 441p. 1985. 57.50 (ISBN 0-521-30312-5). Cambridge U Pr.

Schiwetz Legacy: An Artist's Tribute to Texas, 1910-1971. E. M. Schiwetz. (Illus.). 144p. 1972. 32.50 (ISBN 0-292-77502-4). U of Tex Pr.

Schizoaffective Psychosis. Ed. by A. Marneros & M. T. Tsuang. (Illus.). 330p. 1986. 88.00 (ISBN 0-387-16895-8). Springer-Verlag.

Schizoid Phenomena, Object Relations & the Self. Harry Guntrip. LC 68-56426. 438p. 1969. text ed. 50.00x (ISBN 0-8236-5985-2). Intl Univs Pr.

Schizophrenia. John S. Strauss & William T. Carpenter. (Critical Issues In Psychiatry Ser.). 232p. 1981. 29.50x (ISBN 0-306-40704-3, Plenum Med Bk). Plenum Pub.

Schizophrenia. Maryellen Walsh. 272p. 1986. pap. 3.95 (ISBN 0-446-34160-6). Warner Bks.

Schizophrenia. Patrick Young. (Psychological Disorders & Their Treatments Ser.). (Illus.). 116p. 1988. lib. bdg. 17.95x (ISBN 0-7910-0052-4). Chelsea Hse.

Schizophrenia: A Biblio of Books in English. Mark Weiman. 146p. 1981. Repr. of 1981 ed. lib. bdg. 32.00 (ISBN 0-8414-2826-3). Folcroft.

Schizophrenia: A Developmental Analysis. Sidney J. Blatt & Cynthia Wild. 1976. 44.50 (ISBN 0-12-105050-5). Acad Pr.

Schizophrenia: A Guide for Sufferers, Family & Friends. Jacqueline M. Atkinson. 144p. (Orig.). 1985. pap. 8.99 (ISBN 0-85500-216-6, Pub. by Turnstone Pr England). Sterling.

Schizophrenia: A Multinational Study, Initial Evaluation Phase: Summary. International Pilot Study of Schizophrenia. (Public Health Paper Ser.: No. 63). (Also avail. in French & Spanish). 1975. pap. 6.40 (ISBN 92-4-130063-9). World Health.

Schizophrenia: An International Follow-Up Study. World Health Organization. LC 78-17808. 438p. 1979. 97.95 (ISBN 0-471-99623-8, Pub. by Wiley-Interscience). Wiley.

Schizophrenia: An International Follow-up Study. World Health Organization Staff. LC 78-17808. 456p. pap. 118.60 (2030448). Bks Demand UMI.

Schizophrenia: An Introduction to Research & Theory. 2nd ed. Glenn Shean. 284p. 1987. pap. text ed. 14.75 (ISBN 0-8191-6476-3). U Pr of Amer.

Schizophrenia & Aging: Schizophrenia, Paranoia, & Schizophreniform Disorders in Later Life. Ed. by Nancy E. Miller & Gene D. Cohen. LC 87-14852. (Guilford Psychiatry Ser.). 367p. 1987. lib. bdg. 40.00 (ISBN 0-89862-228-X). Guilford Pr.

Schizophrenia & Civilization. E. Fuller Torrey. LC 79-51931. 240p. 1979. 25.00x (ISBN 0-87668-380-4). Aronson.

Schizophrenia & Genetics. Irving I. Gottesman & James Shields. (Personality & Psychopathology Ser.: Vol. 13). 1972. 85.00 (ISBN 0-12-293450-4). Acad Pr.

Schizophrenia & Human Value. Peter Barham. 232p. 1986. pap. text ed. 14.95 (ISBN 0-631-15016-1). Basil Blackwell.

Schizophrenia & Human Value: Chronic Schizophrenia, Science & Society. Peter Barham. 232p. 1985. 24.95 (ISBN 0-631-13474-3). Basil Blackwell.

Schizophrenia & Madness. Andrew C. Smith. 176p. 1982. text ed. 27.95x (ISBN 0-04-157008-1). Unwin Hyman.

Schizophrenia & the Family. rev. ed. Theodore Lidz & Stephen Fleck. LC 65-23613. 494p. 1985. text ed. 42.50x (ISBN 0-8236-6001-X, 06001). Intl Univs Pr.

Schizophrenia & the Family: A Practitioner's Guide to Psychoeducation & Management. Carol M. Anderson et al. LC 85-17218. 365p. 1986. text ed. 26.95 (ISBN 0-89862-065-1). Guilford Pr.

Schizophrenia & the Poor. Paul M. Roman & Harrison M. Trice. LC 67-63483. (ILR Paperback Ser.: No. 3). 96p. 1967. pap. 3.00 (ISBN 0-87546-028-3); special hard bdg. 7.00 (ISBN 0-87546-270-7). ILR Pr.

Schizophrenia As a Brain Disease. Ed. by Fritz A. Henn & Henry A. Nasrallah. (Illus.). 1982. text ed. 35.00x (ISBN 0-19-503088-5). Oxford U Pr.

Schizophrenia As a Human Process. Harry S. Sullivan. 400p. 1974. pap. 10.95x (ISBN 0-393-00721-9, Norton Lib). Norton.

Schizophrenia at Home. Jacqueline M. Atkinson. 200p. 1986. 35.00x (ISBN 0-8147-0586-3). NYU Pr.

Schizophrenia: Biological & Psychological Perspectives. Ed. by Gene Usdin. LC 75-20118. 1975. 17.50 (ISBN 0-87630-110-3). Brunner-Mazel.

Schizophrenia: Current Concepts & Research. D. Siva Sankar. LC 70-95390. 1969. 21.50 (ISBN 0-9600290-0-1). PJD Pubns.

Schizophrenia in Focus: Guidelines for Treatment & Rehabilitation. David Dawson et al. 190p. 1983. 26.95 (ISBN 0-89885-096-7). Human Sci Pr.

Schizophrenia: Medical & Psychological Subject Index with Bibliography. Harold P. Drummond. 150p. 1987. 34.50 (ISBN 0-88164-496-X); pap. 26.50 (ISBN 0-88164-497-8). ABBE Pubs Assn.

Schizophrenia: New Pharmacological & Clinical Developments. Ed. by A. A. Schiff et al. (International Congress & Symposium Ser.: No. 94). 121p. 1985. pap. 18.00 (ISBN 1-85315-069-X, Pub. by Royal Society of Medicine Services Ltd). Longwood Pub Group.

Schizophrenia, Paranoid Conditions, Depression see Teaching Program in Psychiatry.

Schizophrenia: Recent Biosocial Developments. Costas N. Stefanis & Andreas D. Rabavilas. LC 86-27353. 286p. 1987. text ed. 36.95 (ISBN 0-89885-345-1). Human Sci Pr.

Schizophrenia: Science & Practice. Ed. by John C. Shershow. LC 78-6317. (Illus.). 1978. 19.50x (ISBN 0-674-79112-6). Harvard U Pr.

Schizophrenia: Selected Papers. David Shakow. LC 76-45548. (Psychological Issues Monograph: No. 38). 354p. 1977. text ed. 32.50x (ISBN 0-8236-6003-6); pap. text ed. 25.00x (ISBN 0-8236-6002-8). Intl Univs Pr.

Schizophrenia: Straight Talk for Families & Friends. Maryellen Walsh. LC 84-20558. 288p. 1985. 17.95 (ISBN 0-688-04178-7). Morrow.

Schizophrenia: Symptoms, Causes, Treatments. Kayla F. Bernheim & Richard R. J. Lewine. (Illus.). 1979. pap. 9.95x (ISBN 0-393-09017-5). Norton.

Schizophrenia: The Epigenetic Puzzle. Irving I. Gottesman & James Shields. LC 81-18181. (Illus.). 275p. 1982. o. p. 39.50 (ISBN 0-521-22573-6); pap. 14.95 (ISBN 0-521-29559-9). Cambridge U Pr.

Schizophrenia: The Experience & Its Treatment. Werner M. Mendel. LC 76-20083. (Social & Behavioral Science Ser.). 1976. 25.95x (ISBN 0-87589-296-5). Jossey-Bass.

Schizophrenia: The Facts. Ming T. Tsuang. (Facts Ser.). (Illus.). 1982. text ed. 13.95x (ISBN 0-19-261336-7). Oxford U Pr.

Schizophrenia: The First Ten Dean Award Lectures. Ed. by Stanley R. Dean. LC 73-6815. 1973. text ed. 29.50x (ISBN 0-8422-7115-5). Irvington.

Schizophrenia: The Sacred Symbol of Psychiatry. Thomas Szasz. LC 87-26769. (Illus.). 237p. 1988. pap. 12.95 (ISBN 0-8156-0224-3). Syracuse U Pr.

Schizophrenia: Theory, Diagnoses & Treatment. Ed. by Herman Denber. 1978. 65.00 (ISBN 0-8247-6711-X). Dekker.

Schizophrenia Today. Ed. by D. Kemali et al. 1976. 65.00 (ISBN 0-08-020928-9). Pergamon.

Schizophrenia: Towards a New Synthesis. J. Wing. 304p. 1978. 39.50 (ISBN 0-8089-1140-6, 794857). Grune.

Schizophrenia: Treatment, Management, & Rehabilitation. Ed. by Alan S. Bellack. 432p. 1984. 43.50 (ISBN 0-8089-1640-8, 790497). Grune.

Schizophrenia: Treatment Process & Outcome. Thomas H. McGlashan & Christopher J. Keats. 250p. 1989. text ed. price not set (ISBN 0-88048-281-8). Am Psychiatric.

Schizophrenia: Understanding Its Management: A Guide to the Medical, Legal & Social Complexities. Ed. by J. F. Thornton & M. V. Seeman. 130p. 1988. text ed. write for info. (ISBN 0-920887-17-1, Pub. by H Huber Canada). Hogrefe Intl.

Schizophrenias. Ed. by Frederic Flach. (Directions in Psychiatry Ser.: No. 4). 1988. 29.95 (ISBN 0-393-70062-3). Norton.

Schizophrenias: Ours to Conquer. rev. ed. Carl C. Pfeiffer et al. LC 87-72306. (Illus.). 365p. 1988. pap. 11.95 (ISBN 0-942333-02-0). Bio-Comns Pr.

Schizophrenic: A Fresh Approach. Gwen Howe. 176p. 1987. pap. 13.95 (ISBN 0-7153-8871-1). David & Charles.

Schizophrenic Child: A Primer for Parents & Professionals. Shelia Cantor. 130p. 1982. pap. 8.95 (ISBN 0-920792-13-8). Eden Pr.

Schizophrenic Disorders: Long-Term Patient & Family Studies. Manfred Bleuler. Tr. by Siegfried M. Clemens. LC 75-43303. 1978. 64.00x (ISBN 0-300-01663-8). Yale U Pr.

Schizophrenic Disorders: Theory & Treatment from a Psychodynamic Point of View. Ping-Nie Pao. LC 77-92180. 456p. 1979. text ed. 50.00x (ISBN 0-8236-5990-9). Intl Univs Pr.

Schizophrenics in the Community: An Experimental Study in the Prevention of Hospitalization. Benjamin Pasamanick et al. LC 66-25455. (Illus.). 1967. 29.50x (ISBN 0-89197-390-7). Irvington.

Schizophrenics in the New Custodial Community: Five Years after the Experiment. Ann E. Davis et al. LC 74-11383. 242p. 1974. 12.00 (ISBN 0-8142-0215-2). Ohio St U Pr.

Schizophyceen der Plankton-Expedition der Hunboldt-Stiftung. N. Wille. (Illus.). 1968. Repr. of 1904 ed. 22.50x (ISBN 3-7682-0808-7). Lubrecht & Cramer.

Schlag Nach Uber Rotary. David H. Bailey & Louise Gottlieb. Ed. by Willmon L. White & Mark Perlberg. (Illus.). 506p. (Ger.). 1982. 16.75 (ISBN 0-915062-11-9). Rotary Intl.

Schlagwortregister SFB-ASB-SSD (Arbeitstitel) Ed. by Verein der Bibliothekare & Offentlichen V Bibliotheken. 500p. (Ger.). 1986. lib. bdg. 39.00 (ISBN 3-598-10632-7). K G Saur.

Schlei & Grossman's Employment Discrimination Law: 1983-85 Cumulative Supplement. Ed. by Mark S. Dichter et al. 468p. 1987. pap. 30.00 (ISBN 0-87179-524-8, 0524). BNA.

Schleiermacher the Theologian: The Construction of the Doctrine of God. Robert R. Williams. LC 77-78650. pap. 54.50 (2026892). Bks Demand UMI.

Schleiermachers Predigt. 2nd ed. Wolfgang Trillhaas. (Theologische Bibliothek Toepelmann, Vol. 28). 1975. 20.80x (ISBN 3-11-005739-5). De Gruyter.

Schleiermacher's Soliloques. Friedrich E. Schleiermacher. Tr. by Horace L. Friess. LC 78-59040. 1984. Repr. of 1926 ed. 23.00 (ISBN 0-88355-712-6). Hyperion Conn.

Schleiermachers System als Philosophie und Theologie see Leben Schleiermachers.

Schleitheim Confession. Tr. by John H. Yoder. 32p. 1977. pap. 1.95 (ISBN 0-8361-1831-6). Herald Pr.

Schlemiel As Metaphor: Studies in the Yiddish & American Jewish Novel. Sanford Pinsker. LC 77-132487. (Crosscurrents-Modern Critiques Ser.). 185p. 1971. 6.95x (ISBN 0-8093-0480-5). S Ill U Pr.

Schlemiel As Modern Hero. Ruth R. Wisse. LC 72-160841. 1980. pap. 3.95X (ISBN 0-226-90312-5, P881, Phoen). U of Chicago Pr.

Schlemiel Comes to America. Ezra Greenspan. LC 83-14399. 258p. 1983. 20.00 (ISBN 0-8108-1646-6). Scarecrow.

Schlieffen Plan & the Strategy of the Central Powers in the East. Graydon A. Tunstal, Jr. (Atlantic Studies, No. 45 - War & Society in East Central Europe, Vol. XXVI). write for info. Brooklyn Coll Pr.

Schliemann's Troy: One Hundred Years after. M. I. Finley. (Mortimer Wheeler Archaeological Lectures). 1974. pap. 2.50 (ISBN 0-85672-111-5, Pub. by British Acad). Longwood Pub Group.

Schliemann's Excavations. Carl Schuchhardt. Tr. by Eugenie Sellers. LC 74-77893. (Illus.). 419p. 1975. 15.00 (ISBN 0-89005-034-1). Ares.

Schliemann's Excavations: An Archaeological & Historical Study. C. Schuchardt. LC 74-173145. (Illus.). Repr. of 1891 ed. 25.00 (ISBN 0-405-08938-4). Ayer Co Pubs.

Schliemann's Excavations: An Archaeological & Historical Study. C. Schuchhardt. (Illus.). 1978. Repr. of 1891 ed. lib. bdg. 97.50 (ISBN 0-8492-8076-1). R West.

Schliemann's First Visit to America. Ed. by Shirley H. Weber. (Gennadeion Monographs: Vol. 2). 1942. 7.50x (ISBN 0-87661-402-0). Am Sch Athens.

Schlieren Methods. L. A. Vasil'Ev. 367p. 1972. 51.95x (ISBN 0-470-90335-X). Halsted Pr.

Schlosser Und Garten Um Dresden. K. Kempe. 242p. (Ger.). 1981. 57.00x (ISBN 0-317-57346-2, Pub. by Collets UK). State Mutual Bk.

Schluessel Fuer Die Ggattung Hygrophorus Nach Exsikkatenmerkmalen. A. Bresinsky & J. Huber. (Illus.). 1967. 12.00x (ISBN 3-7682-0536-3). Lubrecht & Cramer.

Schluesselelemente. W. Pies & A. Weiss. (Landolt-Boernstein New Ser, Crystal Structure Data of Inorganic Compounds, Group 3: Vol. 7e). (Illus.). 780p. 1975. 463.20 (ISBN 0-387-07334-5). Springer-Verlag.

Schlumberger, the History of a Technique. Louis Allaud & Maurice H. Martin. LC 77-23566. 333p. 1977. 49.95x (ISBN 0-471-01667-5, Pub. by Wiley-Interscience). Wiley.

Schmitty's Short Stories & Poems, Vol. II. Lloyd Schmidt. LC 86-90506. 128p. 1987. write for info. (ISBN 0-8187-0100-5). Harlo Pr.

Schmuck-und Schauaquarium see Aquarium Decorating & Planning.

Schnabel's Interpretation of Piano Music. Konrad Wolff. (Illus.). 1979. pap. 4.95 (ISBN 0-393-00929-7). Norton.

Schnauzer Grooming Made Easy. Mario Migliorini. LC 82-22799. (Illus.). 104p. 1983. spiral 11.95 (ISBN 0-668-05419-0, 5419). Arco.

Schnitt Entlang Der Zeit. John Heartfield. 608p. (Ger.). 1981. 19.00x (ISBN 0-317-57350-0, Pub. by Collets UK). State Mutual Bk.

Schnitzer-Intensive Nutrition, Schnitzer-Normal Nutrition: 14 Day Menu Plan for Both Nutrition Forms. 10th, rev. ed. J. G. Schnitzer & Mechthilde Schnitzer. (Illus.). 186p. 19.95 (ISBN 3-922894-75-5). Medicina Bio.

Schnitzer O'Shea. Donall MacAmhlaigh. 192p. 1986. 15.95 (ISBN 0-86322-079-7, Pub. by Brandon Bks). Longwood Pub Group.

Schnitzer O'Shea. Donall MacAmhlaigh. 192p. 1987. pap. 7.95 (ISBN 0-86322-090-8, Pub. by Brandon Bks). Longwood Pub Group.

Schockwaves. Thomas Tessier. 1987. pap. 3.50 (ISBN 0-425-09477-4). Berkley Pub.

Schoderbek-Cosier-Aplin: Management: Instructor's Resource Manual. S. Alexander Billon et al. 1988. pap. text ed. 8.75 net, 243p. (ISBN 0-15-554661-9); net study guide, 290p. 10.00 (ISBN 0-15-554663-5); net test bk., 306p. 8.00 (ISBN 0-15-554662-7). HarBraceJ.

Schoenberg. Malcolm MacDonald. (Master Musicians Ser.). (Illus.). 304p. 1976. 17.95x (ISBN 0-460-03143-0, Pub. by J M Dent England). Biblio Dist.

Schoenberg. Anthony Payne. (Oxford Studies of Composers). 1968. pap. 11.95x (ISBN 0-19-314116-7). Oxford U Pr.

Schoenberg: A Critical Biography. Willi Reich. Tr. by Leo Black from Ger. LC 81-1163. (Music Ser.). (Illus.). xi, 268p. 1981. Repr. of 1968 ed. lib. bdg. 35.00 (ISBN 0-306-76104-1). Da Capo.

Schoenberg & His Circle: A Viennese Portrait. Joan A. Smith. (Illus.). 320p. 1986. 24.95 (ISBN 0-02-872620-0). Schirmer Bks.

Schoenberg & His School: The Contemporary Stage of the Language of Music. Rene Leibowitz. LC 75-14128. (Qualty Paperbacks Ser.). 1975. pap. 5.95 (ISBN 0-306-80020-9). Da Capo.

Schoenberg & His School: The Contemporary Stage of the Language of Music. Rene Leibowitz. Tr. by Dika Newlin from Fr. LC 75-115338. (Music Ser). 1970. Repr. of 1949 ed. lib. bdg. 37.50 (ISBN 0-306-71930-4). Da Capo.

Schoenberg & the God-Idea: The Opera "Moses und Aron". Pamela C. White. Ed. by George Buelow. LC 85-1033. (Studies in Musicology: No. 83). 340p. 1985. 54.95 (ISBN 0-8357-1647-3). UMI Res Pr.

Schoenberg & the New Music. Carl Dahlhaus. Tr. by Derrick Puffett & Alfred Clayton. (Illus.). 300p. 1987. 44.00 (ISBN 0-521-33251-6). Cambridge U Pr.

Schoenberg: Articles by Arnold Schoenberg, Erwin Stein & Others, 1929-1937. Ed. by Merle Armitage. LC 79-106709. 1977. Repr. of 1937 ed. lib. bdg. 35.00x (ISBN 0-8371-3439-0, ARSC); fiche 11.80 (ISBN 0-8371-9600-0); fiche & cloth 20.65 (ISBN 0-8371-9599-3). Greenwood.

Schoenberg Discography. R. Wayne Shoaf. (Fallen Leaf Reference Book in Music: No. 5). (Orig.). 1987. pap. 19.95 (ISBN 0-914913-04-2). Fallen Leaf.

Schoenberg: Nineteen Twenty-Nine to Nineteen Thirty-Seven. facsimile ed. Ed. by Merle Armitage. LC 77-157360. (Select Bibliographies Reprint Ser.). Repr. of 1937 ed. 21.00 (ISBN 0-8369-5783-0). Ayer Co Pubs.

Schoenberg Remembered: Diaries & Recollections (Nineteen Thirty-Eight to Nineteen Seventy-Six) Dika Newlin. LC 79-19128. (Illus.). 1980. 28.00 (ISBN 0-918728-14-2). Pendragon NY.

Schoenberg's Twelve-Tone Harmony: The Suite Op. 29 & the Compositional Sketches. Martha M. Hyde. LC 81-16369. (Studies in Musicology: No. 49). pap. 44.50 (2070030). Bks Demand UMI.

Schoensten Gerichte. Nora Richter. (Illus.). 128p. (Ger.). 1984. pap. text ed. 7.95x (ISBN 3-923090-12-9). Lubrecht & Cramer.

Schoepenhauer-Literature. Ferdinand Laban. (Ger). 1970. Repr. of 1880 ed. 21.00 (ISBN 0-8337-1968-8). B Franklin.

Schoepfung aus dem Nichts: Die Entstehung der Lehre von der Creatio Ex Nihilo. Gerhard May. (Arbeiten zur Kirchengeschichte: Vol. 48). 1978. 34.40 (ISBN 3-11-007204-1). De Gruyter.

Schoffler-Weis German & English Dictionary. 1062p. (Ger. & Eng.). 1983. 19.95 (ISBN 0-8442-2878-8, Passport Bks.). Natl Textbk.

Scholae Academicae: Some Account of Studies at English Universities in the 18th Century. Christopher Wordsworth. LC 79-93271. 1969. Repr. of 1877 ed. 39.50x (ISBN 0-678-05085-6). Kelley.

Scholae Academicae: Some Account of the Studies at the English Universities in the Eighteenth Century. Christopher Wordsworth. 435p. 1968. Repr. of 1877 ed. 35.00x (ISBN 0-7146-1450-5, F Cass Co). Biblio Dist.

Scholae Palatinae: The Palace Guards of the Later Roman Empire. R. I. Frank. (Papers & Monographs: No. 23). 260p. 1969. 15.00 (ISBN 0-318-12334-7). Am Acad Rome.

Scholae Palatinae: The Palace Guards of the Later Roman Empire. R. I. Frank. 260p. 1969. 30.00x (ISBN 0-271-00471-1). Pa St U Pr.

Scholar Adventurer: A Tribute to John D. Gordan (1907-1968) on the Eightieth Anniversary of His Birth with Six of His Essays. John D. Gordan. LC 87-18136. (Illus.). xxvi, 132p. (Orig.). 1987. pap. 10.00x (ISBN 0-87104-294-0). NY Pub Lib.

Scholar Adventurers. Richard D. Altick. 1966. pap. text ed. 9.95 (ISBN 0-02-900580-9). Free Pr.

Scholar Adventurers. Richard D. Altick. LC 87-11064. 340p. 1987. pap. 9.95 (ISBN 0-8142-0435-X). Ohio St U Pr.

Scholar & the State: And Other Orations & Addresses. Henry C. Potter. LC 72-4509. (Essay Index Reprint Ser.). Repr. of 1897 ed. 21.00 (ISBN 0-8369-2969-1). Ayer Co Pubs.

TITLE INDEX SCHOMER LICHTNER DRAWINGS.

Scholar Collects: Selections from the Anthony Morris Clark Bequest. Ed. by Ulrich W. Hiesinger & Ann Percy. LC 80-82234. (Illus.). 171p. (Orig.). 1980. pap. 14.95 (ISBN 0-87633-036-7). Phila Mus Art.
Scholar Painters of Japan: The Nanga School. James Cahill. LC 74-27413. (Asia Society Ser.). (Illus.). 1979. Repr. of 1972 ed. lib. bdg. 33.00x (ISBN 0-405-06562-0). Ayer Co Pubs.
Scholar Personal Computing Handbook. Bryan Pfaffenberger. (Microcomputer Bookshelf Ser.). 320p. (Orig.). 1985. pap. write for info. (ISBN 0-673-39109-4). Scott F.
Scholarly Communication: The Report of the National Enquiry. LC 79-51420. 1979. 19.50x (ISBN 0-8018-2267-X); pap. 8.95x (ISBN 0-8018-2268-8). Johns Hopkins.
Scholarly Disciplines see Asia in the Making of Europe.
Scholarly Editing in the Computer Age: Theory & Practice. Peter L. Shillingsburg. LC 85-16544. 176p. 1986. 22.00x (ISBN 0-8203-0828-5); pap. 11.95x (ISBN 0-8203-0889-7). U of GA Pr.
Scholarly Means to Evangelical Ends: The New Haven Scholars & the Transformation of Higher Learning in America, 1830-1890. Louise L. Stevenson. LC 85-27502. (New Studies in American Intellectual & Cultural History). 240p. 1986. text ed. 29.50x (ISBN 0-8018-2695-0). Johns Hopkins.
Scholarly Priviledges in the Middle Ages. Pearl Kibre. LC 60-16435. 1962. 12.00x (ISBN 0-910956-46-4). Medieval Acad.
Scholarly Publishing in an Era of Change. Ed. by Ethel G. Langlois. 86p. 18.00 (ISBN 0-318-16605-4); members 9.00 (ISBN 0-318-16606-2). Soc Schol Pub.
Scholarly Reporting in the Humanities. 4th ed. Roy M. Wiles. LC 68-102276. 1968. pap. 4.95c (ISBN 0-8020-1497-6). U of Toronto Pr.
Scholarly Writing & Publishing: Issues, Problems, & Solutions. Ed. by Mary Frank Fox. 130p. 1985. 39.00x (ISBN 0-8133-0038-X); pap. 17.95x (ISBN 0-8133-0039-8). Westview.
Scholarmanship: Or How to Succeed in College Without Really Trying. John Fox. 9.95 (ISBN 0-940416-04-2). Bacchus Pr.
Scholars. 3rd ed. Ching-Tzu Wu. Tr. by Hsien-Yi Yang et al from Chinese. (Illus.). 607p. 1973. 15.95 (ISBN 0-917056-64-7, Pub. by Foreign Lang Pr China). Cheng & Tsui.
Scholars. Wu Ching-Tsu. silk 15.95 (ISBN 0-8351-0316-1). China Bks.
Scholars & Dollars: Politics, Economics, & the Universities of Ontario 1945-1980. Paul Axelrod. (State & Economic Life Ser.). 388p. 1982. o. p. 35.00x (ISBN 0-8020-5609-1); pap. 15.95c (ISBN 0-8020-6492-2). U of Toronto Pr.
Scholars & Gentlemen: A Biography of the Mackerras Family. Joan Priest. 330p. 1986. 22.95 (ISBN 0-86439-013-0, Pub. by Boolarong Pubns Australia). Intl Spec Bk.
Scholars & Gentlemen: The Library of the New York Historical Society 1804-1982. Pamela S. Richards. LC 83-15876. vxii, 144p. 1984. 22.50 (ISBN 0-208-02039-X, Archon). Shoe String.
Scholars & Personal Computers: Microcomputing in the Human & Social Sciences. George M. Kren & George Christakes. LC 86-27615. 176p. 1988. text ed. 29.95 (ISBN 0-89885-358-3). Human Sci Pr.
Scholars & Priests. Irene M. Franck & David M. Brownstone. (Work Throughtout History Ser.). (Illus.). 208p. (YA) (gr. 7 up). 1988. 16.95 (ISBN 0-8160-1449-3). Facts on File.
Scholars & the Indian Experience: Critical Reviews of Recent Writings in the Social Sciences. Ed. by W. R. Swagerty. LC 83-49510. (Newbury Library D'Arcy Center for the History of the American Indian Bibliographical). 280p. 1984. 22.50x (ISBN 0-253-35095-6); pap. 9.95x (ISBN 0-253-35096-4). Ind U Pr.
Scholars & Their Publishers. Ed. by Weldon A. Kefauver. LC 77-91126. 59p. (Orig.). 1977. pap. 7.50x (ISBN 0-87352-005-X, S31). Modern Lang.
Scholars, Dollars, & Bureaucrats. Chester E. Finn, Jr. LC 78-13363. (Studies in Higher Education Policy). 238p. 1978. 26.95 (ISBN 0-8157-2828-X); pap. 9.95 (ISBN 0-8157-2827-1). Brookings.
Scholars, Dollars & Public Policy: New Frontiers in Corporate Giving. Ernest W. Lefever & Raymond English. LC 82-25126. 62p. 1983. pap. 7.00 (ISBN 0-89633-065-6). Ethics & Public Policy.
Scholar's Glossary of Sex. Roy Goliard. (Illus., Orig.). 1968. pap. 4.95 (ISBN 0-685-11982-3, 20). Heineman.
Scholars' Guide to Humanities & Social Sciences in the Soviet Union. Ed. by Blair A. Ruble & Mark H. Teeter. LC 85-12002. 336p. 1985. 75.00 (ISBN 0-87332-335-1). M E Sharpe.
Scholars Guide to Intelligence Literature. Russell Bowen. 1986. 39.95 (ISBN 0-89568-501-9). Spec Learn Corp.
Scholar's Guide to Intelligence Literature: Bibliography of the Russell J. Bowen Collection. Ed. by Marjorie W. Cline et al. LC 83-80922. 256p. 1983. 40.00 (ISBN 0-89093-540-8, Pub. by National Intelligence Study Center). U Pubns Amer.
Scholars' Guide to Washington D. C. Film & Video Collections. Bonnie Rowan. LC 80-607014. (Scholars' Guide to Washington D. C. Ser.: No. 6). 282p. 1980. pap. text ed. 10.95 (ISBN 0-87474-819-4, ROFVP). Smithsonian.
Scholars' Guide to Washington, D. C. for African Studies. Purnima M. Bhatt. LC 79-607774. (Scholars' Guide to Washington D.C. Ser.: No. 4). 348p. (Orig.). 1980. text ed. 29.95x (ISBN 0-87474-238-2, BHAF); pap. text ed. 12.95x (ISBN 0-87474-239-0, BHAFP). Smithsonian.
Scholars' Guide to Washington D. C. for Central & East European Studies. Kenneth J. Dillon. LC 80-607019. (Scholars' Guide to Washington D. C. Ser.: No. 5). 330p. 1980. text ed. 27.50 (ISBN 0-87474-368-0, DICE); pap. text ed. 11.95 (ISBN 0-87474-367-2, DICEP). Smithsonian.
Scholars' Guide to Washington, D. C. for Cartography & Remote Sensing. Ralph E. Ehrenberg. LC 86-600371. (Scholars' Guides to Washington, D. C. Ser.). 420p. 1987. 29.95x (ISBN 0-87474-406-7); pap. 15.00x (ISBN 0-87474-407-5). Smithsonian.
Scholars' Guide to Washington, D. C. for East Asian Studies. Hong N. Kim. LC 79-17344. (Scholars' Guide to Washington, D. C. Ser.: No. 3). 414p. 1979. pap. text ed. 12.95x (ISBN 0-87474-581-0). Smithsonian.
Scholars' Guide to Washington, D. C., for Latin American & Caribbean Studies. Michael Grow. LC 78-21316. (Scholar's Guide to Washington, D. C. Ser.: No. 2). 346p. 1979. pap. text ed. 10.95x (ISBN 0-87474-487-3, GRLAP). Smithsonian.
Scholar's Guide to Washington, D. C. for Middle Eastern Studies. Steven R. Dorr. LC 81-607073. (Scholar's Guides to Washington, D. C. Ser.: No. 7). 564p. 1981. text ed. 29.95x (ISBN 0-87474-372-9, DOME); pap. text ed. 15.00x (ISBN 0-87474-371-0, DOMEP). Smithsonian.
Scholar's Guide to Washington, D. C. for South Asian Studies. Enayetur Rahim. LC 81-607847. (Scholar's Guides to Washington, D. C. Ser.: No. 8). 438p. 1982. text ed. 29.95x (ISBN 0-87474-778-3, RASA); pap. 12.95 (ISBN 0-87474-777-5, RASAP). Smithsonian.
Scholar's Guide to Washington, D.C. for Audio Resources: Sound Recordings in the Arts, Humanities, & Social, Physical, & Life Sciences. James R. Heintze. Contrib. by Trudi W. Olivetti. LC 84-600234. (Scholar's Guides to Washington, D.C. Series). 396p. 1985. 29.95x (ISBN 0-87474-516-0, HEAR); pap. 15.00x (ISBN 0-87474-517-9, HEARP). Smithsonian.
Scholars' Guide to Washington, D.C. for Russian-Soviet Studies. 2nd ed. Steven A. Grant. Ed. by Patrick M. Mayerchak. LC 83-600231. (Scholars' Guides to Washington, D.C.). 432p. 1983. 29.95x (ISBN 0-87474-490-3, GRSR); pap. 15.00x (ISBN 0-87474-489-X, GRSRP). Smithsonian.
Scholars' Guide to Washington DC for Southeast Asian Studies. Ed. by Patrick M. Mayerchak. LC 82-19454. (Scholars' Guides to Washington, D.C. Series: Vol. 9). 442p. 1983. text ed. 29.95x (ISBN 0-87474-626-4, MASE); pap. text ed. 12.95x (ISBN 0-87474-625-6, MASEP). Smithsonian.
Scholars in Foxholes: The Story of the Army Specialized Training Program in World War Two. Louis E. Keefer. LC 88-42518. 275p. 1988. lib. bdg. 24.95x (ISBN 0-89950-346-2). McFarland & Co.
Scholar's Odyssey. Ference A. Vali. Ed. by Karl W. Ryavec. 408p. 1989. 24.95 (ISBN 0-8138-1533-9). Iowa St U Pr.
Scholars of Byzantium. N. G. Wilson. LC 83-195. 272p. 1983. 34.50x (ISBN 0-8018-3052-4). Johns Hopkins.
Scholars of Night. John M. Ford. 288p. 1988. 16.95x (ISBN 0-312-93051-8). Tor Bks.
Scholars of Night. John M. Ford. 320p. 1989. pap. price not set. Tor Bks.
Scholars, Saints & Sufis: Muslim Religious Institutions Since 1500. Ed. by Nikki R. Keddie. LC 77-153546. (Near Eastern Center, UCLA: No. 9). 350p. 1972. pap. 10.95x (ISBN 0-520-03644-1). U of Cal Pr.
Scholars, Saints & Sufis: Muslim Religious Institutions since 1500. Ed. by Nikki R. Keddie. 1983. 14.50 (ISBN 0-8446-5970-3). Peter Smith.
Scholar's Song. Ken Stone. 24p. 1984. 2.50 (ISBN 0-942432-09-6). M O P Pr.
Scholar's Testament. George E. Woodberry. LC 76-45773. 1977. Repr. of 1931 ed. lib. bdg. 20.50 (ISBN 0-8414-9500-9). Folcroft.
Scholars Who Teach: The Art of College Teaching. Ed. by Steven M. Cahn. LC 78-944. 258p. 1978. 22.95x (ISBN 0-88229-373-7); pap. 11.95x (ISBN 0-88229-598-5). Nelson-Hall.
Scholarship. (Illus.). 64p. (gr. 6-12). 1970. pap. 1.25x (ISBN 0-8395-3384-5, 3384). BSA.
Scholarship & Education in Bengal. Katharine S. Diehl. (Printers & Printing in the East Indies to 1850 Ser.: Vol. VII). Date not set. write for info. (ISBN 0-89241-396-4). Caratzas.
Scholarship & Its Survival: Questions on the Idea of Graduate Education. Jaroslav Pelikan. LC 83-15211. 100p. 1983. pap. text ed. 6.95 (ISBN 0-931050-24-3). Carnegie Found.
Scholarship & Nation Building: The Universities of Strasbourg & Alsatian Society, 1871-1939. John E. Craig. LC 83-24341. 432p. 1984. lib. bdg. 30.00x (ISBN 0-226-11670-0). U of Chicago Pr.
Scholarship & Partisanship: Essays on Max Weber. Reinhard Bendix & Guenther Roth. (California Library Reprint Ser.: No. 110). 1980. Repr. of 1971 ed. 35.00x (ISBN 0-520-04171-2). U of Cal Pr.
Scholarship & Service: The Policies & Ideals of a National University in a Modern Democracy. facsimile ed. Nicholas M. Butler. LC 78-134066. (Essay Index Reprint Ser). Repr. of 1921 ed. 21.50 (ISBN 0-8369-2220-4). Ayer Co Pubs.
Scholarship & Social Action. Gerald M. Reagan & Elizabeth Steiner. (SPE Monograph Ser.). 1979. 2.50 (ISBN 0-933669-17-8). Soc Profs Ed.
Scholarship Book: The Complete Guide to Private-Sector Scholarships, Grants, & Loans for Undergraduates. 2nd ed. Daniel J. Cassidy & Michael J. Alves. 1987. 29.95 (ISBN 0-13-792425-9); pap. 19.95 (ISBN 0-13-792417-8). P-H.
Scholarship Guide to Commonwealth Universities, 1985-87. 35.00 (ISBN 0-8002-3996-2). Intl Pubns Serv.
Scholarship of Dr. Samuel Belkin. pap. cancelled (ISBN 0-686-76254-1). Feldheim.
Scholarships & Grants for Study or Research in U. S. A. A Scholarship Handbook for Foreign Nationals. Ed. by Walter Wickremasinghe. 146p. (Orig.). 1986. pap. 21.95x (ISBN 0-940937-00-X). Amer Coll Serv.
Scholarships & Loans for Nursing Education 1986-1987. 65p. (Orig.). 1986. pap. 8.95 (41-1964). Natl League Nurse.
Scholarships & Loans for Nursing Education 1987-1988. 65p. 1987. pap. 9.95 (ISBN 0-88737-380-1). Natl League Nurse.
Scholarships, Fellowships & Loans, Vol. 7. S. Norman Feingold & Marie Feingold. LC 49-49180. 804p. 1982. 75.00 (ISBN 0-87442-007-5). Bellman.
Scholarships, Fellowships & Loans, Vol. 8. S. Norman Feingold & Marie Feingold. LC 49-49180. 496p. 1987. 80.00 (ISBN 0-87442-008-3). Bellman.
Scholarships, Fellowships, Grants & Loans. 5th ed. LC 79-66191. (College Blue Book Ser.). 1981. 40.00 (ISBN 0-02-695310-2). Macmillan.
Scholarships for International Students: A Complete Guide to U. S. Colleges & Universities. Ed. by Anna Leider. (Illus.). 248p. (Orig.). 1986. pap. 14.95 (ISBN 0-917760-84-0). Octameron Assocs.
Scholary Publishers Guide: Financial & Legal Aspects. Ed. by Primary Comm. Research Centre. 1979. 40.00x (ISBN 0-906083-08-7, Pub. by Primary Com England). State Mutual Bk.
Scholastic Aptitude Test. Jack Rudman. (Admission Test Ser.: ATS-21). 300p. (Cloth bdg. avail. on request). pap. 13.95 (ISBN 0-8373-5021-2). Natl Learning.
Scholastic Aptitude Test (SAT) Edward C. Gruber & Morris Bramson. (Exam Prep. Ser.). 1975. pap. 7.95 (ISBN 0-671-18969-7). Monarch Pr.
Scholastic Aptitude Test (SAT) Practice Examination Number 1. David M. Tarlow. (Practice Examination Ser.). 40p. 1986. pap. 16.95 (ISBN 0-931572-61-4). Datar Pub.
Scholastic Aptitude Test (SAT) Practice Examination Number 3. David M. Tarlow. (Practice Examination Ser.). 40p. 1986. pap. 16.95 (ISBN 0-931572-62-2). Datar Pub.
Scholastic Aptitude Test (SAT) Practice Examination Number 5. David M. Tarlow. (Practice Examination Ser.). 40p. 1986. pap. 16.95 (ISBN 0-931572-63-0). Datar Pub.
Scholastic Aptitude Test (SAT) Preparation for College Entrance. 5th ed. Brigitte Saunders et al. LC 83-15672. 560p. (Orig.). (gr. 9-12). 1984. pap. 7.95 (ISBN 0-668-05898-6). Arco.
Scholastic Aptitude Test (SAT) Student Guide. David M. Tarlow. (Student Guide Ser.). 120p. 1986. pap. 12.95 (ISBN 0-931572-60-6). Datar Pub.
Scholastic Behavior of a Selected Group of Undergraduate Home Economics Students. Ruth Connor. LC 70-176667. (Columbia University. Teachers College. Contributions to Education: No. 497). Repr. of 1931 ed. 22.50 (ISBN 0-404-55497-0). AMS Pr.
Scholastic Culture of the Middle Ages: 1000-1300. John W. Baldwin. LC 70-120060. (Civilization & Society Ser). 192p. 1971. pap. 9.50x (ISBN 0-669-62059-9). Heath.
Scholastic Dictionary of Synonyms, Antonyms & Homonyms. 220p. (YA) (gr. 7 up). pap. 1.95 (ISBN 0-590-01483-8). Scholastic Inc.
Scholastic Journalism. 7th ed. Earl English & Clarence Hach. 332p. 1984. text ed. 18.95x (ISBN 0-8138-1400-6); pap. text ed. 14.95x (ISBN 0-8138-1390-5). Iowa St U Pr.
Scholastic Medicine & Philosophy. Per-Gunner Ottosson. 340p. 1984. pap. text ed. 25.00x (ISBN 88-7088-108-3, Pub. by Bibliopolis Italy). Humanities.
Scholastic Miscellany: Anselm to Ockham. Ed. by Eugene R. Fairweather et al. LC 56-5104. (Library of Christian Classics). 454p. 1982. pap. 12.95 (ISBN 0-664-24418-1). Westminster John Knox.
Scholastic Newspaper Fundamentals. Ed. by Helen F. Smith. (Illus.). 48p. (Orig.). 1986. pap. text ed. 8.50 (ISBN 0-916084-16-7). Columbia Scholastic.
Scholastic Philosophy. Jack Rudman. (Undergraduate Program Field Test Ser.: UPFT-22). (Cloth bdg. avail. on request). pap. 13.95 (ISBN 0-8373-6022-6). Natl Learning.
Scholastic Rabbinism: A Literary Study of the Fathers According to Rabbi Nathan. Anthony J. Saldarini. LC 81-13564. (Brown Judaic Studies). 1982. pap. text ed. 12.00 (ISBN 0-89130-523-8, 14-00-14). Scholars Pr GA.
Scholastic Roots of the Spanish American Revolution. O. Carlos Stoetzer. LC 77-75797. xii, 300p. 1979. 50.00x (ISBN 0-8232-1027-8). Fordham.
Scholastic School Fun Pack. (Illus.). 16p. (gr. 2-4). 1986. pap. 3.95 (ISBN 0-590-40370-2). Scholastic Inc.
Scholastic World Atlas: No. 9552. American Map Corp. Staff. (gr. 7-9). 1981. pap. 2.75 (ISBN 0-8416-9552-0). Am Map.
Scholastic Yearbook Fundamentals. Ed. by Charles E. Savedge. (Illus.). 68p. (Orig.). 1985. pap. text ed. 8.50 (ISBN 0-916084-13-2). Columbia Scholastic.
Scholastica Commentaria in Primam Partem Summae Theologicae S. Thomae Aquinatis, De Deo Uno. F. Dominico Banes. Ed. by Luis Urbano. (Medieval Studies Reprint Ser.). (Lat. & Span.). Repr. of 1934 ed. lib. bdg. 45.00x (ISBN 0-697-00028-1). Irvington.
Scholasticism. Josef Pieper. 1964. pap. text ed. 5.95 (ISBN 0-07-049930-6). McGraw.
Scholasticism & Politics. Jacques Maritain. LC 72-353. (Essay Index Reprint Ser.). Repr. of 1940 ed. 15.00 (ISBN 0-8369-2805-9). Ayer Co Pubs.
Scholasticism in the Modern World. Ed. by George F. McLean. (Proceedings of the American Catholic Philosophical Association: Vol. 40). 1966. pap. 15.00 (ISBN 0-918090-00-8). Am Cath Philo.
Scholastic's A-Plus Guide to Good Writing. Louise Colligan. (Junior A-Plus Guides). 112p. (Orig.). (gr. 4-6). 1988. pap. 2.50 (ISBN 0-590-40591-8). Scholastic Inc.
Scholastic's A-Plus Jr. Guide to Studying. Louise Colligan. (Junior A Plus Guides Ser.). 96p. (Orig.). (gr. 4-7). 1987. pap. 2.50 (ISBN 0-590-40590-X). Scholastic Inc.
Scholemaster. Roger Ascham. Ed. by J. E. Mayor. LC 75-161717. Repr. of 1863 ed. 14.00 (ISBN 0-404-00409-1). AMS Pr.
Scholemaster. Roger Ascham. Ed. by Edward Arber. LC 76-13152. Repr. of 1870 ed. lib. bdg. 17.00 (ISBN 0-8414-2976-6). Folcroft.
Scholemaster: Or, Plaine & Perfite Way of Teachyng Children the Latin Tong. Roger Ascham. LC 68-54609. (English Experience Ser.: No. 15). 134p. 1968. Repr. of 1570 ed. 54.00 (ISBN 90-221-0015-4). Walter J Johnson.
Scholia Ad Libros K-(Z) Continens see Scholia Graeca in Homeri Iliadem: Scholia Vetera.
Scholia Bembina in Terentium. J. F. Mountford. 140p. 1934. text ed. 41.40x (ISBN 0-576-72270-7, Pub. by Gregg Intl Pubs England). Gregg Intl.
Scholia Graeca in Homeri Iliadem: Scholia Vetera, 6 vols. Ed. by Hartmut Erbse. Incl. Vol 1. Praefationem et Scholia ad libros A-D continens. 545p. 1969. 80.00 (ISBN 3-11-002558-2); Vol 2. Scholia Ad Libros E - I Continens. 550p. 1971. 99.20x (ISBN 3-11-003882-X); Vol. 3. Scholia Ad Libros K-(Z) Continens. 1974. 152.00x (ISBN 3-11-004641-5); Vol. 4. Scholia Ad Libros Y-Continens. 1977. 192.00x (ISBN 3-11-005770-0); Vol. 5. Volumen Quintum, Scholia ad Libros y Continens. 1977. 232.00 (ISBN 3-11-006911-3). De Gruyter.
Scholia in Aristophanem, Pars II: Scholia in 'Vespas', 'Aves', et Lysistratam. Ed. by D. Holwerda. (Fasc. 2: Scholia Vetera et Recentiora in Aristophanis 'Pacem' Ser.). (Illus.). xxxii, 194p. 1982. 72.00x (ISBN 90-6088-076-5, Pub. by Boumas Boekhuis Netherlands). Benjamins North AM.
Scholia in Aristophanem, Pars, II: Scholia in 'Vespas', 'Aves', et 'Lysitratem' Ed. by D. Holwerda & W. J. Koster. (Fasc I: Scholia Vetera et Recentiora in Aristophanis 'Vespas' Ser.). (Illus.). li, 248p. 1978. 82.00x (ISBN 90-6088-058-7, Pub. by Boumas Boekhuis Netherlands). Benjamins North AM.
Scholia in Thucydidem: Ad Optimos Codices Collata, Edidit Carolus Hude. Thucydides. LC 72-7895. (Greek History Ser.). (Gr.). Repr. of 1927 ed. 32.00 (ISBN 0-405-04801-7). Ayer Co Pubs.
Scholia on the Aves of Aristophanes. John W. White. 438p. Repr. of 1914 ed. lib. bdg. 78.50x (ISBN 3-487-05318-7, Pub. by G Olms BRD). Coronet Bks.
Scholia Platonica. Ed. by William C. Greene. LC 81-16610. (American Philological Association Monograph Ser.). 1981. pap. 37.50 (ISBN 0-89130-541-6, 40 00 08). Scholars Pr GA.
Schollers Purgatory, Discovered in the Stationers Common-Wealth. George Wither. LC 77-7441. (English Experience Ser: No. 900). 1977. Repr. of 1625 ed. lib. bdg. 14.00 (ISBN 90-221-0900-3). Walter J Johnson.
Scholtes: Fonck Family History. Jean S. Zielinski. LC 88-50096. (Illus.). 250p. Date not set. 39.00 (ISBN 0-9620035-0-6). J S Zielinski.
Schomburg Library of Nineteenth-Century Black Women Writers, 30 vols. Ed. by Henry L. Gates, Jr. 1988. Set. 595.00 (ISBN 0-19-505267-6). Oxford U Pr.
Schomer Lichtner Drawings. Schomer Lichtner. (Illus.). 72p. (Orig.). 1964. pap. 5.00 (ISBN 0-941074-00-5). Lichtner.

Schone Schusterinn, Oder die Puecefarbnen Schube: Vienna, 1779. Ignaz Umlauf. Ed. by Thomas Bauman. (German Opera Ser., 1770-1800). 425p. 1986. lib. bdg. 95.00 (ISBN 0-8240-8862-X). Garland Pub.

schone Schusterinn, ofer puecefarbnen Schube see German Opera.

School. John Burningham. LC 75-4611. (Illus.). (ps-1). 1975. (Crowell Jr Bks); PLB 11.89 (ISBN 0-690-00903-8). HarpJ.

School. A. Gaidar. 159p. 1982. pap. 3.50 (ISBN 0-8285-2427-0, Pub. by Progress Pubs USSR). Imported Pubns.

School. Ed Kelleher & Harriette Vidal. 368p. (Orig.). 1988. pap. 3.95 (ISBN 0-8439-2567-1). Leisure NY.

School. Emily A. McCully. LC 87-156. (Illus.). 32p. (ps-2). 1987. 11.95i (ISBN 0-06-024132-2); PLB 12.89 (ISBN 0-06-024133-0). HarpJ.

School. Tanya Maiboroda. (Hidden Pictures Coloring Bks.). (Illus.). 48p. (gr. 4-7). 1987. pap. 2.95 (ISBN 0-8431-1881-4). Price Stern.

School. Henry Viscardi, Jr. LC 64-22735. 1964. 6.95 (ISBN 0-8397-7400-1). Eriksson.

School, Vol. 1 (incl. 1976-1978 Supplements) Ed. by Eleanor C. Goldstein. (Social Issues Resources Ser.). 1979. 75.00 (ISBN 0-89777-015-3). Soc Issues.

School, Vol. 2 (incl. 1979-1983 Supplements) Ed. by Eleanor C. Goldstein. (Social Issues Resources Ser.). 1984. 75.00 (ISBN 0-89777-047-1). Soc Issues.

School Achievement of Minority Children: New Perspectives. Ed. by Ulric Neisser. 208p. 1986. text ed. 19.95 (ISBN 0-89859-685-8). L Erlbaum Assocs.

School Activities & the Law. John L. Strope, Jr. Ed. by Patricia L. George. LC 84-174586. 80p. (Orig.). 1984. pap. 7.00 (ISBN 0-88210-158-7). Natl Assn Principals.

School Administration & Supervision: Leadership Challenges & Opportunities. 2nd ed. Richard A. Gorton. 576p. 1982. pap. text ed. write for info (ISBN 0-697-06246-5). Wm C Brown.

School Administration: Its Development, Principles, & Function in the United States. 2nd ed. Arthur B. Moehlman. LC 75-94590. (Illus.). 514p. 1970. Repr. lib. bdg. 35.00x (ISBN 0-8371-3988-0, MOSA). Greenwood.

School Administration: Leadership & Interaction. Stanley W. Williams. 380p. 1984. text ed. 24.50x (ISBN 0-8290-0533-1). Irvington.

School Administrative Aide. Jack Rudman. (Career Examination Ser.: C-1069). (Cloth bdg. avail. on request). 1988. pap. 14.00 (ISBN 0-8373-1069-5). Natl Learning.

School Administrative & Supervisory Organizations in Cities of 20,000 to 50,000 Population. William N. McGinnis. LC 71-177024. (Columbia University. Teachers College. Contributions to Education: No. 392). Repr. of 1929 ed. 22.50 (ISBN 0-404-55392-3). AMS Pr.

School Administrator's Complete Letter Book. Gerald Tomlinson. LC 83-24409. 294p. 1984. 29.95 (ISBN 0-13-792367-8, Busn). P-H.

School Administrator's Encyclopedia. P. Susan Mamchak & Steven R. Mamchek. LC 81-22492. 414p. 1982. 27.50x (ISBN 0-13-792390-2, Parker). P-H.

School Administrator's Faculty Supervision Handbook. Ronald T. Hyman. LC 85-28249. 223p. 1986. 24.95 (ISBN 0-13-792409-7, Busn). P-H.

School Administrator's Guide to Computers in Education. Cheever et al. LC 85-19969. 1985. pap. text ed. write for info. Addison-Wesley.

School Administrator's Guide to Early Childhood Programs. Lawrence J. Schweinhart. LC 88-11073. 60p. 1988. pap. text ed. write for info. (ISBN 0-931114-77-2). High-Scope.

School Administrator's Guide to Evaluating Library Media Programs. Bernice L. Yesner & Hilda L. Jay. LC 87-3118. xii, 244p. 1987. 26.00 (ISBN 0-208-02147-7, Lib Prof Pubns); pap. 19.50x (ISBN 0-208-02148-5, Lib Prof Pubns). Shoe String.

School Administrator's Public Speaking Portfolio: With Model Speeches & Anecdotes. P. Susan Mamchak & Steven R. Mamchak. 360p. 1983. 34.95x (ISBN 0-13-792556-5, Parker). P-H.

School Administrator's Resource Guide. Katherine Clay. 112p. 1987. pap. 22.00 (ISBN 0-89774-446-2). Oryx Pr.

School Administrator's Staff Development Activities Manual. Ronald T. Hyman. LC 85-28250. 153p. 1986. pap. 16.95 (ISBN 0-13-792607-3, Busn). P-H.

School-Age Child Care: An Action Manual. M. Seligson Seltzer & R. Kramer Baden. 486p. (Orig.). 1982. pap. 16.95 (ISBN 0-86569-112-6). Auburn Hse.

School-Age Pregnancy & Parenthood: Biosocial Dimensions. Ed. by Jane B. Lancaster & Beatrix A. Hamburg. (Social Science Research Council Bk.). (Illus.). 1986. lib. bdg. 39.95x (ISBN 0-202-30321-7). Aldine de Gruyter.

School Ain't No Way: Appalachian Consciousness. Ronald V. Iannone. 1972. 5.95 (ISBN 0-87012-135-9). McClain.

School: All about Language Ser. Harris Winitz. (Illus.). 50p. (Orig.). (YA) (gr. 7 up). 1987. pap. text ed. 5.45 (ISBN 0-939990-49-0); cassette tape 12.00 (ISBN 0-317-46300-4). Intl Linguistics.

School & College: Partnerships in Education. Gene I. Maeroff. LC 83-70359. 83p. 1983. pap. text ed. 4.95 (ISBN 0-931050-22-7). Carnegie Found.

School & College Speaker. Ed. by Wilmot B. Mitchell. LC 78-74820. (Granger Poetry Library). 1979. Repr. of 1901 ed. 29.50x (ISBN 0-89609-139-2). Roth Pub Inc.

School & Commonwealth. facs. ed. Henry C. Morrison. LC 73-142673. (Essay Index Reprint Ser). 1937. 18.00 (ISBN 0-8369-2063-5). Ayer Co Pubs.

School & Community, Vol. II. OECD. (Illus.). 129p. 1980. pap. 8.00x (ISBN 92-64-12082-3, 96-80-01-1). OECD.

School & Community, Vol. I. OECD & CERI. 145p. (Orig.). 1975. pap. 6.00x (ISBN 92-64-11413-0). OECD.

School & Community in Less Developed Areas. Ed. by Kevin M. Lillis. LC 85-6678. 281p. 1985. 31.00 (ISBN 0-7099-1655-8, Pub. by Croom Helm Ltd). Routledge Chapman & Hall.

School & Community in the Third World. M. E. Sinclair & Kevin Lillis. 188p. 1980. 28.50 (ISBN 0-7099-0323-5, Pub. by Croom Helm Ltd). Routledge Chapman & Hall.

School & Community Relations. 3rd ed. Leslie W. Kindred et al. (Illus.). 350p. 1984. 35.00 (ISBN 0-13-792283-3). P-H.

School & Community Resources for the Behaviorally Handicapped. Ed. by Thomas J. Kelly et al. 333p. 1974. text ed. 29.50x (ISBN 0-8422-5163-4); pap. text ed. 9.75x (ISBN 0-8422-0392-3). Irvington.

School & Continuing Education: Four Studies. LC 72-88520. 256p. (Orig.). 1972. pap. 5.25 (ISBN 92-3-100944-3, U566, UNESCO). UNIPUB.

School & Government Labor Relations: A Guide for Living with & Without Unions. Richard G. Neal. Ed. by Frances I. Felts. LC 82-61295. 266p. 1982. pap. text ed. 25.00 (ISBN 0-9605018-3-5). Neal Assoc.

School & Home Enrichment Program for Severely Handicapped Children. Robert P. Hawkins et al. LC 82-62571. 432p. 1983. 3-ring binder 75.00 ea. (ISBN 0-87822-272-3). Res Press.

School & Home Guide to Apple Macintosh Computer. Everett E. Murdock & Susan Sudbury. LC 85-530. (Illus.). 204p. 1985. pap. 15.95 (ISBN 0-13-793605-2). P-H.

School & Home Guide to IBM Compatible Personal Computers. Everett E. Murdock & Susan Sudbury. LC 84-24786. 292p. 1985. pap. 18.95 (ISBN 0-13-793662-1). P-H.

School & Home Guide to the IBM PCjr. Everett E. Murdock & Susan Sudbury. (Illus.). 224p. 1985. text ed. 29.00 (ISBN 0-13-793654-0); pap. text ed. 15.95 (ISBN 0-13-793647-8). P-H.

School & Society. John Dewey. LC 79-26919. (Arcturus Paperbacks). 124p. 1980. pap. 7.95 (ISBN 0-8093-0967-X). S Ill U Pr.

School & Society. Walter Feinberg & Jonas F. Solitis. (Thinking about Education Ser.). 160p. 1985. pap. 8.95x (ISBN 0-8077-2785-7). Tchrs Coll.

School & Society in Chicago. George S. Counts. LC 71-165715. (American Education Ser, No. 2). 1971. Repr. of 1928 ed. 27.50 (ISBN 0-405-03704-X). Ayer Co Pubs.

School & Society: Learning Content Through Culture. Ed. by Henry T. Trueba & Concha Delgado-Gaitan. 239p. 1988. lib. bdg. 39.95 (ISBN 0-275-92860-8, C2860). Praeger.

School & Society Through Science Fiction. Ed. by Joseph D. Olander et al. LC 81-40587. (Illus.). 404p. 1982. lib. bdg. 34.00 (ISBN 0-8191-1996-2); pap. text ed. 15.25 (ISBN 0-8191-1997-0). U Pr of Amer.

School & the Community: A Case Study of an Open-Plan School in Sri Lanka. (Educational Building Reports: No. 16). 70p. 1980. pap. 5.00 (ISBN 0-686-60291-9, UB79, UB). UNIPUB.

School & the Democratic Environment. Ed. by Danforth Foundation & the Ford Foundation. LC 70-111071. 115p. 1970. 23.00x (ISBN 0-231-03427-X). Columbia U Pr.

School & the Immigrant. Herbert A. Miller. LC 71-129507. (American Immigration Collection, Ser. 2). 1970. Repr. of 1916 ed. 11.00 (ISBN 0-405-00561-X). Ayer Co Pubs.

School & the Law. I. K. Birch. (Second Century in Australian Education Ser.: No. 13). 1976. pap. 7.50x (ISBN 0-522-84103-1, Pub. by Melbourne U Pr). Intl Spec Bk.

School & the Social Order. Frank Musgrave. LC 79-40738. 210p. pap. 54.60 (2030532). Bks Demand UMI.

School & the Social Order. Frank Musgrove. LC 79-40738. 204p. 1980. 76.00x (ISBN 0-471-27651-0, Pub. by Wiley-Interscience); (Pub. by Wiley-Interscience). Wiley.

School & the University: An International Perspective. Ed. by Burton R. Clark. LC 85-1158. 400p. 1985. pap. text ed. 37.50x; pap. 11.95. U of Cal Pr.

School Answers Back: Responding to Student Drug Abuse. Richard Hawley. LC 83-73198. 148p. 1984. pap. 5.00 (ISBN 0-942348-14-1). Am Council Drug Ed.

School Apperception Method (SAM) Irving L. Solomon & Bernard D. Starr. LC 68-23549. 1968. pkg. of 24 cards & manual 25.50 (ISBN 0-8261-0961-6). Springer Pub.

School at Home: An Alternative to the Public School System. Darcy Williamson. LC 79-55830. 100p. (Orig.). 1980. pap. 9.95 (ISBN 0-89288-022-8). Maverick.

School at Home, Teach Your Own Child. Ingeborg U. Kendall. LC 80-85435. 190p. 1982. 6.95 (ISBN 0-914704-03-6). ICER Pr.

School at Mopass: A Problem of Identity. A. Richard King. Ed. by George Spindler & Louise Spindler. (Case Studies in Education & Culture). 112p. 1983. pap. text ed. 6.95x (ISBN 0-8290-0319-3). Irvington.

School at Thrush Green. Read. (Illus.). 272p. 1988. 17.95 (ISBN 0-395-46108-1). HM.

School Attendance Aide. (Career Examination Ser.: C-3264). Date not set. pap. 14.00 (ISBN 0-8373-3264-8). Natl Learning.

School Attendance As a Factor in School Progress. Carl W. Ziegler. LC 70-177608. (Columbia University. Teachers College. Contributions to Education: No. 297). Repr. of 1928 ed. 22.50 (ISBN 0-404-55297-8). AMS Pr.

School Attendance in London Eighteen Seventy to Nineteen Four. David Rubinstein. LC 75-86243. 1969. 22.50x (ISBN 0-678-08000-3). Kelley.

School Attorney: A Practical Guide to Employing School District Legal Counsel. 75p. 1986. 7.00 (ISBN 0-88364-111-9). Natl Sch Boards.

School Bag. Illus. by Tony Tallarico. (Take Me Along Ser.). (Illus.). 12p. (ps-1). 1985. bds. 2.95 (ISBN 0-89828-229-2, 82292). Tuffy Bks.

School-Based Affective & Social Interventions. Ed. by Susan G. Foreman. LC 87-25151. (Special Services in the Schools Ser.). 170p. 1988. text ed. 29.95 (ISBN 0-86656-702-X). Haworth Pr.

School-Based Clinics. Ed. by Barrett Mosbacker. 192p. (Orig.). 1987. pap. 8.95 (ISBN 0-89107-453-8, Crossway Bks). Good News.

School-Based Curriculum Development. 284p. 1979. 12.00x (ISBN 92-64-11985-X). OECD.

School-Based Evaluation. John W. Wick. 1987. lib. bdg. 42.50 (ISBN 0-89838-178-9, Pub. by Kluwer-Nijhoff (Netherlands)). Kluwer Academic.

School Begins at Two. Harriet M. Johnson. Ed. by Barbara Biber. LC 70-108765. 1970. Repr. of 1936 ed. 15.00x (ISBN 0-87586-022-2). Agathon.

School Behavior & School Discipline: Coping with Deviant Behavior in the Schools. Eve E. Gagne. LC 82-15912. 176p. 1983. lib. bdg. 27.50 (ISBN 0-8191-2748-5); pap. text ed. 12.00 (ISBN 0-8191-2749-3). U Pr of Amer.

School Bell Memories: Horse & Buggy to Space Age. Ferol M. Slotte. Intro. by Jeanne Blend. (Illus.). 57p. 1986. pap. text ed. 7.00 private ed. (ISBN 0-9617960-0-6). Del Monte Pr.

School Board Primer: A Guide for School Board Members. John Wiles & Joseph Bondi. 300p. 1985. 34.95x (ISBN 0-205-08331-5, 238331, Pub. by Longwood Div). Allyn.

School Board Spending Priorities Profile. 3rd ed. Raymond G. Taylor & Gordon E. Bryant. 1985. incl. manual, profiles & sofware instrument 100.00 (ISBN 0-931265-03-7). Felicity Pr NC.

School Board Spending Priorities Profile. 2nd ed. Ed. by Raymond G. Taylor & Gordon Bryant. 14p. 1985. 50.00 (ISBN 0-931265-02-9); manual, wkbk. & profiles incl. Felicity Pr NC.

School Board Studies. Maurice E. Stapley. 1957. pap. 3.00 (ISBN 0-931080-00-2). U Chicago Midwest Admin.

School Board Study Programs: Board Members Manual, Series I. Daniel Brent & Carolyn Jurkowitz. 1983. 6.00 (ISBN 0-318-00790-8). Natl Cath Educ.

School Board Study Programs: Board Member's Manual, Series II. Daniel Brent & Carolyn Jurkowitz. 55p. 1988. pap. 6.60 (ISBN 1-558-33004-6). Natl Cath Educ.

School Board Study Programs, Series II: Board Members Manual. Carolyn Jurkowitz & Daniel Brent. 58p. 1984. 6.00 (ISBN 0-318-17910-5). Natl Cath Educ.

School Boards & School Policy: An Evaluation of Decentralization in New York City. Marilyn Gittell et al. LC 72-92475. (Special Studies in U. S. Social, Political & Economic Issues Ser.). (Illus.). 1973. text ed. 29.00x (ISBN 0-89197-929-8). Irvington.

School Boards & the Communities They Represent. Ross Zerchykov. 79p. (Orig.). 1983. pap. text ed. 7.00x (ISBN 0-917754-21-2). Inst Responsive.

School Budget & Business Administration: A Bibliography. Mary Vance. (Public Administration Ser.: P 1972). 13p. 1986. 3.75 (ISBN 0-89028-932-8). Vance Biblios.

School Budget: It's Your Money-It's Your Business. Rhoda Dersh. LC 79-90677. 1979. pap. 4.95 (ISBN 0-934460-10-8). NCCE.

School Budgeting: Problems & Solutions. 1981. 10.95 (ISBN 0-318-01773-3, 021-00900). Am Assn Sch Admin.

School Building Architectural Directory, 1986. Date not set. cancelled (ISBN 0-317-61181-X, 021-00159). Am Assn Sch Admin.

School Building Program for Cities. Nickolaus L. Engelhardt. LC 76-176753. (Columbia Univ. Teachers College Contribs. Ser.: No. 96). Repr. of 1918 ed. 22.50 (ISBN 0-404-55096-7). AMS Pr.

School Buildings & Natural Disasters. D. J. Vickery. (Educational, Buildings & Equipment: No. 4). (Illus.). 85p. 1982. pap. 5.25 (ISBN 92-3-102031-5, U1237, UNESCO). UNIPUB.

School Buildings: Monographs Published 1976-1987. Mary Vance. (Architecture Ser.: A 1940). 23p. 1987. 6.25 (ISBN 1-55590-550-1). Vance Biblios.

School Bus. Donald Crews. LC 83-18681. (Illus.). 32p. (gr. k-3). 1984. 11.75 (ISBN 0-688-02807-1); PLB 11.88 (ISBN 0-688-02808-X). Greenwillow.

School Bus. Donald Crews. LC 85-576. (Illus.). 32p. (ps-1). 1985. pap. 3.95 (ISBN 0-14-050549-0, Puffin). Penguin.

School Bus Law: A Case Study in Education, Religion & Politics. Theodore Powell. LC 60-13155. 1960. 28.95x (ISBN 0-89197-392-3); pap. text ed. 6.95x (ISBN 0-8290-2016-0). Irvington.

School Business Administration. Guilbert C. Hentschke. LC 84-61507. 580p. 1986. 35.00x (ISBN 0-8211-0768-2); text ed. 32.00x (ISBN 0-317-46835-9). McCutchan.

School Business Administration. K. Forbis Jordon et al. LC 84-24877. 416p. 1985. 29.95 (ISBN 0-8039-2417-8). Sage.

School Business Administration: A Planning Approach. 3rd ed. I. Carl Candoli et al. 421p. 1984. 38.95x (ISBN 0-205-08152-5, 238152, Pub. by Longwood Div). Allyn.

School Business Administrator. 3rd ed. Hill. 1982. 8.95 (ISBN 0-910170-26-6). Assn Sch Busn.

School Business Executive. Jack Rudman. (Career Examination Ser.: C-2887). (Cloth bdg. avail. on request). pap. 16.00 (ISBN 0-8373-2887-X). Natl Learning.

School Choral Program. Don Besig et al. Ed. by Jay Althouse. (Roundtable Sessions Ser.). 88p. (Orig.). 1987. pap. 9.95 (ISBN 0-939139-05-7). Music In Action.

School Class Size: Research & Policy. Gene V. Glass et al. (Illus.). 176p. 1982. 25.00 (ISBN 0-8039-1805-4). Sage.

School Clerk. Jack Rudman. (Career Examination Ser.: C-1984). (Cloth bdg. avail. on request). pap. 14.00 (ISBN 0-8373-1984-6). Natl Learning.

School Closing & Declining Enrollment. Ellen Bussard. 1981. pap. 3.50 (ISBN 0-934460-12-4). NCCE.

School-College Cooperative Programs in English. Ed. by Ronald J. Fortune. LC 86-711. (Options for Teaching Ser.: No. 8). 250p. (Orig.). 1986. 32.50x (ISBN 0-87352-360-1); pap. text ed. 17.50x (ISBN 0-87352-361-X). Modern Lang.

School-College Partnerships: A Look at the Major National Models. Franklin P. Wilbur et al. 55p. (Orig.). 1988. pap. 7.00 (ISBN 0-88210-207-9). Natl Assn Principals.

School Communication Workshop Kit. 1986. 119.00 (ISBN 0-87545-049-0, 418-13950). Natl Sch Pr.

School Community Interaction. Richard Saxe. LC 74-13595. 288p. 1975. 25.25x; text ed. 22.50x ten or more copies. McCutchan.

School-Community Relations in Transition. rev. ed. Richard W. Saxe. LC 83-62771. 361p. 1984. 25.50x (ISBN 0-8211-1859-5); text ed. 23.25 10 or more copies. McCutchan.

School Consultation: A Guide to Practice & Training. Jane C. Conoley & Collie W. Conoley. (Pergamon General Psychology Ser.: No. 111). (Illus.). 260p. 1982. text ed. 39.00 (ISBN 0-08-027566-4); pap. 16.95 (ISBN 0-08-027565-6). Pergamon.

School Consultation: Readings about Preventive Techniques for Pupil Personnel Workers. Joel Meyers et al. (Illus.). 368p. 1977. spiral bdg. 43.50x (ISBN 0-398-03485-0). C C Thomas.

School Contract Language. Donald W. Brodie & Peg A. Williams. 414p. 1983. 20.00. Butterworth Legal Pubs.

School Controversy Eighteen Ninety-One to Eighteen Ninety-Three. Daniel F. Reilly. LC 76-89221. (American Education: Its Men, Institutions & Ideas, Ser. 1). 1969. Repr. of 1943 ed. 24.00 (ISBN 0-405-01460-0). Ayer Co Pubs.

School Costs & School Accounting. J. H. Hutchinson. LC 78-176889. (Columbia University. Teachers College. Contributions to Education: No. 62). Repr. of 1914 ed. 22.50 (ISBN 0-404-55062-2). AMS Pr.

School Counseling Assistant. (Career Examination Ser.: C-3469). Date not set. pap. 14.00 (ISBN 0-8373-3469-1). Natl Learning.

School, Court, Public Administration: Judaism & Its Institutions in Talmudic Babylonia. Jacob Neusner. LC 87-4632. (Brown Judaic Studies). 306p. 1987. 34.95 (ISBN 1-55540-115-5, 14-00-83). Scholars Pr Ga.

School Crime & Violence: Problems & Solutions. Joseph I. Grealy. LC 79-55399. 1980. 29.95 (ISBN 0-918214-05-X). F E Peters.

School Crossing Guard. Jack Rudman. (Career Examination Ser.: C-702). (Cloth bdg. avail. on request). pap. 12.00 (ISBN 0-8373-0702-3). Natl Learning.

School Curriculum. Arthur Ellis et al. 450p. 1988. pap. text ed. 34.00 (ISBN 0-205-11172-6). Allyn.

School, Curriculum, & the Individual. John I. Goodlad. LC 66-17796. (Blaisdell Book in Education). pap. 66.80 (ISBN 0-317-09498-X, 2055148). Bks Demand UMI.

School Curriculum in the Context of Lifelong Learning. Uwe Hameyer. (UIE Monographs: Unesco Institute for Education: No. 9). 112p. 1979. pap. 5.00 (ISBN 92-820-1023-6, U931, UNESCO). UNIPUB.

School Curriculum Planning. Denis Lawton. (Studies in Teaching & Learning). 122p. (Orig.). 1986. pap. text ed. 16.95 (ISBN 0-340-38249-X). Princeton Bk Co.

School Custodial Supervisor. Jack Rudman. (Career Examination Ser.: C-1581). (Cloth bdg. avail. on request). pap. 14.00 (ISBN 0-8373-1581-6). Natl Learning.

School Custodian. Jack Rudman. (Career Examination Ser.: C-799). (Cloth bdg. avail. on request). pap. 12.00 (ISBN 0-8373-0799-6). Natl Learning.

School Custodian-Engineer. Jack Rudman. (Career Examination Ser.: C-701). (Cloth bdg. avail. on request). pap. 14.00 (ISBN 0-8373-0701-5). Natl Learning.

School Days: An Original Compilation. Clare V Dwiggins. Ed. by Bill Blackbeard. LC 76-53039. (Classic American Comic Strips). 1977. 16.45 (ISBN 0-88355-633-2); pap. 10.00 (ISBN 0-88355-632-4). Hyperion Conn.

School Days: For the Commodore 64. Claire Passantino. (Creative Pastimes Bk.). 1984p. pap. 6.95 (ISBN 0-8359-6886-3). P-H.

School Days, Rule Days: The Legalization and Regulation of Education. Ed. by David L. Kirp & Donald Jessen. LC 85-1537. (Stanford Series on Education & Public Policy: Vol. 1). 390p. 1986. (Falmer Pr); pap. 22.00x (ISBN 1-85000-018-2, Falmer Pr). Taylor & Francis.

School Daze. Charles Keller. (Illus.). (gr. 2-5). 1981. pap. 3.95 (ISBN 0-13-793612-5, Pub. by Treehouse). P-H.

School Desegregation. Yehuda Amir & Shlomo Sharan. 288p. 1984. text ed. 29.95 (ISBN 0-89859-335-2). L Erlbaum Assocs.

School Desegregation in Texas: The Implementation of United States vs. State of Texas. LC 82-82981. (Policy Research Project Report Ser.: No. 51). 75p. 1982. 6.50 (ISBN 0-89940-653-X). LBJ Sch Pub Aff.

School Desegregation: Past, Present, & Future. Ed. by Walter G. Stephan & Joe R. Feagin. LC 79-23436. (Perspectives in Social Psychology Ser.). (Illus.). 370p. 1980. 37.50x (ISBN 0-306-40378-1, Plenum Pr). Plenum Pub.

School Desegregation Plans That Work. Charles V. Willie. LC 83-12685. (Contributions to the Study of Education Ser.: No. 10). (Illus.). xi, 239p. 1984. lib. bdg. 35.00 (ISBN 0-313-24051-5, WDP/). Greenwood.

School Desegregation Research: New Directions in Situational Analysis. Ed. by Jeffrey Prager et al. (Critical Issues in Social Justice Ser.). 284p. 1986. 29.50x (ISBN 0-306-42151-8, Plenum Pr). Plenum Pub.

School Desegregation: Shadow & Substance. Ed. by Florence H. Levinsohn & Benjamin D. Wright. LC 76-17291. pap. 56.00 (2026781). Bks Demand UMI.

School Desegregation: The Continuing Challenge. new ed. Thomas F. Pettigrew et al. Ed. by Harvard Educational Review Editorial Board. (HER Reprint Ser.: No. 11). 1976. pap. text ed. 4.95x (ISBN 0-916690-13-X). Harvard Educ Rev.

School Discipline-A Planning & Resource Guide. James K. Nighswander. 500p. 1987. tchr's. manual 2.50 (ISBN 0-932957-92-7); instr's. manual 200.00 (ISBN 0-932957-93-5). Natl School.

School Discipline & Student Rights: An Advocate's Manual. Paul Weckstein. LC 83-111264. ix, 544p. 1982. 25.00 (ISBN 0-912585-00-5). Ctr Law & Ed.

School Discipline Desk Book: With Model Programs & Tested Procedures. Eugene R. Howard. (Illus.). 1977. 18.50x (ISBN 0-13-793000-3, Parker). P-H.

School Discourse Problems. Ed. by Danielle N. Ripich & Francesca M. Spinelli. LC 85-12754. 279p. (Orig.). 1985. pap. text ed. 20.50 (ISBN 0-316-74680-0, 746800). College-Hill.

School District Budgeting. William T. Hartman. (Illus.). 304p. 1988. text ed. 32.00 (ISBN 0-13-792292-2). P-H.

School District Library Media Director's Handbook. Betty Martin & Frances Hatfield. LC 81-14292. (Illus.). x, 236p. 1982. 23.00 (ISBN 0-208-01889-1, Lib Prof Pubns); pap. 16 50x (ISBN 0-208-01890-5, Lib Prof Pubns). Shoe String.

School Dividend: An Ethnography of Bilingual Education in a Chinese Community. Grace P. Guthrie. (Psychology of Reading & Reading Instruction Ser.). 264p. 1985. text ed. 29.95 (ISBN 0-89859-576-2). L Erlbaum Assocs.

School Drama in England. Thomas H. Motter. LC 67-27628. 1968. Repr. of 1929 ed. 28.50x (ISBN 0-8046-0325-1, Pub. by Kennikat). Assoc Faculty Pr.

School Drama Including Palsgrave's Introduction to Acolastus. James L. McConaughy. LC 79-177018. (Columbia University. Teachers College. Contributions to Education: No. 57). Repr. of 1913 ed. 22.50 (ISBN 0-404-55057-6). AMS Pr.

School Dropouts: Everybody's Problem. Sheppard Rambon. Ed. by Anne Lewis. 58p. (Orig.). 1986. pap. 7.50 (ISBN 0-937846-91-0). Inst Educ Lead.

School Dropouts: Patterns & Policies. enl. ed. Ed. by Gary Natriello. 192p. 1986. pap. 13.95x (ISBN 0-8077-2835-7). Tchrs Coll.

School Economy. Jelinger C. Symons. LC 71-78973. (Social History of Education). 1973. Repr. of 1852 ed. 25.00x (ISBN 0-678-08460-2). Kelley.

School Education of Girls: An International Comparative Study on School Wastage Among Girls & Boys at the First & Second Levels of Education. Isabell Deble. (Illus.). 180p. 1980. pap. 6.00 (ISBN 92-3-101782-9, U1058, UNESCO). UNIPUB.

School Effectiveness: A Reassessment of the Evidence. George F. Madaus et al. 1980. text ed. 21.95 (ISBN 0-07-039378-8). McGraw.

School Effectiveness: The Key Ingredients of School with Heart. G. Thomas Houlihan. (Illus.). 150p. 1988. text ed. 24.75x (ISBN 0-398-05402-9). C C Thomas.

School Energy Crisis: Problems & Solutions. Shirley B. Neill. (Critical Issues Reports: No. 1). (Illus.). 1977. pap. 8.95 (ISBN 0-686-10937-6, 02100380). Am Assn Sch Admin.

School Energy Management. American Association of School Administrators Staff. Ed. by Shirley Hanson Associates, Inc. 10.00 (ISBN 0-318-01749-0, 021-00520). Am Assn Sch Admin.

School Enrollment in Indonesia. Dov Chernichovsky & Oey A. Meesook. (Working Paper: No. 746). 38p. 1985. 3.50 (ISBN 0-8213-0584-0, WP 0746). World Bank.

School Enrollment, Social & Economic Characteristics of Students: October 1983. Robert Kominski. (Current Population Reports Series P-20, Population Characteristics: No.413). (Illus.). 93p. 1987. pap. 4.50 (ISBN 0-318-22743-6, S/N 803-005-00006-1). USGPO.

School Evaluation for the Catholic Elementary School: An Overview. Carleen Reck & Judith Coreil. 56p. 1983. 3.00 (ISBN 0-318-00791-6). Natl Cath Educ.

School Evaluation: Politics & Process. Ed. by Ernest R. House. LC 72-91622. 370p. 1973. 26.75x (ISBN 0-8211-0750-X); text ed. 24.75x 10 or more copies. McCutchan.

School Events. (Skyview Ser.). (gr. 2-4). wkbk. 3.95 (ISBN 0-317-42450-5). Learning Well.

School Experience. Ed. by Peter Woods & Martyn Hammersley. LC 76-44644. 1977. 26.00x (ISBN 0-312-70140-3). St Martin.

School Facilities Maintenance & Operations Manual. Irene Lober. 96p. (Orig.). 1988. pap. text ed. 15.95 (ISBN 0-910170-51-7). Assn Sch Busn.

School Failure. Ed. by D. W. Kaplan. (Journal: Pediatrician Ser.: Vol. 13, No. 2-3, 1986). (Illus.). 88p. 1987. pap. 39.50 (ISBN 3-8055-4550-9). S Karger.

School Fair. Althea. (Cambridge Information Books for Children). (Illus.). 26p. (gr. 2-5). 1983. pap. 2.50 (ISBN 0-521-27166-5). Cambridge U Pr.

School, Family, & Neighborhood. Eugene Litwak & Henry Meyer. LC 73-17274. 300p. 1974. 28.00x (ISBN 0-231-03354-0). Columbia U Pr.

School Finance & School Improvement: Linkages for the 1980s. Ed. by Allan Odden & Dean Webb. LC 83-11815. (American Education Finance Association). 284p. 1983. 32.95x (ISBN 0-88410-399-4). Ballinger Pub.

School Finance Manager. Jack Rudman. (Career Examination Ser.: C-2886). (Cloth bdg. avail. on request). pap. 16.00 (ISBN 0-8373-2886-1). Natl Learning.

School Finance Policies & Practices: The Nineteen-Eighties: Decade of Conflict. James W. Guthrie. LC 80-19707. (American Education Finance Association). 312p. 1981. pap. 16.95x (ISBN 0-88410-396-X). Ballinger Pub.

School Finance Reform in the States. 58p. 1981. 4.00 (ISBN 0-318-17956-3, F-81-1). Ed Comm States.

School Finance: The Economics & Politics of Public Education. Walter I. Garms et al. (Illus.). 1978. text ed. write for info (ISBN 0-13-793315-0). P-H.

School Financing in Nepal. 22p. 1981. pap. 3.00 (ISBN 0-318-23182-4). Am-Nepal Ed.

School-Focused Inservice: Description & Discussions. Ed. by Howey & Bents. 1981. 6.00 (ISBN 0-686-38076-2). Assn Tchr Ed.

School-Focused Staff Development: Guidelines for Policy Makers. Eric Hewton. 155p. 1988. 36.00x (ISBN 1-85000-273-8, Falmer Pr); pap. 18.00x (ISBN 1-85000-274-6, Falmer Pr). Taylor & Francis.

School Foodservice. 3rd ed. Dorothy VanEgmond-Pannell. (Illus.). 1985. 24.95 (ISBN 0-87055-463-8). AVI.

School Foodservice Handbook. Dorothy V. Pannell. 98p. (Orig.). 1987. pap. text ed. 11.95 (ISBN 0-910170-48-7). Assn Sch Busn.

School for Ambassadors & Other Essays. facs. ed. Jean A. Jusserand. LC 68-57325. (Essay Index Reprint Ser). 1925. 20.00 (ISBN 0-8369-0581-4). Ayer Co Pubs.

School for Angels. (Drama Pak Ser.). 1984. 9.95 (ISBN 0-89273-304-7). Educ Serv.

School for Coeds. Edmund Miller. 1972. pap. 1.25 (ISBN 0-9600486-1-8). Edmund Miller.

School for Colored Girls in Washington, D. C. see Myrtilla Miner: A Memoir.

School for Crusoes (School for Robinsons) Jules Verne. 4.95 (ISBN 0-685-27951-0). Assoc Bk.

School for Fools. Sasha Sokolov. Tr. by Carl Proffer. LC 87-33009. 246p. 1988. pap. 9.95 (ISBN 0-941423-07-7). FWEW.

School for Girls. Michel Mellot. Tr. by Mary Glavin. (Orig.). 1970. pap. 1.50 (ISBN 0-87067-413-7, BH413). Holloway.

School for Husbands. (Illus.). 43p. (Director's Production Script). 1966. pap. 6.00 (ISBN 0-88680-170-2). I E Clark.

School for Masters. Herbert L. Beierle. 1979. 1.00 (ISBN 0-940480-11-5). U of Healing.

School for Murder. Robert Barnard. 1985. pap. 3.50 (ISBN 0-440-17605-0). Dell.

School for Scandal. Frederick Cyr. LC 85-70198. 200p. 1985. pap. 3.95 (ISBN 0-394-62057-7, B-523, BC). Grove.

School for Scandal. Richard B. Sheridan. Ed. by John Loftis. LC 66-12977. (Crofts Classics Ser.). 1966. pap. text ed. 3.95x (ISBN 0-88295-092-4). Harlan Davidson.

School for Scandal. Richard B. Sheridan. Ed. by F. W. Bateson. (New Mermaids Ser.). 1979. pap. 6.95x (ISBN 0-393-90043-6). Norton.

School for Scandal. Richard B. Sheridan. Ed. by C. J. Price. 1971. pap. 4.95x (ISBN 0-19-911008-5). Oxford U Pr.

School for Scandal. Richard B. Sheridan. Ed. by Richard Adams. 1988. pap. 3.95 (ISBN 0-582-33149-8). Longman.

School for Secretaries. Gilbert Preston. 256p. 1984. 15.95 (ISBN 0-312-70146-2). St Martin.

School for Soldiers: An Inquiry into West Point. Josephy Ellis & Robert Moore. 1974. 21.95x (ISBN 0-19-501843-5). Oxford U Pr.

School for Soldiers: West Point & the Profession of Arms. Joseph Ellis & Robert Moore. LC 74-79638. (Illus.). 1974. pap. 5.95 (ISBN 0-19-502022-7). Oxford U Pr.

School for Tomorrow. Jack R. Frymier. LC 72-10647. 286p. 1973. 25.25x (ISBN 0-8211-0505-1); text ed. 22.50x 10 or more copies. McCutchan.

School for Wives. Moliere, pseud. Ed. by Richard Wilbur. LC 70-153693. 1972. pap. 4.95 (ISBN 0-15-679501-9, HB228, Harv). HarBraceJ.

School for Wives: An Adaptation in Rhymed Verse. Moliere, pseud. Tr. by Eric M. Steel. LC 75-154426. 1977. pap. 4.95 (ISBN 0-8120-0436-1). Barron.

School for Wives-Robert-Genevieve or the Unfinished Confidence. Andre Gide. Tr. by Dorothy Bussy from Fr. LC 79-23993. 1980. Repr. of 1929 ed. lib. bdg. 12.50x (ISBN 0-8376-0454-0). Bentley.

School Fun. Al Hartley. (Barbour Activity Bks.). (Illus.). (gr. 1). 1988. pap. text ed. 0.99 (ISBN 1-55748-003-6). Barbour & Co.

School Funds & Their Apportionment, a Consideration of the Subject with Reference to a More General Equalization of Both the Burdens & the Advantages of Education. Ellwood P. Cubberley. LC 72-176681. (Columbia University. Teachers College. Contributions to Education: No. 2). Repr. of 1906 ed. 22.50 (ISBN 0-404-55002-9). AMS Pr.

School Funds in the Province of Quebec. George J. Trueman. LC 75-177695. (Columbia University. Teachers College. Contributions to Education: No. 106). Repr. of 1920 ed. 22.50 (ISBN 0-404-55106-8). AMS Pr.

School Furniture. David Medd. (OECD Programme on Educational Building). (Illus.). 173p. (Orig.). 1981. pap. text ed. 12.50x (ISBN 92-64-12222-2). OECD.

School Furniture Development: An Evaluation. Scriven, F. B. & Associates. (Educational Studies & Documents: No. 16). (Illus.). 54p. 1975. pap. 5.00 (ISBN 92-3-101233-9, U567, UNESCO). UNIPUB.

School Furniture Handbook, 2 Vols. Incl. Vol. 1. General & Specific Aspects, 2 Vols. 258p. 1980 (ISBN 0-686-65828-0, U985). UNIPUB; Vol. 2. Practical Examples & Illustrations, 2 Vols. 246p. 1980 (ISBN 0-686-61618-9, U989). UNIPUB. (Educational Buildings & Equipment Ser.). 1979. pap. 17.00 (UNESCO). UNIPUB.

School Governing Bodies. Ed. by Maurice Kogan et al. 220p. (Orig.). 1984. pap. text ed. 20.00x (ISBN 0-435-82512-7). Heinemann Ed.

School Grievance Arbitration: What the Arbitrators Are Doing. Donald W. Brodie & Peg A. Williams. LC 82-71021. 248p. 1982. Incl. pocket supplement. 20.00 (ISBN 0-409-24965-3). Butterworth WA.

School Guard. Jack Rudman. (Career Examination Ser.: C-1923). (Cloth bdg. avail. on request). pap. 12.00 (ISBN 0-8373-1923-4). Natl Learning.

School Guidance Services: A Career Development Approach. 2nd ed. Thomas H. Hohenshil & Johnnie H. Miles. 336p. 1979. pap. text ed. 21.95 (ISBN 0-8403-2044-2). Kendall-Hunt.

School Health: A Guide for Health Professionals. rev. ed. American Academy of Pediatrics, Committee on School Health Staff. 216p. 1987. pap. 25.00 (ISBN 0-910761-14-0). AM Acad Pediat.

School Health Handbook: A Ready Reference for School Nurses & Educators. Jerry Newton. LC 84-8382. 300p. 1984. 27.95x (ISBN 0-13-793639-7, Busn). P-H.

School Health in America. 4th ed. 1986. write for info. (ISBN 0-917160-00-2). Am Sch Health.

School Health Practice. 9th ed. Creswell et al. 544p. 1989. 33.95 (ISBN 0-8016-2560-2). Mosby.

School Health Practice. 8th ed. William H. Creswell & C. L. Anderson. 1984. text ed. 27.95 (ISBN 0-8016-0217-3). Mosby.

School Health Program. 3rd ed. Jessie H. Haag. LC 70-175461. (Health Education, Physical Education, & Recreation Ser.). pap. 74.30 (2056187). Bks Demand UMI.

School Health Program. 5th ed. Warren Schaller. 574p. 1981. text ed. write for info. (ISBN 0-697-06304-6). Wm C Brown.

School History of Mississippi. Franklin L. Riley. LC 76-68. (Illus.). 448p. 1976. Repr. of 1900 ed. 15.00 (ISBN 0-87152-219-5). Reprint.

School History of the Negro Race in America, 2 Vols. in 1. Edward A. Johnson. LC 73-100532. Repr. of 1911 ed. 26.50 (ISBN 0-404-00176-9). AMS Pr.

School House at Pine Tree Corner, North Salem, N. Y. 1784-1916: Teaching & Administrative Practices in a One-Room Rural School in Westchester County. Helen G. Trager. LC 76-41367. (Illus.). 1976. pap. 7.95 (ISBN 0-916346-24-2). Harbor Hill Bks.

School House in the Wind. Anne Treneer. 224p. 1982. pap. 7.50 (ISBN 0-907746-03-9, Pub. by A Mott Ltd). Longwood Pub Group.

School Improvement: Theory & Practice: A Book of Readings. Ed. by Robert V. Carlson & Edward R. Ducharme. (Illus.). 1228p. (Orig.). 1987. lib. bdg. 55.00 (ISBN 0-8191-5815-1). U Pr of Amer.

School in Question: A Comparative Study of School & Its Future in Western Societies. Torstein Husen. (Illus.). 1979. 29.95x (ISBN 0-19-874085-9); pap. 13.95x (ISBN 0-19-874086-7). Oxford U Pr.

School in Rose Valley: A Parent Venture in Education. Grace Rotzel. LC 70-144200. (Illus.). Repr. of 1971 ed. 39.80 (ISBN 0-8357-9284-6, 2015739). Bks Demand UMI.

School in Society: Studies in the Sociology of Education. Ed. by Sam D. Sieber & David E. Wilder. LC 72-80079. (Illus.). 1973. text ed. 14.95 (ISBN 0-02-928680-8). Free Pr.

School in the Social Setting. Alan Gorr. 392p. 1974. text ed. 37.50x (ISBN 0-8422-5162-6); pap. text ed. 14.95x (ISBN 0-8422-0177-7). Irvington.

School Inspection System. R. P. Singhal et al. 176p. 1987. text ed. 22.50x (ISBN 0-7069-3200-5, Pub. by Vikas India). Advent NY.

School Is Hell. Matt Groening. LC 86-62859. (Illus.). 48p. 1987. pap. 5.95 (ISBN 0-394-75091-8). Pantheon.

School Laboratory Assistant. (Career Examination Ser.: C-3333). Date not set. pap. 14.00 (ISBN 0-8373-3333-4). Natl Learning.

School Language Policy for Puerto Rico. Pedro A. Cebollero. LC 74-14224. (Puerto Rican Experience Ser). (Illus.). 148p. 1975. Repr. 10.00x (ISBN 0-405-06214-1). Ayer Co Pubs.

School Law: Cases & Concepts. Michael W. La Morte. (Illus.). 448p. 1982. write for info. (ISBN 0-13-793695-8). P-H.

School Law: Cases & Concepts. 2nd ed. Michael W. La Morte. (Illus.). 448p. 1987. text ed. write for info. (ISBN 0-13-793720-2). P-H.

School Law: Cases & Materials. Robert E. Phay. 1986. 20.00. U of NC Inst Gov.

School Law for the Practitioner. Robert C. O'Reilly & Edward T. Green. LC 82-11982. (Contributions to the Study of Education Ser.: No. 6). (Illus.). xiv, 314p. 1983. lib. bdg. 36.95 (ISBN 0-313-23639-9, ORS/). Greenwood.

School Law, Georgia. 292p. 1981. 4.50 (ISBN 0-318-02437-3). ICLE Georgia.

School Law, Georgia. 444p. 1984. 9.00 (ISBN 0-318-02438-1). ICLE Georgia.

School Law in Review 1985, Vol. 1. 165p. 1985. 30.00 (ISBN 0-88364-106-2). Natl Sch Boards.

School Law in Review, 1986, Vol. II. 125p. 1986. 30.00. Natl Sch Boards.

School Law in Review, 1987. 156p. 1987. 30.00 (ISBN 0-88364-123-2). Natl Sch Boards.

School Law Seminar Proceedings. 1983. 20.00 (ISBN 0-686-89423-5). Natl Sch Boards.

School Law Seminar Proceedings. 170p. 1982. 15.00 (ISBN 0-686-89312-3). Natl Sch Boards.

School Law Seminar Proceedings. 125p. 1981. 10.00 (ISBN 0-686-89313-1). Natl Sch Boards.

School Law Seminar Proceedings. 1984. 20.00 (ISBN 0-88364-103-8). Natl Sch Boards.

School Law: Theoretical & Case Perspectives. Julius Menacker. 480p. 1987. text ed. write for info. (ISBN 0-13-793753-9). P-H.

School Law Update: Preventive School Law. Ed. by D. Semler & T. Jones. 1984. 17.95 (ISBN 0-318-02065-3). NOLPE.

School Law Update 1985: Addresses from 1984 NOLPE Convention. 1985. 19.95 (ISBN 0-318-20264-6). NOLPE.

School Law Update, 1986. Ed. by D. Selmer & T. Jones. 1986. 19.95 (ISBN 0-318-23628-1). NOLPE.

School Leadership: A Contemporary Reader. Ed. by Joel L. Burdin. 464p. 1988. text ed. 36.00 (ISBN 0-8039-3362-2); pap. text ed. 17.95 (ISBN 0-8039-3363-0). Sage.

School Leadership & Administration: Important Concepts, Case Studies, & Simulations. 3rd ed. Richard Gorton. 352p. 1987. pap. text ed. write for info. (ISBN 0-697-00975-0). Wm C Brown.

School Leadership & Instructional Improvement. Daniel L. Duke. 280p. 1987. pap. text ed. write for info. (ISBN 0-394-35474-5, RanC). Random.

School Leadership: Handbook for Survival. Ed. by Stuart C. Smith et al. (Illus.). xx, 343p. (Orig.). 1981. pap. 13.95 (ISBN 0-86552-078-X). U of Oreg ERIC.

School Learning, with Various Methods of Practice & Rewards. George Forlano. LC 74-176782. (Columbia University. Teachers College. Contributions to Education: No. 688). Repr. of 1936 ed. 22.50 (ISBN 0-404-55688-4). AMS Pr.

School Leavers & Their Prospects: Youth & the Labor Market in the 1980's. Kenneth Roberts. 169p. 1984. pap. 21.00x (ISBN 0-335-10418-5, Pub. by Open Univ Pr). Taylor & Francis.

School-Leaving Youth & Employment: Some Factors Associated with the Duration of Early Employment of Youth Whose Formal Education Ended at High School Graduation or Earlier. Cloyd D. Long. LC 74-177006. (Columbia University. Teachers College. Contributions to Education: No. 845). Repr. of 1941 ed. 22.50 (ISBN 0-404-55845-3). AMS Pr.

School Liability for Injuries to Pupils. Arthur C. Poe. LC 79-177156. (Columbia University. Teachers College. Contributions to Education: No. 828). Repr. of 1941 ed. 22.50 (ISBN 0-404-55828-3). AMS Pr.

School Librarian As Educator. 2nd ed. Lillian B. Wehmeyer. LC 84-19367. (Library Science Text Ser.). 477p. 1984. lib. bdg. 22.50 (ISBN 0-87287-372-2). Libs Unl.

School Librarian's Day: An Investigation into the Role & Functions of the School Librarian. Ann Irving. (British Library Research Paper: No. 9). 1986. pap. 7.50 (ISBN 0-7123-3099-2, Pub. by British Lib). Longwood Pub Group.

School Librarian's Grade-by-Grade Activities Program. Carol Kuhlthau. LC 81-10121. 1981. 23.50x (ISBN 0-87628-744-5). Ctr Appl Res.

School Librarianship. Ed. by John Cook. (Illus.). 272p. 1981. 31.00 (ISBN 0-08-024814-4); pap. 19.25 (ISBN 0-08-024813-6). Pergamon.

School Librarianship. James E. Herring. 116p. 1982. 16.50 (ISBN 0-85157-347-9, Pub. by Bingley England). ALA.

School Librarianship in the United Kingdom. Helen Pain. (British Library Information Guide: No. 4). 1987. pap. 20.00 (ISBN 0-7123-3089-5, Pub. by British Lib). Longwood Pub Group.

School Libraries: International Developments. Jean E. Lowrie. LC 72-3440. 1972. 13.00 (ISBN 0-8108-0505-7). Scarecrow.

School Library. Ralph E. Ellsworth & Hobart E. Wagener. LC 63-19903. (Illus.). 144p. 1963. pap. 2.50 (ISBN 0-89192-039-0). Interbk Inc.

School Library & Media Center Acquisitions Policies & Procedures. 2nd ed. Ed. by Betty Kamp. LC 86-42752. 280p. 1986. 44.50 (ISBN 0-89774-160-9). Oryx Pr.

School Library & Media Center Acquisitions Policies & Procedures. Ed. by Mary M. Taylor. 312p. 1981. lib. bdg. 36.00x (ISBN 0-912700-70-X). Oryx Pr.

School Library As Part of the Instructional System. Charlene R. Swarthout. LC 67-10194. 235p. 1967. lib. bdg. 16.00 (ISBN 0-8108-0026-8). Scarecrow.

School Library at Work: Acquisition, Organization, Use & Maintenance of Materials in the School Library. Azile Wofford. LC 59-6611. (Illus.). 256p. 1959. 12.00 (ISBN 0-8242-0045-4). Wilson.

School Library Media Annual 1984. 2nd., 2nd Annual Vol. ed. Ed. by Shirley L. Aaron & Pat R. Scales. 528p. 1984. lib. bdg. 35.00 (ISBN 0-87287-434-6). Libs Unl.

School Library Media Annual, 1985, Vol. 3. Ed. by Shirley L. Aaron & Pat R. Scales. 450p. 1985. lib. bdg. 40.00 (ISBN 0-87287-475-3). Libs Unl.

School Library Media Annual, 1986, Vol. 4. Ed. by Shirley L. Aaron. Pat R. Scales. 450p. 1986. lib. bdg. 40.00 (ISBN 0-87287-520-2). Libs Unl.

School Library Media Annual 1987, Vol. 5. Ed. by Shirley L. Aaron & Pat R. Scales. 400p. 1987. lib. bdg. 40.00 (ISBN 0-87287-567-9). Libs Unl.

School Library Media Annual, 1988, Vol. 6. Ed. by Jane B. Smith. 300p. 1988. lib. bdg. 29.50 (ISBN 0-87287-635-7). Libs Unl.

School Library Media Center. 3rd ed. Emanuel T. Prostano & Joyce S. Prostano. LC 82-7193. (Library Science Text). 200p. 1982. 28.00 (ISBN 0-87287-286-6); pap. text ed. 20.00 (ISBN 0-87287-334-X). Libs Unl.

School Library Media Center. 4th ed. Emanuel T. Prostano & Joyce S. Prostano. 250p. 1987. lib. bdg. 28.50 (ISBN 0-87287-568-7); pap. text ed. 21.50 (ISBN 0-87287-569-5). Libs Unl.

School Library Media Center Management Case Book. Ed. by Daniel Callison & Jacqueline Morris. 192p. 1988. pap. 24.50 (ISBN 0-89774-441-1). Oryx Pr.

School Library Media Centers & Networking. Mary R. Sive. 85p. 1982. 4.75 (ISBN 0-937597-01-5, IR-60). ERIC Clear.

School Library Media Program: Instructional Force for Excellence. 3rd ed. Ruth A. Davies. LC 79-20358. 580p. 1979. 20.00 (ISBN 0-8352-1244-0). Bowker.

School Library Media Services to the Handicapped. Ed. by Myra Macon. LC 81-4262. (Illus.). xii, 208p. 1982. lib. bdg. 35.00 (ISBN 0-313-22684-9, MAL/). Greenwood.

School Library-Media Skills Test. Anne M. Hyland. LC 86-7249. 8p. 1986. pap. text ed. 25.00 (ISBN 0-87287-521-0). Libs Unl.

School Library Service & the Curriculum. Scottish Library Association Staff. 1987. 29.00x (ISBN 0-317-59228-9, Pub. by Scottish Libr Assn). State Mutual Bk.

School Life & Organizational Psychology. American Psychological Association Staff. (Human Behavior Curriculum Project Ser.). 64p. (Orig.). 1981. pap. text ed. 3.95x (ISBN 0-8077-2617-6); tchrs. manual & duplication masters 9.95x (ISBN 0-8077-2618-4). Tchrs Coll.

School Life in Paris & Lovely Nights of Young Girls. 288p. 1984. pap. 8.95 (ISBN 0-394-62348-7, E-968, Ever). Grove.

School Life in Paris & Lovely Nights of Young Girls. Illus. by Tomi Ungerer. (Victorian Library). (Illus.). 288p. 1984. 19.95 (ISBN 0-394-54268-1, GP953). Grove.

School Literary Magazine. Ed. by B. Jo Kinnick. 1966. pap. 5.75 (ISBN 0-8141-4269-9). NCTE.

School Loan Program Guide. LC 84-148652. 1984. pap. 7.75 (ISBN 0-934338-51-5). NAIS.

School Lunch Coordinator: C-317. Jack Rudman. (Career Examination Ser.). (Cloth bdg. avail. on request). pap. 16.00 (ISBN 0-8373-0317-6). Natl Learning.

School Lunch Director. Jack Rudman. (Career Examination Ser.: C-2088). (Cloth bdg. avail. on request). 1988. pap. 16.00 (ISBN 0-8373-2088-7). Natl Learning.

School Lunch Manager. Jack Rudman. (Career Examination Ser.: C-703). (Cloth bdg. avail. on request). pap. 14.00 (ISBN 0-8373-0703-1). Natl Learning.

School-Maister to the Art of Stenographie. John Willis. LC 74-80225. (English Experience Ser.: No. 702). 176p. 1974. Repr. of 1622 ed. 11.50 (ISBN 90-221-0702-7). Walter J Johnson.

School Makes Sense...Sometimes. Jean Gatch. LC 80-10281. (Human Sciences Books for Young Readers). (Illus.). 32p. (gr. k-5). 1980. 13.95 (ISBN 0-87705-494-0). Human Sci Pr.

School Management. Alan Paisey. 1984. pap. text ed. 13.50 (ISBN 0-06-318283-1). Har-Row.

School Management in Nepal. 25p. 1981. pap. 3.00 (ISBN 0-318-23181-6). Am-Nepal Ed.

School Management Library: Ten volume School Management Model, Plus Two Books: Effective Schools & Improving School Performances, 12 vols. Fredric H. Genck. 1391p. 1986. Set. pap. text ed. 335.00 (ISBN 0-935807-04-7). Inst Pub Mgmt.

School Management Model: How-to-Do-It-Yourself Handbooks & Case Studies, 10 vols. Fredric H. Genck. 875p. (Orig.). 1985. Set. pap. 295.00 (ISBN 0-318-03999-0). Inst Pub Mgmt.

School Management Model: How-to-Do-It-Yourself Handbooks & Case Studies, 8 vols. Fredric H. Genck. 650p. (Orig.). 1984. Set. pap. 185.00 (ISBN 0-318-04000-X). Inst Pub Mgmt.

School Management Model: How-to-Do-It-Yourself Handbooks & Case Studies, 12 vols. Fredric H. Genck. 1068p. 1987. Set. pap. text ed. 355.00 (ISBN 0-935807-05-5). Inst Pub Mgmt.

School Management Model: Overview, Vol. 1. Fredric H. Genck. (School Management Model Ser.). 90p. (Orig.). 1984. pap. 34.00 (ISBN 0-318-04001-8). Inst Pub Mgmt.

School Management Model Self Study Guide. Fredric H. Genck. (School Management Model How-To-Do-It-Yourself Handbooks & Case Studies: Vol. 11). 48p. 1986. pap. text ed. 18.00 (ISBN 0-935807-01-2). Inst Pub Mgmt.

School Materials Safety Manual: A Collection of Material Safety Data Sheets (Plus Updating Service) John H. Bartsch. Ed. by Elizabeth Coccio & Joseph Accrocco. LC 87-14889. 439p. 1987. 195.00x (ISBN 0-931690-22-6). Genium Pub.

School Media Policy Development: A Practical Process for Small Districts. Helen R. Adams. LC 86-185879. 250p. 1986. lib. bdg. 23.50 (ISBN 0-87287-450-8). Libs Unl.

School-Mistress. William Shenstone. LC 75-19183. 1975. Repr. of 1924 ed. lib. bdg. 27.50 (ISBN 0-8414-7602-0). Folcroft.

School Music Program: Description & Standards. Music Educators National Conference Committee on Standards. 56p. 1986. 9.95 (ISBN 0-317-60250-0, 1039). Music Ed Natl.

School Myth-Takes (Myths & Mistakes About School) Margarita V. Hamada. 219p. pap. 10.25x (ISBN 971-10-0320-1, Pub. by New Day Pub Philippines). Cellar.

School Newspaper. Serena K. Bond. (Language Arts Ser.). 24p. (gr. 8-12). 1982. wkbk. 5.00 (ISBN 0-8209-0328-0, J-1). ESP.

School Newspaper Management. Campbell. 0.50 (ISBN 0-318-19222-5). Quill & Scroll.

School Nurse Practitioner. Jack Rudman. (Certified Nurse Examination Ser.: CN-3). 25.95 (ISBN 0-8373-6153-2); pap. 13.95 (ISBN 0-8373-6103-6). Natl Learning.

School of Abuse. Stephen Gosson. Ed. by John P. Collier. LC 77-126658. Repr. of 1841 ed. 12.00 (ISBN 0-404-02886-1). AMS Pr.

School of Abuse: A Pleasant Invective Against Poets, Pipers, Players, Jesters, Etc; see Stage Attacked. Northbrooke & Gosson: A Treatise Against Dicing, Dancing, Plays & Interludes.

School of Athens: The Conflict Between Idolatry & Imagination, 2 vols. John Ruskin. (Illus.). 167p. 1987. Repr. of 1885 ed. 146.55 (ISBN 0-86650-225-4). Gloucester Art.

School of Bowing for Violin, 2 bks, Op. 2. Otakar Sevcik..(Carl Fischer Music Library: Nos. 291 & 292). 1904. Bk. 1. pap. 4.00 (ISBN 0-8258-0038-2, L291); Bk. 2, 42p. pap. 4.00 (ISBN 0-8258-0039-0, L292). Fischer Inc NY.

School of Chartres. Pierre Morizot. 1987. pap. 5.95 (ISBN 0-916786-97-8). St George Bk Serv.

School of Chemical Engineering at Cornell: A History of the First Fifty Years. Julian C. Smith. 101p. Date not set. price not set (ISBN 0-918531-02-0). Cornell Coll Eng.

School of Christian Rejections see Twelve Steps ot Holiness & Salvation.

School of Clavier Playing; or, Instructions in Playing the Clavier for Teachers & Students. Daniel G. Turk. Tr. by Raymond H. Haggh. LC 81-14626. xxxvi, 563p. 1982. 50.00x (ISBN 0-8032-2316-1). U of Nebr Pr.

School of Cyrus: William Barker's Translation of Xeonophon's Cyropaedeia (The Education of Cyrus) London, 1567. Ed. by Stephen Orgel. (Reniassance Imagination Ser.). 500p. 1987. lib. bdg. 75.00 (ISBN 0-8240-8417-9). Garland Pub.

School of Darkness. Bella V. Dodd. 1963. pap. 6.95 (ISBN 0-8159-6804-3). Devin.

School of Education As a Workplace. Ed. by Ayers Bagley. 1986. 5.50 (ISBN 0-933669-36-4). Soc Profs Ed.

School of Femininity. Margaret Lawrence. LC 76-29673. 1976. Repr. of 1936 ed. lib. bdg. 39.00 (ISBN 0-8414-5806-5). Folcroft.

School of Fencing. Domenico Angelo. (Illus.). 104p. 1982. Repr. 200.00 (ISBN 0-88254-718-6, Pub. by Edita SA); Half Leather 400.00 (ISBN 0-686-99271-7). Hippocrene Bks.

School of Hawthorne. Richard H. Brodhead. 276p. 1986. 24.95x (ISBN 0-19-504022-8). Oxford U Pr.

School of Jesus. new ed. James A. Mohler. LC 72-11835. 280p. 1973. 5.95 (ISBN 0-8189-0262-0). Alba.

School of Kabbalah. Z'ev Ben Shimon Halevi. LC 85-50635. (Illus.). 288p. (Orig.). 1985. pap. 8.95 (ISBN 0-87728-648-5). Weiser.

School of Manners or Rules for Children's Behaviour. Joyce Whalley. (Illus.). 36p. 1984. 5.95 (ISBN 0-905209-36-2, Pub. by Victoria & Albert Mus UK). Faber & Faber.

School of Mechanism: Fifteen Etudes for the Piano, Op. 120. J. B. Duvernoy. Ed. by Hans. Seifert. (Carl Fischer Music Library: No. 361). 1904. pap. 5.00 (ISBN 0-8258-0112-5, L361). Fischer Inc NY.

School of Medieval England. Arthur F. Leach. 1976. lib. bdg. 59.95 (ISBN 0-8490-2570-2). Gordon Pr.

School of Names. M. B. Goffstein. LC 85-45419. (Charlotte Zolotow Bks.). (Illus.). 32p. (ps up). 1986. 11.70i (ISBN 0-06-021984-X); PLB 11.89 (ISBN 0-06-021985-8). HarpJ.

School of Obedience. Andrew Murray. (Andrew Murray Ser.). pap. 3.50 (ISBN 0-8024-7627-9). Moody.

School of Obedience see Escuela de la Obediencia.

School of Obedience; Believer's Secret of Obedience see Blessings of Obedience.

School of Paris: Paintings from the Florene May Schoenborn & Samuel A. Marx Collection. James T. Soby. LC 65-25727. (Illus.). 56p. 1965. pap. 7.95 (ISBN 0-87070-575-X). Museum Mod Art.

School of Practical Composition, 3 vols. Carl Czerny. LC 79-21105. (Music Reprint Ser.). 1979. Repr. of 1848 ed. Set. lib. bdg. 110.00 (ISBN 0-306-79595-7). Da Capo.

School of Prague: Painting at the Court of Rudolf II. Thomas D. Kaufmann. (Illus.). xxx, 306p. 1988. 45.00x (ISBN 0-226-42727-7). U of Chicago Pr.

School of Salernum. Regimen Sanitatis Salernitanum et al. LC 79-95627. (Illus.). 1970. Repr. of 1920 ed. 25.00x (ISBN 0-678-03751-5). Kelley.

School of Salernum: Regimen Sanitatis Salernitanum: the English Version. John Harington. 1979. Repr. of 1920 ed. 45.00 (ISBN 0-8492-5284-9). R West.

School of Salernum: Regimen Sanitatis Salernitanum: the English Version. Tr. by John Harington. 1978. Repr. of 1920 ed. lib. bdg. 35.00 (ISBN 0-8495-2336-2). Arden Lib.

School of Shakespeare. D. L. Frost. LC 68-11283. 1968. 52.50 (ISBN 0-521-05044-8). Cambridge U Pr.

School of Shakespeare, 2 vols. Ed. by Richard Simpson. LC 78-176026. Repr. of 1878 ed. Set. 47.50 (ISBN 0-404-06058-7). AMS Pr.

School of Technic for Violin, Op. 1, Pt. 3. O. Sevcik. (Carl Fischer Music Library: No. 284). pap. 6.50 (ISBN 0-8258-0036-6, L284). Fischer Inc NY.

School of Technic for Violin, Op. 1, Part 2. Otakar Sevcik. (Carl Fischer Music Library: No. 283). 49p. (Eng., Fr. & Ger.). 1900. pap. 6.50 (ISBN 0-8258-0035-8, L 283). Fischer Inc NY.

School of Technic for Violin: Op. 1 Part 1. Otakar Sevcik. (Carl Fischer Music Library: No. 282). (Eng., Ger. & Fr.). (gr. 6-12). 1900. pap. 6.50 (ISBN 0-8258-0034-X, L 282). Fischer Inc NY.

School of Technic for Violin, Op. 1, Pt. 4: Exercises in Double Stops. O. Sevcik. (Carl Fischer Music Library: No. 285). 1964. pap. 6.50 (ISBN 0-8258-0037-4, L285). Fischer Inc NY.

School of the French Revolution: A Documentary History of the College of Louis-le-Grand & Its Director, Jean-Francois Champagne, 1762-1814. R. R. Palmer. 1975. 40.00x (ISBN 0-691-05229-8). Princeton U Pr.

School of Velocity for Piano, Op. 299, Complete Edition. Carl Czerny. 101p. 1903. pap. 6.00 (ISBN 0-8258-0108-7, L 338). Fischer Inc NY.

School of Violin-Technic, Bk. 2: Exercises in Double Stops. H. Schradieck. (Carl Fischer Music Library: No. 178). pap. 4.00 (ISBN 0-8258-0031-5, L178). Fischer Inc NY.

School of Visual Arts Guide to Careers. D. Ito. 312p. 1987. text ed. 24.95 (ISBN 0-07-032117-5); pap. text ed. 12.95 (ISBN 0-07-032057-8). McGraw.

School Officials & the Courts: Update 1987. Joseph Beckham. (ERS Monograph Ser.). 66p. 1987. 18.00. Ed Research.

School Organization: A Sociological Analysis. William Tyler. (Croom Helm Social Analysis Ser.). 272p. 1988. lib. bdg. 55.00 (ISBN 0-7099-4333-4, Pub. by Croom Helm UK). Routledge Chapman & Hall.

School Organization & Black Childrens' Esteem & Future-Focused Role Images. Roy A. Weaver. LC 78-68444. 1979. perfect bdg. 12.95 (ISBN 0-88247-576-2). R & E Pubs.

School Partnerships Handbook: How to Set up & Administer Programs with Business, Government & Your Community. Susan D. Otterbourg. 336p. 1986. 29.95 (ISBN 0-13-793852-7). P-H.

School Personnel Management System: 1982. 2nd, Rev. ed. Ed. by Diane E. Kirrane. 500p. 140.00 (ISBN 0-88364-117-8). Natl Sch Boards.

School Phobia & Its Treatment. Nigel Blagg. 240p. 1987. lib. bdg. 49.95x (ISBN 0-7099-3938-8, Pub. by Croom Helm UK). Routledge Chapman & Hall.

School Picnic. Jan Steffy. (Illus.). (ps-3). Date not set. 12.95 (ISBN 0-934672-52-0). Good Bks PA.

School Play: A Source Book. James H. Block & Nancy R. King. LC 86-33491. (Source Books on Education Reference, Library of Social Sciences: Vol. 10). 250p. 1987. lib. bdg. 40.00 (ISBN 0-8240-8632-5). Garland Pub.

School Politics, Chicago Style. Paul E. Peterson. LC 76-603. 320p. 1981. pap. 10.00x (ISBN 0-226-66289-6). U of Chicago Pr.

School Politics, Chicago Style. Paul E. Peterson. LC 76-603. (Illus.). 1976. 20.00x (ISBN 0-226-66288-8). U of Chicago Pr.

School Power: Implications of an Intervention Project. James P. Comer. LC 80-757. 1980. 14.95 (ISBN 0-02-906550-X). Free Pr.

School PR: The Complete Book. National School Public Relations Association Staff. 1986. 29.95 (ISBN 0-87545-051-2, 411-13346). Natl Sch Pr.

School Prayer & Other Religious Issues in American Public Education: A Bibliography. Albert J. Menendez. LC 84-48756. (Reference Library of Social Science). 178p. 1985. lib. bdg. 20.00 (ISBN 0-8240-8775-5). Garland Pub.

School Prayer Decisions: From Court Policy to Local Practice. Kenneth M. Dolbeare & Philip E. Hammond. LC 70-140461. 1971. 8.00x (ISBN 0-226-15515-3). U of Chicago Pr.

School Prayers. John H. Laubach. 1969. 9.00 (ISBN 0-8183-0206-2). Pub Aff Pr.

School Principal. Jalal Al-e Ahmad. Tr. by John K. Newton. (Studies in Middle Eastern Literatures: No. 4). 1983. pap. 12.00 (ISBN 0-88297-032-1). Bibliotheca.

School Programs for Disruptive Adolescents. Daniel J. Safer. LC 81-16446. (Illus.). 384p. 1982. text ed. 24.00x (ISBN 0-8391-1698-5, 1224). Pro Ed.

School Programs in Speech-Language: Organization & Management. Elizabeth A. Neidecker. (Illus.). 1980. text ed. write for info. (ISBN 0-13-794321-0). P-H.

School Programs in Speech Language: Organization & Management. 2nd ed. Elizabeth A. Neidecker. (Illus.). 272p. 1987. text ed. write for info. (ISBN 0-13-794330-X). P-H.

School Promotion, Publicity & Public Relations...Nothing but Benefits. Tracey H. MacPhee & Robert L. DeBruyn. LC 86-63812. 320p. (Orig.). 1987. text ed. 29.95 (ISBN 0-914607-24-3). Master Tchr.

School Provision for Individual Differences. K. O. Broady. LC 71-176591. (Columbia University. Teachers College. Contributions to Education: No. 395). Repr. of 1930 ed. 22.50 (ISBN 0-404-55395-8). AMS Pr.

School Psychologist. Jack Rudman. (Teachers License Examination Ser.: GT-4). (Cloth bdg. avail. on request). pap. 15.95 (ISBN 0-8373-8124-X). Natl Learning.

Schooling of the Creative Animal: A New Theory of the Homo Sapiens. Eugene M. Boyce. 104p. (Orig.). 1988. pap. text ed. 8.75 (ISBN 0-8191-6727-4). U Pr of Amer.

Schooling of the Horse. rev. ed. John R. Young. LC 81-11539. (Illus.). 376p. 1982. 28.95 (ISBN 0-8061-1787-7). U of Okla Pr.

Schooling of the Immigrant see Americanization Studies: The Acculturation of Immigrant Groups into American Society.

Schooling of the Western Horse. Richard Young. (Illus.). Repr. write for info. (ISBN 0-85131-182-2, NL51, Pub. by J A Allen U K). S R Smith Sporting Bks.

Schooling the Daughters of Marianne: Textbooks & the Socialization of Girls in Modern French Primary Schools. Linda L. Clark. LC 83-5035. (European Social History Ser.). 224p. 1984. 54.50 (ISBN 0-87395-787-3); pap. 18.95 (ISBN 0-87395-786-5). State U NY Pr.

Schooling the Violent Imagination. John Schostak. 208p. 1986. 35.00 (ISBN 0-7102-0365-9, 03659). Routledge Chapman & Hall.

Schooling Your Young Horse. George Wheatley. pap. 5.00 (ISBN 0-87980-201-4). Wilshire.

Schoolkeuze-Adviezen: Resultatencontrole Na Vijf Jaar. D. J. Bos. 1974. 18.80x (ISBN 90-2797-302-4). Mouton.

Schoolland. Max Martinez. LC 87-35127. 250p. (Orig.). 1988. pap. 8.50 (ISBN 0-934770-87-5). Arte Publico.

Schoolma'am. Frances R. Donovan. LC 74-3943. (Women in America Ser). 368p. 1974. Repr. of 1938 ed. 27.00x (ISBN 0-405-06087-4). Ayer Co Pubs.

Schoolmaker: Sawney Webb & the Bell Buckle Story. Laurence McMillin. xxiv, 186p. 1979. pap. 8.95 (ISBN 0-8078-1395-8). U of NC Pr.

Schoolmarms. Helen G. Rees. LC 83-73080. 1983p. pap. 4.95 (ISBN 0-8323-0423-9). Binford-Metropolitan.

Schoolmaster. Earl Lovelace. (Caribbean Writers Ser.: No. 20). xvii, 171p. 1983. pap. text ed. 6.00 (ISBN 0-435-98550-7). Heinemann Ed.

Schoolmaster & Other Stories. Anton Chekhov. Tr. by Constance Garnett from Rus. (Tales of Anton Chekhov Ser.: Vol. 11). 302p. 1986. pap. 9.50 (ISBN 0-88001-058-4). Ecco Pr.

Schoolmaster in Comedy & Satire. 592p. 1981. Repr. of 1894 ed. lib. bdg. 65.00 (ISBN 0-8495-5046-7). Arden Lib.

Schoolmaster Ni Huan-Chi. 2nd ed. Yeh Sheng-Tao. Tr. by A. C. Barnes from Chinese. 335p. 1978. 7.95 (ISBN 0-917056-98-1, Pub. by Foreign Lang Pr China). Cheng & Tsui.

Schoolmaster (1570) Roger Ascham. Ed. by Lawrence V. Ryan. (Paperback Ser). 1978. 7.90x (ISBN 0-918016-64-9). Folger Bks.

Schoolmasters. Leonard E. Fisher. LC 67-18896. 48p. 1986. pap. 4.95 (ISBN 0-87923-610-8). Godine.

Schoolmasters of the Tenth Century. Cora E. Lutz. LC 76-29644. xi, 202p. 1977. 22.50 (ISBN 0-208-01628-7, Archon). Shoe String.

Schoolmaster's Stories for Boys & Girls. Edward Eggleston. (Collected Works of Edward Eggleston). 1988. Repr. of 1874 ed. lib. bdg. 59.00x. Am Biog Serv.

Schoolmaster's Stories for Boys & Girls see Collected Works.

Schoolmistress & Other Stories. Anton Chekhov. Tr. by Constance Garnett from Rus. (Tales of Chekhov Ser.: Vol. 9). 305p. 1986. pap. 8.50 (ISBN 0-88001-056-8). Ecco Pr.

Schoolmistress in History, Poetry & Romance. T. W. Field. 59.95 (ISBN 0-8490-0998-7). Gordon Pr.

Schoolproof: How to Help Your Family Beat the System & Learn to Love Learning the Easy, Natural Way. Mary Pride. 1988. pap. 7.95 (ISBN 0-317-68113-3, Crossway Bks). Good News.

Schoolroom Poets: A Bibliography of Bryant, Holmes, Longfellow, Lowell & Whittier with Selective Annotation. Jeanetta Boswell. LC 83-19276. 311p. 1983. 22.50 (ISBN 0-8108-1659-8). Scarecrow.

Schools. Ed. by The Truman & Knightly Educational Service. 1986. 40.00x (ISBN 0-686-87281-9, Pub. by Truman & Knightly). State Mutual Bk.

Schools Abroad of Interest to Americans. 6th ed. Ed. by Porter Sargent Staff. (Handbook Ser.). (Illus.). 464p. 1985. 29.00 (ISBN 0-87558-111-0). Porter Sargent.

Schools Across Frontiers: The Story of International Baccalaureate & the United World Colleges. A. D. Peterson. 256p. 1987. 22.95 (ISBN 0-8126-9046-X). Open Court.

Schools & Careers. Ed. by Edwin L. Herr. (Cooperative Work Experience Education for Careers Program Ser.). (Illus.). (gr. 11-12). 1976. pap. 17.96 (ISBN 0-07-028325-7). McGraw.

Schools & Disruptive Pupils. Galloway & Ball. LC 81-15601. 1982. pap. 10.95x (ISBN 0-582-49707-8). Longman.

Schools & Drugs: A Handbook for Parents & Educators. Joyce M. Tobias. LC 86-25238. 30p. (Orig.). 1986. pap. 2.00 (ISBN 0-9616700-1-0). Panda Press VA.

Schools & Education in Denmark. 3rd ed. Ed. by Kamma Struwe. Tr. by Geoffrey French from Danish. (Danish Information Handbooks). 178p. 1981. pap. text ed. 10.95x (ISBN 87-7429-043-6, Pub. by Det Danske Selskab Denmark). Nordic Bks.

Schools & Families: Issues & Actions. Dorothy Rich. 128p. 1987. 9.95 (ISBN 0-8106-0276-8). NEA.

Schools & Inequality. Ed. by James W. Guthrie et al. 1971. pap. 6.95x (ISBN 0-262-57047-5). MIT Pr.

Schools & Meaning: Essays on the Moral Nature of Schooling. Ed. by David E. Purpel & Svi Shapiro. 278p. (Orig.). 1985. lib. bdg. 29.00 (ISBN 0-8191-4438-X); pap. text ed. 13.50 (ISBN 0-8191-4439-8). U Pr of Amer.

Schools & Persistent Absentees. D. Galloway. LC 84-14913. (Illus.). 200p. 1985. text ed. 40.00 (ISBN 0-08-030834-1, Pub. by Aberdeen Scotland); pap. text ed. 21.00 (ISBN 0-08-030833-3, Pub. by Aberdeen Scotland). Pergamon.

Schools & Politics: The Kaum Muda Movement in West Sumatra 1927-1933. Taufik Abdullah. 257p. 1971. pap. 6.00 (ISBN 0-87763-010-0). Cornell Mod Indo.

Schools & Scholars in Fourteenth-Century England. William J. Courtenay. (Illus.). 416p. 1988. text ed. 48.00 (ISBN 0-691-05500-9). Princeton U Pr.

Schools & Scholars in History, from the Renaissance to the Nineteenth Century. Charles Sarolea. Repr. lib. bdg. 29.50 (ISBN 0-8414-8038-9). Folcroft.

Schools & School Days in Riverdale, Kingsbridge, Spuyten Duyvil: New York City. William A. Tieck. LC 77-149738. (Illus.). 1971. 24.50x (ISBN 0-9600398-1-3). W A Tieck.

Schools & Society: A Reader in Education & Sociology. Jeanne A. Ballantine. 576p. (Orig.). 1985. pap. text ed. 19.95 (ISBN 0-87484-707-9). Mayfield Pub.

Schools & the Challenge of Innovation. Ed. by Sterling M. McMurrin. LC 68-59385. 358p. 1969. lib. bdg. 7.95. Comm Econ Dev.

Schools & the Cloister: The Life & the Writings of Alexander Nequam, 1157-1217. R. W. Hunt & Margaret Gibson. 1984. 49.00x (ISBN 0-19-822398-6). Oxford U Pr.

Schools & the Culturally Diverse Exceptional Student: Promising Practices & Future Directions. Ed. by Bruce Ramirez & Alba A. Ortiz. 176p. 1988. 16.00 (ISBN 0-86586-182-X, 326). Coun Exc Child.

Schools & the Laws. 5th ed. E. F. Reutter, Jr. LC 70-12249. (Legal Almanac Ser.: No.17). 128p. 1981. 6.95 (ISBN 0-379-11139-X); pap. write for info. (ISBN 0-379-11141-1). Oceana.

Schools & Universities on the Continent see Complete Prose Works of Matthew Arnold.

Schools As Sorters: Lewis M. Terman, Applied Psychology, & the Intelligence Testing Movement, 1890-1930. Paul D. Chapman. (American Social Experience Ser.: No. 11). (Illus.). 284p. 1988. 40.00x (ISBN 0-8147-1420-X). NYU Pr.

Schools, Conflict & Change. Ed. by Mike M. Milstein. LC 79-30327. 1980. 21.95x (ISBN 0-8077-2571-4). Tchrs Coll.

Schools, Conflict, & Change. Ed. by Mike M. Milstein. LC 79-20327. pap. 83.20 (2031205). Bks Demand UMI.

Schools for All: The Blacks & Public Education in the South, 1865-1877. William P. Vaughn. LC 73-86408. Repr. of 1974 ed. 48.00 (ISBN 0-8357-9713-7, 2013517). Bks Demand UMI.

Schools for the Boys? Co-Education Re-Assessed. Pat Mahoney. LC 84-28949. (Explorations in Feminism Ser.). (Illus.). 118p. (Orig.). 1985. pap. 5.95 (ISBN 0-09-160841-4, Pub. by Hutchinson Educ). Longwood Pub Group.

Schools for the Shires: The Reform of Middle-Class Education in Mid-Victorian England. David Allsobrook. 200p. 1986. 60.00 (ISBN 0-7190-1972-9, Pub. by Manchester Univ Pr). St Martin.

Schools for Tomorrow. Ed. by Bernadette O'Keefe. 200p. 1988. 40.00x (ISBN 1-85000-287-8, Falmer Pr); pap. 19.00x (ISBN 1-85000-288-6, Falmer Pr). Taylor & Francis.

Schools for Young Disadvantaged Children. Ruth Hamlin et al. LC 67-21504. (Early Childhood Education Ser.). pap. 46.50 (ISBN 0-317-41960-9, 2026019). Bks Demand UMI.

Schools in Central Cities. Kathryn M. Borman & Joel H. Spring. (Structure & Process Ser.). 304p. 1984. pap. text ed. 17.95 (ISBN 0-582-28405-8). Longman.

Schools in Cities: Consensus & Conflict in American Educational History. Ed. by Ronald K. Goodenow & Diane Ravitch. 326p. 1983. 45.00 (ISBN 0-8419-0850-8). Holmes & Meier.

Schools in Conflict: The Politics of Education. Rev. ed. Frederick Wirt & Michael Kirst. LC 81-83250. (Education Ser.). 336p. 1982. 26.00x (ISBN 0-8211-2261-4); text ed. 23.75x 10 or more copies. McCutchan.

Schools in Crisis: Training for Success or Failure? 2nd ed. Carl Sommer. LC 83-71106. 335p. (Orig.). 1984. pap. 8.95 (ISBN 0-9610810-0-7); lib. bdg. 13.95 (ISBN 0-9610810-1-5). Cahill Pub Co.

Schools in Tudor England. Craig R. Thompson. LC 59-1347. (Folger Guides to the Age of Shakespeare). 1959. 3.95 (ISBN 0-918016-28-2). Folger Bks.

Schools Information Retrieval (SIR) Project. M. E. Rowbottom et al. (LIR Report 15). (Illus.). 106p. (Orig.). 1983. pap. 14.25 (ISBN 0-7123-3020-8, Pub. by British Lib). Longwood Pub Group.

Schools of Charles the Great & the Restoration of Education in the Ninth Century. James B. Mullinger. LC 77-450. 1977. lib. bdg. 39.50 (ISBN 0-8414-6193-7). Folcroft.

Schools of Cincinnati & Its Vicinity. John P. Foote. LC 75-112545. (Rise of Urban America). (Illus.). 1970. Repr. of 1855 ed. 15.00 (ISBN 0-405-02454-1). Ayer Co Pubs.

Schools of Democracy: An Englishman's Impressions of Secondary Education in the American Middlewest. John N. Wales. xviii, 161p. 1962. 3.95 (ISBN 0-87013-066-8). Mich St U Pr.

Schools of Griswold, Connecticut: An Historical Perspective. Lucille A. Lupinacci. (Connecticut Educational History Ser.: No. 5). 16p. 1987. pap. 1.50 (ISBN 0-317-58291-7). I N Thut World Educ Ctr.

Schools of Hellas. Kenneth J. Freeman. LC 73-101040. 1969. Repr. of 1907 ed. 28.00x (ISBN 0-8046-0706-0, Pub. by Kennikat). Assoc Faculty Pr.

Schools of Linguistics. Geoffrey Sampson. LC 80-81140. 283p. 1980. 27.50x (ISBN 0-8047-1084-8); pap. 9.95 (ISBN 0-8047-1125-9, SP-72). Stanford U Pr.

Schools of Medieval England. A. F. Leach. LC 68-56478. (Illus.). 1968. Repr. of 1915 ed. 20.00 (ISBN 0-405-08740-3). Ayer Co Pubs.

Schools of the Future. Marvin Cetron. 1985. 7.50 (ISBN 0-317-61178-X, 021-00184). Am Assn Sch Admin.

Schools of Thought. Olga Amsterdamska. 1987. lib. bdg. 64.00 (ISBN 90-277-2391-5, Pub. by Reidel Holland). Kluwer academic.

Schools of Thought in the Christian Tradition. Ed. by Patrick Henry. LC 84-47924. 208p. 1984. 3.95 (ISBN 0-8006-0730-9, 1-730). Fortress.

Schools on Trial: An Inside Account of the Boston Desegregation Case. Robert A. Dentler & Marvin B. Scott. LC 80-69662. (Illus.). 264p. 1981. 28.00 (ISBN 0-89011-555-9). Abt Bks.

Schools on Trial: An Inside Account of the Boston Desegregation Case. Robert A. Dentler & Marvin B. Scott. 258p. 1984. Repr. of 1981 ed. lib. bdg. 29.25 (ISBN 0-8191-4071-6). U Pr of Amer.

Schools on Trial: The Trials of Democratic Comprehensives. Colin Fletcher et al. 128p. 1985. pap. 15.00x (ISBN 0-335-15022-5, Open Univ Pr). Taylor & Francis.

School's Out! Alison Blair. (Roommates Ser.). 192p. 1987. pap. 2.50 (ISBN 0-8041-0059-4, Pub. by Ivy). Ballantine.

School's Out. Allison Blair. (Roommates Ser.). (YA) (gr. 10 up). Date not set. pap. 2.50 (ISBN 0-317-61892-X). Ivy Books.

School's Out: Now What? Joan M. Bergstrom. LC 84-51171. (Illus.). 224p. (Orig.). 1984. pap. 11.95 (ISBN 0-89815-131-7). Ten Speed Pr.

Schools, Parents & Governors: A New Approach to Accountability. Joan Sallis. 256p. 1988. lib. bdg. 35.00x (ISBN 0-7099-4420-9, Pub. by Croom Helm UK). Routledge Chapman & Hall.

Schools, Pupils, & Special Educational Needs. David Galloway. LC 84-23077. 186p. 1985. 26.00 (ISBN 0-7099-1160-2, Pub. by Croom Helm Ltd); pap. 12.00 (ISBN 0-7099-1175-0). Routledge Chapman & Hall.

School's Responsibility for Sex Education. Elizabeth Mooney. LC 74-83886. (Fastback Ser.: No. 47). (Orig.). 1974. pap. 0.90 (ISBN 0-87367-047-7). Phi Delta Kappa.

School's Role in Educating Severely Handicapped Students. Barbara L. Ludlow & Richard Sobsey. LC 84-61199. (Fastback Ser.: No. 213). 50p. (Orig.). 1984. pap. 0.90 (ISBN 0-87367-213-5). Phi Delta Kappa.

School's Role in the Prevention of Child Abuse. Samuel B. London & Stephen W. Stile. LC 81-86312. (Fastback Ser.: No. 172). 50p. (Orig.). 1982. pap. 0.90 (ISBN 0-87367-172-4). Phi Delta Kappa.

Schools, Space & Social Policy: Educational Provision for the Children of Migrant Workers in Munich. Robert H. Geipel. Tr. by N. M. Bealtie. (International Monographs in Community & Educational Policy Studies). 48p. 1986. pap. text ed. 9.95 (ISBN 0-85323-415-9, Pub. by Liverpool U Pr). Humanities.

Schools, Teachers & Teaching. Len Barton & Stephen Walker. 258p. 1981. text ed. 38.00x (ISBN 0-905273-23-0, Falmer Pr); pap. 25.00x (ISBN 0-905273-22-2). Taylor & Francis.

Schools That Fear Built: Segregationist Academies in the South. new ed. David Nevin & Robert E. Bills. LC 76-27582. 1977. 12.50 (ISBN 0-87491-177-X). Acropolis.

Schools We Deserve: Reflections on the Educational Crisis of Our Time. Diane Ravitch. LC 84-45303. 300p. 1985. 19.95 (ISBN 0-465-07236-4). Basic.

Schools We Deserve: Reflections on the Educational Crisis of Our Time. Diane Ravitch. LC 84-45303. 352p. 1987. pap. 8.95 (ISBN 0-465-07235-6, PL 5177). Basic.

Schools Where Children Learn. Joseph Featherstone. LC 75-148664. 1971. pap. 2.95 (ISBN 0-87140-251-3). Liveright.

Schools Without Counselors: Guidance Practices for Teachers. William B. Stafford. LC 73-90567. 200p. 1974. 21.95x (ISBN 0-911012-52-4). Nelson-Hall.

Schools Without Failure. William Glasser. 320p. 1975. pap. 7.95 (ISBN 0-06-090421-6, CN421, PL). Harrow.

Schoolteacher: A Sociological Study. Dan C. Lortie. LC 74-11428. 1977. pap. 10.00x (ISBN 0-226-49354-7, P748, Phoen). U of Chicago Pr.

Schoolteacher Stands Up. Ruth B. Lehenbauer. 1986. 7.95 (ISBN 0-533-06830-4). Vantage.

SchoolTechNews Editors. 127p. 21.95 (ISBN 0-317-64210-3). Ed News Serv.

Schoolwide Enrichment Model: A Comprehensive Plan for Educational Excellence. Joseph S. Renzulli & Sally M. Reis. 522p. (Orig.). 1985. pap. 39.95 (ISBN 0-936386-34-7). Creative Learning.

Schoolwide Positive Activities. Carol Provisor. Ed. by Linda Brookover & Barbara Schadlow. 63p. 1987. 8.95 (ISBN 0-939007-03-7). Canter & Assoc.

Schoolwise: A Parent Guide to Getting the Best Education for Your Child. Martha C. Brown. 266p. 1985. pap. 9.95 (ISBN 0-87477-364-4, Dist. by St. Martin's). J P Tarcher.

Schoolwork: Approaches to the Labor of Teaching, Vol. 1. Ed. by Jenny Ozga. 224p. 1987. 65.00x (ISBN 0-335-15554-5, Open Univ Pr); pap. 26.00x (ISBN 0-335-15544-8). Taylor & Francis.

Schoolworlds - Microworlds: Computers & the Culture of the Classroom. J. Olson. LC 88-11739. 148p. 1988. text ed. 29.01 (ISBN 0-08-034985-4); pap. text ed. 14.51 (ISBN 0-08-034984-6). Pergamon.

Schoolyard Tunes. Sheila Wenz. (Illus.). 136p. Date not set. pap. cancelled (ISBN 0-911137-13-0). Imagine.

Schooner Bay. Jack Neilson. 1977. 7.50 (ISBN 0-682-48930-1). Exposition-Phoenix.

Schooner Days in Door County. Walter M. Hirthe & Mary K. Hirthe. (Illus.). 160p. 1986. 19.95 (ISBN 0-89658-061-X). Voyageur Pr Inc.

Schooner from Windward: Two Centuries of Hawaiian Interisland Shipping. Mifflin Thomas. LC 83-5955. (Kolowalu Bk.). (Illus.). 239p. 1983. 21.95 (ISBN 0-8248-0799-5). UH Pr.

Schooner Integrity. Frank Mulville. (Illus.). 169p. 1979. pap. 12.50 (ISBN 0-87556-475-5). Saifer.

Schooners & Schooner Barges. Paul C. Morris. LC 84-81110. (Illus.). 160p. 1984. 25.00 (ISBN 0-936972-06-8). Lower Cape.

Schooners in Four Centuries. David R. MacGregor. LC 82-73779. (Illus.). 144p. 1983. 15.95 (ISBN 0-87021-958-8). Naval Inst Pr.

Schopenhauer. David W. Hamlyn. (Arguments of the Philosophers Ser.). 224p. 1980. 26.95x (ISBN 0-7100-0522-9). Routledge Chapman & Hall.

Schopenhauer. David W. Hamlyn. (Arguments of the Philosophers Ser.). 192p. 1985. pap. 14.95 (ISBN 0-7102-0543-0). Routledge Chapman & Hall.

Schopenhauer. Vivian J. McGill. LC 77-159487. (Studies in Philosophy, No. 40). 1971. lib. bdg. 56.95x (ISBN 0-8383-1258-6). Haskell.

Schopenhauer & Nietzsche. Georg Simmel. Tr. by Helmut Loiskandl et al from Ger. LC 85-28869. 248p. 1986. lib. bdg. 25.00x (ISBN 0-87023-515-X). U of Mass Pr.

Schopenhauer As Educator. Friedrich Nietzsche. LC 65-16282. 1965. pap. 3.95 (ISBN 0-89526-950-3). Regnery Gateway.

Schopenhauer As Transmitter of Buddhist Ideas. Dorothea W. Dauer. (European University Studies: Series 1, German Language & Literature: Vol. 15). 39p. 1969. 6.55 (ISBN 3-261-00014-7). P Lang Pubs.

Schopenhauer: Essays & Aphorisms. Arthur Schopenhauer. Tr. by R. J. Hollingdale. (Classics Ser.). 1973. pap. 4.95 (ISBN 0-14-044227-8). Penguin.

Schopenhauer: His Philosophical Achievement. Ed. by Michael Fox. 276p. 1980. 29.50x (ISBN 0-389-20097-2). B&N Imports.

Schopenhauer's Interpretation of the History of Philosophy. Arthur Schopenhauer. (Essential Library of the Great Philosophers). (Illus.). 129p. 1983. 117.75 (ISBN 0-89901-093-8). Found Class Reprints.

Schopenhauer's Theory of the Essence of Man & of Life. Arthur Schopenhauer. (Essential Library of the Great Philosophers). (Illus.). 109p. 1983. 117.75 (ISBN 0-89901-094-6). Found Class Reprints.

Schott at Sunrise. Carol Schott. (Orig.). 1987. pap. 4.00 (ISBN 0-944754-00-7). Pudding Hse Pubns.

Schott Guide to Glass. H. Pfaender. 1983. 19.95 (ISBN 0-442-27432-7). Van Nos Reinhold.

Schottky Groups & Mumford Curves. L. Gerritzen & M. Van Der Put. (Lecture Notes in Mathematics: Vol. 817). 317p. 1980. pap. 23.00 (ISBN 0-387-10229-9). Springer-Verlag.

Schpountz. Marcel Pagnol. pap. 9.95 (ISBN 0-685-37008-9). French & Eur.

Schprountz. Marcel Pagnol. (Illus.). 288p. 1976. 15.00 (ISBN 0-686-54842-6). French & Eur.

Schreber Case: Psychoanalytic Profile of a Paranoid Personality. William G. Niederland. (Illus.). 200p. 1984. Repr. 14.95 (ISBN 0-88163-025-X). Analytic Pr.

Schreber: Father & Son. Hans Israels. 300p. 1988. 30.00x (ISBN 0-8236-6011-7, BN#06011). Intl Univs Pr.

Schwierige. Hugo Von Hofmannsthal. Ed. by W. E. Yates. 1966. text ed. 7.50x (ISBN 0-521-05283-1). Cambridge U Pr.

Schwiering & the West. Robert Wakefield. LC 73-77752. (Illus.). 1973. 40.00 (ISBN 0-87970-128-5). North Plains.

Schwingen: The Official Austrian Ski Method. Franz Hoppichler. 1983. pap. 12.95 (ISBN 0-935240-07-1). Poudre Pr.

Schwirrholz. Otto Zerries. 19.00 (ISBN 0-384-70880-3). Johnson Repr.

Sci-Fi. William Marshall. LC 80-27264. (Yellowthread Street Mystery Ser.). 192p. 1981. 10.95 (ISBN 0-03-047486-8). H Holt & Co.

Sci-Tech Libraries in Museums & Aquariums. Ed. by Ellis Mount. LC 85-16436. (Science & Technology Libraries: Vol. 6, Nos. 1-2). 204p. 1985. text ed. 29.95 (ISBN 0-86656-484-5). Haworth Pr.

Sci-Tech Libraries Servng Zoological Gardens. Intro. by Ellis Mount. (Science & Technology Libraries: Vol. 8, No. 4). (Illus.). 178p. 1988. text ed. 22.95 (ISBN 0-86656-837-9). Haworth Pr.

Sci-Tech Library Networks Within Organizations. Ed. by Ellis Mount. LC 88-540. (Science & Technology Libraries Ser.: Vol. 8, No. 2). (Illus.). 170p. 1988. text ed. 22.95 (ISBN 0-86656-747-X). Haworth Pr.

Sci Tech: Reading & Writing the English of Science & Technology. Karl Drobnic et al. 132p. (Orig.). (gr. 10-12). 1981. pap. text ed. 4.95 (ISBN 0-89285-156-2). ELS Educ Servs.

Sci-Tech Selling. Michael Wayne. (Illus.). 192p. 1987. 26.95 (ISBN 0-13-794587-6). P-H.

Science. Richard L. Allington & Kathleen Krull. LC 82-101711. (Beginning to Learn about Ser.). (Illus.). 32p. (gr. 1-2). 1982. PLB 15.33 (ISBN 0-8172-1387-2). Raintree Pubs.

Science. Richard L. Allington & Kathleen Krull. LC 82-10171. (E. G. Beginning to Learn about... Ser.). (Illus.). 32p. (gr. 1-2). 1985. pap. 9.27 (ISBN 0-8172-2486-6). Raintree Pubs.

Science. J. Sheen. 250p. 1987. 39.50x (ISBN 1-85313-002-8, Checkmate Pubs). State Mutual Bk.

Science. Steve Woolgar. 160p. 1988. text ed. 19.95 (ISBN 0-7458-0041-6, Pub. by Tavistock England); pap. 8.95 (ISBN 0-317-67408-0, Pub. by Tavistock England). Routledge Chapman & HAll.

Science - The False Messiah. C. E. Ayres. Bd. with Holier Than Thou; Way of the Righteous. LC 71-130660. 1973. Repr. of 1927 ed. 45.00x (ISBN 0-678-00774-8). Kelley.

Science a Road to Wisdom: Collected Philosophical Studies. E. W. Beth. Tr. by Peter Wesly from Dutch. 123p. 1968. lib. bdg. 21.00 (ISBN 90-277-0003-6, Pub. by Reidel Holland). Kluwer Academic.

Science Achievement in Seventeen Countries. International Association for the Evaluation of Educational Achievement Staff. LC 88-3487. (Illus.). 125p. 1988. pap. text ed. 8.00 (ISBN 0-08-036563-9, PBL). Pergamon.

Science, Action, & Fundamental Theology: Toward a Theology of Communicative Action. Helmut Peukert. Tr. by James Bohman from Ger. (German Social Thought Ser.). 364p. 1984. text ed. 42.50x (ISBN 0-262-16095-1). MIT Pr.

Science, Action, & Fundamental Theology: Toward a Theology of Communicative Action. Helmut Peukert. Tr. by James Bohman. (Studies in Contemporary German Social Thought Ser.). 360p. 1986. pap. text ed. 12.50x (ISBN 0-262-66060-1). MIT Pr.

Science, Action, & Reality. Raimo Tuomela. 1985. text ed. 38.00 (ISBN 90-277-2098-3, Pub. by Reidel Holland). Kluwer Academic.

Science Activities for Children. Willard J. Jacobson & Abby B. Bergman. (Illus.). 256p. 1983. 26.00 (ISBN 0-13-794594-9). P-H.

Science Activities: For Children Three to Nine Years Old. Bonnie E. Nelson. (Illus.). 102p. (ps-4). 1982. 22.50 (ISBN 0-931642-12-4). Lintel.

Science Activities for Christian Children. rev. ed. Clifton Keller & Jeanette Appel. 112p. (gr. k-6). 1986. pap. 5.50 (ISBN 0-930192-15-X). Gazelle Pubns.

Science Activities for Elementary Children. 8th ed. Leslie W. Nelson & George C. Lorbeer. 416p. 1984. write for info. wire coil (ISBN 0-697-06192-2). Wm C Brown.

Science Activities with Simple Things. Howard R. Munson. (gr. 4-8). 1972. pap. 5.25 (ISBN 0-8224-6320-2). D S Lake Pubs.

Science Adventures. Fred Justus. (Science Ser.). 24p. (gr. 4). 1977. wkbk. 5.00 (ISBN 0-8209-0142-3, S-4). ESP.

Science Adventures in Children's Play. rev. ed. Edythe Rieger. 1978. 2.50 (ISBN 0-936426-09-8). Play Schs.

Science Advice to the President. Ed. by William T. Golden et al. LC 79-28743. (Pergamon Policy Studies on Science Policy). 256p. 1980. text ed. 67.00 (ISBN 0-08-025963-4); pap. text ed. 13.25 (ISBN 0-08-026349-6). Pergamon.

Science, Agriculture, & Government: The Politics of Research. Lawerence Busch & William B. Lacy. LC 82-15923. (WVSS in Agriculture Aquaculture Science & Policy Ser.). (Illus.). 325p. (Orig.). 1982. lib. bdg. 42.00x (ISBN 0-86531-225-7); pap. text ed. 17.95x (ISBN 0-86531-230-3). Westview.

Science All Around Us. Jack Myers et al. (Illus.). (gr. 2-6). 1978. pap. 2.50 (ISBN 0-87534-123-3). Highlights.

Science & Agricultural Development. Ed. by Lawrence Busch. LC 81-65005. 198p. 1981. text ed. 31.50x (ISBN 0-86598-022-5, Pub. by Allanheld). Rowman.

Science & Art of Dental Ceramics, Vol. I. John McLean. (Illus.). 334p. 1979. 58.00 (ISBN 0-931386-04-7). Quint Pub Co.

Science & Art of Dental Ceramics, Vol. II. John McLean. (Illus.). 496p. 1980. 144.00 (ISBN 0-931386-11-X). Quint Pub Co.

Science & Art of Elocution. facs. ed. Frank H. Fenno. LC 78-139760. (Granger Index Reprint Ser). 1878. 23.50 (ISBN 0-8369-6214-1). Ayer Co Pubs.

Science & Art of Hot Air Ballooning. John P. Jackson & Rudolph J. Dichtl. (Illus.). 1977. pap. 4.50 (ISBN 0-89540-038-3, SB-038). Sun Pub.

Science & Art of Self-Care. Ed. by Joan Riehl. 320p. 1985. pap. 24.00 (ISBN 0-8385-8494-2). Appleton & Lange.

Science & Art of the Pendulum: A Complete Course in Radiesthesia. Gabriele Blackburn. LC 83-83220. (Illus.). 96p. (Orig.). 1984. pap. 10.00 (ISBN 0-9613054-1-X). Idylwild Bks.

Science & Astrology: The Relationship Between the Measure Formulae & the Zodiac. Arthur M. Young. (Broadside Editions Ser.). (Illus.). 47p. (Orig.). 1988. pap. 4.95 (ISBN 0-931191-06-8). Rob Briggs.

Science & Behavior: An Introduction to Methods of Research. 3rd ed. John M. Neale & Robert M. Liebert. (Illus.). 304p. 1986. text ed. write for info (ISBN 0-13-795139-6). P-H.

Science & Beyond. Ed. by Steven Rose & Lisa Appignanesi. 204p. 1986. 24.95 (ISBN 0-631-14483-8). Basil Blackwell.

Science & Blindness: Retrospective & Prospective. Ed. by Milton D. Graham. LC 72-82240. 212p. 1972. pap. 3.60 (ISBN 0-89128-052-9, PIP052). Am Foun Blind.

Science & Ceremony: The Institutional Economics of C. E. Ayres. Ed. by William Breit & William P. Culbertson, Jr. LC 76-8238. 228p. 1976. text ed. 14.95x (ISBN 0-292-77523-7). U of Tex Pr.

Science & Change. Hugh Kearney. LC 76-96433. (World University Library). (Illus., Orig.). 1971. pap. text ed. 7.95 (ISBN 0-07-033425-0). McGraw.

Science & Characters of the Middle Ages. Edward L. Cutts. 552p. 1981. Repr. of 1926 ed. lib. bdg. 40.00 (ISBN 0-8495-0876-2). Arden Lib.

Science & Christian Faith. William H. Davis. LC 68-21524. (Way of Life Ser: No. 104). 1968. pap. 3.95 (ISBN 0-89112-104-8). Abilene Christ U.

Science & Christian Tradition. Thomas H. Huxley. 419p. 1981. Repr. of 1894 ed. lib. bdg. 45.00 (ISBN 0-89984-285-2). Century Bookbindery.

Science & Christianity. 2nd ed. John D. Callahan. (Illus.). 120p. 1986. pap. 5.95 (ISBN 0-9615767-0-7). Callahan CA.

Science & Civic Life in the Italian Renaissance. Eugenio Garin. Tr. by Peter Munz. 11.50 (ISBN 0-8446-2110-2). Peter Smith.

Science & Civilisation in China, Vol. LX. Dieter Khun. 400p. 1987. 200.00x (ISBN 0-317-68621-6, Pub. by Han-Shan Tang Ltd). State Mutual Bk.

Science & Civilisation in China, 6 vols. Joseph Needham. Incl. Vol. 1. Introductory Orientations. (Illus.). xxxiv, 318p. 1954. 70.00 (ISBN 0-521-05799-X); Vol. 2. History of Scientific Thought. (Illus.). xxiv, 698p. 120.00 (ISBN 0-521-05800-7); Vol. 3. Mathematics & the Sciences of the Heavens & the Earth. (Illus.). xlviii, 878p. 177.50 (ISBN 0-521-05801-5); Vol. 4. Physics & Physical Technology: Part 1 Physics. (Illus.). xxxiv, 434p. 1962. 100.00 (ISBN 0-521-05802-3); Vol. 4. Physics & Physical Technology: Part 2 Mechanical Engineering. (Illus.). lvi, 760p. 1965. 137.50 (ISBN 0-521-05803-1); Vol. 4. Physics & Physical Technology: Part 3 Civil Engineering & Nautics. (Illus.). lviii, 932p. 177.50 (ISBN 0-521-07060-0); Vol. 5. Chemistry & Chemical Technology: Part 1 Paper & Printing. (Illus.). 350p. 1985. 92.50 (ISBN 0-521-08690-6); Vol. 5. Chemistry & Chemical Technology: Part 2 Spagyrical Discovery & Invention: Magisteries of Gold & Immortality. (Illus.). xlviii, 600p. 105.00 (ISBN 0-521-08571-3); Vol. 5. Chemistry & Chemical Technology: Part 3 Spagyrical Discovery & Invention: Historical Survey from Cinnabar Elixirs to Synthetic Insulin. (Illus.). xxxv, 481p. 100.00 (ISBN 0-521-21028-3); Vol. 4. Chemistry & Chemical Technology: Part 4 Spagyrical Discovery & Invention: Apparatus & Theory. (Illus.). xlviii, 756p. 1980. 150.50 (ISBN 0-521-08573-X); Vol. 5. Chemical & Chemical Technology: Part 5 Spagyrical Discovery & Invention: Physiological Alchemy. (Illus.). 550p. 1980. 115.00 (ISBN 0-521-08574-8); Vol. 5. Military Technology: The Gunpowder Epic: Part 7. (Illus.). 600p. 1986. 99.50 (ISBN 0-521-30358-3); Vol. 6. Biology & Biological Technology: Part 1 Botany. (Illus.). 756p. 1986. 100.00 (ISBN 0-521-08731-7); Vol. 6. Biology & Biological Technology: Part 2 Agriculture. (Illus.). 724p. 1984. 110.00 (ISBN 0-521-25076-5). Cambridge U Pr.

Science & Civilisation in China, Vol. VII. Joseph Needham. 703p. 1986. 350.00x (Pub. by Han-Shan Tang Ltd). State Mutual Bk.

Science & Civilisation in China: Textile Technology: Spinning & Reeling, Vol. 5, Pt. 7. Dieter Kuhn. (Illus.). 900p. 1988. 110.00 (ISBN 0-521-32021-6). Cambridge U Pr.

Science & Civilization. Ed. by Francis S. Marvin. LC 70-105030. (Essay Index Reprint Ser.). 1923. 20.00 (ISBN 0-8369-1581-X). Ayer Co Pubs.

Science & Civilization in India, Vol. 1: Harappan Period, c. 3000 BC-1500 BC. A. K. Bag. 175p. 1986. 32.50x (ISBN 0-8364-1549-3, Pub. by Navrang). South Asia Bks.

Science & Civilization in India, Vol. 1: Harappan Period (c.3000-c.1500 B. C.) A. K. Bag. (Illus.). 175p. 1985. 28.00 (ISBN 0-317-69951-2). Orient Bk Dist.

Science & Colonial Expansion: The Role of the British Royal Botanic Gardens. Lucile H. Brockway. LC 79-51669. (Studies in Social Discontinuity). 1979. 25.00 (ISBN 0-12-134150-X). Acad Pr.

Science & Complexity. Ed. by Sara Nash. (Illus.). 165p. 1985. text ed. 39.50x (ISBN 0-905927-32-X, Pub. by Sci Reviews UK). Sheridan.

Science & Computer Literacy Audiovisuals: A Teacher's Sourcebook. NICEM Staff. Ed. by J. C. Johnstone. 275p. (Orig.). 1986. pap. 49.95 (ISBN 0-89320-101-4). Natl Info Ctr NM.

Science & Computers: A Volume Dedicated to Nicholas Metropolis. Gian-Carlo Rota. (Advances in Mathematics Supplementary Studies: Vol. 10). 1986. 79.50 (ISBN 0-12-598545-2). Acad Pr.

Science & Computers in Primary Education: A Report of the Educational Research Workshop Held in Edinburgh, 3-6 September 1984. Ed. by F. Adams. 187p. 1985. pap. text ed. 19.95x (ISBN 0-947833-07-2, Pub. by Scot Council Research). Humanities.

Science & Conscience. Milton R. Wessel. LC 80-12780. 312p. 1980. 35.00x (ISBN 0-231-04746-0). Columbia U Pr.

Science & Consciousness: Two Views of the Universe. Ed. by Cazenave. Tr. by A. Hall & E. Callender. (Illus.). 550p. 1984. 85.00 (ISBN 0-08-028127-3, 0720, 2601, 3505, 3506). Pergamon.

Science & Convention: Essays on the Origin & Significance of the Conventionalist Philosophy of Science. Jerzy Giedymin. (Foundations & Philosophy of Science & Technology Ser.). 260p. 1981. 42.00 (ISBN 0-08-025790-9). Pergamon.

Science & Corporate Strategy: Du Pont R&D, 1902-1980. David A. Hounshell & John K. Smith, Jr. (Studies in Economic History & Policy: The United States in the Twentieth Century). (Illus.). 832p. Date not set. 34.50 (ISBN 0-521-32767-9). Cambridge U Pr.

Science & Creation: Geological, Theological & Educational Perspectives. Ed. by Robert W. Hanson. LC 83-50822. (AAAS Ser. on Issues in Science & Technology). 288p. 1985. text ed. 24.95x (ISBN 0-02-949870-8). Macmillan.

Science & Creation in the Middle Ages: Henry of Langenstein (D. 1397) on Genesis. Nicholas H. Steneck. LC 75-19881. 256p. 1976. text ed. 19.95x (ISBN 0-268-01672-0). U of Notre Dame Pr.

Science & Creation in the Middle Ages: Henry of Langenstein (D. 1397) on Genesis. Nicholas H. Steneck. LC 75-19881. 1977. pap. 9.95x (ISBN 0-268-01691-7). U of Notre Dame Pr.

Science & Creationism. Ed. by Ashley Montagu. LC 82-14173. 434p. 1984. 35.00 (ISBN 0-19-503252-7); pap. 13.95x (ISBN 0-19-503253-5). Oxford U Pr.

Science & Creationism: A View from the National Academy of Sciences. National Research Council. 28p. 1984. pap. 4.00 (ISBN 0-309-03440-X). Natl Acad Pr.

Science & Culture in the Western Tradition: Sources & Interpretations. Ed. by John G. Burke. 1987. pap. text ed. 14.00 (ISBN 0-89787-810-8). Gorsuch Scarisbrick.

Science & Earth History: The Evolution-Creation Controversy. Arthur N. Strahler. 552p. 1988. 39.95 (ISBN 0-87975-414-1). Prometheus Bks.

Science & Egyptology. Ed. by A. Rosalie David. 640p. 1986. 90.00 (ISBN 0-7190-2204-5, Pub. by Manchester Univ Pr). St Martin.

Science & Engineering Applications on the IBM-PC. R. Bartel. 260p. 1986. pap. 19.95 (ISBN 0-916439-65-8). Abacus Soft.

Science & Engineering Dictionary: Russian-English. Eugene A. Carpovich & Vera V. Carpovich. (Rus. & Eng.). 1988. 90.00 (ISBN 0-911484-05-1). Tech Dict.

Science & Engineering for the Commodore. Ranier Bartel. Tr. by Greg Dykema from Ger. 343p. (Orig.). 1985. pap. text ed. 19.95. Abacus Soft.

Science & Engineering Literature: A Guide to Reference Sources. 3rd ed. H. Robert Malinowsky & Jeanne M. Richardson. LC 80-21290. (Library Science Text Ser.). 342p. 1980. lib. bdg. 33.00x (ISBN 0-87287-230-0); pap. text ed. 21.00 (ISBN 0-87287-245-9). Libs Unl.

Science & Engineering of Materials. alt. ed. Donald R. Askeland. 1985. text ed. 34.00 (ISBN 0-534-05034-4, 21R7100, Pub. by PWS Engineering). PWS Kent Pub.

Science & Engineering Programs for the PCjr. Cass Lewart. 200p. 1985. pap. 14.95 (ISBN 0-13-794942-1); incl. disk 29.95 (ISBN 0-13-794975-8). P-H.

Science & Engineering Sourcebook. Cass Lewart. LC 82-80269. (Illus.). 96p. (Orig.). 1982. pap. 9.95 (ISBN 0-942412-02-8); Pre-recorded cass. 8.95 (ISBN 0-686-98227-4). Micro Text Pubs.

Science & English Poetry: A Historical Sketch, 1590-1950. Douglas Bush. LC 80-18161. (Patten Lectures Ser., 1949, Indiana Univ.). viii, 166p. 1980. Repr. of 1950 ed. lib. bdg. 35.00x (ISBN 0-313-22654-7, BUSC). Greenwood.

Science & Epilepsy: Neuroscience Gains in Epilepsy Research. James L. O'Leary & Sidney Goldring. LC 75-21860. 303p. 1976. 43.00 (ISBN 0-89004-072-9). Raven.

Science & Ethical Values. Hiram B. Glass. LC 81-13170. ix, 101p. 1981. Repr. of 1965 ed. lib. bdg. 35.00x (ISBN 0-313-23141-9, GLSE). Greenwood.

Science & Ethics. Ed. by R. Haller. (Grazer Philosophische Studien: Vol. 12-13). 298p. 1981. text ed. 32.50x (ISBN 90-6203-913-8, Pub. by Rodopi Holland). Humanities.

Science & Ethics. Ed. by Keith Lehrer & Rudolf Haller. (Grazer Philosophische Studien: Vol. 30, 1987). 256p. 1988. pap. text ed. 65.00 (ISBN 90-6203-670-8, Pub. by Rodopi Holland). Humanities.

Science & Ethics in American Medicine, 1800-1914 see Divided Legacy: A History of the Schism in Medical Thought.

Science & Everyday Life. J. B. Haldane. LC 74-26267. (History, Philosophy & Sociology of Science Ser). 1975. Repr. 25.50x (ISBN 0-405-06595-7). Ayer Co Pubs.

Science & Fiction. Patrick Moore. 1957. lib. bdg. 35.50 (ISBN 0-8414-6347-6). Folcroft.

Science & Fine Art of Fasting. rev. ed. Herbert M. Shelton. LC 77-99219. 1978. pap. 7.95 (ISBN 0-914532-21-9). Natural Hygiene.

Science & Fine Art of Food & Nutrition. 6th, rev. ed. Herbert M. Shelton. LC 84-60828. 1984. pap. 10.95 (ISBN 0-914532-32-4). Natural Hygiene.

Science & First Principles. F. S. Northrop. LC 79-89840. 1979. 22.00 (ISBN 0-918024-08-0); pap. 12.00 (ISBN 0-918024-09-9). Ox Bow.

Science & Food: The CGIAR & Its Partners. Jock R. Anderson et al. 152p. 1988. 14.95 (ISBN 0-8213-0947-1, BK0947). World Bank.

Science & Football. Ed. by T. Reilly et al. 500p. 1988. text ed. 44.00 (ISBN 0-419-14360-2, Pub. by E FN Spon). Routledge Chapman & Hall.

Science & Freedom. facsimile ed. Ed. by Lyman Bryson. LC 71-156620. (Essay Index Reprint Ser). Repr. of 1947 ed. 18.00 (ISBN 0-8369-2385-5). Ayer Co Pubs.

Science & Future Choice, 2 vols. Ed. by P. W. Hemily & M. N. Ozdas. Incl. Vol. 1. Building on Scientific Achievement. 45.00x (ISBN 0-19-858162-9); Vol. 2. Technological Challenge for Social Changes. 49.50x (ISBN 0-19-858169-6). 1979. Oxford U Pr.

Science & Gender: A Critique of Biology & Its Theories on Women. Ruth Bleier. (Athene Ser.). (Illus.). 250p. 1984. text ed. 34.00 (ISBN 0-08-030972-0); pap. text ed. 15.95 (ISBN 0-08-030971-2). Pergamon.

Science & Health in with Key to the Scriptures. Mary Baker Eddy. 700p. Standard ed., blue, side-indexed. 27.50 (ISBN 0-87952-002-7). First Church.

Science & Health with Key to the Scriptures. Mary Baker Eddy. 1875. standard ed. 13.50 (ISBN 0-87952-001-9); new type ed. 22.50 (ISBN 0-87952-010-8); new type lea. bdg. 60.00 (ISBN 0-87952-015-9); readers ed. 35.00 (ISBN 0-87952-019-1); lea. bdg. 85.00 (ISBN 0-87952-020-5); Century ed. brown lea. bdg 50.00 (ISBN 0-87952-007-8); pap. 5.50 (ISBN 0-87952-000-0). First Church.

Science & Health with Key to the Scriptures. Mary Baker Eddy. (Pol.). 25.00 (ISBN 0-87952-200-3). First Church.

Science & Health with Key to the Scriptures. Mary Baker Eddy. pap. 10.50 Spanish ed. (ISBN 0-87952-225-9); pap. 10.50 German ed. (ISBN 0-87952-150-3); pap. 10.50 French ed. (ISBN 0-87952-116-3). First Church.

Science & Health with Key to the Scriptures. Mary Baker Eddy. Indonesian 25.00 (ISBN 0-87952-175-9); Japanese 25.00 (ISBN 0-87952-190-2). First Church.

Science & Health with Key to the Scriptures. Mary Baker Eddy. Incl. Vol. 1. Danish Ed. 25.00 (ISBN 0-87952-103-1); Vol. 2. Dutch Ed. 25.00 (ISBN 0-87952-109-0); Vol. 3. French Ed. 25.00 (ISBN 0-87952-117-1); Vol. 4. German Ed. 25.00 (ISBN 0-87952-151-1); Vol. 5. Norwegian Ed. 25.00 (ISBN 0-87952-195-3); Vol. 6. Swedish Ed. 25.00 (ISBN 0-87952-250-X); Vol. 7. Russian Ed. 25.00 (ISBN 0-87952-220-8); Vol. 8. Greek Ed. 25.00 (ISBN 0-87952-170-8); Vol. 9. Italian Ed. 25.00 (ISBN 0-87952-180-5); Vol. 10. Spanish Ed. 25.00 (ISBN 0-87952-226-7). First Church.

Science & Health with Key to the Scriptures. Mary Baker Eddy. 700p. Hardcover cloth. 25.00 (ISBN 0-87952-205-4). First Church.

Science & Health with Key to the Scriptures. Mary Baker Eddy. 700p. Flex blue. 49.50 (ISBN 0-87952-124-4). First Church.

Science & Health with Key to the Scriptures. Mary Baker Eddy. 700p. Travel ed. 11.75 (ISBN 0-87952-028-0). First Church.

Science & Health with Key to the Scriptures. Mary Baker Eddy. 700p. Braille ed. 65.00 (ISBN 0-87952-021-3). First Church.

Science & Religion in the Thought of Nicolas Malebranche. Michael E. Hobart. LC 81-7419. x, 196p. 1982. 22.50x (ISBN 0-8078-1487-3). U of NC Pr.

Science & Religion: Towards the Restoration of an Ancient Harmony. Anjam Khursheed. 144p. (Orig.). 1988. pap. 7.50 (ISBN 1-85168-005-5, Pub. by Oneworld Pubns). Alpha NY.

Science & Religious Thought: A Darwinism Case Study. Walter J. Wilkins. Ed. by Margaret R. Miles. LC 86-24946. (Studies in Religion: No. 3). 224p. 1986. 39.95 (ISBN 0-8357-1778-X). UMI Res Pr.

Science & Rice in Indonesia. William B. Ward. LC 85-7281. (AID Science & Technology in Development Ser.). 160p. 1985. text ed. 25.00 (ISBN 0-89946-194-8). Oelgeschlager.

Science & Romance of Selected Herbs Used in Medicine & Religious Ceremony. Anthony K. Andoh. (Illus.). 350p. 1986. 27.95 (ISBN 0-916299-01-5). North Scale Co.

Science & Sanity: An Introduction to Non-Aristotelian Systems & General Semantics. 4th ed. Alfred Korzybski. LC 58-6260. 806p. 1980. 23.50x (ISBN 0-937298-01-8). Inst Gen Seman.

Science & Scepticism. John Watkins. LC 84-42555. (Illus.). 450p. 1984. text ed. 44.00x (ISBN 0-691-07294-9); pap. 15.95x (ISBN 0-691-10171-X). Princeton U Pr.

Science & Scholarship in Hungary. 2nd ed. Ed. by Tibor Erdey-Gruz & Kalman Kulcsar. 1975. 19.95 (ISBN 0-8464-0816-3). Beekman Pubs.

Science & Science Education in Egyptian Society. Yusef S. Kotb. LC 79-176944. (Columbia University. Teachers College. Contributions to Education: No. 967). Repr. of 1951 ed. 22.50 (ISBN 0-404-55967-0). AMS Pr.

Science & Science Policy in the Arab World. A. B. Zahlan. LC 79-3380. 1980. 26.00x (ISBN 0-312-70232-9). St Martin.

Science & Scientific Researchers in Modern Society. 2nd ed. John P. Dickinson. 260p. (Orig.). 1986. pap. text ed. 19.00 (ISBN 92-3-102427-2, U1521, UNESCO). UNIPUB.

Science & Scientists in an Agricultural Research Organization: A Sociological Study. Norman W. Storer. Ed. by Harriet Zuckerman & Robert K. Merton. LC 79-9029. (Dissertations on Sociology Ser.). 1980. lib. bdg. 21.00x (ISBN 0-405-12996-3). Ayer Co Pubs.

Science & Scientists in the Nineteenth Century. Robert H. Murray. 468p. Repr. of 1925 ed. text ed. 62.10x (ISBN 0-576-29220-6, Pub. by Gregg Intl Pubs England). Gregg Intl.

Science & Secrets of Wheat Trading, Vol. 6. Burton H. Pugh. 234p. pap. text ed. 25.00 (ISBN 0-939093-10-3). Lambert Gann Pub.

Science & Security: The Future of Arms Control - Colloquium Proceedings 1986. Ed. by W. Thomas Wander & Kenneth N. Luongo. 326p. 1987. pap. 15.00 (ISBN 0-87168-325-3). AAAS.

Science & Security: The Future of Arms Control (Precolloquium Reader) Ed. by W. Thomas Wander et al. 205p. 1986. pap. 8.00 (ISBN 0-87168-289-3). AAAS.

Science & Sensations of Vocal Tone. Edgar F. Herbert-Caesari. 1968. 7.50 (ISBN 0-8008-7003-4, Crescendo). Taplinger.

Science & Sensibility. G. R. Dunstan & F. D. Maruice. 1982. 20.00x (ISBN 0-317-43865-4, Pub. by Univ Federation Animal). State Mutual Bk.

Science & Sentiment in America: Philosophical Thought from Jonathan Edwards to John Dewey. Morton White. 1972. 25.00x (ISBN 0-19-501519-3). Oxford U Pr.

Science & Service in Mental Retardation: Proceedings of the Seventh Congress of the International Association for the Scientific Study of Mental Deficiency. Ed. by Joseph M. Berg. 512p. 1986. text ed. 66.00 (ISBN 0-416-40650-5, 1042). Routledge Chapman & Hall.

Science & Singing. Ernest G. White. LC 68-59104. 1970. 6.95 (ISBN 0-8008-7006-9, Crescendo). Taplinger.

Science & Social Change. Compiled by Jesse E. Thornton. LC 72-357. (Essay Index Reprint Ser.). Repr. of 1939 ed. 29.00 (ISBN 0-8369-2830-X). Ayer Co Pubs.

Science & Social Change in Britain, 1700-1900. Colin Russell. LC 83-11021. (Illus.). 260p. 1984. 29.95 (ISBN 0-312-70239-6). St Martin.

Science & Social Needs. Julian S. Huxley. Repr. of 1935 ed. 29.00 (ISBN 0-527-43820-0). Kraus Repr.

Science & Social Structure: A Festschrift for Robert K. Merton. LC 80-13464. (N.Y. Academy of Sciences Transactions: Vol. 39). 173p. 1980. 17.00x (ISBN 0-89766-043-9). NY Acad Sci.

Science & Social Studies Workbook for the GED Test. David A. Herzog. LC 82-24441. (Arco's Preparation for the GED Examination Ser.). 224p. 1983. pap. 5.95 (ISBN 0-668-05541-3, 5541). Arco.

Science & Socialist Construction in China. Xu Liangying & Fan Dianian. Ed. by Pierre M. Perrolle. Tr. by John C. Hsu from Chinese. LC 81-23250. 230p. 1982. 37.50 (ISBN 0-87332-189-8). M E Sharpe.

Science & Societal Issues: A Guide for Science Teachers. Charles R. Barman et al. (Illus.). 154p. 1981. pap. text ed. 9.95x (ISBN 0-8138-0485-X). Iowa St U Pr.

Science & Society. Ed. by Norman Kaplan. LC 74-26271. (History, Philosophy & Sociology of Science Ser). 1975. Repr. 46.50x (ISBN 0-405-06599-X). Ayer Co Pubs.

Science & Society in Early America: Essays in Honor of Whitfield J. Bell, Jr. Ed. by Randolph S. Klein. LC 85-71740. (Memoirs Ser.: Vol. 166). 300p. 1986. 30.00 (ISBN 0-87169-166-3). Am Philos.

Science & Society in Modern Japan. Ed. by Shigeru Nakayama et al. 1974. 45.00x (ISBN 0-262-14022-5). MIT Pr.

Science & Society in Restoration England. Michael Hunter. LC 80-41071. 224p. 1981. 47.50 (ISBN 0-521-22866-2); pap. 16.95 (ISBN 0-521-29685-4). Cambridge U Pr.

Science & Society: Knowing, Teaching, Learning. Cheryl Charles. Ed. by Bob Samples & Cheryl Charles. LC 78-70847. (National Council for the Social Studies Ser.: No. 57). pap. 24.00 (ISBN 0-317-39643-9, 2023190). Bks Demand UMI.

Science & Society: Past, Present, & Future. Ed. by Nicholas H. Steneck. 422p. 1975. pap. text ed. 9.95x (ISBN 0-472-08820-3). U of Mich Pr.

Science & Society: Selected Essays. Ed. by Alexander Vavoulis & A. Wayne Colver. LC 66-15005. 1966. pap. text ed. 7.50x (ISBN 0-8162-9172-1). Holden-Day.

Science & Society: Selected Essays in the Sociology of Science. Joseph Agassi. 539p. 1981. 79.00 (ISBN 90-277-1244-1, Pub. by Reidel Holland). Kluwer Academic.

Science & Society Sixteen Hundred to Nineteen Hundred. Ed. by Peter Mathias. LC 76-172833. pap. 45.30 (2031688). Bks Demand UMI.

Science & Sociological Practice. Steven Yearley. 160p. 1984. 59.00x (ISBN 0-335-10584-X, Pub. by Open Univ Pr); pap. 24.00x (ISBN 0-335-10581-5, Pub. by Open Univ Pr). Taylor & Francis.

Science & Speculation. Ed. by Jonathan Barnes et al. LC 82-4221. (Studies in Hellinistic Theory & Practice). 352p. 1983. 47.50 (ISBN 0-521-24689-X). Cambridge U Pr.

Science & Spirit: The Meaning of Psychical Research for Religion. Ed. by Frank C. Tribbe. (Spiritual Frontiers Fellowship Thirtieth Anniversary Booklet Ser.: Vol. I, No. 3). 1986. Set. 12.00 (ISBN 0-317-68876-6). Spirit Front Fellow.

Science & Sporting Performance: Management or Manipulation? Ed. by Bruce Davies & Geoffrey Thomas. (Illus.). 1982. 35.00x (ISBN 0-19-857594-7). Oxford U Pr.

Science & Sports. Robert Gardner. Ed. by Henry Rasof. (Venture Ser.). (Illus.). 112p. (YA) (gr. 7-12). 1988. 11.90 (ISBN 0-531-10593-8). Watts.

Science & Starvation. D. J. Hughes. 1968. pap. 14.25 (ISBN 0-08-012326-0). Pergamon.

Science & State: Monographs. Mary Vance. (Public Administration Ser.: P 1910). 79p. 1986. 18.50 (ISBN 0-89028-830-5). Vance Biblios.

Science & Subjectivity. 2nd ed. Israel Scheffler. LC 81-85414. 178p. 1982. lib. bdg. 22.50 (ISBN 0-915145-31-6); pap. text ed. 8.50 (ISBN 0-915145-30-8). Hackett Pub.

Science & Superstition in the Eighteenth Century: A Study of the Treatment of Science in Two Encyclopedias of 1725-1750. Philip Shorr. LC 33-3916. (Columbia University. Studies in the Social Sciences: No. 364). Repr. of 1932 ed. 10.00 (ISBN 0-404-51364-6). AMS Pr.

Science & Synthesis: An International Colloquium Organized by UNESCO on the Tenth Anniversary of the Death of Albert Einstein & Teilhard De Chardin. UNESCO Colloqium, 10th Anniversary of the Death of Albert Einstein & Teilhard De Charden. Tr. by B. M. Crook. LC 77-143044. 1971. 35.10 (ISBN 0-387-05344-1). Springer-Verlag.

Science & Technical English & Polish Dictionary. Czerni et al. 1986. 50.00x (ISBN 83-204-0763-X, P536). Vanous.

Science & Technlogy in China, Vol. II. Chinese Academy of Sciences Staff. (IAPS Ser.). (Illus.). 550p. 1988. 100.00 (ISBN 0-08-036386-5). Pergamon.

Science & Technology. Ed. by David L. Bender & Bruno Leone. (Opposing Viewpoints Sources Ser.). 1987. lib. bdg. 39.95 (ISBN 0-89908-533-4). Greenhaven.

Science & Technology Advice to the President, Congress & Judiciary. William T. Golden. 475p. 1988. text ed. 49.95 (ISBN 0-08-036126-9); pap. text ed. 24.95 (ISBN 0-08-036125-0). Pergamon.

Science & Technology: An Introduction to the Literature. 4th ed. Denis Grogan. 400p. 1982. 27.50 (ISBN 0-85157-315-0, Pub. by Bingley England); pap. 18.50 (Pub. by Bingley England). ALA.

Science & Technology Annual, 1988. Ed. by David L. Bender & Bruno Leone. (Opposing Viewpoints Sources Ser.). (gr. 4-11). 1988. pap. 9.95 (ISBN 0-89908-542-3). Greenhaven.

Science & Technology As an Organic Part of Contemporary Culture. 12p. 1980. pap. 5.00 (ISBN 92-808-0186-4, TUNU124, UNU). UNIPUB.

Science & Technology Centers. Victor J. Danilov. (Illus.). 416p. 1982. 50.00x (ISBN 0-262-04068-9). MIT Pr.

Science & Technology Education & Future Human Needs, Vol. 1. Ed. by J. L. Lewis & P. J. Kelly. (STEF Ser.: No. 1). (Illus.). 130p. 1987. 28.00 (ISBN 0-08-033909-3, PBL); pap. 16.00 (ISBN 0-08-033910-7, PBL). Pergamon.

Science & Technology Education for Civic & Professional Life: The Undergraduate Years. Association of American Colleges. vi, 32p. 1983. pap. 3.50 (ISBN 0-911696-34-2). Assn Am Coll.

Science & Technology for Development: Corporate & Government Policies & Practices. Jack N. Behrman & William A. Fischer. LC 79-27213. 160p. 1980. text ed. 35.00 (ISBN 0-89946-023-2). Oelgeschlager.

Science & Technology for Development. 784p. 1979. pap. 26.00 (ISBN 92-1-002020-0, MULT.79.1.15). UN.

Science & Technology for Development: Technology Policy & Industrialization in the People's Republic of China. G. C. Dean. 108p. 1979. pap. 8.50 (ISBN 0-88936-210-6, IDRC130, IDRC). UNIPUB.

Science & Technology for Development: The Role of U. S. Universities. Robert P. Morgan et al. (Policy Studies). (Illus.). 1979. 78.00 (ISBN 0-08-025107-2). Pergamon.

Science & Technology for International Development: An Assessment of U. S. Policies & Programs. Robert P. Morgan. (Replica Edition). 115p. 1985. pap. 22.50x (ISBN 0-86531-838-7). Westview.

Science & Technology in a Changing International Order: The United Nations Conference on Science & Technology for Development. Ed. by Volker Rittberger. (Special Studies in Social, Political, & Economic Development). 200p. 1982. lib. bdg. 42.00 (ISBN 0-86531-146-3). Westview.

Science & Technology in Africa. 1988. 115.00 (ISBN 0-582-00086-6). Gale.

Science & Technology in Agriculture. Ed. by Jones & Socolofsky. 1980. cancelled (ISBN 0-87461-034-6). McNally & Loftin.

Science & Technology in an Era of Independence. UNA-USA National Policy Panel. LC 74-29459. (Illus.). 1975. pap. text ed. 2.00x (ISBN 0-934654-12-3). UNA-USA.

Science & Technology in Australasia, Antartica, & Pacific Islands. Ed. by D. Alsmeyer & A. G. Atkins. 540p. 1988. 95.00x (ISBN 0-582-90060-3, Pub. by Longman). Gale.

Science & Technology in China, Vol. I. Chinese Academy of Sciences Staff. (IAPS Ser.). 560p. 1988. write for info. (ISBN 0-08-036379-2). Pergamon.

Science & Technology in Chinese Civilization: Proceedings of the Workshop held at the University of California, San Diego, California, September 1985. Ed. by C-Y Chen. 372p. 1987. 48.00 (ISBN 9971-50-192-9, Z0351G-P). World Scientific Pub.

Science & Technology in Development: A UNESCO Approach. Daniel Behrman. (Illus.). 104p. 1979. pap. 5.00 (ISBN 92-3-101726-8, U947, UNESCO). UNIPUB.

Science & Technology in East Asia. Ed. by Nathan Sivin. (Illus.). 1977. 15.00 (ISBN 0-88202-162-1, Sci Hist); pap. 8.95 (ISBN 0-88202-161-3). Watson Pub Intl.

Science & Technology in Eastern Europe. Ed. by Gyorgy Darvas. 283p. 1988. 114.00x (ISBN 0-582-90054-9, Longman). Gale.

Science & Technology in India. Ed. by Vadilal Dagli. 345p. 1982. text ed. 22.00x. Coronet Bks.

Science & Technology in India. B. R. Nanda. 1977. 11.00x. Intl Bk Dist.

Science & Technology in India. Ed. by B. R. Nanda. 1978. 9.00x (ISBN 0-8364-0170-0). South Asia Bks.

Science & Technology in Japan. Alun M. Anderson. 350p. 1984. text ed. 75.00 (ISBN 0-582-90015-8). Gale Res.

Science & Technology in Korea: Traditional Instruments & Techniques. Sang-Woon Jeon. (East Asian Science Ser). 448p. 1974. 39.50x (ISBN 0-262-10014-2). MIT Pr.

Science & Technology in Latin America. 1983. pap. text ed. 88.00x (ISBN 0-582-90057-3, Pub. by Longman). Gale.

Science & Technology in Medieval Society. Intro. by Pamela O. Long. (Annals of The New York Academy of Sciences: Vol. 441). 224p. 1984. lib. bdg. 50.00x (ISBN 0-89766-276-8); pap. 50.00x (ISBN 0-89766-277-6). NY Acad Sci.

Science & Technology in Post-Mao China. Ed. by Denis F. Simon & Merle Goldman. (Contemporary China Ser.: No. 5). 450p. 1988. pap. text ed. 14.00 (ISBN 0-674-79475-3, Pub. by Coun East Asian Stud). Harvard U Pr.

Science & Technology in Providence, 1760-1914: An Essay in the History of Brown University in the Metropolitan Community. Donald Fleming. LC 52-9555. (Brown University Papers: No. 26). Repr. of 1952 ed. 20.00 (2027504). Bks Demand UMI.

Science & Technology in Scandinavia. 1988. 115.00 (ISBN 0-582-01892-7, Pub. by Longman). Gale.

Science & Technology in South Asia. Ed. by Peter Gaeffke & David A. Utz. LC 85-29476. (Proceedings of the South Asia Seminar: No. 2). (Illus.). x, 171p. (Orig.). 1985. pap. text ed. 10.00 (ISBN 0-936115-01-7). U Penn South Asia.

Science & Technology in the Development of Modern China: An Annotated Bibliography. Genevieve C. Dean. LC 74-76296. 279p. 1974. 32.00x (ISBN 0-7201-0376-2). Mansell.

Science & Technology in the History of Modern Japan: Imitation or Endogenous Creativity? 22p. 1981. pap. 5.00 (ISBN 92-808-0185-6, TUNU134, UNU). UNIPUB.

Science & Technology in the Middle East: A Guide to Issues, Organizations & Institutions. Ed. by Ziauddin Sardar. (Longman Guide to World Science & Technology Ser.: Vol. 1). 324p. 88.00x (ISBN 0-582-90052-2, Pub. by Longman). Gale.

Science & Technology in the Primary School of Tomorrow. G. Orpwood & I. Werdelin. (Studies & Surveys in Comparative Education). 216p. 1987. pap. 15.50 (ISBN 92-3-102502-3, U1648, UNESCO). UNIPUB.

Science & Technology in the Transformation of the World. Ed. by Anouar Abdel-Malek & Gregory Blue. 497p. 1982. 36.25 (ISBN 92-808-0339-5, TUNU193, UNU). UNIPUB.

Science & Technology in the Transformation of the World. Ed. by Miroslav Pecujlic et al. LC 83-40706. 174p. 1984. 19.95 (ISBN 0-312-70265-5). St Martin.

Science & Technology in World Development. Robin Clarke. (OPUS). 208p. 1985. 26.00x (ISBN 0-19-219195-0); pap. 8.95x (ISBN 0-19-289176-6). Oxford U Pr.

Science & Technology Indicators for Development. Ed. by Hiroko Morita-Lou. 150p. 1985. pap. 30.50x (ISBN 0-8133-0294-3). Westview.

Science & Technology of Advanced LMFBR Fuels: A Monograph on Solid State Physics, Chemistry & Technology of Carbides, Nitrides & Carbonitrides of Uranium & Plutonium. Hj Matzke. 755p. 1986. 205.25 (ISBN 0-444-86997-2, North-Holland). Elsevier.

Science & Technology of Building Materials. Henry Cowa & Peter Smith. (Illus.). 288p. 1987. text ed. 34.95 (ISBN 0-442-21799-4). Van Nos Reinhold.

Science & Technology of Coal & Coal Utilization. Ed. by Bernard R. Cooper & William A. Ellingson. 682p. 1984. 95.00x (ISBN 0-306-41436-8, Plenum Pr). Plenum Pub.

Science & Technology of Gelatin. Ed. by A. G. Ward & A. Courts. (Food & Technology Ser.). 1977. 60.00 (ISBN 0-12-735050-0). Acad Pr.

Science & Technology of Microfabrication: Proceedings of Symposium Held at Mrs Fall Meeting, Boston, MA, Dec. 1-6, 1986. Ed. by R. E. Howard et al. (MRS Symposia Proceedings Ser.: Vol. 76). 1987. text ed. 46.00 (ISBN 0-931837-42-1). Materials Res.

Science & Technology of Polymer Colloids. Ed. by R. Buscall et al. (Illus.). 336p. 1985. 77.50 (ISBN 0-85334-312-8, Pub. by Elsevier Applied Sci England). Elsevier.

Science & Technology of Polymer Processing: Proceedings of the International Conference on Polymer Processing. Ed. by Nam P. Suh & Nak-Ho Sung. (Illus.). 1979. 80.00x (ISBN 0-262-19179-2). MIT Pr.

Science & Technology of Rapidly Quenched Alloys: Proceedings of Symposium Held at Mrs Fall Meeting, Boston, MA, Dec. 1-6, 1986. Ed. by M. Tenhover et al. (MRS Symposia Proceedings Ser.: Vol. 80). 1987. text ed. 44.00 (ISBN 0-931837-45-6). Materials Res.

Science & Technology of Rare Earth Materials. Ed. by E. C. Subbarao & W. E. Wallace. 1980. 52.50 (ISBN 0-12-675640-6). Acad Pr.

Science & Technology of Resists. Reiser. 1988. price not set (ISBN 0-471-85550-2). Wiley.

Science & Technology of Rubber. Ed. by Frederick R. Eirich. 1978. 102.00 (ISBN 0-12-234360-3). Acad Pr.

Science & Technology of the Undercooled Melt: Rapid Solidification Materials & Technologies. Ed. by P. R. Sahm et al. 1986. lib. bdg. 68.00 (ISBN 90-247-3386-3, Pub. by Martinus Nijhoff Netherlands). Kluwer Academic.

Science & Technology of Tributyl Phosphate, 2 vols. Ed. by Wallace W. Schulz. 1987. Set. 190.00 (ISBN 0-317-63005-9). Vol. I: Synthesis, Properties, Reactions, & Analysis, 352 pgs (ISBN 0-317-63006-7). Vol. II: Selected Technical & Industrial Uses, 295 pgs (ISBN 0-8493-6397-7). CRC Pr.

Science & Technology of Zirconia. Ed. by A. H. Heuer & L. W. Hobbs. (Advances in Ceramics Ser.: Vol. 3). (Illus.). 1981. 65.00 (ISBN 0-916094-43-X). Am Ceramic.

Science & Technology of Zirconia, II. Ed. by A. H. Heuer & M Ruhie. (Advances in Ceramics Ser.: Vol. 12). 840p. 1985. 120.00 (ISBN 0-916094-64-2). Am Ceramic.

Science & Technology of Zirconia III. Ed. by S. Somiya et al. (Advances in Ceramics Ser.: Vol. 24). Date not set. price not set (ISBN 0-916094-87-1). Am Ceramic.

Science in Schools. Ed. by Joan Brown et al. LC 86-16336. 416p. 1987. 65.00x (ISBN 0-335-15982-6, Open Univ Pr); pap. 26.00x (ISBN 0-335-15981-8). Taylor & Francis.

Science in Science Fiction. Ed. by Peter Nicholls & David Langford. LC 82-14834. 208p. 1983. 24.50 (ISBN 0-394-53010-1); pap. 14.95 (ISBN 0-394-71364-8). Knopf.

Science in Society. Science Education Assoc. London. Ed. by John L. Lewis. 1981. complete pack 100.00x (ISBN 0-686-79369-2, 00407); tchrs. manual o.p. 20.00x (ISBN 0-435-54043-2); Omnibus reader's pack 36.00x (ISBN 0-435-54042-4). Heinemann Ed.

Science in Soviet Russia. National Council of American Soviet Friendship. LC 74-25151. (History, Philosophy & Sociology of Science Ser). 1975. Repr. 16.00x (ISBN 0-405-06635-X). Ayer Co Pubs.

Science in Special Places. Lucia K. Henry. (gr. 1-3). 1988. pap. 5.95 (ISBN 0-8224-6457-8). D S Lake Pubs.

Science in the British Colonies of America. Raymond P. Stearns. LC 78-122915. (Illus.). 780p. 1970. 34.95 (ISBN 0-252-00120-6). U of Ill Pr.

Science in the Changing World. facs. ed. Ed. by Mary Adams. LC 68-29188. (Essay Index Reprint Ser). 1968. Repr. of 1933 ed. 18.00 (ISBN 0-8369-0136-3). Ayer Co Pubs.

Science in the Changing World: (Julian Huxley, Bertrand Russell & J. B. S. Haldane) Ed. by Mary Adams. 1979. Repr. of 1933 ed. lib. bdg. 35.00 (ISBN 0-8495-0204-7). Arden Lib.

Science in the Early Roman Empire: Pliny the Elder, His Sources & His Influence. Ed. by Roger French & Frank Greenaway. LC 86-7919. (Illus.). 298p. 1986. 28.50x (ISBN 0-389-20634-2). B&N Imports.

Science in the Federal Government: A History of Policies & Activities to 1940. A. Hunter Dupree. Ed. by I. Bernard Cohen. LC 79-7959. (Three Centuries of Science in America Ser.). (Illus.). 1980. Repr. of 1957 ed. lib. bdg. 39.00x (ISBN 0-405-12540-2). Ayer Co Pubs.

Science in the Federal Government: A History of Policies & Activities. A. Hunter Dupree. LC 86-45456. 488p. 1986. pap. text ed. 16.95x (ISBN 0-8018-3381-7). Johns Hopkins.

Science in the Making. Joel H. Hildebrand. LC 84-25250. (Bempton Lectures in America Ser.: No. 9). viii, 116p. 1985. Repr. of 1957 ed. lib. bdg. 35.00x (ISBN 0-313-24737-4, HISC). Greenwood.

Science in the MarketPlace. 3rd. ed. Florence G. Korchin. 20.00x (ISBN 0-9611318-2-9). Tiger Pubn.

Science in the Middle Ages. Ed. by David C. Lindberg. LC 78-5367. (Chicago History of Science & Medicine Ser.). (Illus.). 1979. pap. 16.95x (ISBN 0-226-48233-2, P870, Phoen). U of Chicago Pr.

Science in the Provinces: Scientific Communities & Provincial Leadership in France, 1860-1930. Mary Jo Nye. LC 85-8503. 1986. text ed. 42.00x (ISBN 0-520-05561-6). U of Cal Pr.

Science in the Streets: Report of the Twentieth Century Fund Task Force on the Communication of Scientific Risk. Dorothy Nelkin. 97p. (Orig.). 1984. pap. text ed. 7.50x (ISBN 0-87078-154-5). Priority Pr Pubns.

Science in the Twentieth Century. Walter Sullivan. LC 77-18144. 35.00 (ISBN 0-405-06672-4, 1754). Ayer Co Pubs.

Science in the University. facs. ed. University Of California - Members Of The Faculties. LC 68-20331. (Essay Index Reprint Ser). 1944. 20.00 (ISBN 0-8369-0856-2). Ayer Co Pubs.

Science in Traditional China. Joseph Needham. (Illus.). 144p. 1982. text ed. 12.50x (ISBN 0-674-79438-9); pap. 5.95 (ISBN 0-674-79439-7). Harvard U Pr.

Science in Utopia: A Mighty Design. Nell Eurich. LC 67-14339. pap. 65.40 (ISBN 0-317-09457-2, 2017014). Bks Demand UMI.

Science in Victorian Manchester: Enterprise & Expertise. Robert H. Kargon. LC 77-4556. 1978. text ed. 32.50x (ISBN 0-8018-1969-5). Johns Hopkins.

Science in Your Backyard. Robert Gardner & David Webster. LC 86-21817. (Illus.). 128p. (gr. 4-7). 1987. 9.79 (ISBN 0-671-55565-0); pap. 4.95 (ISBN 0-671-63835-1). Messner.

Science Indicators NSB 85-1: The 1985 Rept. (Illus.). 330p. 1985. 15.00. USGPO.

Science Instruction in the Middle & Secondary Schools. Alfred T. Collette & Eugene L. Chiapetta. 1984. text ed. 34.95 (ISBN 0-675-20581-6). Merrill.

Science Instruction of Visually Impaired Youth. Dean R. Brown. 20p. 1978. 4.00 (ISBN 0-89128-969-0, PEP969). Am Foun Blind.

Science, Internationalism & War: An Original Anthology. Ed. by Yehuda Elkana et al. LC 74-25185. (History, Philosophy & Sociology of Science Ser). 1975. Repr. 16.00x (ISBN 0-405-06633-3). Ayer Co Pubs.

Science Is a Sacred Cow. Anthony Standen. 75p. 1950. pap. 5.50. Select Bks.

Science: It's Changing Your World. Paul D. Martin. Ed. by Donald J. Crump. LC 85-2936. (Books for World Explorers Series 6: No. 3). (Illus.). 104p. (gr. 3-8). 1985. 6.95 (ISBN 0-87044-516-2); PLB 8.50 (ISBN 0-87044-521-9). Natl Geog.

Science: Its History & Development among the World's Cultures. Colin A. Ronan. (Illus.). 528p. 1983. 29.95 (ISBN 0-87196-745-6); pap. 14.95 (ISBN 0-8160-1165-6). Facts on File.

Science, Language & the Human Condition. rev. ed. Morton A. Kaplan. 250p. 1989. pap. 14.95 (ISBN 1-55778-147-8). Paragon Hse.

Science Learning Centers for the Primary Grades. C. Poppe & N. Van Matre. 1985. pap. 17.95 (ISBN 0-87628-749-6). Ctr Appl Res.

Science Lecture Room: A Planning Study to Examine the Principles of Location & Design of Lecture Rooms in the Development of University Science Areas. Jeremy R. Taylor. LC 67-24941. pap. 31.80 (ISBN 0-317-27100-8, 2024548). Bks Demand UMI.

Science Library, 6 vols. 1987. Set. 79.95 (ISBN 0-89434-076-X). Ency Brit Ed.

Science Made Stupid! Tom Weller. 1985. pap. 6.95 (ISBN 0-395-36646-1). HM.

Science Magic. Alison Alexander & Susie Bower. (Illus., Orig.). (ps-3). 1988. pap. 5.95 (ISBN 0-13-795022-5). S&S.

Science Magic. 1987. write for info. P-H.

Science Magic: One Hundred One Experiments You Can Do. Ormond McGill. (Illus.). 164p. 1984. lib. bdg. 11.95 (ISBN 0-668-05849-8); pap. 7.95 (ISBN 0-668-05853-6). Arco.

Science Magic Tricks: Over 50 Fun Tricks That Mystify & Dazzle. Nathan Shalit. LC 79-18645. (Illus.). 128p. (gr. 4-9). 1981. 9.95 (ISBN 0-03-047116-8); pap. 4.95 (ISBN 0-8050-0234-0). H Holt & Co.

Science, Medicine, & History, 2 vols. Ed. by E. Ashworth Underwood. LC 74-26300. (History, Philosophy & Sociology of Science Ser). (Illus.). 1975. Repr. Set. 99.00x (ISBN 0-405-06624-4); 49.50x ea. Vol. 1 (ISBN 0-405-06640-6). Vol. 2 (ISBN 0-405-06641-4). Ayer Co Pubs.

Science, Medicine & Psychology of Automobiles: Subject Analysis & Research Guide. Edith Marie Christos et al. LC 83-45545. 140p. 1984. 34.50 (ISBN 0-88164-112-X); pap. 26.50 (ISBN 0-88164-113-8). ABBE Pubs Assn.

Science, Medicine & Psychology of Personality: Subject Analysis with Bibliography. American Health Research Institute Staff. Ed. by John C. Bartone. LC 83-45529. 145p. 1985. 34.50 (ISBN 0-88164-124-3); pap. 26.50 (ISBN 0-88164-125-1). ABBE Pubs Assn.

Science, Medicine & Technology: English Grammar & Technical Writing. Peter A. Master. (Illus.). 320p. 1986. pap. text ed. write for info (ISBN 0-13-795469-7). P H.

Science, Medicine & the Community: The Last Hundred Years: Proceedings of Boehringer Ingelheim Symposium, 5th, Kronberg, Taunus, 8-11 May, 1985. Boehringer Ingelheim Symposium Staff. Ed. by A. Briggs & J. Shelley. (International Congress Series: No. 728). 252p. 1986. 110.75 (ISBN 0-444-80807-8, Excerpta Medica). Elsevier.

Science, Metaphysics, & the Chance of Salvation: An Interpretation of the Thought of William James. Henry S. Levinson. LC 78-7383. 1978. pap. 9.95 (ISBN 0-89130-234-4, 01-01-24). Scholars Pr GA.

Science Mind Stretchers. Imogene Forte & Sandra Schurr. (Illus.). 128p. (gr. 4-7). 1987. pap. text ed. 8.95 (ISBN 0-86530-165-4, 165-4). Incentive Pubns.

Science Mini-Mysteries. Sandra Markle. LC 87-17420. (Illus.). 72p. (gr. 3-7). 1988. 12.95 (ISBN 0-689-31291-1, Atheneum Childrens Bks). Macmillan.

Science Moderne, de 1450 a 1800 see Histoire Generale des Sciences.

Science, Myth, & the Fictional Creation of Alien Worlds. Albert Wendland. Ed. by Robert Scholes. LC 84-16474. (Studies in Speculative Fiction: No. 12). 208p. 1984. 39.95 (ISBN 0-8357-1608-2). Univ Microfilms.

Science, Myth, Reality: The Black Family in One-Half Century of Research. Eleanor Engram. LC 81-1262. (Contributions in Afro-American & African Studies: No. 64). (Illus.). xviii, 216p. 1982. lib. bdg. 35.00 (ISBN 0-313-22835-3, ESM/). Greenwood.

Science Now. Ed. by James Harrison. LC 84-6437. (Illus.). 192p. 1984. 21.95 (ISBN 0-668-06209-6, 6209). Arco.

Science Observed: New Perspectives on the Social Study of Science. Ed. by Karin Knorr-Cetina & Michael Mulkay. 272p. 1983. 39.95 (ISBN 0-8039-9782-5). Sage.

Science of a Legislator: The Natural Jurisprudence of David Hume & Adam Smith. Knud Haakonssen. LC 80-42001. (Illus.). 256p. 1981. 44.50 (ISBN 0-521-23891-9). Cambridge U Pr.

Science of Accepting a Spiritual Master: A Handbook for the Beginning Student of Spiritual Life. Vaishnava Dasa. 95p. (Orig.). 1987. pap. text ed. 9.95 (ISBN 0-941345-00-9). Transcend Chicago.

Science of Alchymy. William W. Westcott. 1983. pap. 2.95 (ISBN 0-916411-02-8, Pub. by Alchemical Pr). Holmes Pub.

Science of Allelopathy. Ed. by A. R. Putnam & C. S. Tang. LC 86-7822. 317p. 1986. 54.95 (ISBN 0-471-83027-5). Wiley.

Science of Animal Behaviour. P. L. Broadhurst. 1963. lib. bdg. 15.00x (ISBN 0-88307-035-9). Gannon.

Science of Animal Husbandry. 4th ed. James Blakely & David Bade. 1985. text ed. write for info. (ISBN 0-8359-6897-9, Reston); instr's. manual avail. (ISBN 0-8359-6898-7). P-H.

Science of Animals That Serve Humanity. 3rd ed. John R. Campbell & John F. Lasley. LC 84-7950. 880p. 1985. text ed. 49.95 (ISBN 0-07-009700-3). McGraw.

Science of Animals That Serve Mankind. 2nd ed. John R. Campbell & John F. Lasley. (Agricultural Science Ser.). (Illus.). 736p. 1975. text ed. 42.95 (ISBN 0-07-009696-1). McGraw.

Science of Artificial Intelligence. Fred D'Ignazio & Allen L. Wold. (Computer-Awareness First Books Ser.). 96p. (gr. 5 up). 1984. lib. bdg. 10.40 (ISBN 0-531-04703-2). Watts.

Science of Becoming Oneself. Haroutiun T. Saraydarian. LC 71-97402. 1969. 11.00 (ISBN 0-911794-26-3); pap. 9.00 (ISBN 0-911794-27-1). Aqua Educ.

Science of Being Great. Wallace D. Wattles. Date not set. pap. 4.95. CSA Pr.

Science of Being Great. Wallace D. Wattles. 1982. pap. 3.95 (ISBN 0-932298-28-1). Copple Hse.

Science of Biological Specimen Preparation for Microscopy & Microanalysis 1985. Ed. by Martin Mueller et al. (Proceedings of 4th Pfefferkorn Conference Ser.). (Illus.). xii, 308p. 1986. text ed. 46.00 (ISBN 0-931288-37-1). Scanning Microscopy.

Science of Biological Specimen Preparation for Microscopy & Microanalysis. Ed. by J. P. Revel et al. (Proceedings of 2nd Pfefferkorn Conference Ser.). (Illus.). x, 246p. 1984. text ed. 40.00 (ISBN 0-931288-32-0). Scanning Microscopy.

Science of Biology. 4th ed. Paul B. Weisz. 1971. text ed. 39.95 (ISBN 0-07-069132-0, C). McGraw.

Science of Biology. 5th ed. Paul B. Weisz & Richard N. Keogh. 1982. text ed. 42.95 (ISBN 0-07-069145-2). McGraw.

Science of Breath. Yogi Ramacharaka. 6.00 (ISBN 0-911662-00-6). Yoga.

Science of Breath: A Practical Guide. Swami Rama et al. (Illus.). 166p. 1979. pap. 7.95 (ISBN 0-89389-057-X). Himalayan Pubs.

Science of Business Negotiation. Philip Sperber. LC 78-26565. 79p. 1979. pap. 10.00 (ISBN 0-87576-077-5). Pilot Bks.

Science of Ceramic Chemical Processing. Ed. by Larry L. Hench & Donald R. Ulrich. LC 85-22490. 594p. 1986. 59.95 (ISBN 0-471-82645-6, Pub. by Wiley-Interscience). Wiley.

Science of Child Development. Stanley K. Fitch. 496p. 1985. pap. 28.00x (ISBN 0-256-03156-8); study guide 11.00 (ISBN 0-256-03447-8). Dorsey.

Science of Chromatography: Lectures Presented at the A. J. P. Martin Honorary Symposium Urbino, Italy May 27-31, 1985. Ed. by F. Bruner. (Journal of Chromatography Library: No. 32). 476p. 1985. 131.75 (ISBN 0-444-42443-1). Elsevier.

Science of Color. Optical Society of America, Committee on Colorimetry. LC 52-7039. (Illus.). 385p. 1963. 29.00x (ISBN 0-9600380-1-9). Optical Soc.

Science of Command & Control: Coping with Uncertainty. Ed. by Stuart E. Johnson & Alexander H. Levis. (AIP Information Systems Ser.). (Illus., Orig.). 1988. pap. text ed. 18.95 (ISBN 0-916159-16-7). AFCEA Intl Pr.

Science of Composite Materials. Bascom. 1991. price not set (ISBN 0-471-60915-3). Wiley.

Science of Conflict. James A. Schellenberg. (Illus.). 1982. 19.95x (ISBN 0-19-502973-9); pap. text ed. 11.95 (ISBN 0-19-502974-7). Oxford U Pr.

Science of Creating Ideas for Industry. Richard E. Paige. 114p. 4.95 (ISBN 0-930317-28-9, B-1605). Mindsight Pub.

Science of Creating Ideas for Industry. Richard E. Paige. 114p. pap. 7.50 (ISBN 0-318-23170-0). Geothermal World.

Science of Criminal Justice. James R. Davis. LC 85-43575. 191p. 1986. lib. bdg. 24.95x (ISBN 0-89950-202-4). McFarland & Co.

Science of Cycling. Edmund R. Burke. LC 86-10246. (Illus.). 223p. 1986. text ed. 18.00x (ISBN 0-87322-048-X, BBUR0048). Human Kinetics.

Science of Cycling. Edmund R. Burke. LC 86-10246. (Illus.). 224p. 1988. pap. 12.95x (ISBN 0-87322-181-8). Human Kinetics.

Science of Dance Training. Ed. by Priscilla M. Clarkson & Margaret Skrinar. LC 87-3370. (Illus.). 312p. 1987. text ed. 33.00x (ISBN 0-87322-122-2, BCLA0122). Human Kinetics.

Science of Design. Gordon L. Glegg. (Illus.). 112p. 1973. 18.95 (ISBN 0-521-20327-9). Cambridge U Pr.

Science of Dreamology: How to Interpret Dreams Correctly & Enjoy Greater Happiness. Bobby A. La Loge. (Illus.). 84p. (Orig.). 1987. pap. text ed. 10.00 (ISBN 0-938147-17-X). Namaste Pubns.

Science of Ecology. Paul R. Erlich & Jonathan Roughgraden. 1987. text ed. write for info. (ISBN 0-02-331700-0). Macmillan.

Science of Education, 3 vols. Caleb Gattegno. Bd. with Facts of Awareness (ISBN 0-87825-125-1); Affectivity & Learning (ISBN 0-87825-073-5); Awareness of Awareness (ISBN 0-87825-126-X). 1977. 3.00 ea. Ed Solutions.

Science of Education. J. F. Herbart. Bd. with Education of Man. LC 77-72191. (Contributions to the History of Psychology Ser.: Pt. B, Vol. I). 226p. 1978. Repr. of 1902 ed. 30.00 (ISBN 0-89093-161-5). U Pubns Amer.

Science of Education & the Professoriate of Education. Ed. by Edwin Johanningmeier. (Occasional Paper: No. 10). 1978. pap. 4.00 (ISBN 0-933669-13-5). Soc Profs Ed.

Science of Education: Awareness of Mathematics - Part IIB, Chapters 10-12. Caleb Gattegno. 1988. pap. 9.95 (ISBN 0-87825-195-2). Ed Solutions.

Science of Education: Awareness of One's Native Language - Part IIA, Chapters 7-9. Caleb Gattegno. 1988. pap. 9.95 (ISBN 0-87825-194-4). Ed Solutions.

Science of Education: Theoretical Considerations - Part I, Chapters 1-6. Caleb Gattegno. 1987. pap. 14.95 (ISBN 0-87825-192-8). Ed Solutions.

Science of Engineering Materials. 3rd ed. Charles O. Smith. (Illus.). 560p. 1986. text ed. write for info (ISBN 0-13-794884-0). P-H.

Science of Engineering Materials. C. M. Srivastava & C. Srinivansan. 462p. 1987. 39.95 (ISBN 0-470-20859-7). Wiley.

Science of English Verse. Sidney Lanier. LC 79-304. 1973. lib. bdg. 35.00 (ISBN 0-8414-5844-8). Folcroft.

Science of Entomology. 2nd ed. William S. Romoser. (Illus.). 544p. 1981. write for info. (ISBN 0-02-403410-X). Macmillan.

Science of Ethics. Leslie Stephen. LC 72-4214. (Select Bibliographies Reprint Ser.). 1972. Repr. of 1882 ed. 25.50 (ISBN 0-8369-6892-1). Ayer Co Pubs.

Science of Etymology. Walter W. Skeat. 16.00 (ISBN 0-405-18877-3). Ayer Co Pubs.

Science of Experience: A Direction for Psychology. Stanton Peele. LC 81-48555. 160p. 1983. 25.00x (ISBN 0-669-05420-8). Lexington Bks.

Science of Fairy Tales. E. S. Hartland. 59.95 (ISBN 0-8490-1001-2). Gordon Pr.

Science of Food. Marion Bennion. 1980. text ed. write for info. (ISBN 0-471-60379-1). Wiley.

Science of Food: An Introduction to Food Science, Nutrition & Microbiology. 2nd ed. P. M. Gaman & K. B. Sherrington. (Illus.). 224p. 1981. pap. text ed. 17.75 (ISBN 0-08-025895-6). Pergamon.

Science of Food & Cooking. 3rd ed. Allan Cameron. (Illus.). 1973. pap. 19.95x (ISBN 0-7131-1791-5). Trans-Atl Phila.

Science of Galileo, Level 3. Michael Bernkopf. Ed. by Jean McConochie. (Regents Readers Ser.). (Illus.). 80p. 1983. pap. text ed. 2.50 (ISBN 0-88345-457-2, 21092). Prentice ESL.

Science of Genetics. 5th ed. George W. Burns. 624p. 1983. write for info. solns. manual (ISBN 0-02-317130-8). Macmillan.

Science of Genetics. 6th ed. George W. Burns & Paul J. Bottino. 333p. 1989. write for info. (ISBN 0-02-317400-5). Macmillan.

Science of Getting Rich. Wallace D. Wattles. (Fictioneer Fact Bk.: No. 1). 1980. pap. text ed. 4.95 (ISBN 0-934882-06-1). Fictioneer Bks.

Science of Getting Rich. Wallace D. Wattles. 1982. pap. 3.95 (ISBN 0-932298-27-3). Copple Hse.

Science of Getting Rich Being Great. Wallace D. Wattles. 168p. 1985. pap. 4.95 (ISBN 0-317-20881-0). CSA Pr.

Science of Goodbyes. Myra Sklarew. LC 81-16023. (Contemporary Poetry Ser.). 96p. 1982. 9.95x (ISBN 0-8203-0603-7); pap. 5.95 (ISBN 0-8203-0604-5). U of Ga Pr.

Science of Grammar. Wilson O. Clough. 1942. 17.50 (ISBN 0-8274-3337-9). R West.

Science of Hair Care. Zviak. (Dermatology Ser.). 752p. 1986. 99.75 (ISBN 0-8247-7378-0). Dekker.

Science of Hard Materials. Ed. by R. K. Viswanadham et al. LC 82-22450. (Illus.). 1022p. 1983. 145.00x (ISBN 0-306-41100-8, Plenum Pr). Plenum Pub.

Science of Hard Materials 1984. Ed. by E. A. Almond et al. R. R. Warren. (Institute of Conference Ser.: 75). 1000p. 1986. 214.00x (ISBN 0-85498-166-7, Pub. by A Hilger U. K.). Taylor & Francis.

Science of Hardness Testing & Its Research Applications: Papers Presented at a Symposium of the American Society for Metals, Oct. 18-20, 1971. Ed. by J. H. Westbrook & H. Conrad. LC 72-95851. (Illus.). pap. 133.50 (ISBN 0-317-08332-5, 2019482). Bks Demand UMI.

Science of Hi-Fidelity. Kenneth W. Johnson-Walker et al. LC 81-81012. (Illus.). 1986. pap. text ed. 25.95 (ISBN 0-8403-2297-6). Kendall-Hunt.

Science of Hi-Fidelity Laboratory Manual. Kenneth W. Johnson & Willard C. Walker. 1978. pap. text ed. 5.95 (ISBN 0-8403-1815-4). Kendall-Hunt.

Science of High Explosives. Melvin A. Cook. LC 58-10260. (A C S Ser: No. 139). 456p. 1971. Repr. of 1958 ed. 39.50 (ISBN 0-88275-010-0). Krieger.

Science of History: A Cybernetic Approach. William J. Chandler. (Studies in Cybernetics: Vol. 7). 160p. 1984. text ed. 37.00 (ISBN 2-88124-012-7). Gordon & Breach.

Science of Hitting, Revised & Updated. Ted Williams & John Underwood. 1986. pap. 9.95 (ISBN 0-671-62103-3, Fireside). S&S.

Science of Homeopathy. George Vithoulkas. 1980. pap. 12.50 (ISBN 0-394-17560-3, E746, Ever). Grove.

Science of Human Existence see Salvation Is a Necessary Evil.

Science of Human Progress. Robin Holliday. 1981. 19.95x (ISBN 0-19-854711-0). Oxford U Pr.

Science of Human Regeneration (Postgraduate Orthopathy) see Secret of Regeneration.

Science of Humanity. David Oberman. 359p. 1985. 59.00x (ISBN 0-7212-0716-2, Pub. by Regency Pr). State Mutual Bk.

Science of International Law. Thomas A. Walker. xvi, 544p. 1984. Repr. of 1893 ed. lib. bdg. 45.00x (ISBN 0-8377-1331-5). Rothman.

Science of Investment. F. H. George. (Information Technology Ser.). 251p. 1984. 29.00 (ISBN 0-85626-422-9). Abacus Pr.

Science of Judo. 8.95x (ISBN 0-685-88122-9). Wehman.

Science of Jurisprudence. A Treatise in Which the Growth of Positive Law Is Unfolded by the Historical Method & Its Elements Classified & Defined by the Analytical. Hannis Taylor. ixv, 676p. 1986. Repr. of 1908 ed. lib. bdg. 65.00x (ISBN 0-8377-1209-2). Rothman.

Science of Knowledge: With First & Second Introductions. J. G. Fichte. Ed. by Peter Heath & John Lachs. Tr. by Peter Heath & John Lachs. LC 82-4536. (Texts in German Philosophy Ser.). 298p. 1982. o. p. 42.50 (ISBN 0-521-25018-8); pap. 16.95 (ISBN 0-521-27050-2). Cambridge U Pr.

Science of Kriya Yoga. Roy E. Davis. 192p. 1984. 7.95 (ISBN 0-317-20860-8). CSA Pr.

Science of Labour & Its Organization. Josefa Ioteyko. LC 73-9710. (Management History Ser.: No. 47). 208p. 1973. Repr. of 1919 ed. 22.50 (ISBN 0-87960-050-0). Hive Pub.

Science of Language. J. J. Callahan. 1938. 15.00 (ISBN 0-8274-3338-7). R West.

Science of Language, 2 vols. Friedrich M. Mueller. LC 73-18817. Repr. of 1891 ed. 94.50 (ISBN 0-404-11441-5). AMS Pr.

Science of Law. Sheldon Amos. (International Scientific Ser.: Vol. X). xx, 417p. 1982. Repr. of 1875 ed. lib. bdg. 32.50x (ISBN 0-8377-0209-7). Rothman.

Science of Law According to the American Theory of Government. E. L. Campbell. viii, 375p. 1981. Repr. of 1887 ed. lib. bdg. 32.50x (ISBN 0-8377-0433-2). Rothman.

Science of Law & Lawmaking: Being an Introduction to Law, a General View of Its Forms & Substance, & a Discussion of the Question of Codification. R. Floyd Clarke. xvi, 473p. 1982. Repr. of 1898 ed. lib. bdg. 37.50x (ISBN 0-8377-0437-5). Rothman.

Science of Learning Disabilities. Kenneth Kavale & Steven Forness. LC 84-17008. (Illus.). 200p. 1984. pap. text ed. 23.50 (ISBN 0-316-48372-9). College-Hill.

Science of Legal Judgment: A Treatise Designed to Show the Materials Whereof, & the Process by Which, Courts Construct Their Judgments; & Adapted to Practical & General Use in the Discussion & Determination of Questions of Law. James Ram. 456p. 1988. Repr. of 1871 ed. lib. bdg. 42.50x (ISBN 0-8377-2539-9). Rothman.

Science of Legal Method. Ed. by E. Brunsken & L. B. Register. 1977. lib. bdg. 59.95 (ISBN 0-8490-2571-0). Gordon Pr.

Science of Legal Method. LC 68-54756. (Modern Legal Philosophy Ser.: Vol. 9). 1969. Repr. of 1917 ed. 35.00x (ISBN 0-678-04520-8). Kelley.

Science of Legal Method: Select Essays. Tr. by Ernest Bruncken & Layton B. Register. (Modern Legal Philosophy Ser: Vol. 9). lxxxvi, 593p. 1969. Repr. of 1917 ed. 37.50x (ISBN 0-8377-2600-X). Rothman.

Science of Lighting & Illumination: General Principles, Vol. 1. Blackwell. 1988. write for info. (ISBN 0-471-88305-0). Wiley.

Science of Linguistics in the Art of Translation: Some Tools from Linguistics for the Analysis & Practice of Translation. Joseph L. Malone. (Linguistics Ser.). 320p. 1988. 59.50 (ISBN 0-88706-653-4); pap. 24.50x (ISBN 0-88706-654-2). State U NY Pr.

Science of Logic: or, An Analysis of the Laws of Thought: Or, An Analysis of the Laws of Thought. Asa Mahan. Repr. of 1857 ed. 18.95x (ISBN 0-935005-84-6). Ibis Pub VA.

Science of Man in the World Crisis. Ed. by Ralph Linton. 1980. lib. bdg. 34.50x (ISBN 0-374-95021-0, Octagon). Hippocrene Bks.

Science of Materials. Witold Brostow. LC 84-15484. 460p. 1985. Repr. of 1979 ed. lib. bdg. 49.50 (ISBN 0-89874-780-5). Krieger.

Science of Materials Used in Advanced Technology. Ed. by Earl R. Parker & Umberto Colombo. LC 73-1065. pap. 143.00 (ISBN 0-317-08187-X, 2015173). Bks Demand UMI.

Science of Mechanics. 6th ed. Ernst Mach. Tr. by T. J. McCormack from Ger. (Illus.). 634p. 1960. pap. 12.95 (ISBN 0-87548-202-3). Open Court.

Science of Mechanics in the Middle Ages. Marshall Clagett. (Illus.). 742p. 1959. text ed. 50.00X (ISBN 0-299-01900-4). U of Wis Pr.

Science of Meditation. Rohit Mehta. 199p. 1987. 13.50 (ISBN 81-208-0297-7, Pub. by Motilal Banarsidass India); pap. 9.00 (ISBN 81-208-0298-5, Pub. by Motilal Banarsidass India). Orient Bk Dist.

Science of Meditation. Rohit Mehta. 199p. 1978. 10.95. Asia Bk Corp.

Science of Meditation. Haroutiun T. Saraydarian. LC 77-158995. 1971. 11.00 (ISBN 0-911794-29-8); pap. 9.00 (ISBN 0-911794-30-1). Aqua Educ.

Science of Mind Hymnal. Thomas L. McClellan. 9.50 (ISBN 0-87516-343-2). DeVorss.

Science of Mind in Daily Living. Donald Curtis. 1975. pap. 5.00 (ISBN 0-87980-299-5). Wilshire.

Science of Minerals in the Age of Jefferson. John C. Greene & John G. Burke. LC 78-50195. (Transactions Ser.: Vol. 68, Pt. 4). (Illus.). 1978. pap. 10.00 (ISBN 0-87169-684-3). Am Philos.

Science of Money. 2nd ed. Alexander Del Mar. LC 68-5846. (Research & Source Ser.: No. 322). 1969. Repr. of 1896 ed. 20.50 (ISBN 0-8337-0830-9). B Franklin.

Science of Money. Alexander Del Mar. 59.95 (ISBN 0-8490-1002-0). Gordon Pr.

Science of Music in Britain, 1714-1830: A Catalogue of Writings, Lectures & Inventions, 2 vols. Jamie C. Kassler. LC 76-52675. (Reference Library of the Humanities: Vol. 79). 1977. Set. lib. bdg. 140.00 (ISBN 0-8240-9894-3). Garland Pub.

Science of Musical Sound. John R. Pierce. LC 82-21427. (Scientific American Library). (Illus.). 242p. 1983. 32.95 (ISBN 0-7167-1508-2). W H Freeman.

Science of Musical Sounds. 2nd ed. Dayton C. Miller. LC 76-181211. 286p. 1926. Repr. 39.00x (ISBN 0-403-01622-3). Scholarly.

Science of Musical Sounds. Dayton C. Miller. 1988. Repr. of 1926 ed. lib. bdg. 49.00x. Am Biog Serv.

Science of Natural Theology. Asa Mahan. LC 75-3273. Repr. of 1867 ed. 27.50 (ISBN 0-404-59261-9). AMS Pr.

Science of Negotiations. David Eary. 240p. 1987. perf. bdg. 69.95 (ISBN 0-912702-37-0). Global Eng.

Science of Numbers. Gopi Sharma. 1984. 11.50x (ISBN 0-8364-1133-1, Pub. by Ajanta). South Asia Bks.

Science of Numerology. Sepharial. LC 86-33462. 128p. 1986. lib. bdg. 19.95x (ISBN 0-89370-692-2). Borgo Pr.

Science of Numerology. Sepharial. 128p. 1986. pap. 7.95 (ISBN 0-87877-092-5). Newcastle Pub.

Science of Nutrition & Its Application in Clinical Dentistry. 2nd ed. Abraham E. Nizel. LC 66-18501. (Illus.). pap. 122.50 (ISBN 0-317-07920-4, 2013534). Bks Demand UMI.

Science of Opticianry see Opticianry: The Practice & the Art.

Science of Ornithology. Fretwell. 1988. price not set (ISBN 0-471-89107-X). Wiley.

Science of Personal Success: How to Turn Your Life into a World of Endless Success. rev., 2nd ed. Leroy Smith, Jr. Ed. by Carolyn McKay. (Illus.). 101p. (Orig.). 1985. pap. 6.95x (ISBN 0-915455-01-3). Prestige Ent.

Science of Philosophy. F. H. George. 336p. 1981. 57.00 (ISBN 0-677-05550-1). Gordon & Breach.

Science of Photobiology. Ed. by K. C. Smith. LC 77-2130. 442p. 1977. 55.00x (ISBN 0-306-31051-1, Plenum Pr.); pap. 29.50x (ISBN 0-306-20029-5). Plenum Pub.

Science of Photobiology. Ed. by K. C. Smith. (Illus.). 470p. Date not set. price not set (ISBN 0-306-43049-5, Plenum Pr); pap. price not set (ISBN 0-306-43059-2, Plenum Pr). Plenum Pub.

Science of Photomedicine. Ed. by James D. Regan & John A. Parrish. LC 82-9072. (Photobiology Ser.). 680p. 1982. 95.00x (ISBN 0-306-40924-0, Plenum Pr). Plenum Pub.

Science of Physiognomy. John C. Lavater. (Most Meaningful Classics in World Culture Ser.). (Illus.). 156p. 1983. Repr. of 1810 ed. 187.45 (ISBN 0-89901-100-4). Found Class Reprints.

Science of Political Economy. Henry George. LC 81-5939. 545p. (Also avail. in Span.). 1981. Repr. of 1898 ed. 10.00x (ISBN 0-911312-51-X). Schalkenbach.

Science of Politics: An Introduction to Hypothesis Formation & Testing. William H. Coogan & Oliver H. Woshinsky. 242p. (Orig.). 1982. lib. bdg. 29.75 (ISBN 0-8191-2652-7); pap. text ed. 13.00 (ISBN 0-8191-2653-5). U Pr of Amer.

Science of Popular Voice: Voice Production for the Pop Singer. Al Berkman. 1979. 15.95 (ISBN 0-934972-09-5); pap. 12.95. Melrose Bk Co.

Science of Programming. D. Gries. (Texts & Monographs in Computer Science). xiii, 366p. 1987. pap. text ed. 19.00 (ISBN 0-387-96480-0). Springer-Verlag.

Science of Programming. David Gries. (Texts & Monographs in Computer Science). 366p. 1981. 29.00 (ISBN 0-387-90641-X). Springer-Verlag.

Science of Providing Milk for Man. John R. Campbell & R. T. Marshall. (Agricultural Sciences Ser). 1975. text ed. 46.95 (ISBN 0-07-009690-2). McGraw.

Science of Psi: ESP & PK. Carroll B. Nash. 308p. 1978. 18.75 (ISBN 0-398-03803-1). C C Thomas.

Science of Psychic Phenomena. Swami Abhedananda. 101p. 1987. 6.95 (ISBN 0-87581-642-8, Ramakrishna Vedanta Math). Vedanta Pr.

Science of Psychology: An Interbehavioral Survey. J. R. Kantor & N. W. Smith. (Illus.). 500p. 1975. text ed. 20.00 (ISBN 0-911188-20-7). Principia Pr.

Science of Religion. LC 84-71200. pap. 10.95 (ISBN 0-937134-16-3). Amrita Found.

Science of Religion. Paramahansa Yogananda. LC 81-52892. (Illus.). 102p. 1982. 6.00 (ISBN 0-87612-004-4); Span. ed. 1.50x (ISBN 0-87612-001-X); pap. 5.00x German ed. (ISBN 3-87041-225-9); pap. 3.95 English ed. (ISBN 0-87612-005-2). Self Realization.

Science of Religion. Paramahansa Yogananda. (Dutch.). 1974. 6.50x (ISBN 90-202-45-465). Self Realization.

Science of Religion & the Sociology of Knowledge: Some Methodological Questions. Ninian Smart. LC 72-12115. 176p. 1973. 22.00x (ISBN 0-691-07191-8); pap. 9.50x (ISBN 0-691-01997-5). Princeton U Pr.

Science of Religion, Studies in Methodology. Ed. by Lauro Honko. (Religion & Reason Ser.). 1979. text ed. 50.50x (ISBN 90-279-7854-9). Mouton.

Science of Revolution: An Introduction. Lenny Wolff. LC 80-51229. 252p. (Orig.). 1983. 15.95 (ISBN 0-89851-035-X); pap. 7.95 (ISBN 0-89851-036-8). RCP Pubns.

Science of Revolution: Fundamentals of Marxism-Leninism, Mao Tse Tung Thought & the Line of the Revolutionary Communist Party, U. S. A. Victor Wild. (Orig.). 1980. pap. 1.50 (ISBN 0-89851-038-4). RCP Pubns.

Science of Self Realization. Swami Bhaktivedanta. (Illus.). 1977. 3.95 (ISBN 0-89213-101-2). Bhaktivedanta.

Science of Selling Alarm Systems. Norman C. Eisenstat. 180p. 1984. text ed. 22.95 (ISBN 0-409-95118-8). Butterworth.

Science of Social Redemption: McGill, The Chicago School, & the Origins of Social Research in Canada. Marlene Shore. 1987. 37.50x (ISBN 0-8020-5733-0); pap. 16.95 (ISBN 0-8020-6645-3). U of Toronto Pr.

Science of Society. Stephen P. Andrews. 69.95 (ISBN 0-8490-1003-9). Gordon Pr.

Science of Society. Stephen Pearl Andrews. Ed. by Charles Shively. 184p. 1970. 15.00X (ISBN 0-87730-004-6). M&S Pr.

Science of Society: Toward an Understanding of the Life & Work of Karl August Wittfogel. G. L. Ulmen. 1978. 97.50 (ISBN 90-279-7766-6). Mouton.

Science of Sound: Musical, Electronic, Environmental. Thomas D. Rossing. LC 80-12028. (Chemistry Ser.). (Illus.). 512p. 1982. text ed. write for info. (ISBN 0-201-06505-3). Addison-Wesley.

Science of Space-Time. Derek J. Raine & Michael Heller. (Astronomy & Astrophysics Ser.: Vol. 9). (Illus.). 256p. 1981. text ed. 38.00 (ISBN 0-912918-12-8, 0012). Pachart Pub Hse.

Science of Speech. B. Dunville. 1909. 12.50 (ISBN 0-8274-3339-5). R West.

Science of Speleology. Ed. by T. D. Ford. 1976. 80.50 (ISBN 0-12-262550-1). Acad Pr.

Science of Spiritual Alchemy. R. Swinburne Clymer. 235p. 1959. 9.95 (ISBN 0-932785-44-1). Philos Pub.

Science of Spirituality. M. K. Khan. 135p. 1983. text ed. 15.00x (ISBN 0-86590-164-3). Apt Bks.

Science of Sports. Ed. by Knowledge Unlimited Staff. (Illus.). 26p. (gr. 7-12). Tchr's guide & color filmstrip 13.00 (ISBN 0-317-14844-3). Know Unltd.

Science of Sports Training: How to Plan & Control Training for Peak Preformance. Thomas Kurz. 300p. (Orig.). Date not set. lib. bdg. price not set (ISBN 0-940149-00-1); pap. price not set (ISBN 0-940149-01-X). Stadion Pub.

Science of Stretching. Michael J. Alter. LC 87-2952. 256p. 1988. text ed. 26.00x (ISBN 0-87322-090-0, BALT0090). Human Kinetics.

Science of Structures & Materials. J. E. Gordon. LC 87-35412. 240p. 1988. 32.95 (ISBN 0-7167-5022-8). W H Freeman.

Science of Successful Living. Raymond C. Barker. LC 57-11392. 145p. 1984. pap. 5.50 (ISBN 0-87516-536-2). DeVorss.

Science of Survival. L. Ron Hubbard. 31.00 (ISBN 0-686-30779-8). Church Scient NY.

Science of Survival: Prediction of Human Behavior. L. Ron Hubbard. LC 51-5566. (Illus.). 550p. 1951. 47.16 (ISBN 0-88404-001-1). Bridge Pubns Inc.

Science of Swimming. James Counsilman. 1968. ref. ed. 34.00 (ISBN 0-13-795385-2). P-H.

Science of Teaching Art. Mitchell Terry. 1986. 20.00x (ISBN 0-931510-14-7). Hi Willow.

Science of Tennis. David J. Anderson & Robert M. Anderson. (Illus.). 146p. (Orig.). 1985. pap. 12.75 (ISBN 0-9617528-0-7). Racquet Pr.

Science of the Amazon. Anthony Smith. Date not set. write for info. (ISBN 0-670-81311-7). Viking.

Science of the Early American Indians. Beulah Tannenbaum & Harold E. Tannenbaum. Ed. by Henry Rasof. (First Bk.). (Illus.). 96p. (gr. 5-8). 1988. 9.90 (ISBN 0-531-10488-5). Watts.

Science of the Mind. Owen J. Flanagan, Jr. (Illus.). 384p. (Orig.). 1984. (Pub. by Bradford Bks); pap. text ed. 13.50x (ISBN 0-262-56031-3). MIT Pr.

Science of the Oneness of Being in the Christian Science Textbook. Max Kappeler. LC 82-81131. 300p. 1983. 22.00 (ISBN 0-942958-03-9). Kappeler Inst Pub.

Science of the Paranormal: The Last Frontier. Lawrence LeShan. (Illus.). 208p. (Orig.). 1987. pap. 12.95 (ISBN 0-85030-628-0, Pub. by Aquarian Pr). Sterling.

Science of the Sacraments. Leadbeater. 17.95 (ISBN 0-8356-7126-7). Theos Pub Hse.

Science of the Singing Voice. Johan Sundberg. LC 87-5499. 1987. 35.00 (ISBN 0-87580-120-X). N Ill U pr.

Science of the Soul. R. Swinburne Clymer. 1944. 4.95 (ISBN 0-686-00828-6). Philos Pub.

Science of the Spoken Word. Mark Prophet & Elizabeth Prophet. LC 74-82293. (Illus.). 242p. 1974. pap. 7.95 (ISBN 0-916766-07-1). Summit Univ.

Science of the Times: No. 4. 1981. write for info. Ayer Co Pubs.

Science of the Times, Vol. 3: A New York Times Survey. Ed. by Arleen Keylin. 16.95 (ISBN 0-405-13094-5). Ayer Co Pubs.

Science of Thought. Friedrich M. Mueller. LC 73-18813. Repr. of 1887 ed. 42.75 (ISBN 0-404-11453-9). AMS Pr.

Science of Trapping. E. Kreps. (Illus.). 229p. pap. 3.50 (ISBN 0-936622-19-9). A R Harding Pub.

Science of Triathlon Training & Competition. Glenn P. Town. LC 84-25259. 154p. 1985. text ed. 16.00x (ISBN 0-931250-82-X, BTOW0082). Human Kinetics.

Science of Triathlon Training & Competition. Glenn P. Town. LC 87-25259. (Illus.). 160p. 1988. pap. 11.95x (ISBN 0-87322-182-6). Human Kinetics.

Science of Violin Playing. 2nd ed. Raphael Bronstein. 288p. 1981. 25.00 (ISBN 0-87666-638-1, Z-10). Paganiniana Pubns.

Science of Vocal Pedagogy: Theory & Application. D. Ralph Appelman. LC 67-10107. (Illus.). 448p. 1967. 40.00x (ISBN 0-253-35110-3); companion cassettes of 3 tapes 17.95 (ISBN 0-253-35115-4); Tape 1 Soprano & Mezzo Soprano. 7.95x (ISBN 0-253-35112-X); Tape 2 Tenor & Bass. 7.95x (ISBN 0-253-35113-8); Tape 3 Two Songs. 7.95x (ISBN 0-253-35114-6). Ind U Pr.

Science of Vocal Pedagogy: Theory & Application. D. Ralph Appelman. LC 67-10107. (Midland Bks Ser.: No. 378). (Illus.). 448p. 1986. pap. 17.50x (ISBN 0-253-20378-3). Ind U Pr.

Science of War. G. F. Henderson. 1977. lib. bdg. 59.95 (ISBN 0-8490-2572-9). Gordon Pr.

Science of Wealth. 7th ed. A. Walker. 1874. 32.00 (ISBN 0-527-93980-3). Kraus Repr.

Science of Yoga. Taimni. 13.95 (ISBN 0-8356-7140-2). Theos Pub Hse.

Science of Yoga. I. K. Taimni. LC 67-4112. pap. 7.50 (ISBN 0-8356-0023-8, Quest). Theos Pub Hse.

Science of Zoology. 2nd ed. Paul B. Weisz. LC 72-4172. (Illus.). 1972. text ed. 42.95 (ISBN 0-07-069135-5). McGraw.

Science Off the Pedestal: Social Perspectives on Science & Technology. Daryl E. Chubin & Ellen W. Chu. Date not set. pap. text ed. write for info. (ISBN 0-534-09858-4). Wadsworth Pub.

Science on Form. Ed. by S. Ishizaka et al. 1987. lib. bdg. 129.00 (ISBN 90-277-2390-7, Pub. by Reidel Holland). Kluwer Academic.

Science on Trial. Douglas Futuyma. 1982. 16.00 (ISBN 0-394-52371-7); pap. 8.95 (ISBN 0-394-70679-X). Pantheon.

Science, Order, Creativity. David Bohm & F. David Peat. LC 87-47570. 1250p. (Orig.). 1987. pap. 8.95 (ISBN 0-553-34449-8, New Age Bks). Bantam.

Science Parks & Innovation Centres: Their Economic & Social Impact: Proceedings of the International Conference Held in Berlin, 13-15 Feb. 1985. Ed. by J. M. Gibb. 478p. 1985. 92.00 (ISBN 0-444-42544-6). Elsevier.

Science Parks & the Growth of High Technology Firms. C. S. Monck et al. 224p. 1988. lib. bdg. 69.50 (ISBN 0-415-00092-0). Routledge Chapman & Hall.

Science: People, Concepts, Processes see Gateways to Science.

Science, Philosophy & ESP. Charles McCreery. 1977. 20.00x (ISBN 0-900076-03-8, Pub. by Inst Psych Res). State Mutual Bk.

Science, Philosophy, & Human Behavior in the Soviet Union. Loren R. Graham. LC 86-26357. 672p. 1987. 45.00 (ISBN 0-231-06442-X). Columbia U Pr.

Science, Philosophy & Religion. John Bascom. LC 75-3041. Repr. of 1871 ed. 36.00 (ISBN 0-404-59039-X). AMS Pr.

Science, Philosophy & Religion. 559p. 1985. Repr. of 1942 ed. lib. bdg. 85.00 (ISBN 0-8492-3208-2). R West.

Science, Philosophy, & Religion: Proceedings. Conference on Science, Philosophy & Religion in Their Relation to the Democratic Way of Life. 3rd. 1943. 40.00 (ISBN 0-527-00650-5). Kraus Repr.

Science, Philosophy, & Religion: Proceedings. Conference on Science, Philosophy & Religion in Their Relation to the Democratic Way of Life, 2nd. 1942. 40.00 (ISBN 0-527-00649-1). Kraus Repr.

Science, Philosophy, & Religion: Proceedings. Conference on Science, Philosophy & Religion & Their Relation to the Democratic Way of Life, 1st. 1941. 40.00 (ISBN 0-527-00648-3). Kraus Repr.

Science Plus Sentiment: Cesar Daly's Formula for Modern Architecture. Richard Becherer. Ed. by Stephen C. Foster. LC 84-2453. (Architecture & Urban Design Ser.: No. 7). 452p. 1984. 54.95 (ISBN 0-8357-1566-3). UMI Res Pr.

Science Policy & Business: The Changing Relations of Europe & the United States. Ed. by David W. Ewing. LC 72-86387. 140p. 1973. 8.95x (ISBN 0-674-79460-5, Pub. by Harvard Busn. School). Harvard U Pr.

Science Policy & Development. E. Tal & Y. Ezrachi. 362p. 1971. 62.00x (ISBN 0-677-60185-9). Gordon & Breach.

Science Policy & National Development. Vikram A. Sarabhai. Ed. by Kamla Chowdhry. LC 74-903458. 1974. 9.00x (ISBN 0-333-90057-X). South Asia Bks.

Science Policy, Ethics, & Economic Methodology. Kristin S. Shrader-Frechette. 1985. lib. bdg. 39.50 (ISBN 90-277-1806-7, Pub. by Reidel Holland); pap. text ed. 19.50 (ISBN 90-277-1845-8, Pub. by Reidel Holland). Kluwer Academic.

Science Policy for Britain. Tam Dalyell. LC 83-190946. pap. 35.30 (2027714). Bks Demand UMI.

Science Policy from Ford to Reagan: Change & Continuity. Claude E. Barfield. 142p. 1983. 19.75 (ISBN 0-8447-3495-0); pap. 9.00 (ISBN 0-8447-3494-2). Am Enterprise.

Science Policy Making in the United States & the Batavia Accelerator. Anton G. Jachim. LC 74-26633. 220p. 1975. 9.95x (ISBN 0-8093-0674-3). S Ill U Pr.

Science Policy Perspectives U. S. A.: The U. S. & Japan (Symposium) Ed. by Arthur Gerstenfeld. LC 82-18159. 1982. 34.50 (ISBN 0-12-281280-8). Acad Pr.

Science Policy Studies. A. Rahman & K. D. Sharma. 1974. 11.25 (ISBN 0-89684-555-9). Orient Bk Dist.

Science, Politics & Gnosticism. Eric Voegelin. LC 68-14367. 128p. 4.95 (ISBN 0-89526-964-3). Regnery Gateway.

Science, Politics, & International Conferences: A Functional Analysis of the Moscow Political Science Congress. Richard L. Merritt & Elizabeth C. Hanson. (GSIS Monograph Series in World Affairs). 1988. lib. bdg. 18.00 (ISBN 1-55587-134-8). Lynne Rienner.

Science, Politics, & International Ocean Management: The Uses of Scientific Knowledge in International Negotiations. Edward L. Miles. LC 87-81999. (Policy Papers in International Affairs: No. 33). (Illus.). viii, 70p. 1987. pap. 6.50x (ISBN 0-87725-533-4). U of Cal Intl St.

Science, Politics, & the Agricultural Revolution in Asia. Ed. by Robert S. Anderson et al. (Selected Symposium Ser.: No. 70). 450p. 1982. lib. bdg. 47.50x (ISBN 0-86531-320-2). Westview.

Science, Politics & the Cold War. Greta Jones. 208p. 1988. lib. bdg. 55.00 (ISBN 0-415-00356-3). Routledge Chapman & Hall.

Science, Politics & the Great Deception, Religion. Ruth Norman. 530p. (Orig.). 1989. text ed. 14.95 (ISBN 0-932642-93-4). Unarius Pubns.

Science Pratique de l'Imprimerie. Martin D. Fertel. (Illus.). 322p. Date not set. Repr. of 1723 ed. text ed. 53.00x (ISBN 0-576-72151-4, Pub. by Gregg Intl Pubs England). Gregg Intl.

Science Profession in the Third World: Studies from India & Kenya. Thomas O. Eisemon. Ed. by Philip G. Altbach. LC 82-7662. (Special Studies in Comparative Education). 186p. 1982. 35.00 (ISBN 0-275-90785-6, C0785). Praeger.

Science Project Puzzlers: Starter Ideas for the Curious. John G. Clark. Harris Stone. (Illus.). 61p. (gr. 7 up). 1981. pap. 4.95 (ISBN 0-13-795450-6, Pub. by Treehouse). P-H.

Science Projects & Activities. Helen J. Challand. LC 84-23252. (Science Activities Ser.). (Illus.). 93p. (gr. 5-8). 1985. lib. bdg. 14.60 (ISBN 0-516-00569-3). Childrens.

Science Projects for the Intermediate Grades. Maxine S. Schneider. LC 70-132146. (gr. 4-6). 1971. pap. 5.95 (ISBN 0-8224-6310-5). D S Lake Pubs.

Science Projects for Young People. George Barr. 153p. (gr. 5 up). 1986. pap. 3.50 (ISBN 0-486-25235-3). Dover.

Science Projects Ser. Mirrors. Hy Ruchlis. (Science-Math Projects Ser.). (Illus.). (gr. 4-9). pap. 3.50 (ISBN 0-87594-014-5). Book-Lab.

Science Projects with Computers. Elayne Schulman et al. Date not set. price not set. S&S.

Science Projects You Can Do. George K. Stone. Orig. Title: One Hundred One Science Projects. (Illus.). 101p. (gr. 7-9). 1963. (Pub. by Treehouse); pap. 4.95 (ISBN 0-13-795328-3). P-H.

Science Proves the Bible. George Carman. Ed. by Mason De Witt. 190p. 1986. 12.00 (ISBN 0-936749-00-8). Zytech Western Pub.

Science, Pseudo-Science & Society. Ed. by Marsha P. Hanen et al. 303p. 1980. pap. text ed. 17.95x (ISBN 0-88920-100-5, Pub. by Wilfrid Laurier Canada). Humanities.

Science, Psychology & Communication: Essays Honoring William Stephenson. Ed. by Steven R. Brown & Donald J. Brenner. LC 73-165607. (Foresight Books in Psychology Ser.). pap. 123.30 (ISBN 0-317-42024-0, 2025996). Bks Demand UMI.

Science Puzzlers see Entertaining Science Experiments with Everyday Objects.

Science Puzzles. Jim Anton & Jean Anton. 64p. (gr. 3-7). 1988. pap. 1.95 (ISBN 0-590-41434-8). Scholastic Inc.

Science Question in Feminism. Sandra Harding. LC 85-48197. (Paperback Ser.). 296p. 1986. 37.95x (ISBN 0-8014-1880-1); pap. 9.95x (ISBN 0-8014-9363-3). Cornell U Pr.

Science Race: Training & Utilization of Scientists & Engineers, U. S. A. & U. S. S. R. Catherine P. Ailes & Francis W. Rushing. LC 81-17516. 280p. 1982. 30.00x (ISBN 0-8448-1407-5, Pub. by Crane Russak & Co). Taylor & Francis.

Science, Reason & Religion. Derek Stanesby. 210p. 1985. 34.50 (ISBN 0-7099-3360-6, Pub. by Croom Helm Ltd). Routledge Chapman & Hall.

Science, Religion & Tradition. Charles R. Cantonwine. 1986. 7.95 (ISBN 0-533-06727-8). Vantage.

Science Restated: Physics & Chemistry for the Non-Scientist. Harold G. Cassidy. LC 72-119371. (Illus.). 538p. 1970. text ed. 12.00x (ISBN 0-87735-007-8). Freeman Cooper.

Science Safety for Elementary Teachers. Ed. by Gary E. Downs & Jack A. Gerlovich. (Illus.). 102p. 1983. pap. text ed. 10.95x (ISBN 0-8138-1641-6). Iowa St U PR.

Science Sampler. Sandra Markle. (Computers & Science Ser.). 112p. (gr. 4-8). 1980. 8.95 (ISBN 0-88160-031-8, LW 216). Learning Wks.

Science, Scientists & Public Policy. D. Schooler. LC 70-122274. 1971. pap. text ed. 4.50 (ISBN 0-02-928010-9). Free Pr.

Science Secrets. Robyn Supraner. LC 80-23794. (Illus.). 48p. (gr. 1-5). 1981. PLB 9.49 (ISBN 0-89375-426-9); pap. 1.95 (ISBN 0-89375-427-7). Troll Assocs.

Science Sensations: An Activity Book from the Children's Museum, Boston. Diane Willow & Emily Curran. 1988. pap. 8.95 (ISBN 0-201-07189-4). Addison-Wesley.

Science: Sense & Nonsense. John L. Synge. LC 72-8534. (Essay Index Reprint Ser.). 1972. Repr. of 1951 ed. 17.00 (ISBN 0-8369-7332-1). Ayer Co Pubs.

Science Serving Faith. Henry N. Wieman. Ed. by Creighton Peden & Charles L. Willig. LC 87-9441. (American Academy of Religion Studies in Religion). 200p. 1987. 19.95 (ISBN 1-55540-131-7, 01-00-46); pap. 14.95 (ISBN 1-55540-132-5). Scholars Pr GA.

Science, Sin & Scholarship: The Politics of Reverend Moon & the Unification Church. Ed. by Irving L. Horowitz. 312p. 1978. pap. 7.95x (ISBN 0-262-58042-X). MIT Pr.

Science since Babylon. enl. ed. Derek D. Price. 1975. pap. 9.95x (ISBN 0-300-01798-7). Yale U Pr.

Science since Fifteen-Hundred: A Short History of Mathematics, Physics, Chemistry, Biology. H. T. Pledge. 11.75 (ISBN 0-8446-0850-5). Peter Smith.

Science Sketches. new & enl. ed. David S. Jordan. (Essay Index Reprint Ser.). Repr. of 1896 ed. 18.00 (ISBN 0-518-10181-9). Ayer Co Pubs.

Science, Society & Philosophy: A New Radical Humanist Approach. Oroon K. Ghosh. 1986. 28.00x (ISBN 0-8364-1563-9, Pub. by Ajanta). South Asia Bks.

Science Speaks to Power: The Role of Experts in Policymaking. David Collingridge & Colin Reeve. LC 86-3907. 180p. 1986. 27.50 (ISBN 0-312-70274-4). St Martin.

Science, Students, & Schools: A Guide for the Middle & Secondary Teacher. Ronald D. Simpson & Norman D. Anderson. LC 80-23124. 558p. 1981. write for info. (ISBN 0-02-410530-9). Macmillan.

Science: Studies in the Life Sciences in Ancient Greece. G. E. Lloyd. LC 82-19808. 300p. 1983. 57.50 (ISBN 0-521-25314-4); pap. 19.95 (ISBN 0-521-27307-2). Cambridge U Pr.

Science Studies Yoga. James Funderburk. 270p. (Orig.). pap. 8.95 (ISBN 0-89389-026-X). Himalayan Pubs.

Science Study Skills Workshop Kit. HM Study Skills Group. (gr. 7-9). 1983. pap. 18.75 (ISBN 0-88210-152-8). Natl Assn Principals.

Science Surprises. (First Science Ser.). (Illus.). 32p. (gr. 2-5). 1986. pap. 3.95 (ISBN 0-86020-914-8). EDC.

Science, Synthesis, & Sanity. G. Scott Williamson & Innes H. Pearse. 352p. 1980. pap. 13.00x (ISBN 0-7073-0259-5, Pub. by Scot Acad Pr). Longwood Pub Group.

Science Teacher Education at Museums: A Resource Guide. Ed. & frwd. by Jacalyn Bedworth. LC 20-80737. (Illus.). 48p. (Orig.). 1985. pap. 12.00 (ISBN 0-944040-06-3). AST Ctrs.

Science Teaching: A Profession Speaks: 1983 NSTA Yearbook. Ed. by David P. Butts & Faith K. Brown. 122p. (Orig.). 1983. pap. text ed. 6.00 (ISBN 0-87355-041-2). Natl Sci Tchrs.

Science Teaching & Career Awareness. Ed. by John Penick. 34p. 1987. pap. 7.00 (ISBN 0-317-66010-1). Natl Sci Tchrs.

Science Teaching in Schools. R. C. Das. 1986. text ed. 30.00x (ISBN 81-207-0037-6, Pub. by Sterling Pubs India). Apt Bks.

Science Teaching: Junior & Senior High School Levels. George W. Hunter. 1978. Repr. of 1934 ed. lib. bdg. 35.00 (ISBN 0-8495-2320-6). Arden Lib.

Science Teaching Methods in the Elementary School. Harold Hungerford & A. Tomera. 1985. pap. 12.80x (ISBN 0-87563-260-2). Stipes.

Science, Technology, & American Foreign Policy. Eugene B. Skolnikoff. 1967. pap. 6.95x (ISBN 0-262-69019-5). MIT Pr.

Science, Technology & China's Drive for Modernization. Richard P. Suttmeier. LC 79-88587. (Publication: No. 223). 133p. 1980. pap. 8.95x (ISBN 0-8179-7232-3). Hoover Inst Pr.

Science, Technology, & Culture. Ed. by Henry J. Steffens & H. N. Mueller, III. LC 74-580. (Studies in Modern Society: Political & Social Issues: No. 5). 32.50 (ISBN 0-404-11275-7). AMS Pr.

Science, Technology, & Development. Atul Wad. (Special Studies in Social, Political, & Economic Development). 300p. 1988. 28.50 (ISBN 0-8133-7410-3, Published in Cooperation with the Third World Foundation). Westview.

Science, Technology & Development in Afghanistan. D. Gopa & M. A. Qureshi. 1987. 25.00x (ISBN 81-7013-042-5, Pub. by Navrang). South Asia Bks.

Science, Technology & Development: Political Economy of Technical Advance in Underdeveloped Countries. Ed. by Charles Cooper. 204p. 1973. 29.50x (ISBN 0-7146-2999-5, F Cass Co). Biblio Dist.

Science, Technology & Development: The Consensus of Brasilia see Americas: Supplement Series.

Science, Technology & Development: The Politics of Modernization. Thomas W. Wilson, Jr. LC 79-53795. (Headline Ser.: No. 245). (Illus., Orig.). 1979. pap. 4.00 (ISBN 0-87124-055-6). Foreign Policy.

Science, Technology & Economic Development in China. V. P. Karbandha. 226p. 1987. 31.00x (ISBN 81-7013-043-3, Pub. by Navrang). South Asia Bks.

Science, Technology & Economic Growth in the Developing Countries. Ed. by G. E. Skorov. 1978. text ed. 42.00 (ISBN 0-08-022223-4). Pergamon.

Science, Technology & Global Problems: Issues of Development: Towards a New Role for Science & Technology. International Symposium on Science & Technology for Development, Singapore, 1979. Ed. by Maurice Goldsmith & Alexander King. LC 79-40879. (Illus.). 200p. 1979. 77.00 (ISBN 0-08-024691-5). Pergamon.

Science, Technology & Global Problems, 4 vols. 1980. Set. 250.00 (ISBN 0-08-025235-4, PBL). Pergamon.

Science, Technology & Global Problems: Science & Technology in Development Planning. International Symposium on Science & Technology for Development, Mexico City, 1979. Ed. by Victor L. Urquidi. LC 79-40912. 200p. 1979. 63.00 (ISBN 0-08-025227-3). Pergamon.

Science, Technology & Global Problems: The United Nations Advisory Committee on the Application of Science & Technology to Development. Office for Science & Technology. 62p. 1979. 25.00 (ISBN 0-08-025131-5). Pergamon.

Science Technology & Global Problems-Views from the Developing World. Ed. by S. Radhakrishna. (Illus.). 1980. 69.00 (ISBN 0-08-024489-0). Pergamon.

Science, Technology & Governmental Policy: A Ministerial Conference for Europe & North America (Minespol II) (Science Policy Studies & Documents: No. 44). 183p. 1979. pap. 7.50 (ISBN 92-3-101718-7, U943, UNESCO). UNIPUB.

Science, Technology & Innovation: A Research Bibliography. Ed. by Felicity Henwood & Graham Thomas. LC 83-40179. 264p. 1984. 27.95 (ISBN 0-312-70281-7). St Martin.

Science, Technology & National Policy. Thomas J. Kuehn & Alan L. Porter. (Illus.). 608p. 1981. 46.50x (ISBN 0-8014-1343-5); pap. 15.95x (ISBN 0-8014-9876-7). Cornell U Pr.

Science, Technology & Policy Decisions. Anne L. Hiskes & Richard P. Hiskes. 194p. 1986. 35.00 (ISBN 0-86531-631-7); pap. 15.95 (ISBN 0-86531-632-5). Westview.

Science, Technology, & Politics in a Changing World. 9p. 1980. pap. 5.00 (ISBN 92-808-0243-7, TUNU123, UNU). UNIPUB.

Science, Technology, & Public Policy. Richard Barke. 245p. 1986. pap. 11.95 (ISBN 0-87187-394-X). Congr Quarterly.

Science Technology & Social Change. 1985. 2.50 (ISBN 0-471-63895-1). Wiley.

Science, Technology & Society. Ed. by Lynchburg College Faculty Staff. LC 81-71947. (Classical Selections on Great Issues, Symposium Readings: Series 2, Vol. 2). 468p. 1982. lib. bdg. 25.25 (ISBN 0-8191-2297-1); pap. text ed. 9.75 (ISBN 0-8191-2298-X). U Pr of Amer.

Science, Technology, & Society Education & Citizen Participation. Leonard J. Waks. (Working Papers on Citizenship). Date not set. 2.50 (PC1). IPPP.

Science, Technology, & Society: Emerging Relationships. Ed. by Rosemary Chalk. 300p. 1988. pap. 14.95 (ISBN 0-87168-332-6). AAAS.

Science, Technology & Society in Seventeenth Century England. R. Merton. LC 79-82308. 1970. 35.00x (ISBN 0-86527-178-X). Fertig.

Science, Technology & Society in the Modern Age. S. P. Gupta. 1977. 18.00x (ISBN 0-686-22672-0). Intl Bk Dist.

Science, Technology & Society in the Time of Alfred Nobel: Proceedings of a Nobel Symposium held at Bjorkborn, Karlskoga, Sweden, August 17-22, 1981. Ed. by C. G. Bernhard & E. Crawford. LC 82-11254. (Illus.). 440p. 1982. 87.00 (ISBN 0-08-027939-2). Pergamon.

Science, Technology & Society-Needs, Challenges & Limitations: Proceedings. International Colloquium on Science, Technology & Society, Vienna, 1979. Ed. by Klaus-Heinrich Standke. (Pergamon Policy Studies on International Development). 656p. 1980. 155.00 (ISBN 0-08-025947-2). Pergamon.

Science, Technology & Society Today. Ed. by Michael Gibbons & Philip Gummett. LC 83-20639. 192p. 1984. 25.00 (ISBN 0-7190-1090-X, Pub. by Manchester Univ Pr); pap. text ed. 9.00 (ISBN 0-7190-0878-6). St Martin.

Science, Technology, & the First Amendment, Special Report. LC 87-619879. (OTA-CIT Ser.: No. 369). (Illus.). 78p. (Orig.). 1988. pap. 3.50 (S/N 052-003-01090-9). USGPO.

Science, Technology & the Future: Soviet Scientists Analysis of the Problems of & Prospects for the Development of Science & Technology & Their Role in Society. Ed. by E. P. Velikhov et al. LC 79-40113. (Illus.). 480p. 1980. 52.00 (ISBN 0-08-024743-1). Pergamon.

Science, Technology & the Modern Industrial State. Keith Pavitt & Michael Worboye. (Sicon Bks.). 1977. pap. 6.95 (ISBN 0-408-71299-6). Butterworth.

Science, Technology & the Nuclear Arms Race. Dietrich Schroeer. LC 84-7379. 432p. 1984. pap. write for info. (ISBN 0-471-88141-4). Wiley.

Science, Technology & the Social Order. Ed. by Ward Morehouse. LC 79-65035. (Illus.). 150p. 1979. pap. text ed. 4.95 (ISBN 0-87855-797-0). Transaction Bks.

Science-Technology-Society. Ed. by John Penick & Richard Meinhard-Pellens. 104p. 1984. pap. 7.00 (ISBN 0-317-65996-0). Natl Sci Tchrs.

Science-Technology-Society: A Framework for Curriculum Reform in Secondary School Science & Social Studies. Faith M. Hickman et al. 58p. (Orig.). 1987. pap. 6.95 (ISBN 0-89994-313-6). Soc Sci Ed.

Science-Technology-Society: Model Lessons for Secondary Science Classes. Ed. by Janice V. Pearson. (Orig.). 1988. pap. 15.95 (ISBN 0-89994-316-0). Soc Sci Ed.

Science-Technology-Society: Model Lessons for Secondary Social Studies Classes. Ed. by Robert D. LaRue, Jr. (Orig.). 1988. pap. 15.95 (ISBN 0-89994-315-2). Soc Sci Ed.

Science-Technology-Society: Training Manual. Ed. by Laurel R. Singleton. (Orig.). 1988. pap. 9.95 (ISBN 0-89994-314-4). Soc Sci Ed.

Science-Technology-Society: 1985 NSTA Yearbook. Ed. by Rodger Bybee. 268p. (Orig.). 1986. pap. text ed. 7.50 (ISBN 0-87355-056-0). Natl Sci Tchrs.

Science Test. rev. ed. Harriet Diamond & Physsil Dutwin. (GED Ser.). 202p. 1985. pap. 7.65 (ISBN 0-8092-5586-3). Contemp Bks.

Science Tests & Reviews. Ed. by Oscar K. Buros. LC 75-8114. xxiii, 296p. 1975. 25.00x (ISBN 0-910674-21-3). U of Nebr Pr.

Science the Endless Frontier: A Report to the President. Vannevar Bush. Ed. by I. Bernard Cohen. LC 79-7953. (Three Cneturies of Science in America Ser.). 1980. Repr. of 1945 ed. lib. bdg. 16.00x (ISBN 0-405-12534-8). Ayer Co Pubs.

Science, Theology & Einstein. Iain Paul. (Theology & Scientific Culture Ser.). 1982. 16.95x (ISBN 0-19-520378-X). Oxford U Pr.

Science Through the Seasons. Lucia K. Henry. (gr. 1-3). 1989. pap. 5.95 (ISBN 0-8224-6304-0). D S Lake Pubs.

Science Time. Jean Warren. 80p. (gr. k-2). 1984. 7.95 (ISBN 0-912107-18-9). Monday Morning Bks.

Science To-Day & To-Morrow, Compiled from a Series of Lectures Delivered at Morley College. facs. ed. Morley College for Working Men & Women, London Staff. LC 67-30231. (Essay Index Reprint Ser). 1932. 17.00 (ISBN 0-8369-0857-0). Ayer Co Pubs.

Science Toys & Tricks. Laurence B. White. LC 84-40787. 1980. pap. 4.95 (ISBN 0-201-08659-X, Lipp Jr Bks). HarpJ.

Science Travel Guide: The Guide to Technological Expositions, Museums, Landmarks, & Science Originals. Fred W. Decker. 1971. pap. 1.95X (ISBN 0-88246-017-X). Oreg St U Bkstrs.

Science Treasures: Let's Repeat the Great Experiments. Bob Brown. LC 68-23980. (Illus.). (gr. 7-12). 1968. 10.50 (ISBN 0-8303-0052-X). Fleet.

Scientific Basis for Nuclear Waste Management, VI. Ed. by D. G. Brookins. (Materials Research Society Symposia Proceedings Ser.: Vol. 15). 808p. 1983. 131.50 (ISBN 0-444-00780-6, North Holland). Elsevier.

Scientific Basis for Nuclear Waste Management. W. Lutze. (Materials Research Society Ser.: Vol. 11). 906p. 1982. 142.50 (ISBN 0-444-00725-3, North-Holland). Elsevier.

Scientific Basis for Nuclear Waste Management. Topp. (Materials Research Society Symposia Ser.: Vol. 6). 768p. 1982. 142.25 (ISBN 0-444-00699-0, North-Holland). Elsevier.

Scientific Basis for Nuclear Waste Management, Vol. 1. Ed. by Gregory J. McCarthy. LC 79-12440. 582p. 1979. 79.50x (ISBN 0-306-40181-9, Plenum Pr). Plenum Pub.

Scientific Basis for Nuclear Waste Management, Vol. 2. Ed. by Clyde J. Northrup, Jr. et al. LC 79-12440. 956p. 1980. 110.00x (ISBN 0-306-40550-4, Plenum Pr). Plenum Pub.

Scientific Basis for Nuclear Waste Management, Vol. 3. Ed. by John G. Moore. LC 81-10663. 650p. 1981. 89.50x (ISBN 0-306-40803-1, Plenum Pr). Plenum Pub.

Scientific Basis for Nuclear Waste Management IX, Vol. 50. Ed. by Lars O. Werme. (Materials Research Society Symposia Proceedings Ser.). 1986. text ed. 55.00 (ISBN 0-931837-15-4). Materials Res.

Scientific Basis for Nuclear Waste Management VIII, Vol. 44. Ed. by C. M. Jantzen et al. LC 85-5023. (Materials Research Society Symposia Proceedings Ser.). 1985. text ed. 55.00 (ISBN 0-931837-09-X). Materials Res.

Scientific Basis for Nuclear Waste Management VII: Proceedings of the 7th International Symposium on the Scientific Basis for Nuclear Waste Management, Boston, MA, Nov. 14-17, 1983. Gary L. McVay. (Material Research Society Symposia Ser.: Vol. 26). 1121p. 1984. 139.50 (ISBN 0-444-00906-X, North Holland). Elsevier.

Scientific Basis for Nuclear Waste Management X: Proceedings of Symposium Held at Mrs Fall Meeting, Boston, MA, Dec. 1-6, 1986. Ed. by J. K. Bates & W. B. Seefeldt. (MRS Symposia Proceedings Ser.: Vol. 84). 1987. text ed. 55.00 (ISBN 0-931837-49-9). Materials Res.

Scientific Basis for Soil Protection in the European Community. Ed. by H. Barth & P. L'Hermite. 629p. 1987. 115.50 (ISBN 1-85166-109-3, Pub. by Elsevier Applied Sci England). Elsevier.

Scientific Basis for the Conservation of Non-Ocean Living Aquatic Resources. (Fisheries Reports: No. 82). 19p. 1968. pap. 5.75 (ISBN 0-686-92705-2, F1740, FAO). UNIPUB.

Scientific Basis of Air Conditioning. Ken-Ichi Kimura. (Illus.). vii, 273p. 1977. 58.00 (ISBN 0-85334-732-8, Pub. by Elsevier Applied Sci England). Elsevier.

Scientific Basis of Antimicrobial Chemotherapy. Ed. by D. Greenwood & F. O'Grady. (Society for General Microbiology Symposium: No. 38). 300p. 1985. 75.00 (ISBN 0-521-30653-1). Cambridge U Pr.

Scientific Basis of Cancer Chemotheraphy. Ed. by G. Mathe. (Recent Results in Cancer Research: Vol. 21). (Illus.). 1969. 22.00 (ISBN 0-387-04683-6). Springer-Verlag.

Scientific Basis of Dermatology: A Practical Approach. Ed. by A. J. Thody & P. S. Friedman. LC 85-29930. (Illus.). 375p. 1986. text ed. 75.00 (ISBN 0-443-03013-8). Churchill.

Scientific Basis of E.D.T.A. Chelation Therapy. Bruce W. Halstead. LC 79-50861. (Illus.). 1979. 29.50 (ISBN 0-933904-03-7). Gold Quill Pubs CA.

Scientific Basis of Filtration, No. 2. Ed. by K. J. Ives. (NATO Advanced Study, Applied Science Ser.). 450p. 1975. 45.00x (ISBN 90-286-0523-1, Pub. by Sijthoff & Noordhoff). Kluwer Academic.

Scientific Basis of Flocculation. Ed. by K. J. Ives. 375p. 1978. 36.00x (ISBN 90-286-0758-7, Pub. by Sijthoff & Noordhoff). Kluwer Academic.

Scientific Basis of Flotation. K. J. Ives. 1984. lib. bdg. 56.00 (ISBN 90-247-2907-6, Pub. by Martinus Nijhoff Netherlands). Kluwer Academic.

Scientific Basis of Health & Safety Regulation. Ed. by Robert W. Crandall & Lester B. Lave. LC 81-10227. (Studies in the Regulation of Economic Activity). 309p. 1981. 32.95t (ISBN 0-8157-1600-1); pap. 12.95t (ISBN 0-8157-1599-4). Brookings.

Scientific Basis of Joint Replacement. Ed. by Sydney A. Swanson et al. LC 76-51524. (Illus.). pap. 47.50 (ISBN 0-317-07938-7, 2020342). Bks Demand UMI.

Scientific Basis of Medical Imaging. Ed. by P. N. Wells. (Illus.). 284p. 1982. text ed. 72.00 (ISBN 0-443-01986-X). Churchill.

Scientific Basis of National Progress, Including That of Morality. G. Gore. 218p. 1970. Repr. of 1882 ed. 26.00x (ISBN 0-7146-2407-1, BHA-02407, F Cass Co). Biblio Dist.

Scientific Basis of Orthopaedics. 2nd ed. James A. Albright & Richard A. Brand. 544p. 1987. 85.00 (ISBN 0-8385-8504-3, Dist. by Prentice-Hall). Appleton & Lange.

Scientific Basis of Psychiatry. Timothy G. Dinan. (Examination Notes). 144p. 1986. pap. 16.00 (ISBN 0-7236-0838-5). PSG Pub Co.

Scientific Basis of Psychiatry. Malcolm P. Weller. (Illus.). 452p. 1983. 52.00 (ISBN 0-7216-0814-0, Bailliere-Tindall). Saunders.

Scientific Basis of Social Work. Maurice J. Karpf. 424p. 1981. Repr. of 1931 ed. lib. bdg. 45.00. Arden Lib.

Scientific Basis of the Art of Teaching. N. L. Gage. LC 78-6250. 1978. pap. text ed. 8.95x (ISBN 0-8077-2537-4). Tchrs Coll.

Scientific Basis of the Care of the Critically Ill. Ed. by R. A. Little & K. N. Frayn. 432p. 1986. 66.00 (ISBN 0-7190-1769-6, Pub. by Manchester Univ Pr). St Martin.

Scientific Basis of Toxicity Assessment. Ed. by H. R. Witschi. (Developments in Toxicology & Environmental Science Ser.: Vol. 6). 330p. 1980. 95.25 (ISBN 0-444-80200-2). Elsevier.

Scientific Basis of Urology. Ed. by A. R. Mundy. LC 86-24491. (Illus.). 409p. 1987. text ed. 110.00 (ISBN 0-443-03228-9). Churchill.

Scientific Betting. pap. 2.25 (ISBN 0-685-19497-3). Powner.

Scientific Blacksmith. Mortimer E. Cooley. LC 72-5041. (Technology & Society Ser.). (Illus.). 290p. 1972. Repr. of 1947 ed. 18.00 (ISBN 0-405-04693-6). Ayer Co Pubs.

Scientific Blacksmith: An Autobiography of Mortimer E. Cooley. Mortimer E. Cooley. 290p. 1947. 4.50 (ISBN 0-317-33611-8, A00010). ASME.

Scientific Books, Libraries, & Collectors. 3rd ed. John L. Thorton & R. I. Tully. 1971. 41.50x (ISBN 0-85365-424-7, Pub. by Library Assn Pub London); suppl. 1978 24.00x (ISBN 0-85365-920-6). ALA.

Scientific Case for Creation. Bert Thompson. (That You May Believe Ser.). 47p. (Orig.). 1985. pap. 1.50 (ISBN 0-932859-03-8). Apologetic Pr.

Scientific Chiropractic. Paul Smallie. LC 84-62211. 200p. 1985. text ed. 20.00x (ISBN 0-9614296-3-1). Wrld-Wide Bks.

Scientific Christian Mental Practice. Emma C. Hopkins. 1974. pap. 8.95 (ISBN 0-87516-199-5). DeVorss.

Scientific Colonialism: A Cross-Cultural Comparison, Papers at a Conference at Melbourne, 1981. Ed. by Nathan Reingold & Marc Rothenberg. LC 85-43238. 264p. (Orig.). 1986. pap. 29.95x (ISBN 0-87474-785-6). Smithsonian.

Scientific Communications & Informatics. A. I. Mikhailov et al. Tr. by Robert H. Burger. LC 83-81012. xxxi, 402p. 1984. text ed. 55.50 (ISBN 0-87815-046-3). Info Resources.

Scientific Communications & National Security. National Academy of Science Staff. 188p. 1982. 14.50x (ISBN 0-309-03332-2). Natl Acad Pr.

Scientific Communism: A Textbook. 334p. 1982. 5.95 (ISBN 0-8285-2475-0, Pub. by Progress Pubs USSR). Imported Pubns.

Scientific Community. Warren O. Hagstrom. LC 74-18379. (Arcturus Books Paperbacks). 319p. 1975. pap. 6.95x (ISBN 0-8093-0720-0). S Ill U Pr.

Scientific Companion: Exploring the Physical World with Facts, Figures & Formulas. Cesare Emiliani. (Illus.). 256p. 1988. pap. 14.95 (ISBN 0-471-62484-5). Wiley.

Scientific Companion: Exploring the Physical World with Facts, Figures, & Formulas. Cesare Emiliani. LC 87-3010. (Science Editions Ser.). 287p. 1988. 24.95 (ISBN 0-471-62483-7). Wiley.

Scientific Computing on Vector Computers. W. Schonauer. (Special Topics in Supercomputing Ser.: No. 2). 488p. 1987. 88.00 (ISBN 0-444-70288-1, North Holland). Elsevier.

Scientific Computing: Proceedings of the IMACS World Congress on Systems, Simulation, & Scientific Computation, Tenth, Montreal, Canada, 8-13 Aug., 1982. Ed. by W. F. Ames et al. (IMACS Transactions on Scientific Computation Ser.: Vol. 1). 364p. 1983. 68.50 (ISBN 0-444-86607-8, North Holland). Elsevier.

Scientific Conference Papers & Proceedings: Contents, Influence, Value, Availability. 29p. (Orig.). 1963. pap. 5.00 (U585, UNESCO). UNIPUB.

Scientific Conscience. Catherine Roberts. 1985. 30.00x (ISBN 0-900000-82-1, Pub. by Centaur Bks). State Mutual Bk.

Scientific Conscience: Reflections on the Modern Biologist & Humanism. Catherine Roberts. 1974. 17.95 (ISBN 0-8464-0819-8). Beekman Pubs.

Scientific Consideration in Monitoring & Evaluating Toxicological Research. E. J. Gralla. 1981. text ed. 29.50 (ISBN 0-07-024047-7). McGraw.

Scientific Considerations in Monitoring & Evaluating Toxicological Research. Ed. by E. J. Gralla. LC 80-21367. (Chemical Industry Institute of Toxicology Ser.). (Illus.). 221p. 1980. text ed. 46.75 (ISBN 0-89116-209-7). Hemisphere Pub.

Scientific Controversies: Case Studies in the Resolution & Closure of Disputes in Sciences & Technology. Ed. by H. Tristram Engelhardt, Jr. & Arthur Caplan. 704p. 1987. 59.50 (ISBN 0-521-25565-1); pap. 19.95 (ISBN 0-521-27560-1). Cambridge U Pr.

Scientific Cooperation for Development: Search for New Directions. Ed. by P. J. Lavakare et al. 216p. 1980. text ed. 16.95x (ISBN 0-7069-0955-0, Pub. by Vikas India). Advent NY.

Scientific Correspondence: Ninety-Seven Letters. Joseph Priestley. LC 5-5452. 1968. Repr. of 1892 ed. 29.00 (ISBN 0-527-72728-8). Kraus Repr.

Scientific Creationism. Ed. by Henry M. Morris et al. LC 74-14160. 1974. pap. 8.95 (ISBN 0-89051-003-2). Master Bks.

Scientific Creativity. Calvin W. Taylor. LC 74-12118. 444p. 1975. Repr. of 1963 ed. 27.50 (ISBN 0-88275-182-4). Krieger.

Scientific Credibility of Freud's Theories & Therapy. Seymour Fisher & Roger P. Greenberg. LC 85-9722. 502p. 1985. 32.50x (ISBN 0-231-06214-1); pap. 15.00x (ISBN 0-231-06215-X). Columbia U Pr.

Scientific Death Investigation: Proceedings, 47th Annual Anatomic Pathology Slide Seminar. Charles S. Petty et al. LC 83-12272. (Proceedings of AP Slide Seminar Ser.). (Illus.). 145p. 1983. pap. 28.00 (ISBN 0-89189-175-7, 50-1-048-00). Am Soc Clinical.

Scientific Demonstration of the Future Life. Thomas Hudson. 1979. pap. 2.50 (ISBN 0-89083-464-4). Zebra.

Scientific Design of Exhaust & Intake Systems. 3rd rev. ed. Philip H. Smith & John C. Morrison. LC 72-86569. (Illus.). 294p. 1972. 16.95 (ISBN 0-8376-0309-9). Bentley.

Scientific Diet Management for Business Executives. (Illus.). 131p. 1985. 97.75 (ISBN 0-86654-149-7). Inst Econ Finan.

Scientific Discoveries & Soviet Law: A Sociohistorical Analysis. James M. Swanson. LC 84-12020. (University of Florida Social Sciences Monographs: No. 70). viii, 150p. 1985. pap. 13.50x (ISBN 0-8130-0805-0). U Presses Fla.

Scientific Discovery: Case Studies. Ed. by Thomas Nickles. (Boston Studies in the Philosophy of Science: No. 60). 386p. 1980. lib. bdg. 36.50 (ISBN 90-277-1092-9, Pub. by Reidel Holland); pap. 16.00 (ISBN 90-277-1093-7). Kluwer Academic.

Scientific Discovery: Computational Explorations of the Creative Processes. Patrick Langley et al. (Illus.). 344p. 1987. text ed. 25.00x (ISBN 0-262-12116-6); pap. 9.95 (ISBN 0-262-62052-9). MIT Pr.

Scientific Discovery, Logic & Rationality. Ed. by Thomas Nickles. (Boston Studies in the Philosophy of Science: No. 56). 400p. 1980. lib. bdg. 36.50 (ISBN 90-277-1069-4, Pub. by Reidel Holland); pap. 16.00 (ISBN 90-277-1070-8). Kluwer Academic.

Scientific Dressing: Your Precise Image. Marilyn Curtin & Mary B. Hall. (Illus.). 104p. (Orig.). 1985. pap. 9.95 (ISBN 0-9615141-9-1). Ro Lyn Pub.

Scientific Elite: Nobel Laureates in the United States. Harriet Zuckerman. LC 76-26444. (Illus.). 1979. 14.95 (ISBN 0-02-935760-8); pap. text ed. 7.95 (ISBN 0-02-935880-9). Free Pr.

Scientific Encounters of Curious Kind. Lynn Embry. (Illus.). 64p. (gr. 4-7). 1984. wkbk 6.95 (ISBN 0-86653-176-9). Good Apple.

Scientific Encounters of the Endangered Kind. Lynn Embry. 64p. (gr. 4-7). 1986. 6.95wkbk. (ISBN 0-86653-353-2). Good Apple.

Scientific Encounters of the Insect World. Lynn Embry. 64p. (gr. 4-7). Date not set. wkbk. 6.95 (ISBN 0-86653-424-5, GA1039). Good Apple.

Scientific Encounters of the Mysterious Sea. Lynn Embry. (Illus.). 64p. (gr. 4-7). 1987. pap. 6.95 (ISBN 0-86653-407-5, GA1013). Good Apple.

Scientific Endeavor. Ed. by H. Jordan & E. Kone. LC 65-18302. (Illus.). 340p. 1965. 6.00x (ISBN 0-87470-004-3); pap. 3.50x. Rockefeller.

Scientific Enigmas. Robert B. Downs. xiv, 154p. 1987. lib. bdg. 17.50 (ISBN 0-87287-617-9). Libs Unl.

Scientific Enterprise, Today & Tomorrow. Adriano A. Buzzati-Traverso. (Illus.). 439p. 1978. 33.75 (ISBN 92-3-101268-1, U865, UNESCO). UNIPUB.

Scientific Establishments & Hierarchies. N. Elias & R. Whitley. 1982. 42.50 (ISBN 90-277-1322-7, Pub. by Reidel Holland); pap. 19.95 (ISBN 90-277-1323-5). Kluwer Academic.

Scientific Estate. Don K. Price. LC 65-22047. 1965. 29.95x (ISBN 0-674-79485-0, Belknap Pr). Harvard U Pr.

Scientific Evidence. Paul C. Giannelli & Edward J. Imwinkelried. (Contemporary Litigation Ser.). 1252p. 1986. with 1987 supplement 75.00x (ISBN 0-87215-936-1). Michie Co.

Scientific Evidence for Dietary Targets in Europe. Ed. by J. C. Somogyi & A. Trichopoulou. (Bibliotheca Nutritio et Dieta: No. 37). (Illus.). vi, 162p. 1985. 100.00 (ISBN 3-8055-4161-9). S Karger.

Scientific Evidence in Criminal Cases. 3rd ed. Andre A. Moenssens & Fred E. Inbau. 815p. 1986. text ed. 32.95 (ISBN 0-88277-281-3). Foundation Pr.

Scientific Evidence of the Existence of the Soul. Benito F. Reyes. LC 70-122432. 259p. Date not set. 10.00. World Univ Amer.

Scientific Evolution of Psychology, 2 Vols. J. R. Kantor. 1963-1969. Set. 40.00 (ISBN 0-911188-25-8). Principia Pr.

Scientific Examination of Questioned Documents. rev. ed. O. Hilton. (Forensic & Police Science Ser.: Vol. 2). 424p. 1981. 62.50 (ISBN 0-444-00628-1). Elsevier.

Scientific Excellence: Origins & Assessment. Ed. by Douglas N Jackson. LC 86-1839. 360p. text ed. 28.00 (ISBN 0-8039-2724-X). Sage.

Scientific Exercise Training. 2nd ed. Zebas-Thomas. 192p. 1987. pap. text ed. 15.95 (ISBN 0-8403-4184-9). Kendall-Hunt.

Scientific Experiments for Manned Orbital Flight: Proceedings of the Goddard Memorial Symposium, 3rd, Washington, D.C., 1965. Ed. by P. C. Badgley. (Science & Technology Ser.: Vol. 4). 1965. 30.00x (ISBN 0-87703-032-4, Pub. by Am Astronaut). Univelt Inc.

Scientific Explanation. Nicholas Rescher. LC 71-80675. 1970. 14.95 (ISBN 0-02-926330-1). Free Pr.

Scientific Explanation & Atomic Physics. Edward M. MacKinnon. LC 82-2702. (Illus.). 464p. 1982. lib. bdg. 31.00X (ISBN 0-226-50053-5). U of Chicago Pr.

Scientific Explanation & the Causal Structure of the World. Wesley C. Salmon. LC 84-42562. 304p. 1984. text ed. 39.00x (ISBN 0-691-07293-0); pap. 15.95x (ISBN 0-691-10170-1). Princeton U Pr.

Scientific Explanation & Understanding: Essays on Reasoning & Rationality. Ed. by Nicholas Rescher. LC 83-14815. (CPS Publications in Philosophy of Science). 156p. (Orig.). 1983. lib. bdg. 26.25 (ISBN 0-8191-3465-1); pap. text ed. 11.25 (ISBN 0-8191-3466-X). U Pr of Amer.

Scientific Explanation of Sex. Walter Russell. (Massage of the Divine Ilaid Ser.: Vol. II). (Illus.). 42p. Date not set. pap. 3.00. U Sci & Philos.

Scientific Explanation, Space & Time. Ed. by Herbert Feigl & G. Maxwell. LC 57-12861. (Studies in the Philosophy of Science Ser: Vol. 3). 1962. 25.00 (ISBN 0-8166-0266-2). U of Minn Pr.

Scientific Farm Animal Production. 3rd ed. Robert E. Taylor & Ralph Bogart. 642p. 1988. text ed. write for info (ISBN 0-02-311750-8). Macmillan.

Scientific Forecasting & Human Needs: Trends, Methods & Message. Ed. by Augusto Forti. 204p. 1984. pap. 19.00 (ISBN 92-3-102134-6, U1403 5071, UNESCO). UNIPUB.

Scientific Formation. Adrian van Kaam. (Formative Spirituality Ser.: Vol. 4). 272p. 1987. 27.50x (ISBN 0-8245-0841-6). Crossroad NY.

Scientific Foundations of Anaesthesia. 3rd ed. Scurr & Feldman. 1982. 106.00 (ISBN 0-8151-7628-7). Year Bk Med.

Scientific Foundations of Business Administration. Ed. by Henry C. Metcalf. LC 77-18084. (Management History Ser.: No. 68). 341p. Repr. of 1926 ed. 25.00 (ISBN 0-87960-074-8). Hive Pub.

Scientific Foundations of Cardiology. Ed. by P. Sleight & J. Vann Jones. 560p. 1984. 90.00x (ISBN 0-433-30415-4, Pub. by W Heinemann Med Bks). Sheridan Med Bks.

Scientific Foundations of Coaching. Russell Pate et al. 344p. 1984. text ed. write for info. (ISBN 0-697-06302-X). Wm C Brown.

Scientific Foundations of Developmental Psychiatry. Ed. by Michael Rutter. 400p. 1987. pap. text ed. 24.95x (ISBN 0-88048-271-0, 48-271-0). Am Psychiatric.

Scientific Foundations of Orthopaedics & Traumatology. Robert Owen et al. (Illus.). 531p. 1981. text ed. 74.00 (ISBN 0-7216-7029-6). Saunders.

Scientific Foundations of Psychiatry. Ed. by Michael Shepherd. (Handbook of Psychiatry Ser.: Vol. 5). 350p. 1985. 65.00 (ISBN 0-521-23304-6); pap. 24.95 (ISBN 0-521-29896-2). Cambridge U Pr.

Scientific Foundations of Space Manufacturing. V. S. Avduyevsky. 173p. 1985. pap. 5.95 (ISBN 0-8285-2949-3, Pub. by Mir Pubs USSR). Imported Pubns.

Scientific Foundations of Space Manufacturing. V. S. Avduyevsky. 170p. 1984. 23.00x (ISBN 0-317-46719-0, Pub. by Collets (UK)). State Mutual Bk.

Scientific Foundations of Urology. 3rd ed. Chisholm & Williams. 1988. 164.00 (ISBN 0-8151-1675-6). Year Bk Med.

Scientific Foundations of Vacuum Technique. 2nd ed. Ed. by Saul Dushman & J. M. Lafferty. LC 61-17361. 1962. 81.95x (ISBN 0-471-22803-6, Pub. by Wiley-Interscience). Wiley.

Scientific French: A Concise Description of the Structural Elements of Scientific & Technical French. William N. Locke. LC 78-11669. 124p. 1979. pap. 6.50 (ISBN 0-88275-771-7). Krieger.

Scientific Fundamentals of Robotics I: Dynamics of Manipulation, Theory & Application. M. Vukobratovic & V. Potkonjak. (Communications & Control Engineering Ser.). (Illus.). 303p. 1982. pap. 41.00 (ISBN 0-387-11628-1). Springer-Verlag.

Scientific Fundamentals of Robotics 2: Control of Manipulation Robots, Theory & Application. M. Vukobratovic & D. Stokic. (Communications & Control Engineering Ser.). (Illus.). 363p. 1982. 49.00 (ISBN 0-387-11629-X). Springer-Verlag.

Scientific Fundamentals of Robotics 3: Kinematics & Trajectories Synthesis of Manipulation Robots. M. Vukobratovic & M. Kircanski. (Communications & Control Engineering Ser.). (Illus.). x, 267p. 1985. 45.50 (ISBN 0-387-13071-3). Springer-Verlag.

Scientific Fundamentals of Robotics 4: Real-Time Dynamics of Manipulation Robots. M. Vukobratovic & N. Kircanski. (Communications & Control Engineering). (Illus.). xii, 239p. 1985. 45.00 (ISBN 0-387-13072-1). Springer-Verlag.

TITLE INDEX SCIENTIFIC PUBLICATION SYSTEM IN

Scientific Fundamentals of Robotics 5. M. Vukobratovic & D. Stokic. (Communications & Control Engineering Ser.). (Illus.). x, 383p. 1985. 64.00 (ISBN 0-387-13073-X). Springer-Verlag.
Scientific Fundamentals of Robotics 6. M. Vukobratovic & V. Potkonjak. (Communications & Control Engineering Ser.). (Illus.). xiii, 305p. 1985. 56.00 (ISBN 0-387-13074-8). Springer-Verlag.
Scientific Fur Servicing: Storage, Cleaning, Repairing & Restyling. Gaetan J. Lapick & Jack Geller. (Illus.). pap. 36.30 (ISBN 0-317-10808-5, 2011751). Bks Demand UMI.
Scientific Genius: A Psychology of Science. Dean K. Simonton. (Illus.). 200p. 1988. 27.95 (ISBN 0-521-35287-8). Cambridge U Pr.
Scientific Genius & Creativity. Owen Gingerich. LC 86-31920. (Illus.). 110p. 1987. pap. 11.95 (ISBN 0-7167-1858-8). W H Freeman.
Scientific German. George E. Condoyannis. LC 77-16570. 174p. 1978. pap. 10.50 (ISBN 0-88275-644-3). Krieger.
Scientific German by the Method of Discovery. Kurt F. Leidecker. 1947. 10.95x (ISBN 0-913298-67-0). S F Vanni.
Scientific Graphics with Lotus 1-2-3. Oleg D. Jefimenko. (Illus.). 194p. 1987. pap. 16.00 (ISBN 0-917406-05-2). Electret Sci.
Scientific Greenhouse Gardening. P. K. Willmott. 200p. 1982. 40.00x (ISBN 0-7158-0663-7, Pub. by EP Pub England). State Mutual Bk.
Scientific Guide to Peaceful Living. Betty Yu-Lin Ho. LC 77-142457. (Illus.). 170p. (Orig.). 1973. pap. 10.00 (ISBN 0-9600148-2-9). Juvenescent.
Scientific Guidebook to Astrological Prediction. Light Simon. (Illus.). 135p. 1982. Repr. of 1935 ed. 117.75 (ISBN 0-89901-058-X). Found Class Reprints.
Scientific Habit of Thought. Frederick Barry. Repr. of 1927 ed. 26.00 (ISBN 0-404-00666-3). AMS Pr.
Scientific Handicapping: Tested Way to Win at the Race Track. Ira S. Cohen. (Illus., Orig.). 1966. pap. 5.95 (ISBN 0-13-795880-3). P-H.
Scientific Healing Affirmations. LC 84-71199. pap. 8.95 (ISBN 0-937134-15-5). Amrita Found.
Scientific Healing Affirmations. 11th ed. Paramahansa Yogananda. LC 81-53040. (Illus.). 100p. 1981. pap. 1.95 (ISBN 0-87612-144-X); pap. 1.25x Span. ed. (ISBN 0-87612-141-5); pap. 5.00x German ed. (ISBN 3-87041-241-0); pap. 2.50x Italian ed. (ISBN 0-87612-143-1). Self Realization.
Scientific Ideas of G.K. Gilbert. Ed. by Ellis L. Yochelson. LC 80-67676. (Special Paper: No. 183). (Illus., Orig.). 1980. pap. 12.50 (ISBN 0-8137-2183-0). Geol Soc.
Scientific Identification of Disputed Documents, Fingerprints & Ballistics. R. A. Gregory. 155p. 1984. 105.00x (ISBN 0-317-54703-8, Pub. by Eastern Bk India). State Mutual Bk.
Scientific Illustration. John L. Ridgway. (Illus.). 1938. 17.50x (ISBN 0-8047-0996-3). Stanford U Pr.
Scientific Illustration: A Guide for the Beginning Artist. Zbigniew T. Jastrzebski. (Illus.). 336p. 1985. pap. 24.95 (ISBN 0-13-795931-1). P H.
Scientific Illustration: A Guide to Biological, Zoological, & Medical Rendering Techniques, Design, Printing, & Display. Phyllis Wood. 152p. 1982. pap. 19.95 (ISBN 0-442-29307-0). Van Nos Reinhold.
Scientific Image. B. C. VanFrassen. (Clarendon Library of Logic & Philosophy Ser.). 248p. 1980. text ed. 45.00x (ISBN 0-19-824424-X); pap. text ed. 14.95x (ISBN 0-19-824427-4). Oxford U Pr.
Scientific Industrial Efficiency. Dwight T. Farnham. LC 73-9692. (Management History Ser.: No. 36). (Illus.). 101p. 1973. Repr. of 1917 ed. 22.50 (ISBN 0-87960-039-X). Hive Pub.
Scientific Inference. 3rd ed. Harold Jeffreys. LC 71-179159. (Illus.). 280p. 1973. 52.50 (ISBN 0-521-08446-6). Cambridge U Pr.
Scientific Inference: Data Analysis & Robustiness (Symposium) Ed. by G. E. Box & Chien-Fu-Wu Leonard. LC 82-22755. 1983. 28.50 (ISBN 0-12-121160-6). Acad Pr.
Scientific Information & Society. Gyorgy Rozsa. 1973. bds. 15.20x (ISBN 90-2797-181-1). Mouton.
Scientific Information Systems & the Principle of Selectivity. William Goffman & Kenneth Warren. LC 80-49. 202p. 1980. 35.00 (ISBN 0-275-90489-X, C0489). Praeger.
Scientific Information Systems in Japan. Ed. by H. Inose. 260p. 1981. 73.75 (ISBN 0-444-86151-3, North-Holland). Elsevier.
Scientific Information Transfer: The Editor's Role. Ed. by Miriam Balaban. 1978. lib. bdg. 37.00 (ISBN 90-277-0917-3, Pub. by Reidel Holland). Kluwer Academic.
Scientific Inquiry & the Social Sciences: A Volume in Honor of Donald T. Campbell. Ed. by Marilynn B. Brewer & Barry E. Collins. LC 81-6023. (Social & Behavioral Science Ser.). 1981. text ed. 45.00x (ISBN 0-87589-496-8). Jossey-Bass.
Scientific Inquiry: Design & Analysis Issues in Occupational Therapy. Kenneth J. Ottenbacher & Bette Bonder. 196p. 1986. pap. text ed. 16.00 (ISBN 0-910317-30-5). Am Occup Therapy.
Scientific Inquiry in Philosophical Perspective. Ed. by Nicholas Rescher. (CPS Publications in Philosophy of Science). (Illus.). 308p. (Orig.). 1987. lib. bdg. 28.00 (ISBN 0-8191-5798-8, Pub. by Ctr Philos Sci); pap. text ed. 14.75 (ISBN 0-8191-5799-6). U Pr of Amer.
Scientific Insights into Yoruba Traditional Medicine. James I. Durodola. (Traditional Healing Ser.). 1985. 27.50 (ISBN 0-686-85813-1). Conch Mag.
Scientific Insights into Yoruba Traditional Medicine. James I. Durodola. (Traditional Healing Ser.). 1984. 27.50 (ISBN 0-932426-17-4). Trado-Medic.
Scientific Institutions of the Future. Ed. by Philip C. Ritterbush. LC 72-3811. (Prometheus Paperback Ser). 164p. 1972. pap. 3.95 (ISBN 0-87491-501-5). Acropolis.
Scientific Instrument Mfr. Ed. by ICC Info. Group Staff. 1987. 695.00x (ISBN 1-85319-044-6, ICC Info Group Ltd UK). State Mutual Bk.
Scientific Intelligentsia in the U. S. S. R. Structure & Dynamics of Personnel. D. M. Gvishiani et al. Tr. by Jane Sayers from Rus. 1976. 15.95 (ISBN 0-8464-0820-1). Beekman Pubs.
Scientific Interfaces & Technological Applications. National Research Council. (Physics Through the 1990's Ser.). 288p. 1986. pap. text ed. 24.95x (ISBN 0-309-03580-5). Natl Acad Pr.
Scientific Interrogation: Hypnosis, Polygraphy, Narcoanalysis, Voice Stress & Pupillometrics. Lawrence Taylor. (Contemporary Litigation Ser.). 378p. 1984. 50.00x (ISBN 0-87215-685-0). Michie Co.
Scientific Inventory Control. 2nd ed. Lewis. 1981. text ed. 29.95 (ISBN 0-408-00595-5). Butterworth.
Scientific Investigations on the Skylab Satellite, PAAS48. Ed. by Marion I. Kent & Ernst Stuhlinger. LC 76-27685. (Illus.). 552p. 1976. 49.50. AIAA.
Scientific Investigator. photocopy ed. Richard O. Arther (Illus.). 248p. 1976. 21.75x (ISBN 0-398-00055-7). C C Thomas.
Scientific Journals: Issues for Library Selection & Management. Ed. by Tony Stankus. LC 87-7047. (Serials Librarian Ser.). 212p. 1987. text ed. 29.95 (ISBN 0-86656-616-3). Haworth Pr.
Scientific Karatedo: Spiritual Development of Individuality in Mind & Body. Masayuki Hisatake. (Illus.). 256p. 1976. 26.00 (ISBN 0-87040-362-1). Japan Pubns USA.
Scientific Knowledge. James Fetzer. 1982. lib. bdg. 49.50 (ISBN 90-277-1335-9, Pub. by Reidel Netherlands); pap. text ed. 14.95 (ISBN 90-277-1336-7, Pub. by Reidel Holland). Kluwer Academic.
Scientific Knowledge & Its Social Problems. Jerome R. Ravetz. 1971. pap. 9.95 (ISBN 0-19-519721-6). Oxford U Pr.
Scientific Knowledge & Philosophic Thought. Harold Himsworth. LC 85-24118. 128p. 1986. text ed. 14.50x (ISBN 0-8018-3316-7). Johns Hopkins.
Scientific Knowledge & Sociological Theory. Barry Barnes. (Monographs in Social Theory). 204p. 1974. pap. 9.95X (ISBN 0-7100-7962-1). Routledge Chapman & Hall.
Scientific Knowledge: Basic Issues in the Philosophy of Science. Ed. by Janet A. Kourany. 399p. 1987. pap. text ed. write for info. (ISBN 0-534-06444-2). Wadsworth Pub.
Scientific Knowledge Socialized. Ed. by Imre Hronszky et al. 1988. lib. bdg. 124.00 (ISBN 90-277-2284-6, Pub. by Reidel Holland). Kluwer Academic.
Scientific London. Bernard H. Becker. 340p. 1968. Repr. of 1847 ed. 29.50x (ISBN 0-7146-2328-8, F Cass Co). Biblio Dist.
Scientific London. Bernard H. Becker. 346p. Repr. of 1874 ed. text ed. 62.10x (ISBN 0-576-29113-7, Pub. by Gregg Intl Pubs England). Gregg Intl.
Scientific Man Versus Power Politics. Hans Morgenthau. (Midway Reprint Ser). 1974. pap. 12.00x (ISBN 0-226-53826-5). U of Chicago Pr.
Scientific Management. 2nd rev. ed. Horace B. Drury. LC 68-56654. (Columbia University. Studies in the Social Sciences: No. 157). 1922. 21.00 (ISBN 0-404-51157-0). AMS Pr.
Scientific Management: A Collection of the More Significant Articles Describing the Taylor System of Management. Ed. by Clarence B. Thompson. LC 72-80596. (Management History Ser.: No. 1). 890p. 1972. Repr. of 1914 ed. 47.50 (ISBN 0-87960-011-X). Hive Pub.
Scientific Management & Labor. Robert F. Hoxie. LC 66-21677. 1966. Repr. of 1915 ed. 35.00x (ISBN 0-678-00169-3). Kelley.
Scientific Management & Railroads. Louis D. Brandeis. Bd. with Higher Railroad Rates vs. Scientific Management. Harry A. Bullock. (Management History Ser.: No. 82). xii, 178p. 1980. lib. bdg. 22.50 (ISBN 0-87960-101-9); pap. 15.00 (ISBN 0-87960-120-5). Hive Pub.
Scientific Management Course. Frank B. Gilbreth et al. LC 79-92317. (Management History Ser.: No. 77). 180p. 1975. Repr. of 1912 ed. 24.00 (ISBN 0-87960-114-0). Hive Pub.
Scientific Management in Action: Taylorism at Watertown Arsenal, 1908-1915. Hugh G. Aitken. (Illus.). 280p. 41.00x (ISBN 0-691-04241-1); pap. 13.50x (ISBN 0-691-00375-0). Princeton U Pr.
Scientific Management in American Industry. Taylor Society. Ed. by H. S. Person. LC 72-89989. (Management History Ser.: No. 11). (Illus.). xix, 479p. 1972. Repr. of 1929 ed. 32.50 (ISBN 0-87960-017-9). Hive Pub.
Scientific Management in Education. J. M. Rice. LC 70-89225. (American Education: Its Men, Institutions & Ideas, Ser. 1). 1969. Repr. of 1914 ed. 21.50 (ISBN 0-405-01462-7). Ayer Co Pubs.
Scientific Management, Job Redesign, & Work Performance. J. E. Kelly. (Organizational & Occupational Psychology Ser.). 1982. 52.00 (ISBN 0-12-404020-9). Acad Pr.
Scientific Management of Library Operations. 2nd ed. Richard M. Dougherty & Fred J. Heinritz. LC 81-18200. 286p. 1982. 16.50 (ISBN 0-8108-1485-4). Scarecrow.
Scientific Management of Society. K. Varlamov. (Library of Political Knowledge: No. 10). 136p. 1983. pap. 7.50x (ISBN 0-317-53774-1, Pub. by Collets (UK)). State Mutual Bk.
Scientific Management of Surgical Patients. Richard M. Peters et al. 499p. 1983. text ed. 64.00 (ISBN 0-316-70201-3). Little.
Scientific Management of Transport Systems: Proceedings International Conference, New Delhi, Nov. 26-28, 1980. Ed. by N. K. Jaiswal. 378p. 1981. 89.50 (ISBN 0-444-86205-6, North-Holland). Elsevier.
Scientific Management since Taylor: A Collection of Authoritative Papers. Ed. by Edward E. Hunt. LC 72-80579. (Management History Ser.: No. 2). 284p. 1972. Repr. of 1924 ed. 25.00 (ISBN 0-87960-010-1). Hive Pub.
Scientific Management, Socialist Discipline, & Soviet Power. Mark R. Beissinger. (Russian Research Center Studies: No. 84). 376p. 1988. text ed. 30.00 (ISBN 0-674-79490-7). Harvard U Pr.
Scientific Marketing Management. Percival White. Ed. by Henry Assael. LC 78-272. (Century of Marketing Ser.). 1978. Repr. of 1927 ed. lib. bdg. 26.50x (ISBN 0-405-11163-0). Ayer Co Pubs.
Scientific Marx. Daniel Little. LC 86-1384. 256p. 1986. 35.00x (ISBN 0-8166-1504-7); pap. 14.95 (ISBN 0-8166-1505-5). U of Minn Pr.
Scientific Materialism. Mario Bunge. 240p. 1981. 48.00 (ISBN 90-277-1304-9, Pub. by Reidel Holland). Kluwer Academic.
Scientific Memoirs. John W. Draper. LC 72-9194. (Literature of Photography Ser.). Repr. of 1878 ed. 32.00 (ISBN 0-405-04904-8). Ayer Co Pubs.
Scientific Memoirs. Ed. by Richard Taylor. 1837-52. Repr. 325.00 (ISBN 0-384-54420-7). Johnson Repr.
Scientific Method & Social Research. 3rd ed. B. N. Ghosh. 254p. 1984. (Sterling Pubs India); text ed. 30.00x (ISBN 0-86590-723-4). Apt Bks.
Scientific Method in Production Management. G. R. Gedye. (Illus.). 1965. 8.50x (ISBN 0-19-859802-5). Oxford U Pr.
Scientific Method in Psychology. Clarence W. Brown & Edwin E. Ghiselli. LC 55-6150. (McGraw-Hill Series in Psychology). pap. 95.50 (ISBN 0-317-08270-1, 2003752). Bks Demand UMI.
Scientific Method: Optimizing Applied Research Decisions. Russell L. Ackoff. LC 83-12060. 476p. 1984. Repr. of 1962 ed. text ed. 38.00 (ISBN 0-89874-661-2). Krieger.
Scientific Methods in Medieval Archaeology. Ed. by Rainer Berger. LC 75-99771. (Center for Medieval & Renaissance Studies, UCLA: Contributions: No. 4). (Illus.). 1971. 58.50x (ISBN 0-520-01626-2). U of Cal Pr.
Scientific Methods of Urban Analysis. Anthony J. Catanese. LC 71-160384. 336p. 1972. 24.95 (ISBN 0-252-00185-0). U of Ill Pr.
Scientific Models & Man. Ed. by Henry Harris. 1979. text ed. 18.95x (ISBN 0-19-857168-2). Oxford U Pr.
Scientific Models for Experimenters. Harry E. Stockman. 400p. 1976. pap. 23.00 (ISBN 0-918332-04-4). Sercolab.
Scientific Monitoring Strategies for Ocean Waste Disposal. Ed. by Hood et al. LC 84-29701. (Oceanic Processes in Marine Pollution Ser.: Vol. 4). 1988. lib. bdg. 49.50 (ISBN 0-89874-813-5). Krieger.
Scientific Movement & Victorian Literature. Tess Cosslett. LC 82-10284. 1983. 25.00x (ISBN 0-312-70298-1). St Martin.
Scientific Objectives, Philosophy & Management of the MOCAT Project. John A. Dutton. LC 77-136104. 141p. 1969. 19.00 (ISBN 0-403-04497-9). Scholarly.
Scientific Organizations in Seventeenth Century France, 1620-1680. Harcourt Brown. LC 66-27046. 1967. Repr. of 1934 ed. 8.50x (ISBN 0-8462-0974-8). Russell.
Scientific Papers, 4 vols. Geoffrey I. Taylor. Ed. by G. K. Batchelor. Incl. Vol. 1. Mechanics of Solids. 95.00 (ISBN 0-521-06608-5); Vol. 2. Meteorology, Oceanography & Turbulent Flow. 1960; Vol. 3. Aerodynamics & the Mechanics of Projectiles & Explosions. 1963. 95.00 (ISBN 0-521-06610-7); Vol. 4. Mechanics of Fluids: Miscellaneous Topics. (Illus.). 1971. 95.00 (ISBN 0-521-07995-0). Cambridge U Pr.
Scientific Papers, Vol. 2. J. Willard Gibbs. 10.75. Peter Smith.
Scientific Papers: Nineteen Seven to Nineteen Sixteen, 5 vols. George Darwin. LC 8-16429. 1976. Set. 300.00 (ISBN 0-527-21620-8). Kraus Repr.
Scientific Papers of Arthur Holly Compton. Arthur H. Compton. Ed. by Robert S. Shankland. 1974. 50.00x (ISBN 0-226-11430-9). U of Chicago Pr.
Scientific Papers of Tjalling C. Koopmans, Vol. 2. Tjalling Koopmans. 320p. 1985. text ed. 37.50x (ISBN 0-262-11106-3). MIT PR.
Scientific Papers of William Bateson, 2 Vols. William Bateson. Ed. by R. C. Punnett. Repr. of 1928 ed. Set. 90.00 (ISBN 0-384-03533-7). Johnson Repr.
Scientific PASCAL. Harley Flanders. 1983. text ed. 37.00 (ISBN 0-8359-6932-0, Reston); pap. text ed. write for info. (ISBN 0-8359-6931-2). P-H.
Scientific Perspectives in Animal Welfare: Symposium. Ed. by W. Jean Dodds & F. Barbara Orlans. LC 82-24375. 1983. 25.50 (ISBN 0-12-219140-4). Acad Pr.
Scientific Philosophy Today. Ed. by Joseph Agassi & Robert Cohen. 1982. lib. bdg. 69.50 (ISBN 90-277-1262-X, Pub. by Reidel Netherlands); pap. text ed. 34.50 (ISBN 90-277-1263-8, Pub. by Reidel Holland). Kluwer Academic.
Scientific Poetry of Madeline Goldstein. Madeline Goldstein. 80p. 1988. 7.95 (ISBN 0-8062-3215-3). Carlton.
Scientific Principles & Methods of Strength Fitness. 2nd ed. John P. O'Shea. LC 75-18158. (Physical Education Ser.). (Illus.). 160p. 1976. pap. text ed. 12.00 (ISBN 0-394-34892-3, RanC). Random.
Scientific Principles of Coaching. 2nd ed. John Bunn. LC 70-159445. (Illus.). 1972. write for info. (ISBN 0-13-796177-4). P-H.
Scientific Principles of Psychopathology. P. McGuffin et al. 780p. 1984. 69.50 (ISBN 0-8089-1667-X, 792837). Grune.
Scientific Problem Solving: An Introduction to Technology. John Aitken & George Mills. (gr. 4-6). 1989. pap. 10.95 (ISBN 0-8224-6324-5). D S Lake Pubs.
Scientific Problems of Coal Utilization: Proceedings. Ed. by Bernard R. Cooper. LC 78-9553. (DOE Symposium Ser.). 424p. 1978. pap. 18.50 (ISBN 0-87079-400-0, CONF-770509); microfiche 6.50 (ISBN 0-87079-378-0, CONF-770509). DOE.
Scientific Problems of the Humid Tropical Zone Deltas & Their Implications. Symposium on Scientific Problems of the Humid Tropical Zone Deltas and Their Implications, Dacca, 1964. 1966. 11.50 (ISBN 92-3-000620-3, U587, UNESCO). UNIPUB.
Scientific Proceedings American Animal Hospital Association Annual Meeting. 704p. 1985. 42.00 (ISBN 0-9616498-9-5). Am Animal Hosp Assoc.
Scientific Proceedings American Animal Hospital Association Annual Meeting. 662p. 1986. 42.00 (ISBN 0-9616498-5-2). Am Animal Hosp Assoc.
Scientific Proceedings of the Annual Meeting of the American Animal Hospital Association, 1981. American Animal Hospital Association Staff. 408p. 9.50; members 3.50 (ISBN 0-9616498-2-8). Am Animal Hosp Assoc.
Scientific Proceedings of the Annual Meeting of the American Animal Hospital Association. American Animal Hospital Association Staff. 467p. 1984. 9.50 (ISBN 0-9616498-7-9); members 3.50. Am Animal Hosp Assoc.
Scientific Process & the Computer. Donald N. Streeter. LC 73-21744. pap. 120.00 (ISBN 0-317-08515-8, 2007078). Bks Demand UMI.
Scientific Productivity: The Effectiveness of Research Groups in Six Countries. Ed. by Frank M. Andrews. 469p. (Co-published with Cambridge University Press). 1979. pap. 29.95 (ISBN 92-3-101599-0, UM42, UNESCO). UNIPUB.
Scientific Programming with MAC Pascal: Self-Teaching Guide. Richard E. Crandall & Marianne M. Colgrove. LC 85-19083. 279p. 1986. pap. 18.95 (ISBN 0-471-82176-4, Pub. by Wiley Press). Wiley.
Scientific Progress. 2nd ed. Craig Dilworth. 1986. lib. bdg. 44.95 (ISBN 90-277-2215-3, Pub. by Reidel Holland); pap. 19.95 (ISBN 90-277-2216-1, Pub. by Reidel Holland). Kluwer Academic.
Scientific Progress: A Philosophical Essay on the Economics of Research in Natural Science. Nicholas Rescher. LC 77-74544. 1977. 26.95x (ISBN 0-8229-1128-0). U of Pittsburgh Pr.
Scientific Progress: A Study Concerning the Nature of the Relation Between Successive Scientific Theories. Craig Dilworth. 160p. 1982. 29.95 (ISBN 90-277-1311-1, Pub. by Reidel Holland). Kluwer Academic.
Scientific Proof of the Existence of God Will Soon Be Announced by the White House! Da Free John. LC 80-81175. 432p. 1980. pap. 19.95 (ISBN 0-913922-48-X). Dawn Horse Pr.
Scientific Proof of the Existence of Reincarnation & Transmigration. Richard Van Den Tak. (Illus.). 1981. 16.50 (ISBN 0-89962-015-9). Todd & Honeywell.
Scientific Publication System in Social Science: A Study of the Operation of Leading Professional Journals in Psychology, Sociology, & Social Work. Duncan Lindsey. LC 78-62570. (Social & Behavioral Science Ser.). (Illus.). 1978. text ed. 28.95x (ISBN 0-87589-390-2). Jossey-Bass.

Scientific Publications of Charles Wilkins Short: Original Anthology. Ed. by Keir B. Sterling. LC 77-81125. (Biologists & Their World Ser.). 1978. lib. bdg. 32.00x (ISBN 0-405-10721-8). Ayer Co Pubs.
Scientific Quests & Political Customs: The Current Crises of Discovery & Government. Gerald M. Edelman. 16p. (Orig.). 1976. pap. text ed. 5.00 (ISBN 0-8191-5826-7, Pub. by Aspen Inst for Humanistic Studies). U Pr of Amer.
Scientific Rationality: Studies in the Foundations of Science & Ethics. Ed. by Risto Hilpinen. (Philosophical Studies in Philosophy: No. 21). 247p. 1980. lib. bdg. 45.00 (ISBN 90-277-1112-7, Pub. by Reidel Holland). Kluwer Academic.
Scientific Realism. Ed. by Jarrett Leplin. LC 84-40311. 250p. 1985. 33.00x (ISBN 0-520-05155-6); pap. 11.95x (ISBN 0-520-05326-5). U of Cal Pr.
Scientific Realism & the Plasticity of Mind. P. M. Churchland. LC 78-73240. (Cambridge Studies in Philosophy). (Illus.). 1979. 37.50 (ISBN 0-521-22632-5). Cambridge U Pr.
Scientific Realism & the Plasticity of Mind. Paul M. Churchland. (Cambridge Studies in Philosophy). 157p. 1986. pap. 12.95 (ISBN 0-521-33827-1). Cambridge U Pr.
Scientific Reasoning & Epistemic Attitudes. L. Harsing. 1982. cancelled 10.00 (ISBN 963-05-3003-1, Pub. by Akademiai Kaido Hungary). IPS.
Scientific Reasoning & Epistemic Attitudes. Laszlo Harsing. 148p. 1982. 31.25x (ISBN 0-317-53773-3, Pub. by Collets (UK)). State Mutual Bk.
Scientific Reasoning: The Bayesian Approach. Colin Howson & Peter Urbach. 272p. (Orig.). 1989. 34.95 (ISBN 0-8126-9084-2); pap. 16.95 (ISBN 0-8126-9085-0). Open Court.
Scientific Reinterpretation of Form. Norma E. Emerton. LC 84-45139. (Cornell History of Science Ser.). 320p. 1984. 33.50x (ISBN 0-8014-1583-7). Cornell U Pr.
Scientific Renaissance, Fourteen Fifty to Sixteen Thirty. Marie Boas. (Illus.). pap. 9.95x (ISBN 0-06-130583-9, TB583, Torch). Har-Row.
Scientific Report: A Guide for Authors. W. Clements & R. Berlo. Ed. by Society for Technical Communication Staff. 52p. (Orig.). 1984. pap. text ed. 15.00x (ISBN 0-914548-41-7). Soc Tech Comm.
Scientific Report of the Intercalibration Exercise: The IOC-WMO-UNEP, Pilot Project on Monitoring Background Levels of Selected Pollutants in Open Ocean Waters. (Intergovernmental Oceanographic Commission Technical Ser.: No. 22). 91p. 1983. pap. 5.00 (ISBN 92-3-102077-3, U1260, UNESCO). UNIPUB.
Scientific Research & Social Goals: Toward a New Development Model. Ed. by F. Mayor. 248p. 1982. 50.00 (ISBN 0-08-028118-4). Pergamon.
Scientific Research: Its Administration & Organization. George P. Bush. LC 50-8690. 198p. 1950. 14.95 (ISBN 0-87419-006-1, U Pr of Wash). Larlin Corp.
Scientific Research: Statistical Analysis Module (SR: SAM) Myra J. Halpin. Ed. by Alice Z. Greiner. (Illus.). 220p. 1988. pap. text ed. 12.95 (ISBN 0-944620-01-9); 15.95 (ISBN 0-944620-04-3); IBM diskette 49.95 (ISBN 0-944620-02-7); Apple disk 49.95 (ISBN 0-944620-03-5). M J Halpin.
Scientific Results of Cruise VII of the "Carnegie" During 1928-1929, under Command of Captain J. P. Ault: The Work of the Carnegie & Suggestions for Future Scientific Cruises. 1946. pap. 7.00 (ISBN 0-87279-582-9). Carnegie Inst.
Scientific Results of Viking Project. Ed. by E. Flinn. (Illus.). 725p. 1977. 15.00 (ISBN 0-87590-207-3). Am Geophysical.
Scientific Revolution. Peter Amey. Ed. by Malcolm Yapp et al. (World History Ser.). (Illus.). (gr. 6-11). 1980. lib. bdg. 6.95 (ISBN 0-89908-132-0); pap. text ed. 2.45 (ISBN 0-89908-107-X). Greenhaven.
Scientific Revolution. P. M. Harman. (Lancaster Pamphlet Ser.). 48p. 1983. pap. 3.95 (ISBN 0-416-35040-2, NO. 3851). Routledge Chapman & Hall.
Scientific Revolution. Jayawardene. 1986. lib. bdg. 26.00 (ISBN 0-8240-9063-2). Garland Pub.
Scientific Revolution & Inter-Paradigmatic Dialogues. 30p. 1979. pap. 5.00 (ISBN 92-808-0075-2, TUNU028, UNU). UNIPUB.
Scientific Revolution, Fifteen Hundred to Eighteen Hundred: The Formation of the Modern Scientific Attitude. Alfred R. Hall. pap. 14.95x (ISBN 0-8070-5093-8, BPA4, Pub. by Ariadne Bks). Beacon Pr.
Scientific Revolution in Victorian Medicine. A. J. Youngson. LC 78-31705. 237p. 1979. 32.50 (ISBN 0-8419-0479-0). Holmes & Meier.
Scientific Revolutions. Ian Hacking. (Oxford Readings in Philosphy Ser.). 1981. pap. text ed. 9.95x (ISBN 0-19-875051-X). Oxford U Pr.
Scientific Romance in Britain Eighteen Ninety to Nineteen Fifty. Brian Stableford. LC 85-14610. 288p. 1985. 29.95 (ISBN 0-312-70305-8). St Martin.
Scientific Romances: First & Second Series, 2 vols, in 1. Howard C. Hinton. LC 75-36841. (Occult Ser.). 1976. Repr. of 1922 ed. 31.00x (ISBN 0-405-07954-0). Ayer Co Pubs.
Scientific Russian. George E. Condoyannis. LC 77-16615. 238p. 1978. pap. 11.50 (ISBN 0-88275-643-5). Krieger.
Scientific Russian Reader. Ed. by Nina Syniawska. LC 61-7717. 1961. 27.00x (ISBN 0-231-02453-3). Columbia U Pr.
Scientific Satellite Programmed During the International Magnetospheric Study: Proceedings, Vol. 57. Astrophysics & Space Science Staff. Ed. by K. Knott & B. Battrick. LC 75-44353. 1976. lib. bdg. 58.00 (ISBN 90-277-0688-3, Pub. by Reidel Holland). Kluwer Academic.
Scientific Satellites. Symposium On Scientific Satellites. Ed. by I. E. Jeter. (Advances in the Astronautical Sciences Ser.: Vol. 12). 1962. 25.00x (ISBN 0-87703-013-8, Pub. by Am Astronaut). Univelt Inc.
Scientific Selection of Catalysts. Ed. by A. A. Balandin et al. 288p. 1968. text ed. 56.00x (ISBN 0-7065-0594-8, Pub. by Keter Pub Jerusalem). Coronet Bks.
Scientific Socialism & Self-Reliance. Jan M. Haakonsen. (Bergen Studies in Social Anthropology: No. 34). (Illus.). 172p. 1985. pap. text ed. 10.50x (ISBN 0-936508-66-3, Pub. by Dept Soc Anthropology, University of Bergen, Norway). Barber Pr.
Scientific Space Selection. Audit Bureau of Circulations Staff. LC 75-22798. (America in Two Centuries Ser). 1976. Repr. of 1921 ed. 15.00x (ISBN 0-405-07669-X). Ayer Co Pubs.
Scientific Spirit & Democratic Faith. facs. ed. Conference On The Scientific Spirit And Democratic Faith-1st-New York-1943. LC 72-121457. (Essay Index Reprint Ser). 1944. 14.00 (ISBN 0-8369-1872-X). Ayer Co Pubs.
Scientific Strategies. Bross. (Statistics: Textbooks & Monographs: Vol. 35). 1981. 39.75 (ISBN 0-8247-1273-0). Dekker.
Scientific Stream Pollution Analysis. Nemerov. 358p. 1974. 37.50 (ISBN 0-89116-519-3). Hemisphere Pub.
Scientific Studies in Mental Retardation. Ed. by John Dobbing et al. (Illus.). 400p. 1984. text ed. 110.00x (ISBN 0-333-35454-0). Sheridan Med Bks.
Scientific Study of Flint & Chert: Proceedings of the Fourth International Flint Symposium. Ed. by G. Sieveking & M. B. Hart. 350p. 1986. 85.00 (ISBN 0-521-26252-6). Cambridge U Pr.
Scientific Study of Foreign Policy. 2nd ed. James N. Rosenau. (Essays on the Analysis of World Politics). 577p. 1980. 39.50x (ISBN 0-89397-074-3); pap. 23.50x (ISBN 0-89397-075-1). Nichols Pub.
Scientific Study of Human Society. Franklin H. Giddings. LC 73-14155. (Perspectives in Social Inquiry Ser.). 264p. 1974. Repr. 13.00x (ISBN 0-405-05501-3). Ayer Co Pubs.
Scientific Study of Marihuana. Ed. by Ernest L. Abel. LC 76-4508. 320p. 1976. 24.95x (ISBN 0-88229-144-0). Nelson-Hall.
Scientific Study of Personality. Hans J. Eysenck. LC 81-20077. xiii, 320p. 1982. Repr. of 1952 ed. lib. bdg. 41.50x (ISBN 0-313-23241-5, EYSS). Greenwood.
Scientific Study of Political Leadership. Glenn D. Paige. LC 76-50464. (Illus.). 1977. 25.00 (ISBN 0-02-923630-4). Free Pr.
Scientific Study of Social Behaviour. Michael Argyle. LC 73-13021. (Illus.). 239p. 1974. Repr. of 1957 ed. lib. bdg. 35.00x (ISBN 0-8371-7108-3, ARSS). Greenwood.
Scientific Study of the College Student. Harry D. Kitson. Bd. with Whole vs. Part Methods in Motor Learning. L. A. Pechstein; Vol. 2, No. 2. Yale Psychology Studies. Ed. by R. P. Angier; Vertical-Horizontal Illusion. S. M. Ritter. (Psychology Monographs, General & Applied: Vol. 23). pap. 29.00 (ISBN 0-8115-1422-6). Kraus Repr.
Scientific-Technical Progress & the Revolution in Military Affairs: A Soviet View. N. A. Lomov. LC 74-601912. 287p. 1980. pap. 7.00 (ISBN 0-318-21897-6, S/N 008-070-00340-6). USGPO.
Scientific-Technological Change & the Role of Women in Development. (Special Studies in Social, Political, & Economic Development). 200p. 1981. 37.50 (ISBN 0-86531-145-5). Westview.
Scientific Technological Dictionary. R. Popic et al. 1140p. (Eng., Serbian & Croatian.). 1980. 195.00 (ISBN 0-686-97432-8, M-9688). French & Eur.
Scientific-Technological Revolution & Soviet Foreign Policy. Erik P. Hoffmann & Robbin F. Laird. LC 81-19924. (Pergamon Policy Studies on International Politics). (Illus.). 256p. 1982. 45.00 (ISBN 0-08-028065-X, K125). Pergamon.
Scientific Temperaments. Philip J. Hilts. 1982. 15.50 (ISBN 0-671-22533-2). S&S.
Scientific Temperaments: Three Lives in Contemporary Science. Philip J. Hilts. 1984. pap. 7.95 (ISBN 0-671-50590-4, Touchstone Bks). S&S.
Scientific Terms, Aeronautics: Japanese-English, English-Japanese. Ministry of Education. 235p. (Japanese & Eng.). 1973. leatherette 39.95 (ISBN 0-686-92173-9, M-9347). French & Eur.
Scientific Terms, Chemistry: Japanese-English, English-Japanese. Ministry of Education. 630p. (Japanese & Eng.). 1974. 75.00 (ISBN 0-686-92209-3, M-9335). French & Eur.
Scientific Terms Electrical Engineering. Ministry of Education Science & Culture. 675p. (Eng. & Japanese.). 1979. 125.00 (ISBN 0-686-97433-6, M-9330). French & Eur.
Scientific Terms Mathematics: Japanese-English, English-Japanese. Ministry of Education. 146p. (Japanese & Eng.). 1954. Leatherette 49.95 (ISBN 0-686-92202-6, M__9346). French & Eur.
Scientific Terms Meteorology: Japanese-English, English-Japanese. Ministry of Education. 140p. (Japanese & Eng.). 1975. Leatherette 35.00 (ISBN 0-686-92205-0, M-9338). French & Eur.
Scientific Terms Naval Architecture & Marine Engineering: Japanese-English, English-Japanese. Ministry of Education. 526p. (Japanese & Eng.). 1955. leatherette 59.95 (ISBN 0-686-92523-8, M-9337). French & Eur.
Scientific Terms Nuclear Engineering: Japanese-English, English-Japanese. Ministry of Education Sciences. 282p. (Japanese & Eng.). 1977. leatherette 49.95 (ISBN 0-686-92519-X, M-9336). French & Eur.
Scientific Terms Physics: Japanese-English, English-Japanese. Ministry of Education. 221p. (Japanese & Eng.). 1954. 49.95 (ISBN 0-686-92514-9, M-9343). French & Eur.
Scientific Terms Spectroscopy: Japanese-English, English-Japanese. Ministry of Education. 165p. (Japanese & Eng.). 1974. leatherette 35.00 (ISBN 0-686-92512-2, M-9341). French & Eur.
Scientific Theism. Francis E. Abbot. LC 75-3012. (Philosophy in America Ser.). Repr. of 1885 ed. 27.50 (ISBN 0-404-59004-7). AMS Pr.
Scientific Theism. Arvid Reuterdahl. 1926. 10.00 (ISBN 0-8159-6805-1). Devin.
Scientific Theist: A Life of Francis Ellingwood Abbot. Sydney E. Ahlstrom & Robert B. Mullin. LC 86-33128. 208p. 1987. 29.95 (ISBN 0-86554-236-8, H208). Mercer Univ Pr.
Scientific Themes in the Popular Literature & the Poetry of the German Enlightenment, 1720-1760. Walter Schatzberg. (Germanic Studies in America: Vol. 12). 349p. 1973. 37.85 (ISBN 3-261-00317-0). P Lang Pubs.
Scientific Theory & Religion. Ernest W. Barnes. LC 77-27198. (Gifford Lectures: 1927-29). Repr. of 1933 ed. 42.50 (ISBN 0-404-60483-8). AMS Pr.
Scientific Theory of Culture. Bronislaw Malinowski. x, 228p. 1944. 15.00x (ISBN 0-8078-0433-9). U of NC Pr.
Scientific Thought. Charles D. Broad. (Quality Paperback: No. 208). 555p. 1959. Littlefield.
Scientific Thought & Social Reality: Essays by Michael Polanyi. Michael Polanyi. Ed. by Fred Schwartz. LC 74-5420. (Psychological Issues Monograph: No. 32, Vol. 8, No. 4). 168p. 1974. text ed. 20.00x (ISBN 0-8236-6005-2). Intl Univs Pr.
Scientific Thought in Poetry. Ralph B. Crum. LC 31-29142. Repr. of 1931 ed. 16.50 (ISBN 0-404-01868-8). AMS Pr.
Scientific Thought in the American College 1638-1800. Theodore Hornberger. 1968. lib. bdg. 14.50x (ISBN 0-374-93952-7, Octagon). Hippocrene Bks.
Scientific Thought: Some Underlying Concepts, Methods & Procedures. (New Babylon, Studies in the Social Sciences: No. 9). (Illus.). 1972. 19.20x (ISBN 90-2797-145-5). Mouton.
Scientific Thought: Some Underlying Concepts, Methods & Procedures. LC 72-79987. 252p. (Co-published with Mouton, The Hague). 1972. 13.75 (ISBN 92-3-101023-9, U589, UNESCO). UNIPUB.
Scientific Training of One's Will for the Achievement of Business & Political Success. Frank C. Haddock. (Illus.). 149p. 1983. 137.45 (ISBN 0-89920-060-5). Am Inst Psych.
Scientific Truth & Statistical Method. M. Boldrini. 1971. 20.25 (ISBN 0-02-841610-4). Hafner.
Scientific Truth & Statistical Method. M. Boldrini. 1972. 28.95x (ISBN 0-85264-197-4). Lubrecht & Cramer.
Scientific Use of Factor Analysis in Behavioral & Life Sciences. Ed. by Raymond B. Cattell. LC 77-10695. (Illus.). 640p. 1978. 65.00x (ISBN 0-306-30939-4, Plenum Pr). Plenum Pub.
Scientific Uses of Earth Satellites. James A. Van Allen. LC 56-11813. pap. 81.50 (ISBN 0-317-07811-9, 2055659). Bks Demand UMI.
Scientific Vedanta. Kashinath. LC 73-900893. 129p. 1974. 7.50x (ISBN 0-89684-451-X). Orient Bk Dist.
Scientific Vegetarianism. Edmond B. Szekely. (Illus.). 56p. 1977. pap. 2.95 (ISBN 0-89564-041-4). IBS Intl.
Scientific Ways in the Study of Ego Development. Ed. by J. Loevinger. (Heinz Werner Lecture: No. 12). 1978. pap. 6.00 (ISBN 0-914206-14-1). Clark U Pr.
Scientific Weed Management. rev. ed. O. P. Gupta. vii, 474p. 1984. 35.00 (ISBN 1-55528-050-1, Pub. by Messers Today & Tomorrow Printers & Publishers). Scholarly Pubns.
Scientific Words: Their Structure & Meaning. W. E. Flood. LC 74-6707. 220p. 1974. Repr. of 1960 ed. lib. bdg. 35.00x (ISBN 0-8371-7541-0, FLOW). Greenwood.
Scientific Work of John Winthrop: An Original Anthology. Michael Shute. Ed. by I. Bernard Cohen. LC 79-8005. (Three Centuries of Science in America Ser.). (Illus.). 1980. lib. bdg. 23.00x (ISBN 0-405-12593-3). Ayer Co Pubs.
Scientific Work of Rene Descartes, 1596-1650. J. F. Scott. Ed. by Willis Doney. (Philosophy of Descartes Ser.). 220p. 1987. lib. bdg. 40.00 (ISBN 0-8240-4672-2). Garland Pub.
Scientific Works. David R. Iriarte. LC 82-82544. (Illus.). 544p. (Orig.). 1983. pap. 39.00 (ISBN 0-89729-316-9). Ediciones.
Scientific World of Copernicus. Ed. by B. Bienkowska. Tr. by K. Cekalska from Pol. LC 73-85712. 1973. lib. bdg. 29.00 (ISBN 90-277-0353-1, Pub. by Reidel Holland). Kluwer Academic.
Scientific World Perspective & Other Essays: 1931-1963. Kazimierz Ajdukiewicz. Ed. by Jerzy Giedymin. (Synthese Library: No. 108). 1977. lib. bdg. 66.00 (ISBN 90-277-0527-5, Pub. by Reidel Holland). Kluwer Academic.
Scientific World View in Dystopia. Alexandra Aldridge. Ed. by Robert Scholes. LC 84-2724. (Studies in Speculative Fiction: No. 3). 108p. 1984. 37.95 (ISBN 0-8357-1572-8). UMI Res Pr.
Scientific Worldview. Glenn Borchardt. (Illus.). xiii, 343p. (Orig.). 1984. 49.95 (ISBN 0-917929-01-2); pap. 29.95 (ISBN 0-917929-00-4). Progressive Sci Inst.
Scientific Writing for Graduate Students. 5th ed. CBE Committee on Graduate Training in Scientific Writing. LC 68-56104. (Illus.). 187p. 1968. pap. text ed. 12.95x (ISBN 0-914340-06-9). Coun Biology Eds.
Scientific Writings of David Rittenhouse: An Original Authology. Ed. by Brooke Hindle & I. Bernard Cohen. LC 79-7987. (Three Centuries of Science in America Ser.). (Illus.). 1980. lib. bdg. 45.00x (ISBN 0-405-12568-2). Ayer Co Pubs.
Scientific Yoga for the Man of Today. Sri S. Chakravarti. 1971. pap. 3.50 (ISBN 0-685-58385-6). Ranney Pubns.
Scientism & Values. Ed. by Helmut Schoeck & James W. Wiggins. LC 78-172228. (Right Wing Individualist Tradition in America Ser). Repr. of 1960 ed. 20.00 (ISBN 0-405-00436-2). Ayer Co Pubs.
Scientism in Chinese Thought, Nineteen Hundred to Nineteen Fifty. D. W. Kwok. LC 73-162297. 231p. 1972. Repr. of 1965 ed. 18.00 (ISBN 0-8196-0275-2). Biblo.
Scientist: A Metaphysical Autobiography. rev. ed. LC 78-3545. (Illus.). 224p. 1988. Repr. 9.95 (ISBN 0-914171-21-6). Ronin Pub.
Scientist & Activist, Phyllis Stearner. Mary E. Verheyden-Hilliard. LC 87-82597. (American Women in Science Biographies Ser.). (Illus.). 32p. (Orig.). (gr. 1-4). 1988. pap. 4.50 (ISBN 0-932469-15-9). Equity Inst.
Scientist & Administrator, Antoinette Rodez Schiesler. Mary E. Verheyden-Hilliard. LC 84-25978. (American Women in Science Biographies Ser.). (Illus.). 32p. (Orig.). (gr. 1-4). 1985. pap. 4.50 (ISBN 0-932469-08-6). Equity Inst.
Scientist & Astronaut, Sally Ride. Mary E. Verheyden-Hilliard. LC 84-25940. (American Women in Science Biographies Ser.). (Illus.). 32p. (Orig.). (gr. 1-4). 1985. pap. 4.50 (ISBN 0-932469-07-8). Equity Inst.
Scientist & Engineer in Court. Michael D. Bradley. LC 83-10582. (Water Resources Monograph: Vol. 8). (Illus.). 111p. (Orig.). 1983. pap. 14.00 (ISBN 0-87590-309-6). Am Geophysical.
Scientist & Governor, Dixy Lee Ray. Mary E. Verheyden-Hilliard. LC 84-25986. (American Women in Science Biographies Ser.). (Illus.). 32p. (Orig.). (gr. 1-4). 1985. pap. 4.50 (ISBN 0-932469-06-X). Equity Inst.
Scientist & Physician, Judith Pachciarz. Mary E. Verheyden-Hilliard. LC 87-82599. (American Women in Science Biographies Ser.). (Illus.). 32p. (Orig.). (gr. 1-4). 1988. pap. 4.50 (ISBN 0-932469-13-2). Equity Inst.
Scientist & Planner, Ru Chih Cheo Huang. LC 84-25982. (American Women in Science Biographies Ser.). (Illus.). 32p. (Orig.). (gr. 1-4). 1985. pap. 4.50 (ISBN 0-932469-03-5). Equity Inst.
Scientist & Puzzle Solver, Constance Tom Noguchi. Mary E. Verheyden-Hilliard. LC 84-25924. (American Women in Science Biographies Ser.). (Illus.). 32p. (Orig.). (gr. 1-4). 1985. pap. 4.50 (ISBN 0-932469-05-1). Equity Inst.
Scientist & Strategist, June Rooks. Mary E. Verheyden-Hilliard. LC 87-82596. (American Women in Science Biographies Ser.). (Illus.). 32p. (Orig.). (gr. 1-4). 1988. pap. 4.50 (ISBN 0-932469-14-0). Equity Inst.
Scientist & Teacher, Anne Barrett Swanson. Mary E. Verheyden-Hilliard. LC 87-82598. (American Women in Science Biographies Ser.). (Illus.). 32p. (Orig.). (gr. 1-4). 1988. pap. 4.50 (ISBN 0-932469-16-7). Equity Inst.
Scientist As Editor. Ed. by Maeve O'Connor. LC 78-60428. 224p. 1979. 19.50 (ISBN 0-471-04932-8, JW). Krieger.
Scientist at the Seashore. James Trefil. (Illus.). 224p. 1987. 8.95 (ISBN 0-02-025920-4, Collier). Macmillan.

Scope of Music. facsimile ed. Percy C. Buck. LC 70-93321. (Essay Index Reprint Ser). 1924. 14.00 (ISBN 0-8369-1276-4). Ayer Co Pubs.

Scope of Political Theology. Kee. Date not set. 9.50 (Pub. by SCM Pr England). Fortress.

Scope of Reincarnation. William. 98p. 1987. pap. 3.00 (ISBN 0-938998-30-7). Theosophy.

Scope of Renaissance Humanism. Charles Trinkaus. 480p. 1983. text ed. 32.50x (ISBN 0-472-10031-9). U of Mich Pr.

Scope of Shelley's Philosophical Thinking. Alexander Cappon. 1938. lib. bdg. 12.50 (ISBN 0-8414-3646-0). Folcroft.

Scope of Shelley's Philosophical Thinking. Alexander P. Cappon. 1978. Repr. of 1935 ed. lib. bdg. 17.00 (ISBN 0-8495-0809-6). Arden Lib.

Scope of Slavic Aspect. Ed. by Michael S. Flier & Alan Timberlake. (UCLA Slavic Studies: Vol. 12). 295p. 1985. 19.95 (ISBN 0-89357-150-4). Slavica.

Scope of Social Architecture. Richard Hatch. LC 81-11437. 362p. 1984. 49.95 (ISBN 0-442-26153-5). Van Nos Reinhold.

Scope of Social Theory: Essays & Sketches, 2 vols. Don Martindale. LC 82-72537. 640p. 1984. Set. pap. text ed. 29.95x (ISBN 0-88105-006-7). Cap & Gown.

Scope of Sociology. Milton M. Gordon. 270p. 1988. pap. text ed. 9.95 (ISBN 0-19-505303-6). Oxford U Pr.

Scope of State Power in China. Ed. by Stuart R. Schram. LC 85-8299. 1985p. 1986. 35.00 (ISBN 0-312-70338-4). St Martin.

Scope of the Fantastic-Culture, Biography, Themes, Children's Literature: Selected Essays from the First International Conference on the Fantastic in Literature & Film. Ed. by Robert A. Collins & Howard D. Pearce. LC 84-530. (Contributions to the Study of Science Fiction & Fantasy Ser.: No. 11). (Illus.). xiii, 284p. 1985. lib. bdg. 36.95 (ISBN 0-313-23448-5, COF/02). Greenwood.

Scope of the Fantastic-Theory, Technique, Major Authors: Selected Essays from the First International Conference on the Fantastic in Literature & Film. Ed. by Robert A. Collins & Howard D. Pearce. LC 84-538. (Contributions to the Study of Science Fiction & Fantasy Ser.: No. 10). (Illus.). xii, 295p. 1985. lib. bdg. 36.95 (ISBN 0-313-23447-7, COF/01). Greenwood.

Scope Twenty Methods for Assessing the Effects of Chemicals on Reproductive Functions. Velimir B. Vouk & Patrick J. Sheehan. LC 82-13529. (Scientific Committee on Problems of the Environment Ser.). 541p. 1983. 87.95x (ISBN 0-471-10538-4, Pub. by Wiley-Interscience). Wiley.

Scope V of the Nursey Industry. 32p. 1985. pap. text ed. 12.95 (ISBN 0-935336-06-0). Horticult Research.

Scopes II-The Great Debate. Bill Keith. LC 82-82837. 193p. (Orig.). pap. 5.95 (ISBN 0-910311-01-3). Huntington Hse Inc.

Scorable Self-Care Evaluation. E. Nelson Clark & Mary Peters. LC 82-61954. 64p. 1984. pap. text ed. 19.95 (ISBN 0-943432-24-3). Slack Inc.

Scorched Earth. (Able Team Ser.: No. 13). Date not set. pap. 2.25 (ISBN 0-317-63976-5, Pub. by Worldwide). Harlequin Bks.

Scorcher. John Lutz. LC 87-221. 272p. 1987. 16.95 (ISBN 0-8050-0411-4). H Holt & Co.

Scorcher. John Lutz. 256p. 1988. pap. 3.95 (ISBN 0-380-70526-5). Avon.

Scorching Wind. Walter Macken. 304p. 1966. pap. 9.95 (ISBN 0-330-30326-0). Bks Britain.

Score. Richard Stark. 1981. lib. bdg. 11.50 (ISBN 0-8398-2711-3, Gregg). G K Hall.

Score. Richard Stark. (Parker Mysteries Ser.). 160p. 1985. 13.95 (ISBN 0-8052-8230-0, Pub. by Allison & Busby England). Schocken.

Score & More: The Sandy Jardine Story. Sandy Jardine & Michael Aitken. 192p. 1987. 50.00x (ISBN 1-85158-078-6, Pub. by Mainstream Scotland). State Mutual Bk.

Score & Podium: A Complete Guide to Conducting. Frederick Prausnitz. 1983. 24.95x (ISBN 0-393-95154-5). Norton.

Score for Lovers Made Men, a Masque by Ben Jonson: The Music Adapted & Arranged for Dramatic Performance from Compositions by Nicholas Lanier, Alphonso Ferrabosco, & Their Contemporaries. Ed. by Andrew J. Sabol. LC 63-8400. (Illus.). 117p. 1963. pap. 12.00x (ISBN 0-87057-073-0). U Pr of New Eng.

Score of Composers see Famous Composers.

Score Reading, 4 vols. Roger Fiske. Incl. Vol. 1. Orchestration. 1958. 8.95x (ISBN 0-19-321301-X); Vol. 2. Musical Form. 1958. 8.95x (ISBN 0-19-321302-8); Vol. 3. Concertos. 1960. 8.95x (ISBN 0-19-321303-6); Vol. 4. Oratorios. 1955. 8.95x (ISBN 0-19-321304-4). (YA) (gr. 9up). Oxford U Pr.

SCORE: Solving Community Obstacles & Restoring Employment. Lynn Wechsler Kramer. LC 83-26555. (Occupational Therapy in Mental Health Ser.: Vol. 4, No. 1). 135p. 1984. text ed. 22.95 (ISBN 0-86656-295-8). Haworth Pr.

Scorebuilder for Financial Accounting. Bruce Baldwin. 1988. pap. 12.95 (ISBN 0-256-06691-4). Irwin.

Scorebuilder for Managerial Accounting. Bruce Baldwin & Diane Pattison. 1988. pap. 12.95 (ISBN 0-256-06692-2). Irwin.

Scorecard. J. Richard Aronson. 1979. Set of 5. pap. 12.95x (ISBN 0-7216-1409-4). Dryden Pr.

Scores: An Anthology of New Music. Commentary by Roger Johnson. LC 80-53302. (Illus.). 450p. 1981. pap. text ed. 19.95 (ISBN 0-02-871190-4). Schirmer Bks.

Scoring Guidelines for the Home Care Accreditation Program. 120p. Date not set. pap. 35.00 (ISBN 0-86688-168-9). Joint Comm Hlthcare.

Scoring High in Addition & Subtracting. Susan Fineman & Susan Ricciardi. (gr. 1-2). 1987. pap. 5.95 (ISBN 0-8224-2726-5). D S Lake Pubs.

Scoring High on Analogy Tests. Eve P. Steinberg. 144p. 1985. pap. 5.95 (ISBN 0-668-06249-5). Arco.

Scoring High on College Entrance Examinations. Nicholas S. Vazzana & Carol J. Theil. (gr. 11-12). 1976. tchrs ed 39.95 (ISBN 0-89507-000-6); wkbk. 5.50 (ISBN 0-685-85067-6). Multi Dimen.

Scoring High on Medical & Health Sciences Exams. Fred A. Anderson. 48p. (Orig.). 1983. pap. 5.95 (ISBN 0-939570-02-5). Skills Improvement.

Scoring High on Reading Tests. 4th ed. LC 77-28477. 1978. pap. 5.00 (ISBN 0-668-00731-1). Arco.

Scoring High on the Armed Forces Test. E. P. Steinberg. LC 83-21395. 288p. (Orig.). 1984. pap. 3.95 (ISBN 0-668-05930-3). Arco.

Scoring: The Shots. Gilbert. LC 76-12423. (Sports Instruction Ser.). (Illus.). (gr. 4 up). 1976. PLB 8.95 (ISBN 0-87191-526-X). Creative Ed.

Scornful Simkin. Lee Lorenz. 1980. 8.95x (ISBN 0-13-796664-4). P-H.

Scornful Simkin. Lee Lorenz. (Illus.). 30p. (Orig.). (gr. k-3). 1982. pap. 3.95 (ISBN 0-13-796730-6, Pub. by Treehouse). P-H.

Scornfyl Lady. Francis Beaumont & John Fletcher. LC 73-38152. (English Experience Ser.: No. 432). 70p. 1972. Repr. of 1616 ed. 9.50 (ISBN 90-221-0432-X). Walter J Johnson.

Scorpio. (Day by Day Horoscopes 1988 Ser.). 192p. 1987. pap. 2.95 (ISBN 0-425-10125-8). Berkley Pub.

Scorpio. (Super Horoscope 1987 Ser.). 1987. pap. 3.95 (ISBN 0-441-79319-3, Pub. by Charter Bks). Ace Bks.

Scorpio. (Astroanalysis Ser.). 1987. pap. 8.95 (ISBN 0-317-63342-2, Charter Pub). Berkley Pub.

Scorpio. 1987. pap. 3.95 (ISBN 0-441-79365-7, Pub. by Charter Bks). Ace Bks.

Scorpio. 3.50 (ISBN 0-515-09128-6). Jove Pubns.

Scorpio. 1988. pap. 8.95 (ISBN 0-425-11213-6). Berkley Pub.

Scorpio see Astroanalysis.

Scorpio: Astro-Numerology. Michael J. Kurban. (Illus.). 50p. (Orig.). 1986. pap. 8.00 (ISBN 0-938863-16-9). Libra Press Chi.

Scorpio-Astroanalysis. 360p. 1984. pap. 8.95. Ace Bks.

Scorpio Cipher. Ralph Hayes. 320p. (Orig.). 1983. pap. 3.25 (ISBN 0-8439-1060-7, Leisure Bks). Leisure NY.

Scorpio Ghosts & the Black Hole Gang. Kathy K. Tapp. LC 86-45492. 192p. (gr. 4-7). 1987. 11.70i (ISBN 0-06-026171-4); PLB 11.89 (ISBN 0-06-026172-2). HarpJ.

Scorpio Rising. R. G. Vliet. 247p. 1985. 16.45 (ISBN 0-394-50616-2). Random.

Scorpio Rising. R. G. Vliet. (Contemporary American Fiction Ser.). 256p. 1986. pap. 6.95 (ISBN 0-14-008513-0). Penguin.

Scorpio Summer. Jacqueline Gilbert. (Harlequin Romances Ser.). (Orig.). 1980. pap. 1.25 (ISBN 0-373-02308-1). Harlequin Bks.

Scorpio: Through the Numbers. Paul Rice & Valeta Rice. 40p. 1983. pap. 2.50 (ISBN 0-87728-572-1). Weiser.

Scorpio, 1987. Sydney Omarr. 1987. pap. 2.95 (ISBN 0-451-14410-4, Sig). NAL.

Scorpion. Katina Alexis. 288p. (Orig.). 1986. pap. 3.50 (ISBN 0-8439-2400-4, Leisure Bks). Leisure NY.

Scorpion. Mildred Davis. 1979. pap. 1.95 (ISBN 0-671-82113-X). PB.

Scorpion. Andrew Kaplan. 336p. 1987. pap. 3.95 (ISBN 0-446-34433-8). Warner Bks.

Scorpion. 2nd ed. Albert Memmi. LC 79-114950. 242p. 1975. 9.95 (ISBN 0-87955-908-X); pap. 7.95 (ISBN 0-87955-906-3). O'Hara.

Scorpion. facsimile ed. Anna E. Weirauch. Tr. by Whittaker Chambers from Ger. LC 75-12357. (Homosexuality Ser.). (Eng.). 1975. Repr. of 1908 ed. 15.00x (ISBN 0-405-07375-5). Ayer Co Pubs.

Scorpion: A Good Bad Horse. Will James. LC 36-23527. (Illus.). vi, 312p. 1975. pap. 8.95 (ISBN 0-8032-5822-4, BB 604, Bison). U of Nebr Pr.

Scorpion-Fish. Nicolas Bouvier. Tr. by Robyn Marsack from Fr. 123p. 1987. 17.95 (ISBN 0-85635-551-8). Carcanet.

Scorpion God. William Golding. (Portway Ser.). 264p. 1988. lib. bdg. 18.50x (ISBN 0-7451-7104-4, Pub. by Chivers Pr UK). G K Hall.

Scorpion God: Three Short Novels. William Golding. 1984. pap. 3.95 (ISBN 0-15-679658-9, Harv). HarBraceJ.

Scorpion: The CVR(T) Range. Simon Dunstanx. (Tanks Illustrated Ser.: No. 22). (Illus.). 72p. (Orig.). 1986. pap. 9.95 (ISBN 0-85368-747-1, Pub. by Arms & Armour). Sterling.

Scorpions. Robert Kelly. LC 84-8785. 192p. (Orig.). 1985. pap. 7.95 (ISBN 0-88268-018-8). Station Hill Pr.

Scorpions. Walter D. Myers. LC 85-45815. 224p. (YA) (gr. 7 up). 1988. 12.95i (ISBN 0-06-024364-3); PLB 12.89 (ISBN 0-06-024365-1). HarpJ.

Scorpions. (Metal Mania Ser.). (Illus.). 48p. (gr. 4-12). 1984. 6.95 (ISBN 0-88188-330-1, Robus Books). H Leonard Pub Corp.

Scorpion's Tail. William Haggard. 15.95 (ISBN 0-88411-669-7, Pub. by Aeonian Pr). Amereon Ltd.

Scorpion's Tail. Antony Sharples. LC 75-26100. 194p. 1976. 8.95 (ISBN 0-8008-7004-2). Taplinger.

Scorpio's Class Act. Margie Palatini. (No. 11). 160p. 1985. pap. 2.25 (ISBN 0-425-08406-X, Pub. by Berkley-Pacer). Berkley Pub.

Scorpius. John Gardner. (James Bond Ser.). 320p. 1988. 12.95 (ISBN 0-399-13347-X). Putnam Pub Group.

Scorpius. John Gardner. LC 88-16066. 402p. 1988. Repr. of 1988 ed. lib. bdg. 17.95 (ISBN 0-89621-176-2). Thorndike Pr.

Scot & His Oats: A Survey of the Part Played by Oats & Oatmeal in Scottish History, Legend, Romance, & the Scottish Character. G. W. Lockhart. 72p. 1986. pap. 11.00x (ISBN 0-946487-05-7, Pub. by Luath Pr UK). State Mutual Bk.

Scot Free. Ivy Strick. LC 78-66809. 1979. 8.95 (ISBN 0-8008-7012-3). Taplinger.

Scot in History. Wallace Notestein. LC 76-104225. xvii, 371p. 1970. Repr. of 1946 ed. lib. bdg. 35.00x (ISBN 0-8371-3342-4, NOSH). Greenwood.

Scot of the Eighteenth Century. John Watson. LC 76-47571. 1976. Repr. of 1907 ed. lib. bdg. 49.50 (ISBN 0-8414-9459-2). Folcroft.

Scotch. 2nd ed. John Kenneth Galbraith. 176p. 1985. 14.95 (ISBN 0-395-39382-5). HM.

Scotch & Holy Water. John D. Tumpane. LC 81-84788. (Illus.). 348p. (Orig.). 1981. pap. 8.00 (ISBN 0-9607382-0-7). St Giles.

Scotch in Miniature. rev. ed. Picton Publishing Staff & Alan Keegan. (Illus.). 1987. 18.00x (Pub. by Picton UK). State Mutual Bk.

Scotch-Irish. James G. Leyburn. LC 68-14360. 1962. 19.95 (ISBN 0-8078-0843-1). U of NC Pr.

Scotch-Irish Americans. Peter Guttmacher. (Peoples of North America Ser.). (Illus.). 112p. 1988. lib. bdg. 16.95 (ISBN 0-87754-875-7). Chelsea Hse.

Scotch-Irish & Their First Settlements on the Tyger River. George D. Howe. 31p. pap. 5.00 (ISBN 0-686-47728-6, SC 53). Southern Hist Pr.

Scotch-Irish Family Research Made Simple. rev. ed. R. G. Campbell. 65p. 1987. 6.00. Summit Pubns.

Scotch-Irish in America. H. J. Ford. 59.95 (ISBN 0-8490-1004-7). Gordon Pr.

Scotch-Irish in America. Henry J. Ford. LC 69-18775. (American Immigration Collection Ser., No. 1). 1969. Repr. of 1915 ed. 20.00 (ISBN 0-405-00523-7). Ayer Co Pubs.

Scotch-Irish of Colonial Pennsylvania. Wayland F. Dunaway. LC 79-52943. 273p. 1985. Repr. of 1944 ed. 17.50 (ISBN 0-8063-0850-8). Genealog Pub.

Scotch Paisano in Old Los Angeles: Hugo Reid's Life in California, 1832-1852. Susanna B. Dakin. 1979. pap. 7.95x (ISBN 0-520-03717-0). U of Ca[illegible]

Scotch Reels: Scotland in Cinema & Television. Ed. by Colin McArthur. (Illus.). 96p. 1982. pap. 7.95 (ISBN 0-85170-121-3, Pub. by British Film Inst England). U of Ill Pr.

Scotch Verdict: Dame Gordon vs. Pirie & Woods. Lillian Faderman. LC 83-7989. (Illus.). 388p. 1983. 17.50 (ISBN 0-688-01559-X). Morrow.

Scotch Verdict: Dame Gordon vs. Pirie & Woods. Lillian Faderman. LC 83-8620. (Illus.). 388p. 1983. pap. 8.45 (ISBN 0-688-02054-2, Quill NY). Morrow.

Scotia Pontificia: Papal Letters to Scotland Before the Pontificate of Innocent III, 1198 to 1216. Ed. by Robert Somerville. 1981. 65.00x (ISBN 0-19-822433-8). Oxford U Pr.

Scotichronicon: Books XV & XVI, Vol. 8. Ed. by D. R. Watt. Walter Bower. 440p. 1987. text ed. 37.50 (ISBN 0-08-034527-1, AUP). Pergamon.

Scotichronicon, Vol. 8: Books XV & XVI. Ed. by D. R. Watt. Date not set. 30.01 (ISBN 0-317-59594-6, AUP). Pergamon.

Scoticisms, Arranged in Alphabetical Order, Designed to Correct Improprieties of Speech & Writing. James Beattie. LC 78-67647. (Scottish Enlightenment Ser.). Repr. of 1779 ed. 18.50 (ISBN 0-404-17177-X). AMS Pr.

Scotish Poems, 3 vols. Ed. by John Pinkerton. LC 70-144531. Repr. of 1792 ed. Set. 60.00 (ISBN 0-404-08680-2); 20.00 ea. AMS Pr.

Scotland. Eric G. Grant. (World Bibliographical Ser.: No. 34). 408p. 1982. lib. bdg. 55.00 (ISBN 0-903450-64-X). ABC-Clio.

Scotland. Richenda Miers. (Cadogan Guides Ser.). (Illus.). 350p. (Orig.). 1987. pap. 12.95 (ISBN 0-87106-834-6). Globe Pequot.

Scotland. Graham Ritchie & Anna Ritchie. LC 80-52043. (Ancient Peoples & Places Ser.). (Illus.). 192p. 1985. pap. 10.95f (ISBN 0-500-27365-0). Thames Hudson.

Scotland. (New Michael's Guides). 224p. 1988. 7.95 (ISBN 965-288-032-9). Hunter Pub NY.

Scotland. (AA Holiday Guides). (Illus.). 192p. 1988. pap. 11.95 (ISBN 0-317-67813-2, Pub. by British Tour). Salem Hse Pubs.

Scotland. (Let's Visit Places & Peoples - - Nations, Dependencies, & Sovereignties of the World Ser.). (Illus.). (gr. 5 up). 1988. 12.95 (ISBN 0-222-01021-5). Chelsea Hse.

Scotland. Dorothy B. Sutherland. LC 84-23227. (Enchantment of the World Ser.). (Illus.). 128p. (gr. 5-9). 1985. lib. bdg. 22.60 (ISBN 0-516-02787-5). Childrens.

Scotland. 9th ed. John Tomes. (Blue Guides Ser.). 1986. pap. 19.95 (ISBN 0-393-30370-5). Norton.

Scotland: A New Study. Ed. by Chalmers Clapperton. (Illus.). 344p. 1983. 18.95 (ISBN 0-7153-8489-9). David & Charles.

Scotland & England, 1286-1815. Ed. by Roger Mason. 280p. 1987. text ed. 39.95 (ISBN 0-85976-177-0, Pub. by John Donald UK). Humanities.

Scotland & Europe: 1200-1850. T. C. Smout. 250p. 1986. text ed. 32.50x (ISBN 0-85976-112-6, Pub. by John Donald Pub UK). Humanities.

Scotland & Its First American Colony, 1683-1760. Ned Landsman. LC 84-42891. (Illus.). 352p. 1985. text ed. 39.00x (ISBN 0-691-04724-3). Princeton U Pr.

Scotland & Nationalism: Scottish Society & Politics, 1707-1977. Christopher Harvie. 318p. 1986. pap. 35.00x (Pub. by S P A Bks Ltd). State Mutual Bk.

Scotland & Nationalism: Scottish Society & Politics, 1707-1977. Christopher T. Harvie. LC 77-368131. pap. 79.50 (ISBN 0-317-20063-1, 2023328). Bks Demand UMI.

Scotland & Scotsmen in the Eighteenth Century: From the Memoirs of John Ramsay Esq. of Ochtertyre, 2 vols. John Ramsay. Ed. by Alexander Allardyce. LC 78-67537. Repr. of 1888 ed. 97.50 (ISBN 0-404-17520-1). AMS Pr.

Scotland & the Crusades: 1095-1560. Alan Macquarrie. 300p. 1985. text ed. 35.00x (ISBN 0-85976-115-0, Pub. by John Donald Pub UK). Humanities.

Scotland & the French Revolution. Henry W. Meikle. LC 68-56255. 1969. Repr. of 1912 ed. 35.00x (ISBN 0-678-00588-5). Kelley.

Scotland & the Lowland Tongue: Studies in the Language & Literature of Lowland Scotland in Honour of David Donald Murison. Ed. by J. D. McClure. 248p. 1983. text ed. 35.00 (ISBN 0-08-028482-5). Pergamon.

Scotland & the Union. 1978. 15.00 (ISBN 0-7195-3391-0). Transatl Arts.

Scotland & Wales on Forty Dollars a Day. (Frommer's Dollar-a-Day Guides). (Illus.). 1988. pap. 11.95 (ISBN 0-13-796574-5). Prentice Hall Pr.

Scotland & Wales on Twenty-Five Dollars a Day. Darwin Porter. 300p. 1986. pap. 10.95. S&S.

Scotland; Archaeology & Early History. Anna Ritchie & Graham Ritchie. LC 81-50799. (Ancient People & Places Ser.). (Illus.). 192p. 1981. 19.95 (ISBN 0-500-02100-7). Thames Hudson.

Scotland Before History. Stuart Piggott. 200p. 1981. 25.00x (ISBN 0-85224-348-0, Pub. by Edinburgh Univ England). State Mutual Bk.

Scotland Before History. Stuart Piggott. (Illus.). 193p. 1983. 21.00x (Pub. by Edinburgh U Pr Scotland). Columbia U Pr.

Scotland Before Seventeen Hundred: From Contemporary Documents. Ed. by Peter H. Brown. LC 77-87675. Repr. of 1893 ed. 27.50 (ISBN 0-404-16467-6). AMS Pr.

Scotland Bloody Scotland. Frank Renwick. LC 86-72909. (Illus.). 92p. 1987. pap. 6.95 (ISBN 0-86241-116-5, Pub. by Canongate Pub Ltd). Dufour.

Scotland: Camping & Caravan Parks. 96p. Date not set. pap. 6.95 (ISBN 0-85419-301-4, Pub. by British Tour). Salem Hse Pubs.

Scotland Discovered. Harry Boyne. (Illus.). 128p. 1986. 19.95 (ISBN 0-88162-202-8). Salem Hse Pubs.

Scotland, Europe & the American Revolution. Ed. by George A Shepperson & Owen D. Edwards. LC 76-48756. 1977. 20.00x (ISBN 0-312-70402-X). St Martin.

Scotland for Fishing. 180p. 1987. pap. 4.95 (ISBN 0-907212-46-8, Pub. by British Tour). Salem Hse Pubs.

Scotland for the Motorist. 184p. 1987. pap. 4.95 (ISBN 0-907212-47-6, Pub. by British Tour). Salem Hse Pubs.

Scotland Forever Home: An Introduction to the Homeland for American & Other Scots. Geddes MacGregor. (Illus.). 288p. 1985. pap. 11.95 (ISBN 0-396-08733-7). Dodd.

Scotland from the Air. James Campbell. 160p. 1984. 25.00 (ISBN 0-517-55527-1). Crown.

Scotland: From the Earliest Times to the Present Century. John Mackintosh. LC 75-39198. (Select Bibliographies Reprint Ser.). Repr. of 1890 ed. 27.00 (ISBN 0-8369-6800-X). Ayer Co Pubs.

Scotland from the Earliest Times to 1603. 3rd ed. W. Croft Dickinson. Ed. by Archibald A. Duncan. (Illus.). 1977. text ed. 49.95x (ISBN 0-19-822453-2). Oxford U Pr.

Scotland from the Eleventh Century to 1603. Bruce Webster. (Sources of History Ser.). 240p. 1975. 33.50x (ISBN 0-8014-0942-X). Cornell U Pr.

Scottish Ballad Operas, Three: Farce & Satire. Ed. by Walter H. Rubsamen. (Ballad Opera Ser.). 1974. lib. bdg. 61.00 (ISBN 0-8240-0925-8). Garland Pub.

Scottish Ballad Operas, Two: History & Politics. Ed. by Walter H. Rubsamen. (Ballad Opera Ser.). 1974. lib. bdg. 61.00 (ISBN 0-8240-0924-X). Garland Pub.

Scottish Ballads. Robert Chambers. LC 77-144549. Repr. of 1829 ed. 24.50 (ISBN 0-404-08628-4). AMS Pr.

Scottish Ballads. Lauchlan Watt. 1979. 42.50 (ISBN 0-911156-32-1). Bern Porter.

Scottish Ballads & Ballad Writing. Lauchlan M. Watt. LC 71-144542. Repr. of 1923 ed. 14.00 (ISBN 0-404-08616-0). AMS Pr.

Scottish Ballads & Ballad Writing. Laughlan M. Watt. 1923. lib. bdg. 35.00 (ISBN 0-8414-9681-1). Folcroft.

Scottish Ballads & Songs, Historical & Traditionary, 2 Vols. James Maidment. LC 78-144497. Repr. of 1868 ed. Set. 57.50 (ISBN 0-404-08670-5). Vol. 1 (ISBN 0-404-08671-3). Vol. 2 (ISBN 0-404-08672-1). AMS Pr.

Scottish Ballads & Writing. Laughlan M. Watt. 1978. Repr. of 1923 ed. lib. bdg. 35.50 (ISBN 0-8495-5800-X). Arden Lib.

Scottish Book. Ed. by D. Mauldin. 320p. 1981. 27.95x (ISBN 0-8176-3045-7). Birkhauser.

Scottish Books: A Brief Bibliography. 51p. 1985. 22.00x (ISBN 0-317-39144-5, Pub. by Saltire Soc.). State Mutual Bk.

Scottish Borders & Edinburgh. Roger Smith. (Visitor's Guides). (Illus.). 160p. 1986. pap. 9.95 (ISBN 0-935161-36-8). Hunter Pub NY.

Scottish Burgh & County Heraldry. R. M. Urquhart. LC 72-12491. (Illus.). 272p. 1973. 38.00x (ISBN 0-8103-2005-3). Gale.

Scottish Capital on the American Credit Frontier. W. G. Kerr. LC 75-16575. (Illus.). xviii, 246p. 1976. 16.95 (ISBN 0-87611-035-9). Tex St Hist Assn.

Scottish Cat: An Anthology. Hamish Whyte. (Illus.). 192p. 1987. 23.50 (ISBN 0-08-035077-1, AUP); pap. 12.50 (ISBN 0-08-035078-X, AUP). Pergamon.

Scottish Chapbook Literature. William Harvey. LC 75-154643. (Research & Source Works Ser: No. 695). (Illus.). 1971. lib. bdg. 19.50 (ISBN 0-8337-1590-9). B Franklin.

Scottish Chiefs. Jane Porter. (Illus.). 520p. 1982. pap. 16.95 (ISBN 0-684-17620-3, ScribT). Scribner.

Scottish Church History. Gordon Donaldson. (Illus.). 256p. 1986. text ed. 25.00 (ISBN 0-7073-0361-3, Pub. by Scot Acad Pr). Longwood Pub Group.

Scottish Churchmen & the Council of Basle. J. H. Burns. LC 64-7472. 1962. 15.00 (ISBN 0-8023-9034-X). Dufour.

Scottish Clans & Tartans. Ian Grimble. (Illus.). 272p. 1982. pap. 9.95 (ISBN 0-517-54827-5, Harmony). Crown.

Scottish Coalmining Ancestors. Lindsay S. Reeks. LC 86-81614. (Illus.). 1986. 25.00 (ISBN 0-9616950-0-5). L S Reeks.

Scottish Coinage. I. H. Stewart. 1977. 15.00 (ISBN 0-685-51519-2, Pub by Spink & Son England). S J Durst.

Scottish Cooking for American Kitchens: The Caledonian Cook. Caledonian Cook Staff. 44p. 1985. pap. 3.95 (ISBN 0-912951-34-6). ScotPr.

Scottish Country Life. Alexander Fenton. 266p. 1982. 39.00x (ISBN 0-85976-011-1, Pub. by Donald Pubs Scotland). State Mutual Bk.

Scottish Country Life. Alexander Fenton. (Illus.). 266p. 1977. Repr. of 1976 ed. text ed. 19.50 (Pub. by John Donald Pub UK). Humanities.

Scottish Crafts. Ian Finlay. (Illus.). 1977. Repr. of 1948 ed. 29.00x (ISBN 0-7158-1171-1). Charles River Bks.

Scottish Declaration of Independence. E. Raymond Capt. (Illus.). 32p. 1983. pap. 2.00 (ISBN 0-934666-11-3). Artisan Sales.

Scottish Eccentrics. Hugh Mac Diarmid. 320p. 1982. Repr. of 1936 ed. lib. bdg. 50.00 (ISBN 0-8495-3535-2). Arden Lib.

Scottish Economic Bulletin, December 1987, No. 36. 66p. (Orig.). 1988. pap. text ed. 16.00 (ISBN 0-11-493430-4, HM2070, Pub. by Her Maj Station Ofc). UNIPUB.

Scottish Economic Literature to 1800. William R. Scott. 1971. Repr. of 1911 ed. lib. bdg. 17.50 (ISBN 0-8337-3215-3). B Franklin.

Scottish Economic Literature to 1800. William R. Scott. LC 77-125362. 1971. Repr. of 1911 ed. lib. bdg. 19.50x (ISBN 0-678-00717-9). Kelley.

Scottish Embroidery: Medieval to Modern. Margaret Swain. (Illus.). 192p. 1987. 42.50 (ISBN 0-7134-4638-2, Pub. by Batsford England). David & Charles.

Scottish Enlightenment. David Daiches. 48p. 1986. 15.00x (ISBN 0-85411-032-1, Pub. by Saltire Soc). State Mutual Bk.

Scottish Enlightenment: An AMS Press Reprint Series. Ed. by Coleman O. Parsons. (39 titles in 51 vols.). Repr. of 1888 ed. write for info. (ISBN 0-404-17120-6). AMS Pr.

Scottish Enlightenment & Early Victorian English Society. Anand C. Chitnis. LC 85-22379. 224p. 1986. 34.50 (ISBN 0-85664-580-X, Pub. by Croom Helm Ltd). Routledge Chapman & Hall.

Scottish Enlightenment & the Theory of Spontaneous Order. Ronald Hamowy. (Journal of the History of Philosophy Monograph Ser.). 96p. 1987. pap. text ed. 10.95x (ISBN 0-8093-1383-9). S Ill U Pr.

Scottish Fairy & Folk Tales. Ed. by George B. Douglas & Richard M. Dorson. LC 77-70591. (International Folklore Ser.). (Illus.). 1977. Repr. of 1901 ed. lib. bdg. 23.00x (ISBN 0-405-10092-2). Ayer Co Pubs.

Scottish Family History. David Moody. 224p. 1988. 39.95 (ISBN 0-7134-5724-4, Pub. by Batsford England); pap. 22.95 (ISBN 0-7134-5725-2, Pub. by Batsford England). David & Charles.

Scottish Family History: A Guide to Works of Reference on the History & Genealogy of Scottish Families. Margaret Stuart. LC 77-90813. 386p. 1983. Repr. of 1930 ed. 17.50 (ISBN 0-8063-0795-1). Genealog Pub.

Scottish Fare. Norma Latimer & Gordon Latimer. (Traditional Cooking of Great Britain Ser.). (Illus.). 105p. (Orig.). 1983. pap. 5.95 (ISBN 0-941869-02-4). Latimers.

Scottish Farm Animals. Picton Publishing Staff. 1987. 7.00x (Pub. by Picton UK). State Mutual Bk.

Scottish Feilde & Flodden Feilde: Two Flodden Poems. Ed. by San F. Baird. (Medieval Literature Ser.). 112p. 1982. lib. bdg. 24.00 (ISBN 0-8240-9449-2). Garland Pub.

Scottish Fiddlers & Their Music. Mary A. Alburger. (Illus.). 224p. 1983. 35.95 (ISBN 0-575-03174-3, Pub. by Gollancz England). David & Charles.

Scottish Finance Sector. Neil Hood et al. (Scottish Industrial Policy Ser.: No. 4). 300p. 1987. 55.00 (ISBN 0-85224-550-5, Pub. by Edinburgh U Pr Scotland). Columbia U Pr.

Scottish Firsts: Innovation & Achievement. Elspeth Wills. 104p. 1987. 35.00x (ISBN 1-85158-060-3, Pub. by Mainstream Scotland). State Mutual Bk.

Scottish Folk Songs for the Young. Derek Pearson. 1983. 25.00x (ISBN 0-904265-27-7, Pub. by Macdonald Pub UK). State Mutual Bk.

Scottish Folk Tales. Ruth Ratcliff. 1977. 19.00 (ISBN 0-685-87557-1). State Mutual Bk.

Scottish Football: A Pictorial History from 1867 to the Present Day. Kevin McCarra. 132p. 1984. 29.00x (Pub. by Third Eye Centre). State Mutual Bk.

Scottish Forester. John Davies. 69p. 1981. 10.00x (ISBN 0-85158-130-7, Pub. by Blackwood & Sons England). State Mutual Bk.

Scottish Gael. James Logan. Ed. by Alex Stewart. 880p. 1982. 90.00x (ISBN 0-85976-021-9, Pub. by Donald Pubs Scotland). State Mutual Bk.

Scottish Gael: Or, Celtic Manners As Preserved among the Highlanders, 2 vols. James Logan. LC 77-87679. Repr. of 1876 ed. Set. 59.50 (ISBN 0-404-16560-5). AMS Pr.

Scottish Gold & Silver Work. Ian Finlay. Rev. by Henry Fothringham. 280p. 1988. 125.00x (Pub. by S P A Bks Ltd). State Mutual Bk.

Scottish Gypsies under the Stewarts. David MacRitchie. LC 75-3463. Repr. of 1894 ed. 14.50 (ISBN 0-404-16892-2). AMS Pr.

Scottish Hand Loom Weavers: A Social History 1790-1850. Norman Murray. 300p. 1982. 59.00x (ISBN 0-85976-028-6, Pub. by Donald Pubs Scotland). State Mutual Bk.

Scottish Highland Games in America. Emily A. Donaldson. LC 85-28479. (Orig.). 1986. 15.95 (ISBN 0-88289-474-9). Pelican.

Scottish Highlands. (AA Ordinance Survey Leisure Guides Ser.). (Illus.). 120p. 1986. pap. 18.95 (ISBN 0-86145-235-6, Pub. by Automobile Assn Brit); bds. 22.95 laminated (ISBN 0-86145-236-4). Salem Hse Pubs.

Scottish History & Literature. John M. Ross. 1973. Repr. of 1884 ed. 35.00 (ISBN 0-8274-0940-0). R West.

Scottish History of James the Fourth. Robert Greene. LC 82-45781. (Malone Society Reprint Ser.: No. 50). Repr. of 1921 ed. 40.00 (ISBN 0-404-63050-2). AMS Pr.

Scottish Housing Statistics 1986. 46p. (Orig.). 1987. pap. text ed. 20.00 (ISBN 0-11-493395-2, HM1050, Pub. by Her Maj Station Ofc). UNIPUB.

Scottish Internationalists' Who's Who, 1872-1986. Douglas Lamming. 250p. 1987. 60.00x (ISBN 0-907033-47-4, Hutton Pr). State Mutual Bk.

Scottish Journey. Edwin Muir. 250p. 1981. 29.75x (ISBN 0-906391-04-0, Pub. by Mainstream). State Mutual Bk.

Scottish Juvenile Justice System. F. M. Martin & K. Murray. 224p. 1983. 17.00x (ISBN 0-7073-0296-X, Pub. by Scot Acad Pr); pap. 9.00x (ISBN 0-7073-0337-0). Longwood Pub Group.

Scottish Law Commission, Annual Report. 29p. (Orig.). 1987. pap. 10.50 (HM1484, Pub. by Her Maj Station Ofc). UNIPUB.

Scottish Legal Tradition. 4th ed. Lord Cooper. Ed. by Michael C. Meston. 36p. 1986. 15.00x (ISBN 0-85411-023-2, Pub. by Saltire Soc). State Mutual Bk.

Scottish Legends, Folklore & Superstitiion. Christian H. McKee. LC 83-80904. (Illus.). 56p. (Orig.). 1983. pap. 4.75 (ISBN 0-9611046-0-0). C H McKee.

Scottish Life & Poetry. Lauchlan M. Watt. LC 75-144543. Repr. of 1912 ed. 23.00 (ISBN 0-404-08617-9). AMS Pr.

Scottish Life & Poetry. Lauchlan M. Watt. 1973. lib. bdg. 39.00 (ISBN 0-8414-9682-X). Folcroft.

Scottish Lifestyle 300 Years Ago New Light on Edinburgh & Border Families. Keith Kelsall & Helen Kelsall. 236p. 1986. 19.95 (ISBN 0-85976-167-3, Pub. by John Donald Pub UK). Humanities.

Scottish Literacy & the Scottish Identity: Illiteracy & Society in Scotland & Northern England, 1600-1800. Rab Houston. (Cambridge Studies in Population, Economy & Society in Past Time: No. 4). (Illus.). 336p. 1985. 49.50 (ISBN 0-521-26598-3). Cambridge U Pr.

Scottish Literature. G. Gregory Smith. 1919. lib. bdg. 39.50 (ISBN 0-8414-0429-1). Folcroft.

Scottish Literature & the Scottish People 1680 to 1830. David Craig. 340p. 1980. Repr. of 1961 ed. lib. bdg. 39.50 (ISBN 0-89987-102-X). Darby Bks.

Scottish Literature in English & Scots: A Guide to Information Sources. Ed. by W. R. Aitken. LC 73-16971. (American Literature, English Literature, & World Literature in English Ser.: Vol. 37). 448p. 1982. 68.00x (ISBN 0-8103-1249-2). Gale.

Scottish Literature's Debt to Italy. R. D. Jack. 86p. 1987. 10.00 (ISBN 0-85224-526-2, Pub. by Edinburgh U Pr Scotland). Columbia U Pr.

Scottish Local Government Elections 1974. J. M. Bochel & D. T. Denver. 1974. pap. 12.50x (ISBN 0-7073-0111-4, Pub. by Scot Acad Pr). Longwood Pub Group.

Scottish Local History: An Introductory Guide. David Moody. (Illus.). 160p. 1987. 35.95 (ISBN 0-7134-5220-X, Pub. by Batsford England); pap. 18.95 (ISBN 0-7134-5221-8, Pub. by Batsford England). David & Charles.

Scottish Local Studies Resources: Directory of Publications from Scottish Public Libraries. Brian D. Osborne. 1987. 29.00x (ISBN 0-900649-59-3, Pub. by Scottish Libr Assn). State Mutual Bk.

Scottish Lord. Joan Wolf. 1988. pap. 2.95 (ISBN 0-451-15288-3, Sig). NAL.

Scottish Mediaeval Churches. Stewart Cruden. (Illus.). 400p. 1986. text ed. 55.00x (ISBN 0-85976-104-5, Pub. by John Donald Scotland). Humanities.

Scottish Medieval Town. Ed. by Michael Lynch et al. 300p. 1987. text ed. 50.00 (ISBN 0-85976-170-3, Pub. by John Donald Pub UK). Humanities.

Scottish Men of Letters in the Eighteenth Century. Henry G. Graham. 1973. Repr. of 1908 ed. 35.00 (ISBN 0-8274-1568-0). R West.

Scottish Methodism in the Early Victorian Period: The Scottish Correspondence of the Reverend Jabez Bunting, 1800-1857. A. J. Hayes & D. A. Gowland. 143p. 1981. 20.00x (Pub. by Edinburgh U Pr Scotland). Columbia U Pr.

Scottish Methodism in the Early Victorian Period: The Scottish Correspondence of the Rev. Jabez Bunting 1800-57. Ed. by A. J. Hayes & D. A. Gowland. 1981. 40.00x (Pub. by Edinburgh Univ England). State Mutual Bk.

Scottish Metrical Romance of Lancelot Du Lak with Miscellaneous Poems. Ed. by Joseph Stevenson. LC 70-165337. Repr. of 1839 ed. 12.00 (ISBN 0-404-53029-X). AMS Pr.

Scottish Military Dress. Peter Cochrane. (Illus.). 128p. 1988. 24.95 (ISBN 0-7137-1738-6, Pub. by Blandford Pr England). Sterling.

Scottish Minstrel: (the Songs of Scotland Subsequent to Burns with Memoirs of the Poets) Charles Rogers. 1978. lib. bdg. 100.00 (ISBN 0-8414-7298-X). Folcroft.

Scottish Moralists on Human Nature & Society. Louis Schneider. LC 67-15316. (Heritage of Sociology). pap. 89.50 (ISBN 0-317-26687-X, 2025113). Bks Demand UMI.

Scottish Museums & Galleries Guide. Ed. by British Tourist Authority Staff. (Illus.). 112p. (Orig.). 1987. pap. 8.95 (ISBN 0-948275-15-4, Pub. by Automobile Assn Brit). Salem Hse Pubs.

Scottish Nationalism. Henry J. Hanham. 1969. 18.50x (ISBN 0-674-79580-6). Harvard U Pr.

Scottish Nationalism & Cultural Identity in the Twentieth Century: An Annotated Bibliography of Secondary Sources. Compiled by Gordon Bryan. LC 84-4667. (Bibliographies & Indexes in Law & Political Science Ser.: No. 1). (Illus.). xii, 180p. 1984. lib. bdg. 40.95 (ISBN 0-313-23998-3, BNA/). Greenwood.

Scottish Novel: From Smollett to Spark. Francis R. Hart. LC 77-20680. 1978. 32.00x (ISBN 0-674-79584-9). Harvard U Pr.

Scottish Nursery Rhymes. Ed. by Nora Montgomerie & William Montgomerie. (Illus.). 158p. 1988. pap. 8.95 (ISBN 0-550-20480-6, Pub. by W & R Chambers). Cambridge U Pr.

Scottish Office & Other Scottish Government Departments. David Milne. LC 84-24792. (New Whitehall Ser.). v, 140p. 1986. Repr. of 1957 ed. lib. bdg. 41.50x (ISBN 0-313-23655-0, MISO). Greenwood.

Scottish Pageant. Agnes M. MacKenzie. Repr. of 1946 ed. lib. bdg. 30.50 (ISBN 0-8414-6316-6). Folcroft.

Scottish People. James A. Rennie. 350p. 1983. pap. 8.75 (ISBN 0-912951-08-7). Scotpr.

Scottish Philosophy. Andrew Seth. LC 82-48346. (Philosophy of David Hume Ser.). 236p. 1983. lib. bdg. 33.00 (ISBN 0-8240-5417-2). Garland Pub.

Scottish Philosophy: A Comparison of the Scottish & German Answers to Hume. Andrew Seth Pringle Pattison. 1971. Repr. of 1890 ed. lib. bdg. 20.50 (ISBN 0-8337-3237-4). B Franklin.

Scottish Philosophy, Biographical, Expository, Critical, from Hutcheson to Hamilton. James McCosh. LC 75-3266. (Philo. in Amer Ser.). 496p. 1980. Repr. of 1875 ed. 41.50 (ISBN 0-404-59254-6). AMS Pr.

Scottish Poetry Book. Ed. by Alan Bold. (Illus.). 128p. (gr. k-3). 1987. 11.95 (ISBN 0-19-916029-5); pap. 5.95 (ISBN 0-19-916030-9). Oxford U Pr.

Scottish Poetry: Drummond of Hawthornden to Fergusson. George Douglas. LC 74-13044. 1973. lib. bdg. 35.00 (ISBN 0-8414-3777-7). Folcroft.

Scottish Poetry of the Eighteenth Century, 2 vols. Ed. by George Eyre-Todd. LC 74-98755. 1971. Repr. of 1896 ed. Vol. 1. lib. bdg. 18.75 (ISBN 0-8371-5836-2, EYED); Vol. 2. lib. bdg. 18.75 (ISBN 0-8371-5837-0, EYEF). Greenwood.

Scottish Poetry of the Seventeenth Century: Robert Aytoun, David Murray, Robert Ker, William Alexander, William Drummond, Marquis of Montrose, The Samples of Beltress. Ed. by George Eyre-Todd. 296p. 1983. Repr. of 1895 ed. lib. bdg. 45.00 (ISBN 0-89987-220-4). Darby Bks.

Scottish Poets in America. Compiled by John D. Ross. LC 72-80502. 1972. Repr. of 1889 ed. lib. bdg. 22.00 (ISBN 0-405-08899-X, Pub. by Blom). Ayer Co Pubs.

Scottish Political System. 3rd ed. James G. Kellas. LC 83-24085. 1985. o. p. 49.50 (ISBN 0-521-26249-6). Cambridge U Pr.

Scottish Poor Law 1745-1845. R. A. Cage. 216p. 1981. 20.00x (ISBN 0-7073-0289-7, Pub. by Scot Acad Pr). Longwood Pub Group.

Scottish Population History: From the Seventeenth Century to the 1930s. Michael W. Flinn. LC 76-11060. (Illus.). 1978. 79.50 (ISBN 0-521-21173-5). Cambridge U Pr.

Scottish Population Statistics. James Kyd. 1976. 12.50x (ISBN 0-7073-0105-X, Pub. by Scot Acad Pr). Longwood Pub Group.

Scottish Postbag. Ed. by Paul Scott & George Bruce. 270p. 1987. 17.95 (ISBN 0-550-20490-3). Cambridge U Pr.

Scottish Postgraduate Research into Maladjustment 1974-1983. A. Peacock & K. Denvir. 30p. 1985. pap. text ed. 6.95x (ISBN 0-947833-08-0, Pub. by Scot Council Research). Humanities.

Scottish Pottery. J. Arnold Flemming. (Illus.). 1976. Repr. 24.00x (ISBN 0-85409-778-3). Charles River Bks.

Scottish Prose. H. J. Millar. 1973. Repr. of 1912 ed. 39.50 (ISBN 0-8274-0126-4). R West.

Scottish Prose of the Seventeenth & Eighteenth Centuries. John H. Millar. LC 74-5384. 1912. Repr. lib. bdg. 47.50 (ISBN 0-8414-6128-7). Folcroft.

Scottish Proverbs. A. Henderson. 59.95 (ISBN 0-8490-1005-5). Gordon Pr.

Scottish Proverbs. Andrew Henderson. LC 70-75962. 230p. 1969. Repr. of 1881 ed. 40.00x (ISBN 0-8103-3894-7). Gale.

Scottish Proverbs. Julie McDonald. Ed. by John Zug & Joan Liffring-Zug. (Illus.). 30p. (Orig.). 1987. pap. 6.50 (ISBN 0-941016-42-0). Penfield.

Scottish Radicals: Tried & Transported to Australia for Treason in 1820. Margaret Macfarlane & Alastair Macfarlane. 78p. 1986. 39.00x (ISBN 0-907590-00-4, Pub. by S P A Bks Ltd). State Mutual Bk.

Scottish Reformation. Ian B. Cowan. LC 82-5834. 256p. 1982. 26.50x (ISBN 0-312-70519-0). St Martin.

Scottish Regiments. P. J. Mileham. (Illus.). 256p. 1987. 70.00 (ISBN 0-87052-361-9). Hippocrene Bks.

Scottish Rite Masonry, 2 vols. E. A. Cook. Set. 22.50x (ISBN 0-685-22097-4). Wehman.

Scottish Rite Masonry, 2 vols. Set. 22.50 (ISBN 0-685-19498-1). Powner.

Scottish Roots: A Step-by-Step Guide for Ancestor-Hunters. Alwyn James. LC 81-23455. 181p. 1982. Repr. of 1981 ed. 13.95 (ISBN 0-88289-334-3). Pelican.

Scottish Salt Industry, 1570-1850: An Economic & Social History. C. A. Whately. 200p. 1987. text ed. 22.35 (ISBN 0-08-034528-X, AUP). Pergamon.

Scottish Seaside Towns. Brian Edward. (Illus.). 128p. (Orig.). 1987. pap. 9.95 (ISBN 0-563-20452-4, Pub. by BBC). Parkwest Pubns.

Scottish Short Stories. Ed. by James Campbell. 240p. pap. 5.95 (Pub. by Granada England). Academy Chi Pubs.

Scottish Short Stories. Ed. by Hendry. 1986. pap. 6.95 (ISBN 0-14-003128-6). Penguin.

Scottish Short Stories, Eighteen Hundred to Nineteen Hundred. Ed. by Douglas Gifford. (Orig.). pap. 11.95 (ISBN 0-7145-0657-5). Riverrun NY.

Scottish Sketches. facsimile ed. Amelia Barr. LC 70-157771. (Short Story Index Reprint Ser.). Repr. of 1883 ed. 19.00 (ISBN 0-8369-3883-6). Ayer Co Pubs.

Scottish Sketches of R. B. Cunningham Graham. John Walker. (Illus.). 232p. 1982. 15.00 (ISBN 0-7073-0288-9, Pub. by Scot Acad Pr). Longwood Pub Group.

Scraps: The Ragtime Girl of Oz. Glasgow V. Koste. (Children's Theatre Playscript Ser.). 1986. write for info. (ISBN 0-88020-127-4). Coach Hse.
Scratch. Archibald MacLeish. 1971. 5.95 (ISBN 0-395-12346-1). HM.
Scratch a Lover. Ed Hertzog. LC 81-86717. 80p. 1982. 6.50 (ISBN 0-937894-08-7); pap. 4.50 (ISBN 0-937894-09-5). Life Arts.
Scratch Modelers Log. Henry Bridenbecker. Ed. by Ernest J. Gentle. (Moonraker Ser.). 112p. 1985. 17.95 (ISBN 0-8168-0014-6, 20014, TAB-Aero). TAB Bks.
Scratch Music. Ed. by Cornelius Cardew. 128p. 1974. pap. 7.95x (ISBN 0-262-53025-2). MIT Pr.
Scratchbuilding & Kitbashing Model Railroad Stations. Ed. by Bob Hayden. LC 77-86282. 1978. pap. 4.95 (ISBN 0-89024-533-9). Kalmbach.
Scratchbuilding Model Cars. Saul Santos. (Illus.). 224p. (Orig.). 1983. pap. 10.95 (ISBN 0-8306-2085-0). TAB Bks.
Scratches on Our Minds: American Images of China & India. Harold R. Isaacs. LC 73-9211. (Illus.). 416p. 1973. Repr. of 1958 ed. lib. bdg. 35.00x (ISBN 0-8371-6983-6, ISSM). Greenwood.
Scratches on Our Minds: American Views of China & India. Harold R. Isaacs. LC 80-65695. 452p. 1980. pap. 13.95 (ISBN 0-87332-161-8). M E Sharpe.
Scratching the Beat Surface. Michael McClure. LC 81-86249. (Illus.). 176p. 1982. 17.50 (ISBN 0-86547-073-1). N Point Pr.
Scratching the Surface of Creative Problem Solving. Ruth B. Noller & Ernest Mauthe. (Illus.). 1977. 2.95 (ISBN 0-914634-39-9). DOK Pubs.
Scrawny Sonnets & Other Narratives. Poems. Robert Bagg. LC 72-93266. 54p. 1973. 11.95 (ISBN 0-252-00317-9); pap. 8.95 (ISBN 0-252-00330-6). U of Ill Pr.
Scream. John Skipp & Craig Spector. 384p. (Orig.). 1988. pap. 3.95 (ISBN 0-553-26798-1). Bantam.
Scream Cheese & Jelly. Victoria Gomez. 64p. (gr. 3-7). 1981. pap. 1.50 (ISBN 0-590-31266-9, Schol Pap). Scholastic Inc.
Scream Machines: Roller Coasters Past, Present & Future. Herma Silverstein. (Illus.). 128p. (gr. 3 up). 1986. 13.95 (ISBN 0-8027-6618-8); lib. bdg. 13.95 (ISBN 0-8027-6619-6). Walker & Co.
Scream Quietly or the Neighbors Will Hear. Erin Pizzey. LC 77-23406. 1978. 14.95 (ISBN 0-89490-005-6). Enslow Pubs.
Screaming High. David Line. 176p. (gr. 6 up). 1985. 12.95 (ISBN 0-316-52682-7). Little.
Screaming High. David Line. (Lythway Ser.). (gr. 4-8). 1987. lib. bdg. 14.95x (ISBN 0-7451-0628-5, Pub. by Chivers Pr UK). G K Hall.
Screaming Mimi. Fredric Brown. 166p. 1989. pap. 3.50 (ISBN 0-88184-449-7). Carroll & Graf.
Screaming Room: A Mother's Journal of Her Son's Struggle with AIDS. Barbara Peabody. LC 86-768. 384p. 1986. 15.95 (ISBN 0-86679-030-6, Pub. by Oak Tree). Oak Tree Pubns.
Screaming Room: A Mother's Journal of Her Son's Struggle with AIDS. Barbara Peabody. 288p. 1987. pap. 3.95 (ISBN 0-380-70345-9). Avon.
Screaming Skull: True Stories of the Unexplained. William E. Warren. (Illus.). (gr. 5 up). Date not set. 10.95 (ISBN 0-13-796699-7). P-H.
Screams from the Backroom. Bob Millard. 1977. pap. 1.50 (ISBN 0-917838-02-5). Brevity.
Screams of Protest. Spurgeon E. Crayton. (Illus.). 1982. 10.00 (ISBN 0-8315-0188-X). Speller.
Screamy Mimi. Robert Kraus. (ps-3). Date not set. 7.95 (ISBN 0-317-62460-1, Little Simon). S&S.
Screed. Jack Saunders. LC 80-53288. 250p. 1981. 12.95 (ISBN 0-912824-23-9); pap. 5.95 (ISBN 0-912824-24-7). Vagabond Pr.
Screen Acting. Mae Marsh. 1976. lib. bdg. 59.95 (ISBN 0-8490-2575-3). Gordon Pr.
Screen Acting: How to Succeed in Motion Pictures. Brian Adams. (Illus.). 378p. 1987. pap. 12.95 (ISBN 0-943728-20-7). Lone Eagle Pub.
Screen & Society: The Impact of Television upon Aspects of Contemporary Civilization. Ed. by Frank J. Coppa. LC 79-13500. 248p. 1980. 22.95x (ISBN 0-88229-413-X). Nelson-Hall.
Screen Deco. Howard Mandelbaum & Eric Myers. (Illus.). 224p. 1987. pap. 15.95 (ISBN 0-312-01087-7). St Martin.
Screen Deco: A Celebration of High Style in Hollywood. Howard Mandelbaum & Eric Myers. (Illus.). 176p. 1985. 24.95 (ISBN 0-312-70590-5). St Martin.
Screen Design Strategies for Computer-Assisted Instruction. Jesse M. Heines. 150p. 1983. 29.00 (ISBN 0-932376-28-2, EY-00028-DP). Digital Pr.
Screen Education: Teaching a Critical Approach to Cinema & Television. A. W. Hodgkinson. (Reports & Papers on Mass Communication: No. 42). (Orig., 5th Printing 1975). 1964. pap. 5.00 (ISBN 92-3-100554-5, U591, UNESCO). UNIPUB.
Screen Greats: Hollywood Nostalgia. M. Samuels. 1980. pap. 2.00 (ISBN 0-931064-30-9). Starlog Pr.
Screen Image of Youth: Movies about Children & Adolescents. Ruth M. Goldstein & Edith Zornow. LC 80-14053. (Illus.). xxi, 363p. 1980. 25.00 (ISBN 0-8108-1316-5). Scarecrow.
Screen Input-Output Programming Techniques Using Turbo Pascal. Andy Stuart. 457p. (Orig.). 1987. pap. 24.95 (ISBN 0-943518-28-8); book & disk 44.95 (ISBN 0-317-57999-1). MIS Press.
Screen Lovers. Anne Billson. (Illus.). 208p. 1988. 27.95 (ISBN 0-312-02073-2). St Martin.
Screen Monographs One. LC 75-124020. (Literature of Cinema, Ser. 1). Repr. of 1970 ed. 5.00 (ISBN 0-405-01626-3). Ayer Co Pubs.
Screen Monographs Two. LC 75-124020. (Literature of Cinema, Ser. 1). Repr. of 1970 ed. 7.00 (ISBN 0-405-01627-1). Ayer Co Pubs.
Screen Personalities of 1933. V. Trotta & C. Lewis. 1976. lib. bdg. 75.95 (ISBN 0-8490-2576-1). Gordon Pr.
Screen Printer's Production Manual. Richard Webb. 100p. (Orig.). Date not set. pap. 14.95 (ISBN 0-911380-78-7). Signs of Times.
Screen Printing. J. I. Biegeleisen. (Illus.). 160p. 1971. 27.50 (ISBN 0-8230-4665-6). Watson-Guptill.
Screen Printing Electronic Circuits. Albert Kosloff. (Illus.). 1980. 15.95 (ISBN 0-911380-49-3). Signs of Times.
Screen Printing Electronic Circuits. Albert Kosloff. (Illus.). 140p. 1984. 24.95 (ISBN 0-317-57914-2, 10006). Bishop Graphics.
Screen Printing: Photostencil Methods. Date not set. text ed. write for info. (ISBN 0-88362-100-2, 0801); write for info. instr's. guide (ISBN 0-88362-101-0, 0800). Graphic Arts Tech Found.
Screen Printing Primer. Babette Magee. LC 85-71229. (Illus.). 92p. 1985. 28.00 (1331). Graphic Arts Tech Found.
Screen Printing Techniques. Albert Kosloff. (Illus.). 1981. 17.95 (ISBN 0-911380-52-3). Signs of Times.
Screen Printing Techniques. Silvie Turner. LC 75-18636. (Illus.). 1979. pap. 7.95 (ISBN 0-8008-7008-5, Pentalic). Taplinger.
Screen Process Printing. Robert A. Banzhaf. 1983. text ed. 14.00 (ISBN 0-02-672270-4). Glencoe Bennett & McKnight.
Screen World, 10 vols. 1949, 1951-1959. Daniel Blum. LC 70-84068. (Illus.). 1969. Set. 200.00 (ISBN 0-8196-0255-8); 22.50 ea. Biblo.
Screen World, Nineteen Eighty-Six, Vol. 37. John Willis. (Illus.). 256p. 1986. 24.95 (ISBN 0-517-56257-X). Crown.
Screen World: Volumes 11-20, 1960 to 1969, The Complete Pictorial & Statistical Record of the Movies. Incl. Vol. 11. Daniel Blum. (Illus.). 240p. 1960 (ISBN 0-8196-0301-5); Vol. 12. Daniel Blum. (Illus.). 240p. 1961 (ISBN 0-8196-0302-3); Vol. 13. Daniel Blum. (Illus.). 240p. 1962 (ISBN 0-8196-0303-1); Vol. 14. Daniel Blum. 240p. 1963 (ISBN 0-8196-0304-X); Vol. 15. Daniel Blum. 240p. 1964 (ISBN 0-8196-0305-8); Vol. 16. Daniel Blum. 240p. 1965 (ISBN 0-8196-0307-4); Vol. 17. John Willis. 256p. 1966; Vol. 18. John Willis. 256p. 1967 (ISBN 0-8196-0308-2); Vol. 19. John Willis. 256p. 1968 (ISBN 0-8196-0309-0); Vol. 20. John Willis. 256p. 1969 (ISBN 0-8196-0310-4). LC 75-612827. (Illus.). 256p. 1983. Repr. of 1960 ed. Set, 10 vols. 200.00 (ISBN 0-517-52583-6); 22.50 ea. Biblo.
Screen World 1983. John Willis. 1983. 19.95 (ISBN 0-517-55067-9). Crown.
Screen World: 1984, Vol. 35. John Willis. (Illus.). 1984. 19.95 (ISBN 0-517-55437-2). Crown.
Screen World, 1985: 1985, Vol. 36. 1985. 22.50 (ISBN 0-517-55821-1). Crown.
Screen World, 1987, Vol. 38. John Willis. (Illus.). 256p. 1987. 29.95 (ISBN 0-517-56615-X). Crown.
Screen World, 1988, Vol. 39. John Willis. (Illus.). 256p. 1988. 29.95 (ISBN 0-517-56963-9). Crown.
Screening America: Using Hollywood Films to Teach History. Marlette Rebhorn. (American University Studies. Series IX, History: Vol. 42). 211p. 1988. 34.50 (ISBN 0-8204-0726-7). P Lang Pubs.
Screening & Diagnosis of Children with Learning Disabilities. Ronald A. Berk. 296p. 1984. 32.75x (ISBN 0-398-04925-4). C C Thomas.
Screening & Diagnostic Procedures. 1983. 1.50 (ISBN 0-939418-50-9). Ferguson Florissant.
Screening & Evaluation in Centralized Forensic Mental Health Facilities. National Center for State Courts Staff. 108p. 1981. manuscript 6.48 (OPS-005). Natl Ctr St Courts.
Screening & Management of Potentially Treatable Genetic Metabolic Disorders. Ed. by P. F. Benson. 176p. 1984. lib. bdg. 57.50 (ISBN 0-85200-784-1, Pub. by MTP Pr England). Kluwer Academic.
Screening & Summary Calendar Procedures at the District of Columbia Court of Appeals: An Evaluation. National Center for State Courts Staff. 42p. 1978. manuscript 2.52 (MARO-005). Natl Ctr St Courts.
Screening Candidates for the Priesthood & Religious Life. Vincent V. Herr et al. (Illus.). 1964. 2.80 (ISBN 0-8294-0038-9). Loyola.
Screening Deep Test of Articulation. Eugene T. McDonald. 69p. (Orig.). 1976. pap. text ed. 35.00 (ISBN 0-88450-912-5, 7230-B). Communication Skill.
Screening for Biological Response Modifiers: Methods & Rationale. James E. Talmadge et al. (Developments in Oncology Ser.). 1985. lib. bdg. 32.50 (ISBN 0-89838-712-4, Pub. by Martinus Nijhoff Netherlands). Kluwer Academic.
Screening for Brain Impairment: A Manual for Mental Health Practice. Berg et al. 256p. 1987. pap. 24.95 (ISBN 0-8261-5740-8). Springer Pub.
Screening for Breast Cancer. Ed. by N. E. Day & A. B. Miller. 160p. 1988. text ed. 26.00 (ISBN 0-920887-26-0, Pub. by H Huber Canada). Hogrefe Intl.
Screening for Cancer. Ed. by Anthony B. Miller. 1985. 77.00 (ISBN 0-12-496720-5). Acad Pr.
Screening for Cancer: General Principles on Evaluation of Screening for Cancer & Screening for Lung, Bladder & Oral Cancer. P. C. Prorok & A. B. Miller. (UICC Technical Report Ser.: Vol. 78). 186p. 1984. pap. text ed. 18.00 (Pub. by UICC Switzerland). Hogrefe Intl.
Screening for Cancer of the Uterine Cervix. Ed. by M. Hakama et al. (IARC Scientific Publications: No. 76). 300p. 1987. 55.00 (ISBN 92-832-1176-6). Oxford U Pr.
Screening for Children with Special Needs: Multidisciplinary Approaches. Ed. by Geoff Lindsay. 202p. 1984. 25.00 (ISBN 0-7099-1636-1, Pub. by Croom Helm Ltd); pap. 15.50 (ISBN 0-7099-4130-7). Routledge Chapman & Hall.
Screening for Gastrointestinal Cancer. Ed. by Jocelyn Chamberlain & Anthony B. Miller. 160p. 1987. text ed. 19.00x (ISBN 0-920887-24-4, Pub. by H Huber Canada). Hogrefe Intl.
Screening for Hearing Impairment: A Practical Guide. Barry McCormack. (Illus.). 128p. 1988. pap. text ed. 19.95x (ISBN 0-7099-4643-0, Pub by Croom Helm England). Sheridan.
Screening Growth & Development of Preschool Children: A Guide for Test Selection. Sharon Stangler et al. (Illus.). 1979. text ed. 25.95 (ISBN 0-07-060780-X). McGraw.
Screening in Chronic Disease. Alan S. Morrison. (Monographs in Epidemiology & Biostatistics: Vol. 7). (Illus.). 1985. 35.00x (ISBN 0-19-503505-4). Oxford U Pr.
Screening Methods in Pharmacology, Vol. 2. Robert A. Turner & Peter Hebborn. 1971. 81.00 (ISBN 0-12-704252-0). Acad Pr.
Screening of Inborn Errors of Metabolism: A Report. WHO Scientific Group, Geneva, 1967. (Technical Report Ser: No. 401). 57p. 1968. pap. 2.00 (ISBN 92-4-120401-X, 701). World Health.
Screening Out the Past: The Birth of Mass Culture & the Motion Picture Industry, with a New Preface. Lary May. LC 83-4927. (Illus.). 1983. pap. 11.95 (ISBN 0-226-51173-1). U of Chicago Pr.
Screening Out the Past: The Birth of Mass Culture & the Motion Picture Industry. Lary L. May. LC 80-11889. (Illus.). 1980. 29.95x (ISBN 0-19-502762-0). Oxford U Pr.
Screening Red Blood Cell Glucose-6 Phosphate Dehydrogenase Activity: Approved Standard, Vol. 4. National Committee for Clinical Laboratory Standards. 1984. 20.00 (ISBN 0-318-19438-4, H12-A). Natl Comm Clin Lab Stds.
Screening Requests for Corporate Contributions. Anne Klepper & Selma Mackler. (Report Ser.: No. 887). (Illus.). vi, 31p. (Orig.). 1986. pap. text ed. 75.00 (ISBN 0-8237-0329-0). Conference Bd.
Screening Space: The American Science Fiction Film. Vivian Sobchack. 1986. cancelled (ISBN 0-8044-2814-X); pap. 14.95 (ISBN 0-8044-6886-9). Ungar.
Screening Techniques for Determining Compliance with Environmental Standards. (Commentary Ser.: No. 3). 1986. 12.00. NCRP Pubns.
Screening Test for Auditory Perception Manual. rev. ed. Geraldine M. Kimmell & Jack Wahl. 48p. 1981. pap. 24.00 incl. manual, 50 recording forms & scoring template (ISBN 0-87879-254-6). Acad Therapy.
Screening Test of Adolescent Language (STAL) rev. ed. Elizabeth M. Prather et al. 1987. 35.00 (ISBN 0-295-77002-3); Additional test forms, pkg. of 50. 7.50 (ISBN 0-295-77003-1). U of Wash Pr.
Screening Test of Spanish Grammar. Allen S. Toronto. 1973. 24.95 (ISBN 0-8101-0435-0); extra answer forms (200 pack) 22.95 (ISBN 0-8101-0436-9). Northwestern U Pr.
Screening Tests in Chemical Carcinogenesis. Ed. by R. Montesano et al. (IARC Scientific Publications: No.12). (Illus.). 666p. 1986. pap. 21.50 (ISBN 0-19-723051-2). Oxford U Pr.
Screening Tests in Chemical Carcinogenesis: Proceedings. International Agency for Research on Cancer Workshop. Brussels, Belgium, June 9-12, 1975 & Commission of the European Communities. Ed. by R. Montesano et al. (IARC Scientific Pub.: No. 12). 1976. 48.00 (ISBN 0-686-16923-9). World Health.
Screening the Holocaust: Cinema's Images of the Unimaginable. Ilan Avisar. LC 87-45400. 256p. 1988. 35.00x (ISBN 0-253-30376-1); pap. 12.50 (ISBN 0-253-20475-5). Ind U Pr.
Screenplay As Literature. Douglas G. Winston. LC 72-654. 240p. 1973. 22.50 (ISBN 0-8386-1200-8). Fairleigh Dickinson.
Screenplay: The Foundations of Screenwriting. enl. ed. Ed. by Syd Field. 246p. 1984. pap. 8.95 (ISBN 0-440-57647-4, Dell Trade Pbks). Dell.
Screenplays. Werner Herzog. Tr. by Alan Greenberg from Ger. 208p. 1980. 12.95 (ISBN 0-934378-02-9); pap. 5.95 osi. Tanam Pr.
Screens. Jean Genet. Tr. by Bernard Frechtman from Fr. 1962. pap. 4.95 (ISBN 0-394-17245-0, E374, Ever). Grove.
Screens. Jean Genet. Tr. by Bernard Frechtman. 1987. 7.95 (ISBN 0-394-62381-9). Grove.
Screenwriter As Collaborator. Kent R. Brown. Ed. by Garth S. Jowett. LC 79-6669. (Dissertations on Film, 1980 Ser.). 1980. lib. bdg. 26.50x (ISBN 0-405-12903-3). Ayer Co Pubs.
Screenwriter: The Life & Times of Nunnally Johnson. Tom Stempel. LC 78-75339. (Illus.). 1980. 14.95 (ISBN 0-498-02362-1). A S Barnes.
Screenwriter: Words Become Pictures. Lee Server. LC 87-5510. (Illus.). 288p. 1987. 22.50 (ISBN 1-55562-018-3); pap. 14.95 (ISBN 1-55562-017-5). Main Street.
Screenwriters Guide. rev. ed. Joseph Gillis. LC 87-43023. 172p. 1987. pap. 10.95 (ISBN 0-918432-81-2). NY Zoetrope.
Screenwriter's Handbook: What to Write, How to Write It, Where to Sell It. Constance Nash & Virginia Oakey. LC 77-76031. 160p. pap. 6.95 (ISBN 0-06-463454-X, EH 454, B&N Bks). Har-Row.
Screenwriter's Workbook. Syd Field. (Orig.). 1988. pap. 8.95 (ISBN 0-440-58225-3, Dell Trade Pbks). Dell.
Screenwriting for Narrative Film & Television. William Miller. (Communication Arts Bks.). 320p. 1980. 17.00x (ISBN 0-8038-6772-7); pap. 10.00x (ISBN 0-8038-6773-5). Hastings.
Screenwriting for Narrative Film & Television. William Miller. 1988. 49.00x (ISBN 0-86287-419-X, Pub. by Harrap Ltd England). State Mutual Bk.
Screenwriting: The Art, Craft & Business of Film & Television Writing. Richard Walter. LC 88-1813. 224p. 1988. pap. 8.95 (ISBN 0-452-26086-8, Plume). NAL.
Screeton, Shelton, Byrd & Sanders Families: Past & Present. rev. ed. Mary L. Lamb. LC 87-80049. (Illus.). 1987. 25.00 (ISBN 0-9618278-0-7). M L Lamb.
Screw: A Guard's View of Bridgewater State Hospital. Tom Ryan & Bob Casey. 250p. (Orig.). 1982. pap. 7.00 (ISBN 0-89608-098-6). South End Pr.
Screw Conveyors. American National Standard Institute Staff. (CEMA Standards: No. 350). (Illus.). 150p. 1981. 12.50 (ISBN 0-318-13805-0); CEMA Standards No. 300: "Screw Conveyor Standards", q.v. incl. Conveyor Equip Mfrs.
Screw Joints in Aluminium Components. C. O. Bauer. 1983. cancelled 30.00 (ISBN 3-87017-166-9, Pub. by Aluminium W Germany). IPS.
Screw Reader. Goldstein & Buckley. 12.50 (ISBN 0-8184-0073-0). Lyle Stuart.
Screw-Retained Dental Prostheses. Shimegi & Matsuo. 140p. 1981. 78.00 (ISBN 0-931386-35-7). Quint Pub Co.
Screw Thread Standards for Federal Services. Ed. by Jerome H. Lieblich. 582p. 1978. loose-leaf 119.95 (ISBN 0-912702-11-7, FED-STD-H28). Global Eng.
Screw Threads & Gaskets for Fire Hose Connections. National Fire Protection Association Staff. 1985. 10.50 (ISBN 0-317-63568-9, 1963-85). Natl Fire Prot.
Screw Threads & Gaskets for Fire Hose Connections. (Ten Ser). 1974. pap. 2.00 (ISBN 0-685-58131-4, 194). Natl Fire Prot.
Screw Unto Others: Revenge Tactics for All Occasions. George Hayduke. 252p. 1987. pap. 16.95 (ISBN 0-87364-405-0). Paladin Pr.
Screwball Comedy: A Genre of Madcap Romance. Wes D. Gehring. LC 85-12703. (Contributions to the Study of Popular Culture Ser.: No. 13). (Illus.). 228p. 1986. lib. bdg. 35.00 (ISBN 0-313-24650-5, GSE/). Greenwood.
Screwdriver Expert's Guide to Peaking Out & Repairing CB Radios. Lou Franklin. (Illus.). 105p. (Orig.). 1983. pap. 19.95 (ISBN 0-943132-39-8). CB City Intl.
Screwed with Abandon. Rae Sturmans. (Illus.). 112p. 1987. 9.95 (ISBN 0-89962-603-3). Todd & Honeywell.
Screwge. Bob Tramonte. Ed. by Barbara Paturick. (Illus.). 44p. (Orig.). 1982. pap. 2.25 (ISBN 0-939602-01-6). Blue Star.
Screwtape Letters. C. S. Lewis. Bd. with Screwtape Proposes a Toast. 1964-67. 14.95 (ISBN 0-02-571240-3). Macmillan.
Screwtape Letters. C. S. Lewis. (Illus.). 144p. 1978. pap. 3.50 (ISBN 0-8007-8336-0, Spire Bks). Revell.
Screwtape Letters. rev. ed. C. S. Lewis. 1982. pap. 1.95 (ISBN 0-02-086740-9, Collier). Macmillan.
Screwtape Letters. C. S. Lewis. 14.95 (ISBN 0-89190-989-3, Pub. by Am Repr). Amereon Ltd.
Screwtape Letters. C. S. Lewis. 1984. pap. 3.50 (ISBN 0-553-26369-2). Bantam.
Screwtape Letters. C. S. Lewis. 160p. 1988. pap. 2.95 (ISBN 0-451-62610-9, Ment). NAL.
Screwtape Proposes a Toast see Screwtape Letters.
Screwtop. Vonda N. McIntyre. Bd. with Girl Who Was Plugged In. James Tiptree, Jr. 1989. price not set. Tor Bks.
Scriabin. Ye. Rudakova & A. I. Kandinsky. Tr. by Tatyana Chistyakova from Rus. (Illus.). 143p. 1984. 19.95 (ISBN 0-86622-006-2, Z-82). Paganiniana Pubns.
Scriabin. Alfred J. Swan. LC 75-76423. (Music Ser.). 1969. Repr. of 1928 ed. lib. bdg. 22.50 (ISBN 0-306-71322-5). Da Capo.
Scriabin. Alfred J. Swan. 1970. Repr. of 1923 ed. lib. bdg. 35.00x (ISBN 0-8371-4350-0, SWSC). Greenwood.

Scroll of Time. J. A. Savage. 6.50 (ISBN 0-88172-120-4). Believers Bkshelf.

Scroll Ornaments of the Early Victorian Period. F. Knight. LC 77-88652. (Pictorial Archive Ser.). (Illus.). 1978. pap. 3.50 (ISBN 0-486-23596-3). Dover.

Scroll Ornaments of the Early Victorian Period. F. Knight. 11.25 (ISBN 0-8446-5689-5). Peter Smith.

Scroll Saw Handbook. Patrick Spielman. LC 86-14352. (Illus.). 256p. (Orig.). 1986. pap. 12.95 (ISBN 0-8069-4770-5). Sterling.

Scroll Saw Pattern Book. Patrick Spielman & Patricia Spielman. LC 86-14358. (Illus.). 256p. (Orig.). 1986. pap. 12.95 (ISBN 0-8069-4772-1). Sterling.

Scroll Saw Projects, Bk. 756. Donald R. Brann. LC 75-3911. 1975. lib. bdg. 5.95 (ISBN 0-87733-056-5); pap. 7.95 (ISBN 0-87733-756-X). Easi-Bild.

Scroll Saw Puzzle Patterns. Patrick Spielman. (Illus.). 264p. (Orig.). 1988. pap. 12.95 (ISBN 0-8069-6586-X). Sterling.

Scrolls & Christian Origins: Studies in the Jewish Background of the New Testament. Matthew Black. LC 83-11519. (Brown Judaic Studies). 232p. 1983. pap. 14.00 (ISBN 0-89130-639-0, 14 00 48). Scholars Pr GA.

Scrolls from Qumran Cave I: The Great Isaiah Scroll the Order of the Community, the Pesher to Habakkuk. John C. Trever. 82p. 1974. pap. text ed. 6.00x (ISBN 0-89757-001-4). Am Sch Orient Res.

Scrolls of Edessa. Robert L. Wise. 216p. 1987. pap. 7.95 (ISBN 0-89693-343-1). Victor Bks.

Scroobious Pip. Edward Lear. LC 68-10373. (Trophy Picture Bks.). (Illus.). 32p. (ps up). 1987. pap. 5.95 (ISBN 0-06-443132-0, Trophy). HarpJ.

Scroobious Pip. Edward Lear & Ogden Nash. LC 68-10373. (Illus.). (gr. 3 up). 1968. 14.70 (ISBN 0-06-023764-3); PLB 13.89 (ISBN 0-06-023765-1). HarpJ.

Scrophulariaceae of Eastern Temperate North America. Francis W. Pennell. (Monograph: No. 1). (Illus.). 650p. (Orig.). 1935. pap. 13.00 (ISBN 0-910006-08-3). Acad Nat Sci Phila.

Scrophulariaceae of the Western Himalayas. Francis W. Pennell. (Monograph: No. 5). (Illus.). 163p. (Orig.). 1943. pap. 8.00 (ISBN 0-910006-14-8). Acad Nat Sci Phila.

Scrubber Strategy: The How & Why of Flue Gas Desulfurization. Mary A. Baviello & Alexandra Bowie. LC 82-81547. 180p. 1982. 37.50x (ISBN 0-918780-19-5). INFORM.

Scruffy. Peggy Parish. LC 87-45564. (I Can Read Book). (Illus.). 64p. (gr. k-3). 1988. 9.95i (ISBN 0-06-024659-6); PLB 10.89 (ISBN 0-06-024660-X). HarpJ.

Scruffy. Jack Stoneley. (Bullseye Bks.). (gr. 3-7). 1989. pap. 2.95 (ISBN 0-394-82039-8). Knopf.

Scruffy. Jack Stonely. (gr. 5 up). 1981. pap. 1.95 (ISBN 0-671-41096-2). Archway.

Scruffy Scoundrels (Gli Straccioni) Annibal Caro. Tr. by M. Ciavolella & Donald Beecher. (Carleton Renaissance Plays in Translation). 95p. 1980. pap. text ed. 6.95x (ISBN 0-88920-103-X, Pub. by Dovehouse Editions Canada). Humanities.

Scrumptious. Houston Junior Forum Staff. (Illus.). 373p. 1980. 11.95. Cookbook Collection Inc.

Scruples. Gilbert Kilpack. 1956. pap. 2.50x (ISBN 0-87574-089-8). Pendle Hill.

Scruples. Judith Krantz. 576p. 1988. pap. 4.95 (ISBN 0-446-34327-7). Warner Bks.

Scrupules de Maigret. Georges Simenon. pap. 3.95 (ISBN 0-685-11557-7). French & Eur.

Scrupulous Meanness: A Study of Joyce's Early Work. Edward Brandabur. LC 71-131057. pap. 49.30 (ISBN 0-317-28998-5, 2020241). Bks Demand UMI.

Scrut. George Roberts. LC 82-81349. 64p. 1983. pap. 4.00 (ISBN 0-930100-10-7). Holy Cow.

Scrutanda. M. G. Balme & M. C. Greenstock. 1973. pap. 7.95x (ISBN 0-19-831777-8). Oxford U Pr.

Scrutinies by Various Writers, Vol. 1. Edell Rickward. LC 76-23140. 1928. lib. bdg. 35.00 (ISBN 0-8414-7239-4). Folcroft.

Scrutinies by Various Writers (T. S. Eliot, Aldous Huxley, James Joyce, D H Lawrence, Wyndham Lewis, the Sitwells, Virginia Woolf, Vol. II. Edell Rickward. LC 76-23331. 1973. lib. bdg. 35.00 (ISBN 0-8414-7241-6). Folcroft.

Scrutinies of Simon Iff. Aleister Crowley. Ed. by Martin P. Starr. LC 87-7122. (Illus.). 200p. 1987. 19.95 (ISBN 0-933429-02-9). Teitan Pr.

Scrutinizing Science. Arthur Donovan et al. 1988. lib. bdg. 98.00 (ISBN 90-277-2608-6, Pub. by Reidel Holland). Kluwer Academic.

Scrutiny at a Glance. (Illus.). 60p. (Orig.). 1980. pap. 6.95 (ISBN 0-9616013-3-7). Midwest Media.

Scrutiny of Cinema. William Hunter. LC 70-169328. (Literature of Cinema, Series 2). (Illus.). 92p. 1972. Repr. of 1932 ed. 15.00 (ISBN 0-405-03896-8). Ayer Co Pubs.

Scrutton on Charter Parties & Bills of Lading. 19th ed. A. A. Mocatta. 1984. 190.00 (ISBN 0-421-29710-7). Heinman.

Scryer. Linda C. Gray. 352p. (Orig.). 1987. pap. 3.95 (ISBN 0-8125-1872-1, Dist. by St Matin's Pr & Warner Pub Servs). Tor Bks.

Scuba Diving. Joan Deakin. (Illus.). 160p. 1981. 16.95 (ISBN 0-7153-7952-6). David & Charles.

Scuba Diving in Safety & Health. Christopher W. Dueker. LC 85-12906. (Illus.). 224p. 1985. pap. 11.98 (ISBN 0-9614638-0-5). Diving Safety.

Scuba Diving Safety. Christopher W. Dueker. LC 78-55789. 200p. 1979. pap. 6.95 (ISBN 0-89037-135-0). Anderson World.

Scuba Diving with Disabilities. Jill Robinson & A. Dale Fox. LC 86-18532. (Illus.). 144p. (Orig.). 1987. pap. 16.00x (ISBN 0-88011-280-8, PROB0280). Leisure Pr.

Scuba Equipment Care & Maintenance. Michael Farley. (Illus.). 176p. 1980. pap. text ed. 9.95 (ISBN 0-932248-01-2). Marcor Pub.

Scuba Handbook for Humans. 2nd ed. Scott Ascher & William Shadburne. LC 75-3832. (Illus.). 1978. pap. text ed. 4.95 (ISBN 0-8403-1126-5). Kendall-Hunt.

Scuba Life Saving. Albert Pierce. (Illus.). 192p. 1986. pap. 14.95x (ISBN 0-88011-279-4, 0279). Leisure Pr.

Scuba Lifesaving & Accident Management. Tom Leaird. 1987. pap. text ed. 9.00 (ISBN 0-87322-132-X, Pub. by YMCA USA). Human Kinetics.

Scuba Northeast, Vol. 2: Shipwrecks, Dive Sites & Dive Activities-Rhode Island to New Jersey. Robert G. Bachand. 130p. (Orig.). 1986. pap. 9.95 (ISBN 0-9616399-0-3). Sea Sports Pubns.

Scuba Regulators: Air Pressure Reduction Valves for Diving. Robert Gonsett. (Illus.). 65p. 1975. text ed. 4.50 (ISBN 0-916974-08-1). NAUI.

Scuba Safe & Simple. John Reseck, Jr. 1976. pap. 7.95 (ISBN 0-13-796680-6, Parker). P-H.

Scuba Tanks: High Pressure Cylinders for Diving. Robert Gonsett. (Illus.). 1973. 4.50 (ISBN 0-916974-07-3). NAUI.

Scuderia Ferrari. Luigi Orsini. (Illus.). 1981. 99.00 (ISBN 0-85045-378-X, Pub. by Osprey England). Motorbooks Intl.

Scuff Marks on the Ceiling: Surviving & Enjoying Your Child's Early Years. Denise Turner. 192p. 1986. 11.95 (ISBN 0-8499-0513-3). Word Bks.

Scuffy Sandals: A Guide for Church Visitation in the Community. Mary M. Eakin. LC 81-15824. 96p. (Orig.). 1982. pap. 5.95 (ISBN 0-8298-0490-0). Pilgrim NY.

Scuffy the Tugboat. Gertrude Crampton. (Big Golden Storybooks). (Illus.). 24p. (ps-k). 1986. Repr. of 1946 ed. 2.95 (ISBN 0-307-10490-7, Pub. by Golden Bks); (Pub. by Golden Bks). Western Pub.

Sculler, Rowing from Tiber to Thames. John Taylor. LC 72-235. (English Experience Ser.: No. 283). 48p. 1970. Repr. of 1612 ed. 9.50 (ISBN 90-221-0283-1). Walter J Johnson.

Sculpted Saints of a Borderland Mission. Richard Ahlborn. LC 74-18171. (Illus.). 124p. 1974. pap. 7.50 (ISBN 0-915076-03-9). SW Mission.

Sculpted Word: Epicureanism & Philosophical Recruitment in Ancient Greece. Bernard Frischer. LC 81-13143. (Illus.). 340p. 1982. 40.00x (ISBN 0-520-04190-9). U of Cal Pr.

Sculpting in Clay. Janice Lovoos. pap. 9.95 (ISBN 0-8306-1344-7, 1344). TAB Bks.

Sculpting in Time: Reflections on the Cinema. Audrey Tarkovsky. Tr. by Kitty Hunter-Blair. 1987. 22.95 (ISBN 0-394-55599-6). Knopf.

Sculpting with Cement: Direct Modeling in a Permanent Medium. Lynn Olson. LC 81-708. (Illus.). 109p. (Orig.). 1987. pap. 14.95 (ISBN 0-9605678-0-1). Steelstone.

Sculpting Wood. Mark Lindquist. LC 86-70901. (Illus.). 304p. 1987. 32.95 (ISBN 0-87192-177-4). Davis Mass.

Sculptor Giovanni Bologna. James Holderbaum. LC 76-23626. (Outstanding Dissertations in the Fine Arts Ser.). 1985. lib. bdg. 66.00x (ISBN 0-8240-2696-9). Garland Pub.

Sculptor Speaks: A Series of Conversations on Art. Jacob Epstein & Arnold L. Haskell. LC 73-172922. (Illus.). Repr. of 1932 ed. 22.00 (ISBN 0-405-08487-0). Ayer Co Pubs.

Sculptor's Eye: The African Art Collection of Chaim Gross. Arnold Rubin. (Illus.). 1976. 9.00 (ISBN 0-686-25966-1). Mus African Art.

Sculptor's Eye: The African Art Collection of Mr. & Mrs. Chaim Gross. (Illus.). 80p. 1976. pap. 8.00 (ISBN 0-89192-169-9, Pub. by Museum of African Art). Interbk Inc.

Sculptors of the Cyclades: Individual & Tradition in the Third Millennium B.C. Pat Getz-Preziosi. (Illus.). 288p. 1987. text ed. 65.00x (ISBN 0-472-10067-X). U of Mich Pr.

Sculptors of the West Portals of Chartres Cathedral. Whitney S. Stoddard. (Illus.). 1987. 65.00 (ISBN 0-393-02365-6). Norton.

Sculptors of the West Portals of Chartres Cathedral. Whitney S. Stoddard. 1988. pap. 11.95x (ISBN 0-393-30043-9). Norton.

Sculptors on Paper: New York. Rene P. Barilleaux. (Illus.). 48p. (Orig.). 1987. pap. 19.95 (ISBN 0-913883-16-6). Madison Art.

Sculptural Forms in Terra Cotta from Chinese Tombs. Toledo Museum of Art Staff. 58p. 1939. 168.00x (Pub. by Han-Shan Tang Ltd). State Mutual Bk.

Sculptural Monuments in an Outdoor Environment. Ed. by Virginia N. Naude. (Illus.). 116p. (Orig.). 1985. pap. write for info. (ISBN 0-943836-04-2). Penn Acad Art.

Sculptural Programs of Chartres Cathedral: Christ, Mary, Ecclesia. Adolf E. Katzenellenbogen. LC 59-14894. pap. 57.50 (ISBN 0-317-10764-X, 2007368). Bks Demand UMI.

Sculptural Programs of Chartres Cathedral. Adolf Katzenellenbogen. (Illus.). 1964. pap. 6.95x (ISBN 0-393-00233-0, Norton Lib). Norton.

Sculpture. Mark Mandel. Ed. by Jim Connor. 256p. (Orig.). 1988. pap. 4.50 (ISBN 0-7701-0879-2). PaperJacks US.

Sculpture. (Illus.). 24p. (gr. 6-12). 1969. pap. 1.25x (ISBN 0-8395-3322-5, 3322). BSA.

Sculpture: A Basic Handbook for Students. 2nd ed. Ronald L. Coleman. 336p. 1980. text ed. write for info. (ISBN 0-697-03335-X). Wm C Brown.

Sculpture: A Fifteen-Week Multimedia Program. Judith Peck. (Illus.). 144p. 1986. pap. 14.95 (ISBN 0-671-61426-6). P-H.

Sculpture & Casting of Equestrian Statues. Tr. by Helen Tullberg. 8p. 1987. pap. 42.00x (Pub. by Picton UK). State Mutual Bk.

Sculpture & Ceramics of Paul Gauguin. Christopher Gray. LC 79-91819. (Illus.). 330p. 1980. Repr. of 1963 ed. lib. bdg. 75.00 (ISBN 0-87817-263-7). Hacker.

Sculpture & Ceramics of Paul Gauguin. Christopher Gray. (Illus.). 330p. 50.00 (ISBN 0-317-54965-0). Apollo.

Sculpture & Enlivened Space: Aesthetics & History. F. David Martin. LC 79-4006. (Illus.). 352p. 1981. 30.00x (ISBN 0-8131-1386-5). U Pr of Ky.

Sculpture & Sculptors of Yazilikaya. Robert L. Alexander. LC 84-40804. (Illus.). 168p. 1986. 29.50x (ISBN 0-87413-279-7). U Delaware Pr.

Sculpture & the Federal Triangle. George Gurney. LC 84-40206. (Illus.). 464p. 1985. text ed. 45.00 (ISBN 0-87474-492-X, GUSF). Smithsonian.

Sculpture by Anna Hyatt Huntington. Beatrice G. Proske. (Illus.). 24p. 1957. pap. text ed. 0.50 (ISBN 0-87535-093-3). Hispanic Soc.

Sculpture by Antoine-Louis Bayre in the Collection of the Fogg Art Museum. Jeanne L. Wasserman & Arthur Beale. (Fogg Art Museum Handbooks Ser.: Vol. IV). (Illus.). 103p. (Orig.). 1983. pap. 14.95 (ISBN 0-916724-53-0). Harvard Art Mus.

Sculpture by Bill Woodrow: Natural Product, Armed Response. Hugh Davies. LC 85-81552. (Illus.). 20p. 1985. 5.00 (ISBN 0-934418-24-1). La Jolla Mus Contemp Art.

Sculpture City: St. Louis: Public Sculpture & Statuary in the "Gateway to the West". George McCue. (Illus.). 192p. 1988. 35.00 (ISBN 0-933920-62-8); pap. 25.00 (ISBN 0-933920-63-6). Hudson Hills.

Sculpture Contemporaine en Belgique. Euginie De Keyser. (Illus.). 259p. (Fr.). 30.00 (ISBN 0-912729-22-8). Newbury Bks.

Sculpture Francais au XIX Siecle. (Illus.). 502p. 1988. 75.00 (ISBN 0-8109-0923-5). Abrams.

Sculpture from Germany. Michael R. Klein & Paul Moor. LC 83-81688. (Illus.). 68p. 1983. 10.00 (ISBN 0-916365-01-8). Ind Curators.

Sculpture from Sardis: The Finds Through 1975. George M. Hanfmann & Nancy H. Ramage. 1978. 37.00x (ISBN 0-674-79588-1). Harvard U Pr.

Sculpture Gardens: A Bibliography of Periodical Literature. Edward H. Teague. (Architecture Ser.: A 1429). 4p. 1985. 2.00 (ISBN 0-89028-479-2). Vance Biblios.

Sculpture in America. 2nd ed. Wayne Craven. LC 82-40439. (Illus.). 808p. 1983. 50.00 (ISBN 0-87413-225-8). U Delaware Pr.

Sculpture in America. 2nd. ed. Wayne Craven. LC 82-40439. (Illus.). 808p. 1983. 50.00 (ISBN 0-8453-4776-4, Cornwall Bks). Assoc Univ Prs.

Sculpture in America. rev. ed. Wayne Craven. (Illus.). 782p. 50.00 (ISBN 0-317-54879-4). Apollo.

Sculpture in Britain, Fifteen Thirty to Eighteen Thirty. rev. ed. Margaret Whinney. Rev. by John Physick. LC 87-62945. (Illus.). 528p. Date not set. 40.00 (ISBN 0-14-056023-8). Penguin.

Sculpture in Britain, Fifteen Thirty to Eighteen Thirty. Margaret Whinney & John Physick. (Illus.). 528p. 1988. pap. 18.95 (ISBN 0-14-056123-4). Penguin.

Sculpture in California Nineteen Seventy-Five to Nineteen-Eighty. Richard Armstrong. LC 80-51414. (Illus.). 96p. 1982. pap. 10.00 (ISBN 0-295-95917-7, Pub. by San Diego Museum Art). U of Wash Pr.

Sculpture in Siam. Alfred Salmony. LC 79-143362. (Illus.). 1972. Repr. of 1925 ed. 50.00 (ISBN 0-87817-081-2). Hacker.

Sculpture in Stone: Museum of Fine Arts Boston. M. B. Comstock & C. C. Vermeule. (Illus.). 296p. 35.00 (ISBN 0-686-47011-7). Apollo.

Sculpture in Stone: The Greek, Roman & Etruscan Collections of the Museum of Fine Arts Boston. Mary B. Comstock & Cornelius C. Vermeule. LC 76-40711. (Illus.). 1978. pap. 15.00 (ISBN 0-87846-103-5, Pub. by Mus Fine Arts Boston). C E Tuttle.

Sculpture in the Huntington Collection. Henry E. Huntington Library & Art Gallery & R. R. Wark. LC 58-10419. (Huntington Library Publications). pap. 21.30 (2027300). Bks Demand UMI.

Sculpture in the Isabella Stewart Gardner Museum. Cornelius C. Vermeule, Jr. et al. LC 77-94517. (Illus.). 1978. 15.00 (ISBN 0-914660-03-9); pap. 10.00 (ISBN 0-914660-04-7). I S Gardner Mus.

Sculpture in the Kingdom of Quito. Gabrielle G. Palmer. LC 86-24959. (Illus.). 181p. 1987. 39.95 (ISBN 0-8263-0930-5). U of NM Pr.

Sculpture in the Peshawar Museum. rev. ed. H. Hargreaves. 1977. 15.95 (ISBN 0-89684-348-3). Orient Bk Dist.

Sculpture in the Sun: Hawaii's Art for Open Spaces. Georgia F. Radford & Warren H. Radford. LC 77-92972. 117p. 1978. pap. 3.95 (ISBN 0-8248-0526-7). UH Pr.

Sculpture in Wood. Jack C. Rich. LC 76-30520. (Quality Paperbacks Ser.). 1977. pap. 9.95 (ISBN 0-306-80052-7). Da Capo.

Sculpture in Wood. John Rood. LC 50-9725. pap. 47.80 (ISBN 0-317-39699-4, 2055902). Bks Demand UMI.

Sculpture Inside Outside. Douglas Dreishpoon et al. (Illus.). 284p. 1989. 50.00 (ISBN 0-8478-1004-6); pap. 29.95 (ISBN 0-8478-1005-4). Rizzoli Intl.

Sculpture Inspired by Kalidasa. C. Sivaramamurti. (Illus.). 1986. 29.95. Asia Bk Corp.

Sculpture, Metalwork, Gem & Stone, Glass Textile. Yamato Bunkakan. 120p. 1976. 100.00x (Pub. by Han-Shan Tang Ltd). State Mutual Bk.

Sculpture of Africa. Eliot Elisofon & William Fagg. LC 76-50293. (Illus.). 1978. Repr. of 1958 ed. lib. bdg. 50.00 (ISBN 0-87817-210-6). Hacker.

Sculpture of Africa: Selections from a Private Collection. Intro. by Evan E. Maurer. (Illus.). 52p. 1984. 5.00 (ISBN 0-912303-41-7). Michigan Mus.

Sculpture of Andrea & Nino Pisano. Anita F. Moskowitz. (Illus.). 504p. 1987. 145.00 (ISBN 0-521-30754-6). Cambridge U Pr.

Sculpture of Anthony Caro, Nineteen Forty-Two to Nineteen Eighty: A Catalogue Raisonne, 4 Vols. Dieter Blume. (Illus.). 736p. (Orig.). 1983. Set. pap. 85.00 (ISBN 0-8390-0299-8). Abner Schram Ltd.

Sculpture of Bernard Rossellino & His Workshop. A. M. Schulz. LC 75-3473. 1976. 61.50x (ISBN 0-691-03886-4). Princeton U Pr.

Sculpture of David Smith: A Catalogue Raisonne. Rosalind Krauss. LC 76-24753. (Reference Library of the Humanities Ser.: Vol. 73). (Illus.). 1977. lib. bdg. 91.00 (ISBN 0-8240-9924-9). Garland Pub.

Sculpture of Donatello. H. W. Janson. LC 62-7041. 1979. 61.50x (ISBN 0-691-03528-8). Princeton U Pr.

Sculpture of Edgar Degas. Charles W. Millard. LC 75-2485. 1976. 55.00x (ISBN 0-691-03898-8); pap. 14.50x (ISBN 0-691-00318-1). Princeton U Pr.

Sculpture of Epstein. Evelyn Silber. LC 85-41060. (Illus.). 240p. 1986. 80.00x (ISBN 0-8387-5103-2). Bucknell U Pr.

Sculpture of Gaspard & Balthazard Marsy: Art & Patronage in the Early Reign of Louis XIV. Thomas Hedin. LC 82-17415. (Illus.). 264p. 1983. text ed. 55.00x (ISBN 0-8262-0395-7). U of Mo Pr.

Sculpture of Giovanni & Bartolomeo Bon & Their Workshop. Anne Schulz. LC 78-50190. (Transactions Ser.: Vol. 68, Pt. 3). (Illus.). 1978. pap. 12.00 (ISBN 0-87169-683-5). Am Philos.

Sculpture of Henri Matisse. Isabelle Monot-Fontaine. LC 84-50422. (Illus.). 160p. 1984. 24.95f (ISBN 0-500-23400-0). Thames Hudson.

Sculpture of India, Three Thousand BC-AD Thirteen Hundred. Pramod Chandra. (Illus.). 224p. 1985. 60.00 (ISBN 0-674-79590-3). Harvard U Pr.

Sculpture of Isamu Noguchi, Nineteen Twenty-Four to Nineteen Seventy-Nine: A Catalogue. Nancy Grove & Diane Botnick. LC 70-28698. (Garland Reference Library of the Humanities: Vol. 207). 625p. 1980. lib. bdg. 73.00 (ISBN 0-8240-9550-2). Garland Pub.

Sculpture of Jacob Epstein. (Publication of the Museum of African Art). (Illus.). 1973. pap. 2.00 (ISBN 0-89192-191-5). Interbk Inc.

Sculpture of Jacob Epstein. LC 76-28788. (Smithsonian Institution Traveling Exhibition Service Ser.). (Illus.). 1976. pap. 2.00x (ISBN 0-913060-25-9). Norton Art.

Sculpture of John Cunningham: Image-Space-Interval. Richard H. Love. LC 83-22553. (Illus.). 15p. (Orig.). 1983. pap. 5.00 (ISBN 0-940114-15-1). Haase Mumm Pub Co.

Sculpture of Jose De Creeft. Jules Campos. LC 72-16688. (Illus.). 238p. 1972. lib. bdg. 59.50 (ISBN 0-306-70294-0). Da Capo.

Sculpture of Julio Gonzalez. Rosalind Krauss. (Illus.). 36p. (Orig.). 1981. pap. 9.00 (ISBN 0-938608-05-3). Pace Pubns.

Sculpture of Life. Ernest Borek. LC 73-6831. (Illus.). 181p. 1973. 27.50x (ISBN 0-231-03425-3); pap. 5.00. Columbia U Pr.

Sculpture of Marshall Fredericks. Marshall Fredericks. (Great Lakes Bks.). (Illus.). 288p. 1988. 60.00x (ISBN 0-8143-1969-6). Wayne St U Pr.

Sculpture of Moissac. Meyer Schapiro & David Finn. 152p. 1985. 35.00 (ISBN 0-8076-1119-0); pap. 20.00 (ISBN 0-8076-1120-4). Braziller.

Sculpture of Nancy Graves: A Catalogue Raisonne. E. A. Carmean, Jr. et al. LC 86-29970. (Illus.). 192p. 1987. 50.00 (ISBN 0-933920-77-6, Dist. by Rizzoli); pap. 25.00 museum distribution only (ISBN 0-933920-78-4). Hudson Hills.

Sea Creatures Do Amazing Things. Arthur Myers. LC 80-20089. (Step-Up Bks.: No. 34). (Illus.). 72p. (gr. 2-5). 1981. 5.95 (ISBN 0-394-84487-4); lib. bdg. 8.99 (ISBN 0-394-94487-9). Random.

Sea-Crossed Fisherman. Yashar Kemal. 286p. 1985. 16.95 (ISBN 0-8076-1122-0). Braziller.

Sea Dangers: The Affair of the Somers. Philip McFarland. LC 85-1852. (Illus.). 320p. 1985. 19.95 (ISBN 0-8052-3990-1). Schocken.

Sea Defense & Coast Protection Works: A Guide to Design. R. Berkeley Thorn & A. G. Roberts. 232p. 1981. 35.00 (ISBN 0-7277-0085-5, Pub. by T Telford UK). Am Soc Civil Eng.

Sea Defense Works: Design, Construction & Emergency. 2nd ed. R. B. Thorn & J. C. Simmons. (Illus.). 128p. 1971. 11.00 (ISBN 0-8088-7020-3). Davey.

Sea Demons. Victor Rousseau. LC 75-28861. (Classics of Science Fiction Ser.). 254p. 1976. 15.00 (ISBN 0-88355-375-9); pap. 10.00 (ISBN 0-88355-462-3). Hyperion Conn.

Sea Disasters. Walter R. Brown. LC 84-40788. (Illus.). 1981. 9.70i (ISBN 0-201-09154-2, Lipp Jr Bks). HarpJ.

Sea Disasters & Inland Catastrophes. Edward R. Snow. LC 80-23876. (Illus.). 288p. 1980. 9.95 (ISBN 0-396-07908-3). Dodd.

Sea Dreamer: A Definitive Biography of Joseph Conrad. Gerard Jean-Aubry. Tr. by Helen Sebba. 1985. Repr. of 1957 ed. lib. bdg. 40.00 (ISBN 0-89984-747-1). Century Bookbindery.

Sea Dyaks of Borneo. Benedict Sandin. (Illus.). xx, 134p. 1968. 7.50 (ISBN 0-87013-122-2). Mich St U Pr.

Sea Edge. W. Phillip Keller. 120p. 1985. 9.95 (ISBN 0-8499-0457-9, 0457-9). Word Bks.

Sea Egg. Lucy M. Boston. LC 67-10200. (Illus.). (gr. 2-5). 1967. 8.95 (ISBN 0-15-271050-7, HJ). HarBraceJ.

Sea Elves: A Complete Culture for Elfquest. Elizabeth Cerriteli. Ed. by Sherman Kahn. (Illus.). 48p. 1985. pap. 6.00 incl. Elfquest roleplaying game supplement (ISBN 0-933635-24-9). Chaosium.

Sea: Excerpts from Herman Melville. Illus. by Joyce Alexander & Dorsey Alexander. (Illus., Calligraphy & Illus.). 1970. pap. 5.00 (ISBN 0-912020-15-6). Turtles Quill.

Sea Experience: The Educational Use of Sailing School Vessels. Ed. by Albert E. Hickey. (Illus.). 144p. (Orig.). 1987. pap. text ed. 37.50 (ISBN 0-87567-085-7). Entelek.

Sea Exploring Manual. Boy Scouts of America. 272p. (gr. 6-12). 1987. flexible bdg. 5.95x (ISBN 0-8395-3229-6, 3239). BSA.

Sea Exploring Manual. rev. ed. Boy Scouts of America. (Illus.). 272p. (gr. 6-12). 1987. pap. 5.95 (ISBN 0-8395-3239-3, 3239). BSA.

Sea Farmers. John F. Waters. LC 71-98059. (Illus.). 128p. (gr. 6-9). 1970. PLB 8.95 (ISBN 0-8038-6690-9). Hastings.

Sea Fighters from Drake to Farragut. facs. ed. Jessie P. Frothingham. LC 67-26743. (Essay Index Reprint Ser). 1902. 19.00 (ISBN 0-8369-0461-3). Ayer Co Pubs.

Sea Fighters from Drake to Farragut. facsimile ed. Jessie P. Frothingham. LC 67-26743. (Essay Index Reprint Ser.). Repr. of 1902 ed. lib. bdg. 18.00 (ISBN 0-8290-0838-1). Irvington.

Sea Fire. Karen Robards. 416p. 1988. pap. 3.95 (ISBN 0-8439-2641-4, Pub. by Leisure Bks CT). Leisure NY.

Sea Fisheries Research. F. R. Harden-Jones. 510p. 1974. 62.95x (ISBN 0-470-35142-X). Halsted Pr.

Sea Fishes Brit. & N. E. Europe. Mirus & Dahlstrom. 1987. pap. 29.95 (ISBN 0-00-219008-7). Greene.

Sea Flavor. facs. ed. Haydn S. Pearson. LC 68-58809. (Essay Index Reprint Ser). 1948. 17.00 (ISBN 0-8369-0051-0). Ayer Co Pubs.

Sea Floor: An Introduction to Marine Biology. E. Seibold & W. Berger. (Illus.). 288p. 1982. pap. 32.00 (ISBN 0-387-11256-1). Springer-Verlag.

Sea Floor Development: Moving into Deep Water. Pref. by Angus Paton. LC 79-670284. (Royal Society). (Illus.). 1978. text ed. 45.00x (ISBN 0-85403-100-6, Pub. by Royal Soc London). Scholium Intl.

Sea Floor Spreading & Continental Drift. J. Coulomb. Tr. by R. W. Tanner from Fr. LC 79-179891. (Geophysics & Astrophysics Monographs: No. 2). 184p. 1972. lib. bdg. 31.50 (ISBN 90-277-0232-2, Pub. by Reidel Holland); pap. 18.50 (ISBN 90-277-0238-1). Kluwer Academic.

Sea Fog. B. Wang. (Illus.). 336p. 1985. 87.00 (ISBN 0-387-13150-7). Springer-Verlag.

Sea Gate. Jacqueline Aeby. 1977. pap. 1.75 (ISBN 0-8439-0509-3, Leisure Bks). Leisure NY.

Sea Gate. Maura Seger. (Intimate Moments Ser.). pap. 2.75 (ISBN 0-373-07209-0). Harlequin Bks.

Sea Gems. Beverly Rowe. LC 82-60557. (Illus.). 64p. 1982. 22.00 (ISBN 0-88014-046-1). Mosaic Pr OH.

Sea Gifts. George Shannon. (gr. 2-4). Date not set. 10.95. Godine.

Sea Glass. Laurence Yep. LC 78-22487. 224p. (YA) (gr. 7 up). 1979. 12.70i (ISBN 0-06-026744-5). HarpJ.

Sea Grammar. John Smith. LC 68-54664. (English Experience Ser.: No. 5). 76p. 1968. Repr. of 1627 ed. 30.00 (ISBN 90-221-0005-7). Walter J Johnson.

Sea Gull. Anton Chekhov. Tr. by Fred Eisemann & Oliver F. Murphy. Bd. with Tragedian in Spite of Himself. (Orig.). pap. 3.00 (ISBN 0-8283-1454-3). Branden Pub Co.

Sea Gypsies of Malaya: An Account of the Nomadic Mawken Pople of the Mergui Archipelago. Walter G. White. LC 77-87082. (Illus.). 318p. Repr. of 1922 ed. 34.50 (ISBN 0-404-16878-7). AMS Pr.

Sea Hag. David Drake. 352p. (Orig.). 1988. pap. 3.95 (ISBN 0-671-65424-1). Baen Bks.

Sea-Harrower. Abigail Clements. (Orig.). 1980. pap. 2.25 (ISBN 0-449-14326-0, GM). Fawcett.

Sea Hawk. Ed. by Rudy Behlmer. LC 81-70418. (Wisconsin-Warner Bros. Screenplay Ser.). (Illus.). 244p. 1982. 18.95x (ISBN 0-299-09010-8); pap. 8.95 (ISBN 0-299-09014-0). U of Wis Pr.

Sea Hawk. Manohar Malgonkar. (Orient Paperbacks Ser.). 293p. 1980. pap. 4.95 (ISBN 0-86578-069-2); 9.95 (ISBN 0-86578-136-2). Ind-US Inc.

Sea Hawk. Raphael Sabatini. 20.95 (ISBN 0-89190-312-7, Pub. by Am Repr). Amereon Ltd.

Sea Horse. Harold B. Clifford. Pref. by & illus. by Alta Ashley. LC 87-81502. 67p. (gr. 6-8). 1987. pap. 5.95 (ISBN 0-9614592-3-9). Grey Gull Pubns.

Sea Ice Biota. Ed. by Rita A. Horner. LC 85-3807. 224p. 1985. 95.00 (ISBN 0-8493-6578-3). CRC Pr.

Sea Ice Processes & Models: Proceedings of the AIDJEX-ICSI Symposium. Ed. by Robert S. Pritchard. LC 78-21760. (Illus.). 536p. 1980. 40.00x (ISBN 0-295-95658-5). U of Wash Pr.

Sea: Ideas & Observations on Progress in the Study of the Seas; The Oceanic Lithosphere, Vol. 7. Ed. by Cesare Emiliani. LC 62-18366. 1738p. 1981. 225.00x (ISBN 0-471-02870-3). Wiley.

Sea in Soviet Strategy. Bryan Ranft & Geoffrey Till. 275p. 1983. 21.95 (ISBN 0-87021-957-X). Naval Inst Pr.

Sea in Soviet Strategy. 2nd ed. Bryan Ranft & Geoffrey Till. (Illus.). 275p. 1988. 21.95 (ISBN 0-87021-992-8). Naval Inst Pr.

Sea in the Pre-Columbian World: Conference at Dumbarton Oaks, October 26 & 27, 1974. LC 76-58217. (Illus.). 188p. 1977. 18.00x (ISBN 0-88402-071-1). Dumbarton Oaks.

Sea Is All about Us: A Guide to Marine Environments of Cape Ann & Other Northern New England Waters. Sarah F. Robbins & Clarice Yentsch. 1973. pap. 10.95 (ISBN 0-87577-046-0, Cape Ann Soc. for Marine Research, Inc.). Peabody Mus Salem.

Sea Is Calling Me. Lee Bennett Hopkins. LC 85-16412. (Illus.). (gr. 4-6). 1986. 14.95 (ISBN 0-15-271155-4, HJ). Harbracej.

Sea Is for Sailing. Peter Pye. 192p. 1987. pap. 12.95 (ISBN 0-246-13164-0, Pub. by Collins England). Sheridan.

Sea Is My Blanket. Helen Webber. (Illus.). (gr. k-6). 1968. 8.95 (ISBN 0-8392-3057-5). Astor-Honor.

Sea Island Dairy: A History of St. Helena Island. Edith M. Dabbs. LC 83-8995. (Illus.). 344p. 1983. 27.50 (ISBN 0-87152-379-5). Reprint.

Sea Island Lady. Francis Griswold. 19.95 (ISBN 0-685-06833-1). Beaufort SC.

Sea Island Roots: African Presence in the Carolinas & Georgia: Testimonies of African Cultural Continuity. Keith E. Baird & Mary A. Twining. 325p. 1988. 35.00 (ISBN 0-86543-068-3); pap. 11.95 (ISBN 0-86543-069-1). Africa World.

Sea Island Sanctuary. Jean E. Holmes. Ed. by Raymond H. Woolsey. 128p. (Orig.). (gr. 6-8). 1988. pap. write for info. (ISBN 0-8280-0436-6). Review & Herald.

Sea Island Seasons. Beaufort County Open Land Trust Staff. 366p. 1980. 9.95 (ISBN 0-918544-40-8). Wimmer Bks.

Sea Island Seasons Cookbook. 368p. 1980. pap. 11.95 (ISBN 0-686-31490-5). Beaufort County.

Sea Island to City: A Study of St. Helena Islanders in Harlem & Other Urban Centers. Clyde V. Kiser. LC 32-34112. (Columbia University Studies in the Social Sciences: No. 368). Repr. of 1932 ed. 16.50 (ISBN 0-404-51368-9). AMS Pr.

Sea Island to City: A Study of St. Helena Islanders in Harlem & Other Urban Centers. Clyde V. Kiser. LC 69-15525. (Studies in American Negro Life Ser). 1969. pap. 3.45 (ISBN 0-689-70118-7, NL16). Atheneum.

Sea Island Yankee. Clyde Bresee. (American Places of the Heart Ser.). (Illus.). 264p. 1986. 16.95 (ISBN 0-912697-37-7). Algonquin Bks.

Sea: Its History & Romance, 4 vols. F. Bowen. 1977. lib. bdg. 400.00 (ISBN 0-8490-2581-8). Gordon Pr.

Sea Jade. Phyllis A. Whitney. 224p. 1985. pap. 2.95 (ISBN 0-449-20870-2, Crest). Fawcett.

Sea Jewel. Penelope Neri. 496p. 1986. pap. 3.95 (ISBN 0-8217-1888-6). Zebra.

Sea Kayaking. rev., enl. ed. John Dowd. 298p. 1988. 14.95. U of Wash Pr.

Sea Kayaking: A Manual for Long-Distance Touring. rev. ed. John Dowd. LC 81-186. (Illus.). 240p. 1983. pap. 9.95 (ISBN 0-295-96047-7). U of Wash Pr.

Sea Kayaking: A Manual for Long-Distance Touring. rev. ed. John Dowd. (Illus.). 272p. 1988. pap. 9.95 (ISBN 0-295-96630-0). U of Wash Pr.

Sea King. (Super Profile CAR Ser.). 8.95 (ISBN 0-85429-377-9, F377, Pub. by G T Foulis Ltd). Haynes Pubns.

Sea Lady; a Tissue of Moonshine. H. G. Wells. LC 75-28862. (Classics of Science Fiction Ser.). (Illus.). vii, 300p. 1976. 15.00 (ISBN 0-88355-376-7); pap. 10.00 (ISBN 0-88355-465-8). Hyperion Conn.

Sea Language Comes Ashore. Joanna C. Colcord. Ed. by Richard M. Dorsen. (International Folklore Ser.). 1977. Repr. of 1945 ed. lib. bdg. 17.00x (ISBN 0-405-10089-2). Ayer Co Pubs.

Sea Language Comes Ashore. Joanna C. Colcord. LC 45-966. 222p. 1945. pap. 5.00 (ISBN 0-87033-095-0). Cornell Maritime.

Sea Lawyer: A Guide for Yachtsmen. 2nd ed. Brian Calwell. (Illus.). 152p. 1986. 14.95 (ISBN 0-229-11762-7). Sheridan.

Sea Level Changes. E. Lisitzin. (Oceanography Ser.: Vol. 8). 286p. 1974. 92.00 (ISBN 0-444-41157-7). Elsevier.

Sea-Level Changes. Ed. by Michael J. Tooley & Ian Shennan. (Illus.). 320p. Date not set. text ed. 49.95 (ISBN 0-631-15402-7). Basil Blackwell.

Sea-Level Changes: North-West England During the Flandrian Stage. M. J. Tooley. (Research Studies in Geography Ser.). (Illus.). 1979. 39.00x (ISBN 0-19-823228-4). Oxford U Pr.

Sea-Level Fluctuations & Coastal Evolution. Ed. by Dag Nummedal et al. (Special Publications Ser.: No. 41). 276p. 1987. 40.00 (ISBN 0-918985-71-4). SEPM.

Sea Life. 85p. 1981. write for info. (ISBN 0-9607580-3-8). S Stafford.

Sea Life in Nelson's Time. facs. ed. John Masefield. LC 75-75513. (Select Bibliographies Reprint Ser). 1905. 22.00 (ISBN 0-8369-5011-9). Ayer Co Pubs.

Sea Lion Caves & Other Poems. Nelson Bentley. LC 70-179835. (New Poetry Ser.). Repr. of 1966 ed. 16.00 (ISBN 0-404-56035-0). AMS Pr.

Sea Lions. James Fenimore Cooper. Ed. by Warren S. Walker. LC 65-18416. (Illus.). Repr. of 1965 ed. 133.30 (ISBN 0-8357-9714-7, 2016027). Bks Demand UMI.

Sea-Lords of Gondor. John B. Morin. Ed. by Peter Fenlon. (Middle-Earth Campaign Ser.). 64p. (Orig.). (YA) (gr. 10-12). 1987. pap. 12.00 (ISBN 0-915795-88-4). Iron Crown Ent Inc.

Sea-Lulled Rocky Mountain Isle. Cynthia Frank. Ed. by Stella Monday. (Illus.). 1977. pap. 2.00 (ISBN 0-918510-00-7). Monday Bks.

Sea Mammals. Dorothy C. Hogner. LC 78-22503. (Illus.). (gr. 4 up). 1979. (Crowell Jr Bks); PLB 12.89 (ISBN 0-690-03950-6). HarpJ.

Sea Mammals. Bernard Stonehouse. 1985. pap. 8.95 (ISBN 0-14-007081-8). Penguin.

Sea Mammals: The Warm-Blooded Ocean Explorers. Jean H. Sibbald. LC 87-33291. (Ocean World Library). (Illus.). 128p. (gr. 4 up). 1988. PLB 11.95 (ISBN 0-87518-372-7). Dillon.

Sea-Mans Practice. Richard Norwood. LC 74-28877. (English Experience Ser.: No. 755). 1975. Repr. of 1637 ed. 30.00 (ISBN 90-221-0755-8). Walter J Johnson.

Sea Marine Atlas: Southern California. rev. ed. William P. Crawford. (Illus.). 1979. 19.95 (ISBN 0-393-03219-1). Norton.

Sea: Marine Chemistry. Ed. by Edward D. Goldberg. LC 62-18366. (Ideas & Observations on Progress in the Study of the Seas Ser.: Vol. 5). 895p. 1974. 94.95x (ISBN 0-471-31090-5, Pub. by Wiley-Interscience). Wiley.

Sea: Marine Modeling. Ed. by Edward D. Goldberg et al. LC 62-18366. (Ideas & Observations on Progress in the Study on the Seas Ser.: Vol. 6). 1048p. 1977. 100.00x (ISBN 0-471-31091-3, Pub. by Wiley-Interscience). Wiley.

Sea Master. Sally Wentworth. (Harlequin Presents Ser.). 192p. 1982. pap. 1.75 (ISBN 0-373-10512-6). Harlequin Bks.

Sea Microbes. John M. Sieburth. (Illus.). 1979. text ed. 70.00x (ISBN 0-19-502419-2). Oxford U Pr.

Sea Monsters, Ancient Reptiles That Ruled the Sea. David Eldridge. LC 79-87964. (Illus.). 32p. (gr. 3-6). 1980. PLB 9.79 (ISBN 0-89375-240-1); pap. 2.50 (ISBN 0-89375-244-4). Troll Assocs.

Sea Monsters of Long Ago. Millicent E. Selsam. LC 78-5385. (Illus.). 32p. (gr. k-3). 1978. 8.95 (ISBN 0-02-778050-3, Four Winds). Macmillan.

Sea Nation. Karl Roebling. (Illus.). 245p. 1987. 14.95 (ISBN 0-942910-14-1). Dynapress.

Sea of Cortez: A Leisurely Journal of Travel & Research. John Steinbeck & Edward F. Ricketts. (Illus.). 640p. Repr. of 1941 ed. 30.00 (ISBN 0-911858-08-3). Appel.

Sea of Cortez Guide: For Fishermen, Cruisers, Trailerboaters & Cartoppers in Mexico's Gulf of California. New ed. Dix Brow. LC 82-15877. (Illus.). 272p. (Orig.). 1987. pap. 19.95 (ISBN 0-930030-26-5). Western Marine Ent.

Sea of Death. Jorge Amado. Tr. by Gregory Rabassa from Port. 288p. 1984. pap. 4.50 (ISBN 0-380-88559-X, Bard). Avon.

Sea of Energy. 5th ed. John E. Moray. (Illus.). 275p. 1978. 22.50 (ISBN 0-9606374-0-0, 264-334); pap. 9.35 (ISBN 0-9606374-1-9). Cosray Res.

Sea of Faith. Don Cupitt. (Illus.). 286p. 1988. 29.95 (ISBN 0-521-34420-4). Cambridge U Pr.

Sea of Glass. Barry B. Longyear. 384p. 1988. pap. 3.50 (ISBN 0-380-70055-7). Avon.

Sea of Grass. Conrad Richter. 1937. 13.45 (ISBN 0-394-44397-7). Knopf.

Sea of Grass. Conrad Richter. 128p. 1984. pap. 3.50 (ISBN 0-345-31778-5). Ballantine.

Sea of Memories. Stan Smith. 144p. 1986. 33.00x (ISBN 0-946771-18-9, Pub. by Spellmount Ltd Pubs). State Mutual Bk.

Sea of Sadness. Alma Guadalupe. 64p. 1984. 5.95 (ISBN 0-89962-041-8). Todd & Honeywell.

Sea of Silence. Niel Hancock. (Windameir Circle: No. 2). 384p. (Orig.). 1987. pap. 3.50 (ISBN 0-445-20565-2, Pub. by Popular Lib). Warner Bks.

Sea of Slaughter. Farley Mowat. 448p. 1986. pap. 9.95 (ISBN 0-553-34269-X). Bantam.

Sea of the Bear. M. A. Ransom & Eloise K. Engle. LC 79-6122. (Navies & Men Ser.). (Illus.). 1980. Repr. of 1964 ed. lib. bdg. 22.00x (ISBN 0-405-13076-7). Ayer Co Pubs.

Sea Otter: Core of Conflict, Loved or Loathed. Jane H. Bailey. (Illus.). 173p. (Orig.). 1985. pap. 7.95x (ISBN 0-9602484-1-2). El Moro.

Sea Otters. Evelyn Shaw. LC 79-2017. (Nature I Can Read Bks.). (Illus.). 64p. (gr. k-3). 1980. PLB 9.89 (ISBN 0-06-025614-1). HarpJ.

Sea Otters: A Natural History & Guide. Roy Nickerson. LC 84-19955. (Illus.). 112p. (Orig.). 1984. pap. 7.95 (ISBN 0-87701-309-8). Chronicle Bks.

Sea Otters & Seaweed. Patricia Lauber. LC 76-17796. (Good Earth Ser.). (Illus.). 64p. (gr. 2-6). 1976. lib. bdg. 7.22 (ISBN 0-8116-6106-7). Garrard.

Sea Peoples: Warriors of the Ancient Mediterranean 1250 to 1150. N. K. Sandars. (Illus.). 140p. 1985. pap. 11.95 (ISBN 0-500-27387-1). Thames Hudson.

Sea Plays. Ed. by Colin C. Clements. LC 79-50022. (One-Act Plays in Reprint Ser.). (Illus.). 1980. Repr. of 1925 ed. 23.50x (ISBN 0-8486-2046-1). Roth Pub Inc.

Sea Power: A Naval History. 2nd, rev. ed. Ed. by E. B. Potter. (Illus.). 432p. 1981. 21.95 (ISBN 0-87021-607-4); bulk rates avail. Naval Inst Pr.

Sea Power & the Nuclear Fallacy: A Reevaluation of Global Strategy. Robert E. Walters. LC 75-15754. 214p. 1975. Repr. of 1974 ed. 22.50 (ISBN 0-8419-0214-3). Holmes & Meier.

Sea Power in Its Relations to the War of 1812, 2 Vols. Alfred Mahan. LC 68-26362. (World History Ser. No. 48). 1969. Repr. of 1905 ed. lib. bdg. 99.95x (ISBN 0-8383-0181-9). Haskell.

Sea Power in Its Relations to the War of 1812, 2 Vols. Alfred T. Mahan. LC 69-10129. 1969. Repr. of 1905 ed. Vol. 2. lib. bdg. 16.00 (ISBN 0-8371-0825-X, MAWB). Greenwood.

Sea Power in the Machine Age. Bernard Brodie. LC 69-13840. 1969. Repr. of 1943 ed. lib. bdg. 27.50x (ISBN 0-8371-1445-4, BRSP). Greenwood.

Sea Power in the Mediterranean: Political Utility & Military Constraints. Edward N. Luttwak & Robert G. Weinland. (Washington Papers: Vol. VI, No. 61). 96p. (Orig.). 1979. pap. text ed. 7.95 (ISBN 0-8191-6010-5, Pub. by CSIS). U Pr of Amer.

Sea Power in the Modern World. Herbert W. Richmond. LC 72-4293. (World Affairs Ser.: National & International Viewpoints). 318p. 1972. Repr. of 1934 ed. 21.00 (ISBN 0-405-04585-9). Ayer Co Pubs.

Sea Power in the Nineteen Seventies. Ed. by George Quester. LC 73-88666. 1975. 23.95x (ISBN 0-8046-7088-9, Pub. by Kennikat). Assoc Faculty Pr.

Sea-Power in the Pacific: A Study of the American-Japanese Naval Problem. Hector C. Bywater. LC 75-111749. (American Imperialism: Viewpoints of United States Foreign Policy, 1898-1941). 1970. Repr. of 1921 ed. 22.00 (ISBN 0-405-02006-6). Ayer Co Pubs.

Sea Power of the State. S. G. Gorshkov. (Illus.). 1979. 59.00 (ISBN 0-08-021944-6). Pergamon.

Sea Priestess. Dion Fortune. (Orig.). 1979. pap. 8.95 (ISBN 0-87728-424-5). Weiser.

Sea Psalms: A Book of Uncommon Prayers for Sailors. John Jay Hughes. LC 88-50446. (Illus.). 48p. (Orig.). 1988. pap. 7.95 (ISBN 0-89622-361-2). Twenty Third.

Sea Remembers: Shipwrecks & Archaeology. Ed. by Peter Throckmorton. LC 87-14273. (Illus.). 240p. 1987. 29.95 (ISBN 1-55584-093-0). Weidenfeld.

Sea Rescue. D. Pike. (Dangerous Jobs Ser.). (Illus.). 32p. (gr. 4 up). Date not set. PLB 13.27 (ISBN 0-86592-411-2). Rourke Corp.

Sea Road to the Indies: An Account of the Voyages & Exploits of the Portuguese Navigators, Together with the Life & Times of Dom Vasco De Gama, Capitao-Mor, Viceroy of India & Count of Vidigueira. Henry H. Hart. LC 70-135246. (Illus.). 1971. Repr. of 1950 ed. lib. bdg. 35.00x (ISBN 0-8371-5165-1, HARO). Greenwood.

Sea Routes to the Gold Fields. Oscar Lewis. 256p. 1987. Repr. 4.50 (ISBN 0-89174-044-9). Comstock Edns.

Sea Rover: A Seaman's Life Aboard Scandinavian Ships During the Fifties & Sixties. Ingvar S. Bergquist. 1987. 14.95 (ISBN 0-533-07348-0). Vantage.

Sea Rovers: Pirates, Privateers & Buccaneers. Albert Marrin. LC 83-15886. (Illus.). 224p. (gr. 5 up). 1984. 14.95 (ISBN 0-689-31029-3, Atheneum Childrens Bks). Macmillan.

Sea Run. Les Johnson. (Illus.). 77p. (Orig.). 1979. pap. 9.95 (ISBN 0-936608-02-1). F Amato Pubns.

Sea Runners. Ivan Doig. 288p. 1983. pap. 5.95 (ISBN 0-14-006780-9). Penguin.

Sea Runners. Ralph Hayes. (Orig.). 1981. pap. 2.50 (ISBN 0-505-51647-0, Pub. by Tower Bks). Leisure NY.

Sea Sailing. Ed. by Wang Tuoming. (Illus.). 18p. (ps). 1986. pap. 1.95 (ISBN 0-8351-1569-0). China Bks.

Sea, Sails & Shipwreck: The Career of the Four Masted Schooner Purnell T. White. Robert H. Burgess. LC 73-124313. (Illus.). 144p. 1970. 6.00 (ISBN 0-87033-147-7). Tidewater.

Sea Serpent Journal: Hugh McCulloch Gregory's Voyage Around the World in a Clipper Ship, 1854-55. Hugh M. Gregory. Ed. by Robert H. Burgess. LC 74-12382. (Illus.). 1975. 12.95 (ISBN 0-8139-0589-3). U Pr of Va.

Sea Serpent: The Yarns of Jean-Marie Cabidoulin. Jules Verne. 4.95 (ISBN 0-87497-035-0). Assoc Bk.

Sea Serpents of Coastal New England. L. D. Geller. 0.35 (ISBN 0-940628-37-6). Pilgrim Soc.

Sea Shells of Southern Africa. Richard Kelburn & Elizabeth Rippery. (Illus.). 264p. 1982. 49.95 (ISBN 0-86954-094-7, Pub. by Macmillan S Africa). Intl Spec Bk.

Sea Shells of Sri Lanka: Including Forms Scattered Throughout the Indian & Pacific Oceans. Parakrama Kirtisinghe. LC 77-72607. (Illus.). 1978. 12.50 (ISBN 0-8048-1189-X). C E Tuttle.

Sea Shells of the West Indies: A Guide to the Marine Molluscs of the Caribbean. Michael Humfrey. LC 74-20213. (Illus.). 352p. 1975. 19.95 (ISBN 0-8008-7014-X). Taplinger.

Sea Shells of the World with Values. A. Gordon Melvin. LC 66-18967. (Illus.). (YA) (gr. 9 up). 1966. 19.50 (ISBN 0-8048-0512-1). C E Tuttle.

Sea Shells of Tropical West America: Marine Mollusks from Baja California to Peru. 2nd ed. A. Myra Keen & James H. McLean. (Illus.). 1971. 47.50 (ISBN 0-8047-0736-7). Stanford U Pr.

Sea Siege. Andre Norton. 224p. 1981. pap. 2.25 (ISBN 0-449-24293-5, Crest). Fawcett.

Sea Siege. Andre Norton. 224p. 1987. pap. 2.95 (ISBN 0-345-34364-6, Del Rey). Ballantine.

Sea Signalling Simplified. J. Russell. (Illus.). 84p. 1973. 10.95 (ISBN 0-8464-0826-0). Beekman Pubs.

Sea Signalling Simplified. rev. ed. P. J. Russell. 1977. 5.95 (ISBN 0-8286-0072-4). J De Graff.

Sea Skater. Helen Dunmore. 72p. 1986. pap. 10.95 (ISBN 1-85224-006-7, Pub. by Bloodaxe Bks). Dufour.

Sea, Sky & Stars: An Illustrated History of Grumman Aircraft. M. J. Hardy. (Illus.). 160p. 1987. 29.95 (ISBN 0-85368-832-X, Pub. by Arms & Armour). Sterling.

Sea-Slug Gastropods. Wesley M. Farmer. (Illus.). 157p. (Orig.). 1980. pap. 5.00 (ISBN 0-937772-00-3). W M Farmer.

Sea Snakes. Harold Heatwole. (Illus.). 85p. 1987. pap. 12.95 (ISBN 0-86840-218-4, Pub. by New South Wales Univ Pr Australia). Intl Spec Bk.

Sea Songs. Myra C. Livingston. LC 85-16422. (Illus.). 32p. (gr. 1-4). 1986. reinforced bdg. 14.95 (ISBN 0-8234-0591-5). Holiday.

Sea Squirts of the Atlantic Continental Shelf from Maine to Texas. Harold H. Plough. LC 76-47388. (Illus.). pap. 32.00 (ISBN 0-317-41676-6, 2025851). Bks Demand UMI.

Sea Star. Pamela Jekel. 384p. 1984. pap. 3.95 (ISBN 0-515-07729-1). Jove Pubns.

Sea Star. Diana L. Paxson. 384p. 1988. pap. 3.95 (ISBN 0-8125-4864-7, Dist. by St Martin's Pr & Warner Pub Servs). Tor Bks.

Sea Star: Orphan of Chincoteague. Marguerite Henry. LC 49-11474. (Illus.). 176p. (gr. 2-9). 1949. 8.95 (ISBN 0-528-82370-1, Checkerboard Pr); pap. 2.95 (ISBN 0-528-87687-2, Checkerboard Pr). Macmillan.

Sea Star: Orphan of Chincoteague. Marguerite Henry. (Illus.). (gr. k-9). 1988. pap. 2.25. Scholastic Inc.

Sea Stories. Joseph Conrad. 272p. (Orig.). 1984. pap. 12.95 (ISBN 0-246-12426-1, Pub. by Granada England). Sheridan.

Sea Stories. Joseph Conrad. 272p. 1985. pap. 8.95 (ISBN 0-88184-177-3). Carroll & Graf.

Sea Stories: Of Dolphins & Dead Sailors. John P. Barrett & Fred Wolleson. LC 87-82430. (Illus.). 128p. 1988. 10.00 (ISBN 0-9619629-0-9). Gaff Pr.

Sea Story. Sam Llewellyn. 400p. 1988. 18.95 (ISBN 0-312-01814-2, Pub. by Thomas Dunne Bks). St Martin.

Sea Surface Studies: A Global View. Ed. by R. J. Devoy. 650p. 1987. lib. bdg. 95.00x (ISBN 0-7099-0871-7, Pub. by Croom Helm UK). Routledge Chapman & Hall.

Sea Surveying, 2 vols. Alan E. Ingham. LC 74-3066. (Illus.). Vol. 1. pap. 82.20 (ISBN 0-317-58206-2, 2052215); Vol. 2. pap. 61.70 (ISBN 0-317-58207-0). Bks Demand UMI.

Sea Survival: The Boatman's Emergency Manual. Robb Huff & Michael Farley. (Illus.). 224p. 1989. pap. 14.95 (3077). TAB Bks.

Sea Swan. Kathryn Lasky. LC 88-1444. (Illus.). 32p. (gr. k-3). 1988. PLB 13.95 (ISBN 0-02-751700-4). Macmillan.

Sea: The Earth Beneath the Sea; History, Vol. 3. Ed. by M. N. Hill. LC 80-248. 980p. 1980. Repr. of 1963 ed. lib. bdg. 65.00 (ISBN 0-89874-099-1). Krieger.

Sea, the Land, the Life Through the Cameras of The Cape Codder. The Cape Codder Staff. (Illus.). 120p. (Orig.). 1988. pap. 14.95 (ISBN 0-9619737-0-6). Cape Codder Pr.

Sea, the Sea. Iris Murdoch. 1980. pap. 7.95 (ISBN 0-14-005199-6). Penguin.

Sea, the Sea. Iris Murdoch. 1978. 12.95 (ISBN 0-670-62651-1). Viking.

Sea to Shining Sea: People, Travel, Places. Berton Roueche. 288p. 1987. pap. 4.50 (ISBN 0-380-70265-7). Avon.

Sea to the West. Norman Nicholson. 64p. (Orig.). 1987. pap. 6.95 (ISBN 0-571-11729-5). Faber & Faber.

Sea Tramps. Robert H. Freeman. 250p. 1985. 9.95 (ISBN 0-931099-01-3). Shellback Pr.

Sea Transport: Operation & Economics. 3rd ed. Patrick M. Alderton. (Illus.). 1984. 20.00 (ISBN 0-900335-93-9). Heinman.

Sea Trout Fishing. Hugh Falkus. (Illus.). 448p. 1986. Repr. of 1983 ed. 43.95 (ISBN 0-85493-115-5). Greycliff Pub.

Sea Turn, & Other Matters. facs. ed. Thomas B. Aldrich. LC 76-81258. (Short Story Index Reprint Ser.). 1902. 18.00 (ISBN 0-8369-3010-X). Ayer Co Pubs.

Sea Turtle: So Excellent a Fishe. rev. ed. Archie Carr. 1986. pap. 9.95 (ISBN 0-292-77595-4). U of Tex Pr.

Sea Turtles & the Turtle Industry of the West Indies, Florida, & the Gulf of Mexico. Thomas P. Rebel. LC 73-159293. 224p. 1974. 10.95 (ISBN 0-87024-217-2). U of Miami Pr.

Sea Urchin Development Cell Use. L. Stearns. 58.95 (ISBN 0-317-64273-1). Van Nos Reinhold.

Sea Urchin Embryoas: A Developmental Biology System. G. Giudice. (Illus.). 260p. 1985. 67.50 (ISBN 0-387-15353-5). Springer-Verlag.

Sea Urchin Harakiri. Bernard Bador. Tr. by Clayton Eshleman. (Illus.). 120p. 1986. 16.95 (ISBN 0-915572-77-X); pap. 6.95 (ISBN 0-915572-76-1). Panjandrum.

Sea Urchin: Molecular Biology, 3 vols, Vol. 2. John B. Chamberlain et al. 188p. 1973. text ed. 28.50x (ISBN 0-8422-7121-X). Irvington.

Sea Urchin: Molecular Biology, Vol. 3. S. A. Terman et al. 1973. 28.50x (ISBN 0-8422-7122-8). Irvington.

Sea Vegetable Gelatin Cookbook. Judith Cooper Madlener. LC 80-29228. (Illus., Orig.). 1981. pap. 7.95 (ISBN 0-912800-76-3). Woodbridge Pr.

Sea Vegetables: Harvesting Guide & Cookbook. Evelyn McConnaughey. (Illus.). 239p. 13.95 (ISBN 0-87961-150-2); pap. 8.95 (ISBN 0-87961-151-0). Naturegraph.

Sea Venture. F. Van Wyck Mason. 1976. Repr. of 1961 ed. lib. bdg. 20.95 (ISBN 0-89190-353-4, Pub. by River City Pr). Amereon Ltd.

Sea Venture: The Downing Wreck Revisted. A. Mardis. (Illus.). 80p. 1983. pap. text ed. 7.95x (ISBN 0-910651-05-1). Fathom Eight.

Sea Verse in a Sailor's Locker. James Tazelaar. LC 72-13085. (Illus.). 63p. 1972. pap. 3.00 (ISBN 0-87033-179-5). Tidewater.

Sea View Hotel. James Stevenson. LC 78-2749. (Illus.). 48p. (gr. k-3). 1978. 11.75 (ISBN 0-688-80168-4); PLB 11.88 (ISBN 0-688-84168-6). Greenwillow.

Sea Vixen. Brian Fiddler. 24p. 1987. pap. 21.00x (ISBN 0-948251-03-4, Pub. by Picton UK). State Mutual Bk.

Sea: Vol. 1, Physical Oceanography. Ed. by M. N. Hill. LC 80-248. 880p. 1982. Repr. of 1962 ed. lib. bdg. 65.00 (ISBN 0-89874-097-5). Krieger.

Sea: Vol. 2, Composition of Sea Water. Ed. by M. N. Hill. LC 80-248. 570p. 1982. Repr. of 1963 ed. lib. bdg. 55.00 (ISBN 0-89874-098-3). Krieger.

Sea Wall. Marguerite Duras. Tr. by Herma Briffault. 288p. 1985. pap. 7.95 (ISBN 0-374-51945-5). FS&G.

Sea Wall. Marguerite Duras. LC 86-45092. 288p. 1986. pap. 6.95 (ISBN 0-06-097053-7, PL-7053, PL). Har-Row.

Sea War in Korea. Malcolm W. Cagle & Frank A. Manson. LC 79-6104. (Navies & Men Ser.). (Illus.). 1980. Repr. of 1957 ed. lib. bdg. 57.50x (ISBN 0-405-13033-3). Ayer Co Pubs.

Sea War: Nineteen Thirty-Nine to Nineteen Forty-Five. Janusz Piekalkiewicz. Tr. by Tek Translation & International Print Ltd. Orig. Title: Seekrieg 1939-1945. (Illus.). 353p. 1987. 19.95 (ISBN 0-918678-17-X). Historical Times.

Sea War 1939-1945. Janusz Piekalkiewicz. (Illus.). 354p. 1987. 29.95 (ISBN 0-7137-1665-7, Pub. by Blandford Pr England). Sterling.

Sea Warfare: Weapons, Tactics & Strategy. H. P. Willmott. (Illus.). 165p. 1981. 22.50 (ISBN 0-917319-02-8). Sheridan.

Sea Was Our Village. Miles Smeeton. (Illus.). 224p. 1986. pap. 12.95 (ISBN 0-246-12922-0, Pub. by Collins England). Sheridan.

Sea Water: Cycles of the Major Elements. Ed. by James I. Drever. (Bench Mark Papers in Geology Ser.). 1977. 40.00 (ISBN 0-12-786383-4). Acad Pr.

Sea Waves, Winds & Stars: True Story of the First Waves Approved by the Navy. 1988. write for info. Interspace Bks.

Sea Wedding & Other Stories from Estonia. Peggy Hoffmann & Selve Maas. LC 75-9623. (Illus.). 104p. (gr. 4 up). 1978. 9.95 (ISBN 0-87518-112-0). Dillon.

Sea Wife. Laird Koenig. 272p. (Orig.). 1986. pap. 3.50 (ISBN 0-446-34244-0). Warner Bks.

Sea Within. Ed. by Onesimo Almeida. Tr. by George Monteiro from Port. LC 83-80877. (Illus.). 115p. (Orig.). 1983. pap. 3.50 (ISBN 0-943722-09-8). Gavea-Brown.

Sea Within. Louise Murphy. 288p. 1985. 16.95 (ISBN 0-399-12998-7, Putnam). Putnam Pub Group.

Sea Wolf. Jack London. (Airmont Classics Ser.). (gr. 6 up). pap. 1.95 (ISBN 0-8049-0064-7, CL-64). Airmont.

Sea Wolf. Jack London. 351p. Repr. of 1904 ed. lib. bdg. 20.95x (ISBN 0-89190-657-6, Pub. by River City Pr). Amereon Ltd.

Sea Wolf. Jack London. (Bantam Classics Ser.). 256p. (gr. 7 up). 1984. pap. 1.95 (ISBN 0-553-21225-7). Bantam.

Sea Wolf. Jack London. Ed. by John C. Fago. (Now Age Illustrated IV Ser.). (Illus.). (gr. 4-12). 1978. text ed. 7.50 (ISBN 0-88301-334-7); pap. text ed. 2.95 (ISBN 0-88301-322-3); activity bk. 1.25 (ISBN 0-88301-346-0). Pendulum Pr.

Sea Wolf. Jack London. (Regents Illustrated Classics Ser.). (Illus.). 62p. (gr. 7-12). 1981. pap. text ed. 3.50 (ISBN 0-13-796798-5, 20545). Prentice ESL.

Sea Wolf. Jack London. (Illus.). 370p. 1981. pap. 7.95 (ISBN 0-932458-05-X). Star Rover.

Sea Wolf. Jack London. 256p. pap. 1.75 (ISBN 0-553-21161-7, Bantam Classics). Bantam.

Sea Wolf see Novels & Stories.

Sea Wolf & Selected Stories. Jack London. 352p. (RL 8). pap. 1.95 (ISBN 0-451-51965-5, CW1552, Sig Classics). NAL.

Sea Wolf, No. 2: Shark North. Bruno Krauss. 1981. pap. 2.25 (ISBN 0-89083-782-1). Zebra.

Sea Wolf: Shark Raid, No. 6. Bruno Krauss. (Sea Wolf Ser.). 1982. pap. 2.25 (ISBN 0-8217-1043-5). Zebra.

Sea Wolves. Wolfgang Frank. 224p. 1981. pap. 2.50 (ISBN 0-345-29504-8). Ballantine.

Sea Wolves. Edwin P. Hoyt. 208p. 1987. pap. 3.95 (ISBN 0-380-75249-2). Avon.

Sea World Alphabet Book. Sea World Press & Alan Sloan, Inc. LC 79-65202. (Sea World Press Ser.). (Illus.). 32p. (ps-3). 1980. 4.95 (ISBN 0-15-271946-6, HJ). HarBraceJ.

Sea World Book of Dolphins. Stephen Leatherwood & Randall Reeves. LC 86-46212. (Illus.). 96p. (Orig.). (gr. 4-8). 1987. 12.95 (ISBN 0-15-271956-3, VoyB); pap. 6.95 (ISBN 0-317-59229-7, VoyB). HarBraceJ.

Sea World Book of Dolphins. Stephen Leatherwood & Randall Reeves. LC 86-46212. 96p. (gr. 4-7). 1987. pap. 9.95 (ISBN 0-15-271957-1, VoyB). HarBraceJ.

Sea World Book of Penguins. Frank S. Todd. LC 86-25588. (Sea World Press Ser.). (Illus.). 96p. (gr. 4-6). 1981. 12.95 (ISBN 0-15-271949-0, HJ). HarBraceJ.

Sea World Book of Penguins. Frank S. Todd. LC 80-25588. (Sea World Press Ser.). (Illus.). 96p. (gr. 4-7). 1984. pap. 6.95 (ISBN 0-15-271951-2, VoyB). HarBraceJ.

Sea World Book of Seals & Sea Lions. Phyllis Roberts Evans. LC 85-27100. (Illus.). (gr. 4-6). 1986. 15.95 (ISBN 0-15-271954-7, HJ); pap. 8.95 (ISBN 0-15-271955-5). HarBraceJ.

Sea World Book of Sharks. Eve Bunting. LC 79-63920. (Sea World Press Ser.). (Illus.). 80p. (gr. 4-6). 1980. 12.95 (ISBN 0-15-271947-4, HJ). HarBraceJ.

Sea World Book of Sharks. Eve Bunting. LC 79-639201. (Sea World Press Ser.). (Illus.). 80p. (gr. 4-7). 1984. pap. 8.95 (ISBN 0-15-271952-0, VoyB). HarBraceJ.

Sea World Book of Whales. Eve Bunting. LC 85-16409. (Sea World Press Ser.). (Illus.). 96p. (gr. 4-6). 1986. 14.95 (ISBN 0-15-271948-2, HJ); pap. 7.95 (ISBN 0-15-271953-9). HarBraceJ.

Sea World, No. 4: Shark Hunt. Bruno Krauss. pap. 2.25 (ISBN 0-89083-833-X). Zebra.

Sea-Wyf & Biscuit. J. M. Scott. 1988. 30.00x (ISBN 0-86025-043-1, Pub. by Ian Henry Pubns England). State Mutual Bk.

Seabed Disposal of High-Level Radioactive Waste: Nuclear Energy Agency. OECD Staff. 246p. (Orig.). 1984. pap. 28.00x (ISBN 92-64-12576-0). OECD.

Seabed Energy & Mineral Resources & the Law of the Sea, 1 vol. E. D. Brown. 1985. 71.50 (ISBN 0-86010-460-5). pap. 97.00 looseleaf (ISBN 0-317-47351-4); pap. 260.00 looseleaf incl. first annual update (ISBN 0-317-47352-2). Graham & Trotman.

Seabed Mechanics. Ed. by Bruce Denness. 296p. 1985. 88.50 (ISBN 0-86010-504-0). Graham & Trotman.

Seabed Minerals Series: Analysis of Exploration, Vol. 2. Ed. by Graham & Trotman, Ltd. Staff. 144p. 1985. 35.00. Graham & Trotman.

Seabed Minerals Series: Vol. 3, Analysis of Processing Technology for Manganese Nodules. Ed. by Graham & Trotman, Ltd. Staff. 104p. 1985. 35.00 (ISBN 0-86010-349-8). Graham & Trotman.

Seabed Pockmarks & Seepages: Geological, Ecological & Environmental Implication. Martin Hovland & Alan G. Judd. 1988. lib. bdg. 112.00 (ISBN 0-86010-948-8, Pub. by Graham & Trotman UK). Kluwer Academic.

Seabed Reconnaissance & Offshore Soil Mechanics for the Installation of Petroleum Structures. Pierre Le Tirant. (Illus.). 508p. 1980. 95.00x (ISBN 0-87201-794-X). Gulf Pub.

Seabewitched. Eileen Akester. 179p. 1985. 34.00x (ISBN 0-901976-88-1, Pub. by United Writers Pubns England). State Mutual Bk.

Seabird. Holling C. Holling. (Illus.). (gr. 4-6). PLB 15.95 (ISBN 0-395-18230-1). HM.

Seabird. Holling C. Holling. (Illus.). (gr. 4-6). 1978. pap. 5.95 (ISBN 0-395-26681-5). HM.

Seabird Ecology. R. W. Furness & P. Monaghan. (Tertiary Level Biology Ser.). 1987. 45.00 (ISBN 0-412-01451-3, 1193, Pub. by Chapman & Hall England); pap. 23.00 (ISBN 0-317-56153-7, 1201). Routledge Chapman & Hall.

Seabird Energetics. Ed. by G. Causey Whittow & Herman Rahn. LC 84-15998. 340p. 1984. 65.00x (ISBN 0-306-41819-3, Plenum Pr). Plenum Pub.

Seabird on Ocean Routes. Gerald Turb. 1987. pap. 14.95 (ISBN 0-00-219403-1). Greene.

Seabirds. J. P. Mackenzie. (Illus.). 144p. Date not set. 19.95 (ISBN 1-55013-025-0, Pub. by Key Porter Canada). U of Toronto Pr.

Seabirds. John P. Mackenzie. (Birds of the World Ser.). 144p. 1987. 19.95 (ISBN 0-942802-52-7). Northword.

Seabirds. John P. Mackenzie. 1987. 65.00x (ISBN 0-245-54593-X, Pub. by Harrap Ltd England). State Mutual Bk.

Seabirds: An Identification Guide. Peter Harrison. LC 82-15564. 1983. 29.95 (ISBN 0-395-33253-2). HM.

Seabirds & Other Marine Vertebrates: Competition, Predation, & Other Interactions. Ed. by Joanna Burger. 312p. 1988. 35.00x (ISBN 0-231-06362-8). Columbia U Pr.

Seabirds: Feeding Ecology & Role in Marine Ecosystems. Ed. by J. P. Croxall. (Illus.). 350p. 1987. 59.50 (ISBN 0-521-30178-5). Cambridge U Pr.

Seabirds of Britian & World. Turb & Heinzel. 1987. pap. 16.95 (ISBN 0-00-219286-1). Greene.

Seabirds of Eastern North Pacific & Arctic Waters. Ed. by Delphine Haley. LC 83-19411. (Illus.). 216p. 1984. 22.95 (ISBN 0-914718-86-X). Pacific Search.

Seabirds of the World. Ronald M. Lockley. (Illus.). 160p. 1984. 24.95 (ISBN 0-87196-249-7). Facts on File.

Seaboard Air Line Motive Power. Paul K. Withers & Warren C. Calloway. 240p. 1988. 39.95 (ISBN 0-9618503-1-0). Paul K Withers.

Seaboard Air Line Railway Album. Albert M. Langley, Jr. et al. LC 88-50417. (Illus.). 184p. (Orig.). 1988. pap. 27.95 (ISBN 0-9615257-2-X). Union Sta.

Seaboard Coastline in Florida. Warren & Clark. (Illus.). 116p. 1985. pap. 15.95 (ISBN 0-911868-46-1). Carstens Pubns.

Seaboard Parish. George MacDonald. 240p. 1985. pap. 5.95 (ISBN 0-89693-329-6). Victor Bks.

Seaborne Commerce of Ancient Rome: Studies in Archaeology & History. J. H. D'Arms & E. C. Kopff. 397p. 1980. 50.00x (ISBN 0-271-00459-2). Pa St U Pr.

Seabrook & the Nuclear Regulatory Commission: The Licensing of a Nuclear Power Plant. Donald W. Steven. LC 79-56160. pap. 66.00 (ISBN 0-317-39645-5, 2023233). Bks Demand UMI.

Seacliff. Felicia Andrews. 368p. 1984. pap. 3.50 (ISBN 0-441-75640-9). Ace Bks.

Seacliff. John W. De Forest. (Collected Works of John W. De Forest). 1988. Repr. of 1859 ed. lib. bdg. 59.00x. Am Biog Serv.

Seacliff see Collected Works.

Seacoast Fortifications of the United States: An Introductory History. Emmanuel R. Lewis. (Illus.). 147p. 1985. pap. 9.95 (ISBN 0-89141-257-3). Presidio Pr.

Seacoast Life: An Ecological Guide to Natural Seashore Communities in North Carolina. Judith M. Spitsbergen. LC 83-80687. (Illus.). 114p. 1983. pap. 5.95 (ISBN 0-8078-4109-9). U of NC Pr.

Seacoast Maine: People & Places. rev. ed. Martin Dibner & George Tice. LC 87-80782. 208p. 1987. 35.00 (ISBN 0-88448-042-9); pap. 17.95 (ISBN 0-88448-043-7). Harpswell Pr.

Seacook: A Guide to Good Living Afloat. Bob Heppel. (Illus.). 122p. 1986. pap. 14.95 (ISBN 0-229-11784-8, Pub. by Adlar Coles). Sheridan.

Seacraft of Prehistory. Paul Johnstone. Ed. by Sean McGrail. (Illus.). 320p. 1980. 29.50 (ISBN 0-674-79595-4). Harvard U Pr.

Seadrift House. Clare Hamilton. 256p. (Orig.). 1981. pap. 2.25 (ISBN 0-505-51746-9, Pub. by Tower Bks). Leisure NY.

Seafarer. O. S. Anderson. 1978. Repr. lib. bdg. 20.00 (ISBN 0-8495-0110-5). Arden Lib.

Seafarer. Ed. by I. L. Gordon. (Old English Ser.). 1966. pap. text ed. 6.95x (ISBN 0-89197-570-5). Irvington.

Seafarer: A Interpretation. O. S. Anderson. LC 73-9785. 1937. lib. bdg. 25.00 (ISBN 0-8414-2866-2). Folcroft.

Seafarers. William Long. (Australians Ser.: No. 13). (Illus.). 1988. pap. 4.95 (ISBN 0-440-20112-8). Dell.
Seafarers' Conditions in India & Pakistan see Labour Courts in Latin America.
Seafarers (Poetry) Wayland W. Williams. 1924. 29.50x (ISBN 0-686-83730-4). Elliots Bks.
Seafaring in Colonial Massachusetts. Ed. by Philip C. Smith. LC 80-51256. (Illus.). xvii, 240p. 1980. 30.00 (ISBN 0-8139-0897-3, Colonial Soc MA). U Pr of Va.
Seafaring in English. 232p. Date not set. incl. 2 cassettes 35.00 (ISBN 0-88432-194-0, S32550). J Norton Pubs.
Seafaring Woman. Dorothy Dowdell. 1988. pap. 3.95 (ISBN 0-449-13181-5, GM). Fawcett.
Seafaring Women. Linda G. De Pauw. (gr. 7 up). 1982. 10.95 (ISBN 0-395-32434-3). HM.
Seafishing Yarns. Zane Grey. 276p. Repr. lib. bdg. 18.95x (ISBN 0-89190-766-1, Pub. by River City Pr). Amereon Ltd.
Seafloor Scour: Design Guidelines for Ocean Founded Structures. Herbich. (Ocean Engineering Ser.). 288p. 1984. 65.00 (ISBN 0-8247-7095-1). Dekker.
Seafood. Bon Appetit Magazine Editors. LC 83-9828. (Cooking with Bon Appetit Ser.). (Illus.). 144p. 1984. 12.95 (ISBN 0-89535-120-X). Knapp Pr.
Seafood. (Spotlight on Resources Ser.). (Illus.). (gr. 5 up). Date not set. write for info. Rourke Corp.
Seafood: A Collection of Heart-Healthy Recipes. Janis Harsila & Evie Hansen. (Illus.). 224p. (Orig.). 1986. pap. 11.95 (ISBN 0-9616426-0-2). Nat Seafood Educ.
Seafood & Health. Joyce A. Nettleton. Ed. by Ian Dore. LC 86-23467. 1987. 22.95x; pap. 15.95x (ISBN 0-943738-21-0). Osprey Bks.
Seafood As We Like It. Anthony Spinazolla & Jean-Jaques Paimblanc. LC 85-9768. (Illus.). 512p. (Orig.). 1985. pap. cancelled (ISBN 0-87106-858-3); casebound 14.95 (ISBN 0-87106-862-1). Globe Pequot.
Seafood Cook Book. 4th ed. Sunset Editors. LC 80-53482. (Illus.). 128p. 1981. pap. 6.95 (ISBN 0-376-02587-5, Sunset Bks.). Sunset-Lane.
Seafood Cookbook. Pierre Franey. LC 86-5779. (Illus.). 296p. 1986. 22.50 (ISBN 0-8129-1604-2). Times Bks.
Seafood Cookbook. Shirley Ross. 1978. text ed. 12.95 (ISBN 0-07-053881-6). McGraw.
Seafood Cookbook: A Complete Guide to Preparing & Cooking Fish & Shellfish. Shirley Ross. (Illus.). 192p. 1980. pap. text ed. 5.95 (ISBN 0-07-053889-1). McGraw.
Seafood Creations by an Italian Gourmet. Nicholas T. Castellucci. 1978. 7.95 (ISBN 0-682-49141-1, Banner). Exposition-Phoenix.
Seafood Dishes. Bianco. 1983. 5.95 (ISBN 0-8120-5530-6). Barron.
Seafood Exporter's Handbook. Ian Dore. (Osprey Seafood Handbooks). 1984. cancelled (ISBN 0-943738-06-7). Osprey Bks.
Seafood Favorites: Recipes from Authors & Staff of International Marine Publishing Company. LC 83-49419. (Illus.). 128p. 1984. pap. 4.95 (ISBN 0-87742-180-3, S630). Intl Marine.
Seafood Fishing for Amateur & Professional. R. C. O'Farrell. 1978. 25.00 (ISBN 0-685-63452-3). State Mutual Bk.
Seafood Heritage Cookbook. Adam Starchild. LC 83-40549. 188p. 1984. 11.95 (ISBN 0-87033-312-7). Tidewater.
Seafood Industry's Almanac. Ed. by Ian Dore. (Osprey Seafood Handbooks Ser.). (Orig.). 1988. price not set (ISBN 0-943738-14-8); pap. price not set (ISBN 0-943738-15-6). Osprey Bks.
Seafood Nutrition: Facts, Issues & Marketing of Nutrition in Fish & Shellfish. Joyce Nettleton. Ed. by Ian Dore. LC 85-15297. (Osprey Seafood Handbooks Ser.). 1986. 59.00x (ISBN 0-943738-12-1). Osprey Bks.
Seafood of South-East Asia. Alan Davidson. (Illus.). 366p. 1985. 15.95x (ISBN 0-8139-1073-0). U Pr of Va.
Seafood Processing & Distribution Market Opportunities. Int'l. Resource Development, Inc. Staff. 243p. 1986. 495.00x (ISBN 0-88694-715-4). Intl Res Dev.
Seafood Quality Determination: Proceedings of the International Symposium, Anchorage, AK. D. E. Kramer & J. Liston. (Developments in Food Science Ser.: Vol. 15). 1987. 207.50 (ISBN 0-444-42895-X). Elsevier.
Seafood Restaurant Operations. Ad Wittemann. 59p. (Orig.). 1988. pap. 25.00 (ISBN 0-938481-49-5). Camelot Consult.
Seafood Smoking. R. Marilyn Schmidt. (Illus.). 58p. (Orig.). 1987. pap. 5.95 (ISBN 0-937996-09-2). Barnegat.
Seafood Sourcebook: A Consumer's Guide to Information on Food from Our Oceans & Lakes. New England Marine Advisory Service. 46p. 1978. 1.00 (ISBN 0-686-36979-3, P762). Sea Grant Pubns.
Seafood Toxins. Edward P. Ragelis. LC 84-18551. (Symposium Ser.: No. 262). 470p. 1984. lib. bdg. 79.95x (ISBN 0-8412-0863-8). Am Chemical.
Seafoods see Cooking with Bon Appetit.
Seagrass Ecosystems: A Scientific Perspective. Ed. by C. Peter McRoy & Carla Helfferich. LC 76-9466. (Marine Science Ser.: No. 4). pap. 85.30 (2030868). Bks Demand UMI.
Seagrave Fire Apparatus. Richard Baker. Date not set. price not set. E Hass.
Seagull see Five Major Plays.
Seagull-Anton Chekhov. Thomas Kilroy. 44p. 1981. pap. 4.95 (ISBN 0-413-49100-5, NO. 3511). Heinemann Ed.
Seagull Produced by Stanislavski. Constantin Stanislavski. Ed. by S. D. Balukhaty. 1984. pap. write for info. (ISBN 0-317-11832-3). Theatre Arts.
Seagull Story. Mac Muehlman. LC 86-51516. (Illus.). 25p. (gr. 6). 1987. 9.95 (ISBN 0-9617854-0-3). J M Muehlman Pubns.
Seahb Siwash. Leon L. Stock. (Illus.). 352p. 1981. 15.00 (ISBN 0-89962-227-5). Todd & Honeywell.
Seahorse. Robert A. Morris. LC 70-146004. (Nature I Can Read Bks.). (Illus.). 64p. (gr. k-3). 1972. PLB 9.89 (ISBN 0-06-024339-2). HarpJ.
Seal. Illus. by Lynne Cherry. LC 86-24030. (Illus.). (ps). 1987. bds. 3.50 (ISBN 0-525-44304-5); book & toy package 13.95. Dutton.
Seal. Mary Hoffman. LC 86-17806. (Animals in the Wild Ser.). (Illus.). 24p. (gr. k-3). 1987. PLB 11.33 (ISBN 0-8172-2702-4). Raintree Pubs.
Seal Called Andre. Dietz & Goodridge. 1980. pap. 6.95 (ISBN 0-89272-076-X). Down East.
Seal Cylinders of Western Asia. William H. Ward. LC 78-72772. (Ancient Mesopotamian Texts & Studies). Repr. of 1910 ed. 72.50 (ISBN 0-404-18228-3). AMS Pr.
Seal for a Pal. Paul E. Layman. (Indian Culture Ser.). (gr. 4-9). 1972. pap. 1.95 (ISBN 0-89992-029-2). Coun India Ed.
Seal Islands of Alaska. Henry W. Elliott. (Alaska History Ser: No. 9). (Illus.). 1976. Repr. 16.50x (ISBN 0-919642-72-1). Limestone Pr.
Seal Mother. Mordicai Gerstein. LC 82-29295. (Illus.). 32p. (ps-3). 1986. 10.95 (ISBN 0-8037-0302-3, 01063-320); PLB 10.89 (ISBN 0-8037-0303-1). Dial Bks Young.
Seal of Approval: A Spontaneous Unfoldment. Kenneth G. Mills. 1979. pap. 12.99 incl. cassette (ISBN 0-919842-03-8). Sun-Scape Pubns.
Seal of Renewal. Catharose De Petri. (Orig.). 1986. pap. 7.50 (ISBN 90-70196-39-5). Rozekruis Pr.
Seal Oil Lamp. Dale DeArmond. (Illus.). 48p. (gr. k-4). 1988. 13.95 (ISBN 0-316-17786-5). Little.
Seal-Oil System. Center for Occupational Research & Development Staff. (EUTEC Power Plant Operator Curriculum Ser.). (Illus.). 20p. 1985. pap. text ed. write for info. (ISBN 1-55502-214-6). Ctr Res & Dev.
Seal on the Rocks. Doug Allan. LC 87-9950. (Animal Habitats Ser.). (Illus.). 32p. (gr. 4-6). 1988. PLB 9.95 (ISBN 1-55532-271-9). Stevens Inc.
Seal Rock. John Haislip. LC 85-72583. 52p. (Orig.). 1987. pap. 5.95 (ISBN 0-935306-40-4). Barnwood Pr.
Seal Secret. Aidan Chambers. LC 80-8456. 128p. (gr. 5 up). 1981. PLB 12.89 (ISBN 0-06-021259-4). HarpJ.
Seal Users Handbook. 2nd ed. R. M. Austin et al. 1979. text ed. 65.00x (ISBN 0-900983-90-6, Dist. by Air Science Co.). BHRA Fluid.
Seal Users Handbook. 3rd ed. Ed. by R. K. Flitney et al. 160p. 1985. 66.00 (ISBN 0-906085-99-3, Dist. by Air Science Co.). BHRA Fluid.
Sealand of Ancient Arabia. Raymond P. Dougherty. LC 78-63564. (Yale Oriental Ser. Researches: No. 19). Repr. of 1932 ed. 40.00 (ISBN 0-404-60289-4). AMS Pr.
Sealant Technology in Glazing Systems: A Symposium. American Society for Testing & Materials Staff. LC 77-83433. (ASTM Special Technical Publication: 638). pap. 29.00 (ISBN 0-317-20575-7, 2022516). Bks Demand UMI.
Sealants: Formulations & Applications, 1973-Jan. 1983. 147p. 1983. pap. 85.00 (ISBN 0-686-48312-X, LS112). T-C Pubns CA.
Sealantsin Construction. Klosowski. (Civil Engineering Ser.). 312p. 1988. 85.00 (ISBN 0-8247-7677-1). Dekker.
Sealed Angel & Other Stories. Nikolay Leskov. Tr. by K. A. Lantz. LC 83-14547. 268p. 1984. text ed. 25.95x (ISBN 0-87049-411-2). U of Tenn Pr.
Sealed Glass Tube Method to Test the Chemical Stability of Material for Use Within Refrigerant Systems, 1983. (ASHRAE Standards Ser.: No. 97). pap. text ed. 18.00 (ISBN 0-910110-31-X). Am Heat Ref & Air Eng.
Sealed Nickel Cadmium Batteries. Varta Batterie. 1982. pap. 34.00 (ISBN 3-18-419071-4, Pub. by VDI W Germany). IPS.
Sealed Orders. facsimile ed. Elizabeth S. Ward. 1972. Repr. of 1879 ed. lib. bdg. 29.00 (ISBN 0-8422-8123-1). Irvington.
Sealed Orders. Elizabeth S. Ward. 1986. pap. text ed. 7.95x (ISBN 0-8290-1876-X). Irvington.
Sealed Orders: The Autobiography of a Christian Mystic. Agnes Sanford. LC 72-76592. 312p. 1972. pap. 7.95 (ISBN 0-88270-048-0). Bridge Pub.
Sealed with a Kiss: Couples Special Edition. M. E. Cooper. 288p. (Orig.). (gr. 7 up). 1988. pap. 2.95 (ISBN 0-590-41263-9). Scholastic Inc.
Sealers. Peter Tutein. Tr. by Eugene Gay-Tifft. (Seafaring Men: Their Ships & Times Ser.). (Illus.). 1980. Repr. of 1938 ed. text ed. 22.50 (ISBN 0-930576-28-4). E M Coleman Ent.
Sealing & Self-Similarity in Physics. Jurg Frohlich. (Progress in Physics Ser.: Vol. 7). 434p. 1983. text ed. 39.50 (ISBN 0-8176-3168-2). Birkhauser.
Sealing Mechanisms of Flexible Packings. White & Denny. 1947. 16.00x (ISBN 0-686-71062-2). BHRA Fluid.
SeAlphabet Encyclopedia. Keith McConnell. (NaturEncyclopedia Ser.). (Illus.). 48p. (gr. 4 up). 1982. pap. 5.95 (ISBN 0-88045-016-9). Stemmer Hse.
Seals. L. Martin. (Wildlife in Danger Ser.). (Illus.). 24p. (gr. k-5). Date not set. PLB 11.33 (ISBN 0-86592-999-8). Rourke Corp.
Seals. 1984. 24.00 (ISBN 0-89883-800-2, SP579). Soc Auto Engineers.
Seals & Man: A Study of Interactions. W. Nigel Bonner. LC 81-69684. (Illus.). 184p. (Orig.). 1982. pap. 9.95x (ISBN 0-295-95890-1, Pub. by Wash Sea Grant). U of Wash Pr.
Seals & Sea Lions. Vicki Leon. (Illus.). 40p. (Orig.). 1988. pap. 4.95 (ISBN 0-918303-15-X). Blake Print Pub.
Seals & Sea Lions. Wildlife Education, Ltd. (Illus.). 20p. (Orig.). (YA) (gr. 5 up). 1985. pap. 1.95 (ISBN 0-937934-33-X). Wildlife Educ.
Seals & Sealing. R. H. Warring. 272p. 1981. 79.50x (ISBN 0-85461-072-3, Pub. by Trade & Tech England). Brookfield Pub Co.
Seals & Sealing Handbook. 2nd ed. 550p. 1986. text ed. 130.00x (ISBN 0-85461-082-0, Pub. by Trade & Tech England). Brookfield Pub Co.
Seals & Sealing Handbook. R. H. Warring. LC 80-85238. (Illus.). 438p. 1981. 67.00x (ISBN 0-87201-801-6). Gulf Pub.
Seals & Sealing in the Ancient Near East. Ed. by M. Gibson & R. D. Biggs. LC 76-44923. (Bibliotheca Mesopotamica Ser: Vol. 6). 160p. 1978. pap. 29.00x (ISBN 0-89003-022-7); cloth & microfiche 39.00. Undena Pubns.
Seals: Design & Performance. 1986. 50.00 (ISBN 0-89883-922-X, SP 651). Soc Auto Engineers.
Seals in the Inner Harbor. Brendan Galvin. LC 85-71692. (Poetry Ser.). 1985. 14.95 (ISBN 0-88748-075-6); pap. 6.95 (ISBN 0-88748-076-4). Carnegie Mellon.
Seals No. Seven: Recon. Steve Mackenzie. 160p. 1988. pap. 2.95 (ISBN 0-380-75529-7). Avon.
SEALS No. 3: Rescue! Steve MacKenzie. 176p. (Orig.). 1987. pap. 2.50 (ISBN 0-380-75191-7). Avon.
Seals No. 4: Target. Steve Mackenzie. 192p. 1987. pap. 2.95 (ISBN 0-380-75193-3). Avon.
Seals, No. 5: Breakout. Steve MacKenzie. 176p. 1988. pap. 2.95 (ISBN 0-380-75194-1). Avon.
Seals No. 6: Desert Rain. Steve Mackenzie. 176p. 1988. pap. 2.95 (ISBN 0-380-75195-X). Avon.
Seals No. 8: Infiltrate. Steve Mackenzie. 160p. (Orig.). 1988. pap. 2.95 (ISBN 0-380-75530-0). Avon.
Seals No. 9. Steve Mackenzie. 160p. 1988. pap. 2.95 (ISBN 0-380-75532-7). Avon.
Seals of Chinese Painters & Collectors. Victoria Contag & Chi-Chuan Wang. 726p. 1966. 220.00x (ISBN 0-317-68622-4, Pub. by Han-Shan Tang Ltd). State Mutual Bk.
Seals of Chinese Painters & Collectors. Victoria Contag & Chi-Chuan Wang. 726p. 1982. 140.00x (ISBN 0-317-68625-9, Pub. by Han-Shan Tang Ltd). State Mutual Bk.
Seals of the Order of St. John of Jerusalem, 3 vols. Edwin J. King. LC 78-63355. (Crusades & Military Orders: Second Ser.). (Illus.). Repr. of 1932 ed. 24.50 set (ISBN 0-404-16248-7). AMS Pr.
Seals of the World. 2nd ed. Judith E. King. LC 82-73980. (Illus.). 240p. 1983. 24.50x (ISBN 0-8014-1568-3). Cornell U Pr.
Seals of Wisdom. Muhyiddin Al-Arabi. (Sacred Texts Ser.). (Illus., Orig.). 1983. pap. 8.75 (ISBN 0-88695-010-4). Concord Grove.
Seals, Sea Lions & Walruses: A Review of the Pinnipedia. Victor B. Scheffer. (Illus.). 1958. 17.50x (ISBN 0-8047-0544-5). Stanford U Pr.
Sealskin & Shoddy: Working Women in the American Nineteenth Century Labor Press, 1870-1920. Intro. by Ann Schofield. LC 87-36065. (Contributions in Women's Studies: No. 96). 272p. 1988. lib. bdg. 39.95 (ISBN 0-313-25453-2, SSK/). Greenwood.
Sealyham Terrier Champions, 1952-1987. Camino E. E. & B. Co. Staff. 175p. (YA) 1988. pap. 29.95 (ISBN 0-940808-90-0). Camino E E & B.
Seam Gas Drainage. Ed. by A. J. Hargraves. 370p. 1982. pap. text ed. 39.00x (ISBN 0-909520-74-7, Pub. by Australian Inst M & M). Brookfield Pub Co.
Seaman. rev. ed. Educational Research Council of America Staff. Ed. by Jack R. Braverman & John P. Marchak. (Real People at Work Ser.: B). (Illus.). 36p. 1977. pap. text ed. 2.70 (ISBN 0-89247-016-X, 9226). Changing Times.
Seaman A. Knapp: Schoolmaster of American Agriculture. Joseph C. Bailey. LC 73-165702. (American Education, Ser. 2). 1971. Repr. of 1945 ed. 17.00 (ISBN 0-405-03691-4). Ayer Co Pubs.
Seaman Speculum, or Complete School-Master. John Davis. Intro. by Merritt A. Edson, Jr. (Illus.). iv, 164p. 1985. pap. 45.00 (ISBN 0-9603456-1-2). Nautical Res.
Seaman's Friend. Richard Dana. LC 79-4623. 1979. Repr. of 1841 ed. lib. bdg. 35.00x (ISBN 0-8201-1330-1). Schol Facsimiles.
Seaman's Guide to the Rules of the Road. 3rd ed. Ed. by J. W. Ford. (Illus.). 300p. 1984. pap. 14.95 (ISBN 0-87021-865-4). Naval Inst Pr.
Seamanship. Robin Knox-Johnston. (Illus.). 1987. 22.50 (ISBN 0-393-03318-X). Norton.
Seamanship: A Handbook for Oceanographers. Carvel H. Blair. LC 76-56349. (Illus.). 238p. 1977. 9.00x (ISBN 0-87033-228-7). Cornell Maritime.
Seamanship, Eighteen Sixty-Two. J. G. Nares. 368p. 1984. 49.00x (ISBN 0-905418-37-9, Pub. by Gresham England). State Mutual Bk.
Seamanship for New Skippers. George H. Ludins. (Illus.). 1980. pap. 5.95 (ISBN 0-916224-54-6). Banyan Bks.
Seamanship for Yachtsmen. Francis B. Cooke. 1977. lib. bdg. 69.95 (ISBN 0-8490-2582-6). Gordon Pr.
Seamanship: Fundamentals for the Deck Officer. 2nd ed. David O. Dodge & S. E. Kyriss. LC 80-5684. (Fundamentals of Naval Science: Vol. 2). 272p. 1981. text ed. 16.95x (ISBN 0-87021-613-9); bulk rates avail. Naval Inst Pr.
Seamanship Handbook. 7th ed. P. H. Adlam. cancelled (ISBN 0-540-07376-8). Sheridan.
Seamanship in the Age of Sail: An Account of the Sailing Man-of-War 1600-1860. John Harland. (Illus.). 200p. 1984. 39.95 (ISBN 0-87021-955-3). Naval Inst Pr.
Seamanship Notes. 4th ed. John Kemp. (Kemp & Young Ser.). (Illus.). 100p. (Orig.). 1983. pap. text ed. 12.95x (ISBN 0-540-07357-1, Pub. by Stanford Maritime). Sheridan.
Seamanship Techniques, Vol. 1. D. J. House. (Illus.). 384p. 1986. text ed. 55.00x (ISBN 0-434-90780-4). Sheridan.
Seamanship Techniques, Vol. 2. D. J. House. (Illus.). 504p. 1986. text ed. 65.00x (ISBN 0-434-90781-2). Sheridan.
Seamarks: Their History & Development. John M. Naish. (Illus.). 200p. 1985. 29.50 (ISBN 0-540-07309-1, Pub. by Stanford Maritime). Sheridan.
Seamen Ashore: A Study of the United Seamen's Service & of Merchant Seamen in Port. Elmo P. Hohman. (Merchant Seamen's Ser.: Vol. 2). 1952. 15.00x (ISBN 0-686-17410-0). R S Barnes.
Seamen Ashore: A Study of the United Seamen's Service & of Merchant Seamen in Port. Elmo P. Hohman. 1952. 10.00x (ISBN 0-317-27582-8). Elliots Bks.
Seamen's Articles of Agreement, Vol. 64. International Labour Office Studies & Reports. (International Labour Office Studies & Reports, P: No. 1). Repr. of 1926 ed. bds. 80.00 (ISBN 0-8115-3296-8). Kraus Repr.
Seamen's Missions: Their Origins & Early Growth. Roald Kverndal. LC 85-25508. (Illus.). 903p. 1986. text ed. 29.95x (ISBN 0-87808-440-1, WCL440-1); pap. text ed. cancelled (ISBN 0-87808-439-8, WCL439-8). William Carey Lib.
Seamless. Ralph Wright. LC 87-83500. 96p. 1988. 9.00x (ISBN 0-8233-0441-8). Golden Quill.
Seamless Robe. Lillian De Waters. 5.95 (ISBN 0-686-17826-2). L De Waters.
Seamless Web. Stanley Burnshaw. LC 71-97603. 1970. text ed. 6.50 (ISBN 0-8076-0535-2). Braziller.
Seamounts, Islands, & Atolls. Ed. by B. H. Keating et al. (Geophysical Monograph Ser.: Vol. 43). (Illus.). 400p. 1987. 31.00 (ISBN 0-87590-068-2). Am Geophysical.
Seams: Poetry. Kerry S. Keys. 1985. pap. 12.95 (ISBN 0-930502-05-1). Pine Pr.
Seams, Threads & Needles. 1976. 39.00x (ISBN 0-317-43774-7, Pub. by F I R A). State Mutual Bk.
Seamstress. Jack Rudman. (Career Examination Ser.: C-1619). (Cloth bdg. avail. on request). pap. 16.00 (ISBN 0-8373-1619-7). Natl Learning.
Seamus Heaney. Ed. & intro. by Harold Bloom. (Modern Critical Views Ser.). 199p. 1986. lib. bdg. 24.50x (ISBN 0-87754-702-5). Chelsea Hse.
Seamus Heaney. Robert Buttel. (Irish Writers Ser.). 88p. 1975. 4.50 (ISBN 0-8387-1567-2). Bucknell U Pr.
Seamus Heaney. Blake Morrison. (Contemporary Writers Ser.). 96p. 1982. pap. 5.95 (ISBN 0-416-31900-9, NO. 3670). Routledge Chapman & Hall.
Seamus Heaney: A Faber Student Guide. Neil Corcoran. 160p. (Orig.). 1986. pap. 9.95 (ISBN 0-571-13955-8). Faber & Faber.
Sean Kelley: A Biography. D. Walsh. 1986. 44.75X (ISBN 0-245-54331-7, Pub. by Harrap Ltd England). State Mutual Bk.
Sean Mooney's Practical Guide to Running a Pub. Sean Mooney & George Green. LC 78-27436. 252p. 1979. 21.95x (ISBN 0-88229-400-8). Nelson-Hall.
Sean O'Casey. Bernard Benstock. LC 72-124101. (Irish Writers Ser). 123p. 1971. 4.50 (ISBN 0-8387-7748-1); pap. 1.95 (ISBN 0-8387-7618-3). Bucknell U Pr.
Sean O'Casey. Intro. by Harold Bloom. (Modern Critical Views Ser.). 194p. 1987. 19.95 (ISBN 0-87754-647-9). Chelsea Hse.

Search for Effectiveness & Efficiency in Government: Policy Analysis, Program Evaluation, Social Indicator, & Quality of Life Research. Mitchel J. Beville & Kenneth Meyer. 1983. 5.00 (ISBN 1-55614-112-2). U of SD Gov Res Bur.

Search for Efficiency in the Adjustment Process: Spain in the 1980's. Augusto Lopez-Claros. (Occasional Papers: No. 57). 40p. 1988. pap. 7.50 (ISBN 1-55775-009-2). Intl Monetary.

Search for Emma's Story: A Model For Humanities Detective Work. Marian L. Martinello. LC 86-30005. (Illus.). 223p. (Orig.). 1987. pap. 12.95 (ISBN 0-87565-070-8). Tex Christian.

Search for Enchantment. Shirley F. Sanders. (YA) (gr. 7 up). 1978. 9.95 (ISBN 0-685-86142-2, Avalon). Bouregy.

Search for English-Canadian Literature: An Anthology of Critical Articles from the Nineteenth & Early Twentieth Centuries. Ed. by Carl Ballstadt. LC 75-15779. (Literature of Canada, Poetry & Prose in Reprint Ser.: No. 16). pap. 65.80 (ISBN 0-317-26829-5, 2023490). Bks Demand UMI.

Search for Environmental Ethics: An Initial Bibliography. Compiled By Mary Anglemyer et al. LC 80-15026. 120p. 1980. Repr. text ed. 17.50x (ISBN 0-87474-212-9, ANSE). Smithsonian.

Search for Equality: The National Urban League, 1910-1961. Jesse T. Moore, Jr. LC 80-24302. (Illus.). 264p. 1981. 24.50x (ISBN 0-271-00302-2). Pa St U Pr.

Search for Equity in School Finance. Rand Corporation Staff & S. J. Carroll. LC 82-11510. 200p. 1983. prof ref 29.95x (ISBN 0-88410-840-6). Ballinger Pub.

Search for Evidence. Art Buckwalter. LC 83-15424. (Library of Investigation). 1984. text ed. 22.95 (ISBN 0-409-95097-1). Butterworth.

Search for Excellence: The Christian College in an Age of Educational Competition. Robert T. Sandin. LC 82-12482. vi, 242p. 1982. text ed. 13.50x (ISBN 0-86554-037-3, MUP-H39). Mercer Univ Pr.

Search for Existential Identity: Patient-Therapist Dialogues in Humanistic Psychotherapy. James F. T. Bugental. LC 75-44882. (Social & Behavioral Science Ser.). 1976. 24.95x (ISBN 0-87589-273-6). Jossey-Bass.

Search for Explanation: Studies in Natural Science Vol. 3. Ed. by Walter C. Blinn. (Illus.). 409p. 1969. text ed. 5.75x (ISBN 0-87013-132-X). Mich St U Pr.

Search for Extraterrestrial Intelligence. D. Fradin. LC 87-14618. (New True Bks.). (Illus.). 48p. (gr. k-4). 1987. PLB 12.60 (ISBN 0-516-01242-8); pap. 3.95 (ISBN 0-516-41242-6). Childrens.

Search for Extraterrestrial Intelligence. National Aeronautics & Space Administration. (Illus.). 190p. 1980. pap. 3.95 (ISBN 0-486-23890-3). Dover.

Search for Extraterrestrial Intelligence: Listening for Life in the Cosmos. Thomas R. McDonough. LC 86-15905. (Science Editions Ser.). 244p. 1986. 19.95 (ISBN 0-471-84684-8). Wiley.

Search for Extraterrestrial Intelligence: Listening for Life in the Cosmos. Thomas R. McDonough. 244p. 1988. pap. 14.95 (ISBN 0-471-84683-X). Wiley.

Search for Extraterrestrial Life. Ed. by J. S. Hanrahan. (Advances in the Astronautical Sciences Ser.: Vol. 22). 1967. 30.00x (ISBN 0-87703-025-1, Pub. by Am Astronaut); microfiche suppl. 5.00x (ISBN 0-87703-132-0). Univelt Inc.

Search for Extraterrestrial Life: Recent Developments. Ed. by Michael Papagiannis. 1985. lib. bdg. 64.00 (ISBN 90-277-2113-0, Pub. by Reidel Holland). Kluwer Academic.

Search for Faith & Justice in the 20th Century. Ed. by Gene G. James. LC 86-30352. 221p. 1987. 22.95 (ISBN 0-913757-78-0); pap. 12.95 (ISBN 0-913757-80-2). Paragon Hse.

Search for Form in Art & Architecture. Eliel Saarinen. 377p. 1985. pap. 7.95 (ISBN 0-486-24907-7). Dover.

Search for Freedom: America & Its People. William J. Jacobs. 1973. 10.68 (ISBN 0-02-645180-8, 64518); tchr's annot. ed. o.p. 10.24 (ISBN 0-02-645190-5, 64519); strategies man. o.p. 3.40 (ISBN 0-02-645220-0, 64522). Glencoe.

Search for Gainsborough. Adrienne Corri. (Illus.). 286p. 1985. 17.50 (ISBN 0-8149-0906-X). Vanguard.

Search for God. David M. White. 448p. 1983. 24.95 (ISBN 0-02-627110-9). Macmillan.

Search for God in Time & Memory. John S. Dunne. LC 76-20165. 1977. pap. 10.95 (ISBN 0-268-01673-9). U of Notre Dame Pr.

Search for God: Nineteen Forty-Two to Nineteen Fifty, 2 Bks. Ed. by Association for Research & Enlightenment, Inc. Virginia Beach, Va. Study Groups et al. 1942-1950. 4.95 ea. Bk. 1 (ISBN 0-87604-000-8). Bk. 2 (ISBN 0-87604-001-6). ARE Pr.

Search for Government Efficiency: From Hubris to Helplessness. George W. Downs & Patrick D. Larkey. LC 85-20798. 288p. 1986. 27.95 (ISBN 0-87722-409-9). Temple U Pr.

Search for Gravity Waves. P. C. Davies. (Illus.). 160p. 1980. 18.95 (ISBN 0-521-23197-3). Cambridge U Pr.

Search for Grissi. Mary F. Shura. 128p. 1987. pap. 2.75 (ISBN 0-380-70305-X, Camelot). Avon.

Search for Grissi. Mary F. Shura. (Illus.). (gr. k-9). 1988. pap. 2.75. Scholastic Inc.

Search for Haigwood-Hagood-Haygood, Et Cetera, 1650-1984, Vol. 1. John E. Haigwood. LC 84-63018. (Illus.). 850p. 1985. 65.00 (ISBN 0-9614500-0-2). J E Haigwood.

Search for Help: A Study of the Retarded Child in the Community. Jerry Jacobs. LC 82-13535. 150p. 1983. pap. text ed. 10.00 (ISBN 0-8191-2680-2). U Pr of Amer.

Search for Historical Meaning: Hegel & the Postwar American Right. Paul Gottfried. LC 86-5279. 1986. 27.00 (ISBN 0-87580-114-5). N Ill U Pr.

Search for Holmes, Robson, Hind, Steele & Graham Families of Cumberland & Northumberland, England. Anne H. Christian. (Illus.). 184p. 1985. 17.95 (ISBN 0-9613723-0-3). Search CA.

Search for Home. Sashthi Brata. 152p. 1975. pap. 2.50 (ISBN 0-88253-771-7). Ind-US Inc.

Search for Human Values. Cornelius J. Van Der Poel. LC 75-161445. 192p. 1973. pap. 3.95 (ISBN 0-8091-1781-9, Deus). Paulist Pr.

Search for Identity. Robert L. Friedly & D. Duane Cummins. Ed. by Herbert H. Lambert. 192p. (Orig.). 1987. pap. 11.95 (ISBN 0-8272-3427-9). CBP.

Search for Identity. Ed. by Arnold T. Olson. LC 80-66030. (Heritage Ser.: Vol. 1). 160p. 1980. 8.95 (ISBN 0-911802-46-0). Free Church Pubns.

Search for Intimacy. Stackhouse & Saunders. 1981. pap. 3.30 (ISBN 0-8298-0438-2). Pilgrim NY.

Search for Jewish Theology. new ed. Bernard J. Bamberger. LC 77-28457. 1978. pap. 4.95x (ISBN 0-87441-300-1). Behrman.

Search for Justice. William H. Webster et al. (Andrew R. Cecil, Lectures on Moral Values in a Free Society: Vol. IV). 191p. 1983. 14.50x (ISBN 0-292-77579-2). U of Tex Pr.

Search for King Pup's Tomb. Jim Razzi & Mary Razzi. (Sherluck Bones Mystery Ser.). 64p. (gr. 3). 1985. pap. 2.25 (ISBN 0-553-15312-9). Bantam.

Search for Labour Market Flexibility: The European Economies in Transition. Ed. by Robert Boyer. (Illus.). 328p. 1988. 59.00 (ISBN 0-19-828560-4). Oxford U Pr.

Search for Leadership. Allen E. Roberts. 236p. 1987. 15.95 (ISBN 0-935633-05-7). Anchor Comm.

Search for Life. Kim Unsong. 303p. 1987. 10.00 (ISBN 0-942049-01-2). One Mind Pr.

Search for Literary Meaning. Ed. by A. P. Foulkes. 159p. 1975. pap. 22.85 (ISBN 3-261-01536-5). P Lang Pubs.

Search for Love. Matthew O. Emiohe. 224p. 1983. 11.00 (ISBN 0-682-49954-4). Exposition-Phoenix.

Search for Love & Achievement: Marriage & the Family in a Changing World. rev., 2nd ed. David S. Shapiro & Elaine S. Shapiro. 278p. 1985. pap. text ed. 16.95x (ISBN 0-88133-155-4). Sheffield Wisc.

Search for Man's Sanity. Trigant Burrow. Ed. by Gerald N. Grob. LC 78-22553. (Historical Issues in Mental Health Ser.). 1979. Repr. of 1958 ed. lib. bdg. 46.00x (ISBN 0-405-11907-0). Ayer Co Pubs.

Search for Meaning. John U. Nef. 1973. 15.00 (ISBN 0-685-57347-8). Pub Aff Pr.

Search for Meaning. John U. Nef. 1979. pap. 7.50 (ISBN 0-8183-0259-3). Pub Aff Pr.

Search for Meaning. Wendy Robinson & Christopher Bryant. 1985. 10.00x (ISBN 0-317-62147-5, Guild of Pastoral Psych). State Mutual Bk.

Search for Meaning in Love, Sex, & Marriage. rev. ed. Hugo Hurst. LC 75-9961. 232p. (gr. 11-12). 1975. pap. text ed. 6.00x (ISBN 0-88489-063-5); teaching manual 3.00x (ISBN 0-88489-119-4). St. Marys.

Search for Mind: Ch'en Pai-Sha, Philosopher-Poet. Paul Y. Jiany. 1981. 18.00x (ISBN 9971-69-006-3, Pub. by Singapore U Pr); pap. 11.00x (ISBN 9971-69-019-5, Pub. by Singapore U Pr). Ohio U Pr.

Search for More Effective State Policy Leadership in Higher Education. 31p. 1986. 2.50 (ISBN 0-318-22551-4, PS-86-1). Ed Comm States.

Search for National Integration in Africa. David R. Smock & Kwamina Bentsi-Enchill. LC 74-33090. 1976. 22.50 (ISBN 0-02-929560-2). Free Pr.

Search for New Antibiotics: Problems & Perspectives. G. F. Gause. 1960. 39.50x (ISBN 0-686-83732-0). Elliots Bks.

Search for New Arts. Charles Biederman. LC 79-90835. 1979. 20.00 (ISBN 0-9605614-0-4); pap. 15.00 (ISBN 0-9605614-1-2). Art History.

Search for New Insights in Librarianship: A Day of Comparative Studies--Proceedings. Library School Commons Conference, University of Wisconsin, Wisconsin, April 25, 1975. Ed. by William L. Williamson. 106p. 1976. pap. 4.00 (ISBN 0-936442-04-2). U Wis Sch Lib.

Search for Nirvana. Kwan-Jo Lee. (Illus.). 124p. 1984. 24.00 (ISBN 0-8048-1417-1, Pub. by Seoul Intl Publishing House). C E Tuttle.

Search for Nothing: Life of John of the Cross. Richard P. Hardy. 160p. 1987. pap. 8.95 (ISBN 0-8245-0815-7). Crossroad NY.

Search for Oil: Some Statistical Methods and Techniques. Ed. by D. B. Owen. (Statistics: Textbooks & Monographs Ser.: Vol.13). 208p. 1975. 49.75 (ISBN 0-8247-6342-4). Dekker.

Search for Omm Sety: A Story of Eternal Love. Jonathan Cott. LC 86-24095. (Illus.). 264p. 1987. 17.95 (ISBN 0-385-23746-4). Doubleday.

Search for Oneness. Lloyd H. Silverman et al. LC 82-4658. x, 306p. 1983. text ed. 35.00x (ISBN 0-8236-6013-3). Intl Univs Pr.

Search for Order: 1877-1920. Robert H. Wiebe. LC 66-27609. (Making of America Ser.). 333p. 1966. pap. 7.95 (ISBN 0-8090-0104-7). Hill & Wang.

Search for Our Beginning. Robert Hutchison. (Illus.). 1983. 24.95 (ISBN 0-19-858505-5). Oxford U Pr.

Search for Peace. F. Longford. 1986. 54.75X (ISBN 0-245-54259-0, Pub. by Harrap Ltd England). State Mutual Bk.

Search for Peace. Hassan Bin Talal. LC 84-51212. (Illus.). 196p. 1984. 16.95 (ISBN 0-312-70821-1). St Martin.

Search for Peace & Unity in the Sudan. Francis M. Deng & Prosser Gifford. LC 87-50714. (Illus.). 208p. (Orig.). 1987. PLB 24.75 (ISBN 0-943875-01-3); pap. text ed. 12.95 (ISBN 0-943875-00-5). Wilson Ctr Pr.

Search for Peace in the Middle East: The Story of President Bourguiba's Campaign for a Negotiated Peace Between Israel & the Arab States. 490p. 1968. 17.50 (ISBN 0-318-04370-X). Inst Medit Affairs.

Search for Personal Freedom. brief ed. Robert C. Lamm et al. 672p. 1985. pap. write for info. (ISBN 0-697-00499-6); write for info. (ISBN 0-697-03142-X); write for info. instr's manual; write for info. test item file (ISBN 0-697-00904-1); write for info. transparencies. Wm C Brown.

Search for Power: The "Weaker Sex" in Seventeenth Century New England. Lyle Koehler. LC 80-16666. 569p. 1980. 32.50 (ISBN 0-252-00808-1). U of Ill Pr.

Search for Principle. Robert Goff. (Maccabaean Lectures in Jurisprudence). 1985. pap. 5.50 (ISBN 0-85672-490-4, Pub. by British Acad). Longwood Pub Group.

Search for Public Administration: The Ideas & Career of Dwight Waldo. Brack Brown & Richard J. Stillman, II. LC 85-40744. 206p. 1986. 22.50x (ISBN 0-89096-252-9). Tex A&M Univ Pr.

Search for Public Policy: Regional Politics & Government Finances in Ecuador, 1830-1940. Linda Rodriguez. LC 84-2446. (Illus.). 290p. 1985. 35.00x (ISBN 0-520-05150-5). U of Cal Pr.

Search for Pure Food: A Sociology of Legislation in Britain. Ingeborg Paulus. (Law in Society Ser.). 144p. 1974. text ed. 8.50x (ISBN 0-85520-076-6). Rothman.

Search for Purpose. Arthur Morgan. LC 55-10426. 1957. 5.00 (ISBN 0-317-06070-8). Comm Serv OH.

Search for Quality Integrated Education: Policy & Research on Minority Students in School & College. Meyer Weinberg. LC 82-12016. (Contributions to the Study of Education: No. 7). (Illus.). xv, 354p. 1983. lib. bdg. 36.95 (ISBN 0-313-23714-X, WEI/). Greenwood.

Search for Relevance: The Campus in Crisis. Joseph Axelrod et al. LC 72-75941. (Jossey-Bass Higher Education Ser.). Repr. of 1969 ed. 48.70 (ISBN 0-8357-9346-X, 2013946). Bks Demand UMI.

Search for St. Truth. Mary Carruthers. 1974. 22.95x (ISBN 0-8101-0422-9). Northwestern U Pr.

Search for Sam. Neil Morris & Ting Morris. (Mystery Picture Bks.). (Illus.). 24p. (gr. k-3). 1983. PLB 6.95 (ISBN 0-316-58377-4). Little.

Search for Sam Goldwyn. Carol Easton. 1988. 10.45 (ISBN 0-688-08666-7, Quill). Morrow.

Search for Sanctuary: Brigham Young & the White Mountain Expedition. Clifford L. Stott. (American West Ser.: Vol. 19). (Illus.). 272p. 1984. 19.95 (ISBN 0-87480-237-7). U of Utah Pr.

Search for Sanity: The Politics of Nuclear Weapons & Disarmament. Ed. by Paul Joseph & Simon Rosenblum. 600p. 1984. 25.00 (ISBN 0-89608-205-9); pap. 12.50 (ISBN 0-89608-204-0). South End Pr.

Search for Sara: A Novel. Martin Russell. 184p. 1986. pap. 3.95 (ISBN 0-394-62331-2, BC). Grove.

Search for Sara Sanderson. Thomas McKean. 160p. (gr. 3-7). 1987. pap. 2.50 (ISBN 0-380-75295-6, Camelot). Avon.

Search for "Satori" & Creativity. E. Paul Torrance. LC 79-65469. 1979. pap. 9.50 (ISBN 0-930222-04-0). Creat Educ Found.

Search for Security. M. J. Field. 478p. 1962. 15.00x (ISBN 0-89771-009-6). State Mutual Bk.

Search for Security: A Study in Baltic Diplomacy, 1920-1934. Hugh I. Rodgers. LC 74-16366. xi, 181p. (Orig.). 1975. 21.50 (ISBN 0-208-01478-0, Archon). Shoe String.

Search for Security: An Ethno-Psychiatric Study of Rural Ghana. Margaret J. Field. 1970. pap. 2.95x (ISBN 0-393-00508-9, Norton Lib). Norton.

Search for Security: An Ethno-psychiatric Study of Rural Ghana. Margaret J. Field. LC 60-14408. (Northwestern University African Studies: No. 5). pap. 117.80 (ISBN 0-317-27793-6, 2015294). Bks Demand UMI.

Search for Shelter. N. Richter Greer. 1986. 15.00 (ISBN 0-913962-82-1). Am-Inst Arch.

Search for Significance. Donald Lombardi. LC 75-17676. (Illus.). 152p. 1975. 17.95x (ISBN 0-88229-109-2). Nelson-Hall.

Search for Significance. Robert S. McGee. 184p. (Orig.). 1985. pap. 6.95 (ISBN 0-318-20049-X). Morgan Pr TX.

Search for Significance. rev. ed. Robert S. McGee. (Illus.). 168p. 1988. 12.00 (ISBN 0-945276-00-1); pap. 6.00. Rapha Pub.

Search for Signs of Intelligent Life in the Universe: The Broadway Smash Starring Lily Tomlin. Jane Wagner. LC 86-45435. (Illus.). 256p. 1986. 15.95i (ISBN 0-06-015673-2, HarpT); Special boxed ed. 49.50i (ISBN 0-06-015723-2, HarpT). Har-Row.

Search for Signs of Intelligent Life in the Universe: The Broadway Smash Starring Lily Tomlin. Jane Wagner. LC 86-54435. (Illus.). 224p. 1987. pap. 7.95 (ISBN 0-06-091431-9, PL/1431, PL). Har-Row.

Search for Silence. rev. ed. Elizabeth O'Connor. Ed. by Marcia Broucek. LC 86-114. 192p. 1986. pap. 8.95 (ISBN 0-931055-07-5). LuraMedia.

Search for Social Peace: Reform Legislation in France, 1890-1914. Judith F. Stone. LC 84-20531. 260p. 1985. 59.50 (ISBN 0-88706-022-6); pap. 17.95 (ISBN 0-88706-023-4). State U NY Pr.

Search for Solutions. Horace F. Judson. LC 87-2856. 288p. 1987. pap. 9.95 (ISBN 0-8018-3526-7). Johns Hopkins.

Search for Solvency: Bretton Woods & the International Monetary System, 1941-1971. Alfred E. Eckes, Jr. LC 75-14433. 369p. 1975. 20.00x (ISBN 0-292-70712-6). U of Tex Pr.

Search for Speed under Sail, 1700-1855. Howard I. Chapelle. (Illus.). 1984. 50.00 (ISBN 0-393-03127-6). Norton.

Search for Spock. Vonda N. McIntyre. (Star Trek Ser.). 1984. lib. bdg. 12.95 (ISBN 0-8398-2839-X, Gregg). G K Hall.

Search for Spring. Moira Miller. LC 86-32898. (Illus.). 32p. (ps-3). 1988. 11.95 (ISBN 0-8037-0445-3, 01160-350). Dial Bks Young.

Search for Stability: United States Diplomacy Toward Nicaragua 1925-1933. William Kamman. (International Studies Ser). 1968. 21.95 (ISBN 0-268-00249-5). U of Notre Dame Pr.

Search for Stable Money: Essays on Monetary Reform. Ed. by James A. Dorn & Anna J. Schwartz. LC 86-25654. xviii, 410p. 1987. text ed. 35.00x (ISBN 0-226-15829-2); pap. 13.95x (ISBN 0-226-15830-6). U of Chicago Pr.

Search for Steam. Joe G. Collias. LC 72-86957. (Illus.). 1972. 29.95 (ISBN 0-8310-7092-7). Howell-North.

Search for Structure: A Report on American Youth Today. Francis A. Ianni. 352p. 1989. 22.50 (ISBN 0-02-915360-3). Free Pr.

Search for Structure: Selected Essays on Science, Art & History. Cyril Stanley Smith. (Illus.). 410p. 1981. 45.00x (ISBN 0-262-19191-1); pap. 17.59 (ISBN 0-262-69082-9). MIT Pr.

Search for Successful Secondary Schools. Bruce Wilson & Thomas Corcoran. 250p. 1987. 38.00x (ISBN 1-85000-200-2, Falmer Pr.); pap. 19.00x (ISBN 1-85000-201-0). Taylor & Francis.

Search for Successful Secondary Schools: The First Three Years of the Secondary School Recognition Program. Thomas B. Corcoran & Bruce L. Wilson. (Education Department Publication PIP Ser.: No. 86-300). (Illus.). 70p. 1986. pap. 8.50 (ISBN 0-318-21896-8, S/N 065-000-00270-1). USGPO.

Search for Sybaris, 1960-1965. Froelich G. Rainey & Carlo M. Lerici. (University Museum Monographs: No. 29). (Illus.). xix, 313p. 1967. pap. 25.00 (ISBN 0-934718-21-0). Univ Mus of U PA.

Search for Synthesis: A Contemporary Re-Interpretation of Classicism, the Neo-Classical Synthesis & Post-Keynesian Economics. Ching Yao-Hsieh & Stephen L. Mangum. LC 82-63152. 360p. 1983. 10.95 (ISBN 0-913420-16-6). Olympus Pub Co.

Search for Synthesis in Economic Theory. Ching-Yao Hsieh & Stephen L. Mangum. LC 84-29816. 320p. 1985. 35.00 (ISBN 0-87332-328-9); pap. 14.95 (ISBN 0-87332-329-7). M E Sharpe.

Search for Tax Principles in the European Economic Community. Clara K. Sullivan. LC 63-22649. (Illus.). 104p. (Orig.). 1963. pap. 4.50x (ISBN 0-915506-04-1). Harvard Law Intl Tax.

Search for the Absolute in Neo-Vedanta. K. C. Bhattacharyya. Ed. by George B. Burch. LC 75-17740. 202p. 1976. text ed. 14.00x (ISBN 0-8248-0296-9). UH Pr.

Search for the Ancient Order, Vol. 1. Earl I. West. 18.95 (ISBN 0-89225-154-9). Gospel Advocate.

Search for the Atocha. rev., 2nd ed. Eugene Lyon. LC 75-25049. (Florida Classics Ser.). (Illus.). 288p. (Orig.). 1985. pap. 9.95 (ISBN 0-912451-15-7). Florida Classics.

Search for the Atocha Treasure. Fran Pelham & Bernadette Balcer. (Illus.). 128p. (gr. 4 up). 1988. PLB 12.95 (ISBN 0-87518-399-9). Dillon.

Search for the Beloved. Jean Houston. 320p. 1987. 19.95 (ISBN 0-87477-450-0). J P Tarcher.

Search for the Beloved Community: The Thinking of Martin Luther King, Jr. Kenneth L. Smith & Ira G. Zepp, Jr. LC 86-24570. 160p. 1987. pap. text ed. 8.25 (ISBN 0-8191-5718-X). U Pr of Amer.

Search for the Cause of Multiple Sclerosis & Other Chronic Diseases of the Central Nervous System. Ed. by A. Boese. (Illus.). 502p. (Orig.). 1980. pap. 73.00 (ISBN 3-527-25875-2). VCH Pubs.

Search for the Causes of Schizopherenia. Ed. by H. Hafner et al. (Illus.). 420p. 1987. 78.00 (ISBN 0-387-17376-5). Springer-Verlag.
Search for the Doctor. David C. Martin. (Doctor Who Ser.: No. 1). pap. 2.50 (ISBN 0-345-33224-5). Ballantine.
Search for the Eighteenth Century Village at Michilimackinac: A Soil Resistivity Survey. J. Mark Williams & Gary Shapiro. LC 83-199521. (Archaeological Completion Report Ser.: No. 4). (Illus.). 79p. (Orig.). 1982. pap. 5.00 (ISBN 0-911872-43-4). Mackinac Island.
Search for the Gold of Tutankhamen. Arnold C. Brackman. 1979. pap. 2.50 (ISBN 0-671-83027-9). PB.
Search for the Great Valley. Adapted by Jim Razzi. (Illus.). 24p. (ps-3). 1988. pap. 2.25 (ISBN 0-448-09357-X, G&D); pap. 5.95 incl. audio cassette (ISBN 0-448-09353-7, G&D). Putnam Pub Group.
Search for the King. Gore Vidal. 208p. 1986. pap. 4.95 (ISBN 0-345-33272-5). Ballantine.
Search for the Liberal College: The Beginning of the St. John's Program. J. Winfree Smith. (Illus.). 136p. 1984. 11.00x (ISBN 0-9603690-0-7). SJC Annapolis.
Search for the "Manchurian Candidate" The CIA & Mind Control. John Marks. 1988. pap. 4.95 (ISBN 0-440-20137-3). Dell.
Search for the Mountain Gorillas. Jim Wallace. (Choose Your Own Adventure Ser.: No. 41). 128p. (gr. 6 up). 1985. pap. 2.25 (ISBN 0-553-26062-6). Bantam.
Search for the Nile. Robert W. Walker. (Time Machine Ser.: No. 12). 144p. 1986. pap. 2.25 (ISBN 0-553-25538-X). Bantam.
Search for the Northwest Passage. Alan E. Day. LC 83-48202. (Garland Reference Library of Social Science: Vol. 186). 600p. 1986. lib. bdg. 78.00 (ISBN 0-8240-9288-0). Garland Pub.
Search for the Northwest Passage. Lucile McDonald. LC 58-11860. (Illus.). (gr. 4-9). 1958. 7.50 (ISBN 0-8323-0029-2). Binford-Metropolitan.
Search for the Northwest Passage. Lucile McDonald. LC 58-11860. (Illus.). 142p. (gr. 4-9). 1975. pap. 5.95 (ISBN 0-8323-0253-8). Binford-Metropolitan.
Search for the Passengers of the Mary & John 1630, Vols. I to X. Burton W. Spear. (Illus.). 1440p. 1987. Set. pap. 145.50 (ISBN 0-941273-10-5). M & J Clear Hse.
Search for the Passengers of the Mary & John 1630, Vol. I: Passengers & Their Children. Burton W. Spear. (Illus.). 82p. (Orig.). 1985. pap. 12.00 (ISBN 0-941273-00-8). M & J Clear Hse.
Search for the Passengers of the Mary & John 1630, Vol. II: Return to the Ancestral Homes-1985. Burton W. Spear. (Illus.). 134p. (Orig.). 1986. pap. 12.50 (ISBN 0-941273-01-6). M & J Clear Hse.
Search for the Passengers of the Mary & John 1630, Vol. III: Updated Ancestries. Burton W. Spear. 73p. 1987. pap. 13.50 (ISBN 0-941273-02-4). M & J Clear Hse.
Search for the Passengers of the Mary & John 1630, Vol. IV: Allen Thru Fyler. Burton W. Spear. (Illus.). 156p. 1987. pap. 14.00 (ISBN 0-941273-03-2). M & J Clear Hse.
Search for the Passengers of the Mary & John 1630, Vol. V: Gallop Thru Greenway. Burton W. Spear. (Illus.). 136p. 1987. pap. 13.50 (ISBN 0-941273-04-0). M & J Clear Hse.
Search for the Passengers of the Mary & John 1630, Vol. VI: Hannum Thru Ludlow. Burton W. Spear. (Illus.). 154p. 1987. pap. 14.00 (ISBN 0-941273-05-9). M & J Clear Hse.
Search for the Passengers of the Mary & John 1630, Vol. VII: Maverick Thru Stoughton. Burton W. Spear. (Illus.). 190p. 1987. pap. 14.50 (ISBN 0-941273-06-7). M & J Clear Hse.
Search for the Passengers of the Mary & John 1630, Vol. VIII: Strong & Fyler. Burton W. Spear. (Illus.). 144p. 1987. pap. 13.50 (ISBN 0-941273-07-5). M & J Clear Hse.
Search for the Passengers of the Mary & John 1630, Vol. VIIII: Terry Thru Wolcott. Burton W. Spear. (Illus.). 114p. 1987. pap. 13.00 (ISBN 0-941273-08-3). M & J Clear Hse.
Search for the Passengers of the Mary & John 1630, Vol. X: Master Index Vol's. IV-VIII. Burton W. Spear. 257p. 1987. pap. 25.00 (ISBN 0-941273-09-1). M & J Clear Hse.
Search for the Past, 6 bks. Robin Place. (Illus., Orig.). (gr. 2-4). 1986. Set. pap. text ed. 16.80 incl. teacher's notes (ISBN 1-55624-010-4). Wright Group.
Search for the Past: An Introduction to Archaeology. Michael Avi-Yonah. LC 72-10791. (Lerner Archaeology Ser.). (Illus.). 96p. (gr. 5 up). 1974. PLB 8.95 (ISBN 0-8225-0826-5). Lerner Pubns.
Search for the Past: An Introduction to Paleontology. 2nd ed. James R. Beerbower. LC 68-18060. (Illus.). 1968. write for info. ref. ed. (ISBN 0-13-797316-0). P-H.
Search for the Pegasus. Roger E. Moore. LC 84-91362. (Crimson Crystal Adventures Ser.). (Illus.). 160p. (gr. 4-6). 1985. pap. 2.95 (ISBN 0-394-73981-7). Random.
Search for the Perfect Chocolate Chip Cookie. Gwen W. Steege. LC 87-46082. (Illus.). 144p. 1988. pap. 7.95 (ISBN 0-88266-478-6); 15.95 (ISBN 0-88266-520-0). Storey Comm Inc.
Search for the Picturesque Landscape: Aesthetics & Tourism in Britain, 1760-1800. Malcolm Andrews. LC 68-63668. (Illus.). 287p. 1988. text ed. 49.50x (ISBN 0-8047-1402-9). Stanford U Pr.
Search for the Rabbit. P. Luc Valloglise. 138p. (YA) (gr. 7 up). 1988. pap. 8.00 (ISBN 0-934852-55-3). Lorien Hse.
Search for the Rainbow. Sharon Brondos. (Superromance Ser.: No. 266). 308p. Date not set. pap. 2.75 (ISBN 0-317-63884-X). Harlequin Bks.
Search for the Rare Plumidor. Ken Kirkwood & Ray Marshall. (Illus.). (gr. 1-7). 1983. 9.95 (ISBN 0-399-20967-0, Philomel). Putnam Pub Group.
Search for the Real & Other Essays. rev. ed. Ed. by Hans Hofmann & Sara T. Weeks. (Illus.). 1967. pap. 5.95 (ISBN 0-262-58008-X). MIT Pr.
Search for the Real Jesus. David Winter. 160p. (Orig.). 1982. pap. 6.95 (ISBN 0-8192-1318-7). Morehouse.
Search for the Real Nancy Reagan. Frances Leighton. 1987. 19.95 (ISBN 0-02-570210-6). Macmillan.
Search for the Real Self: Unmasking the Personality Disorders of Our Age. James F. Masterson. 288p. 1988. 21.63 (ISBN 0-02-920291-4). Free Pr.
Search for the Self: Selected Writings of Heinz Kohut, Vols. 3 & 4. Ed. by Paul H. Ornstein. 1988. Vol. 3. text ed. 35.00x; Vol. 4. text ed. 40.00x. Intl Univs Pr.
Search for the Self: Selected Writings of Heinz Kohut 1950-1978, 2 vols. Ed. by Paul H. Ornstein. LC 77-90229. 1978. text ed. 47.50x ea. (ISBN 0-8236-6015-X). Vol. 1. Vol. 2 (ISBN 0-8236-6016-8). Intl Univs Pr.
Search for the Solar System: The Role of Unmanned Interplanetary Probes. James Strong. (Illus.). 1973. 15.95 (ISBN 0-8464-0827-9). Beekman Pubs.
Search for the Tall Ships. Frank Braynard. (Illus.). 144p. 1986. 20.00 (ISBN 0-317-39399-5). F O Braynard.
Search for the True Meaning of Christmas: Christmas Program. Joyce Reynolds. (Illus.). 32p. 1977. pap. text ed. 2.25 (ISBN 0-88243-100-5, 30-0100). Gospel Pub.
Search for the Truth. Ruth Montgomery. 256p. (Orig.). 1985. pap. 3.50 (ISBN 0-449-21085-5, Crest). Fawcett.
Search for the Twelve Apostles. William S. McBirnie. 1979. pap. 4.50 (ISBN 0-8423-5839-0). Tyndale.
Search for the Universal Ancestors: The Origins of Life. Ed. by H. Hartman et al. LC 86-31685. (Illus.). 127p. 1987. pap. text ed. 17.95 (ISBN 0-86542-328-8). Blackwell Pubns.
Search For the Word of God: A Defense of King James Version. Daniel Segraves. Ed. by Mary Wallace. 328p. (Orig.). 1984. pap. 7.95 (ISBN 0-912315-70-9). Word Aflame.
Search for the Word of God: A Defense of the King James Versions. Daniel L. Segraves. 1982. pap. 10.00x. Freedom Univ-FSP.
Search for Treasure, 5 vols. Thomas P. Terry. (Illus.). 625p. (Orig.). 1980. pap. 24.75 (ISBN 0-939850-15-X). Spec Pub.
Search for Treasure, Vol. 1. Thomas P. Terry. (Illus.). 125p. (Orig.). 1975. pap. 4.95 (ISBN 0-939850-10-9). Spec Pub.
Search for Treasure, Vol. 2. Thomas P. Terry. (Illus.). 125p. (Orig.). 1977. pap. 4.95 (ISBN 0-939850-11-7). Spec Pub.
Search for Treasure, Vol. 3. Thomas P. Terry. (Illus.). 125p. (Orig.). 1977. pap. 4.95 (ISBN 0-939850-12-5). Spec Pub.
Search for Treasure, Vol. 4. Thomas P. Terry. (Illus.). 125p. (Orig.). 1980. pap. 4.95 (ISBN 0-939850-13-3). Spec Pub.
Search for Treasure, Vol. 5. Thomas P. Terry. (Illus.). 125p. (Orig.). 1980. pap. 4.95 (ISBN 0-939850-14-1). Spec Pub.
Search for Truth. Anas Khalid. Ed. by Aliyah F. Abdal-aziz. LC 86-51061. 56p. 1986. pap. 5.00 (ISBN 0-9617422-0-8). A Khalid.
Search for Truth. Natasha Rawson. LC 80-85047. 150p. 1981. 14.95 (ISBN 0-89896-149-1, Pub. by the Linolean Press). Larksdale.
Search for Truth. A. T. Ronk. LC 73-82191. 1973. pap. 1.00x (ISBN 0-934970-04-1). Brethren Ohio.
Search for Truth. John Shirn. 1988. 10.95 (ISBN 0-533-07410-X). Vantage.
Search for Two Bad Mice. Eleanor Clymer. LC 80-12789. (Illus.). 80p. (gr. 2-5). 1980. 9.95 (ISBN 0-689-30771-3, Atheneum Childrens Bks). Macmillan.
Search for Understanding: Selected Writings of Scientists of the Carnegie Institution. Ed. by Caryl P. Haskins. (Illus.). 330p. 1967. 5.00 (ISBN 0-87279-954-9). Carnegie Inst.
Search for Wisdom & Spirit: Thomas Merton's Theology of the Self. Anne E. Carr. LC 87-40352. 176p. 1988. text ed. 17.95x (ISBN 0-268-01727-1). U of Notre Dame Pr.
Search for World Order. Cornelius F. Murphy, Jr. 1986. lib. bdg. 43.00 (ISBN 90-247-3188-7, Pub. by Martinus Nijhoff Netherlands). Kluwer-Academic.
Search for Yesterday: A Critical Examination of the Evidence for Reincarnation. D. Scott Rogo. 288p. 1985. 22.95 (ISBN 0-13-797036-6); pap. 10.95 (ISBN 0-13-797028-5). P H.
Search Government Efficiency. George Downs & Patrick Larkey. 275p. 1986. pap. text ed. write for info (ISBN 0-394-35213-0, RanC). Random.
Search Heaven & Hell. Mark Donnelly & Nina Fenton. Ed. by Jon Rappaport. LC 86-81968. 500p. 1986. pap. 10.95 (ISBN 1-55666-001-4). Authors Unltd.
Search in Secret Egypt. rev. ed. Paul Brunton. LC 83-50399. 288p. (Orig.). 1984. pap. 9.95 (ISBN 0-87728-603-5). Weiser.
Search in Secret India. Paul Brunton. LC 83-160558. (Illus.). 314p. (Orig.). 1985. pap. 9.95 (ISBN 0-87728-602-7). Weiser.
Search INFORM. 3rd ed. Dennis Auld. 1986. 65.00 (ISBN 0-914604-28-7). UMI Data Courier.
Search Is an Emergency: Field Coordinator's Handbook. Patrick Lavalla et al. (Illus.). 136p. pap. 6.00 (ISBN 0-913724-30-0). Emerg Response Inst.
Search Is an Emergency: Text for Emergency Response by Agencies to Persons in Distress, Lost or Injured. Patrick Lavalla & Wade. (Illus.). 480p. 25.00x (ISBN 0-913724-28-9); instr's. manual 25.00 (ISBN 0-913724-29-7); Pocket Field Guide 8.00 (ISBN 0-686-79844-9). Emerg Response Inst.
Search Is Within. Subramuniya. (On the Path Ser.). (Illus.). 1973. pap. 2.00 (ISBN 0-87516-349-1). DeVorss.
Search Manual. Archie A. Silver & Rosa A. Hagin. LC 81-70482. 112p. 1981. pap. text ed. 14.80 (ISBN 0-8027-9035-6). Walker & Co.
Search Mechanisms for Large Files. Marie-Anne K. Neimat. LC 81-13036. (Computer Science: Distributed Database Systems Ser.: No. 11). pap. 33.80 (2070064). Bks Demand UMI.
Search N Shade. Pat Cornell. Ed. by Alan Jacobs. (Illus.). (gr. 4-9). 1979. pap. 7.50 (ISBN 0-918272-07-6). Jacobs.
Search of Gravitational Waves: Proceedings of the Workshop Held in Bogota, Columbia, March 30-April 7, 1982. Ed. by E. Posada & G. Violini. (ACIF Ser.: Vol. 2). vi, 238p. 1983. 32.00 (ISBN 9971-950-78-2). World Scientific Pub.
Search of Mavin Manyshaped. Sheri S. Tepper. 176p. 1985. pap. 2.95 (ISBN 0-441-75712-X). Ace Bks.
Search of the Past: An Introduction to Archaelogy. John Bower. 1986. 33.00x (ISBN 0-256-02215-1). Dorsey.
Search Problems. Rudolf Ahlswede & Ingo Wegener. LC 87-8240. (Discrete Mathematics Ser.). 284p. 1987. 61.95 (ISBN 0-471-90825-8). Wiley.
Search Strategies in Mass Communication. Jean Ward & Kathleen A. Hansen. (Illus.). 274p. 1986. text ed. 35.95 (ISBN 0-582-99851-4); pap. text ed. 15.95 (ISBN 0-582-28596-8). Longman.
Search Sweet Country. B. Kojo Laing. LC 86-32030. 288p. 1987. 18.95 (ISBN 0-688-06905-3, Pub. by Beech Tree Bks). Morrow.
Search Sweet Country. B. Kojo Laing. 308p. 1988. pap. 9.95 (ISBN 0-571-12996-X). Faber & Faber.
Search the Scriptures. Clarence Hyde. (Illus.). 112p. (Orig.). 1986. pap. 9.95 (ISBN 1-55630-014-X). Brentwood Comm.
Search the Scriptures. rev. ed. Ed. by Alan M. Stibbs. 11.95 (ISBN 0-87784-856-4). Inter-Varsity.
Search the Scriptures Illustrated: Modern Medicine & Biblical Personages. Robert B. Greenblatt. (Illus.). 238p. 1985. special illus. ed. 16.00x (ISBN 0-389-20545-1, BNB-08106). B&N Imports.
Search the Seven Hills. Barbara Hambly. 320p. 1987. pap. 3.95 (ISBN 0-345-34438-3). Ballantine.
Search the Shadows. Barbara Michaels. LC 87-11565. 384p. 1987. 17.95 (ISBN 0-689-11906-2). Atheneum.
Search the Shadows. Barbara Michaels. 438p. 1988. lib. bdg. 19.95x (ISBN 0-8161-4429-X, Large Print Bks). G K Hall.
Search the Shadows. Barbara Michaels. Date not set. price not set. Berkley Pub.
Search the Sky. Frederick Pohl & C. M. Kornbluth. 2.95 (ISBN 0-317-38027-3, Pub. by Bean Books). PB.
Search the Word Bible Puzzles. Alice Bostrom. (Illus.). 48p. (gr. 7 up). 1983. pap. 2.50 (ISBN 0-87239-589-8, 2787). Standard Pub.
Search Theory. Chudnovsky & Chudnovsky. (Lecture Notes in Pure & Applied Mathematics). 312p. 1988. 89.75 (ISBN 0-8247-8000-0). Dekker.
Search Warrant Law Deskbook. John M. Burkoff. LC 86-26336. 1987. ring binder 55.00 (ISBN 0-87632-530-4). Clark Boardman.
Search Warrant Process: Preconceptions, Perceptions, & Practices. Richard Van Duizend & L. Paul Sutton. LC 85-21482. xvi, 205p. pap. 15.75 (ISBN 0-89656-080-5, R-094). Natl Ctr St Courts.
Search Within. Humphreys. pap. 10.50 (ISBN 0-8356-5143-6). Theos Pub Hse.
Search Within. D. Gaynell Lawson. 1979. 7.00 (ISBN 0-682-49350-3). Exposition-Phoenix.
Search Within. Theodor Reik. LC 74-997. 657p. 1974. Repr. 30.00x (ISBN 0-87668-138-0). Aronson.
Searcher. F. M. Parker. 1986. pap. 2.75 (ISBN 0-451-14126-1, Pub. by Sig). NAL.
Searcher for God (Isabel Kuhn) Joyce Reason. 1963. pap. 3.50 (ISBN 0-87508-621-7). Chr Lit.
Searchers. Will C. Knott. (Golden Hawk Ser.: No. 9). 176p. 1988. pap. 2.95 (ISBN 0-451-15556-4, Sig). NAL.
Searchers. Alan LeMay. 352p. 1987. pap. 3.50 (ISBN 0-515-09229-0). Jove Pubns.
Searchers. Allan Lemay. Repr. lib. bdg. 15.95x (ISBN 0-88411-179-2, Pub. by Aeonian Pr). Amereon Ltd.
Searchers. Gustaf Stromberg. 256p. 1967. pap. 7.50 (ISBN 0-911336-16-8). Sci of Mind.
Searcher's Path: A Composer's Ways. Roger Reynolds. LC 87-82698. (Monographs: No. 25). 74p. (Orig.). 1988. pap. 12.00 with tape cassette (ISBN 0-914678-28-0). Inst Am Music.
Searches & Seizures, Arrests & Confessions, 2 looseleaf vols. 2nd ed. William E. Ringel. LC 79-22482. 1980. 165.00 (ISBN 0-87632-079-5). Clark Boardman.
Searches for an Imaginary Kingdom: The Legend of the Kingdom of Prester John. L. N. Gumilev. Tr. by R. E. Smith. (Past & Present Publications). (Illus.). 420p. 1988. 54.50 (ISBN 0-521-32214-6). Cambridge U Pr.
Searching America: History & Life (AHL) & Historical Abstracts (HA) on Dialog. Joyce D. Falk & Susan K. Kinnell. (ABC-CLIO Guides to Online Searching Ser.). 103p. 1987. pap. 35.00 (ISBN 0-87436-091-9). ABC-Clio.
Searching Analysis of the Action of Paper Money Upon the Trade & Prosperity of the United States see Financial Economy of the United States Illustrated & Some of the Causes Which Retard the Progress of California Demonstrated.
Searching Between the Stars. Lyman Spitzer, Jr. LC 81-13138. (Stilliman Lectures Ser.). (Illus.). 232p. 1982. 33.00x (ISBN 0-300-02709-5). Yale U Pr.
Searching Between the Stars. Lyman Spitzer, Jr. LC 81-13138. (Silliman Memorial Lectures Ser.). (Illus.). 232p. 1984. pap. 10.95x (ISBN 0-300-03247-1, Y-506). Yale U Pr.
Searching, Exploring, Pondering. Kenneth E. Sibley. (Illus.). 41p. (Orig.). 1988. pap. 5.95 (ISBN 0-9619934-0-5). K E Sibley.
Searching for a Better Way. Monroe E. Hawley. 1980. pap. 5.50 (ISBN 0-89137-525-2). Quality Pubns.
Searching for a Cure. Jonas Morris. LC 83-40568. 236p. 1984. 27.50x (ISBN 0-87663-741-1, Pica Spec Stud). Universe.
Searching for a New You. Denise Richards. Tr. by Media-Siegel Graphics. LC 85-61014. (Illus.). 109p. 1985. pap. 7.95 (ISBN 0-9614714-0-9). Pavillion Fashion.
Searching for a Viable Alternative: The Macedonia Cooperative Community, 1937 to 1958. W. Edward Orser. (American Cultural Heritage Ser.). 1979. 18.95 (ISBN 0-89102-197-3). B Franklin.
Searching for Aboriginal Languages: Memoirs of a Field Worker. Bob Dixon. LC 83-5919. (Illus.). 330p. 1984. text ed. 32.50 (ISBN 0-7022-1713-1); pap. 14.95 (ISBN 0-7022-1933-9). U of Queensland Pr.
Searching for Academic Excellence. J. Wade Gilley. 192p. 1986. 24.95 (ISBN 0-317-59338-2). ACE.
Searching for Academic Excellence: Twenty Outstanding Colleges & Their Leaders. Wade J. Gilley et al. 192p. 1986. 24.95x (ISBN 0-02-911830-1). Macmillan.
Searching for Answers. Wayne T. Gise. LC 85-14993. (Orig.). 1985. pap. 2.95 (ISBN 0-8054-9111-2). Broadman.
Searching for Bobby Fischer: The World of Chess Observed by the Father of a Child Prodigy. Fred Waitzkin. 1988. 17.95 (ISBN 0-394-54455-2). Random.
Searching for Caleb. Anne Tyler. 320p. 1987. pap. 3.95 (ISBN 0-425-09876-1). Berkley Pub.
Searching for Cultural Foundations. Philip McShane. LC 83-23594. 224p. (Orig.). 1984. lib. bdg. 26.75 (ISBN 0-8191-3727-8); pap. text ed. 13.00 (ISBN 0-8191-3728-6). U Pr of Amer.
Searching for Fifth Mesa. Juana Foust. LC 78-31284. (Orig.). 1979. pap. 4.95 (ISBN 0-913270-81-4). Sunstone Pr.
Searching for Healing Through Reincarnation. Robert P. Smith. LC 84-62946. 100p. (Orig.). 1985. pap. 4.50 (ISBN 0-9614477-0-2). Hi Barbaree Pr.
Searching for Health. Robert J. Peshek. 1982. 15.95 (ISBN 0-9605902-4-2). Color Coded Charting.
Searching for Home: Three Families from the Orphan Trains, a True Story. Martha N. Vogt & Christina Vogt. (Illus.). 240p. (Orig.). 1979. pap. 6.95 (ISBN 0-931515-00-9). Triumph Pr.
Searching for Lost Coins: Explorations in Christianity & Feminism. Ann Loades. LC 88-1056. (Princeton Theological Monograph Ser.: Vol. 14). 128p. (Orig.). 1988. pap. 12.00 (ISBN 0-317-66740-8). Pickwick.
Searching for Love. Andrea Warren. (Sweet Dreams Special Ser.: No. 3). 240p. (Orig.). (YA) (gr. 7-12). 1987. pap. 2.95 (ISBN 0-553-26292-0). Bantam.
Searching for My Brother. Tr. by Jan Feidel. (Illus.). 1973. pap. 5.95 (ISBN 0-685-78994-2, Pub. by Mushinsha Bks). Small Pr Dist.
Searching for My Way Home: Poems of a Filipina in the United States. Date not set. price not set. Trudco Pub.
Searching for Perfection. Aaron H. Shovers. (Illus.). 161p. (Orig.). 1985. pap. 6.75 (ISBN 0-9613613-3-6). Three Dimensional.
Searching for Rural Development: Labor Migration & Employment in Mexico. Merilee S. Grindle. LC 87-47970. (Illus.). 216p. 1988. 24.95x (ISBN 0-8014-2109-8). Cornell U Pr.
Searching for Safety. Aaron Wildavsky. 356p. 1988. 32.95 (ISBN 0-88738-192-8); pap. 16.95 (ISBN 0-88738-714-4). Transaction Bks.

Searching for Scottish Ancestors. A. Maxim Coppage. 28.35 (ISBN 0-318-03039-X); pap. 28.25 (ISBN 0-318-03040-3). A M Coppage.

Searching for Shona. Margaret J. Anderson. LC 77-17056. (gr. 5-8). 1978. Knopf.

Searching for Someone. Jim Wortham. LC 76-47781. 1976. pap. 2.95 (ISBN 0-915216-11-6). Marathon Intl Pub Co.

Searching for Spring. Patricia A. Murphy. 256p. 1987. pap. 8.95 (ISBN 0-941483-00-2). Naiad Pr.

Searching for Structure. rev. ed. John A. Sonquist et al. LC 73-620236. 236p. 1974. 15.00x (ISBN 0-87944-110-0); pap. 10.00x (ISBN 0-87944-109-7). Inst Soc Res.

Searching for Survivors. Russell Banks. LC 74-24911. 153p. 1975. pap. 5.95 (ISBN 0-914590-06-5). Fiction Coll.

Searching for the Emperor: A Novel. Roberto Pazzi. Tr. by M. J. Fitzgerald from Ital. LC 88-45220. 160p. 1988. 17.95 (ISBN 0-394-55998-3). Knopf.

Searching for the Figure in the Carpet in the Tales of Henry James: Reflections of an Ordinary Reader. Benjamin Newman. (American University Studies IV: English Language & Literature: Vol. 49). 194p. 1987. text ed. 39.00 (ISBN 0-8204-0442-X). P Lang Pubs.

Searching for the Invisible Man: Slaves & Plantation Life in Jamaica. Michael M. Craton. LC 76-48281. 1978. 37.00x (ISBN 0-674-79629-2). Harvard U Pr.

Searching for the Real China. David Ng. (Orig.). 1978. pap. 2.25 (ISBN 0-377-00073-6). Friendship Pr.

Searching for the Stork. Marion L. Wasserman. LC 87-28221. 208p. 1988. 17.95 (ISBN 0-453-00594-2). NAL.

Searching for Watt. Jessie R. Prosco. 32p. 1988. 6.95 (ISBN 0-8062-3324-9). Carlton.

Searching for World Security. Curt Gasteyger. LC 85-14375. 260p. 1985. 29.95 (ISBN 0-312-70823-8). St Martin.

Searching for Your Ancestors: The How & Why of Geneaology. 5th ed. Gilbert H. Doane & James B. Bell. 1980. 14.95 (ISBN 0-8166-0934-9). U of Minn Pr.

Searching Heart. Ralph W. Neighbour, Sr. 1986. pap. 5.95 (ISBN 0-937931-05-5). Global TN.

Searching in Florida: A Reference Guide to Public & Private Records. Diane C. Robie. (ISC State Search Bks.: No. 2). (Orig.). 1982. 10.95 (ISBN 0-942916-01-8). ISC Pubns.

Searching in God's Word-New Testament. Richard Grunze. (Lutheran Elementary Schools' Religion Curriculum Ser.). 142p. (gr. 5-6). 1986. 4.95 (ISBN 0-938272-41-1). WELS Board.

Searching in God's Word-Old Testament. Richard Grunze. (Lutheran Elementary Schools' Religion Curriculum Ser.). 140p. (gr. 5-6). 1986. 4.95 (ISBN 0-938272-40-3). WELS Board.

Searching in Illinois: A Reference Guide to Public & Private Records. Gayle Beckstead & Mary L. Kozub. LC 84-80217. (ISC State Search Bks.: No. 3). 210p. (Orig.). 1984. pap. text ed. 12.95 (ISBN 0-942916-05-0). ISC Pubns.

Searching in Indiana: A Reference Guide to Public & Private Records. Mickey D. Carty. LC 85-60284. (ISC State Search Bks.: No. 4). 278p. (Orig.). 1985. pap. text ed. 14.95 (ISBN 0-942916-06-9). ISC Pubns.

Searching in New York: A Reference Guide to Public & Private Records. Kate Burke. (ISC State Search Bks.: No. 5). 270p. (Orig.). 1987. pap. text ed. 15.95 (ISBN 0-942916-10-7). ISC Pubns.

Searching in the Syntax of Things: Experiments in the Study of Religion. Maurice S. Friedman & T. Patrick Burke. LC 70-171494. pap. 40.00 (2026864). Bks Demand UMI.

Searching Mind: An Introduction to a Philosophy of God. Joseph F. Donceel. LC 79-18166. 1979. text ed. 6.95 (ISBN 0-268-01700-X). U of Notre Dame Pr.

Searching: Practices & Beliefs of the Religious Cults & Human Potential Movements. Harriet S. Mosatche. LC 83-4829. (Illus.). 437p. 1984. 14.95 (ISBN 0-87396-092-0). Stravon.

Searching, Teaching, Healing: American Indians & Alaskan Natives In Biomedical Research Careers. Ed. by Edwin W. Haller & Ruth A. Myers. (Illus.). 176p. 1986. pap. 9.95 (ISBN 0-87993-292-9). Futura Pub.

Searching the Drowned Man: Poems. Sydney Lea. LC 79-26565. 86p. 1980. 11.95 (ISBN 0-252-00796-4); pap. 8.95 (ISBN 0-252-00798-0). U of Ill Pr.

Searching the Eighteenth Century: Papers Presented at a Colloquium. Ed. by M. Crump & M. Harris. (Illus.). 104p. (Orig.). 1983. pap. 11.95 (ISBN 0-7123-0020-1, Pub. by British Lib). Longwood Pub Group.

Searching the Law. Edward J. Bander et al. 260p. 1987. lib. bdg. 45.50 (ISBN 0-941320-27-8). Transnatl Pubs.

Searching the Law - The States. Francis R. Doyle. 600p. Date not set. lib. bdg. 65.00 (ISBN 0-941320-47-2). Transnatl Pubs.

Searching the Limits of Love. David H. Hassel. 1985. 15.95 (ISBN 0-8294-0461-9). Loyola.

Searching the Medical Literature: A Guide to Printed & Online Sources. J. Welch & T. A. King. 154p. 1985. text ed. 34.50x (ISBN 0-412-25610-X, Pub. by Chapman & Hall UK). Sheridan Med Bks.

Searching the Prophets for Values. Balfour Brickner & Albert Vorspan. 1981. 6.95 (ISBN 0-8074-0047-5). UAHC.

Searching the Scriptures: A History of the Society of Biblical Literature 1880-1980. Ernest W. Saunders. LC 82-10818. (Society of Biblical Literature - Biblical Scholarship in North America Ser.). 1982. 15.00 (ISBN 0-89130-591-2, 06-11-08). Scholars Pr GA.

Searching the Shadows. Ella Blanche. (Contemporary Poets Ser.: No. 1). 48p. (Orig.). 1983. pap. 2.95 (ISBN 0-916982-26-2, RL226). CCR Pubns.

Searching with 1 & 2 Sensor-Location Magnetometers. rev. ed. Murphy L. Dalton, Jr. (One Hundred Forty-Eight Ser.). (Illus.). 144p. pap. text ed. 19.00 (ISBN 0-317-19114-4). M L Dalton Res.

Searching Writing. Ken Macrorie. LC 86-16064. 352p. 1980. pap. 14.00x (ISBN 0-86709-141-X). Boynton Cook Pubs.

Searching Years. Lee Bryan. 1981. pap. 2.25 (ISBN 0-8439-0871-8, Leisure Bks). Leisure NY.

Searchlight. rev. ed. Roger E. Van Harn. 84p. 1980. pap. 3.65 (ISBN 0-933140-16-9). CRC Pubns.

Searchlight on Peace Plans: Choose Your Road to World Government. Edith Wynner & Georgia Lloyd. 532p. 1944. 15.00 (ISBN 0-318-13669-4). Campaign World Gvt.

Searchlight on Spurgeon: Spurgeon Speaks for Himself. Eric W. Hayden. 1973. pap. 4.25 (ISBN 0-686-09108-6). Pilgrim Pubns.

Searchlights on Delinquency. Ed. by Kurt R. Eissler. 1967. text ed. 47.50x (ISBN 0-8236-6020-6). Intl Univs Pr.

Searcy County Arkansas Marriages, Vol. III. Ruby Lacy. 53p. (Orig.). 1987. pap. write for info. (ISBN 0-942977-25-4). Lacy Pubs.

Seargent S. Prentiss: Whig Orator of the Old South. D. C. Dickey. 1988. 11.25 (ISBN 0-8446-0583-2). Peter Smith.

Searing. John Coyne. 272p. 1987. pap. 3.50 (ISBN 0-441-75694-8, Pub. by Charter Bks). Ace Bks.

Searle's Cats. Ronald Searle. (Illus.). 48p. (Orig.). 1988. pap. 9.95 (ISBN 0-89815-263-1). Ten Speed Pr.

Searoom Handbook with Radar Anti-Collision Tables. E. S. Quilter. LC 76-240. 177p. 1976. spiral 15.00x (ISBN 0-87033-221-X). Cornell Maritime.

Sears & Roebuck C1910 Ammunition Catalog: Chicago, Ill. (Illus.). soft bdg 2.00 (ISBN 0-686-20760-2). Sand Pond.

Sears Financial Network Guide to Personal Financial Planning. Bob Storall. (Orig.). 1986. pap. write for info. (ISBN 0-671-60095-8). PB.

Sears List of Subject Headings. 13th ed. LC 86-7734. 681p. 1986. 30.00 (ISBN 0-8242-0730-0). Wilson.

Sears List of Subject Headings: Canadian Companion. Compiled by Ken Haycock & Lynne Lighthall. 72p. 1987. 15.00 (ISBN 0-8242-0754-8). Wilson.

Sears: Lista de Encabezamientos de Materia. Ed. & tr. by Carmen Rovira. LC 84-19619. 798p. (Span.). 1984. 45.00x (ISBN 0-8242-0704-1). Wilson.

Seas. Tyler. (Children's Guides Ser.). (gr. 3-6). 1976. pap. 4.95 (ISBN 0-86020-064-7, Usborne-Hayes). EDC.

Seas & Inland Journeys: Landscape & Consciousness from Wordsworth to Roethke. James Applewhite. LC 85-1165. 328p. 1985. 25.00x (ISBN 0-8203-0795-5). U of Ga Pr.

Seas & Oceans. David Lambert. (Our World Ser.). (Illus.). 48p. (gr. 5-8). 1987. PLB 12.96 (ISBN 0-382-09503-0). Silver.

Seas & Oceans. David Lambert & Anita McConnell. LC 84-1654. (World of Science Ser.). (Illus.). 64p. (YA) (gr. 7 up). 1985. 12.95 (ISBN 0-8160-1064-1). Facts on File.

Seas & Oceans. Imelda Updegraff & Robert Updegraff. (Turning Points Ser.). (Illus.). (gr. 4 up). PLB 9.95. Creative Ed.

Seas & Oceans. Imelda Updegraffe & Robert Updegraffe. (Turning Points Ser.). (Illus.). 24p. (gr. 4-6). 1983. pap. 3.50 (ISBN 0-14-049193-7, Puffin). Penguin.

Seas of Blood. Steve Jackson & Ian Livingstone. (Fighting Fantasy Gamebooks: No. 16). (Orig.). (gr. 5 up). 1986. pap. 2.50 (ISBN 0-440-97708-8, LFL). Dell.

Seas of Fortune. Simon McKay. 368p. 1983. pap. 3.50 (ISBN 0-441-75699-9). Ace Bks.

SEASA Seventy-Nine Proceedings. Ed. by Don Harkness. 111p. 1979. pap. 3.50 (ISBN 0-934996-05-9). American Studies Pr.

Seasa Story: A History of the Southeastern American Studies Association. Gerald E. Critoph. LC 85-72894. 65p. (Orig.). 1986. pap. 5.00 (ISBN 0-934996-35-0). American Studies Pr.

Seasalt's Hidden Power: The Scientific Proof Finding & Identifying & Usage Manual. Jacques De Langre. 1984. pap. 6.00 (ISBN 0-916508-35-8). Happiness Pr.

Seascape see Plays.

Seascape with Dead Figures. Roy Hart. 192p. 1987. 13.95 (ISBN 0-312-01088-5). St Martin.

Seascape with Snow. E. Harrod. LC 75-179823. (New Poetry Ser.). Repr. of 1960 ed. 16.00 (ISBN 0-404-56023-7). AMS Pr.

Seascapes. Jerry Hutchins. Ed. by Anne Hutchins. LC 85-82006. (Illus.). 56p. 1985. pap. 7.50 (ISBN 0-9615989-0-5). J Hutchins.

Seascapes. Judith Shepard. LC 78-58642. (Illus.). 68p. 1978. 14.95 (ISBN 0-932966-01-2). Permanent Pr.

Seascapes. Judith Shepard. LC 78-58642. (Illus.). 68p. 1984. pap. 6.95 (ISBN 0-932966-56-X). Permanent Pr.

Seascapes: A Collection of Photographs of the Jersey Shore. Joseph Paduano. LC 83-91284. (Illus.). 48p. (Orig.). 1983. pap. 9.95x (ISBN 0-9612590-0-0, TR 24.N5). J Paduano.

Seashell Magic. (Beginning to Read Ser.). (gr. 2 up). 1988. PLB 5.95 (ISBN 0-8136-5191-3); pap. 2.95 (ISBN 0-317-66765-3). Modern Curr.

Seashell Parade: Fascinating Facts, Pictures, & Stories. A. Gordon Melvin. LC 72-96776. (Illus.). 1973. 11.50 (ISBN 0-8048-0971-2). C E Tuttle.

Seashells & Laughing Gulls. Patricia Leonard. LC 84-60342. (Illus.). 74p. 1984. 5.95 (ISBN 0-938232-38-X). Winston-Derek.

Seashells & Sunsets. Nan Chalat. Ed. by Don Weller & David Hampshire. LC 86-50559. (Illus.). 72p. 1986. write for info. (ISBN 0-916873-51-X); pap. write for info. (ISBN 0-916873-52-8). Weller Inst.

Seashells in My Pocket: A Child's Guide to Exploring the Atlantic Coast from Maine to North Carolina. Judith Hansen. (Illus.). 128p. (Orig.). (gr. 1 up). 1988. pap. 8.95 (ISBN 0-910146-72-1). Appalach Mtn.

Seashells of Brazil. Eliezer Rios. 328p. 1986. pap. 30.50 (ISBN 0-915826-19-4). Am Malacologists.

Seashells of North America. R. Tucker Abbott. Ed. by Herbert S. Zim. (Golden Field Guide Ser.). (Illus.). (gr. 9 up). 1969. (Golden Pr); pap. 9.95 (ISBN 0-307-13657-4). Western Pub.

Seashells of Oman. Donald Bosch & Eloise Bosch. LC 81-14236. (Illus.). 1982. text ed. 35.00x (ISBN 0-582-78309-7). Longman.

Seashells of the Arabian Gulf. Kathleen Smythe. (Natural History of the Arabian Gulf Ser.). (Illus.). 180p. 1982. text ed. 24.95x (ISBN 0-04-594001-0). Unwin Hyman.

Seashells of the Northeast Coast. Julius Gordon & Townsend E. Weeks. (Illus.). 64p. pap. 5.95 (ISBN 0-317-65669-4). Hancock House.

Seashells of the Pacific Northwest. James White. LC 73-892391. (Illus.). 1976. 11.95 (ISBN 0-8323-0232-5). Binford-Metropolitan.

Seashells of the World. Rev. ed. R. Tucker Abbott. Ed. by Herbert S. Zim. (Golden Guide Ser.). (Illus.). (gr. 9 up). 1985. pap. 3.95 (ISBN 0-307-24410-5, Golden Pr). Western Pub.

Seashore. Victor Mitchell. (Coloring Bks.). (Illus.). 16p. (gr. k up). 1988. pap. 1.75 (ISBN 0-7459-1471-3). Lion USA.

Seashore & Wading Birds of Florida. Patricia Pope. LC 75-2036. (Illus.). 48p. (Orig.). 1975. pap. 2.95 (ISBN 0-8200-0903-2). Great Outdoors.

Seashore Animals of the Pacific Coast. Myrtle E. Johnson & H. J. Snook. (Illus.). 16.50 (ISBN 0-8446-2336-9). Peter Smith.

Seashore Animals of the Southeast. Edward E. Ruppert & Richard S. Fox. (Illus.). 350p. 1988. 34.95x (ISBN 0-87249-534-5); pap. 24.95 (ISBN 0-87249-535-3). U of SC Pr.

Seashore Biology Notes: A New Guide to the Common Animals in the Northern Gulf of California Tidepools. Diana Warr & Albert Collier. (Illus., Orig.). 1982. 7.95 (ISBN 0-938372-02-5). Winter Pub Co.

Seashore Book. E. Boyd Smith. LC 84-22483. (Illus.). 56p. (gr. k-12). 1985. Repr. of 1912 ed. 12.95 (ISBN 0-395-38015-4). HM.

Seashore Discoveries. Wesley M. Farmer. (Illus.). 124p. (Orig.). (YA) (gr. 9 up). 1986. pap. text ed. 7.95x (ISBN 0-937772-01-1). W M Farmer.

Seashore Entertaining. Naomi Black. LC 86-28051. (Illus.). 128p. 1987. 22.50 (ISBN 0-89471-506-2). Running Pr.

Seashore Life. Gerald Cox. 1989. pap. 5.95 (ISBN 0-935576-31-2). Kesend Pub Ltd.

Seashore Life. Cricket Harris. (Orig.). pap. 3.95 (ISBN 0-8200-0205-4). Great Outdoors.

Seashore Life of Florida & the Caribbean. rev. ed. Gilbert L. Voss. LC 80-20172. (Illus.). 199p. 1980. pap. 8.95 (ISBN 0-916224-58-9). Banyan Bks.

Seashore Life of Southern California. rev. & enl. ed. Sam Hinton. (Illus.). 256p. 1987. 27.50x (ISBN 0-520-05923-9); pap. 10.95 (ISBN 0-520-05924-7). U of Cal Pr.

Seashore Life of the Northern Pacific Coast: An Illustrated Guide to Northern California, Oregon, Washington, & British Columbia. Eugene N. Kozloff. LC 83-1130. (Illus.). 378p. 1983. 40.00x (ISBN 0-295-96030-2); pap. 19.95 (ISBN 0-295-96084-1). U of Wash Pr.

Seashore Plants of California. E. Yale Dawson & Michael S. Foster. LC 81-19690. (California Natural History Guides: No. 47). (Illus.). 226p. 1982. 22.50 (ISBN 0-520-04138-0); pap. 7.95 (ISBN 0-520-04139-9). U of Cal Pr.

Seashore Plants of Southern California. E. Yale Dawson. (California Natural History Guides: No. 19). 1966. pap. 5.95 (ISBN 0-520-00300-4). U of Cal Pr.

Seashore Seasonings. 1983. 8.50 (ISBN 0-9608326-0-2). B T Memorial.

Seashores. Joyce Pope. (Action Science Ser.). (Illus.). 32p. (gr. 1-8). 1985. PLB 11.90 (ISBN 0-531-04951-5). Watts.

Seashores. Herbert S. Zim & Lester Ingle. (Golden Guide Ser.). (Illus.). (gr. 5 up). 1955. pap. 3.95 (ISBN 0-307-24496-2, Golden Pr). Western Pub.

Seaside. Amery. (What's Happening Ser.). (Illus.). 20p. (ps). 1985. 3.95 (ISBN 0-86020-855-9, Pub. by Usborne). EDC.

Seaside. David Mohney & Keller Easterling. 1989. pap. 20.00 (ISBN 0-910413-26-6). Princeton Arch.

Seaside. Maria Rius & J. M. Parramon. (Let's Discover Ser.). (ps). 1986. 6.95 (ISBN 0-8120-5747-3); pap. 3.95 (ISBN 0-8120-3699-9). Barron.

Seaside Adventure. (Teddies Ser.). (Illus.). 32p. (gr. k-3). 1987. PLB 13.31 (ISBN 0-8172-2743-1); pap. 9.27 (ISBN 0-8172-2745-8). Raintree Pubs.

Seaside & Lakeside Domestic Architecture: A Bibliography. Mary E. Huls. (Architecture Ser.: A 1486). 6p. 1985. 2.00 (ISBN 0-89028-616-7). Vance Biblios.

Seaside Children's Republic. V. Golyshin. 87p. 1985. 6.95 (ISBN 0-8285-3142-0, Pub. by Raduga Pubs USSR). Imported Pubns.

Seaside Enterprises: Practice Set, No. 5. Wiley Staff. (Series for Principles of Accounting). 1988. pap. price not set (ISBN 0-471-61960-4). Wiley.

Seaside Gardening: Plantings, Procedures, & Design. Susan S. Littlefield. (Garden Design Ser.). (Illus.). 96p. 1987. 19.95 (ISBN 0-671-62222-6, Fireside); pap. 12.95 (ISBN 0-671-60242-X). S&S.

Seaside Kisses. Margaret M. Jensen. (YA) (gr. 7 up). 1982. 9.95 (ISBN 0-686-84711-3, Avalon). Bouregy.

SeaSide Marina. Harry D. Dickinson et al. (A Computer-based Collegiate Accounting Practice Set Ser.). 48p. (Orig.). 1986. tchr's ed. 34.95 (ISBN 0-934427-10-0); 19.95 (ISBN 0-934427-09-7). Ivy Soft.

Seaside Murders: Ten Classic True Crime Stories. Ed. by Jonathan Goodman. 192p. 1985. 13.95 (ISBN 0-8052-8248-3, Pub. by Allison & Busby England). Schocken.

Seaside Naturalist: A Guide to Nature at the Seashore. Deborah Coulombe. 256p. 1984. pap. 12.95 (ISBN 0-13-797242-3). P-H.

Seaside Picture Book. H. Amery. (What's Happening? Ser.). 12p. (ps up). 1988. 3.50 (ISBN 0-7460-0137-1). EDC.

Seaside Sparrow, Its Biology & Management. Ed. by Thomas L. Quay et al. (Occasional Papers of the North Carolina Biological Survey: 1983-5). (Illus.). 174p. 1983. pap. 15.00 (ISBN 0-917134-05-2). NC Natl Sci.

Seaside Studies in Natural History: Marine Animals of Massachusetts Bay. Elizabeth Agassiz & Alexander Agassiz. LC 75-125726. (American Environmental Studies). (Illus.). 1970. Repr. of 1865 ed. 23.50 (ISBN 0-405-02651-X). Ayer Co Pubs.

Season: A Candid Look at Broadway. Rev. ed. William Goldman. LC 84-4409. 448p. 1984. pap. 8.95 (ISBN 0-87910-023-0). Limelight Edns.

Season Abroad. Rebecca Baldwin. 224p. 1981. pap. 1.50 (ISBN 0-449-50215-5, Crest). Fawcett.

Season & Strategy: The Changing Organization of the Rural Water Sector in Botswana. Emery Roe & Louise Fortmann. (Special Series on Resource Management: No. 1). 257p. (Orig.). 1982. pap. text ed. 10.00 (ISBN 0-86731-082-0). Cornell CIS RDC.

Season at Coole. Michael Stephens. LC 84-21373. 176p. 1984. 20.00 (ISBN 0-916583-02-3); pap. 4.50 (ISBN 0-916583-03-1). Dalkey Arch.

Season at the Bass Wars. Nick Taylor. 192p. 1987. text ed. 16.95 (ISBN 0-07-062994-3). McGraw.

Season Clock. Valerie Littlewood. (Viking Kestrel Picture Bks.). (Illus.). (ps-3). 1987. 10.95 (ISBN 0-670-81433-4, Viking Kestrel). Viking.

Season for All Men. E. Valentine Joyce. 1986. 43.00x (ISBN 0-86332-112-7, Pub. by Book Guild Ltd). State Mutual Bk.

Season for Death. Ray Harrison. 288p. 1988. 15.95 (ISBN 0-312-01815-0, Pub. by Thomas Dunne Bks). St Martin.

Season for Healing: Reflections on the Holocaust. Anne Roiphe. 256p. 1988. 17.95 (ISBN 0-671-66753-X). Summit Bks.

Season for Roses. Barbara Kaye. (Superromance Ser.: No. 257). 308p. Date not set. pap. 2.75 (ISBN 0-317-63875-0). Harlequin Bks.

Season for Tenure. John Thomchick. LC 83-90278. 1984. 15.00 (ISBN 0-87212-176-3). Libra.

Season for Unicorns. Sonia Levitin. LC 85-20051. 204p. (gr. 5-9). 1986. 13.95 (ISBN 0-689-31113-3, Atheneum Childrens Bks). Macmillan.

Season for Unicorns. Sonia Levitin. 144p. 1987. pap. text ed. 2.50 (ISBN 0-317-57397-7, Juniper). Fawcett.

Season for Unnatural Causes: Stories. Philip F. O'Connor. LC 75-2289. (Illinois Short Fiction Ser.). 124p. 1975. pap. 8.95 (ISBN 0-252-00531-7). U of Ill Pr.

Season for War. P. F. Kluge. 244p. 1984. 15.95 (ISBN 0-88191-017-1). Freundlich.

Season for War. P. F. Kluge. 272p. 1988. pap. 3.50 (ISBN 1-55547-231-1). Critics Choice Paper.

Season In-Between. Jan Greenberg. LC 79-17997. 120p. (gr. 5 up). 1980. 9.95 (ISBN 0-374-36524-5). FS&G.

Season in Hell. A. Michael Edwardes. LC 72-11088. (Illus.). 326p. 1973. 12.95 (ISBN 0-8008-7015-8). Taplinger.

Seasonings Cookbook for Quantity Cuisine. Jule Wilkinson. LC 80-14412. (Illus.). 208p. 1983. 27.95 (ISBN 0-8436-2188-5). Van Nos Reinhold.

Seasonings for Sermons. Phillip H. Barnhart. 88p. (Orig.). 1980. pap. text ed. 6.25 (ISBN 0-89536-451-4, 1967). CSS of Ohio.

Seasonings for Sermons, Vol. 2. Lynn Ridenhour. 1982. 4.75 (ISBN 0-89536-577-4, 1916). CSS of Ohio.

Seasonings for Sermons, Vol. 3. John H. Krahn. 1983. 4.50 (ISBN 0-89536-585-5, 1922). CSS of Ohio.

Seasons. Illus. by Aurelius Battaglia. LC 76-43128. (Cricket Bk.). (Illus.). (ps-1). 1978. 2.50 (ISBN 0-448-46514-0, G&D). Putnam Pub Group.

Seasons. David Bennett. (Bear Facts Bks.). (Illus.). 32p. (ps up). 1988. pap. 3.95 (ISBN 0-553-05480-5). Bantam.

Seasons. Paul Caponigro. (Illus.). 1988. 35.00 (ISBN 0-8212-1703-8). NYGS.

Seasons. Judith B. Cohen. LC 83-63240. 224p. 1984. 16.95 (ISBN 0-932966-38-1). Permanent Pr.

Seasons. Sue Crawford. Ed. by Janet Caulkins. (Topics Ser.). (Illus.). 32p. (gr. 1-6). 1988. 10.40 (ISBN 0-531-18210-X, Pub. by Bookwright Pr). Watts.

Seasons. Heidi Goennel. LC 85-31226. (Illus.). (gr. k-2). 1986. 14.95 (ISBN 0-316-31836-1). Little.

Seasons. Suzanne Green. LC 86-16193. (Perlorians Ser.). (Illus.). 32p. (ps-3). 1987. pap. 5.95 (ISBN 0-385-23506-2); pap. 5.95 (ISBN 0-385-24007-4). Doubleday.

Seasons. Kathy Holler. (Science Ser.). 24p. (gr. 3-6). 1982. wkbk. 5.00 (ISBN 0-8209-0163-6, S-25). ESP.

Seasons. David Lambert. (Easy-Read Fact Bks.). (Illus.). 32p. (gr. k-3). 1983. PLB 10.90 (ISBN 0-531-04620-6). Watts.

Seasons. Louis Lawrence. (Illus.). 128p. 1983. pap. 9.95 (ISBN 0-03-064171-3). H Holt & Co.

Seasons. Colin McNaughton. Incl. Winter. LC 83-45236; Spring. LC 83-45226; Summer. LC 83-45324; Autumn. LC 83-45235. (Very First Bks.). (Illus.). 12p. (ps-k). 1984. 4.95 ea. (0481-140). Dial Bks Young.

Seasons. Illa Podendorf. LC 81-7751. (New True Bks.). (Illus.). 48p. (gr. k-4). 1981. PLB 12.60 (ISBN 0-516-01647-4); pap. 3.95 (ISBN 0-516-41647-2). Childrens.

Seasons. Ellin Pollachek. (Orig.). 1980. pap. 2.50 (ISBN 0-89083-578-0). Zebra.

Seasons. Ellin R. Pollachek. 352p. 1986. pap. 3.95 (ISBN 0-8217-1928-9). Zebra.

Seasons. Francene Sabin. LC 84-2713. (Illus.). 32p. (gr. 3-6). 1985. PLB 8.45 (ISBN 0-8167-0308-6); pap. text ed. 1.95 (ISBN 0-8167-0309-4). Troll Assocs.

Seasons. 1979. pap. 6.00 (ISBN 0-686-98155-3). Konglomerati.

Seasons. (Shorewood Art Programs for Education Ser.). 1974. tchr's. ed. 86.00 (ISBN 0-88185-003-9); mounted prints 119.00. Shorewood Fine Art.

Seasons. (Electric Company Color & Learn Bks.). (Illus.). 48p. (gr. 1-5). 1985. pap. 1.29 (ISBN 0-317-28611-0). Crown.

Seasons. Tony Tallarico. (Tote Bks.). (Illus.). 12p. (ps). 1982. pap. 3.95 (ISBN 0-89828-301-9). Tuffy Bks.

Seasons. James Thomson. Ed. by James Sanbrook. (Oxford English Texts). (Illus.). 1981. 129.00x (ISBN 0-19-812713-8). Oxford U Pr.

Seasons. James Thomson & Henry D. Roberts. 184p. 1982. Repr. of 1939 ed. lib. bdg. 30.00 (ISBN 0-89987-820-2). Darby Bks.

Seasons. Brian Wildsmith. (Illus.). (ps-3). 1980. 7.95 (ISBN 0-19-279730-1). Oxford U Pr.

Seasons & Celebrations. Rosalie F. Gaziano. LC 84-4226. 144p. 1984. pap. 7.95 (ISBN 0-88289-443-9). Pelican.

Seasons & Concepts. Anita Malnig. (gr. k-2). 1985. pap. 5.95 (ISBN 0-318-04684-9). D S Lake Pubs.

Seasons & Creatures. Lauris Edmond. 56p. 1988. pap. 9.95 (ISBN 0-19-558159-8). Oxford U Pr.

Seasons & Love. Faith T. Allum. (Illus.). 44p. (Orig.). (gr. 6 up). 1984. pap. 3.00 (ISBN 0-9613349-1-6). F T Allum.

Seasons & Other Times. Donna Weissenbrunner. Ed. by Ruth G. Brant & Victoria Fairham. LC 86-90266. (Illus.). 96p. 1987. pap. 8.95 (ISBN 0-9610156-3-2). Rainbow Clackamas.

Seasons & Saints. Anita L. Wheatcroft. (Illus.). 112p. (Orig.). (gr. 6-7). 1974. pap. text ed. 4.25x (ISBN 0-8192-4050-8); tchrs'. ed. 4.75x (ISBN 0-8192-4049-4). Morehouse.

Seasons & Surroundings, Pt. 2. John Anson. 20p. 1984. pap. 4.00 (ISBN 0-941150-28-3). Barth.

Seasons & Symbols. Robert Wetzler & Helen Huntington. LC 62-9094. (Illus., Orig.). 1962. pap. 7.95 (ISBN 0-8066-0221-X, 10-5625). Augsburg.

Seasons & the Castle of Indolence. James Thomson. Ed. by James Sambrook. 1972. pap. 10.95 (ISBN 0-19-871070-4). Oxford U Pr.

Seasons at Eagle Pond. Donald Hall. (Illus.). 96p. 1987. 19.95 (ISBN 0-89919-542-3). Ticknor & Fields.

Seasons Calling: American Haiku & Western-Style Verse. James M. McCready. LC 74-182063. (Illus.). 1972. bds. 3.75 (ISBN 0-8048-1021-4). C E Tuttle.

Seasons Come Spring. Paul A. Giffin. 1979. 5.00 (ISBN 0-682-49491-7). Exposition-Phoenix.

Season's Edge. Edith Hodgkinson. 1980. pap. 4.00 (ISBN 0-914610-22-8). Hanging Loose.

Season's Edge: And Other Poems. Mary Nyman. (Illus.). 64p. 1984. 5.95 (ISBN 0-89962-384-0). Todd & Honeywell.

Season's Greetings: Cooking & Entertaining for Thanksgiving, Christmas & New Year's. Marlene Sorosky. LC 85-30559. (Illus.). 128p. 1986. 20.00i (ISBN 0-06-181782-1, HarpT). Har-Row.

Seasons Hereafter. Elizabeth Ogilvie. Repr. lib. bdg. 19.95x (ISBN 0-88411-337-X, Pub. by Aeonian Pr). Amereon Ltd.

Seasons, Holidays & Anytime: Choral Readings & Action Verses for Fun & Learning. Margaret Hiller. 1987. pap. 8.95 (ISBN 0-933212-26-7). Partner Pr.

Seasons in Fern Hollow. John Patience. (Illus.). 64p. (ps-1). 2.98 (ISBN 0-517-45857-8). Outlet Bk Co.

Seasons in Flight. Brian W. Aldiss. LC 84-24329. 160p. 1986. 10.95 (ISBN 0-689-11538-5). Atheneum.

Seasons in God's World. Beverly Beckmann. (In God's World Ser.). (Illus.). 24p. (gr. 2-5). 1985. 5.95 (ISBN 0-570-04127-9, 56-1538). Concordia.

Seasons in Life. Bonnie Gear. Ed. by Mosazelle N. White. LC 82-62324. 61p. (Orig.). 1983. pap. 5.95x (ISBN 0-936026-19-7). R&M Pub Co.

Seasons in the Shores. Deborah D. Powell. 1987. 10.00 (ISBN 0-533-07389-8). Vantage.

Seasons in the Sun. 5th ed. Beaux Arts Staff. 302p. Repr. spiral bdg. 12.95 (ISBN 0-9607010-0-1). Beaux Arts.

Seasons in the Sun. Ragna Dahl & Mary E. Gilliland. 9.95 (ISBN 0-9603624-4-4). Alpenrose Pr.

Seasons in the Sun. Rod McKuen. (gr. 8 up). 1981. pap. 2.95 (ISBN 0-671-44741-6). PB.

Seasons in Vermont. John Engels. (Illus.). 28p. 1982. pap. 5.00 (ISBN 0-918092-36-1); signed cloth 25.00 (ISBN 0-918092-35-3). Tamarack Edns.

Seasons of a Man's Life. Daniel Levinson et al. 1979. pap. 10.95 (ISBN 0-345-33901-0). Ballantine.

Seasons of a Man's Life. Daniel J. Levinson et al. LC 77-20978. 1978. 18.95 (ISBN 0-394-40694-X). Knopf.

Seasons of a Marriage. H. Norman Wright. LC 82-80010. 1983. pap. 6.95 (ISBN 0-8307-0912-6, 5418058). Regal.

Seasons of Arnold's Apple Tree. Gail Gibbons. LC 84-4484. (Illus.). 32p. (ps-3). 1988. 13.95 (ISBN 0-15-271246-1, HJ). HarBraceJ.

Seasons of Arnold's Apple Tree. Gail Gibbons. 1988. 3.95 (ISBN 0-15-271245-3, HJ). HarBraceJ.

Seasons of Celebration. Thomas Merton. 256p. 1978. pap. 7.95 (ISBN 0-374-51419-4). FS&G.

Seasons of Celebration. Thomas Merton. 1983. 16.00 (ISBN 0-8446-5990-8). Peter Smith.

Season's of Change. Margaret Carpenter. 56p. 1983. 22.00 (ISBN 0-942494-60-1). Coleman Pub.

Seasons of Change. Sherrie Householder. 83p. 1984. 4.13 (ISBN 0-89697-192-9). Intl Univ Pr.

Seasons of Change. Jeri Lee-Hostetler. 192p. (Orig.). 1988. pap. 8.95 (ISBN 0-87178-774-1). Brethren.

Seasons of Delight: A Year on an Old-Fashioned Farm. Tasha Tudor. (Illus.). 12p. (gr. 1 up). 1986. 13.95 (ISBN 0-399-21308-2, Philomel). Putnam Pub Group.

Seasons of Fear. Philip McFarland. LC 83-42713. 288p. 1983. 15.95 (ISBN 0-8052-3850-6). Schocken.

Seasons of Friendship: Naomi & Ruth As a Pattern. Marjory Z. Bankson. Ed. by Marcia Broucek. 160p. (Orig.). 1987. pap. 10.95 (ISBN 0-931055-41-5). LuraMedia.

Seasons of God's Love: The Church Year. Jeanne S. Fogle. Ed. by Mary J. Duckert & Ben Lane. (Illus.). 32p. 1988. pap. 6.95 (ISBN 0-664-25032-7). Westminster John Knox.

Seasons of Grief. Donna Gaffney. LC 87-2832. 176p. 1988. 17.95 (ISBN 0-453-00591-8). NAL.

Seasons of Heron Pond: Wildings of Air, Earth, & Water. Mary Leister. LC 81-9408. (Illus.). 192p. 1981. 10.95 (ISBN 0-916144-84-4). Stemmer Hse.

Seasons of Jesse Stuart: An Autobiography in Poetry 1907-1976. Jesse Stuart & Wanda Hicks. LC 76-49171. (Illus.). 1976. 20.00 (ISBN 0-89097-009-2); ltd ed. 45.00 (ISBN 0-89097-008-4); deluxe ed. 150.00 (ISBN 0-89097-007-6). Archer Edns.

Seasons of Jupiter, a Novel of India. Anand Lall. 1971. Repr. of 1958 ed. lib. bdg. 35.00x (ISBN 0-8371-3837-X, LASJ). Greenwood.

Seasons of Life. Frank Harrington. 55p. 1986. 9.95 (ISBN 0-9616001-0-1). Pr Peachtree.

Seasons of Life. E. James Rohn & Ronald L. Reynolds. (Illus.). 117p. 1981. text ed. 9.95 (ISBN 0-939490-00-5). Jim Rohn Prod.

Seasons of Light. Peter Brown. LC 88-42688. (Illus.). 142p. 1988. 19.95 (ISBN 0-89263-269-0). Rice Univ.

Seasons of Love. June M. Bacher. pap. 4.95 (ISBN 0-89081-504-6). Harvest Hse.

Seasons of Love. rev. ed. George Betts & Donni Betts. LC 86-11733. (Illus.). 80p. (Orig.). 1986. pap. 5.95 (ISBN 0-89087-477-8). Celestial Arts.

Seasons of Mind. Roger Bower. LC 82-90178. (Illus.). 73p. 1982. 8.95 (ISBN 0-9608748-0-1). Marcourt Pr.

Seasons of My Mind. Lorenzo Fitzpatrick. 48p. (Orig.). 1984. pap. 3.00 (ISBN 0-9613323-0-1). Pat Pub Co.

Seasons of Our Joy: A Handbook of Jewish Festivals. Arthur I. Waskow. 1986. 17.95 (ISBN 0-671-61865-2). Summit Bks.

Seasons of Peace. Ed. by Beth Richardson. 72p. (Orig.). 1986. pap. 4.95 (ISBN 0-8358-0548-4). Upper Room.

Seasons of Rebellion: Protest & Radicalism in Recent America. Ed. by Joseph Boskin & Robert A. Rosenstone. LC 79-9678. 349p. 1980. pap. text ed. 14.00 (ISBN 0-8191-0977-0). U Pr of Amer.

Seasons of Sacred Lust. Kazuko Shiraishi. Ed. by Kenneth Rexroth. LC 77-14936. 1978. 4.95 (ISBN 0-8112-0687-4). New Directions.

Seasons of Splendor. Madhur Jaffrey. (Illus.). (ps up). Date not set. pap. 7.95 (ISBN 0-317-62172-6, Puffin Bks). Penguin.

Seasons of Splendor: Tales, Myths, & Legends from India. Madhur Jaffrey. (Illus.). 128p. 1985. 15.95 (ISBN 0-689-31141-9, Atheneum Childrens Bks). Macmillan.

Seasons of Strength: New Visions of Adult Christian Maturing. Evelyn E. Eaton & James D. Whitehead. LC 84-4199. 240p. 1986. pap. 7.95 (ISBN 0-385-19680-6, Im). Doubleday.

Seasons of Success. Valerie Sokolosky. 1985. pap. 3.95 (ISBN 0-89274-382-4). Harrison Hse.

Seasons of the Angler: A Fisherman's Anthology. Ed. by David Seybold. LC 87-33978. (Illus.). 256p. 1988. 19.95 (ISBN 1-55584-091-4). Weidenfeld.

Seasons of the Blood. Lewis Turco. 40p. (Orig.). 1980. pap. 3.50. Mathom.

Seasons of the Crane. Dale Stahleker & Martin Frentzel. (Illus.). 64p. (Orig.). 1986. 6.95 (ISBN 0-910467-07-2). Heritage Assocs.

Seasons of the Family: An Introduction to Marriage & Family Life. William R. Garrett. LC 81-7240. 532p. 1982. text ed. 33.95 (ISBN 0-03-057281-9); instr's. manual 25.00 (ISBN 0-03-057282-7). HR&W.

Seasons of the Heart. Susan Feldhake. 224p. 1988. pap. 5.95 (ISBN 0-310-47752-2, 15631P). Zondervan.

Seasons of the Heart. Cynthia Freeman. 399p. 1986. 17.95 (ISBN 0-399-13107-8). Putnam Pub Group.

Seasons of the Heart. Cynthia Freeman. LC 86-5914. 577p. 1986. 18.95 (ISBN 0-89621-727-2). Thorndike Pr.

Seasons of the Heart. Cynthia Freeman. 352p. 1987. pap. 4.50 (ISBN 0-425-09557-6). Berkley Pub.

Seasons of the Heart. Kay Rizzo. (Destiny Ser.). 96p. 1987. pap. 6.95 (ISBN 0-8163-0703-2). Pacific Pr Pub Assn.

Seasons of the Heart. Ramona Stewart. 304p. 1986. pap. 3.50 (ISBN 0-8439-2335-0, Leisure Bks). Leisure NY.

Seasons of the Hunter. Ed. by Robert Elman et al. LC 85-40088. (Illus.). 320p. 1985. 17.45 (ISBN 0-394-54213-4). Knopf.

Seasons of the Mind. Arlene Zekowski. LC 69-20441. (Archives of Post-Modern Literature). (Illus.). 1969. pap. 9.95 (ISBN 0-913844-06-3). Am Canadian.

Seasons of the Mind. Arlene Zekowski. 304p. 1973. pap. 9.95 (ISBN 0-8180-0617-X). Horizon.

Seasons of the River. Dan Jaffe. Ed. by Pat Huyett. LC 86-71748. 64p. (Orig.). 1987. pap. 14.95 (ISBN 0-933532-58-X). BKMK.

Seasons of the Salt Marsh. David A. Gates. LC 74-27956. (Illus.). 128p. 1975. 12.95 (ISBN 0-85699-121-X). Chatham Pr.

Seasons of the Seal. Fred Bruemmer. (Illus.). 160p. 1988. 29.95 (ISBN 0-942802-93-4). Northword.

Seasons of the Self. Max Coots. LC 71-158676. (Illus.). 1971. 3.50 (ISBN 0-687-37140-6). Unitarian.

Seasons of the Soul: Religious, Historical, & Philosophical Perspectives on the Jewish Year. Nisson Wolpin. (ArtScroll Judaica Scope Ser.). 288p. 1981. 15.95 (ISBN 0-89906-852-9); pap. 12.95 (ISBN 0-89906-853-7). Mesorah Pubns.

Seasons of the Spirit: The Archbishop of Canterbury at Home & Abroad. Robert A. Runcie. LC 83-1734. pap. 68.00 (ISBN 0-317-30160-8, 2025342). Bks Demand UMI.

Seasons of the Sun, Phases of the Moon: Celestial Influences on Plants & Gardens. Diane Martin. (Illus.). 50p. 1988. pap. 7.95 (ISBN 0-931485-11-8). Scriptorium Pr.

Seasons of the Wind: A Naturalist's Look at the Plant Life of Southwestern Sand Dunes. Janice Bowers. LC 85-61939. (Illus.). 174p. (Orig.). 1986. pap. 10.95 (ISBN 0-87358-393-0). Northland.

Seasons of the Year: Poems. Frank Ebersole. 64p. 1983. pap. 5.00 (ISBN 0-941452-15-8). Acheron Pr.

Seasons of Thomas Tebo. John Nagenda. (African Writers Ser.). 156p. (Orig.). 1986. pap. 7.50 (ISBN 0-435-90824-3). Heinemann Ed.

Seasons of Woman: Song, Poetry, Ritual, Prayer, Myth, Story. Ed. by Penelope Washbourn. LC 78-3359. (Illus.). 128p. (Orig.). 1982. pap. 7.95 (ISBN 0-06-250930-6, CN4042, HarpR). Har-Row.

Seasons on a Ranch. Cynthia Vannoy-Rhoades. LC 86-16875. (Illus.). 162p. 1986. 14.95 (ISBN 0-87108-711-1). Pruett.

Seasons on Earth: Ko, or a Season on Earth; & the Duplications. Kenneth Koch. (Elizabeth Sifton Bks.). 288p. 1987. pap. 12.95 (ISBN 0-14-058576-1). Penguin.

Seasons on the Farm. Jane Miller. (Illus.). 32p. (gr. k-3). 1986. PLB 10.95 (ISBN 0-13-797275-X). P-H.

Season's Premiere. Theatre Guild Members. (Illus.). 456p. (Orig.). 1986. pap. 15.00 (ISBN 0-9614424-0-9). Theatre Guild.

Seasons Such As These: Two Novels, New Letters. Natalie L. Petesch. LC 78-67506. 163p. 1979. 15.95 (ISBN 0-8040-0803-5, Pub. by Swallow). Ohio U Pr.

Seasons That Laugh or Weep: Musings on the Human Journey. Walter J. Burghardt. LC 83-60655. 144p. (Orig.). 1983. 4.95 (ISBN 0-8091-2533-1). Paulist Pr.

Seasons: Women's Search for Self Through Life's Stages. Anita Spencer. LC 81-85379. 128p. (Orig.). 1982. pap. 4.95 (ISBN 0-8091-2437-8). Paulist Pr.

Seaspeak Reference Manual: Recommendations for Maritime Communication, Principally by VHF Radio. Ed. by P. Weeks. (Essential English for Maritime Use Ser.). 160p. 1984. text ed. 39.50 (ISBN 0-08-031056-7). Pergamon.

Seaspeak Training Manual. Ed. by F. Weeks et al. (Essential English for Maritime Use Ser.). (Illus.). 180p. 1987. text ed. 19.50 (ISBN 0-08-031071-0, Pub. by PPL); pap. text ed. 13.50 (ISBN 0-08-031555-0). Pergamon.

Seaswept Abandon. Jo Goodman. 496p. 1986. pap. 3.95 (ISBN 0-8217-1905-X). Zebra.

Seat at the Circus. rev. ed. Antony D. Coxe. Ed. by Arthur Saxon. LC 79-19155. (Archon Bks. on Popular Entertainments). (Illus.). 258p. 1980. 24.50 (ISBN 0-208-01766-6, Archon). Shoe String.

Seat Belt Issue: A Bibliography. The Information Access Group Staff. (Public Administration Ser.: P 2041). 12p. 1986. 3.75 (ISBN 1-55590-081-X). Vance Biblios.

Seat in a Wild Place. Erik Brown. LC 81-15017. (Illus.). 128p. 1983. 8.95 (ISBN 0-87233-059-1). Bauhan.

Seat Weaving. C. Perry. 1940. pap. 6.00 (ISBN 0-02-665670-1). Bennett IL.

Seat Yourself: The Complete Guide to Twin Cities Theaters, Arenas & Auditoriums. Anastasia Mickelson & Marlys Mickelson. 50p. 1988. price not set. Mickelsons.

Seat Yourself: The Ticket Buyers Handbook. Emil Krause. LC 87-71204. (Illus.). 150p. (Orig.). Date not set. pap. 6.95 (ISBN 0-89708-163-3). And Bks.

Seated in Heavenly Places. Richard Booker. LC 85-72460. 135p. 1986. pap. 5.95 (ISBN 0-88270-600-4). Bridge Pub.

Seated Liberty Dollars, 1985. W. White. lib. bdg. 18.00 ltd. ed (ISBN 0-942666-42-9); pap. 10.00. S J Durst.

Seats of the Mighty. Gilbert Parker. 1976. lib. bdg. 16.75x (ISBN 0-89968-077-1). Lightyear.

Seats of the Nobility & Gentry in a Collection of Most Interesting Picturesque Views. W. Watts. Ed. by John D. Hunt. LC 79-56982. (English Garden Ser.). 170p. 1982. lib. bdg. 26.00 (ISBN 0-8240-0169-9). Garland Pub.

Seats of the Nobility & Gentry in Great Britain & Wales. W. Angus. Ed. by John D. Hunt. LC 79-56977. (English Landscape Garden Ser.). 190p. 1982. lib. bdg. 33.00 (ISBN 0-8240-0172-9). Garland Pub.

Seats, Votes & the Spatial Organization of Elections. Graham Gudgin & Peter J. Taylor. 254p. 1979. 27.00x (ISBN 0-85086-073-3, NO. 6380, Pub. by Pion England). Routledge Chapman & Hall.

Seatticus Knight. Ralph La Charity. 110p. 1985. pap. 10.00 (ISBN 0-930773-02-0). Black Heron Pr.

Seattle. Photos by David Barnes. LC 80-60. (Illus.). 80p. 1980. pap. 12.95 (ISBN 0-914718-50-9). Pacific Search.

Seattle. Photos by Charles Krebs. LC 86-80096. (Illus.). 160p. (Text by Timothy Egan). 1986. 34.95 (ISBN 0-932575-09-9). Gr Arts Ctr Pub.

Seattle. Jack Lynch. 256p. (Orig.). 1985. pap. 2.95 (ISBN 0-446-32749-2). Warner Bks.

Seattle. Charlotte Paul. 1987. pap. 3.95 (ISBN 0-451-14644-1, Sig). NAL.

Seattle see Trolley Trails Through the West.

Seattle & Its People. Pace International Research, Inc. Staff. (AAA Video Ser.). (Illus.). 135p. 1984. text ed. 8.95 (ISBN 0-89209-048-0); pap. text ed. 4.25 (ISBN 0-89209-078-2); audiocassette 3.25 (ISBN 0-89209-079-0); videocassette 125.00 (ISBN 0-89209-045-6). Pace Intl Res.

Seattle Best Places. 3rd ed. David Brewster. (Best Places Ser.). (Illus.). 312p. 1986. pap. 8.95 (ISBN 0-912365-08-0). Sasquatch Bks.

Seattle Best Places. 4th ed. Brewster David & Robinson Kathryn. (Best Places Ser.). 310p. (Orig.). 1988. pap. 10.95 (ISBN 0-912365-15-3). Sasquatch Bks.

Seattle Bicycle Atlas. (Illus.). 66p. 1985. pap. write for info. (ISBN 0-939116-16-2). Frontier WA.

Seattle Career Hunter's Guide. Sheri Raders & Peggy Newsom. (Illus.). 1978. pap. 5.95 (ISBN 0-918480-07-8). Victoria Hse.

Seattle Celebrity Chefs. Bill Schwartz & Mike McCormick. 200p. (Orig.). 1986. pap. 9.95 (ISBN 0-89716-149-1). Peanut Butter.

Seattle Center. Loralie Cecotti. (Color-A-Story Ser.). (Illus.). 24p. (Orig.). (gr. 1-4). 1983. pap. 2.75 (ISBN 0-933992-30-0). Coffee Break.

Seattle Cheap Eats: Two Hundred Thirty Terrific Bargain Eateries. 3rd ed. Ed. by Kathryn Robinson. (Illus.). 200p. 1988. pap. 7.95 (ISBN 0-912365-13-7). Sasquatch Bks.

Second Annual Internships in Congress. 125p. 1988. pap. 25.00 (ISBN 0-317-58993-8). Graduate Group.

Second Annual Outstanding Resumes of Two-Year College & College Graduates. 125p. 1988. pap. 25.00 (ISBN 0-317-58983-0). Graduate Group.

Second Annual Securities Activities of Banks. Ed. by Law & Business Inc. Staff & Legal Times Seminars Staff. (Seminar Course Handbooks). 1983. pap. 35.00 (ISBN 0-686-89350-6, C01376, Law & Business). HarBraceJ.

Second Annual Securities Law & Enforcement Institute. 35.00 (ISBN 0-317-29533-0, #CO1848, Law & Business). HarBraceJ.

Second Annual Seminar on Grant Law. 222p. 25.00 (ISBN 0-686-40861-6). Federal Bar.

Second Anthology of Atheism & Rationalism. Ed. by Gordon Stein. 442p. 1988. 22.95 (ISBN 0-87975-415-X). Prometheus Bks.

Second Anti-Coloring Book. Susan Striker & Edward Kimmel. (Illus.). 96p. (Orig.). (gr. 2 up). 1979. pap. 5.95 (ISBN 0-03-052496-2, Owl Bks). H Holt & Co.

Second Ark Book of Riddles. Myra Shofner. (Illus.). (gr. 3-7). 1981. pap. 3.50 (ISBN 0-89191-531-1, 55319). Cook.

Second Asia Pacific Physics Conference: Proceedings, Bangalore, India, January 13-17, 1986, 2 vols. Ed. by S. Chandrasekhar. 1232p. 1987. Set. 85.00 (ISBN 9971-50-268-2, Z0385P-P). World Scientific Pub.

Second Asian Regional Workshop on Injectable Contraceptives. Ed. by Edwin B. McDaniel. (Illus.). 93p. 1982. pap. 5.00 (ISBN 0-942716-04-3). World Neigh.

Second Assault: Rape & Public Attitudes. Joyce E. Williams & Karen A. Holmes. LC 81-339. (Contributions in Women's Studies: No. 27). (Illus.). 256p. 1981. lib. bdg. 35.00 (ISBN 0-313-22542-7, WIA/). Greenwood.

Second Assembling. Ed. by Richard Kostelanetz & Henry J. Korn. (Illus., Orig.). 1971. pap. 10.00 (ISBN 0-685-00930-0). Assembling Pr.

Second Assembly Data Book. Ed. by Charles M. Kavanagh. 1987. pap. 9.00 (ISBN 0-317-65730-5). Natl Cath Educ.

Second Athenian League: Empire or Free Alliance? Jack Cargill. 325p. 1981. 38.00x (ISBN 0-520-04069-4). U of Cal Pr.

Second Avenue Rag. Allan Knee. (Phoenix Theatre Ser.). 1980. pap. 2.95x (ISBN 0-912262-71-0). Proscenium.

Second Baldwin Government & the United States, 1924-1929: Attitudes & Diplomacy. B. J. McKercher. (International Studies). 272p. 1984. 44.50 (ISBN 0-521-25802-2). Cambridge U Pr.

Second Bar-Ilan Conference on the Physics of Disordered Systems: Special Issue of Philosophical Magazine, Pt. B, Vol. 56, No. 6. Ed. by E. A. Davis & C. Domb. 414p. 1988. pap. 58.00x (ISBN 0-85066-907-3). Taylor & Francis.

Second Battle of New Orleans: A History of the Vieux Carre Riverfront Expressway Controversy. Richard O. Baumbach, Jr. & William E. Borah. (Illus.). 384p. 1981. 27.50x (ISBN 0-8173-4840-9); pap. 12.95 (ISBN 0-8173-4841-7). U of Ala Pr.

Second Beginner's Guide to Personal Computers for the Blind. 2nd, rev. ed. Ed. by Diane L. Croft. (Illus.). 130p. 1987. pap. text ed. 14.00 (ISBN 0-939173-09-3); Braille 11.00 (ISBN 0-939173-10-7); tape 11.00 (ISBN 0-939173-11-5). Natl Braille Pr.

Second Beginner's Guide to Personal Computers for the Blind & Visually Impaired. National Braille Press Inc. Ed. by Diane L. Croft. (Illus.). 208p. (Orig.). 1984. pap. 14.95 (ISBN 0-939173-03-4); braille 12.95 (ISBN 0-939173-04-2); cassette 12.95 (ISBN 0-939173-05-0). Natl Braille Pr.

Second Berkshire Authology, 2 vols. Ed. by Dana Collins & Mark Canner. LC 74-78475. (Illus.). 230p. 1975. pap. 10.00 boxed set (ISBN 0-912846-10-0). Bookstore Pr.

Second Best. Elizabeth Bernard. (Satin Slippers Ser.). (gr. 6 up). 1988. pap. 2.95 (ISBN 0-449-13308-7). Fawcett.

Second Best. Helen Cavanagh. (YA) (gr. 7 up). 1979. pap. 2.25 (ISBN 0-590-32313-X, Wildfire). Scholastic Inc.

Second-Best Friend. Elizabeth B. Keeton. LC 84-21561. 180p. (gr. 4-7). 1985. 11.95 (ISBN 0-689-31096-X, Atheneum Childrens Bks). Macmillan.

(Second) Best of Everything. David Reid & John Jerald. 1987. 14.95 (ISBN 0-15-179950-4, Harv); pap. 6.95 (ISBN 0-317-64179-4); 10-copy prepack 89.50. HarBraceJ.

Second Best of Granny: Family Recipes. Georgia H. Carter. LC 84-90207. 67p. 1986. 7.95 (ISBN 0-533-06268-3). Vantage.

Second Best Sister. Carol Stanley. 192p. (YA) (gr. 6-9). 1988. pap. 2.50 (ISBN 0-590-40052-5). Scholastic Inc.

Second Best Wife. (Harlequin Presents Ser.). 1982. pap. 1.75 (ISBN 0-373-10555-X). Harlequin Bks.

Second Billion. Penny Kane. 296p. 1988. pap. 7.95 (ISBN 0-14-008657-9). Penguin.

Second Birth. Omraam M. Aivanhov. (Complete Works of O. M. Aivanhov: Vol. 1). 210p. 1981. pap. 11.95 (ISBN 0-87516-418-8). DeVorss.

Second Black Lizard Anthology of Crime Fiction. Ed. by Ed Gorman. Date not set. 13.95 (Pub. by Black Lizard Bks). Creative Arts Bk.

Second Black Renaissance: Essays in Black Literature. C. W. Bigsby. LC 79-7723. (Contributions in Afro-American & African Studies: No. 50). 1980. lib. bdg. 38.95 (ISBN 0-313-21304-6, BNB/). Greenwood.

Second Body. Sue Payer. 1979. pap. 1.95 (ISBN 0-505-51381-1, Pub. by Tower Bks). Leisure NY.

Second Book in English. Robert J. Dixson. 128p. 1983. pap. text ed. 5.25 (ISBN 0-13-797283-0, 21179). Prentice ESL.

Second Book of Broadsheets. Geoffrey Dawson. 1975. Repr. of 1929 ed. 35.00 (ISBN 0-8274-4081-2). R West.

Second Book of Broadsheets. Ed. by Geoffrey Dawson. 301p. 1980. Repr. lib. bdg. 40.00 (ISBN 0-89987-152-6). Darby Bks.

Second Book of Chronicles. John A. Grindel. (Bible Ser.: Vol. 18). (Orig.). 1974. pap. 1.00 (ISBN 0-8091-5171-5). Paulist Pr.

Second Book of Danish Verse. C. W. Stork. 69.75 (ISBN 0-8490-1008-X). Gordon Pr.

Second Book of Danish Verse. facs. ed. Tr. by Charles W. Stork. LC 68-57067. (Granger Index Reprint Ser). 1947. 17.00 (ISBN 0-8369-6044-0). Ayer Co Pubs.

Second Book of Easy-to-Build Electronic Projects. Elementary Electronics Editors. 192p. (Orig.). 1984. 17.95 (ISBN 0-8306-0679-3, 1679H); pap. 14.95 (1999P). TAB Bks.

Second Book of Irish Myths & Legends. Eoin Neeson. 128p. 1981. pap. 7.95 (ISBN 0-85342-131-5, Pub. by Mercier Pr Ireland). Irish Bks Media.

Second Book of Kings. Ed. by J. Robinson. LC 75-39371. (Cambridge Bible Commentary on the New English Bible, Old Testament Ser.). (Illus.). 1976. pap. 14.95x (ISBN 0-521-09774-6). Cambridge U Pr.

Second Book of Kings. Geoffrey Wood. (Bible Ser.: Vol. 16). (Orig.). 1974. pap. 1.00 (ISBN 0-8091-5169-3). Paulist Pr.

Second Book of Lost Swords. Fred Saberhagen. 256p. 1988. pap. 3.95 (ISBN 0-8125-5331-4, Dist. by Warner Pub Services & Saint Martin's Press). Tor Bks.

Second Book of Lost Swords: Sightblinder's Story. Fred Saberhagen. 256p. 1987. 14.95 (ISBN 0-312-93032-1, Dist. by Warner Pub Servs & St Martin Pr). Tor Bks.

Second Book of Maccabees. Neil J. McEleney. (Bible Ser.: Vol. 23). (Orig.). 1974. pap. 1.00 (ISBN 0-8091-5167-7). Paulist Pr.

Second Book of Machine Language. Richard Mansfield. 446p. (Orig.). 1984. pap. 14.95 (ISBN 0-942386-53-1). Compute Pubns.

Second Book of Mathematical Bafflers. Angela Dunn. (Puzzles, Amusements, Recreations Ser.). (Illus.). 192p. (Orig.). 1983. pap. 4.50 (ISBN 0-486-24352-4). Dover.

Second Book of Modern Electronics Fun Projects. Art Salsberg. 192p. 1986. pap. 12.95 (ISBN 0-672-22504-2). Sams.

Second Book of Modern Lace Knitting. rev. ed. Marianne Kinzel. LC 72-86064. (Illus.). 128p. 1973. pap. 4.95 (ISBN 0-486-22905-X). Dover.

Second Book of Modern Lace Knitting. Marianne Kinzel. (Illus.). 8.25 (ISBN 0-8446-4763-2). Peter Smith.

Second Book of Modern Verse. Jessie B. Rittenhouse. 1919. 11.00 (ISBN 0-8274-3342-5). R West.

Second Book of Modern Verse. facs. ed. Ed. by Jessie B. Rittenhouse. LC 75-149113. (Granger Index Reprint Ser.). 1919. 16.00 (ISBN 0-8369-6238-9). Ayer Co Pubs.

Second Book of Operas, Their Histories, Their Plots & Their Music. Henry E. Krehbiel. LC 80-2280. Repr. of 1917 ed. 36.50 (ISBN 0-404-18852-4). AMS Pr.

Second Book of Poems. Harland Sleight. 93p. 1986. 32.00x (ISBN 0-7223-2037-X, Pub. by A H Stockwell England). State Mutual Bk.

Second Book of Samuel. Frederick Moriarty. (Bible Ser.). pap. 1.00 (ISBN 0-8091-5136-7). Paulist Pr.

Second Book of Samuel: Cambridge Bible Commentary on the New English Bible. Peter R. Ackroyd. LC 76-58074. (Cambridge Bible Commentary on the New English Bible, Old Testament Ser.). (Illus.). 1977. 32.50 (ISBN 0-521-08633-7); pap. 13.95 (ISBN 0-521-09754-1). Cambridge U Pr.

Second Book of the Bible: Exodus. Walter Jacob. 1983. 59.50x (ISBN 0-88125-028-7). Ktav.

Second Book of the Lamb. Peter C. Stone. 233p. 1987. 22.00 (ISBN 0-934469-02-4). Gabriel Pr CA.

Second Book of the Rhymers Club. William B. Yeats et al. 1987. pap. 12.95 (ISBN 0-89979-033-X). British Am Bks.

Second Book of the Rhymer's Club see Book of the Rhymer's Club.

Second Book of the Strange. World Almanac Editors & Laurence D. Gadd. LC 81-82644. (Science & the Paranormal Ser.). (Illus.). 341p. 1981. 18.95 (ISBN 0-87975-170-3). Prometheus Bks.

Second Book of the Travels of Nicander Nucius, of Corcyra. Nicander Nucius. Tr. by J. A. Cramer. (Camden Society, London. Publications, First Ser.: No. 17). Repr. of 1841 ed. 19.00 (ISBN 0-404-50117-6). AMS Pr.

Second Book of the Travels of Nicander Nucius of Corcyra. Nicander Nucius. Repr. of 1841 ed. 19.00 (ISBN 0-384-42240-3). Johnson Repr.

Second Book of VIC. 270p. 1983. 12.95 (ISBN 0-942386-16-7). Compute Pubns.

Second Booke Teaching the Composing of Fireworks. facs. ed. John Bate. (Shorey Lost Arts Ser.). 45p. pap. 2.95 (ISBN 0-8466-0120-6, S120). Shorey.

Second Bridge. Gary Gildner. 216p. 1987. 15.95 (ISBN 0-912697-44-X). Algonquin Bks.

Second British Empire: Trade, Philanthropy, & Good Government, 1820-1890. John P. Halstead. LC 82-20965. (Contributions in Comparative Colonial Studies: No. 14). (Illus.). xiii, 261p. 1983. lib. bdg. 56.95 (ISBN 0-313-23519-8, HBE/). Greenwood.

Second Brother. David Guy. 264p. 1985. 14.50 (ISBN 0-453-00497-0). NAL.

Second Brother. David Guy. 1986. pap. 6.95 (ISBN 0-452-25887-1, Plume). NAL.

Second Canadian-American Conference on Hydrogeology: Proceedings. 1986. 43.75 (ISBN 0-318-23039-9). Natl Water Well.

Second Cancer in Relation to Radiation Treatment for Cervical Cancer: Results of a Cancer Registry Collaboration. Ed. by N. E. Day & J. C. Boice, Jr. (Illus.). 1984. 30.00x (ISBN 0-19-723052-0). Oxford U Pr.

Second Catalogue of Variable Stars in Globular Clusters, Comprising 1,421 Entries. Helen B. Sawyer. (University of Toronto, David Dunlap Observatory Ser.: Vol. 2, No. 2). pap. 20.00 (2026544). Bks Demand UMI.

Second Census of Kentucky: 1800. G. Glenn Clift. LC 66-19191. 333p. 1982. Repr. of 1954 ed. 18.50 (ISBN 0-8063-0077-9). Genealog Pub.

Second Centering Book: More Awareness Activites for Children, Parents, & Teachers. C. Gaylord Hendricks & T. Roberts. 1977. (Spec); pap. 8.95 (ISBN 0-13-797324-1, Spec). P-H.

Second Century of Charades. William Bellamy. 1979. Repr. of 1896 ed. lib. bdg. 20.00 (ISBN 0-8495-0527-5). Arden Lib.

Second Century of Charades. William Bellamy. 1977. Repr. of 1896 ed. 15.00. Century Bookbindery.

Second Century of Humor. Anthony Armstrong et al. 30.00 (ISBN 0-8495-6264-3). Arden Lib.

Second Century of New & Rare Indian Plants, Vol. IX, Pt. 1. Royal Botanic Garden, Calcutta, Annals of et al. (Illus.). 80p. 1972. Repr. of 1901 ed. 50.00 (ISBN 0-88065-012-5, Pub. by Messers Today & Tomorrows Printers & Publishers India). Scholarly Pubns.

Second Century of the English Parliament. Goronwy Edwards. 1979. 27.95x (ISBN 0-19-822479-6). Oxford U Pr.

Second Century of the Skyscraper. Council on Tall Buildings & Urban Habitat Staff. (Illus.). 1056p. 1988. text ed. 82.95 (ISBN 0-442-22116-9). Van Nos Reinhold.

Second Certification of Changes to Schedules to the GATT. (Eng. & Fr.). 1974. pap. 10.00 (ISBN 0-686-93130-0, G1, GATT). UNIPUB.

Second Chamber of India Parliament. N. K. Trikha. 1984. 15.00x (ISBN 0-8364-1180-3, Pub. by Allied India). South Asia Bks.

Second Chambers. John A. Marriott. LC 78-102250. (Select Bibliographies Reprint Ser). 1910. 26.50 (ISBN 0-8369-5135-2). Ayer Co Pubs.

Second Chance. Walter J. Adams, Jr. 40p. 1987. 7.95 (ISBN 0-8062-3070-3). Carlton.

Second Chance. E. Manklow. 1985. 24.95x (ISBN 0-7090-2002-3, Pub. by R Hale Ltd UK). State Mutual Bk.

Second Chance. Joan Oppenheimer. 176p. (Orig.). (gr. 7 up). 1982. pap. 1.95 (ISBN 0-590-32173-0, Wishing Star Bks). Scholastic Inc.

Second Chance. Nancy B. Peck. 1981. pap. 2.50 (ISBN 0-89083-745-7). Zebra.

Second Chance. Hildegarde Schneider. 104p. 1987. 6.95 (ISBN 0-8059-3063-9). Dorrance.

Second Chance. Ed. by John B. Whitton. LC 77-111874. (Essay Index Reprint Ser). 1944. 19.00 (ISBN 0-8369-1735-9). Ayer Co Pubs.

Second Chance for Families: Five Years Later. Mary A. Jones. 161p. 1985. 26.95 (ISBN 0-87868-229-5, F-68, 2295); pap. 21.95 (ISBN 0-317-55858-7). Child Welfare.

Second Chance for Ruth. Janet P. Gortsema. 1985. pap. 3.95 (ISBN 0-87162-407-9, D3735). Warner Pr.

Second Chance: Men, Women & Children a Decade after Divorce. Judith Wallerstein & Sandra Blakeslee. 1988. price not set. Ticknor & Fields.

Second Chance: New Hampshire's Electricity Future As A Model for the Nation. 72p. 1983. 1.50 (ISBN 0-938987-02-X). Union Conc Sci.

Second Chance to Live: The Suicide Syndrome. George Alpert & Ernest Leogrande. LC 75-20452. (Photography Ser.). (Illus.). 90p. 1976. lib. bdg. 22.50 (ISBN 0-306-70751-9); pap. 6.95 (ISBN 0-306-80023-3). Da Capo.

Second Chance: Training for Jobs. Sar A. Levitan & Frank Gallo. LC 87-37266. 220p. 1988. text ed. 22.95 (ISBN 0-88099-057-0); pap. text ed. 15.95 (ISBN 0-88099-056-2). W E Upjohn.

Second Chances. Alice Adams. LC 87-46016. 272p. 1988. 18.95 (ISBN 0-394-56824-9). Knopf.

Second Chances. Florine De Veer. 233p. (Orig.). 1985. pap. 6.95 (ISBN 0-932870-69-4). Alyson Pubns.

Second Chances. Nancy Levinson. (Sweet Dreams Ser.: No. 94). 176p. 1985. pap. 2.25 (ISBN 0-553-25132-5). Bantam.

Second Chances. Marcia Rose. 440p. 1982. pap. 2.95 (ISBN 0-345-31918-4). Ballantine.

Second Chances: Men, Women & Children a Decade after Divorce. Judith Wallerstein & Sandra Blakeslee. 1989. 19.95 (ISBN 0-89919-648-9). Ticknor & Fields.

Second Chapter. John P. Splinter. 144p. 1987. pap. 12.95 (ISBN 0-8010-8269-2). Baker Bk.

Second Chapter Leader's Guide: New Beginnings after Divorce or Separation. John P. Splinter. 18p. Date not set. pap. 2.95 (ISBN 0-8010-8280-3). Baker Bk.

Second Characters or the Language of Forms. Anthony A. Shaftesbury. Ed. by Benjamin Rand. 1970. Repr. of 1914 ed. lib. bdg. 25.00 (ISBN 0-8371-2357-7, SHSC). Greenwood.

Second Checklist of French Political Pamphlets, 1560-1653. Ed. by Doris V. Welsh. 1955. pap. 5.00 (ISBN 0-911028-22-6). Newberry.

Second Childhood: Hypno-Play Therapy with Age-Regressed Adults. Marian K. Shapiro. (Professional Bks.). 1988. 22.95 (ISBN 0-393-70053-4). Norton.

Second China War, Eighteen Fifty-Six to Eighteen Sixty. Ed. by David B. Smith & E. W. Lumby. LC 79-2839. (Illus.). 413p. 1985. Repr. of 1954 ed. 32.45 (ISBN 0-8305-0016-2). Hyperion Conn.

Second Christianity. Hick. Date not set. pap. 5.95 (Pub. by SCM Pr England). Fortress.

Second Chronicles of Thomas Covenant, 3 vols. Stephen R. Donaldson. pap. 14.85 boxed set (ISBN 0-345-32963-5, Del Rey). Ballantine.

Second City. Donna McCrohan. (Illus.). 272p. 1987. pap. 9.95 (ISBN 0-399-51339-6, Perigee). Putnam Pub Group.

Second-Class Citizen. Buchi Emecheta. LC 82-24355. 175p. 1983. pap. 6.95 (ISBN 0-8076-1066-6). Braziller.

Second Class Suburbanites: White Blue-Collar Suburbs & Black White-Collar Suburbs, No. 739. Marcelion Cox. 1975. 6.00 (ISBN 0-686-20337-2). CPL Biblios.

Second Class Township Code. Pennsylvania State Legislature. 176p. (Orig.). 1982. text ed. 6.25 (ISBN 0-8182-0001-4). Commonweal PA.

Second Collection: Sing a Song for Sixpence, the Three Jovial Hunters. Randolph Caldecott. (Picture Bk.). (Illus.). 64p. 1986. 4.95 (ISBN 0-7232-3433-7). Warne.

Second Colloquium in Biological Sciences. Ed. by Craig D. Burrell & Fleur L. Strand. (Annals of the New York Academy of Sciences: Vol. 463). 422p. 1986. text ed. 106.00x (ISBN 0-89766-321-7); pap. text ed. 106.00x (ISBN 0-89766-322-5). NY Acad Sci.

Second Coming. David A. Hubbard. LC 84-694. 96p. 1984. pap. 4.95 (ISBN 0-87784-968-4). Inter-Varsity.

Second Coming. William Kelly. 375p. 7.25 (ISBN 0-88172-108-5). Believers Bkshelf.

Second Coming. Walker Percy. LC 80-12899. 368p. 1980. 12.95 (ISBN 0-374-25674-8). FS&G.

Second Coming. Walker Percy. 1982. pap. 4.95 (ISBN 0-671-60104-0). PB.

Second Coming. Walker Percy. 416p. 1981. pap. 4.95. WSP.

Second Coming Anthology: Ten Years in Retrospect. Ed. by A. D. Winans. (Illus.). 240p. 1984. lib. bdg. 15.00 (ISBN 0-915016-32-X); pap. 6.95 (ISBN 0-915016-33-8). Second Coming.

Second Coming Bible Commentary. William E. Biederwolf. (Paperback Reference Library). 728p. 1985. pap. 17.95 (ISBN 0-8010-0887-5). Baker Bk.

Second Coming Bible Study Guide, No. 1. William J. Krutza. (Contemporary Discussion Ser.). 96p. 1973. pap. 0.95 (ISBN 0-8010-5329-3). Baker Bk.

Second Coming Bible Study Guide, No. 2. William J. Krutza. (Contemporary Discussion Ser.). (Orig.). 1973. pap. 0.95 (ISBN 0-8010-5330-7). Baker Bk.

Second Coming: More Computing Projects Which Failed. Robert L. Glass. 1980. 9.00 (ISBN 0-686-26939-X). Computing Trends.

Second Coming of Christ. I. M. Haldeman. 326p. 1986. 12.95 (ISBN 0-8254-2844-0). Kregel.

Second Coming of Christ. Gordon Lindsay. (Prophecy Ser.). 0.95 (ISBN 0-89985-061-8). Christ Nations.

Second Coming of Christ, Vol. II. Paramhansa Yogananda. LC 79-50352. 1984. pap. 14.95 (ISBN 0-937134-05-8). Amrita Found.

Second Coming of Christ, Vol. I. Paramhansa Yogananda. LC 79-50352. 1979. pap. 14.95 (ISBN 0-937134-00-7). Amrita Found.

Second Coming of Christ, 3 vols, Vol. 3. Paramhansa Yogananda. 240p. pap. 14.45 ea. (ISBN 0-937134-12-0). Amrita Found.

Second Coming of Jesus. G. F. Taylor. 3.95 (ISBN 0-911866-63-9); pap. 2.00 (ISBN 0-911866-62-0). Advocate.

Second Coming: Popular Millenarianism 1780-1850. John F. Harrison. 1979. 35.00x (ISBN 0-8135-0879-7). Rutgers U Pr.

Second Coming: Why Jesus Christ Became a Carpenter Instead of an Electrician. Judy L. Bacci. 110p. (Orig.). 1981. pap. 5.95 (ISBN 0-940002-00-0). Studio J Pub.

Second Common Reader. Annotated ed. Virginia Woolf. 1986. pap. 7.95 (ISBN 0-15-619808-8). HarBraceJ.

TITLE INDEX SECOND INTELLECTUAL LIST OF

Second Concerto for Piano & Orchestra, Op. 18. S. Rachmaninoff. (Carl Fischer Music Library: No. 1060). 63p. pap. 7.50 (ISBN 0-8258-0180-X, L1060). Fischer Inc NY.
Second Conference on Faint Blue Stars. Ed. by A. Davis Philip. D. S. Hayes & J. Liebert. 700p. 1987. 47.00; pap. 37.00. L Davis Pr.
Second Conference on Theoretical Aspects of Reasoning about Knowledge: Proceedings. Ed. by Moshe Vardi. 402p. (Orig.). 1988. pap. text ed. 19.95 (ISBN 0-934613-66-4). Morgan Kaufmann.
Second Congress of Polish American Scholars & Scientists: Program & Abstracts of Papers. Ed. by Damian Wandycz. 100p. 1971. 5.00 (ISBN 0-940962-37-3). Polish Inst Art & Sci.
Second Congress of the Communist International. Vladimir I. Lenin. 1980. pap. 1.95 (ISBN 0-8285-1880-7, Pub. by Progress Pubs USSR). Imported Pubns.
Second Conquest. (Storytrails Ser.). 96p. (gr. 6-9). 1985. pap. 1.95 (ISBN 0-521-31705-3). Cambridge U Pr.
Second Cooperative Sports & Games Book. Terry Orlick. (Illus.). 1982. 18.00 (ISBN 0-394-51430-0); pap. 9.95 (ISBN 0-394-74813-1). Pantheon.
Second Cooperative Sports & Games Book: Over 200 Brand-New Noncompetitive Games for Kids & Adults Both. Terry Orlick. 255p. 1982. 9.95 (ISBN 0-318-18138-X). NASCO.
Second Corinthians. Ernest Best. Ed. by James L. Mays & Paul J. Achtemeier. LC 86-45404. (Interpretation: A Bible Commentary for Teaching & Preaching Ser.). 156p. 1987. 15.95 (ISBN 0-8042-3135-4, John Knox). Westminster John Knox.
Second Corinthians. Francis T. Fallon. LC 80-80319. (New Testament Message Ser.: Vol. 11). 12.95 (ISBN 0-89453-199-9); pap. 7.95 (ISBN 0-89453-134-4). M Glazier.
Second Corinthians. Robert B. Hughes. (Everyman's Bible Commentary Ser.). 1983. pap. 6.95 (ISBN 0-8024-0241-0). Moody.
Second Corinthians. Irving Jensen. (Bible Self-Study Ser). (Illus.). 108p. 1972. pap. 3.50 (ISBN 0-8024-1047-2). Moody.
Second Corinthians. Colin Kruse. (Tyndale New Testament Commentaries). 224p. 1987. pap. 6.95 (ISBN 0-8028-0318-0). Eerdmans.
Second Corinthians. Handley Moule. 1976. pap. 4.95 (ISBN 0-87508-359-5). Chr Lit.
Second Corinthians. (Erdmans Commentaries Ser.). pap. 3.50 (ISBN 0-8010-3395-0). Baker Bk.
Second Corinthians. Knofel Staton. (Standard Bible Studies). 208p. 1988. pap. text ed. price not set (ISBN 0-87403-168-0, 11-40108). Standard Pub.
Second Corinthians. Geoffrey Wilson. 1979. pap. 5.95 (ISBN 0-85151-295-X). Banner of Truth.
Second Corinthians, Vol. 40, WBC. Ralph P. Martin. 380p. 1985. 25.95 (ISBN 0-8499-0239-8, 0239-8). Word Bks.
Second Corinthians Eight & Nine: A Commentary on Two Administrative Letters of the Apostle Paul. Hans D. Betz. LC 84-48904. (Hermeneia Ser.). 288p. 1985. 29.95 (ISBN 0-8006-6014-5, 1-6014). Fortress.
Second Corinthians: Keys to Triumphant Living. Edgar C. James. (Teach Yourself the Bible Ser.). 1964. pap. 2.95 (ISBN 0-8024-7680-5). Moody.
Second Corinthians: Message of the New Testament. J. D. Thomas. (Way of Life Ser.). 60p. 1986. pap. text ed. 3.95 (ISBN 0-89112-168-4, 929). Abilene Christ U.
Second Corinthians, Timothy, Titus. & Philemon see Calvin's New Testament Commentaries.
Second Corinthians: Where Life Endures. Roy L. Laurin. LC 85-8154. 248p. 1985. pap. 9.95 (ISBN 0-8254-3129-8). Kregel.
Second Courante of Newes from the East India in Two Letters. LC 74-28849. (English Experience Ser.: No. 730). 1975. Repr. of 1622 ed. 3.50 (ISBN 90-221-0730-2). Walter J Johnson.
Second Course in Business Statistics: Regression Analysis. William Mendenhall & James T. McClave. (Illus.). 637p. 1981. text ed. 25.95x (ISBN 0-02-380470-X). Dellen Pub.
Second Course in Calculus. John M. Olmsted. LC 68-14041. (Century Mathematics Ser.). (Illus.). 336p. 1968. 39.50x (ISBN 0-89197-395-8). Irvington.
Second Course in Computer Science with Modula-2. Daniel D. McCracken. 1987. write for info. Wiley.
Second Course in Computer Science with Pascal. Daniel D. McCracken. LC 86-32586. (Illus.). 432p. 1987. write for info. (ISBN 0-471-01062-6); tchr's. manual avail. (ISBN 0-471-01061-8). Wiley.
Second Course in Elementary Differential Equations. Paul Waltman. 1985. text ed. 36.50 (ISBN 0-12-733910-8). Acad Pr.
Second Course in Linear Algebra. William C. Brown. LC 87-23117. 264p. 1987. 34.95 (ISBN 0-471-62602-3). Wiley.
Second Course in Mathematical Analysis. John C. Burkhill & H. Burkhill. LC 69-16278. (Illus.). 1970. text ed. 47.50 (ISBN 0-521-07519-X); pap. 34.50 (ISBN 0-521-28061-3). Cambridge U Pr.
Second Course in Ordinary Differential Equations for Scientists & Engineers. M. Huni & W. Miller. (Illus.). xi, 441p. 1988. pap. 49.00 (ISBN 0-387-96676-5). Springer-Verlag.
Second Course in Stochastic Processes. Samuel Karlin & Howard M. Taylor. LC 80-533. 1981. 49.00 (ISBN 0-12-398650-8). Acad Pr.
Second Course on Computer Science with MODULA 2. Daniel D. McCracken & William Salmon. LC 87-14230. 496p. 1987. write for info. (ISBN 0-471-63111-6); tchr's. manual avail. (ISBN 0-471-63515-4). Wiley.
Second Course on Real Functions. A. C. Van Rooij & W. H. Schikhof. LC 81-9933. 200p. 1982. 34.50 (ISBN 0-521-23944-3); pap. 13.95 (ISBN 0-521-28361-2). Cambridge U Pr.
Second Creation: Makers of the Revolution in Twentieth Century Physics. Robert P. Crease & Charles C. Mann. 475p. 1985. 25.00 (ISBN 0-02-521440-3). Macmillan.
Second Creation: Makers of the Revolution in 20th Century Physics. Robert P. Crease & Charles C. Mann. 496p. 1987. pap. 11.95 (ISBN 0-02-084550-2, Collier). Macmillan.
Second Crossing. N. A. Diaman. LC 82-7564. (Illus.). 240p. (Orig.). 1982. pap. 9.95 (ISBN 0-931906-03-2). Persona Pr.
Second Curtain. Roy Fuller. 192p. 1986. pap. 4.95 (ISBN 0-89733-197-4). Academy Chi Pubs.
Second Daffodil Poetry Book. facs. ed. Ed. by Ethel L. Fowler. LC 75-123389. (Granger Index Reprint Ser). 1931. 17.00 (ISBN 0-8369-6177-3). Ayer Co Pubs.
Second Deadly Sin. Lawrence Sanders. 448p. 1985. pap. 4.95 (ISBN 0-425-10428-1). Berkley Pub.
Second Defence of the Short View of the English Stage. Jeremy Collier. LC 76-170445. (English Stage Ser.: Vol. 34). lib. bdg. 61.00 (ISBN 0-8240-0617-8). Garland Pub.
Second Deluge. Garrett P. Serviss. LC 73-13266. (Classics of Science Fiction Ser.). (Illus.). 412p. 1973. 15.25 (ISBN 0-88355-120-9); pap. 10.00 (ISBN 0-88355-149-7). Hyperion Conn.
Second Deluge. Garrett P. Serviss. 1976. lib. bdg. 12.95x (ISBN 0-89968-172-7). Lightyear.
Second "Did I Ever Tell You...?". Iris Grender. (Did I Ever Tell You? Ser.). (Illus.). 64p. (gr. 1-3). 1987. 12.95 (ISBN 0-09-133970-7, Pub. by Century Hutchinson). David & Charles.
Second Diesel Spotter's Guide. Jerry A. Pinkepank. LC 66-22894. (Illus.). 459p. 1973. 12.75 (ISBN 0-89024-025-6); pap. 12.75 (ISBN 0-89024-026-4). Kalmbach.
Second Digest of Investigations in the Teaching of Science. Francis D. Curtis. LC 74-153694. pap. 111.50 (ISBN 0-317-42010-0, 2026001). Bks Demand UMI.
Second Dinosaur Action Set. Malcolm Whyte. (Illus.). 20p. (YA) (gr. 7-11). 1987. 4.95 (ISBN 0-8431-1951-9). Price Stern.
Second Duma: A Study of the Social-Democratic Party & the Russian Constitutional Experiment. 2nd ed. Alfred Levin. LC 66-13342. xii, 422p. 1966. 37.50 (ISBN 0-208-00539-0, Archon). Shoe String.
Second Earth. Patrick Woodroffe. (Illus.). 144p. (Orig.). 1988. pap. 15.95 (ISBN 1-85028-043-6, PTB UK). Avery Pub.
Second Empire & Its Downfall. facsimile ed. Napoleon, 3rd. Tr. by Herbert Wilson. LC 74-126266. (Select Bibliographies Reprint Ser). Repr. of 1925 ed. 16.00 (ISBN 0-8369-5464-5). Ayer Co Pubs.
Second Empire, Eighteen Fifty-Two to Eighteen Seventy: Art in France under Napoleon III. Philadelphia Museum of Art & Detroit Institute of Arts, Grand Palais, Paris. LC 78-60516. (Illus.). 464p. 1978. 29.95x (ISBN 0-8143-1630-1, Pub. by Phila Mus Art). Wayne St U Pr.
Second Empire Opera. T. J. Walsh. (History of Opera Ser.). (Illus.). 1981. 35.00 (ISBN 0-7145-3659-8). Riverrun NY.
Second Encore. Ed. by Alice Briley. (Illus.). 128p. 1988. pap. 6.95 (ISBN 0-910042-54-3). Allegheny.
Second Enlargement of the EEC: The Integration of Unequal Partners. Ed. by Dudley Seers & Constantine Vaitsos. LC 81-8750. 312p. 1982. 32.50 (ISBN 0-312-70830-0). St Martin.
Second Enlargement of the European Community: Adjustments Requirements & Challenges for Policy Reform. Juegen B. Donges et al. 263p. 1982. lib. bdg. 62.50x (Pub. by J C B Mohr BRD). Coronet Bks.
Second Epistle Peter & Epistle of Jude. M. Green. (Tyndale Bible Commentaries: Vol. 18). 1988. pap. 6.95. Eerdmans.
Second Epistle to the Corinthians. Charles K. Barrett. LC 73-18682. 366p. 1974. 19.95 (ISBN 0-06-060552-9, HarpR). Har-Row.
Second Epistle to the Corinthians see New Testament for Spiritual Reading.
Second Essays on Literature. facs. ed. Edward B. Shanks. LC 68-20334. (Essay Index Reprint Ser). 1937. 17.00 (ISBN 0-8369-0869-4). Ayer Co Pubs.
Second Essays on Literature. Edward B. Shanks. LC 72-195238. lib. bdg. 25.00 (ISBN 0-8414-8112-1). Folcroft.
Second European Glacoma Symposium Helsinki, May 1984. Ed. by E. L. Greve & C. Raitta. (Documenta Ophthalmica Prooceedings Ser.). 1985. lib. bdg. 69.50 (ISBN 90-6193-526-1, Pub. by Junk Pubs Netherlands). Kluwer Academic.
Second Ewings. John O'Hara. 1977. boxed 40.00 (ISBN 0-89723-012-4). Bruccoli.
Second Expert Consultation on Environmental Criteria for Registration of Pesticides: Rome, May 1981. (Plant Production & Protection Papers: No. 28). 64p. (Eng., Fr. & Span.). 1981. pap. 7.50 (ISBN 92-5-101131-1, F2258, FAO). UNIPUB.
Second Fatherland: The Life & Fortunes of a German Immigrant. Max A. Krueger. Ed. by Marilyn Sibley. LC 76-17975. (Centennial Ser. of the Association of Former Students: No. 4). (Illus.). 186p. 1976. 13.95 (ISBN 0-89096-017-8). Tex A&M Univ Pr.
Second Federalist: Congress Creates a Government. Ed. by Charles S. Hyneman & George W. Carey. LC 66-27380. (Orig.). 1966. pap. text ed. 9.95x (ISBN 0-89197-510-1). Irvington.
Second Federalist: Congress Creates a Government. Ed. by Charles S. Hyneman & George W. Carey. LC 74-119334. xviii, 326p. 1970. lib. bdg. 24.95x (ISBN 0-87249-173-0). U of SC Pr.
Second Fiber Optics & Communications Exposition: FOC '79, Chicago, Ill. 125.00 (ISBN 0-686-33021-8). Info Gatekeepers.
Second Fiddle: A Sizzle & Splat Mystery. Ronald Kidd. 160p. (YA) (gr. 7 up). 1988. 12.95 (ISBN 0-525-67252-4, 01258-370). Lodestar Bks.
Second Fifteen Years in Space. Ed. by S. Ferdman. (Science & Technology Ser.: Vol. 31). 1973. lib. bdg. 25.00x (ISBN 0-87703-064-2, Pub. by Am Astronaut). Univelt Inc.
Second Five-Year Annotated Index to Media Report to Women, 1977-1981. 48p. 1982. 5.00 (ISBN 0-930470-09-5). Womens Inst Free Press.
Second Flight of the Starfire. Edwin Mumford. 1972. 4.00 (ISBN 0-682-47462-2). Exposition-Phoenix.
Second Flowering: Works & Days of the Lost Generation. Malcolm Cowley. 1980. pap. 7.95 (ISBN 0-14-005498-7). Penguin.
Second Folio of Shakespeare. William Shakespeare. (Books of the Monarchs of England). 920p. 1987. Repr. of 1632 ed. 315.00 (ISBN 1-85297-011-1). Archival Facsimiles.
Second Forty Years. Edward J. Stieglitz. Ed. by Robert Kastenbaum. LC 78-22218. (Aging & Old Age Ser.). (Illus.). 1979. Repr. of 1946 ed. lib. bdg. 25.50x (ISBN 0-405-11831-7). Ayer Co Pubs.
Second Forum on International Family Medicine for the Americas, Spain, Portugal: Proceedings-August 14-17, 1984. Compiled by STFM. 347p. 1985. 5.00 (ISBN 0-942295-11-0). Soc Tchrs Fam Med.
Second Foundation. Isaac Asimov. (Foundation Ser.: Bk. 3). 1987. pap. 3.95 (ISBN 0-345-33629-1, Del Rey). Ballantine.
Second Front. D. Botting. Ed. by Time-Life Books Staff. (World War II). (Illus.). 1979. 14.95 (ISBN 0-8094-2498-3). Time-Life.
Second Front. Douglas Botting. LC 78-3405. (World War II Ser.). (Illus.). (gr. 7 up). 1978. lib. bdg. 22.60 (ISBN 0-8094-2499-1, Pub. by Time-Life). Silver.
Second Frutes. John Florio. LC 53-11448. 1977. Repr. of 1591 ed. 35.00x (ISBN 0-8201-1222-4). Schol Facsimiles.
Second Garfield Treasury. Jim Davis. 120p. 1983. pap. 8.95 (ISBN 0-345-33276-8). Ballantine.
Second Generation. Howard Fast. 1978. 10.95 (ISBN 0-395-26683-1). HM.
Second Generation. Howard M. Fast. 1987. pap. 4.50 (ISBN 0-440-17915-7). Dell.
Second Generation. Esther McCoy. LC 83-14898. (Illus.). 200p. 1984. 27.50 (ISBN 0-317-65616-3). Hennessey.
Second Generation. David C. Phillips. (Collected Works of David G. Phillips). 1988. Repr. of 1981 ed. lib. bdg. 59.00x. Am Biog Serv.
Second Generation. David G. Phillips. (American Author Ser.). 1981. Repr. lib. bdg. 29.00 (ISBN 0-686-71943-3). Scholarly.
Second-Generation Japanese Problem. Edward K. Strong. pap. 30.00 (ISBN 0-317-29833-X, 2051956). Bks Demand UMI.
Second-Generation Japanese Problem. Edward K. Strong, Jr. LC 73-129415. (American Immigration Collection, Ser. 2). 1970. Repr. of 1934 ed. 22.00 (ISBN 0-405-00569-5). Ayer Co Pubs.
Second Generation of Multivariate Analysis: Measurement & Evaluation, 2 Vols. Fornell. LC 82-11273. 444p. 1982. Vol. 1. 56.95 (ISBN 0-275-90792-9, C07921); Vol. 2. 54.00 (ISBN 0-275-90793-7, C07932); 91.50 set (ISBN 0-275-90794-5, C07940). Praeger.
Second Generation TMS20 User's Guide. Texas Instruments Inc. Staff. 1988. pap. 18.95 (ISBN 0-13-797374-8). Prentice Hall Pr.
Second Genesis. Donald Moffit. pap. 3.50 (ISBN 0-345-33804-9). Ballantine.
Second Great Awakening in Connecticut. Charles R. Keller. LC 68-26923. ix, 275p. 1968. Repr. of 1942 ed. 25.00 (ISBN 0-208-00662-1, Archon). Shoe String.
Second Greates Commandment see Nouveau Commandement.
Second Greatest Commandment see Segundo Grande Mandamento.
Second Greek Reader. G. Constantopoulos. (Illus.). 96p. 3.70 (ISBN 0-686-79627-6). Divry.
Second Growth. Dale Hobson. (Illus.). 36p. (Orig.). 1980. pap. 3.50 (ISBN 0-918092-09-4). Tamarack Edns.
Second Growth. Wallace Stegner. LC 85-8540. xii, 240p. 1985. 22.50x (ISBN 0-8032-4162-3); pap. 6.95 (ISBN 0-8032-9157-4). U of Nebr Pr.
Second Guesses. James Richardson. 66p. 1984. 17.00x (ISBN 0-8195-5107-4); pap. 8.95 (ISBN 0-8195-6100-2). Wesleyan U Pr.
Second Hand Coat. Ruth Stone. LC 86-46260. 128p. 1987. 14.95 (ISBN 0-87923-679-5); pap. 10.95 (ISBN 0-87923-680-9). Godine.
Second-Hand Dog: How to Turn Yours into a First-Rate Pet. Carol L. Benjamin. LC 88-748. (Illus.). 96p. 1988. pap. 4.95 (ISBN 0-87605-735-0). Howell Bk.
Second-Hand Knowledge: An Inquiry into Cognitive Authority. Patrick Wilson. LC 82-21069. (Contributions in Librarianship & Information Science Ser.: No. 44). vii, 211p. 1983. lib. bdg. 35.00 (ISBN 0-313-23763-8, WWK/). Greenwood.
Second Hand Life: Discussions with Bill Barber. Bill Barber. 144p. (Orig.). 1986. pap. 8.95 (ISBN 0-87418-025-2, 163). Coleman Pub.
Second-Hand Magic. Ruth Chew. 128p. (gr. 2-5). 1986. pap. 2.25 (ISBN 0-590-40118-1, Lucky Star). Scholastic Inc.
Second Handbook on Parent Education: Contemporary Perspectives. Ed. by Marvin J. Fine. (Educational Psychology Ser.). 651p. 1988. price not set (ISBN 0-12-256482-0). Acad Pr.
Second Handshake. Will Fowler. (Illus.). 1980. 12.50 (ISBN 0-8184-0287-3). Lyle Stuart.
Second Harmony. Barbara Bretton. (American Romance Ser.: No. 211). 245p. Date not set. pap. 2.50 (ISBN 0-317-63702-9). Harlequin Bks.
Second Harvest. Denis Rogers. Ed. by Owen Davis. LC 81-84333. 196p. (Orig.). 1981. 12.95 (ISBN 0-935400-07-9); pap. 7.95 (ISBN 0-935400-08-7). News & Observer.
Second Harvest: More Life Stories of the Twentieth Century. Ed. by Ann Davidson et al. 352p. (Orig.). 1988. pap. 8.00 (ISBN 0-945131-00-3). Terrace Pr.
Second Heaven. Judith Guest. LC 82-70124. 336p. 1982. 14.95 (ISBN 0-670-62830-1). Viking.
Second Heaven. Judith Guest. 384p. (YA) (gr. 7 up). pap. 3.95 (ISBN 0-451-12499-5, Sig). NAL.
Second Helpings of Cream & Bread. Janet L. Martin & Allen Todnem. Ed. by Eunice W. Pearson. (Illus., Orig.). 1986. pap. 6.95 (ISBN 0-9613437-1-0). Redbird Prods.
Second Herman Treasury. Jim Unger. LC 80-67423. 225p. 1980. pap. 7.95 (ISBN 0-8362-1155-3). Andrews & McMeel.
Second Hoeing. Hope W. Sykes. LC 82-8424. xviii, 309p. 1982. 26.50x (ISBN 0-8032-4136-4); pap. 7.50 (ISBN 0-8032-9129-9, BB 806, Bison). U of Nebr Pr.
Second Home Handbook: Everything You Need to Know When You Buy, Build, Rent, or Own a Second Home. Beatrice O. Freeman. LC 86-40101. (Illus.). 288p. 1987. pap. 12.95 (ISBN 0-394-74768-2, Pub. by Villard Bks). Random.
Second Homes: Curse or Blessing. Ed. by J. T. Coppock. 1977. 31.00 (ISBN 0-08-021371-5); pap. 11.25 (ISBN 0-08-021370-7). Pergamon.
Second Hulbert Financial Digest Almanac. Mark J. Hulbert. 400p. (Orig.). 1988. pap. text ed. 39.95 (ISBN 0-9620125-0-5). Minerva Bks.
Second Hundred Years of Hancock, New Hampshire. Ed. by Hancock History Committee. LC 79-14026. (Illus.). 1979. 15.00x (ISBN 0-914016-61-X). Phoenix Pub.
Second Hundred Years War, Sixteen Eighty-Nine to Eighteen Fifteen. Arthur H. Buffinton. LC 75-14080. 114p. 1975. Repr. of 1929 ed. lib. bdg. 35.00x (ISBN 0-8371-8204-2, BUSYW). Greenwood.
Second Hunting Book of Wolfgang Birkner. Commentary by Kurt Lindner. LC 77-98938. (Illus.). 1976. ltd. ed. (250 copies) 175.00 (ISBN 0-87691-000-2). Arma Pr.
Second IEEE Conference on Computer Workstations: Proceedings. 188p. 1988. 50.00 (ISBN 0-8186-0810-2, EZ810). IEEE Comp Soc.
Second Impressions (Butler, Stevenson, Wilde, Pater, Henry James, Gissing, Yeats, Browning) T. Earle Welby. 1973. lib. bdg. 27.00 (ISBN 0-8414-9594-7). Folcroft.
Second India Studies: Food. V. M. Rao. 1975. text ed. 5.50x (ISBN 0-333-90116-9). South Asia Bks.
Second India Studies: Overview. H. Ezekiel. 1978. 4.50x (ISBN 0-8364-0251-0). South Asia Bks.
Second India Studies: Services. Hannan Ezekiel & Madhoo Pavaskar. 1976. 4.50x (ISBN 0-333-90155-X). South Asia Bks.
Second Indochina War. William S. Jurley. 272p. 1987. pap. 4.95 (ISBN 0-451-62546-3, Ment). NAL.
Second Indochina War: A Short Political & Military History, 1954-1975. William S. Turley. 176p. 1986. 27.50x (ISBN 0-8133-0308-7); pap. write for info. Westview.
Second Industrial Divide: Possibilities for Prosperity. Michael J. Piore & Charles F. Sabel. LC 83-46080. 355p. 1984. 21.95 (ISBN 0-465-07562-2). Basic.
Second Industrial Divide: Possibilities for Prosperity. Michael J. Piore & Charles F. Sabel. LC 83-46080. 368p. 1986. pap. 9.95 (ISBN 0-465-07563-0, PL 5170). Basic.
Second Intellectual List of Leaders Year Book. 54p. irregular 35.00 (ISBN 0-318-13349-0, 1790900895). Arcane Order.

Second International Aphasia Rehabilitation Congress: Proceedings of the Conference, Goteborg, Sweden, June 1986. Ed. by Chris Code & Dave J. Muller. (Aphasiology Special Issue Ser.: Vol. 1, No. 3, May-June 1987). 116p. 1987. pap. 22.00x (ISBN 0-85066-913-8). Taylor & Francis.
Second International Conference on Austempered Duchle Iron. Sharon Schaefers. 428p. 1986. 60.00 (ISBN 0-317-67962-7). ASME Gear Res.
Second International Conference on Architectural Support for Programming Languages & Operating Systems (ASPLOS II) Proceedings. 306p. 1987. 56.00 (ISBN 0-8186-0805-6, EZ805). IEEE Comp Soc.
Second International Conference on Shot. Peening. 1985. 60.00 (ISBN 0-89883-735-9, P 171). Soc Auto Engineers.
Second International Congress on Advances in Non-Impact Printing Technologies: Advance Printing of Paper Summaries. International Congress on Advances in Non-Impact Printing Technology (2nd: 1984: Arlington, VA) pap. 77.50 (ISBN 0-317-29115-7, 2025037). Bks Demand UMI.
Second International Congress on Organ Procurement. Luis Toledo-Pereyra. 256p. 1986. 54.75 (ISBN 0-8089-1822-2, 795613). Grune.
Second International Exhibition of Holography. Tung H. Jeong. LC 85-80923. (Illus.). 24p. 1985. pap. text ed. 12.00 (ISBN 0-910535-03-5). Lake Forest.
Second International Round Table Conference on Historical Lexicography: Proceedings. Ed. by W. Pynenburg & F. De Tollenaere. viii, 353p. 1980. pap. write for info. (ISBN 90-70176-21-1). Foris Pubns.
Second International Seminar on the Transformation of the World: Report of Proceedings, Madrid, Spain, September 1980. (Unup Ser.). 75p. 1982. pap. 13.50 (ISBN 92-808-0383-2, TUNU191, UNU). UNIPUB.
Second International Symposium on Information Theory. B. Petrov & F. Csaki. 457p. 1973. 89.00x (ISBN 0-569-08075-4, Pub. by Collets (UK)). State Mutual Bk.
Second International Symposium on Metallurgical Slags & Fluxes. Ed. by H. A. Fine & D. R. Gaskell. LC 84-62011. 1984. 72.00 (ISBN 0-89520-483-5). Metal Soc.
Second Irish Christmas Book. John Killen. LC 86-17620. (Illus.). 1986. pap. 15.95 (ISBN 0-85640-371-7, Pub. by Blackstaff Ireland). Irish Bks Media.
Second Jeopardy. Roger Ormerod. (Crime Club Ser.). 1989. 12.95 (ISBN 0-385-24613-7). Doubleday.
Second Jewish Book of Why. A. J. Kolatch. LC 84-21477. 432p. 1985. 13.95 (ISBN 0-8246-0305-2). Jonathan David.
Second Jewish Catalog: Sources & Resources. Ed. by Michael Strassfeld & Sharon Strassfeld. LC 73-11759. (Illus.). 464p. 1976. 12.95 (ISBN 0-8276-0084-4, 391). JPS Phila.
Second Jewish Trivia & Information Book. Ian Shapolsky. 400p. 1986. pap. 6.95 (ISBN 0-933503-45-8). Shapolsky Pubs.
Second Journey. Gerald O'Collins. LC 77-99303. 96p. 1978. pap. 3.95 (ISBN 0-8091-2209-X). Paulist Pr.
Second Jungle Book. Rudyard Kipling. 19.95 (ISBN 0-8488-0092-3, Pub. by Amereon Hse). Amereon Ltd.
Second Jungle Book. Rudyard Kipling. (gr. 5 up). Date not set. pap. 2.25 (ISBN 0-317-62282-X, Puffin Bks). Penguin.
Second Jungle Book. Rudyard Kipling. Ed. by Wallace Robson. (World's Classics Ser.). 320p. 1987. pap. 4.95 (ISBN 0-19-281655-1). Oxford U Pr.
Second Jungle Book see Jungle Book.
Second Kids' World Almanac of Records & Facts. Margo McLoone-Basta & Alice Siegel. Ed. by The World Almanac Staff. 288p. (gr. 3-9). 1987. 11.95 (ISBN 0-345-34979-2); pap. 6.95 (ISBN 0-345-34883-4). Pharos Bks NY.
Second Kings. G. H. Jones. (New Century Bible Commentary Ser.). 352p. 1984. pap. 9.95 (ISBN 0-8028-0040-8). Eerdmans.
Second Kings, Vol. 13, WBC. T. R. Hobbs. 380p. 1985. 22.95 (ISBN 0-8499-0212-6, 0212-6). Word Bks.
Second Kings with Chronicles. rev. ed. Ed. by Irving L. Jensen. (Bible Self-Study Ser.). (Illus., Orig.). 1968. pap. 3.50 (ISBN 0-8024-1012-X). Moody.
Second Lady. Irving Wallace. 352p. 1981. pap. 4.95 (ISBN 0-451-13827-9, Sig). NAL.
Second Lady Cameron. Frieda Thomsen. 1977. pap. 1.50 (ISBN 0-505-51204-1, Pub. by Tower Bks). Leisure NY.
Second Language Acquisition. Wolfgang Klein. (Cambridge Textbooks in Linguistics Ser.). 200p. 1986. 37.50 (ISBN 0-521-26879-6); pap. 13.95 (ISBN 0-521-31702-9). Cambridge U Pr.
Second Language Acquisition: A Book of Readings. Evelyn Hatch. 1978. pap. 19.95 (ISBN 0-88377-086-5). Newbury Hse.
Second Language Acquisition by Adult Immigrants: A Field Manual. Ed. by Clive Perdue. 1984. pap. text ed. 18.95 (ISBN 0-88377-281-7). Newbury Hse.
Second Language Acquisition in Childhood: Preschool Children, 2 vols, Vol.1. 2nd ed. Barry McLaughlin. (Child Psychology Ser.). 256p. 1984. text ed. 24.95 (ISBN 0-89859-378-6); pap. text ed. 30.00 set (ISBN 0-8058-0097-2); pap. text ed. 19.95. L Erlbaum Assocs.
Second Language Acquisition in Childhood: School Age Children, Vol. 2. 2nd ed. Barry McLaughlin. 304p. 1987. pap. text ed. 19.95 (ISBN 0-8058-0096-4); pap. 30.00set (ISBN 0-317-59894-5). L Erlbaum Assocs.
Second Language Acquisition in Childhood: School-Age Children, Vol. 2. Ed. by Barry McLaughlin. (Child Psychology Ser.). 304p. 1985. 29.95 (ISBN 0-89859-565-7); Set 42.50 (ISBN 0-89859-822-2). L Erlbaum Assocs.
Second Language Acquisition Research: Issues & Implications. Ed. by William C. Ritchie. (Perspectives in Neurolinguistics & Psycholinguistics Ser.). 1978. 29.95 (ISBN 0-12-589550-X). Acad Pr.
Second Language Classroom: Directions for the 1980's. Ed. by James E. Alatis et al. Howard B. Altman & Penelope M. Alatis. (Illus.). 1981. pap. text ed. 9.95x (ISBN 0-19-502929-1). Oxford U Pr.
Second Language Classrooms: Research on Teaching & Learning. Craig Chaudron. (Cambridge Applied Linguistics Ser.). (Illus.). 224p. 1988. 29.95 (ISBN 0-521-32775-X); pap. 11.95 (ISBN 0-521-33980-4). Cambridge U Pr.
Second Language Discourse: A Textbook of Current Research. Jonathan Fine. Ed. by Roy O. Freedle. LC 87-19702. (Advances in Discourse Processes Ser.). 208p. 1988. text ed. 34.50 (ISBN 0-89391-413-4). Ablex Pub.
Second Language Learning. Ed. by Frank M. Grittner. LC 79-91182. (National Society for the Study of Education Ser.). 242p. 1980. lib. bdg. 12.00x (ISBN 0-226-60129-3). U of Chicago Pr.
Second Language Learning: A Review of Related Studies. Suzanne Izzo. LC 81-82494. 84p. (Orig.). 1981. pap. 6.00 (ISBN 0-89763-058-0). Natl Clearinghse Bilingual Ed.
Second Language Learning among Young Children: A Bibliography of Research. Emma G. Stupp & Jennifer Gage. 71p. 1981. 7.40 (ISBN 0-317-15109-6). Natl Clearinghse Bilingual Ed.
Second Language Learning: Contrastive Analysis, Error Analysis & Related Aspects. Betty W. Robinett & Jacqueline Schachter. 432p. 1983. text ed. 34.50x (ISBN 0-472-10027-0); pap. text ed. 14.95x (ISBN 0-472-08033-4). U of Mich Pr.
Second Language Learning for American Indians: A Topical Bibliography. Douglas Knox et al. 43p. 1982. 5.65 (ISBN 0-317-15113-4). Natl Clearinghse Bilingual Ed.
Second Language, Poems. Lisel Mueller. LC 86-7246. 72p. 1986. text ed. 14.95 o. p. (ISBN 0-8071-1336-0); pap. 7.95 (ISBN 0-8071-1337-9). La State U Pr.
Second Languages: A Cross-Linguistic Perspective. Ed. by Roger W. Andersen. 440p. 1984. pap. text ed. 25.95. Newbury Hse.
Second Latin. Cora C. Scanlon & Charles L. Scanlon. LC 48-746. 1976. pap. 9.00 (ISBN 0-89555-003-2). TAN Bks Pubs.
Second Law. P. W. Atkins. LC 84-5377. 230p. 1984. 32.95 (ISBN 0-7167-5004-X). W H Freeman.
Second Law: An Introduction to Classical & Statistical Thermodynamics. Henry A. Bent. 1965. 18.95x (ISBN 0-19-500829-4). Oxford U Pr.
Second Law of Thermodynamics. Ed. by Joseph Kestin. (Benchmark Papers on Energy: Vol. 5). 1976. 81.00 (ISBN 0-12-786839-9). Acad Pr.
Second Letter of Paul to the Corinthians. James Thompson. 1970. 12.95 (ISBN 0-915547-28-7). Abilene Christ U.
Second Letter to the Corinthians. Rudolf Bultmann. Tr. by Roy A. Harrisville. LC 83-70517. 272p. 1985. 19.95 (ISBN 0-8066-2023-4, 10-5633). Augsburg.
Second Level see Competency Tests for Basic Reading Skills.
Second-Level Basic Electronics. U. S. Navy (Bureau of Naval Personnel) Orig. Title: Basic Electronics Vol. 2. (Illus.). 352p. 1971. pap. text ed. 6.50 (ISBN 0-486-22841-X). Dover.
Second Life. Stephanie Cook. 384p. 1982. pap. 3.95 (ISBN 0-345-30675-9). Ballantine.
Second Life of Art: Selected Essays. Eugenio Montale. Ed. by Jonathan Galassi. LC 81-9861. 375p. 1982. 17.50 (ISBN 0-912946-84-9). Ecco Pr.
Second Life of Art: Selected Essays. Eugenio Montale. Ed. by Jonathan Galassi. LC 81-9861. 350p. 1985. pap. 9.50 (ISBN 0-912946-85-7). Ecco Pr.
Second Light: Selected Writings of Vilhelm Ekelund. Vilhelm Ekelund. Tr. by Lennart Bruce. LC 85-72987. 256p. 1986. 22.50 (ISBN 0-86547-218-1). N Point Pr.
Second Livre. Ed. by Albert Seay. (Transcriptions Ser.: No. 3). ii, 64p. 1980. pap. 4.00 (ISBN 0-933894-05-8, Pub. by Attaingnant). Colo Coll Music.
Second Livre des Amours. Pierre de Ronsard. 227p. 1951. 9.95 (ISBN 0-686-55331-4). French & Eur.
Second livre des Amours de Pierre de Ronsard see Monuments de la musique francaise au temps de la Renaissance.
Second Logo Book: Advanced Techniques in Logo. Dan Weston. (Illus.). 224p. 1985. pap. 12.95 (ISBN 0-673-18079-4). Scott F.
Second Long Walk: The Navajo-Hopi Land Dispute. Jerry Kammer. LC 80-52273. (Illus.). 258p. 1982. pap. 11.95 (ISBN 0-8263-0642-X). U of NM Pr.
Second Look. Gerhard E. Frost. (Orig.). 1984. pap. 6.95 (ISBN 0-86683-935-6, 8513, HarpR). Har-Row.
Second Look at Agathis. M. R. Bowmen & T. C. Whitmore. 1980. 30.00x (ISBN 0-85074-053-3, Pub. by For Lib Comm England). State Mutual Bk.
Second Look at America. Emilio Aguinaldo & Vicente A. Pacis. 9.95 (ISBN 0-8315-0051-4). Speller.
Second Look at Harmony. Tibor Serly. 8.95 (ISBN 0-317-40588-8, Pub. by Modus Assoc). Tritone Music.
Second Look at White Ironstone. Jean Wetherbee. LC 85-51342. 192p. 1985. 14.95 (ISBN 0-87069-444-8); price guide 2.50 (ISBN 0-87069-448-0). Wallace-Homestead.
Second Look: The Nonprofit Arts & Cultural Industry of New York State 1975-76. National Research Center of the Arts, Inc. 308p. 1978. pap. 8.50x (ISBN 0-89062-072-5, Pub. by NY Found Arts). Pub Ctr Cult Res.
Second Look: The Reconstruction of Personal History in Psychiatry & Psychoanalysis. Samuel Novey. Ed. by Chicago Institute for Psychoanalysis Staff The & Bertram D. Lewin. LC 85-10884. (Classics in Psychoanalysis Monograph: Monograph 3). xiv, 162p. 1986. Repr. of 1968 ed. text ed. 25.00x (ISBN 0-8236-6022-2, 06022). Intl Univs Pr.
Second Love. Anne Warner. LC 63-8068. 172p. (gr. 7-10). 1963. Westminster John Knox.
Second Loves: A Guide for Women Involved with Divorced Men. Gerald A. Silver & Myrna Silver. 192p. 1984. 35.00 (ISBN 0-275-91748-7, C1748). Praeger.
Second Loves: A Guide for Women Involved with Divorced Men. Gerald A. Silver & Myrna Silver. 208p. 1986. pap. 3.95 (ISBN 0-425-09085-X). Berkley Pub.
Second Maiden's Tragedy. Ed. by W. W. Greg. LC 82-45751. (Malone Society Reprint Ser.: No. 17). 1909. 40.00 (ISBN 0-404-63017-0). AMS Pr.
Second Maiden's Tragedy. Ed. by David Hoeniger et al. LC 77-4604. (Revels Plays Ser.). 1978. text ed. 20.00x (ISBN 0-8018-2011-1). Johns Hopkins.
Second Man. Edward Grierson. LC 80-8411. 320p. 1981. pap. 2.25 (ISBN 0-06-080528-5, P 528, PL). Har-Row.
Second Man. Edward Grierson. Ed. by J. Barzun & W. H. Taylor. LC 81-47400. (Crime Fiction 1950-1975 Ser.). 308p. 1982. lib. bdg. 18.00 (ISBN 0-8240-4969-1). Garland Pub.
Second Man. Mae Urbanek. 182p. 3.50x (ISBN 0-940514-06-0). Urbanek.
Second Man, & Other Poems. Louis O. Coxe. LC 55-9369. pap. 20.00 (ISBN 0-317-27945-9, 2055851). Bks Demand UMI.
Second Man in Us. Maria Roeschl & Ernst Lehrs. pap. cancelled (ISBN 0-904822-07-9, Pub by Henry Goulden, Ltd.). St George Bk Serv.
Second Man: Monster, Myth, or Minister. Blaine Hughes. 20p. 1976. pap. text ed. 0.95 (ISBN 0-89265-110-5). Randall Hse.
Second Man: The Changing Role of the Vice Presidency. Michael Dorman. LC 67-19765. (gr. 7 up). 1968. pap. 6.95 (ISBN 0-440-07703-6). Delacorte.
Second Manual for the Calligraphic Arts. Ed. by M. Jane Van Milligan. (Illus.). 156p. 1987. pap. 9.95 (ISBN 0-9617137-1-2). Ctr Callig KS.
Second Marriage. Frederick Barthelme. 204p. 1984. 15.95 (ISBN 0-671-47441-3). S&S.
Second Marriage. Frederick Barthelme. (Contemporary American Fiction Ser.). 224p. 1985. pap. 6.95 (ISBN 0-14-008274-3). Penguin.
Second Marriage Guidebook. George W. Knight. 96p. (Orig.). 1984. pap. 7.95 (ISBN 0-939298-23-6, 236). J M Prods.
Second Marriage: Make it Happy! Make it Last! Richard B. Stuart & Barbara Jacobson. 1985. 15.95 (ISBN 0-393-01910-1). Norton.
Second Marxian Invasion: The Dialectical Fables of Arkady & Boris Strugatsky. Stephen W. Potts. LC 84-309. (Milford Series: Popular Writers of Today: Vol. 50). 96p. (Orig.). Date not set. lib. bdg. 16.95x (ISBN 0-89370-179-3); pap. 7.95x (ISBN 0-89370-279-X). Borgo Pr.
Second Math Helper. Evelyn Farmer. (Classroom Pairing: Math Tutorial Program Ser.). 64p. (gr. k-1). 1975. 2.95 (ISBN 0-87594-141-9). Book-Lab.
Second Medical Revolution: From Biomedicine to Infomedicine. Laurence Foss & Kenneth Rothenberg. LC 86-29652. (New Science Library). (Illus.). 335p. 1987. 29.95 (ISBN 0-87773-394-5). Shambhala Pubns.
Second Medical Revolution: From Biomedicine to Info medicine. Laurence Foss & Kenneth Rothenberg. LC 86-29652. (New Science Library). (Illus.). 352p. (Orig.). 1988. pap. 15.95 (ISBN 0-87773-459-3). Shambhala Pubns.
Second Mercury Story Book. facsimile ed. London Mercury. LC 79-37553. (Short Story Index Reprint Ser.). Repr. of 1931 ed. 23.50 (ISBN 0-8369-4112-8). Ayer Co Pubs.
Second Message of Islam. Mahmoud M. Taha. Tr. by Abdullahi Ahmid An Na'im from Arabic. (Contemporary Issues in the Middle East Ser.). 192p. 1987. text ed. 29.95x (ISBN 0-8156-2407-7). Syracuse U Pr.
Second Midlife Crisis Relating to Aging Parents - Visions of Our Future. James S. Powers et al. 84p. 1988. 10.00 (ISBN 0-533-07442-8). Vantage.
Second Midnight. Andrew Taylor. 368p. 1987. 16.95 (ISBN 0-396-09193-8). Dodd.
Second Mile. Roger Prescott. 1985. 4.95 (ISBN 0-89536-739-4, 5823). CSS of Ohio.
Second Mile. 10th ed. Sarah H. Terry. 96p. 1982. pap. 4.00 (ISBN 0-88053-322-6, S-305). Macoy Pub.
Second Mile: Contemporary Approaches in Counseling Young Women. Ed. by Sue Davidson. 185p. (Orig.). 1983. pap. 8.00 (ISBN 0-9608696-2-X). New Dir Young Women.
Second-Mile People. Isobel Kuhn. 1982. pap. 3.50 (ISBN 0-85363-145-X). OMF Bks.
Second Mrs. Giaconda. E. L. Konigsburg. LC 75-6946. (Illus.). (gr. 5-9). 1978. pap. 1.95 (ISBN 0-689-70450-X, Aladdin). Macmillan.
Second Mrs. Hardy. Robert Gittings & Jo Manton. LC 79-63567. (Illus.). 1979. 14.95x (ISBN 0-295-95668-2). U of Wash Pr.
Second National Ground Water Quality Symposium: Proceedings. Date not set. 43.75 (ISBN 0-318-23003-8). Natl Water Well.
Second Navy Reader. facs. ed. Ed. by William H. Fetridge. LC 71-142627. (Essay Index Reprint Ser). 1944. 26.50 (ISBN 0-8369-2156-9). Ayer Co Pubs.
Second Nine Months. Judith M. Gansberg & Arthur M. Mostel. 1985. pap. 3.95 (ISBN 0-671-54154-4). PB.
Second Novel. Norbert Blei. LC 77-91291. (Illus.). 245p. 1978. pap. 12.50 (ISBN 0-913204-09-9). December Pr.
Second Nuclear Era: A New Start for Nuclear Power. Alvin M. Weinberg et al. LC 85-26613. 460p. 1985. 44.95 (ISBN 0-275-90183-1, C0183). Praeger.
Second Official I Hate Cats Book. Skip Morrow. LC 81-47461. (Illus.). 64p. 1981. pap. 3.95 (ISBN 0-03-059359-X, Owl Bks). H Holt & Co.
Second Oldest Profession. Jess Carr. LC 70-172277. 252p. 1978. 12.95 (ISBN 0-89227-031-4). Commonwealth Pr.
Second Oldest Profession, New York 1931. Ben L. Reitman. Ed. by David J. Rothman & Sheila M. Rothman. (Women & Children First Ser.). 266p. 1986. 35.00 (ISBN 0-8240-7671-0). Garland Pub.
Second Oldest Profession: Spies & Spying in the Twentieth Century. Philip Knightley. (Illus.). 436p. 1987. 19.95 (ISBN 0-393-02386-9). Norton.
Second Oldest Profession: Spies & Spying in the Twentieth Century. Phillip Knightley. 1988. pap. 7.95 (ISBN 0-14-010655-3). Penguin.
Second Omni Book of Science Fiction. Ed. by Ellen Datlow. 1984. pap. 3.95 (ISBN 0-8217-1320-5). Zebra.
Second Opinion Elective Surgery. Eugene McCarthy & Madelon Finkel. LC 81-3471. 193p. 1981. 26.95 (ISBN 0-86569-079-0). Auburn Hse.
Second Opinion Handbook: A Guide for Medical Self Defense. Eugene McCarthy et al. (Illus.). 96p. (Orig.). 1987. pap. 5.95 (ISBN 0-941130-25-8). N Lyons Bks.
Second Opinion: Your Comprehensive Guide to Alternative Treatments. Isadore Rosenfeld. LC 87-47787. 432p. 1988. pap. 10.95 (ISBN 0-553-34478-1). Bantam.
Second Order Linear Differential Equations in Banach Spaces. H. O. Fattorini. (Mathematical Studies: Vol. 108). 1985. 60.75 (ISBN 0-444-87698-7, North-Holland). Elsevier.
Second Order Systems of Partial Differential Equations in the Plane. Hua L. Keng. 312p. 1986. pap. 37.95 (ISBN 0-470-20497-4, Co-Pub. with Longman). Wiley.
Second Pacific Chemical Engineering Congress (PAChEC '77) Proceedings, Vols. 1 & 2. LC 77-82322. 1420p. 1977. pap. 50.00 (ISBN 0-8169-0047-7, P-17). Am Inst Chem Eng.
Second Part of the Anatomie of Abuses. Philip Stubbes. LC 71-170409. (English Stage Ser.: Vol. 8). lib. bdg. 62.00 (ISBN 0-8240-0591-0). Garland Pub.
Second Part of the Booke of Battailes, Fought in Our Age. John Polemon. LC 78-38219. (English Experience Ser.: No. 483). 196p. 1972. Repr. of 1587 ed. 13.00 (ISBN 90-221-0483-4). Walter J Johnson.
Second Part of the Institute of the Laws of England, 2 vols. Edwardo Coke. Ed. by Bernard D. Reams, Jr. (Historical Writing in Law & Jurisprudence. Second Ser.: No. 5B). 1986. Repr. of 1797 ed. Set. 170.00 (ISBN 0-89941-520-2). Vol. I, Third Part. Vol. II, Fourth Part. W S Hein.
Second Part of the Secretes of Maister Alexis of Piemont. Piemontese Alessio. Tr. by W. Ward. LC 77-6843. (English Experience Ser.: No. 839). 1977. Repr. of 1563 ed. lib. bdg. 17.50 (ISBN 90-221-0839-2). Walter J Johnson.
Second Parting. Oral Bullard. 80p. (Orig.). 1980. pap. 4.95 (ISBN 0-918688-04-3). Touchstone Oregon.
Second Partition of Poland. Robert H. Lord. LC 73-101268. 1970. Repr. 38.45 (ISBN 0-404-04009-8). AMS Pr.

Second Passive Solar Catalog. David A. Bainbridge. (Illus.). 110p. (Orig.). 1981. pap. 12.50 (ISBN 0-933490-02-X). Passive Solar.

Second Paycheck: An Analysis of the Employment & Earnings of Wives Compared with Unmarried Women & Men. Alice Nakamura & Masao Nakamura. 1985. 45.50 (ISBN 0-12-513820-2). Acad Pr.

Second Person. Lehman Strauss. 1951. 7.95 (ISBN 0-87213-826-7). Loizeaux.

Second Person Rural. Noel Perrin. LC 80-66193. (Illus.). 176p. 1980. 13.95 (ISBN 0-87923-341-9). Godine.

Second Person Rural: More Essays of a Sometime Farmer. Noel Perrin. 166p. 1981. pap. 6.95 (ISBN 0-14-005920-2). Penguin.

Second Person Singular, & Other Essays. Alice Meynell. 1979. Repr. of 1922 ed. lib. bdg. 20.00 (ISBN 0-8495-3760-6). Arden Lib.

Second Person Singular, & Other Essays. facs. ed. Alice C. Meynell. LC 68-55851. (Essay Index Reprint Ser.). 1922. 13.75 (ISBN 0-8369-0706-X). Ayer Co Pubs.

Second Peter. Thomas A. Bolten. 177p. 1988. 12.95 (ISBN 0-533-07576-9). Vantage.

Second Peter. Jimmy Lebos. 286p. 1988. 16.95 (ISBN 0-533-07465-7). Vantage.

Second Peter. D. Martyn Lloyd-Jones. 18.95 (ISBN 0-85151-379-4). Banner of Truth.

Second Peters Black & Blue Guide to Current Literary Journals. Robert Peters. LC 84-19998. (Illus.). 120p. (Orig.). 1985. pap. 5.00 (ISBN 0-916156-76-1). Cherry Valley.

Second Piatigorsky Cup. Ed. by Isaac Kashdan. LC 77-84070. (Illus.). 1978. pap. 3.95 (ISBN 0-486-23572-6). Dover.

Second Plantation Village Cookbook. Compiled by Friends of Waipahu Cultural Garden Park. (Illus.). 200p. (Orig.). 1987. pap. 8.00x (ISBN 0-930117-04-2). Wonder View Pr.

Second Pond. Ray Smith. (Illus.). 1979. pap. 3.00 (ISBN 0-686-02398-6). Kirk Pr.

Second Quantization Based Methods in Quantum Chemistry. Ed. by Poul Jorgensen & John P. Simons. LC 81-12880. 1981. 47.50 (ISBN 0-12-390220-7). Acad Pr.

Second Quiltmaker's Handbook. Michael James. (Creative Handcrafts Ser.). 208p. 1981. (Spec); pap. 12.95 (ISBN 0-13-797787-5). P-H.

Second Raffi Songbook. (Raffi Bks.). 1987. 15.95 (ISBN 0-517-56637-0). Crown.

Second Rainbow Book of Adventures. Ed. by Charles L. Springer. (Illus.). 333p. (Orig.). 1985. pap. 13.95 (ISBN 0-932471-03-X). Falsoft.

Second Rainbow Book of Simulations. Ed. by Tamara Dunn. (Illus.). 200p. (Orig.). 1986. pap. 9.95 (ISBN 0-932471-06-4). Falsoft.

Second Ralliement: The Rapprochement Between Church & State in France in the Twentieh Century. Harry W. Paul. LC 67-14435. pap. 61.50 (2029503). Bks Demand UMI.

Second Reader for Deaf Children. National Association for Teaching of the Deaf. 59.95 (ISBN 0-8490-1009-8). Gordon Pr.

Second Reading Helper. rev. ed. Gloria Orlick. (Classroom Pairing: Reading Tutorial Program Ser.). (Illus., Orig., Prog. Bk.). (gr. 1). 1983. pap. 3.45 (ISBN 0-87594-003-X). Book-Lab.

Second Reference Catalogue of Bright Galaxies. Gerald H. De Vaucouleurs & Antoinette De Vaucouleurs. LC 75-44009. (Texas University Monographs in Astronomy: No. 2). pap. 101.00 (ISBN 0-317-08632-4, 2021153). Bks Demand UMI.

Second Regional Groundnut Workshop for Southern Africa: Proceedings. 159p. (Orig.). 1987. pap. text ed. 24.60 (ISBN 92-9066-125-9, Pub. by ICRISAT India). Agribookstore.

Second Regional Plan: A Draft for Discussion. (Illus.). 103p. (B). 1968. 3.00 (ISBN 0-318-16384-5, 110); members 2.00 (ISBN 0-318-16385-3). Regional Plan Assn.

Second Regional Symposium on Endogenous Intellectual Creativity: Culture & Intellectual Creativity in Latin America. (Unup Ser.: No. 361). 43p. 1982. pap. 8.50 (ISBN 92-808-0361-1, TUNU190, UNU). UNIPUB.

Second Republic. Theodore Prochazka, Sr. (East European Monograph: No. 90). 231p. 1981. 24.00x (ISBN 0-914710-84-2). East Eur Quarterly.

Second Republic & Napoleon Third. Rene Arnaud. LC 70-158271. Repr. of 1930 ed. 45.00 (ISBN 0-404-50799-9). AMS Pr.

Second Review & Bibliography on Aspects of Fluid Sealing. 1975. text ed. 43.00x (ISBN 0-900983-49-3, Dist. by Air Science Co.). BHRA Fluid.

Second Ring of Power. Carlos Castaneda. (gr. 10-12). 1981. pap. 4.95 (ISBN 0-671-54995-2). PB.

Second Rising. Ed. by Stacy Tuthill. LC 79-64998. (SCOP Ser.: No. IV). (Illus.). 1979. pap. 5.00 (ISBN 0-930526-03-1). SCOP Pubns.

Second Round. Lenrie Peters. (African Writers Ser.). 1966. pap. text ed. 6.00 (ISBN 0-435-90022-6). Heinemann Ed.

Second Rumpole Omnibus. John Mortimer. 672p. 1988. pap. 9.95 (ISBN 0-14-008958-6). Penguin.

Second Rumpole Omnibus: Rumpole & the Golden Thread, Rumpole for the Defence, & Rumpole's Last Case. John Mortimer. 672p. 1987. 18.95 (ISBN 0-670-81125-4). Viking.

Second St. Poems. Beverly Silva. LC 83-70276. 85p. 1983. pap. 7.00x (ISBN 0-916950-39-5). Biling Rev-Pr.

Second Scientific American Book of Mathematical Puzzles & Diversions. Martin Gardner. LC 87-10760. (Illus.). 256p. 1987. pap. 10.95 (ISBN 0-226-28253-8). U of Chicago Pr.

Second Scientific American Book of Mathematical Puzzles & Diversions. Ed. by Martin Gardner. 1965. pap. 6.95 (ISBN 0-671-63653-7, Fireside). S&S.

Second Scroll. A. M. Klein. LC 85-61442. 1985. pap. 8.95 (ISBN 0-910395-15-2). Marlboro Pr.

Second Season. Therese Alderton. 416p. 1988. pap. 3.95 (ISBN 0-8217-2431-2). Zebra.

Second Season. Pauline D. Marrs. 1979. pap. 1.75 (ISBN 0-449-50012-8, Coventry). Fawcett.

Second Season. Joseph Monninger. LC 87-12542. 320p. 1987. 19.95 (ISBN 0-689-11936-4). Atheneum.

Second Season: Lent, Easter, Ascension. Wayne Saffen. LC 72-87064. pap. 24.00 (2026827). Bks Demand UMI.

Second Season: Virginia's Rise to the Final Four. Roland Lazenby. 1984. pap. 9.95 (ISBN 0-913767-02-6). Full Court VA.

Second Seasonal Political Palate. Bloodroot Collective Staff. LC 84-52064. 200p. 1984. pap. 10.95 (ISBN 0-9605210-2-X). Sanguinaria.

Second Seasons. Coburn Britton. LC 82-48443. (Illus.). 80p. (Orig.). 1982. pap. 6.95 (ISBN 0-8180-1584-5). Horizon.

Second Seed. M. D. Polan. 1988. pap. 3.95 (ISBN 0-312-91017-7). St Martin.

Second Seed. Mary L. Polan. 288p. 1987. 17.95 (ISBN 0-684-18735-3). Scribner.

Second Selected Poems. Alfredo O. Cuenca, Jr. 84p. (Orig.). 1982. pap. 6.00x (ISBN 0-686-37567-X, Pub. by New Day Philippines). Cellar.

Second Selections from Modern Poets. Ed. by John Squire. 1978. Repr. of 1948 ed. lib. bdg. 12.50 (ISBN 0-8492-2577-9). R West.

Second Self: Computers & the Human Spirit. Sherry Turkle. 352p. 1984. 17.95 (ISBN 0-671-46848-0). S&S.

Second Self: Computers & the Human Spirit. Sherry Turkle. 1985. pap. 9.95 (ISBN 0-671-60602-6, Touchstone). S&S.

Second Session of the Permanent Migration Committee. Bd. with Training Problems in the Far East. Marguerite Thibert. (I.L.O. Studies & Reports New Series: No. 10). Repr. of 1948 ed. 51.00 (ISBN 0-8115-3334-4). Kraus Repr.

Second Session of the Second National People's Congress of the People's Republic of China, 1949: Documents. Tai Piao Ta Hui Staff. LC 79-38053. (China: Classic & Contemporary Works in Reprint Ser.). Repr. of 1960 ed. 23.00 (ISBN 0-404-56907-2). AMS Pr.

Second Settlement, Eighteen Seventy-Five to Nineteen Twenty-Five: A Case Study in the Development of Victorian Boston. Douglass S. Tucci. (Illus.). 165p. 1974. pap. 10.00 (ISBN 0-686-12061-2). St. Margaret's.

Second Sex. Simone De Beauvoir. Tr. by H. M. Parshley. 1953. 24.50 (ISBN 0-394-44415-9). Knopf.

Second Sex. Simone De Beauvoir. LC 74-4241. 1974. pap. 5.95 (ISBN 0-394-71227-7, V-227, Vin). Random.

Second Shepherd's Play. Ed. by Lisl Beer. (Silver Mosque Ser.). pap. 2.00 (ISBN 0-8283-1246-X). Branden Pub Co.

Second Shopper's Guide to Museum Stores. Compiled by Shelley Hodupp. LC 78-52191. (Illus.). 1978. pap. 7.95 (ISBN 0-87663-983-X). Universe.

Second Sickle. Ursula Curtiss. (Black Dagger Crime Ser.). 224p. 1988. text ed. 14.95x (ISBN 0-86220-724-X, Pub. by Firecrest Pub Ltd). Prescott Pr NH.

Second Sickness: Contradictions of Capitalist Health Care. Howard Waitzkin. 282p. 1986. pap. 11.95 (ISBN 0-02-933810-7). Free Pr.

Second Sickness: Contradictions of Capitalist Health Care. Howard B. Waitzkin. (Illus.). 320p. 1986. text ed. 19.95 (ISBN 0-02-933750-X); pap. 12.95. Free Pr.

Second Sight. Kate Jennings. 28p. (Orig.). 1976. pap. 5.00 (ISBN 0-686-36708-1). Iron Mtn Pr.

Second Sight. A. K. Ramanujan. 72p. 1986. pap. 5.95x (ISBN 0-19-561874-2). Oxford U Pr.

Second Sight. Anne Redmon. 240p. 1988. 17.95 (ISBN 0-525-24605-3). Dutton.

Second Sight. Mary Tannen. LC 87-45119. 288p. 1988. 16.95 (ISBN 0-394-56204-6). Knopf.

Second Sight: Biennial. Graham W. Beal. LC 86-17839. (No. IV). (Illus.). 76p. 1986. pap. 14.95 (ISBN 0-918471-08-7). San Fran MOMA.

Second Sight: The Photographs of Sally Mann. Sally Mann. LC 82-49339. (Contemporary Photographers Ser.: No. 4). (Illus.). 72p. 1983. flexi-bound 25.00 (ISBN 0-87923-471-7). Godine.

Second Sister. Leslie O'Grady. 352p. 1984. 14.95 (ISBN 0-312-70845-9). St Martin.

Second Skin. John Hawkes. LC 64-10674. 1964. pap. 6.95 (ISBN 0-8112-0067-1, NDP146). New Directions.

Second Skin: An Interdisciplinary Study of Clothing. 3rd ed. Marilyn J. Horn & Lois M. Gurel. LC 80-81918. (Illus.). 480p. 1981. text ed. 38.36 (ISBN 0-395-28974-2); instr's. manual 1.56 (ISBN 0-395-28963-7). HM.

Second Slump: A Marxist Analysis of Recession in the Seventies. Ernest Mandel. 226p. Date not set. pap. 13.95 (ISBN 0-86091-728-2, Pub. by Verso). Routledge Chapman & Hall.

Second Son. Robert Ferro. 224p. 1988. 17.95 (ISBN 0-517-56815-2). Crown.

Second Son. Charles Sailor. 1979. pap. 2.75 (ISBN 0-380-45567-6, 45567-6). Avon.

Second Sourcebook for Science Supervisors. rev. ed. Ed. by Mary Harbeck. 258p. 1976. pap. 4.00 (ISBN 0-87355-004-8). Natl Sci Tchrs.

Second Southern Legislative Dictionary. Richard Allin & Goerge Fisher. (Illus.). 36p. 1984. pap. 3.95 (ISBN 0-914546-56-2). Rose Pub.

Second Stage. Betty Friedan. 320p. 1981. 14.95 (ISBN 0-671-41034-2). Summit Bks.

Second Stage. Betty Friedan. 352p. 1982. pap. 8.95 (ISBN 0-671-45951-1). Summit Bks.

Second Stage. rev. ed. Betty Friedan. 1986. pap. 8.95 (ISBN 0-671-63064-4). Summit Bks.

Second Stage Advanced Model Rocketry. Michael Banks. Ed. by Burr Angle. (Illus., Orig.). 1985. pap. 8.50 (ISBN 0-89024-057-4). Kalmbach.

Second Stage Lensman. E. E. Smith. (Lensman Ser.: No. 5). 1987. pap. 2.95 (ISBN 0-425-09787-0). Berkley Pub.

Second Star to the Right. Deborah Hautzig. LC 81-1589. 160p. (gr. 7 up). 1981. reinforced bdg. 11.75 (ISBN 0-688-00498-9). Greenwillow.

Second Star to the Right. Deborah Hautzig. 160p. 1982. pap. 2.50 (ISBN 0-380-60343-8, 60105-2, Flare). Avon.

Second Star to the Right. Deborah Hautzig. (Borzoi Sprinters Ser.). (YA) (gr. 7 up). 1989. pap. 2.95 (ISBN 0-394-82028-2). Knopf.

Second Start: A Widow's Guide to Financial Survival at a Time of Emotional Crisis. Judith N. Brown & Christina Baldwin. 224p. 1987. pap. 7.95 (ISBN 0-671-63515-8, Fireside). S&S.

Second Start: A Widow's Guide to Financial Survival at a Time of Emotional Crisis. Judith N. Brown & Christine Baldwin. 1986. 16.95 (ISBN 0-671-60349-3). S&S.

Second Step: Baccalaureate Education for Registered Nurses. Mary Searight. LC 76-3499. (Illus.). 252p. 1976. text ed. 16.50x (ISBN 0-8036-7780-4). Davis Co.

Second Steps in Ballet: Basic Center Exercises. Thalia Mara. (Illus.). 64p. (Orig.). (gr. 4-6). 1987. pap. 6.95 (ISBN 0-916622-54-1). Princeton Bk Co.

Second Story Man. Mimi Albert. LC 75-10743. 106p. 1975. 10.95 (ISBN 0-914590-12-X); pap. 5.95 (ISBN 0-914590-13-8). Fiction Coll.

Second-String Nobody. H. R. Sheffer. Ed. by Howard Schroeder. LC 80-28767. (Teamates Ser.). (Illus.). 48p. (gr. 3 up). 1981. PLB 7.95 (ISBN 0-89686-101-5). Crestwood Hse.

Second Sun. Bill Tremblay. LC 84-26102. (Poetry Ser.). 84p. (Orig.). 1986. pap. 6.95 (ISBN 0-934332-42-8). L'Epervier Pr.

Second Sunrise: Nuclear War-The Untold Story. Michael Pogodzinski. LC 83-9317. 236p. (Orig.). 1983. 12.95 (ISBN 0-89621-072-3). Thorndike Pr.

Second Supplement see Children's Literature: A Guide to Reference Sources.

Second Supplementary Catalogue of Arabic Books, 1927-1957. A. S. Fulton & M. Lings. 576p. 1960. 52.50 (ISBN 0-7141-0606-2, Pub. by British Lib). Longwood Pub Group.

Second Supplementary Catalogue of Printed Books in Hindi, Bihari (Including Bhojpuria, Kaurmali & Maithili) & Pahari (Including Nepali or Khaskura, Jaunsari, Mandeali, etc.) in the Library of the British Museum. L. D. Barnett et al. 848p. 1957. 67.50 (ISBN 0-7141-0622-4, Pub. by British Lib). Longwood Pub Group.

Second Supplementary Catalogue of Tamil Books in the British Library. Albertine Gaur. 512p. 1980. 142.50 (ISBN 0-904654-18-4, Pub. by British Lib). Longwood Pub Group.

Second Symposium on American Cuisine. Ed. by Phillip S. Cooke. 256p. 1984. pap. 43.95 (ISBN 0-442-21743-9). Van Nos Reinhold.

Second Symposium on Biotechnology in Energy Production & Conservation. Charles D. Scott. 353p. 1980. pap. 62.95 (ISBN 0-471-09015-8, Pub. by Wiley-Interscience). Wiley.

Second Symposium on Integrated Environmental Controls for Coal Fired Power Plants. Ed. by H. E. Hesketh. 139p. 1983. pap. text ed. 25.00 (ISBN 0-317-02646-1, H00252). ASME.

Second Symposium on Laser Technology. Ed. by Wolinski & Romaniuk. 1988. 43.00 (ISBN 0-89252-894-X, 859). SPIE.

Second Ten Years of the World Health Organization, 1958-1967. (Also avail. in French, Russian & Spanish). 1968. 11.60 (ISBN 92-4-156015-0). World Health.

Second Texas Infantry: From Shiloh to Vicksburg. Joseph E. Chance. 192p. 1984. 12.95 (ISBN 0-89015-435-X). Eakin Pr.

Second Thoughts. Katie F. Wiebe. LC 81-80122. 201p. (Orig.). 1981. pap. 6.95 (ISBN 0-937364-01-0, Dist. by Herald Pr.). Kindred Pr.

Second Thoughts. Katie F. Wiebe. LC 81-80122. 201p. 1981. pap. 6.95 (ISBN 0-317-64789-X). Herald Pr.

Second Thoughts: Former Radicals Look Back at the Sixties. Ed. by Peter Collier & David Horowitz. 1988. 16.95 (ISBN 0-937047-12-0). United Comns.

Second Thoughts on Marketing Co-Operatives in Tanzania: Background to Their Reinstatement. Deborah F. Bryceson. 46p. 20.00x (ISBN 0-85042-056-3, Pub. by Plunkett Foundation). State Mutual Bk.

Second Thoughts on Missions. 2nd ed. W. C. Lees. 1965. pap. 0.95 (ISBN 0-87508-908-9). Chr Lit.

Second Thoughts on Work. Sar A. Levitan & Clifford M. Johnson. LC 82-13532. 241p. 1982. text ed. 20.95 (ISBN 0-88099-000-7); pap. text ed. 13.95 (ISBN 0-88099-001-5). W E Upjohn.

Second Thoughts: Reflections on Literature & on Life. Francois Mauriac. LC 72-13201. (Essay Index Reprint Ser.). Repr. of 1961 ed. 12.50 (ISBN 0-8369-8169-3). Ayer Co Pubs.

Second Thoughts: Selected Papers on Psycho-Analysis. Wilfred Bion. LC 77-11749. 192p. 1984. 20.00x (ISBN 0-87668-330-8). Aronson.

Second Thoughts: Where the Christian Right Went Wrong. Colonel V. Doner. 1988. 13.95 (ISBN 0-317-68189-3). Wolgemuth & Hyatt.

Second Time. Janet Dailey. 1986. pap. 2.95 (ISBN 0-671-61212-3). PB.

Second Time Around. Elizabeth Oldfield. (Harlequin Presents Ser.). 192p. 1983. pap. 1.95 (ISBN 0-373-10608-4). Harlequin Bks.

Second Time Around: An Honest Widow Reveals Her Intimate & Humorous Experiences in the Dating & Mating Game. LC 80-27189. 240p. 1981. 12.95 (ISBN 0-934878-03-X, Dist. by Dembner Bks). Norton.

Second Time of Asking. 1982. 15.00x (ISBN 0-903653-63-X, Pub. by New Playwrights Network). State Mutual Bk.

Second Timothy. D. Edmond Hiebert. (Everyman's Bible Commentary Ser). 1958. pap. 5.95 (ISBN 0-8024-2055-9). Moody.

Second to None: American Companies. Robert C. Christopher. 1987. pap. 8.95 (ISBN 0-449-90273-0, Columbine). Fawcett.

Second to None: American Companies in Japan. Robert C. Christopher. 212p. 16.95 (ISBN 0-517-56286-3). Crown.

Second Tongue: An Anthology of Poetry from Malaysia & Singapore. Ed. by Edwin Thumboo. (Writing in Asia Ser.). 1976. pap. text ed. 6.50x (ISBN 0-686-60465-2, 00234). Heinemann Ed.

Second Touch. Keith Miller. LC 67-31340. 1982. 7.95 (ISBN 0-8499-0338-6, 80036). Word Bks.

Second Touring Guide to Britain. British Tourist Authority Staff. 192p. 1987. pap. 18.95 (ISBN 0-86145-080-9, Pub. by British Tour). Salem Hse Pubs.

Second Treasure Chest of Tales. Paul Stroyer. (Illus.). (gr. 3 up). 1960. 12.95 (ISBN 0-8392-3032-X). Astor-Honor.

Second Treasury of Christmas Music. Ed. by Will L. Reed. LC 68-16193. (gr. 9 up). 1968. 15.95 (ISBN 0-87523-165-9). Emerson.

Second Treasury of Kahlil Gibran. Kahlil Gibran. 7.95 (ISBN 0-8065-0230-4, Pub. by Citadel Pr); pap. 5.95 (ISBN 0-8065-0411-0). Lyle Stuart.

Second Treasury of Knitting Patterns. Barbara G. Walker. (Illus.). 433p. 1985. pap. 19.95 (ISBN 0-684-16938-X, ScribT). Scribner.

Second Treatise of Government. John Locke. Ed. by Thomas P. Peardon. LC 52-14648. (gr. 11 up). 1952. pap. 5.99 scp (ISBN 0-672-60193-1, LLA31). Bobbs.

Second Treatise of Government. John Locke. Ed. by C. B. Macpherson. LC 80-15057. (HPC Philosophical Classsics Ser.). 148p. 1980. lib. bdg. 17.50 (ISBN 0-915144-93-X); pap. text ed. 3.95 (ISBN 0-915144-86-7). Hackett Pub.

Second Treatise of Government: Locke. Ed. by Thomas P. Peardon. 1952. pap. text ed. write for info. (ISBN 0-02-393300-3). MacMillan.

Second Treatise on Civil Government. John Locke. 132p. 1986. pap. 3.95 (ISBN 0-87975-337-4). Prometheus Bks.

Second Tree from the Corner. E. B. White. LC 84-47609. 272p. 1984. 16.95i (ISBN 0-06-015354-7, HarpT). Har-Row.

Second Trimester Abortion. Ed. by G. Berger & W. Brenner. 1981. lib. bdg. 50.00 (ISBN 90-247-2487-2, Pub. by Martinus Nijhoff Netherlands). Kluwer Academic.

Second Trimester Abortion: Perspectives after a Decade of Experience. Ed. by Gary S. Berger et al. 364p. 1981. text ed. 42.00 (ISBN 0-88416-256-7). PSG Pub Co.

Second Trimester Pregnancy Termination. Ed. by M. Keirse & Bennebroek J. Gravenhorst. 1982. lib. bdg. 49.50 (ISBN 90-6021-490-0, Pub. by Martinus Nijhoff Netherlands). Kluwer Academic.

Second Trip. Robert Silverberg. 192p. 1987. pap. 2.95. Avon.

Second Tripartite Technical Meeting for the Printing & Allied Tra des, Geneva, 22 September-1 October 1981: Note on the Proceedings. iii, 86p. 1982. 10.50 (ISBN 92-2-102936-0). Intl Labour Office.

Second Try: Labour & the EEC. U. Kitzinger. 1969. 33.00 (ISBN 0-08-012961-7). Pergamon.

Second Twelve Months of Life. Frank Caplan & Theresa Caplan. LC 77-78748. (Illus.). 1979. pap. 13.95 (ISBN 0-399-50776-0, G&D). Putnam Pub Group.
Second Twelve Months of Life. Ed. by Frank Caplan. 1982. pap. 5.95 (ISBN 0-553-26438-9). Bantam.
Second United Order among the Mormons. Edward J. Allen. LC 73-38483. (Columbia University Studies in the Social Sciences: No. 419). Repr. of 1936 ed. 15.00 (ISBN 0-404-51419-7). AMS Pr.
Second U. S. - Japan Science & Technology Exchange Symposium: Patterns of Interdependence. 1987. write for info. Japan Am Soc.
Second Vatican Council: Studies by Eight Anglican Observers. B. Pawley. 12.00 (ISBN 0-8446-2713-5). Peter Smith.
Second Vendee: The Continuity of Counter-Revolution in the Department of the Gard 1789-1815. Gwynne Lewis. (Illus.). 1978. 49.95x (ISBN 0-19-822544-X). Oxford U Pr.
Second Vespers. Ralph McInerny. LC 79-56379. (Father Dowling Mystery Ser.). 256p. 1980. 14.95 (ISBN 0-8149-0837-3). Vanguard.
Second Victory: The Marshall Plan & the Postwar Revival of Europe. Robert J. Donovan. (Illus.). 128p. 1988. 22.95 (ISBN 0-8191-6498-4, Pub. by Madison Bks). U Pr of Amer.
Second Vienna School. Luigi Rognoni. Tr. by Robert Mann from Ger. (Illus.). 448p. (Orig.). 1977. pap. 14.95 (ISBN 0-7145-3865-5). Riverrun NY.
Second View. The Rephotographic Survey Project Staff. LC 84-3600. (Illus.). 223p. 1984. 65.00 (ISBN 0-8263-0751-5). U of NM Pr.
Second Viewtext Exposition VT'82. Information Gatekeepers, Inc. 1981. 125.00 (ISBN 0-686-38471-7). Info Gatekeepers.
Second Virginia Infantry. Dennis Frye. (Virginia Regimental Histories Ser.). (Illus.). 146p. 1984. 16.45 (ISBN 0-930919-06-8). H E Howard.
Second Virial Coefficients of Pure Gases & Mixtures: A Critical Compilation. J. H. Dymond & E. B. Smith. (Oxford Science Research Papers Ser.). (Illus.). 1980. pap. text ed. 89.00x (ISBN 0-19-855361-7). Oxford U Pr.
Second Visit to North America, 2 Vols. Charles B. Lyell. 1855. Set. 69.00x (ISBN 0-403-00357-1). Scholarly.
Second Visit to North America, 2 vols. Charles B. Lyell. 1988. Repr. of 1855 ed. Set. lib. bdg. 98.00x. Am Biog Serv.
Second Vocation. Date not set. 3.30. Coun Soc Wk Ed.
Second Volume de Bouvard et Pecuchet. Gustave Flaubert. 8.95 (ISBN 0-686-55989-4). French & Eur.
Second Voyage. Eilean Ni Chuilleanain. 1977. pap. 4.25 (ISBN 0-916390-05-5). Wake Forest.
Second Voyage. Eilean Ni Chuilleanain. 68p. Date not set. 22.50 (ISBN 1-85224-015-6, Pub. by Bloodaxe Bks); pap. 11.95 (ISBN 1-85224-016-4, Pub. by Bloodaxe Bks). Dufour.
Second War, 6 vols. Winston S. Churchill. 1985. write for info. HM.
Second Wave: Japan's Global Assault on Financial Services. Richard W. Wright & Gunter A. Pauli. LC 87-27138. 140p. 1987. 19.95 (ISBN 0-312-01558-5). St Martin.
Second Wave: Japan's Global Attack on Financial Services. R. W. Wright & G. A. Pauli. 148p. 1987. 19.75 (ISBN 0-08-033090-8, Pub. by Waterlow). Pergamon.
Second Wave: Pinay & Pinoy. Caridad C. Vallangca. Ed. by Jody B. Larson. (Illus.). 286p. (Orig.). 1987. pap. 9.95 (ISBN 0-89407-043-6). Strawberry Hill.
Second Wedding. Delsa Walton. (Orig.). 1981. pap. 1.75 (ISBN 0-8439-8019-2, Tiara Bks). Leisure NY.
Second Wedding Handbook: A Complete Guide to the Options. Judith Slawson. 1989. pap. 7.95 (ISBN 0-385-24677-3). Doubleday.
Second Wife, Second Best? Glynnis Walker. Ed. by Jim Connor. 274p. 1988. pap. 3.95 (ISBN 0-7701-0331-6). Paperjacks US.
Second Wind. Bill Russell & Taylor Branch. pap. 2.75 (ISBN 0-345-28897-1). Ballantine.
Second Wind after Age Sixty. Mister Dee. 1988. price not set (ISBN 0-533-07805-9). Vantage.
Second Wind: Selected Poems, 1968-1986. Phil Weidman & Kirk Robertson. LC 87-70383. (Windriver Ser.). 192p. (Orig.). 1987. pap. 14.00 (ISBN 0-916918-34-3); 26 lettered signed ed. 25.00 (ISBN 0-916918-35-1). Duck Down.
Second Witch. Jack Sendak. LC 65-20255. (Illus.). (gr. 2-6). 1965. PLB 11.89 (ISBN 0-06-025476-9). HarpJ.
Second Wooing of Salina Sue & Other Stories. facsimile ed. Ruth M. Stuart. 1972. Repr. of 1905 ed. lib. bdg. 24.00 (ISBN 0-8422-8114-2). Irvington.
Second Wooing of Salina Sue & Other Stories. Ruth M. Stuart. 1986. pap. text ed. 6.95x (ISBN 0-8290-2018-7). Irvington.
Second Words: Selected Critical Prose. Margaret Atwood. 448p. 1982. 9.95 (ISBN 0-88784-095-7, Pub. by Hse Anansi Pr Canada). U of Toronto Pr.
Second Words: Selected Critical Prose. Margaret Atwood. LC 83-71983. 1984. 18.95x (ISBN 0-8070-6358-4); pap. 9.95 (ISBN 0-8070-6359-2, BP669). Beacon Pr.
Second Workshop on Grand Unification: University of Michigan, Ann Arbor, April 24-26,1981. Ed. by J. P. Leveille et al. 350p. 1981. text ed. 27.50x (ISBN 0-8176-3055-4). Birkhauser.
Second Workshop on Measurement of Microbial Activity in the Carbon Cycle of Aquatic Ecosystems: Proceedings. Ed. by J. Overbeck & M. G. Hoefle. (Advances in Limnology Ser.: No. 19). (Illus.). 316p. 1984. pap. text ed. 89.70x (ISBN 3-510-47017-6). Lubrecht & Cramer.
Second World Almanac Book of Inventions. Valerie-Anne Giscard d'Estaing. (Illus.). 362p. 1986. pap. 12.95 (ISBN 0-345-33730-1, Dist. by Ballantine). Pharos Bks NY.
Second World & Green World: Studies in Renaissance Fiction-Making. Harry Berger, Jr. 1988. 45.00x (ISBN 0-520-05826-7). U of Cal Pr.
Second World Conference on Adult Education (UNESCO) (Education Studies & Documents: No. 46). pap. 16.00 (ISBN 0-8115-1370-X). Kraus Repr.
Second World Conference on Detergents: Proceedings. Ed. by A. R. Baldwin. 302p. 1987. 95.00 (ISBN 0-935315-14-4). Am Oil Chemists.
Second World Congress on Land Policy. Ed. by Matthew Cullen & Sharon Woolery. LC 85-10455. (Lincoln Institute of Land Policy Bk.). 320p. 1985. text ed. 35.00x (ISBN 0-89946-195-6). Oelgeschlager.
Second World War, 6 vols. Winston S. Churchill. Incl. Gathering Storm. 1948. 19.95 (ISBN 0-395-07537-8); Their Finest Hour. 1949. 19.95 (ISBN 0-395-07536-X); Grand Alliance. 1950. 19.95 (ISBN 0-395-07538-6); Hinge of Fate. 1960. 19.95 (ISBN 0-395-07539-4); Closing the Ring. 1951. 19.95 (ISBN 0-395-07535-1); Triumph & Tragedy. 1953. 19.95 (ISBN 0-395-07540-8). 22.95 ea.; Set. 134.70 (ISBN 0-395-07541-6). HM.
Second World War, Set Vols. I-VI. Winston S. Churchill. 1986. pap. 59.70 (ISBN 0-395-41685-X). HM.
Second World War, Vol. I. Liliane Funcken & Fred Funcken. write for info. P-H.
Second World War. C. A. Hills. (Living Through History Ser.). (Illus.). 72p. (gr. 7-12). 1985. 17.95 (ISBN 0-7134-4531-9, Pub. by Batsford England). David & Charles.
Second World War. Charles Messenger. LC 86-62905. (Conflict in the 20th Century Ser.). (Illus.). 64p. (gr. 4-12). 1987. lib. bdg. 12.90 (ISBN 0-531-10321-8). Watts.
Second World War. Michel Pierre & Annette Wieviorka. Ed. by Walter Kossmann & Joanne Fink. LC 86-42662. (Events of Yesteryear Ser.). (Illus.). 69p. (gr. 6 up). 1987. 12.96 (ISBN 0-382-09298-8). Silver.
Second World War: A Military History. Basil Collier. 19.00 (ISBN 0-8446-4724-1). Peter Smith.
Second World War: A Select Bibliography of Books in English since 1975. Compiled by Arthur L. Funk. LC 85-143644. 200p. 1985. lib. bdg. 24.95x (ISBN 0-941690-15-6). Regina Bks.
Second World War: An Illustrated History. A. J. Taylor. (Illus.). 1979. pap. 9.95 (ISBN 0-399-50434-6). Putnam Pub Group.
Second World War & the Atomic Age, 1940-1973. Compiled by E. David Cronon & Theodore D. Rosenof. LC 74-28589. (Goldentree Bibliographies in American History Ser). (Orig.). 1975. pap. 14.95x (ISBN 0-88295-538-1). Harlan Davidson.
Second World War: Asia & the Pacific. Ed. by Thomas Griess. (The West Point Military History Ser.). (Illus.). 356p. (Orig.). 1986. 25.00 (ISBN 0-89529-313-7); pap. 18.00 (ISBN 0-89529-243-2). Avery Pub.
Second World War: Chartwell Edition, 6 Vols. Winston S. Churchill. 1983. 300.00 set (ISBN 0-395-34929-X). HM.
Second World War: Europe & the Mediterranean. new ed. Ed. by Thomas Griess. (The West Point Military History Ser.). 446p. (Orig.). 1986. 25.00 (ISBN 0-89529-314-5); pap. 20.00 (ISBN 0-89529-242-4). Avery Pub.
Second World War in History, Biography, Diary, Poetry, Literature, & Film: A Bibliography. Jill M. Phillips. 1983. lib. bdg. 79.95 (ISBN 0-8490-3231-8). Gordon Pr.
Second World War in Literature: Eight Essays. Ed. by Ian Higgins. 130p. 1987. 14.00 (ISBN 0-7073-0427-X, Pub. by Scot Acad Pr). Longwood Pub Group.
Second Writers Workshop Literary Reader: An Anthology. Ed. by P. Lal. 72p. 1975. 15.00 (ISBN 0-88253-624-9); pap. text ed. 6.75 (ISBN 0-88253-623-0). Ind-US Inc.
Second X: Sex Role & Social Role. Judith L. Laws. LC 75-4069. 415p. 1979. pap. 32.95 (ISBN 0-444-99023-2, LSX/). Elsevier.
Second Year As Reflected in the Media. 1978. write for info. Comm Present Danger.
Second Year Ashore. Jules Verne. 4.95 (ISBN 0-87497-036-9). Assoc Bk.
Second Year Evaluation of the Florida Public Guardianship Pilot Program. K. Miller et al. 1984. write for info. FSU CSP.
Second-Year French. Alice C. Omaggio et al. 416p. (Fr.). 1984. pap. text ed. write for info (ISBN 0-394-33642-9, RanC); 7.25 (ISBN 0-394-33643-7, RanC); write for info (ISBN 0-394-33646-1). Random.
Second-Year Spanish. Shirley Williams. 352p. (Span.). 1984. pap. text ed. write for info (ISBN 0-394-33647-X, RanC); write for info (ISBN 0-394-33648-8); write for info (ISBN 0-394-33651-8). Random.
Second Year: The Emergence of Self-Awareness. Jerome Kagan. LC 81-4214. (Illus.). 240p. 1981. text ed. 18.50x (ISBN 0-674-79662-4). Harvard U Pr.
Second Year: The Emergence of Self-Awareness. Jerome Kagan. 176p. 1986. pap. text ed. 8.95x (ISBN 0-674-79663-2). Harvard U Pr.
Second Zen Reader: The Tiger's Cave & Translations of other Zen Writings. Trevor Leggett. Ed. by Florence Sakade. LC 87-50163. (Illus.). 196p. (Orig.). 1988. pap. 7.50 (ISBN 0-8048-1525-9). C E Tuttle.
Secondary Accent in Modern English Verse. Raymond D. Miller. LC 72-192019. 1904. lib. bdg. 16.50 (ISBN 0-8414-6617-3). Folcroft.
Secondary Analysis in Social Research: A Guide to Data Services & Methods with Examples. Catherine Hakim. (Contemporary Social Research Ser.: No. 5). 224p. 1982. text ed. 28.50x (ISBN 0-04-312015-6). Unwin Hyman.
Secondary Analysis of Available Data Bases. Ed. by David J. Bowering. LC 83-82735. (Program Evaluation Ser.: No. 22). (Orig.). 1984. pap. text ed. 14.95x (ISBN 0-87589-783-5). Jossey-Bass.
Secondary Analysis of Sample Surveys. Herbert Hyman. xxvi, 368p. 1987. pap. 16.50x (ISBN 0-8195-6153-3). Wesleyan U Pr.
Secondary Analysis of Survey Data. K. Jill Kiecolt & Laura E. Nathan. (Quantitative Applications in the Social Sciences Ser.: Vol. 53). 96p. 1985. pap. text ed. 6.50 (ISBN 0-8039-2302-3). Sage.
Secondary & Functional Rhinoplasty: The Difficult Nose. Meyer. 1988. write for info. (ISBN 0-8089-1879-6). Grune.
Secondary & Middle School Teaching Methods. 5th ed. Leonard H. Clark & Irving S. Starr. xii, 973p. 1986. text ed. write for info. (ISBN 0-02-322600-5). Macmillan.
Secondary Attachments. Greg Herriges. 243p. 1986. 15.95 (ISBN 0-688-06171-0). Morrow.
Secondary Cities in Developing Countries: Policies for Diffusing Urbanization. Dennis A. Rondinelli. (Sage Library of Social Research: No. 145). (Illus.). 256p. 1983. 35.00 (ISBN 0-8039-1945-X); pap. 16.95 (ISBN 0-8039-1946-8). Sage.
Secondary Cities of Argentina: The Social History of Corrientes, Salta, & Mendoza, 1850-1910. James R. Scobie. Ed. by Samuel L. Baily. LC 87-18093. (Illus.). 312p. 1988. text ed. 42.50x (ISBN 0-8047-1419-3). Stanford U Pr.
Secondary Detachment of the Retina: Proceedings of the Collogue du Club Jules Gonin, 7th & the Assemblee de la Societe Suisse d'Ophthalmologie, 63rd, Lausanne, 1970. Colloque du Club Jules Gonin Staff & Assemblee de la Societe Suisse d'Ophthalmologie Staff. Ed. by R. Dufour. (Modern Problems in Ophthalmology Ser.: Vol. 10). (Illus.). 1972. 106.75 (ISBN 3-8055-1300-3). S Karger.
Secondary Diabetes: The Spectrum of the Diabetic Syndromes. Ed. by Stephen Podolsky & M. Viswanathan. (Illus.). 624p. 1980. 93.00 (ISBN 0-89004-372-8). Raven.
Secondary Education: An Introduction. 1st ed. David G. Armstrong & Tom V. Savage. 576p. 1983. write for info. (ISBN 0-02-304070-X). Macmillan.
Secondary Education & the Formation of an Elite: The Impact of Education on Gwembe District, Zambia. Thayer Scudder & Elizabeth Colson. (Studies in Anthropology). 1980. 19.95 (ISBN 0-12-634280-6). Acad Pr.
Secondary Education for the Future Report of a Forum Meeting on New Trends & Processes of Secondary Education: Port Moresby - Papua, New Guinea, Nov. 27 - Dec. 4, 1985. (APEID Ser.). 85p. (Orig.). 1986. pap. text ed. 10.00 (ISBN 0-318-21534-9, UB213, UB). UNIPUB.
Secondary Education in Ireland Eighteen Seventy to Nineteen Twenty-One. T. J. McElligott. 200p. 1981. 37.50x (ISBN 0-7165-0074-4, BBA 03856, Pub. by Irish Academic Pr England). Biblio Dist.
Secondary Education in Nepal. 39p. 1981. pap. 4.00 (ISBN 0-318-23180-8). Am-Nepal Ed.
Secondary Education in the South. facsimile ed. Ed. by Will. C. Ryan et al. LC 70-134132. (Essay Index Reprint Ser). Repr. of 1946 ed. 20.00 (ISBN 0-8369-2519-X). Ayer Co Pubs.
Secondary Education in the 19th Century. R. L. Archer. 363p. 1966. Repr. of 1921 ed. 26.00x (ISBN 0-7146-1446-7, BHA 01446, F Cass Co). Biblio Dist.
Secondary Education under Different Types of District Organization. T. B. Bernard. LC 71-176559. (Columbia University. Teachers College. Contributions to Education: No. 642). Repr. of 1935 ed. 22.50 (ISBN 0-404-55642-6). AMS Pr.
Secondary Emission & Structural Properties of Solids. Ed. by Ubai A. Arifov. Tr. by Geoffrey C. Archard from Rus. LC 78-157931. pap. 38.50 (ISBN 0-317-08295-7, 2020683). Bks Demand UMI.
Secondary Epileptogenesis. Ed. by Assa Mayersdorf & Richard P. Schmidt. 188p. 1982. text ed. 39.00 (ISBN 0-89004-578-X). Raven.
Secondary Heroes of Shakespeare & Other Essays. Lucie Simpson. 1951. Repr. 17.50 (ISBN 0-8274-3344-1). R West.
Secondary Hypertension. Ed. by H. Vetter. (Journal: Cardiology: Vol. 72; Suppl. 1 1985). (Illus.). iv, 196p. 1985. pap. 39.50 (ISBN 3-8055-4079-5). S Karger.
Secondary Ion Mass Spectrometry: Basic Concepts, Instrumental Aspects, Applications & Trends. A. Benninghoven et al. LC 86-11014. (Monographs on Analytical Chemistry & Its Applications). 1227p. 1987. 150.00 (ISBN 0-471-01056-1). Wiley.
Secondary Ion Mass Spectrometry: Proceedings of the Sixth International Conference on Secondary Ion Mass Spectrometry (SIMS Six), Palais des Congre Versailles, France, September 13-18th, 1987. Ed. by G. Slodzian et al. 1200p. 1988. write for info. (ISBN 0-471-91832-6). Wiley.
Secondary Ion Mass Spectrometry: SIMS V. Ed. by R. J. Colton et al. (Series in Chemical Physics: Vol. 44). (Illus.). 590p. 1986. 49.00 (ISBN 0-387-16263-1). Springer-Verlag.
Secondary Ion Mass Spectrometry SIMS III: Proceedings. Ed. by A. Benninghoven et al. (Springer Series in Chemical Physics: Vol. 19). (Illus.). 444p. 1982. 44.00 (ISBN 0-387-11372-X). Springer-Verlag.
Secondary Ion Mass Spectrometry SIMS-II: Proceedings of the International Conference on Secondary Ion Mass Spectrometry. Ed. by A. Benninghoven et al. LC 79-23997. (Springer Ser. in Chemical Physics: Vol. 9). (Illus.). 298p. 1979. 51.00 (ISBN 3-540-09843-7). Springer-Verlag.
Secondary Ion Mass Spectroscopy of Solid Surfaces. V. T. Cherepin. viii, 138p. 1987. lib. bdg. 87.50x (ISBN 90-6764-078-6). Coronet Bks.
Secondary Learning Centers. Clifford Bee. 1980. pap. 11.95 (ISBN 0-673-16428-4). Scott F.
Secondary Manufacturing in the Glass Industry. Alexis G. Pincus & S. H. Chang. LC 78-55369. (Processing in the Glass Industry Ser.). 314p. 1978. 34.95 (ISBN 0-911993-14-2). Ashlee Pub Co.
Secondary Metabolism. J. Mann. (Chemistry Ser.: No. 33). (Illus.). 1987. text ed. 55.00x (ISBN 0-19-855506-7); pap. 29.95x (ISBN 0-19-855513-X). Oxford U Pr.
Secondary Metabolism & Cell Differentiation. M. Luckner et al. (Molecular Biology, Biochemistry & Biophysics Ser.: Vol. 23). 1977. 31.00 (ISBN 0-387-08081-3). Springer-Verlag.
Secondary Metabolism & Differentiation in Fungi. Bennett & Ciegler. (Mycology Ser.). 472p. 1983. 95.00 (ISBN 0-8247-1819-4). Dekker.
Secondary Metabolism in Microorganisms, Plants & Animals. 2nd, rev. ed. M. Luckner. (Illus.). 570p. 1984. 66.00 (ISBN 0-387-12771-2). Springer-Verlag.
Secondary Metabolism in Plant Cell Cultures. Ed. by P. Morris et al. (Illus.). 300p. 1986. 39.50 (ISBN 0-521-32889-6). Cambridge U Pr.
Secondary Mortgage Market: A Handbook of Strategies, Techniques & Critical Issues in Contemporary Mortgage Finance. Ed. by Jess Lederman. 600p. 1987. 60.00 (ISBN 0-917253-74-4). Probus Pub Co.
Secondary Mortgage Market Guide. Charles L. Edson & Barry Jacobs. LC 84-73156. 1985. looseleaf 85.00 (668); 1986 updates 25.00. Bender.
Secondary Power: A Primary Function. (Third Garrett Lecture). 1987. 7.00 (ISBN 0-89883-994-7, SP723). Soc Auto Engineers.
Secondary Prevention in Coronary Artery Disease & Myocardial Infarction. Ed. by P. Mathes. (Developments in Cardiovascular Medicine Ser.). 1985. lib. bdg. 84.50 (ISBN 0-89838-736-1, Pub. by Martinus Nijhoff Netherlands). Kluwer Academic.
Secondary Prevention of Colorectal Cancer. Ed. by P. Rozen & S. J. Winawer. (Frontiers of Gastrointestinal Research Ser.: Vol. 10). (Illus.). xiv, 274p. 1986. 132.00 (ISBN 3-8055-4252-6). S Karger.
Secondary Programs for the Gifted-Talented. Allyn Arnold et al. 67p. 10.95 (ISBN 0-318-02148-X). NSLTIGT.
Secondary Progressions: Time to Remember. Nancy Hastings. LC 84-50243. 324p. 1984. pap. 10.95 (ISBN 0-87728-599-3). Weiser.
Secondary Progressions: Using the Adjusted Calculating Date. Laurel Lowell. LC 73-76620. 96p. pap. 4.75 (ISBN 0-88053-762-0, A-313). Macoy Pub.
Secondary Radar. P. Honold. 1976. 69.95 (ISBN 0-471-25772-9, Wiley Heyden). Wiley.
Secondary (Reciprocal) Trigonometric Ratios: Unit 4. Rudolph A. Zimmer. 48p. 1980. pap. text ed. 5.00 (ISBN 0-8403-2277-1). Kendall-Hunt.
Secondary Reclamation of Plastics Waste, Vol. 1. Ed. by Albert Spaak. LC 87-50953. 331p. 1987. pap. 150.00 (ISBN 0-87762-570-0). Technomic.

Secondary Reclamation of Plastics Waste, Vol. 2. Ed. by Albert Spaak. LC 87-50954. 234p. 1987. pap. 150.00 (ISBN 0-87762-571-9). Technomic.
Secondary Research. David W. Stewart. 135p. 1984. 19.95 (ISBN 0-8039-2338-4); pap. 9.95 (ISBN 0-8039-2339-2). Sage.
Secondary School Administration: A Management Approach. 2nd ed. Ed. by M. G. Hughes. LC 74-4453. 1974. pap. text ed. 12.75 (ISBN 0-08-018011-6). Pergamon.
Secondary School Admissions Test - H.S. Entrance Exam. Jack Rudman. (Admission Test Ser.: ATS-80). (Cloth bdg. avail. on request). pap. 13.95 (ISBN 0-8373-5080-8). Natl Learning.
Secondary School Curriculum Improvement: Meeting Challenges of the Times. 3rd ed. J. Lloyd Trump & Delmas F. Miller. 1979. text ed. 39.00 (ISBN 0-205-06600-3, 2366002). Allyn.
Secondary School Evaluative Criteria. 186p. 8.00 (ISBN 0-318-17479-0). Mid St Coll & Schl.
Secondary School Graduation: University Entrance Qualification in Socialist Countries. new ed. Wolfgang Mitter. LC 77-30471. 1979. 36.00 (ISBN 0-08-022237-4); pap. 22.00 (ISBN 0-08-022238-2). Pergamon.
Secondary School Library Management Manual. 2nd ed. LaVerne H. Ireland. 202p. 1987. pap. 30.00 (ISBN 0-943932-27-0). Petervin Pr.
Secondary School Mathematics Curriculum: 1985 Yearbook. Ed. by Christopher R. Hirsch. LC 84-29622. (Illus.). 250p. 1985. 18.00 (ISBN 0-87353-217-1). NCTM.
Secondary School Principal: Manager & Supervisor. 2nd ed. Wood. 1985. 40.00 (ISBN 0-205-08376-5, 238376). Allyn.
Secondary School Reading Instruction: The Content Areas. 3rd ed. Betty D. Roe et al. LC 86-81608. 480p. 1987. text ed. 36.76 (ISBN 0-395-35806-X); instr's. manual 2.36 (ISBN 0-395-42548-4). HM.
Secondary School Reading: Process-Program-Procedure. Walter R. Hill. 1978. text ed. 38.00 (ISBN 0-205-06129-X, 2361299). Allyn.
Secondary School Reading: What Research Reveals for Classroom Practices. Ed. by Allen Berger & H. Alan Robinson. 206p. (Orig.). 1982. pap. 12.95 (ISBN 0-8141-4295-8). NCTE.
Secondary School Reform in Imperial Germany. James C. Albisetti. LC 82-12223. 392p. 1983. 43.50x (ISBN 0-691-05373-1). Princeton U Pr.
Secondary Schools at the Turn of the Century. Theodore R. Sizer. LC 76-43028. 1976. Repr. of 1964 ed. lib. bdg. 35.00x (ISBN 0-8371-8972-1, SISS). Greenwood.
Secondary Schools for American Youth. L. A. Williams. 529p. 1980. Repr. of 1944 ed. lib. bdg. 25.00 (ISBN 0-89984-524-X). Century Bookbindery.
Secondary Social Science Workbook. Satish K. Bajaj. (Illus.). 236p. 1981. pap. text ed. 7.95x (ISBN 0-86131-271-6, Pub. by Orient Longman Ltd India). Apt Bks.
Secondary Social Studies Curriculum, Activities, & Materials. James L. Barth. 342p. (Orig.). 1984. pap. text ed. 16.75 (ISBN 0-8191-3797-9). U Pr of Amer.
Secondary Social Studies Introduction, Curriculum, Evaluation. John U. Michaelis & J. Nelson. (Illus.). 1980. text ed. write for info. (ISBN 0-13-797753-0). P-H.
Secondary Sonnets. Anthony Stowell. 1986. 30.00x (ISBN 0-86332-047-3, Pub. by Book Guild Ltd). State Mutual Bk.
Secondary Sources in the History of Canadian Medicine: A Bibliography. Compiled by C. Roland. 190p. 1984. text ed. 23.95x (ISBN 0-88920-182-X, Pub. by Wilfrid Laurier Canada). Humanities.
Secondary Spread of Cancer. Ed. by R. W. Baldwin. 1978. 66.00 (ISBN 0-12-076850-X). Acad Pr.
Secondary Steelmaking for Product Improvement. 256p. 1985. pap. text ed. 35.00x (ISBN 0-904357-73-2, Pub. by Inst Metals). Brookfield Pub Co.
Secondary Surveillance Radar. Michael Stevens. 320p. 1988. text ed. 66.00 (ISBN 0-89006-292-7). Artech Hse.
Secondary Technical & Vocational Education in Underdeveloped Countries (UNESCO) (Education Studies & Documents: No. 33). pap. 16.00 (ISBN 0-8115-1357-2). Kraus Repr.
Secondary Triad Model: A Practical Plan for Implementing Gifted Programs at the Junior & Senior High School Levels. Sally M. Reis & Joseph S. Renzulli. 1985. pap. 14.95 (ISBN 0-936386-33-9). Creative Learning.
Secondary Vocational Education. Rosemary Kolde. 16p. 1986. 3.00 (ISBN 0-318-22196-9, OC119). Natl Ctr Res Voc Ed.
Secondary Vocational Education: Imperative for Excellence. Ruth P. Hughes. 36p. 1984. 4.95 (ISBN 0-318-22197-7, IN277). Natl Ctr Res Voc Ed.
Secondary Worlds. W. H. Auden. 127p. 1985. pap. 6.95 (ISBN 0-571-13221-9). Faber & Faber.
Seconde. Sidonie-Gabrielle Colette. 1955. pap. 8.95 (ISBN 0-685-11558-5). French & Eur.
Secondhand Bride. Gwen Westwood. (Harlequin Romances Ser.). 192p. 1983. pap. 1.75 (ISBN 0-373-02586-6). Harlequin Bks.
Secondhand Life: Discussions with Bill Barber. 135p. 1985. pap. 7.95 (ISBN 0-9617944-0-2). Akwenasa Pubns.
Secondhand Shopping in Washington, D. C., & Suburban Maryland. Linda C. White. (Illus.). 40p. (Orig.). 1983. pap. 3.75 (ISBN 0-915499-01-0). Prudent Pubs.
Seconds. Nick Wayte. 1969. pap. 3.00 (ISBN 0-686-05259-5, Pub. by Ferry Pr); pap. 9.00 signed ed (ISBN 0-686-05260-9). Small Pr Dist.
Seconds City. Susan Wolfson. 400p. (Orig.). 1986. pap. 8.95 (ISBN 0-8092-5179-5). Contemp Bks.
Secre de Secrez. Pierre D'Abernun of Fetcham. Ed. by Oliver A. Beckerlegge. 1944. 14.00 (ISBN 0-384-54695-1). Johnson Repr.
Secrecy: A Crosscultural Perspective. Ed. by Stanton K. Tefft. LC 79-25454. 351p. 1980. text ed. 39.95 (ISBN 0-87705-442-8); pap. text ed. 19.95 (ISBN 0-87705-443-6). Human Sci Pr.
Secrecy & Democracy: The CIA in Transition. Stansfield Turner. 306p. 1985. 16.95 (ISBN 0-395-35573-7). HM.
Secrecy & Democracy: The CIA in Transition. Stansfield Turner. LC 85-45666. 320p. 1986. pap. 7.95 (ISBN 0-06-097025-1, PL 7025, PL). Har-Row.
Secrecy & Foreign Policy. Ed. by Thomas M. Franck & Edward Weisband. 1974. 29.95x (ISBN 0-19-501746-3). Oxford U Pr.
Secrecy & Power: The Life of J. Edgar Hoover. Richard G. Powers. 600p. 1988. 27.95 (ISBN 0-02-925060-9); pap. 12.95. Free Pr.
Secrecy & Power: The Life of J. Edgar Hoover. Richard G. Powers. (Illus.). 656p. 1988. pap. 12.95 (ISBN 0-02-925061-7). Free Pr.
Secrecy & the Arms Race: A Theory of the Accumulation of Strategic Weapons & How Secrecy Affects It. Martin C. McGuire. LC 65-22062. (Economic Studies: No. 125). (Illus.). 1965. 16.50x (ISBN 0-674-79665-9). Harvard U Pr.
Secret. Mary B. Crabtree. 120p. (Orig.). 1985. pap. 2.95 (ISBN 0-88120-734-9). SRA.
Secret. Gloria M. Guenther. Ed. by Norma Harris. (Contemporary Problems Reading Ser). (Illus.). 86p. (gr. 7-12). 1974. pap. 4.95 (ISBN 0-914296-20-5); tchr's. guide avail. Ed Activities.
Secret. Adrian Malone. 352p. 1988. pap. 3.95 (ISBN 1-55547-214-1). Critics Choice Paper.
Secret. Adrian Malone et al. 403p. 1984. 15.95 (ISBN 0-395-35356-4). HM.
Secret. A. A. Milne. (Perfect Presents Story-Gifts Ser.). (Illus.). 32p. 1986. pap. 5.95 (ISBN 0-317-52324-4). Redpath Pr.
Secret. Bhagwan S. Rajneesh. Ed. by Swami P. Chinmaya. LC 83-185068. (Sufi Ser.). (Illus.). 760p. (Orig.). 1980. 10.95 (ISBN 0-88050-127-8). Chidvilas Inc.
Secret. Carol B. York. 192p. (Orig.). (gr. 7 up). 1984. pap. 1.95 (ISBN 0-590-33098-5, Windswept Bks). Scholastic Inc.
Secret: A Child's Story of Sex Abuse, Ages 7-10. Diana L. McCoy. 32p. (Orig.). (gr. 2-5). 1986. pap. text ed. 6.00 (ISBN 0-9619250-1-9). Magic Lantrn.
Secret Admirer. Created by Francine Pascal. (Sweet Valley High Ser.: No. 39). 160p. (YA) (gr. 7 up). 1987. pap. 2.95 (ISBN 0-553-27691-3). Bantam.
Secret Admirer. Francine Pascale. (Sweet Valley High Ser.: No. 39). (gr. k-9). 1988. pap. 2.75. Scholastic Inc.
Secret Admirer. Debra Spector. (Sweet Dreams Ser.: No. 81). 160p. (gr. 6 up). 1985. pap. 2.25 (ISBN 0-553-24688-7). Bantam.
Secret Adversary. Agatha Christie. 1983. pap. 3.50 (ISBN 0-553-26477-X). Bantam.
Secret Adversary. Agatha Christie. (Popular Author Ser.). 363p. 1988. lib. bdg. 16.95 (ISBN 0-8161-4464-8, Large Print Bks). G K Hall.
Secret Affairs. Larry Hancock & Michael Cherkas. (Silent Invasion Ser.). 80p. (Orig.). 1988. pap. 8.95x (ISBN 0-918348-50-1). NBM.
Secret Affinities: Words & Images by Rene Magritte. Ed. by Dominique De Menil. LC 76-45518. 1976. 2.00 (ISBN 0-914412-12-4). Inst for the Arts.
Secret Agent. Joseph Conrad. lib. bdg. 17.95x (ISBN 0-89966-058-4). Buccaneer Bks.
Secret Agent. Joseph Conrad. 240p. (Orig.). 1984. pap. text ed. 2.50 (ISBN 0-553-21134-X, Bantam Classics). Bantam.
Secret Agent. Joseph Conrad. 240p. 1983. pap. 2.50 (ISBN 0-451-51804-7, Sig Classics). NAL.
Secret Agent. Joseph Conrad. Ed. by Martin Seymour-Smith. (English Library). 272p. 1985. pap. 2.50 (ISBN 0-14-043228-0). Penguin.
Secret Agent on Flight 101. Franklin W. Dixon. (Hardy Boys Ser: Vol. 46). (gr. 5-9). 1967. 4.50 (ISBN 0-448-08946-7, G&D). Putnam Pub Group.
Secret Agent X-9. Dashiell Hammett & Alex Raymond. 225p. 1985. pap. 9.95 (ISBN 0-930330-05-6). Intl Polygonics.
Secret Agents Four. Donald J. Sobol. 144p. (gr. 3-7). 1988. pap. 2.50 (ISBN 0-590-40565-9). Scholastic Inc.
Secret Agents in Fiction: Ian Fleming, John Le Carre & Len Deighton. Lars O. Sauerberg. LC 84-3327. 192p. 1985. 22.50 (ISBN 0-312-70846-7). St Martin.
Secret Alliance: A Study of the Danish Resistance Movement, 1940-1945, Vols. I, II, & III. Jorgen Haestrup. 1162p. 1985. Set. 150.00x (ISBN 0-8147-3431-6). Vol. I (ISBN 0-8147-3428-6). Vol. II (ISBN 0-8147-3429-4). Vol. III (ISBN 0-8147-3430-8). NYU Pr.
Secret among the Ruins. Jean McConochie. (Readers Ser.). 1984. pap. text ed. 2.25 (ISBN 0-88345-575-7). Prentice ESL.
Secret & Lily Hart: Two Tales. Charlotte Bronte. Ed. by William Holtz. LC 78-19645. 96p. 1979. pap. 5.95 (ISBN 0-8262-0268-3). U of Mo Pr.
Secret & Sacred: The Diaries of James Henry Hammond, a Southern Slaveholder. Ed. by Carol K. Bleser. (Illus.). 352p. 1988. 22.95 (ISBN 0-19-505308-7). Oxford U Pr.
Secret & Secure: Privacy, Cryptography & Secure Communication. C. C. Pierce. LC 77-73804. (Illus.). 84p. 1977. pap. 4.95x (ISBN 0-9601564-1-0); Pages 32. pap. supplement incl. (ISBN 0-9601564-3-7). C C Pierce.
Secret & Silent in the Earth. Del Sneller. (Stone Country Poetry Ser.: No. 2). 1976. pap. text ed. 3.95x (ISBN 0-930020-01-4). Stone Country.
Secret & Survival Radio Frequencies & Methods. John J. Williams. Ed. by Laurie Williams. (Illus.). 78p. (Orig.). 1987. pap. 25.00 (ISBN 0-934274-23-1). Consumertronics.
Secret Annexe Three. Colin Dexter. 224p. 1988. pap. 3.95 (ISBN 0-553-27549-6). Bantam.
Secret Annie Oakley. Marcy Heidish. LC 82-22498. (Illus.). 240p. 1983. 14.95 (ISBN 0-453-00437-7); pap. 6.95 (ISBN 0-452-25514-7). NAL.
Secret Armies. Tim Healey. LC 81-50556. (Armies of the Past Ser.). (Illus.). 80p. (gr. 5 up). PLB 14.96 (ISBN 0-382-06587-5); pap. 8.75 (ISBN 0-382-09156-6). Silver.
Secret Armies: Inside the Soviet, American & European Special Forces. James Adams. (Illus.). 448p. 1988. 19.95 (ISBN 0-87113-223-0). Atlantic Monthly.
Secret Armies: Spies, Counterspies, & Saboteurs in World War II. Albert Marrin. LC 85-7944. (Illus.). 192p. (gr. 5 up). 1985. 13.95 (ISBN 0-689-31165-6, Atheneum Childrens Bks). Macmillan.
Secret Army. Tadeusz Bor-Komorowski. (Allied Forces Ser.: No. 2). (Illus.). 408p. 1984. Repr. of 1951 ed. 18.95x (ISBN 0-89839-082-6). Battery Pr.
Secret Army: The IRA, 1916-1979. rev. ed. J. Bowyer Bell. 496p. 1980. pap. 15.00 (ISBN 0-262-52090-7). MIT Pr.
Secret Arts. (Enchanted World Ser.). 144p. 1987. 14.95 (ISBN 0-8094-5285-5); lib. bdg. write for info. (ISBN 0-8094-5286-3). Time-Life.
Secret Ascension. Michael Bishop. 352p. 1987. 16.95 (ISBN 0-312-93031-3, Dist. By Warner Pub Servs & St Martin Pr). Tor Bks.
Secret Ascension. Michael Bishop. 352p. 1989. pap. price not set. Tor Bks.
Secret at Pheasant Cottage. Patricia St. John. LC 78-24384. (gr. 6-8). 1979. pap. 3.95 (ISBN 0-8024-7683-X). Moody.
Secret at Robert's Roost. Mary M. Tallent. 180p. (Orig.). (gr. 4-8). 1988. pap. 3.95 (ISBN 0-941711-05-6). Wyrick & Co.
Secret at Shadow Ranch. Carolyn Keene. (Nancy Drew Ser: Vol. 5). (gr. 4-7). 1931. 4.50 (ISBN 0-448-09505-X, G&D). Putnam Pub Group.
Secret at Summerhaven. Lucy A. Nolan. LC 83-15568. (Escapade Ser.). 128p. (gr. 4-6). cancelled (ISBN 0-689-31383-7, Atheneum Childrens Bks). Macmillan.
Secret at Summerhaven. Lucy A. Nolan. LC 83-15568. 144p. (gr. 3-7). 1987. 12.95 (ISBN 0-689-31336-5, Atheneum Childrens Bks). Macmillan.
Secret at the Polk Street School. Patricia R. Giff. (Polka Dot Private Eye Ser.: No. 3). (Orig.). (gr. k-6). 1987. pap. 2.50 (ISBN 0-440-47696-8, YB). Dell.
Secret Band of Brothers: A Full & True Exposition of All the Various Crimes, Villainies, & Misdeeds of This Powerful Organization in the United States. Jonathan H. Green. (Illus.). 1980. 9.50 (ISBN 0-682-49368-6, University). Exposition-Phoenix.
Secret Baseball Challenge. Jerry Jenkins. (Dallas O'Neil & the Baker Street Sports Club Ser.). (Orig.). (YA) (gr. 9-12). 1986. pap. text ed. 3.95 (ISBN 0-8024-8232-5). Moody.
Secret Behind the Blue Door. Frances C. Matranga. (Voyager Ser.). 96p. (Orig.). (gr. 4-9). 1981. pap. 3.45 (ISBN 0-8010-6121-0). Baker Bk.
Secret Below 103rd Street. Roland Jefferson. pap. 2.25 (ISBN 0-686-45871-0). Holloway.
Secret Bible Prophecies. DeWitt B. Lucas. 1965. pap. 2.50 (ISBN 0-910140-10-3). C & R Anthony.
Secret Birthday Gift. Dandi D. Knorr. (Jenny & Josh Bks.). (Illus.). 32p. (gr. 1-3). 1987. 4.95 (ISBN 0-87403-314-4, 3544). Standard Pub.
Secret Birthday Message. Eric Carle. LC 75-168726. (Illus.). (ps-3). 1972. 12.70i (ISBN 0-690-72347-4, Crowell Jr Bks); PLB 12.89 (ISBN 0-690-72348-2). HarpJ.
Secret Birthday Message. Eric Carle. LC 85-45403. (Trophy Picture Bks.). (Illus.). 24p. (ps-3). 1986. pap. 4.95 (ISBN 0-06-443099-5, Trophy). HarpJ.
Secret Book, Vol. 1. Edmund L. Pearson. LC 72-3419. (Short Story Index Reprint Ser). Repr. of 1914 ed. 18.00 (ISBN 0-8369-4159-4). Ayer Co Pubs.
Secret Book of Artephius. Ed. by Francis Barrett. 1984. pap. 2.95 (ISBN 0-916411-28-1, Pub. by Alchemical Pr). Holmes Pub.
Secret Books of the Egyptian Gnostics. Jean Doresse. LC 79-153316. Repr. of 1960 ed. 27.50 (ISBN 0-404-04646-0). AMS Pr.
Secret Books of the Egyptian Gnostics. Jean Doresse. (Illus.). 446p. 1986. pap. 14.95 (ISBN 0-89281-107-2). Inner Tradit.
Secret Brother & Other Poems. Elizabeth Jennings. LC 69-14765. (Illus.). (gr. 1-5). 1966. 11.95 (ISBN 0-8023-1194-6). Dufour.
Secret Camera: Issues in Doubt. Terence S. Kirk. Ed. by Pauline Jones. LC 87-62825. (Illus.). 248p. 1988. 17.95 (ISBN 0-944531-00-8). Owl Wise Pub.
Secret Careers of Samuel Roth. Leo Hamalian. pap. 2.00 (ISBN 0-911906-08-8). Harian Creative.
Secret Cargo. Carolyn Keene & Franklin W. Dixon. Ed. by Betty Schwartz. (Nancy Drew-The Hardy Boys Be a Detective Mystery Stories Ser.: No. 4). (Illus.). 128p. (Orig.). 1984. pap. 2.95 (ISBN 0-671-49922-X). Wanderer Bks.
Secret Carousel. Mills. (ps-7). 1987. pap. 2.50 (ISBN 0-553-15499-0, Skylark). Bantam.
Secret Carousel. Claudia Mills. LC 82-20938. 144p. (gr. 3-7). 1983. 8.95 (ISBN 0-02-767050-3, Four Winds). Macmillan.
Secret Cause: A Discussion of Tragedy. Normand Berlin. LC 81-4089. 208p. 1983. lib. bdg. 17.50x (ISBN 0-87023-336-X); pap. text ed. 11.95x. U of Mass Pr.
Secret Chambers & Hiding-Places. rev. ed. 3rd ed. Allan Fea. LC 79-155739. 320p. 1971. Repr. of 1901 ed. 43.00x (ISBN 0-8103-3385-6). Gale.
Secret Church. Louise A. Vernon. LC 67-15988. (Illus.). 128p. (gr. 3-8). 1967. pap. 4.50 (ISBN 0-8361-1783-2). Herald Pr.
Secret City: A History of Race Relations in the Nation's Capital. Constance M. Green. 1967. 42.00x (ISBN 0-691-04563-1). Princeton U Pr.
Secret City: Photographs from the U. S. S. R. Photos by Boris Savelev. LC 87-51635. (Illus.). 80p. (Orig.). 1988. pap. 15.95 (ISBN 0-500-27504-1). Thames Hudson.
Secret Code: The Lost & Hidden Language of the Bible, Vol. 1. Thierry Gaudin. LC 85-70031. 300p. (Orig.). 1985. pap. 12.95 (ISBN 0-933357-05-2). Bret Pubns.
Secret Codes & Ciphers. 1986. lib. bdg. 79.95 (ISBN 0-8490-3529-5). Gordon Pr.
Secret Conan Doyle Correspondence. Ed. by Leslie V. Harper. Orig. Title: Secret Holmes-Doyle Correspondence. 224p. (Orig.). 1986. pap. 10.95 (ISBN 0-935927-77-8). Hascom Pubs.
Secret Constitution & the Need for Constitutional Change. Arthur S. Miller. LC 87-235. (Contributions in American Studies: No. 90). 1987. lib. bdg. 12.89 (ISBN 0-313-25745-0, MCG/). Greenwood.
Secret Contenders: The Myth of Cold War Counterintelligence. Melvin Beck. (Illus.). 192p. 1984. 14.95 (ISBN 0-940380-05-6); pap. 7.95 (ISBN 0-940380-04-8). Sheridan Square Pubns.
Secret Corners of the World. Ed. by Donald J. Crump. LC 81-48073. (Special Publications Series 17: No. 1). 200p. 1982. 7.95 (ISBN 0-87044-412-3); lib. bdg. 9.50. Natl Geog.
Secret Country. Janet Bord & Colin Bord. (Illus.). 247p. 1981. pap. 7.95 (ISBN 0-586-08267-0, Pub. by Granada England). Academy Chi Pubs.
Secret Country. Pamela C. Dean. 304p. 1986. pap. 2.95 (Pub. by Ace Science Fiction). Ace Bks.
Secret Country. Frank O'Neill. 1988. 17.95 (ISBN 0-517-56728-8). Crown.
Secret Cross of Lorraine. Thea J. Brow. (gr. 5-8). 1981. 8.95 (ISBN 0-395-30344-3). HM.
Secret Crush. Christie Wells. LC 88-16941. (Cranberry Cousins Ser.). 128p. (gr. 4-8). 1988. lib. bdg. 9.49 (ISBN 0-8167-1498-3); pap. text ed. 2.95 (ISBN 0-8167-1499-1). Troll Assocs.
Secret Cult of the Order. Anthony C. Sutton. 140p. (Orig.). 1984. pap. text ed. 9.95 (ISBN 0-914981-09-9). Res Pubns AZ.
Secret Cult of the Order. Antony Sutton. (Order Ser.: Vol. 4). 1983. 6.50 (ISBN 0-949667-19-6). Concord Bks.
Secret Dakini Oracle. Nik Douglas & Penny Slinger. (Illus.). 224p. 1979. pap. 8.95 (ISBN 0-89281-005-X, Destiny Bks). Inner Tradit.
Secret Dangers. John Preston. (Mission of Alex Kane Ser.: Vol. 5). 117p. (Orig.). 1986. pap. 4.95 (ISBN 0-932870-91-0). Alyson Pubns.
Secret De Gulliver see Gulliver's Secret.
Secret de la licorne. Herge. (Illus., Fr.). (gr. 7-9). looseleaf bdg. 15.95 (ISBN 0-685-28414-X). French & Eur.
Secret de Maitre Cornille. Alphonse Daudet. (Illus.). 32p. 1964. 8.95 (ISBN 0-686-55598-8). French & Eur.
Secret de Wilhelm Storitz. Jules Verne. (Illus.). 192p. 1977. 8.95 (ISBN 0-686-55949-5). French & Eur.
Secret Destinations. Charles Causley. 1988. 9.95 (ISBN 0-87923-739-2); 15.95 (ISBN 0-87923-738-4). Godine.
Secret Destiny of America. Manly P. Hall. 7.95 (ISBN 0-89314-521-1); pap. 5.95 (ISBN 0-89314-388-X). Philos Res.

Secret Diary of Adrian Mole, Aged 13: The Play. Sue Townsend. 65p. pap. 7.95 (ISBN 0-413-59250-2, 9801). Heinemann Ed.

Secret Diary of Adrian Mole, Aged 13 3-4. Sue Townsend. 208p. (gr. 8 up). 1987. pap. 3.50 (ISBN 0-380-86876-8, Flare). Avon.

Secret Diary of Harold L. Ickes, 3 vols. Harold L. Ickes. LC 73-21721. (FDR & the Era of the New Deal Ser.). 1974. Repr. of 1954 ed. Set. lib. bdg. 175.00 (ISBN 0-306-70626-1); lib. bdg. 79.50 ea. Vol. 1, The First Thousand Days, 1933-1936 (ISBN 0-306-70627-X). Vol. 2, The Inside Struggle, 1936-1939 (ISBN 0-306-70628-8). Vol. 3, The Lowering Clouds, 1939-1941 (ISBN 0-306-70629-6). Da Capo.

Secret Diary of Katie Dinkerhoff. Lila Perl. LC 86-31654. 176p. (YA) (gr. 7 up). 1987. 11.95 (ISBN 0-590-41131-4). Scholastic Inc.

Secret Diary of William Byrd of Westover 1709-1712. William Byrd. LC 72-141097. Repr. of 1941 ed. 38.50 (ISBN 0-405-03304-4, Blom Pubns). Ayer Co Pubs.

Secret Diplomacy of the Vietnam War: The Negotiating Volumes of the Pentagon Papers. Ed. by George C. Herring. 915p. 1983. text ed. 47.50x (ISBN 0-292-77573-3). U of Tex Pr.

Secret: Do Not Let Your Body Die. Jahangir Mirala. (Illus.). 48p. 1984. 5.95 (ISBN 0-89962-418-9). Todd & Honeywell.

Secret Doctrine, 3 vols. 7th ed. Helena P. Blavatsky. Ed. by Boris De Zirkoff. (Illus.). 1980. 57.50 ea. (ISBN 0-8356-7525-4). Theos Pub Hse.

Secret Doctrine, 2 vols. facsimile reprint of 1888 ed. Helena P. Blavatsky. LC 74-76603. 1988. Set. 28.00 (ISBN 1-55700-001-8); Set. pap. 17.00 (ISBN 1-55700-002-6); 20.00. Theos U Pr.

Secret Doctrine, 2 vols. Helene P. Blavatsky. 250.00 (ISBN 0-8490-1010-1). Gordon Pr.

Secret Doctrine of H. P. Blavatsky: First International Symposium, July 1984. Ed. by Richard I. Robb. 112p. 1984. pap. 7.00 (ISBN 0-913510-52-1). Wizards.

Secret Doctrine of the Rosicrucians. Magnus Incognito. 8.00 (ISBN 0-911662-30-8). Yoga.

Secret Doctrine: The Synthesis of Science, Religion, & Philosophy, 2 vols. in 1. Helena P. Blavatsky. xci, 1474p. 1925. Repr. of 1888 ed. 18.50 (ISBN 0-938998-00-5). Theosophy.

Secret Doctrines of Jesus. 19th ed. H. Spencer Lewis. LC 37-22922. 237p. 1965. 10.95 (ISBN 0-912057-14-9, G-504). AMORC.

Secret Documents of America. Mark McCloskey. 1976. pap. 1.50 (ISBN 0-88031-032-4). Invisible-Red Hill.

Secret Door to Success. F. Shinn. 4.95x (ISBN 0-685-70721-0). Wehman.

Secret Door to Success. Florence S. Shinn. 1978. pap. 3.50 (ISBN 0-87516-258-4). DeVorss.

Secret Drama of Shakspeare's Sonnets Unfolded. 2nd enl. ed. Gerald Massey. LC 74-172854. Repr. of 1872 ed. 39.75 (ISBN 0-404-04237-6). AMS Pr.

Secret du Masque de Fer. Marcel Pagnol. (Illus.). 416p. 1977. 9.95 (ISBN 0-686-54843-4). French & Eur.

Secret Ecstasy. Rochelle Wayne. 496p. 1986. pap. 3.95 (ISBN 0-8217-1859-2). Zebra.

Secret Enemy: Austria-Hungary & the German Alliance, 1914-1918. Gary W. Shanafelt. 320p. 1985. 30.00x (ISBN 0-88033-080-5, Dist. by Columbia U Pr). East Eur Quarterly.

Secret Essex. Glyn Morgan. 1985. 21.00x (ISBN 0-86025-859-9, Pub. by Ian Henry Pubns England). State Mutual Bk.

Secret Essex. Glyn Morgan. 1988. 30.00x (Pub. by Ian Henry Pubns England). State Mutual Bk.

Secret Exodus. Claire Safran. (Illus.). 192p. 1987. 17.95 (ISBN 0-13-798182-1). P-H.

Secret Families. John Gardner. 400p. 1989. 18.95 (ISBN 0-399-13397-6, Putnam). Putnam Pub Group.

Secret Family. T. Noel Stern. (Illus.). 197p. (Orig.). 1988. pap. 15.00 (ISBN 0-9619733-0-7). T N Stern.

Secret Field. James Wright. Ed. by Anne Wright. 16p. (Orig.). 1985. pap. 3.25. Logbridge Rhodes.

Secret Fighting Arts of the World. John F. Gilbey. LC 63-7910. (Illus.). 1963. bds. 9.75 (ISBN 0-8048-0515-6). C E Tuttle.

Secret Fighting Arts of World. J. F. Gilbey. 9.75x (ISBN 0-685-63779-4). Wehman.

Secret Files of Dakota King. Louise Coligan & Linda Aber. (No. 1). (gr. 4-6). 1987. pap. 2.50. Scholastic Inc.

Secret Files of Solar Pons. Basil Copper. 218p. 1988. pap. 5.95 (ISBN 0-89733-328-4). Academy Chi Pubs.

Secret Fire. Johanna Lindsey. 384p. 1987. pap. 4.50 (ISBN 0-380-75087-2). Avon.

Secret Fire: How Women Live Their Sexual Fantasies. Rosemarie Santini. LC 81-48538. 320p. 1982. pap. 3.95 (ISBN 0-394-17979-X, B-469, BC). Grove.

Secret Flower of Ranatan. Herbert L. McClelland. LC 82-71949. (Illus.). 60p. (gr. 3-5). pap. 3.50x (ISBN 0-943864-09-7). Davenport.

Secret for a Nightingale. Victoria Holt. 408p. 1987. pap. 4.95 (ISBN 0-449-21296-3, Crest). Fawcett.

Secret for Grandmother's Birthday. Franz Brandenberg. LC 75-10606. (Illus.). 32p. (gr. k-3). 1985. 10.25 (ISBN 0-688-05781-0); lib. bdg. 10.88 (ISBN 0-688-05782-9). Greenwillow.

Secret Forces of Nature. Karl Von Eckarthausen. (Rosicrucian - Alchemy Ser.). (Orig.). pap. write for info. Rozekruis Pr.

Secret Forces of the Pyramids. Warren Smith. 220p. 1975. pap. 1.75 (ISBN 0-89083-114-9). Zebra.

Secret Forces: The Technique of Underground Movements. Ferdinand O. Miksche. LC 73-110273. (Illus.). 181p. 1971. Repr. of 1950 ed. lib. bdg. 35.00x (ISBN 0-8371-4499-X, MISF). Greenwood.

Secret Forest of Dean. Fay Godwin. 128p. 39.75x (ISBN 0-948265-65-5, Pub. by Redcliffe Pr Ltd). State Mutual Bk.

Secret Formulas & Techniques of the Masters. Jacques Maroger. Tr. by Eleanor Beckham from Fr. LC 79-83840. (Illus.). 1979. Repr. of 1948 ed. lib. bdg. 25.00 (ISBN 0-87817-245-9). Hacker.

Secret Freedom Fighter: Fighting Tyranny Without Terrorizing the Innocent. Jefferson Mack. 168p. (Orig.). 1986. pap. text ed. 8.95 (ISBN 0-87364-392-5). Paladin Pr.

Secret Friend. Marilyn Sachs. 128p. (gr. 3-7). 1987. pap. 2.50 (ISBN 0-590-40403-2, Apple Paperback). Scholastic Inc.

Secret Friendship. Virginia Brosseit. LC 87-40254. 127p. 1987. 8.95 (ISBN 1-55523-094-6). Winston-Derek.

Secret Garden. Helen P. Avery. (Orig.). (gr. k-3). 1987. pap. 3.50 playscript (ISBN 0-87602-271-9). Anchorage.

Secret Garden. Frances Burnett. 302p. 1981. Repr. PLB 17.95x (ISBN 0-89966-326-5). Buccaneer Bks.

Secret Garden. Frances Burnett. 1977. 17.95 (ISBN 0-89967-001-6). Harmony Raine.

Secret Garden. Frances H. Burnett. (gr. k-6). 1987. pap. 4.95 (ISBN 0-440-47709-3, Pub. by Yearling Classics). Dell.

Secret Garden. Frances H. Burnett. LC 62-17457. (Illus.). 240p. (gr. 5-9). 1962. 8.95 (ISBN 0-397-30632-6, Lipp Jr Bks); PLB 12.89 (ISBN 0-397-32162-7). HarpJ.

Secret Garden. Frances H. Burnett. (Dent's Illustrated Children's Classics Ser.). 256p. (gr. 4 up). 1975. 11.00x (ISBN 0-460-05101-6, Pub. by J. M. Dent England). Biblio Dist.

Secret Garden. Frances H. Burnett. (Puffin Classics Ser.). (gr. 4-6). 1987. pap. 2.25 (ISBN 0-14-035004-7, Puffin). Penguin.

Secret Garden. Frances H. Burnett. (Illustrated Junior Library). (Illus.). 320p. (gr. 4 up). 1987. 12.95 (ISBN 0-448-06029-9, G&D). Putnam Pub Group.

Secret Garden. Frances H. Burnett. LC 62-17457. (Trophy I Can Read Bks.). (Illus.). 321p. (gr. 5-9). 1987. pap. 2.95 (ISBN 0-06-440188-X, Trophy). HarpJ.

Secret Garden. Frances H. Burnett. 1987. pap. 2.50 (ISBN 0-451-52080-7, Sig Classics). NAL.

Secret Garden. Frances H. Burnett. LC 86-17788. (Illus.). 72p. (gr. k-5). 1987. 10.95 (ISBN 0-394-86467-0, BYR); lib. bdg. 12.99 (ISBN 0-394-96467-5). Random.

Secret Garden. Frances H. Burnett. (Illus.). 224p. 1986. 16.95 (ISBN 0-87923-649-3). Godine.

Secret Garden. Frances H. Burnett. (Children's Classics Ser.). (gr. k-6). 8.98 (ISBN 0-517-63225-X). Outlet Bk Co.

Secret Garden. Frances H. Burnett. LC 86-22780. 240p. (gr. 4-6). 1987. 18.95 (ISBN 0-8050-0277-4). H Holt & Co.

Secret Garden. Frances H. Burnett. 304p. (Orig.). (gr. 4-6). 1987. pap. 2.95 (ISBN 0-590-40720-1, Pub. by Apple Classics). Scholastic Inc.

Secret Garden. Frances H. Burnett. (Classics Ser.). 256p. 1987. pap. 2.95 (ISBN 0-553-21201-X, Bantam Classics). Bantam.

Secret Garden. Frances H. Burnett. LC 85-10291. (Illus.). 240p. (gr. 5-9). 1987. 8.95 (ISBN 0-694-00239-9, Lipp Jr Bks). HarpJ.

Secret Garden. Frances H. Burnett. Adapted by Louise Betts. LC 87-15490. (Troll Illustrated Classics Ser.). (Illus.). (gr. 3-6). 1987. PLB 11.89 (ISBN 0-8167-1203-4); pap. 3.95 (ISBN 0-8167-1204-2). Troll Assocs.

Secret Garden. Frances H. Burnett. (World's Classics Ser.). 360p. 1987. pap. 4.95 (ISBN 0-19-281772-8). Oxford U Pr.

Secret Garden. Frances H. Burnett. LC 86-46002. (Knopf Children's Classics). (Illus.). 240p. 1988. 17.95 (ISBN 0-317-65684-8). Knopf.

Secret Garden. Mahmud Shabistari. 1969. 10.95 (ISBN 0-900860-38-3). Ins Study Human.

Secret Garden. (Classics Ser.). (gr. 4 up). 1988. pap. 3.95 (ISBN 0-582-54152-2). Longman.

Secret Garden see New Method Supplementary Readers.

Secret Garden see New Method Supplementary Readers: Bestseller Pack.

Secret Gardens. Alan Toogood. (Illus.). 128p. 1988. 19.95 (ISBN 0-943955-01-7). Trafalgar Sq.

Secret Gardens: A Study of the Golden Age of Children's Literature. Humphrey Carpenter. (Illus.). 235p. 1985. 16.95 (ISBN 0-395-35293-2). HM.

Secret Gardens of Watergate. Pauline Innis. (Illus.). 1986. 9.95 (ISBN 0-914440-91-8). EPM Pubns.

Secret Generations. John Gardner. LC 85-6520. 384p. 1985. 17.95 (ISBN 0-399-13037-3). Putnam Pub Group.

Secret Generations. John Gardner. 496p. 1986. pap. 4.50 (ISBN 0-441-75760-X, Pub. by Charter Bks). Ace Bks.

Secret Go the Wolves. R. D. Lawrence. 240p. 1983. pap. 2.95 (ISBN 0-345-33200-8). Ballantine.

Secret Gold Mine. Stephen Mooser. LC 87-16151. (Treasure Hounds Ser.). (Illus.). 96p. (gr. 3-6). 1987. PLB 9.49 (ISBN 0-8167-1179-8); pap. text ed. 2.95 (ISBN 0-8167-1180-1). Troll Assocs.

Secret Gospel: The Discovery & Interpretation of the Secret Gospel According to Mark. Morton Smith. LC 82-73215. 157p. pap. 7.95 (ISBN 0-913922-55-2). Dawn Horse Pr.

Secret Government. Bill Moyers. Ed. by Calvin Kytle. 152p. 1988. 14.95 (ISBN 0-932020-61-5); pap. 16.95 (ISBN 0-932020-60-7). Seven Locks Pr.

Secret Hearts. Jane Pitt. (Heartlines Ser.: No. 2). (Orig.). (gr. 6 up). 1986. pap. 2.50 (ISBN 0-440-97722-3, LFL). Dell.

Secret Hide-Out. John Peterson. (Illus.). 48p. (gr. 2-4). 1988. pap. 2.50 (ISBN 0-590-41353-8, Lucky Star). Scholastic Inc.

Secret Hiding-Places: The Origins, Histories & Descriptions of English Secret Hiding-Places Used by Priests, Cavaliers, Jacobites, & Smugglers. Granville Squiers. LC 70-157499. (Tower Bks). (Illus.). 288p. 1971. Repr. of 1934 ed. 43.00x (ISBN 0-8103-3920-X). Gale.

Secret Historical Facts: Events of October 15, 1944; Record of Evidence of Interrogations at Sopronkohida, Hungary. Hungarian Historical Research Society Staff. LC 77-95241. Orig. Title: Titkos Tortenelmi Adatok Az 1944 Oktober 15.-I Esemenyek Sopronkohidai Kihallhatasok. 422p. 1978. pap. 15.95 (ISBN 0-935484-02-7). Universe Pub Co.

Secret History. Procopius. Tr. by Richard Atwater. 1961. pap. 4.95x (ISBN 0-472-08728-2, AA). U of Mich Pr.

Secret History. facsimile ed. LC 73-161273. (Black Heritage Library Collection). Repr. of 1808 ed. 16.00 (ISBN 0-8369-8832-9). Ayer Co Pubs.

Secret History. G. A. Williamson. (Penguin Classics). 1982. pap. 6.95 (ISBN 0-14-044182-4). Penguin.

Secret History: An Eyewitness Expose of the Rise of Mormonism. John Ahmanson. Tr. by Gleason L. Archer from Danish. 1984. 9.95 (ISBN 0-8024-0277-1). Moody.

Secret History of Grammar: An Epic Fantasy. Russell Shorto & Robert Cwiklik. (Storytexts Ser.). (Illus.). 160p. (gr. 5 up). 1988. pap. 8.95 (ISBN 0-943718-06-6). Kipling Pr.

Secret History of Queen Zarah & the Zarazians. Mary D. Manley. LC 79-170514. (Foundations of the Novel Ser.: Vol. 10). 1972. lib. bdg. 61.00 (ISBN 0-8240-0522-8). Garland Pub.

Secret History of the American Revolution. Carl Van Doren. LC 76-122062. (Illus.). 1973. Repr. of 1941 ed. 39.50x (ISBN 0-678-03176-2). Kelley.

Secret History of the English Occupation of Egypt. Wilfred S. Blunt. 1967. 45.00x (ISBN 0-86527-179-8). Fertig.

Secret History of the English Occupation in Egypt. Wilfrid S. Blunt. 662p. Repr. of 1907 ed. text ed. 124.20x (ISBN 0-576-03574-2, Pub. by Gregg Intl Pubs England). Gregg Intl.

Secret History of the Jesuits. rev. ed. Edmond Paris. 208p. 1982. pap. 5.95 (ISBN 0-937958-10-7). Chick Pubns.

Secret History of the Lord of Musashi & Arrowroot. Junichiro Tanizaki. 224p. (Orig.). 1983. pap. 5.95 (ISBN 0-399-50860-0, Wideview). Putnam Pub Group.

Secret History of the Lord of Musashi & Arrowroot: Two Novellas. Junichiro Tanizaki. 1982. 12.45 (ISBN 0-394-52454-3). Knopf.

Secret History of the Mongols. Ed. & tr. by Francis W. Cleaves. (Harvard-Yenching Institute Ser.). 344p. 1982. text ed. 22.50x (ISBN 0-674-79670-5). Harvard U Pr.

Secret History of the Mongols: An Adaptation. Ed. by Paul Kahn. Tr. by Francis W. Cleaves from Chinese. LC 83-61394. (Illus.). 256p. (Orig.). 1984. pap. 14.00 (ISBN 0-86547-138-X). N Point Pr.

Secret History of the Oil Companies in the Middle East, 2 vols. new ed. Ed. by William J. Kennedy. 1979. 49.95x set (ISBN 0-89712-078-7). Documentary Pubns.

Secret History of the Oxford Movement. Walter Walsh. LC 73-101915. Repr. of 1898 ed. 25.00 (ISBN 0-404-06819-7). AMS Pr.

Secret History of the Oxford Movement. Walter Walsh. 1977. lib. bdg. 59.95 (ISBN 0-8490-2583-4). Gordon Pr.

Secret History of World War II. Ed. by Sandy Richardson. 304p. 1987. pap. 3.50 (ISBN 0-425-10045-6). Berkley Pub.

Secret History of World War II: The Uncoded Wartime Cables & Letters of, Roosevelt, Stalin, & Churchill. 277p. 1986. 22.50. Richardson & Steirman.

Secret Holmes-Doyle Correspondence see Secret Conan Doyle Correspondence.

Secret Horse. Marion Holland. 160p. (gr. 3-7). 1988. pap. 2.50 (ISBN 0-590-41796-7, Apple Paperbacks). Scholastic Inc.

Secret House. David Bodanis. (Illus.). 224p. 1987. pap. 9.95 (ISBN 0-671-65718-6, Touchstone Bks). S&S.

Secret House of Death. Ruth Rendell. Repr. lib. bdg. 15.95x (ISBN 0-88411-144-X, Pub. by Aeonian Pr). Amereon Ltd.

Secret House of Death. Ruth Rendell. 240p. 1987. pap. 3.50 (ISBN 0-345-34950-4). Ballantine.

Secret House: Twenty-Four Hours in the Strange & Unexpected World in Which We Spend Our Nights & Days. David Bodanis. (Illus.). 224p. 1986. 19.95 (ISBN 0-671-60032-X). S&S.

Secret Houses. John Gardner. 384p. 1987. 18.95 (ISBN 0-399-13311-9, Putnam). Putnam Pub Group.

Secret Houses of the Rose-Croix. 5th ed. Raymond Bernard. Tr. by Amorc Staff. Orig. Title: Fr. 120p. (Orig.). Date not set. pap. price not set (ISBN 0-912057-50-5, G-667). AMORC.

Secret Hunters. Anthony Kemp. 128p. 1986. 39.00x (ISBN 0-948397-35-7, Pub. by M O'Mara UK). State Mutual Bk.

Secret in Miranda's Closet. Sheila Greenwald. (gr. k-6). 1989. pap. price not set (ISBN 0-440-40128-3, YB). Dell.

Secret in the Bird. Camarin Grae. 352p. 1988. pap. 8.95 (ISBN 0-941483-05-3). Naiad Pr.

Secret in the Dungeon. Fernando Krahn. (Illus.). 32p. (gr. 2). 1983. 9.95 (ISBN 0-89919-148-7, Clarion). HM.

Secret in the Garden. Winifred B. Newman. (Illus.). 32p. (Orig.). (gr. k-5). 1980. 6.95 (ISBN 0-87743-151-5, 353-013); pap. 3.95 (ISBN 0-87743-159-0, 353-014). Baha'i.

Secret in the Matchbox. Val Willis. LC 87-46000. (Illus.). 32p. (gr. 3 up). 1988. 12.95 (ISBN 0-374-36603-9). FS&G.

Secret in the Old Attic. rev. ed. Carolyn Keene. LC 78-100118. (Nancy Drew Ser.: Vol. 21). (Illus.). (gr. 4-7). 1955. 4.50 (ISBN 0-448-09521-1, G&D). Putnam Pub Group.

Secret in the Old Mansion. Stephen Mooser. LC 87-15456. (Treasure Hounds Ser.). (Illus.). 96p. (gr. 3-6). 1987. PLB 9.49 (ISBN 0-8167-1175-5); pap. text ed. 2.95 (ISBN 0-8167-1176-3). Troll Assocs.

Secret in the Stlalakum Wild. Christie Harris. LC 72-175554. (Illus.). (gr. 4-6). 1972. 1.29 (ISBN 0-689-30027-1, Atheneum Childrens Bks). Macmillan.

Secret in the Toy Room. Pat Zawadsky. 28p. (Orig.). (gr. 2-7). 1984. pap. 2.50 (ISBN 0-88680-225-3). I E Clark.

Secret in the Toy Room: Musical Score. Pat Zawadsky. 25p. (Orig.). (gr. 2-7). 1984. pap. 7.50 (ISBN 0-88680-226-1). I E Clark.

Secret Incomes of the Soviet State Budget. Igor Birman. 330p. 1981. lib. bdg. 78.50 (ISBN 90-247-2550-X, Pub. by Martinus Nijhoff Netherlands). Kluwer Academic.

Secret Ingredient. Sarah H. Phillips & Mary H. Williams. (Illus.). 179p. 1987. 10.00 (ISBN 0-9619306-0-8). M H Williams.

Secret Ingredients. Michael Roberts. LC 88-47354. (Illus.). 320p. 1988. 21.95 (ISBN 0-553-05320-5). Bantam.

Secret Ingredients: Inactive Ingredients in Drugs. Jeffrey Brown. 1985. 15.95 (ISBN 0-8016-0865-1). Mosby.

Secret Inner Order Rituals of the Golden Dawn. Ed. by Patrick Zalewski et al. (Illus.). 200p. (Orig.). 1988. pap. 12.95 (ISBN 0-941404-65-X). Falcon Pr AZ.

Secret Intelligence: Inside the American Espionage Empire. Ernest Volkman & Blaine Baggett. 1989. 19.95 (ISBN 0-385-24590-4). Doubleday.

Secret Intimacy. Charlotte Lamb. (Harlequin Presents Ser.). 192p. 1984. pap. 1.95 (ISBN 0-373-10658-0). Harlequin Bks.

Secret Invasion. Dave Hunt & Hans Kristian. LC 86-62981. 224p. 1987. pap. 5.95 (ISBN 0-89081-560-7). Harvest Hse.

Secret Iron of the Heart. Arvia McKaye-Ege. 192p. 1982. 12.00 (ISBN 0-932776-05-1); pap. 8.50 (ISBN 0-932776-06-X). Adonis Pr.

Secret Is in the Rainbow. Ruth Berger. 128p. 1986. pap. 6.95 (ISBN 0-87728-638-8). Weiser.

Secret Islands. Franklin Russell. (Illus.). 1966. 5.95 (ISBN 0-393-07381-5). Norton.

Secret Journal & Other Writings. Pierre Drieu La Rochelle. Tr. by Alastair Hamilton from Fr. 1974. 21.50x (ISBN 0-86527-300-6). Fertig.

Secret Journal & Other Writings. Pierre Drieu La Rochelle. Tr. by Alastair Hamilton from Fr. 112p. 1980. 9.95 (ISBN 0-903747-02-2). Writers & Readers.

Secret Journal 1836-1837. Aleksandr Pushkin. LC 86-27858. 104p. 1987. pap. 19.00 (ISBN 0-916201-03-1). M I P Co.

Secret Journals of the Acts & Proceedings of Congress, 4 Vols. U. S. Continental Congress. Repr. of 1821 ed. 165.00 (ISBN 0-384-62910-5). Johnson Repr.

Secret Journey: Mary & Joseph see Baby Born in a Stable: The Christmas Story.

Secret Joy of Repentance. 3.50 (ISBN 0-8198-6863-9); 2.25 (ISBN 0-8198-6864-7). Dghtrs St Paul.

Secret Keeper. Shirley Eskapa. 220p. 1985. pap. 4.95 (ISBN 0-89733-126-5). Academy Chi Pubs.

Secret Kills. William Beechcroft. 208p. 1988. 15.95 (ISBN 0-396-09062-1). Dodd.

Secret of Instantaneous Healing. Harry D. Smith. 1965. 8.95 (ISBN 0-13-797951-7, Reward); pap. 5.95 (ISBN 0-13-797936-3). P-H.

Secret of Intercession. Andrew Murray. (Secret Ser.). (Orig.). 1980. pap. 1.95 (ISBN 0-87508-391-9). Chr Lit.

Secret of Isaac. Jerome Charyn. 240p. 1984. pap. 2.75 (ISBN 0-380-47126-4, 47126, Bard). Avon.

Secret of Israel's Victories-Past, Present, & Future. Moshe M. Maggal. (Illus.). 74p. 7.95 (ISBN 0-533-04986-5, Pub. by Vantage Pr.). Natl Jewish Info.

Secret of Jewish Femininity: Insights into the Practice of Taharat Hamishpachah. Tehilla Abramov & Malka Touger. 176p. 1988. 10.95 (ISBN 0-944070-04-3). Targum Pr.

Secret of John Milton. H. Mutschmann. LC 72-194771. 1925. lib. bdg. 20.50 (ISBN 0-8414-6694-7). Folcroft.

Secret of Jonestown: The Reason Why. Ed Dieckmann, Jr. 176p. (Orig.). 1982. pap. 6.00 (ISBN 0-939482-02-9). Noontide.

Secret of Jungle Park. Laura L. Hope. (Bobbsey Twins Ser.: No. 1). (Illus.). (gr. 2-4). 1987. pap. 2.95 (ISBN 0-671-62651-5, Minstrel Bks). S&S.

Secret of Laughter. A. M. Ludovici. 35.00 (ISBN 0-8490-1011-X). Gordon Pr.

Secret of Laughter. Anthony M. Ludovici. LC 74-8681. 1932. lib. bdg. 35.00 (ISBN 0-8414-5727-1). Folcroft.

Secret of Laughter. Anthony M. Ludovici. 1979. Repr. of 1932 ed. lib. bdg. 39.50 (ISBN 0-8492-1613-3). R West.

Secret of Life. Marvin H. Jackson. 1985. 6.95 (ISBN 0-533-06406-6). Vantage.

Secret of Life. Roy Masters. LC 77-9148. 1972. pap. 9.95 (ISBN 0-933900-02-3). Foun Human Under.

Secret of Life. Rudy Rucker. 240p. 1985. 14.95 (ISBN 0-312-94398-9, Dist. by St. Martin). Bluejay Bks.

Secret of Life & Death: Nineteen Sixty-Nine to Nineteen Eighty-Four, Vol. 1. Allen Ruppersberg. Ed. by Julia Brown. (Illus.). 127p. 1985. incl. computer chip 50.00 (ISBN 0-317-39252-2). Los Angeles Mus Contemp.

Secret of Life: Electricity, Radiation & Your Body. Georges Lakhovsky. Tr. by Mark Clement from Fr. (Illus.). 1988. pap. 9.95 (ISBN 0-939482-08-8). Noontide.

Secret of Life: Perspectivism in Science. Jerry Jacobson. 121p. 1983. 10.95 (ISBN 0-8022-2400-8). Philos Lib.

Secret of Light. Walter Russell. Ed. by Lao Russell. (Illus.). 288p. 1947. text ed. 28.00x. U Sci & Philos.

Secret of Love. Glenna Finley. 192p. 1987. pap. 2.50 (ISBN 0-451-14885-1, Sig). NAL.

Secret of Loving. Josh McDowell. 200p. 1985. 11.95 (ISBN 0-86605-157-0). Campus Crusade.

Secret of Loving. Josh McDowell. (Living Bks.). 240p. Repr. 4.50 (ISBN 0-8423-5845-5). Tyndale.

Secret of Mirror Bay. Carolyn Keene. (Nancy Drew Ser.: Vol. 49). (Illus.). 196p. (gr. 4-7). 1972. 4.50 (ISBN 0-448-09549-1, G&D). Putnam Pub Group.

Secret of Mojo. Regina W. McCally. Ed. by James Baldwin. LC 86-90445. 236p. (YA) (gr. 7 up). 1986. 20.00 (ISBN 0-9619703-0-8). R W McCally.

Secret of Montoya Mission. Dorothy Baughman. (YA) (gr. 7 up). 1981. 9.95 (ISBN 0-686-73950-7, Avalon). Bouregy.

Secret of My Success. Martin Owens. 224p. (Orig.). 1987. pap. 3.95 (ISBN 0-345-34462-6). Ballantine.

Secret of NIMH. Robert C. O'Brien. (Illus.). 264p. (gr. 4-6). 1982. pap. 2.25 (ISBN 0-590-33894-3, Apple Paperbacks). Scholastic Inc.

Secret of Peace & the Environmental Crisis. John F. Gardner. 40p. 1978. pap. 1.50 (ISBN 0-913098-15-9). Myrin Institute.

Secret of Perfect Putting. Horton Smith & Dawson Taylor. pap. 5.00 (ISBN 0-87980-133-6). Wilshire.

Secret of Peter & Jacob. Riva Sepia. 80p. 1988. 7.95 (ISBN 0-89962-696-3). Todd & Honeywell.

Secret of Petrarch. Edmund J. Mills. 1973. Repr. of 1904 ed. 29.50 (ISBN 0-8274-0127-2). R West.

Secret of Pirates' Cave. Dayle Courtney. (Thorne Twins Adventure Bks.). (Illus.). 192p. (Orig.). (gr. 6-10). 1984. pap. 2.98 (ISBN 0-87239-758-0, 2908). Standard Pub.

Secret of Pirates' Hill. rev. ed. Franklin W. Dixon. (Hardy Boys Ser.: Vol. 36). (Illus.). 196p. (gr. 5-9). 1957. 4.50 (ISBN 0-448-08936-X, G&D). Putnam Pub Group.

Secret of Pooduck Island. new ed. Alfred Noyes. Ed. by Albert Stein & George N. Schuster. (Illus., Orig.). (gr. 6-9). 1959. pap. text ed. 3.95 (ISBN 0-910334-22-6). Cath Authors.

Secret of Positive Praying. John Bisagno. Ed. by Jim Ruark. 128p. 1986. pap. 4.50 (ISBN 0-310-21152-2, 9239). Zondervan.

Secret of Power from on High. Andrew Murray. (Secret Ser.). (Orig.). 1980. pap. 1.95 (ISBN 0-87508-392-7). Chr Lit.

Secret of Quaking ASP Cabin & Other Stories. Zane Grey. 1983. pap. 2.50 (ISBN 0-671-45782-9). PB.

Secret of Red Gate Farm. Carolyn Keene. (Nancy Drew Ser.: Vol. 6). (gr. 4-7). 1931. 4.50 (ISBN 0-448-09506-8, G&D). Putnam Pub Group.

Secret of Regeneration. Hilton Hotema. Orig. Title: Science of Human Regeneration (Postgraduate Orthopathy) (Illus.). 900p. 1963. pap. 59.95 (ISBN 0-88697-019-9). Life Science.

Secret of Rejuvenation: Professor Brown Squad's Great Discovery of the Fountain of Youth. Raymond Bernard. 39p. 1956. pap. 7.95 (ISBN 0-88697-036-9). Life Science.

Secret of Right Activity. 4th ed. Swami Paramananda. 1964. 4.50 (ISBN 0-911564-12-8). Vedanta Ctr.

Secret of Room 401. Judith A. Green. (Adult Learner Ser.). (Illus.). 223p. (Orig., Reading level gr. 2, Interest level gr. 9-12, ABE). 1980. pap. text ed. 4.80x (ISBN 0-89061-210-2, 204). Jamestown Pubs.

Secret of Salvation. E. E. Byrum. 264p. pap. 2.50 (ISBN 0-686-29166-2). Faith Pub Hse.

Secret of Sambatyon. Gershon Winkler. Ed. by Bonnie Goldman. 132p. (gr. 4 up). 1987. 6.95 (ISBN 0-910818-68-1); pap. 5.95 (ISBN 0-910818-69-X). Judaica Pr.

Secret of Santa Vittoria. Robert Crichton. 416p. 1986. pap. 3.95 (ISBN 0-88184-267-2). Carroll & Graf.

Secret of Secrets. Uell S. Andersen. pap. 7.00 (ISBN 0-87980-134-4). Wilshire.

Secret of Secrets, Vol. 1. Bhagwan S. Rajneesh. Ed. by Rajneesh Foundation International. LC 82-50464. (Tao Ser.). 588p. (Orig.). 1982. pap. 10.95 (ISBN 0-88050-628-8). Chidvilas Inc.

Secret of Secrets, Vol. 2. Bhagwan S. Rajneesh. Ed. by Ma Y. Sudha. LC 82-50464. (Tao Ser.). 528p. (Orig.). 1983. pap. 4.95 (ISBN 0-88050-629-6). Chidvilas Inc.

Secret of Secrets: Spiritual Discourses. 3rd ed. Darshan Singh. LC 78-69930. (Illus.). 1982. pap. 7.50 (ISBN 0-918224-06-3). Sawan Kirpal Pubns.

Secret of Secrets: The Unwritten Mysteries of Esoteric Qabbalah. Michael-Albion Macdonald. LC 86-81789. (Illus.). 96p. 1986. 20.00 (ISBN 0-935214-08-9). Heptangle.

Secret of Selecting Stocks for Immediate & Substantial Gains. Larry Williams. 1986. 25.00 (ISBN 0-930233-05-0). Windsor.

Secret of Self-Realization. Taimni. 4.50 (ISBN 0-8356-7640-4). Theos Pub Hse.

Secret of Self-Transformation: A Synthesis of Tantra & Yoga. Rohit Mehta. 1987. 21.00x (ISBN 81-208-0381-7, Pub. by Motilal Banarsidass); pap. text ed. 10.00x (ISBN 81-208-0402-3, Pub. by Motilal Banarsidass). South Asia Bks.

Secret of Selling Inventions. 2nd ed. Richard C. Levy. Ed. by Sheryl Levy. 200p. (Orig.). 1986. 49.50 (ISBN 0-931347-00-9). Ricsher Pub Ltd.

Secret of Shakespeare. Martin Lings. 144p. (Orig.). 1984. pap. 8.95 (ISBN 0-89281-059-9). Inner Tradit.

Secret of Shao-Ling Ring: Advanced Chi-Kung, Vol. 1. Thanh-Liem Tran & Duc V. Dao. LC 87-50969. (Illus.). 132p. (Orig.). 1987. pap. 12.95 (ISBN 0-944211-00-3). Vo Lam Pub.

Secret of Sherwood Forest: Oil Production in England During World War Two. Guy H. Woodward & Grace S. Woodward. LC 72-12546. (Illus.). Repr. of 1973 ed. 54.00 (ISBN 0-8357-9741-4, 2016280). Bks Demand UMI.

Secret of Skull Mountain. Franklin W. Dixon. (Hardy Boys Ser: Vol. 27). (gr. 5-9). 1948. 4.50 (ISBN 0-448-08927-0, G&D). Putnam Pub Group.

Secret of Somerset Place. Carol Marsh. (History Mystery Ser.). (Illus.). 160p. (Orig.). (gr. 3-9). 1980. pap. 4.95 (ISBN 0-935326-02-2). Gallopade Pub Group.

Secret of Somerset Place S. P. A. R. K. Kit. Carole Marsh. (S. P. A. R. K. Ser.). (Illus.). 50p. (Orig.). (gr. 3-9). 1986. pap. 24.95 (ISBN 0-935326-20-0). Gallopade Pub Group.

Secret of Squash: How to Win Using the 4-CRO System. John O. Truby, Jr. & John O. Truby. (Illus.). 192p. pap. 8.95 (ISBN 0-316-85353-4). Little.

Secret of Staying in Love. John Powell. LC 74-84712. (Illus.). 1974. pap. 4.95 (ISBN 0-913592-29-3). Tabor Pub.

Secret of Staying Together. John P. Zahody. LC 85-82014. 116p. 1985. deluxe ed. 10.95 (ISBN 0-9615911-0-2). HeartLight Pubns.

Secret of Stonehenge. I. L. Cohen. Ed. by G. Murphy. LC 82-19107. (Illus.). 310p. 1982. 16.95 (ISBN 0-910891-01-X). New Research.

Secret of Success. R. C. Allen. 192p. 1965. 8.95 (ISBN 0-910228-01-9); pap. 4.95 (ISBN 0-910228-02-7). Best Bks.

Secret of Success in Wall Street. Tumbridge & Co. Staff. LC 87-80247. (Illus.). 48p. 1987. pap. 6.00 (ISBN 0-87034-083-2). Fraser Pub Co.

Secret of Swedenborg: Being an Elucidation of His Doctrine of the Divine Humanity. Henry James, Sr. LC 72-914. (Selected Works of Henry James, Sr.: Vol. 7). 264p. 1983. Repr. of 1869 ed. 30.00 (ISBN 0-404-10087-2). AMS Pr.

Secret of Telfair Inn. Idella Bodie. LC 79-177909. (Illus.). 98p. (gr. 5-9). 1983. pap. 6.95 (ISBN 0-87844-050-X). Sandlapper Pub Co.

Secret of Terror Castle see Alfred Hitchcock & the Three Investigators.

Secret of the Abiding Presence. Andrew Murray. (Secret Ser.). (Orig.). 1979. pap. 1.95 (ISBN 0-87508-382-X). Chr Lit.

Secret of the Ages. rev. ed. Robert Collier. 1984. deluxe ed. 15.95 (ISBN 0-912576-12-X); pap. 7.95 (ISBN 0-912576-11-1). R Collier.

Secret of the Andes. Ann N. Clark. (Puffin Story Ser). (Illus.). (gr. 3-7). 1976. pap. 3.95 (ISBN 0-14-030926-8, Puffin). Penguin.

Secret of the Andes. Ann N. Clark. (Illus.). (gr. 4-8). 1952. 13.95 (ISBN 0-670-62975-8). Viking.

Secret of the Andes. Philip. 1976. pap. 5.95 (ISBN 0-915070-02-2). Leaves of Grass.

Secret of the Barbican, & Other Stories. Joseph S. Fletcher. LC 79-121543. (Short Story Index Reprint Ser). 1925. 19.00 (ISBN 0-8369-3499-7). Ayer Co Pubs.

Secret of the Bitter Sweets: A Solve-It-Yourself Whodunit Party for 8 Players. Penny Warner & Tom Warner. (Murder Mystery Parties Ser.). 128p. 1986. pap. 7.95 (ISBN 0-312-35029-5). St Martin.

Secret of the Black Chrysanthemum. Charles Stein. LC 85-14781. (Illus.). 232p. (Orig.). 1987. 27.50 (ISBN 0-88268-017-X, Pub. by Clinamen Studies). Station Hill Pr.

Secret of the Caves. rev. ed. Franklin W. Dixon. (Hardy Boys Ser: Vol. 7). (gr. 5-9). 1929. 4.50 (ISBN 0-448-08907-6, G&D). Putnam Pub Group.

Secret of the Cibolo. Billie P. Matthews & A. Lee Chichester. Ed. by Melissa Roberts. (Illus.). 104p. (gr. 4-7). 1988. 8.95 (ISBN 0-89015-638-7). Eakin Pr.

Secret of the Crater. Duffield Osborn. 1979. Repr. of 1900 ed. 8.50 (ISBN 0-686-65259-2). Bookfinger.

Secret of the Cross. Andrew Murray. (Secret Ser.). (Orig.). 1980. pap. 1.95 (ISBN 0-87508-389-7). Chr Lit.

Secret of the Dark. Barbara Steiner. 176p. (Orig.). (gr. 7-12). 1984. pap. 1.95 (ISBN 0-590-33252-X, Windswept Bks). Scholastic Inc.

Secret of the Diamond Fireside. Ann Terry. (Illus.). 161p. (YA) (gr. 11 up). 1981. pap. 2.95 (ISBN 0-942241-19-3, 8678). Pubs Bk Sales.

Secret of the Drumstick Tree. Jane D. Mook. (Orig.). (gr. 1-3). 1972. pap. 1.95 (ISBN 0-377-12701-9). Friendship Pr.

Secret of the Earth. Charles W. Beale. LC 74-15950. (Science Fiction Ser). 256p. 1975. Repr. of 1899 ed. 21.00x (ISBN 0-405-06276-1). Ayer Co Pubs.

Secret of the Earth Star. Henry Kuttner. Compiled by & intro. by Sheldon Jaffery. (Facsimile Fiction Ser.: No. 6). Date not set. 19.95; pap. 9.95. Starmont Hse.

Secret of the East Wind. Carole G. Page & Doris E. Fell. pap. 5.95 (ISBN 0-89081-514-3). Harvest Hse.

Secret of the Faith Life. Andrew Murray. (Secret Ser.). (Orig.). 1979. pap. 1.95 (ISBN 0-87508-387-0). Chr Lit.

Secret of the Flying T. Charles E. Wheeler. (YA) (gr. 7 up). 1979. 9.95 (ISBN 0-685-65275-0, Avalon). Bouregy.

Secret of the Forest. Jeanne Bowmann. (Contemporary Teens Ser.). 224p. (Orig.). 1981. pap. 2.25 (ISBN 0-89531-146-1, 0146-96). Sharon Pubns.

Secret of the Forest. Neil Morris & Ting Morris. LC 85-40300. (Tales of the Blue Banner Ser.). (Illus.). 24p. (gr. 4-6). 1986. PLB 6.48 (ISBN 0-382-09108-6); pap. 3.95 (ISBN 0-382-09112-4). Silver.

Secret of the Forest. (Sharazad Stories Ser.). (Illus., Arabic.). (gr. 4-6). pap. 3.50x (ISBN 0-86685-266-2). Intl Bk Ctr.

Secret of the Forgotten City. new ed. Carolyn Keene. LC 74-10461. (Nancy Drew Ser.: Vol. 52). (Illus.). 196p. (gr. 4-7). 1975. 4.50 (ISBN 0-448-09552-1, G&D). Putnam Pub Group.

Secret of the Fourth Candle. Patricia St. John. LC 81-22400. 128p. 1981. pap. 3.95 (ISBN 0-8024-7681-3). Moody.

Secret of the Ghost Piano. Elizabeth Bolton. LC 84-8745. (Illus.). 48p. (gr. 2-4). 1985. PLB 9.29 (ISBN 0-8167-0410-4); pap. text ed. 1.95 (ISBN 0-8167-0411-2). Troll Assocs.

Secret of the Golden Flower: A Chinese Book of Life. Richard Wilhelm & C. G. Jung. LC 62-10499. (Illus.). 149p. 1970. pap. 4.95 (ISBN 0-15-679980-4, Harv). HarBraceJ.

Secret of the Golden Hours. Ed. by Regency Press Ltd. Staff. 112p. 1984. 40.00 (ISBN 0-7212-0656-5, Pub. by Regency Pr). State Mutual Bk.

Secret of the Golden Pavilion. Carolyn Keene. (Nancy Drew Ser.: Vol. 36). (Illus.). (gr. 4-7). 1959. 4.50 (ISBN 0-448-09536-X, G&D). Putnam Pub Group.

Secret of the Haunted Chimney. Adrian Robert. LC 84-8763. (Illus.). 48p. (gr. 2-4). 1985. PLB 9.29 (ISBN 0-8167-0408-2); pap. text ed. 1.95 (ISBN 0-8167-0409-0). Troll Assocs.

Secret of the Haunted House. Fran Sabin & Lou Sabin. LC 81-8751. (Easy-To-Read Mystery Ser.). (Illus.). 48p. (gr. 2-4). 1982. PLB 9.29 (ISBN 0-89375-598-2); pap. text ed. 1.95 (ISBN 0-89375-599-0). Troll Assocs.

Secret of the Ice Curtain. Mandy Bruce & Jane Launchbury. (Adventures of the Sunset Patrol Ser.). (Illus.). 32p. (ps-3). cancelled (ISBN 0-8120-6096-2). Barron.

Secret of the Immortal Liquor Called Alkahest. Eirenaeus Philalethes. 1984. pap. 2.95 (ISBN 0-916411-40-0, Pub. by Alchemical). Holmes Pub.

Secret of the Invisible City. Dale Carlson. LC 84-80178. (Jenny Dean Mystery Ser.). (Illus.). (gr. 3-7). 1984. pap. 2.95 (ISBN 0-448-19004-4, G&D). Putnam Pub Group.

Secret of the Island. Jules Verne. 1959. 4.95 (ISBN 0-685-06596-0). Assoc Bk.

Secret of the Kara Sea. Eric Collenette. 1987. 16.95 (ISBN 0-8027-0990-7). Walker & Co.

Secret of the Knights. Byron Preiss & Jim Gasperini. (Time Machine Bk.: No. 1). (Illus.). 144p. (gr. 4 up). 1984. pap. 2.25 (ISBN 0-553-25368-9). Bantam.

Secret of the Knight's Sword. Franklin W. Dixon & Carolyn Keene. Ed. by Betty Schwartz. (Nancy Drew & The Hardy Boys Be a Detective Mystery Stories Ser.: No. 1). (Illus.). 128p. (Orig.). (gr. 3-7). 1984. pap. 3.50 (ISBN 0-671-49919-X). Wanderer Bks.

Secret of the Long-Lost Cousin & Other Mysteries. M. Masters. Ed. by Louise Delagran & Kathe Grooms. LC 83-5392. (Can You Solve the Mystery? Ser.: Vol. 1). (Illus.). 108p. (Orig.). (gr. 2-6). 1983. pap. 1.95 (ISBN 0-671-54489-6). Meadowbrook.

Secret of the Loon Lake Monster & Other Mysteries. M. Masters. Ed. by Mariellen Hanrahan & Kathe Grooms. LC 83-23676. (Can You Solve the Mystery? Ser.: Vol. 10). (Illus.). 108p. (Orig.). (gr. 2-6). 1984. pap. 1.95 (ISBN 0-671-54490-X). Meadowbrook.

Secret of the Lost Lake. Carolyn Keene. (Dana Girls Ser.: Vol. 11). (gr. 4-7). 2.95 (ISBN 0-448-09091-0, G&D). Putnam Pub Group.

Secret of the Lost Tunnel. rev. ed. Franklin W. Dixon. (Hardy Boys Ser: Vol. 29). (Illus.). (gr. 5-9). 1950. 4.50 (ISBN 0-448-08929-7, G&D). Putnam Pub Group.

Secret of the Magic Potion. Elizabeth Bolton. LC 84-8881. (Illus.). 48p. (gr. 2-4). 1985. PLB 9.29 (ISBN 0-8167-0420-1); pap. text ed. 1.95 (ISBN 0-8167-0421-X). Troll Assocs.

Secret of the Minstrel's Guitar. Carolyn Keene. (Dana Girls Ser.: Vol. 5). (Illus.). 192p. (gr. 4-7). 1972. 2.95 (ISBN 0-448-09085-6, G&D). Putnam Pub Group.

Secret of the Missing Camel. Page McBrier. LC 86-887. (Oliver & Company Ser.). (Illus.). 96p. (Orig.). (gr. 3-6). 1986. PLB 9.49 (ISBN 0-8167-0816-9); pap. text ed. 2.95 (ISBN 0-8167-0817-7). Troll Assocs.

Secret of the Mountain. Esther Linfield. LC 85-9912. 144p. (gr. 5 up). 1986. reinforced trade ed. 10.25 (ISBN 0-688-05992-9). Greenwillow.

Secret of the Night. Gaston Leroux. 1975. lib. bdg. 16.70x (ISBN 0-89966-139-4). Buccaneer Bks.

Secret of the Nile. Jack Long. (O'Reilly Mysteries Ser.). (Illus.). 24p. (ps-3). 1987. 3.95 (ISBN 0-02-688777-0, Checkerboard Pr). Macmillan.

Secret of the Nile: Missing Mystery. Doug Cushman. (O'Reilly Mysteries Ser.). (Illus.). 24p. (ps-3). 1987. 3.95 (ISBN 0-02-688778-9). Macmillan.

Secret of the Ninja. Montgomery. (Choose Your Own Adventure Ser.: No. 66). (ps-7). 1987. pap. 2.25 (ISBN 0-553-26484-2). Bantam.

Secret of the Old Barn. Adrian Robert. LC 84-8743. (Illus.). 48p. (gr. 2-4). 1985. PLB 9.29 (ISBN 0-8167-0412-0); pap. text ed. 1.95 (ISBN 0-8167-0413-9). Troll Assocs.

Secret of the Old Clock. Carolyn Keene. (Nancy Drew Ser.: Vol. 1). (gr. 4-7). 1930. 4.50 (ISBN 0-448-09501-7, G&D). Putnam Pub Group.

Secret of the Old Garage. Page McBrier. LC 85-16505. (Oliver & Company Ser.). (Illus.). 96p. (gr. 3-6). 1986. PLB 9.49 (ISBN 0-8167-0543-7); pap. text ed. 2.95 (ISBN 0-8167-0544-5). Troll Assocs.

Secret of the Old House, No. 1. Peggy Albrecht. (gr. 6-8). 1983. pap. 2.95 (ISBN 0-87508-653-5). Chr Lit.

Secret of the Old Mill. Franklin W. Dixon. (Hardy Boys Ser: Vol. 3). (gr. 5-9). 1927. 4.50 (ISBN 0-448-08903-3, G&D). Putnam Pub Group.

Secret of the Old Museum. Roy Wandelmaier. LC 85-2533. (Illus.). 112p. (gr. 3-6). 1985. lib. bdg. 9.49 (ISBN 0-8167-0531-3); pap. text ed. 2.95 (ISBN 0-8167-0532-1). Troll Assocs.

Secret of the Orient: Dwarf Rhapis Excelsa. Lynn McKamey. LC 85-50589. (Illus.). 52p. (Orig.). 1983. pap. 3.95 (ISBN 0-9612130-0-0). Rhapis Gardens.

Secret of the Pacific: Origins of the Toltecs, Aztecs, Mayas, & Incas. C. Reginald Enock. 1977. lib. bdg. 59.95 (ISBN 0-8490-2584-2). Gordon Pr.

Secret of the Painted Idol. Margaret M. Wallworth. LC 85-16574. (Pennypinchers Ser.). 128p. (gr. 4-9). 1985. pap. 2.95 (ISBN 0-89191-902-3, 59022, Chariot Bks). Cook.

Secret of the Past. Ann Gabhart. (YA) (gr. 7 up). 1988. pap. 2.50 (ISBN 0-380-75497-5, Flare). Avon.

Secret of the Peruvian Quipus, 2 pts. in 1 vol. Erland Nordenskiold. LC 75-46059. (Comparative Ethnographical Studies Ser.: Vol. 6). Repr. of 1925 ed. 39.50 (ISBN 0-404-15146-9). AMS Pr.

Secret of the Poison Ring. Dorothy Y. Croman. (Outlands Adventure Ser.). 128p. (Orig.). (gr. 3-6). 1986. 3.50 (ISBN 0-8423-5898-6). Tyndale.

Secret of the Pyramids. Brightfield. (Choose Your Own Adventure Ser.: No. 19). (ps-7). 1987. pap. 2.25 (ISBN 0-553-25761-7). Bantam.

Secret of the Radiant Life. W. E. Sangster. 192p. 1988. pap. 6.95 (ISBN 0-310-51381-2, Pub. by Asbury Pr). Zondervan.

Secret of the Rosary. St. Louis De Monfort. Tr. by Mary Barbour from Fr. 1976. pap. 1.00 (ISBN 0-89555-056-3). TAN Bks Pubs.

Secret of the Rosary. St. Louis De Montfort. pap. 1.00 (ISBN 0-910984-04-2). Montfort Pubns.

Secret of the Rothschilds. M. Hobart. 69.95 (ISBN 0-8490-1012-8). Gordon Pr.

Secret of the Round Beast. John Forrester. LC 86-11800. 192p. (gr. 7 up). 1986. 12.95 (ISBN 0-02-735380-X). Bradbury Pr.

Secret of the Round Beast. John Forrester. LC 87-45281. 160p. (YA) (gr. 7 up). 1988. pap. 2.75 (ISBN 0-694-05622-7, Starwanderer). HarpJ.

Secret of the Royal Treasure. Carol Gaskin. (Time Machine Ser.: No. 13). 144p. (Orig.). 1986. pap. 2.50 (ISBN 0-553-25729-3). Bantam.

Secret of the Runes. Ed. & tr. by Stephen E. Flowers. 196p. 1988. pap. 9.95 (ISBN 0-89281-207-9). Inner Tradit.

Secret of the Sabbath Fish. Ben Aronin. LC 78-63437. (Illus.). (gr. k-4). 1979. 8.95 (ISBN 0-8276-0110-7, 433). JPS Phila.

Secret of the Sachem's Tree. F. N. Monjo. (Illus.). 64p. (gr. 1-5). 1973. pap. 0.75 (ISBN 0-440-47634-8, Yearling). Dell.

Secret of the Sands. Catherine West. (Illus.). 60p. (Orig.). 1987. pap. 6.95 (ISBN 0-944153-00-3). Crosing Pub.

Secret of the Satin Doll. Jean Sprouse. (YA) (gr. 7 up). 1978. 9.95 (ISBN 0-685-87349-8, Avalon). Bouregy.

Secret of the Sea & C. facsimile ed. Brander Matthews. LC 74-160942. (Short Story Index Reprint Ser). Repr. of 1886 ed. 17.00 (ISBN 0-8369-3921-2). Ayer Co Pubs.

Secret of the Seven Crows. Wylly F. St. John. (Illus.). (gr. 3-5). 1981. pap. 1.95 (ISBN 0-380-00433-X, 55244-2, Camelot). Avon.

Secret of the Siddhas. Swami Muktananda. LC 80-53590. 256p. 1980. pap. 6.50 (ISBN 0-914602-52-7). SYDA Found.

Secret of the Sierra Madre: The Man Who Was B. Traven. Will Wyatt. LC 84-21722. (Illus.). 384p. 1985. pap. 9.95 (ISBN 0-15-679999-5, Harv). HarBraceJ.

Secret of the Silver Candlestick. Margaret Wallworth. (Pennypinchers Ser.). 127p. (gr. 5-10). 1984. pap. 2.95 softcover (ISBN 0-89191-832-9). Cook.

Secret of the Silver Dolphin. Carolyn Keene. (Dana Girls Ser.: Vol. 3). (Illus.). 192p. (gr. 4-7). 1972. 2.95 (ISBN 0-448-09083-X, G&D). Putnam Pub Group.

Secret of the Singing Strings. Kate Chambers. (Diana Winthrop Mystery Ser.: No. 1). 1983. pap. 2.25 (ISBN 0-451-12391-3, Sig Vista). NAL.

Secret of the Sixth Magic. Lyndon Hardy. 1988. pap. 3.95 (ISBN 0-345-00764-6, Del Rey). Ballantine.

Secret of the Slight Edge. Dan Zadra. (Self-Esteem Ser.). 1987. lib. bdg. 11.65 (ISBN 0-88682-154-1). Creative Ed.

Secret of the Software Spy & Other Mysteries. M. Masters. Ed. by Louise Delagran et al. LC 83-17319. (Can You Solve the Mystery Ser.: Vol. 8). (Illus.). 108p. (gr. 2-6). 1983. pap. 1.95 (ISBN 0-671-54491-8). Meadowbrook.

Secret of the Spanish Treasure. Jan Washburn. (gr. 4-7). 1980. pap. 2.50 (ISBN 0-89191-245-2). Cook.

Secret of the Spotted Horse. Elizabeth Van Steenwyk. LC 83-7291. (Sports Mysteries Ser.). (Illus.). 64p. (gr. 3-7). 1983. PLB 11.93 (ISBN 0-516-04477-X). Childrens.

Secret of the Spotted Shell. Phyllis A. Whitney. LC 67-10016. (Illus.). 256p. (gr. 6-9). 1967. Westminster John Knox.

Secret of the Stone Face. Phyllis A. Whitney. (YA) (gr. 7 up). 1981. pap. 1.75 (ISBN 0-451-11032-3, Sig). NAL.

Secret of the Sun God. Edward Packard. (Choose Your Adventure Ser.: No. 68). (ps-7). 1987. pap. 2.25 (ISBN 0-553-26529-6). Bantam.

Secret of the Swiss Chalet. rev ed. Carolyn Keene. LC 72-90827. (Dana Girls Ser.: Vol. 7). (Illus.). 196p. (gr. 4-7). 1973. 2.95 (ISBN 0-448-09087-2, G&D). Putnam Pub Group.

Secret of the Syndicate: Nancy Drew, the Hardy Boys, & the Stratemeyer Mystery Factory. Carol Billman. 250p. 1986. 16.95x (ISBN 0-8044-2055-6); pap. cancelled (ISBN 0-8044-6052-3). Ungar.

Secret of the Target. Jackson S. Morisawa. 144p. 1988. pap. 14.95 (ISBN 0-415-00194-3, Pub. by Routledge UK). Routledge Chapman & Hall.

Secret of the Throne of Grace. Andrew Murray. (Secret Ser.). (Orig.). 1980. pap. 1.95 (ISBN 0-87508-393-5). Chr Lit.

Secret of the Totem. Andrew Lang. LC 70-115094. 1970. Repr. of 1905 ed. 16.75 (ISBN 0-404-03866-2). AMS Pr.

Secret of the Twenty-Third Psalm. Joel S. Goldsmith. 1972. pap. 1.50 (ISBN 0-87516-140-5). DeVorss.

Secret of the Unicorn. Herge. (Illus.). 62p. 15.95 (ISBN 0-416-92530-8); pap. 4.95 (ISBN 0-416-80020-3). French & Eur.

Secret of the Unicorn. Herge. LC 73-21250. (Adventures of Tintin Ser.). (Illus.). 64p. (Orig.). (gr. k up). 1974. pap. 6.95 (ISBN 0-316-35832-0, Joy St Bks). Little.

Secret of the Unicorn Queen: Final Test. Dory Perlman. 128p. (YA) 1988. pap. 3.95 (ISBN 0-449-90298-6, Columbine). Fawcett.

Secret of the Unicorn Queen: Sun Blind. Gwen Hansen. 128p. (YA) 1988. pap. 3.95 (ISBN 0-449-90297-8, Columbine). Fawcett.

Secret of the Unicorn Queen: Swept Away. Josepha Sherman. 128p. (YA) 1988. pap. 3.95 (ISBN 0-449-90295-1, Columbine). Fawcett.

Secret of the Universe: New Discoveries on God, Man & the Eternity of Life. William S. Brandall. (Illus.). 119p. 1985. 127.45 (ISBN 0-89266-535-1). Am Classical Coll Pr.

Secret of the Untroubled Mind. Manly P. Hall. pap. 2.50 (ISBN 0-89314-352-9). Philos Res.

Secret of the Veda. Sri Aurobindo. (Sanskrit & Eng.). 1979. oversize ed. 40.00 (ISBN 0-89744-975-4, Pub. by Sri Aurobindo Ashram Trust India); pap. 30.00. Auromere.

Secret of the Veda. Sri Aurobindo. 581p. 1982. 15.00 (ISBN 0-89071-303-0, Pub. by Sri Aurobindo Ashram India); (Pub. by Sri Aurobindo Ashram India). Aurobindo Assn.

Secret of the Video Game Scores & Other Mysteries. M. Masters. Ed. by Mariellen Hanrahan et al. LC 83-26554. (Can You Solve the Mystery? Ser.: Vol. 12). (Illus.). 108p. (gr. 2-6). 1984. pap. 1.95 (ISBN 0-671-54466-7). Meadowbrook.

Secret of the Wooden Lady. Carolyn Keene. (Nancy Drew Ser.: Vol. 27). (gr. 4-7). 1950. 4.50 (ISBN 0-448-09527-0, G&D). Putnam Pub Group.

Secret of the Zodiac. N. H. Webster. 1979. lib. bdg. 59.95 (ISBN 0-8490-3004-8). Gordon Pr.

Secret of Thirteen. B. B. Hiller. (Pick-a-Path Bks.). (Illus.). 64p. (Orig.). (gr. 2-4). 1984. pap. 1.95 (ISBN 0-590-33294-5). Scholastic Inc.

Secret of Thut-Mouse III: or Basil Beaudesert's Revenge. Mansfield Kirby. LC 85-47588. (Illus.). 64p. (ps up). 1985. 10.95 (ISBN 0-374-36677-2). FS&G.

Secret of United Prayer. Andrew Murray. (Secret Ser.). (Orig.). 1980. pap. 1.95 (ISBN 0-87508-394-3). Chr Lit.

Secret of Unlimited Prosperity. Catherine Ponder. 60p. 1981. pap. 3.00 (ISBN 0-87516-419-6). DeVorss.

Secret of Van Rink's Cellar. Beverly Lee. LC 79-52909. (Books for Adults & Young Adults). 180p. (gr. 4-9). 1979. 8.95 (ISBN 0-8225-0763-3). Lerner Pubns.

Secret of Vatican Hill. Charles A. Berry. (Illus.). 296p. (Orig.). 1987. pap. 10.00 (ISBN 0-943625-00-9). Allen & Nurri.

Secret of Weifang. James J. Hannon. 325p. 1988. 19.95. New Cntry Pub Co.

Secret of Wildcat Swamp. Franklin W. Dixon. (Hardy Boys Ser: Vol. 31). (gr. 5-9). 1952. 4.50 (ISBN 0-448-08931-9, G&D). Putnam Pub Group.

Secret of Wilhelm Storitz. Jules Verne. 1964. 4.95 (ISBN 0-685-06597-9). Assoc Bk.

Secret of Windthorn. Bea Carlton. LC 86-72812. 196p. 1987. pap. 6.95 (ISBN 0-89636-231-0). Accent Bks.

Secret of Wing Chun Butterfly Knives Form. rev. ed. Austin Goh. (Illus.). 88p. 1986. pap. text ed. 12.00 (ISBN 0-87364-380-1). Paladin Pr.

Secret Offensive. Chapman Pincher. (Illus.). 320p. 1986. 15.95 (ISBN 0-312-70865-3). St Martin.

Secret Oral Teachings in Tibetan Buddhist Sects. Alexandra David-Neel. 1967. pap. 4.95 (ISBN 0-87286-012-4). City Lights.

Secret Orchard of Roger Ackerley. Diana Petre. (Illus.). 183p. 1985. pap. 11.95 (ISBN 0-241-11408-X, Pub. by Hamish Hamilton England). David & Charles.

Secret Panel. rev. ed. Franklin W. Dixon. LC 74-86693. (Hardy Boys Ser.: Vol. 25). (Illus.). (gr. 5-9). 1946. 4.50 (ISBN 0-448-08925-4, G&D). Putnam Pub Group.

Secret Papers of Camp Get Around. Rose Blue. 160p. 1988. pap. 2.50 (ISBN 0-451-15301-4, Sig). NAL.

Secret Papers of Julia Templeton. Peter Cooper. 160p. (gr. 6-9). 1985. pap. 7.95 (ISBN 0-89272-197-9). Down East.

Secret Paris of the Thirties. Brassai. Tr. by Richard Miller. LC 76-9976. 1977. pap. 17.95 (ISBN 0-394-73384-3). Pantheon.

Secret Passages: A Trilogy of Thought. Philip Robinson. LC 85-91378. 86p. 1987. 7.95 (ISBN 0-533-06885-1). Vantage.

Secret Passions, Secret Remedies: Narcotic Drugs in British Society, 1820-1930. Terry M. Parssinen. LC 82-15571. (Illus.). 250p. 1983. text ed. 17.50 (ISBN 0-89727-043-6). ISHI PA.

Secret Past. Arnold Marmor. (Private Library Collection). 208p. 1986. mini-bound 6.95 (ISBN 0-938422-23-5). SOS Pubns CA.

Secret Path. Paul Brunton. LC 85-50917. 128p. 1985. pap. 4.95 (ISBN 0-87728-652-3). Weiser.

Secret Petrarch. Edmund J. Mills. 219p. 1980. Repr. lib. bdg. 45.00 (ISBN 0-89984-336-0). Century Bookbindery.

Secret Place. Richard McKenzie. 4.95 (ISBN 0-913343-21-8). Inst Psych Inc.

Secret Place of the Most High. Frank E. Stranges. 12p. 1985. pap. text ed. 2.00 (ISBN 0-933470-09-6). Intl Evang.

Secret Places. Rome A. Hanks. Ed. by John R. Pearson. (Illus.). 32p. 1983. pap. 3.50 (ISBN 0-912001-09-7). Big Bend.

Secret Places of Donegal. John M. Feehan. 200p. (Orig.). 1988. pap. 12.95 (ISBN 0-946645-07-8, Pub. by Mercier Pr Ireland). Irish Bks Media.

Secret Places of the Heart. H. G. Wells. 287p. 1986. Repr. of 1922 ed. lib. bdg. 40.00 (ISBN 0-89984-984-9). Century Bookbindery.

Secret Places of the Lion. George H. Williamson. LC 82-2374. 240p. 1983. pap. 8.95 (ISBN 0-89281-039-4, Destiny Bks). Inner Tradit.

Secret Places of the Stairs. Susan Sallis. LC 83-48442. (Charlotte Zolotow Bks.). 160p. (YA) (gr. 7 up). 1984. 11.70i (ISBN 0-06-025142-5); PLB 11.89g (ISBN 0-06-025147-6). HarpJ.

Secret Places: The Winter of My Life. Donna K. Shuman. (Illus.). 55p. (Orig.). 1986. pap. 5.95 (ISBN 0-9616669-0-0). Shades Blue Pubns.

Secret Plague: Venereal Disease in Canada, 1838-1939. Jay Cassel. 35.00x (ISBN 0-8020-2593-5); pap. 17.95 (ISBN 0-8020-6617-8). U of Toronto Pr.

Secret Political Memoirs of the Count of Mirabeau from the German & the Russian Courts, 2 vols. (Illus.). 320p. 1985. Repr. of 1907 ed. 217.85 set (ISBN 0-89901-372-4). Found Class Reprints.

Secret Power. Marie Corelli. pap. 5.95 (ISBN 0-910122-07-5). Amherst Pr.

Secret Power. rev. ed. Dwight L. Moody & Walter Martin. 1987. pap. 7.95 (ISBN 0-8307-1219-4, 5419181). Regal.

Secret Power of Music: The Transformation of Self & Society Through Musical Energy. David Tame. 304p. (Orig.). 1984. pap. 9.95 (ISBN 0-89281-056-4, Destiny Bks). Inner Tradit.

Secret Power of the Pyramids. U. S. Andersen. 1977. pap. 7.00 (ISBN 0-87980-343-6). Wilshire.

Secret Powers Behind the Revolution. Leon V. DePoncins. 59.95 (ISBN 0-8490-1013-6). Gordon Pr.

Secret Proceedings & Debates of the Convention Assembled at Philadelphia in the Year 1787. Ed. by Robert Yates. 1987. 35.00x (ISBN 0-318-21454-7); pap. 17.50x (ISBN 0-318-21455-5). Birm Pub Lib.

Secret Proceedings & Debates of the Convention to Form the U. S. Constitution Philadelphia 1787. Robert Yates. Ed. by George R. Stewart. LC 87-80615. 344p. 1987. lib. bdg. 35.00x (ISBN 0-942301-00-5); pap. 17.50x (ISBN 0-942301-01-3). Birm Pub Lib.

Secret Protocol. Johannes M. Simmel. Tr. by Ivanka Roberts. 544p. (Orig.). 1987. pap. 4.50 (ISBN 0-446-34066-9). Warner Bks.

Secret Raft. Hazel Krantz. LC 65-17372. (Illus.). (gr. 5-8). 1965. 8.95 (ISBN 0-8149-0343-6). Vanguard.

Secret Rendezvous. Kobo Abe. Tr. by Juliet W. Carpenter. (Perigee Japanese Library). 192p. 1981. pap. 4.95 (ISBN 0-399-50501-6, Perigee). Putnam Pub Group.

Secret River. 3rd ed. Marjorie K. Rawlings. (Illus.). 57p. (gr. 3-6). Date not set. Repr. of 1955 ed. PLB 9.95x (ISBN 0-935259-02-3). San Marco Bk.

Secret Road. Bruce Lancaster. 19.95 (ISBN 0-89190-217-1, Pub. by Am Repr). Amereon Ltd.

Secret Roads: The Illegal Migration of a People. Jon Kimche & David Kimche. LC 75-6442. (Rise of Jewish Nationalism & the Middle East Ser.). 223p. 1976. Repr. of 1954 ed. 23.00 (ISBN 0-88355-329-5). Hyperion Conn.

Secret Rose. Laura Parker. 384p. (Orig.). 1987. pap. 3.95 (ISBN 0-446-32639-9). Warner Bks.

Secret Rose Garden. Sa'd Ud Din Mahmud Shabistari. Ed. by Florence Lederer. 92p. 1985. pap. 5.95 (ISBN 0-933999-26-7). Phanes Pr.

Secret Rose, Stories by W. B. Yeats: A Variorum Edition. William B. Yeats. Ed. by Pillip L. Marcus. (Yeats Ser.). 312p. 1981. 39.50x (ISBN 0-8014-1194-7). Cornell U Pr.

Secret Saga of Five-Sack. Henry L. Reimers. 25p. 1975. pap. 4.95 (ISBN 0-87770-145-8). Ye Galleon.

Secret Scandal: Battered Wives. Pascal. pap. 1.75 (ISBN 0-318-18184-3). WCTU.

Secret Scars: A Guide for Survivors of Child Sexual Abuse. Cynthia C. Tower. 1988. 16.95 (ISBN 0-670-82214-0). Viking.

Secret Science at Work. Max F. Long. 1953. pap. 8.95 (ISBN 0-87516-046-8). DeVorss.

Secret Science Behind Miracles. Max F. Long. 1948. pap. 8.95 (ISBN 0-87516-047-6). DeVorss.

Secret Science: For the Physical & Spiritual Transformation of Man--Hermetic Philosophy. John Baines. (Bk. 1). 200p. 1980. pap. 5.95 (ISBN 0-87542-025-7). Llewellyn Pubns.

Secret Science of Covert Inks. Samuel Rubin. LC 86-82957. 138p. (Orig.). 1987. pap. 9.95 (ISBN 0-915179-44-X). Loompanics.

Secret Sciences in the Light of Our Time: Genesis, Golgotha's Mystery, Occultism, Philosopher's Stone, Rudolf Steiner. Hans Liebstoeckl. 59.95 (ISBN 0-8490-1014-4). Gordon Pr.

Secret Seed: Stories & Poems. Sidney Sulkin. 1983. 12.95 (ISBN 0-931848-48-2); pap. 5.95 (ISBN 0-931848-47-4). Dryad Pr.

Secret Self. Orlo Strunk, Jr. LC 76-14780. Repr. of 1976 ed. 27.50 (ISBN 0-8357-9025-8, 2016404). Bks Demand UMI.

Secret Self: A Complete Guide to Handwriting Analysis. Anna Koren. 224p. 1987. 16.95 (ISBN 0-915361-37-X, Dist. by Watts). Adama Pubs Inc.

Secret Selves. Judie Angell. 192p. (gr. 7 up). 1981. pap. 2.25 (ISBN 0-440-97716-9, LE). Dell.

Secret Servant. Cavin Lyall. 1981. pap. 2.95 (ISBN 0-345-33823-5). Ballantine.

Secret Servant: My Life With the KGB & the Soviet Elite. Ilya Dzhirvelov. LC 87-46134. 400p. 1988. 22.50 (ISBN 0-06-015912-X, HarpT). Har-Row.

Secret Service. Duncan Campbell. Ed. by Franklin Watts Ltd. (Illus.). 32p. (YA) (gr. 7-9). 1988. 10.90 (ISBN 0-531-17079-9, Gloucester Pr). Watts.

Secret Service Agent (Uniformed) Jack Rudman. (Career Examination Ser.: C-3255). 1988. pap. 15.00 (ISBN 0-8373-3255-9). Natl Learning.

Secret Service in Action. Harry E. Neal. (Illus.). (gr. 7 up). 1980. 8.95 (ISBN 0-525-66665-6). Lodestar Bks.

Secret Service of the Confederate States in Europe: Or How the Confederate Cruisers Were Equipped, 2 vols. James D. Bulloch. 918p. 1972. Repr. of 1883 ed. Set. lib. bdg. 47.50 (ISBN 0-8337-4555-7). B Franklin.

Secret Service of the Post Office Department. P. H. Woodward. (Illus.). 1978. Repr. of 1885 ed. lib. bdg. 35.00 (ISBN 0-915262-23-1). S J Durst.

Secret Service Story. Michael Dorman. 1967. 5.00 (ISBN 0-440-07716-8). Delacorte.

Secret Service: The Field, the Dungeon, & the Escape. Albert D. Richardson. LC 77-173119. Repr. of 1865 ed. 22.00 (ISBN 0-405-08888-4, Pub. by Blom). Ayer Co Pubs.

Secret Service, the Field, the Dungeon, & the Escape. facsimile ed. Albert D. Richardson. LC 70-37315. (Black Heritage Library Collection). Repr. of 1865 ed. 27.25 (ISBN 0-8369-8952-X). Ayer Co Pubs.

Secret Sex: Male Erotic Fantasies. Tom Anicar. 256p. 1987. pap. 3.95 (ISBN 0-451-14815-0, Sig). NAL.

Secret Shaolin Formulae for the Treatment of External Injury. De Chan & De Quan. Tr. by Zhang Ting-Liang & Bob Flaws. (Illus.). 150p. (Orig.). 1987. pap. 14.95 (ISBN 0-317-64757-1). Blue Poppy.

Secret Sharer. Robert Silverberg. 128p. 1988. 14.95 (ISBN 0-88733-057-6); deluxe ed. 40.00 (ISBN 0-88733-056-8). Underwood Miller.

Secret Sharer & Other Great Stories. Ed. by Abraham Lass & Norma Tasman. (Orig.). 1969. pap. 4.50 (ISBN 0-451-62540-4, ME2084, Ment). NAL.

Secret Sharer Notes see Heart of Darkness Notes.

Secret Sharers: Studies in Contemporary Fictions. Bruce Bassoff. LC 82-20766. (Ars Poetica Ser.: No. 1). (Illus.). 152p. 1983. 34.50 (ISBN 0-404-62501-0). AMS Pr.

Secret, Silent Screams. Joan L. Nixon. (YA) (gr. 7 up). 1988. 14.95 (ISBN 0-440-50059-1). Delacorte.

Secret Singing. Richard C. Smith. 1988. 16.95 (ISBN 0-453-00581-0). NAL.

Secret Sins of British Noblewomen, 2 vols. J. M. Craven. (Illus.). 237p. 1987. Set. 197.50 (ISBN 0-89266-585-8). Am Classical Coll Pr.

Secret Sins of the Most Beautiful European Noblewomen of the 18th & 19th Centuries, 2 Vols. Jerome L. Nash. (Illus.). 217p. 1984. Repr. of 1907 ed. 135.45 set (ISBN 0-89901-143-8). Found Class Reprints.

Secret Sketchbook of Bloomsbury Lady. Kenneth Mahood. (Illus.). 64p. 1982. pap. 10.95 (ISBN 0-312-70873-4). St Martin.

Secret Societies. Arkon Daraul. 1983. Repr. of 1961 ed. 18.95 (ISBN 0-86304-024-1, Pub. by Octagon Pr England). Ins Study Human.

Secret Societies & Subversive Movements. Nesta H. Webster. 419p. 1972. pap. 6.00 (ISBN 0-913022-05-5). Angriff Pr.

Secret Societies & the French Revolution. Una Birch. 1976. lib. bdg. 59.95 (ISBN 0-8490-2585-0). Gordon Pr.

Secret Societies: Can a Christian Belong to Them & Still Honor Christ? George L. Hunt. pap. 1.50 (ISBN 0-87213-338-9). Loizeaux.

Secret Soldier: The Story of Deborah Sampson. Ann McGovern. (gr. 4-6). 1977. pap. 2.25 (ISBN 0-590-32176-5). Scholastic Inc.

Secret Soldier: The Story of Deborah Sampson. Ann McGovern. LC 75-15819. (Illus.). 64p. (gr. 1-5). 1987. 10.95 (ISBN 0-02-765780-9, Pub. by Four Winds Pr). Macmillan.

Secret Sources & Techniques for Locating Missing Persons see How to Find Anyone Anywhere.

Secret South Island. Geoff Cloake & Marthy Cloake. (Illus.). 103p. pap. 14.95 (ISBN 0-86863-419-0, Pub. by Heinemann Pubs New Zealand). Intl Spec Bk.

Secret Spaces, Imaginary Places: Creating Your Own Worlds for Play. Elin McCoy. LC 85-23089. (Illus.). 80p. (gr. 2-6). 1986. 11.95 (ISBN 0-02-765460-5). Macmillan.

Secret Spells & Curious Charms. Monika Beisner. LC 85-45323. (Illus.). 32p. (ps up). 1985. 12.95 (ISBN 0-374-36692-6). FS&G.

Secret Spells & Curious Charms. Monika Beisner. (Illus.). 32p. 1988. pap. 3.95 (ISBN 0-374-46600-9, Sunburst). FS&G.

Secret Spinner: Tales of Rav Gedalia. Howard Cushnir. LC 85-5782. (Illus.). 48p. (gr. 2-5). 1985. pap. 5.95 (ISBN 0-930494-47-4). Kar Ben.

Secret Splendor. Charles E. Essert. 147p. 1973. 7.95 (ISBN 0-8022-2107-6). Philos Lib.

Secret Splendor. Anne Powers. 384p. 1986. pap. 3.95 (ISBN 0-8439-2322-9, Leisure Bks). Leisure NY.

Secret Splendor. Gina Robins. 512p. 1988. pap. 3.95 (ISBN 0-8217-2254-9). Zebra.

Secret Splendors of the Chinese Court: Qing Dynasty Costume from the Charlotte Hill Grant Collection. Emma C. Bunker et al. LC 81-70586. (Illus.). 80p. (Orig.). 1981. pap. 12.95 (ISBN 0-914738-25-9). Denver Art Mus.

Secret Staircase. Jill Barklem. LC 83-6270. (Brambly Hedge Ser.). (Illus.). (ps-3). 1986. pap. 9.95 (ISBN 0-399-20994-8, Philomel). Putnam Pub Group.

Secret Strength. Joni E. Tada. Ed. by Larry Libby. LC 88-12053. 1988. pap. 15.95 (ISBN 0-88070-238-9); journal 6.95 (ISBN 0-88070-244-3). Multnomah.

Secret Strength of Depression. Rev. ed. Frederic F. Flach. 272p. 1986. pap. 3.95 (ISBN 0-553-25935-0). Bantam.

Secret Surrealist: The Paintings of Desmond Morris. Desmond Morris. (Illus.). 112p. 1987. 29.95 (ISBN 0-7148-2448-8, Pub. by Salem House-Phaidon). Salem Hse Pubs.

Secret Symbolism in Occult Art. Fred Gettings. (Illus.). 160p. 1988. 26.00 (ISBN 0-517-56718-0, Harmony). Crown.

Secret Symbols of the Rosicrucians of the 16th & 17th Centuries. 2nd ed. 1987. 20.00 (ISBN 0-912057-44-0, G-301). AMORC.

Secret Symmetry: Sabina Spielrein Between Jung & Freud. Aldo Carotenuto. Commentary by Bruno Bettelheim. Tr. by Arno Pomerans et al. 1984. pap. 8.95 (ISBN 0-394-72295-7). Pantheon.

Secret Table. Mark Mirsky. LC 74-24914. 167p. 1975. 9.95 (ISBN 0-914590-10-3); pap. 5.95 (ISBN 0-914590-11-1). Fiction Coll.

Secret Talents. LC 83-81369. (Grove Press Victorian Library). 320p. 1983. pap. 3.95 (ISBN 0-394-62483-1, B496, BC). Grove.

Secret Talents. 1988. pap. 3.95 (ISBN 0-8216-5007-6). Blue Moon Bks.

Secret Task of Nurse Cavell: A Story about Edith Cavell. Jan Johnson. LC 77-86604. (Stories About Christian Heroes Ser.). (Illus.). (gr. 1-5). 1977. pap. 1.95 (ISBN 0-03-041661-2, HarpR). Har-Row.

Secret Teachings in the Art of Japanese Gardens: Design Principles, Aesthetic Values. David A. Slawson. LC 86-45723. (Illus.). 232p. 1987. 34.95 (ISBN 0-87011-799-8). Kodansha.

Secret Teachings of All Ages: An Encyclopedic Outlines of Masonic, Hermetic, Quabbalistic & Rosicrucian Symbolical Philosophy. Manly P. Hall. (Illus.). 1978. 150.00; pap. 24.95; 35.00. Philos Res.

Secret Teachings of Jesus: Four Gnostic Gospels. Tr. by Marvin W. Meyer. LC 84-42528. 224p. 1984. 15.45 (ISBN 0-394-52959-6). Random.

Secret Teachings of the Vedas: The Ancient Knowledge of the East. Sri Nanda-Nandana. LC 86-51209. 320p. (Orig.). 1987. pap. 14.95 (ISBN 0-9617410-0-7). World Relief.

Secret Techniques of Erotic Delight. Vyvyan Howarth. (Illus.). 1968. 6.00 (ISBN 0-8184-0074-9). Lyle Stuart.

Secret Three. Mildred Myrick. LC 63-13323. (Harper I Can Read Bks.). (Illus.). 64p. (gr. k-3). 1963. 9.89 (ISBN 0-06-024356-2). HarpJ.

Secret to Overcoming Fear. Mike Hernacki. 31p. 1984. pap. 2.00 (ISBN 0-917115-01-5). Secret Library.

Secret Tradition in Arthurian Legend. Gareth Knight. (Illus.). 288p. 1984. pap. 11.95 (ISBN 0-85030-293-5, Pub. by Thorsons UK). Weiser.

Secret Trauma: Incest in the Lives of Girls & Women. Daina E. Russell. LC 85-43107. (Illus.). 448p. 1987. pap. 12.95 (ISBN 0-465-07596-7, PL-5198). Basic.

Secret Treasure of Tibet. Richard Brightfield. (Choose Your Own Adventure Ser.: No. 36). 128p. (Orig.). (gr. 4). 1984. pap. 2.25 (ISBN 0-553-25501-0). Bantam.

Secret Trees. Luci Shaw. LC 76-1342. (Wheaton Literary Ser.). (Illus.). 78p. 1976. cloth 6.95 (ISBN 0-87788-909-0). Shaw Pubs.

Secret Truths for Teens & Twenties. Ed. by Virginia Essene. 120p. (Orig.). 1986. pap. 7.95 (ISBN 0-937147-01-X). SEE Pub Co.

Secret Understandings. Morris Philipson. LC 87-46165. 288p. 1988. pap. 7.95 (ISBN 0-06-097128-2, PL-7128, PL). Har-Row.

Secret Valentine. Laura Damon. LC 87-13736. (Giant First-Start Readers Ser.). (Illus.). 32p. (gr. k-2). 1987. PLB 9.89 (ISBN 0-8167-1101-1); pap. text ed. 2.95 (ISBN 0-8167-1102-X). Troll Assocs.

Secret Vice Exposed. LC 73-20648. (Sex, Marriage & Society Ser.). 470p. 1974. Repr. of 1839 ed. 26.00x (ISBN 0-405-05816-0). Ayer Co Pubs.

Secret Villages. Douglas Dunn. 224p. 1985. 15.95 (ISBN 0-396-08606-3). Dodd.

Secret Vineyards of France. Christine Atkinson. (Illus.). 124p. 1988. 24.95 (ISBN 0-87052-585-9). Hippocrene Bks.

Secret Visitor. Grace Patterson. (Illus.). 96p. (YA) (gr. 7up). 1982. 6.00 (ISBN 0-682-49860-2). Exposition-Phoenix.

Secret War. Frank C. Hanighen. LC 75-6476. (History & Politics of Oil Ser.). 316p. 1976. Repr. of 1934 ed. 21.65 (ISBN 0-88355-294-9). Hyperion Conn.

Secret War. Patsy McArdle. (Make up Your Mind Ser.). 104p. (Orig.). 1984. pap. 9.95 (ISBN 0-85342-724-0, Pub. by Mercier Pr Ireland). Irish Bks Media.

Secret War. F. Russell. LC 81-9382. (World War II Ser.). (gr. 7 up). lib. bdg. 22.60 (ISBN 0-8094-2547-5, Pub. by Time-Life). Silver.

Secret War. Francis Russell. Ed. by Time-Life Books Editors. (World War II Ser.). (Illus.). 208p. 1982. 14.95 (ISBN 0-8094-2546-7). Time-Life.

Secret War. Russell J. Smith. 224p. (Orig.). 1986. 19.95 (ISBN 0-89754-051-4); pap. 19.95 (ISBN 0-89754-050-6); pap. 9.95. Dan River Pr.

Secret War Against Hitler. William Casey. LC 88-2013. 304p. 1988. 19.95 (ISBN 0-89526-563-X). Regnery Gateway.

Secret War: Americans in China, 1944-1945. Oliver J. Caldwell. LC 73-7755. (Arcturus Books Paperbacks). 1973. pap. 2.65x (ISBN 0-8093-0650-6). S Ill U Pr.

Secret War in Central America: Sandinista Assault on World Order. John N. Moore. LC 86-28092. 204p. 1987. 17.95 (ISBN 0-89093-961-6). U Pubns Amer.

Secret War in Mexico: Europe, the United States, & the Mexican Revolution. Friedrich Katz. LC 80-26607. 1981. lib. bdg. 40.00x; pap. 20.00x (ISBN 0-226-42589-4). U of Chicago Pr.

Secret War in the Sudan, Nineteen Fifty-Five to Nineteen Seventy-Two. Edgar O'Ballance. LC 77-1732. 174p. 1977. 23.00 (ISBN 0-208-01692-9, Archon). Shoe String.

Secret War of Captain Johnny Mitchell. Johnny Mitchell. LC 76-2963. 103p. 1976. 12.00x (ISBN 0-88415-802-0, Pub. by Pacesetter Pr). Gulf Pub.

Secret War with Germany: Deception, Espionage, & Dirty Tricks, 1939-1945. William B. Breuer. (Illus.). 278p. 1988. 17.95 (ISBN 0-89141-298-0). Presidio Pr.

Secret Warfare: Battle of Codes & Ciphers. Bruce Norman. 1987. 17.95 (ISBN 0-88029-160-5, Pub. by Dorset Pr). Hippocrene Bks.

Secret Warning. Franklin W. Dixon. (Hardy Boys Ser: Vol. 17). (gr. 5-9). 1938. 4.50 (ISBN 0-448-08917-3, G&D). Putnam Pub Group.

Secret Warriors. Alex Baldwin. 1985. pap. 3.50 (ISBN 0-317-38839-8). PB.

Secret Warriors: Inside the Covert Military Operations of the Reagan Era. Steven Emerson. LC 88-2419. 256p. 1988. 17.95 (ISBN 0-399-13360-7). Putnam Pub Group.

Secret Wars: A Guide to Sources in English, 3 vols. Mryon J. Smith, Jr. Set. 29.00 (ISBN 0-317-58805-2); Vol 1., 1980, 312p. write for info.; Vol 2., 1981, 389p. write for info.; Vol. 3., 1980, 237p. write for info. Regina Bks.

Secret Wars: Covert Operations in Vietnam. (Vietnam Experience). (Illus.). 192p. 16.95 (ISBN 0-201-11944-7). Addison-Wesley.

Secret Waters: A Guide to the Quiet & Unspoilt Rivers, Lakes & Canals of Britain & Ireland. John Watney. (Illus.). 160p. Date not set. 24.95 (ISBN 0-86350-144-3, Pub. by Michael Joseph). Viking.

Secret Ways. Alistair MacLean. 1976. Repr. of 1959 ed. lib. bdg. 17.95 (ISBN 0-89190-172-8, Pub. by River City Pr). Amereon Ltd.

Secret Ways. Alistair MacLean. 1985. pap. 3.50 (ISBN 0-449-21044-8, GM). Fawcett.

Secret Weapon & Other Stories of Faith & Valor. A. Eisenberg & Leah A. Globe. (Illus.). (gr. 4-6). 1971. 9.95x (ISBN 0-685-01035-X). Bloch.

Secret Weapon in Africa. Oleg Ignatyev. 190p. 1977. 10.00x (Pub. by Collets (UK)). State Mutual Bk.

Secret Weapons of World War II. Gerald Pawle. pap. 1.95 (ISBN 0-345-27895-X). Ballantine.

Secret Web. (Red Stripe Ser.). 1988. pap. 4.50 (ISBN 0-8216-5059-9, Univ Bks). Lyle Stuart.

Secret Window. Betty R. Wright. LC 82-80816. 160p. (gr. 3-7). 1982. 10.95 (ISBN 0-8234-0464-1). Holiday.

Secret Window. Betty R. Wright. 176p. (gr. 4-6). 1984. pap. 2.50 (ISBN 0-590-40561-6, Apple Paperbacks). Scholastic Inc.

Secret Wisdom of Qabalah. J. F. C. Fuller. 1976. Repr. 7.00 (ISBN 0-911662-63-4). Yoga.

Secret Wishes. Lou Kassem. 144p. (gr. 3-7). 1989. pap. 2.50 (ISBN 0-380-75544-0, Camelot). Avon.

Secret Wishes, Secret Fears. Dorothy Baughman. 1986. 9.95 (ISBN 0-8034-8628-6, Avalon). Bouregy.

Secret Woman. Victoria Holt. 352p. 1985. pap. 3.95 (ISBN 0-449-20878-8, Crest). Fawcett.

Secret World. Ray Palmer & Richard S. Shaver. (Illus.). 1975. 10.95 (ISBN 0-910122-39-3). Amherst Pr.

Secret World, No. 21. Peter Deriabin. (Espionage-Intelligence Library). 416p. 1982. pap. 3.95 (ISBN 0-345-34923-7). Ballantine.

Secret World Government: Or, the Hidden Hand of the Unrevealed in History. Count Cherep-Spiridovich. 1977. lib. bdg. 69.95 (ISBN 0-8490-2586-9). Gordon Pr.

Secret World of Animals. Ed. by Donald J. Crump. (Books for World Explorers Ser. 7: No. 3). (Illus.). 104p. 1986. 6.95 (ISBN 0-87044-575-8); lib. bdg. 8.50 (ISBN 0-87044-580-4). Natl Geog.

Secret World of Interpol. Omar V. Garrison. cancelled (ISBN 0-686-74638-4). Church of Scient Info.

Secret World of Interpol. Omar V. Garrison. LC 76-24523. 1976. 8.95 (ISBN 0-931116-00-7). Ralston-Pilot.

Secret World of Interpol. Omar V. Garrison. 238p. 1982. 32.00x (ISBN 0-85335-227-5, Pub. by Maclellan Sales Ltd). State Mutual Bk.

Secret World of Men: A Girl's Eye View. Cathy Crimmins. 1987. pap. 6.95 (ISBN 0-452-25919-3, Plume). NAL.

Secret World of Polly Flint. Helen Cresswell. LC 83-24861. (Illus.). 176p. (gr. 4-7). 1984. 11.95 (ISBN 0-02-725400-3). Macmillan.

Secret World of Polly Flint. Helen Cresswell. (Illus.). 178p. (gr. 4-6). 1985. pap. 3.50 (ISBN 0-14-031542-X, Puffin). Penguin.

Secret World of Teddy Bears. Pamela Prince. LC 83-27. (gr. k up). 1983. 9.95 (ISBN 0-517-55022-9, Harmony). Crown.

Secret World of Underground Creatures. Dorothy Leon. LC 82-8185. (Illus.). 64p. (gr. 4-6). 1982. PLB 8.79 (ISBN 0-671-42403-3). Messner.

Secret Writing: An Introduction to Cryptograms, Ciphers, & Codes. Henry Lysing, pseud. LC 74-75261. 128p. 1974. pap. 2.50 (ISBN 0-486-23062-7). Dover.

Secret Writing: An Introduction to Cryptograms, Ciphers & Codes. Henry Lysing, pseud. (Illus.). 11.25 (ISBN 0-8446-5060-9). Peter Smith.

Secret Writing-Codes & Messages. Eugene Baker. LC 80-11416. (Junior Detective Ser.). (Illus.). 32p. (gr. 2-5). 1980. PLB 6.95 (ISBN 0-89565-150-5). Childs World.

Secret Writing: Keys to the Mysteries of Reading & Writing. Peter Sears. 180p. (gr. 9-12). 1986. pap. text ed. 10.95 (ISBN 0-915924-86-2). Tchrs & Writers Coll.

Secret Zodiac: The Hidden Art in Medieval Astrology. Fred Gettings. (Illus.). 224p. 1987. 39.95 (ISBN 0-7102-1147-3, Pub. by Routledge UK). Routledge Chapman & Hall.

Secreta Secretorum. Aristotle. Tr. by Robert Copland. LC 71-26095. (English Experience Ser.: No. 220). 72p. Repr. of 1528 ed. 11.50 (ISBN 90-221-0220-3). Walter J Johnson.

Secreta: Three Methods of Laying Gold Leaf. Joyce Grafe. (Illus.). 112p. 1986. pap. 9.95 (ISBN 0-8008-7023-9). Taplinger.

Secretarial Administration. Ed. by J. Birds & J. Yelland. 1986. 500.00x (ISBN 0-85308-074-7, Pub. by Jordan & Sons UK); First suppl. 50.00 (ISBN 0-317-54475-6); Second suppl. 60.00 (ISBN 0-317-54476-4). State Mutual Bk.

Secretarial Administration & Management. Daniel R. Boyd & Stephen D. Lewis. (Illus.). 550p. 1985. text ed. write for info (ISBN 0-13-798265-8); wkbk. 8.95 (ISBN 0-13-798315-8). P-H.

Secretarial & Administrative Procedure. 2nd ed. Lucy M. Jennings. (Illus.). 560p. 1983. write for info (ISBN 0-13-797746-8). P-H.

Secretarial & General Office Procedures. Lucy M. Jennings. (Illus.). 400p. 1981. write for info (ISBN 0-13-797803-0). P-H.

Secretarial Assistance in Teachers Colleges & Normal Schools. L. J. Bennett. LC 73-176554. (Columbia University. Teachers College. Contributions to Education: No. 724). Repr. of 1937 ed. 22.50 (ISBN 0-404-55724-4). AMS Pr.

Secretarial Assistant. Jack Rudman. (Career Examination Ser.: C-1464). (Cloth bdg. avail. on request). pap. 12.00 (ISBN 0-8373-1464-X). Natl Learning.

Secretarial Dental Assistant. Mary A. Douglas. LC 75-19522. 1976. instr's. guide 5.00 (ISBN 0-8273-0350-5). Delmar.

Secretarial Duties. 5th ed. John Harrison. (Pitman Secretarial Science Ser.). (Illus.). 328p. (Orig.). 1975. pap. text ed. 16.95 (ISBN 0-8464-0829-5). Beekman Pubs.

Secretarial Duties. 8th ed. John Harrison. 1988. pap. 23.50x (ISBN 0-273-02665-8, Pub. by Pitman Pub Ltd London). Trans-Atl Phila.

Secretarial English. Donald A. Sheff. (gr. 9-12). 1964. pap. text ed. 7.00 (ISBN 0-13-797770-0, 17512). Prentice ESL.

Secretarial Handbook for the Modern Office. Fred N. Grayson. LC 85-16889. 256p. 1985. pap. 9.95 (ISBN 0-399-51138-5). Putnam Pub Group.

Secretarial Handbook on Planning & Organizing Work. 1975. pap. 5.95 (ISBN 0-917386-79-5). Exec Ent Pubns.

Secretarial Management. Josephine Shaw. 256p. (Orig.). 1978. pap. text ed. 16.95x. Trans-Atl Phila.

Secretarial Office Procedures. 2nd, ed. Dorothy E. Lee & Walter A. Brower. (Illus.). 416p. 1981. pap. 29.00 (ISBN 0-07-037037-0). McGraw.

Secretarial Office Procedures. Dorothy E. Lee et al. (Illus.). 400p. 1988. pap. 27.45 (ISBN 0-07-037050-8). McGraw.

Secretarial Practice. 10th ed. M. C. Kuchhal. 632p. 1984. text ed. 40.00x (Pub. by Vikas India); pap. text ed. 25.00x (ISBN 0-7069-2638-2). Advent NY.

Secretarial Practice Made Simple. Betty Hutchinson. LC 84-18787. (Made Simple Ser.). 176p. 1985. pap. 6.95 (ISBN 0-385-19430-7). Doubleday.

Secretarial Practice: Syllabus. 2nd ed. Carl Salser & Charlotte Butsch. 1977. pap. text ed. 6.25 (ISBN 0-89420-044-5, 218505); cassette recordings 101.00 (ISBN 0-89420-183-2, 186700). Natl Book.

Secretarial Procedures & Administration. 9th ed. Rita S. Tilton et al. 1987. text ed. write for info. (ISBN 0-538-11790-7, K79). SW Pub.

Secretarial Procedures for the Electronic Office. Rita C. Kutie & Joan L. Rhodes. LC 82-11047. 371p. 1983. text ed. 19.95x (ISBN 0-471-89042-1); tchrs.' manual avail. Wiley.

Secretarial Procedures for the Electronic Office. 2nd ed. Rita C. Kutie & Joan L. Rhodes. LC 85-13841. 462p. 1986. pap. write for info. (ISBN 0-471-82156-X). Wiley.

Secretarial Services. Evelyn Austin. 208p. 1982. pap. text ed. 16.95x (ISBN 0-7121-1984-1). Trans-Atl Phila.

Secretarial Specialist. Alfred C. Pascale. LC 73-34193. (Illus.). 216p. 1968. pap. text ed. 15.95 (ISBN 0-913310-02-6). PAR Inc.

Secretarial Stenographer. Jack Rudman. (Career Examination Ser.: C-1465). (Cloth bdg. avail. on request). pap. 12.00 (ISBN 0-8373-1465-8). Natl Learning.

Secretarial Training for the Changing Office. Norma Curchack & Patricia A. Parzych. (Illus., Orig.). 1977. pap. text ed. 14.00 net (ISBN 0-15-579280-6, HC); instr's. manual avail. (ISBN 0-15-579281-4). HarBraceJ.

Secretarial Training for the Changing Office. Norma Curchack & Patricia A. Parzych. 1986. text ed. 12.00 (ISBN 0-12-200060-9); instr's. manual 2.50 (ISBN 0-12-200061-7). Acad Pr.

Secretarial Word Finder. Ed. by Linnea L. Ochs & Susan Van Der Reyden. LC 83-8640. 540p. 1983. 19.95x (ISBN 0-13-798157-0, Busn). P-H.

Secretariat of the United Nations. Sydney D. Bailey. LC 78-2880. (Carnegie Endowment for International Studies: No. 11). 1978. Repr. of 1964 ed. lib. bdg. 19.75 (ISBN 0-313-20338-5, BASU). Greenwood.

Secretariat: The Making of a Champion. William Nack. (Quality Paperbacks Ser.). 342p. 1988. pap. 10.95 (ISBN 0-306-80317-8). Da Capo.

Secretaries, Management & Organizations. S. Vinnicombe. (Orig.). 1980. pap. text ed. 11.50x (ISBN 0-435-82896-7). Gower Pub Co.

Secretaries of Death: Accounts by Former Prisoners Who Worked in the Administrative Offices of Auschwitz. Ed. by Lore Shelley. LC 85-43608. 450p. 1986. 20.00 (ISBN 0-88400-123-7). Shengold.

Secretaries of State for Scotland, Nineteen Twenty-Six to Nineteen Seventy-Six. George Pottinger. 220p. 1979. 12.50x (ISBN 0-7073-0230-7, Pub. by Scot Acad Pr). Longwood Pub Group.

Secretaries of State, Sixteen Eighty-One to Seventeen Eighty-Two. Mark A. Thomson. 206p. 1968. Repr. of 1932 ed. 32.50x (ISBN 0-7146-1521-8, BHA-01521, F Cass Co). Biblio Dist.

Secretaries of State, Sixteen Eighty-One to Seventeen Eighty-Two. Mark A. Thomson. LC 68-11126. 1968. Repr. of 1932 ed. 27.50x (ISBN 0-678-05089-9). Kelley.

Secretaries of the Moon: The Letters of Wallace Stevens & Jose Rodriguez Feo. Ed. by Beverly Coyle & Alan Filreis. LC 86-16835. x, 210p. 1987. 19.95 (ISBN 0-8223-0670-0). Duke.

Secretaries Study: Directions for the Inditing of Letters. Thomas Gainsford. LC 74-80177. (English Experience Ser.: No. 658). 1974. Repr. of 1616 ed. 14.00 (ISBN 90-221-0658-6). Walter J Johnson.

Secretary. Jack Rudman. (Career Examination Ser.: C-1466). (Cloth bdg. avail. on request). pap. 12.00 (ISBN 0-8373-1466-6). Natl Learning.

Secretary - General & Satellite Diplomacy. Thomas E. Boudreau. 1984. pap. (ISBN 0-87641-311-4). Carnegie Ethics & Intl Affairs.

Secretary Grid: A Program for Increasing Office Synergy. Robert R. Blake & Jane Srygley. 208p. 1983. 14.95 (ISBN 0-8144-5762-2). AMACOM.

Secretary, Martin Bormann: The Man Who Manipulated Hitler. Jochen Von Lang & Claus Sibyll. Tr. by Christa Armstrong & Peter White. LC 81-80847. (Illus.). x, 430p. 1981. pap. 9.95x (ISBN 0-8214-0615-9). Ohio U Pr.

Secretary of Defense. Douglas Kinnard. LC 80-5178. 264p. 1981. 24.00x (ISBN 0-8131-1434-9). U Pr of Ky.

Secretary of Europe: The Life of Fredrich Gentz, Enemy of Napoleon. Golo Mann. 1946. 27.50x (ISBN 0-686-83734-7). Elliots Bks.

Secretary of Europe: The Life of Friedrich Gentz, Enemy of Napoleon. Golo Mann. LC 77-122395. xvi, 323p. 1970. Repr. of 1946 ed. 29.50 (ISBN 0-208-00957-4, Archon). Shoe String.

Secretary of Praise: The Poetic Vocation of George Herbert. Diana Benet. LC 83-1080. 232p. 1984. text ed. 23.00x (ISBN 0-8262-0408-2); pap. text ed. write for info. U of Mo Pr.

Secretary of State. facs. ed. American Assembly Staff. LC 73-133511. (Select Bibliographies Reprint Ser). 1960. 17.00 (ISBN 0-8369-5543-9). Ayer Co Pubs.

Secretary of State, Jan. 1, 1828 - March 4, 1829 see Papers of Henry Clay.

Secretary of State, 1826 see Papers of Henry Clay.

Secretary of State, 1827 see Papers of Henry Clay.

Secretary of the Interior's Standards for Rehabilitation & Guidelines for Rehabilitating Historic Buildings. (Illus.). 58p. 1983. pap. 2.00 (ISBN 0-318-21310-9, S/N 024-005-01003-3). USGPO.

Secretary on the Job. 3rd ed. Mary Witherow. 1983. text ed. 16.40 practice set (ISBN 0-07-071187-9). McGraw.

Secrets of Cuban Entertaining: A Menu Cookbook. Rico Lamadriz et al. 133p. 5.95 (ISBN 0-941072-00-2). Kennedy & Co.

Secrets of dBASE. Christopher White. 350p. (Orig.). 1987. pap. 16.95 (ISBN 1-55519-024-3). Ashton-Tate Pub.

Secrets of Doc Savage. Will Murray. (Illus.). pap. 2.95x (ISBN 0-933752-23-7). Odyssey MA.

Secrets of Dr. Taverner. 4th rev. ed. Dion Fortune. 277p. 1979. pap. 3.95 (ISBN 0-87542-227-6). Llewellyn Pubns.

Secrets of Earth & Sea. Edwin R. Lankester. LC 76-93352. (Essay Index Reprint Ser). 1920. 19.00 (ISBN 0-8369-1301-9). Ayer Co Pubs.

Secrets of Effective Leadership: A Practical Guide to Success. Fred A. Manske, Jr. LC 87-16870. (Illus.). 206p. 1988. 17.95 (ISBN 0-943703-00-X); pap. 9.95. Leader Educ Dev.

Secrets of Eskimo Skin Sewing. Edna Wilder. LC 76-3783. (Illus., Orig.). 1976. pap. 6.95 (ISBN 0-88240-026-6). Alaska Northwest.

Secrets of Eternity. Annalee Skarin. 287p. pap. 5.95 (ISBN 0-87516-092-1). DeVorss.

Secrets of Financial Success. Wallace D. Wattles. 96p. (Orig.). 1986. pap. 14.95 incl. audio cassette (ISBN 0-930298-26-8). Westwood Pub Co.

Secrets of French Hors D'Oeuvres. Ed. by Beverly LeBlanc. (Illus.). 96p. 1988. 15.95x (ISBN 0-356-15580-3, Pub. by Mcdonald & Jone's England). Hippocrene Bks.

Secrets of French Sauces. Ed. by Beverly LeBlanc. (Illus.). 96p. (Orig.). 1988. pap. 15.95x (ISBN 0-356-15318-5, Pub. by Mcdonald & Jone's England). Hippocrene Bks.

Secrets of Graceful Living. Boye De Mente. LC 78-71128. 1980. pap. 4.95 (ISBN 0-914778-22-6). Phoenix Bks.

Secrets of Grandmaster Play: Tournament Level. John Nunn. Ed. by Peter Griffiths. (Chess Library). (Illus.). 176p. 1987. pap. 8.95 (ISBN 0-02-053130-3, Collier). Macmillan.

Secrets of Green-Sand Casting. 1983. pap. 8.95 (ISBN 0-917914-08-2). Lindsay Pubns.

Secrets of Gypsy Fortunetelling. Raymond Buckland. Ed. by Phyllis Galde. LC 88-45196. (New Age Ser.). (Illus.). 1988. pap. 3.95 (ISBN 0-87542-051-6). Llewellyn Pubns.

Secrets of Hakkoryu Jujutsu: Shodan Tactics. Dennis G. Palumbo. (Illus.). 144p. (Orig.). 1987. pap. text ed. 12.50 (ISBN 0-87364-422-0). Paladin Pr.

Secrets of Ham Radio DXing. Dave Ingram. (Illus.). 176p. 1981. 12.95 (ISBN 0-8306-9618-0, 1259). TAB Bks.

Secrets of Happiness: One for Each Day of the Month. J. Donald Walters. (Illus.). 68p. (Orig.). 1987. pap. 4.95 (ISBN 0-916124-39-8, CH2). Crystal Clarity.

Secrets of Harry Bright. Joseph Wambaugh. LC 85-10453. 320p. 1986. pap. 4.95 (ISBN 0-553-26021-9). Bantam.

Secrets of Harry Bright. Joseph Wambaugh. 403p. 1986. 18.95 (ISBN 0-8161-4066-9, Large Print Bks); pap. 10.95 (ISBN 0-8161-4069-3). G K Hall.

Secrets of Health & Beauty: How to Make Yourself Over. Linda A. Clark. 1969. 9.95 (ISBN 0-8159-6807-8). Devin.

Secrets of Herbs. Rita Schnitzer. (Illus.). 64p. (Orig.). 1986. pap. 5.95 (ISBN 0-85613-874-6). Salem Hse Pubs.

Secrets of Hidden Creek. Wylly F. St. John. (Illus.). (gr. 3-7). 1981. pap. 1.75 (ISBN 0-380-00746-0, 51359, Camelot). Avon.

Secrets of Houdini. J. Cannell. 5.95x (ISBN 0-685-47573-5). Wehman.

Secrets of Houdini. J. C. Cannell. LC 72-93609. (Illus.). 288p. 1973. pap. 5.95 (ISBN 0-486-22913-0). Dover.

Secrets of Hypnotism. Sydney J. Van Pelt. pap. 5.00 (ISBN 0-87980-135-2). Wilshire.

Secrets of Italian Meat & Poultry Dishes. Ed. by Beverly LeBlanc. (Illus.). 96p. 1988. 15.95x (ISBN 0-356-15581-1, Pub by Mcdonald & Jone's England). Hippocrene Bks.

Secrets of Italian Pasta. Ed. by Beverly LeBlanc. (Illus.). 96p. (Orig.). 1988. pap. 15.95x (ISBN 0-356-15317-7, Pub. by Mcdonald & Jone's England). Hippocrene Bks.

Secrets of Judo. Jiichi Watanabe & Lindy Avakian. LC 59-14089. (Illus.). 1959. 12.95 (ISBN 0-8048-0516-4). C E Tuttle.

Secrets of Kung-Fu: A Complete Guide to the Fundamentals of Shaolin Kung-Fu & the Principles of Inner Power (Ch'i) George R. Parulski, Jr. (Illus.). 160p. (Orig.). 1984. pap. 11.95 (ISBN 0-8092-5438-7). Contemp Bks.

Secrets of Life Extension. John A. Mann. 192p. 1980. pap. 7.95. And-Or Pr.

Secrets of Lock Picking. Steven Hampton. (Illus.). 72p. (Orig.). 1987. pap. text ed. 15.00 (ISBN 0-87364-423-9). Paladin Pr.

Secrets of Mabel Eastlake. Donald S. Olson. LC 85-7604. 304p. (Orig.). 1986. pap. 7.95 (ISBN 0-915175-15-0). Knights Pr.

Secrets of MacWrite, MacPaint, & MacDraw. David Busch. (Microcomputer Bookshelf Ser.). 225p. (Orig.). 1986. pap. 15.95 (ISBN 0-673-39098-5). Scott F.

Secrets of Magical Seals. Anna Riva. (Illus.). 64p. 1975. pap. 3.95 (ISBN 0-943832-04-7). Intl Imports.

Secret's of Maine's Master Anglers. Harry Vanderweide. (Illus.). 150p. 1984. pap. 8.95 (ISBN 0-930096-54-1). G Gannett.

Secrets of Making Layouts for Quick Printing. Ruth Minshull. (Illus.). 34p. (Orig.). 1982. pap. 3.98 (ISBN 0-937922-06-4). SAA Pub.

Secrets of Management Excellence. John J. McCarthy. LC 84-29381. 248p. 1984. 50.00 (ISBN 0-932648-60-6). Boardroom.

Secrets of Marie Antoinette: A Collection of Letters. Ed. & tr. by Oliver Bernier. LC 86-12117. 336p. 1986. pap. 10.95 (ISBN 0-88064-064-2). Fromm Intl Pub.

Secrets of Mental Magic. Vernon Howard. 1974. pap. 5.95 (ISBN 0-13-797985-1, Reward). P-H.

Secrets of Mental Supremacy. W. R. Latson. 138p. 1968. pap. 7.95 (ISBN 0-88697-028-8). Life Science.

Secrets of Metals. Wilhelm Pelikan. Tr. by Charlotte Lebensart from Ger. 189p. pap. 10.95 (ISBN 0-88010-257-8). Anthroposophic.

Secrets of Methamphetamine Manufacture. Uncle Fester. LC 86-82671. (Illus.). 120p. 1986. pap. text ed. 14.95 (ISBN 0-915179-55-5). Loompanics.

Secrets of Money. Lawrence Kirk. Ed. by Carole A. Kirk. 80p. 1986. 15.95 (ISBN 0-936761-00-8). Alta Vista Bks.

Secrets of My Heart. Cassie Edwards. 416p. 1983. pap. 3.75 (ISBN 0-8439-2048-3, Leisure Bks). Leisure NY.

Secrets of My Heart. Cassie Edwards. 416p. 1987. pap. 3.95 (ISBN 0-8439-2525-6). Leisure NY.

Secrets of Natural New Zealand. Betty Brownlie & Ronald Lockley. LC 87-51088. (Illus.). 176p. 1988. 40.00 (ISBN 0-670-81248-X). Viking.

Secrets of Naturally Youthful Health & Vitality. Samuel Homola. LC 70-152523. (Illus.). 1971. 14.95 (ISBN 0-13-797514-7, Parker). P-H.

Secrets of One Hundred Twenty-Three Classic Science Tricks & Experiments. Edi Lanners. (Illus.). 196p. (Orig.). 1987. pap. 7.95 (ISBN 0-8306-2821-5). TAB Bks.

Secrets of Our National Literature. William P. Courtney. 1908. Repr. 25.00 (ISBN 0-8274-3346-8). R West.

Secrets of Our National Literature: Chapters in the History of the Anonymous & Pseudonymous Writings of Our Countrymen. William P. Courtney. LC 68-21761. 264p. 1968. Repr. of 1908 ed. 43.00x (ISBN 0-8103-3140-3). Gale.

Secrets of Personal Persuasion. William Turner. 19.95 (ISBN 0-13-798687-4); pap. 6.95 (ISBN 0-13-798679-3). P-H.

Secrets of Photographing Women. Peter Gowland. Ed. by Herbert Michelman. (Illus.). 224p. 1981. 14.95 (ISBN 0-517-54180-7, Michelman Books). Crown.

Secrets of Piano Construction. American Steel & Wire Co. Staff. LC 85-9122. Orig. Title: Piano Tone Building. (Illus.). 292p. 1985. pap. 12.95 (A-132). Vestal.

Secrets of Plant Propagation: Starting Your Own Flowers, Vegetables, Fruits, Berries, Shrubs, Trees, & Houseplants. Lewis Hill. LC 84-47788. (Illus.). 208p. 1985. 20.00 (ISBN 0-88266-371-2, Garden Way Pub); pap. 12.95 (ISBN 0-88266-370-4). Storey Comm Inc.

Secrets of Ponds & Lakes. John Snow. Ed. by Susan Jack. (Secrets of... Ser.). (Illus.). 96p. (Orig.). (gr. 4-10). 1982. pap. 3.95 (ISBN 0-930096-30-4). G Gannett.

Secrets of Potfishing. Ed Ricciuti. (Illus.). 74p. pap. 3.50 (ISBN 0-88839-085-8). Hancock House.

Secrets of Power Golf. Gary Wiren. 1988. 9.95 (ISBN 1-55525-201-X). Nightingale-Conant.

Secrets of Practical Marketing for Small Business. Herman Holtz. (Illus.). 192p. 1982. pap. 8.95 (ISBN 0-13-798215-1). P-H.

Secrets of Prayer see Secretos de la Oracion.

Secrets of Professional Cartooning. Kenneth Muse. (Applied Arts & Sciences Ser.). (Illus.). 336p. 1981. pap. text ed. 20.25 (ISBN 0-13-798132-5). P-H.

Secrets of Rivers & Streams. Peter J. Swenson. Ed. by Susan Jack. (Secrets of... Ser.). (Illus.). 90p. (gr. 4-10). 1982. pap. 3.95 (ISBN 0-930096-31-2). G Gannett.

Secrets of Romanism. Joseph Zacchello. 232p. 1981. pap. 4.95 (ISBN 0-87213-981-6). Loizeaux.

Secrets of Sales Champions. Dorothy M. Walters. (Illus.). 323p. 1986. 29.95 (ISBN 0-934344-20-5). Royal Pub.

Secrets of Samurai. Westbrook & Ratti. 35.00x (ISBN 0-685-47575-1). Wehman.

Secrets of Service (How to Make Money in the Restaurant Business) Dixie L. Chavez-Irvin & Thomas O'Malley. 1978. pap. 12.95 (ISBN 0-931976-01-4). Inst Pr Sta Monica.

Secrets of Shamanism: Tapping the Spirit Power Within You. Jose Stevens & Lena S. Stevens. 249p. 1988. pap. 3.95 (ISBN 0-380-75607-2). Avon.

Secrets of Shaolin Temple Boxing. Robert W. Smith. LC 64-22002. (Illus.). 1964. 7.95 (ISBN 0-8048-0518-0). C E Tuttle.

Secrets of Shellfishing. Edward Ricciuti. (Illus.). 70p. pap. 3.50 (ISBN 0-88839-140-4). Hancock House.

Secrets of Show Dog Handling. 2nd ed. Mario Migliorini. LC 81-3627. (Illus.). 136p. 1982. 11.95 (ISBN 0-668-05314-3). Arco.

Secrets of Shuffleboard Strategy. 2nd enl ed. Omero C. Catan. LC 72-91761. (Illus.). 224p. 1973. lib. bdg. 6.00 buckram (ISBN 0-9600618-1-9). Catan.

Secrets of Siena. E. C. Curtsinger. LC 84-81376. 1985. pap. 20.00 (ISBN 0-317-60612-3). Latitudes Pr.

Secrets of Silver Valley. Zeno Zeplin. 89p. (Orig.). 1985. pap. 7.95 library quality, acid-free bond (ISBN 0-9615760-1-4). Nel-Mar Enter.

Secrets of Silver Valley. 2nd ed. Zeno Zeplin. (Illus.). 130p. 1987. 10.95 (ISBN 0-9615760-4-9); pap. 7.95 (ISBN 0-9615760-5-7). Nel-Mar Enter.

Secrets of Sleep. Alexander Borbely. LC 85-73887. (Illus.). 240p. 1986. 19.95 (ISBN 0-465-07592-4). Basic.

Secrets of Sleep. Alexander Borbely. LC 85-83887. (Illus.). 240p. 1988. pap. 8.95 (ISBN 0-465-07593-2, PL 5217). Basic.

Secrets of Smart Airline Travelers. Richard A. Bodner. LC 86-18837. (Illus.). 128p. (Orig.). 1986. pap. 4.95 (ISBN 0-932620-65-5). Betterway Pubns.

Secrets of Sorcery Spells & Pleasure Cults of India. P. Thomas. (Illus.). 284p. 1983. Repr. of 1966 ed. text ed. 45.00x (ISBN 0-86590-237-2, Pub. by Taraporevala India). Apt Bks.

Secrets of Soviet Sports Fitness & Training. Michael Yessis. 1988. 9.70 (ISBN 0-688-08246-7, Quill). Morrow.

Secrets of Soviet Sports Fitness & Training. Michael Yessis & Richard Trubo. (Illus.). 192p. 1987. 17.95 (ISBN 0-87795-900-5, Arbor Hse). Morrow.

Secrets of Spanish Pool Checkers, 2 Bks. Clyde Black & Archie Waters. Bk. 1. pap. 5.00 (ISBN 0-685-20862-1). Univ Place.

Secrets of Spirulina. Ed. by C. Hills. LC 80-22087. 224p. 1980. 6.95 (ISBN 0-916438-38-4). Univ of Trees.

Secrets of State: The State Department & the Struggle over U. S. Foreign Policy. Barry Rubin. 1985. 25.00 (ISBN 0-19-503397-3). Oxford U Pr.

Secrets of State: The State Department & the Struggle over U. S. Foreign Policy. Barry Rubin. 351p. 1987. pap. 8.95 (ISBN 0-19-505010-X). Oxford U Pr.

Secrets of Staying Power. Kevin A. Miller. (Leadership Library Ser.). 175p. 1988. pap. 9.95 (ISBN 0-917463-19-6). Chr Today.

Secrets of Staying Young & Living Longer. 1981. 4.95 (ISBN 0-686-42901-X). Harian.

Secrets of Striped Bass Fishing. D. W. Bennett. (Illus.). 80p. pap. 3.50 (ISBN 0-88839-103-X). Hancock House.

Secrets of Strong Families. Nick Stinnett & John DeFrain. 208p. 1986. pap. 3.50 (ISBN 0-425-09485-5). Berkley Pub.

Secrets of Studio Still Life Photography. Gary Perweiler. (Illus.). 144p. 1984. pap. 18.95 (ISBN 0-8174-5898-0, Amphoto); 27.50 (ISBN 0-8174-5897-2). Watson-Guptill.

Secrets of Success. Lloyd K. Ulery. 96p. 1986. 6.95 (ISBN 0-930984-04-8). Psychic Bks.

Secrets of Success in Your Own Business. James Silvester. 288p. 1986. 20.00 (ISBN 0-8184-0418-3). Lyle Stuart.

Secrets of Successful Big Game Fishing: The Blue Water Bait Book Revised & Updated. rev. ed. Samuel A. Earp & William J. Wildeman. 1986. pap. 11.95 (ISBN 0-316-20331-9). Little.

Secrets of Successful Humor. Rusty Wright & Linda R. Wright. 256p. 1985. 13.95 (ISBN 0-89840-086-4). Heres Life.

Secrets of Successful Insurance Sales: Incorporating an Original Unpublished Work by Napoleon Hill. Jack Kinder et al. (Positive Mental Attitude Ser.). 288p. 1988. 17.95 (ISBN 0-396-09329-9). Dodd.

Secrets of Successful Project Management. Ralph L. Kliem. LC 86-5567. 172p. 1986. 16.50 (ISBN 0-471-83670-2). Wiley.

Secrets of Successful Public Relations. Charles S. Phillips. LC 85-6426. 315p. 1985. 49.95 (ISBN 0-317-39230-1). P-H.

Secrets of Successful Qsl'ing. Gerry L. Dexter. 130p. (Orig.). 1986. pap. 7.96 (ISBN 0-936653-00-0). Tiare Pubns.

Secrets of Successful RVing. John Thompson. 309p. 1981. 12.95 (ISBN 0-318-17004-3). RV Indus Assn.

Secrets of Successful Songwriting. Carl E. Bolte. LC 84-6391. 208p. (Orig.). 1984. pap. 7.95 (ISBN 0-668-06170-7, 6170-7). Arco.

Secrets of Successful Speaking. Maureen Hanigan. LC 84-111243. 176p. 1984. pap. 5.95 (ISBN 0-02-012420-1, Collier). Macmillan.

Secrets of Successful Writing, Speaking, & Listening. David V. Lewis. 200p. 1982. 16.95 (ISBN 0-8144-5685-5). AMACOM.

Secrets of Suntanning. Jerold Buishas & Joseph Buishas. 106p. (Orig.). (YA) (gr. 8 up). 1988. pap. 4.95 (ISBN 0-929509-00-5). J & J Pub IL.

Secrets of Taming the Wild Food Bill. Joe Urshan. 72p. 1983. pap. 6.95 (ISBN 0-318-00153-5). PDQ Printers.

Secrets of the ABCs. D. Dowdell. LC 65-22301. (Illus.). 64p. (gr. 2 up). 1968. PLB 10.95 (ISBN 0-87783-035-5). Oddo.

Secrets of the American Wheel. Randy Roberts. Date not set. pap. price not set (ISBN 0-9618985-1-8). Info Pr Nv.

Secrets of the Andes. Brother Philip. 6.95x (ISBN 0-685-22100-8). Wehman.

Secrets of the Bible People. Kamal Salibi. LC 87-21920. (Illus.). 210p. 1988. 16.95 (ISBN 0-940793-16-4). Interlink Pub.

Secrets of the Blessed Man. Paul Tassell. 1971. pap. 2.95 (ISBN 0-87227-033-5). Reg Baptist.

Secrets of the Blue Jean Millionaire. Gary C. Jones & Rick Huemoller. 158p. 1988. 12.95 (ISBN 0-533-07622-6). Vantage.

Secrets of the Chinese Drama. Cecilia S. Zung. LC 63-23194. (Illus.). 1937. 23.00 (ISBN 0-405-09112-5). Ayer Co Pubs.

Secrets of the Chinese Drama: A Complete Explanatory Guide. Cecilia S. Zung. 59.95 (ISBN 0-8490-1016-0). Gordon Pr.

Secrets of the Chinese Herbalists. rev. ed. Richard Lucas. 252p. 1987. 19.95 (ISBN 0-13-797879-0); pap. 8.95 (ISBN 0-13-798174-0). P-H.

Secrets of the Congdon Mansion. Joe Kimball. (Illus.). 64p. 1985. pap. 4.95 (ISBN 0-9613778-0-1). Jaykay Pub Inc.

Secrets of the Forest. Olive Evans. (gr. 3-12). 1985. pap. text ed. 6.00 (ISBN 0-88734-502-6). Players Pr.

Secrets of the Great Italian Dames at the Court of the De'Medicis. Mark Tracy. (Memoirs Collections of Significant Historical Personalities Ser.). (Illus.). 119p. 1983. Repr. of 1916 ed. 137.50 (ISBN 0-89901-085-7). Found Class Reprints.

Secrets of the Great Magicians. Carrie Carmichael. LC 77-13297. (Myth, Magic & Superstition Ser.). (Illus.). 48p. (gr. 4-5). 1977. PLB 14.65 (ISBN 0-8172-1031-8). Raintree Pubs.

Secrets of the Great Pyramid. Peter Tompkins. LC 74-88639. (Illus.). 416p. 1978. pap. 15.95 (ISBN 0-06-090631-6, CN631, PL). Har-Row.

Secrets of the Great Whiskey Ring, with Documentary Proofs. John McDonald. (Illus.). 1969. Repr. of 1880 ed. 23.50 (ISBN 0-8337-2329-4). B Franklin.

Secrets of the Hand. Maria Gardini. (Illus.). 160p. 1985. pap. 12.95 (ISBN 0-02-011450-8, Collier). Macmillan.

Secrets of the Heart. Mary Balogh. 1988. pap. 3.95 (ISBN 0-451-15289-1, Sig). NAL.

Secrets of the Heart. Pearl S. Buck. LC 76-6550. (John Day Bk.). 1965. o.s.i 14.45i (ISBN 0-381-98287-4). T Y Crowell.

Secrets of the Heart. Kahlil Gibran. Tr. by Anthony R. Ferris from Arabic. 1978. pap. 5.95 (ISBN 0-8065-0062-X, Pub. by Citadel Pr). Lyle Stuart.

Secrets of the Heart. Janet Joyce. (Tapestry Ser.: No. 59). (Orig.). 1985. pap. 2.95 (ISBN 0-671-52677-4). PB.

Secrets of the Hidden Job Market. Bill Rogers et al. Ed. by Phillip Schmitz. LC 86-18799. 144p. (Orig.). 1986. pap. 6.95 (ISBN 0-932620-62-0). Betterway Pubns.

Secrets of the I Ching. Murphy. pap. 5.95 (ISBN 0-13-798694-7). P-H.

Secrets of the Ice Age: A Reappraisal of Prehistoric Man. Evans Hadingham. 342p. 1981. pap. 9.95 (ISBN 0-8027-7192-0). Walker & Co.

Secrets of the Inner Circle. 3rd ed. Harry C. Pellow. 450p. 1983. perfect bd. 29.95 (ISBN 0-941210-06-5). HCP Res.

Secrets of the Knights. Jim Gasperini. (Time Machine Ser.: No. 1). (ps-7). 1984. pap. 2.50 (ISBN 0-553-26960-7). Bantam.

Secrets of the Lost Island. Lynn Beach. (Twistaplot Ser.: No. 16). (Illus.). 96p. (Orig.). (gr. 4 up). 1985. pap. 1.95 (ISBN 0-590-33233-3). Scholastic Inc.

Secrets of the Lost Races. Rene Noorbergen. LC 77-76883. (Illus.). 1977. 12.95 (ISBN 0-672-52289-6). Bobbs.

Secrets of the Master Sellers. J. Porter Henry. 208p. 1987. pap. 12.95 (ISBN 0-8144-7688-0). AMACOM.

Secrets of the Millionaires. Bernard H. Porter. 1986. 42.50 (ISBN 0-317-55085-3). Bern Porter.

Secrets of the Millionaires. 1987. lib. bdg. 69.95 (ISBN 0-8490-3881-2). Gordon Pr.

Secrets of the Millionaires. George Sterne et al. Ed. by Russ Von Hoelscher. 138p. 1981. 14.95 (ISBN 0-940398-02-8). Profit Ideas.

Secrets of the Mummies. Joyce Milton. LC 84-1963. (Step-up Bks). (Illus.). 72p. (gr. 2-5). 1984. 4.95 (ISBN 0-394-86769-6, Pub. by BYR); lib. bdg. 8.99 (ISBN 0-394-96769-0). Random.

Secrets of the Ninja. Ashida Kim. (Illus.). 168p. 1981. 16.95 (ISBN 0-87364-234-1). Paladin Pr.

Secrets of the Ninja. Ashida Kim. 152p. 1983. pap. 7.95 (ISBN 0-8065-0866-3, Pub. by Citadel Pr). Lyle Stuart.

Secrets of the Ninja. Ashida Kim. 224p. 1985. pap. 3.95 (ISBN 0-425-10148-7). Berkley Pub.

Secrets of the Old Milton Cemetery. Bebe Morrell. Ed. by Jill Tyrer. (Illus.). 96p. (Orig.). 1988. pap. 6.00 (ISBN 0-942467-03-5). Cardinal Bks.

Secrets of the Palm. Darlene Hansen. LC 83-70662. 192p. (Orig.). 1985. pap. 9.95 (ISBN 0-917086-52-X). A C S Pubns Inc.

Secrets of the Past see Family Favorites from Reader's Digest.

Secrets of the Past, Bridges to the Future. Annette Labovitz. Ed. by Jerome Hershon. (Illus.). 190p. (Orig.). 1983. pap. text ed. 11.95x (ISBN 0-930029-00-3, TX1-317-473-TXV); tchr's. ed. 9.95x (ISBN 0-930029-01-1). Central Agency.

Secular Mind: Transformations of Faith in Modern Europe. Ed. by W. Warren Wagar. LC 81-20019. 275p. 1982. 42.50 (ISBN 0-8419-0766-8). Holmes & Meier.

Secular Movements in Production & Prices. Simon Kuznets. LC 67-16341. 1967. Repr. of 1930 ed. 45.00x (ISBN 0-678-00318-1). Kelley.

Secular Music in Colonial Annapolis: The Tuesday Club, 1745-56. John B. Talley. LC 86-24992. (Music in American Life Ser.). 304p. 1987. 29.95 (ISBN 0-252-01402-2). U of Ill Pr.

Secular Pilgrims of Victorian Fiction: The Novel as Book of Life. Barry Qualls. LC 82-1165. (Illus.). 234p. 1982. pap. 13.95 (ISBN 0-521-27201-7). Cambridge U Pr.

Secular Poems of Henry Vaughan. Ed. by E. L. Marilla. (Essays & Studies on English Language & Literature: Vol. 21). pap. 31.00 (ISBN 0-8115-0219-8). Kraus Repr.

Secular Ritual: A Working Definition of Ritual. Ed. by Sally F. Moore & Barbara G. Myerhoff. 306p. 1977. text ed. 32.00 (ISBN 90-232-1457-9, Pub. by Van Gorcum Holland). Longwood Pub Group.

Secular Sanctity. rev. ed. Edward Hays. LC 84-81954. (Illus.). 176p. 1984. pap. 7.95 (ISBN 0-939516-05-5). Forest Peace.

Secular Scripture: A Study of the Structure of Romance. Northrop Frye. (Charles Eliot Norton Lectures Ser.). 192p. 1976. 16.00x (ISBN 0-674-79675-6); pap. 7.95x (ISBN 0-674-79676-4, HP 127). Harvard U Pr.

Secular Socialists: The CCF-NDP in Ontario, a Biography. J. T. Morley. 283p. 1984. 25.00X (ISBN 0-7735-0389-7); pap. 12.95 (ISBN 0-7735-0390-0). McGill Queens U Pr.

Secular State & Religious Institutions in India: A Study of the Administration of Hindu Public Religious Trusts in Madras. Chandra Y. Mudaliar. 273p. (Orig.). 1974. pap. 28.50x (ISBN 3-515-01991-X, Pub by Franz Steiner). Coronet Bks.

Secular Word Is Full-Time Service Study Guide. Larry Peabody. 1976. pap. 1.50 (ISBN 0-87508-449-4). Chr Lit.

Secular Work Is Full Time Service. Larry Peabody. 1974. pap. 3.25 (ISBN 0-87508-448-6). Chr Lit.

Secularism in India. V. K. Sinha. 1968. 6.25 (ISBN 0-89684-521-4). Orient Bk Dist.

Secularization & Spirituality. Christian Duquoc. LC 76-103390. (Concilium Ser.: Vol. 49). 187p. 7.95 (ISBN 0-8091-0136-X). Paulist Pr.

Secularization in the U. S. S. R. Shams-ud-din. 336p. 1981. text ed. 27.50x (ISBN 0-7069-1274-8, Pub. by Vikas India). Advent NY.

Secularization of American Education As Shown by State Legislation, State Constitutional Provisions & State Supreme Court Decisions. S. W. Brown. LC 70-176600. (Columbia University. Teachers College. Contributions to Education: No. 49). Repr. of 1912 ed. 22.50 (ISBN 0-404-55049-5). AMS Pr.

Secularization of Leisure: Culture & Communication in Israel. Elihu Katz & Michael Gurevitch. (Illus.). 296p. 1976. 20.00x (ISBN 0-674-79677-2). Harvard U Pr.

Secularization of Modern Cultures. Bernard E. Meland. 1966. 3.50x (ISBN 0-912182-04-0). Seminary Co-Op.

Secularization of the California Missions (1810-1846) Gerald J. Geary. LC 73-3572. (Catholic University of America. Studies in American Church History: No. 17). Repr. of 1934 ed. 26.00 (ISBN 0-404-57767-9). AMS Pr.

Secularization of the European Mind in the Nineteenth Century. Owen Chadwick. LC 77-88670. (Gifford Lectures in the University of Edinburgh Ser.: 1973-1974). 278p. 1976. pap. 14.95 (ISBN 0-521-29317-0). Cambridge U Pr.

Secularization of the Soul: Psychical Research in Modern Britain. John J. Cerullo. LC 81-13322. 200p. 1982. text ed. 21.00 (ISBN 0-89727-028-2). ISHI PA.

Secundus the Silent Philosopher. Ben E. Perry. (APA Philological Monographs). 1983. 30.00 (ISBN 0-89130-744-3, 40-00-22). Scholars Pr GA.

Secure & Rejoicing. George E. Failing. 1980. 0.95 (ISBN 0-937296-03-1, 223-A). Presence Inc.

Secure Arrangement. JoAnn Robb. (Rapture Romance Ser.: No. 70). 1984. pap. 1.95 (ISBN 0-451-12908-3, Sig). NAL.

Secure Base: Parent-Child Attachment & Healthy Human Development. John Bowlby. LC 88-47669. 216p. 1988. 16.95 (ISBN 0-465-07598-3). Basic.

Secure Communication Systems: Related Conference Proceedings. Ed. by J. E. Flood & C. J. Hughes. (IEE Conference Publication). 1986. 44.00 (ISBN 0-85296-339-4, 1C269). Inst Elect Eng.

Secure Communication Systems: Related Conference Proceedings. Ed. by J. E. Flood & C. J. Hughes. (IEE Conference Publication: No. 231). 78p. 1984. pap. 41.00 (ISBN 0-85296-288-6, IC231). Inst Elect Eng.

Secure Communications & Asymetric Crypto-Systems. Ed. by Gustavus J. Simmons. (Selected Symposium Ser. 69). 225p. 1982. lib. bdg. 44.50x (ISBN 0-86531-338-5). Westview.

Secure Digital Communications. Ed. by G. Longo. (CISM International Centre for Mechanical Sciences, Courses & Lectures Ser.: No. 279). (Illus.). v, 332p. 1983. pap. 31.00 (ISBN 0-387-81784-0). Springer-Verlag.

Secure Executive: The Secret of Becoming One, Being One, Staying One. Steve Kahn. 1987. pap. 5.95 (ISBN 0-425-10418-4). Berkley Pub.

Secure Executive: The Secret of Becoming One, Being One, Staying One. Steven Kahn. 128p. 1986. 10.00 (ISBN 0-399-13213-9, Putnam); 10-copy counterpack 129.50 (ISBN 0-399-13217-1). Putnam Pub Group.

Secure Forever. Harold Barker. LC 73-81552. 192p. 1974. pap. 5.95 (ISBN 0-87213-017-7). Loizeaux.

Secure Speech Communications: A Monograph. H. J. Beker & F. C. Piper. (Microelectronics & Signal Processing Ser.). 1985. 49.00 (ISBN 0-12-084780-9). Acad Pr.

Secure the Blessings of Liberty: American Constitutional Law & the New Religious Movement. William C. Shepherd. LC 84-1347. (American Academy of Religion Studies in Religion: No. 35). 1984. 16.95 (ISBN 0-89130-733-8, 01-00-35); pap. 9.95 (ISBN 0-89130-824-5). Scholars Pr GA.

Secured Creditor in Court 1985. Practising Law Institute. 560p. 1985. pap. 15.00 (A4-411 4). PLI.

Secured Creditors & Lessore under the Bankruptcy Reform Act 1985. 477p. 1985. 15.00 (A4-4129). PLI.

Secured Creditors & Lessors under the Bankruptcy Reform Act, 1986. Patrick A. Murphy et al. (Course Handbook Ser.: No. 3). 487p. 1986. pap. 45.00 (A4-4159). PLI.

Secured Creditors & Lessors under the Bankruptcy Reform Act, 1987. (Commercial Law & Practice Ser.). 578p. 1987. 45.00 (A4-4203). PLI.

Secured Transactions. William B. Davenport & Daniel R. Murray. 457p. 1978. 40.00 (ISBN 0-317-32259-1, B388). Am Law Inst.

Secured Transactions. (Sum & Substance Ser.). 1981. write for info (ISBN 0-940366-12-6). Herbert Legal Ser.

Secured Transactions. 2nd ed. (Sum & Substance Ser.). 1987. write for info. (ISBN 0-940366-21-5). Herbert Legal Ser.

Secured Transactions Handbook for the Texas Attorney. Thomas Black. LC 81-85831. 171p. 1982. incl. supplement 36.00 (ISBN 0-938160-27-3, 6241). State Bar TX.

Secured Transactions Handbook for the Texas Attorney: 1986 Supplement. Thomas B. Black. LC 81-85831. 64p. 1986. 15.00 (ISBN 0-938160-43-5, 6243). State Bar TX.

Secured Transactions in a Nutshell. 2nd ed. Henry J. Bailey, III. LC 81-7404. (Nutshell Ser.). 391p. 1981. pap. text ed. 9.95 (ISBN 0-314-59846-4). West Pub.

Secured Transactions in a Nutshell. 3rd ed. Henry J. Bailey, III & Richard B. Hagedorn. (Nutshell Ser.). 390p. 1988. pap. text ed. write for info. (ISBN 0-314-41445-2). West Pub.

Secured Transactions in Arizona: A Lawyer's Guide to Article Nine of the UCC. William E. Boyd. 106p. 1984. 3 ring binder 18.20 (ISBN 0-910039-10-0). Az Law Inst.

Secured Transactions in California Commercial Law Practice. John D. Ayer et al. 363p. 1986. text ed. 90.00 (ISBN 0-88124-142-3). Cal Cont Ed Bar.

Secured Transactions in Florida. Florida Bar Staff. LC 81-71838. 1982. casebound 35.00 (ISBN 0-910373-51-5, 239). FL Bar Legal Ed.

Secured Transactions in Personal Property. Robert L. Jordan & William D. Warren. LC 83-80833. (University Casebook Ser.). 489p. 1983. text ed. 20.00 (ISBN 0-88277-135-3). Foundation Pr.

Secured Transactions in Personal Property. 2nd ed. Robert L. Jordan & William D. Warren. (University Casebook Ser.). 530p. 1987. 25.50 (ISBN 0-88277-575-8). Foundation Pr.

Secured Transactions in Personal Property. Brian N. Siegel. 1979. pap. 26.50 (ISBN 0-89074-067-4). Lega Bks.

Secured Transactions Law & Documentation: A Guide for Loan Officers. William C. Hillman. 1986. 59.95 (ISBN 0-88057-314-7). Exec Ent Pubns.

Secured Transactions, Problems & Materials. Robert J. Nordstrom et al. (American Casebook Ser.). 594p. 1986. text ed. 29.95 (ISBN 0-314-28463-X). West Pub.

Secured Transactions: Teaching Materials. Richard E. Speidel et al. (American Casebook Ser.). 485p. 1987. text ed. 23.95 (ISBN 0-314-61284-X). West Pub.

Secured Transactions, Teaching Notes. Richard E. Speidel et al. (University Casebook Ser.). 1987. write for info. tchr's manual (ISBN 0-314-64772-4). West Pub.

Secured Transactions under the Revised Uniform Commercial Code, 1985. William A. Dreier et al. LC 86-104417. Date not set. price not set. NJ Inst CLE.

Secured Transactions under the Uniform Commercial Code, 4 vols. Peter Coogan & William E. Hogan. (Bender's Uniform Commercial Code Service: Volumes 1, 1A, 1B & 1C). 1963. Set, updates avail. looseleaf 320.00 (615); Updates 1985. 208.50; Supplement 1986. looseleaf 232.00. Bender.

Secured Transactions under the Uniform Commercial Code. William Dreier et al. 226p. 1985. pap. 35.00. NJ Inst CLE.

Secured Transactions under the Uniform Commercial Code. 2nd ed. Ray D. Henson. LC 78-26098. (Hornbook Ser). 504p. 1979. text ed. 22.95 (ISBN 0-8299-2023-4). West Pub.

Securing a Safer Blood Supply: Two Views. Ross D. Eckert & Edward L. Wallace. 1985. 16.95 (ISBN 0-8447-3571-X); pap. 11.00 (ISBN 0-8447-3572-8). Am Enterprise.

Securing & Using Medical Evidence in Personal Injury & Healthcare Cases. Robert C. Strodel. 340p. 1988. 49.95 (ISBN 0-13-050303-7, Busn). P-H.

Securing Europe's Future: Changing Elements of European Security. Ed. by Stephen J. Flanagan & Fen O. Hampson. 334p. 1986. 32.50 (ISBN 0-86569-135-5). Auburn Hse.

Securing Open Spaces for Urban America: Conservation Easements. William H. Whyte. LC 60-4745. (Urban Land Institute, Technical Bulletin Ser.: 36). pap. 20.00 (ISBN 0-317-20032-1, 2023240). Bks Demand UMI.

Securing Our Planet: How to Succeed When Threats Are Too Risky & There's Really No Defense. Ed. by Don Carlson & Craig Comstock. 368p. 1986. 18.95 (ISBN 0-87477-437-3); pap. 11.95 (ISBN 0-87477-407-1). J P Tarcher.

Securing Resources by Force: The Need for Raw Materials & Military Intervention by Major Powers in Less Developed Countries. Mats Hammarstrom. 184p. (Orig.). 1986. pap. text ed. 20.00x (ISBN 91-506-0496-1, Pub. by Uppsala Universitet (Uppsala Sweden)). Coronet Bks.

Securing the Seas: The Soviet Naval Challenge & Western Alliance Options. Paul H. Nitze & Leonard Sullivan. 464p. 1979. 22.50 (ISBN 0-317-33696-7, Pub. by Westview Press); members 12.50 (ISBN 0-317-33697-5). Atlantic Council US.

Securing the Seas: The Soviet Naval Challenge & Western Alliance Options. Paul H. Nitze et al. LC 78-10423. (Illus.). 1979. pap. text ed. 23.00x (ISBN 0-89158-360-2). Westview.

Securing Your Organization's Future: A Complete Guide to Fundraising Strategies. Michael Seltzer. LC 86-31843. 514p. 1987. 19.95 (ISBN 0-87954-190-3). Foundation Ctr.

Securitech. Portcullis Press, Ltd. Staff. 300p. 1986. 150.00x (ISBN 0-317-54376-8, Pub. by Protcullis Pr UK). State Mutual Bk.

Securities. 1981. text ed. 9.95 (66418); pap. text ed. 7.95 (66426). Natl Textbk.

Securities Activities of Commercial Banks. Ed. by Arnold Sametz. LC 80-8339. 208p. 1981. 33.00x (ISBN 0-669-04031-2). Lexington Bks.

Securities Acts: Federal & Pennsylvania. Pennsylvania Bar Institute. 349p. 1985. 60.00 (ISBN 0-318-19074-5, 309). PA Bar Inst.

Securities Analysis: A Personal Seminar. New York Institute of Finance Staff. (Illus.). 240p. 1988. pap. 24.95 (ISBN 0-13-658204-4, Busn). P-H.

Securities & Exchange Commission. Ed. by Arthur M. Schlesinger, Jr. (Know Your Government Ser.). (Illus.). (gr. 5 up). 1989. 14.95 (ISBN 1-55546-119-0). Chelsea Hse.

Securities & Exchange Commission: A Case Study in the Use of Accounting As an Instrument of Public Policy. new ed. Charles W. Lamden. Ed. by Richard P. Brief. LC 77-87302. (Development of Contemporary Accounting Thought Ser). 1978. lib. bdg. 34.50x (ISBN 0-405-10941-5). Ayer Co Pubs.

Securities & Exchange Commission Docket: Cumulative Index. U. S. Securities & Exchange Commission. LC 73-643813. 1983. Repr. of 1980 ed. Index v.1-20, 1973-1980 with 1983 supplement. lib. bdg. 45.00 (ISBN 0-89941-193-2). W S Hein.

Securities & Federal Corporate Law, 4 vols. Harold S. Bloomenthal. LC 72-90956. (Securities Law Ser.). 1972. looseleaf 365.00 (ISBN 0-87632-086-8). Clark Boardman.

Securities & Litigation. Theodore A. Levine & Harvey L. Pitt. LC 83-234302. (Illus.). iv, 714p. Date not set. price not set (Law & Business). HarBraceJ.

Securities & Partnership Law for MLPs & Other Investment Limited Partnerships, Vol. 14. Linda A. Wertheimer. LC 87-25067. (Securities Law Ser.). Date not set. looseleaf 95.00 (ISBN 0-87632-577-0, SE). Clark Boardman.

Securities Arbitration, 1988. David E. Robbins. 705p. 1988. pap. 45.00 (B4-6836). PLI.

Securities: Buying & Selling Discipline. Earl J. Weinreb. LC 86-61264. 221p. 1986. 24.95 (ISBN 0-9616896-0-9). Multi Strategy Pubs.

Securities Enforcement Institute 1986, 2 vols. Gary G. Lynch & Arthur F. Mathews. (Course Handbook Ser.). 1026p. 1986. Set. pap. 45.00 (B4-6762). PLI.

Securities Enforcement Institute, 1987. (Corporate Law & Practice Handbook Ser.: No. 561). 1072p. 1987. 45.00 (B46791). PLI.

Securities Filings, 1987: Review & Update. (Corporate Law & Practice Ser.). 567p. 1987. 45.00 (B4-6805). PLI.

Securities Fraud & Commodities Fraud, 5 vols. Alan R. Bromberg & Lewis D. Lowenfels. (Securities Law Publications). 1750p. 1980. 375.00. Shepards-McGraw.

Securities Handbook. Martin Torosian. 1986.. 38.00 (ISBN 0-9603592-2-2). MTA Financial Servs.

Securities Industry Glossary. 2nd ed. New York Institute of Finance. 1988. pap. 12.95 (ISBN 0-13-798778-1). Prentice Hall Pr.

Securities Industry Glossary. 216p. (Orig.). 1985. pap. text ed. 14.95 (ISBN 0-13-798836-2). NY Inst Finance.

Securities Industry Yearbook, 1987-88. 732p. 90.00. Securities Industry.

Securities Law & Enforcement: 1982. Ed. by Law & Business Inc. Staff & Legal Times Seminars Staff. (Seminar Course Handbooks). 1983. pap. 30.00 (ISBN 0-686-89351-4, C01147, Law & Business). HarBraceJ.

Securities Law Considerations Affecting Employee Benefits Plans. Simon M. Lorne. (Corporate Practice Ser.: No. 44). 1985. 92.00 (ISBN 0-317-55348-8). BNA.

Securities Law for the Non-Securities Professional in State. LC 86-165922. 1987. 30.00. Natl Busn Inst.

Securities Law Handbook, 1987-88. Harold S. Bloomenthal. (Securities Law Ser.). 1988. pap. 85.00 (ISBN 0-87632-554-1). Clark Boardman.

Securities Law Review, 1987. Ed. by Donald C. Langevoort. 1987. 85.00 (ISBN 0-87632-545-2). Clark Boardman.

Securities Law Series, 25 vols. 1986. Set. 1325.00 (ISBN 0-317-09383-5). Clark Boardman.

Securities Law Techniques, 5 vols. Ed. by A. A. Sommer, Jr. 1985. Updates avail. looseleaf set 390.00 (636); 1986 updates 59.00. Bender.

Securities Litigation. 3rd ed. (Resource Materials Ser.). 1032p. 1979. pap. 40.00 (ISBN 0-317-55926-5, R103). Am Law Inst.

Securities Litigation: Prosecution & Defense Strategies. 1033p. 1986. pap. 45.00 (H4-5003). PLI.

Securities Litigation, 1987: Prosecution & Defense Strategies, 2 vols. (Litigation & Administrative Practice Ser.). 1353p. 1987. Set. 45.00 (H4-5028). PLI.

Securities Market. Sidney M. Robbins. LC 66-15499. 1966. 12.95 (ISBN 0-02-926570-3). Free Pr.

Securities Markets. K. Garbade. (Finance Ser.). 1982. text ed. 40.95 (ISBN 0-07-022780-2). McGraw.

Securities Practice: Federal & State Enforcement. Marc I. Steinberg & Ralph C. Ferrara. LC 85-25526. 1985. 170.00. Callaghan.

Securities Practice Handbook. 5th ed. Robert E. Shields & Robert H. Strouse. 350p. 1987. 70.00 (ISBN 0-8318-0460-2, B460). Am Law Inst.

Securities: Public & Private Offerings. William Prifti. LC 82-24495. 1983. 85.00 (ISBN 0-317-11924-9). Callaghan.

Securities: Public & Private Offerings. William M. Prifti. (West's Handbook Ser.). write for info. West Pub.

Securities Regulation, 6 vols. 2nd ed. Louis Loss. Incl. 1969 Supplement, 3 vols. 2053p. 1969. 325.00 (ISBN 0-316-53320-3). 2199p. 1961. Little.

Securities Regulation, 3 vols. 3rd ed. Louis Loss & Joel Seligman. 1800p. 1988. Set. 240.00. Little.

Securities Regulation. Ed. by Prentice-Hall Editorial Staff. 1984. write for info. P-H.

Securities Regulation. Marc I. Steinberg. LC 87-101219. (Analysis & Skills Ser.). 1177p. Date not set. price not set. Bender.

Securities Regulation: A Problem Approach. Larry D. Soderquist. LC 81-9895. (University Casebook Ser.). 1043p. 1981. text ed. 26.50 (ISBN 0-88277-041-1). Foundation Pr.

Securities Regulation: A Problem Approach. Larry D Soderquist. 503p. 1988. text ed. write for info. (ISBN 0-88277-632-0). Foundation Pr.

Securities Regulation: A Problem Approach, 1985 Supplement. Larry D. Soderquist. (University Casebook Ser.). 1985. pap. 14.95 (ISBN 0-88277-253-8). Foundation Pr.

Securities Regulation: Adaptable to Courses Utilizing Materials By Jennings. 5th ed. Richard W. Jennings. LC 83-112301. (Legalines Ser.). 1981. write for info. (Law & Business). HarBraceJ.

Securities Regulation: Adaptable to Courses Utilizing Ratner's Casebook on Securities Regulation. Casenotes Publishing Co., Inc. Staff. Ed. by Norman S. Goldenberg et al. (Legal Brief Ser.). 1986. pap. write for info. (ISBN 0-87457-124-3, 1271). Casenotes Pub.

Securities Regulation & Law Report. BNA's Business & Economic Services Staff. 676.00. BNA.

Securities Regulation & the New Deal. Michael E. Parrish. LC 70-118735. (Yale Historical Publication. Miscellany Ser.: No. 93). pap. 70.50 (ISBN 0-317-09459-9, 2022027). Bks Demand UMI.

Securities Regulation: Cases & Materials. Martin L. Budd & Nicholas Wolfson. (Contemporary Legal Education Ser.). xvii, 970p. 1984. 32.00x (ISBN 0-87215-778-4). Michie Co.

Securities Regulation, Cases & Materials. 5th ed. Richard W. Jennings & Harold Marsh, Jr. LC 82-11075. (University Casebook Ser.). 1432p. 1982. text ed. 30.00 (ISBN 0-88277-054-3). Foundation Pr.

Securities Regulation: Cases & Materials. 6th ed. Richard W. Jennings & Harold Marsh, Jr. (University Casebook Ser.). 1702p. 1987. text ed. 37.00 (ISBN 0-88277-559-6). Foundation Pr.

Security Manager's Desk Reference. Richard Post & David Schachtsiek. 448p. 1986. text ed. 49.95 (ISBN 0-409-90014-1). Butterworth.

Security Manual. 4th ed. Eric Oliver & John Wilson. 244p. (Orig.). 1983. pap. text ed. 12.50x (ISBN 0-566-02415-2). Gower Pub Co.

Security Manual. 5th ed. Eric Oliver & John Wilson. 256p. 1988. text ed. 13.00 (ISBN 0-566-02779-8, Pub. by Gower Pub England). Gower Pub Co.

Security Markets: Findings & Recommendations of a Special Staff of the Twentieth Century Fund. facsimile ed. Twentieth Century Fund. LC 75-2675. (Wall Street & the Security Market Ser.). 1975. Repr. of 1935 ed. 66.00x (ISBN 0-405-07237-6). Ayer Co Pubs.

Security Markets: Stochastic Models. Darrell Duffie. (Economic Theory, Econometrics, & Mathematical Economics Ser.). 350p. 1988. 39.50 (ISBN 0-12-223345-X). Acad Pr.

Security of Buildings. Underwood. 1987. 38.95 (ISBN 0-85139-613-5). Van Nos Reinhold.

Security of Computer Based Information Systems. V. P. Lane. (Computer Science Ser.). (Illus.). 192p. (Orig.). 1985. pap. text ed. 21.50x (ISBN 0-333-36437-6, Pub. bu Macmillan England). Scholium Intl.

Security of Data in Networks. Donald W. Davies. (Tutorial Texts Ser.). 241p. 1981. 20.00 (ISBN 0-8186-0366-6, Q366). IEEE Comp Soc.

Security of Employment & Income in the Light of Structural Changes in the Textile Industry: Textiles Committee Report II. (Programme of Industrial Activities). 64p. 1985. pap. 7.15 (ISBN 92-2-103752-5, ILO358, ILO). UNIPUB.

Security of Englishmen's Lives, or the Trust Power & Duty of Grand Juries. John Somers. (Civil Liberties in American History Ser.). 1974. Repr. of 1681 ed. lib. bdg. 12.50 (ISBN 0-306-70604-0). Da Capo.

Security of Infants. Betty M. Flint. LC 59-40393. (Illus.). 1959. pap. 36.00 (ISBN 0-317-08106-3, 2014209). Bks Demand UMI.

Security of Personal Computer Systems: A Management Guide. 1986. lib. bdg. 79.95 (ISBN 0-8490-3741-7). Gordon Pr.

Security of Personal Computer Systems: A Management Guide. Dennis D. Steinauer. LC 84-601156. (Computer Science & Technology Ser.). 68p. (Orig.). 1985. pap. 3.00 (S/N 003-003-02627-1). USGPO.

Security of Premises: A Manual for Managers. Stanley Lyons. (Illus.). 152p. 1988. text ed. 22.95 (ISBN 0-408-01367-2). Butterworth.

Security of Salvation. Richard C. Nies. LC 78-17523. (Waymark Ser.). 1978. pap. 2.50 (ISBN 0-8127-0187-9). Review & Herald.

Security of South Asia: American & Asian Perspectives. Ed. by Stephen P. Cohen. LC 87-10772. 280p. 1987. text ed. 29.95 (ISBN 0-252-01394-8). U of Ill Pr.

Security of Southwest Asia. Zalmay Khalilzad et al. LC 83-13837. 425p. 1984. 37.50 (ISBN 0-312-70914-5). St Martin.

Security of Taiwan: Unravelling the Dilemma. Martin L. Lasater. LC 82-71154. (Significant Issues Ser.: Vol. 4, No. 1). 85p. 1982. 5.95 (ISBN 0-89206-035-2). CSI Studies.

Security of the Persian Gulf. Ed. by Hossein Amirsadeghi. LC 80-28780. 320p. 1981. 35.00x (ISBN 0-312-70915-3). St Martin.

Security of Western Europe: The European Communities As an Alternative to NATO? Joseph C. Rallo. 272p. 1986. 29.95 (ISBN 0-312-70911-0). St Martin.

Security Officer. Jack Rudman. (Career Examination Ser.: C-1467). (Cloth bdg. avail. on request). pap. 12.00 (ISBN 0-8373-1467-4). Natl Learning.

Security Options Strategy. Albert I. Bookbinder. LC 76-46120. 201p. 1976. 15.00 (ISBN 0-916106-01-2). Prog Pr.

Security or Armageddon: Israel's Nuclear Strategy. Ed. by Louis R. Beres. LC 84-48505. 256p. 1985. 29.00x (ISBN 0-669-09566-4); pap. 12.95 (ISBN 0-669-11131-7). Lexington Bks.

Security Police Officer (U.S.P.S.) Jack Rudman. (Career Examination Ser.: C-2211). (Cloth bdg. avail. on request). pap. 12.00 (ISBN 0-8373-2211-1). Natl Learning.

Security Policy: Dilemmas of Using & Controlling Military Power. Robert Harkavy & Edward Kolodziej. 1979. pap. 8.00 (ISBN 0-918592-34-8). Policy Studies.

Security Practices at Soviet Scientific Research Facilities. Irina Dunskaya. Ed. by Barbara Dash. 143p. (Orig.). Date not set. pap. text ed. 35.00 (ISBN 1-55831-007-X). Delphic Associates.

Security Prices in a Competitive Market: More About Risk & Return from Common Stocks. Richard A. Brealey. 1971. 24.75x (ISBN 0-262-02077-7). MIT Pr.

Security Problems: An African Predicament. Francis Deng. LC 81-71701. (Hans Wolff Memorial Lecture Ser.). 1982. pap. text ed. 5.00 (ISBN 0-941934-36-5). Indiana Africa.

Security Regulations in Hong Kong, Nineteen Seventy-Two to Nineteen Seventy-Seven. M. F. Higgins. 192p. 1978. 25.00x (ISBN 90-286-0948-2, Pub. by Sijthoff & Noordhoff). Kluwer Academic.

Security Safeguards in Computer Operations. Charles F. Hemphill, Jr. & Robert D. Hemphill. 1979. pap. 7.50 (ISBN 0-8144-2232-2). AMACOM.

Security Services Assistant. Jack Rudman. (Career Examination Ser.: C-2204). 1988. pap. 12.00 (ISBN 0-8373-2204-9). Natl Learning.

Security, Strategy, & Policy Responses in the Asian Pacific Region. rev. ed. Ed. by Young W. Kihl & Lawrence E. Grinter. 280p. 1989. lib. bdg. 35.00 (ISBN 1-55587-131-3). Lynne Rienner.

Security, Strategy, & the Logic of Chinese Foreign Policy. Jonathan D. Pollack. LC 82-80971. (Research Papers & Policy Studies (Rpps): No. 5). 66p. 1981. 2.50x (ISBN 0-912966-34-3). IEAS.

Security Supervisor's Handbook: A Guide for the Private Security Primary Manager. John L. Coleman. (Illus.). 122p. 1987. 25.25x (ISBN 0-398-05291-3). C C Thomas.

Security Survey. Denis Hughes & Peter Bowler. 260p. 1982. text ed. 34.25x (ISBN 0-566-02291-5). Gower Pub Co.

Security Syndicate Operations: Organization, Management & Accounting. enl. & rev. ed. Arthur Galston. LC 75-2634. (Wall Street & the Security Market Ser.). 1975. Repr. of 1928 ed. 21.00x (ISBN 0-405-06959-6). Ayer Co Pubs.

Security Through Science & Engineering: Proceedings. International Carnahan Conference. Ed. by J. S. Jackson & R. William De Vore. LC 82-646157. (Illus.). 278p. (Orig.). 1983. pap. 33.50 (ISBN 0-89779-057-X, UKY BU 132). OES Pubns.

Security Through Science & Engineering: Proceedings, Third International Conference. Ed. by R. William De Vore & J. S. Jackson. LC 80-83300. (Illus.). 313p. 1980. pap. 33.50 (ISBN 0-89779-042-1, UKYBU122). OES Pubns.

Security Training & Education: A Handbook with Questions & Answers. David Y. Coverston & Sam S. Coverston. (Illus.). 1988. 12.00 (ISBN 0-936101-05-9); pap. 10.00 (ISBN 0-936101-04-0). Security Seminars.

Security Training: Readings from Security Management Magazine. Shari Gallery. (Illus.). 328p. Date not set. pap. 24.95 (ISBN 0-409-90122-9). Butterworth.

Security Transactions-1985. 1985. pap. 2.00 (ISBN 0-317-44618-5, 4366). Commerce.

Security Transactions-1986. Commerce Clearing House, Inc. 32p. 1986. 2.00 (ISBN 0-317-47514-2, 4367). Commerce.

Security Transactions, 1987. 32p. (Orig.). 1987. pap. 2.50 (4368). Commerce.

Security Transactions, 1988. Clark. 32p. Date not set. pap. 2.50 (4369). Commerce.

Security vs. Liberty: Analyzing Social Structure & Policy. Wolfgang L. Grichting. LC 84-15321. (Illus.). 274p. (Orig.). 1985. lib. bdg. 26.75 (ISBN 0-8191-4223-9); pap. text ed. 14.25 (ISBN 0-8191-4224-7). U Pr of Amer.

Security vs. Survival: The Nuclear Arms Race. Ed. by Theresa C. Smith & Indu B. Singh. LC 84-27521. (Illus.). 195p. 1985. lib. bdg. 30.00x (ISBN 0-931477-13-1). Lynne Rienner.

Security Within the Pacific Rim. Douglas Stuart. 250p. 1987. text ed. 43.95 (ISBN 0-566-05246-6, Pub. by Gower Pub England). Gower Pub Co.

Security Without Nuclear Weapons - Indo-Soviet Dialogue. K. Subrahmanyam & Jasjit Singh. 218p. 1986. 26.00x (ISBN 81-7062-012-0, Pub. by Lancer India). South Asia Bks.

Security Without Starwars: Verifying a Ban on Ballistic Missle Defense. Betty G. Lall. 106p. 1987. pap. 5.00 (ISBN 0-87871-052-3). CEP.

Security Work & Relief Policies. United States National Resources Planning Board. LC 72-2385. (FDR & the Era of the New Deal Ser.). 640p. 1973. Repr. of 1942 ed. lib. bdg. 75.00 (ISBN 0-306-70520-6). Da Capo.

Securityland's Safety. Karl Kratz. Ed. by Cal Lum & Sherrey Bussey. (Illus.). 150p. (Orig.). 1987. pap. 9.95 (ISBN 0-941201-01-5); incl. kit 19.95 (ISBN 0-941201-00-7). INNPRO.

Sed Llenos del Espiritu Santo. rev. ed. John R. Stott. Tr. by David A. Cook from Eng. LC 77-162. 112p. (Span.). 1977. pap. 4.25 (ISBN 0-89922-084-3). Edit Caribe.

Sedad Eldem: Modernity in Tradition. Text by Sibel Bozdogan. (Illus.). 176p. 1988. 40.00 (ISBN 0-89381-292-7). Aperture.

Sedation. Harold L. Hamburg. (Illus.). 198p. 1980. pap. 20.00 (ISBN 0-931386-07-1). Quint Pub Co.

Sedation: A Guide to Patient Management. Malamed. 1985. pap. 36.95 (ISBN 0-8016-3089-4). Mosby.

Sedation: A Guide to Patient Management. Malamed. (Illus.). 640p. 1988. pap. text ed. 33.95 (ISBN 0-8016-3210-2). Mosby.

Seder for Tu B'Shevat. Harlene Appleman & Jane Shapiro. (Illus.). 32p. (ps up). pap. 2.95 (ISBN 0-930494-39-3). Kar Ben.

Seder Mincha U'Maariv. 1982. pap. 0.99 (ISBN 0-686-76256-8). Feldheim.

Seder R. Armram Gaon: The Order of the Sabbath Prayer. Tryggve Kronholm. 238p. (Orig.). 1974. pap. 27.50x (ISBN 0-317-65773-9). Coronet Bks.

Sedge Moths of North America. John B. Heppner. LC 85-13087. (Handbook Ser.: No. 1). (Illus.). 262p. (Orig.). 1985. pap. 27.95 (ISBN 0-916846-32-6). Flora & Fauna.

Sedgemoor, Sixteen Eighty-Five. John Whiles. 52p. 1987. pap. 21.00x (ISBN 0-948251-00-X, Pub. by Picton UK). State Mutual Bk.

Sedgemoor Sixteen Eighty-Five: An Account & an Anthology. David G. Chandler. LC 85-14599. 240p. 1985. 29.95 (ISBN 0-312-70918-8). St Martin.

Sedges: Cyperus to Scleria. Robert H. Mohlenbrock. LC 76-15267. (Illustrated Flora of Illinois Ser.). (Illus.). 208p. 1976. 24.95x (ISBN 0-8093-0604-2). S Ill U Pr.

Sedgewood Book of Baking. LC 82-51036. (Illus.). 192p. 1983. 18.95 (ISBN 0-02-496630-4). Macmillan.

Sediment Diagenesis. Ed. by A. Parker & B. W. Sellwood. pap. text ed. 24.50 (ISBN 90-277-1874-1, Pub. by Reidel Holland). Kluwer Academic.

Sediment-Freshwater Interaction. Peter G. Sly. 1982. text ed. 125.00 (ISBN 90-6193-760-4, Pub. by Junk Pubs Netherlands). Kluwer Academic.

Sediment Kds & Concentration Factors for Radionuclides in the Marine Environment. (Technical Reports Ser.: No. 247). 73p. 1986. pap. 21.00 (ISBN 92-0-125085-1, IDC247, IAEA). UNIPUB.

Sediment Microbiology. Ed. by D. B. Nedwell & C. M. Brown. (Special Publication Ser.: No. 7). 1982. 43.50 (ISBN 0-12-515380-5). Acad Pr.

Sediment Oxygen Demand: Processes, Modeling & Measurement. Ed. by Kathryn J. Hatcher. LC 85-82274. (Illus.). 448p. (Orig.). 1986. pap. write for info. (ISBN 0-935835-00-8). Univ GA Nat Res.

Sediment Transport in Alluvial Streams. Janos Bogardi. 826p. 1974. 230.00x (ISBN 0-569-08252-8, Pub. by Collets (UK)). State Mutual Bk.

Sediment Transport in Alluvial Streams. John L. Bogardi. 68.00 (ISBN 9-6305-1826-0). WRP.

Sediment Transport in the Near-Shore Zone. Ed. by William F. Tanner. 147p. 1974. pap. 20.00 (ISBN 0-686-83994-3). FSU Geology.

Sediment Transport Technology. Daryl B. Simons & Fuat Senturk. LC 76-19737. 1977. 40.00 (ISBN 0-918334-14-4). WRP.

Sedimentary & Evolutionary Cycles. Ed. by U. Bayer & A. Seilacher. (Lecture Notes in Earth Sciences: Vol. 1). vi, 465p. 1985. pap. 32.50 (ISBN 0-387-13982-6). Springer-Verlag.

Sedimentary Cover - North American Craton: U. S. Ed. by L. L. Sloss. (DNAG, Geology of North America Ser.: Vol. D-2). (Illus.). 1988. write for info. Geol Soc.

Sedimentary Dynamics of Continential Shelves. Ed. by C. A. Nittrouer. (Developments in Sedementology Ser.: Vol. 32). 450p. 1981. 105.25 (ISBN 0-444-41962-4). Elsevier.

Sedimentary Environments. 2nd ed. Reading. Date not set. price not set (ISBN 0-444-00861-6). Elsevier.

Sedimentary Environments & Facies. 2nd ed. H. G. Reading. (Illus.). 680p. 1986. text ed. 90.00 (ISBN 0-632-01572-1); pap. text ed. 39.95X (ISBN 0-632-01223-4). Blackwell Pubns.

Sedimentary Environments & Facies. Ed. by H. G. Reading. 558p. 1979. pap. 35.25 (ISBN 0-444-00293-6). Elsevier.

Sedimentary Environments from Wireline Logs. O. Serra. (Illus.). 211p. (Orig.). Date not set. pap. text ed. 20.00 (ISBN 0-929119-01-0, SMP-7008). Schlumberger Educ.

Sedimentary Geology of the Himalaya. Ed. by R. A. Srivastava. (Current Trends in Geology Ser.: Vol. 5). xii, 250p. 1985. 50.00 (ISBN 1-55528-051-X, Pub. by Messers Today & Tomorrow Printers & Publishers). Scholarly Pubns.

Sedimentary Gradients in a High Energy Carbonate Lagoon, Snow Bay, San Salvador, Bahamas. C. B. Anderson & M. R. Boardman. (Occasional Papers: No. 1). 25p. 1987. pap. text ed. 4.00 (ISBN 0-935909-25-7). CCFL Bahamian.

Sedimentary Petrology. Harvey Blatt. LC 81-22147. (Illus.). 564p. 1982. text ed. 39.95 (ISBN 0-7167-1354-3). W H Freeman.

Sedimentary Petrology: An Introduction, Vol.3. M. E. Tucker. (Geoscience Texts Ser.). 252p. 1981. pap. 28.95x (ISBN 0-470-27160-4). Halsted Pr.

Sedimentary Petrology & History of the Haymond Formation (Pennsylvanian), Marathon Basin, Texas. E. F. McBride. (Report of Investigations Ser.: RI 57). 101p. 1966. 2.50 (ISBN 0-686-29339-8). Bur Econ Geology.

Sedimentary Processes, Carbonate Sedimentology: Selected Papers Reprinted from Journal of Sedimentary Petrology. Clif Jordon. LC 79-116635. (Society of Economic Paleontologists & Mineralogists, SEPM Reprint Ser.: No. 5). pap. 60.50 (2026654). Bks Demand UMI.

Sedimentary Processes: Depositional Processes in Ancient Carbonates. Society of Economic Paleontologists & Mineralogists Staff. Compiled by John M. Cys & S. J. Mazzullo. (Society of Economic Paleontologists & Mineralogists Ser.: No. 7). (Illus.). pap. 62.20 (ISBN 0-317-58121-X, 2029674). Bks Demand UMI.

Sedimentary Processes: Diagenesis. Doris M. Curtis. (Society of Economic Paleontologists & Mineralogists, Reprint Ser.: No. 1). pap. 55.50 (ISBN 0-317-27145-8, 2024747). Bks Demand UMI.

Sedimentary Processes on the Amazon Continental Shelf. Ed. by C. A. Nittrouer & D. J. Demaster. (Illus.). 336p. 1987. 39.50 (ISBN 0-08-033928-X, PBL). Pergamon.

Sedimentary Structures, 2 Vols. J. R. Allen. (Developments in Sedimentology Ser.: Vol. 30B). 594p. 1982. Vol. 1. 110.75 (ISBN 0-444-41935-7); Vol. 2. 110.75 (ISBN 0-444-41945-4). Elsevier.

Sedimentary Structures & Facies Analysis of Shallow Marine Carbonates. H. U. Schwarz. (Contributions to Sedimentology Ser.: No. 3). (Illus.). 100p. 1975. pap. text ed. 35.00x (ISBN 3-510-57003-0). Lubrecht & Cramer.

Sedimentary Structures in Dunes of the Namib Desert, South West Africa. Edwin D. McKee. (Special Paper Ser.: No. 188). (Illus.). 1982. 6.40 (ISBN 0-8137-2188-1). Geol Soc.

Sedimentary Structures: Their Character & Physical Basis, Pts. A & B. J. R. Allen. (Developments in Sedimentology Ser.: Vol. 30). 1984. pap. 57.50 (ISBN 0-444-42232-3). Elsevier.

Sedimentary Structuress. J D. Collinson & D B. Thompson. (Illus.). 240p. 1982. text ed. 50.00x (ISBN 0-04-552017-8); pap. text ed. 19.95x (ISBN 0-04-552018-6). Unwin Hyman.

Sedimentation & Mineral Deposits in the Southwestern Pacific Ocean. Ed. by D. S. Cronan. (Ocean Science, Resources & Technology). 1986. 67.50 (ISBN 0-12-195870-1). Acad Pr.

Sedimentation & Tectonics of the Welsh Basin. Ed. by W. R. Fitches & N. H. Woodcock. 1987. 90.00 (ISBN 0-471-91546-7). Wiley.

Sedimentation-Consolidation Models: Predictions & Validation: Proceedings of a Symposium Sponsored by the Geotechnical Engineering Division. Ed. by Raymond N. Yong & Frank C. Townsend. 610p. 1984. 49.00x (ISBN 0-87262-429-3). Am Soc Civil Eng.

Sedimentation Engineering. (Manual & Report on Engineering Practice Ser.: No. 54). 761p. 1975. 39.00x (ISBN 0-87262-001-8). Am Soc Civil Eng.

Sedimentation in the Mississippi River Between Davenport, Iowa, & Cairo, Illinois. Alvin L. Lugn. LC 28-14418. (Augustana College Library Publication Ser.: No. 11). 104p. 1927. pap. 1.00 (ISBN 0-910182-08-6). Augustana Coll.

Sedimentation in the World Ocean with Emphasis on the Nature, Distribution & Behavior of Marine Suspensions. Alexander P. Lisitzin. Ed. by Kelvin S. Rodolfo. LC 72-172081. (Society of Economic Paleontologists & Mineralogists, Special Publication: No. 17). pap. 58.00 (ISBN 0-317-27149-0, 2024744). Bks Demand UMI.

Sedimentation Models & Quantitative Stratigraphy. W. Schwarzacher. 384p. 1975. 116.00 (ISBN 0-444-41302-2). Elsevier.

Sedimentation of Oblique-Slip Mobile Zones. Ed. by Peter F. Ballance & Harold G. Reading. (International Association of Sedimentologists & the Societ As Internationalis Limnological Symposium). 265p. 1980. pap. 74.95x (ISBN 0-470-26927-8). Halsted Pr.

Sedimentation of the Modern Carbonate Tidal Flats of Northwest Andros Island, Bahamas. Lawrence A. Hardie. LC 76-47389. (Johns Hopkins University Studies in Geology: No. 22). (Illus.). 232p. 1977. 32.00x (ISBN 0-8018-1895-8). Johns Hopkins.

Sedimentology & Stratigraphy. Sam Boggs, Jr. 800p. 1986. text ed. 43.95 (ISBN 0-675-20487-9). Merrill.

Sedimentology of Coal & Coal-Bearing Sequences. Ed. by Ray A. Rahmani & Romeo M. Flores. 396p. 1985. pap. 65.00x (ISBN 0-632-01286-2). Blackwell Pubns.

Sedimentology of Shale: Study Guide & Reference Source. P. E. Potter et al. (Illus.). 316p. 1980. pap. 39.50 (ISBN 0-387-90430-1). Springer-Verlag.

Sedimentology: Proceedings of the 27th International Geological Congress, Vol. 4. International Geological Congress Staff. 262p. 1984. lib. bdg. 77.50x (ISBN 90-6764-013-1). Coronet Bks.

Sedimentology: Process & Product. M R. Leeder. (Illus.). 528p. 1982. text ed. 60.00x (ISBN 0-04-551053-9); pap. text ed. 34.95x (ISBN 0-04-551054-7). Unwin Hyman.

Sedimentology: Recent Developments & Applied Aspects. Ed. by P. J. Brenchley & B. P. Williams. (Illus.). 320p. 1985. text ed. 67.00 (ISBN 0-632-01192-0); pap. 37.00 (ISBN 0-632-01418-0). Blackwell Pubns.

Sediments & Sedimentary Rocks 1. Hans Fuechtbauer. (Sedimentary Petrology Ser.: Pt. 2). (Illus.). 464p. 1974. lib. bdg. 62.50x (ISBN 3-510-65007-7). Lubrecht & Cramer.

Sediments & Water Interactions. Ed. by P. G. Sly. (Illus.). 575p. 1986. 105.00 (ISBN 0-387-96293-X). Springer-Verlag.

Sedition Case of Nineteen Forty-Four. Lutheran Research Society. 1979. lib. bdg. 59.95 (ISBN 0-8490-3005-6). Gordon Pr.

Seditious Mandibles: Surrealist Drawings & Poems. Robert Green. (Illus.). 24p. 1981. pap. 3.50 (ISBN 0-941194-13-2). Black Swan Pr.

Sedlacek Technique: Finding the Calm Within You. Keith Sedlacek. 1988. text ed. 17.95 (ISBN 0-07-056521-X). McGraw.

Sedona: Psychic Energy Vortexes. Dick Sutphen. LC 86-50562. 180p. 1986. 7.95 (ISBN 0-87554-049-X). Valley Sun.

Seeburg Jukebox Model SS 160 "Stereo Showcase" Trouble Shooting Guide: Manual No. 55904. 66p. 1983. Repr. of 1967 ed. 10 mil. laminated spiral bdg. 24.50 (ISBN 0-913698-56-3, R-212). AMR Pub Co.

Seeburg Jukebox Model U-100 "Mustang" Parts Catalog of 1965-1966. Seeburg Corp. Ed. by Frank Adams. 62p. 1984. Repr. of 1965 ed. 10 mil laminated spiral bdg. 24.50 (ISBN 0-913599-33-6, R-275). AMR Pub Co.

Seeburg Jukebox Models, LPCI & LPCIR: Installation & Operations Manual & Trouble Shooting Guide of 1963-64. Seeburg Company Staff. 90p. 1983. Repr. of 1964 ed. 10 mil laminated covers, spiral bdg. 26.50 (ISBN 0-913599-17-4, R-255). AMR Pub Co.

Seeburg Jukebox Models M100B & M100BL Service & of 1951: Includes Trouble Shooting Charts. Seeburg Company Staff. 236p. 1984. 10 mil laminated covers, spiral bdg. 37.50 (ISBN 0-913599-16-6, R-258). AMR Pub Co.

Seeburg Jukebox Models of the 146,147 & 148 Series: Service, Parts Manual & Trouble Shooting Charts of 1946, 47 & 48. Seeburg Company Staff. Ed. by Frank Adams. 330p. 1984. Repr. of 1948 ed. spiral bound, laminated covers 44.50 (ISBN 0-913599-25-5, R-265). AMR Pub Co.

Seeburg Jukebox Models Q100 & Q160 Service & Parts Manual. 146p. 1982. pap. 32.50 (ISBN 0-913698-54-7, R-162). AMR Pub Co.

Seeburg Jukebox Models VL-200 & VL-200-D Installation & Operation Manual: Part No. 408785. 32p. 1982. Repr. of 1956 ed. spiral bdg. 9.50 (ISBN 0-913698-57-1). AMR Pub Co.

Seeburg Jukebox Models, VL-200-N & VL-200: Service Parts Manual 1955-56. Seeburg Company Staff. 260p. 1983. Repr. of 1955 ed. 10 mil laminated covers, spiral bdg. 37.50 (ISBN 0-913599-12-3, R-263). AMR Pub Co.

Seeburg Jukebox Service Manual & Parts List for 1940 Models Concert Master, Commander & Cadet: Electric Selector & Mechanical Selector. Seeburg Corp. Ed. by Frank Adams. 148p. 1984. Repr. of 1940 ed. 10 mil lamianted covers, spiral bound 32.50 (ISBN 0-913599-35-2, R-276). AMR Pub Co.

Seeburg Jukebox Service Manual, Brochure & Trouble-Shooting Guide for 1958 Models 101, 161 & 201. Seeburg Corp. Ed. by Frank Adams. 180p. 1984. Repr. of 1958 ed. 10 mil laminated covers. Spiral bound 35.00 (ISBN 0-913599-37-9, R-278). AMR Pub Co.

Seeburg Jukebox Service Manual: Models LPCI & LPCIR of 1963. Seeburg Company Staff. 119p. 1984. Repr. of 1963 ed. 10 mil laminated covers 29.50 (ISBN 0-913599-02-6, R-249). AMR Pub Co.

Seeburg Jukebox Service Manual, Parts List, Installation & Operation Manual for the Models of the AY Series of 1961. Seeburg Co. Staff. Ed. by Frank Adams. 182p. 1984. Repr. of 1961 ed. spiral bound, laminated covers 35.00 (ISBN 0-913599-23-9, R-273). AMR Pub Co.

Seeburg Jukebox Service Parts Manual, Trouble Shooting Guide & Brochure for the Seeburg Selectomatic Models W100 & HF100G. 265p. 1983. Repr. of 1953 ed. 10 mil. laminated spiral bdg. 39.50 (ISBN 0-913698-53-9, R-266). AMR Pub Co.

Seeburg Jukebox 220 & 222: Service, Parts Manual & Trouble Shooting Chart of 1959. Seeburg Company Staff. Ed. by Frank Adams. 222p. 1984. Repr. of 1959 ed. spiral bound, laminated covers 36.50 (ISBN 0-913599-24-7, R-274). AMR Pub Co.

Seeburg Jukeboxes: Sixty Year Pictorial Presentation of this Transition from a Pneumatic Operated Jukebox to the Current Laser Presentation. Frank Adams. 136p. (Orig.). 1986. 24.50 (ISBN 0-939971-07-0, R-400). AMR Pub Co.

Seeburg Library Unit Model 200LU-3 Installation & Service Manual. rev. ed. Seeburg Co. Ed. by Frank Adams. 100p. 1986. Repr. 29.50 (ISBN 0-939971-11-9, R-369). AMR Pub Co.

Seeburg Library Unit Model 200LU1 Installation & Service Manual. Seeburg Co. Ed. by Frank Adams. 118p. 1986. Repr. 32.50 (ISBN 0-939971-10-0, R-368). AMR Pub Co.

Seeburg LPC480 Series Jukebox Service Manual, Trouble Shooting Charts, Installation & Operation Manual. Seeburg Corporation. Ed. by AMR Publishing Company Staff. 258p. 1984. Repr. of 1965 ed. deluxe ed. 39.50 spiral bdg. (ISBN 0-913599-31-X, R-298). AMR Pub Co.

Seeburg LS111 "Apollo" Service Manual of 1970. Seeburg Co. Staff. Ed. by Frank Adams. 130p. 1986. Repr. of 1970 ed. 29.50 (ISBN 0-913599-72-7, R-333). AMR Pub Co.

Seeburg Operation & Adjustments Manual for Types 160ST26, 160ST26-5, 160ST27, 160ST27-5, 160ST28 & 160ST28-5 & Parts Catalog Models SPS-2. rev ed. Seeburg Co. Staff. Ed. by Frank Adams. 152p. 1986. Repr. of 1973 ed. spiral bd. 32.50 (ISBN 0-913599-83-2, R-343). AMR Pub Co.

Seeburg Parts Catalog for Model LS1. Seeburg Co. Staff. 68p. 1986. Repr. 24.50 (ISBN 0-913599-70-0, R-331). AMR Pub Co.

Seeburg Parts Catalog for Model USC-2. rev. ed. Seeburg Company Staff. Ed. by Frank Adams. 100p. 1986. 27.50 (ISBN 0-913599-80-8, R-338). AMR Pub Co.

Seeburg Parts Catalog for Models SPS160 & ESPS160: Olympian. rev. ed. Seeburg Company Staff. Ed. by Frank Adams. 100p. 1986. 27.50 (ISBN 0-913599-79-4, R-337). AMR Pub Co.

Seeburg Parts Catalog: Installation & Operation Manual for Models STD4 & ESTD4. rev. ed. Seeburg Co. Staff. 90p. 1986. Repr. of 1977 ed. 24.50 (ISBN 0-939971-00-3, R-359). AMR Pub Co.

Seeburg Phonograph Service Manual for Models SX100, ESX100-5, ESX100-H5. rev. ed. Seeburg Co. Staff. Ed. by Frank Adams. 100p. 1986. Repr. of 1972 ed. spiral bd. 29.50 (ISBN 0-913599-94-8, R-354). AMR Pub Co.

Seeburg Remote Equipment Service Manuals for the Wall-O-Matic Types 3W-1 & 3W-d. Seeburg Co. Staff. Ed. by Frank Adams. (Installation, Operation, Servicing, Maintence Manual Ser.). 42p. 1986. Repr. 15.00 (ISBN 0-913599-74-3, R-328). AMR Pub Co.

Seeburg SB100 & ESB100 "Magnastar" Installation & Operation Manual, Service Manual & Console Parts Catalog of 1974. rev. ed. Seeburg Company Staff. Ed. by Frank Adams. 80p. 1986. Repr. of 1974 ed. 24.50 (ISBN 0-939971-04-6, R-363). AMR Pub Co.

Seeburg Select-O-Matic Mechanism Service & Parts Catalog for Types 160ST29, 160ST29-5, 145ST16 & 145ST16-5, for Models SMC1, SMC2, SMC3 & 100-77D & 100-78D3 Manuals. rev. ed. Seeburg Co. Staff. Ed. by Frank Adams. 120p. 1986. Repr. of 1978 ed. spiral bd. 29.50 (ISBN 0-913599-90-5, R-347). AMR Pub Co.

Seeburg Service Manual for Models STD160, STD2, STD3, STD4, FC2, EFC2, ESTD4. rev ed. Seeburg Co. Staff. Ed. by Frank Adams. 60p. 1986. Repr. of 1974 ed. spiral bd. 24.50 (ISBN 0-913599-87-5, R-345). AMR Pub Co.

Seeburg Service Manual for the Phono-Jet of 1967-68 Models S100, S100-5, S100-H5. rev. ed. Seeburg Co. Staff. Ed. by Frank Adams. 100p. 1986. Repr. of 1967 ed. spiral bd. 27.50 (ISBN 0-913599-84-0, R-341). AMR Pub Co.

Seeburg Service Manual Supplement for Model LS2. rev. ed. Seeburg Company Staff. Ed. by Frank Adams. 64p. 1986. 24.50 (ISBN 0-913599-76-X, R-334). AMR Pub Co.

Seeburg SL100 & ESL100 "Carnival" & "Magnastar" SB100 & ESB100 Electronic Units Service Manual & Parts Catalog. rev. ed. Seeburg Co. Ed. by Frank Adams. 70p. 1986. Repr. of 1973 ed. 24.50 (ISBN 0-939971-16-X, R-374). AMR Pub Co.

Seeburg SL100 & ESL100 "Carnival" Installation & Operation Manual, Service Manual & Parts Catalog 1973. rev. ed. Seeburg Co. Ed. by Frank Adams. 82p. 1986. Repr. of 1973 ed. 27.50 (ISBN 0-939971-08-9, R-366). AMR Pub Co.

Seeburg SS160 Stereo Showcase Service Manual & Brochure of 1967. Seeburg Co. Staff. 190p. 1986. Repr. 35.00 (ISBN 0-913599-21-2, R-297). AMR Pub Co.

Seeburg STD2 & ESTD2 Entertainer: Installation & Operation Manual & Console Parts Catalog of 1975. Seeburg Co. Staff. Ed. by Frank Adams. 90p. 1986. Repr. of 1975 ed. 24.50 (ISBN 0-939971-01-1, R-360). AMR Pub Co.

Seeburg STD3 & ESTD3 "Sunstar": Installation & Operation Manual & Console Part Catalog of 1976. rev. ed. Seeburg Co. Staff. Ed. by Frank Adams. 84p. 1986. Repr. of 1976 ed. 24.50 (ISBN 0-939971-02-X, R-361). AMR Pub Co.

Seeburg Stereo Consolette, Type SC1 & Type SC11 & the Consolette Intercom Master, Type CIM-1. Seeburg Company Staff. Ed. by Frank Adams. (Installation, Operation, Adjustments, Service & Parts Manual Ser.). 80p. 1986. Repr. 21.50 (ISBN 0-913599-75-1, R-317). AMR Pub Co.

Seeburg Technical Data for All SMC Model Phonographs & Microcomputer Control System. rev. ed. Seeburg Co. Staff. Ed. by Frank Adams. 104p. 1986. Repr. of 1978 ed. spiral bd. 35.00 (ISBN 0-913599-91-3, R-350). AMR Pub Co.

Seeburg USC1 "Musical Bandshell" Service Manual of 1971. Seeburg Co. Staff. Ed. by Frank Adams. 146p. 1986. Repr. of 1971 ed. 32.50 (ISBN 0-913599-66-2, R-321). AMR Pub Co.

Seeburg 100-77D & E-10077D "Topaz" Installation & Operation Manual & Console Parts Catalog of 1976. rev. ed. Seeburg Co Staff. Ed. by Frank Adams. 68p. 1986. Repr. of 1976 ed. 24.50 (ISBN 0-939971-09-7, R-367). AMR Pub Co.

Seeburg 100-78 D & E-10078D "Celestia": Installation & Operation Manual & Console Parts Catalog of 1977. rev. ed. Seeburg Co. Staff. Ed. by Frank Adams. 64p. 1986. Repr. of 1977 ed. 24.50 (ISBN 0-939971-03-8, R-362). AMR Pub Co.

Seeburg 160 Phonograph 160 & 100 Phonographs & Speakers Accessories Parts Catalog for Models SPS160 & 8SX8100. rev. ed. Seeburg Co. Staff. Ed. by AMR Publising Company Staff. 82p. 1986. Repr. of 1972 ed. spiral bd. 19.50 (ISBN 0-913599-92-1, R-356). AMR Pub Co.

Seeburg 160 Selection Stereo Phonograph for the Seeburg CPA Installation & Operation Manual for Models SMC2 & ESMC2 & Console Parts Catalog. rev. ed. Seeburg Co. Staff. Ed. by Frank Adams. 74p. 1986. Repr. of 1979 ed. spiral bd. 24.50 (ISBN 0-913599-88-3, R-348). AMR Pub Co.

Seed. Ann Cameron. LC 74-15296. (Illus.). 36p. (gr. k-4). 1975. Pantheon.

Seed Aging: Implications for Seed Storage & Persistence in the Soil. David A. Priestly. LC 85-21334. (Comstock Bk.). (Illus.). 304p. 1986. 39.95x (ISBN 0-8014-1865-8). Cornell U Pr.

Seed & Nut Cookery. Margaret Eastman. LC 82-3027. 144p. 1982. Greene.

Seed & the Tree: Reflections on Nonviolence. Daniel A. Seeger. (Orig.). 1986. pap. 2.50x (ISBN 0-87574-269-6). Pendle Hill.

Seed Dispersal. Ed. by David Murray. LC 86-72353. 322p. 1987. 49.95 (ISBN 0-12-511900-3). Acad Pr.

Seed Dormancy & Germination. J. W. Bradbeer. (Tertiary Level Biology Ser.). 192p. 1988. text ed. 59.95 (ISBN 0-412-00611-1); pap. text ed. 24.00 (ISBN 0-412-00621-9). Routledge Chapman & Hall.

Seed Ecology. Ed. by W. Heydecker. LC 73-1459. 488p. 1973. 34.50x (ISBN 0-271-01158-0). Pa St U Pr.

Seed Ecology. Micheal Fenner. (Outline Studies in Ecology). 150p. 1985. pap. text ed. 16.95 (ISBN 0-412-25930-3, 9639, Pub. by Chapman & Hall England). Routledge Chapman & Hall.

Seed Finder. John Jeavons et al. LC 83-40023. (Illus.). 160p. (Orig.). 1983. pap. 4.95 (ISBN 0-89815-100-7). Ten Speed Pr.

Seed Gift Greeting Directory, No. 1. Greetings Etc. by Alfreda Staff. 1984. pap. text ed. 9.95 (ISBN 0-318-04378-5, Pub. by Greetings). Prosperity & Profits.

Seed Grower's List of Vegetable Varieties Grown in the United States in 1906, with Descriptions & Synonyms. Charles Johnson. 45p. (Orig.). 1986. pap. 3.95 (ISBN 0-933421-07-9). Redwood Seed.

Seed Legislation. Luis M. Bombin-Bombin. (Legislative Studies: No. 16). 121p. (Eng., Fr. & Span.). 1978. pap. 8.25 (ISBN 92-5-100832-9, F2083, FAO). UNIPUB.

Seed Money in Action. Jon P. Speller. LC 65-26790. 1965. pap. 3.00 (ISBN 0-8315-0007-7). Speller.

Seed of a Woman. Ruth Geller. LC 79-53219. 314p. (Orig.). 1979. pap. 5.95 (ISBN 0-9603008-0-5). Imp Pr.

Seed of Abraham: Arabs & Jews in Conflict. Raphael Patai. 416p. 1987. pap. 11.95 (ISBN 0-684-18752-3). Scribner.

Seed of Abraham: Jews & Arabs in Contact & Conflict. Raphael Patai. 384p. 1986. 29.95 (ISBN 0-87480-251-2). U of Utah Pr.

Seed of Evil. Petrina Crawford. 1976. pap. 1.25 (ISBN 0-685-73459-5, LB410, Leisure Bks). Leisure NY.

Seed of Evil. Edmund Plante. 368p. (Orig.). 1988. pap. 3.95 Mass Market (ISBN 0-8439-2581-7). Leisure NY.

Seed of Redemption. Francis M. Deng. LC 86-7673. 320p. 1986. text ed. 17.95x (ISBN 0-936508-17-5). Barber Pr.

Seed of Sally Good'n: A Black Family of Arkansas, 1833-1953. Ruth P. Patterson. LC 85-6117. 200p. 1985. 19.00 (ISBN 0-8131-1541-8). U Pr of Ky.

Seed of Suspicion. Juanita T. Osborne. 1986. 9.95 (ISBN 0-8034-8619-7, Avalon). Bouregy.

Seed of the Divine Fruit. Enrico Rihaldi. LC 86-91340. 1987. 18.95 (ISBN 0-87212-200-X). Libra.

Seed of the Sun. Wallace Irwin. Ed. by Roger Daniels. LC 78-54342. (Asian Experience in North America Ser.). 1979. Repr. of 1921 ed. lib. bdg. 24.50x (ISBN 0-405-11308-0). Ayer Co Pubs.

Seed of Wisdom: Essays in Honour of T. J. Meek. Ed. by W. S. McCullough. pap. 53.00 (ISBN 0-317-11296-1, 2014302). Bks Demand UMI.

Seed Pathology. D. Suryanarayana. 111p. 1978. 7.95. Asia Bk Corp.

Seed Physiology, Vol. 1. Ed. by David R. Murry. 267p. 1985. 59.00 (ISBN 0-12-511901-1). Acad Pr.

Seed Physiology: Germination & Reserve Mobilization, Vol. 2. David R. Murray. 1985. 59.00 (ISBN 0-12-511902-X). Acad Pr.

Seed Portions. J. Daussant. LC 82-71240. 1983. 75.00 (ISBN 0-12-204380-4). Acad Pr.

Seed Production of Agricultural Crops. Arthur F. Kelly. 227p. 1988. 77.95 (ISBN 0-470-20861-9). Wiley.

Seed Program: Songs for Elementary Emotional Development. Marie Hartwell-Walker & Wayne S. Friedman. 100p. 1982. 47.50 (ISBN 0-913636-13-4); cassettes, sheet music. Educ Res MA.

Seed Propagated Geraniums. Allan Armitage. (Growing Guide Ser.). (Illus.). 86p. 1986. pap. 9.95x (ISBN 0-88192-064-9). Timber.

Seed Propagation of Native California Plants. Dara E. Emery. LC 87-12903. 1988. pap. 9.95 (ISBN 0-916436-11-X). Santa Barb Botanic.

Seed Protein Improvement by Nuclear Techniques. (Panel Proceedings Ser.). (Illus.). 582p. 1978. pap. 59.25 (ISBN 92-0-111078-2, ISP479, IAEA). UNIPUB.

Seed Protein Improvement in Cereals & Grain Legumes: Proceedings of Symposium, Neuherburg 4-8 Sept. 1978, 2 Vols. 1979. pap. 59.25 (ISBN 92-0-010079-1, ISP496-1, IAEA); pap. 65.50 (ISBN 92-0-010179-8, ISP496-2). UNIPUB.

Seed Regeneration in Cross-Pollinated Species: Proceedings of the C. E. C. - Eucarpia Seminar, Nyborg, Denmark, 15-17 July 1981. Ed. by E. Porceddu & G. Jenkins. 302p. 1982. text ed. 48.50 (ISBN 90-6191-244-X, Pub. by A A Balkema). Brookfield Pub Co.

Seed Royale. Guy E. Giovanni. write for info. (ISBN 0-912981-19-9). Hse Bon Giovanni.

Seed Savers Exchange: The First Ten Years. Ed. by Kent Whealy & Arllys Adelmann. LC 86-61687. (Orig.). 1986. pap. 16.00 (ISBN 0-9613977-2-1). Seed Saver Pubns.

Seed Storage Proteins. Ed. by Leslie Fowden & B. J. Miflin. (Philosophical Transactions of The Royal Society of London: Ser. B, Vol. 304). (Illus.). 137p. 1984. Repr. lib. bdg. 52.00x (ISBN 0-85403-225-8, Pub. by Royal Soc London). Scholium Intl.

Seed Syllables. Pieter Dominick. Intro. by Lillian Morrison & Mura D. Thomas. (Poetry Ser.). 40p. (Orig.). 1986. pap. 5.00 (ISBN 0-9608706-1-X, WP-0110). Waterford Pr.

Seed Testing Handbook. Craig C. Dremann. 1987. pap. price not set (ISBN 0-933421-22-2). Redwood Seed.

Seed Thoughts for Public Speakers. Arthur T. Pierson. 1983. Repr. of 1907 ed. lib. bdg. 65.00 (ISBN 0-8495-4416-5). Arden Lib.

Seed-Time & Harvest of Ragged Schools: Three Pleas for Ragged Schools. Thomas Guthrie. LC 75-172569. (Criminology, Law Enforcement, & Social Problems Ser.: No. 150). (With a new chapter & index added). 1973. Repr. of 1860 ed. lib. bdg. 10.00x (ISBN 0-87585-150-9). Patterson Smith.

Seed-Time & Harvest; or, During My Apprenticeship. Fritz Reuter. 292p. 1976. Repr. of 1871 ed. 23.50x (ISBN 0-86527-301-4). Fertig.

Seed Vigor. Woodstock. 1988. write for info. (ISBN 0-471-01076-6). Wiley.

Seed Was Sown: Life of Oscar H. Geiger. Robert Clancy. (Illus.). 124p. 1964. pap. 1.00 (ISBN 0-911312-41-2). Schalkenbach.

Seedburts: Life Principles for Personal Growth. Strephon K. Williams. (Illus.). 128p. (Orig.). 1984. pap. 6.95 (ISBN 0-918572-27-4). Journey Pr.

Seeding Program for Fertilizer Marketing. Lewis B. Williams. Ed. by E. N. Roth & M. K. Thompson. (Illus., Orig.). 1984. pap. text ed. 4.00 (ISBN 0-88090-054-7). Intl Fertilizer.

Seedling Child. Ruth L. Bornstein. LC 86-19581. (Illus.). 40p. (ps-2). 1987. 12.95 (ISBN 0-15-272459-1). HarBraceJ.

Seedling Physiology & Reforestation Success. Ed. by Mary L. Duryea & Gregory N. Brown. (Forestry Sciences Ser.). 1984. lib. bdg. 45.50 (ISBN 90-247-2949-1, Pub. by Martinus Nijhoff Netherlands). Kluwer-Academic.

Seedlings. E. A. Gloeggler. LC 87-83070. 100p. 1987. write for info. Eaglo Bks.

Seedlings of Dicotyledons. 1980. 92.00 (ISBN 90-220-0o96-4, PDC167, Pudoc). UNIPUB.

Seedlings of Some Tropical Trees & Shrubs Mainly of South East Asia. D. Berger Hzn. 1972. pap. 35.00 (ISBN 90-220-0416-3, PDC81, PUDOC). UNIPUB.

Seedlings of the North-Western European Lowland. F. M. Muller. 1978. lib. bdg. 79.00 (ISBN 90-6193-588-1, Pub. by Junk Pubs Netherlands). Kluwer Academic.

Seedlings of the North-Western European Lowland: A Flora of Seedlings. F. M. Muller. (Illus.). 660p. (1209 descriptions & drawings). 1978. 92.00 (ISBN 90-220-0616-6, PDC8, PUDOC). UNIPUB.

Seeds. Terry Jennings. Ed. by Franklin Watts Ltd. (Junior Science Ser.). (Illus.). 24p. (gr. k-3). 1988. 9.90 (ISBN 0-531-17087-X, Gloucester Pr). Watts.

Seeds & Fruits of Plants of Eastern Canada & Northeastern United States. F. H. Montgomery. LC 76-23241. 1976. 37.50x (ISBN 0-8020-5341-6). U of Toronto Pr.

Seeds & Other Stories. Hung-Shan Chen et al. 193p. 1972. 5.95 (ISBN 0-917056-42-6, Pub. by Foreign Lang Pr China). Cheng & Tsui.

Seeds & Sovereignty: Debate over the Use & Control of Plant Genetic Resources. Ed. by Jack R. Kloppenburg, Jr. (Illus.). viii, 369p. 1988. lib. bdg. 47.50 (ISBN 0-8223-0756-1). Duke.

Seeds & Their Uses. C. M. Duffus & J. C. Slaughter. LC 80-40283. 154p. 1980. 59.95x (ISBN 0-471-27799-1, Pub. by Wiley-Interscience). Wiley.

Seeds & their Uses. C. M. Duffus & J. C. Slaughter. LC 80-40283. pap. 41.00 (2026674). Bks Demand UMI.

Seeds As Food Use, 2 vols. A. C. Doyle. 1984. pap. 1.95 ea. (ISBN 0-913597-70-8, Pub. by Alpha Pyramis). Vol. 1. Vol. 2. Prosperity & Profits.

Seeds As They Fall: Poems. Helen Sorrells. LC 76-150329. 1971. 7.95 (ISBN 0-8265-1168-6). Vanderbilt U Pr.

Seeds Beneath the Snow: Vignettes from the South. Arthenia J. Bates. LC 69-18851. 146p. 1975. 8.95 (ISBN 0-88258-046-9). Howard U Pr.

Seeds for Sermons. Hyman Appelman. (Sermon Outline Ser.). 1980. pap. 2.50 (ISBN 0-8010-0026-2). Baker Bk.

Seeing Stars. Charles L. Wagner. Ed. by Andrew Farkas. LC 76-29976. (Opera Biographies). (Illus.). 1977. Repr. of 1940 ed. lib. bdg. 32.00x (ISBN 0-405-09714-X). Ayer Co Pubs.

Seeing Stick. Jane Yolen. LC 75-6946. (Illus.). (gr. k up). 1977. (Crowell Jr Bks); PLB 13.89 (ISBN 0-690-00596-2). HarpJ.

Seeing Summer. Jeannette Eyerly. LC 81-47440. (Illus.). 128p. (gr. 4-6). 1981. 12.70i (ISBN 0-397-31965-7, Lipp Jr Bks); PLB 11.89g (ISBN 0-397-31966-5). HarpJ.

Seeing the Desert Green. Sybil Estess. 1987. pap. 7.00 (ISBN 0-941179-02-8). Latitudes Pr.

Seeing the Insane. Sander L. Gilman. 241p. 1985. pap. 19.95 (ISBN 0-471-82457-7). Wiley.

Seeing the Insane: A Cultural History of Psychiatric Illustration. Sander L. Gilman. LC 79-21933. (Illus.). 500p. 1980. 45.00 (ISBN 0-87630-233-9); pap. 25.00. Brunner-Mazel.

Seeing the Invisible. Mary Irwin. (Orig.). 1987. pap. 3.95 (ISBN 0-8054-5057-2). Broadman.

Seeing the Light. James Broughton. LC 76-30681. 1977. pap. 3.00 (ISBN 0-87286-090-6). City Lights.

Seeing the Light: Optics in Nature, Photography Color, Vision, & Holography. Falk R. David et al. 464p. 1985. text ed. write for info. (ISBN 0-471-60385-6). Wiley.

Seeing the Multitudes Delayed. Lissa McLaughlin. (Burning Deck Fiction Ser.). (Illus.). 1979. 15.00 (ISBN 0-930900-75-8); pap. 4.00 (ISBN 0-930900-76-6). Burning Deck.

Seeing the Story of the Bible. Myer Pearlman. 128p. 1930. pap. 2.95 (ISBN 0-88243-581-7, 02-0581). Gospel Pub.

Seeing the World. Dick Davis. 56p. (Orig.). 1984. pap. 7.95 (ISBN 0-85646-061-3, Pub. by Anvil Pr Poetry). Longwood Pub Group.

Seeing Things. John M. Brown. LC 75-138209. viii, 341p. 1971. Repr. of 1946 ed. lib. bdg. 35.00x (ISBN 0-8371-5564-9, BRST). Greenwood.

Seeing Things. Robert Froman. LC 73-18494. (Illus.). 64p. (gr. 4-8). 1987. 12.70 (ISBN 0-317-61082-1, Crowell Jr Bks); lib. bdg. 12.89 (ISBN 0-690-04625-1). HarpJ.

Seeing Things. rev. ed. Charlotte Painter. (Illus.). 235p. 1984. pap. 5.00 (ISBN 0-932654-02-9). Garden Bks.

Seeing Things. 3rd ed. Charlotte Painter. (Illus.). 236p. 1987. pap. 8.95 (ISBN 0-936784-47-4). J Daniel.

Seeing Things. Frances Thomas. 176p. 1987. 18.95 (ISBN 0-575-03757-1, Pub. by Gollancz England). David & Charles.

Seeing Things: A Book of Poems. Robert Froman. LC 73-18494. 64p. (gr. 4-8). 1987. 13.95i (ISBN 0-690-00291-2, Crowell Jr Bks); PLB 13.89 (Crowell Jr Bks). HarpJ.

Seeing Things: A Chronicle of Surprises. Richard A. Hawley. 1987. 17.95 (ISBN 0-8027-0987-7). Walker & Co.

Seeing Through Clothes. Anne Hollander. (Illus.). 528p. pap. 14.95 (ISBN 0-14-011084-4). Penguin.

Seeing Through Everything: English Literature Between the Wars. William Pritchard. LC 76-47434. 1977. 18.95x (ISBN 0-19-519951-0). Oxford U Pr.

Seeing Through Photographs. Michael Hiley. 144p. 1983. 50.00x (ISBN 0-86092-055-0, Pub. by Fraser Bks); pap. 35.00x (ISBN 0-86092-069-0). State Mutual Bk.

Seeing Through Shuck. Ed. by Richard Kostelanetz. 1978. pap. 20.00 (ISBN 0-932360-14-9). RK Edns.

Seeing Through the Sun. Linda Hogan. LC 84-28019. 88p. 1985. lib. bdg. 16.00x (ISBN 0-87023-471-4); pap. 7.95 (ISBN 0-87023-472-2). U of Mass Pr.

Seeing Through Words: The Scope of Late Renaissance Poetry. Elizabeth Cook. LC 85-29502. 192p. 1986. 22.50x (ISBN 0-300-03675-2). Yale U Pr.

Seeing Through Writing. William E. Coles, Jr. et al. 223p. 1987. pap. text ed. 18.95 (ISBN 0-06-041332-8, HarpC). Har-Row.

Seeing with a Native Eye: Contributions to the Study of Native American Religion. Ed. by Walter H. Capps. LC 76-9980. 1976. pap. 6.95xi (ISBN 0-06-061312-2, RD-177, HarpR). Har-Row.

Seeing with an Eye of Faith. Grant Von Harrison. 73p. (Orig.). (YA) (gr. 11 up). 1986. pap. 3.95 (ISBN 0-942241-04-5, 8680). Pubs Bk Sales.

Seeing with the Heart. Dick Dilley. (Illus.). 48p. (ps-1). 1985. 9.95 (ISBN 0-936535-00-8). People Patch.

Seeing with the Mind's Eye. Mike Samuels & Nancy Samuels. 1975. pap. 14.95 (ISBN 0-394-73113-1). Random.

Seeing Writing. Lewis Meyers. 226p. 1980. pap. text ed. 11.00 net (ISBN 0-15-579420-5, HC). HarBraceJ.

Seeing Young Children: A Guide for Observing & Recording Behavior. Warren R. Bentzen. LC 85-1564. 272p. 1985. pap. text ed. 15.95 (ISBN 0-8273-2329-8); instr's. guide 6.95 (ISBN 0-8273-2330-1). Delmar.

Seek-a-Word, No. 1. 128p. 1982. pap. 1.50 (ISBN 0-505-51777-9, Pub. by Tower Bks). Leisure NY.

Seek-a-Word, No. 2. Ed. by Anita Pfouts. 128p. 1982. pap. 1.50 (ISBN 0-505-51792-2, Pub. by Tower Bks). Leisure NY.

Seek-a-Word, No. 3. 128p. 1982. pap. 1.50 (ISBN 0-505-51811-2, Pub. by Tower Bks). Leisure NY.

Seek & Destroy. Alan Evans. 256p. 1986. 15.95 (ISBN 0-8027-0928-1). Walker & Co.

Seek & Destroy. Alan Evans. 251p. 1987. pap. 3.50 (ISBN 1-55547-211-7). Critics Choice Paper.

Seek & Solve: Addition No. 1 Series 1, Level 1. Ruth L. Perle. (Tool Box Ser.). (Illus.). (gr. k-2). 1976. wkbk. 1.95 (ISBN 0-89796-848-4, SSW 01). Arista Corp NY.

Seek & Solve: Subtraction No. 1, Series 1, Level 1. Ruth L. Perle. (Tool Box Ser.). (Illus.). (gr. k-2). 1976. wkbk. 1.95 (ISBN 0-89796-849-2, SSW 02). Arista Corp NY.

Seek Beauty of the Spring, in Mother Nature. Ed. by Thomas L. Hakes. 9p. 1984. pap. 3.75x (ISBN 0-915020-29-7). Bardic.

Seek First His Kingdom. Roger Thomas. 144p. 1987. pap. 5.95 (ISBN 0-87403-210-5, 39960). Standard Pub.

Seek Good, Not Evil (That You May Live) Paul Harms. 1985. 6.25 (ISBN 0-89536-754-8, 5860). CSS of Ohio.

Seek His Face. Anthony J. Pfarr. LC 73-86211. 1973. 4.95 (ISBN 0-8198-0353-7); pap. 3.95 (ISBN 0-8198-0354-5). Dghtrs St Paul.

Seek It Lovingly. James W. Angell. (Illus.). 1974. pap. 3.95 (ISBN 0-87516-184-7). DeVorss.

Seek, Strike, & Destroy: United States Army Tank Destroyer Doctrine in the World War 2. Christopher R. Gabel. LC 85-21296. (Leavenworth Papers: No. 12). (Illus.). 98p. (Orig.). 1985. pap. 2.50 (ISBN 0-318-19899-1, S/N 008-020-01060-0). USGPO.

Seek Student Activity Booklet. Paul Downes & Marjorie Layton. 20p. (Orig.). 1982. 1.00 (ISBN 0-912578-54-8); tchrs guide 5.50 (ISBN 0-912578-55-6). Chron Guide.

Seek That Which Is Above. Cardinal J. Ratzinger. Tr. by Graham Harrison from Ger. LC 86-81553. 132p. 1986. 9.95 (ISBN 0-89870-101-5). Ignatius Pr.

Seek the Fair Land. Walter Macken. 300p. 1962. pap. 9.95 (ISBN 0-330-30327-9). Bks Britain.

Seek the Truth. Albert Krassner. 1985. pap. 4.95 (ISBN 0-934805-00-8). Gray Pubns WV.

Seek-the-Verses Bible Puzzles. David Gasperson. 48p. 1986. pap. 2.50 (ISBN 0-87403-045-5, 2689). Standard Pub.

Seek Ye First. William MacDonald. pap. 1.95 (ISBN 0-937396-38-9). Walterick Pubs.

Seek Ye First. Elva Martin. 1973. pap. 1.65 (ISBN 0-915374-32-3, 32-3). Rapids Christian.

Seeker after Truth. Idries Shah. 1982. 18.95 (ISBN 0-900860-91-X, Pub. by Octagon Pr England). Ins Study Human.

Seeker: D. S. Merezhkovskiy. C. Harold Bedford. LC 74-28496. x, 222p. 1975. 25.00x (ISBN 0-7006-0131-7). U Pr of KS.

Seeker of the Gentle Heart. Blaine M. Yorgason & Brenton G. Yorgason. 156p. 1982. 6.95 (ISBN 0-88494-456-5). Bookcraft Inc.

Seekers. Eilis Dillon. LC 85-43347. 144p. (gr. 5-9). 1986. 11.95 (ISBN 0-684-18595-4, Pub. by Scribner). Macmillan.

Seekers. David Dvorkin. 288p. 1988. 16.95 (ISBN 0-531-15088-7). Watts.

Seekers. John Jakes. (Kent Family Chronicles: No. 3). 640p. (Orig.). 1983. pap. 4.95 (ISBN 0-515-09038-7). Jove Pubns.

Seekers. Philip Kime. LC 84-90215. 61p. 1985. 6.95 (ISBN 0-533-06269-1). Vantage.

Seekers & Saviors. Time-Life Books Editors. (Enchanted World Ser.). (Illus.). 144p. (YA) (gr. 7 up). 1986. 19.93; lib. bdg. 23.93. Time-Life.

Seekers & the Sword. Michael J. Friedman. 272p. pap. 2.95 (ISBN 0-445-20139-8, Pub. by Popular Lib). Warner Bks.

Seeker's Guide. Alex Sandri-White. 1970. 5.60x (ISBN 0-685-22751-0). Aurea.

Seekers in Sneakers: A Children's Devotional. Sharron Oyer et al. (Vol. 1). 128p. (Orig.). (gr. 2-5). 1988. pap. 4.95 (ISBN 0-89081-611-5). Harvest Hse.

Seekers Long Ago & Now. Louise Griffith. (FGC). 148p. (gr. 7-8). 1965. 2.00 (ISBN 0-318-14153-1). Friends Genl Conf.

Seekers of the Horizon: An Anthology of Sea Kayaking Adventures. Will Norby. (Illus.). 1989. pap. price not set (ISBN 0-87106-634-3). Globe Pequot.

Seekers of Tomorrow. Sam Moskowitz. LC 73-15073. (Classics of Science Fiction Ser.). 441p. 1986. 26.00 (ISBN 0-88355-129-2). Hyperion Conn.

Seekers of Truth. Allen E. Roberts. (History of the Philalethes Society Ser.). (Illus.). 218p. 1988. 17.95 (ISBN 0-935633-06-5). Anchor Comm.

Seeking a Faith for a New Age: Essays on the Interdependence of Religion, Science & Philosophy. Henry N. Wieman. Ed. & intro. by Cedric L. Hepler. 313p. 1988. Repr. of 1975 ed. text ed. 14.95 (ISBN 0-913029-18-1). Stevens Bk Pr.

Seeking a Great Perhaps. Bruce L. Marcoon. 126p. 1987. 6.95 (ISBN 0-8059-3077-9). Dorrance.

Seeking a Just Society: An Educational Design. Edward Van Merrienboer et al. Incl. Elementary Edition. (gr. k-8). 42.00 (ISBN 0-318-00795-9); Secondary Edition. (gr. 9-12). 42.00 (ISBN 0-318-00796-7). (gr. k up). Total Edition. 72.00 (ISBN 0-318-00793-2); faculty unit 4.00 (ISBN 0-318-00794-0). Natl Cath Educ.

Seeking a Living Faith. W. Frank Harrington. Ed. by Michael L. Sherer. (Orig.). 1987. pap. 7.50 (ISBN 1-55673-022-5, 8806). CSS of Ohio.

Seeking a New Accommodation in World Commodity Markets. Carl E. Beigie et al. 1976. 15.00 (ISBN 0-318-02784-4); pap. 4.95 (ISBN 0-318-02785-2). Trilateral Comm.

Seeking a New Accommodation in World Commodity Markets see Trilateral Commission Task Force Reports.

Seeking a Newer World: Memoirs of a Black American Teacher. Nick A. Ford. (Illus.). 320p. 1982. 12.95 (ISBN 0-89962-277-1). Todd & Honeywell.

Seeking a Scientific Explanation for Adaptation. Golden & Rhyne. 124p. (Orig.). 1986. Lab Manual 13.95x (ISBN 0-88725-075-0). Hunter Textbks.

Seeking Air. Barbara Guest. LC 77-17340. 260p. (Orig.). 1978. 14.00 (ISBN 0-87685-352-1); signed 17.50 (ISBN 0-87685-328-9); pap. 5.00 (ISBN 0-87685-327-0). Black Sparrow.

Seeking & Finding Manual. 1970. pap. 7.95 (ISBN 0-913308-03-X). Fordham Pub.

Seeking & Finding Workbook. 1970. pap. 18.95 (ISBN 0-913308-02-1). Fordham Pub.

Seeking First the Kingdom. Robert A. Yoder. LC 83-16618. 104p. (Orig.). 1983. pap. 4.50 (ISBN 0-8361-3349-8). Herald Pr.

Seeking for the Kingdom of God: Origins of the Bruderhof Communities. Eberhard Arnold & Emmy Arnold. LC 74-6317. 200p. 1974. 7.00 (ISBN 0-87486-133-0). Plough.

Seeking Foreign Trouble. Ralph Townsend. 1984. lib. bdg. 79.95 (ISBN 0-87700-609-1). Revisionist Pr.

Seeking Foundation Grants. Barbara S. Gary. 1985. 5.65 (ISBN 0-318-18574-1). Natl Cath Educ.

Seeking God: The Way of St. Benedict. Esther De Waal. 160p. 1984. pap. 4.95 (ISBN 0-8146-1388-8). Liturgical Pr.

Seeking God's Face. Joseph Cardinal Ratzinger. 1982. 6.95 (ISBN 0-8199-0774-X). Franciscan Herald.

Seeking God's Peace in a Nuclear Age. Leaders of the Christian Church Staff & Kenneth L. Teegarden. Ed. by Ronald Osborn. LC 85-7836. 96p. (Orig.). 1985. pap. 2.50 (ISBN 0-8272-3422-8). CBP.

Seeking Heart: Prayer Journal of Mae Yoho Ward. Mae Y. Ward. Ed. by Don Ward. LC 84-23836. 144p. (Orig.). 1985. pap. 7.95 (ISBN 0-8272-3420-1). CBP.

Seeking Jesus in Contemplation & Discernment. Robert Faricy. 111p. 1987. pap. 6.95 (ISBN 0-87061-142-9). Chr Classics.

Seeking Light in the Darkness of the Unconscious. John Yungblut. LC 77-71933. (Orig.). 1977. pap. 2.50x (ISBN 0-87574-211-4). Pendle Hill.

Seeking Many Inventions: The Idea of Community in America. Philip Abbott. LC 86-11338. 224p. 1987. text ed. 19.95x (ISBN 0-87049-514-3). U of Tenn Pr.

Seeking Purity of Heart: The Gift of Ourselves to God. Joseph Breault. (Illus.). 96p. (Orig.). 1975. pap. 2.95 (ISBN 0-914544-07-1). Living Flame Pr.

Seeking Safe Haven. 100p. 1983. 5.00 (ISBN 0-318-17313-1). Lutheran Coun US.

Seeking Shelter: Cambodian Refugees in Thailand. Lawyers Committee for Human Rights Staff. (Orig.). 1986. pap. 7.00 (ISBN 0-934143-14-5). Lawyers Comm Intl.

Seeking Spiritual Meaning: The World of Vedanta. Joseph D. Damrell. LC 77-9145. (Sociological Observations Ser.: No. 2). pap. 63.00 (ISBN 0-317-08760-6, 2021885). Bks Demand UMI.

Seeking Stability in Space: Anti-Satelite Weapons & the Evolving Space Regime. Ed. by Joseph S. Nye, Jr. & James A. Shear. LC 87-21619. (Illus.). 184p. (Orig.). 1988. lib. bdg. 22.75 (ISBN 0-8191-6421-6, Aspen Stragety Group); pap. text ed. 9.75 (ISBN 0-8191-6422-4). U Pr of Amer.

Seeking Sword. Jaan Kangilaski. 352p. (Orig.). 1981. pap. 2.25 (ISBN 0-345-29073-9, Del Rey). Ballantine.

Seeking the Best. Otis M. Shackelford. LC 73-18606. Repr. of 1911 ed. 16.00 (ISBN 0-404-11416-4). AMS Pr.

Seeking the Common Ground Protestant Christianity, the Three-Self Movement & China's United Front. Phillip Wickeri. 400p. 1988. 27.95 (ISBN 0-88344-441-0). Orbis Bks.

Seeking the Heart of Wisdom: The Path of Insight Meditation. Joseph Goldstein & Jack Kornfield. LC 87-9710. (Dragon Editions Ser.). 195p. (Orig.). 1987. pap. 10.95 (ISBN 0-87773-327-9). Shambhala Pubns.

Seeking the Light: Essays in Quaker History, in Honor of Edwin B. Bronner. Ed. by William J. Frost & John M. Moore. 214p. 1986. pap. 16.00 (ISBN 0-87574-909-7). Friends Hist Assn.

Seeking the Personality of Public Enterprise. Ed. by Praxy Fernandes & Pavle Sicheri. 214p. 1981. pap. 20.00x (ISBN 92-9038-030-6, Pub. by Intl Ctr Pub Yugoslavia). Kumarian Pr.

Seeking the Spirit. Joseph F. McConkie. LC 78-13372. 122p. 1985. pap. 4.95 (ISBN 0-87747-818-X). Deseret Bk.

Seeking the Spirit. John Mahoney. 11.95 (ISBN 0-87193-187-7). Dimension Bks.

Seeking Wisdom. N. Sri Ram. 1969. 2.95 (ISBN 0-8356-7194-1). Theos Pub Hse.

Seeking Wisdom: The Sufi Path. Stuart Litvak. LC 82-60163. 128p. (Orig.). 1984. pap. 6.95 (ISBN 0-87728-543-8). Weiser.

Seeking World Order: The United States & International Organization to 1920. Warren F. Kuehl. LC 69-19952. 1969. 17.50x (ISBN 0-8265-1137-6). Vanderbilt U Pr.

Seekrieg 1939-1945 see Sea War: Nineteen Thirty-Nine to Nineteen Forty-Five.

Seelenleben des Kruppels: Kruppelseelen Kundliche Erziehung und das Gesetz Betr. Hans Wurtz. Ed. by William R. Phillips & Janet Rosenberg. LC 79-6007. (Physically Handicapped in Society Ser.). (Ger.). 1980. Repr. of 1921 ed. lib. bdg. 12.00x (ISBN 0-405-13138-0). Ayer Co Pubs.

Seemaennisches Woerterbuch. Wolfram Claviez. (Ger.). 1973. 75.00 (ISBN 3-7688-0166-7, M-7620, Pub. by Delius, Klaving & Co.). French & Eur.

Seemingly Unrelated Regression Equations Models: Estimation & Reference. Srivastava & Giles. (Statistics: Textbooks & Monographs). 352p. 1987. 69.75 (ISBN 0-8247-7610-0). Dekker.

Seems Like Old Times. Cassie Miles. (Temptation Ser.: No. 170). 224p. Date not set. pap. 2.25 (ISBN 0-317-63865-3). Harlequin Bks.

Seems Like This Road Goes on Forever. Jean Van Leeuwen. LC 78-72201. (YA) (gr. 8 up). 1979. 8.95 (ISBN 0-8037-7687-X). Dial Bks Young.

Seems Like Time. Kevin Urick. LC 76-62813. (Illus.). 1977. pap. 3.00 (ISBN 0-917976-00-2, White Ewe Pr). Thunder Baas Pr.

Seems Like Yesterday: A Surgeon's Odyssey. Charles C. Kissinger. Ed. by Anna M. Nesmith. LC 88-81078. (Illus.). 254p. (Orig.). 1988. pap. write for info. (ISBN 0-9620330-0-6). Henderson Pr.

Seen & Heard: New Possibilities for Children in the Church. Ron Buckland & John Lane. (Illus.). 56p. (Orig.). 1986. pap. 4.95 (ISBN 0-85819-593-3, Pub. by JBCE). ANZ Religious Pubns.

Seen & Not Heard. Anne Stuart. 288p. (Orig.). 1988. pap. 3.95 (ISBN 0-671-64249-9). PB.

Seen & Unseen: A Biologist Views the Universe. Edward McCrady. 1988. 10.95 (ISBN 0-918769-16-7). Univ South.

Seen & Unseen: A Story of Psychic Experiences. E. Katharine Bates. LC 75-32535. 1908. lib. bdg. 25.00 (ISBN 0-8414-3234-1). Folcroft.

Seen & Unseen in Browning. Emma J. Burt. LC 73-2639. 1973. lib. bdg. 22.00 (ISBN 0-8414-1785-7). Folcroft.

Seen Any Cats? Frank Modell. LC 79-11607. (Illus.). 32p. (gr. k-3). 1979. 10.25 (ISBN 0-688-80229-X); PLB 10.88 (ISBN 0-688-84229-1). Greenwillow.

Seen from Space. M. Winslow Chapman. 1972. 4.00. Golden Quill.

Seen on the Stage. Clayton Hamilton. 1975. Repr. of 1920 ed. 25.00 (ISBN 0-8274-4121-5). R West.

Seepage & Groundwater. M. A. Marino & Luthin. (Developments in Water Science Ser.: Vol. 13). 490p. 1982. 147.50 (ISBN 0-444-41975-6). Elsevier.

Seepage & Groundwater Flow: Numerical Analysis by Analog & Digital Methods. K. R. Rushton & S. C. Redshaw. LC 78-23359. (Geotechnical Engineering Ser.). 339p. 1979. 97.95 (ISBN 0-471-99754-4). Wiley.

Seepage & Leakage from Dams & Impoundments: Proceedings of a Symposium Sponsored by the Geotechnical Engineering Division. Ed. by Richard L. Volpe & William E. Kelly. 317p. 1985. 30.00x (ISBN 0-87262-448-X). Am Soc Civil Eng.

Seepage, Drainage & Flow Nets. 2nd ed. Harry R. Cedergren. LC 77-3664. 534p. 1977. 60.95 (ISBN 0-471-14179-8, Pub. by Wiley-Interscience). Wiley.

Seepage, Drainage & Flow Nets. 3rd ed. Harry R. Cedergren. 1988. 69.95 (ISBN 0-471-61178-6). Wiley.

Seepage Hydraulics. G. Kovacs. (Developments in Water Science Ser.: Vol. 10). 730p. 1981. 166.00 (ISBN 0-444-99755-5). Elsevier.

Seer. G. Clifton Wisler. Ed. by Rosemary Brosnan. 128p. (gr. 5-9). 1988. 12.95 (ISBN 0-525-67262-1). Lodestar Bks.

Seer: Joseph Smith. Ron Jackson. Orig. Title: Joseph Smith: the Seer. 1977. 6.95 (ISBN 0-89036-088-X). Hawkes Pub Inc.

Seer Out of Season: The Life of Edgar Cayce. Harmon H. Bro. 320p. 1988. 17.95 (ISBN 0-453-00625-6). NAL.

Seerat-un-Nabi: 2 Vols-Shibli Numani. M. T. Badauni. 19.95 ea. (ISBN 0-686-18339-8). Kazi Pubns.

Seers & Scientists: Can the Future Be Predicted? Ann E. Weiss. (Illus.). 96p. (gr. 6 up). 1986. 13.95 (ISBN 0-15-272850-3, HJ). HarBraceJ.

Seers & Singers: A Study of Five English Poets. Arthur D. Innes. 1973. Repr. of 1893 ed. 25.00 (ISBN 0-8274-0354-2). R West.

Seership. Swami Bhakta Vishita. 7.00 (ISBN 0-911662-33-2). Yoga.

Seersucker Whipsaw. Ross Thomas. LC 84-47676. 304p. 1987. pap. 3.50 (ISBN 0-06-080849-7, P 849, PL). Har-Row.

Seismic Response Analysis of Nuclear Power Plant Systems. Ed. by Folker H. Wittmann. (Structural Mechanics in Reactor Technology Ser.: Vol. K1). 608p. 1987. text ed. 63.00 (ISBN 90-6191-771-9, Pub. by A A Balkema). Brookfield Pub Co.

Seismic Response Analysis of Nuclear Power Plant Systems. Ed. by Folker H. Wittmann. (Structural Mechanics in Reactor Technology Ser.: Vol. K2). 670p. 1987. text ed. 63.00 (ISBN 90-6191-772-7, Pub. by A A Balkema). Brookfield Pub Co.

Seismic Response of Buried Pipes & Structural Components. ASCE Committee on Seismic Analysis. 58p. 1983. pap. 12.00x (ISBN 0-87262-368-8). Am Soc Civil Eng.

Seismic Risk & Engineering Decisions. C. Lomnitz & E. Rosenblueth. (Developments in Geotechnical Engineering Ser.: Vol. 15). 426p. 1976. 110.75 (ISBN 0-444-41494-0). Elsevier.

Seismic Sea Waves. 1978. pap. 18.50 (ISBN 0-660-00565-4, SSC105, SSC). UNIPUB.

Seismic Signal Analysis & Discrimination. C. H. Chen. (Methods in Geochemistry & Geophysics: Vol. 17). 196p. 1983. 76.50 (ISBN 0-444-42136-X). Elsevier.

Seismic Signal Analysis & Discrimination III. Ed. by C. H. Chen. (Methods in Geochemistry & Geophysics Ser.: Vol. 22). 170p. 1985. Repr. 76.50 (ISBN 0-444-42430-X). Elsevier.

Seismic Stratigraphy. Robert E. Sheriff. LC 80-83974. (Illus.). 227p. 1980. text ed. 32.00 (ISBN 0-934634-08-4); pap. 25.00 (ISBN 0-934634-51-3). Intl Human Res.

Seismic Strong Motion Synthetics. Ed. by Bruce A. Bolt. (Computational Techniques Ser.). 302p. 1987. 65.00 (ISBN 0-12-112251-4). Acad Pr.

Seismic Studies in Physical Modeling. Ed. by John A. McDonald et al. LC 82-81374. (Illus.). 284p. 1983. text ed. 54.00 (ISBN 0-934634-39-4). Intl Human Res.

Seismic Tomography: With Applications in Global Seismology & Exploration Geophysics. Ed. by Guust Nolet. 1987. lib. bdg. 79.00 (ISBN 90-277-2521-7, Pub. by Reidel Holland); pap. text ed. 38.00 (ISBN 90-277-2583-7, Pub. by Reidel Holland). Kluwer Academic.

Seismic Traveltime Inversion. S. V. Goldin. Ed. by Peter Hubral. Tr. by Alfred Hermont from Rus. (Investigations in Geophysics: No. 1). (Illus.). 363p. 1986. text ed. 110.00 (ISBN 0-931830-38-9). Soc Expl Geophys.

Seismic Velocity Analysis & the Convolutional Model. Enders A. Robinson. LC 83-12631. (Illus.). 290p. 1983. 46.00 (ISBN 0-934634-63-7). Intl Human Res.

Seismic Wave Attenuation. Ed. by M. N. Toksoz & D. H. Johnston. LC 81-50381. (Geophysics Reprint Ser.: No. 2). (Illus.). 465p. 1981. 15.00 (ISBN 0-931830-16-8). Soc Expl Geophys.

Seismic Wave Propagation in Stratified Media. B. L. Kenneth. (Cambridge Monographs on Mechanics & Applied Mathematics). 342p. 1985. pap. 29.95 (ISBN 0-521-31219-1). Cambridge U Pr.

Seismic Wave Propagation in the Earth. Ed. by A. Hanyga. (Physics & Evolution of Earth's Interior Ser.: Vol. 2). 488p. 1985. 129.00 (ISBN 0-444-99611-7). Elsevier.

Seismic Waves & Sources. A. Ben-Menahem & S. Singh. (Illus.). 1000p. 1981. 109.00 (ISBN 0-387-90506-5). Springer-Verlag.

Seismicity of the European Area, Part 1. V. Karnik. 364p. 1969. lib. bdg. 45.00 (ISBN 90-277-0121-0, Pub. by Reidel Holland). Kluwer Academic.

Seismicity of the European Area, Part 2. V. Karnik. LC 78-468652. (Illus.). 218p. 1971. lib. bdg. 60.50 (ISBN 90-277-0179-2, Pub. by Reidel Holland). Kluwer Academic.

Seismics of Heterogeneous & Turbid Media. A. V. Nikolaev. 184p. Repr. of 1975 ed. text ed. 39.00X (ISBN 0-7065-1535-8). Coronet Bks.

Seismologica Bulletin 1975: Station Moxa(Mox) Johannes Stelzner. 318p. 1981. pap. 112.00x (Pub. by Collets (UK)). State Mutual Bk.

Seismological Algorithms: Computational Methods & Computer Programs. Ed. by Durk J. Doornbos. 450p. 1988. price not set (ISBN 0-12-220770-X). Acad Pr.

Seismology of the Sun & the Distant Stars. Ed. by D. O. Gough. (NATO Advanced Science Institutes Series C: Mathematical & Physical Sciences). 1986. lib. bdg. 79.00 (ISBN 90-277-2196-3, Pub. by Reidel Holland). Kluwer-Academic.

Seisomasaurus: The Longest Dinosaur. Elizabeth Sandell. Ed. by Marjorie Oelerich & Howard Schroeder. LC 88-963. (Dinosaur Discovery Era Ser.). (Illus.). 32p. (gr. k-5). 1988. PLB 9.95 (ISBN 0-944280-03-X); pap. 4.95 (ISBN 0-944280-09-9). BSP Pub Inc.

Seitseman Retkea Itaan see Seven Journeys Eastward Eighteen Ninety-Eight to Nineteen Twelve.

Seiuchin Kata. Steve Armstrong. (Illus.). 221p. 1976. pap. text ed. 6.95 (ISBN 0-9614350-2-X). Dlaw Pubns.

Seival Collection, Vol. 1: The Greek Minor Prophets Scroll from Nahal Hever (8 Hev XII gr) Ed. by Emanuel Tov & R. A. Kraft. (Discoveries in the Judaean Desert Ser.). (Illus.). 192p. 1988. 125.00 (ISBN 0-19-826327-9). Oxford U Pr.

Seiyu Roku: On Oil Manufacturing. Nagatsune Okura. Tr. by Eiko Ariga. LC 74-6761. (Illus.). 79p. 1974. 20.00 (ISBN 0-917526-01-5). Olearius Edns.

Seize & Ravage. Richard Hall. 1985. 24.95x (ISBN 0-7090-2123-2, Pub. by R Hale Ltd UK). State Mutual Bk.

Seize the Day. Saul Bellow. 1984. pap. 4.95 (ISBN 0-14-007285-3). Penguin.

Seize the Day. Saul Bellow. 1956. 7.95 (ISBN 0-670-63176-0). Viking.

Seizing of Yankee Green. Ridley Pearson. 384p. 1987. 18.95 (ISBN 0-312-00703-5). St Martin.

Seizing of Yankee Green Mall. Ridley Pearson. 304p. Date not set. pap. 3.95 (ISBN 0-373-97076-5, Pub. by Worldwide). Harlequin Bks.

Seizing Our Bodies: The Politics of Women's Health Care. Ed. by Claudia Dreifus. 1978. pap. 5.95 (ISBN 0-394-72360-0, Vin). Random.

Seizing the Apple: A Feminist Spirituality of Personal Growth. Denise L. Carmody. 176p. (Orig.). 1984. pap. 10.95 (ISBN 0-8245-0652-9). Crossroad NY.

Seizing the Day: How to Take the Day Off & Change Your Life. Harold Henderson. 172p. 1983. pap. 7.95 (ISBN 0-87243-120-7). Templegate.

Seizing the Moments. James W. Moore. 144p. 1988. 11.95 (ISBN 0-687-37152-X). Abingdon.

Seizing the Torch: Leadership for a New Generation. Ted W. Engstrom & Robert C. Larson. Ed. by Mary Beckwith. 240p. 1988. pap. 7.95 (ISBN 0-8307-1195-3, 5419045). Regal.

Seizure. Betty M. Groce. (Better Living Ser.). 1977. pap. 1.25 (ISBN 0-8127-0142-9). Review & Herald.

Seizure Disorders in Children. Peggy C. Ferry et al. (Illus.). 270p. 1985. text ed. 32.50 (ISBN 0-397-50617-1, Lippincott Medical). Lippincott.

Seizure of Power. Czeslaw Milosz. Tr. by Celina Wieniewska from Pol. 259p. 1982. 14.95 (ISBN 0-374-25788-4); pap. 6.95 (ISBN 0-374-51697-9). FS&G.

Seizure of Power: Fascism in Italy, 1919-1929. 2nd ed. Adrian Lyttelton. 546p. 1988. pap. text ed. 18.50 (ISBN 0-691-02278-X). Princeton U Pr.

Sejanus. Ben Jonson. Ed. by W. D. Briggs. 1977. Repr. of 1911 ed. lib. bdg. 27.50 (ISBN 0-8495-2701-5). Arden Lib.

Sejanus: The Secret Ruler of Rome. John W. Graham. (Golden Age of Rome Ser.). 1978. pap. 2.50 (ISBN 0-89083-353-2). Zebra.

Sejarah Melayu or Malay Annals. Tr. by C. C. Brown. (Oxford in Asia Historical Reprints). 1970. 10.50x (ISBN 0-19-638106-1). Oxford U Pr.

Sejatel. Claudia Loukashevitch. (Illus.). 462p. 1966. 20.00 (ISBN 0-317-30416-X); pap. 15.00 (ISBN 0-317-30417-8). Holy Trinity.

Sejour a Clifftop. Christine H. Cott. (Harlequin Seduction Ser.). 332p. 1984. pap. 3.25 (ISBN 0-373-45034-6). Harlequin Bks.

Sek Says. M. Seklemian. Ed. by Carole A. Miller. 1979. 15.95 (ISBN 0-934590-00-1). Retail Report.

Sekai No Naka No Nihon Bijutsu see Japanese Art in World Perspective.

Sekai Toji Zenshu, 1-16: Collection of World's Ceramics. 1961. 3000.00x (ISBN 0-317-45193-6, Pub. by Han-Shan Tang Ltd). State Mutual Bk.

Sekai Toji Zenshu, 10: Ceramic Art of the World 10-Chinese Prehistoric & Ancient Periods. The Zauho Press Staff & Takashi Okazeki. 334p. 1982. 175.00x (ISBN 0-317-45197-9, Pub. by Han-Shan Tang Ltd). State Mutual Bk.

Sekai Toji Zenshu, 11: Ceramic Art of the World 11-Sui & T'ang Dynasties. The Zauho Press Staff & Mashiko Sato. 334p. 1976. 175.00 (ISBN 0-317-45201-0, Pub. by Han-Shan Tang Ltd). State Mutual Bk.

Sekai Toji Zenshu, 11: Chugoku Gendai & Mindai (World Ceramics 11-Yuan & Ming) Fujio Koyama. 307p. 1955. 100.00x (ISBN 0-317-45199-5, Pub. by Han-Shan Tang Ltd). State Mutual Bk.

Sekai Toji Zenshu, 12: Ceramic Art of the World 12-Sung Synasty. The Zauho Press Staff & Gakuji Hasebe. 350p. 1977. 175.00x (ISBN 0-317-45205-3, Pub. by Han-Shan Tang Ltd). State Mutual Bk.

Sekai Toji Zenshu, 13: Ceramic Art of the World 13-Liao, Chin & Yuan Dynasties. The Zauho Press Staff & Tsugio Mikami. 336p. 1981. 175.00x (ISBN 0-317-45216-9, Pub. by Han-Shan Tang Ltd). State Mutual Bk.

Sekai Toji Zenshu, 14: Ceramic Art of the World 14-Ming Dynasty. The Zauho Press Staff & Ryoichi Tujioka. 350p. 1976. 175.00x (ISBN 0-317-45218-5, Pub. by Han-Shan Tang Ltd). State Mutual Bk.

Sekai Toji Zenshu, 15: Ceramic Art of the World 15-Ch'ing Dynasty. John Ayers & Masahiko Sta. 297p. 1983. 175.00x (ISBN 0-317-45220-7, Pub. by Han-Shan Tang Ltd). State Mutual Bk.

Sekai Toji Zenshu, 8: Chugoku Jodial World Ceramics 8-Early China. Fujio Koyama. 328p. 1956. 150.00x (ISBN 0-317-45195-2, Pub. by Han-Shan Tang Ltd). State Mutual Bk.

Sekani's Solution. Tito Banda. (Malawian Writers Ser.). (Illus.). 112p. (Orig.). (gr. 9-12). 1979. pap. 6.00x (ISBN 0-686-63966-9). Three Continents.

Sel-La-V. Jim Findlay. (Life on the Earth Ser.). 1987. 30.00x (ISBN 0-900323-73-6, Pub. by Wm Culross & Son Ltd UK). State Mutual Bk.

Seladon-Keramik Der Koryo-Dynastie, 918-1392. Soontaek Choi-Bae. 247p. 1984. pap. 60.00x (ISBN 0-317-68628-3, Pub. by Han-Shan Tang Ltd). State Mutual Bk.

Seladon Swatow Blauweiss: Chinese Ceramics from the Collection of Ignazio Vok. Ulrich Wiesner. 219p. 1983. 60.00x (ISBN 0-317-45223-1, Pub. by Han-Shan Tang Ltd). State Mutual Bk.

Selberg Trace Formula & Related Topics. Ed. by D. Hejhal et al. LC 86-3512. (Contemporary Mathematics Ser.: Vol. 53). 568p. 1986. pap. text ed. 43.00 (ISBN 0-8218-5058-X). Am Math.

Selberg Trace Formula for PSL; 2, IR, Vol. 2. D. A. Hejhal. (Lecture Notes in Mathematics: Vol. 1001). 806p. 1983. pap. 44.50 (ISBN 0-387-12323-7). Springer-Verlag.

Selberg Trace Formula for PSLR. Efrat. LC 86-28808. (Memoirs of the American Mathematical Society Ser.: Vol. 359). 111p. 1987. pap. text ed. 16.00 (ISBN 0-8218-2424-4). Am Math.

Selberg Trace Formula for PSL(2,R) D. A. Hejhal. (Lecture Notes in Mathematics: Vol. 548). 1976. soft cover 24.00 (ISBN 0-387-07988-2). Springer-Verlag.

Selberg Trace Formula III: Inter Product Formulae (Initial Considerations) M. Scott Osborne et al. LC 83-3918. (Memoirs of the American Mathematical Society Ser.: No. 283). 209p. 1983. pap. 20.00 (ISBN 0-8218-2283-7). Am Math.

Selberg's Zeta-, L-, & Eisensteinseries. U. Christian. (Lecture Notes in Mathematics: Vol. 1030). 196p. 1983. pap. 14.00 (ISBN 0-387-12701-1). Springer Verlag.

Selbourne Year: The "Naturalist's Journal" for 1784. Ed. by Edward Dadswell. (Illus.). 128p. 1987. 17.95 (ISBN 0-86350-098-6). Viking.

Selbstbewusstsein und Unbewusstes: Studien Zu Freud und Heidegger. Martin Bartels. (Quellen und Studien Zur Philosophie Ser.: Vol. 10). 1976. 36.40x (ISBN 3-11-005778-6). De Gruyter.

Selbstbindung des Gesetzgebers. Regine Rausch-Gast. (European University Studies: No. 2, Vol. 322). 547p. (Ger.). 1983. 24.75 (ISBN 3-8204-7518-4). P Lang Pubs.

Selbstmord als Sociale Massenerscheinung der Modernen Civilisation. Thomas G. Masaryk. Ed. & intros. by J. C. Nyiri. (Philosophia Resources Library). xvi, 245p. (Ger.). 1982. lib. bdg. 58.00 (ISBN 0-317-57770-0). Philosophia Pr.

Selbstverstaendnis des Modernen Algeriens: Die Historisch-Nationalen und Islamischen Elemente, Vol. 14. Helga Walter. (Schriften zum Staats - und Volkerrecht). 216p. (Ger.). 1983. 26.85 (ISBN 3-8204-7125-1). P Lang Pubs.

Selchie's Seed. Shulamith Oppenheim. (Illus.). (gr. 8-12). 1983. pap. 1.25 (ISBN 0-380-01727-X, 34165, Camelot). Avon.

Seldens of Virginia & Allied Families, 2 vols. Mary S. Kennedy. Repr. of 1911 ed. 100.00 (ISBN 0-686-19841-7). Ridgeway Bks.

Seldom Sung Songs. Ray Locke. LC 83-63200. 183p. 1984. 13.95 (ISBN 0-915677-02-4). Roundtable Pub.

Seldom-Told Bible Tales. James McKarns. 1985. 4.95 (ISBN 0-89536-738-6, 5821). CSS of Ohio.

Seldwyla Folks: Three Singular Tales by the Swiss Poet. facsimile ed. Gottfried Keller. Tr. by Wolf Von Schierbrand from Ger. LC 70-150545. (Short Story Index Reprint Ser.). Repr. of 1919 ed. 17.00 (ISBN 0-8369-3842-9). Ayer Co Pubs.

Seleccion De Personal En el Servicio Publico De Puerto Rico. Irma G. De Serrano. 5.60 (ISBN 0-8477-2204-X); pap. 4.35 (ISBN 0-8477-2205-8). U of PR Pr.

Seleccion de Romances. (Span.). 9.95 (ISBN 84-241-5619-6). E Torres & Sons.

Selecciones de "Mi Camino a Rotary". Paul Harris. 58p. (Span.). 1984. 3.00 (ISBN 0-915062-21-6). Rotary Intl.

Selecciones Teologias Anabautista. Walter Klaassen. Tr. by C. Arnoldo Snyder from Eng. LC 85-81079. 280p. (Orig., Span.). 1985. pap. 4.50x (ISBN 0-8361-1281-4). Herald Pr.

Select Annotated Bibliography on Women & the Ethnic Minorities of Color in Social Work Education. Houda S. Abdul-Baki. 1985. 10.00 (ISBN 0-533-05934-8). Vantage.

Select Architecture. Robert Morris. LC 72-87427. (Architecture & Decorative Art Ser.). 102p. 1973. Repr. of 1757 ed. lib. bdg. 35.00 (ISBN 0-306-71573-2). Da Capo.

Select Bibliography: Asia, Africa, Eastern Europe, Latin America. American Universities Field Staff. LC 60-10482. 358p. (Orig.). 1960. 8.50 (ISBN 0-910116-50-4); Cumulative Suppl. 1961-71. 12.50 (ISBN 0-910116-85-7). U Fleld Staff Intl.

Select Bibliography for the Study of Anglo-Irish Literature & Its Backgrounds. Maurice Harmon. (Illus.). 192p. 1977. (Pub. by Wolfhound Pr Ireland); pap. 7.95 (ISBN 0-905473-05-1). Irish Bks Media.

Select Bibliography for the Study, Sources & Literature of English Medieval Economic History. Ed. by Hubert Hall. 1960. Repr. of 1914 ed. 23.50 (ISBN 0-8337-1548-8). B Franklin.

Select Bibliography of Books on World War II: Published in the United States 1966-1975. Compiled by A. L. Funk. 33p. 1975. pap. 2.50x (ISBN 0-89126-074-9). MA-AH Pub.

Select Bibliography of British History, 1660-1760. Clyde L. Grose. 1967. lib. bdg. 31.50x (ISBN 0-374-93306-5, Octagon). Hippocrene Bks.

Select Bibliography of Chemistry. H. C. Bolton. Incl. 1492-1892. 1893. 128.00 (ISBN 0-527-09400-5); First Supplement, 1492-1897, Section 1-7. 1899. 35.00 (ISBN 0-527-09420-X); First Supplement, 1492-1897, Section 8: Academic Dissertations. 1901. 35.00 (ISBN 0-527-09426-9); Second Supplement, 1492-1902. 1904. 35.00 (ISBN 0-527-09432-3). (Smithsonian Miscellaneous Collections Ser: No. 36). Kraus Repr.

Select Bibliography of European Folk Music. Ed. by Karel Vetterl. 144p. 1966. 5.00 (ISBN 0-318-17463-4). Intl Coun Trad.

Select Bibliography of Gunter Grass from 1956 to 1973, Including the Works, Editions, Translations & Critical Literature. George A. Everett, Jr. LC 74-1420. 1974. 15.00 (ISBN 0-89102-041-1). B Franklin.

Select Bibliography of Italy. William O. Hassal. LC 83-45436. Repr. of 1946 ed. 20.00 (ISBN 0-404-20118-0). AMS Pr.

Select Bibliography of Music in Africa. International African Institute & L. J. Gaskin. LC 66-36908. (Africa Bibliography Ser.: No. 8). pap. 23.80 (ISBN 0-317-10104-8, 2007644). Bks Demand UMI.

Select Bibliography of Philosophical Logic, Vol. 1. 4th ed. Richardson, J. & Co. Staff. 1984. Supplement to Vol. 1. 35.00x (ISBN 0-317-54316-4, Pub. by J Richardson UK); Supplement to Vol. 1. pap. 22.50x (ISBN 0-317-54317-2, Pub. by J Richardson UK). State Mutual Bk.

Select Bibliography of Philosophical Logic, Vol. 1. 4th ed. Richardson, J. & Co. Staff. 1986. 62.50x (ISBN 0-317-54320-2, Pub. by J Richardson UK); pap. 47.50x (ISBN 0-317-54321-0, Pub. by J Richardson UK). State Mutual Bk.

Select Bibliography of Revisionist Books. rev. ed. Harry E. Barnes. 59.95 (ISBN 0-685-26300-2). Revisionist Pr.

Select Bibliography of the Negro American. Ed. by W. E. B. Dubois. (Atlanta Univ. Publ. Ser.: No. 10). (Orig.). 1905. pap. 14.00 (ISBN 0-527-03112-7). Kraus Repr.

Select Bibliography of the Principal Modern Presses, Public & Private, in Great Britain & Ireland. G. S. Tomkinson. LC 75-2752. (Illus.). 1975. Repr. of 1928 ed. 25.00 (ISBN 0-915346-00-1). A Wofsy Fine Arts.

Select Bibliography on the Selection & Administration of Government Documents. Tim J. Watts. (Public Administration Ser.: P 2179). 45p. 1987. 11.25 (ISBN 1-55590-359-2). Vance Biblios.

Select Bibliography on Women in India. 131p. 1978. 7.95. Asia Bk Corp.

Select British Documents of the Canadian War of 1812, Vol. 1. Ed. by William C. Wood. LC 68-28604. 1968. Repr. of 1920 ed. lib. bdg. 51.25x (ISBN 0-8371-5051-5, WOBA). Greenwood.

Select British Documents of the Canadian War of 1812, Vol. 2. Ed. by William C. Wood. Repr. of 1923 ed. lib. bdg. 32.25x (ISBN 0-8371-5052-3, WOBB). Greenwood.

Select British Documents of the Canadian War of 1812, Vol. 3, Pt. 2. Ed. by William C. Wood. Repr. of 1928 ed. lib. bdg. 32.00x (ISBN 0-8371-5054-X, WOBD). Greenwood.

Select British Documents of the Canadian War of 1812, Vol. 3, Pt. 1. Ed. by William C. Wood. Repr. of 1926 ed. lib. bdg. 32.75x (ISBN 0-8371-5053-1, WOBC). Greenwood.

Select Catalog of Language Universals. Ed. by Gyuia Decsy. (Bibliotheca Nostratica Ser.: Vol. 8). 141p. 1988. pap. 26.00 (ISBN 0-931922-29-1). Eurolingua.

Select Charters & Other Illustrations of English Constitutional History from the Earliest Times to the Reign of Edward the First. 9th ed. William Stubbs. LC 85-28220. xix, 528p. 1985. Repr. of 1921 ed. lib. bdg. 47.50x (ISBN 0-8377-2609-3). Rothman.

Select Charters of Trading Companies A.D. 1530-1707. Ed. by Cecil T. Carr. LC 76-130593. (Research & Source Works: No. 551). 1970. Repr. of 1913 ed. lib. bdg. 24.00 (ISBN 0-8337-0479-6). B Franklin.

Select Circles. Kathryn Junsen. 1987. pap. 3.95 (ISBN 0-8041-0055-1, Pub. by Ivy). Ballantine.

Select Collection of Old English Plays, 15 Vols. in 7. Ed. by Robert Dodsley. LC 64-14702. Repr. of 1876 ed. Set. 305.00 (ISBN 0-405-08452-8, Blom Pubns); 44.00 ea. Vol. 1 (ISBN 0-405-08453-6). Vol. 2 (ISBN 0-405-08454-4). Vol. 3 (ISBN 0-405-08455-2). Vol. 4 (ISBN 0-405-08456-0). Vol. 5 (ISBN 0-405-08457-9). Vol. 6 (ISBN 0-405-08458-7). Vol. 7 (ISBN 0-405-08459-5). Ayer Co Pubs.

Select Collection of Poems, with Notes Biographical & Historical, 8 vols. Ed. by John Nichols. LC 11-29585. Repr. of 1782 ed. 320.00 (ISBN 0-404-04750-5). AMS Pr.

Select Collection of Poems, with Notes Biographical & Historical, 8 vols. Ed. by John Nichols. Repr. of 1782 ed. Set. 360.00 (ISBN 0-527-67180-0). Kraus Repr.

Select Collection of Scarce & Valuable Tracts & Other Publications on the National Debt & the Sinking Fund. Ed. by John R. McCulloch. LC 65-16989. 1966. Repr. of 1857 ed. 50.00x (ISBN 0-678-00148-0). Kelley.

Select Committee on Small Business: Hearing 89th Congress 1st Session. U. S. Congress. 1982. Repr. of 1966 ed. Set. lib. bdg. 180.00 (ISBN 0-89941-232-7); Ea. vol. lib. bdg. 40.00. W S Hein.

S.E.L.E.C.T. Creative-Innovative Approaches. John G. Young. 110p. (Orig.). 1986. pap. 12.95 (ISBN 0-943456-13-4). Bearly Ltd.

Select Developments in Soviet Airborne Computer Technology, 1958-1977. Andrew Michta & John F. Passafiume. 76p. (Orig.). Date not set. pap. text ed. 42.50. Delphic Associates.

Select Discourses. John Smith. Ed. by Rene Wellek. LC 75-11252. (British Philosophers & Theologians of the 17th & 18th Centuries Ser.). 1978. Repr. of 1660 ed. lib. bdg. 51.00 (ISBN 0-8240-1803-6). Garland Pub.

Select Discourses. John Smith. Ed. by C. A. Patrides. LC 79-15690. 1979. Repr. of 1660 ed. 75.00x (ISBN 0-8201-1335-2). Schol Facsimiles.

Select Discussions of Race Problems. Ed. by J. A. Bigham. (Atlanta Publication Ser.: No. 20). (Orig.) 1916. pap. 16.00 (ISBN 0-527-03121-6). Kraus Repr.

Select Dissertations from the Amoenitates Academicae: Supplement to Mr. Stillingfleet's Tracts, Relating Natural History. Carl Linnaeus. Ed. by Frank N. Egerton, 3rd. Tr. by F. J. Brand. LC 77-74238. (History of Ecology Ser.). 1978. Repr. of 1781 ed. lib. bdg. 38.50x (ISBN 0-405-10407-3). Ayer Co Pubs.

Select Documents for Queen Anne's Reign Down to the Union with Scotland, 1702-07. Ed. by George M. Trevelyan & Gerald M. Straka. LC 72-83173. (English Studies Ser.). 1972. Repr. of 1929 ed. lib. bdg. 23.00 (ISBN 0-8420-1429-2). Scholarly Res Inc.

Select Documents Illustrative of the History of the United States, 1776-1861. William MacDonald. LC 68-57913. (Research & Source Works Ser: No. 308). 1969. Repr. of 1898 ed. 29.00 (ISBN 0-8337-2164-X). B Franklin.

Select Documents in Canadian Economic History, 2 vols. Ed. by Harold A. Innis & A. R. Lower. LC 77-8258. 1977. Repr. of 1933 ed. Set. lib. bdg. 95.00x (ISBN 0-87991-132-8); Vol. 1. lib. bdg. 50.00x (ISBN 0-87991-133-6); Vol. 2. lib. bdg. 57.50x (ISBN 0-87991-134-4). Porcupine Pr.

Select Documents on India's Foreign Policy & Relations, Vol. 2. Ed. by Angadipuram Appadorai. 1985. 42.00x (ISBN 0-19-561496-8). Oxford U Pr.

Select Documents on India's Foreign Policy & Relations, 1947-72, Vol. 1. Ed. by Angadipuram Appadorai. 1982. 45.00x (ISBN 0-19-561309-0). Oxford U Pr.

Select Documents Relating to the Unification of South Africa. Ed. by A. P. Newton. 574p. 1968. Repr. of 1924 ed. 45.00x (ISBN 0-7146-1777-6, F Cass Co). Biblio Dist.

Select English Songs & Dialogues of the 16th & 17th Centuries, 2 vols. in 1. Ed. by A. Dolmetsch. LC 74-24070. Repr. of 1898 ed. 34.50 (ISBN 0-404-12897-1). AMS Pr.

Select Epigrams from the Greek Anthology. J. W. Mackail. 1911. 30.00 (ISBN 0-686-20110-8). Quality Lib.

Select Epigrams of Martial. Donald C. Goertz. LC 74-127795. 128p. 1971. 5.95 (ISBN 0-8216-0150-4, Pub. by Univ Bks). Lyle Stuart.

Select Essays of Sainte-Beuve: Chiefly Bearing on English Literature. Tr. by A. J. Butler. 1978. lib. bdg. 25.00 (ISBN 0-8495-4830-6). Arden Lib.

Select Fables of Esop & Other Fabulists. Aesopus. Ed. by Robert Dodsley. LC 70-161796. (Augustan Translators Ser.). Repr. of 1781 ed. 31.50 (ISBN 0-404-54101-1). AMS Pr.

Select Glossary of English Words Used Formerly in Senses Different from Their Present. Richard C. Trench. Ed. by A. Smythe Palmer. 1979. Repr. of 1906 ed. lib. bdg. 25.00 (ISBN 0-8495-5138-2). Arden Lib.

Select Greek Coins. George F. Hill. (Illus.). 64p. 1974. 20.00 (ISBN 0-89005-001-5). Ares.

Select Greek Inscriptions: Auswahl Aus Griechischen Inschriften. R. Helbing. 138p. 1980. 10.00 (ISBN 0-89005-202-6). Ares.

Select Guide to Area Studies Resources. L. Robert Kohls & V. Lynn Tyler. 47p. (Orig.). 1988. pap. write for info. (ISBN 0-912575-08-5). D M Kennedy Ctr Brigham.

Select Guide to California Catholic History. Francis J. Weber. 12.50 (ISBN 0-87026-001-4). Westernlore.

Select Historical Documents of the Middle Ages. Ed. by Ernest F. Henderson. LC 68-57867. (Bohn's Antiquarian Library Ser). 1968. Repr. of 1892 ed. 34.50 (ISBN 0-404-50016-1). AMS Pr.

Select Historical Documents of the Middle Ages. Ed. by Ernest F. Henderson. LC 65-15247. 1892. 15.00 (ISBN 0-8196-0149-7). Biblo.

Select Letters. St. Aurelius Augustine. Tr. by James H. Baxter. LC 75-41012. Repr. of 1930 ed. 37.50. AMS Pr.

Select Letters. Saint Augustine. (Loeb Classical Library: No. 239). 13.95x (ISBN 0-674-99264-4). Harvard U Pr.

Select Letters. Cicero. Ed. by D. R. Bailey. LC 78-67430. (Cambridge Greek & Latin Classics). 250p. 1980. 44.50 (ISBN 0-521-22492-6); pap. 19.95x (ISBN 0-521-29524-6). Cambridge U Pr.

Select Letters, 2 vols. Cicero. Ed. by W. W. How. Vol. 1. 1925 Text. 19.95x (ISBN 0-19-814403-2); Vol. 2. 1926 Notes. 26.00x (ISBN 0-19-814404-0). Oxford U Pr.

Select Letters. Saint Jerome. (Loeb Classical Library: No. 262). 13.95x (ISBN 0-674-99288-1). Harvard U Pr.

Select Letters of English Poets. Ed. by Kochi Doi. 1978. Repr. of 1935 ed. lib. bdg. 40.00 (ISBN 0-8495-1031-7). Arden Lib.

Select Letters of Major Jack Downing. facsimile ed. Seba Smith. LC 77-104567. (Illus.). 223p. Repr. of 1834 ed. lib. bdg. 26.50 (ISBN 0-8398-1868-8). Irvington.

Select Letters of Major Jack Downing. Seba Smith. 223p. 1986. pap. text ed. 6.95x (ISBN 0-8290-2393-3). Irvington.

Select Letters of Seneca. Lucius Annaeus Seneca. Ed. & intro. by Walter C. Summers. (College Classical Ser.). vii, 380p. pap. text ed. 20.00x (ISBN 0-89241-385-9). Caratzas.

Select List of British Parliamentary Papers 1833-1899. P. Ford & G. Ford. 188p. 1969. Repr. of 1953 ed. 30.00x (ISBN 0-7165-0574-6, Pub. by Irish Academic Pr Ireland). Biblio Dist.

Select List of British Parliamentary Papers 1955-1964. P. Ford et al. 128p. 1970. 30.00x (ISBN 0-7165-0884-2, Pub. by Irish Academic Pr Ireland). Biblio Dist.

Select List of Reports of Inquiries of the Irish Dail & Senate: Fifty Years of Policy Making, 1922-72. P. Ford & G. Ford. 64p. 1974. 25.00x (ISBN 0-7165-2254-3, Pub. by Irish Academic Pr Ireland). Biblio Dist.

Select Medieval Documents & Other Material Illustrative in the History of Church & Empire, 754 A.D.-1254 A.D. Shailer Mathews. LC 70-178566. (Lat.). Repr. of 1900 ed. 21.00 (ISBN 0-404-56628-6). AMS Pr.

Select Passages Illustrating Neoplatonism. E. R. Dodds. 128p. 1980. 12.50 (ISBN 0-89005-302-2). Ares.

Select Plays. Francis Beaumont & John Beaumont. Repr. of 1911 ed. 49.00 (ISBN 0-403-04257-7). Somerset Pub.

Select Poems Divine & Humane. Thomas Beedome. LC 75-17757. 1973. lib. bdg. 12.50 (ISBN 0-8414-3228-7). Folcroft.

Select Poetry, Chiefly Devotional, of the Reign of Queen Elizabeth, 2 Vols. Ed. by Edward Farr. 1845. Vol. 1. 41.00 (ISBN 0-384-15165-5); Vol. 2. 41.00 (ISBN 0-384-15166-3). Johnson Repr.

Select Private Orations of Demosthenes, 2 vols. in 1, Pts. I & II. Demosthenes. Ed. by W. R. Connor. LC 78-18601. (Greek Texts & Commentaries Ser.). (Illus.). 1979. Repr. of 1898 ed. lib. bdg. 48.50 (ISBN 0-405-11442-7). Ayer Co Pubs.

Select Readings in Hebrew Literature. Harry Blumberg & Mordecai H. Lewittes. 224p. 1942. 6.95 (ISBN 0-88482-669-4). Hebrew Pub.

Select Remains of the Ancient Popular & Romantic Poetry of Scotland. Ed. by David Laing. LC 77-94594. 1979. Repr. of 1885 ed. lib. bdg. 45.00 (ISBN 0-89341-185-X). Longwood Pub Group.

Select Scottish Ballads, 2 vols. 2nd corr. & enl. ed. Ed. by John Pinkerton. LC 72-144529. Repr. of 1783 ed. Set. 20.00 (ISBN 0-404-08674-8); 10.50 ea. Vol. 1 (ISBN 0-404-08675-6). Vol. 2 (ISBN 0-404-08676-4). AMS Pr.

Select Sermons of Benjamin Whichcote. Benjamin Whichcote. LC 77-16025. 1977. Repr. of 1742 ed. 50.00x (ISBN 0-8201-1306-9). Schol Facsimiles.

Select Sermons of George Whitefield. George Whitefield. 200p. 1985. pap. 4.95 (ISBN 0-85151-454-5). Banner of Truth.

Select Speeches for Declamation. facsimile ed. Ed. by John H. Bechtel. LC 75-103083. (Granger Index Reprint Ser). 1898. 17.00 (ISBN 0-8369-6098-X). Ayer Co Pubs.

Select Statutes & Other Constitutional Documents Illustrative of the Reigns of Elizabeth & James I. 4th ed. Ed. by George W. Prothero. LC 83-1740. cxxv, 490p. 1983. Repr. of 1913 ed. lib. bdg. 79.50x (ISBN 0-313-23973-8, PRSE). Greenwood.

Select Statutes, Documents & Reports Relating to British Banking: 1832-1928, 2 vols. Ed. by Theodore Gregory. (Illus.). 1964. Repr. of 1929 ed. 85.00x set (ISBN 0-7146-1225-1, BHA-01225, F Cass Co). Biblio Dist.

Select Statutes, Documents & Reports Relating to British Banking, 1832-1928, 2 Vols. Ed. by Theodore E. Gregory. LC 67-93658. 1964. Repr. of 1929 ed. 75.00x (ISBN 0-678-05169-0). Kelley.

Select Tracts & Documents Illustrative of English Monetary History 1626-1730. William A. Shaw. LC 67-19743. 1967. Repr. of 1896 ed. 29.50x (ISBN 0-678-00251-7). Kelley.

Select Translations from Old English Poetry. Albert S. Cook. 1902. lib. bdg. 25.00 (ISBN 0-8414-2381-4). Folcroft.

Select Translations from Old English Poetry. rev. ed. Ed. by Albert S. Cook & Chauncey B. Tinker. LC 68-59036. 195p. 1968. Repr. of 1902 ed. 20.00x (ISBN 0-87752-024-0). Gordian.

Select Translations from Old English Prose. Ed. by Albert S. Cook & Chauncey B. Tinker. LC 68-57700. 304p. 1968. Repr. of 1908 ed. 30.00x (ISBN 0-87752-025-9). Gordian.

Select Treatises of St. Athanasius in Controversy with the Arians, 2 vols. 5th ed. St. Athanasius. Tr. by John H. Newman. LC 77-84694. (Heresies of the Early Christian & Medieval Era Ser.). Repr. of 1890 ed. 72.00 set (ISBN 0-404-16100-6). AMS Pr.

Select Trials at the Sessions House in the Old Bailey. LC 83-48613. (Marriage, Sex & the Family in England Ser.). 1488p. 1985. lib. bdg. 193.00 (ISBN 0-8240-5920-4). Garland Pub.

Select Washington Lobbyists. Ed. by Nancy F. Smith. 450p. 1989. pap. text ed. 35.00 (ISBN 0-933833-13-X). Beacham Pub.

Select Works of Antony Van Leeuwenhook: His Microscopical Discoveries in Many Works of Nature, 2 vols in 1. Antony Van Leeuwenhoek. Ed. by Frank N. Egerton. Tr. by Samuel Hoole. LC 77-74236. (History of Ecology Ser.). (Illus.). 1978. Repr. of 1807 ed. lib. bdg. 54.00x (ISBN 0-405-10405-7). Ayer Co Pubs.

Select Works of John Bale, Bishop of Ossory. John Bale. 51.00 (ISBN 0-384-03135-8). Johnson Repr.

Select Works of Robert Crowley, Printer, Archdeacon of Hereford, Vicar of St. Lawrence, Jewry. Robert Crowley. Ed. by J. M. Cowper. (EETS, ES Ser.: No. 15). Repr. of 1872 ed. 43.00 (ISBN 0-527-00230-5). Kraus Repr.

Select Your Own Tree & Shrubbery Locations with a Tree & Shrubbery Care Information Locator Guide. Center for Self-Sufficiency, Research Division Staff. 50p. 1984. pap. text ed. 6.95 (ISBN 0-910811-58-X, Pub. by Center Self Suff). Prosperity & Profits.

Selecta: Selected Papers of D. C. Spencer, 3 vols. D. C. Spencer. LC 85-3338. 1800p. 1985. Vol. I. write for info. (ISBN 9971-978-02-4); Vol. II. write for info. (ISBN 9971-978-03-2); Vol. III. write for info. (ISBN 9971-978-04-0); Set. 197.00. World Scientific Pub.

Selecta Volume One: Research Contributions. P. R. Halmos. (Illus.). 458p. 1983. 46.00 (ISBN 0-387-90755-6). Springer-Verlag.

Selecta Volume Two: Expository Writing. P. R. Halmos. (Illus.). 256p. 1983. 28.00 (ISBN 0-387-90756-4). Springer-Verlag.

Selected Abstracts on Biological Markers of Central Nervous System Neoplasms. Herbert A. Fritsche, Jr. (Oncology Overview Ser.). 1987. pap. 4.00 (ISBN 0-318-23443-2, S/N 017-042-00211-7). USGPO.

Selected Abstracts on Bone Marrow Transplantation in Cancer. (Oncology Overview Ser.). 101p. 1987. pap. 5.50 (ISBN 0-318-22941-2, S/N 017-042-00201-0). USGPO.

Selected Abstracts on Cancer Biology, 1986: Recent Reviews. Jon Palmer. 1987. pap. 10.00 (ISBN 0-318-23523-4, S/N 017-042-00220-6). USGPO.

Selected Abstracts on Cancer Diagnosis & Therapy, 1986: Recent Reviews. Ed. by Ronal D. Hutchins. 167p. 1986. pap. 8.50 (ISBN 0-318-23524-2, S/N 017-042-00221-4). USGPO.

Selected Abstracts on Cancer Prevention. Guy R. Newell. (Oncology Overview Ser.). 83p. 1987. pap. 4.25 (ISBN 0-318-23444-0, S/N 017-042-00210-9). USGPO.

Selected Abstracts on Carcinogenesis, 1986. Ester I. Chow. (Recent Reviews Ser.). 154p. 1987. pap. 8.00 (ISBN 0-318-23525-0, S/N 017-042-00219-2). USGPO.

Selected Abstracts on Chemopreventive Agents. Clement Ip. (Oncology Overview Ser.). 140p. 1987. pap. 6.50 (ISBN 0-317-62881-X, S-N 017-042-00204-4). USGPO.

Selected Abstracts on Childhood Nervous System Neoplasms. Jan Van Eys. (Oncology Overview Ser.). 87p. 1987. pap. 4.50 (ISBN 0-318-23526-9, S/N 017-042-00217-6). USGPO.

Selected Abstracts on Diagnosis & Therapy of Large Bowel Cancer. Bernard Levin. (Oncology Overview Ser.). 103p. 1987. pap. 5.00 (ISBN 0-318-23445-9, S/N 017-042-00216-8). USGPO.

Selected Abstracts on Diagnosis & Treatment of the Acquired Immunodeficiency Syndrome. Evan M. Hersh. (Oncology Overview Ser.). 116p. 1987. pap. 5.50 (ISBN 0-318-23446-7, S/N 017-042-00214-1). USGPO.

Selected Abstracts on Dioxins & Dibenzofurans in Carcinogenesis: 1980-1986. Ed. by William F. Greenlee. (Oncology Overview Ser.). 118p. 1987. pap. 5.50 (017-042-00206-1). USGPO.

Selected Abstracts on Idiotypes, Anti-Idiotypes & Network Regulation. (Oncology Overview Ser.). 116p. 1987. pap. 6.00 (ISBN 0-318-22942-0, S/N 017-042-00202-8). USGPO.

Selected Abstracts on Oncogene Protein Products. Ed. by R. A. Weinberg. (Oncology Overview Ser.). 116p. 1987. pap. 5.50 (017-042-00205-2). USGPO.

Selected Abstracts on Potential Occupational Causes of Cancer 2: The Urinary Tract. Richard R. Monson. (Oncology Overview Ser.). 104p. 1987. pap. 4.75 (ISBN 0-317-62882-8, S-N 017-042-00203-6). USGPO.

Selected Abstracts on Radioprotectors: Experimental Studies & Clinical Applications. Theodore L. Phillips. (Oncology Overview Ser.). 129p. 1987. pap. 6.50 (ISBN 0-317-62894-1, S-N 017-042-00207-9). USGPO.

Selected Abstracts on Recent Advances in the Systemic Therapy of Genitourinary Malignancies. Christopher J. Logothetis & Douglas E. Johnson. (Oncology Overview Ser.). 91p. 1987. pap. 4.50 (ISBN 0-318-23447-5, S/N 017-042-00218-4). USGPO.

Selected Abstracts on Structural Applications of Plastics. (Manual & Report on Engineering Practices Ser.: No. 47). 80p. 1967. pap. 4.00x (ISBN 0-87262-221-5). Am Soc Civil Eng.

Selected Abstracts on Transforming Growth Factors & Other Autocrine Growth Factors. (Oncology Overview Ser.). 84p. 1987. pap. 5.00 (ISBN 0-318-22943-9, S/N 017-042-00200-1). USGPO.

Selected Abstracts on Translocation & Amplification of Oncogenes. (Oncology Overview Ser.). 113p. 1987. pap. 6.00 (ISBN 0-318-22944-7, S/N 017-042-00198-6). USGPO.

Selected Abstracts on Viral Etiology of Human Cancer, No. 3: Hepatitis B Virus. W. Thomas London. (Oncology Overview Ser.). 122p. (Orig.). 1987. pap. 6.50 (ISBN 0-318-22946-3, S/N 017-042-00197-8). USGPO.

Selected Abstracts on Viral Etiology of Human Cancer, No. 2: Papillomaviruses, No. 2. (Oncology Overview Ser.). 106p. 1987. pap. 5.50 (ISBN 0-318-22945-5, S/N 017-042-00199-4). USGPO.

Selected Addresses & Essays. Richard B. Haldane. LC 71-107704. (Essay Index Reprint Ser.). 1928. 18.00 (ISBN 0-8369-1507-0). Ayer Co Pubs.

Selected Addresses of a Southern Lawyer. Aubrey L. Brooks. ix, 165p. 1954. 15.00x (ISBN 0-8078-0657-9). U of NC Pr.

Selected American Game Birds. David Hagerbaumer. LC 74-137773. 1972. 30.00 (ISBN 0-87004-213-0). Caxton.

Selected Analytes in Clinical Chemistry. Ed. by Jocelyn M. Hicks & K. Michael Parker. LC 84-71707. 218p. 1984. 22.00 (ISBN 0-915274-25-6). Am Assn Clinical Chem.

Selected Analytical Concepts in Command & Control. Ed. by John Hwang & Daniel Schutzer. (Military Operations Research Ser.: Vol. 2). 180p. 1982. 77.00 (ISBN 0-677-16420-3). Gordon & Breach.

Selected Ancient Chinese Bronzes. C. F. Yau. 1960. 175.00x (ISBN 0-317-69029-9, Pub. by Han-Shan Tang Ltd). State Mutual Bk.

Selected & Annotated Bibliography for Consultants in the Health Care Field. Jack Ellis & Susan Helbig. 32p. 1980. 3.00 (ISBN 0-318-19157-1, 1009). Am Med Record Assn.

Selected & Annotated Bibliography of American Naval History. Compiled by Paolo E. Coletta. 548p. 1988. lib. bdg. 39.50 (ISBN 0-8191-7111-5). U Pr of Amer.

Selected & Annotated Bibliography of Books & Periodicals in Western Languages Dealing with the Near & Middle East, with Special Emphasis on Medieval & Modern Times. Richard Ettinghausen. LC 70-180337. Repr. of 1954 ed. 24.50 (ISBN 0-404-56249-3). AMS Pr.

Selected & Annotated Bibliography of Bicultural Classroom Materials for Mexican American Studies. Robert P. Reilly. LC 77-81027. 1977. soft bdg. 9.95 (ISBN 0-88247-484-7). R & E Pubs.

Selected & Annotated Bibliography of Chicano Studies. 2nd ed. Charles M. Tatum. LC 79-64044. 1979. pap. 12.00 (ISBN 0-89295-011-0). Society Sp & Sp-Am.

Selected & Annotated Bibliography of Economic Literature in the Arabic Countries of the Middle East, 2 vols. Vol. 1, 1938-1952. pap. 10.00x (ISBN 0-8156-6020-0, Am U Beirut); Vol. 2, 1953-1965. pap. 14.95x (ISBN 0-8156-6021-9). Syracuse U Pr.

Selected & Annotated Bibliography of the Republic of China, 1958-59, & 1959-60, 2 vols. in 1. Tai-Pei National Central Library. Chung-Yang T'u-Shu Kuan. LC 75-38403. Repr. of 1962 ed. 40.00 (ISBN 0-404-56921-8). AMS Pr.

Selected & Annotated Resource List of Materials on the Holocaust. Pref. by Elie Wiesel. 65p. 5.00 (ISBN 0-686-74934-0). ADL.

Selected & Collected Poems. Bill Knott. LC 77-3473. 1977. 12.00 (ISBN 0-915342-17-0); pap. 8.00 (ISBN 0-915342-16-2). SUN.

Selected & New Poems. Sam Cornish. 150p. (Orig.). 1986. 20.00 (ISBN 0-87775-195-1); pap. 8.00 (ISBN 0-87775-196-X). Unicorn Pr.

Selected & New Poems. Norman Dubie. LC 83-42686. 160p. 1983. 14.95 (ISBN 0-393-01817-2); pap. 5.95 (ISBN 0-393-30140-0). Norton.

Selected & New Poems. 1989. pap. 8.95 (ISBN 0-440-55020-3, Delta). Dell.

Selected & New Poems Nineteen Thirty-Nine to Eighty-Four. J. C. Hall. 96p. 1985. pap. 9.95 (ISBN 0-436-19052-4, Pub. by Secker & Warburg UK). David & Charles.

Selected Annotated Bibliography of Ohio Raptors. Jeffery R. Stenzel. Ed. by Veda M. Cafazzo. (Informative Circular Ser.: No. 13). 11p. 1984. 3.00 (ISBN 0-86727-097-7). Ohio Bio Survey.

Selected Annotated Bibliography of Tropical Africa. International African Institute. Ed. by Daryll Forde. 1956. 58.00 (ISBN 0-527-44450-2). Kraus Repr.

Selected Annotated Bibliography of the Physician Assistant Profession. 2nd ed. 119p. 1980. pap. 20.00 (ISBN 0-318-13477-2). Assn Phys Asst Prog.

Selected Annotated Bibliography of Vocational Education: Planning & Implementaion in Developing Countries, with Special Reference to Nepal. Lekh Belbase et al. 49p. 1982. 8.00 (ISBN 0-318-04180-4, 48). Am-Nepal Ed.

Selected Anthropological Papers: 1928-1949. Franz Weidenreich. LC 78-72708. Repr. of 1980 ed. 57.50 (ISBN 0-404-18279-8). AMS Pr.

Selected Antitrust Cases: Landmark Decisions. 7th ed. Irwin M. Stelzer & Howard Kitt. 1986. pap. 19.95x (ISBN 0-256-03222-X). Irwin.

Selected Applications of the Unesco Educational Simulation Model. (Reports & Papers in the Social Sciences: No. 34). (Illus.). 1977. pap. 5.00 (U596, UNESCO). UNIPUB.

Selected Applications of the UNESCO Educational Simulation Model. (Reports & Papers in the Social Sciences: No. 34). (Illus.). 74p. 1977. pap. 5.00 (U596, UNESCO). UNIPUB.

Selected Archaeological Papers of Frederic Ward Putnam. Frederic W. Putnam. LC 76-178419. (Harvard University. Peabody Museum of Archaeology & Ethnology. Antiquities of the New World: No. 5). (Illus.). Repr. of 1973 ed. 54.00 (ISBN 0-404-57305-3). AMS Pr.

Selected Architecture Books Published in Canada 1974-1984. Mary Vance. (Architecture Ser., Bibliography: A 1478). 62p. 1985. pap. 9.00 (ISBN 0-89028-608-6). Vance Biblios.

Selected Articles. Sam Marcy. Incl. 1976-1977. 78p. 2.00 (ISBN 0-317-37252-1); 1977-1978. 72p. 2.00 (ISBN 0-89567-029-1); 1978-1979. 62p. 2.00 (ISBN 0-89567-032-1); 1979-1980. 73p. 2.00; 1980-1981. 64p. 2.00 (ISBN 0-89567-004-6); 1982-1983. 111p. 2.50. World View Forum.

Selected Articles by Harry Gunnison Brown: The Case for Land Value Taxation. Harry G. Brown. LC 80-25662. 245p. 1980. 5.00 (ISBN 0-911312-50-1). Schalkenbach.

Selected Articles in Social Ecology. Ed. by James S. Wittman. LC 73-609. 295p. 1973. text ed. 39.50x (ISBN 0-8422-5086-7); pap. text ed. 14.50x (ISBN 0-8422-0293-5). Irvington.

Selected Articles on Capital Punishment. Lamar T. Beman. LC 82-45654. (Capital Punishment Ser.). 1983. Repr. of 1925 ed. 42.50 (ISBN 0-404-62401-4). AMS Pr.

Selected Articles on Censorship of Speech & the Press. Ed. by Lamar T. Beman. LC 77-95404. (BCL Ser. I). 1969. Repr. of 1930 ed. 14.00 (ISBN 0-404-00747-3). AMS Pr.

Selected Articles on Censorship of Speech & the Press. Compiled by Lamar T. Beman. LC 76-98813. 1971. Repr. of 1930 ed. lib. bdg. 35.00x (ISBN 0-8371-3073-5, BECE). Greenwood.

Selected Articles on Censorship of the Theater & Moving Pictures. Ed. by Lamar T. Beman. LC 78-160229. (Moving Pictures Ser). 385p. 1971. Repr. of 1931 ed. lib. bdg. 22.95x (ISBN 0-89198-030-X). Ozer.

Selected Articles on Corporate Law. 1181p. 1977. 25.00 (ISBN 0-686-47850-9). Amer Bar Assn.

Selected Articles on Local Government Law. 394p. 1984. 10.00 (ISBN 0-318-02419-5). ICLE Georgia.

Selected Articles: 1981-82. Sam Marcy. 89p. 1982. pap. 2.50 (ISBN 0-89567-078-X). World View Forum.

Selected Aspects of Financial Management in Rehabilitation Facilities: A Resource Manual. Jerome R. Lorenz et al. (Illus.). 128p. (Orig.). 1981. pap. 21.50x (ISBN 0-916671-10-0). Material Dev.

Selected ASTM Standards for Agricultural Engineering Students. 264p. 1981. pap. 9.50 (ISBN 0-8031-0820-6, 03-000181-38). ASTM.

Selected ASTM Standards for Fence Materials & Products. 181p. 1984. 15.00 (ISBN 0-8031-0824-9, 03-601483-02). ASTM.

Selected ASTM Standards for the Purchasing Community. 796p. 1983. 50.00 (ISBN 0-8031-0836-2, 03-080083-47). ASTM.

Selected ASTM Standards on Packaging. American Society for Testing & Materials Staff. (Illus.). pap. 62.20 (ISBN 0-317-58777-3, 2029660). Bks Demand UMI.

Selected Attempts at Stereoscopic Moving Pictures & Their Relationship to the Motion Picture Technology, 1852-1903. H. Mark Gosser. 26.50 (ISBN 0-405-09890-1, 11485). Ayer Co Pubs.

Selected Austrian Short Stories. facsimile ed. Tr. by Marie Busch. LC 70-37260. (Short Story Index Reprint Ser). Repr. of 1928 ed. 18.00 (ISBN 0-8369-4071-7). Ayer Co Pubs.

Selected AV Recipes: Materials, Equipment Use & Maintenance. Donald E. Bumpass. 208p. 1981. pap. text ed. 16.95 (ISBN 0-8403-2518-5). Kendall-Hunt.

Selected Basic Agreements & Joint Declarations on Labour-Management Relations. Ed. by Efren Cordova. (Labour-Management Relations Ser.: No. 63). 299p. (Orig.). 1984. pap. 14.25 (ISBN 92-2-103460-7, ILO300, ILO). UNIPUB.

Selected Basic Agreements & Joint Declarations on Labour-Management Relations. (Labour-management Ser.: No. 63). 299p. 1983. pap. 17.50 (ISBN 92-2-103460-7). Intl Labour Office.

Selected Bible Readings. 1962. pap. 3.95 (ISBN 0-686-24354-4); spiral bdg. 4.95 (ISBN 0-686-24355-2); Fabrikoid 5.95 (ISBN 0-686-28567-0). Divine Sci Fed.

Selected Bibliographies of Hydrothermal & Magmatic Mineral Deposits. John D. Ridge. LC 59-1279. (Geological Society of America Memoir Ser.: No. 75). pap. 52.30 (ISBN 0-317-10309-1, 2004397). Bks Demand UMI.

Selected Bibliography: Color Scanners, Vol. 1. Ed. by Patrica Cost. LC 84-40400. 50p. 1984. pap. 15.00 (ISBN 0-89938-018-2). Tech & Ed Ctr Graph Arts RIT.

Selected Bibliography: Computer Graphics. Ed. by Patricia Cost. 1984. pap. 30.00 (ISBN 0-89938-021-2). Tech & Ed Ctr Graph Arts RIT.

Selected Bibliography: Energy Conservation in the Graphic Arts, Vol. 1. Ed. by Patricia Knittel. 41p. (Orig.). 1981. pap. 20.00 (ISBN 0-89938-006-9). Tech & Ed Ctr Graph Arts RIT.

Selected Bibliography: Flexography. Christopher Losee. 1985. pap. 22.00 (ISBN 0-317-27406-6). Tech & Ed Ctr Graph Arts RIT.

Selected Bibliography for Chicano Studies. Juan Gomez-Quinones & Albert Camarillo. (Bibliographic & Reference Ser: No. 3). 1977. pap. 2.50 (ISBN 0-89551-009-X). UCLA Chicano Stud.

Selected Bibliography for Washington & Descriptions of Major Local Collections. Fisher & Lear. 6.00 (ISBN 0-318-21777-5). G Washington Univ.

Selected Bibliography: Gravure, Vol. 1. Ed. by Patricia Knittel. 47p. (Orig.). 1983. pap. 15.00 (ISBN 0-89938-015-8). Tech & Ed Ctr Graph Arts RIT.

Selected Bibliography: Ink Jet Printing, Vol. 1. Ed. by Patricia Knittel & Lily Shung. 17p. 1981. 15.00. Tech & Ed Ctr Graph Arts RIT.

Selected Bibliography: Laser Applications in the Grapic Arts, Vol. 2. 46p. 1981. pap. 20.00 (ISBN 0-317-14990-3). Tech & Ed Ctr Graph Arts RIT.

Selected Bibliography: Materials Handling. Ed. by Patricia Cost. 1984. pap. 22.00 (ISBN 0-89938-020-4). Tech & Ed Ctr Graph Arts RIT.

Selected Bibliography of Applied Ethics in the Professions, 1950-1970: A Working Sourcebook. Daniel L. Gothie. LC 73-80627. 176p. 1973. 14.95x (ISBN 0-8139-0412-9). U Pr of Va.

Selected Bibliography of Books & Articles on Censorship (1950-1983) Compiled by Denise Rogers. LC 83-204879. (Washington University Law Library Bibliography Ser.: No. 4). vi, 22p. (Orig.). 1983. pap. text ed. 8.00. Wash U Law Lib.

Selected Bibliography of Books, Reports & Articles on Crime & the Criminal Justice System in Chicago & Cook County. 2nd ed. Ed. by Gad J. Bensinger. 101p. 1984. 5.00 (ISBN 0-942854-04-7). Loyola U Crim.

Selected Bibliography of Minnesota Government, Politics, & Public Finance Since 1900. G. Theodore Mitau. (Studies in Minn. Govt. & Politics). 94p. 1960. pap. 2.50 (ISBN 0-685-47099-7). Minn Hist.

Selected Bibliography of Missouri Archaeology. Randy L. Cottier et al. Ed. by W. Raymond Wood. LC 72-619659. (Research Ser.: No. 10). (Illus.). 34p. (Orig.). 1973. pap. 2.00 (ISBN 0-943414-11-3). MO Arch Soc.

Selected Bibliography of Monographs & Some Serials on Child Abuse & Neglect Held at the Main Library of the University of Saskatchewan. Edward Stanek. (Public Administration Ser.: P 2161). 8p. 1987. 3.00. Vance Biblios.

Selected Bibliography of Music Librarianship. Don Phillips. (Illinois University Graduate School of Library Science Occassional Papers: No.113). pap. 20.00 (ISBN 0-317-10108-0, 2007257). Bks Demand UMI.

Selected Bibliography of Natal Maps. C. E. Merrett. 1979. lib. bdg. 53.00 (Hall Reference). G K Hall:

Selected Bibliography of Pediatric Orthopaedics. 2nd ed. Ed. by Brian L. Hotchkiss. 170p. 1985. 15.00 (ISBN 0-89203-008-9, 4000020). Amer Acad Ortho Surg.

Selected Bibliography of Significant Works about Adam Smith. Martha B. Lightwood. LC 84-3718. 144p. 1984. 29.95 (ISBN 0-8122-7930-1). U of Pa Pr.

Selected Bibliography of Slavic Linguistics, 2 Vols. Ed. by Edward Stankiewicz & Dean S. Worth. (Slavistic Printings & Reprintings Ser: No. 2). 1966. Vol. 1. text ed. 32.80x (ISBN 0-686-22457-4); Vol. 2. text ed. 60.80x (ISBN 0-686-22458-2). Mouton.

Selected Bibliography of Utah Archaeology. Alan R. Schroedl. (University of Utah Anthropological Papers: No. 102). (Orig.). 1979. pap. text ed. 5.00x (ISBN 0-87480-141-9). U of Utah Pr.

Selected Bibliography on Detection of Dependence-Producing Drugs in Body Fluids. T. L. Chruscie & M. Chrusciel. (Offset Pub.: No. 17). (Also avail. in France). 1975. pap. 6.00 (ISBN 92-4-052004-X). World Health.

Selected Bibliography on East-West Trade & Investment. Julian D. Lew et al. LC 76-3482. 100p. 1976. lib. bdg. 20.00 (ISBN 0-379-00495-X). Oceana.

Selected Bibliography on Employee Attitude Surveys. Margaret C. Blasingame. (Special Report Ser.: No. 2). 42p. 1983. pap. 15.00 (ISBN 0-912879-51-3). Ctr Creat Leader.

Selected Bibliography on Legal & Related Matters Affecting Business in Latin America. Ed. by Raoul Gordon. 1976. lib. bdg. 59.95 (ISBN 0-8490-2587-7). Gordon Pr.

Selected Bibliography on Major African Reservoirs. (Commission for Inland Fisheries of Africa (CIFA): Technical Papers: No. 10). 58p. (Eng. & Fr.). 1984. pap. 7.50 (ISBN 92-5-001349-3, F2482, FAO). UNIPUB.

Selected Bibliography on Social Control Approaches to Community Crime Prevention. Richard C. Rich. (Public Administration Ser.: P 1846). 15p. 1986. 3.75 (ISBN 0-89028-716-3). Vance Biblios.

Selected Bibliography on Studies & Research Relevant to Pollution in the Mediterranean. D. Calimari. (Fisheries Technical Papers: No. 165). 100p. (Eng. & Fr.). 1977. pap. 7.50 (ISBN 92-5-000253-X, F897, FAO). UNIPUB.

Selected Bibliography on the American Jail with Special Emphasis on Illinois Jails, No. 821. Hans W. Mattick. 1975. 8.50 (ISBN 0-686-20357-7). CPL Biblios.

Selected Bibliography on the Asians in America. James I. Wong. LC 81-70526. 140p. 1981. perfect bound 12.95 (ISBN 0-88247-605-X). R & E Pubs.

Selected Bibliography on the Economic Geography of Canada: Agriculture, Land Use, Resources, Energy, Development, Recreation & Tourism. Thomas A. Rumney. (Public Administration Ser.: P 1761). 25p. 1985. 3.75 (ISBN 0-89028-561-6). Vance Biblios.

Selected Bibliography on the Economic Geography of Canada: Industry, Transportation, Urban, & Tertiary Systems. Thomas A. Rumney. (Public Administration Ser.: P 1762). 25p. 1985. 3.75 (ISBN 0-89028-562-4). Vance Biblios.

Selected Bibliography on the Geography of Brazil. Thomas Rumney. (Public Administration Ser.: P 2096). 48p. 1987. 12.50 (ISBN 1-55590-176-X). Vance Biblios.

Selected Bibliography on Work Time Options. 1985. 4.50 ea. (ISBN 0-940173-00-X). New Ways Work.

Selected Bibliography: Packaging & Package Printing. 23p. 1975. pap. 10.00 (ISBN 0-317-14986-5). Tech & Ed Ctr Graph Arts RIT.

Selected Bibliography: Paper Conservation, Vol. 1. Ed. by Patricia Knittel. 20p. (Orig.). 1983. pap. 15.00 (ISBN 0-89938-011-5). Tech & Ed Ctr Graph Arts RIT.

Selected Bibliography: Photographic Conservation, Vol. 1. Ed. by Thomas W. Orth. 8p. 1979. pap. 10.00 (ISBN 0-317-14995-4). Tech & Ed Ctr Graph Arts RIT.

Selected Bibliography: Photographic Processes in Use Before 1880. Ed. by Susan M. Barger. LC 84-84390. 149p. 1980. pap. 37.50 (ISBN 0-89938-003-4). Tech & Ed Ctr Graph Arts RIT.

Selected Bibliography: Printing Inks, Vol. I. Ed. by Patricia Knittel. (Orig.). 1982. pap. 15.00 (ISBN 0-89938-010-7). Tech & Ed Ctr Graph Arts RIT.

Selected Bibliography: Printing Inks, Vol.2. Ed. by Patricia Cost. 1984. pap. 22.00 (ISBN 0-89938-019-0). Tech & Ed Ctr Graph Arts RIT.

Selected Bibliography: Quality Control, Vol. II. Ed. by Patricia Knittel. 85p. (Orig.). 1982. pap. 15.00 (ISBN 0-89938-007-7). Tech & Ed Ctr Graph Arts RIT.

Selected Bibliography: Quality Control, Vol. 1. Ed. by James E. Sutherland. 37p. 1982. pap. 10.00 (ISBN 0-317-14984-9). Tech & Ed Ctr Graph Arts RIT.

Selected Bibliography: Robotics, Vol. I. Patricia Knittel. 14p. 1983. pap. 15.00 (ISBN 0-89938-012-3). Tech & Ed Ctr Graph Arts RIT.

Selected Bibliography: Screen Printing, Vol II. Christopher Losee. 1985. pap. 22.00 (ISBN 0-89938-023-9). Tech & Ed Ctr Graph Arts RIT.

Selected Bibliography: Screen Printing, Vol. 1. 37p. 1976. pap. 10.00 (ISBN 0-317-14992-X). Tech & Ed Ctr Graph Arts RIT.

Selected Bibliography: Universal Product Code, Vol. I. Ed. by Patricia Knittel. 30p. 1983. pap. 15.00 (ISBN 0-89938-017-4). Tech & Ed Ctr Graph Arts RIT.

Selected Bibliography: Videotex, Vol. I. Ed. by Patricia Knittel. 1983. pap. 15.00 (ISBN 0-89938-016-6). Tech & Ed Ctr Graph Arts RIT.

Selected Bird & Flower Paintings from the Palace Museum. (Illus.). 200p. 1981. 450.00 (ISBN 0-8351-1141-5). China Bks.

Selected Black American, African & Caribbean Authors: A Bio-Bibliography. Ed. by James A. Page & Jae M. Roh. LC 85-5225. 402p. 1985. lib. bdg. 55.00 (ISBN 0-87287-430-3). Libs Unl.

Selected Books for Social Workers. rev. ed. 1982. pap. 6.00 (ISBN 0-942644-10-7). Univ Bk Serv.

Selected Bronte Poems. Ed. by Edward Chitham & Tom Winnifrith. 262p. 1986. 34.95x (ISBN 0-631-14564-8); pap. 12.95 (ISBN 0-631-14565-6). Basil Blackwell.

Selected Byzantine Hymns. 2nd ed. Holy Transfiguration Monastery Staff. 120p. (Orig.). 1987. pap. 10.00x (ISBN 0-913026-59-X, Holy Transfiguration). St Nectarios.

Selected Cantos. Ezra Pound. LC 75-11446. 1970. pap. text ed. 5.95 (ISBN 0-8112-0160-0, NDP304). New Directions.

Selected Cases in Fashion Marketing, 2 vols. 3rd ed. Nathan Axelrod. 1968. pap. 13.50 ea.; Vol. 2. pap. 16.33 scp (ISBN 0-672-96038-9). Bobbs.

Selected Cases in Labor Relations: An Experiential Approach. Finston & Porter. 1983. pap. text ed. write for info. (ISBN 0-8359-6981-9, Reston); instr's. manual avail. (ISBN 0-8359-6982-7). P-H.

Selected Catalogue of the Museum Yamato Bunkakan. Yamato Bunkakan. pap. 40.00x (ISBN 0-317-69031-0, Pub. by Han-Shan Tang Ltd). State Mutual Bk.

Selected Catalogue of the Museum Yamato Bunkakan. Yamato Bunkakan. 1964. pap. 100.00x (Pub. by Han-Shan Tang Ltd). State Mutual Bk.

Selected Chapters from the Autobiography of Andrew D. White. Andrew D. White. 253p. (Orig.). pap. 6.50x (ISBN 0-8014-9841-4). Cornell U Pr.

Selected Chapters from the Writings of the Maya Indians. Ed. by Yuri V. Knorozov & Tatiana Proskouriakoff. Tr. by Sophie Coe. LC 70-38502. (Harvard University. Peabody Museum of Archaeology & Ethnology. Russian Translation Ser.: No. 4). Repr. of 1967 ed. 28.00 (ISBN 0-404-52647-0). AMS Pr.

Selected Characteristics of Occupations Defined in the Dictionary of Occupational Titles. 489p. 1981. pap. 11.50 (ISBN 0-318-22431-3, S/N 029-014-00202-0). USGPO.

Selected Chinese Texts in the Classical & Colloquial Styles. Ed. by Lien-Sheng Yang. LC 53-5949. (Harvard-Yenching Institute Publications Ser). 1953. pap. 6.95x (ISBN 0-674-79710-8). Harvard U Pr.

Selected Climatic Data for a Global Set of Standard Stations for Vegetation Science. Manfred J. Muller. 1982. 87.00 (ISBN 90-6193-945-3, Pub. by Junk Pubs. Netherlands). Kluwer Academic.

Selected Comedies: Elizabeth Inchbald. Intro. by Roger Manvell. (Illus.). 372p. (Orig.). 1988. lib. bdg. 24.75 (ISBN 0-8191-6635-9). U Pr of Amer.

Selected Commercial Statutes: 1987. 1987. pap. write for info. West Pub.

Selected Computer Programs in Fortran for Fish Stock Assessment. (FAO Fisheries Technical Paper Ser.: No. 259). 183p. 1986. pap. text ed. 10.00 (ISBN 92-5-102272-0, F2812, FAO). UNIPUB.

Selected Concepts from Educational Psychology & Adult Education for Extension & Continuing Educators. J. P. Leagans et al. LC 74-171881. (Notes & Essays Series, No. 71). 1971. pap. text ed. 3.50 (ISBN 0-87060-046-X, NES 71). Syracuse U Cont Ed.

Selected Concrete Poems. Michael J. Phillips. (Cambric Poetry Ser.). 108p. (Orig.). 1986. pap. 11.95 (ISBN 0-918342-25-2). Cambric.

Selected Conjurations from the Lemegeton (& Other Sources) large type ed. Nelson White & Anne White. LC 81-51403. 50p. (Orig.). 1981. pap. 13.00 (ISBN 0-939856-16-6). Tech Group.

Selected Contributions of Ukrainian Scholars to Economics. Ed. by I. S. Koropeckyj. LC 84-80076. (Sources & Documents Ser.). 244p. 1984. text ed. 20.95x (ISBN 0-916458-10-5). Harvard Ukrainian.

Selected Coolwater Fishes of North America. Ed. by R. L. Kendall. (AFS Special Publications: No. 11). 437p. 1978. text ed. 18.00 (ISBN 0-913235-08-3). Am Fisheries Soc.

Selected Corporation & Partnership Statutes, Rules & Forms: 1987. 1987. pap. write for info. West Pub.

Selected Correspondance of Kenneth Burke & Malcolm Cowley. Ed. by Paul Jay. 1988. 24.95 (ISBN 0-670-81336-2). Viking.

Selected Correspondence. Karl Marx & Friedrich Engels. 552p. 1975. 4.45 (ISBN 0-8285-0048-7, Pub. by Progress Pubs USSR). Imported Pubns.

Selected Correspondence: Eighteen Forty-Six to Eighteen Ninety-Five. Karl Marx & Frederick Engels. LC 75-25261. 551p. 1975. Repr. of 1942 ed. lib. bdg. 35.00x (ISBN 0-8371-8385-5, MAKMF). Greenwood.

Selected Correspondence of Dr. Karl A. Menninger, 1919-1945. Howard J. Faulkner & Virginia D. Pruitt. LC 88-5502. 1989. text ed. 40.00t (ISBN 0-300-03978-6). Yale U Pr.

Selected Correspondence of Fryderyk Chopin. Ed. by Arthur Hedley. LC 79-17655. (Music Reprint Ser.). 1980. Repr. of 1963 ed. 45.00 (ISBN 0-306-79579-5). Da Capo.

Selected County Government Bibliography with Annotations, Nos. 1233- 1234. Cortus T. Koehler. 1977. 9.00 (ISBN 0-686-19691-0). CPL Biblios.

Selected Critical Studies of Baudelaire. Charles P. Baudelaire. Ed. by D. Parmee. LC 76-29452. Repr. of 1949 ed. 21.00 (ISBN 0-404-15300-3). AMS Pr.

Selected Critical Writings of George Santayana, Vol. 1. George Santayana. Ed. by Norman Henfrey. LC 68-21394. pap. 87.00 (ISBN 0-317-28141-0, 2022470). Bks Demand UMI.

Selected Critical Writings of George Santayana, Vol. 2. George Santayana. Ed. by Norman Henfrey. LC 68-21394. pap. 64.30 (ISBN 0-317-26410-9, 2024466). Bks Demand UMI.

Selected Criticism. Nicolas Boileau-Despreaux. Tr. by Ernest Dilworth from Fr. LC 65-26530. 1965. pap. text ed. 8.95x (ISBN 0-672-60471-X). Irvington.

Selected Criticism. John Dryden. Ed. by James Kinsley & G. A. Parfitt. (Orig.). 1970. pap. text ed. 8.95x (ISBN 0-19-871051-8). Oxford U Pr.

Selected Film Criticism: Nineteen Thirty-One to Nineteen Hundred Forty. Ed. by Anthony Slide. LC 82-10642. 292p. 1982. 20.00 (ISBN 0-8108-1570-2). Scarecrow.

Selected Film Criticism: Nineteen Twenty-One to Nineteen Hundred Thirty. Ed. by Anthony Slide. LC 81-23344. 335p. 1982. 22.00 (ISBN 0-8108-1551-6). Scarecrow.

Selected Film Criticism: Nineteen Twelve to Nineteen Hundred Twenty, Vol. 2. Ed. by Anthony Slide. LC 81-23344. 325p. 1982. 22.00 (ISBN 0-8108-1525-7). Scarecrow.

Selected Film Criticism, 1951-1960, Vol. 7. Ed. by Anthony Slide. LC 81-23344. 198p. 1985. 16.50 (ISBN 0-8108-1763-2). Scarecrow.

Selected Flowers of Evil. rev. ed. Charles Baudelaire. Ed. by Marthiel Mathews & Jackson Mathews. LC 58-9276. (Eng & Fr). 1946. pap. 5.95 (ISBN 0-8112-0006-X, NDP71). New Directions.

Selected for Persecution. 2nd, rev. ed. Gene W. King. Tr. by Haydee Sieger from Eng. 82p. (Orig., Span. & Fr.). 1982. pap. 5.95 (ISBN 0-9616448-0-X). Vetco Printing.

Selected from Bless Me, Ultima. abr. ed. Literacy Volunteers of New York City Staff & Rudolfo A. Anaya. (Writers' Voices Ser.). (Illus.). 64p. (Orig.). 1988. pap. text ed. 2.95 (ISBN 0-929631-06-4). Lit Vols NYC.

Selected from Fatherhood & Time Flies. Bill Cosby. Suppl. by Literacy Volunteers of New York City Staff. (Writers' Voices Ser.). (Illus.). 64p. (Orig.). 1988. pap. text ed. 2.95 (ISBN 0-929631-00-5). Lit Vols NYC.

Selected from I Know Why the Caged Bird Sings & The Heart of a Woman. Maya Angelou. Suppl. by Literacy Volunteers of New York City Staff. (Writers' Voices Ser.). (Illus.). 64p. 1988. pap. text ed. 2.95 (ISBN 0-929631-04-8). Lit Vols NYC.

Selected from Kramer vs. Kramer. abr. ed. Avery Corman. Suppl. by Literacy Volunteers of New York City Staff. (Writers' Voices Ser.). (Illus.). 64p. 1988. pap. text ed. 2.95 (ISBN 0-929631-01-3). Lit Vols NYC.

Selected from Love Medicine. abr. ed. Louise Erdrich. Suppl. by Literacy Volunteers of New York City Staff. (Writers' Voices Ser.). (Illus.). 64p. 1988. pap. text ed. 2.95 (ISBN 0-929631-02-1). Lit Vols NYC.

Selected from One More Time: A Memoir. abr. ed. Carol Burnett. Suppl. by Literacy Volunteers of New York City Staff. (Writers' Voices Ser.). (Illus.). 64p. 1988. pap. text ed. 2.95 (ISBN 0-929631-03-X). Lit Vols NYC.

Selected Games. V. V. Smyslov. LC 81-23466. (Russian Chess Ser.). 250p. 1983. 27.95 (ISBN 0-08-026912-5). Pergamon.

Selected Games Nineteen Sixty-Seven to Nineteen Seventy. M. M. Botvinnik. Tr. by K. P. Neat. (Pergamon Russian Chess Ser.). (Illus.). 318p. 1981. 32.00 (ISBN 0-08-024124-7); pap. 17.95 (ISBN 0-08-024123-9). Pergamon.

Selected Garlands. Philipa Jones. 160p. 1986. pap. 30.00x (ISBN 0-947939-02-4, Pub. by Elmcrest UK). State Mutual Bk.

Selected Garlands. Phillipa Jones. 160p. 1987. pap. 30.00x (ISBN 0-317-62100-9, Michael Gardener Pubs). State Mutual Bk.

Selected Gastrointestinal Disorders: Intractibility & Its Management. Ward O. Griffen, Jr. (Illus.). 280p. 1986. 58.50 (ISBN 0-683-03736-6). Williams & Wilkins.

Selected Genetic Markers of Blood & Secretions for Youth 12-17 Years of Age, United States. Bernice H. Cohen et al. (Ser. 11: No. 168). 1979. pap. text ed. 1.75 (ISBN 0-8406-0171-9). Natl Ctr Health Stats.

Selected Groups of Bones from Skeldergate & Walmgate. T. P. O'Connor. (Archaeology of York - The Animal Bones). 60p. 1984. pap. text ed. 12.50x (ISBN 0-906780-39-X, Pub. by Council British Archaeology). Humanities.

Selected Guide to Make-It, Fix-It, Do-It-Yourself Books. Ed. by Susan Nueckel. LC 72-82609. (Selected Guide Ser.). 300p. 1973. 14.50 (ISBN 0-8303-0125-9); pap. 7.50 (ISBN 0-8303-0123-2). Fleet.

Selected Guide to Periodical Literature on Coalitions: 1974-1984. Joseph C. Santora. (Public Administration Ser.: P 1851). 10p. 1986. 3.00 (ISBN 0-89028-721-X). Vance Biblios.

Selected Guide to Sports & Recreation Books. Ed. by Susan Nueckel. LC 73-3735. (Selected Guides Ser). 213p. 1974. 10.50 (ISBN 0-8303-0128-3); pap. 7.50 (ISBN 0-8303-0127-5). Fleet.

Selected Guide to Travel Books. Ed. by Susan Nueckel. LC 73-92718. (Selected Guide Ser). 200p. 1974. 10.50 (ISBN 0-8303-0131-3); pap. 7.50 (ISBN 0-8303-0132-1). Fleet.

Selected Health Characteristics by Occupation: United States, 1975-1976. Charles S. Wilder. Ed. by Klaudia Cox. (Ser. 10: No. 133). 1979. pap. text ed. 1.75 (ISBN 0-8406-0174-3). Natl Ctr Health Stats.

Selected Historical Essays of F. W. Maitland. F. W. Maitland, pseud. LC 85-12552. xxx, 278p. 1985. Repr. of 1957 ed. lib. bdg. 52.50x (ISBN 0-313-24954-7, MSHE). Greenwood.

Selected Imaginary Conversations of Literary Men & Statesmen. Walter S. Landor. Ed. by Charles L. Proudfit. LC 69-10272. xxx, 270p. 1969. 24.95x (ISBN 0-8032-0097-8). U of Nebr Pr.

Selected Indices of Industrial Characteristics for U. S. SMSA. Robert C. Douglas. (Discussion Paper Ser.: No. 20). 1967. pap. 6.50 (ISBN 0-686-32189-8). Regional Sci Res Inst.

Selected Issues in American Education. Samuel E. Beckles. LC 85-90190. 1986. 10.00 (ISBN 0-533-06690-5). Vantage.

Selected Issues in Logic & Communication. Ed. by Trudy Govier. 207p. 1988. pap. text ed. write for info. (ISBN 0-534-08694-2). Wadsworth Pub.

Selected Issues in Mathematics Education. Ed. by Mary M. Lindquist. LC 80-82903. (National Society for the Education Series on Contemporary Education Issues). 250p. 1981. 21.50x (ISBN 0-8211-1114-0); text ed. 20.50x 10 or more copies. McCutchan.

Selected Journals of Henry David Thoreau. Henry David Thoreau. Ed. by Carl Bode. (Illus., Orig.). 1967. pap. 3.95 (ISBN 0-452-00749-6, Mer). NAL.

Selected Journals of L. M. Montgomery, Vol. 2: 1910-1921. Ed. by Mary Rubio & Elizabeth Waterston. 464p. 1988. 27.95 (ISBN 0-19-540586-2). Oxford U Pr.

Selected Journals of L. M. Montgomery, Vol. 1: 1889-1910. Ed. by Lucy M. Montgomery et al. (Illus.). 424p. 1986. 24.95 (ISBN 0-19-540503-X). Oxford U Pr.

Selected Judgments of the Supreme Court of Israel: Special Volume. Asher F. Landau. 191p. 1971. 34.95x (ISBN 0-87855-175-1). Transaction Bks.

Selected Judgments of the Supreme Court of Israel, 4 vols. Israel - State of - Ministry of Justice. 1976. 30.00 ea.; Vol. 1 o.p. 120.00 (ISBN 0-379-13901-4). Vol. 2 o.p (ISBN 0-379-13902-2). Vol. 3 (ISBN 0-379-13903-0). Vol. 4 (ISBN 0-379-13905-7). Oceana.

Selected Kentucky Literature. Ed. by Joy Pennington. 272p. 1980. text ed. 15.00 (ISBN 0-89097-019-X); pap. text ed. 8.95 (ISBN 0-89097-020-3). Archer Edns.

Selected Later Poems of Marie Luise Kaschnitz. Mary L. Kaschnitz. Tr. by Lisel Mueller from Ger. LC 80-7537. (Lockert Library of Poetry Translation). 128p. 1980. 18.00x (ISBN 0-691-06442-3); pap. 8.50 (ISBN 0-691-01374-8). Princeton U Pr.

Selected Latin American One-Act Plays. Tr. by Francesca Colecchia & Julio Matas. LC 72-92696. (Pitt Latin American Ser.). 1974. pap. 10.95x (ISBN 0-8229-5241-6). U of Pittsburgh Pr.

Selected Legal Documents of the People's Republic of China: Volume II. Ed. by Joseph E. Wang. LC 76-5167. (Studies in Chinese Government & Law). 564p. 1979. 32.50 (ISBN 0-89093-241-7). U Pubns Amer.

Selected Legal Papers, 3 vols. 25.00 ea. Vol. 1, No.1 (P-3). Vol. 1, No. 2 (P-4). Vol. 2, No. 1 (P-5). Vol. 2, No. 2 (P-6). Vol. 3, No.1 (P-7). Am IPLA.

Selected Letters. Stephen V Benet. Ed. by Charles A. Fenton. LC 78-52735. (BCL Ser.: Vol. I & II). Repr. of 1960 ed. AMS Pr.

Selected Letters. Witter Bynner. Ed. by James Kraft. 328p. 1981. 30.00 (ISBN 0-374-18504-2). FS&G.

Selected Letters. Cicero. Tr. by D. R. Shackleton-Bailey. (Classics Ser.). 208p. 1986. pap. 5.95 (ISBN 0-14-044458-0). Penguin.

Selected Letters. John Clare. Ed. by Mark Storey. 340p. 1988. 44.00 (ISBN 0-19-818585-5). Oxford U Pr.

Selected Letters. Marquis De Sade. 188p. 1965. 19.95 (ISBN 0-8464-0833-3). Beekman Pubs.

Selected Letters. facsimile ed. Gustave Flaubert. Tr. by Francis Steegmuller. LC 78-160919. (Biography Index Reprint Ser.). Repr. of 1953 ed. 17.50 (ISBN 0-8369-8082-4). Ayer Co Pubs.

Selected Letters. Federico Garcia Lorca. Tr. by David Gershator from Span. LC 83-4006. 172p. (Orig.). 1984. 15.00 (ISBN 0-8112-0872-9); pap. 6.95 (ISBN 0-8112-0873-7, NDP557). New Directions.

Selected Letters. D. H. Lawrence. 1978. pap. 5.95 (ISBN 0-14-000759-8). Penguin.

Selected Letters. Thomas E. Lawrence. Ed. by David Garnett. LC 78-20478. 1980. Repr. of 1952 ed. 29.00 (ISBN 0-88355-856-4). Hyperion Conn.

Selected Letters. Edward Lear. Ed. by Vivien Noakes. (Illus.). 368p. 1988. 29.95 (ISBN 0-19-818601-0). Oxford U Pr.

Selected Letters. St. Leo The Great. LC 63-18826. (Fathers of the Church Ser: Vol. 34). 312p. 1957. 15.95x (ISBN 0-8132-0034-2). Cath U Pr.

Selected Letters. Friedrich Nietzche. Ed. by Oscar Levy. Tr. by A. N. Ludovici from Ger. 364p. 1985. pap. 15.95 (ISBN 0-948166-01-0, Pub. by Soho Bk Co UK). Dufour.

Selected Letters. Dylan Thomas. Ed. by Constantine FitzGibbon. LC 67-14560. 1967. 10.00 (ISBN 0-8112-0399-9). New Directions.

Selected Letters. C. F. Walther. Tr. by Roy A. Sueflow. (Selected Writings of C. F. W. Walther Ser.). 1981. 12.95 (ISBN 0-570-08279-X, 15-2737). Concordia.

Selected Letters, Vol. 4. H. P. Lovecraft. Ed. by August Derleth & James Turner. (Illus.). 424p. 1976. 12.50 (ISBN 0-87054-035-1). Arkham.

Selected Letters, Vol. 5. H. P. Lovecraft. Ed. by August Derleth & James Turner. (Illus.). 400p. 1976. 12.50 (ISBN 0-87054-036-X). Arkham.

Selected Letters & Journals. Fanny Burney. Ed. by Joyce Hemlow. 410p. 1987. 11.95 (ISBN 0-19-281433-8). Oxford U Pr.

Selected Letters & Journals of George Crabbe. George Crabbe. Ed. by Thomas C. Faulkner & Rhonda L. Blair. (Illus.). 1985. 74.00x (ISBN 0-19-812570-4). Oxford U Pr.

Selected Letters, Eighteen Eighty to Nineteen Hundred Three. Marcel Proust. Ed. by Philip Kolb. Tr. by Ralph Manheim. Intro. by Cocking J. M. (Illus.). xxviii, 376p. 1988. pap. 16.95 (ISBN 0-226-68459-8). U of Chicago Pr.

Selected Letters Nineteen Twenty-four to Nineteen Fifty. Cesare Pavese. Tr. by A. E. Murch from Ital. 19.95 (ISBN 0-7206-1520-8). Dufour.

Selected Letters of Albert Jay Nock. Albert J. Nock. 1986. lib. bdg. 79.95 (ISBN 0-8490-3848-0). Gordon Pr.

Selected Letters of Albert Jay Nock. Frances J. Nock. 201p. Date not set. 10.00 (ISBN 0-317-53210-3). Noontide.

Selected Letters of Anton Chekhov. Anton Chekhov. Ed. by Lillian Hellman. Tr. by Sidonie K. Lederer from Rus. 366p. 1955. 16.95 (ISBN 0-374-25800-7); pap. 7.95, 1984 (ISBN 0-374-51838-6). FS&G.

Selected Letters of Byron. Ed. by V. H. Collins. 1928. 17.50 (ISBN 0-8274-3350-6). R West.

Selected Letters of C. G. Jung, 1909-1961. Ed. by Gerhard Adler & Aniela Jaffe. 256p. 1984. 25.00x (ISBN 0-691-09955-3); pap. 9.95 (ISBN 0-691-01860-X). Princeton U Pr.

Selected Letters of Charles Baudelaire: The Conquest of Solitude. Charles Baudelaire. Ed. & tr. by Rosemary Lloyd. LC 85-16461. xxxii, 268p. 1986. lib. bdg. 24.95x (ISBN 0-226-03928-5). U of Chicago pr.

Selected Letters of Charles Dickens. David Paroissien. LC 84-19270. (Critical Editions Program Ser.). 1985. lib. bdg. 39.00 (ISBN 0-8057-8536-1, Twayne); pap. 12.95 o.s.i (ISBN 0-8057-8537-X). G K Hall.

Selected Letters of Conrad Aiken. Aiken. Ed. by Joseph R. Killorin. LC 77-20620. (Illus.). 1978. 32.00x (ISBN 0-300-02180-1). Yale U Pr.

Selected Letters of Cotton Mather. Cotton Mather. Ed. by Kenneth Silverman. LC 78-142338. pap. 118.00 (ISBN 0-317-29860-7, 2019565). Bks Demand UMI.

Selected Letters of E. M. Forster: Vol. II, 1921-1970. E. M. Forster. Ed. by Mary Lago & P. N. Furbank. (Illus.). 352p. 1984. 20.00 (ISBN 0-674-79827-9, Belknap). Harvard U Pr.

Selected Letters of E. M. Forster: Vol. 1, 1879-1920. E. M. Forster. Ed. by Mary Lago & P. N. Furbank. LC 83-4376. (Illus.). 352p. 1983. 22.95 (ISBN 0-674-79825-2, Belknap). Harvard U Pr.

Selected Letters of Edmund Burke. Edmund Burke. Ed. by Harvey C. Mansfield, Jr. LC 83-18138. 1984. lib. bdg. 32.50x (ISBN 0-226-08068-4). U of Chicago Pr.

Selected Letters of Edmund Burke. Ed. by Edmund Burke & Harvey C. Mansfield, Jr. 32.50x. U of Chicago Pr.

Selected Letters of Edwin Arlington Robinson. Edwin A. Robinson. LC 79-15514. (Illus.). 1980. Repr. of 1940 ed. lib. bdg. 35.00x (ISBN 0-313-21266-X, ROSL). Greenwood.

Selected Letters of E.T.A. Hoffman. E. T. A. Hoffman. Tr. by Johanna C. Sahlin from Ger. LC 76-8096. 1978. Repr. of 1967 ed. lib. bdg. 23.50x (ISBN 0-226-34790-7). U of Chicago Pr.

Selected Letters of Eugene O'Neill. Travis Bogard & Jackson Bryer. 1988. 35.00 (ISBN 0-300-04374-0). Yale U Pr.

Selected Letters of Ezra Pound & Louis Zukofsky. Ezra Pound & Louis Zukofsky. Intro. by Barry Ahearn. LC 86-19181. (Correspondence of Ezra Pound Ser.). 384p. 1987. 38.50 (ISBN 0-8112-1013-8). New Directions.

Selected Letters of Ezra Pound, 1907-1941. Ezra Pound. Ed. by D. D. Paige. LC 71-145933. 1971. pap. 6.95 (ISBN 0-8112-0161-9, NDP317). New Directions.

Selected Letters of Fyodor Dostoyevsky. Ed. by Joseph Frank & David I. Goldstein. 533p. 1987. 29.95 (ISBN 0-8135-1185-2). Rutgers U Pr.

Selected Letters of Gustav Mahler. Ed. by Knud Martner & Alma Mahler. Tr. by Eithne Wilkins et al from Ger. (Illus.). 480p. 1979. 30.00 (ISBN 0-374-25846-5). FS&G.

Selected Letters of Henry James. Leon Edel. 17.95 (ISBN 0-89190-316-X, Pub. by Am Repr). Amereon Ltd.

Selected Letters of Henry James to Edmund Gosse, 1882-1915: A Literary Friendship. Ed. by Rayburn S. Moore. (Illus.). 360p. 1988. text ed. 35.00 (ISBN 0-8071-1439-1). La State U Pr.

Selected Letters of Horace Walpole. Horace Walpole. Ed. by W. S. Lewis. LC 72-91300. pap. 86.00 (ISBN 0-317-29273-0, 2022013). Bks Demand UMI.

Selected Letters of Ivan Turgenev, 2 vols. Ivan S. Turgenev. Ed. & tr. by David Lowe. 1983. 50.00 set (ISBN 0-686-75359-3). Vol. 1, 276p (ISBN 0-88233-735-1). Vol. 2, 234p (ISBN 0-88233-736-X). Ardis Pubs.

Selected Letters of James Joyce. James Joyce. LC 71-83240. 440p. 1975. 25.00 (ISBN 0-670-63190-6). Viking.

Selected Letters of James Thurber. James Thurber. Ed. by Helen Thurber & Edward Weeks. 1982. pap. 7.95 (ISBN 0-14-006353-6). Penguin.

Selected Letters of John Crowe Ransom. John Crowe Ransom. Ed. by Thomas D. Young & George Core. LC 84-10006. (Southern Literary Studies). 430p. 1985. text ed. 35.00 (ISBN 0-8071-1168-6). La State U Pr.

Selected Letters of John O'Hara. John O'Hara. Ed. by Matthew J. Bruccoli. 1978. 17.95 (ISBN 0-394-42133-7). Random.

Selected Letters of Lady Mary Wortley Montagu. Lady Mary W. Montagu. Ed. by Robert Halsband. 1986. pap. 6.95 (ISBN 0-14-057026-8). Penguin.

Selected Letters of Lidian Jackson Emerson. Delores B. Carpenter. LC 86-16102. 384p. 1987. text ed. 42.00 (ISBN 0-8262-0610-7, 83-36240). U of Mo Pr.

Selected Letters of Louisa May Alcott. Louisa May Alcott. Ed. by Joel Myerson et al. 1987. 24.95 (ISBN 0-316-59361-3). Little.

Selected Letters of Marjorie Kinnan Rawlings. Ed. by Gordon E. Bigelow & Laura V. Monti. LC 82-2674. (Illus.). vi, 414p. 1983. 30.00 (ISBN 0-8130-0728-3); pap. 15.00 (ISBN 0-8130-0899-9). U Presses Fla.

Selected Letters of Mark Twain. Charles Neider. LC 81-47669. 320p. 1982. 16.45i (ISBN 0-06-014946-9, HarpT). Har-Row.

Selected Letters of Mark Van Doren. Mark Van Doren. Ed. by George Hendrick. LC 86-7456. x, 280p. 1986. text ed. 30.00 (ISBN 0-8071-1317-4). La State U Pr.

Selected Letters of Oscar Wilde. Oscar Wilde. Ed. by Rupert Hart-Davis. 1979. pap. 9.95 (ISBN 0-19-281218-1). Oxford U Pr.

Selected Letters of P. T. Barnum. Arthur H. Saxon. LC 82-12843. (Illus.). 360p. 1983. 27.50 (ISBN 0-231-05412-2). Columbia U Pr.

Selected Letters of Raymond Chandler. Ed. by Frank MacShane. LC 81-4852. 616p. 1981. 29.50 (ISBN 0-231-05080-1). Columbia U Pr.

Selected Letters of Raymond Chandler. Ed. by Frank MacShane. 526p. 1987. pap. 11.95 (ISBN 0-385-29531-6, Delta). Dell.

Selected Letters of Richard Wagner. Richard Wagner. Ed. by Stewart Spencer & Barry Millington. 1988. 35.00 (ISBN 0-393-02500-4). Norton.

Selected Letters of Robert Bridges, 2 vols. Ed. by Donald E. Stanford. LC 80-54789. (Illus.). 960p. 1983. Vol. 1. (ISBN 0-87413-177-4); Vol. 2. 65.00 (ISBN 0-87413-204-5). U Delaware Pr.

Selected Letters of Robert Frost. Robert Frost. Ed. by L. Thompson. LC 64-10767. 1964. 10.00 (ISBN 0-03-043155-7). H Holt & Co.

Selected Letters of Samuel Johnson. Samuel Johnson. LC 76-29446. Repr. of 1925 ed. 23.00 (ISBN 0-404-15312-7). AMS Pr.

Selected Letters of Samuel Taylor Coleridge. Samuel Taylor Coleridge. Ed. by H. J. Jackson. 280p. 1988. pap. 11.95 (ISBN 0-19-282140-7). Oxford U Pr.

Selected Letters of Stephane Mallarme. Stephane Mallarme. Ed. & tr. by Rosemary Lloyd. 272p. 1988. 27.50x (ISBN 0-226-48841-1). U of Chicago Pr.

Selected Letters of Sydney Smith. Sydney Smith. Ed. by Nowell C. Smith. (World's Classics Ser.). 1981. pap. 6.95 (ISBN 0-19-281535-0). Oxford U Pr.

Selected Letters of Theodore Roethke. Theodore Roethke. Ed. by Ralph J. Mills, Jr. LC 68-11045. (Illus.). 295p. 1968. 20.00x (ISBN 0-295-97892-9). U of Wash Pr.

Selected Letters of Thomas Babington Macaulay. Thomas B. Macaulay. Ed. by Thomas Pinney. LC 81-10016. 350p. 1983. 42.50 (ISBN 0-521-24009-3). Cambridge U Pr.

Selected Letters of Virgil Thomson. Virgil Thomson. 1988. 22.95. Summit Bks.

Selected Letters of W. D. Howells: Vol. 5, 1902-1911. William C. Fischer & Christopher K. Lohmann. (Critical Editions Program Ser.). 1983. lib. bdg. 45.95 (ISBN 0-8057-8531-0, Twayne). G K Hall.

Selected Letters of W. D. Howells: Vol. 6, 1912-1920. Ed. by William M. Gibson & Christoph K. Lohmann. (Critical Editions of American Literature Ser.). 270p. 1983. lib. bdg. 40.50 (ISBN 0-8057-8532-9, Twayne). G K Hall.

Selected Letters of Wilfred Owen. Wilfred Owen. Ed. by John Bell. 300p. 1986. pap. 12.95x (ISBN 0-19-281914-3). Oxford U Pr.

Selected Letters of William Carlos Williams. William Carlos Williams. Ed. by John C. Thirwall. 1957. 19.95 (ISBN 0-8392-1098-1). Astor-Honor.

Selected Letters of William Carlos Williams. William Carlos Williams. Ed. by John C. Thirlwall. LC 84-20550. 352p. 1985. pap. 9.95 (ISBN 0-8112-0934-2, NDP589). New Directions.

Selected Letters of William Faulkner. Ed. by Joseph Blotner. 1978. pap. 4.95 (ISBN 0-394-72505-0, Vin). Random.

Selected Letters of William James. Williams James. LC 80-66463. 304p. 1981. pap. 8.95 (ISBN 0-87923-348-6, Nonpareil Bks). Godine.

Selected Papers of Jerzy Neyman & E. S. Pearson, 3 vols. Jerzy Neyman & E. S. Pearson. Incl. Vol. 1. The Selected Papers of E. S. Pearson. 1966; Vol. 2. Joint Statistical Papers. 1967. 46.50x (ISBN 0-520-00991-6); Vol. 3. A Selection of Early Statistical Papers of J. Neyman. 1967. 47.50x (ISBN 0-520-00992-4). U of Cal Pr.

Selected Papers of Julian Schwinger. C. Fronsdal et al. (Mathematical Physics & Applied Mathematics Ser.: No. 4). 1979. lib. bdg. 29.50 (ISBN 90-277-0974-2, Pub. by Reidel Holland); pap. 11.95 (ISBN 90-277-0975-0, Pub. by Reidel Holland). Kluwer Academic.

Selected Papers of Lionel Pearson. Ed. by Donald Lateiner & Susan Stephens. LC 83-16485. (Homage Ser.). 282p. 1983. 14.95 (ISBN 0-89130-646-3, 00 16 04). Scholars Pr GA.

Selected Papers of Ludwig Jekels. Ludwig Jekels. 1970. pap. text ed. 13.95 (ISBN 0-8236-8305-2, 26025). Intl Univs Pr.

Selected Papers of Margaret S. Mahler. Margaret S. Mahler. LC 79-51915. 608p. 1982. Repr. of 1979 ed. 50.00x (ISBN 0-87668-371-5). Vol. I: Infantile Psychosis & Early Contributions. Vol. II: Separation-Individuation. Aronson.

Selected Papers of Morris B. Bender: Memorial Volume. Ed. by Robert P. Friedland. 464p. 1983. text ed. 41.50 (ISBN 0-89004-710-3). Raven.

Selected Papers of Robert S. Mulliken. Robert S. Mulliken. Ed. by J. Hinze & D. A. Ramsay. LC 74-11633. xvi, 1128p. 1975. lib. bdg. 55.00x (ISBN 0-226-54847-3). U of Chicago Pr.

Selected Papers of the International Migraine-Headache Symposium: Proceedings. International Migraine-Headache Symposium, Florence, 1970. Ed. by F. Sicuteri. (Pain & Headache Ser.: Vol. 3). 1972. 93.50 (ISBN 3-8055-1295-3). S Karger.

Selected Papers of Theodore S. Motzkin. Ed. by D. Cantor et al. 1983. text ed. 74.50 (ISBN 0-8176-3087-2). Birkhauser.

Selected Papers of Turner Alfrey. Boyer & Mark. 536p. 1986. 95.00 (ISBN 0-8247-7464-7). Dekker.

Selected Papers of William Clayton. William Clayton. Ed. by Frederick J. Dobney. LC 70-164565. pap. 80.00 (ISBN 0-317-19877-7, 2023093). Bks Demand UMI.

Selected Papers of Wolfgang Kohler. Wolfgang Kohler. Ed. by Solomon E. Asch & Mary Henle. 1971. 15.95x (ISBN 0-87140-505-9); pap. 4.95 (ISBN 0-87140-253-X). Liveright.

Selected Papers of Yano Kentaro. Ed. by M. Obata. (North-Holland Mathematics Studies: No. 70). 366p. 1982. 84.25 (ISBN 0-444-86495-4, North Holland). Elsevier.

Selected Papers on Accounting, Auditing, & Professional Problems with an Autobiographical Introduction. Edward Stamp. LC 83-49446. (Accounting History & the Development of a Profession Ser.). 650p. 1985. lib. bdg. 65.00 (ISBN 0-8240-6313-9). Garland Pub.

Selected Papers on Analog Fault Diagnosis. Ruey-Wen Liu. LC 87-3957. 148p. 1987. 24.25 (ISBN 0-87942-222-X, PCO2139). Inst Electrical.

Selected Papers on Anthropology, Travel & Exploration. Richard Burton. LC 72-80499. Repr. of 1924 ed. 22.00 (ISBN 0-405-08335-1, Blom Pubns). Ayer Co Pubs.

Selected Papers on Clinical Chemistry Instrumentation. Ed. by Henry C. Nipper. LC 85-26814. 230p. 1985. 30.00 (ISBN 0-915274-26-4). Am Assn Clinical Chem.

Selected Papers on Comparative Tai Studies. William J. Gedney. Ed. by Robert J. Bickner et al. LC 85-48239. (Michigan Papers on South & Southeast Asia: No. 29). 450p. 1988. price not set (ISBN 0-89148-037-4); pap. price not set (ISBN 0-89148-038-2). Ctr S&SE Asian.

Selected Papers on Desalination & Ocean Technology. S. N. Levine. (Illus.). 11.25 (ISBN 0-8446-2459-4). Peter Smith.

Selected Papers on Direct Psychoanalysis, Vol. 2. John N. Rosen. 172p. 1968. 31.00 (ISBN 0-8089-0387-X, 793622). Grune.

Selected Papers on Economic Theory. Knut Wicksell. Ed. by Erik Lindhal. LC 68-58667. (Illus.). 1969. Repr. of 1958 ed. 35.00x (ISBN 0-678-00493-5). Kelley.

Selected Papers on Folklore. Carl W. Von Sydow. Ed. by Richard Dorson. LC 77-70623. (International Folklore Ser.). 1977. lib. bdg. 23.50x (ISBN 0-405-10125-2). Ayer Co Pubs.

Selected Papers on Infrared Design. Ed. by R. B. Johnson & W. L. Wolfe. 1032p. Date not set. 80.00 (ISBN 0-89252-548-7, 513). SPIE.

Selected Papers on Laser Scanning & Recording. Ed. by L. Beiser. 504p. Date not set. 72.00 (ISBN 0-89252-413-8, 378). SPIE.

Selected Papers on Molecular Genetics. Ed. by J. Herbert Taylor. (Perspectives in Modern Biology). (Illus., Orig.). 1965. pap. 52.50 (ISBN 0-12-684456-9). Acad Pr.

Selected Papers on New Techniques for Energy Conversion. Ed. by Sumner N. Levine. 11.25 (ISBN 0-8446-2460-8). Peter Smith.

Selected Papers on Noise & Stochastic Processes. Ed. by Nelson Wax. 1954. pap. 8.95 (ISBN 0-486-60262-1). Dover.

Selected Papers on Noise in Circuits & Systems. Madhu S. Gupta. LC 87-32427. 110p. 1988. 19.90 (ISBN 0-87942-239-4, PCO2303). Inst Electrical.

Selected Papers on Optomechanical Design. Ed. by O'Shea. (Milestone Ser.). 1988. write for info. (ISBN 0-89252-805-2, 770). SPIE.

Selected Papers on Physical Processes in Ionized Plasmas. Ed. by Donald H. Menzel. (Orig.). 1962. pap. text ed. 5.95 (ISBN 0-486-60060-2). Dover.

Selected Papers on Quantum Electrodynamics. Ed. by Julian Schwinger. 1958. pap. text ed. 9.95 (ISBN 0-486-60444-6). Dover.

Selected Papers on Soil Mechanics. A. W. Skempton. 282p. 1984. 43.00 (ISBN 0-7277-0205-X, Pub. by T Telford UK). Am Soc Civil Eng.

Selected Papers on the History of Psychology. Robert Watson. Ed. by Josef Brozek & Rand B. Evans. LC 76-11675. pap. 86.80 (ISBN 0-317-39648-X, 2023235). Bks Demand UMI.

Selected Papers on the Pathogenic Rickettsiae. Ed. by Nicholas Hahon. LC 68-17625. (Illus.). 1968. 27.00x (ISBN 0-674-79890-2). Harvard U Pr.

Selected Papers: Saunders MacLane. Saunders MacLane. Ed. by I. Kaplansky. LC 79-10105. 1979. 48.00 (ISBN 0-387-90394-1). Springer-Verlag.

Selected Papers: Studies in Greek & Roman History & Historiography. F. W. Walbank. 400p. 1986. 72.50 (ISBN 0-521-30752-X). Cambridge U Pr.

Selected Passages from Correspondence with Friends. Nikolai Gogol. Tr. by Jesse Zeldin. LC 69-14661. 1969. 14.95x (ISBN 0-8265-1126-0). Vanderbilt U Pr.

Selected Passages from the Works of Bernard Shaw. Charlotte F. Shaw. 1979. Repr. of 1912 ed. lib. bdg. 35.00 (ISBN 0-8492-8229-2). R West.

Selected Passages from the Works of Bernard Shaw. Ed. by Charlotte F. Shaw. 294p. 1983. lib. bdg. 45.00 (ISBN 0-8495-5058-0). Arden Lib.

Selected Paul Durcan. 2nd ed. Paul Durcan. Ed. by Edna Longley. 141p. 1986. pap. 7.50 (ISBN 0-85640-354-7, Pub. by Blackstaff Pr). Longwood Pub Group.

Selected Philosophical Essays. Nikolai G. Chernyshevskii. LC 79-2896. 610p. 1983. Repr. of 1953 ed. 45.25 (ISBN 0-8305-0064-2). Hyperion Conn.

Selected Philosophical Essays. Nikolai A. Dobroliubov. Tr. by J. Finberg. LC 79-2899. 659p. 1983. Repr. of 1956 ed. 51.70 (ISBN 0-8305-0070-7). Hyperion Conn.

Selected Philosophical Essays. Max Scheler. Tr. by David Lachterman from Ger. LC 70-186550. (Studies in Phenomenology & Existential Philosophy). 400p. 1973. 14.95 (ISBN 0-8101-0619-1). Northwestern U Pr.

Selected Philosophical Russian Contemporary Essays. N. A. Dobrolyubov. 174p. 1985. 89.45x (ISBN 0-86722-090-2). Inst Econ Pol.

Selected Philosophical, Social, & Political Essays. Dimitri I. Pisarev. Tr. by R. Dixon & J. Katzer. LC 79-2919. (Illus.). 711p. 1982. Repr. of 1958 ed. 49.50 (ISBN 0-8305-0089-8). Hyperion Conn.

Selected Philosophical Works. Vissarion G. Belinskii. LC 79-2893. li, 552p. 1982. Repr. of 1948 ed. 48.00 (ISBN 0-8305-0061-8). Hyperion Conn.

Selected Philosophical Works, Vol. II. G. V. Plekhanov. 736p. 1976. 9.95 (ISBN 0-8285-0208-0, Pub. by Progress Pubs USSR). Imported Pubns.

Selected Philosophical Works, Vol. III. G. V. Plekhanov. 696p. 1976. 9.95 (ISBN 0-8285-0209-9, Pub. by Progress Pubs USSR). Imported Pubns.

Selected Philosophical Works, Vol. IV. G. V. Plekhanov. 783p. 1980. 9.95 (ISBN 0-8285-1594-8, Pub. by Progress Pubs USSR). Imported Pubns.

Selected Philosophical Works, Vol. V. G. V. Plekhanov. 735p. 1981. 9.95 (ISBN 0-8285-1895-5, Pub. by Progress Pubs USSR). Imported Pubns.

Selected Philosophical Works, Vol. I. G. V. Plekhanov. 808p. 1977. 9.95 (ISBN 0-8285-0207-2, Pub. by Progress Pubs USSR). Imported Pubns.

Selected Philosophical Writings. Rene Descartes. Ed. by John Cottingham & Dugald Murdoch. 150p. Date not set. 6.95 (ISBN 0-521-35264-9); pap. 6.95 (ISBN 0-521-35812-4). Cambridge U Pr.

Selected Philosophical Writings. Denis Diderot. Ed. by J. Lough. LC 86-25774. 232p. 1987. Repr. of 1953 ed. lib. bdg. 39.75x (ISBN 0-313-25228-9, DISE). Greenwood.

Selected Physical & Chemical Standard Methods for Students. American Public Health Assn. Staff et al. 515p. 1986. 45.00 (ISBN 0-87553-144-X). Am Pub Health.

Selected Piano Compositions. Cesar Franck. Ed. by Vincent D'Indy. LC 75-27672. 192p. 1976. pap. 7.50 (ISBN 0-486-23269-7). Dover.

Selected Piano Compositions. Cesar Franck. Ed. by Vincent D'Indy. 10.25 (ISBN 0-8446-5457-4). Peter Smith.

Selected Piano Music. Clara Schumann. LC 78-31836. (Women Composers Ser.: No. 4). 1979. Repr. of 1846 ed. lib. bdg. 27.50 (ISBN 0-306-79554-X). Da Capo.

Selected Piano Works for Four Hands. Franz Schubert. 273p. 1977. pap. 8.95 (ISBN 0-486-23529-7). Dover.

Selected Piano Works for Four Hands. Franz Schubert. 16.50 (ISBN 0-8446-5607-0). Peter Smith.

Selected Plays. Christopher Fry. 1985. pap. 8.95x (ISBN 0-19-281873-2). Oxford U Pr.

Selected Plays. John Marston. Ed. by M. Jackson & M. Neill. (Plays by Renaissance & Restoration Dramatists Ser.). (Illus.). 500p. 1986. 57.50 (ISBN 0-521-21746-6); pap. 19.95 (ISBN 0-521-29247-6). Cambridge U Pr.

Selected Plays. Philip Massinger. Ed. by C. Gibson. LC 77-80835. (Plays by Renaissance & Restoration Dramatists Ser.). 1978. 49.50 (ISBN 0-521-21728-8); pap. 13.95x (ISBN 0-521-29243-3). Cambridge U Pr.

Selected Plays. Thomas Middleton. LC 77-23339. (Plays by Renaissance & Restoration Dramatists Ser.). 1978. 52.50 (ISBN 0-521-21698-2); pap. 14.95 (ISBN 0-521-29236-0). Cambridge U Pr.

Selected Plays. Frank O'Hara. LC 78-9658. 1978. 17.95 (ISBN 0-916190-08-0); pap. 8.95 (ISBN 0-916190-09-9). Full Court NY.

Selected Plays. August Strindberg. Tr. by Evert Sprinchorn from Swedish. LC 85-8742. 848p. 1986. 39.50x (ISBN 0-8166-1506-3). U of Minn Pr.

Selected Plays. John Webster & John Ford. 1974. 14.95x (ISBN 0-460-00899-4, Evman); pap. 4.95x (ISBN 0-460-01899-X, Evman). Biblio Dist.

Selected Plays. Oscar Wilde. Incl. The Importance of Being Earnest; An Ideal Husband; Lady Windermere's Fan; A Woman of No Importance; Salome. (Penguin Plays Ser.). 1986. pap. 2.95 (ISBN 0-14-048209-1). Penguin.

Selected Plays & Libretti see Selected Writing.

Selected Plays & Poems. Cale Y. Rice. LC 27-16490. xviii, 786p. 1972. Repr. of 1926 ed. 79.00x (ISBN 0-403-01174-4). Scholarly.

Selected Plays from Bell's British Theatre, 16 vols. Ed. by John Bell. LC 76-44553. (Illus.). Repr. of 1802 ed. Set. 680.00 (ISBN 0-404-00840-2); 42.50 ea. Ams Pr.

Selected Plays of Aleksei Arbuzov. Tr. by A. Nicolaeff. LC 82-364. (Illus.). 336p. 1982. text ed. 28.00 (ISBN 0-08-024548-X). Pergamon.

Selected Plays of Brian Friel. Brian Friel. (Irish Drama Selections Ser.: No. 6). 1986. 33.50x (ISBN 0-8132-0626-X); pap. 11.95 (ISBN 0-8132-0627-8). Cath U Pr.

Selected Plays of Denis Johnston. Ed. by Joseph Ronsley. (Irish Drama Selections Ser.: No. 2). 416p. 1983. 33.50x (ISBN 0-8132-0576-X); pap. 9.95 (ISBN 0-8132-0577-8). Cath U Pr.

Selected Plays of Lady Gregory. Ed. by Mary FitzGerald. LC 82-22013. (Irish Drama Selections Ser.: No. 3). 376p. 1983. 29.95x (ISBN 0-8132-0582-4); pap. 9.95 (ISBN 0-8132-0583-2). Cath U Pr.

Selected Plays of Lennox Robinson. Ed. by Christopher Murray. LC 82-71455. (Irish Drama Selections Ser.: No. 1). (Illus.). 288p. 1982. 27.95x (ISBN 0-8132-0574-3); pap. 9.95 (ISBN 0-8132-0575-1). Cath U Pr.

Selected Plays of Padraic Colum. Padraic Colum. Ed. by Sanford Sternlicht. (Irish Studies). (Illus.). 128p. 1986. text ed. 18.00x (ISBN 0-8156-2386-0). Syracuse U Pr.

Selected Plays of Severino Montano, Vol. 1 & 2. Severino Montano. (Illus., Orig.). 1982. Vol. 1, 234. pap. 8.25 (ISBN 0-686-37565-3, Pub. by New Day Philippines); Vol. 2, 319. pap. 10.50 (ISBN 0-686-37566-1). Cellar.

Selected Plays of Severino Montano, Vol. 3. Severino Montano. (Illus.). 64p. 1983. pap. 4.50x (ISBN 971-10-0046-6, Pub. by New Day Philippines). Cellar.

Selected Plays: The Broken Heart, 'Tis Pity She's a Whore, Perkin Warbeck. John Ford. Ed. by C. Gibson. (Plays by Renaissance & Restoration Dramatists Ser.). (Illus.). 352p. 1986. 52.50 (ISBN 0-521-22543-4); pap. 20.95 (ISBN 0-521-29545-9). Cambridge U Pr.

Selected Plays: The White Devil; The Duchess of Malfi; The Devil's Law Case. John Webster. Ed. by Jonathan Dollimore & Alan Sinfield. LC 82-22094. (Plays by Renaissance & Restoration Dramatists Ser.). 370p. 1983. 42.50 (ISBN 0-521-24927-9). Cambridge U Pr.

Selected Poemas Selecciones. Angela de Hoyos. 84p. 1979. 6.00 (ISBN 0-934770-65-4). Arte Publico.

Selected Poems. Fleur Adcock. 144p. 1986. pap. 9.95 (ISBN 0-19-558100-8). Oxford U Pr.

Selected Poems. Expanded ed. A. R. Ammons. 1987. 15.95 (ISBN 0-393-02411-3); pap. 9.95 (ISBN 0-393-30396-9). Norton.

Selected Poems. Guillaume Apollinaire. Tr. by Oliver Bernard. (Poetry in Translation Ser.). 176p. 1985. 18.95 (ISBN 0-85646-154-7, Pub. by Anvil Pr Poetry); pap. 9.95 (ISBN 0-85646-155-5). Longwood Pub Group.

Selected Poems. Mirella Aquila. 120p. 1981. pap. 5.00 (ISBN 0-682-49666-9). Exposition-Phoenix.

Selected Poems. John Ashbery. LC 85-40549. 368p. 1985. 22.95 (ISBN 0-670-80917-9, E Sifton Bks). Viking.

Selected Poems. John Ashbery. 352p. 1986. pap. 9.95 (ISBN 0-14-058553-2). Penguin.

Selected Poems. Charles Baudelaire. Tr. by Geoffrey Wagner from Fr. LC 74-7679. 1974. pap. 4.95 (ISBN 0-394-17831-9, B375, BC). Grove.

Selected Poems. Thomas L. Beddoes. Ed. by Judith Higgens. (Fyfield Ser.). 120p. 1976. 7.50 (ISBN 0-85635-192-X). Carcanet.

Selected Poems. Edmund Blunden. Ed. by Robyn Marsack. 107p. 1982. pap. 8.50 (ISBN 0-85635-425-2). Carcanet.

Selected Poems. Robert Bly. LC 84-47556. 224p. 1986. 18.45 (ISBN 0-06-015334-2, HarpT). Har-Row.

Selected Poems. Bronte Sisters. Ed. by Stevie Davies. (Fyfield Ser.). 123p. pap. 7.50 (ISBN 0-85635-131-8). Carcanet.

Selected Poems. Gwendolyn Brooks. 1963. 11.45i (ISBN 0-06-010535-6, HarpT). Har-Row.

Selected Poems. Gwendolyn Brooks. 1963. pap. 6.95 (ISBN 0-06-090989-7, PL). Har-Row.

Selected Poems. Elizabeth Barrett Browning. Ed. by Malcolm Hicks. (Fyfield Ser.). 119p. 1983. pap. 7.50 (ISBN 0-85635-412-0). Carcanet.

Selected Poems. Witter Bynner. Ed. by Richard Wilbur. 384p. 1978. 20.00 (ISBN 0-374-25863-5). FS&G.

Selected Poems. Thomas Chatterton. Ed. by Grevel Lindop. (Fyfield Ser.). 96p. (Orig.). 1986. pap. 7.50 (ISBN 0-85635-694-8). Carcanet.

Selected Poems. John Ciardi. LC 83-24254. 222p. 1984. 21.00 (ISBN 0-938626-29-9); pap. 8.95 (ISBN 0-938626-30-2). U of Ark Pr.

Selected Poems. John Clare. Ed. by J. W. Tibble. 1965. 14.95x (ISBN 0-460-00563-4, Evman); pap. 4.95x (ISBN 0-460-01563-X, Evman). Biblio Dist.

Selected Poems. Austin Clarke. Ed. by Thomas Kinsella. 207p. 1976. 13.95 (ISBN 0-916390-04-7); pap. 7.95 (ISBN 0-916390-03-9). Wake Forest.

Selected Poems. Gillian Clarke. 112p. 1985. pap. 8.50 (ISBN 0-85635-594-1). Carcanet.

Selected Poems. Jack Clemo. 80p. 1988. pap. 14.95 (ISBN 1-85224-052-0, Pub. by Bloodaxe Bks). Dufour.

Selected Poems. Arthur H. Clough. Ed. by Shirley Chew. (Fyfield Ser.). 240p. (Orig.). 1987. pap. 9.50 (ISBN 0-85635-622-0). Carcanet.

Selected Poems. Brian Coffey. (Belacqua Ser.). 68p. 1971. 15.95 (ISBN 0-906897-62-9); pap. 12.95 (ISBN 0-906897-61-0). Dufour.

Selected Poems. Charles Cotton. Ed. by Ken Robinson. (Fyfield Ser.). 136p. 1983. pap. 7.50 (ISBN 0-85635-413-9). Carcanet.

Selected Poems. William Cowper. Ed. by Nick Rhodes. (Fyfield Ser.). 119p. 1984. pap. 7.50 (ISBN 0-85635-414-7). Carcanet.

Selected Poems. George Crabbe. Ed. & intro. by Jem Poster. (Fyfield Ser.). 168p. (Orig.). 1986. pap. 7.50 (ISBN 0-85635-621-2). Carcanet.

Selected Poems. I. Crichton-Smith. LC 74-135657. 1971. 12.95 (ISBN 0-8023-1160-1). Dufour.

Selected Poems. Tony Curtis. 1986. pap. 9.95 (ISBN 0-907476-59-7, Pub. by Poetry Wales Pr UK). Dufour.

Selected Poems. Donald Davie. 124p. 1985. pap. 7.50 (ISBN 0-85635-595-X). Carcanet.

Selected Poems. Walter De La Mare. 208p. 1973. pap. 5.95 (ISBN 0-571-10401-0). Faber & Faber.

Selected Poems. Pierre De Ronsard. Ed. by Christine M. Scollen. 184p. (Fr.). 1974. 14.95 (ISBN 0-485-13807-7, Pub. by Athlone Pr UK). Humanities.

Selected Poems. Bishnu Dey. Ed. by Samir Dasgupta. (Writers Workshop Saffronbird Ser). 1975. 12.00 (ISBN 0-88253-626-5); pap. text ed. 4.80 (ISBN 0-88253-625-7). Ind-US Inc.

Selected Poems. Hilda Doolittle, pseud. Intro. by Louis L. Martz. LC 88-1460. 224p. 1988. 18.95 (ISBN 0-8112-1065-0); pap. 8.95 (ISBN 0-8112-1066-9, NDP658). New Directions.

Selected Poems. Edward Dorn. Ed. by Donald Allen. LC 78-2925. 108p. 1978. pap. 3.50 (ISBN 0-912516-32-1). Grey Fox.

Selected Poems. Michael Drayton. Ed. by Vivien Thomas. (Fyfield Ser.). 96p. 1977. pap. 7.50 (ISBN 0-85635-225-X). Carcanet.

Selected Poems. Lauris Edmond. (Orig.). 1984. pap. 12.95x (ISBN 0-19-558126-1). Oxford U Pr.

Selected Poems. Gunter Eich. Tr. by Teo Savory. LC 69-13015. (German Ser: Vol. 3). (Ger. & Eng.). 1975. 15.00 (ISBN 0-87775-020-3); pap. 5.00 (ISBN 0-87775-090-4). Unicorn Pr.

Selected Poems. Larry Eigner. 1972. 6.00 (ISBN 0-685-29871-X); pap. 2.50 (ISBN 0-685-29872-8). Oyez.

Selected Poems. T. S. Eliot. LC 67-23064. 127p. (gr. 7-12). 1967. pap. 3.95 (ISBN 0-15-680647-9, Harv). HarBraceJ.

Selected Poems. T. S. Eliot. 1988. pap. 4.95. HarBraceJ.

Selected Poems. Dave Etter. 240p. 1987. 14.95 (ISBN 0-933180-91-8). Spoon Riv Poetry.

Selected Poems. Vincent Ferrini. Ed. & intro. by George F. Butterick. LC 76-463360. (Orig.). 1976. pap. 3.95 (ISBN 0-917590-00-7). Univ Conn Lib.

Selected Poems. Anne Finch. Ed. by Denys Thompson. (Fyfield Ser.). 90p. (Orig.). 1987. pap. 7.50 (ISBN 0-85635-624-7). Carcanet.

Selected Poems. Peter Finch. LC 87-60973. 151p. 1987. pap. 11.95 (ISBN 0-907476-74-0, Pub. by Poetry Wales Pr UK). Dufour.

Selected Poems. Lincoln Fitzell. 88p. 1955. 5.95 (ISBN 0-8040-0269-X, Pub. by Swallow). Ohio U Pr.

Selected Poems. dual language ed. R. Gamzatov. 347p. 1974. text ed. 3.95 (ISBN 0-8285-0628-0, Pub. by Progress Pubs USSR). Imported Pubns.

Selected Poems & Three Plays. rev., 3rd ed. William B. Yeats. Ed. by M. L. Rosenthal. 288p. 1987. 10.95 (ISBN 0-02-071560-9, Collier). Macmillan.

Selected Poems & Verse Fables, Seventeen Eighty-Four to Seventeen Ninety-Two. William H. Brown. Ed. by Richard Walser. LC 82-2660. 94p. 1982. 16.50 (ISBN 0-87413-223-1). U Delaware Pr.

Selected Poems by Fernando Pessoa. Tr. by Edwin Honig. LC 75-150758. (Poetry in Europe Ser.). 170p. 1974. pap. 6.95 (ISBN 0-8040-0521-4, Pub. by Swallow). Ohio U Pr.

Selected Poems by Fernando Pessoa. Tr. by Edwin Honig from Port. LC 75-150758. (Poetry in Europe Ser.). 170p. 1971. 10.95 (ISBN 0-8040-0520-6, Pub. by Swallow). Ohio U Pr.

Selected Poems by Jay Wright. Ed. by Robert B. Stepto. LC 86-43128. 130p. 1987. 26.50 (ISBN 0-691-06687-6); pap. 10.50 (ISBN 0-691-01435-3). Princeton U Pr.

Selected Poems by Laurence Housman. Laurence Housman. LC 75-41142. Repr. of 1908 ed. 14.50 (ISBN 0-404-14672-4). AMS Pr.

Selected Poems, Fragments & Fictions. Glyn Jones. LC 88-70902. 146p. (Orig.). 1988. pap. 14.95 (ISBN 0-907476-85-6, Pub. by Poetry Wales Pr UK). Dufour.

Selected Poems II: Poems Selected & New, Nineteen Seventy-Six to Nineteen Eighty-Six. Margaret Atwood. 160p. 1987. 16.95 (ISBN 0-395-40423-1); pap. 9.95 (ISBN 0-395-45406-9). HM.

Selected Poems Including the Woman at the Washington Zoo. Randall Jarrell. LC 64-54618. 1964. pap. 5.95 (ISBN 0-689-70109-8, 66). Atheneum.

Selected Poems: Nineteen Fifty-Eight to Nineteen Eighty. Gilbert Sorrentino. LC 81-1094. 271p. (Orig.). 1981. 20.00 (ISBN 0-87685-502-8); pap. 8.50 (ISBN 0-87685-501-X). Black Sparrow.

Selected Poems: Nineteen Fifty-Eight to Nineteen Eighty-Four. John Wieners. Ed. by Raymond Foye. LC 86-1046. 322p. 1986. pap. 12.50 (ISBN 0-87685-661-X). Black Sparrow.

Selected Poems Nineteen Fifty Five to Nineteen Eighty. Lain C. Smith. 1983. 42.00x (ISBN 0-904265-55-2, Pub. by Macdonald Pub UK); pap. 30.00x (ISBN 0-904265-56-0). State Mutual Bk.

Selected Poems: Nineteen Fifty One-Nineteen Seventy Seven. A. R. Ammons. 1977. pap. 5.95 (ISBN 0-393-04470-X). Norton.

Selected Poems, Nineteen Fifty-Seven to Nineteen Eighty-Seven. W. D. Snodgrass. LC 87-9463. 270p. 1987. 19.95 (ISBN 0-939149-04-4). Soho Press.

Selected Poems: Nineteen Fifty-Six to Nineteen Seventy-Six. Diane Di Prima. LC 76-39890. 1977. 40.00 (ISBN 0-913028-48-7). North Atlantic.

Selected Poems, Nineteen Fifty to Nineteen Eighty-Two. Kenneth Koch. 1985. 9.95 (ISBN 0-394-73771-7, Vin). Random.

Selected Poems, Nineteen Fifty to Nineteen Seventy-Five. Thom Gunn. 140p. 1979. 12.95 (ISBN 0-374-25865-1); pap. 5.95 (ISBN 0-374-51595-6). FS&G.

Selected Poems, Nineteen Forty to Nineteen Eighty-Two. Normon Nicholson. 272p. 1983. pap. 6.95 (ISBN 0-571-11950-6). Faber & Faber.

Selected Poems, Nineteen Seventy to Nineteen Eighty. Andrei Codrescu. LC 82-19532. 137p. 1983. pap. 7.00 (ISBN 0-915342-38-3). SUN.

Selected Poems, Nineteen Seventy to Nineteen Eighty-Three. Lance Henson. LC 85-70355. 64p. (Orig.). 1985. pap. 5.00x (ISBN 0-912678-62-3). Greenfld Rev Pr.

Selected Poems, Nineteen Sixty-Nine to Nineteen Eighty-One. Richard Shelton. LC 82-2680. (Pitt Poetry Ser.). 233p. (YA) 1982. 17.95x (ISBN 0-8229-3470-1); pap. 9.95 (ISBN 0-8229-5343-9). U of Pittsburgh Pr.

Selected Poems Nineteen Sixty-Three to Nineteen Eighty. Michael Longley. LC 80-52997. 63p. 1981. pap. 5.95 (ISBN 0-916390-14-4). Wake Forest.

Selected Poems: Nineteen Sixty-Three to Nineteen Eighty-Three. Charles Simic. 186p. 1985. 14.95 (ISBN 0-8076-1129-8); pap. 8.95 (ISBN 0-8076-1130-1). Braziller.

Selected Poems Nineteen Sixty to Nineteen Eighty. Andrew Taylor. 182p. 1982. text ed. 17.95 (ISBN 0-7022-1661-5). U of Queensland Pr.

Selected Poems Nineteen Sixty to Nineteen Seventy-Five. Paul Mariah. 1978. 6.95 (ISBN 0-686-18930-2). Man-Root.

Selected Poems, Nineteen Thirty-Three to Nineteen Eighty-Seven. Gavin Ewart. LC 87-26873. 128p. 1988. 18.95 (ISBN 0-8112-1054-5); pap. 8.95 (ISBN 0-8112-1055-3, NDP655). New Directions.

Selected Poems, Nineteen Twenty-Three to Nineteen Seventy-Five. Robert Penn Warren. 1976. 17.95 (ISBN 0-394-40531-5); pap. 9.95 (ISBN 0-394-73264-2). Random.

Selected Poems of Albert Steffen, Vol. 1. Albert Steffen. Tr. by Daisy Aldan. (Ger). 1968. 6.00 (ISBN 0-913152-13-7). Folder Edns.

Selected Poems of Anne Sexton. Anne Sexton. Ed. by Diane W. Middlebrook & Diana H. George. LC 87-34253. 320p. 1988. 21.95 (ISBN 0-395-44595-7); pap. 11.95 (ISBN 0-395-47782-4). HM.

Selected Poems of Antonio Machado. Antonio Machado. Tr. by Betty J. Craige. LC 78-57504. 192p. 1978. 22.50 (ISBN 0-8071-0456-6). La State U Pr.

Selected Poems of Barnabe Googe. Barnabe Googe. Ed. by Alan Stephens. LC 80-29155. (Books of the Renaissance Ser.). 60p. 1981. Repr. of 1961 ed. lib. bdg. 35.00x (ISBN 0-313-22830-2, GOSEP). Greenwood.

Selected Poems of Cesar Vallejo. Cesar Vallejo. Tr. by H. R. Hays from Span. LC 81-159. 122p. 1981. 13.50 (ISBN 0-937584-01-0); pap. 6.95 (ISBN 0-937584-02-9). Sachem Pr.

Selected Poems of Claude McKay. Claude McKay. LC 70-78698. 110p. 1969. pap. 3.95 (ISBN 0-15-680649-5, Harv). HarBraceJ.

Selected Poems of Diana Kearny Powell. Diana K. Powell. LC 85-51971. 79p. 1986. 6.95 (ISBN 1-55523-005-9). Winston-Derek.

Selected Poems of E. A. Robinson. Edward A. Robinson. Ed. by Morton D. Zabel. 1966. pap. 9.95 (ISBN 0-02-070530-1, Collier). Macmillan.

Selected Poems of Francis Jammes. Francis Jammes. Tr. by Barry Gifford & Bettina Dickie. LC 76-21760. 97p. (Fr. & Eng.). 1976. 7.95 (ISBN 0-87421-086-0). Utah St U Pr.

Selected Poems of Friedrich Holderlin & Eduard Morike. Friedrich Holderlin & Eduard Morike. Tr. by Christopher Middleton from Ger. LC 72-79570. (German Literary Classics in Translation Ser.). 304p. 1973. pap. 3.75x (ISBN 0-226-34934-9, P487, Phoen). U of Chicago Pr.

Selected Poems of Gabriela Mistral. Ed. & tr. by Doris Dana. LC 77-137467. (Hispanic Foundation Ser). (Illus.). 272p. 1971. 28.50x (ISBN 0-8018-1197-X). Johns Hopkins.

Selected Poems of George Faludy. George Faludy. Ed. & tr. by Robin Skelton. LC 85-16397. 224p. 1985. 18.95x (ISBN 0-8203-0809-9); pap. 8.95 (ISBN 0-8203-0814-5). U of Ga Pr.

Selected Poems of Gunnar Ekelof. Gunnar Ekelof. Tr. by Muriel Rukeyser & Leif Sjoberg. LC 66-16109. (Library of Scandinavian Literature). 1971. lib. bdg. 26.50x (ISBN 0-8057-5852-6). Irvington.

Selected Poems of H. D. H. D. 1957. pap. 8.95 (ISBN 0-394-17329-5, E71, Ever). Grove.

Selected Poems of H. L. Davis. 2nd ed. H. L. Davis. Ed. by O. Burmaster. LC 77-83226. (Ahsahta Press Modern & Contemporary Poets of the West). (Orig.). 1978. pap. 4.50 (ISBN 0-916272-07-9). Ahsahta Pr.

Selected Poems of Henry Newbolt. Henry Newbolt. Ed. by Patric Dickinson. 158p. 1984. 16.95 (ISBN 0-340-26388-1, Pub. by Hodder & Stoughton UK). David & Charles.

Selected Poems of Henry Vaughan. Henry Vaughan. LC 75-43096. 79p. pap. 3.50 (ISBN 0-317-61301-4). Dufour.

Selected Poems of Irving Layton. Irving Layton. LC 76-54704. 1977. 8.50 (ISBN 0-8112-0641-6); pap. 2.25 (ISBN 0-8112-0642-4, NDP431). New Directions.

Selected Poems of Jacob Glatstein. Jacob Glatstein. Tr. by Ruth Whitman. 1973. 9.50 (ISBN 0-8079-0176-8); pap. 5.95 (ISBN 0-8079-0175-X). October.

Selected Poems of Jacques Prevert. Tr. by Carol Poster. 1987. 7.50. White Pine.

Selected Poems of Jehudah Halevi. Jehudah Halevi. LC 73-2203. (Jewish People; History, Religion, Literature Ser.). Repr. of 1924 ed. 32.00 (ISBN 0-405-05268-5). Ayer Co Pubs.

Selected Poems of Jehudah Halevi. Judah Halevi. 59.95 (ISBN 0-8490-1019-5). Gordon Pr.

Selected Poems of John Gould Fletcher. Ed. by Lucas Carpenter & Leighton Rudolph. LC 87-19245. 330p. (Orig.). 1988. 24.95 (ISBN 0-938626-66-3); pap. 14.95 (ISBN 0-938626-67-1). U of Ark Pr.

Selected Poems of John Knoepfle. John Knoepfle. LC 85-70735. (Selected Poems Ser.). 96p. (Orig.). 1985. pap. 6.50. BKMK.

Selected Poems of John Oxenham. John Oxenham. Ed. by Charles L. Wallis. LC 71-179735. (Biography Index Reprint Ser). Repr. of 1948 ed. 15.00 (ISBN 0-8369-8103-0). Ayer Co Pubs.

Selected Poems of Jorge Carrera Andrade. Ed. by H. R. Hays. LC 72-161498. 259p. 1972. 34.50x (ISBN 0-87395-067-4). State U NY Pr.

Selected Poems of Langston Hughes. Langston Hughes. (Illus.). 1959. 19.45 (ISBN 0-394-40438-6). Knopf.

Selected Poems of Langston Hughes. Langston Hughes. LC 73-14913. 1974. pap. 5.95 (ISBN 0-394-71910-7, Vin). Random.

Selected Poems of Leah Goldberg. Leah Goldberg. Tr. by Robert Friend. 64p. 1977. pap. 6.00 (ISBN 0-915572-27-3). Panjandrum.

Selected Poems of Luis Cernuda. Luis Cernuda. Tr. by Reginald Gibbons from Span. LC 75-3767. 1978. 29.95x (ISBN 0-520-02984-4). U of Cal Pr.

Selected Poems of Matthew Arnold. Matthew Arnold. 1878. 15.00 (ISBN 0-932062-06-7). Sharon Hill.

Selected Poems of May Sarton. Ed. by May Sarton & Serena S. Hilsinger. 1978. pap. 8.95 (ISBN 0-393-04512-9). Norton.

Selected Poems of Mbembe. Milton Smith. LC 85-70737. 96p. (Orig.). 1986. pap. 7.95 (ISBN 0-933532-50-4). BkMk.

Selected Poems of Miltos Sahtouris. Miltos Sahtouris. Tr. by Kimon Friar from Gr. LC 81-21374. 125p. 1982. 13.50 (ISBN 0-937584-03-7); pap. 6.95 (ISBN 0-937584-04-5). Sachem Pr.

Selected Poems of Norman Macleod. 3rd ed. Norman W. Macleod. Intro. by Tom Trusky. LC 75-21690. (Modern & Contemporary Western Poets Ser.). 60p. (Orig.). 1975. pap. 4.50 (ISBN 0-916272-00-1). Ahsahta Pr.

Selected Poems of Octavio Paz. Octavio Paz. Intro. by Eliot Weinberger. Tr. by G. Aroul et al from Span. LC 84-9856. 160p. 1984. 14.95 (ISBN 0-8112-0903-2); pap. 6.95 (ISBN 0-8112-0899-0, NDP574). New Directions.

Selected Poems of Osip Mandelstam. Osip Mandelstam. Tr. by Clarence Brown et al. LC 83-6373. 128p. 1984. pap. 6.95 (ISBN 0-689-11425-7). Atheneum.

Selected Poems of Pablo Neruda. Pablo Neruda. 1973. pap. 9.95 (ISBN 0-385-28906-5, Delta). Dell.

Selected Poems of Phillips Kloss. Phillips Kloss. LC 82-19131. 120p. 1983. cloth 10.95 (ISBN 0-686-82374-5). Sunstone Pr.

Selected Poems of Rainer Maria Rilke: A Translation from the German & Commentary. Ed. by Robert Bly. LC 78-2114. 192p. 1981. 15.45 (ISBN 0-06-010432-5, HarpT). Har-Row.

Selected Poems of Richard Hugo. Richard Hugo. 1979. 6.95 (ISBN 0-393-00936-X). Norton.

Selected Poems of Robert Burns. Hugh MacDiarmid. 64p. 1982. Repr. of 1949 ed. lib. bdg. 15.00 (ISBN 0-89987-592-0). Darby Bks.

Selected Poems of Robert Watson. Robert Watson. LC 73-93706. (Orig.). 1974. 10.00 (ISBN 0-689-10602-5). Atheneum.

Selected Poems of Rosario Castellanos. Ed. by Cecilia Vicuna & Magda Bogin. 1988. pap. 9.50 (ISBN 1-55597-112-1). Graywolf.

Selected Poems of Rosemary Thomas. Rosemary Thomas. LC 67-25189. 161p. 1968. 19.50 (ISBN 0-8290-0204-9). Irvington.

Selected Poems of Roy Campbell. Ed. by Roy Campbell & Peter Alexander. 1982. 22.50x (ISBN 0-19-211946-X). Oxford U Pr.

Selected Poems of Ruben Dario. Tr. by Lysander Kemp from Span. (Texas Pan American Ser.). (Illus.). 149p. 1988. pap. 6.95 (ISBN 0-292-77615-2). U of Tex Pr.

Selected Poems of Salvador Espriu. Salvador Espriu. Tr. by Magda Bogin from Catalan. 1989. 15.95 (ISBN 0-393-02608-6). Norton.

Selected Poems of Theo. Marzials. Ed. by John M. Munro. 1973. 10.00x (ISBN 0-8156-6040-5, Am U Beirut). Syracuse U Pr.

Selected Poems of Thomas Gray & William Collins. Ed. by Arthur Johnston. LC 72-116475. (English Library). 222p. (Orig.). 1970. pap. 5.95x (ISBN 0-87249-163-3). U of SC Pr.

Selected Poems of Thomas Hardy. Thomas Hardy. Ed. by J. C. Ransom. 1961. pap. 8.95 (ISBN 0-02-070490-9, Collier). Macmillan.

Selected Poems of Thomas Hardy. Ed. by James Reeves & Robert Gittings. (Poetry Bookself Ser.). 140p. 1981. 13.50x (ISBN 0-389-20080-8, 06991). B&N Imports.

Selected Poems of Thomas Hardy. 204p. 1981. Repr. of 1953 ed. lib. bdg. 20.00 (ISBN 0-8495-6127-2). Arden Lib.

Selected Poems of Tomas Transtromer, 1954-1986. Tomas Transtromer. Ed. by Robert Hass. Tr. by May Swenson et al from Swedish. (Modern European Poets Ser.). 1989. pap. 10.95 (ISBN 0-88001-113-0). Ecco Pr.

Selected Poems of Tudor Arghezi. Tudor Arghezi. Tr. by Michael Impey & Brian Swann. LC 75-30185. (Lockert Library of Poetry in Translation). 1976. pap. 9.50 (ISBN 0-691-01328-4). Princeton U Pr.

Selected Poems of Vesna Parun. Dasha C. Nisula. 175p. 1985. pap. 10.00 (ISBN 0-940580-33-0). Green River.

Selected Poems of W. H. Auden. W. H. Auden. Ed. by Edward Mendelson. LC 78-55719. 1979. pap. 8.95 (ISBN 0-394-72506-9, V-506, Vin). Random.

Selected Poems of Walter Von der Vogel Weide. Ed. by W. A. Phillips. 69.95 (ISBN 0-8490-1020-9). Gordon Pr.

Selected Poems of William Vaughn Moody. William V. Moody. Ed. by Robert M. Lovett. LC 83-45819. Repr. of 1931 ed. 30.00 (ISBN 0-404-20182-2). AMS Pr.

Selected Poems of Yankev Glatshteyn. Richard Fein. 456p. 1988. 39.95 (ISBN 0-8276-0299-5). JPS Phila.

Selected Poems, Old & New. Osbert Sitwell. LC 75-41253. Repr. of 1943 ed. 11.00 (ISBN 0-404-14603-1). AMS Pr.

Selected Poems: Pascoli. G. Pascoli. Ed. by P. R. Horne. (Italian Texts Ser.). 192p. (Ital.). 1983. pap. text ed. 11.00 (ISBN 0-7190-0870-0, Pub. by Manchester Univ Pr). St Martin.

Selected Poems: Pasternak. Boris Pasternak. Tr. by Jon Stallworthy & Peter France. 1983. 15.00 (ISBN 0-393-01819-9). Norton.

Selected Poems: Six Sets, 1951-1983. Howard Hart. LC 84-70011. 88p. 1984. 12.50 (ISBN 0-933944-05-5); pap. 6.95 (ISBN 0-933944-06-3); signed 25.00. City Miner Bks.

Selected Poems: Summer Knowledge. Delmore Schwartz. LC 59-10689. 1967. pap. 6.95 (ISBN 0-8112-0191-0, NDP241). New Directions.

Selected Poems: Thomas. D. M. Thomas. 130p. 1983. pap. 8.95 (ISBN 0-14-042306-0). Penguin.

Selected Poems: William Blake. William Blake. Ed. by P. H. Butter. (Everyman Library). 302p. 1982. pap. text ed. 6.00x (ISBN 0-460-01125-1, Evman). Biblio Dist.

Selected Poems: Zbigniew Herbert. Zbigniew Herbert. Tr. by Czeslaw Milosz & Peter D. Scott. 139p. 1986. pap. 7.50 (ISBN 0-88001-099-1). Ecco Pr.

Selected Poems: 100 Poems Translated from the Norwegian with 8 Poems in the Original Nynorsk. Tarjei Vesaas. Tr. by Anthony Barnett. 128p. (Orig., Norwegian & Eng.). 1988. pap. 15.00 (ISBN 0-907954-12-X, Pub. by Allardyce & Barnett). Small Pr Dist.

Selected Poems 1938-1988. Thomas McGrath. Ed. by Sam Hamill. LC 87-172648. 208p. 1988. 15.00 (ISBN 1-55659-011-3); pap. 10.00 (ISBN 1-55659-012-1). Copper Canyon.

Selected Poems, 1943-1966. Philip Lamantia. LC 67-22807. (Pocket Poets Ser.: No. 20). (Orig.). pap. 3.95 (ISBN 0-87286-029-9). City Lights.

Selected Poems, 1954-1982. John Fuller. 175p. 1987. 25.95 (ISBN 0-436-16754-9, Pub. by Secker & Warburg UK). David & Charles.

Selected Poems: 1956-1986. Anne Stevenson. 160p. pap. 9.95 (ISBN 0-19-282062-1). Oxford U Pr.

Selected Poems: 1964-1983. Douglas Dunn. 175p. 1986. 18.94 (ISBN 0-571-14619-8); pap. 9.95 (ISBN 0-571-14620-1). Faber & Faber.

Selected Poems, 1965-1973. Marin Sorescu. 1983. pap. 8.95 (ISBN 0-906427-48-7, Pub. by Bloodaxe Bks). Dufour.

Selected Poems, 1965-1975. Margaret Atwood. 1987. pap. 9.95 (ISBN 0-395-40422-3). HM.

Selected Poems, 1968-1986. Paul Muldoon. 128p. 1987. 16.50 (ISBN 0-88001-154-8). Ecco Pr.

Selected Poems, 1981-1984. Malcolm S. MacKenzie. 103p. 1984. 4.95 (ISBN 0-89697-180-5). Intl Univ Pr.

Selected Poetry. S. Esenin. 383p. 1981. 8.45 (ISBN 0-8285-2518-8, Pub. by Progress Pubs USSR). Imported Pubns.

Selected Poetry. John Gower. Ed. by Carole Weinberg. (Fyfield Ser.). 184p. 1983. pap. 7.50 (ISBN 0-85635-415-5). Carcanet.

Selected Poetry. Nazim Hikmet. Tr. by Randy Blasing & Mutlu Konuk. (Persea Series of Poetry in Translation). 175p. (Orig.). 1987. pap. 9.95 (ISBN 0-89255-101-1). Persea Bks.

Selected Poetry. Robinson Jeffers. 1938. 24.95 (ISBN 0-394-40442-4). Random.

Selected Poetry. Lenrie Peters. (African Writers Ser.: No. 238). 143p. (Orig.). 1981. pap. text ed. 9.00 (ISBN 0-435-90238-5). Heinemann Ed.

Selected Poetry. T. G. Shevchenko. 333p. 1977. 10.00 (ISBN 0-8285-1031-8, Pub. by Progress Pubs USSR). Imported Pubns.

Selected Poetry. Alfred Tennyson. Ed. by Douglas Bush. (Modern Library College Editions Ser.). 1951. pap. write for info (ISBN 0-394-30960-X, T60, RanC). Random.

Selected Poetry. William Wordsworth. Ed. by Mark Van Doren. (Modern Library College Editions). 1950. pap. write for info (ISBN 0-394-30941-3, T41, RanC). Random.

Selected Poetry & Critical Prose. Charles G. Roberts. LC 73-91558. (Literature of Canada, Poetry & Prose in Reprint Ser.: No. 9). pap. 91.50 (ISBN 0-317-27000-1, 2023662). Bks Demand UMI.

Selected Poetry & Prose. Ilse Aichinger. Tr. by Allen H. Chappel from Ger. LC 83-14867. 141p. 1983. 18.00 (ISBN 0-937406-25-2); pap. 6.50 (ISBN 0-937406-24-4). Logbridge-Rhodes.

Selected Poetry & Prose. William Blake. Ed. by Northrop Frye. (Modern Library College Editions). 1966. pap. text ed. write for info (ISBN 0-394-30986-3, T86, RanC). Random.

Selected Poetry & Prose. Samuel Taylor Coleridge. Ed. by Donald Stauffer. (Modern Library College Editions). 1951. pap. text ed. write for info (ISBN 0-394-30952-9, T52, RanC). Random.

Selected Poetry & Prose. John Dryden. LC 69-17414. (Modern Library College Editions). 1969. pap. text ed. write for info (ISBN 0-394-30063-7, RanC). Random.

Selected Poetry & Prose. Stephane Mallarme. Ed. & intro. by Mary A. Caws. LC 81-18899. 128p. 1982. 6.95 (ISBN 0-8112-0822-2). New Directions.

Selected Poetry & Prose. Edgar Allan Poe. Ed. by T. O. Mabbott. (Modern Library College Editions Ser.). 1951. pap. 3.75 (ISBN 0-394-30958-8, RanC). Random.

Selected Poetry & Prose. Michael Roberts. Ed. by Frederick Grubb. 208p. 1980. 15.00 (ISBN 0-85635-263-2). Carcanet.

Selected Poetry & Prose of Byron. Ed. by W. H. Auden. 1983. pap. 7.95 (ISBN 0-452-00658-9, Mer). NAL.

Selected Poetry & Prose of Shelley. Ed. by Harold Bloom. 1978. pap. 7.95 (ISBN 0-452-00659-7, F491, Mer). NAL.

Selected Poetry & Prose of Wordsworth. Ed. by Geoffrey H. Hartman. 1980. pap. 9.95 (ISBN 0-452-00837-9, Mer). NAL.

TITLE INDEX SELECTED SONGS.

Selected Poetry of Andrea Zanzotto. Andrea Zanzotto. Ed. by Ruth Feldman & Brian Swann. LC 75-2990. (Lockert Library of Poetry in Translation). 376p. 1975. 41.00x (ISBN 0-691-06290-0); pap. 11.95 (ISBN 0-691-01323-3). Princeton U Pr.

Selected Poetry of Browning. Robert Browning. Ed. by George Ridenour. pap. 2.95 (ISBN 0-451-51599-4, CE1599, Sig Classics). NAL.

Selected Poetry of Browning. Ed. by George Widenour. 1984. pap. 8.95 (ISBN 0-452-00711-9, Mer). NAL.

Selected Poetry of F. S. Hermann. F. S. Hermann. 1988. write for info. (ISBN 0-911323-11-2). Concourse Pr.

Selected Poetry of Faye Kicknosway. Faye Kicknosway. (Selected Poetry Series of Poets at Mid-Career). 208p. (Orig.). 1986. 19.95 (ISBN 0-918273-27-7); pap. 9.95 (ISBN 0-918273-26-9). Coffee Hse.

Selected Poetry of Hayden Carruth. Hayden Carruth. 160p. 1986. 18.95 (ISBN 0-02-522290-2); pap. 10.95 (ISBN 0-02-069310-9). Macmillan.

Selected Poetry of Jaroslav Seifert. Jaroslav Seifert. Tr. by Ewald Osers & George Gibian. 240p. 1986. 17.95 (ISBN 0-02-609150-X). Macmillan.

Selected Poetry of Jaroslav Seifert. Jaroslav Seifert. Tr. by Ewald Osers & George Gibian. 208p. 1987. Repr. 9.95 (ISBN 0-02-070760-6, Collier). Macmillan.

Selected Poetry of John Donne. Ed. by Marius Bewley. 1979. pap. 4.95 (ISBN 0-452-00517-5, F517, Mer). NAL.

Selected Poetry of Keats. John Keats. Ed. by John Artos. pap. 3.50 (ISBN 0-451-52035-1, CE1568, Sig Classics). NAL.

Selected Poetry of M. Kianush. M. Kianush. 1988. write for info. (ISBN 0-911323-09-0). Concourse Pr.

Selected Poetry of Pope. Ed. by Martin Price. 1980. pap. 7.95 (ISBN 0-452-00812-3, F607, Mer). NAL.

Selected Poetry of Rainer Maria Rilke. Ed. by Stephen Mitchell. LC 83-47799. 400p. 1984. pap. 8.95 (ISBN 0-394-71636-1, Vin). Random.

Selected Poetry of Rainer Maria Rilke. Rainer M. Rilke. Ed. by Stephen Mitchell. (Illus.). 315p. 1982. 24.50 (ISBN 0-394-52434-9). Random.

Selected Poetry of Rosario Castellanos. Tr. by Bogin. 1988. pap. write for info. Graywolf.

Selected Poetry of Vicente Huidobro. Vicente Huidobro. Ed. by David M. Guss. Tr. by Stephen Fredman et al from Span. LC 81-4305. (Illus.). 288p. 1981. 18.95 (ISBN 0-8112-0804-4); pap. 6.95 (ISBN 0-8112-0805-2, NDP520). New Directions.

Selected Poetry of William Blake. David V. Erdman. 1981. pap. 9.95 (ISBN 0-452-00863-8, F569, Mer). NAL.

Selected Poetry of Yehudah Amichai. Yehudah Amichai. Tr. by Stephen Mitchell & Chana Bloch. 256p. 1986. 22.45i (ISBN 0-06-055001-5, HarpT). Har-Row.

Selected Polish Tales. Tr. by Else C. Benecke & Marie Busch. 1978. Repr. of 1921 ed. lib. bdg. 27.50 (ISBN 0-8495-0417-1). Arden Lib.

Selected Political Speeches. Cicero. Tr. by Michael Grant. (Classics Ser.). 1977. pap. 5.95 (ISBN 0-14-044214-6). Penguin.

Selected Political Writings of Rosa Luxemburg. Rosa Luxemburg. Ed. by Dick Howard. LC 75-142991. 448p. 1971. pap. 8.50 (ISBN 0-85345-197-4). Monthly Rev.

Selected Ponds. Ian H. Finlay. 1975. pap. 10.00 (ISBN 0-915596-10-5). West Coast.

Selected Population, Housing & Economic Characteristics in Kalamazoo County by Tracts: 1960-1970. Katherine Ford & Phyllis Buskirk. 63p. 1973. pap. 0.50 (ISBN 0-911558-46-2). W E Upjohn.

Selected Post-War Lithuanian Poetry. Ed. by Jonas Zdanys. (Illus.). 1978. 12.00 (ISBN 0-87141-056-7). Manyland.

Selected Pottery Groups AD 650-1780. Jane Holdsworth. (Archaeology of York - the Pottery: Vol. 16, Fas. 1). 43p. 1978. pap. text ed. 9.95x (ISBN 0-900312-70-X, Pub. by Council British Archaeology). Humanities.

Selected Power Reactor Projects in Canada & the United States of America. (Technical Reports Ser.: No. 36). 74p. 1964. pap. 11.50 (ISBN 92-0-155264-5, IDC36, IAEA). UNIPUB.

Selected Prayers by Robert Louis Stevenson. Robert Louis Stevenson, (Illus.). 1980. Repr. of 1904 ed. 97.75 (ISBN 0-89901-004-0). Found Class Reprints.

Selected Prefaces & Introductions. W. Somerset Maugham. LC 75-25375. (Works of W. Somerset Maugham Ser.). 1977. Repr. of 1963 ed. 20.00x (ISBN 0-405-07828-5). Ayer Co Pubs.

Selected Private Speeches. Demosthenes. Ed. by C. Carey & R. A. Reid. (Cambridge Greek & Latin Classics Ser.). 250p. 1985. 44.50 (ISBN 0-521-23960-5); pap. 16.95 (ISBN 0-521-28373-6). Cambridge U Pr.

Selected Problems in Ground Lease Practice. 343p. 1986. pap. 30.00 (RE-49035). Cal Cont Ed Bar.

Selected Problems in the Law of Corporate Practice. Ed. by Thomas G. Roady, Jr. & William R. Andersen. LC 60-53097. 1960. 22.50x (ISBN 0-8265-1056-6). Vanderbilt U Pr.

Selected Problems in Yavapai Syntax: The Verde Valley Dialect. Martha B. Kendall. LC 75-25118. (American Indian Linguistics Ser.). 1976. lib. bdg. 51.00 (ISBN 0-8240-1969-5). Garland Pub.

Selected Problems of Adolescence: With Emphasis on Group Formation. Helene Deutsch. LC 67-28587. (Psychoanalytic Study of the Child Monographs: No. 3). 246p. (Orig.). 1967. text ed. 20.00x (ISBN 0-8236-6040-0). Intl Univs Pr.

Selected Problems of Weighted Approximation & Spectral Analysis: Proceedings. Steklov Institute of Mathematics Staff. Ed. by N. K. Nikolskii. LC 76-46375. (Proceeding of the Steklov Institute of Mathematics: No. 120). 1976. 74.00 (ISBN 0-8218-3020-1, STEKLO-120). Am Math.

Selected Procedures in Teaching Biology. E. Irene Hollenbeck & Elmo N. Stevenson. (Studies in Education & Guidance: No. 3). 58p. 1970. pap. 4.95x (ISBN 0-87071-043-5). Oreg St U Pr.

Selected Proceedings from the First & Second Delft Pain Symposia: Journal: Applied Neurophysiology. Ed. by Janine M. Pernak et al. (Vol. 47, No. 4-6). (Illus.). 112p. 1986. pap. 49.50 (ISBN 3-8055-4044-2). S Karger.

Selected Proceedings of the Mid-America Conference on Hispanic Literature. Ed. by Luis T. Gonzalez-del-Valle & Catherine Nickel. LC 85-61851. 200p. 1986. pap. 30.00 (ISBN 0-89295-039-0). Society Sp & Sp-Am.

Selected Proceedings of the Mountain Interstate Foreign Conference, 32nd. Ed. by Gregorio C. Martin. 415p. (Orig.). 1984. pap. text ed. write for info. (ISBN 0-918401-00-3). U Wake Forest.

Selected Prose. Matthew Arnold. Ed. by P. J. Keating. (Penguin Classics Ser.). 480p. 1971. pap. 7.95 (ISBN 0-14-043058-X). Penguin.

Selected Prose. John Donne. Ed. & intro. by Neil Rhodes. 352p. 1987. pap. 7.95 (ISBN 0-14-043239-6). Penguin.

Selected Prose. Jean Follain. Tr. by Mary Feeney & Louise Guiney. 1985. 18.00 (ISBN 0-937406-32-5); pap. 5.00 (ISBN 0-937406-34-1). Logbridge-Rhodes.

Selected Prose. Charles Lamb. Intro. by Adam Phillips. 416p. 1986. pap. 6.95 (ISBN 0-14-043238-8). Penguin.

Selected Prose. Alexander Pope. Ed. by Paul Hammond. LC 86-8295. 336p. 1987. 39.50 (ISBN 0-521-25011-0). Cambridge U Pr.

Selected Prose. John H. Reynolds. Ed. by Leonidas M. Jones. LC 66-15653. (Illus.). 1966. 34.50x (ISBN 0-674-79935-6). Harvard U Pr.

Selected Prose see Selected Writing.

Selected Prose & Poetry. Mikhail Kuzmin. Ed. by Michael Green. 1980. 22.50 (ISBN 0-88233-417-4). Ardis Pubs.

Selected Prose Nineteen Nine to Nineteen Sixty-Five. Ezra Pound. Ed. by William Cookson. LC 72-93978. 480p. 1975. pap. 12.95 (ISBN 0-8112-0574-6, NDP396). New Directions.

Selected Prose of N. M. Karamzin. N. M. Karamzin. Tr. by Henry M. Nebel, Jr. (Publications of 18th Cent. Russ. Lit. Ser). 1969. 22.95x (ISBN 0-8101-0021-5). Northwestern U Pr.

Selected Prose of T. S. Eliot. T. S. Eliot. 320p. 1975. 10.95 (ISBN 0-15-180702-7, Co-Pub by FS&G). HarBraceJ.

Selected Prose of T. S. Eliot. T. S. Eliot. Ed. by Frank Kermode. 313p. 1975. pap. 9.95 (ISBN 0-15-680654-1, Harv). HarBraceJ.

Selected Prose of T. S. Eliot. T. S. Eliot. 1988. pap. 9.95. HarBraceJ.

Selected Prose Writings. William Wordsworth. Ed. by John O. Hayden. 528p. 1988. pap. 7.95 (ISBN 0-14-043292-2). Penguin.

Selected Prose Writings of John Milton. Ed. by Ernest Myers. 1973. Repr. of 1904 ed. lib. bdg. 35.50 (ISBN 0-8414-6695-5). Folcroft.

Selected Publications of Wilhelm Nusselt & Ernst Schmidt. Ed. by U. Griqull. LC 82-9199. 272p. 1982. pap. text ed. 21.95 (ISBN 0-89116-329-8). Hemisphere Pub.

Selected Quotations for the Ideological Skeptic: A Compendium of Epigrams, Aphorisms, Observations & Commentary on Ideologues, True Believers, Fanatics, Crusaders, Partisans & Zealots. Laird Wilcox. (Orig.). 1987. pap. 14.95 (ISBN 0-933592-46-9). L Wilcox.

Selected Quotations from the Sermons of A. W. Tozer see Tozer Pulpit.

Selected Rabbinical Response see Jewish Law & Jewish Life.

Selected Radio & Television Criticism. Ed. by Anthony Slide. LC 86-27891. 213p. 1987. 19.50 (ISBN 0-8108-1942-2). Scarecrow.

Selected Readings from Military Thought: 1963-1973, Vol. 5, Pt. 1. Ed. by Joseph D. Douglass, Jr. Amoretta M. Hoeber. 258p. (Orig.). 1982. pap. 7.50 (ISBN 0-318-21895-X, S/N 008-070-00471-2). USGPO.

Selected Readings in Business & Office Occupations, 1967. (Yearbooks). 351p. 5.75 (ISBN 0-933964-05-6). Natl Busn Ed Assoc.

Selected Readings in Chinese Communist Literature. rev ed. Compiled by Tien-Yi Li. 6.00 (ISBN 0-88710-080-5); tapes avail. (ISBN 0-88710-081-3). Yale Far Eastern Pubns.

Selected Readings in Creativity, 2 vols. Ed. by Stanley S. Gryskievicz. (Creativity Week Ser.). 1983. Set. 40.00 (ISBN 0-912879-81-5). Ctr Creat Leader.

Selected Readings in Mineral Economics. Ed. by F. J. Anderson. 400p. 1987. 52.00 (ISBN 0-08-035864-0, Pub. by PBI, Pub. by PBI). Pergamon.

Selected Readings in Quantitative Urban Analysis. Samuel J. Bernstein & W. Giles Mellon. LC 77-30458. 1978. 45.00 (ISBN 0-08-019593-8); pap. 29.00 (ISBN 0-08-019592-X). Pergamon.

Selected Readings in Scholasticism & Education. Ed. by Vincent J. Colimore. 115p. 1971. pap. text ed. 9.95x (ISBN 0-8422-0142-4). Irvington.

Selected Readings in the History of Physiology. John F. Fulton. 317p. 1983. lib. bdg. 85.00 (ISBN 0-89987-283-2). Darby Bks.

Selected Readings in the Issues of Day Care. Ed. by James A. Harrell. (Illus.). 84p. pap. 5.25 (ISBN 0-936746-24-6, L50). Day Care Coun.

Selected Readings in the Philosophy of Education. 4th ed. Joe Park. (Illus.). 367p. 1974. pap. text ed. write for info. (ISBN 0-02-391650-8). Macmillan.

Selected Readings in Traditional Healing. Philip Singer & Elizabeth M. Titus. (Traditional Healing Ser.: Vol. 2). Date not set. text ed. 15.75x (ISBN 0-932426-01-8); pap. text ed. 10.00x (ISBN 0-932426-05-0). Trado-Medic.

Selected Readings on Ozone in Water Treatment. 35.00 (ISBN 0-317-07469-5). Pan Am Intl Ozone.

Selected References on Reliability Growth. LC 62-38584. 414p. (Orig.). 1988. pap. text ed. 50.00 (ISBN 0-915414-40-6). Inst Environ Sci.

Selected Religious Poems of Solomon Ibn Gabiro. Solomon I. Gabirol. LC 73-2210. (Jewish People; History, Religion, Literature Ser.). Repr. of 1923 ed. 32.00 (ISBN 0-405-05274-X). Ayer Co Pubs.

Selected Reports in Ethnomusicology, Vol. II, No. 1. Ed. by Peter Crossley-Holland. LC 73-620035. vii, 125p. (Orig.). 1974. pap. text ed. 7.50 (ISBN 0-88287-004-1). UCLA Dept Ethnom.

Selected Reports in Ethnomusicology, Vol. III, No. 1. Ed. by James Porter. LC 76-640181. (Illus.). vii, 260p. 1978. pap. text ed. 11.95 (ISBN 0-88287-011-4). UCLA Dept Ethnom.

Selected Reports in Ethnomusicology, Vol. III, No. 2. Ed. by Charlotte Heth. LC 76-640181. (Illus.). xii, 202p. 1980. pap. text ed. 11.95 (ISBN 0-88287-012-2). UCLA Dept Ethnom.

Selected Reports in Ethnomusicology, Vol. II, No. 2. Ed. by David Morton. LC 75-24270. (Illus.). xii, 259p. (Orig.). 1975. pap. text ed. 9.50 (ISBN 0-88287-005-X). UCLA Dept Ethnom.

Selected Reports in Ethnomusicology: Essays in Honour of Peter Crossley-Holland on His 65th Birthday, Vol. IV. Ed. by Nazir A. Jairazbhoy & Nicole Marzac-Holland. LC 76-640181. xxv, 300p. 1983. pap. text ed. 12.95 (ISBN 0-88287-016-5). UCLA Dept Ethnom.

Selected Reports in Ethnomusicology: Studies in African Music, Vol. V. Ed. by J. H. Nketia & Jacqueline C. Dje Dje. LC 76-640181. (Illus.). xx, 387p. (Orig.). 1984. pap. text ed. 18.95 (ISBN 0-88287-017-3). UCLA Dept Ethnom.

Selected Reprints in Software. 3rd ed. Marvin V. Zelkowitz. 400p. (Orig.). 1987. pap. 40.00 (ISBN 0-8186-0789-0, EK789). IEEE Comp Soc.

Selected Reprints on Dataflow & Reduction Architectures. S. S. Thakkar. 454p. 1987. pap. 39.00 (EK759). IEEE Comp Soc.

Selected Reprints on Logic Design for Testability. Constantin C. Timoc. 324p. 1984. 25.00 (ISBN 0-8186-0573-1, EZ573). IEEE Comp Soc.

Selected Reprints on Microprocessors & Microcomputers. 3rd ed. J. T. Cain. 342p. 1984. 20.00 (ISBN 0-8186-0585-5, EZ585). IEEE Comp Soc.

Selected Reprints on VLSI Technologies & Computer Graphics. Henry Fuchs. 490p. 1983. 36.00 (ISBN 0-8186-0491-3). IEEE Comp Soc.

Selected Revisionist Pamphlets: An Original Arno Press Compilation. Harry E. Barnes. LC 72-172205. (Right Wing Individualist Tradition in America Ser). 1972. Repr. of 1971 ed. 19.00 (ISBN 0-405-00415-X). Ayer Co Pubs.

Selected Roy McFadden. Roy McFadden. 112p. (Orig.). 1983. pap. 6.75 (ISBN 0-85640-282-6, Pub. by Blackstaff Pr). Longwood Pub Group.

Selected Salary Data: Massachusetts Judicial Department. National Center for State Courts Staff. 185p. 1978. manuscript 11.10 (NERO-026). Natl Ctr St Courts.

Selected Satires of Lucian. Lucian. Ed. & tr. by Lionel Casson. 1968. pap. 10.95 (ISBN 0-393-00443-0, Norton Lib). Norton.

Selected Scientific Papers of Alfred Lande. Ed. by Asim O. Barut & A. van der Merwe. 1987. lib. bdg. 99.00 (ISBN 90-277-2594-2, Pub. by Reidel Holland). Kluwer Academic.

Selected Scientific Papers of Shanghai Chaio Tung University-Books, 1984. Ed. by Collet's Holdings, Ltd. Staff. 162p. 1984. 66.00x (ISBN 0-317-46721-2, Pub. by Collets (UK)). State Mutual Bk.

Selected Securities & Business Planning Statutes: Rules & Forms, 1987 Edition. David L. Ratner. 493p. 1987. pap. text ed. 10.95 (ISBN 0-314-60645-9). West Pub.

Selected Securities & Business Planning Statutes, Rules & Forms: 1987. 1987. pap. write for info. West Pub.

Selected Sensory Methods Problems & Approaches to Measuring Hedonics - STP 773. Ed. by Kuznicki & Rutkiewic. 113p. 1982. pap. 11.95 (ISBN 0-8031-0782-X, 04-773000-36). ASTM.

Selected Sentences from L. Annaeus Seneca & Publius Syrus the Mime. Emanuel Swedenborg. Tr. by Alfred Acton from Lat. 64p. 1967. pap. 1.50 (ISBN 0-915221-14-4). Swedenborg Sci Assn.

Selected Sermons. facs. ed. Phillips Brooks. Ed. by William Scarlett. LC 79-142610. (Essay Index Reprint Ser). 1949. 19.50 (ISBN 0-8369-2146-1). Ayer Co Pubs.

Selected Sermons. C. F. Walther. Tr. by Herbert J. Bouman. (Selected Writings of C. F. W. Walther Ser.). 1981. 12.95 (ISBN 0-570-08276-5, 15-2734). Concordia.

Selected Sermons of Hugh Latimer. Hugh Latimer. Ed. by Allan G. Chester. (Documents Ser). 1978. 16.00x (ISBN 0-918016-43-6). Folger Bks.

Selected Sermons of the French Baroque. Peter Bayley. LC 82-48767. 326p. 1983. lib. bdg. 85.00 (ISBN 0-8240-9218-X). Garland Pub.

Selected Shelburne Essays. Paul E. More. Repr. of 1935 ed. 39.00x (ISBN 0-403-07240-9). Somerset Pub.

Selected Short Fiction. Charles Dickens. Ed. by Deborah Thomas. (English Library Ser.). 432p. 1976. pap. 4.95 (ISBN 0-14-043103-9). Penguin.

Selected Short Plays. George Bernard Shaw. 384p. 1988. pap. 6.95 (ISBN 0-14-045024-6). Penguin.

Selected Short Stories. E. J. Arnold. Ed. by A. W. Hornsey. 1964. 3.35 (ISBN 0-08-010714-1); pap. 3.45 (ISBN 0-08-010713-3). Pergamon.

Selected Short Stories. Guy De Maupassant. Tr. by Roger Colet. (Classics Ser). 1971. pap. 4.95 (ISBN 0-14-044243-X). Penguin.

Selected Short Stories. Maxim Gorky. 410p. 1975. 14.95 (ISBN 0-8464-0834-1). Beekman Pubs.

Selected Short Stories. Alexander Grin. Ed. & tr. by Nicholas Luker. 250p. 1987. 22.00 (ISBN 0-88233-684-3). Ardis Pubs.

Selected Short Stories. facsimile ed. Per Hallstrom. Tr. by F. J. Fielden from Swedish. LC 77-144155. (Short Story Index Reprint Ser.). Repr. of 1922 ed. 12.00 (ISBN 0-8369-3770-8). Ayer Co Pubs.

Selected Short Stories. Gwyn Jones. 1974. pap. 4.95x (ISBN 0-19-281162-2). Oxford U Pr.

Selected Short Stories. H. G. Wells. 352p. 1988. pap. 4.95 (ISBN 0-14-008247-6). Penguin.

Selected Short Stories from Pakistan. Intro. by Ahmed Ali. 232p. 1988. 16.95 (ISBN 0-19-577382-9). Oxford U Pr.

Selected Short Stories of Franz Kafka. Franz Kafka. Tr. by Willa Muir & Edwin Muir. LC 52-9771. 7.95 (ISBN 0-394-60422-9). Modern Lib.

Selected Short Stories of Mulk Raj Anand. Ed. by M. K. Naik. 296p. 1984. 12.00 (ISBN 0-86578-233-4). Ind-US Inc.

Selected Short Stories of Padraic Colum. Ed. by Sanford Sternlicht. LC 84-20522. (Irish Studies). (Illus.). 160p. 1985. text ed. 19.95x (ISBN 0-8156-2327-5); pap. 12.95 1986 (ISBN 0-8156-0202-2). Syracuse U Pr.

Selected Short Stories of the Supernatural. Margaret Oliphant. Ed. by Margaret K. Gray. 256p. 1985. 12.75 (ISBN 0-7073-0478-4, Pub. by Scot Acad Pr). Longwood Pub Group.

Selected Short Stories of William Faulkner. William Faulkner. LC 62-9690. 306p. 1962. 7.95 (ISBN 0-394-60456-3). Modern Lib.

Selected Short Subjects: From Spanky to the Three Stooges. Leonard Maltin. LC 83-7580. (Quality Paperbacks Ser.). (Illus.). 236p. 1983. pap. 12.95 (ISBN 0-306-80204-X). Da Capo.

Selected Shorter Poems. Donald Finkel. LC 86-47700. 128p. 1987. 21.00 (ISBN 0-689-11855-4); pap. 12.95 (ISBN 0-689-11856-2). Atheneum.

Selected Shorter Writings of Mark Twain. Mark Twain. Ed. by Walter Blair. LC 62-51467. (YA) (gr. 9 up). 1962. pap. 6.50 (ISBN 0-395-05155-X, RivEd). HM.

Selected Sites in the Hill Lake Locality, Vol. 13. Andrew C. Fortier. (American Bottom Archaeology, Selected FAI-270 Site Reports Ser.: Vol. 13). (Illus.). 350p. 1985. pap. 17.50 (ISBN 0-252-01075-2). U of Ill Pr.

Selected Small Homes...Keyed to the Times. rev. ed. Ed. by National Plan Service, Inc. Staff. (Illus.). 32p. Date not set. pap. 3.95 (ISBN 0-934039-11-9, A37). Natl Plan Serv.

Selected Social Studies Skills: Eighty-Eight Reinforcement Lessons for Secondary Students. Ed. by Stuart Stockhaus. 282p. 1979. pap. 19.95 (ISBN 0-89994-236-9). Soc Sci Ed.

Selected Solutions for Semiconductor Devices: Physics & Technology. S. M. Sze. (Illus.). 70p. 1985. pap. 8.95 (ISBN 0-471-82953-6). Wiley.

Selected Songs. Augusta Holmes. LC 85-2532. (Women Composers Ser.: No. 13). 100p. 1983. lib. bdg. 27.50 (ISBN 0-306-76170-X). Da Capo.

Selected Songs. Jeanne Singer. LC 82-71820. (Living Composers' Ser.: No. 3). 1982. pap. 12.50 (ISBN 0-934218-26-9). Dragons Teeth.

Selected Songs for Solo Voice & Piano. Robert Schumann. Tr. by Stanley Appelbaum. 256p. (Repr. of 1882-87 eds.). 1981. pap. 9.95 (ISBN 0-486-24202-1). Dover.

Selected Songs for Solo Voice & Piano: From the Complete Works Edition. Robert Schumann. Ed. by Clara Schumann. Tr. by Stanley Applebaum. 20.25 (ISBN 0-8446-5914-2). Peter Smith.

Selected Songs of Eliakum Zunser. facsimile ed. Eliakum Zunser. LC 74-29534. (Modern Jewish Experience Ser.). 1975. Repr. of 1928 ed. 24.50x (ISBN 0-405-06757-7). Ayer Co Pubs.

Selected Songs of Thomas Campion. Thomas Campion. Ed. by W. H. Auden. LC 71-152794. (Illus.). 168p. 1972. 15.00x (ISBN 0-87923-037-1); ltd. ed. 40.00 (ISBN 0-87923-036-3); pap. 10.00 (ISBN 0-87923-091-6). Godine.

Selected Sonnets of Khawju of Kirman. Khawju of Kirman. Ed. & tr. by Mehdi Nakosteen. LC 78-65312. 118p. 1979. 17.95x. Iran Bks.

Selected Spanish Stories of the Nineteenth & Twentieth Centuries. Robert R. Ashburn. Repr. of 1943 ed. 25.00. Darby Bks.

Selected Specimens of Chinese Porcelain. Danjong Tan. 125p. 1959. 315.00x (ISBN 0-317-45225-8, Pub. by Han-Shan Tang Ltd). State Mutual Bk.

Selected Speeches & Interviews. J. Kadar. (Illus.). 475p. 1985. 28.00 (ISBN 0-08-028178-8, Pub. by PPL). Pergamon.

Selected Speeches & Statements of General of the Army George C. Marshall. George C. Marshall. Ed. by H. A. DeWeerd. LC 72-10365. (FDR & the Era of the New Deal Ser.). 1973. Repr. of 1945 ed. lib. bdg. 37.50 (ISBN 0-306-70556-7). Da Capo.

Selected Speeches & Writings. V. V. Grishin. LC 84-3042. (World Leaders Ser.). 300p. 1984. 51.00 (ISBN 0-08-030856-2). Pergamon.

Selected Speeches & Writings. A. N. Kosygin. LC 80-41077. 352p. 1981. 52.00 (ISBN 0-08-023610-3). Pergamon.

Selected Speeches & Writings. Boris N. Ponomarev. LC 80-40182. 384p. 1981. 57.00 (ISBN 0-08-023606-5). Pergamon.

Selected Speeches & Writings. N. A. Tikhonov. (Illus.). 420p. 1982. 61.00 (ISBN 0-08-023613-8). Pergamon.

Selected Speeches & Writings on Foreign Affairs. Leonid I. Brezhnev. LC 78-40614. 1979. 58.00 (ISBN 0-08-023569-7). Pergamon.

Selected Speeches from the Nineteen Seventy-Five National Marketing Conference. 1975. 15.00 (ISBN 0-89982-047-6, 245300). Am Bankers.

Selected Speeches from the Nineteen Seventy-Four National Marketing Conference: Action or Reaction. 1974. 15.00 (ISBN 0-89982-048-4, 244800). Am Bankers.

Selected Speeches: Including an Interview with Robert Maxwell. Wojciech Jaruzelski. (Leaders of the World Ser.). (Illus.). 200p. 1985. pap. 28.00 (ISBN 0-08-033366-4, Pub. by P P L). Pergamon.

Selected Speeches of a Wake Forest University Law Professor & Dean. Ed. by Wake Forest University School of Law Staff. 1984. 10.00 (ISBN 0-942225-09-0). Wake Forest Law.

Selected Speeches of Mason Gross. Ed. by Richard P. McCormick & Richard Schlatter. 160p. 1980. 24.95 (ISBN 0-87855-388-6). Transaction Bks.

Selected Standards & Policy Statements of Special Interest to Women Workers Adopted under the Auspices of International Labour Office. 132p. (Orig.). 1980. pap. 15.75 (ISBN 92-2-102441-5). Intl Labour Office.

Selected Standards & Policy Statements of Special Interest to Women Workers Adopted under the Auspices of the International Labour Organization. v, 32p. 1980. pap. 8.75 (ISBN 92-2-102441-5, ILO150, ILO). UNIPUB.

Selected Standards on Professional Responsibility Including California Rules, 1986. Thomas D. Morgan & Ronald D. Rotunda. 357p. 1985. pap. text ed. 10.95 (ISBN 0-88277-278-3). Foundation Pr.

Selected Standards on Professional Responsibilty Including California Rules, 1987. Thomas D. Morgan & Ronald D. Rotunda. 431p. 1986. pap. text ed. 11.75 (ISBN 0-88277-544-8). Foundation Pr.

Selected Statistics on the Office of Attorney General. 86p. 1979. 4.50 (ISBN 0-318-15227-4). Natl Attys General.

Selected Statutes & International Agreements on Unfair Competition, Trademarks, Copyrights & Patents, 1987 Edition. Edmund Kitch & Paul Goldstein. 312p. 1987. pap. text ed. write for info. (ISBN 0-88277-590-1). Foundation Pr.

Selected Statutes & International Agreements on Unfair Competition, Trademarks, Copyrights & Patents. Edmund Kitch et al. (University Casebook Ser.). 322p. 1986. pap. text ed. 9.95 (ISBN 0-88277-331-3). Foundation Pr.

Selected Statutes, Rules & Forms, Under the Federal Securities Laws, 1987 Edition. Richard W. Jennings & Harold Marsh, Jr. 1100p. 1987. pap. text ed. write for info. (ISBN 0-88277-580-4). Foundation Pr.

Selected Statutes, Rules & Forms, under the Federal Securities Law, 1988 Edition. Richard W. Jennings & Harold Marsh, Jr. 1988. pap. text ed. write for info. (ISBN 0-88277-670-3). Foundation Pr.

Selected Still Projection Apparatus for Scenic Effects Projection. 2nd ed. Mark Lipschutz. 1976. pap. 5.95x (ISBN 0-685-83023-3). Scenographic.

Selected Stories. Benny Andersen. LC 82-23459. 120p. 1983. pap. 6.00 (ISBN 0-915306-25-5). Curbstone.

Selected Stories. L. N. Andreyev. Ed. by M. H. Shotton. (Library of Russian Classics). 112p. pap. text ed. 9.95x (ISBN 0-900186-10-0). Basil Blackwell.

Selected Stories. Elizabeth Bowen. LC 83-45415. Repr. of 1946 ed. AMS Pr.

Selected Stories. George M. Brown. Date not set. 19.50 (ISBN 0-8149-0929-9). Vanguard.

Selected Stories. Guy De Maupassant. Tr. by Andrew R. MacAndrew. 288p. 1984. pap. 4.95 (ISBN 0-452-00686-4, Mer). NAL.

Selected Stories. Nadine Gordimer. 448p. 1983. pap. 6.95 (ISBN 0-14-006737-X). Penguin.

Selected Stories. Rudyard Kipling. Intro. by Sandra Kemp. 384p. 1987. pap. 7.95 (ISBN 0-460-01584-2, Evman). Biblio Dist.

Selected Stories. Mary Lavin. 272p. 1984. pap. 6.95 (ISBN 0-14-005602-5). Penguin.

Selected Stories. 3rd ed. Lu Hsun. 1972. 10.95 (ISBN 0-8351-0326-9). China Bks.

Selected Stories. K. Paustovsky. 335p. 1974. 5.45 (ISBN 0-8285-1020-2, Pub. by Progress Pubs USSR). Imported Pubns.

Selected Stories. I. L. Peretz. Ed. by Irving Howe & Eliezer Greenberg. LC 73-91342. 159p. 1975. pap. 6.95 (ISBN 0-8052-0496-2). Schocken.

Selected Stories. Robert Walser. Tr. by Christopher Middleton from Ger. LC 82-9257. 203p. 1982. 16.50 (ISBN 0-374-25901-1). FS&G.

Selected Stories. Robert Walser. Tr. by Christopher Middleton et al from Ger. 208p. 1987. pap. 7.95 (ISBN 0-374-52054-2). FS&G.

Selected Stories. Eudora Welty. LC 83-5466. 8.95 (ISBN 0-394-60445-8). Modern Lib.

Selected Stories see Diviner.

Selected Stories from the Southern Review, 1965-1985. Ed. by Lewis P. Simpson et al. LC 87-21383. 384p. 1988. 24.95 (ISBN 0-8071-1443-X); pap. 14.95 (ISBN 0-8071-1490-1). La State U Pr.

Selected Stories of Andre Dubus. Andre Dubus. 1988. 19.95. Godine.

Selected Stories of Bret Harte. Bret Harte. Repr. lib. bdg. 45.50 (ISBN 0-8414-5012-9). Folcroft.

Selected Stories of Julio Ricci. Julio Ricci. Tr. by Clark Zlotchew. 1988. 8.00. White Pine.

Selected Stories of Lu Hsun. 3rd ed. Lu Hsun. Tr. by Gladys Yang & Hsien-Yi. (Illus.). 255p. 1978. pap. 7.95 (ISBN 0-917056-71-X, Pub. by Foreign Lang Pr China). Cheng & Tsui.

Selected Stories of Mary E. Wilkins Freeman. Ed. by Marjorie Pryse. 1983. 27.50 (ISBN 0-393-01726-5). Norton.

Selected Stories of Robert Bloch, 3 vols. Robert Bloch. LC 87-34267. 1200p. 1988. Set. 80.00 (ISBN 0-88733-055-X); deluxe ed. 125.00x. Vol. 1: Final Reckonings. Vol. 2: Bitter Ends. Vol. 3: Last Rites. Underwood-Miller.

Selected Stories of Sean O'Faolain. Sean O'Faolain. LC 78-5780. 1978. 14.95 (ISBN 0-316-63285-6, Pub. by Atlantic Monthly Pr.). Little.

Selected Stories of Sylvia Townsend Warner. Syvia T. Warner. 1988. 19.95 (ISBN 0-670-82467-4). Viking.

Selected Stories of V. S. Pritchett. V. S. Pritchett. 1978. 11.95 (ISBN 0-394-50128-4). Random.

Selected Stories of Xiao Hong. Xiao Hong. Tr. by Howard Goldbratt from Chinese. 220p. 1982. pap. 4.95 (ISBN 0-8351-1049-4). China Bks.

Selected Studies. Ernst H. Kantorowicz. LC 65-25431. 12.50 (ISBN 0-685-71745-3). J J Augustin.

Selected Studies in Bibliography. G. Thomas Tanselle. LC 79-12476. 506p. 1979. 25.00x (ISBN 0-8139-0829-9). U Pr of Va.

Selected Studies in Highway Law, 3 Vols. 1037p. 1976. Set Vols. I & II. 60.00 (ISBN 0-309-02434-X); Vol. III. 30.00 (ISBN 0-317-36103-1). Transport Res Bd.

Selected Studies of Archean Gneisses & Lower Proterozoic Rocks, Southern Canadian Shield. Ed. by G. B. Morey & Gilbert N. Hanson. LC 80-67113. (Special Paper Ser.: No. 182). (Illus., Orig.). 1980. pap. 20.80 (ISBN 0-8137-2182-2). Geol Soc.

Selected Studies on the Dynamics, Patterns & Consequences of Migration: Mexico City: Industrialization, Migration & the Labour Force, 1930-1970, Vol. 1. Humberto Munoz et al. (Reports & Papers in the Social Sciences: No. 46). (Illus.). 87p. 1983. pap. text ed. 5.00 (ISBN 92-3-101855-8, U1276, UNESCO). UNIPUB.

Selected Studies on the Dynamics, Patterns & Consequences of Migration: Migration & Development: Major Features of Migratory Movement in India, Vol. 3. Biplab Dasgupta. (Reports & Papers in the Social Sciences: No. 52). (Illus.). 39p. 1983. pap. text ed. 5.00 (ISBN 92-3-102011-0, U1279, UNESCO). UNIPUB.

Selected Studies on the Dynamics, Patterns & Consequences of Migration: Medium-Sized Towns in Nigeria, Research & Policy Prospects, Vol. 4. Aderanti Adepoju. (Reports & Papers in the Social Sciences: No. 53). 56p. 1983. pap. text ed. 5.00 (ISBN 92-3-102035-8, U1277, UNESCO). UNIPUB.

Selected Subaltern Studies. Ed. by Ranajit Guha & Gayatri C. Spivak. 416p. 1988. pap. 9.95 (ISBN 0-19-505289-7). Oxford U Pr.

Selected Summaries of Court Decisions Relating to the Provision of Library Services in Institutions. Compiled by Arthur J. Moen. 46p. 10.00 (ISBN 0-8389-6539-3); members 9.00 (ISBN 0-318-13354-7). ASCLA.

Selected Tables for Mathematical Statistics. Incl. Vol. 1. LC 71-111981. 1973. 27.00 (ISBN 0-8218-1901-1, TABLES-1); Vol. 2. W. G. Bulgren. Ed. by Institute of Mathematical Statistics. LC 74-6283. 1974. 33.00 (ISBN 0-8218-1902-X, TABLES-2); Vol. 3. Bernard Harris et al. Ed. by Institute of Mathematical Statistics. LC 74-6283. 1975. 43.00 (ISBN 0-8218-1903-8, TABLES-3); Vol. 5. LC 74-6283. 1977. 30.00 (ISBN 0-8218-1905-4, TABLES-5); Vol. 6, The Distribution of the Size of the Maximum Cluster of Points on a Line. Norman D. Neff & Joseph I. Naus. LC 74-6283. 1980. 21.00 (ISBN 0-8218-1906-2); Vol. 7, Product of Two Normally Distributed Random Variables. William Q. Meeker, Jr. et al. LC 74-6283. 1981. 26.00 (ISBN 0-8218-1907-0, TABLES SER.); Vol. 8. 1985. 33.00 (ISBN 0-8218-1908-9); Vol. 4. M. Sobel et al. LC 74-6283. 1977. 33.00 (ISBN 0-8218-1904-6, TABLES-4). Am Math.

Selected Tales. Nikolai Leskov. Tr. by David Magarshack from Rus. 300p. 1987. pap. 7.95. FS&G.

Selected Tales. Edgar Allan Poe. Ed. by Julian Symons. (World's Classics Paperback Ser.). 1980. pap. 2.95 (ISBN 0-19-281522-9). Oxford U Pr.

Selected Tales & Poems. Herman Melville. 24.95 (ISBN 0-89190-681-9, Pub. by Am Repr). Amereon Ltd.

Selected Tales & Sketches. Nathaniel Hawthorne. LC 83-45781. Repr. of 1950 ed. 37.00 (ISBN 0-404-20120-2). AMS Pr.

Selected Tales & Sketches. Nathaniel Hawthorne. 484p. 1987. pap. 5.95 (ISBN 0-14-039057-X). Penguin.

Selected Tales of Grim & Grue from the Horror Pulps. Sheldon Jaffery. LC 87-72859. 186p. 1987. 31.95 (ISBN 0-87972-391-2); pap. 15.95 (ISBN 0-87972-392-0). Bowling Green Univ.

Selected Tales of Jacques Ferron. Jacques Ferron. Tr. by Betty Bednarski from Fr. (Anansi Fiction Ser.: AF 48). 192p. (Orig.). 1984. pap. 9.95 (ISBN 0-88784-140-6, Pub. by Hse Anansi Pr Canada). U of Toronto Pr.

Selected Tales of Laiozhai. Pu Songling. (Panda Bks.). 151p. (Orig.). 1981. pap. 4.95 (ISBN 0-8351-0943-7). China Bks.

Selected Temple Documents of the Ur Dynasty. Clarence E. Keiser. LC 78-63533. (Yale Oriental Series: Babylonian Texts: No. 4). (Illus.). 240p. Repr. of 1919 ed. 42.50 (ISBN 0-404-60254-1). AMS Pr.

Selected Terms in Fish Culture. (Terminology Bulletins: No. 19). 158p. (Eng., Fr., Span. & Arabic.). 1981. pap. 11.25 (ISBN 92-5-000910-0, F2277, FAO). UNIPUB.

Selected Terms in Remote Sensing. (Terminology Bulletins: No. 36). 374p. (Eng., Fr. & Span.). 1985. pap. 28.75 (ISBN 92-5-002248-4, F2783, FAO). UNIPUB.

Selected Terms of Irrigation. (Terminology Bulletins: No. 34). 94p. (Eng., Fr., Span. & Arabic.). 1978. pap. 9.00 (ISBN 92-5-000668-3, F1544, FAO). UNIPUB.

Selected Texts on Prayer. Nilus of Sinai. pap. 0.25 (ISBN 0-317-11390-9). Eastern Orthodox.

Selected Theatre Criticism, Vol. 2: Nineteen Twenty to Nineteen Thirty. Ed. by Anthony Slide. LC 85-2266. 1985. 22.50 (ISBN 0-8108-1844-2). Scarecrow.

Selected Theatre Criticism, Vol 1: Nineteen Hundred to Nineteen-Nineteen. Ed. by Anthony Slide. LC 85-2266. 395p. 1985. 29.50 (ISBN 0-8108-1811-6). Scarecrow.

Selected Theatre Criticism: Volume 3: Nineteen Thirty-One to Nineteen Fifty. Ed. by Anthony Slide. LC 85-2266. 297p. 1986. 21.50 (ISBN 0-8108-1846-9). Scarecrow.

Selected Theses & Dissertations on Washington, D.C. Region. Calvan. 1.00 (ISBN 0-318-21783-X). G Washington Univ.

Selected Titles in Chemistry. 4th ed. 1977. pap. 1.25 (ISBN 0-8412-0413-6). Am Chemical.

Selected Topics from Neurochemistry. Ed. by N. N. Osborne. (Illus.). 580p. 1985. 105.00 (ISBN 0-08-031994-7, Pub. by PPL). Pergamon.

Selected Topics in Algebra. Ionel Bucur. LC 83-24609. 1984. lib. bdg. 79.00 (ISBN 90-277-1671-4, Pub. by Reidel Holland). Kluwer Academic.

Selected Topics in Algebraic Geometry, 2 Vols in 1. 2nd ed. Virgil Snyder et al. LC 78-113149. 1970. text ed. 16.95 (ISBN 0-8284-0189-6). Chelsea Pub.

Selected Topics in Clinical Enzymology: Proceedings of the Third International Congress of Clinical Enzymology, Salzburg, Austria, September 6-9, 1981. Ed. by D. M. Goldberg & M. Werner. 362p. 1983. 104.00 (ISBN 3-11-009688-9). De Gruyter.

Selected Topics in Clinical Enzymology: Vol. 2, Proceedings (Selected) of the 4th International Congress on Clinical Enzymology, Washington, D.C., July 30 - August 2, 1983. Ed. by M. Werner & D. M. Goldberg. (Illus.). xxii, 667p. 1985. 168.00 (ISBN 3-11-010233-1). De Gruyter.

Selected Topics in Electroweak Interactions: Proceedings of the 2nd Lake Louise Winter Institute on New Frontiers in Particle Physics. Ed. by A. Kamal et al. 600p. 1987. 75.00x (ISBN 9971-50-302-6); pap. 37.00 (ISBN 9971-50-303-4). World Scientific Pub.

Selected Topics in Elementary Number Theory. Charles R. Wall. 1974. 34.95 (ISBN 0-87249-311-3). U of SC Pr.

Selected Topics in Gauge Theories. W. Dittrich & M. Reuter. (Lecture Notes in Physics Ser.: Vol. 244). v, 315p. 1986. pap. 18.60 (ISBN 0-387-16064-7). Springer-Verlag.

Selected Topics in Graph Theory, Vol. 2. Lowell W. Beineke & Robin J. Wilson. 1983. 69.00 (ISBN 0-12-086202-6). Acad Pr.

Selected Topics in Graph Theory, Vol. 3. Ed. by Lowell W. Beineke & Robin J. Wilson. 210p. 1988. 53.75 (ISBN 0-12-086203-4). Acad Pr.

Selected Topics in Graphs Theory. Ed. by Lowell Beineke & Robin Wilson. 1979. 98.00 (ISBN 0-12-086250-6). Acad Pr.

Selected Topics in Harmonic Maps. James Eells & Luc Lemaire. LC 82-25526. (Conference Board of the Mathematical Sciences Ser.: No. 50). 86p. 1983. pap. 19.00 (ISBN 0-8218-0700-5). Am Math.

Selected Topics in Human Sexuality. Ed. by A. R. Cavaliere & Janet M. Riggs. 180p. (Orig.). 1988. pap. 14.25 (ISBN 0-8191-6718-5). U Pr of Amer.

Selected Topics in Image Science. Ed. by O. Nalcioglu & Z. H. Cho. (Lecture Notes in Medical Informatics: Vol. 23). ix, 308p. 1984. 34.50 (ISBN 0-387-12898-0). Springer-Verlag.

Selected Topics in Information Theory: Proceedings of CISM, Department of Hydro & Gas Dynamics, 1970. CISM (International Center for Mechanical Sciences), Department of Automation & Information Staff. Ed. by G. Longo. (CISM International Center for Mechanical Sciences Ser.: No. 18). (Illus.). 111p. 1974. pap. 15.70 (ISBN 0-387-81166-4). Springer-Verlag.

Selected Topics in Medical Artificial Intelligence. Ed. by P. L. Miller. (Computers & Medicine Ser.). (Illus.). 220p. 1988. 39.95 (ISBN 0-387-96701-X). Springer-Verlag.

Selected Topics in Nuclear Theory. (Proceedings Ser.). (Illus.). 452p. 1963. 23.50 (ISBN 92-0-030563-6, ISP67, IAEA). UNIPUB.

Selected Topics in Number Theory. H. Gupta. 394p. 1980. 42.00 (ISBN 0-85626-177-7). Abacus Pr.

Selected Topics in Operations Research & Mathematical Economics: Proceedings of the Eighth Symposium on Operations Research Held at the University of Karlsruhe, West Germany, August 22-25, 1984. Ed. by G. Hammer & D. Pallaschke. (Lecture Notes in Economics & Mathematical Systems). ix, 478p. 1984. pap. 35.00 (ISBN 0-387-12918-9). Springer-Verlag.

Selected Topics in Physics: Astrophysics & Biophysics, Proceedings. Latin School of Physics, 14th Caracas, Venezuela July 10-28, 1972. Ed. by E. Abecassis De Laredo & N. K. Jurisic. LC 73-83563. 420p. 1973. lib. bdg. 71.00 (ISBN 90-277-0367-1, Pub. by Reidel Holland). Kluwer Academic.

Selected Topics in Preventive Cardiology. Ed. by A. Raineri & J. J. Kellerman. LC 83-8989. (Ettore Majorana International Science Series, Life Sciences: Vol. 12). 286p. 1983. 65.00x (ISBN 0-306-41375-2, Plenum Pr). Plenum Pub.

Selected Topics in Solid State & Theoretical Physics. M. Bemporad & E. Ferreira. 482p. 1968. 167.00 (ISBN 0-677-11900-3). Gordon & Breach.

Selected Topics in Statistical Mechanics. John G. Kirkwood. Ed. by R. W. Zwanzig. LC 68-6792. (Documents on Modern Physics Ser.). (Illus.). 288p. 1967. 88.00 (ISBN 0-677-00330-7). Gordon & Breach.

Selected Topics in the History of Biochemistry. Ed. by G. Semenza. (Comprehensive Biochemistry Ser.: Vol. 35). 400p. 1984. 126.50 (ISBN 0-444-80507-9). Elsevier.

Selected Topics in Thermodynamics. Ed. by B. M. Goodwin. LC 80-25560. (AIChEMI Modular Instruction D Ser.: Vol. 4: Thermodynamics). 34p. 1983. pap. 30.00 (ISBN 0-8169-0238-0, J-22). Am Inst Chem Eng.

Selected Topics in Transport Phenomena. 100p. 1965. pap. 22.00 (ISBN 0-8169-0305-0, S-58). Am Inst Chem Eng.

Selected Topics in Venous Disorders: Pathophysiology, Diagnosis & Treatment. D. E. Strandness & Brian L. Thiele. LC 80-69527. (Illus.). 270p. 1981. 29.50 (ISBN 0-87993-154-X). Futura Pub.

Selected Works: Volume 5: Poetry & Experience. Wilhelm Dilthey. Ed. by Rudolf A. Makkreel & Rodi Frithjof. LC 84-4200. 432p. 1985. 36.50x (ISBN 0-691-07297-3). Princeton U Pr.

Selected Writing, 3 vols. H. Von Hofmannsthal. Ed. by M. Hamburger. Incl. Vol. 1. Selected Prose. 1952 (ISBN 0-691-09748-8). 41.00x; Vol. 2. Poems & Verse Plays. 1961; Vol. 3. Selected Plays & Libretti. 1963 (ISBN 0-691-09747-X). 52.50x. (Bollingen Ser.: No. 33). Princeton U Pr.

Selected Writings. John M. Addey. LC 76-46204. 232p. 1976. 8.75 (ISBN 0-86690-057-8, 1011-01). Am Fed Astrologers.

Selected Writings. Christopher A. Anderson. LC 88-71661. (Illus.). 270p. (Orig.). Date not set. pap. text ed. 17.50 (ISBN 0-931353-15-7). Andersons Pubns.

Selected Writings. Joe Brainard. pap. 3.50 (ISBN 0-686-09752-1). Kulchur Foun.

Selected Writings. Thomas Carlyle. Ed. by Alan Shelston. (Penguin English Library). 310p. 1980. pap. 6.95 (ISBN 0-14-043065-2). Penguin.

Selected Writings. John J. Chapman. LC 83-45729. Repr. of 1957 ed. AMS Pr.

Selected Writings. Lama Dalai. 1973. lib. bdg. 79.95 (ISBN 0-87968-508-5). Krishna Pr.

Selected Writings. Emile Durkheim. Ed. by Anthony Giddens. 288p. 1972. o. p. 44.50 (ISBN 0-521-08504-7); pap. 14.95 (ISBN 0-521-09712-6). Cambridge U Pr.

Selected Writings. Ralph Waldo Emerson. 1981. pap. 4.00x (T14, Mod LibC). Modern Lib.

Selected Writings. Ralph Waldo Emerson. Ed. by Donald McQuade. LC 80-27210. (Modern Library College Editions). 911p. 1981. pap. text ed. write for info (ISBN 0-394-32662-8, RanC). Random.

Selected Writings. Klement Gottwald. 112p. 1981. 21.25x (ISBN 0-317-53772-5, Pub. by Collets (UK)). State Mutual Bk.

Selected Writings. Hazlitt. (Classics Ser.). 1982. pap. 7.95 (ISBN 0-14-043050-4). Penguin.

Selected Writings. Abram S. Hewitt. Ed. by Allan Nevins. LC 64-24462. 1965. Repr. of 1937 ed. 24.50x (ISBN 0-8046-0203-4, Pub. by Kennikat). Assoc Faculty Pr.

Selected Writings, 8 vols. Roman Jakobson. Incl. Vol. 1. Phonological Studies. 2nd ed. 1971. 94.00 (ISBN 90-2791-662-4); Vol. 2. Word & Language. 1971. 91.00 (ISBN 90-2791-766-3); Vol. 4. Slavic Epic Studies. 1966. 91.00 (ISBN 90-2791-003-0). 72.00x ea. Mouton.

Selected Writings. J. R. Kantor. 1984. 20.00 (ISBN 0-911188-65-7). Principia Pr.

Selected Writings. Thomas B. Macaulay. Ed. by John Clive & Thomas Pinney. LC 78-171350. (Classics of British Historical Literature Ser). 544p. 1972. 25.00x (ISBN 0-226-49996-0). U of Chicago Pr.

Selected Writings. Filippo T. Marinetti. Tr. by R. W. Flint & Arthur A. Coppotelli. (Illus.). 400p. 1972. 12.95 (ISBN 0-374-20290-7). FS&G.

Selected Writings. Marquis de Sade. Tr. by L. St. Ives. 306p. 1987. pap. 20.00 (ISBN 0-87556-698-7). Saifer.

Selected Writings. Karl Marx. Ed. by David McLellan. 1977. pap. text ed. 12.95x (ISBN 0-19-876038-8). Oxford U Pr.

Selected Writings. Giuseppe Mazzini. Ed. by N. Gangulee. LC 74-9397. (Illus.). 253p. 1974. Repr. of 1945 ed. lib. bdg. 35.00x (ISBN 0-8371-7664-6, MASW). Greenwood.

Selected Writings. Philipp Melanchthon. Ed. by Elmer E. Flack & Lowell J. Satre. Tr. by Charles L. Hill. LC 78-5175. 1978. Repr. of 1962 ed. lib. bdg. cancelled (ISBN 0-313-20384-9, MESW). Greenwood.

Selected Writings. Robert Musil. (German Library: Vol. 72). 320p. 1986. 27.50x (ISBN 0-8264-0305-0); pap. 10.95 (ISBN 0-8264-0304-2). Continuum.

Selected Writings. Charles Olson. Ed. by Robert Creeley. LC 66-27613. (Orig.). 1967. pap. 6.95 (ISBN 0-8112-0128-7, NDP231). New Directions.

Selected Writings. Franz Oppenheimer. 69.95 (ISBN 0-8490-1022-5). Gordon Pr.

Selected Writings. Walter Raleigh. Ed. by Gerald Hammond. (Fyfield Ser.). 296p. 1984. 21.00 (ISBN 0-85635-440-6). Carcanet.

Selected Writings. Walter Raleigh. Ed. by Gerald Hammond. 304p. 1986. pap. 6.95 (ISBN 0-14-043257-4). Penguin.

Selected Writings. Ed. by H. P. Rickman. W. Diltlhey. LC 75-23530. 280p. 1976. 44.50 (ISBN 0-521-20966-8); pap. 16.95x (ISBN 0-521-29588-2). Cambridge U Pr.

Selected Writings. Josiah Royce. 59.95 (ISBN 0-8490-1023-3). Gordon Pr.

Selected Writings. Claude H. Saint-Simon. Intro. by F. M. Markham. LC 78-14140. 1985. Repr. of 1952 ed. 18.25 (ISBN 0-88355-814-9). Hyperion Conn.

Selected Writings. Philip Sidney. Ed. by Richard Dutton. (Fyfield Ser.). 178p. (Orig.). 1987. pap. 7.50 (ISBN 0-85635-625-5). Carcanet.

Selected Writings. Sydney Smith. Ed. by W. H. Auden. LC 83-45472. Repr. of 1956 ed. 37.50 (ISBN 0-404-20238-1, PR5456). AMS Pr.

Selected Writings. facs. ed. Robert Louis Stevenson. Ed. by Saxe Commins. LC 70-37157. (Essay Index Reprint Ser.). Repr. of 1947 ed. 42.50 (ISBN 0-8369-2523-8). Ayer Co Pubs.

Selected Writings. Jules Supervielle. LC 66-11415. (Orig., Fr. & Eng.). 1967. 4.95 (ISBN 0-8112-0389-1). New Directions.

Selected Writings. Arthur Symons. Ed. by R. V. Holdsworth. (Fyfield Ser.). 98p. pap. 7.50 (ISBN 0-85635-059-1). Carcanet.

Selected Writings. Thomas Traherne. Ed. by Dick Davis. (Fyfield Ser.). 93p. 1980. pap. 7.50 (ISBN 0-85635-231-4). Carcanet.

Selected Writings. Paul Valery. LC 50-7546. (Fr. & Eng.). 1964. pap. 6.95 (ISBN 0-8112-0213-5, NDP184). New Directions.

Selected Writings. Zwingli. 1972. 11.95x (ISBN 0-8122-1049-2). U of Pa Pr.

Selected Writings: An Introduction to Orgonomy. Wilhelm Reich. 576p. 1973. 15.00 (ISBN 0-374-26084-2); pap. 8.95 (ISBN 0-374-50197-1). FS&G.

Selected Writings & Speeches. Edmund Burke. Ed. by J. P. Stanlis. 12.75 (ISBN 0-8446-1094-1). Peter Smith.

Selected Writings & Speeches. Abraham Lincoln. Ed. by T. Harry Williams. 334p. 1980. pap. 5.95 (ISBN 0-87532-136-4). Hendricks House.

Selected Writings & Speeches of Alexander Hamilton. Morton J. Frisch. 1985. 25.95 (ISBN 0-8447-3553-1); pap. 17.75 (ISBN 0-8447-3551-5). Am Enterprise.

Selected Writings: Aquinas. Robert P. Goodwin. 1965. pap. text ed. write for info. (ISBN 0-02-345050-9). Macmillan.

Selected Writings by Cardinal Mercier. Desire Mercier. (Illus.). 128p. 1984. 117.75 (ISBN 0-89901-136-5). Found Class Reprints.

Selected Writings: Contributions to Comparative Mythology, Vol. 7. (Studies in Linguistics & Philology 1972-1982). xxiv, 405p. 1985. text ed. 69.95 (ISBN 0-89925-051-3). Mouton.

Selected Writings: Early Slavic Paths & Crossroads, 2 pts, Vol. 6. Roman Jacobson. 1985. Set. text ed. 161.00 (ISBN 0-89925-062-9). Pt. 1: Comparative Slavic Studies-The Cyrillo-Methodian Tradition (xxvi, 401 pg.) Pt. 2: Medieval Slavic Studies (viii, 541 pg.) Mouton.

Selected Writings Eighteen Seventy-Seven to Nineteen Thirty. D'Arcy Power. LC 78-95632. (Illus.). 1970. Repr. of 1931 ed. 39.50x (ISBN 0-678-03750-7). Kelley.

Selected Writings from a Connectionist's Psychology. Edward L. Thorndike. Repr. of 1949 ed. lib. bdg. 35.00x (ISBN 0-8371-2570-7, THWP). Greenwood.

Selected Writings, George Herbert Mead. George H. Mead. Ed. by Andrew J. Reck. LC 80-27048. lxxii, 416p. 1981. 30.00x (ISBN 0-226-51672-5); pap. 10.95x (ISBN 0-226-51671-7). U of Chicago Pr.

Selected Writings in British Intellectual History. Leslie Stephen. Ed. by Noel Annan. LC 78-13218. (Classics of British Historical Literature). 1979. lib. bdg. 22.00x (ISBN 0-226-77255-1). U of Chicago Pr.

Selected Writings in English & General Linguistics. Josef Vachek. (Janual Linguarum, Series Maior: No. 92). 451p. 1976. text ed. 53.60x (ISBN 0-686-22609-7). Mouton.

Selected Writings in Sociology & Social Philosophy. Karl Marx. 1963. pap. text ed. 6.95 (ISBN 0-07-040672-3). McGraw.

Selected Writings: Including Scarlet Letter. Nathaniel Hawthorne. Ed. by Gordon Roper. 480p. 1949. 6.45 (ISBN 0-87532-112-7). Hendricks House.

Selected Writings, Nineteen Eighty to Nineteen Eighty-Three. Robin Williamson. (Illus.). 52p. 1984. pap. 6.00 (ISBN 0-9602874-1-8). Pigs Whisker.

Selected Writings of A. T. Vanderbilt, 2 vols. Ed. by F. J. Klein & J. S. Lee. LC 65-14216. (Classic Ser.). 1965. 15.00 ea. (ISBN 0-379-00226-4); Set. 30.00. Oceana.

Selected Writings of Alexandra Kollontai. Alexandra Kollontai. Intro. by Alix Holt. 336p. 1980. pap. 7.95 (ISBN 0-393-00974-2). Norton.

Selected Writings of Anne Martin, Pioneer Nevada Feminist. Anne Martin. Ed. by Dave Basso. 1986. pap. 10.00. Falcon Hill Pr.

Selected Writings of Apollinaire. rev. ed. Guillaume Apollinaire. Tr. by Roger Shattuck from Fr. LC 72-145928. 1971. pap. 8.95 (ISBN 0-8112-0003-5, NDP310). New Directions.

Selected Writings of Artaud. Antonin Artaud. Ed. by Susan Sontag. Tr. by Helen Weaver from Fr. LC 79-143303. 661p. 1976. 20.00 (ISBN 0-374-26048-6); pap. 9.95 (ISBN 0-374-51399-6). FS&G.

Selected Writings of August Cieszkowski. August Cieszkowski. Ed. by Andre Liebich. LC 77-94371. (Studies in the History & Theory of Politics). 1979. 32.50 (ISBN 0-521-21986-8). Cambridge U Pr.

Selected Writings of Baha'u'llah. Baha'u'llah. LC 79-15136. 1979. 16.95 (ISBN 0-87743-133-7, 303-042). Baha'i.

Selected Writings of Benjamin N. Cardozo. Benjamin N. Cardozo. 1947. 15.50 (ISBN 0-685-02517-9). Bender.

Selected Writings of Bertram D. Lewin, M. D. Ed. & intro. by Jacob A. Arlow. LC 72-94802. (Illus.). 608p. 1973. 25.00 (ISBN 0-911194-02-9). Psych Qtly.

Selected Writings of Blaise Cendrars. Blaise Cendrars. Ed. by Walter Albert. LC 78-14223. 1978. Repr. of 1966 ed. lib. bdg. 29.75x (ISBN 0-313-21020-9, CESW). Greenwood.

Selected Writings of C. L. James. C. L. James. 1977. lib. bdg. 59.95 (ISBN 0-8490-2588-5). Gordon Pr.

Selected Writings of Caroline Norton. Caroline S. Norton. LC 78-18828. 1978. 100.00x (ISBN 0-8201-1312-3). Schol Facsimiles.

Selected Writings of Cunningham Graham. Ed. by Cedric Watts. LC 80-70682. 140p. 1981. 22.50 (ISBN 0-8386-3087-1). Fairleigh Dickinson.

Selected Writings of Edgar Allan Poe. Edgar Allan Poe. Ed. by E. H. Davidson. LC 56-13895. 1956. pap. 6.95 (ISBN 0-395-05110-X, RivEd). HM.

Selected Writings of Edward S. Curtis. 3rd ed. Edward S. Curtis. Ed. by Barry Gifford. LC 76-7891. (Illus.). 192p. 1976. pap. 6.95 (ISBN 0-916870-00-6). Creative Arts Bk.

Selected Writings of Edward Sapir in Language, Culture, & Personality. Edward Sapir. Ed. by David G. Mandelbaum. 1985. 42.00x (ISBN 0-520-01115-5); pap. 15.95x (ISBN 0-520-05594-2, CAMPUS 342). U of Cal Pr.

Selected Writings of E.T.A. Hoffmann, 2 Vols. E. T. Hoffmann. Ed. by Elizabeth C. Knight & Leonard J. Kent. LC 73-88790. (Illus.). 1969. Set. boxed 30.00 (ISBN 0-226-34788-5). U of Chicago Pr.

Selected Writings of Fulke Greville. Ed. by Joan Rees. 182p. 1973. 32.50 (ISBN 0-485-13603-1, Pub. by Athlone Pr UK); pap. 14.95 (ISBN 0-485-12603-6, Pub. by Athlone Pr UK). Humanities.

Selected Writings of Gertrude Stein. Gertrude Stein. 736p. 1972. pap. 8.95 (ISBN 0-394-71710-4, Vin). Random.

Selected Writings of Gyula Laziczius. Ed. by Thomas A. Sebeok. (Janua Linguarum, Series Minor: No. 55). 1966. pap. 25.60x (ISBN 90-2790-603-3). Mouton.

Selected Writings of Hans Denck. Ed. & tr. by E. J. Furcha. LC 76-7057. (Pittsburgh Original Texts & Translations Ser.: No. 1). 1976. 5.50 (ISBN 0-915138-15-8). Pickwick.

Selected Writings of Henri Michaux. Henri Michaux. Tr. by Richard Ellmann. LC 68-25545. (Eng. & Fr.). 1968. 7.50 (ISBN 0-8112-0316-6). New Directions.

Selected Writings of Henry Hughes: Antebellum Southerner, Slavocrat, Sociologist. Ed. by Stanford M. Lyman. LC 84-23702. 1985. 20.00x (ISBN 0-87805-250-X). U Pr of Miss.

Selected Writings of Hiram Bingham - Missionary to the Hawaiian Islands, 1814-1869: To Raise the Lord's Banner. Char Miller. (Studies in American Religion: Vol. 31). 540p. 1988. lib. bdg. 79.95 (ISBN 0-88946-675-0). E Mellen.

Selected Writings of Holbrook Working. Chicago Board of Trade, Education Department Staff. (Readings in Futures Markets Ser.: Bk. 1). pap. 12.00 (ISBN 0-317-46965-7, 52-35). Chicago Bd Trade.

Selected Writings of Isaac Mayer Wise. Ed. by David Phillipson & Louis Grossman. LC 71-83433. (Religion in America, Ser. 1). 1969. Repr. of 1900 ed. 29.00 (ISBN 0-405-00258-0). Ayer Co Pubs.

Selected Writings of J. Potapenko, 3 vols. J. Potapenko. 1976. Set. lib. bdg. 350.00 (ISBN 0-8490-2589-3). Gordon Pr.

Selected Writings of Jawaharlal Nehru. Vol. 12. cancelled (ISBN 0-8364-0346-0, Orient Longman). South Asia Bks.

Selected Writings of Jawaharlal Nehru, Vol. 3. Ed. by J. Nehru & B. R. Nanda. cancelled (ISBN 0-8364-0672-9, Orient Longman). South Asia Bks.

Selected Writings of Joaquin Miller. Joaquin Miller. Ed. by Alan Rosenus. LC 73-88918. (Urion Primary Source Book). (Illus.). 1976. 14.95 (ISBN 0-913522-05-8); pap. 7.95 (ISBN 0-913522-06-6). Urion Pr CA.

Selected Writings of Joel Augustus Rogers. Joel A. Rogers. Ed. by Kinya Kiongozi. 100p. (Orig.). 1988. price not set (ISBN 0-939841-04-5); pap. price not set (ISBN 0-939841-03-7). Pyramid MD.

Selected Writings of John & John Quincy Adams. Ed. by Adrienne Koch & William Peden. LC 83-45687. Repr. of 1946 ed. 40.00 (ISBN 0-404-20002-8). AMS Pr.

Selected Writings of John Keracher: Pioneer American Communist. John Keracher. 208p. 1985. lib. bdg. 24.95x (ISBN 0-88286-109-3). C H Kerr.

Selected Writings of Jonathan Edwards. Jonathan Edwards. Ed. by Harold P. Simonson. LC 78-115064. (Milestones of Thought Ser.). 1970. pap. 7.95x (ISBN 0-8044-6132-5). Ungar.

Selected Writings of Julius Guttmann: An Original Anthology. Ed. by Steven Katz. LC 79-7175. (Jewish Philosophy, Mysticism & History of Ideas Ser.). 1980. lib. bdg. 34.50x (ISBN 0-405-12232-2). Ayer Co Pubs.

Selected Writings of Lafcadio Hearn. Henry Goodman. (Illus.). 566p. 1983. 35.00 (ISBN 0-89984-219-4). Century Bookbindery.

Selected Writings of Lafcadio Hearn. Lafcadio Hearn. Ed. by Henry Goodman. 1971. pap. 5.95 (ISBN 0-8065-0245-2, Pub. by Citadel Pr). Lyle Stuart.

Selected Writings of Lafcadio Hearn. Lafcadio Hearn. 576p. 1988. pap. 12.95 (ISBN 0-8065-1107-9, Citadel Pr). Lyle Stuart.

Selected Writings of Lewis Hanke. Lewis Hanke. LC 77-5582. 497p. 1979. pap. text ed. 14.95x (ISBN 0-87918-036-6). ASU Lat Am St.

Selected Writings of Lord Acton, Vol. III: Essays in Religion, Politics & Morality. John E. Aston. Ed. by J. Rufus Fears. 776p. 1988. 22.50 (Liberty Pr); pap. 7.50 (Liberty Pr). Liberty Fund.

Selected Writings of Mary E. Amtman Berc. Berc. 1984. 20.00x (ISBN 0-86516-052-X); pap. 9.95x (ISBN 0-86516-051-1). Bolchazy-Carducci.

Selected Writings of Ralph Waldo Emerson. Ralph Waldo Emerson. Ed. by William H. Gilman. (Orig.). pap. 4.50 (ISBN 0-451-52047-5, CE1832, Sig Classics). NAL.

Selected Writings of Ralph Waldo Emerson. Ralph Waldo Emerson. Ed. by Brooks Atkinson. LC 83-42942. 930p. 1940. 12.95 (ISBN 0-394-60418-0). Modern Lib.

Selected Writings of St. Thomas Aquinas. St. Thomas Aquinas. Tr. by Robert P. Goodwin. Incl. Principles of Nature; On Being & Essence; On the Virtues in General; On Free Choice. LC 65-26529. (Orig.). 1965. pap. 4.24 scp (ISBN 0-672-60469-8, LLA217). Bobbs.

Selected Writings of Samuel Johnson. Samuel Johnson. LC 77-25885. 1977. 35.00x (ISBN 0-8201-1305-0). Schol Facsimiles.

Selected Writings of Samuel Johnson. Ed. by Katherine Rogers. pap. 3.95 (ISBN 0-451-51468-8, CE 1468, Sig Classics). NAL.

Selected Writings of Selma Fraiberg. Selma Fraiberg. Intro. by Louis Fraiberg. LC 86-23454. 728p. 1987. text ed. 39.50x (ISBN 0-8142-0417-1); pap. text ed. 17.50x (ISBN 0-8142-0427-9). Ohio St U Pr.

Selected Writings of Shoghi Effendi. rev. ed. Shoghi Effendi. 1975. pap. 1.00 (ISBN 0-87743-079-9, 308-043). Baha'i.

Selected Writings of Sidney H. Morse. Sidney H. Morse. 1977. lib. bdg. 59.95 (ISBN 0-8490-2590-7). Gordon Pr.

Selected Writings of Sir Charles Sherrington. Charles Sherrington. Ed. by D. Denny-Brown. (Illus.). 1979. 42.00x (ISBN 0-19-920104-8). Oxford U Pr.

Selected Writings of Sir Thomas Browne. Thomas Browne. Ed. by Geoffrey Keynes. LC 68-55536. (Illus.). 1970. pap. 3.25x (ISBN 0-226-07636-9, P347, Phoen). U of Chicago Pr.

Selected Writings of the Ingenious Mrs. Aphra Behn. Aphra Behn. LC 69-13815. 1970. Repr. of 1950 ed. lib. bdg. 35.00 (ISBN 0-8371-1070-X, BESW). Greenwood.

Selected Writings of Truman Capote. Truman Capote. 1963. 16.45 (ISBN 0-394-44467-1). Random.

Selected Writings of Walter Pater. Ed. by Harold Bloom. LC 81-17099. (Morningside Book). 304p. 1982. pap. 14.00x (ISBN 0-231-05481-5). Columbia U Pr.

Selected Writings of William C. Owen. William C. Owen. 1977. lib. bdg. 69.95 (ISBN 0-8490-2591-5). Gordon Pr.

Selected Writings of William Dwight Whitney. William Dwight Whitney. Ed. by Michael Silverstein. 1971. 35.00x (ISBN 0-262-19087-7). MIT Pr.

Selected Writings of Zoltan Kodaly. Zoltan Kodaly. 239p. 1974. 12.00 (ISBN 0-85162-021-3). Boosey & Hawkes.

Selected Writings on Agricultural Policy & Economic Analysis. Frederick V. Waugh. Ed. by Martin E. Abel & James P. Houck. LC 83-6963. 482p. 1984. 29.50x (ISBN 0-8166-1202-1). U of Minn Pr.

Selected Writings on Art & Artists. Charles Baudelaire. Tr. by P. E. Charvet. 460p. 1981. pap. 23.95 (ISBN 0-521-28287-X). Cambridge U Pr.

Selected Writings on Asian Law. Chin Kim. xiv, 572p. 1982. lib. bdg. 37.50x (ISBN 0-8377-0741-2). Rothman.

Selected Writings on Computing: A Personal Perspective. Edsger W. Dijkstra. (Texts & Monographs in Computer Science Ser.). (Illus.). 272p. 1982. 39.00 (ISBN 0-387-90652-5). Springer-Verlag.

Selected Writings on Drama in Education. Gavin Bolton. Ed. by David Davies & Chris Lawrence. 280p. 1986. pap. text ed. 11.95 (ISBN 0-582-36206-7). Longman.

Selected Writings on Economics, Eighteen Twenty-Seven to Eighteen Fifty-Two. Nassau W. Senior. LC 65-26381. 1966. 45.00x (ISBN 0-678-00151-0). Kelley.

Selected Writings on Feminism & Socialism. Lily Braun. Ed. & tr. by Alfred G. Meyer. LC 86-45942. 256p. 1987. 29.95 (ISBN 0-253-35101-4). Ind U Pr.

Selected Writings on Futures Markets: Basic Research in Commodity Markets. Chicago Board of Trade, Education Department Staff. (Readings in Futures Markets Ser.: Bk. 2). pap. 12.00 (ISBN 0-317-46966-5, 52-36). Chicago Bd Trade.

Selected Writings on Futures Markets: Explorations in Financial Futures Markets. Chicago Board of Trade, Education Department Staff. (Readings in Futures Markets Ser.: Bk. 5). pap. 12.00 (ISBN 0-317-46970-3, 52-86). Chicago Bd Trade.

Selected Writings on Futures Markets: Research Directions in Commodity Markets, 1970-1980. Chicago Board of Trade, Education Department Staff. (Readings in Futures Markets Ser.: Bk. 4). pap. 12.00 (ISBN 0-317-46968-1, 52-14). Chicago Bd Trade.

Selected Writings on Philosophy, Religion & Politics. J. Bodin. Ed. by Paul L. Rose. xiv, 94p. (Orig.). 1980. pap. text ed. 23.00x (ISBN 0-317-56046-8, Pub. by Droz Switzerland). Coronet Bks.

Selected Writings on Religion & Society. Edward Bellamy. Ed. by Joseph Schiffman. LC 74-40. (American Heritage Ser.: No. 11). 139p. 1974. Repr. of 1955 ed. lib. bdg. 35.00 (ISBN 0-8371-7359-0, BEWR). Greenwood.

Selected Writings on the Constitution. Raoul Berger. LC 86-27632. vii, 314p. 1987. 28.95 (ISBN 0-940973-00-6). James River Pr.

Selected Writings on the History of Science. William Whewell. Ed. by Yehuda Elkana. (Classics of British Historical Literature Ser.). 452p. 1984. lib. bdg. 35.00x o.s.i (ISBN 0-226-89433-9); pap. 15.00x (ISBN 0-226-89434-7). U of Chicago Pr.

Selected Writings on the Philosophy of Adult Education. Sharan B. Merriam. LC 83-22187. 196p. 1984. 16.00 (ISBN 0-89874-600-0); pap. 8.50. Krieger.

Selected Writings on the State & the Transition to Socialism. Nikolai I. Bukharin. Ed. & tr. by Richard B. Day. LC 82-851. 416p. 1982. 37.50 (ISBN 0-87332-190-1). M E Sharpe.

Selected Writings: Poetry of Grammar, Grammar of Poetry, Vol. 3. Roman Jakobson. Ed. by Stephan Rudy. 814p. 1981. 113.00x (ISBN 90-279-3178-X). Mouton.

Selected Writings: To Commemorate the 60th Birthday of Kenneth Lee Pike. Kenneth L. Pike. Ed. by Ruth M. Brend. (Janua Linguarum, Series Maior: No. 55). (Illus.). 1972. 40.80x (ISBN 0-686-21824-8). Mouton.

Selected Writings, Vol. 1: Sex. Edward Carpenter. (Gay Modern Classics Ser.). 320p. (Orig.). 1984. 32.50 (ISBN 0-907040-44-6, Pub. by GMP England); pap. 10.95 (ISBN 0-907040-43-8). Alyson Pubns.

Selected Writings: Vol. 5: On Verse, Its Masters & Explorers. Roman Jakobson. 1979. text ed. 75.00x (ISBN 90-279-7686-4). Mouton.

Selecting a Computer-Assisted System for Volume Food Service. Thomas W. Pellegrino. (Illus.). 136p. (Orig.). 1986. 31.25 (ISBN 0-939450-78-X, AHA CATALOG NO. 046176). AHPI.

Selecting a Nursing Home. Nanette Craig. 1987. 8.95 (ISBN 0-533-07167-4). Vantage.

Selecting a Superintendent. (Superintendent Career Development Ser.). 3.50 (ISBN 0-686-36521-6, 021-00817). Am Assn Sch Admin.

Selecting a Translation of the Bible. Lewis Foster & Jon Stedman. LC 83-4689. (Illus.). 128p. (Orig.). 1983. pap. 3.95 (ISBN 0-87239-645-2, 39975). Standard Pub.

Selecting an Ada Environment. Ed. by T. G. Lyons & J. C. Nissen. (Ada Companion Ser.). 250p. 1986. 29.95 (ISBN 0-521-32594-3). Cambridge U Pr.

Selecting, Analyzing, & Displaying Planning Information. Harold Starr et al. 164p. 1979. 9.75 (ISBN 0-318-15555-9, RD164). Natl Ctr Res Voc Ed.

Selecting & Developing Media for Instruction. 2nd ed. Ronald H. Anderson. 192p. 1983. 27.95 (ISBN 0-442-20976-2). Van Nos Reinhold.

Selecting & Installing Software Packages: New Methodology for Corporate Implementation. Jud Breslin. LC 86-12403. 260p. 1986. 40.95 (ISBN 0-89930-158-4, BSG/, Quorum). Greenwood.

Selecting & Ordering Populations: A New Statistical Methodology. Jean D. Gibbons et al. LC 77-3700. (Probability & Mathematical Statistics Ser.). 569p. 1977. 55.50x (ISBN 0-471-02670-0, Pub. by Wiley-Interscience). Wiley.

Selecting & Organizing State Government Publications. Margaret T. Lane. LC 87-1341. 244p. 1987. pap. text ed. 35.00x (ISBN 0-8389-0477-7). ALA.

Selecting & Orienting Staff for Service Overseas. Burton W. Teague. LC 76-53078. (Report Ser.: No. 705). 60p. 1977. pap. 30.00 (ISBN 0-8237-0139-5). Conference Bd.

Selecting & Storing Fuels & Lubricants. (Illus.). 55p. 1983. 6.50 (ISBN 0-89606-123-X, 102). Am Assn Voc Materials.

Selecting Business Software. John W. Yu & David Harrison. 1988. 24.95 (ISBN 1-55623-103-2). Dow Jones-Irwin.

Selecting Business Software: A Guide to Success with Microcomputing. E. D. Berman & Leslie Dewhurst. (Illus.). 167p. 1984. pap. 9.00 (ISBN 0-86187-488-9, Pub. by Frances Pinter). Longwood Pub Group.

Selecting College & University Personnel: The Quest & the Questions. Richard A. Kaplowitz. Frwd. by Jonathan D. Fife. LC 87-70537. (ASHE-ERIC Higher Education Report, 1986: No. 8). 113p. (Orig.). 1987. pap. 10.00x (ISBN 0-913317-35-7). Assn Study Higher Ed.

Selecting Colour for Packaging. E. P. Danger. 224p. 1986. text ed. 99.95 (ISBN 0-291-39716-6, Pub. by Technical Pr England). Gower Pub Co.

Selecting Colour for Print. E. P. Danger. 184p. 1986. text ed. 75.50 (ISBN 0-291-39715-8, Pub. by Technical Pr England). Gower Pub Co.

Selecting Computers for Ministry. Robert H. Iles & William L. Callison. LC 84-62333. (Illus.). 160p. (Orig.). 1985. pap. 13.95 (ISBN 0-932489-00-1). New Begin Co.

Selecting, Designing, & Using Speech Recognizers. Wayne A. Lea. (Speech Technology Ser.). (Illus.). 400p. 1982. 74.00 (ISBN 0-686-37644-7); Student Ed. 49.00 (ISBN 0-686-37645-5). Speech Science.

Selecting Educational Equipment & Materials for School & Home, 1986. Rev. ed. Ed. by Joan Moyer & Lucy P. Martin. LC 86-1116. (Illus.). 1986. pap. 8.45 (ISBN 0-87173-111-8). ACEI.

Selecting Effective Insurance Agents. Didactic Systems Staff. (Simulation Game Ser.). 1973. pap. 24.90 (ISBN 0-89401-090-5); pap. 21.50 two or more (ISBN 0-685-78096-1); pap. 24.90 french ed. (ISBN 0-89401-091-3). Didactic Syst.

Selecting Effective People. Didactic Systems Staff. (Simulation Game Ser.). 1970. pap. 24.90 (ISBN 0-89401-087-5); pap. 21.50 two or more (ISBN 0-685-78133-X); pap. 24.90 portuguese ed. (ISBN 0-89401-089-1). Didactic Syst.

Selecting Employees Safely under the Law. K. McCulloch. 1981. 40.00 (ISBN 0-13-802959-8). P-H.

Selecting Financial Services for Government. Government Finance, Officers Association Staff & Girard Miller. LC 84-80555. ix, 115p. Date not set. price not set (ISBN 0-89125-084-0). Municipal.

Selecting Foster Parents: The Ideal & the Reality. Martin Wolins. LC 63-19855. 237p. pap. 61.70 (2029831). Bks Demand UMI.

Selecting-Implementing Educational Software. Miller. 1986. 25.95 (ISBN 0-205-10468-1, Pub. by Longwood Div). Allyn.

Selecting Instructional Media: A Guide to Audiovisual & Other Instructional Media Lists. 3rd ed. Mary R. Sive. LC 82-21675. 330p. 1983. 22.50 (ISBN 0-87287-342-0). Libs Unl.

Selecting Interventions for Nutritional Improvement - A Manual. (Nutrition in Agriculture Ser.: No. 3). 85p. 1984. pap. 7.50 (ISBN 92-5-101402-7, F2489, FAO). UNIPUB.

Selecting Learning Experiences: Linking Theory & Practice. Bruce R. Joyce. LC 78-60734. 55p. 1978. pap. text ed. 4.75 (ISBN 0-87120-091-0, 611-78138). Assn Supervision.

Selecting Library Materials. 3rd rev. ed. Arthur W. Swarthout. LC 74-10504. (Guide Ser.: No. 4). 14p. 1986. pap. 3.95 (ISBN 0-915324-07-5); pap. 3.00 members. CSLA.

Selecting Materials for & about Hispanic & East Asian Children & Young People. Patricia F. Beilke & Frank J. Sciara. LC 85-23920. xii, 178p. 1986. 26.00 (ISBN 0-208-01993-6, Lib Prof Pubns). Shoe String.

Selecting Materials for Libraries. 2nd ed. Robert N. Broadus. LC 81-650. xiv, 464p. 1981. 22.00 (ISBN 0-8242-0659-2). Wilson.

Selecting Media for Instruction. Robert A. Reiser & Robert M. Gagne. LC 83-5686. (Illus.). 136p. 1983. 32.95 (ISBN 0-87778-187-7). Educ Tech Pubns.

Selecting Media for Learning. 96p. 1974. pap. 10.95 (ISBN 0-89240-022-6, 906); pap. 8.95. Assn Ed Comm Tech.

Selecting Microform Readers & Reader-Printers. Francis F. Spreitzer. (Consumer Ser.). (Illus.). 16p. (Orig.). 1983. pap. 7.50 (ISBN 0-89258-082-8, C102). Assn Inform & Image Mgmt.

Selecting Proper Marshall Procedures for Optimum Asphalt Content of Dense Graded Paving Mixtures. (Information Ser.: No. 85). 1982. 10.00 (ISBN 0-317-58410-3). Natl Asphalt Pavement.

Selecting Radio Control Systems & Components for Your Airplane, Boat & Buggy. Douglas Pratt. (Illus.). 112p. (Orig.). 1988. pap. 11.95 (ISBN 0-87938-287-2). Motorbooks Intl.

Selecting Retirement Plan. Isidore Goodman. (Pension & ERISA Ser.). 24p. 1986. 2.00 (ISBN 0-317-47598-3, 5453). Commerce.

Selecting Subsets of Maximum Diversity. Fred Glover et al. 1977. 2.50 (ISBN 0-686-64186-8). U CO Busn Res Div.

Selecting the Administrative Team. American Association of School Administrators Staff & National School Boards Association Staff. (Administrative Team Career Development Ser.: Bk. 1). 9.95 (ISBN 0-318-01721-0, 021-00846). Am Assn Sch Admin.

Selecting the Best Franchises. Gregory Kravitt. 1986. cancelled (ISBN 0-87094-531-9). Dow Jones-Irwin.

Selecting the Church Computer. William R. Johnson. 160p. (Orig.). 1984. pap. 8.95 (ISBN 0-687-37135-X). Abingdon.

Selecting the College Student in America: A Study of Theory & Practice. Habib A. Kurani. LC 79-176936. (Columbia University. Teachers College. Contributions to Education: No. 503). Repr. of 1931 ed. 22.50 (ISBN 0-404-55503-9). AMS Pr.

Selecting the Form of a Small Business Entity. Harry J. Haynsworth, IV. 203p. 1985. 65.00 (ISBN 0-317-39449-5, B472). Am Law Inst.

Selecting the President: The Nominating Process in Transition. Howard L. Reiter. 160p. 1985. text ed. 26.95 (ISBN 0-8122-7990-5); pap. text ed. 10.95 (ISBN 0-8122-1217-7). U of Pa Pr.

Selecting the Right Supervisor. Desk Top Seminar Staff. (Professional Development Program Ser.). 176p. 1983. 95.00 (ISBN 0-471-88880-X). Wiley.

Selecting Thermoplastics for Engineering Applications. MacDermott. (Plasitics Engineering Ser.). 184p. 1984. 45.00 (ISBN 0-8247-7099-4). Dekker.

Selecting Your Accountant. Paul F. Rice. 8p. (Orig.). 1988. bklet. 3.95 (ISBN 0-9620188-2-1). Lifestyle Group.

Selecting Your Financial Advisors: Keys to Choosing a Good Accountant, Lawyer, Securities Broker, Financial Planner & Other Sources of Financial Advice. Paul F. Rice. 52p. (Orig.). 1988. pap. 7.95 (ISBN 0-318-23895-0). Lifestyle Group.

Selecting Your First Telescope. Sherwood Harrington. (Illus.). 16p. 1982. 3.00 (ISBN 0-937707-06-6, IP 300). Astron Soc Pacific.

Selecting Your Lawyer. Paul F. Rice. 8p. (Orig.). 1988. bklet. 3.95 (ISBN 0-9620188-1-3). Lifestyle Group.

Selecting Your Securities Broker & Financial Planner. Paul F. Rice. 8p. (Orig.). 1988. bklet. 3.95 (ISBN 0-9620188-3-X). Lifestyle Group.

Selection. Roberto Sanesi. Tr. by Cid Corman et al. 1975. signed 6.00 (ISBN 0-685-78960-8, Pub. by Grosseteste); sewn in wrappers 2.00 (ISBN 0-685-78961-6). Small Pr Dist.

Selection Among Alternates in Language Standardization: The Case of Albanian. Janet Byron. (Contributions to the Sociology of Language Ser.: No. 12). 1976. pap. text ed. 14.00x (ISBN 90-2797-542-6). Mouton.

Selection & Appointment of School Heads. 3rd. ed. Eileen R. Driscoll. 1982. pap. 7.75 (ISBN 0-934338-47-7). NAIS.

Selection & Breeding to Improve Some Tropical Conifers, 2 Vols, Vol. 1. J. Burley & D. C. Nikles. 1972. Vol. 1. 90.00x (ISBN 0-85074-026-6, Pub. by For Lib Comm England); Vol. 2. 95.00x (ISBN 0-85074-027-4). State Mutual Bk.

Selection & Care of Cleaning Equipment. American Institute of Maintenance Staff. 86p. 1982. pap. 3.00 (ISBN 0-9609052-3-5). Clean Mgmt Inst.

Selection & Election. Ali Shariati. Tr. by Ali A. Ghasemy from Persian. 12p. 1980. pap. 0.75 (ISBN 0-941722-13-9). Book-Dist-Ctr.

Selection & Evaluation of Teachers. Dale Bolton. LC 72-10648. 260p. 1973. 23.00x (ISBN 0-8211-0123-4). McCutchan.

Selection & Installation of Well Screens & Gravel Packs. 1982. 6.25 (ISBN 0-318-23055-0). Natl Water Well.

Selection & Performance of Radiologic Equipment. William R. Hendee. 400p. 1985. 54.95 (ISBN 0-683-03958-X). Williams & Wilkins.

Selection & Promotion of the Successful Police Officer. Lawrence R. O'Leary. (Illus.). 200p. 1979. 24.00 (ISBN 0-398-03805-8). C C Thomas.

Selection & Tenure of Judges. Evan Haynes. xix, 308p. 1981. Repr. of 1944 ed. lib. bdg. 30.00x (ISBN 0-8377-0636-X). Rothman.

Selection & Use of Engineering Materials. J. A. Charles & F. A. Crane. (Illus.). 328p. 1984. text ed. 49.95 (ISBN 0-408-10858-4); pap. text ed. 32.95 (ISBN 0-408-10859-2). Butterworth.

Selection & Use of Instructional Media. 2nd ed. A. J. Romiszowski. 320p. 1988. 41.50 (ISBN 0-89397-281-9). Nichols Pub.

Selection & Use of Wear Tests for Coatings - STP 769. Ed. by R. Bayer. 179p. 1982. 21.00 (ISBN 0-8031-0710-2, 04-769000-29). ASTM.

Selection & Use of Wear Tests for Metals - STP 615. Ed. by R. G. Bayer. 111p. 1977. pap. 10.75 (ISBN 0-8031-0563-0, 04-615000-23). ASTM.

Selection, Certification & Control: Social Issues in Educational Assessment. Ed. by Patricia Broadfoot. (Politics & Education Monograph). 270p. 1984. 36.00x (ISBN 0-905273-78-8, Falmer Pr); pap. 20.00x (ISBN 0-905273-77-X). Taylor & Francis.

Selection-Election: A Forum on the American Presidency. Ed. by Robert S. Hirschfield. LC 81-67957. 1982. lib. bdg. 24.95x (ISBN 0-202-24161-0); pap. text ed. 12.95 (ISBN 0-202-24163-7). Aldine de Gruyter.

Selection for Parole. Lloyd E. Ohlin. (Russell Sage Foundation Reprint Ser). Repr. of 1951 ed. lib. bdg. 34.50 (ISBN 0-697-00207-1). Irvington.

Selection for Secondary Education. Peter Gordon. 269p. 1980. 25.00x (ISBN 0-7130-0157-7, Pub. by Woburn Pr England) (ISBN 3-7165-0122-0). Biblio Dist.

Selection from Our Shelves: Books, Manuscripts & Drawings from the Rosenbach Foundation Museum. Clive E. Driver. 1972. pap. 12.50x (ISBN 0-939084-08-2, Pub. by Rosenbach Mus & Lib). U Pr of Va.

Selection from Poems of Rural Life in the Dorset Dialect. William Barnes. 1977. Repr. of 1909 ed. 20.00. Century Bookbindery.

Selection from Scrutiny, 2 vols. Ed. by Frank R. Leavis. 1968. Vol. 1. 49.50- (ISBN 0-521-06953-X); Vol. 1. pap. 13.95 (ISBN 0-521-09508-5); Vol. 2. pap. 12.95 (ISBN 0-521-09509-3). Cambridge U Pr.

Selection from the Best English Essays, Illustrative of the History of English Prose Style. facs. ed. Ed. by Sherwin Cody. LC 68-8448. (Essay Index Reprint Ser.). 1903. 21.50 (ISBN 0-8369-0320-X). Ayer Co Pubs.

Selection from The Birds of America by John J. Audubon. North Carolina Museum of Art. LC 76-46336. (Illus.). 1976. pap. 4.00x (ISBN 0-88259-084-7). NCMA.

Selection from the Great English Poets. facs. ed. Ed. by Sherwin Cody. LC 76-128152. (Granger Index Reprint Ser). 1905. 32.00 (ISBN 0-8369-6179-X). Ayer Co Pubs.

Selection from the Great English Poets. facsimile ed. Ed. by Sherwin Cody. LC 76-128152. (Granger Index Reprint Ser.). 576p. Repr. of 1905 ed. lib. bdg. 17.50 (ISBN 0-8290-0516-1). Irvington.

Selection from the Letters of Lewis Carroll to His Child-Friends. Evelyn M. Hatch. LC 73-2835. 1973. lib. bdg. 35.50 (ISBN 0-8414-3650-9). Folcroft.

Selection from the Love Poetry of William Butler Yeats. William B. Yeats. 40p. 1970. Repr. of 1913 ed. 15.00x (ISBN 0-7165-1344-7, BBA 02112, Pub. by Cuala Press Ireland). Biblio Dist.

Selection from Writings of... Henry W. Massingham. Ed. by H. J. Massingham. 1925. Repr. 20.00 (ISBN 0-8274-3352-2). R West.

Selection I: American Drawings & Watercolors from the Museum Collection. 76p. 1972. 1.50 (ISBN 0-911517-33-2). Mus of Art RI.

Selection II: British Watercolors & Drawings from the Museum's Collection. Malcolm Cormack. (Illus.). 181p. 1972. 6.50 (ISBN 0-911517-34-0). Mus of Art RI.

Selection III: Contemporary Graphics from the Museum's Collection. Diana L. Johnson. LC 73-76521. 67p. 1973. 5.00 (ISBN 0-911517-35-9). Mus of Art RI.

Selection in Mutation Breeding. (Panel Proceedings Ser.). (Illus.). 180p. 1985. pap. 29.00 (ISBN 92-0-111284-X, ISP665, IAEA). UNIPUB.

Selection in One-&-Two-Locus Systems. T. Nagylaki. (Lecture Notes in Biomathematics: Vol. 15). 1977. 18.00 (ISBN 0-387-08247-6). Springer-Verlag.

Selection Indices in Plant Breeding. Robert J. Baker. 240p. 1986. 115.00 (ISBN 0-8493-6377-2). CRC Pr.

Selection Interviewing: A Management Psychologist's Recommended Approach. Bradford D. Smart. LC 82-23887. 292p. 1983. text ed. 29.95 (ISBN 0-471-87351-9). Wiley.

Selection Interviewing for Managers. Thomas L. Moffatt. LC 86-26313. 208p. 1987. Repr. of 1979 ed. 16.95x (ISBN 0-910239-08-8). Sci Tech Pubs.

Selection IV: Glass from the Museum's Collection. Hedy B. Landman. LC 73-94132. (Illus.). 144p. 1974. 6.50 (ISBN 0-911517-36-7). Mus of Art RI.

Selection of a Court Recording Method for the District Courts of Oregon. National Center for State Courts Staff. 29p. (On loan through the NCSC Library). 1973. pap. write for info. (R-003). Natl Ctr St Courts.

Selection of American Art: The Skowhegan School. Bernard B. Shan. (Illus.). 1976. 5.00 (ISBN 0-910663-11-4). ICA Inc.

Selection of Ancient Slav Literary Monuments. Compiled by Thomas A. Lysaght. 184p. (Eng. & Rus.). 1982. 195.00 (ISBN 0-317-40872-0, Pub. by Collets (UK)). State Mutual Bk.

Selection of Archaeological Finds of the People's Republic of China. Wenwu Press Staff. 54p. 1976. 38.00x (ISBN 0-317-68568-6, Pub. by Han-Shan Tang Ltd). State Mutual Bk.

Selection of Automatic Control Valves. EEMUA Staff. 1969. 75.00x (ISBN 0-85931-087-6, Pub. by EEMUA). State Mutual Bk.

Selection of Behavior: The Operant Behaviorism of B. F. Skinner: Comments & Consequences. Ed. by A. Charles Catania & Stevan Harnad. (Illus.). 640p. 1988. 75.00 (ISBN 0-521-34388-7); pap. 29.95 (ISBN 0-521-34861-7). Cambridge U Pr.

Selection of Books for Adult Study Groups. Margaret C. Lyon. LC 74-177014. (Columbia University. Teachers College. Contributions to Education: No. 695). Repr. of 1937 ed. 22.50 (ISBN 0-404-55696-5). AMS Pr.

Selection of British Paintings. Sara Cannon et al. 32p. Date not set. 7.50 (ISBN 0-945192-00-2). USC Fisher Gallery.

Selection of Calligraphy & Painting. Chi M. Tung. (Illus.). 60p. 1965. pap. 56.00x (ISBN 0-317-69178-3, Pub. by Han-Shan Tang Ltd). State Mutual Bk.

Selection of College & University Presidents. Joseph F. Kauffman. 82p. 1974. 6.00 (ISBN 0-911696-35-0). Assn Am Coll.

Selection of Contemporary Chinese Paintings. Song Wenzhi. (Illus.). 112p. 1981. 60.00 (ISBN 0-8351-0950-X). China Bks.

Selection of Control Valves & Other Final Control Devices. L. R. Driskell. (Instructional Resource Package Ser.). 1982. Instr's Guide: 56p. pap. text ed. 10.00x (ISBN 0-87664-619-4); Student Text: 142p. pap. text ed. 26.50x (ISBN 0-87664-618-6); Slides (set of 59) 160.00x (I524-4SL); Classroom pkg.(10 student texts, instr. guide, 1 set slides) 320.00x (ISBN 0-87664-524-4). Instru Soc.

Selection of Design. Gordon L. Glegg. LC 72-80591. (Illus.). 96p. 1972. Cambridge U Pr.

Selection of Doses in Chronic Toxicity-Carcinogenicity Studies. Ed. by H. C. Grice. (Current Issues in Toxicology Ser.). (Illus.). 130p. 1984. pap. 19.00 (ISBN 0-387-12845-X). Springer-Verlag.

Selection of Etchings by John Sloan. Ed. by Robert F. Bussabarger & Frank Stack. LC 67-22228. (Illus.). 62p. 1967. pap. 13.00x (ISBN 0-8262-0059-1). U of Mo Pr.

Selection of Four-Hand Duets (Seventeen Seventy-Seven to Eighteen Thirty-Eight) Nicholas Temperley. (London Pianoforte School Ser., 1770-1860). 310p. 1986. lib. bdg. 75.00 (ISBN 0-8240-6168-3). Garland Pub.

Selection of Graphic Art of XVI-XIII Century at the Scientific Library of the Tartu State University. Tiina Nuik. 142p. 1981. 29.00x (ISBN 0-317-14297-6, Pub. by Collets (UK)). State Mutual Bk.

Selection of Greek Historical Inscriptions to the End of the 5th Century, B. C. Ed. by Russell Meiggs & David Lewis. 1969. 39.95x (ISBN 0-19-814266-8). Oxford U Pr.

Selection of Hebrew Melodies, Ancient & Modern by Isaac Nathan & Lord Byron. Frederick Burwick & Paul Douglass. LC 87-750758. 250p. 1988. 25.95 (ISBN 0-8173-0373-1). U of Ala Pr.

Selection of His Works: Bacon. Ed. by Sidney Warhaft. 497p. 1965. pap. text ed. write for info. (ISBN 0-02-424530-5). Macmillan.

Selection of His Works: Mill. Ed. by John M. Robson. 505p. 1966. pap. text ed. write for info. (ISBN 0-02-402570-4). Macmillan.

Selection of Historic American Papers on Concrete, 1876-1926. 1st ed. Ed. by Howard Newlon, Jr. LC 76-47294. (American Concrete Institute, Publication: SP-52). pap. 85.50 (ISBN 0-317-27231-4, 2025081). Bks Demand UMI.

Selection of Isadora Duncan Dances: The Schubert Selection, Written in Sutton Dance Writing. Sylvia Gold. Ed. by Valerie Sutton. 100p. (Orig.). 1984. 30.00x (ISBN 0-914336-20-7). Ctr Sutton Movement.

Selection of Japan's Emergency Legislation. Tr. by William J. Sebald. (Studies in Japanese Law & Government). 177p. 1979. Repr. of 1937 ed. 16.00 (ISBN 0-89093-219-0). U Pubns Amer.

Selection of Library Materials in Applied & Interdisciplinary Fields. Ed. by Beth Shapiro & John Whaley. LC 86-32101. 352p. 1987. 42.00x (ISBN 0-8389-0466-1). ALA.

Selection of Library Materials in the Humanities, Social Sciences, & Sciences. Ed. by Patricia A. McClung. LC 85-20084. 1985. 49.00x (ISBN 0-8389-3305-X). ALA.

Selection of Load-Bearing Structures for Buildings. K. Z. Horvath. (Developments in Civil Engineering Ser.: No. 12). 380p. 1986. 129.00 (ISBN 0-444-99557-9). Elsevier.

Selection of Masterworks in the Collection of the National Palace Museum. National Palace Museum Staff. 214p. 1974. pap. 60.00x (ISBN 0-317-69448-0, Pub. by Han-Shan Tang Ltd). State Mutual Bk.

Selection of Materials for Component Design, Source Book. 412p. 1986. 55.00 (ISBN 0-87170-256-8, 6267). ASM.

Selection of Materials for Service Environments: Source Book. 450p. 1987. 55.00 (ISBN 0-87170-239-8). ASM.

Selection of Memorable Objects in the Walters Art Gallery: A Picture Book. (Illus.). 1964. pap. 3.50 (ISBN 0-911886-18-4). Walters Art.

Selection of Methods & Instruments for Blood Banks. Ed. by Morris R. Dixon & Sandra Ellisor. 1987. text ed. 18.00 (ISBN 0-915355-48-5). Am Assn Blood.

Selection of Models by Forecasting Intervals. A. H. Merkies. Tr. by M. Van Holten-De Wolff. LC 73-83565. 1973. lib. bdg. 26.00 (ISBN 90-277-0342-6, Pub. by Reidel Holland). Kluwer Academic.

Selection of Narrative Verse. C. J. Power. 1977. Repr. of 1931 ed. 15.00. Century Bookbindery.

Selection of National Party Leaders in Canada. John C. Courtney. LC 72-14046. xiv, 278p. 1973. 27.50 (ISBN 0-208-01393-8, Archon). Shoe String.

Selection of Nineteenth Century Paintings in the Walters Art Gallery: A Picture Book. LC 66-58391. (Illus.). 1965. pap. 3.00 (ISBN 0-911886-19-2). Walters Art.

Selection of Oils for Carbureted Water Gas. E. S. Pettyjohn & H. R. Linden. (Research Bulletin Ser.: No. 9). iv, 51p. 1952. write for info.; supplement 1.50. Inst Gas Tech.

Selection of Oils for High-Btu Oil Gas. H. R. Linden & E. S. Pettyjohn. (Research Bulletin Ser.: No. 12). iv, 48p. 1952. 5.00 (ISBN 0-317-56810-8); Supplement 1.50 (ISBN 0-317-56811-6). Inst Gas Tech.

Selection of Paintings from the Gerald Peters Collection. Gayle Maxon. LC 83-62810. 94p. 1983. pap. 25.00 (ISBN 0-935037-05-5). Peters Corp NM.

Selection of Papers from Info II, 3 vols. Ed. by D. G. Lainiotis & N. S. Tzannes. 1980. lib. bdg. 47.50 ea. (Pub. by Reidel Holland). Vol. 1, 530p (ISBN 90-277-1140-2). Vol. 2, 600p (ISBN 90-277-1129-1). Vol. 3, 530p (ISBN 90-277-1143-7). Kluwer Academic.

Selection of Patients for X-Ray Examinations: Denial Radiographic Examinations. 40p. 1987. pap. 2.00 (ISBN 0-318-23843-8, 017-015-00236-5). USGPO.

Selection of Patients for X-Ray Examinations: Skull X-ray Examinations for Trauma. (HHS Publication FDA 86-8263). 30p. 1986. pap. 1.75 (ISBN 0-318-21571-3, S/N 017-015-00233-1). USGPO.

Selection of Portrait Miniatures in the Walters Art Gallery: A Picture Book. LC 66-2790. (Illus.). 1966. pap. 3.00 (ISBN 0-911886-20-6). Walters Art.

Selection of Primary Sources for the History of Pharmacy in the United States. Nydia M. King. 123p. (Orig.). 1987. pap. 10.00 (ISBN 0-931292-16-6). Am Inst Hist Pharm.

Selection of Production Processes for the Manufacturing Subsidiaries of U. S. - Based Multinational Corporations. Wayne A. Yeoman. Ed. by Stuart Bruchey & Eleanor Bruchey. LC 76-5044. (American Business Abroad Ser.). (Illus.). 1976. 17.00x (ISBN 0-405-09309-8). Ayer Co Pubs.

Selection of Secondary School Headteachers. Colin Morgan et al. 192p. 1983. pap. 21.00x (ISBN 0-335-10410-X, Open Univ Pr). Taylor & Francis.

Selection of Shorter Poems. Michael Drayton. LC 77-18727. 1927. 25.00 (ISBN 0-8414-0109-8). Folcroft.

Selection of Some of the Most Interesting Narratives of Outrages Committed by the Indians in Their Wars with the White People, 2 Vols. in 1. Archibald Loudon. LC 76-106124. (First American Frontier Ser). 1971. Repr. of 1808 ed. 36.00 (ISBN 0-405-02866-0). Ayer Co Pubs.

Selection of Spanish Masterworks from the Meadows Museum. Marcus Burke et al. LC 86-62402. (Illus.). 16p. (Orig.). 1986. pap. 4.00 (ISBN 0-935937-01-3). Meadows Mus.

Selection of State Roadside Cross Sections. (National Cooperative Highway Research Program Report). 57p. 1975. 4.40 (ISBN 0-309-02335-1). Transport Res Bd.

Selection of Teachers in Large City School Systems. John Coulbourn. LC 72-176673. (Columbia University. Teachers College. Contributions to Education: No. 740). Repr. of 1938 ed. 22.50 (ISBN 0-404-55740-6). AMS Pr.

Selection of Teaching-Learning Materials in Health Sciences Education: Report. WHO Study Group. Geneva, 1973. (Technical Report Ser.: No. 538). (Also avail. in French & Spanish). 1974. pap. 1.60 (ISBN 92-4-120538-5). World Health.

Selection of Technology for Food Processing in Developing Countries. Domien H. Bruinsma et al. 199p. 1984. pap. text ed. 7.50 (ISBN 90-220-0837-1, PDC264, Pudoc). UNIPUB.

Selection of Telegu Proverbs: Translated & Explained. M. W. Carr. 1986. 9.00X (ISBN 0-8364-1874-3, Pub. by Usha). South Asia Bks.

Selection of the Correspondence of Linnaeus & Other Naturalists: From Original Manuscripts, 2 vols. James E. Smith. Ed. by Keir B. Sterling. LC 77-81132. (Biologists & Their World Ser.). (Illus.). 1978. Repr. of 1821 ed. Set. lib. bdg. 99.00x (ISBN 0-405-10730-7); lib. bdg. 49.50x ea. Vol. 1 (ISBN 0-405-10731-5). Vol. 2 (ISBN 0-405-10732-3). Ayer Co Pubs.

Selection of the Political Pamphlets of Charles Bradlaugh 1865-1891. Charles Bradlaugh. LC 77-104611. 1970. lib. bdg. 49.50x (ISBN 0-678-00604-0). Kelley.

Selection of the Social & Political Pamphlets of Annie Besant 1874-1890. Annie Besant. LC 78-114024. 1970. 50.00x (ISBN 0-678-00638-5). Kelley.

Selection of Treatment for Alcoholics. Ed. by E. Mansell Pattison. LC 79-620007. (NIAAA-RUCAS Alcoholism Treatment Ser.: No. 1). 1982. pap. 22.50 (ISBN 0-911290-47-8). Rutgers Ctr Alcohol.

Selection of 16th & 17th-Century Woodcuts from Gesner & Topsell's Natural Histories see Curious Woodcuts of Fanciful & Real Beasts.

Selection Procedures & Personnel Records. (Personnel Policies Forum Surveys Ser.: No. 114). 1976. 30.00 (ISBN 0-686-88626-7). BNA.

Selection, Social Origins, Education & Training of East Central European Office Corps. Ed. by Bela K. Kiraly & Scott W. Dillard. (Atlantic Studies, No. 43 - War & Society in East Central Eruope, Vol. XXIV). write for info. Brooklyn Coll Pr.

Selection, Social Origins, Education, & Training of the East Central European Officers Corps & Their Affects on Politics. Ed. by Bela Kiraly & Walter S. Dillard. (East Central European Militarism Ser.). 320p. 1988. 35.00 (ISBN 0-88033-138-0). East Eur Quarterly.

Selection Tests & Sex Bias: The Impact of Selection Testing on the Employment Opportunities of Women & Men. 132p. 1987. pap. 24.00 (ISBN 0-11-710335-7, HM1724, Pub. by Her Maj Station Ofc). UNIPUB.

Selection Theorems & Their Applications. T. Parthasarathy. LC 72-78192. (Lecture Notes in Mathematics: Vol. 263). 108p. 1972. pap. 13.00 (ISBN 0-387-05818-4). Springer-Verlag.

Selection VII: American Paintings from the Museum's Collection 1800-1930. Patricia Mandel. LC 77-70393. (Illus.). 243p. 1977. 22.00 (ISBN 0-911517-37-5). Mus of Art RI.

Selections. Lucretius. Ed. by G. E. Benfield & R. C. Reeves. 1967. 7.95x (ISBN 0-19-831768-9). Oxford U Pr.

Selections. Ovid. Ed. & intro. by Freeman. 1972. pap. 10.95x (ISBN 0-19-912032-3). Oxford U Pr.

Selections & Essays. John Ruskin. Ed. by Frederick W. Roe. LC 77-145274. 1971. Repr. of 1918 ed. 69.00x (ISBN 0-403-01189-2). Scholarly.

Selections & Essays. John Ruskin. 1988. Repr. of 1918 ed. lib. bdg. 69.00x. Am Biog Serv.

Selections for Developing English Language Skills. rev. ed. Mary Finocchiaro & Violet H. Lavenda. 230p. (gr. 6 up). 1973. pap. 8.75 (ISBN 0-88345-195-6, 18078); cassettes 30.00 (ISBN 0-13-802182-1, 58193); ans. key 1.50 (ISBN 0-13-802174-0, 18161). Prentice ESL.

Selections from A. C. Swinburne. Ed. by Edmund Goose & Thomas J. Wise. 288p. 1985. lib. bdg. 25.00 (ISBN 0-8495-2101-7). Arden Lib.

Selections from A. C. Swinburne. Ed. by Edmund Gosse & Thomas J. Wise. 1979. Repr. of 1919 ed. lib. bdg. 20.00 (ISBN 0-8495-2011-8). Arden Lib.

Selections from a Van Rensselaer Family Library, 1536-1799. Joyce Jackson & Melissa Perlman. 17p. 1979. pap. 2.50 (ISBN 0-943366-03-8). Hist-Cherry Hill.

Selections from Aeneid II. Virgil. Ed. by C. H. Craddock. (Cambridge Latin Texts Ser.). 1975. pap. 4.95 (ISBN 0-521-20827-0). Cambridge U Pr.

Selections from Aeneid IV. Virgil. (Cambridge Latin Texts Ser.). 1977. limp bdg 4.50 (ISBN 0-521-21581-1). Cambridge U Pr.

Selections from Aeneid VI. Virgil. Ed. by Anne Haward. LC 82-12760. (Cambridge Latin Texts Ser.). 64p. 1983. pap. 3.50 (ISBN 0-521-28694-8); pap. 8.95 (ISBN 0-521-28695-6). Cambridge U Pr.

Selections from Aeneid VIII. Virgil. Ed. by C. H. Craddock. (Cambridge Latin Texts Ser.). 48p. 1973. pap. 4.50 (ISBN 0-521-20280-9). Cambridge U Pr.

Selections from American Poetry. Charles Gaston. Repr. of 1908 ed. 20.00 (ISBN 0-686-18788-1). Scholars Ref Lib.

Selections from American Poetry. Frederick Law. 1977. Repr. 15.00. Century Bookbindery.

Selections from Ancient Irish Poetry. Tr. by Kuno Meyer. LC 75-28829. Repr. of 1911 ed. 20.00 (ISBN 0-404-13819-5). AMS Pr.

Selections from Aristophanes & Lucian: Breviary Treasures. Lucian. Tr. by F. A. Paley. 1904. Repr. 30.00 (ISBN 0-8274-3354-9). R West.

Selections from Aristophanes & Lucian. Tr. by F. A. Paley. 1979. Repr. of 1904 ed. lib. bdg. 30.00 (ISBN 0-8492-2157-9). R West.

Selections from Arthur D. Graeff's Scholla. Ed. by Larry M. Neff. LC 79-166008. (Penn. German Ser.: Vol. 5). 1971. 15.00 (ISBN 0-911122-27-3). Penn German Soc.

Selections from Barbour's Bruce, Pts. 1 & 4. John Barbour. Ed. by W. W. Skeat. (EETS, ES: No. 11). Repr. of 1900 ed. Set. 23.00 (ISBN 0-527-00225-9). Kraus Repr.

Selections from Berkeley. George Berkeley. LC 72-4216. (Select Bibliographies Reprint Ser.). 1972. Repr. of 1899 ed. 22.00 (ISBN 0-8369-6873-5). Ayer Co Pubs.

Selections from Catullus. Catullus. Ed. by R. O. Lyne. (Latin Texts Ser.). 48p. 1973. 4.95 (ISBN 0-521-20267-1). Cambridge U Pr.

Selections from Chaucer: Including His Earlier & Later Verse & an Example of His Prose. Clarence G. Child. LC 74-16296. 74. Repr. of 1912 ed. lib. bdg. 22.50 (ISBN 0-8414-3578-2). Folcroft.

Selections from Cicero. Robert P. Sonkowsky. (Living Voice of Greek & Latin Literature Ser.). 1985. incl. 2 audio cassettes 29.95 (ISBN 0-88432-126-6, 23680, Audio-Forum). J Norton Pubs.

Selections from Contemporary Portugese Poetry. Jean Longland. 1966. 3.50 (ISBN 0-87535-143-3). Hispanic Soc.

Selections from Cowper's Poems. Oliphant. 234p. 1983. Repr. lib. bdg. 20.00. Century Bookbindery.

Selections from Cultural Writings. Antonio Gramsci. Ed. by David Forgacs & Geoffrey Nowell-Smith. Tr. by William Boelhower from Ital. 464p. 1985. text ed. 22.00x (ISBN 0-674-79985-2). Harvard U Pr.

Selections from Discoveries in Pharmacology. Ed. by M. J. Parnham & J. Bruinvels. 240p. 1987. pap. 35.00 (ISBN 0-444-80922-8). Elsevier.

Selections from Dr. Johnson's Rambler. W. Hale White. 1907. lib. bdg. 25.50 (ISBN 0-8414-9703-6). Folcroft.

Selections from Dryden. John Dryden. Ed. by G. E. Hadow. 1908. 15.00 (ISBN 0-8274-3355-7). R West.

Selections from Early American Writers 1607-1800. William B. Cairns. 1973. lib. bdg. 30.00 (ISBN 0-8414-1562-5). Folcroft.

Selections from Early American Writers 1607-1800. Ed. by William B. Cairns. 493p. 1981. Repr. of 1925 ed. lib. bdg. 50.00 (ISBN 0-8495-0862-2). Arden Lib.

Selections from Early American Writers: 1607-1800. Ed. by William B. Cairns. 493p. Repr. of 1927 ed. lib. bdg. 50.00. Century Bookbindery.

Selections from Early Greek Philosophy. 4th ed. Ed. by Milton C. Nahm. (Orig.). 1964. pap. text ed. write for info. (ISBN 0-13-800508-7). P-H.

Selections from Enclyclopaedia of Accounting, 1903: Original Anthology. new ed. Ed. by George Lisle & Richard P. Brief. LC 77-87310. (Contemporary Accounting Thought Ser.). 1978. lib. bdg. 37.50x (ISBN 0-405-10923-7). Ayer Co Pubs.

Selections from English Dramatists. Geoffrey H. Crump. 1978. Repr. of 1927 ed. lib. bdg. 27.00 (ISBN 0-8495-0848-7). Arden Lib.

Selections from English Wycliffite Writings. Ed. by Anne Hudson. LC 77-1506. 234p. 1981. pap. 18.95 (ISBN 0-521-28258-6). Cambridge U Pr.

Selections from Erasmus,...Principally from his Epistles. Erasmus. Ed. by P. S. Allen. (College Classical Ser.). 610p. 1982. 22.50 (ISBN 0-89241-361-1); pap. 11.50 (ISBN 0-89241-116-3). Caratzas.

Selections from Fornander's Hawaiian Antiquities & Folk-Lore. Ed. by Samuel H. Elbert. (Illus.). 297p. 1959. pap. text ed. 12.00x (ISBN 0-87022-213-9). UH Pr.

Selections from Free America & Other Works. Bolton Hall. 208p. 1987. pap. text ed. 8.95 (ISBN 0-915179-65-2). Loompanics.

Selections from George Eliot's Letters. George Eliot. Ed. by Gordon S. Haight. LC 84-13222. 585p. 1985. 35.00 (ISBN 0-300-03326-5). Yale U Pr.

Selections from George Eliot's Letters. Ed. by Gordon S. Haight. LC 84-13222. 578p. 1987. pap. 19.95x (ISBN 0-300-04050-4, Y-674). Yale U Pr.

Selections from Ghalib & Iqbal. Tr. by K. N. Sud from Urdu. 106p. 1978. pap. 2.50 (ISBN 0-86578-220-2). Ind-US Inc.

Selections from Greek Historians. Xenophon & Diodorus. (College Classical Ser.). viii, 407p. 1983. lib. bdg. 27.50 (ISBN 0-89241-362-X); pap. text ed. 14.00 (ISBN 0-89241-109-0). Caratzas.

Selections from Greek Papyri. George Milligan. 152p. 1980. 15.00 (ISBN 0-89005-335-9). Ares.

Selections from Hellenistic Philosophy. Ed. by Gordon H. Clark. LC 40-31306. 1964. pap. text ed. 11.95x (ISBN 0-89197-396-6). Irvington.

Selections from Henry Thoreau's Walden. Henry David Thoreau. 2.25 (ISBN 0-87505-315-7, Pub. by Lawrence). Borden.

Selections from Herodotus. Ed. by Amy L. Barbour. (Illus.). 1977. pap. 12.95x (ISBN 0-8061-1427-4). U of Okla Pr.

Selections from His Historie of the World, His Letters, Etc. Walter Raleigh. 1917. Repr. 22.50 (ISBN 0-8274-3357-3). R West.

Selections from Hoccleve. Hoccleve. Ed. by M. C. Seymour. (Illus.). 1981. 28.50x (ISBN 0-19-871083-6); pap. 12.95x (ISBN 0-19-871084-4). Oxford U Pr.

Selections from Homer's Iliad. Homer. Ed. by Allen R. Benner. (Illus.). 522p. (Gr.). 1976. Repr. of 1931 ed. text ed. 29.75x (ISBN 0-89197-636-1). Irvington.

Selections from Johnson on Shakespeare. Samuel Johnson. LC 86-9105. 384p. 1986. text ed. 40.00t (ISBN 0-300-03707-4); pap. 12.95x (ISBN 0-300-03708-2, Y-611). Yale U Pr.

Selections from Juan Montalvo. Tr. by Frank M. Spindler & Nancy C. Brooks. LC 84-23229. 123p. 1985. pap. 12.95 (ISBN 0-87918-056-0). ASU Lat Am St.

Selections from Managing the Human Climate. Philip Lesly. 178p. (Orig.). 1979. pap. 9.00 (ISBN 0-9602866-0-8). Lesly Co.

Selections from "Minnesota History" A Fiftieth Anniversary Anthology. Ed. by Rhoda R. Gilman & June D. Holmquist. LC 65-25992. (Illus.). 369p. (Twenty-eight articles by noted authors). 1965. Repr. 8.95 (ISBN 0-87351-025-9). Minn Hist.

Selections from Modern Poets. John Squire. Repr. of 1948 ed. lib. bdg. 15.00 (ISBN 0-8495-5007-6). Arden Lib.

Selections from "My Road to Rotary". Paul Harris. 58p. 1984. 3.00 (ISBN 0-915062-18-6). Rotary Intl.

Selections from "My Road to Rotary". Paul Harris. 58p. (Japanese.). 1984. 3.00 (ISBN 0-915062-19-4). Rotary Intl.

Selections from Ovid. rev. ed. Charles W. Dunmore. LC 63-12153. 1969. pap. text ed. 15.25 (ISBN 0-582-28131-8). Longman.

Selections from Ovid's Metamorphoses. Frederic J. DeVeau & Norris M. Getty. (gr. 10-12). 1969. text ed. 11.95 (ISBN 0-88334-010-0). Ind Sch Pr.

Selections From Paroles. Jacques Prevert. Tr. by Lawrence Ferlinghetti. LC 56-8586. (Pocket Poets Ser.: No. 9). 1958. pap. 3.00 (ISBN 0-87286-042-6). City Lights.

Selections from Pindar: An Introduction & Commentary. Gordon M. Kirkwood. LC 80-23801. 1982. 26.00 (ISBN 0-89130-430-4, 400307). Scholars Pr GA.

Selections from Pliny's Letters. Pliny. Ed. by M. B. Fisher & M. R. Griffen. LC 73-80489. (Latin Texts Ser.). (Illus.). 64p. 1973. 4.95 (ISBN 0-521-20298-1). Cambridge U Pr.

Selections from Poe's Marginalia. Edgar Allan Poe. 1973. lib. bdg. 35.50 (ISBN 0-8414-9263-8). Folcroft.

Selections from Public Health in Reports and Papers: American Public Health Association (1873-1883) an original anthology ed. Ed. by Barbara G. Rosenkrantz. LC 76-4065. (Public Health in America Ser.). 1977. Repr. lib. bdg. 31.00x (ISBN 0-405-09838-3). Ayer Co Pubs.

Selective Admissions in Higher Education: Public Policy & Academic Policy, the Pursuit of Fairness in Admissions to Higher Education, the Status of Selective Admissions. 1st ed. Carnegie Council on Policy Studies in Higher Education Staff. LC 77-88501. pap. 68.00 (ISBN 0-317-27211-X, 2023874). Bks Demand UMI.

Selective Affinities: Comparative Essays from Goethe to Arden. Carol Wootton. LC 83-48709. (American University Studies III: Vol. 3). 183p. 1983. pap. text ed. 17.35 (ISBN 0-8204-0032-7). P Lang Pubs.

Selective Antibiotic Use in Respiratory Illness. Dr. M. T. Everett. 1986. lib. bdg. 39.75 (ISBN 0-85200-933-X, Pub. by MTP Pr England). Kluwer Academic.

Selective Arteriography of the Spinal Cord. John L. Doppman et al. LC 68-58106. (Illus.). 248p. 1969. 14.50 (ISBN 0-87527-006-9). Green.

Selective Attention & the Control of Binocular Rivalry. Leon C. Lack. (Psychological Studies: No. II). 1978. pap. text ed. 25.20x (ISBN 90-279-7644-9). Mouton.

Selective Awareness. Peter H. Mutke. 197p. 1984. pap. 7.95 (ISBN 0-930298-07-1). Westwood Pub Co.

Selective Awareness: The New Mind-Body Answer to Self Healing. rev. ed. Peter H. Mutke. Ed. by Suzanne Mikesell. 193p. 1987. pap. 7.95 (ISBN 0-914629-50-6, Dist. by St. Martin). Prima Pub Comm.

Selective Bibliography for the Study of English & American Literature. 6th ed. Richard D. Altick & Andrew Wright. 1978. pap. text ed. write for info (ISBN 0-02-302110-1). Macmillan.

Selective Bibliography in Science & Engineering. Northeastern University - Dodge Library, Boston. 1964. 78.00 (ISBN 0-8161-0701-7, Hall Library). G K Hall.

Selective Bibliography of Bibliographies of Hispanic American Literature. 2nd ed. Shasta M. Bryant. (Ilas Guides & Bibliographies Ser.: No. 8). 110p. 1976. pap. 4.95x (ISBN 0-292-77522-9). U of Tex Pr.

Selective Bibliography of Guides to Research in Foreign Law. Tim J. Watts. (Public Administration Ser.: P 2163). 17p. 1987. 5.00 (ISBN 1-55590-323-1). Vance Biblios.

Selective Bibliography of Outer Space Law: A Bibliography of Materials in the English Language. L. Scott Rawnsley. (Collection of Bibliographic & Research Resources Ser.). 280p. 1987. pap. 50.00 (ISBN 0-379-20910-1); with other biliographies in looseleaf 300.00. Oceana.

Selective Bibliography of Shakespeare: Editions, Textual Studies, Commentary. James G. McManaway & Jeanne A. Roberts. (Special Publications Ser). 1978. 15.00x (ISBN 0-918016-02-9); pap. 5.95x (ISBN 0-918016-03-7). Folger Bks.

Selective Bibliography on Imagery Reconnaissance & Related Matters. 3rd ed. Robert A. McDonald. 108p. 1987. pap. 5.50 (S/N 008-000-00491-9). USGPO.

Selective Bibliography on Oil & Gas. Edward Reiter. (Collection of Bibliographic & Research Resources Ser.). 29p. (Orig.). 1985. included among other biliographies in looseleaf 300.00; pap. 35.00 (ISBN 0-379-20901-2). Oceana.

Selective Bibliography on the Conservation of Research Library Materials. Paul N. Banks. (Orig.). 1981. pap. 5.00 (ISBN 0-911028-26-9). Newberry.

Selective Bibliography on the Conservation of Research Library Materials. Paul N. Banks. 150p. 1981. 10.00 (ISBN 0-686-95761-X, 5003) (ISBN 0-686-99604-6). Soc Am Archivists.

Selective Bronchography & Bronchial Brushing. F. Pinet et al. LC 78-21627. (Illus.). 1979. 120.00 (ISBN 0-387-09084-3). Springer-Verlag.

Selective Character of American Secondary Education. George S. Counts. LC 75-89166. (American Education: Its Men, Institutions & Ideas, Ser. 1). 1969. Repr. of 1922 ed. 14.00 (ISBN 0-405-01404-X). Ayer Co Pubs.

Selective Check Lists of Bibliographical Scholarship, 2 Vols. Vol. 1 1949-55. Ed. by Rudolf Hirsch & Howell J. Heaney. LC 58-10164. 25.00x (ISBN 0-8139-0041-7). Vol. No. 2 (1956-62) 1966. 25.00 (ISBN 0-8139-0119-7). U Pr of Va.

Selective Computation. R. Bellman. LC 85-10696. (Series in Modern Applied Mathematics: Vol. 4). 250p. 1985. 31.00 (ISBN 9971-966-86-7). World Scientific Pub.

Selective Conscientious Objection: Accomodating Conscience & Security. Ed. by Michael F. Noone, Jr. 160p. 1988. pap. 18.95 (ISBN 0-8133-7570-3). Westview.

Selective English Old-French Glossary As a Basis for Studies in Old French Onomatology & Synonymics. Joseph P. Murray. LC 77-128932. (Carl Ser.: No. 40). (Fr. & Eng.). Repr. of 1950 ed. 21.00 (ISBN 0-404-50340-3). AMS Pr.

Selective Exposure to Communication. Ed. by Dolf Zillmann & Jennings Bryant. (Communication Ser.). 264p. 1985. text ed. 29.95 (ISBN 0-89859-585-1). L Erlbaum Assocs.

Selective Gas Chromatographic Detectors. M. Dressler. (Journal of Chromatography Library Ser.: No. 36). 334p. 1986. 102.75 (ISBN 0-444-42488-1). Elsevier.

Selective Guide to Chinese Literature 1900-1949. Milena Dolezelova-Velingerova. 240p. 1987. 210.00x (Pub. by Han-Shan Tang Ltd). State Mutual Bk.

Selective Guide to Chinese Literature, 1900-1949. Zbigniew Slupski. 300p. 1987. 294.00x (Pub. by Han-Shan Tang Ltd). State Mutual Bk.

Selective Guide to Colleges 1984-85. Edward B. Fiske. LC 83-45117. 483p. 1983. pap. 9.95 (ISBN 0-8129-1087-7). Times Bks.

Selective Guide to Colleges 1986-87. 3rd ed. Edward B. Fiske. LC 85-40267. 524p. (Orig.). 1985. pap. 10.95 (ISBN 0-8129-1263-2). Times Bks.

Selective Guide to Colleges 1988. 4th, rev. ed. Edward B. Fiske. LC 86-30102. 672p. 1987. pap. 10.95 (ISBN 0-8129-1702-2). Times Bks.

Selective Guide to Women-Related Records in the North Carolina State Archives. Catherine E. Thompson. 77p. pap. 3.00 (ISBN 0-86526-167-9). NC Archives.

Selective Heat Sensitivity of Cancer Cells. Ed. by A. Rossi-Fanelli et al. (Recent Results in Cancer Research: Vol. 59). 1977. 39.00 (ISBN 0-387-07973-4). Springer-Verlag.

Selective Incapacitation Revisited: Why the High Rate Offenders are Hard to Predict. Peter W. Greenwood & Susan Turner. LC 86-33845. 1987. 7.50. Rand Corp.

Selective Inhibitors of Viral Functions. Ed. by W. A. Carter. LC 73-81479. (Uniscience Ser.). 377p. 1973. 70.50 (ISBN 0-87819-027-9). CRC Pr.

Selective Inventory of Information Services. (World Social Science Information Services: No. 3). 140p. 1981. pap. 9.00 (ISBN 92-3-001848-1, U1135, UNESCO). UNIPUB.

Selective Inventory of Information Services 1985. 247p. 1986. pap. 12.75 (ISBN 92-3-002343-4, U1480, UNESCO). UNIPUB.

Selective Laser Spectroscopy of Activated Crystals & Glasses. Ed. by V. V. Osiko. (Proceedings of the Institute of General Physics of the Academy of Sciences of the U. S. S. R.: Vol. 9). 210p. (Rus.). 1989. text ed. 62.00 (ISBN 0-941743-31-4). Nova Sci Pubs.

Selective Music Bibliography from the Period 1663-1763. James Pruett & Lee Rigsby. (Illus.). vii, 53p. 1962. pap. 2.00 (ISBN 0-86526-109-1). NC Archives.

Selective Mutism: Implications for Research & Treatment. Thomas R. Kratochwill. LC 80-18631. 208p. 1981. text ed. 29.95x (ISBN 0-89859-064-7). L Erlbaum Assocs.

Selective Neuronal Death: Symposium, No. 126. CIBA Staff. LC 86-28082. (CIBA Foundation Symposia Ser.). 270p. 1987. 47.00 (ISBN 0-471-91092-9). Wiley.

Selective Nontreatment of Handicapped Newborns: Moral Dilemmas in Neonatal Medicine. Robert F. Weir. LC 83-19376. 292p. 1984. 35.00x (ISBN 0-19-503396-5); pap. 14.95x (ISBN 0-19-504881-4). Oxford U Pr.

Selective, Open Pit Gold Mining Seminar. 174p. 1986. pap. text ed. 33.00x (ISBN 0-909520-97-6, Pub. by Australian Inst M & M). Brookfield Pub Co.

Selective Optical Surfaces for Solar Energy Converters. M. M. Koltun. Ed. by D. P. Siddons. Tr. by S. Chomet from Rus. LC 81-69401. vi, 239p. 1981. 42.50 (ISBN 0-89864-003-2). Allerton Pr.

Selective Oxidation of Hydrocarbons. D. J. Hucknall. 1974. 63.00 (ISBN 0-12-358950-9). Acad Pr.

Selective Plasma Component Removal. Ed. by Alvaro A. Pineda. LC 84-80840. (Illus.). 232p. 1984. 35.00 (ISBN 0-87993-228-7). Futura Pub.

Selective Practice Typing Drills. Alan C. Lloyd et al. 1974. text ed. 10.16 (ISBN 0-07-038147-X). McGraw.

Selective Safeguard Measures in Multilateral Trade Relations: Issues of Protectionism in GATT, European Community, & United States Law. M. C. Bronckers. LC 85-5587. 1985. 50.00 (ISBN 9-06-544222-7). Kluwer Academic.

Selective Safeguards in Multilateral Trade Relations. M. Bronckers. write for info. Kluwer Academic.

Selective Sample Handling & Detection in High Performance Liquid Chromatography. R. W. Frei & K. Zech. (JCL Ser.: Vol. 39, No. 1). 1987. 117.00 (ISBN 0-444-42881-X). Elsevier.

Selective Service & American Society. Ed. by Roger W. Little. LC 68-54411. 220p. 1969. 18.00x (ISBN 0-87154-548-9). Russell Sage.

Selective Survey of English Language Studies on Scandinavian Law. Ruth B. Ginsburg. vi, 53p. (Orig.). 1970. pap. text ed. 4.50x (ISBN 0-8377-0600-9). Rothman.

Selective Toxicity: The Physico-Chemical Basis of Theory. 6th ed. Adrien Albert. LC 78-15491. 1979. pap. text ed. 19.95x (ISBN 0-412-23650-8). Halsted Pr.

Selective Toxicity: The Physico-Chemical Basis of Therapy. 7th Ed ed. Adrien Albert. 792p. 1985. text ed. 69.95 (ISBN 0-412-26010-7, NO. 9126, Pub. by Chapman & Hall England); pap. text ed. 34.95 (ISBN 0-412-26020-4, NO. 9127). Routledge Chapman & Hall.

Selective 5-HT Reuptake Inhibitors: Novel on Commonplace Agents? Ed. by M. Gastpar & Jennifers S. Wakelin. (Advances in Biological Psychiatry Ser.: No. 17). (Illus.). viii, 160p. 1988. 93.50 (ISBN 3-8055-4776-5). S Karger.

Selectivity & Detectability Optimazations in HPLC. Ahuja. (Chemical Analysis Ser.). 1988. price not set (ISBN 0-471-62645-7). Wiley.

Selectivity & Molecular Mechanisms of Toxicology. F. DeMatteis & E. A. Lock. 280p. 1987. 65.00 (ISBN 0-02-329861-8). Macmillan.

Selectivity in Information Systems: Survival of the Fittest. Kenneth S. Warren. LC 84-11607. 188p. 1985. 36.95 (ISBN 0-275-90180-7, C0180). Praeger.

Selectre. S. Mandelbrojt. 640p. 1981. pap. 58.00 cancelled (ISBN 2-04-011310-X, Pub. by Bordas Dunod Gauthier-Villars FR). IPS.

Selenium. 2nd ed. Irene Rosenfeld & O. A. Beath. 1964. 80.00 (ISBN 0-12-597550-3). Acad Pr.

Selenium. (Environmental Health Criteria Ser.: No. 58). 276p. 1987. pap. 13.20 (ISBN 92-4-154258-6). World Health.

Selenium. Ralph Zingaro & Charles W. Cooper. LC 74-1246. 856p. 1974. 59.50 (ISBN 0-442-29575-8, VN). Krieger.

Selenium & Tellurium. I. I. Nazarenk & A. N. Ermakov. (Analytical Chemistry of the Elements Ser.). 249p. 1970. text ed. 50.00x (ISBN 0-7065-1256-1, Pub. by Keter Pub Jerusalem). Coronet Bks.

Selenium As Food & Medicine. Richard A. Passwater. LC 80-82325. 200p. 1981. 10.95 (ISBN 0-87983-237-1); pap. 2.95 (ISBN 0-87983-229-0). Keats.

Selenium in Biology & Medicine III, 2 vols. Ed. by Gerald F. Combs, Jr. et al. 1134p. 1987. Set. 99.95 (ISBN 0-442-22108-8). AVI.

Selenium in Natural Products Synthesis. K. C. Nicolaou & N. A. Petasis. LC 83-72883. (Illus.). 300p. 1984. 37.50 (ISBN 0-914891-00-6). C I S.

Selenium in Nutrition. rev. ed. National Research Council. 1983. pap. text ed. 14.50x (ISBN 0-309-03375-6). Natl Acad Pr.

Selenium: The Trace Element for Health & Life Extension. Eric Trimmer. 96p. Date not set. pap. 3.99 (ISBN 0-7225-1388-7, Pub. by Thorsons (England)). Sterling.

Selenium-Update: Good Health Guide. Richard Passwater. 1987. 1.95 (ISBN 0-87983-393-9). Keats.

Selenographia, Sive Lunae Descriptio. Johann Hevelius. 1968. Repr. 120.00 (ISBN 0-384-22820-8). Johnson Repr.

Seleted Essays & Reviews, 1948-1968. Richard F. Goldman. Ed. by Dorothy Klotzman. LC 79-56152. (I. S. A. M. Monographs: No. 13). 262p. 1980. pap. 10.00 (ISBN 0-914678-13-2). Inst Am Music.

Seleucid Army. B. Bar-Kochva. (Cambridge Classical Studies Ser.). 1976. 39.50 (ISBN 0-521-20667-7). Cambridge U Pr.

Seleucid Mint of Antioch. E. T. Newell. (Illus.). 1980. 50.00 (ISBN 0-89005-268-9). Ares.

Seleucid Mint of Antioch. E. T. Newell. (Illus.). 1978. 50.00 (ISBN 0-916710-38-6). Obol Intl.

Self. Anthony Kenny. LC 88-60191. (Aquinas Lecture Ser.: No. 52). 33p. 1988. 7.95 (ISBN 0-87462-155-0). Marquette.

Self-Abandonment to Divine Providence: Abandonment to Divine Providence. J. P. De Caussade. Tr. by Algar Thorold from Fr. LC 86-51602. 450p. 1987. pap. 15.00 (ISBN 0-89555-312-0). Tan Bks Pubs.

Self-Actualization: An Annotated Bibliography of the Theory & Research. David Welch & George A. Tate. LC 86-31996. (Reference Library of Social Science). 300p. 1987. lib. bdg. 40.00 (ISBN 0-8240-8568-X). Garland Pub.

Self-Actualization for Nurses: Issue, Trends, & Strategies for Job Enrichment. Barbara Fuszard. 252p. 1984. 42.50 (ISBN 0-89443-871-9). Aspen Pub.

Self-Actuated Healing: The Alternative to Doctors & Drugs Is Within You. Lonny Brown. 176p. (Orig.). 1988. 13.95 (ISBN 0-87961-184-7); pap. 7.95 (ISBN 0-87961-185-5). Naturegraph.

Self-Adjoint Operators. W. G. Faris. (Lecture Notes in Mathematics Ser.: Vol. 433). vii, 115p. 1975. pap. 13.00 (ISBN 0-387-07030-3). Springer-Verlag.

Self Affirmation: Perception Techniques That Can Work for You. Guy Greenfield. 176p. (Orig.). 1988. pap. 7.95 (ISBN 0-8010-3820-0). Baker Bk.

Self-Aligning Mechanisms. L. Reshetov. 528p. 1982. 12.95 (ISBN 0-8285-2339-8, Pub. by Mir Pubs USSR). Imported Pubns.

Self-Analysis. Karen Horney. pap. 5.95 (ISBN 0-393-00134-2). Norton.

Self Analysis. L. Ron Hubbard. 20.00 (ISBN 0-686-30780-1). Church Scient NY.

Self Analysis. L. Ron Hubbard. 254p. 1983. pap. 8.95 (ISBN 0-88404-109-3). Bridge Pubns Inc.

Self Analysis. L. Ron Hubbard. 1987. pap. 4.95 (ISBN 0-88404-264-2). Bridge Pubns Inc.

Self Analysis: The Book about Life. James J. Carter. (Illus., Orig.). 1979. pap. 4.95 (ISBN 0-937004-00-6). Unicorn NJ.

Self & Cinema: A Transformalist Perspective. Beverle Houston & Marsha Kinder. (Illus.). vi, 474p. (Orig.). 1980. pap. 14.75 (ISBN 0-913178-62-4). Redgrave Pub Co.

Self & Community in the City. Jerome Krase. LC 81-1430. (Illus.). 232p. (Orig.). 1982. pap. text ed. 13.25 (ISBN 0-8191-2284-X). U Pr of Amer.

Self & Emotion. Ed. by Robert I. Levy & Michelle Z. Rosaldo. (Ethos Ser.: Vol. 11, No. 3). 1983. 10.00 (ISBN 0-317-66364-X). Am Anthro Assn.

Self & Family. Jane C. Peck. LC 84-13166. (Choices: Guides for Today's Woman Ser.: Vol. 11). 118p. 1984. pap. 6.95 (ISBN 0-664-24547-1). Westminster John Knox.

Self & Identity: Perspectives across the Lifespan. T. Honess & K. M. Yardley. (International Library of Psychology Ser.). 416p. 1987. lib. bdg. 67.50x (ISBN 0-7102-0829-4, Pub. by Routledge UK). Routledge Chapman & Hall.

Self & Identity: Psychosocial Perspectives. Yardley. 1986. write for info. (ISBN 0-471-91125-9). Wiley.

Self & Image in Juan Ramon Jiminez: Modern & Post Modern Readings. John C. Wilcox. LC 86-1460. 232p. 1987. 21.95 (ISBN 0-252-01331-X). U of Ill Pr.

Self & Its Brain. rev. ed. K. R. Popper & J. C. Eccles. (Illus.). 597p. 1978. 39.00 (ISBN 0-387-08307-3). Springer-Verlag.

Self & Its Brain: An Argument for Interactionism. Karl Popper & John Eccles. 616p. 1984. pap. 14.95 (ISBN 0-7100-9584-8). Routledge Chapman & Hall.

Self & Nature. De Witt Parker. LC 75-3306. Repr. of 1917 ed. 22.50 (ISBN 0-404-59291-0). AMS Pr.

Self & Nature in Kant's Philosophy. Ed. by Allen W. Wood. LC 84-7678. (Paperback Ser.). 240p. 1984. pap. 9.95x (ISBN 0-8014-9268-8). Cornell U Pr.

Self & Non-Self in Early Buddhism. Joacquin Perez-Ramon. (Religon & Society Ser.: No. 17). 1980. 58.00x (ISBN 90-279-7987-1). Mouton.

Self & Object Constancy: Clinical & Theoretical Perspectives. Ed. by Ruth F. Lax et al. LC 85-27365. (Guilford Psychiatry Ser.). 355p. 1985. text ed. 35.00 (ISBN 0-89862-226-3). Guilford Pr.

Self & Others. R. D. Laing. 1972. pap. 5.95 (ISBN 0-14-021376-7, Pelican). Penguin.

Self & Others. Jan Osterberg. 1988. lib. bdg. 69.00 (ISBN 90-277-2648-5, Pub. by Reidel Holland). Kluwer Academic.

Self & Others: Object Relations Theory in Pratice. N. Gregory Hamilton. LC 87-19479. 338p. 1988. 30.00x (ISBN 0-87668-961-6). Aronson.

Self & Self-Management. Arnold Bennett. LC 74-16345. (Collected Works of Arnold Bennett: Vol. 73). 1976. Repr. of 1918 ed. 16.75 (ISBN 0-518-19154-0). Ayer Co Pubs.

Self & Sequence: The Poetry of D. H. Lawrence. Holly A. Laird. LC 87-23047. 228p. 1988. 35.00x (ISBN 0-8139-1147-8). U Pr of Va.

Self & Social Context. Ray Holland. LC 77-27530. 1978. 27.50x (ISBN 0-312-71229-4). St Martin.

Self & Social Life. Barry R. Schlenker. (Social Psychology & Personality Ser.). 416p. 1985. text ed. 38.95 (ISBN 0-07-055307-6). McGraw.

Self & Society: A Study of Gandhian Thought. Ramashray Roy. 205p. 1985. text ed. 25.00 (ISBN 0-8039-9484-2, Pub. by Sage India). Sage.

Self & Society: A Symbolic Interactionist Social Psychology. 4th ed. John Hewitt. 312p. (Orig.). 1988. pap. text ed. 30.00 (ISBN 0-205-10585-8). Allyn.

Self & Society in Medieval France: The Memories of Abbot Guibert of Nogent. Ed. by John F. Benton. (Medieval Academy Reprints for Teaching Ser.). 260p. 1984. pap. text ed. 9.95c (ISBN 0-8020-6550-3). U of Toronto Pr.

Self & Society in Ming Thought. William T. De Bary. LC 78-101229. (Studies in Oriental Culture: No. 4). pap. 147.20 (2029702). Bks Demand UMI.

Self & Society in the Poetry of Nicholas Guillen. Lorna V. Williams. LC 81-8404. 192p. 1982. text ed. 21.50x (ISBN 0-8018-2666-7). Johns Hopkins.

Self & Society: Narcissism, Collectivism, & the Development of Morals. Drew Westen. LC 84-28478. 430p. 1985. 57.50 (ISBN 0-521-30171-8); pap. 19.95 (ISBN 0-521-31770-3). Cambridge U Pr.

Self & the Dramas of History. Reinhold Niebuhr. 264p. 1988. pap. text ed. 12.75 (ISBN 0-8191-6690-1). U Pr of Amer.

Self & the Environment, Pack 3. Alan Stoker & Bruce Burgess. 170p. 1987. 150.00x (ISBN 1-85008-026-7, Pub. by Framework UK). State Mutual Bk.

Self & the Object World. Edith Jacobson. LC 64-15489. (Journal of the American Psychoanalytic Association Monograph Ser.: No. 2). 250p. 1964. text ed. 30.00x (ISBN 0-8236-6060-5). Intl Univs Pr.

Self & the Other. Ed. by Anna-Teresa Tymieniecka. (Analecta Husserliana: No. 6). 1977. lib. bdg. 31.50 (ISBN 90-277-0759-6, Pub. by Reidel Holland). Kluwer Academic.

Self & the Other in the Ontologies of Sartre & Buber. Sylvain Boni. LC 82-20130. 202p. (Orig.). 1983. lib. bdg. 29.00 (ISBN 0-8191-2852-X); pap. text ed. 13.25 (ISBN 0-8191-2853-8). U Pr of Amer.

Self & World. Eli Siegel. LC 75-44647. 1981. pap. 9.95 (ISBN 0-910492-28-X). Definition.

Self & World: Readings in Philosophy. 2nd ed. James A. Ogilvy. 507p. 1981. pap. text ed. 14.00 net (ISBN 0-15-579628-3, HC). HarBraceJ.

Self-Directed Learning in Nursing. Ed. by Signe S. Cooper. LC 80-80088. 160p. 1980. pap. 32.95 (ISBN 0-913654-64-7). Aspen Pub.
Self-Directed Study Guide on the Education of the Gifted & the Talented. Donald J. Treffinger & Clifford D. Curl. 180p. 17.50 (ISBN 0-318-02125-0). NSLTIGT.
Self-Directed Systematic Desensitization. Wes W. Wenrich et al. LC 76-9019. (Illus.). 95p. 1976. pap. 7.00 (ISBN 0-917472-05-5). F Fournies.
Self-Direction & Political Legitimacy: Rousseau & Herder. F. M. Barnard. 368p. 1988. 65.00 (ISBN 0-19-827327-4). Oxford U Pr.
Self-Discipline: Helping Students Succeed. Kris Amundson. 16p. 1987. pap. text ed. write for info. (ISBN 0-87652-115-4, 021-00196). Am Assn Sch Admin.
Self Disclosure: An Experimental Analysis of the Transparent Self. Sidney Jourard. LC 78-10576. 264p. 1979. Repr. of 1971 ed. lib. bdg. 19.50 (ISBN 0-88275-767-9). Krieger.
Self-Disclosure: Origins, Patterns, & Implications of Openness in Interpersonal Relationships. Gordon J. Chelune et al. LC 79-88766. (Social & Behavioral Science Ser.). 1979. text ed. 42.95x (ISBN 0-87589-433-X). Jossey-Bass.
Self-Disclosure: Theory, Research, & Therapy. Ed. by V. J. Derlega & J. H. Berg. LC 87-18654. (Perspectives in Social Psychology Ser.). (Illus.). 380p. 1987. 39.50x (ISBN 0-306-42635-8, Plenum Pr). Plenum Pub.
Self-Discovery. Thomas Langan. LC 84-82059. 64p. (Orig.). 1985. pap. text ed. 3.50 (ISBN 0-910727-06-6). Golden Phoenix.
Self-Discovery & Authority in Afro-American Narrative. Valerie Smith. LC 87-11950. 179p. 1987. text ed. 22.50x (ISBN 0-674-80087-7). Harvard U Pr.
Self-Discovery in Recovery. Abraham J Twerski. 128p. (Orig.). 1984. pap. 3.95 (ISBN 0-89486-238-3). Hazelden.
Self-Education-Self Assessment in Thoracic Surgery. 3rd ed. Coordinating Committee for Continuing Education in Thoracic Surgery Staff. LC 80-84130. 256p. 1987. pap. 105.00 (ISBN 0-8403-4370-1, 40315601). Kendall-Hunt.
Self, Ego, & Identity. Ed. by D. K. Lapsley & F. C. Power. (Illus.). 280p. 1988. 37.00 (ISBN 0-387-96588-2). Springer-Verlag.
Self-Embodiment of God. Thomas J. Altizer. LC 87-13365. (Brown Classics in Judaica). 114p. 1987. pap. text ed. 9.75 (ISBN 0-8191-6467-4). U Pr of Amer.
Self-Employed Educator see Educators Financial Kit.
Self-Employed Woman: How to Start Your Own Business & Gain Control of Your Life. Jeanette R. Scollard. 288p. 1986. 17.95 (ISBN 0-671-50084-8). S&S.
Self Employment, Self Starter, & Start Your Own: A How to Reference Guide. Center For Self Sufficiency, Research Division Staff. LC 83-90708. 200p. 1983. write for info. (ISBN 0-910811-12-1, Pub. by Center Self Suff). Prosperity & Profits.
Self-Esteem. Joan L. Guest. (Orig.). 1984. pap. 0.75 (ISBN 0-87784-066-0). Inter-Varsity.
Self-Esteem. McKay & Fanning. 1988. pap. 4.50 (ISBN 0-312-90443-6). St Martin.
Self-Esteem. Matthew McKay & Patrick Fanning. 272p. 1987. 19.95 (ISBN 0-934986-42-8); pap. 10.95 (ISBN 0-934986-41-X). New Harbinger.
Self-Esteem. Robert Schuller. 176p. 1985. pap. 3.50 (ISBN 0-515-08912-5). Jove Pubns.
Self-Esteem: A Classroom Affair, Vol. 1. Michele Borba & Craig Borba. 140p. 1978. pap. 8.95 (ISBN 0-86683-612-8, AY8939, HarpR). Har-Row.
Self-Esteem: A Classroom Affair, Vol. 2. Michele Borba & Craig Borba. 144p. (Orig.). 1982. pap. 9.95 (ISBN 0-86683-675-6, AY8210, HarpR). Har-Row.
Self Esteem: A Declaration. Virginia Satir. LC 75-9447. (Illus.). 1975. pap. 4.95 (ISBN 0-89087-109-4). Celestial Arts.
Self-Esteem: A Family Affair. Jean I. Clarke. 280p. 1980. pap. 8.95 (ISBN 0-86683-615-2, HarpR). Har-Row.
Self-Esteem: A Family Affair Leader Guide. Jean Clarke. 1974. pap. 14.95 (ISBN 0-86683-976-3, RD639, HarpR). Har-Row.
Self Esteem: A Family Affair Leader Guide. Jean I. Clarke. 280p. 1981. pap. 14.95 (ISBN 0-03-059064-7, AY8948, HarpR). Har-Row.
Self Esteem: A Gift from God. Ruth M. Ward. (YA) (gr. 9 up). 1984. pap. 7.95 (ISBN 0-8010-9664-2). Baker Bk.
Self-Esteem & Adjusting with Blindness: The Process of Responding to Life's Demands. Dean W. Tuttle. (Illus.). 336p. 1984. 32.75 (ISBN 0-398-04887-8). C C Thomas.
Self-Esteem & Meaning: A Life Historical Investigation. Michael R. Jackson. LC 83-18248. (Transpersonal & Humanistic Psychology Ser.). 228p. 1984. 54.50 (ISBN 0-87395-852-7); pap. 19.95 (ISBN 0-87395-853-5). State U NY Pr.
Self-Esteem & Social Anchorage of Adolescent White, Black & Mexican American Students. Janet D. Ockerman. LC 79-65267. 135p. 1979. perfect bdg. 11.95 (ISBN 0-88247-587-8). R & E Pubs.
Self-Esteem & the Physical You. Anita Canfield. 293p. 1983. 8.95 (ISBN 0-934126-21-6). Randall Bk Co.
Self-Esteem & the Social You. Anita Canfield. 140p. 1983. 7.95 (ISBN 0-934126-26-7). Randall Bk Co.
Self-Esteem at Work: Research, Theory, & Practice. Joel Brockner. LC 84-48747. (Issues in Organization & Management Ser.). 320p. 1988. 39.00x (ISBN 0-669-09755-1). Lexington Bks.
Self-Esteem Discussion Guide. Steele & Maloney. 1987. pap. text ed. 3.00 (ISBN 0-317-59344-7). Ann Arbor FL.
Self-Esteem Enhancement with Children & Adolescents. A. W. Pope & S. M. McHale. 160p. 1988. text ed. 22.50 (ISBN 0-08-032765-6); pap. text ed. 12.95 (ISBN 0-08-032764-8). Pergamon.
Self-Esteem for the Latter-Day Saint Woman. 2nd ed. Anita Canfield. 135p. 1983. 7.95 (ISBN 0-934126-15-1). Randall Bk Co.
Self-Esteem for Tots to Teens: Five Principles for Raising Confident Children. Eugene Anderson et al. 207p. (Orig.). 1984. pap. 4.95 (ISBN 0-671-54467-5). Meadowbrook.
Self-Esteem in Children with Special Educational Needs. Peter W. Gurney. 160p. 1988. text ed. 37.50 (ISBN 0-415-00599-X). Routledge Chapman & Hall.
Self Esteem in the Classroom. Lawrence. 1987. pap. text ed. 12.00 (ISBN 0-06-318393-5, Pub. by Har-Row Ltd England). Har-Row.
Self-Esteem: Overcoming Inferiority Feelings. Cecil G. Osborne. 176p. 1986. pap. 12.95 (ISBN 0-687-37136-8). Abingdon.
Self-Esteem Passport. Krawetz. 1984. pap. 2.95 (ISBN 0-8050-0218-9). H Holt & Co.
Self-Esteem Passport. Michael Krawetz. 1984. pap. 2.95 (ISBN 0-03-069846-4). H Holt & Co.
Self Esteem: The Key to Success in Work & Love. Frieda Porat. Ed. by Estella Krebs. LC 87-90732. 176p. (Orig.). 1988. pap. 9.95 (ISBN 0-88247-778-1). R & E Pubs.
Self-Esteem: The Key to Your Child's Well-Being. Harris Clemes & Reynold Bean. 1982. pap. 3.50 (ISBN 0-8217-1096-6). Zebra.
Self-Esteem: The New Reformation. Robert H. Schuller. 144p. 1982. 3.95 (ISBN 0-8499-4172-5). Word Bks.
Self-Esteem Tools for Recovery. Lindsey Hall & Leigh Cohn. 128p. 1988. pap. 8.95 (ISBN 0-936077-15-8). Gurze Bks.
Self Esteem: You're Better Than You Think. Ray Burwick. 1983. pap. 5.95 (ISBN 0-8423-5865-X). Tyndale.
Self-Evaluation. S. L. Groves & D. L. Groves. 20p. 1978. pap. text ed. 4.00 (ISBN 0-940414-01-5). Appalach Assoc.
Self Evaluation & Exploration Kit. Ed. by Marjorie Layton. (Illus., Orig.). (gr. 5-9). 1982. kit 75.00 (ISBN 0-912578-53-X). Chron Guide.
Self-Evaluation Career Guide. Ruth Crane & Marcine H. Goad. LC 78-1362. 79p. 1978. pap. 3.50 (ISBN 0-87576-067-8). Pilot Bks.
Self-Evaluation for Planning in Human Services Organizations. Harvey Newman et al. LC 86-48283. 160p. 1986. 59.95 (ISBN 0-8144-1945-3). AMACOM.
Self-Evaluation for Primary Schools. I. A. Rodger & J. A. Richardson. (Studies in Teaching & Learning). 216p. (Orig.). 1985. pap. text ed. 20.95 (ISBN 0-340-36933-7). Princeton Bk Co.
Self-Evaluation: Ideas for Participatory Evaluation of Rural Community Development Projects. Jim Rugh. (Illus.). 43p. (Orig.). 1986. pap. 5.00 (ISBN 0-942716-05-1). World Neigh.
Self-Excellence: Key to Preventive Stress Management & Goal-Oriented Living. S. A. Swami. (Illus.). 198p. 1987. 19.95 (ISBN 0-941553-00-0). Minibook Pub.
Self-Expression in Early Greek Lyric, Elegiac & Iambic Poetry. Odsseus Tsagarakis. 181p. (Orig.). 1977. pap. text ed. 33.00x (ISBN 3-515-02488-3, Pub by Franz Steiner). Coronet Bks.
Self-Financing Road System. G. J. Roth. (Institute of Economic Affairs, Research Monographs: No. 3). pap. 2.50 technical (ISBN 0-255-69585-3). Transatl Arts.
Self-Focusing: Experimental & Theory see Progress in Quantum Electronics.
Self-Fulfilling Prophecies: Readership & Authority in the First Roman de la Rose. David F. Hult. (Illus.). 400p. 1986. 47.50 (ISBN 0-521-32014-3). Cambridge U Pr.
Self-Fulfilling Prophecies: Social, Psychological, & Physiological Effects of Expectancies. Russell A. Jones. 288p. 1977. text ed. 29.95x (ISBN 0-89859-126-0). L Erlbaum Assocs.
Self-Fulfilling Prophecy: Exile & Return As the History of Judaism. Jacob Neusner. LC 86-47756. 320p. 1987. 25.00 (ISBN 0-8070-3606-4). Beacon Pr.
Self-Fulfillment in Aging: Avocational Psychology in the Management of a Tri-Powered Life. G. L. Freeman. LC 73-88439. (Illus.). 224p. 1973. 15.00 (ISBN 0-87282-040-8). Am Life Foun.
Self-Fulfillment Through Zionism: A Study in Jewish Adjustment. Ed. by Shlomo Bardin. LC 70-142605. (Biography Index Reprint Ser). Repr. of 1943 ed. 17.00 (ISBN 0-8369-8076-X). Ayer Co Pubs.
Self-Funding of Welfare Benefits. Carlton Harker. 169p. (Orig.). 1981. pap. 15.00 (ISBN 0-89154-162-4). Intl Found Employ.
Self-Funding Your Employee Medical Benefits: A Survival Guide & How-To-Do-It Book. Thomas R. Young. Ed. by Gulf Coast Offset, Inc. Staff. (Orig.). 1985. lib. bdg. write for info. (ISBN 0-9614151-0-X); pap. write for info. (ISBN 0-9614151-1-8). Young.
Self, Global Issues & Ethics. Howard L. Parsons. (Praxis, Philosophical & Scientific Reprints: Vol. 4). 209p. 1980. pap. text ed. 22.50 (Pub. by Gruner Holland). Humanities.
Self God. Subramuniya. (On the Path Ser.). 72p. 1959. pap. 2.00 (ISBN 0-87516-353-X). DeVorss.
Self, God & Immortality: A Jamesian Investigation. Eugene Fontinell. 320p. 1986. 34.95 (ISBN 0-87722-428-5). Temple U Pr.
Self-Governing Dominion: California, 1849-1860. William H. Ellison. (California Library Reprint Ser.: Vol. 95). 1978. Repr. of 1950 ed. 33.00x (ISBN 0-520-03713-8). U of Cal Pr.
Self-Governing Socialism: A Reader, 2 vols. Ed. by Branko Horvat et al. Incl. Vol. 1. 497p. text ed. 35.00 (ISBN 0-87332-050-6); Vol. 2. 330p. text ed. 35.00 (ISBN 0-87332-061-1). LC 73-92805. 1975. Set (ISBN 0-87332-048-4). M E Sharpe.
Self-Government & Freedom in Russia. Sergie Pushkarev. (CCRS Series on Change in Contemporary Soviet Society). 176p. 1988. pap. 15.95 (ISBN 0-8133-7476-6). Westview.
Self-Government in Industry. facsimile ed. George D. Cole. LC 71-152979. (Select Bibliographies Reprint Ser). Repr. of 1918 ed. 21.00 (ISBN 0-8369-5731-8). Ayer Co Pubs.
Self-Government in Modernizing Nations. facsimile ed. Ed. by James R. Pennock. LC 77-167401. (Essay Index Reprint Ser). Repr. of 1964 ed. 15.00 (ISBN 0-8369-2517-3). Ayer Co Pubs.
Self-Government of the Jews in Palestine Since 1900. Moshe Burstein. LC 75-6426. (Rise of Jewish Nationalism & the Middle East Ser.). 298p. 1976. Repr. of 1934 ed. 25.00 (ISBN 0-88355-313-9). Hyperion Conn.
Self-Government with Union. Verna M. Hall. LC 61-16012. (Illus.). 1962. lib. bdg. 15.00 (ISBN 0-912498-01-3). Found Am Christ.
Self-Growth in Families: Kinetic Family Drawings (K-F-D Research & Application) Robert C. Burns. LC 81-21659. (Illus.). 220p. 1982. pap. 19.95 (ISBN 0-87630-305-X). Brunner-Mazel.
Self Guide for Linguistic Fieldwork. Paul R. Turner. 1984. pap. 10.00 (ISBN 0-318-04184-7); cassette 4.00. Impresora Sahuaro.
Self-Guided Architectural Tours of Cape May, NJ. Marsha Cudworth. LC 84-81044. (Illus.). 1985. pap. 6.95 (ISBN 0-9608554-2-4). Lady Raspberry.
Self Guided Architectural Tours of Cape May, N.J. An Illustrated Guide to Cape Mays Rich Architectural Heritage - 2 Walking Tours & 1 Auto Tour Featuring over 100 Historical Sights. Marsha Cudworth. LC 84-81044. 82p. 1987. pap. 7.95 (Pub. by Lady Raspberry Press). Bric A Brac.
Self-Guiding Society. Warren Breed. LC 75-128472. 1971. pap. text ed. 6.95 (ISBN 0-02-904650-5). Free Pr.
Self Healing. Meir Schneider. 224p. 1987. pap. 9.95 (ISBN 0-7102-1084-1, Pub. by Routledge UK). Routledge Chapman & Hall.
Self-Healing Cookbook: A Macrobiotic Primer for Healing Body, Mind & Moods with Whole, Natural Foods. 2nd, rev. ed. Kristina Turner. (Illus.). 216p. (Orig.). 1988. pap. 15.00 (ISBN 0-945668-10-4). Earthtones Pr.
Self Healing Yoga & Destiny. 1983. 4.95 (ISBN 0-943358-06-X). Aurora Press.
Self-Health Guide: A Personal Program for Holistic Living. Kripalu Center for Holistic Health. LC 80-82166. (Illus.). 207p. (Orig.). 1980. pap. 9.95 (ISBN 0-940258-00-5). Kripalu Pubns.
Self Heating: Evaluation & Controlling the Hazards. P. C. Bowes. 1984. 129.00 (ISBN 0-444-99624-9, I-099-84). Elsevier.
Self Help. Lorrie Moore. Ed. by Victoria Wilson. LC 84-48498. 158p. 1985. 13.45 (ISBN 0-394-53921-4). Knopf.
Self-Help. Lorrie Moore. LC 85-28527. 176p. 1986. pap. 6.95 (ISBN 0-452-25821-9, Plume). NAL.
Self-Help. Samuel Sailes. Ed. by George Bull & Keith Joseph. 240p. 1986. pap. 6.95 (ISBN 0-14-009100-9). Penguin.
Self-Help a Hundred Years Ago. 3rd ed. George J. Holyoake. LC 76-47881. Repr. of 1891 ed. 19.50 (ISBN 0-404-60084-0). AMS Pr.
Self-Help & Opportunities, 2 Vols. Samuel Smiles. (Illus.). 177p. 1987. 137.75 (ISBN 0-89920-148-2). Am Classical Coll Pr.
Self-Help & Popular Participation in Rural Water Systems. Duncan Miller. (Development Center Studies). (Illus.). 150p. (Orig.). 1980. pap. text ed. 9.00x (ISBN 92-64-12027-0, 4180011). OECD.
Self-Help Barangay High Schools. rev. ed. Pedro T. Orata. (Illus.). pap. 6.50x (ISBN 0-686-24652-7, Pub. by New Day Pub Philippines). Cellar.
Self-Help by the People: The History of the Rochdale Pioneers, 1844-1892. 10th rev. & enl. ed. George J. Holyoake. LC 76-47882. Repr. of 1893 ed. 27.50 (ISBN 0-404-60085-9). AMS Pr.
Self-Help Clothing for Children Who Have Physical Disabilities. Eleanor B. Hotte. 64p. 1979. 1.50 (ISBN 0-933851-03-0, E-32313). Natl Easter Seal.
Self-Help for Premenstrual Syndrome. Michelle Harrison. (Illus.). 49p. 1982. perfect bound 4.50 (ISBN 0-9610964-0-3). Matrix Pr MA.
Self-Help for Premenstrual Syndrome. rev. ed. Michelle Harrison. LC 84-23723. 169p. 1985. 9.95 (ISBN 0-394-73502-1, RanC). Random.
Self Help for Seniors. National Council of Jewish Women. 30p. (Orig.). 1983. pap. text ed. 4.00 (ISBN 0-941840-14-X). NCJW.
Self-Help: Fourteen Hundred Best Books on Personal Growth. Bill Katz & Linda S. Katz. 225p. 1984. 34.95 (ISBN 0-8352-1939-9). Bowker.
Self-Help Groups & Human Service Agencies: How They Work Together. Daniel Remine et al. LC 83-48645. 109p. (Orig.). 1984. pap. text ed. 13.95 (ISBN 0-87304-204-2). Family Serv.
Self-Help Groups & Voluntary Action: International Perspectives. Alfred H. Katz & David H. Smith. 250p. Date not set. text ed. price not set (ISBN 0-8290-1274-5). Irvington.
Self-Help Groups for Coping with Crisis: Origins, Members, Processes, & Impact. Morton A. Lieberman et al. LC 79-88772. (Social & Behavioral Science Ser.). 1979. text ed. 34.95x (ISBN 0-87589-435-6). Jossey-Bass.
Self-Help Groups: Index of Modern Information with Bibliography. Judy G. Whitefield. LC 88-47792. 150p. (Orig.). 1988. 34.50 (ISBN 0-88164-892-2); pap. 26.50 (ISBN 0-88164-893-0). ABBE Pubs Assn.
Self-Help Handbook of Symptoms & Treatment. Joel N. Shlian & Deborah M. Shlian. 256p. (Orig.). 1986. pap. 8.95 (ISBN 0-8092-5146-9). Contemp Bks.
Self-Help Housing: A Critique. Ed. by Peter M. Ward. 304p. 1982. 37.00x (ISBN 0-7201-1636-8). Mansell.
Self-Help Housing Project in Rural Tunisia in Retrospect. Mirina Curuchet. 137p. 1988. pap. 22.50 (ISBN 0-8419-9790-X). Holmes & Meier.
Self Help in Health & Social Welfare. Ed. by Stephen Humble & Judith Unell. 160p. 1988. text ed. 37.50 (ISBN 0-7099-5726-2, Pub. by Croom Helm UK). Routledge Chapman & Hall.
Self Help in Soweto. Julian Y. Kramer. (Bergen Studies in Social Anthropology: No. 12). 172p. (Orig.). 1985. pap. text ed. 9.95x (ISBN 0-936508-55-8, Pub. by Dept Soc Anthropology, University of Bergen, Norway). Barber Pr.
Self-Help in the Human Services. Alan Gartner & Frank Riessman. LC 77-79483. (Social & Behavioral Science Ser). 1977. text ed. 28.95x (ISBN 0-87589-338-4). Jossey-Bass.
Self-Help in the 1890's Depression. H. Roger Grant. (Illus.). 164p. 1983. text ed. 13.95x (ISBN 0-8138-1634-3). Iowa St U Pr.
Self-Help in Urban America: Patterns of Minority Business Enterprise. Ed. by Scott Cummings. (National University Publications, Interdisciplinary Urban Ser.). 1980. 25.95x (ISBN 0-8046-9251-3, Pub. by Kennikat). Assoc Faculty Pr.
Self-Help Organizations & Professional Practice. Thomas J. Powell. LC 86-21761. 365p. 1987. 16.95x (ISBN 0-87101-133-6). Natl Assn Soc Wkrs.
Self-Help Revolution. Ed. by Alan Gartner & Frank Riessman. (Community Psychology Ser.: Vol. 10). 304p. 1984. 34.95 (ISBN 0-89885-070-3). Human Sci Pr.
Self-Help Wells. R. G. Koegel. (Irrigation & Drainage Papers: No. 30). 86p. 1977. pap. 7.50 (ISBN 92-5-100398-X, F1416, FAO). UNIPUB.
Self Help: Your Strategy for Living with COPD. Christmas Seal League of South Western Pennsylvania Staff. 1984. 3.95 (ISBN 0-915950-64-2). Bull Pub.
Self-Hypnosis. Henry L. Bolduc. 165p. (Orig.). 1985. pap. 8.95 (ISBN 0-87604-160-8). ARE Pr.
Self-Hypnosis. C. F. Freimuth. 12p. 1979. pap. 9.95 (ISBN 0-933992-07-6). Coffee Break.
Self Hypnosis. Leandro Katz. (Viper's Tongue Books Ser.). 1975. 8.00 (ISBN 0-931106-11-7, Dist. by Printed Matter). TVRT.
Self-Hypnosis. Annellen Simpkins & Alex Simpkins. 1988. text ed. 39.50x includes audio cassette (ISBN 0-8290-1369-5). Irvington.
Self-Hypnosis: A Complete Manual for Health & Self-Change. Brian M. Alman. LC 83-17173. (Illus.). 280p. 1983. pap. 19.95 (ISBN 0-913801-05-4). Intl Health Pub.
Self-Hypnosis: A Conditioned-Response Technique. Laurence Sparks. pap. 7.00 (ISBN 0-87980-139-5). Wilshire.
Self Hypnosis: A Method of Improving your Life. 140p. (Orig.). 1984. 6.95 (ISBN 0-9610480-1-8). Park West.
Self Hypnosis & Other Mind Expanding Techniques. Charles Tebbetts. 1977. pap. 5.95 (ISBN 0-685-57682-5). Borden.
Self-Hypnosis & Other Mind Expanding Techniques. 2nd ed. Charles Tebbetts. 141p. 1977. pap. 5.95x (ISBN 0-930298-18-7). Westwood Pub Co.
Self Hypnosis & Other Mind Expanding Techniques. rev. ed. Charles Tebbetts. 141p. 1985. pap. 9.95 (ISBN 0-930298-19-5). Westwood Pub Co.
Self Hypnosis & Other Mind Expanding Techniques. rev. ed. Charles Tebbetts. Ed. by Suzanne Mikesell. 140p. 1987. pap. 7.95 (ISBN 0-914629-41-7, Dist. by St. Martin's). Prima Pub Comm.

Self-Portrait of a Holocaust Survivor. Werner Weinberg. LC 84-43236. 224p. 1985. lib. bdg. 19.95x (ISBN 0-89950-173-7). McFarland & Co.

Self-Portrait with Hand Microscope. Lucille Day. 52p. 1982. pap. 4.95 (ISBN 0-917658-18-3). BPW & P.

Self-Portraits. Tom Ahern. (Illus.). 7p. 1980. 4.99 (ISBN 0-933442-04-1). Dianas Bimonthly.

Self Portraits of Great Artists. Ed. by Stephen Longstreet. (Master Draughtsman Ser.). (Illus.). treasure trove bdg. 10.95x (ISBN 0-87505-048-4); pap. 4.95 (ISBN 0-87505-201-0). Borden.

Self-Portraits, the Gide-Valery Letters, 1890-1942. Andre Gide. Ed. by Robert Mallet. Tr. by June Guicharnaud. LC 65-25125. pap. 86.50 (ISBN 0-317-26503-2, 2024041). Bks Demand UMI.

Self Portraits: Viewing Myself As an Adult Child of an Alcoholic. Jenny Wrenn. LC 86-61851. (Illus.). 73p. (Orig.). 1986. pap. text ed. 11.95 (ISBN 0-9616572-1-9). Clothespin Fever Pr.

Self-Portraiture: From Ancient Egypt to World War II. Carla Gottlieb. 1987. cancelled (ISBN 0-525-93298-4). Dutton.

Self Possession. Marion Halligan. 1988. pap. 8.95 (ISBN 0-7022-2209-7). U of Queensland Pr.

Self Power. Paul H. Skinner. 194p. pap. 7.95 (ISBN 0-942494-44-X). Coleman Pub.

Self-Production of Society. Alain Touraine. Tr. by Derek Coltman from Fr. LC 76-611. (Illus.). 1977. lib. bdg. 11.00x (ISBN 0-226-80858-0). U of Chicago Pr.

Self Profile: The Me Nobody Knows. Lyman Coleman. (Free University - Lay Academy in Christian Discipleship Ser.). (Orig.). 1981. pap. 4.95 leader's guide (ISBN 0-687-37346-8); pap. 1.25 (ISBN 0-687-37347-6). Abingdon.

Self-Propelled in the Southern Sierra: Vol. 1, The Sierra Crest & the Kern Plateau. 2nd ed. J. C. Jenkins. LC 81-70346. (Illus.). 304p. (Orig.). 1982. pap. 12.95 (ISBN 0-89997-016-8). Wilderness Pr.

Self-Propelled in the Southern Sierra: Vol. 2, The Great Western Divides. 2nd new ed. J. C. Jenkins. LC 81-70346. (Illus.). 308p. (Orig.). 1984. pap. 12.95 (ISBN 0-89997-042-7). Wilderness Pr.

Self-Protection Guide-Book for Girls & Women. Fred Neff. LC 75-38477. (Fred Neff's Self-Defense Library). (Illus.). 56p. (gr. 5 up). 1977. PLB 7.95 (ISBN 0-8225-1156-8). Lerner Pubns.

Self Psychology & the Humanities: Reflections on a New Psychoanalytic Approach. Heinz Kohut. Ed. by Charles B. Strozier. 333p. 1985. 27.95 (ISBN 0-393-70000-3). Norton.

Self Psychology in Clinical Social Work. Miriam Elson. (Professional Bks.). 1986. text ed. 24.95 (ISBN 0-393-70015-1). Norton.

Self Psychotherapy, Vol. 1. Albert V. Steinkirchner. LC 75-760. 159p. 1974. 12.00 (ISBN 0-915352-00-1); pap. 7.00 (ISBN 0-915352-01-X). Aquin Pub.

Self Publish to Sucess: Make Money Publishing. Shami Maxwell & Kathryn Maxwell. (Illus.). 128p. (Orig.). 1988. pap. 9.95 (ISBN 0-940649-03-9). Parnell Pub.

Self-Publish Your Own Picture Book. Howard Gregory. 1989. price not set (ISBN 0-9607086-6-9); pap. price not set (ISBN 0-9607086-5-0). H Gregory.

Self-Publisher's Opportunity Kit. 176p. (Orig.). 1985. pap. 30.00 (ISBN 0-933301-10-3). Lion Pub.

Self-Publishing. Date not set. price not set (ISBN 0-937571-03-2). Trudco Pub.

Self-Publishing Handbook. David M. Brownstone & Irene M. Franck. 224p. 1985. pap. 7.95 (ISBN 0-452-25685-2, Plume). NAL.

Self-Publishing: How to Cash in on Your Writing Ability Now. Raymond C. Van Dusen. (Royal Court Reports Ser.: No. 3). (Illus.). 67p. (Orig.). 1982. pap. 3.95 (ISBN 0-941354-02-4). Royal Court.

Self-Publishing Manual: How to Write, Print & Sell Your Own Book. 4th rev. ed. Dan Poynter. LC 84-7632. (Illus.). 352p. 1986. pap. 14.95 (ISBN 0-915516-37-3). Para Pub.

Self-Purification. Jaina Sutra. (Illus.). 8.75 (ISBN 0-88695-020-1). Concord Grove.

Self-Realignment. Robert E. Birdsong. (Aquarian Academy Monograph, Series E: Lecture No. 1). 1974. pap. 1.25 (ISBN 0-917108-01-9). Sirius Bks.

Self-Realization. Satguru S. Keshavadas. (Illus.). 131p. (Orig.). 1976. pap. 3.50. Vishwa.

Self-Realization & Self-Defeat. Samuel J. Warner. LC 66-24911. 1966. pap. 12.50 (ISBN 0-394-62434-3, E453, Ever). Grove.

Self-Realization of Noble Wisdom. Lankavatara-Sutra. Ed. by Dwight Goddard. Tr. by D. T. Suzuki. LC 78-72461. Repr. of 1932 ed. 23.00 (ISBN 0-404-17333-0). AMS Pr.

Self-Realization Through Love. Taimni. 4.75 (ISBN 0-8356-7522-X). Theos Pub Hse.

Self-Reconstruction of Maryland: 1864-1867. William S. Myers. LC 78-63931. (Johns Hopkins University. Studies in the Social Sciences. Twenty-Eighth Ser. 1910: 1-2). Repr. of 1909 ed. 16.00 (ISBN 0-404-61180-X). AMS Pr.

Self-Reference & Modal Logic. C. Smorynski. (Universitext Ser.). xii, 333p. 1985. pap. 33.00 (ISBN 0-387-96209-3). Springer-Verlag.

Self-Reflection in the Arts & Sciences. A Blum & P. McHugh. 159p. 1984. text ed. 15.00x (ISBN 0-391-02877-4). Humanities.

Self Reflections. Intro. by Shirley I. Fisher. Tr. by Gabriela Sanchez-Diaz from Span. (Illus.). 80p. (Orig., Eng.). 1987. pap. 10.00 (ISBN 0-942607-01-5). Hispanic Anglo Pubns.

Self-Regulation: Is It Working, Vol. 3. Peter F. Rousmaniere. (Municipal Securities Regulation Ser.). 1977. pap. text ed. 40.00 (ISBN 0-916450-10-4). Nat Civic League.

Self-Regulation of the Brain & Behavior. Ed. by T. Elbert et al. (Illus.). 385p. 1984. 49.00 (ISBN 0-387-12854-9). Springer Verlag.

Self-Related Cognitions in Anxiety & Motivation. Ed. by Ralf Schwarzer. 360p. 1985. text ed. 39.95 (ISBN 0-89859-513-4). L Erlbaum Assocs.

Self Relaxation: Comfort in Times of Tension. Harley D. Christiansen. (Illus.). 96p. (Orig.). 1981. pap. 11.95 (ISBN 0-915456-02-8). P Juul Pr.

Self-Reliance. Ralph Waldo Emerson. 1967. 5.95 (ISBN 0-88088-149-6). Peter Pauper.

Self Reliance. 2nd ed. Ralph Waldo Emerson. Ed. by Gene Dekovic. LC 75-12544. (Illus.). 96p. 1983. 12.00 (ISBN 0-937088-07-2); pap. 8.00 o.s. (ISBN 0-937088-08-0). Illum Pr.

Self Reliance & Foreign Policy in Tanzania. Okwudiba Nnoli. LC 73-91415. (Studies in East African Society & History). 1977. text ed. 21.50x (ISBN 0-88357-014-9); pap. text ed. 8.95 (ISBN 0-88357-039-4). NOK Pubs.

Self-Reliance & National Resilience. K. Subrahamanayam. LC 75-907181. 1975. 11.50x (ISBN 0-88386-676-5). South Asia Bks.

Self-Reliance & Social Security, 1870-1917. Hace S. Tishler. LC 79-139361. (National University Publications). 1971. 21.95x (ISBN 0-8046-9012-X, Pub. by Kennikat). Assoc Faculty Pr.

Self Reliance in Kenya: The Case of Harambee. Philip M. Mbithi & Rasmus Rasmusson. (Scandinavian Institute of African Studies, Uppsala). (Illus.). 1978. pap. 14.50 (ISBN 0-8419-9729-2). Holmes & Meier.

Self-Reliance vs. Power Politics: American & Indian Experiences in Building Nation - States. J. Ann Tickner. LC 86-12989. (Political Economy of International Change Ser.). 352p. 1986. 35.00 (ISBN 0-231-06272-9). Columbia U Pr.

Self-Reliant Academic. W. Todd Furniss. 80p. 1984. 7.50 (ISBN 0-02-910940-X). ACE.

Self-Reliant Cities: Energy & the Transformation of Urban America. David Morris. LC 81-18301. (Illus.). 256p. 1982. 19.95 (ISBN 0-87156-296-0); pap. 8.95 (ISBN 0-87156-309-6). Sierra.

Self Reliant Development in Europe. E. Brugger & B. Stuckey. 300p. 1986. text ed. 38.00 (ISBN 0-566-05095-1). Gower Pub Co.

Self-Reliant Potter Refractories & Kilns. H. Norsker. (GATE Ser.). (Illus.). 134p. 1987. pap. 14.50 (ISBN 3-528-02031-8, Pub. by Vieweg & Sohn). IPS.

Self-Renewal: The Individual & the Innovative Society. John W. Gardner. 168p. 1983. pap. 6.95 (ISBN 0-393-30112-5). Norton.

Self-Reported Health Characteristics, Behavior, & Attitudes of Youths: U. S., 1966-70. James Scanlon. LC 75-12433. (Data from the Health Examination Survey Ser. 11: No. 147). 80p. 1974. pap. text ed. 1.50 (ISBN 0-8406-0026-7). Natl Ctr Health Stats.

Self Revealing Light. Lillian De Waters. (I Am That I Am Ser). pap. 1.25 (ISBN 0-686-05725-2). L De Waters.

Self Rule-Shared Rule: Federal Solutions to the Middle East Conflict. A Colloquium. Ed. by Daniel J. Elazar. 276p. 1985. pap. text ed. 13.25 (ISBN 0-8191-4355-3, Pub. by Jerusalem Ctr Public). U Pr of Amer.

Self-Schedule System for Instructional Learning Management in Adaptive School Learning Environments. Ed. by Margaret C. Wang. 117p. 2.00 (ISBN 0-318-14736-X, ED 127 299). Learn Res Dev.

Self Science: The Subject Is Me. Karen Stone & Hal Dillehunte. LC 78-4545. 1978. 14.95 (ISBN 0-673-16431-4); pap. 12.95 (ISBN 0-673-16430-6). Scott F.

Self-Scoring I.Q. Test. Alfred W. Munzert. Ed. by Karen K. Elskamp. 1977. pap. 1.95 (ISBN 0-917292-00-6). H-U Public.

Self-Selected Essays. facs. ed. J. B. Priestley. (Essay Index Reprint Ser). 1932. 18.00 (ISBN 0-8369-0801-5). Ayer Co Pubs.

Self-Service Storage: The Handbook for Investors & Managers. rev. ed. Richard E. Cornwell & Buzz Victor. Ed. by Betty T. Moore. LC 81-86050. (Institute of Real Estate Management Monographs: Series on Specific Property Types). (Illus.). 208p. 1983. pap. 25.95 (ISBN 0-912104-54-6, 853). Inst Real Estate.

Self, Sex, & Gender in Cross-Cultural Fieldwork. Ed. by Tony L. Whitehead & Mary E. Conaway. LC 85-8597. (Illus.). 320p. 1986. 39.95 (ISBN 0-252-01248-8); pap. 14.95 (ISBN 0-252-01324-7). U of Ill Pr.

Self, Sign, & Symbol. Ed. by Mark Nueman & Michael Payne. LC 86-47606. (Bucknell Review Ser.: Vol. 30, No. 2). 184p. 1987. 16.50x (ISBN 0-8387-5108-3). Bucknell U Pr.

Self, Society, & Womankind: The Dialectic of Liberation. Kathy E. Ferguson. LC 79-6831. (Contributions in Women's Studies: No. 17). xii, 200p. 1980. lib. bdg. 35.00 (ISBN 0-313-22245-2, FSS/). Greenwood.

Self, Society, Existence: Human Nature & Dialogue in the Thought of George Herbert Mead & Martin Buber. Paul Pfuetze. 400p. 1973. Repr. of 1961 ed. lib. bdg. 35.00x (ISBN 0-8371-6708-6, PFSS). Greenwood.

Self-Splitting Atom: A History of the Rutherford-Soddy Collaboration. T. J. Trenn. 176p. 1977. 42.00x (ISBN 0-85066-109-9). Taylor & Francis.

Self Starvation. Mara S. Palazzoli. LC 78-60671. 320p. 1985. 30.00x (ISBN 0-87668-757-5). Aronson.

Self Storage & Mini Storage: Data Notes. Data Notes Publishing Staff. 30p. 1983. pap. text ed. 4.75 (ISBN 0-911569-52-9, Pub. by Data Notes). Prosperity & Profits.

Self Storage Units or Warehouses: An International Directory. Alpha Pyramis Research Division Staff. 300p. 1983. text ed. 17.95 (ISBN 0-913597-12-0, Pub. by Alpha Pyramis). Prosperity & Profits.

Self Study Bible Course. Derek Prince. 1969. pap. 5.95 (ISBN 0-934920-08-7, B-90). Derek Prince.

Self Study Books in Electrical & Semiconductor Engineering: P3 The Magnetic Field. 1978. pap. 4.95 (ISBN 0-471-25970-5). Wiley.

Self-Study Guide for Catholic High Schools. 76p. 1981. 9.00 (ISBN 0-318-00792-4). Natl Cath Educ.

Self-Study Guide for Catholic High Schools. 98p. 7.50 (ISBN 0-318-17481-2). Mid St Coll & Schl.

Self-Study Guide for Catholic High Schools. 76p. 1981. 9.00 (ISBN 0-318-20605-6). Natl Cath Educ.

Self-Study Guide for Nutrition & Diet Therapy. 4th ed. Williams. 1986. pap. 11.95 (ISBN 0-8016-5570-6). Mosby.

Self Study Guide to DMSMH. B. Robert Ross. 100p. 1986. pap. cancelled (ISBN 0-87916-011-X). Upstat.

Self-Study Guide to Galatians & Romans. rev. ed. J. D. Thomas. (Way of Life Ser: No. 122). Orig. Title: Self-Study Guide to Romans. (Orig.). 1971. pap. text ed. 3.95 (ISBN 0-89112-122-6). Abilene Christ U.

Self-Study Guide to Romans see Self-Study Guide to Galatians & Romans.

Self-Study Guide to the Corinthian Letters. J. D. Thomas. (Way of Life Ser: No. 123). (Orig.). 1972. pap. text ed. 3.95 (ISBN 0-89112-123-4). Abilene Christ U.

Self-Study Processes: A Guide for Postsecondary Institutions. 2nd ed. H. R. Kells. 156p. 1983. 15.95 (ISBN 0-02-916520-2). ACE.

Self-Study Processes: A Guide for Postsecondary Institutions. 2nd ed. H. R. Kells. (Higher Education Ser.). 1983. 16.00 (ISBN 0-02-918060-0). Macmillan.

Self-Study Processes: A Guide for Postsecondary Institutions. 2nd ed. 156p. 1983. 15.95 (ISBN 0-318-17484-7). Mid St Coll & Schl.

Self Sufficiency Continuing Education Alternatives. Center for Self-Sufficiency, Research Division Staff. 200p. 1984. pap. text ed. 5.95 (ISBN 0-910811-73-3, Pub. by Center Self Suff). Prosperity & Profits.

Self-Sufficiency Encyclopaedia. Center for Self-Sufficiency, Research Division Staff. LC 83-90715. 75p. 1983. pap. text ed. 6.95 (ISBN 0-910811-00-8, Pub. by Center Self Suff). Prosperity & Profits.

Self-Sufficient Gardener: A Complete Guide to Growing & Preserving All Your Own Food. John Seymour. LC 78-19223. 1979. pap. 14.95 (ISBN 0-385-14671-X, Dolp). Doubleday.

Self-Sufficient Homestead: Site Selection. Randy Kidd. (Illus.). 69p. (Orig.). 1981. pap. 10.50 spiral bdg. (ISBN 0-936352-05-1). U of KS Cont Ed.

Self-Sufficient House. Frank Coffee. LC 80-13434. (Illus.). 1981. 17.95 (ISBN 0-03-053611-1); pap. 9.95 (ISBN 0-03-059171-6). H Holt & Co.

Self-Sufficient Sailor. Larry Pardey & Lin Pardey. (Illus.). 1982. 19.95 (ISBN 0-393-03269-8). Norton.

Self-Sufficient Suburban Gardener: A Step-by-Step Planning & Management Guide to Backyard Food Production. Jeff Ball. Ed. by Anne Halpin. (Illus.). 256p. 1983. 14.95 (ISBN 0-87857-457-3, 01-083-0). Rodale Pr Inc.

Self-Suggestion & Its Influence on the Human Organism. A. S. Romen. Ed. by A. S. Lewis & V. Forsky. LC 80-28703. Orig. Title: Samovnushenie I Ego Vliianie Na Organizm Cheloveka. (Illus.). 456p. 1981. 40.00 (ISBN 0-87332-195-2). M E Sharpe.

Self-Suggestion & the New Huna Theory of Mesmerism & Hypnosis. Max F. Long. 1958. pap. 4.95 (ISBN 0-87516-048-4). DeVorss.

Self-Supporting City. Gilbert Tucker. 100p. 1958. pap. 1.00 (ISBN 0-911312-56-0). Schalkenbach.

Self-Supporting Scenery for Children's Theatre & Grown-Ups' Too. 4th ed. James H. Miller. Ed. by Arthur L. Zapel. LC 81-84402. (Illus.). 120p. 1982. pap. text ed. 8.95 (ISBN 0-916260-15-1). Meriwether Pub.

Self, Symbols & Society: An Introduction to Mass Communication. Stanley J. Baran et al. (Illus.). 336p. 1984. pap. text ed. write for info (ISBN 0-394-35002-2, RanC). Random.

Self, Symptoms & Psychotherapy. Ed. by Neil Cheshire & Helmut Thomae. LC 86-32565. (Methods in Psychotherapy Ser.). 300p. 1987. 59.95 (ISBN 0-471-90548-8). Wiley.

Self Talk. David Stoop. 160p. 1981. pap. 6.95 (ISBN 0-8007-5074-8, Power Bks). Revell.

Self-Talk, Prayer & Imagery in Counseling (RCC) Norman Wright. 192p. 1986. 12.95 (ISBN 0-8499-0585-0). Word Bks.

Self-Talk Solution. Shad Helmstetter. 320p. 1987. 16.95 (ISBN 0-688-07193-7). Morrow.

Self-Talk Solution. Shad Helmstetter. 1988. pap. 4.50. PB.

Self Taught-Self Help. Rachel Rowlson & Dusty Staub. Ed. by Tim Williams. 75p. (Orig.). 1984. pap. 7.95 (ISBN 0-9614201-0-3). Dragonlord Pr.

Self-Taught Sparrow. Angus L. Jamieson. 29p. 1986. 14.00X (ISBN 0-7223-1925-8, Pub. by A H Stockwell England). State Mutual Bk.

Self-Teaching Process in Higher Education. P. J. Hills. LC 75-44716. 144p. (Orig.). 1976. 13.00 (ISBN 0-470-15024-6, Pub. by John Wiley). Krieger.

Self-Teaching Process in Higher Education. P. J. Hills. 160p. 1976. 21.25 (ISBN 0-85664-288-6, Pub. by Croom Helm Ltd). Routledge Chapman & Hall.

Self-Teaching Study Guide & Workbook for the Sensation of Being Somebody. 3rd. ed. Maurice E. Wagner. 148p. 1985. saddle stitch 10.00 (ISBN 0-940445-00-X). Mid Coast Cnslng.

Self-Teaching Study Guide & Workbook for "The Sensation of Being Somebody". 4th ed. Maurice E. Wagner. 148p. 1986. pap. 10.95 oversized (ISBN 0-940445-02-6). Mid Coast Cnslng.

Self-Testing & Monitoring Products Markets. 200p. 1985. 1800.00 (ISBN 0-86621-415-1, A1490). Frost & Sullivan.

Self, Text, & Romantic Irony: The Example of Byron. Frederick Garber. 358p. 1988. text ed. 37.00 (ISBN 0-691-06730-9). Princeton U Pr.

Self, the Individual, & the Community: Liberalism in the Political Thought F. A. Hayek & Sidney & Beatrice Webb. Brian L. Crowley. 304p. 1987. 59.00 (ISBN 0-19-827497-1). Oxford U Pr.

Self Therapy. Muriel Schiffman. LC 73-75227. 176p. (Orig.). 1980. pap. 15.95 (ISBN 0-914640-01-1, Pub. by Self Therapy Pr). Wingbow Pr.

Self Therapy for Sex Problems. Daniel Steele. LC 86-62950. 211p. (Orig.). 1987. pap. 20.00 (ISBN 0-9618277-0-X). Human Res Pub.

Self-Therapy for the Stutterer. Malcolm Fraser. 1985. pap. 3.00 (ISBN 0-87980-415-7). Wilshire.

Self Therapy for the Stutterer, No. 12. 6th ed. Malcolm Fraser. LC 86-63599. 192p. 1987. write for info. (ISBN 0-933388-26-8); pap. 2.50. Speech Found Am.

Self to the Self. Dora Wilson. 1947. pap. 2.50x (ISBN 0-87574-035-9, 035). Pendle Hill.

Self-Tormenter see Lady of Andros.

Self-Transcendence. Thomas Hora. 35p. 1987. pap. 4.00 (ISBN 0-913105-07-4). PAGL Pr.

Self Transcendence Workbook. T. D. Lingo. 55p. (Orig.). 1982. pap. 11.00 (ISBN 0-686-37712-5). Dormant Brain Res.

Self-Transformation Through Music. Joanne Crandall. (Illus.). 165p. (Orig.). 1986. pap. 6.95 (ISBN 0-8356-0608-2). Theos Pub Hse.

Self Treatment for AIDS: Oxygen Therapy. Betsy Russell-Manning. 1988. pap. 12.95 perfect bdg. (ISBN 0-930165-12-8). Greensward Pr.

Self-tuning & Adaptive Control: Theory & Applications. rev. ed. C. J. Harris & S. A. Billings. (Control Ser.). 352p. 1985. pap. 55.00 (ISBN 0-86341-036-7, CER15). Inst Elect Eng.

Self-Understanding: An Introduction to Transactional Analysis. David Sheinkin. 86p. 1973. pap. text ed. 5.00x (ISBN 0-89039-061-4); instr's. guide 2.00 (ISBN 0-89039-062-2). Ann Arbor FL.

Self-Understanding in Childhood & Adolescence. William Damon & Daniel Hart. (Cambridge Studies in Social & Emotional Development). (Illus.). 280p. Date not set. price not set (ISBN 0-521-30791-0). Cambridge U Pr.

Self Understanding: The Foundation of New Civilization. Ekerete Ekpo. LC 81-83574. 144p. (Orig.). 1981. pap. 6.50x (ISBN 0-935834-05-2). Rainbow Books.

Self-Unfoldment. Manly P. Hall. 10.95 (ISBN 0-89314-524-6). Philos Res.

Self-Validating Numerics For Function Space Problems: Computation With Guarantees For Differential & Integral Equations. Monograph ed. Edgar W. Kaucher & Willard L. Miranker. (Notes & Reports in Computer Science & Applied Mathematics Ser.). 1984. 39.50 (ISBN 0-12-402020-8). Acad Pr.

Self-Views in Historical Perspective in Egypt & Israel. Ed. by Shimon Shamir. (Books from the American University of Beirut Press). 132p. (Orig.). 1988. pap. text ed. 7.95 (ISBN 0-8156-7053-2). Syracuse U Pr.

Self-Winding Circle: A Study of Hegel's System. Mitchell Aboulafia. LC 82-210652. 124p. 1982. 14.75 (ISBN 0-87527-307-6). Green.

Selling the Goods see Markets & Bagmen: Studies in the History of Marketing & British Industrial Performance, 1830-1931.

Selling-the How & Why: A Comprehensive Introduction to Salesmanship. James S. Norris. (Illus.). 304p. 1982. 19.95 (ISBN 0-13-805986-1). P-H.

Selling the People's Cadillac: The Edsel & Corporate Responsibility. Jan G. Deutsch. LC 75-37292. 300p. 1976. 40.00x (ISBN 0-300-01950-5). Yale U Pr.

Selling: The Personal Force in Marketing. Donald W. Jackson et al. LC 87-29438. 506p. 1988. write for info. (ISBN 0-471-86400-5). Wiley.

Selling the Rope to Hang Capitalism? The Debate on West-East Trade & Technology Transfer. Ed. by C. M. Perry & R. L. Pfaltzgraff, Jr. 216p. 1987. 30.00 (ISBN 0-08-034959-5, PDP). Pergamon.

Selling the Smokeless Society: Fifty-six Evaluated Mass Media Programs & Campaigns Worldwide. Brian R. Flay. LC 87-30641. 150p. 1987. 10.00 (ISBN 0-87553-153-9). Am Pub Health.

Selling the Top Brass. Robert K. Weill. 1977. 59.50 (ISBN 0-13-806000-2). Exec Reports.

Selling the Volume Retailer: A Practical Plan for Success. Edwin E. Bobrow. LC 75-1168. 126p. 1975. 15.95 (ISBN 0-86730-511-8). Lebhar Friedman.

Selling the Wild West: Popular Western Fiction, 1860-1960. Christine Bold. 1987. 27.50 (ISBN 0-253-35151-0). Ind U Pr.

Selling Through Independent Reps. Harold J. Novick. 300p. 1988. 49.95 (ISBN 0-8144-5931-5). AMACOM.

Selling Through Negotiation: The Handbook of Sales Negotiation. Homer B. Smith. LC 87-10998. 192p. (Orig.). 1987. 19.95 (ISBN 0-9618228-0-5); pap. 12.95 (ISBN 0-9618228-1-3). Outlook Assocs.

Selling Through Negotiation: The Handbook of Sales Negotiation. Homer B. Smith. 192p. 1988. 12.95 (ISBN 0-8144-7707-0). AMACOM.

Selling Through Photography: How the Pros Use Photography to Sell Ideas. Bob Shafer. LC 83-2738. 250p. cancelled (ISBN 0-87491-704-2). Acropolis.

Selling to a Group: Presentation Strategies. Paul LeRoux. LC 84-47586. (Illus.). 176p. 1984. 14.37 (ISBN 0-06-015345-8, B&N Bks); pap. 8.95 (ISBN 0-06-463598-8, EH 598, B&N Bks). Har-Row.

Selling to Catalog Houses. 1987. lib. bdg. 69.95 (ISBN 0-8490-3888-X). Gordon Pr.

Selling to Consumers: Complete Training Book. Zack Right. 350p. (Orig.). 1984. pap. 18.00 (ISBN 0-9604554-1-8). Talmud Pr.

Selling to NASA. (Illus.). 44p. (Orig.). 1986. pap. 3.25 (ISBN 0-318-22432-1, S/N 033-000-00995-0). USGPO.

Selling to the Federal Government Through Schedule Contracts. Gloria Gamble. Ed. by Global Engineering Documents Staff. 303p. 1987. 59.95 (ISBN 0-912702-34-6). Global Eng.

Selling to the Government: A Complete Step-by-Step Guide to Doing Business with U. S. Government Departments & Agencies. F. Peter Wigginton. 450p. 1988. looseleaf 95.00 (ISBN 1-55738-029-5). Probus Pub Co.

Selling to the Military. 3rd ed. 161p. 1987. pap. 8.00 (ISBN 0-318-22947-1, S/N 008-000-00479-0). USGPO.

Selling Today: A Personal Approach - An Extension of the Marketing Concept. 3rd ed. Gerald L. Manning & Barry L. Reece. 552p. 1987. 38.00 (ISBN 0-205-11477-6, H1477-2); instr's. manual avail. (ISBN 0-205-11478-4, H1478-0). Allyn.

Selling Training Programs Face-to-Face. Don M. Schrello. (Illus.). 50p. (Orig.). 1988. pap. 17.95 (ISBN 0-935823-07-7). Schrello Market.

Selling Your City, No. M-1. Peter F. Rousmaniere. (Practitioner Manuals Ser.). 1978. pap. text ed. 8.00x (ISBN 0-916450-22-8). Nat Civic League.

Selling Your Graphic Design & Illustration. Tad Crawford & Arie Kopelman. 272p. 1981. 15.95 (ISBN 0-312-71252-9). St Martin.

Selling Your Home Sweet Home. Sloan Bashinsky. 160p. 1985. 10.95 (Dist. by Prentice Hall). Menasha Ridge.

Selling Your Home Sweet Home. Sloan Bashinsky. 1985. 12.95 (ISBN 0-671-60213-6). S&S.

Selling Your House Without a Broker. Dale Chaney & Mary B. Libbey. 1986. pap. 4.95 (ISBN 0-8092-4833-6). Contemp Bks.

Selling Your Photography. Arie Kopelman & Tad Crawford. (Illus.). 288p. 1980. 15.95 (ISBN 0-312-71255-3). St Martin.

Selling Your Screenplay: A Successful Hollywood Screenwriter Tells You How to Break into the Business... & Stay There. Cynthia Whitcomb. 224p. 1988. 15.95 (ISBN 0-517-57008-4). Crown.

Selling Your Service: How to Sell It When You Can't See It, Taste It or Touch It. Karen Johnston & Jean Withers. 152p. 1988. pap. 12.95 (ISBN 0-88908-685-0, 9567). ISC Pr.

Selling Your Software. Robert E. Davis, Jr. (General Trade Books). 224p. 1985. pap. 16.95 (ISBN 0-471-80737-0, Pub. by Wiley Pr.). Wiley.

Selling Yourself. Michael C. Downs. LC 70-502897. (Guide to Improved-Career Selection Interviewing-Company Selection Ser.). 1985. 4.95 (ISBN 0-9618713-0-X). Step Up Pubns.

Selling Yourself on You: Discovering God's Plan for Your Life. Mary Ann L. Diorio. 224p. (Orig.). 1988. pap. 9.95 (ISBN 0-930037-02-2). Daystar Comm.

Selling Yourself on You: Discovering God's Will for Your Life. Mary Ann L. Diorio. LC 88-70291. 224p. (Orig.). 1988. 19.95 (ISBN 0-930037-03-0). Daystar Comm.

Selling Yourself: The Way to a Better Job. William R. Jeffers. (Illus.). 1979. (Spec); pap. 6.95 (ISBN 0-13-806075-4). P-H.

Selling's Magic Words. Lester N. Pope. (Illus.). 202p. 1986. 14.95 (ISBN 0-937105-34-1); pap. 9.95 (ISBN 0-937105-33-3). Lokman Pub Co.

Sell's British Exporters 1987. 1987. pap. 75.00 (ISBN 0-85499-553-6, Pub. by Sell's Pubns Ltd (UK)). Taylor & Francis.

Sell's Directory. 1000p. 1985. 250.00 (ISBN 0-85499-519-6, Pub by Sells Pubns England). State Mutual Bk.

Sell's Directory of Products & Services, 1986. 101st ed. 1986. 77.00 (ISBN 0-85499-512-9). Intl Pubns Serv.

Selma Erving Collection: Modern Illustrated Books. Intro. by Ruth Mortimer. 60p. 1977. pap. 7.00 (ISBN 0-87391-037-0). Smith Coll Mus Art.

Selma Erving Collection: Nineteenth & Twentieth Century Prints. Ed. by N. Sojka & C. Swenson. LC 85-80045. 140p. 1985. pap. 12.00 (ISBN 0-87391-036-2). Smith Coll Mus Art.

Selma: Her Institutions & Her Men. John Hardy. LC 78-7915. 1978. Repr. of 1879 ed. 16.50 (ISBN 0-87152-275-6). Reprint.

Selma Kurz: The Singer & Her Time. Desi Halban. (Illus.). 1983. 30.00 (ISBN 3-7630-9028-2). Kraus Repr.

Selma Lagerloef. Hanna A. Larsen. LC 36-27415. 1975. Repr. of 1936 ed. 21.00 (ISBN 0-527-54880-4). Kraus Repr.

Selma Lagerlof. Walter A. Berendsohn. 136p. 1979. Repr. of 1931 ed. lib. bdg. 25.00 (ISBN 0-89984-050-7). Century Bookbindery.

Selma Lagerlof, Her Life & Work. Walter A. Berendsohn. LC 67-27576. (Illus.). 1931. Repr. 15.00x (ISBN 0-8046-0027-9, Pub. by Kennikat). Assoc Faculty Pr.

Selma, Lord, Selma: Girlhood Memories of the Civil-Rights Days. Sheyann Webb & Rachel W. Nelson. LC 79-19327. (Illus.). 163p. 1980. 9.95 (ISBN 0-8173-0031-7). U of Ala Pr.

Selma, Nineteen Sixty-Five: The March That Changed the South. Charles Fager. LC 85-35221. (Illus.). 271p. 1985. pap. 10.95 (ISBN 0-8070-0405-7, BP 695). Beacon Pr.

Selma: The Gospel at Work. F. Wilbur Helmbold. 1983. 12.50; pap. 8.50. Banner Pr AL.

Selma Zaetz's Favorite Ethnic Recipes. Selma Zaetz. LC 82-61686. (Illus.). 272p. (Orig.). 1983. pap. 9.95 (ISBN 0-933050-15-1). New Eng Pr Vt.

Selma's Peacemaker: Ralph Smeltzer & Civil Rights Mediation. Stephen Longenecker. 272p. 1987. 34.95 (ISBN 0-87722-489-7). Temple U Pr.

Selo Stepanchikovo see Village of Stepanchikovo & Its Inhabitants.

Selvages & Biases: The Fabric of History in American Culture. Michael Kammen. LC 87-5285. (Illus.). 352p. 1987. 24.95x (ISBN 0-8014-1924-7). Cornell U Pr.

Selves in Relation: An Introduction to Psychotherapy & Groups. Keith Oatley. Ed. by Peter Herriot. LC 83-19525. (New Essential Psychology Ser.). 175p. 1984. pap. 6.50x (ISBN 0-416-33630-2, NO. 4057). Routledge Chapman & Hall.

Selves Inside You. Stewart B. Shapiro & James Elliot. pap. 4.95 (ISBN 0-685-85016-1). Explorations Inst.

Selwym Image, Previously Unpublished Poems. Selwyn Image. 1987. pap. 5.00 (ISBN 0-89979-050-X). British Am Bks.

Selye's Guide to Stress Research, Vol. 1. Selye. (Van Nostrand Reinhold Stress Research & Management Ser.). 450p. 1980. 33.95 (ISBN 0-442-27483-1). Van Nos Reinhold.

Selye's Guide to Stress Research, Vol. 2. Ed. by Hans Selye. 432p. 1983. 43.95 (ISBN 0-442-26264-7). Van Nos Reinhold.

Selye's Guide to Stress Research, Vol. 3. H. Selye. 1983. 39.95 (ISBN 0-442-28139-0). Van Nos Reinhold.

Selznick. Bob Thomas. LC 82-49237. (Cinemas Classics Ser.). 381p. 1985. lib. bdg. 50.00 (ISBN 0-8240-5780-5). Garland Pub.

SEM: A User's Manual for Materials Science. Barbara L. Gabriel. 1985. 67.00 (ISBN 0-87170-202-9). ASM.

Sema-Kanda: Threshold Memories. Coulson Turnbul. 254p. Date not set. pap. 15.00 (ISBN 0-89540-131-2, SB-131). Sun Pub.

Semaine De Bonte: A Surrealistic Novel in Collage. 2nd ed. Max Ernst. LC 75-17362. (Illus.). 224p. 1976. pap. 7.95 (ISBN 0-486-23252-2). Dover.

Semaine De Mai. Camille Pelletan. LC 75-173941. (Fr.). Repr. of 1880 ed. 41.00 (ISBN 0-404-07163-5). AMS Pr.

Semana de la Pasion, Muerte y Resurreccion: Muerte y Resurreccion. Ed. by Laura Disselkoen. 75p. 1984. pap. 2.25 (ISBN 0-311-08501-6). Casa Bautista.

Semantic Analysis of the Old Russian Finite Preterite System. C. H. Van Schooneveld. 1959. text ed. 20.80x (ISBN 90-2790-164-3). Mouton.

Semantic & Conceptual Development: An Ontological Perspective. Frank C. Keil. LC 79-10491. 1979. 18.95x (ISBN 0-674-80100-8). Harvard U Pr.

Semantic & Pragmatic Language Disorders: Assessment & Remediation. Ellyn Lucas. LC 80-24120. 264p. 1981. text ed. 34.00 (ISBN 0-89443-327-X). Aspen Pub.

Semantic Anthropology. Ed. by David Parkin. 1983. 34.00 (ISBN 0-12-545180-6). Acad Pr.

Semantic Anthropology, Vol. 22. Ed. by David Parkin. (Serial Publication). 1984. pap. 22.00 (ISBN 0-12-545182-2). Acad Pr.

Semantic Behavior & Decision Making. William J. Williams. LC 78-23923. pap. 41.30 (ISBN 0-317-10025-4, 2022587). Bks Demand UMI.

Semantic Confusion: A Report from Atlas Files. Harold B. Allen. (Publications of the American Dialect Society: No. 33). 24p. 1960. pap. 2.20 (ISBN 0-8173-0633-1). U of Ala Pr.

Semantic Constraints on Relevance. Diane Blakemore. 192p. Date not set. text ed. 37.50 (ISBN 0-631-15644-5). Basil Blackwell.

Semantic Development of Words for "Eating" & "Drinking" in Germanic. Henry O. Schwabe. LC 70-173195. (Chicago. University. Linguistic Studies in Germanic: No. 1). Repr. of 1915 ed. 18.00 (ISBN 0-404-50281-4). AMS Pr.

Semantic Development of Words for Walk, Run in the Germanic Languages, No. 4. Roscoe M. Ihrig. LC 71-170058. (Chicago. University. Linguistic Studies in Germanic). Repr. of 1916 ed. 23.00 (ISBN 0-404-50284-9). AMS Pr.

Semantic Divergence in Anglo-French Cognates: A Synchronic Study in Contrastive Lexicography. Jean-Luc Garneau. (Edward Sapir Monograph Series in Language, Culture, & Cognition: No. 14). x, 128p. (Orig.). 1985. pap. 10.00x (ISBN 0-933104-20-0). Jupiter Pr.

Semantic Information Processing. Ed. by Marvin L. Minsky. LC 68-18239. 440p. 1969. 37.50x (ISBN 0-262-13044-0). MIT Pr.

Semantic Interpretation & the Resolution of Ambiguity. Graeme Hirst. (Studies in Natural Language Processing). (Illus.). 275p. 1987. 39.50 (ISBN 0-521-32203-0). Cambridge U Pr.

Semantic Interpretation in Generative Grammar. Ray S. Jackendoff. (Studies in Linguistics). 384p. 1972. pap. 14.95x (ISBN 0-262-60007-2). MIT Pr.

Semantic Mapping: Classroom Applications. Joan E. Heimlich & Susan D. Pittelman. 52p. 1986. pap. 5.00 (ISBN 0-87207-230-4). Intl Reading.

Semantic Organizer Approach to Writing & Reading Instruction. Robert S. Pehrsson & H. Allan Robinson. 190p. 1985. 36.00 (ISBN 0-89443-866-2). Aspen Pub.

Semantic Problems of Translated Subject Headings. Gertrude Soonja Lee Koh. 1979. 20.00 (ISBN 0-686-25169-5). Chinese Cult Serv.

Semantic Relationships of Gahuku Verbs. Ellis Deibler. (SIL Linguistic & Related Fields Ser.: No. 48). 159p. 1976. pap. 8.00x (ISBN 0-88312-058-5); microfiche (2) 4.00 (ISBN 0-88312-458-0). Summer Inst Ling.

Semantic Structure Analysis of Colossians. John Callow. Ed. by Michael F. Kopesec. (Semantic Structure Analysis Ser.). (Illus.). iv, 246p. 1983. pap. 7.80x (ISBN 0-88312-675-3); pap. 6.00 microfiche (3) (ISBN 0-88312-570-6). Summer Inst Ling.

Semantic Structure Analysis of Second Peter. Edna Johnson. Intro. by John Callow. LC 88-60915. (Illus.). 180p. (Orig.). 1988. pap. text ed. write for info. (ISBN 0-88312-922-1). Summer Inst Ling.

Semantic Structure Analysis of Second Thessalonians. John Callow. Ed. by Michael F. Kopesec. (Semantic Structure Analysis Ser.). (Illus.). v, 113p. (Orig.). 1982. pap. 4.30x (ISBN 0-88312-923-X); microfiche (2) 4.00 (ISBN 0-88312-571-4). Summer Inst Ling.

Semantic Structure Analysis of Titus. John Banker. Ed. by John Callow. (Semantic Structure Analysis Ser.). (Illus.). 155p. (Orig.). 1987. pap. 7.80x (ISBN 0-88312-916-7); microfiche (3) 6.00 (ISBN 0-88312-572-2). Summer Inst Ling.

Semantic Structure & Word Formation: Verb-Particle Constructions in Contemporary English. Leonard Lipka. 1973. bds. 47.25x (ISBN 3-7705-0947-1). Adlers Foreign Bks.

Semantic Structures & Relations in Dutch: An Introduction to Case Grammar. Stephen T. Moskey. 165p. 1979. pap. text ed. 7.95 (ISBN 0-87840-176-8). Georgetown U Pr.

Semantic Syntax. Ed. by Pieter A. Seuren. (Oxford Readings in Philosophy Ser.). (Illus.). 1974. pap. text ed. 8.95x (ISBN 0-19-875028-5). Oxford U Pr.

Semantic Theories & Language Teaching. Ed. by V. Prakashan. 1986. 17.50x (ISBN 81-7023-080-2, Pub. by Allied India). South Asia Bks.

Semantic Theory of Evolution. Marcello Barbieri. (Models of Scientific Thought Ser.: Vol. 2). 200p. 1985. text ed. 39.00 (ISBN 3-7186-0243-1). Harwood Academic.

Semantic Theory of the English Auxiliary System. Erich Woisetschlaeger. Ed. by Jorge Hankamer. (Outstanding Dissertations in Linguistics Ser.). 127p. 1985. 26.00 (ISBN 0-8240-5479-2). Garland Pub.

Semantic Transmutations: Prolegomena to a Calculus of Meaning, Vol. 1: The Cardinal Semantic Structure of Prepositions, Cases & Paratactic Conjunctions in Contemporary Standard Russian. C. H. Van Schooneveld. LC 77-80437. (Physsardt Ser. in Prague Linguistics: No. 1-1). (Illus.). 1978. pap. 10.00 (ISBN 0-916062-01-5). Physsardt.

Semantic Variability of Absolute Constructions. Gregory T. Stump. 1985. lib. bdg. 66.50 (ISBN 90-277-1895-4, Pub. by Reidel Holland); pap. 26.00 (ISBN 90-277-1896-2). Kluwer Academic.

Semantical Essays. M. J. Cresswell. 1988. lib. bdg. 64.00 (ISBN 1-55608-061-1, Pub. by Reidel Holland). Kluwer Academic.

Semantical Investigation in Heyting's Intuitionistic Logic. Dov Gabbay. 297p. 1981. 52.50 (ISBN 90-277-1202-6, Pub. by Reidel Holland). Kluwer Academic.

Semantics. 2nd ed. F. R. Palmer. LC 80-42318. (Illus.). 170p. 1981. 37.50 (ISBN 0-521-23966-4); pap. 12.95 (ISBN 0-521-28376-0). Cambridge U Pr.

Semantics: A Bibliography Nineteen Sixty-Five to Nineteen Seventy-Eight. W. Terrence Gordon. LC 79-24719. 321p. 1980. 25.00 (ISBN 0-8108-1300-9). Scarecrow.

Semantics: A Bibliography, 1979-1985. W. Terrence Gordon. LC 87-16344. 304p. 1987. 27.50 (ISBN 0-8108-2055-2). Scarecrow.

Semantics: A Coursebook. James R. Hurford & Brendan Heasley. LC 82-22005. (Illus.). 256p. 1983. pap. 14.95 (ISBN 0-521-28949-1). Cambridge U Pr.

Semantics: An Interdisciplinary Reader in Philosophy, Linguistics & Psychology. Ed. by Danny D. Steinberg & Leon A. Jakobovits. LC 78-123675. pap. 153.80 (ISBN 0-317-20822-5, 2024539). Bks Demand UMI.

Semantics: An Introduction to the Science of Meaning. Stephen Ullmann. LC 78-67169. 278p. 1978. pap. text ed. 9.95x (ISBN 0-06-497076-0). B&N Imports.

Semantics & Cognition. Ray S. Jackendoff. Ed. by Bresnan et al. (Current Studies in Linguistics). (Illus.). 304p. 1985. pap. 9.95x (ISBN 0-262-60013-7). MIT Pr.

Semantics & Communications. 3rd ed. John C. Condon, Jr. 160p. 1985. pap. text ed. write for info. (ISBN 0-02-324200-0). Macmillan.

Semantics & Comprehension. Herbert H. Clark. (Janua Linguarum, Series Minor: No. 187). 148p. 1976. pap. text ed. 15.60x (ISBN 90-2793-384-7). Mouton.

Semantics & Language Analysis. Robert L. Benjamin. 128p. 1970. pap. text ed. 9.95x (ISBN 0-8290-0330-4). Irvington.

Semantics & Syntactic Regularity. Georgia M. Green. LC 74-9947. 256p. 1974. 22.50x (ISBN 0-253-35160-X). Ind U Pr.

Semantics & Syntax. Jim Miller. (Cambridge Studies in Linguistics: 41). 350p. 1985. 39.50 (ISBN 0-521-26265-8). Cambridge U Pr.

Semantics & the Philosophy of Language. 2nd ed. Ed. by Leonard Linsky. LC 52-10465. 304p. 1952. pap. 9.95 (ISBN 0-252-00093-5). U of Ill Pr.

Semantics & the Social Sciences. Graham MacDonald & Philip Pettit. 224p. 1981. pap. 11.95x (ISBN 0-7100-0784-1). Routledge Chapman & Hall.

Semantics-Directed Compiler Generation: Proceedings. Ed. by N. D. Jones. (Lecture Notes in Computer Science Ser.: Vol. 94). 489p. 1980. pap. 31.00 (ISBN 0-387-10250-7). Springer-Verlag.

Semantics from Different Points of View. Ed. by R. Bauerie et al. (Springer Series in Language & Communication: Vol. 6). (Illus.). 1979. 31.00 (ISBN 0-387-09676-0). Springer-Verlag.

Semantics in Biblical Research: New Methods of Defining Hebrew Words for Salvation. John F. Sawyer. LC 72-75901. (Studies in Biblical Theology, Second Ser.: No. 24). 1972. pap. text ed. 12.00x (ISBN 0-8401-3074-0). A R Allenson.

Semantics of Air Passenger Transportation. Edward MacNeal. LC 80-85432. (Illus.). 132p. 1981. 19.95 (ISBN 0-9605682-0-4). Norfolk Port.

Semantics of Bible Language. Barr. Date not set. 19.50 (Pub. by SCM Pr England). Fortress.

Semantics of Choice & Chance. Jorma Suokko. (Janua Linguarum, Ser. Minor: No. 131). 1972. pap. text ed. 7.20x (ISBN 0-686-22553-8). Mouton.

Semantics of Coordination. Ewald Lang. LC 84-14541. (Studies in Language Companion: No. 9). 300p. 1984. 56.00x (ISBN 90-272-3008-0). Benjamins North Am.

Semantics of Desire: The Changing Roles of Identity from Dickens to Joyce. Philip Weinstein. LC 83-43098. 336p. 1984. 36.50x (ISBN 0-691-06594-2). Princeton U Pr.

Semantics of Destructive Lisp. Ian A. Mason. LC 86-72170. (Center for the Study of Language & Information Lecture Notes: No. 5). 300p. 28.95 (ISBN 0-937073-05-9); pap. 14.95 (ISBN 0-937073-06-7). Ctr Study Language.

Semantics of Digital Circuts. C. Delgado Kloos. (Lecture Notes in Computer Science Ser.: Vol. 285). ix, 124p. 1987. pap. 16.40 (ISBN 0-387-18540-2). Springer-Verlag.

Semiconductor Devices & Circuits. Henry Zanger. LC 83-1190. (Electronic Technology Ser.: 1-325). 588p. 1984. write for info. (ISBN 0-471-05323-6, 1-325). Wiley.

Semiconductor Devices & Integrated Electronics. A. G. Milnes. 1008p. 1980. 36.95 (ISBN 0-442-23660-3). Van Nos Reinhold.

Semiconductor Devices & Integrated Electronics. A. G. Milnes. 1008p. 1983. pap. 25.95 (ISBN 0-442-26217-5). Van Nos Reinhold.

Semiconductor Devices for Optical Communication. 2nd, updated ed. Ed. by H. Kressel. (Topics in Applied Physics Ser.: Vol. 39). (Illus.). 325p. 1982. pap. 35.00 (ISBN 0-387-11348-7). Springer-Verlag.

Semiconductor Devices for Power Conditioning. Ed. by P. Roggwiller & Roland Sittig. LC 82-16167. (Brown Boveri Symposia Ser.). 384p. 1982. 65.00x (ISBN 0-306-41131-8, Plenum Pr). Plenum Pub.

Semiconductor Electrodes. Ed. by H. O. Finklea. (Studies in Physical & Theoretical Chemistry: Vol. 55). 520p. 1988. 179.00 (ISBN 0-444-42926-3). Elsevier.

Semiconductor Fundamentals. Robert F. Coughlin & F. F. Driscoll. (Illus.). 336p. 1976. 40.00 (ISBN 0-13-806406-7). P-H.

Semiconductor Fundamentals. 2nd ed. Robert F. Pierret. (Modular Series on Solid State Devices). (Illus.). 128p. 1988. pap. text ed. write for info. (ISBN 0-201-12295-2). Addison-Wesley.

Semiconductor General-Purpose Replacements. 6th ed. HWS Engineering Staff. 432p. (Orig.). 1986. pap. 12.95 (ISBN 0-672-22540-9). Sams.

Semiconductor Industry. Ed. by Peter Allen. 310p. 1984. pap. 295.00 (ISBN 0-931634-40-7). FIND SVP.

Semiconductor Industry: Trade Related Issues. OECD. (Orig.). 1985. pap. 19.00x (ISBN 92-64-12687-2). OECD.

Semiconductor Injection Lasers. Ed. by J. K. Butler. LC 79-91615. 408p. 1980. 52.05 (ISBN 0-87942-133-9, PC01248). Inst Electrical.

Semiconductor Interfaces: Formation & Properties. G. Le Lay et al. (Proceedings in Physics Ser.: Vol. 22). (Illus.). 420p. 1987. 59.40 (ISBN 0-387-18328-0). Springer-Verlag.

Semiconductor Laser Diodes: A User's Handbook. M. E. Fabian. 1981. 159.00x (ISBN 0-686-71789-9, Pub. by Electrochemical Scotland). State Mutual Bk.

Semiconductor Lasers. LC 86-63939. (Technical Digest Series 1987: Vol. 6). 184p. (Orig.). 1987. lib. bdg. 62.00 postconference ed. (ISBN 0-936659-39-4); pap. 35.00 conference ed. (ISBN 0-936659-19-X). Optical Soc.

Semiconductor Lasers & LED's. H. Kressel & J. K. Butler. 1977. 84.00 (ISBN 0-12-426250-3). Acad Pr.

Semiconductor Lithography. Wayne M. Moreau. (Illus.). 1500p. cancelled (ISBN 0-913811-02-5). Northeast A S.

Semiconductor Lithography: Principles, Practices, & Materials. W. M. Moreau. LC 87-29077. (Microdevices: Physics & Fabrication Technologies Ser.). (Illus.). 952p. 1988. 125.00x (ISBN 0-306-42185-2, Plenum Pr). Plenum Pub.

Semiconductor Memories. Betty Prince & Gunnar Due-Gundersen. LC 82-24804. 201p. 1983. 35.95x (ISBN 0-471-90146-6, Pub. by Wiley-Interscience). Wiley.

Semiconductor Microdevices & Materials. David H. Navon. 464p. 1986. text ed. 43.95 (ISBN 0-03-063983-2, HoltC). HR&W.

Semiconductor Nuclear Particle Detectors. (Bibliographical Ser.: No. 8). 95p. 1962. pap. 5.00 (ISBN 92-0-034262-0, ISP21 8, IAEA). UNIPUB.

Semiconductor-On-Insulator & Thin Film Transistor Technology, Vol. 53. Ed. by A. Chiang et al. (Materials Research Society Symposia Proceedings Ser.). 1986. text ed. 46.00 (ISBN 0-931837-18-9). Materials Res.

Semiconductor Opto-Electronics. Trevor S. Moss et al. LC 73-167813. pap. 113.30 (ISBN 0-317-41852-1, 2025735). Bks Demand UMI.

Semiconductor Optoelectronics: Proceedings. Ed. by Marian A. Herman. 648p. 1981. 67.95 (ISBN 0-471-27589-1, Pub. by Wiley-Interscience). Wiley.

Semiconductor Particle Detectors. James M. Taylor. LC 64-9673. (Semiconductor Monographs). pap. 49.00 (ISBN 0-317-09005-4, 2051333). Bks Demand UMI.

Semiconductor Photoelectric Devices. A. Ambroziak. 344p. 1970. 128.00 (ISBN 0-677-61800-X). Gordon & Breach.

Semiconductor Photoelectrochemistry. Yu. V. Pleskov & Yu. Ya. Gurevich. Tr. by P. N. Bartlett from Rus. 426p. 1985. 69.50x (ISBN 0-306-10983-2, Plenum Pr). Plenum Pub.

Semiconductor Physics. 3rd, rev. ed. K. Seeger. (Series in Solid-State Sciences: Vol. 40). (Illus.). 490p. 1985. 35.00 (ISBN 0-387-15578-3). Springer-Verlag.

Semiconductor Physics. Sze. 1987. write for info. (ISBN 0-471-84040-8). Wiley.

Semiconductor Physics. Ed. by V. M. Tuchkevich & V. Ya Frenkel. 556p. 1986. 89.50x (ISBN 0-306-10987-5, Consultants). Plenum Pub.

Semiconductor Physics: Proceedings of the Third Brazilian School. Ed. by C. E. Goncalves da Silva et al. 328p. 1987. 75.00x (ISBN 9971-50-331-X); pap. 44.00 (ISBN 9971-50-332-8). World Scientific Pub.

Semiconductor Power Electronics. Richard G. Hoft. (Illus.). 384p. 1986. 49.95 (ISBN 0-442-22543-1). Van Nos Reinhold.

Semiconductor Processing - STP 850. Ed. by D. C. Gupta. 700p. 1984. 60.00 (ISBN 0-8031-0403-0, 04-850000-46). ASTM.

Semiconductor Sensor Market. (Market Research Reports). 1986. write for info. (ISBN 0-86621-848-3, A1668). Frost & Sullivan.

Semiconductor Silicon Crystal Technology. Fumio Shimura. 598p. 1988. price not set (ISBN 0-12-640045-8). Acad Pr.

Semiconductor Silicon: 1973 International Symposium. International Symposium on Silicon Materials, Science & Technology (2d: 1973: Chicago) Ed. by Howard R. Huff & Ronald R. Burgess. (Illus.). pap. 160.00 (ISBN 0-317-08778-9, 2051088). Bks Demand UMI.

Semiconductor Statistics. J. S. Blakemore. 416p. 1987. pap. text ed. 9.95 (ISBN 0-486-65362-5). Dover.

Semiconductor Technologies. Ed. by J. Nishizawa. (Japan Annual Reviews in Electronics, Computers & Telecommunications Ser.: No. 19). 345p. 1987. 95.00 (ISBN 0-444-87934-X, North Holland). Elsevier.

Semiconductor Technologies: Japan Annual Reviews in Electronics, Computers & Telecommunications. Ed. by J. Nishizawa. (Jarect Ser.: Vol. 13). 1985. 95.00. Elsevier.

Semiconductor Technologies 1982 see Japan Annual Reviews in Electronics, Computers & Telecommunications, 1982.

Semiconductors. F. J. Hyde. (Illus.). 324p. 1969. 14.95x (ISBN 0-8464-0836-8). Beekman Pubs.

Semiconductors. 2nd ed. OAS General Secretariat Department of Scientific & Technological Affairs. (Serie De Fisica (Monograph on Physics): No. 6). 63p. 1980. Repr. text ed. 3.50 (ISBN 0-8270-1068-0). OAS.

Semiconductors. 2nd ed. R. A. Smith. LC 77-82515. 1978. pap. 39.50 (ISBN 0-521-29314-6). Cambridge U Pr.

Semiconductors. Helmut F. Wolf. LC 71-160211. 552p. 1971. 69.95x (ISBN 0-471-95949-9, Pub. by Wiley-Interscience). Wiley.

Semiconductors. Helmut F. Wolf. LC 77-159286. (Illus.). pap. 143.00 (ISBN 0-317-09131-X, 2055668). Bks Demand UMI.

Semiconductors & Semimetals, Vols. 1-12. Ed. by R. K. Willardson & A. C. Beer. Incl. Vol. 1. Physics of III-V Compounds. 1967. 83.00 (ISBN 0-12-752101-1); Vol. 2. Physics of III-V Compounds. 1966. 83.00 (ISBN 0-12-752102-X); Vol. 3. Optical Properties of III-V Compounds. 1967. 83.00 (ISBN 0-12-752103-8); Vol. 4. Physics of III-V Compounds. 1968. 83.00 (ISBN 0-12-752104-6); Vol. 5. Infrared Detectors. 1970. 83.00 (ISBN 0-12-752105-4); Vol. 6. Injection Phenomena. 1970. 83.00 (ISBN 0-12-752106-2); Vol. 7A. Semiconductor Applications & Devices. 1971. 83.00 (ISBN 0-12-752107-0); Vol. 7B. Applications & Devices. 1971. 83.00 (ISBN 0-12-752147-X); Vol. 8. Techniques for Studying Semiconducting Materials. 1972. 83.00 (ISBN 0-12-752108-9); Vol. 9. Modulation Techniques. 1972; Vol. 10. 1975; Vol. 11. 1976. 30.00 (ISBN 0-12-752111-9); Vol. 12. 1977. 78.00 (ISBN 0-12-752112-7). Acad Pr.

Semiconductors & Semimetals, Vol. 17. Ed. by R. K. Willardson & A. C. Beer. 1984. 77.50 (ISBN 0-12-752117-8). Acad Pr.

Semiconductors & Semimetals, Vol. 20. Ed. by R. K. Willardson & Albert C. Beer. LC 65-20648. 1984. 91.50 (ISBN 0-12-752120-8). Acad Pr.

Semiconductors & Semimetals, Vol. 23. Willardson. 1985. 75.00 (ISBN 0-12-752123-2). Acad Pr.

Semiconductors & Semimetals, Vol. 24. Ed. by R. K. Willardson & A. C. Beer. 511p. 1987. 75.00 (ISBN 0-12-752124-0). Acad Pr.

Semiconductors & Semimetals, Vol. 26. Ed. by R. K. Willardson & A. C. Beer. 360p. 1988. price not set (ISBN 0-12-752126-7). Acad Pr.

Semiconductors & Semimetals: Cadmium Telluride. Ed. by R. K. Willardson et al. 1978. Vol. 13. 77.50 (ISBN 0-12-752113-5); Vol. 14. 1979. 77.50 (ISBN 0-12-752114-3). Acad Pr.

Semiconductors & Semimetals: Contacts, Junctions, Emitters, Vol. 15. Ed. by Robert Willardson & A. C. Beer. 1981. 77.50 (ISBN 0-12-752115-1). Acad Pr.

Semiconductors & Semimetals: Deep Levels, Gas Alloys, Photochemistry, Vol. 19. Ed. by Robert K. Willardson & Albert C. Beer. LC 65-26048. 1983. 77.50 (ISBN 0-12-752119-4). Acad Pr.

Semiconductors & Semimetals: Hydrogenated Amorphous Silicon, Pt. C: Electronic & Transport Properties, Vol. 21C. Ed. by R. K. Willardson & A. C. Beer. 1984. 84.00 (ISBN 0-12-752149-6). Acad Pr.

Semiconductors & Semimetals: Hydrogenated Amorphous Silicon, Pt. D: Device Applications, Vol. 21D. Ed. by R. K. Willardson & A. C. Beer. 1984. 73.50 (ISBN 0-12-752150-X). Acad Pr.

Semiconductors & Semimetals: Lightwave Communication Technology: Pt. B, Material Growth Technologies, Vol. 22. Ed. by R. K. Willardson & A. Beer. 1985. 65.00 (ISBN 0-12-752151-8). Acad Pr.

Semiconductors & Semimetals, Vol. 16: Defects, HgCd, Se, HgCdO & Te. Ed. by Robert Willardson & A. Beer. 1981. 77.50 (ISBN 0-12-752116-X). Acad Pr.

Semiconductors & Semimetals, Vol. 18: Mercury Cadmium Telluride. Ed. by Robert Willardson & A. C. Beer. 1981. 77.50 (ISBN 0-12-752118-6). Acad Pr.

Semiconductors & Semimetals, Vol. 21B: Hydrogenated Amorphous Silicon: Optical Properties. R. K. Willardson & Albert C. Beer. 1984. 84.50 (ISBN 0-12-752148-8). Acad Pr.

Semiconductors & Semimetals, Vol. 21A: Hydrogenated Amorphous Silicon: Preparation & Structure. R. K. Willardson & Albert C. Beer. 1984. 77.50 (ISBN 0-12-752121-6). Acad Pr.

Semiconductors & Semimetals, Vol. 22: Lightwave Communications Technology, Pt. E. Integrated Optoelectronics. Ed. by Willardson & Beer. 1985. 65.00 (ISBN 0-12-752154-2). Acad Pr.

Semiconductors & Semimetals Vol. 22 (Pt. A) Lightwave Communications Technology: Part A, Material Growth Technologies. Ed. by W. T. Tsang. 1985. 77.50 (ISBN 0-12-752122-4). Acad Pr.

Semiconductors & Semimetals, Vol. 22, (Pt. C) Lightwave Communications Technology: Semiconductor Inject Lasers II; Light Emitting Diodes. Ed. by R. K. Willardson & A. C. Beer. 1985. 65.00 (ISBN 0-12-752152-6). Acad Pr.

Semiconductors & Semimetals, Vol. 22, Pt. D: Lightwave Communications Technology: Photodetectors. Ed. by W. T. Tsang. 454p. 1985. 79.50 (ISBN 0-12-752153-4). Acad Pr.

Semiconductors & Semimetals, Vol. 27: Highly Conducting Quasi-One-Dimemsional Organic Crystals. Ed. by Esther M. Conwell et al. 540p. 1988. price not set (ISBN 0-12-752127-5). Acad Pr.

Semiconductors: Circuits & Devices. National Education Training Corporation Staff. 1986. write for info. (ISBN 0-471-84861-1) (ISBN 0-471-84869-7). Wiley.

Semiconductors Made Simple. A. Polyakov. 240p. 1985. pap. 4.95 (ISBN 0-8285-3002-5, Pub. by Mir Pubs USSR). Imported Pubns.

Semiconductors: Physics of Group IV Elements & III-V Compounds. Ed. by O. Madelung. (Landolt-Boernstein Ser.: Group III, Vol. 17, Pt. a). (Illus.). 670p. 1982. 615.80 (ISBN 0-387-10610-3). Springer-Verlag.

Semiconductors Probed by Ultrafast Laser Spectroscopy, Vol. 1. R. R. Alfano. 1985. 89.50 (ISBN 0-12-049901-0). Acad Pr.

Semiconductors Probed by Ultrafast Laser Spectroscopy, Vol. 2. R. R. Alfano. 1985. 96.00 (ISBN 0-12-049902-9). Acad Pr.

Semiconductors, Subvolume B: Physics of II-VI & I-VII Compounds, Semimagnetic Conductors. Ed. by K. H. Hellwege. (Landolt-Berstein, Numerical Data & Functional Relationships in Science & Technology, New Series: Group III, Vol. 17, Subvolume b). (Illus.). 540p. 1982. 484.20 (ISBN 0-387-11308-8). Springer-Verlag.

Semiconductors: Subvolume E-Physics of Non-Tetrahodrally Bonded Elements & Binary Compounds I. (Landolt-Boernstein, New Series-Group III: Vol. 17). (Illus.). 410p. 1983. 505.30 (ISBN 0-387-11780-6). Springer-Verlag.

Semidynamical Systems in Infinite Dimensional Spaces. S. H. Saperstone. (Applied Mathematical Sciences Ser.: Vol. 37). 474p. 1981. pap. 40.00 (ISBN 0-387-90643-6). Springer-Verlag.

Semiempirical Methods of Electronic Structure Calculation, 2 pts. Ed. by Gerald A. Segal. Incl. Pt. A, Techniques. 274p (ISBN 0-306-33507-7); Pt. B, Applications. 308p (ISBN 0-306-33508-5). LC 76-48060. (Modern Theoretical Chemistry Ser.: Vols. 7 & 8). (Illus.). 1977. 59.50x ea. (Plenum Pr). Plenum Pub.

Semiempirical Wave-Mechanical Calculations Polyatomic Molecules: A Current Review. Raymond Daudel & Camille Sandorfy. LC 74-140525. (Yale Series in the Sciences). (Illus.). pap. 36.80 (ISBN 0-317-13001-3, 2016797). Bks Demand UMI.

Semigroup Compactifications: Analysis & Applications. Milnes et al. LC 88-14292. 1988. price not set (ISBN 0-471-61208-1). Wiley.

Semigroups. Ed. by T. E. Hall et al. LC 80-23748. 1980. 44.50 (ISBN 0-12-319450-4). Acad Pr.

Semigroups. 4th ed. E. S. Ljapin et al. LC 63-15659. (Translations of Mathematical Monographs: Vol. 3). 519p. 1978. pap. 50.00 (ISBN 0-8218-1553-9, MMONO-3). Am Math.

Semigroups & Their Applications. Ed. by Simon M. Goberstein & Peter M. Higgins. 1987. lib. bdg. 69.00 (ISBN 90-277-2463-6, Pub. by Reidel Holland). Kluwer Academic.

Semigroups of Linear Operators: An Introduction. A. C. McBride. (Research Notes in Mathematics Ser.). 289p. 1987. pap. 37.95 (ISBN 0-470-20824-4, Co-Pub. with Longman). Wiley.

Semigroups of Linear Operators & Applications. Jerome A. Goldstein. (Mathematical Monographs). 1985. 42.50x (ISBN 0-19-503540-2). Oxford U Pr.

Semigroups of Linear Operators & Applications to Partial Differential Equations. A. Pazy. (Applied Mathematical Sciences Ser.: Vol. 44). 288p. 1983. 38.00 (ISBN 0-387-90845-5). Springer-Verlag.

Semigroups: Proceedings. Ed. by H. Juergensen et al. (Lecture Notes in Mathematics Ser.: Vol. 855). 221p. 1981. pap. 16.00 (ISBN 0-387-10701-0). Springer-Verlag.

Semigroups: Structure & Universal Algebraic Problems. Ed. by G. Pollak et al. 502p. 1986. 131.75 (ISBN 0-444-87553-0). Elsevier.

Semigroups: Theory & Applications, 2 vols. Ed. by H. Brezis et al. LC 86-10649. (Research Notes in Mathematics Ser.). 252p. 1986. Vol. 1. pap. 34.95 (ISBN 0-470-20372-2, Co-Pub. with Longman); Vol. 2. pap. 36.95 (ISBN 0-470-20383-8). Wiley.

Semigroups Theory & Applications. Ed. by H. Jurgensen et al. (Lecture Notes in Mathematics Ser.: Vol. 1320). 416p. 1988. pap. 39.40 (ISBN 0-387-19347-2). Springer-Verlag.

Semimartingales: A Course on Stochastic Processes. Michel Metivier. (De Gruyter Studies in Mathematics). 287p. 1982. 44.95 (ISBN 3-11-008674-3). De Gruyter.

Semimetals & Narrow-Bandgap Semiconductors. D. R. Lovett. 1977. 29.00x (ISBN 0-85086-060-1, NO. 2939, Pub. by Pion England). Routledge Chapman & Hall.

Semimetals, Part One: Graphite & Its Compounds. N. B. Brandt et al. (Modern Problems in Condensed Matter Sciences Ser.: Vol. 20). 456p. 1988. 156.00 (ISBN 0-444-87049-0, North Holland). Elsevier.

Seminaire d'Algebre Paul Dubreil et Marie-Paule Malliavin. M. P. Malliavin. (Lecture Notes in Mathematics Ser.: Vol. 1146). iv, 420p. (Fr. & Eng.). 1985. pap. 28.50 (ISBN 0-387-15686-0). Springer-Verlag.

Seminaire d'Algebre Paul Dubreil et Marie-Paule Malliavin. Ed. by M. P. Malliavin. (Lecture Notes in Mathematics: Vol. 1029). 339p. 1983. pap. 19.50 (ISBN 0-387-12699-6). Springer-Verlag.

Seminaire D'Algebre Paul Dubreil: Proceedings, Paris 1976-1977. Ed. by M. P. Malliavin. (Lecture Notes in Mathematics: Vol. 641). 1978. pap. 23.10 (ISBN 0-387-08665-X). Springer-Verlag.

Seminaire d'Analyse. Ed. by P. Lelong et al. (Lecture Notes in Mathematics Ser.: Vol. 1198). x, 260p. 1986. pap. 21.30 (ISBN 0-387-16762-5). Springer-Verlag.

Seminaire de Probabilites XIX 1983-84. Ed. by J. Azema & M. Yor. (Lecture Notes in Mathematics: Vol. 1123). iv, 504p. (Eng. & Fr.). 1985. pap. 36.00 (ISBN 0-387-15230-X). Springer-Verlag.

Seminaire de Probabilities XX 1984-85. Ed. by J. Azema & M. Yor. (Lecture Notes in Mathematics Ser.: Vol. 1204). v, 639p. 1986. pap. 51.60 (ISBN 0-387-16779-X). Springer-Verlag.

Seminaire de Theorie des Nombres: Nineteen Eighty-Two to Nineteen Eighty-Three. Ed. by Marie-Jose Bertin & Catherine Goldstein. (Progress in Mathematics Ser.: No. 51). 312p. 1984. text ed. 34.50 (ISBN 0-8176-3261-1). Birkhauser.

Seminaire De Theorie Des Nombres, Paris 1979-1980. Ed. by M. J. Bertin. (Progress in Mathematics Ser.: Vol. 12). 404p. (Fr. & Eng.). 1981. 34.50x (ISBN 0-8176-3035-X). Birkhauser.

Seminaire de Theorie des Nombres: Paris 1980-1981. Ed. by M. J. Bertin. (Progress in Mathematics Ser.: Vol. 22). 360p. 1982. text ed. 28.50 (ISBN 0-8176-3066-X). Birkhauser.

Seminaire de Theorie des Nombres, Paris 1981-1982. Marie-Jose Bertin. (Progress in Mathematics Ser.: Vol. 38). 359p. 1983. text ed. 34.50 (ISBN 0-8176-3155-0). Birkhauser.

Seminaire de Theorie des Nombres, Paris 1983-84. Ed. by Catherine Goldstein. (Progress in Mathematics Ser.: Vol. 59). 289p. (Eng. & Fr.). 1985. 39.95x (ISBN 0-8176-3315-4). Birkhauser.

Seminaire de Theorie des Nombres, Paris 1984-85. Ed. by Catherine Goldstein. (Progress in Mathematics Ser.: Vol. 63). 252p. 1986. 39.95 (ISBN 0-8176-3347-2). Birkhauser.

Seminaire de Theorie des Nombres, Paris 1985-86. Ed. by Catherine Goldstein. (Progress in Mathematics Ser.: No. 71). 224p. 1987. 35.00 (ISBN 0-8176-3369-3). Birkhauser.

Seminaire de Theorie des Nombres, Paris, 1986-87. Ed. by Catherine Goldstein. (Progress in Mathematics Ser.: No. 75). 480p. 1988. 42.00 (ISBN 0-8176-3414-2). Birkhauser.

Seminaire de Theorie du Potentiel, Paris, No. 8. Ed. by F. Hirsch & G. Mokobodzki. (Lecture Notes in Mathematics Ser.: Vol. 1235). iii, 209p. 1987. pap. 19.40 (ISBN 0-387-17210-6). Springer-Verlag.

Seminal Cases & Contemporary Commentaries: The United States. Ed. by Daniel N. Robinson. (Insanity & Jurisprudence). 1980. 30.00 (ISBN 0-89093-330-8). U Pubns Amer.

Seminal Research Papers. D. A. Spalding et al. LC 77-72191. (Contributions to the History of Psycholgy Ser.: No. 11, Pt. A Orientations). 532p. 1978. Repr. of 1873 ed. 30.00 (ISBN 0-89093-160-7). U Pubns Amer.

TITLE INDEX SEMIOTIC & SIGNIFICS: THE

Seminal Vesicles & Fertility. Ed. by C. Bollack & A. Clavert. (Progress in Reproductive Biology & Medicine: Vol. 12). (Illus.). x, 182p. 1984. 99.50 (ISBN 3-8055-3907-X). S Karger.
Seminar Basics Manual. Wyatt. 1986. write for info. (ISBN 0-88462-584-2, 5606-20, Pub. by Longman Fin Serv Pub). Longman Finan.
Seminar for Murder. B. M. Gill. 192p. 1987. pap. text ed. 2.95 (ISBN 0-345-33978-9). Ballantine.
Seminar in Stochastic Processes: 1983. Ed. by E. Cinlar et al. (Progress in Probability & Statistics Ser.: Vol. 7). 290p. 1985. text ed. 39.50x (ISBN 0-8176-3293-X). Birkhauser.
Seminar Leader's Kit: Statement Analysis Books I-IV. 15.00 (ISBN 0-686-95606-0, 167401); members 10.00. Am Bankers.
Seminar Leader's Kit: Statement Analysis Book V. members 10.00 (ISBN 0-686-95609-5, 167501); non-members 15.00 (ISBN 0-686-99546-5). Am Bankers.
Seminar Market. Don M. Schrello. (Illus.). 125p. 1981. pap. 19.95 (ISBN 0-935823-01-8). Schrello Market.
Seminar Material for Child Custody Workshop. Howard P. Danzig. LC 86-211079. Date not set. price not set. NJ Inst CLE.
Seminar Material for Civil RICO. Harold A. Ackerman. LC 86-207208. 197p. Date not set. price not set. NJ Inst CLE.
Seminar Material for Complying with ECRA in Real Estate Sales & Leases. Institute for Continuing Legal Education Staff & David B. Farer. LC 86-101207. (Illus.). 330p. 1985. looseleaf 35.00. NJ Inst CLE.
Seminar Material for Real Estate Tax Appeals. Saul A. Wolfe. LC 86-206170. Date not set. price not set. NJ Inst CLE.
Seminar on AACR2. Ed. by Graham Roe. 96p. 1980. pap. 20.00 (ISBN 0-85365-593-6, Pub. by Library Assn Pub London). ALA.
Seminar on Ambulatory Pediatrics. Ed. by G. D. Maragos. (Journal: Paediatrician Ser.: Vol. 5, No. 3). (Illus.). 1977. 20.00 (ISBN 3-8055-2433-1). S Karger.
Seminar on Bibliotherapy: Proceedings. Sessions in Madison, Madison, Wisconsin, June 21-23 1978. Ed. by Margaret E. Monroe. 180p. 1978. pap. 5.00 (ISBN 0-936442-07-7). U Wis Sch Lib.
Seminar on Blasting & Overbreak Control see Rock Blasting.
Seminar on Childhood Poisoning. Ed. by G. D. Maragos. (Journal: Paediatrician Ser.: Vol. 6, No. 3-5). (Illus.). 1978. 62.00 (ISBN 3-8055-2863-9). S Karger.
Seminar on Children at Risk. Ed. by O. Wasz-Hoeckert. (Journal: Paediatrician Ser., 1979: Vol. 8, No. 4). (Illus.). 1979. soft cover 22.00 (ISBN 3-8055-3073-0). S Karger.
Seminar on Concurrrency, Vol. 197. Ed. by S. D. Brookes et al. (Lecture Notes in Computer Science: Vol. 197). xi, 523p. 1985. pap. 30.00 (ISBN 0-387-15670-4). Springer-Verlag.
Seminar on Deformations. Ed. by J. Lawrynowicz. (Lecture Notes in Mathematics Ser.: Vol. 1165). ix, 331p. 1985. pap. 23.00 (ISBN 0-387-16050-7). Springer-Verlag.
Seminar on Delivery of Child Health Care. Ed. by O. P. Petersson. (Journal: Paediatrician: Vol. 9, No. 1, 1980). 52p. 1979. pap. 22.00 (ISBN 3-8055-0800-X). S Karger.
Seminar on Differential Geometry. Ed. by Shing-Tung Yau. LC 81-8631. (Annals of Mathematics Studies: No. 102). 832p. 1981. 73.00x (ISBN 0-691-08268-5); pap. 15.00x (ISBN 0-691-08296-0). Princeton U Pr.
Seminar on Emergency Pediatrics. Ed. by George D. Maragos. (Journal: Paediatrician Ser.: Vol. 7, No. 4-5). 1978. pap. 41.50 (ISBN 3-8055-2948-1). S Karger.
Seminar on Empirical Processes. P. Gaenssler & W. Stute. (DMV Seminar Ser.: No. 9). 114p. 1987. 25.00 (ISBN 0-8176-1921-6). Birkhauser.
Seminar on Environmental Pharmacology. Ed. by Ryuta Ito. (Journal: Paediatrician Ser.: Vol. 6, No. 1). (Illus.). 1977. 20.75 (ISBN 3-8055-2794-2). S Karger.
Seminar on Geographical Pediatrics. Ed. by G. D. Maragos. (Journal: Paediatrician Ser.: Vol. 6, No. 2). (Illus.). 1977. 20.75 (ISBN 3-8055-2795-0). S Karger.
Seminar on Geometric Measure Theory. R. Hardt & L. Simon. (DMV Seminars Ser.: Vol. 7). 118p. 1986. 19.95 (ISBN 0-8176-1815-5). Birkhauser.
Seminar on Haematology & Oncology. Ed. by H. Ekert. (Journal: Paediatrician: Vol. 9, No. 2). (Illus.). 88p. 1980. softcover 22.00 (ISBN 3-8055-1302-X). S Karger.
Seminar on Human Genetics. Ed. by George D. Maragos. (Journal: Paediatrician Ser.: Vol. 6, No. 6). (Illus.). 1978. 20.75 (ISBN 3-8055-2909-0). S Karger.
Seminar on Immunological Aspects of Kidney Diseases in Children. Ed. by G. D. Maragos. (Journal: Paediatrician Ser.: Vol. 10, No. 5-6). (Illus.). 164p. 1981. pap. 46.75 (ISBN 3-8055-3488-4). S Karger.
Seminar on Infectious Diseases in Childhood. Ed. by G. D. Maragos. (Journal: Paediatrician Ser.: Vol. 8, No. 1-2). (Illus.). 1979. pap. 44.00 (ISBN 3-8055-3027-7). S Karger.
Seminar on Jewish Art: Proceedings. Ed. by Vivian B. Mann & Gordon Tucker. 37p. (Orig.). 1985. pap. 6.00 (ISBN 0-87334-029-9). Jewish Sem.
Seminar on Kidney Diseases in Children. Ed. by F. Mota-Hernandez. (Journal: Paediatrician: Vol. 8, No. 5-6, 1979). 1979. pap. 44.00 (ISBN 3-8055-0344-X). S Karger.
Seminar on Mechanical Engineering in a Marine Environment. 45p. 1983. pap. text ed. 12.00x (ISBN 0-85825-192-2, Pub. by Inst Engineering Australia). Brookfield Pub Co.
Seminar on Micro-Local Analysis. Victor Guillemin et al. LC 78-70609. (Annals of Mathematics Studies: No. 93). 1979. 29.50x (ISBN 0-691-08228-6); pap. 13.50x (ISBN 0-691-08232-4). Princeton U Pr.
Seminar on Minimal Submanifolds. Enrico Bombieri. LC 82-61356. (Annals of Mathematics Studies: No. 103). 500p. 1983. 52.50x (ISBN 0-691-08324-X); pap. 17.95 (ISBN 0-691-08319-3). Princeton U Pr.
Seminar on National Development & Regional Policy: Nagoya, Japan, Oct. 31-Nov. 4, 1979. (Meeting Report Ser.: No. 1). 17p. 1979. pap. 6.75 (ISBN 0-686-96526-4, CRD134, UNCRD). UNIPUB.
Seminar on Neonatology. Ed. by G. D. Maragos. (Journal: Paediatrician Ser.: Vol. 5, No. 5). (Illus.). 1977. 20.00 (ISBN 3-8055-2702-0). S Karger.
Seminar on New Results in Nonlinear Partial Differential Equations. A. J. Tromba. (Aspects of Mathematics Ser.: Vol. 10). 198p. 1987. pap. 25.00 (ISBN 3-528-08975-X, Pub. by Vieweg & Sohn). IPS.
Seminar on Nonlinear Partial, & Differential Equations. Ed. by S. S. Cherm. (Mathematical Sciences Research Institute Publications: Vol. 2). (Illus.). 373p. 1984. 29.50 (ISBN 0-387-96079-1). Springer-Verlag.
Seminar on Office Pediatrics, Part I. Ed. by G. D. Maragos. (Journal: Paediatrician Ser.: Vol. 7, No. 6). (Illus.). 1979. pap. 20.75 (ISBN 3-8055-3010-2). S Karger.
Seminar on Office Pediatrics, Part II. Ed. by G. G. Maragos. (Journal: Paediatrician Ser., 1979: Vol. 8, No. 3). (Illus.). 1979. soft cover 22.00 (ISBN 3-8055-3074-9). S Karger.
Seminar on Organism-Sediment Interrelationships, 1970. Fred T. Mackenzie et al. (Bermuda Biological Station Special Pubn.: No. 7). (Illus.). iv, 170p. pap. 7.50 (ISBN 0-917642-07-4). Bermuda Bio.
Seminar on Pediatric Allergy. Ed. by G. D. Maragos. (Journal: Paediatrician Ser.: Vol. 5, No. 4). (Illus.). 80p. 1977. 20.00 (ISBN 3-8055-2648-2). S Karger.
Seminar on Pediatric Cardiology. Ed. by George D. Maragos. (Journal: Paediatrician Ser.: Vol. 7, No. 1-3). (Illus.). 1978. soft cover 62.00 (ISBN 3-8055-2912-0). S Karger.
Seminar on Pediatric Cardiology. Ed. by J. G. Shakibi. (Journal: Paediatrician: Vol. 10, No. 1-3). (Illus.). 180p. 1981. pap. 70.00 (ISBN 3-8055-2675-X). S Karger.
Seminar on Phosphate Rock for Direct Application. Ed. by M. Thompson. (Special Publication Ser.: SP-1). (Illus.). 472p. (Orig.). 1979. pap. 10.00 (ISBN 0-88090-022-9). Intl Fertilizer.
Seminar on Public Health, Pt. I. Ed. by G. D. Maragos. (Journal: Paediatrician: Vol. II, No. 1-2, 1982). (Illus.). iv, 120p. 1982. pap. 51.50 (ISBN 3-8055-3533-3). S Karger.
Seminar on Public Health, Pt. 2. Ed. by G. D. Maragos. (Journal: Paediatrician: Vol. II, No. 3-4). (Illus.). 126p. 1982. pap. 43.00 (ISBN 3-8055-3532-5). S Karger.
Seminar on Reliability Growth, Management, Testing & Modeling: Proceedings. LC 62-38584. (Illus.). 1978. pap. text ed. 10.00 (ISBN 0-915414-57-0). Inst Environ Sci.
Seminar on River Basin Management & Development: Blantyre, Malawi, December 8-10, 1980. Ed. by J. M. Kapetsky. (Commission for Inland Fisheries of Africa (CIFA): Technical Papers: No. 8). 313p. (Eng. & Fr.). 1981. pap. 21.25 (ISBN 92-5-001159-8, F2295, FAO). UNIPUB.
Seminar on Singularities of Solutions of Linear Partial Differential Equations. Ed. by Lars Hormander. LC 78-70300. (Annals of Mathematics Studies: No. 91). 1979. 37.00x (ISBN 0-691-08221-9). Princeton U Pr.
Seminar on Spinal Cord Stimulation for the Control of Pain & other Neurological Disorders. Ed. by P. L. Gildenberg & D. M. Long. (Journal: Applied Neurophysiology: Vol. 44, No. 4). (Illus.). vi, 84p. 1982. pap. 32.75 (ISBN 3-8055-3531-7). S Karger.
Seminar on Stochastic Processes, 1981. Ed. by E. Cinlar et al. (Progress in Probability & Statistics Ser.: Vol. 1). 248p. 1982. text ed. 19.95 (ISBN 0-8176-3072-4). Birkhauser.
Seminar on Stochastic Processes, 1982. E. Cinlar et al. (Progress in Probability & Statistics Ser.: Vol. 5). 310p. 1983. text ed. 29.50 (ISBN 0-8176-3131-3). Birkhauser.
Seminar on Stochastic Processes, 1984. Ed. by E. Cinlar et al. (Progress in Probability & Statistics Ser.: Vol. 9). 258p. 1986. 42.00 (ISBN 0-8176-3327-8). Birkhauser.
Seminar on Stochastic Processes, 1985. Ed. by E. Cinlar. (Progress in Probability & Statistics Ser.: Vol. 12). 336p. 1986. 32.00 (ISBN 0-8176-3331-6). Birkhauser.
Seminar on Stochastic Processes: 1987. Ed. by Cinlar et al. (Progress in Probability & Statistics Ser.: No. 15). 250p. 1988. 32.50 (ISBN 0-8176-3381-2). Birkhauser.
Seminar on Technological Development & the Traditional Performing Arts. Seameo Project in Archaeology & Fine Arts Staff. 80p. 1981. 53.00x (Pub. by Han-Shan Tang Ltd). State Mutual Bk.
Seminar on the Ethics in Government Act. 344p. 25.00 (ISBN 0-318-14096-9). Federal Bar.
Seminar on Time. A. G. Blake. LC 79-52756. 1980. 5.95 (ISBN 0-934254-00-1). Claymont Comm.
Seminar on Tubal Physiology & Biochemistry. Ed. by C. J. Pauerstein. (Gynecologic Investigation Ser.: Vol. 6, Nos. 3-4). iv, 160p. 1975. Repr. 37.50 (ISBN 3-8055-2252-5). S Karger.
Seminarians in Theology: A National Profile. Eugene F. Hemrick et al. 128p. 1986. pap. 8.95 (ISBN 1-55586-978-5). US Catholic.
Seminarians of the Eighties: A National Survey. Raymond H. Potvin. 64p. 1986. 5.65 (ISBN 0-318-20579-3). Natl Cath Educ.
Seminaries in Dialogue, No. 1. 1980. 2.40 (ISBN 0-318-20625-0). Natl Cath Educ.
Seminaries in Dialogue, No. 2. 24p. 1981. 2.40 (ISBN 0-318-20624-2). Natl Cath Educ.
Seminaries in Dialogue, No. 3. 20p. 1982. 2.40 (ISBN 0-318-20623-4). Natl Cath Educ.
Seminaries in Dialogue, No. 4. 1982. 2.40 (ISBN 0-318-20622-6). Natl Cath Educ.
Seminaries in Dialogue, No. 5. 20p. 1983. 2.40 (ISBN 0-318-20621-8). Natl Cath Educ.
Seminaries in Dialogue, No. 6. 24p. 1984. 2.40 (ISBN 0-318-20620-X). Natl Cath Educ.
Seminaries in Dialogue, No. 7. 24p. 1984. 2.40 (ISBN 0-318-20619-6). Natl Cath Educ.
Seminaries in Dialogue, No. 8. 24p. 1984. 2.40 (ISBN 0-318-20618-8). Natl Cath Educ.
Seminaries in Dialogue, No. 9. 24p. 1985. 2.40 (ISBN 0-318-20617-X). Natl Cath Educ.
Seminaries in Dialogue, No. 10. 24p. 1985. 2.40 (ISBN 0-318-20616-1). Natl Cath Educ.
Seminaries Without Walls. Ed. by Alex S. White. 1980. 8.00x (ISBN 0-317-47276-3). Aurea.
Seminars As a Selling Tool. Dean L. Smith. 170p. (Orig.). 1987. wkbk. 20.00x (ISBN 0-918699-10-X). D L Smith.
Seminars Directory. 1000p. 1988. 125.00 (ISBN 0-8103-2842-9). Gale.
Seminars of Jacques Lacan: Freud's Writings on Technique 1953-1954. Jacques Lacan. Ed. by Jacques-Alain Miller. Tr. by John Forrester & Sylvana Tomaselli. (Lacan's Series of Seminars: Bk. 1). 1988. 24.95 (ISBN 0-393-01895-4). Norton.
Seminars of Jacques Lacan: The Theory of the Ego in Psychoanalytic Theory & Practice 1954-1955. Jacques Lacan. Ed. by Jacques-Alain Miller. 1988. 24.95 (ISBN 0-393-01897-0). Norton.
Seminary. 2nd ed. Alanson E. Russell & Joan M. Russell. 128p. (Orig.). 1987. pap. 12.95 (ISBN 0-9619115-0-6). Seminary Pubn.
Seminary: A Search. Paul Hendrickson. 320p. 1983. 14.95 (ISBN 0-671-42030-5). Summit Bks.
Seminary: A Search. Paul Hendrickson. 320p. 1987. pap. 6.95 (ISBN 0-671-63586-7). Summit Bks.
Seminary Addresses. Solomon Schechter. 1959. pap. 2.45 (ISBN 0-8381-2109-8). United Syn Bk.
Seminary Addresses & Other Papers. Solomon Schechter. LC 79-83435. (Religion in America, Ser. 1). 1969. Repr. of 1915 ed. 19.00 (ISBN 0-405-00260-2). Ayer Co Pubs.
Seminary Addresses & Other Papers. Solomon Schechter. 270p. Date not set. Repr. of 1915 ed. text ed. 62.10x (ISBN 0-576-80119-4, Pub. by Gregg Intl Pubs England). Gregg Intl.
Seminary Education & Christian-Jewish Relations. Eugene J. Fisher. 100p. 1983. 4.80 (ISBN 0-318-20615-3). Natl Cath Educ.
Seminary Education & Christian-Jewish Relations. 2nd ed. Eugene J. Fisher. 96p. 1988. pap. 4.80 (ISBN 1-55833-005-4). Natl Cath Educ.
Seminary in the City: A Study of New York Theological Seminary. Robert W. Pazmino. LC 88-17250. 146p. (Orig.). 1988. lib. bdg. 20.50 (ISBN 0-8191-7073-9); pap. text ed. 10.25 (ISBN 0-8191-7074-7). U Pr of Amer.
Seminary Libraries & University Extension. Herbert B. Adams. LC 78-63777. (Johns Hopkins University. Studies in the Social Sciences. Fifth Ser. 1887: 11). Repr. of 1887 ed. 11.50 (ISBN 0-404-61043-9). AMS Pr.
Seminary Libraries & University Extension. Herbert B. Adams. pap. 9.00 (ISBN 0-384-00328-1). Johnson Repr.
Seminary Libraries & University Extension. Herbert B. Adams. (Works of Herbert B. Adams). 33p. 1985. Repr. of 1887 ed. lib. bdg. 39.00 (ISBN 0-318-03785-8, Pub. by Am Repr Serv). Am Biog Serv.
Seminary Notes & Historical Literature. Herbert B. Adams et al. LC 78-63798. (Johns Hopkins University. Studies in the Social Sciences. Eighth Ser. 1890: 11-12). Repr. of 1890 ed. 24.50 (ISBN 0-404-61063-3). AMS Pr.
Seminary Notes on Recent Historical Literature. Herbert B. Adams et al. Repr. of 1890 ed. 12.00 (ISBN 0-384-00327-3). Johnson Repr.
Seminary Priests: A Dictionary of the Secular Clergy of England & Wales, 1558-1850, 4 vols. Godfrey Anstruther. Incl. Vol. 1. Elizabethan, 1558-1603. 1968 (ISBN 0-87921-059-1); Vol. 2. Early Stuarts, 1603-1659. 1975 (ISBN 0-85597-082-0); Vol. 3 Paperback. 660-1715. 1976 (ISBN 0-85597-116-9); Vol. 4 Paperback. 1716-1800. 1977 (ISBN 0-85597-118-5). text ed. 18.50x ea. Attic Pr.
Seminary Priests: A Dictionary of the Secular Clery of England & Wales, 1558 to 1800, Vols. 1-4. Godfrey Anstruther. Incl. Vol. 1. Elizabethan 1558-1603. 1969. text ed. 21.50x (ISBN 0-8401-0071-X); Vol. 2. Early Stuarts 1603-1659. 1975. text ed. 21.50x (ISBN 0-8401-0072-8); Vol. 3. 1660-1715. 1976. text ed. 27.50x (ISBN 0-8401-0073-6); Vol. 4. 1716-1800. 1977. text ed. 27.50x (ISBN 0-8401-0074-4). LC 76-441910. A R Allenson.
Seminole. Merwin S. Garbarino. (Indians of North America Ser.). (Illus.). 112p. (YA) (gr. 7-12). 1989. 16.95 (ISBN 1-55546-729-6). Chelsea Hse.
Seminole. Merwin S. Garbarino. (Indians of North America Ser.). (Illus.). 112p. (Orig.). (YA) (gr. 7-12). 1989. pap. 9.95 (ISBN 0-7910-0367-1). Chelsea Hse.
Seminole. Emilie U. Lepthien. LC 84-23141. (New True Bks.). (Illus.). 45p. (gr. 2-4). 1985. lib. bdg. 12.60 (ISBN 0-516-01941-4); pap. 3.95 (ISBN 0-516-41941-2). Childrens.
Seminole. Donald C. Porter. (White Indian Ser.). 1986. pap. 3.95 (ISBN 0-553-25353-0). Bantam.
Seminole & Miccosukee Tribes: A Critical Bibliography. Harry A. Kersey, Jr. 1987. pap. 7.95x (ISBN 0-253-30662-0). Ind U Pr.
Seminole History: A Pictorial History of Florida State University. Martee Wills & Joan P. Morris. Ed. by Susan A. Brady. (Famous Universities of the USA Ser.: No. 2). (Illus.). 240p. 1987. 37.95 (ISBN 0-938637-01-0). South Star Pub.
Seminole Music. Frances Densmore. LC 72-1878. (Music Ser.). (Illus.). 276p. 1972. Repr. of 1956 ed. lib. bdg. 27.50 (ISBN 0-306-70506-0). Da Capo.
Seminole Patchwork. Margaret Brandebourg. (Illus.). 96p. 1987. pap. 9.95 (ISBN 0-8069-6616-5). Sterling.
Seminole Patchwork Book. Cheryl G. Bradkin. (Illus.). 48p. 1980. pap. 8.00 (ISBN 0-932946-03-8). Burdett CA.
Seminole Seed. Robert N. Peck. LC 83-61758. 400p. 1983. 14.95 (ISBN 0-910923-03-5). Pineapple Pr.
Seminole Skies. Paul J. Lederer. (Indian Heritage Ser.: No. 3). 256p. 1983. pap. 2.95 (ISBN 0-451-12263-1, Sig). NAL.
Seminole Sourcebook. Ed. by William C. Sturtevant. LC 83-47632. (North American Indian Ser.). 856p. 1985. lib. bdg. 90.00 (ISBN 0-8240-5885-2). Garland Pub.
Seminoles. Edwin C. McReynolds. LC 57-11198. (Civilization of the American Indian Ser.: No. 47). (Illus.). 1984. pap. 10.95 (ISBN 0-8061-1255-7). U of Okla Pr.
Seminoles! The First Forty Years. Bill McGrotha. LC 87-51238. (Illus.). 256p. 1987. 20.95 (ISBN 0-9613040-1-4). Talla Dem.
Seminormal Operators. K. Clancey. (Lecture Notes in Mathematics: Vol. 742). 1979. pap. 13.00 (ISBN 0-387-09547-0). Springer-Verlag.
Semiochemicals: Their Role in Pest Control. Ed. by Donald A. Nordlund et al. 306p. 1981. 56.00 (ISBN 0-471-05803-3, Pub. by Wiley-Interscience). Wiley.
Semiochemistry - Flavors & Pheromones: Proceedings of American Chemical Society Symposium, Washington, D. C. August 1983. Ed. by Terry E. Acree & David M. Soderlund. (Illus.). x, 289p. 1985. 104.00 (ISBN 3-11-010120-3). De Gruyter.
Semiogenesis: Kultur und Evolution, Vol. 1. Ed. by Walter A. Koch. (Kuetur und Evolution Ser.). 565p. 1981. pap. 48.30 (ISBN 3-8204-5938-3). P Lang Pubs.
Semiologie & Linguistique: Reflexions Preparadigmatiques. J. J. Spa. (Faux Titre: No. 17). 80p. (Fr.). 1985. pap. text ed. 17.50x (ISBN 90-6203-547-7, Pub. by Rodopi Holland). Humanities.
Semiology. Pierre Guiraud. 1975. 18.00x (ISBN 0-7100-8005-0); pap. 7.95x (ISBN 0-7100-8011-5). Routledge Chapman & Hall.
Semiology & Parables: Exploration of the Possibilities Offered by Structuralism for Exegesis. Papers of the Vanderbilt University Conference, May 15-17, 1975. Ed. by Daniel Patte. LC 76-20686. (Pittsburgh Theological Monographs: No. 9). 1976. pap. 9.95 (ISBN 0-915138-11-5). Pickwick.
Semiology, Symbolism & Architecture: A Selected & Partially Annotated Bibliography. William Gwin & Mary M. Gwin. (Architecture Ser.: Bibliography A 1346). 1985. pap. 3.00 (ISBN 0-89028-316-8). Vance Biblios.
Semiosis: Semiotics & the History of Culture. Ed. by Merris Halle et al. (Michigan Slavic Contributions Ser.: No. 10). 1984. pap. 15.00 (ISBN 0-930042-55-7). Mich Slavic Pubns.
Semiotic & Significs: The Correspondence Between Charles S Peirce & Victoria Lady Welby. Ed. by Charles S. Hardwick. LC 77-12369. 240p. 1977. 22.50x (ISBN 0-253-35163-4). Ind U Pr.

Semiotic & Structuralist Analyses of Fiction: An Introduction & a Survey of Applications. Leonard Orr. LC 86-50685. 224p. 1986. 30.00x (ISBN 0-87875-331-1). Whitston Pub.
Semiotic Approaches to Human Relations. Jurgen Ruesch. 1972. 73.60x (ISBN 90-2792-299-3). Mouton.
Semiotic Approaches to Psychiatry. Harley C. Shands. (Approaches to Semiotics Ser: No. 2). 1970. text ed. 33.60x (ISBN 90-2790-506-1). Mouton.
Semiotic Challenge. Roland Barthes. Tr. by Richard Howard from Fr. 288p. 1988. 18.95 (ISBN 0-8090-8529-1); pap. 12.95 (ISBN 0-8090-1538-2). Hill & Wang.
Semiotic Foundations: Steps toward an Epistemology of Written Texts. Floyd Merrell. LC 81-48631. (Advances in Semiotics Ser.). (Illus.). 192p. 1983. 25.00x (ISBN 0-253-35161-8). Ind U Pr.
Semiotic Landscape-Panorama Semiotique. Ed. by Seymour Chatman et al. (Approaches to Semiotics Ser.: No. 29). (Fr.). 1979. text ed. 100.00x (ISBN 90-279-7928-6). Mouton.
Semiotic Perspectives. Sandor Hervey. 304p. 1982. text ed. 15.95x (ISBN 0-04-400026-X). Unwin Hyman.
Semiotic Phenomenology of Rhetoric: Eidetic Practice in Henry Grattan's Discourse on Tolerance. Richard L. Lanigan. (Current Continental Research Ser.: No. 203). (Illus.). 248p. (Orig.). 1984. 28.75 (ISBN 0-8191-4294-8, Pub. by Ctr Adv Res); pap. 14.00 (Pub. by Ctr Adv Res). U Pr of Amer.
Semiotic Praxis: Studies in Pertinence & in the Means of Expression & Communication. Georges Mounin. Tr. by Catherine Tihanyi. (Topics in Contemporary Semiotics Ser.). 226p. 1985. 35.00x (ISBN 0-306-41767-7, Plenum Pr). Plenum Pub.
Semiotic Principles in Semantic Theory. Neal R. Norrick. (Current Issues in Linguistic Theory: No. 20). xiii, 252p. 1981. 36.00x (ISBN 90-272-3513-9). Benjamins North Am.
Semiotic Sphere. Ed. by Thomas A. Sebeok & Jean Umiker-Sebeok. (Topics in Contemporary Semiotics Ser.). 618p. 1986. 85.00x (ISBN 0-306-41765-0, Plenum Pr). Plenum Pub.
Semiotic Theory of Language. Sebastian Shaumyan. (Advances in Semiotics Ser.). 352p. 1987. 57.50x (ISBN 0-253-30472-5). Ind U Pr.
Semiotic Theory of Texts. Floyd Merrell. (Approaches to Semiotics Ser.: No. 70). x, 234p. 1985. 63.50 (ISBN 0-89925-035-1). Mouton.
Semiotic Web. Ed. by Thomas A. Sebeok & Jean Umiker-Sebeok. (Approaches to Semiotics Ser.). 732p. 1987. lib. bdg. 160.00x (ISBN 0-89925-215-X). Mouton.
Semiotica del Dialogo. Ed. by Henk Haverkate. (Dialogos Hispanicos de Amsterdam Ser.: No. 6). 224p. (Span.). 1987. pap. text ed. 75.00 (ISBN 90-6203-510-8, Pub. by Rodopi Holland). Humanities.
Semiotics: An Introductory Anthology. Ed. by Robert E. Innis. LC 84-47700. (Advances in Semiotics: Midland Bks: No. 344). (Illus.). 352p. 1985. 27.50x (ISBN 0-253-35162-6); pap. 12.95x (ISBN 0-253-20344-9). Ind U Pr.
Semiotics & Dialectics: Ideology & the Text. Ed. by Peter V. Zima. (Linguistic & Literary Studies in Eastern Europe: Vol. 5). vi, 573p. 1981. 76.00x (ISBN 90-272-1505-7). Benjamins North Am.
Semiotics & Fieldwork. Peter K. Manning. (Qualitative Research Methods Ser.: Vol. 7). 96p. 1987. text ed. 12.50 (ISBN 0-8039-2761-4); pap. text ed. 6.00 (ISBN 0-8039-2640-5). Sage.
Semiotics & Human Sign Languages. William C. Stokoe, Jr. LC 71-173380. (Approaches to Semiotics Ser: No. 21). (Illus.). 177p. 1972. text ed. 22.40x (ISBN 90-2792-096-6). Mouton.
Semiotics & International Scholarship: Towards a Language of Theory. Ed. by Jonathan D. Evans. 1986. lib. bdg. 68.00 (ISBN 90-247-3391-X, Pub. by Martinus Nijhoff Netherlands). Kluwer Academic.
Semiotics & Interpretation. Robert Scholes. LC 81-15971. 21.00x (ISBN 0-300-02798-2); pap. 8.95 (ISBN 0-300-03093-2, Y-465). Yale U Pr.
Semiotics & Language: An Analytical Dictionary. A. J. Greimas & J. Courtes. Tr. by Larry Crist et al. LC 81-47828. (Advances in Semiotics Ser.). (Illus.). 432p. 1983. 45.00x (ISBN 0-253-35169-3). Ind U Pr.
Semiotics & Legal Theory. Bernard Jackson. pap. 14.95 (ISBN 0-317-65240-0, Pub. by Routledge UK). Routledge Chapman & Hall.
Semiotics & Legal Theory. Bernard S. Jackson. 350p. 1985. 27.50x (ISBN 0-7100-9719-0). Routledge Chapman & Hall.
Semiotics & Lighting: A Study of Six Modern French Cameramen. Sharon A. Russell. LC 81-3377. (Studies in Photography & Cinematography: No. 2). pap. 48.10 (2070215). Bks Demand UMI.
Semiotics & Linguistic Structure. R. M. Martin. LC 78-6873. 321p. 1978. 54.50 (ISBN 0-87395-381-9). State U NY Pr.
Semiotics & Literary Criticism. Cesare Segre. 1973. text ed. 14.00x (ISBN 90-2792-620-4). Mouton.
Semiotics & Pragmatics: An Evaluative Comparison of Conceptual Frameworks. Herman Parret. (Pragmatics & Beyond (P & B), Ser.: Vol. iv, No. 7). xii, 136p. (Orig.). 1983. pap. 30.00x (ISBN 90-272-2532-X). Benjamins North Am.
Semiotics & the Philosophy of Language. Umberto Eco. LC 82-49016. (Advances in Semiotics Ser.). (Illus.). 256p. 1984. 25.00x (ISBN 0-253-35168-5). Ind U Pr.
Semiotics & the Philosophy of Language. Umberto Eco. LC 82-49016. (Midland Bks: No. 398). (Illus.). 256p. 1986. pap. 10.95x (ISBN 0-253-20398-8). Ind U Pr.
Semiotics & Thematics in Hermeneutics. T. K. Seung. LC 82-4345. 256p. 1982. 30.00 (ISBN 0-231-05410-6). Columbia U Pr.
Semiotics from Peirce to Barthes: A Conceptual Introduction to the Study of Communication, Interpretation & Expression. V. Tejera. ix, 201p. 1988. 25.00 (ISBN 90-04-08597-1, Pub. by E J Brill). Heinman.
Semiotics in Poland, 1894-1969. Ed. by Jerzy Pelc. Tr. by Oligierd A. Wojtasiewicz from Pol. (Synthese Library: No. 119). 1978. lib. bdg. 55.00 (ISBN 90-277-0811-8, Pub. by Reidel Holland). Kluwer Academic.
Semiotics, Nineteen Eighty-Four: Proceedings of the Ninth Annual Meeting of the Semiotic Society of America, 11-14 October 1984, Bloomington, Indiana. Ed. by John Deely. LC 84-640162. (Illus.). 754p. (Orig.). 1985. lib. bdg. 51.25 (ISBN 0-8191-4879-2); pap. text ed. 34.50 (ISBN 0-8191-4880-6). U Pr of Amer.
Semiotics of Art: Prague School Contributions. Ed. by Ladislav Matejka & Irwin R. Titunik. 1984. pap. text ed. 10.95 (ISBN 0-262-63065-6). MIT Pr.
Semiotics of Cinema. Jurij Lotman. (Michigan Slavic Contributions Ser.: No. 5). 1976. pap. 6.00 (ISBN 0-930042-13-1). Mich Slavic Pubns.
Semiotics of Culture. Ed. by Irene P. Winner & Jean Rmiker-Sebeok. (Approaches to Semiotics: No. 53). 1979. text ed. 121.00 (ISBN 90-279-7988-X). Mouton.
Semiotics of Culture & Language Vol. 1: Language As Social Semiotic. Ed. by Robin P. Fawcett et al. LC 83-242230. (Open Linguistics Ser.). 166p. 1984. 28.75 (ISBN 0-86187-295-9, Pub. by Frances Pinter). Longwood Pub Group.
Semiotics of Culture & Language Vol. 2: Language & Other Semiotic Systems of Culture. Ed. by Robin P. Fawcett et al. LC 83-242230. (Open Linguistics Ser.). 179p. 1984. 28.75 (ISBN 0-86187-469-2, Pub. by Frances Pinter). Longwood Pub Group.
Semiotics of Deceit: Language, Drama, & Culture in Maistre Pierre Pathelin. Donald Maddox. LC 82-74491. (Illus.). 232p. 1984. 28.50 (ISBN 0-8387-5040-0). Bucknell U Pr.
Semiotics of Drama & Theatre. Ed. by Herta Schmid & Aloysius Van Kesteren. LC 84-14518. (Linguistic & Literary Studies in Eastern Europe: 10). 548p. 1985. 66.00x (ISBN 90-272-1513-8). Benjamins North Am.
Semiotics of Human Sound. Peter F. Ostwald. 1973. text ed. 47.20x (ISBN 90-2792-522-4). Mouton.
Semiotics of Poetry. Michael Riffaterre. LC 78-3245. (No. 332). 224p. 1978. 25.00x (ISBN 0-253-35165-0); pap. 10.95X (ISBN 0-253-20332-5). Ind U Pr.
Semiotics of Russian Cultural History: Essays by Lotman, Uspenskii, Ginsburg. Ed. by Alexander D. Nakhimovsky & Alice S. Nakhimovsky. LC 84-45152. 248p. 1984. 29.95x (ISBN 0-8014-1183-1); pap. 10.95x (ISBN 0-8014-9294-7). Cornell U Pr.
Semiotics of Russian Culture. Ju M. Lotman & B. A. Uspenskij. Ed. by Ann Shukman. (Michigan Slavic Contributions Ser.: No. 11). 356p. 1984. pap. 15.00 (ISBN 0-930042-56-5). Mich Slavic Pubns.
Semiotics of the Built Environment: An Introduction to Architectonic Analysis. Donald Preziosi. LC 78-20404. (Advances in Semiotics Ser.). (Illus.). 128p. 1979. 20.00x (ISBN 0-253-17638-7). Ind U Pr.
Semiotics of the Passion Narratives. Louis Marin. Tr. by Alfred M. Johnson, Jr. (Pittsburgh Theological Monographs: No. 25). 1980. 12.95 (ISBN 0-915138-23-9). Pickwick.
Semiotics of Theatre & Drama. Kier Elam. 1980. 25.00 (ISBN 0-416-72050-1, NO. 6391); pap. 9.95 (ISBN 0-416-72060-9, NO. 6392). Routledge Chapman & Hall.
Semiotics Two: Communication in Man & Beast. Donald W. Thomas. (Illus.). 248p. (Orig.). 1983. pap. text ed. 10.95 (ISBN 0-536-03133-9). Ginn Pr.
Semiotics Unfolding, 3 vols. Ed. by Tasso Borbe. LC 83-13439. (Approaches to Semiotics Ser.: No. 68). 1983. Set. 271.00x (ISBN 3-11-009779-6). Mouton.
Semiotics 1: Signs, Language & Reality. 2nd ed. Donald W. Thomas. (Illus.). 239p. (Orig.). 1980. pap. text ed. 7.95 (ISBN 0-536-03240-8); handbk., 78p. 2.95 (ISBN 0-536-03250-5). Ginn Pr.
Semiotics 1980. Ed. by Michael Herzfeld & Margot D. Lenhart. LC 81-23386. 606p. 1982. 85.00x (ISBN 0-306-40827-9, Plenum Pr). Plenum Pub.
Semiotics 1981. Ed. by John N. Deely & Margot D. Lenhart. LC 81-23386. 570p. 1983. 89.50x (ISBN 0-306-41270-5, Plenum Pr). Plenum Pub.
Semiotics 1982. Ed. by John Deely & Jonathan Evans. (Sources in Semiotics Ser.). 682p. 1987. lib. bdg. 49.50 (ISBN 0-8191-5107-6, Pub. by Semiotic Society of America). U Pr of Amer.
Semiotics 1983. Ed. by Jonathan Evans & John Deely. (Sources in Semiotics Ser.). 712p. 1987. lib. bdg. 54.25 (ISBN 0-8191-5352-4, Pub. by Semiotic Society of America). U Pr of Amer.
Semiotics, 1985. Ed. by John Deely. (Illus.). 800p. 1987. lib. bdg. 45.00 (ISBN 0-8191-5690-6). U Pr of Amer.
Semiotics, 1986. Ed. by John Deely & Jonathan Evans. LC 84-640162. (Sources in Semiotics Ser.). (Illus.). 472p. 1988. lib. bdg. 38.75 (ISBN 0-8191-6672-3, Pub. by Semiotic Society of America). U Pr of Amer.
Semiotics 3: Communication, Codes & Culture. Donald W. Thomas. (Illus.). 58p. (Orig.). 1982. pap. text ed. 3.95 (ISBN 0-536-03997-6). Ginn Pr.
Semiotika J Khudozhsestvennoe Tvorchestvo. Ed. by Collet's Holdings, Ltd. Staff. 368p. (Rus.). 1977. 39.00x (ISBN 0-317-40805-4, Pub. by Collets (UK)). State Mutual Bk.
Semiotique en Jeu: A Partir et Autour de l'Oeuvre d'A. J. Greimas. Michel Arrive & Jean-Claude Coquet. LC 87-30930. (Actes Semiotiques: Vol. 5). 334p. (Orig., Fr.). 1987. pap. 54.00x (ISBN 90-272-2264-9, Hades-Benjamins). Benjamins North Am.
Semiotique et philosophie. Georges Kalinowski. (Actes Semiotiques: No. 3). 293p. (Fr.). 1985. pap. 40.00x (ISBN 90-272-2263-0). Benjamins North Am.
Semiperipheral Development: The Politics of Southern Europe in the Twentieth Century. Giovanni Arrighi. (Explorations in the World-Economy Ser.). 320p. 1985. text ed. 29.95 (ISBN 0-8039-2473-9). Sage.
Semiprecious Stones. (Latin American Products Included in the U. S. General System of Preferences Ser.). 39p. 1978. pap. text ed. 3.00 (ISBN 0-8270-3395-8). OAS.
Semiramis. Voltaire. Ed. by Jean Jacques Olivier. 95p. 1946. 6.50 (ISBN 0-686-55759-X). French & Eur.
Semiramis see Poesies Album De Vers Anciens Avec.
Semirings, Automata & Languages. W. Kuich & A. Salomaa. (EATCS Monographs on Theoretical Computer Science: Vol. 5). (Illus.). 490p. 1985. 50.00 (ISBN 0-387-13716-5). Springer-Verlag.
Semisimple Lie Algebras. Gotto & Grosshan. (Lecture Notes: Vol. 38). 1978. 79.75 (ISBN 0-8247-6744-6). Dekker.
Semisynthetic Proteins. Robin E. Offord. LC 79-40521. (Illus.). 247p. pap. 64.30 (2030535). Bks Demand UMI.
Semites & Anti-Semites. Bernard W. Lewis. LC 85-26021. 1986. 18.95 (ISBN 0-393-02314-1). Norton.
Semites & Anti-Semites. Bernard W. Lewis. 1987. pap. 7.95 (ISBN 0-393-30420-5). Norton.
Semites in Ancient History. S. Moscati. 142p. 1959. text ed. 10.50x (ISBN 0-7083-0074-X, Pub. by U of Wales). Humanities.
Semitic & Oriental Studies: A Volume Presented to William Popper, on the Occasion of His 75th Birthday, October 29, 1949. Ed. by Walter J. Fischel. LC 51-9375. (University of California Publications in Semitic Philology Ser.: Vol. 11). pap. 119.00 (ISBN 0-317-29578-0, 2021490). Bks Demand UMI.
Semitic Influence in Hellenic Mythology. Robert Brown. LC 65-27053. (Library of Religious & Philosophical Thought). 1966. Repr. of 1898 ed. lib. bdg. 27.50x (ISBN 0-678-09952-9, Reference Bk Pubs). Kelley.
Semitic Influence in Hellenic Mythology. Robert Brown. 19.00 (ISBN 0-405-10084-1, 14709). Ayer Co Pubs.
Semitic Interference in Marcan Syntax. Elliott C. Maloney. LC 80-13016. (Society of Biblical Literature Dissertation Ser.: No. 51). 1981. pap. 15.00 (ISBN 0-89130-406-1, 06-01-51). Scholars Pr GA.
Semitic Magic: Its Origins & Development. Reginald C. Thompson. LC 73-18858. Repr. of 1908 ed. 24.50 (ISBN 0-404-11361-3). AMS Pr.
Semitic Mythology. Stephen H. Langdon. LC 63-19090. (Mythology of All Races Ser.: Vol. 5). (Illus.). Repr. of 1932 ed. 30.00x (ISBN 0-8154-0133-7). Cooper Sq.
Semitic Writing. 21.50 (ISBN 0-317-70067-7, Pub. by British Acad). Longwood Pub Group.
Semitic Writing: From Pictograph to Alphabet. G. R. Driver. (British Academy, London, Schweich Lectures on Biblical Archaeology Series, 1944). Repr. of 1948 ed. 12.00 (ISBN 0-8115-1286-X). Kraus Repr.
Semja Pravoslavnago Khristjanina. 569p. 1958. Repr. 15.00 (ISBN 0-317-30248-5). Holy Trinity.
Semocratie et Societe Internationale see Cahiers de l'Institut de Science Economique Appliquee.
Semper Fi, Mac. Henry Berry. 448p. 1987. pap. 3.95 (ISBN 0-425-09724-2). Berkley Pub.
Semper Fidelis. Johnnie Clark. 1988. pap. 4.95. Ballantine.
Semper Fidelis: The History of the United States Marine Corps. Allan R. Millett. LC 80-1059. (Macmillan Wars of the United States Ser.). (Illus.). 1980. 29.95 (ISBN 0-02-921590-0); pap. 18.95 (ISBN 0-02-921570-6). Free Pr.
Semper Fidelis: The History of the U. S. Marine Corps. Allan R. Millett. 1982. pap. 10.95x (ISBN 0-317-30521-2). Free Pr.
Sempreviva. Antonio Callado. Ed. by Erroll McDonald. Tr. by Ellen Watson from Port. LC 87-45933. (Aventura Ser.). 288p. (Orig.). pap. 10.95 (ISBN 0-394-74759-3, Vin). Random.
Semrad: The Heart of a Therapist. Ed. by Susan Rako & Harvey Mazer. LC 84-45091. 208p. 1983. 20.00 (ISBN 0-87668-684-6). Aronson.
Sen-OKU Sei-Sho. Sueji Umehara. 64p. 1961. 140.00x (ISBN 0-317-69038-8, Pub. by Han-Shan Tang Ltd). State Mutual Bk.
Senat De la Republique Romaine: Sa Composition et Ses Attributions, 3 vols. in 2. Pierre Willems. LC 75-7350. (Roman History Ser.). (Fr.). 1975. Repr. Set. 122.00x (ISBN 0-405-07071-3); 61.00x ea. Vol. 1 (ISBN 0-405-07072-1). Vol. 2 (ISBN 0-405-07073-X). Ayer Co Pubs.
Senate. Donald A. Ritchie. (Know Your Government Ser.). (Illus.). 96p. (gr. 5 up). 1988. lib. bdg. 12.95 (ISBN 1-55546-121-2). Chelsea Hse.
Senate & General: Individual Decision-Making & Roman Foreign Relations, 264-194 B. C. Arthur Eckstein. (Illus.). 530p. 1987. text ed. 39.95x (ISBN 0-520-05582-9). U of Cal Pr.
Senate & National Security: A New Mood. Joshua Muravchik. (Washington Papers: Vol. VIII, No. 80). 88p. 1980. pap. text ed. 7.95 (ISBN 0-8191-6024-5, Pub. by CSIS). U Pr of Amer.
Senate & the Versailles Mandate System. Rayford W. Logan. LC 74-14357. 112p. 1975. Repr. of 1945 ed. lib. bdg. 35.00x (ISBN 0-8371-7798-7, LOVM). Greenwood.
Senate & Treaties, Seventeen Eighty-Nine to Eighteen Seventeen. Ralston Hayden. LC 73-127295. (Law, Politics, & History Ser). 1970. Repr. of 1920 ed. lib. bdg. 32.50 (ISBN 0-306-71164-8). Da Capo.
Senate & U. S. Troops in Europe. Phil Williams. LC 84-22851. 224p. 1985. 27.50 (ISBN 0-312-71300-2). St Martin.
Senate Documents, Treaties, Conventions, International Acts, Protocols, & Agreements Between the United States of America & Other Powers, 4 vols. William M. Malloy. Repr. Set. lib. bdg. 195.00x. Scholarly.
Senate Establishment. Joseph S. Clark et al. LC 83-26395. 138p. 1984. Repr. of 1963 ed. lib. bdg. 35.00x (ISBN 0-313-24285-2, CLSE). Greenwood.
Senate Executive Journal & Related Documents see Documentary History of the First Federal Congress of the United States of America, March 4, 1789-March 3,1791.
Senate Journal, Nineteen Forty-Three to Nineteen Forty-Five. Allen Drury. LC 76-38824. (FDR & the Era of the New Deal Ser.). 1972. Repr. of 1963 ed. lib. bdg. 59.50 (ISBN 0-306-70448-X). Da Capo.
Senate Legislative Journal see Documentary History of the First Federal Congress of the United States of America, March 4, 1789-March 3,1791.
Senate Nobody Knows. Bernard Asbell. LC 80-8928. 480p. 1981. pap. text ed. 10.95x (ISBN 0-8018-2620-9). Johns Hopkins.
Senate of Imperial Rome. Richard J. Talbert. LC 83-42580. (Illus.). 576p. 1984. 63.00x (ISBN 0-691-05400-2). Princeton U Pr.
Senate of Imperial Rome. Richard J. Talbert. 608p. 1987. pap. text ed. 22.50 (ISBN 0-691-10238-4). Princeton U Pr.
Senate of Lilliput. Edward Pearce. 242p. (Orig.). 1983. pap. 8.95 (ISBN 0-571-13158-1). Faber & Faber.
Senate of the United States. Richard A. Baker. LC 87-3740. (Anvil Ser.). 272p. 1988. pap. 11.50 (ISBN 0-89874-865-8, (K)). Krieger.
Senate, One Hundredth Congress. Robert S. Smith. LC 86-62570. 200p. 1987. 29.95 (ISBN 0-940441-00-4). Madison Pub AL.
Senate Politics: Operating Within the System. Ralph K. Huitt. (Government & Politics Ser.). 160p. 1987. cancelled (ISBN 0-08-033164-5, PBI); pap. cancelled (ISBN 0-08-033163-7). Pergamon.
Senate Rubberstamp Machine. 150p. 1977. 1.00 (ISBN 0-914389-09-2). Common Cause.
Senate vs. Governor, Alabama 1971: Referents for Opposition in a One-Party Legislature. Harold W. Stanley. LC 74-23369. (Illus.). 126p. 1975. 9.75 (ISBN 0-8173-4827-1). U of Ala Pr.
Senator & Bull Moose Manager 1867-1917 see Joseph M. Dixon of Montana.
Senator Arthur H. Vandenberg: The Evolution of a Modern Republican. C. David Tompkins. 300p. 1970. 9.00 (ISBN 0-87013-145-1). Mich St U Pr.
Senator Joe McCarthy. Richard Rovere. 1973. pap. 5.95x (ISBN 0-06-131970-8, TB1970, Torch). Har-Row.
Senator John Sherman Cooper: Consummate Statesman. Clarice J. Mitchner. 35.00 (ISBN 0-405-14099-1). Ayer Co Pubs.
Senator John Slidell & the Community He Represented in Washington, 1853-1861. A. L. Diket. LC 81-43676. 278p. (Orig.). 1982. lib. bdg. 30.50 (ISBN 0-8191-2547-4); pap. text ed. 14.00 (ISBN 0-8191-2548-2). U Pr of Amer.
Senator Joseph McCarthy & the American Labor Movement. David M. Oshinsky. LC 75-23426. 216p. 1975. 24.00x (ISBN 0-8262-0188-1). U of Mo Pr.
Senator Josiah William Bailey of North Carolina: A Political Biography. John R. Moore. LC 68-24639. Repr. of 1968 ed. 51.50 (ISBN 0-8357-9118-1, 2017914). Bks Demand UMI.

Senior Auditor. Jack Rudman. (Career Examination Ser.: C-2059). (Cloth bdg. avail. on request). 1988. pap. 16.00 (ISBN 0-8373-2059-3). Natl Learning.

Senior Automotive Facilities Inspector. Jack Rudman. (Career Examination Ser.: C-2214). (Cloth bdg. avail. on request). pap. 16.00 (ISBN 0-8373-2214-6). Natl Learning.

Senior Automotive Mechanic. (Career Examination Ser.: C-3472). Date not set. pap. 14.00 (ISBN 0-8373-3472-1). Natl Learning.

Senior Automotive Serviceman. Jack Rudman. (Career Examination Ser.: C-1869). (Cloth bdg. avail. on request). pap. 14.00 (ISBN 0-8373-1869-6). Natl Learning.

Senior Bay Constable. Jack Rudman. (Career Examination Ser.: C-2525). (Cloth bdg. avail. on request). pap. 16.00 (ISBN 0-8373-2525-0). Natl Learning.

Senior Beverage Control Investigator. Jack Rudman. (Career Examination Ser.: C-2823). (Cloth bdg. avail. on request). 1988. pap. 16.00 (ISBN 0-8373-2823-3). Natl Learning.

Senior Blues. Frances L. Lantz. (Caprice Romance Ser.: No. 46). 176p. 1984. pap. 2.25 (ISBN 0-441-75889-4, Pub by Tempo). Ace Bks.

Senior Boiler Inspector. Jack Rudman. (Career Examination Ser.: C-1629). (Cloth bdg. avail. on request). pap. 16.00 (ISBN 0-8373-1629-4). Natl Learning.

Senior Bookkeeper. Jack Rudman. (Career Examination Ser.: C-1751). (Cloth bdg. avail on request). 1988. pap. 14.00 (ISBN 0-8373-1751-7). Natl Learning.

Senior Bookkeeping Machine Operator. Jack Rudman. (Career Examination Ser.: C-3097). 1988. pap. 14.00 (ISBN 0-8373-3097-1). Natl Learning.

Senior Bridge & Tunnel Maintainer. Jack Rudman. (Career Examination Ser.: C-1472). (Cloth bdg. avail. on request). pap. 14.00 (ISBN 0-8373-1472-0). Natl Learning.

Senior Budget Analyst. Jack Rudman. (Career Examination Ser.: C-2415). (Cloth bdg. avail. on request). pap. 16.00 (ISBN 0-8373-2415-7). Natl Learning.

Senior Budget Examiner. Jack Rudman. (Career Examination Ser.: C-2528). (Cloth bdg. avail. on request). pap. 16.00 (ISBN 0-8373-2528-5). Natl Learning.

Senior Budget Officer. Jack Rudman. (Career Examination Ser.: C-2683). (Cloth bdg. avail. on request). pap. 16.00 (ISBN 0-8373-2683-4). Natl Learning.

Senior Building Construction Engineer. Jack Rudman. (Career Examination Ser.: C-3171). (Cloth bdg. avail. on request). 1988. pap. 16.00 (ISBN 0-8373-3171-4). Natl Learning.

Senior Building Custodian. Jack Rudman. (Career Examination Ser.: C-997). (Cloth bdg. avail. on request). pap. 14.00 (ISBN 0-8373-0997-2). Natl Learning.

Senior Building Electrical Engineer. Jack Rudman. (Career Examination Ser.: C-1916). (Cloth bdg. avail. on request). pap. 16.00 (ISBN 0-8373-1916-1). Natl Learning.

Senior Building Guard. Jack Rudman. (Career Examination Ser.: C-2529). (Cloth bdg. avail. on request). pap. 14.00 (ISBN 0-8373-2529-3). Natl Learning.

Senior Building Inspector. Jack Rudman. (Career Examination Ser.: C-2113). (Cloth bdg. avail. on request). 1988. pap. 16.00 (ISBN 0-8373-2113-1). Natl Learning.

Senior Building Mechanical Engineer. Jack Rudman. (Career Examination Ser.: C-2572). (Cloth bdg. avail. on request). pap. 16.00 (ISBN 0-8373-2572-2). Natl Learning.

Senior Building Rehabilitation Specialist. Jack Rudman. (Career Examination Ser.: C-1933). (Cloth bdg. avail. on request). pap. 16.00 (ISBN 0-8373-1933-1). Natl Learning.

Senior Building Structural Engineer. Jack Rudman. (Career Examination Ser.: C-2569). (Cloth bdg. avail. on request). pap. 18.00 (ISBN 0-8373-2569-2). Natl Learning.

Senior Business Consultant. Jack Rudman. (Career Examination Ser.: C-1983). (Cloth bdg. avail. on request). pap. 16.00 (ISBN 0-8373-1983-8). Natl Learning.

Senior Business Machine Operator. Jack Rudman. (Career Examination Ser.: C-1896). (Cloth bdg. avail. on request). pap. 14.00 (ISBN 0-8373-1896-3). Natl Learning.

Senior Business Manager. Jack Rudman. (Career Examination Ser.: C-2359). (Cloth bdg. avail. on request). pap. 16.00 (ISBN 0-8373-2359-2). Natl Learning.

Senior Buyer. Jack Rudman. (Career Examination Ser.: C-2254). (Cloth bdg. avail. on request). 1988. pap. 14.00 (ISBN 0-8373-2254-5). Natl Learning.

Senior Campus Security Officer. Jack Rudman. (Career Examination Ser.: C-2265). (Cloth bdg. avail. on request). 1988. pap. 14.00 (ISBN 0-8373-2265-0). Natl Learning.

Senior Capital Police Officer. Jack Rudman. (Career Examination Ser.: C-2070). (Cloth bdg. avail. on request). 1988. pap. 14.00 (ISBN 0-8373-2070-4). Natl Learning.

Senior Care Directory. rev. ed. Jerry Beigel. (Illus.). 112p. 1988. pap. 2.00 (ISBN 0-941335-01-1). Senior Media.

Senior Care Directory. rev. ed. Dawn Merrill. (Illus.). 256p. 1987. pap. text ed. 2.00 (ISBN 0-941335-00-3). Senior Media.

Senior Caseworker. Jack Rudman. (Career Examination Ser.: C-2931). (Cloth bdg. avail. on request). pap. 14.00 (ISBN 0-8373-2931-0). Natl Learning.

Senior Cashier. Jack Rudman. (Career Examination Ser.: C-860). (Cloth bdg. avail. on request). 1988. pap. 14.00 (ISBN 0-8373-0860-7). Natl Learning.

Senior Chemist. Jack Rudman. (Career Examination Ser.: C-2402). (Cloth bdg. avail. on request). pap. 16.00 (ISBN 0-8373-2402-5). Natl Learning.

Senior Children's Counselor. Jack Rudman. (Career Examination Ser.: C-1601). (Cloth bdg. avail. on request). 1988. pap. 16.00 (ISBN 0-8373-1601-4). Natl Learning.

Senior Citizen Aide. Jack Rudman. (Career Examination Ser.: C-1473). (Cloth bdg. avail. on request). pap. 12.00 (ISBN 0-8373-1473-9). Natl Learning.

Senior Citizen Education Programs: Opportunities on College Campuses in the Southeast. Diane Sudak & Phyllis Kozokoff. LC 87-20789. (Illus.). 300p. 1988. 32.00 (ISBN 0-8108-2063-3). Scarecrow.

Senior Citizen Handbook: A Self-Help & Resource Guide. Marjorie Stokell & Bonnie Kennedy. LC 84-22353. 260p. 1985. 21.95 (ISBN 0-13-806522-5, Busn); pap. 9.95 (ISBN 0-13-806514-4). P-H.

Senior Citizen Law, 1984. Hamline University, Advanced Legal Education Staff. 622p. 1984. 42.40 (ISBN 0-317-42994-9). Hamline Law.

Senior Citizen Participation in the Courts. National Center for State Courts Staff. (Paul Reardon Ser.). 11p. 1981. manuscript 0.66 (PRS-024). Natl Ctr St Courts.

Senior Citizen School Volunteer Program: A Manual for Program Implementation. Cynthia Kramer & Sally Newman. 1986. 8.95 (ISBN 0-937829-01-3); prepub. 7.95. Ctr Study Aging.

Senior Citizen Sourcebook: A Complete Guide to Services, Organizations, Opportunities & Ideas for Your Retirement Years. Marjorie Stokell & Bonnie Kennedy. write for info. P-H.

Senior Citizens' Activities Specialist. Jack Rudman. (Career Examination Ser.: C-900). (Cloth bdg. avail. on request). pap. 12.00 (ISBN 0-8373-0900-X). Natl Learning.

Senior Citizens' Cartoons. 2nd ed. William Armstrong. (Armstrong Cartoon Ser.). (Illus.). 48p. (Orig.). (ps up). 1971. pap. 1.00 (ISBN 0-913452-12-2). Jesuit Bks.

Senior Citizens Club Leader. Jack Rudman. (Career Examination Ser.: C-2745). (Cloth bdg. avail. on request). 1988. pap. 12.00 (ISBN 0-8373-2745-8). Natl Learning.

Senior Citizen's Guide to Budget Travel in Europe. rev. ed. Paige Palmer. LC 82-441. 48p. 1988. pap. 3.95 (ISBN 0-87576-099-6). Pilot Bks.

Senior Citizens Guide to Budget Travel in the United States & Canada. rev. ed. Paige Palmer. LC 83-3949. 64p. 1988. pap. 3.95 (ISBN 0-87576-103-8). Pilot Bks.

Senior Citizens Handbook: Laws & Programs Affecting Senior Citizens in Missouri. 5th ed. Legal Services of Eastern Missouri, Elderly Law Unit & Older Americans Advocacy Assistance Project Staff, Missouri. LC 86-235512. 67p. Date not set. price not set, St Louis Metro Bar.

Senior Citizens Information & Referral Specialist. Jack Rudman. (Career Examination Ser.: C-2814). (Cloth bdg. avail. on request). 1988. pap. 14.00 (ISBN 0-8373-2814-4). Natl Learning.

Senior Citizens on Stage. John J. Murray. 1980. pap. 3.00 (ISBN 0-686-30558-2). Eldridge Pub.

Senior Citizens Program Coordinator. Jack Rudman. (Career Examination Ser.: C-2811). (Cloth bdg. avail. on request). 1988. pap. 14.00 (ISBN 0-8373-2811-X). Natl Learning.

Senior Citizens Program Supervisor. Jack Rudman. (Career Examination Ser.: C-2360). (Cloth bdg. avail. on request). pap. 14.00 (ISBN 0-8373-2360-6). Natl Learning.

Senior Citizens Services Coordinator. Jack Rudman. (Career Examination Ser.: C-2117). (Cloth bdg. avail. on request). 1988. pap. 14.00 (ISBN 0-8373-2117-4). Natl Learning.

Senior Citizen's Survival Manual. William Kaysing. Ed. by Donna LaBrecque. 250p. (Orig.). 1987. pap. 19.95 (ISBN 0-944136-00-1). Bellwether Venice.

Senior Citizen's Ten Minutes a Day Fitness Plan. Paige Palmer. LC 83-17331. 40p. 1986. pap. 3.50 (ISBN 0-87576-107-0). Pilot Bks.

Senior Civil Engineer. Jack Rudman. (Career Examination Ser.: C-998). (Cloth bdg. avail. on request). pap. 16.00 (ISBN 0-8373-0998-0). Natl Learning.

Senior Civil Engineer (Structures) Jack Rudman. (Career Examination Ser.: C-1917). (Cloth bdg. avail. on request). pap. 16.00 (ISBN 0-8373-1917-X). Natl Learning.

Senior Claim Examiner. Jack Rudman. (Career Examination Ser.: C-1716). (Cloth bdg. avail. on request). pap. 14.00 (ISBN 0-8373-1716-9). Natl Learning.

Senior Class. Jane C. Miner. 144p. (Orig.). (gr. 7 up). 1982. pap. 2.25 (ISBN 0-590-31931-0, Wildfire). Scholastic Inc.

Senior Clerical Examinations. 3rd ed. Harry W. Koch. 1985. 8.00 (ISBN 0-910553-02-5). Ken Bks.

Senior Clerical Series. 4th ed. Hy Hammer. LC 82-11412. 272p. 1982. pap. 8.95 (ISBN 0-668-05523-5, 5523). Arco.

Senior Clerical Series. (Career Examination Ser.: C-3473). Date not set. pap. 14.00 (ISBN 0-8373-3473-X). Natl Learning.

Senior Clerk. Jack Rudman. (Career Examination Ser.: C-707). (Cloth bdg. avail. on request). pap. 14.00 (ISBN 0-8373-0707-4). Natl Learning.

Senior Clerk-Stenographer. Jack Rudman. (Career Examination Ser.: C-2633). (Cloth bdg. avail. on request). pap. 14.00 (ISBN 0-8373-2633-8). Natl Learning.

Senior Clerk (Surrogate) Jack Rudman. (Career Examination Ser.: C-2128). (Cloth bdg. avail. on request). 1988. pap. 14.00 (ISBN 0-8373-2128-X). Natl Learning.

Senior Clerk-Typist. Jack Rudman. (Career Examination Ser.: C-1936). (Cloth bdg. avail. on request). pap. 14.00 (ISBN 0-8373-1936-6). Natl Learning.

Senior Clinical Psychologist. Jack Rudman. (Career Examination Ser.: C-1906). (Cloth bdg. avail. on request). pap. 18.00 (ISBN 0-8373-1906-4). Natl Learning.

Senior Commercial Loan Officer Survey. 61p. 1979. 35.00 (ISBN 0-317-32417-9, 168300); members 20.00 (ISBN 0-317-32418-7). Am Bankers.

Senior Commissary Clerk. Jack Rudman. (Career Examination Ser.: C-2050). (Cloth bdg. avail. on request). pap. 14.00 (ISBN 0-8373-2050-X). Natl Learning.

Senior Communications Technician. Jack Rudman. (Career Examination Ser.: C-2412). (Cloth bdg. avail. on request). pap. 16.00 (ISBN 0-8373-2412-2). Natl Learning.

Senior Community Liasion Worker. Jack Rudman. (Career Examination Ser.: C-2995). 1988. pap. 14.00 (ISBN 0-8373-2995-7). Natl Learning.

Senior Community Narcotic Education Representative. Jack Rudman. (Career Examination Ser.: C-1942). (Cloth bdg. avail. on request). pap. 16.00 (ISBN 0-8373-1942-0). Natl Learning.

Senior Community Service Worker. Jack Rudman. (Career Examination Ser.: C-2676). (Cloth bdg. avail. on request). pap. 14.00 (ISBN 0-8373-2676-1). Natl Learning.

Senior Compensation Claims Auditor. Jack Rudman. (Career Examination Ser.: C-2127). (Cloth bdg. avail. on request). 1988. pap. 14.00 (ISBN 0-8373-2127-1). Natl Learning.

Senior Compensation Claims Clerk. Jack Rudman. (Career Examination Ser.: C-867). (Cloth bdg. avail. on request). pap. 14.00 (ISBN 0-8373-0867-4). Natl Learning.

Senior Compensation Claims Examiner. Jack Rudman. (Career Examination Ser.: C-1702). (Cloth bdg. avail. on request). 14.00 (ISBN 0-8373-1702-9). Natl Learning.

Senior Compensation Claims Investigator. Jack Rudman. (Career Examination Ser.: C-2613). 1988. pap. 14.00 (ISBN 0-8373-2613-3). Natl Learning.

Senior Compensation Investigator. Jack Rudman. (Career Examination Ser.: C-2609). (Cloth bdg. avail. on request). 1988. pap. 14.00 (ISBN 0-8373-2609-5). Natl Learning.

Senior Compliance Investigator. Jack Rudman. (Career Examination Ser.: C-2422). (Cloth bdg. avail. on request). pap. 14.00 (ISBN 0-8373-2422-X). Natl Learning.

Senior Computer Operator. Jack Rudman. (Career Examination Ser.: C-708). (Cloth bdg. avail. on request). pap. 14.00 (ISBN 0-8373-0708-2). Natl Learning.

Senior Computer Programmer. Jack Rudman. (Career Examination Ser.: C-1630). (Cloth bdg. avail. on request). pap. 16.00 (ISBN 0-8373-1630-8). Natl Learning.

Senior Computer Programmer-Analyst. Jack Rudman. (Career Examination Ser.: C-1030). (Cloth bdg. avail. on request). 1988. pap. 14.00 (ISBN 0-8373-1030-X). Natl Learning.

Senior Computer Systems Analyst. Jack Rudman. (Career Examination Ser.: C-999). (Cloth bdg. avail. on request). pap. 16.00 (ISBN 0-8373-0999-9). Natl Learning.

Senior Construction Inspector. Jack Rudman. (Career Examination Ser.: C-709). (Cloth bdg. avail. on request). pap. 16.00 (ISBN 0-8373-0709-0). Natl Learning.

Senior Consumer Affairs Inspector. Jack Rudman. (Career Examination Ser.: C-1656). (Cloth bdg. avail. on request). pap. 14.00 (ISBN 0-8373-1656-1). Natl Learning.

Senior Consumer Affairs Investigator. Jack Rudman. (Career Examination Ser.: C-2376). (Cloth bdg. avail. on request). pap. 14.00 (ISBN 0-8373-2376-2). Natl Learning.

Senior Consumer Frauds Representative. Jack Rudman. (Career Examination Ser.: C-877). (Cloth bdg. avail. on request). pap. 14.00 (ISBN 0-8373-0877-1). Natl Learning.

Senior Correction Counselor. Jack Rudman. (Career Examination Ser.: C-3263). (Cloth bdg. avail. on request). 1988. pap. 16.00 (ISBN 0-8373-3263-X). Natl Learning.

Senior Court Clerk. Jack Rudman. (Career Examination Ser.: C-2704). (Cloth bdg. avail. on request). 1988. pap. 16.00 (ISBN 0-8373-2704-0). Natl Learning.

Senior Court Officer. Jack Rudman. (Career Examination Ser.: C-710). (Cloth bdg. avail. on request). pap. 14.00 (ISBN 0-8373-0710-4). Natl Learning.

Senior Custodial Assistant (Men) Jack Rudman. (Career Examination Ser.: C-1001a). (Cloth bdg. avail. on request). pap. 14.00 (ISBN 0-8373-1001-6). Natl Learning.

Senior Custodial Assistant (Women) Jack Rudman. (Career Examination Ser.: C-1001b). (Cloth bdg. avail. on request). 14.00. Natl Learning.

Senior Custodial Foreman. Jack Rudman. (Career Examination Ser.: C-2271). (Cloth bdg. avail. on request). 1988. pap. 14.00 (ISBN 0-8373-2271-5). Natl Learning.

Senior Data Entry Machine Operator. Jack Rudman. (Career Examination Ser.: C-3063). 1988. pap. 14.00 (ISBN 0-8373-3063-7). Natl Learning.

Senior Data Processing Control Clerk. Jack Rudman. (Career Examination Ser.: C-2484). (Cloth bdg. avail. on request). pap. 14.00 (ISBN 0-8373-2484-X). Natl Learning.

Senior Data Processing Equipment Operator. Jack Rudman. (Career Examination Ser.: C-2302). (Cloth bdg. avail. on request). 1988. pap. 14.00 (ISBN 0-8373-2302-9). Natl Learning.

Senior Demolition Inspector. Jack Rudman. (Career Examination Ser.: C-1475). (Cloth bdg. avail. on request). pap. 16.00 (ISBN 0-8373-1475-5). Natl Learning.

Senior Dental Hygienist. Jack Rudman. (Career Examination Ser.: C-2855). (Cloth bdg. avail. on request). 1988. pap. 18.00 (ISBN 0-8373-2855-1). Natl Learning.

Senior Dentist. Jack Rudman. (Career Examination Ser.: C-711). (Cloth bdg. avail. on request). pap. 29.95 (ISBN 0-8373-0711-2). Natl Learning.

Senior Deputy Sheriff. Jack Rudman. (Career Examination Ser.: C-1665). (Cloth bdg. avail. on request). pap. 16.00 (ISBN 0-8373-1665-0). Natl Learning.

Senior Detective Investigator. Jack Rudman. (Career Examination Ser.: C-2038). (Cloth bdg. avail. on request). pap. 16.00 (ISBN 0-8373-2038-0). Natl Learning.

Senior Dietitian. Jack Rudman. (Career Examination Ser.: C-1985). (Cloth bdg. avail. on request). pap. 14.00 (ISBN 0-8373-1985-4). Natl Learning.

Senior Dog Warden. Jack Rudman. (Career Examination Ser.: C-2646). (Cloth bdg. avail. on request). pap. 14.00 (ISBN 0-8373-2646-X). Natl Learning.

Senior Drafting Technician. Jack Rudman. (Career Examination Ser.: C-2679). (Cloth bdg. avail. on request). pap. 14.00 (ISBN 0-8373-2679-6). Natl Learning.

Senior Draftsman. Jack Rudman. (Career Examination Ser.: C-1575). (Cloth bdg. avail. on request). pap. 14.00 (ISBN 0-8373-1575-1). Natl Learning.

Senior Dreams Can Come True. Jane C. Miner. 176p. (Orig.). (gr. 7 up). 1985. pap. 2.25 (ISBN 0-590-33180-9, Wildfire). Scholastic Inc.

Senior Drug Abuse Educator. Jack Rudman. (Career Examination Ser.: C-2520). (Cloth bdg. avail. on request). pap. 16.00 (ISBN 0-8373-2520-X). Natl Learning.

Senior Drug Abuse Rehabilitation Counselor. Jack Rudman. (Career Examination Ser.: C-2928). (Cloth bdg. avail. on request). pap. 16.00 (ISBN 0-8373-2928-0). Natl Learning.

Senior Drug & Alcohol Counselor. Jack Rudman. (Career Examination Ser.: C-2742). (Cloth bdg. avail. on request). 1988. pap. 16.00 (ISBN 0-8373-2742-3). Natl Learning.

Senior Duplicating Machine Operator. Jack Rudman. (Career Examination Ser.: C-1899). (Cloth bdg. avail. on request). pap. 14.00 (ISBN 0-8373-1899-8). Natl Learning.

Senior Economist. Jack Rudman. (Career Examination Ser.: C-3252). (Cloth bdg. avail. on request). 1988. pap. 16.00 (ISBN 0-8373-3252-4). Natl Learning.

Senior Editorial Clerk. Jack Rudman. (Career Examination Ser.: C-2565). (Cloth bdg. avail. on request). pap. 14.00 (ISBN 0-8373-2565-X). Natl Learning.

Senior Educational Personnel: New Functions & Training, Vol. II: From Theory to Practice: Policy & Training Papers. (Educational Studies & Documents: No. 55). 66p. (Orig.). 1987. pap. 5.50 (ISBN 92-3-102425-6, U1625, UNESCO). UNIPUB.

Senior Electrical Engineer. Jack Rudman. (Career Examination Ser.: C-1631). (Cloth bdg. avail. on request). pap. 16.00 (ISBN 0-8373-1631-6). Natl Learning.

Senior Electrical Inspector. Jack Rudman. (Career Examination Ser.: C-712). (Cloth bdg. avail. on request). pap. 16.00 (ISBN 0-8373-0712-0). Natl Learning.

Senior Electronic Computer Operator. Jack Rudman. (Career Examination Ser.: C-1002). (Cloth bdg. avail. on request). pap. 14.00 (ISBN 0-8373-1002-4). Natl Learning.

Senior Medical Social Worker. Jack Rudman. (Career Examination Ser.: C-2629). (Cloth bdg. avail. on request). pap. 14.00 (ISBN 0-8373-2629-X). Natl Learning.

Senior Medical Stenographer. Jack Rudman. (Career Examination Ser.: C-2940). (Cloth bdg. avail. on request). pap. 14.00 (ISBN 0-8373-2940-X). Natl Learning.

Senior Menagerie Keeper. Jack Rudman. (Career Examination Ser.: C-1971). (Cloth bdg. avail. on request). pap. 14.00 (ISBN 0-8373-1971-4). Natl Learning.

Senior Mental Health Worker. Jack Rudman. (Career Examination Ser.: C-1925). (Cloth bdg. avail. on request). 14.00 (ISBN 0-8373-1925-0). Natl Learning.

Senior Meteorologist. Jack Rudman. (Career Examination Ser.: C-2201). (Cloth bdg. avail. on request). pap. 16.00 (ISBN 0-8373-2201-4). Natl Learning.

Senior Methods Analyst. Jack Rudman. (Career Examination Ser.: C-1014). (Cloth bdg. avail. on request). pap. 16.00 (ISBN 0-8373-1014-8). Natl Learning.

Senior Microbiologist. Jack Rudman. (Career Examination Ser.: C-1945). (Cloth bdg. avail. on request). pap. 16.00 (ISBN 0-8373-1945-5). Natl Learning.

Senior Micrographics Operator. Jack Rudman. (Career Examination Ser.: C-2760). (Cloth bdg. avail. on request). 1988. pap. 14.00 (ISBN 0-8373-2760-1). Natl Learning.

Senior Micrographics Technician. Jack Rudman. (Career Examination Ser.: C-2762). (Cloth bdg. avail. on request). 1980. pap. 12.00 (ISBN 0-8373-2762-8). Natl Learning.

Senior Minister. Lyle Shaller. 192p. 1988. pap. 10.95 (ISBN 0-687-37180-5). Abingdon.

Senior Mortuary Caretaker. Jack Rudman. (Career Examination Ser.: C-721). (Cloth bdg. avail. on request). pap. 14.00 (ISBN 0-8373-0721-X). Natl Learning.

Senior Motor Vehicle License Clerk. Jack Rudman. (Career Examination Ser.: C-2611). (Cloth bdg. avail. on request). pap. 14.00 (ISBN 0-8373-2611-7). Natl Learning.

Senior Multiple Residence Inspector. Jack Rudman. (Career Examination Ser.: C-2843). (Cloth bdg. avail. on request). 1988. pap. 16.00 (ISBN 0-8373-2843-8). Natl Learning.

Senior Museum Curator. Jack Rudman. (Career Examination Ser.: C-2374). (Cloth bdg. avail. on request). pap. 16.00 (ISBN 0-8373-2374-6). Natl Learning.

Senior Museum Instructor. Jack Rudman. (Career Examination Ser.: C-1016). (Cloth bdg. avail. on request). pap. 16.00 (ISBN 0-8373-1016-4). Natl Learning.

Senior Narcotics Investigator. Jack Rudman. (Career Examination Ser.: C-2531). (Cloth bdg. avail. on request). pap. 16.00 (ISBN 0-8373-2531-5). Natl Learning.

Senior Neighborhood Aide. Jack Rudman. (Career Examination Ser.: C-2911). (Cloth bdg. avail. on request). pap. 14.00 (ISBN 0-8373-2911-6). Natl Learning.

Senior Nurse. 1986. write for info. Wiley.

Senior Nutritionist. Jack Rudman. (Career Examination Ser.: C-1419). (Cloth bdg. avail. on request). 1988. pap. 14.00 (ISBN 0-8373-1419-4). Natl Learning.

Senior Occupational Analyst. Jack Rudman. (Career Examination Ser.: C-2549). (Cloth bdg. avail. on request). pap. 16.00 (ISBN 0-8373-2549-8). Natl Learning.

Senior Occupational Therapist. Jack Rudman. (Career Examination Ser.: C-2174). (Cloth bdg. avail. on request). pap. 16.00 (ISBN 0-8373-2174-3). Natl Learning.

Senior Office Appliance Operator. Jack Rudman. (Career Examination Ser.: C-1677). (Cloth bdg. avail. on request). pap. 14.00 (ISBN 0-8373-1677-4). Natl Learning.

Senior Office Assistant. Jack Rudman. (Career Examination Ser.: C-2594). (Cloth bdg. avail. on request). pap. 14.00 (ISBN 0-8373-2594-3). Natl Learning.

Senior Office Machine Operator. Jack Rudman. (Career Examination Ser.: C-1480). (Cloth bdg. avail. on request). pap. 14.00 (ISBN 0-8373-1480-1). Natl Learning.

Senior Office Manager. Jack Rudman. (Career Examination Ser.: C-2399). (Cloth bdg. avail. on request). pap. 16.00 (ISBN 0-8373-2399-1). Natl Learning.

Senior Office Stenographer. (Career Examination Ser.: C-3376). Date not set. pap. 14.00 (ISBN 0-8373-3376-8). Natl Learning.

Senior Office Worker. Jack Rudman. (Career Examination Ser.: C-2519). (Cloth bdg. avail. on request). pap. 14.00 (ISBN 0-8373-2519-6). Natl Learning.

Senior Offset Printing Machine Operator. Jack Rudman. (Career Examination Ser.: C-3334). Date not set. pap. 14.00 (ISBN 0-8373-3334-2). Natl Learning.

Senior Olympics, Preventive Medicine, & Findings Pertaining to Health & Longevity. C. Antonio Provost & Worth Blaney. 1981. 6.00x (ISBN 0-686-32025-5). Provost.

Senior Operations Review Specialist. (Career Examination Ser.: C-3261). Date not set. pap. 16.00 (ISBN 0-8373-3261-3). Natl Learning.

Senior Park Attendant. Jack Rudman. (Career Examination Ser.: C-1542). (Cloth bdg. avail. on request). pap. 14.00 (ISBN 0-8373-1542-5). Natl Learning.

Senior Park Engineer. Jack Rudman. (Career Examination Ser.: C-3192). (Cloth bdg. avail. on request). 1988. pap. 16.00 (ISBN 0-8373-3192-7). Natl Learning.

Senior Park Foreman. Jack Rudman. (Career Examination Ser.: C-1562). (Cloth bdg. avail. on request). pap. 14.00 (ISBN 0-8373-1562-X). Natl Learning.

Senior Park Supervisor. Jack Rudman. (Career Examination Ser.: C-2356). (Cloth bdg. avail. on request). pap. 14.00 (ISBN 0-8373-2356-8). Natl Learning.

Senior Parking Enforcement Agent. Jack Rudman. (Career Examination Ser.: C-793). (Cloth bdg. avail. on request). pap. 14.00 (ISBN 0-8373-0793-7). Natl Learning.

Senior Parole Officer. Jack Rudman. (Career Examination Ser.: C-2466). (Cloth bdg. avail. on request). pap. 14.00 (ISBN 0-8373-2466-1). Natl Learning.

Senior Payroll Audit Clerk. Jack Rudman. (Career Examination Ser.: C-2085). (Cloth bdg. avail. on request). 1988. pap. 14.00 (ISBN 0-8373-2085-2). Natl Learning.

Senior Personnel Administrator. Jack Rudman. (Career Examination Ser.: C-2410). (Cloth bdg. avail. on request). pap. 16.00 (ISBN 0-8373-2410-6). Natl Learning.

Senior Personnel Analyst. Jack Rudman. (Career Examination Ser.: C-2345). (Cloth bdg. avail. on request). pap. 16.00 (ISBN 0-8373-2345-2). Natl Learning.

Senior Personnel Clerk. Jack Rudman. (Career Examination Ser.: C-2867). (Cloth bdg. avail. on request). pap. 14.00 (ISBN 0-8373-2867-5). Natl Learning.

Senior Personnel Examiner. Jack Rudman. (Career Examination Ser.: C-1017). (Cloth bdg. avail. on request). pap. 10.00 (ISBN 0-8373-1017-2). Natl Learning.

Senior Pesticide Control Inspector. Jack Rudman. (Career Examination Ser.: C-2562). (Cloth bdg. avail. on request). pap. 14.00 (ISBN 0-8373-2562-5). Natl Learning.

Senior Pharmacist. Jack Rudman. (Career Examination Ser.: C-722). (Cloth bdg. avail. on request). pap. 18.00 (ISBN 0-8373-0722-8). Natl Learning.

Senior Pharmacy Inspector. Jack Rudman. (Career Examination Ser.: C-2532). (Cloth bdg. avail. on request). pap. 20.00 (ISBN 0-8373-2532-3). Natl Learning.

Senior Photographic Machine Operator. Jack Rudman. (Career Examination Ser.: C-2882). (Cloth bdg. avail. on request). pap. 14.00 (ISBN 0-8373-2882-9). Natl Learning.

Senior Physical Therapist. Jack Rudman. (Career Examination Ser.: C-1018). (Cloth bdg. avail. on request). pap. 16.00 (ISBN 0-8373-1018-0). Natl Learning.

Senior Plan Examiner. Jack Rudman. (Career Examination Ser.: C-1481). (Cloth bdg. avail. on request). pap. 16.00 (ISBN 0-8373-1481-X). Natl Learning.

Senior Planner. Jack Rudman. (Career Examination Ser.: C-1019). (Cloth bdg. avail. on request). pap. 14.00 (ISBN 0-8373-1019-9). Natl Learning.

Senior Plumbing Inspector. Jack Rudman. (Career Examination Ser.: C-1740). (Cloth bdg. avail. on request). 16.00 (ISBN 0-8373-1740-1). Natl Learning.

Senior Police Administrative Aide. Jack Rudman. (Career Examination Ser.: C-1020). (Cloth bdg. avail. on request). pap. 14.00 (ISBN 0-8373-1020-2). Natl Learning.

Senior Probation Officer. Jack Rudman. (Career Examination Ser.: C-1594). (Cloth bdg. avail. on request). pap. 14.00 (ISBN 0-8373-1594-8). Natl Learning.

Senior Professional Conduct Investigator. Jack Rudman. (Career Examination Ser.: C-2298). (Cloth bdg. avail. on request). 1988. pap. 14.00 (ISBN 0-8373-2298-7). Natl Learning.

Senior Program Evaluation Specialist. Jack Rudman. (Career Examination Ser.: C-2700). (Cloth bdg. avail. on request). 1988. pap. 16.00 (ISBN 0-8373-2700-8). Natl Learning.

Senior Program Examiner. Jack Rudman. (Career Examination Ser.: C-2755). (Cloth bdg. avail. on request). 1988. pap. 16.00 (ISBN 0-8373-2755-5). Natl Learning.

Senior Program Research Analyst. Jack Rudman. (Career Examination Ser.: C-2219). (Cloth bdg. avail. on request). 1988. pap. 16.00 (ISBN 0-8373-2219-7). Natl Learning.

Senior Program Specialist. Jack Rudman. (Career Examination Ser.: C-2862). (Cloth bdg. avail. on request). 1988. pap. 16.00 (ISBN 0-8373-2862-4). Natl Learning.

Senior Program Specialist (Correction) Jack Rudman. (Career Examination Ser.: C-1998). (Cloth bdg. avail. on request). pap. 16.00 (ISBN 0-8373-1998-6). Natl Learning.

Senior Programmer. Jack Rudman. (Career Examination Ser.: C-2580). (Cloth bdg. avail. on request). pap. 16.00 (ISBN 0-8373-2580-3). Natl Learning.

Senior Project Coordinator. Jack Rudman. (Career Examination Ser.: C-1482). (Cloth bdg. avail. on request). pap. 16.00 (ISBN 0-8373-1482-8). Natl Learning.

Senior Project Development Coordinator. Jack Rudman. (Career Examination Ser.: C-2898). (Cloth bdg. avail. on request). pap. 16.00 (ISBN 0-8373-2898-5). Natl Learning.

Senior Project Services Specialist. Jack Rudman. (Career Examination Ser.: C-1662). (Cloth bdg. avail. on request). pap. 16.00 (ISBN 0-8373-1662-6). Natl Learning.

Senior Prom. Patricia Aks. 176p. (Orig.). (gr. 7 up). 1985. pap. 2.25 (ISBN 0-590-33553-7, Wildfire). Scholastic Inc.

Senior Psychiatric Social Worker. Jack Rudman. (Career Examination Ser.: C-2487). (Cloth bdg. avail. on request). pap. 16.00 (ISBN 0-8373-2487-4). Natl Learning.

Senior Psychologist. Jack Rudman. (Career Examination Ser.: C-2173). (Cloth bdg. avail. on request). pap. 18.00 (ISBN 0-8373-2173-5). Natl Learning.

Senior Public Health Adviser. Jack Rudman. (Career Examination Ser.: C-3175). (Cloth bdg. avail. on request). 1988. pap. 14.00 (ISBN 0-8373-3175-7). Natl Learning.

Senior Public Health Educator. (Career Examination Ser.: C-3475). Date not set. pap. 16.00 (ISBN 0-8373-3475-6). Natl Learning.

Senior Public Health Engineer. (Career Examination Ser.: C-3346). Date not set. pap. 16.00 (ISBN 0-8373-3346-6). Natl Learning.

Senior Public Health Nutritionist. Jack Rudman. (Career Examination Ser.: C-1592). (Cloth bdg. avail. on request). pap. 14.00 (ISBN 0-8373-1592-1). Natl Learning.

Senior Public Health Representative. Jack Rudman. (Career Examination Ser.: C-2385). (Cloth bdg. avail. on request). pap. 14.00 (ISBN 0-8373-2385-1). Natl Learning.

Senior Public Health Sanitarian. Jack Rudman. (Career Examination Ser.: C-2002). (Cloth bdg. avail. on request). pap. 14.00 (ISBN 0-8373-2002-X). Natl Learning.

Senior Public Information Assistant. Jack Rudman. (Career Examination Ser.: C-2957). (Cloth bdg. avail. on reques). pap. 14.00 (ISBN 0-8373-2957-4). Natl Learning.

Senior Pump Operator. Jack Rudman. (Career Examination Ser.: C-2951). (Cloth bdg. avail. on request). pap. 16.00 (ISBN 0-8373-2951-5). Natl Learning.

Senior Purchase Inspector. Jack Rudman. (Career Examination Ser.: C-1483). (Cloth bdg. avail. on request). pap. 14.00 (ISBN 0-8373-1483-6). Natl Learning.

Senior Quantitative Analyst. Jack Rudman. (Career Examination Ser.: C-1718). (Cloth bdg. avail. on request). pap. 16.00 (ISBN 0-8373-1718-5). Natl Learning.

Senior Radio Operator. Jack Rudman. (Career Examination Ser.: C-2551). (Cloth bdg. avail. on request). pap. 14.00 (ISBN 0-8373-2551-X). Natl Learning.

Senior Radiologic Technologist. Jack Rudman. (Career Examination Ser.: C-1545). (Cloth bdg. avail. on request). pap. 16.00 (ISBN 0-8373-1545-X). Natl Learning.

Senior Real Estate Agent. Jack Rudman. (Career Examination Ser.: C-1941). (Cloth bdg. avail. on request). pap. 14.00 (ISBN 0-8373-1941-2). Natl Learning.

Senior Real Estate Appraiser. Jack Rudman. (Career Examination Ser.: C-569). (Cloth bdg. avail. on request). pap. 14.00 (ISBN 0-8373-0569-1). Natl Learning.

Senior Real Estate Manager. Jack Rudman. (Career Examination Ser.: C-1021). (Cloth bdg. avail. on request). pap. 14.00 (ISBN 0-8373-1021-0). Natl Learning.

Senior Real Property Recorder. Jack Rudman. (Career Examination Ser.: C-3103). 1988. pap. 14.00 (ISBN 0-8373-3103-X). Natl Learning.

Senior Records Center Assistant. Jack Rudman. (Career Examination Ser.: C-1919). (Cloth bdg. avail. on request). pap. 14.00 (ISBN 0-8373-1919-6). Natl Learning.

Senior Recreation Leader. Jack Rudman. (Career Examination Ser.: C-1938). (Cloth bdg. avail. on request). pap. 14.00 (ISBN 0-8373-1938-2). Natl Learning.

Senior Recreation Therapist. Jack Rudman. (Career Examination Ser.: C-2974). 1988. pap. 16.00 (ISBN 0-8373-2974-4). Natl Learning.

Senior Rehabilitation Counselor. Jack Rudman. (Career Examination Ser.: C-1952). (Cloth bdg. avail. on request). pap. 14.00 (ISBN 0-8373-1952-8). Natl Learning.

Senior Rent Examiner. Jack Rudman. (Career Examination Ser.: C-1022). (Cloth bdg. avail. on request). pap. 14.00 (ISBN 0-8373-1022-9). Natl Learning.

Senior Rent Inspector. Jack Rudman. (Career Examination Ser.: C-2721). (Cloth bdg. avail. on request). 1980. pap. 14.00 (ISBN 0-8373-2721-0). Natl Learning.

Senior Rent Research Associate. Jack Rudman. (Career Examination Ser.: C-1023). (Cloth bdg. avail. on request). pap. 16.00 (ISBN 0-8373-1023-7). Natl Learning.

Senior Research Analyst. Jack Rudman. (Career Examination Ser.: C-1543). (Cloth bdg. avail. on request). pap. 16.00 (ISBN 0-8373-1543-3). Natl Learning.

Senior Research Assistant. Jack Rudman. (Career Examination Ser.: C-2717). (Cloth bdg. avail. on request). 1988. pap. 16.00 (ISBN 0-8373-2717-2). Natl Learning.

Senior Right-of-Way Aide. Jack Rudman. (Career Examination Ser.: C-2736). (Cloth bdg. avail. on request). 1988. pap. 14.00 (ISBN 0-8373-2736-9). Natl Learning.

Senior Safety & Health Engineer. Jack Rudman. (Career Examination Ser.: C-3204). 1988. pap. 16.00 (ISBN 0-8373-3204-4). Natl Learning.

Senior Safety Coordinator. Jack Rudman. (Career Examination Ser.: C-2668). (Cloth bdg. avail. on request). pap. 16.00 (ISBN 0-8373-2668-0). Natl Learning.

Senior Sanitarian. Jack Rudman. (Career Examination Ser.: C-2430). (Cloth bdg. avail. on request). pap. 14.00 (ISBN 0-8373-2430-0). Natl Learning.

Senior Sanitary Engineer. Jack Rudman. (Career Examination Ser.: C-2446). (Cloth bdg. avail. on request). pap. 16.00 (ISBN 0-8373-2446-7). Natl Learning.

Senior Secretarial Duties & Office Organisation. 3rd ed. Evelyn Austin. 432p. (Orig.). 1983. pap. text ed. 24.95x (ISBN 0-7121-1983-3). Trans-Atl Phila.

Senior Security Hospital Treatment Assistant. Jack Rudman. (Career Examination Ser.: C-1617). 1988. pap. 16.00 (ISBN 0-8373-1617-0). Natl Learning.

Senior Security Officer. Jack Rudman. (Career Examination Ser.: C-2449). (Cloth bdg. avail. on request). pap. 14.00 (ISBN 0-8373-2449-1). Natl Learning.

Senior Settlers: Social Integration in Retirement Communities. Ed. by Nancy J. Osgood. LC 82-13352. 304p. 1982. 36.95 (ISBN 0-275-90873-9, C0873). Praeger.

Senior Sewage Treatment Plant Operator. Jack Rudman. (Career Examination Ser.: C-1556). (Cloth bdg. avail. on request). pap. 14.00 (ISBN 0-8373-1556-5). Natl Learning.

Senior Sewage Treatment Worker. Jack Rudman. (Career Examination Ser.: C-791). (Cloth bdg. avail. on request). pap. 14.00 (ISBN 0-8373-0791-0). Natl Learning.

Senior Shape-Up: An Exercise Guide for the Very Active to the Physically Restricted. Carley McBride & Kate Lefler. LC 86-20141. (Illus.). 130p. (Orig.). 1986. pap. 9.95 (ISBN 0-933703-12-0). Loiry Pubs Hse.

Senior Shorthand Reporter. Jack Rudman. (Career Examination Ser.: C-724). (Cloth bdg. avail. on request). pap. 14.00 (ISBN 0-8373-0724-4). Natl Learning.

Senior Social Case Worker. Jack Rudman. (Career Examination Ser.: C-1555). (Cloth bdg. avail. on request). pap. 14.00 (ISBN 0-8373-1555-7). Natl Learning.

Senior Social Services Employment Specialist. Jack Rudman. (Career Examination Ser.: C-2817). (Cloth bdg. avail. on request). 1988. pap. 16.00 (ISBN 0-8373-2817-9). Natl Learning.

Senior Social Services Management Specialist. Jack Rudman. (Career Examination Ser.: C-2579). (Cloth bdg. avail. on request). pap. 16.00 (ISBN 0-8373-2579-X). Natl Learning.

Senior Social Services Medical Assistance Specialist. Jack Rudman. (Career Examination Ser.: C-2432). (Cloth bdg. avail. on request). pap. 16.00 (ISBN 0-8373-2432-7). Natl Learning.

Senior Social Services Program Specialist. Jack Rudman. (Career Examination Ser.: C-2236). (Cloth bdg. avail. on request). pap. 16.00 (ISBN 0-8373-2236-7). Natl Learning.

Senior Social Welfare Examiner. Jack Rudman. (Career Examination Ser.: C-2320). (Cloth bdg. avail. on request). pap. 14.00 (ISBN 0-8373-2320-7). Natl Learning.

Senior Social Welfare Examiner (Spanish Speaking) Jack Rudman. (Career Examination Ser.: C-2321). (Cloth bdg. avail. on request). pap. 16.00 (ISBN 0-8373-2321-5). Natl Learning.

Senior Social Worker. Jack Rudman. (Career Examination Ser.: C-2488). (Cloth bdg. avail. on request). pap. 14.00 (ISBN 0-8373-2488-2). Natl Learning.

Senior Special Investigator. Jack Rudman. (Career Examination Ser.: C-1589). (Cloth bdg. avail. on request). pap. 16.00 (ISBN 0-8373-1589-1). Natl Learning.

Senior Special Officer. Jack Rudman. (Career Examination Ser.: C-725). (Cloth bdg. avail. on request). pap. 14.00 (ISBN 0-8373-0725-2). Natl Learning.

Senior Speech & Hearing Therapist. Jack Rudman. (Career Examination Ser.: C-2273). (Cloth bdg. avail. on request). 1988. pap. 16.00 (ISBN 0-8373-2273-1). Natl Learning.

Sense & Sensibility. Jane Austen. 352p. (YA) (gr. 9-12). 1983. pap. 2.95 (ISBN 0-553-21334-2, Bantam Classics). Bantam.

Sense & Sensibility see Oxford Illustrated Jane Austen.

Sense & Sensibility in Childbirth: A Guide to Negotiating Supportive Obstetrical Care. Judith Hertzfeld. LC 84-25564. (Illus.). 1985. 12.95 (ISBN 0-393-01983-7). Norton.

Sense & Sensibility in Childbirth: A Guide to Supportive Obstetrical Care. Judith Herzfeld. (Illus.). 176p. 1987. pap. 6.95 (ISBN 0-393-30381-0). Norton.

Sense & Sensibility in Modern Poetry. William Van O'Connor. LC 71-180986. 291p. 1973. Repr. of 1948 ed. text ed. 30.00x (ISBN 0-87752-157-3). Gordian.

Sense & Sensibility in Twentieth Century Writing: A Gathering in Memory of William Van O'Conner. Ed. by Brom Weber. LC 75-112395. (Crosscurrents-Modern Critiques Ser.). 191p. 1970. 6.95x (ISBN 0-8093-0448-1). S Ill U Pr.

Sense & Sensuality. Rosalind Brackenbury. 256p. 1987. 14.95 (ISBN 0-8008-7062-X). Taplinger.

Sense, Antisense, Nonsense. Robert Champigny. LC 83-26007. (University of Florida Humanities Monographs: No. 57). 128p. 1986. pap. 14.00x (ISBN 0-8130-0791-7). U Presses Fla.

Sense of an Audience: Dickens, Thackeray & George Eliot at Mid-Century. Janice Carlisle. LC 81-435. 262p. 1981. 22.00x (ISBN 0-8203-0559-6). U of Ga Pr.

Sense of an Ending: Studies in the Theory of Fiction. Frank Kermode. (YA) (gr. 10 up). 1967. pap. 8.95 (ISBN 0-19-500770-0). Oxford U Pr.

Sense of Animals. E. T. Burtt. (Wykeham Science Ser.: No. 26). 128p. 1974. pap. 18.00x (ISBN 0-85109-370-1). Taylor & Francis.

Sense of Asher 1984. Richard Asher. 97p. 14.00x (ISBN 0-7279-0136-2, Pub. by British Med Assoc UK). Taylor & Francis.

Sense of Balance. Nancy Meltzoff. LC 77-18508. 160p. (YA) (gr. 6-9). 1978. 7.50 (ISBN 0-664-32629-3). Westminster John Knox.

Sense of Beauty. George Santayana. 1896. pap. text ed. 3.95 (ISBN 0-486-20238-0). Dover.

Sense of Beauty: Critical Edition. George Santayana. Ed. by Herman Saatkamp, Jr. & William Holzberber. (Complete Works of George Santayana Ser.). 250p. 1988. write for info. (Pub. by Bradford). MIT Pr.

Sense of Direction. Louis Cameli et al. (Illus.). 128p. 1987. pap. 6.95 (ISBN 0-89505-447-7). Tabor Pub.

Sense of Direction: Some Obervations on the Art of Directing. William Ball. LC 84-8104. 208p. 1984. pap. text ed. 12.95x (ISBN 0-89676-082-0). Drama Bk.

Sense of Europe. Raymond Garlick. 106p. 1985. 25.00x (ISBN 0-85088-415-2, Pub. by Gomer Pr). State Mutual Bk.

Sense of Form in Art. Heinrich Woelfflin. LC 57-12877. (Illus., Orig.). pap. 6.50 (ISBN 0-8284-0153-5). Chelsea Pub.

Sense of Glory. Herbert Read. LC 76-21818. 1929. lib. bdg. 35.50 (ISBN 0-8414-7342-0). Folcroft.

Sense of Glory: Essays in Criticism. facs. ed. Herbert E. Read. LC 67-26773. (Essay Index Reprint Ser). 1930. 17.00 (ISBN 0-8369-0814-7). Ayer Co Pubs.

Sense of Grace: Celebrating the Life of the Honorable Grace Olivier Peck. Thomas Vaughan et al. LC 80-84479. (Illus.). 72p. 1981. pap. 25.00 (ISBN 0-87595-096-5). Oregon Hist.

Sense of Grammar: Language As Semeiotic. Michael Shapiro. LC 82-49244. (Advance in Semiotic Ser.). (Illus.). 256p. 1983. 27.50x (ISBN 0-253-35173-1). Ind U Pr.

Sense of History in Greek & Shakespearean Drama. Tom F. Driver. LC 59-15146. 1960. pap. 15.00x (ISBN 0-231-08576-1). Columbia U Pr.

Sense of Honor. James Webb. 1981. pap. 4.50 (ISBN 0-553-24104-4). Bantam.

Sense of Humour. Stephen Potter. Repr. of 1954 ed. lib. bdg. 30.00 (ISBN 0-8495-4331-2). Arden Lib.

Sense of Injustice: A Social Psychological Perspective. Ed. by Robert G. Folger. LC 84-2068. (Critical Issues in Social Justice Ser.). 1984. 32.50x (ISBN 0-306-41459-7, Plenum Pr.). Plenum Pub.

Sense of Irony: An Examination of the Tragedies of Franz Grillparzer, Vol. 4. Bruce Thompson. (Literaturwissenschaftliche Texte). x, 213p. 1976. pap. 27.40 (ISBN 3-261-01775-9). P Lang Pubs.

Sense of Living. Mildred Tonge. 1954. pap. 2.50x (ISBN 0-87574-079-0, 079). Pendle Hill.

Sense of Loyalty. Jeffrey Ashford. LC 83-40400. 192p. 1984. Walker & Co.

Sense of Loyalty. Jeffrey Ashford. 192p. 1986. Walker & Co.

Sense of Mission: Guidance from the Gospel of John. Albert C. Winn. LC 80-28000. 118p. 1981. pap. 6.95 (ISBN 0-664-24365-7). Westminster John Knox.

Sense of Movement. Thom Gunn. 62p. 1968. pap. 3.95 (ISBN 0-571-08530-X). Faber & Faber.

Sense of Music. Stephen Brown. 395p. 1988. text ed. 24.00 net (ISBN 0-15-579637-2, HC). HarBraceJ.

Sense of Music. rev. ed. Victor Zuckerkandl. (Illus.). 1970. 30.50x (ISBN 0-691-09102-1); pap. 12.95x (ISBN 0-691-02700-5); reel to reel tapes o.p. 52.50 (ISBN 0-691-03838-4); cassette tapes o.p. 40.00x (ISBN 0-691-09128-5). Princeton U Pr.

Sense of Occasion. Chester Kallman. LC 71-160132. (Poetry Ser). 1971. 5.95 (ISBN 0-8076-0625-1); pap. 2.95 (ISBN 0-8076-0624-3). Braziller.

Sense of Order: A Study in the Psychology of Decorative Art. E. H. Gombrich. LC 77-83898. (Illus.). 422p. 1984. pap. 24.95x (ISBN 0-8014-9249-1). Cornell U Pr.

Sense of Order: A Study in the Psychology of Decorative Art. Ernst H. Gombrich. LC 77-83898. (Illus.). 1979. 50.00x (ISBN 0-8014-1143-2). Cornell U Pr.

Sense of Performance in the Post-Art Theatre. S. Tharu. 210p. 1983. text ed. 12.50x (ISBN 0-391-03050-7). Humanities.

Sense of Place. Richard Cobb. 135p. 1978. 15.50 (ISBN 0-8419-7100-5). Holmes & Meier.

Sense of Place. Ed. by Robert McDonald. 24p. (Orig.). 1987. 12.50 (ISBN 0-9602974-8-0). USC Fisher Gallery.

Sense of Place. Steele. 21.95 (ISBN 0-317-64277-4). Van Nos Reinhold.

Sense of Place. Fritz Steele. (Illus.). 272p. 1983. 26.95 (ISBN 0-8436-0135-3). Van Nos Reinhold.

Sense of Place: In Centerville & Washington Township. Ed. by Howard R. Houser. (Illus.). 240p. 1986. 20.00 (ISBN 0-913428-59-0). Landfall Pr.

Sense of Place in the New Literatures in English. Ed. by Peggy Nightingale. 252p. 1986. text ed. 32.50x (ISBN 0-7022-1849-9). U of Queensland Pr.

Sense of Place: Mississippi. Ed. by Peggy W. Prenshaw & Jesse O. McKee. LC 79-26098. (Southern Quarterly Ser.). 1980. 6.95x (ISBN 0-87805-110-4); pap. 3.95 (ISBN 0-87805-111-2). U Pr of Miss.

Sense of Place: Small Communitites Near Ithaca, New York. Andrea F. Clardy. (Illus.). 96p. 1982. pap. 9.95 (ISBN 0-935526-09-9). McBooks Pr.

Sense of Place: The Life & Work of Forrest Shreve. Janice E. Bowers. LC 88-14014. 220p. 1988. 19.95x (ISBN 0-8165-1072-5). U of Ariz Pr.

Sense of Power: Studies in the Ideas of Canadian Imperialism, 1867-1914. Carl Berger. LC 79-470040. 1970. pap. 11.95c (ISBN 0-8020-6113-3). U of Toronto Pr.

Sense of Pride: The Story of Gay Games II. Roy M. Coe. (Illus.). 128p. 1986. pap. 14.95 (ISBN 0-940681-00-5). Pride Pubns.

Sense of Sentences. Wilbert J. Levy. (Orig.). (gr. 9-12). 1976. wkbk. 10.00 (ISBN 0-87720-336-9). AMSCO Sch.

Sense of Sexuality: Christian Love & Intimacy. James D. Whitehead & Evelyn E. Whitehead. 1988. 15.95 (ISBN 0-385-23614-X). Doubleday.

Sense of Shakespeare's Sonnets. Edward Hubler. LC 76-3790. 169p. 1976. Repr. of 1952 ed. lib. bdg. 35.00x (ISBN 0-8371-8815-6, HUSSS). Greenwood.

Sense of Sight. John Berger. Ed. by Lloyd Spencer. (Illus.). 1986. 18.45 (ISBN 0-394-54287-8); pap. 8.95 (ISBN 0-394-74206-0). Pantheon.

Sense of Slavery. Phil Hruskocy. 1978. pap. 5.00 (ISBN 0-910122-51-2). Amherst Pr.

Sense of Smell. Ed. by R. H. Wright. 248p. 1982. 78.50 (ISBN 0-8493-5232-0). CRC Pr.

Sense of Society: A History of the American Novel of Manners. Gordon Milne. 305p. 1977. 25.00 (ISBN 0-8386-1927-4). Fairleigh Dickinson.

Sense of Sociology. rev. ed. Lee Braude. LC 79-20785. 160p. 1981. pap. 7.50 (ISBN 0-89874-016-9). Krieger.

Sense of Story: Essays on Contemporary Writers for Children. John R. Townsend. 216p. 1973. pap. 6.95 (ISBN 0-87675-276-8). Horn Bk.

Sense of Style: Reading in English Prose. James Thorpe. LC 87-17498. vi, 185p. 1987. 25.00 (ISBN 0-208-02181-7, Archon Bks). Shoe String.

Sense of Survival. J. Allan South. 336p. (Orig.). 1985. pap. 10.95 (ISBN 0-935329-00-5). Timpanogos Pub.

Sense of Text: The Art of Language in the Study of Biblical Literature. Stephen A. Geller et al. 113p. 1983. pap. text ed. 12.50 (ISBN 0-9602686-1-8). Dropsie Coll.

Sense of the Cosmos: The Encounter of Modern Science with Ancient Truth. Jacob Needleman. 192p. 1988. pap. text ed. 12.95 (ISBN 1-85063-105-0). Routledge Chapman & Hall.

Sense of the Earth. David J. Leveson. LC 82-11437. (Illus.). 176p. Repr. of 1972 ed. 18.00 (ISBN 0-404-19149-5). AMS Pr.

Sense of the Future: Essays in Natural Philosophy. Jacob Bronowski. Ed. by Piero Ariotti & Rita Bronowski. LC 77-9292. 1977. pap. 8.95 (ISBN 0-262-52050-8). MIT Pr.

Sense of the Morning: Nature Through New Eyes. David Hopes. (Teale Bks.). 256p. 1988. 18.95 (ISBN 0-396-09128-8, Teale Bk). Dodd.

Sense of the Past. Henry James. 1973. lib. bdg. 47.00 (ISBN 0-8414-5363-2). Folcroft.

Sense of the Past. Henry James. LC 73-158805. (Novels & Tales of Henry James: Vol. 26). 1976. Repr. of 1917 ed. lib. bdg. 27.50x (ISBN 0-678-02826-5). Kelley.

Sense of the Past in Victorian Literature. Raymond Chapman. LC 85-6594. 224p. 1986. 27.50 (ISBN 0-312-71301-0). St Martin.

Sense of the Past: Three Twentieth Century British Poets. C. Tomlinson. (Kenneth Allott Lectures). 24p. 1983. pap. text ed. 6.95 (ISBN 0-85323-444-2, Pub. by Liverpool U Pr). Humanities.

Sense of the Sacred: The Life of Bede Griffiths. Kathryn Spink. 140p. 1988. 16.95 (ISBN 0-88344-442-9, 442-9). Orbis Bks.

Sense of the Self: From Self-Portrait to Autobiography. Richard King et al. LC 78-10863. (Illus.). 40p. 1978. 6.00 (ISBN 0-916365-06-9). Ind Curators.

Sense of the Seventies: A Rhetorical Reader. Ed. by Paul J. Dolan & Edward Quinn. 1978. pap. 9.95x (ISBN 0-19-502309-9). Oxford U Pr.

Sense of the Sixties. Edward G. Quinn & Paul J. Dolan. LC 68-12834. (Orig.). 1968. pap. text ed. 7.95 (ISBN 0-02-925560-0). Free Pr.

Sense of the "Song of Roland". Robert F. Cook. LC 87-5407. 296p. 1987. 34.50x (ISBN 0-8014-1930-1). Cornell U Pr.

Sense of Touch. Tr. by E. H. Weber. (Experimental Psychology Ser.). 1978. 55.50 (ISBN 0-12-740550-X). Acad Pr.

Sense of Unity: The Sufi Tradition in Persian Architecture. Nader Ardalan & laleh Bakhtiar. LC 72-92278. (Illus.). xx, 152p. 1986. pap. 29.95 (ISBN 0-226-02560-8). U of Chicago Pr.

Sense of Where You Are: A Profile of William Warren Bradley. 2nd ed. John McPhee. (Illus.). 206p. 1978. 9.95 (ISBN 0-374-26093-1); pap. 7.95 (ISBN 0-374-51485-2). FS&G.

Sense of Wonder. Edgar J. Saxon. 64p. 1980. pap. 3.95x (ISBN 0-8464-1048-6). Beekman Pubs.

Sense of Wonder. Edgar J. Saxon. 1980. 17.50x (ISBN 0-85207-136-1, Pub. by Daniel Co England). State Mutual Bk.

Sense of Wonder: A Spiritual Guidebook. Alison Davis. LC 84-81421. 96p. (Orig.). 1987. pap. 5.95 (ISBN 0-9619499-5-3). Little River Pr.

Sense Organs. Ed. by M. S. Laverack & D. J. Cosens. (Illus.). 394p. 1982. 85.00x (ISBN 0-216-91094-3). Trans-Atl Phila.

Sense Relaxation. Bernard Gunther. 144p. 1986. pap. 9.95 (ISBN 0-87877-093-3). Newcastle Pub.

Sense Relaxation. Bernard Gunther. LC 86-33448. 150p. 1986. lib. bdg. 24.95x (ISBN 0-89370-693-0). Borgo Pr.

Sense You. 2nd ed. Ginger Lox. (Illus.). 42p. (Orig.). 1981. pap. 3.50 (ISBN 0-9604178-0-X). G Rose Pr.

Sensei. David Charney. 448p. 1984. pap. 3.95 (ISBN 0-441-75886-X, Pub by Charter Bks). Ace Bks.

Sensei Book II: Swordmaster. David Charney. 384p. 1984. pap. 3.95 (ISBN 0-441-79264-2, Pub. by Charter Bks). Ace Bks.

Senseless. J. Douglas Burtt. 224p. 1985. pap. 2.50 (ISBN 0-8439-2241-9, Leisure Bks). Leisure NY.

Senses. Ed. by H. B. Barlow & J. D. Mollon. LC 81-17007. (Cambridge Texts in the Physiological Sciences Ser.: No. 3). (Illus.). 400p. 1982. pap. 24.95 (ISBN 0-521-28714-6). Cambridge U Pr.

Senses. Ed. by Dale C. Garell & Solomon H. Snyder. (Encyclopedia of Health Ser.). (Illus.). (YA) (gr. 7-12). 1989. 17.95 (ISBN 0-7910-0027-3). Chelsea Hse.

Senses. John Gaskin. LC 84-52328. (Your Body Ser.). (Illus.). 32p. (gr. 1-6). 1985. PLB 11.90 (ISBN 0-531-10051-0). Watts.

Senses & the Intellect. Alexander Bain. LC 77-72191. (Contributions to the History of Psychology Ser.: No. 4, Pt. A Orientations). 496p. 1978. Repr. of 1855 ed. 30.00 (ISBN 0-89093-153-4). U Pubns Amer.

Senses Considered As Perceptual Systems. James J. Gibson. LC 83-1716. (Illus.). xiv, 335p. 1983. Repr. of 1966 ed. lib. bdg. 59.50x (ISBN 0-313-23961-4, GISE). Greenwood.

Senses in God's World. Beverly Beckman. 24p. (ps). 1986. 5.95 (ISBN 0-570-04150-3, 56-1604). Concordia.

Senses of Animals. E. T. Burtt & A. Pringle. LC 73-77794. (Wykeham Science Ser.: No. 26). 168p. 1974. 18.00x (ISBN 0-8448-1153-X, Pub. by Crane Russak & Co). Taylor & Francis.

Senses of Walden. expanded ed. Stanley Cavell. LC 80-28315. 184p. 1981. 15.00 (ISBN 0-86547-031-6); pap. 9.50. N Point Pr.

Sensibility: An Introduction. Janet Todd. 120p. 1986. 27.50 (ISBN 0-416-37710-6, 1023); pap. 9.95 (ISBN 0-416-37720-3, 1037). Routledge Chapman & Hall.

Sensibility & Criticism: A Study of the Interrelation of Verbal Acts & Visual Acts. Marcus B. Hester. LC 83-14580. 178p. (Orig.). 1983. lib. bdg. 26.00 (ISBN 0-8191-3457-0); pap. text ed. 11.50 (ISBN 0-8191-3458-9). U Pr of Amer.

Sensibility & English Song: Critical Studies of the Early 20th Century, 2 vols. Stephen Banfield. 1985. Vol. I, 336p. 57.50 (ISBN 0-521-23085-3); Vol. 2, 320p. 52.50 (ISBN 0-521-30360-5). Cambridge U Pr.

Sensibility in English Prose Fiction: 1760-1814. 158p. 1980. Repr. of 1937 ed. lib. bdg. 25.00 (ISBN 0-8495-5652-X). Arden Lib.

Sensibility in English Prose Fiction 1760-1814: A Reinterpretation. Walter F. Wright. LC 76-40187. 1937. lib. bdg. 25.00 (ISBN 0-8414-9504-1). Folcroft.

Sensible Cruising: The Thoreau Approach, a Philosophic & a Practical Approach to Cruising. Don Casey & Lew Hackler. LC 86-60480. (Illus.). 364p. 1986. 24.95 (ISBN 0-931595-01-0). Seascape Enters.

Sensible Fitness. Jack H. Wilmore. LC 85-30927. 312p. (Orig.). 1986. pap. 11.95 (ISBN 0-88011-270-0, PWIL0270). Leisure Pr.

Sensible Living. Virgil Herbert. 1988. 15.45 (ISBN 0-688-07821-4). Morrow.

Sensible Living: Winning Your Fight Against Arthritis. Virgil Harbert. (Illus.). 150p. 1988. 15.95 (ISBN 0-688-07195-3). Morrow.

Sensible Solutions How to Get Happily Published Handbook. 2nd ed. Judith Appelbaum et al. 68p. 1988. looseleaf wkbk. 27.50. Sensible Sol.

Sensible Spirit: Walter Pater & the Modernist Paradigm. F. C. McGrath. LC 85-29503. 320p. 1986. 30.00x (ISBN 0-8130-0829-8). U Presses Fla.

Sensible Words: Linguistic Practice in England, 1640-1785. Murray Cohen. LC 77-1856. (Illus.). 1977. text ed. 24.50x (ISBN 0-8018-1924-5). Johns Hopkins.

Sensibly Thin. Stanley H. Title & Charles M. Klein. LC 78-27039. 192p. 1979. 18.95x (ISBN 0-88229-446-6); pap. 9.95 (ISBN 0-88229-665-5). Nelson-Hall.

Sensing & Communication Between Vehicles. (National Cooperative Highway Research Program Report). 105p. 1968. 5.00 (ISBN 0-317-36104-X, 1585). Transport Res Bd.

Sensing & Response in Microorganisms. Ed. by M. Eisenbach & M. Balaban. 316p. 1986. 149.50 (ISBN 0-444-80758-6). Elsevier.

Sensing, Discrimination, & Signal Processing & Superconducting Materials & Instrumentation. Ed. by Nichols & Ionson. 1988. 50.00 (ISBN 0-89252-914-8, 879). SPIE.

Sensing the Spirit. Richard H. Bell. LC 84-5158. (Spirituality & the Christian Life Ser.: Vol. 6). 120p. 1984. pap. 7.95 (ISBN 0-664-24632-X). Westminster John Knox.

Sensing the World. Moreland Perkins. LC 83-10825. 352p. 1983. lib. bdg. 30.00 (ISBN 0-915145-74-X); text ed. 14.50 (ISBN 0-915145-75-8). Hackett Pub.

Sensing Your Hidden Presence: Toward Intimacy With God. Ignacio Larranaga. Tr. by John Diercksmeier & Rigoberto Caloca Rivas. LC 87-5232. 288p. 1987. pap. 7.95 (ISBN 0-385-24021-X, Im). Doubleday.

Sensism, the Philosophy of the West, 2 vols. Charles Smith. 1611p. Set. 6.00 (ISBN 0-318-16739-5). Truth Seeker.

Sensism, the Philosophy of the West, 2 Vols. Charles Smith. 1612p. 12.00 (ISBN 0-318-17126-0); members 8.00 (ISBN 0-318-17127-9). Atheist Assn.

Sensitisation of the Nervous System. Ed. by Charles Barnes & Peter W. Kaliuas. (Illus.). 300p. 1988. 27.50 (ISBN 0-936923-12-1). Telford Pr.

Sensitive Crystallization Processes. Pfeiffer. LC 68-31125. 1975. pap. 16.00 (ISBN 0-910142-66-1). Anthroposophic.

Sensitive Leader. Dennis L. Lythgoe. LC 86-24202. 160p. 1986. 9.95 (ISBN 0-87579-061-5). Deseret Bk.

Sensitive Man: And It's OK to Be Feminine. Richard E. Petitti. (Self Realization Ser.: Bk. II). (Illus.). 150p. 1986. pap. 10.00 (ISBN 0-938582-03-8). Sensitive Man.

Sensitive Periods in Development: Interdisciplinary Perspectives. Ed. by Marc Bornstein. (Crosscurrents in Contemporary Psychology). 304p. 1987. text ed. 32.50 (ISBN 0-89859-696-3). L Erlbaum Assocs.

Sensitive Plant. Percy Bysshe Shelley. LC 72-4547. (Studies in Shelley, No. 25). (Illus.). 1972. Repr. of 1898 ed. lib. bdg. 29.95x (ISBN 0-8383-1612-3). Haskell.

Sensitive Populations & Environmental Standards: An Issue Report. Robert D. Friedman. LC 80-69127. 54p. (Orig.). 1981. pap. 5.00 (ISBN 0-89164-063-0). Conservation Foun.

Sensitive Spots: Nine Drawings. Douglas C. Laudies. (Illus.). 1978. 3.00 (ISBN 0-686-75952-4). Luna Bisonte.

Sensitive Thoughts for the New Wave Soul. Denise A. Reynolds. 1984. 6.95 (ISBN 0-8062-2291-3). Carlton.

Sensitives. Herbert Burkholz. LC 86-2645. 288p. 1987. 18.95 (ISBN 0-689-11842-2). Atheneum.

Sensitivity: Agony or Ecstacy. G. Burton Appleford. (Illus.). 72p. (Orig.). 1988. pap. 7.95 (ISBN 0-8059-3133-3). Dorrance.

Sensitivity Analysis in Linear Regression. Samprit Chatterjee & Ali S. Hadi. LC 87-28580. (Probability & Mathematical Statistics Ser.). 315p. 1988. 29.95 (ISBN 0-471-82216-7). Wiley.

Sensitivity Analysis in Linear Systems. A. Deif. (Illus.). 260p. 1986. 56.00 (ISBN 0-387-16312-3). Springer-Verlag.

Sentence Composing Eleven. Don Killgallon. 160p. (gr. 10-12). 1980. pap. text ed. 9.00x (ISBN 0-86709-125-8). Boynton Cook Pubs.
Sentence Composing Ten. Don Killgallon. 144p. (gr. 10). 1979. pap. text ed. 9.00x (ISBN 0-86709-123-1). Boynton Cook Pubs.
Sentence Composing: The Complete Course. Don Killgallon. 176p. (Orig.). 1987. pap. text ed. 12.50x (ISBN 0-86709-183-5). Boynton Cook Pubs.
Sentence Composing Twelve. Don Killgallon. 160p. (gr. 10-12). 1979. pap. 9.00x; tchr's guide 1.75 (ISBN 0-8104-6121-8). Boynton Cook Pubs.
Sentence Composition. Wilbert J. Levy. (Orig.). 1976. wkbk. 9.33 (ISBN 0-87720-950-2). AMSCO Sch.
Sentence Construction: Writing & Combining Standard English Sentence, Bk. I. Alice C. Pack & Lynn E. Henrichsen. 176p. 1980. pap. text ed. 11.50 (ISBN 0-88377-173-X). Newbury Hse.
Sentence Dynamics: An English Skills Workbook. 2nd ed. Constance Immel & Florence Sacks. 1987. pap. text ed. write for info. (ISBN 0-673-18531-1). Scott F.
Sentence in Biblical Hebrew. Francis I. Andersen. (Janua Linguarum, Ser. Practica: No. 231). 209p. 1974. pap. text ed. 23.20x (ISBN 90-2792-673-5). Mouton.
Sentence Initial Devices. Ed. by Joseph E. Grimes. LC 83-51455. (Publications in Linguistics: No. 75). 350p. (Orig.). 1986. pap. 30.00x (ISBN 0-88312-096-8); microfiche (4) 8.00 (ISBN 0-88312-414-9). Summer Inst Ling.
Sentence Intonation of Contemporary Standard Russian As a Linguistic Structure. J. E. Buning & C. H. van Schooneveld. (Description & Analysis of Contemporary Standard Russian: No. 3). 1961. 23.20x (ISBN 0-686-20924-9). Mouton.
Sentence Making: A Writing Workbook in English As a Second Language. Robert G. Bander. 335p. 1982. pap. text ed. 14.95 (ISBN 0-03-050631-X). HR&W.
Sentence Mastery. 2nd ed. Jack S. Romine. 1966. text ed. write for info. (ISBN 0-13-806695-7). P-H.
Sentence Mastery, Bks. A & B. Edgar H. Schuster. Ed. by Hester E. Weeden. (Sentence Mastery Ser.). (Illus.). 160p. (gr. 7) 1980. Bk. A. 6.64 (ISBN 0-07-055621-0); Bk. B. 6.64 (ISBN 0-07-055622-9); Bk. C. 6.64 (ISBN 0-07-055623-7). McGraw.
Sentence Patterns & Reality. Janos Zsilka. 1973. pap. text ed. 23.20x (ISBN 90-2792-447-3). Mouton.
Sentence Patterns of Indonesian. Soenjono Dardjowidjojo. LC 78-6687. (Pali Language Texts: Indonesia). 447p. 1978. pap. text ed. 17.50x (ISBN 0-8248-0418-X). UH Pr.
Sentence Play. Levy. (gr. 7-9). 1984. pap. 7.83 (ISBN 0-87720-681-3). AMSCO Sch.
Sentence Production: Developments in Research & Theory. Ed. by Sheldon Rosenberg. LC 77-1754. 323p. 1977. 21.95x (ISBN 0-470-99114-3). Halsted Pr.
Sentence Sense: A Writer's Guide. Evelyn Farbman. LC 88-81329. 352p. 1989. pap. text ed. price not set (ISBN 0-395-38004-9). HM.
Sentence Skills: A Workbook for Writers, Form A. 2nd ed. John Langan. 432p. 1983. pap. 17.95 (ISBN 0-07-036267-X). McGraw.
Sentence Skills: A Workbook for Writers, Form B. 2nd ed. John Langan. 1984. text ed. 17.95 (ISBN 0-07-036269-6). McGraw.
Sentence Skills: A Workbook for Writers, Form A. 3rd ed. John Langan. 496p. 1986. pap. text ed. 19.95 (ISBN 0-07-036305-6). McGraw.
Sentence Skills Form C. 3rd ed. 496p. 1987. pap. text ed. 18.95 (ISBN 0-07-036323-4). McGraw.
Sentence Structure. Philip Lutgendorf & Mary Jane Gray. LC 77-730353. (Illus.). (gr. 7-9). 1977. pap. text ed. 209.00 (ISBN 0-89290-119-5, A144). Soc for Visual.
Sentence Structure & Characterization in the Tragedies of Jean Racine: A Computer-Assisted Study. Mary L. Flowers. LC 76-50284. 223p. 1978. 20.00 (ISBN 0-8386-2056-6). Fairleigh Dickinson.
Sentence Structure & the Reading Process. I. M. Schlesinger. LC 68-23200. (Janua Linguarum Ser: No. 69). (Orig.). 1968. pap. text ed. 13.20x (ISBN 90-2790-596-7). Mouton.
Sentence Structure of Japanese: Viewed in the Light of Dialectology. Yoichi Fujiwara. Ed. by Noah S. Brannen & Scott J. Baird. LC 73-78976. pap. 43.80 (ISBN 0-317-10167-6, 2020443). Bks Demand UMI.
Sentence Writing. William Klink. LC 80-5805. (Illus.). 141p. (Orig.). 1981. pap. text ed. 9.25 (ISBN 0-8191-1430-8). U Pr of Amer.
Sentenced & Other Stories. Vladimir Soloukhin. Tr. by D. W. Martin from Rus. 200p. cancelled (ISBN 0-88233-802-1); pap. cancelled (ISBN 0-88233-803-X). Ardis Pubs.
Sentenced to Hospital: Offenders at Broadmoor. Susanne Dell & Graham Robertson. (Maudsley Monographs: 32). 176p. 1988. 45.00 (ISBN 0-19-712156-X). Oxford U Pr.
Sentenced to Life in a Cell. Daniel Valone. (Illus.). 90p. 1975. pap. 1.50 (ISBN 0-942788-02-8). Marginal Med.
Sentenced to Life: 50 Years of Missionary Life in Japan. Leone Cole. 288p. 1987. pap. write for info. (ISBN 0-9618026-1-8). Natl Design Assocs.
Sentenced to Live. Nora Norden. 280p. (Orig.). 1986. pap. 7.00 (ISBN 0-934145-47-4). Airborne Pr.
Sentenced to Prism. Alan D. Foster. 288p. (Orig.). 1985. pap. 3.50 (ISBN 0-345-31980-X, Del Rey). Ballantine.
Sentences. Howard Nemerov. LC 80-17702. 86p. 1980. pap. 4.95 (ISBN 0-226-57262-5). U of Chicago Pr.
Sentences. 1981. 3.00 (ISBN 0-939418-40-1). Ferguson-Florissant.
Sentences & Other Systems: A Language & Learning Curriculum for Hearing-Impaired Children. Peter M. Blackwell et al. LC 78-51922. 1978. pap. text ed. 16.95 (ISBN 0-88200-118-3, C2557). Alexander Graham.
Sentences Children Use. Paula Menyuk. (Press Research Monographs: No. 52). 176p. 1972. pap. 6.95x (ISBN 0-262-63043-5). MIT Pr.
Sentences in Dialog. Richard Gunter. 1975. pap. 11.50 (ISBN 0-917496-03-5). Hornbeam Pr.
Sentences in Small Spaces. Richard Schain. 36p. (Orig.). 1985. pap. 2.00 (ISBN 0-9609922-5-1). Garric Pr.
Sentences Undecidable in Formalized Arithmetic: An Exposition of the Theory of Kurt Godel. Andrej Mostowski. LC 82-11886. (Studies in Logic & the Foundations of Mathematics). viii, 117p. 1982. Repr. of 1952 ed. lib. bdg. 35.00x (ISBN 0-313-23151-6, MOSU). Greenwood.
Sentences Undecidable in Formalized Arithmetic. A. Mostowski. 118p. 1952. 25.00 (ISBN 0-7204-2220-5, North Holland). Elsevier.
Sentencing. Ed. by Hyman Gross & Andrew Von Hirsch. 1981. pap. text ed. 11.95x (ISBN 0-19-502764-7). Oxford U Pr.
Sentencing. Dale G. Parent. 1988. pap. text ed. 15.00 (ISBN 0-88063-102-3). Butterworth Legal Pubs.
Sentencing & Penal Policy. Andrew Ashworth. (Law in Context Ser.). xx, 500p. 1983. 30.00x (ISBN 0-297-78236-3, Pub. by Weidenfeld & Nicholson England). Rothman.
Sentencing As a Human Process. John Hogarth. LC 73-151374. (Canadian Studies in Criminology: No. 1). pap. 112.00 (ISBN 0-317-27028-1, 2023637). Bks Demand UMI.
Sentencing by Mathematics: An Evaluation of the Early Attempts to Develop & Implement Sentencing Guidelines. William D. Rich & L. Paul Sutton. LC 82-42713. 240p. 1982. pap. 20.00 (R-071). Natl Ctr St Courts.
Sentencing Commission & Its Guidelines. Andrew Von Hirsch et al. 215p. 1987. text ed. 30.00x (ISBN 1-55553-009-5). NE U Pr.
Sentencing Dispositions of New York City Lower Court Criminal Judges. James R. Davis. LC 82-45016. (Illus.). 230p. (Orig.). 1982. pap. text ed. 13.25 (ISBN 0-8191-2567-9). U Pr of Amer.
Sentencing Felons in New Mexico: A Proposal for Guidelines Committee to the New Mexico Supreme Court. National Center for State Courts Staff. 81p. 1985. manuscript 5.00 (WRO-062). Natl Ctr St Courts.
Sentencing Guidelines & Policy Statements, 3 Bks. 215p. (Orig.). 1987. pap. 16.00 (ISBN 0-318-22948-X, S/N 052-070-06305-0). USGPO.
Sentencing in the Courts. E. Stockdale. (Criminal Law Library). 352p. 1987. 45.00 (ISBN 0-08-039248-2, Pub. by WAT); 40.50 (ISBN 0-08-033066-5, Pub. by WAT). Pergamon.
Sentencing in Victoria: State & Federal Law. Richard Fox & Arie Freiberg. 1985. 125.00x (ISBN 0-19-554656-3). Oxford U Pr.
Sentencing in Washington. David Boerner. 833p. 1985. 120.00. Butterworth WA.
Sentencing in Washington-A Legal Analysis of the Sentencing Reform Act of 1981. David Boerner. LC 84-72824. 833p. 1985. postbound 120.00 (ISBN 0-409-20152-9). Butterworth WA.
Sentencing of Sex Offenders. James A. Black. LC 74-28602. 1975. soft bdg. 11.95 (ISBN 0-88247-324-7). R & E Pubs.
Sentencing Problems & Remedies of Sentenced Prisoners: A Handbook for Illinois State Prisoners. rev. ed. Mariann Twist & Catherine M. Ryan. LC 82-181619. (Illus.). 48p. 1980. write for info. Illinois Bar.
Sentencing Procedures & Practices: An Annotated Bibliography. National Center for State Courts Staff. 31p. 1979. manuscript 1.86 (FR-003). Natl Ctr St Courts.
Sentencing: Process & Purpose. Gerhard O. Mueller. (Illus.). 228p. 1977. 28.50 (ISBN 0-398-03591-1). C C Thomas.
Sentencing Reform: A Canadian Approach. 592p. (Orig.). 1987. pap. text ed. 30.00 (ISBN 0-660-12245-6, SSC225, CCS). UNIPUB.
Sentencing Reform: A Review & Annotated Bibliography. J. L. Miller & Charlotte A. Carter. 147p. 1981. pap. 10.00 (ISBN 0-89656-056-2, R-061). Natl Ctr St Courts.
Sentencing Reform: Guidance or Guidelines? Ed. by Ken Pease & Martin Wasik. 224p. 1987. 55.00 (ISBN 0-7190-1890-0, Pub. by Manchester Univ Pr). St Martin.
Sentencing Reform Impacts. Michael H. Tonry. (Issues & Practices in Criminal Justice). 113p. 1987. pap. 3.25 (ISBN 0-317-62896-8, S-N 027-000-01276-1). USGPO.
Sentencing Young People: The Effects of the Criminal Justice Act 1982. Elizabeth Burney. 120p. 1985. 27.95 (ISBN 0-566-05127-3). Gower Pub Co.
Sententiae. Richard Schain. 36p. (Orig.). 1984. pap. 2.00 (ISBN 0-9609922-3-5). Garric Pr.
Sentential Complementation in Spanish: A Lexico-Grammatical Study of Three Classes of Verbs. Carlos Subirats-Ruggeberg. LC 86-26865. (Lingvisticae Investigationes Supplementa Ser.: No. 14). xii, 290p. 1987. 38.00x (ISBN 90-272-3123-0). Benjamins North Am.
Sententiousness & the Novel: Laying Down the Law in Eighteenth Century French Fiction. Geoffrey Bennington. (Cambridge Studies in French). 280p. 1986. 42.50 (ISBN 0-521-30246-3). Cambridge U Pr.
Sentido, Forma y Estilo de "Redentores" de Manuel Zeno Gandia. Rosa M. Palmer de Dueno. (UPREX, E. Literarios: No. 34). pap. 1.85 (ISBN 0-8477-0034-8). U of PR Pr.
Sentience. Terry A. Adams. 1986. pap. 3.50 (ISBN 0-88677-108-0). DAW Bks.
Sentience. Wallace I. Matson. (Illus.). 200p. 1976. 28.00x (ISBN 0-520-02987-9); pap. 8.95x (ISBN 0-520-04776-1). U of Cal Pr.
Sentiers et les Routes de la Poesie. Paul Eluard. 176p. 1954. 8.95 (ISBN 0-686-55981-9). French & Eur.
Sentimens sur la distinction des divers es manieres de peinture, dessein et graveure. Abraham Bosse. (Documents of Art & Architectural History Series 2: Vol. 5). 142p. (Fr.). 1981. Repr. of 1649 ed. 27.50x (ISBN 0-89371-205-1). Broude Intl Edns.
Sentiment & Romance in the Poetry by Shakespeare. Benedetto Croce. 139p. 1983. 89.85x (ISBN 0-89266-414-2). Am Classical Coll Pr.
Sentiment & Sensibility, Their Use & Significance in English Literature. S. C. Chakraborty. lib. bdg. 12.50 (ISBN 0-685-25637-5). Folcroft.
Sentiment & Sociability: The Language of Feeling in the Eighteenth Century. John Mullan. 272p. 1988. 45.00 (ISBN 0-19-812865-7). Oxford U Pr.
Sentiment De la Nature En France Dans la Premiere Moitie Du Dix-Septieme Siecle. Grace L. Morley. LC 75-168927. (Research & Source Works Ser.). 211p. (Fr.). 1972. Repr. of 1926 ed. lib. bdg. 21.00 (ISBN 0-8337-4292-2). B Franklin.
Sentiment De la Nature En France De J. J. Rousseau a Bernardin De Saint-Pierre. Daniel Mornet. LC 70-164483. (Research & Source Works Ser.: No. 59). 31.50 (ISBN 0-8337-2468-1). B Franklin.
Sentimental Education. Gustave Flaubert. Tr. by Robert Baldick. (Classics Ser.). (Orig.). 1964. pap. 3.95 (ISBN 0-14-044141-7). Penguin.
Sentimental Education. Gustave Flaubert. 1984. pap. 4.95 (ISBN 0-452-00852-2, Mer). NAL.
Sentimental Education: Stories. Joyce Carol Oates. 192p. 1982. pap. 4.95 (ISBN 0-525-48021-8, Obelisk). Dutton.
Sentimental Feelings. Pat Kowalkowski & Eden Yount. (Illus.). 32p. (Orig.). 1986. pap. 5.95 (ISBN 0-9616583-0-4). P Kowalkowski.
Sentimental Imperialists. James C. Thomson, Jr. et al. LC 79-1689. 347p. 1982. pap. 8.95x (ISBN 0-06-131998-8, TB 1998, Torch). Har-Row.
Sentimental Imperialists: The American Experience in East Asia. James C. Thomson, Jr et al. LC 79-1689. 352p. 1981. 17.50i (ISBN 0-06-014282-0, HarpT). Har-Row.
Sentimental Jewelry. Shirley Bury. (V & A Intruductions to the Decorative Arts Ser.). (Illus.). 48p. 1985. 9.95 (ISBN 0-88045-076-2). Stemmer Hse.
Sentimental Journey. Viktor Shklovsky. Ed. by Richard Sheldon. LC 71-87022. (Paperback Ser.). 352p. 1984. pap. 10.95x (ISBN 0-8014-9291-2). Cornell U Pr.
Sentimental Journey (Dickens) Hugh Kingsmill. LC 72-13526. 1973. Repr. of 1934 ed. lib. bdg. 37.50 (ISBN 0-8414-1228-6). Folcroft.
Sentimental Journey Through France & Italy. Laurence Sterne. Ed. by Graham Petrie. (English Library Ser.). 1967. pap. 3.95 (ISBN 0-14-043026-1). Penguin.
Sentimental Journey Through France & Italy. Laurence Sterne. Ed. by Ian Jack. Bd. with Journal to Eliza; A Political Romance. (World's Classics Paperback Ser.). 1984. pap. 3.95 (ISBN 0-19-281685-3). Oxford U Pr.
Sentimental Journey Through France & Italy. Laurence Sterne. 140p. Repr. of 1925 ed. lib. bdg. 20.00 (ISBN 0-317-19009-1). R West.
Sentimental Journeys: Reminiscences of a Street Kid. Farrellinea. (Illus.). 115p. (YA) (gr. 7-12). 1988. pap. 7.95 (ISBN 0-8059-3100-7). Dorrance.
Sentimental Memoirs of John Seaborne. Oswald De Andrade. Tr. by Albert Bork & Ralph Niebuhr. write for info. (ISBN 0-918722-04-7); pap. 3.95 (ISBN 0-918722-05-5). Nefertiti.
Sentimental Memory Pieces. Dorothy Radcliffe & Carolyn Cook. (Illus.). 32p. Date not set. pap. 4.95 (ISBN 0-87588-304-4). Hobby Hse.
Sentimental Novel in America, 1789-1860. facsimile ed. Herbert R. Brown. LC 75-107685. (Essay Index Reprint Ser). Repr. of 1940 ed. 22.00 (ISBN 0-8369-1490-2). Ayer Co Pubs.
Sentimental Novel in America, 1789-1860. Herbert R. Brown. 1972. lib. bdg. 29.00x (ISBN 0-374-91032-4, Octagon). Hippocrene Bks.
Sentimental Revolution: French Writers of 1690-1740. Geoffroy Atkinson. Ed. by Abraham C. Keller. LC 64-18424. 200p. 1966. 20.00x (ISBN 0-295-74024-8). U of Wash Pr.
Sentimental Talk see Sentimental Talks.
Sentimental Talks. Daniel Castelain. Tr. by Patrick Bowles from Fr. Incl. Unlikely Meeting; Sentimental Talk. LC 79-131217. 128p. (Orig.). 1971. 4.95 (ISBN 0-87376-014-X). Red Dust.
Sentimental Tommy. J. M. Barrie. 16.95 (ISBN 0-8488-0192-X). Amereon Ltd.
Sentimental Tommy see Works of J. M. Barrie.
Sentimental Venture. new ed. E. I. Edwards. LC 76-21423. (Illus.). 71p. 1976. 10.00 (ISBN 0-914224-06-9). Tales Mojave Rd.
Sentiments & Activities: Essays in Social Science. George C. Homans. 342p. (Orig.). 1988. pap. 19.95 (ISBN 0-88738-725-X). Transaction Bks.
Sentiments et Coutumes. Andre Maurois. pap. 17.50 (ISBN 0-685-36959-5). French & Eur.
Sentinel. Arthur C. Clarke. 272p. 1986. pap. 3.50 (ISBN 0-425-09389-1). Berkley Pub.
Sentinel. Emerson Daggett. 12p. (Orig.). 1981. pap. 2.00 (ISBN 0-932942-01-6). Pacific NW Labor.
Sentinel. Jeffrey Konvitz. 1977. pap. 2.50 (ISBN 0-345-30437-3). Ballantine.
Sentinel at Dawn. Louella Nelson. (Superromances Ser.). 384p. pap. 2.95 (ISBN 0-373-70096-2, Pub. by Worldwide). Harlequin Bks.
Sentinel at Ellwood: The Barnsdall-Rio Grande Gasoline Station. Gary B. Coombs & Phyllis Jean Olsen. (Illus.). 24p. 1985. pap. 2.50 (ISBN 0-911773-06-1). Inst Am Res.
Sentinel Diesel Lorries: A Pictorial Record. Trent Valley Publications Staff. (Illus.). 1988. 59.00x (ISBN 0-948131-22-5, Pub. by Trent Valley UK); cardcover 39.00x (Pub. by Trent Valley UK). State Mutual Bk.
Sentinel: Masterworks of Science Fiction & Fantasy. Arthur C. Clarke. 1987. pap. 6.95 (ISBN 0-425-06183-3). Berkley Pub.
Sentinel of the East. Durlab Singh. LC 74-7099. (Studies in Asiatic Literature, No. 57). 1974. lib. bdg. 47.95x (ISBN 0-8383-1975-0). Haskell.
Sentinel of the Southern Plains: Fort Richardson & the Northwest Texas Frontier, 1866-1878. Allen L. Hamilton. LC 87-17379. (Chisholm Trail Ser.: No. 5). (Illus.). 268p. (Orig.). 1988. pap. 14.95 (ISBN 0-87565-073-2). Tex Christian.
Sentinels from Space. Eric F. Russell. 240p. pap. 2.95 (ISBN 0-345-32758-6, Del Rey). Ballantine.
Sentinels of Empire: The United States & Latin American Militarism. Jan K. Black. LC 85-21850. (Contributions in Political Science: No. 144). 249p. 1986. lib. bdg. 36.95 (ISBN 0-313-25155-X, BKS/). Greenwood.
Sentinels of Order: A Study of Social Control & the Minneapolis Settlement House Movement, 1915-1950. Howard J. Karger. LC 87-2208. 202p. 1987. lib. bdg. 22.75 (ISBN 0-8191-6275-2). U Pr of Amer.
Sentinels of Peace: The Soviet Armed Forces. Collets Staff. 208p. 1980. 47.50x (ISBN 0-317-53820-9, Pub. by Collets (UK)). State Mutual Bk.
Sentinels of the North Pacific. James A. Gibbs. (Illus.). 1955. 10.95 (ISBN 0-8323-0011-X). Binford-Metropolitan.
Sentinels of Time: Vermont's Covered Bridges. Phil Ziegler. (Illus.). 1983. pap. 8.95 (ISBN 0-89272-160-X). Down East.
Sentries. Ed McBain. 304p. 1988. pap. 3.50 (ISBN 0-380-70489-7). Avon.
Sentries. Gary Paulsen. LC 85-26978. 160p. (gr. 7 up). 1986. 11.95 (ISBN 0-02-770100-X). Bradbury Pr.
Sentries. Gary Paulsen. (gr. 5-9). Date not set. pap. 3.95 (ISBN 0-317-62279-X, Puffin Bks). Penguin.
Sentry & Other Tales. Nikolai S. Leskov. Tr. by A. Chamot from Rus. LC 76-23888. (Classics of Russian Literature Ser.). (Illus.). 1987. Hyperion Conn.
Sentry Hill: An Ulster Farm & Family. rev. ed. Brian M. Walker. (Illus.). 184p. 1983. pap. 10.50 (ISBN 0-85640-254-0, Pub. by Blackstaff Pr). Longwood Pub Group.
S'Envoler pour Toujours. Valarie Lafargue. (Collection Colombine Ser.). 192p. 1983. pap. 1.95 (ISBN 0-373-48082-2). Harlequin Bks.
Senya. Senya Darklight. Ed. by Marty Campbell. (Illus.). 200p. (Orig.). 1989. pap. 7.00. Mar Crafs.
Seostri, re d'Egitto. Domenico Terradellas. LC 79-20971. (Italian Opera Ser.). 1978. lib. bdg. 83.00 (ISBN 0-8240-2642-X). Garland Pub.
Seoul. (Times Travel Library). (Illus.). 104p. (Orig.). 1988. pap. 10.95 (ISBN 1-55650-090-4). Hunter Pub NY.
Seoul: Nineteen Eighty-Eight Olympic Site. Edward B. Adams. (Illus.). 57p. (Orig.). 1984. pap. 4.00 (ISBN 0-8048-1425-2, Pub. by Seoul Intl Publishing House). C E Tuttle.
Seoul Shopping Guide. Richard B. Rucci. (Illus.). 64p. 1983. pap. 3.50 (ISBN 0-8048-1418-X, Pub. by Seoul Intl Publishing House). C E Tuttle.
Seoul Sketches: A Visual Sketch of the Yi Dynasty. Charlotte Rountree. (Illus.). 84p. 1985. 19.50 (ISBN 0-930878-43-4). Hollym Intl.
Seoul Travel Guide: What to See & Where to Go. rev. ed. Joyce Ryan & Charlotte Rountree. (Illus.). 96p. (Orig.). 1987. pap. 10.95 (ISBN 0-939077-01-9). Butterfly Bks.

Sept Femmes. Guy Des Cars. 384p. 1970. 3.95 (ISBN 0-686-55660-7). French & Eur.
Sept Femmes de la Barbe-Bleue. Anatole France. 224p. 1975. 9.95 (ISBN 0-686-55877-4). French & Eur.
Sept Lecons sur l'etre: Avec: Les Premiers Principes de la Raison Speculative. Jacques Maritain. 166p. 1935. 9.95 (ISBN 0-686-56368-9). French & Eur.
Sept Lilas. Violet Winspear. (Harlequin Romantique Ser.). 192p. 1983. pap. 1.95 (ISBN 0-373-41208-8). Harlequin Bks.
Sept Psaumes de la Penitence. Paul Claudel. 1945. 8.95 (ISBN 0-686-54435-8). French & Eur.
Sept Sentiers du Desert. Vercors. 244p. 1972. 10.95 (ISBN 0-686-55137-0). French & Eur.
Septem Quae Supersunt Tragoedias. Aeschylus. Ed. by Denys L. Page. (Oxford Classical Texts). 1973. 14.95x (ISBN 0-19-814570-5). Oxford U Pr.
September - October. Barbara Gruber. (Instant Idea Bks.). (Illus.). 64p. 1988. 6.95 (ISBN 0-86734-098-3, FS8311). Schaffer Pubns.
September Blackberries. Michael McClure. LC 73-89482. 160p. 1974. pap. 3.25 (ISBN 0-8112-0524-X, NDP370). New Directions.
September Blood: The Battle of Carnifex Ferry. Terry Lowry. LC 85-60320. (Illus.). 168p. (Orig.). 1985. pap. 9.95 (ISBN 0-933126-59-X). Pictorial Hist.
September Echoes: A Study of the Maryland Campaign of 1862. John W. Schildt. (Illus.). 140p. (Orig.). 1984. pap. 6.95 (ISBN 0-932751-01-6). Beidel Printing Hse.
September Faces. Seymour Epstein. LC 87-45000. 329p. 1987. 17.95 (ISBN 1-55611-038-3). D I Fine.
September Idea Book: A Creative Idea Book for the Elementary Teacher. Karen Sevaly. (Illus.). 112p. (Orig.). 1986. pap. 8.95 (ISBN 0-943263-00-X, TF-900). Teachers Friend Pubns.
September Light. Horst Bienek. Tr. by Ralph R. Read. LC 86-47670. 273p. 1987. 17.95 (ISBN 0-689-11848-1). Atheneum.
September Moon. Constance O'Banyon. 1986. pap. 3.95 (ISBN 0-8217-1838-X). Zebra.
September Morning: A Practical Guide for the Middle Years. Mildred Tengbom. Ed. by David Eller. 1985. pap. 9.95 (ISBN 0-87178-776-8). Brethren.
September Nineteenth, Seventeen Seventy-Seven to January Thirty First, Seventeen Seventy-Eight see Letters of Delegates to Congress, Seventeen Seventy-Four to Seventeen Eighty-Nine.
September, September. Shelby Foote. 1978. 10.95 (ISBN 0-394-40721-0). Random.
September Stars. Fred F. Forner. 1988. 6.95 (ISBN 0-533-07683-8). Vantage.
September Storm. Glyn Partos. 1982. 15.00x (ISBN 0-906660-32-7, Pub. by New Playwrights Network). State Mutual Bk.
September to December Seventeen Seventy-Five see Letters of Delegates to Congress, Seventeen Seventy-Four to Seventeen Eighty-Nine.
September to September: Poems for All Year Round. Dee Lillegard. LC 86-13622. (Poetry Ser.). (Illus.). 128p. (ps-5). 1986. 23.93 (ISBN 0-516-03297-6). Childrens.
September's Bonfire. Theodore Enslin. 32p. (Orig.). 1981. pap. 3.00 (ISBN 0-937013-05-6). Potes Poets.
Septemlingual Dictionary of the Names of European Animals, 2 vols. Ed. by L. Gozmany et al. 2232p. (Eng., Rus., Span., Ger., Hungarian., Fr. & Lat.). 1979. Set. cancelled 230.00 (ISBN 963-05-1381-1, Pub. by Akademiai Kaido Hungary). IPS.
Septemlingual Dictionary of the Names of European Animals, 2 vols. Laslo Gozmany. 2188p. 1980. 847.00x (ISBN 0-569-08577-2, Pub. by Collets (UK)). State Mutual Bk.
Septic Shock. Ed. by Richard K. Root & Merle A. Sande. (Contemporary Issues in Infectious Diseases Ser.: Vol. 4). (Illus.). 281p. 1985. text ed. 45.00 (ISBN 0-443-08397-5). Churchill.
Septic Shock. Ed. by J. L. Vincent & L. G. Thijs. (Intensive Care & Emergency Medicine Ser.: Vol. 4). (Illus.). 335p. 1987. pap. 61.70 (ISBN 0-387-17861-9). Springer-Verlag.
Septic Systems & Ground-Water Protection: A Program Manager's Guide & Reference Book. 79p. 1986. pap. 8.00 (ISBN 0-318-21577-2, S/N 055-000-00256-8). USGPO.
Septic Systems Handbook. O. Benjamin Kaplan. LC 86-27339. (Illus.). 300p. 1987. 44.95 (ISBN 0-87371-095-9). Lewis Pubns Inc.
Septic Tank System Effects on Ground Water. Larry W. Canter & R. C. Knox. LC 84-23280. (Illus.). 336p. 1985. 39.95 (ISBN 0-87371-012-6). Lewis Pubs Inc.
Septic Tank Systems: A Consultant's Toolkit. Winneberger & John H. Timothy. 1985. pap. text ed. 42.95. Butterworth.
Septic Tanks & Aqua-Privies from Ferrocement. S. B. Watt. (Illus.). 98p. (Orig.). 1984. pap. 9.75 (ISBN 0-903031-95-7, Pub. by Intermediate Tech England). Intermediate Tech.
Septicemia: Subject, Reference & Research Guidebook. Lucia M. Wilfred. LC 87-47638. 160p. 1987. 34.50 (ISBN 0-88164-578-8); pap. 26.50 (ISBN 0-88164-579-6). ABBE Pubs Assn.
Septieme Cours Sur la Planification Agricole, 1974, Vol. 2. (Agricultural Planning Ser.: No. 19). 232p. (Fr.). 1974. pap. 17.50 (ISBN 92-5-201992-8, F699, FAO). UNIPUB.
Septima Conferencia Interamericana De Estadistica. Santo Domingo, Republica Dominicana. 22 et 28 de Noviembre de 1977, Informe Final. OAS General Secretariat Planning & Statistics. 133p. 1981. pap. 7.00 (ISBN 0-8270-1342-6). OAS.
Septimius Felton see Dolliver Romance.
Septimo Curso de Derecho Internacional Organizado por el Comite Juridico Interamericano: Agosto 1980. (Conferencias e Informes Ser: OEA/CJI-44). pap. text ed. 38.00 (ISBN 0-8270-1460-0). OAS.
Septoria Disease of Gramineae in Western United States. Roderick Sprague. (Studies in Botany: No. 6). (Illus.). 152p. 1944. pap. 4.95x (ISBN 0-87071-016-8). Oreg St U Pr.
Septoria Diseases of Wheat: Concepts & Mehtods of Disease Management. Z. Eyal et al. (Illus.). 45p. (Orig.). 1987. pap. text ed. 15.00X (ISBN 968-6127-06-2, Pub. by Intl Maize & Wheat Mexico). Agribookstore.
Septuagint & Apocrypha in Greek & English. Charles Brenton. 1390p. 1972. 38.95 (ISBN 0-310-20430-5, 6239). Zondervan.
Septuagint & Modern Study. Sidney Jellicoe. 1978. Repr. of 1968 ed. 15.00x (ISBN 0-931464-00-5). Eisenbrauns.
Septuagint of Jewish Worship. H. St. J. Thackeray. (British Academy of London Ser.). pap. 19.00 (ISBN 0-8115-1262-2). Kraus Repr.
Septuagint Translation of the Hebrew Terms in Relation to God in the Book of Jeremiah. Bernard M. Zlotowitz. 1981. 25.00x (ISBN 0-87068-704-2). Ktav.
Septuagint Translation Technique in the Book of Job. Homer Heater. LC 81-10085. (Catholic Biblical Quarterly Monographs: No. 11). xiv, 152p. 1982. pap. 4.00 (ISBN 0-915170-10-8). Catholic Biblical.
Septuagint with Apocrypha: Greek & English. Sir Lancelot C. Brenton. 1408p. 1986. 39.95 (ISBN 0-913573-44-2). Hendrickson MA.
Septuaginta, 1 vol. Ed. by A. Rahlfs. ixix, 1184p. 1979. Repr. of 1935 ed. 16.00x (ISBN 3-438-05120-6, 56404, Pub. by United Bible). Am Bible.
Septuagintal Lexicography. Robert A. Kraft. LC 75-15894. (Society of Biblical Literature. Septuagint & Cognate Studies). 1975. pap. 9.95 (ISBN 0-89130-008-2, 060401). Scholars Pr GA.
Sepulchre. James Herbert. 320p. 1988. 17.95 (ISBN 0-399-13365-8). Putnam Pub Group.
Sepulchre of Christ in Art & Liturgy. Neil C. Brooks. pap. 9.00 (ISBN 0-384-05925-2). Johnson Repr.
Sequatchie: A Story of the Southern Cumberlands. J. Leonard Raulston & James W. Livingood. LC 73-17360. (Illus.). 286p. 1974. 14.95 (ISBN 0-87049-151-2). U of Tenn Pr.
Sequatchie County. Henry R. Camp. Ed. by Robert B. Jones. (Tennessee County History Ser.: No. 77). (Illus.). 144p. 1985. 12.50x (ISBN 0-87870-166-4). Memphis St Univ.
Sequel: Handbook for the Critical Analysis of Literature. 2nd ed. Richard C. Guches. 274p. 1988. pap. text ed. 14.95x (ISBN 0-917962-88-5). T H Peek.
Sequel of Appomattox. Walter L. Fleming. 1919. 8.50x (ISBN 0-686-83736-3). Elliots Bks.
Sequel of Appomattox see No Break Here.
Sequel to an Enquiry: The Forgeries of Forman & Wise Re-examined. Nicolas Barker & John Collins. (Illus.). 368p. 1984. 70.00 (ISBN 0-85967-638-2). Scolar.
Sequel to Bretton Woods: A Proposal to Reform the World Monetary System. Lawrence B. Krause. LC 71-180726. (Brookings Institution Staff Paper Ser.). pap. 20.00 (ISBN 0-317-26729-9, 2025386). Bks Demand UMI.
Sequel to Colonialism: The Nineteen Fifty-Seven to Nineteen Sixty Foundations for Malaysia. Willard A. Hanna. LC 65-12895. 288p. 1965. 7.50 (ISBN 0-910116-59-8). U Field Staff Intl.
Sequel to Riley's Narrative. W. Willshire Riley. 1979. Repr. of 1851 ed. lib. bdg. 49.00x (ISBN 0-403-00317-2). Scholarly.
Sequelae of Low Birthweight: The Vancouver Study. Henry G. Dunn. LC 65-80534. (Illus.). 306p. 1986. text ed. 64.50 (ISBN 0-397-48002-4, Lippincott Medical). Lippincott.
Sequels: An Annotated Guide to Novels in Series. Janet Husband. LC 82-16309. 368p. 1982. 25.00x (ISBN 0-8389-0368-1). ALA.
Sequence. Elinor Glyn. (Barbara Cartland's Library of Love: No. 17). 1980. 12.95 (ISBN 0-7156-1477-0, Pub. by Duckworth London). Longwood Pub Group.
Sequence. 2nd ed. Rory D. Stephens. 416p. 1986. pap. text ed. 16.95 (ISBN 0-03-001519-7, HoltC). HR&W.
Sequence: A Basic Writing Course. Rory D. Stephens. 1982. pap. text ed. 14.95 (ISBN 0-03-055256-7). HR&W.
Sequence Analysis. Michael Proctor & Peter Abell. 133p. 1985. text ed. 32.95x (ISBN 0-566-00686-3). Gower Pub Co.
Sequence Analysis in Molecular Biology: Treasure Trove or Trivial Pursuit. Gunnar Von Heijne. 188p. 1987. 27.95 (ISBN 0-12-725130-8). Acad Pr.
Sequence Dances of 1982, 1983, 1984: 128 from Rumba Amour to Zara Tango, Abbeydale Foxtrot to Wiclif Waltz & Saunter Adele to Wentworth Waltz Ballroom Dance Ser. (Ballroom Dance Ser). 1985. lib. bdg. 74.50 (ISBN 0-87700-716-0). Revisionist Pr.
Sequence Dancing. 2nd ed. Michael Gwynne. 232p. 1985. 20.95 (ISBN 0-7136-2750-6). Princeton Bk Co.
Sequence of Plumages & Moults of the Passerine Birds of New York, Vol. 13. Jonathan Dwight, Jr. (Annals of the New York Academy of Sciences). Repr. of 1900 ed. 10.00x (ISBN 0-89072-004-5). NY Acad Sci.
Sequence of the Supernatural. J. Robert Ashcroft. 80p. 1972. pap. 1.00 (ISBN 0-88243-748-8, 02-0748). Gospel Pub.
Sequence Spaces & Theory. Kamthan. (Lecture Notes in Pure & Applied Mathematics Ser.: Vol. 65). 1981. 69.75 (ISBN 0-8247-1224-2). Dekker.
Sequence Specificity in Transcription & Translation. Richard Calendar & Larry Gold. LC 85-19686. (UCLA Ser.: Vol. 30). 736p. 1985. 88.00 (ISBN 0-8451-2629-6). A R Liss.
Sequence Transformations. J. P. Delahaye. (Computational Mathematics Ser.: Vol. 11). (Illus.). 250p. 1988. 79.50 (ISBN 0-387-15283-0). Springer-Verlag.
Sequence Transformations & Their Applications. Jet Wimp. LC 80-68564. (Mathematics in Science & Engineering Ser.). 1981. 59.00 (ISBN 0-12-757940-0). Acad Pr.
Sequenced Inventory of Communication Development. rev. ed. Dona L. Hedrick et al. 1984. Complete kit. 250.00 (ISBN 0-295-77005-8); instr. manual 20.00 (ISBN 0-295-77004-X); test manual 20.00 (ISBN 0-295-77010-4); Pkg. of both manuals. 30.00 (ISBN 0-295-77013-9); Receptive Scales & Profiles, pkg. of 50. 25.00 (ISBN 0-295-77011-2); Expressive Scales & Profiles, pkg. of 50. 25.00 (ISBN 0-295-77012-0); Spanish-language forms, pkg. of 25. 25.00 (ISBN 0-295-77014-7). U of Wash Pr.
Sequences. H. Halberstam & K. Roth. 293p. 1983. Repr. of 1966 ed. 38.00 (ISBN 0-387-90801-3). Springer-Verlag.
Sequences. Leslie Norris. 64p. 1988. pap. 9.95 (ISBN 0-87905-303-8). Gibbs Smith Pub.
Sequences: An Annotated Guide to Children's Fiction in Series. Susan Roman. LC 84-24447. 116p. 1985. 17.50x (ISBN 0-8389-0428-9). ALA.
Sequences & Combinatorial Problems. S. I. Gelfand et al. (Pocket Mathematical Library). 92p. 1968. 44.00 (ISBN 0-677-20730-1). Gordon & Breach.
Sequences & Series in Banach Spaces. J. Diestel. (Graduate Texts in Mathematics Ser.: Vol. 92). 280p. 1984. 46.00 (ISBN 0-387-90859-5). Springer-Verlag.
Sequences of Convergence for Series: Proceedings. Steklov Institute of Mathematics, Academy of Sciences, U S S R et al. (Proceedings of the Steklov Institute of Mathematics: No. 86). 1967. 28.00 (ISBN 0-8218-1886-4, STEKLO-86). Am Math.
Sequencing. Gail Aemmer. (Stick-Out-Your-Neck Ser.). (Illus.). 20p. (gr. 3-4). 1985. pap. 5.95 (ISBN 0-88724-146-8, CD-0555). Carson-Dellos.
Sequencing. Gail Aemmer. (Stick-Out-Your-Neck Ser.). (Illus.). 20p. (gr. 5-6). 1985. pap. 5.95 (ISBN 0-88724-147-6, CD-0556). Carson-Dellos.
Sequencing. Arlene Cardozo. LC 86-47663. 224p. 1986. 16.95 (ISBN 0-689-11608-X). Atheneum.
Sequencing. Sharon Wheeler. (Preschool Express Ser.). (Illus.). (ps). 1984. wkbk 1.95 (ISBN 0-916119-10-6). Creat Teach Pr.
Sequencing & Scheduling: An Introduction to the Mathematics of the Job-Shop. Simon French. (Mathematics & Its Applications Ser.). 245p. pap. 39.95 (ISBN 0-470-27456-5). Halsted Pr.
Sequencing Seal. Betty Isaak. (Parents & Preschoolers Ser). (Illus.). 24p. (ps). 1982. wkbk. 2.95 (ISBN 0-88160-090-3, LW 124). Learning Wks.
Sequency Theory Foundations & Applications see Advances in Electronics & Electron Physics: Supplements.
Sequential Analysis. John M. Gottman & Anup K. Roy. (Illus.). 230p. Date not set. price not set (ISBN 0-521-34665-7). Cambridge U Pr.
Sequential Analysis & Optimal Design. Herman Chernoff. (CBMS-NSF Regional Conference Ser.: No. 8). (Illus.). v, 119p. (Orig.). 1972. pap. text ed. 14.50 (ISBN 0-89871-006-5). Soc Indus-Appl Math.
Sequential Analysis: Tests & Confidence Intervals. D. Siegmund. (Statistic Ser.). (Illus.). xi, 272p. 1985. 35.50 (ISBN 0-387-96134-8). Springer-Verlag.
Sequential Curriculum for the Severely & Profoundly Mentally Retarded-Multi-Handicapped. Ellen M. Kissinger. 276p. 1981. spiral 31.75x (ISBN 0-398-04145-8). C C Thomas.
Sequential Estimation. Ghosh et al. (Probability & Mathematical Statistics Ser.). 1987. write for info. (ISBN 0-471-81271-4). Wiley.
Sequential Identification & Ranking Procedures: With Special Reference to Koopman-Darmois Populations. Robert E. Bechhofer et al. LC 67-28463. (Statistical Research Monographs Ser.: Vol. 3). pap. 109.50 (ISBN 0-317-09299-5, 2019954). Bks Demand UMI.
Sequential Methods in Statistics. 2nd ed. G. Barrie Wetherill. (Monographs in Applied Probability & Statistics). 1975. pap. 17.95x (ISBN 0-412-21810-0, NO. 6317, Pub. by Chapman & Hall). Routledge Chapman & Hall.
Sequential Methods in Statistics. G. Barrie Wetherill. (Monographs in Statistics & Applied Probability). 288p. 1986. text ed. 33.00 (ISBN 0-412-28150-3, 9981, Pub. by Chapman & Hall England). Routledge Chapman & Hall.
Sequential Nonparametrics: Invariance Principles & Statistical Inference. Pranab K. Sen. LC 81-4432. (Probability & Mathematical Statistics Ser.). 421p. 1981. 59.95x (ISBN 0-471-06013-5). Wiley.
Sequential Optimization. Joseph Burstein. LC 85-61000. (Illus.). 74p. 1985. pap. 26.32 (ISBN 0-9607126-2-3). Metrics Pr.
Sequential Sourcebook for Elementary School Music: A Curriculum Guide & Sourcebook Combined. 2nd ed. Laura Hochheimer. (Illus.). 1979. pap. 13.50 spiral binding (ISBN 0-918812-12-7). MMB Music.
Sequential Spanish Readers, 3 bks. Homero Castillo et al. Incl. Bk. 1. Primeras Lecturas en Espanol. LC 72-11246. pap. text ed. 5.24 (ISBN 0-395-13389-0); Bk. 2. Aventuras en la Ciudad. LC 72-11248. pap. text ed. 8.96 (ISBN 0-395-14737-9); Bk. 3. Hidalgo de la Mancha: Aventuras de Don Quijote. LC 72-11249. pap. text ed. 8.68 (ISBN 0-395-13390-4). (Span.). 1973. pap. HM.
Sequential Statistical Analysis of Hypothesis Testing, Point & Interval Estimation, & Decision Theory. Ed. by Zakkula Gobidarajulu. (Mathematical & Management Sciences Ser.: Vol. 5). 1987. 48.50 (ISBN 0-935950-17-6). Am Sciences Pr.
Sequential Statistical Analysis of Hypothesis Testing, Point & Interval Estimation, & Decision Theory. Zakkula Govindarajulu. LC 80-68287. (American Sciences Press Ser. in Mathematical & Management Sciences: Vol. 5). 1981. text ed. 48.50 (ISBN 0-935950-02-8). Am Sciences Pr.
Sequential Techniques in Bioassay. Z. Govindarajulu. (Illus.). xiv, 166p. 1988. 46.00 (ISBN 3-8055-4630-0). S Karger.
Sequential Tests. Ed. by Collet's Holdings, Ltd. Staff. 1986. 42.00x (ISBN 0-317-46722-0, Pub. by Collets (UK)). State Mutual Bk.
Sequentics en Formuleringen. Ten P. Have. (Studies Over Taalgebruik). xi, 367p. 1987. pap. write for info. (ISBN 90-6765-315-2). Foris Pubns.
Sequestres d'Altona. Jean-Paul Sartre. (Folio Ser.: No. 938). 1972. 7.95 (ISBN 0-686-54991-0). Schoenhof.
Sequins & Shades: The Michael Jackson Reference Guide. Carol D. Terry. (Rock & Roll Reference Ser.: No. 22). (Illus.). 542p. 1987. 29.50 (ISBN 0-87650-205-2, 3380). Pierian.
Sequoia: Kings Canyon National Parks. Randy Collings. 1982. 7.95 (ISBN 0-933692-23-4). A R Collings.
Sequoia-Kings Canyon: The Story Behind the Scenery. William C. Tweed. LC 79-87571. (Illus.). 64p. 1980. pap. 4.50 (ISBN 0-916122-65-4). KC Pubns.
Sequoias of Yosemite National Park. H. T. Harvey. (Illus.). 36p. 1978. pap. 2.95 (ISBN 0-939666-14-6). Yosemite Assn.
Sequoyah. Grant Foreman. (Civilization of the American Indian Ser.: No. 16). (Illus.). 85p. 1984. pap. 4.50 (ISBN 0-8061-1056-2). U of Okla Pr.
Sequoyah. Jan Geitler & Kathleen Thompson. (Raintree Stories Ser.). (Illus.). 32p. (Orig.). (gr. 2-3). 1988. PLB 15.33 (ISBN 0-8172-2678-8); pap. text ed. 9.26 (ISBN 0-8173-3682-6). Raintree Pubs.
Sequoyah, Cherokee Hero. new ed. Joanne Oppenheim. LC 78-60117. (Illus.). 48p. (gr. 4-6). 1979. PLB 9.59 (ISBN 0-89375-159-6); pap. 1.95 (ISBN 0-89375-149-9). Troll Assocs.
Sequoyah: The Cherokee Who Captured Words. Lillie Patterson. LC 74-20966. (Indians Ser.). (Illus.). 80p. (gr. 2-5). 1975. PLB 6.69 (ISBN 0-8116-6612-3). Garrard.
Ser Algo: E. U.-Cuba-Puerto Rico (Federalismo: Union para la Defensa para la Union) Jose R. Goldaras. LC 79-53923. 1979. pap. 7.00 (ISBN 0-89729-201-4). Ediciones.
Ser o No Ser una Madre un Padre. rev. ed. 24p. (Span.). 1981. pap. 0.75 (ISBN 0-934586-20-9, 951). Plan Parent.
Ser y el Mesias see Being & the Messiah: The Message of St. John.
Seraffyn's European Adventure. Lin Pardey & Larry Pardey. (Illus.). 1984. pap. 12.95 (ISBN 0-393-30191-5). Norton.
Seraffyn's Oriental Adventure. Lin Pardey & Larry Pardey. (Illus.). 1983. 19.95 (ISBN 0-393-03281-7). Norton.
Seraglio. James Merrill. LC 87-17548. 336p. 1987. 19.95 (ISBN 0-689-11924-0). Atheneum.
Seraph on the Suwanee: A Novel. Zora N. Hurston. LC 73-18580. Repr. of 1948 ed. 24.50 (ISBN 0-404-11391-5). AMS Pr.
Seraphim Code. Robert Liston. 352p. 1988. pap. 3.95 (ISBN 0-8125-0616-2). Tor Bks.
Seraphim Grosse Pointe. Oswald De Andrade. Tr. by Kenneth D. Jackson & Albert Bork. LC 78-70340. 1979. 8.95 (ISBN 0-918722-08-X). Nefertiti.
Seraphim of Sarov see St. Seraphim of Sarov.

Seraphim's Seraphim: The Life of Pelagia Ivanovna Serebrenikova, Fool for Christ's Sake of the Seraphim-Diveyevo Convent. Tr. by Holy Transfiguration Monastery. LC 79-90720. (Illus.). 184p. (Orig.). 1980. pap. 4.50x (ISBN 0-913026-08-5). St Nectarios.

Seraphina. Jean Merrill. 224p. (Orig.). 1980. pap. 1.75 (ISBN 0-449-50124-8, Coventry). Fawcett.

Seraphita. facs. ed. Honore De Balzac. LC 73-134961. (Short Story Index Reprint Ser). 1889. 18.00 (ISBN 0-8369-3691-4). Ayer Co Pubs.

Seraphita. Honore De Balzac. 303p. 1950. 14.95 (ISBN 0-686-53926-5). French & Eur.

Seraphita. Honore De Balzac. LC 76-12203. (Spiritual Science Library). 184p. Repr. of 1976 ed. cancelled (ISBN 0-8334-0734-1, Steinerbks). Garber Comm.

Seraphita. 3rd ed. Honore De Balzac. LC 85-80912. (Spiritual Fiction Ser.). 216p. 1986. pap. 10.50 (ISBN 0-8334-0015-0, Freedeeds Bks). Garber Comm.

SERB Official Reporter. 1987. 155.00 (ISBN 0-8322-0235-5). Banks-Baldwin.

Serber Says: About Nuclear Physics. R. Serber. 308p. 1987. 53.00 (ISBN 9971-50-158-9); pap. 28.00 (ISBN 9971-50-376-X). World Scientific Pub.

Serbia Between East & West, The Events of 1903-1908. Wayne S. Vucinich. LC 68-54304. (Stanford University. Stanford Studies in History, Economics, & Political Science: No. 9). Repr. of 1954 ed. 31.00 (ISBN 0-404-50973-8). AMS Pr.

Serbian Folk Lore. Elodie Mijatovic. Ed. by W. Denton. LC 68-56477. 1968. Repr. of 1874 ed. 22.00 (ISBN 0-405-08788-8, Pub. by Blom). Ayer Co Pubs.

Serbian Folk Poetry: Ancient Legends, Romantic Songs. Zora D. Zimmerman. xii, 343p. 1986. 11.95 (ISBN 0-915887-07-X). Kosovo Pub Co.

Serbian Poetry & Milutin Bojic. Mihailo Dordevic. (East European Monographs: No. 4). 113p. 1977. 20.00x (ISBN 0-914710-27-3). East Eur Quarterly.

Serbian Poetry from the Beginning to the Present: An Historical Anthology. Milne Holton & Vasa D. Mihailovich. (Yale Russian & East European Publications: No. 11). 400p. Date not set. price not set. Y Cent Inter Area.

Serbian Village in Historical Perspective. Joel M. Halpern & Barbara K. Halpern. (George & Louise Spindler Case Studies in Cultural Anthropology Ser.). (Illus.). 156p. 1983. pap. text ed. 7.95x (ISBN 0-8290-0585-4). Irvington.

Serbian Village in Historical Perspective. Joel M. Halpern & Barbara K. Halpern. (Illus.). 152p. 1986. pap. text ed. 8.50x (ISBN 0-88133-209-7). Waveland Pr.

Serbo Croat for Foreigners: Vocabulary & Grammar. 2nd ed. Slavna Babic. (Illus.). 233p. 1985. pap. text ed. 18.50x (ISBN 0-89918-702-1, Y702). Vanous.

Serbo-Croatian. Berlitz Editors. (Travel Guides Ser.). 1983. pap. 14.95 (ISBN 0-317-12086-7, Berlitz). Macmillan.

Serbo-Croatian, Vol. I. Foreign Service Institute Staff. 633p. (Serbian & Croatian.). 1980. 175.00x (ISBN 0-88432-042-1, Y601); 12 audio cassettes incl. J Norton Pubs.

Serbo-Croatian Basic Course, Vol. II. Foreign Service Institute Staff. 677p. 1981. includes 24 cassettes 195.00x (ISBN 0-88432-101-0, Y650). J Norton Pubs.

Serbo-Croatian, English: English-Serbo Croatian Dictionary, 2 vols. Morton Benson. 1373p. 1987. 55.00 ea. (ISBN 0-87052-399-6) (ISBN 0-87052-398-8). Hippocrene Bks.

Serbo-Croatian-English, English-Serbo-Croatian Dictionary. (Hippocrene Foreign Language Dictionaries Ser.). 550p. 1986. 19.95 (ISBN 0-87052-139-X). Hippocrene Bks.

Serbo-Croatian for Foreigners. Slauna Babic. 240p. 1987. 9.95 (ISBN 0-87052-397-X). Hippocrene Bks.

Serbo-Croatian for Foreigners, Vol. 1. Rev. & enl. ed. S. Babic. (Illus.). 1981. pap. 25.00. Heinman.

Serbo-Croatian for Travellers. Berlitz Editors. LC 73-2272. (Travellers Ser. for English Speakers). (Illus.). 1974. pap. 4.95 (ISBN 0-02-964150-0, Berlitz); cassettepak, 1976 14.95 (ISBN 0-02-962150-X). Macmillan.

Serbo-Croatian Grammar & Reader. Oton Grozdic. 1969. 12.95x (ISBN 0-02-845540-1). Hafner.

Serbo-Croatian Heroic Songs: Bijelo Polje: Three Texts from Avdo Mededovic, Vol. 6. new ed. Compiled By Milman Parry et al. (Publications of the Milman Parry Collection Texts; & Translation: No. 4). (Illus.). 383p. 1980. text ed. 25.00x (ISBN 0-674-80166-0). Harvard U Pr.

Serbo-Croatian Reading Passages, with Comments, Exercises, Vocabulary. S. Babic. 1975. 10.00 (ISBN 0-88431-623-8). Heinman.

Serbo-Croation Reading Passages. Sluna Bahic. 210p. 1983. pap. 7.50x (ISBN 0-89918-732-3, Y-732). Vanous.

Serbocroatian-English - English-Serbocroatian Dictionary. 1985. 32.50. Saphrograph.

Serbocroatian-English Dictionary. M. Benson. 770p. (Serbian, Croatian & Eng.). 1980. 95.00 (ISBN 0-686-97438-7, M-9630). French & Eur.

Serbocroatian-English Dictionary. Ed. by Morton Benson. LC 79-146959. (Eng., Serbian & Croatian.). 1971. text ed. 48.95x (ISBN 0-8122-7636-1). U of Pa Pr.

Serbocroatian-English Dictionary. S. Brkic. 416p. (Serbian, Croatian & Eng.). 1980. pap. 14.95 (ISBN 0-686-97436-0, M-9631). French & Eur.

Serbocroatian-English Dictionary. M. Drvodelic. 847p. (Serbian, Croatian & Eng.). 1978. 69.95 (ISBN 0-686-92510-6, M-9707). French & Eur.

Serbocroatian-English, English-Serbocroatian Dictionary. Rev. & enl. ed. B. Grujic. (Serbo., Croatian. & Eng.). 15.00. Heinman.

Serbocroatian Heroic Songs: Bihacka Krajina: Epics from Bihac, Cazin, & Kulen Vakuf, Vol. XIV. Milman Parry. Ed. by David E. Bynum. (Milman Parry Collection, Texts & Translations Ser.). (Illus.). 529p. 1980. text ed. 22.50x (ISBN 0-674-80165-2). Harvard U Pr.

Serbocroatian-Slovene Dictionary. J. Jurancic. 1320p. (Serbian, Croatian & Slovene.). 1972. 49.95 (ISBN 0-686-92509-2, M-9698). French & Eur.

Serbocroatian Heroic Songs, Vol. III: Wedding of Smailagic Meho. Millman Parry. Ed. & tr. by Albert B. Lord. 1974. text ed. 22.50x (ISBN 0-674-80163-6). Harvard U Pr.

Serbocroatian Heroic Songs, Vol. IV: Zenidba Smailagina sina: Wedding of Smailagic Meho in Original Serbo-Croatian. Millman Parry. Ed. & tr. by Albert B. Lord. 1974. text ed. 20.00x (ISBN 0-674-80164-4). Harvard U Pr.

Serbokraotischen Dialekte, Ihre Struktur und Entwicklung. P. Ivic. (S P R Ser: No. 18). 1958. text ed. 32.80x (ISBN 0-686-22459-0). Mouton.

Serbs & Byzantium During the Reign of Tsar Stephen Dusan (1331-1355) & His Successors. George Soulis. LC 84-1662. (Illus.). 392p. 1984. 15.00x (ISBN 0-88402-137-8). Dumbarton Oaks.

Serenade. James M. Cain. LC 78-63982. (Gay Experience). Repr. of 1937 ed. 26.00 (ISBN 0-404-61502-3). AMS Pr.

Serenade. James M. Cain. 1978. pap. 3.95 (ISBN 0-394-72585-9, Vin). Random.

Serenade. Bernard Welt. Ed. by Kenward Elmslie. (Orig.). 1980. pap. 5.00 (ISBN 0-915990-15-6). Z Pr.

Serenade for a Lost Love. Jocelyn Haley. (Super Romances Ser.). 384p. 1983. pap. 2.95 (ISBN 0-373-70054-7, Pub. by Worldwide). Harlequin Bks.

Serenade Pour Anne. Flora Kidd. (Collection Harlequin Ser.). 192p. 1983. pap. 1.95 (ISBN 0-373-49324-X). Harlequin Bks.

Serenade: The Stories of Joseph A. L. Poitras. Joseph A. Poitras. 130p. 1985. 10.95 (ISBN 0-533-06213-6). Vantage.

Serenading Louie. Lanford Wilson. 1976. pap. 3.50x (ISBN 0-685-74730-1). Dramatists Play.

Serenading Louie. rev. ed. Lanford Wilson. 64p. 1985. 12.95 (ISBN 0-8090-8538-0); pap. 6.95 (ISBN 0-8090-1249-9). Hill & Wang.

Serenading the Reluctant Eagle: American Musical Life During Crisis, 1925-1945. Nicholas E. Tawa. 272p. 1984. text ed. 19.95 (ISBN 0-02-871760-0). Schirmer Bks.

Serena's Secret. Bryan Strong & Christine DeVault. Ed. by Mary Nelson. (Illus.). (gr. 5-8). 1987. pap. 3.95 (ISBN 0-941816-32-X). Network Pubns.

Serendipity. Scholasticus Chimpus. 215p. 1988. 9.95 (ISBN 0-945268-00-9). Drone Pub Co.

Serendipity. (gr. 1-6). pap. 2.50 (ISBN 0-8431-0562-3). Price Stern.

Serendipity, 5 vols. write for info. (ISBN 0-8431-0605-0). Price Stern.

Serendipity Bible Study Book of Acts. Abr. ed. Lyman Coleman. 64p. 1988. pap. price not set (ISBN 0-310-59011-6). Zondervan.

Serendipity Bible Study Book of John. abr. ed. Lyman Coleman. 64p. 1988. pap. 2.50 (ISBN 0-310-59001-9, 12028P). Zondervan.

Serendipity Bible Study Book of Revelation. Abr. ed. Lyman Coleman. 48p. 1988. pap. price not set (ISBN 0-310-59031-0). Zondervan.

Serendipity Bible Study Book of Romans. Abr. ed. Lyman Coleman. 32p. 1988. lib. bdg. 2.50 (ISBN 0-310-59021-3, 12030P). Zondervan.

Serendipity Group Study Book. Ed. by Lyman Coleman et al. 496p. 1986. kivar 11.95 (ISBN 0-310-25081-1, 12032P). Zondervan.

Serendipity in St. Helena. I. Shine. 1970. 51.00 (ISBN 0-08-012794-0). Pergamon.

Serendipity: When Good Things Happen to You Unexpectedly. Uriah J. Fields. 34p. 1983. pap. 3.00 (ISBN 0-938844-09-1). Am Mutuality.

Serene Life. A. Pupil. 1981. pap. 2.00 (ISBN 0-911794-47-6). Aqua Educ.

Serengeti: Dynamics of an Ecosystem. A. R. Sinclair & M. Norton-Griffiths. LC 79-10146. (Illus.). 384p. 1979. lib. bdg. 35.00x (ISBN 0-226-76028-6). U of Chicago Pr.

Serengeti: Dynamics of an Ecosystem. Ed. by A. R. Sinclair & M. Norton-Griffiths. LC 79-10146. (Illus.). xii, 390p. 1984. pap. text ed. 15.00x (ISBN 0-226-76029-4). U of Chicago Pr.

Serengeti Lion: A Study of Predator-Prey Relations. George B. Schaller. LC 78-180043. (Wildlife Behavior & Ecology Ser.). (Illus.). 472p. 1976. pap. 16.95 (ISBN 0-226-73640-7, P661, Phoen). U of Chicago Pr.

Serengeti: Natural Order on the African Plain. Mitsuaki Iwago. LC 87-6393. (Illus.). 328p. 1987. 35.00 (ISBN 0-87701-441-8); pap. 19.95 (ISBN 0-87701-432-9). Chronicle Bks.

Serengeti Wind. Russ Thomas. LC 87-40252. 115p. (Orig.). 1987. pap. 7.95 (ISBN 1-55523-093-8). Winston-Derek.

Serenissima. Erica Jong. 1987. 17.95. HM.

Serenissima. Erica Jong. 1988. pap. 4.95 (ISBN 0-440-20104-7). Dell.

Serenity. Paul Reed. 112p. (Orig.). 1987. pap. 5.95 (ISBN 0-89087-506-5). Celestial Arts.

Serenity. (Pocket Power Ser.). 16p. (Orig.). 1986. pap. 0.50 (ISBN 0-89486-355-X). Hazelden.

Serenity: Living with Equanimity, Zest, & Fulfilment by Applying the Wisdom of the World's Greatest Thinkers. William Gerber. 464p. (Orig.). 1986. lib. bdg. 41.50 (ISBN 0-8191-5019-3, North Amer Soc Social Philosophy); pap. text ed. 19.75 (ISBN 0-8191-5020-7). U Pr of Amer.

Serenity Principle: Finding Inner Peace in Recovery. Joseph Bailey. LC 87-46195. 144p. 1988. pap. 7.95 (ISBN 0-06-255481-6, PL 4286, HarpR). Har-Row.

Serente. Curt Nimuendaju. Tr. by Robert H. Lowie. LC 76-44769. Repr. of 1942 ed. 22.50 (ISBN 0-404-15873-0). AMS Pr.

Serente. Curt Nimuendaju. Ed. by Robert H. Lowie. Tr. by Curt Lowrie. (Illus.). xii, 106p. 1967. pap. 5.00 (ISBN 0-916561-58-5). Southwest Mus.

Serf Actor: The Life & Art of Mikhail Shchepkin. Laurence Senelick. LC 83-12593. (Contributions in Drama & Theatre Studies: No. 9). xvi, 305p. 1984. lib. bdg. 36.95 (ISBN 0-313-22494-3, SSF/). Greenwood.

Serf & Crusader. Philip Sauvain. 1984. pap. 9.95 (ISBN 0-7175-1238-X). Dufour.

Serf & State Peasant Agriculture: Kharkov Province, 1842-1861. Zack J. Deal, III. Ed. by Stuart Bruchey. LC 80-2803. (Dissertations in European Economic History II). (Illus.). 1981. lib. bdg. 43.00x (ISBN 0-405-13987-X). Ayer Co Pubs.

Serf Population in Russia: A Statistical Survey According to the Tenth National Census 1858. A. Troynitskii. Tr. by Elaine Herman. 160p. 1982. 21.00 (ISBN 0-89250-061-1). Orient Res Partners.

Serf, Seigneur, & Sovereign: Agrarian Reform in Eighteenth-Century Bohemia. William E. Wright. LC 66-29653. pap. 56.80 (2056205). Bks Demand UMI.

Serfdom & Social Control in Russia: Petrovskoe, a Village in Tambov. Stephen L. Hoch. LC 86-6915. (Illus.). x, 220p. 1986. lib. bdg. 25.00x (ISBN 0-226-34583-1). U of Chicago Pr.

Serfs, Peasants, & Socialists: A Former Serf Village in the Republic of Guinea. William Derman. LC 78-117148. 1973. 40.00x (ISBN 0-520-01728-5). U of Cal Pr.

Serge Diaghilev: His Life, His Work, His Legend. Serge Lifar. LC 76-25041. (Series in Dance). 1976. Repr. of 1940 ed. lib. bdg. 32.50 (ISBN 0-306-70839-6). Da Capo.

Serge Koussevitsky, the Boston Symphony Orchestra & the New American Music. Hugo Leichtentritt. LC 75-41172. Repr. of 1946 ed. 16.45 (ISBN 0-404-14680-5). AMS Pr.

Serge Lifar Collection of Ballet & Costume Design. (Illus.). 84p. 1965. pap. 5.00 (ISBN 0-317-13580-5). Wadsworth Atheneum.

Sergeant Bilko. Nat Hiken. 12.95 (ISBN 0-89190-168-X, Pub. by Am Repr). Amereon Ltd.

Sergeant-Bridge & Tunnel Authority. Jack Rudman. (Career Examination Ser.: C-732). (Cloth bdg. avail. on request). pap. 15.00 (ISBN 0-8373-0732-5). Natl Learning.

Sergeant Getulio. Joao U. Ribeiro. 144p. 1984. pap. 2.95 (ISBN 0-380-67082-8, 67082, Bard). Avon.

Sergeant Gringo. Jack Cummings. 184p. 1987. pap. 2.95 (ISBN 1-55547-139-0). Critics Choice Paper.

Sergeant Lamb's America. Robert Graves. 339p. 1986. pap. 7.95 (ISBN 0-89733-213-X). Academy Chi Pubs.

Sergeant Lawrence Goes France. Ed. by Peter Yule. 207p. 1987. 19.95 (ISBN 0-522-84320-4, Pub. by Melbourne U Pr). Intl Spec Bk.

Sergeant Marco. Anthony Mercadante. 195p. 1986. 12.95 (ISBN 0-533-06487-2). Vantage.

Sergeant Ola & His Followers. David Lan. 1981. pap. 4.95 (ISBN 0-413-47590-5, NO. 6383). Heinemann Ed.

Sergeant, P. D. Ed. by Hy Hammer. LC 81-10897. 304p. (Orig.). 1982. pap. 12.00 (ISBN 0-668-05278-3, 5278). Arco.

Sergeant, P.D. 8th ed. Anthony S. Mazzara. (ARCO Civil Service Test Tutor Ser.). 1988. pap. 11.95 (ISBN 0-13-806993-X). Prentice Hall Pr.

Sergeant Pepper's Lonely Hearts Club Band: The Beatles. (Illus.). 72p. 1987. pap. 9.95 perfect bd. (ISBN 0-88188-771-4). H Leonard Pub Corp.

Sergeant-Police Department. Jack Rudman. (Career Examination Ser.: C-733). (Cloth bdg. avail. on request). pap. 15.00 (ISBN 0-8373-0733-3). Natl Learning.

Sergeant Shakespeare. Duff Cooper. LC 76-30696. (Studies in Shakespeare, No. 24). 1977. lib. bdg. 46.95x (ISBN 0-8383-2152-6). Haskell.

Sergeant, Sheriff's Department. Jack Rudman. (Career Examination Ser.: C-874). 1988. pap. 15.00 (ISBN 0-8373-0874-7). Natl Learning.

Sergeant York: An American Hero. David D. Lee. LC 84-10465. (Illus.). 184p. 1985. 18.00 (ISBN 0-8131-1517-5). U Pr of Ky.

Sergeant's Cat. Janwillem Van de Wetering. LC 87-2411. 224p. 1987. 16.95 (ISBN 0-394-54925-2). Pantheon.

Sergeant's Colonel. Walter C. Krause. LC 85-91003. (Illus.). 224p. 1985. 13.50 (ISBN 0-682-40241-9). Exposition-Phoenix.

Sergei Aksakov & Russian Pastoral. Andrew R. Durkin. 421p. 1983. 37.00 (ISBN 0-8135-0954-8). Rutgers U Pr.

Sergei Kirov & the Struggle for Soviet Power in the Terek Region, 1917-1918. Richard D. King. Ed. by William H. McNeill & Barbara Jelavich. (Modern European History Ser.). 430p. 1987. lib. bdg. 65.00 (ISBN 0-8240-8056-4). Garland Pub.

Sergei Koussevitsky & His Epoch. Arthur Lourie. LC 78-121287. Repr. of 1931 ed. 17.50 (ISBN 0-404-04036-5). AMS Pr.

Sergei Koussevitzky & His Epoch. Arthur Lourie. Tr. by S. W. Pring. LC 78-94276. (Select Bibliographies Reprint Ser). 1931. 24.50 (ISBN 0-8369-5050-X). Ayer Co Pubs.

Sergei M. Eisenstein: A Biography. Marie Seton. 533p. 1981. 60.00x (ISBN 0-234-77440-1, Pub. by Dobson Bks England). State Mutual Bk.

Sergei Nechaev. Philip Pomper. (Illus.). 1979. 35.00x (ISBN 0-8135-0867-3). Rutgers U Pr.

Sergei Prokofiev: A Biography. Harlow Robinson. (Illus.). 592p. 1987. 29.95 (ISBN 0-670-80419-3). Viking.

Sergei Prokofiev: A Biography. Harlow Robinson. LC 87-21007. (Illus.). 573p. 1988. pap. 12.95 (ISBN 1-55778-009-9). Paragon Hse.

Sergei Prokofiev: A Soviet Tragedy. Victor Seroff. LC 78-73657. 1979. 14.95 (ISBN 0-8008-7067-0, Crescendo); pap. 7.95 (ISBN 0-8008-7068-9, Crescendo). Taplinger.

Sergei Prokofiev: Materials, Articles, Interviews. D. Shostakovich et al. 257p. 1978. 9.45 (ISBN 0-8285-1618-9, Pub. by Progress Pubs USSR). Imported Pubns.

Sergei Vasilievich Rachmaninoff: A Guide to Research. Robert Palmieri. LC 83-49315. (Reference Library of the Humanities: Composer Resource Manuals). 357p. 1985. lib. bdg. 49.00 (ISBN 0-8240-8996-0). Garland Pub.

Sergei Yesenin: The Man, the Verse, the Age. Y. Prokushev. 309p. 1979. 9.45 (ISBN 0-8285-1567-0, Pub. by Progress Pubs USSR). Imported Pubns.

Sergengeti Sunrise. (Superromance Ser.). 384p. 1983. pap. 2.95 (ISBN 0-373-70092-X, Pub. by Worldwide). Harlequin Bks.

Sergison Papers. Ed. by R. D. Merriman. 1985. 69.00x (ISBN 0-317-44232-5, Pub. by Navy Rec Soc). State Mutual Bk.

Seri. A. L. Kroeber. (Illus.). 60p. 1964. pap. 3.50 (ISBN 0-916561-59-3). Southwest Mus.

Seri. Alfred L. Kroeber. LC 76-43764. (Southwest Museum, Papers: No. 6). Repr. of 1931 ed. 11.50 (ISBN 0-404-15619-3). AMS Pr.

Seri Indians of Sonora, Mexico. Bernice Johnston. (Illus.). 16p. 1980. pap. 3.95 (ISBN 0-8165-0711-2). U of Ariz Pr.

Seri Prehistory: The Archaeology of the Central Coast of Sonora, Mexico. Thomas Bowen. LC 74-29360. (Anthropological Papers: No. 27). 120p. 1976. pap. 10.95x (ISBN 0-8165-0358-3). U of Ariz Pr.

Serial. Cyra MacFadden. 1977. pap. 4.95 spiral bound (ISBN 0-394-73361-4). Knopf.

Serial Arrangement of Chinese Characters. George A. Kennedy. 2.00 (ISBN 0-88710-087-2). Yale Far Eastern Pubns.

Serial Bibliographies & Abstracts in History: An Annotated Guide. David Henige. LC 85-27178. (Bibliographies & Indexes in World History: No. 2). 234p. 1986. lib. bdg. 36.95 (ISBN 0-313-25070-7, HSE/). Greenwood.

Serial Bibliographies for Medieval Studies. Ed. by Richard H. Rouse. LC 68-31637. (Center for Medieval & Renaissance Studies, UCLA: Publications: No. 3). 1969. 36.50x (ISBN 0-520-01456-1). U of Cal Pr.

Serial Bibliographies in the Humanities & Social Sciences. Ed. by Richard A. Gray. LC 68-58895. 1969. 29.50 (ISBN 0-87650-004-1). Pierian.

Serial Biography. Tom Raworth. LC 77-82307. (New World Writing Ser.). 1977. pap. 9.95 (ISBN 0-913666-16-5). Turtle Isl Foun.

Serial Changes in Subcutaneous Fat Thicknesses of Children & Adults. A. F. Roche et al. (Monographs in Paediatrics: Vol. 17). (Illus.). x, 110p. 1982. pap. 52.75 (ISBN 3-8055-3496-5). S Karger.

Serial Composition. Reginald S. Brindle. (YA) (gr. 9 up). 1966. 14.50x (ISBN 0-19-311906-4). Oxford U Pr.

Serial Compositon & Atonality: An Introduction to the Music of Schoenberg, Berg, & Webern. 5th ed. George Perle. 1981. 25.00x (ISBN 0-520-04365-0). U of Cal Pr.

Serial Connection: People, Information, Communication. Ed. by Leigh Chatterton & Mary E. Clack. LC 86-32021. (Serials Librarian Ser.). 200p. 1987. text ed. 34.95 (ISBN 0-86656-654-6). Haworth Pr.

Serial-Data Computation. Stewart G. Smith & Peter B. Denyer. 1987. lib. bdg. 42.50 (ISBN 0-89838-253-X). Kluwer Academic.

Serial Issue Identification: Code & Symbol Guidelines. Joint Committee of the Book Industry Study Group & Serials Industry Advisory Committee. (Illus.). 36p. 1987. pap. 5.00 (ISBN 0-940016-26-5). Bk Indus Study.

Serial Killers: The Causes of a Growing Menace. Joel Norris. LC 87-32537. (Illus.). 192p. 1988. 18.95 (ISBN 0-385-23730-8, Dolp). Doubleday.

Serial Murder. Ronald M. Holmes & James DeBurger. (Studies in Crime, Law, & Justice: Vol. 2). 160p. 1987. text ed. 27.50 (ISBN 0-8039-2840-8); pap. text ed. 12.95 (ISBN 0-8039-2841-6). Sage.

Serial Music: A Classified Bibliography of Writings on 12 Tone & Electronic Music. Ann Basart. LC 75-45460. 151p. 1976. Repr. of 1961 ed. lib. bdg. 35.00x (ISBN 0-8371-8753-2, BASM). Greenwood.

Serial Numbers of U. S. Martial Arms. Franklin B. Mallory. LC 82-63083. 112p. 1983. 10.00 (ISBN 0-9603306-1-5). Springfield Res Serv.

Serial Numbers of U. S. Martial Arms, Vol. 2. Franklin B. Mallory. 209p. 1986. 15.00 (ISBN 0-9603306-3-1). Springfield Res Serv.

Serial Publications. Marine Biological Laboratory. 1983. 10.00 (ISBN 0-685-52862-6). Marine Bio.

Serial Publications Containing Medical Classics. 2nd ed. Lee Ash. 1979. 35.00 (ISBN 0-9603990-0-3). Antiquarium.

Serial Publications in Anthropology. 2nd ed. Ed. by Library-Anthropology Resource Group (LARG) et al. v, 177p. (Orig.). 1982. pap. 17.50 (ISBN 0-913178-64-0). Redgrave Pub Co.

Serial Publications: Their Place & Treatment in Libraries. 3rd ed. Andrew D. Osborn. LC 80-11686. 486p. 1980. 25.00x (ISBN 0-8389-0299-5). ALA.

Serial Reactions Considered As Conditioned Reactions. William M. Lepley. Bd. with Classified Bibliography of Psychodietetics. M. F. Frtiz. Repr. of 1934 ed; Development of Alfred Binet's Psychology. E. J. Varon. Repr. of 1935 ed; Autistic Gestures, an Experimental Study in Symbolic Movement. M. H. Krout. Repr. of 1935 ed; Nightmare Dream. H. Cason. Repr. of 1935 ed; Studies in Psychology from Smith College. Ed. by J. J. Gibson. Repr. of 1935 ed. (Psychology Monographs General & Applied: Vol. 46). pap. 36.00 (ISBN 0-8115-1445-5). Kraus Repr.

Serial Verb Formation in the Dravidian Languages. Sanford B. Steever. 1987. 24.00 (ISBN 81-208-0378-7, Pub. by Motilal Banarsidass). South Asia Bks.

Serials & Microforms: Patron Oriented Management: Proceedings. Ed. by Nancy J. Melin. 100p. 1983. 35.00x (ISBN 0-930466-65-9). Meckler Corp.

Serials Automation for Acquisition & Inventory Control. William G. Potter & Arlene F. Sirkin. 192p. 1981. pap. text ed. 15.00x (ISBN 0-8389-3267-3). ALA.

Serials Automation in the United States: A Bibliographic History. Gary M. Pitkin. LC 76-18116. 157p. 1976. 16.50 (ISBN 0-8108-0955-9). Scarecrow.

Serials Cataloging: The State of the Art. Jim E. Cole & Jackie Zajanc. LC 87-2877. (Serials Librarian). 100p. 1987. text ed. 29.95 (ISBN 0-86656-619-8). Haworth Pr.

Serials Collection Development: Choices & Strategies. Ed. by Sul H. Lee. LC 81-84645. (Library Management Ser.: No. 5). 1981. 30.00 (ISBN 0-87650-136-6). Pierian.

Serials Collection: Organization & Administration. Ed. by Nancy J. Melin. LC 82-81133. (Current Issues In Serials Management Ser.: No. 1). 1982. 30.00 (ISBN 0-87650-140-4). Pierian.

Serials Control, Vol. I. Ed. by James E. Rush. LC 83-9584. (Library Systems Evaluation Guide Ser.). (Illus.). 194p. 1983. velo bound 59.50 (ISBN 0-912803-01-0). Rush Assoc.

Serials Directory: An International Reference Book, 3 vols. EBSCO Publishing Staff. 4119p. 1987. Set. 289.00 (ISBN 0-913956-22-8). Vol. 1 (ISBN 0-913956-23-6). Vol. 2 (ISBN 0-913956-24-4). Vol. 3 (ISBN 0-913956-25-2). EBSCO Ind.

Serials for Libraries: An Annotated Guide to Continuations, Annuals, Yearbooks, Almanacs, Transactions, Proceedings, Directories, Services. 2nd ed. Ed. by John Ganly. Diane Sciattara. LC 85-4997. 442p. 1985. lib. bdg. 75.00 (ISBN 0-918212-85-5). Neal-Schuman.

Serials in Psychology & Allied Fields. Margaret Tompkins & Norma Shirley. LC 75-38213. 475p. 1976. 22.50 (ISBN 0-87875-083-5). Whitston Pub.

Serials Information Chain: Discussion, Debate & Dialoge Proceeding of the North American Serials Interest Group. Leigh Chatterton & Mary E. Clack. LC 87-31063. (The Serial Librarian Ser.). (Illus.). 170p. 1988. text ed. 29.95 (ISBN 0-86656-744-5). Haworth Pr.

Serials Librarianship. Ross Bourne. 270p. 1980. 25.00 (ISBN 0-85365-631-2, Pub. by Library Assn Pub London); pap. 13.50 (ISBN 0-85365-721-1, Pub. by Library Assn Pub London). ALA.

Serials Librarianship in Transition: Issues & Developments. Ed. by Peter Gellatly. LC 85-16439. (Serials Librarian Ser.: Vol. 10, Nos. 1-2). 305p. 1986. text ed. 38.95 (ISBN 0-86656-497-7, B497). Haworth Pr.

Serials Management & Microforms. Ed. by Patricia M. Walsh. LC 78-13179. (Meckler Publishing's Series in Library Micrographics Management: No. 4). 1979. 21.50x (ISBN 0-913672-11-4). Meckler Corp.

Serials Management in an Automated Age: Proceedings, Serials Conference. Ed. by Nancy J. Melin. 1982. 35.00x (ISBN 0-930466-48-9). Meckler Corp.

Serials on Aging: An Analytical Guide. Compiled by Shirley B. Hesslein. LC 86-14969. (Annotated Bibliographies of Serials: A Subject Approach: No. 9). 197p. 1986. lib. bdg. 35.00 (ISBN 0-313-24709-9, HSA/). Greenwood.

Serials Review, Vol. 13. 1987. quarterly 30.00 (ISBN 0-685-70329-0); yearly 55.00. Pierian.

Serials: Suspense & Drama by Installment. 2nd, rev. & enl. ed. Raymond W. Stedman. LC 76-62516. 574p. 1981. pap. 12.95 (ISBN 0-8061-1695-1). U of Okla Pr.

Serials: Suspense & Drama by Installment. 2nd, rev. & enl. ed. Raymond W. Stedman. LC 76-62516. (Illus.). 1977. 27.95x (ISBN 0-8061-1403-7). U of Okla Pr.

Serie Illustrada, "Now Age". Ed. by Sr. Teresa Agnes. Tr. by Rudolf Heller from Eng. Incl. Veinte Mille Leguas de Viaje Submarino. Jules Verne. Orig. Title: Twenty Thousand Leagues Under the Sea. (ISBN 0-88301-455-6); wkbk. (ISBN 0-88301-575-7); Viaje al centro de la tierra. Jules Verne. Orig. Title: Journey to the Center of the Earth. (ISBN 0-88301-456-4); wkbk. (ISBN 0-88301-576-5); Moby Dick. Herman Melville. (ISBN 0-88301-454-8); wkbk. (ISBN 0-88301-574-9); Isla del Tesoro. Robert Louis Stevenson. Orig. Title: Treasure Island. (ISBN 0-88301-451-3); wkbk. (ISBN 0-88301-571-4); Mejores Cuentos de O. Henry. William S. Porter. Orig. Title: Best of O. Henry. (ISBN 0-88301-453-X); wkbk. (ISBN 0-88301-573-0); Huckleberry Finn. Samuel Clemens. (ISBN 0-88301-450-5); wkbk. (ISBN 0-88301-570-6); Frankenstein. Mary Wollstonecraft Shelley. (ISBN 0-88301-448-3); wkbk. (ISBN 0-88301-568-4); Llamado de la Selva. Jack London. Orig. Title: Call of the Wild. (ISBN 0-88301-452-1); wkbk. (ISBN 0-88301-572-2); Hombre Invisible. H. G. Wells. Orig. Title: Invisible Man. (ISBN 0-88301-449-1); wkbk. (ISBN 0-88301-569-2); Extrano Casa de Dr Jekyll y Mister Hyde. Robert Louis Stevenson. Orig. Title: Dr. Jekyll & Mr. Hyde. (ISBN 0-88301-447-5); wkbk. (ISBN 0-88301-567-6); Azabache. Anna Sewell. Orig. Title: Black Beauty. (ISBN 0-88301-445-9); wkbk. (ISBN 0-88301-565-X); Dracula. Bram Stoker. (ISBN 0-88301-446-7); wkbk. (ISBN 0-88301-566-8). (Illus.). 64p. (Orig., Span., For students with 1 1/2-2 yrs. of spanish). 1979. pap. text ed. 3.95 ea.; wkbk. 1.50 ea. Pendulum Pr.

Series & Approximation, Vol. 3. N. K. Bari et al. (Translations Ser.: No. 1). 1962. 27.00 (ISBN 0-8218-1603-9, TRANS 1-3). Am Math.

Series C. (Requirements for Qualification of Plans Ser.). Eleven Folios (1978-79) pap. 15.00 (ISBN 0-317-31123-9, B348-351; B353-359). Am Law Inst.

Series Chronologica Patriarcharum Antiochiae. Joseph S. Assemani. 100p. Repr. of 1881 ed. text ed. 33.12x (ISBN 0-576-99725-0, Pub. by Gregg Intl Pubs England). Gregg Intl.

Series D, 6 folios. (Rules for Operation of Qualified Plans Ser.). 1978-82. pap. 10.00x (ISBN 0-317-55931-1, B360-B365). Am Law Inst.

Series E. (Tax & Estate Planning Considerations for Qualified Plans Ser.). Four Folios (1978-1980) pap. 6.00 (ISBN 0-317-31194-8, B366-B369). Am Law Inst.

Series Eighty Software Catalog. 4th ed. Hewlett-Packard Company Staff. 15.95 (ISBN 0-317-13082-X). P-H.

Series G, 3 folios. (Procedural Law Affecting Qualified Plans Ser.: G). 1978. pap. 4.00x (ISBN 0-317-55932-X, B373-B375). Am Law Inst.

Series in Connecticut History, 5 vols. Ed. by David M. Roth. Incl. Vol. 1. Puritans Against the Wilderness: Connecticut History to 1763. Albert E. Van Dusen (ISBN 0-87106-128-7); Vol. 2. From Revolution to Constitution: Connecticut 1763 to 1818. David M. Roth & Freeman Meyer (ISBN 0-87106-129-5); Vol. 3. Preachers, Rebels, & Traders: Connecticut 1818 to 1865. Janice L. Trecker (ISBN 0-87106-130-9); Vol. 4. From Yankee to American: Connecticut 1865 to 1914. Ruth O. Andersen (ISBN 0-87106-131-7); Vol. 5. Diverse People: Connecticut 1914 to the Present. Herbert F. Janick, Jr (ISBN 0-87106-132-5). LC 73-83257. 1978. 3.50 ea. Ctr CT Studies.

Series in Mathematics Modules, 5 Modules. Leon Ablon et al. 1981. pap. Module 1. pap. 8.95 (ISBN 0-8053-0131-3); Module 2. pap. 8.95 (ISBN 0-8053-0132-1); Module 3. pap. 8.95 (ISBN 0-8053-0133-X); Module 4. pap. 8.95 (ISBN 0-8053-0134-8); Module 5. pap. 8.95 (ISBN 0-8053-0135-6). Benjamin-Cummings.

Series in Mathematics Modules: Practical Mathematics, Module 2A. Helen B. Siner. Ed. by Leon J. Ablon. LC 75-12083. 1975. Module 2A. pap. text ed. 7.95 (ISBN 0-8465-6714-8). Benjamin-Cummings.

Series of Elementary Exercises upon Geological Maps. John Platt. 1974. pap. text ed. 6.95x (ISBN 0-04-550019-3). Unwin Hyman.

Series of Etchings: Chiefly of Views in Scotland. John Clerk. Ed. by David Laing. LC 72-963. (Bannatyne Club, Edinburgh. Publications: No. 98). Repr. of 1855 ed. 85.00 (ISBN 0-404-52854-6). AMS Pr.

Series of Irregular Observations. R. Azencott & D. Dacunha-Castelle. Tr. by D. McHale from Fr. (Applied Probability Ser.). 250p. 1986. 32.00 (ISBN 0-387-96263-8). Springer-Verlag.

Series of Lectures on Social Justice. C. E. Coughlin. LC 71-173652. (FDR & the Era of the New Deal). 242p. 1971. Repr. of 1935 ed. lib. bdg. 32.50 (ISBN 0-306-70373-4). Da Capo.

Series of Letters Between Mrs. Elizabeth Carter & Miss Catherine Talbot from the Year 1741 to 1770, 4 vols. Elizabeth Carter. Repr. of 1809 ed. Set. 170.00 (ISBN 0-404-56730-4); 42.50 ea. AMS Pr.

Series of Letters from Feargus O'Connor Esq., Barrister-at-Law, to Daniel O'Connell... Containing a Review of Mr. O'Connell's Conduct During the Agitation of the Question of Catholic Emancipation etc. Feargus O'Connor. Ed. by Dorothy Thompson. (Chartism, Working-Class Politics in the Industrial Revolution Ser.). 200p. 1987. lib. bdg. 30.00 (ISBN 0-8240-5590-X). Garland Pub.

Series of Old Welsh Texts, 11 vols. in 14. Ed. by John Rhys & John G. Evans. Repr. Set. 600.00 (ISBN 0-404-60580-X). AMS Pr.

Series of Papers on Shakespeare & the Theatre. Shakespeare Association. LC 74-32229. 1927. lib. bdg. 27.00 (ISBN 0-8414-7529-6). Folcroft.

Series of Public Issues, No. 3. Lawrence C. Wolken. Ed. by Pejovich Svetozar & Janet G. Joyce. Orig. Title: Japan: The Modernization of Ancient Culture. 1983. pap. 2.00 (ISBN 0-86599-012-3). Ctr Educ Res.

Series of Suggestions. Ed. by Bibliotheca Press Research Division Staff. 300p. 1983. text ed. 75.00 (ISBN 0-939476-92-4, Pub. by Biblio Pr GA). Prosperity & Profits.

Series of Views of the Collieries in the Counties of Northcumberland & Durham. T. H. Hair. LC 69-11240. (Illus.). 1969. Repr. of 1844 ed. lib. bdg. 37.50x (ISBN 0-678-05581-5). Kelley.

Series on Nursing Administration, Vol. 2. Marion Johnson & Joanne McCloskey. 1988. write for info. (ISBN 0-201-12928-0). Addison-Wesley.

Series on Public Issues, No. 2. S. Charles Maurice & Jane Hobson. Ed. by Svetozar Pejovich. Orig. Title: Minimum Wage Law: Who Benefits, Who Loses? 1983. pap. 2.00 (ISBN 0-86599-009-3). Ctr Educ Res.

Series One: Poverty & Wealth, Vol. IV. Ed. by Lynchburg College Faculty Staff. LC 82-45155. (Classical Selections on Great Issues, Symposium Readings Ser.). 532p. (Orig.). 1982. lib. bdg. 25.25 (ISBN 0-8191-2468-0); pap. text ed. 9.75 (ISBN 0-8191-2469-9). U Pr of Amer.

Series Program: One Student's Behavior. Richard A. Roman & Joan I. Heller. 51p. 1976. 1.50 (ISBN 0-318-14737-8). Learn Res Dev.

Series Seven Made Ridiculously Simple. Martin Torosian. 1987. 295.00 (ISBN 0-9603592-3-0). MTA Financial Servs.

Series Seven Typing Complete Course, Gregg Typing. Alan C. Lloyd et al. 496p. (gr. 11-12). 1982. text ed. 27.08 (ISBN 0-07-038280-8). McGraw.

Series Summa Izbu. E. V. Leichty. LC 66-25697. 24.00 (ISBN 0-685-71732-1). J J Augustin.

Series TV: How a Show Is Made. Malka Drucker & Elizabeth James. LC 83-2119. (Illus.). 112p. (gr. 4up). 1983. 11.95 (ISBN 0-89919-142-8, Clarion). HM.

Series 32000, Programmer's Reference Manual. National Semiconductor Staff. (Illus.). 323p. 1987. pap. 20.95 (ISBN 0-13-806936-0). P-H.

Serigamy of Stories. Kathryn T. Windham. LC 88-5461. (Muscadine Bk.). (Illus.). 1988. 14.95 (ISBN 0-87805-354-9). U Pr of Miss.

Serigraphy: Silk Screen Techniques for the Artist. Kenneth W. Auvil. (Illus., Orig.). 1965. 21.00 (ISBN 0-13-807164-0). P-H.

Serious & Tragic Elements in the Comedy of Thomas Dekker. Peggy F. Shirley & James Hogg. (Jacobean Drama Studies). 132p. (Orig.). 1975. pap. 15.00 (ISBN 3-7052-0345-2, Salzburg Studies). Longwood Pub Group.

Serious Assembler. pap. 8.95 (ISBN 0-671-55963-X). PB.

Serious Breach of National Security As Occurred: Some Game!!! (Analysis Ser.: No. 9). 1982. pap. 10.00 (ISBN 0-686-42844-7). Inst Analysis.

Serious Business of Growing Up: A Study of Children's Lives Outside School. Elliott A. Medrich & Judith A. Roizen. LC 81-7650. 412p. 1981. 35.00x (ISBN 0-520-04296-4); pap. 11.95 (ISBN 0-520-05071-1). U of Cal Pr.

Serious Call to a Devout & Holy Life. William Law. 1967. Repr. of 1906 ed. 12.95x (ISBN 0-460-00091-8, Evman). Biblio Dist.

Serious Call to a Devout & Holy Life. William Law. Ed. by John Meister et al. LC 55-5330. 156p. 1968. pap. 6.25 (ISBN 0-664-24833-0). Westminster John Knox.

Serious Call to a Devout & Holy Life. William Law. LC 82-80470. (Treasures from the Spiritual Classics Ser.). 64p. 1982. pap. 2.95 (ISBN 0-8192-1306-3). Morehouse.

Serious Call to Holy Living. Abriged by ed. William Law. 96p. 1985. pap. 3.95 (ISBN 0-8423-5861-7). Tyndale.

Serious Character: The Life of Ezra Pound. Humphrey Carpenter. (Illus.). 976p. 1988. 40.00 (ISBN 0-395-41678-7). HM.

Serious Cycling for the Beginner. Ray Adams. LC 77-73654. (Illus.). 88p. 1977. pap. 4.95 (ISBN 0-89037-115-6). Anderson World.

Serious Cycling for the Beginner. Ray Adams. 1984. pap. 5.95 (ISBN 0-02-028220-6, Collier). Macmillan.

Serious Drama & the London Stage: 1729-1739. Bonnie A. Nelson. Ed. by James Hogg. (Poetic Drama & Poetic Theory Ser.). 278p. (Orig.). 1981. pap. 15.00 (ISBN 3-7052-0898-5, Pub. by Salzburg Studies). Longwood Pub Group.

Serious Entertainments: The Writing of History in Twelfth-Century England. Nancy F Partner. LC 77-4402. 1977. lib. bdg. 20.00x (ISBN 0-226-64763-3). U of Chicago Pr.

Serious Fun. David R. Veerman. 128p. (YA) (gr. 7 up). 1987. pap. 10.95 (ISBN 0-89693-017-3). Victor Bks.

Serious Games. Clark C. Abt. LC 86-34021. 196p. (Orig.). 1987. lib. bdg. 24.50 (ISBN 0-8191-6147-0); pap. text ed. 9.95 (ISBN 0-8191-6148-9). U Pr of Amer.

Serious Juvenile Offender: The/Scope of the Problem & the Response of Juvenile Courts. Howard N. Snyder & John L. Hutzler. 10p. 1981. 2.50. Natl Juv & Family Ct Judges.

Serious Living. Tom Lorenz. 1988. 17.95 (ISBN 0-670-81060-6). Viking.

Serious Money. Caryl Churchill. (Royal Court Writer's Ser.). 50p. 1987. pap. 8.95 (ISBN 0-413-16660-0). Heinemann Ed.

Serious Programming for the Commodore 64. Henry Simpson. (Illus.). 176p. (Orig.). 1984. pap. 10.95 (ISBN 0-8306-1821-X). TAB Bks.

Serious Programming for the IBM PC, XT, AT. Henry Simpson. (Illus.). 208p. (Orig.). 1985. pap. 15.95 (ISBN 0-8306-1921-6, 1921P). TAB Bks.

Serious Programming for Your Apple II, IIe, IIc. Henry Simpson. LC 85-17320. (Illus.). 192p. (Orig.). 1985. 18.95 (ISBN 0-8306-0960-1, 1960); pap. 12.95 (ISBN 0-8306-1960-7, 1960P). Tab Bks.

Serious Programming in BASIC. Henry Simpson. (Illus.). 224p. 1986. pap. 14.95 (ISBN 0-8306-2650-6, 2650P). Tab Bks.

Serious Questions: An ABC of Skeptical Reflections. Erwin Chargaff. 304p. 1986. 40.00 (ISBN 0-8176-3337-5). Birkhauser.

Serious Reduction of Hazardous Waste for Pollution Prevention & Industrial Efficiency. LC 86-600571. (OTA-ITE-317 Ser.). 264p. (Orig.). 1986. pap. 12.00 (ISBN 0-318-21557-8, S/N 052-003-01048-8). USGPO.

Serious Reflections During the Life & Surprising Adventures of Robinson Crusoe, with His Vision of the Angelic World. Daniel Defoe. LC 74-13445. (Illus.). Repr. of 1895 ed. 32.50 (ISBN 0-404-07913-X). AMS Pr.

Serious Reflections on the Scandalous Abuse & Effects of the Stage. Arthur Bedford. Bd. with Second Advertisement Concerning the Profaneness of the Play-House; Sermon Preached in the Parish-Church of St. Butolph's Algate, in the City of London: Occasioned by the Erecting of a Play-House in the Neighborhood. (English Stage Ser.: Vol. 41). 1974. lib. bdg. 61.00 (ISBN 0-8240-0624-0). Garland Pub.

Serious Remonstrance in Behalf of the Christian Religion Against English Play-Houses. Arthur Bedfrod. LC 79-170478. (English Stage Ser.: Vol. 42). lib. bdg. 61.00 (ISBN 0-8240-0625-9). Garland Pub.

Serious Runner's Handbook. Tom Osler. LC 78-367. (Illus.). 187p. 1978. pap. 5.95 (ISBN 0-89037-126-1). Anderson World.

Serious Season. Ed. by Roger Swenson. LC 86-25876. 116p. (Orig.). 1987. pap. 7.95 (ISBN 0-8189-0512-3). Alba.

Serious Shopper's Guide to Italy. Robert Tine. (Serious Shopper's Guides). (Illus.). 384p. (Orig.). 1988. pap. 15.95 (ISBN 0-13-806894-1). Prentice Hall Pr.

Serious Shopper's Guide to London. Beth Reiber. (Serious Shopper's Guides). (Illus.). 384p. 1987. pap. 15.95 (ISBN 0-13-806852-6). Prentice Hall Pr.

Serious Shopper's Guide to Los Angeles. Jennifer Merin. (Illus.). 312p. (Orig.). 1987. pap. 14.95 (ISBN 0-13-806878-X). Prentice Hall Pr.

Serious Shopper's Guide to Paris. Jennifer Merin. (Serious Shopper's Guides). (Illus.). 384p. 1987. pap. 14.95 (ISBN 0-317-62462-8). Prentice Hall Pr.

Serious Social Problems. Jerome G. Manis. 1983. text ed. 37.00 (ISBN 0-205-08044-8, 818044); write for info. tchrs' manual (ISBN 0-205-08045-6, 818045). Allyn.

Serious Trouble Stories: Stories. Paul Friedman. LC 85-28843. (Illinois Short Fiction Ser.). 168p. 1986. 11.95 (ISBN 0-252-01310-7). U of Ill Pr.

Serious Whimsey. George J. Seidel. 1987. 35.70 (ISBN 0-926725-05-X). Scaramouche.

Seris. David Burckhalter. LC 75-44915. 80p. 1976. pap. 7.50 (ISBN 0-8165-0517-9). U of Ariz Pr.

Serizawa: A Living Treasure of Japan. Commentary by Martha Longenecker. LC 79-90086. (Illus.). 45p. 1979. 7.50 (ISBN 0-317-68014-5). Mingei Intl Mus.

TITLE INDEX SERMONS OF ST. ALPHONSUS

Serjeant Musgrave's Dance see John Arden: Plays One.
Serjeant Musgraves Dance & Notes. Date not set. pap. price not set (ISBN 0-413-49260-5). Heinemann Ed.
Sermo Lupi Ad Anglos. Wulfstan. Ed. by Dorothy Whitelock. (Old English Ser.). 1967. pap. text ed. 4.95x (ISBN 0-89197-575-6). Irvington.
Sermon a Day Keeps the Devil Away. Bob Jones, III. 208p. (Orig.). 1980. pap. 3.15 (ISBN 0-89084-114-4). Bob Jones Univ Pr.
Sermon Analysis. Jay Adams. LC 85-73072. (Pastor's Library). 224p. 1986. 17.95 (ISBN 0-89636-193-4). Accent Bks.
Sermon As God's Word: Theologies for Preaching. Robert W. Duke. LC 80-18094. (Abingdon Preacher's Library). 128p. (Orig.). 1980. pap. 7.95 (ISBN 0-687-37520-7). Abingdon.
Sermon Charts & Outlines, 3 vols. W. E. Skipper. spiral bdg. 3.50 ea. (ISBN 0-685-70356-8). Vol. 1 (ISBN 0-89315-253-6). Vol. 2 (ISBN 0-89315-254-4). Vol. 3 (ISBN 0-89315-255-2). Lambert Bk.
Sermon-Conferences of St. Thomas Aquinas on the Apostles' Creed. Ed. by Nicholas R. Ayo. LC 87-40620. 176p. 1988. text ed. 21.95x (ISBN 0-268-01728-X). U of Notre Dame Pr.
Sermon del Monte. Emmet Fox. 1984. 5.95 (ISBN 0-87159-034-4). Unity School.
Sermon del Monte. D. M. Lloyd-Jones. 1978. Vol. 2. 7.95. Banner of Truth.
Sermon del Monte. J. Dwight Pentecost. Orig. Title: Sermon on the Mount. (Span.). 1981. pap. 4.75 (ISBN 0-8254-1556-X). Kregel.
Sermon Eficaz. James D. Crane. 308p. (Span.). 1986. pap. 5.95. Casa Bautista.
Sermon Illustrations for the Gospel Lessons. LC 12-2968. 1983. pap. 5.75 (ISBN 0-570-03875-8). Concordia.
Sermon in the Desert: Belief and Behavior in Early St. George, Utah. Larry Logue. LC 87-19181. (Illus.). 200p. 1986. 19.95 (ISBN 0-252-01474-X). U of Ill Pr.
Sermon Joyeux et Truanderie: Villon, Nemo, Ulespiegle. Jelle Koopmans & Paul Verhuyck. (Faux Titre: Vol. 29). (Illus.). 260p. 1987. pap. text ed. 39.95 (Pub. by Rodopi Holland). Humanities.
Sermon Notes on the Psalms. David Thomas. Ed. by Herbert Lockyer. 320p. (Orig.). Date not set. pap. 10.95 (ISBN 0-8254-3116-6). Kregel.
Sermon of Repentance. John Bradford. LC 74-28835. (English Experience Ser.: No. 716). 1975. Repr. of 1553 ed. 25.00 (ISBN 90-221-0716-7). Walter J Johnson.
Sermon on the Decollation of St. John the Baptist, & on Herodias, & on Good & Evil Women. St. John Chrysostom. (Early Slavic Literatures, Studies, Texts, & Seminar Materials: Vol. 3). Orig. Title: V 29 den' mesiatsa avgusta slovo Ioanna Zlatoustogo na useknovenie glavy. 45p. (Slavic & Gr.). 1982. pap. 4.00 (ISBN 0-933884-23-0). Berkeley Slavic.
Sermon on the Mount. Clovis G. Chappell. (Pulpit Library Ser). 1979. pap. 4.95 (ISBN 0-8010-2363-7). Baker Bk.
Sermon on the Mount. William D. Davies. (Orig.). 1966. pap. 9.95 (ISBN 0-521-09384-8). Cambridge U Pr.
Sermon on the Mount. Emmet Fox. 1934. 14.45 (ISBN 0-06-062950-9, HarpR). Har-Row.
Sermon on the Mount. Robert Guelich. 448p. 1982. 19.95 (ISBN 0-8499-0110-3). Word Bks.
Sermon on the Mount. Manly P. Hall. pap. 2.50 (ISBN 0-89314-353-7). Philos Res.
Sermon on the Mount. Herman Hendrickx. (Commentary on the Synoptic Gospels Ser.). 228p. 1984. pap. 9.95 (8526, HarpR). Har-Row.
Sermon on the Mount. Joachim Jeremias. Ed. by John Reumann. Tr. by Norman Perrin from Ger. LC 63-17882. (Facet Bks.). (Orig.). 1963. pap. 2.50 (ISBN 0-8006-3002-5, 1-3002). Fortress.
Sermon on the Mount. Clarence Jordan. 1970. pap. 4.95 (ISBN 0-8170-0501-3). Judson.
Sermon on the Mount. Anton Morgenroth. 150p. (Orig.). 1987. pap. 5.95 (ISBN 0-937495-19-0). Trinity Comns.
Sermon on the Mount. Roger L. Shinn. LC 62-19785. 112p. (Orig.). 1984. pap. 3.95 (ISBN 0-8298-0120-0). Pilgrim NY.
Sermon on the Mount. John R. Stott. (LifeGuide Bible Studies). 64p. 1987. pap. 2.95 (ISBN 0-8308-1036-6). Inter-Varsity.
Sermon on the Mount. Richard Teed. 91p. pap. 2.75 (ISBN 0-87785-124-7). Swedenborg.
Sermon on the Mount. Ed. by Thomas B. Warren & Garland Elkins. 1982. pap. 15.00 (ISBN 0-934916-00-4). Natl Christian Pr.
Sermon on the Mount see Sermon del Monte.
Sermon on the Mount: A History of Interpretation & Bibliography. Warren S. Kissinger. LC 75-29031. (ATLA Bibliography Ser.: No. 3). 309p. 1975. 22.50 (ISBN 0-8108-0843-9). Scarecrow.
Sermon on the Mount: A Study Guide. Dale Cooper. (Revelation Series for Adults). 1981. pap. text ed. 2.75 (ISBN 0-933140-22-3). CRC Pubns.
Sermon on the Mount: A Theological Interpretation. Carl G. Vaught. LC 86-14500. (Religious Studies). 217p. (Orig.). 1987. 34.50x (ISBN 0-88706-364-0); pap. 10.95x (ISBN 0-88706-365-9). State U NY Pr.
Sermon on the Mount According to Vedanta. Swami Prabhavananda. 1972. pap. 3.95 (ISBN 0-451-62509-9, ME2338, Ment). NAL.
Sermon on the Mount According to Vedanta. Swami Prabhavananda. LC 64-8660. 6.95 (ISBN 0-87481-002-7). Vedanta Pr.
Sermon on the Mount: An Evangelical Exposition of Matthew 5-7. D. A. Carson. LC 77-93260. 1978. pap. 5.95 (ISBN 0-8010-2480-3). Baker Bk.
Sermon on the Mount: An Exegetical Commentary. Georg Strecker. Tr. by O. C. Dean. 1988. pap. 13.95 (ISBN 0-687-37560-6). Abingdon.
Sermon on the Mount: An Exposition. John M. Boice. 328p. (Orig.). 1981. pap. 12.95 (ISBN 0-310-21511-0, 10360P). Zondervan.
Sermon on the Mount As an Ideological Intervention: A Reconstruction of Meaning. Sjef Van Tilborg. 324p. 1986. 30.00 (ISBN 90-232-2243-1, Pub. by Van Gorcum Holland). Longwood Pub Group.
Sermon on the Mount: Authentic Human Values. Oscar S. Brooks. 124p. (Orig.). 1985. lib. bdg. 23.25 (ISBN 0-8191-4740-0); pap. text ed. 9.25 (ISBN 0-8191-4741-9). U Pr of Amer.
Sermon on the Mount for Today. Thomas Coates. LC 77-184. 1979. pap. 2.95x (ISBN 0-915644-13-4). Clayton Pub Hse.
Sermon on the Mount: From the Translation Prepared at Cambridge in 1611 for King James I. Illus. by Judith A. Duncan. LC 81-211201. (Illus.). 1978. 15.00 (ISBN 0-9606844-0-9). Mac Col MN.
Sermon on the Mount Interpreted by Paramhansa Yogananada. Yogananda Paramhansa. LC 79-91531. 1980. pap. 10.95 (ISBN 0-937134-01-5). Amrita Found.
Sermon on the Mount: Proclamation & Exhortation. Jan Lambrecht. LC 85-47751. (Good News Studies: Vol. 14). 1985. pap. 12.95 (ISBN 0-89453-467-X). M Glazier.
Sermon on the Mount: Utopia or Program for Action? Pinchas Lapide. Tr. by Arlene Swindler from Ger. 160p. (Orig.). 1986. pap. 9.95 (ISBN 0-88344-248-5, 85-29810). Orbis Bks.
Sermon on the Mount: Wisdom of the Kingdom. Ed. by Gary Wilde. (Basic Bible Ser.). 96p. 1986. pap. 4.95 (ISBN 0-89191-521-4). Cook.
Sermon on the Mountain. Carol Gonsalves. (Arch Books Supplement Ser.). (gr. k-4). 1981. pap. 1.29 (ISBN 0-570-06149-0, 59-1304). Concordia.
Sermon Outline Bible, 12 vols. Ed. by W. Robertson Nicoll. 1987. Repr. Set. text ed. 195.00 (ISBN 0-8010-6749-9). Baker Bk.
Sermon Outline Series, 6 vols. John Ritchie. 1987. pap. 27.50 (ISBN 0-8254-3624-9). Kregel.
Sermon Outlines. W. A. Schultz. 3.95 (ISBN 0-88027-092-6). Firm Foun Pub.
Sermon Outlines for Evangelism. H. Lee Mason. (Sermon Outline Ser.). (Orig.). 1981. pap. 2.50 (ISBN 0-8010-6120-2). Baker Bk.
Sermon Outlines for Funeral Services. Ed. by Charles R. Wood. 64p. 1970. pap. 2.95 (ISBN 0-8254-4007-6). Kregel.
Sermon Outlines for Funerals. C. W. Keiningham. (Sermon Outline Ser.). (Orig.). 1981. pap. 2.50 (ISBN 0-8010-5427-3). Baker Bk.
Sermon Outlines for Funerals, No. 2. C. W. Keiningham. (Sermon Outline Ser.). 64p. (Orig.). 1988. pap. 2.95 (ISBN 0-8010-5493-1). Baker Bk.
Sermon Outlines for Revival Preaching. James H. Bolick. (Pulpit Library). 106p. 1986. pap. 2.95 (ISBN 0-8010-0922-7). Baker Bk.
Sermon Outlines for Special Days. Croft M. Pentz. (Sermon Outline Ser.). 1979. pap. 2.50 (ISBN 0-8010-7046-5). Baker Bk.
Sermon Outlines for Special Days & Occasions. Ed. by Charles R. Wood. 64p. 1970. pap. 2.95 (ISBN 0-8254-4006-8). Kregel.
Sermon Outlines from Acts. Croft M. Pentz. (Sermon Outline Ser.). 1978. pap. 2.50 (ISBN 0-8010-7039-2). Baker Bk.
Sermon Outlines from Proverbs. Charles R. Wood. LC 83-25569. 88p. (Orig.). 1984. pap. 3.95 (ISBN 0-8254-4023-8). Kregel.
Sermon Outlines from the Sermon on the Mount. Charles R. Wood. LC 85-23734. 64p. (Orig.). 1986. pap. 2.95 (ISBN 0-8254-4032-7). Kregel.
Sermon Outlines from the Word. James H. Bolick. (Sermon Outline Ser.). (Orig.). 1980. pap. 2.50 (ISBN 0-8010-0528-0). Baker Bk.
Sermon Outlines on Christian Living. George W. Lockaby. LC 81-68536. 1981. pap. 2.95 (ISBN 0-8054-2244-7). Broadman.
Sermon Outlines on Christian Living. W. H. Griffith Thomas. LC 87-29888. 128p. 1988. pap. 5.95 (ISBN 0-8254-3830-6). Kregel.
Sermon Outlines on Key Bible Themes. Hyman Appelman. (Sermon Outline Ser.). pap. 1.95 (ISBN 0-8010-0003-3). Baker Bk.
Sermon Outlines on the Person & Work of Christ. George W. Lockaby. LC 80-67916. 1981. pap. 2.95 (ISBN 0-8054-2238-2). Broadman.
Sermon Outlines on the Psalms. Charles R. Wood. LC 85-23735. 64p. (Orig.). 1986. pap. 2.95 (ISBN 0-8254-4033-5). Kregel.
Sermon Preached at Pauls Crosse Touching the Supposed Apostasie of J. King, Late Bishop of London. Henry King. LC 76-57392. (English Experience Ser.: No. 809). 1977. Repr. of 1621 ed. lib. bdg. 9.50 (ISBN 90-221-0809-0). Walter J Johnson.
Sermon Preached at Pawles Crosse, 3 November 1577 see Godly Exhortation.
Sermon Preached at the Cross, February 14, 1607. William Crashaw. Repr. of 1608 ed. 27.00 (ISBN 0-384-10125-9). Johnson Repr.
Sermon Preached in the Parish-Church of St. Butolph's Algate, in the City of London: Occasioned by the Erecting of a Play-House in the Neighborhood see Serious Reflections on the Scandalous Abuse & Effects of the Stage.
Sermon Preached upon the Anniversary of the Gunpowder Treason. Jeremy Taylor. LC 78-25673. (English Experience Ser.: No. 354). 64p. 1971. Repr. of 1638 ed. 11.50 (ISBN 90-221-0354-4). Walter J Johnson.
Sermon Seeds from Psalms. William G. Heslop. LC 76-12080. (W. G. Heslop Bible Study Aids Ser.). 144p. 1976. pap. 4.50 (ISBN 0-8254-2831-9). Kregel.
Sermon Starters from the Greek New Testament. Gerald Cowen. LC 84-27448. 1985. pap. 5.95 (ISBN 0-8054-1397-9). Broadman.
Sermon Struggles: Four Methods of Sermon Preparation. Ernest E. Hunt, III. 160p. (Orig.). 1982. pap. 8.95 (ISBN 0-8164-2375-X, HarpR). Har-Row.
Sermon Studies on the Gospels. Ed. by E. H. Wendland. (Series C). 1982. 12.95 (ISBN 0-8100-0149-7, 15NO378). Northwest Pub.
Sermon Studies on the Old Testament. Ed. by E. H. Wendland. (Series B). 1984. 12.95 (ISBN 0-8100-0192-6, 15N0412). Northwest Pub.
Sermon Texts. Ed. by E. H. Wendland. 1984. 9.95 (ISBN 0-8100-0186-1, 15N0409). Northwest Pub.
Sermon under Attack. Ruhia Klaas. 110p. pap. 9.50 (ISBN 0-85364-341-5, Pub. by Paternoster UK). Attic Pr.
Sermones para Dias Especiales, Tomo II. Adolfo Robleto. 96p. 1985. Repr. of 1984 ed. 2.95 (ISBN 0-311-07011-6). Casa Bautista.
Sermones para Dias Especiales, Tomo I. Adolfo Robleto. 112p. (Span.). 1986. Repr. of 1983 ed. 2.95 (ISBN 0-311-07009-4). Casa Bautista.
Sermones Ratherii Episcopi Veronensis. Benny R. Reece. 5.00 (ISBN 0-686-23377-8). Classical Folia.
Sermones Sobre Job. John Calvin. 250p. (Span.). 1988. 8.95 (ISBN 0-939125-10-2). Evangelical Lit.
Sermones Sobre la Obra Salvadora de Cristo. John Calvin. Tr. by Guillermo Kratzig from Eng. 250p. (Span.). 1988. 8.95 (ISBN 0-939125-11-0). Evangelical Lit.
Sermonic Pictures of a Preacher's Soul. 1981. pap. 4.95 (ISBN 0-933184-32-8). Flame Intl.
Sermons, 2 vols. Charles E. Coughlin. Set. 250.00 (ISBN 0-8490-1025-X). Gordon Pr.
Sermons. Hugh Latimer. LC 76-172301. Repr. of 1906 ed. 23.50 (ISBN 0-404-03886-7). AMS Pr.
Sermons. Thomas Lever. 143p. pap. 15.00 (ISBN 0-87556-200-0). Saifer.
Sermons. Jonathan Mayhew. LC 76-83429. (Religion in America, Ser. 1). 1969. Repr. of 1749 ed. 19.00 (ISBN 0-405-00254-8). Ayer Co Pubs.
Sermons, Nos. 81-186. St. Caesarius Of Arles. LC 56-3628. (Fathers of the Church Ser.: Vol. 47). 495p. 1964. 25.95x (ISBN 0-8132-0047-4). Cath U Pr.
Sermons see Oeuvres.
Sermons, Addresses & Reminiscences & Important Correspondence, with a Picture Gallery of Eminent Ministers & Scholars. Elias C. Morris. Ed. by Edwin S. Gaustad. LC 79-52598. (Baptist Tradition Ser.). (Illus.). 1980. Repr. of 1901 ed. lib. bdg. 27.50x (ISBN 0-405-12465-1). Ayer Co Pubs.
Sermons & Addresses, 1853-1891. Daniel A. Payne. LC 70-38458. (Religion in America, Ser. 2). 1972. 19.00 (ISBN 0-405-04079-2). Ayer Co Pubs.
Sermons & Cannonballs. LC 81-13594. (Sermon in America Series, 1620-1800). 1982. Repr. 60.00x (ISBN 0-8201-1370-0). Schol Facsimiles.
Sermons & Epistles. Horace. Ed. by John C. Rolfe. (College Classical Ser). 1977. pap. text ed. 17.50 (ISBN 0-89241-026-4). Caratzas.
Sermons & Homilies of the Christ of Elqui. Nicanor Parra. Tr. by Sandra Reyes. LC 84-2187. 120p. 1984. 13.50x (ISBN 0-8262-0451-1). U of Mo Pr.
Sermons & Illustrations for Every Occasion. Willie White. LC 88-71158. 164p. (Orig.). 1988. pap. 4.95 (ISBN 0-89900-306-0). College Pr Pub.
Sermons & Memoirs of Christmas Evans. Christmas Evans. LC 86-7108. 320p. 1986. Repr. 12.95 (ISBN 0-8254-2522-0). Kregel.
Sermons & Soda-Water, 3 Vols. John O'Hara. 1960. Set. 12.50 (ISBN 0-394-44480-9). Random.
Sermons & Soda Water. John O'Hara. 336p. 1986. pap. 4.95 (ISBN 0-88184-271-0). Carroll & Graf.
Sermons & Speeches of Gerrit Smith. Gerrit Smith. LC 73-82222. (Anti-Slavery Crusade in America Ser). 1969. Repr. of 1861 ed. 11.50 (ISBN 0-405-00660-8). Ayer Co Pubs.
Sermons Capitulaires de la Chartreuse de Mayence du Debut du XV Siecle. Dom P. Dupont. Ed. by James Hogg. (Analecta Cartusiana Ser.: No. 46). 193p. (Orig., Fr.). 1978. pap. 25.00 (ISBN 3-7052-0062-3, Pub by Salzburg Studies). Longwood Pub Group.
Sermons de Marcel Pagnol. Marcel Pagnol. Ed. by Calmels. 12.50 (ISBN 0-685-37009-7). French & Eur.
Sermons for Celebrating. Landrum P. Leavell. LC 77-90220. 1978. pap. 4.95 (ISBN 0-8054-2231-5). Broadman.
Sermons for Christians Seasons. Merle A. Johnson. LC 75-44210. Repr. of 1976 ed. 21.10 (ISBN 0-8357-9026-6, 2016406). Bks Demand UMI.
Sermons for Eighteen Special Occasions. LC 12-2963. 1982. pap. 5.75 (ISBN 0-570-03870-7). Concordia.
Sermons for Funeral Occasions. B. L. Bedwell. 1960. pap. 2.00 (ISBN 0-88027-029-2). Firm Foun Pub.
Sermons for Special Occasions. 1981. pap. 5.95 (ISBN 0-570-03825-1, 12-2790). Concordia.
Sermons for Special Occasions. Charles H. Spurgeon. Ed. by Charles T Cook. 256p. 1977. Repr. of 1958 ed. limp bk. 7.50 (ISBN 0-551-05573-1). Attic Pr.
Sermons for the Seasons. C. W. Bess. LC 84-23226. 1985. pap. 4.95 (ISBN 0-8054-2256-0). Broadman.
Sermons for the Seventies. Alfred J. Kolatch. LC 75-164518. 1971. 7.95x (ISBN 0-8246-0122-X). Jonathan David.
Sermons for Today. Gary R. Beauchamp. LC 80-70788. 1981. 11.95 (ISBN 0-89112-403-9). Abilene Christ U.
Sermons for Today. Prentice A. Meador, Jr. LC 80-70788. 1981. 11.95 (ISBN 0-89112-402-0). Abilene Christ U.
Sermons for Today, No. 1. Rex P. Kyker. LC 80-50106. 196p. 1980. 11.95 (ISBN 0-89112-401-2). Abilene Christ U.
Sermons from Early America. 2nd ed. 1974. 6.00 (ISBN 0-9606952-0-6). PBBC Pr.
Sermons from Luke. C. M. Ward. 96p. (Orig.). 1983. pap. 2.25 (ISBN 0-89274-260-7). Harrison Hse.
Sermons from the Black Pulpit. Samuel D. Proctor & William D. Watley. 128p. 1984. pap. 7.95 (ISBN 0-8170-1034-3). Judson.
Sermons from the Parables. James Bailey. 104p. (Orig.). 1981. pap. 2.95 (ISBN 0-8341-0730-9). Beacon Hill.
Sermons in a Monastery: Chapter Talks by Matthew Kelty Ocso, No. 59. Ed. by William O. Paulsell. (Cistercian Studies Series). 1983. 14.95 (ISBN 0-87907-858-8); pap. 6.00 (ISBN 0-87907-958-4). Cistercian Pubns.
Sermons in Candles. C. H. Spurgeon. 1971. 3.95 (ISBN 0-686-09093-4). Pilgrim Pubns.
Sermons in Science Fiction: The Novels of S. Fowler Wright. Mary S. Weinkauf. (Milford Ser.: Popular Writers of Today: Vol. 51). 144p. Date not set. lib. bdg. 16.95x (ISBN 0-89370-180-7); pap. 7.95x (ISBN 0-89370-280-3). Borgo Pr.
Sermons in Stones. Bhagwan Rajneesh. Ed. by Ma D. Sarito. LC 87-42569. (University of Mysticism Ser.). 900p. (Orig.). 1987. pap. 9.95 (ISBN 3-907757-04-1). Chidvilas Inc.
Sermons, Nos. 187-238. St. Caesarius Of Arles. LC 56-3628. (Fathers of the Church Ser.: Vol. 66). 303p. 1973. 17.95x (ISBN 0-8132-0066-0). Cath U Pr.
Sermons of a Buddhist Abbot. Soyen Shaku. 35.00 (ISBN 0-8490-1026-8). Gordon Pr.
Sermons of Athens Clay Pullias. Athens C. Pullias. Ed. by J. D. Thomas. (Great Preachers Ser). 1962. 11.95 (ISBN 0-89112-203-6). Abilene Christ U.
Sermons of Batsell Barrett Baxter. Ed. by J. D. Thomas. (Great Preachers Ser). 1960. 11.95 (ISBN 0-89112-201-X). Abilene Christ U.
Sermons of Charles F. Parham. Ed. by Donald W. Dayton. (Higher Christian Life Ser.). 261p. 1985. lib. bdg. 35.00 (ISBN 0-8240-6413-5). Garland Pub.
Sermons of Edwin Sandys D. D. Edwin Sandys. Repr. of 1841 ed. 41.00 (ISBN 0-384-53200-4). Johnson Repr.
Sermons of Frank Pack. Ed. by J. D. Thomas. (Great Preachers Ser). 1963. 11.95 (ISBN 0-89112-205-2). Abilene Christ U.
Sermons of George W. Bailey. Ed. by J. D. Thomas. (Great Preachers Ser). 1961. 11.95 (ISBN 0-89112-202-8). Abilene Christ U.
Sermons of Gus Nichols. Ed. by J. D. Thomas. (Great Preachers Ser). 1966. 11.95 (ISBN 0-89112-209-5). Abilene Christ U.
Sermons of John Alexander Dowie. Gordon Lindsay. (Champion of the Faith Ser.). 2.50 (ISBN 0-89985-193-2). Christ Nations.
Sermons of John Donne: In Ten Volumes. John Donne. Ed. by Evelyn M. Simpson & George R. Potter. LC 52-7179. 4365p. 1984. lib. bdg. 450.00x set (ISBN 0-520-05255-2). U of Cal Pr.
Sermons of John H. Banister. Ed. by J. D. Thomas. (Great Preachers Ser). 1965. 11.95 (ISBN 0-89112-208-7). Abilene Christ U.
Sermons of Joseph R. Narot. Joseph R. Narot. 6.00 (ISBN 0-686-15812-1). Rostrum Bks.
Sermons of Laurence Sterne. Melvyn New. (Orig.). 1989. pap. price not set (ISBN 0-8130-0860-3). U Presses Fla.
Sermons of Martin Luther: On the New Testament, 8 vols. Martin Luther. Ed. by John N. Lenker. 1983. Repr. of 1904 ed. 125.00 (ISBN 0-8010-5626-8). Baker Bk.
Sermons of Metropolitan Philaret of Moscow. pap. 3.95 (ISBN 0-686-17311-2). Eastern Orthodox.
Sermons of R. M. M'Cheyne. R. M. M'Cheyne. 1985. pap. 5.95 (ISBN 0-85151-165-1). Banner of Truth.
Sermons of St. Alphonsus Liguori for All the Sundays of the Year. Alphonsus de Liguori. LC 82-50894. 408p. 1982. pap. 12.50 (ISBN 0-89555-193-4). TAN Bks Pubs.

Sermons of St. Francis de Sales for Advent & Christmas. St. Francis de Sales. Ed. by Lewis S. Fiorelli. Tr. by Nuns of the Visitation Staff. LC 87-50748. 135p. 1987. pap. 7.00 (ISBN 0-89555-261-2). TAN Bks Pubs.

Sermons of St. Francis de Sales for Lent Given in 1622. St. Francis de Sales. Ed. by Lewis S. Fiorelli. Tr. by Nuns of the Visitation Staff. LC 87-50084. 226p. (Orig.). 1987. pap. 8.00 (ISBN 0-89555-260-4). TAN Bks Pubs.

Sermons of St. Francis de Sales on Our Lady. St. Francis of Sales. Ed. by Lewis S. Fiorelli. LC 85-51662. 197p. 1985. pap. 8.00 (ISBN 0-89555-259-0). TAN Bks Pubs.

Sermons of St. Francis de Sales on Prayer. Francis De Sales. Ed. by Lewis Fiorelli. Tr. by Visitation Nuns. LC 84-52310. 51p. 1985. pap. 3.00 (ISBN 0-89555-258-2). TAN Bks Pubs.

Sermons of the American Revolution see Millennium in America: From the Puritan Migration to the Civil War.

Sermons of Thomas Foxcroft of Boston: 1697-1769. Thomas Foxcroft. LC 82-10457. 1983. 50.00x (ISBN 0-8201-1387-5). Schol Facsimiles.

Sermons of William S. Banowsky. Ed. by J. D. Thomas. (Great Preachers Ser). 1967. 11.95 (ISBN 0-89112-211-7). Abilene Christ U.

Sermons on Biblical Characters. Clovis G. Chappell. (Pocket Pulpit Lib.). 192p. 1981. pap. 4.95 (ISBN 0-8010-2330-0). Baker Bk.

Sermons on Deuteronomy. John Calvin. Tr. by Arthur Golding from Fr. (Sixteenth-Seventeenth Century Facsimile Editions Ser.). 1408p. 1987. 79.95 (ISBN 0-85151-511-8). Banner-of-Truth.

Sermons on Ephesians. John Calvin. 1979. 23.95 (ISBN 0-85151-170-8). Banner of Truth.

Sermons on Prayer. Ronald E. Wall. (Pulpit Library). 144p. 1986. pap. 6.95 (ISBN 0-8010-9672-3). Baker Bk.

Sermons on Religion & Life. Frederick W. Robertson. 332p. 1983. Repr. of 1982 ed. lib. bdg. 33.50 (ISBN 0-89987-731-1). Darby Bks.

Sermons on Revival: Kelvedon. Charles H. Spurgeon. Ed. by Charles T. Cook. 256p. 1977. Repr. of 1958 ed. limp bk. 7.50 (ISBN 0-551-05575-8). Attic Pr.

Sermons on Shalom. Steve Clapp. 79p, (Orig.). 1982. pap. 8.00 (ISBN 0-914527-37-1). C-Four Res.

Sermons on Special Days: Preaching Through the Year in the Black Church. William D. Watley. 128p. 1987. pap. 6.95 (ISBN 0-8170-1089-0). Judson.

Sermons on the Christian Household. Friedrich Schleiermacher. Tr. & intro. by Dietrich Seidel. (Schleiermacher Studies & Translations: Vol. 3). 1988. lib. bdg. 59.95x (ISBN 0-88946-360-3). E Mellen.

Sermons on the Final Verses of the Song of Songs. (Cistercian Fathers Ser.: Nbr. 43). 1982. 21.95 (ISBN 0-87907-643-7). Cistercian Pubns.

Sermons on the Final Verses of the Song of Songs, Vol. 1. John of Ford. (Cistercian Fathers Ser.: No. 29). 14.95. Cistercian Pubns.

Sermons on the Final Verses of the Song of Songs, Vol. 2. John Of Ford. Tr. by Wendy M. Beckett from Lat. (Cistercian Fathers Ser.: No. 39). 1982. 21.95 (ISBN 0-87907-639-9). Cistercian Pubns.

Sermons on the Final Verses of the Song of Songs, Vol. 4. John of Ford. (Cistercian Fathers Ser.: No. 44). 24.95 (ISBN 0-87907-644-5). Cistercian Pubns.

Sermons on the Final Verses of the Song of Songs, Vol. 5. John of Ford. (Cistercian Fathers Ser.: No. 45). 24.95 (ISBN 0-87907-645-3). Cistercian Pubns.

Sermons on the Final Verses of the Song of Songs, Vol. 6. John of Ford. 24.95 (ISBN 0-87907-646-1). Cistercian Pubns.

Sermons on the Final Verses of the Song of Songs, Vol. 7. John of Ford. 24.95. Cistercian Pubns.

Sermons on the Liturgical Seasons. St. Augustine. (Fathers of the Church Ser.: Vol. 38). 1959. 29.95x (ISBN 0-8132-0038-5). Cath U Pr.

Sermons on the Major Holy Days of the Orthodox Church. A. Coniaris. 1978. pap. 5.95. Light&Life Pub Co MN.

Sermons on the Miracles. Charles H. Spurgeon. Ed. by Charles T Cook. 256p. 1977. Repr. of 1958 ed. limp bk. 7.50 (ISBN 0-551-05576-6). Attic Pr.

Sermons on the Parables. Charles H. Spurgeon. Ed. by Charles T Cook. 256p. 1977. Repr. of 1958 ed. limp bk. 7.50 (ISBN 0-551-05574-X). Attic Pr.

Sermons on the Saving Work of Christ. John Calvin. 1980. pap. 11.95 (ISBN 0-87552-980-1, Evangel Pr Uk). Presby & Reformed.

Sermons on the Song of Songs, Vol. 1. Bernard of Clairvaux. (Cistercian Fathers Ser.: No. 4). pap. 5.00 (ISBN 0-87907-704-2). Cistercian Pubns.

Sermons on the Song of Songs, 3 vols, Vols. 1-3. Gilbert of Hoyland. Set. 30.00. Cistercian Pubns.

Sermons on the Song of Songs, Vol. 4. Bernard of Clairvaux. (Cistercian Fathers Ser.: No. 40). 15.95. Cistercian Pubns.

Sermons on Timothy & Titus. facsmilie ed. John Calvin. 1983. 48.95 (ISBN 0-85151-374-3). Banner of Truth.

Sermons on Unusual Occasions. C. H. Spurgeon. 1978. pap. 6.25 (ISBN 0-686-00494-9). Pilgrim Pubns.

Sermons on War by Theodore Parker. Blanche Cook et al. LC 70-149546. (Library of War & Peace; Relig. & Ethical Positions on War). 1973. lib. bdg. 46.00 (ISBN 0-8240-0499-X). Garland Pub.

Sermons-One to Eighty. St. Caesarius Of Arles. (Fathers of the Church Ser.: Vol. 31). 1956. 34.95x (ISBN 0-8132-0031-8). Cath U Pr.

Sermons Outline Series, 8 vols. Charles R. Wood. pap. 22.00 (ISBN 0-8254-4035-1). Kregel.

Sermons Preached at the Church of St. Paul the Apostle, New York, During the Year, 1863. Church of St. Paul the Apostle, New York Staff. 32.00 (ISBN 0-405-10851-6, 11854). Ayer Co Pubs.

Sermons Preached in the African Protestant Episcopal Church of St. Thomas' Philadelphia. facs. ed. William Douglass. LC 79-157366. (Black Heritage Library Collection Ser). 1854. 20.00 (ISBN 0-8369-8804-3). Ayer Co Pubs.

Sermons Preached on Plantations to Congregations of Negroes. facsimile ed. Alexander Glennie. LC 75-161260. (Black Heritage Library Collection). Repr. of 1844 ed. 16.25 (ISBN 0-8369-8819-1). Ayer Co Pubs.

Sermons Preached upon Various Occasions, 8 vols. Robert South. LC 73-175991. Repr. of 1842 ed. Set. 155.00 (ISBN 0-404-06180-X). AMS Pr.

Sermons, Speeches, Letters on Slavery & Its War 1850-1868. Gilbert Haven. LC 74-82197. (Anti-Slavery Crusade in America Ser). 1969. Repr. of 1869 ed. 26.00 (ISBN 0-405-00637-3). Ayer Co Pubs.

Sermons That Demand a Decision. Edward Fudge. pap. 2.00 (ISBN 0-686-12681-5). E Fudge.

Sermons That Save. Robert R. Taylor. 1984. 10.95 (ISBN 0-317-16702-2). Firm Foun Pub.

Sermons That Should Be in Print. John Stacy. (Illus.). 104p. (Orig.). 1986. pap. 9.95 (ISBN 0-317-55027-6). Brentwood Comm.

Sermons That Strengthen. Edward Fudge. pap. 2.00 (ISBN 0-686-12682-3). E Fudge.

Sermons: The Yale Edition of the Works of Samuel Johnson, Vol. 14. Samuel Johnson. Ed. by Jean H. Hagstrum & James Gray. LC 57-918. (Illus.). 1978. 45.00t (ISBN 0-300-02104-6). Yale U Pr.

Sermons to Grow on. Edward Fudge. pap. 2.00 (ISBN 0-686-12683-1). E Fudge.

Sermons to the Natural Man. W. G. Shedd. 1977. 17.95 (ISBN 0-85151-260-7). Banner of Truth.

Sermons to the Twelve. Jung L. Lee. 144p. 1988. pap. 9.95 (ISBN 0-687-38001-4). Abingdon.

Sermons with Life Sketh. B. H. Carroll. 1986. Repr. of 1893 ed. 19.50 (ISBN 0-317-47643-2). Church History.

Sermons You Can Preach. W. Herschel Ford. (Simple Sermon Ser.). 384p. 1983. pap. 12.95 (ISBN 0-310-46971-6, 9833P). Zondervan.

Sermons You Can Preach on Acts. W. Herschel Ford. 352p. 1987. pap. 11.95 (ISBN 0-310-38461-3, 9832P). Zondervan.

Sermons You Can Preach on John: Simple Sermons. W. Herschel Ford. 432p. pap. 12.95 (ISBN 0-310-38451-6, 9835P). Zondervan.

Sermons You Can Preach on Matthew. W. Herschel Ford. 240p. (Orig.). 1985. pap. 9.95 (ISBN 0-310-45521-9, 9834P). Zondervan.

Sermons You Should Preach. J. J. Turner. 1984. pap. 3.95 (ISBN 0-89137-547-3). Quality Pubns.

Serodiagnostics & Vaccines: Proceedings. International Symposium on Fish Biologics. Ed. by D. P. Andersen et al. (Developments in Biological Standardization Ser.: Vol. 49). (Illus.). xii, 496p. 1981. pap. text ed. 62.75 (ISBN 3-8055-3471-X). S Karger.

Serological Methods in Forensic Science. Ed. by Susan D. Rolih & W. John Judd. LC 85-18595. (Illus.). 1985. 22.00 (ISBN 0-915355-19-1). Am Assn Blood.

Serological Tests for Syphilis, Vol. 2. Takayuki Tomizawa. Ed. by Nozomu Kosakai. LC 81-83037. (Illustrated Laboratory Techniques Ser.). 62p. 1981. 11.00 (ISBN 0-89640-063-8). Igaku-Shoin.

Serology & Immunochemistry of Plant Viruses. M. H. Van Regenmortal. LC 81-17631. 1982. 55.50 (ISBN 0-12-714180-4). Acad Pr.

Serology & Immunology. Stansfield. 1981. write for info. (ISBN 0-02-415740-6). Macmillan.

Serology of Tuberculosis & BCG Vaccination. Ed. by W. Fox. (Advances in Tuberculosis Research Ser.: Vol. 21). (Illus.). viii, 192p. 1983. 110.00 (ISBN 3-8055-3855-3). S Karger.

Serotonin & Microcirculation. Ed. by R. S. Reneman & A. Bollinger. (Mikrozirkulation in Forschung und Klinik; Progess in Applied Microcirculation Ser.: Vol. 10). (Illus.). x, 92p. 1986. pap. 44.00 (ISBN 3-8055-4163-5). S Karger.

Serotonin in Affective Disorders. Ed. by J. Menlewicz et al. (Advances in Biological Psychiatry Ser.: Vol. 14). (Illus.). vi, 90p. 1984. 36.00 (ISBN 3-8055-3898-7). S Karger.

Serotonin in Biological Psychiatry: Advances in Biochemical Psychopharmacology, Vol. 34. Ed. by Beng T. Ho et al. 352p. 1982. text ed. 55.00 (ISBN 0-89004-803-7). Raven.

Serotonin in Mental Abnormalities. Ed. by David J. Boullin. LC 77-18281. pap. 82.00 (ISBN 0-317-07778-3, 2019207). Bks Demand UMI.

Serotonin Neurotoxins. Ed. by J. H. Jacoby & L. D. Lytle. (Annals of the New York Academy of Sciences: Vol. 305). 702p. 1978. 68.00x (ISBN 0-89072-061-4); pap. write for info. (ISBN 0-89072-078-9). NY Acad Sci.

Serotonin Neurotransmission & Behavior. Ed. by Barry L. Jacobs & Alan Gelperin. 430p. 1981. text ed. 65.00x (ISBN 0-262-10023-1). MIT Pr.

Serotonin, New Vistas: Biochemistry & Behavioral & Clinical Studies. Ed. by E. Costa et al. LC 73-91166. (Advances in Biochemical Psychopharmacology Ser.: Vol. 11). 446p. 1974. 58.00 (ISBN 0-911216-69-3). Raven.

Serotonin, New Vistas: Histochemistry & Pharmacology. Ed. by E. Costa et al. LC 73-91165. (Advances in Biochemical Psychopharmacology Ser.: Vol. 10). 345p. 1974. 58.00 (ISBN 0-911216-68-5). Raven.

Serotoninergic System, Feeding & Body Weight Regulation. Ed. by Stylianos Nicolaidis. 170p. 1988. pap. 29.00 (ISBN 0-12-518175-2). Acad Pr.

Serowe: Village of the Rain-Wind. Bessie Head. (African Writers Ser.: No. 220). (Orig.). 1981. pap. text ed. 8.00 (ISBN 0-435-90220-2). Heinemann Ed.

Serpe d'Or. De Goscinny. (gr. 7-9). 15.95 (ISBN 0-685-33971-8). French & Eur.

Serpe d'Or. R. Goscinny & M. Uderzo. (Illus., Fr.). 15.95 (ISBN 0-686-56240-2). French & Eur.

Serpent see America Hurrah & Other Plays.

Serpent & Columbine: Four Chapters on Francis Bacon & "The Advancement of Learning". Shanti Padhi. 1969. 17.50x (ISBN 0-8046-8820-6, Pub. by Kennikat). Assoc Faculty Pr.

Serpent & Lily: A Novella, with a Manifesto: The Sickness of the Age. Nikos Kazantzakis. Tr. by Theodora Vasils from Gr. LC 78-68832. 1980. 12.95x (ISBN 0-520-03885-1). U of Cal Pr.

Serpent & the Eagle. Daniel Spicehandler. LC 83-70293. 309p. 1983. 14.95 (ISBN 0-937444-05-7); pap. 9.95 (ISBN 0-937444-06-5). Caislan Pr.

Serpent & the Rainbow. E. Wades Davis. 288p. 1986. 17.95 (ISBN 0-671-50247-6). S&S.

Serpent & the Rainbow: A Harvard Scientist Uncovers the Startling Truth about the Secret World of Haitian Voodoo & Zombis. Wade Davis. 384p. (Orig.). 1987. pap. 4.95 (ISBN 0-446-34387-0). Warner Bks.

Serpent & the Rope. Raja Rao. 408p. 1968. pap. 6.00 (ISBN 0-88253-766-0). Ind-US Inc.

Serpent & the Rope. Raja Rao. LC 85-13628. 408p. 1986. 22.50 (ISBN 0-87951-220-2). Overlook Pr.

Serpent & the Rope. Raja Rao. (Illus.). 408p. 1988. pap. 9.95 (ISBN 0-87951-243-1). Overlook Pr.

Serpent & the Stag: The Saga of England's Powerful & Glamourous Cavendish Family from the Age of Henry the Eighth to the Present. John Pearson. 1984. 19.95 (ISBN 0-03-055431-4, William Abrahams Bk). H Holt & Co.

Serpent de Mer. Jules Verne. 254p. 1976. 8.95 (ISBN 0-686-55950-9). French & Eur.

Serpent d'Etoiles. Jean Giono. 192p. 1962. 8.95 (ISBN 0-686-53989-3). French & Eur.

Serpent for a Dove: The Suppression of the American Indian. Noel Grisham. (Illus.). 168p. 8.50 (ISBN 0-8363-0089-0). Jenkins.

Serpent Imagery & Symbolism. Lura Pedrini & Duilio T. Pedrini. 1966. 10.95 (ISBN 0-8084-0274-9); pap. 6.95x (ISBN 0-8084-0275-7). New Coll U Pr.

Serpent in Eden: H. L. Mencken & the South. Fred C. Hobson, Jr. LC 73-15674. xv, 242p. 1974. pap. text ed. 8.95x (ISBN 0-8071-0455-8). La State U Pr.

Serpent in Eden: H. L. Mencken & the South. Fred C. Hobson, Jr. LC 73-15674. xvi, 242p. 1974. 25.00x (ISBN 0-8078-1224-2). U of NC Pr.

Serpent in Paradise. Rosemary Carter. (Harlequin Presents Ser.). 192p. 1984. pap. 1.95 (ISBN 0-373-10664-5). Harlequin Bks.

Serpent in the Sky: The High Wisdom of Ancient Egypt. John A. West. (Illus.). 256p. 1987. pap. 12.95 (ISBN 0-517-56635-4, Julian Pr). Crown.

Serpent Is Shut out from Paradise: A Revaluation of Romantic Love in Shelley. Seraphia D. Leyda. Ed. by James Hogg. (Romantic Reassessment Ser.). 300p. (Orig.). 1972. pap. 15.00 (ISBN 0-317-40093-2, Pub. by Salzburg Studies). Longwood Pub Group.

Serpent, la Femme et l'Epee: Recherches sur l'Imagination Symbolique d'un Romancier Medieval--Chretien de Troyes. Gerard Chandes. (Faux Titre Ser.: Vol. 27). 312p. 1986. pap. text ed. 75.00 (ISBN 90-6203-788-7, Pub. by Rodopi). Humanities.

Serpent Mage. Greg Bear. 352p. (Orig.). 1986. pap. 3.50 (ISBN 0-425-09337-9). Berkley Pub.

Serpent Mage. Greg Bear. 1987. pap. 3.50 (ISBN 0-441-79066-6, Pub. by Ace Science Fiction). Ace Bks.

Serpent Mound. Lloyd St. Alcorn. (Dreamquest Ser.: No. 3). 1989. pap. 3.50 (ISBN 0-451-15766-4, Sig). NAL.

Serpent Never Sleeps: A Novel of Jamestown & Pocahontas. Scott O'Dell. (Illus.). 240p. (gr. 5 up). 1987. 15.95 (ISBN 0-395-44242-7). HM.

Serpent Power. Arthur Avalon. LC 74-75259. (Illus.). 1974. pap. 8.95 (ISBN 0-486-23058-9). Dover.

Serpent Power (Sat-Chakra-Nirupana & Paduka-Panchaka) Tr. by John Woodroffe from Sanskrit. (Illus.). 512p. (Eng. only). 1973. 24.00 (ISBN 0-89744-117-6, Pub. by Ganesh & Co. India). Auromere.

Serpent Ring. Barbara H. Withey. LC 87-32458. (Illus.). 192p. (gr. 5 up). 1988. 10.95 (ISBN 0-87518-378-6, Gemstone Bks). Dillon.

Serpent Symbol & the Worship of the Reciprocal Principles of Nature in America. Ephraim G. Squier. LC 17-25223. 1975. Repr. of 1851 ed. 21.00 (ISBN 0-527-03228-X). Kraus Repr.

Serpent: The Atlan Cycle, No. 1. Jane Gaskell. 1986. pap. 2.95 (ISBN 0-87997-990-9). DAW Bks.

Serpent under It: A Novel. Edith Taylor. 256p. 1973. 5.95 (ISBN 0-393-08673-9). Norton.

Serpent Worship in Africa - the Ovimbundu of Angola: Culture Areas of Nigeria. W. D. Hambly. (Chicago Field Museum of Natural History Fieldiana Anthropology Ser). Repr. of 1935 ed. 56.00 (ISBN 0-527-01881-3). Kraus Repr.

Serpent Worship in Ancient India. B. C. Sinha. xvi, 87p. 1979. 16.00 (ISBN 1-55528-052-8, Pub. by Messers Today & Tomorrow Printers & Publishers). Scholarly Pubns.

Serpentes. Jean-Claude Rage. (Encyclopedia of Paleoherpetology: Pt. 11). (Illus.). 80p. 1984. pap. text ed. 60.50x (ISBN 3-437-30448-8). Lubrecht & Cramer.

Serpentine. Thomas Thompson. 1981. pap. 4.95 (ISBN 0-440-17611-5). Dell.

Serpentine & Its Vegetation: A Multi-disciplinary Approach. Robert R. Brooks. (Ecology, Phytogeography & Physiology Ser.: Vol. 1). (Illus.). 454p. 1987. 47.50 (ISBN 0-931146-04-6). Dioscorides Pr.

Serpentine Futures. Lewis Packer. LC 85-14139. 63p. 1987. 12.50 (ISBN 0-7022-1906-1). U of Queensland Pr.

Serpentine Rouletted Stamps of Finland: Issues of 1860 & 1866. Leo Linder & D. A. Dromberg. Ed. by G. B. Koplowitz. Tr. by Kauko Aro from Finnish. (Illus.). 106p. (Orig.). 1983. pap. text ed. 17.50 (ISBN 0-936493-00-3). Scand Philatelic.

Serpentine Rouletted Stamps of Finland-Issues of 1860 & 1866, Vol. 2: Cancellations & Roulette Varieties, Vol. 2. Mikka Ossa. Ed. by G. B. Koplowitz. Tr. by Kauko I. Aro from Finnish. (Illus.). 116p. (Orig.). 1985. pap. text ed. 18.50 (ISBN 0-936493-08-9). Scand Philatelic.

Serpentine Wall. James DeBrosse. 336p. 1988. 17.95 (ISBN 0-312-02278-6). St Martin.

Serpentor & the Mummy Warrior. R. L. Stine. (G.I. Joe - Find Your Fate Ser.: No. 20). (Orig.). 1987. pap. text ed. 2.50 (ISBN 0-345-34069-8). Ballantine.

Serpent's Children. Laurence Yep. LC 82-48855. 288p. (YA) (gr. 7 up). 1984. 13.70i (ISBN 0-06-026809-3); PLB 13.89g (ISBN 0-06-026812-3). HarpJ.

Serpent's Circle. Patick Harpur. 272p. 1986. pap. 3.50 (ISBN 0-446-30026-8). Warner Bks.

Serpents Coil. Farley Mowat. 224p. 1982. pap. 3.50 (ISBN 0-7704-2098-2). Bantam.

Serpent's Coil. Farley Mowat. 224p. (Orig.). Date not set. pap. 3.50. Bantam.

Serpent's Egg: A Collection of Literature & Art. LC 79-84549. 1979. pap. 10.00 (ISBN 0-931350-02-6). Moonlight Pubns.

Serpent's Eye. Wade Barker. 288p. 1985. pap. 2.95 (ISBN 0-446-32394-2). Warner Bks.

Serpent's Reach. C. J. Cherryh. (Science Fiction Ser.). 1985. pap. 3.50 (ISBN 0-88677-088-2). DAW Bks.

Serpent's Silver. Piers Anthony. 320p. 1989. 17.95. Tor Bks.

Serpent's Tooth. Christopher P. Andersen. 1988. pap. 3.95 (ISBN 0-312-90541-6). St Martin.

Serpent's Tooth: The True Story of the Benson Family Murders. Christopher Andersen. LC 86-46040. (Illus.). 288p. 1987. 16.45i (ISBN 0-06-015746-1, HarpT). Har-Row.

Serr-ol Hajar: Secret of Hajar. Sadegh M. Angha. LC 82-84673. 161p. (Orig., Persian.). 1983. 75.00 (ISBN 0-910735-43-3); pap. 35.00 (ISBN 0-910735-42-5). MTO Printing & Pubn Ctr.

Serrano Indians of Southern California. Frank Johnston. 1967. 1.75 (ISBN 0-939046-22-9). Malki Mus Pr.

Serra's San Diego: Father Junipero Serra & California's Beginnings. Iris H. Engstrand. (Illus.). 16p. 1982. 2.95 (ISBN 0-918740-02-9). San Diego Hist.

Serres Chaudes: Chansons Completes. Maurice Maeterlinck. 144p. 1955. 28.95 (ISBN 0-686-52690-9). French & Eur.

Serta Turyniana: Studies in Greek Literature & Palaeography in Honor of Alexander Turyn. Ed. by John L. Heller. LC 73-81567. (Illus.). 633p. 1974. 42.50 (ISBN 0-252-00405-1). U of Ill Pr.

Sertoli Cells & Leydig Cells in Man. C. Schulze. (Advances in Anatomy, Embryology & Cell Biology Ser.: Vol. 88). (Illus.). 120p. 1984. pap. 29.00 (ISBN 0-387-13603-7). Springer-Verlag.

Sertones. Euclides Da Conha. (Ayacucho Library Collection Ser.: Vol. 79). (Span.). 1980. 35.00 (ISBN 0-317-56600-8, Pub. by Biblioteca Ayacucho); pap. 17.50 (ISBN 0-317-56601-6, Pub. by Biblioteca Ayacucho). Humanities.

Sertorius. Pierre Corneille. 160p. 1959. 5.95 (ISBN 0-686-54622-9). French & Eur.

Sertorius. Adolf Schulten. LC 75-7340. (Roman History Ser.). (Ger.). 1975. Repr. 16.00x (ISBN 0-405-07061-6). Ayer Co Pubs.

Sertum Austro-Caledonicum. J. J. De La Billardiere. (Illus.). 1968. Repr. of 1825 ed. 92.50x (ISBN 3-7682-0541-X). Lubrecht & Cramer.

Sertum Orchidaceum. John Lindley. 300.00. Johnson Repr.

Serum Cholesterol Level of Adults 18-74 Years in the United States, 1971-1974. Sidney Abraham et al. Ed. by Taloria Stevenson. (Series Eleven: No. 205). 1977. pap. text ed. 1.50 (ISBN 0-8406-0111-5). Natl Ctr Health Stats.

Serum Cholesterol Levels of Persons Aged 4-74 Years by Socioeconomic Characteristics, United States, 1971-74. Ed. by Audrey Shipp. (Series 11: No. 217). 1979. pap. text ed. 1.75 (ISBN 0-8406-0180-8). Natl Ctr Health Stats.

Serum of the Water. Dean Phelps. LC 78-12785. 1978. pap. 3.95 (ISBN 0-914974-17-3). Holmgangers.

Serum Protein Abnormalities: Diagnostic & Clinical Aspects. Ed. by Stephan E. Ritzmann & Jerry C. Daniels. LC 82-18001. 572p. 1982. 66.00 (ISBN 0-8451-2799-3). A R Liss.

Serum Uric Acid Values of Youth 12 to 17 Years, U. S. Paul S. Levy et al. Ed. by Taloria Stevenson. LC 75-619039. (Data from the Health Examination Survey Ser. 11: No. 152). 50p. 1975. pap. 1.50 (ISBN 0-8406-0041-0). Natl Ctr Health Stats.

Servant see Five Screenplays.

Servant & Son: Jesus in Parable & Gospel. J. Ramsey Michaels. LC 80-84651. 322p. 1982. pap. 9.95 (ISBN 0-8042-0409-8, John Knox). Westminster John Knox.

Servant As His Lord. Oswald Chambers. 1973. pap. 3.95 (ISBN 0-87508-137-1). Chr Lit.

Servant Church: Diaconal Ministry & the Episcopal Church. John E. Booty. LC 82-81429. (Orig.). 1982. pap. 7.95 (ISBN 0-8192-1316-0). Morehouse.

Servant Girl Question. Harriet P. Spofford. Ed. by Leon Stein. LC 77-70535. (Work Ser.). 1977. Repr. of 1881 ed. lib. bdg. 20.00x (ISBN 0-405-10203-8). Ayer Co Pubs.

Servant Leadership: A Journey into the Nature of Legitimate Power & Greatness. Robert K. Greenleaf. LC 76-45678. 348p. 1977. 9.95 (ISBN 0-8091-2527-7). Paulist Pr.

Servant of God's Servants: The Work of a Christian Minister. Paul M. Miller. LC 63-15499. (Conrad Grebel Lectures: 1963). pap. 59.00 (ISBN 0-317-26613-6, 2025423). Bks Demand UMI.

Servant of Jehovah. H. L. Ellison. 32p. 1983. pap. 2.95 (ISBN 0-85364-254-0, Pub. by Paternoster UK). Attic Pr.

Servant of Love: Mother Teresa & Her Missionaries of Charity. Edward Le Joly. LC 77-15874. (Illus.). 1978. 4.95 (ISBN 0-06-065215-2, HarpR). Har-Row.

Servant of Power: A Political Biography of Senator William M. Stewart. Russell R. Elliott. (History & Political Science Ser.: No. 18). (Illus., Orig.). 1983. pap. 12.95x (ISBN 0-87417-076-1). U of Nev Pr.

Servant of Quality. Eileen Jackson. 224p. (Orig.). 1988. pap. 2.95 (ISBN 0-451-15582-3, Sig). NAL.

Servant of the Muse: A Garland for Peter Russell on His Sixtieth Birthday. James Hogg. (Poetic Drama & Poetic Theory). 224p. (Orig.). 1981. pap. 15.00 (ISBN 3-7052-0897-7, Pub. by Salzburg Studies). Longwood Pub Group.

Servant of the Shogun. Richard Tames. 132p. 1985. pap. 25.00x (ISBN 0-904404-39-0, Pub. by Norbury Pubns Ltd). State Mutual Bk.

Servant of the Shogun: Being the True Story of William Adams, Pilot & Samurai, First Englishman in Japan. Richard Tames. LC 87-28348. 144p. 1988. 19.95 (ISBN 0-312-01603-4). St Martin.

Servant of the Stuarts. Moyra Cimino. 1982. 32.00x (ISBN 0-7223-1557-0, Pub. by A H Stockwell England). State Mutual Bk.

Servant of the Word. Dawn De Vries. LC 86-45902. 240p. 1987. pap. 14.95 (ISBN 0-8006-3203-6). Fortress.

Servant of Truth: Messages of John Paul II. Pope John Paul II. 1979. 9.95 (ISBN 0-8198-0595-5); pap. 8.95 (ISBN 0-8198-0596-3). Dghtrs St Paul.

Servant of Two Masters. Carlo Goldoni. Tr. by Frederick H. Davies. (Orig.). 1961. pap. 3.50x (ISBN 0-87830-537-8). Theatre Arts.

Servant of Two Masters & Other Italian Classics. Ed. by Eric Bentley. (Eric Bentley's Dramatic Repertoire Ser.). 272p. (Orig., Ital.). 1986. pap. 7.95 (ISBN 0-936839-20-1). Applause Theatre Bk Pubs.

Servant Problem: Domestic Workers in North America. Linda Martin & Kerry Segrave. LC 84-43214. 175p. 1985. lib. bdg. 18.95x (ISBN 0-89950-135-4). McFarland & Co.

Servant Story (Mark) Leader's Guide. (New Horizons Bible Study Ser.). 48p. 1980. pap. 1.95 (ISBN 0-89367-050-2). Light & Life.

Servant Story (Mark) Study Guide. (New Horizons Bible Study Ser.). 64p. 1980. pap. 2.50 (ISBN 0-89367-049-9). Light & Life.

Servant with a Smile. Marsha Barrett. (Illus.). 40p. (Orig.). (gr. 1-3). 1985. pap. 2.00 (ISBN 0-317-18029-0). Home Mission.

Servants & Masters in 18th Century France: The Uses of Loyalty. Sarah C. Maza. LC 83-42566. (Illus.). 320p. 1983. 38.50x (ISBN 0-691-05394-4). Princeton U Pr.

Servants & Stewards. Everett L. Fullam. Ed. by Shelli Hendrican & Lynda Barnes. (Tips for the Church Ser.). 31p. (Orig.). 1987. pap. 3.50 (ISBN 0-943525-33-0). St Pauls Ctr.

Servant's Call. Knofel Staton. LC 75-7462. (Illus.). 96p. 1976. pap. 2.25 (ISBN 0-87239-051-9, 40024). Standard Pub.

Servants for Christ: The Adventist Church Facing the 80's. Gottfried Oosterwal & Russell L. Staples. vi, 162p. 1980. pap. 3.95 (ISBN 0-943872-78-2). Andrews Univ Pr.

Servant's Hand: English Fiction from Below. Bruce Robbins. LC 85-14955. 256p. 1986. 27.50 (ISBN 0-231-05966-3). Columbia U Pr.

Servants in Charge. Keith M. Bailey. 123p. 1979. pap. 4.95 (ISBN 0-87509-160-1); Leader's Guide. 0.95 (ISBN 0-87509-261-6). Chr Pubns.

Servants in Husbandry in Early Modern England. Ann Kussmaul. (Interdisciplinary Perspectives on Modern History Ser.). (Illus.). 240p. 1981. 34.50 (ISBN 0-521-23566-9). Cambridge U Pr.

Servants Like Him. Phyllis Thompson et al. (Illus.). 1985. pap. 3.25 (ISBN 0-937170-30-5). Home Mission.

Servants, Not Celebrities. Nelson L. Price. (Orig.). 1989. pap. 6.95 (ISBN 0-8054-5068-8). Broadman.

Servants of All. Chiara Lubich. Tr. by Hugh Moran from Ital. LC 78-59470. 176p. 1978. pap. 3.50 (ISBN 0-911782-05-2). New City.

Servants of All. Wilbert L. Walker. LC 82-81162. 244p. 1982. 12.00 (ISBN 0-935428-02-X). Heritage Pr.

Servants of God: The Lives of the 10 Gurus of the Sikhs. Jon Engle. LC 79-63457. (Illus.). 192p. 1980. pap. 6.00 (ISBN 0-89142-035-5). Sant Bani Ash.

Servants of Post-Industrial Power: Sociologie Du Travail in Modern France. Michael Rose. LC 78-65594. 244p. 1979. 40.00 (ISBN 0-87332-130-8). M E Sharpe.

Servants of Power: The Role of the English-Speaking Churches 1903-1930. James Cochrane. 304p. 1987. pap. text ed. 21.95x (ISBN 0-317-59569-5, Pub. by Ravan Pr.). Ohio U Pr.

Servants of Satan: The Age of the Witch Hunts. Joseph Klaits. LC 84-48252. (Illus.). 224p. 1987. 24.95X (ISBN 0-253-35182-0); pap. 7.95x (ISBN 0-253-20422-4). Ind U Pr.

Servants of the Goddess: The Priest of a South Indian Temple. Christopher J. Fuller. LC 83-14369. (Cambridge Studies in Social Anthropology: No. 47). (Illus.). 240p. 1984. 44.50 (ISBN 0-521-24777-2). Cambridge U Pr.

Servants of the People: The Uncertain Future of the Federal Civil Service. Howard Rosen. LC 85-7266. 1985. pap. 12.95 (ISBN 0-913420-55-7). Olympus Pub Co.

Servants of the State: The Contested Control of Teaching 1900-1930. Martin Lawn. 180p. 1987. 37.00x (ISBN 1-85000-257-6, Falmer Pr); pap. 18.00x (ISBN 1-85000-258-4, Falmer Pr). Taylor & Francis.

Servants of Twilight. Dean R. Koontz. 1988. 18.95 (ISBN 0-913165-24-7). Dark Harvest.

Servant's Tale. Paula Fox. LC 84-60679. 336p. 1984. 16.50 (ISBN 0-86547-164-9). N Point Pr.

Servant's Tale. Paula Fox. (Contemporary American Fiction Ser.). 336p. 1986. pap. 6.95 (ISBN 0-14-008386-3). Penguin.

Serve: Older Volunteers in Community Service, a New Role & a New Resource. Janet S. Sainer & Mary L. Sander. 347p. 1971. pap. 14.00 (ISBN 0-88156-090-1). Comm Serv Soc NY.

Serve the Lord with Your Heart. Grant Von Harrison. 28p. (Orig.). (YA) (gr. 11 up). 1981. pap. 1.95 (ISBN 0-910558-07-8, 8679). Pubs Bk Sales.

Serve Together with Generosity & Forgiveness 1987: Cathechetical Sunday. Department of Education. Tr. by Marina Herrera. 48p. (Orig., Eng. & Span.). 1987. Bilingual Publication. pap. 4.95 (ISBN 1-55586-140-7). US Catholic.

Serve with Champagne. Hilde G. Lee. 288p. 1988. 19.95 (ISBN 0-89815-274-7); pap. 14.95 (ISBN 0-89815-262-3). Ten Speed Pr.

Serve with Love. Ed. by Gale Clausen. (Illus.). 416p. 1982. plastic spine 9.95 (ISBN 0-943980-02-X). AIGA Pubns.

SerVermont - the First Year: 1986. Cynthia Parsons. 50p. (Orig.). 1986. pap. 5.00 (ISBN 0-9617872-1-X). VT Schoolhse Pr.

Servermont & the U. S. A. Cynthia Parsons. 70p. (Orig.). 1988. pap. 1000.00 (ISBN 0-9617872-2-8). VT Schoolhse Pr.

Serviani in Aeneidem Commentarii: Editio Harvardiana, Vol. 3 - Aeneid III-V. E. K. Rand et al. (American Philological Association Special Publications Ser.). 1974. 37.50 (ISBN 0-89130-718-4, 40 05 01). Scholars Pr GA.

Service. Henry David Thoreau. 59.95 (ISBN 0-87968-441-0). Gordon Pr.

Service: A Trilogy on Colonization. Martha Rosler. 36p. 1978. pap. 5.00 (ISBN 0-89439-007-4). Printed Matter.

Service America: Doing Business in the New Economy. Karl Albrecht & Ron Zemke. 235p. 1985. 20.95 (ISBN 0-87094-659-5). Dow Jones-Irwin.

Service & a Smile. Nancy Beck-Irland. (Hall of Faith Ser.). 75p. 1987. pap. 6.95 (ISBN 0-8163-0704-0). Pacific Pr Pub Assn.

Service & Development Process. 80p. 12.50 (ISBN 92-1-112200-7, E.85.11.D.13). UN.

Service & Spirituality. Swami Swahananda. 211p. (Orig.). 1980. pap. 3.95 (ISBN 0-87481-500-2). Vedanta Pr.

Service Banking: The All Purpose Bank. D. G. Hanson. 1987. 75.00x (ISBN 0-85297-192-3, Pub. by Inst of Bankers). State Mutual Bk.

Service Banking: The Arrival of the All Purpose Bank. Derrek Hanson. 1985. 75.00x (ISBN 0-85297-066-8, Pub. by Inst of Bankers). State Mutual Bk.

Service Book. Tr. by Laurence Mancuso from Slavic & Gr. (New Skete). (Illus.). 214p. 1978. 20.00x (ISBN 0-9607924-4-9). Monks of New Skete.

Service Business: A Guide to Winning Customers & Making Profits. Fred E. Jandt. 1988. write for info. (ISBN 0-471-85944-3). Wiley.

Service-Center-Produced-Records. (American Institute of CPAs Audit Guides Ser.). 1987. pap. 10.50 (ISBN 0-87051-036-3). Am Inst CPA.

Service Centers & Consumer Trips: Studies on the Philadelphia Metropolitan Fringe. John E. Brush & Howard L. Gautier, Jr. LC 67-25274. (Research Papers: No. 113). 182p. 1968. pap. 12.00 (ISBN 0-89065-021-7). U Chicago Comm Geo.

Service Centres in Rural India: Policy, Theory & Practice. Sudhir Wanmali. 236p. 1983. text ed. 35.00x (ISBN 0-86590-131-7). Apt Bks.

Service Charges in Gas & Electric Rates. Hubert F. Havlik. LC 68-58590. (Columbia University. Studies in the Social Sciences: No. 435). Repr. of 1938 ed. 20.00 (ISBN 0-404-51435-9). AMS Pr.

Service City: State & Townsmen in Russia, 1600-1800. J. Michael Hittle. LC 79-10909. 1979. text ed. 24.50x (ISBN 0-674-80170-9). Harvard U Pr.

Service Contract Act Directory of Occupations. 2nd ed. Emanuel Weinstein. 143p. 1986. pap. 7.00 (ISBN 0-318-21558-6, S/N 029-016-00091-7). USGPO.

Service Corporation Manual. 350p. 1985. 75.00 (ISBN 0-929097-26-2, 12872). US League Savi Inst.

Service Delivery in Intermediate-Size Jewish Communities. Gary Tobin & Jan Rothschild. 61p. 1986. write for info. Coun Jewish Feds.

Service Dog Goes to School: The Story of a Dog Trained to Help the Disabled. Elizabeth S. Smith. (Illus.). 64p. (gr. 1-4). 1988. 11.95 (ISBN 0-688-07648-3); PLB 11.88 (ISBN 0-688-07649-1). Morrow.

Service Economies in Europe: Opportunities for Growth. Wolfgang Ochel & Manfred Wegner. 220p. 1988. 37.50 (ISBN 0-8133-0580-2). Westview.

Service Economy. Victor R. Fuchs & Irving F. Leveson. (General Ser.: No. 87). 308p. 1968. 18.50 (ISBN 0-87014-475-8, 62, Dist. by Columbia UPr); pap. 9.00 (ISBN 0-87014-476-6). Natl Bur Econ Res.

Service Encounter. Ed. by John A. Czepiel et al. LC 83-49532. (Advances in Retailing Ser.). 352p 1984. 40.00x (ISBN 0-669-08273-2). Lexington Bks.

Service Etiquette. 3rd ed. Oretha D. Swartz. LC 76-47995. 582p. 1977. 17.95 (ISBN 0-87021-624-4). Naval Inst Pr.

Service Etiquette. 4th ed. Oretha D. Swartz. (Illus.). 576p. 1988. 17.95 (ISBN 0-87021-620-1). Naval Inst Pr.

Service Evangelism. Richard S. Armstrong. LC 78-26701. 198p. 1979. pap. 8.95 (ISBN 0-664-24252-9). Westminster John Knox.

Service Excellence: The Customer Relations Strategy for Health Care. Ed. by Wendy Leebov. LC 87-30631. 348p. (Orig.). 1988. pap. 37.50 (ISBN 1-55648-019-9, 136104). AHPI.

Service Fatigue Loads Monitoring, Simulation, Analysis- STP 671. Ed. by P. R. Abelkis & J. M. Potter. 298p. 1979. 29.50x (ISBN 0-8031-0721-8, 04-671000-30). ASTM.

Service for the Dead. Robert A. Anderson. 288p. 1986. 16.95 (ISBN 0-87795-812-2). Morrow.

Service for the Dead. Robert A. Anderson. 288p. 1987. pap. 3.95 (ISBN 0-380-89980-9). Avon.

Service for the Hanging of the Greens. 1984. 2.75 (ISBN 0-89536-709-2, 4890). CSS of Ohio.

Service for the High Holy Days Adapted for Youth. Adapted by Hyman Chanover. LC 72-2058. 192p. (gr. 8 up). 1972. pap. 4.95x (ISBN 0-87441-123-8). Behrman.

Service for the Lord's Day: The Worship of God. LC 84-5220. (Supplemental Liturgical Resource Ser.: No. 1). 192p. (Orig.). 1984. text ed. 7.95 kivar (ISBN 0-664-24643-5); pap. 14.75 pack of five, pew edition (ISBN 0-664-24641-9). Westminster John Knox.

Service Hotline Handbook, Vol. II. Compiled by Phil Roman. 160p. 1986. 12.95 (ISBN 0-912524-34-0). Busn News.

Service Hotline Handbook, Vol. III. Compiled by Phil Roman. 160p. 1987. 12.95 (ISBN 0-912524-35-9). Busn News.

Service Ideals. Tom Evans. (Illus.). 100p. (Orig.). 1987. pap. text ed. 22.95 (ISBN 0-944947-01-8). Busn Knowledge.

Service Imperative for Libraries: Essays in Honor of Margaret E. Monroe. Ed. by Gail A. Schlachter. LC 82-8991. 215p. 1982. text ed. 28.50 (ISBN 0-87287-272-6). Libs Unl.

Service Improvement of the State Teachers College Faculty: A Study of the Efforts at in-Service Improvement of the Faculties of State Teachers Colleges in the United States. Adolph Linscheid. LC 70-176998. (Columbia University. Teachers College. Contributions to Education: No. 309). Repr. of 1928 ed. 22.50 (ISBN 0-404-55309-5). AMS Pr.

Service in Siberia. Ned E. Wick. LC 75-29500. 1976. write for info (ISBN 0-686-17444-5). Fennwyn Pr.

Service in Siberia. Ned E. Wick. LC 72-29500. 1975. 4.00 (ISBN 0-685-64827-3). Honor Bks.

Service in the Roman Army. Roy Davies. Ed. by David Breeze & Valerie Maxfield. (Illus.). 256p. 1987. 42.50 (ISBN 0-85224-495-9, Pub. by Edinburgh U Pr Scotland). Columbia U Pr.

Service Industries. Valorie Grigoli. (First Books-Economic Ser.). 72p. (gr. 4-8). 1984. lib. bdg. 10.40 (ISBN 0-531-04832-2). Watts.

Service Industries: A Geographical Appraisal. Peter Daniels. 300p. 1986. text ed. 55.00 (ISBN 0-416-34530-1, 9793). Routledge Chapman & Hall.

Service Industries: A WEP Study. Yves Sabolo. xv, 238p. 1975. 24.50 (ISBN 92-2-101300-6); pap. 17.50 (ISBN 92-2-101133-X). Intl Labour Office.

Service Industries & Economic Development: Case Studies in Technology Transfer. Ronald K. Shelp et al. LC 84-8304. 192p. 1984. 35.00 (ISBN 0-275-91265-5, C1265). Praeger.

Service Industries: Growth & Location. 2nd ed. P. W. Daniels. LC 82-4260. (Cambridge Topics in Geography Ser.). (Illus.). 96p. 1982. 14.95 (ISBN 0-521-23730-0). Cambridge U Pr.

Service Industries in Developing Countries. Ed. by Erdener Kaynak. 224p. 1986. 32.50x (ISBN 0-7146-3291-0, F Cass Co). Biblio Dist.

Service Inutile. Henry De Montherlant. 9.95 (ISBN 0-685-36986-2). French & Eur.

Service Is No Inheritance, or Rules to Servants According to the Rev. Dr. J. Swift. Jonathan Swift. Ed. by Simona Draghici. LC 87-15113. Orig. Title: Directions to Servants. (Illus.). 80p. (Orig.). 1987. pap. text ed. 4.95 (ISBN 0-943045-01-0). Plutarch Pr DC.

Service-Led Growth: The Role of the Service Sector in World Development. Dorothy I. Riddle. LC 85-16743. 304p. 1987. lib. bdg. 37.95 (ISBN 0-275-92041-0, C2041); pap. 16.95 (ISBN 0-275-92728-8, B2728). Praeger.

Service Load in Teacher Training Institutions of the United States. Lynn B. McMullen. LC 73-177038. (Columbia University. Teachers College. Contributions to Education: No. 244). Repr. of 1927 ed. 22.50 (ISBN 0-404-55244-7). AMS Pr.

Service Load of a Staff Nurse in One Official Public Health Agency. Marion Ferguson. LC 71-176768. (Columbia University. Teachers College. Contributions to Education: No. 915). Repr. of 1945 ed. 22.50 (ISBN 0-404-55915-8). AMS Pr.

Service Management: Operating Decisions. David C. Collier. (Illus.). 240p. 1987. pap. write for info. (ISBN 0-13-806977-8). P-H.

Service Management: Principles & Practices. 2nd ed. W. H. Bleuel & J. D. Patton, Jr. 288p. 1986. text ed. 36.50x (ISBN 0-87664-941-X); instr's. manual 10.00x (ISBN 0-87664-982-7). Instru Soc.

Service Management: Strategy & Leadership in Service Business. R. Normann. LC 84-3711. 143p. 1984. 34.95 (ISBN 0-471-90403-1). Wiley.

Service Management Systems: How to Create Competitive Advantages Through Integrated Work Management, Materials Management, & Cost Management Systems. David P. Vondle. (Illus.). 256p. 1988. 39.95 (ISBN 0-07-067577-5). McGraw.

Service Manual for J-3 Piper Cub. Piper Aircraft Corporation. 1979. pap. 5.95 (ISBN 0-686-74080-7). Aviation.

Service Marks. 1987. 190.00x (ISBN 0-948641-95-9, Pub. by ESC Ltd UK). State Mutual Bk.

Service Marks: A Guide to the New Law. Christopher Morcom. 1987. 95.00x (ISBN 0-906214-48-3, Pub. by ESC Ltd UK). State Mutual Bk.

Service Monographs of the United States Government, No. 1-66. Brookings Institution, Washington, D.C., Institute for Government Research Staff. Repr. of 1934 ed. 1760.00 (ISBN 0-404-57100-X). AMS Pr.

Service Music for the Adult Choir. Ed. by W. Lawrence Curry. 3.50 ea. (ISBN 0-664-10059-7). Westminster John Knox.

Service Occupations. Sara Throop & Kathryn Hunter. 104p. 1983. wkbk. 4.25 (ISBN 0-88323-189-1, 202); tchr's. key .50 (275). Richards Pub.

Service of All the Dead. Colin Dexter. 224p. 1988. pap. 3.95 (ISBN 0-553-27239-X). Bantam.

Service of Clinical Laboratory Instruments: Approved Guideline, Vol. 4. National Committee for Clinical Laboratory Standards. 1984. 20.00 (16-A). Natl Comm Clin Lab Stds.

Service of Colored Americans in the Wars of 1776 & 1812. William C. Nell. LC 78-144663. Repr. of 1851 ed. 10.00 (ISBN 0-404-00202-1). AMS Pr.

Service of God. William H. Willimon. 240p. 1983. pap. 11.50 (ISBN 0-687-38094-4). Abingdon.
Service of God in Man. Swami Akhandananda. 186p. 2.95 (ISBN 0-87481-503-7). Vedanta Pr.
Service of Humanity. Damodar K. Mavalankar. (Sangam Texts). 132p. 1986. pap. 8.75 (ISBN 0-88695-025-2). Concord Grove.
Service of North Carolina Prison & Jail Sentences: Parole Eligibility, Good Time, & Gain Time. Stevens H. Clarke. LC 84-621823. 1984. 2.50. U of NC Inst Gov.
Service of the Cavalry in the Army of the Potomac. Edward P. Tobie. Ed. by George R. Stewart. 62p. 1988. pap. 10.00x (ISBN 0-942301-13-7). Birm Pub Lib.
Service of the Heart. Evelyn Garfiel. pap. 7.00 (ISBN 0-87980-140-9). Wilshire.
Service of the Heart: A Guide to the Jewish Prayer Book. Evelyn Garfiel. 275p. 1989. 22.00 (ISBN 0-87668-873-3). Aronson.
Service of the Small Paraklesis to the Most Holy Theotokos. Tr. by Demetri Kangelaris & Nicholas Kasemeotes. 38p. 1984. pap. 2.00 (ISBN 0-917651-01-4). Holy Cross Orthodox.
Service Operations Management. J. A. Fitzsimmons & R. S. Sullivan. 464p. 1982. text ed. 43.95 (ISBN 0-07-021215-5). McGraw.
Service Operations Supervisor. Jack Rudman. (Career Examination Ser.: C-1880). (Cloth bdg. avail. on request). pap. 16.00. Natl Learning.
Service Parts Management. Joseph D. Patton, Jr. LC 84-19163. 320p. 1984. text ed. 39.50x (ISBN 0-87664-811-1). Instru Soc.
Service Parts Management: Principles & Practices. William B. Lee & Earle Steinberg. LC 84-70976. 129p. 1984. pap. 20.00 (ISBN 0-935406-47-6). Am Prod & Inventory.
Service Parts Management Reprints. Ed. by David C. Davis et al. LC 82-72118. 123p. 1982. pap. 11.00 (ISBN 0-935406-19-0). Am Prod & Inventory.
Service Parts Seminar Proceedings: September 1983. Ed. by American Production & Inventory Control Society Staff. LC 83-72512. 90p. 1983. pap. 5.00 (ISBN 0-935406-31-X, 40631). Am Prod & Inventory.
Service Project Ideas. Sandra Ziegler. (Ideas Ser.). (Illus.). 48p. 1977. pap. text ed. 1.95 (ISBN 0-87239-122-1, 7962). Standard Pub.
Service Quality: A Profit Strategy for Financial Institutions. Leonard L. Berry et al. 300p. 1988. 35.00 (ISBN 1-55623-094-X). Dow Jones-Irwin.
Service Sector in Soviet Economic Growth: A Comparative Study. Gur Ofer. LC 72-87775. (Economic Studies: No. 141-Russian Research Center Studies: No. 71). (Illus.). 224p. 1973. 16.50x (ISBN 0-674-80180-6). Harvard U Pr.
Service Sector in the United States Eighteen Thirty-Nine Through Eighteen Ninety-Nine. Thomas J. Weiss. LC 75-2602. (Dissertations in American Economic History). (Illus.). 1975. 25.50x (ISBN 0-405-07223-6). Ayer Co Pubs.
Service Sector Workers in a Manufacturing City: A Study of Work Histories & Attitudes in a Coventry Service Industry. Ian Procter. 191p. 1988. text ed. 44.40 (ISBN 0-566-05618-6, Pub. by Gower Pub England). Gower Pub Co.
Service Shop School. Peter T. Kulak. (Illus.). 92p. (Orig.). 1985. pap. text ed. 24.95 (ISBN 0-943876-02-8). Barks Pubns.
Service Station. Philippe Dupasquier. (Busy Places Ser.). (Illus.). 24p. (gr. k-1). 1984. pap. 3.95 (ISBN 0-448-21501-2, G&D). Putnam Pub Group.
Service Station Recordkeeping: A Practice Set. N. Fritz. 1968. text ed. 19.20 (ISBN 0-07-022474-9). McGraw.
Service: The Joy of Sweat. Ed. by Paul Woods. (Bible Basics Youth Electives Ser.). 96p. (Orig.). 1988. tchr's. ed. 9.95 (ISBN 1-55513-875-6, 68759). Cook.
Service to a Fool for Christ Sake. Orthodox Eastern Church. pap. 0.75 (ISBN 0-686-05663-9). Eastern Orthodox.
Service to St. Tikhon of Kaluga. (Church Slavic.). pap. 5.00 (ISBN 0-686-16368-0). Eastern Orthodox.
Service to the Nation Through Photo-Optical Instrumentation: 13th Annual Technical Symposium. Society of Photo-Optical Instrumentation Engineers. LC 79-8810. (SPIE Ser.: Vol. 1). (Illus.). pap. 121.50 (ISBN 0-317-41788-6, 2025646). Bks Demand UMI.
Service Trap: From Altruism to Dirty Work. Paula Dressel. 178p. 1984. spiral bdg. 19.75x (ISBN 0-398-04975-0). C C Thomas.
Serviceability-Based Design of Partially Prestressed Beams. (PCI Journal Reprints Ser.). 47p. pap. 8.00 (JR209). Prestressed Concrete.
Servicemember's Legal Guide: Everything You & Your Family Need to Know about the Law. Jonathan Tomes. LC 86-30053. (Illus.). 224p. (Orig.). 1987. pap. 14.95 (ISBN 0-8117-2204-X). Stackpole.
Services, Pt. 1. Thomas Tomkins. Ed. by P. C. Buck. (Tudor Music Ser.: Vol.8). 1963. Repr. of 1928 ed. 85.00x. Broude.
Services - The Second Industrial Revolution: Business, Technology & Employment Outlook for U. K. Growth Industries. Ed. by Amin Rajan. (Illus.). 304p. 1987. text ed. 80.00 (ISBN 0-408-02003-2). Butterworth.
Services Administration by Local Authorities. Philip L. Lloyd. LC 85-5349. 324p. 1985. 41.25 (ISBN 0-902197-22-3, Pub. by Woodhead-Faulkner); pap. 24.75 (ISBN 0-902197-32-0). Longwood Pub Group.
Services & Circuses: Community & the Welfare State. Frederic Lesemann. Tr. by Lorne Huston & Margaret Heap. Orig. Title: Du Pain et des Services. 277p. 1984. 29.95 (ISBN 0-920057-06-3, Pub. by Black Rose Bks); pap. 12.95 (ISBN 0-920057-05-5, Pub. by Black Rose Bks). U of Toronto Pr.
Services & Maintenance for Hotels & Residential Establishments. Rosemary Hurst. 152p. 1981. pap. 16.95 (ISBN 0-434-90793-6, Pub. by W Heinemann Ltd). David & Charles.
Services & Uneven Development. Ed. by J. N. Marshall. (Illus.). 224p. 1988. 39.95 (ISBN 0-19-823285-3). Oxford U Pr.
Services & U. S. Trade Policy. John N. Yochelson & Gordon J. Cloney. 31p. 1982. 6.00 (ISBN 0-89206-037-9). CSI Studies.
Services & Urbanization at the Turn of the Century: The Diffusion of Innovations. M. Hietala. (Studia Historica: No. 23). 481p. (Orig.). 1987. pap. 57.50x (ISBN 951-9254-88-9). Coronet Bks.
Services Around the World, Vol. 7. Ed. by Wesley F. Craven & James L. Cate. (Army Air Forces in World War II Ser.). (Illus.). 667p. 1983. Repr. of 1958 ed. write for info. (ISBN 0-912799-09-9). Off Air Force.
Services, Branches, Productivity, Software-Hardware Requirements. Business Communications Staff. 1988. 2450.00 (ISBN 0-89336-661-7, G-113B). BCC.
Services Challenge: Integrating for Competitive Advantage - Proceedings. Ed. by Carole Congram et al. LC 87-12543. (Illus.). 125p. 1987. pap. text ed. 18.00 (ISBN 0-87757-188-0). Am Mktg.
Services for Cardiovascular Emergencies: Report. WHO Expert Committee. Geneva, 1974. (Technical Report: No. 562). (Also avail. in French & Spanish). 1975. pap. 4.00 (ISBN 92-4-120562-8). World Health.
Services for Children & Their Families. T. Stroud. 1973. pap. 23.00 (ISBN 0-08-016605-9). Pergamon.
Services for Developmentally Disabled Adults. Robert L. Schalock. LC 82-246798. (Illus.). 281p. 1983. text ed. 29.00x (ISBN 0-936104-75-9, 1232). Pro-Ed.
Services for Employees. (Personnel Policies Forum Surveys Ser.: No. 133). 58p. 1981. 30.00 (ISBN 0-87179-973-1). BNA.
Services for Sexually Active, Pregnant, & Parenting Adolescents in New York City: Planning for the Future, Vol. 1. Camille Bristow & Marian R. Cohn. LC 82-71262. (Illus.). 140p. (Orig.). 1982. pap. write for info. (ISBN 0-943138-01-9). Ctr Pub.
Services for the Chemical Industry. J. Davidson Pratt & T. F. West. 1968. pap. 14.75 (ISBN 0-08-012664-2). Pergamon.
Services for the Mentally Handicapped in Britain. Nigel Malin et al. 266p. 1980. 30.00 (ISBN 0-85664-869-8, Pub. by Croom Helm Ltd); pap. 11.50 (ISBN 0-85664-870-1, Pub. by Croom Helm Ltd). Routledge Chapman & Hall.
Services in the Global Market. Jacques A. Nusbaumer. 1987. lib. bdg. 45.00 (ISBN 0-89838-198-3). Kluwer Academic.
Services in Transition: The Impact of Information Technology on the Service Sector. Ed. by Gerald R. Faulhaber et al. LC 86-7918. 240p. 1987. prof. ref. 34.95x (ISBN 0-88730-092-8). Ballinger Pub.
Services Marketing: A Selective Bibliography. Sarojini Balachandra. (Public Administration Ser.: P 1969). 18p. 1986. 5.00 (ISBN 0-89028-929-8). Vance Biblios.
Services Marketing: An Annotating Bibliography. Ed. by Raymond P. Fisk & Patriya S. Tansuhaj. LC 84-3028. 256p. (Orig.). 1985. pap. text ed. 16.00 (ISBN 0-87757-167-8). Am Mktg.
Services Marketing in a Changing Environment: Proceedings. Ed. by Thomas M. Bloch et al. LC 84-24307. (Illus.). 138p. (Orig.). 1985. pap. text ed. 18.00 (ISBN 0-87757-174-0). Am Mktg.
Services Marketing: Texts, Cases & Readings. Christopher H. Lovelock. (Illus.). 624p. 1983. 39.00 (ISBN 0-13-806786-4). P-H.
Services of Colored Americans in the War of 1776 & 1812. William C. Nell. 120p. Date not set. pap. text ed. price not set (ISBN 0-933121-21-0). Black Classic.
Services of Graduates of West Point in Indian Wars. Eben Swift. (Guidon Monograph). 1976. 7.00 (Pub. by J M C & Co). Amereon Ltd.
Services of Our Lady. Ed. by Sten Von Krusenstierna. 70p. 1982. pap. text ed. 2.75 (ISBN 0-918980-11-9). St Alban Pr.
Services of Secondary School Media Centers: Evaluation & Development. Mary V. Gaver. LC 77-165675. 144p. 1971. pap. 7.00x (ISBN 0-8389-0095-X). ALA.
Services: Regulation Reporter. 90.00 (ISBN 0-317-40253-6, 2=005). Am Prepaid.
Services: The Driving Force of the European Economy. G. A. Pauli. 144p. 1987. 19.75 (ISBN 0-08-033091-6, Pub. by Waterlow). Pergamon.
Services to Jewish Adolescents in the New York Metropolitan Area: A Planning Study & Needs Assessment Summary of Findings & Recommendations. Jacqueline Goldstein & Joan Jacobson. 1986. write for info. Coun Jewish Feds.
Services to People, Pack 4. Bruce Burgess & Alan Stoker. 170p. 1987. 150.00x (ISBN 1-85008-031-3, Pub. by Framework UK). State Mutual Bk.
Services to Teen Mothers in New York City: Needs, Resources, Issues & Trends. 1982. 3.50 (ISBN 0-686-40510-2). Comm Coun Great NY.
Services to the Orthopedically Handicapped. Louis Hoyer & Charles K. Hay. Ed. by William R. Phillips & Janet Rosenberg. LC 79-6906. (Physically Handicapped in Society Ser.). (Illus.). 1980. Repr. of 1942 ed. lib. bdg. 14.00x (ISBN 0-405-13115-1). Ayer Co Pubs.
Servicing Careers in the Post-Employment Society. Stewart Ranson & Peter Ribbins. 250p. 1988. 42.00x (ISBN 1-85000-390-4, Falmer Pr); pap. 22.00x (ISBN 1-85000-391-2, Falmer Pr). Taylor & Francis.
Servicing Electrical Appliances. National Radio Institute Staff. Ed. by O. J. Ruel & R. C. Nolte. Incl. Vol. 1. Electrical Fundamentals & Heat-Producing Items. 1972. text ed. 32.95 (ISBN 0-07-046128-7); Vol. 2. Motor Theory & Motor-Driven Items. 1972. text ed. 32.95 (ISBN 0-07-046129-5). 1972. McGraw.
Servicing Rig Task Details & Performance Standards, 4 vols. Canadian Association of Oilwell Drilling Contractors Staff. (Orig.). 1982. Set. pap. 40.00x (ISBN 0-87201-928-4). Rig Manager (ISBN 0-87201-934-9). Rig Operator (ISBN 0-87201-935-7). Derrickhand (ISBN 0-87201-936-5). Floorhand (ISBN 0-87201-937-3). Gulf Pub.
Servile Estate see Slaves & Slavery in Muslim Africa.
Servile State. Hilaire Belloc. LC 77-2914. 1977. 8.00 (ISBN 0-913966-31-2, Liberty Clas); pap. 3.00 (ISBN 0-913966-32-0). Liberty Fund.
Servility & Service: The Life & Work of Sir John Coke, No. 45. Michael B. Young. (Royal Historical Society Ser.). 297p. 1986. 51.00 (ISBN 0-86193-202-1, Pub. by Boydell & Brewer). Longwood Pub Group.
Serving Adult Learners: A Public Library Tradition. 230p. 1981. pap. text ed. 20.00x (ISBN 0-8389-0346-0). ALA.
Serving Adult Learners: Collaborative Approaches in Five Communities. Stephanie L. Barton. 63p. 1983. 6.50 (ISBN 0-86510-047-0). Natl Inst Work.
Serving & Returning. Paul J. Deegan. LC 75-31813. (Sports Instruction Ser.). (Illus.). (gr. 4 up). 1976. PLB 8.95 (ISBN 0-87191-495-6). Creative Ed.
Serving & Surviving As a Human-Service Worker. J. Robert Russo. 168p. 1985. pap. text ed. 11.95x (ISBN 0-88133-167-8). Waveland Pr.
Serving Children & Adolescents with Developmental Disabilities in the Special Education Classroom: Proven Methods. Sebastian Striefel & Mary J. Cadez. LC 83-3632. (Illus.). 276p. (Orig.). 1983. pap. text ed. 18.95 (ISBN 0-933716-32-X, 32X). P H Brookes.
Serving Church. 2nd ed. L. T. Johnson. LC 83-80609. (Enabling Ser.). (Illus.). 104p. (Orig.). 1984. pap. 5.95 (ISBN 0-935797-01-7). Harvest IL.
Serving Crime Victims and Witnesses. Peter Finn & Beverly N. Lee. (Issues & Practices in Criminal Justice Ser.). (Illus.). 225p. (Orig.). 1987. pap. 11.00 (ISBN 0-318-22949-8, S/N 027-000-01275-2). USGPO.
Serving End-Users in Sci-Tech Libraries. Ed. by Ellis Mount. LC 84-10789. (Science & Technology Libraries: Vol. 5, No. 1). 122p. 1984. text ed. 22.95 (ISBN 0-86656-327-X, B327). Haworth Pr.
Serving God. Z. W. Swafford. (God & Us Ser.). 32p. (gr. k-2). 1981. pap. 2.00 (ISBN 0-89114-097-2); pap. 0.69 coloring bk. (ISBN 0-89114-098-0). Baptist Pub Hse.
Serving God Always. Arnold G. Kuntz. 1966. pap. text ed. 3.00 (ISBN 0-570-06645-X, 22-2014); pap. 5.85 manual (ISBN 0-570-06646-8, 22-2015). Concordia.
Serving God & Mammon: William Juxon, 1582-1663. Thomas Mason. LC 83-40507. (Illus.). 208p. 1985. 29.50 (ISBN 0-87413-251-7). U Delaware Pr.
Serving God First. Sighard Kleiner. 1985. 14.95 (ISBN 0-87907-883-9). Cistercian Pubns.
Serving Grace. Michael Griffiths. 1986. pap. 2.95 (ISBN 9971-972-40-9). OMF Bks.
Serving Humanity: A Compilation. Alice A. Bailey. 1987. pap. 9.00 (ISBN 0-85330-133-6). Lucis.
Serving in the City: Nurturing the Poor to Independence. Monroe Ballard & JoeAnn Ballard. 88p. 1986. 3 ring binder 10.95 (S-350). Beacon Hill.
Serving Learners at a Distance: A Guide to Program Practices. Charles E. Feasley. Ed. & frwd. by Jonathan D. Fife. LC 84-160901. (ASHE-ERIC Higher Education Report Ser.: No. 5, 1983). 69p. (Orig.). 1983. pap. 7.50x (ISBN 0-913317-04-7). Assn Study Higher Educ.
Serving Life & Faith: Adult Religious Education & the American Catholic Community. Ed. by Neil A. Parent. 72p. 1986. pap. 6.95 (ISBN 1-55586-982-3). US Catholic.
Serving Mentally Impaired People. Gerald Oosterveen & Bruce L. Cook. 56p. 1983. pap. 5.95 (ISBN 0-89191-764-0). Cook.
Serving More Than Students: A Critical Need for College Student Personnel Services. Peter H. Garland. Frwd. by Jonathan D. Fife. LC 86-70252. (ASHE-ERIC Higher Education Report No. 7, 1985). 160p. (Orig.). 1985. pap. 10.00 (ISBN 0-913317-26-8). Assn Study Higher Ed.
Serving Older Adults: Policy, Programs, & Professional Activities. Andrew J. Dobelstein & Ann Johnson. (Illus.). 272p. 1985. text ed. write for info. (ISBN 0-13-806860-7). P-H.
Serving Older School-Aged Children. Vicki L. Larson et al. 52p. 1987. audio cassette tapes in an album 40.00 (ISBN 0-930599-21-7, 2701). Thinking Pubns.
Serving One Another. Gene Getz. 156p. 1984. pap. 5.95 (ISBN 0-88207-612-4). Victor Bks.
Serving Personal & Community Needs Through Adult Education. Edgar J. Boone et al. LC 79-9664. (Higher Education Ser.). 1980. text ed. 28.95x (ISBN 0-87589-451-8). Jossey-Bass.
Serving Physically Disabled People: An Information Handbook for All Libraries. Ruth A. Velleman. LC 79-17082. (Serving Special Populations Ser.). 392p. 1979. 29.95 (ISBN 0-8352-1167-3). Bowker.
Serving Planet Earth. John S. Haigh. 112p. 1986. pap. 7.95 (ISBN 0-87516-568-0). DeVorss.
Serving Power: The Making of the Academic Social Science Expert. Edward T. Silva & Sheila A. Slaughter. LC 83-18518. (Contributions to the Study of Education Ser.: No. 11). xi, 346p. 1984. lib. bdg. 35.00 (ISBN 0-313-24058-2, SSG/). Greenwood.
Serving Sunday School. Wayne Goodwin & Gregory D. Cook. (Complete Teacher Training Meeting Ser.). 48p. 1986. tchr's ed 9.95 (ISBN 0-89191-315-7). Cook.
Serving the Geriatric Market. Business Communications Staff. 1988. pap. 1750.00 (ISBN 0-89336-530-0, GB-096). BCC.
Serving the Good Life in Rancho Bernardo. Rancho Bernardo Junior Woman's Club. (Illus.). 310p. 1982. Easel Binder 12.95 (ISBN 0-686-36317-5). Rancho Bern.
Serving the Hispanic Elderly of the United States: A National Community Service Directory. Carmela G. Lacayo. 234p. 1982. 5.00 ea. Assn Personas Mayores.
Serving the Homeland & the Cause of Communism. D. F. Ustinov. (World Leaders Speeches & Writings Ser.). 96p. 1983. 36.00 (ISBN 0-08-028174-5). Pergamon.
Serving the Jewish Family. Ed. by G. B. Bubis. 25.00x (ISBN 0-87068-439-6). Ktav.
Serving the Mentally Ill Elderly: Problems & Perspectives. Ed. by Elinor E. Lurie & James H. Swan. 272p. 1987. 32.00x (ISBN 0-669-14113-5). Lexington Bks.
Serving the Older Adult: A Guide to Library Programs & Information Services. Betty J. Turock. (Serving Special Populations Ser.). 277p. 1983. 34.95 (ISBN 0-8352-1487-7). Bowker.
Serving the People: Social Services & Social Change. Ann Withorn. LC 84-3160. 288p. 1984. 37.00x (ISBN 0-231-05560-9). Columbia U Pr.
Serving the Public-Building the Union: The History of the National Union of Public Employees, Vol. 1: The Forerunners 1889-1928. Bernard Dix & Stephen Williams. (Illus.). 244p. 1987. 29.95 (ISBN 0-85315-645-X, Pub. by Lawrence Wishart Publishers UK); pap. 12.50 (ISBN 0-85315-646-8). Humanities.
Serving the Republic: Memoirs of the Civil & Military Life of Nelson A. Miles. facsimile ed. Nelson A. Miles. LC 74-147786. (Select Bibliographies Reprint Ser). Repr. of 1911 ed. 25.50 (ISBN 0-8369-5632-X). Ayer Co Pubs.
Serving the Salesian Family: A Resource Manual for Salesians. (Salesian Family Ser.). 88p. 1983. pap. 3.50 (ISBN 0-89944-076-2). Don Bosco Multimedia.
Serving the Word: Lutheran Women Consider Their Calling. Ed. by Marilyn Preus. LC 88-14537. 176p. (Orig.). 1988. pap. 11.95 (ISBN 0-8066-2357-8, 10-5726). Augsburg.
Serving Time Together: Men & Women in Prison. Charles Campbell. LC 79-22496. 1980. pap. 10.00X (ISBN 0-912646-54-3). Tex Christian.
Serving Two Masters: The Law of Lawyer Disqualification. American Bar Association Staff. 54p. 1984. 7.95 (ISBN 0-89707-149-2). Amer Bar Assn.
Serving with Joy: A Study in Philippians. Stephen A. Grunlan. LC 85-71352. 107p. (Orig.). 1985. pap. 5.45 (ISBN 0-87509-371-X); leader's guide 2.95 (ISBN 0-87509-372-8). Chr Pubns.
Serving Women: Household Service in Nineteenth-Century America. Faye E. Dudden. 352p. 1983. 20.00x (ISBN 0-8195-5072-8); pap. 12.95 (ISBN 0-8195-6109-6). Wesleyan U Pr.
Servings with Love; Seasonal. Elizabeth Pistole. 1981. gift, padded cover 6.95 (ISBN 0-87162-244-0, J1013). Warner Pr.
Servings with Love; Special Days. Elizabeth Pistole. 1981. gift, padded cover 6.95 (ISBN 0-87162-245-9, J1014). Warner Pr.
Servitude Et Grandeur Militaires. Alfred De Vigny. Ed. by Germain. 1965. pap. 09.95 (ISBN 0-685-11560-7). French & Eur.

Set Theory & Metric Spaces. 2nd ed. Irving Kaplansky. LC 77-7344. 1977. text ed. 10.95 (ISBN 0-8284-0298-1). Chelsea Pub.

Set Theory & Model Theory: Proceedings. Ed. by R. R. Jensen & A. Prestel. (Lecture Notes in Mathematics Ser.: Vol. 872). 174p. 1981. pap. 13.00 (ISBN 0-387-10849-1). Springer-Verlag.

Set Theory & Related Topics. Seymour Lipschutz. (Orig.). 1964. pap. text ed. 8.95 (ISBN 0-07-037986-6). McGraw.

Set Theory & Syntactic Description. William S. Cooper. (Janua Linguarum, Ser. Minor: No. 34). 52p. 1974. pap. text ed. 6.80x (ISBN 90-2792-704-9). Mouton.

Set Theory & the Continuum Hypothesis. Paul J. Cohen. (Math Lecture Notes Ser.: No. 3). (Orig.). 1966. pap. write for info. (ISBN 0-8053-2327-9, Adv Bk Prog MSP). Addison-Wesley.

Set Theory with Applications. You-Feng Lin & Shwu Yeng T. Lin. (Illus.). ix, 221p. 1985. pap. text ed. 19.75 (ISBN 0-931541-04-2). Bk Pubs.

Set This House on Fire. William Styron. 1960. 15.00 (ISBN 0-394-44482-5). Random.

Set Up. Brian Austin. 1982. 15.00x (ISBN 0-906660-37-8, Pub. by New Playwrights Network). State Mutual Bk.

Set Up. Robin Moore & Milt Machlin. 320p. 1988. pap. 3.95 (ISBN 1-55785-035-6). Bart Books.

Set Up, No. 6. (All That Glitters Ser.). 176p. (YA) 1988. pap. 2.50 (ISBN 0-553-26670-5). Bantam.

Set up Your Home Studio. (Kodak Library of Creative Photography). 1985. lib. bdg. 17.27 (ISBN 0-86706-238-X, Pub. by Time-Life). Silver.

Set up Your Home Studio. (Kodak Library of Creative Photography). 1988. 11.95 (ISBN 0-86706-236-3). Time-Life.

Set Valued Dynamical Systems & Economic Flow. L. J. Cherene, Jr. (Lecture Notes in Economics & Mathematical Systems: Vol. 158). 1978. pap. 12.00 (ISBN 0-387-08847-4). Springer-Verlag.

Set-Valued Mappings, Selections & Topological Properties of 2x: Proceedings. Conference on Set-Valued Mappings, SUNY, Buffalo, 1969. Ed. by W. M. Fleischman. (Lecture Notes in Mathematics: Vol. 171). 1970. pap. 11.00 (ISBN 0-387-05293-3). Springer-Verlag.

Set Your Mind Free. N. Douglas Wiegand & Bob Ebaugh. 192p. (Orig.). 1988. pap. 6.95 (ISBN 0-8007-5270-8). Revell.

Set Your Sights: A Guide to Handgun Basics. (Illus.). 1982. 1.95 (ISBN 0-916682-34-X). Outdoor Empire.

Seth. Roy F. Wood. LC 87-12050. 249p. (Orig.). 1987. pap. 8.50 (ISBN 0-915175-24-X). Knights Pr.

Seth & Me & Rebel Make Three. Jeannette Eyerly. LC 82-48463. 128p. (YA) (gr. 7 up). 1983. 11.25i (ISBN 0-397-32042-6, Lipp Jr Bks); PLB 9.89g (ISBN 0-397-32043-4). HarpJ.

Seth Bullock: Frontier Marshall. Kenneth C. Kellar. LC 72-92726. 191p. 1972. 4.95 (ISBN 0-87970-126-9). North Plains.

Seth, Dreams & Projection of Consciousness. Jane Roberts. LC 86-60443. 350p. (Orig.). 1986. 15.95 (ISBN 0-913299-25-1, Dist. by NAL). Stillpoint.

Seth, Dreams & Projection of Consciousness. Jane Roberts. 360p. 1987. pap. 9.95 (ISBN 0-913299-42-1, Dist. by NAL). Stillpoint.

Seth Eastman, Pictorial Historian of the Indian. 1st ed. John F. McDermott. LC 61-15145. (Illus.). pap. 75.50 (2005846). Bks Demand UMI.

Seth Eastman's Mississippi: A Lost Portfolio Recovered. John F. McDermott. LC 73-2457. (Illus.). 166p. 1973. 15.50 (ISBN 0-252-00192-3). U of Ill Pr.

Seth Harding, Mariner. James L. Howard. 1930. 59.50x (ISBN 0-685-69827-0). Elliots Bks.

Seth Low. Benjamin R. Low. LC 70-137256. Repr. of 1925 ed. 11.50 (ISBN 0-404-04037-3). AMS Pr.

Seth Low: The Patrician As Social Reformer; the Patrician As Social Architect--a Biography. Gerald Kurland. LC 76-125816. 405p. 1971. Repr. of 1886 ed. 39.50 (ISBN 0-8290-0205-7). Irvington.

Seth Material. Jane Roberts. 352p. 1976. pap. 4.50 (ISBN 0-553-24910-X). Bantam.

Seth Material. Jane Roberts. LC 75-112971. (Illus.). 1970. pap. 9.95 (ISBN 0-13-807180-2). P-H.

Seth Speaks. Jane Roberts. (Illus.). 512p. 1985. pap. 4.95 (ISBN 0-553-25592-4). Bantam.

Seth Speaks. Jane Roberts. 552p. 1981. pap. 8.95 (ISBN 0-13-807222-1). P-H.

Seth Thomas Clocks & Movements: A Guide to Identification & Prices. Tran Duy Ly. (Illus.). 275p. (Orig.). 1985. pap. 19.95 (ISBN 0-930163-26-5). Arlington Bk.

Seth's Brother's Wife. facsimile ed. Harold Frederic. LC 68-23720. (Americans in Fiction Ser.). lib. bdg. 29.50 (ISBN 0-8398-0565-9); pap. text ed. 4.95x (ISBN 0-89197-934-4). Irvington.

Seth's Brother's Wife. Harold Frederic. (Collected Works of Harold Frederic). 1988. Repr. of 1887 ed. lib. bdg. 59.00x. Am Biog Serv.

Seth's Brother's Wife see Collected Works.

Seti (Pervaya Kniga Stikhov) 3rd ed. Mikhail A. Kuzmin. LC 78-68927. 1979. pap. 5.95 (ISBN 0-89830-003-7). Russica Pubs.

Setpoint Diet. Gilbert A. Leveille. 272p. (Orig.). 1985. pap. 3.50 (ISBN 0-345-32196-0). Ballantine.

Sets & Boolean Algebra. Marcel Rueff & Max Jeger. Ed. by A. G. Howson. LC 72-189267. (Mathematical Studies: A Series for Teachers & Students: No. 4). pap. 48.00 (ISBN 0-317-20064-X, 2023329). Bks Demand UMI.

Sets & Borders. Gwen Marston & Joe Cunningham. (Illus.). 104p. 1987. pap. 14.95 (ISBN 0-89145-923-5, 1821). Collector Bks.

Sets & Groups: A First Course in Algebra. J. A. Green. 256p. 1988. pap. text ed. 15.95 (ISBN 0-7102-1227-5, Pub. by Kegan Paul). Routledge Chapman & Hall.

Sets, Functions & Logic. K. J. Devlin. 90p. 1981. (Pub. by Chapman & Hall England); pap. 9.95x (ISBN 0-412-22670-7, NO. 2048). Routledge Chapman & Hall.

Sets, Logic, & Axiomatic Theories. 2nd ed. Robert R. Stoll. LC 74-8932. pap. 61.00 (ISBN 0-317-08628-6, 2055554). Bks Demand UMI.

Sets: Naive, Axiomatic & Applied. D. Van Dalen et al. 1978. text ed. 68.00 (ISBN 0-08-021166-6); pap. text ed. 32.00 (ISBN 0-08-023047-4). Pergamon.

Sets, Series & Ensembles in African Art. George N. Preston. LC 85-7791. (Illus.). 96p. 1986. 19.95 (ISBN 0-8109-1637-1). Abrams.

Sette Racconti. Moravia. (EMC Easy Readers: Series C). (YA) (gr. 7-12). pap. 4.95 (ISBN 0-88436-060-1, 55258). EMC.

Sette Sfere di Cristallo. Herge. (Illus.). 62p. (Ital.). pap. 15.95 (ISBN 0-686-54357-2). French & Eur.

Settecento Musicale in Europa. Antonio Capri. LC 77-5523. (Music Reprint Ser). 1977. Repr. of 1936 ed. lib. bdg. 49.50 (ISBN 0-306-77413-5). Da Capo.

Settin' Hen Never Gets Fat. J. C. Miller. 15.00 (ISBN 0-9614177-0-6). Mill Press.

Setting a Course: American Women in the 1920s. Dorothy M. Brown. (American Women in the Twentieth Century Ser.). 328p. 1987. lib. bdg. 18.95x (ISBN 0-8057-9906-0, Twayne). G K Hall.

Setting a Course: American Women in the 1920s. Dorothy M. Brown. (American women in the Twentieth Century Ser.). 328p. 1987. pap. 9.95x (ISBN 0-8057-9908-7, Twayne). G K Hall.

Setting a Target Date: Report of a PSSC Study Group. 1980. 22.00x (ISBN 0-317-05769-3, Pub. by Natl Inst Social Work). State Mutual Bk.

Setting & Controlling the Hot Bins. (Training Aids Ser.: No. 10). 1975. Package: instr's. manual, student wkbk, slides, tape. 400.00 (ISBN 0-317-58411-1); Instr's. manual, 48 pg. 12.00 (ISBN 0-317-58412-X); Student wkbk., 38 pg. 8.00 (ISBN 0-317-58413-8). Natl Asphalt Pavement.

Setting Ceramic Tile. Michael Byrne. LC 86-51320. (Illus.). 240p. 1987. pap. 17.95 (ISBN 0-918804-55-8, Dist. by W.W Norton). Taunton.

Setting Credit Lines. Credit Research Foundation. 17p. 1982. 40.00 (ISBN 0-939050-39-0). Credit Res NYS.

Setting Environmental Standards: Guidelines for Decision-Making. de H. W. Koning. 105p. 1987. pap. 10.20 (ISBN 92-4-154214-4). World Health.

Setting for Black Business Development: A Study in Sociology & Political Economy. Roy F. Lee. LC 72-619630. 272p. 1973. pap. 7.00 (ISBN 0-87546-039-9); special hard bdg 11.00 (ISBN 0-87546-275-8). ILR Pr.

Setting Free the Bears. John Irving. 1982. pap. 3.95 (ISBN 0-671-46534-1). PB.

Setting Free the Bears. John Irving. LC 68-28537. 1968. 8.95 (ISBN 0-394-44496-5). Random.

Setting Goals. 3rd ed. John Renesch. 170p. 1983. 9.95 (ISBN 0-932654-08-8). Context Pubns.

Setting in the American Short Story of Local Color, 1865-1900. Robert D. Rhode. (Studies in English Literature: No. 30). 190p. (Orig.). 1975. pap. text ed. 20.80x (ISBN 90-2793-281-6). Mouton.

Setting Limits: Medical Goals in an Aging Society. Daniel Callahan. LC 87-13029. 256p. 1987. 18.95 (ISBN 0-671-22477-8). S&S.

Setting Limits: Medical Goals in an Aging Society. Daniel Callahan. 256p. 1988. pap. 8.95 (ISBN 0-671-66831-5, Touchstone Bks). S&S.

Setting Limits: Parents, Kids & Drugs. William LaFountain. 36p. 1.15 (ISBN 0-89486-145-X). Hazelden.

Setting Limits: The Battle for the Balanced Budget - Tax Limitation Amendments. Lewis K. Uhler. 144p. 1989. pap. 6.95 (ISBN 0-915463-43-1, Pub. by Jameson Bks). Green Hill.

Setting Municipal Priorities: American Cities & the New York Experience. Ed. by Charles Brecher & Raymond D. Horton. 560p. 1985. 50.00 (ISBN 0-8147-1066-2); pap. text ed. 25.00x (ISBN 0-8147-1067-0). NYU Pr.

Setting Municipal Priorities, 1980. Ed. by Raymond D. Horton & Charles Brecher. LC 79-88261. 224p. 1979. text ed. 24.00x (ISBN 0-916672-37-9, Pub. by Allanheld). Rowman.

Setting Municipal Priorities, 1981. Ed. by Charles Brecher & Raymond D. Horton. LC 80-67392. 212p. 1981. text ed. 25.00x (ISBN 0-86598-010-1, Pub. by Allanheld). Rowman.

Setting Municipal Priorities, 1984. Ed. by Charles Brecher & Raymond D. Horton. 250p. (Orig.). 1984. pap. 15.00 (ISBN 0-8147-1054-9). NYU Pr.

Setting Municipal Priorities, 1986. Ed. by Charles Brecher & Raymond D. Horton. 476p. 1985. 60.00x (ISBN 0-8147-1081-6); pap. 30.00x (ISBN 0-8147-1082-4). NYU Pr.

Setting Municipal Priorities, 1988. Ed. by Charles Brecher & Raymond D. Horton. 320p. 1987. 50.00x (ISBN 0-8147-1103-0); pap. 25.00x (ISBN 0-8147-1104-9). NYU Pr.

Setting National Priorities: Agenda for the 1980s. Ed. by Joseph A. Pechman. Incl. Agenda for the 1980's. Ed. by Joseph A. Pechman. 1980. 29.95 (ISBN 0-8157-6988-1); pap. 11.95 (ISBN 0-8157-6987-3); The Next Ten Years. Ed. by Henry Owen & Charles L. Schultze. 325p. 1976; The 1971 Budget. Ed. by Charles Schultze et al. 192p. 1970. 18.95 (ISBN 0-8157-7750-7); pap. 7.95 (ISBN 0-8157-7749-3); The 1972 Budget. Ed. by Charles Schultze et al. LC 74-161599. 336p. 1971. 22.95 (ISBN 0-8157-7756-6); pap. 8.95 (ISBN 0-8157-7755-8); The 1973 Budget. Ed. by Charles Schultze et al. LC 74-161599. 468p. 1972. 26.95 (ISBN 0-8157-7758-2); pap. 9.95 (ISBN 0-8157-7757-4); The 1974 Budget. Ed. by Edward R. Fried et al. LC 73-1076. 446p. 1974. 16.95 (ISBN 0-8157-2934-0); pap. 9.95 (ISBN 0-8157-2933-2); The 1975 Budget. Ed. by Barry M. Blechman et al. 200p. 1975. pap. 9.95.; The 1978 Budget. Ed. by Joseph A. Pechman. LC 77-81316. 443p. 1977. 26.95 (ISBN 0-8157-6980-6); pap. 8.95 (ISBN 0-8157-6979-2); The 1979 Budget. Ed. by Joseph A. Pechman. LC 77-91837. 319p. 1978. 22.95 (ISBN 0-8157-6984-9); pap. 8.95 (ISBN 0-8157-6983-0); The 1980 Budget. Ed. by Joseph A. Pechman. LC 76-27205. 229p. 1979. 22.95 (ISBN 0-8157-6986-5); pap. 8.95 (ISBN 0-8157-6985-7); The 1982 Budget. Ed. by Joseph A. Pechman. LC 76-27205. 275p. 1981. 26.95 (ISBN 0-8157-6990-3); pap. 9.95 (ISBN 0-8157-6989-X); The 1983 Budget. Ed. by Joseph A. Pechman. 268p. 1982. 26.95 (ISBN 0-8157-6992-X); pap. 9.95 (ISBN 0-8157-6991-1); The 1984 Budget. Ed. by Joseph A. Pechman. LC 76-27205. 248p. 1983. 26.95 (ISBN 0-8157-6994-6); pap. 9.95 (ISBN 0-8157-6993-8). 1980. Brookings.

Setting Objectives for College Reading & Study Skills. Clifford C. Brooks. 173p. 1983. pap. text ed. 17.95x (ISBN 0-912855-39-8). E Bowers Pub.

Setting of the Sermon on the Mount. William Davies. LC 64-630. pap. 140.80 (ISBN 0-317-26320-X, 2024449). Bks Demand UMI.

Setting Out. Andrea Breese. 1984. 20.00x (ISBN 0-906549-21-3, Pub. by J Clare Bks). State Mutual Bk.

Setting Out: A Guide for Site Engineers. S. Brighty. (Illus.). 264p. 1975. text ed. 22.00. Beekman Pubs.

Setting-Out Procedures. Barry Sadgrove. (Illus.). 136p. 1988. text ed. 24.95 (ISBN 0-408-02837-8). Butterworth.

Setting Rates for Hospital & Nursing Home Care. Paul L. Grimaldi. LC 84-17838. 360p. 1985. text ed. 27.50 (ISBN 0-88331-196-8). Luce.

Setting Sail: How to Buy a Boat & Cruise the World on 300 Dollars a Month. Lawrence Taylor. (Illus.). 176p. 1982. 14.95 (ISBN 0-89651-700-4). B L Pub.

Setting Sails. Derek Maitland. 174p. 1981. 53.00x (ISBN 0-317-69048-5, Pub. by Han-Shan Tang Ltd). State Mutual Bk.

Setting Standards for Professional Nursing: The Marker Model. Carolyn Smith-Marker. 1987. 39.00 (ISBN 0-932491-84-7). Res Appl Inc.

Setting Sun. rev. ed. Osamu Dazai. Tr. by Donald Keene from Japanese. LC 56-13350. (Illus.). 1968. pap. 6.95 (ISBN 0-8112-0032-9, NDP258). New Directions.

Setting the Agenda for the Year 2000: Knowledge Development in Nursing. American Academy of Nursing Staff. 57p. (Orig.). 1986. pap. 11.50 (ISBN 0-317-60339-6, G-170). ANA.

Setting the Captives Free. Bob Buess. LC 42-1127. 1975. pap. 2.50 (ISBN 0-934244-02-2). Sweeter Than Honey.

Setting the Captives Free! A Practical Guide to Breaking the Power of Satan over Your Life. Marc W. Farschman. LC 85-61138. 146p. (Orig.). 1985. pap. 4.95 (ISBN 0-934285-00-4). New Life Faith.

Setting the East Ablaze. Peter Hopkirk. 252p. 1984. 44.00x (ISBN 0-317-68629-1, Pub. by Han-Shan Tang Ltd). State Mutual Bk.

Setting the East Ablaze: Lenin's Dream of an Empire in Asia. Peter Hopkirk. (Illus.). 1985. 17.95 (ISBN 0-393-01943-8). Norton.

Setting the Field for a New E. D. E. N. Gateway of Wholeness Evolutionary Dynamics & the Energies of Number. Kathryn Chardin. LC 86-82102. (Illus., Orig.). 1986. pap. 6.95 (ISBN 0-939385-00-7). Eden Project Pubs.

Setting the Heart to Understand. Jane Kopp. 1987. pap. 7.00 (ISBN 0-941179-03-6). Latitudes Pr.

Setting the Mould: The United States & Britain, 1945-50. Robin Edmonds. 1987. 22.95 (ISBN 0-393-02382-6). Norton.

Setting the Pace: A Speed, Comprehension & Study Skills Program. William Brozo & Ron Schmelzer. (No. 174). 208p. 1984. pap. text ed. 20.95 (ISBN 0-675-20152-7). Merrill.

Setting the Seen: Creative Visualization for Healing. Alan Cohen. (Illus.). 36p. (Orig.). 1982. pap. 2.95 (ISBN 0-910367-33-7). A Cohen.

Setting the Stage, Vol. I. Edward G. Doyle & Samuel Lipsman. LC 81-65796. (Vietnam Experience Ser.). (Illus.). 192p. 1981. 16.95 (ISBN 0-939526-00-X). Boston Pub Co.

Setting the Tone: Essays & a Diary. Ned Rorem. LC 82-14427. 384p. 1983. 18.95 (ISBN 0-698-11234-2, Coward). Putnam Pub Group.

Setting the Tone: Essays & a Diary. Ned Rorem. LC 84-4374. 384p. 1984. pap. 9.95 (ISBN 0-87910-024-9). Limelight Edns.

Setting the Tone for Future Trends. Ed. by Julia Elam. (NAFEO Conference Ser.). 286p. 1987. pap. text ed. 27.95 (ISBN 0-695-60054-0). Follett Pr.

Setting up a Library: How to Begin or Begin Again. Rev, 2nd ed. Ruth S. Smith. LC 79-15630. (Guide Ser.: No. 1). 23p. 1987. pap. 4.95x (ISBN 0-915324-16-4); pap. 3.95 members. CSLA.

Setting up a Small Workers' Co-Operative. Derek Smith. 127p. 1984. Repr. of 1971 ed. 17.00x (ISBN 0-317-54695-3, Pub. by Plunkett Foundation). State Mutual Bk.

Setting up an Effective Marketing Operation. Peter J. Youdale. (Illus.). 168p. 1972. 25.00 (ISBN 0-8464-0840-6). Beekman Pubs.

Setting up an Office. D. W. Logan. (Illus.). 232p. 1968. 17.95 (ISBN 0-8464-1135-0). Beekman Pubs.

Setting Up & Executing Trusts. Arthur D. Sederbaum. 160p. 1987. 50.00 (Q1-3005). PLI.

Setting up & Running Non Resident Companies. 250p. 1985. 415.00x (Pub. by ESC Ltd UK). State Mutual Bk.

Setting up Home. Mary Gilliatt. 24.95 (ISBN 0-316-31381-5); pap. 14.95 (ISBN 0-316-31383-1). Little.

Setting up Shop. Randy B. Smith. 288p. 1983. pap. 7.95 (ISBN 0-446-38277-9). Warner Bks.

Setting up Shop: The Do's & Dont's of Starting a Small Business. R. B. Smith. LC 81-8146. 256p. 1981. text ed. 29.95 (ISBN 0-07-058531-8). McGraw.

Setting Your Weight. Time-Life Books Editors. (Fitness, Health & Nutrition Ser.). 144p. 1988. 17.27 (ISBN 0-8094-6191-9); lib. bdg. 21.27 (ISBN 0-8094-6192-7). Time-Life.

Settings & Costumes of the Modern Stage. Ed. by Theodore Komisarjevsky & Lee Simonson. LC 65-19618. (Illus.). Repr. of 1933 ed. 33.00 (ISBN 0-405-08716-0). Ayer Co Pubs.

Settle It Yourself: Who Needs a Lawyer. Fred Benjamin & Dorothea Kaplan. LC 85-71295. (Illus.). 104p. 1985. pap. 9.95 (ISBN 0-933893-01-9). Bonus Books.

Settled Out of Court: The Social Process of Insurance Claims Adjustment. 2nd ed. H. Laurence Ross. LC 80-68523. 1980. lib. bdg. 34.95x (ISBN 0-202-30286-5); pap. text ed. 17.95x (ISBN 0-202-30296-2). Aldine de Gruyter.

Settlement. Henry G. Miller. (Art of Advocacy Ser.). 1983. looseleaf 90.00 (041); Updates avail. 1985 30.00; 1986 39.00. Bender.

Settlement after the War in South Africa. M. J. Farrelly. LC 78-118468. 1971. Repr. of 1900 ed. 28.50x (ISBN 0-8046-1217-X, Pub. by Kennikat). Assoc Faculty Pr.

Settlement & Growth of Copper-Tolerant Populations of Ectocarpus Siliculosus (Dillw.) Lyngbye on Different Antifouling Surfaces & Coatings. 66p. 1982. write for info. (306). Intl Copper.

Settlement & Metamorphosis of Marine Invertebrate Larvae: Proceedings of a Symposium Held at Toronto, Canada, Dec. 27-28, 1977. Ed. by F. Chia & M. E. Rice. 290p. 1979. 57.75 (ISBN 0-444-00277-4, Biomedical Pr). Elsevier.

Settlement & Social Change in Asia, Vol. 1. Wolfram Eberhard. pap. 134.00 (ISBN 0-317-11153-1, 2020775). Bks Demand UMI.

Settlement & Society: Aspects of West Europe Prehistory in the First Millennnium B.C. Ed. by T. C. Champion & J. V. Megaw. LC 85-2112. 238p. 1985. 29.95 (ISBN 0-312-71317-7). St Martin.

Settlement & Society in Wales. D. Huw Owen. (Illus.). 444p. 1988. text ed. 60.00 (ISBN 0-7083-0985-2, Pub. by U of Wales). Humanities.

Settlement & Unsettlement in Early America: The Crisis of Political Legitimacy Before the Revolution. Kenneth A. Lockridge. LC 80-25658. (Illus.). 96p. 1981. 15.95 (ISBN 0-521-23707-6). Cambridge U Pr.

Settlement Conference: Experimenting with Appellate Justice, Final Report. 168p. 1986. manuscript 10.00 (ISBN 0-317-59206-8, NERO-185). Natl Ctr St Courts.

Settlement Cookbook. 3rd rev. ed. 576p. 1976. 17.95 (ISBN 0-671-22087-X). S&S.

Settlement Costs. (Housing & Urban Development Dept Ser.: 398-H (3)). 45p. 1987. pap. 1.50 (ISBN 0-318-23448-3, S/N 023-000-00721-5). USGPO.

Settlement Excavations at Borgo Le Ferriere - Satricum, Vol. 1. M. Maaskant-Kleibrink. (Illus.). viii, 356p. 1987. 75.00 (ISBN 90-6980-013-6, Pub. by Egbert Forsten Holland). Benjamins North Am.

Settlement Geography of the Indian Desert. R. C. Sharma. LC 72-906182. (Illus.). 209p. 1974. 12.50x (ISBN 0-89684-452-8). Orient Bk Dist.

Settlement History & Rise of Civilisation in Ganga-Yamuna Doab from 1500 B.C.-300 A.D. Makkhan Lal. (Illus.). 400p. text ed. 100.00x (ISBN 0-86590-380-8, Pub. by B R Pub Corp Delhi). Apt Bks.

Settlement Horizon: A National Estimate. Robert A. Woods & Albert J. Kennedy. LC 79-112562. (Rise of Urban America). 1970. Repr. of 1922 ed. 28.00 (ISBN 0-405-02488-6). Ayer Co Pubs.

Settlement House Movement in New York City, 1886-1914. Harry P. Kraus. Ed. by Francesco Cordasco. LC 80-872. (American Ethnic Groups Ser.). 1981. lib. bdg. 32.00x (ISBN 0-405-13434-7). Ayer Co Pubs.

Settlement Houses & the Great Depression. Judith A. Trolander. LC 74-20994. 205p. 1975. text ed. 21.50x (ISBN 0-8143-1529-1). Wayne St U Pr.

Settlement Idea: A Vision of Social Justice. Arthur C. Holden. LC 70-112549. (Rise of Urban America). 1970. Repr. of 1922 ed. 16.00 (ISBN 0-405-02455-X). Ayer Co Pubs.

Settlement of Disputes in Early Medieval Europe. Wendy Davies & Paul Fouracre. LC 86-6783. 324p. 1986. 52.50 (ISBN 0-521-30788-0). Cambridge U Pr.

Settlement of Disputes on the New Natural Resources: Workshop 1982. Rene-Jean Dupuy. 1983. lib. bdg. 43.50 (ISBN 90-247-2901-7, Pub. by Martinus Nijhoff Netherlands). Kluwer Academic.

Settlement of Estates in Massachusetts. 4th ed. 193.50 (ISBN 0-318-11944-7); Suppl. 1987. 50.00 (ISBN 0-318-11945-5) (ISBN 0-318-11946-3). Lawyers Co-Op.

Settlement of Germantown, Pennsylvania, & the Beginning of German Emigration to North America. Samuel W. Pennypacker. LC 69-13248. (Illus.). 1969. Repr. of 1899 ed. 24.50 (ISBN 0-405-08847-7). Ayer Co Pubs.

Settlement of Illinois, 1778-1830. facs. ed. Arthur C. Boggess. LC 71-128873. (Select Bibliographies Reprint Ser). 1908. 18.00 (ISBN 0-8369-5493-9). Ayer Co Pubs.

Settlement of International Disputes Between Canada & the U. S. A. LC 79-56149. 113p. 1979. pap. 7.00 (ISBN 0-89707-015-1). Amer Bar Assn.

Settlement of John Batman. John Batman. 24p. 1986. pap. 7.95 (ISBN 0-949230-04-9, Pub. by Quest Pub Australia). Intl Spec Bk.

Settlement of Labor Disputes on Rights in Australia. Paul F. Brissenden. (Monograph & Research Ser.: No.13). 131p. 1966. 5.00 (ISBN 0-89215-014-9). U Cal LA Indus Rel.

Settlement of Polynesia: A Computer Simulation. Michael Levison et al. LC 72-92337. pap. 36.30 (ISBN 0-317-39704-4, 2055888). Bks Demand UMI.

Settlement of Shallow Foundations on Cohesionless Soils: Design & Performance. Ed. by William O. Martin. (Sessions Proceedings, Geotechnical Special Publication: No. 5). 93p. 1986. 12.00x (ISBN 0-87262-535-4). Am Soc Civil Eng.

Settlement of the Israelite Tribes in Palestine. Manfred Weippert. Tr. by James Martin from Ger. LC 74-131587. (Studies in Biblical Theology, 2nd Ser.: No. 21). (Orig.). 1970. pap. 12.00x (ISBN 0-8401-3071-6). A R Allenson.

Settlement of the Jews in North America. C. P. Daly. 59.95 (ISBN 0-8490-1027-6). Gordon Pr.

Settlement Out of Court: The Disposition of Medical Malpractice Claims. Patricia M. Danzon & Lee A. Lillard. LC 83-114134. (Rand Papers: P-6800). 54p. 1982. 7.50. Rand Corp.

Settlement Pattern Excavations at Kaminajuyu, Guatemala. Ed. by Joseph W. Michels. LC 77-14659. (Monograph Ser. on Kaminaljuyu). (Illus.). 1979. text ed. 32.00x (ISBN 0-271-00536-X). Pa St U Pr.

Settlement Patterns in Missouri: A Study of Population Origins with a Wall Map. Russel L. Gerlach. LC 84-23454. 96p. 1986. text ed. 22.00 (ISBN 0-8262-0473-2). U of Mo Pr.

Settlement Patterns in the Oxford Region. H. J. Case & A. W. Whittle. 1982. 90.00x (ISBN 0-900090-85-5, Pub. by Ashmolean Museum). State Mutual Bk.

Settlement Patterns in the Oxford Region: The Abingdon Causeway Enclosure & Other Sites. Ed. by H. J. Case & A. W. Whittle. (CBA Research Report Ser.: No. 44). 170p. 1982. pap. text ed. 40.00x (ISBN 0-906780-14-4, Pub. by Council British Archaeology). Humanities.

Settlement Statement: HUD Form 1. bulk rates avail. 0.60 (261002). Am Bankers.

Settlement, Subsistence, & Society in Late Zuni Prehistory. Keith W. Kintigh. LC 84-22769. (Anthropological Papers: No. 44). 132p. 1985. pap. 19.95x (ISBN 0-8165-0831-3). U of Ariz Pr.

Settlement Systems in Sparsely Populated Regions: The United States & Australia. Ed. by Richard E. Lonsdale & John H. Holmes. LC 80-27278. (Pergamon Policy Studies on Urban Affairs; Comparative Rural Transformation Ser.). (Illus.). 360p. 1981. 61.00 (ISBN 0-08-023111-X). Pergamon.

Settlement, the Immigrant & the Public School: A Study of the Influence of the Settlement Movement & the New Migration Upon Public Education, 1890-1924. Morris I. Berger. Ed. by Francesco Cordasco. LC 80-841. (American Ethnic Groups Ser.). 1981. lib. bdg. 22.00x (ISBN 0-405-13405-3). Ayer Co Pubs.

Settlements & the Law: A Juridicial Analysis of the Israeli Settlements in the Occupied Territories. Sally V. Mallison & Thomas W. Mallison. (Illus.). 1982. pap. 1.00x (ISBN 0-318-01027-5). Am Educ Trust.

Settlements Including Deferred Payments. 206p. 1984. pap. 15.00 (ISBN 0-317-27558-5, #H4-4953). PLI.

Settlements of the Kuro-Araxes Culture. L. Ghlonti & A. Djavakhishvili. (Occasional Papers on the Near East: Vol. 2 & 3). (Illus.). 42p. Date not set. 10.00x (ISBN 0-89003-196-7). Undena Pubns.

Settlements to Society, 1607-1763: A Documentary History of Colonial America. Ed. by Jack P. Greene. 400p. 1975. pap. 10.95x (ISBN 0-393-09232-1). Norton.

Settlements, Trade & Polities in the Seventeenth-Century Gold Coast. Ray A. Kea. LC 81-23609. (Johns Hopkins University Studies in Atlantic History & Culture). 315p. 1982. text ed. 48.50x (ISBN 0-8018-2310-2). Johns Hopkins.

Settler Capitalism: The Dynamics of Dependent Development in the Southern Hemisphere. Donald Denoon. (Illus.). 1983. 49.50x (ISBN 0-19-828291-5). Oxford U Pr.

Settler Economies: Studies in the Economic History of Kenya & Southern Rhodesia, 1900-1963. Paul Mosley. LC 82-12896. (African Studies: No. 35). (Illus.). 336p. 1983. 49.50 (ISBN 0-521-24339-4). Cambridge U Pr.

Settler Mac & the Charmed Quarter-Section. Mrs. Hal Russell. 159p. 1956. 6.95 (ISBN 0-8040-0271-1, Pub. by Swallow). Ohio U Pr.

Settler Regimes in Africa & the Arab World: The Illusion of Endurance. Ed. by Ibrahim Abu-Lughod & Baha Abu-Laban. (Monograph: No. 4). 255p. 1974. 10.95 (ISBN 0-914456-06-7); pap. text ed. 6.95 (ISBN 0-914456-07-5). Assn Arab-Amer U Grads.

Settlers. Meyer Levin. 832p. 1987. pap. 5.95 (ISBN 0-553-26349-8). Bantam.

Settlers. William S. Long. (Australians Ser.: Vol. II). (Orig.). 1982. pap. 4.50 (ISBN 0-440-17929-7). Dell.

Settlers. Vilhelm Moberg. 480p. 1983. pap. 4.95 (ISBN 0-446-31129-4). Warner Bks.

Settlers & Convicts. rev ed. Alexander Harris. 1969. pap. 10.50x (ISBN 0-522-83944-4, Pub. by Melbourne U Pr). Intl Spec Bk.

Settlers & the Agrarian Question: Foundations of Capitalism in Colonial Australia. Philip McMichael. (Illus.). 320p. 1984. 42.50 (ISBN 0-521-26570-3). Cambridge U Pr.

Settlers by the Long Grey Trail: Some Pioneers to Old Augusta County, Virginia, & Their Descendants, of the Family of Harrison & Allied Lines. J. Houston Harrison. LC 75-636. (Illus.). 665p. 1975. Repr. of 1935 ed. 35.00 (ISBN 0-8063-0664-5). Genealog Pub.

Settlers in America. Lowrie & Stein. 64p. 1977. 4.75 (ISBN 0-88336-498-0). New Readers.

Settlers of Bajavista. James F. Hopgood. LC 79-21191. (Papers in International Studies: Latin America Ser.: No. 7). 1979. pap. 11.00x (ISBN 0-89680-101-2, Ohio U Ctr Intl). Ohio U Pr.

Settlers of Rensselaerswyck, 1630-1658. Ed. by Arnold J. Van Laer. LC 65-29272. 54p. 1980. pap. 6.00 (ISBN 0-8063-0359-X). Genealog Pub.

Settlers of the Okefenokee. Lois B. Mays. 208p. 1975. 7.95x (ISBN 0-9601606-0-4). Okefenokee Pr.

Settlers on a Strange Shore. Edith McCall. LC 60-11154. (Frontiers of America Ser.). (Illus.). 128p. (gr. 3-10). 1980. PLB 11.93 (ISBN 0-516-03367-0). Childrens.

Settlers, Southerners, Americans: The History of Essex County, Virginia, 1608-1984. James B. Slaughter. LC 84-81011. (Illus.). 400p. 1984. 34.50 (ISBN 0-9613549-0-9). Essex Cty Bd Sup.

Settling & Safeguarding Estates in California Without an Attorney: With Forms. rev. ed. Clive Hinkley. LC 79-74698. 1988. pap. 20.00. C Hinckley.

Settling Civil Suits: Litigators' Views about Appropriate Roles & Effective Techniques for Federal Judges. Wayne D. Brazil. LC 84-72690. (Illus.). 180p. 1984. 15.00. Amer Bar Assn.

Settling Claims under Government Contracts: Avoiding Litigation. 160p. 1981. 20.00 (ISBN 0-686-48259-X). Amer Bar Assn.

Settling Claims under Government Contracts: Avoiding Litigation. 160p. 1981. 20.00 (ISBN 0-317-37307-2). Amer Bar Assn.

Settling Disputes in Soviet Society: The Formative Years of Legal Institutions. John N. Hazard. 1978. Repr. of 1960 ed. lib. bdg. 37.50x (ISBN 0-374-93758-3, Octagon). Hippocrene Bks.

Settling into Routine: Human Rights Abuses in Duarte's Second Year. Jemera Rone & Aryeh Meier. LC 86-202472. 162p. 1986. 10.00 (ISBN 0-938579-19-3). Fund Free Expression.

Settling of Copper City, Michigan. (Copper Country Local History Ser.: Vol. 21). (Illus.). 92p. 1983. 2.50 (ISBN 0-942363-20-5). C J Monette.

Settling the Desert. Ed. by Louis Berkofsky et al. 290p. 1981. 66.00 (ISBN 0-677-16280-4). Gordon & Breach.

Settling the Dust. Robert J. Ege. 1981. pap. 3.95 (ISBN 0-933147-03-1). Werner Pubn.

Settling the Score: Essays on Music. Ned Rorem. 352p. 1988. 27.95 (ISBN 0-15-180895-3). HarBraceJ.

Settling Things: Six Case Studies in Environmental Mediation. Allan R. Talbot. LC 82-25255. 101p. 1983. pap. 8.50 (ISBN 0-89164-077-0). Conservation Foun.

Settlings. Frank Fleckenstein. (Illus.). 32p. (Orig.). 1988. pap. 2.50 (ISBN 0-945073-03-8). Nightsun MD.

Setups: Representation in the United States Congress-1973. Ray A. Geigle & Peter G. Hartjens. LC 75-22542. 1975. pap. 4.00 (ISBN 0-915654-10-5). Am Political.

Seul Instant Suffit. Penny Jordan. (Harlequin Romantique Ser.). 192p. 1984. pap. 1.95 (ISBN 0-373-41240-1). Harlequin Bks.

Seule Sans Lui. Anne Hampson. (Harlequin Romantique Ser.). 192p. pap. 1.95 (ISBN 0-373-41178-2). Harlequin Bks.

Seumas O'Kelly. George B. Saul. LC 74-126030. (Irish Writers Ser.). 101p. 1971. 4.50 (ISBN 0-8387-7765-1); pap. 1.95 (ISBN 0-8387-7661-2). Bucknell U Pr.

Seumas O'Kelly's the Weaver's Grave. Michael O. Aodha. (New Abbey Theatre Ser.). 1984. pap. 2.95x (ISBN 0-912262-81-8). Proscenium.

Seurat. Sarane Alexandrian. (QLP Ser.). (Illus.). 96p. 1980. 12.95 (ISBN 0-517-54106-8). Crown.

Seurat. Pierre Courthion. 1988. 19.95 (ISBN 0-8109-1519-7). Abrams.

Seurat. John Russell. (World of Art Ser.). (Illus.). 286p. 1985. pap. 11.95 (ISBN 0-500-20032-7). Thames Hudson.

Seurat: A Sunday Afternoon on the Grande Jatte. (Let's Get Lost in a Painting Ser.). 1983. write for info. Garrard.

Seurat & the Science of Painting. William I. Homer. LC 84-80600. (Illus.). 327p. 1985. Repr. of 1964 ed. lib. bdg. 35.00 (ISBN 0-87817-295-5). Hacker.

Seurat's Complete Paintings. John Rewald & Henri Dorra. (Illus.). 311p. (Fr.). 1988. 225.00 (ISBN 1-55660-010-0). A Wofsy Fine Arts.

Seve: The Young Champion. Severiano Ballesteros & Dudley Doust. LC 83-83248. (Illus.). 156p. 1984. 14.95 (ISBN 0-914178-67-9). Golf Digest.

Seven. John MacDonald. 15.95 (ISBN 0-89190-775-0, Pub. by AM Repr). Amereon Ltd.

Seven Against Thebes. Aeschylus. Tr. by Anthony Hecht & Helen Bacon. (Greek Tragedy Ser.). 1973. 19.95x (ISBN 0-19-501732-3). Oxford U Pr.

Seven Against Thebes. Henry David Thoreau. Ed. by Leo Kaiser. LC 80-2522. (Emerson Society Quarterly No. Seventeen; Nineteen Fifty-Nine, 1-30). Repr. of 1959 ed. 14.00 (ISBN 0-404-19070-7). AMS Pr.

Seven Ages. Eva Figes. LC 86-42643. 192p. 1987. 14.95 (ISBN 0-394-55540-6). Pantheon.

Seven Ages. Eva Figes. 288p. 1988. pap. 3.95 (ISBN 0-345-35199-1). Ballantine.

Seven Ages of a Medical Scientist: An Autobiography. George W. Corner, Sr. LC 81-51143. (Illus.). 406p. 1981. 35.95x (ISBN 0-8122-7811-9). U of Pa Pr.

Seven Ages of Childhood. Carolyn Wells. (Envelope Library). (Illus.). 12p. (Orig.). (YA) (gr. 7-9). 1982. pap. 2.50 (ISBN 0-914676-98-9). Green Tiger Pr.

Seven Ages of Man: A Survey of Human Development. Ed. by Robert R. Sears & S. Shirley Feldman. LC 73-12029. 155p. 1973. pap. 6.95x (ISBN 0-913232-06-8). W Kaufmann.

Seven Ages of the British Army. Field Marshall Lord Carver. (Illus.). 344p. 1985. 22.50 (ISBN 0-8253-0241-2). Beaufort Bks NY.

Seven Ages of the Theatre. Richard Southern. (Illus.). 312p. (Orig.). 1961. pap. 9.95 (ISBN 0-8090-0534-4, Drama). Hill & Wang.

Seven Ages of Venice. C. M. Smith. 1977. lib. bdg. 59.95 (ISBN 0-8490-2594-X). Gordon Pr.

Seven Ages of Woman. Elizabeth Parker. Ed. by Evelyn Breck. LC 60-8739. pap. 155.30 (ISBN 0-317-07935-2, 2014853). Bks Demand UMI.

Seven Altars of Dusarra, Bk. 2: The Lords of Dus. Lawrence Watt-Evans. 1987. pap. 3.50 (ISBN 0-345-33961-4, Del Rey). Ballantine.

Seven Amana Villages: Recipes, Crafts, Folk Arts. Joan Liffring-Zug. (Illus.). 36p. 1981. pap. 1.85 (ISBN 0-9603858-7-8). Penfield.

Seven American Nights - Sailing to Byzantium. Gene Wolfe. 1989. pap. price not set. Tor Bks.

Seven American Poets from Macleish to Nemerov: An Introduction. Ed. by Denis Donoghue. LC 74-22560. (Library on American Writers: Vol. 9). 320p. 1975. 16.95x (ISBN 0-8166-0739-7). U of Minn Pr.

Seven American Stories. Walter D. Edmonds. 22.95 (ISBN 0-88411-442-2, Pub. by Aeonian Pr). Amereon Ltd.

Seven American Stylists from Poe to Mailer: An Introduction. Ed. by George T. Wright. LC 72-95441. (Minnesota Library on American Writers). pap. 78.50 (2056206). Bks Demand UMI.

Seven & One Half Sins of Stacey Kendall. Nancy J. Hopper. 112p. (gr. 4-7). 1982. 9.95 (ISBN 0-525-45115-3). Dutton.

Seven & One-Half Sins of Stacey Kendall. Nancy J. Hopper. (gr. 5-9). 1983. pap. 2.75 (ISBN 0-440-47736-0, YB). Dell.

Seven Archbishops. Sidney Dark. Repr. of 1944 ed. 25.00 (ISBN 0-686-19840-9). Ridgeway Bks.

Seven Arias con Tromba Sola. Alessandro Scarlatti. Ed. by Henry Meredith. LC 80-28901. 1980. pap. text ed. 24.00x (ISBN 0-914282-51-4). Brass Pr.

Seven Arrows. Hyemeyohsts Storm. 1988. pap. 14.95 (ISBN 0-345-32901-5). Ballantine.

Seven Arts, Vols. 1-2. Repr. of 1917 ed. Set. lib. bdg. 82.00 (ISBN 0-404-19551-2). AMS Pr.

Seven Bamboo Tablets of the Cloudy Satchel. Deng Ming-Dao. (Illus.). 275p. 1987. 15.95 (ISBN 0-06-250227-1). Har-Row.

Seven Basic Export Products. (Eng. & Span.). 1972. pap. 1.00 Eng. ed. (ISBN 0-8270-3755-4); Span. ed. 1.00 (ISBN 0-8270-3750-3). OAS.

Seven Basic Export Products: Sugar, Petroleum, Tin, Coffee, Copper, Beef, Bananas see Americas: Supplement Series.

Seven Beginnings. Walker Knight & Ken Touchton. LC 75-44496. (Human Torch Ser.: 2nd). (Illus.). 1976. 5.95 (ISBN 0-937170-17-8). Home Mission.

Seven Bible Ways to Properly Relate to Your Pastor. Mark Barclay. 32p. 1982. pap. 2.25 (ISBN 0-88144-024-8). Christian Pub.

Seven Books for Grossman. Morris Lurie. 128p. 1984. pap. 5.95 (ISBN 0-14-006837-6). Penguin.

Seven Books of History Against the Pagans. Paulus Orosius. LC 64-8670. (Fathers of the Church Ser: Vol. 50). 414p. 1964. 22.95x (ISBN 0-8132-0050-4). Cath U Pr.

Seven Boy Romance. Jan Gelman. 1986. pap. 2.25 (ISBN 0-671-60299-3). PB.

Seven Britons in Imperial Russia, Sixteen Ninety to Eighteen Twelve. Ed. by Peter Putman. (Princeton Studies in History: Vol. 7). 1970. Repr. of 1952 ed. 28.00 (ISBN 0-384-48290-2). Johnson Repr.

Seven by Seven: Interviews with American Science Fiction Writers of the West & Southwest. Neal Wilgus. LC 87-814. (Milford Series: Popular Writers of Today: Vol. 44). 96p. (Orig.). Date not set. lib. bdg. 16.95x (ISBN 0-89370-173-4); pap. 7.95x (ISBN 0-89370-273-0). Borgo Pr.

Seven Candles. Winfield B. Sutphin. 98p. 4.55 (ISBN 0-89697-257-7). Intl Univ Pr.

Seven Cardinal Virtues of Science Fiction. Ed. by Isaac Asimov et al. 1981. pap. 2.50 (ISBN 0-449-24440-7, Crest). Fawcett.

Seven Celtic Macrobiotic Principles. Jacques de De Langre. (Illus.). 64p. 1984. pap. 4.50 (ISBN 0-916508-30-7). Happiness Pr.

Seven Centuries of Poetry. Ed. by A. N. Jeffares. (Granger Index Reprint Ser). 1955. 29.00 (ISBN 0-8369-6068-8). Ayer Co Pubs.

Seven Centuries of the Problem of Church & State. Frank Gavin. 1938. 22.50x (ISBN 0-86527-180-1). Fertig.

Seven Chinese Stories. T. J. Sheridan. (Oxford Progressive English Readers Ser.). (Illus.). 1972. pap. 3.75x (ISBN 0-19-638230-0). Oxford U Pr.

Seven Chocolate Sins. Ruth Moorman & Lalla Williams. (Cookbook Ser.: No. 2). (Illus.). 80p. 1979. pap. 5.95 (ISBN 0-937552-01-1). Quail Ridge.

Seven Churches. Marshall Neal. (Illus.). 108p. (Orig.). 1977. pap. 3.15 (ISBN 0-89084-062-8). Bob Jones Univ Pr.

Seven Churches. 36p. (Orig.). pap. 0.95 (ISBN 0-937408-20-4). GMI Pubns Inc.

Seven Churches of Prophecy, 2 vols. Gordon Lindsay. (Revelation Ser.). 1.25 ea. Vol. 1 (ISBN 0-89985-977-1). Vol. 2 (ISBN 0-89985-978-X). Christ Nations.

Seven Clam Sisters. Xia Qing. (Illus.). 18p. (Orig.). (gr. 5-7). 1982. pap. 1.95 (ISBN 0-8351-1143-1). China Bks.

Seven Clues to the Origin of Life: A Scientific Detective Story. A. G. Cairns-Smith. 143p. 1987. pap. 8.95 (ISBN 0-521-33793-3). Cambridge U Pr.

Seven Comedies by Marivaux. Pierre De Marivaux. Ed. by Oscar Mandel & Adrienne Mandel. LC 68-16386. (Illus.). 380p. 1968. 39.00x (ISBN 0-686-60850-X); pap. text ed. 14.50x (ISBN 0-8290-2023-3). Irvington.

Seven Comedies by Marivaux. Marivaux. (Illus.). 380p. 1984. pap. text ed. 16.50 (ISBN 0-8191-4121-6). U Pr of Amer.

Seven Concentric Circles. Jim Goure. 56p. (Orig.). 1983. pap. 5.00 (ISBN 0-915235-05-6). United Res.

Seven Conquests. Poul Anderson. 1984. pap. 2.95 (ISBN 0-671-55914-1, Pub. by Baen Bks). PB.

Seven Contemporary Chinese Women Writers. Gladys Yang. (Panda Ser.). (Illus.). 280p. (Orig.). 1982. pap. 5.95 (ISBN 0-8351-0962-3). China Bks.

Seven Contemporary Chinese Women Writers. Intro. by Gladys Yang. 282p. 1982. pap. 4.95 (ISBN 0-295-96017-5, Pub. by Chinese Lit Beijing). U of Wash Pr.

Seven Contemporary Short Novels. 3rd ed. Charles Clerc & Louis Leiter. 1982. pap. text ed. write for info. (ISBN 0-673-15569-2). Scott F.

Seven Contemporary Short Novels. 2nd ed. Charles Clerc & Louis H. Leiter. 1975. pap. write for info. (ISBN 0-673-07971-6). Scott F.

Seven Conundrums. facs. ed. Edward P. Oppenheim. LC 78-134973. (Short Story Index Reprint Ser). (Illus.). 1923. 18.00 (ISBN 0-8369-3704-X). Ayer Co Pubs.

Seven Conversations with Jorge Luis Borges. Fernando Sorrentino. Tr. by Clark M. Zlotchew from Span. LC 80-54425. 235p. 1981. 18.50x (ISBN 0-87875-214-5). Whitston Pub.

Seven Countries: A Multivariate Analysis of Death & Coronary Heart Disease. Ancel Keys. LC 79-9163. (Illus.). 1980. 30.00x (ISBN 0-674-80237-3). Harvard U Pr.

Seven Cream Jugs. David Coe. 15.00x (ISBN 0-903653-76-1, Pub. by New Playwrights Network). State Mutual Bk.

Seven Crystal Balls. Herge. (Illus.). 62p. (gr. 3-8). 15.95 (ISBN 0-416-92610-X); pap. 4.95 (ISBN 0-416-78000-8). French & Eur.

Seven Crystal Balls. Herge. (Adventures of Tintin). (Illus., Eng.). 1975. pap. 6.95 (ISBN 0-316-35840-1, Joy St Bks). Little.

Seven Curses of London. James Greenwood. LC 83-48479. (World of Labour-English Workers 1850-1890 Ser.). 336p. 1984. lib. bdg. 40.00 (ISBN 0-8240-5707-4). Garland Pub.

Seven Cycles: Public Rituals. Mary B. Edelson. (Illus.). 64p. (Orig.). 1980. pap. 10.00x (ISBN 0-9604650-0-6). Edelson.

Seven Dada Manifestos. Tristan Tzara. Tr. by Barbara Wright from Fr. (Orig.). 1979. pap. 5.95 (ISBN 0-7145-3762-4). Riverrun NY.

Seven Daily Sins & What to Do about Them. Cecil Murphey. 112p. (Orig.). 1981. pap. 2.95 (ISBN 0-89283-101-4). Servant.

Seven Daughters & Seven Sons. Barbara Cohen & Bahija Lovejoy. LC 81-8092. 216p. (gr. 5-9). 1982. 12.95 (ISBN 0-689-30875-2, Atheneum Childrens Bks). Macmillan.

Seven Daughters of the Theater. Edward Wagenknecht. (Quality Paperbacks Ser.). (Illus.). 234p. 1981. pap. 7.95 (ISBN 0-306-80153-1). Da Capo.

Seven-Day Afghans. Jean Leinhauser & Rita Weiss. (Illus.). 144p. 1985. 19.95 (ISBN 0-8069-5708-5). Sterling.

Seven Day Circle: The History & Meaning of the Week. Eviatar Zerubavel. 206p. 1985. 19.95 (ISBN 0-02-934680-0). Free Pr.

Seven-Day Magic. Edward Eager. LC 62-17040. (Illus.). 183p. (gr. 4-6). 1986. 4.95 (ISBN 0-15-272922-4, VoyB). HarBraceJ.

Seven Day Rice Diet. Ed. by Consumer Guide Editors. 128p. 1987. pap. 3.50 (ISBN 0-451-14800-2, Sig). NAL.

Seven Days a Week. Lion The Printer. (Illus.). (gr. k-5). 1977. spiral 2.00 (ISBN 0-914080-62-8). Shulsinger Sales.

Seven Days a Week: Faith in Action. Nelvin Vos. LC 84-47937. 144p. 1985. pap. 2.95 (ISBN 0-8006-1658-8, 1-1658). Fortress.

Seven Days a Week: Women & Domestic Service in Industrializing America. David M. Katzman. 1978. 27.95x (ISBN 0-19-502368-4). Oxford U Pr.

Seven Days a Week: Women & Domestic Service in Industrializing America. David M. Katzman. (Illus.). 402p. 1981. pap. 10.95 (ISBN 0-252-00882-0). U of Ill Pr.

Seven Days at Jericho & Rachel Meets the Healer. Joann Knox. (Junior Adventure Ser.). 64p. (gr. 4-8). 1973. pap. 1.00 (ISBN 0-88243-774-7, 02-0774). Gospel Pub.

Seven Days for Ruby. Blaine M. Yorgason & Brenton G. Yorgason. LC 86-72357. 190p. 1986. 9.95 (ISBN 0-87579-066-6). Deseret Bk.

Seven Days in May. Fletcher Knebel & Charles Bailey, II. 384p. 1988. pap. 4.50 (ISBN 0-553-26956-9). Bantam.

Seven Days in Nicaragua Libre. Lawrence Ferlinghetti. (Illus.). 112p. (Orig.). 1984. pap. 6.95 (ISBN 0-87286-160-0). City Lights.

Seven Days of Creation. Sara Aronow. (Bible Stories in Rhymes Ser.: Vol. 1). (Illus.). 32p. (ps-2). 1985. 4.95 (ISBN 0-87203-119-5). Hermon.

Seven Days of Creation. Illus. & adapted by Leonard E. Fisher. LC 81-2952. (Illus.). 32p. (ps-3). 1981. reinforced bdg. 12.95 (ISBN 0-8234-0398-X). Holiday.

Seven Days of the Beginning. Eli Munk. 8.95 (ISBN 0-87306-028-8). Feldheim.

Seven Days to a Brand-New Me. Ellen Conford. 96p. (gr. 5 up). 1981. 14.95 (ISBN 0-316-15311-7). Little.

Seven Days to a Brand-New Me. Ellen Conford. 120p. (gr. 7 up). 1982. pap. 2.50 (ISBN 0-590-40729-5, Point). Scholastic Inc.

Seven Days to Better Discipline. Jean Anderson. (Lifeline Ser.). 95p. 1987. pap. 6.95 (ISBN 0-8163-0709-1). Pacific Pr Pub Assn.

Seven Days to Faster Reading. William S. Schaill. pap. 5.00 (ISBN 0-87980-141-7). Wilshire.

Seven Days to Petrograd. Tom Hyman. 1988. 18.95 (ISBN 0-670-80865-2). Viking.

Seven Deadly Sins. Anthony Campolo. 156p. 1987. 10.95 (ISBN 0-89693-533-7). Victor Bks.

Seven Deadly Sins. Sunday Times, London. LC 75-117848. (Essay Index Reprint Ser). 1962. 14.00 (ISBN 0-8369-1722-7). Ayer Co Pubs.

Seven Deadly Sins & Cardinal Virtues of Science Fiction, 2 vols. Ed. by Isaac Asimov et al. 672p. 1982. cancelled (ISBN 0-517-38595-3, Bonanza). Outlet Bk Co.

Seven Deadly Sins of Science Fiction. Ed. by Isaac Asimov et al. 1980. pap. 2.50 (ISBN 0-449-24349-4, Crest). Fawcett.

Seven Deadly Sins Today. Henry Fairlie. LC 79-893. (Illus.). 1979. pap. 6.95 (ISBN 0-268-01698-4). U of Notre Dame Pr.

Seven Deadly Virtues. Forester F. Church. LC 87-45729. 128p. 1988. 13.45 (ISBN 0-06-061373-4, HarpR). Har-Row.

Seven Decades of Rural Social Work: From Country Life Commission to Rural Caucus. Emilia E. Martinez-Brawley. LC 80-24185. 288p. 1981. 36.95 (ISBN 0-275-90678-7, C0678). Praeger.

Seven Decades of the Union: The Humanities & Materialism. facsimile ed. Henry A. Wise. LC 72-154164. (Select Bibliographies Reprint Ser). Repr. of 1871 ed. 20.00 (ISBN 0-8369-5780-6). Ayer Co Pubs.

Seven Decades That Changed America. 440p. 10.00 (ISBN 0-916150-17-8, HO579). Am Soc Ag Eng.

Seven Decisive Battles of the Middle Ages. Joseph Dahmus. LC 83-13490. (Illus.). 270p. (Orig.). 1983. lib. bdg. 23.95X (ISBN 0-8304-1030-9). Nelson-Hall.

Seven Delivery Systems for God's Healing Power. Peter Popoff. Ed. by Don Tanner. LC 81-69730. (Illus.). 70p. 1981. pap. 1.50 (ISBN 0-938544-07-1). Faith Messenger.

Seven Detective Stories see New Method Supplementary Readers.

Seven Detective Stories see New Method Supplementary Readers: Bestseller Pack.

Seven Dialogues. Bernardino Ochino. Ed. by Rita Belladonna. (Renaissance & Reformation Texts in Translation Ser.: No. 3). 1988. pap. text ed. 12.50 (ISBN 0-317-69304-2, Pub. by Dovehouse Editions Canada). Humanities.

Seven Dials Mystery. Agatha Christie. 224p. 1983. pap. 3.50 (ISBN 0-553-26896-1). Bantam.

Seven Dirty Words & Six Other Stories: Controlling the Content of Print & Broadcast. Matthew L. Spitzer. LC 86-9158. 192p. 1987. 16.95x (ISBN 0-300-03568-3). Yale U Pr.

Seven Diving Ducks. Margaret Friskey. LC 65-20889. (Easy Reading Picture Bks.). (Illus.). 32p. (gr. k-3). 1965. PLB 11.93 (ISBN 0-516-03605-X). Childrens.

Seven Dreamers. Annie T. Slosson. LC 79-98602. (Short Story Index Reprint Ser.). 1890. 18.00 (ISBN 0-8369-3168-8). Ayer Co Pubs.

Seven Early Churches of Nashville. H. T. Tipps et al. (Illus.). 1972. 30.00x (ISBN 0-918450-07-1). C Elder.

Seven Edwards of England. K. A. Patmore. LC 71-118493. 1971. Repr. of 1911 ed. 26.00x (ISBN 0-8046-1241-2, Pub.by Kennikat). Assoc Faculty Pr.

Seven Eggs. Meredith Hooper. LC 84-43159. (Illus.). 20p. (ps-3). 1985. 3.95 (ISBN 0-694-00144-9). HarpJ.

Seven Eighteenth Century Bibliographies. Iolo A. Williams. LC 68-56585. (Bibliography & Reference Ser.: No. 108). 1969. Repr. of 1924 ed. 22.50 (ISBN 0-8337-3806-2). B Franklin.

Seven Eighty Five or Some of the Digits Method. Ed. by Financial Publishing Co. Staff. 36p. 1986. pap. 6.25 (ISBN 0-87600-004-9). Finan Pub.

Seven Eleven. Douglas M. Holly. 270p. 1982. 12.50 (ISBN 0-682-49895-5). Exposition-Phoenix.

Seven-Eleven Diet. Bill Adler. (Critic's Choice Paperbacks Ser.). 1988. pap. 3.50 (ISBN 1-55547-280-X, Univ Bks). Lyle Stuart.

Seven Enemies of the Arabs & the Absolute Final Problem of Life & Death in the Middle East & Throughout the World, 2 vols. Eugenius Von Ricthofen. (Illus.). 1984. 198.75 (ISBN 0-86722-076-7). Inst Econ Pol.

Seven Essays. George Sampson. LC 79-115398. Repr. of 1947 ed. 11.00 (ISBN 0-404-05556-7). AMS Pr.

Seven Everyday Collisions in American Higher Education. Harlan Cleveland. (Occasional Paper of ICED). 1974. pap. 1.00 (ISBN 0-89192-154-0). Interbk Inc.

Seven Exegetical Works: Isaac, or the Soul, Death As a Good, Jacob & the Happy Life, Joseph, the Patriarchs, Flight from the World, the Prayer of Job & David. St. Ambrose. (Fathers of the Church Ser.: Vol. 65). 447p. 1972. 34.95x (ISBN 0-8132-0065-2). Cath U Pr.

Seven Expressionist Plays: Squire of Blue Bell (Barlach); Wolves (Brust); Methusalem (Goll); Protagonist (Kaiser); Murder Hope of Womankind (Kokoschka); Guardian of the Tomb (Kafka); Awakening (Stramm) Tr. by J. M. Richtie & H. F. Barten. (Orig.). 1980. pap. 7.95 (ISBN 0-7145-0521-8). Riverrun NY.

Seven Faces of Love. Andre Maurois. Repr. of 1944 ed. 17.75 (ISBN 0-518-10169-X). Ayer Co Pubs.

Seven Fallen Pillars. Jon Kimche. LC 76-6848. (Middle East in the 20th Century). 1976. Repr. of 1950 ed. lib. bdg. 49.50 (ISBN 0-306-70820-5). Da Capo.

Seven Families in Pueblo Pottery. Maxwell Museum of Anthropology, Univ. of New Mexico. LC 75-17376. (Illus.). 115p. 1975. pap. 7.95 (ISBN 0-8263-0388-9). U of NM Pr.

Seven Famous Greek Plays. Ed. by Whitney J. Oates & Eugene O'Neill, Jr. Incl. Prometheus Bound. Aeschylus; Agamemnon. Aeschylus; Oedipus the King. Sophocles; Medea. Euripides; Frogs. Aristophanes; Antigone. Sophocles; Alcestis. Euripides. 1955. pap. 4.95 (ISBN 0-394-70125-9, RanC). Random.

Seven Famous Plays. Henrik Ibsen. Ed. by William Archer. Tr. by P. F. Tennant et al. 634p. 1961. Repr. of 1950 ed. 12.95 (ISBN 9-9940967-4-5, Pub. by Duckworth London). Longwood Pub Group.

Seven Feet Four & Growing. H. Alton Lee. LC 77-13923. 96p. (gr. 6-9). 1978. 8.95 (ISBN 0-664-32623-4). Westminster John Knox.

Seven Financial Conspiracies Which Have Enslaved the American People. Sarah E. Emery. LC 75-112. (Radical Tradition in America Ser). 112p. 1975. Repr. of 1891 ed. 15.00 (ISBN 0-88355-216-7). Hyperion Conn.

Seven Firefights in Vietnam. John A. Cash et al. (War Ser.). 208p. (Orig.). 1985. pap. 3.50 (ISBN 0-553-26875-9). Bantam.

Seven for Oregon. Cornelia Shields. 1986. 9.95 (ISBN 0-9617393-0-4). Green Springs Pr.

Seven for Oregon. Cornelia Shields. 1988. Repr. of 1986 ed. 9.95 (ISBN 0-9617393-1-2). Green Springs Pr.

Seven for the Road see And We're Off!.

Seven French Chroniclers: Witnesses to History. Paul Archambault. LC 73-16652. 224p. 1974. 15.95x (ISBN 0-8156-0099-2). Syracuse U Pr.

Seven Friends. Louis Marlow. LC 76-58445. (English Biography Ser, No. 31). 1977. lib. bdg. 48.95x (ISBN 0-8383-2132-1). Haskell.

Seven Froggies Went to School. Kate Duke. LC 84-1371. (Illus.). 32p. (ps-1). 1985. 11.95 (ISBN 0-525-44160-3). Dutton.

Seven Generations of the Descendants of Aquila & Thomas Chase. John C. Chase & George W. Chamberlain. LC 83-60849. (Illus.). 650p. 1983. Repr. of 1928 ed. 35.00x (ISBN 0-89725-038-9). NE History.

Seven Gifts of the Holy Spirit. 1980. plastic 1.75 (ISBN 0-8198-6807-8); pap. 1.00 (ISBN 0-8198-6808-6). Dghtrs St Paul.

Seven Golden Candlesticks. Wade H. Horton. 7.95 (ISBN 0-87148-767-5); pap. 6.95 (ISBN 0-87148-768-3). Pathway Pr.

Seven Golden Chapters of Hermes. Hermes Trismegistus. 1984. pap. 2.95 (ISBN 0-916411-82-6, Pub by Alchemical Pr). Holmes Pub.

Seven Good Years & Other Stories of I. L. Peretz. Tr. by Esther Hautzig from Yiddish. (Illus.). 96p. (gr. 3-6). 1984. 10.95 (ISBN 0-8276-0244-8). JPS Phila.

Seven Gothic Tales. Isak Dinesen. LC 39-27353. 420p. 6.95 (ISBN 0-394-60496-2). Modern Lib.

Seven Graves to Laredo, No. 97. Jake Logan. 192p. 1987. pap. 2.50 (ISBN 0-425-09479-0). Berkley Pub.

Seven Great Religions. Besant. 6.75 (ISBN 0-8356-7218-2). Theos Pub Hse.

Seven Guides to Effective Prayer. Colin Whittaker. 224p. (Orig.). 1988. pap. 5.95 (ISBN 1-55661-011-4). Bethany Hse.

Seven Half-Miles from Home. Mary Back. LC 85-81264. (Illus.). 200p. 1985. pap. 9.95 (ISBN 0-933472-90-0). Johnson Bks.

Seven-Headed Luther: Essays in Commemoration of Quincentenary, 1483-1983. Ed. by Peter N. Brooks. (Illus.). 1983. 49.95x (ISBN 0-19-826648-0). Oxford U Pr.

Seven-Headed Serpent. Ali Ghanem. Tr. by Alan Sheridan. 352p. 1986. 17.95 (ISBN 0-15-181200-4). HarBraceJ.

Seven Herbs: Plants As Teachers. Matthew Wood. (Illus.). 132p. (Orig.). pap. 8.95 (ISBN 0-938190-91-1). North Atlantic.

Seven Hills of the Dove. Scharmen Iris. 25.00 (ISBN 0-8283-1391-1). Branden Pub Co.

Seven Hindrances to Healing. Kenneth Hagin, Jr. 1980. pap. 0.50 mini bk. (ISBN 0-89276-705-7). Hagin Ministries.

Seven Hued Rainbow. Norimoto Iino. 1967. 5.95 (ISBN 0-8022-0771-5). Philos Lib.

Seven Human Temperaments. 6th ed. Geoffrey Hodson. 1977. 5.75 (ISBN 0-8356-7222-0). Theos Pub Hse.

Seven Hundred Fifty Over-the-Counter Stocks. Carol Mull. LC 84-71342. 438p. 1986. 25.00 (ISBN 0-86690-279-1, 2614-01). Am Fed Astrologers.

Seven Hundred Fifty Years of a Scottish School. John Strawhorn. 112p. 1985. 39.00x (ISBN 0-907526-10-1, Pub. by Alloway Pub). State Mutual Bk.

Seven Hundred MB Atlas for the Northern Hemisphere: Five-Day Mean Heights, Standard Deviations, & Changes for the 700 mb. Pressure Surface. Eberhard W. Wahl & James F. Lahey. LC 69-5. 152p. 1969. plastic comb. bdg. 50.00x (ISBN 0-299-05383-0). U of Wis Pr.

Seven Hundred Science Experiments for Everyone. rev. ed. UNESCO Staff. LC 64-10638. (Illus.). 252p. (gr. 5-9). 1964. pap. 12.95 (ISBN 0-385-05275-8). Doubleday.

Seven Hundred Sixty Four Helpful Hints for Model Railroaders. Ed. by Bob Warren & Model Railroader Staff. LC 65-22095. (Illus.). 64p. 1965. pap. 5.00 (ISBN 0-89024-505-3). Kalmbach.

Seven Icelandic Short Stories. 2nd ed. 1961. 6.95x (ISBN 0-89067-037-4). Am Scandinavian.

Seven Ideas That Shook the Universe. Nathan Spielberg & Bryon D. Anderson. 288p. 1986. pap. 14.95 (ISBN 0-471-84816-6). Wiley.

Seven Ideas That Shook the Universe. Nathan Spielberg & Bryon D. Anderson. 272p. 1987. 22.95 (ISBN 0-471-85974-5). Wiley.

Seven Ideas That Shook the Universe. Nathan Spielberg & Byron D. Anderson. LC 85-6442. 291p. 1985. write for info. (ISBN 0-471-81477-6). Wiley.

Seven in One Blow. Friere Wright & Michael Foreman. (Pictureback Ser.). (Illus.). 32p. (ps-3). 1981. lib. bdg. 4.99 (ISBN 0-394-93805-4). Random.

Seven Interpretive Essays on Peruvian Reality. Jose C. Mariategui. Tr. by Marjory Urquidi. 335p. 1988. pap. 9.95 (ISBN 0-292-77611-X). U of Tex Pr.

Seven Irish Plays, Nineteen Forty-Six to Nineteen Sixty-Four. Ed. by Robert Hogan. LC 67-20594. pap. 119.50 (ISBN 0-317-39702-8, 2055878). Bks Demand UMI.

Seven Is Heaven. Compiled by Treld Bicknell. LC 86-45415. (Illus.). (gr. 2). 1986. 8.95 (ISBN 0-15-200580-3, Gulliver Bks). HarBraceJ.

Seven Japanese Tales. Junichiro Tanizaki. Tr. by Howard Hibbett from Japanese. (Perigee Japanese Library). 320p. 1981. pap. 9.95 (ISBN 0-399-50523-7, Perigee). Putnam Pub Group.

Seven "Jesus Only" Tracts. Ed. by Donald W. Dayton. (Higher Christian Life Ser.). 379p. 1985. lib. bdg. 45.00. Garland Pub.

Seven Journeys Eastward Eighteen Ninety-Eight to Nineteen Twelve. Gustav J. Ramstedt. Tr. by John R. Krueger from Swedish. (Occasional Papers, the Mongolia Society: No. 9). Orig. Title: Seitseman Retkea Itaan. 1978. pap. 15.00 (ISBN 0-910980-19-5). Mongolia.

Seven Keys to Baldpate. Earl D. Biggers. 1976. Repr. of 1917 ed. lib. bdg. 21.95x (ISBN 0-89966-076-2). Buccaneer Bks.

Seven Keys to Color Healing: Successful Treatment Through Color. Roland Hunt. LC 81-47849. (Library of Spiritual Wisdom). 128p. 1982. pap. 7.95 (ISBN 0-06-064080-4, CN 4028, HarpR). Har-Row.

Seven Keys to Colour Healing. Roland Hunt. 124p. 1971. 8.95x (ISBN 0-8464-1063-X). Beekman Pubs.

Seven Keys to Happiness. Don J. Black. (Illus.). 87p. (Orig.). 1972. pap. 4.50 (ISBN 0-8425-1451-1, 8681). Pubs Bk Sales.

Seven Keys to Power. Lewis De Claremont. 4.95x (ISBN 0-685-22105-9). Wehman.

Seven Keys to Texas. T. R. Fehrenbach. 148p. 1983. 15.00 (ISBN 0-87404-069-8); pap. 8.00 (ISBN 0-87404-098-1). Tex Western.

Seven Keys to the Rocky Mountains. Richard M. Pearl. LC 68-55439. 1968. 5.00 (ISBN 0-940566-09-5). R M Pearl Bks.

Seven Keys to Triumphant Christian Living. Gordon Lindsay. 1.25 (ISBN 0-89985-006-5). Christ Nations.

Seven Kings of England. Geoffrey Trease. LC 55-7892. 320p. (gr. 6 up). 1955. 12.95 (ISBN 0-8149-0432-7). Vanguard.

Seven Kisses in a Row. Patricia MacLachlan. LC 82-47718. (Charlotte Zolotow Bks.). (Illus.). 64p. (gr. 2-5). 1983. 8.70i (ISBN 0-06-024083-0); PLB 9.89g (ISBN 0-06-024084-9). HarpJ.

Seven Kisses in a Row. Patricia MacLachlan. LC 82-47718. (Charlotte Zolotow Bk.: Trophy Bk.). (Illus.). 64p. (gr. 2-5). 1988. pap. 2.50 (ISBN 0-06-440231-2, Trophy). HarpJ.

Seven Lady Godivas. Dr. Seuss. LC 86-31541. (Illus.). 80p. 1987. 9.95 (ISBN 0-394-56269-0); ltd. ed. 50.00 (ISBN 0-394-56779-X). Random.

Seven Lamps of Advocacy. facs. ed. Edward A. Parry. LC 68-16965. (Essay Index Reprint Ser). 1968. Repr. of 1923 ed. 14.00 (ISBN 0-8369-0773-6). Ayer Co Pubs.

Seven Lamps of Architecture. John Ruskin. 210p. 1961. pap. 8.95 (ISBN 0-374-50188-2). FS&G.

Seven Last Objects of Jesus Christ. Edward F. Sundberg. (Illus.). 18p. (Orig.). 1985. 10.95 (ISBN 0-933499-01-9); pap. 5.95 (ISBN 0-933499-00-0). Seabird.

Seven Last Words. Fulton J. Sheen. 1982. pap. 2.95 (ISBN 0-8189-0438-0). Alba.

Seven Last Words of the Church. Ralph W. Neighbour, Jr. LC 79-51937. 1979. pap. 4.95 (ISBN 0-8054-5527-2). Broadman.

Seven Laws of Money. Michael Phillips et al. 1974. pap. 6.00 (ISBN 0-394-70686-2). Random.

Seven Laws of Teaching. John M. Gregory. 1954. 7.95 (ISBN 0-8010-3652-6). Baker Bk.

Seven Laws of Teaching. John M. Gregory. (Orig.). 1886. 1.95x (ISBN 0-9606952-1-4). PBBC Pr.

Seven Lean Years. Thomas J. Woofter & Ellen E. Winston. LC 79-39479. (FDR & the Era of the New Deal Ser). 1972. Repr. of 1939 ed. lib. bdg. 25.00 (ISBN 0-306-70463-3). Da Capo.

Seven Lectures on Shakespeare & Milton. Samuel Taylor Coleridge. Ed. by John P. Collier. LC 72-962. Repr. of 1856 ed. 12.50 (ISBN 0-404-01617-0). AMS Pr.

Seven Lectures on Shakespeare & Milton. Samuel Taylor Coleridge. LC 68-56787. (Research & Source Works Ser.: No. 276). 1969. Repr. of 1856 ed. 13.50 (ISBN 0-8337-0618-7). B Franklin.

Seven Lectures on the Law & History of Copyright in Books. Augustine Birrell. 228p. 1971. Repr. of 1899 ed. 20.00x (ISBN 0-8377-1929-1). Rothman.

Seven Short Novels. Anton Chekhov. Tr. by Barbara Makanowitzky from Rus. 1971. pap. 10.95 (ISBN 0-393-00552-6, Norton Lib). Norton.
Seven Short Plays. Gregory. 204p. 1982. Repr. of 1915 ed. lib. bdg. 30.00 (ISBN 0-8495-2130-0). Arden Lib.
Seven Short Plays. Isabella A. Gregory. LC 77-131727. 1970. Repr. of 1909 ed. 29.00x (ISBN 0-403-00614-7). Scholarly.
Seven Short Plays. Isabella A. Gregory. 1988. Repr. of 1909 ed. lib. bdg. 49.00x. Am Biog Serv.
Seven Short Plays. Isabelle A. Gregory. LC 76-40386. (One-Act Plays in Reprint Ser.). 1976. Repr. of 1903 ed. 18.50x (ISBN 0-8486-2002-X). Roth Pub Inc.
Seven Short Stories. Anton Chekhov. Tr. & intro. by Ronald Hingley. (Oxford Paperbacks Ser). 1974. 7.95x (ISBN 0-19-281159-2). Oxford U Pr.
Seven Signs of a Born Again Person. Wim Malgo. 1.45 (ISBN 0-937422-14-2). Midnight Call.
Seven Silent Men. Noel Behn. 1985. pap. 3.95 (ISBN 0-671-54390-3). PB.
Seven Silly Circles. Pam Conrad. LC 85-45835. (Illus.). 64p. (gr. 2-5). 1987. 10.95i (ISBN 0-06-021333-7); PLB 10.89 (ISBN 0-06-021334-5). HarpJ.
Seven Sinners in Grand Opera: Level 6. Bruce Barkman. Ed. by Jean McConochie. (Regents Readers Ser.). 1985. pap. text ed. 3.25 (ISBN 0-13-807389-9, 21066). Prentice ESL.
Seven Sins. Sax Rohmer. 1972. 6.50 (ISBN 0-685-33437-6). Bookfinger.
Seven Sister-Folk Tales, No. 6. (Chinese Folk Tales' Ser.). (Illus.). 122p. 1982. pap. 2.95 (ISBN 0-8351-1037-0). China Bks.
Seven Six-Gunners. Nelson Nye. 144p. 1987. pap. 2.50 (ISBN 0-441-75972-6, Pub. by Charter Bks). Ace Bks.
Seven Sixes Are Forty-Three: A Novel. Kiran Nagarkar. Tr. by Shubha Slee from Marathi. (Vikas Library of Modern Indian Writing: No. 15). 175p. 1981. text ed. 15.95x (ISBN 0-7069-1346-9, Pub. by Vikas India). Advent NY.
Seven Sketchbooks of Vincent Van Gogh. facsimile ed. Johannes Van der Wolk. LC 87-1351. (Illus.). 320p. 1987. 40.00 (ISBN 0-8109-1731-9). Abrams.
Seven Slayers. rev. ed. Paul Cain. LC 87-70576. 160p. 1987. pap. 3.95 (ISBN 0-88739-077-3, Pub. by BlackLizard). Creative Arts Bk.
Seven Slayers. Paul Cain. 194p. 1987. 14.95 (ISBN 0-940941-03-1); ltd. ed. 35.00 (ISBN 0-940941-04-X). Blood & Guts Pr.
Seven Sleepers. Phyllis S. Busch. LC 84-42984. (Illus.). 64p. (gr. 2-6). 1985. 11.95 (ISBN 0-02-715650-8). Macmillan.
Seven Sloppy Days of Phineas Pig. Mitchell Sharmat. LC 81-6954. (Illus.). 48p. (ps-3). 1983. 12.95 (ISBN 0-15-272936-4, HJ). HarBraceJ.
Seven Songs for the Harpsichord or Forte Piano. Francis Hopkinson. (Illus.). 1954. pap. 10.00x (ISBN 0-8450-2597-X, Musical Americana). Broude.
Seven South: The Adventures & Times of a Small Vermont Restaurant, 1972-1982. Roy M. Newton. (Illus.). 250p. 1985. 14.95 (ISBN 0-930721-00-4). Newton Pub.
Seven Soviet Plays. Vladimir Solovyov et al. Tr. by J. J. Robbins et al from Rus. LC 78-21619. 1980. Repr. of 1946 ed. lib. bdg. 41.50x (ISBN 0-313-20785-2, SSPL). Greenwood.
Seven Soviet Poets. Ed. by R. C. Porter. 128p. Date not set. pap. text ed. 15.00 (ISBN 0-631-15567-8). Basil Blackwell.
Seven Spanish Realists. LC 86-60887. (Illus.). 52p. (Orig.). 1986. pap. 12.00 (ISBN 0-936827-02-5). C Bernard Gallery Ltd.
Seven Sparrows & the Motor Car Picnic. Joan Hickson. (Illus.). 32p. (ps-2). 1982. 9.95 (ISBN 0-233-97363-X). Andre Deutsch.
Seven Spears of the W'dch'ck. Lionel Fenn. 384p. 1988. pap. 3.95 (ISBN 0-8125-3791-2). Tor Bks.
Seven Special Days. Henrietta D. Gambill. (Happy Day Bks.). (Illus.). 32p. (gr. k-2). 1987. 1.59 (ISBN 0-87403-281-4, 3781). Standard Pub.
Seven Spells to Farewell. Betty Baker. LC 81-19305. 123p. (gr. 5-9). 1982. 8.95 (ISBN 0-02-708150-8). Macmillan.
Seven Spirits. William Booth. 128p. 1984. Repr. of 1890 ed. 3.95 (ISBN 0-86544-026-3). Salv Army Suppl South.
Seven Spiritual Works of Mercy. Daughters of St. Paul. 1979. 1.75 (ISBN 0-8198-6805-1); pap. 1.00 (ISBN 0-8198-6806-X). Dghtrs St Paul.
Seven Stages. Geoffrey Trease. LC 65-26138. (Illus.). 256p. (gr. 7-9). 1965. 12.95 (ISBN 0-8149-0425-4). Vanguard.
Seven Stars & Orion: Reflections of the Past. Esther H. Mumford. (Illus.). 112p. (Orig.). 1986. pap. 7.95 (ISBN 0-9605670-1-1). Ananse Pr.
Seven Stars for Catfish Bend. Ben L. Burman. (Illus.). 88p. (gr. 3-5). 1981. pap. 1.95 (ISBN 0-380-53488-6, 53488-6, Camelot). Avon.
Seven Stars for Catfish Bend see Three from Catfish Bend.
Seven Steps along the Way. F. Dale Simpson. 1981. pap. 7.45 (ISBN 0-89137-527-9). Quality Pubns.
Seven Steps for Judging Prophecy. Kenneth E. Hagin. 1982. pap. 1.00 (ISBN 0-89276-024-9). Hagin Ministries.
Seven Steps to Effective Prayer. William L. Asher, Jr. 36p. (Orig.). 1978. pap. 2.00 (ISBN 0-915235-01-3). United Res.
Seven Steps to Freedom. Derin Carmack. 31p. 1986. pap. 3.00 (ISBN 0-937093-25-4). Jewel Pr.
Seven Steps to God's Healing Power. Shy Mackes. pap. 0.95 (ISBN 0-910924-28-7). Macalester.
Seven Steps to Peak Performance. Richard M. Suinn. 60p. 1986. pap. text ed. 12.90 (ISBN 0-920887-12-0, H Huber Canada). Hogrefe Intl.
Seven Steps to Treason. Michael Hartland. 304p. 1986. pap. 3.95 (ISBN 0-515-08490-5). Jove Pubns.
Seven Steps Toward God. Bill Beatty. LC 85-82315. 102p. (Orig.). 1986. pap. 5.95 (ISBN 0-937779-01-6). Greenlawn Pr.
Seven Stones: A Portrait of Arthur Erickson, Architect. Edith Iglauer. LC 81-13154. (Illus.). 120p. 1981. 29.95 (ISBN 0-295-95882-0). U of Wash Pr.
Seven Storey Mountain. Thomas Merton. LC 78-7109. 429p. 1978. pap. 7.95 (ISBN 0-15-680679-7, Harv). HarBraceJ.
Seven Storey Mountain. Thomas Merton. 1978. Repr. lib. bdg. 32.00x (ISBN 0-88254-843-3, Octagon). Hippocrene Bks.
Seven Storey Mountain. Thomas Merton. 429p. 1948. 15.95 (ISBN 0-15-181353-1). HarBraceJ.
Seven Stories. James Hall. Ed. by Mary Burtschi. LC 75-23549. 114p. 1975. 7.00 (ISBN 0-9601642-1-9). Little Brick Hse.
Seven Stories by Marie von Ebner-Eschenbach. Tr. & intro. by Helga Harriman. LC 86-70738. (Studies in German Literature, Linguistics & Culture: Vol. 26). (Illus.). 180p. 1986. 27.00x (ISBN 0-938100-45-9). Camden Hse.
Seven Stories from Spanish America. Ed. by G. Brotherston & M. V. Llosa. 1968. pap. text ed. 4.60 (ISBN 0-08-012675-8). Pergamon.
Seven Stories of Christmas Love. Leo Buscaglia. (Illus.). 112p. 1987. 12.95 (ISBN 0-688-07521-5). Slack Inc.
Seven Stories of Christmas Love. Leo Buscaglia. 1987. write for info. Morrow.
Seven Stories with Basement & Attic. Donald G. Mitchell. 1972. lib. bdg. 29.50 (ISBN 0-8422-8096-0); pap. text ed. 8.95x (ISBN 0-8290-0672-9). Irvington.
Seven Stranded Coal Towns: A Study of an American Depressed Area. Malcolm Brown & John N. Webb. LC 76-165680. (Research Monograph: Vol. 23). 1971. Repr. of 1941 ed. lib. bdg. 25.00 (ISBN 0-306-70355-6). Da Capo.
Seven Strategies for Wealth & Happiness: Power Ideas from America's Foremost Business Philosopher. E. James Rohn. Ed. by Nancy D. Dominitz. 160p. (Orig.). 1986. 13.95 (ISBN 0-914629-02-6, Dist. by St. Martin); pap. 7.95. Prima Pub Comm.
Seven Strategies for Wealth & Happiness: Power Ideas from America's Foremost Business Philosopher. Jim Rohn. 160p. 1988. pap. 8.95 (ISBN 0-914629-73-5, Dist. by St. Martins). Prima Pub Comm.
Seven Streets by Seven Streets. Evelyn Richardson. (Illus.). 172p. (Orig.). 1984. pap. write for info (ISBN 0-914110-15-2). Blyden Pr.
Seven Studies in Medieval English History & Other Historical Essays. Ed. by Richard H. Bowers. LC 83-3530. 208p. 1983. 15.00x (ISBN 0-87805-183-X). U Pr of Miss.
Seven Summers. Mulk-Raj Anand. 242p. 1973. pap. 3.00 (ISBN 0-88253-124-7). Ind-US Inc.
Seven Summits. Dick Bass et al. 1986. 19.95 (ISBN 0-446-51312-1). Warner Bks.
Seven Summits. Dick Bass et al. 352p. 1988. pap. 12.95 (ISBN 0-446-38517-4). Warner Bks.
Seven Supreme Poets: Homer, Aeschylus, Sophocles, Vergil, Dante, Shakespeare, Milton. Robert P. Downes. 1973. 25.00 (ISBN 0-8274-1701-2). R West.
Seven Suspects. Michael Innes. (Crime Ser.). 288p. 1984. pap. 3.95 (ISBN 0-14-006886-4). Penguin.
Seven Swedes: Sweden's Top Multinational Companies. Reinhold Von Essen. 140p. (Orig.). 1984. pap. text ed. 23.00x (Pub. by Almqvist & Wiksell). Coronet Bks.
Seven Symphonies. Carlo D'Ordonez. Ed. by Peter Brown & Barry S. Brook. LC 79-12057. (Symphony 1720-1840, Ser. B: Vol. IV). 255p. 1980. lib. bdg. 90.00 (ISBN 0-8240-3800-2). Garland Pub.
Seven Synonyms for God. Max Kappeler. Tr. by Kathleen Lee from Ger. LC 83-83266. 400p. 35.00 (ISBN 0-942958-09-8). Kappeler Inst Pub.
Seven Systems of Indian Philosophy. Pandit R. Tigunait. 250p. (Orig.). pap. 9.95 (ISBN 0-89389-076-6). Himalayan Pubs.
Seven Tablets of Creation, 2 vols. Enuma Elish. LC 73-18850. (Luzac's Semitic Text & Translation Ser.: Nos. 12 & 13). (Illus.). Repr. of 1902 ed. Set. 45.00 (ISBN 0-404-11344-3). AMS Pr.
Seven Tears for Apollo. Phyllis A. Whitney. 224p. 1985. pap. 2.95 (ISBN 0-449-20871-0, Crest). Fawcett.
Seven Tell Their Story. Robert J. Mueller. Ed. by Michael L. Sherer. (Orig.). 1988. pap. 3.25 (ISBN 1-55673-019-5, 8803). CSS of Ohio.
Seven Theories of Human Nature. Leslie Stevenson. 1974. pap. text ed. 6.95x (ISBN 0-19-875034-X). Oxford U Pr.
Seven Theories of Human Nature. 2nd ed. Leslie Stevenson. 160p. 1987. 14.95 (ISBN 0-19-505291-9). Oxford U Pr.
Seven Theories of Human Nature. 2nd ed. Leslie Stevenson. 160p. 1987. pap. text ed. 7.95 (ISBN 0-19-505214-5). Oxford U Pr.
Seven Theories of Human Society. Tom Campbell. 1981. text ed. 22.50x (ISBN 0-19-876104-X); pap. text ed. 9.95x (ISBN 0-19-876105-8). Oxford U Pr.
Seven Things Children Need. 2nd ed. John M. Drescher. LC 88-10173. 144p. 1988. pap. 5.95 (ISBN 0-8361-3475-3). Herald Pr.
Seven Things You Should Know about Divine Healing. Kenneth E. Hagin. 1979. pap. 2.50 (ISBN 0-89276-400-7). Hagin Ministries.
Seven Thousand Days in Siberia. Karlo Stajner. Tr. by Joel Agee from Rus. 560p. 1987. 30.00 (ISBN 0-374-26126-1). FS&G.
Seven Thunderers Utter Their Voices: History & Verse by Verse Study in the Book of Revelation of the Bible. 2nd ed. E. Warren Anglin. 176p. (Orig.). pap. 7.95 (ISBN 0-318-04199-5). Total Comm Ministries.
Seven Times Seven. Maria T. Daviess. Ed. by Annette K. Baxter. LC 79-8786. (Signal Lives Ser.). (Illus.). 1980. Repr. of 1924 ed. lib. bdg. 34.50x (ISBN 0-405-12834-7). Ayer Co Pubs.
Seven Towers. Patricia C. Wrede. 272p. 1984. pap. 2.95 (ISBN 0-441-75976-9, Pub. by Ace Science Fiction). Ace Bks.
Seven Trails. Max Brand. 1988. 30.00x (ISBN 0-86025-208-6, Pub. by Ian Henry Pubns England). State Mutual Bk.
Seven Training Sketches for the Painter by Rudolf Steiner. Marie Groddeck. Ed. by John Fletcher. Tr. by Inge Martin from Ger. 23p. 1982. pap. 1.95 (ISBN 0-88010-059-1, Pub. by Steinerbooks). Anthroposophic.
Seven True Bear Stories. Laura Geriner. (Illus.). (gr. 2-5). 1979. 8.95 (ISBN 0-8038-6747-6). Hastings.
Seven True Dog Stories. Margaret Davidson. (Illus.). 96p. (gr. 2-5). 1986. Repr. of 1977 ed. 9.95 (ISBN 0-8038-6738-7). Hastings.
Seven Types of Ambiguity. William Empson. 1947. pap. 7.95 (ISBN 0-8112-0037-X, NDP204). New Directions.
Seven Valleys & the Four Valleys. 3rd rev. ed. Baha'u'llah. Tr. by Marzieh Gail. LC 77-23326. 1978. 7.95 (ISBN 0-87743-113-2, 103-015); pap. 4.95 (ISBN 0-87743-114-0, 103-016). Baha'i.
Seven Verdi Librettos. Tr. by William Weaver. (Illus.). 1975 30.00x (ISBN 0-393-02181-5, N852, Norton Lib); pap. 12.951977 (ISBN 0-393-00852-5). Norton.
Seven Victorian Architects. Ed. by Jane Fawcett. LC 76-42090. (Illus.). 1977. 19.75x (ISBN 0-271-00500-9). Pa St U Pr.
Seven Views of Hudson's River. Harry Waitzman. Ed. by Alana Sherman. (Chapbooks Second Ser.). 20p. (Orig.). 1987. pap. 3.95 (ISBN 0-939689-04-9). Alms Hse Pr.
Seven Viking Romances. Tr. by Hermann Palsson & Paul Edwards. (Penguin Classics Ser.). 304p. 1986. pap. 5.95 (ISBN 0-14-044474-2). Penguin.
Seven Visions & Other Poems. Arthur Johnson. (Illus., Orig.). 1987. pap. 4.95 (ISBN 0-942943-00-7). Silent Hse Pubns.
Seven Vital Steps to Publishing Reports & Booklets. 1987. lib. bdg. 59.00 (ISBN 0-8490-3870-7). Gordon Pr.
Seven Vital Steps to Receiving the Holy Spirit. 2nd ed. Kenneth E. Hagin. 1980. pap. 1.00 (ISBN 0-89276-003-6). Hagin Ministries.
Seven Voices Speak. Catharose De Petri. Ed. by Lectorium Rosicrucianum. Orig. Title: Zeven Stemmen Spreken. 79p. (Dutch.). Date not set. pap. 8.00 (ISBN 0-317-55565-0). Rozekruis Pr.
Seven Was the Padre's Number. Henry James. 1973. 6.00 (ISBN 0-682-47784-2). Exposition-Phoenix.
Seven Ways Jesus Heals. Norvel Hayes. 142p. (Orig.). 1982. pap. 4.95 (ISBN 0-89274-235-6, HH-235). Harrison Hse.
Seven Ways to Get More from Your Bible. Terry Hall. (Orig.). 1987. pap. 2.95 (ISBN 0-8024-7676-7). Moody.
Seven Who Fled. Frederic Prokosch. 496p. 1984. 18.95 (ISBN 0-374-26128-8); pap. 9.95 (ISBN 0-374-51831-9). FS&G.
Seven Wild Pigs. Helme Heine. LC 87-3448. (Illus.). 120p. (gr. k up). 1988. Repr. of 1986 ed. 18.95 (ISBN 0-689-50439-X, M K McElderry). Macmillan.
Seven Winters. Elizabeth Bowen. 72p. 1971. Repr. of 1942 ed. 15.00x (ISBN 0-7165-1397-8, BBA 02047, Pub. by Cuala Press Ireland). Biblio Dist.
Seven Wise Men of Colonial America. Richard M. Gummere. LC 67-27084. 1967. 11.00x (ISBN 0-674-80250-0). Harvard U Pr.
Seven Wives of Bluebeard. facsimile ed. Anatole France. LC 73-144154. (Short Story Index Reprint Ser.). Repr. of 1923 ed. 17.00 (ISBN 0-8369-3769-4). Ayer Co Pubs.
Seven Women Against the World. Margaret Goldsmith. LC 75-21989. (Pioneers of the Woman's Movement Ser.). (Illus.). ix, 236p. 1976. Repr. of 1894 ed. 21.00 (ISBN 0-88355-316-3). Hyperion-Conn.
Seven Women: Portraits from the American Radical Tradition. Judith Nies. 1978. pap. 5.95 (ISBN 0-14-004792-1). Penguin.
Seven Wonders of New Jersey--& Then Some. Thomas C. Murray & Valerie Barnes. LC 80-16424. (Illus.). 128p. (gr. 7-12). 1981. pap. 7.95 (ISBN 0-89490-017-X). Enslow Pubs.
Seven Wonders of the Ancient World. Ed. by Peter A. Clayton & Martin J. Price. 192p. 1988. text ed. 32.50 (ISBN 0-415-00279-6). Routledge Chapman & Hall.
Seven Wonders of the World. Kenneth McLeish. 32p. (gr. 4-7). 1986. 11.95 (ISBN 0-521-26538-X). Cambridge U Pr.
Seven Words from the Cross: A Commentary. Charles E. Wolfe. 1980. pap. 4.65 (ISBN 0-89536-420-4, 1962). CSS of Ohio.
Seven Words: The Words of Jesus on the Cross Reveal the Heart of the Christian Faith. Clovis G. Chappell. (Pocket Pulpit Library). 80p. 1976. pap. 2.95 (ISBN 0-8010-2387-4). Baker Bk.
Seven Works of Vasubandhu: The Buddhist Psychological Doctor. Stefan Anacker. (Religion of Asia Ser.: No. 4). 491p. 1986. Repr. of 1984 ed. 24.00x (ISBN 81-208-0203-9, Pub. by Motilal Banarsidass India). Orient Bk Dist.
Seven Works of Vasubandhu: The Buddhist Psychological Doctor. Stefan Anacker. x, 493p. 1986. 23.00x (ISBN 0-317-61124-0, Pub. by Motilal Banarsidass). South Asia Bks.
Seven Worlds to Win. Morris Watkins. 240p. (Orig.). (YA) (gr. 7 up). 1987. pap. 19.95 (ISBN 0-939925-00-1). R C Law & Co.
Seven Writers in the English Left: A Bibliography of Literature & Politics, 1916-1980. Alan Munton & Alan Young. 1983. lib. bdg. 55.00 (ISBN 0-8240-9777-7). Garland Pub.
Seven Year Balance Sheet of the Sovereign, Military & Hospitaller Order of St. John of Jerusalem, of Rhodes & of Malta: From May 1st, 1778 to end of April 1785. Chevalier Bosredon de Ransijat. Ed. by Marcel V. Dingli-Attard-Inguanez. (Illus.). 79p. (Orig.). pap. 10.00 (ISBN 0-9610740-2-7). U Intel Data Bank.
Seven Years among the Freedmen. 2nd, rev. & enl ed. M. Waterbury. LC 79-178484. (Black Heritage Library Collection). Repr. of 1890 ed. 18.50 (ISBN 0-8369-8934-1). Ayer Co Pubs.
Seven Years at Sea. Manuel Alvarez. 220p. 1983. lib. bdg. 16.95 (ISBN 0-919573-20-7); pap. 7.95 (ISBN 0-919573-21-5). Left Bank.
Seven Years Conversing with Spirits. Paul Lojnikov. 1987. 6.95 (ISBN 0-533-07213-1). Vantage.
Seven Years from Somewhere. Philip Levine. LC 78-20595. 1979. pap. 4.95 (ISBN 0-689-10974-1). Atheneum.
Seven Years Harvest. Henry S. Canby. LC 66-25902. Repr. of 1936 ed. 24.95x (ISBN 0-8046-0065-1, Pub. by Kennikat). Assoc Faculty Pr.
Seven Years in France: Change & Stability under Mitterrand. Julius W. Friend. 250p. 1988. 34.95 (ISBN 0-8133-0610-8). Westview.
Seven Years in Russia & Siberia, Nineteen Fourteen to Nineteen Twenty-One. Roman Dyboski. Tr. by Marion M. Coleman from Pol. LC 79-137001. (Illus., Orig.). 1971. pap. 5.00 (ISBN 0-910366-09-8). Alliance Coll.
Seven Years in South Africa, 2 Vols. Emil Holub. 1881. Set. 49.00x (ISBN 0-403-00390-3). Scholarly.
Seven Years in Soviet Russia. Paul Scheffer. Tr. by Arthur Livingston from Ger. LC 73-853. (Russian Studies: Perspectives on the Revolution Ser.). 357p. 1973. Repr. of 1932 ed. 29.35 (ISBN 0-88355-050-4). Hyperion Conn.
Seven Years in the Soudan... Romolo Gessi-Pasha. 492p. Repr. of 1892 ed. text ed. 99.36x (ISBN 0-576-79105-9, Pub. by Gregg Intl Pubs England). Gregg Intl.
Seven Years in Tibet. Heinrich Harrer. Tr. by Richard Graves. LC 81-23244. (Illus.). 336p. 1982. pap. 8.95 (ISBN 0-87477-217-6). J P Tarcher.
Seven Years of the King's Theatre. John Ebers. LC 79-88490. Repr. of 1828 ed. 24.50 (ISBN 0-405-08481-1, Blom Pubns). Ayer Co Pubs.
Seven Years of the New Copyright Act: Report, Analysis, & Predictions for the Future, October 26-27, 1984. American Bar Association Forum Committee on Entertainment & Sports Industries Staff & American Bar Association Section of Patent Trademark & Copyright Law Staff. write for info. Amer Bar Assn.
Seven Years War & the Old Regime in France: The Economic & Financial Toll. James C. Riley. 256p. 1987. text ed. 32.50x (ISBN 0-691-05488-6). Princeton U Pr.
Seven Years with God. 2nd ed. Frank W. Sandford. (Illus.). 1957. 4.00 (ISBN 0-910840-02-4). Kingdom.
Seven You Will Remember. Peter Tarnov. 162p. 1983. pap. 8.00 (ISBN 0-911109-00-5). Oxymora Bk Pr.
Sevenfold Path to Peace. Alan Bond. 1986. 4.50 (ISBN 0-89536-774-2, 6801). CSS of Ohio.

Seventeenth Century Songs & Lyrics. facsimile ed. Ed. by John P. Cutts. LC 70-80373. (Granger Index Reprint Ser). 1959. 21.00 (ISBN 0-8369-6055-6). Ayer Co Pubs.

Seventeenth-Century Stage. Ed. by Gerald E. Bentley. LC 68-26759. (Patterns of Literary Criticism Ser.). 1968. 20.00x (ISBN 0-226-04308-8). U of Chicago Pr.

Seventeenth Century Studies. Edmund Gosse. 1897. Repr. 10.95 (ISBN 0-8274-3366-2). R West.

Seventeenth Century Studies. Edmund W. Gosse. LC 70-136381. Repr. of 1914 ed. 18.50 (ISBN 0-404-02885-3). AMS Pr.

Seventeenth Century Studies. Edmund W. Gosse. 1971. Repr. of 1913 ed. 16.00x (ISBN 0-403-00995-2). Scholarly.

Seventeenth Century Studies, 2 vols. Robert Shafer. text ed. 36.00 (ISBN 0-8369-9354-3, 19725). Ayer Co Pubs.

Seventeenth Century Studies. First Series. facs. ed. Ed. by Robert Shafer. LC 68-16976. (Essay Index Reprint Ser). 1933. 18.00 (ISBN 0-8369-0866-X). Ayer Co Pubs.

Seventeenth Century: Studies in the History of English Thought & Literature from Bacon to Pope. Richard F. Jones et al. 1951. 35.00x (ISBN 0-8047-0408-2); pap. 12.95 (ISBN 0-8047-0409-0, SP93). Stanford U Pr.

Seventeenth Century Studies Presented to Sir Herbert Grierson. Herbert Grierson. 1967. Repr. lib. bdg. 24.50x (ISBN 0-374-93268-9, Octagon). Hippocrene Bks.

Seventeenth Century Studies. Second Series. facs. ed. Ed. by Robert Shafer. LC 68-16976. (Essay Index Reprint Ser). 1937. 18.00 (ISBN 0-8369-0867-8). Ayer Co Pubs.

Seventeenth Century, the Intellectual & Cultural Context of English Literature, 1603-1700. Graham Parry. (Literature in Eneglish Ser.). 336p. (Orig.). 1988. text ed. 32.95 (ISBN 0-582-49377-3); pap. text ed. 16.95 (ISBN 0-582-49376-5). Longman.

Seventeenth Century Tokens of the British Isles & Their Values. Michael Dickinson. (Illus.). 288p. 1986. 65.00 (ISBN 0-900652-78-0, Pub. by Seaby UK). Numismatic Fine Arts.

Seventeenth-Century Writings on the Kievan Caves Monastery. Intro. by Paulina Lewin. LC 87-83705. (Library of Early Ukrainian Literature: Texts: Vol. IV). 468p. 1988. text ed. 35.00x (ISBN 0-916458-24-5). Harvard Ukrainian.

Seventeenth Degree. Mary McCarthy. LC 74-1065. 451p. 1974. pap. 3.95 (ISBN 0-15-680680-0, Harv). HarBraceJ.

Seventeenth International Byzantine Congress: Major Papers. Compiled by The U. S. National Committee for Byzantine Studies. (Illus.). 736p. 1986. lib. bdg. 75.00x (ISBN 0-89241-443-X). Caratzas.

Seventeenth International Congress on High Speed Photography & Photonics. Ed. by McDowell & Hollingworth. 600p. 1986. 79.00 (ISBN 0-89252-709-9, 674). SPIE.

Seventeenth Special Report of the Director-General on the Application of the Declaration Concerning the Policy of Apartheid of the Republic of South Africa: 67th session, 1981. International Labour Office Staff. 102p. (Orig.). 1981. pap. 12.25 (ISBN 92-2-102395-8). Intl Labour Office.

Seventeenth-Street Gang. Emily C. Neville. LC 66-7116. (Trophy I Can Read Bks.). (Illus.). 160p. (gr. 5-7). 1966. pap. 2.95 (ISBN 0-06-440019-0, Trophy). HarpJ.

Seventeenth Summer. Maureen Daly. (gr. 7-9). 1968. pap. 2.95 (ISBN 0-671-61931-4). Archway.

Seventeenth Summer. Maureen Daly. 293p. 1981. Repr. PLB 19.95x (ISBN 0-89966-355-9). Buccaneer Bks.

Seventeenth Summer. Maureen Daly. 288p. (YA) 1981. Repr. PLB 19.95x (ISBN 0-89967-029-6). Harmony Raine.

Seventeenth Swap. Eloise McGraw. (gr. 4-8). 1987. pap. 2.95 (ISBN 0-8167-1050-3). Troll Assocs.

Seventeenth Swap. Eloise J. McGraw. LC 86-8791. 160p. (gr. 4-7). 1986. 11.95 (ISBN 0-689-50398-9, M K McElderry). Macmillan.

Seventeenth Virginia Cavalry: Or Wildcat Cavalry. John Dawson. 1982. 15.00 (ISBN 0-89029-310-4). Pr of Morningside.

Seventh. Richard Stark. LC 80-39928. 158p. 1981. 15.00 (ISBN 0-317-43332-6). Ultramarine Pub.

Seventh American Checker Tourney, Chicago 1929. 7.50 (ISBN 0-685-02659-0). Univ Place.

Seventh & Walnut, Life in Colonial Philadelphia. James E. Knight. LC 81-24036. (Illus.). 32p. (gr. 5-9). 1982. PLB 9.79 (ISBN 0-89375-740-3); pap. text ed. 1.95 (ISBN 0-89375-741-1). Troll Assocs.

Seventh Annual Acquisition & Takeovers. 35.00 (ISBN 0-317-29535-7, #CO3514, Law & Business). HarBraceJ.

Seventh Annual Banking Expansion Institute. Michael Bradfield & Law & Business Inc. Staff. LC 86-217817. 481p. Date not set. price not set (Law & Business). HarBraceJ.

Seventh Annual Institute on Proxy Statements, Annual Meeting, & Disclosure Documents. Edward F. Greene. LC 86-187495. iv, 628p. Date not set. price not set. HarBraceJ.

Seventh Annual Review, North Carolina, 1987. Ed. by Wake Forest University School of Law - Continuing Legal Education. (Orig.). 1987. pap. 80.00 (ISBN 0-942225-29-5). Wake Forest Law.

Seventh Assembling. Richard Kostelanetz & Henry J. Korn. (Illus.). 1977. pap. 10.00 (ISBN 0-685-81580-3). Assembling Pr.

Seventh Babe. Jerome Charyn. 352p. 1984. pap. 2.95 (ISBN 0-380-51540-7, 51540, Bard). Avon.

Seventh Candle & Other Folk Tales of Eastern Europe. David Einhorn. Tr. by Gertrude Pashin. LC 68-10968. (Illus.). (gr. 6-8). 1968. 7.95x (ISBN 0-87068-369-1). Ktav.

Seventh Carrier. Peter Albano. 1983. pap. 3.25. Zebra.

Seventh Cavalry's Own Colonel Tommy Tompkins: A Military Heritage & Tradition. John M. Carroll. (Illus.). 26.95 (ISBN 0-8488-0013-3, Pub. by J M C & Co). Amereon Ltd.

Seventh Census of the United States. U. S. Census Office, 1850. LC 75-22851. (America in Two Centuries Ser). 1976. Repr. of 1853 ed. 97.00x (ISBN 0-405-07718-1). Ayer Co Pubs.

Seventh Census, 1850: Message of the President of the U. S. Communicating a Digest of the Statistics of Manufacturing see American Industry & Manufactures in the Nineteenth Century.

Seventh Continent: Antarctica in a Resource Age. Deborah Shapley. LC 85-5581. 350p. 1986. lib. bdg. 40.00 (ISBN 0-915707-17-9). Resources Future.

Seventh Cross. Anna Seghers. Tr. by James A. Galston from Ger. (Voices of Resistance Ser.). 384p. 1987. pap. 7.50 (ISBN 0-85345-712-3). Monthly Rev.

Seventh Day. Gordon Lindsay. 1.25 (ISBN 0-89985-116-9). Christ Nations.

Seventh-Day Adventism. Anthony A. Hoekema. 1974. pap. 4.95 (ISBN 0-8028-1490-5). Eerdmans.

Seventh-Day Adventism in a Nutshell. D. M. Canright. 2.75 (ISBN 0-89225-162-X). Gospel Advocate.

Seventh-Day Adventism Renounced. D. M. Canright. 1982. pap. 5.95. Gospel Advocate.

Seventh-Day Adventist Family: An Empirical Study. Charles C. Crider & Robert C. Kistler. 296p. 1979. pap. 3.95 (ISBN 0-943872-77-4). Andrews Univ Pr.

Seventh-Day Adventists: A History. Anne D. Jordan. 150p. 1988. 14.95 (ISBN 0-87052-562-X). Hippocrene Bks.

Seventh-Day Baptists in Europe & America: A Series of Historical Papers Written in Commemoration of the One Hundred Anniversary of the Organization, 2 vols. Seventh-Day Baptist General Conference. Ed. by Edwin S. Gaustad. LC 79-52605. (Baptist Tradition Ser.). (Illus.). 1980. Repr. of 1910 ed. lib. bdg. 160.00x set (ISBN 0-405-12470-8). Ayer Co Pubs.

Seventh-Day Baptists in Europe & America, Vol. 1. Seventh-Day Baptists General Conference. 80.00 (ISBN 0-405-12478-3). Ayer Co Pubs.

Seventh-Day Baptists in Europe & America, Vol. 2. Seventh-Day Baptists General Conference. 80.00 (ISBN 0-405-12479-1). Ayer Co Pubs.

Seventh Day: The Story of the Jewish Sabbath. Miriam Chaikin & David Frampton. LC 82-16987. (Illus.). 48p. (Orig.). 1983. pap. 4.95 (ISBN 0-8052-0743-0). Schocken.

Seventh Day: The Story of the Seventh-Day Adventists. Booton Herndon. LC 78-11705. 1979. Repr. of 1960 ed. lib. bdg. 35.00x (ISBN 0-313-21054-3, HESD). Greenwood.

Seventh Division 1888. 60p. 5.50 (ISBN 0-318-18049-9). Mobile PO.

Seventh Dragon: The Riddle of Equal Temperment. new ed. Anita T. Sullivan. LC 84-22627. (Illus.). 100p. (Orig.). 1985. 12.95 (ISBN 0-943920-22-1). Metamorphous Pr.

Seventh E. C. Photovoltaic Solar Energy Conference. Ed. by A. Goetzberger et al. 1987. lib. bdg. 174.00 (ISBN 90-277-2449-0, Pub. by Reidel Holland). Kluwer Academic.

Seventh Fiber Optics & Communications & Local Area Networks Exposition, 1983. 1983. 125.00. Info Gatekeepers.

Seventh Fleet Super Carriers: U. S. Naval Air Power in the Pacific. Tony Holmes. (Osprey Color Library). (Illus.). 128p. (Orig.). 1987. pap. 14.95 (ISBN 0-85045-815-3, Pub. by Osprey England). Motorbooks Intl.

Seventh Gate. Carlin Aden. 1973. pap. 3.00 (ISBN 0-686-05617-5). Goliards Pr.

Seventh Gate. Dolores Hall. (Harlequin Category Romances Ser.). 224p. 1983. pap. 2.25 (ISBN 0-373-33001-4). Harlequin Bks.

Seventh Gate, No. 4. Geraldine Harris. (Seven Citadels Ser.). (gr. k-12). 1987. pap. 2.95 (ISBN 0-440-97747-9, LFL). Dell.

Seventh Gate: Pt. 4. Geraldine Harris. LC 83-14084. (Seven Citadels Ser.). 256p. (gr. 7 up). 1984. reinforced bdg. 10.25 (ISBN 0-688-01759-2). Greenwillow.

Seventh Generation. Hal Renko et al. Date not set. cancelled. Addison-Wesley.

Seventh Generation of One Hundred & One Aggie Jokes. Illus. by Bob Taylor. (One Hundred & One Aggie Jokes Ser.). (Illus.). 50p. (Orig.). 1977. write for info. (ISBN 0-945430-07-8). Gigem Pr.

Seventh Grade: Most Extreme Climbing. Reinhold Messner. (Illus.). 1982. pap. 11.95 (ISBN 0-19-520373-9). Oxford U Pr.

Seventh-Grade Rumors: The Fabulous Five, No. 1. Betsy Haynes. (gr. 4-7). 1988. pap. 2.75 (ISBN 0-553-15625-X, Skylark). Bantam.

Seventh Grade Soccer Star. Gail Roper. LC 88-9496. 132p. (gr. 3-7). 1988. pap. 3.95 (ISBN 1-55513-507-2, Chariot Bks). Cook.

Seventh Hero: Thomas Carlyle & the Theory of Radical Activism. Phillip Rosenberg. LC 73-87659. 288p. 1974. 18.50x (ISBN 0-674-80260-8). Harvard U Pr.

Seventh Horse & Other Tales. Leonora Carrington. (Illus.). 224p. 1988. 16.95 (ISBN 0-525-24651-7, Obelisk); pap. 7.95 (ISBN 0-525-48384-5, Obelisk). Dutton.

Seventh Hour. Grace L. Hill. 17.95 (ISBN 0-317-27917-3, Pub. by Amereon Hse). Amereon Ltd.

Seventh International Conference on Distributed Computing Systems (ICDCS) Proceedings. 588p. 1987. 70.00 (ISBN 0-8186-0801-3, EZ801). IEEE Comp Soc.

Seventh International Conference on High Energy Physics & Nuclear Structure. Ed. by M. P. Locher. (Experientia Supplementa: 31). 436p. 1978. 78.95x (ISBN 0-8176-0987-3). Birkhauser.

Seventh International Conference on Sarcoidosis & Other Granulomatous Disorders, Vol. 278. Ed. by Louis E. Siltzbach. (Annals of the New York Academy of Sciences). 1976. 55.00x (ISBN 0-89072-057-6). NY Acad Sci.

Seventh International Congress - Cold Forging. Ed. by Portcullis Press Ltd. Staff. 1985. 395.00x (Pub. by Portcullis Pr UK). State Mutual Bk.

Seventh International Congress of Endocrinology Abstracts: Proceedings of Congress Held 1-7 July, 1984, in Quebec City, Canada. Ed. by F. Labrie. (International Congress Ser.: No. 652). 1708p. 1984. 157.00 (ISBN 0-444-80587-7, Excerpta Medica). Elsevier.

Seventh International Light Metals Congress, Vienna, Austria, 1981. 114.00 (Pub. by Aluminium W Germany). IPS.

Seventh International Mineral Processing Congress: Proceedings, 1965. Ed. by Nathaniel Arbiter. 625p. 1965. 175.00 (ISBN 0-677-10690-4). Gordon & Breach.

Seventh International Technical Conference on Slurry Transportation: Proceedings. LC 82-6012. (Illus.). 454p. 1982. 75.00 (ISBN 0-932066-07-0). Slurry Tech.

Seventh Judicial Circuit, South Dakota: A Caseflow Management System. National Center for State Courts Staff. 58p. 1976. manuscript 3.48 (NCRO-005). Natl Ctr St Courts.

Seventh Judicial District Requirements Analysis: State of Iowa. National Center for State Courts Staff. 317p. 1984. manuscript 19.00 (NERO-167). Natl Ctr St Courts.

Seventh Man. John Berger. 1981. pap. 6.95 (ISBN 0-906495-90-3). Writers & Readers.

Seventh Man. Max Brand. 240p. 1987. pap. 2.75 (ISBN 0-515-08939-7). Jove Pubns.

Seventh Man. Max Brand. LC 88-19971. 386p. 1988. Repr. of 1974 ed. lib. bdg. 15.95 (ISBN 0-89621-179-7). Thorndike Pr.

Seventh National Ground Water Quality Symposium. 1984. 43.75 (ISBN 0-318-23006-2). Natl Water Well.

Seventh Night of July. Retold by Paula Franklin. LC 84-40798. (Stories from Around the World Ser.). (Illus.). 28p. (ps-3). 1985. pap. 3.75 (ISBN 0-382-09047-0). Silver.

Seventh Nizam. Aubaida Yazdani & Mary Chrystal. 1986. 44.00 (ISBN 0-9510819-0-X, Pub. by British Library). South Asia Bks.

Seventh North American Ginseng Conference: Proceedings. Ed. by Arthur Rashap & Beverly Braly. 200p. 1986. pap. text ed. 10.00x (ISBN 0-9613800-1-2). Ginseng Res Inst.

Seventh of Joyce. Ed. by Bernard Benstock. LC 81-47775. (Midland Bks: No. 282). 288p. (Orig.). 1982. 25.00X (ISBN 0-253-35184-7); pap. 12.50X (ISBN 0-253-20282-5). Ind U Pr.

Seventh Penguin Book of the Times Crosswords. Ed. by Edmund Akenhead. 144p. 1986. pap. 3.50 (ISBN 0-14-007918-1). Penguin.

Seventh Phoenix Conference on Computers & Communications: Proceedings. 540p. 1988. 80.00 (ISBN 0-8186-0830-7, EZ830). IEEE Comp Soc.

Seventh Plan Perspectives, India. Malcolm S. Adiseshiah. 1985. 26.00x (ISBN 0-8364-1449-7, Pub. by Lancer India). South Asia Bks.

Seventh Raven. Peter Dickinson. 192p. (gr. 7 up). 1981. 11.50 (ISBN 0-525-39150-9). Dutton.

Seventh Reading Helper. Gloria Orlick. (Classroom Pairing: Reading Tutorial Program Ser.). (Illus., Orig., Prog. Bk.). (gr. 3). 1970. pap. 3.45 (ISBN 0-87594-021-8). Book-Lab.

Seventh Report of FAO International Food Technology Training Centre. 81p. 1982. pap. 7.50 (ISBN 92-5-100201-0, F2112, FAO). UNIPUB.

Seventh Royale. Donald Stanwood. LC 83-45495. 395p. 1987. 19.95 (ISBN 0-689-11449-4). Atheneum.

Seventh Royale. Donald Stanwood. 448p. 1988. pap. 4.50 (ISBN 0-440-17750-2). Dell.

Seventh Sanctuary. Daniel Easterman. LC 86-19880. 456p. 1987. 17.95 (ISBN 0-385-19814-0). Doubleday.

Seventh Sanctuary. Daniel Easterman. 608p. 1988. pap. 4.50 (ISBN 0-8217-2451-7). Zebra.

Seventh Secret. Irving Wallace. 1986. pap. 4.95 (ISBN 0-451-14557-7, Sig). NAL.

Seventh Secret. Irving Wallace. (Large Print Bks (Special Editions)). 515p. 1986. lib. bdg. 19.95 (ISBN 0-8161-4148-7). G K Hall.

Seventh Sense. Paul Economos. (Illus.). 24p. 1981. pap. 3.00 (ISBN 0-932662-36-6). St Andrews NC.

Seventh Sense: A Study of Francis Hutcheson's Aesthetics & Its Influence in Eighteenth Century Britain. Peter Kivy. 241p. 1976. lib. bdg. 19.95 (ISBN 0-89102-044-6). B Franklin.

Seventh Sense: Reflections on Learning to Learn. J. Nisbet & J. Shucksmith. 82p. 1984. pap. text ed. 6.95x (ISBN 0-947833-00-5, Pub. by Scot Council Research). Humanities.

Seventh Sinner. Elizabeth Peters. 256p. 1986. pap. 3.95 (ISBN 0-445-40225-3). Mysterious Pr.

Seventh Sister. Lou Graham. 480p. (Orig.). 1985. pap. 3.95 (ISBN 0-8439-2266-4, Leisure Bks). Leisure NY.

Seventh Solitude: Metaphysical Homelessness in Kierkegaard, Dostoevsky, & Nietzsche. Ralph Harper. LC 65-11662. 163p. 1965. pap. 6.95x (ISBN 0-8018-0257-1). Johns Hopkins.

Seventh Son. Orson S. Card. LC 86-51490. (Tales of Alvin Maker Ser.: Vol. I). 1987. 17.95 (ISBN 0-312-93019-4). St Martin.

Seventh Son. Orson S. Card. 256p. 1988. pap. 3.95 (ISBN 0-8125-3353-4, Dist. by St Martin's Pr & Warner Pub Servs). Tor Bks.

Seventh Son. Orson S. Card. 256p. 1987. pap. 17.95. Tor Bks.

Seventh Station. Ralph McInerny. LC 77-77417. (Father Dowling Mystery Ser.). 224p. 1977. 14.95 (ISBN 0-8149-0787-3). Vanguard.

Seventh Stone. Warren Murphy & Richard Sapir. (Destroyer Ser.: No. 62). 1985. pap. 2.95 (ISBN 0-451-13756-6, Sig). NAL.

Seventh Swan. Nicholas S. Gray. (Magic Quest Ser.: No. 3). 208p. 1984. pap. 2.25 (ISBN 0-441-75955-6). Ace Bks.

Seventh Symposium on Biotechnology for Fuels & Chemicals. Ed. by Charles D. Scott. 741p. 1986. pap. 89.95 (ISBN 0-471-85103-5). Wiley.

Seventh Tennessee Cavalry. John P. Young. (Illus.). 1975. Repr. 17.50 (ISBN 0-89029-026-1). Pr of Morningside.

Seventh Trumpet. Mark Link. LC 78-53943. 1978. 9.95 (ISBN 0-89505-014-5). Tabor Pub.

Seventh Trumpet. Mark Link. 207p. (YA) (gr. 9-12). 1978. 16.95 (ISBN 0-89505-030-7). Tabor Pub.

Seventh Virginia Infantry. David Riggs. (Virginia Regimental Histories Ser.). (Illus.). 107p. 1982. 16.45 (ISBN 0-930919-02-5). H E Howard.

Seventh Workshop on Grand Unification: Proceedings of Workshop, Toyama, Japan, April 16-18, 1986. Ed. by J. Arafune. 572p. 1987. 71.00 (ISBN 9971-50-130-9); pap. 34.00 (ISBN 9971-50-131-7). World Scientific Pub.

Seventh World Congress on Animal, Plant & Microbial Toxins: Proceedings. Seventh International Symposium on Animal, Plant, & Microbial Toxins, Brisbane, Australia, 11-16 July, 1982 & R. Endean. (Illus.). 544p. 1983. pap. 120.00 (ISBN 0-08-029803-6). Pergamon.

Seventh Year: Industrial Civilization in Transition. W. Jackson Davis. (Illus.). 1979. 19.95 (ISBN 0-393-05693-7); pap. text ed. 7.95x (ISBN 0-393-09027-2). Norton.

Seventh Year of the Manna Bird. Lou Vertolli & Frederick Biro. (Eden Entertainment Ser.). 258p. (Orig.). Date not set. pap. 5.95 (ISBN 0-920792-76-0). Eden Pr.

Seventies. John Edwards. LC 80-54638. (History of the Modern World Ser.). 64p. (gr. 5 up). 14.96 (ISBN 0-382-06448-8). Silver.

Seventies: Counterfeit Decade. Herbert London. LC 79-65632. 1979. pap. text ed. 11.25 (ISBN 0-8191-0788-3). U Pr of Amer.

Seventies into Eighties: Printmaking Now. Clifford S. Ackley. Ed. by Cynthia Purvis. LC 86-62526. (Illus.). 32p. (Orig.). 1986. pap. 2.95 (ISBN 0-87846-277-5). Mus Fine Arts Boston.

Seventies No. 1: An Anthology of Leaping Poetry. Ed. by Robert Bly. pap. 10.00 (ISBN 0-685-31525-8). Eighties Pr.

Seventieth Steelmaking Conference Proceedings. 512p. 1987. 60.00 (ISBN 0-932897-20-7). Iron & Steel.

Seventrees. Janice Y. Brooks. 1986. pap. 3.95 (ISBN 0-451-14592-5, Sig). NAL.

Seventy Birth Control Clinics: A Survey & Analysis Including the General Effects of Control on Size & Quality of Population. Caroline H. Robinson. LC 71-169398. (Family in America Ser). 380p. 1972. Repr. of 1930 ed. 16.00 (ISBN 0-405-03875-5). Ayer Co Pubs.

Seventy Classic Quilting Patterns: Ready-to-Use Designs & Instructions. Gwen Marston & Joe Cunningham. (Illus.). 96p. (Orig.). 1987. pap. 4.50 (ISBN 0-486-25474-7). Dover.

Seventy-Eight Degrees of Wisdom, 2 pts. Pt. 1. pap. 8.99 (ISBN 0-85030-220-X, Pub. by Aquarium Pr in England); Pt. 2. pap. 9.99 (ISBN 0-85030-339-7). Sterling.

Severing the Cause; or, Wandering Mindless Through Reindeer Passes. Richard Boyles. 56p. 1975. 5.50 (ISBN 0-87881-022-6). Mojave Bks.

Severinis Graphic Work. Francesco Meloni. (Illus.). 218p. (Ital.). 1982. 125.00x (ISBN 1-55660-001-1). A Wofsy Fine Arts.

Severity Weighting of Data on Accidents Involving Consumer Products. (Document Ser.). 68p. 1979. 4.50x (ISBN 92-64-11980-9). OECD.

Severn & Avon. Lawrence Garner. (Vistor's Guide Ser.). (Illus.). 144p. (Orig.). 1986. pap. 8.95 (ISBN 0-935161-19-8). Hunter Pub NY.

Severn Barrage: Conference Proceedings. 246p. 1982. 50.00 (ISBN 0-7277-0156-8, Pub. by T Telford UK). Am Soc Civil Eng.

Severn Bore. Fred Rowbotham. (Illus.). 108p. 1983. 14.95 (ISBN 0-7153-8508-9). David & Charles.

Severn Enterprise. Christopher Jordan. 112p. 1985. 80.00x (ISBN 0-317-57716-6, Pub. by A H Stockwell England); pap. 22.00x (ISBN 0-7223-1536-8). State Mutual Bk.

Severo Bonini's Discorsi e Regole: A Bilingual Edition. Don Severo Bonini. Ed. & tr. by MaryAnn Bonino. LC 77-18514. (Illus.). 1979. text ed. 24.95x (ISBN 0-8425-0997-6). Brigham.

Severo Sarduy & the Religion of the Text. Rolando Perez. LC 87-37160. 50p. (Orig.). 1988. pap. text ed. 8.25 (ISBN 0-8191-6861-0). U Pr of Amer.

Severus Scroll & 1QISA. Jonathan P. Siegel. LC 75-28372. (Society of Biblical Literature, Masoretic Studies). 1975. pap. 8.95 (ISBN 0-89130-028-7, 060502). Scholars Pr GA.

Sevilla of Carmen. Robert Vavra. (Illus.). 196p. 1985. 29.95 (ISBN 0-688-05880-9). Morrow.

Sevilla, 5-I-43 & Paris N. A. Frc. 439. Ed. by Dragan Plamenac. (Veroffentlichungzen Mittlelalterlicher Musikhandschriften-Publications of Mediaeval Musical Manuscripts: Vol. 8). (Eng. & Ger.). 1964. pap. 36.00 (ISBN 0-912024-08-9). Inst Mediaeval Mus.

Sevka Wants to Live Somewhere Else. G. Yurmin. 18p. 1975. pap. 0.99 (ISBN 0-8285-1225-6, Pub. by Progress Pubs USSR). Imported Pubns.

Sevres Egyptian Service: 1810-12. Charles Truman. (Orig.). pap. 7.95 (ISBN 0-905209-24-9, Pub. by Victoria & Albert Mus UK). Faber & Faber.

Sevres Porcelain: Makers & Marks of the Eighteenth Century. Carl C. Dauterman. (Illus.). 264p. 1986. 45.00 (ISBN 0-87099-227-9). Metro Mus Art.

Sevres Porcelain: Vincennes & Sevres 1740-1800. Svend Erikson & Geoffrey De Bellaigue. (Illus.). 320p. 1986. 135.00 (ISBN 0-571-09354-X). Faber & Faber.

Sevukakmet: Ways of Life on St. Lawrence Island. Helen S. Carius. (Alaskana Book Ser.: No. 36). 56p. (Orig.). 1979. pap. 9.95 (ISBN 0-935094-00-8). Alaska Pacific.

Sew a Beautiful Gift. Claire B. Shaeffer. LC 86-1796. (Illus.). 200p. (Orig.). 1986. pap. 12.95 (ISBN 0-8069-6314-X). Sterling.

Sew a Beautiful Wedding. Karen Dillon & Gail Brown. 1980. pap. 6.95 (ISBN 0-935278-05-2). Palmer-Pletsch.

Sew & Know: Puppet Projects to Teach Beginning Sounds. Esther Hornnes & Eunice Magos. Ed. by Ellen Sussman. (Illus.). 32p. (Orig.). (gr. k-1). 1982. pap. 4.95 (ISBN 0-933606-16-8, MS-614). Monkey Sisters.

Sew & Know: Puppet Projects to Teach numbers, 1-12. Esther Hornnes & Eunice Magos. Ed. by Ellen Sussman. (Illus.). 28p. (Orig.). (gr. k-1). 1982. pap. text ed. 4.95 (ISBN 0-933606-17-6, MS-615). Monkey Sisters.

Sew & Know: Puppet Projects to Teach Vowel Sounds. Esther Hornnes & Eunice Magos. Ed. by Ellen Sussman. (Illus.). 40p. (Orig.). (gr. k-2). 1984. pap. text ed. 4.95 (ISBN 0-933606-29-X, MS-628). Monkey Sisters.

Sew & Save Source Book: Your Guide to Supplies for Creative Sewing. Margaret A. Boyd. LC 83-11888. (Illus.). 216p. (Orig.). 1984. pap. 9.95 (ISBN 0-932620-23-X). Betterway Pubns.

Sew Big: A Fashion Guide for the Fuller Figure. rev. ed. Marilyn Thelen. (Illus.). 128p. 1981. pap. 6.95 (ISBN 0-935278-06-0). Palmer-Pletsch.

Sew-Fit Manual. Ruth Oblander et al. LC 77-84538. (Illus.). 1978. 26.95x (ISBN 0-933956-03-7). Sew-Fit.

Sew for Toddlers. Kerstin Martensson. (Illus.). 1979. pap. 8.95 (ISBN 0-913212-08-3). Kwik Sew.

Sew It Yourself Home Decorating. LC 84-9358. (Illus.). 168p. 1984. 19.95 (ISBN 0-668-06247-9, 6247). Arco.

Sew It Yourself Home Decorating: Creative Ideas for Beautiful Interiors. (Illus.). 168p. 1986. pap. 14.95 (ISBN 0-13-807264-7). P-H.

Sew Romantic. Ruth Seeley-Scheel. (Illus.). 1988. pap. 6.95 (ISBN 0-9619815-3-9). Laugh Goose.

Sew Simply, Sew Right. Mini Rhea & Frances Leighton. LC 72-76031. (Illus.). 1969. 10.95 (ISBN 0-8303-0069-4). Fleet.

Sew Smart with Ultra Suede Fabric & Other Luxury Suedes. Judy Lawrence & Clotilde Yurick. (Illus.). 106p. 1981. pap. 5.95x (ISBN 0-9605860-0-8). Sewing Knits.

Sew Special. Susan A. Grosskopf. (Illus.). 52p. 1984. pap. 6.00 (ISBN 0-943574-25-0). That Patchwork.

Sew Successfully with Style. Leila Aitken. (Illus.). 96p. (Orig.). 1987. pap. 11.95 (ISBN 0-8069-6634-3). Sterling.

Sew Wonderful Gourmet Garments. Cheryl Arrants. Ed. by Kristi St. Amant. (Illus.). 96p. (Orig.). 1982. pap. text ed. 6.95 (ISBN 0-943704-01-4). Arrants & Assoc.

Sew Wonderful Silk: The Guide to Gourmet Sewing with Silk & Silk-like Fabrics. rev. ed. Cheryl Arrants & Jan Asbjornsen. Ed. by Kristi Amant. (Illus.). 128p. 1981. pap. text ed. 5.95 (ISBN 0-943704-02-2). Arrants & Assoc.

Sew Your Own Outdoor Wear & Gear: Expert Tips on Today's Materials, Design & Construction Techniques. Louise Sumner. (Illus.). 160p. (Orig.). 1988. pap. 14.95 (ISBN 0-89886-057-1). Mountaineers.

Sewage District Superintendent. (Career Examination Ser.: C-3343). Date not set. pap. 18.00 (ISBN 0-8373-3343-1). Natl Learning.

Sewage Organisms: A Color Atlas. J. Carl Fox et al. (Illus.). 116p. 1981. 79.95 (ISBN 0-87371-031-2). Lewis Pubs Inc.

Sewage Plant Operator. Jack Rudman. (Career Examination Ser.: C-2443). (Cloth bdg. avail. on request). pap. 14.00 (ISBN 0-8373-2443-2). Natl Learning.

Sewage Plant Operator Trainee. Jack Rudman. (Career Examination Ser.: C-2281). (Cloth bdg. avail. on request). 1988. pap. 12.00 (ISBN 0-8373-2281-2). Natl Learning.

Sewage Pump Operator. Jack Rudman. (Career Examination Ser.: C-3018). (Cloth bdg. avail. on request). 1988. pap. 16.00 (ISBN 0-8373-3018-1). Natl Learning.

Sewage Sludge Treatment & Disposal. R. W. James. LC 76-17939. (Pollution Technology Review: No. 29). (Illus.). 339p. 1977. 39.00 (ISBN 0-8155-0630-9). Noyes.

Sewage Treatment Construction Grants Manual. BNA's Environment & Safety Services Staff. looseleaf 424.00. BNA.

Sewage Treatment Operator. Jack Rudman. (Career Examination Ser.: C-1488). (Cloth bdg. avail. on request). pap. 14.00 (ISBN 0-8373-1488-7). Natl Learning.

Sewage Treatment Operator Trainee. Jack Rudman. (Career Examination Ser.: C-1489). (Cloth bdg. avail. on request). pap. 12.00 (ISBN 0-8373-1489-5). Natl Learning.

Sewage Treatment Plant Supervisor. Jack Rudman. (Career Examination Ser.: C-1490). (Cloth bdg. avail. on request). pap. 14.00 (ISBN 0-8373-1490-9). Natl Learning.

Sewage Treatment Worker. Jack Rudman. (Career Examination Ser.: C-734). (Cloth bdg. avail. on request). pap. 14.00 (ISBN 0-8373-0734-1). Natl Learning.

Sewage Treatment Worker Trainee. Jack Rudman. (Career Examination Ser.: C-735). (Cloth bdg. avail. on request). pap. 12.00 (ISBN 0-8373-0735-X). Natl Learning.

Sewall Wright & Evolutionary Biology. William B. Provine. LC 85-24651. (Illus.). xvi, 546p. 1986. lib. bdg. 30.00x (ISBN 0-226-68474-1). U of Chicago Pr.

Sewanee. William A. Percy. LC 82-60214. (Illus.). 40p. 1982. 12.95 (ISBN 0-913720-37-2). Beil.

Sewanee. William A. Percy. 14p. 1968. pap. 15.00 (ISBN 0-918769-04-3). Univ South.

Sewanee in Ruins. Richard Tillinghast. 39p. 1983. pap. 15.00 (ISBN 0-918769-05-1). Univ South.

Sewanee Review: A Forty-Year Index. Mary Lucia Snyder & Cornelius Engsberg. 200p. 1983. 45.00 (ISBN 0-938734-06-7). Learned Info.

Sewanee-the University of the South. William Strode. (Illus.). 96p. 1984. 30.00 (ISBN 0-916509-01-X). Harmony Hse Pub Lo.

Seward, Alaska, a History of the Gateway City, Volume 1: Prehistory to 1914, Vol. 1 of 2. Mary J. Barry. LC 86-71202. (Illus.). 182p. (Orig.). 1987. pap. 25.00 (ISBN 0-9617009-0-4). M J P Barry.

Sewer Charges for Wastewater Collection & Treatment. 46p. (Orig.). 1982. pap. 9.00 (ISBN 0-943244-39-0). Water Pollution.

Sewer, Class. 138p. 1984. loose-leaf ed. 12.00 (ISBN 0-318-15027-1). NARUC.

Sewer Inspector. Jack Rudman. (Career Examination Ser.: C-2454). (Cloth bdg. avail. on request). pap. 14.00 (ISBN 0-8373-2454-8). Natl Learning.

Sewer Socialists: A History of the Socialist Party of Wisconsin, 1897-1940, 2 Vols. Ed. by Elmer A. Beck & John Westburg. Incl. Vol. 1. The Socialist Trinity of the Party, the Unions & the Press. 204p; Vol. 2. The Nineteen Twenties & Nineteen Thirties. (Illus.). 168p. LC 82-70072. (Illus.). 1982. Set. pap. 20.00 (ISBN 0-87423-031-4). Westburg.

Sewerage & Sewage Treatment: International Practice. Leonard B. Escritt. LC 83-1300. 450p. 1984. 79.95x (ISBN 0-471-10339-X, Pub. by Wiley-Interscience). Wiley.

Sewering the Cities: An Original Anthology. Ed. by Barbara G. Rosenkrantz. LC 76-40352. (Public Health in America Ser.). (Illus.). 1977. Repr. of 1977 ed. lib. bdg. 20.00x (ISBN 0-405-09879-0). Ayer Co Pubs.

Sewing. Linda Gong & Susan Echaore-Yoon. (Home Economics in Action Ser.). (Illus.). 80p. (YA) (gr. 7-12). 1988. 14.95 (ISBN 0-88102-109-1); 3-ring bdg. 4.95 (ISBN 0-88102-110-5). Janus Bks.

Sewing Activewear. Cy DeCosse Inc. Staff. LC 85-29362. (Singer Sewing Reference Library). (Illus.). 128p. 1986. 14.95 (ISBN 0-86573-211-6); pap. 11.95 (ISBN 0-86573-212-4). Cy De Cosse.

Sewing As a Home Business. Mary A. Roehr. (Illus.). 135p. (Orig.). 1987. pap. 11.95 (ISBN 0-9619229-2-3). M Roehr Cust Tailor.

Sewing As a Home or Small Business - Possibilities. Carrol, Frieda, Research Division Staff. 1984. pap. text ed. 3.25 (ISBN 0-910811-65-2). Prosperity & Profits.

Sewing Classic Clothes for Children. Kitty Benton. 160p. 1981. 20.50 (ISBN 0-87851-204-7). Hearst Bks.

Sewing Easy Garments Without a Pattern. Carol Handley Little. (Illus.). 160p. 1985. 18.95 (ISBN 0-9613962-1-0). Cal Creative Pubns.

Sewing Essentials. Cy De Cosse Inc. Staff. LC 84-42637. (Singer Sewing Reference Library). (Illus.). 128p. 1984. 14.95 (ISBN 0-86573-201-9); pap. 11.95 (ISBN 0-86573-202-7). Cy De Cosse.

Sewing Essentials. LC 84-42637. (Illus.). 17.45 (ISBN 0-394-54051-4); pap. 9.95 (ISBN 0-394-72757-6). Random.

Sewing Etc. Donna L. Salyers. Ed. by Lynda Watcke. LC 84-40063. (Illus.). 120p. (Orig.). 1984. pap. 14.95 (ISBN 0-916525-00-7). A Scott Pub Co.

Sewing for Baby. Kerstin Martensson. (Illus.). 128p. 1987. pap. 11.95 (ISBN 0-913212-10-5). Kwik Sew.

Sewing for Children. Cy DeCosse Incorporated Staff. (Singer Sewing Reference Library). (Illus.). 128p. 1988. 14.95 (ISBN 0-86573-243-4); pap. 11.95 (ISBN 0-86573-244-2). Cy De Cosse.

Sewing for Fashion Design. reference ed. Nurie Relis & Gail Strauss. (Illus.). 1978. write for info. (ISBN 0-87909-755-8, Reston). P-H.

Sewing for Profits. rev. ed. Judith Smith & Allan Smith. (Illus.). 150p. 1984. pap. 10.00 (ISBN 0-931113-01-6). Success Publ.

Sewing for Style. Cy De Cosse Inc. Staff. LC 85-13074. (Singer Sewing Reference Library). (Illus.). 128p. 1985. 14.95 (ISBN 0-86573-207-8); pap. 11.95 (ISBN 0-86573-208-6). Cy De Cosse.

Sewing for Style: Details & Techniques Beyond the Basics. (Singer Reference Library). 1985. pap. 11.95 (ISBN 0-394-73411-4). Random.

Sewing for the Home. Cy De Cosse Inc. Staff. LC 84-42638. (Singer Sewing Reference Library). (Illus.). 128p. 1984. 14.95 (ISBN 0-86573-203-5); pap. 11.95 (ISBN 0-86573-204-3). Cy De Cosse.

Sewing Machine. Beatrice Siegel. LC 83-40397. (Inventions That Changed Our Lives Ser.). 64p. (gr. 5 up). 1984. PLB 10.85 (ISBN 0-8027-6532-7). Walker & Co.

Sewing Machine Handbook. Peter Lucking. (Illus.). 112p. 1986. 11.95 (ISBN 0-668-06556-7); pap. 6.95 (ISBN 0-668-06562-1). Arco.

Sewing Machine: Its Invention & Development. Grace R. Cooper. LC 75-619415. (Illus.). 238p. 1977. 29.95x (ISBN 0-87474-330-3, COIS). Smithsonian.

Sewing No-No's & Know Hows. Mary J. Wadlington. LC 83-20782. (Illus.). 136p. 1983. pap. 7.95 (ISBN 0-941832-01-5). Gem Pubns.

Sewing Publications, Pattern Companies, Fabric Outlets, Etc. A How to Find or Locate Guide. Center for Self Sufficiency, Research Division Staff. LC 83-90722. 60p. 1983. pap. text ed. 3.95 (ISBN 0-910811-30-X, Pub. by Center Self Suff). Prosperity & Profits.

Sewing Sculpture: Sewn Art in Three Dimensions. Charlene Kinser. LC 76-56736. (Illus.). 144p. 1977. 12.50 (ISBN 0-87131-215-8); pap. 6.95 o. p. (ISBN 0-87131-236-0). M Evanș.

Sewing Skinner Ultrasuede Fabric. rev. ed. Pati Palmer & Susan Pletsch. LC 76-151841. 1976. pap. 4.95 (ISBN 0-935278-01-X). Palmer-Pletsch.

Sewing Specialty Fabrics. Cy De Cosse Inc. Staff. LC 85-13050. (Singer Sewing Reference Library). (Illus.). 128p. 1986. 14.95 (ISBN 0-86573-209-4); pap. 11.95 (ISBN 0-86573-210-8). Cy De Cosse.

Sewing Specialty Fabrics. The Singer Sewing Co. LC 85-13050. (Illus.). 128p. 1986. 10.95 (ISBN 0-394-74416-0). Random.

Sewing Update 1988. Cy DeCosse Inc. Staff. LC 87-27284. (Singer Sewing Reference Library) (Illus.). 128p. 1988. 14.95 (ISBN 0-86573-237-X); pap. 11.95 (ISBN 0-86573-238-8). Cy De Cosse.

Sewing Update, 1989. Cy DeCosse Incorporated Staff. (Singer Sewing Reference Library). (Illus.). 128p. 1989. 14.95 (ISBN 0-86573-245-0); pap. 11.95 (ISBN 0-86573-246-9). Cy De Cosse.

Sewing with Scraps. Phyllis Guth & Georgeanna Goff. (Illus.). (YA) (gr. 10 up). 1977. pap. 6.95 (ISBN 0-8306-6878-0, 878). TAB Bks.

Sewing with Sergers: The Complete Handbook for Overlock Sewing. Gail Brown & Pati Palmer. LC 85-60347. (Illus.). 128p. (Orig.). 1985. pap. 6.95 (ISBN 0-935278-11-7). Palmer-Pletsch.

Sewing Without Pins. Ruth Oblander. LC 76-53269. 1986. 4.95 (ISBN 0-933956-01-0). Sew-Fit.

Sex. J. G. Bennett. 128p. 1981. pap. 4.95 (ISBN 0-87728-533-0). Weiser.

Sex: A User's Manual. The Diagram Group. 352p. 1988. pap. 4.95 (ISBN 0-425-08972-X). Berkley Pub.

Sex: A User's Manual. The Diagram Group. (Illus.). 196p. 1981. pap. 9.95 (ISBN 0-399-50517-2, Perigee). Putnam Pub Group.

Sex: A User's Manual. Diagram Group. (Illus.). 192p. 1987. pap. 10.95 (ISBN 0-399-51353-1, Perigee). Putnam Pub Group.

Sex Abuse Legitimacy Scale (Sal Scale) Richard A. Gardner. 8p. 1987. 12.50 (ISBN 0-933812-19-1). Creative Therapeutics.

Sex, Age & Work: The Changing Composition of the Labor Force. Juanita Kreps & Robert Clark. LC 75-34452. (Policy Studies in Employment & Welfare: No. 23). (Illus.). 108p. 1976. 12.50x (ISBN 0-8018-1806-0). Johns Hopkins.

Sex & Advantage: A Comparative, Macro-Structural Theory of Sex Stratification. Janet S. Chafetz. LC 83-19077. 142p. 1984. 23.50x (ISBN 0-86598-159-0, Rowman & Allanheld); pap. 11.95x (ISBN 0-86598-161-2). Rowman.

Sex & Age As Principles of Social Differentiation. Ed. by J. S. LaFontaine. (ASA Monograph). 1978. 36.00 (ISBN 0-12-433050-9). Acad Pr.

Sex & All You Can Eat. Louise D. Campanelli. 1975. 7.95 (ISBN 0-8184-0202-4). Lyle Stuart.

Sex & Behavior: Status & Prospect. T. E. McGill et al. LC 77-17840. (Illus.). 458p. 1978. 55.00x (ISBN 0-306-31084-8, Plenum Pr). Plenum Pub.

Sex & Birth Control: A Guide for the Young. rev. ed. E. J. Lieberman & Ellen Peck. LC 81-16674. 304p. (Orig.). (gr. 9-12). 1982. pap. 4.95 (ISBN 0-8052-0701-5). Schocken.

Sex & Broadcasting: A Handbook on Building a Radio Station for the Community. Lorenzo W. Milam. (Illus.). 375p. 1988. pap. 12.95 (ISBN 0-917320-01-8). Mho & Mho.

Sex & Character. Otto Weininger. LC 72-11295. Repr. of 1906 ed. 40.00 (ISBN 0-404-57507-2). AMS Pr.

Sex & Character: The Intimate Psychology of Males & Females, 2 vols. Otto Weininger. (Illus.). 411p. 1988. 187.50 (ISBN 0-89920-192-X). Am Inst Psych.

Sex & Character: The Laws of Male & Female Psychology, 2 vols. Otto Weininger. (Illus.). 375p. 1988. Set. 227.45 (ISBN 0-89266-630-7). Am Classical Coll Pr.

Sex & Circumstance: Humanity in History Ser. Robert B. Greemblatt. LC 86-27728. (Illus.). 339p. 1987. 14.95 (ISBN 0-933703-36-8). Loiry Pubs Hse.

Sex & Class in Women's History. Ed. by Judith L. Newton et al. (History Workshop Ser.). (Illus.). 224p. 1983. pap. 9.95x (ISBN 0-7100-9529-5). Routledge Chapman & Hall.

Sex & Death to the Age Fourteen. Spalding Gray. LC 85-40682. 272p. 1986. pap. 6.95 (ISBN 0-394-74257-5, Vin). Random.

Sex & Disease in a Mountain Community. Paul Hockings. 1980. 15.00x (ISBN 0-8364-0625-7). South Asia Bks.

Sex & Drugs. M. Laurence Lieberman. 1987. pap. 12.95 (ISBN 0-452-26004-3, Plume). NAL.

Sex & Drugs. 2nd ed. Robert A. Wilson. 220p. 1987. pap. 9.95 (ISBN 0-941404-48-X). Falcon Pr Az.

Sex & Education: A Reply to Dr. E. H. Clarke's Sex in Education, Ed. by Julia W. Howe. LC 72-2608. (American Women Ser: Images & Realities). 208p. 1972. Repr. of 1874 ed. 16.00 (ISBN 0-405-04463-1). Ayer Co Pubs.

Sex & Enlightenment: Women in Richardson & Diderot. Rita Goldberg. LC 83-23210. 264p. 1984. 44.50 (ISBN 0-521-26069-8). Cambridge U Pr.

Sex & Equality: An Original Anthology. Ed. by Annette K. Baxter. LC 74-3972. (Women in America Ser). 220p. 1974. Repr. of 1974 ed. 20.00x (ISBN 0-405-06121-8). Ayer Co Pubs.

Sex & Evolution. George C. Williams. LC 74-2985. (Monographs in Population Biology: No. 8). 200p. 1974. 32.00x (ISBN 0-691-08147-6); pap. 13.95 (ISBN 0-691-08152-2). Princeton U Pr.

Sex & Friendship in Baboons. Barbara B. Smuts. (Biological Foundations of Human Behavior Ser.). (Illus.). 320p. 1985. lib. bdg. 39.95x (ISBN 0-202-02027-4). Aldine de Gruyter.

Sex & Gender. John Archer & Barbara Lloyd. (Illus.). 228p. 1985. 39.50 (ISBN 0-521-26497-9); pap. 11.95 (ISBN 0-521-31921-8). Cambridge U Pr.

Sex & Gender. Ed. by Phillip Shaver & Clyde Hendrick. (Review of Personality & Social Psychology Ser.: Vol. 7). (Illus.). 328p. (Orig.). 1987. text ed. 35.00 (ISBN 0-8039-2929-3); pap. text ed. 16.95 (ISBN 0-8039-2930-7). Sage.

Sex & Gender: A Theological & Scientific Inquiry. Ed. by Mark F. Schwartz et al. 385p. (Orig.). 1984. pap. 19.95 (ISBN 0-935372-13-X). Pope John Ctr.

Sex & Gender: An Introduction. Hilary Lips. 416p. 1988. pap. text ed. 22.95 (ISBN 0-87484-764-8). Mayfield Pub.

Sex and Gender in the Social Sciences: Reassessing the Introductory Courses. Judith Gappa & Janice Pearce. 176p. 1982. 10.50 (ISBN 0-317-36342-5). Am Sociological.

Sex & Gender: The Human Experience. James A. Doyle. 432p. 1985. pap. text ed. write for info. (ISBN 0-697-00304-3); instr's. manual avail. (ISBN 0-697-00571-2). Wm C Brown.

Sex & Generation. Diana Leonard. LC 79-40816. 315p. 1982. (Pub. by Tavistock England); pap. 12.95x (ISBN 0-422-78220-3, NO. 3691). Routledge Chapman & Hall.

Sex Differences in the Professional Life Changes of Chemists. Barbara F. Reskin. Ed. by Harriet Zuckerman & Robert K. Merton. LC 79-9041. (Dissertations on Sociology Ser.). 1980. lib. bdg. 40.00x (ISBN 0-405-12987-4). Ayer Co Pubs.

Sex Differentiation & Chromosomal Abnormalities. Ed. by Robert Summit & Daniel Bergsma. (Alan R. Liss, Inc. Ser.: Vol. 14, No. 6c). 1978. 61.00 (ISBN 0-686-23951-2). March of Dimes.

Sex Differentiation & Chromosomal Abnormalities see Annual Review of Birth Defects, 1977: Proceedings of the Birth Defects Annual Conference, 10th, Memphis, Tenn., June, 1977.

Sex Differentiation & Schooling. Ed. by Michael Marland. (Organization in Schools Ser.). vi, 250p. 1984. text ed. 27.50x (ISBN 0-435-80592-4). Heinemann Ed.

Sex Directory. Compiled by Ann Darnbrough & Derek Kinrade. 224p. 1985. 21.50 (ISBN 0-85941-162-1, Pub. by Woodhead-Faulkner); pap. 15.95 (ISBN 0-85941-163-X). Longwood Pub Group.

Sex Discrimination: Adaptable to Courses Utilizing Babcock, Freedman, Norton & Ross Casebook on Sex Discrimination & the Law. Casebooks Publishing Co., Inc. Staff. Ed. by Norman S. Goldenberg et al. (Legal Briefs Ser.). 1979. pap. write for info. (ISBN 0-87457-125-1, 1530). Casenotes Pub.

Sex Discrimination & Equal Opportunity: The Labor Market & Employment Policy. Ed. by Gunther Schmid & Renate Weitzel. LC 84-11450. 320p. 1984. 29.95 (ISBN 0-312-71333-9). St Martin.

Sex Discrimination & Law: A Selected Bibliography. Dittakavi N. Rao. (Public Administration Series: Bibliography: No. P 1830). 1985. pap. 3.75 (ISBN 0-89028-680-9). Vance Biblios.

Sex Discrimination & the Law in Hawaii: A Guide to Your Legal Rights. Judith Gething. LC 78-10636. 122p. 1979. pap. 3.95 (ISBN 0-8248-0620-4). UH Pr.

Sex Discrimination & the Law (1975) Causes & Remedies. Barbara A. Babcock & Ann. E. Freedman. 1092p. 1975. 35.00 (ISBN 0-316-07420-9); Supplement, 1978. pap. 7.95 (ISBN 0-316-07421-7). Little.

Sex Discrimination in a Nutshell. Claire S. Thomas. LC 82-2657. (Nutshell Ser.). 399p. 1982. pap. text ed. 9.95 (ISBN 0-314-65663-4). West Pub.

Sex Discrimination in Educational Employment: Legal Alternatives & Strategies. Cynthia Stoddard. LC 80-82019. 125p. 1981. text ed. 11.95x (ISBN 0-918452-26-0); pap. 8.95 (ISBN 0-918452-27-9). Learning Pubns.

Sex Discrimination in Higher Education: Strategies for Equality. Ed. by Jennie Farley. LC 81-9604. 168p. 1981. pap. 7.50 (ISBN 0-87546-089-5). ILR Pr.

Sex Discrimination Law. Evelyn Ellis. 1988. text ed. 45.00x (ISBN 0-566-05355-1, Pub. by Gower Pub England). Gower Pub Co.

Sex Discrimination Law. David Pannick. 288p. 1986. 55.00x (ISBN 0-19-825481-4). Oxford U Pr.

Sex Discrimination Law in Higher Education: The Lessons of the Past Decade. J. Ralph Lindgren et al. Ed. by Jonathan D. Fife. LC 84-72774. (ASHE-ERIC Higher Education Report Ser.: No. 4, 1984). 85p. (Orig.). 1984. pap. 7.50x (ISBN 0-913317-13-6). Assn Study Higher Ed.

Sex Discrimination Law of the European Community. Sacha Prechal & N. Burrows. 1988. text ed. 60.00 (ISBN 0-566-05365-9, Pub. by Gower Pub England). Gower Pub Co.

Sex Disorders: Medical Subject Analysis & Research Guidebook with Bibliography. American Health Research Institute Staff. Ed. by John C. Bartone. LC 84-45866. 150p. 1987. 34.50 (ISBN 0-88164-288-6); pap. 26.50 (ISBN 0-88164-289-4). ABBE Pubs Assn.

Sex, Drink & Fast Cars. Stephen Bayley. LC 86-42976. (Illus.). 192p. 1987. 7.95 (ISBN 0-394-75046-2). Pantheon.

Sex, Drugs & AIDS. Oralee Wachter. LC 87-977. 80p. 1987. pap. 3.95 (ISBN 0-553-34454-4). Bantam.

Sex, Drugs, Death & the Law: An Essay on Human Rights & Overcriminalization. David A. Richards. LC 81-23392. (Philosphy & Society Ser.). 328p. 1982. 28.95 (ISBN 0-8476-7063-5). Rowman.

Sex During Pregnancy & after Childbirth. Sylvia Close. LC 86-34326. 144p. 1986. Repr. of 1984 ed. lib. bdg. 19.95x (ISBN 0-8095-7032-7). Borgo Pr.

Sex Education. Julie Becker. 1983. pap. 12.50x (ISBN 0-931460-26-3). Bieler.

Sex Education. Jenny Davis. LC 87-30441. 160p. (YA) (gr. 7 up). 1988. 13.95 (ISBN 0-531-05756-9); PLB 13.99 (ISBN 0-531-08356-X). Orchard Bks Watts.

Sex Education. U. Shankar & L. Shankar. 1978. 15.00 (ISBN 0-89684-529-X). Orient Bk Dist.

Sex Education & Counseling of Special Groups: The Mentally & Physically Disabled, Ill & Elderly. 2nd ed. Warren R. Johnson & Winifred Kempton. 274p. 1981. 27.25x (ISBN 0-398-04501-1). C C Thomas.

Sex Education & Counselling for Mentally Handicapped People. Ed. by Ann Craft & Michael Craft. LC 82-50831. 322p. 1983. pap. 21.00x (ISBN 0-8391-1773-6, 1252). Pro Ed.

Sex Education & Family Life for Visually Hanicapped Children & Youth: A Resource Guide. Ed. by Irving R. Dickman. pap. 24.00 (2027352). Bks Demand UMI.

Sex Education Books for Young Adults, 1892-1979. Patricia J. Campbell. LC 79-1535. 1979. 24.95 (ISBN 0-8352-1157-6). Bowker.

Sex Education for Adolescents: A Bibliography of Low Cost Materials. Young Adult Services Division. 32p. 1980. pap. 3.00x (ISBN 0-8389-3248-7). ALA.

Sex Education for Physically Handicapped Youth. C. Edmund Hopper & William A. Allen. (Illus.). 154p. 1980. pap. 15.75 (ISBN 0-398-03935-6). C C Thomas.

Sex Education for the Health Professional: A Curriculum Guide. Ed. by Norman Rosenzweig & F. Paul Pearsall. (Seminars in Psychiatry Ser.). 352p. 1978. 44.50 (ISBN 0-8089-1100-7, 793645). Grune.

Sex Education for the Visually Handicapped in Schools & Agencies: Selected Papers. 76p. 1975. pap. 5.00 (ISBN 0-89128-071-5, PEP071). Am Foun Blind.

Sex Education in a Church Setting: The OCTOPUS Training Manual. Fred Isberner et al. 128p. (Orig.). 1986. pap. text ed. 9.95x (ISBN 0-8093-1315-4). S Ill U Pr.

Sex Education in the Classroom. J. C. Willke & Mrs. Willke. 1977. 4.95 (ISBN 0-910728-11-9). Hayes.

Sex Education in the Eighties: The Challenge of Healthy Sexual Evolution. Ed. by Lorna Brown. LC 81-15738. (Perspectives in Sexuality Ser.). 278p. 1981. 35.00x (ISBN 0-306-40762-0, Plenum Pr). Plenum Pub.

Sex Education in the Public Schools. 124p. (Reprint from Journal of School Health). 1981. 5.50 (ISBN 0-317-33171-X). Am Sch Health.

Sex Education: Index of Modern Information. Peter J. Kasnevitch. LC 88-47622. 150p. 1988. 34.50 (ISBN 0-88164-756-X); pap. 26.50 (ISBN 0-88164-757-8). ABBE Pubs Assn.

Sex Education Is for the Family. Tim LaHaye. 192p. (gr. 9-12). 1985. 12.95 (ISBN 0-310-27010-3, 18343). Zondervan.

Sex Education on Film: A Guide to Visual Aids & Programs. Laura J. Singer & Judith Buskin. LC 75-154694. pap. 44.00 (2026230). Bks Demand UMI.

Sex Education: Political Issues in Britain & Europe. Philip Meredith & Alan Beattie. 250p. 1988. lib. bdg. 49.95 (ISBN 0-415-00604-X). Routledge Chapman & Hall.

Sex Education, Rationale & Reaction. Ed. by Rex S. Rogers. LC 73-89764. pap. 73.80 (ISBN 0-317-26377-3, 2024519). Bks Demand UMI.

Sex Education: Syllabus. Lester A. Kirkendall & Ruth F. Osborne. 1971. pap. text ed. 4.65 (ISBN 0-89420-087-9, 216786); cassette recordings 82.60 (ISBN 0-89420-184-0, 180800). Natl Book.

Sex Education: Teacher's Guide & Resource Manual. Rev. ed. Steven Bignell. Ed. by Jane Hiatt & Mary Nelson. 277p. 1982. 29.95 (ISBN 0-941816-08-7); avail. tchr's guide (ISBN 0-941816-03-6). Network Pubns.

Sex Education Within the Family. Ed. by David M. Thomas. LC 80-69136. (Marriage & Family Living in Depth Bk.). 80p. 1980. pap. 2.45 (ISBN 0-87029-171-8, 20248-1). Abbey.

Sex Energy: The Sexual Force in Man & Animals. Robert S. De Ropp. 1969. pap. 6.95 (ISBN 0-440-07818-0, Sey Lawr). Delacorte.

Sex Equity in Education: Readings & Strategies. Ed. by Anne O. Carelli. (Illus.). 412p. 1988. text ed. 42.75x (ISBN 0-398-05415-0). C C Thomas.

Sex Equity Strategies. 2nd ed. Louise Vetter et al. 192p. 1980. 11.00 (ISBN 0-318-22198-5, RD144). Natl Ctr Res Voc Ed.

Sex, Eros & Marital Love. Gerhard Gollwitzer. pap. 0.75 (ISBN 0-87785-104-2). Swedenborg.

Sex Errors of the Body: Dilemmas, Education, Counseling. Ed. by John Money. LC 68-15447. 145p. 1968. 16.50x (ISBN 0-8018-0467-1). Johns Hopkins.

Sex Ethics in the Writings of Moses Maimonides. Fred Rosner. LC 74-75479. 225p. 1974. 7.95x (ISBN 0-8197-0365-6). Bloch.

Sex Etiquette: Should I? Can I? May I? Must I? Or, The Modern Woman's Guide to Mating Manners. Marilyn Hamel. 254p. 1984. 13.95 (ISBN 0-385-29331-3). Delacorte.

Sex, Evolution, & Behavior. 2nd ed. Martin Daly & Margo Wilson. 402p. 1983. pap. text ed. write for info. (ISBN 0-87150-767-6). Wadsworth Pub.

Sex Factor & the Management of Schools. Neal Gross & Anne E. Trask. LC 75-34337. Repr. of 1976 ed. 71.50 (ISBN 0-8357-9977-8, 2055256). Bks Demand UMI.

Sex: Facts, Fantasy, Hogwash, & the Urologic Backwash. Harold Lipshutz. (Illus.). 192p. 1984. 10.95 (ISBN 0-8059-2897-9). Dorrance.

Sex Fair Career Counseling. Peggy Hawley. 58p. 1980. pap. text ed. 6.25 (ISBN 0-911547-66-5, 72195W34). Am Assn Coun Dev.

Sex, Family & the Woman in Society. Torkom Saraydarian. LC 86-71759. 1988. 25.00 (ISBN 0-911794-53-0); pap. 20.00 (ISBN 0-911794-54-9). Aqua Educ.

Sex for Beginners. Erroll Selkirk. (Writers & Readers Documentary Comics Ser.). (Illus., Orig.). 1987. pap. 7.95 (ISBN 0-86316-011-5). Writers & Readers.

Sex for Christians. Lewis B. Smedes. 176p. 1976. pap. 6.95 (ISBN 0-8028-1618-5). Eerdmans.

Sex for One: The Joy of Selfloving. Betty Dodson. (Illus.). 192p. 1987. 15.95 (ISBN 0-517-56676-1, Harmony). Crown.

Sex for the Common Man. LC 73-20654. 222p. 1974. Repr. 13.00x (ISBN 0-405-05819-5). Ayer Co Pubs.

Sex for the Handicapped Man: An Educational Booklet. Weldon L. Sutton. Ed. by Christine Merriman. (Illus.). 56p. 1981. self-help manual 15.00 (ISBN 0-686-36408-2). W Sutton.

Sex for Women Who Want to Have Fun & Loving Relationships with Equals. Carmen Kerr. LC 76-14509. 1977. pap. 7.95 (ISBN 0-394-17035-0, E705, Ever). Grove.

Sex from a Different Position. Cyrus Bass. 320p. (Orig.). 1984. pap. 11.00 (ISBN 0-915911-01-9). Publishers Assocs.

Sex Game: Communication Between the Sexes. Jessie Bernard. LC 68-13219. 1972. pap. 4.95 (ISBN 0-689-70293-0, 187). Atheneum.

Sex, Gender & Care Work. Ed. by Gordon Horobin. LC 87-9787. (Research Highlights in Social Work Ser.). 112p. 1987. 25.00 (ISBN 0-312-01141-5). St Martin.

Sex, Gender & Care Work. Ed. by Gordon Horobin. (Research Highlights in Social Work Ser.: No. 15). 180p. 1987. write for info. (ISBN 1-85302-001-X, HV41, Pub. by J Kingsley Pubs UK). UNIPUB.

Sex, Gender & Society. Ann Oakley. (Towards a New Society Ser.). 1985. pap. text ed. 10.95x (ISBN 0-85117-020-X, Pub. by Gower Pub England). Gower Pub Co.

Sex God's Creative Gift. Vickrey Dougherty. 216p. 1988. pap. 6.95 (ISBN 1-55523-155-1). Winston-Derek.

Sex Guides: Books & Films about Sexuality for Young Adults, 1986. Patty Campbell. write for info. (ISBN 0-8240-8693-7). Garland Pub.

Sex, Hormones & Behaviour. CIBA Foundation Staff. (CIBA Foundation Symposium: No. 62). 1979. 47.00 (ISBN 0-444-90045-4). Elsevier.

Sex, Hormones & Behaviour. Ciba Foundation Staff. (Ciba Foundation Symposium, New Ser.: 62). pap. 97.50 (ISBN 0-317-29765-1, 2022185). Bks Demand UMI.

Sex: Hot, Love: Warm. Jim DeWitt. (Illus.). 64p. (Orig.). 1978. pap. 3.95 (ISBN 0-915199-97-1). Pen-Dec.

SEX-I-CON! Poetry. Philip L. Sherrod. 81p. (Orig.). 1985. pap. 7.95 (ISBN 0-317-18741-4). Carrousel Pubns.

Sex, Ideology & Religion: The Representation of Women in the Bible. Kevin Harris. LC 84-12413. 144p. 1984. 22.50x (ISBN 0-389-20509-5, BNB08067). B&N Imports.

Sex in Civilization. Ed. by Victor F. Calverton & S. D. Schmalhausen. LC 72-9630. Repr. of 1929 ed. 75.00 (ISBN 0-404-57429-7). AMS Pr.

Sex in Development. Carney Landis. 232p. 1984. Repr. of 1940 ed. lib. bdg. 65.00 (ISBN 0-8495-3414-3). Arden Lib.

Sex in Education; or, a Fair Chance for the Girls. Edward Clarke. LC 74-180566. (Medicine & Society in America Ser.). 190p. 1972. Repr. of 1873 ed. 14.00 (ISBN 0-405-03943-3). Ayer Co Pubs.

Sex in Groups. J. N. Galena. 1974. pap. 1.25 (ISBN 0-685-51414-5, LB221ZK, Leisure Bks). Leisure NY.

Sex in Human Relationships. Magnus Hirschfeld. LC 72-9649. Repr. of 1935 ed. 39.00 (ISBN 0-404-57459-9). AMS Pr.

Sex in Industry: A Plea for the Working Girl. Azel Ames, Jr. Ed. by David J. Rothman & Sheila M. Rothman. (Women & Children First Ser.). 158p. 1986. lib. bdg. 25.00 (ISBN 0-8240-7650-8). Garland Pub.

Sex in Literature, Vol. 2. John Atkins. (Orig.). 1980. pap. 6.95 (ISBN 0-7145-1138-2). Riverrun NY.

Sex in Literature, Vol. 3. John Atkins. 1981. pap. 12.95 (ISBN 0-7145-3861-2); 25.00 (ISBN 0-7145-3668-7). Riverrun NY.

Sex in Literature, Vol. 1. John Atkins. (Orig.). 1981. pap. 9.95 (ISBN 0-7145-0523-4). Riverrun NY.

Sex in Literature, Vol. 4: The Eighteenth Century. John Atkins. 400p. (Orig.). 1982. pap. 12.95 (ISBN 0-7145-3977-5). Riverrun NY.

Sex in Middlesex: Popular Mores in a Massachusetts County, 1649-1699. Roger Thompson. LC 85-24630. (Illus.). 272p. 1989. lib. bdg. 30.00x (ISBN 0-87023-516-8); pap. 11.95 (ISBN 0-87023-656-3). U of Mass Pr.

Sex in Nature. Chris Catton & James Gray. (Illus.). 224p. 1985. 18.95 (ISBN 0-8160-1294-6). Facts on File.

Sex in Prison: The Mississippi Experiment with Conjugal Visiting. Columbus B. Hopper. LC 70-86491. pap. 33.50 (ISBN 0-317-28745-1, 2051649). Bks Demand UMI.

Sex in Society. Alex Comfort. 172p. 1975. pap. 2.95 (ISBN 0-8065-0064-6, Pub. by Citadel Pr). Lyle Stuart.

Sex in the Bible. Tom Horner. LC 73-87676. 1974. 8.50 (ISBN 0-8048-1124-5). C E Tuttle.

Sex in the Bible: An Introduction to What the Scriptures Teach Us about Sexuality. Michael Cosby. LC 83-16090. 182p. 1984. 12.95 (ISBN 0-13-807280-9). P-H.

Sex in the Christian Marriage. 2nd ed. Richard Meier et al. (Life Enrichment Ser.). 144p. 1988. pap. 5.95 (ISBN 0-8010-6204-7). Baker Bk.

Sex in the Light of Reincarnation & Freedom. Alan Howard. 1980. pap. 5.95 (ISBN 0-916786-48-X). St George Bk Serv.

Sex in the Marketplace: American Women at Work. Juanita Kreps. LC 77-155165. (Policy Studies in Employment & Welfare: No. 11). 117p. 1971. pap. 4.95x (ISBN 0-8018-1277-1). Johns Hopkins.

Sex in the Movies. Sam Frank. (Illus.). 288p. 1986. 19.95 (ISBN 0-8065-0999-6, Pub. by Citadel Pr). Lyle Stuart.

Sex in the Talmud. Reuven P. Bulka. (Illus.). 64p. 1979. 5.95 (ISBN 0-88088-488-6). Peter Pauper.

Sex in the Therapy Hour: A Case of Professional Incest. Carolyn Bates & Annette Brodsky. 260p. 1988. lib. bdg. 25.00 (ISBN 0-89862-726-5, 2726). Guilford Pr.

Sex in the World's Religions. Geoffrey Parrinder. 1980. pap. 9.95x (ISBN 0-19-520202-3). Oxford U Pr.

Sex Inequalities in Urban Employment in the Third World. Richard Anker & Catherine Hein. LC 85-27781. 304p. 1986. 32.50 (ISBN 0-312-71341-X). St Martin.

Sex Is God's Idea. Earl Paulk. 175p. (Orig.). 1985. pap. 5.95 (ISBN 0-917595-04-1). K-Dimension.

Sex Is Holy. Mary Rousseau & Chuck Gallagher. (Wellspring Bk). 160p. (Orig.). 1986. pap. 9.95 (ISBN 0-916349-11-X). Amity Hse Inc.

Sex Is More Than a Word. Andrew Lester. (Sexuality in Christian Living Ser). 80p. (gr. 10-12). 1973. pap. 5.95 (ISBN 0-8054-5313-X). Broadman.

Sex Joke Book. Max Brodnick. (Illus., Orig.). 1975. pap. 1.25 (ISBN 0-685-52937-1, LB264ZK, Leisure Bks). Leisure NY.

Sex Jokes & Male Chauvinism. George Fine. (Illus.). 192p. 1981. 9.95 (ISBN 0-8065-0753-5, Pub. by Citadel Pr). Lyle Stuart.

Sex Law in England. Tony Honore. 200p. 1978. 26.00 (ISBN 0-208-01764-X, Archon). Shoe String.

Sex Life in Europe. Max Hodann. LC 72-9652. Repr. of 1932 ed. 40.00 (ISBN 0-404-57461-0). AMS Pr.

Sex Life in Marriage. Oliver M. Butterfield. (Illus.). 9.95 (ISBN 0-87523-035-0). Emerson.

Sex Life of a Football Referee. Allan Kent. 37p. 1987. 6.95 (ISBN 0-533-07399-5). Vantage.

Sex Life of Flowers. Bastiaan Meeuse & Sean Morris. (Illus.). 160p. 19.95 (ISBN 0-87196-907-6). Facts on File.

Sex Life of the Unmarried Adult: An Inquiry into & an Interpretation of Current Sex Practices, New York 1934. Ira S. Wile. Ed. by David J. Rothman & Sheila M. Rothman. (Women & Children First Ser.). 320p. 1986. lib. bdg. 40.00 (ISBN 0-8240-7680-X). Garland Pub.

Sex, Literature & Censorship. D. H. Lawrence. 122p. 1953. 19.50 (ISBN 0-8290-0206-5); pap. text ed. 8.95x (ISBN 0-8290-2394-1). Irvington.

Sex Lives of Animals Without Backbones. Haig H. Najarian. LC 75-4447. 125p. (Orig.). 1976. lib. bdg. 6.95 (ISBN 0-684-14613-4). Krieger.

Sex, Love & Procreation: Synthesis Ser. William E. May. 1976. pap. 0.75 (ISBN 0-8199-0711-1). Franciscan Herald.

Sex-Love-Marriage & Divorce: A Male Primer. Joseph H. Hughes, Jr. 1977. pap. 4.95 (ISBN 0-686-28626-X). Aaron Jenkins.

Sex, Love, or Infatuation: How Can I Really Know? Ray E. Short. LC 78-52180. 1978. pap. 4.50 (ISBN 0-8066-1653-9, 10-5650). Augsburg.

Sex Magazines in the Library Collection: A Scholarly Study of Sex in Serials & Periodicals. Ed. by Peter Gellatly. LC 80-15011. (Supplement to Serials Librarian Ser.: Vol. 4). 142p. 1981. text ed. 24.95 (ISBN 0-917724-16-X, B16). Haworth Pr.

Sex Magick. rev. ed. Louis T. Culling. LC 85-45955. 160p. 1986. pap. 6.95 (ISBN 0-87542-110-5). Llewellyn Pubns.

Sex Manual for People over Thirty. Ira Alterman. 96p. 1984. pap. 3.95 (ISBN 0-8092-5354-2). Contemp Bks.

Sex, Marriage & Chastity: Reflections of a Catholic Layman, Spouse & Parent. William E. May. 1981. 6.95 (ISBN 0-8199-0821-5). Franciscan Herald.

Sex, Marriage & Society, 35 bks. Ed. by Charles E. Rosenberg & Carroll Smith-Rosenberg. 1974. 832.00x (ISBN 0-405-05790-3). Ayer Co Pubs.

Sex, Mind & Habit Compatibility. Marc Robertson. 56p. 1975. 4.50 (ISBN 0-86690-148-5). Am Fed Astrologers.

Sex, Money & Power: An Essay on Christian Social Ethics. Philip Turner. LC 84-72481. 135p. (Orig.). 1985. pap. 8.95 (ISBN 0-936384-22-0). Cowley Pubns.

Sex, Motivation, & the Criminal Offender. photocopy ed. Robert H. Morneau, Jr. & Robert R. Rockwell. (Illus.). 416p. 1980. 50.50x (ISBN 0-398-03933-X). C C Thomas.

Sex Mythology. Sha Rocco. (Illus.). 55p. 1982. Repr. of 1874 ed. 3.00 (ISBN 0-911826-34-3). Am Atheist.

Sex, Nutrition & You. Author-Gordon S. Tessler et al. (Illus.). 256p. 1986. 16.95 (ISBN 0-932213-61-8). Better Health.

Sexes Throughout Nature. Antoinette B. Blackwell. LC 75-7714. (Pioneers of the Woman's Movement: an International Perspective Ser.). 240p. 1985. Repr. of 1875 ed. 24.00 (ISBN 0-88355-349-X). Hyperion Conn.

Sexism & God-Talk: Toward a Feminist Theology. Rosemary R. Ruether. LC 82-72502. 300p. (Orig.). 1984. pap. 10.95 (ISBN 0-8070-1105-3, BP680); 24.95x (ISBN 0-8070-1104-5). Beacon Pr.

Sexism & Language. Alleen Pace Nilsen et al. LC 76-58260. 203p. 1977. pap. 10.50 (ISBN 0-8141-4373-3). NCTE.

Sexism & Science. Evelyn Reed. LC 77-92144. (Illus.). 1978. pap. 6.95 (ISBN 0-87348-541-6). Path Pr NY.

Sexism & Science. Evelyn Reed. LC 77-92144. (Illus.). 1977. cloth 20.00 (ISBN 0-87348-540-8). Path Pr NY.

Sexism & the Law: Male Beliefs & Legal Bias in Britain & the United States. Albie Sachs & Joan H. Wilson. LC 78-63402. 1979. 15.95 (ISBN 0-02-927640-3). Free Pr.

Sexism & the War System. Betty Reardon. LC 85-12619. 128p. (Orig.). 1985. pap. text ed. 10.95x (ISBN 0-8077-2769-5). Tchrs Coll.

Sexism in Award-Winning Picture Books. Suzanne M. Czaplinski. (Illus.). 1973. pap. 2.50x (ISBN 0-912786-21-3). Know Inc.

Sexism in Indian Education. N. N. Kalia. 193p. 1979. 15.95. Asia Bk Corp.

Sexism in Indian Education: Lies We Tell Our Children. Narendra N. Kalia. 1979. text ed. 20.00x (ISBN 0-7069-0809-0, Pub. by Vikas India). Advent NY.

Sexism in Secondary Schools. Whyld. 1983. pap. text ed. 14.50 (ISBN 0-06-318251-3). Har-Row.

Sexism in the Computer Industry. Dick Whitson. 1984. looseleaf 74.95 (ISBN 0-917194-16-0). Prog Studies.

Sexism in the Computer Industry: Startling Report. Dick Whitson. 1984. 9.95 (ISBN 0-917194-18-7). Prog Studies.

Sexism: New Issue in American Education. Pauline Gough. LC 76-16876. (Fastback Ser.: No.81). (Orig.). 1976. pap. 0.90 (ISBN 0-87367-081-7). Phi Delta Kappa.

Sexism of Social & Political Theory: Women & Reproduction from Plato to Nietzsche. Ed. by Lorenne Clark & Lynda Lange. LC 79-17862. 1979. o. p. 20.00x (ISBN 0-8020-5459-5); pap. 10.95c (ISBN 0-8020-6375-6). U of Toronto Pr.

Sexism, Racism & Oppression. Arthur Brittan & Mary Maynard. 220p. 1984. pap. 14.95 (ISBN 0-85520-675-6). Basil Blackwell.

Sexism: The Male Monopoly on History & Thought. Marielouise Janssen-Jurreit. Tr. by Verne Moberg from Ger. 384p. 1982. 25.00 (ISBN 0-374-26167-9); pap. 12.95 (ISBN 0-374-51683-9). FS&G.

Sexist Language: A Modern Philosophical Analysis. Mary Vetterling-Braggin. LC 80-26248. (Quality Paperbacks Ser.: No. 353). 344p. 1981. pap. 8.95 (ISBN 0-8226-0353-5). Littlefield.

Sexist Language: A Modern Philosophical Analysis. Ed. by Mary Vetterling-Braggin et al. LC 80-26263. 344p. 1981. 15.00x (ISBN 0-8476-6293-4). Rowman.

SEX...Now that I've Got Your Attention, Let Me Answer Your Questions! Judith Kuriansky. LC 84-2153. 256p. 1984. 15.95 (ISBN 0-399-12891-3, Putnam). Putnam Pub Group.

Sexo, Dinero y Balas. new ed. Glenn Chase. Tr. by Danilo Cesto from Eng. (Cereza Delicias: No.7). Orig. Title: Chuck You Farley! (Illus.). 160p. (Span.). 1975. pap. 1.25 (ISBN 0-88473-241-X). Fiesta Pub.

Sexo y Mas: Guia Para la Juventud. Michael Lawson & David Skipp. (Illus.). 110p. (Orig., Span.). (YA) (gr. 10-12). 1988. pap. write for info. (ISBN 0-945792-02-6). Editorial Unilit.

Sexocize. Janan Clark. (Illus.). 39p. (Orig.). 1988. pap. text ed. 12.95 (ISBN 0-929593-00-6). West Pine Pub.

Sexologia para Cristianos. Lewis Smedes. Tr. by Jorge Sanchez from Eng. 288p. 1982. pap. 6.25 (ISBN 0-89922-175-0). Edit Caribe.

Sexology. Ed. by Z. Hoch & H. I. Lief. (International Congress Ser.: Vol. 566). 422p. 1982. 145.25 (ISBN 0-444-90260-0, Excerpta Medica). Elsevier.

Sexology. William H. Walling. LC 73-20641. (Sex, Marriage & Society Ser.). 238p. 1974. Repr. 21.00x (ISBN 0-405-05822-5). Ayer Co Pubs.

Sexplicitly Yours: The Trial of Cynthia Payne. Gloria Walker & Lynn Daly. 128p. 1988. pap. 4.95 (ISBN 0-14-010543-3). Penguin.

S'Expliquer (Myself Freud Explained) Stephen N. Stivers. 64p. 1985. 12.95 (ISBN 0-9615274-0-4); pap. 4.95 (ISBN 0-9615274-1-2). Stivers.

Sexta Reunion de la Conferencia Permanente de Organismos Nacionales de Politica Cientifica y Tecnologica en America Latina y el Caribe. (Estudios & Documentos de Politica Cientifica). 201p. (Span.). 1984. pap. 12.50 (ISBN 92-3-302084-3, U1372, UNESCO). UNIPUB.

Sextant Handbook: Adjustment, Repair, Use & History. Bruce Bauer. 194p. (Orig.). 1987. text ed. 19.95 (ISBN 0-87742-956-1). Intl Marine.

Sextant Handbook: Adjustment, Repair, Use & History. Bruce A. Bauer. LC 85-73594. (Illus.). 192p. 1986. 19.95 (ISBN 0-913179-09-4). Azimuth Pr.

Sextet. Henry Miller. LC 77-20795. (Illus.). 1977. pap. 7.95 (ISBN 0-88496-111-7). Capra Pr.

Sextet: His Later Writings under One Cover. Henry Miller. 188p. 1988. Repr. lib. bdg. 19.95x (ISBN 0-8095-4046-0). Borgo Pr.

Sextet in a Minor: A Novella & Thirteen Stories. Norma Klein. 224p. 1983. 12.95 (ISBN 0-312-71348-7, Pub. by Marek). St Martin.

Sextet: Six Story Discoveries in the Novella Form. Ed. by Hallie Burnett & Whit Burnett. LC 51-13446. 1968. Repr. of 1951 ed. 20.00 (ISBN 0-527-13700-6). Kraus Repr.

Sextette: Translations from the French Symbolists. Tr. by Dorothy Martin. LC 80-10539. (Symbolists Ser.). Repr. of 1928 ed. 18.50 (ISBN 0-404-16331-9). AMS Pr.

Sexto Curso de Derecho International Organizado por el Comite Juridico Interamericano: Julio-Agosto de 1979, Conferencias e Informes. OAS General Secretariat, Dept. of Publications. 630p. (Span.). 1979. pap. text ed. 25.00 (ISBN 0-8270-1144-X). OAS.

Sexton: Selected Criticism. Ed. by Diana H. George. 352p. 1988. 29.95 (ISBN 0-252-01552-5). U of Ill Pr.

Sextus Aurelius Victor: A Historiographical Study. H. W. Bird. (ARCA Classical & Medieval Texts, Papers, & Monographs: No. 14). 175p. 1984. text ed. 32.00 (ISBN 0-905205-21-9, Pub. by F Cairns). Longwood Pub Group.

Sextus Empiricus: Selections from the Major Writings on Scepticism, Man, & God. rev. ed. Sextus Empiricus. Ed. by Phillip P. Hallie. Tr. by Sanford G. Etheridge from Gr. LC 85-27059. (HPC Philosophical Classics Ser.). 256p. 1985. lib. bdg. 27.50 (ISBN 0-87220-007-8); pap. 6.95 (ISBN 0-87220-006-X). Hackett Pub.

Sextus Pompey. Moses Hadas. LC 72-181935. Repr. of 1930 ed. 19.50 (ISBN 0-404-03020-3). AMS Pr.

Sexual Abuse: Causes, Consequences & Treatment of Incestuous & Pedophilic Acts. Adele Mayer. LC 84-80657. 176p. 1985. pap. text ed. 19.95 casebound (ISBN 0-918452-80-5). Learning Pubns.

Sexual Abuse: Incest Victims & Their Families. 2nd ed. Jean M. Goodwin. (Illus.). 288p. 1988. pap. 31.50 (ISBN 0-88416-588-4). PSG Pub Co.

Sexual Abuse: Let's Talk about It. rev. & enl. ed. Margaret O. Hyde. LC 87-133328. 112p. (gr. 5 up). 1987. 8.95. Westminster John Knox.

Sexual Abuse of Children: A Comprehensive Guide to Current Knowledge & Intervention Strategies. Jeffrey J. Haugaard & N. Dickon Reppucci. LC 87-46345. (Social & Behavioral Science Ser.). 1988. 27.95x (ISBN 1-55542-077-X). Jossey-Bass.

Sexual Abuse of Children: A Resource Guide & Annotated Bibliography. Benjamin Schlesinger. 212p. 1982. pap. 10.95c (ISBN 0-8020-6481-7). U of Toronto Pr.

Sexual Abuse of Children: Implications from the Sexual Trauma Treatment Program of Connecticut-Special Report of Two Research Utilization Workshops. 1979. 3.00 (ISBN 0-86671-048-5). Comm Coun Great NY.

Sexual Abuse of Young Children. Kee MacFarlane & Jill Waterman. 355p. 1988. pap. 14.95 (ISBN 0-89862-703-6, 2703). Guilford Pr.

Sexual Abuse of Young Children: Evaluation & Treatment. Kee MacFarlane et al. LC 85-30539. 355p. 1986. text ed. 27.95 (ISBN 0-89862-675-7). Guilford Pr.

Sexual Abuse Prevention: A Study for Teenagers. Marie M. Fortune. (Orig.). 1984. pap. 3.95 (ISBN 0-8298-0711-X). Pilgrim NY.

Sexual Abuse Prevention Education: An Annotated Bibliography. Ed. by Kay Clark. 68p. 1986. pap. text ed. 9.95 (ISBN 0-941816-21-4). Network Pubns.

Sexual Adjustment: A Guide for the Spinal Cord Injured. Martha F. Gregory. Ed. by Raymond C. Cheever. 70p. 1974. pap. 4.95 (ISBN 0-915708-00-0, #1410). Cheever Pub.

Sexual Aggressor: Current Perspectives on Treatment. Ed. by Joanne G. Greer & Irving R. Stuart. 384p. 1983. 36.95 (ISBN 0-442-22855-4). Van Nos Reinhold.

Sexual Aliveness: A Reichian Gestalt Perspective. Edward W. Smith. LC 87-42521. 140p. 1987. lib. bdg. 16.95x (ISBN 0-89950-268-7). McFarland & Co.

Sexual & Gender Harassment in the Academy: A Guide for Faculty, Students, & Administrators. Phyllis Franklin et al. LC 81-14059. iii, 75p. (Orig.). 1981. pap. 9.50x (ISBN 0-87352-333-4, B811). Modern Lang.

Sexual Animosity Between Men & Women. Gerald Schoenewolf. LC 88-19353. 230p. 1988. 25.00x (ISBN 0-87668-933-0). Aronson.

Sexual Anomalies: The Origin, Nature, & Treatment of Sexual Disorders. Magnus Hirschfeld. 538p. 1948. 9.95 (ISBN 0-317-39779-6). Brown Bk.

Sexual Anxiety: A Study of Male Impotence. Eric Carlton. LC 79-56651. 197p. 1980. 27.50x (ISBN 0-06-490960-3, 06386). B&N Imports.

Sexual Archetypes: East & West. Ed. by Bina Gupta. LC 86-25441. (God: The Contemporary Discussion Ser.). (Illus.). 344p. 1986. 22.95 (ISBN 0-913757-59-4, Pub. by New Era Bks); pap. 12.95 (ISBN 0-913757-68-3, Pub. by New Era Bks). Paragon Hse.

Sexual Arena & Women's Liberation. Edward J. Bardon. LC 77-23937. 260p. 1978. 20.95x (ISBN 0-88229-219-6). Nelson-Hall.

Sexual Arousal: New Concepts in Basic Sciences, Diagnosis, & Treatment. Ed. by Miguel Ficher et al. (Illus.). 290p. 1984. 32.50x (ISBN 0-398-04962-9). C C Thomas.

Sexual Assault: A Guide for Community Action. Barbara J. Rodabaugh & Melanie Austin. 1981. lib. bdg. 33.00 (ISBN 0-8240-7197-2). Garland Pub.

Sexual Assault among Adolescents. Suzanne S. Ageton. LC 82-48573. 208p. 1983. 29.00x (ISBN 0-669-06322-3). Lexington Bks.

Sexual Assault of Children & Adolescents. Ann W. Burgess & Groth A. Nichols. 245p. 1978. postpaid 16.00 (ISBN 0-318-17072-8). Kempe Nat Ctr.

Sexual Assault of Children & Adolescents. Ann W. Burgess et al. LC 77-10217. 1978. 29.00x (ISBN 0-669-01890-2); pap. 14.00x (ISBN 0-669-01892-9). Lexington Bks.

Sexual Astrology. Martine. 1977. pap. 3.95 (ISBN 0-440-18020-1). Dell.

Sexual Asymmetry: Studies in Ancient Society. Ed. by Josine Blok & Peter Mason. (Illus.). ix, 298p. (Orig.). 1987. pap. 40.00 (ISBN 90-5063-018-9, Pub. by Gieben Amsterdam). Humanities.

Sexual Attack & the Crime of Rape. rev. ed. Joseph S. Roucek. Ed. by D. Steve Rahmas. (Topics of Our Times Ser.: No. 13). 32p. 1980. lib. bdg. 3.75 incl. catalog cards (ISBN 0-87157-814-X); pap. 2.50 vinyl laminated covers (ISBN 0-87157-314-8). SamHar Pr.

Sexual Attraction. Mark Cook & R. McHenry. 1978. pap. text ed. 11.00 (ISBN 0-08-022230-7). Pergamon.

Sexual Aversion, Sexual Phobias & Panic Disorder: Integration of Medication & Psychodynamic Sex Therapy. Helen S. Kaplan & Donald F. Klein. LC 86-28311. 168p. 1987. 27.50 (ISBN 0-87630-450-1). Brunner-Mazel.

Sexual Awareness. Barry W. McCarthy & Emily McCarthy. LC 84-9502. 320p. 1984. pap. 9.95 (ISBN 0-88184-100-5). Carroll & Graf.

Sexual Bargaining: Power Politics in the American Marriage. 2nd ed. John Scanzoni. LC 81-16222. xvi, 180p. 1982. lib. bdg. 15.00x (ISBN 0-226-73564-8); pap. 5.95 (ISBN 0-226-73565-6, Phoen). U of Chicago Pr.

Sexual Barrier: Legal, Medical, Economic & Social Aspects of Sex Discrimination. Marija M. Hughes. LC 77-83214. 1977. 70.00 (ISBN 0-912560-04-5). Hughes Pr.

Sexual Behavior & Family Life in Transition. T. M. Kando. 27.95 (ISBN 0-444-99049-6, KSB/, Pub. by Elsevier). Greenwood.

Sexual Behavior in the Human Male. Alfred C. Kinsey et al. LC 48-5195. (Illus.). 1948. write for info. (ISBN 0-7216-5445-2). Saunders.

Sexual Behaviour in Canada: Patterns & Problems. Benjamin Schlesinger. 1977. pap. 8.95 (ISBN 0-8020-6314-4). U of Toronto Pr.

Sexual Body: An Interdisciplinary Perspective. Arthur Efron. LC 82-642121. 314p. 1985. pap. 13.00 (ISBN 0-930195-01-9). Inst Mind Behavior.

Sexual Celibate. Don Goergen. 272p. 1975. 5.00 (ISBN 0-8164-0268-X, HarpR). Har-Row.

Sexual Chaos: The Personal & Social Consequences of the Sexual Revolution. John S. Vertefeuille. LC 87-71891. 192p. (Orig.). 1988. pap. 7.95 (ISBN 0-89107-430-9, Crossway Bks). Good News.

Sexual Chemistry. Julius Fast & Meredith Bernstein. 1984. pap. 3.50 (ISBN 0-671-49934-3). PB.

Sexual Circus: Wedekind's Theatre of Subversion. Elizabeth Boa. Date not set. text ed. 29.95 (ISBN 0-631-14234-7). Basil Blackwell.

Sexual Compatibility: A Practical Approach to Solving Problems. John F. O'Connor. 1985. 8.95 (ISBN 0-317-17527-0, Perigee). Putnam Pub Group.

Sexual Conduct & the Law. 2nd ed. Gerhard O. Mueller. Ed. by Irving J. Sloan. LC 79-28180. 128p. 1980. lib. bdg. 6.95 (ISBN 0-379-11129-2). Oceana.

Sexual Conduct: The Social Sources of Human Sexuality. John H. Gagnon & William Simon. 328p. 1973. text ed. 29.95x (ISBN 0-202-30261-X). Aldine de Gruyter.

Sexual Connection. John Sparks. 1978. text ed. 8.95 (ISBN 0-07-059908-4). McGraw.

Sexual Consequences of Disability. Alex Comfort. LC 78-62810. (Illus.). 296p. 1978. text ed. 19.50x (ISBN 0-89313-008-7). G F Stickley Co.

Sexual, Contraceptive, & Pregnancy Choices: Counseling Adolescents. Julie Spain. 156p. 1988. text ed. 24.95; pap. 14.95 (ISBN 0-317-59429-X). Gardner Pr.

Sexual Contract. Carole Pateman. LC 87-63007. 300p. 1988. text ed. 39.00x (ISBN 0-8047-1476-2); pap. text ed. 12.95x (ISBN 0-8047-1477-0). Stanford U Pr.

Sexual Contradictions: Psychology, Psychoanalysis, & Feminism. Janet Sayers. 250p. 1986. 29.95 (ISBN 0-422-78780-9, 9791, Pub. by Tavistock England); pap. 11.95 (ISBN 0-422-78790-6, 9804). Routledge Chapman & Hall.

Sexual Counseling: A Practical Guide for Non-Professional Counselors. Eugene Kennedy. 216p. 1980. pap. 12.95 (ISBN 0-8264-0021-3). Continuum.

Sexual Counseling for Ostomates: A Resource Book for Health Care Professionals. Ellen A. Shipes & Sally T. Lehr. (Illus.). 118p. 1980. spiral bdg. 16.25 (ISBN 0-398-03950-X). C C Thomas.

Sexual Counseling Skills Workshop: A Trainers' Handbook. Robert R. Wilson. 1977. pap. 2.00 (ISBN 0-89055-120-0). Carolina Pop Ctr.

Sexual Creators: An Ethical Proposal for Concerned Christians. Andre Guindon. 256p. (Orig.). 1986. lib. bdg. 29.50 (ISBN 0-8191-5239-0); pap. text ed. 13.75 (ISBN 0-8191-5240-4). U Pr of Amer.

Sexual Crimes & Confrontations: A Criminological Perspective. Donald J. West. (Cambridge Studies in Criminology: Vol. 56). 1987. text ed. 59.50 (ISBN 0-566-05380-2, Pub. by Gower Pub England). Gower Pub Co.

Sexual Desire: A Moral Philosophy of the Erotic. Roger Scruton. 428p. 1986. 25.00 (ISBN 0-02-929280-8). Free Pr.

Sexual Desire & Love: Origins & History of the Christian Ethic of Sexuality & Marriage. Eric Fuchs. Tr. by Marsha Daigle. 320p. (Fr.). 1983. pap. 15.95 (ISBN 0-8164-2467-5, HarpR). Har-Row.

Sexual Desire Disorders. Ed. by Sandra R. Leiblum & Raymond C. Rosen. 470p. 1988. lib. bdg. 35.00 (ISBN 0-89862-714-1). Guilford Pr.

Sexual Deviancy & Social Proscription. Clifton Bryant. LC 81-6216. 432p. 1982. text ed. 44.95x (ISBN 0-89885-024-X); pap. text ed. 19.95x (ISBN 0-89885-094-0). Human Sci Pr.

Sexual Deviation. 2nd ed. Ed. by Ismond Rosen. (Illus.). 1979. text ed. 60.00x (ISBN 0-19-263208-6). Oxford U Pr.

Sexual Deviation in American Society: A Social-Psychological Study of Sexual Nonconformity. Bernard J. Oliver, Jr. 1967. 13.95x (ISBN 0-8084-0276-5); pap. 9.95x (ISBN 0-8084-0277-3). New Coll U Pr.

Sexual Deviations & Paraphilias: Medical Analysis Index with Research Bibliography. Harold P. Drummond. LC 85-47570. 150p. 1987. 34.50 (ISBN 0-88164-314-9); pap. 26.50 (ISBN 0-88164-315-7). ABBE Pubs Assn.

Sexual Deviations in the Criminal Law: Homosexual, Exhibitionistic, & Pedophilic Offences in Canada. Alex K. Gigeroff. LC 79-364215. (Clarke Institute of Psychiatry. Monograph Ser.: No. 2). pap. 57.50 (2026432). Bks Demand UMI.

Sexual Differentiation: Basic & Clinical Aspects. Ed. by M. Serio et al. (Serono Symposia Publications: Vol. 11). 384p. 1984. text ed. 66.00 (ISBN 0-89004-316-7). Raven.

Sexual Differentiation of the Brain. Ed. by Robert W. Goy & Bruce S. McEwen. (Illus.). 1980. text ed. 30.00x (ISBN 0-262-07077-4). MIT Pr.

Sexual Difficulties in Marriage. David R. Mace. LC 72-75652. (Pocket Counsel Books). pap. 20.00 (2027178). Bks Demand UMI.

Sexual Dilemmas for the Helping Professional. Jerry Edelwich & Archie Brodsky. LC 82-9491. 250p. 1982. 25.00 (ISBN 0-87630-314-9). Brunner-Mazel.

Sexual Dimension: A Guide for the Mental Health Practitioner. Herbert S. Strean. LC 83-47512. 1983. 24.95x (ISBN 0-02-932170-0). Free Pr.

Sexual Dimension in Literature. Ed. by Alan Bold. LC 82-13894. (Critical Studies Ser.). 224p. 1983. text ed. 28.50x (ISBN 0-389-20314-9, 07152). B&N Imports.

Sexual Dimorphism in Homo Sapiens: A Question of Size. Ed. by Robert L. Hall. LC 81-5907. 446p. 1982. 67.95 (ISBN 0-275-91365-1, C1365). Praeger.

Sexual Dimorphism in Human & Mammalian Biology & Pathology. A. Glucksmann. LC 80-42373. 374p. 1981. 84.00 (ISBN 0-12-286960-5). Acad Pr.

Sexual Dimorphism, Ontogeny, & Functional Morphology of Rutiderma Hartmanni Poulsen, 1965 (Crustacea: Ostracoda) Louis S. Kornicker. LC 84-600218. (Smithsonian Contributions to Zoology Ser.: No. 408). pap. 20.00 (ISBN 0-317-30425-9, 2024936). Bks Demand UMI.

Sexual Disorders: Treatment, Theory & Research. C. David Tollison & Henry E. Adams. 1979. text ed. 32.00 (ISBN 0-89876-029-1). Gardner Pr.

Sexual Distinctions in the Law: Early Maximum Hour Decisions of the United States Supreme Court, 1905-1917. Candice Dalrymple. Ed. by Harold Hyman & Stuart Bruchey. (American Legal & Constitutional History Ser.). 325p. 1987. lib. bdg. 40.00 (ISBN 0-8240-8257-5). Garland Pub.

Sexual Division of Labour: The Italian Case. Francesca Bettio. (Illus.). 288p. 1988. 59.00 (ISBN 0-19-828544-2). Oxford U Pr.

Sexual Divisions & Society. Diana L. Barker. Ed. by Allen Barker. 1976. 12.95x (ISBN 0-422-74820-X, NO. 2616, Pub. by Tavistock England); (Pub. by Tavistock England). Routledge Chapman & Hall.

Sexual Divisions in Law. Katherine O'Donovan. (Law in Context Ser.). 272p. 1986. 27.95x (ISBN 0-297-78664-4, Pub. by Weidenfeld & Nicolson England). Biblio Dist.

Sexual Divisions: Patterns & Processes. Ed. by Mary Evans & Clare Ungerson. 224p. 1983. pap. 13.50 (ISBN 0-422-78440-0, NO. 3835, Pub. by Tavistock). Routledge Chapman & Hall.

Sexual Dynamics of Antisocial Behavior. Louis B. Schlesinger & Eugene Revitch. (Illus.). 332p. 1983. 34.75 (ISBN 0-398-04802-9). C C Thomas.

TITLE INDEX SEXUAL REVOLUTION: CHALLENGE &

Sexual Dynamics of History: Men's Power, Women's Resistance. The London Feminist History Group. 226p. (Orig.). 1983. pap. 13.00 (ISBN 0-86104-711-7, Pub by Pluto Pr). Longwood Pub Group.
Sexual Dysfunction. Ben N. Ard, Jr. LC 73-17735. 300p. 1975. 30.00x (ISBN 0-87668-113-5). Aronson.
Sexual Dysfunction in Neurological Disorders: Diagnosis, Management & Rehabilitation. Francois Boller & Ellen Frank. 108p. 1982. text ed. 22.50 (ISBN 0-89004-500-3). Raven.
Sexual Endocrinology: Proceedings of the Foundation pour la recherche en endocrinologie sexuelle et la reproduction humaine. Ed. by R. Vokaer & G. De Bock. 252p. 1975. 69.00 (ISBN 0-08-018170-8). Pergamon.
Sexual Energy & the Old Religion: Red Dragon Power of Witchcraft. Rhuddlwm Gawr. LC 85-73748. (Illus.). 156p. (Orig.). 1988. text ed. 15.95 (ISBN 0-931760-03-8); pap. 12.95 (ISBN 0-931760-11-9). Camelot Ga.
Sexual Energy & Yoga. Elisabeth Haich. 160p. 1983. 8.95 (ISBN 0-943358-03-5). Aurora Press.
Sexual Energy Ecstasy: A Guide to the Ultimate Intimate Sexual Experience. David A. Ramsdale & Ellen J. Dorfman. LC 84-60801. (Illus.). 288p. (Orig.). 1985. pap. 9.95 (ISBN 0-917879-00-7). Peak Skill.
Sexual Enhancement for Men. Judith L. Silverstein. 1986. 10.00 (ISBN 0-533-06904-1). Vantage.
Sexual Enlightenment of Children. Sigmund Freud. 1963. pap. 4.95 (ISBN 0-02-076500-2, Collier). Macmillan.
Sexual Equation. J. Dudley Chapman. LC 77-75256. (Illus.). 446p. 1977. 17.95 (ISBN 0-8022-2201-3). Philos Lib.
Sexual Ethics. Philip Turner. 1988. pap. price not set (ISBN 0-88028-085-9). Forward Movement.
Sexual Excitement: Dynamics of Erotic Life. Robert J. Stoller. LC 86-17316. 304p. 1986. pap. text ed. 16.95x (ISBN 0-88048-263-X, 48-263-X). Am Psychiatric.
Sexual Exercises for Women. Anthony Harris. (Illus.). 104p. 1986. pap. 11.95 (ISBN 0-7043-3480-1, Pub. by Quartet Bks). Salem Hse Pubs.
Sexual Exercises for Women. Anthony Harris. 145p. 1988. pap. 8.95 (ISBN 0-88184-412-8). Carroll & Graf.
Sexual Exploitation. Diane E. Russell. LC 84-6950. 319p. 1984. 35.00 (ISBN 0-8039-2354-6); pap. 16.95 (ISBN 0-8039-2355-4). Sage.
Sexual Exploitation of Children. Judith Ennew. LC 86-15510. 200p. 1986. 25.00 (ISBN 0-312-71353-3). St Martin.
Sexual Exploitation of Children. S. Goldstein. (Elsevier Series in Practical Aspects of Criminal & Forensic Investigation). 440p. 1986. 37.75 (ISBN 0-444-01117-X). Elsevier.
Sexual Exploitation of Patients by Health Professionals. Ed. by Ann W. Burgess & Carol R. Hartman. LC 86-9318. (Series in Sexual Medicine: Vol. 4). 207p. 1986. lib. bdg. 40.95 (ISBN 0-275-92171-9, C2171). Praeger.
Sexual Exploitation of the Child. Thomas M. Frost & Magnus J. Seng. LC 86-7009. 95p. 1986. pap. 4.50 (ISBN 0-911531-14-9). Loyola U Ctr Urban.
Sexual Expression: A Manual for Trainers. Carl Hartman et al. LC 81-6760. (Illus.). 152p. 1981. pap. text ed. 14.95 (ISBN 0-89885-053-3). Human Sci Pr.
Sexual Fiction. Maurice Charney. 200p. 1981. 22.00x (ISBN 0-416-31930-0, NO. 6519); pap. 8.95 (ISBN 0-416-31940-8, NO. 6518). Routledge Chapman & Hall.
Sexual Fitness. Time-Life Books Editors. (Fitness, Health & Nutrition Ser.). 144p. 1988. 17.27 (ISBN 0-8094-6110-2); lib. bdg. 21.27 (ISBN 0-8094-6111-0). Time-Life.
Sexual Force or the Winged Dragon. rev. ed. Omraam M. Aivanhov. (Izvor Collection: Vol. 205). 138p. (Orig.). 1987. pap. 5.95 (ISBN 2-85566-299-0, Pub. by Prosveta France). Prosveta USA.
Sexual Freedom. V. Mary Stewart. pap. 0.75 (ISBN 0-87784-111-X). Inter-Varsity.
Sexual Friendship: A New Dynamics in Relationships. Richard Walters. LC 87-91726. 1988. pap. 12.95 (ISBN 0-87212-208-5). Libra.
Sexual Geometry. Charlie Clark, III. Ed. by Rose E. Sanfilippo. LC 82-91125. (Illus.). 112p. 1983. 8.95 (ISBN 0-9609808-0-6). New Pen Pub Co.
Sexual Happiness: A Practical Approach. Maurice Yaffe & Elizabeth Fenwick. LC 87-45839. 318p. 1988. 24.95 (ISBN 0-8050-0691-5). H Holt & Co.
Sexual Happiness in Marriage. Herbert J. Miles. 160p. 1985. pap. 2.95 (ISBN 0-515-08172-8). Jove Pubns.
Sexual Harassment. Hamline University Advanced Legal Education Staff. 102p. 1986. 42.40. Hamline Law.
Sexual Harassment: A Guide to Resources. M. Dawn McCaghy. 200p. 1985. lib. bdg. 28.00 (ISBN 0-8161-8669-3). G K Hall.
Sexual Harassment: A Management Issue. Sandra H. Carey. Date not set. price not set (ISBN 0-8290-1055-6). Irvington.
Sexual Harassment at Work. Mary C. Meyer et al. (Illus.). 256p. 1981. 17.50 (ISBN 0-89433-156-6). Petrocelli.
Sexual Harassment at Work. Ann Sedley & Melissa Benn. 1982. 20.00x (ISBN 0-946088-00-4, Pub. by NCCL UK). State Mutual Bk.
Sexual Harassment: Employer Policies & Problems. (PPF Survey Ser.: No. 144). 54p. 1987. 30.00 (ISBN 0-87179-975-8). BNA.
Sexual Harassment in the Workplace. rev. ed. Ralph H. Baxter, Jr. LC 85-81035. 100p. 1986. pap. 9.95 (ISBN 0-88057-407-0). Exec Ent Pubns.
Sexual Harassment in the Workplace. 14p. 1981. 1.00 (ISBN 0-317-67865-5). Women's Legal Defense.
Sexual Harassment in the Workplace: Conference Report. Patricia Stover & Yvonne Giles. (Program on Women & Work Ser.). 67p. 1980. pap. 5.00 (ISBN 0-87736-346-3). U of Mich Inst Labor.
Sexual Harassment in the Workplace: The Management View. Iris McQueen. Ed. by Joan Levers & Lowell Moss. LC 82-99921. (Illus.). 138p. (Orig.). 1983. text ed. 24.95 (ISBN 0-9609354-1-X); pap. 14.95 (ISBN 0-9609354-0-1). McQueen & Son.
Sexual Harassment Issues & Answers: A Guide for Education, Business, Industry. Ed. by Nancy H. Deane. LC 87-106408. 39p. 1986. 25.00; 16.00. Coll & U Personnel.
Sexual Harassment of Working Women: A Case of Sex Discrimination. Catharine A. MacKinnon. LC 78-9645. (Fastback Ser.: No. 19). 1979. 37.00x (ISBN 0-300-02298-0); pap. 11.95x (ISBN 0-300-02299-9). Yale U Pr.
Sexual Harassment: The Issues & the Law. members 12.00 (ISBN 0-686-95693-1, 286200); non-members 18.00 (ISBN 0-686-99576-7). Am Bankers.
Sexual Harmony. Edmond B. Szekely. (Illus.). 60p. 1977. pap. 3.50 (ISBN 0-89564-077-5). IBS Intl.
Sexual Harmony in Marriage. Oliver M. Butterfield. LC 84-13625. (Illus.). 1981. pap. 2.95 (ISBN 0-89490-108-7). Enslow Pubs.
Sexual Health in Later Life. Thomas H. Walz & Nancee S. Blum. 144p. 1987. 25.00x (ISBN 0-669-14600-5); pap. 9.95 (ISBN 0-669-14599-8). Lexington Bks.
Sexual Homicide: Patterns, Motives & Procedures for Investigation. Ed. by Robert K. Ressler et al. 256p. 1987. 32.95x (ISBN 0-669-16559-X). Lexington Bks.
Sexual Hormones: Influence on the Electrophysiology of the Brain. Manuel Alcaraz et al. LC 74-4137. 223p. 1974. text ed. 28.00x (ISBN 0-8422-7214-3). Irvington.
Sexual Humor. Baird Jones. LC 86-4927. (Illus.). 364p. 1987. 19.95 (ISBN 0-8022-2478-4). Philos Lib.
Sexual Identity: Implications for Mental Health. Ronald A. LaTorre. LC 78-26442. 184p. 1979. 19.95x (ISBN 0-88229-360-5). Nelson-Hall.
Sexual Identity: Sex Roles & Social Change. Betty Yorburg. LC 80-22489. 240p. 1981. Repr. of 1974 ed. text ed. 16.50 (ISBN 0-89874-265-X). Krieger.
Sexual Impotence in the Male & Female. William A. Hammond. LC 73-20626. (Sex, Marriage & Society Ser.). 310p. 1974. Repr. 24.50x (ISBN 0-405-05802-0). Ayer Co Pubs.
Sexual Imprisonment. Partick G. Oh. 1979. 8.50 (ISBN 0-682-49274-4, Banner). Exposition-Phoenix.
Sexual Indulgence & Denial. Ed. by Charles E. Rosenberg & Carroll-Smith Rosenberg. LC 73-20650. (Sex, Marriage & Society Ser.). 188p. 1974. Repr. 17.00x (ISBN 0-405-05818-7). Ayer Co Pubs.
Sexual Interactions. 2nd ed. Albert R. Allgeier & Elizabeth Allgeier. LC 87-80888. (Illus.). 664p. 1988. text ed. 27.50 (ISBN 0-669-12791-4); study guide 10.50 (ISBN 0-669-12792-2); Instr. Guide file 2.00 (ISBN 0-669-12793-0); Transparencies 80.00 (ISBN 0-669-12794-9); Archive Testing Prog. Apple 150.00 (ISBN 0-669-14771-0); Archive Testing Prog. IBMPC 150.00 (ISBN 0-669-14774-5). Heath.
Sexual Interactions in Eukaryotic Microbes. Ed. by D. H. O'Day & P. A. Horgen. LC 80-39593. (Cell Biology Ser.). 1981. 71.00 (ISBN 0-12-524160-7). Acad Pr.
Sexual Interactions in Plants. Herman Van Den Ende. 1976. 54.50 (ISBN 0-12-711250-2). Acad Pr.
Sexual Intimacy. Andrew Greeley. 200p. 1982. pap. 9.95 (ISBN 0-88347-143-4). Thomas More.
Sexual Intimacy. Andrew M. Greeley. 199p. 1975. pap. 8.95 (ISBN 0-8164-2591-4, HarpR). Har-Row.
Sexual Intimacy Between Therapists & Patients. Kenneth S. Pope & Jacqueline C. Bouhoutsos. LC 86-15165. (Sexual Medicine Ser.: Vol. 5). 197p. 1986. lib. bdg. 29.95 (ISBN 0-275-92253-7, C2253). Praeger.
Sexual Intimacy Between Therapists & Patients. Kenneth S. Pop & Jaxqueline C. Bouhoutsos. LC 86-15165. (Sexual Medicine Ser.: No. 5). 197p. 1988. pap. 14.95 (ISBN 0-275-92953-1, B2953). Praeger.
Sexual Intimacy: Love & Play. Andrew M. Greeley. 1988. pap. 7.95 (ISBN 0-446-38556-5). Warner Bks.
Sexual Inversion. Havelock Ellis & John A. Symonds. LC 75-12312. (Homosexuality: Lesbians & Gay Men in Society, History & Literature Ser.). 1975. Repr. of 1897 ed. 22.00x (ISBN 0-405-07363-1). Ayer Co Pubs.
Sexual Inversion: The Questions-with Catholic Answers. Herbert F. Smith. 1979. 2.95 (ISBN 0-8198-0612-9); pap. 1.95 (ISBN 0-8198-0613-7). Dghtrs St Paul.
Sexual Key to the Tarot. Theodor Laurence. 1973. pap. 3.50 (ISBN 0-451-13301-3, AE3301, Sig). NAL.
Sexual Key to the Tarot. Theodor Lawrence. (Illus.). 1971. 5.95 (ISBN 0-8065-0242-8, Pub. by Citadel Pr). Lyle Stuart.
Sexual Labyrinth of Nikolai Gogol. Simon Karlinsky. 1976. 24.50x (ISBN 0-674-80281-0). Harvard U Pr.
Sexual Landscapes: Why We Are What We Are, Why We Love Whom We Love. James D. Weinrich. 1987. 19.95 (ISBN 0-684-18705-1). Scribner.
Sexual Life in Ancient China. R. H. Van Gulik. 392p. 1981. 525.00x (ISBN 0-317-69050-7, Pub. by Han-Shan Tang Ltd). State Mutual Bk.
Sexual Life in Ancient Egypt. Lise Manniche. (Illus.). 127p. 1987. 29.95 (ISBN 0-7103-0202-9, Routledge UK). Routledge Chapman & Hall.
Sexual Life in Ancient Greece. Hans Licht, pseud. Ed. by Lawrence H. Dawson. Tr. by J. H. Freese from Ger. LC 72-9622. (Illus.). Repr. of 1932 ed. 54.00 (ISBN 0-404-57417-3). AMS Pr.
Sexual Life in Ancient Rome. Otto Kiefer. Tr. by Gilbert Highet & Helen Highet. LC 72-9657. (Illus.). Repr. of 1934 ed. 44.50 (ISBN 0-404-57466-1). AMS Pr.
Sexual Life of Our Time in Its Relation to Modern Civilization. Iwan Bloch. Tr. by M. Eden Paul. LC 72-9619. Repr. of 1910 ed. 80.00 (ISBN 0-404-57415-7). AMS Pr.
Sexual Life of Savages. Bronislaw Malinowski. LC 86-47760. (Illus.). 650p. 1987. pap. 14.95 (ISBN 0-8070-4607-8, BP 740). Beacon Pr.
Sexual Life of Savages in North-Western Melanesia. B. Malinowski. 700p. 1987. pap. text ed. 17.95 (ISBN 0-7100-6659-7, Pub. by Routledge UK). Routledge Chapman & Hall.
Sexual Life of the Child. Albert Moll. Tr. by Eden Paul from Ger. LC 72-11290. Repr. of 1913 ed. 38.50 (ISBN 0-404-57483-1). AMS Pr.
Sexual Life of the Kumaonis: A New Approach to Sexuality. Tribhuwan Kapur. 200p. 1987. text ed. 27.50x (ISBN 0-7069-3292-7, Pub. by Vikas Pub Hse India). Advent NY.
Sexual Love & Western Morality. Ed. by D. P. Verene. pap. 8.95x (ISBN 0-06-131722-5, TB1722, Torch). Har-Row.
Sexual Magic: The S-M Photographs. Michael A. Rosen. (Illus.). 72p. (Orig.). 1986. pap. 25.00 retail (ISBN 0-936705-69-8). Shaynew Pr.
Sexual Maladjustment & Disease: An Introduction to Modern Venereology. Gavin Hart. LC 76-29073. 256p. 1977. 24.95x (ISBN 0-88229-325-7). Nelson-Hall.
Sexual Maturation & the Physical Growth of Girls Age Six to Nineteen. Frank K. Shuttleworth. (SRCD M). 1937. 23.00 (ISBN 0-527-01498-2). Kraus Repr.
Sexual Maturation & the Skeletal Growth of Girls Age Six to Nineteen. Frank K. Shuttleworth. (SRCD M). 1938. pap. 10.00 (ISBN 0-527-01505-9). Kraus Repr.
Sexual Meanings: The Cultural Construction of Gender & Sexuality. Ed. by Sherry Ortner & Harriet Whitehead. LC 80-26655. 448p. 1981. pap. 17.95 (ISBN 0-521-28375-2). Cambridge U Pr.
Sexual Ministry: A Modern Sex Manual. John Bohlen & Karen Bohlen. (Illus.). 345p. 1987. pap. 5.95 (ISBN 0-9607702-2-4). Kingdom God.
Sexual Ministry: Happily Ever After. John Bohlen & Karen Bohlen. (Illus.). 345p. (Orig.). 1987. pap. 5.95. Destiny Image.
Sexual Morality: A Catholic Perspective. Philip Keane. LC 77-83536. 252p. 1978. pap. 9.95 (ISBN 0-8091-2070-4). Paulist Pr.
Sexual Morality: Guidelines for Today's Catholic. Russell M. Abata. 1975. pap. 1.50 (ISBN 0-89243-019-2, 29528). Liguori Pubns.
Sexual Mountain & Black Women Writers: Adventure in Sex, Literature & Real Life. Calvin C. Hernton. LC 87-467. 192p. 1987. pap. 16.95 (ISBN 0-385-23921-1, Anchor Pr). Doubleday.
Sexual Neurasthenia, Its Hygiene, Causes, Symptoms & Treatment with a Chapter on Diet for the Nervous. 5th ed. George M. Beard. Ed. by A. D. Rockwell. LC 76-180553. (Medicine & Society in America Ser). 312p. 1972. Repr. of 1898 ed. 18.00 (ISBN 0-405-03933-6). Ayer Co Pubs.
Sexual Nomenclature: A Thesaurus. Indiana University, Institute for Sex Research Staff. 1977. lib. bdg. 100.00 (ISBN 0-8161-0044-6, Hall Library). G K Hall.
Sexual Nutrition. Morton Walker & Joan Walker. 400p. 1984. pap. 3.95 (ISBN 0-8217-1390-6). Zebra.
Sexual Offences: A Report. F. J. Odgers & F. H. McClintock. Ed. by L. Radzinowicz. (Cambridge Studies in Criminology: Vol. 9). pap. 43.00 (ISBN 0-8115-0423-9). Kraus Repr.
Sexual Offences Against Children, 2 vols. 638p. (Orig.). 1984. pap. text ed. 49.95x (Pub. by Minister Supplies Canada). Brookfield Pub Co.
Sexual Options for Paraplegics & Quadriplegics. Thomas O. Mooney et al. (Illus.). 150p. 1975. pap. 15.00 (ISBN 0-316-57937-8). Little.
Sexual Organism: Its Healthful Management. James C. Jackson. LC 73-20632. (Sex, Marriage & Society Ser.). 296p. 1974. Repr. of 1861 ed. 23.50x (ISBN 0-405-05807-1). Ayer Co Pubs.
Sexual Orientation & the Law. Ed. by Roberta Achtenberg. 75.00. Natl Lawyers Guild.
Sexual Orientation & the Law. National Lawyers Guild, San Francisco Bay Area Chapter, Anti-Sexism Committee & Roberta Achtenberg. LC 84-24213. 1985. 75.00 (ISBN 0-87632-454-5). Clark Boardman.
Sexual Outlaw: A Documentary. John Rechy. LC 83-49452. 320p. 1984. pap. 8.95 (ISBN 0-394-62147-6, E939, Ever). Grove.
Sexual Palmistry: Hand Analysis Techniques for Dealing With Love, Sex & Relationships. Nathaniel Altman. (Illus.). 160p. (Orig.). 1986. pap. 8.99 (ISBN 0-85030-455-5, Pub. by Aquarian Pr England). Sterling.
Sexual Perspective: Homosexuality & Art in the Last 100 Years in the West. Emmanuel Cooper. (Illus.). 320p. 1986. 35.00 (96356, Pub. by Routledge UK); pap. 18.95 (ISBN 0-7102-0902-9, 09029). Routledge Chapman & Hall.
Sexual Perversions & Abnormalities: A Study in the Psychology of Paraphilia. Clifford Allen. LC 78-27783. 1979. Repr. of 1949 ed. lib. bdg. 35.00x (ISBN 0-313-20627-9, ALSP). Greenwood.
Sexual Perversity in Chicago & the Duck Variations. David Mamet. LC 77-91885. 1978. 10.00 (ISBN 0-394-50161-6). Grove.
Sexual Pharmacy: The Complete Guide to Drugs with Sexual Side Effects. M. Laurence Lieberman. 320p. 1988. 18.95 (ISBN 0-317-66926-5). NAL.
Sexual Physiology. R. T. Trall. LC 73-20640. (Sex, Marriage & Society Ser.). 310p. 1974. Repr. 24.50 (ISBN 0-405-05821-7). Ayer Co Pubs.
Sexual Pleasure Enhancement Program. G-Jo Institute Staff. 1980. pap. 4.50 (ISBN 0-916878-12-0). Falkynor Bks.
Sexual Politics. Kate Millett. 1978. pap. 3.95 (ISBN 0-345-29270-7). Ballantine.
Sexual Politics of Jean-Jacques Rousseau. Joel Schwartz. LC 83-18141. xii, 196p. 1985. lib. bdg. 17.00x (ISBN 0-226-74223-7); pap. 7.95x (ISBN 0-226-74224-5). U of Chicago Pr.
Sexual Politics of Reproduction: Feminist Approaches to the Sociology of Human Reproduction. Ed. by Hilary Thomas. 220p. 1985. text ed. 37.95 (ISBN 0-566-00853-X). Gower Pub Co.
Sexual Politics, Sexual Communities: The Making of a Homosexual Minority in the United States, 1940-1970. John D'Emilio. LC 82-16000. 262p. 1983. 20.00x (ISBN 0-226-14265-5). U of Chicago Pr.
Sexual Politics, Sexual Communities: The Making of a Homosexual Minority in the United States, 1940-1970. John D'Emilio. LC 82-16000. 268p. 1984. pap. 9.95 (ISBN 0-226-14266-3). U of Chicago Pr.
Sexual Practices & the Medieval Church. Ed. by Vern Bullough & James Brundage. LC 80-85227. 289p. 1984. pap. 17.95 (ISBN 0-87975-268-8). Prometheus Bks.
Sexual Preference: Its Development in Men & Women. Alan P. Bell et al. 336p. 1981. 20.00x (ISBN 0-253-16674-8). Ind U Pr.
Sexual Problems in Marriage: Help from a Christian Counselor. F. Philip Rice. LC 77-27443. 252p. 1978. softcover 6.95 (ISBN 0-664-24194-8). Westminster John Knox.
Sexual Problems: New Insight, New Solutions. 3.00 (ISBN 0-686-40911-6, SR17). Transitions.
Sexual Problems of Adolescents in Institutions. David A. Shore & Harvey L. Gochros. (Illus.). 262p. 1981. 29.25 (ISBN 0-398-04143-1). C C Thomas.
Sexual Psychology of Males & Females. Otto Weininger. (Illus.). 302p. 1984. Vol.1 & Vol. 2. 247.85 (ISBN 0-89920-103-2). Am Inst Psych.
Sexual Relationship. Gillman Noonan. 148p. 1982. pap. 4.95 (ISBN 0-905169-59-X, Pub. by Poolbeg Pr Ireland). Irish Bks Media.
Sexual Relationship: An Object Relations View of Sex & the Family. David E. Scharff. 288p. 1983. 29.95x (ISBN 0-7100-9072-2). Routledge Chapman & Hall.
Sexual Relationship: An Object Relations View of Sex & the Family. David E. Scharff. (International Library of Group Psychotherapy & Group Processes). 284p. 1988. pap. text ed. 14.95 (ISBN 0-415-00081-5). Routledge Chapman & Hall.
Sexual Repression & Victorian Literature. Russell M. Goldfarb. LC 70-101685. 222p. 1970. 20.00 (ISBN 0-8387-7619-1). Bucknell U Pr.
Sexual Reproduction in the Mucorinaeae. A. F. Blakeslee. (Biblioteca Mycologica Ser: No. 48). 1976. Repr. of 1904 ed. text ed. 24.00x (ISBN 3-7682-1064-2). Lubrecht & Cramer.
Sexual Revolution, Vol 173. Ed. by Gregory Baum & John Coleman. (Concilium Ser.). 128p. pap. 14.95 (ISBN 0-317-31462-9, Pub. by T & T Clark Ltd UK). Fortress.
Sexual Revolution: Challenge & Response. J. Rinzema. Tr. by Lewis B. Smedes. LC 73-14712. pap. 26.80 (ISBN 0-317-09741-5, 2012849). Bks Demand UMI.

Sexual Revolution: Its Impact on Society & a Challenge against the Makers with a Plea for Reforms & Some Recommendations. C. Antonio Provost. write for info. (ISBN 0-318-23066-6). Provost.

Sexual Revolution: Toward a Self-Regulating Character Structure. Wilhelm Reich. Tr. by Therese Pol from Ger. LC 73-76780. 273p. 1974. 12.95 (ISBN 0-374-26172-5); pap. 9.95. FS&G.

Sexual Rights of Adolescents: Competence, Vulnerability, & Parental Control. Hyman Rodman & Susan H. Lewis. LC 83-14440. 183p. 1984. 27.50x (ISBN 0-231-04916-1). Columbia U Pr.

Sexual Rights of Adolescents: Competence, Vulnerability, & Parental Control. Hyman Rodman et al. 183p. 1988. pap. 13.00x (ISBN 0-231-04917-X). Columbia U Pr.

Sexual Sanity. Earl D. Wilson. LC 83-22753. 156p. 1984. pap. 5.95 (ISBN 0-87784-919-6). Inter-Varsity.

Sexual Scarcity: The Marital Mistake & the Communal Alternative. Michael J. Betzold. 1978. pap. 2.50 (ISBN 0-686-10620-2). Betzold.

Sexual Scene. rev. 2nd ed. Ed. by John H. Gagnon & William Simon. LC 72-87668. 150p. 1973. pap. 9.95 (ISBN 0-87855-541-2); 18.95 (ISBN 0-87855-048-8). Transaction Bks.

Sexual Secrets, the Alchemy of Ecstasy. Nik Douglas & Penny Slinger. LC 79-9479. (Illus.). 384p. 1979. 24.95 (ISBN 0-89281-010-6, Destiny Bks); limited signed ed. 250.00 (ISBN 0-89281-009-2); pap. 14.95 (ISBN 0-89281-011-4). Inner Tradit.

Sexual Secrets: When to Keep Them, When & How to Tell. Marty Klein. Ed. by L. Wells. 256p. 1988. 18.95 (ISBN 0-525-24716-5). Dutton.

Sexual Selection & Animal Genetalia. William G. Eberhard. LC 85-907. 256p. 1988. pap. text ed. 14.95 (ISBN 0-674-80284-5). Harvard U Pr.

Sexual Selection & Animal Genitalia. William G. Eberhard. (Illus.). 288p. 1985. text ed. 26.00x (ISBN 0-674-80283-7). Harvard U Pr.

Sexual Selection & Reproductive Competition in Insects. Ed. by Murray S. Blum & Nancy A. Blum. 1979. 56.50 (ISBN 0-12-108750-6). Acad Pr.

Sexual Selection & the Descent of Man. Ed. by Bernard Campbell. LC 70-169510. 388p. 1972. 40.95x (ISBN 0-202-02005-3). Aldine de Gruyter.

Sexual Selection, Lek & Arena Behavior, & Sexual Size Dimorphism in Birds. Robert B. Payne. 52p. 1984. 8.00 (ISBN 0-943610-40-0). Am Ornithologists.

Sexual Selection: Testing the Alternatives. J. W. Bradbury. LC 87-10616. 1988. 81.95 (ISBN 0-471-91624-2). Wiley.

Sexual Self. Avodah K. Offit. 320p. 1983. pap. 9.95 (ISBN 0-312-92766-5). Congdon & Weed.

Sexual Self. Avodah K. Offit. 320p. Date not set. 9.95 (ISBN 0-86553-079-3). Congdon & Weed.

Sexual Self-Destruct: Conscience of the West. Karl K. Lewin. LC 79-54918. 156p. 1980. 15.00 (ISBN 0-87527-197-9). Green.

Sexual Shakedown. Lin Farley. 1980. pap. 2.50 (ISBN 0-446-91251-4). Warner Bks.

Sexual Size Differences in Reptiles. Henry S. Fitch. (Miscellaneous Publications: No. 70). 72p. 1981. 5.25 (ISBN 0-317-04862-7). U of KS Mus Nat Hist.

Sexual Size Differences in the Mainland Anoles. Henry S. Fitch. (Occasional Papers: No. 50). 21p. 1976. pap. 1.25 (ISBN 0-686-80357-4). U of KS Mus Nat Hist.

Sexual Size Dimorphism in Hawks & Owls of North America. Noel F. Snyder & James W. Wiley. 95p. 1976. 7.00 (ISBN 0-943610-20-6). Am Ornithologists.

Sexual Static: How Men Are Confusing the Women They Love. Morton H. Shaevitz. 1987. 14.95 (ISBN 0-316-77292-5). Little.

Sexual Strands: Understanding & Treating Sexual Anomalies in Men. R. Langevin. (Illus.). 560p. 1983. text ed. 49.95x (ISBN 0-89859-205-4). L Erlbaum Assocs.

Sexual Stratagems: The World of Women in Film. Ed. by Patricia Erens. LC 76-20310. (Illus.). 1979. 15.00 (ISBN 0-8180-0706-0); pap. 8.95 (ISBN 0-8180-0707-9). Horizon.

Sexual Strategy. Tim Halliday. LC 82-2607. (Phoenix). (Illus.). 160p. 1982. pap. 12.50 (ISBN 0-226-31387-5). U of Chicago Pr.

Sexual Stratification: A Cross-Cultural View. Ed. by Alice Schlegel. LC 77-2742. 1977. 34.00x (ISBN 0-231-04214-0); pap. 17.00x (ISBN 0-231-04215-9). Columbia U Pr.

Sexual Superstars. R. T. Larkin. 1976. pap. 1.75 (ISBN 0-685-69155-1, LB363KK, Leisure Bks). Leisure NY.

Sexual-Textual Politics. Toril Moi. 200p. 1985. 25.00 (ISBN 0-416-35360-6, 9450); pap. 13.95 (ISBN 0-416-35370-3, 9451). Routledge Chapman & Hall.

Sexual Trafficking in Children: An Investigation of the Child Sex Trade. Daniel S. Campagna & Donald L. Poffenberger. 250p. 1987. 24.95 (ISBN 0-86569-154-1); pap. 17.95 (ISBN 0-86569-155-X). Auburn Hse.

Sexual Trauma in Children & Adolescents: Dynamics & Treatment. Diana S. Everstine & Louis Everstine. 300p. 1989. 32.50 (ISBN 0-87630-529-X). Brunner-Mazel.

Sexual Underworlds of the Enlightenment. Ed. by G. S. Rousseau & Roy Porter. (Illus.). vi, 294p. 1988. 35.00x (ISBN 0-8078-1782-1). U of NC Pr.

Sexual Values: Opposing Viewpoints. 2nd ed. Ed. by Bruno Leone & M. Teresa O'Neill. LC 85-8065. (Opposing Viewpoints Ser.). (Illus.). 160p. (Orig.). 1983. lib. bdg. 13.95 (ISBN 0-89908-344-7); pap. text ed. 6.95 (ISBN 0-89908-319-6). Greenhaven.

Sexual Variance in Society & History. Vern L. Bullough. LC 79-26504. 1980. lib. bdg. 40.00x (ISBN 0-226-07995-3, Phoen); pap. 15.00x (ISBN 0-226-07994-5, P861). U of Chicago Pr.

Sexual Victimisation: Two Recent Researches into Sex Problems & Their Social Effects. Ed. by D. J. West. 194p. 1985. text ed. 29.95 (ISBN 0-566-00832-7). Gower Pub Co.

Sexual Victimization of Adolescents. Ann W. Burgess. 56p. 1985. pap. text ed. 2.00 (ISBN 0-318-22950-1, S/N 017-024-01239-4). USGPO.

Sexual Victimization of Children. Mary De Young. LC 82-17197. 190p. 1982. lib. bdg. 19.95x (ISBN 0-89950-063-3). McFarland & Co.

Sexual Victimology of Youth. LeRoy G. Schultz. (Illus.). 432p. 1980. 51.25 (ISBN 0-398-03925-9). C C Thomas.

Sexual Violence: A Reality for Women. London Rape Crisis Centre Staff. 192p. (Orig.). 1984. pap. 5.95 (ISBN 0-7043-3910-2, Pub. by Quartet Bks). Salem Hse Pubs.

Sexual Violence: The Unmentionable Sin: An Ethical & Pastoral Perspective. Marie M. Fortune. 256p. (Orig.). 1983. pap. 9.95 (ISBN 0-8298-0652-0). Pilgrim NY.

Sexual Woman. Mary A. Mayo & Joseph L. Mayo. LC 87-81048. 240p. (Orig.). 1987. 12.95 (ISBN 0-89081-582-8). Harvest Hse.

Sexualitat des Menschen: Handbuch und Atlas. E. J. Haeberle. 559p. (Ger.). 1983. 21.60 (ISBN 3-11-008753-7). De Gruyter.

Sexuality. Mary Durkin. (Guidelines for Contemporary Catholics Ser.). (Orig.). 1987. pap. 7.95 (ISBN 0-88347-211-2). Thomas More.

Sexuality. Letha D. Scanzoni. LC 83-27375. (Choices: Guides for Today's Woman: Vol. 8). 114p. (Orig.). 1984. pap. 6.95 (ISBN 0-664-24548-X). Westminster John Knox.

Sexuality. Jeffrey Weeks. (Key Ideas Ser.). 128p. 1986. 19.95 (ISBN 0-85312-879-0, 9892, Pub. by Tavistock England); pap. 7.50 (ISBN 0-7458-0002-5, 9876, Pub. by Tavistock England). Routledge Chapman & Hall.

Sexuality, Vol. 1 (incl. 1980-1982 Supplements) Ed. by Eleanor C. Goldstein. (Social Issues Resources Ser.). 1983. 75.00 (ISBN 0-89777-030-7). Soc Issues.

Sexuality: A Health Education Perspective. Mary E. Taylor & Richard St. Pierce. 1988. 12.95 (ISBN 0-910251-26-6). Venture Pub PA.

Sexuality: A Nursing Perspective. Ferm Mims & Melinda Swenson. 1979. pap. text ed. 25.95 (ISBN 0-07-042388-1). McGraw.

Sexuality Alphabet. (Illus.). 24p. 1982. pap. 0.75 (ISBN 0-934586-33-0, 1637). Plan Parent.

Sexuality & Aging. 1978. 4.00 (ISBN 0-938846-04-3). Ebenezer Ctr.

Sexuality & Aging. rev. ed. Robert L. Solnick. LC 78-51932. 1978. pap. 14.00x (ISBN 0-88474-023-4, 05752-5). Lexington Bks.

Sexuality & Aging: An Annotated Bibliography. George F. Wharton. LC 81-5097. 251p. 1981. 19.00 (ISBN 0-8108-1427-7). Scarecrow.

Sexuality & Cancer. Ernest H. Rosenbaum et al. (Orig.). 1980. pap. 2.95 (ISBN 0-915950-39-1). Bull Pub.

Sexuality & Chronic Illness: A Comprehensive Approach. Leslie R. Schover & Soren B. Jensen. 357p. 1988. lib. bdg. 35.00 (ISBN 0-89862-715-X). Guilford Pr.

Sexuality & Dating. Richard Reichert. LC 81-51011. (Illus.). 111p. (gr. 10-11). 1981. pap. 5.00x (ISBN 0-88489-133-X); tchrs' guide 9.00x (ISBN 0-88489-138-0); student workbook 2.00 (ISBN 0-88489-139-9). St Mary's.

Sexuality & Family Planning: Report of a Consultation & Research Findings. T. Langfeldt & M. Porter. 62p. 1986. pap. 4.80 (ISBN 92-890-1042-8). World Health.

Sexuality & Feminism in Shelley. Nathaniel Brown. LC 79-4634. 1979. text ed. 22.50x (ISBN 0-674-80285-3). Harvard U Pr.

Sexuality & Handicap: Problems of Motor Handicapped People. Ed. by B. H. Dechesne et al. (Illus.). 240p. 1986. pap. 38.25x (ISBN 0-398-04746-4). C C Thomas.

Sexuality & Its Discontents: Meaning, Myths & Modern Sexualities. Jeffrey Weeks. 288p. 1985. 25.00s (ISBN 0-7102-0564-3); pap. 13.95 (ISBN 0-7102-0565-1). Routledge Chapman & Hall.

Sexuality & Life-Threatening Illness. Ed. by Margot Tallmer et al. 228p. 1984. 27.25 (ISBN 0-398-05018-X). C C Thomas.

Sexuality & Marriage. James F. Moore. LC 87-12626. 160p. (Orig.). 1987. pap. 8.95 (ISBN 0-8066-2282-2, 10-5729). Augsburg.

Sexuality & Medicine, Vol. I: Conceptual Roots. Ed. by Earl E. Shelp. 1987. lib. bdg. 49.00 (ISBN 90-277-2290-0, Pub. by Reidel Holland). Kluwer Academic.

Sexuality & Mind: The Role of the Father & the Mother in the Psyche. Janine Chasseguet-Smirgel. 167p. 1988. 35.00x; pap. 15.00x (ISBN 0-8147-1414-5). NYU Pr.

Sexuality & Recovery. Barbara McFarland. 20p. (Orig.). 1984. pap. 0.85 (ISBN 0-89486-246-4). Hazelden.

Sexuality & Social Order: The Debate over the Fertility of Women & Workers in France, 1770-1920. Angus McLaren. 240p. 1983. 44.50 (ISBN 0-8419-0744-7). Holmes & Meier.

Sexuality & the Adolescent: A Teaching Guide. Jerelyn Schultz et al. (Contemporary Parenting Choices Ser.: Module 2). 260p. 1981. pap. text ed. 15.95x (ISBN 0-8138-1616-5). Iowa St U Pr.

Sexuality & the Counseling Pastor. Herbert W. Stroup & Norma S. Wood. LC 73-88344. pap. 33.50 (2027176). Bks Demand UMI.

Sexuality & the Genetics of Bacteria. rev. ed. Francois Jacob & E. Wollman. 1961. 39.95 (ISBN 0-12-379450-1). Acad Pr.

Sexuality & the Mentally Retarded: A Clinical & Therapeutic Guidebook. Rosalyn K. Monat. LC 82-9647. (Illus.). 150p. 1982. pap. 20.50 (ISBN 0-316-57820-7). College-Hill.

Sexuality & the Psychology of Love. Sigmund Freud. 1963. pap. 5.95 (ISBN 0-02-076450-2, Collier). Macmillan.

Sexuality & Victorian Literature. Ed. by Don R. Cox. LC 83-21655. (Tennessee Studies in Lit. Ser.: Vol. 27). 280p. 1984. text ed. 12.95x (ISBN 0-87049-424-4); pap. text ed. 12.95 (ISBN 0-87049-438-4). U of Tenn Pr.

Sexuality Counseling: A Training Program. Kay F. Schepp. 400p. text ed. 21.95 (ISBN 0-915202-47-6). Accel Devel.

Sexuality Debates. Sheila Jeffreys. 550p. 1987. 55.00 (ISBN 0-7102-0936-3, 09363, Pub by Pandora Pr). Routledge Chapman & Hall.

Sexuality Education: A Curriculum for Adolescents. Douglas Kirby. 450p. 1984. pap. text ed. 34.95 (ISBN 0-941816-28-1). Network Pubns.

Sexuality Education: A Curriculum for Parent-Child Programs. Douglas Kirby. 212p. 1984. pap. text ed. 29.95 (ISBN 0-941816-29-X). Network Pubns.

Sexuality Education: A Family Life Education Curriculum for Parents & Young Adolescents. Barbara Dawson & Barbara Feibelman. LC 84-61333. 105p. (Orig.). (gr. 4-8). 1984. pap. 9.45 (ISBN 0-934586-14-4). Plan Parent.

Sexuality Education: A Guide to Developing & Implementing Programs. Douglas Kirby. 132p. 1984. pap. text ed. 19.95 (ISBN 0-941816-27-3). Network Pubns.

Sexuality Education: A Handbook for the Evaluation Programs. Douglas Kirby. 192p. 1984. pap. text ed. 24.95 (ISBN 0-941816-30-3). Network Pubns.

Sexuality Education: An Evaluation of Programs & Their Effects. Douglas Kirby. 462p. 1984. pap. text ed. 39.95 (ISBN 0-941816-26-5). Network Pubns.

Sexuality Education for Parents of Young Children: A Facilitator Training Manual. Sally Koblinsky. (Illus.). 300p. (Orig.). 1983. pap. 13.95 (ISBN 0-934978-05-0). Ed U Pr.

Sexuality Education: Theory & Practice. 2nd ed. Clint E. Bruess & Jerrold S. Greenberg. 397p. 1988. text ed. write for info. (ISBN 0-02-315691-0). Macmillan.

Sexuality: God's Good Idea. Carolyn Nystrom & Matthew Floding. (Young Fisherman Bible Studyguides Ser.). 64p. (Orig.). (YA) (gr. 9-12). 1988. pap. 2.95 (ISBN 0-87788-764-0); tchr's. ed. 4.95 (ISBN 0-87788-765-9). Shaw Pubs.

Sexuality: Human Needs & Nursing Practice. Janie S. Weinberg. (Illus.). 352p. 1982. pap. 22.95 (ISBN 0-7216-9152-8). Saunders.

Sexuality in America: Contemporary Perspectives on Sexual Identity, Dysfunction & Treatment. Donald A. Brown & Chanda Clary. LC 81-81824. 1981. 24.50 (ISBN 0-87650-132-3). Pierian.

Sexuality in Eighteenth-Century Britain. Ed. by Paul-Gabriel Bouce. LC 82-8785. (Illus.). 274p. 1982. text ed. 28.50x (ISBN 0-389-20313-0, 07151). B&N Imports.

Sexuality in Islam. Abdelwahab Bouhdiba. 288p. 1985. 42.50x (ISBN 0-7100-9608-9). Routledge Chapman & Hall.

Sexuality in Later Life. L. Croft. (Illus.). 204p. 1981. pap. 24.00 (ISBN 0-7236-7002-1). PSG Pub Co.

Sexuality in Plants & Its Hormonal Regulation. M. K. Chailakhyan & V. N. Khrianin. (Illus.). 175p. 1987. 67.00 (ISBN 0-387-96488-6). Springer-Verlag.

Sexuality in the Later Years: Roles & Behavior. Ed. by Ruth B. Weg. LC 82-11395. 1983. 24.95 (ISBN 0-12-741320-0). Acad Pr.

Sexuality in the Movies. Ed. by Thomas R. Atkins. LC 84-11403. (Quality Paperbacks Ser.). (Illus.). 244p. 1984. pap. 12.95 (ISBN 0-306-80220-1). Da Capo.

Sexuality in the Second Decade. Raymond R. Willoughby. (SRCD M). 1937. pap. 14.00 (ISBN 0-527-01496-6). Kraus Repr.

Sexuality in World Cinema, 2 vols. James L. Limbacher. LC 83-3019. 1535p. 1983. 77.50 (ISBN 0-8108-1609-1). Vol. 1: A-K. Vol. 2: L-Z. Scarecrow.

Sexuality: Insights & Issues. Jerrold S. Greenberg et al. 568p. 1986. text ed. write for info. (ISBN 0-697-00466-X); pap. text ed. write for info. (ISBN 0-697-00482-1); write for info. instr's. manual (ISBN 0-697-00859-2); write for info. transparencies (ISBN 0-697-00858-4). Wm C Brown.

Sexuality, Magic & Perversion. Francis King. (Illus.). 1972. 6.95 (ISBN 0-8065-0289-4, Pub. by Citadel Pr). Lyle Stuart.

Sexuality, Magic & Perversion. Francis King. 208p. 1974. pap. 3.45 (ISBN 0-8065-0454-4, Pub. by Citadel Pr). Lyle Stuart.

Sexuality: New Perspectives. Ed. by Zira DeFries et al. LC 84-28991. (Contributions in Psychology Ser.: No. 6). (Illus.). xii, 362p. 1985. lib. bdg. 46.95 (ISBN 0-313-24207-0, DFS/). Greenwood.

Sexuality, Nursing & Health. C. Webb. LC 85-13627. 1985. pap. 16.60 (ISBN 0-471-90818-5). Wiley.

Sexuality of Christ in Renaissance Art & in Modern Oblivion. Leo Steinberg. (Illus.). 1984. 19.45 (ISBN 0-394-53580-4); pap. 14.95 (ISBN 0-394-72267-1). Pantheon.

Sexuality of Men. Ed. by Andy Metcalf & Martin Humphries. 194p. 1985. pap. 8.50 (ISBN 0-86104-638-2, Pub. by Pluto Pr). Longwood Pub Group.

Sexuality Papers: Male Sexuality & the Social Control of Women. Lal Coveney et al. LC 84-12867. (Explorations in Feminism Ser.). 109p. (Orig.). 1984. pap. 5.95 (ISBN 0-09-156971-0, Pub. by Hutchinson Educ). Longwood Pub Group.

Sexuality-Related Measures: A Compendium. Ed. by Clive M. Davis et al. 280p. 1988. pap. 39.50. Graphic Pub.

Sexuality-Textuality: A Study of the Fabric of Montaigne's "Essais". Robert D. Cottrell. LC 81-2085. 197p. 1981. 18.50 (ISBN 0-8142-0326-4). Ohio St U Pr.

Sexuality, the Bible & Science. Stephen Sapp. LC 76-62617. pap. 38.00 (2026976). Bks Demand UMI.

Sexuality: Theological Voices. Kevin T. McMahon. 350p. (Orig.). 1987. pap. 14.95 (ISBN 0-935372-20-2). Pope John Ctr.

Sexuality Today. Gilbert D. Nass & Mary P. Fisher. 488p. 1988. text ed. 30.00 (ISBN 0-86720-408-7). Jones & Bartlett.

Sexuality Today: The Human Perspective. Gary F. Kelly. LC 88-703137. (Illus.). 512p. 1988. pap. text ed. 15.95 (ISBN 0-87967-750-3). Dushkin Pub.

Sexuality, Vol. 2 (incl. 1983-1987 Supplements) Ed. by Eleanor C. Goldstein. (Social Issues Resources Ser.). 1987. 75.00 (ISBN 0-89777-062-5). Soc Issues.

Sexualleben der Griechen und Roemer von den Anfaengen Bis 6. Jahrhundert nach Christus. Theodor Hopfner. LC 72-9653. Repr. of 1938 ed. 57.50 (ISBN 0-404-57462-9). AMS Pr.

Sexually Abused Children & Their Families. Patricia B. Mrazek & C. H. Kempe. 300p. 1982. pap. text ed. 17.75 (ISBN 0-08-030194-0). Pergamon.

Sexually Abused Children & Their Families. Ed. by Patricia B. Mrazek & C. Henry Kempe. 263p. 1981. soft-cover 18.00 (ISBN 0-318-14676-2). Kempe Nat Ctr.

Sexually Adequate Female. Caprio. pap. 3.00 (ISBN 0-87980-146-8). Wilshire.

Sexually Adequate Male. Caprio. pap. 3.00 (ISBN 0-87980-147-6). Wilshire.

Sexually Dangerous Poet. Walta Borawski. 1984. pap. 5.00 (ISBN 0-915480-16-6). Good Gay.

Sexually Fulfilled Man. Rachel Copeland. pap. 5.00 (ISBN 0-87980-403-3). Wilshire.

Sexually Fulfilled Woman. Rachel Copeland. 1983. pap. 5.00 (ISBN 0-87980-402-5). Wilshire.

Sexually Mature Larval Hemiramphidae from the Hawaiian Islands. O. Schindler. (BMB). pap. 10.00 (ISBN 0-527-02203-9). Kraus Repr.

Sexually Transmissable Diseases: The Facts. 1985. pap. 0.75 (ISBN 0-934586-45-4, 1606). Plan Parent.

Sexually Transmitted Chlamydial Infections: New Approaches to Treatment. Ed. by D. Taylor-Robinson. (International Congress & Symposium Ser.: No. 111). 1987. pap. write for info. (ISBN 0-905958-42-X, Pub. by Royal Society of Medicine Services Ltd). Longwood Pub Group.

Sexually Transmitted Disease Control. Business Communications Staff. 175p. 1984. 1500.00 (ISBN 0-89336-374-X, C-049). BCC.

Sexually Transmitted Disease: Guidelines for Physicians & Health Workers. Alan S. Meltzer. 86p. (Orig.). 1981. handbook 6.95 (ISBN 0-88831-126-5). Eden Pr.

Sexually Transmitted Diseases. Ed. by R. D. Catterall. 1976. 76.00 (ISBN 0-12-164150-3). Acad Pr.

Sexually Transmitted Diseases. Ed. by Yehudi M. Felman. (Illus.). 321p. 1986. text ed. 65.00 (ISBN 0-443-08331-2). Churchill.

Sexually Transmitted Diseases. Ed. by Dale C. Garell & Solomon H. Snyder. (Encyclopedia of Health Ser.). (Illus.). (YA) (gr. 7-12). 1989. 17.95 (ISBN 0-7910-0080-X). Chelsea Hse.

Sexually Transmitted Diseases. D. Goldmeier & S. Barton. 120p. 1986. pap. 12.10 (ISBN 0-387-17056-1). Springer-Verlag.

Sexually Transmitted Diseases. 2nd rev. ed. Gavin Hart. Ed. by J. J. Head. LC 83-70603. (Carolina Biology Readers Ser.). (Illus.). 16p. (gr. 10 up). 1984. pap. 1.65 (ISBN 0-89278-200-5, 45-9695). Carolina Biological.

Sexually Transmitted Diseases. Ed. by King K. Holmes et al. 1108p. 1984. text ed. 85.00 (ISBN 0-07-029675-8). McGraw.

Sexually Transmitted Diseases. Elaine Landau. LC 85-4349. (Illus.). 96p. (gr. 6-12). 1986. lib. bdg. 13.95 (ISBN 0-89490-115-X). Enslow Pubs.

Sexually Transmitted Diseases. 3rd ed. Robert C. Noble. (Vol. 8). 1984. pap. text ed. 38.00 (ISBN 0-87488-436-5). Med Exam.

Sexually Transmitted Diseases. 3rd ed. C. B. Schofield. (Illus.). 1978. pap. text ed. 16.00 (ISBN 0-443-01805-7). Churchill.

Sexually Transmitted Diseases. Spagna. (Reproductive Medicine Ser.). 568p. 1985. 95.00 (ISBN 0-8247-7310-1). Dekker.

Sexually Transmitted Diseases. C. Howard Tseng et al. LC 87-50304. 150p. (Orig.). 1987. pap. 9.95 (ISBN 0-88247-770-6). R & E Pubs.

Sexually Transmitted Diseases: An Annotated Selective Bibliography. Stephen Margolis. LC 83-48248. (Garland Reference Library of Social Science). 200p. (Orig.). 1984. lib. bdg. 23.00 (ISBN 0-8240-9092-6). Garland Pub.

Sexually Transmitted Diseases in Homosexual Men: Diagnosis, Treatment, & Research. Ed. by David G. Ostrow et al. LC 83-10957. (Illus.). 292p. 1983. 45.00x (ISBN 0-306-41337-X, Plenum Pr.). Plenum Pub.

Sexually Transmitted Diseases: The Facts. David Barlow. (Facts Ser.). (Illus.). 1979. text ed. 14.95x (ISBN 0-19-261157-7). Oxford U Pr.

Sexually Transmitted Diseases: The Facts. David Barlow. (Facts Ser.). (Illus.). 1979. pap. 6.95 (ISBN 0-19-520276-7). Oxford U Pr.

Sexually Unusual: Guide to Understanding & Helping. Dennis M. Dailey. (Journal of Social Work & Human Sexuality Ser.: Vol. 7, No. 1). (Illus.). 183p. 1988. pap. text ed. 12.95 (ISBN 0-918393-63-9). Harrington Pk.

Sexually Unusual: Guide to Understanding & Helping. Ed. by Dennis M. Dailey. (Journal of Social Work & Human Sexuality Ser.: Vol. 7, No. 1). (Illus.). 183p. 1988. text ed. 22.95 (ISBN 0-86656-786-0); pap. 12.95 (ISBN 0-86656-847-6). Haworth Pr.

Sexually Victimized Children. David Finkelhor. LC 79-7104. 1979. 19.95 (ISBN 0-02-910210-3); pap. 14.95 1981 (ISBN 0-02-910400-9). Free Pr.

Sexus. Henry Miller. (Orig.). 1965. pap. 5.95 (ISBN 0-394-17430-5, B325, BC). Grove.

Sexus. Henry Miller. LC 86-33723. (Rosy Crucifixion Ser.: Bk. 1). 640p. 1987. pap. 9.95 (ISBN 0-394-62371-1, BC). Grove.

Sexus see Rosy Crucifixion.

Sexy Buttocks: How to Get Them & How to Keep Them. Susan L. Peterson & James A. Peterson. LC 83-80742. (Illus.). 80p. (Orig.). 1983. pap. 4.95 (ISBN 0-88011-163-1). Scribner.

Sexy Legs: How to Get Them & How to Keep Them. Susan L. Peterson & James A. Peterson. LC 83-80741. (Orig.). 1983. pap. 6.95 (ISBN 0-88011-162-3). Scribner.

Sexy Legs in Twenty Days: Spot Reducing the Aerobics Way. Deborah Frichman-McKenzie. (Illus.). 64p. 1983. 2.95 (ISBN 0-399-50780-9, Perigee). Putnam Pub Group.

Sexy Robots: Genkosha (Airbrush, Erotic Female Robots) (Illus.). 1984. 19.95 (ISBN 4-7683-0001-4). Bks Nippan.

Sexy Stomach: How to Get It & How to Keep It. James A. Peterson & Susan L. Peterson. LC 82-83928. (Illus.). 64p. (Orig.). 1983. pap. 4.95 (ISBN 0-88011-096-1). Scribner.

Seychelles. rev. ed. (Hildebrand Travel Guides). 128p. (Orig.). 1988. pap. 8.95 (ISBN 3-88989-069-5). Hunter Pub NY.

Seychelles. (Let's Visit Places & Peoples - - Nations, Dependencies, & Sovereignties of the World Ser.). (Illus.). (gr. 5 up). 1988. 12.95 (ISBN 0-7910-0104-0). Chelsea Hse.

Seychelles: Unquiet Islands. Marcus Franda. LC 82-1979. (Nations of Contemporary Africa Ser.). (Illus.). 140p. 1982. lib. bdg. 28.50x (ISBN 0-86531-266-4). Westview.

Seyidu Kamara Ka Donkiliw. Bourama Soumaoro & Charles S. Bird. (Occasional Papers in Mande Studies). 101p. (Orig.). 1976. pap. text ed. 5.00 (ISBN 0-941934-18-7). Indiana Africa.

Seymore Snake & Friends: Chester Does His Chores Speech Reinforcement for the Ch Sound. Katherine T. McAvoy. (gr. 3-6). 1981. pap. text ed. 9.95 (ISBN 0-86703-034-8). Opportunities Learn.

Seymore Snake & Friends: Complete Program. Katherine T. McAvoy. (gr. 3-6). 1981. pap. text ed. 57.00 (ISBN 0-86703-030-5). Opportunities Learn.

Seymore Snake & Friends: Freddy the Frog Speech Reinforcement for the R Sound. Katherine T. McAvoy. (gr. 3-6). 1981. pap. text ed. 9.95 (ISBN 0-86703-032-1). Opportunities Learn.

Seymore Snake & Friends-Liam the Leprechaun: Speech Reinforcement for the L Sound. Katherine T. McAvoy. (gr. 3-6). pap. text ed. 9.95 (ISBN 0-86703-033-X). Opportunities Learn.

Seymore Snake & Friends: S Sound Reinforcement. Katherine T. McAvoy. (gr. 3-6). 1981. pap. text ed. 9.95 (ISBN 0-86703-031-3). Opportunities Learn.

Seymore Snake & Friends: Shadra O'Shay: Speech Reinforcement for the Sh Sound. Katherine T. McAvoy. (gr. 3-6). 1981. pap. text ed. 9.95 (ISBN 0-86703-035-6). Opportunities Learn.

Seymore Snake & Friends: Theodore Throughly: Speech Reinforcement for the Th Sound. Katherine T. McAvoy. (gr. 3-6). 1981. pap. text ed. 9.95 (ISBN 0-86703-036-4). Opportunities Learn.

Seymour - An Introduction see Raise High the Roof Beam, Carpenters & Seymour: An Introduction.

Sez Who? Sez Me. Mike Royko. 336p. 1983. pap. 3.95 (ISBN 0-446-30896-X). Warner Bks.

Sezz Who? John Lomax. LC 73-83916. 1974. 12.95 (ISBN 0-87949-021-7). Ashley Bks.

SF Book of Lists. Maxim Jakubowski & Malcolm Edwards. 352p. (Orig.). 1983. pap. 7.95 (ISBN 0-425-06187-6). Berkley Pub.

SF in Dimension. 2nd ed. Alexei Panshin & Cory Panshin. LC 80-68572. 1980. pap. 7.00 (ISBN 0-911682-24-4). Advent.

SF One Seventy One: The Federal Employment Application Form. Pauline J. White. 128p. 1988. pap. 4.95 (ISBN 0-13-396672-0). P-H.

SF Published in Nineteen Seventy-Seven. Joanne Burger. (Orig.). 1978. pap. 4.00x (ISBN 0-916188-08-6). J Burger.

SF: the Other Side of Realism. Thomas Clareson. 370p. 14.95 (ISBN 0-87972-022-0); pap. 8.95 (ISBN 0-87972-023-9). Bowling Green Univ.

S.F.B.J.-Captivating Character Children. Ann M. Porot & Jacques Porot. (Illus.). 272p. 1986. 25.00 (ISBN 0-87588-279-X, 3302). Hobby Hse.

SFBRI: Science Fiction Book Review Index, Vols. 1-10. H. W. Hall. Incl. Vol. 1. 1970 (ISBN 0-89370-066-5); Vol. 2. 1971 (ISBN 0-89370-067-3); Vol. 3. 1972 (ISBN 0-89370-068-1); Vol. 4. 1973 (ISBN 0-89370-069-X); Vol. 5. 1974 (ISBN 0-89370-070-3); Vol. 6. 1975 (ISBN 0-89370-071-1); Vol. 7. 1976 (ISBN 0-89370-072-X); Vol. 8. 1977 (ISBN 0-89370-073-8); Vol. 9. 1978 (ISBN 0-89370-074-6); Vol. 10. 1980 (ISBN 0-89370-075-4). LC 72-625320. 64p. Vols. 1-10. lib. bdg. 19.95x ea. Borgo Pr.

SFBRI: Science Fiction Book Review Index, 1975, Vol. 6. H. W. Hall. LC 72-625320. 1976. 5.50x (ISBN 0-935064-01-X). SFBRI.

SFBRI: Science Fiction Book Review Index, Vol. 10, 1979. Ed. by H. W. Hall. LC 72-625320. (Orig.). 1980. pap. 7.50x (ISBN 0-935064-05-2). SFBRI.

SFBRI: Science Fiction Book Review Index, Vol. 11. H. W. Hall. 64p. 1981. lib. bdg. 19.95x (ISBN 0-89370-076-2). Borgo Pr.

SFBRI: Science Fiction Book Review Index, Vol. 11, 1980. H. W. Hall. LC 72-625320. 54p. (Orig.). 1981. pap. text ed. 7.50x (ISBN 0-935064-06-0). SFBRI.

SFBRI: Science Fiction Book Review Index, Vol. 12. H. W. Hall. 64p. 1982. lib. bdg. 19.95x (ISBN 0-89370-077-0). Borgo Pr.

SFBRI: Science Fiction Book Review Index, 1981, Vol. 12. 46p. 1981. 7.50x (ISBN 0-935064-07-9). SFBRI.

SFBRI: Science Fiction Book Review Index, Vol. 13. H. W. Hall. 64p. 1983. lib. bdg. 19.95x (ISBN 0-89370-078-9). Borgo Pr.

SFBRI: Science Fiction Book Review Index, 1982, Vol. 13. Ed. by H. W. Hall. LC 72-625320. 50p. 1983. pap. 7.50 (ISBN 0-935064-08-7). SFBRI.

SFBRI: Science Fiction Book Review Index, Vol. 14. H. W. Hall. 80p. 1984. Repr. of 1984 ed. lib. bdg. 19.95x (ISBN 0-89370-773-2). Borgo Pr.

SFBRI: Science Fiction Book Review Index, 1983, Vol. 14. Ed. by H. W. Hall. LC 72-625320. 61p. (Orig.). 1984. pap. 7.50x (ISBN 0-935064-14-1). SFBRI.

SFBRI: Science Fiction Book Review Index, Vol. 15. H. W. Hall. 80p. 1985. lib. bdg. 19.95x (ISBN 0-89370-570-5). Borgo Pr.

SFBRI: Science Fiction Book Review Index, Vol. 16. H. W. Hall. lib. bdg. 22.95x (ISBN 0-89370-531-4). Borgo Pr.

Sforno: Commentary on the Torah. Raphael Pellcovitz. (ArtScroll Mesorah Ser.: Vol. I - Bereishis-Shmos). 420p. 1987. 19.95 (ISBN 0-89906-238-5); pap. 15.95 (ISBN 0-89906-239-3). Mesorah Pubns.

Sforza Court: Milan in the Renaissance, 1450-1535. Ed. by Andrea S. Norris. (Illus.). 228p. 1989. 50.00 (ISBN 0-935213-13-9). A M Huntington Art.

Sforzando! Music Medicine for String Players. American String Teachers Association Staff. Ed. by Anne Mischakoff. 1985. pap. text ed. 7.95 (ISBN 0-89917-462-0). Am String Tchrs.

SGML Users Guide to ISO 8879. Smith. (Computers & Their Applications Ser.). 168p. 1988. 39.95 (ISBN 0-470-21126-1). Wiley.

Sh-Ko & His Eight Wicked Brothers. Ashley Bryan. LC 88-892. (Illus.). 32p. (ps-3). 1988. 12.95 (ISBN 0-689-31446-9, Atheneum Childrens Bks). Macmillan.

SH Reference Guide. Anatole Olczak. 12p. (Orig.). pap. 7.95 (ISBN 0-935739-05-X). A System Pubns.

Shaanxi Chutu Shang Zhou Qingtongqii. Shaanxi Xian Kaogu Yanjiusuo. 37p. 1979. 161.00x (ISBN 0-317-69051-5, Pub. by Han-Shan Tang Ltd). State Mutual Bk.

Shaanxi Sheng Chutu Tangyong Xuanji: Selection of Tang Figures Unearthed in Shaanxi. 1958. 175.00x (ISBN 0-317-45227-4, Pub. by Han-Shan Tang Ltd). State Mutual Bk.

Shaanxi Tang Sancai Young: Three Colour Tang Pottery Figures Found in Shaanxi Province. 1964. 250.00x (ISBN 0-317-45230-4, Pub. by Han-Shan Tang Ltd). State Mutual Bk.

Shaanxi Tongquan Yaozhou Yao: Excavations of Yaozhou Kiln Sites at Tongquan Shaanxi. 62p. 1965. 240.00x (ISBN 0-317-45232-0, Pub. by Han-Shan Tang Ltd). State Mutual Bk.

Shaare Rahmin: Sermon Material for the High Holidays in Hebrew. P. S. Pollak. 7.50 (ISBN 0-87559-104-3). Shalom.

Shaarei Selicha: Gates of Forgiveness. Ed. by Chaim Stern. 96p. (Eng. & Hebrew.). pap. 1.00 (ISBN 0-317-33900-1, 57-7E, 74-7H). Central Conf.

Shabbat: A Peaceful Island (a Jewish Holidays Book) Malka Drucker. LC 83-7900. (Illus.). 96p. (gr. 5up). 1983. reinforced bdg. 11.95 (ISBN 0-8234-0500-1). Holiday.

Shabbat & the Young Child. 64p. 2.50 (ISBN 0-318-13633-3, 22-051). Board Jewish Educ.

Shabbat Can Be. Audrey F. Marcus & Raymond A. Zwerin. Ed. by Daniel B. Syme. (Illus.). (gr. k-3). 1979. pap. text ed. 7.95 (ISBN 0-8074-0023-8, 102560); tchrs'. guide 3.00 (ISBN 0-8074-0024-6, 208025). UAHC.

Shabbat Cantata see Kadima Kesher Series.

Shabbat Catalogue. Ruth Brin. 1971. 5.00x (ISBN 0-87068-636-4). Ktav.

Shabbat Haggadah for Celebration & Study. Michael Strassfeld. LC 80-83430. 124p. 1980. pap. 5.50 (ISBN 0-87495-025-2). Am Jewish Comm.

Shabbat Manual. 1972. pap. 5.95 (ISBN 0-916694-54-2). Central Conf.

Shabbat Morning Service, Bk. 1: The Shema & Its Blessings. Commentary by Jules Harlow. 96p. 1985. pap. text ed. 3.50x (ISBN 0-87441-417-2); tchr's ed., 86 pps. 14.95x (ISBN 0-87441-430-X). Behrman.

Shabbat Morning Service, Bk. 2: The Shabbat Amidah. Jules Harlow. 96p. 1986. pap. text ed. 3.50x (ISBN 0-87441-432-6); By Roberta O. Baum. tchr's ed.,109p 14.95x (ISBN 0-87441-437-7). Behrman.

Shabbat Shalom: A Renewed Encounter with the Sabbath. Pinchas Peli. 120p. 1986. pap. 7.95 (ISBN 0-940646-37-4). Rossel Bks.

Shabbath, 3 vols. (Hebrew & Eng.). 45.00 (ISBN 0-910218-53-6). Bennet Pub.

Shabbos Is Coming. Ruth Lipson. (Sifrei Rimon Ser.). 1985. pap. 2.95 (ISBN 0-87306-383-X). Feldheim.

Shabono. Florinda Donner. 1983. pap. 3.95 (ISBN 0-440-38276-9, LE). Dell.

Shabtis. W. M. Petrie. 1974. 25.00 (ISBN 0-85668-012-5, Pub. by Aris & Phillips UK). Humanities.

Shabunin Affair: An Episode in the Life of Leo Tolstoy. Walter Kerr. LC 81-70715. (Illus.). 192p. 1982. 25.95x (ISBN 0-8014-1461-X). Cornell U Pr.

Shackelton's Nutrition: Essentials & Diet Therapy. 5th ed. Charlotte L. Poleman & Christine L. Capra. (Illus.). 384p. 1984. pap. 22.95 (ISBN 0-7216-7280-9). Saunders.

Shackle. Colette. 1982. pap. 2.50 (ISBN 0-345-30058-0). Ballantine.

Shackle. Colette. Tr. by Antonia White from Fr. 224p. 1976. 7.95 (ISBN 0-374-26184-9); pap. 3.95 (ISBN 0-374-51311-2). FS&G.

Shackles: A "Nameless Detective" Mystery. Bill Pronzini. 272p. 1988. 16.95 (ISBN 0-312-01818-5, Pub. by Thomas Dunne Bks). St Martin.

Shackleton. Roland Huntford. (Illus.). 452p. 1986. 29.95 (ISBN 0-689-11429-X). Atheneum.

Shackleton. Roland Huntford. 1987. pap. 12.95 (ISBN 0-449-90269-2, Columbine). Fawcett.

Shackleton's Boat Journey. F. A. Worsley. (Illus.). 224p. 1987. pap. 6.95 (ISBN 0-393-30376-4). Norton.

Shade Book. rev. ed. Judy Lindahl. (Illus.). 128p. pap. 6.95 (ISBN 0-9603032-2-7). Lindahl.

Shade Gardening. A. Cort Sinnes. Ed. by Ken Burke. LC 82-82159. (Illus.). 96p. (Orig.). 1982. pap. 6.95 (ISBN 0-89721-005-0). Ortho.

Shade of Difference. Allen Drury. LC 62-8838. 1962. 10.95 (ISBN 0-385-02389-8). Doubleday.

Shade of His Hand. Oswald Chambers. 1961. pap. 3.95 (ISBN 0-87508-127-4). Chr Lit.

Shade of the Balkans. Henry Bernard. 1978. Repr. of 1904 ed. lib. bdg. 50.00 (ISBN 0-8495-0425-2). Arden Lib.

Shade of the Balkans: Being a Collection of Bulgarian Folksongs & Proverbs. Intro. by Henry Bernard. LC 73-15747. Repr. of 1904 ed. lib. bdg. 45.00 (ISBN 0-8414-3331-3). Folcroft.

Shade of the Tree. Piers Anthony. 352p. 1986. 15.95 (ISBN 0-312-93724-5). St Martin.

Shade of the Tree. Piers Anthony. 352p. 1987. pap. 3.95 (ISBN 0-8125-3103-5). Tor Bks.

Shade of the Tree. Jack I. Brown. 176p. 1988. 12.95 (ISBN 0-89962-732-3). Todd & Honeywell.

Shades. Betty Brock. (gr. 3-5). 1983. pap. 1.25 (ISBN 0-380-01545-5, 27888, Camelot). Avon.

Shades. Heather McHugh. viii, 80p. 1988. 18.50x (ISBN 0-8195-2142-6); pap. 9.95 (ISBN 0-8195-1137-4). Wesleyan U Pr.

Shades & Shadows: An Anthology of Modern Poetry. Ed. by Louisa Persing. (Illus.). 1973. 5.50 (ISBN 0-686-05276-5). Palomar.

Shades of Brown: New Perspectives on School Desegregation. Ed. by Derrick Bell. LC 80-21877. 1980. text ed. 13.95x (ISBN 0-8077-2595-1). Tchrs Coll.

Shades of Dark. Ed. by Aidan Chambers. LC 85-45840. (Charlotte Zolotow Bks.). 128p. (YA) (gr. 7 up). 1986. 11.25i (ISBN 0-06-021247-0); PLB 11.89 (ISBN 0-06-021248-9). HarpJ.

Shades of Gray. Mark Denning. (Private Library Collection). 274p. 1986. mini-bound 6.95 (ISBN 0-938422-20-0). SOS Pubns CA.

Shades of Gray. Kay Hooper. (Loveswept Ser.: No. 286). 192p. 1988. pap. 2.50 (ISBN 0-553-21905-7). Bantam.

Shades of Gray. Timothy R. O'Neill. 352p. 1987. 17.95 (ISBN 0-670-81133-5). Viking.

Shades of Gray. Timothy R. O'Neill. 352p. 1988. pap. 3.95 (ISBN 0-345-35425-7). Ballantine.

Shades of Gray: Over a Hundred Years. Robert N. Gray & Joan G. Hull. 312p. (Orig.). 1987. pap. 8.95 (ISBN 0-943087-00-7). Traditional OK.

Shades of Green. Shree Devi. (Writers Workshop Redbird Ser). 1975. 8.00 (ISBN 0-88253-632-X); pap. text ed. 4.00 (ISBN 0-88253-631-1). Ind-US Inc.

Shades of Green & Grey. Barbra Chadwick. (Illus.). 32p. 1980. 5.95 (ISBN 0-89962-033-7). Todd & Honeywell.

Shades of Hades: Ladies in Hades, 2 vols. in 1. Frederic A. Kummer. Ed. by R. Reginald & Douglas Melville. LC 77-84242. (Lost Race & Adult Fantasy Ser.). (Illus.). 1978. Repr. of 1930 ed. lib. bdg. 44.00x (ISBN 0-405-10990-3). Ayer Co Pubs.

Shades of Heathcliffe & Death of Captain Doughty. John Spurling. 96p. 1978. (Dist by Scribner); pap. 5.95 (ISBN 0-7145-2518-9). M Boyars Pubs.

Shades of Lebanon. Debe K. Scott. 48p. 1989. 6.95 (ISBN 0-89962-792-7). Todd & Honeywell.

Shades of Minos. Joe E. Pierce. 146p. 1973. pap. 5.95 (ISBN 0-913244-04-X). Hapi Pr.

Shades of Reckoning. Steve Waterhouse. 1982. 15.00x (ISBN 0-906660-79-3, Pub. by New Playwrights Network). State Mutual Bk.

Shades of Salem. Ruth W. Schuler. (Illus.). 48p. (Orig.). 1987. pap. text ed. 5.00 (ISBN 0-910083-10-X). Heritage Trails.

Shades of the Past; or, Indiscreet Tales of Japan. Harold S. Williams. LC 63-19394. (Illus.). 352p. 1972. pap. 7.95 (ISBN 0-8048-1050-8). C E Tuttle.

Shades of the Sunbelt: Essays on Ethnicity, Race, & the Urban South. Ed. by Randall M. Miller & George E. Pozzetta. LC 87-18164. (Contributions in American History Ser.: No. 128). 240p. 1988. lib. bdg. 39.95 (ISBN 0-313-25690-X, MET/). Greenwood.

Shades of the Wilderness: A Story of Lee's Great Stand. Joseph A. Altsheler. 312p. Repr. of 1916 ed. lib. bdg. 20.95x (ISBN 0-88411-940-8, Pub. by Aeonian Pr). Amereon Ltd.

Shades of Yesteryear. Marion Pond. LC 82-71114. (Illus.). 48p. (Orig.). 1982. pap. 7.50 (ISBN 0-941284-13-1). Deco Design Studio.

Shading TV Guide lack Side: A Book. George Hill & Robert P. Davenport. (Bibliographic Perspective, 1953-1987). 75p. 1987. text ed. 13.00 (ISBN 0-933650-12-4); pap. text ed. 8.00 (ISBN 0-933650-13-2). Daystar Co Carson.

Shadow. Marcia Brown. LC 86-3432. (Illus.). 32p. (gr. k up). 1986. pap. 3.95 (ISBN 0-689-71084-4, Aladdin Bks). Macmillan.

Shadow. Blaise Cendrars. Tr. & illus. by Brown Marcia. LC 81-9424. Orig. Title: Feticheuse. (Illus.). 40p. (gr. 1 up). 1982. 12.95 (ISBN 0-684-17226-7, Pub. by Scribner). Macmillan.

Shadow. Duncan Dave. 1987. pap. 2.95 (ISBN 0-345-34274-7, Del Rey). Ballantine.

Shadow. Benito P. Galdos. Tr. by Karen O. Austin from Span. LC 80-10549. Orig. Title: Sombra. xiv, 58p. 1980. 10.95x (ISBN 0-8214-0553-5). Ohio U Pr.

Shadow. Mary W. Ovington. LC 72-4736. (Black Heritage Library Collection). Repr. of 1920 ed. 20.00 (ISBN 0-8369-9118-4). Ayer Co Pubs.

Shadow. Molly Tuby. 1985. 10.00x (ISBN 0-317-62151-3, Guild of Pastoral Psych). State Mutual Bk.

Shadow & Act. Ralph Ellison. pap. 6.95 (ISBN 0-394-71716-3, V-716, Vin). Random.

Shadow & Evil in Fairytales. Marie-Louise Von Franz. LC 85-30304. (Seminar Ser., No. 9). 284p. 1974. pap. 16.50 (ISBN 0-88214-109-0). Spring Pubns.

Shadow & Flowers. W. Scarfe. 8.00 (ISBN 0-89253-733-7). Ind-US Inc.

Shadow & Light. Katharine J. Bacon. LC 86-23789. 208p. (gr. 6 up). 1987. 12.95 (ISBN 0-689-50431-4, M K McElderry). Macmillan.

Shadow & Light: An Autobiography. Mifflin W. Gibbs. LC 68-28998. (American Negro: His History & Literature Ser., No. 1). 1968. Repr. of 1902 ed. 16.00 (ISBN 0-405-01817-7). Ayer Co Pubs.

Shadow, & Other Stories. Jeffery Farnol. LC 75-122696. (Short Story Index Reprint Ser). 1929. 17.00 (ISBN 0-8369-3529-2). Ayer Co Pubs.

Shadow & Sheen. Carl S. Criswell. 1983. 5.50 (ISBN 0-8233-0360-8). Golden Quill.

Shadow & Sound: The Historical Thought of a Sumatran People. James T. Siegel. LC 78-17963. (Illus.). 1979. lib. bdg. 25.00x (ISBN 0-226-75690-4). U of Chicago Pr.

Shadow & Substance. P. Donizetti. 1967. 23.00 (ISBN 0-08-012182-9); pap. 14.75 (ISBN 0-08-012181-0). Pergamon.

Shadow & Substance: Afro-American Experience in Contemporary Children's Fiction. Rudine Sims. LC 82-6518. (Orig.). 1982. pap. 8.95 (ISBN 0-8141-4376-8). NCTE.

Shadow & Substance: Afro-American Experience in Contemporary Children's Fiction. Rudine Sims. LC 82-6518. 112p. 1982. pap. 9.00x (ISBN 0-8389-3278-9). ALA.

Shadow & Substance in British Foreign Policy, 1895-1939. Ed. by B. J. McKercher & D. J. Moss. x, 280p. 1984. 30.00x (ISBN 0-88864-046-3, Pub. by Univ of Alta Pr Canada); pap. 14.95x (ISBN 0-88864-090-0). U of Nebr Pr.

Shadow & the Fear. Jane Corby. 1977. pap. 1.50 (ISBN 0-505-51174-6, Pub. by Tower Bks). Leisure NY.

Shadow & the Golden Master. Walter Gibson. LC 83-63032. (Shadow Ser.). 1984. 14.95 (ISBN 0-89296-073-6); ltd. ed. 45.00 (ISBN 0-89296-074-4). Mysterious Pr.

Shadow & Whispers: Power Politics Inside the Knowledge from Brezhnev to Gorbachev. Dusko Doder. LC 86-10135. (Illus.). 352p. 1986. 19.45 (ISBN 0-394-54998-8). Random.

Shadow Applique. 5.98 (ISBN 0-317-38602-6). Gick.

Shadow Bands. Jeanne Schinto. 170p. 1988. pap. 9.95 (ISBN 0-86538-065-1). Persea Bks.

Shadow Before. William Rollins, Jr. LC 74-22808. Repr. of 1934 ed. 29.50 (ISBN 0-404-58464-0). AMS Pr.

Shadow Behind Me. Sybil L. Owen. LC 86-90042. 43p. 1987. 6.95 (ISBN 0-533-07001-5). Vantage.

Shadow Behind the Curtain. Velda Johnston. 208p. 1987. pap. 3.95 (ISBN 0-446-34495-8). Warner Bks.

Shadow Boxing. Barbara Condos. Ed. by Pat Golbitz. 356p. 1988. 20.95 (ISBN 0-688-04477-8). Morrow.

Shadow by the Door. Gerardo Di Masso. (New Fiction Ser.). 112p. 1983. 13.95x (ISBN 0-86232-467-X, Pub. by Zed Pr England); pap. 6.95x (ISBN 0-86232-468-8, Pub. by Zed Pr England). Humanities.

Shadow by the Door. Gerardo Di Masso. Tr. by Richard Jacques. LC 87-73441. 96p. 1988. 6.95 (ISBN 0-915306-76-X). Curbstone.

Shadow Cabinet. W. T. Tyler. LC 82-48839. 368p. 1984. 15.00i (ISBN 0-06-015169-2, HarpT). Har-Row.

Shadow Chaser. Stephen Cosgrove. Ed. by Jane Brown. LC 88-1533. (Barely There Ser.). (Illus.). 1988. 8.95 (ISBN 0-88070-220-6); PLB 13.95 (ISBN 0-88070-236-2). Multnomah.

Shadow Climber. Mickey Z. Reicher. 304p. (Orig.). Date not set. pap. 3.50 (ISBN 0-88677-284-2). DAW Bks.

Shadow Club. Neal Shusterman. LC 87-35369. 183p. (YA) (gr. 7-9). 1988. 12.95 (ISBN 0-316-77540-1). Little.

Shadow Country. Paula G. Allen. (Native American Ser.). 149p. 1982. pap. 7.50 (ISBN 0-935626-26-3). U Cal AISC.

Shadow Dance: Poems of the Night for Young People. Adrian Rumble. (Illus.). 112p. 1988. 12.95 (ISBN 0-304-31493-5, Pub. by Cassell UK). Sterling.

Shadow Dancers. Lillian S. Carl. 1987. pap. 2.95 (ISBN 0-441-75988-2, Pub. by Ace Science Fiction). Ace Bks.

Shadow Dancers. Jane L. Curry. LC 83-3733. 204p. (gr. 7 up). 1983. 10.95 (ISBN 0-689-50276-1, M K McElderry). Macmillan.

Shadow Dancers: G. O. D. Inc, No. 2. Jack L. Chaker. 288p. (Orig.). 1987. pap. 3.95 (ISBN 0-8125-3308-9, Dist. by St Martin's Pr & Warner Pub Servs). Tor Bks.

Shadow Dancing. Donna Lynn. 66p. (Orig.). 1983. pap. 3.95 (ISBN 0-912713-00-3). I S C CA.

Shadow Dancing in the U. S. A. Michael Ventura. 240p. 1985. 15.95 (ISBN 0-87477-372-5, Dist. by St Martin). J P Tarcher.

Shadow Dancing in the U. S. A. Michael Ventura. 1986. pap. 7.95 (ISBN 0-87477-394-6). J P Tarcher.

Shadow Eighty One. Lucien Nahum. LC 74-17770. 287p. pap. 8.95 (ISBN 0-931933-27-7). Richardson & Steirman.

Shadow Fall. Rowan Kirby. (Romances Ser.: No. 2873). 192p. Date not set. pap. 1.95 (ISBN 0-317-63930-7). Harlequin Bks.

Shadow Flies. Rose Macaulay. LC 70-145153. (Literature Ser). 484p. 1972. Repr. of 1932 ed. 59.00 (ISBN 0-403-01082-9). Scholarly.

Shadow Forms. Manly P. Hall. pap. 5.95 (ISBN 0-89314-398-7). Philos Res.

Shadow from Ladakh. Bhabani Bhattacharya. 359p. 1969. pap. 3.00 (ISBN 0-88253-018-6). Ind-US Inc.

Shadow Game. Dorinda Kamm. (Orig.). 1979. pap. 1.95 (ISBN 0-89083-492-X). Zebra.

Shadow Games. Glen Cook. 320p. 1989. pap. price not set. Tor Bks.

Shadow Guests. Joan Aiken. (gr. 5 up). 1986. pap. 2.95 (ISBN 0-440-48226-7, YB). Dell.

Shadow Guests: A Novel. Joan Aiken. LC 80-65830. 144p. (gr. 7 up). 1980. pap. 11.95 (ISBN 0-385-28889-1). Delacorte.

Shadow Hawk. Andre Norton. 256p. 1987. pap. 2.95 (ISBN 0-345-34366-2, Del Rey). Ballantine.

Shadow Hill Book of Mix Easy Cakes. Susan Ashby. (Illus.). 64p. (Orig.). 1984. pap. 3.95 (ISBN 0-912661-05-4). Woodsong Graph.

Shadow Hill Book of Squares, Bars & Brownies. Susan Ashby. LC 84-52106. (Illus.). 144p. 1984. pap. 7.95 (ISBN 0-912661-03-8). Woodsong Graph.

Shadow in Hawthorn Bay. Janet Lunn. LC 87-4297. 180p. (YA) (gr. 7 up). 1987. 12.95 (ISBN 0-684-18843-0, Pub. by Scribner). Macmillan.

Shadow in Hawthorn Bay. Janet Lunn. (gr. 5-9). 1988. pap. 3.95 (ISBN 0-14-032436-4, Puffin Bks). Penguin.

Shadow in Red: A Norah Mulcahaney Mystery. Lillian O'Donnell. 240p. 1986. 16.95 (ISBN 0-399-13208-2, Putnam). Putnam Pub Group.

Shadow in the North. Philip Pullman. LC 87-29846. 320p. (gr. 7 up). 1988. 12.95 (ISBN 0-394-89453-7); lib. bdg. 13.99 (ISBN 0-394-99453-1). Knopf.

Shadow in the Pond. Ron Roy. 96p. (gr. 4-6). 1987. pap. 2.25 (ISBN 0-590-31304-5). Scholastic Inc.

Shadow in the Weave. Michael Humfrey. LC 86-18075. 176p. 1987. 15.95 (ISBN 0-87951-265-2). Overlook Pr.

Shadow in the Window: A Book about Caring. Lorayne Mitchell. (Value Teachers Ser.). (Illus.). 32p. (ps-4). 1987. PLB 12.95 (ISBN 0-943491-02-9). Valued Pubns.

Shadow Justice: The Ideology & Institutionalization of Alternatives to Court. Christine B. Harrington. LC 84-27923. (Contributions in Political Science Ser.: No. 133). (Illus.). x, 224p. 1985. lib. bdg. 35.00 (ISBN 0-313-24332-8, HID/). Greenwood.

Shadow Kills. Rodman Philbrick. 288p. 1985. 15.95 (ISBN 0-8253-0283-8). Beaufort Bks NY.

Shadow Kills. W. R. Philbrick. 272p. 1986. pap. 3.50 (ISBN 0-425-09208-9). Berkley Pub.

Shadow Kisses. J. H. Rhodes. 1986. 9.95 (ISBN 0-8034-8607-3, Avalon). Bouregy.

Shadow Knows. Diane Johnson. 288p. 1988. pap. 3.95 (ISBN 0-449-21560-1, Crest). Fawcett.

Shadow Land: Stories of the South. Florence H. Robertson. LC 72-3188. (Black Heritage Library Collection). Repr. of 1905 ed. 13.25 (ISBN 0-8369-9077-3). Ayer Co Pubs.

Shadow Lands. Johannes Bobrowski. Tr. by Ruth Mead & Matthew Mead. (Poetry in Translation Ser.). 208p. 1984. 18.95 (ISBN 0-85646-117-2, Pub. by Anvil Pr Poetry); pap. 10.95 (ISBN 0-85646-118-0). Longwood Pub Group.

Shadow Like a Leopard. Myron Levoy. LC 79-2812. 192p. (YA) (gr. 7 up). 1981. i o.p. 8.95 (ISBN 0-06-023816-X); PLB 12.89 (ISBN 0-06-023817-8). HarpJ.

Shadow Like a Leopard. Myron Levoy. 144p. 1982. pap. 2.50 (ISBN 0-451-13698-5, Sig Vista). NAL.

Shadow Line. Joseph Conrad. Ed. by Jeremy Hawthorn. (WC-P Ser.). 1985. pap. 3.95 (ISBN 0-19-281686-1). Oxford U Pr.

Shadow Lives. Betty Benson. 256p. (Orig.). 1988. pap. 3.95 (ISBN 1-55785-019-4). Bart Books.

Shadow Lord. Laurence Yep. (Star Trek Ser.). 288p. (Orig.). 1985. pap. 3.50 (ISBN 0-671-47392-1). PB.

Shadow Magic. (Beginning to Read Ser.). (gr. 2 up). 1988. PLB 5.95 (ISBN 0-8136-5192-1); pap. 2.95 (ISBN 0-8136-5692-3). Modern Curr.

Shadow Magic. Seymour Simon. LC 84-4433. (Illus.). 48p. (ps-3). 1985. 11.88 (ISBN 0-688-02681-8); PLB 10.88 (ISBN 0-688-02682-6). Lothrop.

Shadow Magic. Patricia C. Wrede. (Lyra Ser.: Bk. 1). (Illus.). 256p. 1987. pap. 2.95 (ISBN 0-441-76014-7). Ace Bks.

Shadow Man. Stephen Gresham. 400p. 1986. pap. 3.95 (ISBN 0-8217-1946-7). Zebra.

Shadow Man. James W. Kunetka. LC 87-40176. 272p. 1988. 17.95 (ISBN 0-446-51358-X). Warner Bks.

Shadow Man. F. M. Parker. 256p. 1988. 16.95 (ISBN 0-453-00619-1). NAL.

Shadow Man: The Life of Dashiell Hammett. Richard Layman. LC 80-8752. 352p. 1981. 14.95 (ISBN 0-15-181459-7). HarBraceJ.

Shadow Man: The Life of Dashiell Hammett. Richard Layman. LC 83-16645. 312p. 1984. pap. 7.95 (ISBN 0-15-681400-5, Harv). HarbraceJ.

Shadow Money. George A. Effinger. 288p. 1988. 16.95x (ISBN 0-312-93054-2). Tor Bks.

Shadow Mountain. Bliss Lomax. 224p. 1986. pap. 2.95 (ISBN 0-445-20225-4, Pub. by Popular Library). Warner Bks.

Shadow Mountain Lodge, Typing Practice Set. Olive Church. (Illus.). (gr. 9-12). 1977. pap. 12.88 (ISBN 0-07-010835-8). McGraw.

Shadow Network: Espionage As an Instrument of Soviet Policy. Edward Van der Rhoer. 352p. 1985. 24.95x (ISBN 0-7090-2155-0, Pub. by R Hale Ltd UK). State Mutual Bk.

Shadow Nose. Elizabeth Levy. LC 83-7925. (Illus.). 64p. (gr. 2-5). 1983. 10.25 (ISBN 0-688-02410-6); lib. bdg. 10.88 (ISBN 0-688-02411-4). Morrow.

Shadow Nose. Elizabeth Levy. (Illus.). 64p. (gr. 2-5). 1985. pap. 2.50 (ISBN 0-590-41060-1, Lucky Star). Scholastic Inc.

Shadow of a Bird. D. M. Toliver. 288p. Date not set. 16.95 (ISBN 0-933031-13-0). Coun Oak Bks.

Shadow of a Broken Man. George C. Chesbro. 1987. pap. 3.50 (ISBN 0-440-17761-8). Dell.

Shadow of a Bull. Maia Wojciechowska. LC 64-12563. (Illus.). 176p. (gr. 5 up). 1964. 10.95 (Atheneum Childrens Bk). Macmillan.

Shadow of a Bull. Maia Wojciechowska. LC 64-12563. (Illus.). 176p. (gr. 5 up). 1964. 10.95 (ISBN 0-689-30042-5, Atheneum Childrens Bks). Macmillan.

Shadow of a Bull. Maia Wojciechowska. LC 86-22199. 160p. (gr. 4). 1987. pap. 3.95 (ISBN 0-689-71132-8, Aladdin Bks). Macmillan.

Shadow of a Dream. William D. Howells. Ed. by Edwin H. Cady. Bd. with Imperative Duty. (Masterworks of Literature Ser.). 1962. pap. 6.95x (ISBN 0-8084-0340-0). New Coll U Pr.

Shadow of a Dream: Economic Life & Death in the South Carolina Low Countries, 1670-1920. Peter Coclanis. (Illus.). 448p. 1988. 39.95 (ISBN 0-19-504420-7). Oxford U Pr.

Shadow of a Man. Rick Bundschuh. LC 86-22048. (Light Force Ser.). 120p. (Orig.). (YA) (gr. 6-9). 1986. pap. 4.95 (ISBN 0-8307-1143-0, S185116). Regal.

Shadow of a Man. Doris M. Disney. Repr. lib. bdg. 15.95x (ISBN 0-88411-840-1, Pub. by Aeonian Pr). Amereon Ltd.

Shadow of a Man. May Sarton. 304p. 1982. pap. 4.95 (ISBN 0-393-30030-7). Norton.

Shadow of a Star. Elmer Kelton. 192p. 1986. pap. 2.50 (ISBN 0-441-76075-9, Pub. by Charter Bks). Ace Bks.

Shadow of a Unicorn. Norma Johnston. 224p. (Orig.). 1987. pap. 2.95 (ISBN 0-553-26475-3, Starfire). Bantam.

Shadow of an Agony. Oswald Chambers. 1965. pap. 3.95 (ISBN 0-87508-128-2). Chr Lit.

Shadow of an Angel. Marion D. Cohen. LC 86-27723. (Woman in History Ser.: Vol. 73). (Illus.). 136p. (Orig.). 1986. pap. 8.95 (ISBN 0-934659-04-4). Liberal Pr.

Shadow of Cain. Vincent Bugliosi & Ken Hurwitz. 1981. 12.95 (ISBN 0-393-01466-5). Norton.

Shadow of Cain. Edith Sitwell. LC 77-7598. 1977. Repr. of 1947 ed. lib. bdg. 27.50 (ISBN 0-8414-7755-8). Folcroft.

Shadow of Calvary. Hugh Martin. 1983. pap. 6.95 (ISBN 0-85151-373-5). Banner of Truth.

Shadow of Dante. Maria F. Rossetti. LC 70-101031. 1969. Repr. of 1901 ed. 23.00x (ISBN 0-8046-0698-6, Pub. by Kennikat). Assoc Faculty Pr.

Shadow of Dark God & the Sin. Indira Goswami. 200p. 1986. text ed. 25.00x (ISBN 81-85006-14-8, Pub. by Gaurav Pubs India). Apt Bks.

Shadow of Death. Thomas C. Callahan & Freda Turner. LC 80-50008. (Illus.). 192p. 1980. 9.95 (ISBN 0-936354-01-1). Val-Hse Pub.

Shadow of Death. William X. Kenzle. 1986. pap. 3.50 (ISBN 0-345-33110-9). Ballantine.

Shadow of Death. Lilli Schultze. 1981. 3.50 (ISBN 0-87813-516-2). Christian Light.

Shadow of Death. Stenbock. LC 82-49099. (Degeneration & Regeneration Ser.). 253p. 1984. lib. bdg. 34.00 (ISBN 0-8240-5561-6). Garland Pub.

Shadow of Deceit. Lizabeth Loghry. (Intrigue Ser.: No. 61). Date not set. pap. 2.25 (ISBN 0-317-63667-7). Harlequin Bks.

Shadow of Dolores. Georgia M. Shewmake. (YA) (gr. 7 up). 1978. 9.95 (ISBN 0-685-86413-8, Avalon). Bouregy.

Shadow of Eternity: Belief & Structure in Herbert, Vaughan, & Traherne. Sharon C. Seelig. LC 80-51018. 200p. 1981. 18.00 (ISBN 0-8131-1444-6). U Pr of Ky.

Shadow of Fear. Dayle Courtney. LC 83-4696. (Thorne Twins Adventure Bks.). (Illus.). 192p. (gr. 7-12). 1983. pap. 2.98 (ISBN 0-87239-682-7, 2902). Standard Pub.

Shadow of Fu Manchu. Sax Rohmer. 272p. 1986. pap. 3.50 (ISBN 0-8217-1870-3). Zebra.

Shadow of God. Versa H. Davidson. 320p. 1980. 7.95 (ISBN 0-89962-026-4). Todd & Honeywell.

Shadow of God & the Hidden Iman: Religion, Political Order & Societal Change in Shi'ite Iran from the Beginning to 1890. Said A. Arjomand. LC 83-27196. (Publications of the Center for the Middle Eastern Studies: No. 17). (Illus.). xii, 356p. 1984. lib. bdg. 28.00x (ISBN 0-226-02782-1). U of Chicago Pr.

Shadow of God & the Hidden Inam: Religion, Political Order, & Societal Change in Shi'ite Iran from the Beginning to 1890. Said A. Arjomand. LC 83-27196. (Publications of the Center for Middle Eastern Studies: No. 17). (Illus.). xii, 356p. 1987. pap. 14.95x (ISBN 0-317-57640-2) (ISBN 0-226-02784-8). U of Chicago Pr.

Shadow of Henry Irving. Henry A. Jones. LC 77-91527. 1931. 16.00 (ISBN 0-405-08674-1, Blom Pubns). Ayer Co Pubs.

Shadow of His Wings. Bruce Fergusson. 1987. 17.95 (ISBN 0-87795-852-1). Morrow.

Shadow of His Wings. Bruce Fergusson. 288p. 1988. pap. 2.95 (ISBN 0-380-70415-3). Avon.

Shadow of Lies. Donald E. McQuinn. 416p. 1985. 15.95 (ISBN 0-312-93726-1). St Martin.

Shadow of Life. David J. Halton. 150p. 1986. 39.00x (ISBN 0-317-59357-9, Pub. by Regency Pr). State Mutual Bk.

Shadow of Light. Bill Brandt. LC 76-52463. (Quality Paperback Ser.). (Illus.). 1977. lib. bdg. 29.50 o. p. (ISBN 0-306-70858-2); pap. 14.50 (ISBN 0-306-80066-7). Da Capo.

Shadow of My Days: A Short-Story Collection. Robert Anjou. 168p. (Orig.). 1984. pap. 8.95 (ISBN 0-9613373-0-3). Jasper Assocs.

Shadow of Our Bones. Keith Wilson. (Illus.). 31p. (Orig.). 1971. pap. 4.00 (ISBN 0-932264-19-0). Trask Hse Bks.

Shadow of Paradise: Sombra Del Paraiso. Vincente Aleixandra. Tr. by Hugh A. Harter. LC 86-6942. 186p. 1986. 25.00x (ISBN 0-520-05599-3). U of Cal Pr.

Shadow of Pearl Harbor: Political Controversy over the Surprise Attack, 1941-1946. Martin V. Melosi. LC 77-23578. 200p. 1977. 17.95 (ISBN 0-89096-031-3). Tex A&M Univ Pr.

Shadow of Reddoch's Landing. Melissa Lee. 1976. pap. 1.25 (ISBN 0-685-74576-7; LB424ZK, Leisure Bks). Leisure NY.

Shadow of Sequoyah: Social Documents of the Cherokees, 1862-1964. Ed. by Jack F. Kilpatrick & Anna G. Kilpatrick. LC 65-24205. (Civilization of the American Indian Ser.: No. 81). pap. 36.00 (ISBN 0-317-27894-0, 2052156). Bks Demand UMI.

Shadow of the Almighty: The Life & Testament of Jim Elliot. Elizabeth Elliot. LC 58-10365. 1979. pap. 7.95 (ISBN 0-06-062211-3, RD 488, HarpR). Har-Row.

Shadow of the Bamboo. Bhagwan Shree Rajneesh. Ed. by Ma Prem Maneesha. LC 84-42807. (Initiation Talks Ser.). 240p. (Orig.). 1984. pap. 3.95 (ISBN 0-88050-630-X). Chidvilas Inc.

Shadow of the Big Horn. E. E. Halleran. 160p. 1981. pap. text ed. 1.75 (ISBN 0-345-29430-0). Ballantine.

Shadow of the Cat. Monique Hara. 400p. 1988. pap. 3.95 (ISBN 0-8217-2359-6). Zebra.

Shadow of the Crescent: The Renaissance Image of the Turk. Robert Schwoebel. (Illus.). 1969. 25.00 (ISBN 0-312-71400-9). St Martin.

Shadow of the Cross. Morton F. Rose. LC 86-9630. (Orig.). 1986. pap. 4.95 (ISBN 0-8054-5030-0). Broadman.

Shadow of the Cross: Studies in Self-denial. Walter J. Chantry. 79p. (Orig.). 1981. pap. 3.95 (ISBN 0-85151-331-X). Banner of Truth.

Shadow of the Dragon: Chinese Domestic & Trade Ceramics. Columbus Museum of Art Staff. (Illus.). 100p. (Orig.). 1982. pap. 10.00x (ISBN 0-918881-10-2). Columbus Mus Art.

Shadow of the Eagle. Judith Hagar. 192p. 1984. 12.95 (ISBN 0-8027-0821-8). Walker & Co.

Shadow of the Eagles. Rebel Montgomery Temple. (Illus.). 157p. (Orig.). 1982. pap. 3.75x (ISBN 0-89279-045-8, TXU 90-499). Rebel Mont Tem.

Shadow of the Earth. Lee Wichelns. 300p. (Orig.). 1987. 18.95 (ISBN 0-941692-07-8). Elysian Pr.

Shadow of the Earth. Lee Wichelns. 300p. (Orig.). 1987. 24.95 (ISBN 0-317-66730-0). Elysian Pr.

Shadow of the East. E. M. Hull. 1976. Repr. of 1921 ed. lib. bdg. 19.95 (ISBN 0-89190-733-5, Pub. by River City Pr). Amereon Ltd.

Shadow of the Gun. Wayne C. Lee. 1981. pap. 1.95 (ISBN 0-89083-758-9). Zebra.

Shadow of the Hawk. Leigh F. James. (Saga of the Southwest Ser.: No. 8). 368p. (Orig.). 1985. pap. 3.95 (ISBN 0-553-25165-1). Bantam.

Shadow of the Hawk. Dan Parkinson. 432p. 1988. pap. 3.95 (ISBN 0-8217-2259-X). Zebra.

Shadow of the Hunter: Stories of Eskimo Life. Richard K. Nelson. LC 80-11091. (Illus.). xiv, 282p. 1980. pap. 10.95 (ISBN 0-226-57180-7). U of Chicago Pr.

Shadow of the Long Knives. Thomas Boyd. 20.95 (ISBN 0-88411-861-4, Pub. by Aeonian Pr). Amereon Ltd.

Shadow of the Lynx. Victoria Holt. 320p. 1982. pap. 3.95 (ISBN 0-449-20231-3, Crest). Fawcett.

Shadow of the Moon. M. M. Kaye. 816p. 1980. pap. 4.95 (ISBN 0-553-25156-2). Bantam.

Shadow of the Moth: A Novel of Espionage with Virginia Woolf. Ellen Hawkes & Peter Manso. 272p. 1983. 12.95 (ISBN 0-312-71414-9, Pub. by Marek). St Martin.

Shadow of the Moth: A Novel of Espionage with Virginia Woolf. Ellen Hawkes & Peter Manso. (Crime Ser.). 288p. 1984. pap. 3.95 (ISBN 0-14-007060-5). Penguin.

Shadow of the Ninja. Toda Katsumi. LC 82-71143. (Illus.). 118p. (Orig.). 1982. pap. 7.95 (ISBN 0-86568-036-1, 513, Pub. by Dragon Bks Ltd). Unique Pubns.

Shadow of the North. Joseph A. Altsheler. 357p. 1976. Repr. of 1917 ed. lib. bdg. 19.95x (ISBN 0-88411-944-0, Pub. by Aeonian Pr). Amereon Ltd.

Shadow of the Object: Psychoanalysis of the Unknown Thought. Christopher Bollas. 368p. 1987. 35.00 (ISBN 0-231-06626-0). Columbia U Pr.

Shadow of the Parthenon: Studies in Ancient History & Literature. Peter Green. LC 72-87205. 1973. 32.00x (ISBN 0-520-02322-6). U of Cal Pr.

Shadows of the Storm. National Historical Society Staff. Ed. by William C. Davis & Bell I. Wiley. LC 80-1659. (Image of War Ser. 1861-1865: Vol. 1). (Illus.). 464p. 1981. pap. 19.95 (ISBN 0-385-15466-6). Doubleday.

Shadows of the Sun: The Diaries of Harry Crosby. Harry Crosby. Ed. by Edward Germain. LC 77-2869. 300p. (Orig.). 1977. 20.00 (ISBN 0-87685-304-1). Black Sparrow.

Shadows of the Voice. E. Robson & L. Wendt. 1982. pap. 14.00 (ISBN 0-934982-09-0); cloth signed ltd. ed. 35.00 (ISBN 0-934982-08-2). Primary Pr.

Shadows of Time. Haig Khatchadourian. LC 83-8755. 64p. 1983. pap. 3.95 (ISBN 0-935102-12-4). Ashod Pr.

Shadows of Time. Mehr N. Masroor. 1988. 31.00x (ISBN 81-7001-030-6, Pub. by Chanakya India). South Asia Bks.

Shadows of Vengeance. David Charles. 384p. 1988. pap. 3.95 (ISBN 0-8125-0136-5). Tor Bks.

Shadows of Villette. Margaret Crompton. 1982. 15.00x (ISBN 0-903653-93-1, Pub. by New Playwrights Network). State Mutual Bk.

Shadows of Yog-Sothoth: A Global Campaign to Save Mankind. Sandy Petersen et al. Ed. by Lynn Willis. (Illus.). 72p. 1982. incl. Call of Cthulhu roleplaying game supplement 10.00 (ISBN 0-933635-03-6, 2302). Chaosium.

Shadows of Your Mind. Tom Johnson. LC 83-762. (Illus.). 207p. (Orig.). 1983. pap. 8.95 (ISBN 0-941992-02-0). Los Arboles Pub.

Shadows on Little Reef Bay. C. S. Adler. LC 83-15207. 180p. (gr. 6 up). 1984. PLB 10.95 (ISBN 0-89919-217-3, Clarion). HM.

Shadows on Our Skin. Jennifer Johnston. 1983. pap. 2.50 (ISBN 0-380-44347-3, Bard). Avon.

Shadows on the Graveyard Trail. Stephen Mooser. (Orig.). (gr. 5-7). 1986. pap. 2.75 (ISBN 0-440-40805-9, YB). Dell.

Shadows on the Ice. Zena Meyler. 416p. (Orig.). 1988. pap. 4.50 (ISBN 1-55785-039-9). Bart Books.

Shadows on the Moon. Nancy Fairweather. 1978. pap. 1.50 (ISBN 0-505-51234-3, Pub. by Tower Bks). Leisure NY.

Shadows on the Moon. David Houston. (Inflation Fighters Ser.). 192p. 1982. pap. 1.50 (ISBN 0-8439-1081-X, Leisure Bks). Leisure NY.

Shadows on the Moon. Myrtle R. Latimer. LC 86-60426. (Illus.). 64p. 1985. 19.95x (ISBN 0-89754-048-4); pap. 7.95 (ISBN 0-89754-047-6); pap. 7.95. Dan River Pr.

Shadows on the Pond. Alison C. Herzig. 200p. (gr. 7 up). 1985. 14.95 (ISBN 0-316-35895-9). Little.

Shadows on the Rock. Willa Cather. (YA) (gr. 7 up). 1931. 13.45 (ISBN 0-394-44506-6). Knopf.

Shadows on the Rock. Willa Cather. 1971. pap. 6.95 (ISBN 0-394-71680-9, Vin). Random.

Shadows on the Sand: The Memoirs of Sir Gawain Bell. Gawain Bell. LC 83-40286. (Illus.). 253p. 1984. 25.00 (ISBN 0-312-71418-1). St Martin.

Shadows on the Shoji. Cynthia Menadue. 104p. 1986. 14.95 (ISBN 0-909134-82-0, Pub. by J Ferguson Australia). Intl Spec Bk.

Shadows on the Wall. Arch Merrill. LC 87-24477. (Arch Merrill's New York Ser.: Vol. 11). (Illus.). 168p. 1987. pap. 7.95 (ISBN 1-55787-000-4, Empire State Bks). Heart of the Lakes.

Shadows on the Wall. facsimile ed. Howard Weeden. LC 72-178485. (Black Heritage Library Collection). Repr. of 1898 ed. 12.00 (ISBN 0-8369-8935-X). Ayer Co Pubs.

Shadows on the Wall: A Century of Film. Jefferson B. Crow, III. (Illus.). 375p. 1990. price not set (ISBN 0-940375-02-8). WindRiver Pub.

Shadows on the Wall: or, Glimpses of the Past. John H. Hewitt. LC 76-166200. Repr. of 1877 ed. 19.00 (ISBN 0-404-07225-9). AMS Pr.

Shadows on This Land. Joyce H. Ranck. (Illus.). 200p. (Orig.). 1985. pap. 6.95 (ISBN 0-9606006-2-0). Ranck.

Shadows Out of Hell, Vol. II. Andrew J. Offutt. (War of the Gods on Earth Ser.). 1983. pap. 2.50 (ISBN 0-441-76077-5, Ace Science Fiction). Ace Bks.

Shadows over Briarcliff. Marilyn Ross. (Gothic Romances Ser.: No. 11). Date not set. pap. 2.25 (ISBN 0-317-63816-5). Harlequin Bks.

Shadows over Nordmaar. Dezra D. Phillips. LC 87-51252. (Advanced Dungeons & Drangons Gamebook Ser.: No. 16). (Illus.). 192p. (Orig.). (gr. 7-12). 1988. pap. 2.95 (ISBN 0-88038-541-3). TSR Inc.

Shadows over Paradise. Hope Goodwin. LC 87-19058. (Starlight Romance Ser.). 192p. 1987. 12.95 (ISBN 0-385-24337-5). Doubleday.

Shadows over Stonewycke. Michael R. Phillips & Judith Pella. (Stonewycke Legacy Fiction Ser.). 356p. (Orig.). 1988. pap. 6.95 (ISBN 0-87123-901-9). Bethany Hse.

Shadows over the Sunshine Act. 73p. 1977. 1.00 (ISBN 0-914389-11-4). Common Cause.

Shadows Seven. Charles L. Grant. 192p. 1987. pap. 2.95 (ISBN 0-425-09564-9). Berkley Pub.

Shadows Six. Ed. by Charles L. Grant. 192p. 1986. pap. 2.95 (ISBN 0-425-08787-5). Berkley Pub.

Shadows Three. Ed. by Charles L. Grant. 224p. 1985. pap. 2.95 (ISBN 0-425-09491-X). Berkley Pub.

Shadows Within. Gershon Shaked. 216p. 1988. 19.95 (ISBN 0-8276-0295-2). JPS Phila.

Shadowshow. Brad Strickland. 1988. pap. 3.95 (ISBN 0-451-40109-3, Onyx). NAL.

Shadowtown. John Lutz. LC 88-40068. 256p. 1988. 16.95 (ISBN 0-89296-221-6). Mysterious Pr.

Shadowy Heroes: Irish Literature of the 1890's. Wayne E. Hall. LC 80-21383. (Irish Studies). (Illus.). 1980. 20.00x (ISBN 0-8156-2231-7). Syracuse U Pr.

Shadowy Third. Marco Page. LC 75-44997. (Crime Fiction Ser). 1976. Repr. of 1946 ed. lib. bdg. 21.00 (ISBN 0-8240-2389-7). Garland Pub.

Shadrach. Meindert DeJong. LC 53-5250. (Illus.). (gr. 1-5). 1953. PLB 13.89 (ISBN 0-06-021546-1). HarpJ.

Shadrach. Meindert DeJong. LC 53-5250. (Trophy I Can Read Bks.). (Illus.). 192p. (gr. 3-6). 1980. pap. 3.50 (ISBN 0-06-440115-4, Trophy). HarpJ.

Shadrach in the Furnace. Ed. by Robert Silverburg. 17.95 (ISBN 0-89190-523-5, Pub. by Am Repr). Amereon Ltd.

Shadrach's Crossing. Avi. LC 82-19008. 192p. (gr. 5 up). 1983. lib. bdg. 10.99 o.p (ISBN 0-394-95816-0). Pantheon.

Shady Affair. Cindy Coleman. (Illus.). 16p. 1983. pap. 5.95 (ISBN 0-910585-01-6). Willcraft.

Shady Grove. Janice H. Giles. LC 78-12454. 260p. 1978. Repr. of 1968 ed. 16.00 (ISBN 0-89783-002-4). Larlin Corp.

Shady Ladies of the West. Ronald D. Miller. LC 64-25860. (Illus.). 9.95 (ISBN 0-87026-023-5). Westernlore.

Shady Lady. Ruth Gordon. 1983. pap. 3.25 (ISBN 0-8217-1187-3). Zebra.

Shady Side of Words. Ray C. Kasper. 64p. 1986. 6.95 (ISBN 0-8059-3009-4). Dorrance.

Shaeffer's Complete Fabric Sewing. Claire Shaeffer. LC 87-48012. (Illus.). 288p. 1988. pap. 14.95 (ISBN 0-8019-7802-5). Chilton.

Shafer: Swamp to Village. Vivian F. Myers. (Illus.). 227p. (Orig.). 1980. pap. 15.50 (ISBN 0-933565-04-6). Porter Pub Co.

Shaft Alignment Handbook. Piotrowski. (Mechanical Engineering Ser.). 224p. 1986. 55.00 (ISBN 0-8247-7432-9). Dekker.

Shaftesbury. H. D. Traill. 1888. Repr. 17.50 (ISBN 0-8274-3367-0). R West.

Shaftesbury & the French Deists. Dorothy B. Schlegel. Repr. of 1956 ed. 24.00 (ISBN 0-384-53930-0). Johnson Repr.

Shaftesbury: The Great Reformer 1801-1885. Georgina Battiscombe. LC 74-32370. 1975. 15.00 (ISBN 0-395-19953-0). HM.

Shaftesbury's Philosophy of Religion & Ethics: A Study in Enthusiasm. Stanley Grean. LC 67-15457. pap. 80.00 (ISBN 0-317-09231-6, 2006441). Bks Demand UMI.

Shaftsbury, Rousseau & Kant: An Introduction to the Conflict Between Aesthetic & Moral Values in Modern Thought. John A. Bernstein. LC 78-75190. 192p. 1980. 19.50 (ISBN 0-8386-2351-4). Fairleigh Dickinson.

Shaggy D.A. Vic Crume. 1981. pap. 1.75 (ISBN 0-449-13642-6, GM). Fawcett.

Shaggy Dog Murder Trial. Joanna H. Kraus. (Orig.). (gr. 4-7). 1988. playscript 3.00 (ISBN 0-87602-274-3). Anchorage.

Shaggy Dog Story. facsimile ed. Eric Partridge. LC 72-117910. (Select Bibliographies Reprint Ser). (Illus.). Repr. of 1953 ed. 14.50 (ISBN 0-8369-5363-0). Ayer Co Pubs.

Shaggy Dog's Animal Alphabet. Donald Charles. LC 78-12904. (Illus.). 32p. (ps-3). 1979. PLB 11.93 (ISBN 0-516-03674-2); pap. 2.95 (ISBN 0-516-43674-0). Childrens.

Shaggy Dog's Birthday. Donald Charles. LC 86-9566. (Shaggy Dog Storybooks). (Illus.). 32p. (ps-3). 1986. PLB 11.93 (ISBN 0-516-03576-2); pap. 2.95 (ISBN 0-516-43576-0). Childrens.

Shaggy Dog's Halloween. Donald Charles. LC 84-5901. (Shagg Dog Storybooks Ser.). (Illus.). 32p. (ps-3). 1984. lib. bdg. 11.93 (ISBN 0-516-03575-4); pap. text ed. 2.95 (ISBN 0-516-43575-2). Childrens.

Shaggy Dog's Tall Tale. Donald Charles. LC 79-26493. (Illus.). 32p. (ps-3). 1980. PLB 11.93 (ISBN 0-516-03616-5); pap. 2.95 (ISBN 0-516-43616-3). Childrens.

Shaggy Little Monster. Stephanie Calmunson. (Illus.). (ps-1). 1986. bds. 4.95 (ISBN 0-671-62738-4, Little Simon). S&S.

Shags Finds a Kitten. Gyo Fujikawa. (Illus.). 32p. (ps-1). 1983. pap. 3.95 (ISBN 0-448-16465-5, G&D). Putnam Pub Group.

Shah Bano Controversy. Ed. by Asghar Ali Engineer. 352p. 1987. text ed. 27.50x (ISBN 0-86131-701-7, Pub. by Orient Longman Ltd India). Apt Bks.

Shah Commission Begins: India Under Emergency. John Dayal & Ajoy Bose. 1978. 13.50x (ISBN 0-8364-0179-4). South Asia Bks.

Shah Diz of Isma'ili Fame, Its Siege & Destruction. C. O. Minasian. 74p. 1985. 52.00x (ISBN 0-317-39149-6, Pub. by Luzac & Co Ltd). State Mutual Bk.

Shah of Iran: Father & Son: Documents on the Rise of the Pahlevi Dynasty in Modern Iran & the Role of the United States in Maintaining That Power, Vol. 1. Ed. by Don McCall. (U. S. National Archives, Document Ser.). cancelled (ISBN 0-89712-200-3). Documentary Pubns.

Shah of Shahs. Ryszard Kapuscinski. Tr. by William R. Brand & Katarzyna Mroczkowska-Brand. (Helen & Kurt Wolff Bk.). 192p. 1985. 12.95 (ISBN 0-15-181483-X). HarBraceJ.

Shahanshah: A Study of Monarchy of Iran. E. Burke Inlow. 1979. 12.50 (ISBN 0-89684-051-4, Pub. by Motilal Banarsidass, India). Orient Bk Dist.

Shahed va Mashhoud & Seyr-al Saer va Teyr-al Nader. Sadegh M. Angha. LC 83-60134. 85p. (Orig., Persian.). 1983. pap. 18.00 (ISBN 0-910735-22-0). MTO Printing & Pubn Ctr.

Shahhat: An Egyptian. Richard Critchfield. 1981. pap. 3.50 (ISBN 0-380-48405-6, Discus). Avon.

Shahhat: An Egyptian. Richard Critchfield. 1978. 19.95x (ISBN 0-8156-2202-3). Syracuse U Pr.

Shahhat: An Egyptian. Richard Critchfield. LC 78-11945. (Contemporary Issues in the Middle East Ser.). (Illus.). 264p. 1984. pap. text ed. 10.95x (ISBN 0-8156-0151-4). Syracuse U Pr.

Shahjahan. Muni Lal. 452p. 1986. text ed. 40.00x (ISBN 0-7069-2929-2, Pub. by Vikas India). Advent NY.

Shahmah in Pursuit of Freedom. facs. ed. Frances H. McDougall. LC 71-154082. (Black Heritage Library Collection). 1858. 31.25 (ISBN 0-8369-8793-4). Ayer Co Pubs.

Shahnameh. Abu'l-Qasem Ferdowsi. Ed. by Djalal Khaleghi-Motlagh. (Persian Text Ser.). 416p. 1988. 88.50x (ISBN 0-88706-770-0). State U NY Pr.

Shah's Last Ride: The True Story of the Emperor's Dreams & Illusions, Exile & Death at the Hands of His Foes & Friends. William Shawcross. (Illus.). 432p. 1988. 19.95 (ISBN 0-671-55231-7). S&S.

Shahsavan: Iranian Rugs & Textiles. Parviz Tanavili. (Illus.). 432p. 75.00 (ISBN 0-317-55101-9). Apollo.

Shai's Shabbat Walk. Ellie Gellman. LC 85-80780. (Illus.). 12p. (ps). 1985. bds. 4.95 (ISBN 0-930494-49-0). Kar Ben.

Shaiva Devotional Songs of Kashmir: A Translation & Study of Utpaladeva's Shivastotravali. Constantina R. Bailly. LC 87-6488. (Shaiva Traditions of Kashmir Ser.). 224p. 1987. 39.50x (ISBN 0-88706-492-2); pap. 12.95x (ISBN 0-88706-493-0). State U NY Pr.

Shaka: King of the Zulus. Diane Stanley. (Illus.). Date not set. price not set. Morrow.

Shaka Zula. E. A. Ritter. (Penguin Nonfiction Ser.). 416p. 1985. pap. 5.95 (ISBN 0-14-004826-X). Penguin.

Shake a Palm Branch: The Story & Meaning of Sukkot. Miriam Chaikin. LC 84-5022. (Illus.). 80p. (gr. 3-6). 1984. PLB 12.95 (ISBN 0-89919-254-8, Pub. by Clarion). Ticknor & Fields.

Shake a Palm Branch: The Story & Meaning of Sukkot. Miriam Chaikin. LC 84-5022. (Illus.). 88p. (gr. 3-6). 1986. pap. 4.95 (ISBN 0-89919-428-1, Pub. by Clarion). Ticknor & Fields.

Shake down the Stars. Frances Donnelly. 608p. 1988. 22.95 (ISBN 0-312-01819-3). St Martin.

Shake Hands Forever. Ruth Rendell. 208p. 1986. pap. 3.50 (ISBN 0-553-25970-9). Bantam.

Shake Hands with a Bum. Philip McGrath. LC 84-14269. 1986. 12.50 (ISBN 0-904573-95-8, Pub. by Caliban Bks). Longwood Pub Group.

Shake Hands with the Devil. Reardon Connor. 312p. Repr. of 1934 ed. lib. bdg. 19.95x (ISBN 0-89190-449-2, Pub. by River City Pr). Amereon Ltd.

Shake Hands with the Dragon. Carl Glick. LC 75-162513. 340p. 1971. Repr. of 1941 ed. 43.00x (ISBN 0-8103-3765-7). Gale.

Shake Hands with the Dragon. Carl Glick. 220p. 1944. 49.00x (Pub. by Han-Shan Tang Ltd). State Mutual Bk.

Shake Heaven & Earth: Peter Bergson & the Rescue of the Jews of Europe. Louis Rapoport. 1988. 21.95 (ISBN 0-940461-06-4). Seth Pr.

Shake My Sillies Out. Bert Simpson & Bonnie Simpson. (Raffi Songs to Read Ser.). (Illus.). 32p. (ps-2). 1987. PLB 9.95 (ISBN 0-517-56646-X). Crown.

Shake Off the Dust. Jay Strack. 1988. 12.95 (ISBN 0-8407-7624-1). Nelson.

Shake-Speare: The Mystery. George E. Sweet. 1985. 13.95 (ISBN 0-533-06203-9). Vantage.

Shake the Anger Habit! Betty Doty & Pat Rooney. LC 87-71633. (Illus.). 172p. (Orig.). 1987. pap. 8.95 (ISBN 0-930822-08-0). Bookery.

Shake the Salt Habit: A Salt Content Guide to Food, Beverages, & Medicine. Kermit R. Tantum. 128p. 1982. pap. 2.50 (ISBN 0-345-35014-6). Ballantine.

Shake Your Head, Darling. Jose Eber. LC 82-50639. (Illus.). 208p. (Orig.). 1983. 17.50 (ISBN 0-446-51250-8); pap. 10.95 (ISBN 0-446-37364-8). Warner Bks.

Shakedown. Gerald Petievich. 240p. 1988. 16.95 (ISBN 0-671-63154-3). S&S.

Shakedown of Elastic-Plastic Structures. J. A. Konig. (Fundamental Studies in Engineering: No. 7). 226p. 1987. 89.50 (ISBN 0-444-98979-X). Elsevier.

Shaken Realist: Essays in Modern Literature in Honor of Frederick J. Hoffman. Ed. by Melvin J. Friedman & John B. Vickery. LC 77-108199. xxvi, 344p. 1970. 35.00 (ISBN 0-8071-0933-9). La State U Pr.

Shaker: A Collector's Source Book, No. 2. Don Raycraft & Carol Raycraft. LC 80-50497. (Illus.). 120p. 1985. pap. 14.95 (ISBN 0-87069-443-X). Wallace-Homestead.

Shaker Adventure. Marguerite F. Melcher. 319p. 1986. pap. 9.95 (ISBN 0-937942-08-1). Shaker Mus.

Shaker Architecture. Herbert Schiffer. LC 79-52439. (Illus.). 190p. 1979. 20.00 (ISBN 0-916838-25-0). Schiffer.

Shaker Architecture: A Brief Bibliography. Anthony G. White. (Architecture Ser.: A 1684). 4p. 1986. 3.00 (ISBN 1-55590-034-8). Vance Biblios.

Shaker Baskets. Martha Wetherbee et al. Ed. by Mary L. Ray. 296p. (Orig.). 1987. pap. price not set. M Wetherbee.

Shaker Chair. Charles R. Muller & Timothy D. Rieman. (Illus.). 268p. 1984. 39.95 (ISBN 0-9611116-0-7). Canal Pr.

Shaker Communism: Or, Tests of Divine Inspiration. Frederick W. Evans. LC 72-2987. Repr. of 1871 ed. 23.50 (ISBN 0-404-10749-4). AMS Pr.

Shaker Communities, Shaker Lives. Priscilla J. Brewer. LC 85-40930. (Illus.). 293p. 1988. pap. 12.95 (ISBN 0-87451-400-2). U Pr of New Eng.

Shaker Cookbook. C. B. Piercy. 1986. 5.98 (ISBN 0-517-62243-2, 014246). Outlet Bk Co.

Shaker Cookbook: Recipes & Lore from the Valley of God's Pleasure. rev. ed. Caroline B. Piercy & Arthur P. Tolve. (Illus.). 192p. 1984. pap. 10.95 (ISBN 0-911861-02-5). Gabriel's Horn.

Shaker Dance Service Reconstucted. J. G. Davies & P. Van Zyl. 1984. pap. 3.00 (ISBN 0-941500-34-9). Sharing Co.

Shaker Days Remembered. Martha Hulings. pap. 5.00 (ISBN 0-317-17252-2). Shaker Her Soc.

Shaker Design. Date not set. 25.00 (ISBN 0-393-30544-9). Norton.

Shaker Design. June Sprigg. 1986. 40.00 (ISBN 0-393-02338-9). Norton.

Shaker Folk Art & Industry. Marion Klamklin. 17.00 (ISBN 0-8446-6128-7). Peter Smith.

Shaker Furniture: The Craftmanship of an American Communal Sect. Edward D. Andrews & F. Andrews. (Illus.). 14.75 (ISBN 0-8446-1537-4). Peter Smith.

Shaker Furniture: The Craftsmanship of an American Communal Sect. Edward D. Andrews & Faith Andrews. (Illus.). pap. 6.95 (ISBN 0-486-20679-3). Dover.

Shaker Gardener's Manual. Charles F. Crosman. 24p. 1986. pap. 4.95 (ISBN 0-918222-85-0). Applewood.

Shaker Herbs & Their Medicinal Uses. Dee Herbrandson. (Illus.). 28p. 1985. pap. 4.00 (ISBN 0-317-56372-6). Shaker Her Soc.

Shaker Holy Land. Edward R. Horgan. LC 87-8542. (Illus.). 256p. (Orig.). 1987. pap. 9.95 (ISBN 0-916782-86-7). Harvard Common Pr.

Shaker Lane. Alice Provensen & Martin Provensen. (ps up). Date not set. 14.95 (ISBN 0-317-62524-1, Viking Kestrel). Viking.

Shaker: Life, Work, & Art. June Sprigg & David Larkin. LC 87-9957. (Illus.). 272p. 1987. 40.00 (ISBN 1-55670-011-3). Stewart Tabori & Chang.

Shaker Light. Robert Peters. 104p. 1987. 19.95 (ISBN 0-87775-200-1); pap. 8.95 (ISBN 0-87775-201-X). Unicorn Pr.

Shaker Literature: A Bibliography, 2 vols. Compiled by Mary L. Richmond. LC 75-41908. 656p. 1976. Set. 60.00x (ISBN 0-87451-117-8). U Pr of New Eng.

Shaker: Masterworks of Utilitarian Design Created Between 1800 & 1875 by the MasterCraftsmen & Craftswomen of America's Foremost Communal Religious Sect. June Sprigg. LC 83-82644. (Illus.). 56p. 1983. Exhibition Catalogue 10.00 (ISBN 0-915171-00-7). Katonah Gal.

Shaker Music: A Manifestation of American Folk Culture. Harold E. Cook. LC 71-161507. (Illus.). 312p. 1973. 25.00 (ISBN 0-8387-7953-0). Bucknell U Pr.

Shaker Music: Inspirational Hymns & Melodies Illustrative of the Resurection, Life & Testimony of the Shakers. Frederick W. Evans. LC 72-2988. Repr. of 1875 ed. 42.50 (ISBN 0-404-10750-8). AMS Pr.

Shaker Religious Concept. John S. Williams. (Illus.). 32p. 1959. pap. 2.50 (ISBN 0-937942-04-9). Shaker Mus.

Shaker Sampler Coloring Book. Kathleen Moriarty. 2.25 (ISBN 0-937942-11-1). Shaker Mus.

Shaker Seed Industry. Margaret F. Sommer. (Illus.). 61p. (Orig.). 1972. pap. text ed. 2.00 (ISBN 0-937942-06-5). Shaker Mus.

Shaker Spiritual. Daniel W. Patterson. LC 77-85557. (Illus.). 1979. text ed. 100.00x (ISBN 0-691-09124-2). Princeton U Pr.

Shaker Spiritual Narrative. Sarah D. Sasson. LC 83-3666. (Illus.). 248p. 1983. text ed. 23.95x (ISBN 0-87049-392-2). U of Tenn Pr.

Shaker Textile Arts. Beverly Gordon. LC 78-69899. (Illus.). 343p. 1985. pap. 15.95 (ISBN 0-87451-242-5). U Pr of New Eng.

Shaker Village. Edmund Gillon. (Illus.). 56p. 1986. pap. 5.95 (ISBN 0-88740-077-9). Schiffer.

Shaker Village Views: Illustrated Maps & Landscape Drawings by Shaker Artists of the Nineteenth Century. Robert P. Emlen. LC 86-40393. (Illus.). 208p. 1987. 35.00 (ISBN 0-87451-397-9). U Pr of New Eng.

Shaker Way. Charles R. Muller. LC 79-89838. (Illus.). 1979. pap. 9.50 (ISBN 0-9603290-0-5). Ohio Antique Rev.

Shakespeare & the Classics. James A. Thomson. 1978. Repr. of 1966 ed. lib. bdg. 35.00x (ISBN 0-313-20388-1, THSC). Greenwood.
Shakespeare & the Classroom. Ed. by A. K. Hudson. 1960. 29.50x (ISBN 0-317-27585-2). Elliots Bks.
Shakespeare & the Common Understanding. Norman Rabkin. LC 67-19237. (Orig.). 1967. pap. 2.95 (ISBN 0-02-925650-X). Free Pr.
Shakespeare & the Common Understanding. Norman Rabkin. LC 83-18153. xii, 268p. 1984. pap. 9.95x (ISBN 0-226-70180-8). U of Chicago Pr.
Shakespeare & the Confines of Art. Philip Edwards. (Methuen Library Reprint Ser.). 176p. 1981. 32.00x (ISBN 0-416-32200-X, NO. 3581). Routledge Chapman & Hall.
Shakespeare & the Courtly Aesthetic. Gary Schmidgall. LC 80-23257. (Illus.). 344p. 1981. 35.95x (ISBN 0-520-04130-5). U of Cal Pr.
Shakespeare & the Critics. A. L. French. LC 75-183221. 224p. 1972. 47.50 (ISBN 0-521-08470-9). Cambridge U Pr.
Shakespeare & the Critics' Debate. Raymond Powell. 167p. 1980. 21.50x (ISBN 0-8476-6227-6). Rowman.
Shakespeare & the Denial of Death. James L. Calderwood. LC 87-5922. 248p. (Orig.). 1988. lib. bdg. 30.00x (ISBN 0-87023-582-6); pap. text ed. 12.95x (ISBN 0-87023-583-4). U of Mass Pr.
Shakespeare & the Diction of Common Life. Frank P. Wilson. LC 77-21976. 1941. lib. bdg. 17.00 (ISBN 0-8414-9624-2). Folcroft.
Shakespeare & the Elizabethan Poetry. Muriel C. Bradbrook. LC 79-2315. (History of Elizabethan Drama Ser.: Vol. 4). (Illus.). 1979. pap. 12.95 (ISBN 0-521-29528-9). Cambridge U Pr.
Shakespeare & the Emblem Writers. Henry Green. (Illus.). 1967. Repr. of 1870 ed. 29.00 (ISBN 0-8337-1440-6). B Franklin.
Shakespeare & the English Romantic Imagination. Jonathan Bate. (Illus.). 320p. 1986. 49.95x (ISBN 0-19-812848-7). Oxford U Pr.
Shakespeare & the Englishman. Josiah H. Symon. LC 77-155114. (Studies in Shakespeare, No. 24). 1972. Repr. of 1929 ed. lib. bdg. 39.95x (ISBN 0-8383-1288-8). Haskell.
Shakespeare & the Experience of Love. Arthur C. Kirsch. LC 81-635. 204p. pap. 53.10 (2030601). Bks Demand UMI.
Shakespeare & the Founders of Liberty in America. Charles M. Gayley. LC 77-26994. 35.00 (ISBN 0-8414-2004-1). Folcroft.
Shakespeare & the Greek Romance: A Study of Origins. Carol Gesner. LC 70-11509. 232p. 1970. 21.00x (ISBN 0-8131-1220-6). U Pr of Ky.
Shakespeare & the Hazards of Ambition. Robert N. Watson. 360p. 1984. text ed. 24.50x (ISBN 0-674-80390-6). Harvard U Pr.
Shakespeare & the Homilies. Alfred Hart. LC 73-144635. Repr. of 1934 ed. 10.00 (ISBN 0-404-03138-2). AMS Pr.
Shakespeare & the Homilies. Alfred Hart. LC 72-120626. 1970. Repr. of 1934 ed. lib. bdg. 16.00x (ISBN 0-374-93699-4, Octagon). Hippocrene Bks.
Shakespeare & the Influence of the Stars. D. Fraser-Harris. 69.95 (ISBN 0-8490-1031-4). Gordon Pr.
Shakespeare & the Ireland Forgeries. D. Bodde. LC 75-22073. (Studies in Shakespeare, No. 24). 1975. lib. bdg. 40.95x (ISBN 0-8383-2084-8). Haskell.
Shakespeare & the Ireland Forgeries. Derk Bodde. LC 73-15741. 1930. lib. bdg. 25.00 (ISBN 0-8414-3300-3). Folcroft.
Shakespeare & the Italian Renaissance. Sidney Lee. 1915. lib. bdg. 17.00 (ISBN 0-8414-5785-9). Folcroft.
Shakespeare & the Jew. G. Friedlander. 59.95 (ISBN 0-8490-1032-2). Gordon Pr.
Shakespeare & the Jew. Gerald Friedlander. LC 74-168084. Repr. of 1921 ed. 18.00 (ISBN 0-404-02579-X). AMS Pr.
Shakespeare & the Late Moral Plays. Alan C. Dessen. LC 85-8625. xii, 196p. 1986. 19.95x (ISBN 0-8032-1671-8). U of Nebr Pr.
Shakespeare & the Makers of Virginia. A. W. Ward. LC 74-20613. Repr. of 1919 ed. lib. bdg. 20.50 (ISBN 0-8414-9550-5). Folcroft.
Shakespeare & the Modern Stage. Sidney Lee. LC 74-172042. Repr. of 1906 ed. 10.00 (ISBN 0-404-03929-4). AMS Pr.
Shakespeare & the Modern Theatre. Margaret Webster. LC 77-22468. 1944. lib. bdg. 18.00 (ISBN 0-8414-9467-3). Folcroft.
Shakespeare & the Mystery of God's Judgments. Robert G. Hunter. LC 75-11449. 224p. 1976. 20.00x (ISBN 0-8203-0388-7). U of Ga Pr.
Shakespeare & the Players. R. David. (Shakespeare Lectures). 1961. pap. 5.50 (ISBN 0-902732-36-6, Pub. by British Acad). Longwood Pub Group.
Shakespeare & the Players. Richard David. LC 74-20519. 1961. lib. bdg. 15.00 (ISBN 0-8414-3787-4). Folcroft.
Shakespeare & the Popular Tradition in the Theater: Studies in the Social Dimension of Dramatic Form & Function. Robert Weimann. Ed. by Robert Schwartz. LC 77-13673. 352p. 1987. pap. text ed. 12.95x (ISBN 0-8018-3506-2). Johns Hopkins.
Shakespeare & the Post Horses: A New Study of the Merry Wives of Windsor. John E. Crofts. LC 78-153313. Repr. of 1937 ed. 19.00 (ISBN 0-404-01856-4). AMS Pr.
Shakespeare & the Problem of Meaning. Norman Rabkin. LC 80-18538. 1981. lib. bdg. 16.00x (ISBN 0-226-70177-8, Phoen); pap. 4.95X (ISBN 0-226-70178-6). U of Chicago Pr.
Shakespeare & the Question of Theory. Ed. by Patricia Parker & Geoffrey Hartman. 300p. 1985. 27.00 (ISBN 0-416-36920-0, 9479); pap. 12.95 (ISBN 0-416-36930-8, 9480). Routledge Chapman & Hall.
Shakespeare & the Reporter. W. Matthews. LC 77-21970. 1935. lib. bdg. 15.00 (ISBN 0-8414-6173-2). Folcroft.
Shakespeare & the Revolution of the Times: Perspectives & Commentaries. Harry Levin. LC 75-16908. 1976. 25.00x (ISBN 0-19-501982-2). Oxford U Pr.
Shakespeare & the Revolution of the Times: Perspectives & Commentaries. Harry Levin. 1976. pap. 9.95 (ISBN 0-19-502362-5). Oxford U Pr.
Shakespeare & the Rhetoricians. Marion Trousdale. LC 81-40703. xiii, 206p. 1982. 22.00x (ISBN 0-8078-1482-2). U of NC Pr.
Shakespeare & the Rival Poet. Arthur Acheson. LC 79-113535. 1903. 12.50 (ISBN 0-404-00277-3). AMS Pr.
Shakespeare & the Rival Poet. Arthur Acheson. 1973. Repr. of 1903 ed. 12.25 (ISBN 0-8274-1599-0). R West.
Shakespeare & the Romance Tradition. E. Pettet. LC 75-30806. (Studies in Shakespeare, No. 24). 1975. lib. bdg. 75.00x (ISBN 0-8383-2081-3). Haskell.
Shakespeare & the Shapes of Time. David S. Kastan. LC 82-40337. 205p. 1982. 25.00x (ISBN 0-87451-237-9). U Pr of New Eng.
Shakespeare & the Sixteenth Century Study of Language. Jane Donawerth. LC 82-21740. 296p. 1984. 29.95 (ISBN 0-252-01038-8). U of Ill Pr.
Shakespeare & the Solitary Man. Janette Dillon. 200p. 1981. 26.50x (ISBN 0-8476-6254-3). Rowman.
Shakespeare & the South Essays on Performance. Ed. by Philip C. Kolin. LC 83-5954. (Illus.). 298p. 1983. 20.00x (ISBN 0-87805-185-6). U Pr of Miss.
Shakespeare & the Soviet Union. Roman Samarin & Alexander Nikolyukin. 1978. Repr. of 1966 ed. 30.00 (ISBN 0-8492-8062-1). R West.
Shakespeare & the Stage. Maurice Jonas. LC 72-193728. 1918. lib. bdg. 52.50 (ISBN 0-8414-5426-4). Folcroft.
Shakespeare & the Story: Aspects of Creation. Joan Rees. 239p. 1978. 42.50 (ISBN 0-485-11179-9, Pub. by Athlone Pr UK); pap. 18.95 (ISBN 0-485-12041-0, Pub. by Athlone Pr UK). Humanities.
Shakespeare & the Supernatural. Cumberland Clark. LC 72-186985. 1931. lib. bdg. 37.50 (ISBN 0-8414-0341-4). Folcroft.
Shakespeare & the Supernatural. Cumberland Clark. LC 72-92957. (Studies in Shakespeare, No. 24). 1970. Repr. of 1931 ed. lib. bdg. 75.00x (ISBN 0-8383-0966-6). Haskell.
Shakespeare & the Supernatural. Cumberland Clark. 346p. Repr. of 1931 ed. 29.00 (ISBN 0-403-04266-6). Somerset Pub.
Shakespeare & the Supernatural. Margaret Lucy. LC 70-144653. Repr. of 1906 ed. 6.50 (ISBN 0-404-04065-9). AMS Pr.
Shakespeare & the Supernatural. Margaret Lucy. LC 73-16087. 1906. lib. bdg. 16.50 (ISBN 0-8414-5699-2). Folcroft.
Shakespeare & the Tempest. Francis Neilson. LC 74-30004. 181p. 1975. Repr. of 1956 ed. lib. bdg. 48.50x (ISBN 0-8371-7385-X, NEST). Greenwood.
Shakespeare & the Tenth Muse. Elizabeth Beach. LC 76-85797. 1969. 6.00 (ISBN 0-686-00965-7). Willoughby.
Shakespeare & the Tragic Pattern. Kenneth Muir. 1958. lib. bdg. 16.50 (ISBN 0-8414-5945-2). Folcroft.
Shakespeare & the Tragic Theme, Arthur H. Fairchild. 1978. Repr. of 1944 ed. lib. bdg. 30.00 (ISBN 0-8495-1617-X). Arden Lib.
Shakespeare & the Triple Play: From Study to Stage to Classroom. Ed. by Sidney Homan. LC 86-73239. (Illus.). 240p. 1988. 32.50x (ISBN 0-8387-5122-9). Bucknell U Pr.
Shakespeare & the Tudor Jaggards. William Jaggard. 1934. lib. bdg. 17.50 (ISBN 0-8414-5414-0). Folcroft.
Shakespeare & the Uses of Comedy. J. A. Bryant, Jr. LC 86-7770. 280p. 1986. 26.00x (ISBN 0-8131-1595-7). U Pr of Ky.
Shakespeare & the Uses of Ideology. Sidney Shanker. (Studies in English Literature: No. 105). 224p. 1975. pap. text ed. 23.60x (ISBN 90-2793-257-3). Mouton.
Shakespeare & the Victorian Stage. Ed. by Richard Foulkes. (Illus.). 340p. 1986. 49.50 (ISBN 0-521-30110-6). Cambridge U Pr.
Shakespeare & the Welsh. Frederick J. Harries. LC 72-1333. (Studies in Shakespeare, No. 24). 1972. Repr. of 1919 ed. lib. bdg. 39.95x (ISBN 0-8383-1444-9). Haskell.
Shakespeare & Tolstoy. G. Wilson Knight. LC 76-41817. 1934. lib. bdg. 20.00 (ISBN 0-8414-5532-5). Folcroft.
Shakespeare & Tolstoy. G. Wilson Knight. LC 77-100769. (Studies in Comparative Literature, No. 35). 1970. pap. text ed. 39.95 (ISBN 0-8383-0050-2). Haskell.
Shakespeare & Tragedy. John Bayley. 224p. 1981. pap. 9.95 (ISBN 0-7100-0607-1). Routledge Chapman & Hall.
Shakespeare & Typography: Being an Attempt to Show Shakespeare's Personal Connection with & Technical Knowledge of the Art of Printing. William Blades. (Illus.). 1969. Repr. of 1872 ed. Set. 11.00 (ISBN 0-8337-0303-X). B Franklin.
Shakespeare & Voltaire. T. R. Lounsbury. 59.95 (ISBN 0-8490-1033-0). Gordon Pr.
Shakespeare & Voltaire. Thomas R. Lounsbury. LC 72-172753. Repr. of 1902 ed. 18.45 (ISBN 0-404-04029-2). AMS Pr.
Shakespeare & Voltaire. Thomas R. Lounsbury. LC 68-20237. 1968. Repr. of 1902 ed. 22.00 (ISBN 0-405-08754-3, Pub. by Blom). Ayer Co Pubs.
Shakespeare & Voltaire. Thomas R. Lounsbury. 463p. 1982. Repr. of 1902 ed. lib. bdg. 40.00 (ISBN 0-89987-523-8). Darby Bks.
Shakespeare Anthology, 1592-1616 A.D. Ed. by Edward Arber. 312p. 1986. Repr. of 1899 ed. lib. bdg. 45.00 (ISBN 0-8495-0236-5). Arden Lib.
Shakespeare Around the Globe: A Guide to Notable Postwar Revivals. Ed. by Samuel L. Leiter. LC 85-27124. 987p. 1986. 95.00 (ISBN 0-313-23756-5, LES/). Greenwood.
Shakespeare As a Dramatic Artist. Richard G. Moulton. 1972. lib. bdg. 49.50 (ISBN 0-8414-6680-7). Folcroft.
Shakespeare As a Dramatic Artist with an Account of His Reputation at Various Periods. Thomas R Lounsbury. 449p. 1981. Repr. of 1901 ed. lib. bdg. 50.00 (ISBN 0-8495-3265-5). Arden Lib.
Shakespeare As a Dramatic Thinker. Richard G. Moulton. 1907. lib. bdg. 49.50 (ISBN 0-8414-6681-5). Folcroft.
Shakespeare As a Dramatist. John Squire. LC 79-159971. (Studies in Shakespeare, No. 24). 1971. lib. bdg. 39.95x (ISBN 0-8383-1221-7). Haskell.
Shakespeare As a Lawyer. Franklin F. Heard. LC 76-51206. (Studies in Shakespeare,No. 24). 1977. lib. bdg. 75.00x (ISBN 0-8383-2156-9). Haskell.
Shakespeare As a Lawyer. Franklin F. Heard. 119p. 1987. Repr. of 1883 ed. lib. bdg. 24.00 (ISBN 0-89941-571-7, 305240). W S Hein.
Shakespeare As a Letter Writer & Artist in Prose. Rodolphe L. Megroz. LC 73-10413. 1927. Repr. lib. bdg. 28.00 (ISBN 0-8414-5958-4). Folcroft.
Shakespeare As a Scientist. Oliver C. Ellis. LC 76-44822. 1933. lib. bdg. 12.50 (ISBN 0-8414-3951-6). Folcroft.
Shakespeare As an Angler. Henry N. Ellacombe. LC 76-166018. Repr. of 1883 ed. 11.50 (ISBN 0-404-02278-2). AMS Pr.
Shakespeare As Poet & Lover. Louis K. Anspacher. LC 73-9528. (Studies in Shakespeare, No. 24). 1973. Repr. of 1944 ed. lib. bdg. 75.00x (ISBN 0-8383-1701-4). Haskell.
Shakespeare As Political Thinker. Ed. by John Alvis & Thomas West. LC 79-51946. 306p. 1980. lib. bdg. 29.75 (ISBN 0-89089-097-8); pap. 12.75 (ISBN 0-89089-096-X). Carolina Acad Pr.
Shakespeare: Aspects of Influence. Ed. by G. B. Evans. (Harvard English Studies: No. 7). 1976. 15.00x (ISBN 0-674-80330-2, EVSA); pap. 5.95x (ISBN 0-674-80331-0, EVSX). Harvard U Pr.
Shakespeare at the Maddermarket: Nugent Monck & the Norwich Players. Franklin J. Hildy. Ed. by Oscar Brockett. LC 86-16155. (Theater & Dramatic Studies: No. 41). 280p. 1986. 44.95 (ISBN 0-8357-1775-5). UMI Res Pr.
Shakespeare, Bacon & the Great Unknown. Andrew Lang. LC 75-75982. Repr. of 1912 ed. 10.00 (ISBN 0-404-03871-9). AMS Pr.
Shakespeare-Bacon Controversy. Arthur M. Young. (Broadside Editions). (Illus.). 24p. (Orig.). 1987. pap. 3.95 (ISBN 0-931191-05-X). Rob Briggs.
Shakespeare, Bacon, Jonson & Greene. Edward J. Castle. LC 77-113363. 1970. Repr. of 1897 ed. 25.00x (ISBN 0-8046-1010-X, Pub. by Kennikat). Assoc Faculty Pr.
Shakespeare Bibliography. Walter Ebisch & Levin L Schucking. 294p. Repr. of 1931 ed. lib. bdg. 150.00 (ISBN 0-918377-99-4). Russell Pr.
Shakespeare Bibliography. Compiled by Walther Ebisch. LC 68-20246. 1968. Repr. of 1930 ed. 24.50 (ISBN 0-405-08482-X, Blom Pubns). Ayer Co Pubs.
Shakespeare Bibliography: A Supplement. Walther Ebisch & Levin L. Schhucking. 1972. 24.50 (ISBN 0-405-08483-8, 901). Ayer Co Pubs.
Shakespeare Biography & Other Papers, Chiefly Elizabethan. facs. ed. Felix E. Schelling. LC 68-26473. (Essay Index Reprint Ser). 1968. Repr. of 1937 ed. 15.00 (ISBN 0-8369-0853-8). Ayer Co Pubs.
Shakespeare by Hilliard. Leslie Hotson. LC 76-24584. 1977. 40.00x (ISBN 0-520-03313-2). U of Cal Pr.
Shakespeare, Chapman & Sir Thomas More. Arthur Acheson. LC 72-113536. Repr. of 1931 ed. 35.00 (ISBN 0-404-00278-1). AMS Pr.
Shakespeare-Characters. Charles C. Clarke. LC 72-961. Repr. of 1863 ed. 22.50 (ISBN 0-404-01567-0). AMS Pr.
Shakespeare Circle. C. M. Mitchell. LC 76-30693. (Studies in Shakespeare, No. 24). 1977. lib. bdg. 46.95x (ISBN 0-8383-2166-6). Haskell.
Shakespeare Commentaries. Georg G. Gervinus. Tr. by Fanny E. Bunnett. LC 74-168112. Repr. of 1877 ed. 37.50 (ISBN 0-404-02716-4). AMS Pr.
Shakespeare: Comtemporary Critical Approaches. Ed. by Harry R. Garvin. LC 79-50103. (Bucknell Review Ser.: Vol. 25, No. 1). 192p. 1980. 16.50 (ISBN 0-8387-2376-4). Bucknell U Pr.
Shakespeare Concordance, 4 vols. John R. Bartlett. Set. 600.00 (ISBN 0-87968-266-3). Gordon Pr.
Shakespeare: Contrasts & Controversies. Kenneth Muir. 256p. 1985. cancelled (ISBN 0-389-20561-3). B&N Imports.
Shakespeare: Contrasts & Controversies. Kenneth Muir. LC 85-40473. 208p. 1985. 18.95 (ISBN 0-8061-1940-3). U of Okla Pr.
Shakespeare Country. John Leyland. Repr. lib. bdg. 27.00 (ISBN 0-8414-5860-X). Folcroft.
Shakespeare Criticism: An Essay in Synthesis. C. Narayana Menon. 276p. 1988. Repr. of 1938 ed. text ed. 30.00 (ISBN 0-89891-030-7, Pub. by Mittal Pubns India). Advent NY.
Shakespeare Criticism: Dryden to Morgann. S. Homchaudhuri. 1979. text ed. 19.00x. Coronet Bks.
Shakespeare Criticism: From the Beginnings to 1765. V. K. Pillai. 1932. lib. bdg. 30.50 (ISBN 0-8414-1685-0). Folcroft.
Shakespeare Criticsm: A Selection. Intro. by Nichol Smith. 416p. 1984. Repr. of 1916 ed. lib. bdg. 47.50 (ISBN 0-89984-623-8). Century Bookbindery.
Shakespeare Cross-Examination Association Staff: A Compilation of Articles First Appearing in the American Bar Association Journal. American Bar Association Staff. 125p. 1961. 5.00 (ISBN 0-686-47950-5). Amer Bar Assn.
Shakespeare Documents: A Chronological Catalogue. D. Lambert. 59.95 (ISBN 0-8490-1034-9). Gordon Pr.
Shakespeare Explained. Forrest S. Hunt. 191p. 1980. Repr. of 1915 ed. lib. bdg. 25.00 (ISBN 0-8495-3255-8). Arden Lib.
Shakespeare Explained. Forrest S. Lunt. 190p. 1981. Repr. of 1915 ed. lib. bdg. 40.00 (ISBN 0-89984-307-7). Century Bookbindery.
Shakespeare-Expositor. Thomas Keightley. LC 54-171550. Repr. of 1867 ed. 26.45 (ISBN 0-404-03642-2). AMS Pr.
Shakespeare Folios: Facsimiles of the Second, Third, & Fourth Folio Editions. Intro. by Marvin Spevack. 1986. facsimile 711.00 (Pub. by Boydell & Brewer). Longwood Pub Group.
Shakespeare for Everyone. William Shakespeare. Retold by Jennifer Mulherin. (gr. 5-12). Date not set. pap. 5.95 ea. Hamlet. Macbeth. The Merchant of Venice. A Midsummer Night's Dream. Romeo & Juliet. Twelfth Night. Silver.
Shakespeare Forgeries in the Revels Accounts. folio ed. Samuel A. Tannenbaum. LC 66-25946. (Illus.). Repr. of 1928 ed. 34.50x (ISBN 0-8046-0458-4, Pub. by Kennikat). Assoc Faculty Pr.
Shakespeare-from Betterton to Irving, 2 Vols. George C. Odell. LC 63-23277. (Illus.). Repr. of 1920 ed. Set. 50.00 (ISBN 0-405-08824-8); 27.50 ea. Vol. 1 (ISBN 0-405-08825-6). Vol. 2 (ISBN 0-405-08826-4). Ayer Co Pubs.
Shakespeare: From Richard II to Henry V. Derek A. Traversi. 1957. 17.50x (ISBN 0-8047-0503-8). Stanford U Pr.
Shakespeare Gallery, Containing the Principle Female Characters in the Plays of the Great Poet. Charles Heath. 1984. Repr. lib. bdg. 150.00 (ISBN 0-89984-930-X). Century Bookbindery.
Shakespeare Garden. Esther Singleton. LC 75-176028. (Illus.). Repr. of 1933 ed. 15.00 (ISBN 0-404-06096-X). AMS Pr.
Shakespeare Garden: With Numerous Illustrations from Photographs & Reproductions of Old Wood Cuts. Esther Singleton. LC 74-8203. 444p. 1974. Repr. of 1922 ed. 46.00x (ISBN 0-8103-4048-8). Gale.
Shakespeare Glossary. 3rd, enl. & rev. ed. C. T. Onions. Ed. by Robert D. Eagleson. 360p. 1986. 34.00 (ISBN 0-19-811199-1); pap. 10.95 (ISBN 0-19-812521-6). Oxford U Pr.
Shakespeare Handbook. facsimile ed. Raymond M. Alden. Ed. by Oscar J. Campbell. LC 75-109639. (Select Bibliographies Reprint Ser). 1932. 22.00 (ISBN 0-8369-5248-0). Ayer Co Pubs.
Shakespeare Handbook. Ed. by Levi Fox. (Illus.). 272p. 1987. lib. bdg. 29.95 (ISBN 0-8161-8905-6, Hall Reference). G K Hall.
Shakespeare: Handwriting & Spelling. Gerald H. Rendall. LC 76-169107. (Studies in Shakespeare, No. 24). 1971. Repr. of 1931 ed. lib. bdg. 40.95x (ISBN 0-8383-1335-3). Haskell.
Shakespeare Hermeneutics. Clement M. Ingleby. LC 73-157552. (Studies in Shakespeare, No. 24). 1971. Repr. of 1875 ed. lib. bdg. 33.95x (ISBN 0-8383-1294-2). Haskell.
Shakespeare, His Ethical Teaching. Harold Ford. 112p. 1980. Repr. lib. bdg. 30.00 (ISBN 0-89987-257-3). Century Bookbindery.
Shakespeare, His Life, Art & Character: An Historical Sketch of the Origin & Growth of the Drama in England, 2 Vols. H. N. Hudson. 495p. 1982. Repr. of 1880 ed. Set. lib. bdg. 100.00 (ISBN 0-89987-394-4). Darby Bks.
Shakespeare: His Life, Art, & Character, 2 Vols. 4th rev. ed. Henry N. Hudson. LC 72-169453. Repr. of 1872 ed. Set. 94.50 (ISBN 0-404-03378-4). AMS Pr.

Shakespeare Studies: An Annual Gathering of Research, Criticism & Reviews, Vol. XI. J. Leeds Barroll. 1978. lib. bdg. 25.00x (ISBN 0-89102-148-5). B Franklin.

Shakespeare Studies: An Annual Gathering of Research, Criticism, Reviews, Vols. I-X & XII. J. Leeds Barroll, 3rd. Incl. Vol. 1. 25.00 (ISBN 0-89102-079-9); Vol. 2. 25.00 (ISBN 0-89102-080-2); Vol. 3. 25.00 (ISBN 0-89102-081-0); Vol. 4. 25.00 (ISBN 0-89102-082-9); Vol. 5. 25.00 (ISBN 0-89102-083-7); Vol. 6. 25.00 (ISBN 0-89102-084-5); Vol. 7. 25.00 (ISBN 0-89102-085-3); Vol. 8. 25.00 (ISBN 0-89102-068-3); Vol. 9. 25.00 (ISBN 0-89102-070-5); Vol. 10. 25.00 (ISBN 0-89102-086-1); Vol. 12. 25.00 (ISBN 0-89102-188-4). 1976. Vol. 13. 29.95 (ISBN 0-89102-229-5). B Franklin.

Shakespeare Studies & an Essay on English Dictionaries. Thomas S. Baynes. Repr. of 1894 ed. 22.50 (ISBN 0-404-00697-3). AMS Pr.

Shakespeare Studies & an Essay on English Dictionaries. Thomas S. Baynes. 1973. Repr. of 1894 ed. 17.45 (ISBN 0-8274-1674-1). R West.

Shakespeare Studies: Biographical & Literary. Edgar I. Fripp. LC 72-168062. Repr. of 1930 ed. 29.50 (ISBN 0-404-07882-6). AMS Pr.

Shakespeare Studies: Historical & Comparative in Method. Edgar E. Stoll. 502p. 1980. lib. bdg. 50.00 (ISBN 0-89984-410-3). Century Bookbindery.

Shakespeare Studies: Julius Caesar. Blanche Coles. LC 72-86174. Repr. of 1940 ed. 21.00 (ISBN 0-404-01597-2). AMS Pr.

Shakespeare Studies: Julius Caesar. Blanche Coles. 281p. 1981. Repr. of 1940 ed. lib. bdg. 35.00 (ISBN 0-89987-127-5). Darby Bks.

Shakespeare Studies: Macbeth. Blanche Coles. LC 70-86176. Repr. of 1938 ed. 21.00 (ISBN 0-404-01598-0). AMS Pr.

Shakespeare Study Guide. Isidore J. Semper. LC 74-8732. 1930. lib. bdg. 29.50 (ISBN 0-8414-7764-7). Folcroft.

Shakespeare Study Today: The Horace Howard Furness Memorial Lectures. Ed. by Georgiana Ziegler. LC 84-45436. (Studies in the Renaissance: No. 13). 1986. 34.50 (ISBN 0-404-62283-6). AMS Pr.

Shakespeare Survey, 32 vols. Kenneth Muir. Set. 595.00 (ISBN 0-317-52152-7, Pub. by S Chand India). State Mutual Bk.

Shakespeare Survey: An Annual Survey of Shakespearian Study & Production, Vol. II. Ed. by Allardyce Nicoll. LC 49-1639. pap. 34.80 (ISBN 0-317-30413-5, 2024944). Bks Demand UMI.

Shakespeare the Aesthete: An Exploration of Literary Theory. Lachlan Mackinnon. LC 87-14378. 176p. 1987. 29.95 (ISBN 0-312-00981-X). St Martin.

Shakespeare the Boy. William J. Rolfe. LC 78-128411. (Studies in Shakespeare, No. 24). 1970. Repr. of 1900 ed. lib. bdg. 49.95x (ISBN 0-8383-1103-2). Haskell.

Shakespeare the Boy. William J. Rolfe. 251p. 1982. Repr. of 1896 ed. 18.95 (ISBN 0-87928-111-1). Corner Hse.

Shakespeare, the Comedies: A Collection of Critical Essays. Ed. by Kenneth Muir. 1965. 15.95 (ISBN 0-13-807693-6, Spec); (Spec). P-H.

Shakespeare: The Complete Works. Ed. by George B. Harrison. (Illus.). 1672p. 1952. text ed. 29.00 net (ISBN 0-15-580530-4, HC). HarBraceJ.

Shakespeare the Craftsman. Muriel C. Bradbrook. LC 79-2316. (History of Elizabethan Drama Ser.: Vol. 5). (Illus.). 1979. pap. 11.95 (ISBN 0-521-29529-7). Cambridge U Pr.

Shakespeare: the Critical Heritage, 4 Vols. Brian Vickers. Incl. Vol. 1. 1623-1692. 40.00x (ISBN 0-7100-7716-5); Vol. 2. 1693-1733. 40.00x (ISBN 0-7100-7807-2); Vol. 3. 1733-1752. 40.00x (ISBN 0-7100-7990-7); Vol. 4. 1753-1765. 1976. 40.00x (ISBN 0-7100-8297-5). (Critical Heritage Ser). 1974. six vols. 230.00x (ISBN 0-7100-0828-7). Routledge Chapman & Hall.

Shakespeare: The Critical Heritage, 1765-1774, Vol. 5. Ed. by Brian Vickers. (Critical Heritage Ser). 1979. 40.00x (ISBN 0-7100-8788-8). Routledge Chapman & Hall.

Shakespeare: The Critical Heritage, 1774-1801, Vol. 6. Ed. by Brian Vickers. (Critical Heritage Ser.). 664p. 1981. 55.00x (ISBN 0-7100-0629-2). Routledge Chapman & Hall.

Shakespeare, the Dark Comedies to the Last Plays: From Satire to Celebration. R. A. Foakes. LC 70-146536. 186p. 1971. 15.95x (ISBN 0-8139-0327-0). U Pr of Va.

Shakespeare the Director. Ann P. Slater. LC 82-6704. 256p. 1982. text ed. 26.50x (ISBN 0-389-20304-1, 07139). B&N Imports.

Shakespeare the Dramatist. Una Ellis-Fermor. LC 73-2638. 1948. lib. bdg. 15.00 (ISBN 0-8414-1900-0). Folcroft.

Shakespeare the Elizabethan. G. Bullough. (Shakespeare Lectures). 1964. pap. 5.50 (ISBN 0-85672-333-9, Pub. by British Acad). Longwood Pub Group.

Shakespeare: The Globe & the World. S. Schoenbaum. (Illus.). 1979. pap. 9.95 (ISBN 0-19-502646-2); ltd. ed., slipcased 90.00x (ISBN 0-19-502731-0). Oxford U Pr.

Shakespeare: The Last Phase. Derek Traversi. 272p. 1984. Repr. of 1954 ed. lib. bdg. 40.00 (ISBN 0-918377-22-6). Russell Pr.

Shakespeare: The Last Phase. Derek A. Traversi. 1955. 25.00x (ISBN 0-8047-0508-9). Stanford U Pr.

Shakespeare: The 'Lost Years' E. A. Honigmann. LC 84-24354. (Illus.). 182p. 1985. 22.50x (ISBN 0-389-20549-4, BNB-08112). B&N Imports.

Shakespeare, the Man. Walter Bagehot. LC 71-126678. Repr. of 1901 ed. 18.00 (ISBN 0-404-00446-6). AMS Pr.

Shakespeare, the Man. E. Lamborn. LC 76-30695. (Studies in Shakespeare, No. 24). 1977. lib. bdg. 39.95x (ISBN 0-8383-2173-9). Haskell.

Shakespeare the Man. Godwin Smith. LC 76-30768. (Studies in Shakespeare, No. 24). 1977. lib. bdg. 75.00x (ISBN 0-8383-2149-6). Haskell.

Shakespeare the Man: An Essay. Walter Bagehot. 66p. 1980. Repr. of 1901 ed. lib. bdg. 17.50 (ISBN 0-8495-0396-5). Arden Lib.

Shakespeare the Man: An Essay. Walter Bagehot. LC 73-4015. 1973. lib. bdg. 17.00 (ISBN 0-8414-1765-2). Folcroft.

Shakespeare: The Man & His Stage. Edmund A. Lamborn & George B. Harrison. LC 73-153336. Repr. of 1923 ed. 21.50 (ISBN 0-404-03805-0). AMS Pr.

Shakespeare: The Man & His Work. Morton Luce. 259p. 1981. Repr. of 1913 ed. lib. bdg. 35.00 (ISBN 0-8495-3264-7). Arden Lib.

Shakespeare: The Play of History. Graham Holderness et al. LC 87-50124. 250p. 1987. text ed. 21.00x (ISBN 0-87745-180-X). U of Iowa Pr.

Shakespeare: The Poet in His World. Muriel C. Bradbrook. LC 78-7611. 272p. 1978. 30.00x (ISBN 0-231-04648-0); pap. 14.50x (ISBN 0-231-04649-9). Columbia U Pr.

Shakespeare: The Roman Plays. Derek A. Traversi. 1963. 25.00x (ISBN 0-8047-0182-2). Stanford U Pr.

Shakespeare: The Theatrical Dimension. Ed. by Philip C. McGuire & David A. Samuelson. LC 77-78320. (Studies in the Renaissance: No. 3). 1979. lib. bdg. 34.50 (ISBN 0-404-16002-6). AMS Pr.

Shakespeare-The Tragedies: A Collection of Critical Essays. Clifford Leech. LC 65-17295. (Midway Reprint Ser.). xxxii, 256p. 1975. pap. 15.00x (ISBN 0-226-47018-0). U of Chicago Pr.

Shakespeare; the Tragedies: Twentieth Century Views, New Perspectives. Robert B. Heilman. 252p. 1984. 14.95 (ISBN 0-13-807918-8). P-H.

Shakespeare, the True Authorship. Douglas Baker. 1987. 60.00x (ISBN 0-9505502-2-1, Pub. by Claregate Coll UK). State Mutual Bk.

Shakespeare Through Eastern Eyes. R. Shahani. 59.95 (ISBN 0-8490-1037-3). Gordon Pr.

Shakespeare Through Eastern Eyes. Ranjee G. Shahani. 1973. lib. bdg. 29.50 (ISBN 0-8414-8116-4). Folcroft.

Shakespeare, Thy Name Is Marlow. David R. Williams. LC 66-16173. 94p. 1966. 5.95 (ISBN 0-8022-1884-9). Philos Lib.

Shakespeare to Hardy. Edmund Blunden. LC 73-16007. 1948. lib. bdg. 19.50 (ISBN 0-8414-9862-8). Folcroft.

Shakespeare to Hardy. A. Methuen. 1977. Repr. of 1922 ed. 12.50 (ISBN 0-89984-064-7). Century Bookbindery.

Shakespeare to Shaw. Cecil F. Armstrong. LC 70-95402. (BCL Ser.: No. 1). Repr. of 1913 ed. 15.00 (ISBN 0-404-00383-4). AMS Pr.

Shakespeare to Shaw: Studies in the Life's Work of Six Dramatists of the English Stage. facs. ed. Cecil F. Armstrong. LC 68-8435. (Essay Index Reprint Ser). 1913. 21.50 (ISBN 0-8369-0157-6). Ayer Co Pubs.

Shakespeare Translation: Annual Publication, 11 vols. Ed. by Toshikazu Oyama et al. 1980. 412.50 set (ISBN 0-686-77269-5); 37.50 ea. AMS Pr.

Shakespeare und Morus. Hans Glunz. Repr. of 1938 ed. 20.00 (ISBN 0-384-18960-1). Johnson Repr.

Shakespeare under Elizabeth. George B. Harrison. Repr. of 1933 ed. 29.00 (ISBN 0-403-04273-9). Somerset Pub.

Shakespeare Versus Shallow. L. Hotson. LC 74-95430. (Studies in Shakespeare, No. 24). 1970. Repr. of 1931 ed. lib. bdg. 49.95x (ISBN 0-8383-0981-X). Haskell.

Shakespeare Versus Shallow. Leslie Hotson. LC 74-109652. (Select Bibliographies Reprint Ser). 1931. 24.50 (ISBN 0-8369-5261-8). Ayer Co Pubs.

Shakespeare Versus Shallow. Leslie Hotson. 1973. Repr. of 1931 ed. 27.00 (ISBN 0-8274-0289-9). R West.

Shakespeare Without Words. A. Harbage. (Shakespeare Lectures). 1969. pap. 5.50 (ISBN 0-85672-337-1, Pub. by British Acad). Longwood Pub Group.

Shakespeare Without Words & Other Essays. Alfred Harbarge. LC 77-188353. 246p. 1972. 15.00x (ISBN 0-674-80395-7). Harvard U Pr.

Shakespeare Word-Book, Being a Glossary of Archaic Forms & Varied Usages of Words Employed by Shakespeare. Compiled by John Foster. LC 68-15123. 1969. Repr. of 1908 ed. 17.50x (ISBN 0-8462-1234-X). Russell.

Shakespeare Workbook, 2 vols. Bertram Joseph. 1980. pap. 12.95 ea. Vol. 1 Tragedies (ISBN 0-87830-566-1). Vol. 2 Comedies & Histories (ISBN 0-87830-571-8). Theatre Arts.

Shakespeare 1564-1964: A Collection of Modern Essays by Various Hands. Ed. by Edward A. Bloom. LC 64-17777. 240p. 1964. 28.00x (ISBN 0-87057-083-8). U Pr of New Eng.

Shakespearean Adaptations. Montague Summers. Incl. The Tempest; The Mock Tempest; King Lear. LC 68-1979. (Studies in Shakespeare, No. 24). (Illus.). 388p. 1969. Repr. of 1922 ed. lib. bdg. 49.95x (ISBN 0-8383-0682-9). Haskell.

Shakespearean Alchemy: Theme & Variations in Literary Criticism. Michael D. Gallatin. LC 85-62988. (Illus.). 84p. 1986. text ed. 16.95 (ISBN 0-9615997-5-8); pap. text ed. 9.95 (ISBN 0-9615997-0-7). QED Pr Ann Arbor.

Shakespearean Comedy. Chintamani N. Desai. LC 79-144595. Repr. of 1952 ed. 19.50 (ISBN 0-404-02099-2). AMS Pr.

Shakespearean Comedy. Thomas M. Parrott. LC 62-13844. 1962. Repr. of 1949 ed. 24.00x (ISBN 0-8462-0253-0). Russell.

Shakespearean Comedy & Other Studies. Amaranatha Jha. LC 77-3410. 1930. lib. bdg. 35.00 (ISBN 0-8414-5255-5). Folcroft.

Shakespearean Criticism, Vol. 1. Ed. by Laurie L. Harris & Mark W. Scott. LC 84-4010. (Literary Criticism Ser.). (Illus.). 680p. 1984. 95.00x (ISBN 0-8103-6125-6). Gale.

Shakespearean Criticism, Vol. 2. Samuel Taylor Coleridge. Ed. by T. M. Raysor. 1980. Repr. of 1960 ed. 14.95x (ISBN 0-460-00183-3, Evman). Biblio Dist.

Shakespearean Criticism, Vol. 2. Ed. by Mark Scott & Laurie L. Harris. 616p. 1985. 95.00x (ISBN 0-8103-6126-4). Gale.

Shakespearean Criticism, Vol. 3. Ed. by Laurie L. Harris & Mark Scott. 600p. 1986. 95.00x (ISBN 0-8103-6127-2). Gale.

Shakespearean Criticism, Vol. 4. Ed. by Mark Scott. (Shakespearean Criticism Ser.). 600p. 1986. 95.00x (ISBN 0-8103-6128-0). Gale.

Shakespearean Criticism, Vol. 5. Ed. by Mark Scott. (Shakespearean Criticism Ser.). 635p. 1987. 95.00x (ISBN 0-8103-6129-9). Gale.

Shakespearean Criticism, Vol. 6. Ed. by Mark W. Scott. 600p. 1987. 95.00x (ISBN 0-8103-6130-2). Gale.

Shakespearean Criticism, Vol. 8. Ed. by Mark Scott. 600p. 1988. 95.00 (ISBN 0-8103-6132-9). Gale.

Shakespearean Criticism, Textual & Literary, from Dryden to the End of the 18th Century. Ernest Walder. LC 76-39969. Repr. of 1895 ed. lib. bdg. 37.00 (ISBN 0-8414-9508-4). Folcroft.

Shakespearean Criticism, Vol. 7. Ed. by Mark W. Scott. 600p. 1988. 95.00 (ISBN 0-8103-6131-0). Gale.

Shakespearean Enigma & an Elizabethan Mania. John F. Forbis. LC 75-136375. Repr. of 1924 ed. 24.50 (ISBN 0-404-02458-0). AMS Pr.

Shakespearean Frauds. William Jaggard. LC 74-20601. 1974. Repr. of 1911 ed. lib. bdg. 17.50 (ISBN 0-8414-5322-5). Folcroft.

Shakespearean Gleanings. Edmund K. Chambers. LC 74-153312. Repr. of 1944 ed. 14.00 (ISBN 0-404-01444-5). AMS Pr.

Shakespearean Gleanings. Edmund K. Chambers. 1944. lib. bdg. 20.00 (ISBN 0-8414-3523-5). Folcroft.

Shakespearean Iconoclasm. James R. Siemon. LC 83-17923. 300p. 1984. 35.00x (ISBN 0-520-05031-2). U of Cal Pr.

Shakespearean Metadrama: The Argument of the Play in Titus Andronicus, Love's Labour's Lost, Romeo & Juliet, a Midsummer Night's Dream & Richard 2nd. James L. Calderwood. LC 71-141839. 1971. 12.95x (ISBN 0-8166-0595-5). U of Minn Pr.

Shakespearean Metaphor: Studies in Language & Form. Ralph Berry. 128p. 1978. 19.50x (ISBN 0-8476-6047-8). Rowman.

Shakespearean Miscellany. Francis G. Waldron. LC 73-131497. (Illus.). Repr. of 1802 ed. 17.50 (ISBN 0-404-06805-7). AMS Pr.

Shakespearean Mob. Frederick Tupper. (Studies in Shakespeare, No. 24). 1970. pap. 39.95x (ISBN 0-8383-0077-4). Haskell.

Shakespearean Motives. Derek Cohen. LC 87-12532. 140p. 29.95 (ISBN 0-312-01267-5). ST Martin.

Shakespearean Music in the Plays & Early Operas. Frederick Bridge. LC 68-358. (Studies in Shakespeare, No. 24). 1969. Repr. of 1923 ed. lib. bdg. 39.95x (ISBN 0-8383-0513-X). Haskell.

Shakespearean Music in the Plays & Early Operas. John F. Bridge. LC 75-153307. Repr. of 1923 ed. 16.50 (ISBN 0-404-07808-7). AMS Pr.

Shakespearean Negotiations: The Circulation of Social Energy in Renaissance England. Stephen Greenblatt. (New Historicism: Studies in Cultural Poetics: No. 4). 1988. 20.00x (ISBN 0-520-06159-4). U of Cal Pr.

Shakespearean Playhouses: A History of English Theatres from the Beginning to the Reformation. Joseph Q. Adams. (Illus.). 1959. 18.00 (ISBN 0-8446-1009-7). Peter Smith.

Shakespearean Politics: Government & Misgovernment in the Great Histories. C. G. Thayer. LC 83-2450. x, 190p. 1983. text ed. 22.95x (ISBN 0-8214-0726-0). Ohio U Pr.

Shakespearean Prompt-Books of the Seventeenth Century. Ed. by Blakemore G. Evans. Vol. III The Comedy of Errors, A Midsummer Night's Dream. boxed 25.00x (ISBN 0-8139-0216-9); Vol. V Smock Alley Macbeth. boxed 25.00x (ISBN 0-8139-0301-7). U Pr of Va.

Shakespearean Prompt-Books of the Seventeenth Century: The Smock Alley Othello, Vol. VI, Part I & II. Ed. by G. Blakemore Evans. LC 60-2680. 1981. 25.00x (ISBN 0-8139-0831-0). U Pr of Va.

Shakespearean Representation: Mimesis & Modernity in Elizabethan Tragedy. Howard Felperin. LC 77-71982. (Princeton Essays in Literature). 1977. 26.50x (ISBN 0-691-06341-9). Princeton U Pr.

Shakespearean Selves. Arthur T. Cadoux. 176p. 1981. Repr. of 1938 ed. lib. bdg. 30.00 (ISBN 0-89984-109-0). Century Bookbindery.

Shakespearean Sentences: A Study in Style & Syntax. John P. Houston. LC 87-28584. 232p. 1988. 27.50x (ISBN 0-8071-1399-9). La State U Pr.

Shakespearean Stage, 1574-1642. 2nd ed. Andrew Gurr. LC 80-40085. (Illus.). 220p. 1981. 57.50 (ISBN 0-521-23029-2); pap. 17.95 (ISBN 0-521-29772-9). Cambridge U Pr.

Shakespearean Structures. Ralph Berry. 164p. 1981. 28.50x (ISBN 0-389-20173-1, 06949). B&N Imports.

Shakespearean Tragedy. J. Leeds Barroll. LC 82-49309. 312p. 1984. 35.00 (ISBN 0-918016-18-5). Folger Bks.

Shakespearean Tragedy. Ed. by Malcolm Bradbury & David Palmer. LC 84-81206. (Stratford-upon-Avon Ser.: Vol. 20). 192p. 1984. 39.50 (ISBN 0-8419-0981-4); Oct. 1984. pap. text ed. 13.95 (ISBN 0-8419-0982-2). Holmes & Meier.

Shakespearean Tragedy & the Elizabethan Compromise. Paul Siegel. LC 78-39208. (Select Bibliographies Reprint Ser.). Repr. of 1957 ed. 19.00 (ISBN 0-8369-6810-7). Ayer Co Pubs.

Shakespearean Tragedy & the Elizabethan Compromise: A Marxist Study. Paul N. Siegel. LC 83-6469. 266p. 1983. pap. text ed. 14.00 (ISBN 0-8191-3243-8). U Pr of Amer.

Shakespearean Tragedy: Lectures on Hamlet, Othello, King Lear, Macbeth. 2nd ed. A. C. Bradley. LC 84-26215. 456p. 1985. 32.50 (ISBN 0-312-71427-0). St Martin.

Shakespeareana Genealogica. George R. French. LC 74-168139. Repr. of 1869 ed. 52.50 (ISBN 0-404-02575-7). AMS Pr.

Shakespeareana Genealogica. 1869. Repr. 20.00 (ISBN 0-8274-3378-6). R West.

Shakespeare's Analogical Scene: Parody as Structural Syntax. Joan Hartwig. LC 83-6845. (Illus.). xii, 243p. 1983. 22.50x (ISBN 0-8032-2324-2). U of Nebr Pr.

Shakespeare's Anonymous Editors: Scribe & Compositor in the Folio Text of "2 Henry IV". Eleanor Prosser. LC 79-66179. (Illus.). xiv, 219p. 1981. 22.50x (ISBN 0-8047-1033-3). Stanford U Pr.

Shakespeare's Apprenticeship. Robert Y. Turner. LC 73-84195. 328p. 1974. 25.00x (ISBN 0-226-81736-9). U of Chicago Pr.

Shakespeare's Art. Ed. by Milton Crane. 210p. 1973. 11.00x (ISBN 0-226-11835-5). U of Chicago Pr.

Shakespeare's Art from a Comparative Perspective. Ed. by Wendell M. Aycock. LC 80-54322. (Proceedings of the Comparitive Literature Symposium, No. 12). (Illus.). 197p. (Orig.). 1981. pap. 12.00 (ISBN 0-89672-081-0). Tex Tech Univ Pr.

Shakespeare's Art of Orchestration: Stage Technique & Audience Response. Jean E. Howard. LC 84-56. 224p. 1984. 16.95 (ISBN 0-252-01116-3). U of Ill Pr.

Shakespeare's Audience. Alfred Harbage. LC 41-26970. 201p. 1941. pap. 13.00x (ISBN 0-231-08513-3). Columbia U Pr.

Shakespeare's Audience. Alfred Harbage. 20.00 (ISBN 0-8446-2203-6). Peter Smith.

Shakespeare's Autobiographical Poems. C. A. Brown. 59.95 (ISBN 0-8490-1038-1). Gordon Pr.

Shakespeare's Autobiographical Poems. Charles A. Brown. LC 76-39541. Repr. of 1838 ed. 21.50 (ISBN 0-404-01127-6). AMS Pr.

Shakespeare's Bad Quartos: Deliberate Abridgements Designed for Performance by Reduced Cast. Robert E. Burkhart. (Studies in English Literature: No. 101). (Illus.). 124p. 1975. pap. text ed. 16.80x (ISBN 90-2793-276-X). Mouton.

Shakespeare's Biblical Knowledge. R. Noble. 59.95 (ISBN 0-8490-1039-X). Gordon Pr.

Shakespeare's Biblical Knowledge & Use of the Book of Common Prayer. Richmond Noble. 1970. lib. bdg. 20.00x (ISBN 0-374-96115-8, Octagon). Hippocrene Bks.

Shakespeare's Biblical Knowledge & Use of the Book of Common Prayer: As Exemplified in the Plays of the First Folio. Richmond S. Noble. 303p. 1980. Repr. of 1935 ed. lib. bdg. 39.50 (ISBN 0-8492-1971-X). R West.

Shakespeare's Birds. Peter Goodfellow. LC 83-42982. (Illus.). 96p. 1988. 14.95 (ISBN 0-87951-201-6). Overlook Pr.

Shakespeare's Land: A Journey Through the Landscape of Elizabethan England. A. L. Rowse. LC 87-6576. (Illus.). 200p. 1987. pap. 16.95 (ISBN 0-87701-462-0). Chronicle Bks.
Shakespeare's Language: An Introduction. N. F. Blake. LC 82-22005. 154p. 1984. pap. 10.95 (ISBN 0-312-71430-0). St Martin.
Shakespeare's Last Plays. Frances A. Yates. 1975. 19.95 (ISBN 0-7100-8100-6). Routledge Chapman & Hall.
Shakespeare's Late Plays: Essays in Honor of Charles Crow. Ed. by Richard C. Tobias & Paul G. Zolbrod. LC 74-27704. xiv, 235p. 1975. 16.00x (ISBN 0-8214-0178-5). Ohio U Pr.
Shakespeare's Legal Acquirements Considered. John C. Campbell. LC 79-39811. Repr. of 1859 ed. 14.50 (ISBN 0-404-01369-4). AMS Pr.
Shakespeare's Legal Maxims. William L. Rushton. LC 70-174795. Repr. of 1907 ed. 14.00 (ISBN 0-404-05456-0). AMS Pr.
Shakespeare's Liars. Inga-Stina Ewbank. (Shakespeare Lectures). 32p. 1985. pap. 5.50 (ISBN 0-85672-489-0, Pub. by British Acad). Longwood Pub Group.
Shakespeare's Library, 6 Vols. 2nd ed. Ed. by William C. Hazlitt. LC 17-24753. Repr. of 1875 ed. Set. 220.00 (ISBN 0-404-03250-8). Vol. 1 (ISBN 0-404-03251-6). Vol. 2 (ISBN 0-404-03252-4). Vol. 3 (ISBN 0-404-03253-2). Vol. 4 (ISBN 0-404-03254-0). Vol. 5 (ISBN 0-404-03255-9). Vol. 6 (ISBN 0-404-03256-7). AMS Pr.
Shakespeare's Life & Work. F. J. Furnivall & John Munro. 1973. lib. bdg. 16.00 (ISBN 0-8414-4290-8). Folcroft.
Shakespeare's Life & Work. Sidney Lee. 1978. Repr. of 1900 ed. lib. bdg. 27.00 (ISBN 0-8414-5754-9). Folcroft.
Shakespeare's Life & Work. Sidney Lee. (Illus.). 231p. 1986. Repr. of 1900 ed. lib. bdg. 50.00 (ISBN 0-8495-3435-6). Arden Lib.
Shakespeare's Life & Work: Being Abridgment, Chiefly for the Use of Students, of a Life of William Shakespear. Sidney Lee. 231p. 1983. Repr. of 1913 ed. lib. bdg. 40.00 (ISBN 0-89987-524-6). Darby Bks.
Shakespeare's Lives. Samuel Schoenbaum. LC 74-118290. 1970. 39.95x (ISBN 0-19-501243-7). Oxford U Pr.
Shakespeare's Lofty Scene. J. I. Stewart. (Shakespeare Lectures). 1971. pap. 5.50 (ISBN 0-902732-08-0, Pub. by British Acad). Longwood Pub Group.
Shakespeare's London. T. P. Ordish. 59.95 (ISBN 0-8490-1043-8). Gordon Pr.
Shakespeare's London. Henry T. Stephenson. LC 74-176435. Repr. of 1905 ed. 24.50 (ISBN 0-404-06258-X). AMS Pr.
Shakespeare's London: A Study of London in the Reign of Queen Elizabeth. Thomas F. Ordish. LC 72-144667. Repr. of 1897 ed. 18.45 (ISBN 0-404-07957-1). AMS Pr.
Shakespeare's Lost Play: Edmund Ironside. Ed. by Eric Sams. LC 85-19579. 416p. 1986. 37.50 (ISBN 0-312-71432-7). St Martin.
Shakespeare's Lost Years in London. Arthur Acheson. LC 79-152552. (Studies in Shakespeare, No. 24). 1971. Repr. lib. bdg. 75.00x (ISBN 0-8383-1235-7). Haskell.
Shakespeare's Lovers: A Text for Performance & Analysis. Libby Appel & Michael Flachmann. LC 82-5444. 156p. 1982. pap. 8.95x (ISBN 0-8093-1072-4). S Ill U Pr.
Shakespeare's Lusty Punning in Love's Labour's Lost. Herbert A. Ellis. LC 73-86159. (Studies in English Literature Ser.: Vol. 81). 239p. 1974. text ed. 29.50x (ISBN 90-2792-616-6). Mouton.
Shakespeare's Macbeth. 2nd ed. Walter S. Dalgliesh. LC 74-163664. Repr. of 1864 ed. 11.50 (ISBN 0-404-01918-8). AMS Pr.
Shakespeare's Magic Circle. facs. ed. Alfred J. Evans. LC 72-128884. (Select Bibliographies Reprint Ser.). 1956. 15.00 (ISBN 0-8369-5504-8). Ayer Co Pubs.
Shakespeare's Marriage. J. W. Gray. 59.95 (ISBN 0-8490-1044-6). Gordon Pr.
Shakespeare's Marriage. Joseph W. Gray. LC 75-168182. Repr. of 1905 ed. 35.00 (ISBN 0-404-02894-2). AMS Pr.
Shakespeare's Mature Tragedies. Bernard McElroy. LC 72-5389. 272p. 1986. pap. 14.50x (ISBN 0-691-10201-5). Princeton U Pr.
Shakespeare's Mediated World. Richard Fly. LC 75-32486. 192p. 1976. 17.50x (ISBN 0-87023-199-5). U of Mass Pr.
Shakespeare's Medical Knowledge. Charles W. Stearns. LC 72-959. Repr. of 1865 ed. 11.50 (ISBN 0-404-06224-5). AMS Pr.
Shakespeare's Melancholics. W. I. Scott. LC 73-18200. 1974. Repr. of 1962 ed. lib. bdg. 29.00 (ISBN 0-8414-7711-6). Folcroft.
Shakespeares Metrical Art. George T. Wright. 1988. 39.95x (ISBN 0-520-06057-1). U of Cal Pr.
Shakespeare's Military World. Paul A. Jorgensen. LC 56-9673. 1974. 42.00x (ISBN 0-520-02519-9). U of Cal Pr.
Shakespeare's Mingled Drama. Prabodh C. Ghose. 1966. Repr. 20.00 (ISBN 0-8274-3381-6). R West.
Shakespeare's Mingled Drama. Prabodh C. Ghosh. 143p. 1986. Repr. of 1966 ed. lib. bdg. 40.00 (ISBN 0-89984-667-X). Century Bookbindery.
Shakespeare's Mingled Yarn & Measure for Measure. E. A. Honigmann. (Shakespeare Lectures). (Illus.). 12p. 1981. pap. 5.50 (ISBN 0-85672-355-X, Pub. by British Acad). Longwood Pub Group.
Shakespeare's Monarchs. J. C. Stobart. 59.95 (ISBN 0-8490-1045-4). Gordon Pr.
Shakespeare's Monologues They Haven't Heard. Ed. by Edith B. Maag. 50p. 1987. pap. 4.95 (ISBN 0-940669-01-3). Dramaline Pubns.
Shakespeare's "More Than Words Can Witness" Essays on Visual & Nonverbal Enactment in the Plays. Ed. by Sidney Homan. LC 77-81576. 240p. 1980. 23.50 (ISBN 0-8387-2153-2). Bucknell U Pr.
Shakespeare's Motley. Leslie Hotson. LC 75-117592. (Studies in Shakespeare, No. 24). 1970. Repr. of 1952 ed. lib. bdg. 49.95x (ISBN 0-8383-1025-7). Haskell.
Shakespeare's Mystery Play. Colin Still. LC 73-4871. 1921. lib. bdg. 38.50 (ISBN 0-8414-7543-1). Folcroft.
Shakespeare's Mystery Play, a Study of the Tempest. Colin Still. LC 71-131842. 247p. 1921. Repr. 39.00x (ISBN 0-403-00729-1). Scholarly.
Shakespeare's Names: A Pronouncing Dictionary. Helge Kokeritz. LC 59-6798. (Shakespeare Supplements Ser.). Repr. of 1959 ed. 22.10 (ISBN 0-8357-9507-1, 2011105). Bks Demand UMI.
Shakespeare's Opening Scenes. Robert F. Willson, Jr. & James Hogg. (Elizabethan & Renaissance Studies). 217p. (Orig.). 1977. pap. 15.00 (ISBN 3-7052-0709-1, Pub. by Salzburg Studies). Longwood Pub Group.
Shakespeare's Othello. Samuel A. Tannenbaum. LC 77-12146. 1977. Repr. lib. bdg. 29.00 (ISBN 0-8414-8638-7). Folcroft.
Shakespeare's "Othello" A Comprehensive Bibliography. John Smith. (Studies in the Renaissance: No. 26). 1988. 57.50. AMS Pr.
Shakespeare's Othello: The Study & the Stage 1604-1904. Gino J. Matteo. Ed. by James Hogg. (Poetic Drama & Poetic Theory ser.). 287p. (Orig.). 1974. pap. 15.00 (ISBN 3-7052-0835-7, Pub. by Salzburg Studies). Longwood Pub Group.
Shakespeare's Other Anne. W. J. Hutcheson. LC 74-1149. (Studies in Shakespeare, No. 24). 1974. lib. bdg. 33.95x (ISBN 0-8383-1793-6). Haskell.
Shakespeare's Other Language. Ruth Nevo. 160p. 1988. text ed. 37.50x (ISBN 0-416-06402-7). Routledge Chapman & Hall.
Shakespeare's Pagan World: The Roman Tragedies. J. L. Simmons. LC 73-80126. 1973. 17.95x (ISBN 0-8139-0488-9). U Pr of Va.
Shakespeare's Pastoral Comedy. Thomas McFarland. LC 72-81325. x, 218p. 1972. 22.00x (ISBN 0-8078-1199-8). U of NC Pr.
Shakespeare's Patterns of Self-Knowledge. Rolf Soellner. LC 72-5804. 476p. 1972. 15.00 (ISBN 0-8142-0171-7). Ohio St U Pr.
Shakespeare's "Pericles" & "Apolonius of Tyre" A Study in Comparative Literature. Albert H. Smyth. LC 79-126696. Repr. of 1898 ed. 11.50 (ISBN 0-404-06129-X). AMS Pr.
Shakespeare's Perjured Eye: The Invention of Poetic Subjectivity in the Sonnets. Joel Fineman. 1985. 37.50x (ISBN 0-520-05486-5); pap. 12.95 (ISBN 0-520-06331-7). U of Cal Pr.
Shakespeare's Philosophical Patterns. Walter C. Curry. 12.50 (ISBN 0-8446-0567-0). Peter Smith.
Shakespeare's Philosophy of Evil. Lloyd C. Sears. LC 73-84911. 256p. 1973. 8.95 (ISBN 0-8158-0309-5). Chris Mass.
Shakespeare's Planet. Clifford D. Simak. 1988. pap. 2.95 (ISBN 0-345-00762-X, Del Rey). Ballantine.
Shakespeare's Play of King Henry IV from a Contemporary Manuscript see Shakesperian Commentary: The Remarks of Karl Simrock on the Plots of Shakespeare's Plays.
Shakespeare's Players. J. Cook. 1986. pap. 29.75X (ISBN 0-245-53825-9, Pub. by Harrap Ltd England). State Mutual Bk.
Shakespeare's Playhouse Practice: A Handbook. Warren D. Smith. LC 74-15448. pap. 33.30 (ISBN 0-317-55652-5, 2029255). Bks Demand UMI.
Shakespeare's Playhouses. Herbert Berry. LC 85-48061. (Studies in the Renaissance: No.19). 1987. 34.50 (ISBN 0-404-62289-5). AMS Pr.
Shakespeare's Plays for Young People. Martha Harris Fair et al. (Illus.). 37p. (Orig.). (gr. 2-9). 1982. pap. 10.00 (ISBN 0-911181-01-6). Harris Academy.
Shakespeare's Plays in Quarto: A Facsimile Edition of Copies Primarily from the Henry E. Huntington Library. William Shakespeare. Ed. by Michael J. Allen & Kenneth Muir. LC 81-40322. 936p. 1982. (boxed) 175.00x (ISBN 0-520-04077-5). U of Cal Pr.
Shakespeare's Plots. W. H. Fleming. 59.95 (ISBN 0-8490-1046-2). Gordon Pr.
Shakespeare's Plots. William H. Fleming. LC 75-131512. Repr. of 1902 ed. 30.00 (ISBN 0-404-02437-8). AMS Pr.
Shakespeare's Plutarch. Ed. by Plutarchus. Walter W. Skeat. 1875. 15.00 (ISBN 0-404-06097-8). AMS Pr.
Shakespeare's Poetics. Ekbert Faas. 279p. 1986. 34.50 (ISBN 0-521-30825-9). Cambridge U Pr.
Shakespeare's Political Drama: The History Plays & the Roman Plays. Alexander Leggatt. 320p. 1988. lib. bdg. 45.00 (ISBN 0-415-00655-4). Routledge Chapman & Hall.
Shakespeare's Political Plays. H. M. Richmond. 11.00 (ISBN 0-8446-2804-2). Peter Smith.
Shakespeare's Politics. Allen Bloom & Harry V. Jaffa. LC 81-10342. x, 150p. 1986. pap. 12.00x (ISBN 0-226-06040-3, Midway Reprint). U of Chicago Pr.
Shakespeare's Politics. L. C. Knights. 1957. lib. bdg. 16.50 (ISBN 0-8414-5596-1). Folcroft.
Shakespeare's Portrayal of Moral Life. Frank Sharp. LC 76-121352. (Studies in Shakespeare, No. 24). 1970. Repr. of 1902 ed. lib. bdg. 49.95x (ISBN 0-8383-1069-9). Haskell.
Shakespeare's Predecessors in the English Drama. John A. Symonds. LC 67-28915. 1967. Repr. of 1883 ed. 25.00x (ISBN 0-8154-0301-1). Cooper Sq.
Shakespeare's Predecessors in the English Drama. John A. Symonds. 1970. Repr. of 1900 ed. lib. bdg. 35.00 (ISBN 0-8371-1154-4, SYSH). Greenwood.
Shakespeare's Primitive Art. M. C. Bradbrook. (Shakespeare Lectures). 1965. pap. 2.25 (ISBN 0-85672-334-7, Pub. by British Acad). Longwood Pub Group.
Shakespeare's Principal Plays. 3rd ed. Ed. by Tucker Brooke et al. (Illus.). 1935. 59.50 (ISBN 0-89197-402-4). Irvington.
Shakespeare's Problem Plays. Eustace M. Tillyard. LC 83-45901. 1950. 21.50 (ISBN 0-404-20258-6, PR2976). AMS Pr.
Shakespeare's Producing Hand. Richard Flatter. 1973. Repr. of 1948 ed. 27.00 (ISBN 0-8274-0540-5). R West.
Shakespeare's Professional Skills. Nevill Coghill. pap. 60.00 (2027277). Bks Demand UMI.
Shakespeare's Pronunciation. Wilhelm Vietor. LC 76-177864. Repr. of 1906 ed. 16.50 (ISBN 0-404-06765-4). AMS Pr.
Shakespeare's Prophetic Mind. A. C. Harwood. 63p. 1977. pap. 7.50 (ISBN 0-85440-318-3, Pub. by Steinerbooks). Anthroposophic.
Shakespeare's Proverbial Language: An Index. R. W. Dent. 378p. 1981. 45.00x (ISBN 0-520-03894-0). U of Cal Pr.
Shakespeare's Puck & His Folkslore, 3 Vols. William Bell. Repr. of 1864 ed. Set. 92.50 (ISBN 0-404-00740-6). AMS Pr.
Shakespeare's Recoil from Romanticism. H. B. Charlton. 1931. lib. bdg. 15.00 (ISBN 0-8414-3493-X). Folcroft.
Shakespeare's Recoil from Romanticism. Henry B. Charlton. 27p. 1980. Repr. of 1931 ed. lib. bdg. 17.00. R West.
Shakespeare's Religious Background. Ed. by Peter Milward. 312p. 1985. Repr. of 1973 ed. 10.95 (ISBN 0-8294-0508-9). Loyola.
Shakespeare's Religious Frontier. Robert Stevenson. LC 73-16102. 1974. Repr. of 1958 ed. lib. bdg. 30.00 (ISBN 0-8414-7699-3). Folcroft.
Shakespeare's Reparative Comedies: A Psychoanalytic View of the Middle Plays. Joseph Westlund. LC 83-9305. 192p. 1984. lib. bdg. 17.50x (ISBN 0-226-89413-4). U of Chicago Pr.
Shakespeare's Repentance Plays: The Search for an Adequate Form. Alan R. Velie. LC 72-422. 127p. 1972. 15.00 (ISBN 0-8386-1126-5). Fairleigh Dickinson.
Shakespeare's Restorations of the Father. David Sundelson. 170p. 1983. text ed. 25.00 (ISBN 0-8135-0980-7). Rutgers U Pr.
Shakespeare's Revision of King Lear. Steven Urkowitz. LC 79-3234. (Princeton Lectures in Literature Ser.). 184p. 1987. 25.00x (ISBN 0-691-06432-6); pap. text ed. 11.50 (ISBN 0-691-10228-7). Princeton U Pr.
Shakespeare's Rhetoric of Comic Character: Dramatic Convention in Classical & Renaisance Comedy. Karen Newman. 128p. 1985. 16.95 (ISBN 0-416-37990-7, 9116). Routledge Chapman & Hall.
Shakespeare's Rival. Robert Gittings. LC 76-3689. (Illus.). 138p. 1976. Repr. of 1960 ed. lib. bdg. 35.00x (ISBN 0-8371-8814-8, GISR). Greenwood.
Shakespeare's Romances. Richard A. Andretta. 152p. 1981. text ed. 15.00x (ISBN 0-7069-1420-1, Pub. by Vikas India). Advent NY.
Shakespeare's Romances: A Study of Some Ways of the Imagination. Hallett Smith. LC 72-79314. 244p. 1972. 29.95 (ISBN 0-87328-052-0); pap. 9.95 (ISBN 0-87328-053-9). Huntington Lib.
Shakespeare's Romances & the Royal Family. David M. Bergeron. LC 85-689. xiv, 256p. 1985. 25.00x (ISBN 0-7006-0271-2). U Pr of KS.
Shakespeare's Romances Reconsidered. Ed. by Carol M. Kay & Henry E. Jacobs. LC 77-17389. xii, 224p. 1978. 19.95x (ISBN 0-8032-0958-4). U of Nebr Pr.
Shakespeare's Romantic Comedies: The Development of Their Form & Meaning. Peter G. Phialas. LC 66-25355. xvi, 314p. 1969. pap. 8.95x (ISBN 0-8078-4043-2). U of NC Pr.
Shakespeare's Rome. Robert S. Miola. LC 83-1777. 244p. 1983. 34.50 (ISBN 0-521-25307-1). Cambridge U Pr.
Shakespeare's "Rough Magic". Ed. by Peter Erickson & Coppelia Kahn. LC 83-40112. (Illus.). 320p. 1985. 37.50 (ISBN 0-87413-247-9). U Delaware Pr.
Shakespeare's Satire. Oscar J. Campbell. LC 74-159036. 239p. 1971. Repr. of 1943 ed. 27.50x (ISBN 0-87752-150-6). Gordian.
Shakespeare's Scepticism. Graham Bradshaw. LC 87-9479. 283p. 1987. 35.00 (ISBN 0-312-00964-X). St Martin.
Shakespeare's Scotland. Sir James Fergusson Of Kilkerran. LC 79-15666. Repr. of 1957 ed. lib. bdg. 17.00 (ISBN 0-8414-4164-2). Folcroft.
Shakespeare's Self. Teighmouth W. Shore. 1920. Repr. 15.00 (ISBN 0-8274-3383-2). R West.
Shakespeare's Self. W. Shore. LC 72-179265. (Studies in Shakespeare, No. 24). 1971. Repr. of 1920 ed. lib. bdg. 49.95x (ISBN 0-8383-1366-3). Haskell.
Shakespeare's Self Portrait: Passages from His Work. Compiled by & notes by A. L. Rowse. 200p. 1985. lib. bdg. 14.95 (ISBN 0-8191-4220-4, Pub. by Madison Bks). U Pr of Amer.
Shakespeare's Seventeenth-Century Editors, 1632-1685. Matthew W. Black & M. A. Shaaber. LC 38-3681. (MLA.MGS). 1937. 40.00 (ISBN 0-527-08600-2). Kraus Repr.
Shakespeare's Sexual Comedy: A Mirror for Lovers. Hugh M. Richmond. LC 77-155437. Date not set. Repr. of 1971 ed. price not set (ISBN 0-8290-2141-8). Irvington.
Shakespeare's Significance. Edmund Blunden. LC 73-9822. 1929. lib. bdg. 15.00 (ISBN 0-8414-3160-4). Folcroft.
Shakespeare's Sisters: Feminist Essays on Women Poets. Ed. by Sandra M. Gilbert & Susan Gubar. LC 78-9510. (Midland Bks.: No. 263). 368p. 1979. 25.00x (ISBN 0-253-11258-3); pap. 12.95x (ISBN 0-253-20263-9). Ind U Pr.
Shakespeare's Soliloquies. Wolfgang Clemen. LC 76-58367. 1977. Repr. of 1964 ed. lib. bdg. 12.00 (ISBN 0-8414-3440-9). Folcroft.
Shakespeare's Soliloquies. Wolfgang Clemen. Tr. by Charity S. Stokes. LC 87-1541. 211p. 1987. 39.95 (ISBN 0-416-05862-0); pap. 13.95 (ISBN 0-416-30460-5). Routledge Chapman & Hall.
Shakespeare's Sonnet Story: 1592-1598. Arthur Acheson. LC 72-164658. (Studies in Shakespeare, No. 24). 1971. Repr. of 1922 ed. lib. bdg. 69.95x (ISBN 0-8383-1322-1). Haskell.
Shakespeare's Sonnets. Commentary by Stephen Booth. LC 76-56161. 1977. 45.00x (ISBN 0-300-01959-9); pap. 16.95 (ISBN 0-300-02495-9). Yale U Pr.
Shakespeare's Sonnets. Tucker Brooke. LC 74-2054. 1936. lib. bdg. 39.00 (ISBN 0-8414-9904-7). Folcroft.
Shakespeare's Sonnets. W. H. Hadow. Bd. with Lover's Complaint. 103p. 1980. Repr. of 1907 ed. lib. bdg. 30.00 (ISBN 0-89987-375-8). Darby Bks.
Shakespeare's Sonnets. Ed. by W. G. Ingram & Theodore Redpath. 1978. 24.50 (ISBN 0-8419-6210-3); pap. 11.50 (ISBN 0-8419-6211-1). Holmes & Meier.
Shakespeare's Sonnets. Kenneth Muir. (Unwin Critical Library). 179p. 1982. pap. 12.95 (ISBN 0-04-821055-2). Unwin Hyman.
Shakespeare's Sonnets. Kenneth Muir. (Unwin Critical Library). 1979. text ed. 22.95 (ISBN 0-04-821042-0). Unwin Hyman.
Shakespeare's Sonnets. William Shakespeare. Ed. by S. C. Campbell. 177p. 1978. 15.00x (ISBN 0-8476-6134-2). Rowman.
Shakespeare's Sonnets. William Shakespeare. Ed. by Louis B. Wright & Virginia LaMar. (Folger Library). 372p. (YA) (gr. 9 up). 1967. pap. text ed. 3.95. WSP.
Shakespeare's Sonnets. C. C. Stopes. 1978. Repr. of 1904 ed. lib. bdg. 30.00 (ISBN 0-8492-8075-3). R West.
Shakespeare's Sonnets: A Record of Twentieth Century Criticism. Tetsumaro Hayashi. LC 77-184764. 163p. 1972. 17.50 (ISBN 0-8108-0462-X). Scarecrow.
Shakespeare's Sonnets & a Lover's Complaint. W. H. Hadow. LC 74-16293. 1907. lib. bdg. 27.00 (ISBN 0-8414-4877-9). Folcroft.
Shakespeare's Sonnets & a Lover's Complaint. William Shakespeare. Ed. by Stanley Wells. 176p. 1986. 9.95 (ISBN 0-19-812946-7). Oxford U Pr.
Shakespeare's Sonnets Dated & Other Essays. Leslie Hotson. 1977. Repr. of 1949 ed. lib. bdg. 39.00 (ISBN 0-8495-2208-0). Arden Lib.
Shakespeare's Sonnets Never Before Interpreted. Gerald Massey. LC 78-172855. Repr. of 1866 ed. 39.75 (ISBN 0-404-04238-4). AMS Pr.
Shakespeare's Sonnets: Notes. James K. Lowers. (Orig.). 1965. pap. 3.25 (ISBN 0-8220-0077-6). Cliffs.
Shakespeare's Sonnets Reconsidered. Ed. by Samuel Butler. LC 76-136416. Repr. of 1899 ed. 15.00 (ISBN 0-404-01249-3). AMS Pr.
Shakespeare's Sonnets: Their Relation to His Life. Barbara A. Mackenzie. LC 78-6965. Repr. of 1946 ed. 11.50 (ISBN 0-404-04135-3). AMS Pr.
Shakespeares Speech-Headings: The Bibliographer, the Editor & the Critic. Ed. by George W. Williams. (Studies in the Renaissance: No. 25). 1988. 34.50. AMS Pr.
Shakespeare's Stage. enl. ed. A. M. Nagler. LC 80-26513. (Shakespeare Supplements Ser.). 152p. 1981. pap. 9.95x (ISBN 0-300-02689-7, Y-400). Yale U Pr.
Shakespeare's Stagecraft. J. L. Styan. (Illus.). 1967. 47.50 (ISBN 0-521-06902-5); pap. 14.95 (ISBN 0-521-09435-6). Cambridge U Pr.

Shallow Grave: A Memoir of the Spanish Civil War. Walter Gregory. (Illus.). 192p. 1987. 25.95 (ISBN 0-575-03790-3, Pub. by Gollancz England). David & Charles.
Shallow Grave at Waiilatpu: The Sagers' West. 2nd ed. Erwin N. Thompson. LC 77-110668. (Illus.). 192p. 1973. pap. 7.95 (ISBN 0-87595-024-8). Oregon Hist.
Shallow Graves: Two Women & Vietnam. Wendy W. Larsen & Tran Thi Nga. LC 85-14534. 288p. 1986. 16.45 (ISBN 0-394-54985-6). Random.
Shallow Graves: Two Women & Vietnam. Wendy W. Larsen & Tran Thi Nga. LC 86-46077. 320p. 1987. pap. 7.95 (ISBN 0-06-097093-6, PL 7093, PL). Har-Row.
Shallow Ground Disposal of Radioactive Wastes: A Guidebook. (Safety Ser.: No. 53). 52p. 1981. pap. 9.75 (ISBN 92-0-123281-0, ISP578, IAEA). UNIPUB.
Shallow Impurity Centers in Semiconductors: Proceedings of the 2nd International Conference, Fourth Trieste IUPAP-ICTP Semiconductor Symposium, International Centre for Theoretical Physics, Trieste, Italy, 28 July to August 1,1986. Ed. by A. Baldereschi & R. Resta. 308p. 1987. 71.00 (ISBN 0-444-87087-3, North Holland). Elsevier.
Shallow Lakes: Contributions to Their Limnology. Ed. by M. Dokulil et al. (Developmrnts in Hydrobiology Ser.: No. 3). 218p. 1981. PLB 59.50 (ISBN 0-686-28842-4, Pub. by Junk Pubs Netherlands). Kluwer Academic.
Shallow-Level Plutonic Complexes in the Eastern Sierra Nevada, California & Their Tectonic Implications. Richard A. Schweickert. LC 76-11570. (Geological Society of America Special Papers: No. 176). pap. 20.00 (ISBN 0-317-29102-5, 2023742). Bks Demand UMI.
Shallow Oil & Gas Resources. UNITAR Staff. LC 85-17592. (Illus.). 600p. 1986. 59.00x (ISBN 0-87201-833-4). Gulf Pub.
Shallow Refraction Seismics. Bengt Sjogren. 256p. 1984. 55.00 (ISBN 0-412-24210-9, NO. 9171, Pub. by Chapman & Hall). Routledge Chapman & Hall.
Shallow Tethys Two: Proceedings of the International Symposium on Shallow Tethys 2, Wagga Wagga, 15-17 September 1986. Ed. by K. G. McKenzie. (Illus.). 587p. 1987. text ed. 58.50 (ISBN 90-6191-647-X, Pub. by A A Balkema). Brookfield Pub Co.
Shallow-Water Asteroidea & Ophiuroidea of Hawaii. C. A. Ely. (BMB Ser.). Repr. of 1942 ed. 13.00 (ISBN 0-527-02284-5). Kraus Repr.
Shallow Water Bass. Larry Larsen. LC 85-82041. (Illus.). 160p. (Orig.). 1986. pap. 7.95 (ISBN 0-936513-00-4). Larsen's Outdoor.
Shallow-Water Crabs. R. W. Engle. LC 82-9706. (Synopses of the British Fauna Ser.: No. 25). (Illus.). 220p. 1983. 42.50 (ISBN 0-521-24963-5). Cambridge U Pr.
Shallow-Water Gammaridean Amphipoda of New England. E. L. Bousfield. 17.50 (ISBN 0-8014-0726-5). Brown Bk.
Shallow-Water Marine Benthic Macroinvertebrates of South Carolina. Richard S. Fox & Edward E. Ruppert. (Belle W. Baruch Library in Marine Science: No. 14). 335p. 1985. 42.95x (ISBN 0-87249-473-X). U of SC Pr.
Shallow-Water Pycnogonida from the Izu Peninsula, Japan. Koichiro Nakamura & C. Allan Child. LC 83-10183. (Smithsonian Contributions to Zoology: No. 386). pap. 20.00 (ISBN 0-317-29735-X, 2022202). Bks Demand UMI.
Shallow-Water Sponges of the Western Bahamas. F. Wiedenmayer. (Experientia Supplementa: No. 28). (Illus.). 332p. 1977. 102.95x (ISBN 0-8176-0906-7). Birkhauser.
Shallow Water Wave Equations: Formulation, Analysis & Application. I. Kinnmark. (Lecture Notes in Engineering: Vol. 15). 187p. 1985. pap. 18.00 (ISBN 0-387-16031-0). Springer-Verlag.
Shallow Waters: A Year on Cape Cod's Pleasant Bay. William Sargent. (Illus.). 168p. 1985. pap. 12.95 (ISBN 0-940160-28-5). Parnassus Imprints.
Shallows. Tim Winton. LC 85-48146. 235p. 1986. 14.95 (ISBN 0-689-11806-6). Atheneum.
Shallows of Night. Eric Van Lustbader. 1987. pap. 3.50 (ISBN 0-425-09964-4). Berkley Pub.
Shalom Aleichem. Noah Golinkin. 77p. 1978. pap. 5.95x (ISBN 0-88482-696-1). Hebrew Pub.
Shalom: Essays in Honor of Dr. Charles H. Shaw. Ed. by Eugene J. Mayhew. 231p. 1983. pap. 11.95 (ISBN 0-912407-01-8). William Tyndale Col Pr.
Shalom Home Study Course in Modern Hebrew. Ehud, pseud. LC 84-90401. 123p. 1984. Repr. of 1978 ed. 19.95 (ISBN 0-9603914-1-X). Kellogg.
Shalom: Hope for the World. Steve Clapp. 178p. (Orig.). 1982. pap. 8.00 (ISBN 0-914527-35-5). C-Four Res.
Shalom Seders. Ed. by New Jewish Agenda. 128p. 1984. pap. 12.95 (ISBN 0-531-09840-0). Watts.
Shalom Seders: Three Passover Haggadahs. Compiled by New Jewish Agenda. LC 83-25857. (Illus.). 104p. 1984. pap. 12.95 (ISBN 0-915361-03-5, 09747-1, Dist. by Watts). Adama Pubs Inc.
Shalom: The Bible's Word for Salvation, Justice & Peace. Perry B. Yoder. LC 86-82879. 161p. 1987. pap. 14.95 (ISBN 0-87303-120-2). Faith & Life.
Sham Flyers. Edward Kissam. 1969. 6.95 (ISBN 0-685-00953-X, Pub. by Anvil Pr); pap. 4.95 (ISBN 0-685-00954-8). Small Pr Dist.
Shamail Tirmidhi. M. Hussain. 16.50 (ISBN 0-317-01594-X). Kazi Pubns.
Shaman. Frank Coffey. Ed. by Jim Connor. 256p. 1988. pap. 3.95 (ISBN 0-7701-0901-2). PaperJacks US.
Shaman. Joan Halifax. LC 87-71938. (Art & Imagination Ser.). (Illus.). 96p. 1988. pap. 11.95 (ISBN 0-500-81029-X). Thames Hudson.
Shaman & the Magician. Nevill Drury. 130p. 1987. pap. 11.95 (ISBN 1-85063-085-2, Pub. by Routledge UK). Routledge Chapman & Hall.
Shaman & the Magician: Journeys Between the Worlds. Nevill Drury. 156p. (Orig.). 1982. pap. 8.95 (ISBN 0-7100-0910-0). Routledge Chapman & Hall.
Shaman & the Medicine Wheel. Evelyn Eaton. LC 81-84490. (Illus.). 206p. (Orig.). 1982. 13.95 (ISBN 0-8356-0566-3). Theos Pub Hse.
Shaman from Elko. Sandner & Oakes. Ed. & frwd. by Gareth Hill. 272p. 1978. pap. 12.00 (ISBN 0-932630-00-6). C G Jung Frisco.
Shaman: His Symbols & His Healing Power. Spencer L. Rogers. (Illus.). 224p. 1982. 27.00 (ISBN 0-398-04594-1). C C Thomas.
Shaman, Housewives, & Other Rest Spirits: Women in Korean Ritual Life. Laurel Kendall. LC 84-24138. (Illus.). 248p. 1987. pap. text ed. 9.95x (ISBN 0-317-66953-2). UH Pr.
Shaman: Patterns of Religious Healing among the Ojibway Indians. John A. Grim. LC 83-47834. (Civilization of the American Indian Ser.: No. 165). (Illus.). 272p. 1988. pap. 8.95 (ISBN 0-8061-2106-8). U of Okla Pr.
Shaman: Patterns of Siberian & Ojibway Healing. John A. Grim. LC 83-47834. (Civilization of the American Indian Ser.: Vol. 165). (Illus.). 264p. 1983. pap. 19.95 (ISBN 0-8061-1809-1). U of Okla Pr.
Shaman Psalm. James Broughton. 1981. 3.00 (ISBN 0-9608372-0-5). Syzygy Pr.
Shaman Sorceress. Dong-Ni Kim. 275p. 1988. text ed. 19.95 (ISBN 0-7103-0280-0, Kegan Paul). Routledge Chapman & Hall.
Shaman Warrior. Gini G. PhD. Scott. LC 87-83637. 250p. (Orig.). (YA) (gr. 9-12). 1988. pap. text ed. 9.95 (ISBN 0-941404-67-6). Falcon Pr AZ.
Shamanic Healer. Ikuko Osumi & Malcolm Ritchie. 240p. 1988. pap. 8.95 (ISBN 0-89281-204-4, Healing Arts Pr). Inner Tradit.
Shamanic Voices: A Survey of Visionary Narratives. Joan Halifax. 1979. pap. 11.95 (ISBN 0-525-47525-7). Dutton.
Shamanism. Compiled by Shirley Nicholson. LC 86-40405. 402p. (Orig.). 1987. pap. 7.50 (ISBN 0-8356-0617-1). Theos Pub Hse.
Shamanism: Archaic Techniques of Ectasy. Mircea Eliade. Tr. by Willard R. Trask. (Bollingen Ser.: Vol. 76). 1964. pap. 14.50x (ISBN 0-691-01779-4). Princeton U Pr.
Shamanism, Colonialism, & the Wild Man: A Study in Terror & Healing. Michael Taussig. LC 86-11410. (Illus.). xx, 518p. 1987. lib. bdg. 29.95 (ISBN 0-226-79012-6). U of Chicago Pr.
Shamanism for the New Age: A Guide to Radionics & Radiesthesia. Jane E. Hartman. LC 86-83375. (Illus.). 157p. (Orig.). 1987. pap. 12.95 (ISBN 0-9618045-0-5). Aquarian Sys.
Shamanism in Siberia. V. Dioszegi & M. Hoppal. 532p. 1978. 150.00x (ISBN 0-569-08451-2, Pub. by Collets (UK)). State Mutual Bk.
Shamanism in Western North America. Willard Z. Park. LC 74-12553. 166p. 1975. Repr. of 1938 ed. lib. bdg. 22.50x (ISBN 0-8154-0497-2). Cooper Sq.
Shamanism: The Foundations of Magic. Date not set. price not set (ISBN 0-85030-453-9, Pub. by Thorsons UK). Weiser.
Shamanism: The Spirit World of Korea. C. S. Yu & R. Guisso. LC 87-71271. (Studies in Korean Religions & Culture). 192p. 1988. 30.00 (ISBN 0-89581-875-2); pap. text ed. 15.00 (ISBN 0-89581-886-8). Asian Human Pr.
Shamanist Folk Paintings: Korea's Eternal Spirits. Alan C. Covell. LC 83-82586. (Illus.). 120p. 1984. 19.50x (ISBN 0-930878-39-6). Hollym Intl.
Shamanistic Healing Within the Medicine Wheel. Marie L. Lorler. 304p. 1988. pap. 15.95. Bro Life Inc.
Shaman's Doorway: Opening Imagination to Power & Myth. Stephen Larsen. (Illus.). 260p. (Orig.). 1988. pap. 10.95 (ISBN 0-88268-072-2). Station Hill Pr.
Shamans Healing Way. Spencer Rogers. 1976. pap. 4.95 (ISBN 0-916552-06-3). Acoma Bks.
Shamans, Lamas & Evangelicals: The English Missionaries in Siberia. C. R. Bawden. (Illus.). 400p. 1985. 50.00x (ISBN 0-7102-0064-1). Routledge Chapman & Hall.
Shamans, Mystics & Doctors: A Psychological Inquiry into India & its Healing Traditions. Sudhir Kakar. LC 82-47806. 312p. 1982. 14.50 (ISBN 0-394-52240-0). Knopf.
Shamans, Mystics, & Doctors: A Psychological Inquiry into India & Its Healing Traditions. Sudhir Kakar. LC 83-70654. 324p. 1983. pap. 12.95x (ISBN 0-8070-2903-3, BPA 22). Beacon Pr.
Shaman's Path: Healing, Personal Growth, & Empowerment. Compiled by Gary Doore. LC 87-32233. 236p. (Orig.). 1988. pap. 10.95 (ISBN 0-87773-432-1). Shambhala Pubns.
Shamans, Prophets, & Sages: An Introduction to World Religions. Denise L. Carmody & John T. Carmody. 320p. 1985. pap. text ed. write for info. (ISBN 0-534-04263-5). Wadsworth Pub.
Shaman's Touch: Otomi Indian Symbolic Healing. James Dow. (Illus.). 180p. (Orig.). 1986. 13.95 (ISBN 0-87480-257-1). U of Utah Pr.
Shambaa Kingdom: A History. Steven Feierman. LC 72-7985. 250p. 1974. 32.50x (ISBN 0-299-06360-7). U of Wis Pr.
Shambala Warriors: Non-Violent Fighters for Peace. Teddy Milne. LC 86-64054. (Illus.). 150p. (Orig.). (gr. 4 up). 1987. pap. 7.95 (ISBN 0-938875-07-8). Pittenbruach Pr.
Shambhala. Nicholas Roerich. softcover 12.00 (ISBN 0-686-79666-7); 16.00. Agni Yoga Soc.
Shambhala: The Sacred Path of the Warrior. Chogyam Trungpa. LC 83-20401. (Dragon Editions Ser.). 201p. 1988. pap. 9.95 (ISBN 0-87773-264-7). Shambhala Pubns.
Shambhala: The Sacred Path of the Warriors. Chogyam Trungpa. 176p. 1986. pap. 3.95 (ISBN 0-553-26172-X). Bantam.
Shame. Salman Rushdie. LC 83-48103. 318p. 1983. 13.45 (ISBN 0-394-53408-5). Knopf.
Shame. Salman Rushdie. LC 84-40223. 336p. 1984. pap. 9.95 (ISBN 0-394-72665-0, Vin). Random.
Shame. 64p. 1982. 3.50 (ISBN 0-89486-131-X). Hazelden.
Shame & Guilt: Characteristics of the Dependency Cycle. Ernest Kurtz. 68p. 4.95 (ISBN 0-89486-132-8, 1940A). Hazelden.
Shame & Guilt in Neurosis. Helen B. Lewis. LC 75-128622. 519p. 1971. text ed. 45.00x (ISBN 0-8236-6075-3); pap. text ed. 17.95 (ISBN 0-8236-8307-9, 026075). Intl Univs Pr.
Shame & the Sacrifice: The Life & Martyrdom of Dietrich Bonhoeffer. Edwin Robertson. 288p. 1988. text ed. 16.95 (ISBN 0-02-603650-9). Macmillan.
Shame Experience. Susan Miller. (Psychoanalytic Monographs: Vol. 1). 160p. 1984. text ed. 29.95 cloth (ISBN 0-88163-017-9); pap. 29.95 (ISBN 0-88163-027-6). Analytic Pr.
Shame Faced: The Road to Recovery. 28p. (Orig.). 1986. pap. 1.75 (ISBN 0-89486-358-4). Hazelden.
Shame of a Nation. Philip Stern & George De Vincent. (Illus.). 1965. 14.95 (ISBN 0-8392-1162-7). Astor-Honor.
Shame of Her Youth. Kathleen Hand-Wheeler. (Destiny Ser.). 96p. 1987. pap. 6.95 (ISBN 0-8163-0707-5). Pacific Pr Pub Assn.
Shame of the Cities. Lincoln Steffens. (American Century Ser.). 214p. 1957. pap. 6.95 (ISBN 0-8090-0008-3). Hill & Wang.
Shame of the Cities. Lincoln Steffens. 14.25 (ISBN 0-8446-3001-2). Peter Smith.
Shame of the Cities. Lincoln Steffens. 16.95 (ISBN 0-89190-719-X, Pub. by Am Repr). Amereon Ltd.
Shame of the States. Albert Deutsch. LC 73-2394. (Mental Illness & Social Policy; the American Experience Ser.). Repr. of 1948 ed. 17.00 (ISBN 0-405-05202-2). Ayer Co Pubs.
Shame the Devil. Alan J. Leavitt. LC 86-82113. 222p. 1987. 17.95 (ISBN 1-55611-006-5). D I Fine.
Shame the Devil. Alan J. Leavitt. 288p. 1988. pap. 3.50 (ISBN 1-55802-179-5). Lynx Bks.
Shame the Devil. Alison McMaster. 1982. 15.00x (ISBN 0-903653-60-5, Pub. by New Playwrights Network). State Mutual Bk.
Shame the Devil. Liam O'Flaherty. 288p. 1981. 18.95 (ISBN 0-905473-64-7, Pub. by Wolfhound Pr Ireland). Irish Bks Media.
Shame: The Power of Caring. 2nd ed. Gershen Kaufman. LC 84-277120. 200p. 1985. 18.25 (ISBN 0-87047-007-8); pap. text ed. 9.95 (ISBN 0-87047-006-X). Schenkman Bks Inc.
Shamela see Joseph Andrews.
Shameless. Diana Sydney. (Orig.). 1988. pap. 3.95 (ISBN 0-553-26994-1). Bantam.
Shameless Desire. Thea Devine. (Heartfire Romance Ser.). 1987. pap. 3.75 (ISBN 0-8217-2105-4). Zebra.
Shamor V'Zachor et Yom Hashabbat L'Kadsho see Mitzvah of the Month.
Shamp of the City-Solo. rev. ed. Jaimy Gordon. LC 79-24979. 131p. 1980. 12.50 (ISBN 0-914232-38-X); pap. 3.95 (ISBN 0-914232-37-1). McPherson & Co.
Shampoo King: F. W. Fitch & His Company. Denny Rehder. (Illus.). 160p. 1982. pap. 12.95 (ISBN 0-942240-05-7). W & M Pr.
Shampooing & Hair Care. Linda Hunter. (Series 941). (Orig.). 1978. pap. 7.00 wkbk. (ISBN 0-8064-0425-6); audio-visual pkg. 279.00 (ISBN 0-8064-0426-4). Bergwall.
Shamrock & the Swastika: German Espionage in Ireland in World War II. Carolle J. Carter. LC 76-14103. (Illus.). 1977. 14.95 (ISBN 0-87015-221-1). Pacific Bks.
Shamrock in the Sun. Patricia Bird. (YA) (gr. 7 up). 1980. 9.95 (ISBN 0-686-73921-3, Avalon). Bouregy.
Shamrock, Rose & Thistle: Folk Singing in North Derry. Hugh Shields. (Illus.). 208p. (Orig.). 1981. pap. 7.50 (ISBN 0-85640-166-8, Pub. by Blackstaff Pr). Longwood Pub Group.
Shamrock Specialties: Trinity High School Family Cookbook. Trinity High School Cookbook Committee. 256p. 1988. pap. 10.00. Trinity HS Cookbook.
Shamrock Trinity: Burke, the Kingpin. Fayrene Preston. (Loveswept Ser.: No. 165). 192p. (Orig.). 1986. pap. 2.50 (ISBN 0-553-21788-7). Bantam.
Shamrock Trinity: Rafe, the Maverick. Kay Hooper. (Loveswept Ser.: No. 163). 192p. (Orig.). 1986. pap. 2.50 (ISBN 0-553-21786-0). Bantam.
Shamrock Trinity: York, the Renegade. Iris Johansen. (Loveswept Ser.: No. 164). 192p. 1986. pap. 2.50 (ISBN 0-553-21787-9). Bantam.
Shamrocks & Sea Silver & Other Illuminations. Leonard Wibberley. Ed. by Christopher Wibberley. LC 84-345. (I. O. Evans Studies in the Philosophy & Criticism of Literature: No. 8). 144p. (Orig.). Date not set. lib. bdg. 19.95x (ISBN 0-89370-302-8); pap. 9.95x (ISBN 0-89370-402-4); limited ed. 29.95x (ISBN 0-89370-009-6). Borgo Pr.
Shamrocks & Shepherds: The Irish of Morrow County. 2nd ed. John F. Kilkenny. (Illus.). 164p. 1981. pap. 3.95 (ISBN 0-87595-099-X). Oregon Hist.
Shamrocks, Harps, & Shillelaghs: The Story of the St. Patrick's Day Symbols. Edna Barth. LC 77-369. (Illus.). 96p. (gr. 3-6). 1982. pap. 4.95 (ISBN 0-89919-038-3, Clarion). HM.
Shamrocks, Harps, & Shillelaghs: The Story of the St. Patrick's Day Symbols. Edna Barth. LC 77-369. (Illus.). 96p. (gr. 3-6). 1977. 9.95 (ISBN 0-395-28845-2, Clarion). HM.
Shams or Uncle Ben's Experience with Hypocrites. John S. Draper. LC 71-166712. (Illus.). 1971. Repr. of 1898 ed. 29.00x (ISBN 0-403-01430-1). Scholarly.
Shan. Eric Van Lustbader. LC 86-10027. 608p. 1987. 18.95 (ISBN 0-394-55640-2). Random.
Shan. Eric Van Lustbader. 544p. 1987. pap. 4.95 (ISBN 0-449-20598-3, Crest). Fawcett.
Shan & English Dictionary. J. N. Cushing. 708p. Repr. of 1914 ed. text ed. 99.36x (ISBN 0-576-03338-3, Pub. by Gregg Intl Pubs England). Gregg Intl.
Shan Chrestomathy: An Introduction to Tai Mau Language & Literature. Linda W. Young. (Monograph Ser.: No. 28). (Illus.). 324p. 1985. lib. bdg. 30.00 (ISBN 0-8191-4808-3, Co-Pub by Center for South & Southeast Asia Studies); pap. text ed. 15.50 (ISBN 0-8191-4809-1). U Pr of Amer.
Shan of Burma: Memoirs of a Shan Exile. Chao Tzang Yawnghwe. 276p. 1988. text ed. 15.00 (ISBN 9971-988-62-3, Pub. by Inst of Southeast Asian Stud). Gower Pub Co.
Shan Phonological Drills. Eileen M. Scott & Sao T. Moeng. 221p. 1987. text ed. 20.00 (ISBN 0-931745-40-3). Dunwoody Pr.
Shan States & the British Annexation. Sao S. Mangrai. 204p. 1965. pap. 4.00 (ISBN 0-87727-057-0, DP 57). Cornell SE Asia.
Shandygraff. Christopher Morley. LC 76-145192. 1971. Repr. of 1920 ed. 25.00 (ISBN 0-403-01116-7). Scholarly.
Shane. Jack Schaefer. (Literature Ser). (gr. 9-12). 1949. pap. text ed. 7.08 (ISBN 0-87720-757-7). AMSCO Sch.
Shane. Jack Schaefer. 128p. 1980. pap. 2.95 (ISBN 0-553-26262-9). Bantam.
Shane. Jack Schaefer. (Illus.). (gr. 7 up). 1954. 12.95 (ISBN 0-395-07090-2). HM.
Shane Notes. Gary Carey & James L. Roberts. (Orig.). 1987. pap. 3.25 (ISBN 0-8220-1190-5). Cliffs.
Shane: The Critical Edition. Jack Schaefer. Ed. by James C. Work. LC 83-25948. xviii, 434p. 1984. pap. 10.95 (ISBN 0-8032-9142-6, Bison). U of Nebr Pr.
Shang Civilization. Kwang-Chih Chang. LC 79-19107. (Illus.). 1980. 47.50x (ISBN 0-300-02428-2); pap. 13.95x (ISBN 0-300-02885-7, Y-435). Yale U Pr.
Shang Civilization. Price N. Thompson. 68p. 1986. pap. 35.00x (ISBN 0-317-69056-6, Pub. by Han-Shan Tang Ltd). State Mutual Bk.
Shang Ritual Bronzes in the Arthur M. Sackler Collections. Robert W. Bagley. LC 86-83376. (Ancient Chinese Bronzes in the Arthur M. Sackler Collections Ser.: Vol. 1). (Illus.). 350p. 1982. text ed. 125.00x (ISBN 0-674-80525-9). Harvard U Pr.
Shang Yang's Reforms & State Control in China. Ed. by Li Yu-Ning. LC 76-4301. (China Book Project). 392p. 1977. 40.00 (ISBN 0-87332-080-8). M E Sharpe.
Shang Zhou Jinwen Luyi. Yu Xingwu. 22p. 1957. 455.00x (ISBN 0-317-69062-0, Pub. by Han-Shan Tang Ltd). State Mutual Bk.
Shanghai. China Guide Series Editors. (Illus.). 144p. 1987. pap. 8.95 (ISBN 0-8442-9816-6, Passport Bks). Natl Textbk.
Shanghai. Christopher New. 1985. 19.95 (ISBN 0-671-42197-2). Summit Bks.
Shanghai. Christopher New. 1986. pap. 4.50 (ISBN 0-553-25781-1). Bantam.
Shanghai & Manchuria Nineteen Thirty-Two: Recollections of a War Correspondent. A. T. Steele. 45p. 1977. 3.00 (ISBN 0-939252-06-6). ASU Ctr Asian.
Shanghai Bildzeitung, 1884-1898. Fritz Van Briessen. (Illus.). 157p. 1977. 98.00x (ISBN 0-317-69192-9, Pub. by Han-Shan Tang Ltd). State Mutual Bk.

Shape Theory & Geometric Topology: Proceedings. Ed. by S. Mardesic & J. Segal. (Lecture Notes in Mathematics Ser.: Vol. 870). 265p. 1981. pap. 19.00 (ISBN 0-387-10846-7). Springer-Verlag.

Shape up for Soccer. Pete Broccoletti & Rich Hunter. (Illus.). 232p. 1981. 14.95 (ISBN 0-89651-750-0); wirebd. 9.95 (ISBN 0-89651-751-9). B L Pub.

Shape up from the Inside Out. John R. Throop. (Living Bks.). 128p. (Orig.). 1986. pap. 2.95 (ISBN 0-8423-5899-4). Tyndale.

Shape up Through Posture, Diet, Exercise & Relaxation. Karren Mazzeo. (Illus.). 208p. 1984. pap. 10.95 (ISBN 0-89582-100-1). Morton Pub.

Shape up with Baby: Exercise Games for the New Parent & Child. Ann Fienup-Riordan. LC 80-82128. (Illus.). 104p. (Orig.). 1980. pap. 4.50 (ISBN 0-937604-04-6). Pennypress.

Shape-Up with Splash: Exercises to Be Done in the Water. Judy D. Conley. (Illus.). 112p. 1988. 10.95 (ISBN 0-9619828-1-0). Judys Splash Aerobics.

Shape Your Body, Shape Your Life: The Weight Training Ways to Total Fitness. Tony Lycholat. (Illus.). 128p. (Orig.). 1987. pap. 6.99 (ISBN 0-85059-869-9, Pub. by PSL P Stephens). Sterling.

Shape Your Body, Shape Your Life: The Weight Training Way to Total Fitness. Tony Lycholat. (Illus.). 128p. 1988. Repr. lib. bdg. 19.95x (ISBN 0-8095-7062-9). Borgo Pr.

Shape Your Swing the Modern Way. rev. ed. Byron Nelson & Larry Dennis. (Classics of Golf Ser.). (Illus.). 126p. 1985. 17.95x (ISBN 0-940889-06-4). Classics Golf.

Shape Your Waist & Hips in Thirty Days: Spot Reducing the Aerobics Way. Deborah Frichman-McKenzie. (Illus.). 64p. 1983. 2.95 (ISBN 0-399-50781-7, Perigee). Putnam Pub Group.

Shapechangers! Jennifer Roberson. (Orig.). 1986. pap. 2.95 (ISBN 0-88677-140-4). DAW Bks.

Shaped & Cut-Out Cakes: The Easy Professional Way. John N. McNamara. (Illus.). 40p. (Orig.). 1984. pap. 9.00 (ISBN 0-932770-04-5). McNamara Pubns.

Shaped by the Word. M. Robert Mulholland. (Orig.). 1985. pap. 7.95 (ISBN 0-8358-0519-0). Upper Room.

Shaped Reflector Antenna Design. Brian S. Westcott. 186p. 1983. 67.95 (ISBN 0-471-90152-0). Wiley.

Shapedown: Weight Management Program for Adolescents. Laurel Mellin. LC 86-71125. (Illus.). 1987. Parent's Guide 2nd ed. 124pp. 16.95 (ISBN 0-935902-09-0); Instr's. Guide 4th ed. 288pp. 29.95 (ISBN 0-935902-08-2); Teen wkbk. 4th ed. 215pp. 16.95 (ISBN 0-935902-07-4). Balboa Pub.

Shapeless God: Essays on Modern Fiction. Ed. by Harry J. Mooney & Thomas F. Staley. LC 68-21630. pap. 58.00 (2026314). Bks Demand UMI.

Shaper Handbook. 2nd ed. Eric Stephenson. (Illus.). 192p. (Orig.). 1987. pap. 15.95 (ISBN 0-941936-09-0). Linden Pub Fresno.

Shaper Poems. James Hoggard. (Illus.). 30p. (Orig.). pap. 6.00 (ISBN 0-912435-00-3). Cedarshouse.

Shapers of American Fiction, Seventeen Ninety Eight to Nineteen Forty Seven. George Snell. LC 61-13269. Repr. of 1947 ed. 23.50x (ISBN 0-8154-0209-0). Cooper Sq.

Shapers of American Health Care Policy: An Oral History. Lewis E. Weeks & Howard J. Berman. LC 85-17687. 376p. 1985. text ed. 29.00x (ISBN 0-910701-09-1, 0660). Health Admin Pr.

Shapers of Baptist Thought. James E. Tull. LC 84-6545. (Reprints of Scholarly Excellence Ser.: No. 8). 255p. 1984. Repr. of 1972 ed. 14.50 (ISBN 0-86554-125-6, MUP-H116). Mercer Univ Pr.

Shapers of Religious Traditions in Germany, Switzerland, & Poland, Fifteen Sixty to Sixteen Hundred. Ed. by Jill Raitt. LC 80-23287. 256p. 1981. text ed. 30.00t (ISBN 0-300-02457-6). Yale U Pr.

Shapes. Richard L. Allington. LC 79-19852. (Beginning to Learn About Ser.). (Illus.). 32p. (gr. k-2). 1979. PLB 15.33 (ISBN 0-8172-1277-9). Raintree Pubs.

Shapes. Richard L. Allington. LC 79-19852. (E. G. Beginning to Learn about... Ser.). (Illus.). 32p. (gr. k-2). 1985. pap. 9.27 (ISBN 0-8172-2487-4). Raintree Pubs.

Shapes. Christopher Carrie. (Crayola Kinder Art Bks.). (Illus.). 12p. (Orig.). (gr. 3-6). 1987. pap. 4.70 (ISBN 0-86696-202-6). Binney & Smith.

Shapes. Richard Delap & Walt Lee. 336p. pap. 3.95 (ISBN 0-441-76103-8, Pub. by Charter). Ace Bks.

Shapes. Mike Gordon. (Lift & Learn Ser.). (Illus.). 12p. (ps-1). 2.95 (ISBN 0-382-09190-6). Silver.

Shapes. Barbara Gregorich. Ed. by Joan Hoffman. (Get Ready! Bks.). (Illus.). 32p. (ps). 1983. wkbk. 1.95 (ISBN 0-938256-63-7). Sch Zone Pub Co.

Shapes. Sara Lynn & Rosalinda Kightley. (Little Bown Primers Ser.). (Illus.). 32p. (ps-1). 1986. 6.95 (ISBN 0-316-54005-6). Little.

Shapes. Jan Pienkowski. (Concept Bks.). (Illus.). 32p. (ps-k). 1981. 3.95 (ISBN 0-671-44455-7, Little Simon). S&S.

Shapes. John J. Reiss. LC 86-22164. (Illus.). 32p. (ps-2). 1987. pap. 3.95 (ISBN 0-689-71121-2, Aladdin Bks). Macmillan.

Shapes. Illus. by John J. Reiss. LC 73-76545. (Illus.). 32p. (ps-2). 1974. 12.95 (ISBN 0-02-776190-8). Bradbury Pr.

Shapes. Illus. by Tony Tallarico. (Tote Bks.). (Illus.). 12p. (ps-1). 1985. bds. 3.95 (ISBN 0-89828-315-9). Tuffy Bks.

Shapes. Illus. by Tony Tallarico. (Preschool See & Say Bks.). (Illus.). 12p. (ps). Date not set. bds. 2.95 (ISBN 0-89828-262-4). Tuffy Bks.

Shapes. C. Watson. (Simple Facts Ser.). (Illus.). 24p. (gr. k-2). 1983. 3.95 (ISBN 0-86020-760-9). EDC.

Shapes. Sharon Wheeler. (Preschool Express Ser.). (Illus.). (ps). 1984. wkbk 1.95 (ISBN 0-916119-00-9). Creat Teach Pr.

Shapes see Let's Learn Set.

Shapes & Colors. (Golden Play Book 'n' Tapes). (Illus.). (ps-3). pap. write for info. incl. cassette (ISBN 0-307-13956-5, Golden Bks). Western Pub.

Shapes & Colors. (Play & Learn Sticker Bks.). 24p. (ps-k). 1988. pap. 2.95 (ISBN 0-8249-8282-7). Ideals.

Shapes & Colors. Annette Taulbee. (Be Smart Bks.). (Illus.). 24p. (ps-k). 1986. 2.50 (ISBN 0-86734-068-1, FS-3061). Schaffer Pubns.

Shapes & Colors, No. 1. (Instructive Play Books for Toddlers). 8p. 1980. pap. 1.95 (ISBN 0-8431-0165-2). Price Stern.

Shapes & Colors, No. 2. (Instructive Play Bks. for Toddlers). 8p. 1980. 1.95 (ISBN 0-8431-0166-0). Price Stern.

Shapes & Colors, No. 3. (Instructive Play Bks. for Toddlers). 8p. 1980. 1.95 (ISBN 0-8431-0167-9). Price Stern.

Shapes & Colors, No. 4. (Instructive Play Bks. for Toddlers). 8p. 1980. 1.95 (ISBN 0-8431-0168-7). Price Stern.

Shapes & Patterns. National Education Association Staff. 1983. pap. 1.95 (ISBN 0-380-82701-8, 82701). Avon.

Shapes & Sizes. (Mr. Men & Little Miss Bks.). (Illus.). 48p. (ps-1). 1982. pap. 1.50 (ISBN 0-8431-1112-7). Price Stern.

Shapes & Sizes. (Questron Electronic Workbook Library Ser.). (Illus.). 32p. (ps). 1985. 3.95 (ISBN 0-394-87704-7). Random.

Shapes & Sounds for the Atari. Herb Moore. (Professional Software Ser.). 1984. incl. disks 45.00 (ISBN 0-471-88547-9, Pub. by Wiley Professional Software). Wiley.

Shapes & Stories: A Book about Pictures. Geoffrey Grigson. LC 65-25262. (Illus.). 72p. (gr. 5 up). 15.95 (ISBN 0-8149-0311-8). Vanguard.

Shapes & Things. Illus. by Tana Hoban. LC 70-102965. (Illus.). 32p. (ps-2). 1970. 12.95 (ISBN 0-02-744060-5). Macmillan.

Shapes & Things. Patricia Mahany. (My Shape Bks.). (Illus.). 12p. (ps-1). 1984. 2.95 (ISBN 0-87239-786-6, 2726). Standard Pub.

Shapes, Animals & Special Creatures. Geoffrey Grigson & Jane Grigson. LC 72-77789. (Illus.). 64p. (gr. 5 up). Date not set. 12.95 (ISBN 0-8149-0717-2). Vanguard.

Shapes Are Everywhere. Another Adventure Staff. (Teddy Ruxpin Answer Box Ser.). (Illus.). 22p. (ps). 1988. write for info. incl. pre-programmed audiotape (ISBN 0-934323-73-9). Alchemy Comms.

Shapes: Circle, Triangle, Square, Rectangle, Diamond. Patti Carson & JAnet Dellosa. (Let's Learn Ser.). (Illus.). 32p. (ps-1). 1983. pap. 1.98 (ISBN 0-88724-006-2, CD-7007). Carson-Dellos.

Shapes: How Do You Say It? Meredith Dunham. LC 86-27740. (Illus.). 24p. (ps up). 1987. 9.25 (ISBN 0-688-06952-5); PLB 9.88 (ISBN 0-688-06953-3). Lothrop.

Shapes in God's World. Beverly Beckman. LC 56-1462. (In God's World Ser.). (ps-k). 1984. 5.95 (ISBN 0-570-04094-9). Concordia.

Shapes of Change. Marcia B. Siegel. 400p. 1984. pap. 3.95 (ISBN 0-380-53892-X, 53892-X, Discus). Avon.

Shapes of Change: Images of American Dance. Marcia B. Siegel. LC 78-23669. 1985. 35.00x (ISBN 0-520-04203-4); pap. 10.95x (ISBN 0-520-04212-3). U of Cal Pr.

Shapes of Culture. Thomas McFarland. LC 86-14670. 201p. 1987. text ed. 22.50x (ISBN 0-87745-162-1). U of Iowa Pr.

Shapes of Philosophical History. Frank E. Manuel. 1965. 13.50x (ISBN 0-8047-0248-9). Stanford U Pr.

Shapes of Power: The Development of Ezra Pound's Poetic Sequences. Bruce Fogelman. Ed. by A. Walton Litz. LC 88-9647. (Studies in Modern Literature: No. 95). 236p. 1988. 44.95 (ISBN 0-8357-1883-2). UMI Res Pr.

Shapes of Structure. Heather Martienssen. (Illus.). 1976. pap. 6.95x (ISBN 0-19-289075-1). Oxford U Pr.

Shapes of Their Thoughts: Reflections of Culture Contact in Northwest Coast Indian Art. Victoria Wyatt. LC 84-40281. (Illus.). 80p. (Orig.). 1984. pap. 9.95 (ISBN 0-8061-1908-X). U of Okla Pr.

Shapes of Time. Peter Munz. LC 77-2459. 400p. 1977. lib. bdg. 20.00x (ISBN 0-8195-5017-5). Wesleyan U Pr.

Shapes, Shapes, Shapes. Tana Hoban. LC 85-17569. (Illus.). 32p. (ps-3). 1986. 11.75 (ISBN 0-688-05832-9); PLB 11.88 (ISBN 0-688-05833-7). Greenwillow.

Shapes, Space, & Symmetry. Alan Holden. LC 71-158459. (Illus.). 1971. pap. 17.50x (ISBN 0-231-08323-8). Columbia U Pr.

Shapes to Show. Karen Gundersheimer. LC 85-45409. (Illus.). 32p. (ps-1). 1986. 3.95 (ISBN 0-694-00067-1); PLB 10.89 (ISBN 0-06-022197-6). HarpJ.

Shaping a Curriculum: For 4's & 5's. 1980. 16.00 (ISBN 0-939418-08-8). Ferguson-Florissant.

Shaping a Healthy Religion. Thomas Aldworth. 132p. 1985. pap. 9.95 (ISBN 0-88347-200-7). Thomas More.

Shaping a Maritime Empire: The Commercial & Diplomatic Role of the American Navy, 1829-1861. John H. Schroeder. LC 85-942. (Contributions in Military Studies: No. 48). (Illus.). ix, 229p. 1985. lib. bdg. 36.95 (ISBN 0-313-24883-4, SSH/). Greenwood.

Shaping a National Housing Policy: Recommendations for State & Federal Action. Rich Jones & Sandra J. Singer. 1988. pap. 10.00 (ISBN 1-55516-947-3). Natl Conf State Legis.

Shaping a New Health Care System: The Explosion of Chronic Illness As a Catalyst for Change. Anselm Strauss & Juliet M. Corbin. LC 88-42801. 1988. 19.95x (ISBN 1-55542-116-4). Jossey-Bass.

Shaping an American Institution: Robert E. Wood & Sears, Roebuck. James C. Worthy. LC 83-18157. (Illus.). 326p. 1984. 18.95 (ISBN 0-252-01051-5). U of Ill Pr.

Shaping an American Institution: Robert E. Wood & Sears, Roebuck. Updated ed. James C. Worthy. 320p. Date not set. pap. 8.95 (ISBN 0-452-00817-4, Plume). NAL.

Shaping an Urban World: Planning in the Twentieth Century. Ed. by Gordon E. Cherry. LC 80-17276. 1980. 30.00 (ISBN 0-312-71618-4). St Martin.

Shaping College Writing: Paragraph & Essay. 4th ed. Joseph D. Gallo & Henry W. Rink. 166p. 1985. pap. text ed. 10.00 net (ISBN 0-15-580863-X, HC); answer key avail. (ISBN 0-15-580864-8). HarBraceJ.

Shaping Education Policy in the States. Ed. by Susan Fuhrman & Alan Rosenthal. 140p. 1981. lib. bdg. 15.00 (ISBN 0-318-03011-X); pap. 9.50 (ISBN 0-318-03625-8). Inst Educ Lead.

Shaping Faith Through Involvement. Sonjia L. Hunt. 72p. (Orig.). 1981. pap. text ed. 2.50 (ISBN 0-87148-796-9). Pathway Pr.

Shaping Forces in Music. Ernst Toch. 1948. 11.95 (ISBN 0-910468-07-9). Criterion Mus.

Shaping Forces in Music: An Inquiry into the Nature of Harmony, Melody, Counterpoint, Form. Ernst Toch. 1977. pap. text ed. 6.95 (ISBN 0-486-23346-4). Dover.

Shaping History Through Prayer & Fasting. Derek Prince. 1973. 9.95 (ISBN 0-934920-23-0, B-24); pap. 5.95 (ISBN 0-686-12766-8, B-25). Derek Prince.

Shaping Identity in Canadian Society. J. Haas et al. 1978. pap. 14.00 (ISBN 0-13-808204-9). P-H.

Shaping Library Collections for the 1980s. Ed. by Peter Spyers-Duran & Thomas Mann, Jr. 222p. 1980. lib. bdg. 37.00x (ISBN 0-912700-58-0). Oryx Pr.

Shaping LOGO on Your Apple. Judith Wild & Mary Zyskowski. (Illus.). 160p. (gr. 3-8). 1984. pap. 7.95 (ISBN 0-88056-315-X). Weber Systems.

Shaping LOGO on Your Apple. Judith Wild & Mary Zyskowski. (Illus.). 160p. pap. 7.95 (ISBN 0-517-56395-9). Crown.

Shaping: New Poems in Traditional Prosodies. Philip Jason. LC 77-13081. 1978. text ed. 10.00x (ISBN 0-931848-10-5); pap. text ed. 5.95 (ISBN 0-931848-11-3). Dryad Pr.

Shaping New Vision: Gender & Values in American Culture. Ed. by Clarissa W. Atkinson et al. LC 87-13854. (Studies in Religion: No. 5). 238p. 1987. 34.95 (ISBN 0-8357-1803-4). UMI Res Pr.

Shaping of a Behaviorist. B. F. Skinner. 384p. 1985. pap. 11.95 (ISBN 0-8147-7844-5). NYU PR.

Shaping of a Behaviorist: Part Two of an Autobiography. B. F. Skinner. LC 78-20620. (Illus.). 1979. 12.95 (ISBN 0-394-50581-6). Knopf.

Shaping of a Family. Egbert S. Oliver. (Illus.). 1979. pap. 8.95 (ISBN 0-913244-19-8). Hapi Pr.

Shaping of a Jewish Identity in Nineteenth Century France. Jay R. Berkovitz. 360p. 1989. 34.95x (ISBN 0-8143-2011-2). Wayne St U Pr.

Shaping of a National Identity: Subcarpathian Rus', 1848-1948. Paul R. Magocsi. (Ukrainian Ser.). 1978. 32.50x (ISBN 0-674-80579-8). Harvard U Pr.

Shaping of Abbasid Rule. Jacob Lassner. LC 79-84000. (Princeton Studies in the Near East). (Illus.). 1980. 41.00x (ISBN 0-691-05281-6). Princeton U Pr.

Shaping of America: A Geographical Perspective on 500 Years of History: Atlantic America, 1492-1800, Vol. 1. D. W. Meinig. LC 85-17962. (Illus.). 512p. 1986. 35.00 (ISBN 0-300-03548-9). Yale U Pr.

Shaping of America: A People's History of the Young Republic. Page Smith. LC 79-13592. 870p. 1980. text ed. 20.00 (ISBN 0-07-059017-6). McGraw.

Shaping of America, Vol. 1: A Geographical Perspective on 500 Years of History. D. W. Meinig. LC 85-17962. 512p. 1988. Repr. of 1986 ed. 19.95 (ISBN 0-300-03882-8). Yale U Pr.

Shaping of Black America. Lerone Bennett, Jr. LC 74-20659. 1975. 15.95 (ISBN 0-87485-071-1). Johnson Chi.

Shaping of British Policy During the Nationalist Revolution in China. Richard Stremski. LC 80-110682. Orig. Title: Soochow University Political Science Series. 179p. 1980. text ed. 20.00x (ISBN 0-931712-02-5). Alpine Guild.

Shaping of Chinese Foreign Policy. Greg O'Leary. LC 80-10231. 320p. 1980. 27.50 (ISBN 0-312-71620-6). St Martin.

Shaping of Fiction. Ed. by Robert M. Bender. (Orig.). 1970. pap. text ed. 0.95 (ISBN 0-671-47802-8). WSP.

Shaping of Foreign Policy. Ed. by Harold K. Jacobson. (Controversy Ser). 214p. 1969. 12.95x (ISBN 0-202-24071-1); pap. 6.95x (ISBN 0-202-24072-X). Lieber-Atherton.

Shaping of France. Isaac Asimov. LC 72-75604. (Illus.). 288p. (gr. 7 up). 1972. 5.95 (ISBN 0-395-13891-4). HM.

Shaping of History & Poetry in Late Medieval France. Cynthia J. Brown. LC 85-61597. 215p. 1985. 18.95 (ISBN 0-917786-10-6). Summa Pubns.

Shaping of Ireland. Ed. by William Nolan. (Thomas David Lecture Ser.). 208p. 1986. pap. 15.95 (ISBN 0-85342-765-8, Pub. by Mercier Pr Ireland). Irish Bks Media.

Shaping of Longfellow's John Endicott: A Textual History, Including Two Early Versions. Edward L. Tucker. LC 84-19652. 1985. 20.00x (ISBN 0-8139-1039-0). U Pr of Va.

Shaping of Middle-Earth. J. R. R. Tolkien. LC 86-10338. (History of Middle Earth Ser.). (Illus.). 380p. (YA) 1986. 16.95 (ISBN 0-395-42501-8). HM.

Shaping of Middle Earth: The Quenta, the Ambarkanta, & the Annals. J. R. R. Tolkien. 1986. 16.95 (ISBN 0-317-47339-5). HM.

Shaping of Modern America: Eighteen Seventy-Seven to Nineteen Sixteen. Vincent P. DeSantis. 1973. pap. text ed. 13.95x (ISBN 0-88273-110-6). Forum Pr IL.

Shaping of Modern India. Ed. by Daniel Thorner. 1981. 28.00x (ISBN 0-8364-0678-8, Pub. by Allied India). South Asia Bks.

Shaping of Modern Psychology: An Historical Introduction. L. S. Hearnshaw. 408p. 1987. text ed. 36.95 (ISBN 0-7102-0576-7, 05767, Pub. by Routledge UK). Routledge Chapman & Hall.

Shaping of Nineteenth Century Aberdeenshire. Sydney Wood. 332p. 1986. 85.00x (ISBN 0-907590-05-5, Pub. by S P A Bks Ltd). State Mutual Bk.

Shaping of North America: From Earliest Times to 1763. Isaac Asimov. LC 72-7931. (Illus.). 272p. (gr. 7-12). 1973. 5.95 (ISBN 0-395-15493-6). HM.

Shaping of Our World: A Human & Cultural Geography. William A. Jackson. LC 84-7518. 622p. 1985. write for info. (ISBN 0-471-88031-0). Wiley.

Shaping of Religion in America. Norman W. Harrington. (Illus.). 168p. 1980. 29.95 (ISBN 0-937692-01-8). Queen Anne Pr.

Shaping of Somali Society: Reconstructing the History of a Pastoral People, 1600 to 1900. Lee V. Cassanelli. LC 81-43520. (Illus.). 328p. 1982. 39.95 (ISBN 0-8122-7832-1). U of Pa Pr.

Shaping of South African Society, 1652-1840. Ed. by Richard Elphick & Hermann Giliomee. 518p. 1988. 40.00x (ISBN 0-8195-5209-7); pap. 15.95. Wesleyan U Pr.

Shaping of Southern Politics: Suffrage Restriction & the Establishment of the One-Party South, 1880-1910. J. Morgan Kousser. LC 73-86905. (Historical Publications, Miscellany Ser.: No. 102). (Illus.). 336p. 1974. 35.00x (ISBN 0-300-01696-4); pap. 11.95x (ISBN 0-300-01973-4). Yale U Pr.

Shaping of the American High School, Vol. 1, 1880-1920. Edward A. Krug. LC 64-12801. 504p. 1974. pap. text ed. 15.00x (ISBN 0-299-05165-X). U of Wis Pr.

Shaping of the American High School, Vol. 2: Nineteen Twenty to Nineteen Forty-One. Edward A. Krug. LC 64-12801. 392p. 1972. 25.00x (ISBN 0-299-05980-4). U of Wis Pr.

Shaping of the American Past. 2nd ed. Robert Kelley. Incl. Combined Edition. 1978; Vol. 1. To 1877. 1978; Vol. 2. 1865 to Pesent. 1978. (Illus.). P-H.

Shaping of the American Past, Vol. II. 4th ed. Robert Kelley. 560p. 1986. pap. text ed. write for info (ISBN 0-13-808247-2). P-H.

Shaping of the American Past, Vol. I. 4th ed. Robert Kelly. 448p. 1986. text ed. write for info (ISBN 0-13-808197-2). P-H.

Shaping of the American Tradition. Louis M. Hacker. LC 47-1257. 1247p. 1947. 75.00x (ISBN 0-231-01574-7). Columbia U Pr.

Shaping of "The Dynasts" A Study in Thomas Hardy. Walter F. Wright. LC 67-19159. (Illus.). xiv, 334p. 1968. 27.95x (ISBN 0-8032-0200-8). U of Nebr Pr.

Shaping of the Elizabethan Regime. Wallace MacCaffrey. 1971. 47.00x (ISBN 0-691-05168-2). Princeton U Pr.

Shaping of the Elizabethan Regime. Wallace MacCaffrey. LC 68-27409. Repr. of 1968 ed. 129.30 (ISBN 0-8357-9513-6, 2014636). Bks Demand UMI.

Shaping of the Foundations: Being at Home in the Transcendental Method. Philip McShane. 13.00 (ISBN 0-8191-0209-1). U Pr of Amer.

Shari'at & Ambiguity in South Asian Islam. Katherine P. Ewing. (Comparative Studies on Muslim Societies: No. 4). 1988. 37.50x (ISBN 0-520-05575-6). U of Cal Pr.

Sharifa. Cornelia Dalenburg & David De Groot. (Historical Series of the Reformed Church in America: Vol. 11). (Orig.). 1983. pap. 11.95 (ISBN 0-8028-1973-7). Eerdmans.

Sharing. Marian Bennett. (Wipe-Clean Bks.). (Illus.). 12p. (ps). 1985. pap. 1.39 (ISBN 0-87239-959-1, 3519). Standard Pub.

Sharing. Dan Carr. (God I Need to Talk to You About...Ser.). (Illus.). (gr. k-4). 1984. pap. 0.89 (ISBN 0-570-08728-7, 56-1472). Concordia.

Sharing. Taro Gomi. (Fun Time Ser.). (Illus.). 22p. (ps-1). 1981. 3.50 (ISBN 0-89346-198-9). Heian Intl.

Sharing. Debbie Pincus. (Illus.). 80p. (gr. 4-8). 1983. wkbk. 7.95 (ISBN 0-86653-117-3, GA 468). Good Apple.

Sharing. Janet Riehecky. LC 87-26811. (What Is It?--A Values Ser.). (Illus.). 32p. (gr. k-3). 1988. PLB 7.95 (ISBN 0-89565-416-4). Childs World.

Sharing. Sue Riley. LC 77-16293. (What Does It Mean? Ser.). (Illus.). (ps-2). 1978. PLB 6.75 (ISBN 0-89565-015-0). Childs World.

Sharing. Sue Riley. LC 77-16293. (What Does it Mean? Ser.). (Illus.). 32p. (ps-2). 1978. 10.33 (ISBN 0-516-06144-5). Childrens.

Sharing. (Tiny Tots World Ser.). 2.95 (ISBN 0-86112-041-8, Brimax Bks). Borden.

Sharing: A Book of Poetry. Carl H. F. Lichtenberg. 1987. 7.95 (ISBN 0-533-07007-4). Vantage.

Sharing a Heritage: American Indian Arts. Charlotte Heth. (Contemporary American Indian Issues ser.). 214p. 1984. pap. 15.00 (ISBN 0-935626-00-X). U Cal AISC.

Sharing: A Manual for Program Directors. Thomas Zanzig. (Sharing Program Ser.). 214p. 1985. pap. 54.00 (ISBN 0-88489-167-4). St Mary's.

Sharing a Vision. Phoebe Willetts. 116p. 1978. pap. 7.50 (ISBN 0-227-67842-7). Attic Pr.

Sharing an Apartment. Durlynn Anema. Ed. by Antonia Padial. (Janus On Your Own Ser.). (Illus.). 64p. (gr. 9 up). 1981. pap. text ed. 3.95 (ISBN 0-915510-60-X). Janus Bks.

Sharing Architecture. Robert L. Vickery. LC 83-13614. 1983. 13.95x (ISBN 0-8139-0973-2). U Pr of Va.

Sharing Authority Effectively: Participation, Interaction, & Discretion. Kenneth P. Mortimer & T. R. McConnell. LC 76-50721. (Higher Education Ser.). 1978. text ed. 27.95x (ISBN 0-87589-357-0). Jossey-Bass.

Sharing Birth: A Father's Guide to Giving Support During Labor. Carl Jones. LC 84-15990. (Illus.). 192p. (Orig.). 1985. pap. 7.95 (ISBN 0-688-04164-7, Quill). Morrow.

Sharing Bulletin Board Ideas. (Illus.). 50p. 1978. 4.00 (ISBN 0-318-15256-8). Natl Busn Ed Assoc.

Sharing Care: The Christian Ministry of Respite Care. Judith K. Murphy. (Illus.). 64p. (Orig.). 1986. pap. 3.95 (ISBN 0-8298-0575-3). Pilgrim NY.

Sharing Child Care in Early Parenthood. Malcolm Hill. 336p. 1987. lib. bdg. 67.00x (ISBN 0-7102-0497-3, Pub. by Routledge UK). Routledge Chapman & Hall.

Sharing Destiny: A Study of Global Integration. Trygve Mathisen. 175p. 1984. 26.00x (ISBN 82-00-06842-0). Oxford U Pr.

Sharing Faith. Beatrice P. Shields. 96p. 1988. 8.95 (ISBN 0-8062-3338-9). Carlton.

Sharing Faith at Home. Jan Hartley. (SPAN Ser.). (Illus.). 31p. (Orig.). 1983. pap. 3.95 (ISBN 0-85819-450-3, Pub. by JBCE). ANZ Religious Pubns.

Sharing from the Psalms. Nelle A. Vander Ark. 64p. 1984. pap. 2.95 (ISBN 0-8010-9295-7). Baker Bk.

Sharing God's Feelings. B. J. Whitley, Jr. LC 84-51661. 201p. (Orig.). 1985. pap. 9.95 (ISBN 0-9615536-0-X). Spirit Christ.

Sharing God's Love. John F. Marshall. LC 81-11794. 108p. 1981. pap. 5.95 (ISBN 0-8146-1068-4). Liturgical Pr.

Sharing God's Love in Marriage. Vern Trocinski. 48p. (Orig.). 1987. pap. 1.25 (ISBN 0-8146-1564-3). Liturgical Pr.

Sharing Ideas: A Rhetoric for Beginning Writers. Robert M. Perrin. 288p. 1985. pap. text ed. 14.95 (ISBN 0-03-062944-6, HoltC). HR&W.

Sharing in Development: A Programme of Employment, Equity & Growth for the Philippines. A WEP Study. 687p. 1974. 29.75 (ISBN 92-2-101111-9). Intl Labour Office.

Sharing in the Kitchen. S. Calwallader. 1979. pap. text ed. 5.95 (ISBN 0-07-009528-0). McGraw.

Sharing International Responsibilities among the Trilateral Countries. Nobuhiko Ushiba et al. 1983. write for info. Trilateral Comm.

Sharing Is Fun. Beverly Amstutz. (Illus.). 24p. (gr. k-7). 1979. pap. 2.50x (ISBN 0-937836-00-1). Precious Res.

Sharing It All: The Rewards & Struggles of Two-Career Families. Lucia A. Gilbert. (Illus.). 205p. 1988. 18.95 (ISBN 0-306-42961-6, Plenum Pr). Plenum Pub.

Sharing Jesus Effectively. Jerry Savelle. 125p. (Orig.). 1982. pap. 3.95 (ISBN 0-89274-251-8). Harrison Hse.

Sharing Literature with Children: A Thematic Anthology. Ed. by Francelia Butler. (English & Humanities Ser.). 1977. pap. text ed. 23.95 (ISBN 0-582-28114-8); instr's. manual avail. Longman.

Sharing Makes Me Happy. Dot Cachiaras. LC 82-80030. (Happy Day Bks.). (Illus.). 24p. (Orig.). (ps-3). 1982. pap. 1.59 (ISBN 0-87239-543-X, 3589). Standard Pub.

Sharing Music: An Introductory Guide to Music Education. J. G. Martin. (Academic Ser.). 260p. 1987. pap. 16.95x (ISBN 0-910075-06-9). Hardin Simmons.

Sharing My Notebook. Raymond J. Reynolds. 1980. 7.50 (ISBN 0-87881-085-4). Mojave Bks.

Sharing Nature with Children. Joseph B. Cornell. LC 78-74650. (Illus.). 143p. 1979. pap. 6.95 (ISBN 0-916124-14-2, Dawn Pubns). Crystal Clarity.

Sharing of My Love. new ed. Sandra J. Lofland. LC 76-27966. (Illus.). 88p. 1977. 2.95 (ISBN 0-910812-20-9); pap. 1.95 (ISBN 0-910812-23-3). Johnny Reads.

Sharing of Productivity Gains in Indian Industry. Nar Singh. 180p. 1984. text ed. 22.50x (ISBN 0-86590-292-5, Pub. by B R Pub Corp Indian). Apt Bks.

Sharing Ownership in the Workplace. Raymond Russell. LC 84-8908. (Series in the Sociology of Work). 267p. 1985. 59.50 (ISBN 0-87395-998-1); pap. 19.95 (ISBN 0-87395-999-X). State U NY Pr.

Sharing Possessions: Mandate & Symbol of Faith. Luke T. Johnson. Ed. by Walter Brueggemann & John R. Donahue. LC 80-2390. (Overtures to Biblical Theology Ser.: No. 9). 176p. (Orig.). 1981. pap. 2.50 (ISBN 0-8006-1534-4, 1-1534). Fortress.

Sharing Prayer: Simple Formats for Small Groups. Mary S. Taylor. 140p. (Orig.). 1988. pap. 5.95 (ISBN 0-86716-086-1, SBN 861). St Anthony Mess Pr.

Sharing Research Data. National Research Council & Commission on Behavioral & Social Sciences & Education. Ed. by Stephen E. Fienberg et al. 240p. 1985. pap. text ed. 17.50 (ISBN 0-309-03499-X). Natl Acad Pr.

Sharing Resources: Post Secondary Education & Industry Cooperation. Catherine P. Warmbrod & Jon J. Persavich. 175p. 1981. 10.00 (ISBN 0-318-15558-3, RD203). Natl Ctr Res Voc Ed.

Sharing Sexual Values: A Parent's Approach. Joan H. Etheredge. 64p. 1986. pap. 1.95 (ISBN 0-89243-252-7). Liguori Pubns.

Sharing Society. Edward Lamb. 1979. 12.00 (ISBN 0-8184-0284-9). Lyle Stuart.

Sharing the Children: How to Resolve Custody Problems & Get on with Your Life. Robert E. Adler. LC 87-19532. 220p. 1988. 17.95 (ISBN 0-917561-50-3); pap. 7.95 (ISBN 0-917561-56-2). Adler & Adler.

Sharing the Eucharistic Bread: The Witness of the New Testament. Xavier Leon-Dufour. 368p. (Orig.). 1987. pap. 12.95 (ISBN 0-8091-2865-9). Paulist Pr.

Sharing the Faith: The Beliefs & Values of Catholic High School Teachers. Peter L. Benson & Michael J. Guerra. 85p. 1985. 11.40 (ISBN 0-318-18578-4); member 8.55. Natl Cath Educ.

Sharing the Faith with Your Child: From Birth to Age Six. Phyllis Chandler & Joan Burney. 96p. 1984. pap. 2.50 (ISBN 0-89243-205-5). Liguori Pubns.

Sharing the Gains of Productivity. Brian F. Moore. (Studies in Productivity: No. 24). 57p. 1982. pap. 39.00 (ISBN 0-08-029505-3). Work in Amer.

Sharing the House. Jan Seale. Ed. by Dorey Schmidt. (River Sedge Poetry Ser.: No. 3). (Illus.). 50p. (Orig.). 1982. pap. 4.00 (ISBN 0-938884-05-0). RiverSedge Pr.

Sharing the Journey. Ellen Cook. 1986. pap. 6.95 (ISBN 0-697-02208-0). Wm C Brown.

Sharing the Light of Faith: National Catechetical Directory for Catholics of the United States. United States Catholic Conference, Conference of Catholic Bishops, Department of Education. (Illus., Orig.). 1979. pap. 7.95 (ISBN 1-55586-001-X). US Catholic.

Sharing the Old, Old Story: Educational Ministry in the Black Community. Nathan Jones. LC 81-86046. (Illus.). 113p. (Orig.). 1982. pap. 8.95 (ISBN 0-88489-144-5). St Mary's.

Sharing the Risk: How the Nation's Businesses, Homes & Autos Are Insured. rev. ed. 192p. 1985. pap. 6.95 (ISBN 0-932387-10-1). Insur Info.

Sharing the Search. Thomas R. Hawkins. LC 87-51424. 112p. 1988. pap. 6.95 (ISBN 0-8358-0583-2). Upper Room.

Sharing the Work: An Analysis of the Issues in Worksharing & Jobsharing. Noah M. Meltz et al. LC 81-188245. pap. 24.50 (ISBN 0-317-39707-9, 2055826). Bks Demand UMI.

Sharing the World's Resources. Oscar Schachter. LC 76-28422. 1977. 21.00x (ISBN 0-231-04110-1). Columbia U Pr.

Sharing Traditions: Five Black Artists in Nineteenth-Century America. Lynda R. Hartigan. LC 84-600335. (Illus.). 120p. 1985. pap. 17.50 (ISBN 0-87474-513-6, HASTP). Smithsonian.

Sharing Treasure, Time, & Talent: A Parish Manual for Sacrificial Giving or Tithing. Joseph M. Champlin. LC 82-16178. 88p. (Orig.). 1982. pap. 4.95 (ISBN 0-8146-1277-6). Liturgical Pr.

Sharing Wisdom. Mary B. Mckinney. 192p. 1987. pap. 7.95 (ISBN 0-89505-449-3). Tabor Pub.

Sharing with Children: New Ideas on the Evolution of Life. Lynn Margulis. (Illus.). 23p. (Orig.). 1985. pap. 3.00 (ISBN 0-918374-21-9). City Coll Wk.

Sharing with Thumpy: My Story of Love & Grief. Jane M. Lamb. (Illus.). 48p. (gr. k-12). 1985. pap. 8.95 workbook (ISBN 0-918533-10-4). Prairie Lark.

Sharing Your Faith. Robert B. Hall. 1981. pap. 4.95 (ISBN 0-686-14949-1). Episcopal Ctr.

Sharing Your Faith. Harold Odor & Ruth Odor. (Illus.). 16p. (gr. 3-7). 1985. 0.75 (ISBN 0-87239-902-8, 3302). Standard Pub.

Sharing Your Faith: Ministry Training Program for Facilitators: Leader's Guide. Gemma Fisher et al. (Illus.). 31p. (Orig.). 1987. pap. 3.95 (ISBN 1-55612-082-6). Sheed & Ward MO.

Sharing Your Faith: Ministry Training Program for Facilitators Participant. Gemma Fisher et al. (Illus.). 35p. (Orig.). 1987. pap. 2.95 (ISBN 1-55612-085-0). Sheed & Ward MO.

Sharing Your Faith with a Muslim. Adiyah Akbar Abdul-Haqq. 192p. (Orig.). 1980. pap. 6.95 (ISBN 0-87123-553-6, 210553). Bethany Hse.

Sharing 1: A Manual for Volunteer Teachers. Thomas Zanzig. (Sharing Program Ser.). (Illus.). 199p. 1985. pap. 18.95 (ISBN 0-88489-163-1). St Mary's.

Sharing 2: A Manual for Volunteer Teachers. Thomas Zanzig. (Sharing Program Ser.). 239p. 1985. pap. text ed. 18.95 (ISBN 0-88489-164-X). St Mary's.

Sharing 3: A Manual for Volunteer Teachers. Thomas Zanzig. (Sharing Program Ser.). 231p. 1985. pap. 18.95 (ISBN 0-88489-165-8). St Mary's.

Sharing 4: A Manual for Volunteer Teachers. Thomas Zanzig. (Sharing Program Ser.). 200p. 1988. pap. 18.95 (ISBN 0-88489-166-6). St Mary's.

Shariyat-Ki-Sugmad. Paul Twitchell. 1971. Vol. 1 1970. kivar bdg 10.95 (ISBN 0-914766-13-9); Vol. 2 1971. 10.95 (ISBN 0-914766-14-7). Illum Way Pub.

Shariyat-Ki-Sugmad, Vol. 2. Paul Twitchell. 189p. (Fr.). 1983. pap. 10.95 (ISBN 0-914766-72-4). Illum Way Pub.

Shariyat-Ki-Sugmad: Buch Eins, Vol. 1. Paul Twitchell. Tr. by Steve DeWitt et al from Ger. 186p. (Orig.). 1980. pap. 8.95 (ISBN 0-914766-56-2, 0538). Illum Way Pub.

Shariyat Ki Sugmad: Buch Zwei, Vol. 2. Paul Twitchell. Tr. by Steve Dewitt & Uli Sacchet. 204p. (Orig., Ger.). 1981. pap. 8.95 (ISBN 0-914766-70-8, 0539). Illum Way Pub.

Shariyat-Ki-Sugmad: Premier Livre, Vol. 1. Paul Twitchell. Tr. by Yves D. Martin from Fr. 190p. (Orig.). 1980. pap. 8.95 (ISBN 0-914766-34-1, 0338). Illum Way Pub.

Shark. Zane Grey. Ed. by Loren Grey. 1978. pap. 1.50 (ISBN 0-505-51265-3, Pub. by Tower Bks). Leisure NY.

Shark: A Photographer's Story. Jeremy Stafford-Deitsch. LC 87-4798. (Illus.). 200p. 1988. pap. 16.95 (ISBN 0-87156-733-4). Sierra.

Shark Africa. Bruno Krauss. (Sea Wolf Ser.: No. 5). (Orig.). 1981. pap. 2.25 (ISBN 0-89083-871-2). Zebra.

Shark & Ray. Vincent Serventy. LC 84-15097. (Animals in the Wild Ser.). (Illus.). 24p. (gr. k-3). 1984. PLB 11.33 (ISBN 0-8172-2402-5). Raintree Pubs.

Shark Attack & Treatment of Victims in Southern African Waters. Tim Wallett. 1980. 50.00x (ISBN 0-686-69986-6, Pub. by Bailey Bros & Swinfen Ltd). State Mutual Bk.

Shark Attack! Greg Norman's Guide to Agressive Golf. Greg Norman & George Peper. (Illus.). 288p. 1988. 19.95 (ISBN 0-671-64316-9). S&S.

Shark Lady. Ann McGovern. (Illus.). 96p. (gr. k-3). 1987. pap. 2.25 (ISBN 0-590-41178-0). Scholastic Inc.

Shark Lady: True Adventures of Eugenie Clark. Ann McGovern. LC 78-22126. (Illus.). 96p. (gr. 1-5). 1979. 10.95 (ISBN 0-02-767060-0, Four Winds). Macmillan.

Shark: Lord of the Sea. 5th ed. Sandra D. Romashko. LC 76-150452. (Illus.). 64p. 1987. pap. 3.95 (ISBN 0-89317-001-1). Windward Pub.

Shark Man: Master Hunter of the Deep. Robert F. Boggs. 1977. 7.95 (ISBN 0-89328-007-0). Lorenz Corp.

Shark Mazes: Educational Activity-Coloring Book. Peter M. Spizzirri. Ed. by Linda Spizzirri. (Illus.). 32p. (gr. k-5). 1984. pap. 0.99 (ISBN 0-86545-056-0). Spizzirri.

Shark Pack. Bruno Krauss. (Sea Wolf Ser.: No. 3). 1981. pap. 2.25 (ISBN 0-89083-817-8). Zebra.

Shark Repellents & Golden Parachutes: A Handbook for the Practitioner. Ed. by Robert H. Winter et al. 590p. 1983. Annual supplements avail. 166.00 (ISBN 0-15-004286-8, Law & Business). HarBraceJ.

Shark Utilization & Marketing. Rudolf Kreuzer et al. 187p. (Eng. & Span.). 1978. pap. 14.00 (ISBN 92-5-100654-7, F1531, FAO). UNIPUB.

Shark Watcher's Guide. Guido Dingerkus. (Illus.). 176p. (gr. 7 up). 1985. 9.79 (ISBN 0-671-50234-4); pap. 5.95 (ISBN 0-671-55038-1). Messner.

Sharkes in the North Woods. Jane Zaring. (gr. 5-8). 1982. 9.95 (ISBN 0-395-32271-5). HM.

Sharks. Gilda Berger. LC 85-29327. (Illus.). 48p. (gr. k-4). 1987. pap. 8.95 (ISBN 0-385-23419-8); pap. 8.95 (ISBN 0-385-23418-X). Doubleday.

Sharks. Rhoda Blumberg. (First Bks.). (Illus.). 72p. (gr. 4 up). 1976. PLB 10.40 (ISBN 0-531-00846-0). Watts.

Sharks. Rhoda Blumberg. 1980. pap. 2.25 (ISBN 0-380-49247-4, 64980-2, Camelot). Avon.

Sharks. Russell Freedman. LC 85-42881. (Illus.). 40p. (gr. 1-4). 1985. reinforced bdg. 12.95 (ISBN 0-8234-0582-6). Holiday.

Sharks. Ann McGovern. LC 76-17122. (Illus.). 48p. (gr. k-3). 1976. 9.95 (ISBN 0-02-765740-X, Four Winds). Macmillan.

Sharks. Ann McGovern. (Illus.). (gr. k-3). 1977. pap. 1.75 (ISBN 0-590-10234-6). Scholastic Inc.

Sharks. Ann McGovern. 48p. (gr. k-3). 1987. 2.25 (ISBN 0-590-41360-0). Scholastic Inc.

Sharks. Kate Petty. LC 85-80638. (First Library). (Illus.). 32p. (gr. 2-4). 1985. PLB 10.90 (ISBN 0-531-10025-1). Watts.

Sharks. Ed. by John Stevens & Saltz. LC 87-601. (Illus.). 240p. 1987. 29.95 (ISBN 0-8160-1800-6). Facts on File.

Sharks. Alwyne Wheeler. (First Sight Ser.). (Illus.). 32p. (gr. 1-6). 1987. lib. bdg. 10.90 (ISBN 0-531-17052-7, Gloucester Pr). Watts.

Sharks. Wildlife Education, Ltd. (Zoobooks). (Illus.). 20p. (YA) (gr. 5 up). 1983. pap. 1.95 (ISBN 0-937934-15-1). Wildlife Educ.

Sharks: An Educational Coloring Book. Henry Berkowitz. (Illus.). 32p. (Orig.). (gr. 1-9). 1988. pap. 2.50 (ISBN 0-938059-01-7). Henart Bks.

Sharks: An Educational Coloring Book. Spizzirri Publishing Co. Staff. Ed. by Linda Spizzirri. (Illus.). 32p. (gr. 1-8). 1981. pap. 1.49 (ISBN 0-86545-029-3). Spizzirri.

Sharks: An Introduction for the Amateur Naturalist. Sanford A. Moss. (Illus.). 240p. 1984. 21.95 (ISBN 0-13-808312-6); pap. 10.95 (ISBN 0-13-808304-5). P-H.

Sharks & Little Fish. Wolfgang Ott. 1982. pap. 2.95 (ISBN 0-345-30390-3). Ballantine.

Sharks & Other Dangerous Sea Creatures. Idaz Greenberg & Jerry Greenberg. (Illus.). 64p. 1981. pap. 5.95 (G-095). Banyan Bks.

Sharks & Other Dangerous Sea Creatures. Idaz Greenberg & Jerry Greenberg. (Illus.). 64p. 1981. saddlestiched 6.00x. Seahawk Pr.

Sharks & Rays: A Handbook of the Sharks & Rays of Hawaii & the Central Pacific Ocean. Spencer W. Tinker & Charles J. DuLuca. LC 73-77578. 1973. 7.25 (ISBN 0-8048-1082-6). C E Tuttle.

Sharks & Shipwrecks. Hugh Edwards. LC 74-33219. (Illus.). 128p. 1975. write for info. (ISBN 0-8129-0559-8, Demeter). Times Bks.

Sharks & Troubled Waters. Margaret Harris. LC 77-10760. (Myth, Magic & Superstition Ser.). (Illus.). 48p. (gr. 4-5). 1977. PLB 14.65 (ISBN 0-8172-1041-5). Raintree Pubs.

Sharks & Whales. Burton Albert. LC 78-66936. (Deluxe Illustrated Ser.). (Illus.). (gr. 1-6). 1979. 5.95 (ISBN 0-448-48990-2, G&D); PLB 5.29 (ISBN 0-448-13620-1). Putnam Pub Group.

Sharks Are People Too! Leigh Rubin. LC 82-99813. (Illus.). 80p. 1982. pap. 4.95 (ISBN 0-943384-02-8). Rubes Pubns.

Sharks Are Us. Edward J. Schuler. 32p. 1987. 6.95 (ISBN 0-8062-3156-4). Carlton.

Sharks of Arabia. John E. Randall. 148p. 1986. 95.00x (ISBN 0-907151-09-4, Pub. by IMMEL UK). State Mutual Bk.

Sharks of North American Waters. Jose I. Castro. LC 82-45892. (W. L. Moody, Jr., Natural History Ser.: No. 5). (Illus.). 194p. (Orig.). 1983. 19.50 (ISBN 0-89096-140-9); pap. 9.95 (ISBN 0-89096-143-3). Tex A&M Univ Pr.

Sharks of the Order Carcharhiniformes. L. J. Compagno. (Illus.). 650p. 1988. text ed. 99.50 (ISBN 0-691-08453-X). Princeton U Pr.

Sharks of the World. Rodney Steel. LC 85-6849. (Illus.). 192p. 1985. 22.95 (ISBN 0-8160-1086-2). Facts on File.

Sharks, Ships & Potato Chips: Curriculum Integrated Library Instruction. Ruth Toor & Hilda K. Weisburg. (Illus.). 260p. 1986. 29.50 (ISBN 0-931315-02-6). Lib Learn Res.

Sharks: Silent Hunters of the Deep. Reader's Digest Editors. LC 87-670009. (Illus.). 208p. 1986. 19.95 (ISBN 0-86438-014-3, Pub. by RD Assn). Random.

Sharks, the Super Fish. Helen R. Sattler. LC 84-4381. (Illus.). 96p. (YA) (gr. 9 up). 1985. 15.00 (ISBN 0-688-03993-6). Lothrop.

Sharks, Wrecks, & Movie Stars: The Adventures of an Underwater Photographer. rev. ed. Jack McKenney. Orig. Title: Dive to Adventure. (Illus.). 1989. pap. 10.95 (ISBN 0-89732-082-4). Menasha Ridge.

Sharky's Machine. William Diehl. 1979. pap. 2.50 (ISBN 0-440-18292-1). Dell.

Sharlot Hall on the Arizona Strip: A Diary of a Journey Through Northern Arizona in 1911. Sharlot Hall. Ed. by C. Gregory Crampton. 108p. 1988. pap. 9.95 (ISBN 0-87358-468-6). Northland.

Sharmanka. Andrei Platonov. (Orig., Rus.). 1979. pap. 25.00 (ISBN 0-88233-156-6). Ardis Pubs.

Sharon: An Israeli Caesar. Uzi Benziman. LC 85-13461. 276p. 1985. 17.95 (ISBN 0-915361-23-X, Dist. by Watts). Adama Pubs Inc.

Sharon, Connecticut, Probate Records 1757-83. 1984. 11.00 (ISBN 0-914385-03-8). Catoctin Pr.

Shawnee Minisink: A Stratified Paleoinidian-Archaic Site in the Upper Delaware Valley of Pennsylvania. Charles W. McNett. (Studies in Archaeology). 1985. 64.50 (ISBN 0-12-485970-4); pap. 24.95 (ISBN 0-12-485971-2). Acad Pr.
Shawnee Prophet. R. David Edmunds. LC 82-23830. (Illus.). xii, 272p. 1983. 23.50x (ISBN 0-8032-1850-8). U of Nebr Pr.
Shawnee Prophet. R. David Edmunds. LC 82-23830. (Illus.). xii, 272p. 1985. pap. 7.95 (ISBN 0-8032-6711-8, BB 906, Bison). U Of Nebr Pr.
Shawnee: The Ceremonialism of a Native Indian Tribe & Its Cultural Background. James H. Howard. LC 80-23752. (Illus.). xvi, 454p. 1981. 28.95 (ISBN 0-8214-0417-2); pap. 14.95 (ISBN 0-8214-0614-0). Ohio U Pr.
Shawnese Traditions. Charles C. Trowbridge. Ed. by Vernon Kinietz & Erminie W. Voegelin. LC 76-43871. (Michigan Univ. Museum of Anthropology. Occasional Contributions: No. 9). Repr. of 1939 ed. 17.00 (ISBN 0-404-15729-7). AMS Pr.
Shawno. George Dennison. LC 84-1434. 96p. 1984. 10.95 (ISBN 0-8052-3917-0). Schocken.
Shawno: Large Print Books. George Dennison. 1985. lib. bdg. 11.95 (ISBN 0-8161-3876-1). G K Hall.
Shaw's Moral Vision: The Self & Salvation. Alfred Turco, Jr. LC 75-36524. 304p. 1976. 29.95x (ISBN 0-8014-0965-9). Cornell U Pr.
Shaw's Music: The Complete Musical Criticism, 3 vols. Ed. by Dan H. Laurence. LC 80-1113. 1981. Boxed Set. 150.00 (ISBN 0-396-07967-9). Dodd.
Shaw's Nam. John Carn. LC 84-70275. 224p. (Orig.). 1984. pap. 3.95 (ISBN 0-916967-00-X). Af Am Artists Sm Pr.
Shaw's Plays in Performance. Daniel J. Leary. LC 83-2188. (Annual of Bernard Shaw Studies: Vol. 3). 268p. 1983. 25.00x (ISBN 0-271-00346-4). Pa St U Pr.
Shaw's Plays in Review. Desmond MacCarthy. LC 75-25542. 1951. lib. bdg. 45.00 (ISBN 0-8414-6039-6). Folcroft.
Shaw's Plays: Man & Superman Notes & Caesar & Cleopatra Notes. James K. Lowers. (Orig.). 1982. pap. 3.95 (ISBN 0-8220-0808-4). Cliffs.
Shaw's Plays: Pygmalion Notes & Arms & the Man Notes. Marilynn O. Harper. (Orig.). 1981. pap. 3.25 (ISBN 0-8220-1103-4). Cliffs.
Shaw's Sense of History. J. L. Wisenthal. 208p. 1988. 45.00 (ISBN 0-19-812892-4). Oxford U Pr.
Shaykh Ahmad Sirhindi: An Outline of His Thought & a Study of His Image in the Eyes of Posterity. Yohanan Friedmann. 136p. 1971. 24.95x (ISBN 0-7735-0068-5). McGill-Queens U Pr.
Shayna Maidel. Barbara Lebow. 1988. pap. 6.95 (ISBN 0-452-26150-3, Plume). NAL.
Shay's Rebellion. Ed. by Frank Feidel & Ernest May. (Harvard Dissertation in American History & Political Science Ser.). 605p. 1988. lib. bdg. 95.00 (ISBN 0-8240-5122-X). Garland Pub.
Shays' Rebellion: The Making of an Agrarian Insurrection. David P. Szatmary. LC 79-22522. 1980. pap. 9.95x (ISBN 0-87023-419-6). U of Mass Pr.
Shcharansky Chronicles: A Complete Documentary. Ed. by Felix Roziner. 1986. cancelled (ISBN 0-318-21399-0); pap. cancelled. Shapolsky Pubs.
Shcharansky: Hero of Our Time. Martin Gilbert. (Illus.). 512p. 1986. 24.95 (ISBN 0-670-81418-0). Viking.
Shcharansky: The Man. Felix Roziner. 326p. 1987. pap. 9.95 (ISBN 0-933503-06-7). Shapolsky Pubs.
She. H. Rider Haggard. (Airmont Classics Ser.). (gr. 8 up). pap. 1.95 (ISBN 0-8049-0146-5, CL-146). Airmont.
She. H. Rider Haggard. 1976. Repr. of 1887 ed. lib. bdg. 20.95 (ISBN 0-89190-705-X, Pub. by River City Pr). Amereon Ltd.
She. Lucille Quinitchette. 16p. (Orig.). 1978. pap. 2.00 (ISBN 0-935252-17-7). Street Pr.
She. M. L. Rosenthal. (American Poets Continuum Ser.: No. 2). 40p. pap. 6.95 (ISBN 0-918526-06-X). Boa Edns.
She & Allan. H. Rider Haggard. Repr. lib. bdg. 22.95 (ISBN 0-89190-706-8, Pub. by River City Pr). Amereon Ltd.
She & Allan. H. Rider Haggard. Ed. by R. Reginald & Douglas Menville. LC 80-19461. (Newcastle Forgotten Fantasy Library Ser.: Vol. 6). 303p. 1980. Repr. of 1977 ed. lib. bdg. 22.95x (ISBN 0-89370-505-5). Borgo Pr.
She Came Back. Patricia Wentworth. 15.95 (ISBN 0-88411-744-8, Pub. by Aeonian Pr). Amereon Ltd.
She Came too Late. Mary Wings. LC 87-21914. (Crossing Press Women-Sleuth Ser.). 208p. 1987. 20.95 (ISBN 0-89594-244-5); pap. 7.95 (ISBN 0-89594-243-7). Crossing Pr.
She Child. Mardiningsih Arquette. (Illus.). 32p. (Orig.). 1982. pap. 4.00 (ISBN 0-9605594-1-8). Monkey Man.
She Come Bringing Me That Little Baby Girl. Eloise Greenfield. LC 74-8104. (Illus.). (gr. k-3). 1974. 12.70i (ISBN 0-397-31586-4, Lipp Jr Bks). HarpJ.
She Comes When You're Leaving. Bruce Boston. 64p. (Orig.). 1982. pap. 3.95 (ISBN 0-917658-14-0). BPW & P.
She Died a Lady. Carter Dickson. 256p. 1987. pap. 3.50 (ISBN 0-8217-2238-7). Zebra.
She Died, She Lives: In Search of Maria Orsola. George Francis. 176p. 1977. pap. 3.95 (ISBN 0-232-51392-9). Attic Pr.
She Fulfilled the Impossible Dream. DeWitt S. Williams. Ed. by Gerald Wheeler. (Banner Ser.). 126p. (Orig.). 1985. pap. 6.95 (ISBN 0-8280-0274-6). Review & Herald.
She Had Some Horses. Joy Harjo. 80p. (Orig.). 1983. text ed. 14.95 (ISBN 0-938410-07-5); pap. 6.95 (ISBN 0-938410-06-7). Thunder's Mouth.
She Hath Done What She Could. Pamela Brubaker. 224p. (Orig.). 1985. pap. 7.95 (ISBN 0-87178-942-6). Brethren.
She Hath Done What She Could. Jane McWhorter. 1973. 4.95 (ISBN 0-89137-405-1). Quality Pubns.
She Is Not Registered. Kenneth B. Pettis. 64p. 1984. 6.95 (ISBN 0-89962-399-9). Todd & Honeywell.
She King, or the Book of Poetry, 4 vols, Vol. 3. Tr. by James Legge. (Chinese Classics Ser.). (Chinese & Eng.). 1983. Repr. of 1893 ed. 35.00x (ISBN 0-89986-355-8); Set. 135.00x. Oriental Bk Store.
She, King Solomon's Mines & Allan Quartermain. H. Rider Haggard. 636p. pap. 7.95 (ISBN 0-486-20643-2). Dover.
She Likes You, Charlie Brown. Charles M. Schulz. (Illus.). 1985. pap. 2.25 (ISBN 0-449-20788-9, Crest). Fawcett.
She Never Looked Back: Margaret Mead in Samoa. Samuel Epstein & Beryl Epstein. LC 78-31821. (Science Discovery Ser.). (Illus.). (gr. 3-7). 1980. PLB 6.99 (ISBN 0-698-30715-1, Coward). Putnam Pub Group.
She-rab Dong-bu, or Prajnya Danda: A Metrical Translation in Tibetan of a Sanskirt Ethical Work. Nagarjuna. Ed. by W. L. Campbell. LC 78-70103. Repr. of 1919 ed. 22.00 (ISBN 0-404-17354-3). AMS Pr.
She Said - He Said. Nancy Henley & Barrie Thorne. 1976. perfect bdg. 3.50 (ISBN 0-912786-36-1). Know Inc.
She Said, Laughing, Moss Herbert. 74p. 1986. 3.72 (ISBN 0-89697-277-1). Intl Univ Pr.
She Shall Be Called Woman. Marsha Newman & Gene Newman. 1981. pap. write for info. Wellspring Utah.
She Stands Accused: Being a Series of Accounts of the Lives & Deeds of Notorious Women Murderesses. Victor MacClure. LC 74-10429. (Classics of Crime & Criminology Ser.). (Illus.). 239p. 1975. Repr. of 1935 ed. 15.40 (ISBN 0-88355-196-9). Hyperion Conn.
She Stoops to Conquer. Oliver Goldsmith. Ed. by Vincent F. Hopper & Gerald B. Lahey. (Illus.). (gr. 9 up). 1958. pap. text ed. 4.95 (ISBN 0-8120-0158-3). Barron.
She Stoops to Conquer. Oliver Goldsmith. Ed. by Katherine G. Balderston. LC 51-6755. (Crofts Classics Ser.). 1951. pap. text ed. 3.95x (ISBN 0-88295-039-8). Harlan Davidson.
She Stoops to Conquer. Oliver Goldsmith. Ed. by J. A. Lavin. (New Mermaids Ser.). 1980. pap. 6.95x (ISBN 0-393-90046-0). Norton.
She Stoops to Conquer. Oliver Goldsmith. Ed. by Harry Shefter. (Illus.). (YA) (gr. 7 up). 1984. pap. 2.95 (Re). PB.
She Stoops to Conquer. Oliver Goldsmith. Ed. by Harry Shefter. (Enriched Classics Edition Ser.). 176p. pap. 2.95. WSP.
She Stoops to Conquer. (Illus.). 34p. (Director's Production Script). 1965. pap. 5.00 (ISBN 0-88680-174-5). I E Clark.
SHE: Subject Headings for Engineering. 1987. 45.00 (ISBN 0-87394-019-9). Eng Info.
She Talks to Herself in the Language of an Educated Woman. Frances Jaffer. (Illus.). 48p. 1981. 4.25 (ISBN 0-932716-13-X). Kelsey St Pr.
SHE: Understanding Feminine Psychology. Robert A. Johnson. LC 86-45122. 80p. 1986. pap. 5.95 (ISBN 0-06-097058-8, PL 7058, PL). Har-Row.
She Waits for Me. Donald G. Finch. (gr. 8-12). 1977. pap. 1.50 (ISBN 0-912472-16-2). Miller Bks.
She Wanted Something Else. Megan Staffel. LC 87-60881. 352p. 1987. 17.95 (ISBN 0-86547-293-9). N Point Pr.
She Wanted to Read: The Story of Mary Macleod Bethune. Ella K. Carruth. (Illus.). (gr. 3-7). 1966. 6.75 (ISBN 0-687-38353-6). Abingdon.
She Wants to Go to Pago-Pago. Bill Sherman. LC 85-72156. (Poetry Ser.: Bk. 1). 48p. (Orig.). 1986. pap. 7.50 (ISBN 0-9615784-0-8). Branch Redd.
She Wears Him Fancy in Her Night Braid. Faye Kicknosway. (Illus.). 48p. 1983. 40.00 (ISBN 0-915124-88-2, Pub. by Toothpaste); pap. 10.00 (ISBN 0-915124-87-4). Coffee Hse.
She Who Remembers. Linda L. Shuler. 432p. 1988. 18.45 (ISBN 0-87795-892-0, Arbor Hse). Morrow.
She Woke Me Up So I Killed Her. Tr. by Paul Bowles. LC 82-71550. 100p. 1986. signed ltd. ed 25.00 (ISBN 0-317-02696-8); pap. 7.95. Cadmus Eds.
She-Wolf & Other Stories. enlarged ed. Giovanni Verga. Tr. by Giovanni Cecchetti from Ital. 315p. 10.95 (ISBN 0-520-04789-3). U of Cal Pr.
She Would If She Could. George Etherege. Ed. by Charlene M. Taylor. LC 76-128913. (Regents Restoration Drama Ser). xxx, 132p. 1971. pap. 3.95x (ISBN 0-8032-6700-2, BB 281, Bison). U of Nebr Pr.
Sheaf of Cinquain. Irene Stanley. 15.00 (ISBN 0-686-00950-9). Wagon & Star.
Sheaf of Japanese Papers: In Tribute to Heinz Kaempfer on His 75th Birthday. Ed. by M. Forrer et al. 116p. (Orig.). 1979. pap. 27.00x (ISBN 90-70265-71-0, Pub. by Gieben Amsterdam). Benjamins North Am.
Sheaf of Papers. Oliver Elton. LC 72-194754. 1923. lib. bdg. 25.00 (ISBN 0-8414-3917-6). Folcroft.
Sheaf of Songs from a Family Garden. C. S. Charlotte. 1985. write for info. Crambruck.
Sheaf of Studies. facsimile ed. Edmund K. Chambers. LC 74-99622. (Essay Index Reprint Ser.). 1942. 18.00 (ISBN 0-8369-1398-1). Ayer Co Pubs.
Sheaf of Studies. Edmund K. Chambers. LC 74-12168. 1942. lib. bdg. 27.00 (ISBN 0-8414-3371-2). Folcroft.
Sheaf Theory. B. R. Tennison. LC 74-31791. (London Mathematical Society Lecture Note Ser.: No. 20). 120p. 1976. pap. 22.95 (ISBN 0-521-20784-3). Cambridge U Pr.
Shear Flow in Surface Oriented Co-Ordinates. Hirschel. 1981. 46.00 (ISBN 3-528-08078-7, Pub. by Vieweg & Sohn Germany). IPS.
Shear in Reinforced Concrete. American Concrete Institute Staff. LC 73-94112. (American Concrete Institute Publication Ser.: SP-42). (Illus.). Vol. 1. pap. 108.30 (ISBN 0-317-10241-9); Vol. 2. pap. 131.00 (ISBN 0-317-10242-7). Bks Demand UMI.
Shear Stability of Multigrade Crankcase Oil-DS49. 1973. pap. 7.75 (ISBN 0-8031-0090-6, 05-049000-12). ASTM.
Shear Stability of Multigrade Oils-IP Fleet Test-DS49-S1. 36p. 1974. pap. 4.00x (ISBN 0-8031-0566-5, 05-049001-12). ASTM.
Shear Strength of Cohesive Soils. Compiled by American Society of Civil Engineers Staff. 1170p. 1960. pap. 38.00x (ISBN 0-87262-004-2). Am Soc Civil Eng.
Shear Strength of Reinforced & Prestressed Concrete Beams: CEB Approach. Bruno Thverlimann. (IBA Ser.: No. 93). 23p. 1979. pap. text ed. 12.95x (ISBN 0-8176-1131-2). Birkhauser.
Shear Wall-Frame Interaction: A Design Aid. 18p. 1970. pap. 3.50 (ISBN 0-89312-111-8, EB066D). Portland Cement.
Shear-Wave Exploration. S. Danbom & S. N. Domenic. LC 87-60488. (Geophysical Developments Ser.: No. 1). 384p. 1987. Set. text ed. 70.00 (ISBN 0-931830-45-1). Soc Expl Geophys.
Shearer Furniture Designs. R. Fastnedge. 1966. 8.95 (ISBN 0-685-52092-7). Transatl Arts.
Shearer's Manual of Human Dissection. 6th ed. Charles E. Tobin & John J. Jacobs. (Illus.). 416p. 1980. pap. 35.00 (ISBN 0-07-064926-X). McGraw.
Sheathing the Sword: The Demilitarization of Post-War Japan. Meirion Harries & Susie Harries. (Illus.). 384p. 1987. 24.95 (ISBN 0-02-548340-4). Macmillan.
Sheaves of Friendship. Ruth Adams Bevell. 256p. 1982. text ed. 8.95 (ISBN 0-88053-325-0, S-100). Macoy Pub.
Sheaves: Poems & Songs. 2nd ed. Rabindranath Tagore. Tr. by Nagendranath Gupta from Indian. LC 78-98878. 1971. Repr. of 1950 ed. lib. bdg. 48.50x (ISBN 0-8371-3149-9, TASH). Greenwood.
Sheba's Daughters. Harris S. Philby. LC 83-45836. Repr. of 1939 ed. 55.00 (ISBN 0-404-20201-2). AMS Pr.
Sheboygan County: One Hundred Fifty Years of Progress: An Illustrated History. Janice Hildebrand. Ed. by Marilyn Horn. (Illus.). 208p. (YA) (gr. 7 up). 1988. 29.95 (ISBN 0-89781-252-2). Windsor Pubns Inc.
Shebu'oth, 1 vol. (Hebrew & Eng.). 18.00 (ISBN 0-910218-75-7). Bennet Pub.
Shebu'oth see Soncino Books of the Bible.
Shechem I: Middle Bronze IIB Pottery. Dan P. Cole. LC 84-3004. (Excavation Reports of the American Schools of Oriental Research). xiv, 203p. 1984. text ed. 30.00 (ISBN 0-89757-206-8, Dist.by Eisenbrauns). Am Sch Orient Res.
Shechita: Religious & Historical Research on the Method of Slaughter. Ed. by Michael L. Munk & Eli Munk. (Illus.). 1976. 10.95 (ISBN 0-87306-992-7). Feldheim.
Shed Light on Death. L. A. Taylor. 183p. 1985. 14.95 (ISBN 0-8027-5630-1). Walker & CO.
Shedding Light on Benefits Issues: Educational Conference Proceedings 1984 Annual, Vol. 26. Ed. by Mary E. Brennan. 342p. 1985. text ed. 35.00 (ISBN 0-89154-281-7). Intl found Employ.
Shedding of Plant Parts. Ed. by T. T. Kozlowski. (Physiological Ecology Ser.). 1973. 93.50 (ISBN 0-12-424250-2). Acad Pr.
Shedding Silence. Janice Mirikitani. 176p. 1987. 14.95 (ISBN 0-89087-496-4); pap. 8.95 (ISBN 0-89087-493-X). Celestial Arts.
Sheds to Shelter: The Modular Approach for Low Cost Construction. H. Siegfried Wentz. (Illus.). 1985. 14.95 (ISBN 0-318-19506-2). Rockcom Pub.
Sheeba. Malinda Mayer. Ed. by Kendra Crossen. LC 85-62138. (Illus.). 32p. (Orig.). (gr. 3). 1986. pap. text ed. 5.00x (ISBN 0-9615163-0-5). Maji Bks.
Sheep. Mark Ahlstrom. Ed. by Howard Schroeder. LC 83-25215. (Wildlife (Habits & Habitat) Ser.). (Illus.). 48p. (gr. 4-5). 1984. PLB 10.95 (ISBN 0-89686-248-8). Crestwood Hse.
Sheep: A Guide to Management. Edward Hart. (Illus.). 1985. 12.95 (ISBN 0-946284-07-5, Pub. by Crowood Pr). Longwood Pub Group.
Sheep among Wolves. Don R. Pegram. 1982. pap. 1.25 (ISBN 0-89265-084-2). Randall Hse.
Sheep & Goat Breeding. (Better Fárming Ser.: No. 12). 51p. 1977. pap. 7.50 (ISBN 92-5-100152-9, F70. FAO). UNIPUB.
Sheep & Goat Breeds of India. R. M. Acharya. (Animal Production & Health Papers: No. 30). 197p. 1982. pap. 13.75 (ISBN 92-5-101212-1, F2340, FAO). UNIPUB.
Sheep & Goat Production. J. E. Coop. (World Animal Science Ser.: Vol. 1C). 492p. 1982. 158.00 (ISBN 0-444-41989-6). Elsevier.
Sheep & Goat Science. 5th ed. Ensminger & Parker. (Illus.). 1986. text ed. 53.25 (ISBN 0-8134-2464-X); pap. text ed. 39.95. Inter Print Pubs.
Sheep & Goats in Developing Countries: Their Present & Potential Role. Winrock International Livestock Research & Training Center Staff. (Technical Paper: No. 15). 109p. 1983. 5.00 (ISBN 0-8213-0272-8, BK 0272). World Bank.
Sheep & Goats in Humid West Africa. Ed. by J. E. Sumberg & K. Cassaday. 74p. (Orig.). 1985. pap. text ed. 12.00x (ISBN 0-318-18376-5, Pub. by Intl Livestock Africa). Agribookstore.
Sheep & Goats in Pakistan. H. U. Hasnain. (FAO Animal Production & Health Paper: No. 56). (Illus.). 135p. (Orig.). 1986. pap. text ed. 11.25 (ISBN 92-5-102346-8, F2916, FAO). UNIPUB.
Sheep & Goats in Turkey. B. C. Yalcin. (FAO Animal Production & Health Paper: No. 60). (Illus.). 168p. (Orig.). 1987. pap. text ed. 13.75 (ISBN 92-5-102449-9, F3045, FAO). UNIPUB.
Sheep & Land: The Economics of Power in a Tribal Society. Jacob Black-Michaud. (Illus.). 246p. 1986. pap. 27.95 (ISBN 0-521-31075-X). Cambridge U Pr.
Sheep & the Rowan Tree. Julia Butcher. LC 83-26423. (Illus.). 32p. (gr. k-2). 1984. 12.50 (ISBN 0-03-071602-0). H Holt & Co.
Sheep & Wool Correspondence of Sir Joseph Banks, 1781-1820. Ed. by Harold B. Carter. (Illus.). xxx, 641p. 1979. 106.50x (ISBN 0-565-00802-1, Pub. by Brit Mus Nat Hist England). Sabbot-Natural Hist Bks.
Sheep & Wool: Science, Production & Management. M. P. Botkin & Ray A. Field. (Illus.). 512p. 1988. text ed. 40.00 (ISBN 0-13-808494-7). P-H.
Sheep As an Experimental Animal. J. F. Hecker. 1983. 48.00 (ISBN 0-12-336050-1). Acad Pr.
Sheep Book. Ron Parker. 368p. 1984. pap. 4.95 (ISBN 0-345-31574-X). Ballantine.
Sheep Boy. Gladys Campbell. 193p. 1984. 7.60 (ISBN 0-317-41421-6). Intl Univ Pr.
Sheep Dog. George Ancona. LC 84-20100. (Illus.). 64p. (gr. 5 up). 1985. 11.75 (ISBN 0-688-04118-3); PLB 11.88 (ISBN 0-688-04119-1). Lothrop.
Sheep from the Goats: Selected Literary Essays. John Simon. 352p. 1988. 19.95 (ISBN 1-55584-180-5). Weidenfeld.
Sheep Housing & Equipment Handbook. 3rd ed. Midwest Plan Service Staff. LC 81-18842. (Illus.). 116p. 1982. 6.00 (ISBN 0-89373-052-1, MWPS-3). Midwest Plan Serv.
Sheep Husbandry & Diseases. 6th ed. Allan Fraser & John Stamp. 350p. 1987. pap. 32.50x (ISBN 0-00-383272-4, Pub. by Collins England). Sheridan.
Sheep Husbandry in India. G. C. Taneja. cancelled (ISBN 0-8364-0315-0, Orient Longman). South Asia Bks.
Sheep in a Jeep. Nancy Shaw. LC 86-3101. (Illus.). 32p. (ps-k). 1986. 12.95 (ISBN 0-395-41105-X). HM.
Sheep in a Jeep. Nancy Shaw. (Illus.). 32p. (ps-k). 1988. pap. 3.95 (ISBN 0-395-47030-7, Sandpiper). HM.
Sheep Is Life: An Assessment of Livestock Reduction in the Former Navajo-Hopi Joint Use Area. rev. ed. John J. Wood et al. (Northern Arizona University Anthropological Papers: No. 1). (Illus.). xxiii, 182p. 1982. pap. 13.50 (ISBN 0-910953-00-7). N Arizona U.
Sheep Look Up. John Brunner. 192p. 1981. pap. 3.50 (Del Rey). Ballantine.
Sheep Management & Production. 2nd ed. Derek H. Goodwin. 224p. (Orig.). 1982. pap. text ed. 12.25 (ISBN 0-317-03049-3, Hutchinson & Co). Brookfield Pub Co.
Sheep of His Pasture: A Study of the Hebrew Noun 'AM(M) & its Semitic Cognates. Robert M. Good. LC 83-90934. (Harvard Semitic Monographs). 214p. 1984. 15.00 (ISBN 0-89130-628-5, 04 00 29). Scholars Pr GA.
Sheep on the Farm. Cliff Moon. LC 83-71628. (Down on the Farm Bks.). (Illus.). 33p. (ps-2). 1983. PLB 8.90 (ISBN 0-531-04698-2). Watts.
Sheep Production. William Haresign. (University of Nottingham Easter School of Agriculture Ser.). 92p. 1983. text ed. 130.00 (ISBN 0-408-10844-4). Butterworth.
Sheep Production. J. B. Owen. (Illus.). 444p. 1976. 20.95 (ISBN 0-7216-0793-4, Bailliere-Tindall). Saunders.
Sheep Production in the Tropics. A. B. Carles. (Tropical Handbooks). (Illus.). 1983. 35.00x (ISBN 0-19-859449-6). Oxford U Pr.
Sheep Production Series: Breeding & Reproduction, Vol. 1. Ed. by G. A. Wickham & M. F. McDonald. (Illus.). 269p. 1985. 37.95x (ISBN 0-908596-13-8, Pub. by Inkata Pr Australia). Intl Spec Bk.

Sheep Raiser's Manual. William K. Kruesi. (Illus.). 288p. (Orig., Includes index, appendix & bibliography). 1985. pap. 13.95 (ISBN 0-913589-10-1). Williamson Pub Co.

Sheep-Rearing & the Wool Trade in Italy During the Roman Period. Joan M. Frayn. (ARCA Classical & Medieval Texts, Papers, & Monographs: No. 15). (Illus.). 208p. 1984. text ed. 40.00 (ISBN 0-905205-22-7, Pub. by F Cairns). Longwood Pub Group.

Sheep-Skin Coat & an Absolutely Happy Village. Boris Vakhtin. Tr. by R. Dessais & M. Ulman. 1988. lib. bdg. 15.00 (ISBN 0-88233-786-6). Ardis Pubs.

Sheep, Stars, & Solitude: Adventure Saga of a Wilderness Trail. Francis R. Line. LC 86-11154. (Illus.). 166p. (Orig.). 1986. pap. 8.95 (ISBN 0-938109-02-2). Wide Horiz Pr.

Sheep Well see Four Plays of Lope de Vega.

Sheepchase. Paul Rogers. LC 85-40387. (Viking Kestrel Picture Bks.). (Illus.). 32p. (ps-k). 1986. 9.95 (ISBN 0-670-80599-8, Viking Kestrel). Viking.

Sheepchase. Paul Rogers. (Illus.). 32p. (Orig.). (ps-k). Date not set. pap. 3.50 (ISBN 0-14-050561-X, Puffin Bks). Penguin.

Sheepdog Training: An All Breed Approach. Mari Taggart. LC 85-52416. (Illus.). 176p. 1986. 17.98 (ISBN 0-931866-24-3). Alpine Pubns.

Sheepen: An Early Roman Industrial Site at Camulodunum. R. Niblett. (CBA Research Reports: No. 57). (Illus.). 176p. 1985. pap. text ed. 35.00x (ISBN 0-906780-46-2, Pub. by Council British Archaeology). Humanities.

Sheepfarmer's Daughter. Elizabeth Moon. (Deed of Paksenarrion Ser.: Bk. 1). (Orig.). 1988. pap. 3.95 (ISBN 0-671-65416-0). Baen Bks.

Sheepherders. Michael Mathers. (Illus.). 1975. 5.95 (ISBN 0-395-20723-1, Pub. by Montana Bks). Madrona Pubs.

Sheep's Clothing. Celia Dale. (Crime Club Ser.). 1989. 12.95 (ISBN 0-385-24607-2). Doubleday.

Sheep's in the Meadow, Raccoon's in the Corn. Marguerite H. Wolf. LC 79-91349. (Illus.). 136p. (Orig.). 1979. pap. 6.95 (ISBN 0-933050-03-8). New Eng Pr VT.

Sheer Anecdotages Leaves from a Reporter's Diary. D. R. Mankekar. 1984. 12.50x (ISBN 0-8364-1167-6, Pub. by Allied India). South Asia Bks.

Sheer Fiction. Paul West. LC 86-33252. 224p. 1987. 17.95 (ISBN 0-914232-82-7). McPherson & Co.

Sheer Fiction. Paul West. 221p. 1988. pap. 10.00 (ISBN 0-914232-98-3). McPherson & Co.

Sheer Romance: The Story of Pierre Dulaine, Yvonne Marceau & the American Ballroom Theatre Company. Lucy Gordon & Herbert Gordon. (Ballroom Dancing Ser.). (Illus.). 1985. lib. bdg. 79.95 (ISBN 0-8490-3245-8); pap. 39.95 (ISBN 0-8490-3246-6). Gordon Pr.

She'erit Yoseph. Yoseph Katz. Ed. by Asher Siev. LC 83-50567. 350p. 1984. 15.00 (ISBN 0-87203-116-0). Hermon.

Sheet Control for a Small Lithographic Offset Press. 30p. 1978. 16.00 (ISBN 0-88362-052-9, 0601). Graphic Arts Tech Found.

Sheet Control on the Offset Press. 48p. 1981. 16.00 (ISBN 0-88362-041-3, 0621). Graphic Arts Tech Found.

Sheet Fed Pressroom Managers Training Guide. Frank Drazan. 120p. pap. 25.00 spiral (ISBN 0-318-23317-7). F Drazan.

Sheet Formability of Alpha-Brass: Effect of Material Properties, Anisotrophy, & Processing Parameters. Drexel Institute of Technology Staff. 127p. 1973. 19.05 (ISBN 0-317-34545-1, 129). Intl Copper.

Sheet Forming on Paper Machines: Drainage & Other Topics, Vol. 1. (Bibliographic Ser.: No. 246). 126p. 1969. 10.00 (ISBN 0-317-34444-7); 1975 supplement 1 10.00 (ISBN 0-317-34445-5). Inst Paper Chem.

Sheet Forming on Paper Machines: Fiber Retention & Sheet Formation, Vol. 2. (Bibliographic Ser.: No. 247). 129p. 1969. 9.00 (ISBN 0-317-34446-3); 1975 supplement 15.00 (ISBN 0-317-34447-1). Inst Paper Chem.

Sheet Metal Blueprint Reading: For the Building Trades. 2nd ed. Claude J. Zinngrabe. LC 79-2748. 138p. 1980. 18.50 (ISBN 0-8273-1352-7); instr's. guide 8.00 (ISBN 0-8273-1353-5). Delmar.

Sheet Metal Drafting. 2nd ed. Melvin L. Betterley. (Illus.). 1977. text ed. 35.95 (ISBN 0-07-005126-7). McGraw.

Sheet Metal Estimating Handbook. Herbert C. Wendes. 250p. 1982. 33.95 (ISBN 0-442-25739-2). Van Nos Reinhold.

Sheet Metal Fabrication. Jack Rudman. (Occupational Competency Examination Ser.: OCE-31). (Cloth bdg. avail. on request). 13.95 (ISBN 0-8373-5731-4). Natl Learning.

Sheet Metal Fabrication. W. Watkins. (Illus.). 263p. 1971. 24.25 (ISBN 0-444-20124-6, Pub. by Applied Sci England). Elsevier.

Sheet Metal Forming & Energy Conservation: Proceedings of the Biennial Congress of the International Deep Drawing Research Group, 9th, Ann Arbor, Michigan, U. S. A., October 13-14, 1976. International Deep Drawing Research Group. LC 76-27547. (Illus.). 1976. pap. 73.00 (ISBN 0-317-10787-9, 2050982). Bks Demand UMI.

Sheet Metal Hand Processes. Claude J. Zinngrabe & F. W. Schumacher. LC 73-2159. 1974. 13.95 (ISBN 0-8273-0220-7). Delmar.

Sheet Metal Industries Year Book. 1986. 115.00x (ISBN 0-686-87230-4, Pub. by Portcullis Pr UK). State Mutual Bk.

Sheet Metal Industries Yearbook, 1988. Ed. by Portcullis Press Ltd. Staff. 1985. 150.00x (Pub. by Portcullis Pr UK). State Mutual Bk.

Sheet Metal Layout. 2nd ed. Leo A. Meyer. (Illus.). 1979. pap. 34.95 (ISBN 0-07-041731-8). McGraw.

Sheet Metal Layout Simplified, 3 vols. Hugh B. Reid. Vol. 1. 1981. 19.50 (ISBN 0-685-77694-8); Vol. 2. 1981. 19.50 (ISBN 0-685-41577-5); Vol. 3. 1981. 19.50 (ISBN 0-685-41578-3). H B Reid.

Sheet Metal Layout Tables for the Heating, Ventilation & Air Conditioning Industry. Richard S. Budzik. 1988. 29.95 (ISBN 0-912914-31-9). Practical Pubns.

Sheet Metal Machine Processes. Claude J. Zinngrabe & F. W. Schumacher. LC 73-2160. 1975. pap. text ed. 14.95 (ISBN 0-8273-0222-3). Delmar.

Sheet Metal Machinery. Leo Rizzo. LC 82-730275. 1982. wkbk. 7.00 (ISBN 0-8064-0253-9, 518); audio visual pkg. 399.00 (ISBN 0-8064-0254-7). Bergwall.

Sheet-Metal Pattern Drafting & Shop Problems. rev. ed. J. S. Daugherty & R. E. Powell. 196p. 1975. pap. text ed. 18.20 (ISBN 0-02-665680-9). Bennett IL.

Sheet Metal Shop Fabrication Projects Including Over Three Hundred Fifty Graded Parts. Richard S. Budzik. LC 80-84009. (Illus.). (gr. 7-12). 1980. 21.95 (ISBN 0-912914-07-6). Practical Pubns.

Sheet Metal Shop Practice. 4th ed. L. A. Meyer. (Illus.). 316p. 1975. 19.96 (ISBN 0-8269-1902-2). Am Technical.

Sheet Metal Technology. 3rd ed. Richard S. Budzik. 1988. 24.95 (ISBN 0-912914-34-3). Practical Pubns.

Sheet Metal Work. John D. Bies. 472p. 1985. lib. bdg. 17.95 (ISBN 0-8161-1706-3, Pub. by Audel). Macmillan.

Sheet Metal Worker. Jack Rudman. (Career Examination Ser.: C-736). (Cloth bdg. avail. on request). pap. 14.00 (ISBN 0-8373-0736-8). Natl Learning.

Sheet Metalwork. John Nagle. LC 79-730773. 1977. wkbk. 9.00 (ISBN 0-8064-0231-8, 507); audio visual pkg. 339.00 (ISBN 0-8064-0232-6). Bergwall.

Sheet Steel Carbon, High Strength Low Alloy, & Alloy Coils & Cut Lengths: Including Coated Products. 140p. 1988. 30.00 (ISBN 0-932897-27-4). Iron & Steel.

Sheetfed Offset Press Operating. Lloyd P. DeJidas & Thomas M. Destree. LC 88-81903. (Illus.). 350p. (Orig.). 1988. pap. text ed. 40.00 (ISBN 0-88362-116-9). Graphic Arts Tech Found.

Sheetfed Pressroom Manager's Guide Book. Date not set. 25.00. F Drazan.

Sheeting & Packaging Seminar, 1986: Notes of TAPPI, Mead Inn, Wisconsin Rapids, WI May 18-21, 1986. Technical Association of the Pulp & Paper Industry. pap. 34.50 (2029190). Bks Demand UMI.

Sheetmetal Occupations 1981: Equipment Planning Guide for Vocational & Technical Training & Education Programmes, Vol. 4. pap. 28.00 (ISBN 92-2-101892-X, ILO238, ILO). UNIPUB.

Sheffield Outrages Inquiry: Report Presented to the Trades Unions Commissioners. Great Britain Poor Law Board Staff. LC 72-108850. Repr. of 1867 ed. lib. bdg. 45.50x (ISBN 0-678-07766-5). Kelley.

Sheffield Site: An Oneota Site on the St. Croix River. Guy E. Gibbon. LC 73-6715. (Minnesota Prehistoric Archaeology Ser., No. 10). (Illus.). 62p. 1973. pap. 4.00x (ISBN 0-87351-079-8). Minn Hist.

Sheffield Steel & America: A Century of Commercial & Technological Interdependence 1830-1930. Geoffrey Tweedale. (Illus.). 320p. 1987. 49.50 (ISBN 0-521-33458-6). Cambridge U Pr.

Sheffield Wednesday: A Complete Record, 1867-1987. Keith Farnsworth. 400p. 1987. 60.00x (ISBN 0-907969-25-9, Pub. by Breedon Bks Pub UK). State Mutual Bk.

Shefford. Judith Grunfeld. 1980. pap. 7.50 (ISBN 0-900689-55-2). Soncino Pr.

Shehu Shegari: My Vision of Nigeria. Ed. by Aminu Tijjani & David Williams. (Illus.). 446p. 1981. 29.50x (ISBN 0-7146-3181-7, F Cass Co). Biblio Dist.

Sheik. E. M. Hull. 1976. Repr. of 1921 ed. lib. bdg. 18.95x (ISBN 0-89190-734-3, Pub. by River City Pr). Amereon Ltd.

Sheikh & Disciple. M. R. Bawa Muhaiyaddeen. LC 83-1565. (Illus.). 120p. 1983. 7.95 (ISBN 0-914390-26-0). Fellowship Pr PA.

Sheikh Mohammad Abdullah: A Political Phoenix. R. N. Kaul. (Illus.). vi, 120p. 1985. text ed. 20.00x (ISBN 0-86590-596-7, Pub. by Sterling Pubs India). Apt Bks.

Sheila Cluff's Aerobic Body Contouring. Sheila Cluff & Eva Shaw. Ed. by Ray Wolf & Catherine Cassidy. (Illus.). 224p. 1987. pap. 14.95 (ISBN 0-87857-698-3). Rodale Pr Inc.

Sheila Rae, the Brave. Kevin Henkes. LC 86-25761. (Illus.). 32p. (gr. k-3). 1987. 11.95 (ISBN 0-317-60820-7); PLB 11.88 (ISBN 0-688-07156-2). Greenwillow.

Sheila Rae, The Brave. Kevin Henkes. (ps-3). 1988. pap. 3.95 (ISBN 0-14-050897-X, Puffin Bks). Penguin.

Sheit: A No-Nonsense Guidebook to Writing & Using Nonsexist Language. Val Dumond. 60p. (Orig.). 1984. pap. 8.95 (ISBN 0-9613673-0-X). V Dumond.

Shek-Wan Pottery. Hong Kong Museum of Art. 234p. 1977. 50.00x (ISBN 0-317-44189-2, Pub. by Han-Shan Tang Ltd). State Mutual Bk.

Shekhina: Forty Poems. Norma Farber. LC 83-73424. 96p. 1984. 15.95 (ISBN 0-9610662-1-0); pap. 9.95 (ISBN 0-9610662-2-9). Capstone Edns.

Shekhinah. Eleanor Wilner. LC 84-2511. (Phoenix Poets Ser.). 80p. 1985. lib. bdg. 15.00x (ISBN 0-226-90025-8); pap. 6.95 (ISBN 0-226-90026-6). U of Chicago Pr.

Shelburne Essays. Paul E. More. 1904. 15.00 (ISBN 0-8274-3895-8). R West.

Shelburne Essays, 11 vols. Ed. by Paul E. More. Incl. Vol. 1. 1904. 253p. (ISBN 0-685-22556-9); Vol. 2. 1905. 253p. (ISBN 0-685-22557-7); Vol. 3. 1906. 265p. (ISBN 0-685-22558-5); Vol. 4. 1906. 286p. (ISBN 0-685-22559-3); Vol. 5. 1908. 216p. (ISBN 0-685-22560-7); Vol. 6. Studies in Religious Dualism, 1909. 355p. (ISBN 0-685-22561-5); Vol. 7. 1910. 272p. (ISBN 0-685-22562-3); Vol. 8. Drift of Romanticism, 1913. 316p. (ISBN 0-685-22563-1); Vol. 9. Aristocracy & Justice, 1915. 253p. (ISBN 0-685-22564-X); Vol. 10. With the Wits, 1919. 323p. (ISBN 0-685-22565-8); Vol. 11. A New England Group & Others, 1921. 300p. (ISBN 0-685-22566-6). LC 67-17764. 1967. Repr. of 1921 ed. 20.00 ea.; Set. 150.00x (ISBN 0-87753-028-9). Phaeton.

Shelburne Essays: Second Series. P. E. More. Repr. 15.00 (ISBN 0-8274-3896-6). R West.

Shelby Mustang Muscle Cars 1965-70. R. M. Clarke. (Illus.). 100p. (Orig.). 1984. pap. 13.95 (ISBN 0-946489-40-8, Pub. by Brooklands Bks England). Motorbooks Intl.

Shelby's Wildlife. 2nd ed. Wallace Wyss. (Illus.). 224p. 1987. pap. 19.95 (ISBN 0-87938-257-0). Motorbooks Intl.

Sheldon Boxed Set: Bloodline, A Stranger in the Mirror, Rage of Angels. Sidney Sheldon. 1988. Set. pap. 14.85 (ISBN 0-446-11284-4). Warner Bks.

Sheldon Memorial Art Gallery Cookbook. Ed. by Jean L. Martin et al. LC 78-10588. (Illus.). 212p. 1978. pap. 13.95 (ISBN 0-9602018-1-5). Nebraska Art.

Sheldon's Retail Directory, 1988. 104th ed. Ed. by Kenneth W. Phelon, Jr. 730p. 1988. pap. 100.00 (ISBN 0-942239-02-4). P S & M Inc.

Sheldon's Retail, 1986. 101st ed. 650p. 1986. 100.00 (ISBN 0-317-55720-3). B Klein Pubns.

Shelf. Kay Dick. 128p. 1986. pap. 6.50 (ISBN 0-85449-002-7, Pub. by GMP England). Alyson Pubns.

Shelf Access in Libraries. Richard J. Hyman. (Studies in Librarianship: No. 9). 190p. 1982. pap. 12.50x (ISBN 0-8389-0357-6, 81-22764). ALA.

Shelf Browsing, Open Access & Storage Capacity in Research Libraries. John J. Boll. (Occasional Papers: No. 169). 1985. pap. 3.00 (ISBN 0-317-59022-7). U of Ill Lib Info Sci.

Shelf Display Pack of Project Plan Book. 1984. 71.10 (ISBN 0-938708-10-4). L F Garlinghouse Co.

Shelf Life: A Key to Sharpening Your Competitive Edge: Proceedings. Food Processors Institute Staff. 64p. (Orig.). 1981. pap. 10.00 (ISBN 0-937774-05-7). Food Processors.

Shelf Life of Foods & Beverages. Ed. by G. Charalambous. (Developments in Food Science Ser.: No. 12). 828p. 1986. 242.00 (ISBN 0-444-42611-6). Elsevier.

Shelf of Lincoln Books: A Critical, Selective Bibliography of Lincolniana. Paul M. Angle. LC 46-25256. pap. 40.50 (ISBN 0-317-10291-5, 2050456). Bks Demand UMI.

Shelf of Old Books. James T. Fields. 215p. 1982. Repr. of 1894 ed. lib. bdg. 50.00 (ISBN 0-89987-267-0). Darby Bks.

Shelf Sands & Sandstone Reservoirs. Roderick W. Tillman et al. (Short Course Notes Ser.: No. 13). 708p. 1985. pap. 44.00 (ISBN 0-918985-57-9). SEPM.

Shelfbreak: Critical Interface on Continental Margins. Ed. by Daniel J. Stanley & George T. Moore. (Special Publication Ser.: No. 33). 467p. 1983. 29.00 (ISBN 0-918985-13-7). SEPM.

Shelflist of Congressional Committee Hearings (Not Confidential in Character) in the United States Senate Library from 86th Congress (January 7, 1959) Through 91st Congress (January 2, 1971) LC 74-22115. 688p. 1975. 38.95 (ISBN 0-8371-7838-X, CHJ/). Greenwood.

Shelflist of Congressional Hearings (Not Confidential in Character) Prior to January 3, 1935 in the United States Senate Library. U. S. Congress-Senate Library. LC 78-159498. 716p. 1971. Repr. lib. bdg. 36.95 (ISBN 0-8371-6187-8, CHF/). Greenwood.

Shelflist on Congressional Hearings (Not Confidential in Character) 74th Through 85th Congress (January 3, 1935 to January 3, 1959) U. S. Congress - Senate Library. LC 72-590. 1108p. 1973. Repr. lib. bdg. 46.95 (ISBN 0-8371-6032-4, CHH/). Greenwood.

Shelia's Dying. Alden R. Carter. LC 86-25129. 208p. (gr. 8 up). 1987. 13.95 (ISBN 0-399-21405-4, Putnam). Putnam Pub Group.

Shelkagari. Harold King. LC 84-81328. 384p. 1987. 18.95 (ISBN 0-917657-09-8). D I Fine.

Shelkagari. Harold King. 608p. 1988. pap. 4.50 (ISBN 1-55802-154-X). Lynx Bks.

Shell Africa: North & West. Date not set. write for info. S&S.

Shell Africa: North & West. (Baedeker-Shell Roadmaps Ser.). 7.95 (ISBN 0-13-808486-6). P-H.

Shell Alps. (Baedeker-Shell Roadmaps Ser.). 6.95 (ISBN 0-317-51998-0). P-H.

Shell & Apatial Structures: Computational Aspects: Proceedings of the International Symposium, Leuven, Belgium, July, 1986. Ed. by G. De Roeck et al. (Lecture Notes in Engineering Ser.: Vol. 26). 495p. 1987. pap. 60.00 (ISBN 0-387-17498-2). Springer-Verlag.

Shell & the Pearl. Roger White. 32p. 1985. pap. 3.00 (ISBN 0-85398-205-8). G Ronald Pub.

Shell & Tube Heat Exchangers. Ed. by William R. Apblett, Jr. 1982. 82.00 (ISBN 0-87170-145-6). ASM.

Shell & Tube Heat Exchangers, Rotating Equipment, Bins, Silos, Stacks see Mechanical Design of Process Systems.

Shell Art: A Handbook for Making Flowers, Mosaics, Jewelry & Other Ornaments. Helen Krauss. 14.00 (ISBN 0-8446-5473-6). Peter Smith.

Shell Art: A Handbook for Making Shell Flowers, Mosaics, Jewelry. rev. ed. Helen K. Krauss. LC 75-21356. (Illus.). 136p. 1976. pap. 3.95 (ISBN 0-486-23255-7). Dover.

Shell Auto Care Guide. Ross R. Olney. 304p. 1986. pap. 8.95 (ISBN 0-671-62788-0, Fireside); 16.45 (ISBN 0-671-61083-X). S&S.

She'll Be Comin' 'round the Mountain. Reissue. ed. Robert Quackenbush. LC 73-2943. (Illus.). 40p. (ps up). 1988. Repr. of 1973 ed. PLB 12.89 (ISBN 0-397-32266-6, Lipp Jr Bks). HarpJ.

Shell-Bearing Land Snails of Ohio. Celeste Taft. 1961. 3.50 (ISBN 0-86727-045-4). Ohio Bio Survey.

Shell Bed to Shell Midden. Betty Meehan. (AIAS New Ser.: No. 37). 187p. 1982. text ed. 22.50x (ISBN 0-391-02243-1); pap. text ed. 15.00x o. p. Humanities.

Shell Book: A Complete Guide to Collecting & Identifying. 5th ed. Sandra D. Romashko. LC 76-360976. (Illus.). 64p. 1984. pap. 3.95 (ISBN 0-89317-000-3). Windward Pub.

Shell Book of Beachcombing. Tony Soper. LC 73-5276. (Illus.). 128p. 1973. 5.50 (ISBN 0-8008-7177-4). Taplinger.

Shell Book of British Buildings. Anthony McIntyre. (Illus.). 384p. 1984. 29.95 (ISBN 0-7153-8122-9). David & Charles.

Shell Book of British Walks. John Whatmore. (Illus.). 368p. 1988. 34.95 (ISBN 0-7153-8810-X). David & Charles.

Shell Book of Inland Waterways. rev. ed. Hugh McKnight. (Illus.). 493p. 1988. 29.95 (ISBN 0-7153-8239-X). David & Charles.

Shell Book of the British Coast. Adrian Robinson & Roy Millward. (Illus.). 496p. (Orig.). 1983. 34.95 (ISBN 0-7153-8150-4). David & Charles.

Shell Book of the Islands of Britain. British Tourist Authority Staff. 198p. 1982. 19.95 (ISBN 0-7112-0087-4, Pub. by British Tour). Salem Hse Pubs.

Shell Burst Pond. Richard E. Baker. (Illus.). 1982. pap. 3.00 (ISBN 0-942648-02-1). Vardaman Pr.

Shell Collector's Field Guide. Idaz Greenberg. (Illus.). 1985. incl. plastic card 5.00x (ISBN 0-913008-16-8). Seahawk Pr.

Shell-Corner Method. Li Kung Shaw. LC 83-60572. 332p. 1984. Standard words ed. 20.00 (ISBN 0-9607806-5-3); Xin hua ed., 1986, 240pps. 20.00 (ISBN 0-9607806-6-1). Li Kung Shaw.

Shell Countryside Book. Richard Muir & Eric Duffey. 318p. 1984. 24.95 (ISBN 0-460-04626-8, BKX 05256, Pub. by J M Dent England). Biblio Dist.

Shell Dredging & Its Influence on Gulf Coast Environments. Ed. by Arnold H. Bouma. LC 75-39416. 464p. 1976. 50.00x (ISBN 0-87201-805-9). Gulf Pub.

Shell Europe. Date not set. write for info. S&S.

Shell Fish. Emile Zola. Repr. lib. bdg. 8.95x (ISBN 0-88411-290-X, Pub. by Aeonian Pr). Amereon Ltd.

Shell France. Baedeker's. 1985. pap. 5.95 (ISBN 0-13-808544-7). P-H.

Shell from Cape Cod to Cape May. Morris Jacobson. 1988. 14.75 (ISBN 0-8446-6329-8). Peter Smith.

Shell Game. Douglas Terman. 448p. 1985. 17.95 (ISBN 0-671-53292-8, Pub. by Poseidon). S&S.

Shell Game. Douglas Terman. 1986. pap. 4.50 (ISBN 0-671-53291-X). PB.

Shell Game: Reflections on Rowing. Stephen Kiesling. LC 81-14187. 192p. 1982. 10.50 (ISBN 0-688-00958-1). Morrow.

Shell Game: Reflections on Rowing & the Pursuit of Excellence. Stephen Kiesling. 208p. 1983. pap. 8.95 (ISBN 0-8092-5570-7). Contemp Bks.

Shell Germany. Baedeker's. 1985. pap. 5.95 (ISBN 0-13-808551-X). P-H.

Shell: Gift of the Sea. Hugh Stix et al. (Illus.). 164p. 1985. 14.98 (ISBN 0-8109-8058-4). Abrams.

Shell Great Britain. Baedeker's. 1985. pap. 5.95 (ISBN 0-13-808569-2). P-H.

Shell Greece. Baedeker's. 1985. pap. 5.95 (ISBN 0-13-808577-3). P-H.

Shell Guide to France. Ed. by Edward Young. (Illus.). 1979. 11.98 (ISBN 0-393-08842-1). Norton.

Shell Guide to the History of London. W. R. Dalzell. (Illus.). 1981. 29.95 (ISBN 0-393-01593-9). Norton.

Shell Guide to the History of London. W. R. Dalzell. (Illus.). 528p. 1988. pap. 22.95 (ISBN 0-7181-2977-6). Penguin.

Shell-Heaps of the Lower Fraser River, British Columbia. Harlan I. Smith. LC 73-3519. (Jesup North Pacific Expedition. Publications: Vol. 2, Pt. 4). Repr. of 1903 ed. 24.50 (ISBN 0-404-58120-X). AMS Pr.

Shell Italy. Baedeker's. 1985. pap. 5.95 (ISBN 0-13-808601-X). P-H.

Shell Lady's Daughter. C. S. Adler. LC 82-19801. 144p. (gr. 6 up). 1983. pap. 10.95 (ISBN 0-698-20580-4, Coward). Putnam Pub Group.

Shell Mexico. Date not set. write for info. S&S.

Shell Mexico. (Baedeker-Shell Roadmaps Ser.). 5.95 (ISBN 0-13-808635-4). P-H.

Shell Middle East. Date not set. write for info. S&S.

Shell Middle East. (Baedeker-Shell Roadmaps Ser.). 7.95 (ISBN 0-13-808643-5). P-H.

Shell Money of the Slave Trade. Jan Hogendorn & Marion Johnson. (African Studies: No. 49). (Illus.). 230p. 1986. 37.50 (ISBN 0-521-32086-0). Cambridge U Pr.

Shell-Mounds of Ogido in Riu-Kiu. Ed. by Matsumura Akira. 66p. 1950. 200.00x (Pub. by Han-Shan Tang Ltd). State Mutual Bk.

Shell Mounds of Omori. Edward S. Morse. 36p. 1879. 2450.00x (Pub. by Han-Shan Tang Ltd). State Mutual Bk.

Shell Process Control Workshop. David M. Prett & Manfred Morari. (Illus.). 336p. 1987. text ed. 45.00 (ISBN 0-409-90136-9). Butterworth.

Shell Process Foundry Practice. 2nd ed. 158p. 1973. 50.00 (ISBN 0-317-32670-8, GM7311); members 25.00 (ISBN 0-317-32671-6). Am Foundrymen.

Shell Scandinavia. (Baedeker-Shell Roadmaps Ser.). 6.95 (ISBN 0-317-52003-2). P-H.

Shell, Sea Shell. Liam Lynch. 192p. 1984. 17.95 (ISBN 0-905473-80-9, Pub. by Wolfhound Pr Ireland); pap. 7.95 (Pub. by Wolfhound Pr Ireland). Irish Bks Media.

Shell Seekers. Rosamunde Pilcher. 560p. 1988. 19.95x (ISBN 0-312-01058-3, Pub. by Thomas Dunne Bks). St Martin.

Shell Seekers. Rosamunde Pilcher. (YA) (gr. 7 up). 1989. pap. price not set (ISBN 0-440-20204-3). Dell.

Shell Seekers. Rosamunde Pilcher. LC 88-14756. 909p. 1988. Repr. of 1987 ed. lib. bdg. 20.95 (ISBN 0-89621-166-5). Thorndike Pr.

Shell-Shock & Other Neuropsychiatric Problems Presented in Five Hundred & Eighty-Nine Case Histories from the War Literature, 1914-1918. Elmer E. Southard. LC 73-2416. (Mental Illness & Social Policy; the American Experience Ser.). Repr. of 1919 ed. 62.00 (ISBN 0-405-05226-X). Ayer Co Pubs.

Shell Spain-Portugal. (Baedeker-Shell Roadmaps Ser.). 4.95 (ISBN 0-13-808676-1). P-H.

Shell Structures: Stability & Strength. Ed. by R. Narayanan. 360p. 1985. 93.75 (ISBN 0-85334-343-8, Pub. by Elsevier Applied Sci England). Elsevier.

Shell Theory. F. I. Niordson. (Applied Mathematics & Mechanics Ser.: Vol. 29). 402p. 1985. 55.00 (ISBN 0-444-87640-5, North Holland). Elsevier.

Shell Theory: General Methods of Construction. I. N. Vekna. 288p. 1986. 120.00 (ISBN 0-470-20653-5, Co-Pub. with Longman). Wiley.

Shell Theory of the Nucleus. Eugene Feenberg. LC 54-9017. (Investigations in Physics: No. 3). pap. 55.80 (ISBN 0-317-09267-7, 2000630). Bks Demand UMI.

Shell Yugoslavia. Date not set. write for info. S&S.

Shell Yugoslavia. (Baedeker-Shell Roadmaps Ser.). 6.95 (ISBN 0-13-808700-8). P-H.

Shellbby Rumford: The Story of a Happy Rabbit. Bernice D. Smith. (Illus.). 64p. (ps-2). 1984. 5.50 (ISBN 0-682-40177-3). Exposition-Phoenix.

Shellcraft Animals. Patricia Pope. LC 75-15906. (Short-Time Projects for Beginners). (Illus.). 32p. (Orig.). 1975. pap. 1.00 (ISBN 0-8200-0507-X). Great Outdoors.

Shellcraft Creations: Short Time Projects for Beginners. Gloria V. Sexton. 1981. pap. 1.00 (ISBN 0-8200-0510-X). Great Outdoors.

Shellcraft Critters: Short Time Projects for Beginners. Kellum. (Illus.). 1977. pap. 1.00 (ISBN 0-8200-0509-6). Great Outdoors.

Shellcraft Instruction. Marjorie Pelosi & Frank Pelosi. (Orig.). pap. 3.95 (ISBN 0-8200-0501-0). Great Outdoors.

Shellcraft Necklaces. Sexton. (Illus.). 1981. pap. 1.00 (ISBN 0-8200-0511-8). Great Outdoors.

Shelley. Ruth Bailey. LC 74-1442. 1934. lib. bdg. 12.50 (ISBN 0-8414-9910-1). Folcroft.

Shelley. Oliver Elton. 1978. Repr. of 1924 ed. lib. bdg. 17.00 (ISBN 0-8495-1314-6). Arden Lib.

Shelley. Oliver Elton. LC 76-17044. 1924. lib. bdg. 15.00 (ISBN 0-8414-3975-3). Folcroft.

Shelley. Adolphus A. Jack. LC 72-193220. 1904. lib. bdg. 16.00 (ISBN 0-8414-5352-7). Folcroft.

Shelley. Compiled by & illus. by Patricia Machin. (Pocket Poets Ser.). (Illus.). 52p. 1987. 4.95 (ISBN 0-88162-299-0). Salem Hse Pubs.

Shelley. David Pirie. (Open Guides to Literature Ser.). 128p. 1988. 46.00x (ISBN 0-335-15091-8, Open Univ Pr); pap. 13.00x (ISBN 0-335-15082-9, Open Univ Pr). Taylor & Francis.

Shelley. Percy Bysshe Shelley. (Plain Texts of the Poets Ser). 1968. pap. 2.50x (ISBN 0-7022-0676-8). U of Queensland Pr.

Shelley. John A. Symonds. LC 68-58400. (English Men of Letters). Repr. of 1887 ed. 12.50 (ISBN 0-404-51732-3). AMS Pr.

Shelley. John A. Symonds. 1979. Repr. of 1881 ed. 17.00 (ISBN 0-8495-4924-8). Arden Lib.

Shelley. John A. Symonds. 1973. lib. bdg. 17.00 (ISBN 0-8414-8025-7). Folcroft.

Shelley. John A. Symonds. 189p. 1983. Repr. of 1879 ed. lib. bdg. 22.50 (ISBN 0-89984-612-2). Century Bookbindery.

Shelley. Sydney Waterlow. LC 71-103216. 1970. Repr. of 1913 ed. 15.00x (ISBN 0-8046-0853-9, Pub. by Kennikat). Assoc Faculty Pr.

Shelley. Sydney Waterlow. 1979. 42.50 (ISBN 0-685-59718-0). Bern Porter.

Shelley. D. Wellesley. (English Poets in Pictures). 1941. Repr. 10.00 (ISBN 0-8274-3388-3). R West.

Shelley: A Critical Biography. George B. Smith. LC 73-16290. (Studies in Shelley, No. 25). 1974. lib. bdg. 49.95x (ISBN 0-8383-1727-8). Haskell.

Shelley: A Critical Reading. Earl R. Wasserman. LC 70-138036. (Illus.). 512p. 1971. pap. 14.95x (ISBN 0-8018-2017-0). Johns Hopkins.

Shelley: A Prelude. Robert Martin-Baynat. LC 72-193207. 1946. lib. bdg. 18.50 (ISBN 0-8414-6483-9). Folcroft.

Shelley Also Known As Shirley. Shelley Winters. 512p. 1981. pap. 3.50 (ISBN 0-345-29506-4). Ballantine.

Shelley: An Essay. A. Jack. 35.00 (ISBN 0-8490-1048-9). Gordon Pr.

Shelley: An Essay. Adolphus A. Jack. LC 70-113337. 1970. Repr. of 1904 ed. 20.00x (ISBN 0-8046-1022-3, Pub. by Kennikat). Assoc Faculty Pr.

Shelley & Browning: A Myth & Some Facts. Frederick A. Pottle. LC 65-18629. (Illus.). 94p. 1965. Repr. of 1923 ed. 16.00 (ISBN 0-208-00545-5, Archon). Shoe String.

Shelley & Byron. Isabel Clarke. LC 74-118006. (English Literature Ser., No. 33). 1970. Repr. of 1934 ed. lib. bdg. 49.95x (ISBN 0-8383-1062-1). Haskell.

Shelley & Byron: The Snake & Eagle Wreathed in Fight. Charles E. Robinson. LC 75-36927. 304p. 1976. 34.50x (ISBN 0-8018-1707-2). Johns Hopkins.

Shelley & His Circle: Seventeen Seventy-Three to Eighteen Twenty-Two, 6 Vols. Ed. by Percy Bysshe Shelley. Incl. Vol. 1. (Illus.). l, 474p. 1961; Vol. 2. Ed. by Kenneth N. Cameron. (Illus.). xvi, 545p. 1961. Vols. 1 & 2. boxed set 85.00x (ISBN 0-674-80610-7); Vol. 3. Ed. by Donald H. Reiman. (Illus.). xxxvi, 485p. 1970; Vol. 4. (Illus.). xviii, 529p. 1970. Vols. 3 & 4. boxed set 85.00x (ISBN 0-674-80611-5); Vols. 5-6. (Illus.). 1973. boxed set 85.00x (ISBN 0-674-80612-3); Ed. by Donald J Reiman. 1308p. 1985. Vols. 7 & 8. boxed set 100.00x (ISBN 0-674-80613-1). LC 60-5393. (Carl H. Pforzheimer Library). Harvard U Pr.

Shelley & His Friends in Italy. H. R. Angeli. LC 72-3197. (Studies in Shelley, No.25). 1972. Repr. of 1911 ed. lib. bdg. 52.95x (ISBN 0-8383-1539-9). Haskell.

Shelley & His Friends in Italy. H. R. Angeli. 1911. Repr. 15.75 (ISBN 0-8274-3391-3). R West.

Shelley & His Poetry. E. W. Edmunds. LC 74-23905. 1911. lib. bdg. 27.50 (ISBN 0-8414-3953-2). Folcroft.

Shelley & His Poetry. Edward W. Edmunds. LC 78-120961. (Poetry & Life Ser.). Repr. of 1912 ed. 7.25 (ISBN 0-404-52511-3). AMS Pr.

Shelley & His Poetry. Edward W. Edmunds. LC 76-52970. (Studies in Shelley, No. 25). 1977. lib. bdg. 39.95x (ISBN 0-8383-2124-0). Haskell.

Shelley & His Writings, 2 vols. Charles S. Middleton. LC 72-11587. 1973. lib. bdg. 97.50 (ISBN 0-8414-0909-9). Folcroft.

Shelley & Keats as They Struck Their Contemporaries. E. Blunden. LC 70-174689. (English Literature Ser., No. 33). 1971. Repr. of 1925 ed. lib. bdg. 39.95x (ISBN 0-8383-1341-8). Haskell.

Shelley & Keats as They Struck Their Contemporaries. Edmund Blunden. LC 74-16306. 1925. lib. bdg. 25.00 (ISBN 0-8414-9878-4). Folcroft.

Shelley, & Other Essays. facs. ed. George H. Cowling. LC 67-23198. (Essay Index Reprint Ser). 1936. 17.00 (ISBN 0-8369-0344-7). Ayer Co Pubs.

Shelley & the Concept of Humanity: A Study of His Moral Vision. James Brazell. Ed. by James Hogg. (Romantic Reassessment Ser.). 300p. (Orig.). 1972. pap. 15.00 (ISBN 0-317-40094-0, Pub. by Salzburg Studies). Longwood Pub Group.

Shelley & the Dramatic Form. Sheila U. Singh. Ed. by James Hogg. (Romantic Reassessment Ser.). 243p. (Orig.). 1972. pap. 15.00 (ISBN 0-317-40095-9, Pub. by Salzburg Studies). Longwood Pub Group.

Shelley & the New Criticism: The Anatomy of a Critical Misvaluation. Wilfred C. Barton. Ed. by James Hogg. (Romantic Reassessment Ser.). 228p. (Orig.). 1973. pap. 15.00 (ISBN 0-317-40096-7, Pub. by Salzburg Studies). Longwood Pub Group.

Shelley & the Oppressors of Mankind. George Gordon. LC 76-15981. 1973. lib. bdg. 16.00 (ISBN 0-8414-4421-8). Folcroft.

Shelley & the Revolutionary Idea. Gerald McNiece. LC 75-88808. Repr. of 1969 ed. 79.30 (ISBN 0-8357-9178-5, 2011601). Bks Demand UMI.

Shelley & the Romantic Revolution. F. Lea. LC 71-164028. (Studies in Shelley, No. 25). 1971. Repr. of 1945 ed. lib. bdg. 52.95x (ISBN 0-8383-1328-0). Haskell.

Shelley & the Romantic Revolution. F. A. Lea. LC 76-23425. 1945. lib. bdg. 39.00 (ISBN 0-8414-5801-4). Folcroft.

Shelley & the Sublime: An Interpretation of the Major Poems. Angela Leighton. LC 83-7818. 208p. 1984. 39.50 (ISBN 0-521-25089-7); pap. 13.95 (ISBN 0-521-27202-5). Cambridge U Pr.

Shelley & the Unromantics. Olwen W. Campbell. LC 68-1189. (Studies in Shelley, No. 25). 1969. Repr. of 1924 ed. lib. bdg. 51.95x (ISBN 0-8383-0652-7). Haskell.

Shelley at Oxford. Thomas J. Hogg. LC 74-17483. 1974. Repr. of 1904 ed. lib. bdg. 29.00 (ISBN 0-8414-4881-7). Folcroft.

Shelley at Oxford: Early Correspondence of P. B. Shelley with His Friend, T. J. Hogg. Walter S. Scott. (Together with letters of Mary Shelley & T. L. Peacock & a hitherto unpublished prose fragment by Shelley). 1944. Repr. 29.50 (ISBN 0-8274-3389-1). R West.

Shelley at Work: A Critical Enquiry. N. Rogers. 1956. Repr. 20.00 (ISBN 0-8274-3390-5). R West.

Shelley: Concept of Nature. R. De Loyola Furtado. 1973. Repr. of 1958 ed. 30.00 (ISBN 0-8274-0411-5). R West.

Shelley Correspondence in the Bodleian Library. Ed. by R. E. Hill. LC 75-30870. (Studies in Shelley, No. 25). 1975. lib. bdg. 46.95x (ISBN 0-8383-2101-1). Haskell.

Shelley Correspondence in the Bodleian Library. R. H. Hill. LC 77-5169. 1926. lib. bdg. 27.00 (ISBN 0-8414-4876-0). Folcroft.

Shelley, Dryden, & Mr. Eliot in Rehabilitations. C. S. Lewis. 1973. 37.00 (ISBN 0-8274-1043-3). R West.

Shelley: His Life & Work, 2 Vols. Walter E. Peck. 1969. Repr. of 1927 ed. 47.00 (ISBN 0-8337-2702-8). B Franklin.

Shelley: His Theory of Poetry. Melvin T. Solve. LC 75-30014. Repr. of 1927 ed. 16.50 (ISBN 0-404-14020-3). AMS Pr.

Shelley: His Thought & Work. 3rd ed. Desmond King-Hele. LC 83-14242. 416p. 1984. 30.00 (ISBN 0-8386-3199-1). Fairleigh Dickinson.

Shelley in America in the Nineteenth Century. J. Power. LC 65-15892. (Studies in Shelley, No. 25). 1969. Repr. of 1940 ed. lib. bdg. 49.95x (ISBN 0-8383-0611-X). Haskell.

Shelley in America in the Nineteenth Century. Julia Power. LC 70-90370. 233p. 1969. Repr. of 1940 ed. 27.50x (ISBN 0-87752-088-7). Gordian.

Shelley in England, 2 vols. Roger Ingpen. 1973. Repr. of 1917 ed. Set. 80.00 (ISBN 0-8274-0014-4). R West.

Shelley in England: New Facts & Letters from the Shelley-Whitton Papers, 3 vols. Roger Ingpen. 711p. 1980. Repr. of 1917 ed. lib. bdg. 125.00 set (ISBN 0-8414-5078-1). Folcroft.

Shelley in English Poets Vol. 4. F. W. Myers. Ed. by T. H. Ward. 20.00 (ISBN 0-8274-3392-1). R West.

Shelley in Germany. Solomon Liptzin. LC 24-14279. (Columbia University. Germanic Studies, Old Series: No. 27). Repr. of 1924 ed. 17.00 (ISBN 0-404-50427-2). AMS Pr.

Shelley in Italy: An Anthology Selected with an Introduction. John Lehman. Repr. of 1947 ed. 25.00 (ISBN 0-8492-9952-7). R West.

Shelley in the Twentieth Century: A Study of the Development of Shelley Criticism in England & America, 1916-1971. Nancy Fogarty. Ed. by James Hogg. (Romantic Reassessment Ser.). 179p. (Orig.). 1976. pap. 15.00 (ISBN 3-7052-0511-0, Pub. by Salzburg Studies). Longwood Pub Group.

Shelley Legend. Robert M. Smith. LC 67-27652. 1945. Repr. 28.50x (ISBN 0-8046-0428-2, Pub. by Kennikat). Assoc Faculty Pr.

Shelley-Leigh Hunt: How Friendship Made History. Reginald Johnson. LC 72-3431. (Studies in Shelley, No. 25). 1972. Repr. of 1929 ed. lib. bdg. 56.95x (ISBN 0-8383-1536-4). Haskell.

Shelley Library. Maurice B. Forman. LC 78-116794. (Studies in Shelley, No. 25). 1970. Repr. of 1886 ed. lib. bdg. 39.95x (ISBN 0-8383-1036-2). Haskell.

Shelley Library. Thomas J. Wise. LC 78-122990. (Studies in Shelley, No. 25). 1970. Repr. of 1924 ed. lib. bdg. 49.95x (ISBN 0-8383-1123-7). Haskell.

Shelley Library, an Essay in Bibliography. H. Buxton Forman. LC 74-30296. (Shelley Society, Fourth Ser.: No. 1). Repr. of 1886 ed. 24.00 (ISBN 0-404-11513-6). AMS Pr.

Shelley Memorials. Jane G. Shelley. 1859. Repr. 24.00x (ISBN 0-403-00299-0). Scholarly.

Shelley Memorials from Authentic Sources. Walter Sidney Scott. (To which is added an Essay on Christianity by percy Bysshe Shelley). 1859. Repr. 25.00 (ISBN 0-8274-3393-X). R West.

Shelley Memorials: From Authentic Sources. Ed. by Lady Shelley. 1978. Repr. of 1859 ed. lib. bdg. 45.00 (ISBN 0-8414-7949-6). Folcroft.

Shelley-Moore Debate (Baptism, Sprinkling or Immersion) pap. 3.95 (ISBN 0-89315-256-0). Lambert Bk.

Shelley Notebook in the Harvard College Library. George E. Woodberry. LC 72-129913. 1929. lib. bdg. 30.00 (ISBN 0-8414-9388-X). Folcroft.

Shelley on Love: An Anthology. Percy Bysshe Shelley. Ed. by Richard Holmes. LC 80-53387. 248p. 1981. 19.95x (ISBN 0-520-04322-7). U of Cal Pr.

Shelley: Poems. Percy Bysshe Shelley. (Poetry Library). 304p. 1985. pap. 4.95 (ISBN 0-14-058504-4). Penguin.

Shelley, Poems Published in 1820. Ed. by A. M. Huges. 224p. 1981. Repr. of 1910 ed. lib. bdg. 25.00 (ISBN 0-8495-5050-5). Arden Lib.

Shelley: Poetry & Prose. Percy Bysshe Shelley. LC 76-29404. Repr. of 1931 ed. 18.50 (ISBN 0-404-15323-2). AMS Pr.

Shelley Potteries: The History & Production of a Staffordshire Family of Potters. Chris Watkins et al. (Illus.). 279p. 1989. 55.00 (Pub. by Century Hutchinson). David & Charles.

Shelley Primer. H. S. Salt. LC 74-30299. (Shelley Society, Fourth Ser.: No. 4). Repr. of 1887 ed. 24.00 (ISBN 0-404-11516-0). AMS Pr.

Shelley Primer. Henry S. Salt. LC 68-26219. Repr. of 1887 ed. 17.50x (ISBN 0-8046-0402-9, Pub. by Kennikat). Assoc Faculty Pr.

Shelley Revalued: Essays from the Gregynog Conference. Ed. by Kelvin Everest. LC 83-3735. 248p. 1983. text ed. 28.50x (ISBN 0-389-20390-4). B&N Imports.

Shelley Society's Papers: Papers Read Before the Society & Abstracts of Any Not Fully Reported. Shelley, Society London. (First Ser.: No. 1). Repr. of 1891 ed. 45.00 (ISBN 0-404-11501-2). AMS Pr.

Shelley: The Critical Heritage. Ed. by James E. Barcus. (Critical Heritage Ser.). 1975. 36.00x (ISBN 0-7100-8148-0). Routledge Chapman & Hall.

Shelley: The Golden Years. Kenneth N. Cameron. LC 73-80566. 1974. text ed. 37.00x (ISBN 0-674-80605-0). Harvard U Pr.

Shelley: The Last Phase. Ivan Roe. LC 72-97078. (Illus.). 256p. 1973. Repr. of 1953 ed. lib. bdg. 25.00x (ISBN 0-8154-0464-6). Cooper Sq.

Shelley, the Man & the Poet. Robert Browning. LC 75-26948. 1975. Repr. of 1908 ed. lib. bdg. 20.00 (ISBN 0-8414-3248-1). Folcroft.

Shelley the Man & the Poet. Arthur Clutton-Brock. 16.25 (ISBN 0-8369-7106-X, 7940). Ayer Co Pubs.

Shelley: The Man & the Poet, 2 vols. Felix Rabbe. 1972. Repr. of 1888 ed. lib. bdg. 87.50 (ISBN 0-8414-7267-X). Folcroft.

Shelley: The Pursuit. Richard Holmes. 11.95 (ISBN 0-7043-3111-X, Pub. by Quartet England). Charles River Bks.

Shelley: The Pursuit. Richard Holmes. (Elizabeth Sifton Bks.). (Illus.). 848p. 1987. pap. 12.95 (ISBN 0-14-058037-9). Penguin.

Shelley the Seagull. Margaret S. Pursell. Tr. by Dyan Hammarberg from Fr. LC 76-29454. (Animal Friends Books). (Illus.). (gr. k-4). 1977. PLB 5.95 (ISBN 0-87614-083-5). Carolrhoda Bks.

Shelley, Trelawney & Henley. Samuel J. Looker. 1950. Repr. 20.00 (ISBN 0-8274-3897-4). R West.

Shelley's Adonais: A Critical Edition. Anthony D. Knerr. LC 83-7451. 360p. 1984. 26.50x (ISBN 0-231-05466-1). Columbia U Pr.

Shelley's Annus Mirabilis: The Maturing of an Epic Vision. Stuart Curran. LC 74-20037. (Illus.). 225p. 1975. 29.95 (ISBN 0-87328-064-4). Huntington Lib.

Shelley's Cenci Scorpions Ringed with Fire. Stuart Curran. LC 71-120753. (Illus.). 1970. 37.00x (ISBN 0-691-06196-3). Princeton U Pr.

Shelley's Critical Prose. Percy Bysshe Shelley. Ed. by Bruce R. McElderry, Jr. LC 66-19856. (Regents Critics Ser.). pap. 53.90 (2031990). Bks Demand UMI.

Shelley's Day: The Day of a Legally Blind Child. Candace C. Hall. (Illus.). 24p. (Orig.). (gr. k-6). 1980. pap. 2.95 (ISBN 0-9603840-0-6). Andrew Mtn Pr.

Shelley's Defence of Poetry & Blunden's Lectures on Defence. Edmund Blunden. LC 73-16387. 1948. lib. bdg. 15.00 (ISBN 0-8414-9852-0). Folcroft.

Shelley's Democracy. Laura J. Wylie. 1973. lib. bdg. 18.00 (ISBN 0-8414-9329-4). Folcroft.

Shelley's Early Life from Original Sources, with Curious Incidents, Letters, & Writings, Now First Published or Collected. Dennis F. MacCarthy. LC 76-18865. 1976. Repr. of 1872 ed. lib. bdg. 55.00 (ISBN 0-8414-6076-0). Folcroft.

Shenandoah National Park: An Interpretive Guide. John A. Conners. LC 87-90429. (Illus.). 200p. (Orig.). 1988. pap. price not set (ISBN 0-939923-02-5). M & W Pub Co.
Shenandoah Noah. Jim Aylesworth. LC 84-22554. (Illus.). 32p. (gr. k-2). 1985. 11.95 (ISBN 0-03-003749-2). H Holt & Co.
Shenandoah Pottery. Alvin H. Rice & John B. Stoudt. LC 29-20412. (Illus.). 277p. Repr. of 1929 ed. write for info. (ISBN 0-685-65083-9). Va Bk.
Shenandoah Saga: A Narrative History of the U. S. Navy's Pioneering Large Rigid Airship. 3rd rev Large Format ed. Thom Hook. Ed. by T. G. Settle. LC 73-86973. (Famous Airships Ser.). (Illus.). 208p. 1981. pap. 8.95 (ISBN 0-9601506-3-3). Airsho Pubs.
Shenandoah: The Story Behind the Scenery. Hugh Crandall. LC 74-30797. (Illus.). 32p. 1975. pap. 4.50 (ISBN 0-916122-15-8). KC Pubns.
Shenandoah Valley Family Data 1799-1813. Johannes Braun. Ed. & tr. by Klaus Wust. 1978. pap. 7.75 (ISBN 0-917968-05-0). Shenandoah Hist.
Shenandoah Valley Pioneers & Their Descendants. Thomas K. Cartmell. LC 64-1062. (Illus.). 572p. Repr. of 1909 ed. write for info. (ISBN 0-686-63647-3). Va Bk.
Shenandoah Vestiges: What the Mountain People Left Behind. Carolyn Reeder & Jack Reeder. LC 80-81761. 72p. 1980. pap. 5.00 (ISBN 0-915746-14-X). Potomac Appalach.
Shenanigan. Howard J. Chesshire. LC 75-5226. (Illus.). pap. 2.75 (ISBN 0-9603226-0-4). Mandala Bks.
Shenanigans of Mr. B. Eleanor Archer-Lofton. 32p. 1986. 6.50 (ISBN 0-8062-2968-3). Carlton.
Shenfan. William Hinllton. 840p. 1983. 160.00x (Pub. by Han-Shan Tang Ltd). State Mutual Bk.
Shenfan: The Continuing Revolution in a Chinese Village. William Hinton. LC 84-40004. 848p. 1984. pap. 10.95 (ISBN 0-394-72378-3, Vin). Random.
Shenstone's Miscellany 1759-1763. Ed. by Ian A. Gordon. 164p. 1983. lib. bdg. 50.00 (ISBN 0-89984-222-4). Century Bookbindery.
Shenzhou Geoguang JI 1-21. 1972. 7000.00x (ISBN 0-317-68860-X, Pub. by Shan-Han Tang Ltd). State Mutual Bk.
Sheolah's Easy Ways to Elegant Cooking. Sheilah Kaufman. 288p. 1983. pap. 7.95 (ISBN 0-671-50383-9). S&S.
Shepard Alonzo Mount: His Life & Art. Deborah J. Johnson. LC 87-36561. (Illus.). 64p. (Orig.). 1988. pap. 16.00 (ISBN 0-943924-12-X). Mus Stony Brook.
Shepard's Acts & Cases by Popular Names: Federal & State. 3rd ed. LC 85-30336. Date not set. write for info. (Shepards-Mcgraw). McGraw.
Shepard's Atlantic Reporter Citations. 3rd ed. Shepard's McGraw-Hill Staff. LC 86-1974. Date not set. price not set (Shepards-McGraw). McGraw.
Shepard's Calendar & the Ruins of Time. Edmund Spenser. (Illus.). 175p. 1986. 147.50 (ISBN 0-89266-558-0). Am Classical Coll Pr.
Shepard's Code of Federal Regulations Citations: A Compilation of Citations to the Code of Federal Regulations, Presidential Proclamations, Executive Orders & Reorganization Plans. 2nd ed. LC 85-30335. Date not set. write for info. (Shepards-McGraw). McGraw.
Shepard's Florida Citations. 5th ed. Shepard's McGraw-Hill Staff. LC 86-3809. Date not set. price not set (Shepards-McGraw). McGraw.
Shepards Handbook. 2nd ed. Ralph W. Neighbour, Jr. (Illus.). 124p. 1987. 9.95 (ISBN 0-937931-27-6). Global TN.
Shepard's Illinois Case Names Citator. Shepard's & McGraw-Hill Staff. LC 85-14612. write for info. (Shepards). McGraw.
Shepard's Iowa Case Names Citator: A Compilation of Case Names & Citations of Iowa Cases Decided from 1925 to the Present: the Case Names & Citations Appear in Iowa Reports, Northwestern Reporter (Iowa Cases), Northwestern Reporter, Second Series (Iowa Cases) Shepard's McGraw-Hill. LC 85-11899. write for info. McGraw.
Shepard's Kansas Citations. Shepard's & McGraw-Hill Staffs. LC 85-18396. write for info. (Shepards). McGraw.
Shepard's Kentucky Case Names Citator: A Compilation of Case Names & Citations of Kentucky Cases Decided from 1940 to the Present. Shepard's McGraw-Hill Staff. LC 86-6450. Date not set. price not set (Shepards-McGraw). McGraw.
Shepard's Law Review Citations: A Compilation of Citations to Law Reviews & Legal Periodicals. 4th ed. Shepard's McGraw-Hill Staff. LC 86-4002. Date not set. price not set (Shepards-McGraw). McGraw.
Shepard's Lawyer's Reference Manual. Shepard's & McGraw-Hill Staffs. LC 83-20035. x, 800p. 1983. text ed. 85.00 (ISBN 0-07-056736-0). Shepards-McGraw.
Shepard's Look at Psalm 23. Phillip Keller. 1976. 9.95 (ISBN 0-310-26790-0, 6780); large print 6.95 (ISBN 0-310-26797-8, 12553L). Zondervan.
Shepard's Manual of Federal Practice. 2nd ed. Shepard's & McGraw-Hill. Ed. by Rudolph W. Fischer & Richard A. Lavine. LC 79-9143. 860p. 1979. 80.00 (ISBN 0-07-056706-9). Shepards-McGraw.
Shepard's Maryland Case Names Citator. LC 85-18385. write for info. McGraw.
Shepard's Mobile Home Parks: Cases, Statutes, Ordinances, Regulations, Opinions, Tables & Schedules. Shepard's Citations, Inc. LC 75-28276. 488p. 1975. text ed. 90.00 (ISBN 0-07-056564-3). Shepards-McGraw.
Shepard's New Jersey Citations Cases. Ed. by Shepard's Citation Inc. Staff. LC 71-1597. Supplements available. 270.00 (ISBN 0-686-89835-4). Shepards-McGraw.
Shepard's New York Locator: A Complete Index to All Modern Sources of New York Law, 7 vols. LC 75-12781. 1975. 275.00 (ISBN 0-686-90059-6). Shepards-McGraw.
Shepard's Northwestern Reporter Citations: A Compilation of Citations to All Cases in the Norhtwestern Reporter, Including Affirmances. Ed. by Shepard's Citation, Inc. Staff. LC 52-2849. Supplements available. 400.00 (ISBN 0-686-90097-9). Shepards-McGraw.
Shepard's Oklahoma Case Names Citator: A Compilation of Case Names & Citations of Oklahoma Cases Decided from 1940 to the Present. LC 85-30335. Date not set. write for info. (Shepard's-McGraw). McGraw.
Shepard's Southern Reporter Citations: A Compilation of Citations to All Cases Reported in the Southern Reporter. 3rd ed. Shepard's McGraw Hill Staff. LC 86-15597. Date not set. write for info. Shepards-McGraw.
Shepard's Texas Case Names Citator. Shepard's-McGraw-Hill. 1983. 75.00 (ISBN 0-07-056743-3). McGraw.
Shepard's United States Citations: Statutes - Court Rules... 7th ed. LC 86-17769. Date not set. write for info. Shepards-McGraw.
Shephard Technologies & Neoclassical Production Functions. T. Junius. (Tilburg Studies in Econometrics: No. 2). lib. bdg. 16.00 (ISBN 90-207-0727-2, Pub. by Martinus Nijhoff Netherlands). Kluwer Academic.
Shepheardes Calendar. Edmund Spenser. 1890. 32.00 (ISBN 0-8337-3349-4). B Franklin.
Shepheardes Calender. Edmund Spenser. LC 79-691. Repr. of 1579 ed. 35.00x (ISBN 0-8201-1328-X). Schol Facsimiles.
Shepherd. Frederick Forsyth. 19.95 (ISBN 0-88411-563-1, Pub. by Aeonian Pr). Amereon Ltd.
Shepherd Boy. Mrs. Marvin Good. 1978. pap. 1.95 (ISBN 0-686-24054-5). Rod & Staff.
Shepherd Boy & the Dancing Dog. M. L. Mortimer. (Illus.). (ps-3). 1.75 (ISBN 0-8198-0187-9); pap. 1.00 (ISBN 0-8198-0188-7). Dghtrs St Paul.
Shepherd Kings. P. Danielson. (Children of the Lion Ser.: Bk. 2). 1985. lib. bdg. 13.95 (ISBN 0-8398-2870-5, Gregg). G K Hall.
Shepherd Kings. Peter Danielson. 448p. (Orig.). 1981. pap. 3.95 (ISBN 0-553-23749-7). Bantam.
Shepherd Moon. H. M. Hoover. LC 83-16784. 180p. (gr. 7 up). 1984. 11.95 (ISBN 0-670-63977-X, Viking Kestrel). Viking.
Shepherd Moon. H. M. Hoover. (gr. 5-9). 1988. pap. 3.95 (ISBN 0-14-032611-1, Puffin Bks). Penguin.
Shepherd of an Immigrant People: The Story of Erland Carlsson. Emory Lindquist. LC 78-108120. (Augustana Historical Society Publication Ser.: No. 26). 236p. 1978. 7.50 (ISBN 0-910184-26-7). Augustana.
Shepherd of Guadaloupe. Zane Grey. 1984. pap. 2.95 (ISBN 0-671-83594-7). PB.
Shepherd of Hermas, Martyrdom of Polycarp, Epistle to Diognetus see Works of Apostolic Fathers.
Shepherd of Jerusalem. Dov P. Elkins. LC 75-39436. (Illus.). (gr. 8-12). 1976. 8.95 (ISBN 0-88400-045-1). Shengold.
Shepherd of My Soul. 1981. 4.95 (ISBN 0-8198-6801-9); pap. 3.50 (ISBN 0-8198-6802-7). Dghtrs St Paul.
Shepherd of the Hills. Harold B. Wright. 1975. lib. bdg. 19.95x (ISBN 0-89966-206-4). Buccaneer Bks.
Shepherd of the Hills. Harold B. Wright. 1958. 6.95 (ISBN 0-448-01056-9, G&D). Putnam Pub Group.
Shepherd of the Hills. rev. ed. Harold B. Wright. Ed. by Michael R. Phillips. 256p. 1988. pap. 6.95 (ISBN 0-87123-916-7). Bethany Hse.
Shepherd of the Sun. Benjamin Appel. (Illus.). (gr. 5 up). 1961. 10.95 (ISBN 0-8392-3033-8). Astor-Honor.
Shepherd Psalm. F. B. Meyer. 1972. pap. 2.95 (ISBN 0-87508-351-X). Chr Lit.
Shepherd Tom. Thomas R. Hazard. 1915. 36.00 (ISBN 0-384-21890-3). Johnson Repr.
Shepherd under Christ. Armin W. Schuetze & Irwin J. Habezk. LC 74-81794. 1974. text ed. 14.95 (ISBN 0-8100-0046-6, 15N0351). Northwest Pub.
Shepherdess of Elk River Valley. 2nd ed. Margaret D. Brown. (Illus.). 1967. 5.50x (ISBN 0-87315-037-6). Golden Bell.
Shepherding God's Flock. Jay E Adams. 1979. pap. 11.95 (ISBN 0-87552-058-8). Presby & Reformed.
Shepherding God's Flock: A Handbook on Pastoral Ministry, Counseling, & Leadership. Jay E. Adams. (Jay Adams Library). 544p. 1986. pap. 11.95 (ISBN 0-310-51071-6, 12119P). Zondervan.
Shepherding the Sheep. Benjamin S. Baker. LC 82-73531. 1983. 9.95 (ISBN 0-8054-2543-8). Broadman.
Shepherding: Workbook, No. 3. Robert D. Noble. 57p. (Orig.). 1987. 10.00 (ISBN 0-944687-03-2). Gather Family Inst.
Shepherds & Bathrobes. Thomas Long. (Orig.). 1987. pap. 7.25 (ISBN 0-89536-869-2, 7855). CSS of Ohio.
Shepherds & Lovers. Brian Hall. LC 81-84352. 144p. (Orig.). 1982. pap. 6.95 (ISBN 0-8091-2425-4). Paulist Pr.
Shepherd's Calendar. John Clare. Ed. by Eric Robinson & Geoffrey Summerfield. (Oxford Paperbacks Ser). 1973. 21.95x (ISBN 0-19-211249-X); pap. 9.95x (ISBN 0-19-281142-8). Oxford U Pr.
Shepherd's Care. William Goulooze. pap. 0.45 (ISBN 0-686-23475-8). Rose Pub MI.
Shepherd's Care: Reflections on the Changing Role of Pastor. NCCB Committee on Priestly Life & Ministry. 96p. (Orig.). 1987. pap. 4.95 (ISBN 1-55586-166-0). US Catholic.
Shepherd's Castle. George MacDonald & Mike Phillips. LC 83-11805. 288p. (Orig.). 1983. pap. 5.95 (ISBN 0-87123-579-X, 210579). Bethany Hse.
Shepherd's Crowns: A Volume of Essays. facs. ed. Pamela G. Grey. LC 67-30216. (Essay Index Reprint Ser). 1923. 15.00 (ISBN 0-8369-0498-2). Ayer Co Pubs.
Shepherd's Delight: A James Hogg Anthology. James Hogg. 167p. 1985. 17.95 (ISBN 0-86241-106-8); pap. 7.95 (ISBN 0-86241-088-6). Dufour.
Shepherds Find a King. Stephanie Caffrey & Timothy Kenslea. (Rainbow Books (Bible Story Books for Children)). 16p. (ps-1). 1978. pap. 1.00 (ISBN 0-8192-1232-6). Morehouse.
Shepherd's Historical Atlas. 9th rev. ed. William R. Shepherd. LC 64-26. (Illus.). (gr. 7 up). 1980. 38.95x (ISBN 0-389-20155-3). B&N Imports.
Shepherd's Life. William H. Hudson. Repr. of 1923 ed. 35.00 (ISBN 0-404-03406-3). AMS Pr.
Shepherds of Britain: Scenes from Shepherd Life Past & Present. Adelaide L. Gosset. LC 78-174415. (Illus.). Repr. of 1911 ed. 24.50 (ISBN 0-405-08565-6, Pub. by Blom). Ayer Co Pubs.
Shepherds of the Night. Jorge Amado. 384p. 1988. pap. 7.95 (ISBN 0-380-75471-1, 58768-8). Avon.
Shepherd's Pipe, & Other Stories. facs. ed. Arthur Schnitzler. Tr. by O. F. Theis. LC 74-140340. (Short Story Index Reprint Ser). 1922. 11.00 (ISBN 0-8369-3732-5). Ayer Co Pubs.
Shepherd's Pipe Songs from the Holy Night: A Christmas Cantata for Children's Voices or Youth Choir. Choral ed. Georg J. Gick & Marlys Swinger. LC 71-85805. (Illus.). 64p. (gr. k up). 1969. pap. 2.50 choral ed. (ISBN 0-87486-011-3); cassette 6.00 (ISBN 0-686-66331-4). Plough.
Shepherd's Purse: Organic Pest Control. Pest Publications. LC 86-73059. 48p. (Orig.). 1987. pap. 5.95 (ISBN 0-913990-52-3). Book Pub Co.
Shepherds Speak: American Bishops Confront the Social & Moral Issues That Challenge Christians Today. Ed. by James F. Hinchey & Dennis Corrado. 240p. (Orig.). 1986. pap. 11.95 (ISBN 0-8245-0737-1). Crossroad NY.
Shepherd's Trade. R. J. Berman. 1984. limited autographed ed. 100.00 (ISBN 0-317-02338-1); 25.00 (ISBN 0-317-02339-X). Rosen Group.
Sheppard-Towner Act: The Record of the Hearings. Ed. by David J. Rothman & Sheila M. Rothman. (Women & Children First Ser.). 490p. 1986. lib. bdg. 60.00 (ISBN 0-8240-7687-7). Garland Pub.
Sheppard's Book Dealers in North America 1986-87: A Directory of Antiquarian & Secondhand Book Dealers in the U. S. A. & Canada. 10th ed. Sheppard. 1986. 40.00 (ISBN 0-8108-1927-9). Scarecrow.
Sheppard's Book Dealers in the British Isles, 1987. 12th ed. 500p. 1987. 40.00 (ISBN 0-946653-24-0, Pub. by Europa England). Intl Pubns Serv.
Sheppard's Book Dealers in the British Isles, 1988: A Directory of Antiquarian & Secondhand Book Dealers in the United Kingdom & Ireland. 13th ed. 468p. 1988. 42.00 (ISBN 0-946653-48-8, Pub. by Europa Pubns Ltd England). Seven Hills Bks.
Sheppard's European Book Dealers. 468p. 1988. 45.00 (Pub. by Europa Pubns Ltd England). Seven Hills Bks.
Sheppard's International Directory of Print & Map Dealers. 250p. 1987. 42.00 (ISBN 0-317-67144-8, Pub. by Europa Pubns Ltd England). Seven Hills Bks.
Sheppard's International Directory of Print & Map Sellers. 1987. 42.00x (ISBN 0-946653-25-9, Pub. by Europa England). Intl Pubns Serv.
Sheppey: A Play in Three Acts. W. Somerset Maugham. LC 75-30396. (Works of W. Somerset Maugham Ser.). 1977. Repr. of 1933 ed. 20.00x (ISBN 0-405-07848-X). Ayer Co Pubs.
Sheraton Furniture. Ralph Fastnedge. (Illus.). 224p. 1983. 49.50. Antique Collect.
Sheraton Furniture. Ralph Fastnedge. (Illus.). 224p. 1985. 49.50 (ISBN 0-907462-47-2). Apollo.
Sheraton World Cookbook. Ed. by Vera Krijn. 304p. (Orig.). 1983. pap. 9.95 (ISBN 0-672-52761-8). Bobbs.
Sheraton World Cookbook: Great Recipes from Great Chefs. 1981. 15.95 (ISBN 0-672-52672-7). Bobbs.
Sherborne; or, the House at the Four Ways, 1875. Edward H. Dering. Ed. by Robert L. Wolff. LC 75-457. (Victorian Fiction Ser.). 1976. lib. bdg. 73.00 (ISBN 0-8240-1536-3). Garland Pub.
Sherbro of Sierra Leone. H. U. Hall. (Illus.). 15p. 1938. pap. 10.00 (ISBN 0-686-17762-2). Univ Mus of U PA.
Sherds. Ray Ragosta. (Burning Deck Poetry Ser.). 32p. (Orig.). 1982. pap. 3.00 (ISBN 0-930901-08-8). Burning Deck.
Sheridan. W. A. Darlington. LC 74-7188. (Studies in Drama, No. 39). 1974. lib. bdg. 39.95x (ISBN 0-8383-1926-2). Haskell.
Sheridan. Lewis Gibbs, pseud. LC 75-103189. 1970. Repr. of 1947 ed. 25.50x (ISBN 0-8046-0826-1, Pub. by Kennikat). Assoc Faculty Pr.
Sheridan. Margaret O. Oliphant. Ed. by John Morley. LC 68-58392. (English Men of Letters). Repr. of 1889 ed. lib. bdg. 12.50 (ISBN 0-404-51724-2). AMS Pr.
Sheridan, 2 vols. W. Fraser Rae. 1973. Repr. of 1896 ed. 100.00 (ISBN 0-8274-1001-8). R West.
Sheridan, 2 vols. Walter Sichel. 1973. Repr. of 1909 ed. Set. 80.00 (ISBN 0-8274-0452-2). R West.
Sheridan & the Drama of Georgian England. John Loftis. 1977. 13.50x (ISBN 0-674-80632-8). Harvard U Pr.
Sheridan: From New & Original Manuscripts Material; Including a Manuscript Diary by Georgiana Duchess of Devonshire, 4 vols. Walter Sichel. 1980. Repr. of 1909 ed. lib. bdg. 160.00 set (ISBN 0-8414-8000-1). Folcroft.
Sheridan le Fanu & Victorian Ireland. W. J. McCormack. (Illus.). 1980. text ed. 45.00x (ISBN 0-19-812629-8). Oxford U Pr.
Sheridan to Robertson: A Study of the Nineteenth-Century London Stage. Ernest B. Watson. LC 63-23191. (Illus.). 1926. 30.00 (ISBN 0-405-09055-2). Ayer Co Pubs.
Sheridaniana; or, Anecdotes of the Life of Richard Brinsley Sheridan. 1973. lib. bdg. 47.50 (ISBN 0-8414-8086-9). Folcroft.
Sheridans, 2 vols. Percy Fitzgerald. 1973. Repr. of 1886 ed. 85.00 (ISBN 0-8274-0417-4). R West.
Sheridan's Comedies: Their Contexts & Achievements. Mark S. Auburn. LC 77-7205. x, 221p. 1977. 19.50x (ISBN 0-8032-0914-2). U of Nebr Pr.
Sheridan's Plays. Ed. by W. Fraser Rae. 1902. Repr. 30.00 (ISBN 0-8274-3396-4). R West.
Sheridan's Plays. Richard B. Sheridan. Ed. by Cecil Price. (Oxford Standard Authors Ser.). 1975. pap. 8.95x (ISBN 0-19-281158-4). Oxford U Pr.
Sheridan's Troopers on the Borders. Deb R. Keim. 308p. 1973. Repr. of 1869 ed. 18.95 (ISBN 0-87928-043-3). Corner Hse.
Sheridan's Troopers on the Borders: A Winter Campaign on the Plains. facsimile ed. Deb. Randolph Keim. LC 78-133523. (Select Bibliographies Ser). (Illus.). Repr. of 1885 ed. 20.00 (ISBN 0-8369-5555-2). Ayer Co Pubs.
Sheridan's Troopers on the Borders: A Winter Campaign on the Plains. DeBenneville R. Keim. LC 84-25754. (Illus.). xvi, 322p. 1985. pap. 7.95 (ISBN 0-8032-7755-5, BB 899, Bison). U of Nebr Pr.
Sheriff. Robert O'Neill. (American Structural Readers Ser.: Stage 1). (Illus.). 16p. (Orig.). 1982. pap. text ed. 3.95 (ISBN 0-582-79819-1). Longman.
Sheriff. Jack Rudman. (Career Examination Ser.: C-794). (Cloth bdg. avail. on request). pap. 15.00 (ISBN 0-8373-0794-5). Natl Learning.
Sheriff & the Branding Iron Murders. D. R. Meredith. 160p. 1986. pap. 2.95 (ISBN 0-380-70050-6). Avon.
Sheriff & the Branding Iron Murders. Doris R. Meredith. 159p. 1985. 14.95 (ISBN 0-8027-4050-2). Walker & Co.
Sheriff & the Folsom Man Murders. D. R. Meredith. 208p. 1987. pap. 2.95 (ISBN 0-380-70364-5). Avon.
Sheriff & the Folsom Man Murders. Doris Meredith. 192p. 1987. 16.95 (ISBN 0-8027-5663-8). Walker & Co.
Sheriff at Waterstop. Andy Thomson. (Light Line Ser.). (Illus.). 133p. (Orig.). (gr. 4-6). 1987. pap. 5.83 (ISBN 0-89084-371-6). Bob Jones Univ Pr.
Sheriff Jory. Milton Bass. 1987. pap. 2.75 (ISBN 0-451-14817-7, Sig). NAL.
Sheriff of Mad River. Dan Roberts. (Orig.). 1980. pap. text ed. 1.75 (ISBN 0-505-51571-7, Pub. by Tower Bks). Leisure NY.
Sheriff of Rottenshot. Jack Prelutsky. LC 81-6420. (Illus.). 32p. (gr. k-3). 1982. PLB 11.88 (ISBN 0-688-00198-X). Greenwillow.
Sheriff of Singing River. Al Cody. 1981. pap. 1.75 (ISBN 0-8439-0862-9, Leisure Bks). Leisure NY.
Sheriff Pat Garrett's Last Days. Colin Richards. LC 85-25020. (Illus.). 96p. (Orig.). 1986. pap. 8.95 (ISBN 0-86534-079-X). Sunstone Pr.
Sheriff Rides. Max Brand. Date not set. pap. 2.95 (ISBN 0-446-32070-6). Warner Bks.
Sheriff Sally Gopher & the Thanksgiving Caper. Robert Quackenbush. LC 82-135. (Illus.). 32p. (gr. 1-3). 1982. PLB 10.88 (ISBN 0-688-01293-0). Lothrop.
Sheriff William Brady: Tragic Hero of the Lincoln County War. Donald R. LaVash. LC 85-8025. (Illus.). 128p. (Orig.). 1986. pap. 10.95 (ISBN 0-86534-064-1). Sunstone Pr.

SHHHH! Suzy W. Kline. Ed. by Ann Fay. LC 84-26032. (Albert Whitman Concept Bks.). (Illus.). (ps). 1984. PLB 10.50 (ISBN 0-8075-7321-3). A Whitman.
Shi ChuChai Chien Pu. text ed. 1250.00. Johnson Repr.
Shi, Its Religion: A History of Islam in Persia & Iraq. Dwight M. Donaldson. 1976. lib. bdg. 59.95 (ISBN 0-8490-2598-2). Gordon Pr.
Shi King. William Jennings. 383p. 58.00x (ISBN 0-317-68634-8, Pub. by Han-Shan Tang Ltd). State Mutual Bk.
Shi Tao Hua Ji. Daoji. 118p. 1968. 245.00x (Pub. by Han-Shan Tang Ltd). State Mutual Bk.
Shia Origin & Faith. Ed. by Kashif Al-Gita. Tr. by M. Fazal Haq from Arabic. 284p. 1984. pap. 7.50 (ISBN 0-941724-23-9). Islamic Seminary.
Shiatsu. T. Namikoshi. (Illus.). 1974. pap. cancelled (ISBN 0-685-52367-5, Pub. by Japan Pubns). Wehman.
Shiatsu & Stretching: A New Method of Stretching Exercise with Finger Pressure. Toru Namikoshi. (Illus.). 128p. (Orig.). 1983. pap. 11.95 (ISBN 0-87040-575-6). Japan Pubns USA.
Shiatsu: Japanese Finger-Pressure Therapy. Tokujiro Namikoshi. LC 68-19983. (Illus.). 84p. 1972. pap. 7.95 (ISBN 0-87040-169-6). Japan Pubns USA.
Shiatsu: Japanese Finger Pressure Therapy. Wi Schultz. 7.95x (ISBN 0-685-70704-0). Wehman.
Shiatsu Therapy: Its Theory & Practice. Toru Namikoshi. (Illus.). 1977. pap. 8.25 (ISBN 0-87040-270-6). Japan Pubns USA.
Shiatsu Therapy: Theory & Practice. Ti Namikoshi. pap. 8.25x (ISBN 0-685-70705-9). Wehman.
Shiatsu Way to Health: Relaxation & Relief at a Touch. Toru Namikoshi. Tr. by Susan K. McCandless. LC 87-81676. (Illus.). 160p. 1988. pap. 14.95 (ISBN 0-87011-796-3). Kodansha.
Shiatzu: Japanese Finger Pressure for Energy. Yukiko Irwin & James Wagenvoord. (Illus.). 240p. 1976. pap. 14.95 (ISBN 0-397-01107-5, LP-093). Har-Row.
Shiba Kokan. Calvin L. French. LC 74-76104. 224p. 1974. 27.50 (ISBN 0-8348-0098-5). Weatherhill.
Shiba Kokan. Calvin L. French. 200p. 1974. 450.00x (Pub. by Han-Shan Tang Ltd). State Mutual Bk.
Shibboleth. Michael D. Aghy. 64p. 1989. pap. 8.95 (ISBN 0-19-282564-X). Oxford U Pr.
Shibori: Japanese Shaped Resist Dyeing. Yoshiko Wada. LC 82-48789. (Illus.). 296p. 1983. 80.00 (ISBN 0-87011-559-6). Kodansha.
Shibumi. Trevanian. 448p. 1983. pap. 3.95 (ISBN 0-345-31180-9). Ballantine.
Shidduchim & Zivugim: The Torah Perspective on Finding Your Mate. Yehuda Lebovits. 1988. 10.95 (ISBN 0-317-68131-1). Feldheim.
Shidduchim & Zivugim: The Torah's Perspective on Choosing Your Mate. Yehudah Lebovits. 168p. (Orig.). 1988. 10.95 (ISBN 0-944070-01-9). Targum Pr.
Shiel in Diverse Hands: A Collection of Essays. Moskowitz et al. LC 82-61695. 501p. 1983. pap. 32.50x. Reynolds Morse.
Shield & Hiding Place: The Religious Life of the Civil War Armies. Gardiner H. Shattuck, Jr. LC 87-11157. (Illus.). 192p. 1987. 24.95 (ISBN 0-86554-273-2, H236). Mercer Univ Pr.
Shield & the Sword. P. S. Bhagat. 1974. 6.00 (ISBN 0-686-20304-6). Intl Bk Dist.
Shield Devices of the Greeks in Art & Literature. G. H. Chase. (Illus.). 1978. Repr. of 1902 ed. 20.00 (ISBN 0-89005-260-3). Ares.
Shield for Murder. William P. McGivern. 192p. 1988. pap. 2.95 (ISBN 0-425-10551-2). Berkley Pub.
Shield of Faith. Martyria Madauss. 1974. gift edition 0.95 (ISBN 3-87209-659-1). Evang Sisterhood Mary.
Shield of Faith: A Chronicle of Strategic Defense, from Zeppelins to Star Wars. B. Bruce-Briggs. 448p. 1988. 19.95 (ISBN 0-671-61086-4). S&S.
Shield of Herakles see Works & Days.
Shield of Perseus: The Vision & Imagination of Howard Nemerov. Julia A. Bartholomay. LC 70-137851. 168p. 1972. 12.00x (ISBN 0-8130-0317-2). U Presses Fla.
Shield of Three Lions. Pamela Kaufman. 528p. 1984. pap. 3.95 (ISBN 0-446-32419-1). Warner Bks.
Shifra Stein's Day Trips from Cincinnati: Getaways Less Than Two Hours Away. David Hunter. Ed. by Shifra Stein. LC 83-49040. (Day Trips America Ser.). 160p. 1984. pap. 8.95 (ISBN 0-88742-005-2). Globe Pequot.
Shifra Stein's Day Trips from Greater Baltimore: Getaways Less than Two Hours Away. Gwyn Willis. Ed. by Shifra Stein. LC 84-48890. (Day Trips American Ser.). 160p. (Orig.). 1985. pap. 7.95 (ISBN 0-88742-023-0). Globe Pequot.
Shifra Stein's Kansas City. Ed. by Shifra Stein. (Illus.). 64p. (Orig.). 1986. pap. 9.95 (ISBN 0-9609752-5-X). S Stein Prods.
Shift. Hugh Cook. 1987. 6.95 (ISBN 0-394-74739-9, Vin). Random.
Shift in Value Added Minus Payroll & the Forecasting of Growth for Industries in Maine. Benjamin H. Stevens & J. R. Rower. (Discussion Paper Ser.: No. 125). 20p. (Orig.). 1981. pap. 6.50 (ISBN 1-55869-002-6). Regional Sci Res Inst.
Shift of Meaning. J. Copley. 1978. Repr. of 1961 ed. lib. bdg. 25.00 (ISBN 0-8495-0719-7). Arden Lib.
Shift Register Sequences. rev. ed. Soloman Golomb. 1981. lib. bdg. 42.80 (ISBN 0-89412-116-2); pap. 34.80 (ISBN 0-89412-048-4). Aegean Park Pr.
Shift Work in the Brewing Industry see Effects of New Technological Change on Shift Work in the Brewing Industry.
Shift Work Swindle. Jean Coussins. 1979. 20.00x (ISBN 0-317-54920-0, Pub. by NCCL UK). State Mutual Bk.
Shifting & Incidence of Taxation. Otto Von Mering. LC 70-137965. (Economic Thought, History & Challenge Ser). 1971. Repr. of 1942 ed. 26.00x (ISBN 0-8046-1466-0, Pub. by Kennikat). Assoc Faculty Pr.
Shifting & Incidence of Taxation. 5th rev. ed. Edwin R. Seligman. LC 68-30543. (Illus.). Repr. of 1927 ed. 45.00x (ISBN 0-678-00478-1). Kelley.
Shifting Balance of World Forces, 1898-1945 see Cambridge New Modern History.
Shifting Contexts: The Generation of Effective Psychotherapy. Bill O'Hanlon & James Wilk. LC 86-26986. 289p. 1987. lib. bdg. 25.00 (ISBN 0-89862-677-3). Guilford Pr.
Shifting Cultivation & Soil Conservation in Africa: Papers Presented at the FAO-SUDA-ARCN Regional Seminar Held in Ibadan, Nigeria, 2-21 July 1973. (Soils Bulletins: No. 24). 254p. (Eng., Fr. & Span.). 1974. pap. 19.50 (ISBN 92-5-100393-9, F1166, FAO). UNIPUB.
Shifting Cultivation in Latin America. (Forestry Development Papers: No. 17). (Span.). pap. 17.00 (F1300, FAO). UNIPUB.
Shifting Cultivation in Northern Thailand: Possibilities for Development. Terry B. Grandstaff. (Resource Systems Theory & Methodology Ser.: No. 3). 44p. 1981. pap. 10.00 (ISBN 92-808-0192-9, TUNU120, UNU). UNIPUB.
Shifting Cultivation in Southeastern Asia. J. E. Spencer. 1978. 35.00x (ISBN 0-520-03517-8). U of Cal Pr.
Shifting Cultivation in Southeastern Asia. Joseph E. Spencer. LC 67-63051. (University of California Publications in Geography Ser.: Vol. 19). pap. 64.00 (ISBN 0-317-29507-1, 2021275). Bks Demand UMI.
Shifting Fires. Eric Helm. (Vietnam: Ground Zero Ser.). 352p. (Orig.). 1989. pap. 3.95 (ISBN 0-373-60502-1, Pub. by Worldwide). Harlequin Bks.
Shifting Frontiers. Peter Jay. 79p. (Orig.). 1980. pap. 7.50 (ISBN 0-85635-323-X). Carcanet.
Shifting Frontiers in Financial Markets. Ed. by D. E. Fair. 1986. lib. bdg. 60.75 (ISBN 90-247-3225-5, Pub. by Martinus Nijhoff Netherlands). Kluwer-Academic.
Shifting Gears: Changing Labor Relations in the U. S. Automobile Industry. Harry C. Katz. 248p. 1987. pap. text ed. 8.95x (ISBN 0-262-61050-7). MIT Pr.
Shifting Gears: Technology, Literature, Culture in Modernist America. Cecelia Tichi. LC 86-16161. (Illus.). xviii, 310p. 1987. 35.00x (ISBN 0-8078-1715-5); pap. 14.95x (ISBN 0-8078-4167-6). U of NC Pr.
Shifting Ground: Exile Literature from the Spanish Civil War. Michael Ugarte. 256p. 1989. lib. bdg. 36.50 (ISBN 0-8223-0857-6). Duke.
Shifting Horizons. Lynn Beaton. 265p. (Orig.). 1985. pap. 13.50 (ISBN 0-9509967-3-4). Left Bank.
Shifting Involvements: Private Interest & Public Action. Albert O. Hirschman. LC 81-47922. (Illus.). 160p. 1981. cloth 20.50x (ISBN 0-691-04231-4); pap. 8.95x (ISBN 0-691-00368-8). Princeton U Pr.
Shifting Landscape. Henry Roth. 448p. 1987. 19.95 (ISBN 0-8276-0292-8). JPS Phila.
Shifting Point: Theatre, Film, Opera, 1946-1987. Peter Brook. LC 87-45026. (Illus.). 320p. 1987. 22.50i (ISBN 0-06-039073-5, HarpT). Har-Row.
Shifting Sands. N. N. Bray. LC 70-180321. Repr. of 1934 ed. 16.00 (ISBN 0-404-56216-7). AMS Pr.
Shifting Sands: The British in South Arabia. D. Ledger. 232p. 1983. 95.00x (ISBN 0-907151-08-6, Pub. by IMMEL UK). State Mutual Bk.
Shifting Scenes of the Modern European Theatre. Hallie Flanagan. LC 79-187832. (Illus.). Repr. of 1929 ed. 31.00 (ISBN 0-405-08522-2, Blom Pubns). Ayer Co Pubs.
Shifting Skies. Ed. by Rita S. Mathur. (Vikas Library & Modern Moian Writing Ser.: No. 7). 192p. 1980. text ed. 15.00x (ISBN 0-7069-1271-3, Pub by Vikas India). Advent NY.
Shifting the Debate: Public-Private Sector Relations in the Modern Welfare State. Ed. by Susan Ostrander et al. 148p. 1987. 29.95 (ISBN 0-88738-185-5). Transaction Bks.
Shifting Town: Glass Plate Images of Clermont & Its People. G. C. Pullar. Compiled by Richard Stringer & Marguerite Stringer. LC 86-16070. (Illus.). 232p. 1987. text ed. 49.50x (ISBN 0-7022-2012-4). U of Queensland Pr.
Shifting World: Social Change & Nostalgia in the American Novel. David C. Stineback. LC 74-31510. 192p. 1976. 20.00 (ISBN 0-8387-1686-5). Bucknell U Pr.
Shifting Worlds, Changing Minds: Where the Sciences & Buddhism Meet. Jeremy W. Hayward. LC 87-9732. (New Science Library Ser.). 310p. (Orig.). 1987. pap. 12.95 (ISBN 0-87773-368-6). Shambhala Pubns.
Shifts in the Functions of Cities & Towns of India, Nineteen Sixty-One to Nineteen Seventy-One. Asok Mitra et al. 1981. 47.50x (ISBN 0-8364-0719-9, Pub. by Abhinav India). South Asia Bks.
Shiftwork: Its Practice & Improvement. Ed. by K. Kogi et al. (Journal of Human Ergology Ser.: Vol. II). (Illus.). 541p. 1982. pap. 60.00x supplement (ISBN 4-905648-02-5, Pub by Japan Sci Soc Japan). Intl Spec Bk.
Shiga Hero. William F. Sibley. LC 79-14120. 1979. lib. bdg. 21.00x (ISBN 0-226-75620-3). U of Chicago Pr.
Shiga the Potter. Jutta Malnic. 75p. 1986. 24.95 (ISBN 0-909134-53-7, Pub. by J Ferguson Australia). Intl Spec Bk.
Shigaraki, Potters' Valley. Shigaraki. LC 79-89265. (Illus.). 428p. 1980. 65.00 (ISBN 0-87011-382-8). Kodansha.
Shih-Ching: The Classic Anthology Defined by Confucius. Tr. by Ezra Pound. 336p. 1954. pap. 4.95 (ISBN 0-674-13397-8). Harvard U Pr.
Shih Tzu. Audrey Dadds. LC 75-13607. (Complete Breed Book Ser). 224p. 1975. 17.95 (ISBN 0-87605-309-6). Howell Bk.
Shih Tzu. Robert P. Parker & Gerarda M. Collins. (Illus.). 1981. 9.95 (ISBN 0-87666-703-5, KW-084). TFH Pubns.
Shih Tzu. Gay Widdrington. Ed. by William W. Denlinger & Annabel Rathman. (Breed Bks.). (Illus.). 1988. write for info. (ISBN 0-87714-073-1). Denlingers.
Shihouette du Scandale. Marcel Ayme. 1973. pap. 14.95 (ISBN 0-686-51905-1). French & Eur.
Shi'ism & Social Protest. Juan R. Cole & Nikki R. Keddie. LC 85-22780. 352p. 1986. text ed. 42.50 (ISBN 0-300-03550-0); pap. 13.95x (ISBN 0-300-03553-5, Y-584). Yale U Pr.
Shi'ism: Doctrines, Thought, & Spirituality. Intros. by Seyyed H. Nasr et al. 432p. 1988. 73.50 (ISBN 0-88706-689-5); pap. 24.50 (ISBN 0-88706-690-9). State U NY Pr.
Shi'ism, Resistance & Revolution. Ed. by Milton Kramer. 350p. 1986. 39.85 (ISBN 0-8133-0453-9). Westview.
Shi'ite Anthology. Ed. by W. C. Chittick & Allamah Tabataba'i. Tr. by W. C. Chittick. 152p. 1980. 40.00x (ISBN 0-317-39150-X, Pub. by Luzac & Co Ltd); pap. 29.00x (ISBN 0-317-39151-8). State Mutual Bk.
Shi'ite Anthology. Allamah Tabataba'l. Ed. by William C. Chittick. 152p. 1986. text ed. 25.00 (ISBN 0-7103-0159-6); pap. text ed. 12.95 (ISBN 0-317-40555-1). Routledge Chapman & Hall.
Shi'ite Anthology: Passages from the Hadith. Tr. by William C. Chittick from Arabic. 152p. 1981. 59.50 (ISBN 0-87395-510-2); pap. 19.95x (ISBN 0-87395-511-0). State U NY Pr.
Shi'ite Islam. Muhammed H. Al-Tabataba'i. Tr. by Seyyed H. Nasr. LC 74-8289. 252p. 1975. 49.50 (ISBN 0-87395-272-3); pap. 16.95x (ISBN 0-87395-390-8). State U NY Pr.
Shi'ite Islam. Muhammad Tabatabai. Tr. by Sayyed H. Nasr from Persian. 253p. 1979. pap. 4.95 (ISBN 0-941722-19-8). Book-Dist-Ctr.
Shi'ite Religion: A History of Islam in Persia & Irak. Dwight M. Donaldson. LC 80-1933. 49.50 (ISBN 0-404-18959-8). AMS Pr.
Shikar. Jamshed Butt. 1967. pap. 2.35 (ISBN 0-88253-128-X). Ind-US Inc.
Shikasta: Canopus in Argos-Archives. Doris Lessing. LC 79-11295. 1979. 13.45 (ISBN 0-394-50732-0). Knopf.
Shikimic Acid Pathway. Ed. by Eric E. Conn. LC 86-8885. (Recent Advances in Phytochemistry Ser.: Vol. 20). 356p. 1986. 59.50x (ISBN 0-306-42283-2, Plenum Pr). Plenum Pub.
Shikitei Sanba & the Comic Tradition in Edo Fiction. Robert W. Leutner. (Harvard-Yenching Institute Monographs: No. 25). 300p. 1985. text ed. 21.00x (ISBN 0-674-80646-8). Harvard U Pr.
Shiksa: A Novel. Barbara Bartlett. Ed. by Pat Golbitz. LC 87-12526. 448p. 1987. 18.95 (ISBN 0-688-04389-5). Morrow.
Shikwa & Jawab-I-Shikwa (Answer) Iqbal's Dialogue with Allah. Mohammed Iqbal. Tr. by Krushwant Singh from Urdu. 96p. (Orig.). 1981. pap. 7.95x (ISBN 0-19-561324-4). Oxford U Pr.
Shilappadikaram: The Ankle Bracelet. Ilango Adigal. Tr. by Alain Danielou. LC 64-16823. (Orig.). 1964. 4.95 (ISBN 0-8112-0246-1). New Directions.
Shilling for Candles. Josephine Tey. 1981. pap. 3.95 (ISBN 0-671-55179-5, RE). WSP.
Shilling for Candles. Josephine Tey. (Josephine Tey Mysteries Ser). 1988. pap. 3.95 (ISBN 0-02-054530-4, Collier). Macmillan.
Shilling for Candles. Josephine Tey. (Portway Ser.). 304p. 1988. lib. bdg. 18.50x (ISBN 0-7451-7114-1, Pub. by Chivers Pr UK). G K Hall.
Shilling for Carmarthen. Pat Molloy. 201p. 1980. 23.00x (ISBN 0-86383-182-6, Pub. by Gomer Pr). State Mutual Bk.
Shiloh. Shelby Foote. 1976. 11.95 (ISBN 0-394-40873-X). Random.
Shiloh. Shelby Foote. 1985. 18.95 (ISBN 0-8488-0158-X, Pub. by J M C & Co). Amereon Ltd.
Shiloh. David G. Martin. (Illus.). 192p. 1987. 9.98 (ISBN 0-914373-08-0). Wieser & Wieser.
Shiloh & Other Stories. Bobbie A. Mason. LC 82-47541. 288p. 1982. 12.45i (ISBN 0-06-015062-9, HarpT). Har-Row.
Shiloh & Other Stories. Bobbie A. Mason. LC 82-47541. 224p. 1983. pap. 7.95 (ISBN 0-06-091330-4, PL1330, PL). Har-Row.
Shiloh: Bloody April. Wiley Sword. (Illus.). 519p. 1983. Repr. 35.00 (ISBN 0-89029-070-9). Pr of Morningside.
Shiloh-in Hell Before Night. James L. McDonough. LC 76-18864. (Illus.). 272p. 1977. 18.95 (ISBN 0-87049-199-7); pap. 9.95 (ISBN 0-87049-232-2). U of Tenn Pr.
Shiloh to Vicksburg, "Dear Eliza" An Eyewitness Account in the Civil War Letters of Major Virgil H. Moats. Edward L. Walker. LC 84-81325. (Illus.). 196p. pap. 10.00 (ISBN 0-943486-01-7). Hedgehog Pr.
Shimmee & the Taste-Me Tree. Sheindel Weinbach. (Illus.). (ps-2). 2.95 (ISBN 0-87306-991-9). Feldheim.
Shimmeree. Stephen Cosgrove. (Serendipity Storybks.). (Illus.). 32p. (gr. k-4). 1980. pap. 1.95 (ISBN 0-8431-0574-7). Price Stern.
Shimmershine Queens. Camille Yarbrough. 128p. (gr. 5-8). 1989. 13.95 (ISBN 0-399-21465-8, Putnam). Putnam Pub Group.
Shimoda Story. Oliver Statler. LC 85-29012. (Illus.). 648p. 1986. pap. 19.95 (ISBN 0-8248-1059-7). UH Pr.
Shimon Peres: A Biography. Matti Golan. Tr. by Ina Friedman. LC 82-7354. (Illus.). 275p. (Hebrew.). 1982. 25.00 (ISBN 0-312-71736-9). St Martin.
Shimoni's Lover. Jenifer Levin. 1987. 18.95 (ISBN 0-15-181990-4). HarBraceJ.
Shin Kage Ryu: The Complete Fighting Art. Robin L. Reilly. 1988. 29.95 (ISBN 0-8048-1536-4). C E Tuttle.
Shin Tzu Heritage. Jon Ferrante et al. (Illus.). 1988. write for info. (ISBN 0-87714-132-0). Denlingers.
Shina Ko Toshi: Ancient Chinese Ceramics. K. Otani. 114p. 1932. 425.00x (ISBN 0-317-45234-7, Pub. by Han-Shan Tang Ltd). State Mutual Bk.
Shina Kodo Seikwa. 10500.00x (Pub. by Han-Shan Tang Ltd). State Mutual Bk.
Shina Komeiki Deizo Zusetsu. Hamada Kosaku. 76p. 1927. 300.00x (ISBN 0-317-44192-2, Pub. by Han-Shan Tang Ltd). State Mutual Bk.
Shina No Toji: Chinese Ceramics. Kushi Takushi. 373p. 1942. 200.00x (ISBN 0-317-44194-9, Pub. by Han-Shan Tang Ltd). State Mutual Bk.
Shina Seiji Shiko: Draft History of Chinese Porcelain. Koyama Fujio. 337p. 1943. 240.00 (ISBN 0-317-44196-5, Pub. by Han-Shan Tang Ltd). State Mutual Bk.
Shina Toji Zatsudan: Chats on Chinese Ceramics. Kyosuke Ueda. 400p. 1930. 175.00x (ISBN 0-317-45235-5, Pub. by Han-Shan Tang Ltd). State Mutual Bk.
Shina Tojiki Shi: A History of Chinese Ceramics. Soshu Watanabe. 223p. 1934. 175.00x (ISBN 0-317-45236-3, Pub. by Han-Shan Tang Ltd). State Mutual Bk.
Shina Toki Zufu. Aoyama Jiro. 36p. 1946. 700.00x (Pub. by Han-Shan Tang Ltd). State Mutual Bk.
Shinano! Joseph F. Enright & James W. Ryan. 1988. pap. 3.95 (ISBN 0-317-67199-5). St Martin.
Shinano! The Sinking of Japan's Secret Supership. Joseph F. Enright & James W. Ryan. (Illus.). 256p. 1987. 18.95 (ISBN 0-312-00186-X). St Martin.
Shinbi Taikan, 20 vols. Ed. by Tajima Shi'ichi. (Illus.). 1908. Set. 21000.00x Japanese style bdg., in slipcase (Pub. by Han-Shan Tang Ltd). State Mutual Bk.
Shindano-Swahili Essays & Other Stories. Alice Grant et al. (Foreign & Comparative Studies Program, African Special Publications Ser.: No.6). 55p. 1971. pap. 3.50x (ISBN 0-686-70992-6). Syracuse U Foreign Comp.
Shine Hawk. Charlie Smith. 368p. 1988. 17.95 (ISBN 0-945167-01-6). British Amer Pub.
Shine On. Fred Pfeil. 1987. 14.95 (ISBN 0-89924-047-X); pap. 7.50. Small Pr Dist.
Shine on, Bright & Dangerous Object. Laurie Colwin. 1979. pap. 1.95 (ISBN 0-345-28415-1). Ballantine.
Shine On, Bright & Dangerous Object. Laurie Colwin. 192p. 1984. pap. 5.95 (ISBN 0-14-007414-7). Penguin.
Shine Perishing Republic. Rudolph Gilbert. LC 65-15883. (Studies in Poetry, No. 38). 1969. Repr. of 1936 ed. lib. bdg. 75.00x (ISBN 0-8383-0556-3). Haskell.
Shine, Shine, Shine: A Book of Black Poetry. Jimmy L. Gravely. 32p. (Orig.). 1986. pap. 3.95 (ISBN 0-936903-03-1). Certified Feelings.
Shine, Sun! Carol Greene. LC 82-19853. (Rookie Readers Ser.). (Illus.). 32p. (ps-2). 1983. PLB 9.93 (ISBN 0-516-02038-2); pap. 2.50 (ISBN 0-516-42038-0). Childrens.
Shingarev Diary: How It Was, Nov. 1917-Jan. 1918. A. I. Shingarev. Tr. by F. Ashbee & I. Tidmarsh. 1978. 11.50x (ISBN 0-931554-06-3); pap. 6.00 (ISBN 0-931554-07-1). Strathcona.
Shingle Style Today, or the Historian's Revenge. Vincent Scully, Jr. LC 74-79058. (Illus.). 112p. 1974. 12.50 (ISBN 0-8076-0759-2); pap. 9.95 (ISBN 0-8076-0760-6). Braziller.
Shingling the Fog & Other Plains Lies. Roger L. Welsch. LC 79-18730. viii, 160p. 1980. 15.95x (ISBN 0-8032-4709-5); pap. 4.95 (ISBN 0-8032-9700-9, Bison). U of Nebr Pr.

Ship Who Sang. Anne McCaffrey. 1976. pap. 2.95 (ISBN 0-345-33431-0). Ballantine.

Shipboard Acoustics. Ed. by J. Buiten. 1987. lib. bdg. 169.00 (ISBN 90-247-3420-7, Pub. by Martinus Nijhoff Netherlands). Kluwer Academic.

Shipboard Antennas. 2nd ed. Preston E. Law, Jr. 575p. 1986. text ed. 67.00 (ISBN 0-89006-211-0). Artech Hse.

Shipboard Damage Control. David Livingston et al. LC 76-4674. 1976. text ed. 15.95x (ISBN 0-87021-627-9). Naval Inst Pr.

Shipboard Electromagnetics. Preston E. Law, Jr. 320p. 1987. text ed. 66.00 (ISBN 0-89006-247-1). Artech Hse.

Shipboard Fish Scouting & Electronavigational Equipment. V. P. Averkiev. Tr. by S. K. Kane from Rus. 485p. 1985. text ed. 48.50 (ISBN 90-6191-436-1, Pub. by A A Balkema). Brookfield Pub Co.

Shipboard Kisses. Patricia Bird. (YA) (gr. 7 up). 1983. 9.95 (ISBN 0-8034-8317-1, Avalon). Bouregy.

Shipboard Operations. H. I. Lavery. (Illus.). 248p. 1984. pap. text ed. 24.50x (ISBN 0-434-91090-2, Pub. by Heinemann Med Bks). Sheridan.

Shipboard Refrigeration & Fish Processing Equipment. Ed. by N. G. Kondrashova. Tr. by B. Karekar from Rus. 266p. 1986. text ed. 41.00 (ISBN 90-6191-432-9, Pub. by A A Balkema). Brookfield Pub Co.

Shipbuilders. Leonard E. Fisher. (Colonial American Craftsmen Ser.). (YA) (gr. 9-12). pap. 4.95 (ISBN 0-317-57048-X). Godine.

Shipbuilders to the World: 125 Years of Harland & Wolff, Belfast. Michael Moss & John Hume. (Illus.). 560p. 1986. 29.95 (ISBN 0-85640-343-1, Pub. by Blackstaff Pr). Longwood Pub Group.

Shipbuilding Contracts. Ed. by M. Clarke. 1982. 45.00 (ISBN 0-907432-25-5). Lloyds London Pr.

Shipbuilding Credit. Ian Riddle. 100p. 1983. pap. text ed. 28.50x (ISBN 0-7083-0843-0, Pub. by U of Wales). Humanities.

Shipbuilding in Colonial America. Joseph A. Goldenberg. LC 74-32136. xiii, 306p. 1976. 16.95x (ISBN 0-8139-0588-5, Mariners Museum). U Pr of Va.

Shipcarvers of North America. M. V. Brewington. LC 79-187020. (Illus.). 190p. 1972. pap. 4.95 (ISBN 0-486-22168-7). Dover.

Shipfitter. Jack Rudman. (Career Examination Ser.: C-1031). (Cloth bdg. avail. on request). pap. 14.00 (ISBN 0-8373-1031-8). Natl Learning.

Shiphandling for the Mariner. 2nd ed. Daniel H. MacElrevey. LC 88-20308. (Illus.). 320p. 1988. text ed. 30.00x (ISBN 0-87033-383-6). Cornell Maritime.

Shiphandling with Tugs. George H. Reid. LC 86-47712. (Illus.). 279p. 1986. text ed. 18.00 (ISBN 0-87033-354-2). Cornell Maritime.

Shipley Associates Style Guide. Terry R. Bacon & Lawrence H. Freeman. 3 ring binder 24.95 (ISBN 0-933427-00-X). Shipley.

Shipley Associates Style Guide for Oil & Gas Professionals. Terry R. Bacon & Lawrence H. Freeman. 1985. 24.95 (ISBN 0-933427-01-8). Shipley.

Shipmaster's Handbook on Ship's Business. 2nd ed. James R. Aragon. LC 87-47998. 288p. 1988. text ed. 24.00x (ISBN 0-87033-378-X). Cornell Maritime.

Shipment Clerk. Jack Rudman. (Career Examination Ser.: C-738). (Cloth bdg. avail. on request). pap. 12.00 (ISBN 0-8373-0738-4). Natl Learning.

Shipowners' Liability for Loss of or Damage to Cargo under the Hague Rules (Gold Clause Agreement) 1987. 18.00x (ISBN 0-317-61474-6, Pub. by Witherby & Co England). State Mutual Bk.

Shipper's Guide to Stowage of Cargo in Marine Containers. (Illus.). 144p. 1982. pap. 5.50 (ISBN 0-318-19900-9, S/N 050-015-00004-1). USGPO.

Shipping & Craft in Silhouette. Charles G. Davis. LC 70-162509. (Tower Bks.). (Illus.). 100p. 1972. Repr. of 1929 ed. 40.00x (ISBN 0-8103-3945-5). Gale.

Shipping & Development Policy: An Integrated Assessment. Alexander J. Yeats. LC 81-4989. 190p. 1981. 35.00 (ISBN 0-275-90745-7, C0745). Praeger.

Shipping & the American War 1775-1783: A Study of British Transport Organization. David Syrett. 274p. 1970. 48.50 (ISBN 0-485-13127-7, Pub. by Athlone Pr UK). Humanities.

Shipping & Trade Between the Baltic Area & Western Europe 1784-95. Hans Johansen. (Odense Studies in History & Social Sciences: No. 82). 139p. (Orig.). 1983. Incl. 4 microfiche. pap. 30.00x (ISBN 87-7492-433-8, Pub. by Odense Universitets Forlag (Odense Denmark)). Coronet Bks.

Shipping Conferences: The Legal Framework & Operation of Shipping Conferences. Amos Herman. 1983. 44.00 (ISBN 90-654-4089-5, Pub. by Kluwer Law Netherlands). Kluwer Academic.

Shipping Days of Old Boothbay (Maine) George W. Rice. LC 84-61955. (Illus.). 464p. 1984. Repr. of 1938 ed. 45.00x (ISBN 0-89725-054-0). NE History.

Shipping in International Trade Relations. Ademuni-Odeke. 600p. 1988. text ed. 90.00x (ISBN 0-566-05371-3, Pub. by Gower Pub England). Gower Pub Co.

Shipping Industry: The Technology & Economics of Specialization. Edmund J. Gubbins. (Transportation Studies: Vol. 5). 140p. 1986. text ed. 40.00 (ISBN 2-88124-063-1). Gordon & Breach.

Shipping Law Consolidated. Ed. by E. R. Ivamy. 1984. wkbk. loose leaf Encyclopedia 140.00 (ISBN 1-850-44011-5). Lloyds London Pr.

Shipping, Maritime Trade, & the Economic Development of Colonial North America. James F. Shepherd. LC 76-176256. pap. 66.30 (ISBN 0-317-20814-4, 2024536). Bks Demand UMI.

Shipping Out: A Sociological Study of the American Merchant Seaman. Mariam G. Sherar. LC 72-78239. 96p. 1973. pap. 6.00x (ISBN 0-87033-173-6). Cornell Maritime.

Shipping Practice: With a Consideration of the Relevant Law. 11th ed. E. F. Stevens. 1981. pap. 25.00 (ISBN 0-273-01616-4). Heinman.

Shipping Regulations: Cases, 22 vols. 1961-1987. Rev ed. Pike & Fischer. LC 61-31808. 1978. Repr. of 1961 ed. lib. bdg. 1265.00 (ISBN 0-89941-206-8); lib. bdg. 55.00 ea. W S Hein.

Shipping Situation Between New York City & Philadelphia: A Survey of the Factors Causing the Growth of Motor Truck Transportation for the Purpose of Presenting Specifications to Be Met in Coordinating Rail & Motor Truck Transportation for Intercity Service. Russell Talbot. 1931. pap. 49.50x (ISBN 0-685-89782-6). Elliots Bks.

Shippo: The Art of Enameling in Japan. George Kuwayama. (Illus.). 56p. (Orig.). 1987. pap. 9.95 (ISBN 0-87587-136-4). LA Co Art Mus.

Ships. N. S. Barrett. (Illus.). 32p. (gr. k-3). PLB 9.90 (ISBN 0-531-03722-3). Watts.

Ships. Jacqueline Dineen. Ed. by Janet Caulkins. (Topics Ser.). (Illus.). 32p. (gr. 1-6). 1988. 10.40 (ISBN 0-531-18212-6, Pub. by Bookwright Pr). Watts.

Ships. National Academy of Sciences Staff. LC 77-79218. (Fire Safety Aspects of Polymeric Materials: Vol. 9). 236p. 1981. 19.00 (ISBN 0-87762-230-2). Technomic.

Ships Afire. J. J. Marcelo. Tr. by Sarah Arvio. 336p. (Orig.). 1988. pap. 7.95 (ISBN 0-380-89741-5). Avon.

Ships: An Educational Coloring Book. Spizzirri Publishing Co. Staff. Ed. by Linda Spizzirri. (Illus.). 32p. (gr. 1-8). 1981. pap. 1.49 (ISBN 0-86545-035-8). Spizzirri.

Ships & Aircraft of the U. S. Fleet: 1939, '41, '42 & '45 Editions, 4 Vols. Ed. by James C. Fahey. (Illus.). 208p. 1976. Set. incl. slipcase 19.95 (ISBN 0-87021-171-4); bulk rates avail. Naval Inst Pr.

Ships & Aircraft of the U. S. Fleet: 1950, '58, & '65 Editions, 3 Vols. James C. Fahey. LC 76-15840. (Illus.). 192p. 1980. Set. 19.95 (ISBN 0-87021-647-3); bulk rates avail. Naval Inst Pr.

Ships & Aircraft of the U. S. Fleet. 13th ed. Ed. by Norman Polmar. LC 76-15840. (Illus.). 456p. 31.95 (ISBN 0-87021-648-1). Naval Inst Pr.

Ships & Aircraft of the U. S. Fleet. 14th ed. Ed. by Norman Polmar. (Illus.). 624p. 1987. 33.95 (ISBN 0-87021-649-X). Naval Inst Pr.

Ships & Fleets of the Ancient Mediterranean. Jean Rouge. Tr. by Susan Frazer from Fr. LC 81-4927. 229p. 1981. 17.50x (ISBN 0-8195-5055-8). Wesleyan U Pr.

Ships & Memories. (Teredo Books Ltd.). 90.00 (ISBN 0-903662-02-7, Teredo Bks England). State Mutual Bk.

Ships & Narrow Gauge Rails: The Story of the Pacific Coast Company. Gerald M. Best. LC 64-19122. (Illus.). 155p. 1981. Repr. of 1964 ed. 19.95 (ISBN 0-8310-7042-0). Howell-North.

Ships & Other Seacraft. Brian Williams. (Gateway Fact Bks.). 96p. (gr. k-8). 1984. lib. bdg. 9.90 (ISBN 0-531-09229-1). Watts.

Ships & Sailors: Ancient & Modern. C. C. Cotterill & E. Little. 1977. lib. bdg. 69.95 (ISBN 0-8490-2599-0). Gordon Pr.

Ships & Sailors: The Story of Our Merchant Marine. William H. Clark. LC 74-22736. (Illus.). Repr. of 1938 ed. 21.00 (ISBN 0-404-58488-8). AMS Pr.

Ships & Seamanship in the Ancient World. Lionel Casson. LC 85-43373. (Illus.). 564p. 1986. pap. 19.50x (ISBN 0-691-00215-0). Princeton U Pr.

Ships & Seaports. Katherine Carter. LC 82-4463. (New True Bks.). (Illus.). (gr. k-4). 1982. PLB 12.60 (ISBN 0-516-01656-3). Childrens.

Ships & Shipping: A Comprehensive Guide. Roy L. Nersesian. 252p. 1981. 49.95 (ISBN 0-87814-148-0, P-4260). Pennwell Bks.

Ships & Shipping of Tomorrow. Rolf Schonknecht et al. LC 82-14209. (Illus.). 240p. 1983. 30.00 (ISBN 0-87033-299-6). Cornell Maritime.

Ships & Shipwrecks of the Americas: A History Based on Underwater Archaeology. Ed. by George F. Bass. (Illus.). 1988. 40.00 (ISBN 0-500-05049-X). Thames Hudson.

Ships & Submarines. Michael Gray. LC 86-50034. (Modern Technology Ser.). (Illus.). 32p. (gr. 4-9). 1986. PLB 11.90 (ISBN 0-531-10201-7). Watts.

Ships & Submarines. Price, Stern & Sloan Staff. (How & Why Wonder Bks.). (Illus.). 32p. (YA) (gr. 7-12). 1987. pap. 1.95 (ISBN 0-8431-4289-8). Price Stern.

Ships & the River. David Canright. Ed. by Janet Cambell. (Illus.). 32p. (gr. 2-6). 1975. pap. 2.00 (ISBN 0-913344-22-2). South St Sea Mus.

Ships & Their Cargoes. 3rd ed. A. N. Cabot. 41p. 1975. pap. 2.50x (ISBN 0-85174-073-1). Sheridan.

Ships & Voyages. Jon Nichol. (Resource Units, Middle Ages, 1066-1485, Ser.). (Illus.). 24p. 1974. pap. text ed. 12.95 10 copies & tchr's guide (ISBN 0-582-39388-4). Longman.

Ship's Bell. Karl Wede. (Illus.). 60p. 1972. 1.00 (ISBN 0-913344-10-9). South St Sea Mus.

Ships Chronometer. Marvin E. Whitney. (Illus.). 490p. 1984. 75.00 (ISBN 0-918845-08-4). Am Watchmakers.

Ships Data 1. Ed. by Arnold S. Lott & Robert F. Sumrall. (Illus.). 32p. 1982. 3.00 (ISBN 0-915268-07-8). USS North Car.

Ship's Doctor. Stephen Kerry. LC 74-164018. 1972. 6.50 (ISBN 0-8008-7179-0). Taplinger.

Ship's Figureheads. M. K. Stammers. 3.25 (ISBN 0-913714-63-1). Legacy Bks.

Ships Fire-Fighting Manual. Ed. by Lorne & MacLean Marine Staff. 1985. 90.00x (ISBN 0-317-43641-4, Pub. by Lorne & MacLean Marine). State Mutual Bk.

Ships in Bottles. Guy De Marco. LC 84-52714. (Illus.). 64p. 1985. pap. 6.95 (ISBN 0-88740-033-7). Schiffer.

Ships in Bottles: A Step-by-Step Guide to a Venerable Nautical Craft. rev. ed. Hubbard Donald. LC 88-90507. (Illus.). 144p. 1988. pap. 14.95 (ISBN 0-943665-00-0). Sea Eagle Pubns.

Ships in Miniature: A New Manual for Modelmakers. Lloyd McCaffery. (Illus.). 144p. 1988. 29.95 (ISBN 0-9615021-3-4). Phoen Pubns.

Ships in the Sky: the Story of the Great Dirigibles see Great Dirigibles: Their Triumph & Disasters.

Ships in the Sky: the Story of the Great Dirigibles see Great Dirigibles, Their Triumphs & Disasters.

Ship's Log. Henry Beard & Roy McKie. (Illus.). 96p. 1984. pap. 6.95 (ISBN 0-89480-574-6). Workman Pub.

Ship's Log Book. Frank F. Farrar. Ed. by Dorothy B. Maxwell. (Tales of Adventure, Mischief Ser.). (Illus.). 287p. (Orig.). 1988. 29.95 (ISBN 0-8200-1037-5); pap. 14.95 (ISBN 0-8200-1036-7). Great Outdoors.

Ships of British Columbia: An Illustrated History of the British Columbia Ferry Corporation. Gary Bannerman & Pat Bannerman. (Illus.). 176p. 1985. 29.95 (ISBN 0-88839-188-9); pap. text ed. 14.95 (ISBN 0-317-39274-3). Hancock House.

Ships of Catalina Island. Martin P. Riegel. LC 88-61279. (California Heritage Ser.: Vol. IV). (Illus.). 88p. (Orig.). 1988. 12.95 (ISBN 0-944871-07-0); pap. 8.95 (ISBN 0-944871-06-2). Riegel Pub.

Ships of China. Valentin A. Sokoloff. LC 82-90290. (Illus.). 54p. 1982. 29.75 (ISBN 0-9607438-0-4). Sokoloff.

Ships of John Paul Jones. William Gilkerson. (Illus.). 88p. 1987. 32.95 (ISBN 0-87021-619-8). Naval Inst Pr.

Ships of the American Revolution. John F. Millar. Ed. by Harry Knill. (Illus.). 48p. (Orig.). 1976. pap. 3.50 (ISBN 0-88388-036-9). Bellerophon Bks.

Ships of the American Revolution & Their Models. Harold M. Hahn. (Illus.). 288p. 1988. 29.95 (ISBN 0-87021-653-8). Naval Inst Pr.

Ships of the French Arm. Timothy B. Brown. (Traveller Ser.: No. 2300). 96p. (Orig.). 1987. pap. 10.00 (ISBN 0-943580-34-X). Game Designers.

Ships of the German Fleet, 1848-1945. rev. ed. Hans J. Hansen. (Illus.). 192p. 1988. Repr. of 1974 ed. 24.95 (ISBN 0-87021-654-6). Naval Inst Pr.

Ships of the Great Lakes in Miniature. John Heinz. Ed. by Jeffrey A. Phillips. (Illus.). 98p. 1987. 19.95 (ISBN 0-9615021-2-6). Phoen Pubns.

Ships of the Inland Sea. 2nd ed. Gordon R. Newell. (Illus.). 1960. 9.95 (ISBN 0-8323-0039-X). Binford-Metropolitan.

Ships of the Panama Canal. James L. Shaw. (Illus.). 192p. 1985. 29.95 (ISBN 0-87021-629-5). Naval Inst Pr.

Ships of the Redwood Coast. Jack McNairn & Jerry MacMullen. (Illus.). 1945. 8.95 (ISBN 0-8047-0386-8). Stanford U Pr.

Ships of the Royal Navy. rev. ed. J. J. Colledge. 450p. 1988. 37.95 (ISBN 0-87021-652-X). Naval Inst Pr.

Ships of the Royal Navy: An Historical Index, 2 vols. James J. Colledge. Incl. Vol. 1. Major Ships. 50.00x (ISBN 0-678-05300-6); Vol. 2. Navy-Built Trawlers, Drifters, Tugs & Requisitioned Ships. 45.00x (ISBN 0-678-05301-4). LC 69-10859. 1969-70. Set. 87.50x (ISBN 0-678-05514-9). Kelley.

Ships of the Texas Navy. David Gracy & Jean Carefoot. (Illus.). 1979. 45.00 (ISBN 0-935978-04-6). Presidial.

Ships of the U. S. Navy. John Kirk & Aaron Klein. (Illus.). 192p. 1987. 14.98 (ISBN 0-671-08913-7, Pub. by Exeter Bks). Bookthrift.

Ships of the Victorian Navy. Conrad Dixon. (Illus.). 170p. 1987. 34.95 (ISBN 1-85253-033-2, Pub. by Ashford Pr Pub); pap. 19.95 (ISBN 1-85253-024-3, Pub. by Ashford Pr Pub). Sheridan.

Ships Passenger Lists, Port of Galveston, Texas: 1846-1871. Galveston County Genealogical Society Staff. 1984. 28.00 (ISBN 0-89308-343-7). Southern Hist Pr.

Ship's Pasture: Poems. Jon Silken. 96p. 1986. pap. 9.95 (ISBN 0-7102-0841-3, 08413). Routledge Chapman & Hall.

Ships, Ports & Pilots: A History of the Piloting Profession. Roger Clancy. LC 84-42600. (Illus.). 223p. 1984. lib. bdg. 16.95x (ISBN 0-89950-125-7). McFarland & Co.

Ships, Saints, & Mariners: A Maritime Encyclopedia of Mormon Migration, 1830-1890. Conway B. Sonne. 256p. 1987. 19.50x (ISBN 0-87480-270-9). U of Utah Pr.

Ships, Seafaring & Society: Essays in Maritime History. Ed. by Timothy J. Runyan. LC 87-17769. 382p. 1987. 22.50x (ISBN 0-8143-1990-4); pap. 14.95x (ISBN 0-8143-1991-2). Wayne St U Pr.

Ships, Submarines & the Sea. P. J. Gates & N. M. Lynn. (SEAP Ser.: No. 2). (Illus.). 200p. 1988. 28.91 (ISBN 0-08-034735-5, BDP); pap. 15.91 (ISBN 0-08-033626-4, BDP). Pergamon.

Ship's Surgeon's Yarn, & Other Stories. facs. ed. Francis B. Young. LC 72-134985. (Short Story Index Reprint Ser). 1940. 18.00 (ISBN 0-8369-3715-5). Ayer Co Pubs.

Ships That Brought Us So Far. Peter Stanford. (Illus.). pap. 2.00 (ISBN 0-686-15903-9). Sea Hist Pr.

Ships that Pass. Frank A. Weaner. 160p. 1987. 9.95 (ISBN 0-317-60465-1). Carlton.

Shipshape: The Art of Sailboat Maintenance. Ferenc Mate. 29.95 (ISBN 0-317-64888-8). Norton.

Shipton Quebec Canada Eighteen Twenty Five Census. Jay M. Hobrook. LC 76-364055. 1976. pap. 5.00 (ISBN 0-931248-07-8). Holbrook Res.

Shipwreck. John Fowles. (Illus.). 48p. 1983. pap. 9.95 (ISBN 0-316-29091-2). Little.

Shipwreck & Adventures among the South Sea Islanders. John P. Twyning. 110p. Date not set. write for info. Ye Galleon.

Shipwrecked. Joann Knox. (Junior Adventure Ser.). 48p. (gr. 4-8). 1973. pap. 1.00 (ISBN 0-88243-773-9, 02-0773). Gospel Pub.

Shipwrecked in the Tunnel of Love. Martha Smith & Maureen Croteau. (Illus.). 96p. (Orig.). 1984. pap. text ed. 4.95 (ISBN 0-932413-00-5). Recreat Pub.

Shipwrecked on Mystery Island. Roy Wandelmaier. LC 85-2531. (Illus.). 112p. (gr. 3-6). 1985. lib. bdg. 9.49 (ISBN 0-8167-0533-X); pap. text ed. 2.95 (ISBN 0-8167-0534-8). Troll Assocs.

Shipwrecks along the Atlantic Coast. William P. Quinn. 240p. 1988. 34.95 (ISBN 0-940160-40-4). Parnassus Imprints.

Shipwrecks & Sea Monsters of California's Central Coast. Randall A. Reinstedt. LC 76-350548. (Illus.). 168p. 1975. pap. 6.95 (ISBN 0-933818-02-5). Ghost Town.

Shipwrecks Around Cape Cod. William P. Quinn. LC 73-92326. (Illus.). 240p. 1973. pap. 19.50 (ISBN 0-936972-01-7). Lower Cape.

Shipwrecks Around Maine. William P. Quinn. LC 83-80403. (Illus.). 200p. 1983. 30.00 (ISBN 0-936972-04-1). Lower Cape.

Shipwrecks Around New England. William P. Quinn. LC 79-88076. (Illus.). 240p. 1984. pap. 19.50 (ISBN 0-936972-05-X). Lower Cape.

Shipwrecks: Diving the Graveyard of the Atlantic. Roderick Farb. LC 85-7233. (Illus.). 278p. (Orig.). 1985. pap. 12.95 (ISBN 0-89732-034-4). Menasha Ridge.

Shipwrecks in Florida Waters: A Billion Dollar Graveyard. Robert F. Marx. LC 78-65775. (Illus.). ix, 147p. 1986. 12.50; pap. 7.95 (ISBN 0-913122-55-6). Mickler Hse.

Shipwrecks in the Americas. Robert F. Marx. (Illus.). 544p. 1987. pap. 10.95 (ISBN 0-486-25514-X). Dover.

Shipwrecks in the Americas. Robert F. Marx. (Illus.). 1988. 18.25 (ISBN 0-8446-6328-X). Peter Smith.

Shipwrecks in the Vicinity of Jupiter Inlet. Bessie W. DuBois. (Illus.). 31p. 1981. pap. 2.95 (ISBN 0-317-19706-1). Florida Classics.

Shipwrecks, Legends & Ghost Stories of Cape May. Charles J. Adams, III & David J. Seibold. (Illus.). 115p. 1987. pap. 5.95 (ISBN 0-9610008-5-6). C J Adams.

Shipwrecks of Barnegat Inlet. Charles J. Adams & David J. Seibold. (Illus.). 85p. 1984. pap. 4.95 (ISBN 0-9610008-3-X). C J Adams.

Shipwrecks of Lake Huron: The Great Sweet Water Sea. Jack Parker. (Illus.). 175p. (Orig.). 1986. pap. 7.49 (ISBN 0-932212-45-X). Avery Color.

Shipwrecks of Lake Superior. James R. Marshall. (Illus.). 100p. (Orig.). 1987. pap. 11.95 (ISBN 0-942235-00-2). LSPC Inc.

Shipwrecks of New Jersey. Gary Gentile. (Illus.). 172p. (Orig.). 1988. pap. 14.95 (ISBN 0-9616399-2-X). Sea Sports Pubns.

Shipwrecks of North Wales. Ivor W. Jones. (Illus.). 192p. 1986. 18.95 (ISBN 0-7153-8864-9). David & Charles.

Shipwrecks of the Lakes. Dana T. Bowen. 1952. 9.75 (ISBN 0-912514-21-3). Freshwater.

Shipwrecks of the Pacific Coast. 2nd rev. & enl. ed. James A. Gibbs. LC 57-13208. (Illus.). 1971. pap. 9.95 (ISBN 0-8323-0391-7). Binford-Metropolitan.

Shipwrecks of the Straits of Mackinac. Charles E. Feltner & Jeri Baron Felter. LC 87-60808. (Illus.). 128p. (Orig.). 1987. pap. 9.95 (ISBN 0-9609014-1-8). Seajay.

Shipwrecks off Central New Jersey Coast. William O. Davis. 1987. write for info. Wm O Davis.

Shipwrecks off Juan De Fuca. James A. Gibbs. LC 68-28924. (Illus.). 1968. 10.95 (ISBN 0-8323-0012-8); map 2.00 (ISBN 0-8323-0051-9). Binford-Metropolitan.

Shipwrecks off Ocean City (N. J.) David J. Seibold & Charles J. Adams, III. (Illus.). 112p. 1986. pap. 5.95 (ISBN 0-9610008-4-8). C J Adams.

Shipwrecks on the Chesapeake: Maritime Disasters on Chesapeake Bay & Its Tributaries, 1608-1978. Donald G. Shomette. LC 81-85606. (Illus.). 336p. 1982. 18.50 (ISBN 0-87033-283-X). Tidewater.

Shipwrecks on the Virginia Coast & the Men of the United States Life Saving Service. Richard A. Pouliot & Julie J. Pouliot. LC 85-41004. (Illus.). 240p. 1986. 16.95 (ISBN 0-87033-352-6). Tidewater.

Shipwrecks, Smugglers & Maritime Mysteries. 2nd rev. ed. Eugene D. Wheeler & Robert E. Kallman. LC 84-25106. (Illus.). 160p. (Orig.). 1986. pap. 8.95 (ISBN 0-934793-03-4). Pathfinder CA.

Shir Hama Alot L'Davd (Song of the Steps) & Ktav Hitzazzelut L'Darshanim (In Dengese of Preachers) by David Darshan. Perelmutter. Date not set. 20.00. Ktav.

Shir Hashirim-Song of Songs. Meir Zlotowitz. (Art Scroll Tanach Ser.). 224p. 1977. 11.95 (ISBN 0-89906-008-0); pap. 8.95 (ISBN 0-89906-009-9). Mesorah Pubns.

Shira: A Legacy of Courage. Sharon Grollman. LC 87-13456. (Illus.). 96p. (YA) (gr. 6-12). 1988. pap. 12.95 (ISBN 0-385-24114-3). Doubleday.

Shira's Summer. Libby Lazewnik. (YA) (gr. 6-9). Date not set. 12.95; pap. 9.95. Feldheim.

Shiraz, Persian City of Saints & Poets. Arthur J. Arberry. LC 60-8752. (Centers of Civilization Ser.: No.2). (Illus.). pap. 47.80 (ISBN 0-317-11173-6, 2016192). Bks Demand UMI.

Shire Horse. Keith Chivers. (Illus.). 36.00 (ISBN 0-85131-245-4, BL176, Pub. by J A Allen U K). S R Smith Sporting Bks.

Shirim: Songs of My Jewishness. LC 85-62081. 64p. 1986. 4.95 (ISBN 0-9615631-0-9). Almin.

Shirim U-Zemirot: Songs & Hymns for Gates of Prayer. Ed. by Cantor Raymond Smolover & Malcolm Stern. (Illus.). 121p. 3.95 (ISBN 0-317-33901-X, 33-X). Central Conf.

Shirkutu of Babylonian Deities. Raymond P. Dougherty. LC 78-63548. (Yale Oriental Ser. Researches: 5, Pt. 2). Repr. of 1923 ed. 25.00 (ISBN 0-404-60295-9). AMS Pr.

Shirley. Charlotte Bronte. (Clarendon Edition of the Novels of Brontes). (Illus.). 1981. text ed. 98.00x (ISBN 0-19-812565-8). Oxford U Pr.

Shirley. Charlotte Bronte. Ed. by Andrew Hook & Judith Hook. (English Library Ser.). (Orig.). 1974. pap. 4.95 (ISBN 0-14-043095-4). Penguin.

Shirley. Charlotte Bronte. Ed. by Margaret Smith & Herbert Rosengarten. (World's Classics-Paperback Ser.). 1981. pap. 4.95 (ISBN 0-19-281562-8). Oxford U Pr.

Shirley Chisholm: A Bibliography of Writings by & about Her. Compiled by Susan Duffy. LC 88-2073. 143p. 1988. 17.50 (ISBN 0-8108-2105-2). Scarecrow.

Shirley Family. G. T. Ridlon. LC 79-138076. (Saco Valley Settlements Ser). 1970. pap. 1.50 (ISBN 0-8048-0833-3). C E Tuttle.

Shirley Holmquist & Aunt Wilma, Who Dunit? Janet L. Martin. Ed. by Eunice W. Pearson. (Illus.). 120p. (Orig.). 1988. pap. 7.95 (ISBN 0-9613437-2-9, Martin Hse Pubns). Redbird Prods.

Shirley Jackson. Lenemaja Friedman. (United States Authors Ser.: No. 253). 1975. lib. bdg. 14.95 (ISBN 0-8057-0402-7, Twayne). G K Hall.

Shirley Jackson Case & the Chicago School: The Socio-Historical Method. William J. Hynes. Ed. by Kent Richards. LC 81-8973. (Society of Biblical Literature Biblical Scholarship in North America Ser.). 1981. pap. text ed. 15.00 (ISBN 0-89130-510-6, 06-11-05). Scholars Pr GA.

Shirley Letters. Louise Clappe. LC 77-141468. (Illus.). 224p. 1970. pap. 5.95 (ISBN 0-87905-004-7, Peregrine Smith). Gibbs Smith Pub.

Shirley Maclaine. Roy Pickard. (Film Stars Ser.). (Illus.). 96p. 1985. 7.95 (ISBN 0-87052-122-5). Hippocrene Bks.

Shirley MacLaine & the New Age Movement. James W. Sire. (Viewpoint Pamphlet Ser.). 32p. (Orig.). 1988. pap. 1.95 (ISBN 0-8308-1106-0). Inter-Varsity.

Shirley Muldowney. Jane Duden. Ed. by Carnival Enterprises Staff. LC 87-27570. (Sports Close-Ups Ser.). (Illus.). 48p. (gr. 5-6). 1988. PLB 10.95 (ISBN 0-89686-369-7). Crestwood Hse.

Shirley Temple: American Princess. Anne Edwards. (Illus.). 420p. 1988. 22.95 (ISBN 0-688-06051-X). Morrow.

Shirley Temple Black: Actress to Ambassador. James Haskins. (Women of Our Time Ser.). (Illus.). 64p. (gr. 2-7). 1988. 10.95 (ISBN 0-670-81957-3). Viking.

Shirley Temple Scrapbook. Loraine Burdick. 1982. pap. 8.95 (ISBN 0-8246-0277-3). Jonathan David.

Shirlick Holmes & the Case of the Wandering Wardrobe. Jane Yolen. (Illus.). 80p. (gr. 9-12). 1981. 8.95 (ISBN 0-698-20498-0, Coward). Putnam Pub Group.

Shiro in Love. Wendy Tokuda & Richard Hall. (Illus.). 32p. (gr. 1-3). 1988. 11.95 (ISBN 0-89346-306-X). Heian Intl.

Shiro to Shoin see Feudal Architecture of Japan.

Shirot Bialik: A New & Annotated Translation of Chaim Nachman Bialik's Epic Poems. Steven L. Jacobs. LC 87-11383. (Hebraica-Judaica Bookshelf Ser.). 1988. 22.95 (ISBN 0-933771-03-7). Alpha Pub Co.

Shirt Drafting & Grading Book, No. 1. rev. ed. L. H. Warmkessel. (Illus.). 1977. spiral binding 12.00 (ISBN 0-686-21214-2). Master Design.

Shirt Shoppe. 1987. pap. 5.95 (ISBN 0-256-06492-X). Irwin.

Shirt Sleeve Approach to Long Range Planning for the Smaller Growing Corporation. R. Linneman. 1980. 39.00 (ISBN 0-13-808972-8). P-H.

Shirt-Sleeve Diplomacy. facs. ed. Jonathan B. Bingham. LC 77-133512. (Select Bibliographies Reprint Ser). 1954. 19.00 (ISBN 0-8369-5544-7). Ayer Co Pubs.

Shirt-Sleeve Diplomat. Josephus Daniels. LC 73-11621. (Illus.). 547p. 1973. Repr. of 1947 ed. lib. bdg. 35.00x (ISBN 0-8371-7082-6, DASD). Greenwood.

Shirt-Sleeves Management. James F. Evered. 160p. 1981. 14.95 (ISBN 0-8144-5636-7). AMACOM.

Shirt-Sleeves Management. James F. Evered. LC 80-67962. pap. 47.00 (ISBN 0-317-10215-X, 2022625). Bks Demand UMI.

Shirt-Sleeves Management. James F. Evered. LC 80-67962. 192p. 1984. pap. 9.95 (ISBN 0-8144-7626-0); pap. 7.95. AMACOM.

Shish Mahal Cook Book. 88p. 1985. 20.00x (ISBN 0-907526-08-X, Pub. by Alloway Pub). State Mutual Bk.

Shisha Embroidery: Traditional Mirrorwork of India, Pakistan & Afghanistan. Nancy D. Gross & Frank Fontana. (Illus.). 80p. (Orig.). 1981. pap. 3.50 (ISBN 0-486-24043-6). Dover.

Shishapangma Expedition. Doug Scott & Alex MacIntyre. (Illus.). 322p. 1985. 18.95 (ISBN 0-89886-098-9). Mountaineers.

Shit on My Shoes. Duncan McNaughton. (Illus.). 1979. pap. 5.00 (ISBN 0-939180-12-X). Tombouctou.

Shitkickers & Other Texas Stories. Carolyn Weathers. LC 87-72599. 85p. (Orig.). 1987. pap. 6.95 (ISBN 0-9616572-2-7). Clothespin Fever Pr.

Shito-Ryu Karate. Fumio Demura. LC 74-169720. (Japanese Arts Ser.). (Illus.). 1971. pap. text ed. 6.95x (ISBN 0-89750-005-9, 110, Dist. by Wehman). Ohara Pubns.

Shitra Stein's Day Trips from Houston. rev. ed. Carol Barrington. Ed. by Shifra Stein. LC 85-71256. (Day Trips America Ser.). 192p. 1985. pap. 7.95 (ISBN 0-88742-055-9). Globe Pequot.

Shitra Stein's Day Trips from Phoenix-Tucson & Flagstaff. Pam Hait. Ed. by Shifra Stein. LC 85-71255. (Day Trips America Ser.). (Illus.). 192p. 1986. pap. 9.95 (ISBN 0-88742-056-7). Globe Pequot.

Shitsu-Gei. Jo Okada. 199p. 1961. 350.00x (ISBN 0-317-68496-5, Pub. by Han-Shan Tang Ltd). State Mutual Bk.

Shiur Qomah: Liturgy & Theurgy in Pre-Kabbalistic Jewish Mysticism. Martin S. Cohen. 300p. (Orig.). 1983. lib. bdg. 29.00 (ISBN 0-8191-3272-1). U Pr of Amer.

Shiva & Dionysus. Alain Danielou. 250p. (Orig.). 1984. pap. 8.95 (ISBN 0-89281-057-2). Inner Tradit.

Shiva Descending. Gregory Benford & William Rotsler. 400p. 1985. pap. 3.95 (ISBN 0-8125-3183-3, Dist. by Warner Pub Services & St. Martin's Press). Tor Bks.

Shiva's Pigeons: An Experience of India. Jon Godden & Rumer Godden. (Illus.). 384p. 1972. 25.00 (ISBN 0-670-64055-7, Studio). Viking.

Shivering Babe, Victorious Lord: The Nativity in Poetry & Art. Linda C. Sledge. LC 81-9728. pap. 49.80 (ISBN 0-317-30162-4, 2025344). Bks Demand UMI.

Shivers. William Schoell. 400p. (Orig.). 1985. pap. 3.75 (ISBN 0-8439-2235-4, Leisure Bks). Leisure NY.

Shivers. William Schoell. 400p. 1988. pap. 3.95 (ISBN 0-8439-2607-4, Pub. by Leisure Bks CT). Leisure NY.

Shivers & Goose Bumps: How We Keep Warm. Franklyn M. Branley. LC 82-45921. (Illus.). 96p. (gr. 5 up). 1984. 12.70 (ISBN 0-690-04334-1, Crowell Jr Bks); PLB 12.89 (ISBN 0-690-04335-X). HarpJ.

Shiv'im: Essays & Studies in Honor of Ira Eisenstein. Ed. by R. A. Brauner. 20.00x (ISBN 0-87068-442-6). Ktav.

Shiwan Gujin Taoyi: Ancient & Modern Shekwan Pottery. Ed. by He Bingen. 196p. 1981. 75.00x (ISBN 0-317-44198-1, Pub. by Han-Shan Tang Ltd). State Mutual Bk.

Shiyak! Tom Anderson & Helane Anderson. (Illus.). 325p. 1988. 24.95; lib. bdg. 24.95 (ISBN 0-9619474-9-7). Windship Pr.

Shizuo Kakutani: Collected Mathematical Papers, 2 Vols. Robert Kallman. (Contemporary Mathematics Ser.). 1987. Vol. 1. lib. bdg. 139.50 (ISBN 0-8176-3277-8); Vol. 2. lib. bdg. 137.00 (ISBN 0-8176-3278-6); Set. 230.50. Birkhauser.

Shkola Dlya Durakov. 2nd & rev. ed. Sasha Sokolov. 1983. 19.50 (ISBN 0-88233-884-6); pap. 8.95 (ISBN 0-88233-885-4). Ardis Pubs.

Shlamo Homelich & the Ashmedai. Illus. by Rochel Denkels & Miriam Silberman. write for info. (ISBN 0-9614920-0-7). Shain F.

Sh'ma B'ni. M. Lavry. (BJE Choral). 6p. (Hebrew.). 0.65 (ISBN 0-318-13634-1, 44-604). Board Jewish Educ.

Shmittah: What It's All About. Eliezer Gevirtz. (Orig.). 1987. 5.00. Torah Umesorah.

Shmuel Aleph. David Benvenisty. (Illus.). 84p. pap. 1.80 (ISBN 0-318-13635-X, 14-523). Board Jewish Educ.

Shmuel Bet. David Benvenisty. (Illus.). 63p. pap. 1.80 (ISBN 0-318-13636-8, 14-524). Board Jewish Educ.

Shmueli Family, 2 bks. Incl. Bk. 1. Cartoon Adventure. 5.00x (ISBN 0-685-55046-X, 405310); Bk. 2. More Cartoon Adventures. 5.00x (ISBN 0-685-55047-8, 405311). 1975. 6.00. UAHC.

Shnook the Peddler. Maxine Schur. LC 85-6807. (Illus.). 40p. (gr. 3-6). 1985. PLB 8.95 (ISBN 0-87518-298-4, Gemstone Bks). Dillon.

Sho: Japanese Calligraphy. C. J. Earnshaw. 1988. 19.95 (ISBN 0-8048-1568-2). C E Tuttle.

Sho King, or the Book of Historical Documents, 4 vols, Vol. 2. Tr. by James Legge. (Chinese Classics Ser.). (Chinese & Eng.). 1983. Repr. of 1893 ed. 35.00x (ISBN 0-89986-354-X); Set. 125.00x. Oriental Bk Store.

Shoah: An Oral History of the Holocaust. Claude Lanzmann. 228p. 1985. 11.95 (ISBN 0-394-55142-7); pap. 6.95 (ISBN 0-394-74329-6). Pantheon.

Shoal of Time: A History of the Hawaiian Islands. Gavan Daws. LC 73-92053. 507p. 1974. pap. 8.95 (ISBN 0-8248-0324-8). UH Pr.

Shoals of Capricorn. Francis D. Ommanney. LC 74-15555. (Illus.). 322p. 1975. Repr. of 1952 ed. lib. bdg. 35.00x (ISBN 0-8371-7823-1, OMSC). Greenwood.

Shobogenzo: Zen Essays by Dogen. Dogen. Tr. by Thomas Cleary. LC 85-20979. 136p. 1986. 14.00x (ISBN 0-8248-1014-7). UH Pr.

Shock. George T. Shires & Charles J. Carrico. LC 73-85076. (Major Problems in Clinical Surgery Ser.: Vol. 13). pap. 44.50 (ISBN 0-317-08711-8, 2016682). Bks Demand UMI.

Shock: A Nursing Guide. Jacqueline Carolan. 1984. pap. 19.50 (ISBN 0-87489-346-1). Med Economics.

Shock & Detonation Waves. John G. Kirkwood. Ed. by W. W. Wood. LC 68-7145. (Documents on Modern Physics Ser.). (Illus.). 142p. 1967. 59.00 (ISBN 0-677-00380-3). Gordon & Breach.

Shock & the Adult Respiratory Distress Syndrome. Ed. by W. J. Kox & D. J. Bihari. (Current Concepts in Critical Care Ser.). (Illus.). 255p. 1987. 41.20 (ISBN 0-387-17484-2). Springer-Verlag.

Shock & Vibration Control Handbook. 2nd ed. Cyril M. Harris & Charles E. Crede. 1976. text ed. 69.50 (ISBN 0-07-026799-5). McGraw.

Shock & Vibration Engineering. Charles T. Morrow. LC 63-7556. pap. 101.00 (ISBN 0-317-08532-8, 2011956). Bks Demand UMI.

Shock & Vibration Handbook. 3rd ed. Cyril M. Harris. 1344p. 1988. text ed. 76.50 (ISBN 0-07-026801-0). McGraw.

Shock Effect. Glen Ebisch. (Crosswinds Ser.). pap. 2.25 (ISBN 0-373-98011-6). Harlequin Bks.

Shock: Medical Subject Analysis & Research Bibliography. Illie L. Fodor. LC 84-45663. 150p. 1986. 34.50 (ISBN 0-88164-202-9); pap. 26.50 (ISBN 0-88164-203-7). ABBE Pubs Assn.

Shock of Motherhood: The Unexpected Challenge for the New Generation of Mothers. Beppie Harrison. 256p. 1986. 17.95 (ISBN 0-684-18485-0). Scribner.

Shock of the New: Art & the Century of Change. Robert Hughes. 423p. 1981. pap. text ed. 30.95 (ISBN 0-394-32800-0, KnopfC). Knopf.

Shock of the New: The Life & Death of Modern Art. Robert Hughes. LC 80-7631. (Illus.). 400p. 1981. 29.95 (ISBN 0-394-51378-9). Knopf.

Shock: Pathology, Metabolism, Shock Cell, Treatment. I. Suteu. (Illus.). 447p. 1977. cancelled 32.00 (ISBN 0-85626-091-6, Pub. by Abacus England). IPS.

Shock, Physiological Surgery & George Washington Crile: Medical Innovation in the Progressive Era. Peter C. English. LC 79-8579. (Contributions in Medical History: No. 5). xi, 271p. 1980. lib. bdg. 40.95 (ISBN 0-313-21490-5, EMI/). Greenwood.

Shock Research. D. H. Lewis & U. Haglund. (Fernstrom Foundation Ser.: Vol. 3). 1983. 97.00 (ISBN 0-444-80533-8, I-352-83). Elsevier.

Shock Sensitive Industrial Materials: Advanced Improvised Explosives, Vol. Two. Seymour Lecker. (Illus.). 56p. 1988. pap. text ed. 8.00 (ISBN 0-87364-461-1). Paladin Pr.

Shock Tactics. Mary Lee. 1982. 15.00x (ISBN 0-906660-07-6, Pub. by New Playwrights Network). State Mutual Bk.

Shock: The Reversible Stage of Dying. R. M. Hardaway. (Illus.). 568p. 1988. 75.00 (ISBN 0-88416-470-5). PSG Pub Co.

Shock to the System. Simon Brett. 256p. 1985. 13.95 (ISBN 0-684-18351-X, ScribT). Scribner.

Shock to the System. Simon Brett. 1987. pap. 3.50 (ISBN 0-440-18200-X). Dell.

Shock-Trauma Care Plans. Julie M. Strange. LC 87-9922. (Illus.). 382p. 1987. pap. 24.95 (ISBN 0-87434-084-5). Springhouse Pub.

Shock Trauma-Critical Care Handbook. C. Michael Dunham & R. Adams Cowley. 641p. 1986. 39.00 (ISBN 0-87189-359-2). Aspen Pub.

Shock Treatment: A Collection of Short Fiction Thrillers. Ed. by Mary M. Blake & Jacquelyn D. Scheneman. LC 88-90792. 196p. (Orig.). 1988. pap. price not set (ISBN 0-945157-04-5). Peak Output Unltd.

Shock Tube & Shock Wave Research: Proceedings of the Eleventh International Symposium on Shock Tubes & Waves. Ed. by Boye Ahlborn et al. LC 77-20168. (Illus.). 670p. 1978. 60.00x (ISBN 0-295-95582-1). U of Wash Pr.

Shock Value. Karin Berne. 320p. (Orig.). 1985. pap. 2.95 (ISBN 0-445-20136-3, Pub. by Popular Lib). Warner Bks.

Shock Value: A Tasteful Book about Bad Taste. John Waters. 224p. (Orig.). 1981. pap. 14.95 (ISBN 0-385-28903-0, Delta). Dell.

Shock Waves & High-Strain-Rate Phenomena in Metals: Concepts & Applications. Ed. by Marc A. Meyers & Lawrence E. Murr. LC 80-27395. 1116p. 1981. 145.00x (ISBN 0-306-40633-0, Plenum Pr). Plenum Pub.

Shock Waves & Reaction-Diffusion Equations. J. Smoller. (Grundlehren der Mathematischen Wissenschaften: Vol. 258). (Illus.). 581p. 1983. 50.00 (ISBN 0-387-90752-1). Springer-Verlag.

Shock Waves & Shock Tubes: Proceedings of the Fifteenth International Symposium on Shock Waves & Shock Tubes. Ed. by Daniel Bershader & Ronald Hanson. (Illus.). 950p. 1986. 49.50x (ISBN 0-8047-1310-3). Stanford U Pr.

Shock Waves, Explosions & Detonations, PAAS 87. Ed. by J. R. Bowen et al. LC 83-15454. (Illus.). 505p. 59.50 (ISBN 0-915928-76-0). AIAA.

Shock Waves in Chemistry. Lifshitz. 400p. 1981. 95.00 (ISBN 0-8247-1331-1). Dekker.

Shock Waves in Collisionless Plasmas. D. A. Tidman. Ed. by N. A. Krali. LC 74-13711. 187p. (Orig.). 1971. 18.50 (ISBN 0-471-86785-3, JW). Krieger.

Shock Waves in Condensed Matter. Ed. by Y. M. Gupta. 940p. 1986. 125.00x (ISBN 0-306-42276-X, Plenum Pr). Plenum Pub.

Shock Waves in Condensed Matter - 1987: Proceedings of the American Physical Society Topical Conference, Monterey, CA, July 20-23, 1987. Ed. by S. C. Schmidt & N. C. Holmes. 804p. 1988. 131.50 (ISBN 0-444-87097-0, North Holland). Elsevier.

Shock Waves in Condensed Matter: 1981 (Menlo Park) Ed. by W. J. Nellis et al. LC 82-70014. (AIP Conference Proceedings: No. 78). 715p. 1982. lib. bdg. 43.00 (ISBN 0-88318-177-0). Am Inst Physics.

Shock Waves in Condensed Matter, 1983: Proceedings of the American Physical Society, Topical Conference, Conference, Sante Fe, Mexico, July 18-21, 1983. Ed. by J. R. Asay et al. 670p. 1985. 68.75 (ISBN 0-444-86904-2, North-Holland). Elsevier.

Shock Waves in Plasmas. Sagdeev. 1987. write for info. (ISBN 0-471-09588-5). Wiley.

Shock Waves: Letter from the Edge. Jonathan Konrad. 1987. 6.95 (ISBN 0-533-07281-6). Vantage.

Shocking & Astounding Rise & Fall of the Educated Fool. George T. Brittain. 1988. 5.95 (ISBN 0-533-07619-6). Vantage.

Shocking Truth about Water. 24th, rev. ed. Paul C. Bragg & Patricia Bragg. (Illus.). pap. 4.95 (ISBN 0-87790-000-0). Health Sci.

Shocktrauma. Jon Franklin & Alan Doelp. 256p. 1981. pap. 2.95 (ISBN 0-449-24387-7, Crest). Fawcett.

Shockwave, Vol. 4. Barbara Siegel & Scott Siegel. (Firebrats Ser.: No. 4). 160p. (Orig.). (YA) (gr. 7 up). pap. 2.50 (ISBN 0-671-60682-4). Archway.

Shockwave Rider. John Brunner. (Del Rey Bk.). 1984. pap. 2.95 (ISBN 0-345-32431-5). Ballantine.

Shoe & Canoe or Pictures of Travel in the Canadas, 2 Vols. John J. Bigsby. LC 69-19549. 1969. Repr. of 1850 ed. Set. 42.50 (ISBN 0-404-00880-1); 22.00 ea. Vol. 1 (ISBN 0-404-00881-X). Vol. 2 (ISBN 0-404-00882-8). AMS Pr.

Shoe City: Growing up in Brockton, Mass. During the Roaring Twenties. Arthur F. Joy. (Illus.). 1978. pap. 5.50 (ISBN 0-317-28503-3). Saturscent Pubns.

Shoe Goes to Wrigley Field. Jeff MacNelly. (Illus.). 64p. (Orig.). 1988. pap. 5.95 (ISBN 0-933893-51-5). Bonus Books.

Shoe Must Go On. Jeff MacNelly. 128p. 1985. pap. 6.95 (ISBN 0-03-000737-2, Owl Bks). H Holt & Co.

Shoe Repairing. Henry Karg. (Illus.). 1975. pap. text ed. 12.00 (ISBN 0-931424-00-3). Shoe Serv Inst.

Shoe Repairing Course see Practical Course in Modern Shoe Repairing.

Shoe Shine Parlor Poems Et Al. W. R. Rodriguez. 48p. 1984. pap. 6.50 (ISBN 0-941160-08-4). Ghost Pony Pr.

Shoe That Wouldn't. Jerry Duris. (Young People Ser.). (Illus.). 60p. (Orig.). 1986. pap. 7.95 (ISBN 0-943920-49-3). Metamorphous Pr.

Shoeblack & the Sovereign: Reflections on Morality & Foreign Policy. George Walden. 192p. 1988. 14.95 (ISBN 0-312-02281-6, Pub. by Thomas Dunne Bks). St Martin.

Shoebox of Desire. Allen Woodman. LC 86-63358. (Illus.). 88p. 1987. lib. bdg. 13.95 (ISBN 0-930501-10-1); pap. 7.95 (ISBN 0-930501-11-X). Swallows Tale Pr.

Shoebox Syndrome (Record-Keeping) Selma H. Lamkin. (Orig.). 15.00 (ISBN 0-686-32948-1). Nikmal Pub.

Shoelace Solution. Ray Broekel. LC 79-52409. (Carolrhoda Mini-Mysteries Ser.). (Illus.). (gr. 1-4). 1980. PLB 5.95 (ISBN 0-87614-115-7). Carolrhoda Bks.

Shoeless Joe. W. P. Kinsella. 224p. 1983. pap. 3.95 (ISBN 0-345-34256-9). Ballantine.

Shoemaker. Flora R. Schreiber. 1984. pap. 4.50 (ISBN 0-451-12855-9, Sig). NAL.

Shoemaker. William Shoemaker & Barney Nagler. 288p. 1988. 17.95 (ISBN 0-385-23945-9). Doubleday.

Shoemaker & the Elves. Adrienne Adams. (Illus.). 32p. (gr. k-3). 1981. pap. 2.95 (ISBN 0-689-70480-1, Aladdin). Macmillan.

Shoemaker & the Elves. Adrienne Adams & Jacob Grimm. LC 60-12607. (Illus.). (gr. k-4). 1960. 12.95 (ISBN 0-684-12982-5, Scribner). Macmillan.

Shoemaker & the Elves. Cynthia Birrer & William Birrer. LC 83-1145. (Illus.). 32p. (gr. k-3). 1983. 11.75 (ISBN 0-688-01988-9); PLB 11.88 (ISBN 0-688-01989-7). Lothrop.

Shoemaker & the Elves. Jacob Grimm & Wilhelm K. Grimm. (Illus.). 16p. 1975. 20.00 (ISBN 0-945303-04-1). Evanescent Pr.

Shoemaker & the Elves. Wilhelm K. Grimm & Jacob Grimm. Adapted by Margaret A. Hughes. (Talking Mother Goose Ser.). (Illus.). 26p. (ps). 1987. Packaged with pre-programmed audio cassette tapes. 9.95 (ISBN 0-934323-65-8). Alchemy Comms.

Shoemaker & the Elves. (Pic-a-Story Bks.). (Illus.). 24p. (Orig.). (gr. k-1). 1981. 4.95 (ISBN 0-89531-103-8, 218-96); pap. 1.95 (ISBN 0-686-79405-2, 0219-48). Sharon Pubns.

Shoemaker Fooze. D. L. Pape. LC 68-56827. (Oddo Sound Ser.). (Illus.). 48p. (gr. 2-5). 1969. PLB 10.95 (ISBN 0-87783-036-3). Oddo.

Shoemaker Martin. Leo Tolstoy. Adapted by Brigitte Hanhart. LC 86-60489. (Illus.). 32p. (gr. k-3). 1986. 12.95 (ISBN 0-8050-0040-2, North South Bks). H Holt & Co.

Shoemaker: The Anatomy of a Psychopath. Flora R. Schreiber. 1983. 16.95 (ISBN 0-671-22652-5). S&S.

Shoemaker's Best Selections, No. 1. facsimile ed. Ed. by J. W. Shoemaker. LC 79-116415. (Granger Index Reprint Ser). 1873. 15.00 (ISBN 0-8369-6156-0). Ayer Co Pubs.

Shoemaker's Best Selections, No. 2. facs. ed. Ed. by J. W. Shoemaker. LC 79-116415. (Granger Index Reprint Ser). 1875. 15.00 (ISBN 0-8369-6185-4). Ayer Co Pubs.

Shoemaker's Best Selections, No. 3. facsimile ed. Ed. by J. W. Shoemaker. LC 79-116415. (Granger Index Reprint Ser). 1875. 15.00 (ISBN 0-8369-6157-9). Ayer Co Pubs.

Shoemaker's Best Selections, No. 4. facsimile ed. Ed. by J. W. Shoemaker. LC 79-116415. (Granger Index Reprint Ser). 1890. 15.00 (ISBN 0-8369-6158-7). Ayer Co Pubs.

Shoemaker's Best Selections, No. 5. facs. ed. Ed. by J. W. Shoemaker. LC 79-116415. (Granger Index Reprint Ser). 1877. 14.00 (ISBN 0-8369-6175-7). Ayer Co Pubs.

Shoemaker's Best Selections, No. 6. facs. ed. Ed. by J. W. Shoemaker. LC 79-116415. (Granger Index Reprint Ser). 1880. 15.00 (ISBN 0-8369-6186-2). Ayer Co Pubs.

Shoemaker's Best Selections, No. 7. facs. ed. Ed. by J. W. Shoemaker. LC 79-116415. (Granger Index Reprint Ser). 1880. 14.00 (ISBN 0-8369-6176-5). Ayer Co Pubs.

Shoemaker's Best Selections, Nos. 9, 10, 11. Compiled by J. W. Shoemaker. LC 79-116415. (Granger Index Reprint Ser.). 1972. 16.00 ea.; No. 9, 1881. (ISBN 0-8369-6378-4); No. 10, 1882. (ISBN 0-8369-6379-2); No. 11, 1883. (ISBN 0-8369-6380-6). Ayer Co Pubs.

Shoemaker's Best Selections: For Readings & Recitations. Incl. No. 25. Compiled by Mrs. J. W. Shoemaker. LC 79-116415. Repr. of 1906 ed (ISBN 0-8369-6414-4); No. 26. Compiled by Mrs. J. W. Shoemaker. LC 79-116415. Repr. of 1901 ed (ISBN 0-8369-6415-2). (Granger Index Reprint Ser.). 1973. 13.50 ea. Ayer Co Pubs.

Shoemaker's Best Selections: For Readings & Recitations. Incl. No. 21. Compiled by Austin H. Merrill. LC 79-116415. Repr. of 1893 ed (ISBN 0-8369-6408-X); No. 22. Compiled by Loraine Immen. LC 79-116415. Repr. of 1894 ed (ISBN 0-8369-6409-8); No. 23. Ed. by Mrs. J. W. Shoemaker. LC 79-116415. 1973. Repr. of 1895 ed (ISBN 0-8369-6410-1). (Granger Index Reprint Ser.). 1973. 13.25 ea. Ayer Co Pubs.

Shoemaker's Best Selections: For Reading & Recitations, No. 14. facsimile ed. Ed. by J. W. Shoemaker. LC 79-116415. (Granger Index Reprint Ser.). Repr. of 1886 ed. 14.00 (ISBN 0-8369-6273-7). Ayer Co Pubs.

Shoemaker's Dream. Mildred Schell. (Illus.). 28p. (ps up). 1982. 6.95. Judson.

Shoemaker's Holiday. Thomas Dekker. Ed. by Merritt Lawlis. LC 78-14915. (gr. 10up). 1979. pap. text ed. 4.95 (ISBN 0-8120-0314-4). Barron.

Shoemakers Holiday. Thomas Dekker. Ed. by R. L. Smallwood et al. LC 79-87579. (Revels Plays Ser.). 244p. 1979. text ed. 20.00x (ISBN 0-8018-2293-9). Johns Hopkins.

Shoemaker's Holiday. Thomas Dekker. Ed. by D. J. Palmer. (New Mermaid Ser.). 1987. pap. 4.95x (ISBN 0-393-90005-3). Norton.

Shoemaker's Prodigious Wife see Five Plays: Comedies & Tragicomedies.

Shoemaker's Wife. Lotte Kramer. Date not set. price not set. Hippopotamus.

Shoemakes: God's Helpers. Elsie Rives. LC 86-4148. (Meet the Missionary Ser.). (gr. 4-6). 1986. pap. 5.95 (ISBN 0-8054-4328-2). Broadman.

Shoes. Robert Novak. 1975. 1.00 (ISBN 0-685-67937-3). Windless Orchard.

Shoes. June Swann. (Illus.). 96p. 1982. text ed. 15.95x (ISBN 0-7134-0942-8). Drama Bk.

Shoes. Elizabeth Winthrop. LC 85-45841. (Illus.). 32p. (ps-2). 1986. 11.95i (ISBN 0-06-026591-4); PLB 11.89 (ISBN 0-06-026592-2). HarpJ.

Shoes. Elizabeth Winthrop. LC 85-45841. (Trophy Picture Book). (Illus.). 32p. (ps-3). 1988. pap. 3.95 (ISBN 0-06-443171-1, Trophy). HarpJ.

Shoes for Everyone: A Story about Jan Matzeliger. Barbara Mitchell. (Creative Minds Ser.). (Illus.). 64p. (gr. 3-6). 1986. PLB 9.95 (ISBN 0-87614-290-0). Carolrhoda Bks.

Shoes for Everyone: A Story about Jan Matzeliger. Barbara Mitchell. (Creative Minds Bks.). (Illus.). (gr. 3-6). 1987. pap. 4.95 (ISBN 0-87614-473-3, First Ave Edns). Lerner Pubns.

Shoes in Vogue since 1910. Christina Probert. LC 81-67880. (Accessories in Vogue Ser.). (Illus.). 96p. 1981. pap. 12.95 (ISBN 0-89659-241-3). Abbeville Pr.

Shoes Never Lie. Mimi Pond. 128p. 1985. pap. 4.95 (ISBN 0-425-08104-4). Berkley Pub.

Shoes of Tanboury. Shimon Ballas. 40p. 1970. 4.95 (ISBN 0-88482-767-4). Hebrew Pub.

Shoes Story. Napoleon E. Fontanosa, II. 32p. (gr. 1-3). 1984. 5.95 (ISBN 0-89962-373-5). Todd & Honeywell.

Shoes That Danced & Other Poems. Anna H. Branch. LC 77-89722. (One-Act Plays in Reprint Ser.). 1977. Repr. of 1905 ed. 19.50x (ISBN 0-8486-2027-5). Roth Pub Inc.

Shoes to Live in Iowa. John Ellerbach. (Illus.). 72p. 1986. pap. 4.95 (ISBN 0-9616813-0-6). J Ellerbach.

Shoeshine Girl. Clyde R. Bulla. LC 75-8516. (Illus.). 80p. (gr. 3 up). 1975. 12.70i (ISBN 0-690-00758-2, Crowell Jr Bks). HarpJ.

Shoestring. Paul Abelman. LC 83-61259. 224p. 1984. 9.95 (ISBN 0-88186-376-9); pap. 3.50 (ISBN 0-88186-875-2). Parkwest Pubns.

Shofar That Lost Its Voice. David E. Fass. (Illus.). 48p. 1982. 6.95 (ISBN 0-8074-0168-4, 103500). UAHC.

Shoghi Effendi: Recollections. Ugo Giachery. (Illus.). 248p. 1973. 19.95 (ISBN 0-85398-050-0). G Ronald Pub.

Shogi: Japan's Game of Strategy. Trevor P. Leggett. LC 66-11011. (Illus.). 1966. 15.95 (ISBN 0-8048-0526-1). C E Tuttle.

Shogun. James Clavell. (YA) 1986. pap. 5.95 (ISBN 0-440-17800-2). Dell.

Shogun. James Clavell. 1983. pap. 21.95 (ISBN 0-385-29224-4). Delacorte.

Shogun. (Span.). 1985. pap. 5.95 (ISBN 0-440-17803-7). Dell.

Shogun see James Clavell Library.

Shogun Age Exhibition. Shogun Age Exhibition Exec. Committee Staff. (Illus.). 280p. 1983. pap. 250.00x (Pub. by Han-Shan Tang Ltd). State Mutual Bk.

Shogun! The Shogun Age Exhibition. The Shogun Age Exhibition Executive Committee. (Illus.). 280p. 1984. 50.00 (ISBN 0-295-96198-8); pap. 24.95 (ISBN 0-295-96197-X). U of Wash Pr.

Shogunal Politics: Arai Hakuseki & the Premises of Tokugawa Rule. Kate W. Nakai. LC 87-30517. (Harvard East Asian Monographs: No. 134). 400p. 1987. text ed. 23.00x (ISBN 0-674-80653-0, Pub. by Coun East Asian Stud). Harvard U Pr.

Shogun's Agents. (Grove Press Victorian Library). 224p. 1986. pap. 3.95 (ISBN 0-394-62252-9, BC). Grove.

Shogun's Reluctant Ambassadors. Katherine Plummer. (Illus.). 317p. 1984. pap. 9.25 (ISBN 4-89788-023-8, Pub. by Lotus Pr Japan). C E Tuttle.

Shoji. Jay Van Arsdale. LC 87-82860. (Illus.). 96p. 1988. pap. 15.95 (ISBN 0-87011-864-1). Kodansha.

Shoji Screens. Glenna Luschei. 1987. Handoriented artist bk. 125.00 (ISBN 0-318-22926-9). Solo Pr.

Shojo O Temmin. T. Volker. 82p. 1953. pap. 214.00x (ISBN 0-317-68412-4, Pub. by Han-Shan Tang Ltd). State Mutual Bk.

Shokuhin No Nenchosei see Consistency of Foodstuffs.

Sholem Aleichem's Wandering Star & Other Plays of Jewish Life. David S. Lifson. LC 86-73240. 216p. 1988. 19.95 (ISBN 0-8453-4810-8, Cornwall Bks). Assoc Univ Prs.

Sholem Aleykhem: Person, Persona, Presence. Dan Miron. LC 73-161969. (Uriel Weinreich Memorial Lecture Ser.: No.1). 45p. 1972. pap. 3.00 (ISBN 0-914512-02-1). Yivo Inst.

Sholom Aleichem: A Non-Critical Introduction. Sol Gittleman. (De Proprietatibus Litterarum Ser. Didactica: No. 3). 1974. pap. text ed. 13.60x (ISBN 90-2792-606-9). Mouton.

Shona & Zimbabwe Nine Hundred to Eighteen Fifty: An Outline of Shona History. D. N. Beach. LC 80-14116. 424p. 1980. 54.50 (ISBN 0-8419-0624-6, Africana). Holmes & Meier.

Shona, Lunch Girls, the Shelter: The 1983 Verity Bargate Award Winning Short Plays. Tony Craze et al. 128p. pap. 6.95 (ISBN 0-413-53850-8, NO. 3939). Heinemann Ed.

Shonto: A Study of the Role of the Trader in a Modern Navaho Community. Ed. by William Y. Adams. 1988. Repr. lib. bdg. 75.00x. Am Biog Serv.

Shoo-Fly & Other Folk Tales from Upstate. Donald J. Sawyer. LC 84-61376. (Illus.). 160p. (Orig.). 1984. pap. 8.75 (ISBN 0-9613682-0-9). Dejay Bks.

Shoot Better with Centerfire Rifle Cartridges-Ballistics Tables. Charles W. Matthews. (Illus.). 560p. (Orig.). 1984. pap. 16.45 (ISBN 0-9613734-0-7). B Matthews Inc.

Shoot-Em-Ups: The Complete Reference Guide to Westerns of the Sound Era. Les Adams & Buck Rainey. LC 78-656. 1985. 49.50 (ISBN 0-8108-1848-5). Scarecrow.

Shoot Low, Boys - They're Ridin' Shetland Ponies. Lewis Grizzard. 1988. pap. 3.95 (ISBN 0-345-00759-X). Ballantine.

Shoot Low, Boys-They're Ridin' Shetland Ponies. Lewis Grizzard. LC 85-61974. 336p. 1985. 13.95 (ISBN 0-931948-79-7). Peachtree Pubs.

Shoot Me While I Watch. Antonio Gambino. 250p. 1987. pap. text ed. write for info. (ISBN 0-9617987-9-3). Gambino West Pub.

Shoot Organization in Vascular Plants. Kenneth J. Dormer. LC 70-39412. (Illus.). 256p. 1972. text ed. 22.95x (ISBN 0-8156-5032-9). Syracuse U Pr.

Shoot Out. James L. Berkman. 32p. (Orig.). 1983. pap. 10.00 (ISBN 0-943662-02-8, 1-166-723). Runaway Pubns.

Shoot-Out. Robert E. Trevathan. 1985. 9.95 (ISBN 0-8034-8555-7, Avalon). Bouregy.

Shoot-Out at Buffalo Gulch. Bernard Palmer. (Living Books). 304p. 1985. pap. 3.95 (ISBN 0-8423-5849-8). Tyndale.

Shoot! (Si Gira) The Notebooks of Serafino Gubbio, Cinematograph Operator. Luigi Pirandello. Tr. by C. K. Moncrieff from Ital. LC 74-12380. 334p. 1975. Repr. of 1926 ed. 17.50x (ISBN 0-86527-302-2). Fertig.

Shoot! (Si Gura) The Notebook of Serafino Gubbio Cinematograph Operator. Luigi Pirandello. Ed. by Bruce S. Kupelnick. LC 76-52123. (Classics of Film Literature Ser.). 1978. lib. bdg. 22.00 (ISBN 0-8240-2889-9). Garland Pub.

Shoot the Piano Player. David Goodis. LC 86-71912. 176p. 1987. pap. 3.95 (ISBN 0-88739-030-7, Pub. by Black Lizard). Creative Arts Bk.

Shoot the Stars: How to Become a Celebrity Photographer. Brad Elterman. LC 85-71055. (Illus.). (gr. 10 up). 1985. pap. 12.95 (ISBN 0-933781-00-8). Cal Features.

Shoot Your Friends & Family for Fun & Profit. Eileen Stanton. (Illus.). 136p. Date not set. 11.95 (ISBN 0-944009-09-3). Compupress.

Shootdown: Flight 007 & the American Connection. R. W. Johnson. LC 86-1647. (Illus.). 352p. 1986. 18.95 (ISBN 0-670-81209-9). Viking.

Shootdown: Flight 007 & the American Connection. R. W. Johnson. (Illus.). 544p. 1987. pap. 4.50 (ISBN 0-14-009474-1). Penguin.

Shooter. Barry Sadler. 288p. (Orig.). 1987. pap. 3.50 (ISBN 0-8125-8831-2, Dist. by St Martin's Pr & Warner Pub Servs). Tor Bks.

Shooters. Leon Metz. LC 76-21578. (Illus.). 300p. 1976. 19.95 (ISBN 0-930208-04-8); Ltd. Silver Bullet Ed. o.p. 50.00 (ISBN 0-930208-05-6). Mangan Bks.

Shooters. Ken Meyer. LC 79-84407. (Illus.). 1979. pap. 12.95 (ISBN 0-87863-187-9, Farnswth Pub). Longman Finan.

Shooters Bible, 1988, No. 79. Ed. by W. S. Jarrett. 576p. 1987. pap. 14.95. Stoeger Pub Co.

Shooter's Bible 1989, No. 80. Ed. by William S. Jarrett. 576p. 1988. pap. 14.95 (ISBN 0-88317-145-7). Stoeger Pub Co.

Shootin' Mad. Sergio Aragones. (Mad Ser.). (Illus.). 192p. (Orig.). 1988. pap. 2.95 (ISBN 0-446-35131-8). Warner Bks.

Shootin' Sheriff & The Bandit of Bloody Run. Nelson Nye. (Two-in One Western Ser.). 1979. pap. 1.95 (ISBN 0-89083-444-X). Zebra.

Shooting: A Complete Guide for Beginners. John Marchington. (Illus.). 184p. (Orig.). 1982. pap. 6.95 (ISBN 0-571-11932-8). Faber & Faber.

Shooting an Elephant. George Orwell. LC 50-10343. 200p. 1956. 12.95 (ISBN 0-15-182043-0). HarBraceJ.

Shooting & Stalking: A Basic Guide. Ed. by Charles Coles. (Illus.). 204p. 1988. 34.95 (ISBN 0-09-173573-4, Pub. by Century Hutchinson). David & Charles.

Shooting & the Countryside. Hunter Adair. (Illus.). 144p. 1984. (Oriel); pap. 9.95 (ISBN 0-85362-215-9). Routledge Chapman & Hall.

Shooting Baskets in a Dark Gymnasium. Carl Linder. LC 84-82946. 64p. 1984. lib. bdg. 7.95 (ISBN 0-943512-03-4, 402W). Linwood Pub.

Shooting Ducks: A History of University of Oregon Basketball. Howard A. Hobson. (Illus.). 272p. (Orig.). 1984. (Western Imprints); pap. 15.95 (ISBN 0-87595-142-2). Oregon Hist.

Shooting Field: One Hundred Fifty Years with Holland & Holland. Peter King. (Illus.). 176p. 1985. 39.95 (ISBN 0-941540-12-X); For U. K. & European orders. (ISBN 0-907621-62-7). Blacksmith Corp.

Shooting for Stock. George Schaub. (Illus.). 144p. 1987. 27.50 (ISBN 0-8174-5870-0, Amphoto); pap. 18.95 (ISBN 0-8174-5871-9, Amphoto). Watson-Guptill.

Shooting for the Gold: A Portrait of America's Olympic Athletes. Walter Iooss, Jr. & Dave Anderson. LC 85-150626. 144p. 1984. 29.95 (ISBN 0-915463-03-2, Pub. by Jameson Bks, Dist. by Kampmann). Green Hill.

Shooting From the Lip: Essay Columns & Quips. Mike Lupica. LC 88-3387. 1988. 15.95 (ISBN 0-933893-60-4). Bonus Books.

Shooting Gallery. Yuko Tsushima. Tr. by Geraldine Harcourt. LC 87-22171. 160p. 1988. 11.95 (ISBN 0-394-56559-2); pap. 7.95 (ISBN 0-394-75743-2). Pantheon.

Shooting Guide for Beginners. Stepheni Slahor et al. LC 85-52428. (Illus.). 144p. 1986. pap. 7.95 (ISBN 0-910042-53-5). Allegheny.

Shooting in a Game. Paul J. Deegan. LC 75-11776. (Creative Education Sports Instructional Bks.). (Illus.). 32p. (gr. 4 up). 1975. PLB 8.95 (ISBN 0-87191-434-4). Creative Ed.

Shooting in the Dark. Carolyn Hougan. 336p. 1985. pap. 3.50 (ISBN 0-449-20633-5, Crest). Fawcett.

Shooting in the Dark: A Novel. Carolyn Hougan. 256p. 1984. 15.95 (ISBN 0-671-46722-0). S&S.

Shooting Made Easy. Mike Reynolds & Mike Barnes. (Illus.). 144p. 1986. 19.95 (ISBN 0-946284-78-4, Pub. by Crowood Pr). Longwood Pub Group.

Shooting of Dan McGrew. Robert W. Service. (Illus.). (gr. 3 up). Date not set. 14.95. Godine.

Shooting Ourselves in the Foot. Bernard J. O'Keefe. LC 85-7651. 294p. 1985. 17.95 (ISBN 0-395-38511-3). HM.

Shooting Party. Isabel Colegate. 208p. 1982. pap. 3.50 (ISBN 0-380-59543-5, 60297-0, Bard). Avon.

Shooting Party: A Novel. Anton Chekhov. LC 86-14605. 220p. 1987. pap. 8.95 (ISBN 0-226-10241-6). U of Chicago Pr.

Shooting Portraits on Location. Lisl Dennis. (Illus.). 144p. 1985. 27.50 (ISBN 0-8174-5875-1, Amphoto); pap. 16.95 (ISBN 0-8174-5876-X). Watson-Guptill.

Shooting Scripts. Adam Cornford. (Illus.). 1979. pap. 10.00 (ISBN 0-686-28251-5). Black Stone.

Shooting Star. Herge. (gr. 3-8). looseleaf bdg. 15.95 (ISBN 0-685-23419-3). French & Eur.

Shooting Star. Herge. (Illus.). 62p. 15.95 (ISBN 0-416-60580-X); pap. 4.95 (ISBN 0-416-24080-1). French & Eur.

Shooting Star. Herge. 1978. pap. 6.95 (ISBN 0-316-35851-7, Joy St Bks). Little.

Shooting Star & Other Poems. Martha LaBare. 64p. (Orig.). 1982. pap. 4.50 (ISBN 0-9609090-2-8). Swollen Magpie.

Shooting Stars. Rod Kierkegaard, Jr. (Illus.). 48p. 1987. 12.95 (ISBN 0-87416-028-6). Catalan Communs.

Shooting Stars: Heroes & Heroines of Western Film. Archie P. McDonald. 1987. 35.00 (ISBN 0-253-36685-2); pap. 12.95 (ISBN 0-253-20415-1). Ind U Pr.

Shooting Stars: Lockheed's Legendary T-Bird. Michael O'Leary. (Illus.). 128p. 1988. pap. 14.95 (ISBN 0-85045-846-3, Pub. by Osprey England). Motorbooks Intl.

Shooting Trail. Jack Bassett. 1986. 12.50 (ISBN 0-8166-0249-2, Large Print Bks). G K Hall.

Shooting Video. Frederic W. Rosen. 220p. 1983. pap. 15.95 (ISBN 0-240-51709-1). Focal Pr.

Shooting War: Photography & the American Experience of Combat. Susan D. Moeller. LC 88-47895. (Illus.). 408p. 1989. 25.95 (ISBN 0-465-07777-3). Basic.

Shootout at Milk River. Lee Floren. 1977. pap. 1.50 (ISBN 0-505-51185-1, Pub. by Tower Bks). Leisure NY.

Shootout at Shiprock. Lee O. Miller. (Orig.). 1981. pap. 1.75 (ISBN 0-505-51630-6, Pub. by Tower Bks). Leisure NY.

Shoowa Design: African Textiles from the Kingdom of Kuba. Georges Meurant. (Illus.). 200p. 1986. 60.00. Thames Hudson.

Shop. Watson. (Picture Word Bks.). (gr. k-2). 1980. 6.95 (ISBN 0-86020-393-X, Usborne-Hayes); PLB 11.96 (ISBN 0-88110-069-2); pap. 2.95 (ISBN 0-86020-390-5). EDC.

Shop Boy: An Autobiography. J. B. Thomas. 182p. 1983. 15.95 (ISBN 0-7100-9347-0). Routledge Chapman & Hall.

Shop by Mail Worldwide. Anne Flato & Marilyn Schiff. LC 86-40159. 224p. 1987. pap. 9.95 (ISBN 0-394-74667-8, Vin). Random.

Shop Carpenter. Jack Rudman. (Career Examination Ser.: C-739). (Cloth bdg. avail. on request). pap. 14.00 (ISBN 0-8373-0739-2). Natl Learning.

Shop Clerk. Jack Rudman. (Career Examination Ser.: C-740). (Cloth bdg. avail. on request). pap. 12.00 (ISBN 0-8373-0740-6). Natl Learning.

Shop Committee in the United States. Carroll E. French. LC 78-641100. (Johns Hopkins University Studies in the Social Sciences, Forty-First Series, 1923: No. 2: 2). 112p. 1982. Repr. of 1923 ed. 24.50 (ISBN 0-404-61225-3). AMS Pr.

Shop Drawings of Shaker Furniture & Woodenware, Vol. 1. Ejner Handberg. LC 73-83797. 96p. 1973. pap. 5.95 (ISBN 0-912944-09-9). Berkshire Traveller.

Shop Drawings of Shaker Furniture & Woodenware, Vol. 2. Ejner Handberg. LC 73-83797. 1975. pap. 5.95 (ISBN 0-912944-29-3). Berkshire Traveller.

Shop Drawings of Shaker Furniture & Woodenware, Vol. 3. Ejner Handberg. LC 73-83797. 1977. pap. 5.95 (ISBN 0-912944-45-5). Berkshire Traveller.

Shop Drawings of Shaker Iron & Tinware. Ejner Handberg. LC 76-12896. 96p. 1976. pap. 5.95 (ISBN 0-912944-36-6). Berkshire Traveller.

Shop Expense: Analysis & Control. Nicholas T. Ficker. Ed. by Richard P. Brief. LC 80-1492. (Dimensions of Accounting Theory & Practice Ser.). 1981. Repr. of 1917 ed. lib. bdg. 25.50x (ISBN 0-405-13522-X). Ayer Co Pubs.

Shop Floor Bargaining & the State: Historical & Comparative Perspectives. Ed. by Steven Tolliday & Jonathan Zeitlin. 268p. 1985. 37.50 (ISBN 0-521-26711-0). Cambridge U Pr.

Shop Floor Control. Steven A. Melnyk et al. LC 85-70568. 1985. 35.00 (ISBN 0-87094-628-5). Dow Jones-Irwin.

Shop Floor Control Principles & Practices & Case Studies. Steven A. Melnyck & Phillip L. Carter. LC 87-72180. Date not set. pap. text ed. price not set (ISBN 0-935406-95-6). Am Prod & Inventory.

Shop Floor Controls Reprints. Ed. by APICS Curriculum & Certification Program Council Committee. 165p. 1973. 14.00 (ISBN 0-935406-17-4). Am Prod & Inventory.

Shop Floor Controls Training Aid. APICS Milwaukee Chapter Staff. 30p. 1979. 25.00 (ISBN 0-935406-08-5). Am Prod & Inventory.

Shop Math. National Machine Tool Builders Association Staff. LC 82-13534. (NMTBA Shop Practices Ser.). 140p. 1982. pap. 13.95 (ISBN 0-471-07841-7). Wiley.

Shop Math. Henry Ortiz. LC 84-730297. (Series 950). (Orig.). 1984. pap. 7.00 wkbk. (ISBN 0-8064-0435-3); audio-visual pkg. 199.00 (ISBN 0-8064-0436-1). Bergwall.

Shop Mathematics. 6th ed. Charles A. Felker. 1984. 18.20 (ISBN 0-02-816310-9); tchr's man 7.80 (ISBN 0-02-816330-3). Glencoe.

Shop Mathematics. Jack Rudman. (Career Examination Ser.: CS-36). (Cloth bdg. avail. on request). pap. 14.00 (ISBN 0-8373-3736-4). Natl Learning.

Shop of the Crafters: At Cincinnati. (Illus.). 72p. 1985. pap. 6.95 (ISBN 0-87905-414-X). Gibbs Smith Pub.

Shop Stewards: Workplace Relations in Industry. Ed. by Michael Terry & P. K. Edwards. 300p. 1988. text ed. 55.00x (ISBN 0-631-15979-7). Basil Blackwell.

Shop Subjects. Jack Rudman. (Teachers License Examination Ser.: T-53). (Cloth bdg. avail. on request). pap. 13.95 (ISBN 0-8373-8053-7). Natl Learning.

Shop Subjects Chairman - Sr. H.S. Jack Rudman. (Teachers License Examination Ser.: CH-24). (Cloth bdg. avail. on request). pap. 15.95 (ISBN 0-8373-8174-6). Natl Learning.

Shop Talk: A Prevocational Language Program for Retarded Students. Louise Kent-Udolf & Eileen R. Sherman. LC 83-61810. 230p. 1983. pap. 25.95 (ISBN 0-87822-229-4). Res Press.

Shop Talk: An Anthology of Poetry. Vancouver Industrial Writers' Union Staff. Ed. by Tom Wayman. 128p. (Orig.). 1985. pap. 8.95 (ISBN 0-88978-169-X). Left Bank.

Shop Talk: Papers on Historical Business & Commercial Records of New England. Ed. by James Lawton. 1975. 3.00 (ISBN 0-89073-003-2). Boston Public Lib.

Shop Testing of Automatic Liquid-Level Gages. 49p. 1961. 3.00 (ISBN 0-317-33099-3, 85225092). Am Petroleum.

Shop Theory. 6th ed. James Anderson & Earl E. Tatro. (Illus.). 576p. (gr. 9-11). 1974. text ed. 29.15 (ISBN 0-07-001612-7). McGraw.

Shopacheck's Rugby League Review, Nineteen Eighty-Four to Nineteen Eighty-Five. Paul Fitzpatrick. (Illus.). 144p. 1985. 23.95 (ISBN 0-571-13687-7); pap. 13.95 (ISBN 0-571-13690-7). Faber & Faber.

Shopaholics: Serious Help for Addicted Spenders. Janet E. Damon. 252p. 1988. 16.95 (ISBN 0-89586-749-4). Price Stern.

ShopFloor Politics of New Technology. Barry Wilkinson. viii, 120p. 1983. pap. text ed. 11.50x (ISBN 0-435-82951-3). Gower Pub Co.

Shopkeepers & Master Artisans in Nineteenth-Century Europe. Ed. by Geoffrey Crossick. 304p. 1984. 39.95 (ISBN 0-416-35660-5, NO. 4153). Routledge Chapman & Hall.

Shopkeeper's Daughter. George MacDonald. 288p. 1986. pap. 5.95 (ISBN 0-89693-270-2). Victor Bks.

Shopkeeper's Millennium: Society & Revivals in Rochester, New York, 1815-1837. Paul E. Johnson. (American Century Ser.). 210p. 1978. 10.95 (ISBN 0-8090-8654-9); pap. 5.95. Hill & Wang.

Shopkeeper's World: 1830-1914. Michael J. Winstanley. LC 83-845. 240p. 1983. pap. 16.00 (ISBN 0-7190-1798-X, Pub. by Manchester Univ Pr). St Martin.

Shoplifter. Richard H. Smithies. 1968. 4.95 (ISBN 0-8180-0601-3). Horizon.

Shoplifting: A Manual for Store Detectives. rev. ed. James Brindy. LC 79-92049. (Illus.). Date not set. pap. 8.00 (ISBN 0-910338-01-9). Cavalier.

Shoplifting & Shrinkage Protection for Stores. Loren E. Edwards. (Illus.). 272p. 1976. 31.50x (ISBN 0-398-00498-6). C C Thomas.

Shoplifting: The Antishoplifting Guidebook. Kathleen L. Farrell & John A. Ferrara. LC 85-3613. 176p. 1985. 35.00 (ISBN 0-275-90096-7, C0096). Praeger.

Shoplifting: The Crime Everybody Pays for. Dorothy B. Francis. LC 79-20807. 1980. 10.95 (ISBN 0-525-66658-3, 01063-320). Lodestar Bks.

Shoplifting: What You Need to Know about the Law. Stanley L. Sklar. 250p. 1981. text ed. 14.50 (ISBN 0-87005-399-X). Fairchild.

Shoppell's Modern Houses 1887. Ed. by Donald J. Berg. (Yesterday's Home Ser.). (Illus.). 48p. (Orig.). 1983. pap. 6.00 (ISBN 0-937214-06-X). Antiquity Re.

Shoppers' Almanac. Donald L. Smith. 1969. pap. 1.84 (ISBN 0-9600270-1-7). Consumer Pub.

Shopper's Choice. Ralph Harris & Arthur Seldon. (Occasional Paper Ser.: No. 68). 36p. (Orig.). 1984. pap. 4.75x (ISBN 0-255-36170-X, Pub. by Inst Econ Affairs UK). Transatl Arts.

Shopper's Guide to Gems. Scott D. Sucher. (Illus.). 32p. (Orig.). 1987. pap. 2.95 (ISBN 0-9619696-0-1). KNS.

Shopper's Guide to Mexico. Steve Rogers & Tina Rosa. Ed. by Richard Harris. 200p. (Orig.). 1988. pap. 9.95 (ISBN 0-912528-90-7). John Muir.

Shopper's Guide to Natural Foods. East West Journal Editors. 252p. 1987. pap. 12.95 (ISBN 0-89529-233-5). Avery Pub.

Shopper's Guide to the Best Buys in England, Scotland, & Wales. Dick Johns & Vicki Johns. Date not set. write for info. S&S.

Shopper's Guide to the Best Buys in England, Scotland & Wales. Vicki Johns & Dick Johns. (Illus.). 1988. write for info. Prentice Hall Pr.

Shopper's Guide to the Caribbean. Jeanne Harman & Harry Harman. 300p. 1986. pap. 12.95 (ISBN 0-671-60743-X). P-H.

Shopper's Guide to the Medical Marketplace. Robert B. Keet & Mary Nelson. 134p. 1986. pap. 11.95 (ISBN 0-915166-52-6). Impact Pubs Cal.

Shopper's Guide, 1978. rev. ed. (Illus.). 1977. pap. 3.00 (ISBN 0-89552-009-5). DMR Pubns.

Shopping. Jean Claverie. (It's Great to Read Ser.). 32p. (ps-1). 1986. 5.95 (ISBN 0-517-56024-0). Crown.

Shopping. Sue Tarsky. (Time to Talk Ser.). (Illus.). 32p. (ps-2). 1983. 2.50 (ISBN 0-671-47110-4, Little Simon). S&S.

Shopping. Diane Wilmer. (Step by Step Bks.). (Illus.). 10p. (ps-2). Date not set. bds. 3.95 (ISBN 0-689-71242-1, Aladdin Bks). Macmillan.

Shopping Arcades: A Gazeteer of Extant British Arcades,1817-1939. Magaret MacKeith. LC 82-257. (Illus.). 166p. 1985. 59.00x (ISBN 0-7201-1758-5). Mansell.

Shopping Bag Design. Judi Radice. (Illus.). 256p. 1987. 49.95 (ISBN 0-86636-053-0). PBC Intl Inc.

Shopping Bag Ladies: Homeless Women Speak about Their Lives. Ann Marie Rousseau & Alix K. Shulman. LC 81-407. (Illus.). 160p. 1982. pap. 9.95 (ISBN 0-8298-0603-2). Pilgrim NY.

Shopping Bag Ladies of New York. Joan Roth. Ed. by Robert Walter. LC 81-85387. (Illus.). 122p. (Orig.). 1982. pap. 10.95 (ISBN 0-942160-00-2). St Joans Pr.

Shopping Bag: Portable Art. Stephen C. Wagner & Michael L. Closen. (Illus.). 1986. 24.95 (ISBN 0-517-56177-8). Crown.

Shopping Basket. John Burningham. LC 80-7987. (Illus.). 32p. (ps-2). 1980. 12.70i (ISBN 0-690-04082-2, Crowell Jr Bks); PLB 12.89 (ISBN 0-690-04083-0). HarpJ.

Shopping Cart Art. abr. ed. James E. Seidelman & Grace Mintonye. LC 78-93279. (Illus.). 48p. (gr. 3-6). 1973. pap. 0.95 (ISBN 0-02-045100-8, Collier). Macmillan.

Shopping Center & Store Leases. Emanuel B. Halper. 1000p. 1979. looseleaf 75.00 (ISBN 0-318-12031-3, 00548). NY Law Pub.

Shopping Center Census 1985. 1986. 250.00 (ISBN 0-912610-13-1). Natl Res Bur.

Shopping Center Census, 1986. 1986. 250.00 (ISBN 0-912610-38-7). Natl Res Bur.

Shopping Center Development. 262p. 1985. 15.00 (N4-4448). PLI.

Shopping Center Development Handbook. 2nd ed. ULI Commercial & Office Development Council. Ed. by Frank H. Spink, Jr. (Community Builders' Handbook Ser.). 338p. 1985. 56.00 (ISBN 0-87420-634-0). Urban Land.

Shopping Center Parking: The Influence of Changing Car Sizes. 97p. 1984. pap. text ed. 28.00 (ISBN 0-317-16406-6); pap. text ed. 14.00 member (ISBN 0-317-16407-4). Intl Coun Shop.

Shopping Center Versus Downtown. C. T. Jonassen. 1955. pap. 3.50 (ISBN 0-87776-075-6, R75). Ohio St U Admin Sci.

Shopping Center Zoning. J. Ross McKeever. LC 73-88224. (Illus.). 73p. 1973. pap. 11.50 (ISBN 0-87420-069-5, S07). Urban Land.

Shopping Centers & Malls. Ed. by Robert D. Rathbun. (Illus.). 192p. 1986. 44.95. Retail Report.

Shopping Centers & Malls, Bk. 2. Ed. by Robert D. Rathbun. (Illus.). 192p. 1988. 44.95 (ISBN 0-934590-25-7). Retail Report.

Shopping Centers & the Accessibility Codes. David Fishman. 1979. nonmembers 14.00 (ISBN 0-913598-12-7); members 7.00. Intl Coun Shop.

Shopping Centers, Nineteen Eighty-Eight: Answers for the Next Decade. Intro. by Albert Sussman. LC 79-84514. 1979. pap. text ed. 32.00 nonmember (ISBN 0-913598-07-0); member 16.00. Intl Coun Shop.

Shopping Centers: Planning, Development & Administration. Edgar Lion. LC 75-33374. 198p. 1976. 39.50x (ISBN 0-471-54020-X, Pub. by Wiley-Interscience). Wiley.

Shopping Centers: Planning, Development, & Administration. Edgar Lion. LC 75-33374. pap. 52.00 (2056295). Bks Demand UMI.

Shopping Centre Development: Policies & Prospects. Ed. by John Dawson & Dennis Lord. 280p. 1985. 38.50 (ISBN 0-89397-225-8). Nichols Pub.

Shopping Centre Management. P. G. Martin. 328p. 1982. 42.00 (ISBN 0-419-11870-5, NO. 6674, Pub. by E & FN Spon England). Routledge Chapman & Hall.

Shopping Day. Illus. by Pam Adams. (Pre-Reading Ser.). (Illus.). 24p. (ps-2). 1974. 4.50 (ISBN 0-85953-033-7, Pub. by Child's Play England). Playspaces.

Shopping for a God. John Allan. 218p. 1987. pap. 6.95 (ISBN 0-8010-0212-5). Baker Bk.

Shopping for Health Care Plans: How to Choose the Insurance Coverage That's Right for You. Henry Berman & Louise Rose. (Illus.). 400p. 1989. pap. 15.00 (ISBN 0-89043-218-X). Consumer Reports.

Shopping for Health Care: The Essential Guide to Products & Services. Harold J. Cornacchia & Stephen Barrett. 1982. pap. 9.95 (ISBN 0-452-25366-7, Plume). NAL.

Shopping in China. R. Stalberg. 1988. 10.95 (ISBN 0-8351-1828-2). China Bks.

Shopping in China: Arts, Crafts & the Unusual. Roberta Stalberg. LC 87-70009. (Illus.). 240p. (Orig.). 1987. pap. text ed. 9.95 (ISBN 0-8351-1811-8). China Bks.

Shopping in Exciting Australia & Papua New Guinea: Your Passport to the Unique & Exotic. Ronald L. Krannich & Caryl R. Krannich. 240p. (Orig.). 1989. pap. 11.95 (ISBN 0-942710-22-3). Impact VA.

Shopping in Exotic Hong Kong: Your Passport to Asia's Most Incredible Shopping Bazaar. Jo Reimer et al. 180p. (Orig.). 1988. pap. 9.95 (ISBN 0-942710-14-2). Impact VA.

Shopping in Exotic Indonesia: Your Passport to the World's Most Exciting Islands & Cultures. Ronald L. Krannich & Caryl R. Krannich. 265p. (Orig.). 1989. pap. 11.95. Impact VA.

Shopping in Exotic Places: Your Passport to Exciting Hong Kong, Korea, Thailand, Indonesia, & Singapore. 2nd ed. Ronald L. Krannich et al. 478p. 1988. pap. 13.95 (ISBN 0-942710-18-5). Impact VA.

Shopping in Exotic Singapore & Malaysia. Ronald L. Krannich & Caryl R. Krannich. 170p. (Orig.). 1989. pap. 9.95. Impact VA.

Shopping in Exotic Thailand: Your Passport to Exciting Bangkok & Chiengnai. Ronald L Krannich & Caryl R. Krannich. LC 87-22582. 112p. (Orig.). 1987. pap. 9.95 (ISBN 0-942710-13-4). Impact VA.

Shopping in Exotic Thailand: Your Passport to Exciting Bangkok, Chiengnai, & Beyond. 2nd ed. Ronald L. Krannich & Caryl R. Krannich. 180p. 1989. pap. 9.95 (ISBN 0-942710-16-9). Impact VA.

Shopping in the Exotic South Pacific: Your Passport to Exciting Australia, New Zealand, Papua New Guinea, Fiji, & Tahiti. Ronald L. Krannich & Caryl R. Krannich. 430p. (Orig.). 1989. pap. 13.95 (ISBN 0-942710-21-5). Impact VA.

Shopping Mall High School. Arthur G. Powell et al. 356p. 1985. 16.95 (ISBN 0-395-37904-0). HM.

Shopping Mall High School: Winners & Losers in the Educational Marketplace. Arthur G. Powell et al. 1986. pap. 8.95 (ISBN 0-395-42638-3). HM.

Shopping Malls: Planning & Design. Barry Maitland. 244p. 1985. 57.50 (ISBN 0-89397-226-6). Nichols Pub.

Shopping Maps & Guides: Milan. Frances Ehrlich. (Shopwalks Ser.). 1987. pap. 5.95 (ISBN 0-517-56528-5). Crown.

Shopping Maps & Guides: Paris. Jane Magidson & Nancy Marshak. (Shopwalks Ser.). 1985. pap. 4.95 (ISBN 0-517-55438-0). Crown.

Shopping the Insider's Way. Leil Lowndes. 192p. 1985. pap. 5.95 (ISBN 0-8065-0939-2, Pub. by Citadel Pr). Lyle Stuart.

Shopping Your Way Around Japan. Boye De Mente. (Illus.). 166p. 1983. pap. 7.25 (ISBN 4-89788-016-5, Pub. by Lotus Pr Japan). C E Tuttle.

Shops: A Manual of Planning & Design. Mun. 1987. 75.95 (ISBN 0-85139-610-0). Van Nos Reinhold.

Shops & Shopkeeping in Eighteenth-Century England. Hoh-cheung Mui & Lorna H. Mui. 435p. 1987. 45.00x (ISBN 0-7735-0620-9). McGill-Queens U Pr.

Shops Bill: The Family Dimension. Melanie Henwood & Malcolm Wicks. 1986. 20.00x (ISBN 0-317-57688-7, Pub. by FPSC UK). State Mutual Bk.

Shopwalks Hong Kong: Shopping Maps & Guide. Corby Kummer. 1986. pap. 4.95 (ISBN 0-517-56326-6, Harmony). Crown.

Shopwalks London. Frances Ehrlich. (Shopwalks Ser.). 1986. pap. 4.95 (ISBN 0-517-56091-7). Crown.

Shopwalks: Montreal. 1988. 5.95 (ISBN 0-517-56633-8, Harmony). Crown.

Shopwalks San Francisco. Judy M. Rheingold. (Illus.). 8p. 1987. pap. 4.95 (ISBN 0-517-56457-2, Harmony). Crown.

Shore. Y. Bondarev. 443p. 1984. 11.95 (ISBN 0-8285-2849-7, Pub. by Raduga Pub USSR). Imported Pubns.

Shore Bird Decoys. Henry Fleckenstein, Jr. LC 80-52024. (Illus.). 144p. 1980. 35.00 (ISBN 0-916838-32-3). Schiffer.

Shore Bird Patterns, Bk. V. William Veasey. LC 83-61646. (Blue Ribbon Pattern Ser.). (Illus.). 64p. 1983. pap. 14.95 (ISBN 0-916838-88-9). Schiffer.

Shore Environment, Vol. 1: Methods. Ed. by J. R. Price et al. (Systematics Association Special Ser.: No.17). 1981. 87.50 (ISBN 0-12-564701-8). Acad Pr.

Shore Environment, Vol. 2: Ecosystems. Ed. by J. H. Price et al. (Systematics Association Special Ser.: No. 17). 1981. 134.00 (ISBN 0-12-564702-6). Acad Pr.

Shore Fishes of Hawaii. David S. Jordan & Barton W. Evermann. LC 73-77578. (Illus.). 1973. pap. 22.50 (ISBN 0-8048-1106-7). C E Tuttle.

Shore Fishing in Hawaii. Edward Hosaka. pap. 8.95 (ISBN 0-912180-20-X). Petroglyph.

Shore Ghosts & Other Stories of New Jersey. Larona Homer. (Illus.). 154p. (gr. 4-8). Date not set. 8.95 (ISBN 0-912608-14-5). Mid Atlantic.

Shore Guide to Flocking Names. Robert Huff. 1985. 12.50 (ISBN 0-9614841-1-X); pap. 8.50 (ISBN 0-9614841-0-1). Fanferon Pr.

Shore of Love. O. Honchar. 259p. 1980. 8.95 (ISBN 0-8285-1876-9, Pub. by Progress Pubs USSR). Imported Pubns.

Shore of Pearls: Hainan Island in Early Times. Edward H. Schafer. LC 78-94990. (Illus.). 1970. 33.00x (ISBN 0-520-01592-4). U of Cal Pr.

Shore of Women. Pamela Sargent. 448p. 1986. 16.95 (ISBN 0-517-55834-3). Crown.

Shore of Women. Pamela Sargent. 512p. 1987. pap. 4.95 (ISBN 0-553-26854-6, Spectra). Bantam.

Shore Protection: A Bibliography. Mary Vance. (Public Administration Ser.: P 2239). 26p. 1987. 7.50 (ISBN 1-55590-479-3). Vance Biblios.

Shore Road Mystery. Franklin W. Dixon. (Hardy Boys Ser: Vol. 6). (Illus.). (gr. 5-9). 1964. 4.50 (ISBN 0-448-08906-8, G&D). Putnam Pub Group.

Shore Wildflowers of California, Oregon, & Washington. Philip A. Munz. (Illus., Orig.). 1965. pap. 8.95 (ISBN 0-520-00903-7). U of Cal Pr.

Shore Writers' Sampler: Best Stories by Eastern Shore Writers. Ed. by George H. Gillelan & Frank Megargee. LC 87-81639. (Illus.). 248p. (Orig.). 1987. pap. 9.50 (ISBN 0-9618993-0-1). Friendly Harbor.

Shorebird: An Identification Guide. John Marchant & Tony Prater. (Illus.). 416p. 1985. 35.00 (ISBN 0-395-37903-2). HM.

Shorebirds. Peter Hayman et al. 1986. write for info. HM.

Shoreline for the Public: A Handbook of Social, Economic, & Legal Considerations Regarding Public Recreational Use of the Nation's Coastal Shoreline. Dennis W. Ducsik. 1974. 22.50x (ISBN 0-262-04045-X). MIT Pr.

Shoreline Protection: Proceedings of a Conference Organized by the Institution of Civil Engineers. 254p. 1983. 63.00 (ISBN 0-7277-0173-8, Pub. by T Telford UK). Am Soc Civil Eng.

Shorelines & Beaches in Coastal Management: A Bibliography, No. 876. Ed. by Joseph M. Heikoff. 1975. 6.50 (ISBN 0-686-20368-2). CPL Biblios.

Shorelines Management: The Washington Experience. Ed. by Roger Leed. (Washington Sea Grant Ser.). 184p. 1973. pap. 7.50x (ISBN 0-295-95309-8). U of Wash Pr.

Shorelines Past & Present, 3 vols. Ed. by William F. Tanner. 745p. 1980. pap. 50.00 (ISBN 0-686-83996-X). FSU Geology.

Shorelines: Poetic Thoughts & Stories. Compiled by DeLong & Associates Staff. (Illus.). 88p. (Orig.). 1986. pap. 6.00 (ISBN 0-9603414-2-0). DeLong & Assocs.

Shoremen: An Anthology of Eastern Shore Prose & Verse. Ed. by Harold D. Jopp & R. H. Ingersoll. LC 74-7497. 336p. 1974. pap. 6.00 (ISBN 0-87033-186-8). Tidewater.

Shores & Headlands. Emily Grosholz. (Series of Contemporary Poets). 80p. 1988. 16.00 (ISBN 0-691-06749-X); pap. 9.95t (ISBN 0-691-01448-5). Princeton U Pr.

Shores of Darkness. facs. ed. Demetrios Capetanakis. LC 73-76897. (Essay Index Reprint Ser). 1949. 17.00 (ISBN 0-8369-0010-3). Ayer Co Pubs.

Shores of Light: A Literary Chronicle of the 1920s & 1930s. Edmund Wilson. 832p. 1985. pap. text ed. 13.50x (ISBN 0-930350-68-5). NE U Pr.

Shores of Refuge: A Hundred Years of Jewish Emigration. Ronald Sanders. (Illus.). 448p. 1988. 27.95 (ISBN 0-8050-0563-3). H Holt & Co.

Shorewood Collection. Shorewood Staff. (Illus.). 216p. 1983. loose leaf binder 15.00 (ISBN 0-88185-000-4). Shorewood Fine Art.

Shorewood Collection Art Reference Guide. Shorewood Staff. 84p. (Orig.). 1985. 16.50 (ISBN 0-88185-026-8). Shorewood Fine Art.

Shorin-Ryu Karate. T. Yamashita. 1976. 7.95x (ISBN 0-685-83536-7). Wehman.

Shorin-Ryu: Okinawan Karate Question & Answer Book. William Cummins & Robert Scaglione. (Illus.). 90p. (Orig.). 1985. pap. 11.95 (ISBN 0-8048-1426-0, Pub. by Person to Person Pub Inc). C E Tuttle.

Short. Charles Doria. 50p. (Orig.). limited ed, signed & lettered 15.00 (ISBN 0-915066-47-5); pap. 3.00 (ISBN 0-915066-48-3). Assembling Pr.

Short a & Long a Play a Game. Jane B. Moncure. LC 79-10300. (Play with Vowel Sounds Ser.). (Illus.). 32p. (gr. k-3). 1981. lib. bdg. 11.93 (ISBN 0-516-06451-7). Childrens.

Short A & Long A Play a Game. Jane B. Moncure. LC 79-10300. (Play with Vowel Sounds Ser.). (Illus.). (gr. k-2). 1979. PLB 7.95 (ISBN 0-89565-089-4). Childs World.

Short Account of Bermudez see Portuguese Expedition to Abyssinia in 1541-1543.

Short Account of Early Muslim Architecture. K. Creswell. 1968. 18.00x (ISBN 0-86685-010-4). Intl Bk Ctr.

Short Account of Old English Pottery: An Introduction to the Study of Chinese Porcelain. Also a Catalogue of Old China Offered for Sale. 124p. 1901. 25.00x (ISBN 0-317-45237-1, Pub. by Han-Shan Tang Ltd). State Mutual Bk.

Short Account of the History of Mathematics. 4th ed. W. W. Ball. 1908. pap. 9.95 (ISBN 0-486-20630-0). Dover.

Short Account of the Malignant Fever, Lately Prevalent in Philadelphia. Mathew Carey. LC 73-112531. (Rise of Urban America). 1970. Repr. of 1794 ed. 12.00 (ISBN 0-405-02441-X). Ayer Co Pubs.

Short & Long. Elizabeth Gregory. (Illus.). 1981. 6.95 (ISBN 0-933184-09-3); pap. 4.95 (ISBN 0-933184-10-7). Flame Intl.

Short & Long Term Changes in Climate, Vol. I. Felix G. Sulman. 192p. 1982. 79.00 (ISBN 0-8493-6420-5). CRC Pr.

Short & Long Term Changes in Climate, Vol. II. Felix G. Sulman. 184p. 1982. 79.00 (ISBN 0-8493-6421-3). CRC Pr.

Short & Profitable Treatise Touching the Cure of the Morbus Gallicus by Unctions. William Clowes. LC 75-38166. (English Experience Ser.: No. 443). 118p. 1972. Repr. of 1579 ed. 16.00 (ISBN 90-221-0443-5). Walter J Johnson.

Short & Shivery: Thirty Chilling Tales. Robert D. San Souci & Katherine Coville. LC 86-29067. 192p. (gr. 4-6). 1987. 10.95 (ISBN 0-385-23886-X). Doubleday.

Short & Simple Annals. Llewellyn McKernan. 40p. (Orig.). 1982. pap. 3.99 (ISBN 0-9615487-0-3). Dickinson WV.

Short & Ultrashort Wavelength Lasers. Ed. by Jones. 1988. 43.00 (ISBN 0-89252-910-5, 875). SPIE.

Short Apologie for School of Abuse. S. Gosson. 80p. 1984. pap. 15.00 (ISBN 0-87556-627-8). Saifer.

Short Audit Case: Pamela's Pottery. 2nd ed. Mattie Porter & Robert Strauser. 1987. 7.95 (ISBN 0-256-06500-4). Irwin.

Short Audit Case: The Valley Publishing Company. 5th ed. Ben Barr et al. 1985. 21.95x (ISBN 0-256-03284-X). Irwin.

Short Baptist Manual of Polity & Practice. Norman H. Maring & Winthrop S. Hudson. 1965. pap. 4.95 (ISBN 0-8170-0338-X). Judson.

Short Bengali-English, English-Bengali Dictionary. 3rd ed. Jack A. Dabbs. LC 78-149931. 5.00 (ISBN 0-911494-01-4). Dabbs.

Short Bible Reference System. Ed. by R. G. Bratcher. 148p. 1961. 7.50x (ISBN 0-8267-0030-6, 08506, Pub. by United Bible). Am Bible.

Short Bike Rides in Connecticut. 3rd ed. Edwin Mullen. (Short Bike Rides Ser.). (Illus.). 1989. pap. price not set (ISBN 0-87106-635-1). Globe Pequot.

Short Bike Rides in Connecticut. 2nd, rev. ed. Edwin Mullen & Jane Griffith. LC 75-1924. (Illus.). 128p. 1983. pap. 6.95 (ISBN 0-87106-930-X). Globe Pequot.

Short Bike Rides in Greater Boston & Central Massachusetts. 3rd ed. Howard Stone. LC 81-86604. (Short Bike Rides Ser.). (Illus.). 592p. 1988. pap. 11.95 (ISBN 0-87106-717-X). Globe Pequot.

Short Bike Rides in Long Island. rev., 3rd ed. Phil Angeillo. (Short Bike Rides Ser.). (Illus.). 1989. pap. price not set (ISBN 0-87106-636-X). Globe Pequot.

Short Bike Rides in New Jersey. Robert Santelli. (Short Bike Rides Ser.). (Illus.). 160p. (Orig.). 1988. pap. 7.95 (ISBN 0-87106-715-3). Globe Pequot.

Short Bike Rides in Rhode Island. 2nd, rev. ed. Howard Stone. LC 78-73547. (Illus.). 248p. 1984. pap. 8.95 (ISBN 0-87106-948-2). Globe Pequot.

Short Bike Rides in Rhode Island. 3rd ed. Howard Stone. (Short Bike Rides Ser.). (Illus.). 248p. 1988. pap. 8.95 (ISBN 0-87106-721-8). Globe Pequot.

Short Bike Rides on Cape Cod, Nantucket, & the Vineyard. 3rd ed. Edwin Mullen & Jane Griffith. LC 76-58214. (Short Bike Rides Ser.). (Illus.). 160p. 1988. pap. 7.95 (ISBN 0-87106-719-6). Globe Pequot.

Short Bike Rides on Long Island. 2nd, rev. ed. Phil Angelillo. LC 76-45045. (Illus.). 160p. 1984. pap. 6.95 (ISBN 0-87106-932-6). Globe Pequot.

Short Biography. Leonid I. Brezhnev. LC 77-30493. 1978. 19.75 (ISBN 0-08-022266-8). Pergamon.

Short Biography of John Leeth, with an Account of His Life Among the Indians. Ewel Jeffries. Ed. by Reuben G. Thwaites. LC 74-180034. 18.00 (ISBN 0-405-08669-5, Pub. by Blom). Ayer Co Pubs.

Short Book on the Subject of Speaking. John Quick. (Illus.). 1978. text ed. 24.95 (ISBN 0-07-051050-4). McGraw.

Short Book on the Subject of Speaking. John Quick. 160p. 1981. pap. 2.25 (ISBN 0-671-42162-X). WSP.

Short Business Letters for Dictation & Transcription. Charles E. Zoubek. (Diamond Jubilee Ser.). 1970. text ed. 27.45 (ISBN 0-07-073075-X). McGraw.

Short Calculus: An Applied Approach. 4th ed. Daniel Saltz. 1985. text ed. write for info. (ISBN 0-673-16625-2). Scott F.

Short Change Game: How to Stop the School from Depriving Your Retarded or Handicapped Child. Maryn Baker. LC 81-3653. Date not set. 17.95 (ISBN 0-87949-211-2). Ashley Bks.

Short Changes for Loretta. Paul Trachtenberg. LC 81-17044. 64p. 1982. pap. 4.00x (ISBN 0-916156-62-1). Cherry Valley.

Short Chic. Leopold & Cloutier. 1984. pap. 10.95 (ISBN 0-553-34570-2). Bantam.

Short Chronology of American History, Fourteen Ninety-Two to Nineteen Fifty. Irving S. Kull & Nell M. Kull. LC 79-24781. 388p. 1980. Repr. of 1952 ed. lib. bdg. 41.50x (ISBN 0-313-22259-2, KUSC). Greenwood.

Short Circuit. Jon Land. (Orig.). 1986. pap. write for info. (GM). Fawcett.

Short Circuit. Michael Mewshaw. 400p. 1984. pap. 6.95 (ISBN 0-14-007278-0). Penguin.

Short-Circuit Currents In Three-Phase Systems. 2nd, rev., enl. ed. Richard Roeper. LC 85-655. 167p. 1985. 39.95 (ISBN 0-471-90707-3). Wiley.

Short Circular Walks Around Nottinghamshire. 64p. 1987. 29.00x (ISBN 0-907496-58-X, Pub. by JNM Pubns UK). State Mutual Bk.

Short Circular Walks on the Northern Moors. 64p. 1987. 29.00x (ISBN 0-907496-59-8, Pub. by JNM Pubns UK). State Mutual Bk.

Short Commentary on Aristotle's Prior Analytics. Al-Farabi. Tr. by Nicholas Rescher. LC 63-10581. pap. 33.00 (ISBN 0-317-09047-X, 2010487). Bks Demand UMI.

Short Commentary on Kant's "Critique of Pure Reason". A. C. Ewing. viii, 278p. 1987. pap. text ed. 16.00x (ISBN 0-226-22779-0, Midway Reprint). U of Chicago Pr.

Short Comparative Grammar of Greek & Latin for Schools & Colleges. Victor Henry. Tr. by R. T. Elliott from Fr. 330p. 1982. Repr. of 1890 ed. lib. bdg. 65.00 (ISBN 0-8495-2431-8). Arden Lib.

Short Constitutional History of England. 3rd ed. H. St. Clair Feilden & W. Gray Etheridge. xx, 358p. 1986. Repr. of 1895 ed. lib. bdg. 42.50x (ISBN 0-8377-2130-X). Rothman.

Short Cornish Dictionary: Gerlyver Ber. Christine Truran. 1985. 10.00x (ISBN 1-85022-015-8, Pub. by Dyllansow & Truran). State Mutual Bk.

Short Course in Algebra & Trigonometry. A. W. Goodman. (Illus.). 139p. 1985. pap. text ed. 9.95x (ISBN 0-912675-11-X). Ardsley.

Short Course in Biochemistry. Albert L. Lehninger. LC 72-93199. (Illus.). 452p. 1973. text ed. 34.95x (ISBN 0-87901-024-X). Worth.

Short Course in Calculus. Bodh R. Gulati. LC 79-67409. 536p. 1981. text ed. 36.95x; solutions manual 20.00 (ISBN 0-03-057434-X). Dryden Pr.

Short Course in Calculus. Bodh R. Gulati. 536p. 1981. text ed. 42.75 (ISBN 0-03-047466-3). SCP.

Short Course in Canon Photography. Barbara London. 1979. 14.95 (ISBN 0-930764-11-0). Curtin & London.

Short Course in Canon Photography. Barbara London. (Illus.). 144p. 1983. pap. 11.95 (ISBN 0-930764-52-8, Co.-Pub. by Van Nos Reinhold). Curtin & London.

Short Course in Cloud Physics. 2nd ed. R. R. Rogers. 1979. text ed. 48.00 (ISBN 0-08-023040-7); pap. text ed. 23.00 (ISBN 0-08-023041-5). Pergamon.

Short Course in Cloud Physics. 3rd ed. R. R. Rogers & M. K. Yau. (International Series on Natural Philosophy). (Illus.). 350p. 1989. 54.00 (ISBN 0-08-034864-5); pap. 27.00 (ISBN 0-08-034863-7). Pergamon.

Short Course in Differential Equations. 6th ed. E. D. Rainville & P. E. Bedient. 1981. write for info. (ISBN 0-02-397760-4). Macmillan.

Short Course in Foundation Engineering. Simons & Menzies. 1977. 27.50 (ISBN 0-408-00295-6). Butterworth.

Short Course in Gold Investing: A Guide to Financial Security. Daniel Rosenthal & Ellen Young. 95p. (Orig.). 1986. pap. text ed. 49.95 (ISBN 0-938689-00-2). Inst Preserv Wealth.

Short Course in Minolta Photography. Barbara London. 1979. 14.95 (ISBN 0-930764-12-9). Curtin & London.

Short Course in Nikon Photography. Barbara London. 1979. 14.95 (ISBN 0-930764-10-2). Curtin & London.

Short Course in Nikon Photography. Barbara London. (Illus.). 144p. 1983. pap. 11.95 (ISBN 0-930764-54-4, Co.-Pub. by Van Nos Reinhold). Curtin & London.

Short Course in Olympus Photography. Barbara London. 1979. 14.95 (ISBN 0-930764-13-7). Curtin & London.

Short Course in Olympus Photography. Barbara London. (Illus.). 144p. 1983. pap. 11.95 (ISBN 0-930764-55-2, Co.-Pub. by Van Nos Reinhold). Curtin & London.

Short Course in Organic Chemistry. Edward E. Burgoyne. (Illus.). 1979. text ed. 36.95 (ISBN 0-07-009171-4). McGraw.

Short Course in Pentax Photography. Barbara London. (Illus., Orig.). 1979. 14.95 (ISBN 0-930764-14-5); pap. 9.95 (ISBN 0-930764-05-6). Curtin & London.

Short Course in Photography. Barbara London. 1979. 14.95 (ISBN 0-930764-09-9). Curtin & London.

Short Course in Photography. Barbara London. 1987. text ed. write for info. (ISBN 0-673-39616-9). Scott F.

Short Course in PL-I PL-C. Ann L. Clark & Steven L. Mandell. (Series in Data Processing & Information Systems). 190p. 1978. pap. text ed. 21.50 (ISBN 0-8299-0219-8); instrs.' manual avail. (ISBN 0-8299-0465-4). West Pub.

Short Course in Remedial English Composition. Renee C. Crauder & Gwendolyn E. Etter-Lewis. 1977. pap. 3.95x (ISBN 0-8134-1938-7, 1938); instructor's manual 1.00 (ISBN 0-8134-1939-5, 1939). Inter Print Pubs.

Short Course in Sheet Metal Shop Theory: Including 25 Practical Projects. Richard S. Budzik. LC 79-93131. (Illus.). (gr. 7-12). 1979. 17.95 (ISBN 0-912914-05-X). Practical Pubns.

Short Course in Spoken English. Ronald Mackin. 1975. pap. 5.95 (ISBN 0-87789-137-0); cassettes 55.00 (ISBN 0-87789-140-0). ELS Educ Servs.

Short Course in Structured BASIC Programming on IBM Personal Computers to Accompany Introducing Computers 1988. Robert H. Blissmer & John E. Castek. 303p. 1988. pap. write for info. (ISBN 0-471-60171-3). Wiley.

Short Course in the Secret War. Christopher Felix. 1988. pap. 3.95 (ISBN 0-440-20085-7). Dell.

Short Course in Writing. 3rd ed. Kenneth A. Bruffee. 1985. pap. text ed. 16.50 (ISBN 0-673-39201-5). Scott F.

Short Course of Economic Science. A. Bogdanoff, pseud. Tr. by J. Fineberg. LC 78-20483. 1980. Repr. of 1923 ed. text ed. 30.25 (ISBN 0-88355-860-2). Hyperion Conn.

Short Course of Geological Prospecting & Exploration. A. Maximov et al. 256p. 1983. text ed. cancelled (ISBN 0-8290-1495-0). Irvington.

Short Course of Political Economy. L. Leontyev. 14.95 (ISBN 0-8464-0844-9). Beekman Pubs.

Short Course on Error Correcting Codes. N. J. Sloane. (CISM International Centre for Mechanical Sciences Ser.: Vol. 188). (Illus.). 76p. 1982. pap. 12.00 (ISBN 0-387-81303-9). Springer-Verlag.

Short Course on Functional Equations: Based upon Recent Applications to the Social & Behavioural Sciences. J. Aczel. 1986. lib. bdg. 49.50 (ISBN 90-277-2376-1, Pub. by Reidel Netherlands); pap. text ed. 24.00 (ISBN 90-277-2377-X, Pub. by Reidel Netherlands). Kluwer Academic.

Short-Cut Building Code Excerpts: South Florida Building Code 1984 Mechanical Section & Contractors Code of Dade County Chapter 10. Ed. by John Gladstone. 64p. 1984. pap. 9.75 (ISBN 0-930644-09-3). Engineers Pr.

Short-Cut Math. Gerard W. Kelly. (Popular Science Ser.). 112p. 1984. pap. 2.95 (ISBN 0-486-24611-6). Dover.

Short Cut to Winning Bridge. Alfred Sheinwold. 1979. 3.00 (ISBN 0-87980-366-5). Wilshire.

Short Cuts for Busy Dressmakers. Ann Ladbury. (Illus.). 192p. 1983. pap. 14.95 (ISBN 0-7134-1812-5, Pub. by Batsford England). David & Charles.

Short-Cuts for Round Layouts. 4th ed. Joseph J. Kaberlein. 1985. 21.00 (ISBN 0-02-819450-0). Glencoe.

Short Cuts: Styling & Caring for Short Hair. Olivier Casanova & Patrice Casanova. 1985. pap. 7.95 (ISBN 0-671-55375-5, Pub. by Fireside). S&S.

Short Cuts to Affective on the Job Writing. Lynn Lamphear. 179p. 1982. pap. 6.95 (ISBN 0-13-809137-4). P-H.

Short Dance in the Sun. George Benet. 160p. 1988. 17.95 (ISBN 0-932499-59-7); pap. 9.95 (ISBN 0-932499-58-9). Lapis Pr.

Short Descriptive Grammar of Middle High German. John A. Asher. 1967. pap. 13.95x (ISBN 0-19-647410-8). Oxford U Pr.

Short Dialysis. Ed. by Vincenzo Cambi. (Topics in Renal Medicine). 1987. lib. bdg. 87.50 (ISBN 0-89838-858-9, Pub. by Kluwer-Nijhoff (Netherlands)). Kluwer Academic.

Short Dictionary of Anglo-Saxon Poetry: In a Normalized Early West-Saxon Orthography. Jess B. Bessinger. LC 61-2144. pap. 26.30 (ISBN 0-317-09527-7, 2020454). Bks Demand UMI.

Short Dictionary of Eighteenth Century Russian. Charles E. Gribble. 103p. (Rus.). 1976. soft cover 8.95 (ISBN 0-89357-172-5). Slavica.

Short Dictionary of Social Science Terms for Swahili Speakers. James L. Brain. (Foreign & Comparative Studies Program, African Special Publications: No. 4). 70p. (Orig., Swahili.). 1969. pap. text ed. 4.50x (ISBN 0-686-74011-4). Syracuse U Foreign Comp.

Short Dictionary of the New Testament. Albert Rouet. (Illus.). 128p. 1982. pap. 6.95 (ISBN 0-8091-2400-9). Paulist Pr.

Short Discourse of the English Stage Appended to Love's Kingdom see Historia Histrionica.

Short Discourse of the Three Kinds of Peppers in Common Use. Walter Bailey. LC 77-38145. (English Experience Ser.: No. 425). 48p. Repr. of 1588 ed. 7.00 (ISBN 90-221-0425-7). Walter J Johnson.

Short Discoverie of the Dangers of Ignorant Practisers of Physicke. John Cotta. LC 72-38168. (English Experience Ser.: No. 445). 144p. 1972. Repr. of 1612 ed. 21.00 (ISBN 90-221-0445-1). Walter J Johnson.

Short-Distance Phenomena in Nuclear Physics. Ed. by David H. Boal & Richard M. Woloshyn. (NATO ASI Series B, Physics: Vol. 104). 438p. 1983. 72.50x (ISBN 0-306-41494-5, Plenum Pr). Plenum Pub.

Short Dramas for the Church. Dorcas D. Shaner. 224p. 1980. pap. 10.95 (ISBN -08170-0883-7). Judson.

Short e & Long e Play a Game. Jane B. Moncure. LC 79-10305. (Play with Vowel Sounds Ser.). (Illus.). 32p. (gr. k-3). 1981. lib. bdg. 11.93 (ISBN 0-516-06452-5). Childrens.

Short E & Long E Play a Game. Jane B. Moncure. LC 79-10305. (Play with Vowel Sounds Ser.). (Illus.). (gr. k-2). 1979. PLB 7.95 (ISBN 0-89565-090-8). Childs World.

Short Economic & Social History of Twentieth Century England. Walford Johnson et al. LC 67-21370. 1967. 19.50x (ISBN 0-678-06002-9). Kelley.

Short Economic & Social History of the Lake Counties, 1500-1830. Charles M. Bouch & G. P. Jones. LC 67-8870. (Illus.). 1962. 39.50x (ISBN 0-678-06786-4). Kelley.

Short Economic History of Modern Japan. 4th ed. C. G. Allen. LC 80-13919. 272p. 1981. 29.95 (ISBN 0-312-71771-7). St Martin.

Short Energy History of the United States & Some Thoughts about the Future. Joseph M. Dukert. (Decisionmakers Bookshelf Ser.: Vol. 7). (Illus.). 88p. (Orig.). 1980. pap. 2.50 (ISBN 0-931032-07-5). Edison Electric.

Short Energy History of the United States... & Some Thoughts About the Future, Vol. 7. 85p. 1980. 2.50 (ISBN 0-317-34110-3, 01078005). Edison Electric.

Short English Handbook. 3rd ed. David E. Fear & Gerald J. Schiffhorst. 1986. pap. text ed. write for info. (ISBN 0-673-18160-X). Scott F.

Short Essays. 4th ed. Gerald Levin. 416p. 1986. pap. text ed. 13.00 net (ISBN 0-15-580918-0, Pub. by HC); instr's. manual avail. (ISBN 0-15-580919-9). HarBraceJ.

Short Eyes. Miguel Pinero. (Mermaid Dramabook Ser.). 128p. 1975. pap. 5.95 (ISBN 0-8090-1232-4). Hill & Wang.

Short Fiber Reinforced Composite Materials - STP 772. Ed. by B. Sanders. 258p. 1982. 27.50 (ISBN 0-8031-0697-1, 04-772000-30). ASTM.

Short Fibre Reinforced Thermoplastics. M. J. Folkes. (Polymer Engineering Research Studies Ser.). 176p. 1982. 57.95x (ISBN 0-471-10209-1, Pub. by Res Stud Pr). Wiley.

Short Fibre Reinforced Thermoplastics. M. J. Folkes. (Illus.). 186p. 1982. 60.00 (ISBN 0-686-48236-0, 0808). T-C Pubns CA.

Short Fiction: A Critical Collection. 2nd ed. James R. Frakes & Isadore Traschen. LC 69-11382. 1968. pap. text ed. write for info. (ISBN 0-13-809178-1). P-H.

Short Fiction of Caroline Gordon: A Symposium. Ed. by Thomas H. Landess. 1972. 4.95x (ISBN 0-918306-02-7). U of Dallas Pr.

Short Fiction of Charles W. Chesnutt. Ed. by Sylvia L. Render. LC 81-6314. 1981. pap. 7.95 (ISBN 0-88258-092-2). Howard U Pr.

Short Fiction of Charles W. Chesnutt. Ed. by Sylvia L. Render. LC 81-6314. 428p. 1974. 15.00 (ISBN 0-88258-012-4). Howard U Pr.

Short Fiction of D. H. Lawrence. Janice H. Harris. 284p. 1984. text ed. 27.00 (ISBN 0-8135-1046-5). Rutgers U Pr.

Short Fiction of Ernest Hemingway: A Study in Major Themes. Syed A. Hamod. ix, 167p. 1985. 16.50 (ISBN 81-7024-008-5, Pub. by Ashish Pub Hse India). Nataraj Bks.

Short Fiction of Jewett & Freeman. Barbara H. Solomon. Date not set. pap. 4.95 (ISBN 0-452-00892-1, Mer). NAL.

Short History of Keyboard Music. F. E. Kirby. LC 66-23081. 1966. 24.95 (ISBN 0-02-917330-2). Free Pr.

Short History of Korea. Davis Rees. (Illus.). 216p. 1988. 16.95 (ISBN 0-87052-575-1). Hippocrene Bks.

Short History of Legal Thinking in the West. Stig Stromholm. 1986. text ed. 37.50x. Rothman.

Short History of Linguistics. 2nd ed. R. H. Robins. (Longman Linguistics Library). (Illus.). 1980. pap. text ed. 14.95x (ISBN 0-582-55288-5). Longman.

Short History of Literary English. 2nd ed. W. F. Bolton. (Quality Paperback: No. 266). 86p. 1973. pap. 1.50 (ISBN 0-8226-0266-0). Littlefield.

Short History of Logic. Robert Adamson. Ed. by W. R. Sorley. (Reprints in Philosophy Ser.). Repr. of 1911 ed. lib. bdg. 39.50 (ISBN 0-697-00001-X). Irvington.

Short History of Los Angeles. Gordon DeMarco. (Illus.). 156p. (Orig.). 1987. pap. 9.95 (ISBN 0-938530-37-2). Lexikos.

Short History of Lyme Regis. John Fowles. (Illus.). 56p. 1983. 13.00 (ISBN 0-316-28987-6). Little.

Short History of Malaysia, Singapore, & Brunei. C. Mary Turnbull. Ed. by J. D. Legge. (Illus.). 320p. 1981. pap. 15.00 (ISBN 9971-947-06-4, Graham Brash Singapore). Three Continents.

Short History of Marriage: Marriage Rites, Customs, & Folklore in Many Countries in All Ages. Ethel L. Urlin. LC 69-16071. 288p. 1969. Repr. of 1913 ed. 44.00x (ISBN 0-8103-3569-7). Gale.

Short History of Medicine 1982. rev. ed. Erwin H. Ackerknecht. LC 81-48194. 304p. 1982. pap. 9.95x (ISBN 0-8018-2726-4). Johns Hopkins.

Short History of Medieval Philosophy. Julius R. Weinberg. 1964. pap. 10.95x (ISBN 0-691-01956-8). Princeton U Pr.

Short History of Modern Bulgaria. R. J. Crampton. (Illus.). 224p. 1987. 34.50 (ISBN 0-521-25340-3); pap. 12.95 (ISBN 0-521-27323-4). Cambridge U Pr.

Short History of Modern Chinese Literature. Ting Yi. LC 76-103236. 1970. Repr. of 1959 ed. 23.00x (ISBN 0-8046-0872-5, Pub. by Kennikat). Assoc Faculty Pr.

Short History of Modern Egypt. Afaf L. Marsot. 168p. 1985. pap. 10.95 (ISBN 0-521-27234-3). Cambridge U Pr.

Short History of Modern English Literature. Edmund Gosse. 1900. 35.00 (ISBN 0-8274-3401-4). R West.

Short History of Modern Greece. 2nd ed. Richard Clogg. (Illus.). 256p. 1986. 44.50 (ISBN 0-521-32837-3); pap. 12.95 (ISBN 0-521-33804-2). Cambridge U Pr.

Short History of Morals. John M. Robertson. LC 73-154648. (Research & Source Works Ser.: No. 701). 1971. Repr. lib. bdg. 24.50 (ISBN 0-8337-3021-5). B Franklin.

Short History of Music. Alfred Einstein. (Illus.). 450p. 1987. 19.95 (ISBN 0-88029-097-8, Pub. by Dorset Pr). Hippocrene Bks.

Short History of Nautical Medicine. Louis H. Roddis. LC 75-23757. Repr. of 1941 ed. 30.50 (ISBN 0-404-13363-0). AMS Pr.

Short History of New Orleans. Mel Leavitt. LC 82-7138. (Illus.). 160p. (Orig.). 1982. pap. 9.95 (ISBN 0-938530-03-8). Lexikos.

Short History of North Africa. Jane S. Nickerson. LC 68-54233. 1961. 20.00 (ISBN 0-8196-0219-1). Biblo.

Short History of Observatories. Marian Donnelly. LC 73-175209. 1973. 7.50. U of Oreg Bks.

Short History of Obstetrics & Gynecology. Theodore Cianfrani. (Illus.). 466p. 1960. photocopy ed. 48.50x (ISBN 0-398-00308-4). C C Thomas.

Short History of Opera. 2nd ed. Donald J. Grout. LC 64-11043. 852p. 1965. 32.00x (ISBN 0-231-02422-3). Columbia U Pr.

Short History of Opera. 3rd ed. Donald J. Grout & Hermine W. Williams. (Illus.). 1120p. 1987. 39.00 (ISBN 0-231-06192-7). Columbia U Pr.

Short History of Paper Money & Banking in the United States. William M. Gouge. LC 65-26366. 1968. Repr. of 1833 ed. 45.00x (ISBN 0-678-00307-6). Kelley.

Short History of Parliament, Twelve Ninety-Five - Sixteen Forty-Two. Faith Thompson. LC 53-10471. pap. 72.50 (ISBN 0-317-28170-4, 2055965). Bks Demand UMI.

Short History of Political Thinking. facs. ed. Paul W. Ward. LC 70-134151. (Essay Index Reprint Ser). 1939. 14.00 (ISBN 0-8369-2080-5). Ayer Co Pubs.

Short History of Psychiatry. 2nd rev. ed. E. H. Ackerknecht. Tr. by Sula Wolff. (Illus.). 1970. pap. 8.95x (ISBN 0-02-840070-4, 84007). Hafner.

Short History of Religion in America. Lester B. Scherer. (Illus.). 145p. (Orig.). 1980. pap. 8.95x (ISBN 0-89894-011-7). Advocate Pub Group.

Short History of Religions. facsimile ed. Ernest E. Kellett. LC 71-156671. (Essay Index Reprint Ser). Repr. of 1934 ed. 30.00 (ISBN 0-8369-2281-6). Ayer Co Pubs.

Short History of Roman Law: Being the First Part of His "Manuel Elementaire De Droit Romain.". Paul F. Girard. Tr. by A. H. Lefroy & J. H. Cameron. LC 79-1603. 1983. Repr. of 1906 ed. 20.35 (ISBN 0-88355-906-4). Hyperion Conn.

Short History of Rosalia, Washington. Alice Campbell. 10p. 1970. pap. 1.00 (ISBN 0-87770-037-0). Ye Galleon.

Short History of Russian Literature. Shakhnovski. 1921. Repr. 15.00 (ISBN 0-8274-3402-2). R West.

Short History of Sacramento. Dorothy K. Leland. (Illus.). 150p. (Orig.). 1988. pap. 9.95 (ISBN 0-938530-40-2). Lexikos.

Short History of San Diego. Michael McKeever. (Short History Ser.). (Illus.). 144p. (Orig.). 1985. pap. 9.95 (ISBN 0-938530-32-1). Lexikos.

Short History of San Francisco. Tom Cole. LC 81-2588. (Illus.). 144p. (Orig.). 1981. pap. 9.95 (ISBN 0-938530-00-3, 00-3). Lexikos.

Short History of San Francisco. 2nd ed. Tom Cole. 144p. 1986. pap. 9.95 (ISBN 0-917583-08-6, Don't Call Frisco). Lexikos.

Short History of Santa Fe. Susan Hazen-Hammond. (Illus., Orig.). 1987. pap. 9.95 (ISBN 0-938530-39-9). Lexikos.

Short History of Science & Scientific Thought. F. Sherwood Taylor. (Illus.). 1963. pap. 8.95x (ISBN 0-393-00140-7). Norton.

Short History of Scotland, 2 vols. Robert L. Mackie. 1980. Repr. of 1931 ed. Set. lib. bdg. 75.00 (ISBN 0-8495-3857-2). Vol. 1, 208 Pp. Vol. 2, 414 Pp. Arden Lib.

Short History of Scotland, 2 vols. Robert L. Mackie. 1979. Repr. of 1931 ed. Set. lib. bdg. 67.00 (ISBN 0-8414-6345-X). Folcroft.

Short History of Sex. Richard Armour. 1970. text ed. 4.95 (ISBN 0-07-002263-1). McGraw.

Short History of Shakespearean Criticism. Arthur M. Eastman. LC 85-3201. 442p. 1985. pap. text ed. 17.75 (ISBN 0-8191-4589-0). U Pr of Amer.

Short History of Sierra Leone. Christopher Fyfe. (Illus.). 1979. pap. text ed. 5.50x (ISBN 0-582-60358-7). Longman.

Short History of Social Life in England. M. B. Synge. 1973. Repr. of 1908 ed. 35.00 (ISBN 0-8274-0846-3). R West.

Short History of Sociological Thought. Alan Swingewood. LC 84-40119. 350p. 1984. 29.95 (ISBN 0-312-72150-1); pap. 12.95 (ISBN 0-312-72151-X). St Martin.

Short History of Sociology. Heinz Maus. 1962. 6.95 (ISBN 0-8022-1095-3). Philos Lib.

Short History of Solicitors. Edmund B. Christian. xiv, 255p. 1983. Repr. of 1896 ed. lib. bdg. 25.00x (ISBN 0-8377-0448-0). Rothman.

Short History of Spanish Literature: Revised & Updated Edition. James R. Stamm. LC 78-53803. (Gotham Library). 1979. 37.50x (ISBN 0-8147-7791-0); pap. 17.50x (ISBN 0-8147-7792-9). NYU Pr.

Short History of Spanish Music. Ann Livermore. LC 72-86597. 262p. 1972. 12.50x (ISBN 0-8443-0077-2). Vienna Hse.

Short History of Spanish Music. Ann Livermore. 262p. 1972. 40.50 (ISBN 0-7156-0634-4, Pub. by Duckworth London); pap. 13.50 (ISBN 0-7156-0898-3). Longwood Pub Group.

Short History of Spanish Music. Ann Livermore. LC 72-196469. pap. 68.00 (ISBN 0-317-42003-8, 2026116). Bks Demand UMI.

Short History of Surgery. D'Arcy Power. LC 75-23751. Repr. of 1933 ed. 20.00 (ISBN 0-404-13357-6). AMS Pr.

Short History of Switzerland. Edgar Bonjour et al. LC 84-25253. viii, 388p. 1985. Repr. of 1952 ed. lib. bdg. 52.50x (ISBN 0-313-24675-0, BOSZ). Greenwood.

Short History of Syriac Christianity to the Rise of Islam. W. Stewart McCullough. LC 80-29297. (Scholars Press Polebridge Bks.). 1982. 21.95 (ISBN 0-89130-454-1, 00-03-04). Scholars Pr GA.

Short History of Syriac Literature. William Wright. LC 78-14330. 1978. Repr. of 1894 ed. lib. bdg. 49.50 (ISBN 0-8414-9709-5). Folcroft.

Short History of Tasmania. Lloyd Robson. (Illus.). 204p. 1986. pap. 14.95x (ISBN 0-19-554651-2). Oxford U Pr.

Short History of the American Bison. rev. facsimile ed. Martin S. Garretson. LC 79-169759. (Select Bibliographies Reprint Ser). Repr. of 1934 ed. 12.00 (ISBN 0-8369-5979-5). Ayer Co Pubs.

Short History of the American Nation, 2 vols. 4th ed. John A. Garraty. 1985. To 1877, 313p. pap. text ed. 12.95 scp (ISBN 0-06-042294-7, HarpC); Since 1865, 315p. pap. text ed. 13.95 (ISBN 0-06-042295-5). Har-Row.

Short History of the American Nation. 4th ed. John A. Garraty. 589p. 1985. scp 25.50 (ISBN 0-06-042293-9, HarpC). Har-Row.

Short History of the American Nation. 5th ed. John A. Garraty. 640p. 1988. pap. text ed. 20.50t (ISBN 0-06-042415-X, HarpC). Har-Row.

Short History of the American Teilhard Association. Winifred McCulloch. 1979. pap. 3.00 (ISBN 0-89012-013-7). Anima Pubns.

Short History of the Art of Distillation from the Beginnings up to the Death of Cellier Blumenthal. Robert J. Forbes. LC 79-8608. Repr. of 1948 ed. 41.00 (ISBN 0-404-18470-7). AMS Pr.

Short History of the Baptists. Henry C. Vedder. 12.95 (ISBN 0-8170-0162-X). Judson.

Short History of the Beginnings & Origins of These Present Wars in Moscow under the Reign of Various Sovereigns Down to the Year 1610. Issac Massa. Tr. by G. Edward Orchard from Dutch. 256p. 1982. 37.50x (ISBN 0-8020-2404-1). U of Toronto Pr.

Short History of the British People. D. Morgan. 182p. 1981. 13.00x (ISBN 0-317-54547-7, Pub. by Collets (UK)). State Mutual Bk.

Short History of the Brontes. K. A. Sugden. LC 72-193758. 1929. lib. bdg. 30.00 (ISBN 0-8414-7990-9). Folcroft.

Short History of the Browntail Moth. William Curtis. 1969. 40.00x (ISBN 0-317-07175-0, Pub. by FW Classey UK). State Mutual Bk.

Short History of the Catholic Church. Derek J. Holmes & Bernard W. Bickers. LC 83-63193. 315p. 1984. pap. 8.95 (ISBN 0-8091-2623-0). Paulist Pr.

Short History of the Catholic Church. Denis Meadows. 246p. 1959. 14.95 (ISBN 0-8159-6813-2). Devin.

Short History of the Catholic Church. Jose Orlandis. 163p. 1985. pap. 7.95 (ISBN 0-912414-43-X). Lumen Christi.

Short History of the Catholic Church. Jose Orlandis. Tr. by Michael Adams from Span. 163p. (Orig.). 1985. pap. 7.95 (ISBN 0-906127-86-6, Pub. by Four Courts Pr Ireland). Scepter Pubs.

Short History of the Clan Robertson. J. Robertson Reid. 64p. 1985. pap. 7.95 (ISBN 0-912951-31-1). ScotPr.

Short History of the Drama. Martha F. Bellinger. 469p. 1980. Repr. lib. bdg. 47.00 (ISBN 0-89984-052-3). Century Bookbindery.

Short History of the Early American Microscopes, Vol. 12. Donald L. Padgitt. LC 74-30750. (Illus.). 1975. 15.00 (ISBN 0-904962-04-0). Microscope Pubns.

Short History of the Early Church. Harry R. Boer. LC 75-25742. pap. 8.95 (ISBN 0-8028-1339-9). Eerdmans.

Short History of the Early Years of Study by Correspondence. Joseph E. Smart. 43p. (Orig.). 1986. pap. 4.95 (ISBN 0-917619-10-2). Smartco.

Short History of the Egyptian People with Chapters on Their Religion, Daily Life, Etc. E. A. Budge. LC 78-14274. 1978. Repr. of 1914 ed. lib. bdg. 35.00 (ISBN 0-8414-0390-2). Folcroft.

Short History of the English Drama. facsimile ed. Benjamin Brawley. LC 71-102227. (Select Bibliographies Reprint Ser). 1921. 24.50 (ISBN 0-8369-5112-3). Ayer Co Pubs.

Short History of the English Microscope, Vol. 11. Harold Malies. LC 80-83457. (Illus.). 1981. 11.00 (ISBN 0-904962-09-1). Microscope Pubns.

Short History of the English Novel. S. Diana Neill. 340p. 1981. Repr. of 1951 ed. lib. bdg. 45.00 (ISBN 0-89984-354-9). Century Bookbindery.

Short History of the English People, 2 Vols. John R. Green. 1980. Repr. of 1960 ed. Vol. 1. 16.95x (ISBN 0-460-00727-0, Evman); Vol. 2. 16.95x (ISBN 0-460-00728-9). Biblio Dist.

Short History of the English People, 3 vols. John Richard Green. 1073p. 1986. Repr. of 1900 ed. lib. bdg. 100.00 (ISBN 0-8495-2145-9). Arden Lib.

Short History of the English Stage: From Its Beginnings to the Summer of the Year of 1908. R. F. Sharp. LC 73-4181. 1973. text ed. 37.50 (ISBN 0-8414-7520-2). Folcroft.

Short History of the English Stage from Its Beginnings to the Summers of the Year 1908. R. Farquharson Sharp. 355p. 1984. Repr. of 1909 ed. lib. bdg. 50.00 (ISBN 0-89987-980-2). Darby Bks.

Short History of the European Working Class. Wolfgang Abendroth. Tr. by Nicholas Jacobs et al from Ger. LC 72-81766. 208p. 1972. pap. 5.95 (ISBN 0-85345-289-X). Monthly Rev.

Short History of the European Working Class. Rev. ed. Wolfgang Abendroth. Tr. by Nicholas Jacobs et al. 240p. (Orig.). Date not set. 25.00 (ISBN 0-85345-694-1); pap. 9.00 (ISBN 0-85345-695-X). Monthly Rev.

Short History of the Fatmid Khalifate. De Lacy O'Leary. 267p. 1988. Repr. of 1923 ed. text ed. 45.00x (ISBN 0-86590-823-0, Pub. by Renaissance New Delhi). Apt Bks.

Short History of the First Liberian Republic. Ed. by Joseph S. Guannu. 1985. pap. 10.00 (ISBN 0-682-40267-2). Exposition-Phoenix.

Short History of the French Revolution, 1789-1799. Albert Soboul. Tr. by Geoffrey Symcox. 1977. o.s.i 23.75x (ISBN 0-520-02855-4); pap. 7.95x (ISBN 0-520-03419-8). U of Cal Pr.

Short History of the Georgian Church. Platon Ioseliani. 208p. 1983. pap. 6.00 (ISBN 0-317-30451-8). Holy Trinity.

Short History of the German Language. W. Walker Chambers & John R. Wilkie. 1970. pap. 12.95x (ISBN 0-416-18220-8, NO. 2130). Routledge Chapman & Hall.

Short History of the Hebrews: From the Patriarchs to Herod the Great. 3rd ed. B. K. Rattey. (Illus.). 1976. pap. 11.50x (ISBN 0-19-832121-X). Oxford U Pr.

Short History of the Hungarian Cinema. Istvan Nemeskurty. (Illus.). 141p. (Orig.). 1981. pap. 4.95 (ISBN 963-13-1101-5). NY Zoetrope.

Short History of the Indians of the United States. Edward H. Spicer. LC 83-11320. 320p. 1983. pap. text ed. 11.25 (ISBN 0-89874-657-4). Krieger.

Short History of the Interpretation of the Bible. 2nd, rev. & enlarged ed. Robert M. Grant & David Tracy. LC 83-18485. 224p. 1984. pap. 10.95 (ISBN 0-8006-1762-2, 1-1762). Fortress.

Short History of the Island of Butterflies. Nicholas Christopher. (Poetry Ser.). 81p. 1986. pap. 8.95 (ISBN 0-14-058554-0). Penguin.

Short History of the Jewish People. rev. ed. Cecil Roth. 1969. 14.95; pap. 6.95 (ISBN 0-87677-183-5). Hartmore.

Short History of the Jews in the United States. Hyman Grinstein. 208p. 1980. 20.00 (ISBN 0-900689-50-1). Soncino Pr.

Short History of the Korean War. James L. Stokesbury. Ed. by Howard Cady. (Illus.). 352p. 1988. 18.95 (ISBN 0-688-06377-2). Morrow.

Short History of the Liberal Party, 1900-1984. 2nd ed. Chris Cook. LC 85-111247. Date not set. price not set. Macmillan.

Short History of the Massachusetts Courts. National Center for State Courts Staff. 74p. 1975. manuscript 4.44 (NERO-042). Natl Ctr St Courts.

Short History of the Movies. 3rd ed. Gerald Mast. LC 80-18024. (Illus.). 516p. 1981. pap. text ed. 19.96 scp. Bobbs.

Short History of the Movies. 3rd ed. Gerald Mast. LC 79-14309. 1981. pap. 19.96scp. Pegasus.

Short History of the Movies. 3rd ed. Gerald Mast. (Illus.). 1981. 20.00 (ISBN 0-226-50982-6). U of Chicago Pr.

Short History of the Movies. 4th ed. Gerald Mast. 451p. 1986. pap. text ed. write for info. (ISBN 0-02-377060-0). Macmillan.

Short History of the Movies. 4th ed. Gerald Mast. (Illus.). 520p. 1986. 35.00 (ISBN 0-02-580500-2). Macmillan.

Short History of the Netherlands Antilles & Surinam. Cornelis C. Goslinga. 1978. pap. 20.00 (ISBN 90-247-2118-0, Pub. by Martinus Nijhoff Netherlands). Kluwer Academic.

Short History of the Papacy in the Middle Ages. Walter Ullmann. 1974. pap. 16.95x (ISBN 0-416-74970-4, NO. 2562). Routledge Chapman & Hall.

Short History of the Printed Word. Warren Chappell. LC 79-90409. (Nonpareil Bks.). (Illus.). 288p. 1980. pap. 9.95 (ISBN 0-87923-312-5). Godine.

Short History of the Printed Word. Warren Chappell. 17.00 (ISBN 0-405-13093-7). Ayer Co Pubs.

Short History of the Renaissance in Italy. John A. Symonds. LC 66-23320. Repr. of 1894 ed. 22.50x (ISBN 0-8154-0227-9). Cooper Sq.

Short History of the Romantic Movement in Spain. Edgar A. Peers. LC 76-28478. Repr. of 1949 ed. 32.50 (ISBN 0-404-15034-9). AMS Pr.

Short History of the Saracens. A. A. Syed. 702p. 1984. 350.00x (ISBN 1-85077-034-4, Pub. by Darf Pubs Ltd). State Mutual Bk.

Short History of the Twelve Buddhist Sects. Tr. by Bunyiu Nanjio from Japanese. LC 79-52924. (Studies in Japanese History & Civilization). 172p. 1979. Repr. of 1886 ed. 19.75 (ISBN 0-89093-252-2). U Pubns Amer.

Short History of the Twelve Japanese Buddhist Sects. Compiled by Bunyiu Nanjio. LC 78-70104. Repr. of 1886 ed. 23.00 (ISBN 0-404-17355-1). AMS Pr.

Short History of the United States. 6th ed. Allan Nevins & Henry S. Commager. (YA) (gr. 7-12). 1976. 22.95 (ISBN 0-394-40892-6). Knopf.

Short History of the United States of America: With the Co-operation of Heinz Forster & Leonard A. Jones. Max Zeuske. 180p. 1984. 25.00x (ISBN 0-317-54539-6, Pub. by Collets (UK)). State Mutual Bk.

Short History of the U. S. S. R. S. Schmidt et al. 304p. 1984. 18.00x (ISBN 0-317-54536-1, Pub. by Collets (UK)). State Mutual Bk.

Short History of the University of Michigan. Wilfred B. Shaw. 1934. 5.00x (ISBN 0-685-21804-X). Wahr.

Short History of the Vietnam War. Ed. by Allan R. Millett. LC 77-23623. (Midland Bks: No. 210). 224p. 1978. 22.50x (ISBN 0-253-35215-0); pap. 6.95X (ISBN 0-253-20210-8). Ind U Pr.

Short History of the West Indies. 4th ed. J. H. Parry & P. M. Sherlock. LC 73-145588. 1988. pap. text ed. write for info. (ISBN 0-312-00443-5). St Martin.

Short History of the Western Liturgy. 2nd ed. Theodor Klauser. Tr. by John Halliburton from Ger. 1979. pap. text ed. 10.95x (ISBN 0-19-213223-7). Oxford U Pr.

Short History of the Yugoslav Peoples. Fred Singleton. (Illus.). 336p. 1985. pap. 13.95 (ISBN 0-521-27485-0). Cambridge U Pr.

Short History of the Zulu. Baso Nebo. (Illus.). 96p. 1987. pap. 9.95 (ISBN 0-941157-06-7). Pride & Co.

Short History of Tompkins County. Jane M. Dieckmann. (Illus.). 229p. (Orig.). 1986. pap. 9.95 (ISBN 0-942690-33-8). Dewitt Hist.

Short History of Tompkins County. Jane M. Dieckmann. LC 85-25440. (Illus.). 229p. (Orig.). 1986. 16.95 (ISBN 0-942690-34-6). Dewitt Hist.

Short History of Tuberculosis. George N. Meachen. LC 75-23738. Repr. of 1936 ed. 20.00 (ISBN 0-404-13295-2). AMS Pr.

Short Stories by Sir Walter Scott. Walter Scott. LC 71-145286. 1971. Repr. of 1934 ed. 39.00x (ISBN 0-403-01200-7). Scholarly.
Short Stories by Sir Walter Scott. Walter Scott. 1988. Repr. of 1934 ed. lib. bdg. 65.00x. Am Biog Serv.
Short Stories for Discussion. Ed. by Albert Ridout & Jesse Stuart. 489p. 1965. pap. text ed. write for info. (ISBN 0-02-400590-8, Pub. by Scribner). Macmillan.
Short Stories for Young & Old. G. Polizoides. (Gr.). 1977. pap. text ed. 2.00 (ISBN 0-685-81640-0). Divry.
Short Stories from the Balkans. Tr. by Edna Underwood. LC 75-122590. Repr. of 1919 ed. 20.50 (ISBN 0-404-06703-4). AMS Pr.
Short Stories: How to Write Them. Cecil Hunt. 1979. Repr. of 1934 ed. lib. bdg. 22.50 (ISBN 0-8495-2259-5). Arden Lib.
Short Stories of Charlie Elliott. Charles Elliott. 1987. 14.95 (ISBN 0-89783-042-3). Larlin Corp.
Short Stories of De Maupassant. Guy De Maupassant. Repr. of 1941 ed. 35.00. Darby Bks.
Short Stories of Ernest Hemingway. Ernest Hemingway. 1938. lib. bdg. 32.50x (ISBN 0-684-15155-3, ScribT); pap. 10.95 (ISBN 0-684-71806-5, ScribT); rack size 7.95 (ISBN 0-684-18356-0). Scribner.
Short Stories of Ernest Hemingway. Ernest Hemingway. 26.95 (ISBN 0-88411-689-1, Pub. by Aeonian Pr). Amereon Ltd.
Short Stories of Ernest Hemingway. Ernest Hemingway. 508p. 1987. pap. 7.95 (ISBN 0-02-051860-9, Collier). Macmillan.
Short Stories of Ernest Hemingway: Critical Essays. Jackson L. Benson. LC 74-75815. xv, 375p. 1986. pap. 14.95x (ISBN 0-8223-0386-8). Duke.
Short Stories of F. Scott Fitzgerald: New Approaches in Criticism. Ed. by Jackson R. Bryer. 416p. 1982. pap. 10.95x (ISBN 0-299-09084-1). U of Wis Pr.
Short Stories of Fray Angelico Chavez. Ed. by Genaro M. Padilla. LC 87-5992. (Illus.). 159p. 1987. 19.95 (ISBN 0-8263-0949-6); pap. 9.95 (ISBN 0-8263-0950-X). U of NM Pr.
Short Stories of Grace Livingston Hill. Grace L. Hill. Ed. by J. E. Clauss. 1976. lib. bdg. 12.95 (ISBN 0-89190-101-9, Pub. by River City Pr). Amereon Ltd.
Short Stories of H. G. Wells. 1148p. 1984. Repr. of 1928 ed. lib. bdg. 40.00 (ISBN 0-8495-5846-8). Arden Lib.
Short Stories of John Galsworthy. J. Henry Smit. LC 68-877. (Studies in Fiction, No. 34). 1969. Repr. lib. bdg. 75.00x (ISBN 0-8383-0681-0). Haskell.
Short Stories of Katherine Mansfield. Katherine Mansfield. (YA) (gr. 7-12). 1947. 22.45 (ISBN 0-394-44532-5). Knopf.
Short Stories of Katherine Mansfield. Katherine Mansfield. LC 83-21012. 688p. 1983. pap. 11.95 (ISBN 0-88001-025-8). Ecco Pr.
Short Stories of Mark Twain. Mark Twain. (Airmont Classics Ser.). (gr. 8 up). 1968. pap. 3.95 (ISBN 0-8049-0171-6, CL-171). Airmont.
Short Stories of Padriac Pearse. Ed. by Desmond Malguire. 117p. (Dual language Irish & Eng.). 1978. pap. 7.95 (ISBN 0-85342-117-X, Pub. by Mercier Pr Ireland). Irish Bks Media.
Short Stories of Saki. Saki. LC 83-5468. 10.95 (ISBN 0-394-60428-8). Modern Lib.
Short Stories of Saki (H. H. Munro) H. H. Munro. 716p. 1986. Repr. of 1930 ed. lib. bdg. 50.00 (ISBN 0-89987-618-8). Darby Bks.
Short Stories of Sean O'Faolain. J. S. Rippier. 1976. 21.00 (ISBN 0-901072-30-3, Pub. by Colin Smythe Ltd Britain). Dufour.
Short Stories of the Australian Outback. Ray E. White. 1987. 10.95 (ISBN 0-533-07409-6). Vantage.
Short Stories of the Far East. Graham Brash Editorial Staff. (Illus.). 184p. 1984. pap. 8.00 (ISBN 9971-947-62-5, Pub. by Graham Brash Singapore). Three Continents.
Short Stories of the Sea. Ed. by George C. Solley et al. LC 78-31843. 584p. 1984. 18.95 (ISBN 0-87021-650-3). Naval Inst Pr.
Short Stories of Thomas Hardy. Kristin Brady. LC 81-5665. 200p. 1982. 23.50 (ISBN 0-312-72219-2). St Martin.
Short Stories of Today & Yesterday. George Gissing. 1929. 25.00 (ISBN 0-8274-3408-1). R West.
Short Stories on Film & Video. 2nd ed. Carol A. Emmens. LC 85-13160. 351p. 1985. lib. bdg. 25.00 (ISBN 0-87287-424-9). Libs Unl.
Short Stories: The Tale of Chloe, The House on the Beach, Farina, The Case of General Ople & Lady Camper. George Meredith. 315p. 1982. Repr. of 1914 ed. lib. bdg. 25.00 (ISBN 0-8495-3936-6). Arden Lib.
Short Stories, Vol. 1: A Sahib's War & Other Stories. Rudyard Kipling. Ed. by Andrew Rutherford. 1977. pap. 5.95. Penguin.
Short Stories, Vol. 2: Friendly Brook & Other Stories. Rudyard Kipling. Ed. by Andrew Rutherford. (Modern Classics Ser.). 1977. pap. 5.95. Penguin.
Short Story. Sean O. Faolain. 269p. 1983. pap. 9.95 (ISBN 0-85342-302-4, Pub. by Mercier Pr Ireland). Irish Bks Media.
Short Story. Sean O'Faolain. pap. 7.95 (ISBN 0-8159-6814-0). Devin.
Short Story. Barry Pain. 1979. Repr. lib. bdg. 20.00 (ISBN 0-8414-6822-2). Folcroft.
Short Story. Barry Pain. 1973. 22.00 (ISBN 0-8274-1253-3). R West.
Short Story. Ian Reid. (Critical Idiom Ser.). 1977. 9.95x (ISBN 0-416-56060-1, NO. 2402); pap. 5.50x (ISBN 0-416-56070-9, NO. 2403). Routledge Chapman & Hall.
Short Story: A Critical Introduction. Valerie Shaw. 304p. 1983. pap. text ed. 15.95 (ISBN 0-582-48687-4). Longman.
Short Story: An Introduction. 2nd ed. Wilfred Stone & N. H. Packer. 640p. 1983. pap. 16.95 (ISBN 0-07-061693-0, +007). McGraw.
Short Story & the Oral Tradition. Paul Sherr. LC 70-101314. 1970. pap. text ed. 15.00x (ISBN 0-87835-002-0). Boyd & Fraser.
Short Story & the Reader: Discovering Narrative Techniques. Ed. by Thomas S. Kane & Leonard J. Peters. 1975. pap. text ed. 10.95x (ISBN 0-19-501960-1); tchr's. manual avail. (ISBN 0-19-502042-1). Oxford U Pr.
Short Story Criticism, Vol. 1. Ed. by Laurie L. Harris & Sheila Fitzgerald. 450p. 1987. 70.00x. Gale.
Short Story Criticism, Vol. 2. Ed. by Sheila Fitzgerald. 550p. 1988. 70.00 (ISBN 0-8103-2551-9). Gale.
Short Story: Fifty Masterpieces. Ed. by Ellen C. Wynn. LC 82-60462. 650p. 1983. pap. text ed. write for info. (ISBN 0-312-72216-8). St Martin.
Short Story: Henry James to Elizabeth Bowen. John Bayley. LC 87-36942. 205p. 1988. 35.00 (ISBN 0-312-01669-7). St Martin.
Short Story in America, 1900-1950. facs. ed. Ray B. West. LC 68-55863. (Essay Index Reprint Ser). 1952. 20.00 (ISBN 0-8369-0982-8). Ayer Co Pubs.
Short Story in English. Walter Allen. 1981. 29.95 (ISBN 0-19-812666-2). Oxford U Pr.
Short Story in Spain in the Seventeenth Century, with a Bibliography of the Novela from 1576-1700. Caroline B. Bourland. LC 73-170183. 1927. 21.00 (ISBN 0-8337-4498-4). B Franklin.
Short Story Index: Basic Volume, 1900-1949. Ed. by Dorothy E. Cook & Isabel S. Monro. Incl. Supplement 1950-1954. Ed. by Dorothy E. Cook & Estelle A. Fidell. 394p. 1956. 25.00 (ISBN 0-8242-0385-2); Supplement 1955-1958. Ed. by Estelle A. Fidell & Esther V. Flory. 341p. 1960. 25.00 (ISBN 0-8242-0386-0); Supplement 1959-1963. Ed. by Estelle A. Fidell. 487p. 1965. 25.00 (ISBN 0-8242-0387-9); Supplement 1964-1968. Ed. by Estelle A. Fidell. 599p. 1969. 30.00 (ISBN 0-8242-0399-2); Supplement 1969-1973. Ed. by Estelle A. Fidell. 639p. 1974. 40.00 (ISBN 0-8242-0497-2); Supplement 1974. Ed. by Gary L. Bogart & Estelle A. Fidell. 1975; 1976; 1977; Supplement, 1974-1978. Ed. by Gary L. Bogart. LC 75-649762. 802p. 70.00 (ISBN 0-686-66656-9); 1979-1983. LC 75-649762. 918p. 1984. 80.00. LC 53-8991. 1553p. 1953. 35.00 (ISBN 0-8242-0384-4). Wilson.
Short Story Index: Collections Indexed 1900-1978. LC 79-24887. 349p. 1979. 30.00 (ISBN 0-8242-0643-6). Wilson.
Short Story Masterpieces. Ed. by Robert Penn Warren & Albert Erskine. 542p. 1954. pap. 5.95 (ISBN 0-440-37864-8, LE). Dell.
Short-Story Masterpieces: Vol. 3, Russian. facsimile ed. Compiled by Joseph B. Esenwein. Tr. by John Cournos from Rus. LC 79-179299. (Short Story Index Reprint Ser.). Repr. of 1913 ed. 14.50 (ISBN 0-8369-4038-5). Ayer Co Pubs.
Short Story Reader. 2nd ed. Berkley & Gould Saundra. 1973. pap. 8.40 scp (ISBN 0-672-73292-0). Bobbs.
Short-Story: Specimens Illustrating Its Development. Ed. by Brander Matthews. 1977. Repr. of 1907 ed. lib. bdg. 20.00 (ISBN 0-8492-1791-1). R West.
Short Story Theories. Ed. by Charles E. May. LC 75-36982. xiv, 251p. 1977. 15.00x (ISBN 0-8214-0189-0); pap. 8.95x (ISBN 0-8214-0221-8). Ohio U Pr.
Short Story Writing. Charls R. Barrett. 257p. 1981. Repr. lib. bdg. 30.00 (ISBN 0-8495-0465-1). Arden Lib.
Short Story Writing. Mary B. Ovis. 291p. 1981. Repr. of 1928 ed. lib. bdg. 35.00 (ISBN 0-8495-4229-4). Arden Lib.
Short Story Writing. pap. 1.25 (ISBN 0-686-32332-7). Rod & Staff.
Short Story Writing for Profit. Michael Joseph. 12.50 (ISBN 0-932062-90-3). Sharon Hill.
Short Story: 30 Masterpieces. Ed. by Beverly Lawn. LC 86-60661. 474p. 1986. pap. text ed. write for info. (ISBN 0-312-72222-2). St Martin.
Short Story's Mutations: From Petronius to Paul Morand. Frances Newman. Repr. of 1924 ed. lib. bdg. 30.00 (ISBN 0-8495-4100-X). Arden Lib.
Short Studies in Shakespeare. G. Bradby. LC 76-30728. (Studies in Shakespeare, No. 24). 1977. lib. bdg. 75.00x (ISBN 0-8383-2169-0). Haskell.
Short Studies of American Authors. enl. ed. Thomas W. Higginson. 78p. 1967. pap. 6.50 (ISBN 0-910120-01-3). Americanist.
Short Studies of American Authors. Thomas W. Higginson. LC 76-25056. 1880. Repr. lib. bdg. 16.00 (ISBN 0-8414-4829-9). Folcroft.
Short Studies of Great Lawyers. Irving Browne. iv, 382p. 1982. Repr. of 1878 ed. lib. bdg. 30.00x (ISBN 0-8377-0330-1). Rothman.
Short Studies of Shakespeare's Plots. Cyril Ransome. 299p. 1981. Repr. of 1911 ed. lib. bdg. 35.00 (ISBN 0-8495-4638-9). Arden Lib.
Short Studies on Great Subjects. James A. Froude. 1964. Repr. of 1906 ed. 8.95x (ISBN 0-460-00013-6, Evman). Biblio Dist.
Short Studies on Great Subjects, 3 vols. James A. Froude. 1878. Set. 75.00 (ISBN 0-8274-3889-3). R West.
Short Survey of Czech Literature. F. Chudoba. 1924. 29.00 (ISBN 0-527-17000-3). Kraus Repr.
Short Survey of Surrealism. David Gascoyne. (Illus.). 162p. 1971. Repr. of 1935 ed. 29.50x (ISBN 0-7146-2262-1, BHA-02262, F Cass Co). Biblio Dist.
Short Survey of Surrealism. David Gascoyne. (Illus.). 164p. 1982. pap. 5.95 (ISBN 0-87286-137-6). City Lights.
Short Survey of the Literature of Rabbinical & Medieval Judaism. William O. Oesterley. LC 72-82352. 328p. 1973. Repr. of 1920 ed. lib. bdg. 24.50 (ISBN 0-8337-3944-1). B Franklin.
Short Synopsis of the Most Essential Points in Hawaiian Grammar. W. C. Alexander. LC 68-13866. pap. 2.95 (ISBN 0-8048-0528-8). C E Tuttle.
Short Syntax of New Testament Greek. 5th ed. Henry P. Nunn. 1931. text ed. 12.95 (ISBN 0-521-09941-2). Cambridge U Pr.
Short-Tailed Fruit Bat: A Study in Plant-Animal Interactions. Theodore H. Fleming. (Wildlife Behavior & Ecology Ser.). (Illus.). 408p. 1988. 49.95x (ISBN 0-226-25328-7). U of Chicago Pr.
Short Takes. Michael Meltsner. LC 79-4778. 1980. 8.95 (ISBN 0-394-50606-5). Random.
Short Takes. Damon Runyon. 278p. 1985. Repr. of 1948 ed. lib. bdg. 35.00 (ISBN 0-89987-414-2). Darby Bks.
Short Takes: A Collection of Short Stories. Elizabeth Segel. (Illus.). 160p. (YA) (gr. 9 up). 1986. 11.75 (ISBN 0-688-06092-7). Lothrop.
Short Takes: Model Essays for Composition. 2nd ed. Elizabeth Penfield. 1987. pap. text ed. write for info. (ISBN 0-673-18397-1). Scott F.
Short Tales One-Six. Geoffrey Summerfield. (Ward Lock Educational Ser.). (gr. 1-5). 12.00x ea. (Pub. by Ward Lock Educ Co Ltd). Bk. 1 (ISBN 0-7062-4017-0, Pub. by Ward Lock Educ Co Ltd). Bk. 2 (ISBN 0-7062-4018-9, Pub. by Ward Lock Educ Co Ltd). Bk. 3 (ISBN 0-7062-4019-7, Pub. by Ward Lock Educ Co Ltd). Bk. 4 (ISBN 0-7062-4020-0, Pub. by Ward Lock Educ Co Ltd). Bk. 5 (ISBN 0-7062-4024-3, Pub. by Ward Lock Educ Co Ltd). Bk. 6 (ISBN 0-7062-4072-3, Pub. by Ward Lock Educ Co Ltd). State Mutual Bk.
Short Talks Around the Lord's Table. Harry L. Thomson. pap. 4.25 (ISBN 0-89137-559-7). Quality Pubns.
Short Talks for Special Occasions, Bk. 1. Mildred Dennis. 64p. 1987. pap. 2.95 (ISBN 0-87403-069-2, 2880). Standard Pub.
Short Talks for Special Occasions, Bk. 2. Mildred Dennis. 64p. 1987. pap. 2.95 (ISBN 0-87403-070-6, 2881). Standard Pub.
Short Talks on Huna. 2nd rev. ed. Max F. Long. 1978. pap. 5.00 (ISBN 0-910764-02-6). Huna Res Inc.
Short Talks on Masonry. Joseph F. Newton. 255p. 1979. Repr. of 1969 ed. text ed. 7.95 (ISBN 0-88053-036-7, M-85). Macoy Pub.
Short Talks with the Dead, & Others. facs. ed. Hilaire Belloc. LC 67-23175. (Essay Index Reprint Ser). 1926. 18.00 (ISBN 0-8369-0192-4). Ayer Co Pubs.
Short-Term Approaches to Psychotheraphy, Vol. III. Ed. by Henry Grayson. LC 78-27605. (New Directions in Psychotherapy Ser.). 285p. 1979. 29.95 (ISBN 0-87705-345-6). Human Sci Pr.
Short-Term Bioassays in the Analysis of Complex Environmental Mixtures, Pt. 5. Ed. by S. S. Sandhu et al. LC 87-27388. (Environmental Science Research Ser.: Vol. 36). (Illus.). 422p. 1987. 75.00x (ISBN 0-306-42772-9, Plenum Pr). Plenum Pub.
Short-Term Bioassays in the Analysis of Complex Environmental Mixtures, Pt. 1. Ed. by Michael D. Waters et al. LC 79-22240. (Environmental Science Research Ser.: Vol. 15). 602p. 1979. 95.00x (ISBN 0-306-40319-6, Plenum Pr). Plenum Pub.
Short-Term Bioassays In the Analysis of Complex Environmental Mixtures, Pt. 3. Ed. by Michael D. Waters et al. LC 82-22323. (Environmental Science Research: Vol. 27). 606p. 1983. 95.00x (ISBN 0-306-41191-1, Plenum Pr). Plenum Pub.
Short-Term Bioassays In the Analysis of Complex Environmental Mixtures, Pt. 2. Ed. by Michael D. Waters et al. LC 81-17839. (Environmental Science Research Ser.: Vol. 22). 540p. 1981. 89.50x (ISBN 0-306-40890-2, Plenum Pr). Plenum Pub.
Short-Term Bioassays in the Analysis of Complex Environmental Mixtures, Pt. 4. Ed. by Michael D. Waters et al. LC 85-9505. (Environmental Science Research Ser.: Vol. 32). 394p. 1985. 69.50x (ISBN 0-306-42015-5, Plenum Pr). Plenum Pub.
Short-Term Counseling: A Psychoanalytic Approach. Barbara W. Tilley. LC 84-9008. xii, 358p. 1985. text ed. 37.50x (ISBN 0-8236-6072-9, BN#06072). Intl Univs Pr.
Short-Term Counseling: Guidelines Based on Recent Research. Irving L. Janis. LC 83-3488. 240p. 1983. text ed. 30.00t (ISBN 0-300-03102-5); pap. 10.95x (ISBN 0-300-03125-4, Y-480). Yale U Pr.
Short-Term Counseling: Theory & Practice. Kathleen Black. 1982. pap. write for info. (ISBN 0-201-00073-3, 00073, Hlth-Sci). Addison-Wesley.
Short-Term Dynamic Psychotherapy. Ed. by H. Davanloo. LC 80-67986. 416p. 1980. 35.00x (ISBN 0-87668-418-5). Aronson.
Short-Term Dynamic Psychotherapy: Evaluation & Technique. 2nd ed. Peter E. Sifneos. LC 87-2346. (Topics in General Psychiatry Ser.). 316p. 1987. 34.50x (ISBN 0-306-42341-3, Plenum Pr). Plenum Pub.
Short-Term Economic Reports: Colombia, Vol. 1. 2nd ed. OAS General Secretariat. (Short Term Economic Reports Ser.). 77p. 1980. pap. text ed. 5.00 (ISBN 0-8270-1261-6). OAS.
Short-Term Economic Reports: Mexico 1980. OAS General Secretariat Executive Secretariat for Economic & Social Affairs. (Sort-Term Economic Report Ser.). 54p. (Span.). 1980. lib. bdg. 4.00 (ISBN 0-8270-1293-4). OAS.
Short-Term Economic Reports, Vol. IV: Brazil-Relatorios Economicos De Curto Prazo, Brazil. (Eng. & Port.). 1978. pap. 2.00 Eng. ed. (ISBN 0-8270-3675-2); pap. 2.00 Port. ed. (ISBN 0-8270-3615-9). OAS.
Short-Term Economic Reports, Vol. V: Venezuela-Informes Economicos De Corto Plazo, Venezuela. (Eng. & Span.). 1978. pap. 2.00 Eng. ed. (ISBN 0-8270-3595-0); pap. 2.00 Span. ed. (ISBN 0-8270-3625-6). OAS.
Short-Term Financial Management. Ned C. Hill & William L. Sartoris. Ed. by Ken MacLeod. (Illus.). 544p. 1988. write for info. (ISBN 0-02-354820-7). Macmillan.
Short Term Forecasting: A Case Study. George Polanyi. (Institute of Economic Affairs-Background Memoranda Ser.: No. 4). pap. 4.25 technical (ISBN 0-685-44124-5). Transatl Arts.
Short-Term Investment Forecasting: An Exploratory Study. Samuel Paul & C. Rangarajan. LC 75-903519. 1974. 12.00 (ISBN 0-8364-0466-1). South Asia Bks.
Short-Term Macroeconomic Policy in Latin America: Conference on Planning & Short-Term Marco-Economic Policy in Latin America. Ed. by Jere R. Behrman & James A. Hanson. LC 78-24053. (Other Conference Ser.: No.14). 416p. 1979. prof ref 35.00x (ISBN 0-88410-489-3, Pub for the National Bureau of Economic Research). Ballinger Pub.
Short-Term Memory. Ed. by D. Deutsch & J. A. Deutsch. 1975. 44.00 (ISBN 0-12-213350-1). Acad Pr.
Short Term Psychotherapies for Depression: Behavioral, Interpersonal, Cognitive, Psychodynamic. Ed. by John A. Rush. LC 81-7058. 339p. 1982. 32.50 (ISBN 0-89862-615-3, 2615). Guilford Pr.
Short-Term Psychotherapy & Brief Treatment Techniques: An Annotated Bibliography, 1920-1980. Harvey P. Mandel. LC 81-221. 704p. 1981. 65.00x (ISBN 0-306-40658-6, Plenum Pr). Plenum Pub.
Short Term Psychotherapy & Emotional Crisis. Peter Sifneos. LC 78-172323. (Illus.). 320p. 1972. 18.50x (ISBN 0-674-80720-0). Harvard U Pr.
Short Term Regulation of Liver Metabolism. Ed. by L. Hue & G. Van de Werve. 464p. 1982. 187.00 (ISBN 0-444-80333-5, Biomedical Pr). Elsevier.
Short-Term Responses to Trade & Incentive Policies in the Ivory Coast: Comparative Static Simulations in a Computable General Equilibrium Model. Gilles Michel & Michel Noel. (Staff Working Paper: No. 647). 108p. 1984. 5.00 (ISBN 0-318-11923-4, WP 0647). World Bank.
Short-Term Sedentism in the American Southwest: The Mimbres Valley Salado. Ben A. Nelson & Steven A. LeBlanc. LC 85-14078. (Illus.). 315p. 1986. pap. 35.00x (ISBN 0-8263-0834-1). U of NM Pr.
Short Term Skill Training: Alternative Approaches for Vocational Education. Russell Paulsen. 20p. 1981. 2.35 (ISBN 0-318-22199-3, IN222). Natl Ctr Res Voc Ed.
Short-Term Surplus Funds Management for the State of Texas, No. 17. (Policy Research Project Reports). 68p. 1977. 3.00 (ISBN 0-89940-610-6). LBJ Sch Pub Aff.
Short Term Survival Techniques. John Tomikel. LC 84-70534. (Illus.). 144p. 1984. pap. 4.95 (ISBN 0-910042-45-4). Allegheny.
Short-Term Tests for Chemical Carcinogens. Ed. by H. F. Stich & R. H. San. (Topics in Environmental Physiology & Medicine). (Illus.). 518p. 1981. 95.00 (ISBN 0-387-90496-4). Springer-Verlag.
Short-Term Trading in Futures: A Manual of Systems, Strategies & Techniques. Jacob Bernstein. 400p. 1987. 3-ring binder 125.00 (ISBN 0-917253-66-3). Probus Pub Co.
Short Term Transit Policies & Downtown Revitalization. F. Ulrich. 29p. 1979. pap. 6.00x (28500). Urban Inst.

Short-Term Treatment in Occupational Therapy. Diane Gibson & Kathy Kaplan. LC 84-9115. (Occupational Therapy in Mental Health Ser.: Vol. 4, No. 3). 114p. 1984. 22.95 (ISBN 0-86656-342-3). Haworth Pr.

Short-Term Visual Information Forgetting. A. H. Van Der Heijden. (International Library of Psychology). 224p. 1982. 29.95x (ISBN 0-7100-0851-1). Routledge Chapman & Hall.

Short Term Vocational Evaluation. Karl F. Botterbusch. (Illus.). 163p. (Orig.). 1983. pap. 16.25x (ISBN 0-916671-05-4). Material Dev.

Short Textbook of Medical Jurisprudence. C. C. Mallik. 1985. 79.00x (ISBN 0-317-38795-2, Pub. by Current Dist). State Mutual Bk.

Short Textbook of Orthopedics & Traumatology. 3rd ed. Rev. by Sean Hughes. 294p. 1983. pap. 19.00 (ISBN 0-668-05911-7). Appleton & Lange.

Short Textbook of Otolaryngology. N. K. Gami. 1983. 59.00x (ISBN 0-317-38793-6, Pub. by Current Dist). State Mutual Bk.

Short Textbook of Otolaryngology. A. L. Mukherjee. 1985. 59.00x (ISBN 0-317-39560-2, Pub. by Current Dist). State Mutual Bk.

Short Textbook of Radiotherapy. 4th ed. J Walter & H. Miller. (Illus.). 1979. 43.00 (ISBN 0-443-01389-6). Churchill.

Short-Time Compensation: A Formula for Work Sharing. Ed. by Ramelle McCoy & Martin J. Morand. LC 83-13265. 223p. 1984. 31.00 (ISBN 0-08-030148-7, 29/59/4). Work in Amer.

Short Time to Stay: Comments on Time, Literature & Oral Performance. Ruth Finnegan. LC 81-70548. (Hans Wolff Memorial Lecture Ser.). 55p. 1982. pap. text ed. 5.00 (ISBN 0-941934-35-7). Indiana Africa.

Short Timers (Full Metal Jacket) Hasford. 1987. pap. 3.50 (ISBN 0-553-26739-6). Bantam.

Short-Title Catalogue of Books Printed in England, Scotland, & Ireland & of English Books Printed Abroad 1475-1640, 2 vols. 2nd ed. Ed. by A. W. Pollard & G. R. Redgrave. (Bibliographical Society Ser.). 1976. Vol. 1: A-H. 195.00x (ISBN 0-19-721789-3); Vol. 2: I-Z. 165.00 (ISBN 0-19-721790-7). Oxford U Pr.

Short-Title Catalogue of Books Printed in England, Scotland, Ireland, Wales & North America & of English Books Printed in Other Countries, 1641-1700, 3 vols. 2nd rev & enl ed. Compiled by Donald Wing. Date not set. Vol. 1, 622 p., Sep. 1972. 175.00x (ISBN 0-87352-044-0, Z21); Vol. 2, Ed. by Timothy J. Crist, 690 p., 1982. 350.00x (ISBN 0-87352-045-9, Z22); Vol. 3, Ed. by John J. Morrison, xvi, 786 June 1988. 350.00x (ISBN 0-87352-046-7). Modern Lang.

Short-Title Catalogue of Books Printed in France & French Books Printed in Other Countries from 1470 to 1600 in the British Library. British Library Staff. 500p. 1983. 45.00 (ISBN 0-7123-0025-2, Pub. by British Lib). Longwood Pub Group.

Short-Title Catalogue of Books Printed in Italy & Italian Books Printed in Other Countries from 1465 to 1600 Now in the British Museum. Ed. by British Library Staff. 1000p. 1958. 90.00 (ISBN 0-7123-0097-X, Pub. by British Lib). Longwood Pub Group.

Short-Title Catalogue of Books Printed in Italy & Other Italian Books Printed in Other Countries from 1465 to 1600 Now in the British Library: Supplement. Ed. by British Library Staff. 208p. 1986. 37.50 (ISBN 0-7123-0094-5, Pub. by British Lib). Longwood Pub Group.

Short-Title Catalogue of Books Printed in the German-Speaking Countries & of German Books Printed in Other Countries from 1455 to 1600 Now in the British Museum. British Library Staff. 1232p. 1962. 45.00 (ISBN 0-7141-0268-7, Pub. by British Lib). Longwood Pub Group.

Short-Title Catalogue of Books Printed in the Netherlands & Belgium & of Dutch & Flemish Books Printed in Other Countries from 1470-1600 Now in the British Museum. British Library Staff. 284p. 1965. 22.50 (ISBN 0-7141-0270-9, Pub. by British Lib). Longwood Pub Group.

Short-Title Catalogue of Books Printed on the Continent of Europe, Fifteen Hundred to Sixteen Hundred, in Aberdeen University Library. Compiled by H. J. Drummond. 1979. text ed. 69.00x (ISBN 0-19-714106-4). Oxford U Pr.

Short-Title Catalogue of Household & Cookery Books Published in the English Tongue, 1701-1800. Virginia Maclean. (Illus.). 197p. 1982. 40.00x (ISBN 0-907325-06-8, Pub. by Prospect England). U Pr of Va.

Short Title Catalogue of the Emblem Books & Related Works in the Stirling Maxwell Collection of Glasgow University Library (1499-1917) Hester M. Black. Ed. by David Weston. 150p. 1988. text ed. 24.00 (ISBN 0-85967-751-6, Pub. by Gower Co England). Gower Pub Co.

Short Title Catalogue of Works on Psychical Research. Harry Price. (Hypnosis & Altered States of Consciousness Ser.). 468p. 1982. lib. bdg. 49.50 (ISBN 0-306-76166-1). Da Capo.

Short Titles of Books Relating to or Illustrating the History & Practice of Psalmody in the U. S., 1620-1820. James Warrington. LC 77-178095. (American Classics in History & Social Science Ser.: No. 218). 102p. 1972. Repr. of 1898 ed. lib. bdg. 19.00 (ISBN 0-8337-5357-6). B Franklin.

Short Topographical Description of His Majesty's Province of Upper Canada in North America. David W. Smith. (Canadiana Before 1867 Ser). 1969. Repr. of 1799 ed. 15.00 (ISBN 0-384-56150-0). Johnson Repr.

Short Treatise Declaringe the Detestable Wickednesse of Magicall Sciences. Francis Coxe. LC 72-5971. (English Experience Ser.: No. 501). 32p. 1972. Repr. of 1561 ed. 20.00 (ISBN 90-221-0501-6). Walter J Johnson.

Short Treatise of Geometrie. John Babington. LC 76-25837. (English Experience Ser.: No. 296). 200p. Repr. of 1635 ed. 50.00 (ISBN 90-221-0296-3). Walter J Johnson.

Short Treatise of Lawfull & Unlawfull Recreations. Dudley Fenner. LC 77-6740. (English Experience Ser.: No. 870). 1977. Repr. of 1590 ed. lib. bdg. 15.00 (ISBN 90-221-0870-8). Walter J Johnson.

Short Trips in & Around Dallas. Laura Trim. (Illus.). 298p. (Orig.). 1984. pap. 11.95x (ISBN 0-317-18943-3). LDT Pr.

Short u & Long u Play a Game. Jane B. Moncure. LC 79-10306. (Play with Vowel Sounds Ser.). (Illus.). 32p. (gr. k-3). 1981. lib. bdg. 11.93 (ISBN 0-516-06455-X). Childrens.

Short U & Long U Play a Game. Jane B. Moncure. LC 79-10306. (Play with Vowel Sounds Ser.). (Illus.). (gr. k-2). 1979. PLB 7.95 (ISBN 0-89565-093-2). Childs World.

Short View of Menckenism. Joseph B. Harrison. LC 77-3997. 1927. lib. bdg. 25.00 (ISBN 0-8414-4918-X). Folcroft.

Short View of the English Stage 1900-1926. James Agate. LC 75-91887. Repr. of 1926 ed. 19.00 (ISBN 0-405-08194-4, Pub. by Blom). Ayer Co Pubs.

Short View of the English Stage, 1900-1926. facsimile ed. James E. Agate. LC 70-94263. (Select Bibliographies Reprint Ser). 1926. 17.00 (ISBN 0-8369-5037-2). Ayer Co Pubs.

Short View of the Immorality, & Profaneness of the English Stage. 3rd ed. Jeremy Collier. LC 74-3401. Repr. of 1698 ed. 21.50 (ISBN 0-404-01619-7). AMS Pr.

Short View of the Immorality & Prophaneness of the English Stage: A Critical Edition. Jeremy Collier. Ed. by Stephen Orgel. (Satire & Sense Ser.). 475p. 1987. lib. bdg. 70.00 (ISBN 0-8240-6015-6). Garland Pub.

Short View of the Profaneness & Immorality of the English Stage. Jeremy Collier. 1969. Repr. of 1730 ed. cancelled (ISBN 3-4870-2589-2). Adlers Foreign Bks.

Short View of Tragedy. Thomas Rymer. LC 79-118069. 1968. Repr. of 1693 ed. 10.00 (ISBN 0-404-05478-1). AMS Pr.

Short View of Tragedy. Thomas Rymer. 184p. 1971. Repr. of 1692 ed. 26.00x (ISBN 0-7146-2519-1, F Cass Co). Biblio Dist.

Short View of Tragedy. Thomas Rymer. LC 78-96341. (Eighteenth Century Shakespeare). 1971. Repr. of 1693 ed. 27.50x (ISBN 0-678-05120-8). Kelley.

Short Vindication of the Relapse & the Provok'd Wife. Sir John Vanbrugh. LC 75-170442. (English Stage Ser.: Vol. 28). 1973. lib. bdg. 61.00 (ISBN 0-8240-0611-9). Garland Pub.

Short Vowel Voyage. Linda Schwartz. (Learning Works Reading Ser.). 20p. (gr. 1-3). 1980. 3.95 (ISBN 0-88160-057-1, LW 605). Learning Wks.

Short Vowels. Barbara Gregorich. Ed. by Joan Hoffman. (I Know It! Bks.). (Illus.). 32p. (gr. 1-3). 1981. wkbk. 1.95 (ISBN 0-938256-40-8). Sch Zone Pub Co.

Short Vowels. Virginia Polish. (Starting off with Phonics Ser.: Bk. 5). (Illus.). (gr. k). 1980. pap. text ed. 2.12; tchrs. ed. 2.00. Modern Curr.

Short Voyages. Stephen Jones. 1985. 19.95 (ISBN 0-393-03303-1). Norton.

Short Walk. Alice Childress. 336p. 1981. pap. 3.95 (ISBN 0-380-54239-0, 64790-7, Bard). Avon.

Short Walk in the Hindu Kush. Ed. by Eric Newby. 1987. pap. 6.95 (ISBN 0-14-009575-6). Penguin.

Short Walks in English Towns. Bryn Frank. (Illus.). 192p. 1988. 19.95 (ISBN 0-517-56755-5, Harmony). Crown.

Short Walks on Cape Cod & the Vineyard. 2nd, rev. ed. Hugh Sadlier & Heather Sadlier. LC 75-34252. (Illus.). 128p. 1983. pap. 5.95 (ISBN 0-87106-921-0). Globe Pequot.

Short Walks on Long Island. 2nd, enl. ed. Rodney Albright & Priscilla Albright. LC 74-75075. 132p. 1983. pap. 5.95 (ISBN 0-87106-920-2). Globe Pequot.

Short Wave Length Microscopy, Vol. 306. Parson. 1978. 45.00 (ISBN 0-89072-062-2). NY Acad Sci.

Short-Wave Mystery. rev. ed. Franklin W. Dixon. (Hardy Boys Ser: Vol. 24). (gr. 5-9). 1928. 4.50 (ISBN 0-448-08924-6, G&D); PLB 3.29 (ISBN 0-448-18924-0). Putnam Pub Group.

Short Wavelength Coherent Radiation: Generation & Applications. Ed. by D. T. Attwood & J. Bokor. LC 86-71674. (AIP Conference Proceedings Ser.: No. 147). 480p. 1986. lib. bdg. 60.00 (ISBN 0-88318-346-3). Am Inst Physics.

Short Wavelength Coherent Radiation: Generation & Applications. LC 88-60866. 180p. (Orig.). 1988. pap. write for info. conference ed. (ISBN 1-55752-052-6). Optical Soc.

Short Way to Lower Scoring. Paul Runyan & Dick Aultman. LC 79-52549. (Illus.). 175p. 1982. pap. 9.95 (ISBN 0-394-75407-7, Dist. by Random House). Golf Digest.

Short Work of It: Selected Writing by Mark Harris. Mark Harris. LC 79-3999. 1979. 19.95 (ISBN 0-8229-3403-5). U of Pittsburgh Pr.

Shortchanged: Minorities & Women in Banking. Ed. by Rodney Alexander & Elizabeth Sapery. LC 73-79033. 190p. 1973. 22.50x (ISBN 0-8046-7066-8, Pub. by Kennikat); pap. 11.95 (ISBN 0-8046-7067-6). Assoc Faculty Pr.

Shortcut Gourmet Cookbook. Leo Kuhle & Debbie Monroe. (Illus., Orig.). pap. cancelled (ISBN 0-933474-20-2, Gabriel Bks). Media Mktg Group.

Shortcut Through Adventureland, Vol. I. Jack Cassidy et al. Date not set. price not set. P-H.

Shortcut Through Adventureland, Vol. II: Infocom. Richard Lynn et al. Date not set. price not set. P-H.

Shortcut to Devil's Claw. William O. Turner. 1988. pap. 2.75 (ISBN 0-515-09818-3). Jove Pubns.

Shortcut to French. Colette Dulac. (gr. 9 up). 1977. pap. text ed. 5.45 (ISBN 0-88345-300-2, 18441); cassettes 25.00 (ISBN 0-685-79306-0, 58442). Prentice ESL.

Shortcut to Peril. James I. Clark. LC 79-22151. (Quest, Adventure, Survival Ser.). (Illus.). 48p. (gr. 4-9). 1982. pap. 9.27 (ISBN 0-8172-2070-4). Raintree Pubs.

Shortcut to Peril. James I. Clark. LC 79-22151. (Quest, Adventure, Survival Ser.). (Illus.). 48p. (gr. 4-8). 1980. PLB 15.33 (ISBN 0-8172-1570-0). Raintree Pubs.

Shortcut to Reading. Richard P. Archer. 29p. 1983. 10.00 (ISBN 0-317-02255-5). Concept Spelling.

Shortcut to the Italian Language. Waldo A. Rigal. (Quality Paperback: No. 165). 286p. 1965. pap. 3.50 (ISBN 0-8226-0165-6). Littlefield.

Shortcuts & Strategies for the GMAT. (Gary Gruber's Shortcuts & Strategies Ser.). 160p. (Orig.). 1982. pap. 6.95 (ISBN 0-671-44818-8). Monarch Pr.

Shortcuts & Strategies for the GRE. (Gary R. Gruber's Shortcuts & Strategies Ser.). 160p. (Orig.). 1982. pap. 7.95 (ISBN 0-671-44815-3). Monarch Pr.

Shortcuts for Teachers: Strategies for Reducing Classroom Workload. Jean Enk & Meg Hendricks. LC 81-81392. (gr. k-6). 1981. pap. 6.95 (ISBN 0-8224-6373-3). D S Lake Pubs.

Shortcuts to Basic Writing Skills. 2nd ed. Gary Steele. 336p. 1985. pap. text ed. 15.95 (ISBN 0-03-069731-X, HoltC). HR&W.

Shortcuts to Becoming Rich. Robert E. Shindler. 1979. 12.00 (ISBN 0-915451-01-8). New Start Pubns.

Shortcuts to Establishing AAA Credit: Even after Bankruptcy. Bruce E. David. Ed. by Craig Fintor. (Illus.). 1984. 12.95 (ISBN 0-9609734-4-3); write for info wkbk. Worthprinting.

Shortcuts to Increase Your Typing Speed. Elza Dinwiddie-Boyd. 96p. (Orig.). 1988. pap. 5.95 (ISBN 0-399-59527-9, Perigee Bks). Putnam Pub Group.

Shortcuts to Macroeconomics. Tosporn Chotigeat. (Illus.). 422p. 1988. pap. text ed. 24.50 (ISBN 0-943437-63-6). CAT Pub.

Shorte & Briefe Narration of the Two Navigations to Newe Fraunce. Jacques Cartier. Tr. by J. Florio. LC 73-6110. (English Experience Ser.: No. 718). 1975. Repr. of 1580 ed. 25.00 (ISBN 90-221-0718-3). Walter J Johnson.

Shorte Introduction of Grammar. William Lily. LC 45-4059. 1977. Repr. of 1567 ed. 40.00x (ISBN 0-8201-1208-9). Schol Facsimiles.

Shorte Treatise of Politike Power. Compiled by John Poynet. LC 72-38220. (English Experience Ser.: No. 484). 184p. 1972. Repr. of 1556 ed. 35.00 (ISBN 90-221-0484-2). Walter J Johnson.

Shortened History of England. G. M. Trevelyan. 1976. pap. 7.95 (ISBN 0-14-020443-1, Pelican). Penguin.

Shortened Path: Autobiography of a Western Yogi. abr. ed. Sri Kriyananda. 209p. 1980. pap. 6.95 (ISBN 0-916124-19-3). Crystal Clarity.

Shortening Manufacturing Cycle Time. 19p. 1970. 15.00 (ISBN 0-318-19678-6). Clothing Mfrs.

Shortening Structures in Eastern & Northwestern Himalayan Rocks. W. Schwan. (Currnt Trends in Geology Ser.: Vol. III). 70p. 1980. 12.00 (ISBN 0-88065-189-X, Pub. by Messers Today & Tomorrows Printers & Publishers India). Scholarly Pubns.

Shorter Aslib Directory. Ellen M. Codlin. 590p. 1986. 95.00 (ISBN 0-85142-199-7). Learned Info.

Shorter Bergey's Manual of Determinative Bacteriology. 8th ed. Ed. by John G. Holt. (Illus.). 400p. 1977. pap. 23.95 (ISBN 0-683-04105-3). Williams & Wilkins.

Shorter Books of the Apochrypha. J. C. Dancy. LC 72-76358. (Cambridge Bible Commentary on the New English Bible Old Testament Ser.). 224p. (Orig.). 1972. pap. 9.95 (ISBN 0-521-09729-0). Cambridge U Pr.

Shorter Cambridge Medieval History, 2 vols. Ed. by C. W. Previte-Orton. Incl. Vol. 1. The Later Roman Empire to the Twelfth Century. (Illus.). 644p. 74.50 (ISBN 0-521-20962-5); Vol. 2. The Twelfth Century to the Renaissance. (Illus.). 558p. 74.50 (ISBN 0-521-20963-3); pap. 23.95 (ISBN 0-521-09977-3). (Medieval History Ser). 1975. pap. 18.95 ea. Set. 137.50 (ISBN 0-521-05993-3). Cambridge U Pr.

Shorter Cambridge Medieval History: The Twelfth Century to the Renaissance, Vol. 2. Charles W. Previte-Orton. LC 75-31398. pap. 150.60 (2031627). Bks Demand UMI.

Shorter Catechism: A Study Manual, 2 vols. G. I. Williamson. LC 77-139855. Vol. 1. pap. 5.95 (ISBN 0-87552-539-3); Vol. 2. pap. 4.95 (ISBN 0-87552-540-7). Presby & Reformed.

Shorter Catechism Explained from Scripture. Thomas Vincent. (Puritan Paperbacks). 282p. (Orig.). 1980. pap. 5.95 (ISBN 0-85151-314-X). Banner of Truth.

Shorter Catechism of the Orthodox Church. pap. 0.50 (ISBN 0-686-05664-7). Eastern Orthodox.

Shorter Catechism with Scripture Proofs. Westminster Assembly. 0.75 (ISBN 0-85151-265-8). Banner of Truth.

Shorter Christian Prayer. National Conference of Catholic Bishops. 670p. 1988. 7.95 (ISBN 0-89942-408-2, 408/10). Catholic Bk Pub.

Shorter Classics of Bohm-Bawerk: Five Essays. Eugen Von Bohm-Bawerk. Incl. The Austrian Economists; Control or Economic Law; Ultimate Standard of Value; Unresolved Contradiction in the Marxian Economic System; Whether Legal Rights & Relationships Are Economic Goods. LC 60-11663. 376p. 1962. 15.95 (ISBN 0-910884-12-9). Libertarian Press.

Shorter College German. 3rd ed. M. Blakemore Evans et al. LC 56-5843. (Illus.). 1956. text ed. 15.95x (ISBN 0-89197-403-2); pap. text ed. 8.95x (ISBN 0-89197-404-0). Irvington.

Shorter Course of Theoretical Physics. L. D. Landau & E. M. Lifshitz. Incl. Vol. 1. Mechanics & Electrodynamics. 1972. text ed. 25.00 (ISBN 0-08-016739-X); Vol. 2. Quantum Mechanics. 1985. pap. 32.00 (ISBN 0-08-032616-1). LC 74-167927. 1989. Set. text ed. write for info. (ISBN 0-08-025049-1). Pergamon.

Shorter Dictionary of English Furniture. Ralph Edwards. (Illus.). 684p. 120.00 (ISBN 0-317-54987-1). Apollo.

Shorter Encyclopaedia of Islam. Ed. by H. A. Gibb & J. H. Kramers. (Illus.). 678p. 1957. 88.50x (ISBN 0-8014-0150-X). Cornell U Pr.

Shorter English-Interlingua Dictionary. Ed. by B. C. Sexton. write for info. (ISBN 0-917848-01-2). Interlingua Inst.

Shorter English Nepali Dictionary. T. Warren. 1988. Repr. 11.50x (ISBN 81-206-0304-4, Pub. by Asian Educ Servs India). South Asia Bks.

Shorter English-Persian Dictionary. Soleyman Haim. 890p. 18.00x (ISBN 0-939214-50-4). Mazda Pubs.

Shorter English Poems. Henry Morley. Repr. of 1889 ed. lib. bdg. 30.00 (ISBN 0-8414-6645-9). Folcroft.

Shorter Finnish-English Dictionary with 80,000 Titlewords & Idioms. R. Hurme et al. 793p. 1987. 97.50x (ISBN 951-0-14031-7). Coronet Bks.

Shorter History of Greek Art. Martin Robertson. (Illus.). 256p. 1981. 80.00 (ISBN 0-521-23629-0); pap. 22.95 (ISBN 0-521-28084-2). Cambridge U Pr.

Shorter Hours: A Study of the Movement Since the Civil War. Marion C. Cahill. LC 68-54258. (Columbia University Studies in the Social Sciences: No. 380). 1971. Repr. of 1932 ed. 17.50 (ISBN 0-404-51380-8). AMS Pr.

Shorter Hours, Shorter Weeks: Spreading the Work to Reduce Unemployment. Sar Levitan & Richard Belous. LC 77-4787. (Johns Hopkins University Policy Studies in Employment & Welfare: No. 30). (Illus.). Repr. of 1977 ed. 26.80 (ISBN 0-8357-9286-2, 2016573). Bks Demand UMI.

Shorter Latin Dicitionary. A. Cree. 1985. 45.00 (ISBN 0-317-68637-2, Pub. by J Richardson); pap. 30.00 (ISBN 0-317-68638-0). State Mutual Bk.

Shorter Latin Poems of Master Henry of Avranches Relating to England. Henry Of Avranches. Ed. by Josiah C. Russell & John P. Heironimus. (Mediaeval Academy of America Publications). (Lat). 1935. 20.00 (ISBN 0-527-01693-4). Kraus Repr.

Shorter Latin Quotations. A. Cree. 1985. 20.00x (ISBN 0-317-54323-7, Pub. by J Richardson UK). State Mutual Bk.

Shorter Lexicon of the Greek New Testament. 2nd, rev. ed. Frederick W. Danker. Rev. by F. Wilbur Gingrich. LC 82-10933. 256p. 1983. lib. bdg. 22.00x (ISBN 0-226-13613-2). U of Chicago Pr.

Shorter Lexicon of the Greek New Testament. 2nd ed. F. Wilbur Gingrich. 256p. 1983. 25.95 (ISBN 0-310-25030-7, 18075). Zondervan.

Shorter Life of Christ. Donald Guthrie. LC 71-120039. (Contemporary Evangelical Perspectives Ser). 1970. kivar 9.95 (ISBN 0-310-25441-8, 6500P). Zondervan.

Shorter Life of D. L. Moody. Arthur P. Fitt. 143p. 1982. pap. 2.00 (ISBN 0-89323-014-6). Bible Memory.

Shorter Lyrics of the Twentieth Century 1900-1922. W. H. Davies. Repr. of 1922 ed. lib. bdg. 15.00 (ISBN 0-8414-2443-8). Folcroft.

Shorter Modern Poems: 1900-1931. Ed. by David Morton. LC 74-116411. (Granger Index Reprint Ser). 1932. 12.00 (ISBN 0-8369-6152-8). Ayer Co Pubs.
Shorter Morning & Evening Prayer. 576p. 1987. 8.95 (ISBN 0-00-599056-4, Pub. by Collins Liturgical). Har Row.
Shorter Mrs. Beeton. 240p. 1987. 59.00x (ISBN 0-7063-6563-1, Pub. by Ward Lock Educ Co Ltd). State Mutual Bk.
Shorter Novels of Herman Melville. Herman Melville. (Black & Gold Lib). 1978. (Co-Pub with Tudor); pap. 7.95 (ISBN 0-87140-122-3). Liveright.
Shorter Novels of Herman Melville. Ed. by Raymond Weaver. 1980. pap. 3.50 (ISBN 0-449-30798-0, Prem). Fawcett.
Shorter Novels: Seventeenth Century. 1967. Repr. of 1930 ed. 14.95x (ISBN 0-460-00841-2, Evman). Biblio Dist.
Shorter Oxford English Dictionary, 2 vols. 1973. 150.00 (ISBN 0-19-861126-9); indexed ed. 160.00 (ISBN 0-19-861127-7). Oxford U Pr.
Shorter Pepys. Samuel Pepys. Ed. & selected by Robert Latham. LC 85-40210. 1152p. 1985. 35.00 (ISBN 0-520-03426-0). U of Cal Pr.
Shorter Persian-English Dictionary. Soleyman Haim. 850p. 18.00x (ISBN 0-939214-49-0). Mazda Pubs.
Shorter Plays & Scenarios of Norm Moser. Ed. by Norm Moser. 48p. (Orig.). 1981. pap. 3.00x (ISBN 0-941442-00-4). Illuminations Pr.
Shorter Poems of Matthew Prior. Matthew Prior. 13.25 (ISBN 0-8369-7120-5, 7954). Ayer Co Pubs.
Shorter Poems of Walter Savage Landor. J. B. Sidgwick. LC 73-13982. 1974. Repr. of 1946 ed. lib. bdg. 17.00 (ISBN 0-8414-7652-7). Folcroft.
Shorter Redhouse Turkish-English Dictionary. (Turkish & Eng.). 1971. 11.50x (ISBN 0-686-16858-5). Intl Learn Syst.
Shorter Science & Civilisation in China, Vol. 1. Colin A. Ronan. LC 77-82513. (Illus.). 337p. 1980. pap. 19.95 (ISBN 0-521-29286-7). Cambridge U Pr.
Shorter Science & Civilisation in China, Vol. 2. Colin A. Ronan. LC 77-82513. (Illus.). 250p. 1982. 47.50 (ISBN 0-521-23582-0). Cambridge U Pr.
Shorter Science & Civilisation in China, Vol. 2. Colin A. Ronan. 400p. 1985. pap. 19.95 (ISBN 0-521-31536-0). Cambridge U Pr.
Shorter Science & Civilisation in China, Vol. 3. Colin A. Ronan. 280p. 1986. 49.50 (ISBN 0-521-25272-5); pap. 19.95 (ISBN 0-521-31560-3). Cambridge U Pr.
Shorter Strachey: Selected Essays of Lytton Strachey. Lytton Strachey. Ed. by Michael Holroyd & Paul Levy. (Illus.). 1980. 22.50x (ISBN 0-19-212211-8). Oxford U Pr.
Shorter Tales. Joseph Conrad. LC 71-128727. (Short Story Index Reprint Ser). 1924. 22.00 (ISBN 0-8369-3618-3). Ayer Co Pubs.
Shorter Working Time: A Dilemma for Collective Bargaining. OECD. 92p. (Orig.). 1984. pap. 12.00x (ISBN 92-64-12640-6). OECD.
Shorter Works for Pianoforte Solo. Franz Schubert. 199p. 1970. pap. 7.95 (ISBN 0-486-22648-4). Dover.
Shorter Works for Pianoforte Solo: From the Breitkopf & Hartel Complete Works Edition. Franz Schubert. Ed. by Julius Epstein. 12.00 (ISBN 0-8446-0250-7). Peter Smith.
Shorter Works of Stephen King. Michael R. Collings & David Engebretson. LC 85-22949. (Starmont Studies in Literary Criticism: No. 9). 202p. 1985. Repr. lib. bdg. 17.95x (ISBN 0-89370-981-6). Borgo Pr.
Shorter Works of Stephen King. Michael R. Collings & David Engebretson. LC 85-2822. (Studies in Literary Criticism: No. 9). (Illus.). 208p. (Orig.). 1985. 17.95x (ISBN 0-930261-03-8); pap. 9.95x (ISBN 0-930261-02-X). Starmont Hse.
Shorter Workweek in the 1980's. William McGaughey, Jr. LC 80-54666. 320p. (Orig.). 1981. pap. 6.95 (ISBN 0-9605630-0-8). Thistlerose.
Shortest Way to Hades. Sarah Caudwell. 208p. 1985. 12.95 (ISBN 0-684-18292-0, ScribT). Scribner.
Shortest Way to Hades. Sarah Caudwell. 1986. pap. 3.50 (ISBN 0-14-009401-6). Penguin.
Shortest Way to the Essay: Rhetorical Strategies. May F. McMillan. LC 84-20567. xxii, 274p. 1984. 19.45x (ISBN 0-86554-132-9, H123). Mercer Univ Pr.
Shortgrass Prairie. Ruth C. Cushman & Stephen R. Jones. (Illus.). 152p. (Orig.). 1988. pap. 17.95 (ISBN 0-87108-736-7). Pruett.
Shorthand. John C. Evans. 1963. pap. 5.95 (ISBN 0-06-463225-3, EH 225, B&N Bks). Har-Row.
Shorthand Collection in the New York Public Library: A Catalogue of Books, Periodicals & Manuscripts. Ed. by Karl Brown & Daniel C. Haskell. LC 77-137704. (New York Public Library Publications in Reprint Ser). 1971. Repr. of 1935 ed. 46.50 (ISBN 0-405-01746-4). Ayer Co Pubs.
Shorthand Fashion Sketching. 4th ed. Patricia L. Rowe. LC 60-6848. 1964. 17.50 (ISBN 0-87005-068-0). Fairchild.
Shorthand in Four Days. rev. ed. Benjamin Friedlander. LC 52-3478. 24p. 1980. pap. 3.95 (ISBN 0-917520-02-5). Fineline.
Shorthand: Learning & Instruction. Susie VanHuss et al. 1980. text ed. write for info. (ISBN 0-538-24110-1, X11). SW Pub.
Shorthand Reporter. Jack Rudman. (Career Examination Ser.: C-741). (Cloth bdg. avail. on request). pap. 12.00 (ISBN 0-8373-0741-4). Natl Learning.
Shorthand Speed Building & Transcription. E. Ray Smith et al. (Shorthand Ser.: 1-577). 269p. 1983. pap. text ed. 15.95 (ISBN 0-471-86533-8). Wiley.
Shorthand, Typewriting & Secretarial Training. Abraham Epstein & Morris White. 1958. pap. 3.95 (ISBN 0-399-50814-7, G&D). Putnam Pub Group.
Shortline Railroads of Arkansas. Clifton E. Hull. LC 68-31376. (Illus.). pap. 112.40 (ISBN 0-317-58128-7, 2029678). Bks Demand UMI.
Shortline Railroads of Arkansas. Clifton E. Hull. LC 87-30080. (Illus.). 432p. (Orig.). 1988. pap. text ed. 24.75 (ISBN 0-944436-00-5). Univ Central AR Pr.
Shortness of Breath: A Guide to Better Living & Breathing. 3rd ed. Kenneth M. Moser & Carol Archibald. (Illus.). 100p. 1983. pap. text ed. 11.50 (ISBN 0-8016-3567-5). Mosby.
Shortridge High School Eighteen Sixty-Four to Nineteen Eighty-One: In Retrospect. Laura S. Gaus. (Illus.). 295p. 1985. 15.00 (ISBN 0-87195-003-0). Ind Hist Soc.
Shorts: An Anthology. Ed. by Octavio Roca & M. Owen Korsmo. 115p. (Orig.). 1987. pap. 7.95 (ISBN 0-9618239-0-9). Thane Pr.
Shorts: For Fun, Not for Instruction. J. Chester Johnson. LC 85-81660. (Orig.). 1986. pap. 6.50 (ISBN 0-914426-02-8). Juliet Pr.
Shorts: On Reaching Forty. J. Chester Johnson. LC 85-82179. (Orig.). 1986. pap. 6.50 (ISBN 0-914426-03-6). Juliet Pr.
Shortstop. Bob Cluck. (Winning Edge Ser.). (Illus.). 96p. (Orig.). 1987. pap. 4.95 (ISBN 0-8092-4785-2). Contemp Bks.
Shortstop from Tokyo. Matt Christopher. (Illus.). (gr. 3-6). 1988. pap. 3.95 (ISBN 0-316-13992-0). Little.
Shortwave Book. Larry Miller & Kenneth D. MacHarg. 1984. 9.99 (ISBN 0-914021-02-8). L Miller Pub.
Shortwave Clandestine Confidential. Gerry L. Dexter. (Illus.). 86p. (Orig.). 1984. pap. 8.95 (ISBN 0-916661-02-4, 203). Universal Elect.
Shortwave Directory. 4th ed. Robert B. Grove. LC 87-51078. (Illus.). 500p. 1988. pap. text ed. 17.95 (ISBN 0-944543-00-6). Grove Enterp.
Shortwave Listener's Antenna Handbook. Robert J. Traister. (Illus.). 304p. (Orig.). 1982. pap. 11.95 (ISBN 0-8306-1487-7). TAB Bks.
Shortwave Listening Handbook. Harry L. Helms. (Illus.). 224p. 1987. pap. 17.95 (ISBN 0-13-809591-4). P-H.
Shortwave Radio Listening with the Experts. Gerry L. Dexter. 518p. 1986. pap. 22.95 (ISBN 0-672-22519-0). Sams.
Shorty. Clifton Adams. (Illus.). 224p. 1982. pap. 2.25 (ISBN 0-441-76174-7, Pub. by Charter Bks). Ace Bks.
Shorty McCabe Gets the Hail. Sewell Ford. LC 79-125211. (Short Story Index Reprint Ser). 1919. 18.00 (ISBN 0-8369-3578-0). Ayer Co Pubs.
Shorty McCabe Looks 'em Over. Sewell Ford. LC 73-122702. (Short Story Index Reprint Ser). (Illus.). 1917. 19.00 (ISBN 0-8369-3535-7). Ayer Co Pubs.
Shosankenshu. L. Joly Henri. 150p. 1985. 80.00x (ISBN 0-317-68639-9, Pub. by Han-Shan Tang Ltd). State Mutual Bk.
Shosankenshu: Japanese Sword Mounts. Henri Joly. 45.00 (ISBN 0-87556-133-0). Saifer.
Shosha. Isaac Bashevis Singer. 1985. pap. 3.95 (ISBN 0-449-20808-7, Crest). Fawcett.
Shosha. Isaac Bashevis Singer. LC 78-6921. 288p. 1978. 8.95 (ISBN 0-374-26336-1). FS&G.
Shosha. Isaac Bashevis Singer. 1988. pap. 8.95 (ISBN 0-374-52142-5, Noonday). FS&G.
Shoshin Issho & Niwano Nikkyo Jiden see Lifetime Beginner: An Autobiography.
Shoshinge: The Heart of Shin Buddhism. Alred Bloom. Tr. by T. Nagatani & Ruth Tabrah. 108p. (Orig.). 1986. pap. 6.95 (ISBN 0-938474-06-5). Buddhist Study.
Shoshone Mike. Frank Bergon. LC 87-40031. 288p. 1987. 17.95 (ISBN 0-670-81563-2). Viking.
Shoshoni-Crow Sun Dance. Fred W. Voget. LC 83-40332. (Civilization of the American Indian Ser.: Vol. 170). (Illus.). 368p. 1984. 19.95 (ISBN 0-8061-1886-5). U of Okla Pr.
Shoshoni Frontier & the Bear River Massacre. Brigham D. Madsen. (Utah Centennial Ser.: Vol.1). (Illus.). 336p. 1985. 19.95 (ISBN 0-87480-099-4). U of Utah Pr.
Shoshoni River Witching Hour. 2nd ed. Dean Phelps. 44p. 1975. pap. 3.00 (ISBN 0-914974-04-1). Holmgangers.
Shoshonis: Sentinels of the Rockies. Virginia C. Trenholm & Maurine Carley. (Civilization of the American Indian Ser.: No. 74). (Illus.). 1964. pap. 12.95 (ISBN 0-8061-1055-4). U of Okla Pr.
Shostakovich. N. V. Lukyanova. Tr. by Yu. Shirokov from Rus. (Illus.). 175p. 1984. 19.95 (ISBN 0-86622-019-4, Z-88). Paganiniana Pubns.
Shostakovich: About Himself & His Times. D. Shostakovich. 343p. 1981. 12.00 (ISBN 0-8285-2140-9, Pub. by Progress Pubs USSR). Imported Pubns.
Shostakovich: The Man & His Music. Christopher Norris. LC 82-4172. 235p. 1983. 25.00 (ISBN 0-7145-2778-5, Dist. by Scribner). M Boyars Pubs.
Shot for Baby Bear. Dorothy Corey. Ed. by Ann Fay. (Illus.). 24p. (ps-1). 1988. 9.95g (ISBN 0-8075-7348-5). A Whitman.
Shot in the Arm: Death at the BBC. John Sherwood. 172p. 1985. pap. 4.95 (ISBN 0-930330-25-0). Intl Polygonics.
Shot into Infinity. Otto W. Gail. Ed. by Lester Del Rey. Tr. by F. Currier from Ger. LC 75-410. (Library of Science Fiction). 1975. lib. bdg. 21.00 (ISBN 0-8240-1415-4). Garland Pub.
Shot Peening: Proceedings of the 1st International Conference, Paris, 14-17 September 1981. Ed. by A. Niku-Lari & S. T. Al-Hassani. 528p. 1982. 145.00 (ISBN 0-08-027599-0). Pergamon.
Shot Peening, Science, Technology, Application: Proceedings of the 3rd International Conference on Shot Peening, 1987. Ed. by H. Wohlfahrt et al. (Illus.). 700p. 1987. 139.00 (ISBN 3-88355-120-1, Pub. by DGM Metallurgy Germany). IR Pubns.
Shot to Hell. (Able Team Ser.: No. 20). Date not set. pap. 2.25 (ISBN 0-317-63983-8, Pub. by Worldwide). Harlequin Bks.
Shotakan Advanced Kata, Vol. 3. Keinosuke Enoeda. 111p. (Orig.). 1986. pap. 14.95 (ISBN 0-86568-048-5, 517, Pub. by Dragon Bks Ltd). Unique Pubns.
Shotcrete for Ground Support. 776p. 1977. pap. 24.00x (ISBN 0-87262-091-3). Am Soc Civil Eng.
Shotcrete for Underground Support, No. IV. Ed. by Elwyn H. King. LC 85-81285. 194p. 1985. pap. 15.00 (ISBN 0-939204-27-4, 82-18). Eng Found.
Shotcrete for Underground Support, Vol. III. Ed. by Robin Mason. 346p. (Orig.). 1980. pap. 20.00x (ISBN 0-939204-04-5, 78-14). Eng Found.
Shotcreting. 224p. 1966. 27.95 (ISBN 0-317-32091-2, SP-14). ACI.
Shotgun. Ed McBain. 1982. pap. 2.50 (ISBN 0-451-11971-1, Sig). NAL.
Shotgun. Ed McBain. 1988. pap. 3.50 (ISBN 0-451-15674-9, Sig). NAL.
Shotgun: A Social History. Macdonald Hastings. (Illus.). 224p. 1981. 34.95 (ISBN 0-7153-8062-1). David & Charles.
Shotgun Book. 2nd, Rev. ed. Jack O'Connor. LC 77-92795. (Illus.). 1978. pap. 13.95 (ISBN 0-394-73562-5). Knopf.
Shotgun Digest. 3rd ed. Ed. by Jack Lewis. LC 74-80333. (Illus.). 256p. (Orig.). 1986. pap. 12.95 (ISBN 0-87349-004-5). DBI.
Shotgun for Hire: The Story of Deacon Jim Miller, Killer of Pat Garrett. Glenn Shirley. (Illus.). 1979. pap. 5.95 (ISBN 0-8061-1646-3). U of Okla Pr.
Shotgun Gap. W. F. Bragg. 1981. pap. 1.75 (ISBN 0-8439-0895-5, Leisure Bks). Leisure NY.
Shotgun in Combat. T. Lesce. (Weaponry Ser.). 1986. lib. bdg. 79.95 (ISBN 0-8490-3725-5). Gordon Pr.
Shotgun in Combat. Tony Lesce. (Illus.). 152p. 1984. pap. text ed. 10.00 (ISBN 0-87364-314-3). Paladin Pr.
Shotgun Law. Max Brand. 1988. pap. 2.75 (ISBN 0-671-66143-4). PB.
Shotgun Man. John Benteen. (Fargo Ser). (Orig.). 1977. pap. 1.25 (ISBN 0-505-51155-X, Pub. by Tower Bks). Leisure NY.
Shotgun Marksmanship. Percy Stanbury & G. L. Carlisle. (Illus.). 188p. 1988. 22.95 (ISBN 0-09-142360-0, Pub. by Century Hutchinson). David & Charles.
Shotgun Marshal. Wade Everett. 1981. pap. 1.75 (ISBN 0-345-29434-3). Ballantine.
Shotgun Saturday Night. Bill Crider. 1987. 16.95 (ISBN 0-8027-5684-0). Walker & Co.
Shotgun Station. Kit Dalton. (Buckskin Ser.: No. 19). 224p. (Orig.). 1987. pap. 2.95 (ISBN 0-8439-2529-9). Leisure NY.
Shotgunner. Ray Hogan. Bd. with Overkill at Saddlerock. 1985. pap. 3.50 (ISBN 0-451-13529-6, Sig). NAL.
Shotgunner's Bible. George Laycock. LC 86-29156. (Illus.). 176p. 1987. pap. 7.95 (ISBN 0-385-23907-6, Pub. by Outdoor Bible). Doubleday.
Shotgunning: The Art & the Science. Bob Brister. LC 82-62603. 1976. 17.95 (ISBN 0-8329-1840-7, Pub. by Winchester Pr). New Century.
Shotguns & Cartridges for Game & Clays. 3rd ed. Gough Thomas. (Illus.). 254p. 1976. 25.00 (ISBN 0-7136-1583-4). Transatl Arts.
Shoto Clay. Robert Slocum & Kenneth Matsen. 1968. pap. 2.00 (ISBN 0-8323-0133-7). Binford-Metropolitan.
Shoto-Kan Karate. P. Ventresca. 12.50x (ISBN 0-685-63780-8). Wehman.
Shoto-Kan Karate: The Ultimate in Self-Defense. Peter Ventresca. LC 71-104205. (Illus.). 1970. 12.50 (ISBN 0-8048-0529-6). C E Tuttle.
Shotokan Advanced Kata, Vol. 1. Keinosuke Enoeda. 132p. (Orig.). 1983. pap. 14.95 (ISBN 0-86568-046-9, 515, Pub by Dragon Bks Ltd). Unique Pubns.
Shotokan Advanced Kata, Vol. 2. Keinosuke Enoeda. 103p. (Orig.). pap. 14.95 (ISBN 0-86568-047-7, 516, Pub by Dragon Bks Ltd). Unique Pubns.
Shotokan Karate: Free Fighting Techniques. rev. ed. C. Mack & K. Enoeda. (Illus.). 96p. 1985. pap. text ed. 12.00 (ISBN 0-87364-365-8). Paladin Pr.
Shotokan Karate: It's History & Evolution. Randall G. Hassell. Ed. by Dale F. Poertner. 150p. (Orig.). 1984. pap. 7.95 (ISBN 0-911921-05-2). Focus Pubns Mo.
Shots for Lower Scoring. Beverly Lewis & Ken Lewis. (Golf Clinic Ser.). (Illus.). 80p. (Orig.). 1988. pap. 7.95 (ISBN 0-8069-6929-6). Sterling.
Shots in the Dark. Edgar Anstey. Ed. by Bruce S. Kupelnick. LC 76-52088. (Classics of Film Literature Ser.). 1978. lib. bdg. 22.00 (ISBN 0-8240-2864-3). Garland Pub.
Shots in the Dark: Films of 1949-1951. Edgar Anstel. 1976. lib. bdg. 59.95 (ISBN 0-8490-2601-6). Gordon Pr.
Shots of Style: Great Fashion Photographs Chosen by David Bailey. David Bailey & Martin Harrison. (Illus.). 224p. 1986. 60.00 (ISBN 0-948107-26-X); pap. 25.00. Faber & Faber.
Should a Christian Be a Mason? E. M. Storms. LC 80-83598. (Orig.). 1980. pap. text ed. 2.50 (ISBN 0-932050-08-5). New Puritan.
Should Christians Attend Movies? Gordon Lindsay. 0.95 (ISBN 0-89985-007-3). Christ Nations.
Should Government Encourage Homeownership? Raymond J. Struyk. 85p. 1977. pap. 6.50 (ISBN 0-87766-192-8, 18700). Urban Inst.
Should I Buy a Home Computer. Lincoln Hallen. (Illus.). 100p. 1984. pap. 4.95 (ISBN 0-89433-257-0). Petrocelli.
Should I Call the Doctor? A Comprehensive Guide to Understanding Your Child's Illnesses & Injuries. Christine A. Nelson & Susan C. Pescar. 1986. 22.50 (ISBN 0-446-51262-1); pap. 12.50 (ISBN 0-446-38189-6). Warner Bks.
Should I Divorce? Robert Lindberg. LC 85-50287. 240p. (Orig.). 1985. pap. 10.95 (ISBN 0-934955-04-2). Watercress Pr.
Should I Have a Baby Test? Joy Grdnic. (Illus.). 48p. 1988. pap. 1.95 (ISBN 0-8431-1861-X). Price Stern.
Should I Keep My Baby? Martha Zimmerman. 112p. (Orig.). 1983. pap. 3.95 (ISBN 0-87123-578-1, 210578). Bethany Hse.
Should I Tithe? Dick Benjamin. 1977. pap. 0.89 (ISBN 0-911739-11-4). Abbott Loop.
Should Land Have Selling Value? John C. Lincoln. 1972. pap. 0.75 (ISBN 0-686-17295-7). Lincoln Inst Land.
Should Medical Care Be Rationed by Age? Ed. by Timothy M. Smeeding et al. 160p. 1987. 34.50 (ISBN 0-8476-7521-1). Rowman.
Should Pension Assets Be Managed for Social-Political Purposes? Employee Benefit Research Institute Staff. Ed. by Dallas L. Salisbury. LC 80-65232. 381p. (Orig.). 1980. pap. 10.00 (ISBN 0-86643-001-6). Employee Benefit.
Should Pension Assets Be Managed for Social Political Purposes? Ed. by Dallas L. Salisbury. (Illus.). 394p. 1986. pap. text ed. 26.25 (ISBN 0-8191-5546-2, Pub. by Employee Benefit Rsch Inst). U Pr of Amer.
Should Students Share the Power? A Study of Their Role in College & University Governance. Earl J. McGrath. 124p. 1971. pap. 9.95 (ISBN 0-87722-003-4). Temple U Pr.
Should the Baby Live? Peter Singer & Helga Kuhse. 280p. 1986. 24.95 (ISBN 0-19-217745-1). Oxford U Pr.
Should the Baby Live? The Problem of Handicapped Infants. Peter Singer & Helga Kuhse. 240p. 1988. pap. 8.95 (ISBN 0-19-286062-3). Oxford U Pr.
Should Trees Have Standing? Toward Legal Rights for Natural Objects. Christopher D. Stone. LC 73-19535. 102p. 1988. pap. 7.95 (ISBN 0-913232-08-4). Tioga Pub Co.
Should United States Immigration Policy Be Changed? Lawrence H. Fuchs et al. 30p. 1980. 5.00 (ISBN 0-8447-2186-7). Am Enterprise.
Should War Be Eliminated? Philosophical & Theological Investigations. Stanley Hauerwas. LC 84-60236. (Pere Marquette Lecture Ser.). 75p. 1984. 7.95 (ISBN 0-87462-539-4). Marquette.
Should We Allow Mother to Die? Dorothea M. Nyberg. 160p. 1988. pap. 7.95 (ISBN 0-89840-203-4). Heres Life.
Should We Disown Milton Friedman? Thomas B. Silver. (Occasional Paper of the Study of Statesmanship & Political Philosophy: No. 6). 14p. (Orig.). 1983. pap. text ed. 2.00 (ISBN 0-930783-12-3). Claremont Inst.
Should We Limit Science & Technology. Ed. by L. Steg. 1976. pap. 19.75 (ISBN 0-08-019981-X). Pergamon.
Should You Become a Brother? Leo Kirby. 1979. pap. 1.95 (ISBN 0-89243-102-4). Liguori Pubns.
Should You Become a Priest? Terence Tierney. 64p. (Orig.). (YA) (gr. 9 up). 1975. pap. 1.50 (ISBN 0-89243-020-6, 29530). Liguori Pubns.
Should You Become a Sister? Marcella Holloway. 1978. pap. 1.95 (ISBN 0-89243-073-7, 29553). Liguori Pubns.
Should You Incorporate? Council of New York Law Associates Staff. 24p. (Eng. & Span.). 1977. 3.00. Coun NY Law.
Shoulder. Rowe. 1987. 140.00 (ISBN 0-443-08457-2). Churchill.
Shoulder. pap. 6.00 (ISBN 0-912452-66-8). Am Phys Therapy Assn.
Shoulder & Elbow, 2 vols. Jules R. Kalisch & Harold Williams. (Courtroom Medicine Ser.: Vols. 5 & 5A). 1971. looseleaf set 180.00 (246); Updates avail. 1985 63.50; 1986 74.50. Bender.

Shrewbetinna's Birthday. John S. Goodall. LC 73-24238. (Illus.). 1971. 7.95 (ISBN 0-15-274080-5, HJ). HarBraceJ.

Shrewbettina's Birthday. John S. Goodall. LC 73-24238. (Illus.). 60p. (ps-3). 1983. pap. 3.95 (VoyB). HarBraceJ.

Shrewsbury As It Was: Third Impression. Hendon Publishing Co., Ltd. Staff. 1986. 22.40x (ISBN 0-317-54177-3, Pub. by Hendon Pub UK). State Mutual BK.

Shrewsdale Exit. John Buell. 279p. 1972. 6.95 (ISBN 0-374-26342-6). FS&G.

Shrewsdale Exit. John Buell. 288p. 1984. pap. 3.50 (ISBN 0-88184-039-4). Carroll & Graf.

Shri Varadrajswamy Temple-Kanchi. N. S. Raman. (Illus.). 206p. 1975. 29.95. Asia Bk Corp.

Shrichakrasambhara Tantra: A Buddhist Tantra. Tr. by Kazi Dawa-Samdup from Tibetan. 255p. 1984. Repr. of 1919 ed. lib. bdg. 22.50x (ISBN 0-88181-000-2). Canon Pubns.

Shrieking Silence: A Library Landscape. David Gerard. LC 87-32248. (Illus.). 297p. 1988. 29.50 (ISBN 0-8108-2069-2). Scarecrow.

Shrieks at Midnight: Macabre Poems, Eerie & Humorous. Ed. by Sara Brewton & John E. Brewton. LC 69-11824. (Illus.). (gr. 4 up). 1969. 13.70i (ISBN 0-690-73518-9, Crowell Jr Bks). HarpJ.

Shrifty Dlia Khudozhnikov-Oformitelei. Ed. by Collet's Holdings, Ltd. Staff. 224p. 1984. 49.00x (ISBN 0-317-40860-7, Pub. by Collets (UK)). State Mutual Bk.

Shrikant. Saratchandra Chattopadhyaya. 168p. 1969. pap. 2.50 (ISBN 0-88253-028-3). Ind-US Inc.

Shrimp Lover's Cookbook. William Flagg. LC 84-7957. 128p. 1984. pap. 8.95 (ISBN 0-88427-055-6). North River.

Shrimps, Lobsters, & Crabs of the Atlantic Coast. rev. ed. Austin B. Williams. LC 83-600095. (Illus.). 568p. 1984. text ed. 45.00 (ISBN 0-87474-960-3, WISL). Smithsonian.

Shrine. James Herbert. 464p. 1984. pap. 3.95 (ISBN 0-451-12724-2, Sig). NAL.

Shrine. John Iorio. (Juniper Bk.: No. 51). 68p. (Orig.). 1987. 15.00 (ISBN 1-55780-092-8); signed ed. 25.00 (ISBN 1-55780-091-X); pap. 8.00 (ISBN 1-55780-080-4). Juniper Pr WI.

Shrine & Choma's Drum: Two Short Novels. Shivram K. Karanth. Tr. by U. R. Kalkur from Kannada. 137p. 1984. 14.95 (ISBN 0-86578-246-6). Ind-US Inc.

Shrine of Party: Congressional Voting Behavior, 1841 to 1852. Joel H. Silbey. LC 81-6341. (Illus.). x, 292p. 1981. Repr. of 1967 ed. lib. bdg. 35.00 (ISBN 0-313-22661-X, SISP). Greenwood.

Shrine of St. Peter & the Vatican Excavations. Jocelyn M. Toynbee. LC 78-63482. Repr. of 1956 ed. 32.00 (ISBN 0-404-16548-6). AMS Pr.

Shrine of the Desert Mage. Stephen Goldin. (Parasina Saga: Vol. 1). 256p. (Orig.). 1988. pap. 3.95 (ISBN 0-553-27212-8, Spectra). Bantam.

Shrine, Shelter, Cave. David McAleavey. LC 80-19572. 72p. 1980. 4.00 (ISBN 0-87886-110-6). Greenfld Rev Pr.

Shringar: The Golden Book of Indian Hair Styles. Earl Cumine. (Illus.). 1975. pap. 2.50 English, Urdu, & Tamil (ISBN 0-88253-454-8). Ind-US Inc.

Shrink. Joel L. Schwartz. (Orig.). (gr. 3-6). 1986. pap. 2.75 (ISBN 0-440-47687-9, YB). Dell.

Shrinkage & Creep in Concrete. ACI Committee Staff. (Bibliography: No. 10). 1972. pap. 42.95 (ISBN 0-685-85150-8, B-10) (ISBN 0-685-85151-6). ACI.

Shrinking. William Lehr. LC 87-7928. 120p. 1987. 13.95 (ISBN 0-916515-23-0). Mercury Hse Inc.

Shrinking Circle: The Commonwealth in British Foreign Policy, 1945-1974. B. Vivekanandan. 1984. 37.50x (ISBN 0-8364-1039-4, Pub. by Somaiya). South Asia Bks.

Shrinking History: On Freud & the Failure of Psychohistory. David E. Stannard. 1980. pap. 8.95 (ISBN 0-19-503044-3). Oxford U Pr.

Shrinking History: On Freud & the Failure of Psychohistory. David E. Stannard. (Illus.). 1980. 24.95x (ISBN 0-19-502735-3). Oxford U Pr.

Shrinking of Treehorn. Florence P. Heide. (gr. k-3). 1979. pap. 0.95 (ISBN 0-440-47684-4, YB). Dell.

Shrinking of Treehorn. Florence P. Heide. LC 78-151753. (Illus.). 64p. (gr. 3-6). 1971. 10.95 (ISBN 0-8234-0189-8). Holiday.

Shrinking Planet: U. S. Information Technology & Sustainable Development. John Elkington. LC 88-50613. 88p. (Orig.). 1988. pap. 10.00 (ISBN 0-915825-20-1). World Resources Inst.

Shrinking Political Arena: Participation & Ethnicity in African Politics, with a Case Study of Uganda. Nelson Kasfir. LC 73-85790. 320p. 1976. 46.50x (ISBN 0-520-02576-8). U of Cal Pr.

Shrinking Shadows of Penporth Island. Serita Stevens. 1984. pap. 2.95 (ISBN 0-8217-1344-2). Zebra.

Shrinking the Federal Government. Irene S. Rubin. 256p. 1985. pap. text ed. 15.95 (ISBN 0-582-28473-2). Longman.

Shrinklits. Maurice Sagoff. LC 79-56532. (Illus.). 112p. 1980. pap. 5.95 (ISBN 0-89480-079-5, 413). Workman Pub.

Shrinkproofing of Wool. Makinson. (Fiber Science Ser.: Vol. 8). 1979. 79.75 (ISBN 0-8247-6776-4). Dekker.

Shrinks & Other Lunatics. Howard Danziger. (Illus.). 32p. (Orig.). 1982. pap. 1.25 (ISBN 0-88009-020-0). Planet Bks.

Shropshire, Vol. III. Ed. by G. C. Baugh. (Victoria History of the Counties of Encland Ser.). (Illus.). 1979. 145.00x (ISBN 0-19-722730-9). Oxford U Pr.

Shropshire Lad. A. E. Housman. 100p. 1981. Repr. lib. bdg. 14.95x (ISBN 0-89966-285-4). Buccaneer Bks.

Shropshire Lad. A. E. Housman. (Illus.). 96p. 1986. pap. 14.95X (ISBN 0-245-54233-7, Pub. by Harrap Ltd England). State Mutual Bk.

Shropshire Lad. Alfred E. Housman. 1950. pap. 0.60 (ISBN 0-380-02139-0, 02139, Bard). Avon.

Shropshire Lad. Alfred E. Housman. (Illus.). pap. 2.50 (ISBN 0-8283-1455-1, 7, IPL). Branden Pub Co.

Shropshire Lad. Alfred E. Housman. 5.95 (ISBN 0-88088-306-5). Peter Pauper.

Shropshire of Mary Webb. W. Reid Chappell. 1930. Repr. 20.00 (ISBN 0-8274-3410-3). R West.

Shroud. John Coyne. 304p. Date not set. pap. 3.50 (ISBN 0-441-76225-5, Pub. by Charter Bks). Ace Bks.

Shroud & the Grail: A Modern Quest for the True Grail. Noel Currer-Briggs. (Illus.). 272p. 1988. 19.95x (ISBN 0-312-01510-0, Pub. by Thomas Dunne Bks). St Martin.

Shroud for a Nightingale. P. D. James. 1982. pap. 2.95 (ISBN 0-446-31006-9). Warner Bks.

Shroud for a Nightingale. P. D. James. 288p. 1987. pap. 3.95 (ISBN 0-446-34829-5). Warner Bks.

Shroud for Aquarius. Max A. Collins. 256p. 1988. pap. 3.95 (ISBN 0-8125-0163-2, Dist. by St Martin Pr & Warner Pub Servs). Tor Bks.

Shroud in the Family. Lionel Garcia. LC 87-70271. 319p. (Orig.). 1987. 9.00 (ISBN 0-934770-71-9). Arte Publico.

Shroud of Sophia: The Secret of Wisdom. Aurora Terrenus. (Orig.). 1988. pap. write for info. (ISBN 0-945717-88-1). Celestial Comns.

Shroud of Turin. Daniel Scavone. (Opposing Viewpoints Sources Ser.). (Illus.). 112p. (gr. 3-8). 1988. PLB 12.95 (ISBN 0-89908-061-8). Greenhaven.

Shroud of Turin: Case History in Chemical Analysis. Jumper. (Chemical Analysis Ser.). 1987. write for info. (ISBN 0-471-87877-4). Wiley.

Shroud of Turin: The Burial Cloth of Jesus Christ. Ian Wilson. LC 77-81551. (Illus.). 1979. pap. 6.95 (ISBN 0-385-15042-3, Im). Doubleday.

Shrouded Planet. Robert Randall. 224p. 1982. pap. 2.50 (ISBN 0-441-76219-0). Ace Bks.

Shrouded Walls. Susan Howatch. 1986. pap. 2.95 (ISBN 0-449-21178-9, Crest). Fawcett.

Shrouded Walls of Boranga. Mike Sirota. (Ro-Lan Ser.: No. 2). 304p. (Orig.). 1980. pap. 1.95 (ISBN 0-89083-677-9). Zebra.

Shrouding of Steel Flow for Casting & Teeming. Collective Work Staff. 110p. 1986. pap. 25.00 (ISBN 0-932897-13-4). Iron & Steel.

Shrovetide in Old New Orleans. Ishmael Reed. 1979. pap. 2.50 (ISBN 0-380-42937-3, Discus). Avon.

Shrub Identification Book. George W. Symonds. LC 63-7388. 1963. 17.95 (ISBN 0-688-00040-1); pap. 12.95 (ISBN 0-688-05040-9). Morrow.

Shrub It Up: A Guide for Pacific Northwest Landscaping. George R. McNair. Ed. by Chris McNair. (Illus.). 66p. 1986. pap. 7.96x (ISBN 0-9619034-0-6). CGM Pub Co.

Shrub Legumes in Indonesia & Australia. Ed. by E. T. Craswell & Budi Tangendaja. 42p. 1985. pap. 9.50x (ISBN 0-949511-08-0, Pub. by Inkata Pr Australia). Intl Spec Bk.

Shrub Roses of Today. Rev. ed. Graham S. Thomas. (Illus.). 242p. 1980. 22.50x (ISBN 0-460-04533-4, Pub. by J M Dent England). Biblio Dist.

Shrubs & Small Trees. David Stuart. (Garden Color Books). (Illus.). 80p. 1985. 11.95 (ISBN 0-668-06408-0). Arco.

Shrubs & Small Trees. David Stuart. (Garden Color Ser.). (Illus.). 1986. pap. 6.95 (ISBN 0-668-06412-9). Arco.

Shrubs & Trees of the Southwest Uplands. 2nd ed. Francis H. Elmore. Ed. by Earl Jackson. LC 76-14115. (Popular Ser: No. 19). (Illus., Orig.). 1976. pap. 9.95 (ISBN 0-911408-41-X). SW Pks Mnmts.

Shrubs and Vines for American Gardens. enl. rev. ed. Donald Wyman. (Illus.). 1969. 29.95 (ISBN 0-02-632160-2). Macmillan.

Shrubs & Vines for Southern Landscapes. William D. Adams. LC 76-15455. (Illus.). 96p. (Orig.). 1979. pap. 6.95x (ISBN 0-88415-804-7, Pub. by Pacesetter Pr). Gulf Pub.

Shrubs for the Landscape. T. Elias. 1986. cancelled (ISBN 0-442-26405-4). Van Nos Reinhold.

Shrubs in the Landscape. Joseph Hudak. (Illus.). 304p. 1984. pap. 39.95 (ISBN 0-07-030842-X). McGraw.

Shrubs of Michigan. 2nd ed. Cecil Billington. LC 44-1024. (Bulletin Ser.: No. 20). (Illus.). 339p. 1949. text ed. 12.00x (ISBN 0-87737-005-2). Cranbrook.

Shrubs of the Great Basin: A Natural History. Hugh N. Mozingo. LC 86-7070. (Great Basin Ser.: No. 4). 342p. (Orig.). 1987. 29.95 (ISBN 0-87417-111-3); pap. 19.95 (ISBN 0-87417-112-1). U of Nev Pr.

Shrubs, Trees & Climbers for Southern Africa. Sima Eliovson. (Illus.). 270p. 1982. 32.50 (ISBN 0-86954-011-4, Pub. by Macmillan S Africa). Intl Spec Bk.

Shrunken Planets. Robert Louthan. LC 79-54883. 64p. 1980. pap. 7.95 (ISBN 0-914086-28-6). Alicejamesbooks.

Shtetl & Other Yiddish Novellas. Ed. by Ruth R. Wisse. LC 86-15794. 344p. 1986. 17.50X (ISBN 0-8143-1848-7); pap. 9.95X (ISBN 0-8143-1849-5). Wayne St U Pr.

Shtetl Book. rev ed. Diane K. Roskies & David G Roskies. pap. 11.95x (ISBN 0-87068-455-8). Ktav.

Shtetl Book. Diane K. Roskies & David G. Roskies. 327p. pap. 5.95 (ISBN 0-686-95146-8). ADL.

Shtetl Finder. Chester G. Cohen. 1980. pap. 8.25 (ISBN 0-9605586-0-8). Periday.

Shtetl Memoirs: Jewish Life in Galicia under the Austro-Hungarian Empire & in the Polish Republic, 1898-1939. Joachim Schoenfeld. 400p. 1985. text ed. 17.50x (ISBN 0-88125-075-9). Ktav.

Shtetl on the Bug River. Adele Mondry. 1979. 11.95 (ISBN 0-87068-657-7). Ktav.

Shtudies Vegn Yidisher Folksshafung. Judah L. Cahan. Ed. by Weinreich. 1952. 20.00 (ISBN 0-914512-05-6). Yivo Inst.

Shua: Discussion Guide. LC 87-70468. 16p. 1987. Inl. video cassette. pap. 3.95. ACTA Pubns.

Shuckin' & Jivin': Folklore from Contemporary Black Americans. Daryl C. Dance. LC 77-23635. (Midland Bks.: No. 265). 416p. 1978. 27.50X (ISBN 0-253-35220-7); pap. 12.50x (ISBN 0-253-20265-5). Ind U Pr.

Shucks, Shocks, & Hominy Blocks: Corn as a Way of Life in Pioneer America. Nicholas P. Hardeman. LC 80-26534. (Illus.). xiv, 270p. 1981. 30.00 (ISBN 0-8071-0793-X). La State U Pr.

Shudder Pulps. Robert K. Jones. LC 74-82614. 1975. 11.95x (ISBN 0-913960-04-7). Fax Collect.

Shudders & Thrills: The Second Oppenheim Omnibus. Phillips E. Oppenheim. 836p. 1985. Repr. of 1908 ed. lib. bdg. 58.50 (ISBN 0-8495-4235-9). Arden Lib.

Shuffleboard: Those Capricious Discs. Floyd Swem. (Illus., Orig.). 1975. pap. 3.95 (ISBN 0-8200-0611-4). Great Outdoors.

Shukar Balan: The White Lamb. Mela M. Lindsay. 1976. 11.95 (ISBN 0-914222-02-3). Am Hist Soc Ger.

Shukis Upsidedown Dream. Yaffa Ganz. (gr. k-3). 1986. 5.95 (ISBN 0-87306-384-8). Feldheim.

Shuktugan. D. Tardzhemanov. (Illus.). 16p. (Span.). 1975. pap. 1.49 (ISBN 0-8285-1303-1, Pub. by Progress Pubs USSR). Imported Pubns.

Shuktugan. D. Tardzhemanov. 16p. 1975. pap. 1.49 (ISBN 0-8285-1226-4, Pub. by Progress Pubs USSR). Imported Pubns.

Shulamith. Meera Mahadevan. 208p. 1980. pap. 3.25 (ISBN 0-86578-061-7). Ind-US Inc.

Shulamith. Meera Mahadevan. (Indian Novel Ser.). 208p. 1976. cancelled (ISBN 0-89253-047-2). Ind-US Inc.

Shulchan Aruch Choshan Mishpot: With Commentaries, 2 Vols. (Hebrew., Heb). 35.00 (ISBN 0-87559-081-0). Shalom.

Shunga. Charles Grosbois. 157p. 1964. 315.00x (ISBN 0-317-69071-X, Pub. by Han-Shan Tang Ltd). State Mutual Bk.

Shunga. 64p. 1979. pap. 140.00x (ISBN 0-317-69073-6, Pub. by Han-Shan Tang Ltd). State Mutual Bk.

Shunga-Erotic Figures in Japanese Art. Gabriele Mandel. 112p. 1983. 40.00x (ISBN 0-317-68641-0, Pub. by Han-Shan Tang Ltd). State Mutual Bk.

Shunga: The Art of Love in Japan. Tom Evans & Mary A. Evans. 285p. 1979. 315.00x (Pub. by Han-Shan Tang Ltd). State Mutual Bk.

Shunpiker's Guide to the Northeast: Washington to Boston Without Turnpikes or Interstates. Peter Exton. (Illus.). 160p. (Orig.). 1988. pap. 9.95 (ISBN 0-939009-10-2). EPM Pubns.

Shunts & Problems in Shunts. Ed. by M. Choux. (Monographs in Neural Sciences: Vol. 8). (Illus.). x, 230p. 1982. pap. 76.75 (ISBN 3-8055-2465-X). S Karger.

Shura. Alexander A. Cooper. 64p. 1986. 6.95 (ISBN 0-8062-3009-6). Carlton.

Shurangama Mantra: A Commentary, Vol. III. bi-lingual ed. Tripitaka Master Hua. Tr. by Buddhist Text Translation Society. (Illus.). 156p. (Orig.). 1982. pap. 7.00 (ISBN 0-917512-36-7). Buddhist Text.

Shurangama Mantra: A Commentary, Vol. I. bi-lingual ed. Tripitaka Master Hua. Tr. by Buddhist Text Translation Society. (Illus.). 296p. (Orig.). 1981. pap. 9.00 (ISBN 0-917512-69-3). Buddhist Text.

Shurangama Mantra: A Commentary, Vol. II. bi-lingual ed. Tripitaka Master Hua. Tr. by Buddhist Text Translation Society. (Illus.). 210p. (Orig.). 1982. pap. 8.00 (ISBN 0-917512-82-0). Buddhist Text.

Shurangama Mantra: A Commentary, Vol. IV. bi-lingual ed. Tripitaka Master Hua. Tr. by Buddhist Text Translation Society. (Illus.). 158p. (Orig.). 1986. pap. 10.00 (ISBN 0-88139-022-4). Buddhist Text.

Shurangama Sutra, Vol. 1. Commentary by Tripitaka Master Hua. Tr. by Buddhist Text Translation Society. (Illus.). 289p. (Orig.). 1977. pap. 9.00 (ISBN 0-917512-17-0). Buddhist Text.

Shurangama Sutra, Vol. 2. Commentary by Tripitaka Master Hua. Tr. by Buddhist Text Translation Society. (Illus.). 212p. (Orig.). 1979. pap. 8.00 (ISBN 0-917512-25-1). Buddhist Text.

Shurangama Sutra, Vol. 3. Commentary by Tripitaka Master Hua. Tr. by Buddhist Text Translation Society. (Illus.). 240p. (Orig.). 1980. pap. 8.50 (ISBN 0-917512-94-4). Buddhist Text.

Shurangama Sutra, Vol. 4. Commentary by Tripitaka Master Hua. Tr. by Buddhist Text Translation Society. (Illus.). 285p. (Orig.). 1980. pap 8.50 (ISBN 0-917512-95-2). Buddhist Text.

Shurangama Sutra, Vol. 5. Commentary by Tripitaka Master Hua. Tr. by Buddhist Text Translation Society. (Illus.). 250p. (Orig.). 1980. pap. 8.50. Buddhist Text.

Shurangama Sutra, Vol. 6. Commentary by Tripitaka Master Hua. Tr. by Buddhist Text Translation Society. (Illus.). 200p. (Orig.). 1981. pap. 8.50. Buddhist Text.

Shurangama Sutra, Vol. 7. Tripitaka Master Hua. Tr. by Buddhist Text Translation Society. (Illus.). 270p. (Orig.). 1982. pap. 8.50 (ISBN 0-917512-97-9). Buddhist Text.

Shurter's Communication in Business. 4th ed. Donald J. Leonard. (Illus.). 1979. text ed. 36.95 (ISBN 0-07-037183-0). McGraw.

Shurtleff & Lawton Families: History & Genealogy. William R. Shurtleff. (Illus.). 336p. 1988. 69.95 (ISBN 0-942515-01-3). Pine Hill CA.

Shussan Shaka-Darstellungen in der Malerei Ostasiens. Helmut Brinker. (Schweizer Asiatische Studien: Vol. 3). 145p. (Ger.). 1983. 44.75 (ISBN 3-261-04806-9). P Lang Pubs.

Shuster Mission & the Persian Constitutional Revolution. Robert A. McDaniel. LC 72-96696. (Studies in Middle Eastern History: No. 1). 1974. 28.00x (ISBN 0-88297-004-6). Bibliotheca.

Shuswap. James A. Teit. LC 73-3522. (Jesup North Pacific Expedition. Publications: No. 2, Pt. 7). Repr. of 1909 ed. 57.50 (ISBN 0-404-58123-4). AMS Pr.

Shuswap Language. Aert H. Kuipers. LC 73-85775. (Janua Linguarum, Ser. Practica: No. 225). 297p. 1974. pap. text ed. 42.40x (ISBN 90-2792-672-7). Mouton.

Shut-Ins. Armand Di. Francesco. LC 84-62171. 160p. (Orig.). 1985. pap. 2.75 (ISBN 0-87973-599-6, 599). Our Sunday Visitor.

Shut the Door. Thelma Burris. 256p. 1985. 12.95 (ISBN 0-89962-496-0). Todd & Honeywell.

Shut Those Thick Lips! A Study of Slum School Failure. Gerry Rosenfeld. 120p. 1983. pap. text ed. 7.95x (ISBN 0-88133-022-1). Waveland Pr.

Shut Up & Sell! Tested Techniques for Closing the Sale. Don Sheehan. 160p. 1981. 13.95 (ISBN 0-8144-5705-3). AMACOM.

Shut up & Sell: Tested Techniques for Closing the Sale. Don Sheehan. LC 81-66235. 160p. 1984. pap. 9.95 (ISBN 0-8144-7615-5). AMACOM.

Shut Up! He Explained: A Writer's Guide to the Uses & Misuses of Dialogue. William Noble. 240p. 1987. 17.95 (ISBN 0-8397-7777-9). Eriksson.

Shutdown at Youngstown: Public Policy for Mass Unemployment. Terry F. Buss & F. Stevens Redburn. LC 82-5686. (Urban Public Policy Ser.). 219p. 1983. 49.50 (ISBN 0-87395-646-X); pap. 16.95x (ISBN 0-87395-647-8). State U NY Pr.

Shutter of Snow. Emily H. Coleman. 232p. 1986. pap. 6.95 (ISBN 0-14-016144-9). Penguin.

Shutterbug. Stan Hayward. (Henry's Cat Ser.). (Illus.). (ps-5). 1987. pap. 2.25 (ISBN 0-671-63776-2). Wanderer Bks.

Shuttered Houses of Paris. LC 86-80161. (Classics of the Victorian Imagination Ser.). 1986. pap. 7.95 (ISBN 0-394-62215-4, Ever). Grove.

Shuttered Houses of Paris. 13.95 (ISBN 0-317-54379-2). Grove.

Shutting Down Utilities' Tax Juice. Joseph Kriesberg. 4p. (Orig.). 1986. pap. 0.75 (ISBN 0-937188-39-5). Critical Mass.

Shuttle. 2nd ed. Nigel MacKnight. (Illus.). 116p. 1988. pap. 9.95 (ISBN 0-87938-305-4). Motorbooks Intl.

Shuttle. David C. Onley. (Orig.). 1982. pap. 3.25 (ISBN 0-89083-951-4). Zebra.

Shuttle Challenger: A Complete History of Space Shuttle Orbiter OV-099. David Shayler. (Illus.). 64p. (YA) (gr. 9-12). 1987. 12.95 (ISBN 0-13-125147-3). P-H.

Shuttle Craft: An Educational Coloring Book. Spizzirri Publishing Co. Staff. Ed. by Linda Spizzirri. (Illus.). 32p. (gr. 1-8). 1986. pap. 1.49 (ISBN 0-86545-077-3). Spizzirri.

Shuttle-Craft Book of American Hand-Weaving. Mary M. Atwater. (Illus.). 352p. 1986. pap. 16.95 (ISBN 0-916658-43-0). Shuttle Craft.

Shuttle Down. Lee Corey. 224p. (Orig.). 1981. pap. 2.95 (ISBN 0-345-33179-6, Del Rey). Ballantine.

Shuttle in the Crypt. Wole Soyinka. 96p. (Orig.). 1972. 12.95 (ISBN 0-8090-8667-0); pap. 7.95 (ISBN 0-8090-1364-9). Hill & Wang.

Shuttle Plus One - A New View of Space: Proceedings of the 12th Conference on Space Simulation, May 1982, Pasadena, California. 363p. 1982. 15.00 (ISBN 0-686-92542-4). Inst Environ Sci.

Shuttle Propulsion Systems. Ed. by J. Robinson. (AD-05 Ser.). 1982. 24.00 (H00243). ASME.

Shuttle Showdown. David Taylor. 288p. 1988. pap. 3.95 (ISBN 0-8125-1263-4, Dist. by St Martin's Pr & Warner Pub Servs). Tor Bks.

Shuttle-Spacelab: The New Transportation System & Its Utilization. Ed. by Dietrich E. Koelle & George V. Butler. LC 57-43769. (Advances in the Astronautical Sciences Ser.: Vol. 43). (Illus.). 342p. 1981. lib. bdg. 45.00x (ISBN 0-87703-144-4, Pub. by Am Astronaut); pap. text ed. 35.00x (ISBN 0-87703-146-0). Univelt Inc.

Shuttle to the Next Space Age. (Illus.). 131p. 18.00 (ISBN 0-317-32189-7). AIAA.

Shuttlecock. Phil Andros. LC 83-18434. (Perineum Press Bk.). 184p. 1984. pap. 7.95 (ISBN 0-912516-78-X). Grey Fox.

Shuttlecock. Graham Swift. 1985. pap. 7.95 (ISBN 0-671-54612-0). WSP.

Shuttleless Weaving Machines. O. Talavasek & V. Svaty. (Textile Science & Technology Ser.: Vol. 3). 622p. 1981. 134.25 (ISBN 0-444-99758-X). Elsevier.

Shu'ubiyya in Al-Andalus: The Risala of Ibn Garcia & Five Refutations. James T. Monroe. LC 77-627464. (University of California Publications, Near Eastern Studies: No. 13). (Illus.). 113p. pap. 29.40 (2030679). Bks Demand UMI.

Shuzo Kuki & Jean Paul Sartre: Influence & Counter-Influence in the Early History of Existential Phenomenology. Stephen Light. (Journal of the History of Philosophy Monographs). 168p. (Orig.). 1987. pap. text ed. 13.95x (ISBN 0-8093-1271-9). S Ill U Pr.

Shy? Michel Girodo. (gr. 10 up). 1981. pap. 2.95 (ISBN 0-671-43061-0). PB.

Shy, but Not Too Shy. Dave Jackson. (Caring ParentsStorybooks Ser.). 32p. (ps-2). 1986. pap. 3.95 (ISBN 0-89191-277-0). Cook.

Shy Charlene & Sharyl. C. A. Nobens. (Illus.). 32p. (ps-3). 1987. 12.95 (ISBN 0-316-61167-0). Little.

Shy Charles. Rosemary Wells. LC 87-27247. (Illus.). 32p. (ps-3). 1988. 11.95 (ISBN 0-8037-0563-8, 01160-350); PLB 11.89 (ISBN 0-8037-0564-6). Dial Bks Young.

Shy Child. Philip G. Zimbardo & Shirley Radl. LC 82-45079. (Illus.). 240p. 1982. pap. 7.95 (ISBN 0-385-18175-2, Dolp). Doubleday.

Shy Dragon. Jindra Strand. 1985. 15.00x (ISBN 0-907349-11-0, Pub by Spindlewood). State Mutual Bk.

Shy Gentle Sheree. Vonna Veray. 288p. 1988. 12.95 (ISBN 0-8062-3205-6). Carlton.

Shy Leopardess: The Neustrian Cycle, Bk. 3. Leslie Barringer. Ed. by R. Reginald & Douglas Menville. LC 80-19240. (Newcastle Forgotten Fantasy Library Ser.: Vol. 13). 392p. 1980. Repr. of 1977 ed. lib. bdg. 19.95x (ISBN 0-89370-512-8). Borgo Pr.

Shy Leopardess: The Neustrian Cycle, Book Three. Leslie Barringer. (Forgotten Fantasy Library: Vol. 13). 1977. pap. 6.95 (ISBN 0-87877-112-3, F-112). Newcastle Pub.

Shy Man Syndrome: Why Men Become Love-Shy & How They Can Overcome It. Brian G. Gilmartin. 336p. 1988. 19.95 (ISBN 0-8191-7009-7). Madison Bks UPA.

Shy Man's Guide to the Secrets of Attracting Women. Dale J. Kroll. 56p. (Orig.). 1986. pap. 5.95 (ISBN 0-9616728-0-3). Randale Resources.

Shy Ones. Lynn Hall. (Illus.). 192p. (YA) (gr. 9-12). 1977. pap. 1.95 (ISBN 0-380-01723-7, 63263-2, Camelot). Avon.

Shy Persons Guide to a Happier Love Life. Eric Weber & Judi Miller. Repr. of 1979 ed. text ed. 13.95 (ISBN 0-914094-17-3). Symphony.

Shyest 'Kid in the 'Patch. Kathleen N. Daly. (Cabbage Patch Kids Ser.). (Illus.). 40p. (gr. 1-5). 1984. 5.95 (ISBN 0-910313-30-X). Parker Bros.

Shylock & Others: Eight Studies. G. H. Radford. LC 72-13311. (Essay Index Reprint Ser.). Repr. of 1894 ed. 16.00 (ISBN 0-8369-8172-3). Ayer Co Pubs.

Shylock & Shakespeare. Abraham Morevski. LC 67-19382. 112p. 1967. 3.95. Fireside Bks.

Shylock & Shakespeare. Abraham Morevski. LC 67-19382. 112p. 1967. 3.95 (ISBN 0-87527-056-5). Green.

Shylock on the Stage. Toby Lelyveld. 148p. 1982. Repr. of 1961 ed. lib. bdg. 25.00 (ISBN 0-89984-907-5). Century Bookbindery.

Shylock: The History of a Character. Hermann Sinsheimer. LC 63-23188. (Illus.). Repr. of 1947 ed. 15.00 (ISBN 0-405-08977-5, Pub. by Blom). Ayer Co Pubs.

Shylock's Rights: A History of Lockian Doctrine. Edward Andrew. 192p. 1987. 35.00x (ISBN 0-8020-2611-7); pap. 15.95 (ISBN 0-8020-6660-7). U of Toronto Pr.

Shyness. Philip Zimbardo. 1987. pap. 3.95 (ISBN 0-515-08919-2). Jove Pubns.

Shyness & Love: Causes, Consequences, & Treatment. Brian G. Gilmartin. LC 86-33658. (Illus.). 726p. 1987. lib. bdg. 32.50 (ISBN 0-8191-6102-0). U Pr of Amer.

Shyness: Perpectives on Reasearch & Treatment. Ed. by Warren H. Jones et al. (Emotion, Personality, & Psychotherapy Ser.). 410p. 1986. 35.00x (ISBN 0-306-42033-3, Plenum Pr). Plenum Pub.

Shyness: What It Is, What to Do About It. Philip Zimbardo. LC 77-73069. 1977. pap. write for info. (ISBN 0-201-08794-4). Addison-Wesley.

Shyp of Folys of the Worlde. Sebastian Brant. Tr. by Alexander Barcley. LC 74-25743. (English Experience Ser.: No. 229). 1970. Repr. of 1509 ed. 76.00 (ISBN 90-221-0229-7). Walter J Johnson.

Shyster. Elizabeth-Ann Sachs. LC 85-7943. (Illus.). 128p. (gr. 2-5). 1985. 10.95 (ISBN 0-689-31161-3, Atheneum Childrens Bks). Macmillan.

Si Amas a Tu Adolescente. Ross Campbell. Tr. by Juan S. Araujo from Eng. 144p. (Span.). 1986. pap. 3.95 (ISBN 0-88113-030-3). Edit Betania.

Si Amas a Tu Hijo. Ross Campbell. Tr. by Juan S. Araujo from Eng. 144p. (Span.). 1986. pap. 3.95 (ISBN 0-88113-031-1). Edit Betania.

SI Chemical Data. 2nd ed. Gordon H. Aylward & Tristan J. Findlay. LC 75-148002. 136p. 1976. pap. 11.95 (ISBN 0-471-03851-2, Pub. by Wiley-Interscience). Wiley.

Si Dios Me Ama, Por Que Me Sale Todo Mal? Lorraine Peterson. Tr. by Rhode F. Ward from Eng. 160p. (Span.). (YA) 1988. pap. 3.95 (ISBN 0-88113-269-1). Edit Betania.

SI Drilling Manual. Canadian Association of Oilwell Drilling Contractors Staff. LC 82-15466. 820p. 1982. three ring binder 195.00x (ISBN 0-87201-211-5). Gulf Pub.

SI Einheiten in der Medizin see SI Units in Medicine.

Si Haulte Architecture: The Design of Sceve's Delie. Doranne Fenoaltea. LC 81-71432. (French Forum Monographs: No. 35). 246p. (Orig.). 1982. pap. 16.95x (ISBN 0-917058-34-8). French Forum.

Si le Grain ne Meurt: Memoires. Andre Gide. (Folio Ser.: No. 875). 1966. 7.95 (ISBN 0-685-11561-5). Schoenhof.

Si loin Pour T'Aimer. Judith Anglars. (Collection Colombine Ser.). 192p. 1983. pap. 1.95 (ISBN 0-373-48087-3). Harlequin Bks.

SI Metric Handbook. John Feirer. (Illus.). 1977. 27.50 (ISBN 0-87002-908-8, ScribT). Scribner.

SI Metric System of Units & SEG Tentative Metric Standard. 158p. 1981. pap. 10.00 (ISBN 0-931830-21-4). Soc Expl Geophys.

Si Nos Chemins se Croisent. Sonia Daquine. (Collection Colombine Ser.). 192p. 1983. pap. 1.95 (ISBN 0-373-48068-7). Harlequin Bks.

Si-Sio2 System. Ed. by P. Balk. 1984. write for info. Elsevier.

SI Statics see ARA Engineering Mechanics.

Si Su Hijo Tartamudea: Una Guia para los Padres. (Publications on Stuttering: No. 15). 48p. (Span.). pap. 1.00 (ISBN 0-933388-12-8). Speech Found Am.

SI-Ten Asme Steam Charts, SI Metric & U. S. Customary Units. J. H. Potter. 128p. 1976. pap. text ed. 25.00 (ISBN 0-685-62575-3, E00090). ASME.

Si tu t'imagines. Raymond Queneau. 348p. 1952. 8.95 (ISBN 0-686-54686-5). French & Eur.

SI Unit Cards: British Journal of Radiology. 35p. 1984. pap. text ed. 1.95 (ISBN 0-444-40824-X). Butterworth.

SI Units in Engineering & Technology. S. H. Qasim. 1977. pap. text ed. 10.75 (ISBN 0-08-021278-6). Pergamon.

SI Units in Medicine. Ed. by Herbert Lippert & H. Peter Lehmann. Tr. by H. L. Lehmann from Ger. LC 77-17354. Orig. Title: SI Einheiten in der Medizin. (Illus.). 220p. 1978. spiral bdg. 24.50 (ISBN 0-8067-1101-9). Urban & S.

SI Units in Radiation Protection & Measurements. LC 85-3052. (NCRP Report Ser.: No. 82). 50p. (Orig.). 1985. pap. text ed. 14.00 (ISBN 0-913392-74-X). NCRP Pubns.

Siah Armajani. Janet Kardon & Kate Linker. (Illus.). 96p. 1985. pap. 20.00 (ISBN 0-88454-039-1). U of Pa Contemp Art.

Sialadenosis & Sialadenitis. Ed. by R. Chilla. (Advances in Oto-Rhino-Laryngology Ser.: Vol. 26). (Illus.). viii, 252p. 1981. 105.50 (ISBN 3-8055-1669-X). S Karger.

Sialic Acids: Chemistry, Metabolism, & Function. Ed. by R. Schauer. (Cell Biology Monographs: Vol. 10). (Illus.). 344p. 1982. 82.00 (ISBN 0-387-81707-7). Springer-Verlag.

Siam in Transition: A Brief Survey of Cultural Trends in the Five Years Since the Revolution of 1932. Kenneth P. Landon. LC 68-57615. (Illus.). 1969. Repr. of 1939 ed. lib. bdg. 25.00x (ISBN 0-8371-0521-8, LASI). Greenwood.

Siam: The Crossroads. Josiah Crosby. LC 72-179186. Repr. of 1945 ed. 25.00 (ISBN 0-404-54817-2). AMS Pr.

Siam: The Land of the White Elephant, As It Was & Is. George B. Bacon. LC 77-87064. Repr. of 1873 ed. 26.50 (ISBN 0-404-16792-6). AMS Pr.

Siam Then: The Foreign Colony in Bangkok Before & After Anna. William L. Bradley. LC 81-12196. (Illus.). 207p. (Orig.). 1981. pap. 8.95 (ISBN 0-87808-185-2). William Carey Lib.

Siamang in Malaya: A Field Study of a Primate in Tropical Rain Forest. D. J. Chivers et al. Ed. by H. Hofer & A. H. Schultz. (Contributions to Primatology Ser.: Vol. 4). (Illus.). 250p. 1974. 114.75 (ISBN 3-8055-1668-1). S Karger.

Siamese Cat. Leila Keane. (American Structural Readers Ser.: Stage 2). (Illus.). 32p. (Orig.). 1985. pap. text ed. 3.95 (ISBN 0-582-79880-9). Longman.

Siamese Cats. Mary Dunnill. (Pet Care Ser.). 1984. pap. 5.95 (ISBN 0-8120-2924-0). Barron.

Siamese Cats. Ron Reagan. (Illus.). 127p. 1981. 9.95 (ISBN 0-87666-860-0, KW-062). TFH Pubns.

Siamese Cats. Loren Spiotta-DiMare. (Illus.). 81p. (Orig.). 1985. pap. 5.95 (ISBN 0-86622-209-X, PB-135). TFH Pubns.

Siamese Cookery. Marie M. Wilson. LC 65-23329. (Illus.). 1965. 12.50 (ISBN 0-8048-0530-X). C E Tuttle.

Siamese-English Dictionary. Edward B. Michell. (Siamese & Eng.). 1976. Repr. of 1958 ed. 39.50 (ISBN 0-518-19004-8). Ayer Co Pubs.

Siamese Mauser. Francis C. Allan & Roger L. Wakelam. Ed. by Joseph P. Koss, Jr. (Illus.). 50p. 1987. pap. 7.95 (ISBN 0-9614814-2-0). AK Enterprises.

Siamese Tales Old & New. Reginald S. Le May. LC 74-16311. 1974. Repr. of 1930 ed. lib. bdg. 39.50 (ISBN 0-8414-5747-6). Folcroft.

Siamese Twin Mystery. Ellery Queen. 360p. 1980. lib. bdg. 16.95x (ISBN 0-89966-145-9). Buccaneer Bks.

Sian Incident: A Pivotal Point in Modern Chinese History. Tien-wei Wu. (Michigan Monographs in Chinese Studies: No. 26). (Illus.). 1976. pap. 8.50 (ISBN 0-89264-026-X). U of Mich Ctr Chinese.

Sian Phillips Needlepoint. Sian Phillips. (Illus.). 120p. 1988. 22.95 (ISBN 0-241-12310-0, Pub. by Hamish Hamilton). David & Charles.

Siaya: A Historical Anthropology of an African Landscape. David W. Cohen & E. S. Odhiambo. (Illus.). 192p. (Orig.). 1988. lib. bdg. 25.95x (ISBN 0-8214-0901-8); pap. text ed. 12.95x (ISBN 0-8214-0902-6). Ohio U Pr.

Sibelius. Rev. ed. Robert Layton. (Master Musicians Ser.). (Illus.). 210p. 1978. 17.95x (ISBN 0-460-03169-4, Pub. by J M Dent England). Biblio Dist.

Sibelius. Robert Layton. (Illus.). 222p. 1984. pap. 7.95 (ISBN 0-8226-0387-X, Helix). Rowman.

Sibelius: A Personal Portrait. Santeri Levas. Tr. by Percy M. Young. LC 73-11556. 165p. 1973. 18.00 (ISBN 0-8387-1411-0). Bucknell U Pr.

Sibelius: A Symposium. G. Abraham. 59.95 (ISBN 0-8490-1051-9). Gordon Pr.

Sibelius: The Symphonies. Cecil Gray. LC 78-114879. (Select Bibliographies Reprint Ser). 1935. 11.00 (ISBN 0-8369-5283-9). Ayer Co Pubs.

Sibelius, Vol. II: 1904-1914. Erik Tawaststjerna. Tr. by Robert Layton. 1986. 27.50 (ISBN 0-520-05869-0). U of Cal Pr.

Sibelius: 1865-1905, Vol. I. Erik Tawaststjerna. LC 75-13147. 330p. 1976. 55.00x (ISBN 0-520-03014-1). U of Cal Pr.

Siberia. G. Markov. 527p. 1975. 8.45 (ISBN 0-8285-1011-3, Pub. by Progress Pubs USSR). Imported Pubns.

Siberia & Central Asia. John Bookwalter. LC 76-27541. (Illus.). 1976. Repr. of 1899 ed. lib. bdg. 55.00 (ISBN 0-89341-041-1). Longwood Pub Group.

Siberia & Northwestern America, Seventeen Eighty-Eight to Seventeen Ninety-Two: The/Journal of Carl Heinrich Merck. Ed. by Richard A. Pierce. Tr. by Fritz Jaensch. (Alaska History Ser.: No. 17). (Illus.). 1980. 16.50x (ISBN 0-919642-93-4). Limestone Pr.

Siberia & the Soviet Economy. J. M. Kaul. 1984. 9.00x (ISBN 0-8364-1225-7, Pub. by Bagchi India). South Asia Bks.

Siberia & the Soviet Far East: Strategic Dimensions in Multinational Perspective. Ed. by Roger Swearingen. 1987. text ed. 32.95x (ISBN 0-8179-8361-9); pap. 16.95x (ISBN 0-8179-8362-7). Hoover Inst Pr.

Siberia and the Soviet Far East: Unmasking the Myths. Abraham Resnick. (Illus.). 115p. 1985. lib. bdg. 10.95 (ISBN 0-86596-075-5). G E McCuen Pubns.

Siberia in the Seventeenth Century: A Study of the Colonial Administration. George V. Lantzeff. LC 75-159205. viii, 235p. 1972. Repr. of 1943 ed. lib. bdg. 19.50x (ISBN 0-374-94774-0, Octagon). Hippocrene Bks.

Siberia: Problems & Prospects for Regional Development. Ed. by Alan Wood. 256p. 1987. 31.50 (ISBN 0-389-20736-5). B&N Imports.

Siberia: Problems & Prospects for Regional Development. Ed. by Alan Wood. 240p. 1987. lib. bdg. 49.95x (ISBN 0-7099-3655-9, Pub. by Croom Helm UK). Routledge Chapman & Hall.

Siberia Today & Tomorrow. Violet Conolly. LC 75-26327. (Illus.). 260p. 1976. 20.00 (ISBN 0-8008-7182-0). Taplinger.

Siberian & Other Folk-Tales: Primitive Literature from the Empire of the Tsars. Charles F. Coxwell. LC 78-67702. (Folktale). 1056p. Repr. of 1925 ed. 74.50 (ISBN 0-404-16076-X). AMS Pr.

Siberian Development & East Asia: Threat or Promise? Allen S. Whiting. LC 81-50057. 296p. 1981. 25.00x (ISBN 0-8047-1109-7). Stanford U Pr.

Siberian Forest Adventure. E. Boronina. Ed. by G. A. Birkett. LC 66-25018. (Rus.). 1966. pap. text ed. 2.75x (ISBN 0-89197-485-7). Irvington.

Siberian Huskies. Beverly Pisano. (Illus.). 128p. 1979. 9.95 (ISBN 0-87666-677-2, KW-068). TFH Pubns.

Siberian Husky Champions, 1952-1980. Jan L. Pata. (Illus.). 151p. 1982. pap. 29.95 (ISBN 0-940808-11-0). Camino E E & B.

Siberian Husky Champions, 1981-1986. Camino E. E. & B. Co. Staff. (Illus.). 114p. 1988. pap. 24.95 (ISBN 0-940808-66-8). Camino E E & B.

Siberian Journey: The Journal of Hans Fries, 1774-1776. Ed. by Walter Kirchner. (Illus.). 183p. 1974. 29.50x (ISBN 0-7146-2964-2, F Cass Co). Biblio Dist.

Siberian Stories. S. Sartakov. 607p. 1979. 9.45 (ISBN 0-8285-1621-9, Pub. by Progress Pubs USSR). Imported Pubns.

Siberians. Farley Mowat. 1984. pap. 3.95 (ISBN 0-553-24896-0). Bantam.

Sibley's Heir: A Volume in Memory of Clifford Kenyon Shipton. F. Allis. LC 81-71840. (Illus.). 635p. 1982. 30.00x (ISBN 0-8139-0972-4, Colonial Soc MA). U Pr of Va.

Sibley's Heir: A Volume in Memory of Clifford Kenyon Shipton. Ed. by Frederick S. Allis, Jr. & Frederick S. Allis, Jr. 1983. 30.00x (ISBN 0-686-89628-9). U Pr of Va.

Sibling Bond. Stephen P. Bank & Michael D. Kahn. LC 81-68401. 1982. 16.95 (ISBN 0-465-07818-4). Basic.

Sibling Bond. Stephen P. Bank & Michael D. Kahn. LC 81-68401. 363p. 1983. pap. 12.95 (ISBN 0-465-07819-2, CN-5106). Basic.

Sibling Relationships: Their Nature & Significance Across the Lifespan. Ed. by Michael E. Lamb & Brian Sutton-Smith. 416p. 1982. 39.95x (ISBN 0-89859-189-9). L Erlbaum Assocs.

Sibling Rivalry. Seymour V. Reit. 208p. 1988. pap. 3.95 (ISBN 0-345-35553-9). Ballantine.

Sibling Rivalry in the Household of God. Jay E. Adams. LC 87-72822. 160p. 1988. pap. 7.95 (ISBN 0-89636-236-1). Accent Bks.

Sibling Rivalry Monster. Ben Ginsberg. LC 85-17474. (Illus.). 48p. (Orig.). (gr. 1-3). 1985. 6.95 (ISBN 0-89594-184-8). Crossing Pr.

Siblings. Robert J. Burger. 256p. 1984. 13.00 (ISBN 0-682-40188-9). Exposition-Phoenix.

Siblings. Robert J. Burger. 296p. 1985. 14.95 (ISBN 0-8059-2980-0). Dorrance.

Siblings in Therapy: Life Span & Clinical Issues. Ed. by Michael D. Kahn & Karen G. Lewis. (Professional Bks.). (Illus.). 1988. 34.95 (ISBN 0-393-70058-5). Norton.

Siblings: Love, Envy, & Understanding. Judy Dunn & Carol Kendrick. LC 81-7251. (Illus.). 304p. 1982. text ed. 22.95x (ISBN 0-674-80735-9). Harvard U Pr.

Siblings of the Mentally Ill. Wendy Carlisle. 160p. (Orig.). 1984. pap. 8.95 (ISBN 0-317-13561-9). R & E Pubs.

Siblings Without Rivalry. Adele Faber & Elaine Mazlish. 1988. 8.95 (ISBN 1-55525-208-7). Nightingale-Conant.

Siblings Without Rivalry: How to Help Your Children Live Together So You Can Live Too. Adele Faber & Elaine Mazlish. (Illus.). 224p. 1987. 14.95 (ISBN 0-393-02441-5). Norton.

Siblings Without Rivalry: How to Help Your Children Live Together So You Can Live Too. Adele Faber & Elaine Mazlish. 1988. pap. 7.95 (ISBN 0-380-70527-3). Avon.

Siblingship in Oceania: Studies in the Meaning of Kin Relations. Ed. by Mac Marshall. LC 83-14516. (ASAO Monograph: No. 8). (Illus.). 434p. 1983. lib. bdg. 36.25 (ISBN 0-8191-3429-5); pap. text ed. 18.75 (ISBN 0-8191-3430-9). U Pr of Amer.

Sibo-American Relations After Normalization. Steven M. Goldstein & Jay Mathews. LC 86-81093. (Headline Ser.: No. 276). (Illus.). 63p. (Orig.). 1985. pap. 4.00 (ISBN 0-87124-105-6). Foreign Policy.

Sibshops: A Handbook for Implementing Workshops for Siblings of Children with Special Needs. Donald J. Meyer et al. 70p. 1986. looseleaf notebook 14.95 (ISBN 0-295-96306-9). U of Wash Pr.

Sibton Abbey Cartularies & Charters, Pt. III. Ed. by Philippa Brown. (Suffolk Records Society-Suffolk Charters Ser.: No. 9). 1987. 36.00 (ISBN 0-85115-474-3, Pub. by Boydell & Brewer). Longwood Pub Group.

Sibton Abbey Cartularies & Charters, Pt. 4. Ed. by Philippa Brown. (Suffolk Records Society - Suffolk Charters Ser.: No. 10). 250p. 1988. 35.00 (ISBN 0-85115-499-9, Pub. by Boydell & Brewer). Longwood Pub Group.

Sibton Abbey Cartularies & Charters I. Ed. by Philippa Brown. (Suffolk Charters: VII). (Illus.). 164p. 1985. 36.00 (ISBN 0-85115-413-1, Pub. by Boydell & Brewer). Longwood Pub Group.

Sibton Abbey Cartularies & Charters: II. Ed. by Philippa Brown. (Suffolk Charters VIII). 192p. 1986. 36.00 (ISBN 0-85115-443-3, Pub. by Boydell & Brewer). Longwood Pub Group.

Sibton Abbey Estates: Selected Documents, 1325-1509. Ed. by A. H. Denney. (Suffolk Records Society Ser.: No. II). 166p. 1962. 18.00 (ISBN 0-900716-12-6, Pub. by Boydell & Brewer). Longwood Pub Group.

Sibyl. Par Lagerkvist. Tr. by Naomi Walford. 1963. pap. 3.95 (ISBN 0-394-70240-9, Vin). Random.

Sibyl see Angelos Sikelianos & the Delphic Idea.

Sibylline Oracles. Tr. by Milton Terry. (Great works of Philosophy Ser.: Vol. 7). 267p. 1987. text ed. 35.00 (ISBN 0-933601-07-7); pap. text ed. 22.50 (ISBN 0-933601-08-5). Selene Bks.

Sibylline Oracles. new ed. Tr. by Milton S. Terry from Gr. LC 72-176141. Repr. of 1899 ed. 21.45 (ISBN 0-404-06362-4). AMS Pr.

Sibyls & Seers. Edwyn R. Bevan. 1979. Repr. of 1928 ed. lib. bdg. 42.50 (ISBN 0-8495-0510-0). Arden Lib.
Sibyls & Sibylline Prophecy in Classical Antiquity. H. W. Parke. Ed. by Brian C. McGing. 256p. 1988. lib. bdg. 37.50 (ISBN 0-415-00343-1). Routledge Chapman & Hall.
Sibyl's Dreams. Mary Helen. 1980. deluxe ed. 14.95x autographed (ISBN 0-912492-18-X). Pyquag.
Sibyl's Legend of Mammy Jane. Sibyl J. Pischke. 1981. 14.95 (ISBN 0-9608532-0-0). S J Pischke.
Sic et Non: A Critical Edition, 7 fascicles. P. Abailard. Ed. by Blanche Boyer & Richard McKeon. Incl. Fascicle 1. (ISBN 0-226-00058-3);;; Fascicle 4. (ISBN 0-226-00061-3); Fascicle 5. (ISBN 0-226-00062-1); (ISBN 0-226-00064-8);. LC 74-7567. 1978. pap. text ed. 16.00x ea. O. P.; fascicles 1-7 complete in one clothbound vol. 130.00x (ISBN 0-226-00066-4). U of Chicago Pr.
Sicconis Polentoni Scriptorum Illustrium Latinaelinguae Libri XVIII. Sicco Polenton. Ed. by B. L. Ullman. LC 29-7429. (American Academy in Rome. Papers & Monographs: Vol. 6). pap. 149.30 (2026721). Bks Demand UMI.
Sich ein Bild Machen. Inge Habig. (Europaisches Forum: Vol. 5). 140p. (Ger.). 1982. 17.35 (ISBN 3-8204-5709-7). P Lang Pubs.
Sichou Zhi Lu. Museum of the Siankiang-Uighur Region. 1973. 175.00x (ISBN 0-317-68498-1, Pub. by Han-Shan Tang Ltd). State Mutual Bk.
Sichuan Taoqi Gongye. Chen Fuwen. 1958. 50.00x (ISBN 0-317-43950-2, Pub. by Han-Shan Tang Ltd.). State Mutual Bk.
Sicilian. Georgette Hall. 1974. 7.95 (ISBN 0-88289-060-3). Pelican.
Sicilian. Mario Puzo. 448p. 1984. 17.95 (ISBN 0-671-43564-7, Linden Pr). S&S.
Sicilian. Mario Puzo. 416p. 1985. pap. 4.95 (ISBN 0-553-25282-8). Bantam.
Sicilian Antigruppo. Ed. by Stanley H. Barkan & Saverio A. Scammacca. (Illus.). 30p. 1976. 5.00 (ISBN 0-89304-008-8). Cross Cult.
Sicilian Carousel. Lawrence Durrell. 1977. 13.95 (ISBN 0-670-64362-9). Viking.
Sicilian Colony Dates: Studies in Chronography One. Molly Miller. LC 69-14646. (Illus.). 287p. 1970. 59.50 (ISBN 0-87395-049-6). State U NY Pr.
Sicilian Comedies. Luigi Pirandello. LC 82-62097. 1983. 18.95 (ISBN 0-933826-50-8); pap. 6.95 (ISBN 0-933826-51-6). PAJ Pubns.
Sicilian Defense Classical Richter Rauzer. Eric Schiller. 65p. (Orig.). 1987. pap. 6.00 (ISBN 0-931462-72-X). Chess Ent Inc.
Sicilian Defense, Velimirovic Attack. Bruce Leverett. (Illus.). 70p. (Orig.). 1983. pap. 5.00 (ISBN 0-931462-23-1). Chess Ent Inc.
Sicilian Defense, Wing Gambits. Thomas Kapitaniak. 71p. (Orig.). 1985. pap. 5.00 (ISBN 0-931462-41-X). Chess Ent Inc.
Sicilian Dragon Jugoslav Attack. Eric Schiller & Jonathan Goldman. 136p. (Orig.). 1987. pap. 6.50 (ISBN 0-931462-68-1). Chess Ent Inc.
Sicilian English Dictionary. Joseph Bellestri. LC 85-73172. 338p. 1985. 20.00 (ISBN 0-9615777-0-3). J Bellestri.
Sicilian Episode. Robert H. Wyatt, Sr. 224p. 1985. 12.95 (ISBN 0-8059-2982-7). Dorrance.
Sicilian Folk Medicine. Giuseppe Pitre. (Illus.). 320p. 1971. 48.50x (ISBN 0-87291-013-X). Coronado Pr.
Sicilian Gentleman's Cookbook. Don Baratta. Ed. by Nancy D. Dominitz. (Illus.). 188p. (Orig.). 1987. pap. 12.95 (ISBN 0-914629-06-9, Dist. by St. Martin). Prima Pub Comm.
Sicilian-Lines with e5: Middle Level. T. D. Harding & P. R. Markland. (Illus.). 128p. 1982. pap. 18.95 (ISBN 0-7134-4020-1, Pub. by Batsford England). David & Charles.
Sicilian Lives. Danilo Dolci. 1982. pap. 5.56 (ISBN 0-394-74938-3). Pantheon.
Sicilian: Modern Richter-Rauzer Systems. Eric Schiller. 59p. (Orig.). 1986. pap. 5.00 (ISBN 0-931462-51-7). Chess Ent Inc.
Sicilian: Poisoned Pawn Variation. L. M. Kovaca. 220p. 1986. 21.00 (ISBN 0-08-029755-2). Pergamon.
Sicilian Richter-Rauzer with...a6. Eric Schiller. 120p. (Orig.). 1987. pap. 5.00 (ISBN 0-931462-66-5). Chess Ent Inc.
Sicilian Romance. Ann Radcliffe. LC 75-131338. (Gothic Novels Ser). 1971. Repr. of 1821 ed. 42.00 (ISBN 0-405-00809-0). Ayer Co Pubs.
Sicilian Scheveningen: Keres Attack. Doug Eckert. 128p. (Orig.). 1986. pap. 5.50 (ISBN 0-931462-54-1). Chess Ent Inc.
Sicilian Specialist. Norman Lewis. 352p. 1986. 3.50 (ISBN 0-88184-279-6). Carroll & Graf.
Sicilian: Sveshnikov Variation. A. Adorjan & T. Horvath. (Pergamon Chess Opening Ser.). 150p. 1987. 23.95 (ISBN 0-08-029735-8, P115); pap. 14.75 (ISBN 0-08-029734-X). Pergamon.
Sicilian Tuna Trap. V. Fodera. (GFCM Studies & Reviews: No. 15). 112p. (2nd Printing 1965). 1961. pap. 8.00 (ISBN 92-5-101933-9, F1779, FAO). UNIPUB.
Sicilian Uncles. Leonardo Sciascia. Tr. by N. S. Thompson from Ital. 205p. 1986. 15.95 (ISBN 0-85635-555-0). Carcanet.
Sicilian Uncles. Leonardo Sciascia. Tr. by N. S. Thompson from Ital. 205p. 1988. pap. 6.95 (ISBN 0-85635-782-0). Carcanet.
Sicilian Vespers. Steven Runciman. 1958. 42.50 (ISBN 0-521-06167-9). Cambridge U Pr.
Sicilian Vespers: A History of the Mediterranean World in the Later Thirteenth Century. Steven Runciman. (Illus.). 370p. 1982. pap. 18.95 (ISBN 0-521-28652-2). Cambridge U Pr.
Sicilian Walks: Exploring the History & Culture of the Two Sicilies. William J. Bonville. (Illus.). 300p. (Orig.). 1988. pap. 9.95 (ISBN 0-938179-15-2). Mills Sanderson.
Sicilian 2C3. Murray Chandler. (Illus.). 128p. 1987. pap. 15.95 (ISBN 0-7134-5651-5, Pub. by Batsford England). David & Charles.
Sicily. Roland Flint. 32p. (Orig.). 1987. pap. 5.00 (ISBN 0-933598-03-3); 10.00 (ISBN 0-317-65523-X). NC Wesleyan Pr.
Sicily. Alta Macadam. (Blue Guide Ser.). (Illus.). 1982. 24.95 (ISBN 0-393-01552-1); pap. 16.95 (ISBN 0-393-30004-8). Norton.
Sicily. 3rd ed. Alta Macadam. (Blue Guides Ser.). (Illus.). 1988. pap. 17.95 (ISBN 0-393-30478-7). Norton.
Sicily. (Panorama Bks.). (Illus., Fr.). 3.95 (ISBN 0-685-11562-3). French & Eur.
Sicily. Pref. by Denis M. Smith. LC 88-5907. (Illus.). 164p. 1988. 60.00 (ISBN 0-8478-0958-7). Rizzoli Intl.
Sicily & Naples, or the Fatal Union: A Tragedy, by S. Harding. Joan W. Roberts. Ed. by Stephen Orgel. LC 86-10300. (Renaissance Imagination Ser.). 296p. 1986. lib. bdg. 41.00 (ISBN 0-8240-5460-1). Garland Pub.
Sicily Enough. Claire Rabe. (Illus.). 1976. pap. 3.75 (ISBN 0-88496-070-6). Capra Pr.
Sicily Enough. Claire Rabe. 74p. 1988. Repr. lib. bdg. 19.95x (ISBN 0-8095-4048-7). Borgo Pr.
Sicily: The Fabulous Island. Edith L. Hough. (Illus.). 1949. 4.00 (ISBN 0-8338-0027-2). M Jones.
Sicily: The Insecure Base: A History of British Occupation of Sicily, 1806-1815. Desmond Gregory. LC 86-46244. (Illus.). 184p. 1987. 27.50x (ISBN 0-8386-3306-4). Fairleigh Dickinson.
Sicily Travel Guide. (Berlitz Travel Guides). (Illus.). 1982. pap. 4.95 (ISBN 0-02-969510-4, Berlitz). Macmillan.
Sicily under the Roman Empire. R. J. Wilson. (Classical Studies). (Illus.). 160p. 1988. text ed. 65.00 (ISBN 0-85668-160-1, Pub. by Aris & Phillips UK). Humanities.
Sick Citadel: The American Academic Medical Center & the Public Interest. Irving J. Lewis & Cecil G. Sheps. LC 82-22448. 224p. 1983. text ed. 27.50 (ISBN 0-89946-173-5). Oelgeschlager.
Sick Day. Patricia MacLachlan. LC 78-11686. (Illus.). (gr. k-3). 1979. Pantheon.
Sick for Justice. Ed. by Joseph Hughes. (Southern Exposure Ser.). (Illus.). 128p. (Orig.). 1978. pap. 3.00 (ISBN 0-943810-06-X). Inst Southern Studies.
Sick Heart of Modern Europe: The Problem of the Danubian Lands. Hugh Seton-Watson. LC 74-30170. 89p. 1975. 12.50x (ISBN 0-295-95360-8). U of Wash Pr.
Sick: How Americans Feel about Being Sick & What They Think of Those Who Care for Them. Robert C. Hardy. LC 77-90162. 1977. o.p 18.95 (ISBN 0-931028-05-1); pap. 14.95 (ISBN 0-931028-04-3). Teach'em.
Sick in Bed. Anne Rockwell & Harlow Rockwell. LC 81-15637. (My World Ser.). (Illus.). 24p. (ps-k). 1982. 8.95 (ISBN 0-02-777730-8). Macmillan.
Sick-in-Bed Birthday Book. Linda Tyler. (Illus.). 32p. (ps-1). 1988. 11.95 (ISBN 0-670-81823-2). Viking.
Sick Newborn Baby. C. J. Kelnar & David Harvey. (Illus.). 360p. 1981. pap. write for info. (ISBN 0-7216-0872-8, Bailliere-Tindall). Saunders.
Sick Newborn Baby. 2nd ed. Christopher J. Kelnar & David Harvey. (Illus.). 360p. 1986. 15.00 (ISBN 0-7020-1185-1, Bailliere-Tindall). Saunders.
Sick of Being Sick Book. Bob Stine & Jane Stine. (Illus.). 96p. (gr. 7 up). 1982. pap. 2.25 (ISBN 0-590-40315-X, Vagabond). Scholastic Inc.
Sick of Being Sick Book. Bob Stine & Jane Stine. 96p. (gr. 6-8). 1988. pap. 2.50 (ISBN 0-590-41865-3). Scholastic Inc.
Sick Story. Linda Hirsch. (Illus.). (gr. k-3). 1976. 7.95 (ISBN 0-8038-6733-6). Hastings.
Sicke Womans Private Looking Glasse Wherein Methodically Are Handled All Uterine Affects, or Diseases Arising from Ye Wombe. John Sadler. LC 77-7430. (English Experience Ser.: No. 891). 1977. Repr. of 1636 ed. lib. bdg. 25.00 (ISBN 90-221-0891-0). Walter J Johnson.
Sickle & Crescent: The Communist Revolt of 1926 in Banten. Michael C. Williams. 81p. 1982. 6.00 (ISBN 0-87763-027-5). Cornell Mod Indo.
Sickle Cell. 2.00 (ISBN 0-685-87401-X). Hippocrene Bks.
Sickle Cell Anemia: A Preliminary Survey, Nos. 1042-1043. 2nd ed. Lenwood G. Davis. 1976. 9.50 (ISBN 0-686-20397-6). CPL Biblios.
Sickle Cell Disease. Graham R. Serjeant. (Illus.). 494p. 1986. text ed. 69.00x (ISBN 0-19-261534-3). Oxford U Pr.
Sickle Cell Disease. Graham R. Serjeant. (Illus.). 496p. 1988. pap. 39.95 (ISBN 0-19-261753-2). Oxford U Pr.
Sickle Cell Disease: Psychological & Psychosocial Issues. Anita L. Hurtig & Carol T. Viera. LC 85-5400. 168p. 1986. 15.95 (ISBN 0-252-01186-4). U of Ill Pr.
Sickle Cell Hemoglobinopathies: A Comprehensive Bibliography 1910-1972. Charles W. Triche & Diane S. Triche. LC 73-85959. v, 434p. 1974. 18.00x (ISBN 0-87875-048-7). Whitston Pub.
Sickle Cell Hemoglobinopathies: A Comprehensive Bibliography 1973-75. Charles W. Triche, 3rd & Diane S. Triche. LC 73-85959. 1976. 9.50x (ISBN 0-87875-104-1). Whitston Pub.
Sickled Cell. Stuart J. Edelstein. LC 86-2003. (Illus.). 224p. 1986. text ed. 27.00x (ISBN 0-674-80737-5). Harvard U Pr.
Sicklets. Pat Anderson. 1987. pap. 3.95 (ISBN 0-425-10399-4). Berkley Pub.
Sickness & Healing. Klaus Seybold & Ulrich B. Mueller. Tr. by Douglas W. Stott from Ger. LC 81-3663. (Biblical Encounter Ser.). 208p. (Orig.). 1981. pap. 9.95 (ISBN 0-687-38444-3). Abingdon.
Sickness & Health: A Novel. Colin Douglas. LC 80-28316. 200p. cancelled (ISBN 0-8008-7178-2). Taplinger.
Sickness & Health in America: Readings in the History of Medicine & Public Health. 2nd, rev. ed. Ed. by Judith W. Leavitt & Ronald L. Numbers. LC 85-40370. (Illus.). 548p. 1985. text ed. 32.50x (ISBN 0-299-10270-X); pap. text ed. 14.95x (ISBN 0-299-10274-2). U of Wis Pr.
Sickness & Sectarianism: Exploratory Studies in Medical & Religious Sectarianism. Ed. by Kenneth Jones. 517p. 1985. text ed. 28.95x (ISBN 0-566-00662-6). Gower Pub Co.
Sickness unto Death. Ed. by Robert L. Perkins. LC 87-5614. (International Kierkegaard Ser.: No. 19). 272p. 1987. 18.95 (ISBN 0-86554-271-6, H234). Mercer Univ Pr.
Sickness Unto Death: A Christian Psychological Exposition for Upbuilding & Awakening. Soren Kierkegaard. Tr. by Howard V. Hong & Edna H. Hong. LC 79-3218. (Kierkegaard's Writings Ser.: Vol. XIX). 216p. 1980. 30.50x (ISBN 0-691-07247-7); pap. 10.00 (ISBN 0-691-02028-0). Princeton U Pr.
SICSA Cookbook. SICSA Staff. LC 85-61448. (Illus.). 1985. write for info. (ISBN 0-9615105-0-1). SICSA.
Sicuanga Runa: The Other Side of Development in Amazonian Ecuador. Norman E. Whitten, Jr. LC 84-155. (Illus.). 328p. 1985. 24.95 (ISBN 0-252-01117-1). U of Ill Pr.
Sid & Nancy: Love Kills. Alex Cox & Abbe Wool. 1986. pap. 8.95 (ISBN 0-571-14545-0). Faber & Faber.
Sid & Sol. Arthur Yorinks. LC 77-24126. (Illus.). 32p. (ps up). 1977. 8.95 (ISBN 0-374-36904-6). FS&G.
SID Internaitonal Symposium Digest of Technical Papers, May 1986. 40.00 (ISBN 0-318-20633-1). SID.
SID International Symposium Digest of Technical Papers, Orlando, April-May 1985. 55.00 (ISBN 0-318-20632-3). SID.
Siddhanta Darsanam of Vyasa. Vyasa. Tr. by Mohan L. Sandal. LC 73-3822. (Sacred Books of the Hindus: No. 29). Repr. of 1925 ed. 17.00 (ISBN 0-404-57829-2). AMS Pr.
Siddhartha. Hermann Hesse. (YA) (gr. 10-12). 1982. pap. 2.95 (ISBN 0-553-20884-5). Bantam.
Siddhartha. Hermann Hesse. Tr. by Hilda Rosner. LC 51-13669. 1951. gift ed. 16.95 (ISBN 0-8112-0292-5); pap. 3.95 (ISBN 0-8112-0068-X, NDP65). New Directions.
Siddhartha. Hermann Hesse. 191p. 1983. Repr. lib. bdg. 16.95x (ISBN 0-89966-447-4). Buccaneer Bks.
Siddhi Kur: Tales of the Bewitched Vampire, the Vetalapan-cavimsatika. (Mongolia Society Special Papers: Issue III). 7.50 (ISBN 0-910980-23-3). Mongolia.
Siddur Leshabbat Veyom Tov: Prayer Book for Sabbath & Festivals with Torah Readings. Philip Birnbaum. 724p. 1950. 17.00 (ISBN 0-88482-062-9). Hebrew Pub.
Siddur Leshabbat Veyom Tov: Prayer Book for Sabbath & Festivals. Philip Birnbaum. 384p. 1978. 19.50 (ISBN 0-88482-126-9). Hebrew Pub.
Siddur Program, II to Hebrew & Heritage. Pearl Tarnor & Norman Tarnor. (Illus.). 128p. 1982. pap. text ed. 3.95x (ISBN 0-87441-330-3); pap. text ed. 3.50x prayer wkbk.; tchr's annotated ed. 14.95. Behrman.
Siddur Program III to Hebrew & Heritage. Pearl Tarnor & Norman Tarnor. (Illus.). 128p. 1983. pap. text ed. 3.95x (ISBN 0-87441-359-1); pap. text ed. 3.50x prayer wkbk.; tchr's annotated ed. 14.95 (ISBN 0-87441-426-1). Behrman.
Siddur: Sabbath Eve Service. Nosson Scherman. 1980. 10.95 (ISBN 0-686-68764-7); pap. 7.95 (ISBN 0-686-68765-5). Mesorah Pubns.
Siddur: The Complete ArtScroll Siddur - Ashkenaz. N. Scherman. Ed. by M. Zlotowitz. (ArtScroll Siddur Ser.). 992p. 17.95 (ISBN 0-89906-650-X); leather 39.95 (ISBN 0-89906-653-4); large print 29.95 (ISBN 0-89906-656-9); Complete Siddur with Telillim. 18.95 (ISBN 0-89906-664-X); Rabbinical Council ed. 18.95 (ISBN 0-89906-662-3); Pocket sized. 13.95 (ISBN 0-89906-655-0); Pocket sized paper. 10.95 (ISBN 0-89906-661-5); Pocket sized leather gift bd. 19.95. Mesorah Pubns.
Siddur: The Prayer Book. Commentary by Ben Z. Bokser. 10.00 (ISBN 0-317-70173-8); pap. 11.95 (ISBN 0-317-70174-6). Behrman.
Siddurenu. Sidney Greenberg & Morris Silverman. (gr. 3-7). 8.95x (ISBN 0-87677-099-5). Prayer Bk.
Side by Side. Norman M. Bradburn et al. 208p. pap. 2.95 (ISBN 0-686-74895-6). ADL.
Side by Side. Martha Humphreys. (First Love Ser.). 186p. 1984. pap. 1.95 (ISBN 0-671-53402-5, Pub. by Silhouette Bks). S&S.
Side by Side. Helen Joseph. LC 86-23747. 256p. 1987. 16.95 (ISBN 0-688-07103-1). Morrow.
Side by Side. Oxford Scientific Films Staff. (Illus.). 32p. (ps up). 1988. 13.95 (ISBN 0-399-21582-4, Putnam). Putnam Pub Group.
Side by Side, Bk. 1. 2nd ed. Molinsky Blise. (Illus.). 130p. 1988. pap. text ed. price not set. P-H.
Side by Side, Bk. 2. 2nd ed. Molinsky Bliss. (Illus.). 130p. Date not set. pap. text ed. price not set (ISBN 0-13-811241-X). P-H.
Side by Side: English Grammar Through Guided Conversations, Bk. I. Steven J. Molinsky & Bill Bliss. 1980. pap. text ed. 115.00 (ISBN 0-13-809848-4); write for info (ISBN 0-13-809830-1). P-H.
Side by Side: English Grammar Through Guided Conversations Bk. II. Steven J. Molinsky & Bill Blass. 1980. pap. text ed. write for info (ISBN 0-13-809855-7). P-H.
Side by Side: English Grammar Through Guided Conversation 1A. Steven J. Molinsky & Bill Bliss. 128p. 1983. pap. text ed. write for info (ISBN 0-13-809715-1); write for info. (ISBN 0-13-809525-6). P-H.
Side by Side: English Grammar through Guided Conversation 1B. Steven J. Molinsky & Bill Bliss. 128p. 1983. pap. text ed. write for info (ISBN 0-13-809723-2); write for info (ISBN 0-13-809582-5). P-H.
Side by Side: English Grammar Through Guided Conversation 2A. Steven J. Molinsky & Bill Bliss. 128p. 1983. pap. text ed. write for info (ISBN 0-13-809772-0); write for info. (ISBN 0-13-809640-6). P-H.
Side by Side: English Grammar Through Guided Conversation 2B. Steven J. Molinsky & Bill Bliss. 128p. 1983. pap. text ed. write for info (ISBN 0-13-809798-4); pap. 3.50 wkbk. (ISBN 0-13-809699-6). P-H.
Side by Side: Poems to Read Together. Ed. by Lee B. Hopkins. (Illus.). 96p. (gr. 1 up). 1988. PLB 14.95 (ISBN 0-671-63579-4). S&S.
Side Effect of Drugs, Vol. 9. 9th ed. Ed. by M. N. Dukes. 860p. 1980. 160.75 (ISBN 0-444-90102-7, Excerpta Medica). Elsevier.
Side Effects. Allen. Date not set. 16.95 (ISBN 0-8488-0365-5). Amereon Ltd.
Side Effects. Woody Allen. 160p. 1981. pap. 3.50 (ISBN 0-345-34335-2). Ballantine.
Side Effects. Woody Allen. 1980. 8.95 (ISBN 0-394-51104-2). Random.
Side Effects. Barbara Betcherman. 1988. pap. 4.95. Tudor Pub NYC.
Side Effects. Karen Silverstein & Mel Silverstein. 1982. pap. 2.95 (ISBN 0-89083-895-X). Zebra.
Side Effects & Drug Design. Lien. (Medicinal Research Ser.). 232p. 1987. 99.75 (ISBN 0-8247-7686-0). Dekker.
Side Effects of Anti-Inflammatory Drugs, Vol. 1. Ed. by K. D. Rainsford & G. P. Velo. (Inflammation & Drug Therapy Ser.). 1987. lib. bdg. 84.25 (ISBN 0-85200-681-0, Pub. by MTP Pr England). Kluwer Academic.
Side Effects of Anti-Inflammatory Drugs, Vol. 2: Studies in Major Organ Systems. Ed. by K. D. Rainsford & G. P. Velo. (Inflammation & Drug Therapy Ser.). 1988. lib. bdg. 123.00 (ISBN 0-85200-693-4, Pub. by MTP Pr England). Kluwer Academic.
Side-Effects of Antiinflammatory-Analgesic Drugs. Ed. by Kim D. Rainsford & Giampaolo Velo. (Advances in Inflammation Research Ser.: Vol. 6). (Illus.). 320p. 1984. text ed. 59.50 (ISBN 0-89004-971-8). Raven.
Side Effects of Drugs: Annual. 9th ed. Ed. by M. N. Dukes. 500p. 1985. 109.50 (ISBN 0-444-90394-1). Elsevier.
Side Effects of Drugs Annual, Vol. 10. Ed. by M. N. Dukes & L. Beeley. 500p. 1986. 110.75 (ISBN 0-444-90451-4). Elsevier.
Side Effects of Drugs Annual: No. 3, 1979. Ed. by M. N. Dukes. 470p. 1979. 109.50 (ISBN 0-444-90072-1, Excerpta Medica). Elsevier.
Side Effects of Drugs: Annual 10, 1986. Ed. by M. Dukes. 500p. 1986. 102.50 (ISBN 0-317-65196-X). Elsevier.
Side Effects of Drugs, Annual 11. Ed. by M. N. Dukes & L. Beeley. 500p. 1987. 116.00 (ISBN 0-444-90473-5). Elsevier.
Side Effects of Drugs, Annual 12. Ed. by M. N. Dukes. 500p. 1988. 131.50 (ISBN 0-444-90491-3). Elsevier.
Side Effects of Drugs: Annual 4, 1980. Ed. by M. N. Dukes. 376p. 1980. 74.50 (ISBN 0-444-90130-2, Excerpta Medica). Elsevier.
Side Effects of Drugs: Annual 6, 1982. Ed. by M. N. Dukes. 478p. 1982. 109.50 (ISBN 0-444-90211-2, Excerpta Medica). Elsevier.
Side Effects of Drugs: Annual 7, 1983. Ed. by M. N. Dukes. 500p. 1983. 109.50 (ISBN 0-444-90279-1, Excerpta Medica). Elsevier.

Siege De Corinthe. Gioachino Rossini. Ed. by Phillip Gossett & Charles Rosen. LC 76-49189. (Early Romantic Opera Ser.: No. 14). 1980. lib. bdg. 99.00 (ISBN 0-8240-2913-5). Garland Pub.
Siege in Peking: China Against the World. William A. Martin. (Illus.). 190p. 1972. Repr. of 1900 ed. 27.50x (ISBN 0-7165-2037-0, BBA 03054, Pub. by Irish Academic Pr). Biblio Dist.
Siege in Peking: China Against the World. William A. Martin. LC 72-79832. (China Library Ser.). 1972. Repr. of 1900 ed. lib. bdg. 23.00 (ISBN 0-8420-1376-8). Scholarly Res Inc.
Siege in the Sun. Dorothy Eden. 1980. pap. 2.25 (ISBN 0-449-23884-9, Crest). Fawcett.
Siege: Malta, Nineteen Forty to Nineteen Forty-Three. Ernle Bradford. LC 85-21503. (Illus.). 320p. 1985. 19.95 (ISBN 0-688-04781-5). Morrow.
Siege of Boston. Allen French. LC 68-58326. (Illus.). 1969. Repr. of 1911 ed. 20.00 (ISBN 0-87152-052-4). Reprint.
Siege of Charleston. Ed. by Bernard A. Uhlendorf. LC 67-29028. (Eyewitness Accounts of the American Revolution Ser., No. 1). 1968. Repr. of 1938 ed. 23.50 (ISBN 0-405-01125-3). Ayer Co Pubs.
Siege of Charleston, 1861-1865. E. Milby Burton. LC 70-120584. xxii, 390p. 1982. pap. 9.95 (ISBN 0-87249-345-8). U of SC Pr.
Siege of Constantinople Fourteen Fifty-Three: Seven Contemporay Accounts. J. R. Jones. 137p. 1973. lib. bdg. 34.00x (Pub. by A M Hakkert). Coronet Bks.
Siege of Derry. Patrick Macrory. 384p. 1988. pap. 12.95 (ISBN 0-19-285182-9). Oxford U Pr.
Siege of Fort Macon. Ed. by Paul R. Branch, Jr. (Illus.). 105p. (Orig.). 1982. pap. 5.00 (ISBN 0-9614000-0-5). P Branch.
Siege of Gibraltar, Seventeen Seventy-Nine to Seventeen Eighty-Three. T. H. McGuffie. LC 64-25508. (Illus.). 1965. 14.95 (ISBN 0-8023-1074-5). Dufour.
Siege of Jerusalem. (EETS OS: No. 188). Repr. of 1932 ed. 30.00 (ISBN 0-527-00188-0). Kraus Repr.
Siege of Krishnapur. J. G. Farrell. 344p. 1985. pap. 4.95 (ISBN 0-88184-195-1). Carroll & Graf.
Siege of Leningrad. Leon Goure. LC 62-8662. 1962. 35.00x (ISBN 0-8047-0115-6). Stanford U Pr.
Siege of Leningrad. R. Conrad Stein. LC 82-17841. (World at War Ser.). (Illus.). 48p. (gr. 4-8). 1983. PLB 12.33 (ISBN 0-516-04773-6); pap. 2.95 (ISBN 0-516-44773-4). Childrens.
Siege of London. Henry James. 59.95 (ISBN 0-8490-1053-5). Gordon Pr.
Siege of London see Lady Barbarina.
Siege of Londonderry. P. Dwyer. 1971. Repr. of 1689 ed. 19.95 (ISBN 0-8464-0847-3). Beekman Pubs.
Siege of Love. Catherine Lyndell. (Tapestry Ser.: No. 58). (Orig.). 1985. pap. 2.95 (ISBN 0-671-54396-2). PB.
Siege of Malta Rediscovered. Donald E. Sultana. 1977. 17.50x (ISBN 0-7073-0131-9, Pub. by Scot Acad Pr). Longwood Pub Group.
Siege of Mobile, Seventeen Eighty in Maps: With Data on Troop Strength, Military Units, Ships, Casualties, & Prisoners of War. William S. Coker & Hazel P. Coker. LC 82-675288. (Spanish Borderlands Ser.: Vol. 9). (Illus.). 131p. (Orig.). 1982. pap. text ed. 12.95x (ISBN 0-933776-11-X). Perdido Bay.
Siege of Orbitor. Richard L. Newman. 1980. pap. 2.25 (ISBN 0-8439-0814-9, Leisure Bks). Leisure NY.
Siege of Paris: Eighteen Seventy to Eighty Seventy-One; a Political & Social History. Melvin Kranzberg. LC 78-112326. 1971. Repr. of 1950 ed. lib. bdg. 15.00x (ISBN 0-8371-4714-X, KRSP). Greenwood.
Siege of Penobscot by the Rebels & the Proceedings of the General Assembly & of the Council of the State of Massachusetts Bay Relating to the Penobscot Expedition. Ed. by John Calef. LC 78-140857. (Eyewitness Accounts of the American Revolution Ser., No. 3). (Illus.). 1970. Repr. of 1780 ed. 9.50 (ISBN 0-405-01226-8). Ayer Co Pubs.
Siege of Pensacola, 1781. William S. Coker & Hazel P. Coker. LC 81-675060. (Spanish Borderlands Ser.: Vol. VIII). (Illus.). 132p. 1981. pap. text ed. 12.00 (ISBN 0-933776-07-1). Perdido Bay.
Siege of Portsmouth in the Civil War. rev. ed. John Webb. 1977. 39.00x (ISBN 0-317-43676-7, Pub. by City of Portsmouth). State Mutual Bk.
Siege of Rhodes see Book of Subtyl Histories & Fables of Esope.
Siege of St. Augustine. Charles W. Arnade. LC 59-63743. (Illus.). 100p. (Orig.). 1959. pap. 3.95 (ISBN 0-917553-00-4). St Augustine Hist.
Siege of Savannah. Franklin B. Hough. LC 77-165683. (Era of the American Revolution Ser.). 187p. 1974. Repr. of 1866 ed. lib. bdg. 27.50 (ISBN 0-306-70619-9). Da Capo.
Siege of Savannah, by the Combined American & French Forces, under the Command of Gen. Lincoln & the Count dEstaing, in the Autumn of 1779. Franklin B. Hough. LC 75-1142. (Illus.). 190p. 1975. Repr. of 1866 ed. 17.50 (ISBN 0-87152-193-8). Reprint.
Siege of Savannah, Eighteen Sixty-Four. 2nd ed. Charles O. Jones, Jr. LC 88-80982. (Ga. Military History Ser.). 184p. 1988. Repr. of 1874 ed. 13.00x (ISBN 0-944259-04-9). Freedom Hill.
Siege of Savannah, in 1779 As Described in Two Contemporaneous Journals of French Officers in the Fleet of Count D'estaing. Ed. by Charles C. Jones, Jr. LC 67-29027. (Eyewitness Accounts of the American Revolution Ser., No. 1). 1968. Repr. of 1874 ed. 13.00 (ISBN 0-405-01115-6). Ayer Co Pubs.
Siege of Serpentor. R. L. Stine. (G. I. Joe Ser.: No. 1). 128p. 1988. pap. 2.95 (ISBN 0-345-35094-4). Ballantine.
Siege of Sevastopol Terrace. John Waterhouse. 1984. 15.00 (Pub. by New Playwrights Network). State Mutual Bk.
Siege of Silence. A. J. Quinnell. 1986. 16.95 (ISBN 0-525-24429-8). Dutton.
Siege of Silence. A. J. Quinnell. 1987. pap. 3.95 (ISBN 0-451-40045-3, Onyx). NAL.
Siege of South Africa: What the Press Doesn't Tell You. Ivor Benson. 1986. lib. bdg. 79.50 (ISBN 0-8490-3820-0). Gordon Pr.
Siege of the Castle of Edinburgh. Ed. by Robert Bell. LC 78-39425. (Bannatyne Club, Edinburgh. Publications: No. 23). Repr. of 1828 ed. 18.50 (ISBN 0-404-52729-9). AMS Pr.
Siege of the Dragonriders. Eric Affabee. (Wizards, Warriors & You Ser.: Bk. 2). (Illus.). 112p. 1984. pap. 2.50 (ISBN 0-380-88054-7, 88054-7). Avon.
Siege of the Peking Legations: A Diary. Lancelot Giles. 1970. 18.50x (ISBN 0-85564-041-3, Pub. by U of W Austral Pr). Intl Spec Bk.
Siege of the Villa Lipp. Eric Ambler. 19.95 (ISBN 0-89190-465-4, Pub. by Am Repr). Amereon Ltd.
Siege of Three Eighteen: Thirteen Mystical Stories. Davis Grubb. LC 78-61067. 180p. 1978. 12.00 (ISBN 0-686-37046-5). Back Fork Bks.
Siege of Wonder. Mark S. Geston. LC 75-36624. 180p. 1976. 15.00 (ISBN 0-385-11359-5). Ultramarine Pub.
Siege Perilous, & Other Stories. Maud Diver. LC 78-122694. (Short Story Index Reprint Ser). 1924. 17.00 (ISBN 0-8369-3527-6). Ayer Co Pubs.
Siege Perilous: Essays in Biblical Anthropology & Kindred Subjects. facsimile ed. Samuel H. Hooke. LC 73-130552. (Select Bibliographies Reprint Ser). Repr. of 1956 ed. 18.00 (ISBN 0-8369-5525-0). Ayer Co Pubs.
Siege: The First Eight Years of an Autistic Child with an Epilogue, Fifteen Years Later. Clara C. Park. 1982. 14.95 (ISBN 0-316-69076-7, Pub. by Atlantic Monthly Pr); pap. 8.95 (ISBN 0-316-69069-4). Little.
Siege: The Saga of Israel & Zionism. Conor C. O'Brien. 200p. 1986. 24.95 (ISBN 0-671-60044-3). S&S.
Siege: The Saga of Israel & Zionism. Conor C. O'Brien. 798p. 1987. pap. 12.95 (ISBN 0-671-63310-4, Touchstone Bks). S&S.
Siege Train: Journal of a Confederate Artilleryman in the Defense of Charleston. Ed. by Warren Ripley. 1986. 24.95 (ISBN 0-87249-491-8). U of SC Pr.
Siege Warfare: The Fortress in the Early Modern World, 1494-1660. Christopher Duffy. (Illus.). 1979. 30.00 (ISBN 0-7100-8871-X). Routledge Chapman & Hall.
Siegel Modular Forms & Representations by Quadratic Forms. Y. Kitaoka. v, 227p. 1986. pap. 11.00 (ISBN 0-387-16472-3). Springer-Verlag.
Siegfried. Jean Giraudoux. pap. 9.50 (ISBN 0-685-33926-2). French & Eur.
Siegfried. Richard Wagner. Ed. by Nicholas John. Tr. by Andrew Porter from Ger. (English National Opera - Royal Opera House Guide Ser.: No. 28, Libretto, Articles). (Illus., Orig.). 1984. pap. 5.95 (ISBN 0-7145-4040-4). Riverrun NY.
Siegfried see Theatre.
Siegfried et le Limousin. Jean Giraudoux. 1956. pap. 9.95 (ISBN 0-685-11563-1). French & Eur.
Siegfried Horn: The Survivor. Joyce Rochat. (Illus.). 325p. 1986. pap. 9.95 (ISBN 0-943872-61-8). Andrews Univ Pr.
Siegfried Sassoon: A Memorial Exhibition. Compiled by David Farmer. LC 77-628295. (Illus.). 1969. pap. 5.00 (ISBN 0-87959-007-6). U of Tex H Ransom Ctr.
Siegfried Sassoon Diaries: Nineteen Fifteen to Nineteen Eighteen. Siegfried Sassoon. Ed. by Rupert Hart-Davis. 296p. 1983. 22.95 (ISBN 0-571-11997-2). Faber & Faber.
Siegfried Sassoon Diaries: Nineteen Twenty to Nineteen Twenty-Two. Seigfried Sassoon. Ed. by Rupert Hart-Davis. 1983. pap. 23.95 (ISBN 0-571-11685-X). Faber & Faber.
Siegfried Sassoon Diaries, Nineteen Twenty-Three to Nineteen Twenty-Five. Ed. by Rupert Hart-Davis. 300p. 1984. 27.95 (ISBN 0-571-13322-3). Faber & Faber.
Siegfried Sassoon's Long Journey: Selections from the Sherston Memoirs. Ed. by Paul Fussell. (Illus.). 1983. 24.95 (ISBN 0-19-503309-4). Oxford U Pr.
Siegfried's Journey. Siegfried Sassoon. 224p. pap. 5.95 (ISBN 0-571-11917-4). Faber & Faber.
Siegfried's Journey: 1916-1920. Siegfried Sassoon. LC 76-6592. (BCL Ser.: No. I & II). Repr. of 1945 ed. 34.50 (ISBN 0-404-15294-5). AMS Pr.
Siegfried's Silent Night. Brad Bluth. (Christmas Bks.). (Illus.). 32p. (gr. k-4). 1983. 11.93 (ISBN 0-516-09159-X). Childrens.
Siegfried's Silent Night. Brad Bluth & Toby Bluth. 32p. (Orig.). (gr. k-6). 1983. 3.95 (ISBN 0-8249-8059-X). Ideals.
Siempre Junto a Ti. Rafael Crespo. (Romance Real). 192p. (Span.). 1981. pap. 1.50 (ISBN 0-88025-004-6). Roca Pub.
Siena: A City & Its History. Judith Hook. (Illus.). 258p. 1980. 30.95 (ISBN 0-241-10297-9, Pub. by Hamish Hamilton England). David & Charles.
Siena & Her Artists. Frederick Seymour. LC 77-9436. 1977. Repr. of 1907 ed. lib. bdg. 25.00 (ISBN 0-89341-201-5). Longwood Pub Group.
Siena Baptistry Font: A Study of an Early Renaissance Collaborative Program, 1416-1434. John T. Paoletti. LC 78-74374. (Fine Arts Dissertations, Fourth Ser.). (Illus.). 1980. lib. bdg. 40.00 (ISBN 0-8240-3961-0). Garland Pub.
Siena: The Story of a Mediaeval Commune. Ferdinand Schevill. 1979. Repr. of 1909 ed. lib. bdg. 40.00 (ISBN 0-8492-8120-2). R West.
Sienese Altarpieces 1215-1460 Form, Content, Function: Vol. I 1215-1344. Henk Van Os. Contrib. by Kees Van Der Ploeg. (Mediaevalia Groningana IV). (Illus.). 163p. 1984. 36.00x (ISBN 90-6088-083-8, Pub. by Boumas Boekhuis Netherlands). Benjamins North AM.
Sienese Painting: From Its Origins to the Fifteenth Century. Bruce Cole. LC 79-3670. (Icon Editions Ser.). (Illus.). 224p. 1980. 25.50i (ISBN 0-06-430901-0, HarpT). Har-Row.
Sienese Painting in the Age of the Renaissance. Bruce Cole. LC 84-48246. (Illus.). 216p. 1985. 37.50x (ISBN 0-253-18130-5). Ind U Pr.
Sienese Paintings. Enzo Carli. (Illus.). 80p. pap. 13.95 (ISBN 0-935748-25-3). Scala Books.
Sieneser Domkanzel des Nicola Pisano. Joachim Poeschke. LC 72-81565. (Beitraege zur Kunstgeschichte Vol. 9). 1973. 23.60x (ISBN 3-11-003961-3). De Gruyter.
Siente Katerine: Re-Edited from Ms Bodley 34 & Other Manuscripts. Ed. by S. R. D'Ardenne & E. J. Doboson. (Early English Text Soc. Ser. Supplementary Texts). 1981. text ed. 47.50x (ISBN 0-19-722407-5). Oxford U Pr.
Sierra Big Trees. abr. ed. John Muir. Ed. by William R. Jones. (Illus.). 80p. 1981. pap. 4.95 (ISBN 0-89646-069-X). Outbooks.
Sierra Club Guide to the National Parks of the Desert Southwest. LC 83-9310. (Sierra Club Guides to the National Parks Ser.). (Illus.). 352p. (Orig.). 1984. pap. 14.95 (ISBN 0-394-72488-7). Stewart Tabori & Chang.
Sierra Club Guide to the National Parks of the Pacific Southwest & Hawaii. LC 83-17848. (Sierra Club Guides to the National Parks Ser.). (Illus.). 261p. (Orig.). 1984. pap. 12.95 (ISBN 0-394-72490-9). Stewart Tabori & Chang.
Sierra Club Guide to the National Parks of the Rocky Mountains & the Great Plains. LC 84-2539. (Sierra Club Guides to the National Parks Ser.). (Illus.). 272p. (Orig.). 1984. pap. 14.95 (ISBN 0-394-72754-1). Stewart Tabori & Chang.
Sierra Club Guide to the Natural Areas of California. John Perry & Jane G. Perry. LC 82-16939. (Sierra Club Guides to the Natural Areas of the United States). (Illus.). 352p. (Orig.). 1983. pap. 9.95 (ISBN 0-87156-333-9). Sierra.
Sierra Club Guide to the Natural Areas of Colorado & Utah. John Perry & Jane G. Perry. LC 84-22215. (Sierra Club Guides to the Natural Areas of the United States Ser.). (Illus.). 416p. (Orig.). 1985. pap. 9.95 (ISBN 0-87156-832-2). Sierra.
Sierra Club Guide to the Natural Areas of Idaho, Montana & Wyoming. John Perry & Jane G. Perry. LC 87-26312. 416p. (Orig.). 1988. pap. 10.95 (ISBN 0-87156-781-4). Sierra.
Sierra Club Guide to the Natural Areas of New Mexico, Arizona, & Nevada. John Perry & Jane G. Perry. LC 85-18481. (Guides to the Natural Areas of the United States). (Illus.). 448p. 1986. pap. 10.95 (ISBN 0-87156-753-9, Dist. by Random). Sierra.
Sierra Club Guide to the Natural Areas of Oregon & Washington. John Perry & Jane G. Perry. LC 82-16937. (Sierra Club Guides to the Natural Areas of the United States). (Illus.). 360p. (Orig.). 1983. pap. 9.95 (ISBN 0-87156-334-7). Sierra.
Sierra Club Guide to the Pacific Northwest & Alaska. LC 84-23971. (Sierra Club Guides Ser.). (Illus.). 400p. (Orig.). 1985. pap. 14.95 (ISBN 0-394-73554-4). Stewart Tabori & Chang.
Sierra Club Handbook of Whales & Dolphins. Stephen Leatherwood & Randall R. Reeves. LC 83-388. (Sierra Club Paperback Library). (Illus.). 320p. 1983. 25.00 (ISBN 0-87156-341-X); pap. 14.95 (ISBN 0-87156-340-1). Sierra.
Sierra Club Naturalist's Guide to Southern New England. Neil Jorgensen. LC 77-28543. (Naturalist's Guide Ser.). (Illus.). 448p. 1978. 25.00 (ISBN 0-87156-190-5); pap. 14.95 (ISBN 0-87156-183-2). Sierra.
Sierra Club Naturalist's Guide to the Middle Atlantic Coast: Cape Hatteras to Cape Cod. Bill Perry. LC 83-18691. (Sierra Club Naturlist's Guide Ser.). (Illus.). 448p. (Orig.). 1985. 25.00 (ISBN 0-87156-810-1); pap. 12.95 (ISBN 0-87156-816-0). Sierra.
Sierra Club Naturalist's Guide to the North Atlantic Coast: Cape Cod to Newfoundland. Michael Berrill & Deborah Berrill. LC 80-23086. (Naturalist's Guides Ser.). (Illus.). 512p. 1981. 24.95 (ISBN 0-87156-242-1); pap. 12.95 (ISBN 0-87156-243-X). Sierra.
Sierra Club Naturalist's Guide to the North Woods of Michigan, Wisconsin, Minnesota & Southern Ontario. Glenda Daniel & Jerry Sullivan. LC 80-28742. (Naturalist's Guide Ser.). (Illus.). 384p. 1981. 24.95 (ISBN 0-87156-248-0); pap. 12.95 (ISBN 0-87156-277-4). Sierra.
Sierra Club Naturalist's Guide to the Piedmont of Eastern North America. Michael A. Godfrey. LC 79-22328. (Naturalists Guide Ser.). (Illus.). 432p. 1980. 19.95 (ISBN 0-87156-268-5); pap. 9.95 (ISBN 0-87156-269-3). Sierra.
Sierra Club Naturalist's Guide to the Sierra Nevada. Stephen Whitney. LC 79-766. (Naturalist's Guide Ser.). (Illus.). 544p. 1979. 14.95 (ISBN 0-87156-215-4); pap. 12.95 (ISBN 0-87156-216-2). Sierra.
Sierra Club Wayfinding Book. Vicki McVey. (Illus.). 96p. (gr. 4-7). 1988. 12.95 (ISBN 0-316-56340-4). Little.
Sierra Club WILDCARDS: Record-Setting Animals. Melinda B. Burgener. (Illus.). 24p. (ps up). 1988. 6.95 (ISBN 0-316-11618-1). Little.
Sierra Club's Growing Up Books. Derek Hall. Incl. Otter Swims. LC 83-22004. 4.95; PLB 6.99; Panda Climbs. LC 83-17462. 4.95; PLB 6.99; Tiger Runs. LC 84-793. 1984. 4.95 (ISBN 0-394-86504-9). (Illus.). 24p. (ps up). 1984. Knopf.
Sierra Flower Finder: A Guide to Sierra Nevada Wildflowers. Glenn Keator. (Illus.). 1980. pap. 3.00 (ISBN 0-912550-09-0). Nature Study.
Sierra Gold. W. S. Brady. 1985. 24.95x (ISBN 0-7090-1277-2, Pub. by R Hale Ltd UK). State Mutual Bk.
Sierra Gold Mystery. new ed. Carolyn Keene. (Dana Girls Ser.: Vol. 10). (Illus.). 192p. (gr. 4-7). 1973. 2.95 (G&D). Putnam Pub Group.
Sierra Leone. (Let's Visit Places & Peoples - - Nations, Dependencies, & Sovereignties of the World Ser.). (Illus.). (gr. 5 up). 1988. 12.95 (ISBN 0-7910-0106-7). Chelsea Hse.
Sierra Leone after a Hundred Years. E. G. Ingham. (Illus.). 368p. 1968. Repr. of 1894 ed. 30.00x (F Cass Co). Biblio Dist.
Sierra Leone As It Was & Is: Its Progress, People, Native Customs, & Undeveloped Wealth. Thomas J. Alldridge. 1976. lib. bdg. 59.95 (ISBN 0-8490-2602-4). Gordon Pr.
Sierra Leone in Maps. Colin G. Clarke & Alan G. Hodgkiss. (Graphic Perspectives of Developing Countries Ser.). 120p. 1972. 34.50 (ISBN 0-8419-0070-1). Holmes & Meier.
Sierra Leone Law Reports: 1960, 1961, 1962, 2 vols. LC 67-26375. 1966. Set. 90.00 (ISBN 0-379-16000-5). Oceana.
Sierra Leone, Seventeen Eighty-Seven to Nineteen Eighty-Seven: Two Centuries of Intellectual Life. Ed. by Murray Last et al. 176p. 1988. pap. 19.95 (ISBN 0-7190-2791-8, Pub. by Manchester Univ Pr). St Martin.
Sierra Leone's Settler Women Traders: Women on the Afro-European Frontier. E. Frances White. (Women & Culture Ser.). (Illus.). 200p. 1987. text ed. 27.50 (ISBN 0-472-10080-7). U of Mich Pr.
Sierra Nevada: A Mountain Journey. Tim Palmer. (Illus.). 300p. 1988. 31.95 (ISBN 0-933280-54-8); pap. 19.95 (ISBN 0-933280-53-X). Island CA.
Sierra Nevada Big Trees: History of the Exhibitions 1850-1903. Dennis G. Kruska. 1985. 30.00 (ISBN 0-87093-188-1). Dawsons.
Sierra Nevada Flora. 3rd ed. Norman Weeden. LC 85-41055. (Illus.). 412p. 1986. pap. 11.95 (ISBN 0-89997-073-7). Wilderness Pr.
Sierra-Nevada Lakes. George Hinkle & Bliss Hinkle. (Vintage West Ser.). (Illus.). 383p. 1987. pap. 8.95 (ISBN 0-87417-123-7). U of Nev Pr.
Sierra Nevada Natural History: An Illustrated Handbook. Tracy I. Storer & Robert L. Usinger. (Illus.). 1963. pap. 10.95 (ISBN 0-520-01227-5). U of Cal Pr.
Sierra Nevadan Wildlife Region. 2nd rev. ed. Vinson Brown & Robert Livezey. (American Wildlife Region Ser.: Vol. 2). (Illus.). 96p. (gr. 4 up). 1962. 11.95 (ISBN 0-911010-03-3); pap. 5.95 (ISBN 0-911010-02-5). Naturegraph.
Sierra North. 5th ed. Thomas Winnett & Jason Winnett. LC 85-40198. (Illus.). 296p. (Orig.). 1985. pap. 12.95 (ISBN 0-89997-054-0). Wilderness Pr.
Sierra Railroad: A Portfolio. Lowell Amrine. LC 86-2307. 32p. 1986. Repr. of 1980 ed. lib. bdg. 19.95x (ISBN 0-89370-554-3). Borgo Pr.
Sierra Railroad: An Adventure in Yesteryear. Larry Jensen. (Illus.). 3.95 (ISBN 0-933506-03-1). Darwin Pubns.
Sierra South. 4th ed. Thomas Winnett & Jason Winnett. LC 85-41024. (Illus.). 1986. pap. 11.95 (ISBN 0-89997-065-6). Wilderness Pr.
Sierra Sunrise. Lynn Wilson & Jim Wilson. Ed. by Vicki Leon. (Illus.). 64p. (Orig.). 1985. pap. 8.95 (ISBN 0-918303-05-2). Blake Print Pub.
Sierra: The Mountain Flower Book. Millie Miller. (Pocket Nature Guides Ser.). (Illus.). 40p. (Orig.). 1981. pap. 4.95 (ISBN 0-933472-58-7). Johnson Bks.
Sierra Trout Guide. Ralph Cutter. (Illus.). 108p. (Orig.). 1984. pap. 7.95 (ISBN 0-936608-23-4). F Amato Pubns.
Sierra Wildflowers: Mt. Lassen to Kern Canyon. Theodore F. Niehaus. (California Natural History Guides: No.32). (Illus., Orig.). 1974. pap. 8.95 (ISBN 0-520-02506-7). U of Cal Pr.

Sign Here: A Contracting Book for Children & Their Parents. 2nd ed. Jill C. Dardig & William L. Heward. LC 76-18757. (Illus.). 166p. 1981. pap. 10.00 (ISBN 0-917472-04-7); leader's manual 3.00 (ISBN 0-914474-27-8). F Fournies.
Sign Here Please. Gordon Ford. 1981. 25.00x (ISBN 0-7223-1377-2, Pub. by A H Stockwell England). State Mutual Bk.
Sign in Mendel's Window. Illus. by Mildred Phillips & Margot Zemach. LC 85-5049. 32p. (gr. k-3). 1985. PLB 12.95 (ISBN 0-02-774600-3). Macmillan.
Sign in Music & Literature. Ed. by Wendy Steiner. 243p. 1981. text ed. 25.00x (ISBN 0-292-77563-6). U of Tex Pr.
Sign in Sidney Brustein's Window see Raisin in the Sun.
Sign in the Straw. Richard C. Hoefler. 128p. (Orig.). 1980. pap. text ed. 6.95 (ISBN 0-89536-465-4, 1969). CSS of Ohio.
Sign Language. Greene & Dicker. 1981. 9.90 (ISBN 0-531-04195-6). Watts.
Sign Language: A Survival Vocabulary, Book A. Jim Richey. (Sign Language Ser.). (Illus.). 52p. (gr. 7-12). 1976. pap. text ed. 2.65 (ISBN 0-915510-08-1). Janus Bks.
Sign Language: A Survival Vocabulary, Book B. Jim Richey. (Sign Language Ser). (Illus.). 52p. (gr. 7-12). 1976. pap. text ed. 2.65 (ISBN 0-915510-09-X). Janus Bks.
Sign Language: A Survival Vocabulary, Book C. Jim Richey. (Sign Language Ser.). (Illus.). 52p. (gr. 7-12). 1977. pap. text ed. 2.65 (ISBN 0-915510-13-8). Janus Bks.
Sign Language: A Survival Vocabulary, Book D. Jim Richey. (Sign Language Ser.). (Illus.). 52p. (gr. 7-12). 1977. pap. text ed. 2.65 (ISBN 0-915510-14-6). Janus Bks.
Sign Language Among North American Indians Compared with That among Other Peoples & Deaf Mutes. (with Articles by A. L. Kroeber & C. F. Vogelin) D. Garrick Mallery. (Approaches to Semiotics Ser: No. 14). (Illus.). 552p. 1972. Repr. of 1881 ed. text ed. 40.80x (ISBN 0-686-22538-4). Mouton.
Sign Language & the Deaf Community: Essays in Honor of William Stokoe. Charlotte Baker & Robbin Battison. (Illus.). 267p. 1981. text ed. 15.00 (ISBN 0-913072-37-0); pap. text ed. 11.00 (ISBN 0-913072-36-2). Natl Assn Deaf.
Sign Language: Contemporary Southwest Native America. Mike Mitchell et al. (Illus.). xx, 80p. 1988. 30.00 (ISBN 0-89381-333-8). Aperture.
Sign Language Dot-to-Dot. new ed. Ed. by J. A. Belcher. 32p. (ps-3). 1979. 2.95 (ISBN 0-917002-40-7). Joyce Media.
Sign Language Flash Cards. Harry Hoemann & Rosemarie Lucafo. (Vol. II). (Illus.). 500p. 1983. pap. text ed. 14.95x (ISBN 0-913072-52-4). Natl Assn Deaf.
Sign Language Flash Cards, Vol. I. rev. ed. Harry W. Hoemann & Shirley A. Hoemann. (Illus.). 120p. 1988. pap. text ed. 14.95 (ISBN 0-9614621-5-9). Bowling Gr Pr.
Sign Language Flash Cards, Vol. II. Harry W. Hoemann et al. (Illus.). 120p. 1988. pap. text ed. 14.95 (ISBN 0-9614621-4-0). Bowling Gr Pr.
Sign Language for Everyone. California State Department of Health Staff & Jeanne Huffmann. LC 75-70066. (Illus.). 11.95 (ISBN 0-917002-02-4). Joyce Media.
Sign Language for Everyone: A Basic Course in Communication with the Deaf. Cathy Rice. LC 77-14592. 1978. 13.95 (ISBN 0-8407-9002-3). Nelson.
Sign Language: Fourth Most Used Language in the U. S. A. Louie J. Fant, Jr. LC 77-93544. (Illus.). 1977. pap. 19.95 (ISBN 0-917002-13-X, 159). Joyce Media.
Sign Language Interpreting: A Basic Resource Book. Sharon Newmann-Solow. (Illus.). 107p. 1981. text ed. 11.95 (ISBN 0-913072-45-1); pap. text ed. 8.95 (ISBN 0-913072-44-3). Natl Assn Deaf.
Sign Language Made Simple. Edgar D. Lawrence. LC 79-10417. (Illus.). 240p. 1975. 12.95 (ISBN 0-88243-604-X, 02-0604). Gospel Pub.
Sign Language Manual. M. Ann Boles. (Illus.). 472p. 1984. pap. 32.75x spiral (ISBN 0-398-04943-2). C C Thomas.
Sign Language of the Deaf: Psychological Linguistic & Sociological Perspectives. I. M. Schlesinger & L. Namir. (Perspectives in Neurolinguistics & Psycholinguistics Ser.). 1978. 39.95 (ISBN 0-12-625150-9). Acad Pr.
Sign Language Talk. Laura Greene & Eva B. Dicker. Ed. by Maury Solomon. (First Book Ser.). (Illus.). 96p. (gr. 5 up). 1988. 9.90 (ISBN 0-531-10597-0). Watts.
Sign Language: The Study of Deaf People & Their Language. Jim Kyle & Bencie Woll. (Illus.). 300p. 1988. pap. 16.95 (ISBN 0-521-35717-9). Cambridge U Pr.
Sign Language: The Study of Deaf People & Their Language. Jim Kyle et al. (Illus.). 300p. 1985. 54.50 (ISBN 0-521-26075-2). Cambridge U Pr.
Sign Languages of Aboriginal Australia: Cultural, Semiotic, & Communicative Perspectives. Adam Kendon. 450p. Date not set. price not set (ISBN 0-521-36008-0). Cambridge U Pr.
Sign Languages Used by Deaf People, & Psycholinguistics. 128p. (Orig.). 1986. pap. 20.00 (ISBN 9-02650-701-1). Hogrefe Intl.
Sign Numbers. Nancy Bartusch. (Illus.). 54p. (Orig.). (ps-3). 1988. pap. 5.00 (ISBN 0-916708-17-9). Modern Signs.
Sign of a Friend. Michelle Baron. Ed. by Ken Forsse & Mary Becker. (Teddy Ruxpin Adventure Ser.). (Illus.). 26p. (ps). 1986. 9.95 (ISBN 0-934323-37-2); pre-programmed audio cassette tapes incl. Alchemy Comms.
Sign of a Promise & Other Stories. James C. Schaap. 263p. (Orig.). 1979. pap. 6.95 (ISBN 0-932914-02-0). Dordt Coll Pr.
Sign of Chaos. Roger Zelazny. (Amber Ser.). 224p. 1987. 15.95 (ISBN 0-87795-926-9). Morrow.
Sign of Chaos. Roger Zelazny. (Amber Ser.: Vol. VIII). 224p. 1988. pap. 3.50 (ISBN 0-380-89637-0). Avon.
Sign of Death. Barbara Merrell. (YA) (gr. 7 up). 1981. pap. 2.50 (ISBN 0-89083-781-3). Zebra.
Sign of Her Heart. John M. Haffert. 270p. 1971. 5.95 (ISBN 0-911988-02-5); pap. 4.50 (ISBN 0-911988-03-3). AMI Pr.
Sign of Jonah in the Theology of the Evangelists & Q. Richard A. Edwards. LC 74-153931. (Studies in Biblical Theology, 2nd Ser.: No. 18). 1971. pap. text ed. 10.00x (ISBN 0-8401-3068-6). A R Allenson.
Sign of Jonas. Thomas Merton. LC 79-10283. 362p. 1979. pap. 6.95 (ISBN 0-15-682529-5, Harv). HarBraceJ.
Sign of Jonas. Thomas Merton. 362p. 1983. Repr. of 1953 ed. lib. bdg. 30.00 (ISBN 0-88254-871-9, Octagon). Hippocrene Bks.
Sign of Reconciliation & Conversion: The Sacrament of Penance for Our Times. Monika Hellwig. LC 82-80404. (Message of the Sacraments Ser.: Vol. 4). 1982. 13.95 (ISBN 0-89453-394-0); pap. 8.95 (ISBN 0-89453-272-3). M Glazier.
Sign of the Beaver. Elizabeth G. Speare. 144p. (gr. 5 up). 1983. 12.95 (ISBN 0-395-33890-5). HM.
Sign of the Beaver. Elizabeth G. Speare. 144p. (gr. 5-9). 1984. pap. 3.20 (ISBN 0-440-47900-2, YB). Dell.
Sign of the Beaver see Newbery Awards Collection.
Sign of the Chrysanthemum. Katherine Paterson. (Illus.). 132p. (gr. 6 up). 1980. pap. 2.50 (ISBN 0-380-49288-1, Camelot). Avon.
Sign of the Chrysanthemum. Katherine Paterson. LC 72-7553. (Illus.). (gr. 5-9). 1973. 12.70i (ISBN 0-690-73625-8, Crowell Jr Bks). HarpJ.
Sign of the Chrysanthemum. Katherine Paterson. LC 72-7553. (Trophy Bk.). (Illus.). 144p. (gr. 3-7). 1988. pap. 3.50 (ISBN 0-06-440232-0, Trophy). HarpJ.
Sign of the Crooked Arrow. rev ed. Franklin W. Dixon. LC 71-100119. (Hardy Boys Ser.: Vol. 28). (Illus.). (gr. 5-9). 1949. 4.50 (ISBN 0-448-08928-9, G&D); PLB 3.29 (ISBN 0-448-18928-3, Putnam). Putnam Pub Group.
Sign of the Cross. John Damascus et al. 1987. pap. 1.00 (ISBN 0-89981-200-7). Eastern Orthodox.
Sign of the Eagle. John J. Peck. Ed. by Richard F. Pourade. LC 79-123643. (Illus.). 184p. 1970. 14.50 (ISBN 0-913938-10-6). Copley Bks.
Sign of the Eighties. Gail Parent. 320p. 1987. 17.95 (ISBN 0-399-13262-7, Putnam). Putnam Pub Group.
Sign of the Eighties. Gail Parent. 1988. pap. 4.50. Jove Pubns.
Sign of the Fish. Peter Quennell. (Illus.). 255p. 1980. Repr. of 1960 ed. lib. bdg. 30.00 (ISBN 0-8492-2209-5). R West.
Sign of the Four. Arthur Conan Doyle. 160p. 1975. pap. 3.95 (ISBN 0-345-35290-4). Ballantine.
Sign of the Four. Arthur Conan Doyle. lib. bdg. 15.95x (ISBN 0-89966-230-7). Buccaneer Bks.
Sign of the Four. Arthur Conan Doyle. 1982. pap. 2.95 (ISBN 0-14-005855-9). Penguin.
Sign of the Green Falcon. Cynthia Harnett. LC 83-24831. (Cynthia Harnett's Adventure Novels Ser.). (Illus.). 288p. (gr. 5 up). 1984. 9.95 (ISBN 0-8225-0888-5). Lerner Pubns.
Sign of the Guardian. John A. Long. 256p. 1987. pap. 3.50 (ISBN 0-8125-2118-8, Dist. by St Martin's Pr & Warner Pub Servs). Tor Bks.
Sign of the Ivory Horn: Eastern African Civilizations. R. Rosenthal. LC 70-132279. (gr. 9 up). 1971. PLB 7.50 (ISBN 0-379-00449-6). Oceana.
"Sign" of the Last Days--When? Carl O. Jonsson & Wolfgang Herbst. LC 86-72140. (Illus.). 288p. 1987. pap. 7.95 (ISBN 0-914675-09-5). Comment Pr.
Sign of the Moonbow. Andrew J. Offutt. 256p. 1982. pap. 2.25 (ISBN 0-441-76353-7). Ace Bks.
Sign of the Praying Tiger. Ben L. Burman. 4.95 (ISBN 0-685-02657-4). Taplinger.
Sign of the Raven. Poul Anderson. (Last Viking Ser.: No. 3). (Orig.). 1981. pap. 2.50 (ISBN 0-686-96926-X). Zebra.
Sign of the Raven. Poul Anderson. (Last Viking Ser.: No. 2). 352p. (Orig.). 1980. pap. 2.50 (ISBN 0-89083-625-6). Zebra.
Sign of the Scorpion. LC 73-111002. 224p. 1981. pap. 2.95 (ISBN 0-394-17894-7, B-450, BC). Grove.
Sign of the Serpent. Sara Hely. 220p. 1984. 11.95 (ISBN 0-312-72426-8). St Martin.
Sign of the Server. Charles DeLuca. 1987. pap. 3.95 (ISBN 0-451-40032-1, Onyx). NAL.
Sign of the Twisted Candle. Carolyn Keene. (Illus.). 180p. (YA) (gr. 3-9). 4.50 (ISBN 0-448-09509-2). Putnam Pub Group.
Sign of the Twisted Candles. rev. ed. Carolyn Keene. (Nancy Drew Ser: Vol. 9). (Illus.). (gr. 4-7). 1959. 2.95 (G&D). Putnam Pub Group.
Sign of the Unicorn. Roger Zelazny. 192p. (YA) (gr. 9 up). 1986. pap. 2.95 (ISBN 0-380-00831-9). Avon.
Sign of the Water Bearer. Heather Buck. 1987. pap. 9.95 (ISBN 0-85646-193-8, Pub. by Anvil Pr Poetry). Longwood Pub Group.
Sign of Three: Dupin, Holmes, Peirce. Ed. by Umberto Eco & Thomas A. Sebeok. LC 82-49207. (Advances in Semiotics Ser.). (Illus.). 256p. 1984. 27.50x (ISBN 0-253-35235-5). Ind U Pr.
Sign of Three: Dupin, Holmes, Pierce. Ed. by Umberto Eco & Thomas A. Sebeok. 1988. pap. 10.95 (ISBN 0-253-20487-9). Ind U Pr.
Sign off: The Last Days of Television. Edwin Diamond. 288p. 1982. 27.50x (ISBN 0-262-04069-7); pap. 7.95 (ISBN 0-262-54039-8). MIT Pr.
Sign on Rosie's Door. Maurice Sendak. LC 60-9451. (Illus.). 48p. (gr. k-3). 1960. 10.70i (ISBN 0-06-025505-6); PLB 10.89 (ISBN 0-06-025506-4). HarpJ.
Sign on the Dotted Line: Two Hundred Years of U. S. Constitution Silly Trivia. Carole Marsh. (Triviatime Ser.). (Illus.). 48p. (Orig.). (gr. 3-9). 1986. pap. 7.95 (ISBN 0-935326-76-6). Gallopade Pub Group.
Sign Painter. Jack Rudman. (Career Examination Ser.: C-2090). (Cloth bdg. avail. on request). 1988. pap. 14.00 (ISBN 0-8373-2090-9). Natl Learning.
Sign Painter. Barbara M. Sutryn. (Living Bks.). 352p. 1985. 3.95 (ISBN 0-8423-5894-3). Tyndale.
Sign Painting & Graphics Course. Lonnie Tettaton. LC 80-12135. (Illus.). 240p. 1981. 33.95x (ISBN 0-88229-478-4); pap. 19.95x (ISBN 0-88229-768-6). Nelson-Hall.
Sign Painting Techniques: Beginner to Professional. Ralph Gregory. (Illus.). 1973. 19.95 (ISBN 0-911380-29-9). Signs of Times.
Sign Says Wet Paint. Donald E. Mansel. (Outreach Ser.). 27p. 1985. pap. 1.25 (ISBN 0-8163-0616-8). Pacific Pr Pub Assn.
Sign, Semiotics Around the World. Ed. by Bailey & Matejka. (Michigan Slavic Contributions Ser.: No. 9). 1980. 10.00 (ISBN 0-930042-28-X). Mich Slavic Pubns.
Sign: Semiotics Around the World. Ed. by R. W. Bailey et al. (Michigan Slavic Contributions Ser.: No. 9). 1980. 10.00 (ISBN 0-930042-39-5). Mich Slavic Pubns.
Sign, Sentence, Discourse: Language in Medieval Thought & Literature. Ed. by Julian N. Wasserman & Lois Roney. 352p. 1988. 39.95x (ISBN 0-8156-2445-X); pap. 18.95x (ISBN 0-8156-2451-4). Syracuse U Pr.
Sign Structures & Foundations: A Guide for Designers & Estimators. Peter Horsley. (Illus.). 1984. 33.95 (ISBN 0-911380-65-5). Signs of Times.
Sign, System & Function: Papers of the First & Second Polish-American Semiotics Colloquia. Ed. by Jerzy Peic et al. LC 84-3288. (Approaches to Semiotics Ser.: No. 67). xiii, 503p. 1984. 84.95x (ISBN 90-279-3270-0). Mouton.
Sign System for Libraries. Mary S. Mallery & Ralph E. DeVore. LC 82-11612. 40p. 1982. pap. 5.00x (ISBN 0-8389-0377-0). ALA.
Sign User-s Guide: A Marketing Aid. rev. ed. James R. Claus & Karen Claus. Ed. by William Dorsey. LC 88-201992. (Illus.). 256p. 1988. text ed. 39.95 (ISBN 0-911380-83-3, 92). Signs of Times.
Sign Writing for Everyday Use. Valerie J. Sutton. (Illus.). 450p. 1981. pap. text ed. 20.00x (ISBN 0-914336-51-7). Ctr Sutton Movement.
Sign Writing Shorthand for Sign Language Stenography. Valerie Sutton. 1982. text ed. 15.00x (ISBN 0-914336-52-5). Ctr Sutton Movement.
Signage. Alan Davies. LC 87-60108. (Roof Bks.). 150p. (Orig.). 1987. pap. 10.95 (ISBN 0-937804-24-X). Segue NYC.
Signage: Communication Standards. Charles McLendon & Mick Blackistone. (Illus.). 192p. 1982. text ed. 46.00 (ISBN 0-07-005740-0). McGraw.
Signal: Access to Communication Tools & Information Frontiers. Ed. by Kevin Kelly. (Whole Earth Catalog Ser.). (Illus.). 1988. 16.95 (ISBN 0-517-57084-X, Harmony). Crown.
Signal Analysis. Athanasios Papoulis. 1977. text ed. 52.95 (ISBN 0-07-048460-0). McGraw.
Signal Analysis & Estimation. Ronald Fante. LC 87-21707. 1987. 39.95 (ISBN 0-471-62425-X). Wiley.
Signal Analysis & Pattern Recognition in Biomedical Engineering. Ed. by G. F. Inbar. 324p. 1975. text ed. 56.00x (ISBN 0-7065-1465-3, Pub. by Keter Pub Jerusalem). Coronet Bks.
Signal, & Other Stories. facsimile ed. Wsewolod M. Garshin. Tr. by Rowland Smith from Rus. LC 77-163027. (Short Story Index Reprint Ser.). Repr. of 1915 ed. 21.00 (ISBN 0-8369-3941-7). Ayer Co Pubs.
Signal Approach to Children's Books. Ed. by Nancy Chambers. LC 81-8824. 352p. 1981. 19.00 (ISBN 0-8108-1447-1). Scarecrow.
Signal Book: Cues & Signals in Broadcasting & Film. Desi K. Bognar. (Illus.). 96p. 1988. price not set. Media Forum.
Signal Coding & Processing: An Introduction Based on Video Systems. J. G. Wade. (Electrical & Electronic Engineering). 256p. 1987. 37.95 (ISBN 0-470-20778-7). Halsted Pr.
Signal Corps, U. S. A. in the War of the Rebellion. Willard J. Brown. LC 74-4670. (Telecommunications Ser). (Illus.). 916p. 1974. Repr. of 1896 ed. 57.50x (ISBN 0-405-06036-X). Ayer Co Pubs.
Signal Detection & ROC-Analysis. James P. Egan. (Academic Press Ser. in Cognition & Perception). 1975. 27.50 (ISBN 0-12-232850-7). Acad Pr.
Signal Detection in Non-Gaussian Noise. S. A. Kassam. (Illus.). ix, 234p. 1988. 48.00 (ISBN 0-387-96680-3). Springer-Verlag.
Signal Driver. Patrick White. (Illus.). 60p. (Orig.). pap. 7.95 (ISBN 0-936839-47-3). Applause Theatre Bk Pubs.
Signal Electrician. Jack Rudman. (Career Examination Ser.: C-2440). (Cloth bdg. avail. on request). pap. 16.00 (ISBN 0-8373-2440-8). Natl Learning.
Signal from Space. Will Eisner. Ed. by Denis Kitchen. (Illus.). 136p. 1983. pap. 6.95 (ISBN 0-317-00648-7). Kitchen Sink.
Signal from Space. Pamale. 1987. 12.95 (ISBN 0-533-07009-0). Vantage.
Signal Lives Series, 51 bks. Ed. by Annette K. Baxter. 1980. Set. lib. bdg. 1889.50x (ISBN 0-405-12815-0). Ayer Co Pubs.
Signal Maintainer. Jack Rudman. (Career Examination Ser.: C-742). (Cloth bdg. avail. on request). pap. 14.00 (ISBN 0-8373-0742-2). Natl Learning.
Signal Message. John Moffitt. 1982. 5.50 (ISBN 0-8233-0346-2). Golden Quill.
Signal Noise. Miriam Goodman. LC 82-71819. 64p. 1982. 14.95 (ISBN 0-914086-40-5); pap. 7.95 (ISBN 0-914086-39-1). Alicejamesbooks.
Signal Processing. Ed. by J. L. Lacoume et al. 900p. 1987. 202.00 (ISBN 0-444-87027-X, North Holland). Elsevier.
Signal Processing, Pt. 1. J. L. Lacoume & R. Stora. (Les Houches Summer School Processing Ser.: Vol. 45, No. 1). 1987. 105.00 (ISBN 0-444-87058-X). Elsevier.
Signal Processing, Pt. 2. J. L. Lacoume & R. Stora. (Les Houches Summer School Processing Ser.: Vol. 45, No. 2). 1987. 117.00 (ISBN 0-444-87059-8). Elsevier.
Signal Processing Algorithms. Samuel D. Stearns & Ruth A. David. (Illus.). 288p. 1987. text ed. 46.00 (ISBN 0-13-809435-7). P-H.
Signal Processing & Pattern Recognition in Nondestructive Evaluation of Materials. Ed. by C. H. Chen. (NATO ASI Series F: Vol. 44). viii, 344p. 1988. 79.50 (ISBN 0-387-19100-3). Springer-Verlag.
Signal Processing Design Techniques. Britt Rorabaugh. (Illus.). 304p. 1986. 32.50 (ISBN 0-8306-0457-X, NO. 2657, TAP-TPR). TAB Bks.
Signal Processing: Discrete Spectral Analysis, Detection & Estimation. Mischa Schwartz & L. Shaw. 1975. text ed. 52.95 (ISBN 0-07-055662-8). McGraw.
Signal Processing for Control. Ed. by K. Godfrey & P. Jones. (Lecture Notes in Control & Information Sciences Ser.: Vol. 79). xviii, 420p. 1986. pap. 31.40 (ISBN 0-387-16511-8). Springer-Verlag.
Signal Processing Handbook. Chen. (Electrical Engineering & Electronics Ser.). 840p. 1988. 125.00 (ISBN 0-8247-7956-8). Dekker.
Signal Processing II - Theories & Applications: Proceedings of the EUSIPCO-83 Second European Signal Processing Conference. Erlangen, W. Germany, Sept. 12-16, 1983. Ed. by H. W. Schussler. 866p. 1984. 118.50 (ISBN 0-444-86743-0, North Holland). Elsevier.
Signal Processing III: Theories & Applications. Ed. by I. T. Young et al. 1420p. 1986. 200.00 (ISBN 0-317-53577-3, North-Holland). Elsevier.
Signal Processing Market Opportunities. 139p. 1985. 1650.00x (ISBN 0-88694-678-6). Intl Res Dev.
Signal Processing: Model Based Approach. J. V. Candy. 256p. 1985. text ed. 48.95 (ISBN 0-07-009725-9). McGraw.
Signal Processing: Principles & Applications. D. Brook & R. J. Wynne. (Illus.). 288p. 1988. pap. text ed. 19.95 (ISBN 0-7131-3564-6, Pub. by E Arnold UK). Routledge Chapman & Hall.
Signal Processing Signals, Filtering & Detection. N. Mohanty. 1987. 59.95 (ISBN 0-442-26476-3). Van Nos Reinhold.
Signal Processing: Theories & Applications. Ed. by M. Kunt & F. De Coulon. 798p. 1980. 144.75 (ISBN 0-444-86050-9, North-Holland). Elsevier.
Signal Processor Chips. David Quarmby. 192p. 1985. 24.95 (ISBN 0-13-809450-0); pap. 14.95 (ISBN 0-13-809443-8). P H.
Signal Recovery from Noise in Electronic Instrumentation. T. H. Wilmshurst. 200p. 1985. 53.00x (ISBN 0-85274-783-7, Pub. by A Hilger UK). Taylor & Francis.
Signal Routing in Integrated Circuit Layout. Chi-Ping Hsu. Ed. by Harold Stone. LC 86-1382. (Computer Science: Very Large Systems Integration: No. 1). 126p. 1986. 44.95 (ISBN 0-8357-1744-5). UMI Res Pr.

Signal Theory & Processing. Frederic De Coulon. 550p. 1986. text ed. 75.00 (ISBN 0-89006-185-8). Artech Hse.

Signal Theory & Random Processes. Harry Urkowitz. LC 83-70360. (Radar Ser.). (Illus.). 715p. 1983. 79.00 (ISBN 0-89006-121-1). Artech Hse.

Signal Through the Flames: Mitch Snyder & America's Homeless. Victoria Rader. LC 86-61655. 272p. (Orig.). 1986. pap. 10.95 (ISBN 0-934134-24-3). Sheed & Ward MO.

Signal Transduction & Protein Phosphorylation. Ed. by L. M. Heilmeyer. LC 87-15398. (NATO ASI Series A, Life Sciences: Vol. 135). (Illus.). 410p. 1987. 75.00x (ISBN 0-306-42615-3, Plenum Pr). Plenum Pub.

Signal Was Spain: The British Aid Spain Movement, 1936-1939. Jim Fryth. LC 86-26200. 340p. 1987. 32.50 (ISBN 0-312-00405-2). St Martin.

Signaling. (Illus.). 32p. (gr. 6-12). 1974. pap. 1.25x (ISBN 0-8395-3237-7, 3237). BSA.

Signaling & Communicating at Sea: An Original Anthology. Ed. by David L. Woods & Christopher Sterling. LC 80-484. (Historical Studies in Telecommunications Ser.). (Illus.). 1981. lib. bdg. 73.00x (ISBN 0-405-13195-X). Ayer Co Pubs.

Signaling & Communicating at Sea, Vol. 1. David L. Woods. 1980. 36.50 (ISBN 0-405-13196-8). Ayer Co Pubs.

Signalled Love. D. W. Hartnett. 64p. (Orig.). 1985. pap. 7.95 (ISBN 0-85646-144-X, Pub. by Anvil Pr Poetry). Longwood Pub Group.

Signalling in Telecommunications Networks. rev. ed. S. Welch. (Illus.). 392p. 1981. pap. 43.00 (ISBN 0-906048-46-X, TEP06). Inst Elect Eng.

Signalling Through Space Without Wires: Being a Description of the Work of Hertz & His Successors. 3rd ed. Oliver J. Lodge. LC 74-9688. (Telecommunications Ser.). (Illus.). 138p. 1974. 14.00x (ISBN 0-405-06051-3). Ayer Co Pubs.

Signalman. Charles Dickens. LC 81-19819. (Illus.). 32p. (gr. 5-10). 1982. PLB 9.79 (ISBN 0-89375-630-X); pap. text ed. 2.50 (ISBN 0-89375-631-8). Troll Assocs.

Signalman & Other Ghost Stories. Charles Dickens. 138p. (Orig.). 1988. pap. 3.95 (ISBN 0-89733-307-1). Academy Chi Pubs.

Signals. Ed. by Jean Keenan & Vonnie Crist. (Illus.). 4.95 (ISBN 0-317-06434-7). New Poets.

Signals. Allan Pease. (Orig.). 1984. pap. 7.95 (ISBN 0-553-34019-0). Bantam.

Signals. Allan Pease. 1984. pap. 7.95 (ISBN 0-553-34366-1). Bantam.

Signals: A Grammar & Guide for Writers. Evelyn Farbman. LC 84-81970. 384p. 1985. pap. text ed. 23.56 (ISBN 0-395-36989-4); instructor's manual 2.36 (ISBN 0-395-37010-8). HM.

Signals & Circuits. S. I. Basakov. 518p. 1986. 14.95 (ISBN 0-8285-3434-9, Pub. by Mir Pubs USSR). Imported Pubns.

Signals & Linear Systems. 3rd ed. Robert A. Gabel & Richard A. Roberts. LC 86-7748. 576p. 1986. write for info. (ISBN 0-471-82513-1). Wiley.

Signals & Systems. B. P. Lathi. LC 86-72954. 531p. 1987. text ed. 44.95 (ISBN 0-941413-33-0). Berkeley-Cambridge.

Signals & Systems. Meade & Dillon. 1986. pap. 19.95 (ISBN 0-442-30633-4). Van Nos Reinhold.

Signals & Systems. Alan V. Oppenheim et al. (Illus.). 464p. 1982. 52.00 (ISBN 0-13-809731-3). P-H.

Signals & Systems: Continuous & Discrete. 1st ed. Rodger Ziemer et al. 624p. 1983. write for info. (ISBN 0-02-431650-4). Macmillan.

Signals & Systems: Continuous & Discrete. 2nd ed. Rodger E. Ziemer, Jr. et al. 279p. 1989. text ed. price not set (ISBN 0-02-431630-X). Macmillan.

Signals From the Flames. Jose E. Pacheco. Ed. by Yvette E. Miller. Tr. by Thomas Hoeksema from Span. LC 80-19979. (Discoveries Ser.). 97p. (Orig.). 1980. pap. 8.50 (ISBN 0-935480-03-X). Lat Am Lit Rev Pr.

Signals, Systems, & the Computer. Paul Chirlian. 615p. 1986. text ed. 42.95 (ISBN 0-938862-81-2). Weber Systems.

Signals, Systems & Transforms. James Cadzow & Hugh Van Landingham. (Illus.). 384p. 1985. text ed. 51.00 (ISBN 0-13-809542-6). P-H.

Signals to the Blind. Danny L. Rendleman. LC 72-19183. 50p. 1972. 2.95 (ISBN 0-87886-015-0). Greenfld Rev Pr.

Signals: What Your Child Is Really Telling You. Paul Ackerman & Murray Kappelman. 1980. pap. 3.95 (ISBN 0-451-12186-4, AE2186, Sig). NAL.

Signaturas Librísticas: Normas para Su Aplicacion en Bibliotecas de Habla. Donald J. Lehnus. (Serie Bibliotecologica). 35p. 1975. pap. text ed. 1.85 (ISBN 0-8477-0903-5). U of PR Pr.

Signature Book of Netsuke, Inro & Ojime Artists in Photographs. George Lazarnick. LC 76-9504. (Illus.). 1976. 85.00 (ISBN 0-917064-01-1). Reed Pubs HI.

Signature in Time: Contemporary Samplers in Stitch. Vanessa-Ann Collection Staff. LC 86-63721. (Illus.). 168p. 1987. 19.95 (ISBN 0-02-496790-4, Pub. by Sedgewood Pr). Macmillan.

Signature Knits: A Designer's Portfolio of Projects, Patterns & Techniques to Create Your Own Classics. Glenora K. Smith. (Illus.). 160p. 1986. 24.95 (ISBN 0-684-18473-7, ScribT). Scribner.

Signature Loans by Mail Broker Success Kit. Tyler G. Hicks. 176p. 1987. pap. 100.00 (ISBN 0-934311-24-2). Intl Wealth.

Signature: New & Selected Poems. Bonaro W. Overstreet. 1978. 9.95 (ISBN 0-393-04504-8); pap. 3.95 (ISBN 0-393-04511-0). Norton.

Signature of All Things: & Other Writings. Jacob Boehme. 307p. 1969. pap. 15.95 (ISBN 0-227-67733-1). Attic Pr.

Signature of God. Dr. Velma Ruch. 1986. pap. 25.00 (ISBN 0-8309-0428-X). Herald Hse.

Signature of God: A Positive Identification of Christ & His Prophets by Computer Wordprints. Robert L. Hamson. LC 81-51809. (Illus.). 111p. 1982. 8.95 (ISBN 0-940356-01-5). Sandpiper CA.

Signature of Jesus. Brennan Manning. 192p. 1988. 8.95 (ISBN 0-8007-9128-2). Revell.

Signature of Power: Buildings, Communication, & Policy. Harold D. Lasswell. 224p. 1978. text ed. 34.95 (ISBN 0-87855-289-8). Transaction Bks.

Signature of the Spiral. Daniel W. Schreck. LC 87-16469. 64p. (Orig.). 1988. pap. 6.95 (ISBN 0-86534-114-1). Sunstone Pr.

Signature One: A Graphic Annual. Mohawk Valley Community College, Advertising Design Department. Ed. by Michael Cavallaro & Pamela Schriber. (Illus.). 32p. 1983. pap. 7.95 (ISBN 0-86610-126-8). Meridian Pub.

Signature Pieces: On the Institution of Authorship. Peggy Kamuf. LC 88-47731. 256p. 1988. 27.95x. Cornell U Pr.

Signatures. Joseph Stroud. (American Poets Continuum Ser.: No. 8). 72p. 1982. 12.95 (ISBN 0-918526-38-8); pap. 6.95 (ISBN 0-918526-39-6). Boa Edns.

Signatures in the First-Journal Book and the Charter-Book of the Royal Society. (Illus.). 192p. 1980. lib. bdg. 139.50x (ISBN 0-85403-115-4, Pub by Royal Soc London). Scholium Intl.

Signboards of Old London Shops. Ambrose Heal. LC 76-174401. (Illus.). 1973. Repr. of 1947 ed. lib. bdg. 18.00 (ISBN 0-405-08608-3, Blom Pubns). Ayer Co Pubs.

Signe Ascendant. Andre Breton. Bd. with Fata Morgana; Etats-generaux; Des epingles tremblantes; Xenophile; Ode a Charles Fourier; Constellation; Le la. (Poesie Ser.). pap. 7.95 (ISBN 0-685-37239-1). Schoenhof.

Signed & Posted. 4th, rev. & enl. ed. A. E. Tomkin. LC 79-84855. 88p. 1980. 11.95 (ISBN 0-8022-2352-4). Philos Lib.

Signed English for the Classroom. Harry Bornstein. LC 75-2974. (Signed English Ser.). 74p. 1979. pap. 6.00 (ISBN 0-913580-37-6, Clerc Bks). Gallaudet Univ Pr.

Signed English for the Residence Hall. Harry Bornstein. (Signed English Ser.). 107p. 1979. pap. 7.00 (ISBN 0-913580-61-9, Clerc Bks). Gallaudet Univ Pr.

Signed English Schoolbook: Signed English Ser. Ed. by Harry Bornstein & Karen L. Saulnier. LC 87-15042. (Illus.). 184p. 1987. pap. text ed. 13.95 (ISBN 0-930323-30-0, Clerc Bks). Gallaudet Univ Pr.

Signed English Starter. Harry Bornstein & Karen L. Saulnier. LC 84-4042. (Signed English Ser.). (Illus.). xxii, 208p. (ps-6). 1984. pap. text ed. 13.95 (ISBN 0-913580-82-1, Clerc Bks). Gallaudet Univ Pr.

Signed Numbers: Level Three Texts. rev. ed. (Math Components Ser.). 48p. 1983. 3.50 (ISBN 0-88336-830-7). New Readers.

Signed, Sealed, Delivered: True Life Stories of Women in Pop. Sue Steward & Sheryl Garratt. (Orig.). 1984. 20.00 (ISBN 0-89608-241-5); pap. 8.00 (ISBN 0-89608-240-7). South End Pr.

Signed with Their Honor: Air Chivalry During the Two World Wars. Hiet H. Meijering. (Illus.). 185p. 1988. 18.95 (ISBN 1-55778-116-8). Paragon Hse.

Signed with Their Honour: The Story of Chivalry in Air Warfare, 1914-1945. Piet H. Meijering. 192p. 1987. 65.00x (ISBN 1-85158-063-8, Pub. by Mainstream Scotland). State Mutual Bk.

Signeponge-Signsponge. Jacques Derrida. Tr. by Richard Rand from Fr. 1984. 27.00x (ISBN 0-231-05446-7); pap. 14.00 (ISBN 0-231-05447-5). Columbia U Pr.

Signers of the Constitution. Robert G. Ferris & James H. Charleton. LC 86-81140. (Illus.). 280p. (Orig.). 1986. pap. 8.95 (ISBN 0-936478-10-1). Interpretive Pubns.

Signers of the Constitution. C. Edward Quinn. (Illus.). 112p. 1986. pap. 9.95 (ISBN 0-941980-18-9). Bronx County.

Signers of the Declaration of Independence. Robert G. Ferris & Richard E. Morris. LC 82-82219. (Illus.). 180p. 1982. pap. 6.95 (ISBN 0-936478-07-1). Interpretive Pubns.

Signes et les Prodiges. Francoise Mallet-Joris. 416p. 1966. 12.50 (ISBN 0-686-56315-8); pap. 3.95 (ISBN 0-686-56316-6). French & Eur.

Signes et Paraboles see Signs & Parables: Semiotics & Gospel Texts.

Signet Book of American Wine. 3rd rev. ed. Peter Quimme. 1980. pap. 2.50 (ISBN 0-451-09178-7, E9178, Sig). NAL.

Signet Classic Book of American Short Stories. Ed. & intro. by Burton Raffel. 1985. pap. 4.95 (ISBN 0-451-52152-8, Sig Classics). NAL.

Signet Classic Book of British Short Stories. Frederick A. Karl. 1985. pap. 4.95 (ISBN 0-451-51948-5, Sig Classics). NAL.

Signet Classic Book of Contemporary American Short Stories. Ed. by Burton Raffel. 1986. pap. 4.95 (ISBN 0-451-51997-3, Sig Classics). Nal.

Signet Classic Book of Eighteenth & Nineteenth Century British Drama. Ed. by Katherine Rogers. (Orig.). 1979. pap. 2.95 (ISBN 0-451-51265-0, CE1265, Sig Classics). NAL.

Signet Classic Book of Mark Twain's Stories. Intro. by Justin Kaplan. 1985. pap. 3.95 (ISBN 0-451-51960-4, Sig Classics). NAL.

Signet Classic Book of Restoration Drama. Ronald Berman. 1980. pap. 3.95 (ISBN 0-451-51402-5, CE1402, Sig Cl). NAL.

Signet Encyclopedia of Wine. E. Frank Henriques. (Orig.). 1975. pap. 4.95 (ISBN 0-451-13211-4, Sig). NAL.

Signet Encyclopedia of Wine. E. Frank Henriques. 1985. pap. 8.95 (ISBN 0-452-25669-0, Plume). NAL.

Signet-Hammond World Atlas. rev. ed. 272p. 1982. pap. 4.50 (ISBN 0-451-12793-5, AE2793, Sig). NAL.

Signet Handbook of Parapsychology. Ed. by Martin Ebon. 528p. (Orig.). 1988. pap. 4.95 (ISBN 0-451-15478-9, Sig). NAL.

Signet Hebrew-English - English-Hebrew Dictionary. Dov Ben Abba. (Orig., Hebrew & Eng.). 1978. pap. 4.95 (ISBN 0-451-14202-0, Sig). NAL.

Signet-Mosby Medical Encyclopedia. C. V. Mosby Company Staff. 704p. 1987. pap. 5.95 (ISBN 0-451-15059-7, Sig). NAL.

Signifcant Name in Terence. James C. Austin. pap. 9.00 (ISBN 0-384-02605-2). Johnson Repr.

Significance & Impact of Gregorio Maranon. Gary D. Keller. LC 76-45295. 1977. lib. bdg. 24.00x (ISBN 0-916950-04-2); pap. 12.00x (ISBN 0-916950-18-2). Biling Rev-Pr.

Significance & Impact of Nuclear Research in Developing Countries: Proceedings of a Symposium Athens, 8-12 September 1986. (Proceedings Ser.). (Illus.). 371p. (Orig.). 1987. pap. text ed. 75.00 (ISBN 92-0-070087-X, ISP720, IAEA). UNIPUB.

Significance of Anthony Trollope. Spencer Nichols. LC 76-27335. 1925. lib. bdg. 16.50 (ISBN 0-8414-6293-3). Folcroft.

Significance of Anthony Trollope. Spencer V. Nichols. 1977. lib. bdg. 59.95 (ISBN 0-8490-2604-0). Gordon Pr.

Significance of Art: A Phenomenological Approach to Aesthetics. Moritz Geiger. Ed. by Klaus Berger. LC 86-13250. (Current Continental Research Ser.: No. 402). 238p. (Orig.). 1987. lib. bdg. 24.75 (ISBN 0-8191-5484-9, Pub. by Ctr Adv Res); pap. text ed. 12.75 (ISBN 0-8191-5485-7). U Pr of Amer.

Significance of ASTM Tests for Petroleum Products - STP-7C. 216p. 1977. pap. 11.75 (ISBN 0-8031-0567-3, 04-007030-12). ASTM.

Significance of ASTM Tests for Petroleum Products-STP-7. 216p. 1977. pap. 11.75 (ISBN 0-8031-0767-6, 04-007030-12). ASTM.

Significance of Children's Play. Joan E. Cass. 1977. 15.95 (ISBN 0-7134-0689-5, Pub. by Batsford England). David & Charles.

Significance of City Incorporation of Unincorporated Areas. (Technical Topics: No. 12). 1979. 2.00 (ISBN 0-318-02026-2). MI Municipal.

Significance of Defects in Welded Structures: Proceedings of the Japan-U. S. Seminar, 1973, Tokyo. Ed. by Takeshi Kanazawa & A. S. Kobayashi. 413p. 1974. 47.50 (ISBN 0-86008-114-1, Pub. by U of Tokyo Japan). Columbia U Pr.

Significance of English Place-Names. K. Cameron. (Sir Israel Gollancz Memorial Lectures in Old English). 1976. pap. 5.50 (ISBN 0-85672-267-7, Pub. by British Acad). Longwood Pub Group.

Significance of Flesh. Joseph P. Clancy. 159p. 1985. 29.00x (ISBN 0-86383-061-7, Pub. by Gomer Pr). State Mutual Bk.

Significance of Jesus. Joyce Marie Smith. 1976. pap. 2.95 (ISBN 0-8423-5887-0). Tyndale.

Significance of Mary. Agnes Cunningham. 1988. 9.95 (ISBN 0-88347-226-0). Thomas More.

Significance of Mineralogy in the Development of Flow Sheets for Processing Uranium Ores. (Technical Reports Ser.: No. 196). (Illus.). 276p. 1980. pap. 44.00 (ISBN 92-0-145080-X, IDC196, IAEA). UNIPUB.

Significance of Names. Leopold Wagner. 1893. Repr. 35.00 (ISBN 0-8274-3412-X). R West.

Significance of Neoplatonism. Ed. by R. Baine Harris. LC 76-21254. 370p. 1976. 34.50x (ISBN 0-87395-800-4). State U NY Pr.

Significance of Organizational Conflict on the Legislative Evolution of the Accounting Profession in the United States. Myron S. Lubell. Ed. by Richard P. Brief. LC 80-1515. (Dimensions of Accounting Theory & Practice Ser.). 1981. lib. bdg. 45.00x (ISBN 0-405-13494-0). Ayer Co Pubs.

Significance of Philosophical Scepticism. Barry Stroud. 294p. 1984. 27.50x (ISBN 0-19-824730-3); pap. 11.95x (ISBN 0-19-824761-3). Oxford U Pr.

Significance of Psychoanalysis for the Mental Sciences. Otto Rank & Hans Sachs. Tr. by Charles R. Payne. (Nervous & Mental Disease Monographs: No. 23). Repr. of 1916 ed. 19.00 (ISBN 0-384-49580-X). Johnson Repr.

Significance of Satan: New Testament Demonology & Its Contemporary Relevance. Trevor O. Ling. LC 79-8110. (Satanism Ser.). 120p. 1985. Repr. of 1961 ed. 21.50 (ISBN 0-404-18424-3). AMS Pr.

Significance of Sense: Meaning, Modality, & Morality. Roger Wertheimer. Ed. by Max Black. LC 70-162541. (Contemporary Philosophy Ser.). 232p. 1971. 28.95x (ISBN 0-8014-0672-2). Cornell U Pr.

Significance of Shakespeare. Felix E. Schelling. LC 77-8416. 1929. lib. bdg. 20.00 (ISBN 0-8414-7658-6). Folcroft.

Significance of Silence. Arnold T. Olson. LC 80-70698. (Heritage Ser.: Vol. 2). 208p. 1981. 8.95 (ISBN 0-911802-49-5). Free Church Pubns.

Significance of Sinclair Lewis. Stuart P. Sherman. LC 73-16169. 1922. lib. bdg. 20.00 (ISBN 0-8414-7693-4). Folcroft.

Significance of Spinoza's First Kind of Knowledge. C. E. Duegd. 291p. 1966. text ed. 38.50x (ISBN 90-232-0449-2, Pub. by Van Gorcum Holland). Coronet Bks.

Significance of Spiritual Research for Moral Action. Rudolf Steiner. Tr. by Alan P. Cottrell from Ger. 17p. 1981. pap. 2.95 (ISBN 0-88010-101-6). Anthroposophic.

Significance of Territory. Jean Gottmann. LC 72-87807. (Page-Barbour Lecture Ser). (Illus.). 169p. 1973. 16.95x (ISBN 0-8139-0413-7). U Pr of Va.

Significance of Tests & Properties of Concrete & Concrete-Making Materials- STP 169B. 882p. 1978. 65.00x (ISBN 0-8031-0612-2, 04-169020-07). ASTM.

Significance of the Bible for the Church. Anders Nygren. Ed. by John Reumann. Tr. by Carl C. Rasmusen. LC 63-17879. (Facet Bks.). 56p. (Orig.). 1963. pap. 2.50 (ISBN 0-8006-3000-9). Fortress.

Significance of the Christian Woman's Veiling. Merle Ruth. 1980. 1.95 (ISBN 0-686-30769-0). Rod & Staff.

Significance of the Church. Robert M. Brown. LC 56-6172. (Layman's Theological Library). 96p. 1956. pap. 2.45 (ISBN 0-664-24001-1). Westminster John Knox.

Significance of the Father: Four Papers from the FSAA Biennial Meeting, Washington, D.C., April, 1959. Family Service Association of America Staff. pap. 20.00 (ISBN 0-317-10308-3, 2007668). Bks Demand UMI.

Significance of the Frontier in American History. Frederick J. Turner. Ed. by Harold P. Simonson. LC 63-12915. (Milestones of Thought Ser). pap. 4.95x (ISBN 0-8044-6919-9). Ungar.

Significance of the Frontier in American History. Frederick J. Turner. 148p. 1984. 75.00 (ISBN 0-318-03521-9). Silver Buckle Pr.

Significance of the Physical Constitution in Mental Disease: Medicine Monographs, Vol. X. F. I. Wertheimer & Florence E. Hesketh. Ed. by Gerald N. Grob. LC 78-22594. (Historical Issues in Mental Health Ser.). (Illus.). 1979. Repr. of 1926 ed. lib. bdg. 12.00x (ISBN 0-405-11944-5). Ayer Co Pubs.

Significance of the Ring & the Book. Roy S. Stowell. LC 77-21914. 1977. lib. bdg. 19.50 (ISBN 0-8414-7702-7). Folcroft.

Significance of the Women's Movement to Marketing. Alladi Venkatesh. LC 85-19106. 224p. 1985. 35.00 (ISBN 0-275-90232-3, C0232). Praeger.

Significance of the Young Child's Motor Development. Ed. by Georgianna Engstrom. LC 70-177238. 55p. (Orig.). 1971. pap. text ed. 3.50 (ISBN 0-912674-32-6, NAEYC #128). Natl Assn Child Ed.

Significance of Various Kinds of Preparation for the City-Elementary School Principalship in Pennsylvania with Implications for a Program for Preparing for the Elementary-School Principalship in. Marion E. Macdonald. LC 77-177020. (Columbia University. Teachers College. Contributions to Education: No. 416). Repr. of 1930 ed. 22.50 (ISBN 0-404-55416-4). AMS Pr.

Significance of Zoochromes. A. E. Needham. (Zoophysiology & Ecology Ser.: Vol. 3). (Illus.). 300p. 1974. 47.50 (ISBN 0-387-06331-5). Springer-Verlag.

Significance Test Controversy: A Reader. Ed. by Denton E. Morrison & Ramon E. Henkel. LC 77-10952. 347p. 1970. text ed. 39.95x (ISBN 0-202-30068-4). Aldine de Gruyter.

Significant Aspects of Early Chinese Ceramic Arts. Sieur Tzen. (Illus.). 102p. (Orig.). 1982. pap. 20.00. China Hse Arts.

Significant Aspects of Early Chinese Ceramic Arts. Sieur Tzen. 100p. 1982. 50.00x (ISBN 0-317-45239-8, Pub. by Han-Shan Tang Ltd). State Mutual Bk.

Significant Decisions of the Supreme Court: 1976-1977 Term. Bruce E. Fein. 168p. 1978. pap. 11.00 (ISBN 0-8447-3289-3). Am Enterprise.

Significant Decisions of the Supreme Court: 1978-1979 Term. Bruce E. Fein. 199p. 1980. pap. 11.00 (ISBN 0-8447-3387-3). Am Enterprise.

Significant Decisions of the Supreme Court, 1979-1980 Term. Bruce E. Fein. 248p. (Orig.). 1985. pap. 22.50x (ISBN 0-317-19290-6). Rothman.
Significant Decisions of the Supreme Court, 1980-1981 Term. Paul B. Stephan, III. 108p. (Orig.). 1985. pap. 15.00x (ISBN 0-8377-1136-3). Rothman.
Significant Decisions of the Supreme Court: 1977-78 Term. Bruce E. Fein. 162p. 1979. 9.00 (ISBN 0-8447-3360-1). Am Enterprise.
Significant Decisions of the Supreme Court, 1971-72 Term. Bruce E. Fein. 65p. 1972. pap. 6.00 (ISBN 0-8447-1072-5). Am Enterprise.
Significant Decisions of the Supreme Court: 1975-76 Term. Bruce E. Fein. 198p. 1977. pap. 11.00 (ISBN 0-8447-3283-4). Am Enterprise.
Significant Developments in Continuing Higher Education. A. A. Liverwright & Freda H. Goldmann. 1965. 2.50 (ISBN 0-87060-016-8, OCP 12). Syracuse U Cont Ed.
Significant Developments in Engineering Practice & Research. Ed. by Mete A. Sozen. LC 81-69911. (SP-72). 425p. (Orig.). 1981. pap. 55.75 (ISBN 0-686-95236-7). ACI.
Significant Irish Educationalist. Seamus O'Buachalla. 415p. 1977. 25.00 (ISBN 0-85342-569-8, Pub. by Mercier Pr Ireland). Irish Bks Media.
Significant Others. Armistead Maupin. LC 86-46088. 192p. (Orig.). 1987. pap. 9.95 (ISBN 0-06-096126-0, PL 6126, PL). Har-Row.
Significant Others. Armistead Maupin. 1987. 18.95 (ISBN 0-06-055086-4). Har-Row.
Significant Phased Array Papers. Ed. by R. C. Hansen. LC 73-81240. (Artech Radar Library). (Illus.). 288p. 1973. pap. 15.00 (ISBN 0-89006-019-3). Artech Hse.
Significant Philosophies & Readings from India. R. N. Vyas. 248p. 1979. 19.50 (ISBN 0-89684-257-6, Pub. by Asian Pubn India). Orient Bk Dist.
Significant Sisters: The Grassroots of Active Feminism, 1839-1939. Margaret Forster. LC 84-48536. (Illus.). 368p. 1985. 17.45 (ISBN 0-394-54153-7). Knopf.
Significant Sisters: The Grassroots of Active Feminism, 1839-1939. Margaret Forster. (Illus.). 368p. 1986. pap. 9.95 (ISBN 0-19-504014-7). Oxford U Pr.
Significantly Improving Instruction. 96p. 1984. 3.00 (ISBN 0-317-36796-X, 611-84320). Assn Supervision.
Signification & Significance: A Study of the Relations of Signs & Values. Charles Morris. 1964. pap. 9.95x (ISBN 0-262-63014-1). MIT Pr.
Significations: Signs, Symbols & Images in the Interpretation of Religion. Charles H. Long. LC 85-45495. 208p. 1986. pap. 12.95 (ISBN 0-8006-1892-0, 1-1892). Fortress.
Significs & Language. Victoria L. Welby. LC 84-28456. (Foundation of Semiotics Ser.: No. 5). cclxvii, 220p. 1985. 58.00x (ISBN 90-272-3275-X). Benjamins North Am.
Significs & Language: The Articulate Form of Our Expressive & Interpretative Resources. V. Welby. 105p. 1981. Repr. of 1911 ed. lib. bdg. 30.00 (ISBN 0-89984-507-X). Century Bookbindery.
Signifier & the Signified. Noske. 1977. lib. bdg. 55.00 (ISBN 90-247-1995-X, Pub. by Martinus Nijhoff Netherlands). Kluwer Academic.
Signifying Acts: Structure & Meaning in Everyday Life. R. S. Perinbanayagam. 205p. 1985. 24.50x (ISBN 0-8093-1181-X). S Ill U Pr.
Signifying Monkey: A Theory of Afro-American Literary Criticism. Henry L. Gates, Jr. (Illus.). 304p. 1988. 29.95 (ISBN 0-19-503463-5). Oxford U Pr.
Signifying Nothing: The Semiotics of Zero. Brian Rotman. LC 87-15632. 210p. 1987. 29.95 (ISBN 0-312-01202-0); pap. 12.95. St Martin.
Signifying Nothing: Truth's True Contents in Shakespeare's Text. Malcolm Evans. LC 85-28945. 256p. 1986. 25.00x (ISBN 0-8203-0837-4). U of GA Pr.
Signing English: Exact or Not - A Collection of Articles. Ed. by G. Gustason. 1988. 17.50 (ISBN 0-916708-18-7). Modern Signs.
Signing Exact English. Gustason et al. 490p. 1980. pap. 19.95 (ISBN 0-317-34989-9, SL025). Natl Assn Deaf.
Signing Exact English. 1980 ed. Gerilee Gustason et al. LC 80-80571. (Illus.). 490p. (gr. k-12). 1980. pap. text ed. 21.50x (ISBN 0-916708-03-9). Modern Signs.
Signing: How to Speak with Your Hands. Elaine Costello. (Illus.). 256p. 1983. pap. 12.95 (ISBN 0-553-34455-2). Bantam.
Signing Made Easy. Rod R. Butterworth & Mickey Flodin. 224p. 1988. pap. 10.95 (ISBN 0-399-51490-2, Perigee Bks). Putnam Pub Group.
Signing Off: How to Have Fun with Names. Homer. 140p. 1980. pap. 3.95 (ISBN 0-936944-00-5). Comm Creat.
Signing On: The Birth of Radio in Canada. Bill McNeil & Morris Wolfe. LC 82-45257. (Illus.). 320p. 1983. 29.95 (ISBN 0-385-17742-9); pap. 19.95 (ISBN 0-385-18379-8). Doubleday.
Signing: Signed English - A Basic Guide. Harry Bornstein & Karen L. Saulnier. (Illus.). 240p. 1986. pap. 6.95 (ISBN 0-517-56132-8). Crown.
Signing With Cindy. Cindy Cochran. LC 81-86529. (Illus.). 96p. (Orig.). (gr. 3-12). 1982. pap. 9.95x (ISBN 0-87201-109-7). Gulf Pub.
Signor Faranta's Iron Theatre. Boyd Cruise & Merle Harton. LC 82-83592. (Illus.). xii, 148p. 1982. 14.95x (ISBN 0-917860-13-6). Historic New Orleans.
Signors of the Night. facs. ed. Max Pemberton. LC 74-132123. (Short Story Index Reprint Ser). 1899. 18.00 (ISBN 0-8369-3680-9). Ayer Co Pubs.
Signos Para el Ingles Exacto: A Book for Spanish-Speaking Families of Deaf Children in Schools Using Signing Exact English. Cargill & Brown. LC 82-61647. (Illus.). 160p. 1983. pap. 10.95 (ISBN 0-916708-06-3). Modern Signs.
Signpost-Middle East. Anne C. Stephens. (Orig.). (gr. 4-6). 1979. pap. 2.95 (ISBN 0-377-00087-6). Friendship Pr.
Signpost to Poetry. Humbert Wolfe. 1931. Repr. 20.00 (ISBN 0-8274-3413-8). R West.
Signpost to Poetry: An Introduction to the Study of Verse. Humbert Wolfe. 228p. 1981. Repr. of 1931 ed. lib. bdg. 25.00 (ISBN 0-89987-871-7). Darby Bks.
Signposts. Roger Hecht. LC 74-112873. 56p. 1973. 7.95 (ISBN 0-8040-0277-0, Pub. by Swallow); pap. 4.25 (ISBN 0-8040-0639-3, 82-71959, Pub. by Swallow). Ohio U Pr.
Signposts. Patricia Loomis. Ed. by Kathleen Muller. (Illus.). 93p. 1982. 19.95 (ISBN 0-914139-06-1). San Jose His Mus Assn.
Signposts for Archeological Publication. 2nd ed. Vincent Megaw. 36p. 1979. pap. 6.95x (ISBN 0-900312-93-9, Pub. by Council British Archaeology). Humanities.
Signposts II. Patricia Loomis. (Illus.). 104p. 1985. 25.00 (ISBN 0-914139-02-9). San Jose His Mus Assn.
Signposts: Nineteen Twelve to Nineteen Seventy-Six. Martin Heidegger. Ed. by Thomas Sheehan et al. 300p. Date not set. text ed. cancelled (ISBN 0-8476-7223-9, Rowman & Littlefield). Rowman.
Signposts of the Sea. Althea. (Cambridge Information Books for Children). (Illus.). 32p. (gr. 5-7). 1983. pap. 2.95 (ISBN 0-521-27171-1). Cambridge U Pr.
Signposts: Theological Reflections in a New Zealand Context. Ed. by Douglas Pratt. (Orig.). 1987. pap. 4.95 (ISBN 0-9597775-7-1, Pub. by Methodist Theol). ANZ Religious Pubns.
Signposts to Criticism of Children's Literature. Robert Bator. 360p. 1983. 30.00x (ISBN 0-8389-0372-X, 82-18498). ALA.
Signposts to the Past: Placenames & the History of England. Margaret Gelling. (Illus.). 256p. 1978. 17.50x (ISBN 0-460-04264-5, Pub. by J. M. Dent England). Biblio Dist.
Signs. Ron Goor & Nancy Goor. LC 83-47649. (Illus.). 40p. (ps-1). 1983. 11.70i (ISBN 0-690-04354-6, Crowell Jr Bks); PLB 12.89g (ISBN 0-690-04355-4). HarpJ.
Signs. Maurice Merleau-Ponty. Tr. by Richard C. McCleary. (Studiesin Phenomenology & Existential Philosophy). 1964. 32.95 (ISBN 0-8101-0168-8); pap. 14.95 (ISBN 0-8101-0253-6). Northwestern U Pr.
Signs Across America. Edgar H. Shroyer & Susan P. Shroyer. LC 84-21219. (Illus.). xviii, 286p. 1984. pap. 15.95x (ISBN 0-913580-96-1, Clerc Bks). Gallaudet Univ Pr.
Signs along Our Way: Biblical Reflections for Charting Life's Journey. Karen Berry. 1987. pap. 4.95 (ISBN 0-317-57177-X). St Anthony Mess Pr.
Signs along the River: Learning to Read the Natural Landscape. Kayo Robertson. 1986. pap. 4.95 (ISBN 0-911797-22-X). R Rinehart Inc.
Signs & Emblems. Erhardt D. Stiebner & Dieter Urban. LC 83-14793. (Illus.). 352p. 1983. pap. 18.95 (ISBN 0-442-28059-9). Van Nos Reinhold.
Signs & Graphics for Health Care Facilities. LC 77-26180. (Illus.). 76p. (Orig.). 1978. pap. 27.50 (ISBN 0-939450-65-8, 043140). AHPI.
Signs & Meaning in the Cinema. Enl. ed. Peter Wollen. LC 72-82722. (Cinema One Ser.: No. 9). (Illus.). 176p. 1973. pap. 6.95 (ISBN 0-253-18141-0). Ind U Pr.
Signs & Parables: Semiotics & Gospel Texts. Entrevernes Group Staff. Tr. by Gary Phillips from Fr. LC 78-12840. (Pittsburgh Theological Monographs: No. 23). Orig. Title: Signes et Paraboles. 1978. pap. 10.00 (ISBN 0-915138-35-2). Pickwick.
Signs & Portents. Chelsea Q. Yarbro. 232p. 1984. lib. bdg. 15.00 (ISBN 0-910489-02-5, Pub by Dream Pr.). Scream Pr.
Signs & Portents. Chelsea Q. Yarbro. 208p. 1987. pap. 2.95 (ISBN 0-515-09345-9). Jove Pubns.
Signs & Seats of Power. (Illus.). 28p. 1986. pap. 2.00 (ISBN 0-912303-36-0). Michigan Mus.
Signs & Symbols. Chris Kiernan et al. (Studies in Education: No. 11). xi, 290p. (Orig.). 1982. pap. text ed. 17.50x (ISBN 0-85473-129-6). Heinemann Ed.
Signs & Symbols in Chaucer's Poetry. John P. Hermann & John J. Burke, Jr. LC 80-11064. 272p. 1981. 21.75 (ISBN 0-8173-0038-4); pap. 9.95 (ISBN 0-8173-0042-2). U of Ala Pr.
Signs & Symbols in Christian Art. George Ferguson. (Illus.). 1966. pap. 8.95 (ISBN 0-19-501432-4). Oxford U Pr.
Signs & Symptoms. Ed. by Matthew Cahill & Minnie B. Rose. LC 85-17353. (Nurse's Reference Library). 842p. 1986. text ed. 27.95 (ISBN 0-916730-96-4). Springhouse Pub.
Signs & Symptoms. Ed. by Susan R. Williams & Barbara McVan. LC 85-17295. (Clinical Pocket Manual Ser.). 187p. 1985. pap. text ed. 13.95 (ISBN 0-87434-005-5). Springhouse Pub.
Signs & Symptoms: Adolescent Drug & Alcohol Use: What to Look for, What to Do. Community Intervention, Inc. Staff. 32p. (Orig.). 1986. pap. 2.95 (ISBN 0-9613416-3-7). Comm Intervention.
Signs & Symptoms in Cardiology. Horwitz & Groves. LC 65-6570. 1984. 39.50 (ISBN 0-397-50512-4, Lippincott Medical). Lippincott.
Signs & Symptoms in Endocrine & Metabolic Disorders. John W. Hare et al. (Illus.). 290p. 1986. text ed. 34.50 (ISBN 0-397-50573-6, Lippincott Medical). Lippincott.
Signs & Symptoms in Gynecology. Ben M. Peckham & Sander S. Shapiro. LC 65-6414. (Illus.). 478p. 1983. text ed. 36.50 (ISBN 0-397-50497-7). Lippincott.
Signs & Symptoms in Nursing: Interpretation & Management. Jacobs & Geels. LC 64-3323. 1984. 22.50 (ISBN 0-397-54391-3, Lippincott Nursing). Lippincott.
Signs & Symptoms in Pediatrics. 3rd ed. Walter W. Tunnessen. LC 65-10283. 1987. 39.50 (ISBN 0-397-50863-8, Lippincott Medical). Lippincott.
Signs & Symptoms in Pulmonary Medicine. Ed. by Frederick L. Glauser. (Illus.). 242p. 1983. text ed. 28.75 (ISBN 0-397-50544-2, 65-06943, Lippincott Medical). Lippincott.
Signs & Symptoms of Chemical Exposure. J. Bradford Block. 164p. 1980. spiral bdg. 20.75x (ISBN 0-398-03958-5). C C Thomas.
Signs & Symptoms: Thomas Pynchon & the Contemporary World. Peter L. Cooper. LC 82-6929. 288p. 1983. 27.50 (ISBN 0-520-04537-8). U of Cal Pr.
Signs & Wonders. Carl Dennis. LC 79-3210. (Princeton Series of Contemporary Poets). 69p. 1979. 18.00x (ISBN 0-691-01363-2); pap. 7.50. Princeton U Pr.
Signs & Wonders. Ralph A. DiOrio. LC 87-6697. 160p. 1987. pap. 4.95 (ISBN 0-385-24289-1, Im). Doubleday.
Signs & Wonders. Norman Geisler. 192p. 1988. pap. 6.95 (ISBN 0-8423-5904-4). Tyndale.
Signs & Wonders. Cecil Michael. 1977. 10.95 (ISBN 0-87881-048-X); pap. 7.95 (ISBN 0-87881-049-8). Mojave Bks.
Signs & Wonders. Dr. G. Wasserzug. 1.95 (ISBN 0-686-12836-2). Midnight Call.
Signs & Wonders Today. Christian Life Magazine Staff & C. Peter Wagner. 1986. write for info. (ISBN 0-8297-0709-3). Life Pubs Intl.
Signs & Wonders Today. 1983. Repr. 4.95 (ISBN 0-88419-189-3, Creation Hse). Strang Comms Co.
Signs & Wonders Today. Peter C. Wanger. 168p. 1987. pap. 7.95 (ISBN 0-88419-205-9, Creation Hse). Strang Comms Co.
Signs Everywhere: A Collection of Signs for Towns, Cities, States, & Provinces in the United States, Canada, & Mexico. Nancy Kelly-Jones & Harley Hamilton. LC 81-80388. (Illus.). 280p. (Orig.). pap. 8.95 (ISBN 0-916708-05-5). Modern Signs.
Signs for All Seasons. Joyce Jillson. (Orig.). 1983. pap. 9.95 (ISBN 0-671-43049-1, Wallaby). S&S.
Signs for All Seasons. Suzie L. Kirchner. Ed. by John Joyce. LC 77-93546. (Illus.). 1981. pap. 10.95 (ISBN 0-917002-19-9, 149). Joyce Media.
Signs for Catholic Liturgy & Education. 61p. pap. 5.00 (ISBN 0-318-16887-1). Natl Cath off Deaf.
Signs for Computing Terminology. Steven Jamison. (Illus.). 182p. (Orig.). 1983. pap. text ed. 11.95x (ISBN 0-913072-63-X). Natl Assn Deaf.
Signs for Me: A Basic Sign Language for Children, Parents & Teachers. Benjamin Bahan et al. (Illus.). 104p. 1987. pap. 10.95 (ISBN 0-915035-27-8). Dawn Sign.
Signs for the Times: Symbolic Realism in the Mid-Victorian World. Christopher L. Brooks. 224p. 1984. text ed. 39.95 (ISBN 0-04-800030-2). Unwin Hyman.
Signs from the Ancestors: Zuni Cultural Symbolism & Perceptions of Rock Art. Jane M. Young. LC 87-30242. (Illus.). 336p. 1988. pap. 24.95 (ISBN 0-8263-1039-7). U of NM Pr.
Signs Getting along. Edward Wilson. LC 83-71741. 144p. 1983. 12.00 (ISBN 0-86690-246-5). Am Fed Astrologers.
Signs in Action. Pound & Michaux. LC 87-42539. 48p. 1987. pap. 4.00 (ISBN 0-87376-057-3). Red Dust.
Signs in Judaism: A Resource Book for the Jewish Deaf Community. Adele K. Shuart. 196p. 1986. pap. 16.95x (ISBN 0-8197-0505-5). Bloch.
Signs in Society: Psychological & Socio-Cultural Studies in Semiotic Mediation. Ed. by Elizabeth Mertz & Richard A. Parmentier. (Language, Thought & Culture Advances in the Study of Cognition Ser.). 1985. 39.95 (ISBN 0-12-491280-X). Acad Pr.
Signs, Letters, Words: Archaeology Discovers Writing. W. John Hackwell. LC 86-26237. (Illus.). 72p. (gr. 7 up). 1987. 13.95 (ISBN 0-684-18807-4, Pub. by Scribner). Macmillan.
Signs of a Friend. Linda Bourke. LC 84-40790. (Illus.). 1982. pap. 2.95 (ISBN 0-201-10094-0, Lipp Jr Bks). HarpJ.
Signs of a Lively Congregation. Richard D. Campbell. 1984. 3.95 (ISBN 0-89536-701-7, 4886). CSS of Ohio.
Signs of Celebration. Edie Lauckner. 1978. 3.50 (ISBN 0-570-03770-0, 12-2706). Concordia.
Signs of Christ. Harold Balyoz. LC 79-64608. 1979. 18.00 (ISBN 0-9609710-0-9). Altai Pub.
Signs of Christ's Return. John MacArthur, Jr. (John MacArthur Bible Studies Ser.). 1987. pap. 5.95 (ISBN 0-8024-5311-2). Moody.
Signs of Crime: A Field of Manual for Police. David Powis. LC 77-30173. (Illus.). 1978. pap. text ed. 5.95 (ISBN 0-89444-007-1). John Jay Pr.
Signs of Drug Use. James Woodward. 1980. pap. 7.95x (ISBN 0-932666-04-3). T J Pubs.
Signs of Faith, Hope, & Love: The Christian Sacraments Today. Ed. by Elizabeth Russell & John Greenhalgh. LC 87-24992. 125p. (Orig.). 1988. pap. 6.95 (ISBN 0-00-599084-X, Pub. by Collins Liturgical). Har Row.
Signs of Fertility: The Personal Science of Natural Birth Control. Margaret Nofziger. LC 86-90578. (Illus.). 100p. (Orig.). 1988. pap. 6.95 (ISBN 0-940847-07-8). MND Publish.
Signs of Glory. Richard Holloway. 96p. 1983. pap. 5.95 (ISBN 0-8164-2412-8, HarpR). Har-Row.
Signs of God's Love: Baptism & Communion. Jeanne S. Fogle. Ed. by Mary J. Duckert & W. Ben Lane. (Illus.). 32p. (Orig.). (gr. 3-8). 1984. pap. 4.50 (ISBN 0-664-24636-2, Geneva Pr). Westminster John Knox.
Signs of Healthy Love. Brenda Schaeffer. 24p. (Orig.). 1986. pap. 1.25 (ISBN 0-89486-374-6). Hazelden.
Signs of His Coming. Arthur E. Bloomfield. LC 57-8724. 160p. 1962. pap. 4.95 (ISBN 0-87123-513-7, 210513). Bethany Hse.
Signs of Immortality. Kathryn Linden. 192p. 1986. 12.95 (ISBN 0-8062-2993-4). Carlton.
Signs of Language. Edward Klima & Ursula Bellugi. LC 78-31820. 1978. 30.00x (ISBN 0-674-80795-2). Harvard U Pr.
Signs of Language. Edward Klima & Ursula Bellugi. 1979. 26.00x (ISBN 0-317-05961-0). Harvard U Pr.
Signs of Language. Edward S. Klima & Ursula Bellugi. 432p. 1988. pap. text ed. 12.95 (ISBN 0-674-80796-0). Harvard U Pr.
Signs of Life: Jews from Wuerttemberg-Reports for the Period after 1933 in Letters & Descriptions. Ed. by Walter Strauss. 35.00x (ISBN 0-87068-201-6). Ktav.
Signs of Love: The Sacraments of Christ. Leonard Foley. (Illus.). 1976. pap. 1.95 (ISBN 0-912228-32-6). St Anthony Mess Pr.
Signs of My Friends. Ed. by Patricia T. Harsch & Leslie K. Harsch. Tr. by Joseph Farley Advertising Associates. (Illus.). 420p. 1984. 9.95 (ISBN 0-931977-00-2); Gift box ed. 14.95 (ISBN 0-931977-01-0); deluxe ed. 19.95 (ISBN 0-931977-02-9). About Faces Pub.
Signs of Our Time. Jack Solomon. 256p. 1988. 18.95 (ISBN 0-87477-479-9). J P Tarcher.
Signs of Our Times: Theological Essays on Art in the Twentieth Century. George S. Heyer. LC 79-26805. (Illus.). pap. 27.00 (ISBN 0-317-10532-9, 2019327). Bks Demand UMI.
Signs of Sexual Behavior. James Woodward. 1979. pap. 7.95x (ISBN 0-932666-02-7). T J Pubs.
Signs of Stress: The Social Problems of Psychiatric Illness. J. Wallace McCulloch & Herschel A. Prins. (Psychiatric Topics for Community Workers Ser.). 207p. 1978. 14.00x (ISBN 0-7130-0165-8, Pub. by Woburn Pr England). Biblio Dist.
Signs of Survival. Nancy L. McKinley. (SOS Ser.: No. I). (Illus.). 1986. box 10.00 (ISBN 0-930599-10-1). Thinking Pubns.
Signs of Survival. Nancy L. McKinley. (SOS Ser.: No. II). (Illus.). 1987. box 10.00 (ISBN 0-930599-15-2). Thinking Pubns.
Signs of Taste. Steven M. Weiss. LC 88-11730. 208p. 1988. pap. 9.95 (ISBN 0-932576-59-1). Breitenbush Bks.
Signs of the Apostles. Walter Chantry. 1979. pap. 4.95 (ISBN 0-85151-175-9). Banner of Truth.
Signs of the Coming of the Antichrist. Gordon Lindsay. (End of the Age Ser.: Vol. 1). 1.25 (ISBN 0-89985-067-7). Christ Nations.
Signs of the Flesh: An Essay on the Evolution of Homonid Sexuality. Daniel Rancour-Laferriere. (Approaches to Semiotics Ser.: No. 71). x, 473p. 1986. 109.00 (ISBN 0-89925-121-8). Mouton.
Signs of the Judgement, Onomastica Sacra & the Generations from Adam. Michael Stone. LC 80-28371. (University of Pennsylvania Armenian Texts & Studies). 1981. text ed. 16.50 (ISBN 0-89130-460-6, 21-02-03); pap. 12.00 (ISBN 0-89130-461-4). Scholars Pr GA.
Signs of the Kingdom in the Secular City: Resources for the Urban Church. Ed. by Helen Ujvarosy. 1984. pap. 6.95 (ISBN 0-910452-56-3). Covenant.
Signs of the Spirit: How God Reshapes the Church. Howard Snyder. 336p. 1988. pap. write for info. (ISBN 0-310-51541-6). Zondervan.
Signs of the Stars. Frederick Davies. (Illus.). 224p. 1987. pap. 12.95 (ISBN 0-13-842808-5). P-H.

Silence of God: Meditations on Prayer. James P. Carse. 128p. 1985. 11.95 (ISBN 0-02-521490-X). Macmillan.
Silence of God: Meditations on Prayer. James P. Carse. 120p. 1987. pap. 5.95 (ISBN 0-02-084270-8, Collier). Macmillan.
Silence of Jesus: The Authentic Voice of the Historical Man. James Breech. LC 82-71825. 192p. 1983. 10.95 (ISBN 0-8006-0691-4, 1-1946). Fortress.
Silence of Love: Twentieth-Century Korean Poetry. Ed. by Peter H. Lee. LC 80-21999. 367p. 1980. text ed. 17.95x (ISBN 0-8248-0711-1); pap. 8.95 (ISBN 0-8248-0732-4). UH Pr.
Silence of Snakes. Lewis Green. LC 84-16804. 350p. 1984. 5.98 (ISBN 0-89587-040-1). Blair.
Silence of Surrendering Love: Body, Soul, Spirit Integration. George A. Maloney. LC 85-28636. 189p. 1986. pap. 7.95 (ISBN 0-8189-0494-1). Alba.
Silence of the "Good" People. Garry De Young. Date not set. pap. 14.95. De Young Pr.
Silence of the Lambs. Thomas Harris. 352p. 1988. 18.95a (ISBN 0-312-02282-4). St Martin.
Silence of the LLano. Rudolfo A. Anaya. LC 82-50703. 1982. pap. 8.00 (ISBN 0-89229-009-9). Tonatiuh-Quinto Sol Intl.
Silence of the North. Olive A. Fredrickson & Ben East. 208p. 1973. pap. 2.75 (ISBN 0-446-85559-6). Warner Bks.
Silence of the Sea. facs. ed. Hilaire Belloc. LC 74-107682. (Essay Index Reprint Ser). 1940. 16.00 (ISBN 0-8369-2038-4). Ayer Co Pubs.
Silence Speaks--from the Chalkboard of Baba Hari Dass. Baba Hari Dass et al. LC 76-53902. (Illus.). 224p. (Orig.). 1977. pap. 5.95 (ISBN 0-918100-01-1). SRI Rama.
Silence Spoken Here. Samuel Hazo. 1988. pap. 16.95 (ISBN 0-910395-38-1). Marlboro Pr.
Silence: The Phenomenon & Its Ontological Significance. Bernard P. Dauenhauer. LC 80-7683. (Studies in Phenomenology & Existential Philosophy). 224p. 1980. 20.00x (ISBN 0-253-11021-1). Ind U Pr.
Silence: The Ultimate Protector of Individual Rights. 3rd, rev. ed. Carl Watner. 1984. 9.95 (ISBN 0-911752-39-0). I & O Pub.
Silence to Be Broken: Hope for Those Caught in the Web of Incest. Earl Wilson. LC 86-21792. (Orig.). 1986. pap. 6.95 (ISBN 0-88070-143-9). Multnomah.
Silence to the Drums. Margaret Perry. LC 74-19806. (Contributions in Afro-American & African Studies: No. 18). 1976. lib. bdg. 35.00 (ISBN 0-8371-7847-9, PSD/). Greenwood.
Silence Was a Weapon: The Vietnam War in the Villages. Stuart A. Herrington. (Illus.). 240p. 1982. cloth 15.95 (ISBN 0-89141-140-2). Presidio Pr.
Silence Was a Weapon: The Vietnam War in the Villages. Stuart A. Herrington. 336p. 1987. pap. 3.95 (ISBN 0-8041-0105-1, Pub. by Ivy). Ballantine.
Silence Will Speak: A Study of the Life of Denys Finch Hatton & His Relationship with Karen Blixen. Errol Trzebinski. LC 77-93000. (Illus.). xx, 348p. 1985. pap. 10.95 (ISBN 0-226-81287-1). U of Chicago Pr.
Silenced Observed: A Sir John Appleby Mystery. Michael Innes. LC 87-45627. 224p. 1988. pap. 3.95 (ISBN 0-06-080879-9, P-879, PL). Har-Row.
Silenced Theatre: Czech Playwrights Without a Stage. Marketa Goetz-Stankiewicz. LC 79-13423. pap. 89.20 (2031931). Bks Demand UMI.
Silenced Vision. Constantin Ponomareff. Ed. by Frankfurt M. Berne. (European University Studies Series 18, Comparative Literature: Vol.20). 102p. 1979. 16.45 (ISBN 3-8204-6463-8). P Lang Pubs.
Silencer Patents, Vol. III: European Patents 1901-1978. Donald G. Thomas. (Illus.). 253p. 1978. pap. 20.00 (ISBN 0-87364-102-7). Paladin Pr.
Silencer Theory. Henry C. Landa. (Illus.). 1979. pap. 4.00 (ISBN 0-931974-09-7). FICOA.
Silencers for Hand Firearms. Siegfried F. Huebner. LC 76-13260. (Illus.). 100p. 1976. pap. 11.95 (ISBN 0-87364-055-1). Paladin Pr.
Silencers in the Nineteen-Eighties: Great Designs, Great Designers. J. David Truby. (Illus.). 120p. 1983. pap. 12.00 (ISBN 0-87364-269-4). Paladin Pr.
Silencers, Patterns, & Principles, Vol. II. American Machines & Foundry Co. Staff. (Illus.). 78p. 1969. pap. 12.95 (ISBN 0-87364-018-7). Paladin Pr.
Silencers, Snipers & Assassins. J. David Truby. LC 72-180079. (Illus.). 214p. 1972. 19.95 (ISBN 0-87364-012-8). Paladin Pr.
Silences. Vijay Munshi. (Redbird Book Ser). 24p. 1975. 8.00 (ISBN 0-88253-846-2); pap. text ed. 4.80 (ISBN 0-88253-715-6). Ind-US Inc.
Silences. Tillie Olsen. 356p. 1979. pap. 6.95 (ISBN 0-385-28893-X, Delta). Dell.
Silences. Tillie Olsen. 1984. 15.75 (ISBN 0-8446-6091-4). Peter Smith.
Silences. Tillie Olsen. 1989. pap. 9.95 (Delta). Dell.
Silences Between: Moeraki Conversations. Hulme. 1985. pap. 6.95x (ISBN 0-19-648007-8). Oxford U Pr.
Silences du Colonel Bramble. Andre Maurois. Bd. with Discours et Nouveaux discours ou Docteur O'Grady. pap. 6.50 (ISBN 0-685-23886-5, 90). French & Eur.
Silences du Colonel Bramble: Avec: Discours, Nouveaux Discours du Dr. O'Grady. Andre Maurois. 14.50 (ISBN 0-686-55498-1). French & Eur.
Silencing of Leonardo Boff: The Vatican & the Future of World Christianity. Harvey Cox. LC 87-43277. 224p. (Orig.). 1988. pap. 9.95 (ISBN 0-940989-35-2). Meyer Stone Bks.
Silencio de Dios. Robert Anderson. Orig. Title: Silence of God. 192p. (Span.). 1981. pap. 3.95 (ISBN 0-8254-1022-3). Kregel.
Silencio Mortal: La Amistad y Los Problemas de la Bebida. Jon R. Weinberg. 12p. (Span.). 1983. pap. 0.95 (ISBN 0-89486-200-6). Hazelden.
Silent Alliance. Michael S. McMahon & James M. Friedman. 112p. 1984. 8.95 (ISBN 0-89526-603-2). Regnery Gateway.
Silent & the Damned: The Murder of Mary Phagan & the Lynching of Leo Frank. Robert S. Frey & Nancy Thompson-Frey. LC 87-24758. (Illus.). 308p. (Orig.). 1988. 15.95 (ISBN 0-8191-6491-7). Madison Bks UPA.
Silent Arrows. 3rd ed. Earl F. Moore. LC 23-939860. 1977. 12.95 (ISBN 0-939860-03-1). Tremaine Graph & Pub.
Silent Boundaries: Cultural Constraints on Sickness & Diagnosis of Iranians in Israel. Karen L. Pliskin. LC 86-32492. 304p. 1987. text ed. 25.00 (ISBN 0-300-03792-9). Yale U Pr.
Silent Builder: Emily Warren Roebling & the Brooklyn Bridge. Marilyn E. Weigold. LC 83-21560. (Illus.). 188p. 1984. 19.95 (ISBN 0-8046-9349-8, 9349, Natl U). Assoc Faculty Pr.
Silent Bullet: The Adventures of Craig Kennedy, Scientific Detective. Arthur B. Reeve. LC 75-32795. (Literature of Mystery & Detection). (Illus.). 1976. Repr. 31.00x (ISBN 0-405-07896-X). Ayer Co Pubs.
Silent but for the Word: Tudor Women as Patrons, Translators & Writers of Religious Works. Margaret P. Hannay. LC 84-27802. (Illus.). 320p. 1985. 27.50x (ISBN 0-87338-315-X). Kent St U Pr.
Silent Children: A Parents Guide to the Prevention of Child Sexual Abuse. Linda T. Sanford. 1982. pap. text ed. 7.95 (ISBN 0-07-054662-2). Mcgraw.
Silent Churches: Persecution of Religions in Soviet Dominated Areas. Peter J. Babris. LC 78-52811. (Illus.). 1978. 19.50 (ISBN 0-911252-02-9). Res Publs.
Silent Cinema: An Annotated Critical Bibliography. Leona R. Phillips. 1977. lib. bdg. 69.95 (ISBN 0-8490-1368-2). Gordon Pr.
Silent Cities: A Tombstone Registry of Old Lexington District South Carolina. June A. Seay. LC 86-114293. (Registry of Tombstone Epitaphs Ser.: Vol. I). (Illus.). 428p. (Orig.). 1984. Set. pap. 32.50 (ISBN 0-9617786-4-4); Vol. pap. (ISBN 0-9617786-5-2). June A Seay.
Silent Cities of Mexico & the Maya. 2nd ed. Norman F. Carver, Jr. (Illus.). 216p. 1986. 26.95 (ISBN 0-932076-06-8); pap. 19.95 (ISBN 0-932076-07-6). Documan.
Silent Clowns. Walter Kerr. 1975. 20.00 (ISBN 0-394-46907-0). Knopf.
Silent Clowns. Walter Kerr. LC 75-8231. (Illus.). 1979. pap. 9.95 (ISBN 0-394-73450-5). Knopf.
Silent Community: Public Homosexual Encounters. Edward W. Delph. LC 78-629. (Sociological Observations Ser.: No. 3). pap. 46.50 (ISBN 0-317-08749-5, 2021886). Bks Demand UMI.
Silent Coping. Linda G. Klein. LC 87-90941. 279p. 1988. 13.95 (ISBN 0-533-07545-9). Vantage.
Silent Courage: The Autobiography of George P. Lee. George P. Lee. LC 86-29324. 1987. 14.95 (ISBN 0-87579-056-9). Deseret Bk.
Silent Crisis: Children in a Troubled World. Pranay Gupte. Date not set. 17.95 (ISBN 0-393-02519-5). Norton.
Silent Cry. Kenzaburo Oe. Tr. by John Bester. LC 80-85382. 274p. 1981. pap. 6.95 (ISBN 0-87011-466-2). Kodansha.
Silent Cry. Kenzaburo Oe. Tr. by John Bester from Japanese. LC 74-77961. 274p. 1974. 14.95x (ISBN 0-87011-232-5). Kodansha.
Silent Death. Y. Fyororov. 141p. 1987. pap. 3.95 (ISBN 0-8285-3488-8, Pub. by Progress Pubs USSR). Imported Pubns.
Silent Dialogue: A Study in the Social Psychology of Professional Socialization. Virginia L. Olesen & Elvi W. Whittaker. LC 68-21320. (Jossey-Bass Behavioral Science Ser.). pap. 82.00 (ISBN 0-317-41981-1, 2025678). Bks Demand UMI.
Silent Dictatorship: The Politics of the German High Command Under Hindenburg & Ludendorff, 1916-1918. Martin Kitchen. LC 76-16055. 301p. 1976. text ed. 34.50 (ISBN 0-8419-0277-1). Holmes & Meier.
Silent Disease: Hypertension. Lawrence Galton. 1974. pap. 3.95 (ISBN 0-451-13702-7, AE2098, Sig). NAL.
Silent Embraces. Debra Z. Patterson. (Illus.). 132p. (Orig.). 1985. write for info. (ISBN 0-933077-01-7); pap. 12.95 (ISBN 0-933077-00-9). Unibra Pub Co.
Silent Encounter. Ed. by Virginia Hanson. LC 74-4168. 240p. (Orig.). 1974. pap. 4.75 (ISBN 0-8356-0448-9, Quest). Theos Pub Hse.
Silent Enemies. Justina H. Hill. LC 79-134093. (Essay Index Reprint Ser). 1942. 20.00 (ISBN 0-8369-1954-8). Ayer Co Pubs.
Silent Enemies: The Story of the Diseases of War & Their Control. Justina H. Hill. (Essay Index Reprint Ser.). 275p. 1982. Repr. of 1942 ed. lib. bdg. 17.00 (ISBN 0-8290-0789-X). Irvington.
Silent Enemy. John Benteen. (Sundance Ser.: No. 21). 1981. pap. 1.75 (ISBN 0-8439-1052-6, Leisure Bks). Leisure NY.
Silent Enemy. Ernest T. Jahn. 1981. pap. 2.75 (ISBN 0-89083-763-5). Zebra.
Silent Epidemic: We Can Stop Teenage Suicide. Mary A. Wilder. LC 85-90257. 94p. 1986. 10.00 (ISBN 0-533-06682-4). Vantage.
Silent Executioner: Being the Second in the Series of Fantomas Adventures. Marcel Allain & Pierre Souvestre. LC 86-33112. (Fantomas Ser.: No. 2). 288p. 1987. 15.95 (ISBN 0-688-07265-8). Morrow.
Silent Fire. Ed. by Walter H. Capps & Wendy M. Wright. LC 78-3366. (Forum Bk.). 1978. pap. 7.95x (ISBN 0-06-061314-9, RD 290, HarpR). Har-Row.
Silent Flight. Lily O'Niel. (Illus.). 25p. (YA) (gr. 6 up). 1988. 5.95 (ISBN 0-533-07328-6). Vantage.
Silent Galaxy. William Tedford. 288p. (Orig.). 1981. pap. 2.50 (ISBN 0-8439-0997-8, Leisure Bks). Leisure NY.
Silent Garden. Paul W. Ogden & Suzanne Lipsett. 1982. 12.95 (ISBN 0-312-72440-3). St Martin.
Silent Garden: Understanding the Hearing-Impaired Child. Paul W. Ogden & Suzanne Lipsett. 240p. 1983. pap. 7.95 (ISBN 0-8092-5571-5). Contemp Bks.
Silent Gondoliers, By S. Morgenstern. William Goldman. 128p. 1985. pap. 3.50 (ISBN 0-345-32583-4, Pub. by Del Rey). Ballantine.
Silent Grief: Living in the Wake of Suicide. Chistopher Lukas & Henry M. Seiden. 240p. 1987. 19.95 (ISBN 0-684-18770-1). Scribner.
Silent Hattie Speaks: The Personal Journal of Senator Hattie Caraway. Hattie W. Caraway. Ed. by Diane D. Kincaid. LC 78-22136. (Contributions in Women's Studies: No. 9). (Illus.). 1979. lib. bdg. 35.00 (ISBN 0-313-20820-4, KSI/). Greenwood.
Silent Heroes. Jack Campbell. 276p. (Orig.). 1987. pap. text ed. 9.95x (ISBN 0-942761-42-1). JONopher Pub.
Silent Horror Film: Three Decades of Unspeakable Terror, Vol. I. Robert G. Marrero. Ed. by Linda Bryant. (Illustrated History of the Horror Film Ser.). (Illus.). 140p. (Orig.). Date not set. pap. 11.95 Cancelled (ISBN 0-942436-09-1). RGM Pubns.
Silent Hunter. Charles D. Taylor. 1987. pap. 3.95 (ISBN 0-441-36934-0, Pub. by Charter Bks). Ace Bks.
Silent Intruder: Surviving the Radiation Age. Charles Panati & Michael Hudson. 224p. 1981. 9.95. HM.
Silent Invaders. Harriette S. Abels. Ed. by Howard Schroeder. LC 79-4644. (Galaxy I Ser.). (Illus.). 48p. (gr. 3-5). 1979. PLB 7.95 (ISBN 0-89686-031-0). Crestwood Hse.
Silent Invaders. Robert Silverberg. 256p. 1985. pap. 2.95 (ISBN 0-8125-5460-4, Dist. by Warner Pub Services & St. Martin's Press). Tor Bks.
Silent Investor, Silent Loser. Martin Sosnoff. write for info. Richardson & Steirman.
Silent Issues of the Church. Carl H. Lundquist. 156p. 1985. pap. 5.95 (ISBN 0-89693-721-6). Victor Bks.
Silent Killers. Kevin Stillwagon. (Illus.). 128p. 1984. 8.95 (ISBN 0-89962-354-9). Todd & Honeywell.
Silent Killers: Radon & Other Hazards. Kathlyn Gay. Ed. by M. Kline. (Impact Ser.). (Illus.). (gr. 6-12). 1988. 12.90 (ISBN 0-531-10598-9). Watts.
Silent Killing. Janice Robinson. 1985. 24.95x (ISBN 0-7090-2083-X, Pub. by R Hale Ltd UK). State Mutual Bk.
Silent Knife: Cesarean Prevention & Vaginal Birth after Cesarean. Nancy Wainer Cohen & Lois J. Estner. (Illus.). 464p. 1983. 34.95 (ISBN 0-89789-026-4); pap. 14.95 (ISBN 0-89789-027-2). Bergin & Garvey.
Silent Knife: Vaginal Birth After Cesarean (VBAC) & Cesarean Prevention. Nancy W. Cohen & Lois J. Estner. 464p. 1983. 13.46 (ISBN 0-318-17499-5). C Sec.
Silent Knives. Laurence Gough. 192p. 1988. 13.95 (ISBN 0-312-01747-2). St Martin.
Silent Language. Edward T. Hall. LC 72-97265. 240p. 1973. pap. 4.95 (ISBN 0-385-05549-8, Anch). Doubleday.
Silent Language in the Classroom. Charles M. Galloway. LC 76-23912. (Fastback: No.86). (Orig.). 1976. pap. 0.90 (ISBN 0-87367-086-8). Phi Delta Kappa.
Silent Language of Psychotherapy: Social Reinforcement of Unconscious Processes. 2nd ed. Ernst G. Beier & David M. Young. LC 84-6287. 318p. 1984. lib. bdg. 34.95x (ISBN 0-202-26097-6); pap. text ed. 17.95x (ISBN 0-202-26098-4). Aldine de Gruyter.
Silent Letters Released. Elwood A. Seaman. 1988. 12.95 (ISBN 0-533-07693-5). Vantage.
Silent Liars. Michael Underwood. (Nightingales Ser.). 318p. 1987. pap. 12.95x (ISBN 0-8161-4223-8, Large Print Bks.). G K Hall.
Silent Life. Thomas Merton. 178p. 1975. pap. 8.25 (ISBN 0-374-51281-7). FS&G.
Silent Life. Thomas Merton. 1983. 12.75 (ISBN 0-8446-5986-X). Peter Smith.
Silent Magic. Ivan Butler. (Illus.). 212p. 1988. 24.95 (ISBN 0-8044-2078-5). Ungar.
Silent Magic: Rediscovering the Silent Film Era. Ivan Butler. 1987. 59.99x (ISBN 0-86287-315-0, Pub. by Harrap Ltd England). State Mutual Bk.
Silent Majority: Families of Emotionally Healthy College Students. William A. Westley & Nathan B. Epstein. LC 77-75937. (Jossey-Bass Behavioral Science Ser.). pap. 52.00 (ISBN 0-8357-9347-8, 2013780). Bks Demand UMI.
Silent Messages: Implicit Communication of Emotions & Attitudes. 2nd ed. Albert Mehrabian. 196p. 1981. pap. text ed. write for info. (ISBN 0-534-00910-7). Wadsworth Pub.
Silent Miaow: A Manual for Kittens, Strays, & Homeless Cats. Paul Gallico & Suzanne Szasz. (Illus.). 160p. 1985. pap. 6.95 (ISBN 0-517-55683-9). Crown.
Silent Minority: Non-Respondents in Sample Surveys. John Goyder. 225p. 1988. 39.00 (ISBN 0-8133-0592-6). Westview.
Silent Moon. William Relling. 352p. 1989. pap. price not set. Tor Bks.
Silent Movies: A Picture Quiz Book. Stanley Appelbaum. 1974. pap. 3.50 (ISBN 0-486-23054-6). Dover.
Silent Music: The Science of Meditation. William Johnston. LC 73-18688. 1979. pap. 7.95 (ISBN 0-06-064196-7, RD 293, HarpR). Har-Row.
Silent Myocardial ISC-INFR. Cohn. (Basic & Clinical Cardiology Ser.). 208p. 1986. 49.75 (ISBN 0-8247-7469-8). Dekker.
Silent Myocardial Ischemia. Ed. by W. Rutishauser & H. Roskamm. (Illus.). 220p. 1984. 34.00 (ISBN 0-387-13193-0). Springer-Verlag.
Silent Night. Illus. by Francesca Crespi. (Illus.). 8p. (ps-k). 1987. 3.95 (ISBN 0-8050-0471-8). H Holt & Co.
Silent Night. Susan Jeffers. LC 84-8113. (Illus.). 32p. (gr. k up). 1984. 12.95 (ISBN 0-525-44144-1). Dutton.
Silent Night. Joseph Mohr. LC 84-8113. (Unicorn Paperbacks Ser.). (Illus.). 32p. (ps up). 1988. pap. 4.95 (ISBN 0-525-44431-9, 0481-140). Dutton.
Silent Night: Written in Sutton Sign Writing. Valerie J. Sutton. 1981. pap. text ed. 3.00 (ISBN 0-914336-38-X). Ctr Sutton Movement.
Silent Nights for You & Your Baby. Jane Asher. (Orig.). 1987. pap. 5.95 (ISBN 0-440-58141-9, Dell Trade Pbks). Dell.
Silent One. Cowley. LC 80-21853. (Illus.). (gr. 4-6). 1981. Knopf.
Silent Ones. Elizabeth Ogilvie. 20.95 (ISBN 0-89190-399-2, Pub. by Am Repr). Amereon Ltd.
Silent Partner. Judith Greber. 320p. 1985. pap. 3.95 (ISBN 0-345-32270-3). Ballantine.
Silent Partner. Elizabeth S. Phelps. Bd. with Tenth of January. 396p. 1983. pap. 8.95 (ISBN 0-935312-08-0). Feminist Pr.
Silent Partner. facsimile ed. Elizabeth S. Ward. (Americans in Fiction Ser.). 310p. lib. bdg. 29.00 (ISBN 0-8398-2151-4); pap. text ed. 10.95x (ISBN 0-89197-936-0). Irvington.
Silent Partner: The History of the American Film Manufacturing Company 1910-1921. Timothy J. Lyons. LC 73-21590. (Vol. 7). 266p. 1974. 25.50 (ISBN 0-405-04872-6). Ayer Co Pubs.
Silent Partner: West Germany & Arms Control. Barry M. Blechman & Cathleen S. Fisher. 312p. 1988. 39.95x (ISBN 0-88730-316-1); pap. text ed. 19.95x (ISBN 0-88730-320-X). Ballinger Pub.
Silent Partners. Albert Kovetz. 400p. (Orig.). 1980. pap. 2.50 (ISBN 0-89083-688-4). Zebra.
Silent Partners: The Legacy of Ape Language Experiments. Eugene Linden. 208p. 1987. pap. text ed. 3.95 (ISBN 0-345-34234-8). Ballantine.
Silent Passage. Photos by Mikael Levin. (Illus.). 52p. 1988. 20.00. Hudson Hills.
Silent Path to God. James E. Griffiss. LC 79-8903. pap. 27.50 (ISBN 0-317-55552-9, 2029620). Bks Demand UMI.
Silent People. Walter Macken. 346p. 1965. pap. 9.95 (ISBN 0-330-30328-7). Bks Britain.
Silent People Dwelling in a World Without Sound: All About Deaf Mutes. J. N. Williams. 69.95 (ISBN 0-8490-1054-3). Gordon Pr.
Silent Picture: Numbers One-Nineteen. 66.00 (ISBN 0-405-09898-7, 11492). Ayer Co Pubs.
Silent Pilgrimage to God: The Spirituality of Charles deFoucauld. Ed. by Rene Voillaume. Tr. by Jeremy Moiser from Fr. LC 74-32516. Orig. Title: Ce Sue Crojart Charles de Foucauld. 100p. (Orig.). 1977. pap. 4.95 (ISBN 0-88344-461-5). Orbis Bks.
Silent Pilots: Figureheads in Mystic Seaport Museum. Georgia W. Hamilton. (Illus.). 116p. 1984. pap. 15.00 (ISBN 0-913372-30-7). Mystic Seaport.
Silent Places. Stewart E. White. 1976. lib. bdg. 14.25x (ISBN 0-89968-123-9). Lightyear.
Silent Pool. Patricia Wentworth. 1976. Repr. of 1953 ed. lib. bdg. 15.95 (ISBN 0-88411-740-5, Pub. by Aeonian Pr). Amereon Ltd.
Silent Power: Japan's Identity & World Role. Ed. by Japan Center for International Exchange. 1976. 13.50x (ISBN 0-89955-245-5, Pub. by Simul). Intl Spec Bk.
Silent Presence. Ernest Larkin. 4.95 (ISBN 0-87193-172-9). Dimension Bks.

Silent Prophet. Joseph Roth. Tr. by David Le Vay from Ger. LC 79-67676. 216p. 1980. 22.50 (ISBN 0-87951-110-9). Overlook Pr.

Silent Pulse: The Search for the Perfect Rhythm that Exists in Each of Us. George Leonard. 1986. pap. 8.95 (ISBN 0-525-48199-0). Dutton.

Silent Raveller in San Francisco. Chiang Yee. 366p. 1964. 105.00x (Pub. by Han-Shan Tang Ltd). State Mutual Bk.

Silent Reading: An Introduction to Its Study & Teaching. A. K. Pugh. 1979. pap. text ed. 17.00x (ISBN 0-435-10719-4). Heinemann Ed.

Silent Recesses. Judith Beckett. 70p. 1984. 3.65 (ISBN 0-89697-222-4). Intl Univ Pr.

Silent Retreats. Philip F. Deaver. LC 87-14313. (Flannery O'Connor Award for Short Fiction Ser.). 240p. 1988. 15.95 (ISBN 0-8203-0981-8). U of Ga Pr.

Silent Revolution: Changing Values & Political Styles among Western Publics. Ronald Inglehart. LC 76-24294. 1977. 61.50x (ISBN 0-691-07585-9); pap. 18.50x (ISBN 0-691-10038-1). Princeton U Pr.

Silent Revolution: The Effects of Modernization on Australian Aboriginal Religion. Erich Kolig. LC 81-6430. (Illus.). 224p. 1981. text ed. 27.50 (ISBN 0-89727-020-7). ISHI PA.

Silent Revolution: The Transformation of Divorce Law in the United States. Herbert Jacob. 224p. 1988. 19.95x (ISBN 0-226-38951-0). U of Chicago Pr.

Silent Rider. Jack Aintry. 256p. 1988. pap. 2.95 (ISBN 0-8217-2385-5). Zebra.

Silent River: A Pastoral Elegy in the Form of a Recollection of Arctic Adventure. Charles R. Metzger. (Illus.). xi, 161p. (Orig.). 1984. pap. 7.95x (ISBN 0-9613094-0-7). Omega LA.

Silent Salesman. 2nd ed. 156p. 1973. text ed. 24.50x (ISBN 0-220-66203-7, Pub. by Busn Bks England). Brookfield Pub Co.

Silent Sam, & Other Stories of Our Day. Harvey J. O'Higgins. 20.00 (ISBN 0-8369-4251-5, 6061). Ayer Co Pubs.

Silent Scenarios. Styne Sandi. 180p. (Orig.). (YA) 1987. pap. 8.95 (ISBN 0-9618923-0-7). Sandi Styne.

Silent Scream. Martha Janssen. LC 83-5714. 112p. 1983. pap. 4.95 (ISBN 0-8006-1722-3, 1-1722). Fortress.

Silent Scream: Alfred Hitchcock's Sound Track. Elisabeth Weis. LC 80-71093. (Illus.). 192p. 1982. 19.50 (ISBN 0-8386-3079-0). Fairleigh Dickinson.

Silent Screams & Hidden Cries: A Compilation & Interpretation of Artwork by Children from Violent Homes. Anges Wohl & Bobbie Kaufman. LC 85-6652. (Illus.). 192p. 1985. 25.00 (ISBN 0-87630-392-0). Brunner-Mazel.

Silent Screen & My Talking Heart: The Autobiography of Nell Shipman. 2nd, rev. ed. Nell Shipman. Ed. by Tom Trusky. (Hemingway Western Studies). (Illus.). 300p. (Orig.). 1988. pap. 15.95. Hemingw Studies.

Silent Season: Fishing Adventures by Seven American Experts. Russell Chatham et al. (Illus.). 300p. (Orig.). 1988. pap. 12.95 (ISBN 0-944439-05-5). Clark City Pr.

Silent Seasons: Fishing Adventures by Seven American Experts. 2nd ed. Russell Chatham et al. (Illus.). 300p. Date not set. pap. 12.95. Clark City Pr.

Silent Selling: A Guide to Fashion Merchandise Presentation. Judith A. Bell. 150p. (Orig.). 1987. 18.95 (ISBN 0-911380-77-9). Signs of Times.

Silent September. Joyce Landorf. 1984. pap. 10.00 (ISBN 0-317-14051-5). Word Bks.

Silent Service: U. S. Submarines in World War II. Hughston E. Lowder. LC 87-90657. 504p. 1987. 24.95 (ISBN 0-9619189-0-X). Silent Serv Bks.

Silent Shame: The Alarming Rise of Child Sexual Abuse & How to Protect Your Children from It. Martin J. Mawyer. LC 86-72062. 160p. (Orig.). 1987. pap. 6.95 (ISBN 0-89107-419-8, Crossway Bks). Good News.

Silent Shame: The Sexual Abuse of Children & Youth. Renitta Goldman & Virginia Wheeler. 192p. 1986. pap. text ed. 14.95x (ISBN 0-8134-2609-X). Inter Print Pubs.

Silent Shofar. Carol K. Hubner. (Devorah Doresh Mysteries). (Illus.). (gr. 3 up). 6.95 (ISBN 0-910818-53-3); pap. 5.95 (ISBN 0-910818-54-1). Judaica Pr.

Silent Shout. Mayland Schurch. (Discovery Ser.). 31p. 1987. pap. 0.75 (ISBN 0-8163-0728-8). Pacific Pr Pub Assn.

Silent Siege II: Japanese Attacks on North America in World War II. Bert Webber. Ed. by Margie Webber. (Illus.). 400p. 1988. pap. 19.95 (ISBN 0-936738-26-X). Webb Research.

Silent Siege: Japanese Attacks Against North America in World War II. Bert Webber. (Illus.). 397p. 1985. o.s.i 22.50 (ISBN 0-87770-315-9); pap. 16.95 (ISBN 0-87770-318-3). Ye Galleon.

Silent Silos: A Counterbomb Haiku Sequence. Johnny Baranski. (Sunburst Matchbooks Ser.: No. 1). (Illus.). 16p. (Orig.). 1985. pap. 3.00x (ISBN 0-934648-10-7). Sunburst Pr.

Silent Sky: The Incredible Extinction of the Passenger Pigeon. Allan W. Eckert. LC 65-20745. 244p. 1973. pap. 4.95 (ISBN 0-913428-15-9). Landfall Pr.

Silent Snow. Oliver Patton. 1988. pap. 3.95 (ISBN 0-451-15283-2, Sig). NAL.

Silent Snow, Secret Snow. Conrad Aiken. LC 83-71788. (Creative's Classic Short Stories Ser.). 48p. (gr. 6 up). 1983. PLB 8.95 (ISBN 0-87191-963-X). Creative Ed.

Silent South see Collected Works.

Silent South: Including the Freedman's Case in Equity, the Convict Lease System & to Which Has Been Added Eight Hitherto Uncollected Essays by Cable on Prison & Asylum Reform & an Essay on Cable by Arlin Turner. George W. Cable. LC 69-14915. (Criminology, Law Enforcement, & Social Problems Ser.: No. 57). 1969. 10.00x (ISBN 0-87585-057-X). Patterson Smith.

Silent Speech of Politicians: Body Language in Government. Miriam D. Blum. Ed. by Lee Rathbone. (Illus.). 128p. (Orig.). 1988. pap. 7.95 (ISBN 0-929535-00-6). Brenner Info Group.

Silent Spring. Rachel Carson. (Illus.). 1962. 16.95 (ISBN 0-395-07506-8). HM.

Silent Spring Revisited. Ed. by Gino J. Marco et al. 1987. 29.95 (ISBN 0-317-59797-3); pap. 17.95 (ISBN 0-317-59798-1). Am Chemical.

Silent Spring: Twenty-Fifth Anniversary Edition. Rachel Carson. (Illus.). 448p. 1987. 17.95 (ISBN 0-395-45389-5); pap. 7.95 (ISBN 0-395-45390-9). HM.

Silent Storm. Marion M. Brown et al. 1985. pap. 6.95 (ISBN 0-8010-0884-0). Baker Bk.

Silent Strength. David M. Masumoto. 90p. (Orig.). 1985. pap. 5.95 (ISBN 0-9614541-1-3, Pub. by New Currents International). Inaka Countryside Pubns.

Silent Tears, Joyous Joys. Jane Blair & Ruth J. Oleksowicz. 18p. (Orig.). 1986. 15.00 (ISBN 0-910147-29-9); pap. 12.00 (ISBN 0-317-60033-8). World Poetry Pr.

Silent Terror. James Ellroy. 288p. 1986. pap. 3.50. Avon.

Silent Terror. James Ellroy. 280p. 1986. 35.00x (ISBN 0-940941-00-7). Blood & Guts Pr.

Silent Thunder. Robert Barnes. (Orig.). 1980. pap. text ed. 1.75 (ISBN 0-505-51551-2, Pub. by Tower Bks). Leisure NY.

Silent Tower. Barbara Hambly. 1988. pap. 3.95 (ISBN 0-345-00691-7, Del Rey). Ballantine.

Silent Track Star. Jerry Jenkins. (Dallas O'Neil & the Baker Street Sports Club Ser.). (Orig.). (YA) (gr. 9-12). 1986. pap. text ed. 3.95 (ISBN 0-8024-8239-2). Moody.

Silent Traveller in Boston. Chiang Yee. (Illus.). 1959. 7.50 (ISBN 0-393-08474-4). Norton.

Silent Traveller in Japan. Chiang Yee. (Illus.). 1972. 15.00 (ISBN 0-393-08642-9). Norton.

Silent Traveller in London. Chiang Yee. 256p. 1940. 56.00x (ISBN 0-317-68584-8, Pub. by Han-Shan Tang Ltd). State Mutual Bk.

Silent Traveller in Oxford. Chiang Yee. 183p. 1944. 84.00x (ISBN 0-317-68586-4, Pub. by Han-Shan Tang Ltd). State Mutual Bk.

Silent Traveller in San Francisco. Chiang Yee. (Illus.). 1964. 12.50 (ISBN 0-393-08422-1). Norton.

Silent Traveller in San Francisco. Chiang Yee. (Illus.). 384p. 1981. pap. 6.95 (ISBN 0-393-00064-8). Norton.

Silent Traveller in War Time. Chiang Yee. 131p. 1939. 70.00x (ISBN 0-317-68588-0, Pub. by Han-Shan Tang Ltd). State Mutual Bk.

Silent Treatment. David Carkeet. LC 87-45567. 288p. (YA) (gr. 7 up). 1988. 13.95i (ISBN 0-06-020978-X); PLB 13.89 (ISBN 0-06-020979-8). HarpJ.

Silent Twins. Marjorie Wallace. (Illus.). 256p. 1986. 16.95 (ISBN 0-13-810276-7). Prentice Hall Pr.

Silent Twins. Marjorie Wallace. 320p. 1987. pap. 3.95 (ISBN 0-345-34802-8). Ballantine.

Silent Victory. Carmen McBride. LC 73-84602. 224p. 1969. 16.95 (ISBN 0-911012-03-6). Nelson-Hall.

Silent Violence: Food, Famine, & Peasantry in Northern Nigeria. Michael J. Watts. LC 82-13384. (Illus.). 500p. 1983. text ed. 42.00x (ISBN 0-520-04323-5). U of Cal Pr.

Silent Voice. Julia Cunningham. 176p. (gr. 5-9). 1981. 11.95 (ISBN 0-525-39295-5). Dutton.

Silent Voices. Jared Angira. (African Writers Ser.). 1972. pap. text ed. 5.50 (ISBN 0-435-90111-7). Heinemann Ed.

Silent Voices. Tr. by Andrea Deletant & Brenda Walker. LC 85-80386. (Illus.). 161p. (Orig.). 1986. pap. 11.00 (ISBN 0-948259-03-5, Pub. by Forest Bks London). Three Continents.

Silent Voices: Recent American Poems on Nature. Ed. by Paul Feroe. LC 78-54317. 1978. pap. 2.95 (ISBN 0-915408-17-1). Ally Pr.

Silent Voyage. James Pattinson. 1959. 10.95 (ISBN 0-8392-1105-8). Astor-Honor.

Silent War. facsimile ed. John A. Mitchell. LC 68-57541. (Muckrakers Ser.). (Illus.). 222p. 1979. Repr. of 1906 ed. lib. bdg. 24.00 (ISBN 0-8398-1263-9). Irvington.

Silent War. John A. Mitchell. (Muckraker Ser.). (Illus.). 222p. 1986. pap. text ed. 6.95x (ISBN 0-8290-2004-7). Irvington.

Silent War: America's Struggle for world Markets. IRA Magaziner Staff & Mark Patinkin. LC 88-42822. 352p. 1989. 19.95 (ISBN 0-394-56979-2). Random.

Silent Warrior. L. E. Modesitt. 1987. pap. 3.50 (ISBN 0-8125-4588-5, Dist. by St Martin's Pr & Warner Pub Servs). Tor Bks.

Silent Way for English. rev. ed. Caleb Gattegno. (Orig.). (gr. k-12). 1977. tchr's. ed 6.95; Worksheets. 2.00 (ISBN 0-87825-086-7); Wall Pictures. 10.00 (ISBN 0-87825-044-1); Word Charts. 60.00 (ISBN 0-87825-133-2); Fidel Charts. 40.00 (ISBN 0-87825-134-0); Sound Color Charts. 5.00 (ISBN 0-87825-137-5); Mini Word Chart Cards. 5.25; Mini Fidel Card. 1.75 (ISBN 0-87825-142-1); one thousand sentences 3.50 (ISBN 0-87825-007-7). Ed Solutions.

Silent Way for French. Caleb Gattegno. (Orig.). (gr. k-12). 1965. tchr's. ed 6.95; Mille Phrases. 2.95 (ISBN 0-87825-082-4); Trente-Six Instantanes. 2.95 (ISBN 0-87825-099-9); Huit Contes. 3.50 (ISBN 0-87825-095-6); Worksheets. 2.00 (ISBN 0-87825-083-2); Wall Pictures. 10.00 (ISBN 0-87825-052-2); Word Charts. 55.00 (ISBN 0-87825-075-1); Fidel Charts. 30.00 (ISBN 0-87825-078-6); Expanded Fidel. 5.00 (ISBN 0-87825-098-0). Ed Solutions.

Silent Way for Spanish. Caleb Gattegno. (Orig.). (gr. k-12). 1965. tchr's. ed 6.95; Mil Frases. 2.95 (ISBN 0-87825-047-6); Narraciones Breves. 2.95 (ISBN 0-87825-048-4); Ocho Cuentos. 3.50 (ISBN 0-87825-049-2); Worksheets. 2.00 (ISBN 0-87825-084-0); Wall Pictures. 10.00 (ISBN 0-87825-045-X); Word Charts. 25.00 (ISBN 0-87825-076-X); Spanish Fidel (European) 5.00 (ISBN 0-87825-079-4); Spanish Fidel (S. American) 5.00 (ISBN 0-87825-080-8). Ed Solutions.

Silent Winds: Poetry of One Hopi. 3rd ed. Ramson Lomatewama. LC 83-61654. 64p. 1983. pap. 5.00 (ISBN 0-935825-00-2). Badger Claw Pr.

Silent Wings. Gordon A. Alcorn. (Illus.). 83p. 1982. pap. 4.95x (ISBN 0-87770-277-2). Ye Galleon.

Silent Wings: The Saga of the U. S. Army & Marine Combat Glider Pilots During World War II. Gerard M. Devlin. (Illus.). 560p. 1985. 27.95 (ISBN 0-312-72460-8). St Martin.

Silent Witness. Edward Yourdon. LC 82-90213. 184p. 1982. 7.95 (ISBN 0-917072-28-6, Yourdon). P-H.

Silent Word. new ed. Francis Brabazon. 1978. text ed. 9.95 (ISBN 0-913078-34-4); pap. text ed. 6.95 (ISBN 0-913078-35-2). Sheriar Pr.

Silent World. Jaques Cousteau & Frederic Dumas. (Illus.). 288p. 1987. pap. 12.95 (ISBN 0-941130-45-2). N Lyons Bks.

Silent World of Doctor & Patient. Jay Katz. LC 83-48830. 240p. 1984. 15.95 (ISBN 0-02-917010-9). Free Pr.

Silent World of Doctor & Patient. Jay Katz. 236p. 1986. pap. 9.95 (ISBN 0-02-918760-5). Free Pr.

Silent World of Nicholas Quinn. Colin Dexter. 224p. 1988. pap. 3.95 (ISBN 0-553-27238-1). Bantam.

Silent Years: An Autobiography with Memoirs of James Joyce & Our Ireland. John F. Byrne. LC 75-11682. xi, 307p. 1975. Repr. of 1953 ed. lib. bdg. 24.50x (ISBN 0-374-91144-4, Octagon). Hippocrene Bks.

Silenus. Thomas Woolner. LC 76-148336. Repr. of 1884 ed. 15.00 (ISBN 0-404-07033-7). AMS Pr.

Siletz: Survival for an Artifact. 2nd ed. Leone L. Kasner. (Illus.). 82p. 1980. pap. text ed. 4.50 (ISBN 0-911443-04-5). Lincoln Coun Hist.

Silhouette Christmas Stories. 1987. pap. 3.95 (ISBN 0-373-48212-4). Harlequin Bks.

Silhouette Crafts. Romilda Dilley. (Illus.). 24p. (YA) (gr. 9-12). 1987. wkbk. 2.95 (ISBN 0-87403-238-5, 2148). Standard Pub.

Silhouette Cutting for Fun & Money. Ann Woodward & Deidre Woodward. LC 87-90602. (Illus.). 102p. (Orig.). 1987. pap. 12.50 (ISBN 0-944095-00-3). Profile VA.

Silhouette in Diamonds: The Life of Mrs. Potter Palmer. facsimile ed. Ishbel Ross. LC 75-1868. (Leisure Class in America Ser.). (Illus.). 1975. Repr. of 1960 ed. 23.50x (ISBN 0-405-06934-0). Ayer Co Pubs.

Silhouette of a Saint: Albert Pepper. Danny R. Morrow. 1985. 4.95 (ISBN 0-86544-027-1). Salv Army Suppl South.

Silhouettes. Edmund Gosse. 1973. Repr. of 1925 ed. 25.00 (ISBN 0-8274-0382-8). R West.

Silhouettes. facsimile ed. Edmund W. Gosse. LC 78-156654. (Essay Index Reprint Ser). Repr. of 1925 ed. 24.50 (ISBN 0-8369-2399-5). Ayer Co Pubs.

Silhouettes: A History & Dictionary of Artists. E. Nevill Jackson. (Illus.). 25.00 (ISBN 0-8446-5895-2). Peter Smith.

Silhouettes: A Pictorial Archive of Varied Illustrations. Ed. by Carol B. Grafton. (Illus.). 1979. pap. 5.95 (ISBN 0-486-23781-8). Dover.

Silhouettes in America, 1790-1840: A Collectors' Guide. Blume J. Rifken. (Illus.). 128p. (Orig.). 1987. pap. 12.95 (ISBN 0-943741-00-9). Paradigm VT.

Silhouettes of American Life. Rebecca H. Davis. 1972. Repr. of 1892 ed. lib. bdg. 26.50 (ISBN 0-8422-8033-2). Irvington.

Silhouettes of American Life. Rebecca H. Davis. 1986. pap. text ed. 6.95x. Irvington.

Silhouettes of Charles S. Thomas, Colorado Governor & United States Senator. Sewell Thomas. LC 59-7608. (Illus.). 228p. 1959. 7.50 (ISBN 0-87004-167-3). Caxton.

Silhouettes of Woman. Phyliss Shanken. (Illus.). 1976. pap. 4.95 (ISBN 0-918836-01-8). Philmer.

Silhouetting Halftones & Making Dropout Masks. 38p. 1981. 16.00 (ISBN 0-88362-029-4, 0431). Graphic Arts Tech Found.

Silica & Me: The Career of an Industrial Chemist. Guy Alexander. LC 73-75723. (Chemistry in Action Ser.). 111p. 1973. pap. 7.95 (ISBN 0-8412-0162-5). Am Chemical.

Silica in Sediments: A Symposium. Symposium on Silica in Sediments,(1958: Los Angeles) Ed. by H. Andrew Ireland. LC 60-50. (Society of Economic Paleontologists & Mineralogists, Special Publication: No. 7). pap. 49.30 (ISBN 0-317-27166-0, 2024734). Bks Demand UMI.

Silica in Sediments: Nodular & Bedded Chert. (Reprint Ser.: No. 8). 184p. 1979. 13.00 (ISBN 0-918985-34-X). SEPM.

Silica, Silicosis & Cancer: Controversy in Occupational Medicine. Ed. by David F. Goldsmith et al. LC 85-640225. (Cancer Research Monographs: Vol. 2). 592p. 1985. 62.95 (ISBN 0-275-91305-8, C1305). Praeger.

Silicate Glass Technology Methods. Clarence L. Babcock. LC 76-30716. (Wiley Series in Pure & Applied Optics). pap. 84.00 (ISBN 0-317-28068-6, 2055768). Bks Demand UMI.

Silicate Melt Equilibria. Wilhelm Eitel. Tr. by J. G. Philips & T. G. Madgwick. LC 51-62230. pap. 42.30 (ISBN 0-317-11176-0, 2050514). Bks Demand UMI.

Silicate Science: A Treatise, 8 vols. Ed. by Wilhelm Eitel. Incl. Vol. 1. Silicate Structures. 1964. 117.50 (ISBN 0-12-236301-9); Vol. 2. Glasses, Enamels, Slags. 1964 (ISBN 0-12-236302-7); Vol. 3. Dry Silicate Systems. 1966 (ISBN 0-12-236303-5); Vol. 4. Hydrothermal Silical Systems. 1966 (ISBN 0-12-236304-3); Vol. 5. Ceramics & Hydraulic Binders. 1966 (ISBN 0-12-236305-1). Vols. 2-5. 129.50; Vol. 6. 113.00; Vol. 7. 117.50; Vol. 8. 102.00. Acad Pr.

Siliceous Deposits in the Pacific Region. Ed. by A. Iijima & J. R. Hein. (Developments in Sedimentology Ser.: No. 36). 472p. 1983. 110.75 (ISBN 0-444-42129-7). Elsevier.

Siliceous Sedimentary Rock-Hosted Ores & Petroleum. James R. Hein. (Evolution of Ore Fields Ser.). (Illus.). 320p. 1987. 42.95 (ISBN 0-442-23250-0). Van Nos Reinhold.

Siliciclastic Shelf Sediments. Ed. by Roderick W. Tillman & Charles T. Siemers. (Special Publications Ser.: No. 34). 268p. 1984. 32.00 (ISBN 0-918985-14-5). SEPm.

Silicides for VLSI Applications. Ed. by S. P Murarka. 1983. 26.00 (ISBN 0-12-511220-3). Acad Pr.

Silicon. Ed. by J. Grabmaier. (Crystals-Growth, Properties, & Applications Ser.: Vol. 5). (Illus.). 215p. 1981. 70.00 (ISBN 0-387-10932-3). Springer-Verlag.

Silicon. L. V. Myshlyaeva. (Analytical Chemistry of the Elements Ser.). 236p. 1970. text ed. 62.00x (ISBN 0-7065-1402-5, Pub. by Keter Pub Jerusalem). Coronet Bks.

Silicon & Siliceous Structures in Biological Systems. Ed. by T. L. Simpson & B. E. Yolcani. (Illus.). 587p. 1981. 145.20 (ISBN 0-387-90592-8). Springer-Verlag.

Silicon & Silicones. E. G. Rochow. (Illus.). 190p. 1987. pap. 16.95 (ISBN 0-387-17565-2). Springer-Verlag.

Silicon Biochemistry: Symposium, No. 121. CIBA Foudation Symposium Staff. LC 86-4095. 264p. 1986. 54.95 (ISBN 0-471-91025-2). Wiley.

Silicon Carbide. Ed. by J. Cawley & C. Semler. Date not set. write for info. (ISBN 0-916094-99-5). Am Ceramic.

Silicon Carbide: Proceedings. Conference on Silicon Carbide, 3rd, 1973. Ed. by R. C. Marshall & John W. Faust, Jr. LC 74-2394. (Illus.). 692p. 1974. 36.95x (ISBN 0-87249-315-6). U of SC Pr.

Silicon-Chemical Etching. Ed. by H. C. Freyhardt. (Crystals-Growth, Properties & Applications Ser.: Vol. 8). (Illus.). 255p. 1982. 87.00 (ISBN 0-387-11862-4). Springer-Verlag.

Silicon Chemistry One. Ed. by F. Boschke. LC 51-5497. (Topics in Current Chemistry: Vol. 50). (Illus.). 180p. 1974. 39.50 (ISBN 0-387-06714-0). Springer-Verlag.

Silicon Chemistry Two. Ed. by F. Boschke. LC 51-5497. (Topics in Current Chemistry Ser.: Vol. 51). (Illus.). 140p. 1974. 36.00 (ISBN 0-387-06722-1). Springer-Verlag.

Silicon Chips: The Magical Mineral in Your Telephone, Calculator, Toys, Automobile, Hospital, Air Conditioning, Factory, Furnace, Sewing Machine, & Countless Other Future Inventions. C. D. Renmore. LC 80-24153. (Illus.). 160p. 1980. 8.95 (ISBN 0-8253-0022-3). Beaufort Bks NY.

Silicon Compilation. Daniel D. Gajski. LC 87-1365. (Illus.). 608p. 1987. text ed. 37.95x (ISBN 0-201-09915-2). Addison-Wesley.

Silicon Compilers: The Technology, the Vendors, the Opportunities. 150p. 1987. 950.00 (ISBN 0-914993-40-2, R-96). Tech Insights.

Silicon English: Business Writing Tools for the Computer Age. Darlene Frank. LC 84-8081. (Illus., Orig.). 1985. pap. 12.95 (ISBN 0-914735-00-4). Royall Pr.

Silicon Geochemistry & Biogeochemistry. S. R. Aston. 1983. 51.50 (ISBN 0-12-065620-5). Acad Pr.

Silicon in Organic Synthesis. Ernest W. Colvin. LC 85-19. 368p. 1985. Repr. of 1981 ed. lib. bdg. 34.50 (ISBN 0-89874-843-7). Krieger.
Silicon Jungle. David H. Rothman. 334p. 1985. pap. 3.95 (ISBN 0-345-32063-8). Ballantine.
Silicon Landscapes. Peter Hall & Ann Markusen. (Illus.). 160p. 1985. text ed. 29.95x (ISBN 0-04-338122-7); pap. 14.95X (ISBN 0-04-338123-5). Unwin Hyman.
Silicon Mage. Barbara Hambly. LC 87-91378. 352p. 1988. pap. 3.95 (ISBN 0-345-33763-8, Del Rey). Ballantine.
Silicon Material Preparation & Economical Wafering Methods. Ed. by Ralph Lutwack & Andrew Morrison. LC 84-5968. (Illus.). 586p. 1984. 54.00 (ISBN 0-8155-0990-1). Noyes.
Silicon-Molecular Beam Epitaxy. Ed. by Erich Kasper & John C. Bean. 1988. Vol. I, 272 pgs. 145.00 (ISBN 0-8493-6830-8, 6830); Vol. II, 256 pgs. 150.00 (ISBN 0-8493-6831-6, 6831). CRC Pr.
Silicon-on-Insulator & Buried Metals in Semiconductors. Ed. by C. K. Chen et al. (Symposium Proceedings Ser.: Vol. 107). 1988. text ed. 46.00 (ISBN 0-931837-75-8). Materials Res.
Silicon Processing for Photovoltaics One: Materials Processing: Theory & Practices, Vol. 5. Ed. by C. P. Khattak & K. V. Ravi. 450p. 1985. 118.50 (ISBN 0-444-86933-6, North-Holland). Elsevier.
Silicon Processing for the VLSI Era: Process Technology, Vol. 1. Stanley Wolf & Richard N. Tauber. (Illus.). 660p. 1986. 54.95x (ISBN 0-9616721-3-7). Lattice Pr.
Silicon Processing-STP 804. Ed. by D. C. Gupta. LC 82-83529. 559p. 1983. text ed. 60.00 (ISBN 0-8031-0243-7, 04-804000-46). ASTM.
Silicon Reagents. E. W. Colvim. 147p. 1988. 54.00 (ISBN 0-12-182560-4). Acad Pr.
Silicon Reagents for Organic Synthesis. William P. Weber. (Reactivity & Structure: Vol. 14). 450p. 1983. 131.00 (ISBN 0-387-11675-3). Springer-Verlag.
Silicon Semiconductor Technology. W. R. Runyan. LC 64-24607. (Texas Instruments Electronics Ser.). (Illus.). pap. 71.00 (ISBN 0-317-09126-3, 2055600). Bks Demand UMI.
Silicon Shock: The Menace of the Computer Invasion. Geoff Simons. 192p. 1985. 24.95 (ISBN 0-631-13835-8). Basil Blackwell.
Silicon Spies. Lauran Paine. 224p. 1987. 14.95 (ISBN 0-312-00183-5). St Martin.
Silicon Syndrome: A Survival Handbook for Couples. Jean Hollands. Ed. by Joan Craig. (Illus.). 222p. 1983. pap. 8.95 (ISBN 0-9606288-1-9). Coastlight PR.
Silicon Syndrome: How to Survive a High-Tech Relationship. Jean Hollands. 240p. (Orig.). 1987. pap. 3.95 (ISBN 0-553-25689-0). Bantam.
Silicon Valley. Michael Rogers. 1982. 15.95 (ISBN 0-671-41030-X). S&S.
Silicon Valley & Beyond: High Technology Growth for the San Francisco Bay Area. (Working Papers . . . Region's Economy: No. 2). 110p. 1981. 20.00 (ISBN 0-318-22694-4). Assn Bay Area.
Silicon Valley As An Advanced Information Society. Everett M. Rogers. (Institute for Urban Studies Monograph Ser.: No. 4). (Illus.). 50p. (Orig.). 1985. pap. 5.00x. U MD Inst.
Silicon Valley As an Advanced Information Society. Everett M. Rogers. (Monograph Ser.: No. 4). 50p. 1985. pap. 5.00. U MD Inst.
Silicon Valley Fever: Growth of High-Technology Culture. Everett M. Rogers & Judith K. Larsen. LC 83-45257. 302p. 1986. pap. 9.95 (ISBN 0-465-07822-2, PL-5156). Basic.
Silicon Visions: The Future of Microcomputer Technology. The Waite Group & Dan Shafer. 320p. 1985. 18.95 (ISBN 0-89303-845-8). Brady Comp Bks.
Silicone Oil in Vitreoretinal Surgery. R. Zivojnovic. (Monographs in Ophthalmology). 1987. lib. bdg. 97.50 (ISBN 0-89838-879-1, Pub. by Martin Nijhoff Netherlands). Kluwer Academic.
Siliconnections: Coming of Age in the Electronic Era. Forrest M. Mims, III. 240p. 1985. text ed. 16.95 (ISBN 0-07-042411-X). McGraw.
Silicosis: Records of International Conference, Johannesburg, August, 1930, (I. L. O. Studies & Reports) (Series F: No. 13, Vol. 31). Repr. of 1930 ed. 65.00 (ISBN 0-8115-3263-1). Kraus Repr.
Silk & Barbed Wire: An A-Z Handoriented Artist's Book. Glenna Luschei. 1986. 125.00 (ISBN 1-318-18355-3). Solo Pr.
Silk & Satin. Marcia Wolfson. 320p. 1986. 18.95 (ISBN 0-399-13192-2, Putnam). Putnam Pub Group.
Silk & Shadow. Aola Vandergriff. 512p. (Orig.). 1981. pap. 3.50 (ISBN 0-446-30856-0). Warner Bks.
Silk & Splendor. Ellen T. Marsh. 432p. 1986. pap. 3.95 (ISBN 0-380-89677-X). Avon.
Silk & Steel. Stephen Alter. 327p. 1980. 11.95 (ISBN 0-374-26411-2). FS&G.
Silk & Steel. Rita Balkey. 496p. 1986. pap. 3.95 (ISBN 0-8217-1949-1). Zebra.
Silk & Steel. Cordia Byers. 352p. 1985. pap. 3.50 (ISBN 0-449-12746-X, GM). Fawcett.
Silk & the Skin. Rodie Sudbery. 144p. (gr. 3-7). 1982. 8.95 (ISBN 0-233-96816-4). Andre Deutsch.
Silk Bonsai. Patricia Ratcliffe. (Illus.). 88p. 1988. 19.95 (ISBN 0-85219-706-3, Pub. by Batsford England). David & Charles.
Silk City: Studies on the Paterson Silk Industry, 1860-1940. Ed. by Philip B. Scranton. LC 85-42869. (Collections of the New Jersey Historical Society Ser.: Vol. 19). (Illus.). 250p. 1985. 19.95 (ISBN 0-911020-12-8). NJ Hist Soc.
Silk Expressions. Deonne B. Wright. 31p. (Orig.). 1986. pap. 4.00 (ISBN 4-151-09253-6). D B Wright.
Silk Flags & Cold Steel: The Civil War in North Carolina, Vol. I: The Piedmont. William Trotter. (Illus.). 350p. Date not set. 18.95 (ISBN 0-929307-01-1). Signal Research Inc.
Silk Glove Hegemony: Finnish-Soviet Relations, 1944-1974: A Case Study of the Theory of the Soft Sphere of Influence. John P. Vloyantes. LC 74-27387. pap. 55.50 (ISBN 0-317-55823-4, 2029409). Bks Demand UMI.
Silk Industry in Ch'ing China. Shih Min-hsiung. Tr. by E-tu Zen Sun from Chinese. (Michigan Abstracts of Chinese & Japanese Works on Chinese History: No. 5). (Illus.). 98p. 1976. pap. 5.00 (ISBN 0-89264-905-4). U of Mich Ctr Chinese.
Silk Industry: Problems & Prospects. Abdul Aziz & H. G. Hanumappa. 1985. 18.50x (ISBN 0-8364-1511-6, Pub. by Ashish India). South Asia Bks.
Silk Lady. Gwen Davis. 427p. 1986. 17.95 (ISBN 0-446-51345-8). Warner Bks.
Silk Lady. Gwen Davis. 416p. 1987. pap. 4.95 (ISBN 0-446-34485-0). Warner Bks.
Silk on the Skin, No. 247. Linda Cajio. 192p. (Orig.). 1988. pap. 2.50 (ISBN 0-553-21887-5, Loveswept). Bantam.
Silk Road. I. Franck & D. Brownstone. 356p. 1987. 119.00x (ISBN 0-317-69076-0, Pub. by Han-Shan Tang Ltd). State Mutual Bk.
Silk Road. Irene M. Franck & David M. Brownstone. (Illus.). 304p. 1986. 24.95 (ISBN 0-8160-1122-2). Facts on File.
Silk Road. Guan Weiran. 11p. 1986. 126.00x (ISBN 0-317-69079-5, Pub. by Han-Shan Tang Ltd). State Mutual Bk.
Silk Road & the Shoso-In. Ryoichi Hayashi. Tr. by Robert Ricketts from Japanese. LC 75-23081. (Heibonsha Survey of Japanese Art Ser.: Vol. 6). (Illus.). 184p. 1975. 20.00 (ISBN 0-8348-1022-0). Weatherhill.
Silk Road & the Shoso-In. Ryoichi Hayashi. 181p. 1975. 91.00x (Pub. by Han-Shan Tang Ltd). State Mutual Bk.
Silk Route & the Diamond Path. Deborah E. Klimburg-Salter. (Illus.). 256p. 1982. 192.00x (Pub. by Han-Shan Tang Ltd). State Mutual Bk.
Silk-Screen Printing for Artists & Craftsmen. Mathilda V. Schwalbach & James A. Schwalbach. (Illus.). 150p. 1981. pap. 7.95 (ISBN 0-486-24046-0). Dover.
Silk Screen Techniques. J. I. Biegeleisen & J. A. Cohn. (Illus.). 1958. pap. 4.50 (ISBN 0-486-20433-2). Dover.
Silk Screen Techniques. J. I. Biegeleisen & M. A. Cohn. (Illus.). 14.75 (ISBN 0-8446-0491-7). Peter Smith.
Silk Stalkings: A Survey of Series Characters Created by Women Authors in Crime & Mystery Fiction. Victoria Nichols & Susan Thompson. 448p. (Orig.). 1988. pap. 12.95 (ISBN 0-88739-096-X, Pub. by Black Lizard Bks). Creative Arts Bk.
Silk Stocking Street. Rachel Paris. (Illus.). 120p. 1972. Repr. of 1970 ed. 10.00 (ISBN 0-87797-020-3). Cherokee.
Silk Textiles of Spain, Eighth-Fifteenth Century. Florence L. May. (Illus.). 296p. 1957. 14.00 (ISBN 0-317-00613-4, Pub. by Hispanic Soc). Interbk Inc.
Silk Textiles of Spain: Eighth to Fifteenth Century. Florence L. May. (Illus.). 1957. 14.00 (ISBN 0-87535-092-5). Hispanic Soc.
Silk: The Luxurious Fabric, Vol. 1, No. 1. S. Jill Miller-Lewis. (Illus.). 34p. (Orig.). 1987. pap. text ed. 8.00 (ISBN 0-934155-04-6). Miller Des.
Silk Town: Industry & Culture in Macclesfield, 1750-1835. Gail Malmgreen. (Illus.). 272p. 1985. pap. text ed. 18.50x (ISBN 0-85958-447-X, Pub. by U of Hull of UK). Humanities.
Silk Vendetta. Victoria Holt. LC 87-5266. 432p. 1987. 17.95 (ISBN 0-385-24299-9). Doubleday.
Silk Vendetta. Victoria Holt. 1989. pap. 4.95 (Crest). Fawcett.
Silk Worker's Notebook. rev. ed. Cheryl Kolander. LC 85-80616. (Illus.). 168p. 1985. pap. 12.00 (ISBN 0-934026-18-1). Interweave.
Silken Barbarity. Violet Winspear. (Harlequin Presents Ser.: No. 1006). 192p. Date not set. pap. 1.95 (ISBN 0-317-63752-5). Harlequin Bks.
Silken Rapture. Cassie Edwards. 1983. pap. 3.50 (ISBN 0-8217-1172-5). Zebra.
Silken Savage. Catherine Hart. 480p. (Orig.). 1985. pap. 3.95 (ISBN 0-8439-2226-5, Leisure Bks). Leisure NY.
Silken Secrets. Joan Smith. 1988. pap. 2.95 (ISBN 0-449-21372-2, Crest). Fawcett.
Silken Sorcery see Handkerchief Magic.
Silken Thread. Cora Sandel. Tr. by Elizabeth Rokkan. 176p. 1987. text ed. 17.95x (ISBN 0-8214-0864-X); pap. text ed. 8.95 (ISBN 0-8214-0865-8). Ohio U Pr.
Silkies. Charlotte Koplinka. LC 77-79123. (Illus.). 1978. 7.95 (ISBN 0-8397-7810-4). Eriksson.
Silko. Alfred Konner. Tr. by Richard Sadler. (Day in the Life of...Ser.). (Illus.). (gr. 2-4). 1977. 2.00 (ISBN 0-905778-01-4). Academy Chi Pubs.
Silkroads & Shadows. Susan Shawartz. 352p. 1988. pap. 3.95 (ISBN 0-8125-5411-6). Tor Bks.
Silkworm Story. Jennifer Coldrey. LC 85-71250. (Illus.). 32p. (ps-3). 1985. 9.95 (ISBN 0-233-97553-5). Andre Deutsch.
Silkworms. Sylvia A. Johnson. LC 82-250. (Lerner Natural Science Bks.). (Illus.). 48p. (gr. 4-10). 1982. PLB 12.95 (ISBN 0-8225-1478-8). Lerner Pubns.
Silky, Smooth & Strong: Natural Care for Your Hair, Skin & Nails. Stella Weller. (Illus.). 160p. (Orig.). 1988. pap. 5.99 (ISBN 0-7225-1502-2, Pub. by Thorsons (England)). Sterling.
Silky Terriers. Martin Weil. (Illus.). 128p. 1981. 9.95 (ISBN 0-87666-730-2, KW-115). TFH Pubns.
Sillages. Vercors. 190p. 1972. 8.95 (ISBN 0-686-55138-9). French & Eur.
Sillas. (Productos Latinoamericanos Incluidos en el Sistema Generalizado de Preferencias de los Estados Unidos Ser.). 36p. 1977. pap. text ed. 3.00 (ISBN 0-8270-3505-5). OAS.
Sills Family & Related Lines. Louise J. Sills. 1969. pap. 8.00 (ISBN 0-686-05558-6). L C Bryant.
Silly Aunt Sally. Jan Holstock. (Ward Lock Educational Ser.). 96p. 29.00x (ISBN 0-7062-4313-7, Pub. by Ward Lock Educ Co Ltd). State Mutual Bk.
Silly Baby. Judith Caseley. LC 87-4097. (Illus.). 24p. (ps-3). 1988. 11.95 (ISBN 0-688-07355-7); lib. bdg. 11.88 (ISBN 0-688-07356-5). Greenwillow.
Silly Circus. (Surprise Bks.). (Illus.). 22p. (ps-1). 1983. 5.95 (ISBN 0-8431-0643-3). Price Stern.
Silly Egg. Nancy Reese. Ed. by Alton Jordan. (I Can Read Underwater Bks.). (Illus.). (gr. k-3). 1974. PLB 3.95 (ISBN 0-89868-004-2, Read Res); pap. text ed. 1.75 (ISBN 0-89868-037-9). ARO Pub.
Silly Ghost Riddles. Roger Salinas. (Illus.). 32p. (Orig.). (gr. 3-5). 1987. pap. 2.95 (ISBN 0-942673-00-X). Salinas Salinas & Matthews.
Silly Goose. Jack Kent. LC 82-21441. (Illus.). 32p. (ps-3). 1983. PLB 10.95 (ISBN 0-13-809947-2). P-H.
Silly Goose. Jack Kent. (Illus.). 32p. (Orig.). (gr. k-3). 1986. pap. 5.95 (ISBN 0-13-810177-9). P-H.
Silly Goose. Jan Ormerod. LC 85-17131. (Illus.). 24p. (ps). 1986. 4.95 (ISBN 0-688-04209-0). Lothrop.
Silly Joke Book. Victoria G. Hartman. (Illus.). 96p. (gr. 4-6). 1987. pap. 1.95 (ISBN 0-590-33846-3). Scholastic Inc.
Silly Kid Joke Book. Caroline A. Levine. LC 82-17727. (Illus.). 64p. (gr. 1-3). 1983. 10.95 (ISBN 0-525-44039-9). Dutton.
Silly Mother Hubbard. Leonard Kessler. LC 79-18776. (Young Mother Goose Bks.). (Illus.). 32p. (gr. k-3). 1980. PLB 7.12 (ISBN 0-8116-7401-0). Garrard.
Silly Rhymes. Mik Brown. Ed. by JV-Warwick Press Staff. (Illus.). 32p. (gr. 1-6). 1988. 7.90 (ISBN 0-531-19047-1, Warwick). Watts.
Silly Riddles. Mik Brown. Ed. by JV-Warwick Press Staff. (Illus.). 32p. (gr. 1-6). 1988. 7.90 (ISBN 0-531-19048-X, Warwick). Watts.
Silly Sandwich Book. Randa Rasmussen & Rick Rasmussen. (Illus.). 30p. pap. cancelled (ISBN 0-932967-10-8). Pacific Shoreline.
Silly School Riddles & Other Classroom Crack-Ups. Caroline Levine. Ed. by Abby Levine. LC 84-17300. (Illus.). 32p. (gr. 1-5). 1984. 7.75 (ISBN 0-8075-7359-0). A Whitman.
Silly Scribbles: A Complete Readiness Program for Young Children. Shirley A. Steinmetz. 272p. (ps-k). 1988. pap. 24.95x (ISBN 0-87628-776-3). Ctr Appl Res.
Silly Sidney. Morgan Matthews. LC 85-14063. (Illus.). 48p. (Orig.). (gr. 1-3). 1986. PLB 9.49 (ISBN 0-8167-0610-7); pap. text ed. 1.95 (ISBN 0-8167-0611-5). Troll Assocs.
Silly Song. Shaerie Cosgrove. (Sing! Ser.). 32p. (ps-3). 1988. pap. 7.95 (ISBN 0-8249-7275-9). Ideals.
Silly Songbook. Esther L. Nelson. LC 81-50989. (Illus.). 128p. (ps up). 1981. PLB 16.79 (ISBN 0-8069-4651-2); spiral pap. 9.95 (ISBN 0-8069-7552-0). Sterling.
Silly Tail Book. Marc Brown. LC 83-2250. (Illus.). 48p. (ps-3). 1983. 5.95 (ISBN 0-8193-1109-X). Parents.
Silly Tail Book. Marc Brown. (ps-2). 1987. pap. 2.95 (ISBN 0-517-56746-6). Crown.
Silly Tillie. Jeanine Wine. (gr. k-3). 1988. 12.95 (ISBN 0-317-69022-1). Good Bks PA.
Silly Tilly & the Easter Bunny. Lillian Hoban. LC 86-7682. (Early I Can Read Bks.). (Illus.). 32p. (ps-3). 1987. 7.70i (ISBN 0-06-022392-8); PLB 8.89 (ISBN 0-06-022393-6). HarpJ.
Sillycomb. Hunce Voelcker. 136p. 1973. 6.95 (ISBN 0-915572-10-9). Panjandrum.
Silmarillion. J. R. R. Tolkien. 1985. pap. 3.95 (ISBN 0-345-32581-8). Ballantine.
Silmarillion. J. R. R. Tolkien. LC 77-8025. 1983. 7.95 (ISBN 0-395-34646-0). HM.
Silo Site. R. G. Chenhall. (Arizona Archaeologist Ser.: No. 2). (Illus.). 56p. (Orig.). 1977. pap. 4.00 (ISBN 0-939071-01-0). AZ Archaeol.
Silos: Theory & Practice. M. Reimbert & A. Reimbert. (Bulk Materials Handling Ser: Vol.1, No. 3). (Illus.). 251p. 1976. text ed. 60.00 (ISBN 0-87849-014-0, Trans Tech Germany). Trans Tech.
Siloxane Bond: Physical Properties & Chemical Transformations. M. G. Voronkov et al. LC 78-16675. (Studies in Soviet Science--Physical Sciences). (Illus.). 506p. 1978. 95.00x (ISBN 0-306-10940-9, Consultants). Plenum Pub.
Silt & Sky. Romein-Verschoor. LC 74-86058. Repr. of 1950 ed. 21.50x (ISBN 0-8046-0636-6, Pub. by Kennikat). Assoc Faculty Pr.
Silurian & Lower Devonian Basin & Basin-Slope Limestones, Copenhagen Canyon, Nevada. Jonathan C. Matti et al. LC 74-19734. (Geological Society of America Special Papers: No. 159). pap. 20.00 (ISBN 0-317-28377-4, 2025458). Bks Demand UMI.
Silurian Conodonts from Wills Mountain Anticline, Virginia. Charles T. Helfrich. LC 74-28984. (Geological Society of America Special Papers: No. 161). pap. 49.50 (ISBN 0-317-28375-8, 2025456). Bks Demand UMI.
Siluro-Devonian Microfaunal Biostratigraphy in Nevada see Bulletins of American Paleontology.
Silva Mind Control Method. Jose Silva & Philip Miele. 1978. pap. 4.50 (ISBN 0-671-62610-8). PB.
Silva Mind Control Method for Business Managers. Jose Silva & Robert B. Stone. LC 83-13888. 241p. 1983. 16.95 (ISBN 0-13-811018-2, Busn); pap. 7.95 (ISBN 0-13-811000-X). P-H.
Silva Mind Control Method for Business Managers. Jose Silva & Robert B. Stone. Date not set. pap. 3.95 (ISBN 0-671-61110-0). PB.
Silva Mind Control Through Psychorientology. Harry F. McKnight. 5.95 (ISBN 0-913343-40-4). Inst Psych Inc.
Silvae Mycologicae Berolinensis. C. G. Ehrenberg. 1972. Repr. of 1818 ed. 25.00x (ISBN 90-6123-253-8). Lubrecht & Cramer.
Silvae, Thebaid, Achilleid, 2 Vols. Statius. (Loeb Classical Library: No. 206-207). 1928. 13.95x ea. Vol. 1 (ISBN 0-674-99226-1). Vol. 2 (ISBN 0-674-99228-8). Harvard U Pr.
Silver. Jessie McNab. Ed. by Brenda Gilchrist. LC 78-62731. (Smithsonian Illustrated Library of Antiques). (Illus.). 128p. (Orig.). 1981. 9.95 (ISBN 0-910503-37-0). Cooper-Hewitt Museum.
Silver. Norma F. Mazer. 288p. (YA) (gr. 7 up). 1988. 11.95 (ISBN 0-688-06865-0). Morrow.
Silver. G. Rickard. (Spotlight on Resources Ser.). (Illus.). 48p. (gr. 5 up). Date not set. PLB 14.60 (ISBN 0-86592-273-X). Rourke Corp.
Silver. Gloria Whelan. LC 87-26612. (Stepping Stone Bks.). (Illus.). 64p. (Orig.). (gr. 2-4). 1988. lib. bdg. 5.99 (ISBN 0-394-99611-9, BYR); pap. 1.95 (ISBN 0-394-89611-4). Random.
Silver. Hilma Wolitzer. 352p. 1988. 18.95 (ISBN 0-374-26422-8). FS&G.
Silver see Antiques & Their Values.
Silver Age of the Greek World. John P. Mahaffy. 1978. Repr. of 1911 ed. lib. bdg. 65.00 (ISBN 0-8495-3718-5). Arden Lib.
Silver Age: Russian Art in the Early Twentieth Century & the World Art Group. 2nd ed. John Bowlt. (Illus.). 456p. 1982. 36.00 (ISBN 0-89250-063-8). Orient Res Partners.
Silver Amalgam in Clinical Practice. 2nd ed. I. Gainsford. (Illus.). 120p. 1976. pap. 16.00 (ISBN 0-7236-0372-3). PSG Pub Co.
Silver: An Analysis of Factors Affecting Its Price. 2nd ed. Y. S. Leong. (Brookings Institution Reprint Ser.). Repr. of 1934 ed. lib. bdg. 39.50 (ISBN 0-697-00162-8). Irvington.
Silver: An Illustrated Guide to Collecting Silver. Margaret Holland. (Illus.). 144p. 20.00 (ISBN 0-317-55086-1). Apollo.
Silver & Carving of the Old China Trade. Ed. by Neville J. Irons. (Illus.). 280p. 1983. 406.00x (Pub. by Han-Shan Tang Ltd). State Mutual Bk.
Silver & Entrepreneurship in Seventeenth-Century Potosi: The Life & Times of Antonio Lopez de Quiroga. Peter Bakewell. LC 84-7582. (Illus.). 272p. (Orig.). 1988. 35.00x (ISBN 0-8263-1097-4); pap. 15.95x (ISBN 0-8263-1098-2). U of NM Pr.
Silver & Gold Investor's Profit Guide. Daniel Rosenthal & Ellen Young. 62p. 1986. pap. text ed. 69.00 (ISBN 0-938689-02-9). Inst Preserv Wealth.
Silver & Information: Poems. Bruce Smith. LC 84-16331. (Contemporary Poetry Ser.). 72p. 1985. 10.95x (ISBN 0-8203-0761-0); pap. 6.95 (ISBN 0-8203-0762-9). U of Ga Pr.
Silver & Politics in Nevada: 1892-1902. Mary E. Glass. LC 72-92547. (Lancehead Ser). (Illus.). xi, 242p. 1970. 8.95 (ISBN 0-87417-026-5). U of Nev Pr.
Silver & Sapphire. Coral S. Saxe. 416p. 1988. pap. 3.95 (ISBN 0-553-27603-4). Bantam.
Silver & the Human Organism. Eugen Kolisko & Lily Kolisko. pap. cancelled (ISBN 0-906492-10-6, Pub by Kolisko Archives). St George Bk Serv.
Silver Angel. Johanna Lindsey. 432p. (Orig.). 1988. pap. 4.50 (ISBN 0-380-75294-8). Avon.
Silver Apples, Golden Apples: Best-Loved Irish Verse. Frank Delaney. (Illus.). 1987. pap. 15.95 (ISBN 0-85640-391-1, Pub. by Blackstaff Ireland). Irish Bks Media.
Silver Arrow & Other Indian Romances of the Dune Country. E. H. Reed. 1977. lib. bdg. 59.95 (ISBN 0-8490-2605-9). Gordon Pr.

Silver Scream. Ed. by David J. Schow. 1988. 19.95 (ISBN 0-913165-27-1). Dark Harvest.
Silver Screen in the Silver City: A History of Cinemas in Aberdeen, 1896-1987. M. Thomson. (Illus.). 350p. 1988. pap. 17.01 (ISBN 0-08-036402-0, AUP). Pergamon.
Silver Setup: A Mike Garrett Mystery. Richard Blaine. 1988. pap. 2.95 (ISBN 0-517-00067-9, Pageant Bks). Crown.
Silver Ships-Green Fields. Sara C. Juengst. (Illus.). 52p. (Orig.). (gr. 1-6). 1986. pap. 5.95 (ISBN 0-377-00161-9). Friendship Pr.
Silver, Sin & Sixpenny Ale: A Social History of Broken Hill 1883-1921. Brian Kennedy. 1978. 20.00x (ISBN 0-522-84141-4, Pub. by Melbourne U Pr). Intl Spec Bk.
Silver Situation in the United States. facsimile ed. Frank W. Taussig. LC 73-95079. (Select Bibliographies Reprint Ser). 1896. 19.00 (ISBN 0-8369-5079-8). Ayer Co Pubs.
Silver Skates. Nancy B. Irland. (Destiny Ser.). 128p. (Orig.). 1987. pap. 6.95 (ISBN 0-8163-0678-8). Pacific Pr Pub Assn.
Silver Skates. William A. Kottmeyer. 1972. text ed. 7.96 (ISBN 0-07-034019-6). McGraw.
Silver Skates: Breaking the Ice. Barbara J. Mumma. (Girls Only Ser.: No. 1). (YA) (gr. 6 up). 1988. pap. 2.95 (ISBN 0-449-13459-8). Fawcett.
Silver Skates: Winner's Waltz. Barbara J. Mumma. (Girls Only Ser.: No. 2). (YA) (gr. 6 up). 1988. pap. 2.95 (ISBN 0-449-13460-1). Fawcett.
Silver Skull. Les Daniel. 240p. 1983. pap. 2.50 (ISBN 0-441-76687-0). Ace Bks.
Silver Slave, Dear Puritan & Rapture of the Desert, 3 Vols. Violet Winspear. (Harlequin Romances Series (3-in-1)). 576p. 1983. pap. 3.50 (ISBN 0-373-20069-2). Harlequin Bks.
Silver Spike. Glen Cook. 288p. 1989. pap. price not set. Tor Bks.
Silver Spoon. John W. Schnurr. 508p. 1984. 16.95 (ISBN 0-89697-157-0). Intl Univ Pr.
Silver Spoon & the Passers by. John Galsworthy. 18.95 (ISBN 0-8488-0064-8, Pub. by Amereon Hse). Amereon Ltd.
Silver Spoon Murders. D. W. Smith. 272p. 1988. 15.95 (ISBN 0-8184-0460-4). Lyle Stuart.
Silver Spur Anthology of Western Fiction. Ed. by Edward Gorman. LC 87-72798. 448p. (Orig.). 1988. pap. 11.95 (ISBN 0-88739-059-5). Creative Arts Bk.
Silver Spurs. R. Knigge. LC 75-10111. 1973. 4.95 (ISBN 0-915614-01-4); incl. record 6.95 (ISBN 0-685-57207-2). Knollwood Pub.
Silver Spurs. Charles A. Seltzer. 277p. 1975. Repr. of 1935 ed. lib. bdg. 18.95x (ISBN 0-88411-109-1, Pub. by Aeonian PR). Amereon Ltd.
Silver Stampede. facsimile ed. Neill C. Wilson. LC 74-165650. (Select Bibliographies Reprint Ser). Repr. of 1937 ed. 24.50 (ISBN 0-8369-5969-8). Ayer Co Pubs.
Silver Stampede: The Career of Death Valley's Hell-Camp, Old Panamint. Neill C. Wilson. (Illus.). 360p. 1986. pap. 10.00 (ISBN 0-87380-156-3). Rio Grande.
Silver Star. Jackson Gregory. 1976. Repr. of 1931 ed. lib. bdg. 19.95x (ISBN 0-88411-285-3, Pub. by Aeonian Pr). Amereon Ltd.
Silver Star. Stirling Silliphant. (Orig.). 1986. pap. 3.50 (ISBN 0-345-32619-9). Ballantine.
Silver Storm. Cynthia Wright. 1981. pap. 2.95 (ISBN 0-345-30333-4). Ballantine.
Silver Street. E. Richard Johnson. 152p. 1988. pap. 4.95 (ISBN 0-930330-78-1). Intl Polygonics.
Silver Sun. Nancy Springer. 1983. pap. 3.50 (ISBN 0-671-61117-8, Timescape). PB.
Silver Sunbeam: A Practical & Theoretical Text-book on Sun Drawing & Photographic Printing. J. Towler. LC 78-88124. 1969. Repr. of 1864 ed. 19.95 (ISBN 0-87100-005-9). Morgan.
Silver Sunset. Alicia Engelhardt. 1986. 9.95 (ISBN 0-8034-8617-0, Avalon). Bouregy.
Silver Swan. Susannah Leigh. 496p. 1988. pap. 3.95 (ISBN 0-451-40063-1, Onyx). NAL.
Silver Swimmer: Poems. Rosalie Boyle. LC 74-33990. 1975. pap. 5.00 (ISBN 0-914562-01-0). Merriam-Eddy.
Silver Sword. Ian Serraillier. LC 59-6556. (Illus.). (gr. 7-9). 1959. 16.95 (ISBN 0-87599-104-1). S G Phillips.
Silver Tombstone of Edward Schieffelin. Lonnie E. Underhill. LC 78-66100. (Illus.). 64p. 1979. 19.95 (ISBN 0-933234-01-5); pap. 10.95 (ISBN 0-933234-00-7). Roan Horse.
Silver Tongues: Famous Speeches from Burke to Baldwin. John Hayward. 1937. 20.00 (ISBN 0-686-17685-5). Quaker City.
Silver Tower. Dale Brown. 1988. 18.95 (ISBN 1-55611-060-X). D I Fine.
Silver Toys. Miranda Poliakoff. (Illus.). 64p. (Orig.). 1985. pap. 5.95 (ISBN 0-905209-94-X, Pub. by Victoria & Albert Mus UK). Faber & Faber.
Silver Treasure from Early Byzantium: The Kaper Karaon & Related Treasures. Marlia Mundell Mango. Frwd. by Gary Vikan. LC 86-50138. (Illus.). 125p. (Orig.). 1986. pap. 45.00 (ISBN 0-911886-32-X). Walters Art.
Silver Treasury of English Lyrics. Ed. by T. Earle Welby. 1979. Repr. of 1926 ed. lib. bdg. 25.00 (ISBN 0-8495-5722-4). Arden Lib.
Silver Trumpet. Owen Barfield. LC 85-71803. (Illus.). 156p. (gr. 3-8). 1986. 16.95 (ISBN 0-917665-05-8). Bookmakers Guild.
Silver Twilight. Leigh Bristol. 384p. (Orig.). 1987. pap. 3.95 (ISBN 0-446-34695-0). Warner Bks.
Silver Veil. Margaret Way. (Harlequin Romances Ser.). 192p. 1983. pap. 1.75 (ISBN 0-373-02539-4). Harlequin Bks.
Silver Vessels of the Sansanian Period, Royal Imagery, Vol. I. Prudence Harper. LC 80-26188. (Illus.). 272p. 1982. 47.00x (ISBN 0-691-03973-9). Princeton U Pr.
Silver Wands. Marion M. Boyd. LC 70-144724. (Yale Ser. of Younger Poets: No. 17). Repr. of 1923 ed. 18.00 (ISBN 0-404-53817-7). AMS Pr.
Silver Warriors. Michael Moorcock. 224p. 1985. pap. 2.95 (ISBN 0-425-10146-0). Berkley Pub.
Silver Web. Jean Nash. (Last of the Lattimers Ser.). 352p. 1984. pap. 3.50 (ISBN 0-8439-2064-5, Leisure Bks). Leisure NY.
Silver Whistle. Patrick B. Mace. (Orig.). (gr. k up). pap. 3.50 (ISBN 0-87602-250-6). Anchorage.
Silver Whistle. Ann Tompert. LC 88-1446. (Illus.). 32p. (gr. k-3). 1988. PLB 14.95 (ISBN 0-02-789160-7). Macmillan.
Silver Wings. Grace L. Hill. Repr. lib. bdg. 18.95 (ISBN 0-89190-030-6, Pub. by River City Pr). Amereon Ltd.
Silver Wings & Leather Jackets. C. T. Westcott. (Eagleheart Ser.: No. 1). (Orig.). (YA) 1989. pap. price not set (ISBN 0-440-20239-6). Dell.
Silver Wings, Santiago Blue. Janet Dailey. 480p. 1984. 15.95 (ISBN 0-671-50405-3, Pub. by Poseidon); deluxe ed. 40.00 (ISBN 0-671-50906-3). S&S.
Silver Wings, Santiago Blue. Janet Dailey. (General Ser.). 1984. lib. bdg. 15.95 (ISBN 0-8161-3725-0, Large Print Bks). G K Hall.
Silver Wings, Santiago Blue. Janet Dailey. 1985. pap. 4.50 (ISBN 0-671-60072-9). PB.
Silver Wood. James Facos. 1977. pap. 1.75 (ISBN 0-686-38383-4). Eldridge Pub.
Silver-Zinc Batteries. Himy. (Electrochemical Society Ser.). 1985. write for info. (ISBN 0-471-89315-3). Wiley.
Silver-Zinc Battery: Phenomena & Design Principles. Albert Himy. 1986. 15.00 (ISBN 0-317-28947-0). Vantage.
Silverado. Logan Winters. (Spectros Ser.: No. 1). (Orig.). 1981. pap. 1.75 (ISBN 0-505-51612-8, Pub. by Tower Bks). Leisure NY.
SilverFlatware - English, Irish & Scottish: 1660-1980. Ian Pickford. (Illus.). 232p. 1983. 59.50 (ISBN 0-907462-35-9). Antique Collect.
Silvergirl's Surgery: Plastic Surgery. Frank McDowell. 475p. 1987. text ed. 43.00 (ISBN 0-317-55942-7). Year Bk Med.
Silverhair the Wanderer. Diana Paxson. 320p. (Orig.). 1986. pap. 2.95 (ISBN 0-8125-4860-4, Dist. by Warner Publisher Services & St. Martin's Press). Tor Bks.
Silverhawks: The Menace of Mon Star. Adapted by Michael J. Pellowski. (Illus.). (gr. k-5). 1987. pap. 1.95 (ISBN 0-448-48634-2). Putnam Pub Group.
Silverhawks: The Planet-Eater. Adapted by Michael J. Pellowski. (Illus.). (gr. k-5). 1987. pap. 1.95 (ISBN 0-448-48631-8). Putnam Pub Group.
Silverhawks: The Sun Bandits. Adapted by Michael J. Pellowski. (Illus.). (gr. k-5). 1987. pap. 1.95 (ISBN 0-448-48632-6). Putnam Pub Group.
Silverhawks: The Terror of the Time-Stopper. Adapted by Michael J. Pellowski. (Illus.). (gr. k-5). 1987. pap. 1.95 (ISBN 0-448-48633-4). Putnam Pub Group.
Silverless Mirrors: Book, Self, & Postmodern American Fiction. Charles Caramello. LC 83-14841. 1983. o. p. 25.00 (ISBN 0-8130-0769-0); pap. 21.00x. U Presses Fla.
Silverlock. John M. Myers. LC 83-1039. (Bk. 5). 544p. (Orig.). (gr. 3-5). 1984. pap. 4.95x (ISBN 0-441-76674-9). Ace Bks.
Silvermine Trail. Virgil Hart. 224p. 1985. pap. 2.25 (ISBN 0-8439-2273-7, Leisure Bks). Leisure NY.
Silverplated Flatware. 3rd., rev. ed. Tere Hagan. (Illus.). 368p. 1987. pap. 14.95 (ISBN 0-89145-351-2, 1816). Collector Bks.
Silverplated Flatware. rev. ed. Tere Hagen. 352p. 1984. pap. 14.95 (ISBN 0-89145-257-5). Collector Bks.
Silversmith in Eighteenth Century Williamsburg. Colonial Williamsburg Foundation Staff. (Williamsburg Craft Ser). (Illus.). 37p. (Orig.). 1956. pap. 1.50 (ISBN 0-910412-21-9). Williamsburg.
Silversmithing & Art Metal for Schools, Tradesmen, Craftsmen. Murray Bovin. LC 64-2766. (Illus.). 176p. 1977. 18.95 (ISBN 0-910280-04-5); pap. 14.95 (ISBN 0-910280-03-7). Bovin.
Silversmithing (FET) Seitz & Finegold. LC 82-70657. 480p. 1983. 35.00 (ISBN 0-8019-7232-9). Chilton.
Silversmith's Manual. 2nd ed. Bernard Cuzner. 416p. 1987. 125.00x (Pub. by E Bruton Assocs Ltd UK). State Mutual Bk.
Silversmiths of Birmingham & Their Marks 1750-1980. Ed. by A. K. Jones. 416p. 1987. 125.00x (ISBN 0-7198-0002-1, Pub. by E Bruton Assocs Ltd UK). State Mutual Bk.
Silversmiths of Lancaster, Pennsylvania 1730-1850. Vivian S. Gerstell. LC 72-86855. (Illus.). 160p. 1972. 9.50 (ISBN 0-915010-17-8). Sutter House.
Silversmiths of North Carolina,1696-1860. Rev. ed. Mary Reynolds Peacock. (Illus.). xxix, 301p. 1984. 15.00 (ISBN 0-86526-201-2); pap. 8.00 (ISBN 0-86526-215-2). NC Archives.
Silversmiths of Virginia. George B. Cutten. (Illus.). 1976. Repr. 17.50 (ISBN 0-87517-040-4). Dietz.
Silverstreet. Thomas E. Williams. (Illus.). 240p. 1983. 15.00 (ISBN 0-682-49929-3). Exposition-Phoenix.
Silverswept. Linda Ladd. (Avon Romance Ser.). 368p. 1987. pap. 3.95 (ISBN 0-380-75204-2). Avon.
Silversword. Phyllis Whitney. 1988. lib. bdg. 19.95x (ISBN 0-8161-4368-4, Large Print Bks); pap. 12.95x (ISBN 0-8161-4369-2, Large Print Bks). G K Hall.
Silversword. Phyllis A. Whitney. LC 86-4471. 312p. 1987. 15.95 (ISBN 0-385-23666-2). Doubleday.
Silversword. Phyllis A. Whitney. 1987. pap. 4.50 (ISBN 0-449-21278-5). Fawcett.
Silverthorn. Raymond E. Feist. LC 83-27471. 360p. 1985. 15.95 (ISBN 0-385-19210-X). Doubleday.
Silverthorn. Raymond E. Feist. 336p. 1986. pap. 3.95 (ISBN 0-553-25928-8, Spectra). Bantam.
Silvertip's Roundup. Max Brand. Date not set. pap. 2.95 (ISBN 0-446-32023-4). Warner Bks.
Silvertip's Search. Max Brand. 1978. pap. 1.50 (ISBN 0-671-81762-0). PB.
Silvertip's Search. Max Brand. 144p. 1987. pap. 2.75 (ISBN 0-671-63987-0). PB.
Silvertip's Strick. Max Brand. pap. 2.75 (ISBN 0-515-08898-6). Jove Pubns.
Silvertip's Trap. Max Brand. 1979. pap. 1.50 (ISBN 0-671-81763-9). PB.
Silverton. rev. ed. Jack L. Benham. (Illus.). 64p. (Orig.). 1981. pap. 3.95 (ISBN 0-941026-02-7). Bear Creek Pub.
Silvertown, Nineteen Seventeen. Michael Paris. 1988. 30.00x (Pub. by Ian Henry Pubns England). State Mutual Bk.
Silverwood. Joanna Barnes. 432p. 1985. 16.95 (ISBN 0-671-45940-6, Linden Pr). S&S.
Silverwood. Joanna Barnes. 1986. pap. 3.95 (ISBN 0-671-60776-6). PB.
Silverwood. Joanna Barnes. (Large Print Books (General Ser.)). 558p. 1985. lib. bdg. 18.95 (ISBN 0-8161-3936-9). G K Hall.
Silverwork & Jewelery. Henry Wilson. 1978. pap. 9.95 (ISBN 0-8008-7192-8, Pentalic). Taplinger.
Silverwork & Jewelry Handbook. W. R. Lethaby. (Illus.). 343p. 1988. pap. 25.00 (ISBN 0-87556-362-7). Saifer.
Silvery Past. Candice F. Ransom. 208p. (Orig.). (gr. 7 up). 1982. pap. 1.95 (ISBN 0-590-32514-0, Windswept). Scholastic Inc.
Silvia Dubois: A Biografy of the Slav Who Whipt Her Mistres & Gand Her Fredom. C. W. Larison. Tr. & intro. by Jared C. Lobdell. (Schomburg Library of Nineteenth-Century Black Women Writers). 288p. 1988. 19.95 (ISBN 0-19-505239-0). Oxford U Pr.
Silvio Gesell: Money Reformer. L Wise. 1982. lib. bdg. 59.95 (ISBN 0-87700-393-9). Revisionist Pr.
Silyated Surfaces, Vol. 7. D. Leyden & W. Collins. (Midland Macromolecular Monographs). 388p. 1980. 105.00x (ISBN 0-677-13370-7). Gordon & Breach.
Simas. Jurgis Gliauda. 1971. 5.00 (ISBN 0-87141-042-7). Manyland.
Simbad the Sailor: Fairy Tales. Ed. by Tony Tallarico. (Tuffy Story Bks). (Illus.). 32p. (ps-3). 1987. pap. text ed. 2.95 (ISBN 0-89828-335-3, 83353). Tuffy Bks.
Simbambene: The Voices of Women at Mboza. Hanlie Griesel et al. 49p. 1988. pap. text ed. 8.95x (ISBN 0-86975-319-3, Pub. by Ravan Pr). Ohio U Pr.
Simbi & the Satyr of the Dark Jungle. Amos Tutuola. 144p. (Orig.). 1988. pap. 6.95 (ISBN 0-87286-214-3). City Lights.
Simbolos - Fechas - Biografias. Rolando Espinosa. (Illus.). 168p. (Span.). 1969. pap. 3.00 (ISBN 0-89729-414-9). Ediciones.
Simca's Cuisine. Simone Beck. (Illus.). 1972. 17.45 (ISBN 0-394-47449-X). Knopf.
Simenon. De Fallois. pap. 11.50 (ISBN 0-685-36579-4). French & Eur.
Simenon: A Critical Biography. Stanley G. Eskin. LC 86-43084. 320p. 1987. lib. bdg. 24.95x (ISBN 0-89950-281-4). McFarland & Co.
Simeon & the Baby Jesus. Evelyn Marxhausen. (Arch Bks.). (Illus.). 24p. (gr. k-4). 1986. pap. 1.29 saddlestitched (ISBN 0-570-06202-0, 59-1425). Concordia.
Simeon Mountain-A Biography: Nulato. Yvonne Yarber & Curt Madison. (YKSD Biography Ser.). 80p. 1983. pap. 8.95 (ISBN 0-910871-05-1). Spirit Mount Pr.
Simeon North: First Official Pistol Maker of the United States. North & North. Repr. 12.95 (ISBN 0-88227-001-X). Gun Room.
Simhat Torah. Norma Simon. (Festival Series of Picture Storybooks). (Illus.). (ps-k). 1960. bds. 4.50 lam. (ISBN 0-8381-0704-4). United Syn Bk.
Simian Viruses. R. N. Rull. Bd. with Rhinoviruses. D. A. Tyrrell. (Virology Monographs: Vol. 2). (Illus.). iv, 124p. 1968. 21.00 (ISBN 0-387-80890-6). Springer-Verlag.
Similarities in Physics. John N. Shive & Robert L. Weber. 277p. 1982. pap. 31.50 (ISBN 0-471-89795-7, Pub. by Wiley-Interscience). Wiley.
Similarity & Analogical Reasoning. Ed. by Stella Vosniadou & Andrew Ortony. (Illus.). 410p. Date not set. price not set (ISBN 0-521-36295-4). Cambridge U Pr.
Similarity & Choice: Papers in Honour of Clyde Coombs. Ed. by E. D. Lantermann & H. Feger. 392p. 1980. pap. text ed. 39.95x (ISBN 0-89859-198-8). L Erlbaum Assocs.
Similarity & Clustering in Chemical Information Systems. Willett. LC 86-31433. (Chemometrics Research Studies). 254p. 1987. 54.95 (ISBN 0-471-91463-0). Wiley.
Similarity in Visually Perceived Forms. Erich Goldmeier. LC 72-83230. (Psychological Issues Monograph: No. 29, Vol. 8, No. 1). 135p. 1972. text ed. 20.00x (ISBN 0-8236-6077-X). Intl Univs Pr.
Similarity Laws & Modeling. Jhurgen Zierep. LC 74-157835. (Gasdynamics: Vol. 2). pap. 42.80 (ISBN 0-317-28555-6, 2055016). Bks Demand UMI.
Similarity of Automorphisms of the Torus. R. L. Adler & B. Weiss. LC 52-42839. (Memoirs: No. 98). 43p. 1970. pap. 11.00 (ISBN 0-8218-1298-X, MEMO-98). Am Math.
Similarity, Self-Similarity & Intermediate Asymptotics. Ed. by G. I. Barenblatt. LC 79-14621. (Illus.). 236p. 1980. 65.00x (ISBN 0-306-10956-5, Consultants). Plenum Pub.
Simile & Metaphor in the English & Scottish Ballads. George C. Odell. 107p. 1980. Repr. of 1892 ed. lib. bdg. 17.50 (ISBN 0-8495-4215-4). Arden Lib.
Simile & Metaphor in the English & Scottish Ballads. George C. O'Dell. LC 74-28467. 1892. lib. bdg. 29.50 (ISBN 0-8414-6512-6). Folcroft.
Similes & Their Use. Grenville Kleiser. (Illus.). 381p. 1981. Repr. of 1925 ed. lib. bdg. 45.50 (ISBN 0-8495-3131-4). Arden Lib.
Similes & Their Use. Grenville Kleiser. 1973. Repr. of 1925 ed. 39.00 (ISBN 0-8274-0092-6). R West.
Similes: As Gentle As a Lamb, Spin Like a Top, & Other "Like" or "As" Comparisons Between Unlike Things. Joan Hanson. LC 76-22433. (Joan Hanson Word Bks.). (Illus.). (ps-3). 1976. PLB 4.95 (ISBN 0-8225-1108-8). Lerner Pubns.
Similes Dictionary. Lawrence Urdang. 1988. 68.00x (ISBN 0-8103-4361-4). Gale.
Similia Dissimilia. Rainer Crone. LC 87-63250. (Illus.). 188p. 1988. 45.00 (ISBN 0-8478-0922-6). Rizzoli Intl.
Similitude & Approximation Theory. S. J. Kline. (Illus.). 250p. 1986. Repr. of 1965 ed. 39.50 (ISBN 0-387-16518-5). Springer-Verlag.
Similitude & Modelling. E. Szucs. LC 79-10177. (Fundamental Studies in Engineering: Vol. 2). 1980. 84.25 (ISBN 0-444-99780-6). Elsevier.
Similkameen Country. N. L. Barlee. Ed. by Herb Bryce. (Illus.). 96p. Date not set. 9.95 (ISBN 0-88839-990-1). Hancock House.
Siminare des Probabilites XXI. Ed. by J. Azema et al. (Lecture Notes in Mathematics Ser.: Vol. 1247). iv, 579p. 1987. pap. 54.40 (ISBN 0-387-17768-X). Springer-Verlag.
Siminov-SKS-46 Type Carbines. Wyatt J. Lamont. 1981. 21.95 (ISBN 0-87505-281-9). Borden.
Simkin's Soldiers - The British Army in 1890, Vol. II: The Infantry. P. S. Walton. (Illus.). 134p. 1987. 91.00x (ISBN 0-948251-02-6, Pub. by Picton UK). State Mutual Bk.
Simkin's Soldiers - The British Army in 1890, Vol. 1: The Cavalry & the Royal Artillery with a Special Section on the Royal Marines. Ed. by P. S. Walton. (Illus.). 112p. 1987. pap. 461.00x (ISBN 0-9506885-1-7, Pub. by Picton UK). State Mutual Bk.
Simla: A Hill Station in British India. Pat Barr & Ray Desmond. 1982. pap. 15.00 (ISBN 0-85967-659-5). Scolar.
Simla Village Tales, or, Folk Tales from the Himalayas. Alice E. Dracott. 1976. lib. bdg. 59.95 (ISBN 0-8490-2606-7). Gordon Pr.
Simmel & Parsons: Two Approaches to the Study of Society. Donald N. Levine. Ed. by Harriet Zuckerman & Robert K. Merton. LC 79-9011. (Dissertations on Sociology). 1980. lib. bdg. 27.50x (ISBN 0-405-12979-3). Ayer Co Pubs.
Simmering Volcano: Study of Jannu's Relations with Kashmir. Balraj Puri. 1983. text ed. 15.95x (ISBN 0-86590-157-0, Pub. by Sterling India). Apt Bks.
Simmons E. C. Hardware Co. 1930 Keen Kutter & Winchester Pocket Knives. 1974. pap. 3.50 (ISBN 0-915706-07-5). Am Reprints.
Simms to McConkey: Blood, Sweat & Gatorade. Phil Simms et al. (Illus.). 224p. 1987. 18.95 (ISBN 0-517-56703-2). Crown.
Simon. Arthur Blessitt. LC 87-7213. 128p. 1987. pap. 5.00 (ISBN 0-934461-04-X). Blessitt Pub.
Simon. Rosemary Sutcliff. (Illus.). (gr. 6 up). 1979. Repr. of 1953 ed. 17.95 (ISBN 0-19-271442-2). Oxford U Pr.
Simon & Halbig Dolls: The Artful Aspect. Jan Foulke. (Illus.). 236p. 1984. 22.95 (ISBN 0-87588-219-6, 2850). Hobby Hse.
Simon & Schuster Book of Cryptic Crossword Puzzles, No. 4. Ed. by Eugene T. Maleska. 64p. 1986. pap. 5.95 (ISBN 0-671-55752-1, Fireside). S&S.

Simon & Schuster Book of Cryptic Crossword Puzzles, No. 5. Ed. by Eugene T. Maleska. (Illus.). 64p. 1987. pap. 5.95 (ISBN 0-671-61816-4, Fireside). S&S.

Simon & Schuster Book of Cryptic Puzzles, No. 3. Ed. by Eugene T. Maleska. 1984. pap. 5.95 (ISBN 0-671-50213-1, Fireside). S&S.

Simon & Schuster Book of Facts & Fallacies. Rhoda Blumberg & Leda Blumberg. Ed. by Betty Schwartz. 160p. (Orig.). (gr. 3-8). Wanderer Bks.

Simon & Schuster Book of Facts & Fallacies. Rhoda Blumberg & Leda Blumberg. (gr. 9-12). 1983. lib. bdg. 9.59 (ISBN 0-671-47612-2). S&S.

Simon & Schuster Book of the Opera. 1985. 14.95 (ISBN 0-671-60438-4, Fireside). S&S.

Simon & Schuster Color Illustrated Question & Answer Book: What Is It? Ed. by Wendy Barish. (Simon & Schuster Question & Answer Books Ser.). (Illus.). 128p. (gr. 8-12). 1984. Repr. of 1984 ed. text ed. 8.95. Wanderer Bks.

Simon & Schuster Complete Guide to Home Repair & Maintenance. Bernard Gladstone. LC 83-20409. 431p. 1984. 24.95 (ISBN 0-671-25601-7). S&S.

Simon & Schuster Complete Guide to Home Repair & Maintenance. Bernard Gladstone. 1987. pap. 12.95 (ISBN 0-671-63940-4, Fireside). S&S.

Simon & Schuster Crossword Book of Quotations. Ed. by Eugene T. Maleska. (Series 12). (Orig.). 1980. pap. 4.95 (ISBN 0-671-24090-0, Fireside). S&S.

Simon & Schuster Crossword from the Times, Series 36: A Daily Collection. Ed. by Margaret P. Farrar. 1979. pap. 3.95 (ISBN 0-671-24795-6, Fireside). S&S.

Simon & Schuster Crossword Puzzle Book, No. 119. Margaret P. Farrar & Eugene T. Maleska. 1979. pap. 4.95 (ISBN 0-671-24098-6, Fireside). S&S.

Simon & Schuster Crossword Puzzle Book, No. 120. Margaret P. Farrar & Eugene T. Maleska. 1979. 5.95 (ISBN 0-671-24099-4, Fireside). S&S.

Simon & Schuster Crossword Puzzle Book, No. 121. Margaret P. Farrar & Eugene T. Maleska. 1980. 4.95 (ISBN 0-671-24100-1, Fireside). S&S.

Simon & Schuster Crossword Puzzle Book. Ed. by Margaret P. Farrar & Eugene T. Maleska. (Series: No. 132). 64p. 1983. spiral bound 5.95 (ISBN 0-671-44396-8, Fireside). S&S.

Simon & Schuster Crossword Puzzle Book, No. 139. Ed. by Eugene T. Maleska & John M. Samson. 64p. 1986. pap. 5.95 (ISBN 0-671-60587-9, Fireside). S&S.

Simon & Schuster Crossword Puzzle Book, No. 140. Ed. by Eugene T. Maleska & John M. Samson. 64p. 1986. pap. 5.95 (ISBN 0-671-62758-9, Fireside). S&S.

Simon & Schuster Crossword Puzzle Book, No. 141. Ed. by Eugene T. Maleska & John M. Samson. (Illus.). 64p. 1987. pap. 5.95 (ISBN 0-671-62759-7, Fireside). S&S.

Simon & Schuster Crossword Puzzle Book Series, No. 143. Ed. by Eugene T. Maleska & John M. Samson. 64p. 1987. pap. 5.95 (ISBN 0-671-62761-9, Fireside). S&S.

Simon & Schuster Crossword Puzzle Book, No. 144. Ed. by Eugene T. Maleska & John M. Samson. 1988. 5.95 (ISBN 0-671-62762-7, Fireside). S&S.

Simon & Schuster Crossword Puzzle Book Series, No. 145. Ed. by Eugene T. Maleska & John M. Samson. 1988. 5.95 (ISBN 0-671-62763-5, Fireside). S&S.

Simon & Schuster Crossword Puzzle Book Series, No. 146. Ed. by Eugene T. Maleska & John M. Samson. 64p. 1988. spiral bdg. 5.95 (ISBN 0-671-62764-3, Fireside). S&S.

Simon & Schuster Crossword Puzzle Treasury, No. 25. Ed. by Margaret P. Farrar. 1984. pap. 6.95 (ISBN 0-671-47949-0, Fireside). S&S.

Simon & Schuster Crossword Puzzle Treasury, No. 27. Margaret P. Farrar & Eugene T. Maleska. 1985. pap. 6.95 (ISBN 0-671-55753-X). S&S.

Simon & Schuster Crossword Treasury, No. 26. Ed. by Margaret P. Farrar. 64p. 1985. pap. 6.95 (ISBN 0-671-54195-1, Fireside). S&S.

Simon & Schuster Crossword Treasury, No. 33. Ed. by Margaret Farrar & Eugene T. Maleska. 1988. 6.95 (ISBN 0-671-66406-9, Fireside). S&S.

Simon & Schuster Crossword Treasury 30. Ed. by Margaret P. Farrar & Eugene T. Maleska. 96p. 1986. pap. 6.95 (ISBN 0-671-63025-3, Fireside). S&S.

Simon & Schuster Crossword Treasury, 32. Ed. by Margaret P. Farrar & Eugene T. Maleska. 96p. 1987. pap. 6.95 (ISBN 0-671-64427-0, Fireside). S&S.

Simon & Schuster Crosswords from the Times, Series 38. Ed. by Margaret P. Farrar. (Orig.). 1980. pap. 5.95 (ISBN 0-671-25503-7, Fireside). S&S.

Simon & Schuster Crosswords from the Times, Series 34. Ed. by Margaret P. Farrar. 1979. spiral 3.95 (ISBN 0-686-67343-3, Fireside). S&S.

Simon & Schuster Crosswords from the Times, Series 37: A Daily Collection. Margaret P. Farrar. 1979. 5.95 (ISBN 0-671-25082-5, Fireside). S&S.

Simon & Schuster Crosswords from the Times, Series 35: A Sunday Collection. Ed. by Margaret P. Farrar. 1979. pap. 3.95 (ISBN 0-671-24778-6, Fireside). S&S.

Simon & Schuster Crostics, No. 90. Thomas H. Middleton. (Simon & Schuster Crostics Ser.). (Orig.). 1983. pap. 6.95 (ISBN 0-671-49435-X, Fireside). S&S.

Simon & Schuster Crostics, No. 96. Thomas H. Middleton. 64p. 1986. pap. 6.95 (ISBN 0-671-63018-0, Fireside). S&S.

Simon & Schuster Crostics, No. 99. Thomas H. Middleton. 1988. 6.95 (ISBN 0-671-66405-0, Fireside). S&S.

Simon & Schuster Crostics Ninety-Eight. Thomas H. Middleton. 64p. 1987. pap. 6.95 (ISBN 0-671-64428-9, Fireside). S&S.

Simon & Schuster Crostics, No. 72. Ed. by Thomas H. Middleton. 1974. spiral bdg. 2.95 (ISBN 0-671-21866-2, Fireside). S&S.

Simon & Schuster Crostics, No. 75. Ed. by Thomas H. Middleton. 1976. 4.95 (ISBN 0-671-22266-X, Fireside). S&S.

Simon & Schuster Crostics, No. 77. Ed. by Thomas H. Middleton. 1977. pap. 4.95 (ISBN 0-671-22781-5, Fireside). S&S.

Simon & Schuster Crostics, No. 79. Ed. by Thomas H. Middleton. 1978. spiral bdg. 6.95 (ISBN 0-671-24136-2, Fireside). S&S.

Simon & Schuster Crostics, No. 80. Ed. by Thomas H. Middleton. 1978. spiral 4.95 (ISBN 0-671-24412-4). S&S.

Simon & Schuster Crostics, No. 80. Ed. by Thomas H. Middleton. 1976. pap. 4.95 (ISBN 0-671-22392-5). S&S.

Simon & Schuster Crostics, No. 81. Thomas H. Middleton. 1979. pap. 4.95 (ISBN 0-671-24793-X, Fireside). S&S.

Simon & Schuster Crostics, No. 82. Thomas H. Middleton. 1979. 4.95 (ISBN 0-671-25085-X, Fireside). S&S.

Simon & Schuster Crostics Ominbus, No. 15. Thomas H. Middleton. 1988. 6.95 (ISBN 0-671-64988-4, Fireside). S&S.

Simon & Schuster Crostics Omnibus, No. 8. Ed. by Thomas H. Middleton. 1978. 6.95 (ISBN 0-671-24137-0). S&S.

Simon & Schuster Crostics One Hundred. Thomas H. Middleton. 64p. 1988. spiral bdg. 6.95 (ISBN 0-671-67131-6, Fireside). S&S.

Simon & Schuster Guide to Briefcase Computers. Ashley D. Grayson. 1985. pap. 12.95 (Pub. by Computer Bks). S&S.

Simon & Schuster Guide to Peripherals. Linda G. Christie. 288p. 1985. pap. 14.95 (ISBN 0-671-50628-5, Pub. by Computer Bks). S&S.

Simon & Schuster Guide to Shells. Harold Feinberg. (Illus.). 1980. pap. 11.95 (ISBN 0-671-25320-4). S&S.

Simon & Schuster Guide to the IBM PCjr. Danny Goodman. 160p. 1984. pap. 8.95 (ISBN 0-671-50904-7, Pub. by Computer Bks). S&S.

Simon & Schuster Guide to the TRS-80 Model 100. Danny Goodman. 128p. 1984. pap. 9.95 (ISBN 0-671-49254-3, Pub. by Computer Bks). S&S.

Simon & Schuster Handbook-Dictionary Package. Lynn Q. Troyka. 1987. pap. text ed. write for info. (ISBN 0-13-810656-8). P-H.

Simon & Schuster Handbook for Writers. Lynn Q. Troyka. (Illus.). 750p. 1987. text ed. write for info. (ISBN 0-13-810409-3). P-H.

Simon & Schuster Handbook of Anatomy & Physiology. James Bevan. 8.50 (ISBN 0-671-24998-3); 8.95 (ISBN 0-317-00952-4). S&S.

Simon & Schuster Illustrated Dictionary of Science. (Illus.). (gr. 3 up). 1988. 5.95 (ISBN 0-671-54547-7, Little Simon). S&S.

Simon & Schuster International Dictionary: English-Spanish, Spanish-English. (Eng. & Span.). 1973. thumb-indexed 45.00 (ISBN 0-671-21267-2). S&S.

Simon & Schuster Large Type Crosswords, No. 4. Margaret P. Farrar. 1979. pap. 5.95 (ISBN 0-671-24792-1, Fireside). S&S.

Simon & Schuster Picture Dictionary of Phonics from A to Zh. Linda Hayward. (Illus.). (ps-5). 1984. 10.95 (ISBN 0-671-43102-1, Little Simon). S&S.

Simon & Schuster Pocket Book of the Human Body. (Illus.). (gr. 3 up). 1988. 6.95 (ISBN 0-671-62973-5, Little Simon). S&S.

Simon & Schuster Pocket Companion to Shakespeares' Plays. J. C. Trewin. 1981. 5.95 (ISBN 0-671-42006-2). S&S.

Simon & Schuster Pocket Encyclopedia of Prescription & Nonprescription Drugs. Samuel W. Perry. (Illus.). 1982. 6.25 (ISBN 0-671-42398-3). S&S.

Simon & Schuster Pocket Guide to Antiques. Bevis Hillier. (Illus.). 1981. 7.95 (ISBN 0-671-25250-X). S&S.

Simon & Schuster Pocket Guide to Beer. Michael Jackson. 160p. 1986. pap. 7.95 (ISBN 0-671-61460-6, Fireside). S&S.

Simon & Schuster Pocket Guide to Beer. rev. & exp. ed. Michael Jackson. 1988. 7.95 (ISBN 0-671-66225-2, Fireside). S&S.

Simon & Schuster Pocket Guide to Cognac & Other Brandies. Nicholas Faith. (Illus.). 144p. 1987. pap. 9.95 (ISBN 0-671-64231-6, Fireside). S&S.

Simon & Schuster Pocket Guide to Cheese. Sandy Carr. (Illus.). 1981. 5.95 (ISBN 0-671-42475-0). S&S.

Simon & Schuster Pocket Guide to Drawings. Diana Armfield. 1982. 8.25 (ISBN 0-671-42474-2). S&S.

Simon & Schuster Pocket Guide to French Regional Wines. Roger Voss. (Illus.). 176p. 1988. pap. 8.95 (ISBN 0-671-64233-2, Fireside). S&S.

Simon & Schuster Pocket Guide to German Wines. Ian Jamieson. 144p. 1984. pap. 8.95 (ISBN 0-671-52743-6). S&S.

Simon & Schuster Pocket Guide to German Wines. rev. & updated ed. Ian Jamieson. (Illus.). 160p. 1988. pap. 8.95 (ISBN 0-671-65247-8, Fireside). S&S.

Simon & Schuster Pocket Guide to Home Sewing. Ann Ladbury. (Illus.). 144p. 1988. pap. 8.95 (ISBN 0-671-64234-0, Fireside). S&S.

Simon & Schuster Pocket Guide to Italian Wines. Burton Anderson. 1982. 5.95 (ISBN 0-671-45234-7). S&S.

Simon & Schuster Pocket Guide to Italian Wines. Burton Anderson. (Illus.). 160p. 1987. pap. 8.95 (ISBN 0-671-63843-2, Fireside). S&S.

Simon & Schuster Pocket Guide to Painting in Oils. Diana Armfield. 1982. 8.25 (ISBN 0-671-42473-4). S&S.

Simon & Schuster Pocket Guide to Spanish Wines. Jan Read. (Orig.). 1983. pap. 6.95 (ISBN 0-671-47194-5). S&S.

Simon & Schuster Pocket Guide to Spanish Wines. rev. ed. Jan Read. (Illus.). 144p. 1988. pap. 9.95 (ISBN 0-671-66787-4, Fireside). S&S.

Simon & Schuster Pocket Guide to Trout & Salmon Flies. (Illus.). 192p. 1987. pap. 9.95 (ISBN 0-671-64064-X, Fireside). S&S.

Simon & Schuster Pocket Guide to the Wines of Bordeaux. David Peppercorn. 160p. 1987. pap. 7.95 (ISBN 0-671-63675-8, Fireside). S&S.

Simon & Schuster Pocket Guide to the Wines of Burgundy. Serena Sutcliffe. Date not set. write for info. S&S.

Simon & Schuster Pocket Guide to Wine Tasting. rev. ed. Michael Broadbent. (Illus.). 160p. 1988. pap. 9.95 (ISBN 0-671-66788-2, Fireside). S&S.

Simon & Schuster Question & Answer Book: Computers. Daniel Cohen. (gr. 9-12). 1983. PLB 9.29 (ISBN 0-671-49750-2). S&S.

Simon & Schuster Question & Answer Book. Kathleen N. Daly. Ed. by Wendy Barish. (Illus.). 320p. (gr. 3 up). 1982. 8.95 (ISBN 0-671-44427-1). Wanderer Bks.

Simon & Schuster Workbook for Writers. Emily R. Gordon & Lynn Q. Troyka. (Illus.). 400p. 1987. pap. text ed. write for info. (ISBN 0-13-811191-X). P-H.

Simon & Schuster World Coin Catalogue 1979-1980. Gunter Schon. (Illus.). 1979. pap. 13.25 (ISBN 0-671-24639-9). S&S.

Simon & Schuster World Coin Catalogue: 1982 - 1983 Twentieth Century. Gunter Schon. 1982. 19.95 (ISBN 0-671-45606-7); pap. text ed. 13.50 (ISBN 0-671-45612-1). S&S.

Simon & Schuster World Coin Catalogue, 1986-1987 Edition. Gunter Schon. 1540p. 1986. pap. 14.95 (ISBN 0-671-60416-3, Fireside). S&S.

Simon & Schuster Young Readers' Atlas. Jill Wright & David Wright. Ed. by Wendy Barish. (Illus.). 192p. 1983. pap. 9.79 (ISBN 0-671-50657-9). Wanderer Bks.

Simon & Schuster Young Readers' Guide to Dates & Events. (Illus.). 1988. 6.95 (ISBN 0-671-61226-3, Little Simon). S&S.

Simon & Schuster Young Readers' Illustrated Dictionary. (Illus.). (gr. 3 up). 6.95 (ISBN 0-671-50821-0, Little Simon). S&S.

Simon & Schuster Young Readers' Thesaurus. George Beal. Ed. by Wendy Barish. (Illus.). 192p. (gr. 3-7). 1984. pap. 6.95. Wanderer Bks.

Simon & Schuster's Book of Cryptic Crossword Puzzles, No. 6. Ed. by Eugene T. Maleska. 1988. 5.95 (ISBN 0-671-61817-2, Fireside). S&S.

Simon & Schuster's Book of the Opera. Editore Mondadori. 1979. 32.50 (ISBN 0-671-24886-3). S&S.

Simon & Schuster's Complete Guide to Plants & Flowers. Ed. by Frances Perry. (Illus.). 1976. pap. 11.95 (ISBN 0-671-22247-3). S&S.

Simon' & Schuster's Crossword Book of Quotations, No. 13. Ed. by Eugene T. Maleska. 1981. pap. 4.95 (ISBN 0-686-73805-5, Fireside). S&S.

Simon & Schuster's Crossword Book of Quotations, No. 17. Ed. by Eugene T. Maleska. 64p. 1984. pap. 5.95 (ISBN 0-671-44322-4, Fireside). S&S.

Simon & Schuster's Crossword Book of Quotations, No. 11. Eugene T. Maleska. 1979. 3.95 (ISBN 0-671-24089-7, Fireside). S&S.

Simon & Schuster's Crossword Puzzle Book, No. 134. Ed. by Margaret P. Farrar & Eugene T. Maleska. 1984. 5.95 (ISBN 0-671-50204-2, Fireside). S&S.

Simon & Schuster's Crossword Puzzle Book, No. 135. Ed. by Margaret P. Farrar & Eugene T. Maleska. 64p. 1985. pap. 5.95 (ISBN 0-671-54192-7, Fireside). S&S.

Simon & Schuster's Crossword Puzzle Book: Series No. 136. Ed. by Eugene T. Maleska. 1985. pap. 5.95 (ISBN 0-671-50206-9). S&S.

Simon & Schuster's Crossword Puzzle Book Series 133. Margaret P. Farrar & Eugene T. Maleska. 1984. pap. 5.95 (ISBN 0-671-50202-6, Fireside Bks). S&S.

Simon & Schuster's Crostic Omnibus, No. 13. Ed. by Thomas H. Middleton. 96p. 1984. pap. 6.95 (ISBN 0-671-54194-3, Fireside). S&S.

Simon & Schuster's Crostics, No. 91. Thomas H. Middleton. 1984. 6.95 (ISBN 0-671-50647-1, Fireside). S&S.

Simon & Schuster's Crostics, No. 92. Ed. by Thomas H. Middleton. 96p. 1984. pap. 6.95 (ISBN 0-671-54198-6, Fireside). S&S.

Simon & Schuster's Crostics No. 93. Ed. by Thomas H. Middleton. 1985. pap. 6.95 (ISBN 0-671-55671-1). S&S.

Simon & Schuster's Crostics Omnibus, No. 9. Thomas H. Middleton. 1979. pap. 5.75 (ISBN 0-671-24794-8, Fireside). S&S.

Simon & Schuster's Dur-Acrostics, Series 1. Charles A. Duerr. 64p. 1988. pap. 6.95 spiral bdg. (ISBN 0-671-65755-0, Fireside). S&S.

Simon & Schuster's Dur-Acrostics, Series 2. 64p. 1988. pap. 6.95 spiral bdg. (ISBN 0-671-65756-9, Fireside). S&S.

Simon & Schuster's Guide to Atari's "My First Computer". Danny Goodman. 128p. 1984. pap. 5.95 (ISBN 0-671-49255-1, Pub. by Computer Bks). S&S.

Simon & Schuster's Guide to Butterflies & Moths. Mauro Daccordi et al. 1987. 21.95 (ISBN 0-671-66065-9). S&S.

Simon & Schuster's Guide to Butterflies & Moths. Mauro Daccordi et al. 1988. pap. 11.95 (ISBN 0-671-66066-7, Fireside). S&S.

Simon & Schuster's Guide to Cats. Pugnetti. Ed. by Mordecai Siegal. (Illus.). 256p. 1983. 23.95 (ISBN 0-671-49167-9); pap. 9.95 (ISBN 0-671-49170-9). S&S.

Simon & Schuster's Guide to Dogs. Ed. by Mondadori. pap. 11.95 (ISBN 0-671-25527-4). S&S.

Simon & Schuster's Guide to Fossils. Paolo Arduini & Giorgio Teruzzi. (Nature Guide Ser.). (Illus.). 320p. 1987. 22.95 (ISBN 0-671-63219-1, Fireside); pap. 12.95 (ISBN 0-671-63132-2). S&S.

Simon & Schuster's Guide to Freshwater & Marine Aquarium Fish. LC 76-56863. 1977. pap. 11.95 (ISBN 0-671-22809-9). S&S.

Simon & Schuster's Guide to Garden Flowers. Guido Moggi et al. Ed. by Stanley Schuler. (Illus.). 1983. 19.95 (ISBN 0-671-46674-7); pap. 10.95 (ISBN 0-671-46678-X). S&S.

Simon & Schuster's Guide to Gems & Precious Stones. Curzio Cippriani & Alessando Borelli. Ed. by Kennie Lyman. 384p. 1986. 21.95 (ISBN 0-671-60116-4); pap. 11.95 (ISBN 0-671-60430-9). S&S.

Simon & Schuster's Guide to Horses & Ponies of the World. Maurizio Bonganni. 1988. pap. 9.95 (ISBN 0-671-66068-3, Fireside). S&S.

Simon & Schuster's Guide to Horses & Ponies of the World. Maurizio Bongianni. 1988. 19.95 (ISBN 0-671-66067-5). S&S.

Simon & Schuster's Guide to House Plants. Alessandro Chuisoli & Maria L. Boriani. (Nature Guide Ser.). (Illus.). 320p. 1987. 22.95 (ISBN 0-671-63218-3, Fireside); pap. 12.95 (ISBN 0-671-63131-4). S&S.

Simon & Schuster's Guide to Mammals. Ed. by Sydney Anderson. (Illus.). 512p. 1984. 30.95 (ISBN 0-671-43727-5); pap. 11.95 (ISBN 0-671-42805-5). S&S.

Simon & Schuster's Guide to Pet Birds. Matthew M. Vriends. 320p. 1985. 24.50 (ISBN 0-671-50695-1); pap. 11.95 (ISBN 0-671-50696-X). S&S.

Simon & Schuster's Guide to Rocks & Minerals. Ed. by Mondadori. pap. 12.95 (ISBN 0-671-24417-5). S&S.

Simon & Schuster's Guide to Roses. Stelvio Coggiatti. 1987. pap. 11.95 (ISBN 0-671-63957-9, Fireside). S&S.

Simon & Schuster's Guide to Roses. Stelvo Coggiatti. 1987. 22.95 (ISBN 0-671-63955-2). S&S.

Simon & Schuster's Guide to Shrubs & Vines & Other Small Ornamentals. Constanza Lunardi. 1989. 21.95 (ISBN 0-671-66932-X, Fireside); pap. 11.95 (ISBN 0-671-66933-8, Fireside). S&S.

Simon & Schuster's Guide to Trees. Ed. by Stanley Schuler. (Illus.). 1978. 19.95 (ISBN 0-671-24124-9); pap. 11.95 (ISBN 0-671-24125-7). S&S.

Simon & Schuster's Hooked on Puzzles Series, No. 1. Henry Hook. 1988. 7.95 (ISBN 0-671-64728-8, Fireside). S&S.

Simon & Schuster's Illustrated Young Readers' Dictionary. rev. ed. John Grisewood. Ed. by Wendy Barish. (Illus.). 240p. (gr. 8 up). 1984. pap. 9.79 (ISBN 0-671-50020-1). Wanderer Bks.

Simon & Schuster's Illustrated Young Reader's Dictionary. 1983. pap. 4.95 (ISBN 0-671-47144-9). Wanderer Bks.

Simon & Schuster's Large-Type Crosswords, No. 6. Ed. by Margaret P. Farrar. 96p. (Orig.). pap. 5.95 (ISBN 0-671-43644-9, Fireside). S&S.

Simon & Schuster's Large Type Crosswords, No. 8. Ed. by Eugene T. Maleska. 5.95 (ISBN 0-671-61819-9, Fireside). S&S.

Simon & Schuster's Large Type Crosswords, No. 9. Ed. by Eugene T. Maleska. 1988. 5.95 (ISBN 0-671-61820-2, Fireside). S&S.

Simon & Schuster's Super Crossword Book, No. 4. Ed. by Margaret P. Farrar & Eugene T. Maleska. (Illus.). 256p. 1987. pap. 7.95 (ISBN 0-671-63302-3, Fireside). S&S.

Simon & Shuster's Guide to Cacti & Succulents. Ed. by Stanley Schuler. 1985. 21.95 (ISBN 0-671-55846-3); pap. 10.95 (ISBN 0-671-60231-4). S&S.

Simon & the Snow Flakes. Gilles Tibo. (Illus.). 24p. (gr. 3 up). 1988. 9.95 (ISBN 0-88776-218-2). Tundra Bks.
Simon & the Snowflakes. Gilles Tibo. (ps-3). Date not set. 9.95 (Dist. by U of Toronto Pr). Tundra Bks.
Simon Benson: Northwest Lumber King. Alice B. Allen. LC 77-157143. 1970. 11.95 (ISBN 0-8323-0047-0). Binford-Metropolitan.
Simon Boccanegra. Giuseppe Verdi. Ed. by Nicholas John. Tr. by Sylvia Mulcahy from Ital. LC 85-1831. (English National Opera - the Royal Opera House Opera Guide Ser.: No. 32). (Illus.). 96p. (Orig.). 1985. pap. 5.95 (ISBN 0-7145-4064-1). Riverrun NY.
Simon Bolivar. Dennis Wepman. (World Leaders: Past & Present Ser.). (Illus.). 112p. 1985. lib. bdg. 16.95x (ISBN 0-87754-569-3). Chelsea Hse.
Simon Bolivar: A Bibliography. Ed. by Raoul Gordon. 1976. lib. bdg. 59.95 (ISBN 0-8490-2607-5). Gordon Pr.
Simon Bolivar: The Hope of the Universe. J. L. Salcedo-Bastardo. 308p. 1983. text ed. 15.75 (ISBN 92-3-102103-6, U1303, UNESCO). UNIPUB.
Simon Cameron: Ante Bellum Years. Lee F. Crippen. LC 76-168674. (American Scene Ser). 1972. Repr. of 1942 ed. lib. bdg. 39.50 (ISBN 0-306-70362-9). Da Capo.
Simon Commission & Indian Nationalism. S. R. Bakshi. 1977. 11.50x (ISBN 0-88386-966-7). South Asia Bks.
Simon Commission: Report on India, 3 vols. 1987. Set. 2500.00. Asia Bk Corp.
Simon De Cramaud & The Great Schism. Howard Kaminsky. 363p. 1983. 45.00 (ISBN 0-8135-0949-1). Rutgers U Pr.
Simon De Cramaud, De Substraccione Obediencie. Ed. by Howard Kaminsky. 1984. 37.50x (ISBN 0-910956-84-7). Medieval Acad.
Simon de Montfort & Baronial Reform. R. F. Treharne. 368p. 1986. 40.00 (ISBN 0-907628-70-2). Hambledon Press.
Simon De Montfort, Earl of Leicester, 1208-1265. Charles Bemont. Tr. by E. F. Jacob. LC 74-9223. (Illus.). 303p. 1974. Repr. of 1930 ed. lib. bdg. 35.00x (ISBN 0-8371-7625-5, BESM). Greenwood.
Simon de Puille: Chason de Geste. Ed. by Denis J. Conlon. (Studien und Dokumente zur Geshichte der Romanischen Literatur: Vol. 17). 316p. 1987. pap. 40.65 (ISBN 3-8204-9755-2). P Lang Pubs.
Simon Et Les Flocons de Neige. Gilles Tibo. (Fr.). 1988. 9.95 (ISBN 0-88776-219-0). Tundra Bks.
Simon Girty the Outlaw. Uriah James Jones. 1931. 20.00x (ISBN 0-686-17407-0). R S Barnes.
Simon Gross' U. S. Revenue Cutter Active 1791-1798. Florence Kern. 1977. 3.95 (ISBN 0-913377-05-8). Alised.
Simon: Histoire. A. Cheal Pugh. (Critical Guides to French Texts Ser.: No. 22). 87p. 1982. pap. 4.50 (ISBN 0-7293-0143-5, Pub. by Grant & Cutler). Longwood Pub Group.
Simon J. Ortiz. Andrew Wiget. LC 86-70653. (Western Writers Ser.: No. 74). (Illus.). 53p. (Orig.). 1986. pap. 2.95x (ISBN 0-88430-048-X). Boise St Univ.
Simon Kenton, His Life & Period, 1755-1836. Edna Kenton. LC 70-146406. (First American Frontier Ser). (Illus.). 1971. Repr. of 1930 ed. 26.00 (ISBN 0-405-02865-2). Ayer Co Pubs.
Simon; la Marquise; Monssieur Rousset; Rouny-Robin; Les Sauvages de Paris. George Sand. 313p. 1976. 32.50 (ISBN 0-686-54945-7). French & Eur.
Simon Le Duc & Le Chevalier de Saint-Georges. Simon Le Duc & Le Chevalier de Saint-Georges. Ed. by Barry S. Brook & David Bain. LC 83-1457. (Symphony Ser.). 346p. 1983. lib. bdg. 90.00 (ISBN 0-8240-3823-1). Garland Pub.
Simon le Pathetique. Jean Giraudoux. pap. 9.95 (ISBN 0-685-33927-0). French & Eur.
Simon Magus. G. R. S. Mead. 1978. Repr. of 1892 ed. 10.00 (ISBN 0-89005-258-1). Ares.
Simon Peter. Georges Chevrot. 223p. 1980. pap. 4.95x (ISBN 0-933932-43-X). Scepter Pubs.
Simon Peter. Hugh Martin. 1984. pap. 5.95 (ISBN 0-85151-427-8). Banner of Truth.
Simon Peter: From Galilee to Rome. Carsten P. Thiedee. 272p. 1988. pap. price not set (ISBN 0-310-51561-0). Zondervan.
Simon Pure. Julian F. Thompson. 336p. (YA) (gr. 10-12). 1987. 12.95x (ISBN 0-590-40507-1, Scholastic Hardcover). Scholastic Inc.
Simon Pure. Julian F. Thompson. 336p. (YA) (gr. 7 up). Date not set. pap. 2.75 (ISBN 0-590-41823-8, Point). Scholastic Inc.
Simon Rodia & His Towers in Watts: An Introduction & a Bibliography. Daniel F. Ward. (Architecture Ser.: A 1674). 13p. 1986. 3.75 (ISBN 1-55590-024-0). Vance Biblios.
Simon Says Is Not the Only Game. Compiled by Bernadette Leary & Margaret Von Schneden. LC 82-3943. 148p. 1982. pap. 7.00 (ISBN 0-89128-109-6, PEP109). Am Foun Blind.
Simon Says, "Let's Play Learning Games". Eunice Magos & Esther Hornnes. Ed. by Ellen Sussman. (Illus.). 48p. (Orig.). (ps-1). 1985. tchr's ed. 5.95 (ISBN 0-933606-40-0, MS-640). Monkey Sisters.
Simon Says: The Best of Roger Simon. Roger Simon. 320p. 1986. pap. 8.95 (ISBN 0-8092-4853-0). Contemp Bks.
Simon the Coldheart. Georgette Heyer. 1978. 12.00 (ISBN 0-685-90568-3). Bookfinger.
Simon the Coldheart. Georgette Heyer. 1976. Repr. of 1925 ed. lib. bdg. 19.95x (ISBN 0-89966-118-1). Buccaneer Bks.
Simon the Snake. Alice L. Mason. (Illus.). 16p. (gr. k-6). 1984. pap. 1.50 (ISBN 0-8249-8069-7). Ideals.
Simon Tyssot de Patot & the Seventeenth-Century Background of Critical Deism. David R. McKee. (Johns Hopkins University Studies in Romance Literatures & Languages: Vol. 40). 105p. pap. 14.00 (ISBN 0-384-34885-8). Johnson Repr.
Simon Underground. Joanne Ryder. LC 74-20397. (Illus.). 32p. (YA) (ps-3). 1976. PLB 10.89 (ISBN 0-06-025157-3). HarpJ.
Simon Wheeler, Detective. Mark Twain. Ed. by Franklin R. Rogers. LC 63-18140. (Levy Pub. Ser.: No. 2). 204p. 1965. 15.00 (ISBN 0-87104-161-8). NY Pub Lib.
Simon Wiesenthal Center Annual, Vol. 1. Ed. by Alex Grobman. (Illus.). 256p. 1984. text ed. 17.95x (ISBN 0-940646-30-7). Rossel Bks.
Simon Wiesenthal Center Annual, Vol. 2. Ed. by Sybil Milton et al. 1985. lib. bdg. 30.00 (ISBN 0-527-96489-1). Kraus Intl.
Simon Wiesenthal Center Annual, Vol. 4. Ed. by Sybil Milton & Henry Friedlander. 1986. lib. bdg. 30.00 (ISBN 0-527-96491-3). Kraus Intl.
Simon Willard & His Clocks. John W. Willard. Orig. Title: History of Simon Willard, Inventor & Clockmaker. (Illus.). 1968. pap. 5.95 (ISBN 0-486-21943-7). Dover.
Simon Wolf: Private Conscience & Public Image. Esther L. Panitz. LC 86-45378. (Illus.). 224p. 1987. 29.50x (ISBN 0-8386-3293-9). Fairleigh Dickinson.
Simone. Lion Feuchtwanger. Tr. by G. A. Hermann from Fr. 238p. 1986. Repr. of 1944 ed. lib. bdg. 49.50 (ISBN 0-8495-1745-1). Arden Lib.
Simone de Beauvoir. Lisa Appignanesi. 136p. 1988. pap. 4.95 (ISBN 0-14-008737-0). Penguin.
Simone de Beauvoir. Robert D. Cottrell. LC 74-34131. (Literature and Life Ser.). 176p. 1975. 16.95x (ISBN 0-8044-2132-3). Ungar.
Simone De Beauvoir. Margaret Crosland. 1988. 19.95 (ISBN 0-317-67520-6). Crown.
Simone de Beauvoir. Judith Okely. LC 86-42616. (Illus.). 208p. pap. 7.95 (ISBN 0-394-74765-8). Pantheon.
Simone de Beauvoir. Renee Winegarten. (Berg Women Ser.). 144p. 1987. 25.00 (ISBN 0-85496-151-8, Pub. by Berg Pubs). St Martin.
Simone de Beauvoir: A Feminist Mandarin. Mary Evans. 192p. 1985. pap. 9.95 (ISBN 0-422-79510-0, 9529, Pub. by Tavistock England). Routledge Chapman & Hall.
Simone de Beauvoir: A Life, a Love Story. Claude Francis & Fernande Gontier. (Illus.). 416p. 1987. 25.00 (ISBN 0-312-00189-4). St Martin.
Simone de Beauvoir: A Life...A Love Story. Claude Francis & Fernande Gontier. (Vermilion Bks.). (Illus.). 452p. 1988. pap. 12.95 (ISBN 0-312-02324-3). St Martin.
Simone de Beauvoir: A Study of Her Writings. Terry Keefe. LC 83-6024. (Illus.). 247p. 1983. text ed. 18.50x (ISBN 0-389-20365-3). B&N Imports.
Simone de Beauvoir & the Limits of Commitment. Anne Whitmarsh. 280p. 1981. 39.50 (ISBN 0-521-23669-X). Cambridge U Pr.
Simone de Beauvoir on Women. Jean Leighton. LC 74-3615. 230p. 1975. 22.50 (ISBN 0-8386-1504-X). Fairleigh Dickinson.
Simone de Beauvoir ou le Refus de l'Indifference. Gagnebin. (Collection Celebrites). 13.50 (ISBN 0-685-37194-8). French & Eur.
Simone de Beauvoir: Witness to a Century. Ed. by Helene V. Wenzel. LC 86-26675. (French Studies: No. 72). 272p. 1987. pap. 13.95x (ISBN 0-300-03897-6). Yale U Pr.
Simone Martini. Enrico Castelnuovo. LC 80-82539. (Illus.). 80p. 1988. pap. 13.95 (ISBN 0-935748-79-2). Scala Books.
Simone Martini: Complete Edition. Andrew Martindale. (Illus.). 240p. 1988. 150.00x (ISBN 0-8147-5444-9). NYU Pr.
Simone Weil. John Dunaway. (World Authors Ser.: No. 723). 152p. 1984. lib. bdg. 20.95 (ISBN 0-8057-6570-0, Twayne). G K Hall.
Simone Weil. Pat Little. LC 87-37397. (Women's Ser.). 208p. 1988. 21.95 (ISBN 0-85496-165-8, Pub. by Berg Pubs). St Martin.
Simone Weil. Dorothy T. McFarland. LC 82-25609. (Literature & Life Ser.). 207p. 1983. 16.95x (ISBN 0-8044-2604-X). Ungar.
Simone Weil: A Bibliography. J. P. Little. (Research Bibliographies & Checklists Ser.: No. 5). 91p. (Orig.). 1973. pap. 7.25 (ISBN 0-900411-61-9, Pub. by Grant & Cutler). Longwood Pub Group.
Simone Weil: A Bibliography, Supplement No. 1. J. P. Little. (Research Bibliographies & Checklists Ser.: No. 5a). 91p. (Orig.). 1979. pap. 6.50 (ISBN 0-7293-0085-4, Pub. by Grant & Cutler). Longwood Pub Group.
Simone Weil: A Life. Simone Petrement. LC 87-43117. 592p. 1988. pap. 11.95 (ISBN 0-8052-0862-3). Schocken.
Simone Weil: A Modern Pilgrimage. Robert Coles. LC 86-32292. (Radcliffe Biography Ser.). 224p. 1987. 17.95 (ISBN 0-201-02205-2). Addison-Wesley.
Simone Weil a New York et a Londres. Cabaud. 15.95 (ISBN 0-685-36635-9). French & Eur.
Simone Weil: A Sketch for a Portrait. Richard Rees. LC 66-11154. (Crosscurrents-Modern Critiques Ser.). 215p. 1966. 10.95x (ISBN 0-8093-0191-1). S Ill U Pr.
Simone Weil: A Sketch for a Protrait. Richard Rees. LC 77-24990. (Arcturus Books Paperbacks). 215p. 1978. pap. 6.95x (ISBN 0-8093-0852-5). S Ill U Pr.
Simone Weil: An Anthology. Ed. & intro. by Sian Miles. LC 86-9242. 320p. 1986. 17.95 (ISBN 1-55584-012-4); pap. 8.95 (ISBN 1-55584-021-3). Weidenfeld.
Simone Weil: An Introduction to Her Thought. John Hellman. 170p. 1982. text ed. 17.95x (ISBN 0-88920-121-8, Pub. by Wilfrid Laurier Canada). Humanities.
Simone Weil & the Suffering of Love. Eric O. Springsted. LC 86-2312. 131p. (Orig.). 1986. pap. 8.95 (ISBN 0-936384-33-6). Cowley Pubns.
Simone Weil: Interpretations of a Life. Ed. by George A. White. LC 81-7460. 224p. 1981. lib. bdg. 18.00x (ISBN 0-87023-343-2); pap. 9.95 (ISBN 0-87023-344-0). U of Mass Pr.
Simone Weil Reader. Ed. by George A. Panichas. 529p. 1985. pap. 10.95 (ISBN 0-918825-01-6, Dist. by Kampmann & Co.). Moyer Bell Limited.
Simoniacal Entry into Religious Life, 1000 to 1260: A Social, Economic, & Legal Study. Joseph H. Lynch. LC 76-22670. (Illus.). 286p. 1976. 15.00x (ISBN 0-8142-0222-5). Ohio St U Pr.
Simon's Adventure. Elizabeth Spires. (Illus.). 12p. (ps-4). 1982. pap. 2.95 (ISBN 0-89954-205-0). Antioch Pub Co.
Simon's Book. Henrik Drescher. LC 82-24931. (Illus.). 32p. (gr. k-3). 1983. 11.75 (ISBN 0-688-02085-2); lib. bdg. 11.88 (ISBN 0-688-02086-0). Lothrop.
Simon's Book. Henrik Drescher. 40p. (gr. k-3). 1987. 3.95 (ISBN 0-590-41934-X). Scholastic Inc.
Simons Daughter. Ronald Sandison. 1986. 49.00x (ISBN 0-86332-036-8, Pub. by Book Guild Ltd). State Mutual Bk.
Simon's Masterpiece. James LaVilla-Havelin. 1983. pap. 6.00 (ISBN 0-934834-40-7). White Pine.
Simon's Night. Jon Hassler. 320p. 1986. pap. 3.50 (ISBN 0-345-33374-8). Ballantine.
Simon's Waif. Mira Stables. 224p. 1981. pap. 1.50 (ISBN 0-449-50207-4, Coventry). Fawcett.
Simoon see Plays from the Cynical Life.
Simpco Land Use Planning Information System Design: What to Do When the Data Arrives. Kenneth Meyer et al. (Technical Report Ser.: No. 1). 1978. 5.00 (ISBN 1-55614-113-0). U of SD Gov Res Bur.
Simpkinsville & Vicinity: Arkansas Stories of Ruth McEnery Stuart. Ed. by Ethel C. Simpson. LC 82-16160. 208p. 1983. pap. 8.95 (ISBN 0-938626-16-7). U of Ark Pr.
SIMPL-T: A Structured Programming Language. Victor R. Basili & Albert J. Turner. 1976. coil bdg. 5.50 (ISBN 0-88252-062-8). Paladin Hse.
SIMPLAN: A Computer Based Planning System for Government. Thomas H. Naylor et al. LC 74-75956. pap. 47.30 (ISBN 0-317-20449-1, 2023426). Bks Demand UMI.
Simple Additon & Subtraction. Fred Justus. (Math Ser.). 24p. (gr. k-1). 1982. wkbk. 5.00 (ISBN 0-8209-0089-3, A-K). ESP.
Simple American Cooking. Ed. by Evelyn L. Beilenson. LC 87-60946. (Illus.). 64p. 1987. 5.95 (ISBN 0-88088-500-9). Peter Pauper.
Simple & Complex Vibratory Systems. Eugen Skudrzyk. LC 66-18222. (Illus.). 1968. 36.75x (ISBN 0-271-73127-3). Pa St U Pr.
Simple & Delicious Chinese Cooking. Deh-ta Hsiung. LC 84-81921. (Creative Cuisine Ser.). (Illus.). 80p. 1985. pap. 4.95 (ISBN 0-89586-338-3). Price Stern.
Simple & Direct: A Rhetoric for Writers. rev. ed. Jacques Barzun. LC 83-48936. 256p. 1985. 15.00 (ISBN 0-06-015283-4, HarpT). Har-Row.
Simple & Direct: A Rhetoric for Writers. rev. ed. Jacques Barzun. LC 83-48936. 256p. 1984. pap. 7.95 (ISBN 0-06-091122-0, CN 1122, PL). Har-Row.
Simple & Easy Japanese Cooking. Ed. by Shufunmoto Staff. (Illus.). 42p. (Orig.). 1988. pap. 6.95 (ISBN 4-07-974771-3, Pub. by Shufunmoto Co Ltd Japan). C E Tuttle.
Simple & Easy Way to Study the Bible. Don Gray & Marjorie Gray. (Outreach Ser.). 31p. 1985. pap. 1.25 (ISBN 0-8163-0613-3). Pacific Pr Pub Assn.
Simple & Profound. David Du Plessis. 207p. 1986. pap. 7.95 (ISBN 0-941478-51-3). Paraclete Pr.
Simple & Quick Diet Cookbook: How to Lose Weight & Stay Healthy. Hannelore Blohm & Hans-Diedrich Cremer. 104p. 1985. 10.95 (ISBN 0-8120-5659-0). Barron.
Simple Annals. Eugene Lockhart. 132p. (Orig.). 1987. pap. 7.65 (ISBN 0-9618581-3-3). E Lockhart.
Simple Answer to Fitness for All Ages: How to Lose Weight without Dieting--with Practical Reasons Why--Easily Explainable to Laypersons & Physicans. James W. Fisk. (Illus.). 132p. 1984. spiral bdg. 14.25x (ISBN 0-398-04995-5). C C Thomas.
Simple Art of Murder. Raymond Chandler. 1977. pap. 3.95 (ISBN 0-345-34937-7). Ballantine.
Simple Art of Murder. LC 87-45923. 288p. 1988. 5.95 (ISBN 0-394-75765-3, Vin). Random.
Simple as A, B, C. Charles Hunter & Frances Hunter. 1982. pap. 0.75 (ISBN 0-917726-51-0). Hunter Bks.
Simple Biflagellate Holocarpic Phycomycetes. 2nd ed. J. S. Karling. (Illus.). 1981. lib. bdg. 90.00x. Lubrecht & Cramer.
Simple but Powerful Goal Programming Formula for Problems of Statistical Discrimination & Multi-Dimensional Classification. Ned Freed & Fred Glover. 1977. 2.50 (ISBN 0-686-64911-7). U CO Busn Res Div.
Simple but Powerful Goal Programming Models for Discriminant Problems. Ned Freed & Fred Glover. 1978. 2.50 (ISBN 0-686-64183-3). U CO Busn Res Div.
Simple Checkmates. Tony Gillam. 1978. pap. 11.95 (ISBN 0-7134-1482-0, Pub. by Batsford England). David & Charles.
Simple Chemistry. Neil Ardley. LC 83-51444. (Action Science Ser.). (Illus.). 32p. (gr. 4-6). 1985. PLB 11.90 (ISBN 0-531-03778-9). Watts.
Simple Chess. Michael Stean. 128p. 1987. pap. 6.95 (ISBN 0-571-11257-9). Faber & Faber.
Simple Chess Tactics. Tony Gillam. 1978. pap. 11.95 (ISBN 0-7134-1480-4, Pub. by Batsford England). David & Charles.
Simple Chinese Conversation. Jianyi H. Huihua. (Chinese.). pap. 7.50 (ISBN 0-87557-010-0; 010-0). Saphrograph.
Simple Chinese Phrase Book. rev. ed. Terry C. Shen. (Illus.). 75p. 1986. pap. 2.50 (ISBN 0-935655-01-8). Language Intl.
Simple Chinese Stories. George A. Kennedy. 3.95 (ISBN 0-88710-088-0). Yale Far Eastern Pubns.
Simple Composition. Charles Wuorinen. 168p. 1977. text ed. 15.95 (ISBN 0-02-873210-3). Schirmer Bks.
Simple Computing: What Computers Can Do for You. Chauncey Ching. LC 84-33. (Orig.). 1984. pap. 9.95 (ISBN 0-915805-00-6). Total Concepts.
Simple Conjunctions. Phil Galgiani. (Illus.). 20p. 1986. pap. 6.25 (ISBN 0-317-64325-8). CEPA Gall.
Simple Conjunctions: An Installation by Phillip Galgiani. James Welling. (Illus.). 16p. 1986. pap. 6.50 (ISBN 0-918471-09-5). San Fran MOMA.
Simple Cooking. John Thorne. 1987. 20.00 (ISBN 0-670-81212-9). Viking.
Simple Cooking. John Thorne. 1989. 9.95 (ISBN 0-14-011737-7). Penguin.
Simple Cooperation in the Classroom. Jacqueline Rhoades & Margaret E. McCabe. (Illus.). 165p. (Orig.). 1985. pap. 15.95 (ISBN 0-933935-07-2). ITA Pubns.
Simple Creatures. Lionel Bender. Ed. by Franklin Watts Ltd. (Today's World Ser.). (Illus.). 40p. (YA) (gr. 7-9). 1988. 12.40 (ISBN 0-531-17092-6, Gloucester Pr). Watts.
Simple Creole Cajun. Floyd Babineaux. 165p. 1986. 12.00 (ISBN 0-317-69245-3). F Babineaux.
Simple Curiosity: Letters from George Gaylord Simpson to His Family 1921-197. George G. Simpson. Ed. by Leo F. Laporte. LC 86-25046. (Illus.). 332p. 1987. 29.95 (ISBN 0-520-05792-9). U of Cal Pr.
Simple Data Processing: A Practical Introduction to Business Information Technology. Jackie Chaudhury & Lyn Agley. (Illus.). 60p. 1983. pap. 12.95x (ISBN 0-317-02460-4). Trans-Atl Phila.
Simple Definition of the Feynman Integral, with Applications. R. H. Cameron & D. A. Storvick. LC 83-15605. (Memoirs Ser.: No. 288). 48p. 1983. pap. 11.00 (ISBN 0-8218-2288-8). Am Math.
Simple Dielectric Liquids: Mobility, Conduction, & Breakdown. T. J. Gallagher. (Oxford Science Research Papers Ser). (Illus.). 1975. pap. 56.00x (ISBN 0-19-851933-8). Oxford U Pr.
Simple Electrical Devices. Martin J. Gutnik. LC 85-26369. (First Books Ser.). (Illus.). 72p. (gr. 4-9). 1986. lib. bdg. 10.40 (ISBN 0-531-10127-4). Watts.
Simple Embroidery Designs. Ondori Staff. (Illus.). 103p. (Orig.). 1985. pap. 7.95. Japan Pubns USA.
Simple Estate Planning & Will Writing: A Home Study Course. James E. De Martino. (Home Study Ser.). 41p. 1982. 28.00 (ISBN 0-939926-15-6); audio tape incl. (ISBN 0-939926-14-8). Fruition Pubns.
Simple Etiquette in Arabia & Simple Arabic: Businessman's Guide. 1983. pap. 9.95x (ISBN 0-904404-41-2). Intl Bk Ctr.
Simple Etiquette in Arabia Incorporating Very Simple Arabic. James Peters. 1985. 19.95 (ISBN 0-317-39111-9, Pub. by Norbury Pubns Ltd). State Mutual Bk.
Simple Etiquette in China. Ed. by Paul Norbury. 1985. 19.95x (ISBN 0-317-39114-3, Pub. by Norbury Pubns Ltd). State Mutual Bk.
Simple Etiquette in France. Ed. by Paul Norbury. 1985. 19.95x (ISBN 0-317-39116-X, Pub. by Norbury Pubns Ltd). State Mutual Bk.
Simple Etiquette in Germany. Ed. by Paul Norbury. 1985. 19.95x (ISBN 0-317-39118-6, Pub. by Norbury Pubns Ltd). State Mutual Bk.
Simple Etiquette in Japan. Helmut Morsbach. 48p. 1985. 19.95x (ISBN 0-904404-46-3, Pub. by Norbury Pubns Ltd); pap. 20.00 (Pub. by Norbury Pubns Ltd). State Mutual Bk.

Simple Etiquette in Korea. Tony Michell. 1985. 19.95x (ISBN 0-317-39119-4, Pub. by Norbury Pubns Ltd). State Mutual Bk.

Simple Etiquette in the U. S. A. Ed. by Paul Norbury. 1985. 19.95x (ISBN 0-317-39122-4, Pub. by Norbury Pubns Ltd). State Mutual Bk.

Simple Explanations. Richard Behm. (Juniper Bk: No. 40). 1982. pap. 5.00 (ISBN 1-55780-039-1). Juniper Pr WI.

Simple Fact. Cathy Cockrell. LC 87-8677. 1987. 15.00 (ISBN 0-914610-45-7); pap. 8.00. Hanging Loose.

Simple Feasts: Appetizers, Main Dishes & Desserts. Ed. by Marilee Matteson. (Illus.). 200p. 1983. 21.95 (ISBN 0-395-33102-1). HM.

Simple Food for the Good Life. Helen Nearing. (Orig.). 1982. pap. 7.95 (ISBN 0-385-28929-4, Delta). Dell.

Simple Food for the Good Life. Helen Nearing. 309p. 1985. pap. 9.95 (ISBN 0-913299-24-3, Dist. by NAL). Stillpoint.

Simple Foods for the Pack: The Sierra Club Guide to Delicious Natural Foods for the Trail. rev. ed. Claudia Axcell et al. LC 85-22076. (Outdoor Activities Guides Ser.). (Illus.). 224p. 1986. pap. 8.95 (ISBN 0-87156-757-1, Dist. by Random). Sierra.

Simple Forms & Vivid Colors: Maine Painted Furniture, 1800-1850. Edwin A. Churchill. LC 83-61807. (Illus.). 116p. 1983. pap. 17.95 (ISBN 0-913764-16-7). Maine St Mus.

Simple Fractions. (Math Action Ser.). (Illus.). 64p. 1985. text ed. 4.65 (ISBN 0-88102-044-3); & resource 10.95guide (ISBN 0-88102-045-1). Janus Bks.

Simple French Food. Richard Olney. LC 73-80755. (Illus.). pap. 10.95 (ISBN 0-689-70546-8, 229). Atheneum.

Simple French Phrase Book. Terry C. Shen. Tr. by Sara Mills. (Popular Phrase Bk.). (Illus.). 40p. 1986. pap. 2.50x (ISBN 0-935655-06-9). Language Intl.

Simple Geological Structures. John Platt & John Challinor. 1974. pap. text ed. 7.95x (ISBN 0-04-550020-7). Unwin Hyman.

Simple Gifts. Joanne Greenberg. LC 86-323. 208p. 1987. pap. 7.95 (ISBN 0-8050-0540-4). H Holt & Co.

Simple Gifts, Vols. 1&2. Ed. by Gabe Huck. 1974. pap. 6.50 (ISBN 0-918208-65-3). Liturgical Conf.

Simple Graphical Procedure to Estimate the Minimum Time to Evacuate a Building. R. L. Francis. 1979. 3.50 (ISBN 0-686-25955-6, TR 79-5). Society Fire Protect.

Simple Greenhouse Gardening. Alan Toogood. (Concorde Gardening Ser.). (Illus.). 96p. (Orig.). 1988. pap. 9.95 (ISBN 0-7063-6504-6, Pub. by Ward Lock). David & Charles.

Simple Groups of Lie Type. Roger Carter. LC 72-39228. (Pure & Applied Mathematics Ser.: Vol. 28). pap. 85.80 (ISBN 0-317-26151-7, 2024274). Bks Demand UMI.

Simple Guide to Planning Applications. Ed. by Robert Cooke. 1988. 30.00x (ISBN 0-86025-419-4, Pub. by Ian Henry Pubns England). State Mutual Bk.

Simple Guide to Research Papers. rev. ed. Samuel Draper. 1978. 8.95 (ISBN 0-89529-040-5). Avery Pub.

Simple Guide to Trauma. 4th ed. R. L. Huckstep. (Illus.). 1987. pap. text ed. 14.00 (ISBN 0-443-03350-1). Churchill.

Simple Guide to U. S. Immigration Law. Josef Avesar. 205p. (Orig.). 1986. pap. 9.95 (ISBN 0-9617022-0-6). Univ Pub CA.

Simple Guides to Daily Growth: Problem Solving or Purposeful Relaxation for Comfort or Effectiveness, Set-SG. Russell E. Mason. 1975. pap. 30.00x (ISBN 0-89533-001-6); incl. tape-1a, t-2, t-5a 23.00x, Notes, Clinical Applications, Differential Criteria & Implications for Bioawareness, rev. ed., 1979; tapes only 23.00x. F I Comm.

Simple Harmonies. Ken Stone. 24p. 1987. 2.50 (ISBN 0-942432-12-6). M O P Pr.

Simple Heraldry. new ed. Don Pottinger & Iain Moncreiffe. LC 78-23691. (Illus.). 1979. 6.95 (ISBN 0-8317-7799-0, Mayflower Bks). Smith Pubs.

Simple Home Repairs: Inside. rev. ed. (Illus.). 26p. 1986. pap. 1.50 (ISBN 0-318-22434-8, S/N 001-000-04473-7). USGPO.

Simple Inorganic Substances. R. T. Sanderson. LC 87-35345. (Orig.). 1988. lib. bdg. 38.50 (ISBN 0-89464-232-4). Krieger.

Simple Interest Monthly Payment Tables. Financial Publishing Co. Staff. 288p. 1983. pap. 7.75 (ISBN 0-87600-683-7). Finan Pub.

Simple Interest Monthly Payment Tables. Financial Publishing Co. Staff. 288p. 1984. pap. 7.75 (ISBN 0-87600-686-1). Finan Pub.

Simple Interest Monthly Payment Tables. Financial Publishing Co. Staff. 288p. 1984. pap. 7.75 (ISBN 0-87600-689-6). Finan Pub.

Simple Interest Payment Tables, Biweekly. Ed. by Financial Publishing Co. Staff. (Illus.). 208p. 1985. pap. 7.75 (ISBN 0-87600-681-0). Finan Pub.

Simple Interest Payment Tables, Semimonthly. Ed. by Financial Publishing Co. Staff. (Illus.). 208p. 1985. pap. 7.75 (ISBN 0-87600-682-9). Finan Pub.

Simple Interest Payment Tables, Weekly. Ed. by Financial Publishing Co. Staff. (Illus.). 208p. 1985. pap. 7.75 (ISBN 0-87600-680-2). Finan Pub.

Simple Japanese Phrase Book. rev. ed. Terry C Shen. Tr. by Y. Yang Lai. (Illus.). 79p. 1986. text ed. 21.95 (ISBN 0-935655-02-6); pap. 2.50. Language Intl.

Simple Jitterbug. (Ballroom Dance Ser.). 1985. lib. bdg. 60.00 (ISBN 0-87700-787-X). Revisionist Pr.

Simple Jitterbug. (Ballroom Dance Ser.). 1986. lib. bdg. 59.95 (ISBN 0-8490-3296-2). Gordon Pr.

Simple Joys of Womanhood. Betty J. Busch. 32p. 1988. 7.95. Carlton.

Simple Justice: How Litigants Fare in the Pittsburgh Court Arbitration Program. Jane W. Adler et al. LC 83-16016. 152p. 1983. 15.00 (ISBN 0-8330-0518-9, R-3071-ICJ). Rand Corp.

Simple Justice: The History of Brown v. Board of Education & Black America's Struggle for Equality. Richard Kluger. 1976. 34.50 (ISBN 0-394-47289-6). Knopf.

Simple Justice: The History of Brown V. Board of Education & Black America's Struggle for Equality. Richard Kluger. 1977. pap. 16.95 (ISBN 0-394-72255-8, Vin). Random.

Simple Latin for Family Historians. 1987. 30.00x (Pub. by Birmingham Midland Soc UK). State Mutual Bk.

Simple Life. Belle Burton. 144p. 1981. 8.95 (ISBN 0-89962-213-5). Todd & Honeywell.

Simple Life: C. R. Ashbee in the Cotswolds. Fiona MacCarthy. LC 80-53299. (Illus.). 192p. 1981. 25.00x (ISBN 0-520-04369-3). U of Cal Pr.

Simple Life Coloring Book. Craig Sandberg. 1983. 2.25 (ISBN 0-87813-519-7). Christian Light.

Simple Life: Plain Living & High Thinking in American Culture. David E. Shi. 332p. 1985. 29.95 (ISBN 0-19-503475-9). Oxford U Pr.

Simple Life: Plain Living & High Thinking in American Culture. David E. Shi. 352p. 1986. pap. 8.95 (ISBN 0-19-504013-9). Oxford U Pr.

Simple Living. new ed. Edward K. Ziegler. 128p. 1974. pap. 1.25 (ISBN 0-87178-791-1). Brethren.

Simple Low-Cost Wire Antennas for Radio Amateurs. 2nd ed. William I. Orr & S. D. Cowan. LC 76-190590. (Illus.). 192p. 1972. 11.95 (ISBN 0-933616-02-3). Radio Pubns.

Simple Lust. Dennis Brutus. (African Writers Ser.). 1973. pap. text ed. 7.50 (ISBN 0-435-90115-X). Heinemann Ed.

Simple Man in a Complicated World. Steve Duniphan. LC 85-81164. (Illus.). 1985. 10.00 (ISBN 0-934426-08-2). Napsac Reprods.

Simple Math Programs in Basic for Your Personal Computer. John E. Dadas. Date not set. write for info. S&S.

Simple Matter of Justice: The Phyllis Wheatly YWCA Story. Florence J. Radcliffe. 304p. 1985. 13.00 (ISBN 0-682-40199-4). Exposition-Phoenix.

Simple Methods for Detecting Buying & Selling Points in Securities. James Liveright. LC 68-21699. 1968. Repr. of 1926 ed. flexible cover 8.00 (ISBN 0-87034-028-X). Fraser Pub Co.

Simple Methods for Identification of Plastics: With the Plastics Identification Table by Hansjurgen Saechtling. 2nd ed. D. Braun. (Hanser Publications). (Illus.). 110p. 1987. 22.50 (ISBN 0-19-520725-4). Oxford U Pr.

Simple Methods for the Treatment of Drinking Water. G. Heber. (GATE Ser.). (Illus.). 78p. 1986. pap. 11.00 (ISBN 3-528-02021-0, Pub. by Vieweg & Sohn). IPS.

Simple Minds: An Illustrated Biography. 96p. 1985. 1.95 (ISBN 0-7119-0617-3). Cherry Lane.

Simple Minds: The Race is the Prize. Alfred Bos. 128p. 1986. pap. 10.95 (ISBN 0-88715-014-4). Putnam Pub Group.

Simple Models of Equilibrium & Nonequilibrium Phenomena. Ed. by J. L. Lebowitz. (Studies in Statistical Mechanics: Vol. 13). 272p. 1987. 77.75 (ISBN 0-444-87039-3, North Holland). Elsevier.

Simple Morphisms in Algebraic Geometry. Richard Sot. (Lecture Notes in Mathematics: Vol. 935). 146p. 1982. pap. 11.00 (ISBN 0-387-11564-1). Springer-Verlag.

Simple Noneuclidean Geometry & Its Physical Basis. I. M. Yaglom. (Heidelberg Science Library). (Illus.). 1979. pap. 34.00 (ISBN 0-387-90332-1). Springer-Verlag.

Simple Object Lessons for Children. Tom A. Biller & Martie Biller. (Object Lesson Ser.). 160p. 1980. pap. 4.95 (ISBN 0-8010-0793-3). Baker Bk.

Simple Objects. Illus. by Tony Tallarico. (Preschool See & Say Bks.). (Illus.). 12p. (ps). Date not set. bds. 2.95 (ISBN 0-89828-257-8). Tuffy Bks.

Simple Omnibus. Langston Hughes. 17.95 (ISBN 0-88411-059-1, Pub. by Aeonian Pr). Amereon Ltd.

Simple Outlines on the Christian Faith. Russell E. Spray. (Dollar Sermon Library). 1977. pap. 2.50 (ISBN 0-8010-8120-3). Baker Bk.

Simple Pascal. James J. McGregor & Alan H. Watt. LC 81-5407. 182p. 1981. pap. 21.95 (ISBN 0-914894-72-2, Computer Sci Pr). W H Freeman.

Simple Path: A Guide to Nourishing the Body, Mind & Spirit. Kim Le. 1987. write for info. Scriptorium Pr.

Simple Pictures Are Best. Nancy Willard. LC 76-4923. (Illus.). (gr. 1-4). 1977. 7.95 (ISBN 0-15-274958-6, HJ). HarBraceJ.

Simple Pictures Are Best. Nancy Willard. LC 78-6424. (Illus.). (ps-3). 1978. pap. 3.95 (ISBN 0-15-682625-9, VoyB). HarBraceJ.

Simple Pictures Are Best. Nancy Willard. LC 78-6424. (Voyager Picture Bks.). (Illus.). 32p. (Orig.). (ps-3). 1987. pap. 3.95 (ISBN 0-317-59233-5, VoyB). HarBraceJ.

Simple Pictures Are Best. Nancy Willard. (Illus.). (gr. k-3). 1988. 3.95 (VoyB). HarBraceJ.

Simple Pink Bubble That Ended the Trouble with Jonathan Hubble. Utz. LC 78-190273. (Illus.). 32p. (gr. 2-3). 1972. PLB 9.95 (ISBN 0-87783-062-2); pap. 3.94 deluxe ed. (ISBN 0-87783-108-4). Oddo.

Simple Plant Progagation. Ed. by Jane Courtier. (Concorde Gardening Ser.). (Illus.). 96p. (Orig.). 1988. pap. 9.95 (ISBN 0-7063-6507-0, Pub. by Ward Lock). David & Charles.

Simple Plant Propagation. R. C. Wright. LC 77-70396. (Illus.). 1978. pap. 5.95 (ISBN 0-8120-0795-6). Barron.

Simple Pleasures: Casual Cooking for all Occasions. Helen Hecht. LC 85-48133. 352p. 1986. 16.95 (ISBN 0-689-11523-7). Atheneum.

Simple Pleasures of Japan. Jack Condon & Camy Condon. (Illus.). 148p. (Orig.). 1981. pap. 9.95 (ISBN 4-07-973843-9, Pub. by Shufunmoto Co Ltd Japan). C E Tuttle.

Simple Prayer. John Dalrymple. LC 83-82664. (Ways of Prayer Ser.: Vol. 9). 118p. 1984. pap. 4.95 (ISBN 0-89453-301-0). M Glazier.

Simple Printing Methods. Jeanne Cross. LC 72-39812. (Illus.). 48p. (gr. 6 up). 1972. 14.95 (ISBN 0-87599-192-0). S G Phillips.

Simple Procedure to Speed Disposition of Appealed Civil Cases in Tennessee. National Center for State Courts Staff. (Paul Reardon Ser.). 3p. 1981. manuscript 0.18 (PRS-005). Natl Ctr St Courts.

Simple Processes at the Gas-Solid Interface. C. H. Bamford & C. F. Tipper. (Comprehensive Chemical Kinetics Ser.: Vol. 19). 1984. 202.75 (ISBN 0-444-42287-0, I-147-84). Elsevier.

Simple Progression. Larry Moffi. LC 82-72089. 54p. 1982. pap. 4.95 (ISBN 0-9604740-1-3). Ampersand RI.

Simple Puppets You Can Make. Jennifer MacLennan. LC 87-26691. (Illus.). 132p. 1988. 17.95 (ISBN 0-8069-6816-8). Sterling.

Simple Quantum Physics. P. V. Landshoff & A. J. Metherell. LC 78-73244. (Illus.). 1980. pap. 14.95 (ISBN 0-521-29538-6). Cambridge U Pr.

Simple Repair & Preservation Techniques for Collection Curators, Librarians & Archivists. 3rd ed. Jean Gunner. (Illus.). 22p. 1984. pap. 3.00 (ISBN 0-913196-44-4). Hunt Inst Botanical.

Simple Science. (Disney Begin to Learn Ser.). (Illus.). (ps-7). 1987. 5.95 (ISBN 0-553-05415-5). Bantam.

Simple Science. Wilkes. (Illus.). 38p. (gr. 2-5). 1983. 10.95 (ISBN 0-86020-761-7); PLB 12.96 (ISBN 0-88110-272-5). EDC.

Simple Science Says: Take One Balloon. Melvin Berger. (gr. 2-5). 1988. pap. 2.95 (ISBN 0-590-41612-X). Scholastic Inc.

Simple Screamer: A Guide to the Art of Papier & Cloth Mache. Dan Reeder. (Illus.). 96p. 1984. pap. 14.95 (ISBN 0-87905-163-9, Peregrine Smith). Gibbs Smith Pub.

Simple Scrumptious Microwaving. Mary A. Robinson et al. 224p. (Orig.). 1986. pap. 9.95 (ISBN 0-449-90174-2, Columbine). Fawcett.

Simple Seismics. Nigel A. Anstey. LC 82-80267. (Short Course Handbooks). (Illus.). 168p. 1982. text ed. 29.00 (ISBN 0-934634-37-8); pap. text ed. 21.00 (ISBN 0-934634-43-2). Intl Human Res.

Simple Sermons for Funeral Services. Herschel W. Ford. 54p. 1985. pap. 3.50 (ISBN 0-8010-3514-7). Baker Bk.

Simple Sermons for Midweek Services. W. Herschel Ford. 104p. (Orig.). 1988. pap. 4.95 (ISBN 0-8010-3546-5). Baker Bk.

Simple Sermons for Saints & Sinners. W. Herschel Ford. 152p. 1986. pap. 4.50 (ISBN 0-8010-3522-8). Baker Bk.

Simple Sermons for Special Days & Occasions. W. Herschel Ford. 140p. 1985. pap. 4.95 (ISBN 0-8010-3515-5). Baker Bk.

Simple Sermons for Sunday Evening. W. Herschel Ford. 126p. (Orig.). 1988. pap. 4.95 (ISBN 0-8010-3545-7). Baker Bk.

Simple Sermons for Sunday Morning. W. Herschel Ford. 128p. 1986. pap. 4.50 (ISBN 0-8010-3523-6). Baker Bk.

Simple Sermons for Time & Eternity. W. Herschel Ford. 120p. 1985. pap. 4.95 (ISBN 0-8010-3516-3). Baker Bk.

Simple Sermons for Today's World. W. Herschel Ford. 120p. (Orig.). 1988. pap. 4.95 (ISBN 0-8010-3544-9). Baker Bk.

Simple Sermons of Great Christian Doctrines. W. Herschel Ford. 138p. 1985. pap. 4.95 (ISBN 0-8010-3519-8). Baker Bk.

Simple Sermons on Conversion & Commitment. W. Herschel Ford. (W. Herschel Ford Sermon Library). 128p. 1986. pap. 4.95 (ISBN 0-8010-3524-4). Baker Bk.

Simple Sermons on Evangelistic Themes. W. Herschel Ford. 128p. 1986. pap. 4.95 (ISBN 0-8010-3525-2). Baker Bk.

Simple Sermons on Grace & Glory. W. Herschel Ford. 92p. 1986. pap. 4.50 (ISBN 0-8010-3526-0). Baker Bk.

Simple Sermons on Prayer. W. Herschel Ford. 88p. 1985. pap. 4.50 (ISBN 0-8010-3520-1). Baker Bk.

Simple Sermons on Salvation & Service. W. Herschel Ford. 136p. 1986. pap. 4.95 (ISBN 0-8010-3527-9). Baker Bk.

Simple Sermons on Simple Themes. W. Herschel Ford. 118p. (Orig.). 1988. pap. 4.95 (ISBN 0-8010-3543-0). Baker Bk.

Simple Sermons on the New Testament Texts. W. Herschel Ford. 112p. 1985. pap. 3.95 (ISBN 0-8010-3517-1). Baker Bk.

Simple Sermons on the Saviour Last Words. W. Herschel Ford. 89p. (Orig.). 1988. pap. 4.95 (ISBN 0-8010-3541-4). Baker Bk.

Simple Sermons on the Second Coming. W. Herschel Ford. 104p. (Orig.). 1988. pap. 4.95 (ISBN 0-8010-3542-2). Baker Bk.

Simple Sermons That Demand a Decision. Edward Fudge. 2.00 (ISBN 0-686-12689-0). E Fudge.

Simple Sermons That Say Something. Edward Fudge. pap. 2.00 (ISBN 0-686-12684-X). E Fudge.

Simple Settings of American Folk Songs and Rhymes for Orff Ensemble Book 2. 2nd, rev. ed ed. Isabel M. Carley. 1974. pap. 2.00 (ISBN 0-918812-07-0). MMB Music.

Simple Simon & Other Favorites (Mother Goose) Illus. by Allen Atkinson. (Mother Goose Lil Classics Ser.). (Illus.). 64p. (Orig.). 1986. pap. 2.50 (ISBN 0-553-15322-6). Bantam.

Simple Singularities & Simple Algebraic Groups. P. Slodowy. (Lecture Notes in Mathematics: Vol. 815). 175p. 1980. pap. 15.00 (ISBN 0-387-10026-1). Springer-Verlag.

Simple Soupbook. Adelaide Hechtlinger. LC 69-18890. 1969. pap. 2.50 (ISBN 0-8283-1031-9). Branden Pub Co.

Simple South Indian Savoury Dishes for One & All. Ed. by Regency Press Ltd. Staff. 48p. 1984. 25.00x (ISBN 0-7212-0604-2, Pub. by Regency Pr). State Mutual Bk.

Simple Spanish Phrase Book. Abr. ed. Terry C. Shen. Ed. by Farres. (Popular Phrase Bk.). (Illus., Orig.). 1986. pap. 2.50 (ISBN 0-317-43437-3). Language Intl.

Simple Speaks His Mind. Langston Hughes. (gr. 5-6). Repr. lib. bdg. 17.95x (ISBN 0-88411-061-3, Pub. by Aeonian Pr). Amereon Ltd.

Simple Squeezes. Hugh Kelsey. (Master Bridge Ser.). 128p. 1985. 18.95 (ISBN 0-575-03607-9, Pub. by Gollancz England). David & Charles.

Simple Story. S. Y. Agnon. Tr. & afterword by Hillel Halkin. LC 85-2481. 256p. 1985. 14.95 (ISBN 0-8052-3999-5). Schocken.

Simple Story. S. Y. Agnon. Tr. by Hillel Halkin from Hebrew. LC 85-2481. 250p. 1986. pap. 8.95 (ISBN 0-8052-0820-8). Schocken.

Simple Story. Elizabeth Inchbald. Ed. by J. M. Tompkins & Jane Spencer. (World's Classics Ser.). 384p. 1988. pap. 7.95 (ISBN 0-19-281849-X). Oxford U Pr.

Simple Subs Book. 2nd ed. L. Sellers. 187p. 1985. text ed. 28.00 (ISBN 0-08-031839-8, Pub by PPL); pap. text ed. 13.75 (ISBN 0-08-031840-1). Pergamon.

Simple Sums. Watson. (Simple Facts Ser.). (Illus.). 28p. (ps-2). 1985. 3.95 (ISBN 0-86020-779-X). EDC.

Simple Surgical Emergencies. Douglas Lindsey. (Illus.). 272p. 1982. pap. 14.95 (ISBN 0-668-05472-7). Appleton & Lange.

Simple Systems, Complex Environments: Hospital Financial Information Systems. Mari Malvey. LC 80-29597. (Managing Information Ser.: Vol. 2). (Illus.). 185p. 1981. 25.00 (ISBN 0-8039-1541-1). Sage.

Simple Takes a Wife. Langston Hughes. 17.95 (ISBN 0-88411-062-1, Pub. by Aeonian Pr). Amereon Ltd.

Simple Task-Centered Exercises as an Aid to Social Work Training. Kay McDougall. 1977. 25.00x (ISBN 0-317-42899-3, Pub by Natl Soc Work). State Mutual Bk.

Simple Things of the Christian Life. G. Campbell Morgan. 1984. pap. 2.25 (ISBN 0-915374-40-4). Rapids Christian.

Simple, Thorough & Reliable Course in Pottery Making. Alfred Binsfield. (Illus.). 147p. 1984. 97.75 (ISBN 0-86650-115-0). Gloucester Art.

Simple Thoughts. Mike Hamill. Ed. by Judy L. Wofter. (Illus.). 78p. (Orig.). 1983. pap. 7.95 (ISBN 0-912477-00-8, TX 1-086-794). Ogab Pubs.

Simple Tomato Growing. Ian G. Walls. (Concorde Gardening Ser.). (Illus.). 96p. (Orig.). 1988. pap. 9.95 (ISBN 0-7063-6505-4, Pub. by Ward Lock). David & Charles.

Simple Truth. Elizabeth Hardwick. LC 81-43389. (Neglected Books of the 20th Century Ser.). 278p. 1982. Repr. of 1955 ed. 12.95 (ISBN 0-912946-98-9). Ecco Pr.

Simple Truth. Mary-Alice Jafolla. 90p. (ps up). 1982. 5.95 (ISBN 0-87159-146-4). Unity School.

Simple Vegetarian Cookery. Paul Cartan. 1974. lib. bdg. 69.95 (ISBN 0-685-51356-4). Revisionist Pr.

Simple Vietnamese for Americans. Nguyen Cuong. 12.50 (ISBN 0-87559-169-8). Shalom.

Simple Welcome Speeches & Other Helps. Amy Bolding. (Pocket Pulpit Library). 1973. pap. 4.50 (ISBN 0-8010-0612-0). Baker Bk.
Simple Yet Stunning Quilts. Rita Davis. (Illus.). 80p. 1981. pap. 8.95 (ISBN 0-942152-07-7). R C Pubns OR.
Simple Yoga & Therapy. Yogeswar. (Illus.). 340p. 1987. 16.95. Asia Bk Corp.
Simples Machines. Rae Bains. LC 84-2607. (Illus.). 32p. (gr. 3-6). 1985. PLB 9.49 (ISBN 0-8167-0166-0); pap. text ed. 1.95 (ISBN 0-8167-0167-9). Troll Assocs.
Simple's Uncle Sam. Langston Hughes. (American Century Ser.). 180p. 1965. pap. 7.95 (ISBN 0-8090-0087-3). Hill & Wang.
Simple's Uncle Sam. Langston Hughes. 15.95 (ISBN 0-88411-709-X, Pub. by Aeonian Pr). Amereon Ltd.
Simplest Explanation of God Ever Explained. Nam U. Detacuden. 230p. 1983. 13.50 (ISBN 0-682-49951-X). Exposition-Phoenix.
Simpleton. Aleksei F. Pisemskii. Tr. by I. Litvinova from Rus. LC 76-23893. (Classics of Russian Literature). (Illus.). 1977. 15.00 (ISBN 0-88355-508-5); pap. 10.00 (ISBN 0-88355-507-7). Hyperion Conn.
Simpleton of Naples & Other Italian Folktales. Nonna Maria Scarpato & Camille Fattoross. LC 82-81946. (Illus.). 96p. (gr. 3-8). 1983. 13.95 (ISBN 0-88100-010-8). Capricorn Bks.
Simpleton of Naples & Other Italian Folktales, Bk. 2. 2nd ed. Nonna M. Scarpato. Ed. by Camille Fattoross. (Illus.). 94p. (gr. 3-12). Date not set. text ed. write for info. (ISBN 0-9618462-1-6). Capricorn Bks.
Simplex Method. K. H. Borgwardt. (Algorithms & Combinatorics: Vol. 1). (Illus.). xi, 268p. 1986. pap. 38.00 (ISBN 0-387-17096-0). Springer-Verlag.
Simplical Methods & the Interpretation of "Triple" Cohomolgy. J. Duskin. LC 75-20008. (Memoirs: No. 163). 135p. 1975. pap. 15.00 (ISBN 0-8218-1863-5, MEMO-163). Am Math.
Simplication of American Life: Hollywoods Films of the 1930's. Jeffery M. Paine. 26.50 (ISBN 0-405-09893-6, 11489). Ayer Co Pubs.
Simplicial Objects in Algebraic Topology. J. Peter May. LC 82-51078. vi, 162p. 1983. pap. text ed. 9.00x (ISBN 0-226-51180-4). U of Chicago Pr.
Simplicissimus: One-Hundred Eighty Satirical Drawings from the Famous German Weekly. Ed. & tr. by Stanley Appelbaum. LC 74-79171. (Illus.). 192p. 1975. 14.95 (ISBN 0-486-23099-6); pap. 8.95 (ISBN 0-486-23098-8). Dover.
Simplicities: Poems. Oscar Mandel. LC 74-79131. 64p. 1974. pap. 4.00 (ISBN 0-914502-01-8). Spectrum Prods.
Simplicity. Elliott Sober. (Clarendon Library of Logic & Philosophy). (Illus.). 1975. 27.50x (ISBN 0-19-824407-X). Oxford U Pr.
Simplicity: A Rich Quaker's View. George Peck. LC 72-97851. (Orig.). 1973. pap. 2.50x (ISBN 0-87574-189-4). Pendle Hill.
Simplicity & Ordinariness: Studies in Medieval Cistercian History, Vol. IV. Ed. by John R. Sommerdfeldt. (Cistercian Studies: No. 61). (Orig.). 1980. pap. text ed. 8.95 (ISBN 0-87907-861-8). Cistercian Pubns.
Simplicity & Reality of the Bible: A Revolutionary Bible Handbook. Eric Demaree. LC 87-91608. 97p. (Orig.). 1988. pap. 6.00 (ISBN 0-9619367-0-3). Bible Outreach Pub Co.
Simplicity Fitting Book. Rev. ed. Ed. by Jo Kirshon. (Illus., Orig.). 1978. pap. 3.50. Simplicity.
Simplicity of Comp-Proc. Microform Specialist Group Seminar. British Computer Society Staff. 1976. pap. 24.95 (ISBN 0-471-25611-0, Wiley Heyden). Wiley.
Simplicity of Life As Lived in the Everyday. Kathleen Storms. LC 83-16812. 322p. (Orig.). 1984. lib. bdg. 29.25 (ISBN 0-8191-3601-8). U Pr of Amer.
Simplicity of Mental Aberrations. G. P. Sanderson. 1986. 44.00x (ISBN 0-86332-092-9, Pub. by Book Guild Ltd). State Mutual Bk.
Simplicity of Racine. Cecil M. Bowra. LC 74-14552. 1956. lib. bdg. 15.00 (ISBN 0-8414-9876-8). Folcroft.
Simplicity of Racine. Maurice Bowra. 1978. Repr. of 1956 ed. lib. bdg. 15.50 (ISBN 0-8495-0421-X). Arden Lib.
Simplicity: The Key to Successful Inventions. Richard E. Paige. 185p. 7.50 (ISBN 0-930317-06-8). Mindsight Pub.
Simplicity, the Key to Successful Inventions. 185p. pap. 7.50 (ISBN 0-318-23164-6). Geothermal World.
Simplicity's Simply the Best Sewing Book. Simplicity Pattern Co. Staff. 1988. 29.95 (ISBN 0-06-055049-X, HarpT). Har-Row.
Simplicity's Simply the Best Sewing Book. Simplicity Pattern Co. Staff. (Illus.). 288p. 1988. pap. 14.95 (ISBN 0-06-096125-2, PL-6125, PL). Har-Row.
Simplicius Simplicissimus. Hans J. C. Von Grimmelshausen. Tr. by Lesley Weissenborn & Helmut Weissenborn. (Orig.). 1982. pap. 10.95 (ISBN 0-7145-3910-4). Riverrun NY.
Simplicius Simplicissimus. Johann J. Von Grimmelshausen. LC 86-5646. 610p. (Orig.). 1986. lib. bdg. 36.25 (ISBN 0-8191-5348-6); pap. text ed. 26.00 (ISBN 0-8191-5349-4). U Pr of Amer.
Simplicius Simplicissimus see Adventures of a Simpleton.
Simplified Accounting for Non-Accountants. Rick S. Hayes & C. Richard Baker. LC 80-11267. (Small Business Management Ser.). 291p. 1980. 19.95 (ISBN 0-471-04977-8, Pub. by Ronald Pr). Wiley.
Simplified Accounting for Non-Accountants. Rick S. Hayes & Richard Baker. 304p. 1986. pap. 3.95 (ISBN 0-515-09099-9). Jove Pubns.
Simplified Accounting for the Computer Industry. R. S. Hayes & C. R. Baker. (Wiley Series on Small Business Management). 191p. 1981. 39.95x (ISBN 0-471-05703-7, Pub. by Ronald Pr). Wiley.
Simplified Accounting Systems & Concepts for Lawyers: With a Standard Chart of Accounts. 145p. 1982. pap. 34.00 (ISBN 0-89707-076-3). Amer Bar Assn.
Simplified Approach to Electrocardiography. Richard Johnson & Mark Schwartz. (Illus.). 331p. 1986. pap. 19.95 (ISBN 0-7216-1738-7). Saunders.
Simplified Approach to Planning Estates: Problems & Solutions. Benjamin M. Becker & Ben Roth. LC 82-71022. 204p. 1982. text ed. 14.95 (ISBN 0-87863-144-5, Farnsworth Pub Co). Longman Finan.
Simplified Approach to S-370 Assembly Language Programming. Barbara J. Burian. (Illus.). 1977. write for info (ISBN 0-13-810119-1). P-H.
Simplified Astronomy for Astrologers. David Williams. 108p. 1969. 5.00 (ISBN 0-86690-172-8, 1525-01). Am Fed Astrologers.
Simplified Basic Programming for IBM PCs, Ps-2s, Compatible & Clones. 2nd ed. Gerald A. Silver & Myrna L. Silver. Orig. Title: Simplified Basic Programming for Microcomputers. (Illus.). 350p. 1988. pap. text ed. 21.95x (ISBN 0-912675-26-8); instr's. manual avail. (ISBN 0-912675-27-6). Ardsley.
Simplified Basic Programming for Microcomputers see Simplified Basic Programming for IBM PCs, Ps-2s, Compatible & Clones.
Simplified Behavior & "Feeling" State Change & Goal Accomplishment, Set-SB. Russell E. Mason. 1975. pap. 50.00x Tape (ISBN 0-89533-002-4); incl. tape-1a, t-2, t-5a, t-3, t-16, t-17, Notes, Clinical Applications, rev. ed., 1979, Brief Outlines 3, Substitution Training & Positive Goal Achievement 45.00x. F I Comm.
Simplified Bible Lessons on the Old & New Testaments. G. H. Showalter & W. M. Davis. 1944. pap. 2.75 (ISBN 0-88027-039-X). Firm Foun Pub.
Simplified Boatbuilding: Flat Bottom. Harry V. Sucher. (Illus.). 1973. 24.95 (ISBN 0-393-03173-X). Norton.
Simplified Boatbuilding: The V-Bottom Boat. Harry V. Sucher. LC 73-22340. (Illus.). 458p. 1974. 24.95 (ISBN 0-393-03180-2). Norton.
Simplified Building Design for Wind & Earthquake Forces. James Ambrose & Dimitry Vergun. LC 79-26660. 142p. 1980. 41.95 (ISBN 0-471-05013-X, Pub. by Wiley-Interscience). Wiley.
Simplified Buying Guide. 1988. 2.00 (102). Am Bartenders.
Simplified Chinese Characters. Tan Huay Peng. (Peng's Chinese Treasury Ser.). (Illus.). 128p. 1987. pap. 4.95 (ISBN 0-89346-293-4). Heian Intl.
Simplified Circuit Analysis: Digital-Analog Logic. Richard D. Sacks et al. LC 79-179386. (Illus.). pap. 43.50 (ISBN 0-317-08020-2, 2017857). Bks Demand UMI.
Simplified Computer Programming: Including the Easy RPG Way. Kelton Carson. LC 73-90739. (Illus.). 240p. 1974. pap. 8.95 (ISBN 0-8306-3676-5, 676). TAB Bks.
Simplified Concrete Masonry Planning & Building. 2nd ed. J. Ralph Dalzell. LC 81-385. 398p. 1981. Repr. of 1972 ed. lib. bdg. 23.50 (ISBN 0-89874-278-1). Krieger.
Simplified Consumer Credit Forms. Carl Felsenfeld & Alan Siegel. LC 78-50301. 1978. 64.00 (ISBN 0-88262-184-X). Warren Gorham & Lamont.
Simplified Cost System. 14.95 (ISBN 0-318-02603-1). Print Indus Am.
Simplified Course in Hatha Yoga. Wallace Slater. 1967. pap. 2.75 (ISBN 0-8356-0138-2, Quest). Theos Pub Hse.
Simplified Criminal Case Processing in the Massachusetts District Courts. National Center for State Courts Staff. (Paul Reardon Ser.). 19p. 1982. manuscript 1.14 (PRS-027). Natl Ctr St Courts.
Simplified Design. Portland Cement Association. Ed. by Gerald B. Neville. 200p. 1984. pap. 14.75 (ISBN 0-317-07247-1, EB104D) (ISBN 0-89312-043-X). Portland Cement.
Simplified Design of Building Foundations. 2nd ed. Ambrose. 1988. price not set (ISBN 0-471-85898-6). Wiley.
Simplified Design of Building Foundations. James Ambrose. LC 80-39880. 338p. 1981. 41.95 (ISBN 0-471-06267-7, Pub. by Wiley-Interscience). Wiley.
Simplified Design of Building Structures. 2nd ed. James Ambrose. LC 85-22676. 266p. 1986. 36.95 (ISBN 0-471-80929-2). Wiley.
Simplified Design of Concrete Buildings of Moderate Size & Height. 160p. 1984. 26.95 (ISBN 0-317-37040-5, EB104); 16.75 (ISBN 0-317-37041-3). ACI.
Simplified Design of Reinforced Concrete. 5th ed. Harry Parker. LC 84-10462. 250p. 1984. text ed. 38.95x (ISBN 0-471-80349-9, Pub. by Wiley-Interscience). Wiley.
Simplified Design of Roof Trusses Architects & Builders. 3rd ed. Harry Parker & James Ambrose. LC 81-19800. 301p. 1982. 32.50x (ISBN 0-471-07722-4, Pub. by Wiley-Interscience). Wiley.
Simplified Design of Structural Steel. 5th ed. Harry Parker & James Ambrose. LC 83-1180. 401p. 1983. 32.95 (ISBN 0-471-89766-3, Pub. by Wiley-Interscience). Wiley.
Simplified Design of Structural Wood. 4th ed. Harry Parker. LC 88-154. 240p. 1988. 34.95 (ISBN 0-471-85134-5). Wiley.
Simplified Dictionary. Compiled by C. W. Airne & O. Harland. 1987. 25.00x (ISBN 0-7217-0122-1, Pub. by Schofield & Sims). State Mutual Bk.
Simplified Dictionary of Modern Samoan. R. W. Allardice. 288p. 1985. pap. text ed. 26.95x (ISBN 0-908597-02-9, Pub. by Polynesian Soc). UH Pr.
Simplified Diet Manual Study Guide. 3rd ed. Martha Spillman. (Illus.). 80p. 1985. pap. 7.95x (ISBN 0-8138-1435-9). Iowa St U Pr.
Simplified Diet Manual with Meal Patterns. 5th ed. Iowa Dietetic Association Staff. 108p. 1984. pap. text ed. 12.95 (ISBN 0-8138-1430-8). Iowa St U Pr.
Simplified Digital Automation with Microprocessors. James T. Arnold. LC 78-51242. 1979. 53.00 (ISBN 0-12-063750-2). Acad Pr.
Simplified Drugs & Solutions for Nurses: Including Mathematics. 9th ed. Dison. 176p. 1987. pap. 15.95 (ISBN 0-8016-2467-3). Mosby.
Simplified Energy Analysis Using the Modified Bin Method. (Illus.). 240p. 1984. pap. text ed. 45.00 nonmember price (ISBN 0-910110-39-5). Am Heat Ref & Air Eng.
Simplified Energy Calculations. (Professional Development Ser.: No. 5). 329p. 1983. 125.00 (ISBN 0-317-58765-X, PDST-5). Am Heat Ref & Air Eng.
Simplified Engineering for Architects & Builders. 6th ed. Harry Parker & James Ambrose. 447p. 1984. 33.95x (ISBN 0-471-86611-3). Wiley.
Simplified Estimating for Builders & Engineers. Joseph Helton. (Illus.). 208p. 1985. text ed. 34.00 (ISBN 0-13-810144-2). P-H.
Simplified Extended, Deep, & or Meditative Relaxation, Set-R. rev. ed. Russell E. Mason. 1975. 30.00x (ISBN 0-89533-004-0); tape-1a, t-l, t-6 incl., Clinical Applications, Brief Outlines, Relaxation Training, rev. ed., 1979. (ISBN 0-89533-026-1). F I Comm.
Simplified Fly Fishing: It Gets You on the Water & Fishing with Flies in Half an Hour. S. R. Slaymaker, II. LC 87-7088. (Illus.). 160p. 1988. pap. 10.95 (ISBN 0-8117-2279-1). Stackpole.
Simplified Golf: There's No Trick to It! 2nd ed. Peter Longo. Ed. by Boye De Mente. (Illus.). 144p. (Orig.). 1984. pap. 9.95 (ISBN 0-914778-34-X). Phoenix Bks.
Simplified Governmental Budgeting. Edward A. Lehan. LC 81-82463. (Illus.). 86p. 1981. nonmemeber 30.00 (ISBN 0-686-84272-3); member 25.00 (ISBN 0-686-84273-1); students manual 15.00. Municipal.
Simplified Guide to BHS (Biblia Hebraica Stuttgartensia) William R. Scott. LC 87-51113. 1987. write for info. (ISBN 0-941037-04-5). Bibal Pr.
Simplified Guide to Bishops' Transcripts & Marriage Licenses, Their Location & Indexes in England, Wales, & Ireland. J. S. Gibson. LC 82-82482. 33p. 1984. pap. 4.00 (ISBN 0-8063-0995-4). Genealog Pub.
Simplified Guide to Computerized Perimetry. Marc F. Lieberman & Michael Drake. LC 86-42789. 202p. 1987. pap. text ed. 40.00 (ISBN 0-943432-90-1). Slack Inc.
Simplified Guide to FORTRAN Programming. Daniel McCracken. LC 74-876. 278p. 1974. pap. write for info. (ISBN 0-471-58292-1); tchr's manual avail. (ISBN 0-471-58293-X). Wiley.
Simplified Guide to FORTRAN Programming. (Arabic.). 1985. pap. 15.00 (ISBN 0-471-82382-1). Wiley.
Simplified Guide to Microcomputers with Practical Programs & Applications. William A. Bocchino. LC 82-3671. 256p. 1982. 19.95 (ISBN 0-13-810085-3, Busn). P-H.
Simplified Guide to Probate Jurisdictions: Where to Look for Wills in Great Britain & Ireland. J. S. Gibson. LC 82-82481. (Illus.). 72p. 1982. pap. 5.00 (ISBN 0-8063-0994-6). Genealog Pub.
Simplified Guide to Structured COBOL Programming. 2nd ed. Donald Golden. 1988. pap. write for info. (ISBN 0-471-61054-2). Wiley.
Simplified Guide to Structured COBOL Programming. Daniel McCracken. LC 75-44339. 390p. 1976. pap. write for info. (ISBN 0-471-58284-0). Wiley.
Simplified Guide to Structured COBOL Programming. 2nd ed. Daniel D. McCracken & Donald G. Golden. LC 87-34608. 630p. 1988. pap. text ed. write for info. (ISBN 0-471-88658-0); tchr's. manual avail. (ISBN 0-471-60019-9). Wiley.
Simplified Guide to Structured COBOL Programming. 400p. (Arabic.). 1987. pap. write for info. (ISBN 0-471-87968-1). Wiley.
Simplified Guide to Using Statistical Techniques with Computer Applications. Margaret N. Morrison. LC 86-3242. 206p. 1986. pap. 24.95 (ISBN 0-13-810185-X, Busn). P-H.
Simplified Hairdressing Science. David Salinger & Jon Williams. (Illus.). 180p. 1986. pap. text ed. 15.95 (ISBN 0-9614548-4-9). Intl Assn Trichologists.
Simplified Independence Proofs: Boolean Valued Models of Set Theory. Barkley J. Rosser. (Pure & Applied Mathematics Ser: Vol. 31). 1969. 59.00 (ISBN 0-12-598050-7). Acad Pr.
Simplified Indian Cookery. Rebecca Joseph. 1970. pap. 3.00 (ISBN 0-88253-144-1). Ind-US Inc.
Simplified Introduction to the Wisdom of St. Thomas. Peter A. Redpath. LC 80-5230. 180p. 1980. lib. bdg. 25.25 (ISBN 0-8191-1058-2); pap. text ed. 11.25 (ISBN 0-8191-1059-0). U Pr of Amer.
Simplified Inventory System: For Collectors, Investors & Dealers. E. R. Jones. (Illus.). 68p. 1982. 6.75 (ISBN 0-9600934-3-5). E R Jones.
Simplified Job-Resume Preparation. 5th ed. Ray G. Hadley. LC 56-1958. 1981. perfect bdg. 2.97 (ISBN 0-9600988-1-X). R G Hadley.
Simplified Keyboarding for Data Entry. Sheryl L. LIndsell. 96p. 1985. Reference Text 9.95 (ISBN 0-668-06087-5); pap. 5.95 (ISBN 0-668-06091-3). Arco.
Simplified Laboratory Procedures for Wastewater Examination. 3rd ed. Water Pollution Control Federation. LC 85-51664. (Special Publication Ser.). 105p. 1985. pap. 10.00 (ISBN 0-943244-62-5, MOO18). Water Pollution.
Simplified Low-Cost Maintenance Control. rev. ed. W. Colebrook Cooling. 128p. 1983. 24.95 (ISBN 0-8144-5657-X). AMACOM.
Simplified Low-cost Maintenance Control. Wilmer Cooling. LC 82-18380. pap. 30.50 (ISBN 0-317-20412-2, 2023501). Bks Demand UMI.
Simplified Mail Order Bookkeeping System. 1987. lib. bdg. 79.95 (ISBN 0-8490-3863-4). Gordon Pr.
Simplified Masonry Skills. 2nd ed. R. T. Kreh. 336p. 1982. 24.95 (ISBN 0-442-25337-0). Van Nos Reinhold.
Simplified Mechanics & Strength of Materials. 4th ed. Harry Parker & James Ambrose. LC 86-11004. 355p. 1986. 35.95 (ISBN 0-471-82269-8). Wiley.
Simplified Mechanics & Strength of Materials. 3rd ed. Harry Parker & Harold D. Hauf. LC 76-56465. 325p. 1977. 36.95x (ISBN 0-471-66562-2). Wiley.
Simplified Medical Dictionary. R. Franks & H. Swartz. 276p. 1977. casebound 27.50 (ISBN 0-87489-054-3). Med Economics.
Simplified Methodology for Community Energy Management Planning. (Technical Report). 116p. 1981. 20.00 (ISBN 0-318-17715-3, DG 81-310). Pub Tech Inc.
Simplified Methods for Estimating Vapor Concentration & Dispersion Distances for Continuous LNG Spills into Dikes with Flat or Sloping Floors. 103p. 1978. pap. 6.00 (ISBN 0-318-12699-0, X50978). Am Gas Assn.
Simplified Nursing. 9th ed. Claire P. Hoffman & Gladys B. Lipkin. (Illus.). 500p. 1981. pap. text ed. 16.50 (ISBN 0-397-54364-6, Lippincott Nursing); wkbk. 9.50 (ISBN 0-686-86026-8). Lippincott.
Simplified Painless Endodontics for the General Dentist: The Alternative to N 2. David Pyner. (Illus.). 171p. 1980. 62.00 (ISBN 0-931386-12-8). Quint Pub Co.
Simplified Precision Bridge. C. C. Wei. Ed. by Robert B. Ewen. (Illus.). 64p. 1972. pap. 1.95 (ISBN 0-87643-006-X). Barclay Bridge.
Simplified Procedures for Water Examination, Including Supplement on Instrumental Methods - M12. American Water Works Association Staff. (AWWA Manuals). (Illus.). 190p. 1978. pap. text ed. 20.40 (ISBN 0-89867-070-5). Am Water Wks Assn.
Simplified Proofreading. 2nd ed. Peggy Smith. 103p. 1984. pap. text ed. 14.00 (ISBN 0-935012-01-X). Edit Experts.
Simplified Purposeful Relaxation for Comfort or Effectiveness, Set-PR. Russell E. Mason. 1975. pap. 30.00x (ISBN 0-89533-003-2); Tapes only. incl. tape-1a, t-2, t-6, Notes, Clinical Applications, rev. ed., 1979 23.00. F I Comm.
Simplified Quantity Recipes: Nursing-Convalescent Homes & Hospitals. Mabel Caviani & Muriel Urbashich. 310p. 1986. pap. 24.95 (ISBN 0-317-57875-8, FP783). Natl Restaurant Assn.
Simplified Radiation Heat Transfer Calculations from Large Open Hydrocarbon Fires. Philip J. DiNenno. 1982. 5.35 (ISBN 0-686-37674-9, TR 82-9). Society Fire Protect.
Simplified Real Estate Examination. John L. Edmonds. LC 86-91854. 256p. (Orig.). 1986. pap. 25.00 (ISBN 0-9617949-0-9). J L Edmonds Pub Co.
Simplified Recipes for Adult Care Centers. Lila M. Jones & Barbara R. Fischer. 224p. 1983. 26.95 (ISBN 0-8436-2203-2). Van Nos Reinhold.
Simplified Recipes for Day Care Centers. Patricia D. Asmussen. LC 74-222. 224p. 1983. spiral bdg. 20.95 (ISBN 0-8436-0590-1). Van Nos Reinhold.
Simplified Reinforced Concrete. Edward G. Nawy. (Illus.). 320p. 1986. text ed. 29.95 (ISBN 0-317-29670-1). P-H.

Simulation of Control Systems: Proceedings of the IFAC-IMACS Symposium, Vienna, 22-26 September, 1986. I. Troch et al. (IFAC Proceedings Ser.: No. 8713). 470p. 1987. 120.00 (ISBN 0-08-034349-X). Pergamon.
Simulation of Control Systems With Special Emphasis on Modelling & Redundancy. Ed. by I. Troch. 312p. (Proceedings). 1978. 79.00 (ISBN 0-444-85199-2, North-Holland). Elsevier.
Simulation of Distributed-Parameter & Large-Scale Systems. S. G. Tzafestas. 380p. 1980. 92.00 (ISBN 0-444-85447-9, North-Holland). Elsevier.
Simulation of Ecological Processes. 2nd ed. C. T. DeWit & J. Goudriaan. 1978. pap. 11.50 (ISBN 90-220-0652-2, PDC144, PUDOC). UNIPUB.
Simulation of Ecological Processes. 2nd ed. C. T. DeWit & J. Houdriaan. LC 78-5408. (Simulation Monographs). 174p. 1978. pap. 34.95x (ISBN 0-470-26357-1). Halsted Pr.
Simulation of Energy Systems. Ed. by Kenneth E. Watt. (SCS Simulation Ser.: Vol. 8, Nos. 1 & 2). 1978. No.1. 36.00 ea. (ISBN 0-911801-00-6); No.2. (ISBN 0-911801-01-4). Soc Computer Sim.
Simulation of Field Water Use & Crop Yield. 1979. pap. 18.00 (PDC142, PUDOC). UNIPUB.
Simulation of Grazing Systems. K. R. Christian et al. 121p. 1978. pap. 9.50 (ISBN 0-686-93181-5, PDC106, Pudoc). UNIPUB.
Simulation of Infectious Disease Epidemics. Eugene Ackerman et al. (Illus.). 210p. 1984. 32.75x (ISBN 0-398-04900-9). C C Thomas.
Simulation of Large Stat Variations in Steam Power Plants. R. Dolezal. (Lecture Notes in Engineering Ser.: Vol. 30). x, 120p. 1987. pap. 21.70 (ISBN 0-387-18053-2). Springer-Verlag.
Simulation of Liquids & Solids: Molecular Dynamics & Monte Carlo Methods in Statistical Mechanics. Ed. by G. Ciccotti et al. 490p. 1987. 58.75 (ISBN 0-444-87062-8, North Holland); pap. 36.75 (ISBN 0-444-87061-X). Elsevier.
Simulation of Manufacturing Systems. Allan Carrie. LC 87-35562. 200p. 1988. write for info. (ISBN 0-471-91574-2). Wiley.
Simulation of Natural Language. Fernard J. Vandamme. (Janua Linguarum, Ser Major: No. 50). 1972. text ed. 25.60x (ISBN 90-2792-106-7). Mouton.
Simulation of Plant Growth & Crop Production. Ed. by F. W. T. Penning de Vries & H. H. Van Laar. (Simulation Monographs). 308p. (20 papers, index). 1982. pap. 35.50 (ISBN 90-220-0809-6, PDC250, PUDOC). UNIPUB.
Simulation of Recreational Use for Park & Wilderness Management. Mordechai Shechter & Robert C. Lucas. LC 78-17920. (Resources for the Future). 1979. 25.00x (ISBN 0-8018-2160-6). Johns Hopkins.
Simulation of Systems, 1979. Ed. by L. Dekker & G. Savastano. 1170p. 1980. 171.00 (ISBN 0-444-86123-8, North-Holland). Elsevier.
Simulation of the Denver Fire Department for Development Policy Analysis. Donald R. Plane et al. 1975. 2.50 (ISBN 0-686-64196-5). U CO Busn Res Div.
Simulation of the Maneuverability of Inland Waterway Tows. George L. Petrie. (University of Michigan, Dept. of Naval Architecture & Marine Engineering, Report: No. 186). pap. 23.30 (ISBN 0-317-27207-1, 2023871). Bks Demand UMI.
Simulation of Waiting-Line Systems. Susan L. Solomon. (Illus.). 464p. 1983. text ed. 52.00 (ISBN 0-13-810044-6). P-H.
Simulation of Water Use & Herbage Growth in Arid Regions. H. Van Keulen. (Illus.). 150p. 1975. pap. 15.50 (ISBN 90-220-0557-7, PDC88, PUDOC). UNIPUB.
Simulation of Water Use, Nitrogen Nutrition & Growth of a Spring Wheat Crop. H. Van Keulen & N. G. Seligman. 250p. 1987. text ed. 50.00 (ISBN 90-220-0905-X, PDC322, Pub. by PUDOC). UNIPUB.
Simulation of Wave Processes in Excitable Media. V. Zykov. Ed. by A. T. Winfree & P. N. Nandapurkas. 384p. 1988. 49.95 (ISBN 0-7190-2472-2, Pub. by Manchester Univ Pr). St Martin.
Simulation Profession (ESC '85) 16.00 (ISBN 0-317-60960-2). Soc Computer Sim.
Simulation: Programming Techniques. Ed. by Blaise W. Liffick. LC 78-8649. 1979. pap. text ed. 15.95 (ISBN 0-07-037826-6, BYTE Bks). McGraw.
Simulation Software & Ada. Unger et al. 1984. pap. 16.00 (ISBN 0-911801-03-0). Soc Computer Sim.
Simulation: Statistical Foundations & Methodology. G. Arthur Mihram. (Mathematics in Science & Engineering Ser: Vol. 92). 1972. 95.00 (ISBN 0-12-495950-4). Acad Pr.
Simulation Studies. Ed. by Ian Hodder. LC 78-51670. (Illus.). 1979. 34.50 (ISBN 0-521-22025-4). Cambridge U Pr.
Simulation Teaching of Library Administration. Martha J. Zachert. LC 74-32041. pap. 78.80 (ISBN 0-317-10402-0, 2004384). Bks Demand UMI.
Simulation Techniques for Discrete Event Systems. I. Mitrani. LC 82-4549. (Cambridge Computer Science Texts Ser.: No. 14). (Illus.). 200p. 1983. 29.95 (ISBN 0-521-23885-4); pap. 13.95 (ISBN 0-521-28282-9). Cambridge U Pr.
Simulation Technology & Traffic Accident Record Systems. (Transportation Research Record Ser.). 76p. 1979. 3.00 (ISBN 0-309-02952-X). Transport Res Bd.
Simulation Using GPSS. Thomas J. Schriber. LC 73-21896. 533p. 1974. write for info. (ISBN 0-471-76310-1). Wiley.
Simulation with GASP-PL-I: A PL-I Based Continuous-Discrete Simulation Language. Alan B. Pritsker & Robert E. Young. LC 75-23182. pap. 87.80 (ISBN 0-317-11035-7, 2022490). Bks Demand UMI.
Simulation with Gpss & Gpssv. P. A. Bobillier et al. LC 75-40316. 1976. 48.00 (ISBN 0-13-810549-9). P-H.
Simulator GPSS-FORTRAN: Version 3. B. Schmidt. 350p. 1987. 29.00 (ISBN 0-387-96504-1). Springer-Verlag.
Simulator Market. 169p. 1983. 1285.00x (ISBN 0-88694-549-6). Intl Res Dev.
Simulators. Ed. by M. Sage et al. (IEE Conference Publication: No. 226). 344p. 1983. pap. 99.00 (ISBN 0-85296-279-7, IC226). Inst Elect Eng.
Simulators. (IEE Conference Publication). 1986. 62.00 (ISBN 0-85296-335-1, IC267). Inst Elect Eng.
Simulators (ESC '85) 36.00 (ISBN 0-317-60978-5). Soc Computer Sim.
Simulators III (ESC '86) 36.00 (ISBN 0-317-60985-8). Soc Computer Sim.
Simulators IV (ESC '87) 1987. 36.00 (ISBN 0-911801-15-4). Soc Computer Sim.
Simulators V (ESC 1988, Orlando) (Simulation Ser.: Vol. 19, No. 4). Date not set. 40.00 (ISBN 0-911801-34-0). Soc Computer Sim.
Simuliation of Operations in Space: Capabilities & Requirements. 1988. 36.00 (ISBN 0-89883-995-5, SP724). Soc Auto Engineers.
Simuliide of the Ethiopian Region. Paul Freeman & Botha De Meillon. (Illus.). vii, 224p. 1953. Repr. of 1968 ed. 26.00x (ISBN 0-565-00194-9, Pub. by Brit Mus Nat Hist). Sabbot-Natural Hist Bks.
Simultaneous see Three Paths to the Lake.
Simultaneous & Successive Cognitive Processes. J. P. Das et al. LC 78-20039. (Educational Psychology Ser.). 1979. 43.50 (ISBN 0-12-203150-4). Acad Pr.
Simultaneous Equation Model of Price & Quantity Adjustments in World Primary Commodity Markets. Erh-Cheng Hwa. (Working Paper: No. 499). 48p. 1981. pap. 5.00 (ISBN 0-686-39661-8, WP-0499). World Bank.
Simultaneous Equation Models with Measurement Error. Vincent J. Geraci. LC 79-53208. (Outstanding Dissertations in Economics Ser.). 180p. 1984. lib. bdg. 29.00 (ISBN 0-8240-4158-5). Garland Pub.
Simultaneous Rapid Combustion see Methods in Microanalysis.
Simultaneous Statistical Inference. Rupert Miller, Jr. (Springer Series in Statistics). (Illus.). 299p. 1981. 32.00 (ISBN 0-387-90548-0). Springer-Verlag.
Sin. J. Keith Miller. 240p. 1987. 14.95 (ISBN 0-06-065713-8, HarpR). Har-Row.
Sin. Robert Vaughan. (Orig.). 1979. pap. 2.50 (ISBN 0-89083-479-2). Zebra.
Sin see Studies in Dogmatics: Theology.
Sin: A Christian View for Today. Xavier Thevenot. Ed. by Roger Marchand. Tr. by Simone Inkel from Fr. 80p. 1984. pap. 2.95 (ISBN 0-89243-218-7). Liguori Pubns.
Sin Ai. 80p. 13.95 (ISBN 0-395-37907-5); pap. 5.95 (ISBN 0-395-37908-3). HM.
Sin & Forgiveness. Michael J. Beers. (Fathers of the Church Ser.: Vol. 12). 1988. 12.95 (ISBN 0-89453-352-5); pap. 8.95 (ISBN 0-89453-323-1). M Glazier.
Sin & Hoodoo Memory. W. Gellis. 44p. 1987. pap. 10.00 (ISBN 0-917455-04-5). Big Foot Ny.
Sin & Its Consequences. rev. ed. Cardinal Henty E. Manning. LC 86-50420. 200p. 1986. pap. 5.00 (ISBN 0-89555-299-X). Tan Bks Pubs.
Sin & Judgment in the Prophets. Patrick D. Miller. LC 81-8950. (SBL Monograph Ser.). 1982. 19.50 (ISBN 0-89130-514-9, 06-00-27); pap. 16.00 (ISBN 0-89130-515-7). Scholars Pr GA.
Sin & Sanction in Israel & Mesopotamia: A Comparative Study. K. Van der Toorn. (Studia Semitica Neerlandica: No. 22). 213p. 1985. pap. 20.00 (ISBN 90-232-2166-4, Pub. by Van Gorcum Holland). Longwood Pub Group.
Sin & Scientism. Jacob Needleman. (Broadside Editions Ser.). 26p. (Orig.). 1986. pap. 3.95 (ISBN 0-9609850-7-7). Rob Briggs.
Sin & Sex. R. Briffault. LC 72-6300. (Studies in Philosophy, No. 40). 228p. 1972. Repr. of 1931 ed. lib. bdg. 49.95x (ISBN 0-8383-1631-X). Haskell.
Sin & Sex. Robert Briffault. LC 72-9623. (Human Sexual Behavior Ser.). Repr. of 1931 ed. 22.50 (ISBN 0-404-57418-1). AMS Pr.
Sin & Temptation. John Owen. Ed. by James M. Houston. LC 83-791. (Classics of Faith & Devotion). 1983. 13.95 (ISBN 0-88070-013-0). Multnomah.
Sin at Easter. Tumas J. Vaizgantas. 1971. 5.95 (ISBN 0-87141-038-9). Manyland.
Sin Bearer. Tom Taylor. 192p. 1986. 10.95 (ISBN 0-8499-0573-7). Word Bks.
Sin-Eater. Fiona Macleod. (H. P. Lovecraft's Favorite Horror Stories Ser.). 26p. (Orig.). 1985. pap. 2.00 (ISBN 0-318-04719-5). Necronomicon.
Sin-Eater, & Other Tales & Episodes. facsimile ed. William Sharp. LC 74-167470. (Short Story Index Reprint Ser.). Repr. of 1895 ed. 19.00 (ISBN 0-8369-3996-4). Ayer Co Pubs.
Sin: Its Reality & Nature. Ed. by Pietro Palazzini. 238p. 1964. 9.95 (ISBN 0-933932-25-1). Scepter Pubs.
Sin Loi. Arthur B. Greathead. (Illus.). 50p. (Orig.). 1988. pap. 5.95 (ISBN 0-945670-00-1). Greathead Pub.
Sin of Father Mouret. Emile Zola. Tr. by Sandy Petrey from Fr. LC 83-10436. viii, 310p. 1983. 25.00x (ISBN 0-8032-4902-0); pap. 7.50 (ISBN 0-8032-9901-X, BB 862, Bison). U of Nebr Pr.
Sin of Henry R. Luce: An Anatomy of Journalism. David Cort. 480p. 1974. 12.50 (ISBN 0-8184-0201-6). Lyle Stuart.
Sin of Monsieur Pettipon & Other Humorous Stories. facsimile ed. Richard E. Connell. LC 77-106273. (Short Story Index Reprint Ser.). 1922. 18.00 (ISBN 0-8369-3310-9). Ayer Co Pubs.
Sin of Obedience. Willard Beecher & Marguerite Beecher. 88p. (Orig.). 1982. pap. 4.75 (ISBN 0-942350-00-6). Beecher Found.
Sin of Origin. John Barnes. (Isaac Asimov Presents Ser.). 256p. 1988. 15.95 (ISBN 0-86553-195-1). Congdon & Weed.
Sin of the Book: Edmond Jabes. Ed. by Eric Gould. LC 84-5270. (Illus.). xxvi, 252p. 1985. 23.95x (ISBN 0-8032-2115-0). U of Nebr Pr.
Sin of Unbelief. C. H. Spurgeon. 1977. pap. 0.95 (ISBN 0-686-23224-0). Pilgrim Pubns.
Sin Reconsidered. James Gaffney. LC 82-61424. 96p. (Orig.). 1983. pap. 3.95 (ISBN 0-8091-2516-1). Paulist Pr.
Sin Redemption & Sacrifice: A Biblical & Patristic Study. Stanislas Lyonnet & Leopold Sabarin. (Analecta Biblica: Vol. 48). 1971. pap. 26.00 (ISBN 88-7653-048-7, Biblical Inst. Press). Loyola.
Sin, Salvation & Service. Henry Stob. (Orig.). 1984. pap. 2.95 (ISBN 0-933140-98-3). CRC Pubns.
Sin, Salvation, & the Spirit. Ed. & pref. by Daniel Durken. LC 79-20371. (Illus.). 368p. 1979. text ed. 6.00 (ISBN 0-8146-1078-1); pap. text ed. 10.00 (ISBN 0-8146-1079-X). Liturgical Pr.
Sin, Sex & Self-Control. Norman V. Peale. 1981. pap. 2.95 (ISBN 0-449-23921-7, Crest). Fawcett.
Sin, Sickness & Sanity: A History of Sexual Attitudes. Vern Bullough & Bonnie Bullough. (Orig.). 1977. pap. 9.95 (ISBN 0-452-00794-1, F562, Mer). NAL.
Sin, Suffering & God. Thomas B. Warren. 1980. pap. 15.00 (ISBN 0-934916-25-X). Natl Christian Pr.
Sin, Suffering & Sickness. David Cox. 1985. 10.00x (ISBN 0-317-62161-0, Guild of Pastoral Psych). State Mutual Bk.
Sin Tactics. David Ganz. 54p. 1988. 12.00 (ISBN 0-916258-19-X); pap. 7.50. Mercury Print.
Sinagua Social Differentiation: Inferences Based on Prehistoric Mortuary Practices. John W. Hohman. (Arizona Archaeologist Ser.: No. 17). (Illus.). 115p. (Orig.). 1983. pap. 6.00 (ISBN 0-939071-12-6). AZ Archaeol.
Sinai: A Photographic Portfolio. Neil Folberg. (Illus.). 1986. 60.00 (ISBN 0-915361-05-1, Dist. by Watts). Adama Pubs Inc.
Sinai Accord As a Phase of the U. S. Containment Policy. Naseer Aruri. (Occasional Papers: No. 2). 7p. 1976. pap. 1.00 (ISBN 0-937694-41-X). Assn Arab-Amer U Grads.
Sinai & Palestine. A. P. Stanley. 646p. 1986. 350.00x (ISBN 1-85077-088-3, Pub. by Darf Pubs Ltd). State Mutual Bk.
Sinai & Zion: An Entry into the Jewish Bible. Jon D. Levenson. 240p. (Orig.). 1985. 16.95 (ISBN 0-86683-961-5, AY8551, HarpR). Har-Row.
Sinai Blunder. Indar Jit Rikhje. 200p. 1978. 25.50 (ISBN 0-937722-19-7). Intl Peace.
Sinai Blunder: Withdrawal of the United Nations Emergency Force Leading to the Six-Day War of June 1967. Indar J. Rikhye. 240p. 1980. 27.50x (ISBN 0-7146-3136-1, F Cass Co). Biblio Dist.
Sinai Strategy: Economics & the Ten Commandments. Gary North. 368p. (Orig.). 1986. pap. 12.50 (ISBN 0-930464-07-9). Inst Christian.
Sinai Victory: Command Decisions in History's Shortest War, Israel's Hundred Hour Conquest of Egypt East of Suez, Autumn 1956. Samuel L. Marshall. (Combat Arms Ser.: 11th). (Illus.). 280p. 1958. Repr. of 1958 ed. 18.95 (ISBN 0-89839-085-0). Battery Pr.
Sinan, Ottoman, Architect. Lamia Doumato. (Architecture Ser.: A 1803). 7p. 1987. 3.00 (ISBN 1-55590-273-1). Vance Biblios.
Sinatra, Sinatra. Paul Fericano. 16p. (Orig.). 1982. Chapbook 200.00 (ISBN 0-916296-06-7). Poor Souls Pr.
Sinbad & the Evil Genii. Jack Melanos. (Orig.). (gr. k up). 1985. pap. 3.50 (ISBN 0-87602-251-4). Anchorage.
Sinbad the Sailor. Patricia Daniels. LC 79-28588. (Fairy Tales Ser.). (Illus.). 24p. (gr. k-3). 1980. PLB 13.31 (ISBN 0-8393-0256-8). Raintree Pubs.
Sinbad the Sailor. Patricia Daniels. LC 79-28588. (Fairy Tale Clippers Ser.). (Illus.). 24p. (gr. k-4). 1980. PLB 27.99 incl. cassette (ISBN 0-8172-1835-1). Raintree Pubs.
Sinbad, the Sailor. (MacDonald Educational Ser.). (Illus., Arabic.). (gr. 4-6). 3.95x (ISBN 0-86685-267-0). Intl Bk Ctr.
Since Aquino: The Philippine Tangle & the United States. Justus M. Van der Kroef. (Contemporary Asian Studies: No. 6-1987). 1987. pap. text ed. 3.00 (ISBN 0-942182-80-4). Occasional Papers.
Since Cezanne. facs. ed. Clive Bell. (Essay Index Reprint Ser). 1922. 16.00 (ISBN 0-8369-0034-0). Ayer Co Pubs.
Since Cumorah. Hugh Nibley. 450p. 1988. 16.95 (ISBN 0-87579-139-5). Deseret Bk.
Since Daisy Creek. W. O. Mitchell. LC 85-9088. 288p. 1985. 16.95 (ISBN 0-8253-0303-6). Beaufort Bks NY.
Since Dallas: Images of John F. Kennedy in Popular & Scholarly Literature, 1963-1973. Vincent L. Toscano. LC 77-81013. 1978. soft cover 13.95 (ISBN 0-88247-493-6). R & E Pubs.
Since Debussy: A View of Contemporary Music. Andre Hodeir. Tr. by Noel Burch. LC 74-28310. (Music Ser.). (Illus.). 256p. 1975. Repr. of 1961 ed. lib. bdg. 29.50 (ISBN 0-306-70662-8). Da Capo.
Since Flannery O'Connor: Essays on the Contemporary American Short Story. Ed. by Loren Logsdon & Charles W. Mayer. LC 87-61274. (Essays in Literature Book Ser.: No. 7). (Illus.). 152p. (Orig.). 1987. pap. 8.00 (ISBN 0-934312-06-0). WIU Essays Lit.
Since Gandhi: India's Sarvodaya Movement. Mark Shepard. 40p. 1984. pap. 3.50 (ISBN 0-934676-63-1). Greenlf Bks.
Since Jesus Passed By. Charles Hunter & Frances Hunter. 199p. 1986. pap. 3.00 (ISBN 0-917726-76-6). Hunter Bks.
Since Jesus Passed By. Frances Hunter & Charles Hunter. 1973. pap. 4.95 (ISBN 0-917726-38-3). Hunter Bks.
Since Lenin Died. Max. F. Eastman. LC 73-839. (Russian Studies: Perspectives on the Revolution Ser.). 158p. 1973. Repr. of 1925 ed. 17.60 (ISBN 0-88355-035-0). Hyperion Conn.
Since Nineteen Sixty-Four: New & Selected Poems. Peter Schjeldahl. LC 78-15572. 1978. pap. 7.00 (ISBN 0-915342-26-X). SUN.
Since O'Casey: And Other Essays on Irish Drama. Robert Hogan. LC 82-22813. (Irish Literary Studies: No. 15). 176p. 1983. text ed. 28.50x (ISBN 0-389-20346-7). B&N Imports.
Since Seventeen Eighty-Seven: The Franklin & Marshall College Story. Frederic S. Klein. 1968. 2.00 (ISBN 0-685-10974-7); pap. 1.00 (ISBN 0-685-10975-5). Franklin & Marsh.
Since Socrates: Studies in the History of Western Educational Thought. Henry J. Perkinson. LC 79-9150. 222p. 1980. pap. text ed. 16.95 (ISBN 0-582-28098-2). Longman.
Since Stanislavski & Vakhtangov: The Method As a System for Today's Actor. Lawrence Parke. 272p. (Orig.). 1986. pap. 12.95 (ISBN 0-9615288-8-5). Acting World Bks.
Since the Civil War see Growth of American Politics: A Modern Reader.
Since the Civil War see Synopsis of American History.
Since the Filer Commission..., 1983. (Working Papers for Spring Research Forum). 569p. Date not set. 75.00 ea. Ind Sector.
Since the Harlem Renaissance: Fifty Years of Afro-American Art. Joseph Jacobs. LC 85-71056. (Illus.). 124p. 1985. pap. 17.50 (ISBN 0-916279-02-2). Cntr Gallery Buck Univ.
Since Time Immoral: The Kipper Family Song Book. 64p. (Orig.). 1986. pap. 12.95 (ISBN 0-85418-149-0). Princeton Bk Co.
Since Yesterday - the Nineteen Thirties in America: September 3, 1929 to September 3, 1939. Frederick L. Allen. LC 86-45060. 304p. 1986. pap. 7.95 (ISBN 0-06-091322-3, PL1322, PL). Har-Row.
Since You Asked. Bill Flatt. pap. 5.95 (ISBN 0-89137-544-9). Quality Pubns.
Since You've Been Gone. Michael P. Jones. (Illus.). 155p. 1984. text ed. 20.00 (ISBN 0-89904-016-0). Crumb Elbow Pub.
Sincere Faith. C. M. Wagner. 75p. Date not set. pap. 4.00. Tru-Faith.
Sincerely, Lyndon: The Handwriting of Lyndon Baines Johnson. Jennifer Casoni. LC 83-6956. 100p. (Orig.). 1983. pap. 14.95 (ISBN 0-9608816-1-1). Univ Autograph.
Sincerely Peg. Peggy R. Dobler. (Illus.). 1976. pap. 4.95 (ISBN 0-686-17611-1). New Expressions.
Sincerity: A Story of Our Time. John Erskine. 356p. 1983. Repr. of 1929 ed. lib. bdg. 20.00 (ISBN 0-8495-1431-2). Arden Lib.
Sincerity & Authenticity. Lionel Trilling. LC 80-7945. 192p. 1980. Repr. of 1972 ed. 12.95 (ISBN 0-15-182645-5). HarBraceJ.
Sincerity & Authenticity: Six Lectures. Lionel Trilling. LC 72-83468. (Charles Eliot Norton Lectures Ser: 1969-1970). 1972. pap. 5.95 (ISBN 0-674-80861-4). Harvard U Pr.
Sincerity & Insincerity in Charles James Fox. H. Butterfield. (Raleigh Lectures on History). 1971. pap. 5.50 (ISBN 0-85672-050-X, Pub. by British Acad). Longwood Pub Group.
Sincerity & Truth: Essays on Arnauld, Bayle, & Toleration. John Kilcullen. 240p. 1988. 39.95 (ISBN 0-19-826691-X). Oxford U Pr.

TITLE INDEX

SING WHEN YOU'RE WINNING.

Sinclair Lewis. Intro. by Harold Bloom. (Modern Critical Views Ser.). 144p. 1987. 19.95 (ISBN 0-87754-628-2). Chelsea Hse.
Sinclair Lewis. Sheldon N. Grebstein. (Twayne's United States Authors Ser). 1962. pap. 8.95x (ISBN 0-8084-0278-1, T14, Twayne). New Coll U Pr.
Sinclair Lewis. Sheldon N. Grebstein. (United States Authors Ser.). 1987. lib. bdg. 16.95 (ISBN 0-8057-0448-5, Twayne). G K Hall.
Sinclair Lewis. Oliver Harrison. LC 73-3461. 1925. lib. bdg. 17.00 (ISBN 0-8414-2065-3). Folcroft.
Sinclair Lewis. James Lundquist. LC 72-76774. (Literature and Life Ser.). 159p. 16.95x (ISBN 0-8044-2562-0). Ungar.
Sinclair Lewis. Mark Schorer. (Pamphlets on American Writers Ser: No. 27). (Orig.). 1963. pap. 1.25x (ISBN 0-8166-0290-5, MPAW27). U of Minn Pr.
Sinclair Lewis' Arrowsmith. Intro. by Harold Bloom. (Modern Critical Interpretations Ser.). 112p. 1988. lib. bdg. 19.95 (ISBN 1-55546-046-1). Chelsea Hse.
Sinclair Lewis: Home at Last. John J. Koblas. (Illus.). 172p. 1981. 12.95 (ISBN 0-89658-024-5). Voyageur Pr Inc.
Sinclair Lewis: Our Own Diogenes. Vernon Parrington. LC 73-11205. (American Literature Ser., No. 49). 1974. lib. bdg. 75.00x (ISBN 0-8383-1720-0). Haskell.
Sinclair Lewis: Our Own Diogenes. Vernon L. Parrington. LC 77-9602. 1977. Repr. of 1930 ed. lib. bdg. 17.00 (ISBN 0-8414-6794-3). Folcroft.
Sinclair Lewis: Twentieth Century American Author & Nobel Prize Winner. Alan L. Paley. Ed. by D. Steve Rahmas. LC 73-87626. (Outstanding Personalities Ser.: No. 67). 32p. (Orig.). (YA) (gr. 7-12). 1974. lib. bdg. 3.75 incl. catalog cards (ISBN 0-87157-567-1); pap. 2.50 vinyl laminated covers (ISBN 0-87157-067-X). SamHar Pr.
Sinclair ZX-81: Programming for Real Applications, Also for the Timex-Sinclair 1000-1500. Randle Hurley. 170p. 1983. pap. 11.95 (ISBN 0-88056-090-8); incl. cassette o.p. 29.95 (ISBN 0-88056-155-6). Dilithium Pr.
Sinclair's Double War. Terrell L. Bowers. (YA) (gr. 9-12). 1985. 9.95 (ISBN 0-8034-8505-0, Avalon). Bouregy.
Sind Through the Centuries. Hamida Khuro. (Illus.). 1981. 55.00x (ISBN 0-19-577250-4). Oxford U Pr.
Sindell Negligence Folio. rev. ed. Joseph M. Sindell & I. David. 24p. 1970. pap. 3.35 (ISBN 0-88450-101-9, 6105). Lawyers & Judges.
Sindhi Short Stories. Ed. by Moti L. Jotwani. (Vikas Library of Modern Indian Writing). 160p. 1984. text ed. 20.00x (ISBN 0-7069-2637-4, Pub. by Vikas India). Advent NY.
Sindicalizacion de Trabajadores Agricolas en Mexico: La Experiencia de la Confederacion Nacional Campesina (CNC) Heladio R. Lopez. (Research Report Ser.: No. 26). 16p. (Orig.). 1981. pap. 5.50 (ISBN 0-935391-25-8, RR-26). Ctr Mex Studies.
Sindon: A Layman's Guide to the Shroud of Turin. Frank O. Adams. Ed. by John A. DeSalvo. LC 82-90138. (Illus.). 1982. 12.50 (ISBN 0-86700-008-2, Synergy Bks). P Walsh Pr.
Sindrome de la Borrachera Seca. R. J. Solberg. 12p. (Orig., Span.). 1983. pap. 0.95 (ISBN 0-89486-219-7). Hazelden.
Sindrome de Marfan. Reed E. Pyeritz & Julia Conant. Tr. by Marta Sozzi. (Illus.). 22p. (Orig., Span.). Date not set. pap. 1.00 (ISBN 0-918335-04-3). Natl Marfan Foun.
Sine Qua Nun. Monica Quill. Date not set. 14.95 (ISBN 0-8149-0926-4). Vanguard.
Sinequan: Doxepin HC1. Mendels. (International Congress Ser.: No. 385). 1976. pap. 25.25 (ISBN 0-444-15215-6, Excerpta Medica). Elsevier.
Sinews of Independence. Charles H. Lesser. LC 75-12227. 288p. 1976. 20.00x (ISBN 0-226-47332-5). U of Chicago Pr.
Sinews of Peace, Post-War Speeches. Winston L. Churchill. Ed. by Randolph S. Churchill. LC 83-45733. Repr. of 1949 ed. 30.00 (ISBN 0-404-20059-1). AMS Pr.
Sinews of the Spirit: The Ideal of Christian Manlines in Victorian Literature & Religious Thought. Norman Vance. 256p. 1985. 34.50 (ISBN 0-521-30387-7). Cambridge U Pr.
Sinews of Ulysses: Form & Convention in Milton's Works. Michael Lieb. (Language & Literature Ser.: Vol. 9). 250p. 1988. text ed. 29.95x (ISBN 0-8207-0205-6). Duquesne.
Sinews of War. Arnold Bennett. LC 74-17139. (Collected Works of Arnold Bennett: Vol. 74). 1976. Repr. 24.25 (ISBN 0-518-19155-9). Ayer Co Pubs.
Sinfonia Sexual. Hugo Escamilla. (Pimienta Collection Ser). (Span.). 1977. pap. 1.00 (ISBN 0-88473-259-2). Fiesta Pub.
Sinfonias Do Otono (Symphonies of Autumn) Enrique Aguilar. 1962. 3.50 (ISBN 0-686-17964-1). Franciscan Inst.
Sinful Tunes & Spirituals: Black Folk Music to the Civil War. Dena J Epstein. LC 77-6315. (Music in American Life Ser.). (Illus.). 460p. 1981. pap. 10.95 (ISBN 0-252-00875-8). U of Ill Pr.
Sinful Woman. James M. Cain. LC 87-72701. 144p. 1988. pap. 4.95 (ISBN 0-88739-089-7, Pub. by Black Lizard Bks). Creative Arts Bk.
Sinfully Good Cookbook. Gayle E. Salvatore. 256p. (Orig.). 1986. pap. text ed. 10.00 (ISBN 0-87507-035-3). Cath Lib Assn.
Sing. Ed. by American Camping Association Publications Committee. 95p. 1978. pap. 2.50 (ISBN 0-87603-037-1, SO 01). Am Camping.
Sing a Fun Song. Burl Ives. pap. 8.95 (ISBN 0-686-09069-1, Pub. by Peer-Southern). Columbia Pictures.
Sing-a-Long Christmas Carols. 40p. 1987. pap. text ed. 7.95 (ISBN 0-88188-626-2). H Leonard Pub Corp.
Sing a Message to Freedom: The Freedom Man. Anthony E. McAden. Ed. by Alexis Satchell. (Illus.). 50p. (Orig.). 1986. pap. 6.25 (ISBN 0-931841-07-0). Satchells Pub.
Sing a New Song. Charles Allums. Ed. by Betty Allums. (Illus.). 135p. (Orig.). 1984. pap. 8.75 (ISBN 0-932211-00-3). Bay Area Cross.
Sing a New Song. Andrea J. Shepard. 96p. (Orig.). 1986. pap. 5.95 (ISBN 0-310-34302-X, 12352P). Zondervan.
Sing a New Song. H. Lynn Stone. LC 81-85596. 123p. (Orig.). 1981. pap. text ed. 3.00 (ISBN 0-87148-798-5). Pathway Pr.
Sing a New Song unto the Lord: Poems of Joyful Praise. John C. Biardo. LC 86-83240. 80p. (Orig.). 1987. pap. 3.95 (ISBN 0-933181-03-5). Elmwood Park Pub.
Sing a New Song! Worship Renewal for Adventists Today. C. Raymond Holmes. LC 84-70077. xii, 190p. 1984. pap. 9.95 (ISBN 0-943872-88-X). Andrews Univ Pr.
Sing a Rainbow: Musical Activities with Mentally Handicapped Children. David Ward. (Illus., Orig.). 1979. pap. text ed. 8.95x (ISBN 0-19-317416-2). Oxford U Pr.
Sing a Sad Song: The Life of Hank Williams. 2nd ed. Roger M. Williams. LC 80-15520. (Music in American Life Ser.). 328p. 1981. pap. 9.95 (ISBN 0-252-00861-8). U of Ill Pr.
Sing a Song for Sixpence: The English Picture Book Tradition & Randolph Caldecott. Brian Alderson. (Illus.). 112p. 1987. 24.95 (ISBN 0-521-33179-X). Cambridge U Pr.
Sing a Song of Concepts. Dina Zeese. LC 87-83701. 112p. (Orig.). 1988. pap. 16.95 (ISBN 0-936485-01-9). Lkng Glass Pubns.
Sing a Song of Friendship. Irving Caesar. Repr. 1.95 (ISBN 0-686-95023-2). ADL.
Sing a Song of Gladness. C. Clayton. (Arch Bks.). (Illus.). 32p. (gr. k-4). 1974. pap. 1.29 (ISBN 0-570-06087-7, 59-1302). Concordia.
Sing a Song of Halloween: With Communication, Arts & Nutrition Activities. Julie Strand & Juanita Boggs. (Illus.). 133p. 1982. pap. text ed. 10.95 (ISBN 0-910817-00-6). Collaborative Learn.
Sing a Song of Halloween: With Communication, Arts & Nutrition Activities. rev. ed. Julie Strand et al. (Illus.). 133p. pap. text ed. write for info. (ISBN 0-910817-03-0). Collaborative Learn.
Sing a Song of Love. Judith Enderle. 160p. 1984. pap. 1.95 (ISBN 0-441-76726-5). Ace Bks.
Sing a Song of Mother Goose: Yellow Ladder Books for Toddlers Through 4 Years. Illus. by Cheryl Harte. (Learning Ladders Ser.). (Illus.). 16p. (ps). 1988. pap. 5.95 bk. & cassette pkg. (ISBN 0-394-89404-9, BYR). Random.
Sing a Song of Murder. Jan Michaels. (Mystery Puzzler Ser.: No. 12). (Illus.). 1978. pap. 1.95 (ISBN 0-89083-424-5). Zebra.
Sing a Song of People. Lois Lenski. (ps-3). 1987. 14.95 (ISBN 0-316-52074-8). Little.
Sing a Song of People. Roberta McLaughlin & Lucille Wood. (ps-3). 1973. songbook 9.63 (ISBN 0-8372-2375-X); 3 l p records 10.98ea.; sets 1-3, incl. 2 filmstrips, lp record & 20 minibks 59.85 ea.; minibks. sep. sets of 10 12.99; complete kit cassette ed. 229.95 (ISBN 0-8372-0219-1); complete kit record ed. 229.95 (ISBN 0-8372-0218-3). Bowmar-Noble.
Sing a Song of Popcorn: Every Child's Book of Poems. Ed. by Beatrice De Regniers. (Illus.). 160p. 1988. 16.95 (ISBN 0-590-40645-0, Scholastic Hardcovers). Scholastic Inc.
Sing a Song of Silence: A Deaf Girl's Odyssey. Jessica Rees. 164p. 1986. 51.80x (ISBN 0-946041-17-2, Pub. by Kensal Pr UK). State Mutual Bk.
Sing a Song of Sixpence. Illus. by Randolph Caldecott. (Picture Classic Ser.). (ps up). 1988. Repr. of 1888 ed. 8.95 (ISBN 0-8120-5900-X). Barron.
Sing a Song of Sixpence. Illus. by Margaret Chamberlain. LC 83-22510. (Nursery Rhyme Press-Out Bks.). (Illus.). 8p. (gr. k-2). 1984. bds. 4.95 (ISBN 0-911745-29-7, Bedrick Blackie). P Bedrick Bks.
Sing a Song of Sixpence. Leonard Lubin. LC 86-10337. (Illus.). 32p. (ps-2). 1987. 11.75 (ISBN 0-688-00544-6); PLB 11.88 (ISBN 0-688-00545-4). Lothrop.
Sing a Song of Sixpence. Ray Marshall & Korky Paul. Ed. by Kate Klimo. (Chubby Pop-Ups Ser.). (Illus.). 10p. (ps-k). 1983. 3.95 (ISBN 0-671-46237-7, Little Simon). S&S.
Sing a Song of Sixpence. Tracey C. Pearson. LC 84-14206. (Pied Piper Bk.). (Illus.). 32p. (ps-2). 1988. pap. 3.95 (ISBN 0-8037-0492-5, 0383-120). Dial Bks Young.
Sing a Song of Sixpence. Illus. by Tracey C. Pearson. LC 84-14206. (Illus.). 32p. (ps-2). 10.95 (ISBN 0-8037-0151-9, 01063-320); PLB 10.89 (ISBN 0-8037-0152-7). Dial Bks Young.
Sing a Song of Sixpence. Ferelith E. Williams. (Nursery Rhyme Board Bks.). (Illus.). 8p. (ps-k). 1985. 4.95 (ISBN 0-437-86002-7, Pub. by Worlds Work). David & Charles.
Sing a Song of Social Significance. rev ed. R. Serge Denisoff. LC 78-186631. 1983. 19.95 (ISBN 0-87972-036-0); pap. 6.95 (ISBN 0-87972-272-X). Bowling Green Univ.
Sing a Song of Sound. Vicki Silvers. LC 72-90695. (Illus.). 32p. (ps-2). 1973. 7.95 (ISBN 0-87592-046-2). Scroll Pr.
Sing about Us. Winifred Madison. 192p. (Orig.). (gr. 7 up). 1982. pap. 1.95 (ISBN 0-590-32191-9, Wildfire). Scholastic Inc.
Sing-Along Favorites. (Golden Song Book 'n' Tapes). (Illus.). (ps-3). pap. 5.45 (ISBN 0-307-13977-8, Golden Bks). Western Pub.
Sing Along-Senior Citizens. Ed. by R. E. Grant. 108p. 1973. spiral 14.25x (ISBN 0-398-02722-6). C C Thomas.
Sing along with Mad. Ed. by William M. Gaines. 1970. pap. 1.25 (ISBN 0-451-06826-2, Y6826, Sig). NAL.
Sing along with Mad. Frank Jacobs. 192p. 1987. pap. 2.95 (ISBN 0-446-34855-4). Warner Bks.
Sing along with Mad. Frank Jacobs & Al Jaffee. (Illus.). 192p. (Orig.). 1977. pap. 1.75 (ISBN 0-446-94440-8). Warner Bks.
Sing Along with Me. Frank DiSilvestro. (Illus.). 52p. (YA) (gr. 8-10). 1985. pap. 7.95 (ISBN 0-934591-00-8). Songs & Stories.
Sing & Be Happy: Songs for the Young Child. Clara B. Baker. LC 80-13421. (Illus.). 96p. 1980. pap. 1.50 spiral (ISBN 0-687-38547-4). Abingdon.
Sing & Be Joyful: Enjoying Music with Young Children. Compiled by Evelyn Andre. LC 79-14787. 1979. pap. 8.95 (ISBN 0-687-38550-4). Abingdon.
Sing & Play--Preschool Piano Book One. Ann Collins & Linda Clary. (Illus.). 60p. (ps). 1987. spiral bdg. 5.00 (ISBN 0-87563-307-2). Stipes.
Sing & Pray & Shout Hurray. Roger Ortmayer. 1974. pap. 2.75 (ISBN 0-377-00004-3). Friendship Pr.
Sing & Rejoice! Orlando Schmidt. LC 79-84367. 192p. 1979. 6.95x (ISBN 0-8361-1210-5); pap. 5.95x (ISBN 0-8361-1211-3). Herald Pr.
Sing & Rejoice! Introductory Kit. with cassette 8.25 (ISBN 0-8361-1219-9). Herald Pr.
Sing & Scatter Daisies. Louise Lawrence. LC 76-21393. (gr. 7 up). 1977. PLB 11.89 (ISBN 0-06-023773-2). HarpJ.
Sing Around Scotland. Morag Henriksen. (Ward Lock Educational Ser.). (Illus.). 96p. 29.00x (ISBN 0-7062-4481-8, Pub. by Ward Lock Educ Co Ltd). State Mutual Bk.
Sing As You Grow. Brenda Piper. (Ward Lock Educational Ser.). 96p. 29.00x (ISBN 0-7062-4158-4, Pub. by Ward Lock Educ Co Ltd). State Mutual Bk.
Sing Children Sing. Ed. by Carl Miller. (gr. k up). 1972. pap. 3.50 (ISBN 0-935738-05-3, 5027). US Comm Unicef.
Sing, Clap, & Play the Recorder. Heather Cox & Garth Rickard. (Illus.). 1983. pap. 3.50 ea. Book 1, A Soprano Recorder Book for Beginners (ISBN 0-918812-29-1). Book 2, A Soprano Recorder Book for Intermediate Players (ISBN 0-918812-30-5). MMB Music.
Sing, Clean Your Brain & Stay Sound & Sane: Postulate on Mechanical Effect of Vocalization on the Brain. Karel F. Jindrak & Heda Jindrak. LC 86-91345. (Illus.). 204p. 1986. 24.50 (ISBN 0-9617498-0-6). K F Jindrak.
Sing Down the Moon. Scott O'Dell. 138p. (gr. 5 up). 1976. pap. 2.75 (ISBN 0-440-97975-7, LFL). Dell.
Sing Down the Moon. Scott O'Dell. LC 71-98513. (gr. 5 up). 1970. 12.95 (ISBN 0-395-10919-1). HM.
Sing for Peace. Lois Lenski. 16p. (ps-2). 1985. pap. 1.50 (ISBN 0-8361-3396-X). Herald Pr.
Sing High! Sing Low! A Book of Essays. Osbert Sitwell. (Essay Index Reprint Ser.). Repr. of 1944 ed. 16.25 (ISBN 0-518-10171-1). Ayer Co Pubs.
Sing Ho for a Prince (Sleeping Beauty) Joe Grenzeback & Haakon Bergh. (Children's Theatre Musical Playscript Ser.). (gr. k-12). 1957. pap. 2.50x (ISBN 0-88020-054-5); 15.00x (ISBN 0-88020-055-3). Coach Hse.
Sing It! Amy Sit. 1979. pap. 3.50 (ISBN 0-917726-39-1). Hunter Bks.
Sing It Again! J. Irving Erickson. 1985. 12.95 (ISBN 0-910452-58-X). Covenant.
Sing Joyfully. Ed. by Hutterian Society of Brothers Staff. (Illus.). 434p. 1985. 12.00 (ISBN 0-87486-019-9). Plough.
Sing Like the Whippoorwill. Stafford Betty. LC 86-51539. (Illus., Orig.). 1987. pap. 6.95 (ISBN 0-89622-324-8). Twenty-Third.
Sing Long & Loud of Leafy Trees. Laverne Rison. (Illus.). 37p. 1979. pap. 5.00 (ISBN 0-934040-04-4). Quality Ohio.
Sing Me a Murder. Helen Nielsen. LC 87-70477. 176p. 1988. pap. 4.95 (ISBN 0-88739-079-X, Pub. by BlackLizard). Creative Arts Bk.
Sing Me a Sky. John Sherman. 1978. pap. 4.25 (ISBN 0-915358-02-6). Bridgeberg.
Sing Me a Song. William A. Owens. 1983. 9.95x (ISBN 0-292-77574-1). U of Tex Pr.
Sing Me a Song. Joyce S. Whitcomb. 64p. 1982. 4.00 (ISBN 0-682-49849-1). Exposition-Phoenix.
Sing Me Back Home. Merle Haggard & Peggy Russell. 1983. pap. 3.95 (ISBN 0-671-55219-8). PB.
Sing Me No Love Songs. Leon Rooke. 270p. 1986. pap. 9.50 (ISBN 0-88001-047-9). Ecco Pr.
Sing Me No Love Songs, I'll Say You No Prayers. Leon Rooke. 1984. 15.50 (ISBN 0-88001-036-3, Dist. by Norton). Ecco Pr.
Sing Me No Songs: A Novel. Kusum Ansal. (Vikas Library of Modern Indian Writing: No. 22). 1982. text ed. 17.95x (ISBN 0-7069-1771-5, Pub. by Vikas India). Advent NY.
Sing, O Barren One: A Study in Comparative Midrash. Mary Callaway. LC 86-15554. (Society of Biblical Literature Disseration Ser.). 150p. 1986. 14.95 (ISBN 0-89130-994-2, 06-01-91); pap. 10.95 (ISBN 0-89130-995-0). Scholars Pr GA.
Sing of Life & Faith. Ed. by Max B. Miller & Louise C. Drew. LC 68-22233. (Illus.). (gr. k-6). 1969. 5.95 (ISBN 0-8298-0123-5). Pilgrim NY.
Sing Out: For the Reader Who Loves to Explore Life. Annie R. Napier. 40p. 1986. 7.00 (ISBN 0-8062-2561-0). Carlton.
Sing Peace to Cedar River. William Clark. Ed. by Jim Brunelle. (Illus.). 240p. 1983. pap. 10.95 (ISBN 0-930096-41-X). G Gannett.
Sing, Pierrot, Sing. Tomie DePaola. LC 83-8403. (Voyager Picture Bks.). (Illus.). 32p. (Orig.). (ps-3). 1987. pap. 3.95 (ISBN 0-15-274989-6, VoyB). HarBraceJ.
Sing, Pierrot, Sing: A Picture Book in Mime. Tomie DePaola. LC 83-8403. (Illus.). 32p. (ps-3). 1983. 12.95 (ISBN 0-15-274988-8, HJ). HarBraceJ.
Sing Praises! Management of Church Hymns. Dale E. Ramsey. 30p. (Orig.). 1983. pap. 3.50 (ISBN 0-8272-3300-0). CBP.
Sing Praises to His Name. Louis Pratt. Ed. by Michael L. Sherer. (Orig.). 1986. pap. 6.75 (ISBN 0-89536-831-5, 6845). CSS of Ohio.
Sing! Sing! Sing! Music Book for Children. (gr. 1-3). 1.50 (ISBN 0-8198-6836-1). Dghtrs St Paul.
Sing Song: A Nursery Rhyme Book. Christina G. Rossetti. LC 68-55822. (Illus.). x, 130p. (gr. 3-7). 1969. pap. 4.50 (ISBN 0-486-22107-5). Dover.
Sing-Song of Old Man Kangaroo. Rudyard Kipling. LC 85-22920. (Just So Stories Ser.). (Illus.). 32p. (gr. 1-5). 1986. 9.95 (ISBN 0-87226-073-9, Dist. by Har-Row). P Bedrick Bks.
Sing Songs & Some That Don't. Joseph A. Labadie. (Men & Movements in the History & Philosophy of Anarchism Ser.). 1979. lib. bdg. 59.95 (ISBN 0-87700-310-6). Revisionist Pr.
Sing the Cows Home. 2nd rev. & abr. ed. Kerstin Brorson. Ed. by Florence Ekstrand. (Illus.). 176p. 1985. pap. 9.95 (ISBN 0-916871-07-X). Welcome Pr.
Sing the Joys of Mary. Ed. by Costante Berselli & Georges Gharib. Tr. by Phil Jenkins from Ital. 136p. (Orig.). 1983. pap. 7.95 (ISBN 0-8192-1329-2). Morehouse.
Sing the Lord's Song in a Strange Land: The Life of Justin Morgan. Betty Bandel. LC 78-73309. 264p. 1981. 24.50 (ISBN 0-8386-2411-1). Fairleigh Dickinson.
Sing Through the Day: Ninety Songs for Younger Children. 3rd ed. Marlys Swinger. Ed. by Society Of Brothers. LC 68-9673. (Illus.). (gr. 5 up). 1968. 12.00 (ISBN 0-87486-005-9). Plough.
Sing Through the Seasons: Ninety-Nine Songs for Children. Illus. by Susanna Biene & Moneli. LC 70-164916. (Illus.). 190p. (gr. k-6). 1972. 12.00 (ISBN 0-87486-006-7); l.p. record 6.00 (ISBN 0-87486-040-7); cassette 6.00. Plough.
Sing to God: Songs & Hymns for Christian Education. (Orig.). 1984. pap. 9.95 leader's ed. (ISBN 0-8298-0688-1); student's ed. 6.45 (ISBN 0-8298-0689-X); spiral bd. leaders guide 12.95 (ISBN 0-8298-0716-0). Pilgrim NY.
Sing to Me of Heaven: A Study of Folk & Early American Materials in Three Old Harp Books. Dorothy D. Horn. LC 74-99212. (Illus.). 1970. 12.00x (ISBN 0-8130-0293-1). U Presses Fla.
Sing to the Earth. Jane L. Reynolds. 84p. (gr. k-4). 1978. pap. write for info. (ISBN 0-932320-00-7). Solar Studio.
Sing to the Earth. Jane L. Reynolds. 1978. The Orange Book for First Chorus. 16p. write for info. (ISBN 0-932320-01-5); The Yellow Book for Second Chorus. 20p. write for info. (ISBN 0-932320-02-3); The Green Book for Third Chorus. 20p. write for info. (ISBN 0-932320-03-1); The Blue Book for Fourth Chorus & Soloists. 24p. write for info. (ISBN 0-932320-04-X). Solar Studio.
Sing Together: A Girl Scout Songbook. Girl Scouts of the U. S. A. Staff. (Illus.). 192p. (gr. 1-12). 1973. spiral bdg. 5.50 (ISBN 0-88441-309-8, 20-206). Girl Scouts USA.
Sing Unto God. Compiled by Roy A. Strubhar. 1972. pap. 1.00x (ISBN 0-87813-108-6). Park View.
Sing We Noel. Mary Goetze. 1984. 4.50 (ISBN 0-918812-42-9). MMB Music.
Sing When You're Winning. Steve Redhead & Richard Kuper. (Illus.). 128p. (Orig.). 1986. pap. 11.25 (ISBN 0-7453-0144-4, Pub. by Pluto Pr). Longwood Pub Group.

Sing with Me. (gr. 1-6). 5.50 (ISBN 0-87747-362-5). Deseret Bk.

Sing with Me Animal Songs. Illus. by Pat Magers. (Sing with Me Songbooks). (Illus.). (ps-1). 1987. incl. cassette 4.95 (ISBN 0-394-88809-X, BYR). Random.

Sing with Me Christmas Carols. Illus. by Helen Davie. (Sing with Me Songbooks & Cassettes Ser.). (Illus.). 24p. (ps up). 1987. pap. 4.95 incl. cassette (ISBN 0-394-89060-4, BYR). Random.

Sing with Me Lullabies. Illus. by Roberta Collier. (Sing with Me Songbooks). (Illus.). (ps-1). 1987. incl. cassette 4.95 (ISBN 0-394-88811-1, BYR). Random.

Sing with Me Mother Goose. Illus. by Lulu Delacre. (Sing with Me Songbooks). (Illus.). (ps-1). 1987. incl. cassette 4.95 (ISBN 0-394-88812-X, BYR). Random.

Sing with Me Play-along & Counting Songs. Illus. by Betty Reichmeier. (Sing with Me Songbooks). (Illus.). (ps-1). 1987. incl. cassette 4.95 (ISBN 0-394-88810-3, BYR). Random.

Sing with Me Sing-along Take-along Library: Lullabies, Mother Goose, & Play-Along & Counting Songs, 3 bks. (Illus.). 72p. (ps-1). 1988. Set. pap. 9.95 bks. & cassette pkg. (ISBN 0-394-89966-0, BYR). Random.

Sing with the Wind. LC 68-56014. autographed gift ed. 6.95 (ISBN 0-918114-01-2). Inspiration Conn.

Sing with Understanding. Harry Eskew & Hugh T. McElrath. LC 79-55293. 1980. 18.95 (ISBN 0-8054-6809-9). Broadman.

Sing Your Heart Out, Country Boy. rev. ed. Dorothy Horstman. 456p. 1986. 24.95 (ISBN 0-915608-10-3). Country Music Found.

Sing Your Joys: The Complete New York Poems, 1968-1980. James R. Hurst. Compiled by John E. Westburg. LC 80-54736. viii, 120p. 1980. pap. 10.00 (ISBN 0-87423-028-4). Westburg.

Sing Your Song for All You're Worth: A Book on Living Abundantly for the Young at Heart. Leo J. Fishbeck. Ed. by Raylene Fishbeck. 64p. (Orig.). 1988. 5.50 (ISBN 0-9619866-0-3). L J Fishbeck.

Singalong! (Ultimate Ser.). 292p. 1983. plastic comb 17.95 (ISBN 0-88188-128-7, 00361417); pap. 14.95 (ISBN 0-88188-134-1, 00361418). H Leonard Pub Corp.

Singalong Tribe. Kent Ashford. 192p. (Orig.). 1986. pap. 7.50 (ISBN 0-85449-001-9, Pub. by GMP England). Alyson Pubns.

Singapore. John Ball. 224p. 1987. pap. 3.50 (ISBN 0-7701-0509-2). Paperjacks US.

Singapore. Ed. by Harrap Limited Staff. 1986. pap. 49.75X (ISBN 0-245-54120-9, Pub. by Harrap Ltd England). State Mutual Bk.

Singapore. Insight Guides Staff. (Illus.). 240p. 1983. pap. 16.95 (ISBN 0-13-810713-0). P-H.

Singapore. Jon S. T. Quah & Stella R. Quah. (World Bibliographical Ser.: No. 95). 240p. 1988. lib. bdg. 45.00 (ISBN 1-85109-070-3). ABC-Clio.

Singapore. (Baedeker's City Guides Ser.). 1986. pap. 10.95 (ISBN 0-13-058090-2). P-H.

Singapore. (Post Guides Ser.). (Illus.). 144p. (Orig.). 1987. pap. 8.95 (ISBN 0-317-52564-6). Hunter Pub NY.

Singapore. (Times Travel Library). (Illus.). 128p. (Orig.). 1988. pap. text ed. 11.95 (ISBN 1-55650-097-1). Hunter Pub NY.

Singapore. (Let's Visit Places & Peoples - - Nations, Dependencies, & Sovereignties of the World Ser.). (Illus.). (gr. 5 up). 1988. 12.95 (ISBN 0-222-00988-8). Chelsea Hse.

Singapore: A Virgil Tibbs Novel. John Ball. 224p. 1986. 14.95 (ISBN 0-396-08763-9). Dodd.

Singapore & Malaysia. John Platt & Heidi Weber. (Varieties of English Around the World, (VEAW) Text Ser.: T4). iv, 138p. (Orig.). 1983. pap. 22.00x (ISBN 90-272-4712-9). Benjamins North Am.

Singapore & Malaysian Writing, Vol. 4:1. Ed. & Kirpal Singh. (Pacific Moana Quarterly (Special Issue)). 104p. 1979. pap. 10.00 (ISBN 0-686-89171-6, Pub. by Outrigger Pubs New Zealand). Three Continents.

Singapore Books in Print, 1986. 392p. 1987. pap. text ed. 50.00x (ISBN 0-317-54337-7, Pub. by Chopmen Singapore). Advent NY.

Singapore by Night. Harold Stephens. (Asia by Night Ser.). (Illus.). 64p. (Orig.). 1981. pap. 4.95 (ISBN 962-7031-09-7, Pub. by CFW Pubns Hong Kong). C E Tuttle.

Singapore: Development Policies & Trends. Ed. by Peter S. Chen. (Illus.). 1983. 52.00x (ISBN 0-19-582514-4). Oxford U Pr.

Singapore: Dynamics of a Free Trade Regime. Philip J. Deluty & Perry L. Wood. 100p. 1986. pap. text ed. 35.00 (ISBN 1-55813-024-1, HI-3749-2-P). Hudson Inst.

Singapore Grip. J. G. Farrell. 455p. 1986. pap. 4.95 (ISBN 0-88184-124-2). Carroll & Graf.

Singapore: Idealogy, Society, Culture. John Clammer. 178p. 1986. text ed. 32.50x (ISBN 0-317-43158-7, Pub. by Chopmen Pubs Singapore). Advent NY.

Singapore in Focus. Simon Barnes. ("In Focus" Ser.). (Illus.). 64p. (Orig.). 1981. pap. 5.95 (ISBN 962-7031-11-9, Pub. by CFW Pubn Hong Kong). C E Tuttle.

Singapore Master Tax Guide. 6th ed. 500p. 1985. 52.00 (ISBN 0-317-44624-X, 3536). Commerce.

Singapore Master Tax Guide. 7th ed. Soin. 750p. (Orig.). 1986. pap. 65.00 (3411). Commerce.

Singapore Naval Base & the Defense of Britain's Eastern Empire, 1919-1941. James Neidpath. (Illus.). 1981. 63.00x (ISBN 0-19-822474-5). Oxford U Pr.

Singapore, Nineteen Forty-One to Nineteen Forty-Two. Louis Allen. Ed. by Noble Frankland & Christopher Dowling. LC 79-52236. (Politics & Strategy of the Second World War). 343p. 1979. 27.50 (ISBN 0-87413-160-X). U Delaware Pr.

Singapore: Resources & Growth. Chong-Yah Lim & Peter J. LLoyd. (Illus.). 281p. 1986. pap. 24.95 (ISBN 0-19-582675-2). Oxford U Pr.

Singapore Short Stories, Vol. 1. Ed. by Robert Yeo. (Writing in Asia Ser.). 1978. pap. text ed. 5.50x (ISBN 0-686-60470-9, 00242). Heinemann Ed.

Singapore Short Stories, Vol. 2. Ed. by Robert Yeo. (Writing in Asia Ser.). 1978. pap. text ed. 5.50x (ISBN 0-686-60471-7, 00243). Heinemann Ed.

Singapore Studies: Critical Surveys of the Humanities & Social Sciences. Ed. by Basant K. Kapur. 498p. 1987. text ed. 36.00x (ISBN 9971-69-105-1, Pub. by Singapore U Pr). Ohio U Pr.

Singapore Survival Address Guide. Tr. by Alpha Pyramis World Business Division. 15p. 1984. pap. 4.00 (ISBN 0-913597-43-0, Pub. by Alpha Pyramis). Prosperity & Profits.

Singapore: The Chain of Disaster. Stanley W. Kirby. LC 76-853426. pap. 71.50 (ISBN 0-317-26204-1, 2052127). Bks Demand UMI.

Singapore Travel Guide. (Berlitz Travel Guides). (Illus.). 1982. pap. 6.95 (ISBN 0-02-969800-6, Berlitz). Macmillan.

Singapore's Little India: Past, Present & Future. Sharon Siddique & Nirmala P. Shotam. 174p. 1984. pap. text ed. 22.50x (ISBN 9971-902-31-1, Pub. by Inst Southeast Asian Stud). Gower Pub Co.

Singapore's New Education System. Soon Teck Wong. 1988. text ed. 24.00 (ISBN 9971-988-91-7, Pub. by Inst Southeast Asian Stud). Gower Pub Co.

Singaravelu: First Communist in South India. K. Murugesan. LC 75-905821. 1975. 9.00x (ISBN 0-88386-714-1). South Asia Bks.

Singboards & Handbills. Tenri Sankokan Museum Staff. 34p. 1971. pap. 120.00x (Pub. by Han-Shan Tang Ltd). State Mutual Bk.

Singe a la Porte: Vers une Theorie de la Parodie. Groupar Staff. LC 84-47830. 177p. (Fr.). 1984. pap. text ed. 18.50 (ISBN 0-8204-0144-7). P Lang Pubs.

Singer. Calvin Miller. LC 74-20097. 144p. (Orig.). 1975. pap. 6.95 (ISBN 0-87784-639-1). Inter-Varsity.

Singer in the Stone. John Willett. (gr. 5-8). 1981. 6.95 (ISBN 0-395-30374-5). HM.

Singer Instructions for Art Embroidery & Lace Work. Ed. by Jules Kliot & Kaethe Kliot. (Illus.). 224p. 1987. pap. 22.00 (ISBN 0-916896-24-2). Lacis Pubns.

Singer of Tales. Albert B. Lord. (Harvard Studies in Comparative Literature: No. 24). 325p. 1981. pap. text ed. 10.95x (ISBN 0-674-80881-9). Harvard U Pr.

Singer of the Eclogues: A Study of Virgilian Pastoral. Paul Alpers. LC 77-93465. 1979. 30.00x (ISBN 0-520-03651-4). U of Cal Pr.

Singer Trilogy. Calvin Miller. (Illus.). 496p. 1980. boxed set 19.95 (ISBN 0-87784-912-9). Inter-Varsity.

Singer with the High Hat: A Jewish Troubadour in the Germany of the Crusades. Carl H. Kurz. LC 83-73509. 1984. 4.95 (ISBN 0-931926-19-X). Alta Napa.

Singermann. facsimile ed. Myron Brinig. LC 74-27968. (Modern Jewish Experience Ser.). 1975. Repr. of 1929 ed. 36.50x (ISBN 0-405-06698-8). Ayer Co Pubs.

Singer's & Speaker's Handbook. J. A. Fracht & E. Robinson. 1978. text ed. 15.00 (ISBN 0-8206-0238-8). Chem Pub.

Singers & Storytellers. Ed. by Mody C. Boatright et al. LC 60-15894. (Texas Folklore Society Publications: No. 30). 304p. 1961. 14.95 (ISBN 0-87074-019-9). SMU Press.

Singers & the Song. Gene Lees. 272p. 1987. 18.95 (ISBN 0-19-504293-X). Oxford U Pr.

Singers Glossary of Show Business Jargon. Al Berkman. 1961. 3.95 (ISBN 0-934972-06-0). Melrose Bk Co.

Singer's Guide to Writing Arrangements. Leslyn Tepper. (Illus.). 100p. (Orig.). 1985. pap. 7.95 (ISBN 0-930867-03-3). S O S Pubs.

Singers in Late Byzantine & Slavonic Painting. N. K. Moran. (Byzantina Neerlandica Ser.: No. 9). (Illus.). xiv, 173p. 1986. 34.00 (ISBN 90-04-07809-6, Pub. by E J Brill). Heinman.

Singers' Italian: A Manual of Diction & Phonetics. Evelina Colorni. LC 71-113927. 1970. pap. text ed. 9.50 (ISBN 0-02-870620-X). Schirmer Bks.

Singer's Lock: The Revolution in the Understanding of Weather, Pt. 1. Oscar Singer. LC 83-90086. (Illus.). 351p. 1983. 40.00x (ISBN 0-9610922-0-3); computer print-out & plastic transparent tool 10.00x (ISBN 0-9610922-1-1). Singer Pr.

Singer's Manual of English Diction. Madeleine Marshall. 1953. pap. text ed. 8.95 (ISBN 0-02-871100-9). Schirmer Bks.

Singer's Manual of German & French Diction. Richard G. Cox. 1970. pap. text ed. 7.95 (ISBN 0-02-870650-1). Schirmer Bks.

Singers Manual of Latin Diction & Phonetics. Robert S. Hines. LC 74-34130. 1975. 10.95 (ISBN 0-02-870800-8). Schirmer Bks.

Singers of Daybreak: Studies in Black American Literature. Houston A. Baker. LC 82-23280. 107p. 1975. 19.84 (ISBN 0-88258-017-5); pap. 6.95 (ISBN 0-88258-025-6). Howard U Pr.

Singers of the New Song: A Mystical Interpretation of the Song of Songs. George A. Maloney. LC 85-71639. 176p. (Orig.). 1985. pap. 4.95 (ISBN 0-87793-292-1). Ave Maria.

Singers of Today. Donald Brook. LC 70-160917. (Biography Index Reprint Ser). Repr. of 1949 ed. 19.75 (ISBN 0-8369-8080-8). Ayer Co Pubs.

Singers on Singing: Opera. Bernard Jacobson. 224p. Date not set. 18.95. Vanguard.

Singer's Pilgrimage. Blanche Marchesi. Ed. by Andrew Farkas. LC 76-29951. (Opera Biographies). (Illus.). 1977. Repr. of 1923 ed. lib. bdg. 26.50x (ISBN 0-405-09692-5). Ayer Co Pubs.

Singer's Pilgrimage. Blanche Marchesi. LC 77-1941. (Music Reprint Ser.: 1978). (Illus.). 1978. Repr. of 1923 ed. lib. bdg. 37.50 (ISBN 0-306-70878-7). Da Capo.

Singer's Repertoire, 4 vols. 2nd ed. Berton Coffin. Incl. Vol. 1. Coloratura, Lyric & Dramatic Soprano (ISBN 0-8108-0188-4); Vol. 2. Mezzo Soprano & Contralto (ISBN 0-8108-0189-2); Vol. 3. Lyric & Dramatic Tenor (ISBN 0-8108-0190-6); Vol. 4. Baritone & Bass (ISBN 0-8108-0191-4). LC 60-7265. 1960. Set. 59.50 (ISBN 0-8108-2023-4); 18.50 ea. Scarecrow.

Singer's Temple: Prose Fictions of Barthelme, Gaines, Brautigan, Piercy, Kesey, & Kosinski. Jack Hicks. LC 80-26074. vii, 293p. 1982. pap. 9.95x (ISBN 0-8078-4096-3). U of NC Pr.

Singin' & Swingin' & Gettin' Merry Like Christmas. Maya Angelou. (gr. 8-12). 1985. pap. 3.95 (ISBN 0-553-25199-6). Bantam.

Singin' & Swingin' & Gettin' Merry Like Christmas. Maya Angelou. 1976. 13.95 (ISBN 0-394-40545-5). Random.

Singin' in the Rain. Betty Comden & Adolph Green. 1986. pap. 8.95 (ISBN 0-8044-6350-6). Ungar.

Singin' Somebody Else's Song. Mary B. Christian. LC 88-12000. 192p. (gr. 7 up). 1988. 13.95 (ISBN 0-02-718500-1). Macmillan.

Singin' Texas. Francis E. Abernethy. LC 83-80205. (Illus.). 208p. (Orig.). 1983. 29.95 (ISBN 0-935014-07-1); pap. 19.95 (ISBN 0-935014-04-7). E-Heart Pr.

Singing. Dennis Schmitz. (American Poetry Ser.: Vol. 31). 60p. (Orig.). 1985. pap. 7.50 (ISBN 0-88001-068-1). Ecco Pr.

Singing. Herbert Witherspoon. LC 80-12944. (Music Reprint Ser.). (Illus.). 126p. 1980. Repr. of 1925 ed. lib. bdg. 25.00 (ISBN 0-306-76001-0). Da Capo.

Singing--An Extension of Speech. Russell A. Hammar. LC 78-11756. 216p. 1978. lib. bdg. 18.00 (ISBN 0-8108-1182-0). Scarecrow.

Singing: A Fable about What Makes Us Human. Theron Raines. 176p. 1988. 12.95 (ISBN 0-87113-177-3). Atlantic Monthly.

Singing & Dancing. Kenneth McLeish & Valerie McLeish. (Illus.). 1982. pap. 7.95x laminated (ISBN 0-19-321436-9). Oxford U Pr.

Singing & Dancing Games for the Very Young. Esther L. Nelson. LC 77-79513. (Illus.). (ps). 1982. pap. 8.95 (ISBN 0-8069-7572-5). Sterling.

Singing & Playing: The Beginner's Book see Oxford Piano Courses for Class & Individual Instruction.

Singing Bee! A Collection of Favorite Children's Songs. Ed. by Jane Hart. LC 82-15296. (Illus.). 160p. 1982. 17.95 (ISBN 0-688-41975-5). Lothrop.

Singing Black. Homer A. Rodeheaver. LC 72-1681. Repr. of 1936 ed. 12.50 (ISBN 0-404-08330-7). AMS Pr.

Singing Bone. R. Austin Freeman. LC 75-44972. (Crime Fiction Ser.). 1976. Repr. of 1912 ed. lib. bdg. 21.00 (ISBN 0-8240-2367-6). Garland Pub.

Singing Bone. R. Austin Freeman. 1976. lib. bdg. 12.95x (ISBN 0-89968-168-9). Lightyear.

Singing Campaign for Ten Thousand Pounds. rev. ed. Gustavus D. Pike. LC 75-164392. (Black Heritage Library Collection). Repr. of 1875 ed. 18.25 (ISBN 0-8369-8851-5). Ayer Co Pubs.

Singing Canaries. Klaus Speicher. (Illus.). 96p. 1981. 9.95 (ISBN 0-87666-875-9, KW-047). TFH Pubns.

Singing Church. 623p. 1985. 7.95x (ISBN 0-916642-25-9). Hope Pub.

Singing Cowboy. Ed. by Margaret Larkin. LC 78-31779. (Music Reprint Ser.). 176p. 1979. Repr. of 1931 ed. 27.50 (ISBN 0-306-79555-8). Da Capo.

Singing Cowboys. David Rothel. LC 77-89646. 1978. 12.95 (ISBN 0-498-02523-3). A S Barnes.

Singing Cowboys & All That Jazz: A Short History of Popular Music in Oklahoma. William W. Savage, Jr. LC 82-17560. (Illus.). 200p. 1983. 16.95 (ISBN 0-8061-1648-X). U of Okla Pr.

Singing Cowboys & All That Jazz: A Short History of Popular Music in Oklahoma. William W. Savage, Jr. (Illus.). 200p. 1988. pap. 7.95 (ISBN 0-8061-2085-1). U of Okla Pr.

Singing Creek Where the Willows Grow: The Rediscovered Diary of Opal Whiteley. Benjamin Hoff. 384p. 1988. pap. 9.95 (ISBN 0-446-38676-6). Warner Bks.

Singing Creek Where the Willows Grow: The Rediscovered Diary of Opal Whiteley. Ed. by Benjamin Hoff. 288p. 1986. 16.95 (ISBN 0-89919-444-3). Ticknor & Fields.

Singing Detective. Dennis Potter. 300p. 1986. 22.95 (ISBN 0-571-14631-7); pap. 9.95 (ISBN 0-571-14590-6). Faber & Faber.

Singing Detective. Dennis Potter. 1988. 6.95 (ISBN 0-679-72046-4, Vin). Random.

Singing Dog. Valerie Trip. LC 86-14797. (Just One More Ser.). (Illus.). 24p. (ps-2). 1986. PLB 10.60 (ISBN 0-516-01578-8); pap. 2.95 (ISBN 0-516-41578-6). Childrens.

Singing Energy in the Gan-Tone Method of Voice Production. Robert Gansert. Ed. by Carmela Capano. LC 81-80960. 324p. 1981. incl. cassette 38.50 (ISBN 0-939458-00-4). Gan-Tone Pub.

Singing Entertainer: A Contemporary Study of the Art & Business of Being a Professional. John Davidson & Cort Casady. 240p. 1982. pap. 14.95 (ISBN 0-88284-194-7). Alfred Pub.

Singing Faith. Jane P. Huber. LC 86-753277. 142p. (Orig.). 1987. pap. 7.95 (ISBN 0-664-24055-0); spiral bound 10.95 (ISBN 0-664-24056-9). Westminster John Knox.

Singing Family of the Cumberlands. Jean Ritchie. 264p. 1988. 20.00 (ISBN 0-8131-1679-1); pap. 8.00 (ISBN 0-8131-0186-7). U Pr of Ky.

Singing Feather. Vasily Sukhomlinsky. Tr. by James Riordan. (Illus.). 27p. 1984. pap. 1.99 (ISBN 0-8285-2910-8, Pub. by Raduga Pubs USSR). Imported Pubns.

Singing Flame. Ernie O'Malley. 312p. 1978. 17.95 (ISBN 0-900068-40-X, Pub. by Anvil Pr Ireland); pap. 7.95 (ISBN 0-947962-32-8, Pub. by Anvil Pr Ireland). Irish Bks Media.

Singing for My Echo: Memories of a Native Healer of Santa Fe. Gregorita Rodriguez & Edith Powers. (Cota Editions: No. 2). (Illus.). 96p. (Orig.). 1987. pap. 6.95 (ISBN 0-943734-22-3). Ocean Tree Bks.

Singing for Power: The Song Magic of the Papago Indians of Southern Arizona. Ruth M. Underhill. (Library Reprint Ser.). 1977. 25.00x (ISBN 0-520-03310-8). U of Cal Pr.

Singing for the Stars: A Complete Program for Training Your Voice. Seth Riggs. Ed. by John Carratello. (Illus.). 146p. 1986. with cassettes 29.95 (ISBN 0-88284-340-0, 2455). Alfred Pub.

Singing from the Abdomen. Alan Basting. 1976. pap. 2.50 (ISBN 0-685-79281-1). Stone-Marrow Pr.

Singing from the Well. Reinaldo Arenas. 1987. 16.95 (ISBN 0-670-80805-9). Viking.

Singing from the Well. Reinaldo Arenas. 224p. 1988. pap. 7.95 (ISBN 0-14-009444-X). Penguin.

Singing Game. Iona Opie & Peter Opie. 521p. 1985. 29.95x (ISBN 0-19-211562-6). Oxford U Pr.

Singing Game. Iona Opie & Peter Opie. 544p. 1988. pap. 10.95 (ISBN 0-19-284019-3). Oxford U Pr.

Singing Games & Playparty Games. Richard Chase. (Illus.). 63p. (gr. 1-4). 1949. pap. 2.50 (ISBN 0-486-21785-X). Dover.

Singing Games & Playparty Games. Richard Chase. (Illus.). (gr. 4-8). 12.50 (ISBN 0-8446-4721-7). Peter Smith.

Singing Guns. Max Brand. 1983. pap. 2.25 (ISBN 0-671-41571-9). PB.

Singing Guns. Max Brand. 405p. 1988. lib. bdg. 15.95x (ISBN 0-8161-4144-4, Large Print Bks). G K Hall.

Singing Heart. Margaret Clarkson. Intro. by Donald P. Hustad. LC 87-82067. 203p. (Orig.). 1987. pap. 9.95 (ISBN 0-916642-31-3, 390). Hope Pub.

Singing Heart. N. M. Gohagan. LC 85-91001. 96p. 1985. 10.00 (ISBN 0-682-40272-9). Exposition-Phoenix.

Singing in a Dark Language. Terri Drake. 1968. 3.00 (ISBN 0-317-47210-0). New Collage.

Singing in French: A Manual of French Diction & French Vocal Repertoire. Thomas Grubb. LC 77-18473. 1979. pap. text ed. 14.95 (ISBN 0-02-870790-7). Schirmer Bks.

Singing in the Season. Jane Frazee. 1983. pap. 5.00 (ISBN 0-918812-24-0). MMB Music.

Singing in the Shrouds. Ngaio Marsh. 1976. Repr. of 1958 ed. lib. bdg. 18.95x (ISBN 0-88411-494-5, Pub. by Aeonian Pr). Amereon Ltd.

Singing Keys Omnibus. 64p. (Orig.). (gr. 6-12). 1946. pap. text ed. 9.95 (ISBN 0-87487-651-6). Birch Tree Gr.

Singing Knives. Frank Stanford. LC 78-17914. (Lost Roads Poetry Ser.: No. 18). 1979. pap. 6.00 (ISBN 0-918786-19-3). Lost Roads.

Singing Man. Neil Anderson. Ed. by Allen Rinzler. 216p. (Orig.). 1984. pap. 8.95 (ISBN 0-915811-02-2). H J Kramer Inc.

Singing Mouse Stories. Emerson Hough. 1976. lib. bdg. 12.50x (ISBN 0-89968-047-X). Lightyear.

Singing of Birth & Death: Texts in Performance. Stuart H. Blackburn. 296p. 1988. text ed. 31.95x (ISBN 0-8122-8097-0). U of Pa Pr.

Singing of Mount Abora: Coleridge's Use of Biblical Imagery & Natural Symbolism in Poetry & Philosophy. H. W. Piper. LC 86-45480. 128p. 1987. 20.00x (ISBN 0-8386-3295-5). Fairleigh Dickinson.

Singing of the Real World: The Philosophy of Virginia Woolf's Fiction. Mark Hussey. LC 86-12763. 250p. 1986. 25.00x (ISBN 0-8142-0414-7). Ohio St U Pr.

Singing on the Titanic. Perry Glasser. LC 87-1654. (Illinois Short Fiction Ser.). 190p. 1987. 11.95 (ISBN 0-252-01427-8). U of Ill Pr.

Singing Penguins & Puffed-up Toads. William L. Coleman. 125p. (ps-4). 1981. pap. 5.95 (ISBN 0-87123-554-4, 210554). Bethany Hse.

Singing Pope: The Story of Pope John Paul II. Rinna Wolfe. (Illus.). 128p. (gr. 6-8). 1980. 8.95 (ISBN 0-8164-0472-0, HarpR). Har-Row.

Singing Psalms of Joy & Praise. Fred R. Anderson. LC 86-1550. 78p. (Orig.). 1986. pap. 5.95 (ISBN 0-664-24696-6). Westminster John Knox.

Singing Rabbit. G. Menovschchikov. 12p. 1984. pap. 1.99 (ISBN 0-8285-2939-6, Pub. by Raduga Pubs USSR). Imported Pubns.

Singing Rhymes. (Tiny Tots Rhymes Ser.). (ps). 1982. 2.95 (ISBN 0-86112-088-4). Borden.

Singing Ringing Tree. Retold by Selina Hastings. (Illus.). 1988. 13.95 (ISBN 0-8050-0573-0). H Holt & Co.

Singing Road: Medium-High Voice, 3 vols. Arthur E. Ward. Vol. 1, 1939, 95p. pap. 8.95 (ISBN 0-8258-0218-0, 02794); Vol. 2, 1950, 47p. pap. 8.95 (ISBN 0-8258-0219-9, 03516); Vol. 3, 1950. pap. 8.95 (ISBN 0-8258-0221-0, 03652). Fischer Inc NY.

Singing Road: Medium-Low Voice, 3 vols. Ed. by Arthur E. Ward. Vol. 1, 1939, 95p. pap. 8.95 (ISBN 0-8258-0217-2, 02793); Vol. 2, 1950. pap. 8.95 (ISBN 0-8258-0220-2, 03517); Vol. 3, 1950. pap. 8.95 (ISBN 0-8258-0222-9, 03653). Fischer Inc NY.

Singing Sands. Josephine Tey. 224p. 1988. pap. 3.95 (ISBN 0-671-49456-2). PB.

Singing Sands. Josephine Tey. 224p. 1988. pap. 3.95 (ISBN 0-02-008825-6, Collier). Macmillan.

Singing Sands. Josephine Trey. Ed. by J. Barzun & W. H. Taylor. LC 81-47389. (Crime Fiction 1950-1975 Ser.). 192p. 1982. lib. bdg. 18.00 (ISBN 0-8240-5000-2). Garland Pub.

Singing Saying Dancing Playing: Level One. Richard Gill et al. 1984. pap. 32.00 incl. 6 cassettes, Book (ISBN 0-918812-25-9). MMB Music.

Singing Soldiers. John J. Niles. LC 68-26595. 192p. 1968. Repr. of 1927 ed. 35.00x (ISBN 0-8103-3416-X). Gale.

Singing Soldiers: A History of the Civil War in Song. Paul Glass & Louis Singer. LC 75-14127. (Quality Paperback Ser.). Orig. Title: Spirit of the Sixties. (Illus.). xx, 300p. 1975. pap. 13.95 (ISBN 0-306-80021-7). Da Capo.

Singing Stone. O. R. Melling. (YA) (gr. 5-9). 1987. 13.95 (ISBN 0-670-80817-2, Viking Kestrel). Viking.

Singing Swan: An Account of Anna Seward & Her Acquaintance with Dr. Johnson, Etc. Margaret Ashmun. 1931. Repr. 20.00 (ISBN 0-8274-3417-0). R West.

Singing Swan: An Account of Anne Seward & Her Acquaintance with Dr. Johnson, Boswell, & Others of Their Time. Margaret Ashmun. 1931. 19.50x (ISBN 0-686-51310-X). Elliots Bks.

Singing Swans. Dilys Gater. 1982. 15.00x (ISBN 0-906660-56-4, Pub. by New Playwrights Network). State Mutual Bk.

Singing Takes More Than a Voice. Al Berkman. 1985. 4.95 (ISBN 0-934972-00-1). Melrose Bk Co.

Singing the Glory! Georgiana L. Lahr. 3.95 (ISBN 0-533-01211-2). Vantage.

Singing the Glory of Lord Krishna Baru Candidasa's Srikrsnakirtana: Baru Candidasa's Srikrsnakirtana. Tr. by M. H. Klaiman. LC 84-3905. (AAR Classics in Religious Studies). 1984. 28.75 (ISBN 0-89130-736-2, 01 05 05); pap. 20.75 (ISBN 0-89130-737-0). Scholars Pr GA.

Singing: The Mechanism & the Technic. rev ed. William Vennard. (Illus.). 275p. 1967. pap. 25.00 (ISBN 0-8258-0055-2, 04685). Fischer Inc NY.

Singing the Middle Ages. Tom Smith. LC 82-2452. 64p. 1982. 11.95 (ISBN 0-914378-87-2); pap. 5.95 (ISBN 0-914378-88-0). Countryman.

Singing the Mozart Requiem. Ingrid Wendt. LC 87-5133. 1987. 14.95 (ISBN 0-932576-51-6); pap. 7.95 (ISBN 0-932576-52-4). Breitenbush Bks.

Singing the Sacrament. 1987. 25.00x (ISBN 0-947988-16-5, Pub. by Wild Goose Pubns Scotland). State Mutual Bk.

Singing Tradition of Child's Popular Ballads. abr. ed. Ed. by Bertrand H. Bronson. LC 75-2980. 488p. 1976. 64.50x (ISBN 0-691-09119-6). Princeton U Pr.

Singing Tree. Brian Parvin. 192p. 1985. 24.95x (ISBN 0-7090-2159-3, Pub. by R Hale Ltd UK). State Mutual Bk.

Singing Triangle. Brent C. Christensen. 55p. 1988. write for info. BMC Pubns.

Singing Underneath. Jeffrey Harrison. Selected by James Merrill. LC 87-25194. (National Poetry Ser.). 80p. 1988. 13.95 (ISBN 0-525-24640-1); pap. 7.95 (ISBN 0-525-48383-7). Dutton.

Singing Wheels & Circus Wagons. Gene Plowden. LC 75-21135. (Illus.). 1978. pap. 4.95 (ISBN 0-87004-256-4). Caxton.

Singing Wilderness. Sigurd F. Olson. (Illus.). 1956. 17.95 (ISBN 0-394-44560-0). Knopf.

Singing Wind. Marjorie K. Lawrence. 1985. 6.95 (ISBN 0-533-06632-8). Vantage.

Singing Wind. Jennifer Wade. LC 77-23984. 1977. 8.95 (ISBN 0-698-10857-4, Coward). Putnam Pub Group.

Singing Wind & Other Short Stories see New Method Supplementary Readers.

Singing Wind: Five Melodies from Ecuador. Elizabeth V. Brennan. (Illus.). 48p. (Orig., Span. & Eng.). 1988. pap. 5.95 (ISBN 0-937203-25-4); cassette tape 5.00 (ISBN 0-937203-26-2). World Music Pr.

Singing Winds: Stories of Gypsy Life. Konrad Bercovici. LC 79-133814. (BCL Ser. I). 1970. Repr. of 1926 ed. 22.00 (ISBN 0-404-00787-2). AMS Pr.

Singing with the Owls. Michael McPherson. 58p. 1983. pap. 5.95 (ISBN 0-932136-05-2, Dist. by UH). Petronium Pr.

Singing with Understanding: Including 101 Beloved Hymn Backgrounds. Kenneth W. Osbeck. LC 78-19960. 324p. (Orig.). 1979. 14.95 (ISBN 0-8254-3414-9). Kregel.

Singing Words. facsimile ed. Compiled by Alice G. Thorn. LC 79-38605. (Granger Index Reprint Ser.). (Illus.). Repr. of 1941 ed. 16.00 (ISBN 0-8369-6337-7). Ayer Co Pubs.

Single Action. Nelson Nye. 192p. 1984. pap. 2.25 (ISBN 0-8439-2080-7, Leisure Bks). Leisure NY.

Single Adults: Resource & Recipients for Revival. Dan R. Crawford. LC 85-7889. 1985. pap. 5.95 (ISBN 0-8054-3236-1). Broadman.

Single Adults Want to Be the Church, Too. Britton Wood. LC 77-78411. 1977. 10.95 (ISBN 0-8054-3221-3). Broadman.

Single After Fifty: How to Have the Time of Your Life. Adeline P. McConnell & Beverly Anderson. 312p. 1980. pap. text ed. 5.95 (ISBN 0-07-044874-4). McGraw.

Single Again--This Time with Children: A Christian Guide for the Single Parent. Alice S. Peppler. LC 81-52278. 136p. (Orig.). 1982. pap. 6.95 (ISBN 0-8066-1910-4, 10-5802). Augsburg.

Single-Again Man. Jane K. Burgess. LC 86-46342. 224p. 1988. 17.95 (ISBN 0-669-15675-2). Lexington Bks.

Single & Compound Angle Members: Structural Analysis & Design. M. K. Madugula & J. B. Kennedy. (Illus.). 372p. 1985. 86.50 (ISBN 0-85334-364-0, Pub. by Elsevier Applied Sci England). Elsevier.

Single & Feeling Good. Harold I. Smith. 160p. 1987. pap. 9.95 (ISBN 0-687-38552-0). Abingdon.

Single & Multiphase Flows in an Electromagnetic Field: Energy, Metallurgical, & Solar Applications, PAAS 100. Ed. by Herman Branover et al. LC 85-19979. (Illus.). 762p. 1985. 89.50 (ISBN 0-930403-04-5). AIAA.

Single & Multiple Chip Microcomputer Interfacing. G. J. Lipovski. (Illus.). 528p. 1987. text ed. 40.00 (ISBN 0-13-810557-X). P-H.

Single & Pregnant: The Pregnancy Careers of Unmarried Women. Sally Macintyre. LC 77-325. 1977. lib. bdg. 25.00 (ISBN 0-88202-112-5). Watson Pub Intl.

Single & Sober. 48p. (Orig.). 1985. pap. 1.95 (ISBN 0-89486-310-X). Hazelden.

Single & Whole. Rhena Taylor. LC 85-8345. Orig. Title: Every Single Blessing. 96p. 1985. pap. 3.95 (ISBN 0-87784-510-7). Inter-Varsity.

Single Bed Blues. Ellen Leroe. Ed. by Elisa B. Fitzgerald. LC 81-23307. 72p. 1981. pap. 5.95 (ISBN 0-913024-12-0). Tandem Pr.

Single Black Mother. Thelma Williams. (Illus.). 24p. (Orig.). 1988. pap. 2.50 (ISBN 0-945768-00-1). A-Town Pub Co.

Single-Board Computer Application. Joseph J. Carr. (Illus.). 272p. 1986. 24.95 (ISBN 0-8306-9530-3, 1930); pap. 16.95 (ISBN 0-8306-1930-5, 1930P). Tab Bks.

Single But Not Alone. Jane Graver. LC 12-2815. 1983. pap. 2.75 (ISBN 0-570-03880-4). Concordia.

Single But Not Alone. Mary Strebeck. (Illus.). 80p. (Orig.). 1982. pap. 4.95 (ISBN 0-939298-16-3, 163); pap. 2.95 leader's guide, 38pgs. (252). J M Prods.

Single, but Not Sorry. rev. ed. Joyce Parks. 235p. 1986. pap. 4.95 (ISBN 0-89084-307-4). Bob Jones Univ Pr.

Single-Camera Video Production Handbook: Techniques, Equipment, & Resources for Producing Quality Video Programs. Barry Fuller et al. (Illus.). 252p. 1982. 26.95 (ISBN 0-13-810762-9); pap. 18.95 (ISBN 0-13-810754-8). P-H.

Single Case Experimental Designs: Strategies for Studying Behavior Change. 2nd ed. David H. Barlow & Michel Hersen. (Pergamon General Psychology Ser.: No. 56). 432p. 1984. text ed. 55.00 (ISBN 0-08-030136-3); pap. text ed. 22.50 (ISBN 0-08-030135-5). Pergamon.

Single-Case Research Designs: Methods for Clinical & Applied Settings. Alan E. Kazdin. (Illus.). 1982. text ed. 29.95x (ISBN 0-19-503020-6); pap. text ed. 19.95x (ISBN 0-19-503021-4). Oxford U Pr.

Single Cell Marking & Cell Lineage in Animal Development. Ed. by R. L. Gardner & P. A. Lawrence. (Illus.). 187p. 1986. text ed. 99.50X (ISBN 0-85403-261-4, Pub. by Royal Soc London). Scholium Intl.

Single-Cell Mutation Monitoring Systems: Methodologies & Applications. Ed. by Aftab A. Ansari & Frederick De Serres. LC 84-3368. (Topics in Chemical Mutagenesis Ser.: Vol. 2). 308p. 49.50x (ISBN 0-306-41537-2, Plenum Pr). Plenum Pub.

Single Cell Protein. I. Goldberg. (Biotechnology Monographs: Vol. 1). (Illus.). 260p. 1985. 60.00 (ISBN 0-387-15308-X). Springer-Verlag.

Single Cell Protein--Safety for Animal & Human Feeding: Proceedings of the Protein-Calorie Advisory Group of the United Nations System Symposium, Milan, Italy, March-April 1977. S. Garattini et al. LC 78-40993. (Illus.). 220p. 1979. 48.00 (ISBN 0-08-023765-7); pap. 18.75 (ISBN 0-08-023764-9). Pergamon.

Single-Cell Protein II. Ed. by Steven R. Tannenbaum & Daniel I. C. Wang. 1975. text ed. 42.50x (ISBN 0-262-20030-9). MIT Pr.

Single Cell Proteins from Cellulose & Hydrocarbons. P. J. Rockwell. LC 76-9492. (Chemical Technology Review No. 74; Food Technology Review: No. 34). (Illus.). 337p. 1976. 39.00 (ISBN 0-8155-0626-0). Noyes.

Single-Channel Recording. Ed. by Bert Sakmann et al. 526p. 1983. 65.00x (ISBN 0-306-41419-8, Plenum Pr). Plenum Pub.

Single-Child Family. Ed. by Toni Falbo. LC 83-1612. 304p. 1984. 32.50 (ISBN 0-89862-630-7). Guilford Pr.

Single-Chip Computer Cookbook, with 25 One-Evening. Edward V. Hiskes. (Illus.). 224p. 1989. 24.95 (ISBN 0-8306-9135-9, 3135); pap. 16.95 (ISBN 0-8306-3135-6, 3135). TAB Bks.

Single Chip Microcomputer. S. J. Cahill. 352p. 1987. pap. text ed. 44.00 (ISBN 0-13-810581-2). P-H.

Single-Chip Microcomputers. Ed. by P. Lister. (Illus.). 256p. 1985. text ed. 45.95 (ISBN 0-07-038030-9). McGraw.

Single Circles. Martha McKee. 132p. 1982. 8.95 (ISBN 0-913428-42-6); pap. 5.95 (ISBN 0-913428-43-4). Landfall Pr.

Single Combat. Dean Ing. 320p. (Orig.). 1983. pap. 2.95 (ISBN 0-8125-4100-6, Dist. by Warner Pub Services & Saint Martin's Press). Tor Bks.

Single Cook's Book: One Hundred & Six Unusual Recipes for One-Person Servings. Larry Luce. (Illus.). 1976. pap. 3.00 (ISBN 0-686-16919-0). Other Bks.

Single Crystal Diffractometry. Ulrich W. Arndt & B. T. Willis. LC 66-13637. (Cambridge Monographs on Physics). pap. 88.80 (ISBN 0-317-26117-7, 2024404). Bks Demand UMI.

Single Crystal Elastic Constants & Calculated Aggregate Properties. Gene Simmons & Herbert Wang. 1971. 35.00x (ISBN 0-262-19092-3). MIT Pr.

Single Crystals of Refractory Compounds, Vol. 16, Nos. 1-4. V. N. Gurin. (Progress in Crystal Growth & Characterization Ser.). (Illus.). 448p. 1988. 219.00 (ISBN 0-08-036862-X). Pergamon.

Single Cylinder Engine Tests: Caterpillar L38A Test Method - STP 509-A, Pt. 4. 46p. 1980. pap. 7.25x (ISBN 0-8031-0575-4, 04-509040-12); looseleaf 9.50x (ISBN 0-8031-0576-2, 04-509041-12). ASTM.

Single Cylinder Engine Tests: Caterpillar 1G2 Test Method - STP 509-A, Pt. 1. 94p. 1979. pap. 9.75x (ISBN 0-8031-0569-X, 04-509010-12); looseleaf 12.75x (ISBN 0-8031-0570-3, 04-509011-12). ASTM.

Single Cylinder Engine Tests: Caterpillar 1D2 Test Method - STP 509-A, Pt. 3. 86p. 1979. pap. 9.75x (ISBN 0-8031-0573-8, 04-509030-12); looseleaf 12.75x (ISBN 0-8031-0574-6, 04-509031-12). ASTM.

Single Cylinder Engine Tests: Caterpillar 1H2 Test Method, STP 509A, Pt. 2. 94p. 1979. soft cover 9.75 (04-509020-12); looseleaf 12.75 (04-509021-12). ASTM.

Single Cylinder Engine Tests, Part II: Caterpillar 1H2 Test Method - STP 509A. 94p. 1979. looseleaf 12.75 (04-509021-12); pap. 9.75 (04-509020-12). ASTM.

Single Door: Social Work with Families of Disabled Children. Caroline Glendinning. 240p. 1986. text ed. 37.95x (ISBN 0-04-361060-9); pap. text ed. 14.95x (ISBN 0-04-361061-7). Unwin Hyman.

Single-Dose Therapy of Urinary Tract Infections: Modern Trend in the Treatment of Lower Urinary Tract Infections. Ed. by A. Jardin & J. D. Williams. (Journal: European Urology Supplement 1, 1987: Vol. 13). (Illus.). iv, 136p. 1987. pap. 33.50 (ISBN 3-8055-4559-2). S Karger.

Single-Employer Pension Plan Amendments Act of 1986. 160p. (Orig.). 1986. pap. 7.00 (5419). Commerce.

Single Entry Bookkeeping System for Small Scale Manufacturing Businesses. Derry Caye. 55p. 1977. prfct. bnd. 5.50 (ISBN 0-86619-046-5, 11029-BK). Vols Tech Asst.

Single Far Only. Taylor Lowering. 1982. 15.00x (ISBN 0-906660-12-2, Pub. by New Playwrights Network). State Mutual Bk.

Single Fathers. Geoffrey L. Greif. xvi, 544p. 1985. 27.00x (ISBN 0-669-09594-X); pap. text ed. 10.95 (ISBN 0-669-09595-8). Lexington Bks.

Single-Field Isodose Charts for High-Energy Radiation: An International Guide. (Technical Reports Ser.: No. 8). 185p. 1962. pap. 14.00 (ISBN 92-0-115062-8, IDC8, IAEA). UNIPUB.

Single Girls! Twenty-Six to Seventy & Beyond Nice Guys Do Answer Personal Ads: How to Find Excitement, New Friends Maybe Even Love & Marriage - Through the Personal Ads. Sara David. LC 88-70572. 120p. (Orig.). 1988. pap. 8.95 (ISBN 0-929034-00-7). Palmtree Pr.

Single Grandmother. Tracy E. Hyde. LC 73-88510. 250p. 1974. 18.95x (ISBN 0-88229-128-9). Nelson-Hall.

Single-Handed. Ed. by Betty Garee. (Illus.). 32p. 1978. pap. 3.50. Cheever Pub.

Single Handed: Devices & Aids for One Handers & Sources of These Devices. 3.50 (1480). Cheever Pub.

Single in Baltimore. Richard G. Berman. 163p. (Orig.). 1986. pap. 6.95 (ISBN 0-9616388-0-X). Singular Hse Pr.

Single in New York. Charles Oldfield. 1977. pap. 1.50 (ISBN 0-8439-0426-7, LB426DK, Leisure Bks). Leisure NY.

Single Issues. J. Fishman. (International Journal of the Sociology of Language: No. 22). 1979. 19.00x (ISBN 90-279-7938-3). Mouton.

Single Jack. Max Brand. 1980. pap. 1.75 (ISBN 0-671-83417-7). PB.

Single Lady. A Novel. John M. Saunders. LC 75-37829. (Lost American Fiction Ser.). 411p. 1976. Repr. 8.95 (ISBN 0-8093-0761-8). S Ill U Pr.

Single Lens Reflex Camera Handbook. Michael Langford. LC 79-3473. (Illus.). 1980. 8.95 (ISBN 0-394-51090-9). Knopf.

Single Lens: The Story of the Simple Microscope. Brian J. Ford. LC 84-48161. (Illus.). 192p. 1985. 14.45i (ISBN 0-06-015366-0, HarpT). Har-Row.

Single-Level Home Plans. 2nd ed. Ed. by Garlinghouse Co. Staff. LC 84-82406. (Illus.). 112p. 1985. pap. 2.95 (ISBN 0-938708-13-9). L F Garlinghouse Co.

Single Life: A Christian Challenge. Martha M. Niemann. 144p. 1986. pap. 4.25 (ISBN 0-89243-254-3). Liguori Pubns.

Single Life: Unmarried Adults in Social Context. Ed. by Peter J. Stein. 350p. 1981. pap. text ed. write for info. (ISBN 0-312-72597-3). St Martin.

Single Man. Christopher Isherwood. 1985. pap. 2.95 (ISBN 0-380-37689-X, 60251-2, Bard). Avon.

Single Man. Christopher Isherwood. (Michael Di Capua Books). 192p. 1986. pap. 6.95 (ISBN 0-374-52038-0). FS&G.

Single-Mode Fiber Optics. Luc B. Jeunhomme. 296p. 1983. 59.75 (ISBN 0-8247-7020-X). Dekker.

Single Mother by Choice. Jessica Curtis. 224p. 1987. 8.95 (ISBN 0-14-009463-6). Penguin.

Single Mothers & Their Children. Irwin Garfinkel & Sara McLanahan. text ed. 24.95x (ISBN 0-87766-405-6); pap. text ed. 14.95x (ISBN 0-87766-404-8). Urban Inst.

Single Mothers by Choice. Jessica Curtis. 1987. write for info. (ISBN 0-670-80587-4). Viking.

Single Mother's Handbook. Elizabeth S. Greywolf. LC 83-17350. (Orig.). 1984. 12.95 (ISBN 0-688-02260-X); pap. 6.70 (ISBN 0-688-02261-8). Morrow.

Single Mothers Raising Sons. Bobbie Reed. LC 88-1688. 1988. pap. 7.95 (ISBN 0-8407-3113-2). Nelson.

Single Mother's Survival Manual. Barbara Duncan. LC 83-62294. 180p. 1984. pap. 12.95 (ISBN 0-88247-707-2). R & E Pubs.

Single-Movement Pieces, Published & Unpublished in Bach's Lifetime. Carl P. Bach. Ed. by Dorrell Berg. (Carl Bach (Seventeen Fourteen to Seventeen Eighty-Eight): The Collected Works for Solo Keyboard Ser.). 240p. 1986. lib. bdg. 65.00 (ISBN 0-8240-6454-2). Garland Pub.

Single Nature's Double Name: The Collectedness of the Conflicting in British & American Romanticism. Raymond Benoit. (De Proprietatibus Litterarum Ser.: No. 26). 1973. text ed. 16.00x (ISBN 90-2792-599-2). Mouton.

Single Needs Sales. 76p. (Eng., Span. & Fr.). 5.00 ea. Life Ins Mktg Res.

Single on Sunday: A Manual for Successful Single Adult Ministries. Bobbie Reed. 1979. pap. 6.50 (ISBN 0-570-03781-6, 12-2735). Concordia.

Single Operatic Arias. Ed. by Ernest Warburton. (Johann Christian Bach 1735-1782; The Collected Works Ser.). 75.00 (ISBN 0-8240-6061-X). Garland Pub.

Single Out. Ruth Weiss. LC 78-73007. (Illus.). 1978. pap. 7.00 (ISBN 0-933022-01-8); signed & numbered edition 25.00 (ISBN 0-685-90846-1). DAurora Pr.

Single Parent. Coleen Hume. 32p. 1987. pap. 15.00x (ISBN 0-85937-145-X, Pub. by K Mason Pubns Ltd UK). State Mutual Bk.

Single Parent Experience: A Time For Growth. Beverly C. Barnes & Jennifer Coplon. LC 80-5953. 168p. 1980. 15.95 (ISBN 0-86618-002-8). Family Serv.

Single-Parent Families: A Challenge to the Jewish Community. Chaim I. Waxman. 24p. 1980. pap. 1.00 (ISBN 0-87495-020-1). Am Jewish Comm.

Single Parent Families & Housing: A Bibliography. Kathryn H. Anthony & Cynthia L. Cornfield. (Public Administration Ser.: P 2280). 17p. 1987. 5.00 (ISBN 1-55590-560-9). Vance Biblios.

Single-Parent Families at Camp: The Essence of an Experience. Bernard Reisman & Gladys Rosen. LC 84-70480. 54p. 1984. pap. 2.50 (ISBN 0-87495-061-9). Am Jewish Comm.

Single Parent Families: Myths, Realitites, & Social Policy. Elizabeth A. Mulroy. 228p. 1988. 24.95 (ISBN 0-86569-176-2). Auburn Hse.

Single-Parent Family in Children's Books: An Analysis & Annotated Bibliography, with an Appendix on Audiovisual Material. Catherine T. Horner. LC 78-15403. 180p. 1978. 17.50 (ISBN 0-8108-1157-X). Scarecrow.

Single-Parent Family on Children's Books: An Annotated Bibliography. 2nd ed. Catherine T. Horner. LC 87-76403. 349p. 1988. 29.50 (ISBN 0-8108-2065-X). Scarecrow.

Single Parent Housing Guide. Ruth Rejnis. 216p. 1984. pap. 9.95 (ISBN 0-87131-448-7). M Evans.

Single Parent: Revised, Updated & Expanded. Virginia W. Smith. 192p. 1983. pap. 5.95 (ISBN 0-8007-5105-1, Power Bks). Revell.

Single Parenting: A Wilderness Journey. Robert G. Barnes, Jr. 176p. 1984. pap. 5.95 (ISBN 0-8423-5892-7). Tyndale.

Single Parents & Their Families: A Guide to Involving School & Community. 52p. 2.00 (ISBN 0-317-36579-7). Natl PTA.

Single Parents in Black America: A Study in Culture & Legitimacy. Annie S. Barnes. LC 87-51006. 175p. 1987. text ed. 24.95x (ISBN 1-55605-023-2); pap. text ed. 14.95x (ISBN 1-55605-024-0). Wyndham Hall.

Single Parent's Survival Guide: How to Raise the Children. Leroy G. Baruth. 128p. 1979. pap. text ed. 12.95 (ISBN 0-8403-2053-1). Kendall-Hunt.

Single-Particle Density in Physics & Chemistry. Ed. by N. H. March & B. M. Deb. (Techniques of Physics Ser.). 385p. 1988. 79.00 (ISBN 0-12-470518-9). Acad Pr.

Single-Particle Rotations in Molecular Crystals. W. Press. (Springer Tracts in Modern Physics Ser.: Vol. 92). (Illus.). 140p. 1981. 29.00 (ISBN 0-387-10897-1). Springer-Verlag.

Single Pebble. John Hersey. 1989. 6.95 (ISBN 0-394-75697-5, Vin). Random.

Single Pebble. John R. Hersey. 1956. 16.45 (ISBN 0-394-44562-7). Knopf.

Single-Period Stationarity in Open Systems of Regions. Gene E. Smith. (Discussion Paper Ser.: No. 71). 1974. pap. 6.50 (ISBN 0-686-32237-1). Regional Sci Res Inst.

Single-Photon Emission Computed Tomography: A Primer. Robert J. English et al. 148p. (Orig.). 1986. 15.00 (ISBN 0-932004-24-5). Soc Nuclear Med.

Single-Photon Ultrashort-Lived Radionuclides: Proceedings. DOE Technical Information Center Staff. Ed. by Peter Paras & J. W. Thiessen. LC 84-26051. (Symposium Ser.). 359p. 1985. pap. 17.00 (ISBN 0-87079-520-1, CONF-830504); microfiche 6.50 (ISBN 0-87079-521-X, CONF-830504). DOE.

Single Pilot Operations: Flying Without a Copilot. Lee J. Lindo. (Illus.). 176p. (Orig.). 1988. pap. 14.95 (ISBN 0-938051-15-6). Cockpit Mgmt Trng.

Single-Ply Roofing Technology- STP 790. Ed. by W. Gumpertz. 120p. 1982. pap. 14.25 (ISBN 0-8031-0778-1, 04-790000-10). ASTM.

Single Point Morning: Maintenance & Operations Guide. OCIMF Staff. 1985. 162.00x (ISBN 0-317-61479-7, Pub. by Witherby & Co England). State Mutual Bk.

Single Rooms: Stories of an Urban Subculture. Ellie Winberg & Tom Wilson. 192p. 1981. pap. text ed. 9.95 (ISBN 0-87073-496-2). Schenkman Bks Inc.

Single Rose. Barbara Delinsky. (Temptation Ser.: No. 150). 224p. Date not set. pap. 2.25 (ISBN 0-317-63836-X). Harlequin Bks.

Single Salary Schedule: An Analysis & Evaluation. Lyle L. Morris. LC 72-177086. (Columbia University. Teachers College. Contributions to Education: No. 413). Repr. of 1930 ed. 22.50 (ISBN 0-404-55413-X). AMS Pr.

Single Scattering & Transport Theory. A. Ishimaru. (Wave Propagation & Scattering in Random Media: Vol. 1). 1978. 49.50 (ISBN 0-12-374701-5). Acad Pr.

Single Serve Packaging. BCC Staff. 177p. 1987. pap. 1950.00 (ISBN 0-89336-541-6, P-097). BCC.

Single Server Queue. 2nd ed. J Cohen. (Applied Mathematics & Mechanics Ser.: Vol. 8). 694p. 1982. 116.00 (ISBN 0-444-85452-5, North-Holland). Elsevier.

Single Shot. Gart A. Ewing. 144p. 1988. 9.95 (ISBN 0-8062-3265-X). Carlton.

Single-Shot Rifles. James J. Grant. 25.00 (ISBN 0-88227-017-6). Gun Room.

Single? Single Again? A Handbook for Living. Hugh Binford & Helaina Binford. 120p. (Orig.). 1986. pap. 7.00 (ISBN 0-939313-22-7). Joshua-I-Minist.

Single Solution: Taxpayers Guide to Sheltering More of the 20,000 Dollars; 50,000 Dollars; or 100,000 Dollars You Make as a Single Person. Mary J. Parson. (Illus.). 192p. 19.95 (ISBN 0-8160-1406-X); pap. 11.95 (ISBN 0-8160-1597-X). Facts on File.

Single Source: A Reference for Singles. Ed. by Bibliotheca Press Research Division Staff. 75p. 1982. pap. 4.00 (ISBN 0-939476-71-1, Pub. by Biblio Pr GA). Prosperity & Profits.

Single Sparks: China's Rural Revolutions. Ed. by Kathleen J. Hartford & Steven M. Goldstein. 1987. 27.50 (ISBN 0-87332-427-7). M E Sharpe.

Single Speckled Egg. Sonia Levitin. LC 75-4189. (Illus.). 40p. (ps-3). 1976. 6.95 (ISBN 0-87466-074-2, Pub. by Parnassus). HM.

Single Steps Toward Marriage. Jean Lehman. 112p. (Orig.). 1987. pap. price not set (ISBN 0-87227-120-X). Reg Baptist.

Single, Straight Men: One Hundred Fifteen Guaranteed Places to Find Them. Diana Summerfield. 176p. 1986. 9.95 (ISBN 0-312-76381-6). St Martin.

Single-Subject Experimental Designs in Communicative Disorders. Leija V. McReynolds & Kevin R. Kearns. LC 82-8501. (Illus.). 265p. 1983. text ed. 24.00x (ISBN 0-89079-101-5, 1182). Pro Ed.

Single Subject Research in Special Education. James W. Tawney & David L. Gast. 1984. 34.95 (ISBN 0-675-20135-7). Merrill.

Single-System Research Designs. Ed. by Martin Bloom. (Journal of Social Service Research Ser.: Vol. 3, No. 1). 134p. 1979. pap. text ed. 10.00 (ISBN 0-917724-70-4, B70). Haworth Pr.

Single Truth. Bob E. Lyons. 1982. text ed. 5.25 (ISBN 0-87148-801-9); pap. 4.25 (ISBN 0-87148-802-7); instr's. manual 6.95 (ISBN 0-87148-804-3). Pathway Pr.

Single Variable Calculus. H. Flanders. 649p. 1985. pap. 19.95 (ISBN 0-7167-1752-2). W H Freeman.

Single Vessel Midwater Trawling. D. Amos. (Marine Bulletin Ser.: No. 43). 30p. 1980. 2.00 (ISBN 0-938412-26-4, P872). Sea Grant Pubns.

Single Voices. Ed. by Bruce Yoder & Imo J. Yoder. LC 82-3002. 128p. 1982. pap. 6.95 (ISBN 0-8361-1998-3). Herald Pr.

Single vs. Multiple Languages in Secondary Schools see Language Teacher.

Single Wing Offense with the Spinning Fullback. John F. Aldrich. 176p. 1983. text ed. 16.95 (ISBN 0-8138-1643-2). Iowa St U Pr.

Single Woman: A Medical Study in Sex Education. Robert Dickinson & Lura B. Dickinson. Ed. by David J. Rothman & Sheila M. Rothman. (Women & Children First Ser.). 488p. 1986. lib. bdg. 60.00 (ISBN 0-8240-7656-7). Garland Pub.

Single Woman's Vacation Guide. Linda Ledray. 1988. pap. 9.95 (ISBN 0-449-90210-2, Columbine). Fawcett.

Single-Word Usage, Cognitive Development, & the Beginnings of Combinatorial Speech: A Study of Ten English-speaking Children. Maris M. Rodgon. LC 75-7211. pap. 43.30 (ISBN 0-317-26378-1, 2024520). Bks Demand UMI.

Singlehanded Sailing. 2nd ed. Richard Henderson. (Illus.). 320p. 1988. 24.95 (ISBN 0-87742-972-3). Intl Marine.

Singlehanding: A Sailor's Guide. Tony Meisel. (Illus.). 192p. 1986. 16.95 (ISBN 0-02-583930-6). Macmillan.

Singlehood--After the Sexual Revolution: The Complete Guide to Enjoying Life on Your Own. Michael Broder & Edward B. Claflin. 256p. 1988. 16.95 (ISBN 0-89256-333-8). Rawson Assocs.

Singleness. Dorothy Payne. LC 83-10174. (Choices: Guides for Today's Woman Ser.: Vol. 4). 112p. 1983. pap. 7.95 (ISBN 0-664-24541-2). Westminster John Knox.

Singleness: A Guide to Understanding & Satisfaction. Nadine Peterson & Barbara N. Sofie. LC 87-50532. 184p. (Orig.). 1987. pap. 9.95 (ISBN 0-934955-09-3). Watercress Pr.

Singleness: An Opportunity for Growth & Fulfillment. Edward F. Weising & Gwen Weising. LC 82-80197. (Radiant Life Ser.). 128p. (Orig.). 1982. pap. 2.50 (ISBN 0-88243-901-4, 02-0901); teacher's guide 3.95 (ISBN 0-88243-196-X, 32-0196). Gospel Pub.

Singleness of Purpose. Jeffries Tula. LC 85-19525. (Orig.). 1986. pap. 3.95 (ISBN 0-8054-5029-7). Broadman.

Singles. Marlene F. Shyer. (Orig.). 1987. pap. 3.95. Warner Bks.

Singles Alive! Jim Towns. LC 83-23777. 128p. 1984. 9.95 (ISBN 0-88289-421-8). Pelican.

Singles Almanac. Jeffrey Ullman. 224p. (Orig.). 1986. pap. 8.95. Pharos Bks NY.

Single's Almanac. Jeffrey Ullman. pap. 8.95 (ISBN 0-345-32633-4). Ballantine.

Singles Ask: Answers to Questions about Relationships & Sexual Issues. Harold I. Smith. LC 88-6368. 160p. 1988. 8.95 (ISBN 0-8066-2379-9, 10-5803). Augsburg.

Singles Cookbooks: An Index. Ed. by Cookbook Consortium Information Division Staff. 70p. 1984. pap. text ed. 3.95 (ISBN 0-318-00120-9, Pub. by Cookbk Consort). Prosperity & Profits.

Singles Guide to California. Richard Gosse. 252p. 1987. pap. 9.95 (ISBN 0-934377-03-0). Marin Pubns.

Singles Guide to the L. A. Area. Richard Gosse. 160p. 1988. pap. 9.95 (ISBN 0-934377-06-5). Marin Pubns.

Singles Guide to the San Francisco Bay Area. Richard Gosse. 202p. 1988. pap. 9.95 (ISBN 0-934377-05-7). Marin Pubns.

Singles Guide to Tight Spots & Tricky Situations. Jacinth I. Baublitz. LC 86-91044. 168p. 1986. pap. 7.95 (ISBN 0-9610316-1-1). J I Baublitz.

Single's Pocket Guide to Survival: Single's Survival. Mort Buckley. Ed. by Boye DeMente. LC 83-90907. (Illus.). 304p. (Orig.). 1983. pap. 9.95 (ISBN 0-914067-00-1). Single Graph.

Singlet Oxygen. Ed. by Harry H. Wasserman & Robert W. Murray. LC 77-25737. (Organic Chemistry Ser.). 1979. 85.00 (ISBN 0-12-736650-4). Acad Pr.

Singlet Oxygen: Reactions with Organic Compounds & Polymers. Ed. by Bengt G. Ranby & J. F. Rabek. LC 77-2793. 341p. pap. 88.70 (2030475). Bks Demand UMI.

Singlet Oxygen-Two, 4 vols. Ed. by Aryeh A. Frimer. Incl. Vol. I. Physical-Chemical Aspects. 248p; Vol. II, Part I. Reaction Modes & Products. 296p; Vol.III, Reaction Modes & Products-Part II. 288p; Vol. IV. Polymers & Biomolecules. 224p. 1985. Set. 590.00 (ISBN 0-8493-6439-6, 6439FD). CRC Pr.

Singleton. Jack Cady. LC 81-8117. 288p. 1981. 13.95 (ISBN 0-914842-63-3). Madrona Pubs.

Singleton Fontenoy, R. N, 3 vols. in 2. James Hannay. LC 79-8129. Repr. of 1850 ed. Set. 84.50 (ISBN 0-404-61899-5). AMS Pr.

Singualarities des Systemes Differentiels de Gauss-Manin. F. Pham. (Progress in Mathematics Ser.: No. 2). 340p. (Fr.). 1979. pap. 28.50x (ISBN 0-8176-3002-3). Birkhauser.

Singular Homology Theory. W. S. Massey. LC 79-23309. (Graduate Texts in Mathematics: Vol. 70). (Illus.). 280p. 1980. 40.00 (ISBN 3-540-90456-5). Springer-Verlag.

Singular Images. Ansel Adams. LC 73-93872. (Illus.). 76p. 1974. pap. 14.45i (ISBN 0-8212-0728-8, 792896). NYGS.

Singular Integral Operators. S. G. Michlin & S. Prossdorf. Tr. by A. Bottcher & R. Lehmann. (Illus.). 540p. 1986. 49.00 (ISBN 0-387-15967-3). Springer-Verlag.

Singular Integrals & Differentiability Properties of Functions. E. M. Stein. (Mathematical Ser.: No. 30). 1971. 38.50x (ISBN 0-691-08079-8). Princeton U Pr.

Singular Integrals: Proceedings. Symposium in Pure Mathematics - Chicago - 1966. Ed. by A. P. Calderon. LC 67-16553. (Proceedings of Symposia in Pure Mathematics: Vol. 10). 384p. 1982. pap. 41.00 (ISBN 0-8218-1410-9, PSPUM-10). Am Math.

Singular Life. Ed. by Carol Clark & Blythe Thatcher. LC 87-22269. 182p. 1987. 9.95 (ISBN 0-87579-107-7). Deseret Bk.

Singular Life Story of Heedless Hopalong. Hans J. Christoffel von Grimmelshausen. Tr. by Robert L. Hiller & John C. Osborne. LC 81-10446. 160p. 1981. 19.95x (ISBN 0-8143-1688-3). Wayne St U Pr.

Singular Man. J. P. Donleavy. 1989. pap. 7.95 (ISBN 0-87113-265-6). Atlantic Monthly.

Singular Marriage: A Labour Love Story in Letters & Diaries. Jane Cox. 1988. 60.00x (ISBN 0-245-54672-3, Pub. by Harrap Ltd England). State Mutual Bk.

Singular Optimal Control Problems. D. J. Bell & D. H. Jacobson. (Mathematics in Science & Engineering Ser.). 1975. 51.50 (ISBN 0-12-085060-5). Acad Pr.

Singular Ordinary Differential Operators & Pseudodifferential Equations. J. Elschner. (Lecture Notes in Mathematics: Vol. 1128). 200p. 1985. pap. 16.00 (ISBN 0-387-15194-X). Springer-Verlag.

Singular Paths: Old Men Living Alone. Robert L. Rubinstein. LC 85-19063. 1986. 30.00 (ISBN 0-231-06206-0). Columbia U Pr.

Singular Paths: Old Men Living Alone. Robert L. Rubinstein. 265p. 1988. pap. 15.00 (ISBN 0-231-06207-9). Columbia U Pr.

Singular Pertubations & Symptotics. Ed. by Richard Meyer & Seymour Parter. LC 80-24946. 1980. 43.00 (ISBN 0-12-493260-6). Acad Pr.

Singular Perturbation Analysis of Discrete Control Systems. D. S. Naidu & A. K. Rao. (Lecture Notes in Mathematics: Vol. 1154). 195p. 1985. pap. 16.00 (ISBN 0-387-15981-9). Springer-Verlag.

Singular Perturbation Methods in Control: Analysis & Design. Peter Kokotovic et al. (Mathematics in Science & Engineering Candidate). 1986. 69.50 (ISBN 0-12-417635-6). Acad Pr.

Singular Perturbation Theory: An Introduction with Applications. Donald R. Smith. 576p. 1985. 49.50 (ISBN 0-521-30042-8). Cambridge U Pr.

Singular Perturbations & Asymptotic Analysis in Control Systems. Ed. by P. V. Kokotovic et al. (Lecture Notes in Control & Information Sciences: Vol. 90). vi, 419p. 1987. pap. 52.20 (ISBN 0-387-17362-5). Springer-Verlag.

Singular Perturbations & Differential Inequalities. F. A. Howes. LC 75-44235. (Memoirs: No. 168). 75p. 1976. pap. 15.00 (ISBN 0-8218-1868-6, MEMO-168). Am Math.

Singular Perturbations in Control Systems. D. S. Naidv. (IEE Control Engineering Ser.: No. 33). 1987. write for info. (ISBN 0-86341-107-X, CE033). Inst Elect Eng.

Singular Perturbations in Systems & Control. Ed. by M. D. Ardema. (CISM, Courses & Lectures: No. 280). (Illus.). 337p. 1983. pap. 29.00 (ISBN 0-387-81751-4). Springer-Verlag.

Singular Perturbations in Systems & Control. Ed. by Petar V. Kokotovic & Hassan K. Khalil. LC 86-7435. 504p. 1986. 59.10 (ISBN 0-87942-205-X, PC01966). Inst Electrical.

Singular Perturbations: Order Reduction in Control System Design. American Society of Mechnical Engineers Staff. LC 72-87029. pap. 20.00 (ISBN 0-317-08441-0, 2012304). Bks Demand UMI.

Singular Points of Complex Hypersurfaces. John W. Milnor. (Annals of Mathematics Studies: No. 61). 1969. pap. 18.50x (ISBN 0-691-08065-8). Princeton U Pr.

Singular Power: An Essay on American Television News. Robert Hershman. 32p. (Orig.). 1982. pap. text ed. 5.00 (ISBN 0-8191-5850-X, Pub. by Aspen Inst for Humanistic Studies). U Pr of Amer.

Singular Problem of the Epistle to the Galatians. James H. Ropes. (Harvard Theological Studies). 1929. pap. 15.00 (ISBN 0-527-01014-6). Kraus Repr.

Singular Problems of the Single Jewish Parent. Shlomo D. Levine. 39p. (Orig.). 1981. pap. text ed. 1.25 (ISBN 0-8381-2115-2). United Synagogue.

Singular Rebellion. Saiichi Maruya. LC 85-45785. 430p. 1986. 19.95 (ISBN 0-87011-763-7). Kodansha.

Singular Torsion & the Splitting Properties. K. R. Goodearl. LC 72-4344. (Memoirs: No. 124). 89p. 1972. pap. 12.00 (ISBN 0-8218-1824-4, MEMO-124). Am Math.

Singular View: The Art of Seeing with One Eye. 3rd, rev. ed. Frank Brady. (Illus.). 129p. 1985. pap. 12.50 (ISBN 0-9614639-0-2). Frank B Brady.

Singular Visions: Long Island Folk Art from the Late 18th Century to the Present. Alyce Assael. LC 85-70640. (Illus.). 48p. (Orig.). 1985. pap. 6.00 (ISBN 0-933793-00-6). Guild Hall.

Singular Women. Freda Bright. 374p. (Orig.). 1988. pap. 4.50 (ISBN 0-553-27330-2). Bantam.

Singularities. O. Riemenschneider. (Aspects of Mathematics Ser.). 250p. 1987. pap. price not set (ISBN 3-528-08966-0, Pub. by Vieweg & Sohn). IPS.

Singularities & Constructive Methods for Their Treatment. Ed. by P. Grisvard et al. (Lecture Notes in Mathematics: Vol. 1121). ix, 346p. 1985. pap. 26.00 (ISBN 0-387-15219-9). Springer-Verlag.

Singularities & Dynamical Systems: Proceedings of the International Conference Held in Heraklion, Greece, 30 August-6 September 1983. Ed. by S. N. Pnevmatikos. (Mathematics Studies: Vol. 103). 460p. 1985. 84.25 (ISBN 0-444-87641-3, North-Holland). Elsevier.

Singularities & Groups in Bifurcation Theory I. M. Golubitsky & D. Schaeffer. (Applied Mathematical Sciences Ser.: Vol. 51). (Illus.). 320p. 1984. 46.00 (ISBN 0-387-90999-0). Springer-Verlag.

Singularities & Groups in Bifurcation Theory Two. M. Golubitsky et al. (Applied Mathematical Sciences Ser.: Vol. 69). (Illus.). 550p. 1988. 69.50 (ISBN 0-387-96652-8). Springer-Verlag.

Singularities in Boundary Value Problems. Ed. by H. G. Garnir. 370p. 1982. 49.50 (ISBN 90-277-1240-9, Pub. by Reidel Holland). Kluwer Academic.

Singularities in Linear Wave Propagation. L. Garding. (Lecture Notes in Mathematics Ser.: Vol. 1241). iii, 125p. 1987. pap. 13.10 (ISBN 0-387-18001-X). Springer-Verlag.

Singularities of Differentiable Maps. Ed. by Arnold et al. (Monographs in Mathematics Ser.: No. 83, Vol. II). 400p. 1988. 125.00 (ISBN 0-8176-3185-2). Birkhauser.

Singularities of Differentiable Maps: Vol. 1. Arnold et al. (Monographs in Mathematics). 1984. text ed. 49.50 (ISBN 0-8176-3187-9). Birkhauser.

Singularities of Smooth Functions & Maps. Jean Martinet. Tr. by C. P. Simon. LC 81-18034. (London Mathematical Society Lecture Note Ser.: No. 58). 180p. 1982. pap. 22.95 (ISBN 0-521-23398-4). Cambridge U Pr.

Singularities of Smooth Maps. James J. Eells. (Notes on Mathematics & Its Applications Ser.). 114p. (Orig.). 1967. 40.00 (ISBN 0-677-01330-2). Gordon & Breach.

Singularities: Proceedings of Symposia in Pure Mathematics. Ed. by Peter Orlik. LC 83-2529. (Proceedings of Symposia in Pure Mathematics: Vol. 40). Set. text ed. 114.00 (ISBN 0-8218-1443-5); text ed. 65.00 Pt. 1 (ISBN 0-8218-1450-8); text ed. 65.00 Pt. 2 (ISBN 0-8218-1466-4). Am Math.

Singularities, Representation of Algebras, & Vector Bundles. Ed. by G. Greuel & G. Trautmann. (Lecture Notes in Mathematics: Vol.1273). xiv, 383p. 1987. pap. 32.90 (ISBN 0-387-18263-2). Springer-Verlag.

Singularity. William Sleator. LC 84-26075. 192p. (gr. 7 up). 1985. 12.95 (ISBN 0-525-44161-1). Dutton.

Singularity. William Sleator. 208p. 1986. pap. 2.95 (ISBN 0-553-25627-0, Spectra). Bantam.

Singularity of Thomas Nashe. Stephen S. Hilliard. LC 85-16538. x, 260p. 1986. 22.50x (ISBN 0-8032-2326-9). U of Nebr Pr.

Singweisen Bernarts Von Ventadorn nach den Handschriften mitgeteilt. Carl L. Appel. LC 80-2171. Repr. of 1934 ed. 17.50 (ISBN 0-404-19002-2). AMS Pr.

Sinhala Writing & the New Critics. Ranjini Obeyesekere. 1974. 9.00x (ISBN 0-88386-660-9). South Asia Bks.
Sinhalese: An Introductory Course. C. Reynolds. 1980. 38.00x (ISBN 0-8364-0661-3, Pub. by London U England). South Asia Bks.
Sinhalese & Other Island Languages in South Asia. M. W. De Silva. (ARS Linguistica: 3). 75p. (Orig.). 1979. pap. 17.00x (ISBN 3-87808-353-X). Benjamins North Am.
Sining Through the Clouds, Pt. 3. Samuel Lewin. Tr. by Joseph Leftwich. LC 85-22377. (Trilogy Ser.). 160p. 1987. 12.95 (ISBN 0-8453-4805-1, Cornwall Bks). Assoc Univ Prs.
Sinister Abbey. Elsie Lee. 288p. 1988. pap. 2.95 (ISBN 0-8217-2464-9). Zebra.
Sinister Airfield. Alison Prince. LC 82-18877. (Illus.). 128p. (gr. 4-6). 1983. 10.25 (ISBN 0-688-01741-X). Morrow.
Sinister Barrier. Eric F. Russell. 288p. 1986. pap. 2.95 (ISBN 0-345-32760-8, Pub. by Del Rey). Ballantine.
Sinister Circle. Dayle Courtney. LC 83-4699. (Thorne Twins Adventure Bks.). (Illus.). 192p. (Orig.). (gr. 7-12). 1983. pap. 2.98 (ISBN 0-87239-684-3, 2904). Standard Pub.
Sinister Forces. Patrick Anderson. 1987. pap. 3.95 (ISBN 0-515-09475-7). Jove Pubns.
Sinister House. Leland Hall. 1975. 5.00 (ISBN 0-685-72184-1). Bookfinger.
Sinister Ladies of Mystery: The Dark Asteroids of Earth. Ted George & Barbara Parker. LC 87-81809. 145p. 1988. 13.00 (ISBN 0-932782-04-3). Arthur Pubns.
Sinister Madonna. Sax Rohmer. (Sumuru Ser). 1977. Repr. 8.50 (ISBN 0-685-88226-8). Bookfinger.
Sinister Paradise. Carolyn Keene. (Nancy Drew Files Ser.: No. 23). (YA) (gr. 7 up). 1988. pap. 2.75 (ISBN 0-671-64229-4). Archway.
Sinister Purposes. Margot Arnold. 304p. 1988. pap. 3.95 (ISBN 0-449-13284-6, GM). Fawcett.
Sinister Ray. Lester Dent. 175p. (Orig.). 1987. pap. 9.95 (ISBN 0-936071-04-4). Gryphon Pubns.
Sinister Romance. Mary H. Vorse. 1988. 25.00 (ISBN 0-910489-20-3). Scream Pr.
Sinister Sign Post. Franklin W. Dixon. (Hardy Boys Ser: Vol. 15). (gr. 5-9). 1936. 4.50 (ISBN 0-448-08915-7, G&D); PLB 3.29 (ISBN 0-448-18915-1). Putnam Pub Group.
Sinister Stones. Arthur W. Upfield. 192p. 1983. pap. 3.95 rack-size (ISBN 0-684-18021-9, ScribT). Scribner.
Sinister Studios of KESP-TV. Louise M. Foley. (Twistaplot Ser.: No. 5). (Illus.). 96p. (Orig.). (gr. 7 up). 1983. pap. 1.95 (ISBN 0-590-32827-1). Scholastic Inc.
Sinister Touches: The Secret War Against Hitler. Robert Goldston. LC 81-65853. 176p. (gr. 7 up). 1982. 11.95 (ISBN 0-8037-7903-8, 01160-350). Dial Bks Young.
Sink or Float. Elementary Science Study Staff. (gr. 3-8). 1971. tchr's guide 17.40 (ISBN 0-07-017724-4). McGraw.
Sink or Swim. Betty Miles. LC 85-23134. (Illus.). 198p. (gr. 5-9). 1986. 11.95 (ISBN 0-394-85515-9); lib. bdg. 11.99 (ISBN 0-394-95515-3). Knopf.
Sink or Swim. Betty Miles. 208p. (YA) (gr. 3-7). 1987. pap. 2.75 (ISBN 0-380-69913-3, Camelot). Avon.
Sink or Swim: College Lifesavers to Help You Stay Afloat. Priscilla Tanner. 167p. (Orig.). 1986. pap. 6.95 (ISBN 0-9616673-0-3). Wilson Crewe.
Sink the Haguro! The Last Destroyer Action of the Second World War. John Winton. (Illus.). ix, 182p. 1978. 24.00 (ISBN 0-85422-152-2, Seeley Service). Shoe String.
Sink the Tirpitz! Leonce Peillard. 348p. 1983. pap. 6.95 (ISBN 0-583-12384-8, Pub. by Granada England). Academy Chi Pubs.
Sinkholes - Their Geology, Engineering & Environmental Impact: First Multidisciplinary Conference on Sinkholes, Orlando, Florida, 15-17 October 1984. Ed. by F. B Beck. 440p. 1984. text ed. 76.50 (ISBN 90-6191-570-8, Pub. by A A Balkema). Brookfield Pub Co.
Sinkiang Excutive. Adam Hall. 240p. 1986. pap. 3.50 (ISBN 0-515-08678-9). Jove Pubns.
Sinkiang: Pawn or Pivot? Allen S. Whiting & Sheng Shih-Ts'Ai. xxii, 314p. 1958. 5.00 (ISBN 0-87013-039-0). Mich St U Pr.
Sinking Ark: A New Look at the Problem of Disappearing Species. Norman Myers. 1979. 25.00 (ISBN 0-08-024501-3). Pergamon.
Sinking Island: The Modern English Writers. Hugh Kenner. LC 87-45131. 304p. 1988. 22.95 (ISBN 0-394-54254-1). Knopf.
Sinking of Clay City. Robert Wrigley. 1979. pap. 5.00 (ISBN 0-914742-42-6). Copper Canyon.
Sinking of the Belgrano. Desmond Rice & Arthur Gavshon. (Illus.). 218p. 1984. 22.95 (ISBN 0-436-41332-9, Pub. by Secker & Warburg UK). David & Charles.
Sinking of the Kenbane Head. 2nd ed. Sam McAughtry. (Illus.). 152p. 1984. pap. 5.95 (ISBN 0-85640-141-2, Pub. by Blackstaff Pr). Longwood Pub Group.
Sinking of the Merrimac. Richmond P. Hobson. Ed. by Jack Sweetman. (Classics of Naval Literature Ser.). (Illus.). 320p. 1988. Repr. of 1898 ed. 21.95 (ISBN 0-87021-632-5). Naval Inst Pr.
Sinking of the Odradek Stadium. Harry Mathews. 198p. 1985. 14.95 (ISBN 0-85635-572-0); pap. 7.50 (ISBN 0-85635-602-6). Carcanet.
Sinking of the Sarah Diamond. William D. Jennings. LC 73-83220. 416p. 1974. 5.95 (ISBN 0-8397-7814-7). Eriksson.
Sinking of the Titanic. John Dudman. Ed. by Janet Caulkins. (Great Disasters Ser.). (Illus.). 32p. (gr. k-6). 1988. 10.90 (ISBN 0-531-18160-X, Pub. by Bookwright Pr). Watts.
Sinking Spell. Edward Gorey. (Illus.). 1965. pap. 5.95 (ISBN 0-8392-1150-3). Astor-Honor.
Sinking Star; Or, Frank Reade, Jr.'s Trip into Space with His New Air-Ship "Saturn" see Across the Milky Way; Or, Frank Reade, Jr.'s Great Astronomical Trip with His Air-Ship "The Shooting Star".
Sinking-Stealing: A Novel. Jan Clausen. LC 85-4158. (Feminist Ser.). 280p. (Orig.). 1985. 21.95 (ISBN 0-89594-160-0); pap. 8.95 (ISBN 0-89594-159-7). Crossing Pr.
Sinkiria. Gail Walker. (Dest Two Ser.). 1985. pap. 6.95 (ISBN 0-8163-0552-8). Pacific Pr Pub Assn.
Sinks of Gandy Creek. Jack Preble. (Illus.). 1969. 3.00 (ISBN 0-87012-038-7). McClain.
Sinless Season. Damon Galgut. (Penguin Fiction Ser.). 1985. pap. 5.95 (ISBN 0-14-007077-X). Penguin.
Sinn und Inhalt in der Genetischen Phanomenologica E. Husserls. Almeida. (Phaenomenologica Ser: No. 47). 1972. lib. bdg. 31.50 (ISBN 90-247-1318-8, Pub. by Martinus Nijhoff Netherlands). Kluwer Academic.
Sinne: Beitrage Zur Geschichte der Physiologie und Psychologie Im Ittelalter Aus Hebraischen und Arabisch En Quellen. David Kaufmann. Ed. by Steven Katz. LC 79-7141. (Jewish Philosophy, Mysticism & History of Ideas Ser.). 1980. Repr. of 1884 ed. lib. bdg. 17.00x (ISBN 0-405-12267-5). Ayer Co Pubs.
Sinner. Stewart MacGregor. LC 72-95425. 256p. 1973. 7.95 (ISBN 0-87955-903-9). O'Hara.
Sinner from Toledo & Other Stories. Anton Chekhov. Tr. by Arnold Hinchliffe. LC 70-147269. 168p. 1972. 14.50 (ISBN 0-8386-7890-4). Fairleigh Dickinson.
Sinners. Jackie Collins. 1984. pap. 4.50 (ISBN 0-671-62465-2). PB.
Sinners. Yusuf Idris. Tr. by Kristin Peterson-Ishaq from Arabic. LC 84-50630. (Illus.). 120p. 1985. 20.00 (ISBN 0-89410-393-8); pap. 8.00 (ISBN 0-89410-394-6). Three Continents.
Sinner's Comedy. John O. Hobbes. LC 79-8130. Repr. of 1892 ed. 44.50 (ISBN 0-404-61903-7). AMS Pr.
Sinner's Guide. Venerable Louis of Granada. LC 84-51820. 395p. 1985. pap. 9.00 (ISBN 0-89555-254-X). Tan Bks Pubs.
Sinners in the Hands of an Angry God. Jonathan Edwards. pap. 0.50 (ISBN 0-685-00746-4). Reiner.
Sinners Progress: A Study of Madness in English Renaissance Drama. Robert Shenk. Ed. by James Hogg. (Elizabethan & Renaissance Studies). 285p. (Orig.). 1978. pap. 15.00 (ISBN 3-7052-0718-0, Pub. by Salzburg Studies). Longwood Pub Group.
Sinner's Return to God: Or, the Prodigal Son. Michael Mueller. LC 82-74244. 224p. 1983. pap. 7.50 (ISBN 0-89555-205-1). TAN Bks Pubs.
Sinnfrage in Psychotherapie und Theologie: Die Existenzanalyse und Logotherapie Viktor E. Frankls aus theologischer Sicht. Uwe Boeschemeyer. (Theologische Bibliothek Toepelmann Ser.: Vol. 32). 1977. 22.80x (ISBN 3-11-006727-7). De Gruyter.
Sinning Against the Holy Spirit. Don R. Pegram. 1982. pap. 1.25 (ISBN 0-89265-085-0). Randall Hse.
Sinning with Annie. Paul Theroux. 1972. 9.95 (ISBN 0-395-25502-3). HM.
Sino-American Economic Exchanges: The Legal Contributions. Guiguo Wang. LC 84-18108. 236p. 1985. 36.95 (ISBN 0-275-90179-3, C0179). Praeger.
Sino-American Foreign Policy & Relations since World War II. Joseph D. Lowe. LC 88-91014. (Illus.). xii, 60p. 1988. 11.50 (ISBN 0-930325-07-9). Lowe Pub.
Sino-American Normalization & Its Policy Implications. Gene T. Hsiao. 560p. 1983. Praeger.
Sino-German Connection: Alexander von Falkenhausen Between China & Germany 1900-1941. Liang Hsi-Huey. 246p. 1978. pap. text ed. 19.00 (ISBN 90-232-1554-0, Pub. by Van Gorcum Holland). Longwood Pub Group.
Sino-Indian Border Dispute: A Legal Study. Chih Lu. LC 85-12713. (Contributions in Political Science: No. 139). 153p. 1986. lib. bdg. 36.95 (ISBN 0-313-25024-3, LSI/). Greenwood.
Sino-Indian Border Dispute & Its Impact on Indo-Pakistan Relations. Ram Naresh Trivedi. 1977. 21.00x (ISBN 0-686-12058-2). Intl Bk Dist.
Sino Indian Relations. Ed. by Chopra Surendra. 1985. 17.95. Asia Bk Corp.
Sino-Indian Relations, 1948-52: Role of K. M. Panikar. Karunakar Gupta. 1987. 16.00x (ISBN 0-8364-2199-X, Pub. by Minerva India). South Asia Bks.
Sino-Iranica see Beginnings of Porcelain in China: Field Museum of Nautual History.
Sino Iranica: Chinese Contributions to the History of Civilization in Iran. B. Laufer. 1976. lib. bdg. 59.95 (ISBN 0-8490-2608-3). Gordon Pr.
Sino-Japanese Axis: A New Force in Asia? R. Taylor. LC 84-29812. 132p. 1985. 29.95 (ISBN 0-312-72601-5). St Martin.
Sino-Japanese Controversy & the League of Nations. Westel W. Willoughby. LC 68-54995. (Illus.). 1968. Repr. of 1935 ed. lib. bdg. 35.00 (ISBN 0-8371-0755-5, WISJ). Greenwood.
Sino-Japanese Negotiations of 1915: Japanese & Chinese Documents & Chinese Official Statement. Carnegie Endowment for International Peace, Division of International Law Staff. LC 75-36222. Repr. of 1921 ed. 16.50 (ISBN 0-404-14473-X). AMS Pr.
Sino-Japanese Relations, 1862-1927: A Checklist of the Chinese Foreign Ministry Archives. Ting-Yee Kuo & James W. Morley. (Occasional Papers of the East Asian). 245p. 1965. pap. 5.00 (ISBN 0-317-17108-9). Columbia U E Asian Inst.
Sino Japanese War in Woodcuts, 1894-1895. Nathan Chaiken. (Illus.). 203p. 1983. 160.00. Saifer.
Sino-Portuguese Trade from 1514 to 1644: A Synthesis of Portuguese & Chinese Sources. Chang Tien-Tse. LC 78-38052. Repr. of 1934 ed. 20.00 (ISBN 0-404-56906-4). AMS Pr.
Sino-Russian Relations. Rosemary Quested. 200p. 1984. pap. text ed. 10.95 (ISBN 0-86861-255-3). Unwin Hyman.
Sino-Soviet Conflict. Ed. by Leopold Labedz & George Urban. LC 65-18351. 1965. 10.95 (ISBN 0-8023-1070-2). Dufour.
Sino-Soviet Conflict: A Global Perspective. Ed. by Herbert J. Ellison. LC 81-51279. 432p. 1981. 35.00x (ISBN 0-295-95854-5); pap. 17.95x (ISBN 0-295-95873-1). U of Wash Pr.
Sino-Soviet Conflict: A Historical Bibliography. LC 83-27155. (ABC-Clio Research Guides: No. 13). 190p. 1985. lib. bdg. 34.00. ABC-Clio.
Sino-Soviet Conflict: A Historical Bibliography. (Researach Guides). 190p. 1985. 34.00 (ISBN 0-317-69754-4). ABC-Clio.
Sino-Soviet Confrontation since Mao Zedong: Dispute, Detente, or Conflict. Alfred D. Low. (Social Science Monographs Ser.). 400p. 1987. text ed. 40.00 (ISBN 0-88033-958-6, Dist. by Columbia Univ Pr). East Eur Quarterly.
Sino-Soviet Crisis Politics: A Study of Political Change & Communication. Richard Wich. (Harvard East Asian Monographs: No. 96). 315p. 1981. text ed. 21.00x (ISBN 0-674-80935-1). Harvard U Pr.
Sino-Soviet Cultural Frontier: The Ili Kazakh Autonomous Chou. George Moseley. LC 67-827. (East Asian Monographs: No. 22). 1966. pap. 11.00x (ISBN 0-674-80925-4). Harvard U Pr.
Sino-Soviet Diplomatic Relations, 1917-1926. Sow-Theng Leong. LC 76-4960. 382p. 1976. text ed. 17.50x (ISBN 0-8248-0401-5). UH Pr.
Sino-Soviet Dispute: An Analysis of the Polemics. Alfred D. Low. LC 74-2949. 364p. 1976. 28.50 (ISBN 0-8386-1479-5). Fairleigh Dickinson.
Sino-Soviet Intervention in Africa. Ed. by Roger Pearson. 1977. pap. 15.00 (ISBN 0-930690-05-2). Coun Soc Econ.
Sino-Soviet Potentialities. Stuart Wolk. LC 62-16586. (Illus.). 40p. 1962. pap. 3.95 (ISBN 0-87419-021-5, U Pr of Wash). Larlin Corp.
Sino-Soviet Relations: Nineteen Seventeen to Nineteen Forty-Nine; with Emphasis on the Early Period. Joseph D. Lowe. LC 88-91013. (Illus.). xiv, 50p. 1988. 10.00 (ISBN 0-930325-06-0). Lowe Pub.
Sino-Soviet Relations: Re-examining the Prospects for Normalization. T. G. Hart. (Swedish Institute of International Affairs). 150p. 1987. text ed. 38.95 (ISBN 0-566-05449-3, Pub. by Gower Pub England). Gower Pub Co.
Sino-Soviet Relations Since Mao: The Chairman's Legacy. C. G. Jacobsen. LC 80-27319. 176p. 1981. 36.95 (ISBN 0-275-90652-3, C0652). Praeger.
Sino-Thai Ceramics: In the National Museum, Bangkok, Thailand, & in Private Collections. 1982. 145.00 (ISBN 0-317-45243-6, Pub. by Han-Shan Tang Ltd). State Mutual Bk.
Sino-Tibetan: A Conspectus. Paul K. Benedict. LC 78-154511. (Princeton-Cambridge Studies in Chinese Linguistics: No. 2). 1972. 85.00 (ISBN 0-521-08175-0). Cambridge U Pr.
Sino-Vietnamese Conflict. Eugene K. Lawson. LC 84-8329. 336p. 1984. 35.00 (ISBN 0-275-91212-4, C1212). Praeger.
Sino-Vietnamese Territorial Dispute. Pao-min Chang. (Washington Papers: No. 118). 128p. 1985. 35.00 (ISBN 0-275-90022-3, C0022); pap. 9.95 (ISBN 0-275-91456-9, B1456). Praeger.
Sino-Vietnamese Territorial Dispute. Pao-Min Chang. (Washington Papers). 119p. pap. text ed. 9.95 (ISBN 0-317-65579-5). CSI Studies.
Sino-Western Calendar for Two Thousand Years. Chung-san Hsueh. lib. bdg. 90.00 (ISBN 0-87968-096-2). Krishna Pr.
Sinomongolische Glossare One. Erich Haenisch. 37p. 1957. pap. 60.00x (ISBN 0-317-69081-7, Pub. by Han-Shan Tang Ltd). State Mutual Bk.
Sinonimus Castellanos. 17th ed. Roque Barcia. 590p. (Span.). 1978. 27.50 (ISBN 0-686-56660-2, S-11889). French & Eur.
Sinonoma Bartholomei. John Mirfeld. Ed. by J. L. Mowat. (Anecdota Oxoniensia Ser.: No. 1). 1988. Repr. of 1882 ed. 32.50 (ISBN 0-404-63951-8). AMS Pr.
Sinopah, the Indian Boy. James W. Schultz. LC 83-73494. (J. W. Schultz Reprint Ser.: Bk.3). (Illus.). 103p. (gr. 4-7). pap. 7.95; pap. 15.95. Confluence Pr.
Sins for Father Knox. Josef Skvorecky. Tr. by Paul Wilson from Czech. 1988. 17.95 (ISBN 0-393-02512-8). Norton.
Sins of Appu's Mother. T Janakiraman. Tr. by Tamil M. Krishnan from Tamil. 168p. 1972. pap. 2.75 (ISBN 0-88253-042-9). Ind-US Inc.
Sins of Commission. Harold L. Klawans. 336p. 1987. pap. 3.95 (ISBN 0-451-14703-0, Sig). NAL.
Sins of Herod. Frank G. Slaughter. 370p. 1976. Repr. lib. bdg. 21.95 (ISBN 0-89190-284-8, Pub. by River City Pr). Amereon Ltd.
Sins of New York. Edward Van Every. LC 70-177502. (Illus.). Repr. of 1930 ed. 27.50 (ISBN 0-405-09038-2, Pub. by Blom). Ayer Co Pubs.
Sins of New York As "Exposed" by the Police Gazette. Edward Vanevery. LC 70-174130. (Illus.). 318p. 1976. Repr. of 1930 ed. 43.00x (ISBN 0-8103-4038-0). Gale.
Sins of Omission: The Neglected Child. 1982. pap. 5.95 (ISBN 0-686-76259-2). Feldheim.
Sins of Our Fathers. Lillian C. Harris. (Church & the World Ser., The West & the Wider World Ser.). xvi, 230p. 1988. 28.85x (ISBN 0-940121-08-5); lib. bdg. 28.85x. Cross Cultural Pubns.
Sins of Our Fathers: A Profile of Pennsylvania Attorney General LeRoy S. Zimmerman & a Historical Explanation of the Suicide of State Treasurer R. Budd Dwyer. William Keisling & Richard Kearns. Ed. by Cecil Brooks. (Illus.). 108p. (Orig.). 1988. pap. 7.95 (ISBN 0-9620251-0-0). W Keisling.
Sins of Philip Fleming. Irving Wallace. 1985. pap. 3.50 (ISBN 0-451-13760-4, Sig). NAL.
Sins of Saint Anthony: Tales of the Theatre. Charles W. Collins. LC 72-116948. (Short Story Index Reprint Ser). 1925. 18.00 (ISBN 0-8369-3450-4). Ayer Co Pubs.
Sins of Saints. Herbert Lockyer. LC 75-108378. 1970. pap. 5.95 (ISBN 0-87213-532-2). Loizeaux.
Sins of Severac Bablon. Sax Rohmer. 1967. 10.00 (ISBN 0-685-22714-6). Bookfinger.
Sins of Sumuru. Sax Rohmer. 1977. Repr. 8.50 (ISBN 0-685-88227-6). Bookfinger.
Sins of the Fathers. Lawrence Block. 1988. pap. 3.50 (ISBN 0-515-09831-0). Jove Pubns.
Sins of the Fathers. John Gribben. 304p. 1989. pap. price not set. Tor Bks.
Sins of the Fathers. Susan Howatch. 1985. pap. 4.95 (ISBN 0-449-20798-6, Crest). Fawcett.
Sins of the Fathers. (Chief Inspector Wexford Ser.). pap. 3.50 (ISBN 0-345-34253-4). Ballantine.
Sins of the Fathers: Decadence in France, 1870-1914. Jennifer Birkett. (Illus.). 288p. 1987. 22.95 (ISBN 0-7043-2503-9, Pub. by Quartet Bks). Salem Hse Pubs.
Sins of the Flesh. Don Davis. 1989. pap. price not set (ISBN 0-8125-1679-6). Tor Bks.
Sins of War. John R. Zodrow. pap. 3.95 (ISBN 0-671-53272-3). PB.
Sintered Metal-Ceramic Composites. Ed. by G. S. Upadhyaya. (Materials Science Monographs: Vol. 25). 1985. 179.00 (ISBN 0-444-42401-6). Elsevier.
Sintering. M. B. Waldron & B. L. Daniell. LC 79-307614. (Monographs in Powder Science & Technology). pap. 29.50 (ISBN 0-317-10497-7, 2019651). Bks Demand UMI.
Sintering & Catalysis. Ed. by G. C. Kuczynski. LC 75-35639. (Materials Science Research Ser.: Vol. 10). 522p. 1975. 85.00x (ISBN 0-306-38510-4, Plenum Pr). Plenum Pub.
Sintering & Heterogeneous Catalysis. Ed. by G. C. Kuczynski et al. (Materials Science Research Ser.: Vol. 16). 346p. 1984. 65.00x (ISBN 0-306-41666-2, Plenum Pr). Plenum Pub.
Sintering & Plastic Deformation, Proceedings. Symposium on Fundamental Phenomena in the Materials Science, 1st, 1963, Boston. Ed. by L. J. Bonis & H. H. Hausner. LC 64-20752. (Fundamental Phenomena in the Material Sciences Ser.: Vol. 1). pap. 36.50 (ISBN 0-317-09858-6, 2003371). Bks Demand UMI.
Sintering & Related Phenomena. Ed. by G. Kuczynski et al. 904p. 1970. 215.00 (ISBN 0-677-10890-7). Gordon & Breach.
Sintering-New Developments. Ed. by Momcilo M. Ristic. (Materials Science Monographs: Vol. 4). 380p. 1979. 108.00 (ISBN 0-444-41796-6). Elsevier.
Sintering Processes. Ed. by G. C. Kuczynski. LC 79-25813. (Materials Sciences Research Ser.: Vol. 13). 586p. 1980. 95.00x (ISBN 0-306-40336-6, Plenum Pr). Plenum Pub.
Sintering: Theory & Practice. Ed. by D. Kolar et al. (Materials Science Monographs: Vol. 14). 654p. 1983. 179.00 (ISBN 0-444-42122-X). Elsevier.
Sintering '85. Ed. by G. C. Kuczynski et al. 442p. 1987. 79.50x (ISBN 0-306-42541-6, Plenum Pr). Plenum Pub.
Sintesis del Nuevo Testamento. W. M. Dunnett. Tr. by Jose M. Blanch from Eng. (Curso Para Maestros Cristianos: No. 3). 128p. (Span.). 1972. pap. 4.50 (ISBN 0-89922-012-6). Edit Caribe.
Sintigo. Jose L. Ramos-Escobar. LC 85-80225. (Sur Ser.). 121p. (Span.). 1985. pap. 5.95 (ISBN 0-940238-81-0). Ediciones Huracan.

Sintomatologia De la Deficiencia De Vitamin A y Su Relacion Con la Nutricion Aplicada. Elmer J. Ballintine et al. (Illus.). 38p. (Orig., Span.). 1983. pap. text ed. 3.50. Nutrition Found.
Sinus Node: Structure, Function, & Clinical Relevance. Felix I. Bonke. 1978. lib. bdg. 55.00 (ISBN 90-247-2064-8, Pub. by Martinus Nijhoff Netherlands). Kluwer Academic.
Sion Crossing. Anthony Price. 1985. 15.95 (ISBN 0-89296-114-7); limited ed. 45.00 (ISBN 0-89296-111-2). Mysterious Pr.
Sion Crossing. Anthony Price. 1986. pap. 3.95 (ISBN 0-445-40247-4). Mysterious Pr.
Sionisme Contre Israel PT I see Zionism: False Messiah.
SIOR Industrial Real Estate Market Survey: 1986 Review-1987 Forecast. The Economics & Research Division of the National Association of Realtors. 240p. 1987. 10.00 (ISBN 0-939623-06-4). Soc Industrial Realtors.
Siouan Indian Language (Teton & Santee Dialects) Dakota. Franz Boas & John Swanton. (Shorey Indian Ser.). 94p. pap. 7.95 (ISBN 0-8466-4029-5, 129). Shorey.
Siouan Tribes of the East. James Mooney. LC 2-14653. 1971. Repr. of 1895 ed. 12.00 (ISBN 0-384-39935-5). Johnson Repr.
Siouan Tribes of the East. James Mooney. LC 73-108504. (American Indian History Ser). (Illus.). 1970. Repr. of 1894 ed. 39.00x (ISBN 0-403-00348-2). Scholarly.
Sioux. Alice Osinski. LC 84-7629. (New True Bks.). (Illus.). 48p. (gr. k-4). 1984. lib. bdg. 12.60 (ISBN 0-516-01929-5); pap. 3.95 (ISBN 0-516-41929-3). Childrens.
Sioux City District - A History: The United Methodist Church. Lyle Johnston. (Illus.). 90p. (Orig.). 1978. pap. 1.95 (ISBN 0-9616365-0-5). Grt Plains Emporium.
Sioux Indian Religion: Tradition & Innovation. Ed. by Raymond J. DeMallie & Douglas R. Parks. LC 86-40527. (Illus.). 240p. 1987. 17.95x (ISBN 0-8061-2055-X). U of Okla Pr.
Sioux Indians: A Socio-Ethnological History. G. Mallery et al. (Illus.). 1897. 19.50 (ISBN 0-914074-06-7, Pub. by J M C & Co). Amereon Ltd.
Sioux Indians: Hunters & Warriors of the Plains. Sonia Bleeker. (Illus.). (gr. 3-6). 1962. PLB 10.88 (ISBN 0-688-31457-0). Morrow.
Sioux: Life & Customs of a Warrior Society. Royal B. Hassrick. LC 64-11331. (Civilization of the American Indian Ser.: Vol. 72). (Illus.). 400p. 1988. pap. 11.95 (ISBN 0-8061-2140-8). U of Okla Pr.
Sioux: Life & Customs of a Warrior Society. Royal B. Hassrick et al. (Civilization of the American Indian Ser.: No. 72). (Illus.). 1982. Repr. of 1964 ed. 22.50 (ISBN 0-8061-0607-7). U of Okla Pr.
Sioux Music. William N. Fenton. lib. bdg. 29.00 (ISBN 0-403-08975-1). Scholarly.
Sioux of the Rosebud: A History in Pictures. Henry W. Hamilton & Jean T. Hamilton. LC 78-145506. (Civilization of the American Indian Ser.: Vol. 111). (Illus.). 320p. 1981. pap. 19.95 (ISBN 0-8061-1622-6). U of Okla Pr.
Sioux Showdown. Chet Cunningham. (Pony Soldiers Ser.: No. 5). 192p. (Orig.). 1988. pap. 2.75 (ISBN 0-8439-2620-1, Pub. by Leisure Bks CT). Leisure NY.
Sioux Slaughter. Chet Cunningham. (Pony Soldiers Ser.: No. 6). 176p. (Orig.). 1988. pap. 2.75 (ISBN 0-8439-2650-3, Pub. by Leisure Bks CT). Leisure NY.
Sioux Spaceman. Andre Norton. 160p. 1984. pap. 2.50 (ISBN 0-441-76804-0). Ace Bks.
Sioux Spaceman. Andre Norton. 1987. pap. 2.50 (ISBN 0-317-63474-7, Pub.by Ace Science Fiction). Ace Bks.
Sioux Sunrise. Michael J. Stewart. 192p. (Orig.). 1981. pap. 1.95 (ISBN 0-505-51747-7, Pub. by Tower Bks). Leisure NY.
Sioux Uprising of 1862. rev. ed. Kenneth Carley. LC 76-16499. (Illus.). 102p. 1976. pap. 6.50 (ISBN 0-87351-103-4). Minn Hist.
Sioux Wildfire. E. J. Hunter. (White Squaw Ser.: No. 1). (Orig.). 1983. pap. 2.50 (ISBN 0-8217-1205-5). Zebra.
SiO2 & Its Interfaces. Ed. by G. Lucovsky & S. T. Pantelides. (Symposium Proceedings Ser.: Vol. 105). 1988. text ed. 46.00 (ISBN 0-931837-73-1). Materials Res.
Siphonaptera of the Indian Subregion. Ravi Iyenger. 1973. 30.00. Oriental Insects.
Siphre Zutta. Saul Lieberman. 1968. 10.00x (ISBN 0-685-31431-6, Pub. by Jewish Theol Seminary). Ktav.
Sippapu the Kiva. John Campion. 1988. pap. 7.00 (ISBN 0-941179-09-5). Latitudes Pr.
Sippi. John O. Killens. (Classic Reprint Ser.). 420p. lib. bdg. 20.00 (ISBN 0-938410-54-7); pap. 9.95 (ISBN 0-938410-55-5). Thunder's Mouth.
Sippin' Bill Padgett. (Illus.). 52p. 12.95 (ISBN 0-934073-04-X). Rountree Pub NC.
Sipping Saints. David Wilkerson. 128p. 1979. pap. 3.50 (ISBN 0-8007-8339-5, Spire Bks). Revell.
SIPRI Yearbook Nineteen Eighty. Stockholm International Peace Research Institute Staff. 514p. 1980. 42.00x (ISBN 0-85066-201-X). Taylor & Francis.
SIPRI Yearbook: World Armaments & Disarmament, 1984. SIPRI Stockholm International Peace Research Institute. LC 83-643843. (Peace Studies). (Illus.). 650p. 1984. 62.00x (ISBN 0-85066-263-X). Taylor & Francis.
SIPRI Yearbook, 1979: World Armaments & Disarmament. SIPRI. 698p. 1979. 54.00x (ISBN 0-85066-181-1). Taylor & Francis.
SIPRI Yearbook, 1981: World Armaments & Disarmament. SIPRI. 518p. 1981. 50.00x (ISBN 0-85066-215-X). Taylor & Francis.
SIPRI Yearbook, 1982: World Armaments & Disarmament. SIPRI. 516p. 1982. 55.00x (ISBN 0-85066-230-3). Taylor & Francis.
SIPRI Yearbook, 1983: World Armaments & Disarmament. 14th ed. SIPRI. 500p. 1983. 58.00x (ISBN 0-85066-247-8). Taylor & Francis.
SIPRI Yearbook, 1988: World Armaments & Disarmament. Ed. by Stockholm International Peace Research Institute Staff. (Illus.). 500p. 1988. 72.00 (ISBN 0-19-829126-4). Oxford U Pr.
SIPRI Yearbooks, 1968-1979 Cumulative Index: World Armaments & Disarmament. SIPRI. 90p. 1980. 13.00x (ISBN 0-85066-189-7). Taylor & Francis.
Sips of Wein. Anna M. Weinreis. (Illus.). 48p. 1984. pap. 4.00 (ISBN 0-9610130-2-8, Pub. by Wein Cellar). Melius Peterson Pub.
Siquiatria de Dios. Charles L. Allen. 176p. 1975. 2.95 (ISBN 0-88113-280-2). Edit Betania.
Sir. Mildred Cram. 1973. 4.95 (ISBN 0-913270-11-3). Sunstone Pr.
Sir A. Sherley His Relation of Travels into Persia. Anthony Sherley. LC 74-80232. (English Experience Ser.: No. 695). 140p. 1974. Repr. of 1613 ed. 15.00 (ISBN 90-221-0695-0). Walter J Johnson.
Sir Alec Douglas-Home. Kenneth Young. LC 76-167748. (Illus.). 282p. 1971. 22.50 (ISBN 0-8386-1041-2). Fairleigh Dickinson.
Sir Alexander Fleming: Man of Penicillin. John Malkin. 92p. 1985. 30.00x (ISBN 0-907526-06-3, Pub. by Alloway Pub). State Mutual Bk.
Sir Arthur Conan Doyle: L'Homme Et L'Oeuvre. Pierre Nordon. 481p. 1985. Repr. of 1984 ed. lib. bdg. 100.00 (ISBN 0-89987-615-3). Darby Bks.
Sir Arthur Evans: An Illustrated Memoir. D. B. Harden. 52p. 1983. 20.00x (ISBN 0-900090-86-3, Pub. by Ashmolean Museum). State Mutual Bk.
Sir Arthur Evans: An Illustrated Memoir. D. B. Harden. (Illus.). 48p. (Orig.). 1983. pap. 6.50 (ISBN 0-317-58654-8, Pub. by Ashmolean Mus). Longwood Pub Group.
Sir Arthur Pinero, a Critical Biography with Letters. Wilbur D. Dunkel. LC 67-27594. 1941. Repr. 16.50x (ISBN 0-8046-0123-2, Pub. by Kennikat). Assoc Faculty Pr.
Sir Arthur Sullivan. Arthur Lawrence. LC 79-27876. (Music Reprint 1980 Ser.). (Illus.). 340p. 1980. Repr. of 1900 ed. lib. bdg. 39.50 (ISBN 0-306-76029-0). Da Capo.
Sir Arthur Sullivan. Arthur Lawrence. LC 72-3244. (English Biography Ser.: No. 31). 1972. Repr. of 1899 ed. lib. bdg. 56.95x (ISBN 0-8383-1522-4). Haskell.
Sir Arthur Sullivan: An Index to His Vocal Works. Sirvart Poladian. (Detroit Studies in Music Bibliography Ser.: No. 2). 1961. pap. 6.00 (ISBN 0-911772-22-7). Harmonie Pk Pr.
Sir Arthur Sullivan: His Life & Music. Benjamin W. Findon. 1976. Repr. of 1904 ed. 23.00 (ISBN 0-404-12913-7). AMS Pr.
Sir Aurel Stein: A Biography. Jeannette Mirsky. LC 76-17703. 1977. 25.00x (ISBN 0-226-53176-7). U of Chicago Pr.
Sir Baldergog the Great. Ruth Beni. (Illus.). 32p. (gr. 1-3). 1985. 10.95 (ISBN 0-233-97628-0). Andre Deutsch.
Sir Bertie & the Wyvern: A Tale of Heraldry. Nicholas Wilde. LC 84-7779. (Carolrhoda Good Time Library). (Illus.). 64p. (gr. 4 up). 1984. PLB 8.95 (ISBN 0-87614-273-0). Carolrhoda Bks.
Sir Beves of Hamtoun: A Metrical Romance. Ed. by W. B. Turnbull. LC 72-144415. Repr. of 1838 ed. 17.50 (ISBN 0-404-53022-2). AMS Pr.
Sir Brooke Fossbrooke, 3 vols. in 2. Charles J. Lever. LC 79-8422. Repr. of 1866 ed. Set. 84.50 (ISBN 0-404-61971-1). Vol. 1 (ISBN 0-404-61972-X). Vol. 2 (ISBN 0-404-61973-8). AMS Pr.
Sir Cecil & the Bad Blue Beast. Glen Dines. LC 70-125868. (Illus.). (gr. k-2). 1970. 14.95 (ISBN 0-87599-175-0). S G Phillips.
Sir Cedric. Roy Gerrard. LC 84-6111. (Illus.). 32p. (ps up). 12.95 (ISBN 0-374-36959-3). FS&G.
Sir Cedric. Roy Gerrard. (Illus.). 32p. (gr. k-3). 1986. pap. 3.95 (ISBN 0-374-46659-9, Sunburst). FS&G.
Sir Cedric Rides Again. Roy Gerrard. (Illus.). 32p. (ps up). 1986. 12.95 (ISBN 0-374-36961-5). FS&G.
Sir Cedric Rides Again. Roy Gerrard. (Illus.). 32p. (ps up). 1988. 11.95 (ISBN 0-317-69890-7, Sunburst); pap. 4.95 (ISBN 0-374-46662-9, Sunburst). FS&G.
Sir Charles Arden-Clarke. David Rooney. 236p. 1982. text ed. 12.50 (ISBN 0-89874-598-5). Krieger.
Sir Charles Eastlake & the Victorian Art World. David Robertson. LC 75-43797. (Illus.). 1978. text ed. 90.50x (ISBN 0-691-03902-X). Princeton U Pr.
Sir Charles God Damn: The Life of Sir Charles G. D. Roberts. John C. Adams. 264p. 1986. 24.95 (ISBN 0-8020-2595-1). U of Toronto Pr.
Sir Charles Grandison. Jane Austen. Ed. by Brian Southam. (Illus.). 1980. 28.00x (ISBN 0-19-812637-9). Oxford U Pr.
Sir Charles Grandison. Samuel Richardson. Ed. & intro. by Jocelyn Harris. (World's Classics Ser.). 1728p. 1986. pap. 13.95 (ISBN 0-19-281745-0). Oxford U Pr.
Sir Charles Grandison: The Compleat Conduct Book. Sylvia K. Marks. LC 85-47800. 176p. 1986. 27.50x (ISBN 0-8387-5090-7). Bucknell U Pr.
Sir Charles J. Jackson's Silver & Gold Marks of England, Scotland & Ireland. Ed. by Ian Pickford. 1988. 89.50 (ISBN 0-907462-63-4). Antique Collect.
Sir Charles Sedley, 1639-1701. Vivian De Sola Pinto. 1988. Repr. of 1927 ed. lib. bdg. 49.00x. Am Biog Serv.
Sir Charles Sedley, 1639-1701. Vivian De Sola Pinto. (Illus.). 1971. Repr. of 1927 ed. 27.00x (ISBN 0-403-01150-7). Scholarly.
Sir Charles Sedley, 1639-1701: A Study in the Life & Literature of the Restoration. Vivian de Sola Pinto. LC 76-85904. Repr. of 1927 ed. 28.45 (ISBN 0-404-05056-5). AMS Pr.
Sir Charles V. Stanford. J. F. Porte. LC 76-12570. (Music Reprint Ser.). 1976. Repr. of 1921 ed. lib. bdg. 25.00 (ISBN 0-306-70790-X). Da Capo.
Sir Charles V. Stanford. John F. Porte. 1984. Repr. of 1921 ed. lib. bdg. 20.00 (ISBN 0-89341-415-8). Longwood Pub Group.
Sir Claude MacDonald, the Open Door, & British Informal Empire in China, 1895-1900. Mary H. Wilgus. Ed. by William H. McNeill & Peter Stansky. (Modern European History Ser.). 350p. 1987. lib. bdg. 55.00 (ISBN 0-8240-7837-3). Garland Pub.
Sir Cleges: Sir Libeaus. Tr. by Jessie L. Weston. LC 72-141787. Repr. of 1902 ed. 22.50 (ISBN 0-404-00476-8). AMS Pr.
Sir Constantine Huygens & Britain: 1597-1619, Vol. 1. A. G. Bachrach. (Publications of the Sir Thomas Browne Institute Ser: No. 1). 1962. 26.00 (ISBN 90-6021-059-X, Pub. by Leiden Univ Holland). Kluwer Academic.
Sir Cornelius Vermuyden: The Lifework of a Great Anglo-Dutchman in Land-Reclamation & Drainage, with Some Notes by the Author on the Present Condition of Drainage in England & a Resume of the Drainage Legislation in Holland. J. Korthals-Altes. Ed. by Mira Wilkins. LC 76-29751. (European Business Ser.). (Illus.). 1977. Repr. of 1925 ed. lib. bdg. 23.50 (ISBN 0-405-09767-0). Ayer Co Pubs.
Sir Dana - A Knight: As Told by His Trusty Armor. Dana Fradon. (Illus.). 32p. (gr. 3-7). 1988. 13.95 (ISBN 0-525-44424-6, 01354-410). Dutton.
Sir David Salomons: Sound of Bow Bells. Robert D. Abrahams. LC 62-12320. (Covenant Ser.). 158p. (gr. 6-10). 1962. 3.50 (ISBN 0-8276-0159-X, 286). JPS Phila.
Sir David Wilkie of Scotland (1785-1841) William J. Chiego et al. LC 86-63234. (Illus.). xix, 370p. 1987. pap. 24.95 (ISBN 0-88259-953-4). NCMA.
Sir David Wilkie, Seventeen Eighty-Five to Eighteen Forty-One: A Catalogue Raisonne of the Paintings & Drawings in the Ashmolean, to Mark the Bi-Centenary of the Artist's Birth. D. B. Brown. (Illus.). 120p. (Orig.). 1985. pap. 10.50x (ISBN 0-907849-11-3, Pub. by Ashmolean Museum). State Mutual Bk.
Sir David Wilkie (Seventeen Eighty-Five to Eighteen Forty-One: A Catalogue Raisonne of the Paintings & Drawings in the Ashmolean to Mark the Bi-Centenary of the Artist's Birth. D. B. Brown. (Illus.). 120p. (Orig.). 1985. pap. 14.75 (ISBN 0-317-58659-9, Pub. by Ashmolean Mus). Longwood Pub Group.
Sir Don Bradman. David Frith. 192p. 1986. 65.00x (ISBN 0-946771-36-7, Pub. by Spellmount Ltd Pubs). State Mutual Bk.
Sir Donald Cameron: Colonial Governor. Harry A. Gailey. LC 74-7301. (Publications Ser.: No. 139). 181p. 1974. 10.95x (ISBN 0-8179-6391-X). Hoover Inst Pr.
Sir Edmund Gosse. James D. Woolf. LC 79-125822. (English Authors Ser.). lib. bdg. 17.95 (ISBN 0-89197-937-9); pap. text ed. 6.95x (ISBN 0-8290-2024-1). Irvington.
Sir Edmund Orme see Altar of the Dead.
Sir Edward Burne-Jones: A Record & Review. Malcolm Bell. Repr. of 1898 ed. 16.00 (ISBN 0-404-00733-3). AMS Pr.
Sir Edward Coke & "The Grievances of the Commonwealth," 1621-1628. Stephen D. White. LC 78-16418. (Studies in Legal History). xv, 327p. 1979. 32.50x (ISBN 0-8078-1335-4). U of NC Pr.
Sir Edward Elgar. facsimile ed. John F. Porte. LC 75-107827. (Select Bibliographies Reprint Ser). (Illus.). Repr. of 1921 ed. 19.00 (ISBN 0-8369-5194-8). Ayer Co Pubs.
Sir Edward Elgar. John F. Porte. LC 102843. (Illus.). 1970. Repr. of 1921 ed. 22.50x (ISBN 0-8046-0763-X, Pub. by Kennikat). Assoc Faculty Pr.
Sir Edward Seaward's Narrative of His Shipwreck, 3 vols. facsimile ed. Edward Seaward. Ed. by Jane Porter. LC 79-164393. (Black Heritage Library Collection). Repr. of 1831 ed. Set. 71.50 (ISBN 0-8369-8852-3). Ayer Co Pubs.
Sir Edwyn Hoskyns As a Biblical Theologian. Richard E. Parsons. LC 85-25038. 152p. 1986. 25.00 (ISBN 0-312-72647-3). St Martin.
Sir Eglamore & the Dragon. Lisl Beer. (Silver Series of Puppet Plays). pap. 1.50 (ISBN 0-8283-1245-1). Branden Pub Co.
Sir Eglamour. Eglamour. Ed. by Albert S. Cook. 1911. 29.50x (ISBN 0-685-69803-3). Elliots Bks.
Sir Eldon Gorst: The Overshadowed Proconsul. Peter Mellini. LC 76-51878. (Publication Ser: No. 178). (Illus.). 1977. 12.95x (ISBN 0-8179-6781-8). Hoover Inst Pr.
Sir Ferdinando Gorges (1565-1647) & His Province of Maine, 3 vols. James P. Baxter. 1966. Set. 62.00 (ISBN 0-8337-0190-8). B Franklin.
Sir Francis Bacon. Jean O. Fuller. 384p. 1982. 49.00x (ISBN 0-85692-069-X, Pub. by E-W Pubns England). State Mutual Bk.
Sir Francis Bacon. Byron Steel. 1930. 30.00 (ISBN 0-8274-3419-7). R West.
Sir Francis Bacon. Parker Woodward. 1920. 25.00 (ISBN 0-8274-3420-0). R West.
Sir Francis Drake. British Library Staff. (Illus.). 128p. (Orig.). 1977. pap. 6.00 (ISBN 0-7141-0393-4, Pub. by British Lib). Longwood Pub Group.
Sir Francis Drake. J. S. Corbett. LC 68-25228. (English Biography Ser., No. 31). 1969. Repr. of 1890 ed. lib. bdg. 49.95x (ISBN 0-8383-0932-1). Haskell.
Sir Francis Drake. Julian S. Corbett. LC 77-105513. (BCL Ser. II). Repr. of 1890 ed. 10.00 (ISBN 0-404-01725-8). AMS Pr.
Sir Francis Drake. Jason Hook. Ed. by Janet Caulkins. (Great Lives Ser.). (Illus.). 32p. (gr. 1-6). 1988. 10.40 (ISBN 0-531-18202-9, Pub. by Bookwright Pr). Watts.
Sir Francis Drake. George M. Thomson. (Illus.). 368p. (Orig.). 1988. 29.95 (ISBN 0-233-98205-1, Pub. by A Deutsch England); pap. 17.95 (ISBN 0-233-98290-6, Pub. by A Deutsch England). David & Charles.
Sir Francis Drake & the Famous Voyage, 1577-1580: Essays Commemorating the Quadricentennial of Drake's Circumnavigation of the Earth. Ed. by Norman J. Thrower. LC 83-10446. (Center for Medieval & Renaissance Studies, UCLA: Contributions: No. 11). 240p. 1984. 40.00x (ISBN 0-520-04876-8). U of Cal Pr.
Sir Francis Drake: His Daring Deeds. Roy Gerrard. (Illus.). 32p. (gr. 3 up). 1988. 12.95 (ISBN 0-374-36962-3). FS&G.
Sir Francis Drake, His Voyage, Fifteen Ninety-Five. Thomas Maynarde. Ed. by W. D. Cooley. LC 70-141352. (Hakluyt Soc. Ser: No. 4). 1971. Repr. of 1849 ed. lib. bdg. 22.50 (ISBN 0-8337-2308-1). B Franklin.
Sir Francis Galton & the Study of Heredity in the Nineteenth Century. Ruth S. Cowan. Ed. by Charles Rosenberg. LC 83-48624. (History of Hereditarian Thought Ser.). 289p. 1985. lib. bdg. 35.00 (ISBN 0-8240-5802-X). Garland Pub.
Sir Francis Hincks: A Study of Canadian Politics, Railways, & Finance in the Nineteenth Century. Ronald S. Longley. Ed. by Stuart Bruchey. LC 80-1326. (Railroads Ser.). 1981. Repr. of 1943 ed. lib. bdg. 40.00x (ISBN 0-405-13800-8). Ayer Co Pubs.
Sir Frederic Madden: A Bibliography & Biographical Sketch. Robert W. Ackerman & Gretchen P. Ackerman. LC 78-68237. 150p. 1979. lib. bdg. 22.00 (ISBN 0-8240-9819-6). Garland Pub.
Sir Gawain & the Green Knight. Ed. by W. R. Barron. LC 74-21. (Manchester Medieval Classics Ser). 179p. 1976. pap. text ed. 11.95x (ISBN 0-06-490311-7, 06341). B&N Imports.
Sir Gawain & the Green Knight. Tr. by Marie Borroff. (Orig.). 1967. pap. 3.95x (ISBN 0-393-09754-4, NortonC). Norton.
Sir Gawain & the Green Knight. Ed. by J. A. Burrow. Tr. by Stone. (Classics Ser.). 176p. 1987. pap. 5.95 (ISBN 0-14-042295-1). Penguin.
Sir Gawain & the Green Knight. Selina Hastings. LC 80-85379. (Illus.). 32p. (gr. 3-7). 1981. 11.75 (ISBN 0-688-00592-6). Lothrop.
Sir Gawain & the Green Knight. James R. Kreuzer. LC 59-6208. (Rinehart Editions). 1959. pap. text ed. 9.50 (ISBN 0-03-008880-1, HoltC). HR&W.
Sir Gawain & the Green Knight. Burton Raffel. (Orig.). 1970. pap. 2.50 (ISBN 0-451-62456-4, ME2312, Ment). NAL.
Sir Gawain & the Green Knight. Dennis Scott. (gr. k up). 1978. 4.00 (ISBN 0-87602-202-6). Anchorage.
Sir Gawain & the Green Knight. Dennis Scott. (Illus.). 1979. 9.95 (ISBN 0-930970-01-2); pap. 4.95 (ISBN 0-930970-02-0). O'Neill Pr.
Sir Gawain & the Green Knight. 2nd ed. Ed. by J. R. Tolkien & E. V. Gordon. 1967. pap. 8.95x (ISBN 0-19-811486-9). Oxford U Pr.
Sir Gawain & the Green Knight. Ed. by R. A. Waldron. LC 75-129568. (York Medieval Texts Ser). 1970. text ed. 14.95x (ISBN 0-8101-0327-3). Northwestern U Pr.
Sir Gawain & the Green Knight. Tr. by Jessie L. Weston. LC 70-135732. Repr. of 1898 ed. 22.50 (ISBN 0-404-00471-7). AMS Pr.
Sir Gawain & the Green Knight: A New Critical Edition. Ed. by Theodore Silverstein. LC 83-9126. 290p. 1984. lib. bdg. 30.00x (ISBN 0-226-75767-6); pap. text ed. 15.00x (ISBN 0-226-75768-4). U of Chicago Pr.

Sir Gawain & the Green Knight: A Reference Guide. Robert J. Blanch. LC 82-50412. 300p. 1984. 22.50x (ISBN 0-87875-244-7). Whitston Pub.
Sir Gawain & the Green Knight Notes. John C. Gardner. (Orig.). 1967. pap. 3.50 (ISBN 0-8220-0515-8). Cliffs.
Sir Gawain & the Green Knight: Pearl Poet. Pearl Poet. Ed. by J. A. Burrow. (English Poets Ser.: No. 13). 176p. 1982. text ed. 18.00t (ISBN 0-300-02906-3); pap. 6.95x (ISBN 0-300-02907-1, YEP-13). Yale U Pr.
Sir Gawain & the Lady of Lys. Tr. by Jessie L. Weston. LC 70-141789. Repr. of 1907 ed. 22.50 (ISBN 0-404-00478-4). AMS Pr.
Sir Gawain & the Loathly Lady. Selina Hastings. LC 85-63. (Illus.). 32p. (gr. 3-7). 1985. 13.00 (ISBN 0-688-05823-X). Lothrop.
Sir Gawain & the Loathly Lady. (ps-7). 1987. pap. 3.95 (ISBN 0-688-07046-9, Mulberry Bks). Macmillan.
Sir Gawain at the Grail Castle. Tr. by Jessie L. Weston. LC 76-141788. Repr. of 1903 ed. 22.50 (ISBN 0-404-00477-6). AMS Pr.
Sir George Alexander & the St. James' Theatre. Alfred E. Mason. LC 72-84520. (Illus.). 1935. 22.00 (ISBN 0-405-08762-4, Pub. by Blom). Ayer Co Pubs.
Sir George Arthur Bart, Seventeen Eighty-Four to Eighteen Fifty-Four. A. G. Shaw. 1980. 37.50x (ISBN 0-522-84195-3, Pub. by Melbourne Univ Pr Australia). Intl Spec Bk.
Sir George Beaumont: A Collector of Genius. David Brown & Felicity Owen. LC 87-26114. 256p. 1988. text ed. 37.50 (ISBN 0-300-04183-7). Yale U Pr.
Sir George Etheredge Sein Leben, Seine Zeit & Seine Dramen. Vincenz Meindl. pap. 25.00 (ISBN 0-384-38020-4). Johnson Repr.
Sir George Etheredge, Sein Leben, Seine Zeit und Seine Dramen. Vincenz Meindl. (Ger.). 1978. Repr. of 1901 ed. 65.00 (ISBN 0-8492-6749-8). R West.
Sir George Etherege. Arthur R. Huseboe. (Twayne's English Authors Ser.: No. 446). 160p. 1987. lib. bdg. 24.95 (ISBN 0-8057-6946-3, Twayne). G K Hall.
Sir George Etherege. Frances S. McCamic. LC 74-19349. 1931. lib. bdg. 17.50 (ISBN 0-8414-5924-X). Folcroft.
Sir George Etherege: A Reference Guide. David D. Mann. 1981. lib. bdg. 28.00 (ISBN 0-8161-8171-3, Hall Reference). G K Hall.
Sir George Etienne Cartier, Bart. His Life & Times. facsimile ed. John Boyd. LC 74-164590. (Select Bibliographies Reprint Ser.). Repr. of 1914 ed. 44.00 (ISBN 0-8369-5874-8). Ayer Co Pubs.
Sir George Goldie, Founder of Nigeria: A Memoir. Dorothy Violet Wellington. Ed. by Mira Wilkins. LC 76-29765. (European Business Ser.). (Illus.). 1977. Repr. of 1934 ed. lib. bdg. 18.00x (ISBN 0-405-09779-4). Ayer Co Pubs.
Sir George Otto Trevelyan: A Memoir. George M. Trevelyn. 1932. Repr. 25.00 (ISBN 0-8274-3424-3). R West.
Sir Gibbie. George MacDonald. Ed. by Elizabeth Yates. LC 79-64123. (YA) (gr. 7-12). 1979. pap. 8.95 (ISBN 0-8052-0637-X). Schocken.
Sir Giles Goosecap. LC 70-133738. (Tudor Facsimile Texts. Old English Plays: No. 112). Repr. of 1912 ed. 49.50 (ISBN 0-404-53412-0). AMS Pr.
Sir Godfrey Kneller. J. Stewart. (Illus.). 12.00 (ISBN 0-912729-05-8). Newbury Bks.
Sir Godfrey Kneller & the English Baroque Portrait. J. Douglas Stewart. (Oxford Studies in the History of Art & Architecture). 1983. 89.00x (ISBN 0-19-817356-3). Oxford U Pr.
Sir Gyles Goosecappe, 1606, Pt. 1. Ed. by W. Bang & R. Brotanek. (Material for the Study of the Old English Drama Ser.: No. 1, Vol. 26). pap. 11.00 (ISBN 0-8115-0275-9). Kraus Repr.
Sir Hans Sloane & the British Museum. G. R. De Beer. LC 74-26258. (History, Philosophy & Sociology of Science Ser.). (Illus.). 1975. Repr. of 1953 ed. 22.00x (ISBN 0-405-06586-8). Ayer Co Pubs.
Sir Harry Hotspur of Humblethwaite. Anthony Trollope. Ed. by N. John Hall. LC 80-1891. (Selected Works of Anthony Trollope Ser.). 1981. Repr. of 1871 ed. lib. bdg. 35.00 (ISBN 0-405-14158-0). Ayer Co Pubs.
Sir Harry Hotspur of Humblethwaite. Anthony Trollope. 248p. 1985. pap. 5.95 (ISBN 0-486-24953-0). Dover.
Sir Henry. Robert Nathan. LC 79-12787. 187p. 1979. lib. bdg. 17.95x (ISBN 0-89370-136-X); pap. 7.95x (ISBN 0-89370-236-6). Borgo Pr.
Sir Henry Maine: A Brief Memoir of His Life. M. E. Grant Duff. Ed. by Whitley Stokes. 451p. 1979. Repr. of 1892 ed. lib. bdg. 35.00x (ISBN 0-8377-0609-2). Rothman.
Sir Henry Maine: A Study in Victorian Jurisprudence. Raymond Cocks. (Cambridge Studies in English Legal History). 248p. Date not set. price not set (ISBN 0-521-35343-2). Cambridge U Pr.
Sir Henry Morgan, Buccaneer. Cyrus T. Brady. 445p. Repr. of 1903 ed. lib. bdg. 24.95x (ISBN 0-88411-175-X, Pub. by Aeonian Pr). Amereon Ltd.
Sir Henry Morgan, the Buccaneer, 3 vols. in 2. Edward G. Howard. LC 79-8136. Repr. of 1842 ed. Set. 84.50 (ISBN 0-404-61923-1). AMS Pr.
Sir Henry Vane the Younger: A Study in Political & Administrative History. Violet A. Rowe. 298p. 1970. 60.00 (ISBN 0-485-13128-5, Pub. by Athlone Pr UK). Humanities.
Sir Henry Wotton: A Biographical Sketch. Adolphus W. Ward. LC 73-1247. 1973. lib. bdg. 27.50 (ISBN 0-8414-2806-9). Folcroft.
Sir Humfrey Gylberte & His Enterprise of Colonization in America. Ed. by Carlos Slafter. 1966. 24.00 (ISBN 0-8337-3286-2). B Franklin.
Sir Humphrey Davy's Published Works. June Z. Fullmer. LC 69-18029. 1969. text ed. 11.00x (ISBN 0-674-80961-0). Harvard U Pr.
Sir, I Represent Christian Salesmanship. William E. Cox. pap. 1.50 (ISBN 0-686-64392-5). Reiner.
Sir, I'm Worried about Your Mood Swings. G. B. Trudeau. 128p. 1984. pap. 2.25 (ISBN 0-449-20198-8, Crest). Fawcett.
SIR Industrial Real Estate Market Survey, Fall-Winter 1983. Society of Industrial Realtors Staff & National Association of Realtors Staff. 213p. 1984. 10.00 (ISBN 0-939623-12-9). Soc Industrial Realtors.
SIR Industrial Real Estate Market Survey, Fall-Winter 1984. Society of Industrial Realtors Staff & National Association of Realtors Staff. 234p. 1984. 10.00 (ISBN 0-939623-14-5). Soc Industrial Realtors.
SIR Industrial Real Estate Market Survey, Fall-Winter 1985. Society of Industrial Realtors Staff & National Association of Realtors Staff. 226p. 1985. 10.00 (ISBN 0-939623-16-1). Soc Industrial Realtors.
SIR Industrial Real Estate Market Survey, Fall 1981. Society of Industrial Realtors Staff & National Association of Realtors Staff. 106p. 1981. 10.00 (ISBN 0-939623-09-9). Soc Industrial Realtors.
SIR Industrial Real Estate Market Survey, May 1980. Society of Industrial Realtors Staff & National Association of Realtors Staff. 69p. 1980. 10.00 (ISBN 0-939623-07-2). Soc Industrial Realtors.
SIR Industrial Real Estate Market Survey, Spring-Summer 1983. Society of Industrial Realtors Staff & National Association of Realtors Staff. 218p. 1983. 10.00 (ISBN 0-939623-11-0). Soc Industrial Realtors.
SIR Industrial Real Estate Market Survey, Spring-Summer 1984. Society of Industrial Realtors Staff & National Association of Realtors Staff. 196p. 1984. 10.00 (ISBN 0-939623-13-7). Soc Industrial Realtors.
SIR Industrial Real Estate Market Survey, Spring-Summer 1985. Society of Industrial Realtors Staff & National Association of Realtors Staff. 236p. 1985. 10.00 (ISBN 0-939623-15-3). Soc Industrial Realtors.
SIR Industrial Real Estate Market Survey, Spring-Summer 1986. Society of Industrial Realtors Staff & National Association of Realtors Staff. 220p. 1984. 10.00 (ISBN 0-939623-17-X). Soc Industrial Realtors.
SIR Industrial Real Estate Market Survey, Spring 1981. Society of Industrial Realtors Staff & National Association of Realtors Staff. 102p. 1981. 10.00 (ISBN 0-939623-08-0). Soc Industrial Realtors.
SIR Industrial Real Estate Market Survey, Spring 1982. Society of Industrial Realtors Staff & National Association of Realtors Staff. 120p. 1982. 10.00 (ISBN 0-939623-10-2). Soc Industrial Realtors.
Sir Isaac Newton. S. Brodetsky. 1927. Repr. 20.00 (ISBN 0-8274-3425-1). R West.
Sir Isaac Newton's Mathematical Principles of Natural Philosophy & His System of the World. Isaac Newton. Tr. by Andrew Motte. 1962. Greenwood.
Sir J. M. Barrie: His First Editions, Points & Values. Andrew Block. LC 73-15690. 1933. lib. bdg. 15.00 (ISBN 0-8414-3292-9). Folcroft.
Sir Jadunath Sarkar: A Profile in Historiography. Kiran Pawar. 225p. 1986. 19.00X (Pub. by Meenaksi India). South Asia Bks.
Sir James Barrie: A Bibliography with Full Collations of the American Unauthorized Editions. Bradley D. Cutler. 1967. Repr. of 1931 ed. 24.50 (ISBN 0-8337-0748-5). B Franklin.
Sir James Gowans: Romantic Rationalist. Duncan McAra. 1977. 12.95 (ISBN 0-8464-0851-1). Beekman Pubs.
Sir James Y. Simpson. Eve B. Simpson. 160p. 1980. Repr. lib. bdg. 20.00 (ISBN 0-89987-755-9). Darby Bks.
Sir John Betjeman: A Bibliography of Writings by & about Him. Margaret L. Stapleton. (Author Bibliographies Ser.: No. 21). 149p. 1974. 17.50 (ISBN 0-8108-0758-0). Scarecrow.
Sir John Beverley Robinson: Bone & Sinew of the Compact. Patrick Brode. (Publications of the Osgoode Society). 344p. 1984. 45.00x (ISBN 0-8020-3406-3); pap. 15.95 (ISBN 0-8020-3419-5). U of Toronto Pr.
Sir John Chardin's Travels in Persia. John Chardin. LC 76-181928. (BCL Ser.: No. I). Repr. of 1927 ed. 24.50 (ISBN 0-404-01449-6). AMS Pr.
Sir John Davies & the Conquest of Ireland: A Study in Legal Imperialism. Hans H. Pawlisch. (Studies in the History & Theory of Politics). 263p. 1985. 42.50 (ISBN 0-521-25328-4). Cambridge U Pr.
Sir John Falstaff Knight. Rupin W. Desai. LC 75-5210. (Comparative Literature Studies Ser). (Illus.). 133p. pap. 10.00 (ISBN 0-87423-013-6). Westburg.
Sir John Hawkins: Samuel Johnson. C. A. Miller. LC 72-10377. 1951. lib. bdg. 17.00 (ISBN 0-8414-0450-X). Folcroft.
Sir John Hawkins, the Time & the Man. James A. Williamson. 1970. Repr. of 1927 ed. lib. bdg. 35.00 (ISBN 0-8371-4569-4, WIJH). Greenwood.
Sir John Hicks: Critical Assessments, 4 vols. John Cunningham & Ronald N. Woods. (Critical Assessments Ser.). 400p. 1988. Set. lib. bdg. 585.00 (ISBN 0-7099-5243-0). Routledge Chapman & Hall.
Sir John Jeffcott. R. M. Hague. 1963. 11.00x (ISBN 0-522-83623-2, Pub. by Melbourne U Pr). Intl Spec Bk.
Sir John Magill's Last Journey. Freeman W. Crofts. Incl. Vols. 1-3. 72p. 1972-75. Repr. avail. (0039); Vols. 4-7. 120p. 1975-79 (0050). 301p. 1977. Repr. lib. bdg. 13.95x (ISBN 0-89966-274-9). Buccaneer Bks.
Sir John Mandeville: The Man & His Book. Malcolm Letts. 1949. Repr. lib. bdg. 35.00 (ISBN 0-8414-5856-1). Folcroft.
Sir John Mandeville: The Man & His Book. Malcolm Letts. LC 70-161957. 192p. 1949. Repr. 25.00 (ISBN 0-403-01318-6). Scholarly.
Sir John Oldcastle. Michael Drayton et al. LC 72-133657. (Tudor Facsimile Texts. Old English Plays: No. 89). Repr. of 1911 ed. 49.50 (ISBN 0-404-53389-2). AMS Pr.
Sir John Paston's Grete Boke: A Descriptive Catalogue with an Introduction, of British Library Ms. Lansdowne 285. G. A. Lester. 197p. 1984. 36.00 (ISBN 0-85991-161-6, Pub. by Boydell & Brewer). Longwood Pub Group.
Sir John Richardson, FRS (Seventeen Eighty-Seven to Eighteen Sixty-Five) Artic Explorer, Natural Historian, Naval Surgeon. Robert E. Johnson. 300p. 1976. 55.00x (ISBN 0-85066-074-2). Taylor & Francis.
Sir John Robert Seeley: A Study of the Historian. G. A. Rein. Ed. by John L. Herkless. 1983. 25.00 (ISBN 0-89341-550-2). Longwood Pub Group.
Sir John Sloane: Seventeen Fifty-Three to Eighteen Thirty-Seven. John N. Summerson. LC 52-11842. 96p. 1952. Repr. 29.00 (ISBN 0-403-07225-5). Somerset Pub.
Sir John Soane, Architect. Dorothy Stroud. LC 83-11488. (Illus.). 288p. 1984. 73.00 (ISBN 0-571-13050-X). Faber & Faber.
Sir John Soane's Museum. Susan F. Millenson. Ed. by Stephen Foster. LC 86-24926. (Architecture & Urban Design: No. 18). 199p. 1986. 49.95 (ISBN 0-8357-1766-6). UMI Res Pr.
Sir John Vanbrugh: A Biography. Kerry Downes. 560p. 1988. 29.95 (ISBN 0-312-01825-8, Pub. by Thomas Dunne Bks). St Martin.
Sir John Vanbrugh, Architect & Dramatist, 1664-1726. L. Whistler. Repr. of 1938 ed. 23.00 (ISBN 0-527-95850-6). Kraus Repr.
Sir Joseph Banks & Iceland. Halldor Hermannsson. LC 28-11080. (Islandica Ser.: Vol. 18). 1928. 20.00 (ISBN 0-527-00348-4). Kraus Repr.
Sir Joseph Banks & the Plant Collection from Kew Sent to the Empress Catherine II of Russia 1795. H. B. Carter. (Bulletin of the British Museum Natural History, Historical Ser.: Vol. 4, No. 5). (Illus.). 1975. text ed. 26.00x (ISBN 0-565-00768-8, Pub. by Brit Mus Nat Hist); pap. text ed. 20.00x (ISBN 0-8277-4351-3). Sabbot-Natural Hist Bks.
Sir Joshua Reynolds. Claude Phillips. 1980. Repr. of 1894 ed. lib. bdg. 45.00 (ISBN 0-89341-378-X). Longwood Pub Group.
Sir Joshua Reynolds. John Steegman. LC 77-17594. 1977. Repr. of 1933 ed. lib. bdg. 25.00 (ISBN 0-8414-7867-8). Folcroft.
Sir Joshua Reynolds: Discourses on Art. Robert R. Wark. LC 74-17647. (Paul Mellon Center for Studies in British Art Ser.). (Illus.). 384p. 1981. pap. 18.95x (ISBN 0-300-02775-3, Y-411). Yale U Pr.
Sir Joshua's Nephew. Susan M. Radcliffe. 1973. Repr. of 1930 ed. 35.00 (ISBN 0-8274-1399-8). R West.
Sir Josiah Child, Merchant Economist. William Letwin. (Kress Library Publications: No. 14). (Illus.). 1959. pap. 8.95x (ISBN 0-678-09909-X, Baker Lib). Kelley.
Sir Kenelm Digby & His Venetia. E. W. Bligh. 1932. Repr. 20.00 (ISBN 0-8274-3428-6). R West.
Sir Lancelot of the Lake. Lucy A. Paton. LC 74-8340. 1929. lib. bdg. 57.00 (ISBN 0-8414-6774-9). Folcroft.
Sir Lionel. Fred Archer. (Illus.). 339p. 1980. 12.95 (ISBN 0-86595-005-9). Gift Pubns.
Sir Maggie, the Mighty. Michael Waite. LC 87-35527. (Building Christian Character Ser.). (Illus.). 32p. (ps-2). 1988. 5.95 (ISBN 1-55513-616-8, Chariot Bks). Cook.
Sir Mortimer. Mary Johnston. 1978. Repr. of 1904 ed. lib. bdg. 20.00 (ISBN 0-8495-2709-0). Arden Lib.
Sir Mortimer. Mary Johnston. 1904. Repr. lib. bdg. 49.00 (ISBN 0-8414-5422-1). Folcroft.
Sir Moses Montefiore Seventeen Eighty-Four to Eighteen Eighty-Five. Myrtle Franklin & Michael Bor. (Illus.). 129p. 1985. 29.95 (ISBN 0-8149-0902-7). Vanguard.
Sir Nigel. Arthur Conan Doyle. 21.95 (ISBN 0-88411-538-0, Pub. by Aeonian Pr). Amereon Ltd.
Sir Oliver Lodge: Psychical Researcher & Scientist. W. P. Jolly. LC 74-24803. 256p. 1975. 22.50 (ISBN 0-8386-1703-4). Fairleigh Dickinson.
Sir Oliver Lodge Returns. Robert R. Leichtman. (From Heaven to Earth Ser.). (Illus.). 96p. (Orig.). 1979. pap. 3.50 (ISBN 0-89804-056-6). Ariel OH.
Sir Oliver Mowat: A Biographical Sketch, 2 vols. Charles R. Biggar. LC 71-136404. (BCL Ser. I). Repr. of 1905 ed. Set. 75.00 (ISBN 0-404-00858-5). Vol. 1 (ISBN 0-404-08021-9). Vol. 2 (ISBN 0-404-08022-7). AMS Pr.
Sir Orfeo. Ed. by A. J. Bliss. (Illus.). 79p. 1981. Repr. of 1954 ed. lib. bdg. 35.00 (ISBN 0-8495-0486-4). Arden Lib.
Sir Owen Dixon: A Celebration. Stephen Ninian. 41p. 1986. pap. 7.50 (ISBN 0-522-84330-1, Pub. by Melbourne U Pr). Intl Spec BK.
Sir Percy Leads the Band. Orczy. 316p. 1985. Repr. of 1936 ed. lib. bdg. 35.00 (ISBN 0-89987-614-5). Darby Bks.
Sir Peter Scott. Julia Courtney. LC 88-2076. (People Who Have Helped the World Ser.). (Illus.). 68p. (gr. 5-6). 1989. PLB 12.45 (ISBN 1-55532-819-9). Stevens Inc.
Sir Philip Sidney. Percy Addleshaw. LC 77-113304. 1970. Repr. of 1909 ed. 29.75x (ISBN 0-8046-1005-3, Pub. by Kennikat). Assoc Faculty Pr.
Sir Philip Sidney. Henry R. Bourne. LC 73-14433. (Heroes of the Nation Ser.). Repr. of 1901 ed. AMS Pr.
Sir Philip Sidney. Kenneth Muir. Ed. by Bonamy Dobree et al. Bd. with Sir Thomas Wyatt. Sergio Baldi; Edmund Spenser. Rosemary Freeman. LC 63-63096. (British Writers & Their Work Ser: Vol. 8). viii, 125p. 1965. pap. 1.60x (ISBN 0-8032-5658-2, BB 457, Bison). U of Nebr Pr.
Sir Philip Sidney. John A. Symonds. LC 68-58401. (English Men of Letters). Repr. of 1887 ed. lib bdg. 7.80 (ISBN 0-404-51733-1). AMS Pr.
Sir Philip Sidney. John A. Symonds. 1973. lib. bdg. 17.00 (ISBN 0-8414-8026-5). Folcroft.
Sir Philip Sidney. John A. Symonds. LC 67-23878. 216p. 1968. Repr. of 1886 ed. 35.00x (ISBN 0-8103-3056-3). Gale.
Sir Philip Sidney. John A. Symonds. 59.95 (ISBN 0-8490-1055-1). Gordon Pr.
Sir Philip Sidney. John A. Symonds. (English Men of Letters). 1979. Repr. of 1902 ed. lib. bdg. 15.00 (ISBN 0-8492-8101-6). R West.
Sir Philip Sidney. Mona Wilson. LC 72-187163. 1950. lib. bdg. 30.00 (ISBN 0-8414-0525-5). Folcroft.
Sir Philip Sidney: A Concise Bibliography. Samuel A. Tannenbaum. LC 77-2725. 1977. Repr. of 1941 ed. lib. bdg. 25.50 (ISBN 0-8414-8559-3). Folcroft.
Sir Philip Sidney: A Concise Bibliography. Samuel A. Tannenbaum. 1979. Repr. of 1941 ed. lib. bdg. 22.50 (ISBN 0-8492-8400-7). R West.
Sir Philip Sidney: A Study in Colflict. C. Henry Warren. LC 67-30823. (English Biography Ser., No. 31). 1969. Repr. of 1936 ed. lib. bdg. 75.00x (ISBN 0-8383-0737-X). Haskell.
Sir Philip Sidney: An Anthology of Modern Criticism. Ed. by Dennis Kay. 352p. 1988. 72.00 (ISBN 0-19-811204-1). Oxford U Pr.
Sir Philip Sidney: An Apology for Poetry. Ed. by Visvanath Chatterjee. 96p. 1975. pap. 3.95x (ISBN 0-86125-617-4, Pub. by Orient Longman India). Apt Bks.
Sir Philip Sidney & the Arcadia. Marcus S. Goldman. 1934. lib. bdg. 16.00 (ISBN 0-8414-4655-5). Folcroft.
Sir Philip Sidney & the Interpretation of Renaissance Culture: The Poet in His Times & in Ours: A Collection of Critical & Scholarly Essays. Ed. by Gary F. Waller & Michael D. Moore. LC 84-12343. 158p. 1984. 26.50x (ISBN 0-389-20514-1). B&N Imports.
Sir Philip Sidney & the Poetics of Protestantism. Andrew D. Weiner. LC 78-25559. (Illus.). 1979. 19.75x (ISBN 0-8166-0873-3). U of Minn Pr.
Sir Philip Sidney: Arcadia. Philip Sidney. LC 78-85106. (Kent English Reprint Ser.: The Renaissance). 346p. 1971. pap. 7.75x (ISBN 0-87338-044-4). Kent St U Pr.
Sir Philip Sidney As a Literary Craftsman. Kenneth Myrick. LC 35-13065. x, 362p. 1966. pap. 6.95x (ISBN 0-8032-5140-8, BB 312, Bison). U of Nebr Pr.
Sir Philip Sidney En France. Albert W. Osborn. LC 74-30354. 1932. lib. bdg. 37.50 (ISBN 0-8414-6524-X). Folcroft.
Sir Philip Sidney: Rebellion in Arcadia. Richard C. McCoy. 1979. 33.00x (ISBN 0-8135-0869-X). Rutgers U Pr.
Sir Philip Sidney: Representative Elizabethan. Frederick S. Boas. 1955. lib. bdg. 15.00 (ISBN 0-8414-3153-1). Folcroft.
Sir Philip Sidney: Selected Prose & Poetry. 2nd ed. Ed. by Robert Kimbrough. LC 82-51093. 576p. 1983. text ed. 25.00 (ISBN 0-299-09130-9); pap. 12.95x (ISBN 0-299-09134-1). U of Wis Pr.

Sir Philip Sidney: Servant of God. Anna M. Stoddart. 1973. Repr. of 1894 ed. 30.00 (ISBN 0-8274-0418-2). R West.
Sir Philip Sidney: Type of English Chivalry in the Elizabethan Age. H. R. Bourne. 1973. Repr. of 1889 ed. 30.00 (ISBN 0-8274-0070-5). R West.
Sir Philip Sidney's Defense of Poesy. Philip Sidney. Ed. by Lewis Soens. LC 74-108900. (Regents Critics Ser). xlii, 95p. 1970. 13.95x (ISBN 0-8032-0464-7). U of Nebr Pr.
Sir Philip Sidney's Toys. K. Duncan-Jones. (Chatterton Lectures on an English Poet). 1980. pap. 5.50 (ISBN 0-85672-237-5, Pub. by British Acad). Longwood Pub Group.
Sir Philip Sydney & the English Renaissance. 3rd ed. John Buxton. 283p. 1987. 53.00 (ISBN 0-333-43437-4, Pub. by Macmillan Pr Ltd); pap. 23.00 (ISBN 0-333-43438-2). Intl Spec Bk.
Sir Philip Sydney: 1586 & the Creation of a Legend. Jan Van Dorsten et al. (Publications of the Sir Thomas Browne Institute, Leiden, New Ser.: No. 9). (Illus.). x, 246p. 1986. 38.25x (ISBN 90-04-07923-8, Pub. by E J Brill). Heinman.
Sir Pompey & Madame Juno: And Other Tales. facsimile ed. Martin D. Armstrong. LC 75-163021. (Short Story Index Reprint Ser.). Repr. of 1927 ed. 17.00 (ISBN 0-8369-3935-2). Ayer Co Pubs.
Sir Ralph Esher. Leigh Hunt. LC 78-162913. (Bentley's Standard Novels: No. 118). Repr. of 1849 ed. 20.00 (ISBN 0-404-54518-1). AMS Pr.
Sir Randal Cremer: His Life & Work. Howard Evans. LC 74-147455. (Garland Library of War & Peace: Peace Leaders: Biographies & Memoirs). xviii, 356p. 1973. Repr. of 1909 ed. lib. bdg. 42.00 (ISBN 0-8240-0250-4). Garland Pub.
Sir Randal Cremer: His Life & Writings. Howard Evans. 1976. lib. bdg. 59.95 (ISBN 0-8490-2609-1). Gordon Pr.
Sir Raymond Unwin: Architect, Planner & Visionary. Frank Jackson. Ed. by Peter Willis. (Architects in Perspective Ser.). (Illus.). 208p. 1986. pap. 29.95 (ISBN 0-302-00591-9, Pub. by Zwemmer Bks UK). Sotheby Pubns.
Sir Reginald Blomfield: An Edwardian Architect. Richard A. Fellows. Ed. by Peter Willis. (Architects in Perspective Ser.). (Illus.). 184p. 1986. 29.95 (ISBN 0-302-00590-0, Pub. by Zwemmer Bks UK). Sotheby Pubns.
Sir Richard Blackmore & the Wits. Richard C. Boys. 1969. lib. bdg. 18.50x (ISBN 0-374-90912-1, Octagon). Hippocrene Bks.
Sir Richard Burton's Wife. Jean Burton. 1942. 20.00 (ISBN 0-8274-3429-4). R West.
Sir Richard Roos C., Lancastrian, 1410-1482. Ethel Seaton. 1988. Repr. of 1961 ed. lib. bdg. 99.00x. Am Biog Serv.
Sir Richard Roos C. 1410-1482, Lancastrian Poet. Ethel Seaton. LC 78-161959. Repr. of 1961 ed. 69.00x (ISBN 0-403-01322-4). Scholarly.
Sir Richard Steele. Willard Connely. LC 67-27588. 1934. Repr. 34.50x (ISBN 0-8046-0086-4, Pub. by Kennikat). Assoc Faculty Pr.
Sir Richard Steele. Willard Connely. 1973. 30.00 (ISBN 0-8274-0053-5). R West.
Sir Richard Steele. M. P. The Later Career. Calhoun Winston. LC 75-112616. pap. 70.80 (ISBN 0-317-42062-3, 2025882). Bks Demand UMI.
Sir Richard Whittington, Lord Maylor of London. Walter Besant & James Rice. 222p. 1982. Repr. of 1881 ed. lib. bdg. 30.00 (ISBN 0-8495-0608-5). Arden Lib.
Sir Robert Clayton & the Origins of English Deposit Banking, 1658-1685. Frank T. Melton. (Illus.). 232p. 1986. 49.50 (ISBN 0-521-32039-9). Cambridge U Pr.
Sir Robert Cotton, Fifteen Eighty-Six to Sixteen Thirty-One: History & Politics in Early Modern England. Kevin Sharpe. (OHM Ser.). (Illus.). 1979. 39.00x (ISBN 0-19-821877-X). Oxford U Pr.
Sir Robert Falconer: A Biography. James G. Greenlee. (Illus.). 432p. 1988. 37.50x (ISBN 0-8020-2655-9). U of Toronto Pr.
Sir Robert Mackintosh's Lumbar Puncture & Spinal Analgesia. 5th ed. J. Alfred Lee et al. (Illus.). 1985. text ed. 48.00 (ISBN 0-443-02671-8). Churchill.
Sir Robert Peel. facsimile ed. Anna A. Ramsay. LC 72-95076. (Select Bibliographies Reprint Ser). 1928. 22.50 (ISBN 0-8369-5076-3). Ayer Co Pubs.
Sir Robert Peel. facsimile ed. Anna A. Ramsay. LC 72-95076. (Select Bibliographies Reprint Ser.). 1982. Repr. of 1928 ed. lib. bdg. 21.50 (ISBN 0-8290-0839-X). Irvington.
Sir Robert Peel: From His Private Papers, 3 Vols. George Peel & H. J. Palmerston. Ed. by C. Parker. Repr. of 1899 ed. Set. 132.00 (ISBN 0-527-70400-8). Kraus Repr.
Sir Robert Peel: The Life of Sir Robert Peel after 1830. Norman Gash. 745p. (Orig.). 1986. pap. text ed. 32.95 (ISBN 0-582-49722-1). Longman.
Sir Robert Peel's Administration, 1841-1846. Travis L. Crosby. LC 76-927. (Elections & Administrations Ser.). 190p. 1976. 24.50 (ISBN 0-208-01517-5, Archon). Shoe String.
Sir Robert Taylor from Rococco to Neo-Classicism. Binney Marcus. (Genius of Architecture Ser.). 1984. 55.00X (ISBN 0-317-52174-8, Pub. by Pinhorns Uk). State Mutual Bk.
Sir Robert Walpole: The King's Minister, Vol. 2. John H. Plumb. LC 72-128080. (Illus.). xi, 362p. 1973. Repr. of 1961 ed. lib. bdg. 39.50x (ISBN 0-678-03572-5). Kelley.
Sir Roger L'Estrange: A Contribution to the History of the Press in the 17th Century. George Kitchin. LC 74-120325. (English Book Trade). 1971. Repr. of 1913 ed. 45.00x (ISBN 0-678-00703-9). Kelley.
Sir, Said Dr. Johnson. Chartres Biron. 1979. Repr. of 1940 ed. lib. bdg. 17.50 (ISBN 0-8414-9843-1). Folcroft.
Sir Samuel Ferguson. Malcom Brown. (Irish Writers Ser.). 101p. 1973. 4.50 (ISBN 0-8387-1083-2); pap. 1.95 (ISBN 0-8387-1208-8). Bucknell U Pr.
Sir Sayyid Ahmad Khan & Muslim Modernization in India & Pakistan. Hafeez Malik. LC 80-13905. (Illus.). 288p. 1980. 36.00 (ISBN 0-231-04970-6). Columbia U Pr.
Sir Sayyid Ahmad Khan's History of Bijnor Rebellion. Syed A. Khan. Tr. by Hafeez Malik. 1983. 13.50x (ISBN 0-8364-1080-7, Pub. by Idarah). South Asia Bks.
Sir Sham. Marion Devon. 292p. 1988. pap. 2.50 (ISBN 0-449-21339-0, Crest). Fawcett.
Sir Silver Swine. Susan Saunders. (Illus.). 48p. (Orig.). (ps-3). 1986. pap. 2.95 (ISBN 0-590-33586-3). Scholastic Inc.
Sir Small & the Dragonfly. Jane O'Connor. LC 87-35309. (Step into Reading Bks.). (Illus.). 32p. (Orig.). (ps-1). 1988. PLB 6.99 (ISBN 0-394-99625-9, BYR); pap. 2.95 (ISBN 0-394-89625-4, BYR). Random.
Sir Spenser Hayti, Or the Black Republic, 1889. St. John. (Illus.). 389p. 1972. Repr. of 1889 ed. 32.50x (ISBN 0-7146-2705-4, F Cass Co). Biblio Dist.
Sir. Squirrel Starts a Business. (Oak Tree Tales Ser.). (Illus.). (ps-1). 1.98 (ISBN 0-517-45740-7). Outlet Bk Co.
Sir T. Overbury His Observations in His Travailes. Thomas Overbury. LC 70-26399. (English Experience Ser.: No. 154). 28p. 1969. Repr. of 1626 ed. 25.00 (ISBN 90-221-0154-1). Walter J Johnson.
Sir Thomas Beecham Discography. Sir Thomas Beecham Society. LC 78-2261. 1978. Repr. of 1975 ed. lib. bdg. 35.00x (ISBN 0-313-20367-9, STBD). Greenwood.
Sir Thomas Browne. Jonathan F. Post. (English Author Ser.). 1987. lib. bdg. 24.95x (ISBN 0-8057-6948-X, Twayne). G K Hall.
Sir Thomas Browne. Ed. by Alexander Whyte. LC 71-118556. 1971. Repr. of 1898 ed. 21.50x (ISBN 0-8046-1181-5, Pub. by Kennikat). Assoc Faculty Pr.
Sir Thomas Browne & Robert Burton: A Reference Guide. Dennis G. Donovan & Magaretha G. Herman. 1981. lib. bdg. 46.00 (ISBN 0-8161-8018-0, Hall Reference). G K Hall.
Sir Thomas Browne's Pseudodoxia Epidemica, 2 vols. Thomas Browne. Ed. by R. H. Robbins. (Oxford English Texts Ser.). (Illus.). 1981. 195.00x (ISBN 0-19-812706-5). Oxford U Pr.
Sir Thomas Browne's "Religio Medici" & Two Seventeenth-Century Critics. James N. Wise. LC 72-84204. 224p. 1973. 25.00x (ISBN 0-8262-0130-X). U of Mo Pr.
Sir Thomas Drake. Julian Corbett. 1916. lib. bdg. 17.50 (ISBN 0-8414-2388-1). Folcroft.
Sir Thomas Elyot & Renaissance Humanism. John M. Major. LC 64-11351. (Illus.). xii, 276p. 1964. 22.50x (ISBN 0-8032-0108-7). U of Nebr Pr.
Sir Thomas Elyot & Roger Ascham: A Reference Guide. Jerome S. Dees. 1981. 31.50 (ISBN 0-8161-8353-8, Hall Reference). G K Hall.
Sir Thomas Elyot's The Defence of Good Women. Sir Thomas Elyot. Ed. by Edwin J. Howard. 1940. ltd. ed. 15.00x (ISBN 0-686-17401-1). R S Barnes.
Sir Thomas Malory. Edmund K. Chambers. Repr. of 1922 ed. lib. bdg. 17.00 (ISBN 0-8414-3431-X). Folcroft.
Sir Thomas Malory. George L. Kittredge. LC 74-17474. 1974. Repr. of 1925 ed. lib. bdg. 17.50 (ISBN 0-8414-5516-3). Folcroft.
Sir Thomas Malory: An Anecdotal Bibliography of Editions, 1485-1985. Barry Gaines. LC 85-48067. (Studies in the Middle Ages: No. 10). 1986. 42.50 (ISBN 0-404-61440-X). AMS Pr.
Sir Thomas Malory & the Cultural Crisis of the Late Middle Ages. Robert Merrill. LC 86-27318. (American University Studies IV: English Language & Literature: Vol. 39). 469p. 1987. text ed. 59.00 (ISBN 0-8204-0303-2). P Lang Pubs.
Sir Thomas Malory & the Morte D'Arthur: A Survey of Scholarship & Annotated Bibliography. Page W. Life. LC 80-16180. 297p. 1980. 17.50x (ISBN 0-8139-0868-X). U Pr of Va.
Sir Thomas Malory: His Turbulent Career, a Biography. Edward Hicks. LC 78-120630. 1970. Repr. of 1928 ed. lib. bdg. 16.50x (ISBN 0-374-93885-7, Octagon). Hippocrene Bks.
Sir Thomas More. Claude Jenkins. 1935. Repr. 20.00 (ISBN 0-8274-3431-6). R West.
Sir Thomas More. Anthony Munday & William Shakespeare. LC 74-133715. (Tudor Facsimile Texts. Old English Plays: No. 65). Repr. of 1910 ed. 49.50 (ISBN 0-404-53365-5). AMS Pr.
Sir Thomas More. facsimile ed. Leslie Paul. LC 75-128882. (Select Bibliographies Ser). Repr. of 1953 ed. 16.00 (ISBN 0-8369-5502-1). Ayer Co Pubs.
Sir Thomas More Circle: A Program of Ideas & Their Impact on Secular Drama. Pearl Hogrefe. LC 59-10553. 366p. 1959. 29.95 (ISBN 0-252-72653-7). U of Ill Pr.
Sir Thomas More: Selected Letters. Thomas More. LC 61-14944. (Yale Edition of the Works of St. Thomas More: Modernized Ser.). pap. 74.00 (ISBN 0-317-28285-9, 2022022). Bks Demand UMI.
Sir Thomas Overbury's Vision (1616) & Other English Sources of Nathaniel Hawthorne's "The Scarlet Letter.". Richard Niccols. LC 57-6417. 35.00x (ISBN 0-8201-1239-9). Schol Facsimiles.
Sir Thomas Urquhart & Rabelais. F. C. Roe. LC 73-4484. 1973. lib. bdg. 16.00 (ISBN 0-8414-2570-1). Folcroft.
Sir Thomas Urquhart of Cromartie. John Willcock. 1899. 35.00 (ISBN 0-8274-3432-4). R West.
Sir Thomas Urquhart of Cromartie Knight. John Willcock. 1979. Repr. of 1899 ed. lib. bdg. 45.00 (ISBN 0-8495-5749-6). Arden Lib.
Sir Thomas Wyatt. Thomas Dekker & John Webster. LC 75-133655. (Tudor Facsimile Texts. Old English Plays: No. 122). Repr. of 1914 ed. 49.50 (ISBN 0-404-53422-8). AMS Pr.
Sir Thomas Wyatt see Sir Philip Sidney.
Sir Thomas Wyatt: A Literary Portrait. H. A. Mason. 280p. 1980. 20.00 (ISBN 0-906515-65-3, Pub. by Bristol Classical Pr). Focus Info Gr.
Sir Thomas Wyatt: A Literary Portrait. Ed. by H. A. Mason. 344p. 1986. 32.50x (ISBN 0-8453-4512-5, Pub. by Bristol Classical Pr). Assoc Univ Prs.
Sir Thomas Wyatt & Henry Howard, Earl of Surrey: A Reference Guide. Clyde W. Jentoft. 1980. lib. bdg. 28.00 (ISBN 0-8161-8176-4, Hall Reference). G K Hall.
Sir Thomas Wyatt: The Complete Poems. Thomas Wyatt. Ed. by R. A. Rebholz. LC 80-53980. 558p. 1981. text ed. 37.00t (ISBN 0-300-02681-1); pap. 11.95x (ISBN 0-300-02688-9, YEP 5). Yale U Pr.
Sir Tristrem Tristan. Ed. by George P. McNeill. 1886. 24.00 (ISBN 0-384-61600-3). Johnson Repr.
Sir Walter Ralegh. Philip Edwards. LC 76-39784. 1976. Repr. of 1953 ed. lib. bdg. 22.00 (ISBN 0-8414-3969-9). Folcroft.
Sir Walter Ralegh. Robert Lacey. LC 73-80750. (Illus.). 1979. pap. 6.95 (ISBN 0-689-70585-9, 248). Atheneum.
Sir Walter Ralegh: An Annotated Bibliography. Compiled by Christopher M. Armitage. LC 87-40134. xiii, 236p. 1988. 14.95X (ISBN 0-8078-1757-0). U of NC Pr.
Sir Walter Ralegh & the New World. John W. Shirley. (America's 400th Anniversary Ser.). (Illus.). xi, 129p. (Orig.). 1985. pap. 5.00 (ISBN 0-86526-206-3). NC Archives.
Sir Walter Raleigh. John Buchan. 232p. 1983. lib. bdg. 35.00. Century Bookbindery.
Sir Walter Raleigh. H. A. Cruso. 1973. Repr. of 1907 ed. 25.00 (ISBN 0-8274-1789-6). R West.
Sir Walter Raleigh. Eric Ecclestone. 1941. Repr. 20.00 (ISBN 0-8274-3433-2). R West.
Sir Walter Raleigh. Philip Edwards. 1953. Repr. 25.00 (ISBN 0-8274-3434-0). R West.
Sir Walter Raleigh. Rennell Rodd. 1973. Repr. of 1904 ed. 25.00 (ISBN 0-8274-1050-6). R West.
Sir Walter Raleigh. Williamson H. Ross. LC 78-17033. 1978. Repr. of 1951 ed. lib. bdg. 25.00x (ISBN 0-313-20577-9, ROSI). Greenwood.
Sir Walter Raleigh. I. A. Taylor. 1973. Repr. of 1902 ed. 20.00 (ISBN 0-8274-0514-6). R West.
Sir Walter Raleigh. Edward Thompson. Repr. of 1935 ed. 30.00 (ISBN 0-8274-0511-1). R West.
Sir Walter Raleigh. Henry David Thoreau. Ed. by Franklin B. Sanborn. LC 80-2523. Repr. of 1905 ed. 24.50 (ISBN 0-404-19071-5). AMS Pr.
Sir Walter Raleigh. Henry David Thoreau. 59.95 (ISBN 0-87968-442-9). Gordon Pr.
Sir Walter Raleigh. Norman L. Williams. 295p. 1982. Repr. of 1962 ed. lib. bdg. 40.00 (ISBN 0-8495-5821-2). Arden Lib.
Sir Walter Raleigh. Norman Lloyd Williams. 295p. 1982. Repr. of 1962 ed. lib. bdg. 35.00 (ISBN 0-89987-893-8). Darby Bks.
Sir Walter Raleigh: A Reference Guide. Jerry L. Miles. (Reference Guides to Literature Ser.). 148p. 1986. lib. bdg. 35.00 (ISBN 0-8161-8596-4). G K Hall.
Sir Walter Raleigh & His Colony in America. Ed. by Increase N. Tarbox. 1966. 24.00 (ISBN 0-8337-3470-9). B Franklin.
Sir Walter Raleigh & the Age of Discovery. Andrew Sinclair. 96p. 1984. pap. 7.95 (ISBN 0-14-007245-4). Penguin.
Sir Walter Raleigh As Historian: An Analysis of the History of the World. John Racin. Ed. by James Hogg. (Elizabethan & Renaissance Studies). 216p. (Orig.). 1974. pap. 15.00 (ISBN 3-7052-0651-6, Pub. by Salzburg Studies). Longwood Pub Group.
Sir Walter Raleigh, His Family & Private Life. Alfred Rowse. LC 73-21492. (Illus.). 348p. 1975. Repr. of 1962 ed. lib. bdg. 25.00x (ISBN 0-8371-6388-9, ROWR). Greenwood.
Sir Walter Raleigh Selections for His Historie of the World: His Letters, Etc. Intro. by G. E. Hadow. 212p. 1980. Repr. of 1917 ed. lib. bdg. 35.00 (ISBN 0-8495-2376-1). Arden Lib.
Sir Walter Raleigh Selections from His "Historie of the World," His Letters, Etc. Walter Raleigh. Ed. by G. E. Hadow. LC 78-25901. 1978. Repr. of 1917 ed. lib. bdg. 35.00 (ISBN 0-8414-4968-6). Folcroft.
Sir Walter Raleigh: The British Dominion of the West. Martin A. Hume. 1977. Repr. of 1906 ed. lib. bdg. 40.00 (ISBN 0-8492-1143-3). R West.
Sir Walter Raleigh: The British Dominion of the West. Martin A. Hume. 292p. 1985. Repr. of 1926 ed. lib. bdg. 50.00 (ISBN 0-317-37974-7). Century Bookbindery.
Sir Walter Raleigh's Ghost or Englands Forewarner. Thomas Scott. LC 74-80222. (English Experience Ser.: No. 693). 42p. 1974. Repr. of 1626 ed. 5.00 (ISBN 90-221-0693-4). Walter J Johnson.
Sir Walter Raleigh's History of the World. Charles Firth. 49p. 1980. Repr. 7.50 (ISBN 0-8492-4707-1). R West.
Sir Walter Raleigh's History of the World. Charles H. Firth. LC 77-1815. 1918. lib. bdg. 15.00 (ISBN 0-8414-4190-1). Folcroft.
Sir Walter Scott. John Buchan. 1932. lib. bdg. 20.00 (ISBN 0-8414-2515-9). Folcroft.
Sir Walter Scott. John Buchan. LC 67-27580. Repr. of 1932 ed. 21.50x (ISBN 0-8046-0054-6, Pub. by Kennikat). Assoc Faculty Pr.
Sir Walter Scott. John Buchan. 384p. Repr. of 1932 ed. lib. bdg. 40.00. Century Bookbindery.
Sir Walter Scott. W. S. Crockett & James I. Caw. LC 72-12503. 1972. Repr. of 1903 ed. lib. bdg. 16.00 (ISBN 0-8414-0931-5). Folcroft.
Sir Walter Scott. Amy Cruse. 1973. Repr. of 1915 ed. 20.00 (ISBN 0-8274-1766-7). R West.
Sir Walter Scott. Oliver Elton. LC 72-193214. 1924. lib. bdg. 15.00 (ISBN 0-8414-3998-2). Folcroft.
Sir Walter Scott. H. Grierson. LC 72-95427. (English Biography Ser., No. 31). 1969. Repr. of 1938 ed. lib. bdg. 49.95x (ISBN 0-8383-0977-1). Haskell.
Sir Walter Scott. James Hay. 1973. 25.00 (ISBN 0-8274-0280-5). R West.
Sir Walter Scott. William H. Hudson. LC 72-6573. 1901. lib. bdg. 32.00 (ISBN 0-8414-0125-X). Folcroft.
Sir Walter Scott. Richard H. Hutton. Ed. by John Morley. LC 68-58381. (English Men of Letters). Repr. of 1887 ed. lib. bdg 12.50 (ISBN 0-404-51713-7). AMS Pr.
Sir Walter Scott. Richard H. Hutton. 1978. Repr. of 1884 ed. lib. bdg. 20.50 (ISBN 0-8495-2233-1). Arden Lib.
Sir Walter Scott. Richard H. Hutton. 1909. Repr. lib. bdg. 17.00 (ISBN 0-8414-5244-X). Folcroft.
Sir Walter Scott. William Ker. LC 74-7282. (Sir Walter Scott Ser, No. 73). 1974. lib. bdg. 29.95x (ISBN 0-8383-1937-8). Haskell.
Sir Walter Scott. William P. Ker. LC 74-14534. 1974. Repr. of 1919 ed. lib. bdg. 17.00 (ISBN 0-8414-5512-0). Folcroft.
Sir Walter Scott. Andrew Lang. 1973. Repr. of 1906 ed. 15.00 (ISBN 0-8274-0317-8). R West.
Sir Walter Scott. George E. Saintsbury. LC 72-186991. 1897. lib. bdg. 20.00 (ISBN 0-8414-7516-4). Folcroft.
Sir Walter Scott: A Character Study. John A. Patten. 1932. Repr. 40.00 (ISBN 0-8274-3435-9). R West.
Sir Walter Scott: A Lecture. William P. Ker. 65p. 1983. Repr. of 1919 ed. lib. bdg. 10.00 (ISBN 0-8492-1477-7). R West.
Sir Walter Scott: A Reference Guide. Jill Rubenstein. 1978. lib. bdg. 40.50 (ISBN 0-8161-7868-2, Hall Reference). G K Hall.
Sir Walter Scott & Friends. Florence MacCunn. LC 73-17224. 1910. Repr. lib. bdg. 37.50 (ISBN 0-8414-6095-7). Folcroft.
Sir Walter Scott & Scots Law. David Marshall. LC 72-193206. 1932. lib. bdg. 25.50 (ISBN 0-8414-1121-2). Folcroft.
Sir Walter Scott & the Aberdonians. George M. Fraser. LC 76-44855. 1976. Repr. of 1908 ed. lib. bdg. 17.50 (ISBN 0-8414-4182-0). Folcroft.
Sir Walter Scott & the Border Minstrelsy. Andrew Lang. LC 68-59266. Repr. of 1910 ed. 10.00 (ISBN 0-404-03869-7). AMS Pr.
Sir Walter Scott As a Critic of Literature. Margaret Ball. LC 65-27125. 1907. Repr. 23.50x (ISBN 0-8046-0015-5, Pub. by Kennikat). Assoc Faculty Pr.
Sir Walter Scott, Baronet. Herbert J. Grierson. LC 76-153326. Repr. of 1938 ed. 12.50 (ISBN 0-404-02914-0). AMS Pr.
Sir Walter Scott, Bart. Herbert J. Grierson. LC 72-193213. 1938. lib. bdg. 30.00 (ISBN 0-8414-4688-1). Folcroft.
Sir Walter Scott: Broadcast Lectures to the Young. Herbert Grierson. LC 72-194438. 1932. lib. bdg. 25.00 (ISBN 0-8414-4689-X). Folcroft.
Sir Walter Scott: His Life & Personality. Hesketh Pearson. 295p. Repr. of 1954 ed. lib. bdg. 40.00 (ISBN 0-89984-854-0). Century Bookbindery.
Sir Walter Scott in Famous Edinburg Students. George Saintsbury. 1973. Repr. of 1914 ed. 27.00 (ISBN 0-8274-1070-0). R West.
Sir Walter Scott: Landscape & Locality. James Reed. (Illus.). 192p. 1980. 46.50 (ISBN 0-485-11197-7, Pub. by Athlone Pr UK). Humanities.
Sir Walter Scott Lectures: 1940-1948. W. L. Renwick. LC 73-13772. 1950. Repr. lib. bdg. 30.50 (ISBN 0-8414-7238-6). Folcroft.

TITLE INDEX SISTER CARRIE.

Sir Walter Scott: Some Centenary Reflections. Dorothy M. Stuart. LC 77-28863. 1973. Repr. of 1934 ed. 10.00 (ISBN 0-8492-2464-0). R West.
Sir Walter Scott: The Long Forgotten Melody. Ed. by Alan Bold. LC 83-2792. (Critical Studies). 224p. 1983. text ed. 28.50x (ISBN 0-389-20371-8, 07243). B&N Imports.
Sir Walter Scott: The Story of His Life. R. Shelton MacKenzie. LC 77-20999. Repr. of 1871 ed. lib. bdg. 55.00 (ISBN 0-8414-0455-0). Folcroft.
Sir Walter Scott To-Day. Herbert J. Grierson. LC 73-14912. 1832. Repr. lib. bdg. 25.00 (ISBN 0-8414-4462-5). Folcroft.
Sir Walter Scott's Conge. Lord Sands. 1973. Repr. of 1929 ed. 30.00 (ISBN 0-8274-1067-0). R West.
Sir Walter Scott's Edinburgh Annual Register. Kenneth Curry. LC 77-8136. Repr. of 1977 ed. 56.80 (2027563). Bks Demand UMI.
Sir Walter Scott's First Love. Adam Scott. LC 72-2013. (English Literature Ser., No. 33). 1972. Repr. of 1896 ed. lib. bdg. 39.95x (ISBN 0-8383-1450-3). Haskell.
Sir Walter Scott's Tour in Ireland in 1825. David J. O'Donoghue. 96p. 1980. Repr. of 1905 ed. lib. bdg. 25.00 (ISBN 0-8492-7304-8). R West.
Sir Walter Scott's Tour in Ireland in 1852. David J. O'Donoghue. LC 76-10778. 1976. Repr. of 1905 ed. lib. bdg. 27.50 (ISBN 0-8414-6533-9). Folcroft.
Sir Walter Temple: The Man & His Work. Homer E. Woodbridge. 361p. 1980. Repr. lib. bdg. 40.00 (ISBN 0-8492-8849-5). R West.
Sir Walter's Post-Bag: More Stories & Sidelights from His Unpublished Letter-Books. Wilfred Partington. 1973. Repr. of 1932 ed. 35.00 (ISBN 0-8274-1079-4). R West.
Sir Walter's Post-Bag: More Stories & Sidelights from his Unpublished Letter-Books. Wilfred Partington. 402p. 1983. Repr. of 1932 ed. lib. bdg. 50.00 (ISBN 0-89984-950-4). Century Bookbindery.
Sir, We Would Like to See Jesus: Homilies from a Hilltop. Walter J. Burghardt. LC 82-60589. 1983. pap. 8.95 (ISBN 0-8091-2490-4). Paulist Pr.
Sir William Alexander & American Colonization. Ed. by Edmund F. Slafter. 1966. 21.00 (ISBN 0-8337-3292-7). B Franklin.
Sir William & the Pumpkin Monster. Margery Cuyler. LC 84-610. (Illus.). 32p. (gr. k-2). 1984. 9.95 (ISBN 0-8050-0247-2). H Holt & Co.
Sir William Blackstone. David A. Lockmiller. 11.75 (ISBN 0-8446-0776-2). Peter Smith.
Sir William Chambers. John Harris. LC 70-113198. (Illus.). 1971. 65.00x (ISBN 0-271-00133-X). Pa St U Pr.
Sir William Chambers. John Harris. 397p. 1970. 403.00x (Pub. by Han-Shan Tang Ltd). State Mutual Bk.
Sir William Davenant: An Annotated Bibliography. Sophia B. Blaydes & Philip Bordinat. LC 84-45395. (Literature Ser.). 250p. 1985. lib. bdg. 53.00 (ISBN 0-8240-8874-3). Garland Pub.
Sir William Davenant, Poet Venturer, 1606-1668. Alfred Harbage. LC 75-120624. 1970. Repr. lib. bdg. 21.50x (ISBN 0-374-93659-5, Octagon). Hippocrene Bks.
Sir William Davenant: The Siege of Rhodes: A Critical Study. Ann-Mari Hedback. (Studia Anglistica Upsaliensia: No. 14). (Illus.). 121p. (Orig.). 1973. pap. 15.00x (ISBN 0-317-65800-X). Coronet Bks.
Sir William Dawson: A Life in Science & Religion. Charles F. O'Brien. LC 71-153381. (American Philosophical Society, Memoirs: Vol. 84). pap. 54.30 (ISBN 0-317-20673-7, 2025140). Bks Demand UMI.
Sir William Empson: An Annotated Bibliography. Frank Day. Ed. by William E. Cain. LC 82-49130. (Modern Critics & Critical Schools Ser.: vol. 8). 180p. 1984. lib. bdg. 64.00 (ISBN 0-8240-9207-4). Garland Pub.
Sir William Flower. R. Lydekker. Repr. of 1906 ed. 20.00 (ISBN 0-527-58860-1). Kraus Repr.
Sir William Foster, 1863-1951: A Bibliography. Anthony Farrington. (Occasional Publication No. 1). (Illus.). 30p. 1972. 1.50 (ISBN 0-7123-0602-1, Pub. by British Lib). Longwood Pub Group.
Sir William Gilbert. Isaac Goldberg. 59.95 (ISBN 0-8490-2610-5). Gordon Pr.
Sir William Gregory of Coole: The Biography of an Anglo-Irishman. Brian Jenkins. LC 86-63638. (Illus.). 339p. 1987. 50.00 (ISBN 0-86140-175-1, Pub. by Colin Smythe Ltd Britain). Dufour.
Sir William Jones: A Bibliography of Primary & Secondary Sources. Garland Cannon. (Library & Information Sources in Linguistics Ser.: No. 7). xiv, 73p. 1979. 18.00x (ISBN 90-272-0998-7). Benjamins North Am.
Sir William Jones: A Study in Eighteenth-Century British Attitudes to India. S. N. Mukherjee. 184p. 1987. text ed. 22.50x (ISBN 0-86131-581-2, Pub. by Orient Longman Ltd India). Apt Bks.
Sir William Jones: His Mind & Art. Janardan P. Singh. 324p. 27.00 (ISBN 0-317-52155-1, Pub. by S Chand). State Mutual Bk.
Sir William Jones, Orientalist: An Annotated Bibliography of His Works. Garland H. Cannon. LC 52-7595. (Pacific Area Bibliographies Ser.). pap. 26.50 (ISBN 0-317-09239-1, 2001352). Bks Demand UMI.
Sir William Osler: An Annotated Bibliography. Richard L. Golden & Charles G. Roland. LC 87-12209. (Norman Bibliography Ser.). (Illus.). 240p. 1988. Repr. of 1939 ed. 100.00 (ISBN 0-930405-00-5). Norman SF.
Sir William Petty (Sixteen Twenty-Three - Sixteen Eighty-Seven: Ses Idees Economiques. Maurice Pasquier. LC 77-143647. (Research & Source Works Ser.: No. 667). 1971. Repr. of 1903 ed. lib. bdg. 21.00 (ISBN 0-8337-2678-1). B Franklin.
Sir William Rowan Hamilton: A Biography. Thomas L. Hankins. LC 80-10627. 496p. 1980. text ed. 47.50x (ISBN 0-8018-2203-3). Johns Hopkins.
Sir William Scott, Lord Stowell, Judge of the High Court Of Admirality, 1798-1828. Henry J. Bourguignon. LC 87-6377. (Cambridge Studies in English Legal History). 320p. 1987. 49.50 (ISBN 0-521-34076-4). Cambridge U Pr.
Sir William Temple. Murray Beaven. 1973. Repr. of 1908 ed. 20.00 (ISBN 0-8274-1584-2). R West.
Sir William Temple. Clara Marburg. 1973. Repr. of 1932 ed. 29.50 (ISBN 0-8274-0140-X). R West.
Sir William Temple. Homer E. Woodbridge. (MLA Ser.: Vol. 12). 1940. 36.00 (ISBN 0-527-97870-1). Kraus Repr.
Sir William Temple: A Seventeenth Century Libertin. Clara M. Kirk. LC 77-26928. 30.00 (ISBN 0-8414-6232-1). Folcroft.
Sir William Temple's Essays on Ancient & Modern Learning & on Poetry. J. E. Spingarn. 1909. lib. bdg. 27.00 (ISBN 0-8414-1617-6). Folcroft.
Sir William Watson. James G. Nelson. LC 66-28912. (Twayne's English Authors Ser.). 1966. lib. bdg. 17.95 (ISBN 0-89197-938-7); pap. text ed. 6.95x (ISBN 0-8290-2025-X). Irvington.
Sir Williams Gregory K. C. M. G. An Autobiography. 3rd ed. Ed. by Isabella A. Gregory. (Coole Edition of the Works of Lady Gregory). 1981. 59.00x (ISBN 0-19-520282-1). Oxford U Pr.
Sir Winston Churchill: His Life & Times. 2nd ed. Maxwell P. Schoenfeld. LC 85-5245. 1986. pap. text ed. 6.50 (ISBN 0-89874-858-5). Krieger.
Sirach. R. A. MacKenzie. LC 82-83725. (Old Testament Message Ser.: Vol. 19). 12.95 (ISBN 0-89453-419-X); pap. 8.95 (ISBN 0-89453-253-7). M Glazier.
Sirach. Bruce Vawter. (Bible Ser.). Pt. 1. pap. 1.00 (ISBN 0-8091-5138-3); Pt. 2. pap. 1.00 (ISBN 0-8091-5139-1). Paulist Pr.
Sirague City. Photos by Vilem Kriz. LC 75-14371. 64p. 1975. 25.00 (ISBN 0-915756-00-5); pap. 10.00 (ISBN 0-915756-01-3). D McPhail.
Sirdar's Sabre: Being for the Most Part the Adventures of Sirdar Bahadur Mohammed Khan. facsimile ed. Louis Tracy. LC 74-37568. (Short Story Index Reprint Ser.). Repr. of 1920 ed. 19.00 (ISBN 0-8369-4127-6). Ayer Co Pubs.
Sire de Maletroit's Door. Robert Louis Stevenson. Ed. by Ann Redpath. (Creative's Classic Short Stories Ser.). (Illus.). 58p. (gr. 6 up). 1985. PLB 8.95 (ISBN 0-87191-967-2). Creative Ed.
Sire of Champions. Marguerite Henry. (King of the Wind). 24p. (ps-3). 1988. pap. 1.95 (ISBN 0-02-688807-6, Checkerboard Pr). Macmillan.
Siren. Dino Buzzati. Tr. by Lawrence Venuti from Ital. LC 84-60682. 160p. (Orig.). 1984. pap. 10.50 (ISBN 0-86547-159-2). N Point Pr.
Siren. Linda C. Gray. 1989. pap. price not set (ISBN 0-8125-1838-1). Tor Bks.
Siren, 3 vols. in 1. Thomas A. Trollope. LC 75-32787. (Literature of Mystery & Detection). 1976. Repr. 65.00x (ISBN 0-405-07902-8). Ayer Co Pubs.
Siren in the Night. Eddie Iroh. (African Writers Ser.: No. 255). 207p. 1982. pap. text ed. 7.50 (ISBN 0-435-90255-5). Heinemann Ed.
Siren Song. Leslie Stone. 480p. (Orig.). 1985. pap. 3.95 (ISBN 0-445-20000-6, Pub. by Popular Lib). Warner Bks.
Siren Sparks. Rose M. Poole. 203p. 1984. 6.45 (ISBN 0-89697-173-2). Intl Univ Pr.
Sirenian Evolution in the North Pacific Ocean. Daryl P. Domning. LC 77-83099. (University of California Publications in Geological Sciences: No. 118). (Illus.). 208p. pap. 54.10 (2029874). Bks Demand UMI.
Sirenoid Ganoids, Vol. 2. L. C. Mial. Repr. of 1907 ed. 70.00 (ISBN 0-384-38760-8). Johnson Repr.
Sirens. Chris Achilleos. 130p. (Orig.). 1988. pap. 15.95 (ISBN 1-85028-013-4, PTB UK). Avery Pub.
Sirens. Bernard Evslin. (Monsters of Mythology Ser.). (Illus.). 104p. 1987. lib. bdg. 19.95x (ISBN 1-55546-258-8). Chelsea Hse.
Sirens. Eric Van Lustbader. LC 81-1482. 480p. 1981. 13.95 (ISBN 0-87131-346-4). M Evans.
Sirens & Others Stories. Azorin. Tr. by Warre B. Wells. 1978. Repr. of 1931 ed. lib. bdg. 30.00 (ISBN 0-8492-0062-8). R West.
Sirens & Spies. Janet T. Lisle. LC 84-21518. 176p. (gr. 7 up). 1985. 11.95 (ISBN 0-02-759150-6). Bradbury Pr.
Sirens of Song: The Popular Female Vocalist in America. Aida Pavletich. LC 81-22147. (Quality Paperbacks Ser.). (Illus.). 281p. 1982. pap. 7.95 (ISBN 0-306-80162-0). Da Capo.
Sirens of Titan. Kurt Vonnegut, Jr. 1981. 9.95 (ISBN 0-385-28923-5, Sey Lawr). Delacorte.
Sirens of Titan. Kurt Vonnegut, Jr. 320p. 1970. pap. 4.50 (ISBN 0-440-17948-3). Dell.
Sirens' Song: Selected Essays of Maurice Blanchot. Maurice Blanchot. Ed. by Gabriel Josipovici. Tr. by Sacha Rabinovitch. LC 81-48510. 264p. 1982. 22.50 (ISBN 0-253-35255-X). Ind U Pr.
Sires & Dams of Stakes Winners, 1925-1985. Ed. by Blood-Horse, Inc. Staff. 2000p. 1986. 95.00 (ISBN 0-936032-98-7). Blood-Horse.
Sires & Dams of Stakes Winners, 1928-1978. 40.00 (ISBN 0-936032-10-3). Blood-Horse.
Sirfidy Sibiri: (Diptera, Syrphidae) N. A. Violovich. 242p. 1983. 58.00x (Pub. by Collets (UK)). State Mutual Bk.
Sirga. Rene Guillot. LC 59-12198. (Illus.). (gr. 6-9). 1959. 14.95 (ISBN 0-87599-046-0). S G Phillips.
Sirian Experiments. Doris Lessing. LC 79-27710. 304p. 1981. 13.45 (ISBN 0-394-51231-6). Knopf.
Sirian Experiments. Doris Lessing. LC 81-52259. 400p. 1982. 5.95 (ISBN 0-394-75195-7, Vin). Random.
Sirius: A Volume of Fiction. facsimile ed. Ellen T. Fowler. LC 73-150543. (Short Story Index Reprint Ser.). Repr. of 1901 ed. 22.00 (ISBN 0-8369-3840-2). Ayer Co Pubs.
Sirius & Saba. Deborah King. (Illus.). 32p. (gr. 3-6). 1982. 13.95 (ISBN 0-241-10599-4, Pub. by Hamish Hamilton England). David & Charles.
Sirius Mystery. Robert K. Temple. 292p. (Orig.). 1987. pap. 12.95 (ISBN 0-89281-163-3, Destiny Bks). Inner Tradit.
Siroe. Johann A. Hasse. Ed. by Howard M. Brown. LC 76-20985. (Italian Opera 1640-1770 Ser.). 1978. lib. bdg. 77.00 (ISBN 0-8240-2632-2). Garland Pub.
SIRS Digest: Alcohol. Ed. by Eleanor C. Goldstein. (Digest Ser.). 1985. ring binder 35.00 (ISBN 0-89777-110-9). Soc Issues.
SIRS Digest: Drugs. Ed. by Eleanor C. Goldstein. (Digest Ser.). 1987. ring binder 35.00 (ISBN 0-89777-108-7). Soc Issues.
SIRS Digest: Energy. Ed. by Eleanor C. Goldstein. (Digest Ser.). 40p. (YA) (gr. 6-8). 1987. binder 35.00 (ISBN 0-89777-111-7). Soc Issues.
SIRS Digest: Family. Ed. by Eleanor C. Goldstein. (Digest Ser.). 1983. ring binder 35.00 (ISBN 0-89777-105-2). Soc Issues.
SIRS Digest: Food. Ed. by Eleanor C. Goldstein. (Digest Ser.). 1984. ring binder 35.00 (ISBN 0-89777-109-5). Soc Issues.
SIRS Digest: Pollution. Ed. by Eleanor C. Goldstein. (Digest Ser.). 1981. ring binder 35.00 (ISBN 0-89777-106-0). Soc Issues.
SIRS Digest Population. Ed. by Eleanor C. Goldstein. (Digest Ser.). 1985. ring binder 35.00 (ISBN 0-89777-107-9). Soc Issues.
Sis & Chris & the Knowbots in "We Don't Need Drugs to Be O. K. " Educational Coloring Book. Mary L. Pringle & Joseph Ellis. 32p. (Orig.). (gr. k-5). 1985. pap. 1.95 (ISBN 0-935847-02-2). Inst Subs Abuse Res.
Sis & Chris & the Knowbots in "We Need Drugs to Be O. K." Educational Coloring Book. Mary L. Pringle & Joseph Ellis. (gr. k-5). 1987. pap. 1.95 (ISBN 0-935847-03-0). Inst Subs Abuse Res.
SISCIS: Subject Index to Sources of Comparative International Statistics. Ed. by F. C. Pieper. LC 78-323066. 745p. 1978. 200.00x (ISBN 0-900246-23-5). Intl Pubns Serv.
Siskiyou. Richard Hoyt. 304p. (Orig.). 1984. pap. 3.50 (ISBN 0-8125-0487-9, Dist. by Warner Pub Services & Saint Martin's Press). Tor Bks.
Sisley: Q.L.P. Raymond Cogniat. (Illus.). 1978. 14.95 (ISBN 0-517-53321-9). Crown.
Sismonde De Sismondi As an Economist. Tuan Mao-Lan. LC 68-57585. (Columbia University. Studies in the Social Sciences: No. 298). Repr. of 1927 ed. 17.50 (ISBN 0-404-51298-4). AMS Pr.
Sisomicin: An International Round-Table Discussion. Ed. by P. Noone. (International Congress & Symposium Ser.: No. 35). 72p. 1980. pap. 15.00 (ISBN 1-85315-071-1, Pub. by Royal Society of Medicine Services Ltd). Longwood Pub Group.
Sissano, Movements of Migration Within & Through Melanesia. William Churchill. LC 16-23055. (Carnegie Institution of Washington Publications: No. 244). (Illus.). pap. 22.30 (ISBN 0-317-10107-2, 2015706). Bks Demand UMI.
Sissie. (Classic Reprint ser.). 280p. 1988. pap. 9.95 (ISBN 0-938410-66-0). Thunder's Mouth.
Sisson Report on the German Bolshevik Conspiracy. Edgar Sisson & George Creel. 1980. lib. bdg. 59.95 (ISBN 0-8490-3097-8). Gordon Pr.
Sisson's Synonyms: An Unabridged Synonym & Related-Terms Locator. A. F. Sisson. LC 74-77314. 1970. 24.95 (ISBN 0-13-810630-4, Parker). P-H.
Sisson's Word & Expression Locater. A. F. Sisson. 371p. 1966. 18.95 (ISBN 0-13-810671-1, Busn). P-H.
"Sissy Boy Syndrome" & the Development of Homosexuality. Richard Green. LC 85-29489. 432p. 1987. 40.00 (ISBN 0-300-03696-5). Yale U Pr.
Sissy Kid Brother. Amelia Mueller. LC 74-17385. (Illus.). 236p. (YA) (gr. 7-10). 1975. pap. 4.95 (ISBN 0-8361-1754-9). Herald Pr.
Sistema Alimentario Mexicano (SAM) Elements of a Program of Accelerated Production of Basic Foodstuffs in Mexico. Cassio Luiselli. Tr. by David Sweet from Span. (Research Report Ser.: No. 22). 24p. (Orig.). 1982. pap. 5.50 (ISBN 0-935391-21-5, RR-22). Ctr Mex Studies.
Sistema de Clasificacion Decimal, con Adaptaciones para los Paises de Habla Espanola, Basado en la 18a Edicion con Adiciones de la 19a Edicion, 3 vols. Melvil Dewey. Tr. by Jorge Aguayo. LC 80-24527. (Span.). 1980. Set. 65.00x (ISBN 0-910608-26-1); Vol. 1, Introduccion, Tablas Auxiliares. 25.00x (ISBN 0-910608-27-X); Vol. 2, Esquemas. 25.00x (ISBN 0-910608-28-8); Vol. 3, Indice. 25.00x (ISBN 0-910608-29-6). Forest Pr.
Sistema de Evidencias Christianas. Ed. by L. D. Keyser. 172p. (Span.). pap. 4.95 (ISBN 0-87148-885-X). Pathway Pr.
Sistema Expresivo de Ricardo Guiraldes. Miriam Curet De Anda. LC 76-8166. (Coleccion Mente y Palabra). 383p. (Orig., Span.). 1976. 6.25 (ISBN 0-8477-0532-3); pap. 5.00 (ISBN 0-8477-0533-1). U of PR Pr.
Sistema Interamericano a Treaves de Tratados, Convenciones y Otros Documentos: Vol. I, Asuntos Juridicos Politicos. OAS General Secretariat for Juridical Affairs. (Sistema Interamericano). 1040p. 1981. text ed. 60.00 (ISBN 0-8270-1426-0). OAS.
Sistema Judicial de Puerto Rico. Jose Trias-Monge. LC 77-10936. 1978. 20.00 (ISBN 0-8477-3014-X). U of PR Pr.
Sistema Metrico (Modulo) Fe Acosta de Gonzalez. (Coleccion Uprex; Serie Pedagogia: No. 57). (Span.). 1979. pap. text ed. 3.80 (ISBN 0-8477-2743-2). U of PR Pr.
Sistemas de Numeracion. S. V. Fomin. 46p. (Span.). 1975. pap. 1.45 (ISBN 0-8285-1692-8, Pub. by Mir Pubs USSR). Imported Pubns.
Sistemas de Transporte Publico Urbano: Directrices para el Examen de Opciones. Alan Armstrong-Wright. (Urban Transport Ser.). 94p. 1987. 5.00 (ISBN 0-8213-0765-7, BK0875). World Bank.
Sister. Eloise Greenfield. LC 73-22182. (Illus.). (gr. 5-12). 1974. 13.70 (ISBN 0-690-00497-4, Crowell Jr Bks). HarpJ.
Sister. Eloise Greenfield. LC 73-22182. (Trophy Bks.). (Illus.). 96p. (gr. 3-7). 1987. pap. 2.95 (ISBN 0-06-440199-5, Trophy). HarpJ.
Sister Act. Blossom Elfman. 1978. 7.95 (ISBN 0-395-26476-6). HM.
Sister Act. Max F. Harris. 1981. pap. 1.95 (ISBN 0-8439-0907-2, Leisure Bks). Leisure NY.
Sister Age. M. F. Fisher. LC 82-48880. 1983. 12.45 (ISBN 0-394-53066-7). Knopf.
Sister Age. M. F. Fisher. 1984. pap. 7.95 (ISBN 0-394-72385-6, Vin). Random.
Sister Alyonushka & Brother Ivanushka: Bd. with The White Duck. Illus. by I. Bilibin. (Illus.). 16p. 1979. pap. 2.45 (ISBN 0-8285-1227-2, Pub. by Goznak Pubs USSR). Imported Pubns.
Sister Anna: God's Captive to Set Others Free. Dorothy G. Murray. 175p. (Orig.). 1983. pap. 7.95 (ISBN 0-87178-796-2). Brethren.
Sister Arts: The Tradition of Literary Pictorialism & English Poetry from Dryden to Gray. Jean H. Hagstrum. LC 58-11948. (Illus.). xxii, 372p. 1987. pap. 12.95 (ISBN 0-226-31298-4). U of Chicago Pr.
Sister Bond: A Feminist View of a Timeless Connection. Ed. by T. McNaron. (Athene Ser.: No. 6). (Illus.). 142p. 1985. text ed. 24.00 (ISBN 0-08-032367-7); pap. text ed. 11.95 (ISBN 0-08-032366-9). Pergamon.
Sister Carrie. Theodore Dreiser. (Airmont Classics Ser.). (YA) (gr. 11 up). pap. 2.95 (ISBN 0-8049-0147-3, CL-147). Airmont.
Sister Carrie. Theodore Dreiser. (Literature Ser). (gr. 10-12). 1970. pap. text ed. 7.25 (ISBN 0-87720-739-9). AMSCO Sch.
Sister Carrie. Theodore Dreiser. 432p. (gr. 9-12). 1982. pap. 2.95 (ISBN 0-553-21264-8, Bantam Classics). Bantam.
Sister Carrie. Theodore Dreiser. LC 78-183140. 472p. 1971. Repr. lib. bdg. 15.00x (ISBN 0-8376-0401-X). Bentley.
Sister Carrie. Theodore Dreiser. Ed. by Jack Salzman. LC 69-16530. 1970. pap. 6.65 scp (ISBN 0-672-61014-0). Bobbs.
Sister Carrie. Theodore Dreiser. LC 69-13798. (Merrill Standard Ser). 6.00x (ISBN 0-675-09527-1); pap. 4.00x (ISBN 0-675-09528-X). Brown Bk.
Sister Carrie. Theodore Dreiser. Ed. by Claude Simpson. LC 59-1819. (YA) (gr. 9 up). 1959. pap. 6.50 (ISBN 0-395-05134-7, RivEd). HM.
Sister Carrie. abr. ed. Theodore Dreiser. (Belles Lettres in English Ser). 1969. Repr. of 1901 ed. 24.00 (ISBN 0-384-12780-0). Johnson Repr.
Sister Carrie. Theodore Dreiser. 557p. 1980. Repr. of 1907 ed. lib. bdg. 25.95x (ISBN 0-89968-207-3). Lightyear.
Sister Carrie. Theodore Dreiser. 1962. pap. 2.95 (ISBN 0-451-51969-8, CE1725, Sig Classics). NAL.
Sister Carrie. Theodore Dreiser. Ed. by Donald Pizer. (Critical Editions). 1970. pap. text ed. 10.95x (ISBN 0-393-09949-0). Norton.
Sister Carrie. Theodore Dreiser. (Penguin American Library). 488p. 1981. pap. 4.95 (ISBN 0-14-039002-2). Penguin.

Sister Carrie, Jennie Gerhardt, Twelve Men. Theodore Dreiser. Ed. by Richard Lehan. LC 86-27583. 1168p. 1987. 27.50 (ISBN 0-940450-41-0). Library of America.
Sister Carrie Notes. Frederick J. Balling. (Orig.). 1967. pap. 3.50 (ISBN 0-8220-1201-4). Cliffs.
"Sister Carrie" Portfolio. James L. West, III. LC 85-5370. (Bibliographical Society of University of Virgina Ser.). viii, 87p. 1985. 25.00x (ISBN 0-8139-1067-6). U Pr of Va.
Sister Carrie: The Pennsylvania Edition. Theodore Dreiser. Ed. by James L. West et al. (Illus.). 404p. 1981. 52.95 (ISBN 0-8122-7784-8); pap. 21.95x (ISBN 0-8122-1110-3). U of Pa Pr.
Sister Chromatid Exchange. Avery A. Sandberg. LC 82-157. (Progress & Topics in Cytogenetics Ser.: Vol. 2). 724p. 1982. 108.00 (ISBN 0-8451-2401-3). A R Liss.
Sister Chromatid Exchange. Ed. by Sheldon Wolff. LC 81-13102. 306p. 1982. 94.50 (ISBN 0-471-05987-0, Pub. by Wiley-Interscience). Wiley.
Sister Chromatid Exchanges: Twenty-Five Years of Experimental Research, 2 vols, Pts. A & B. Ed. by Raymond R. Tice & Alexander Hollaender. Incl. Pt. A. The Nature of the SCEs. 550p. 85.00x (ISBN 0-306-41881-9, Plenum Pr); Pt. B. Genetic Toxicology & Human Studies. 560p. 85.00x (ISBN 0-306-41882-7, Plenum Pr). (Basic Life Sciences Ser.: Vols. 29A & 29B). Set. 150.00 (ISBN 0-317-17199-2, Plenum Pr). Plenum Pub.
Sister City & Other Tales. Norway Leif. (Illus.). 22p. (Orig.). 1971. pap. 2.50 (ISBN 0-932264-18-2). Trask Hse Bks.
Sister D'Aranyi. Joseph Macleod. 1972. 7.50 (ISBN 0-8008-7223-1, Crescendo). Taplinger.
Sister Fly Goes to Market. Melissa Cannon. LC 80-21120. (Illus., Orig.). 1980. pap. 1.95 (ISBN 0-937212-01-6). Truedog.
Sister for Sam. Evelyn Mason. (Care Bears Ser.). (Illus.). 40p. (ps-3). 1983. cancelled (ISBN 0-910313-03-2, 7005). Parker Bros.
Sister in the Shadow. Anne W. Smith. LC 85-20058. 169p. (gr. 7-10). 1986. 11.95 (ISBN 0-689-31185-0, Atheneum Childrens Bks). Macmillan.
Sister in the Shadow. Anne W. Smith. 176p. (YA) (gr. 7-12). 1988. pap. 2.50 (ISBN 0-380-70378-5, Flare). Avon.
Sister Jennie's Shaker Desserts. Arthur Tolve & James Bissland, III. (Illus.). 48p. 1983. pap. 3.95 (ISBN 0-911861-00-9). Gabriel's Horn.
Sister Kate. Jean Bedford. 160p. 1987. pap. 5.95 (ISBN 0-14-006496-6). Penguin.
Sister Kenny: The Woman Who Challenged the Doctors. Victor Cohn. LC 75-15401. (Illus.). 320p. 1976. 16.50 (ISBN 0-8166-0755-9). U of Minn Pr.
Sister Light, Sister Dark. Jane Yolen. 256p. 1988. 16.95 (ISBN 0-312-93091-7). Tor Bks.
Sister of the Bride. Beverly Cleary. 128p. (gr. 6-9). 1981. pap. 2.75 (ISBN 0-440-97596-4, LE). Dell.
Sister of the Bride. Beverly Cleary. (Illus.). (gr. 7 up). 1963. PLB 12.88 (ISBN 0-688-31742-1). Morrow.
Sister of the Queen. Lorinda Hagen. 1977. pap. 1.95 (ISBN 0-505-51188-6, Pub. by Tower Bks). Leisure NY.
Sister of the Quints. Stella Pevsner. LC 86-17565. (Junior Literary Guild Selections Ser.). 192p. (gr. 5-9). 1987. 12.95 (ISBN 0-89919-498-2, Pub. by Clarion). Ticknor & Fields.
Sister of the Quints. Stella Pevsner. 192p. (YA) (gr. 7 up). 1988. pap. 2.75 (ISBN 0-671-65973-1). PB.
Sister of Wisdom: St. Hildegard's Theology of the Feminine. Barbara Newman. LC 86-16094. 288p. 1987. 35.00x (ISBN 0-520-05810-0). U of Cal Pr.
Sister Outsider: Essays & Speeches. Audre Lorde. LC 84-1844. (Feminist Ser.). 192p. 1984. 21.95 (ISBN 0-89594-142-2); pap. 8.95 (ISBN 0-89594-141-4). Crossing Pr.
Sister Philomene. Edmond De Goncourt & Jules De Goncourt. Tr. by L. Ensor. 292p. 1975. Repr. of 1890 ed. 23.50x (ISBN 0-86527-304-9). Fertig.
Sister Republics: The Origins of French & American Republicanism. Patrice Higonnet. 336p. 1988. text ed. 25.00 (ISBN 0-674-80982-3). Harvard U Pr.
Sister Rose. Darwin Porter. Date not set. price not set. Maxim Bks.
Sister Satan. Dana Reed. 400p. 1987. pap. 3.95 (ISBN 0-8439-2472-1, Leisure Bks). Leisure NY.
Sister Ships: And Other Stories. Joan London. 1988. pap. 5.95 (ISBN 0-14-010571-9). Penguin.
Sister Suzie Cinema. Lee Breuer. LC 87-1955. 160p. 1986. pap. 10.95 (ISBN 0-930452-60-7). Theatre Comm.
Sister Teresita & the Spirit. Fractious. LC 86-81077. 140p. 1986. pap. 7.95 (ISBN 0-89870-088-4). Ignatius Pr.
Sister to the Sioux: The Memoirs of Elaine Goodale Eastman, 1885-91. Elaine G. Eastman. Ed. by Kay Graber. LC 77-25018. (Pioneer Heritage Ser.: Vol. VII). (Illus.). xvi, 183p. 1985. pap. 5.95 (ISBN 0-8032-6713-4, BB 915, Bison). U Of Nebr Pr.
Sister to the Sun. Margaret K. Biggs. Ed. by Barbara Holley. (Earthwise Chapbook Ser.). 32p. 1981. pap. 3.50 (ISBN 0-933494-00-9). Earthwise Pubns.
Sister Trap. Tina Oaks. (Stepsisters Ser.: No. 2). 176p. (Orig.). (YA) (gr. 7 up). 1987. pap. 2.50 (ISBN 0-590-40903-4). Scholastic Inc.
Sister Vayda's Song. Wilma E. McDaniel. 1982. pap. 6.00 (ISBN 0-914610-27-9). Hanging Loose.
Sister Wolf. Ann Arensberg. LC 80-7659. 240p. 1980. 9.95 (ISBN 0-394-51021-6). Knopf.
Sister Wolf. Ann Arensberg. 1987. pap. 5.95 (ISBN 0-671-64507-2). WSP.
Sister X & the Victims of Foul Play. Carlene H. Polite. 145p. 1975. 8.95 (ISBN 0-374-26521-6). FS&G.
Sisterhood & Solidarity: Feminism & Labor in the 1980s. Diane Balser. 250p. (Orig.). 1987. 25.00 (ISBN 0-89608-278-4); pap. 9.00 (ISBN 0-89608-277-6). South End Pr.
Sisterhood & Solidarity: Workers' Education for Women, 1914-1984. Ed. by Joyce L. Kornbluh & Mary Frederickson. 354p. 1984. 29.95 (ISBN 0-87722-328-9). Temple U Pr.
Sisterhood Denied: Race, Gender & Class in a New South Community. Dolores Janiewski. (Class & Culture Ser.). 272p. 1985. 34.95 (ISBN 0-87722-361-0). Temple U Pr.
Sisterhood Is Global: The First Anthology of Writings from The International Women's Movement. Ed. by Robin Morgan. LC 82-45332. 840p. 1984. (Anchor Pr); pap. 14.95 (ISBN 0-385-17797-6). Doubleday.
Sisterhood Is Powerful: An Anthology of Writings from the Women's Liberation Movement. Ed. by Robin Morgan. 1970. 12.95 (ISBN 0-394-45240-2). Random.
Sisterhood Is Powerful: An Anthology of Writings from the Women's Liberation Movement. Ed. by Robin Morgan. 1970. pap. 9.95 (ISBN 0-394-70539-4, Vin). Random.
Sisterhood of Man. Kathleen Newland. 1979. pap. 5.95 (ISBN 0-393-00935-1). Norton.
Sisterhood: The True Story Behind the Women's Movement. Marcia Cohen. 1988. 19.95 (ISBN 0-671-49553-4). S&S.
Sisters. Pat Booth. 1987. 17.95 (ISBN 0-517-56439-4). Crown.
Sisters. Pat Booth. 416p. 1988. pap. 4.95 (ISBN 0-345-34789-7). Ballantine.
Sisters. Suzanne Goodwin. 1988. pap. 3.95 (ISBN 0-312-90281-6). St Martin.
Sisters. Pamela Hill. (Nightingale Ser.). 252p. 1988. pap. 12.95x (ISBN 0-8161-4416-8). G K Hall.
Sisters. 2nd ed. June Levine. 308p. 1985. pap. 7.95 (ISBN 0-907085-43-1, Pub. by Ward River Pr Ireland). Irish Bks Media.
Sisters. Robert Littell. 352p. (Orig.). 1987. pap. 3.95 (ISBN 0-553-25831-1). Bantam.
Sisters. David McPhail. LC 84-3775. (Illus.). 32p. (ps-3). 1984. 10.95 (ISBN 0-15-275319-2, HJ). HarBraceJ.
Sisters. Vikenti V. Veresaev. Tr. by Juliet Soskice from Rus. LC 74-10093. (Soviet Literature in English Translation Ser). 288p. 1974. Repr. of 1934 ed. 21.45 (ISBN 0-88355-179-9). Hyperion Conn.
Sisters. Margaret H. Wright. 80p. 1986. 7.95 (ISBN 0-8062-2911-X). Carlton.
Sisters, No. 3. 224p. 1986. pap. 2.50 (ISBN 0-449-13008-8, Pub. by Girls Only). Ballantine.
Sisters, No. 4. Jennifer Cole. (Orig.). 1986. pap. 2.50 (ISBN 0-449-13011-8, Pub. by Girls Only). Ballantine.
Sisters, No. 5. 1986. pap. 2.50 (ISBN 0-449-13012-6, Pub. by Girls Only). Ballantine.
Sisters, No. 6. (Orig.). 1986. pap. 2.50 (ISBN 0-449-13013-4, Pub. by Girls Only). Ballantine.
Sisters, No. 10. Jennifer Cole. (Orig.). 1987. pap. 2.50 (ISBN 0-449-13210-2). Fawcett.
Sisters, No. 12. Jennifer Cole. (Orig.). 1987. pap. 2.50 (ISBN 0-449-13212-9, Juniper). Fawcett.
Sisters & Brothers. Judy Dunn. LC 84-19343. (Developing Child Ser.). (Illus.). 182p. 1985. text ed. 12.00x (ISBN 0-674-80980-7); pap. 4.95 (ISBN 0-674-80981-5). Harvard U Pr.
Sisters & Strangers. large print ed. Helen Van Slyke. LC 82-3361. 667p. 1982. 15.95 (ISBN 0-89621-356-0). Thorndike Pr.
Sisters & Strangers. Helen Van Slyke. 416p. 1986. pap. 4.50 (ISBN 0-446-31292-4). Warner Bks.
Sisters & Strangers: Women in the Shanghai Cotton Mills, 1919-1949. Emily Honig. LC 84-51711. 320p. 1986. 37.50x (ISBN 0-8047-1274-3). Stanford U Pr.
Sisters: And Then There Were Two. Jennifer Cole. (Girls Only Ser.: No. 14). (YA) (gr. 6 up). 1988. pap. 2.95 (ISBN 0-449-13494-6). Fawcett.
Sisters & Wives: The Past & Future of Sexual Equality. Karen Sacks. LC 78-75241. (Contributions in Women's Studies: No. 10). 1979. lib. bdg. 35.00x (ISBN 0-313-20983-9, SPA/). Greenwood.
Sisters & Wives: The Past & Future of Sexual Equality. Karen Sacks. LC 82-13491. 288p. 1982. pap. 9.95 (ISBN 0-252-01004-3). U of Ill Pr.
Sisters' Arts: The Writing & Painting of Virginia Woolf & Vanessa Bell. Diane F. Gillepsie. LC 88-2086. (Illus.). 360p. 1988. text ed. 32.50x (ISBN 0-8156-2430-1). Syracuse U Pr.
Sisters, Brothers, & Others. Suzanne Szasz & Elizabeth Taleporos. LC 83-42642. (Illus.). 1984. 17.95 (ISBN 0-393-01810-5). Norton.
Sisters by a River. Barbara Comyns. Ed. by Gamel Woolsen. (Virago Modern Classics Ser.). 160p. 1987. pap. 6.95 (ISBN 0-14-016167-8). Penguin.
Sisters Impossible. James D. Landis. 160p. 1981. pap. 2.50 (ISBN 0-553-26013-8). Bantam.
Sisters Impossible. James D. Landis. LC 78-32148. (gr. 4-7). 1979. Knopf.
Sisters in Charge. Tina Oaks. (Stepsisters Ser.: No. 4). 176p. (Orig.). (gr. 7 up). 1988. pap. 2.50 (ISBN 0-590-41300-7). Scholastic Inc.
Sisters in Crime. Freda Adler. 287p. 1985. pap. text 9.95x (ISBN 0-88133-145-7). Waveland Pr.
Sisters in Crime. Carolyn Keene. (Nancy Drew Files Ser.: No. 19). 160p. (Orig.). (YA) (gr. 7 up). 1988. pap. 2.75 (ISBN 0-671-64225-1). Archway.
Sisters in Crime. Ed. by Marilyn Wallace. 1989. price not set. Berkley Pub.
Sisters in Crime: Feminism & the Crime Novel. Maureen T. Reddy. 176p. 1988. 17.95 (ISBN 0-8264-0407-3). Continuum.
Sisters in Spirit: Mormon Women in Historical & Cultural Perspective. Ed. by Maureen U. Beecher & Lavina F. Anderson. LC 86-30757. 304p. 1987. 21.95 (ISBN 0-252-01411-1). U of Ill Pr.
Sisters in the Sky: Vol. I--The WAFS. Adela R. Scharr. (Illus.). ix, 531p. 1986. 27.95 (ISBN 0-935284-46-X). Patrice Pr.
Sisters in the Sky, Vol. II: The WASP. Adela R. Scharr. Ed. by Gregory M. Franzwa. (Illus.). x, 765p. 1988. 29.95 (ISBN 0-935284-55-9). Patrice Pr.
Sisters: New & Selected Poems. Josephine Jacobsen. 132p. 1987. 18.00 (ISBN 0-930769-03-1); pap. 9.00 (ISBN 0-930769-04-X). Bench Pr SC.
Sisters of a Different Dawn. Darcy Williamson. 309p. 1988. 7.95 (ISBN 1-55523-158-6). Winston-Derek.
Sisters of Charity & the Communion of Labour. Anna B. Jameson. LC 74-15087. (Pioneers of the Woman's Movement: an International Perspective Ser.). 1976. Repr. of 1857 ed. 24.75 (ISBN 0-88355-268-X). Hyperion Conn.
Sisters of Liberty: Marseille, Lyon, Paris, & the Reaction to a Centralized State, 1868-1871. Louis M. Greenberg. LC 70-134952. (Historical Monographs Ser: No. 62). 1971. 25.00x (ISBN 0-674-81000-7). Harvard U Pr.
Sisters of Maryknoll: Through Troubled Waters. Sr. Mary De Paul Cogan. LC 72-167329. (Essay Index Reprint Ser.). Repr. of 1947 ed. 18.00 (ISBN 0-8369-2764-8). Ayer Co Pubs.
Sisters of Orleans: A Tale of Race & Social Conflict. LC 72-2025. (Black Heritage Library Collection Ser.). Repr. of 1871 ed. 17.75 (ISBN 0-8369-9063-3). Ayer Co Pubs.
Sisters of Sacred Song: Selected Listing of Women Hymnodists in Great Britain & America. Samuel J. Rogal. LC 80-8482. 180p. 1981. lib. bdg. 28.00 (ISBN 0-8240-9482-4). Garland Pub.
Sisters of the Road. Barbara Wilson. LC 86-20367. 210p. (Orig.). 1986. pap. 8.95 (ISBN 0-931188-45-8). Seal Pr Feminist.
Sisters of the Spirit: Three Black Women's Autobiographies of the Nineteenth Century. Ed. by William L. Andrews. LC 85-42544. (Religion in North America Ser.). 256p. 1986. 29.50x (ISBN 0-253-35260-6); pap. 8.95x (ISBN 0-253-28704-9). Ind U Pr.
Sisters or Citizens? Women & Socialism in France Since 1876. Charles Sowerwine. LC 81-7692. 272p. 1982. 29.95 (ISBN 0-521-23484-0). Cambridge U Pr.
Sisters or Citizens? Women & Socialism in France since 1876. Charles Sowerwine. LC 81-7692. pap. 66.50 (2027253). Bks Demand UMI.
Sisters Rejoice: Paul's Letter to the Philippians & Luke-Acts as Received by First Century Philippian Women. Lilian Portefaix. (Coniectanea Biblica New Testament Ser.: No. 20). (Illus.). 260p. (Orig.). 1988. pap. 34.00x (ISBN 91-22-01201-X, Pub. by Almqvist & Wiksell). Coronet Bks.
Sisters Rondoli, & Other Stories: Collected Novels & Stories, Vol. 5. facsimile ed. Guy De Maupassant. Ed. by Ernest Boyd. LC 79-157792. (Short Story Index Reprint Ser.). Repr. of 1923 ed. 20.00 (ISBN 0-8369-3904-2). Ayer Co Pubs.
Sisters: The Boy Next Door. Jennifer Cole. (Girls Only Ser.: No. 15). (YA) (gr. 6 up). 1988. pap. 2.95 (ISBN 0-449-13497-0). Fawcett.
Sisters: The Story of Olivia de Havilland & Joan Fontaine. Charles Higham. (Illus.). 1984. 15.95 (ISBN 0-698-11268-7, Coward). Putnam Pub Group.
Sisters Tragedy see Five Modern Plays.
Sisters under the Sari. Ruth G. Armstrong. LC 63-22164. pap. 127.00 (ISBN 0-317-11036-5, 2022765). Bks Demand UMI.
Sistine Cartoons. 2nd ed. L. C. Phillips. LC 68-59442. 84p. 1970. 16.95 (ISBN 0-912282-00-2). Pulse-Finger.
Sistine Chapel. Lutz Heuzinger & Fabrizio Mancinelli. LC 84-50553. (Illus.). 96p. (Orig.). 1984. pap. 13.95 (ISBN 0-935748-58-X). Scala Books.
Sistine Chapel: The Art, the History, & the Restoration. Carlo Pietrangeli et al. (Illus.). 272p. 1986. 60.00 (ISBN 0-517-56274-X, Harmony). Crown.
Sisu: Even Through a Stone Wall. Oskari Tokoi. 9.95 (ISBN 0-8315-0008-5). Speller.
Sisyphus; or, the Limits of Education. Siegfried Bernfeld. Tr. by Frederic Lilge from Ger. LC 77-84784. (Quantum Bks.: No. 1). 1973. 30.00x (ISBN 0-520-01407-3). U of Cal Pr.
Sit By Me. Francis H. Wise & Joyce M. Wise. (Phonetic Reader Ser: No. 13). (Illus., Dr. Wise Learn to Read Ser.). (ps-1). 1975. pap. text ed. 1.50 (ISBN 0-915766-33-7). Wise Pub.
Sit Down & Play. Elsa J. Baker. Ed. by Kenneth W. Baker. LC 87-90545. (Illus.). 203p. (Orig.). 1987. pap. 9.95 (ISBN 0-9620178-0-9). Sycamore WA.
Sit Down & Shape Up: Sit & Exercise? Yes You Can. Fairfax Stephenson. LC 78-62586. 1979. pap. 4.95 (ISBN 0-931490-04-9). Gotuit Ent.
Sit-Down: The General Motors Strike of 1936-1937. Sidney Fine. LC 73-83455. 1969. 24.95x (ISBN 0-472-32948-0). U of Mich Pr.
Sit-in: Mini-Play. (Black Americans Ser.). (gr. 7 up). 1977. 6.50 (ISBN 0-89550-309-3). Stevens & Shea.
Sit, Walk, Stand. Watchman Nee. 1964. pap. 2.95 (ISBN 0-87508-419-2). Chr Lit.
Sit, Walk, Stand. Watchman Nee. 1977. pap. 2.95 (ISBN 0-8423-5893-5). Tyndale.
Sita. Kate Millett. 1978. pap. 3.50 (ISBN 0-345-33066-8). Ballantine.
Sitanka: The Full Story of Wounded Knee. Forest W. Seymour. 1981. 10.75 (ISBN 0-8158-0399-0). Chris Mass.
Sitar Technique in Nibaddha Forms. Stephen Slawek. (Illus.). 264p. 1987. 47.50 (ISBN 81-208-0200-4, Pub. by Motilal Banarsidass). South Asia Bks.
Site. Melisand March. 320p. 1988. 17.95x (ISBN 0-312-01512-7, J Kahn). St Martin.
Site Analysis & Evaluation: A Programmed Course. 1971. pap. 30.00 (ISBN 0-88329-016-2). IAAO.
SITE: Buildings & Spaces. LC 80-16394. (Illus.). 48p. (Orig.). 1970. pap. 3.50 (ISBN 0-917046-10-2). Va Mus Arts.
Site Characterization & Exploration. Ed. by C. H. Dowding. 401p. 1979. pap. 15.00x (ISBN 0-87262-186-3). Am Soc Civil Eng.
Site Control of Materials: Handling, Storage, & Security. John E. Johnston. (Illus.). 1981. text ed. 25.95 (ISBN 0-408-00377-4). Butterworth.
Site Design & Construction Detailing. 2nd ed. Theodore D. Walker. LC 77-18668. (Illus.). 506p. 1986. 38.00 (ISBN 0-914886-32-0); instr's manual 19.00 (ISBN 0-914886-25-8). PDA Pubs.
Site Engineering for Landscape Architects. Steven Strom & Kurt Nathan. (Illus.). 1985. 41.95 (ISBN 0-87055-471-9). AVI.
Site Evaluation Workbook. John W. Schafer & Terry Smith. 1979. spiral bdg. 5.00 (ISBN 0-88252-065-2). Paladin Hse.
Site Experience, 2 Vols. (Reports & Papers on Mass Communication: No. 91). 58p. pap. 5.00 (ISBN 92-3-101796-9, U1322, UNESCO). UNIPUB.
Site Graphics. Richard L. Austin. (Illus.). 128p. 1983. 23.95 (ISBN 0-442-21077-9). Van Nos Reinhold.
Site Handling Equipment: Construction Guide. J. R. Illingworth. 69p. 1982. 8.00 (ISBN 0-7277-0141-X, Pub. by T Telford UK). Am Soc Civil Eng.
Site Index Curves for Gmelina Arborea. A. Greaves. 1978. 30.00x (ISBN 0-85074-043-6, Pub. by For Lib Comm England). State Mutual Bk.
Site Investigation: A Handbook for Engineers. Christopher Clayton et al. LC 81-21973. 448p. 1982. 59.95 (ISBN 0-470-27328-3). Halsted Pr.
Site Investigation & the Law. Jack Cottington & Robert Akenhead. 184p. 1984. 26.00 (ISBN 0-7277-0188-6, Pub. by T Telford UK). Am Soc Civil Eng.
Site Investigation: Construction Guide. Andrew D. Robb. 29p. 1982. 8.00 (ISBN 0-7277-0142-8, Pub. by T Telford UK). Am Soc Civil Eng.
Site Investigation Practice. M. Joyce. (Illus.). 300p. 1982. 49.95 (ISBN 0-419-12260-5, NO. 6733, Pub. by E & FN Spon England). Routledge Chapman & Hall.
Site Investigations, Design, Construction, Operation, Shutdown & Surveillance of Repositories for Low & Intermediate Level Radioactive Wastes in Rock Cavities. (Safety Ser.: No. 62). 95p. (Orig.). 1984. pap. 18.50 (ISBN 92-0-123284-5, ISP659, IAEA). UNIPUB.
Site Investigations for Repositories for Solid Radioactive Wastes in Deep Continental Geological Formations. (Technical Reports Ser.: No. 215). (Illus.). 106p. 1983. pap. 25.00 (ISBN 92-0-125282-X, IDC215, IAEA). UNIPUB.
Site Investigations for Repositories for Solid Radioactive Wastes in Shallow Ground. (Technical Reports Ser.: No. 216). (Illus.). 89p. 1982. pap. 18.00 (ISBN 92-0-125382-6, IDC216, IAEA). UNIPUB.
Site of Lesion Testing. Harriet Kaplan et al. LC 83-5852. (Illus.). 344p. 1984. pap. text ed. 22.00x (ISBN 0-8391-4145-9, 1305). Pro Ed.
Site Perspectives. L. Azeo Torre & William L. Douglas. (Illus.). 192p. 1986. 34.95x (ISBN 0-442-21848-6). Van Nos Reinhold.
Site Plan for Architectural Working Drawings. George T. Clayton. (Illus.). 42p. 1973. pap. text ed. 3.00X (ISBN 0-87563-252-1). Stipes.
Site Plan Reviewer. Jack Rudman. (Career Examination Ser.: C-3251). (Cloth bdg. avail. on request). 1988. pap. 16.00 (ISBN 0-8373-3251-6). Natl Learning.
Site Planning. R. G. Brooks. (Illus.). 512p. 1988. 39.33 (ISBN 0-13-811258-4). P-H.
Site Planning. 3rd ed. Kevin Lynch & Gary Hack. (Illus.). 450p. 1984. text ed. 23.95x (ISBN 0-262-12106-9). MIT Pr.
Site Planning: A Bibliography. Edward Teague. (Architecture Ser.: A 1633). 9p. 1986. 3.00 (ISBN 0-89028-943-3). Vance Biblios.

Site Planning: A Bibliography. Mary Vance. (Architecture Ser.: A 1598). 32p. 1986. 8.75 (ISBN 0-89028-868-2). Vance Biblios.

Site Planning & Design for the Elderly: Issues, Guidelines, & Alternatives. Diane Y. Carstens. (Illus.). 176p. 1985. 41.95 (ISBN 0-442-21768-4). Van Nos Reinhold.

Site Planning for Affordable Housing: Four Case Studies in Falmouth, Massachusetts. Bunker Stimson Solien & Jacob, Inc. Staff. (Illus., Orig.). 1988. pap. text ed. write for info. (ISBN 0-929072-00-6). Bunker Stimson.

Site Planning for Cluster Housing. Richard Untermann & Robert Small. 314p. 1981. pap. 24.95 (ISBN 0-442-28677-5). Van Nos Reinhold.

Site Planning Organization for Transport Infrastructures. Corona. 340p. 1985. 92.00 (ISBN 0-444-87600-6). Elsevier.

Site Reconnaissance & Engineering: An Introduction for Architects, Landscape Architects & Planners. H. C. Landphair & J. L. Motloch. xxi, 300p. 1985. 39.25 (ISBN 0-444-00900-0). Elsevier.

Site Sections & Details: A Reference Guide to Site Construction Details. David J. Ciaccio. LC 84-5095. (Illus.). 128p. 1984. pap. 18.95 (ISBN 0-442-23522-4). Van Nos Reinhold.

Site Selection & Evaluation for Nuclear Power Plants. (Safety Ser.: No. 50-SG-S4). (Illus.). 54p. (Fr. , Eng. , Rus. & Span.). 1980. pap. 11.50 (ISBN 92-0-223680-1, ISP569, IAEA). UNIPUB.

Site Selection & Evaluation for Nuclear Power Plants with Respect to Population Distribution: A Safety Guide. (Safety Ser.: No. 50-SG-S4). (Illus.). 51p. (Fr., Rus. & Span. eds. avail.). 1980. pap. 12.00 (ISBN 92-0-123580-1, ISP569, IAEA). UNIPUB.

Site Selection Factors for Repositories of Solid High-Level & Alpha Bearing Wastes in Geological Formations. (Illus.). 64p. 1978. pap. 14.50 (ISBN 92-0-125177-7, IDC177, IAEA). UNIPUB.

Site Selection for Health Care Facilities. James Lifton & Owen B. Hardy. LC 82-13745. 64p. (Orig.). 1982. pap. 18.75 (ISBN 0-87258-382-1, 127200). AHPI.

Site, Space, & Structure. Kim Todd. (Illus.). 192p. 1985. pap. 27.95 (ISBN 0-442-28319-9). Van Nos Reinhold.

Site-Specific Drug Delivery: Cell Biology, Medical & Pharmaceutical Aspects. Ed. by E. Tomlinson & S. S. Davis. LC 86-24686. 164p. 1986. 39.95 (ISBN 0-471-91236-0). Wiley.

Site Supervision. R. H. Clarke. 256p. 1984. 21.00 (ISBN 0-7277-0200-9, Pub. by T Telford UK). Am Soc Civil Eng.

Site Survey for Nuclear Power Plants. (Safety Ser.: No. 50-SG-S9). 48p. 1985. pap. 11.25 (ISBN 92-0-123884-3, ISP682, IAEA). UNIPUB.

Site Surveying & Levelling: Level 2. H. Rawlinson. LC 81-8122. (Longman Technician Series. Construction & Civil Engineering Sector). (Illus.). 173p. pap. 45.00 (2030342). Bks Demand UMI.

Site Value Taxation. Patricia Carmean. (Research & Information Ser.). 67p. 1980. pap. 13.00 (ISBN 0-88329-020-0). IAAO.

Site Work. 20.00 (ISBN 0-317-65068-8). Am Consul Eng.

Sites: A Third Memoir. Wallace Fowlie. LC 86-19760. v, 179p. 1987. 19.95 (ISBN 0-8223-0700-6). Duke.

Sites & Services Approach Renewed. J. Van der Linden. Orig. Title: Sites & Services: Solution or Stopgap? 1986. text ed. 41.50 (ISBN 0-566-05308-X, Pub. by Gower Pub England). Gower Pub Co.

Sites & Services Projects. (Urban Development Technical Paper: No. 1). 47p. (Eng. & Span.). 1974. pap. 5.00 Eng. Ed. (ISBN 0-686-39780-0, BK9180); pap. Span. Ed. avail. World Bank.

Sites & Services: Solution or Stopgap? see Sites & Services Approach Renewed.

Sites & Solutions: Recent Public Art. Judith E. Tannenbaum. LC 85-80210. (Illus.). 36p. (Orig.). 1985. pap. text ed. 8.00x (ISBN 0-941972-02-X). Freedman.

Sites of Action for Neurotoxic Pesticides. Ed. by Robert M. Hollingworth & Maurice B. Green. LC 87-27047. (Symposium Ser.: No. 356). (Illus.). ix, 334p. 1987. 69.95 (ISBN 0-8412-1436-0). Am Chemical.

Sites of Oahu. Compiled by Elspeth P. Sterling & Catherine C. Summers. LC 78-73981. (Special Publications-Anthropology). 372p. 1978. pap. 25.00 (ISBN 0-910240-73-6). Bishop Mus.

Sites, Perceptions & the Nonvisual Experience: Designing & Manufacturing Mobility Maps. Anne M. Kidwell & Peter S. Greer. 210p. 1973. pap. 4.20 (ISBN 0-89128-055-3, PMR055). Am Foun Blind.

Sites to See: Historical Landmarks in Tulane Country. Annie Mitchell. LC 83-62939. 168p. 1983. pap. 9.95 (ISBN 0-914330-63-2). Panorama West.

Siting, Design & Construction of Underground Repositories for Radioactive Wastes: Proceedings of a Symposium Hanover, 3-7 March 1986. (Illus.). 727p. (Orig., Eng. & Fr.). 1986. pap. text ed. 145.00 (ISP715, IAEA). UNIPUB.

Siting Energy Facilities. Ralph L. Keeney. LC 80-764. 1980. 42.50 (ISBN 0-12-403080-7). Acad Pr.

Siting Handbook for Large Wind Energy Systems. T. R. Hiester & W. T. Pennell. Orig. Title: Meteorological Aspects of Siting Large Wind Turbines. (Illus.). 510p. (Orig.). 1983. pap. 59.50 (ISBN 0-88016-004-7). Windbks.

Siting Handbook for Small Wind Energy Conversion Systems. rev. ed. Harry L. Wegley et al. (Illus.). 100p. 1982. pap. 14.95 (ISBN 0-88016-003-9). Windbks.

Siting Hazardous Waste Management Facilities. Hazardous Waste Dialogue Group Staff & J. Bloom. 71p. 1983. 3.00 (ISBN 0-318-20482-7). Natl Resources Defense Coun.

Siting of Hazardous Waste Disposal Facilities in Texas, No. 53. Susan G. Hadden. LC 82-85620. 128p. 1982. 7.50 (ISBN 0-89940-655-6). LBJ Sch Pub Aff.

Siting of Hazardous Waste Facilities & Transport of Hazardous Substances. LC 85-72050. 32p. 1985. pap. 8.00 (ISBN 0-89707-190-5, 359-0012-01). Amer Bar Assn.

Siting of Major Facilities. Edward A. Williams. (Illus.). 288p. 1983. text ed. 51.50 (ISBN 0-07-070420-1). McGraw.

Siting of Radioactive Waste Repositories in Geological Formations. OECD Staff & NEA Staff. 260p. (Orig.). 1981. pap. 15.00x (ISBN 92-6402-186-8). OECD.

Siting of Reactors & Nuclear Research Centres. (Proceedings Ser.). (Illus.). 511p. 1963. 25.25 (ISBN 92-0-020263-2, ISP72, IAEA). UNIPUB.

Siting Procedures for Major Energy Facilities: Some National Cases. OECD. (Illus.). 142p. (Orig.). 1980. pap. text ed. 8.00x (ISBN 92-64-11986-8). OECD.

Sitings: Aycock, Fleischner, Miss, Trakas. Hugh M. Davies & Ronald J. Onorato. Ed. by Sally Yard. LC 86-80303. (Illus.). 149p. (Orig.). 1986. pap. text ed. 19.50 perfect bdg. (ISBN 0-934418-25-X). La Jolla Mus Contemp Art.

Sitio. Theodore Enslin. LC 73-86250. 50p. 1974. pap. 2.00 (ISBN 0-914102-02-8). Bluefish.

Sitio de Mascaras. Milton M. Martinez. LC 87-72348. (Coleccion Caniqui). (Illus.). 208p. (Orig., Span.). 1987. pap. 9.95 (ISBN 0-89729-460-2). Ediciones.

Sitio de Nadie. 3rd ed. Hilda Perera. 329p. (Orig., Span.). 1973. 15.00 (ISBN 0-317-68245-8). Ediciones.

Sitka. Louis L'Amour. 1986. pap. 3.50 (ISBN 0-553-26119-3). Bantam.

Sitka: A Short History. 2nd, rev. ed. Jack Calvin. (Illus.). 48p. 1983. pap. 10.00 (ISBN 0-9615529-0-5); limited ed. 100.00 (ISBN 0-9615529-1-3). Old Harbor Pr.

Sitka Man. Al Brookman, Sr. LC 84-6430. (Illus.). 172p. (Orig.). 1985. pap. 7.95 (ISBN 0-88240-263-3). Alaska Northwest.

Sitkum Siwash. Helen K. Smith. LC 74-33825. (Western Americana Book). (Illus.). 104p. (Orig.). 1976. pap. 5.50 (ISBN 0-913626-29-5). S S S Pub Co.

Sitosterol. O. J. Pollak & D. Kritchevsky. (Monographs on Atherosclerosis: Vol. 10). (Illus.). vii, 220p. 1981. pap. 98.75 (ISBN 3-8055-0568-X). S Karger.

Sitsiy Yugh Noholnik Ts'in: As My Grandfather Told It. Catherine Attla. (Illus.). 258p. (Orig.). 1983. pap. 12.00 (ISBN 0-933769-07-5). Alaska Native.

Sitsiy Yugh Noholnik Ts'in' As My Grandfather Told It: A Teacher's Guide. Niki McCurry & Eliza Jones. (Illus.). vi, 127p. (Orig.). 1985. pap. 6.50 t'chrs guide (ISBN 0-933769-85-7). Alaska Native.

Sitt Marie-Rose. Etel Adnan. Tr. by Georgina Kleege from Fr. 116p. (Orig.). 1982. pap. 7.50 (ISBN 0-942996-02-X, Dist. by Three Continents). Post Apollo Pr.

Sitter for Baby Monster. Emily P. Kingsley. LC 86-72403. (Sesame Street Growing-Up Bks.). (Illus.). 32p. (gr. 2-5). 1987. 2.95 (ISBN 0-307-12022-8, Pub. by Golden Bks). Western Pub.

Sitting at His Feet. Martha Borth. (Illus.). 85p. (Orig.). 1985. pap. 5.95 (ISBN 0-935993-00-2). Clar Call Bks.

Sitting at the Window Looking Out. Grace C. Johnson. 1988. 4.95 (ISBN 0-533-04068-X). Vantage.

Sitting Bull. Kathie Smith. LC 86-33888. (Great Americans Ser.). (Illus.). 24p. (gr. k-4). 1987. 7.79 (ISBN 0-671-64603-6). Messner.

Sitting Bull. Kathie B. Smith. (Great Americans Ser.). (Illus.). (gr. k-5). 1987. pap. 2.25 (ISBN 0-671-64027-5). Wanderer Bks.

Sitting Bull & the Plains Indians. John Hook. (Life & Times Ser.). (Illus.). 64p. (gr. 4-8). 1987. PLB 12.40 (ISBN 0-531-18102-2, Pub. by Bookwright Pr). Watts.

Sitting Bull, Champion of the Sioux: A Biography. rev.ed ed. Stanley Vestal. (Civilization of the American Indian Ser: No. 46). (Illus.). 1980. Repr. of 1957 ed. 22.95 (ISBN 0-8061-0363-9). U of Okla Pr.

Sitting Bull: Great Sioux Chief. LaVere Anderson. LC 70-120462. (Indians Ser.). (Illus.). 80p. (gr. 2-5). 1970. PLB 6.69 (ISBN 0-8116-6608-5). Garrard.

Sitting Bull, Warrior of the Sioux. new ed. Jane Fleischer. LC 78-18047. (Illus.). 48p. (gr. 4-6). 1979. PLB 9.59 (ISBN 0-89375-154-5); pap. 1.95 (ISBN 0-89375-144-8). Troll Assocs.

Sitting by My Laughing Fire. Ruth B. Graham. LC 77-75457. 1977. 10.95 (ISBN 0-8499-2933-4). Word Bks.

Sitting by the Dock of the Bay. Martin Zoltan. 212p. (Orig.). 1987. pap. 8.95 (ISBN 0-935539-33-6). Heroica Bks.

Sitting Down Hug. Marion D. Cohen. 150p. (Orig.). 1988. pap. 9.00 (ISBN 0-934659-14-1). Liberal Pr.

Sitting in a High Chair. Hap Palmer & Martha Palmer. (Baby Songs Ser.). (Illus.). 16p. (ps). 1987. 3.95 (ISBN 0-8431-1774-5); cassette & bk. 6.95 (ISBN 0-8431-1895-4). Price Stern.

Sitting in Darkness: Americans in the Philippines. David H. Bain. LC 84-8945. (Illus.). 500p. 1984. 24.95 (ISBN 0-395-35285-1). HM.

Sitting in Darkness: Americans in the Philippines. David H. Bein. 496p. 1986. pap. 8.95 (ISBN 0-14-008992-6). Penguin.

Sitting in Judgment: The Sentencing of White-Collar Criminals. Stanton Wheeler et al. LC 88-3196. 1988. 28.50 (ISBN 0-300-03983-2). Yale U Pr.

Sitting in Our Treehouse Waiting for the Apocalypse. Leonard Terr. LC 75-319625. 63p. 1975. 3.50 (ISBN 0-87886-064-9). Greenfld Rev Pr.

Sitting In: Selected Writings on Jazz, Blues, & Related Topics. Hayden Carruth. LC 86-7042. 206p. 1986. text ed. 22.50 (ISBN 0-87745-153-2). U of Iowa Pr.

Sitting on the Job. Scot W. Donkin. 1989. pap. 7.95 (ISBN 0-395-50089-3). HM.

Sitting on the Job: A Practical Survival Guide for People Who Earn Their Living While Sitting. Scott W. Donkin. Ed. by Joseph J. Sweere. LC 86-90503. (Illus.). 137p. 1987. pap. 8.95 (ISBN 0-9617281-0-8). Parallel Integ.

Sitting Posture. Ed. by Etienne Grandjean. LC 70-23595. (Illus.). 253p. 1976. 33.00x (ISBN 0-85066-029-7). Taylor & Francis.

Sitting Pretty. Al Young. LC 75-21461. 272p. 1986. pap. 8.95 (ISBN 0-88739-017-X). Creative Arts Bk.

Sitting Pretty, Marmaduke. Brad Anderson. 128p. 1987. pap. 1.95 (ISBN 0-317-58001-9, Dist. by St Martin's Pr & Warner Pub Servs). Tor Bks.

Sittings with Eusapai Palladino & Other Studies. Everard Feilding. (Illus.). 1963. 10.00 (ISBN 0-8216-0153-9, Pub. by Univ Bks). Lyle Stuart.

Situacion y Perspectivas de los Productos Basicos, 1982-83. (Economic & Social Development Ser.). (Illus.). 171p. (Span.). 1983. pap. 37.50 (ISBN 92-5-301272-2, F3165, FAO). UNIPUB.

Situacion y Perspectivas de los Productos Basicos. (Economic & Social Development Ser.). (Illus.). 131p. (Span.). 1984. pap. 37.50 (ISBN 92-5-301434-2, F3166, FAO). UNIPUB.

Situaciones. Nila G. Marrone. 314p. 1987. pap. text ed. write for info. (ISBN 0-394-37385-5, RanC). Random.

Situaciones: Intermediate Spanish. Jean-Paul Valette et al. 465p. 1988. pap. text ed. 18.00 (ISBN 0-669-15959-X); tchr's annotated ed. 18.00 (ISBN 0-669-15960-3); wkbk. 7.00 (ISBN 0-669-15961-1). Heath.

Situatie Van de Mens. Harvey Jackins. Tr. by Erik Fokke & Jaap Sanders. (Dutch.). pap. 6.00 (ISBN 0-911214-88-7). Rational Isl.

Situating Indian History. Ed. by Bhattacharya & Thapar. 463p. 1986. 49.95. Asia Bk Corp.

Situating Indian History: For Sarvepalli Gopal. Ed. by Sabyasachi Bhattacharya & Romila Thapar. 480p. 1987. 24.95 (ISBN 0-19-561842-4). Oxford U Pr.

Situation Actuelle de L'Anthropologie Culturelle en Hollande see Cahiers de l'Institut de Science Economique Appliquee.

Situation Actuelle de L'Ethnographie et de L'Ethonologie en Allemagne Occidentale see Cahiers de L'Institut de Science Economique Appliquee.

Situation Analyst: Business Positioning. James F. Moore et al. 1985. pap. 20.95x (ISBN 0-256-03567-9). Irwin.

Situation Analyst: Stategic Manager. James F. Moore. 1985. 19.95x (ISBN 0-256-03536-9). Irwin.

Situation de la Poesie. 2nd ed. Jacques Maritain. 144p. 1964. 9.95 (ISBN 0-686-56369-7). French & Eur.

Situation de la Terre. Jules Romains. 244p. 1958. 4.95 (ISBN 0-686-55291-1). French & Eur.

Situation des Menschen. Harvey Jackins. Tr. by Dietmar Kreuer from Ger. 1984. pap. 6.00. Rational Isl.

Situation et Signification. Ivan Fonagy. (Pragmatics & Beyond Ser.: III: 1). vi, 160p. (Orig., Fr.). 1982. pap. 32.00 (ISBN 90-272-2504-4). Benjamins North Am.

Situation Ethics: The New Morality. Joseph Fletcher. LC 66-11917. 176p. 1966. pap. 7.95 (ISBN 0-664-24691-5). Westminster John Knox.

Situation in Flushing. Edmund G. Love. (Great Lakes Bks.). 261p. 1987. 25.00x (ISBN 0-8143-1916-5); pap. 13.95x (ISBN 0-8143-1917-3). Wayne St U Pr.

Situation in Logic. Jon Barwise. (CSLI Lecture Notes Ser.). 200p. 1988. 34.95x (ISBN 0-937073-33-4); pap. 14.95x (ISBN 0-937073-32-6). Ctr Study Language.

Situation Is Hopeless. Ronald Searle. 1982. pap. 6.95 (ISBN 0-14-006312-9). Penguin.

Situation Is Hopeless, but Not Serious: The Pursuit of Unhappiness. Paul Watzlawick. 96p. 1983. 14.95 (ISBN 0-393-01821-0). Norton.

Situation of Industrial Property in the Arab States. 1979. pap. 11.00 (ISBN 0-685-96911-8, WIPO59, WIPO). UNIPUB.

Situation of Poetry: Contemporary Poetry & Its Traditions. Robert Pinsky. LC 76-3015. (Princeton Essays in Literature Ser.). 1977. pap. 8.95 (ISBN 0-691-01352-7). Princeton U Pr.

Situation of Poetry: Four Essays on the Relations Between Poetry, Mysticism, Magic & Knowledge. Raissa Maritain & Jacques Maritain. Tr. by Marshall Suther. LC 54-13505. 1968. Repr. of 1955 ed. 18.00 (ISBN 0-527-61400-9). Kraus Repr.

Situation of the Asian-Pacific Elderly. Ed. by Charlotte Nusberg & Masako M. Osako. 116p. (Orig.). 1981. pap. text ed. 5.00 (ISBN 0-910473-10-2). Intl Fed Ageing.

Situation of the Fishing Industry in Italy, Particularly Regarding Distribution. P. Pagliazzi. (General Fisheries Council of the Mediterranean (GFCM): Studies & Reviews: No. 8). 22p. (Eng. & Fr., 2nd Printing 1966). 1959. pap. 7.50 (ISBN 92-5-101926-6, F1772, FAO). UNIPUB.

Situation of Youth in the 1980s & Prospects & Challenges for the Year 2000. 106p. 1987. 11.00 (ISBN 92-1-130117-3, E.86.IV.10). UN.

Situation-Reaction Drills for Offensive Basketball. Richard W. Harvey. LC 83-4084. 228p. 1983. 18.95 (ISBN 0-13-811273-8, Parker). P-H.

Situation Red, The UFO Siege. Leonard H. Stringfield. 1978. pap. 1.75 (ISBN 0-449-23654-4, Crest). Fawcett.

Situation to Sentence: An Evolutionary Method for Descriptive Linguistics. Anoop Chandola. LC 78-7125. 1979. 32.50 (ISBN 0-404-16038-7). AMS Pr.

Situational Anxiety. Herbert J. Freudenberger & Gail North. 336p. 1983. pap. 8.95 (ISBN 0-88184-024-6). Carroll & Graf.

Situational Chinese. Beverly Hong. (Illus.). 335p. (Orig.). 1983. pap. 8.95 (ISBN 0-8351-1386-8). China Bks.

Situational Exercises in Cross-Cultural Awareness. Richard A. Nitsche & Adele Green. (Elementary Education Ser.). 1977. pap. text ed. 19.95 (ISBN 0-675-08472-5). Merrill.

Situational Interviewing. Eric W. Skopec. 172p. 1988. pap. text ed. 9.95x (ISBN 0-88133-370-0). Waveland Pr.

Situational Leader. Paul Hersey. 126p. 13.50 (ISBN 0-317-13971-1). Ctr Leadership.

Situational Leader. Paul Hersey. LC 84-40659. 128p. (Orig.). 1985. 13.50 (ISBN 0-446-51342-3). Warner Bks.

Situational Leadership for Principals: The School Administrator in Action. Kenneth Dunn & Rita Dunn. LC 82-11211. 228p. 1983. 18.95x (ISBN 0-686-84595-1, Parker). P-H.

Situational Selling: An Approach for Increasing Sales Effectiveness. Paul Hersey. LC 85-72476. (Illus.). 169p. 1985. 29.95 (ISBN 0-931619-00-9). Ctr Leadership.

Situational Selling: Six Keys to Handling the Complex Business Sale. Paul Kelly. 224p. 1988. 19.95 (ISBN 0-8144-5938-2). AMACOM.

Situational Writing. Gene H. Krupa. 260p. 1982. pap. text ed. write for info. (ISBN 0-534-01082-2). Wadsworth Pub.

Situationist International Anthology. Situationist International. Ed. by Ken Knabb. LC 81-69735. 406p. (Orig.). 1981. pap. 10.00 (ISBN 0-939682-00-1). Bur Public Secrets.

Situations. Charles Peguy. (Fr.). pap. 4.50 (ISBN 0-685-37040-2). French & Eur.

Situations, Vol. 1. Jean-Paul Sartre. (Blanche Ser.). 338p. 1947. 11.95 (ISBN 0-686-54992-9). Schoenhof.

Situations, Vol. 2. Jean-Paul Sartre. 336p. 1948. 15.95 (ISBN 0-686-54993-7). French & Eur.

Situations, Vol. 3. Jean-Paul Sartre. 320p. 1949. 22.50 (ISBN 0-686-54994-5). French & Eur.

Situations & Attitudes. Jon Barwise & John Perry. 376p. 1985. pap. text ed. 9.95x (ISBN 0-262-52099-0, Pub. by Bradford). MIT Pr.

Situations & Speech Acts: Toward a Formal Semantics of Discourse. Ed. by David A. Evans & Jorge Hankamer. (Outstanding Dissertations in Linguistics Ser.). 225p. 1985. 37.00 (ISBN 0-8240-5446-6). Garland Pub.

Situations: Autour de 1968, Vol. 8. Jean-Paul Sartre. 481p. 1972. 16.95 (ISBN 0-686-54999-6). French & Eur.

Situations: Colonialisme et Neo-Colonialism, Vol. 5. Jean-Paul Sartre. 256p. 1964. 6.95 (ISBN 0-686-54996-1). French & Eur.

Situations, Language & Logic. Ed. by Jens E. Fenstad et al. 1987. lib. bdg. 59.50 (ISBN 1-55608-048-4, Pub. by Reidel Holland); pap. 22.00 (ISBN 1-55608-049-2, Pub. by Reidel Holland). Kluwer Academic.

Situations: Melanges, Vol. 9. Jean-Paul Sartre. 369p. 1972. 13.95 (ISBN 0-686-55000-5). French & Eur.

Situations: Politique et Autobiographie, Vol. 10. Jean-Paul Sartre. 232p. 1976. 14.95 (ISBN 0-686-55001-3). French & Eur.

Situations: Portraits, Vol. 4. Jean-Paul Sartre. 464p. 1964. 16.95 (ISBN 0-686-54995-3). French & Eur.

Situations: Problemes du Marxisme, Pt. 1, Vol. 6. Jean-Paul Sartre. 392p. 1964. 24.95 (ISBN 0-686-54997-X). French & Eur.
Situations: Problemes du Marxisme, Pt. 2, Vol. 7. Jean-Paul Sartre. 352p. 1965. 9.95 (ISBN 0-686-54998-8). French & Eur.
Sitwells. John Pearson. LC 80-14371. 528p. 1980. pap. 7.95 (ISBN 0-15-682676-3, Harv). HarBraceJ.
Sitwells: Edith, Osbert, & Sacheverell. G. A. Cevasco. (Twayne English Author Ser.). 176p. 1987. lib. bdg. 19.95x (ISBN 0-8057-6953-6, Twayne). G K Hall.
Siva & Buddha. Sr. Nivedita. pap. 0.50 (ISBN 0-87481-116-3). Vedanta Pr.
Siva in Dance, Myth & Iconography. Anne-Marie Gaston. (Illus.). 1982. 45.00x (ISBN 0-19-561354-6). Oxford U Pr.
Siva-Mahimna Stotram (the Hymn on the Greatness of Siva) Pushpadanta. Tr. by Swami Pavitrananda. pap. 1.00 (ISBN 0-87481-148-1). Vedanta Pr.
Siva Samhita. Sivasamhita. Tr. by Srisa Chandra Vasu. LC 73-3803. (Sacred Books of the Hindus: Vol. 15, Pt. 1). Repr. of 1914 ed. 18.00 (ISBN 0-404-57815-2). AMS Pr.
Siva! Siva! Cresent & Heart: Selected Poetry of Murshid Samuel L. Lewis. Samuel L. Lewis. (Bismillah Bks.: No. 1). (Illus.). 112p. (Orig.). 1980. pap. 3.50 (ISBN 0-915424-04-5). Sufi Islamia-Prophecy.
Siva Sutras: The Yoga of Supreme Identity. Jaideva Singh. 1979. 18.00 (ISBN 0-89684-057-3, Pub. by Motilal Banarsidass India); pap. 12.50 (ISBN 0-89684-063-8, Pub. by Motilal Banarsidass India). Orient Bk Dist.
Siva: The Erotic Ascetic. Wendy D. O'Flaherty. (Illus.). 1981. pap. 9.95 (ISBN 0-19-520250-3). Oxford U Pr.
Sivalaya: Explorations of the Eight-Thousand Metre Peaks of the Himalaya. Louis Baume. LC 79-20964. 348p. 1979. pap. 9.95 (ISBN 0-916890-71-6). Mountaineers.
Sivananda: Biography of a Modern Sage. Ed. by Swami Venkatesananda. (Life & Works of Swami Sivananda). (Illus.). 448p. (Orig.). 1985. pap. 11.95 (ISBN 0-949027-01-4). Integral Yoga Pubns.
Sivananda Companion to Yoga. The Sivananda Yoga Center. 1983. pap. 11.95 (ISBN 0-671-47088-4). S&S.
Sivananda Lahari of Sri Sankara. Shankara. Tr. by Tapasyananda from Sanskrit. 87p. 1987. pap. 1.95 (ISBN 0-87481-545-2, Pub. by Ramakrishna Math Madras India). Vedanta Pr.
Sivapithecus Palate see New Siwalik Primates: Their Bearing on the Question of Evolution of Man & the Anthropoidea.
Sivastotravali of Utpaladeva. N. K. Kotru. 172p. 1985. 16.00 (ISBN 81-208-0011-7, Pub. by Motilal Banarsidass India). Orient Bk Dist.
Sivastotravali of Utpaladeva. N. K. Kotru. 173p. 1986. 17.00X (ISBN 0-317-53535-8, Pub. by Motilal Banarsidass). South Asia Bks.
Six. David Meltzer. LC 76-40038. (Illus.). 130p. (Orig.). 1976. pap. 4.00 (ISBN 0-87685-270-3). Black Sparrow.
Six. Rudolf Rocker. 69.95 (ISBN 0-87700-079-4). Revisionist Pr.
Six Acts on a Flying Trapeze. Ellen Clarkson. (Illus.). 160p. 1986. pap. text ed. write for info (ISBN 0-13-811308-4). P H.
Six Airs Varies for Violin & Piano, Op. 89. Charles Dancla. (Carl Fischer Music Library: No.125). 1911. pap. 6.50 (ISBN 0-8258-0027-7, L125). Fischer Inc NY.
Six American Poets from Emily Dickinson to the Present: An Introduction. Ed. by Allen Tate. LC 70-172932. (Library on American Writers: No. 5). 1971. 18.95x (ISBN 0-8166-0630-7). U of Minn Pr.
Six & Higher-Membered Monocarbocyclic Compounds see Rodd's Chemistry of Carbon Compounds.
Six & One-Half Ounce Can of Tuna Recipe Ingredient Substitution Cookbook. Alpha Pyramis Research Division Staff. 18p. 1985. pap. text ed. 4.95 (ISBN 0-913597-88-0, Pub. by Alpha Pyramis). Prosperity & Profits.
Six & Silver. Joan Phipson. LC 70-152696. (Illus.). 190p. (gr. 4-6). 1971. 5.95 (ISBN 0-15-275330-3, HJ). HarBraceJ.
Six Answers to the Problem of Taste. Ronald Suter. LC 79-84279. 1979. pap. text ed. 8.25 (ISBN 0-8191-0726-3). U Pr of Amer.
Six Approaches to Child Rearing: Models from Psychological Theory. D. Eugene Mead. LC 76-19040. 1976. pap. 5.95x (ISBN 0-8425-0327-7). Brigham.
Six Archaeological Sites in Sharqiyeh Province. S. R. Nape. (Liverpool University Delta Survey Ser.: Vol. 1). (Illus.). 104p. 1986. pap. text ed. 19.95 (ISBN 0-85323-405-1, Pub. by Liverpool U Pr). Humanities.
Six Architects. facs. ed. Reginald T. Blomfield. LC 78-99682. (Essay Index Reprint Ser.). 1935. 18.00 (ISBN 0-8369-1340-X). Ayer Co Pubs.
Six Armies in Normandy: From D-Day to the Liberation of Paris, June 6th-August 25th, 1944. John Keegan. LC 81-69968. (Illus.). 416p. 1982. 17.95 (ISBN 0-670-64736-5). Viking.
Six Armies in Normandy: From D-Day to the Liberation of Paris. John Keegan. (Illus.). 392p. 1983. pap. 7.95 (ISBN 0-14-005293-3). Penguin.
Six Artists - Six Idioms. Marti Mayo. 48p. (Orig.). Date not set. pap. 8.00 (ISBN 0-941193-01-2). U Houst Sarah.
Six Axle Quartet: An Essay of Diesel Portraiture. Lowell Amrine. LC 86-2246. 96p. 1986. Repr. of 1980 ed. lib. bdg. 19.95x (ISBN 0-89370-553-5). Borgo Pr.
Six Bells off Java & By Eastern Windows, 2 vols. in 1. William H. McDougall. 25.00 (ISBN 0-914740-27-X). Western Epics.
Six Billion People: Demographic Dilemmas & World Politics. Georges Tapinos & Phyllis Piotrow. (Illus.). 1978. McGraw.
Six Blue Horses. Yvonne Escoula. LC 70-103044. (gr. 5-9). 1970. 14.95 (ISBN 0-87599-162-9). S G Phillips.
Six Bookes of Commonweale. Jean Bodin. Ed. by J. P. Mayer. LC 78-67335. (European Political Thought Ser.). 1979. Repr. of 1962 ed. lib. bdg. 66.50x (ISBN 0-405-11680-2). Ayer Co Pubs.
Six Booklets by Verner & Brahma, 6 bks. Alexander Verner & Swami Brahma. Incl. Bk. 1. Medical Hypnotism & Suggestion (ISBN 0-911662-14-6); Bk. 2. Psychometry (Reading by Vibration (ISBN 0-911662-15-4); Bk. 3. How to Converse with Spirit Friends (ISBN 0-911662-16-2); Bk. 4. Table Rapping & Automatic Writing (ISBN 0-911662-28-6); Bk. 5. How to Know Your Future (ISBN 0-911662-29-4); Bk. 6. Success & Happiness (ISBN 0-911662-68-5). Set. pap. 6.00 (ISBN 0-685-24372-9); pap. 1.00 each. Yoga.
Six Brandenburg Concertos & the Four Orchestral Suites in Full Score. Johann S. Bach. 273p. 1976. pap. 9.95 (ISBN 0-486-23376-6). Dover.
Six Brave Explorers. Kees Moerbeek & Carla Dijs. (Illus.). 12p. (ps up). 9.95 (ISBN 0-8431-2253-6). Price Stern.
Six Breeds. Ralph G. Kirk. LC 70-125225. (Short Story Index Reprint Ser). (Illus.). 1923. 17.00 (ISBN 0-8369-3592-6). Ayer Co Pubs.
Six Busy Days. Mary Erickson. LC 88-11803. (Illus.). 32p. (ps-2). 1988. 7.95 (ISBN 1-55513-699-0, Chariot Bks). Cook.
Six by Lewis, 6 vols. C. S. Lewis. 1978. pap. 18.95 (ISBN 0-02-086770-0, Collier). Macmillan.
Six Byzantine Portraits. Dimitri Obolensky. (Illus.). 248p. 1988. 55.00 (ISBN 0-19-821951-2). Oxford U Pr.
Six Cent Sam's. Julian Hawthorne. LC 70-101283. (Short Story Index Reprint Ser.). 1893. 19.00 (ISBN 0-8369-3220-X). Ayer Co Pubs.
Six Central Texas Auto Tours. Myra H McIlvain & Virginia Erickson. (Illus.). 1980. 9.95 (ISBN 0-89015-242-X). Eakin Pr.
Six Centuries at Tunhuang. Lionel Giles. 50p. 1944. 105.00x (ISBN 0-317-69085-X, Pub. by Han-Shan Tang Ltd). State Mutual Bk.
Six Centuries in East Asia: China, Japan & Korea from the 14th Century to 1912. Peter Lum. LC 72-12582. (Illus.). 288p. 1973. 17.95 (ISBN 0-87599-183-1). S G Phillips.
Six Centuries of Verse. Selected by Anthony Thwaite. (Illus.). 224p. (Orig.). 1985. pap. 9.95 (ISBN 0-423-00960-5, NO. 9410). Routledge Chapman & Hall.
Six Chapters from My Life "Downunder". Yang Jiang. Tr. by Howard Goldblatt. (Illus.). 128p. 1988. pap. 8.95 (ISBN 0-295-96644-0). U of Wash Pr.
Six Chapters from My Life "Downunder". Jiang Yang. Tr. by Howard Goldblatt from Chinese. LC 84-2228. (Renditions Bks.). (Illus.). 128p. 1984. 10.95 (ISBN 0-295-96146-5). U of Wash Pr.
Six Chapters of Canada's Prehistory. J. V. Wright. (Canadian Prehistory Ser.). (Illus.). 118p. 1976. pap. text ed. 10.00x (ISBN 0-317-18871-2, 56515-7, Pub. by Natl Mus Canada). U of Chicago Pr.
Six Chapters of Life in a Cadre School. Yang Chiang. Tr. by Chu Djang. 100p. 1985. pap. 11.85x (ISBN 0-8133-7099-X). Westview.
Six Characters in Search of an Author see Naked Masks: Five Plays.
Six Children Draw. Ed. by S. Paine. LC 81-69580. 1982. 17.00 (ISBN 0-12-543950-4). Acad Pr.
Six Collations of New Testament Manuscripts. Ed. by Kirsopp Lake & Silva New. (Harvard Theol Studies). 1932. 26.00 (ISBN 0-527-01017-0). Kraus Repr.
Six Comedies. W. Somerset Maugham. LC 75-25391. (Works of W. Somerset Maugham). 1977. Repr. of 1939 ed. 32.00 (ISBN 0-405-07849-8). Ayer Co Pubs.
Six Concert Etudes, Opus 35 see Three Piano Works.
Six Criminal Women. facs. ed. Elizabeth Jenkins. LC 76-148222. (Biography Index Reprint Ser.). 1949. 18.00 (ISBN 0-8369-8069-7). Ayer Co Pubs.
Six Crows. Leo Lionni. LC 87-3141. (Illus.). 32p. (ps-2). 1988. 11.95 (ISBN 0-317-65686-4); lib. bdg. 12.99 (ISBN 0-394-99572-4). Knopf.
Six Cuban Painters-Working in New York. (Illus.). 1975. pap. 1.50 (ISBN 0-89192-168-0, Pub. by Ctr Inter-Am Rel). Interbk Inc.
Six Dances for Paper Piano. Coco Gordon. (Intimate Ser.: No. 8). 112p. (Orig.). 1987. 32.00 (ISBN 0-943375-08-8). W Space.
Six Days. Elinor Glyn. (Barbara Cartland's Library of Love: No. 12). 213p. 1980. 12.95 (ISBN 0-7156-1471-1, Pub. by Duckworth London). Longwood Pub Group.
Six Days & the Seven Gates. Yitzhak Navon. 1980. 6.00 (ISBN 0-930832-57-4); pap. 4.00 (ISBN 0-686-70336-7). Herzl Pr.
Six Days of Destruction: Meditations Toward Hope. Elie Wiesel & Albert H. Friedlander. 1988. 9.95; pap. 4.95. Paulist Pr.
Six Days or Forever? Tennessee vs. John Thomas Scopes. Ray Ginger. 1974. pap. 8.95x (ISBN 0-19-519784-4). Oxford U Pr.
Six Days to Better Golf: The Secret of Learning the Golf Swing. Harry Obitz et al. LC 76-9196. (Illus.). 1988. 16.95 (ISBN 0-06-013203-5, HarpT). Har-Row.
Six Days to Die. Gus Stevens. (Orig.). 1981. pap. 2.25 (ISBN 0-505-51696-9, Pub. by Tower Bks). Leisure NY.
Six Days to Saturday: Joe Paterno & Penn State. Jack Newcombe. LC 74-11207. (Illus.). 128p. (gr. 7 up). 1974. 6.95 (ISBN 0-374-36975-5). FS&G.
Six Days to Swim-Jeff Farrell: A Story of Olympic Courage. Jean M. Henning. LC 71-103031. (Illus.). (gr. 6-12). 1970. 3.50 (ISBN 0-911822-02-X). Swimming.
Six Demons of Love: A Book about Men & Love. Steve Berman. 144p. 1984. pap. text ed. 6.95 (ISBN 0-07-004915-7). McGraw.
Six Disciplines of Man's Being & Man's Relation to Government. rev. ed. Melvin Gorham. 128p. 1983. pap. 5.00 (ISBN 0-914752-16-2). Sovereign Pr.
Six Distinct Phases in the Stock Market Course As It Moves from Inactivity to Paroxysm & from Paroxysm to its Catastrophic Collapse & How To Master Them, 2 vols. Charles M. Delaferre. (Illus.). 237p. 1988. 247.75 (ISBN 0-86654-245-0). Inst Econ Finan.
Six Dogs, Twenty-Three Cats, Forty-Five Mice, & One Hundred Sixteen Spiders. Mary Chalmers. LC 83-49482. (Illus.). 40p. (gr. k-3). 1986. 11.70i (ISBN 0-06-021188-1); PLB 11.89 (ISBN 0-06-021189-X). HarpJ.
Six Duos for One or Two Violins, Op. 23. L. Pleyel. (Carl Fischer Music Library: Nos. 156 & 156A). 1902. pap. 6.00 (ISBN 0-8258-0173-7); pap. 5.00 Piano Accompaniment (ISBN 0-8258-0205-9, L-156A). Fischer Inc NY.
Six Dutch Hearts. Mac Hammond. 1977. 5.00 (ISBN 0-686-24036-7). Bellevue Pr.
Six Dynasties Poetry. Kang-i Sun Chang. LC 85-43274. 240p. 1986. text ed. 30.00x (ISBN 0-691-06669-8). Princeton U Pr.
Six Elegies. Laurence Josephs. 1973. staple bdg. 0.75 (ISBN 0-912678-04-6). Greenfld Rev Pr.
Six Elizabethan Plays. Ed. by Robert C. Bald. Incl. Tamburlaine, Pt. 1. Christopher Marlowe; Shoemaker's Holiday. Thomas Dekker; Knight of the Burning Pestle. Francis Beaumont & John Fletcher; Epicoene. Ben Jonson; Duchess of Malfi. John Webster; Broken Heart. John Ford. LC 63-4440. (YA) (gr. 9up). 1963. pap. 6.95 (ISBN 0-395-05135-5, RivEd). HM.
Six English Towns. Alec Clifton-Taylor. (Illus.). 176p. (Orig.). 1987. pap. 12.95 (ISBN 0-563-20490-7, Pub. by BBC). Parkwest Pubns.
Six Essays. J. T. Emmett. 270p. 1972. Repr. of 1891 ed. cancelled (ISBN 0-384-14335-0). Johnson Repr.
Six Essays on Depression. Jean Kirkpatrick. 23p. 1980. pap. 1.50 (ISBN 0-686-35775-2). WFS.
Six Essays on Erasmus & a Translation of Erasmus' Letter to Carondelet 1523. John C. Olin. LC 76-18467. (Illus.). xiv, 125p. 1977. 20.00 (ISBN 0-8232-1023-5); pap. 10.00 (ISBN 0-8232-1024-3). Fordham.
Six Essays on the Development of T. S. Eliot. Francis Wilson. LC 76-15345. 1976. Repr. of 1948 ed. lib. bdg. 18.00 (ISBN 0-8414-9516-5). Folcroft.
Six Essays on the Development of T. S. Eliot. Frank Wilson. 67p. 1980. Repr. of 1896 ed. lib. bdg. 17.50 (ISBN 0-8492-8805-3). R West.
Six Existential Heroes: The Politics of Faith. Lucio P. Ruotolo. LC 72-86386. 192p. 1973. 13.50x (ISBN 0-674-81025-2). Harvard U Pr.
Six Existentialist Thinkers. H. J. Blackham. 179p. 1983. pap. 8.95 (ISBN 0-7100-4611-1). Routledge Chapman & Hall.
Six Faces of Mexico: History, People, Geography, Government, Economy, Literature & Art. Ed. by Russell C. Ewing. LC 66-18533. pap. 83.50 (ISBN 0-317-28563-7, 2055251). Bks Demand UMI.
Six Fairy Variations. Marius Petipa. 44p. pap. 15.00 (ISBN 0-932582-66-4). Dance Notation.
Six Families: Macomber, Marr, Mabillard, Campo, Rateaver, Schaffnit. James D. Macomber. LC 81-71950. (Illus.). 466p. 1982. 45.00 (ISBN 0-9608118-0-X). Woodpile Pubs.
Six Famous Living Poets. facs. ed. Coulson Kernahan. LC 68-8475. (Essay Index Reprint Ser). 1968. Repr. of 1922 ed. 18.00 (ISBN 0-8369-0593-8). Ayer Co Pubs.
Six Famous Living Poets: Introductory Studies, Illustrated by Quotation & Comment. Coulson Kernahan. 1977. Repr. of 1926 ed. lib. bdg. 20.00 (ISBN 0-8492-1405-X). R West.
Six Feet of Country. Nadine Gordimer. 1986. pap. 5.95 (ISBN 0-14-006559-8). Penguin.
Six Feet under. Dorothy Simpson. 176p. 1985. pap. 2.95 (ISBN 0-553-25192-9). Bantam.
Six Figure Woman. Lois Wyse. 192p. 1983. 11.95 (ISBN 0-671-47764-1, Linden Pr). S&S.
Six Figure Woman & How to Be One. Lois Wyse. 192p. 1984. pap. 3.50 (ISBN 0-449-20607-6, Crest). Fawcett.
Six Fillious. B. P. Nichol et al. 1978. pap. 7.00x (ISBN 0-87924-032-6). Membrane Pr.
Six Flags over PTL: Fun with Jim & Tammy. Steve Lail. (Illus.). 55p. (Orig.). 1985. pap. 4.95 (ISBN 0-318-22517-4). Lail Press.
Six Foolish Fishermen. Benjamin Elkin. (Illus.). (gr. k-4). 1957. PLB 11.93 (ISBN 0-516-03601-7). Childrens.
Six Foolish Fishermen. Benjamin Elkin. (Illus.). 48p. (gr. k-3). pap. 2.50 (ISBN 0-590-41377-5). Scholastic Inc.
Six for the Charleston. Barry L. Hillman. 1982. 15.00x (ISBN 0-903653-28-1, Pub. by New Playwrights Network). State Mutual Bk.
Six French Poets of Our Time: A Critical & Historical Study. Robert W. Greene. LC 78-70927. (Princeton Essays in Literature Ser.). 1979. 26.50x (ISBN 0-691-06390-7). Princeton U Pr.
Six French Poets: Studies in Contemporary Literature. facs. ed. Amy Lowell. LC 67-28737. (Essay Index Reprint Ser). 1915. 19.50 (ISBN 0-8369-0626-8). Ayer Co Pubs.
Six Galleons for the King of Spain: Imperial Defense in the Early Seventeenth Century. Carla R. Phillips. LC 86-45444. (Illus.). 368p. 1987. text ed. 37.50x (ISBN 0-8018-3092-3). Johns Hopkins.
Six Generations: Life & Work in Ireland from 1790. L. M. Cullen. (Illus.). 120p. 1986. pap. 15.95 (ISBN 0-85342-227-3, Pub. by Mercier Pr Ireland). Irish Bks Media.
Six German Romantic Tales. Heinrich V. Kleist et al. Tr. by Ronald Taylor from Ger. LC 85-73377. 176p. (Orig.). 1986. pap. 10.95 (ISBN 0-946162-17-4, Pub. by Angel Bks). Dufour.
Six Gothic Tales. Ed. by Reader's Digest Editors. LC 77-83406. (Illus.). 640p. 1979. 17.97 (ISBN 0-89577-060-1). RD Assn.
Six Great American Plays. Ed. & intro. by Allan G. Halline. LC 83-42951. 7.95 (ISBN 0-394-60457-1). Modern Lib.
Six Great Englishmen. Aubrey De Selincourt. LC 73-12820. 1953. lib. bdg. 30.00 (ISBN 0-8414-3658-4). Folcroft.
Six Great Englishwomen. Yvonne Ffrench. LC 76-10646. 1953. lib. bdg. 30.00 (ISBN 0-8414-4219-3). Folcroft.
Six Great Ideas. Mortimer J. Adler. 243p. 1981. 12.95 (ISBN 0-02-500560-X). Macmillan.
Six Great Ideas: Truth, Goodness, Beauty, Liberty, Equality, Justice. Mortimer J. Adler. 256p. 1984. pap. 6.95 (ISBN 0-02-072020-3). Macmillan.
Six Great Modern Plays. Laurel Editions Editors. Incl. Three Sisters. Anton Chekhov; Master Builder. Henrik Ibsen; Mrs. Warren's Profession. George Bernard Shaw; Red Roses for Me. Sean O'Casey; Glass Menagerie. Tennessee Williams; Ali My Sons. Arthur Miller. 512p. 1956. pap. 5.95 (ISBN 0-440-37984-9, LE). Dell.
Six Great Modern Short Novels. Incl. Dead. James Joyce; Billy Budd, Foretopman. Herman Melville; Noon Wine. Katherine A. Porter; Overcoat. Nikolai Gogol; Pilgrim Hawks. Glenway Wescott; Bear. William Faulkner. 448p. 1954. pap. 4.95 (ISBN 0-440-37996-2, LE). Dell.
Six Great Novelists. Walter Allen. LC 73-5556. 1955. lib. bdg. 30.00 (ISBN 0-8414-1737-7). Folcroft.
Six Great Novelists. Walter Allen. 1985. 52.50 (ISBN 0-317-19976-5). Bern Porter.
Six Great Novelists. Walter E. Allen. 1978. Repr. of 1955 ed. lib. bdg. 35.00 (ISBN 0-8495-0106-7). Arden Lib.
Six Great Overtures in Full Score. Ludwig van Beethoven. (Music Scores to Play & Study Ser.). 288p. 1985. pap. 9.95 (ISBN 0-486-24789-9). Dover.
Six Great Playwrights. Aubrey De Selincourt. LC 74-17310. 1974. Repr. of 1960 ed. lib. bdg. 30.00 (ISBN 0-8414-3805-6). Folcroft.
Six Great Poets. Aubrey De Selincourt. LC 73-6998. 1956. lib. bdg. 30.00 (ISBN 0-8414-1868-3). Folcroft.
Six Great Poets: Chaucer, Pope, Wordsworth, Shelley, Tennyson, the Brownings. Aubrey De Selincourt. Repr. of 1956 ed. 26.00x (ISBN 0-403-04283-6). Somerset Pub.
Six Great Poets: Chaucer, Pope, Wordsworth, Shelley, Tennyson, the Brownings. Aubrey De Selincourt. 1988. Repr. of 1956 ed. lib. bdg. 49.00x. Am Biog Serv.
Six Great Russian Composers. facs. ed. Donald Brook. LC 73-136643. (Biography Index Reprint Ser). Repr. of 1946 ed. 25.00 (ISBN 0-8369-8038-7). Ayer Co Pubs.
Six Great Secular Cantatas in Full Score. Johann S. Bach. 288p. (Orig.). 1980. pap. 10.95 (ISBN 0-486-23934-9). Dover.
Six Great Thinkers. Aubrey De Selincourt. LC 77-1363. 1977. lib. bdg. 30.00 (ISBN 0-8414-3816-1). Folcroft.
Six Great Victorian Novelists. F. E. Baily. LC 68-8221. 1969. Repr. of 1947 ed. 17.00x (ISBN 0-8046-0013-9, Pub.by Kennikat). Assoc Faculty Pr.

Six Plays for Young People from the Federal Theatre Project (1936-1939) An Introductory Analysis & Six Representative Plays. Ed. by Lowell Swortzell. LC 85-21974. (Documentary Reference Collection Ser.). (Illus.). 258p. 1986. lib. bdg. 38.95 (ISBN 0-313-24780-3, SYO/). Greenwood.

Six Plays of Clifford Odets: Waiting for Lefty, Awake & Sing, Golden Boy, Rocket to the Moon, Till the Day I Die, & Paradise Lost. Clifford Odets. LC 79-52014. 1979. pap. 9.95 (ISBN 0-394-17092-X, B429, BC). Grove.

Six Plays of Strindberg. August Strindberg. LC 55-5504. 1955. pap. 6.95 (ISBN 0-385-09272-5, A54, Anch). Doubleday.

Six Plays of the Yiddish Theatre. Ed. by Isaac Goldberg. 1977. lib. bdg. 59.95 (ISBN 0-8490-2611-3). Gordon Pr.

Six Poets. Charles Bukowski et al. 1979. 3.00 (ISBN 0-912824-21-2). Vagabond Pr.

Six Poets of the San Francisco Renaissance: Portraits & Checklists. David Kherdian. 17.50 (ISBN 0-87791-000-6). Giligia.

Six Point Two Diesel Engine Explained. Daniel Ash. (Orig.). 1985. write for info. wkbk. (ISBN 0-8064-0201-6, 476); audio visual pkg. 239.00 (ISBN 0-8064-0202-4). Bergwall.

Six-Pointed Star. O. J. Graham. LC 84-60276. 1984. pap. text ed. 2.50 (ISBN 0-932050-24-7). New Puritan.

Six Portraits. John M. Bennett. 1975. 2.00 (ISBN 0-686-73434-3). Luna Bisonte.

Six Portraits. facs. ed. Isabel C. Clarke. LC 67-26725. (Essay Index Reprint Ser). 1935. 20.00 (ISBN 0-8369-0309-9). Ayer Co Pubs.

Six Possible Meanings of "Overevaluation" The 1981-85 Dollar, No. 159. Jeffrey A. Frankel. (Essays in International Finance Ser.). 1985. pap. text ed. 4.50. Princeton U Int Finan Econ.

Six Practical Lessons for an Easier Childbirth. Elizabeth Bing. 1982. pap. 3.50 (ISBN 0-553-25984-9). Bantam.

Six Problems for Don Isidro Parodi. Jorge L. Borges & Adolfo Bioy-Cesares. 160p. 1983. pap. 4.95 (ISBN 0-525-48035-8). Dutton.

Six Proud Walkers. Anthea Fraser. (Crime Club Ser.). 1988. 12.95 (ISBN 0-385-24615-3). Doubleday.

Six Psychological Studies. Jean Piaget. Ed. by David Elkind. Tr. by Anita Tenzer. (Orig.). 1968. pap. 3.95 (ISBN 0-394-70462-2, Vin). Random.

Six Quintets see Music of the Moravians in America from the Archives of the Moravian Church at Bethlehem Pa,.

Six Racy Madams of Colorado. Caroline Bancroft. 64p. 1965. pap. 3.95 (ISBN 0-933472-22-6). Johnson Bks.

Six Radical Thinkers: Bentham, J.S. Mill, Codden, Carlyle, Massine, T.H. Green. John MacCunn. Ed. by J. P. Mayer. LC 78-67370. (European Political Thought Ser.). 1979. Repr. of 1907 ed. lib. bdg. 19.00x (ISBN 0-405-11720-5). Ayer Co Pubs.

Six Records of a Floating Life. Shen Fu. Tr. by Leonard Pratt. 176p. 1983. pap. 3.95 (ISBN 0-14-044429-7). Penguin.

Six Red Months in Russia. Louise Bryant. (Illus.). 299p. (Orig.). 1985. pap. 6.95 (ISBN 0-904526-79-8, Pub. by Journeyman Pr England). Riverrun NY.

Six Red Months in Russia: An Observer's Account of Russia Before & During the Proletarian Dictatorship. Louise Bryant. LC 70-115578. (Russia Observed, Series 1). 1970. Repr. of 1918 ed. 23.50 (ISBN 0-405-03006-1). Ayer Co Pubs.

Six Reports from the Select Committee on Artizans & Machinery, 23 February - 21 May 1824. Great Britain, Parliament, House of Commons, Select Committee on Artizans & Machinery. LC 68-110405. 1968. Repr. of 1824 ed. lib. bdg. 67.50x (ISBN 0-678-05229-8). Kelley.

Six Restoration Plays. Ed. by John H. Wilson. Incl. Country Wife. William Wycherley; Man of Mode. George Etherege; All for Love. John Dryden; Venice Preserved. Thomas Otway; Way of the World. William Congreve; Beaux Stratagem. George Farquhar. LC 59-1770. (YA) (gr. 9up). 1959. pap. 6.95 (ISBN 0-395-05136-3, RivEd). HM.

Six Revue Sketches see Complete Works: No. 3.

Six Roundtable Discussions of Corporate Finance with Joel Stern. Ed. by Donald H. Chew, Jr. LC 86-12382. 345p. 1986. lib. bdg. 39.95 (ISBN 0-89930-162-2, SFV/, Quorum Bks). Greenwood.

Six Rural Problem Areas: Relief-Resources-Rehabilitation. P. G. Beck & M. C. Forster. LC 71-165679. (Research Monograph: Vol. 1). 1971. Repr. of 1935 ed. lib. bdg. 22.50 (ISBN 0-306-70333-5). Da Capo.

Six San Francisco Poets. David Kherdian. pap. 6.00 (ISBN 0-685-11738-3). Giligia.

Six Satirists. Carnegie Institute of Technology, Department of English Staff. LC 72-1315. (Essay Index Reprint Ser.). Repr. of 1965 ed. 12.00 (ISBN 0-8369-2838-5). Ayer Co Pubs.

Six Scandinavian Novelists. Alrik Gustafson. LC 40-27695. 1940. 14.50x (ISBN 0-89067-051-X). Am Scandinavian.

Six Scandinavian Novelists: Lie, Jacobsen, Heidenstam, Selma Lagerlof, Hamsun, Sigrid Undset. Alrik Gustafson. LC 69-19835. 1968. Repr. of 1940 ed. 18.00 (ISBN 0-8196-0230-2). Biblo.

Six Sesame Street Golden Super Shape Books. (Golden Boxed Ser.). (Illus.). (gr. 2-5). 1987. pap. write for info. (ISBN 0-307-15533-1, Pub. by Golden Bks). Western Pub.

Six Seventeen Squadron: The Dambusters at War. Tom Bennett. (Illus.). 272p. (Orig.). 1988. pap. 12.95 (ISBN 1-85260-041-1, Pub. by PSL P Stephens England). Sterling.

Six-Shooter Sod-Buster. Russ Kidd. (Lythway Ser.). 176p. 1988. lib. bdg. 17.50 (ISBN 0-7451-0647-1, Pub. by Chivers Pr UK). G K Hall.

Six Short Plays of Eugene O'Neill. Eugene O'Neill. Incl. Dreamy Kid; Before Breakfast; Diff'rent; Welded; Straw; Gold. (Orig.). 1965. pap. 4.95 (ISBN 0-394-70276-X, Vin). Random.

Six Silver Spoons. Janette S. Lowrey. LC 77-105469. (I Can Read History Bks.). (Illus.). 64p. (ps-2). 1971. PLB 9.89 (ISBN 0-06-024037-7). HarpJ.

Six Simple Pumps. Ed. by Margaret Crouch. 94p. 1983. perfect bound 7.65 (ISBN 0-86619-166-6, E-11075). Vols Tech Asst.

Six-Six-One-Nine-Nine. Lloyd Dunn. 28p. (Orig.). 1987. pap. 2.50 (ISBN 0-938309-03-X). Bomb Shelter Prop.

Six Six Six in U. S. A. Dale A. Howard. (Illus.). 52p. (Orig.). 1987. pap. text ed. 4.99 (ISBN 0-940517-00-0). JCMC Louisiana.

Six Sixty-Six. Jay Anson. 1982. pap. 3.50 (ISBN 0-671-83126-7). PB.

Six-Sixty-Six: The Number of a Man. Marvin H. Banta. LC 87-91121. 64p. (Orig.). 1987. pap. 7.95 (ISBN 0-937139-01-7). Grasshopper Pubns.

Six Sketches. Tony Caramia. Ed. by Frances Clark & Louise Goss. (Frances Clark Presents Ser.). 12p. 1985. pap. text ed. 2.95 (ISBN 0-913277-17-7). New Schl Mus Study.

Six Sonatas for Unaccompanied Violin. J. S. Bach. Ed. by Leopold Auer. (Carl Fischer Music Library: No. 788). 1917. pap. 7.00 (ISBN 0-8258-0088-9, L788). Fischer Inc NY.

Six Sonatas for Violin & Piano. Georg F. Handel. Ed. by Leopold Auer & Carl Friedberg. (Carl Fischer Music Library: NO. 846). 51p. 1919. pap. 8.00 (ISBN 0-8258-0091-9, L 846). Fischer Inc NY.

Six Soviet Plays. Ed. by Eugene Lyons. Repr. of 1934 ed. lib. bdg. 48.50x (ISBN 0-8371-0154-9, LYSP). Greenwood.

Six Spanish Missions in Texas: A Portfolio of Paintings. Memorial ed. E. M. Schiwetz. (Illus.). 1984. 60.00 (ISBN 0-292-77597-0). U of Tex Pr.

Six Stages of Parenthood. Ellen Galinsky. LC 87-1800. 384p. 1987. pap. 10.95 (ISBN 0-201-10529-2). Addison-Wesley.

Six Stars. Nelson M. Lloyd. LC 75-125229. (Short Story Index Reprint Ser). 1906. 18.00 (ISBN 0-8369-3596-9). Ayer Co Pubs.

Six Steps in the Treatment of Borderline Personilty Organization. Vamik D. Volkan. LC 87-19475. 250p. 1987. 25.00x (ISBN 0-87668-753-2). Aronson.

Six Steps to a Sustainable Society. Lester R. Brown & Pamela Shaw. LC 81-51798. (Worldwatch Papers). 1982. pap. 4.00 (ISBN 0-916468-47-X). Worldwatch Inst.

Six Steps to Successful Interviewing: How to Build Your Reputation by Picking the Winners. 1986. 14.95 (ISBN 0-317-64342-8). Coll Placement.

Six Stories. Robert Pepper-Smith. 60p. (Orig.). 1987. pap. 7.50 (ISBN 0-936993-15-4, 87-10-X). Europa Media.

Six Stories of Jesus. Peter Enns & Glen Forsberg. (Stories that Live Ser.: Bk. 5). (Illus.). 24p. (ps-5). 1985. 4.95 (ISBN 0-936215-05-4); cassette incl. STL Intl.

Six Stuart Sovereigns, 1512-1701. Eva Scott. LC 73-118499. 1971. Repr. of 1935 ed. 31.50x (ISBN 0-8046-1247-1, Pub.by Kennikat). Assoc Faculty Pr.

Six Stunning Paradoxes: The Present Disadvantages of Certain Unique Improvements. Morris Philipson. 1968. 2.00 (ISBN 0-940550-04-0). Caxton Club.

Six Subjects of Reformation Art: A Preface to Rembrandt. William H. Halewood. (Illus.). 167p. 1982. pap. 14.95 (ISBN 0-8020-6491-4). U of Toronto Pr.

Six Subjects of Reformation Art: A Preface to Rembrandt. William H. Halewood. LC 82-175730. pap. 42.00 (2026410). Bks Demand UMI.

Six Systems of Indian Philosophy. Friedrich M. Mueller. LC 73-18829. Repr. of 1919 ed. 44.50 (ISBN 0-404-11459-8). AMS Pr.

Six Systems of Indian Philosophy. Friedrich M. Muller. 1973. 16.50 (ISBN 0-686-20305-4). Intl Bk Dist.

Six Tales of the Jazz Age & Other Stories. F. Scott Fitzgerald. 1968. 8.95 (ISBN 0-684-10160-2, ScribT); pap. 8.95 (ISBN 0-684-71762-X, ScribT). Scribner.

Six Tales of the Jazz Age & Other Stories. F. Scott Fitzgerald. 15.95 (ISBN 0-88411-597-6, Pub. by Aeonian Pr). Amereon Ltd.

Six Talks on Jung's Psychology. Robert A. Clark. (Orig.). 1953. pap. 4.50 (ISBN 0-910286-07-8). Boxwood.

Six: The Versewagon Poetry Manual. Ed. by Rivelin Grapheme Press Staff. 128p. 40.00x (ISBN 0-947612-13-0, Pub. by Rivelin Grapheme Pr); pap. 20.00x (ISBN 0-947612-14-9, Pub. by Rivelin Grapheme Pr). State Mutual Bk.

Six Theories of Justice: Perspectives from Philosophical & Theological Ethics. Karen Lebacqz. LC 86-26547. 160p. (Orig.). 1986. pap. 9.95 (ISBN 0-8066-2245-8, 10-5820). Augsburg.

Six Things Satan Uses to Rob You of God's Abundant Blessings. Peter Popoff. Ed. by Don Tanner. LC 81-86521. (Illus.). 96p. 1982. pap. 2.00 (ISBN 0-938544-11-X). Faith Messenger.

Six Thinking Hats. Edward De Bono. 207p. 17.95 (ISBN 0-317-47211-9). Intl Ctr Creat Think.

Six Thinking Hats: An Essential Approach to Business Management from the Creator of Lateral Thinking. Edward DeBono. 1986. 16.95 (ISBN 0-316-17791-1). Little.

Six Thousand Five Hundred & Two Applications. Rodnay Zaks. LC 78-73740. (Six Thousand Five Hundred & Two Ser.: No. 2). (Illus.). 278p. 1979. pap. 14.95 (ISBN 0-89588-015-6, D302). SYBEX.

Six Thousand Five Hundred & Two Assembly Language Programming. Judi N. Fernandez et al. LC 82-6917. 277p. 1983. pap. 14.95 (ISBN 0-471-86120-0). Wiley.

Six Thousand Four Hundred Seventy-Four Slack Relatives. Roscoe Keeney. 1983. 17.50 (ISBN 0-9613116-0-6). McClain.

Six Thousand Miles of Fence: Life on the XIT Ranch of Texas. Cordia S. Duke & Joe B. Frantz. (M. K. Brown Range Life Ser.: No. 1). (Illus.). 285p. 1961. pap. 7.95 (ISBN 0-292-77564-4). U of Tex Pr.

Six Thousand Names for Your Baby. expanded ed. 176p. (Orig.). 1983. pap. 2.95 (ISBN 0-440-17956-4). Dell.

Six Thousand Year Old Space Suit. Vaughn Greene. (Illus.). 116p. 1985. 5.95. V Greene.

Six Thousand Year-Old Spacesuit. Vaughn M. Greene. (Illus.). 104p. (Orig.). 1982. pap. 7.95. Merlin Engine Wks.

Six Thousand Years of Seafaring: The Irish Incas King Solomon's Ophir in New Mexico Raleigh's Roanoke Colony Was Not Lost West Virginia, St. Brendan's Promised Land. rev. ed. Orville L. Hope. LC 84-90413. 1984. 10.00 (ISBN 0-318-20082-1). O L Hope.

Six Times True. Mae H. Ashworth. 48p. (Orig.). (gr. 7-9). 1973. pap. 1.95 (ISBN 0-377-03601-3). Friendship Pr.

Six to Five: The Six to Five Exercise Almanac-a Lunch, or other Hour Guide to Fitness & a Longer Life. 3rd, rev. ed. Harvest Staff. 1988. pap. 10.00. Harvest Pubns.

Six Tracts by W. B. Godbey. W. B. Godbey. Ed. by David W. Faupel. (Higher Christian Life Ser.). 479p. 1985. 60.00 (ISBN 0-8240-6420-8). Garland Pub.

Six Tragedies of Shakespeare. John D. Wilson. LC 72-14314. 1973. lib. bdg. 20.00 (ISBN 0-8414-1367-3). Folcroft.

Six Tragedies of Shakespeare. John D. Wilson. 1982. 42.50 (ISBN 0-686-81919-5). Bern Porter.

Six Trees. Mary E. Wilkins Freeman. LC 74-94721. (Short Story Index Reprint Ser.). 1903. 18.00 (ISBN 0-8369-3100-9). Ayer Co Pubs.

Six Vignettes. Robert L. Merriam. (Illus.). 38p. 1981. 6.50x (ISBN 0-686-32492-7). R L Merriam.

Six Vignettes from my life of 88 Years, & Supplement. Samuel E. Burr. (Illus.). 116p. 1968. Ltd. ed. 7.50 (ISBN 0-911994-61-0). Burr Pubns Ltd.

Six Voices: Contemporary Australian Poets. Ed. by Chris Wallace-Crabbe. LC 79-4265. 1979. Repr. of 1977 ed. lib. bdg. 35.00x (ISBN 0-313-21250-3, WCSV). Greenwood.

Six Voyages of Lone Sloane. Philippe Druillet. (Stories of the Fantastic Ser.). 64p. 1987. pap. cancelled. NBM.

Six Wars at a Time. Howard Shaff & Audrey Shaff. LC 85-70296. 1985. 18.95 (ISBN 0-931170-27-3); pap. 12.95 (ISBN 0-931170-26-5). Ctr Western Studies.

Six-Way Paragraphs. Walter Pauk. (Illus.). 224p. (gr. 9 up). 1974. pap. text ed. 6.00x (ISBN 0-89061-009-6, 744). Jamestown Pubs.

Six-Way Paragraphs: Advanced Level. Walter Pauk. 240p. (Reading level gr. 8-12, Interest level gr. 6-12, ABE). 1983. pap. text ed. 7.20 (ISBN 0-89061-303-6, 731). Jamestown Pubs.

Six-Way Paragraphs: Middle Level. Walter Pauk. 240p. (Reading level gr. 4-8, Interest level 6-12, ABE). 1983. pap. 7.20 (ISBN 0-89061-302-8, 730). Jamestown Pubs.

Six Ways to Pray from Six Great Saints. Gloria Hutchinson. (Illus.). 152p. 1982. pap. text ed. 4.95 (ISBN 0-86716-007-1). St Anthony Mess Pr.

Six-Week Fat to Muscle Makeover. Ellington Darden. (Illus.). 160p. 1988. 17.95 (ISBN 0-399-13406-9, Putnam). Putnam Pub Group.

Six Weeks. Fred M. Stewart. pap. 3.50 (ISBN 0-671-54358-X). PB.

Six Weeks in the Life of Fanny Scott. Clara T. Fugate. Ed. by Elizabeth Calvera. Tr. by Gilda Socarras-Roufagalas. (Tales of the Virginia Wilderness Ser.: No. 2). (Illus., Orig., Eng. & Span.). 1988. pap. 6.95 (ISBN 0-936015-08-X). Pocahontas Pr.

Six Weeks in the Sioux Teepees. Sarah F. Wakefield. 1985. 13.00 (ISBN 0-87770-215-2). Ye Galleon.

Six Weeks to Better Parenting. Caryl W. Krueger. LC 85-6489. 1985. pap. 8.95 (ISBN 0-88289-482-X). Pelican.

Six Weeks to Better Parenting. Caryl W. Krueger. 326p. 1984. pap. 8.95 (ISBN 0-317-68235-0). Belleridge.

Six Weeks to Words of Power. Wilfred Funk. (gr. 9 up). 1983. pap. 3.95 (ISBN 0-671-62366-4). PB.

Six Wheel Drive. Ronald T. Martin. 64p. 1986. 6.95 (ISBN 0-8062-3022-3). Carlton.

Six White Horses: Okalahoma. Janet Dailey. (Americana Ser.). pap. 2.75 (ISBN 0-373-89836-3). Harlequin Bks.

Six Who Dared. Michael L. Sherer. 1984. 6.50 (ISBN 0-89536-663-0, 1971). CSS of Ohio.

Six Who Won. Ed. by Coordinating Council of Literary Magazines Staff. 96p. (Orig.). 1987. pap. 6.95 (ISBN 0-317-56483-8, Dist. by Kampmann & Co.). Moyer Bell Limited.

Six Wings: Men of Science in the Renaissance. George Sarton. LC 56-11998. (Illus.). 336p. 1957. 19.50x (ISBN 0-253-35275-4). Ind U Pr.

Six Women Novelists. Merryn Williams. LC 88-6435. (Modern Novelists Ser.). 140p. 1988. 24.95 (ISBN 0-312-02089-9). St Martin.

Six Women's Slave Narratives, 1831-1909. Mary Prince et al. (Schomburg Library of Nineteenth-Century Black Women Writers). 384p. 1988. 22.50 (ISBN 0-19-505262-5). Oxford U Pr.

Six-Won: The Nineteen Eighty-Six Literary Magazine Writers' Awards. 95p. 1986. pap. 6.95 (ISBN 0-942332-11-3). Coord Coun Lit Mags.

Six-Year Experience of Unwed Mothers As Parents: A Continuing Study of These Mothers & Their Children. Mignon Sauber & Eileen M. Corrigan. 177p. 1970. pap. 3.50 (ISBN 0-86671-007-8). Comm Coun Great NY.

Six-Year-Old-Man. Stanley Elkin. LC 86-73201. 140p. 1987. 18.00 (ISBN 0-917453-16-6); 25.00x (ISBN 0-917453-17-4); pap. 10.00 (ISBN 0-917453-15-8). Bamberger.

Six-Year Rural High School: A Comparative Study of Small & Large Units in Alabama. John I. Riddle. LC 70-177191. (Columbia University. Teachers College. Contributions to Education: No. 737). Repr. of 1937 ed. 22.50 (ISBN 0-404-55737-6). AMS Pr.

Six-Year Sequence see Language Learner.

Six Years of Educational Progress in Nepal. University of Oregon Contract. 76p. (Eng. & Nepali.). 1959. 4.00 (ISBN 0-318-12885-3, 17). Am-Nepal Ed.

Six Years on the West Coast of America, 1856-1862. Louis S. Rossi. Tr. by W. Victor Wortley. (Illus.). 376p. 1983. 19.95 (ISBN 0-87770-293-4). Ye Galleon.

Six Years with the Texas Rangers, 1875 to 1881. James B. Gillett. Ed. by Milo M. Quaife. LC 76-4495. (Illus.). xxxvi, 279p. 1976. pap. 8.50 (ISBN 0-8032-5844-5, BB 624, Bison). U of Nebr Pr.

Six Yogas of Naropa & Mahamudra. 2nd ed. Garma C. Chang. LC 86-10020. 128p. 1986. pap. 9.95 (ISBN 0-937938-33-5). Snow Lion.

Six Yuan Plays. Tr. by Liu Jung-En. (Classics Ser.). 288p. 1972. pap. 6.95 (ISBN 0-14-044262-6). Penguin.

Sixe Bookes of Politickes or Civil Doctrine. Justus Lipsius. Tr. by W. Jones. LC 79-25633. (English Experience Ser.: No. 287). 1970. Repr. of 1594 ed. 22.00 (ISBN 90-221-0287-4). Walter J Johnson.

Sixfold Symmetry. 1987. 20.95 (ISBN 0-9617354-0-6). Samara Editions.

Sixgun Cartridges & Loads. Elmer Keith. 1985. Repr. of 1936 ed. 19.95 (ISBN 0-88227-024-9). Gun Room.

Sixgun Cemetry, No. 99. Jake Logan. 100p. 1987. pap. 2.75 (ISBN 0-425-09647-5). Berkley Pub.

Sixgun Circus, No. 2. J. D. Hardin. 192p. 1987. 2.75 (ISBN 0-425-10115-0). Berkley Pub.

Sixgun Law. Jake Logan. Ed. by Tom Colgan. (Slocum Ser.: No. 113). 1988. pap. 2.75 (ISBN 0-425-10850-3). Berkley Pub.

Sixgun Legacy. Evan Evans. 256p. 1983. pap. 2.25 (ISBN 0-441-76858-X). Ace Bks.

Sixgun Legacy. Evans Evans, pseud. 256p. 1986. pap. 2.75 (ISBN 0-515-08711-4). Jove Pubns.

Sixguns & Society: A Structural Study of the Western. Will Wright. 1975. pap. 10.95x (ISBN 0-520-03491-0). U of Cal Pr.

Sixguns at Silverado, No. 107. Jake Logan. 1987. pap. 2.75 (ISBN 0-425-10347-1). Berkley Pub.

Sixteen & Away from Home. Arleta Richardson. (Grandma's Attic Ser.). (gr. 5 up). 1985. pap. 3.50 (ISBN 0-89191-933-3, 59337). Cook.

Sixteen Authors to One: Intimate Sketches of Leading American Storytellers. facs. ed. David Karsner. LC 68-16944. (Essay Index Reprint Ser). 1928. 18.00 (ISBN 0-8369-0584-9). Ayer Co Pubs.

Sixteen-Bit Microprocessor: An 8086-8088 Based Product-Development Approach. Roy W. Goody. LC 85-22419. (Illus.). 496p. 1986. 29.95 (ISBN 0-935397-00-0). CompTech.

Sixteen-Bit Microprocessor Systems. T. Flik & H. Liebig. 300p. 1985. pap. 42.00 (ISBN 0-387-15164-8). Springer-Verlag.

Sixteen-Bit Microprocessor Systems. Texas Instruments Engineering Staff. (Illus.). 592p. 1982. text ed. 58.50 (ISBN 0-07-063760-1). McGraw.

Sixteen-Bit Microprocessors. Ian Whitworth. 300p. 1983. 21.95 (ISBN 0-13-811372-6). P-H.

Sixth International Conference on Collective Phenomena: Reports from the Moscow Refusnik Seminar. Inga Fischer-Hjalmars & Joel L. Lebowitz. (Annals of the New York Academy of Sciences: Vol. 452). 411p. 1985. text ed. 94.00x (ISBN 0-89766-298-9); pap. text ed. 94.00x (ISBN 0-89766-299-7). NY Acad Sci.

Sixth International Conference on Expansive Soils (6eme Conference Internationale des Sols Expansifs: Proceedings, New Delhi, 1-4 December 1987, 2 vols. 700p. 1988. text ed. 115.00 (ISBN 90-6191-923-1, Pub. by A A Balkema). Brookfield Pub Co.

Sixth International Congress on Accounting. (Accounting History & the Development of a Profession Ser.). 718p. 1984. lib. bdg. 90.00 (ISBN 0-8240-6335-X). Garland Pub.

Sixth International Fiber Optics & Communications Exposition: FOC '82, Los Angeles, Calif. Information Gatekeepers, Inc. 1982. 125.00 (ISBN 0-686-38469-5). Info Gatekeepers.

Sixth International Report on the Prevention & Suppression of Dust in Mining, Tunnelling, & Quarrying, 1973-1977. (Occupational Safety & Health Ser.: No. 48). viii, 152p. 1982. pap. 12.25 (ISBN 92-2-103006-7). Intl Labour Office.

Sixth International Visual Field Symposium. Ed. by A. Heijl & E. L. Greve. (Documenta Ophthalmologica Proceedings Ser.). 1985. lib. bdg. 115.00 (ISBN 90-6193-524-5, Pub. by Junk Pubs Netherlands). Kluwer Academic.

Sixth International Workshop on Photon-Photon Collision. Ed. by R. L. Lander. 498p. 1985. 61.00 (ISBN 9971-978-22-9). World Scientific Pub.

Sixth Level see Competency Tests for Basic Reading Skills.

Sixth Mad Spy vs. Spy. Date not set. pap. price not set (ISBN 0-446-35240-3). Warner Bks.

Sixth Man. Dan Marlowe. 61p. 1987. pap. 3.95 (ISBN 0-8224-2398-7). D S Lake Pubs.

Sixth Marine Division Association History. Sixth Marine Division Association Staff. LC 87-50368. 128p. 1987. 45.00 (ISBN 0-938021-12-5). Turner Pub KY.

Sixth Meeting of the Eastern African Sub-Committee for Soil Correlation & Land Evaluation, Maseru, Lesotho, 9-18 October, 1985. FAO Staff. (World Soil Resources Reports: No. 58). (Illus.). 205p. (Orig.). 1987. pap. text ed. 16.25 (ISBN 0-317-55824-2, F2992, FAO). UNIPUB.

Sixth Meeting of the Italian League Against Parkinson's Disease & Extrapyramidal Disorders, 1981. Ed. by A. Agnoli. (Journal: Pharmacology: Vol. 22, No. 1). (Illus.). 96p. 1981. pap. 31.50 (ISBN 3-8055-2322-X). S Karger.

Sixth Merry Adventure of Robin Hood. Howard Pyle. 1986. pap. 2.95 (ISBN 0-317-38208-X, Pub. by Sig Classics). NAL.

Sixth National Ground Water Quality Symposium. 1983. 31.25 (ISBN 0-318-23007-0). Natl Water Well.

Sixth National Symposium & Exposition on Aquifer Restoration: Proceedings. LC 86-18198. 1986. 43.75 (ISBN 0-318-23015-1). Natl Water Well.

Sixth Old House Catalogue. Lawrence Grow. LC 88-13385. (Illus.). 224p. (Orig.). 1988. pap. 12.95 (ISBN 1-55562-065-5). Main Street.

Sixth Patriarch's Sutra: Great Master Hui Neng. Commentary by Tripitaka Master Hua. Tr. by Buddhist Text Translation Society Staff. (Illus.). 235p. (Orig.). 1977. 15.00 (ISBN 0-917512-19-7); pap. 10.00 (ISBN 0-917512-33-2). Buddhist Text.

Sixth Precinct. Christopher Newman. 320p. (Orig.). 1987. pap. 3.95 (ISBN 0-449-13174-2, GM). Fawcett.

Sixth Process Technology Division Conference Proceedings. 780p. 1986. 60.00 (ISBN 0-932897-11-8). Iron & Steel.

Sixth Reading Helper. Gloria Orlick. (Classroom Pairing: Reading Tutorial Program Ser.). (Illus., Orig., Prog. Bk.). (gr. 3). 1970. pap. 3.45 (ISBN 0-87594-020-X, 2160). Book-Lab.

Sixth Report of the United States Geographic Board: 1890-1932. United States Geographic Board. LC 67-8571. 844p. 1967. Repr. of 1933 ed. 48.00x (ISBN 0-685-11676-X). Gale.

Sixth Sense. Larry Kettelkamp. (Illus.). (gr. 5-9). 1970. PLB 11.88 (ISBN 0-688-31463-5). Morrow.

Sixth Sense & Other Stories. Jessie Haas. LC 88-45226. 192p. (gr. 1-5). 1988. 11.95 (ISBN 0-688-08129-0). Greenwillow.

Sixth Sense & Other Stories. Margaret S. Hopkins. LC 71-110199. (Short Story Index Reprint Ser.). 1899. 19.00 (ISBN 0-8369-3350-8). Ayer Co Pubs.

Sixth Sense of Animals. Maurice Burton. LC 72-6622. (Illus.). 192p. 1973. 7.95 (ISBN 0-8008-7232-0). Taplinger.

Sixth Sense: Psychic Powers & Your Five Senses. Jenny Randles. 240p. 1987. 15.95 (ISBN 0-88162-226-5). Salem Hse Pubs.

Sixth Sense: Psychic Powers & Your Five Senses. Jenny Randles. 240p. 1987. 49.00x (ISBN 0-7090-2802-4, Pub. by R Hale Ltd UK). State Mutual Bk.

Sixth Stellation of the Icosahedron. Gerald Jenkins & Magdalen Bear. (Tarquin Polyhedra Ser.). 24p. (Orig.). (gr. 5-9). 1986. pap. 4.50 (ISBN 0-906212-46-4, Pub. by Tarquin). Parkwest Pubns.

Sixth Symposium on Biotechnology for Fuel & Chemicals: Symposium No. 14, Gatlinburg, Tennessee, May 15-18, 1984. C. D. Scott & Elmer L. Gaden. 697p. 1985. pap. 78.95 (ISBN 0-471-81332-X). Wiley.

Sixth Trumpeter Swan Society Conference: Proceedings & Papers. Trumpeter Swan Society Staff. Ed. by David K. Weaver. 101p. (Orig.). 1981. pap. 4.00 (ISBN 0-9619936-1-8). Trumpeter Swan Soc.

Sixth Wisconsin Infantry. Rufus R. Dawes. 1984. 30.00 (ISBN 0-89029-079-2). Pr of Morningside.

Sixth Workshop on Grand Unification: Proceedings of the Workshop held at Minneapolis, April, 1985. Ed. by S. Rudaz & T. Walsh. 500p. 1986. 67.00 (ISBN 9971-978-83-0); pap. 38.00 (ISBN 9971-978-84-9). World Scientific Pub.

Sixties. Todd Gitlin. 528p. 1989. pap. 11.95 (ISBN 0-553-34601-6). Bantam.

Sixties. Ed. by Gerald Howard. 540p. (Orig.). 1982. pap. 5.95 (ISBN 0-671-42389-4). WSP.

Sixties. rev. ed. John Javna & Gordon Javna. (Illus.). 240p. 1988. pap. 14.95 (ISBN 0-312-01725-1). St Martin.

Sixties, No. 4. Ed. by Robert Bly & William Duffy. 1982. pap. 5.95 (ISBN 0-934888-06-X). Hobart & Wm Smith.

Sixties, No. 5. Ed. by Robert Bly & William Duffy. 1982. pap. 5.95 (ISBN 0-934888-07-8). Hobart & Wm Smith.

Sixties, No. 6. Ed. by Robert Bly & William Duffy. 1982. pap. 5.95 (ISBN 0-934888-08-6). Hobart & Wm Smith.

Sixties, No. 7. Ed. by Robert Bly & William Duffy. 1982. pap. 5.95 (ISBN 0-934888-09-4). Hobart & Wm Smith.

Sixties, No. 8. Ed. by Robert Bly & William Duffy. (Junior Literary Guild Ser.). (gr. 4-9). 1982. pap. 5.95 (ISBN 0-934888-10-8). Hobart & Wm Smith.

Sixties, No. 9. Ed. by Robert Bly & William Duffy. 1982. pap. 5.95 (ISBN 0-934888-11-6). Hobart & Wm smith.

Sixties, No. 10. Ed. by Robert Bly & William Duffy. 1982. pap. 5.95 (ISBN 0-934888-12-4). Hobart & Wm Smith.

Sixties As Reported by the New York Times. Ed. by Arlene Keylin & Laurie Barnett. LC 80-84. (Illus.). 256p. 1980. lib. bdg. 11.98 (ISBN 0-405-13085-6). Ayer Co Pubs.

Sixties! Barbie & Batman, Twiggy & Twinkies, Surfing & Star Trek, Mustangs & Mini-Skirts, James Bond & Jimi Hendrix & Chubby Checker & More. Gordon Javna & John Javna. LC 83-428. (Illus.). 224p. 1983. pap. 13.95 (ISBN 0-312-72752-6). St Martin.

Sixties Papers: Documents of a Rebellious Decade. Ed. by Judith C. Albert & Stewart E. Albert. 336p. 1984. 40.95 (ISBN 0-275-91116-0, C1116); pap. 17.95 (ISBN 0-275-91781-9, B1781). Praeger.

Sixties Reader. James Haskins & Kathleen Benson. LC 85-40886. (Viking Kestrel Non-Fiction Ser.). (Illus.). 256p. (YA) (gr. 7 up). 1988. 13.95 (ISBN 0-670-80674-9, Viking Kestrel). Viking.

Sixties Rock: A Listener's Guide. Robert Santelli. (Illus.). 320p. 1985. pap. 10.95 (ISBN 0-8092-5439-5). Contemp Bks.

Sixties: The Decade in Vogue. Ed. by Caroline Hall & Nicholas Drake. 192p. 1988. 35.00 (ISBN 0-13-811647-4). Prentice Hall Pr.

Sixties, Without Apology. Ed. by Sohnya Sayres et al. LC 84-2274. (Illus.). 390p. 1984. 29.50x (ISBN 0-8166-1336-2); pap. 14.95 (ISBN 0-8166-1337-0). U of Minn Pr.

Sixties: Years of Hope, Days of Rage. Todd Gitlin. LC 87-47575. 512p. 1987. 19.95 (ISBN 0-553-05233-0). Bantam.

Sixtieth Anniversary of the U. S. S. R. Greetings from Abroad. Collets Staff. 496p. 1983. 16.25x (ISBN 0-317-53819-5, Pub. by Collets (UK)). State Mutual Bk.

Sixty Alphabets. S. Gunnlaugur Briem. LC 85-5225. (Illus.). 128p. 1986. pap. 12.95 (ISBN 0-500-27414-2). Thames Hudson.

Sixty American Poets, Eighteen Ninety-Six to Nineteen Forty-Four. rev. ed. U. S. Library of Congress, General Reference & Bibliography Division. LC 73-5993. xii, 168p. Repr. of 1954 ed. 35.00x (ISBN 0-8103-3365-1). Gale.

Sixty Bokes Olde & Newe: Manuscripts & Early Printed Books From Libraries in & Near Philadelphia Illustrating Chauncer's Sources, His Works, & Their Influence. Ed. by David Anderson. 123p. 1986. pap. text ed. 9.95X (ISBN 0-317-59565-2, Pub. by Rosenbach Mus & Lib). U Pr of Va.

Sixty Crocheted Snowflakes. Barbara Christopher. 32p. (Orig.). 1987. pap. 2.95 (ISBN 0-486-25393-7). Dover.

Sixty Daily Studies for Piano. Pischna. Ed. by Hans Seifert. (Carl Fischer Music Library: No. 484). 64p. (Eng. & Span.). 1964. pap. 4.50 (ISBN 0-8258-0126-5, L 484). Fischer Inc NY.

Sixty-Day Diet Diary. Karen Kreps & Richard Smith. 144p. (Orig.). 1987. pap. 3.95 (ISBN 0-440-57946-5, Dell Trade Pbks). Dell.

Sixty-Day Fully Financed Fortune Kit: How to Make Money Raising Money for People. 3rd ed. Tyler G. Hicks. 150p. 1987. pap. 29.50 (ISBN 0-934311-16-1). Intl Wealth.

Sixty Dramatic Illustrations in Full Colours of the Cathedral Cities of England. George Gilbert. (Promotion of the Arts Library). (Illus.). 99p. 1983. 297.85 (ISBN 0-86650-046-4). Gloucester Art.

Sixty-Eight Communion Meditations & Prayers. Robert Shannon et al. 120p. (Orig.). 1984. pap. 3.95 (ISBN 0-87239-770-X, 3033). Standard Pub.

Sixty-Eight Great Ideas: The Library Awareness Handbook. Ed. by Peggy Barber. LC 82-11518. 66p. 1982. pap. 7.50x (ISBN 0-8389-0376-2). ALA.

Sixty-Eight Hundred Microprocessor Architecture: Software & Interface Techniques. Walter A. Triebel & Avtar Singh. (Illus.). 336p. 1986. text ed. 40.00 (ISBN 0-13-811357-2). P-H.

Sixty-Eight Hundred Microprocessor: Architecture, Software & Interfacing Techniques. Walter A. Triebel & Avtar Singh. (Illus.). 384p. 1987. Motorola edition. text ed. 21.97 (ISBN 0-13-811290-8). P-H.

Sixty-Eight Hundred Nine Microprocessor. Andrew C. Staugaard, Jr. (Illus.). 421p. 1982. pap. text ed. 24.95 (ISBN 0-87119-080-X, EB-6404); tchr's. ed. 9.95 (ISBN 0-87119-081-8). Heathkit-Zenith Ed.

Sixty Eight Hundred Nine Microprocessor. Andrew C. Staugaard, Jr. (Illus.). 424p. 1982. 99.95 (ISBN 0-87119-092-3, EE-3404). Heathkit-Zenith Ed.

Sixty-Eight Hundred Nine Primer: Assembly Language & Subroutines for the TRS-80 Color Computer. Kenneth Skier. 280p. 1983. pap. 16.95 (ISBN 0-07-057862-1, BYTE Bks). McGraw.

Sixty-Eight Scientific & Engineering Programs for the Apple II & IIe. Joseph J. Carr. 1984. 22.00 (ISBN 0-8359-6920-7, Reston). P-H.

Sixty-Eight Thousand Assembly Language Programming. 2nd ed. Lance A. Levanthal et al. (Illus.). 625p. 1986. pap. text ed. 19.95 (ISBN 0-07-881232-1). Osborne-Mcgraw.

Sixty-Eight Thousand Assembly Language: Techniques for Building Programs. Donald Krantz & James Stanley. 1988. pap. 24.95 (ISBN 0-201-11659-6). Addison-Wesley.

Sixty-Eight Thousand Microcomputer Systems: Designing & Troubleshooting. Alan D. Wilcox. (Illus.). 512p. 1987. text ed. 48.00 (ISBN 0-13-811399-8). P-H.

Sixty-Eight Thousand Microprocessor: Architecture, Programming, & Applications. Michael A. Miller. 640p. 1988. case bound 37.95; supplements avail. Merrill.

Sixty-Eight Thousand: Principles & Programming. Leo Scanlon. LC 81-51553. 240p. 1981. pap. 16.95 (ISBN 0-672-21853-4, 21853). Sams.

Sixty Eight Thousand User Guide. Fleetwood. 182p. 1985. 19.90 (ISBN 1-8505-8001-4, Pub. by Sigma Pr UK). Bk Clearing Hse.

Sixty-Eight Thousand User's Manual. Joseph J. Carr. Date not set. write for info. S&S.

Sixty-Eight Thousand, 68010, 68020 Primer. Kelly-Bottle & Fowler. 368p. 1985. 21.95 (ISBN 0-672-22405-4, 22405-4). Sams.

Sixty Etudes for Violin, Op. 45, 2 bks. (Carl Fischer Music Library: Nos. 122 & 123). (Ger. & Fr.). Bk. 1. pap. 3.50 (ISBN 0-8258-0026-9, L122); Bk. 2. pap. 3.50 (ISBN 0-8258-0141-9, L123). Fischer Inc NY.

Sixty Fairy Tales of the Brothers Grimm. Illus. by Arthur Rackham. (Fairy Tales & Fables Ser.). (Illus.). (gr. 2-7). 8.98 (ISBN 0-517-28525-8). Outlet Bk Co.

Sixty-Fifth Art Directors Annual. Ed. by Miriam L. Solomon. (Illus.). 816p. 1986. 44.95 (ISBN 0-937414-06-9). R Silver.

Sixty-First Art Directors Annual. Art Directors Club of New York Staff. Ed. by Miriam L. Solomon. (Illus.). 672p. 1982. 39.95 (ISBN 0-937414-02-6). ADC Pubns.

Sixty-Five Buttercream Flowers. Richard V. Snyder. (Illus.). 1957. 8.50 (ISBN 0-682-40089-0, Banner). Exposition-Phoenix.

Sixty-Five Pearls. Manohar Kelkar. LC 87-42906. 59p. 1988. 6.95 (ISBN 1-55523-116-0). Winston-Derek.

Sixty Five Press Interviews with Robert G. Ingersoll. Robert Ingersoll. 288p. 1983. 6.00 (ISBN 0-911826-66-1). Am Atheist.

Sixty-Five Songs; Sixty-Five Pesen. Bulat Okudzhava. Ed. by V. Frumkin. (Eng. & Rus.). 1980. pap. 11.00 (ISBN 0-88233-638-X). Ardis Pubs.

Sixty-Five Valiants. Alice H. Luiggi. LC 65-28692. (Illus.). 1965. 10.00x (ISBN 0-8130-0147-1). U Presses Fla.

Sixty-Five Ways to Give Evangelistic Invitations. Faris D. Whitesell. LC 84-11269. 128p. 1984. pap. 5.95 (ISBN 0-8254-4021-1). Kregel.

Sixty-Five Year Index to Physical Therapy. pap. 20.00 (ISBN 0-912452-65-X). Am Phys Therapy Assn.

Sixty-Five Years of Progress & a Record of New York City Banks. Ed. by Stuart Bruchey. LC 80-1189. (Rise of Commercial Banking Ser.). (Illus.). 1981. Repr. of 1935 ed. lib. bdg. 12.00x (ISBN 0-405-13674-9). Ayer Co Pubs.

Sixty Five Zero Two Assembly Language Programming. 2nd ed. Lance A. Leventhal. (Illus.). 650p. 1986. pap. text ed. 19.95 (ISBN 0-07-881216-X). Osborne-McGraw.

Sixty-Five Zero Two Assembly Language Subroutines. Lance A. Leventhal & Winthrop Saville. 546p. (Orig.). 1982. pap. text ed. 19.95 (ISBN 0-07-931059-1). Osborne-McGraw.

Sixty Folk-Tales from Exclusively Slavonic Sources. Ed. by Richard M. Dorson. Tr. by Albert H. Wratislaw. LC 77-70629. (International Folklore Ser.). 1977. Repr. of 1889 ed. lib. bdg. 24.50x (ISBN 0-405-10133-3). Ayer Co Pubs.

Sixty Forms for the Entrepreneur: Forms Generator - Apple II, II Plus, IIc & IIe. Robert V. Burns & Rees C. Johnson. 192p. 1985. pap. cancelled (ISBN 0-88056-256-0). Dilithium Pr.

Sixty Forms for the Entrepreneur: Forms Generator - Commodore 64. Robert V. Burns & Rees C. Johnson. 192p. 1985. pap. cancelled (ISBN 0-88056-257-9). Dilithium Pr.

Sixty Forms for the Entrepreneur: Forms Generator - IBM-PC, PCjr & PC XT. Robert V. Burns & Rees C. Johnson. 192p. 1985. pap. cancelled (ISBN 0-88056-258-7). Dilithium Pr.

Sixty Forms for the Landlord: Forms Generator - Apple II, II Plus, IIc & IIe. Robert V. Burns & Rees C. Johnson. 192p. 1985. pap. cancelled (ISBN 0-88056-253-6). Dilithium Pr.

Sixty Forms for the Landlord: Forms Generator - Commodore 64. Robert V. Burns & Rees C. Johnson. 192p. 1985. pap. cancelled (ISBN 0-88056-254-4). Dilithium Pr.

Sixty Forms for the Landlord: Forms Generator - IBM-PC, PCjr & PC XT. Robert V. Burns & Rees C. Johnson. 192p. 1985. pap. cancelled (ISBN 0-88056-255-2). Dilithium Pr.

Sixty Forms for Your Household: Forms Generator for Your Apple II, Apple II Plus, & Apple IIc & IIe. Robert V. Burns & Rees C. Johnson. 192p. 1985. pap. cancelled (ISBN 0-88056-250-1). Dilithium Pr.

Sixty Forms for Your Household: Forms Generator for Your Commodore 64. Robert V. Burns & Rees C. Johnson. 192p. 1985. pap. cancelled (ISBN 0-88056-251-X). Dilithium Pr.

Sixty Forms for Your Household: Forms Generator for Your IBM-PC, IBM-PCjr & IBM-PC XT. Robert V. Burns & Rees C. Johnson. 192p. 1985. pap. cancelled (ISBN 0-88056-252-8). Dilithium Pr.

Sixty Four Techniques for Coming up with New Ideas. Vernon A. Magnesen & Joanne F. Cucwa. 180p. 1987. pap. 19.95 (ISBN 0-911541-10-1). Gregory Pub.

Sixty Hiking Trails Central Oregon Cascades. Don Lowe & Roberta Lowe. (Trail Guide). (Illus.). 1978. pap. 9.95 (ISBN 0-911518-51-7). Touchstone Pr Ore.

Sixty Hiking Trails, Central Oregon Cascades. Don Lowe & Roberta Lowe. Ed. by Thomas K. Worcester. (Illus.). 128p. (Orig.). 9.95 (ISBN 0-317-65195-1). Touchstone Oregon.

Sixty Jane. John L. Long. LC 76-103524. (Short Story Index Reprint Ser.). 1903. 17.00 (ISBN 0-8369-3266-8). Ayer Co Pubs.

Sixty-Minute Bread Book: And Other Fast-Yeast Recipes You Can Make in One Half the Usual Time. Nancy Baggett. LC 84-24756. 1985. 17.95 (ISBN 0-399-13020-9). Putnam Pub Group.

Sixty-Minute Flower Garden: A Yard Full of Dazzling Flowers in One Hour a Week. Jeff Ball & Charles Cresson. (Illus.). 288p. 1986. 21.95; pap. 13.95 (ISBN 0-87857-637-1). Rodale Pr Inc.

Sixty Minute Gourmet. Pierre Franey. 1987. Boxed Set. pap. 17.90 (ISBN 0-449-90215-3). Fawcett.

Sixty Minutes Verbatim. CBS, Inc. Staff. LC 80-23836. (Illus.). 1981. lib. bdg. 20.00x (ISBN 0-405-13723-0). Ayer Co Pubs.

Sixty-Nine Days of Easter. Todd S. Lawson. LC 76-30786. 1977. ltd. ed. 3.50x (ISBN 0-914024-31-0); pap. 2.00x ltd. ed. (ISBN 0-914024-30-2). SF Arts & Letters.

Sixty-Nine Images...Below the Belt! Poetry. Philip L. Sherrod. LC 84-72169. (Illus.). 79p. (Orig.). 1984. pap. 7.95. Carrousel Pubns.

Sixty-Ninth Steelmaking Conference Proceedings. 600p. 1986. 60.00 (ISBN 0-932897-09-6). Iron & Steel.

Sixty on the Sixties: A Decade's History in Verse. Ed. by Richard Snyder & Robert McGovern. 63p. 1970. pap. 4.25 (ISBN 0-912592-02-8). Ashland Poetry.

Sixty-One. Tony Kubek & Terry Pluto. (Illus.). 352p. 1987. 19.95 (ISBN 0-02-566870-6). Macmillan.

Sixty-One Gospel Talks for Children: With Suggested Objects for Illustration. Eldon Weisheit. LC 70-96217. 1969. pap. 5.50 (ISBN 0-570-03713-1, 12-2615). Concordia.

Sixty-One Talks for Orthodox Funerals. A. Coniaris. 1969. pap. 4.95 (ISBN 0-937032-02-6). Light&Life Pub Co MN.

Sixty-One Ways to Cut Gas Consumption see Up Your Gas: Sixty-One Ways to Cut Gas Consumption, Increase Your Mileage, Chop Costs & Minimize Waiting in Gas Lines! Plus Eleven Ways to Find a Good Mechanic & Save Money!.

Sixty-One Worship Talks for Children. rev. ed. E. Weisheit. LC 68-20728. (gr. 3-6). 1975. pap. 5.50 (ISBN 0-570-03714-X, 12-2616). Concordia.

Sixty-Plus & Fit Again: Exercises for Older Men & Women. Magda Rosenberg. LC 76-49130. (Illus.). 156p. 1977. 6.95 (ISBN 0-87131-224-7); pap. 3.95 (ISBN 0-87131-237-9). M Evans.

Skateboard Practice: Addition & Subtraction. new ed. Mary Laycock et al. (Illus.). (gr. 1-2). 1978. pap. text ed. 6.95 (ISBN 0-918932-55-6). Activity Resources.
Skateboard Practice: Multiplication & Division. Mary Laycock & Peggy McLean. (Illus.). (gr. 3-6). 1979. pap. text ed. 6.95 (ISBN 0-918932-65-3). Activity Resources.
Skateboard Scramble. Barbara Douglass. LC 78-12480. (Illus.). 92p. (gr. 3-6). 1979. Westminster John Knox.
Skateboarding. Dorothy C. Schmitz. Ed. by Howard Schroeder. LC 78-7048. (Funseekers Ser.). (Illus.). 32p. (gr. 3-4). 1978. PLB 8.95 (ISBN 0-913940-91-7). Crestwood Hse.
Skateboarding. (Illus.). 1988. pap. 4.95 (ISBN 0-451-82172-6, Sig). NAL.
Skateboarding Is for Me. Lowell A. Dickmeyer. LC 78-54361. (Sports for Me Bks.). (Illus.). (gr. 2-5). 1978. PLB 7.95 (ISBN 0-8225-1081-2). Lerner Pubns.
Skateboards & Skateboarding: The Complete Beginner's Guide. LaVada Weir. (Illus.). (gr. 4-6). 1977. pap. 1.75 (ISBN 0-671-41136-5). Archway.
Skaters: Profile of a Pair. Lynn Haney. LC 83-13655. (Illus.). (gr. 5 up). 1983. 10.95 (ISBN 0-399-21013-X, Putnam). Putnam Pub Group.
Skater's Waltz: A Novel. Philip Norman. 1985. 15.95 (ISBN 0-671-50379-0, Linden Pr). S&S.
Skates of Uncle Richard. Carol Fenner. LC 78-55910. (Illus.). (gr. 2-5). 1978. (BYR); lib. bdg. 7.99 (ISBN 0-394-93553-5). Random.
Skating. (Illus.). 64p. (gr. 6-12). 1983. pap. 1.25x (ISBN 0-8395-3250-4, 3250). BSA.
Skating Book. Ginny L. Winter. (Illus.). (gr. k-3). 1963. 8.95 (ISBN 0-8392-3035-4). Astor-Honor.
Skating for Cross-Country Skiers. Audun Endestad & John Teaford. LC 86-21298. (Illus.). 160p. (Orig.). 1987. pap. 10.95 (ISBN 0-88011-282-4, PEND0282). Leisure Pr.
Skating Heidens. Mary V. Fox. LC 80-23066. (Illus.). 128p. (gr. 5-12). 1981. PLB 13.95 (ISBN 0-89490-046-3). Enslow Pubs.
Skating on Skis. Dick Mansfield. LC 87-14563. (Illus.). 144p. 1988. pap. 9.95 (ISBN 0-937921-37-8). Acorn Pub.
Skating on Thin Ice. Louise Everett. LC 86-30857. (Illus.). 32p. (gr. k-2). 1987. PLB 5.41 (ISBN 0-8167-0992-0); pap. text ed. 1.50 (ISBN 0-8167-0993-9). Troll Assocs.
Skating Rink. Mildred Lee. LC 69-13443. 128p. (gr. 6 up). 1969. 10.95 (ISBN 0-395-28912-2, Clarion). HM.
Skating Shoes. Noel Streatfeild. (Orig.). (gr. 5 up). 1982. pap. 3.25 (ISBN 0-440-47731-X, YB). Dell.
Skating System: Scrutineering Ballroom Dance Competitions. Imperial Society of Teachers of Dancing Staff. (Ballroom Dance Ser.). 1986. lib. bdg. 69.95 (ISBN 0-8490-3360-8). Gordon Pr.
Skating System: Scrutineering Ballroom Dance Competitions. Ed. by Imperial Society of Teachers of Dancing Staff. (Ballroom Dance Ser.). 1985. lib. bdg. 79.95 (ISBN 0-87700-869-8). Revisionist Pr.
Skating with Heather Grace. Thomas Lynch. 1987. 14.45 (ISBN 0-394-55480-9); pap. 8.95 (ISBN 0-394-74756-9). Knopf.
Skazaiia J Povesti O Kulikovskoi Bitve. Compiled by L. A. Dmitriev & O. O. Likhachev. 424p. (Rus.). 1982. 39.00x (ISBN 0-317-40878-X, Pub. by Collets (UK)). State Mutual Bk.
Skazanije o Khrista Radi Jurodivoj - Pelagiji Ivanovna Serebrennikva. 183p. pap. 7.00 (ISBN 0-317-29280-3). Holy Trinity.
Skazanije o Zemnoj Zhizni Presvjatoj Bogoroditsi. Ed. by Archimandrite Panteleimon Nizhnik. 552p. 1974. pap. 20.00 (ISBN 0-317-29172-6). Holy Trinity.
Skazanije o zhizni i Podvigakh Ieroskimanakha Parthenija, startsa Kievo-Petcherskoj-Lavri. 104p. pap. 4.00 (ISBN 0-317-29270-6). Holy Trinity.
Skazhi Izium. Vasilii Aksenov. 375p. 1985. 25.00 (ISBN 0-88233-518-9); pap. 12.50. Ardis Pubs.
Skazki T Pesni Pozhdennye V. Doroge. 520p. 1985. 39.00x (ISBN 0-317-42706-7, Pub. by Collets (UK)). State Mutual Bk.
Skazki: Tales & Legends of Old Russia. Ida Zeitlin. (Illus.). 1979. Repr. of 1926 ed. lib. bdg. 45.00 (ISBN 0-8492-3155-8). R West.
Skazki Tales & Legends of Old Russia. Ida Zeitlin. (Illus.). 333p. 1985. Repr. of 1984 ed. lib. bdg. 85.00 (ISBN 0-89984-540-1). Century Bookbindery.
SKCALB. Lee O. Lewis. LC 84-91442. 48p. 1985. 6.95 (ISBN 0-533-06510-0). Vantage.
Skeeball & the Secret of the Universe. Barbara Hall. LC 87-7730. 240p. (gr. 7 up). 1987. 12.95 (ISBN 0-531-05722-4); PLB 12.99 (ISBN 0-531-08322-5). Orchard Bks Watts.
Skeen's Leap. Jo Clayton. 320p. 1986. pap. 3.95 (ISBN 0-88677-169-2). DAW Bks.
Skeen's Return. Jo Clayton. 1987. pap. 3.50 (ISBN 0-88677-202-8). DAW Bks.
Skeen's Search. Jo Clayton. 288p. 1987. pap. 3.50 (ISBN 0-88677-241-9). DAW Bks.
Skeet Shooting with D. Lee Braun: A Remington Sportsmen's Library Bk. Ed. by Robert Campbell. LC 67-10528. pap. 4.95 (ISBN 0-87502-068-2). Benjamin Co.
Skeeter & the Computer. Frank Modell. LC 84-1585. (Illus.). 24p. (ps-3). 1988. 11.95 (ISBN 0-688-03703-8); lib. bdg. 11.88 (ISBN 0-688-03706-2). Greenwillow.
Skein of Legends Around Chopin. Adam Harasowski. LC 77-28829. (Music Reprint Ser., 1978). (Illus.). 1980. Repr. of 1967 ed. lib. bdg. 39.50 (ISBN 0-306-77525-5). Da Capo.
Skeletal Dysplasia Syndromes. K. Kozlowski. 150p. 1984. pap. 21.30 (ISBN 0-387-12825-5). Springer-Verlag.
Skeletal Dysplasias. Ed. by Daniel Bergsma. (March of Dimes Ser.: Vol. 10, No. 8). 12.95 (ISBN 0-686-10015-8). March of Dimes.
Skeletal Dysplasias. Ed. by Costas J. Papadatos & Christos S. Bartsocas. LC 82-17277. (Progress in Clinical & Biological Research Ser.: Vol. 104). 572p. 1982. 66.00 (ISBN 0-8451-0104-8). A R Liss.
Skeletal Growth of Aquatic Organisms: Biological Records of Environmental Change. Ed. by Donald C. Rhoads & Richard A. Lutz. LC 79-25825. (Topics In Geobiology Ser.: Vol. I). (Illus.). 762p. 1980. 95.00x (ISBN 0-306-40259-9, Plenum Pr). Plenum Pub.
Skeletal Imaging. L. Rosenthal & R. Lisbona. 320p. 1984. 59.00 (ISBN 0-8385-8563-9). Appleton & Lange.
Skeletal Injury in the Child. John A. Ogden. LC 81-8384. (Illus.). 656p. 1982. text ed. 115.00 (ISBN 0-8121-0809-4). Lea & Febiger.
Skeletal Intermediary Organization, 2 vols. Harold M. Frost. 1986. 350.00 set (ISBN 0-8493-5947-3). Vol. I, 368p. Vol. II, 352p. CRC Pr.
Skeletal Material from San Jose Ruin, British Honduras. W. D. Hambly. Incl. Anthropometry of the Ovimbundu, Angola; Craniometry of New Guinea. (Field Museum of Natural History). 1937-40. 48.00 (ISBN 0-527-01885-6). Kraus Repr.
Skeletal Maturity of Children Six to Eleven Years: Racial, Area, & Socioeconomic Differentials. A. F. Roche et al. LC 74-18049. (Data from the Health Examination Survey Ser. 11: No. 149). 70p. 1975. pap. 1.75 (ISBN 0-8406-0030-5). Natl Ctr Health Stats.
Skeletal Maturity of Children 6-11 Years, U. S. A. F. Roche & Peter V. Hamill. LC 74-3219. (Data from the Health Examination Survey Ser. 11: No. 140). 1974. pap. text ed. 1.50 (ISBN 0-8406-0006-2). Natl Ctr Health Stats.
Skeletal Maturity of Youths 12-17 Years. Alex F. Roche et al. Ed. by Audrey M. Shipp. (Series 11: No. 160). 95p. 1976. pap. text ed. 2.00 (ISBN 0-8406-0070-4). Natl Ctr Health Stats.
Skeletal Maturity of Youths 12-17 Years: Racial, Geographic Area, & Socioeconomic Differentials. Alex F. Roche et al. Ed. by Audrey Shipp. (Ser. 11: No. 167). 1978. pap. 2.50 (ISBN 0-8406-0121-2). Natl Ctr Health Stats.
Skeletal Metastases. C. S. Galasko. (Illus.). 180p. 1986. text ed. 115.00 (ISBN 0-407-00409-2). Butterworth.
Skeletal Muscle. H. Schalmbruch. (Handbuch der Mikroskopischen Anatomie des Menschen: Vol. 2, Pt. 6). (Illus.). 500p. 1985. 290.00 (ISBN 0-387-15608-9). Springer-Verlag.
Skeletal Muscle Microcirculation. Ed. by K. Messmer & F. Hammersen. (Mikrozirkulation in Forschung und Klinik, Progress in Applied Microciculation Ser.: Vol. 5). (Illus.). vii, 148p. 1984. pap. 49.50 (ISBN 3-8055-3920-7). S Karger.
Skeletal Muscle Pathology. F. L. Mastaglia & John Walton. LC 81-21701. (Illus.). 648p. 1983. text ed. 145.00 (ISBN 0-443-02028-0). Churchill.
Skeletal Muscle Pharmacology. W. G. Walter. 474p. 1982. 152.75 (ISBN 0-444-90226-0, Excerpta Medica). Elsevier.
Skeletal Muscle Toxicity of Six Mercaptopurine, Vol. 11, 14. Ed. by C. P. Bianchi et al. (Illus.). 144p. 1986. 45.00 (ISBN 0-911131-95-7). Princeton Sci Pubs.
Skeletal Musculature in Larval Phases of the Beetle Epicauta Segmenta, (Coleoptera, Meloidae) A. Berrios-Ortiz & R. B. Selandev. (Entomologica Ser.: Vol. 16). (Illus.). 1979. lib. bdg. 26.00 (ISBN 90-6193-126-6, Pub. by Junk Pubs Netherlands). Kluwer Academic.
Skeletal Radiography. Sheila Bull. (Illus.). 224p. 1985. pap. text ed. 34.95 (ISBN 0-407-00278-2). Butterworth.
Skeletal Remains from Santa Barbara, California: I. Craniology. Bruno Oetteking. LC 76-43795. (MAI Indian Notes & Monographs: No. 39). Repr. of 1925 ed. 21.50 (ISBN 0-404-15651-7). AMS Pr.
Skeletal Remains of Early Man. Ales Hrdlicka. 1930. 48.00 (ISBN 0-384-24710-5). Johnson Repr.
Skeletal Remains of the Central Eskimos. Knud Fischer-Moller. Tr. by W. E. Calvert. LC 76-22524. (Thule Expedition, 5th, 1921-1924: Vol. 3, No. 1). Repr. of 1937 ed. 32.50 (ISBN 0-404-58311-3). AMS Pr.
Skeletal Research: An Experimental Approach. Ed. by David J. Simmons & Arthur S. Kukin. 1979. 85.00 (ISBN 0-12-644150-2). Acad Pr.
Skeletal Research: An Experimental Approach, Vol. 2. Ed. by Arthur S. Kunin & David J. Simons. 1983. 71.00 (ISBN 0-12-429002-7). Acad Pr.
Skeletal, Skin & Sexual Prostheses. Int'l Resource Development Inc. 157p. 1987. 1285.00x (ISBN 0-88694-737-5). Intl Res Dev.
Skeletal Structures: Matrix. C. M. Bommer & D. A. Symonds. 106p. 1968. 48.00 (ISBN 0-677-61120-X). Gordon & Breach.
Skeletal System see Anatomy & Physiology: A Programmed Approach.
Skeleton. Steve Parker. LC 87-26314. (Eyewitness Bks.). (Illus.). 64p. (gr. 5 up). 1988. 12.95 (ISBN 0-394-89620-3); lib. bdg. 13.99 (ISBN 0-394-99620-8). Knopf.
Skeleton & Movement. Brian Ward. (Human Body Ser.). (Illus.). 48p. (gr. 4 up). 1981. lib. bdg. 12.40 (ISBN 0-531-04291-X). Watts.
Skeleton Boy: The Nuclear Hero. Dane Krogman & Doug Holelson. (Illus.). 80p. (YA) (gr. 6-12). 1982. 8.95 (ISBN 0-910519-00-5). Daneco Pubns.
Skeleton Clocks. 2nd ed. F. B. Royer-Collard. 174p. 1987. 90.00x (ISBN 0-7198-0110-9, Pub. by E Bruton Assocs Ltd UK). State Mutual Bk.
Skeleton Coast. Amy Schoeman. (Illus.). 192p. 17.95 (ISBN 0-86954-213-3, Pub. by Macmillan S Africa). Intl Spec Bk.
Skeleton Construction in Buildings. William H. Birkmire. LC 72-5035. (Technology & Society Ser.). (Illus.). 200p. 1972. Repr. of 1894 ed. 19.00 (ISBN 0-405-04688-X). Ayer Co Pubs.
Skeleton Crew. Stephen King. 512p. 1985. 18.95 (ISBN 0-399-13039-X). Putnam Pub Group.
Skeleton Crew. Stephen King. 576p. 1986. pap. 4.95 (ISBN 0-451-14293-4, Sig). NAL.
Skeleton from Mesa House. Bruno Oetteking. (Illus.). 48p. 1970. pap. 3.50 (ISBN 0-916561-61-5). Southwest Mus.
Skeleton in the Clock. Carter Dickson. 1977. pap. 1.50 (ISBN 0-505-51194-0, Pub. by Tower Bks). Leisure NY.
Skeleton in the Closet see Greatest Thing in the World.
Skeleton in the Darkroom: Stories of Serendipity in Science. Gilbert Shapiro. LC 86-45024. (Illus.). 160p. 1986. 13.95 (ISBN 0-06-250778-8, HarpR). Har-Row.
Skeleton in the Grass. Robert Barnard. 208p. 1988. 15.95 (ISBN 0-684-18948-8). Scribner.
Skeleton in the Grass. Robert Barnard. 1988. Repr. of 1988 ed. lib. bdg. 17.95 (ISBN 0-89621-189-4). Thorndike Pr.
Skeleton Inside You. Philip Balestrino. LC 72-132290. (Let's-Read-&-Find-Out Science Bks.). (Illus.). (gr. k-3). 1971. PLB 12.89 (ISBN 0-690-74123-5, Crowell Jr Bks); pap. 4.95 (ISBN 0-690-01263-2). HarpJ.
Skeleton Inside You. Philip Balestrino. LC 85-42982. (Trophy Let's-Read-&-Find-Out Book). (Illus.). 40p. (ps-3). 1986. pap. 4.95 (ISBN 0-06-445039-2, Trophy). HarpJ.
Skeleton Key. Steven Charles. (Private School Ser.: No. 4). (YA) (gr. 7 up). pap. 2.50 (ISBN 0-671-60329-9). Archway.
Skeleton Key to Finnegans Wake. Joseph Campbell & Henry M. Robinson. (Nonfiction Ser.). 384p. 1977. pap. 8.95 (ISBN 0-14-004663-1). Penguin.
Skeleton Man. Jay Bennett. LC 86-11202. 176p. 1986. 12.95 (ISBN 0-531-15031-3). Watts.
Skeleton Man. Jay Bennett. 1988. pap. 2.95 (ISBN 0-449-70284-7, Juniper). Fawcett.
Skeleton of Chaucer's Canterbury Tales. Henry Bradshaw. LC 70-39518. Repr. of 1871 ed. 16.00 (ISBN 0-404-00929-8). AMS Pr.
Skeleton of Justice. Edith Roper. LC 73-180425. Repr. of 1941 ed. 29.00 (ISBN 0-404-56159-4). AMS Pr.
Skeletons. Marshall Goldberg. 384p. 1986. pap. 3.95 (ISBN 0-8439-2403-9, Leisure Bks). Leisure NY.
Skeletons from the Opera Closet. David Groover & C. C. Conner. 240p. 1986. 15.95 (ISBN 0-312-72762-3, Thomas Dunne Bks). St Martin.
Skeletons of a Course of Theological Lectures see Heart of Truth: Finney's Outlines of Theology.
Skeletons, Word Problems & Dinosaurs. new ed. Connie Johnson. Ed. & illus. by Ruth Roes. (Illus.). (gr. 9-12). 1978. pap. text ed. 6.95 (ISBN 0-918932-53-X). Activity Resources.
Skellig: Island Outpost of Europe. Des Lavelle. (Illus.). 112p. 1987. pap. 15.95 (ISBN 0-86278-139-6, Pub. by O'Brien Pr Ireland). Irish Bks Media.
Skelling: Island Outpost of Europe. Des Lavelle. (Illus.). 112p. 1977. 17.95 (ISBN 0-905140-26-5, Pub. by O'Brien Pr Ireland). Irish Bks Media.
Skelton. facs. ed. H. L. Edwards. LC 77-148879. (Select Bibliographies Reprint Ser.). 1949. 19.00 (ISBN 0-8369-5673-7). Ayer Co Pubs.
Skelton. J. Holloway. (Chatterton Lectures on an English Poet). 1958. pap. 5.50 (ISBN 0-902732-56-0, Pub. by British Acad). Longwood Pub Group.
Skelton Lord's Key. Daniel Moran. 192p. (Orig.). 1987. pap. 2.95 (ISBN 0-8125-4602-4, Dist. by St Martin's Pr & Warner Pub Servs). Tor Bks.
Skelton, the Life & Times of an Early Tudor Poet. H. L. Edwards. 1988. Repr. lib. bdg. 75.00x. Am Biog Serv.
Skepsis, Dogma, & Belief: Uses & Abuses in Medicine. Edmond A. Murphy. LC 80-8870. 176p. 1981. text ed. 22.50x (ISBN 0-8018-2510-5). Johns Hopkins.
Skeptic & the Ten Commandmants. H. M. Richard. (Uplook Ser.). 1981. pap. 0.99 (ISBN 0-686-79998-4). Pacific Pr Pub Assn.
Skeptic Disposition in Contemporary Criticism. Eugene Goodheart. LC 84-15076. (Essays in Literature Ser.). 200p. 1985. text ed. 25.00x (ISBN 0-691-06626-4). Princeton U Pr.
Skeptical Consumer's Guide to Used Computers. Ed Kahn & Charles Seiter. LC 85-50399. 256p. (Orig.). 1985. pap. 9.95 (ISBN 0-89815-141-4). Ten Speed Pr.
Skeptical Dialogue on Induction. Arne Naess. (Methodology & Science Foundation Ser.: No. 3). 70p. 1984. pap. 12.50 (ISBN 90-232-2047-1, Pub. by Van Gorcum Holland). Longwood Pub Group.
Skeptical Economist. Eli Ginzberg. 182p. 1987. 29.95 (ISBN 0-8133-7372-7). Westview.
Skeptical Engagements. Frederick Crews. LC 86-1391. 256p. 1986. 19.95. Oxford U Pr.
Skeptical Engagements. Frederick Crews. 272p. 1988. pap. 9.95 (ISBN 0-19-505660-4). Oxford U Pr.
Skeptical Essays. Benson Mates. LC 80-19553. xii, 176p. 1981. lib. bdg. 17.00x (ISBN 0-226-50986-9). U of Chicago Pr.
Skeptical Feminist. Barbara Walker. 224p. 1987. 16.95 (ISBN 0-06-250932-2, HarpR). Har-Row.
Skeptical Muse: A Study of Gunter Grass' Conception of the Artist. Ann L. Mason. (Stanford German Studies: Vol. 5). 140p. 1975. pap. 21.20 (ISBN 3-261-01009-6). P Lang Pubs.
Skeptical Sociology. Dennis H. Wrong. LC 76-18843. 1976. 35.00x (ISBN 0-231-04014-8). Columbia U Pr.
Skeptical Tradition. Ed. by Myles Burnyeat. LC 78-62833. (Major Thinkers: No. 3). 536p. 1983. text ed. 45.00x (ISBN 0-520-03747-2); pap. text ed. 14.95x (ISBN 0-520-04795-8). U of Cal Pr.
Skepticism & Cognitivism: A Study in the Foundations of Knowledge. Oliver A. Johnson. LC 77-91743. 1978. 30.00x (ISBN 0-520-03620-4). U of Cal Pr.
Skepticism & Dissent: Selected Journalism, 1898-1901. Ambrose Bierce. Ed. by Lawrence I. Berkove. LC 85-24588. (Nineteenth-Century Studies). 336p. 1986. 44.95 (ISBN 0-8357-1727-5). UMI Res Pr.
Skepticism & Ideology: Shelley's Political Prose & Its Philosophical Context from Bacon to Marx. Terence A. Hoagwood. LC 88-17270. 282p. 1988. text ed. 28.00x (ISBN 0-87745-218-0). U of Iowa Pr.
Skepticism & Moral Principles: Modern Ethics in Review. Ed. by Curtis I. Carter & Anthony Flew. 14.95; pap. 8.95. Precedent Pub.
Skepticism & Moral Principles: Modern Ethics in Review. Ed. by Curtis L. Carter. LC 73-79477. (Studies in Ethics & Society Ser.: Vol. 1). 1973. 14.95 (ISBN 0-89044-017-4); pap. 9.95 (ISBN 0-89044-018-2). New Univ Pr.
Skepticism & Moral Principles: Modern Ethics in Review. Ed. by Curtis L. Carter. 143p. 1973. 14.95; pap. 9.95. Transaction Bks.
Skepticism & Naturalism: Some Varieties. P. F. Strawson. LC 84-12659. 100p. 1984. 19.50x (ISBN 0-231-05916-7). Columbia U Pr.
Skepticism & Naturalism: Some Varieties. P. F. Strawson. (Woodbridge Lectures: No. 12). 98p. 1987. pap. text ed. 10.00 (ISBN 0-231-05917-5, Kings Crown Paperbacks). Columbia U Pr.
Skepticism & Reasonable Doubt: The British Naturalist Tradition in Wilkins, Hume, Reid, & Newman. M. Jamie Ferreira. LC 86-18023. 208p. 1987. 45.00x (ISBN 0-19-824912-8). Oxford U Pr.
Skepticism in Cervantes. Maureen Ihrie. (Serie A: Monagrafias, LXXXVI). 122p. 1982. 22.00 (ISBN 0-7293-0119-2, Pub. by Tamesis Bks Ltd). Longwood Pub Group.
Skepticism, Justification, & Explanation. James W. Cornman. (Philosophical Studies Series in Philosophy: No. 18). 368p. 1980. lib. bdg. 39.50 (ISBN 90-277-1041-4, Pub. by Reidel Holland). Kluwer Academic.
Skepticism of Anatole France. Helen B. Smith. 35.00 (ISBN 0-8490-1057-8). Gordon Pr.
Skepticism of Anatole France. Helen B. Smith. LC 76-46532. 1973. Repr. of 1927 ed. 20.00 (ISBN 0-8492-2403-9). R West.
Skeptic's Handbook of Parapsychology. Ed. by Paul Kurtz. LC 85-43082. 727p. 1985. 34.95 (ISBN 0-87975-302-1); pap. 17.95 (ISBN 0-87975-300-5). Prometheus Bks.
Skeptics of the French Renaissance. John Owen. 59.95 (ISBN 0-8490-1058-6). Gordon Pr.
Skeptics of the Italian Renaissance. John Owen. 59.95 (ISBN 0-8490-1059-4). Gordon Pr.
Skeptics Quest. Joe Musser. 224p. (Orig.). 1984. pap. 6.95 (ISBN 0-86605-151-1). Campus Crusade.
Skerrett. Liam O'Flaherty. 288p. 1980. 15.95 (ISBN 0-905473-10-8, Pub. by Wolfhound Pr Ireland); (Pub. by Wolfhound Pr Ireland). Irish Bks Media.
Skerrett. Liam O'Flaherty. 288p. 1988. pap. 8.95 (Pub. by Wolfhound Pr Ireland). Irish Bks Media.
Sketch. Robert S. Oliver. 134p. 1979. pap. 17.95 (ISBN 0-442-26249-3). Van Nos Reinhold.
Sketch & Draw Today. Henry J. Filson. (Illus.). 120p. 1976. plastic bdg. 12.00x (ISBN 0-918554-00-4); library 9.60. Old Violin.
Sketch Book. Washington Irving. 389p. (RL 5). pap. 2.95 (ISBN 0-451-51614-1, CE1614, Sig Classics). NAL.
Sketch Book of Geoffrey Crayon, Gent. Washington Irving. 384p. 1988. pap. 5.95 (ISBN 0-14-039032-4). Penguin.

Sketches of Life in Little Rock: Eighteen Thirty-Six to Eighteen Fifty Based on the F. W. Trapnalls. Rita P. Wooley. LC 81-68284. (Illus.). 48p. (Orig.). pap. 3.95 (ISBN 0-9606278-2-0). AR Commemorative.
Sketches of Mexico. J. Butler. 1976. lib. bdg. 59.95 (ISBN 0-8490-2613-X). Gordon Pr.
Sketches of Mission Life among the Indians of Oregon. Zachariah A. Mudge. 1983. 12.50 (ISBN 0-87770-308-6). Ye Galleon.
Sketches of My Own Times. David Turpie. LC 75-177581. Repr. of 1903 ed. 26.00 (ISBN 0-404-04636-3). AMS Pr.
Sketches of Nebraska. Robert Hanna. LC 84-3722. (Illus.). xx, 124p. 1984. 16.95 (ISBN 0-8032-2328-5). U of Nebr Pr.
Sketches of Negro Life & History in South Carolina. 2nd ed. Asa H. Gordon. LC 76-122358. xxiv, 338p. 1971. pap. 9.95 (ISBN 0-87249-202-8). U of SC Pr.
Sketches of North Carolina. 3rd ed. William H. Foote. 593p. 1965. 12.00. Synod NC Church.
Sketches of Old Warrenton, North Carolina: Traditions & Reminiscences of the Town & People Who Made It. Lizzie W. Montgomery. (Illus.). 488p. 1984. Repr. of 1924 ed. 25.00 (ISBN 0-87152-393-0, 83-23120). Reprint.
Sketches of Orleans, Vermont (Originally Barton Landing) An Informal History. Darrell Hoyt. Ed. by James Hayford. (Illus.). 97p. (Orig.). 1985. pap. 8.00 (ISBN 0-9610860-2-5). Orleans.
Sketches of Places & People Abroad. facs. ed. William W. Brown. LC 71-133149. (Black Heritage Library Collection Ser). 1854. 17.00 (ISBN 0-8369-8705-5). Ayer Co Pubs.
Sketches of Polk County History. Sadie Patton. LC 76-4897. (Illus.). 178p. 1976. Repr. of 1950 ed. 17.50 (ISBN 0-87152-234-9). Reprint.
Sketches of Rabun County: Georgia History 1819-1948. Andrew J. Ritchie. (Illus.). 520p. 1985. Repr. of 1948 ed. 30.00 (ISBN 0-87797-152-8). Cherokee.
Sketches of Reforms & Reformers of Great Britain & Ireland. facs. ed. Henry Stanton. LC 75-89446. (Black Heritage Library Collection Ser). 1849. 17.25 (ISBN 0-8369-8654-7). Ayer Co Pubs.
Sketches of St. Augustine, with a View of Its History & Advantages as a Resort for Invalids. Rufus K. Sewall. Intro. by Thomas Graham. LC 75-44177. (Floridiana Facsimile & Reprint Ser.). 1976. Repr. of 1848 ed. 8.00 (ISBN 0-8130-0419-5). U Presses Fla.
Sketches of Scenery & Manners in the United States. Theodore Dwight. LC 82-10258. 1983. 35.00x (ISBN 0-8201-1383-2). Schol Facsimiles.
Sketches of Some Booksellers of the Time of Dr. Samuel Johnson. Edward Marston. LC 79-107923. (English Book Trade). (Illus.). 1972. Repr. of 1902 ed. lib. bdg. 19.50x (ISBN 0-678-00727-6). Kelley.
Sketches of Southern Mystery, Treason, & Murder. James Brewster. LC 70-39529. Repr. of 1903 ed. 18.50 (ISBN 0-404-00006-1). AMS Pr.
Sketches of Springfield in 1856. Daily Nonpareil Office. (Annual Monograph Ser.). 96p. 1973. pap. 3.00 facsimile reprint (ISBN 0-686-29090-9). Clark County Hist Soc.
Sketches of Summerland: Nassau & the Bahama Islands. G. J. Northcroft. 1976. lib. bdg. 59.95 (ISBN 0-8490-2614-8). Gordon Pr.
Sketches of Tennessee's Pioneer Baptist Preachers: History of Baptist Beginnings in the Several Associations in the State. J. J. Burnett. (Illus.). 576p. 1985. Repr. of 1919 ed. 21.95 (ISBN 0-932807-11-9). Overmountain Pr.
Sketches of the Character, Manner & Present State of the Highlanders of Scotland--with Details of the Military Service of the Highland Regiments, 2 vols set. David Stewart. (Scottish Reprint Library: Vol. 6). 1182p. 1977. Repr. of 1822 ed. text ed. 69.95 (Pub. by John Donald Pub UK). Humanities.
Sketches of the Character, Manners, & Present State of the Highlanders of Scotland, 2 vols. David Stewart of Gart. 1182p. 1985. 159.00x (Pub. by J Donald Pubs Ltd UK). State Mutual Bk.
Sketches of the Christian Life & Public Labors of William Miller. James White. LC 70-134376. Repr. of 1875 ed. 42.50 (ISBN 0-404-08424-9). AMS Pr.
Sketches of the Civil & Military Services of William Henry Harrison. facsimile ed. Charles S. Todd & Benjamin Drake. LC 75-128. (Mid-American Frontier Ser.). 1975. Repr. of 1840 ed. 13.00 (ISBN 0-405-06893-X). Ayer Co Pubs.
Sketches of the Dynasties of Southern India. Robert Sewell. 138p. Repr. of 1883 ed. text ed. 20.00x. Coronet Bks.
Sketches of the Early Catholic Missions of Kentucky; from Their Commencement in 1787 to the Jubilee of 1826-7. Martin Spalding. LC 70-38548. (Religion in America, Ser. 2). 328p. 1972. Repr. of 1844 ed. 22.00 (ISBN 0-405-04087-3). Ayer Co Pubs.
Sketches of the Higher Classes of Colored Society in Philadelphia. Joseph Willson. (Illus.). text ed. 10.00 (ISBN 0-8369-9227-X, 9081). Ayer Co Pubs.
Sketches of the History of Man, 4 Vols. Henry Home. 1968. Repr. of 1778 ed. Set. cancelled (ISBN 0-685-00779-0). Adlers Foreign Bks.
Sketches of the Island of Negros. Robustiano Echau. Tr. by Donn V. Hart. LC 78-13403. (Papers in International Series: Southeast Asia Ser.: No. 50). (Illus.). 1978. pap. 10.00x (ISBN 0-89680-070-9, Ohio U Ctr Intl). Ohio U Pr.
Sketches of the Island of Negros. Robustiano Echau. Tr. by Donn V. Hart. (Papers in International Studies, Southeast Asia Ser.: No. 50). pap. 45.80 (ISBN 0-317-09574-9, 2007466). Bks Demand UMI.
Sketches of the Judicial History of Massachusetts from 1630 to the Revolution in 1775. Emory Washburn. LC 74-6427. (American Constitutional & Legal History Ser.). 407p. 1974. Repr. of 1840 ed. lib. bdg. 49.50 (ISBN 0-306-70616-4). Da Capo.
Sketches of the Life & Character of Patrick Henry. facs. ed. William Wirt. LC 72-130568. (Select Bibliographies Reprint Ser). 1836. 23.50 (ISBN 0-8369-5541-2). Ayer Co Pubs.
Sketches of the Life & Correspondences of Nathanael Green, 2 vols. William Johnson. LC 78-119063. 516p. 1973. Repr. of 1822 ed. Set. lib. bdg. 65.00 (ISBN 0-306-71953-3). Da Capo.
Sketches of the Life, Times, - Character of Right Reverend Benedict Joseph Flaget, First Bishop of Louisville. Martin J. Spalding. LC 71-83441. (Religion in America, Ser. 1). 1969. Repr. of 1852 ed. 21.00 (ISBN 0-405-00266-1). Ayer Co Pubs.
Sketches of the Origin, Process & Effects of Music. R. Eastcott. LC 70-159680. (Music Ser.). 1971. Repr. of 1793 ed. lib. bdg. 37.50 (ISBN 0-306-70184-7). Da Capo.
Sketches of the Philosophy of Apparitions: Or, an Attempt to Trace Such Illusions to Their Physical Causes. Samuel Hibbert. LC 75-7387. (Perspectives in Psychical Research Ser.). 1975. Repr. of 1824 ed. 34.50x (ISBN 0-405-07035-7). Ayer Co Pubs.
Sketches of the Pioneers in Burke County History, North Carolina. Thomas G. Walton. 96p. 1984. pap. 12.50 (ISBN 0-89308-538-3). Southern Hist Pr.
Sketches of the Pioneers of Methodism in North Carolina & Virginia. M. H. Moore. 314p. 1977. Repr. of 1884 ed. 12.50 (ISBN 0-87921-039-7). Attic Pr.
Sketches of the Political Literature of the Past Half-Century. D. M. Moir. 1973. Repr. of 1851 ed. 45.00 (ISBN 0-8274-1201-0). R West.
Sketches of the Rise, Progress, & Decline of Secession. 2nd ed. William G. Brownlow. LC 68-23813. (American Scene Ser). 1968. Repr. of 1862 ed. 55.00 (ISBN 0-306-71137-0). Da Capo.
Sketches of the Royal Society & Royal Society Club. John Barrow. 216p. 1971. Repr. of 1849 ed. 30.00x (ISBN 0-7146-2405-5, F Cass Co). Biblio Dist.
Sketches of the Sixties. Bret Harte & Samuel L. Clemens. LC 73-131734. 1970. Repr. of 1926 ed. 21.00 (ISBN 0-403-00621-X). Scholarly.
Sketches of the Sixties. Bret Harte & Mark Twain. Ed. by John Howell. LC 77-92173. (Illus.). Repr. of 1927 ed. 19.50 (ISBN 0-404-03151-X). AMS Pr.
Sketches of Travel in Oregon & Idaho. Angelo C. Aubrey. Repr. of 1866 ed. 18.95 (ISBN 0-87770-427-9). Ye Galleon.
Sketches of Upper Canada, Domestic, Local, & Characteristic. John Howison. 1965. Repr. of 1821 ed. 25.00 (ISBN 0-384-24490-4). Johnson Repr.
Sketches of Urban & Cultural Life in North America. Ed. & tr. by Stewart A. Stehlin. (Illus.). 288p. 1988. text ed. 38.00 (ISBN 0-8135-1327-8); pap. text ed. 15.00 (ISBN 0-8135-1328-6). Rutgers U Pr.
Sketches of Western Adventure. John A. M'Clung. LC 76-90184. (Mass Violence in America Ser). Repr. of 1832 ed. 13.00 (ISBN 0-405-01326-4). Ayer Co Pubs.
Sketches of Western Methodism: Biographical, Historical & Miscellaneous Illustrative of Pioneer Life. James B. Finley. LC 79-83419. (Religion in America, Ser. 1). 1969. Repr. of 1954 ed. 30.00 (ISBN 0-405-00244-0). Ayer Co Pubs.
Sketches Taken During Ten Voyages to Africa Between the Years 1786 & 1800. John Adams. (Landmarks in Anthropology Ser). (Illus.). Repr. of 1822 ed. 13.00 (ISBN 0-384-00330-3). Johnson Repr.
Sketching & Rendering Interior Spaces. Ivo Drpic. (Illus.). 176p. 1988. 35.00 (ISBN 0-8230-4854-3, Whitney Lib); pap. 24.95 (ISBN 0-8230-4853-5, Whitney Lib). Watson-Guptill.
Sketching for Landscapes. Wilfred Ball. (Illus.). 120p. 1986. 19.95 (ISBN 0-85219-651-2, Pub. by Batsford England). David & Charles.
Sketching Interior Architecture. Norman Diekman & John Pile. (Illus.). 176p. 1985. 32.50 (ISBN 0-8230-7450-1, Whitney Lib); pap. 19.95 (ISBN 0-8230-7459-5). Watson-Guptill.
Sketching Outdoors in Autumn. Jim Arnosky. LC 88-1244. (Illus.). 48p. 1988. 12.95 (ISBN 0-688-06288-1). Lothrop.
Sketching Outdoors in Spring. Jim Arnosky. LC 86-21308. (Illus.). 48p. (gr. 4 up). 1987. 11.75 (ISBN 0-688-06284-9). Lothrop.
Sketching Outdoors in Summer. Jim Arnosky. LC 87-29728. (gr. 5 up). 1988. PLB 11.95 (ISBN 0-688-06286-5). Lothrop.
Sketching Outdoors in Winter. Jim Arnosky. LC 88-2202. (Illus.). 48p. 1988. 12.95 (ISBN 0-688-06290-3). Lothrop.
Sketching Techniques. Ed. by Mary Suffudy. (Illus.). 144p. 1985. pap. 16.95 (ISBN 0-8230-4855-1). Watson-Guptill.
Sketching with Markers. Thomas G. Wang. 108p. 1981. pap. 17.95 (ISBN 0-442-26341-4). Van Nos Reinhold.
Skevington's Daughter. Oliver Reynolds. LC 85-10124. 160p. 1985. 17.95 (ISBN 0-571-13697-4); pap. 8.95 (ISBN 0-571-13546-3). Faber & Faber.
Skew Distributions & Sizes of Business Firms. Y. Ijiri & H. A. Simon. (Studies in Mathematical & Managerial Economics: Vol. 24). 232p. 1977. 58.00 (ISBN 0-7204-0518-1, North-Holland). Elsevier.
Skew Fields. Peter K. Draxl. LC 82-22036. (London Mathematical Society Lecture Note Ser.: No. 81). 194p. 1983. pap. 22.95 (ISBN 0-521-27274-2). Cambridge U Pr.
Skew Linear Groups. M. Shirvani & B. Wehrfritz. (London Mathematical Society Lecture Note Ser.: No. 118). 275p. 1987. pap. 29.95 (ISBN 0-521-33925-1). Cambridge U Pr.
Ski Bum. Helane Zeiger. (Caprice Romance Ser.: No. 54). 160p. pap. 2.25 (ISBN 0-441-76879-2). Ace Bks.
Ski Bum. Helane Zeiger. 1988. pap. 2.50 (Pub. by Berkley-Pacer). Berkley Pub.
Ski! Colorado. David Lissy. (Illus.). 112p. 1988. 29.95. Westcliffe Pubs Inc.
Ski Country: Nordic Skiers Guide to the Minnesota Arrowhead. Robert Beymer. LC 86-81167. 224p. (Orig.). 1986. pap. 8.95 (ISBN 0-933287-01-1). Fisher Co.
Ski Dictionary: German Definitions with English & French Equivalents. F. Fetz. 20.00 (ISBN 3-85-123-0280). Heinman.
Ski Europe: Winter 1987. rev. ed. Charles Leocha & William Walker. LC 85-51209. 280p. (Orig.). 1986. pap. 8.95 (ISBN 0-915009-07-2). World Leis Corp.
Ski Europe: Winter 1987-88. rev. ed. Charles Leocha & William Walker. LC 87-50899. (Illus.). 392p. 1987. pap. 11.95 (ISBN 0-915009-08-0). World Leis Corp.
Ski Europe: Winter 1989. Charles Leocha & William Walker. 1988. pap. 11.95 (ISBN 0-915009-09-9). World Leis Corp.
Ski Faster, Easier. Lee Borowski. LC 85-23211. (Illus.). 325p. (Orig.). 1986. pap. 15.95 (ISBN 0-88011-272-7, PBOR0272). Leisure Pr.
Ski: Fifty Years in North America. Richard Needham. (Illus.). 232p. 1987. 39.95 (ISBN 0-8109-1504-9). Abrams.
Ski Injury Biomechanics. Gerald Essenmacher. (Illus.). 1978. 20.00 (ISBN 0-916750-52-3). Dayton Labs.
Ski Lift to Love. Helen Murray. 1980. pap. 1.75 (ISBN 0-8439-8003-6, Tiara Bks). Leisure NY.
Ski Magazine's Total Skiing. Bob Jonas & Seth Masia. (Illus.). 192p. 1986. 19.95 (ISBN 0-399-13171-X, Putnam). Putnam Pub Group.
Ski Magazine's Total Skiing. Bob Jonas & Seth Masia. (Illus.). 192p. (Orig.). 1988. pap. 8.95 (ISBN 0-399-51495-3, Perigee Bks). Putnam Pub Group.
Ski Maintenance & Repair Handbook. Seth Masia. (Illus.). 192p. 1982. pap. 7.95 (ISBN 0-8092-5737-8). Contemp Bks.
Ski Minnesota. Elizabeth Noren & Gary Noren. (Illus.). 424p. 1985. pap. 11.95 (ISBN 0-931714-25-7). Nodin Pr.
Ski Mountaineering. Peter Cliff. (Illus.). 160p. (Orig.). 1987. pap. 16.95 (ISBN 0-931397-22-7). Pacific Search.
Ski Mountaineering. Peter Cliff. (Illus.). 1988. 16.95 (ISBN 0-317-67796-9). Globe Pequot.
Ski Party! The Skier's Guide to the Good Life. Stephen Deschenes & Jonathan Runge. (Illus.). 224p. 1986. pap. 7.95 (ISBN 0-312-72832-8). St Martin.
Ski Rental Shop Survey. Karen Duea. 38p. 1983. pap. text ed. 25.00 (ISBN 0-89478-102-2). U Co Busn Res Div.
Ski Tips. Suzy Carter. (Illus.). 64p. 1988. pap. 2.95 (ISBN 0-89586-756-7). Price Stern.
Ski Touring - Arizona. Dugald Bremner. (Illus.). 94p. 1988. pap. 11.95 (ISBN 0-87358-461-9). Northland.
Ski Touring: An Introductory Guide. William E. Osgood & Leslie J. Hurley. LC 78-83073. (Illus.). (gr. 6 up). 1969. pap. 3.50 (ISBN 0-8048-1149-0). C E Tuttle.
Ski Touring Guide to New England. 4th ed. Ed. by Katey Ziegler. (Illus.). 1979. pap. 7.95 (ISBN 0-910146-23-3). Eastern Mount.
Ski Touring in California. 3rd ed. David Beck. LC 88-40008. (Illus.). 224p. 1983. pap. 11.95 (ISBN 0-89997-100-8). Wilderness Pr.
Ski Touring Methow Style. Sally Portman. (Illus.). 144p. (Orig.). 1986. pap. 8.95 (ISBN 0-936289-02-3). Wash Trail Assn.
Ski Touring with Kids: A Guide to Winter Activities with Children. Ross Gibb & Laurie Gibb. LC 81-15748. (Illus.). 200p. (Orig.). 1982. pap. 8.95 (ISBN 0-87108-596-8). Pruett.
Ski Tours in the Sierra Nevada: Carson Pass, Bear Valley, Pinecrest, Vol. 2. Marcus Libkind. LC 84-73452. (Illus.). 132p. (Orig.). 1985. pap. 9.95 (ISBN 0-931255-01-5). Bittersweet Pub.
Ski Tours in the Sierra Nevada: East of Sierra Crest, Vol. 4. Marcus Libkind. LC 84-73452. (Illus.). 184p. (Orig.). 1986. pap. 11.95 (ISBN 0-931255-03-1). Bittersweet Pub.
Ski Tours in the Sierra Nevada: Lake Tahoe, Vol. 1. Marcus Libkind. LC 84-73452. (Illus.). 176p. (Orig.). 1985. pap. 11.95 (ISBN 0-931255-00-7). Bittersweet Pub.
Ski Tours in the Sierra Nevada: Yosemite, Kings Canyon, Sequoia, Vol. 3. Marcus Libkind. LC 84-73452. (Illus.). 136p. (Orig.). 1985. pap. 9.95 (ISBN 0-931255-02-3). Bittersweet Pub.
Ski Tours of Southwest Colorado. Thomas Lepisto. (Illus.). 224p. (Orig.). 1987. pap. 13.95 (ISBN 0-87108-748-0). Pruett.
Skibo. Joseph F. Wall. (Illus.). 1984. 29.95x (ISBN 0-19-503450-3). Oxford U Pr.
Skid Resistance. (National Cooperative Highway Research Program Synthesis of Highway Practice). 66p. 1972. 4.00 (ISBN 0-309-02024-7). Transport Res Bd.
Skid Resistance, 16 reports. (Transportation Research Record Ser.). 152p. 1974. 6.60 (ISBN 0-309-02368-8). Transport Res Bd.
Skid Resistance of Highway Pavements. American Society for Testing & Materials Staff. LC 72-97870. (American Society for Testing & Materials. Special Technical Publication Ser.: No. 530). pap. 41.30 (ISBN 0-317-11157-4, 2016438). Bks Demand UMI.
Skid Road. new ed. Murray Morgan. LC 60-9775. 1978. pap. 3.95 (ISBN 0-89174-030-9). Comstock Edns.
Skid Road: An Informal Portrait of Seattle. rev. ed. Murry Morgan. LC 81-11701. (Illus.). 296p. 1982. pap. text ed. 8.95 (ISBN 0-295-95846-4). U of Wash Pr.
Skid Row: A Wide-Ranging Bibliography. J. Randolph Gregson. 1977. 2.50 (ISBN 0-686-19107-2, 1249). CPL Biblios.
Skid Row & Its Alternatives: Research & Recommendations from Philadelphia. Leonard Blumberg et al. LC 72-92877. 350p. 1973. 29.95 (ISBN 0-87722-055-7). Temple U Pr.
Skidding Accidents: Ancillary Papers. 150p. 1976. 6.40 (ISBN 0-309-02580-X). Transport Res Bd.
Skidding Accidents: Pavement Characteristics. (Transportation Research Record Ser.). 110p. 1976. 4.60 (ISBN 0-309-02575-3). Transport Res Bd.
Skidding Accidents: Tires, Vehicles & Vehicle Components. (Transportation Research Record Ser.). 171p. 1976. 7.00 (ISBN 0-309-02574-5). Transport Res Bd.
Skidding Accidents: Wet-Weather, Accident Experience, Human Factors, & Legal Aspects. (Transportation Research Record Ser.). 87p. 1976. 3.60 (ISBN 0-309-02576-1). Transport Res Bd.
Skidmarks in the Sky: An Irreverent Look at Aviation History. Ed Markin & Christian Beloit. Ed. by Pamela Sload. LC 85-807. (Illus.). 152p. (Orig.). 1986. pap. 4.95 (ISBN 0-9615223-0-5). Flaming Hooker Pr.
Skidmore, Owings & Merrill: Architecture & Urbanism 1973-1983. Albert Bush-Brown & Oswald W. Grube. LC 83-16955. (Illus.). 400p. 1984. 55.95 (ISBN 0-442-21169-4). Van Nos Reinhold.
Skidmore's Portland: His Fountain & Its Sculptor. Eugene E. Snyder. LC 73-85142. (Illus.). 1973. pap. 5.95 (ISBN 0-8323-0229-5). Binford-Metropolitan.
Skier's Bible: A Complete Guide to the Sport of Skiing-Eastern & Western. rev. ed. Morten Lund. LC 77-164722. 176p. 1972. pap. 4.50 (ISBN 0-385-04733-9, Pub. by Outdoor Bible). Doubleday.
Skier's Companion. Curtis Casewit. (Illus.). 192p. 1984. pap. 8.95 (ISBN 0-8289-0549-5). Greene.
Skier's Guide to North America. Ed. by Brent K. Pickard. LC 88-50618. (Illus.). 256p. (Orig.). 1988. pap. 11.95 (ISBN 0-944982-01-8). Wise Guide Pub.
Skiers' Song Book. Ed. by David Kemp. (Illus.). 1950. 6.95 (ISBN 0-87015-022-7). Pacific Bks.
Skies Call. Andy Keech. 1975. 30.00 (ISBN 0-9503341-0-3). A C Keech.
Skies Call Three. Andy Keech. (Illus.). 132p. 1981. 30.00 (ISBN 0-9503341-2-X). A C Keech.
Skies Call Two. Andy C. Keech. 1979. 30.00 (ISBN 0-9503341-1-1). A C Keech.
Skies Were Not Cloudy All Day. Denny Redman. LC 83-61228. (Illus.). 96p. (Orig.). 1983. pap. 4.95 (ISBN 0-941104-04-4). Real Comet.
Skiffs & Schooners. R. D. Culler. LC 74-17905. pap. 51.80 (ISBN 0-317-27637-9, 2025076). Bks Demand UMI.
Skiing. (Illus.). 56p. (gr. 6-12). 1980. pap. 1.25x (ISBN 0-8395-3364-0, 3364). BSA.
Skiing. 4th ed. Karl Tucker et al. (Physical Education Activities Ser.). 112p. 1983. pap. text ed. write for info. (ISBN 0-697-07210-X). Wm C Brown.
Skiing--Everyone. Jim Cottrell. 81p. (Orig.). 1981. pap. text ed. 4.95x (ISBN 0-89459-125-8). Hunter Textbks.

Skiing America: Winter 1989. Charles Leocha. 1988. pap. 11.95 (ISBN 0-915009-10-2). World Leis Corp.

Skiing: An Art.....a Technique. Georges Joubert. Ed. by Doug Smith. Tr. by James Major from Fr. LC 79-90394. (Illus., Orig.). 1980. pap. 12.95 (ISBN 0-935240-01-2). Poudre Pr.

Skiing Basics. Alfred Marozzi. (Illus.). 48p. (gr. 3-7). 1984. pap. 4.95 (ISBN 0-13-812264-4). P-H.

Skiing Colorado: A Complete Guide to America's Number 1 Ski State. Curtis W. Casewit. LC 75-21060. 160p. 1975. pap. 4.95 (ISBN 0-85699-123-6). Chatham Pr.

Skiing: Developing Your Skill. John Shedden. (Illus.). 128p. 13.95 (ISBN 0-946284-42-3, Pub. by Crowood Pr). Longwood Pub Group.

Skiing Europe. (Frommer's Dollarwise Guides Ser.). 1988. 13.95 (ISBN 0-13-048570-5). Prentice Hall Pr.

Skiing for Women. Pamela Ammons et al. (Illus.). 1979. 9.95 (ISBN 0-88280-052-3); pap. 9.95 (ISBN 0-88280-053-1). ETC Pubns.

Skiing Freestyle: Official Training Guide of the U. S. Freestyle Ski Team. Hilary Engisch & Park Smalley. LC 85-25104. (Illus.). 192p. 1986. 24.95 (ISBN 0-87833-520-X). Taylor Pub.

Skiing into Wisconsin: A Celebration of Winter. Jerry Apps. (Illus.). 270p. (Orig.). 1985. pap. 10.95 (ISBN 0-9606240-7-4). Pearl-Win.

Skiing Is a Family Sport. John H. Auran. LC 68-31329. 4.95 (ISBN 0-910294-33-X). Brown Bk.

Skiing Is for Me. Annette J. Chappell. LC 78-12411. (Sports for Me Bks.). (Illus.). (gr. 2-5). 1978. PLB 7.95 (ISBN 0-8225-1082-0). Lerner Pubns.

Skiing Mechanics. John G. Howe. 1983. 18.95 (ISBN 0-935240-02-0). Poudre Pr.

Skiing Out of Your Mind: The Psychology of Peak Performance. Leonard A. Loudis et al. Ed. by Kenneth M. Singer. LC 85-18210. (Illus.). 256p. (Orig.). 1986. pap. 12.95 (ISBN 0-88011-268-9, PLOU0268). Leisure Pr.

Skiing Right. Horst Abraham. LC 83-48651. (Illus.). 238p. (Orig.). 1984. pap. 14.95 (ISBN 0-06-250015-5, CN 4093, HarpR). Har-Row.

Skiing School. Mark Heller. (Illus.). 191p. 1987. 19.95 (ISBN 0-8120-5836-4). Barron.

Skiing: Techniques & Training, with a Brief History of Skiing. L. Schaller. Tr. by C. Marsch from Ger. (Illus.). 1984. pap. 20.00 (ISBN 3-85423-032-X). Heinman.

Skiing the Rockies. Photos by Bruce Barthel. LC 80-65133. (Belding Imprint Ser.). (Illus.). 128p. (Text by Charlie Meyers). 1980. 29.50 (ISBN 0-912856-60-2). Gr Arts Ctr Pub.

Skiing Trauma & Safety: Fifth International Symposium - STP 860. Ed. by Robert J. Johnson & C. Daniel Mote, Jr. LC 85-3897. (Illus.). 500p. 1985. text ed. 62.00 (ISBN 0-8031-0429-4, 04-860000-47). ASTM.

Skiing Trauma & Skiing Safety: Sixth International Symposium. Ed. by C. D. Mote, Jr. & Robert J. Johnson. LC 87-1826. (Special Technical Publications: No. 938). (Illus.). 378p. 1987. text ed. 79.00 (ISBN 0-8031-0936-9, 04-938000-47). ASTM.

Skiing Trivia. Lisa Haselton. LC 85-62494. (Illus.). 183p. 1985. pap. 7.95 (ISBN 0-933341-18-0). Quinlan Pr.

Skiing Utah. A. Kelner. (Illus.). 1979. pap. write for info. A Kelner.

Skiing with Kids. Christi M. Northrop. LC 76-18486. (Illus.). 160p. (Orig.). 1976. pap. 5.95 (ISBN 0-85699-136-8). Chatham Pr.

Skilful Means: A Concept in Mahayana Buddhism. Michael Pye. 211p. 1978. 75.00 (Pub. by Duckworth London). Longwood Pub Group.

Skill Acquisition Rates & Patterns. N. E. Lane. (Recent Research in Psychology). (Illus.). 170p. 1987. pap. 27.00 (ISBN 0-387-96579-3). Springer Verlag.

Skill & the English Working Class 1870-1914. Ed. by Charles More. LC 80-51895. 1980. 26.00 (ISBN 0-312-72772-0). St Martin.

Skill Book 1. (Laubach Way to Reading Components Ser.). 80p. 1981. 3.00 (ISBN 0-88336-901-X); tchr's. manual 3.25 (ISBN 0-88336-911-7); checkups 0.30 (ISBN 0-88336-931-1). New Readers.

Skill Book 2. (Laubach Way to Reading Components Ser.). 80p. 1981. 3.00 (ISBN 0-88336-902-8); tchr's. manual 3.25 (ISBN 0-88336-912-5); checkups 0.30 (ISBN 0-88336-932-X). New Readers.

Skill Book 3. (Laubach Way to Reading Components Ser.). 128p. 1982. 4.75 (ISBN 0-88336-903-6); tchr's. manual 4.75 (ISBN 0-88336-913-3); checkups 0.30 (ISBN 0-88336-933-8). New Readers.

Skill Book 4. (Laubach Way to Reading Components Ser.). 144p. 1984. 4.75 (ISBN 0-88336-904-4); tchr's manual 5.75 (ISBN 0-88336-914-1); checkups 0.30 (ISBN 0-88336-934-6). New Readers.

Skill Builders: For Your Apple II, IIe & II Plus, 2 bks. Dan Isaacson et al. (Illus.). 64p. (gr. 1-12). 1984. Bk. 1. pap. cancelled (ISBN 0-88056-209-9); Bk. 2. pap. cancelled (ISBN 0-88056-210-2). Dilithium Pr.

Skill Builders: For Your Commodore 64, 2 bks. Dan Isaacson et al. (Illus.). 64p. (gr. 1-12). 1984. Bk. 1. pap. cancelled (ISBN 0-88056-211-0); Bk. 2. pap. cancelled (ISBN 0-88056-212-9). Dilithium Pr.

Skill Builders: For Your IBM-PC & IBM-PCjr, 2 bks. Dan Isaacson et al. (Illus.). 64p. (gr. 1-12). 1984. Bk. 1. pap. cancelled (ISBN 0-88056-215-3); Bk. 2. pap. cancelled (ISBN 0-88056-216-1). Dilithium Pr.

Skill Builders: For Your TRS-80, 2 bks. Dan Isaacson et al. (Illus.). 64p. (gr. 1-12). 1984. Bk. 1. pap. cancelled (ISBN 0-88056-213-7); Bk. 2. pap. cancelled (ISBN 0-88056-214-5). Dilithium Pr.

Skill Builders: For Your VIC-20, 2 bks. Dan Isaacson et al. (Illus.). 64p. (gr. 1-12). 1984. Bk. 1. pap. cancelled (ISBN 0-88056-226-9); Bk. 2. pap. cancelled (ISBN 0-88056-227-7). Dilithium Pr.

Skill Builders Using Action Math Level A. Caryl K. Pierson et al. 150p. 1987. pap. 29.95 (ISBN 0-933383-23-1). Math Teachers Pr.

Skill Builders Using Action Math Level D. Caryl K. Pierson & Vicki De Voss. (Illus.). 208p. 1988. pap. 29.95 (ISBN 0-933383-29-0). Math Teachers Pr.

Skill Building Dictation & Transcription. Frances Greer. (Stenospeed Ser.). (Illus.). 325p. 1976. pap. text ed. write for info (ISBN 0-574-20830-5, 13-3830); write for info tchr's guide (ISBN 0-574-20831-3, 13-3831); write for info dication cassettes (ISBN 0-574-20835-6, 13-3835). SRA.

Skill Checklists & Criteria for Kindergarten: Language. 1981. 5.00 (ISBN 0-939418-09-6). Ferguson-Florissant.

Skill Checklists & Criteria for Kindergarten: Math. 1981. 5.00 (ISBN 0-939418-10-X). Ferguson-Florissant.

Skill Checklists: Birth Through 5's. rev. ed. 1986. 6.00 (ISBN 0-939418-06-1). Ferguson-Florissant.

Skill in Communication: A Vital Element in Effective Management. David D. Acker. (Illus.). 91p. (Orig.). 1980. pap. 2.00 (ISBN 0-318-18836-8, S/N 008-020-01036-7). USGPO.

Skill in Nonverbal Communication: Individual Differences. Ed. by Robert Rosenthal. LC 79-19063. 288p. 1979. text ed. 35.00 (ISBN 0-89946-000-3); 15.00 (ISBN 0-89946-033-X). Oelgeschlager.

Skill in Trials: Containing a Variety of Civil & Criminal Cases Won by the Art of Advocates; J. W. Donovan. 173p. 1982. Repr. of 1891 ed. lib. bdg. 20.00x (ISBN 0-8377-0515-0). Rothman.

Skill Tester: Computer-Analyzed Arithmetic Test. Wilbur et al. 278p. 1986. pap. text ed. write for info. (ISBN 0-205-08537-7); write for info. Wm C Brown.

Skill with People. Les Giblin. 32p. (Orig.). pap. 2.50 (ISBN 0-9616416-0-6). L Giblin.

Skillbook in Reading. Jack Norman. (gr. 6-12). 1975. wkbk. 9.33 (ISBN 0-87720-322-9). AMSCO Sch.

Skillbooster Series, Level B. Kravitz & Dramer. Incl. Building Word Power. pap. text ed. (ISBN 0-8136-1202-0); Increasing Comprehension. pap. text ed. (ISBN 0-8136-1209-8); Organizing Information. pap. text ed. (ISBN 0-8136-1223-3). pap. text ed. 3.04 ea. Modern Curr.

Skillbooster Series Level C. Alvin Kravitz & Dan Dramer. Incl. Building Wordpower. 1978. pap. text ed. 3.04 (ISBN 0-8136-1203-9); Increasing Comprehension. 1978. pap. text ed. 3.04 (ISBN 0-8136-1210-1); Organizing Information. 1978. pap. text ed. 3.04 (ISBN 0-8136-1224-1); Using References. 1978. pap. text ed. 3.04 (ISBN 0-8136-1231-4); Working with Facts & Details. 1978. pap. text ed. 1.92 (ISBN 0-87895-343-4). 48p. (gr. 3). Modern Curr.

Skillbooster Series, Level D. Brown. Incl. Building Word Power. pap. text ed. 3.04 (ISBN 0-8136-1204-7); Increasing Comprehension. pap. text ed. 3.04 (ISBN 0-8136-1211-X); Organizing Information. pap. text ed. 3.04 (ISBN 0-8136-1225-X); Using References. pap. text ed. 3.04 (ISBN 0-8136-1232-2); Working with Facts & Details. pap. text ed. 3.04 (ISBN 0-8136-1218-7). (gr. 4). 1976. pap. Modern Curr.

Skillbooster Series, Level E. Brown. Incl. Building Word Power. pap. text ed. 3.04 (ISBN 0-8136-1205-5); Increasing Comprehension. pap. text ed. 3.04 (ISBN 0-8136-1212-8); Organizing Information. pap. text ed. 3.04 (ISBN 0-8136-1226-8); Using References. pap. text ed. 3.04 (ISBN 0-8136-1233-0); Working with Facts & Details. pap. text ed. 3.04 (ISBN 0-8136-1219-5). (gr. 5). 1976. pap. Modern Curr.

Skillbooster Series, Level F. Brown. Incl. Building Word Power. pap. text ed. 3.04 (ISBN 0-8136-1206-3); Increasing Comprehension. pap. text ed. 3.04 (ISBN 0-8136-1213-6); Organizing Information. pap. text ed. 3.04 (ISBN 0-8136-1227-6); Using References. pap. text ed. 3.04 (ISBN 0-8136-1234-9); Working with Facts & Details. pap. text ed. 3.04 (ISBN 0-8136-1220-9). (gr. 6). 1976. pap. Modern Curr.

Skilled Based Automated Manufacturing: Proceedings of the IFAC Workshop, Karlsruhe, FRG, 3-5 September 1986. Ed. by P. Brodner. (IFAC Publication). (Illus.). 136p. 1987. 42.00 (ISBN 0-08-034800-9). Pergamon.

Skilled Helper: Model Skills & Methods for Effective Helping. 3rd ed. Gerard Egan. LC 85-14956. (Psychology Ser.). 384p. 1985. pub net 20.00 (ISBN 0-534-05904-X). Brooks-Cole.

Skilled Labor Shortages in the United Kingdom: With Particular Reference to the Engineering Industry. Gerry Eastwood. (British-North American Committee Ser.). 52p. 1976. 3.00 (ISBN 0-902594-28-1). Natl Planning.

Skilled Labour Supply Imbalances: The Canadian Experience. William Dodge. LC 77-93071. (British-North American Committee Ser.). 56p. 1977. 3.00 (ISBN 0-902594-31-1). Natl Planning.

Skilled Participant: A Way to Effective Collaboration. Keith Clark. 112p. (Orig.). 1988. pap. 4.95 (ISBN 0-87793-387-1). Ave Maria.

Skilled Workers in the Class Structure. Roger Penn. LC 84-5796. (Illus.). 270p. 1985. 49.50 (ISBN 0-521-25455-8). Cambridge U Pr.

Skillful Means. R. Tulku. 136p. 1978. 25.00x (ISBN 0-317-39154-2, Pub. by Luzac & Co Ltd). State Mutual Bk.

Skillful Means. Tarthang Tulku. LC 78-73688. (Nyingma Psychology Ser.). 1978. 17.95x (ISBN 0-913546-63-1); pap. 9.95x (ISBN 0-913546-64-X). Dharma Pub.

Skillful Mind: An Introduction of Cognitive Psychology. Ed. by Angus Gellatly. LC 86-8622. 160p. 1986. 65.00x (ISBN 0-335-15336-4, Open Univ Pr); pap. 24.00x (ISBN 0-335-15335-6). Taylor & Francis.

Skillful Reading: A Text & Workbook for Students of English as a Second Language. A. Sonka. 1981. pap. write for info (ISBN 0-13-812404-3). P-H.

Skillful Rugby. Ray Williams. 1977. 12.50 (ISBN 0-285-62233-1, Pub. by Souvenir Pr). Intl Spec Bk.

Skillful Shepherds: An Introduction to Pastoral Theology. Derek J. Tidball. 1986. pap. 13.95 (ISBN 0-310-44631-7, 12600P). Zondervan.

Skills Analysis Model: An Effective Curriculum for Children with Severe Learning Difficulties. J. M. Gardner & N. B. Crawford. 130p. 1985. 30.00x (ISBN 0-906054-41-9, Pub. by British Inst Mental). State Mutual Bk.

Skills & Procedures of Emergency & General Medicine. Harvey W. Meislin & Stephen J. Dresnick. 250p. 1981. text ed. 31.50 (ISBN 0-8359-7009-4, Reston). P-H.

Skills & Strategies for Winning Racquetball. Ed Turner & Marty Hogan. LC 87-2736. (Illus.). 368p. (Orig.). 1987. pap. 12.95 (ISBN 0-88011-289-1, PTUR0289). Leisure Pr.

Skills & Strategies Handbook for Working with People. Robert J. Martin. 228p. 1983. 12.95 (ISBN 0-13-812370-5); pap. 6.95 (ISBN 0-13-812362-4). P-H.

Skills & Tactics of Soccer. Martin Tyler. LC 79-18627. (Skills & Tactics Ser.). (Illus.). 152p. 1983. Repr. of 1980 ed. 6.95 (ISBN 0-668-05884-6, 5884). Arco.

Skills & Vocationalism. Maurice Holt. 172p. 1987. 59.00x (ISBN 0-335-10290-5, Open Univ Pr.); pap. 21.00x (ISBN 0-335-10289-1). Taylor & Francis.

Skills Development for the HMO Managers of the 1980s. Ed. by T. Bell. 310p. 1980. pap. text ed. 15.00 (ISBN 0-936164-01-8). Group Health Assoc of Amer.

Skills Drills: Reading Level 4.5, 3 Vols, Vol. 1. Ed. by Edward Spargo. (Skills Drills Ser.). 100p. 1983. reproducibles 115.00 (ISBN 0-89061-324-9, 121); Set. 295.00 (ISBN 0-89061-352-4, 120). Jamestown Pubs.

Skills Drills: Reading Level 5.5, Vol. 2. Ed. by Edward Spargo. (Skills Drills Ser.). 100p. 1983. reproducibles 115.00 (ISBN 0-89061-350-8, 122). Jamestown Pubs.

Skills Drills: Reading Level 6.5, Vol. 3. Ed. by Edward Spargo. (Skills Drills Ser.). 100p. 1983. reproducibles 115.00 (ISBN 0-89061-351-6, 123). Jamestown Pubs.

Skills For Adolescence. Ed. by Hank Resnik. (Illus.). 436p. 1985. 24.50 (ISBN 0-933419-05-8); activities & assignments wkbk. 4.00 (ISBN 0-933419-09-0). Quest Intl.

Skills for Adolescence: Teachers Manual. rev. ed. Hank Resnik et al. Ed. by Linda Barr. (Skills for Adolescence Ser.). (Illus.). 531p. 1988. 110.00 (ISBN 0-933419-23-6). Quest Intl.

Skills for Everyday living. (Illus.). 480p. 1988. text ed. 22.40 (ISBN 0-87006-611-0); price not set tchr's. resource guide (ISBN 0-87006-658-7); student activity 4.60 (ISBN 0-87006-612-9); answer key 2.00 (ISBN 0-87006-613-7). Goodheart.

Skills for Musicianship, Vol. I. Dan M. Urquhart. 176p. (Orig.). 1983. pap. 13.25 (ISBN 0-9602576-1-6); tchr's. manual avail. High Goals Pr.

Skills for Preschool Teachers. 2nd ed. Janice J. Beaty. 276p. 1984. pap. text ed. 18.95 (ISBN 0-675-20086-5). Merrill.

Skills for Preschool Teachers. 3rd ed. Janice J. Beaty. 288p. 1988. pap. 18.95 (ISBN 0-675-20803-3). Merrill.

Skills for Professional Nursing Practice. Barbara Norton & Anna Miller. 1076p. 1986. pap. 33.95 (ISBN 0-8385-8565-5). Appleton & Lange.

Skills for Radio Broadcasters. 3rd ed. Curtis Holsopple. (Illus.). 208p. 1987. pap. 14.95 (ISBN 0-8306-2930-0, 2930). TAB BKs.

Skills for Success. Adele M. Scheele. 208p. 1981. pap. 3.50 (ISBN 0-345-35371-4). Ballantine.

Skills for Successful School Leaders. John R. Hoyle et al. 265p. (Orig.). 1985. pap. text ed. 16.95 (ISBN 0-87652-083-2). Am Assn Sch Admin.

Skills for the Changing Workplace, 4 vols. Incl. A Marketing Educator's Guide. Marilyn J. Gordon & Catherine P. Warmbrod. 86p (RD253); A Business & Office Educator's Guide. Frieda Bennett & Gail W. Cope. 93p (RD254); An Electronics Instructor's Guide. Robert D. Bhaerman & Larry Oliver. 81p (RD255); An Automotive Repair Instructor's Guide. Robert D. Bhaerman & Ricke A. North. 78p (RD256). 1985. 8.00 ea. Natl Ctr Res Voc Ed.

Skills for the Future. Gary R. Smith. (Illus.). 65p. (gr. 5-12). 1979. pap. 14.95 (ISBN 0-943804-28-0). U of Denver Teach.

Skills in Counseling Women: The Feminist Approach. Mary N. Russell. 240p. 1984. 27.25x (ISBN 0-398-04971-8). C C Thomas.

Skills in Focus: Writing, Rewriting, Proofreading. Thomas Friedmann. LC 87-60509. 320p. 1988. pap. text ed. write for info. (ISBN 0-312-00291-2); write for info. instr's. manual (ISBN 0-312-00292-0). St Martin.

Skills in Language, 2 bks. (Skill Power Ser.). Bk. 1. pap. text ed. 5.95 (ISBN 0-8428-9336-9); Bk. 2. pap. text ed. 5.95 (ISBN 0-8428-9338-5); Key Bk. 1. 1.10 (ISBN 0-8428-9337-7); Key Bk. 2. 1.10 (ISBN 0-8428-9339-3). Cambridge Bk.

Skills in Mathematics, Bks. 1-2. Educational Systems, Inc. Staff. (Cambridge Skill Power Ser.). 192p. Bk. 1. pap. text ed. 5.95 (ISBN 0-8428-2108-2); Bk. 2. pap. text ed. 5.95 (ISBN 0-8428-2110-4); Key Bk. 1. 1.10 (ISBN 0-8428-2109-0). Cambridge Bk.

Skills in Neighbourhood Work. Ed. by Paul Henderson & David Thomas. 1980. 43.75x (ISBN 0-317-05806-1, Pub. by Natl Inst Social Work). State Mutual Bk.

Skills in Reading, 2 bks. Educational Systems, Inc. Staff. (Cambridge Skill Power Ser.). (gr. 9-12). Bk.1 key. pap. text ed. 5.95 (ISBN 0-8428-9004-1); Bk. 2 key. pap. text ed. 5.95 (ISBN 0-8428-9013-0); 1.10 (ISBN 0-8428-9200-1); 1.10 (ISBN 0-8428-9201-X). Cambridge Bk.

Skills in Social & Educational Caring. John M. McMaster. 148p. 1982. text ed. 32.00x (ISBN 0-566-00385-6). Gower Pub Co.

Skills in Volleyball Training. Berthold Frohner. 312p. 1987. pap. 9.95 (ISBN 3-32-800155-7, Pub. by Sportverlag Berlin GDR). Imported Pubns.

Skills Necessary for Contributive Family & Home Living. Cynthia J. Stacy-Scherrer. 390p. 1981. 43.50 (ISBN 0-398-04607-7). C C Thomas.

Skills of Appraisal. John Slater & Peter Packard. LC 87-22388. 1988. pap. text ed. 70.00 (ISBN 0-566-02729-1). Gower Pub Co.

Skills of Communicating. Bill Scott. 250p. 1986. 32.50 (ISBN 0-89397-247-9). Nichols Pub.

Skills of Communicating. Bill Scott. (Managemant Skills Library). 210p. 1987. pap. text ed. 14.00x (ISBN 0-7045-0575-4, Pub. by Gower Pub England). Gower Pub Co.

Skills of Cricket. Keith Andrew. (Illus.). 144p. 1986. pap. 6.50 (ISBN 0-946284-93-8, Pub. by Crowood Pr). Longwood Pub group.

Skills of Helping. Robert R. Carkhuff & William A. Anthony. 220p. Date not set. 15.00. Human Res Dev Pr.

Skills of Helping: An Introduction to Counseling. Robert Carkhuff et al. LC 78-73987. (Illus.). 262p. 1979. pap. 15.00x (ISBN 0-914234-09-9) (ISBN 0-914234-87-0). Human Res Dev.

Skills of Helping Individuals & Groups. 2nd ed. Lawrence Shulman. LC 83-63542. 432p. 1984. text ed. 27.50 (ISBN 0-87581-302-X). Peacock Pubs.

Skills of Human Relations Training: A Guide for Managers & Trainers. Leslie Rae. 300p. 1985. 32.50 (ISBN 0-89397-210-X). Nichols Pub.

Skills of Interviewing. Leslie Rae. 200p. 1988. 27.50t (ISBN 0-89397-293-2). Nichols Pub.

Skills of Leadership. John Adair. 200p. 1984. 39.50 (ISBN 0-89397-195-2). Nichols Pub.

Skills of Living: A Complete Course in You & What You Can Do about Yourself. William L. Mikulas. LC 83-10367. 240p. (Orig.). 1983. lib. bdg. 28.50 (ISBN 0-8191-3340-X); pap. text ed. 13.00 (ISBN 0-8191-3341-8). U Pr of Amer.

Skills of Management. W. David Rees. 199p. 1984. (Pub. by Croom Helm Ltd); pap. 12.00 (ISBN 0-7099-2266-3). Routledge Chapman & Hall.

Skills of Management. A. N. Welsh. 240p. 1981. 15.95 (ISBN 0-8144-5670-7). AMACOM.

Skills of Negotiating. Bill Scott. LC 81-6472. 244p. 1981. 41.95 (ISBN 0-470-27219-8). Halsted Pr.

Skills of Skiing. Walter Snellman. (Illus.). 224p. 1985. pap. 12.95 (ISBN 0-02-029070-5, Collier). Macmillan.

Skills of Supervision & Staff Management. Lawrence Shulman. LC 81-83338. 366p. 1982. text ed. 24.95 (ISBN 0-87581-278-3). Peacock Pubs.

Skills of Teaching: Interpersonal Skills. Robert Carkhuff et al. (Skills of Teaching Series: Vol. 1). (Illus., Orig.). 1977. pap. text ed. 15.00x (ISBN 0-914234-20-X); Tchrs. Guide. pap. text ed. 10.00x (ISBN 0-914234-51-X). Human Res Dev Pr.

Skills of Training: A Guide for Managers & Practitioners. Leslie Rae. 181p. 1983. text ed. 35.00x (ISBN 0-566-02431-4). Gower Pub Co.

Skills, Outlooks, Passions: A Psychoanalytic Contribution to the Study of Politics. 2nd ed. A. F. Davies. LC 78-54575. (Illus.). 456p. 1981. o. p. 64.50 (ISBN 0-521-22081-5); pap. 19.95 (ISBN 0-521-29349-9). Cambridge U Pr.

Skillstreaming the Adolescent: A Structured Learning Approach to Teaching Prosocial Skills. Arnold P. Goldstein et al. LC 79-66179. (Illus.). 232p. (Orig.). 1979. pap. text ed. 13.95 (ISBN 0-87822-205-7, 2057). Res Press.

Skillstreaming the Elementary School Child: A Guide for Teaching Prosocial Skills. Ellen McGinnis et al. LC 84-61282. 256p. (Orig.). 1984. pap. text ed. 13.95 (ISBN 0-87822-235-9, 2359); Program Forms Booklet 11.95 (ISBN 0-87822-236-7, 2360). Res Press.

Skillstuff-Reading. Imogene Forte. LC 79-89158. (Skillstuff Set). (Illus.). 264p. (gr. 2-6). 1979. pap. text ed. 12.95 (ISBN 0-913916-79-X, IP-79X). Incentive Pubns.

Skim. Thomas Henege. 272p. 1986. pap. 4.95 (ISBN 0-89733-190-7). Academy Chi Pubs.

Skimming & Scanning: Advanced Level. Edward Fry. (Illus.). (gr. 9 up). 1978. pap. text ed. 7.20x (ISBN 0-89061-123-8, 781). Jamestown Pubs.

Skimming & Scanning Middle Level. Edward B. Fry. (Illus.). 160p. (Orig.). (gr. 4-8). 1982. pap. text ed. 7.20x (ISBN 0-89061-246-3, 780). Jamestown Pubs.

Skimming the Cream: Fifty Years with "Peggy of the Flint Hills". Zula B. Greene. 214p. 1983. 14.95 (ISBN 0-941974-04-9). Baranski Pub Co.

Skimming the Water: Rent-Seeking & the Performance of Public Irrigation Systems. Robert Repetto. LC 86-51517. 56p. (Orig.). 1986. pap. text ed. 10.00 (ISBN 0-915825-18-X). World Resources Inst.

Skin. Curzio Malaparte. Tr. by David Moore from Ital. LC 87-63048. 344p. 1988. pap. 12.95 (ISBN 0-910395-37-3). Marlboro Pr.

Skin. Philip F. Millington & Rosemary Wilkinson. LC 82-14637. (Biological Structure & Function: No. 9). (Illus.). 300p. 1983. 80.00 (ISBN 0-521-24122-7). Cambridge U Pr.

Skin. (Looking Good Ser.). (Illus.). (gr. 5 up). Date not set. write for info. Rourke Corp.

Skin, 3 Vols. Charles Whitmore. (Courtroom Medicine Ser.). 1971. Set. looseleaf 240.00 (ISBN 0-686-46749-3); looseleaf 1981 67.50 (ISBN 0-686-46750-7); looseleaf 1982 75.00 (ISBN 0-686-46751-5); looseleaf 1983 80.00; looseleaf 1984 87.50. Bender.

Skin see Anatomy & Physiology: A Programmed Approach.

Skin & Aging Processes. Barbara A. Gilchrest. 136p. 1984. 75.00 (ISBN 0-8493-5472-2, 5472FD). CRC Pr.

Skin & Bone. Gwynne Vevers. LC 83-18757. (Your Body Ser.). (Illus.). 24p. (gr. 1-4). 1984. 8.25 (ISBN 0-688-02820-9); lib. bdg. 7.63 (ISBN 0-688-02821-7). Lothrop.

Skin & Bones. Joanne E. DeJonge. 105p. 1985. pap. 6.95 (ISBN 0-8010-2953-8). Baker Bk.

Skin & Scuba Diving. Albert A. Tillman. (Physical Education Activities Ser.). 78p. 1966. pap. text ed. write for info. (ISBN 0-697-07022-0). Wm C Brown.

Skin & Systematic Disease in Children. Hurwitz. 1985. 47.50 (ISBN 0-8151-4784-8). Year Bk Med.

Skin Boats of Saint Lawrence Island, Alaska. Stephen R. Braund. LC 88-10746. (Illus.). 144p. 1988. 19.95 (ISBN 0-295-96674-2). U of Wash Pr.

Skin Book: Looking & Feeling Your Best Through Proper Skin Care. Arnold W. Klein et al. (Illus.). 1981. (Collier); pap. 4.95 (ISBN 0-02-080750-3). Macmillan.

Skin Cancer. R. A. Schwartz. (Illus.). 1005p. 1988. 99.00 (ISBN 0-387-96612-9). Springer-Verlag.

Skin Care. (Fit Self-Improvement Ser.). 1983. pap. 7.95 (ISBN 0-89037-268-3). Anderson World.

Skin Care: For Men & Women Outdoors. Cameron Smith. LC 78-58031. (Illus.). 272p. 1980. 14.95 (ISBN 0-89037-148-2). Anderson World.

Skin Care for Men Only: A Complete Guide. Zia Wesley-Hosford. 1987. pap. 4.95 (ISBN 0-15-682749-2, Harv). HarBraceJ.

Skin Care for Teens. Nelson L. Novick. Ed. by Maury Solomon. (Illus.). 144p. (gr. 7 up). 1988. 12.40 (ISBN 0-531-10521-0). Watts.

Skin Care Products Market. 183p. 1984. 1000.00 (ISBN 0-86621-178-0, A1240). Frost & Sullivan.

Skin Chairs. Barbara Comyns. (Virago Modern Classics Ser.). 208p. 1987. pap. 5.95 (ISBN 0-14-016138-4). Penguin.

Skin Color, Race, & Self-Image: An Exploratory Study of a Group of High School Youths. Zelte Crawford. LC 79-65270. 135p. 1979. perfect bdg. 10.95 (ISBN 0-88247-580-0). R & E Pubs.

Skin Condition of Youths 12-17 Years. Jean Roberts & Jacqueline Ludford. Ed. by Audrey M. Shipp. (Ser. 11: No.157). 75p. 1976. pap. text ed. 2.00 (ISBN 0-8406-0060-7). Natl Ctr Health Stats.

Skin Conditions & Related Need for Medical Care among Persons 1-74 Years, U. S., 1971-74. Marie-Louise T. Johnson & Jean Roberts. Ed. by Taloria Stevenson. (Ser. 11: No. 212). 1978. pap. 1.75 (ISBN 0-8406-0146-8). Natl Ctr Health Stats.

Skin Deep. Annette Capone. (Wildfire Extra Ser.). 96p. (Orig.). (gr. 6 up). 1984. pap. 2.25 (ISBN 0-590-33458-1, Wildfire). Scholastic Inc.

Skin Deep. Guy Garcia. 176p. 1988. 16.95 (ISBN 0-374-26573-9). FS&G.

Skin Deep. Helene Geutary & Patrice Casanova. (Illus.). 1984. 24.95 (ISBN 0-394-53812-9, GP 911). Grove.

Skin Deep. William Harrington. 320p. 1983. 17.95 (ISBN 0-399-31024-X, Seaview). Putnam Pub Group.

Skin Deep. David Peters. Ed. by Susan Allison. (Photon Adventure Novel Ser.: No. IV). 144p. (Orig.). 1988. pap. 2.50 (ISBN 0-425-10612-8, Pub. by Berkley-Pacer). Berkley Pub.

Skin Disease in Old Age. Ronald Marks. LC 65-73331. (Illus.). 276p. 1987. text ed. 44.95 (ISBN 0-397-58306-0, Lippincott Medical). Lippincott.

Skin Disease in the Dog & Cat: The Library of Veterinary Practice. Grant. 1986. 12.50 (ISBN 0-8016-1959-9). Mosby.

Skin Diseases. D. Sharvill. (Pocket Picture Guides to Clinical Medicine Ser.). 100p. 1984. 9.95 (ISBN 0-683-07689-2). Williams & Wilkins.

Skin Disorders. Ed. by Dale C. Garell & Solomon H. Snyder. (Encyclopedia of Health Ser.). (Illus.). (YA) (gr. 7-12). 1989. 17.95 (ISBN 0-7910-0076-1). Chelsea Hse.

Skin Diver Magazine's Book of Fishes. Hilary Hauser. LC 83-63356. (Illus.). 192p. 1984. 24.95 (ISBN 0-86636-021-2). PBC Intl Inc.

Skin Diver's Bible. rev. ed. Owen Lee. LC 85-45522. (Illus.). 192p. 1986. pap. 7.95 (ISBN 0-385-13543-2, Pub. by Outdoor Bible). Doubleday.

Skin Diving in the Virgins & Other Poems. John M. Brinnin. 1970. pap. 4.50 (ISBN 0-440-08031-2, Sey Lawr). Delacorte.

Skin Diving is for Me. Carole S. Briggs. LC 80-27409. (Sports for Me Bks.). (Illus.). (gr. 2-5). 1981. PLB 7.95 (ISBN 0-8225-1132-0, AACR1). Lerner Pubns.

Skin Doctor's Skin Doctoring Book. Thomas Goodman. LC 83-15815. (Illus.). 256p. 1984. pap. 7.95 (ISBN 0-8069-7784-1). Sterling.

Skin: Drug Application & Evaluation of Environmental Hazards. Oholo Biological Conference, 22nd, Ma'alot, March 1977. Ed. by J. W. Mali et al. (Current Problems in Dermatology Ser.: Vol. 7). (Illus.). 1977. 66.00 (ISBN 3-8055-2797-7). S Karger.

Skin Flaps. Ed. by William C. Grabb & M. Bert Myers. LC 74-20219. 440p. 1975. 85.00 (ISBN 0-316-32267-9). Little.

Skin for Skin. Douglas Rutherford. (Black Dagger Crime Ser.). 200p. 1988. text ed. 14.95x (ISBN 0-86220-732-0, Pub. by Firecrest Pub Ltd). Prescott Pr NH.

Skin for Skin. 152p. 1985. 25.00x (ISBN 0-317-38811-8, Pub. by Redcliffe Pr Ltd). State Mutual Bk.

Skin-Freeze Casting. G. F. Balandin. 240p. 1964. text ed. 49.50x (ISBN 0-7065-0531-X, Pub. by Keter Pub Jerusalem). Coronet Bks.

Skin Grafting. Ross Rudolph et al. 1979. 28.00 (ISBN 0-316-76109-5). Little.

Skin, Hair, Nails & Nutrition. Health Media America Staff. (Health Media of America Nutrition Ser.). (Illus.). 80p. 1986. pap. 3.95 (ISBN 0-937325-04-X). Health Med Amer.

Skin in Diabetes. Ed. by J. E. Jelinek. LC 85-6901. (Illus.). 237p. 1986. text ed. 33.50 (ISBN 0-8121-0989-9). Lea & Febiger.

Skin Injuries: Medical Subject Analysis with Reference Bibliography. Charlene P. Singh. LC 85-48100. 150p. 1987. 34.50 (ISBN 0-88164-472-2); pap. 26.50 (ISBN 0-88164-473-0). ABBE Pubs Assn.

Skin Manifestations in Visceral Cancer. V. C. Andreev. (Current Problems in Dermatology Ser.: Vol. 8). (Illus.). 1978. pap. 66.00 (ISBN 3-8055-2878-7). S Karger.

Skin Meat Bones. Anne Waldman. (Illus.). 96p. (Orig.). 1985. pap. 8.95 (ISBN 0-918273-15-3). Coffee Hse.

Skin Microbiology: Relevance to Clinical Infection. Ed. by H. Maibach. R. Aly. 384p. 1981. 55.00 (ISBN 0-387-90528-6). Springer-Verlag.

Skin Models. Ed. by R. Marks & G. Plewig. (Illus.). 380p. 1986. pap. 85.00 (ISBN 0-387-15330-6). Springer-Verlag.

Skin of Dreams. Raymond Queneau. Tr. by H. J. Kaplan from Fr. LC 77-11668. 1979. Repr. of 1948 ed. 19.50x (ISBN 0-86527-305-7). Fertig.

Skin of Vertebrates. Ed. by R. I. Spearman & P. A. Riley. (Linnean Society Symposium Ser.: No. 9). 1981. 138.00 (ISBN 0-12-656950-9). Acad Pr.

Skin Painting Techniques & in vivo Carcinogenesis Bioassays. Ed. by F. Homburger. (Progress in Experimental Tumor Research Ser.: Vol. 26). (Illus.). vi, 314p. 1983. 146.75 (ISBN 3-8055-3556-2). S Karger.

Skin Pathology by Light & Electron Microscopy. Ken Hashimoto & Kan Niizuma. LC 81-13355. (Illus.). 280p. 1983. monograph 99.00 (ISBN 0-89640-080-8). Igaku-Shoin.

Skin Permeability. Hans Schaefer et al. (Illus.). 360p. 1982. pap. 72.00 (ISBN 0-387-11797-0). Springer-Verlag.

Skin Pharmacokinetics. Ed. by B. Shroot & H. Schaefer. (Pharmacology & the Skin Ser.: Vol. 1). (Illus.). x, 266p. 1987. 132.00 (ISBN 3-8055-4555-X). S Karger.

Skin Problems of the Amputee. William S. Levy. LC 78-50196. (Illus.). 320p. 1983. 49.95 (ISBN 0-87527-181-2). Green.

Skin Secrets: A Dermatologist's Prescription for Beautiful Skin at Any Age. Joseph Bark. 1987. text ed. 18.95 (ISBN 0-07-003671-3). McGraw.

Skin Secrets: A Dermatologist's Prescription for Beautiful Skin at Any Age. Joseph Bark. 336p. 1988. pap. text ed. 8.95 (ISBN 0-07-003672-1). McGraw.

Skin Sense: The Complete Guide to Skin Care for Men. Nance Mitchell. (Orig.). 1987. pap. 8.95 (ISBN 0-449-90189-0, Columbine). Fawcett.

Skin-Shadows-Silence. Deena Metzger. 112p. 1975. pap. text ed. 5.00 (ISBN 0-915596-09-1). West Coast.

Skin Surgery. 6th ed. Ervin Epstein, Sr. & Ervin Epstein, Jr. (Illus.). 696p. 1987. 99.00 (ISBN 0-7216-1809-X). Saunders.

Skin Surgery. Marwali Harahap. (Illus.). 1054p. 1985. 125.00 (ISBN 0-87527-317-3). Green.

Skin to Skin: Eroticism in Dress. Prudence Glynn. LC 82-81091. (Illus.). 1982. 39.95 (ISBN 0-19-520391-7). Oxford U Pr.

Skin Troubles. Leon Chaitow. (New Self Help Ser.). 96p. (Orig.). 1988. pap. 2.99 (ISBN 0-7225-1504-9, Pub. by Thorsons (England)). Sterling.

Skindeep. Toeckey Jones. LC 85-45843. (Charlotte Zolotow Bks.). 256p. (YA) (gr. 7 up). 1986. 12.70i (ISBN 0-06-023051-7); PLB 12.89 (ISBN 0-06-023052-5). HarpJ.

Skinflick. Hansen. pap. 3.95 (ISBN 0-8050-0197-2). H Holt & Co.

Skinflick. Joseph Hansen. LC 79-11077. 192p. 1980. pap. 3.50 (ISBN 0-03-057641-5). H Holt & Co.

Skinner. F. M. Parker. 1985. pap. 2.75 (ISBN 0-451-13813-9, Sig). NAL.

Skinner for the Classroom: Selected Papers. B. F. Skinner. Ed. by Robert Epstein. LC 82-80868. (Illus.). 295p. (Orig.). 1982. pap. text ed. 19.95 (ISBN 0-87822-261-8, 2618). Res Press.

Skinner Primer: Behind Freedom & Dignity. Finlay Carpenter. LC 73-16603. 1974. 14.95 (ISBN 0-02-905290-4); pap. 11.95x 1984 (ISBN 0-02-905900-3). Free Pr.

Skinner's Philosophy. Paul T. Sagal. LC 80-5737. 132p. 1981. lib. bdg. 24.25 (ISBN 0-8191-1432-4); pap. text ed. 9.25 (ISBN 0-8191-1433-2). U Pr of Amer.

Skinner's Science of Dental Materials. 8th ed. Ralph W. Phillips. (Illus.). 646p. 1982. 44.95 (ISBN 0-7216-7235-3). Saunders.

Skinny Angel. Thelma Jones. 6.95 (ISBN 0-87018-035-5). Ross.

Skinny Dynamite & Other Short Stories. Jack Micheline. Ed. by A. D. Winans. LC 79-63969. 96p. (Orig.). 1980. pap. 4.95 (ISBN 0-915016-27-3). Second Coming.

Skinny Island. Louis Auchincloss. 1988. pap. 3.95 (ISBN 0-317-67200-2). St Martin.

Skinny Island: More Tales of Manhattan. Louis Auchincloss. 1987. 17.95 (ISBN 0-395-43295-2). HM.

Skinny Malinky Leads the War for Kidness. Stanley Kiesel. 176p. (gr. 7 up). 1984. 12.95 (ISBN 0-525-66918-3, 01258-370). Lodestar Bks.

Skinny Malinky Leads the War for Kidness. Stanley Kiesel. 176p. (gr. 7 up). 1985. pap. 2.50 (ISBN 0-380-69875-7, Flare). Avon.

Skinnybones. Barbara Park. LC 81-20791. 128p. (gr. 3-6). 1982. 9.95 (ISBN 0-394-84988-4); lib. bdg. 9.99 (ISBN 0-394-94988-9). Knopf.

Skins & Bones. Paula G. Allen. 80p. (Orig.). 1988. pap. 6.95 (ISBN 0-931122-50-3). West End.

Skins on the Earth. Primus St. John. LC 75-14652. 74p. 1975. 16.00x (ISBN 0-685-52614-3); pap. 7.00 (ISBN 0-914742-07-8). Copper Canyon.

Skinwalkers. Tony Hillerman. LC 86-45600. 224p. 1987. 15.95i (ISBN 0-06-015695-3, HarpT). Harper Row.

Skinwalkers. Tony Hillerman. LC 86-45600. 1987. pap. 3.95 (ISBN 0-06-080893-4, P/893, PL). Harper Row.

Skip Aboard a Space Ship. Jane B. Moncure. LC 77-12958. (Creative Dramatics Ser.). (Illus.). (ps-3). 1978. PLB 5.95 (ISBN 0-89565-009-6); pap. 2.50 (ISBN 0-89565-042-8). Childs World.

Skip for Fun. Kevin Brooks. 45p. 1985. pap. 3.50 (ISBN 0-908175-79-5, Pub. by Boolarong Pubn Australia). Intl Spec bk.

Skip to a Healthy Heart. Candace L. Hogan. pap. 4.95 (ISBN 0-517-55736-3). Crown.

Skip to My Lou: For Brownies, Juniors, Cadettes, Seniors & Leaders. Girl Scouts of the U. S. A. Staff. 32p. (gr. 1-8). 1958. pap. 1.50 (ISBN 0-88441-307-1, 20-199). Girl Scouts USA.

Skip Tracing. Thomas Stelter. 130p. 1987. pap. 30.00 (ISBN 0-941161-16-1). PES Inc WI.

Skip Trip. John Burningham. LC 83-25981. (Noisy Words Ser.). (Illus.). 24p. (ps). 1984. 4.95 (ISBN 0-670-65016-1, Viking Kestrel). Viking.

Skipped Payment Tables: U. S. Rule Escrow Method. Financial Publishing Co. Staff. 300p. 1979. pap. 29.50 (ISBN 0-87600-768-X). Finan Pub.

Skipper. Paige Dixon. LC 79-10420. 132p. (gr. 5-9). 1979. 8.95 (ISBN 0-689-30706-3, Childrens Bk). Atheneum.

Skipper: Confessions of a Fighter Squadron Commander. T. H. Winters. (Illus.). 160p. 1986. 16.95 (ISBN 0-912173-07-6). Champlin Museum.

Skipper's Course. rev. ed. (Illus.). 113p. 1986. pap. 6.50 (S/N 050-012-00225-8). USGPO.

Skipping a Grade Can Be Fun. Francine Cristel. 1984. 5.00 (ISBN 0-89824-037-9). Trillium Pr.

Skipping Rope. A. Barto. 52p. 1971. pap. 1.99 (ISBN 0-8285-1228-0, Pub. by Progress Pubs USSR). Imported Pubns.

Skippy. Percy L. Crosby. Ed. by Bill Blackbeard. LC 76-53037. (Classic American Comic Strips). (Illus.). 1977. 18.75 (ISBN 0-88355-629-4); pap. 10.00 (ISBN 0-88355-628-6). Hyperion Conn.

Skippy Blair on Contemporary Social Dance. Skippy Blair. 1978. 19.95 (ISBN 0-932980-00-7). Golden St Dance Teach Assn.

Skiptrace. Antoinette Azolakov. 180p. (Orig.). 1988. pap. 8.95 (ISBN 0-934411-09-3, Banned Bks). Edward-William Austin.

Skirmish. Melissa C. Michaels. (Skyrider Ser.: Vol. 1). 256p. 1985. pap. 2.95 (ISBN 0-8125-4566-4, Dist. by Warner Publisher Services & St. Martin's Press). Tor Bks.

Skirmish. Meliza C. Michaels. 1987. pap. 3.50 (ISBN 0-8125-4574-5, Dist. by St Martin's Pr & Warner Pub Servs). Tor Bks.

Skirmishers see Confluence.

Skirmishes. Catherine Hayes. 61p. 1983. pap. 6.95 (ISBN 0-571-11979-4). Faber & Faber.

Skirt Tag: You're It. Juliet Freefoam, pseud. (Adult Poetry Ser.). (Illus.). 96p. (Orig.). 1987. pap. 6.95 (ISBN 0-915199-05-X). Pen Dec.

Skitch. Vincent G. Perry. LC 75-20788. (Other Dog Bks.). 1975. 8.95 (ISBN 0-87714-032-4). Denlingers.

Skiterminology in Six Languages, English, French, German, Czech, Polish. 2nd ed. H. Abraham. (Illus.). 136p. (Orig.). 1986. pap. 15.00 (ISBN 3-85423-056-7, Pub. by Steiger Verlag Austria). Heinman.

Skits, 2 vols. Set. 8.95 (ISBN 0-685-61260-0). Young Life.

Skits & Short Farces for Young Actors. Lewy Olfson. (gr. 4-12). 1985. pap. 9.95 (ISBN 0-8238-0273-6). Plays.

Skits for Seniors Only. Jane L. Reynolds. (Yellow Book of Skits for Seniors Only Ser.). 20p. 1980. write for info. (ISBN 0-932320-06-6). Solar Studio.

Skits for Seniors Only. Jane L. Reynolds. (Green Book of Skits for Seniors Only Ser.). 20p. 1980. write for info. (ISBN 0-932320-07-4). Solar Studio.

Skits for Seniors Only. Jane L. Reynolds. (Orange Book of Skits for Seniors Only Ser.). 20p. 1980. write for info. (ISBN 0-932320-05-8). Solar Studio.

Skits for the Young in Heart. Clay Franklin. 1977. pap. 3.00 (ISBN 0-686-38386-9). Eldridge Pub.

Skits in English. new ed. Mary E. Hines. (Illus.). 121p. (gr. 9-12). 1980. pap. text ed. 6.50 (ISBN 0-13-812397-7, 18854); cassettes 55.00 (ISBN 0-13-812421-3, 58855). Prentice ESL.

Skits That Teach. Colleen Ison. (Illus.). 112p. 1985. pap. 4.95 (ISBN 0-87239-848-X, 3356). Standard Pub.

Skits That Win. Ruth Vaughn. Bd. with More Skits That Win. 128p. pap. 6.95 (ISBN 0-310-33681-3, 10943P). Zondervan.

Skitter Bugs. Illus. by Tony Tallarico. (Baby's First Bks.). (Illus.). 14p. (ps). 1980. 2.25 (ISBN 0-448-16277-6, G&D). Putnam Pub Group.

Skittles in Action. (ps). 1976. 2.00 (ISBN 0-904494-35-7, Brimax Bks). Borden.

Skittles Make Believe School. (ps). 1976. 2.00 (ISBN 0-904494-25-X, Brimax Bks). Borden.

Skittles on the Move. 2.50 (ISBN 0-904494-36-5, Brimax Bks). Borden.

SkiWriter II. Date not set. price not set. P-H.

Sklansky on Poker. David Sklansky. (Illus., Orig.). Date not set. pap. text ed. 9.95 (ISBN 0-89746-069-3). Gambling Times.

Sklaverei, Staatskirche und Freikirche. Adolf Lotz. pap. 10.00 (ISBN 0-384-33770-8). Johnson Repr.

Skolt Lapp Community Suenjelsijd During the Year 1938. Karl Nickul. LC 77-87728. (Acta Lapponica: 5). (Illus.). 160p. 1983. Repr. of 1948 ed. 57.50 (ISBN 0-404-16504-4). AMS Pr.

Skook. J. P. Miller. LC 84-2389. 320p. (Orig.). 1984. 17.00 (ISBN 0-446-51296-6). Warner Bks.

Skook. J. P. Miller. 1985. pap. 3.95 (ISBN 0-446-32861-8). Warner Bks.

Skookum: An Oregon Pioneer Family's History & Lore. Shannon Applegate. (Illus.). 448p. 1988. 19.95 (ISBN 0-688-05350-5, Pub. by Beech Tree Bks). Morrow.

Skopas in Malibu. Andrew Stewart. LC 28-81304. (Illus.). 90p. 1982. 16.00 (ISBN 0-89236-054-2); pap. 9.00 (ISBN 0-89236-036-4). J P Getty Mus.

Skopas in Samothrace. Phyllis W. Lehmann. LC 73-88453. (Katharine Asher Engel Lecture for 1972). (Illus.). 1973. pap. 5.00 (ISBN 0-87391-009-5). Smith Coll.

Skopas of Paros. Ed. by Andrew F. Stewart. LC 77-149. (Illus.). 240p. 1977. 32.00 (ISBN 0-8155-5051-0, NP). Noyes.

Skorpion's Death: A Novel. David Brierly. 256p. 1986. 13.95 (ISBN 0-671-47755-2). Summit Bks.

Skorzeny: Hitler's Commando. Glenn B. Infield. (Dorset Press Reprints Ser.). (Illus.). 266p. 1988. 18.95 (ISBN 0-88029-212-1). Hippocrene Bks.

Skouras, King of Fox Studios. Carlos Curti. (Orig.). 1967. pap. 0.95 (ISBN 0-87067-141-3, BH141). Holloway.

Skruggs & Friends. Glen Hausladen. (Illus.). 100p. (Orig.). 1986. pap. 3.95 (ISBN 0-9617130-0-3). Hausladen Pub.

Skryabin. Hugh MacDonald. (Studies of Composers). 1978. pap. 9.95x (ISBN 0-19-315438-2). Oxford U Pr.

Skrymnikov: Time of Troubles. Ed. by Hugh Graham. 1987. 25.00. Academic Intl.

Skrynnikov - Time of Troubles. Ed. by Hugh F. Graham. 1988. pap. 10.00 (ISBN 0-317-66682-7). Academic Intl.

Skuas. Robert W. Furness. (Illus.). 336p. 1987. 45.00 (ISBN 0-85661-046-1, Pub. by Poyser UK). Buteo.

Skulduggery. William Marshall. 1984. pap. 3.95 (ISBN 0-03-071064-2). H Holt & Co.

Skull Beneath the Skin. P. D. James. 432p. 1983. pap. 3.95 (ISBN 0-446-30606-1). Warner Bks.

Skull Beneath the Skin. P. D. James. 432p. 1987. pap. 3.95 (ISBN 0-446-34830-9). Warner Bks.

Skull Beneath the Skin: The Achievement of John Webster. Charles R. Forker. (Illus.). 648p. 1986. text ed. 50.00x (ISBN 0-8093-1279-4). S Ill U Pr.

Skull Fractures: Medical Research Subject Analysis with Bibliography. Harriet D. Jakhovsky. LC 84-45733. 150p. 1986. 34.50 (ISBN 0-88164-244-4); pap. 26.50 (ISBN 0-88164-245-2). ABBE Pubs Assn.

Skull Gate. Robin Bailey. 288p. (Orig.). 1985. pap. 2.95 (ISBN 0-8125-3139-6, Dist. by Warner Pub Services & St. Martin's Press). Tor Bks.

Skull in Salop & Other Poems. Geoffrey Grigson. LC 68-8309. 1969. 12.95 (ISBN 0-8023-1183-0). Dufour.

Skull Juices. Doug Blazek. (Orig.). 1970. pap. 4.25 (ISBN 0-912136-22-7); pap. 10.00x signed ed. (ISBN 0-685-04867-5). Twowindows Pr.

Skull Mountain Bandit. Terrell L. Bowers. 1985. 9.95 (ISBN 0-8034-8525-5, Avalon). Bouregy.

Skull of Adam. Stanley Moss. 1980. 7.95 (ISBN 0-8180-1578-0); pap. 3.95 (ISBN 0-686-64570-7). Horizon.

Skull of Amiurus. James E. Kindred. (Illus.). 1919. 12.00 (ISBN 0-384-29415-4). Johnson Repr.

Skull of Sinanthropus Pekinensis. Franz Weidenreich. (Paleontologia Sinica). (Illus.). 1943. pap. 15.00x (ISBN 0-934454-88-4). Lubrecht & Cramer.

Skull of "Sinanthropus Pekinensis" A Comparative Study on a Primitive Hominid Skull. Franz Weidenreich. LC 77-86450. (China. Geological Survey. Palaeontologia Sinica. New Ser. D.: No. 10. Whole Ser. No. 127). (Illus.). Repr. of 1943 ed. 59.00 (ISBN 0-404-16693-8). AMS Pr.

Skull of Swift. facsimile ed. Shane Leslie. LC 79-169767. (Select Bibliographies Reprint Ser). Repr. of 1928 ed. 24.50 (ISBN 0-8369-5987-6). Ayer Co Pubs.

Skull of Swift, an Extempore Exhumation. Shane Leslie. 347p. 1983. lib. bdg. 35.00 (ISBN 0-8495-3409-7). Arden Lib.

Skull of Swift: An Extempore Exhumation. Shane Leslie. 347p. Repr. of 1928 ed. lib. bdg. 40.00 (ISBN 0-89984-724-2). Century Bookbindery.

Skull, Spine & Contents: Part 1: Procedures & Indications. Ed. by H. J. Kaufmann. (Progress in Pediatric Radiology Ser.: Vol. 5). 300p. 1976. 86.00 (ISBN 3-8055-1382-8). S Karger.

Skull, Spine & Contents: Part 2: Clinical Aspects. Ed. by H. J. Kaufmann. (Progress in Pediatric Radiology Ser.: Vol. 6). (Illus.). 1977. 107.50 (ISBN 3-8055-2337-8). S Karger.

Skull Worship. Connie Fox. 64p. 1988. 14.95 (ISBN 0-930090-37-3); pap. 6.95 (ISBN 0-930090-38-1); 20.00 (ISBN 0-930090-36-5). Applezaba.

Skullduggery. Peter Marks. LC 87-754. 280p. 1987. 17.95 (ISBN 0-88184-319-9). Carroll & Graf.

Skullduggery. Peter Marks. 1988. pap. 4.50 (ISBN 0-88184-403-9). Carroll & Graf.

Skulls along the River. Quincy Troupe. 144p. (Orig.). 1984. pap. 5.95 (ISBN 0-918408-22-9). Reed & Cannon.

Skulls Are Forever: A Book of Secret Truths. Mary Nash. (Illus.). 35p. (Orig.). 1986. pap. 14.95 (ISBN 0-9618893-0-6). Ichthys VA.

Skulpturen vom 5. Jahrhundert Bis in die Roemische zeit see Kerameikos: Ergebnisse der Ausgrabungen (Deutsches Archaeologisches Institut).

Skungpoomery. Ken Campbell. 47p. 1984. pap. 4.95 (ISBN 0-413-33910-6, 4108). Heinemann Ed.

Skunk Camp Promises. Tom Peters. 1987. flexi-bound 9.95 (ISBN 0-317-56480-3). Knopf.

Skunk for Rent & Other Animal Tails. Grace F. Anderson. 120p. (gr. 1 up). 1982. pap. 3.95 (ISBN 0-88207-493-8). Victor Bks.

Skunk Lane. Brom Hoban. LC 81-47729. (Illus.). 64p. (gr. 2-4). 1983. PLB 10.89g (ISBN 0-06-022348-0). HarpJ.

Skunk Missal see NEA Series.

Skunks & Their Relatives. Wildlife Education Ltd. (Illus.). 20p. (Orig.). 1985. pap. 1.95 (ISBN 0-937934-38-0). Wildlife Educ.

Skutarevsky. Leonid M. Leonov. Tr. by Alec Brown. LC 76-135250. 1971. Repr. of 1936 ed. lib. bdg. 48.50x (ISBN 0-8371-5170-8, LESK). Greenwood.

Sky. Bob Arnold. 1986. 4.00 (ISBN 0-934834-74-1). White Pine.

Sky. George Gessert. (Illus.). 1985. pap. text ed. 7.95 (ISBN 0-9615895-0-7). G Gessert.

Sky above & Worlds Beyond. Judith Herbst. LC 82-13749. (Illus.). 224p. (gr. 5 up). 1983. 14.95 (ISBN 0-689-30974-0, Atheneum Childrens Bks). Macmillan.

Sky & Earth. Ed. by Gakken Co. Ltd. Editors. Tr. by Time-Life Books Inc. Editors. (Child's First Library of Learning). (Illus.). 90p. (gr. k-3). 1988. write for info. (ISBN 0-8094-4837-8); PLB write for info. (ISBN 0-8094-4838-6). Time-Life.

Sky & the Desert. Lionel Folkard. 204p. 1985. 30.00 (ISBN 0-901976-93-8, Pub. by United Writers Pubns England). State Mutual Bk.

Sky at Ashland. Michael Anania. 80p. (Orig.). 1986. 12.95 (ISBN 0-918825-31-8, Dist. by Kampmann & Co.); pap. 7.95 (ISBN 0-918825-32-6). Moyer Bell Limited.

Sky at Night. 1987. 11.95 (ISBN 0-393-30390-X). Norton.

Sky Atlas 2000.0 Color. Wil Tirion. 1981. spiral bound 34.95 (ISBN 0-933346-33-6, 46336). Sky Pub.

Sky Atlas 2000.0 Field: White Stars on Black Backround. Wil Tirion. (Illus.). 1981. 15.95 (ISBN 0-933346-32-8, 46328). Sky Pub.

Sky Atlas 2000.0: Twenty-Six Star Charts Covering Both Hemispheres. Wil Tirion. LC 81-52999. (Illus.). 26p. 1981. 39.50 (ISBN 0-521-24467-6). Cambridge U Pr.

Sky Blew Blue. Cora Brooks. 100p. pap. text ed. 4.95 (ISBN 0-934678-13-8). New Victoria Pubs.

Sky Blue Frame. Franklin W. Dixon. (Hardy Boys Ser.: No. 89). 160p. (Orig.). (gr. 3-6). 1988. pap. 3.50 (ISBN 0-671-64974-4, Minstrel Bks). S&S.

Sky Blue-Grass Green. Susan Kropa. 128p. (gr. 1-3). 1986. wkbk. 8.95 (ISBN 0-86653-355-9, GA 698). Good Apple.

Sky Catalogue 2000, Vol. 1. Alan Hirshfeld & Roger W. Sinnott. 604p. 1982. 49.95. Sky Pub.

Sky Catalogue 2000, Vol. 2. Ed. by Alan Hirshfeld. 1983. 49.95 (ISBN 0-933346-39-5); pap. 29.95 (ISBN 0-933346-38-7). Sky Pub.

Sky Changes. Gilbert Sorrentino. LC 85-72984. 160p. 1986. pap. 12.50 (ISBN 0-86547-243-2). N Point Pr.

Sky Clears: Poetry of the American Indians. A. Grove Day. LC 65-38538. xiv, 204p. 1964. pap. 3.95 (ISBN 0-8032-5047-9, BB 142, Bison). U of Nebr Pr.

Sky Clears: Poetry of the American Indians. Ed. by Arthur G. Day. LC 83-1576. xiii, 204p. 1983. Repr. of 1951 ed. lib. bdg. 35.00x (ISBN 0-313-23883-9, DASK). Greenwood.

Sky Dancer: The Secret Life & Songs of the Lady Yeshe Tsogyel. Ed. by Keith Dowman. (Illus.). 350p. (Orig.). 1984. pap. 14.95 (ISBN 0-7100-9576-7). Routledge Chapman & Hall.

Sky Diggers: Aces of the R.A.A.F. Stanley Brogden. 1944. 15.00 (ISBN 0-913076-02-3). Beachcomber Bks.

Sky Dragons & Flaming Swords: The Story of Eclipses, Comets, & Other Strange Happenings in the Sky. Marietta Moskin. LC 84-22206. 91p. (gr. 5-9). 1985. 11.95 (ISBN 0-8027-6574-2); PLB 12.85 (ISBN 0-8027-6575-0). Walker & Co.

Sky Drift. David Dunn. LC 80-80806. (Illus.). 90p. 1979. soft wrap-around cover 13.50 (ISBN 0-939044-27-7). Lingua Pr.

Sky Explored: Celestial Cartography, 1500-1800. Deborah J. Warner. LC 78-24737. 312p. 1979. 77.00x (ISBN 0-8451-1700-9). A R Liss.

Sky Fighters of France: Aerial Warfare, Nineteen Fourteen to Nineteen Eighteen. Henry Farre. Ed. by James Gilbert. Tr. by Catharine Rush. LC 79-7252. (Flight: Its First Seventy-Five Years Ser.). (Illus.). 1979. Repr. of 1919 ed. lib. bdg. 19.00x (ISBN 0-405-12164-4). Ayer Co Pubs.

Sky for Henry. Chris Strodder. (Illus.). 32p. (ps-3). 1985. pap. 4.95 (ISBN 0-931093-03-1). Red Hen Pr.

Sky Full of Poems. Eve Merriam. (Illus., Orig.). (gr. k-6). 1986. pap. 2.95 (ISBN 0-440-47986-X, YB). Dell.

Sky Giants over Japan. Chester Marshall. (Illus.). 220p. (Orig.). 1984. 12.95 (ISBN 0-9615206-0-4). Marshall Pubs.

Sky-God An-Anu: Head of the Mesopotamian Pantheon in Sumerian Akkadian Literature. Herman Wohlstein. Ed. by E. Curt. Tr. by Salvator Attanasio from Ger. LC 76-10388. 1976. 17.50 (ISBN 0-9601138-0-0). P A Stroock.

Sky Hook. Dan Jorgensen. LC 85-14983. (Pennypinchers Ser.). 128p. (gr. 4-9). 1985. pap. 3.95 (ISBN 0-89191-682-2, 56820, Chariot Bks). Cook.

Sky Hooks & Track Shoes: Climbing the Career Ladder. May Gruber. 200p. 1989. 16.95 (ISBN 0-931790-83-2). Brick Hse Pub.

Sky Hooks: The Autobiography of John Kane see John Kane, Painter.

Sky Is Falling. Barbara Corcoran. LC 87-33358. 192p. (gr. 3-7). 1988. 13.95 (ISBN 0-689-31388-8, Atheneum Childrens Bks). Macmillan.

Sky Is Falling. Warren Murphy & Richard Sapir. (Destroyer Ser.: No. 63). 1986. pap. 3.50 (ISBN 0-451-14039-7, Pub. by Sig). NAL.

Sky Is Falling! Why Buildings Fail. Marvin Hornstein. LC 82-72602. (Illus.). 120p. (Orig.). 1982. pap. 7.95 (ISBN 0-89708-106-4). And Bks.

Sky Is Full of Song. Lee B. Hopkins. LC 82-48263. (Charlotte Zolotow Bks.). (Illus.). 48p. (gr. 3-7). 1983. 11.70i (ISBN 0-06-022582-3); PLB 11.89g (ISBN 0-06-022583-1). HarpJ.

Sky Is Full of Song. Lee B. Hopkins. LC 82-48263. (Trophy Nonfiction Bks.). (Illus.). 48p. (gr. k-3). 1987. pap. 3.95 (ISBN 0-06-446064-9, Trophy). HarpJ.

Sky Is Full of Stars. Franklyn M. Branley. LC 81-43037. (Let's-Read-&-Find-Out Science Bks.). (Illus.). 40p. (gr. k-3). 1981. (Crowell Jr Bks); PLB 12.89 (ISBN 0-690-04123-3). HarpJ.

Sky Is Full of Stars. Franklyn M. Branley. LC 81-43037. (Trophy Let's Read-&-Find-Out Science Bks.). (Illus.). 40p. (gr. k-3). 1983. pap. 4.95 (ISBN 0-06-445002-3, Trophy). HarpJ.

Sky Is Home. John McCollister & Diann Ramsden. LC 86-16661. (Illus.). 128p. 1986. 9.95 (ISBN 0-8246-0321-4). Jonathan David.

Sky Is My Tipi. Ed. by Mody C. Boatright. LC 49-1690. (Texas Folklore Society Publications: No. 22). (Illus.). 256p. 1966. Repr. of 1949 ed. 13.95 (ISBN 0-87074-010-5). SMU Press.

Sky Is Red. Giuseppe Berto. Tr. by Angus Davidson from Ital. LC 76-138575. 1971. Repr. of 1948 ed. lib. bdg. 35.00x (ISBN 0-8371-5774-9, BESR). Greenwood.

Sky Is Still Falling. Donald E. Carr. 1982. 14.95 (ISBN 0-393-01508-4). Norton.

Sky Is the Limit: Strategies for Protecting the Ozone Layer. Alan S. Miller & Irving M. Mintzer. LC 86-51521. 48p. (Orig.). 1986. pap. text ed. 10.00 (ISBN 0-915825-17-1). World Resources Inst.

Sky Jumps into Your Shoes at Night. Jasper Tomkins. (Illus.). 40p. (Orig.). 1986. pap. 7.95 (ISBN 0-88138-068-7). Green Tiger Pr.

Sky-Liners. Louis L'Amour. 1972. pap. 2.95 (ISBN 0-553-25511-8). Bantam.

Sky Observer's Guide. Rev. ed. R. Newton Mayall et al. (Golden Guide Ser.). (Illus.). (gr. 9 up). 1985. pap. 3.95 (ISBN 0-307-24009-6, Golden Pr). Western Pub.

Sky Observer's Guidebook. Charles E. Roth. (PHalarope Bk.). (Illus.). 256p. 1986. 17.95 (ISBN 0-13-812793-X); pap. 10.95 (ISBN 0-13-812785-9). P-H.

Sky of Ashes, Sea of Flames. Kimberleigh Caitlin. 368p. (Orig.). 1987. pap. 3.95 (ISBN 0-515-08975-3). Jove Pubns.

Sky of Late Summer: Poems. Henry Rago. LC 78-92464. (Phoenix Poets Ser). 1970. pap. 1.95 (ISBN 0-226-70309-6, PP13, Phoen). U of Chicago Pr.

Sky over My Head. John Attwood. 96p. 1986. pap. 20.00x (ISBN 0-7212-0791-X, Pub. by Regency Pr). State Mutual Bk.

Sky People. John Emery. LC 87-26525. 357p. (Orig.). 1988. 18.95 (ISBN 0-939149-10-9). Soho Press.

Sky People. Jack Nisbet. LC 84-61542. (Illus.). 128p. (Orig.). 1984. 12.95 (ISBN 0-931849-00-4); pap. 5.95 (ISBN 0-931849-01-2). Quartzite Bks.

Sky Phantom. Carolyn Keene. 4.50 (ISBN 0-448-09553-X, G&D). Putnam Pub Group.

Sky Pilot, a Tale of the Foothills. Ralph Connor. 1976. lib. bdg. 14.25x (ISBN 0-89968-019-4). Lightyear.

Sky Pilot in No Man's Land. Ralph Connor. 1976. lib. bdg. 15.75x (ISBN 0-89968-018-6). Lightyear.

Sky Pioneering: Arizona in Aviation History. Ruth M. Reinhold. LC 81-11514. (Illus.). 232p. 1982. 22.50 (ISBN 0-8165-0737-6); pap. 10.95 (ISBN 0-8165-0757-0). U of Ariz Pr.

Sky Prints Aviation Enroute Atlas. annual 27th ed. Sky Prints Corp. 1988. 69.50 (ISBN 0-911720-64-2, Pub. by FR). Aviation.

Sky Remembers. Dan Brennan. 1977. pap. 1.50 (ISBN 0-8439-0484-4, Leisure Bks). Leisure NY.

Sky Sabotage. Franklin W. Dixon & Wendy Barish. (Hardy Boys Ser.: No. 79). (Illus.). 192p. (Orig.). (gr. 3-7). 1983. 9.95 (ISBN 0-671-47556-8). Wanderer Bks.

Sky Scanner. 2nd ed. Eppler Nowell. (Illus.). 17p. (Orig.). 1980. pap. text ed. 4.95x (ISBN 0-9611454-0-4). E Nowell.

Sky, Sea, Birds, Trees, Earth, House, Beast. 2nd ed. Kenneth Rexroth. LC 76-134750. (Illus.). 30p. 1973. 10.00 (ISBN 0-87775-044-0); pap. 4.00 (ISBN 0-87775-048-3). Unicorn Pr.

Sky Ship: The Akron Era. 2nd ed. Thomas S. Hook. Ed. by T. G. Settle. LC 76-21910. (Famous Airships Ser.). (Illus.). 160p. (Large format). 1985. pap. 9.95 (ISBN 0-9601506-5-X). Airsho Pubs.

Sky Signs: Aratus' Phaenomena. Tr. by Stanley Lombardo. 100p. 1983. 20.00 (ISBN 0-938190-15-6); pap. 7.95 (ISBN 0-938190-16-4). North Atlantic.

Sky Soldiers: An Illustrated History of the Vietnam War, I. John Forbes et al. LC 86-47565. 160p. (Orig.). 1987. pap. 6.95 (ISBN 0-553-34320-3). Bantam.

Sky Songs. Myra C. Livingston. LC 83-12955. (Illus.). 32p. (gr. 1-4). 1984. reinforced bdg 14.95 (ISBN 0-8234-0502-8). Holiday.

Sky Storming Yankee: Life of Glenn Curtis. Clara Studer. LC 76-169438. (Literature & History of Aviation Ser). 1971. Repr. of 1937 ed. 22.00 (ISBN 0-405-03780-5). Ayer Co Pubs.

Sky Truck. Stephen Piercey. (Illus.). 128p. 1984. pap. 14.95 (ISBN 0-85045-552-9, Pub. by Osprey England). Motorbooks Intl.

Sky Was Blue. Charlotte Zolotow. LC 62-13328. (Illus.). (gr. k-3). 1963. PLB 13.89 (ISBN 0-06-027001-2). HarpJ.

Sky Watchers of Ages Past. Malcolm E. Weiss. (Illus.). (gr. 5-9). 1982. 7.95 (ISBN 0-395-29525-4). HM.

Sky Will Be Blue. G Gordon & L. Gordon. 160p. 1984. 5.95 (ISBN 0-8285-2819-5, Pub. by Mir Pubs USSR). Imported Pubns.

Sky with Its Mouth Wide Open. Rocco Scotellaro. 1975. pap. 3.00 (ISBN 0-88031-024-3). Invisible-Red Hill.

Skyclimber. Raymond Z. Gallun. (Orig.). 1981. pap. 2.25 (ISBN 0-505-51682-9, Pub. by Tower Bks). Leisure NY.

Skydancer. Geoffrey Archer. 272p. 1988. 15.95 (ISBN 0-396-09192-X). Dodd.

Skydancer. Geoffrey Arhcer. 340p. 1989. pap. price not set. Tor Bks.

Skydiving. Norman Barrett. Ed. by Franklin Watts Ltd. (Picture Library). (Illus.). 32p. (ps-9). 1988. 9.90 (ISBN 0-531-10352-8). Watts.

Skydiving. Rolf Benson. LC 78-26246. (Superwheels & Thrill Sports Bks.). (Illus.). (gr. 4-9). 1979. PLB 8.95 (ISBN 0-8225-0425-1). Lerner Pubns.

Skydiving. Jerolyn Nentl. Ed. by Howard Schroeder. LC 78-8702. (Funseekers Ser.). (Illus.). 32p. (gr. 3-4). 1978. PLB 8.95 (ISBN 0-913940-87-9). Crestwood Hse.

Skydiving: A Dictionary for the Sport Parachutist. William H. Simons. LC 88-80653. (Orig.). 1988. pap. 8.95 (ISBN 0-940837-14-5). Fodderstack Pr.

Skye. Derek Cooper. (Illus.). 242p. 1983. pap. 11.95 (ISBN 0-7100-9565-1). Routledge Chapman & Hall.

Skye. Lauran Paine. 192p. 1987. pap. 2.75 (ISBN 0-380-70186-3). Avon.

Skye Cameron. Phyllis Whitney. 1981. pap. 2.50 (ISBN 0-449-24100-9, Crest). Fawcett.

Skye Terrier Champions, Nineteen Fifty-Two to Nineteen Eighty-Seven. Camino E. E. & B. Co. Staff. 175p. (YA) 1988. pap. 29.95 (ISBN 0-940808-92-7). Camino E E & B.

Skye: The Island. James Hunter & Cailean Maclean. 192p. 1987. 22.95 (ISBN 0-88162-224-9). Salem Hse Pubs.

Skye: The Island. James Hunter & Cailean Maclean. 192p. 1987. 65.00x (ISBN 1-85158-017-4, Pub. by Mainstream Scotland). State Mutual Bk.

Skyfall. Thomas A. Block. 352p. 1987. pap. 3.95 (ISBN 0-515-09178-2). Jove Pubns.

Skyfall. Harry Harrison. 256p. 1985. pap. 3.50 (ISBN 0-441-76945-4). Ace Bks.

Skyfire. Frank Asch. LC 83-16165. (Illus.). 32p. 1984. 10.95 (ISBN 0-13-812389-6). P-H.

Skyfire. Frank Asch. (Illus.). 32p. (ps-2). 1988. pap. 4.95 (ISBN 0-671-66861-7). S&S.

Skyguide. Mark R. Chartrand. LC 81-70086. (Golden Field Guide Ser.). (Illus.). 280p. 1982. pap. 9.95 (ISBN 0-307-13667-1, Golden Pr). Western Pub.

Skyhawk. Ted Tate & Tom Tweddale. 260p. (Orig.). 1985. pap. 8.95 (ISBN 0-89288-111-9). Maverick.

Skyhooks: Riding the Crest of the Industrial Revolution. Algo D. Henderson. LC 81-53001. (Illus.). 288p. (YA) 1982. 14.95 (ISBN 0-9601902-1-X). Reverchon Pr.

Skyjack. (S.O.B. Ser.: No. 19). Date not set. pap. 2.50 (Pub. by Worldwide). Harlequin BKs.

Skylab. Dennis B. Fradin. LC 83-23180. (Illus.). 48p. (gr. k-4). 1984. lib. bdg. 12.60 (ISBN 0-516-01727-6); pap. 3.95 (ISBN 0-516-41727-4). Childrens.

Skylab & Pioneer Report: Proceedings of the 12th Goddard Memorial Symposium. Ed. by Paul B. Richards & Philip H. Bolger. (Science & Technology Ser: Vol. 36). (Illus.). 160p. 1975. lib. bdg. 20.00x (ISBN 0-87703-071-5, Pub. by Am Astronaut). Univelt Inc.

Skylab Results, 2 pts, Pt. 1 & 2. Ed. by W. C. Schneider & T. E. Hanes. (Advances in the Astronautical Sciences Ser.: Vol. 31). 1975. write for info. (Pub. by Am Astronaut); microfiche 55.00x (ISBN 0-87703-072-3). Univelt Inc.

Skylab: The Story of Man's First Station in Space. William Cromie. LC 74-25983. (Illus.). 192p. (gr. 7 up). 1976. 10.95 (ISBN 0-679-20300-1). McKay.

Skyland: The Heart of the Shenandoah National Park. George F. Pollock. Ed. by Stuart E. Brown, Jr. LC 60-16567. (Illus.). 283p. 1960. pap. 10.00 (ISBN 0-685-65073-1). Va Bk.

Skylark Duquesne. Doc Smith. 240p. 1986. pap. 2.95 (ISBN 0-425-09148-1). Berkley Pub.

Skylark Duquesne. Edward E. Smith. Ed. by Lester Del Rey. LC 75-432. (Library of Science Fiction). 1975. lib. bdg. 21.00 (ISBN 0-8240-1435-9). Garland Pub.

Skylark of Space. E. E. Smith. 160p. 1985. pap. 2.75 (ISBN 0-425-08636-4). Berkley Pub.

Skylark of Space. Edward E. Smith & Lee H. Garby. Ed. by Lester Del Rey. LC 75-427. (Library of Science Fiction). 1975. lib. bdg. 21.00 (ISBN 0-8240-1432-4). Garland Pub.

Skylark of Valeron. E. E. Smith. 208p. 1986. pap. 2.95 (ISBN 0-425-08953-3). Berkley Pub.

Skylark Sing Your Lonely Song. Bobby Sands. 176p. (Orig.). 1988. pap. 9.95 (ISBN 0-85342-726-7, Pub. by Mercier Pr Ireland). Irish Bks Media.

Skylark Soars Again. Kay Powers. 128p. 1987. 9.95 (ISBN 0-89962-605-X). Todd & Honeywell.

Skylark Three. E. E. Smith. 208p. 1984. pap. 2.95 (ISBN 0-425-08730-1). Berkley Pub.

Skylark Three. Edward E. Smith. Ed. by Lester Del Rey. LC 75-429. (Library of Science Fiction). 1975. lib. bdg. 21.00 (ISBN 0-8240-1433-2). Garland Pub.

Skylarks & Lecterns: A Law School Charter. Ron Lansing. LC 86-82416. 244p. (Orig.). 1986. pap. 18.50x (ISBN 0-934355-08-8). Huddleston-Brown Pubs.

Skylighters. Graeme Garden. (Illus.). 32p. (gr. 1 up). 1988. 13.95 (ISBN 0-19-520642-8). Oxford U Pr.

Skylights: A Revision of A-621. Mary Vance. (Architecture Ser.: A 1503). 9p. 1985. 2.00. Vance Biblios.

Skylights: The Definitive Guide to Planning, Installing & Maintaining Skylights & Natural Light Systems. Tom Jensen. LC 83-3089. (Illus.). 112p. (Orig.). 1983. lib. bdg. 19.80 (ISBN 0-89471-195-4); pap. 12.95 (ISBN 0-89471-194-6). Running Pr.

Skylines. Ethel R. Fuller. 1978. pap. 3.95 (ISBN 0-8323-0333-X). Binford-Metropolitan.

Skyraider: The Douglas A-1 "Flying Dump Truck". Rosario Rausa. LC 82-14187. (Illus.). 224p. 1987. Repr. of 1982 ed. 19.95 (ISBN 0-933852-31-2). Nautical & Aviation.

Skyraiders. Robert F. Dorr. LC 87-47956. (Illustrated History of the Vietnam War Ser.: No. 14). (Illus.). 160p. 1988. pap. 6.95 (ISBN 0-553-34548-6). Bantam.

Skyraiders. Alan Marks. 1979. pap. 1.95 (ISBN 0-505-51416-8, Pub. by Tower Bks). Leisure NY.

Skyriders: History of the 327-401 Glider Infantry. James L. McDonough & Richard S. Gardner. LC 80-67956. (Airborne Ser.: No. 11). (Illus.). 176p. 1980. 20.00 (ISBN 0-89839-034-6). Battery Pr.

Skyripper. David Drake. 352p. 1986. pap. 3.50 (ISBN 0-8125-3618-5, Dist. by Warner Pub Services & St. Martin's Press). Tor Bks.

Skyrmions & Anomalies: Proceedings of the Workshops. Ed. by M. Jezabek & M. Prassatowics. 544p. 1987. 75.00 (ISBN 9971-50-350-6). World Scientific Pub.

Skyrocket Your Sales. Raymond A. Slesinski. LC 85-28452. 207p. 1986. 14.95 (ISBN 0-88289-485-4). Pelican.

Sky's the Limit. Wayne Dyer. 384p. 1984. pap. 4.95 (ISBN 0-671-54757-7). PB.

Sky's the Limit: The History of the Airlines. Charles J. Kelly, Jr. LC 70-169423. (Literature & History of Aviation Ser). 1971. Repr. of 1963 ed. 21.00 (ISBN 0-405-03766-X). Ayer Co Pubs.

Skyscraper. Faith Baldwin. 1976. Repr. of 1931 ed. lib. bdg. 19.95x (ISBN 0-88411-623-9, Pub. by Aeonian Pr). Amereon Ltd.

Skyscraper. Paul Goldberger. LC 81-47480. (Illus.). 224p. 1983. pap. 16.95 (ISBN 0-394-71586-1). Knopf.

Skyscraper Book. James C. Giblin. LC 81-43038. (Illus.). 96p. (gr. 3-6). 1981. 12.70 (ISBN 0-690-04154-3, Crowell Jr Bks); PLB 11.89 (ISBN 0-690-04155-1). HarpJ.

Skyscraper Going Up. Vicki Cobb. LC 86-47795. (Illus.). 18p. (gr. 1-5). 1987. 14.95i (ISBN 0-690-04525-5, Crowell Jr Bks). HarpJ.

Skyscraper in American Art, 1890-1931. Merrill Schleier. Ed. by Stephen Foster. LC 86-6986. (Studies in Fine Arts: The Avant-Garde: No. 53). (Illus.). 298p. 1986. 49.95 (ISBN 0-8357-1729-1). UMI Res Pr.

Skyscraper Style: Art Deco New York Photographs by Cervin Robinson. Cervin Robinson & Rosemarie H. Bletter. LC 74-22885. (Illus.). 1976. pap. 19.95 (ISBN 0-19-502112-6). Oxford U Pr.

Skyscrapers. Tim Ostler. Ed. by Franklin Watts Ltd. (Engineers at Work Ser.). (Illus.). 32p. (YA) (gr. 7-9). 1988. 10.90 (ISBN 0-531-17074-8, Gloucester Pr). Watts.

Skyscrapers: A Revision of A-577. Mary Vance. (Architecture Ser.: A 1501). 62p. 1985. 9.00 (ISBN 0-89028-651-5). Vance Biblios.

Skyscrapers, & Other Essays. facs. ed. Lewis B. Namier. LC 68-22113. (Essay Index Reprint Ser). 1931. 14.50 (ISBN 0-8369-0734-5). Ayer Co Pubs.

Skyshooting: Photography for Amateur Astronomers. rev. ed. Robert N. Mayall & Margaret W. Mayall. pap. 4.50 (ISBN 0-486-21854-6). Dover.

Skyshroud. Tom Keene. 336p. 1988. pap. 3.95 (ISBN 0-441-76903-9, Charter Bks). Ace Bks.

Skystalker. Len Nevfield. (Be an Interplanetary Spy Ser.: No. 12). 128p. (Orig.). 1985. pap. 1.95 (ISBN 0-553-24894-4). Bantam.

Skysweeper. (Executioner Ser.: No. 69). Date not set. pap. 2.25 (ISBN 0-317-63938-2, Pub. by Worldwide). Harlequin Bks.

Skytalk: English for Air Communication. L. Leveson. 1985. 40.00x (ISBN 0-317-38816-9, Pub. by S Thornes Pubs England). State Mutual Bk.

Skythen. Alexej P. Smirnov. 216p. (Ger.). 1979. 8.00x (ISBN 0-317-57347-0, Pub. by Collets UK). State Mutual Bk.

Skytrap: An Adventure Novel. John Smith. 1984. 12.95 (ISBN 0-393-01860-1). Norton.

Skywalking: The Life & Films of George Lucas. George Pollack. 1984. pap. 3.50 (ISBN 0-345-31419-0). Ballantine.

Skyward Trend of Thought: The Meta-Physics of the American Skyscraper. Thomas A. Van Leeuwen. (Illus.). 192p. 1988. 25.00 (ISBN 0-262-22034-2). MIT Pr.

Skywarriors: Aviation in the California Army & Air National Guard. Rene Francillon. (Osprey Colour Library). (Illus.). 128p. (Orig.). 1988. pap. 14.95 (ISBN 0-85045-814-5, Pub. by Osprey England). Motorbooks Intl.

Skywatch: The Western Weather Guide. Richard A. Keen. LC 87-11871. (Illus.). 158p. 1987. pap. 13.95 (ISBN 1-55591-019-X). Fulcrum Inc.

Skywatcher's Handbook. Colin Ronan. LC 85-3810. 1985. pap. 13.95 (ISBN 0-517-55703-7). Crown.

Skywatchers of Ancient Mexico. Anthony F. Aveni. (Texas Pan American Ser.). (Illus.). 369p. 1980. text ed. 35.00x (ISBN 0-292-77557-1). U of Tex Pr.

Skywatchers of Ancient Mexico. Anthony F. Aveni. (Texas Pan American Ser.). (Illus.). 369p. 1983. pap. 17.50 (ISBN 0-292-77578-4). U of Tex Pr.

Skywriting by Word of Mouth. John Lennon. LC 86-45312. 160p. 1986. 12.45i (ISBN 0-06-015656-2, HarpT). Har-Row.

Skywriting by Word of Mouth: And Other Short Works, Including the Ballad of John & Yoko. John Lennon. LC 86-54312. (Illus.). 160p. 1987. pap. 5.95 (ISBN 0-06-091444-0, PL/1444, PL). Har-Row.

SL 2 (IR) S. Lang. (Graduate Texts in Mathematics Ser.: Vol. 105). (Illus.). xiv, 428p. 1985. Repr. of 1975 ed. 43.00 (ISBN 0-387-96198-4). Springer-Verlag.

SLA Triennial Salary Survey. SLA Staff. LC 86-1847. 74p. 1986. pap. 25.00 (ISBN 0-87111-316-3). SLA.

Slab Boys. John Byrne. (Paisley Patterns Trilogy). 44p. 1983. pap. 5.95 (ISBN 0-907540-20-1, NO.3990). Routledge Chapman & Hall.

Slab Thickness Design for Industrial Floors on Grade. 1976. pap. 1.25 (ISBN 0-89312-158-4, IS195D). Portland Cement.

Slabs on Grade. 78p. 9.50 (ISBN 0-317-39818-0). ACI.

Slacks for Perfect Fit: Sew-Fit Method. Ruth Oblander. LC 81-50280. (Illus.). 64p. 1981. pap. 4.95x (ISBN 0-933956-07-X). Sew-Fit.

Slade Short Course. 2nd ed. Slade Schuster. 77p. (Orig.). (gr. 8-11). 1982. pap. text ed. 3.75 (ISBN 0-88334-111-5). Ind Sch Pr.

Slade's Glacier. Robert F. Jones. 1982. pap. 3.25 (ISBN 0-440-18441-X). Dell.

Slag. David Hare. 78p. 1971. pap. 5.95 (ISBN 0-571-09643-3). Faber & Faber.

Slag of Creation. Richard Grossinger. 256p. (Orig.). 1975. pap. 5.00 (ISBN 0-913028-32-0). North Atlantic.

Slain by the Doones, & Other Stories. facs. ed. Richard D. Blackmore. LC 74-86137. (Short Story Index Reprint Ser.). 1895. 17.00 (ISBN 0-8369-3041-X). Ayer Co Pubs.

Slain in the Spirit. Ezra M. Coppin. LC 75-36001. 96p. 1976. pap. 2.50 (ISBN 0-89221-010-9). New Leaf.

Slake's Limbo. Felice Holman. LC 74-11675. (gr. 5-9). 1974. 12.95 (ISBN 0-684-13926-X, Pub. by Scribner). Macmillan.

Slake's Limbo. Felice Holman. LC 85-26795. 128p. (gr. 6 up). 1986. pap. 3.95 (ISBN 0-689-71066-6, Aladdin). Macmillan.

SLAM-Addition, 30 wkbks. Set. 15.95 (ISBN 0-86624-031-4, LWB6536TB). Bilingual Ed Serv.

Slam Bang. John Burningham. LC 83-23549. (Noisy Words Ser.). 24p. 1985. 4.95 (ISBN 0-670-65076-5, Viking Kestrel). Viking.

Slam Bidding. Hugh Kelsey. (Master Bridge Ser.). 192p. 1986. pap. 13.95 (ISBN 0-575-03799-7, Pub. by Gollancz England). David & Charles.

Slam Book. Ann M. Martin. LC 87-45335. 160p. (YA) (gr. 7 up). 1987. 12.95 (ISBN 0-8234-0666-0). Holiday.

Slam the Big Door. John D. MacDonald. 272p. 1987. pap. 3.95 (ISBN 0-449-13275-7, GM). Fawcett.

Slam the Big Door. John D. MacDonald. 208p. 1987. 16.95 (ISBN 0-89296-190-2). Mysterious Pr.

Slammin' Sam: An Autobiography. Sam Snead & George Mendoza. LC 86-82381. (Illus.). 1986. 17.95 (ISBN 0-917657-87-X). D I Fine.

Slan. A. E. Van Vogt. 15.95 (ISBN 0-89190-454-9, Pub. by Am Repr). Amereon Ltd.

Slang see **Doughty's English.**

Slang & Euphemism: A Dictionary of Oaths, Curses, Insults, Sexual Slang & Metaphor, Racial Slurs, Drug Talk, Homosexual Lingo, & Related Matters. Richard A. Spears. LC 80-18714. 1981. 24.95 (ISBN 0-8246-0259-5). Jonathan David.

Slang & Euphemism: A Dictionary of Oaths, Curses, Insults, Sexual Slang & Metaphor Racial Slurs, Drug Talk, Homosexual Lingo & Related Matters. Richard A. Spears. 1981. pap. 12.95 (ISBN 0-8246-0273-0). Jonathan David.

Slang & Euphemism: Abridged Edition. Richard A. Spears. 1982. pap. 4.95 (ISBN 0-451-14979-3, Sig). NAL.

Slang & Its Analogues, Past & Present, 7 Vols. in 3. John S. Farmer & W. E. Henley. LC 5-16232. 1890-1904. Set. 210.00 (ISBN 0-527-28300-2). Kraus Repr.

Slang & Jargon of Drugs & Drink. Richard A. Spears. LC 85-26277. 601p. 1986. 42.50 (ISBN 0-8108-1864-7). Scarecrow.

Slang from Shakespeare. Anderson M. Baten. LC 72-6402. 1931. lib. bdg. 20.00 (ISBN 0-8414-0154-3). Folcroft.

Slang Thesaurus. Jonathon Green. 352p. 1988. 29.95 (ISBN 0-241-11851-4, Pub. by Hamish Hamilton). David & Charles.

Slang Today & Yesterday: With a Short Historical Sketch & Vocabularies of English, American & Australian Slang. 4th ed. Eric Partridge. 1970. 30.00 (ISBN 0-7100-6922-7). Routledge Chapman & Hall.

Slanguage. John Artman. (gr. 4-8). 1980. 7.95 (ISBN 0-916456-60-9, GA 175). Good Apple.

Slanidar Neandertals. Erick Trinkaus. LC 83-2488. (Monograph). 1983. 39.95 (ISBN 0-12-700550-1). Acad Pr.

Slant Book. Peter Newell. LC 67-12304. (Illus.). 50p. (gr. k-4). 1967. Repr. of 1910 ed. 12.95 (ISBN 0-8048-0532-6). C E Tuttle.

Slanted Colt. Dan Parkinson. 224p. 1984. pap. 2.25 (ISBN 0-8217-1413-9). Zebra.

Slap in the Farce. Eugene Labiche. Tr. by Norman R. Shapiro from Fr. Bd. with Matter of Wife & Death. (Tour de Farce Ser.: Vol. 3). (Orig.). 1987. pap. 5.95 (ISBN 0-936839-82-1). Applause Theatre Bk Pubs.

Slapstick. Kurt Vonnegut, Jr. 1976. pap. 9.95 (ISBN 0-385-28944-8, Sey Lawr). Delacorte.

Slapstick or Lonesome No More. Kurt Vonnegut, Jr. 1978. pap. 3.95 (ISBN 0-385-28935-9, Delta). Dell.

Slapstick: or, Lonesome No More! Kurt Vonnegut, Jr. 256p. 1977. pap. 4.95 (ISBN 0-440-18009-0). Dell.

Slapstick: The Illustrated Story. Tony Staveacre. (Illus.). 200p. 1987. pap. 14.95 (ISBN 0-207-15493-7, Pub. by Angus & Robertson). Salem Hse Pubs.

Slash & Burn: Farming in the Third World Forest. Leon F. Neuenschwander & William J. Peters. (Illus.). 156p. 1988. lib. bdg. 29.95 (ISBN 0-89301-123-1). U of Idaho Pr.

Slash & Thrust. John Sanchez. 72p. 1980. pap. 8.00 (ISBN 0-87364-188-4). Paladin Pr.

Slashed to Ribbons in Defense of Love & Other Stories. Felice Picano. 192p. (Orig.). 1983. 12.95 (ISBN 0-9604724-4-4); pap. 6.95 (ISBN 0-9604724-2-8). Gay Pr NY.

Slashing the Deficit, Fiscal Year 1987. Stephent Moore. 285p. 1986. pap. 8.00 (ISBN 0-317-47105-8). Heritage Found.

Slat of Wood & Other Poems. Helen M. Brooks 46p. 1976. 5.00 (ISBN 0-686-34466-9). Whimsie Pr.

Slate. Nathan Aldyne. 192p. 1985. pap. 2.95 (ISBN 0-345-31366-6). Ballantine.

Slate Waste: Engineering & Environmental Aspects. K. L. Watson. (Illus.). 195p. 1980. 43.00 (ISBN 0-85334-880-4, Pub. by Elsevier Applied Sci England). Elsevier.

Slater's Planet see **Planeta Fantasma.**

Slaughter & Son. E. B. Majors. 1985. pap. 2.75 (ISBN 0-446-32680-1). Warner Bks.

Slaughter & Son No. 4: Death In Durango. E. B. Majors. 192p. (Orig.). 1986. pap. 2.95 (ISBN 0-446-34097-9). Warner Bks.

Slaughter & Son Number Three: Hair Trigger Kill. E. B. Majors. 192p. (Orig.). 1986. pap. 2.75 (ISBN 0-446-32684-4). Warner Bks.

Slaughter at Buffalo Creek. Chet Cunningham. (Pony Soldiers Ser.: No. 1). 224p. (Orig.). 1987. pap. 2.75 (ISBN 0-8439-2518-3). Leisure NY.

Slaughter by Product: Winning the Products Liability Case. Edward M. Swartz. LC 86-3002. (Kluwer Products Liability Library). 593p. 1986. text ed. 80.00 (ISBN 0-930273-54-0). Kluwer Law Bk.

Slaughter Day, No. 218. Nick Carter. 208p. 1986. pap. 2.50 (ISBN 0-441-57287-1, Pub. by Charter Bks). Ace Bks.

Slaughter Express. Jon Sharpe. (Trailsman Ser.: No. 58). 192p. pap. 2.75 (ISBN 0-451-14524-0, Sig). NAL.

Slaughter of Poultry for Human Consumption. W. N. Scott. 1978. 16.00x (ISBN 0-317-43887-5, Pub. by Univ Federation Animal). State Mutual Bk.

Slaughter of Terrified Beasts: A Biblical Basis for the Humane Treatment of Animals. J. R. Hyland. LC 88-50200. 74p. (Orig.). 1988. pap. 6.95 (ISBN 0-945703-00-7). Viatoris Comns.

Slaughter of the Innocents: A Study of the Battered Child Phenomenon. David Bakan. LC 78-155168. (Social & Behavioral Science Ser.). 1971. 24.95x (ISBN 0-87589-093-8). Jossey-Bass.

Slaughter Run. Axel Kilgore. (They Call Me the Mercenary Ser.). (Orig.). 1981. pap. 2.25 (ISBN 0-89083-719-8). Zebra.

Slaughter Zone. Frank Garrett. (Killsquad Ser.: No. 8). 176p. 1987. pap. 2.50 (ISBN 0-380-75364-2). Avon.

Slaughterhouse Cleaning & Sanitation. Tove Skaarup. (FAO Animal Production & Health Paper: No. 53). 45p. 1986. pap. text ed. 7.50 (ISBN 92-5-102296-8, F2889, FAO). UNIPUB.

Slaughterhouse Five. Kurt Vonnegut, Jr. (Book Notes Ser.). 1985. pap. 2.50 (ISBN 0-8120-3539-9). Barron.

Slaughterhouse Five: Or, The Children's Crusade. Kurt Vonnegut, Jr. 224p. 1978. pap. 4.95 (ISBN 0-440-18029-5). Dell.

Slaughterhouse Five; or, the Children's Crusade. Kurt Vonnegut, Jr. 356p. 1970. pap. 9.95 (ISBN 0-385-28940-5, Delta). Dell.

Slaughterhouse Province: An American Diplomat's Report on the Armenian Genocide of 1914-17. Leslie A. Davis. Intro. by Susan Blair. (Illus.). 224p. 1988. 30.00 (ISBN 0-89241-458-8). Caratzas.

Slav for the Tournament Player. Glenn Flear. (Illus.). 128p. 1989. pap. 10.95 (ISBN 0-7134-5635-3, Pub. by Batsford England). David & Charles.

Slav Soul, & Other Stories. facsimile ed. Alexander I. Kuprin. LC 78-150547. (Short Story Index Reprint Ser.). Repr. of 1916 ed. 17.00 (ISBN 0-8369-3844-5). Ayer Co Pubs.

Slave. Elechi Amadi. (African Writers Ser.). 1979. pap. text ed. 6.00 (ISBN 0-435-90210-5). Heinemann Ed.

Slave. William Malliol. 1986. 16.95 (ISBN 0-393-02268-4). Norton.

Slave. Isaac Bashevis Singer. 1978. pap. 1.95 (ISBN 0-380-01553-6, 26377, Bard). Avon.

Slave. Isaac Bashevis Singer. 1984. pap. 2.95 (ISBN 0-449-20694-7, Crest). Fawcett.

Slave. Isaac Bashevis Singer. Tr. by Cecil Hemley from Yiddish. 311p. 1962. pap. 7.95 (ISBN 0-374-50680-9). FS&G.

Slave & Citizen. Frank Tannenbaum. Date not set. 13.00 (ISBN 0-916304-58-2); pap. 8.00 (ISBN 0-916304-59-0). SDSU Press.

Slave & Citizen: A Critical Annotated Bibliography on Slavery & Race Relations in the Americas. Robert Detweiler & Theodore Kornweibel. 300p. 1983. pap. 6.00 (ISBN 0-686-84758-X). SDSU Press.

Slave & Citizen: The Life of Frederick Douglass. Nathan I. Huggins. (Library of American Biography). 1980. pap. 14.95 (ISBN 0-316-38001-6). Little.

Slave & Freeman: The Autobiography of George L. Knox. George L. Knox. Ed. by Willard B. Gatewood, Jr. LC 78-21058. 256p. 1979. 23.00x (ISBN 0-8131-1384-9). U Pr of Ky.

Slave Catchers: Enforcement of the Fugitive Slave Law, 1850-1860. Stanley W. Campbell. 1972. pap. 1.95x (ISBN 0-393-00626-3, Norton Lib). Norton.

Slave Catchers: Enforcement of the Fugitive Slave Law, 1850-1860. Stanley W. Campbell. LC 79-109463. ix, 236p. 1970. 22.50x (ISBN 0-8078-1141-6). U of NC Pr.

Slave Community: Plantation Life in the Ante-Bellum South. 2nd rev. enl. ed. John W. Blassingame. (Illus.). 1979. 27.95 (ISBN 0-19-502562-8); pap. text ed. 9.95x (ISBN 0-19-502563-6). Oxford U Pr.

Slave Culture: Nationalist Theory & the Foundations of Black America. Sterling Stuckey. 416p. 1987. 27.50 (ISBN 0-19-504265-4). Oxford U Pr.

Slave Culture: Nationalist Theory & the Foundations of Black America. Sterling Stuckey. 416p. 1988. pap. 9.95 (ISBN 0-19-505664-7). Oxford U Pr.

Slave Dancer. Paula Fox. LC 73-80642. (Illus.). 192p. (gr. 5-8). 1973. 10.95 (ISBN 0-02-735560-8). Bradbury Pr.

Slave Dancer. Paula Fox. 128p. (gr. 7 up). 1975. pap. 2.75 (ISBN 0-440-96132-7, LFL). Dell.

Slave Dreads Her Work. Nathan Whiting. 1980. pap. 6.00 (ISBN 0-914610-15-5). Hanging Loose.

Slave Drivers: Black Agricultural Labor Supervisors in the Antebellum South. William L. Van Deburg. LC 78-59261. (Contributions in Afro-American & African Studies: No. 43). 1979. lib. bdg. 35.00x (ISBN 0-313-20610-4, VSD/). Greenwood.

Slave Drivers: Black Agricultural Labor Supervisors in the Antebellum South. William L. Van Deburg. 224p. 1988. pap. text ed. 8.95 (ISBN 0-19-505698-1). Oxford U Pr.

Slave Economy of the Old South: Selected Essays in Economic & Social History. Ulrich B. Phillips. Ed. by Eugene D. Genovese. LC 68-21806. (Illus.). 1968. pap. text ed. 9.95 (ISBN 0-8071-0134-6). La State U Pr.

Slave Emancipation in Cuba: The Transition to Free Labor, 1860-1899. Rebecca J. Scott. LC 85-42703. (Illus.). 352p. 1986. text ed. 49.00x (ISBN 0-691-07667-7); pap. text ed. 14.95x (ISBN 0-691-10157-4). Princeton U Pr.

Slave Genealogy: A Research Guide with Case Studies. David H. Streets. iv, 87p. (Orig.). 1986. pap. 10.00 (ISBN 0-917890-63-9). Heritage Bk.

Slave Girl. Buchi Emecheta. LC 77-77559. 1977. pap. 6.95 (ISBN 0-8076-0952-8). Braziller.

Slave Girl of Gor, No. 11. John Norman. (Science Fiction Ser). 1986. pap. 3.95 (ISBN 0-88677-027-0). DAW Bks.

Slave Lady. Julia Fitzgerald. 352p. (Orig.). 1989. pap. 4.50 (ISBN 1-55785-072-0). Bart Books.

Slave Life in America: A Historiography & Selected Bibliography. James S. Olson. 128p. (Orig.). 1983. lib. bdg. 26.25 (ISBN 0-8191-3285-3); pap. text ed. 10.25 (ISBN 0-8191-3286-1). U Pr of Amer.

Slave Life in Georgia. facsimile ed. John Brown. Ed. by L. A. Chamerovzow. LC 77-168512. (Black Heritage Library Collection). Repr. of 1855 ed. 18.75 (ISBN 0-8369-8865-5). Ayer Co Pubs.

Slave Life in Rio De Janerio, 1808-1850. Mary C. Karasch. LC 85-43290. 1987. 85.00x (ISBN 0-691-07708-8). Princeton U Pr.

Slave Narrative: It's Place in American History. Marion W. Starling. 400p. 1988. pap. 12.95 (ISBN 0-88258-165-1). Howard U Pr.

Slavery in the Arab World. Murray Gordon. 272p. 1988. 24.95 (ISBN 0-941533-30-1). New Amsterdam Bks.
Slavery in the Cities: The South, Eighteen Twenty to Eighteen Sixty. Richard C. Wade. 1965. pap. 9.95x (ISBN 0-19-500755-7). Oxford U Pr.
Slavery in the Colonial Chesapeake. David B. Davis. (Foundations of America Ser.). (Illus.). 48p. (Orig.). 1986. pap. text ed. 5.95 (ISBN 0-87935-115-2). Williamsburg.
Slavery in the Courtroom: An Annotated Bibliography of American Cases. Paul Finkelman. LC 83-600166. (Illus.). xxviii, 313p. 1985. 12.00. Lib Congress.
Slavery in the State of North Carolina. John S. Bassett. LC 79-161726. (John Hopkins University Studies in the Social Sciences Seventeenth Ser.: No. 1899: 7-8). Repr. of 1899 ed. 11.50 (ISBN 0-404-00246-3). AMS Pr.
Slavery in the State of North Carolina. John S. Bassett. Repr. of 1899 ed. 13.00 (ISBN 0-384-03527-2). Johnson Repr.
Slavery in the Structure of American Politics, 1765-1820. Donald Robinson. 1979. pap. 7.95x (ISBN 0-393-00913-0). Norton.
Slavery in the Twentieth Century. Roger Sawyer. 400p. 1986. text ed. 34.95 (ISBN 0-7102-0475-2, 04752, Pub. by Routledge UK). Routledge Chapman & Hall.
Slavery in the U. S. A. Henry Sherman. LC 79-92440. 1858. 14.00x (ISBN 0-403-00172-2). Scholarly.
Slavery in the Union. Gilman M. Ostrander. 1970. pap. text ed. 3.25x (ISBN 0-88273-224-2). Forum Pr IL.
Slavery in the United States: A Narrative of the Life & Adventures of Charles Ball, a Black Man. Charles Ball. LC 71-92414. 1970. Repr. of 1836 ed. 11.00 (ISBN 0-403-00178-1). Scholarly.
Slavery in the United States: Four Views. James C. Morgan. LC 84-43220. 214p. 1985. lib. bdg. 18.95x (ISBN 0-89950-162-1). McFarland & Co.
Slavery Inconsistent with Justice & Good Policy. David Rice. LC 70-82216. (Anti-Slavery Crusade in America Ser). 1969. Repr. of 1804 ed. 9.50 (ISBN 0-405-00655-1). Ayer Co Pubs.
Slavery: Its Origins & Legacy. Ed. by J. B. Duff & Larry A. Greene. LC 74-22308. (Problem Studies in American History Ser.). 1975. pap. 7.95x (ISBN 0-88295-727-9). Harlan Davidson.
Slavery, Law, & Politics: The Dred Scott Case in Historical Perspective. Don E. Fehrenbacher. (Illus.). 1981. 21.95x (ISBN 0-19-502882-1). Oxford U Pr.
Slavery, Law & Politics: The Dred Scott Case in Historical Perspective. Don E. Fehrenbacher. (Illus.). 1981. pap. 9.95 (ISBN 0-19-502883-X). Oxford U Pr.
Slavery: Letters & Speeches. facs. ed. Horace Mann. LC 79-81126. (Black Heritage Library Collection Ser). 1851. 24.50 (ISBN 0-8369-8623-7). Ayer Co Pubs.
Slavery, Letters & Speeches. Horace Mann. LC 70-82205. (Anti-Slavery Crusade in America Ser). 1969. Repr. of 1851 ed. 24.50 (ISBN 0-405-00643-8). Ayer Co Pubs.
Slavery: Letters & Speeches. Horace Mann. 1969. Repr. of 1851 ed. 23.95 (ISBN 0-8337-2205-0). B Franklin.
Slavery of Prostitution: A Plea for Emancipation, New York 1916. Maude E. Miner. Ed. by David J. Rothman & Sheila M. Rothman. (Women & Children First Ser.). 320p. 1986. 40.00 (ISBN 0-8240-7665-6). Garland Pub.
Slavery of Sex: Feminist-Abolitionists in America. Blanch G. Hersh. LC 78-14591. 291p. 1978. 29.95 (ISBN 0-252-00695-X). U of Ill Pr.
Slavery of the British West India Colonies, 2 Vols. in 1. James Stephen. LC 2-7045. 1924-1930. 58.00 (ISBN 0-527-86320-3). Kraus Repr.
Slavery on Louisiana Sugar Plantations. Vernie A. Moody. LC 74-22753. (Labor Movement in Fiction & Non-Fiction). Repr. of 1924 ed. 20.00 (ISBN 0-404-58505-1). AMS Pr.
Slavery on the Spanish Frontier: The Colombian Choco, 1680-1810. William F. Sharp. LC 76-18767. (Illus.). 1976. 16.95x (ISBN 0-8061-1375-8); pap. 8.95 (ISBN 0-8061-1759-1). U of Okla Pr.
Slavery Ordained by God. facs. ed. Frederick A. Ross. LC 74-83876. (Black Heritage Library Collection Ser). 1857. 14.25 (ISBN 0-8369-8647-4). Ayer Co Pubs.
Slavery Ordained of God. Frederick Ross. LC 70-95445. (Studies in Black History & Culture, No. 54). 1970. Repr. of 1959 ed. lib. bdg. 48.95x (ISBN 0-8383-1202-0). Haskell.
Slavery Question. John Lawrence. 14.75 (ISBN 0-8369-9168-0, 9043). Ayer Co Pubs.
Slavery, Race & the American Revolution. D. J. MacLeod. LC 74-77382. 269p. 1975. pap. 13.95x (ISBN 0-521-09877-7). Cambridge U Pr.
Slavery Remembered: A Record of Twentieth Century Slave Narratives. Paul D Escott. LC 78-12198. xv, 221p. 1979. 17.50x (ISBN 0-8078-1340-0); pap. text ed. 8.95x (ISBN 0-8078-1343-5). U of NC Pr.
Slavery, Sabbath, War & Women: Case Issues in Biblical Interpretation. Willard Swartley. LC 82-23417. (Conrad Grebel Lecture Ser.). 320p. (Orig.). 1983. pap. 15.95 (ISBN 0-8361-3330-7). Herald Pr.
Slavery: The Afro-American Experience. Peter Hogg. (Illus.). 52p. (Orig.). 1979. pap. 2.95 (ISBN 0-904654-28-1, Pub. by British Lib). Longwood Pub Group.
Slavery, the Mere Pretext for the Rebellion. John P. Kennedy. 20p. 1967. pap. 3.65 (ISBN 0-910120-02-1). Americanist.
Slavery Times in Kentucky. John W. Coleman, Jr. LC 40-31785. (Basic Afro-American Reprint Library Ser). (Illus.). 1970. Repr. of 1940 ed. 22.00 (ISBN 0-384-09535-6). Johnson Repr.
Slavery Unmasked: Being a Truthful Narrative of A Three Year's Residence & Journeying in Eleven Southern States. Philo Tower. LC 74-104585. (Illus.). 432p. Repr. of 1856 ed. lib. bdg. 18.50 (ISBN 0-8398-1971-4). Irvington.
Slavery Unmasked: Being a Truthful Narrative of a Three Years' Residence & Journeying in Eleven Southern States. Philo Tower. (Illus.). 432p. 1986. pap. text ed. 7.95x (ISBN 0-8290-2005-5). Irvington.
Slavery, War & Revolution: The British Occupation of Saint Dominigue, 1793-1798. David P. Geggus. (Illus.). 1982. 72.00x (ISBN 0-19-822634-9). Oxford U Pr.
Slavery Without Chains, & Other Selected Poems. Tonia R. Lee. LC 87-9058. (Orig.). 1988. pap. 4.50 (ISBN 0-942029-00-3). Price Pub.
Slavery's End in Tennessee, Eighteen Sixty-One to Eighteen Sixty-Five. John Cimprich. LC 84-16200. (Illus.). 191p. 1985. 24.50 (ISBN 0-8173-0257-3). U of Ala Pr.
Slaves & Freedmen in Civil War Louisiana. C. Peter Ripley. LC 75-18043. xvi, 237p. 1976. 27.50 (ISBN 0-8071-0187-7). La State U Pr.
Slaves & Ivory: A Record of Adventure & Exploration in the Unknown Sudan, & Among the Abbyssinia Slave-Raiders. Henry A. Darley. LC 73-99366. (Illus.). xvii, 219p. 1972. Repr. of 1926 ed. lib. bdg. 12.00 (ISBN 0-8411-0037-3). Metro Bks.
Slaves & Masters in the Roman Empire: A Study in Social Control. Keith R. Bradley. 160p. 1987. pap. text ed. 8.95 (ISBN 0-19-520607-X). Oxford U Pr.
Slaves & Missionaries: The Disintegration of Jamaican Slave Society, 1787-1834. Mary Turner. LC 82-6983. (Blacks in the New World Ser.). (Illus.). 240p. 1982. 25.95 (ISBN 0-252-00961-4). U of Ill Pr.
Slaves & Slavery in Ancient Rome. Zvi Yavetz. Tr. by Adam Vital. 206p. 1987. 29.95 (ISBN 0-88738-128-6). Transaction Bks.
Slaves & Slavery in Muslim Africa, 2 vols. Ed. by John R. Willis. Incl. Vol. 1. Islam & the Ideology of Slavery (ISBN 0-7146-3142-6); Vol. 2. Servile Estate (ISBN 0-7146-3201-5). 1985. cloth 36.00x ea. (F Cass Co). Biblio Dist.
Slaves, Citizens, Sons: Legal Metaphors in the Epistles. Francis Lyall. 320p. 1984. pap. 14.95 (ISBN 0-310-45191-4, 12452P). Zondervan.
Slaves in Ancient Greece. Linda C. Reilly. 1978. 25.00 (ISBN 0-89005-223-9). Ares.
Slaves in Red Coats: The British West India Regiments, 1795-1815. Rober N. Buckley. LC 78-16830. (Illus.). 1979. 28.50x (ISBN 0-300-02216-6). Yale U Pr.
Slave's Narrative. Ed. by Charles T. Davis & Henry L. Gates, Jr. (Illus.). 1985. 35.00x (ISBN 0-19-503276-4). Oxford U Pr.
Slaves No More: Letters from Liberia, 1833-1869. Ed. by Bell I. Wiley. LC 79-4015. (Illus.). 360p. 1980. 30.00 (ISBN 0-8131-1388-1). U Pr of Ky.
Slaves of New York. Tama Janowitz. 288p. 1986. 15.95 (ISBN 0-517-56107-7). Crown.
Slaves of New York. Tama Janowitz. 1987. pap. 6.95 (ISBN 0-671-63678-2). WSP.
Slaves of New York. Tama Janowitz. 1988. pap. 3.95. PB.
Slaves of Slaves: The Challenge of Latin American Women. Orig. Title: Mujeres. 240p. 1981. 26.25x (ISBN 0-86232-006-2, Pub. by Zed Pr England); pap. text ed. 9.25 (ISBN 0-86232-001-1). Humanities.
Slaves of Solitude. Patrick Hamilton. (Twentieth-Century Classics Ser.). 1982. pap. 5.95 (ISBN 0-19-281359-5). Oxford U Pr.
Slaves of Sumuru. Sax Rohmer. (Sumuru Ser.). 1979. 8.50 (ISBN 0-686-65266-5). Bookfinger.
Slaves of the Depression: Workers' Letters about Life on the Job. Ed. by Gerald Markowitz & David Rosner. LC 87-6671. (Paperback Ser.). 272p. 1987. 31.50x (ISBN 0-8014-1956-5); pap. 9.95 (ISBN 0-8014-9464-8). Cornell U Pr.
Slaves of the Harvest. Barbara B. Torey. 1978. 10.00. Tanadgusix Corp.
Slaves on Horses. Patricia Crone. LC 79-50234. 1980. 52.50 (ISBN 0-521-22961-8). Cambridge U Pr.
Slaves, Peasants, & Capitalists in Southern Angola: Eighteen Forty to Nineteen Twenty-Six. W. G. Clarence-Smith. LC 78-67805. (African Studies: No. 27). (Illus.). 1979. 27.95 (ISBN 0-521-22406-3). Cambridge U Pr.
Slaves, Peasants, & Capitalists in Southern Angola, 1840-1926. W. G. Clarence-Smith. LC 78-67805. (African Studies Ser.: No. 27). pap. 37.00 (2031633). Bks Demand UMI.
Slaves, Spices & Ivory in Zanzibar: Integration of An East African Commercial Empire into the World Economy 1770-1873. Abdul Sheriff. 297p. 1987. text ed. 29.95x (ISBN 0-8214-0871-2); pap. text ed. 15.95x (ISBN 0-8214-0872-0). Ohio U Pr.
Slaves to Duty. John Badcock, Jr. LC 72-77199. (Libertarian Broadsides Ser: No. 2). 36p. 1972. pap. 0.85 (ISBN 0-87926-013-0). R Myles.
Slaves Today: A Story of Liberia. George S. Schuyler. LC 72-99887. 1969. Repr. 29.50 (ISBN 0-404-00209-9). AMS Pr.
Slaves Without Masters: The Free Negro in the Antebellum South. Ira Berlin. 1981. pap. 10.95x (ISBN 0-19-502905-4). Oxford U Pr.
Slavic Americans: A Study Guide. Joseph Stipanovich & Maria K. Woroby. LC 77-81037. 1977. soft cover, perfect bound 6.00. Ragusan Pr.
Slavic Americans: A Study Guide & Source Book. Joseph Stipanovich. LC 77-81037. 1977. soft bdg. 8.95. R & E Pubs.
Slavic Books & Bookmen: Papers & Essays. Edward Kasinec. LC 83-60970. (Russica Bibliography Ser.: No. 3). 180p. (Orig.). 1984. pap. 13.50 (ISBN 0-89830-069-X). Russica Pubs.
Slavic Element in the Old Prussian Elbing Vocabulary. Jules F. Levin. LC 72-619636. (U. C. Publ. in Linguistics: Vol. 77). Repr. of 1974 ed. 31.00 (ISBN 0-8357-9639-6, 2015116). Bks Demand UMI.
Slavic Epic Studies see Selected Writings.
Slavic Ethnic Libraries, Museums & Archives in the United States. 164p. 1980. 9.00 (ISBN 0-8389-6742-6). Assn Coll & Res Libs.
Slavic Ethnic Libraries, Museums & Archives in the United States: A Guide & Directory. Lubomyr Wynar. 164p. 1980. 9.00x. ALA.
Slavic Forum: Essays in Linguistics & Literature. Michael Flier. LC 72-88178. (Slavistic Printings & Reprintings Ser.: No. 277). 169p. 1974. text ed. 23.20x (ISBN 90-2792-713-8). Mouton.
Slavic History & Literatures, 4 Vols. Harvard University Library Staff. LC 69-10588. (Widener Library Shelflist Ser: No. 28-31). 1971. Set. 200.00x (ISBN 0-674-81090-2). Harvard U Pr.
Slavic Linguistics & Language Teaching. Ed. by Thomas F. Magner. x, 309p. 1976. pap. 18.95 (ISBN 0-89357-037-0). Slavica.
Slavic Literary Languages: Formation & Development. Ed. by Alexander M. Schenker & Edward Stankiewicz. LC 80-51031. (Russian & East European Publications Ser.: No. 1). 287p. 1980. 18.50 (ISBN 0-936586-00-1, Dist. by Slavica). Yale Russian.
Slavic Literatures. Richard C. Lewanski. LC 65-23122. (Literatures of the World in English Translation, Vol. 2). 1967. 60.00x (ISBN 0-8044-3145-0). Ungar.
Slavic Literatures & Modernism. Ed. by Nils A. Nilsson. (Nobel Symposium Ser.: No. 62). 318p. 1986. pap. text ed. 34.00x (ISBN 91-7402-180-X, Pub. by Almqvist & Wiksell). Coronet Bks.
Slavic Manuscripts from the Fekula Collection: A Description. Mateja Matejic. (Illus.). xxvi, 294p. 1983. 24.95 (ISBN 0-915887-03-7). Kosovo Pub Co.
Slavic Poetics: Essays in Honor of Kiril Taranovsky. Roman Jakobson et al. LC 72-88184. (Slavistic Printings & Reprintings: Vol. 267). (Illus.). 1973. 111.00x (ISBN 90-2792-526-7). Mouton.
Slavic Structuralism. Endre Bojtar. (Linguistic & Literary Studies in Eastern Europe: 11). 160p. 1985. 34.00x (ISBN 90-272-1507-3). Benjamins North Am.
Slavonic & Western Music: Essays for Gerald Abraham. Ed. by Malcolm H. Brown & Roland J. Wiley. LC 84-2625. (Russian Music Studies: No. 12). 322p. 1984. 42.95 (ISBN 0-8357-1594-9). UMI Res Pr.
Slavonic Encyclopedia, 4 Vols. Ed. by Joseph S. Roucek. LC 69-19855. 1969. Repr. of 1949 ed. 125.00x (ISBN 0-8046-0537-8, Pub. by Kennikat). Assoc Faculty Pr.
Slavonic Europe: A Political History of Poland & Russia from 1447 to 1796. R. Nisbet Bain. LC 76-135790. (Eastern Europe Collection Ser). 1970. Repr. of 1908 ed. 23.00 (ISBN 0-405-02732-X). Ayer Co Pubs.
Slavonic Europe: A Political History of Russia & Poland, 1447-1796. R. N. Bain. 1976. lib. bdg. 59.95 (ISBN 0-8490-2615-6). Gordon Pr.
Slavonic Fairy Tales: From the Russian, Polish, Serbian & Bohemian. John T. Naake. 59.95 (ISBN 0-8490-1062-4). Gordon Pr.
Slavonic Languages. D. J. Hunns. 1986. 49.00x (Pub. by Drake Educ Assocs). State Mutual Bk.
Slavonic Manuscripts from the British Museum & Library. British Library Staff. (Illus.). 112p. (Orig.). 1978. pap. 4.50 (ISBN 0-7123-0091-0, Pub. by British Lib). Longwood Pub Group.
Slavonic Mutual & Benevolent Society: One Hundred Twenty-Five Years in San Francisco 1857-1985. Adam S. Eterovich. LC 82-62215. 205p. 1984. 20.00 (ISBN 0-918660-23-8). Ragusan Pr.
Slavonic New Testament. 832p. 1983. Repr. of 1751 ed. text ed. 7.00x (ISBN 0-564-02418-X, 81165). Am Bible.
Slavonic Pioneers of California. Vjekoslav Meler. LC 68-57133. 1968. Repr. of 1932 ed. softcover 8.00 (ISBN 0-88247-121-X). Ragusan Pr.
Slavophile Controversy: A History of a Conservative Utopia in Nineteenth-Century Russian Thought. Andrzej Walicki. 1988. pap. text ed. 10.95x (ISBN 0-268-01734-4). U of Notre Dame Pr.
Slavophile Controversy: History of a Conservative Utopia in Nineteenth Century Russian Thought. Andrzej Walicki. Tr. by Hilda Andrews from Pol. 1975. 66.00x (ISBN 0-19-822507-5). Oxford U Pr.
Slavoteutonica: Lexikalische Untersuchungen Zum Slawisch-deutschen Sprachkontakt Im Ostmitteldeutschen. Guenter Bellman. (Studia Linguistica Germanica Ser.: Vol. 4). (Illus.). 356p. 1971. 41.60x (ISBN 3-11-003344-5). De Gruyter.
Slavs Beneath Parnassus. Miodrag Pavlovic. Date not set. pap. price not set (ISBN 0-89823-062-4). New Rivers Pr.
Slavs, Byzance et Rome Au Onzieme Siecle. Francis Dvornik. (Russian Ser.: Vol. 13). Repr. of 1926 ed. 40.00 (ISBN 0-87569-016-5). Academic Intl.
Slavs in European History & Civilization. Francis Dvornik. 726p. 1975. pap. 35.00 (ISBN 0-8135-0799-5). Rutgers U Pr.
Slavs in European History & Civilization. Francis Dvornik. (Illus.). 696p. 1986. text ed. 35.00 (ISBN 0-8135-0403-1); pap. text ed. 15.00. Rutgers U Pr.
Slay Ride. Dick Francis. 272p. 1987. pap. 4.50 (ISBN 0-449-21271-8, Crest). Fawcett.
Slayer of Souls. Robert W. Chambers. Ed. by R. Reginald & Douglas Melville. LC 77-84207. (Lost Race & Adult Fantasy Ser.). 1978. Repr. of 1920 ed. lib. bdg. 26.50x (ISBN 0-405-10963-6). Ayer Co Pubs.
Slayer of the Sacred Cow: A Contemporary Freethought Novel. Carl Shapiro. 185p. (Orig.). 1986. pap. 15.00 (ISBN 0-914937-07-3). Ind Pubns.
Slayers of Moses: The Emergence of Rabbinic Interpretation in Modern Literary Theory. Susan A. Handelman. LC 81-16522. (Modern Jewish Literature & Culture Ser.). 267p. 1983. 56.50 (ISBN 0-87395-576-5); pap. 18.95x (ISBN 0-87395-577-3). State U NY Pr.
Slayers of Superstition. Edgar R. Pike. LC 78-102581. 1970. Repr. of 1931 ed. 16.50x (ISBN 0-8046-0741-9, Pub.by Kennikat). Assoc Faculty Pr.
Slayground. Richard Stark. 176p. 1984. 13.95 (ISBN 0-8052-8181-9, Pub. by Allison & Busby England). Schocken.
Slaying of Joseph Bowne Elwell. Jonathan Goodman. LC 87-27117. 224p. 1988. 15.95x (ISBN 0-312-01513-5, Pub. by Thomas Dunne Bks). St Martin.
Slaying of the Dragon: Modern Tales of the Playful Imagination. Ed. by Franz Rottensteiner. LC 83-26542. 320p. 1984. 14.95 (ISBN 0-15-182975-6). HarbraceJ.
Slaying of the Dragon: Tales of the Hindu Gods. Rosalind Kerven. (Illus.). 100p. (gr. 4 up). 1988. 10.95 (ISBN 0-233-98037-7). Andre Deutsch.
Slaying the English Jargon. Fern Rock. 42p. 1983. pap. text ed. 8.00x (ISBN 0-914548-43-3). Soc Tech Comm.
Slaying the Law School Dragon. George J. Roth. LC 80-16974. 284p. 1980. 10.95 (ISBN 0-396-07880-X); pap. 7.95 (ISBN 0-396-07879-6). Dodd.
Slayride. Dick Francis. 1986. pap. 3.50 (ISBN 0-671-50731-1). PB.
Sled Dog Trails. Mary Shields. (Illus.). 127p. 1984. pap. 8.95 (ISBN 0-88240-258-7). Pyrola Pub.
Sled Dogs. Phyllis R. Emert. Ed. by Howard Schroeder. LC 85-14967. (Working Dogs Ser.). (Illus.). 48p. (gr. 5-6). 1985. 9.95 (ISBN 0-89686-288-7). Crestwood Hse.
Sled Dogs of Denali. Sandy Kogl. Ed. by Charles Gilbert. (Illus.). 20p. 1981. pap. 2.00 (ISBN 0-9602876-3-9). Alaska Natural.
Sledgehammer. Walter Wager. 340p. 1989. pap. price not set. Tor Bks.
Sleek Chic: Head-to-Toe Fashion Strategies for Fixing Figure Flaws. Tracy Hensler & Karla Dougherty. (Illus.). 160p. 1988. pap. 9.95 (ISBN 0-399-51403-1, Perigee Bks). Putnam Pub Group.
Sleek for the Long Flight. William Matthews. 1988. 8.00 (ISBN 0-317-61749-4). White Pine.
Sleende Paris. Charles Baudelaire. 1973. pap. 8.95 (ISBN 0-686-51925-6). French & Eur.
Sleep. Lynn Biederstadt. 320p. 1988. pap. 3.50 (ISBN 0-7701-0502-5). Paperjacks US.
Sleep: A Horror Story. Lynn Biederstadt. 352p. 1985. 16.95 (ISBN 0-312-72849-2, Pub. by Marek). St Martin.
Sleep: A Scientific Perspective. A. Michael Anch et al. 304p. 1988. text ed. 33.33 (ISBN 0-13-812918-5). P-H.
Sleep, Aging & Related Disorders. Ed. by W. Emser et al. (Interdisciplinary Topics in Gerontology Ser.: Vol. 22). (Illus.). x, 166p. 1987. 83.50 (ISBN 3-8055-4451-0). S Karger.
Sleep & Aging: A Research-Based Guide to Sleep in Later Life. Kevin Morgan. LC 87-45486. 160p. 1987. text ed. 27.50x (ISBN 0-8018-3564-X). Johns Hopkins.
Sleep & Breathing. Saunders & Sullivan. (Lung Biology in Health & Disease Ser.). 640p. 1984. 85.00 (ISBN 0-8247-7064-1). Dekker.
Sleep & Dream Research. Research & Education Association Staff. LC 82-62130. (Illus.). 384p. 1982. 14.30 (ISBN 0-87891-545-1). Res & Educ.
Sleep & Dreaming: Origins, Nature, & Functions. D. Cohen. (International Ser. Experimental Psychology: Vol. 23). (Illus.). 315p. 1981. pap. text ed. 22.00 (ISBN 0-08-027400-5). Pergamon.
Sleep & Dreams. Duane Michals. (Illus.). 64p. 1984. pap. 11.95 (ISBN 0-912810-46-7). Lustrum Pr.

Sleepless Green Green Grass & Sixty-Eight Other Poems. Shiang-hua Chang. Tr. by Stephan L. Smith from Chinese. (Illus.). 151p. 1982. 7.95 (ISBN 0-917056-15-9). Cheng & Tsui.

Sleepless Night in a Soundproof Motel. Michael C. Ford. (Rockbook Ser.: No. 6). 16p. (Orig.). 1978. pap. 3.00 (ISBN 0-930012-36-4). J Mudfoot.

Sleepless Nights. Elizabeth Hardwick. LC 79-23246. 1980. pap. 2.50 (ISBN 0-394-74363-6, Vin). Random.

Sleepless Nights. Helmut Newton. (Illus.). 1983. pap. 17.95 (ISBN 0-937950-07-6). Xavier-Moreau.

Sleepless Nights in the Procrustean Bed: Essays. Harlan Ellison. Ed. by Marty Clark. LC 83-27543. (I. O. Evans Studies in the Philosophy & Criticism of Literature: No. 5). 192p. 1984. lib. bdg. 19.95x (ISBN 0-89370-170-X); pap. 9.95x (ISBN 0-89370-270-6). Borgo Pr.

Sleepless Nights in the Procrustean Bed: Essays. Harlan Ellison. 176p. 1984. pap. 7.95 (ISBN 0-87877-270-7). Newcastle Pub.

Sleepside Story. Greg Bear. (Illus.). 84p. 1988. signed numbered slipcased 95.00x (ISBN 0-941826-18-X). Cheap St.

Sleepwalkers: A Trilogy by Hermann Broch. Hermann Broch. Tr. by Willa Muir & Edwin Muir. LC 85-60862. (Broch Novels Ser.). 656p. 1985. pap. 15.50 (ISBN 0-86547-200-9). N Point Pr.

Sleepwalker's Son. William Meissner. 57p. 1987. text ed. 17.95x (ISBN 0-8214-0854-2); pap. 9.95 (ISBN 0-8214-0855-0). Ohio U Pr.

Sleepwalker's World. Gordon R. Dickson. 256p. (Orig.). 1985. pap. 2.95 (ISBN 0-8125-3556-1, Dist. by Warner Pub Services & St. Martin's Press). Tor Bks.

Sleepwalking. Meg Wolitzer. 1982. 12.00 (ISBN 0-394-52155-2). Random.

Sleepwalking. Meg Wolitzer. 224p. 1984. pap. 2.25 (ISBN 0-380-68221-4, 68221, Flare). Avon.

Sleepwalking Nights: Poems, Vol. II. August Strindberg. Tr. by Arvid Paulsen. 1978. 8.95 (ISBN 0-317-67897-3). Law Arts.

Sleepwalking Nights, Poems of August Strindberg. August Strindberg. Tr. by Arvid Paulsen. LC 78-56420. 8.95 (ISBN 0-88238-078-8). Law Arts.

Sleepwalking on the Borders of the Apocylapse. Bruce Braunstein. (Orig.). 1986. 19.95. Tetragrammaton.

Sleepy Bear. Lydia Dabcovich. (Illus.). 32p. (ps-2). 1982. 11.95 (ISBN 0-525-39465-6). Dutton.

Sleepy Bear. Lydia Dabcovich. (Unicorn Paperback Ser.). (Illus.). 32p. (ps-2). 1985. pap. 4.95 (ISBN 0-525-44196-4). Dutton.

Sleepy Book. Charlotte Zolotow. LC 87-45861. (Illus.). 32p. (ps-1). 1988. 12.95i (ISBN 0-06-026967-7); PLB 12.89 (ISBN 0-06-026968-5). HarpJ.

Sleepy Dog: A Step One Book. Harriet Ziefert. LC 84-4775. (Step into Reading Bks). (Illus.). (ps-2). 1984. lib. bdg. 6.99 (ISBN 0-394-96877-8, Pub. by BYR); pap. 2.95 (ISBN 0-394-86877-3). Random.

Sleepy Hollow Restorations: A Cross-Section of the Collection. Joseph T. Butler. LC 82-16774. (Illus.). 344p. 1983. 39.95 (ISBN 0-912882-57-3). Sleepy Hollow.

Sleepy Little Lion. Margaret W. Brown. LC 47-11482. (Illus.). 24p. (gr. k-3). 1947. PLB 12.89 (ISBN 0-06-020771-X). HarpJ.

Sleepy Owl. Marcus Pfister. LC 85-63305. (Illus.). 32p. (gr. k-2). 1986. 10.95 (ISBN 0-8050-0616-8, North South Bks.). H Holt & Co.

Sleepy People. rev. ed. M. B. Goffstein. LC 66-10723. (Illus.). (ps-2). 1979. 6.95 (ISBN 0-374-37030-3). FS&G.

Sleepy, Sleepy. Ann Morris. LC 85-45333. (Illus.). 16p. (ps). 1986. 3.50 (ISBN 0-694-00075-2). HarpJ.

Sleepy Song. Shaerie Cosgrove. (Sing! Ser.). 32p. (ps-3). 1988. pap. 7.95 (ISBN 0-8249-7273-2). Ideals.

Sleepy Squirrel. Amye Rosenberg. (Golden Sturdy Shape Bks.). (Illus.). 14p. (ps-k). 1986. 2.95 (ISBN 0-307-12314-6, Pub. by Golden Bks). Western Pub.

Sleepy Time Bunny. (Peter Curry Board Bks.). (Illus.). 1984. 2.50 (ISBN 0-8431-0997-1). Price Stern.

Sleepytime for Baby Mouse. Margaret Hopkins. (Teddy Board Bks.). (Illus.). 12p. (ps-3). 1985. 3.95 (ISBN 0-448-40875-9, G&D). Putnam Pub Group.

Sleepytime Songs Book & Cassette: Blue Ladder Books for Babies Through 16 Months. Illus. by Cheryl Harte. (Learning Ladders Ser.). (Illus.). 16p. (ps). 1988. pap. 5.95 bk. & cassette pkg. (ISBN 0-394-89947-4, BYR). Random.

Sleeve Puppets. Brenda Morton. LC 77-92754. (Illus.). 1978. 8.50 (ISBN 0-8008-7237-1). Taplinger.

Sleight of Hand. Edwin T. Sachs. 1979. 20.00 (ISBN 0-915926-15-6). Magic Ltd.

Sleight of Hand: A Practical Manual of Legerdemain for Amateurs & Others. Edwin Sachs. (Illus.). 1980. pap. 5.95 (ISBN 0-486-23911-X). Dover.

Slightly Deceived. Patrick A. Kelley. 224p. (Orig.). 1987. pap. 2.95 (ISBN 0-380-75231-X). Avon.

Slightly Guilty. Patrick A. Kelley. 192p. 1988. pap. 3.50 (ISBN 0-380-75240-9). Avon.

Slightly Invisible. Patrick A. Kelley. 224p. (Orig.). 1986. pap. 2.95 (ISBN 0-380-75116-X). Avon.

Slightly Murder. Patrick A. Kelley. (Harry Colderwood Ser.: No. 1). 208p. 1985. pap. 2.75 (ISBN 0-380-89511-0). Avon.

Slender Human Word: Emerson's Artistry in Prose. William J. Scheick. LC 77-27020. 1978. 17.95x (ISBN 0-87049-222-5). U of Tenn Pr.

Slender Is the Thread: Tales from a Country Law Office. Harry M. Caudill. LC 87-1983. 192p. 1987. 18.00 (ISBN 0-8131-1611-2). U Pr of Ky.

Slender Means. 2nd ed. Michael Hannon. 16p. 1986. pap. 10.00 handmade (ISBN 0-918824-41-9). Turkey Pr.

Slender Thread. Aubrey R. McKinney. LC 84-80635. (Illus.). 384p. 1985. 24.95 (ISBN 0-914587-00-5). Helix Pr.

Slender Tree, a Life of Alice Meynell. June Eadeni. 256p. 1981. 25.00x (ISBN 0-907018-01-7, Pub. by Tabb Hse). State Mutual Bk.

Slenderness of Prestressed Concrete Columns. (PCI Journal Reprints Ser.). 30p. pap. 8.00 (ISBN 0-318-19797-9, JR286). Prestressed Concrete.

Sleuth. 2nd ed. Anthony Shaffer. (Illus.). 92p. 1985. pap. 7.95 (ISBN 0-7145-0763-6, Dist. by Kampmann & Co). M Boyars Pubs.

Sleuth & the Scholar: Origins, Evolution, & Current Trends in Detective Fiction. Ed. by Barbara A. Rader & Howard G. Zettler. LC 87-24958. (Contributions to the Study of Popular Culture Ser.: No. 19). 160p. 1988. lib. bdg. 29.95 (ISBN 0-313-26036-2, ZSS/). Greenwood.

Sleuthing in the Stacks. Rudolph Altrocchi. LC 68-26239. 1968. Repr. of 1944 ed. 24.00x (ISBN 0-8046-0009-0, Pub. by Kennikat). Assoc Faculty Pr.

Slice of Country Life, 1902-1915. George F. Walker. (Illus.). 192p. (Orig.). 1984. pap. 7.95 (ISBN 0-89407-037-1). Strawberry Hill.

Slice of Life. James Kisner. (Orig.). 1982. pap. text ed. 2.95 (ISBN 0-8217-1055-9). Zebra.

Slice of Life-Reflections. Claire Schneider. (Illus.). 48p. (Orig.). 1978. pap. 2.95 (ISBN 0-9601982-1-0). Greenwood Hse.

Slice of the Big Apple. American Cancer Society Staff. 192p. 1982. pap. 6.00 (ISBN 0-686-31486-7). Am Cancer Forest Hills.

Slice of Wry. Anne E. Edge. (Illus.). 1981. 20.00x (ISBN 0-918824-28-1). pap. 7.50 (ISBN 0-918824-27-3). Turkey Pr.

Sliced Dog. Frederic Will. LC 84-26135. 40p. (Orig.). 1985. pap. 5.95 (ISBN 0-934332-40-1). L'Epervier Pr.

Slices. McCullough & Baker. pap. 8.95 (ISBN 0-937816-08-6). Tech Data.

Slices of Life. Linda Andersen. 112p. 1986. 6.95 (ISBN 0-8010-0205-2). Baker Bk.

Slices of Life. Hulda Staples. 240p. 1987. 11.95 (ISBN 0-89962-576-2). Todd & Honeywell.

Slicing Eggplant. Phyllis S. Prestia. 32p. 1984. 10.00 (ISBN 0-913719-73-0); pap. 3.50 (ISBN 0-913719-72-2). High Coo Pr.

Slicing, Hooking, & Cooking. rev. ed. Jackie Eddy. Ed. by Nancy D. Dominitz. (Illus.). 200p. 1986. 14.95 (ISBN 0-914629-04-2, Dist. by St. Martin); pap. 9.95 (ISBN 0-914629-05-0). Prima Pub Comm.

Slicing the Health Care Pie. Charles Bruner. 85p. 1987. 8.95 (ISBN 0-317-62692-2). NCPA Washington.

Slick. Whitey Ford & Phil Pepe. 1988. pap. 3.95 (ISBN 0-440-20108-X). Dell.

Slick: My Life in & Around Baseball. Whitey Ford & Phil Pepe. LC 87-1615. 288p. 1987. 16.95 (ISBN 0-688-06690-9). Morrow.

Slick Set of Wheels. Vernon Frazer. 80p. 1987. pap. 6.95 (ISBN 0-934953-15-5). Water Row Pr.

Slickensides: A Derbyshire Mystery. John B. Hilton. 176p. 1987. 13.95 (ISBN 0-312-01091-5). St Martin.

Slickers: Stories from Inside the City. Martin Braune. 1985. 35.80x (ISBN 0-946041-27-X, Pub. by Kensal Pr UK). State Mutual Bk.

Slickrock. Edward Abbey & Philip Hyde. (Illus.). 144p. 1987. pap. 24.95 (ISBN 0-87905-269-4). Gibbs Smith Pub.

Slickrock Reckoning. Randolph Newman. 192p. 1982. pap. 1.95 (ISBN 0-441-77152-1). Ace Bks.

Slide Atlas of Immunology. Roitt et al. 1985. 750.00 (ISBN 0-8016-4285-X). Mosby.

Slide Buyers' Guide: An International Directory of Slide Sources for Art & Architecture. 5th ed. Ed. by Norine D. Cashman & Mark M. Braunstein. (Visual Resources Ser.). 267p. 1985. lib. bdg. 25.00 (ISBN 0-87287-471-0). Libs Unl.

Slide Duplicating. Robert Holmes. (Illus.). 200p. Date not set. 25.95 (ISBN 0-240-51732-6). Focal Pr.

Slide Guitar. Arlen Roth. pap. 12.95 with recording (ISBN 0-8256-0162-2, Oak); recording incl. Music Sales.

Slide Guitar. Straw Dog. LC 72-76529. (Green Note Musical Publications Ser.). (Illus.). 1975. 12.95 (ISBN 0-02-871310-9); pap. 8.95 (ISBN 0-02-871000-2). Schirmer Bks.

Slide Interpretation in Oral Diseases & the Oral Manifestations of Systematic Diseases. Crispian Scully & Jonathan Shepherd. (Illus.). 160p. 1986. 27.95 (ISBN 0-19-261497-5). Oxford U Pr.

Slide Rule for Ohio Criminal Code. annual Gould Editorial Staff. slide rule study guide 5.00 (ISBN 0-87526-273-2). Gould.

Slide Rule for Pennsylvania Crimes Code. annual Gould Editorial Staff. 1982. slide rule study guide 5.00 (ISBN 0-87526-265-1). Gould.

Slide Rule for Pennsylvania Vehicle Law. annual Gould Editorial Staff. 1982. slide rule study guide 5.00 (ISBN 0-87526-290-2). Gould.

Slide Rule Handbook. James O. Perrine. 112p. 1965. 28.00 (ISBN 0-677-01060-5). Gordon & Breach.

Slide Rule in a Nutshell. Stan L. Schirmacher. 1960. pap. 1.25x (ISBN 0-686-08956-1). Azirona Agency.

Slide Rule Simplified. 3rd ed. Charles O. Harris. LC 78-183979. pap. 88.00 (ISBN 0-317-08654-5, 2004578). Bks Demand UMI.

Slide Set to Accompany Fundamentals of Building Construction: Materials & Methods. Allen. 341p. 1986. Set. 350.00 (ISBN 0-471-01156-8). Wiley.

Slide Shows on a Shoe String. Nancy Macduff. Ed. by Janie Millgard. (Illus.). 54p. 1986. pap. 7.95 (ISBN 0-945795-02-5). MBA Pub.

Slide-Sound & Filmstrip Production. John Sunier. (Illus.). 160p. 1981. text ed. 17.95x (ISBN 0-240-51074-7). Focal Pr.

Slide Supply for Organic Chemistry. Frank Cartledge. 1981. spiral bdg. 6.95 (ISBN 0-88252-115-2). Paladin Hse.

Slide Value & Link Motions. William S. Auchincloss. 1983. pap. 9.95 (ISBN 0-917914-13-9). Lindsay Pubns.

Slides. Roger A. Kueter & Janeen Miller. Ed. by James E. Duane. LC 80-21335. (Instructional Media Library: Vol. 13). (Illus.). 112p. 1981. 23.95 (ISBN 0-87778-173-7). Educ Tech Pubns.

Slides in Human Anatomy, 2 vols. Sobotta. Ed. by Walther J. Hild & Helmut Ferner. 778p. 1983. 895.00 set (ISBN 0-317-65613-9); Vol. 495.00. Urban & S.

Slides in Human Arthrology. B. N. Tillman. (Illus.). 32p. 1985. ringbinder 260.00 (ISBN 0-387-00350-9). Springer-Verlag.

Slides in Human Histology. 3rd ed. Sobotta & Hammersen. 1986. slides 595.00 (ISBN 0-8067-1753-X). Urban & S.

Slides in Sectional Human Anatomy. H Sick & J. G. Koritke. 161p. 1983. slide set 185.00 (ISBN 0-8067-1041-1). Urban & S.

Slides Planning & Producing Slide Programs. Ed. by Eastman Kodak Company. LC 81-67828. (Illus.). 70p. (Orig.). 1984. pap. 14.95 (ISBN 0-87985-291-7, S-30). Eastman-Kodak.

Sliding Bearings. V. N. Constantinescu et al. xx, 543p. 1984. 80.00x (ISBN 0-89864-011-3). Allerton Pr.

Sliding Piece Puzzles. Edward Hordern. (Recreations in Mathematics: No. 4). (Illus.). 313p. 1987. 26.95 (ISBN 0-19-853204-0). Oxford U Pr.

Slight Ache see Complete Works: No. 1.

Slight Ache see Three Plays.

Slight Momentary Affliction. Lawrence Dorr. LC 86-34424. 160p. 1987. 15.95 (ISBN 0-8071-1346-8). La State U Pr.

Slightly Beyond Moral Skepticism. Leonard W. Doob. LC 86-22400. 304p. 1987. text ed. 25.00 (ISBN 0-300-03823-2). Yale U Pr.

Slightly Crumpled Survival Flower. Norman Leer. 40p. 1985. pap. 3.00 (ISBN 0-933180-68-3). Spoon Riv Poetry.

Slightly Foxed: By My Theatrical Family. Angela Fox. (Illus.). 224p. 1987. 15.95 (ISBN 0-312-00681-0, Pub. by Thomas Dunne Bks). St Martin.

Slightly Like Strangers. Emily Listfield. LC 88-47518. 208p. 1988. pap. 7.95 (ISBN 0-553-34538-9). Bantam.

Slightly Sexy: Comedy from Europe. Denny Whitelaw. (Illus.). 120p. 1982. pap. 5.00 (ISBN 0-940178-14-1). Sitare Inc.

Slightly to the Right. H. L. Richardson. 1965. pap. 1.50 (ISBN 0-911956-02-6). Constructive Action.

Slim Buttes Battle. Fred H. Werner. 1981. pap. 4.95 (ISBN 0-933147-01-5). Werner Pubn.

Slim Buttes, Eighteen Seventy-Six: An Episode of the Great Sioux War. Jerome A. Greene. LC 81-40291. (Illus.). 208p. 1982. 17.95 (ISBN 0-8061-1712-5). U of Okla Pr.

Slim Chance in a Fat World: Behavioral Control of Obesity. condensed ed. Richard B. Stuart & Barbara Davis. LC 78-62902. (Illus.). 168p. (Orig.). 1978. pap. 8.95 (ISBN 0-87822-193-X, 0623). Res Press.

Slim Chef: A Cookbook for the Healthy Gourmet. Arlyn Hackett. (Illus.). 190p. 1987. pap. 12.95 (ISBN 0-8184-0449-3). Lyle Stuart.

Slim Deception-Fat Reflection: One Woman's Struggle with Bulimia. Deborah Yelinek. 1987. pap. 7.95 (ISBN 0-317-62683-3). Herald Pr.

Slim Down Camp. Stephen Manes. 192p. (gr. 4-6). 1981. 8.95 (ISBN 0-395-30170-X, Clarion). HM.

Slim Fingers Beckon. Arch Merrill. LC 86-33602. (Arch Merril's New York Ser.: Vol. 10). (Illus.). 204p. 1987. pap. 7.95 (ISBN 0-932334-86-5, Empire State Bks). Heart of the Lakes.

Slim for Him: Biblical Devotions on Diet. Patricia B. Kreml. LC 78-53422. 163p. 1978. pap. 4.95 (ISBN 0-88270-300-5). Bridge Pub.

Slim Goodbody: What Can Go Wrong & How to Be Strong. John Burstein. (Illus.). (gr. k-6). 1978. text ed. 9.95 (ISBN 0-07-009242-7). McGraw.

Slim Goodbody: Your Body, Health & Feelings. Good Thing, Inc. Staff & John Burstein. (gr. 1-3). 1978. text ed. 169.00 (ISBN 0-89290-098-9, A443-SA). Soc for Visual.

Slim Gourmet Cookbook. Barbara Gibbons. LC 75-23883. 416p. 1976. 17.95i (ISBN 0-06-011517-3, HarpT). Har-Row.

Slim Gourmet's Soup Book: A Complete Book of Soups. Martin Lederman. 1974. lib. bdg. 69.95 (ISBN 0-685-51364-5). Revisionist Pr.

Slim 'N' Sporty Wallets. Date not set. pap. 4.98 (ISBN 0-317-03197-X). Gick.

Slim Rails Through the Sand. 4th rev. ed. George Turner. LC 76-4633. (Illus.). 15.95 (ISBN 0-87046-040-4, Pub. by Trans-Anglo). Interurban.

Slim Well. Joan Clayton. 32p. 1987. pap. 15.00x (ISBN 0-85937-070-4, Pub. by K Mason Pubns Ltd UK). State Mutual Bk.

Slim Wok Cookery. Ceil Dyer. LC 86-80026. (Illus.). 169p. 1986. pap. 8.95 (ISBN 0-89586-412-6). Price Stern.

Slime. William Essex. 368p. (Orig.). 1988. pap. 3.95 (ISBN 0-8439-2640-6, Pub. by Leisure Bks CT). Leisure NY.

Slime. 2nd ed. John Halkin. 256p. 1988. pap. 3.50 (ISBN 1-55547-261-3). Critics Choice Paper.

Slime Molds of Ohio. E. L. Fullmer. 1921. 1.50 (ISBN 0-86727-010-1). Ohio Bio Survey.

Slimer. Harry A. Knight. 224p. (Orig.). 1989. pap. 3.50 (ISBN 1-55785-076-3). Bart Books.

Slimfit Course. Allison Manley & Vanessa Moore. 1985. 20.00x (ISBN 0-900873-52-3, Pub. by Bishopsgate Pr. Ltd.). State Mutual Bk.

Slimmanship. Dewey Lipe & Jurgen Wolff. LC 74-17808. (Illus.). 257p. 1974. pap. 18.95 (ISBN 0-88229-161-0). Nelson-Hall.

Slimmer's Microwave Cookbook. Margaret Weale. (Illus.). 120p. (Orig.). 1983. 16.95 (ISBN 0-7153-8392-2). David & Charles.

Slimming Down & Growing Up. Neva Coyle & Marie Chapian. 160p. (Orig.). (gr. 4-7). 1985. pap. 4.95 (ISBN 0-87123-833-0, 210833). Bethany Hse.

Slimming Down: The Numbers Game. ECRS Institute Staff. 78p. (Orig.). 1987. pap. 4.95 (ISBN 0-9618644-1-9). ECRS Inc.

Slimming Partner. Donald S. Fitch. (Illus.). 186p. (Orig.). 1988. pap. 9.95 (ISBN 0-9620454-0-3). MicroSkills.

Slimming Your Hips & Thighs. Consumer Guide Editors. 1983. pap. 2.95 (ISBN 0-671-47311-5). PB.

Slimy Book. Babette Cole. LC 85-43357. (Illus.). 40p. (gr. 1-7). 1986. 7.95 (ISBN 0-394-88166-4); lib. bdg. 8.99 (ISBN 0-394-98166-9). Random.

Sling for David. Charles Van Landingham. LC 84-90226. 160p. 1985. 13.95 (ISBN 0-533-06275-6). Vantage.

Sling: For Sport & Survival. Cliff Savage. LC 84-81630. (Illus.). 72p. (Orig.). 1984. pap. 5.95 (ISBN 0-915179-19-9). Loompanics.

Slinging Ink: A Practical Guide to Producing Booklets, Newspapers, & Ephemeral Publications. Jan Sutter. LC 82-15179. (Illus.). 168p. 1982. pap. 7.95 (ISBN 0-86576-037-3). W Kaufmann.

Slip Form Techniques. T. A. Dinescu & C. Radulescu. (Illus.). 488p. 1984. 58.00 (ISBN 0-85626-307-9). Abacus Pr.

Slipcovers & Bedspreads. Sunset Editors. LC 79-88157. (Illus.). 120p. 1979. pap. 6.95 (ISBN 0-376-01513-6, Sunset Bks). Sunset-Lane.

Sliphammer. Brian Garfield. 1979. pap. 1.75 (ISBN 0-449-24215-3, Crest). Fawcett.

Sliphammer. Brian Garfield. 176p. 1987. pap. 2.95 (ISBN 0-553-26855-4). Bantam.

Slipknot. Angus Black. Ed. by M. Batmanglij. LC 88-14716. 1988. 16.95 (ISBN 0-934211-17-5). Mage Pubs Inc.

Slipp' Away: The Loss of Black-Owned Farms. Ed. by David A. Dybiec. (Illus.). 80p. (Orig.). 1988. pap. 4.50 (ISBN 0-914422-16-2). Glenmary Res Ctr.

Slipper. Jennifer Wilde. 352p. 1987. text ed. 16.95 (ISBN 0-07-070216-0). McGraw.

Slipper. Jennifer Wilde. 1988. pap. 4.95. Ballantine.

Slippery & Other Stories. R. A. Lafferty. (Booklet Ser.: No. 19). 39p. (Orig.). 1985. ltd ed., signed 5.00 (ISBN 0-936055-17-0); pap. 2.00 (ISBN 0-936055-18-9). C Drumm Bks.

Slippery Slope: The Long Road to the Breakup of AT&T. Fred W. Henck. LC 87-28043. (Contributions in Economics & Economic History Ser.: No. 80). 288p. 1988. lib. bdg. 37.95 (ISBN 0-313-26025-7, HKO/). Greenwood.

Slipping Down Life. Anne Tyler. 224p. 1987. 3.95 (ISBN 0-425-10362-5). Berkley Pub.

Slipping Through the Cracks: The Status of Black Women. Ed. by Margaret C. Simms & Julianne M. Malveaux. 224p. 1986. pap. 14.95 (ISBN 0-88738-662-8). Transaction Bks.

Slipping, Tripping & Falling Accidents. Ed. by P. R. Davis. (Ergonomics Special Issue Ser.: Vol. 28). 168p. 1985. pap. 23.00x (ISBN 0-85066-950-2). Taylor & Francis.

Slips of Speech. John H. Bechtel. LC 77-159889. 218p. Repr. of 1901 ed. 40.00x (ISBN 0-8103-4041-0). Gale.

Slips of the Tongue & Language Production. Ed. by Anne Cutler. 293p. 1982. pap. 16.95 (ISBN 90-279-3120-8). Mouton.

Slipshod but Not Shabby. Tom Runnels. LC 84-90639. (Illus.). 107p. 1984. 12.00 (ISBN 0-9603710-1-X). T Runnels Pubns.

Slipt. Alan D. Foster. 272p. 1984. pap. 2.95 (ISBN 0-425-08980-0). Berkley Pub.

Slow Start in Paradise. Phyllis Myers. 34p. 1974. pap. 1.50 (ISBN 0-89164-015-0). Conservation Foun.
Slow Stirring Spoon. Al Ortolani. 16p. 1981. 7.00 (ISBN 0-913719-50-1); pap. 2.00 (ISBN 0-913719-49-8). High-Coo-Pr.
Slow Tango to Konigsberg. Norbert Schiller. (Illus.). 1985. 2.50 (ISBN 0-943164-08-7). Geronima.
Slow Tennis: Poems, Nineteen Eighty to Nineteen Eighty-Three. Gary Catalano. LC 84-11980. 62p. 1985. 9.95 (ISBN 0-7022-1775-1). U of Queensland Pr.
Slow Train to Cincinnati. P. J. Blumenthal. 1975. pap. 3.00 (ISBN 0-915572-51-6, Pub by Black Dragon Bks). Panjandrum.
Slow Train to Milan. Lisa St. Aubin de Teran. (Fiction Ser.). 256p. 1985. pap. 6.95 (ISBN 0-14-006954-2). Penguin.
Slow Transmissible Diseases of the Nervous System: Clinical, Epidemiological, Genetic & Pathological Aspects of the Spongiform Encephalopathie, Vol. 1. Ed. by Stanley B. Prusiner & William J. Hadlow. LC 79-18087. 1980. 60.00 (ISBN 0-12-566301-3). Acad Pr.
Slow Transmissible Diseases of the Nervous System: Pathogenesis, Immunology, Virology & Molecular Biology of the Spongiform Encephalopathies, Vol. 2. Ed. by Stanley B. Prusiner & William J. Hadlow. LC 79-18087. 1979. 60.00 (ISBN 0-12-566302-1). Acad Pr.
Slow Transparency. Rachel Hadas. 88p. 1983. 17.00 (ISBN 0-8195-5089-2); pap. 9.95 (ISBN 0-8195-6085-5). Wesleyan U Pr.
Slow Virus Diseases. Ed. by J. Hotchin. (Progress in Medical Virology Ser.: Vol. 18). 380p. 1974. 90.75 (ISBN 3-8055-1700-9). S Karger.
Slow Virus Infections. V. D. Timakov & V. A. Zuev. 246p. 1980. 10.00 (ISBN 0-686-74546-9, Pub. by Mir Pubs USSR). Imported Pubns.
Slow Virus Infections of the Central Nervous System. Ed. by V. Ter Meulen & M. Katz. LC 77-1570. 1977. 55.00 (ISBN 0-387-90188-4). Springer-Verlag.
Slow-Wave Propagation in Plasma Wave-Guides. A. W. Trivelpiece. (Illus.). 1967. 12.50 (ISBN 0-911302-02-6). San Francisco Pr.
Slow Work to the Rhythm of Cicadas. Rebecca Gonzales. (Illus.). 64p. (Orig.). 1985. pap. 9.95 (ISBN 0-933384-13-0); lib. bdg. 13.95 (ISBN 0-933384-14-9). Prickly Pear.
Slowdown: Global Economic Maladies. Andrew Brody. 1985. 19.95 (ISBN 0-8039-2352-X). Sage.
Slower Growth in the Western World. Ed. by R. C. Matthews. (NIESR-PSI-RIIA Joint Studies in Public Policy: No. 6). vi, 176p. 1982. text ed. 35.00x (ISBN 0-435-84515-2); pap. text ed. 15.00x (ISBN 0-435-84516-0). Gower Pub Co.
Slower Runner's Guide. Arthur J. Amchan. (Illus.). 62p. (Orig.). 1985. pap. 5.95 (ISBN 0-9617132-0-8). Amchan Pubns.
Slowly Climbs the Sun. Matt Menger. LC 72-96835. 1973. 5.50 (ISBN 0-685-42651-3). Guild Bks.
Slowly Down the Ganges. Eric Newby. 304p. 1986. pap. 7.95 (ISBN 0-14-009572-1). Penguin.
Slowly, Out of Stones. Edward Zuckrow. LC 80-53432. (Illus.). 80p. (Orig.). 1980. pap. 3.50 (ISBN 0-912292-64-4). The Smith.
Slowly, Slowly I Raise the Gun. Jay Bennett. 128p. 1983. pap. 2.25 (ISBN 0-380-84426-5, 84426-5, Flare). Avon.
Slowly, Slowly in the Wind. Patricia Highsmith. 192p. 14.95 (ISBN 0-89296-116-3, Penzler Bks); ltd. ed 45.00 (ISBN 0-89296-117-1, Dist. by FS&G). Mysterious Pr.
Slowly Strangle All Political Rapists: The Story of the Voters' Vendetta. Ed Hertzog. LC 80-83137. 1981. 15.00 (ISBN 0-937894-00-1); pap. 10.00 (ISBN 0-937894-01-X). Life Arts.
Slowmotional Meditation. Colin F. Howard. LC 85-60092. (Illus.). 359p. (Orig.). 1987. pap. 8.95 perfect bound (ISBN 0-916222-24-1). OLAM.
Slownik Gwar Polskich, 6 vols. Jan Karlowicz. Repr. Set. 450.00 (ISBN 0-318-23362-2). Szwede Slavic.
Slownik Mitologiczny, 3 vols. A. Osinski. Repr. of 1812 ed. Set. 280.00 (ISBN 0-318-23358-4). Szwede Slavic.
Slownik Snow. Adam Potok. 160p. (Orig., Pol.). pap. 10.00 (ISBN 0-930401-02-6). Artex Pr.
Slownik Staropolskich Nazw Osobowych, 6 vols. Ed. by W. Taszycki. Repr. Set. 400.00 (ISBN 0-318-23363-0). Szwede Slavic.
Slowpitch Tips. Glen D. Eley. (Illustrated Instructions Ser.). 1983. pap. 7.95 (ISBN 0-940934-07-8). GDE Pubns OH.
Slowth: The Changing Economy & How You Can Successfully Cope. Martin Kupferman & Maurice D. Levi. LC 80-18863. pap. 66.00 (ISBN 0-317-09675-3, 2022246). Bks Demand UMI.
SLP & the U. S. S. R. Socialist Labor Party. 1978. pap. 0.75 (ISBN 0-935534-26-1). NY Labor News.
SLR Photographer's Handbook. Carl Shipman. LC 85-62316. (Illus.). 160p. pap. 12.95 (ISBN 0-89586-427-4). Price Stern.
SLR Tips & Techniques. Ed. by H P Books Staff. LC 82-82516. 96p. 1982. pap. 9.95 (ISBN 0-89586-187-9). Price Stern.
Sludge. Edward J. Drew. 1988. 12.95 (ISBN 0-533-07480-0). Vantage.
Sludge Dewatering. Water Pollution Control Federation. (Manual of Practice: 20). (Illus.). 164p. 1983. pap. text ed. 35.50 (ISBN 0-943244-42-0). Water Pollution.
Sludge Disinfection: A Review of the Literature. Water Pollution Control Federation Staff. (Manual of Practice Ser.: P0040). 50p. 1984. pap. 29.50 (ISBN 0-943244-55-2). Water Pollution.
Sludge Management & Disposal for the Practicing Engineer. Aarne Vesiland et al. LC 85-24189. 350p. 1986. 49.95 (ISBN 0-87371-060-6). Lewis Pubs Inc.
Sludge Stabilization. Water Pollutions Control Federation Staff. LC 85-51397. (Manual of Practice, Facilities Development Ser.: No. 9). 106p. (Orig.). 1985. pap. 24.00 (ISBN 0-943244-63-3, MOPFD9). Water Pollution.
Sludge Thickening ('80) Water Pollution Control Federation. (Manual of Practice, Facilities & Development Ser.: No. 1). 189p. 1980. pap. 19.00 (ISBN 0-943244-18-8). Water Pollution.
Sludge Treatment. Ed. by W. Eckenfelder & C. Santhanam. (Pollution, Engineering & Technology Ser.: Vol. 14). 1981. 95.00 (ISBN 0-8247-6977-5). Dekker.
Slug Manual: The Rise & Fall of Criticism. rev. ed. Jennifer James. (Illus.). 84p. (Orig.). 1986. pap. text ed. 5.95. Bronwen Pr.
Slugs. David Greenberg. LC 82-10017. (Illus.). 32p. (gr. k-5). 1983. PLB 12.95 (ISBN 0-316-32658-5, Joy St Bks); pap. 4.95i (ISBN 0-316-32659-3, Joy St Bks). Little.
Slugs. Shaun Hutson. 368p. (Orig.). 1987. pap. 3.95 (ISBN 0-8439-2511-6). Leisure NY.
Slum & Squatter Settlements in Sub-Saharan Africa: Toward a Planning Strategy. Ed. by R. A. Obudho & Constance C. Mhlanga. LC 87-11705. 448p. 1988. lib. bdg. 65.00 (ISBN 0-275-92309-6, C2309). Praeger.
Slum & the Ghetto: Neighborhood Deterioration & Middle-Class Reform, Chicago 1880-1930. Thomas L. Philpott. LC 76-57275. (Urban Life in America Ser.). (Illus.). 1978. 25.00x (ISBN 0-19-502276-9). Oxford U Pr.
Slum As a Way of Life: A Study of Coping Behavior in an Urban Environment. F. Landa Jocano. 1976. wrps. 9.00x (ISBN 0-686-09437-9, Pub. by New Day Pub.). Cellar.
Slum Children of India. S. D. Singh & K. P. Pothen. 110p. 1982. 19.95. Asia Bk Corp.
Slum Eradication & Urban Renewal. new ed. Satish Sinha. (Illus.). xix, 205p. 1986. text ed. 50.00x (ISBN 81-210-0045-9, Pub. by Inter India Pubns N Delhi). Apt Bks.
Slum Housing & Residential Renewal: The Case in Urban Britain. David Kirby. LC 77-30748. (Topics in Applied Geography Ser.). pap. 28.00 (ISBN 0-317-20813-6, 2025275). Bks Demand UMI.
Slum Silouette. Leela Dharmaraj. 8.00 (ISBN 0-89253-551-2); flexible cloth 4.00 (ISBN 0-89253-552-0). Ind-US Inc.
Slumber Did My Spirit Seal see Poetry Unfolding.
Slumber of Apollo: Reflections on Recent Art, Literature, Language & the Individual Consciousness. John Holloway. LC 83-14279. (Illus.). 150p. 1984. 32.50 (ISBN 0-521-24804-3). Cambridge U Pr.
Slumber Party. Christopher Pike. LC 84-20238. 170p. (Orig.). (YA) (gr. 7 up). 1985. pap. 2.50 (ISBN 0-590-40927-1, Point). Scholastic Inc.
Slumbering Giant of the Past. 2nd ed. Rodman J. Bethel. Ed. by Louise White. (Illus.). 91p. (Orig.). 1985. lib. bdg. 19.95 (ISBN 0-9614702-1-6). Slumbering.
Slumbering Giant of the Past. Rodman J. Bethel & Louise White. (Illus.). 91p. (Orig.). 1984. pap. 11.95 (ISBN 0-9614702-0-8). Slumbering.
Slump & Reocvery, Nineteen Twenty-Nine to Nineteen Thirty-Seven: A Survey of World Economic Affairs. Henry V. Hodson. LC 82-48208. (Gold, Money, Inflation & Deflation Ser.). 492p. 1983. lib. bdg. 61.00 (ISBN 0-8240-5273-0). Garland Pub.
Slump City: The Politics of Mass Unemployment. Andrew Friend & Andy Metcalf. 194p. 1981. pap. 7.50 (ISBN 0-86104-342-1, Pub. by Pluto Pr). Longwood Pub Group.
Slump in Europe: Reconstruction Open Economy Theory. Jean-Paul Fitoussi & Edmund S. Phelps. text ed. 24.95 (ISBN 0-631-15557-0). Basil Blackwell.
Slumps, Grunts, & Snickerdoodles: What Colonial America Ate & Why. Lila Perl. LC 75-4894. (Illus.). 128p. (gr. 6 up). 1975. 12.95 (ISBN 0-395-28923-8, Clarion). HM.
Slums. Thomas Akare. (African Writers Ser. No. 241). 188p. (Orig.). 1981. pap. 6.50 (ISBN 0-435-90241-5). Heinemann Ed.
Slums & Housing, with Special Reference to New York City. James Ford. LC 76-142935. (Illus.). 1972. Repr. of 1936 ed. Vol. 1. 33.00 (ISBN 0-8371-5937-7, FOU&); Vol. 2. 33.00 (ISBN 0-8371-5938-5, FOV&). Greenwood.
Slums & Slum Clearance in Victorian London. James A. Yelling. (London Research Series in Geography: No. 10). 176p. 1986. text ed. 37.95x (ISBN 0-04-942192-1). Unwin Hyman.
Slums Are for People. rev. ed. Aprodicio A. Laquian. (Illus.). 1971. 15.00x (ISBN 0-8248-0098-2, Eastwest Ctr). UH Pr.
Slums of Baltimore, Chicago, New York, & Philadelphia: Seventh Special Report of the Commissioner of Labor. Carroll D. Wright. LC 71-112587. (Rise of Urban America). 1970. Repr. of 1894 ed. 46.50 (ISBN 0-405-02489-4). Ayer Co Pubs.
Slums of Hope? Shanty Towns of the Third World. Peter C. Lloyd. LC 78-24770. 1979. 22.50x (ISBN 0-312-72963-4). St Martin.
Slums, Projects & People. Kurt W. Back. LC 73-19572. 123p. 1974. Repr. of 1962 ed. lib. bdg. 35.00x (ISBN 0-8371-7289-6, BASL). Greenwood.
Slums, Projects, & People: Social Psychological Problems of Relocation in Puerto Rico. LC 62-15369. (Duke University Press, a Sociological Monograph). pap. 34.30 (ISBN 0-317-41840-8, 2026184). Bks Demand UMI.
Slums, Urban Decline & Revitalization. C. S. Yadav. 1987. 40.00x (ISBN 0-8364-2309-7, Pub. by Concept). South Asia Bks.
Slurry Erosion: Uses, Applications, & Test Methods. Ed. by J. E. Miller & F. E. Schmidt, Jr. LC 87-920. (Special Technical Publications: No. 946). (Illus.). 274p. 1987. text ed. 48.00 (ISBN 0-8031-0941-5, 04-946000-29). ASTM.
Slurry Pipeline Transportation. new ed. Edward J. Wasp et al. (Bulk Materials Handling Ser.: Vol. 1, No. 4). (Illus.). 300p. 1977. text ed. 60.00 (ISBN 0-87849-016-7, Trans Tech Germany). Trans Tech.
Slurry Transportation & Pneumatic Handling. Ed. by E. Hay. 104p. 1983. pap. text ed. 24.00 (ISBN 0-317-03527-4, H00256). ASME.
Slurry Trench Construction for Pollution Migration Control. Philip Spooner et al. LC 84-22747. (Pollution Technology Review Ser.: No. 118). (Illus.). 237p. 1985. 36.00 (ISBN 0-8155-1020-9). Noyes.
Slurry Walls. Petros P. Xanthakos. LC 79-10095. 704p. 1979. text ed. 64.00 (ISBN 0-07-072215-3). McGraw.
Sly Fox. C. A. Shepherd et al. (Orig.). (gr. 3-12). 1985. pap. text ed. 6.00 (ISBN 0-88734-503-4). Players Pr.
Sly Fox & the Little Red Hen in Arabic. (Illus.). (gr. 4-6). 3.50x (ISBN 0-86685-224-7). Intl Bk Ctr.
Sly Old Cat. Beatrix Potter. LC 73-163984. (Illus.). 38p. (ps-2). 1971. 5.95 (ISBN 0-7232-1420-4). Warne.
Sly Spy & Other Stories. Reusable ed. Marjorie T. Olson. (Ann Arbor Educational Ser.). (Illus.). (gr. 2-3). 1979. pap. 6.50 (ISBN 0-89039-242-0). Ann Arbor FL.
Smack. Drury Pifer. (Contemporary Drama Ser.). 1979. 6.95x (ISBN 0-912262-58-3); pap. 2.95 (ISBN 0-912262-59-1). Proscenium.
Smackover & Lower Buckner Formations, Jurassic, South Texas: Depositional Systems on a Carbonate Ramp. D. A. Budd & R. G. Loucks. (Report of Investigations Ser.: No. 112). (Illus.). 38p. 1981. 2.25 (ISBN 0-686-36593-3). Bur Econ Geology.
Small AC Generator Service Manual. 2nd ed. Intertec Publishing Corp. Staff. LC 86-86558. (Illus.). 320p. 1986. pap. 12.95 (ISBN 0-87288-227-6, GSM-2). Intertec Pub.
Small Airport Management Handbook. Jerry A. Singer. 176p. (Orig.). 1985. pap. 15.95 (ISBN 0-89854-099-2). U of GA Inst Govt.
Small Airports Managers Handbook. Earl Seay. (Aviation Management Ser.). 78p. 1980. 9.95 (ISBN 0-89100-140-9, EA-140-9). IAP.
Small Amish Quilt Patterns. Rachel T. Pellman. LC 85-70280. (Illus.). 128p. (Orig.). 1985. pap. 10.95 (ISBN 0-934672-30-X). Good Bks PA.
Small & Beautiful Flower Arrangements: An Idea Book for Miniature Flower Arrangements. Marion Johnson. 1983. 10.95 (ISBN 0-517-54788-0, C N Potter Bks). Crown.
Small & Intermediate Urban Centres: Their Role in Regional & National Development in the Third World. Ed. by Jorge Hardoy & David Satterthwaite. 416p. 1986. pap. 37.50 (ISBN 0-8133-0404-0). Westview.
Small & Medium Enterprises in Southeast Asia. Ronald Clapham. 152p. 1985. pap. text ed. 18.50x (ISBN 9-971902-99-0, Pub. by Inst Southeast Asian Stud). Gower Pub Co.
Small & Medium Power Reactors: 1968. (Panel Proceedings Ser.). (Illus.). 179p. pap. 13.75 (ISP217, IAEA). UNIPUB.
Small & Medium Power Reactors: 1970. (Proceedings Ser.). (Illus.). 536p. 1971. pap. 47.00 (ISBN 92-0-050171-0, ISP267, IAEA). UNIPUB.
Small & Medium Sawmills in Developing Countries: A Guide for Their Planning & Establishment. (Forestry Papers: No. 28). 160p. (Eng. & Span.). 1981. pap. 11.25 (ISBN 92-5-101155-9, F2272, FAO). UNIPUB.
Small & Medium Scale Industries in the ASEAN Countries: Agents or Victims of Economic Development? Mathias Bruch & Ulrich Hiemenz. (Replica Edition Ser.). 130p. 1984. pap. 21.50x (ISBN 0-86531-848-4). Westview.
Small & Medium Size Enterprises & Regional Development. Ed. by Maria Giaoutzi et al. 256p. 1988. lib. bdg. 67.50 (ISBN 0-415-00415-2). Routledge Chapman & Hall.
Small & Medium-Size Power Reactors. (Safety Ser.: No. 50-SG-S4). 51p. 1980. pap. 12.00 (ISBN 92-0-123580-1, ISP569, IAEA). UNIPUB.
Small & Medium-Sized Restaurant Chains. Peter Allen. 250p. 1987. 1250.00 (ISBN 0-941285-10-3). FIND-SVP.
Small & Mini Hydropower Systems: Resource Assessment & Project Feasibility. Jack Fritz. Ed. by Patricia Allen-Browne. (Illus.). 464p. 1984. text ed. 59.50 (ISBN 0-07-022470-6). McGraw.
Small & New Business Development: An Action Guide for State Governments. Roger Vaughan. LC 83-179220. 29p. 1983. pap. text ed. 5.00 (ISBN 0-914193-02-3). Coalition NE Govn.
Small & Specialty Manufacturers Radio Diagrams & Servicing Information, 1946-1950. Hartford Beitmam. (Supreme Specialty Servicing Manuals Ser.). (Illus.). 219p. (Orig.). 1988. pap. text ed. 24.00 (ISBN 0-938630-77-6, SM-18). ARS Enterprises.
Small & Unusual Woodturning Projects. James A. Jacobson. LC 87-9970. (Illus.). 164p. (Orig.). 1987. pap. 12.95 (ISBN 0-8069-6510-X). Sterling.
Small Angle Scattering: Perspectives in Crystallography at Atomic Resolution. American Crystallographic Association Staff. (Program & Abstracts Ser.). 1983. pap. 10.00 (ISBN 0-686-45047-7). Polycrystal Bk Serv.
Small-Angle X-Ray Scattering. Ed. by H. Brumberger. 518p. 1967. 150.00 (ISBN 0-677-11190-8). Gordon & Breach.
Small Angle X-Ray Scattering. Ed. by Otto Glatter & H. C. Kratky. 1982. 102.50 (ISBN 0-12-286280-5). Acad Pr.
Small Animal Clinical Nutrition, No. III. 3rd ed. Lon D. Lewis et al. Tr. by Philippe Moreau from Eng. (Illus.). 470p. Date not set. 18.00 (ISBN 0-945837-00-3). M Morris Assocs.
Small Animal Dermatology. 4th ed. George H. Muller et al. 1216p. 1988. price not set (ISBN 0-7216-2416-2). Saunders.
Small Animal Dermatology. 3rd ed. George H. Muller et al. (Illus.). 906p. 1983. 99.00 (ISBN 0-7216-6609-4). Saunders.
Small Animal Endocrinology. Ed. by Frederick H. Drazner. (Illus.). 508p. 1986. text ed. 69.00 (ISBN 0-443-08256-1). Churchill.
Small Animal Medical Diagnosis. Lorenz & Cornelius. LC 65-7099. 1987. text ed. 39.95 (ISBN 0-397-50555-8, Lippincott Medical). Lippincott.
Small Animal Radiology: A Diagnostic Atlas & Text. Ronald L. Burk & Norman Ackerman. (Illus.). 382p. 1987. text ed. 75.00 (ISBN 0-443-08323-1). Churchill.
Small Animal Reproduction & Infertility: A Clinical Approach to Diagnosis & Treatment. Ed. by Thomas J. Burke. LC 86-10519. (Illus.). 408p. 1986. text ed. 42.50 (ISBN 0-8121-1042-0). Lea & Febiger.
Small Animal Surgery: An Atlas of Operative Techniques. Wayne E. Wingfield & A. Clarence Rawlings. (Illus.). 228p. 1979. 41.95 (ISBN 0-7216-9463-2). Saunders.
Small Animals. Sara Lynn. (Illus.). 14p. (ps). 1987. bds. 2.95 (ISBN 0-689-71099-2, Aladdin Bks). Macmillan.
Small Antennas. K. Fujimoto et al. LC 86-26198. (Antenna Ser.). 300p. 1987. 64.95 (ISBN 0-471-91413-4). Wiley.
Small Apparatus in Practice. John Learmouth. 109p. 1982. 30.00 (ISBN 0-7217-4516-4, Pub. by Schofield & Sims UK). State Mutual Bk.
Small Appliance Industry. Ed. by Peter Allen. 400p. (Orig.). 1983. pap. 295.00 (ISBN 0-931634-30-X). FIND SVP.
Small Appliance Repair. Phyllis Palmore & Nevin Andre. Ed. by Charles A. Schuler. LC 79-19186. (Basic Skills in Electricity & Electronics Ser.). (Illus.). 192p. (gr. 9-12). 1980. text ed. 25.96 (ISBN 0-07-048361-2). McGraw.
Small Appliances. Time-Life Books Editors. (Fix-It-Yourself Ser.). 144p. 1988. 17.27 (ISBN 0-8094-6256-7); lib. bdg. 21.27 (ISBN 0-8094-6257-5). Time-Life.
Small Area Employment Forecasting. Kevin Allen & Douglas Yuill. 264p. 1978. text ed. 44.50x (ISBN 0-566-00201-9). Gower Pub Co.
Small Area Estimation: An Empirical Comparison of Conventional & Synthetic Estimators for States. Wesley L. Schaible et al. Ed. by Audrey Shipp. (Ser. 2: No. 82). 1979. pap. text ed. 1.75 (ISBN 0-8406-0176-X). Natl Ctr Health Stats.
Small Area Statistics: An International Symposium. Ed. by R. Platek et al. (Probability & Mathematical Statistics Ser.). 1986. 39.95 (ISBN 0-471-84456-X). Wiley.
Small Arms & Cannons. D. J. Marchant-Smith & P. R. Haslem. (Brassey's Battlefield Weapons System & Technology: Vol. 5). 160p. 1982. pap. text ed. 16.95 (ISBN 0-08-028331-4). Pergamon.
Small Arms Eighteen Fifty-Six: Reports of Experiments with Small Arms for the Military Service. Officers of the U.S. Army Ordnance Dept. Staff. (Illus.). 168p. 1984. Repr. of 1856 ed. 15.00 (ISBN 0-939631-01-6). Thomas Publications.
Small Arms Identification & Operations Guide: Pistols. 1986. lib. bdg. 79.95 (ISBN 0-8490-3575-9). Gordon Pr.

TITLE INDEX SMALL BUSINESS MANAGEMENT TRAINING

Small Arms Identification & Operation Guide-Submachine Guns. 1986. lib. bdg. 79.95 (ISBN 0-8490-3576-7). Gordon Pr.
Small Arms of the Sea Services: A History of the Firearms & Edged Weapons of the U. S. Navy, Marine Corps & Coast Guard from the Revolution to the Present. Robert H. Rankin. LC 72-186706. (Illus.). 260p. 1972. 14.50 (ISBN 0-910598-10-X). Flayderman.
Small Arms of the World: A Basic Manual of Small Arms. 12th, rev. ed. W. H. Smith. (Illus.). 896p. 49.95 (ISBN 0-317-55095-0). Apollo.
Small Arms of the World: A Basic Manual of Small Arms. 12th ed. W. H. B. Smith. 896p. 1983. 49.95 (ISBN 0-8117-1687-2). Stackpole.
Small Arms Today. Edward C. Ezell. 256p. (Orig.). 1984. pap. 16.95 (ISBN 0-8117-2197-3). Stackpole.
Small Arms Training: Sten Machine Carbine, Vol. 1. 1983. pap. text ed. 0.95 (ISBN 0-86663-990-X). Ide Hse.
Small As a Resurrection. Honor Johnson. LC 82-82498. (Lost Roads Ser.: No. 20). 60p. 1982. pap. 5.95 (ISBN 0-918786-23-1). Lost Roads.
Small Batteries: Primary Cells, Vol. 2. T. R. Crompton. LC 81-11495. 240p. 1983. Repr. 78.95x (ISBN 0-470-27356-9). Halsted Pr.
Small Batteries: Secondary Cells, Vol. 1. T. R. Crompton. LC 81-6990. 226p. 1982. Repr. 83.95x (ISBN 0-470-27267-8). Halsted Pr.
Small Bear & the Secret Surprise. Adelaide Holl. LC 77-17204. (Small Bear Adventure Ser.). (Illus.). 48p. (gr. k-4). 1978. PLB 6.69 (ISBN 0-8116-4455-3). Garrard.
Small Bear Builds a Playhouse. Adelaide Holl. LC 77-11640. (Small Bear Adventures Ser.). (Illus.). 48p. (gr. k-4). 1978. PLB 6.69 (ISBN 0-8116-4454-5). Garrard.
Small Bear Solves a Mystery. Adelaide Holl. LC 78-16727. (Small Bear Adventures Ser.). (Illus.). 48p. (gr. k-4). 1979. PLB 6.69 (ISBN 0-8116-4456-1). Garrard.
Small Bear's Birthday Party. Adelaide Holl. LC 77-5630. (Small Bear Adventures Ser.). (Illus.). 48p. (gr. k-4). 1977. PLB 6.69 (ISBN 0-8116-4453-7). Garrard.
Small Bear's Busy Day. Adelaide Holl. LC 77-910. (Small Bear Adventures Ser.). (Illus.). 48p. (gr. k-4). 1977. 6.69 (ISBN 0-8116-4452-9). Garrard.
Small Bear's Name Hunt. Adelaide Holl. LC 76-56141. (Small Bear Adventures Ser.). (Illus.). 48p. (gr. k-4). 1977. PLB 6.69 (ISBN 0-8116-4451-0). Garrard.
Small Beginnings: New Roles for British Businesses. Alan Bollard. (Illus.). 335p. 1983. 23.50x (ISBN 0-903031-91-4, Pub. by Intermediate Tech England). Intermediate Tech.
Small Beginnings: Things People Say about Babies. Nanette Newman. (Illus.). 64p. 1987. 7.95 (ISBN 0-517-56714-8). Crown.
Small Bequest. Edmund G. Love. LC 87-16202. (Great Lakes Bks.). 238p. 1987. 22.50x (ISBN 0-8143-1925-4); pap. 12.50x (ISBN 0-8143-1926-2). Wayne St U Pr.
Small Birds of the New Zealand Bush. Elaine Power. (Illus.). 27p. 1983. pap. 9.95 (ISBN 0-00-216984-3, Pub. by W Collins New Zealand). Intl Spec Bk.
Small Boat Building. H. Paterson. 144p. 1985. Repr. of 1934 ed. 20.00 (ISBN 0-87556-691-X); 20 folding plates incl. Saifer.
Small Boat Design. Ed. by Johanna M. Reinhart. (Illus.). 79p. 1983. pap. text ed. 12.00x (ISBN 0-89955-393-1, Pub. by ICLARM Philippines). Intl Spec Bk.
Small Boat Law. Herbert L. Markow. LC 77-154289. (Illus.). 435p. (Orig.). 1977. pap. 40.00x (ISBN 0-934108-00-5). H L Markow.
Small Boat Law: Nineteen Seventy-Eight Supplement. Herbert L. Markow. LC 79-88475. 144p. 1979. pap. 20.00x (ISBN 0-934108-01-3). H L Markow.
Small Boat Law: Nineteen Seventy-Nine to Nineteen Eighty Supplement. Herbert L. Markow. LC 77-154289. 174p. 1981. pap. 24.00x (ISBN 0-934108-02-1). H L Markow.
Small Boat Law: 1981-1983 Supplement. Herbert L. Markow. LC 77-154289. 274p. 1984. pap. text ed. 36.00x (ISBN 0-934108-03-X). H L Markow.
Small-Boat Sailing. (Illus.). 80p. (gr. 6-12). 1965. pap. 1.25x (ISBN 0-8395-3319-5, 3319). BSA.
Small Boat Sailing: The Basic Guide. Bob Bond & Steve Sleight. LC 82-48883. (Illus.). 1983. 15.45 (ISBN 0-394-52446-2). Knopf.
Small-Boat Sailor's Bible. rev ed. Hervey G. Smith. LC 73-82247. (Outdoor Bible Ser.). 144p. 1974. pap. 4.95 (ISBN 0-385-05527-7). Doubleday.
Small Boat Through Holland. Roger Pilkinton. 1985. 20.00x (ISBN 0-86025-807-6, Pub. by Ian Henry Pubns England). State Mutual Bk.
Small Bones, Little Eyes. Nila Northsun & Jim Sagel. Ed. by Kirk Robertson. (Windriver Ser.). 72p. (Orig.). 1982. pap. 5.00 (ISBN 0-916918-17-3). Duck Down.
Small Book of Herbs. Karen Feinberg. LC 83-90112. (Illus.). 64p. 1984. 20.00 (ISBN 0-88014-071-2). Mosaic Pr OH.
Small Books & Pleasant Histories: Popular Fiction & Its Readership in Seventeenth-Century England. Margaret Spufford. LC 81-11684. 268p. 1982. 22.00x (ISBN 0-8203-0595-2). U of Ga Pr.
Small Books & Pleasant Histories: Popular Fiction & Its Readership in Seventeenth-Century England. Margaret Spufford. (Past & Present Publications Ser.). 296p. 1985. pap. 14.95 (ISBN 0-521-31218-3). Cambridge U Pr.
Small Bore Liquid Chromatography Columns: Their Properties & Uses. Ed. by Raymond P. W. Scott. LC 84-2393. (Chemical Analysis: A Series of Monographs on Analytical Chemistry & its Applications: 1-075). 271p. 1984. text ed. 58.00 (ISBN 0-471-80052-X). Wiley.
Small Bowel Radiology. G. Antes & F. Eggemann. (Illus.). 210p. 1987. 110.00 (ISBN 0-387-15263-6). Springer-Verlag.
Small-Bowel Transplantation. Ed. by E. Deltz et al. 400p. 1987. 108.90 (ISBN 0-387-16336-0). Springer-Verlag.
Small Boy & Others. Henry James. 419p. 1985. Repr. of 1914 ed. lib. bdg. 100.00. Century Bookbindery.
Small Boy in the Sixties. George Sturt. 257p. 1982. pap. 7.50 (ISBN 0-904573-50-8, Pub. by Caliban Bks). Longwood Pub Group.
Small Bridges to One World: Perspective of a Peace Corps Staff Wife, 1963-1965. (Illus., Orig.). 1986. pap. 12.50. P E Randall Pub.
Small Building Contractor & the Client: How to Run Your Business Successfully. Derek Miles. (Illus.). 270p. (Orig.). 1980. pap. 13.50x (ISBN 0-903031-67-1, Pub. by Intermediate Tech England). Intermediate Tech.
Small Business. Tom Parker. 240p. 1987. pap. 6.95 (ISBN 0-14-009810-0). Penguin.
Small Business: A Novel. Tom Parker. 1986. 14.95 (ISBN 0-393-02254-4). Norton.
Small Business Administration. Ed. by Arthur M. Schlesinger, Jr. (Know Your Government Ser.). (Illus.). (gr. 5 up). 1989. 14.95 (ISBN 1-55546-122-0). Chelsea Hse.
Small Business Agenda: Trends in a Global Economy. Galen S. Hull. 138p. (Orig.). 1986. lib. bdg. 25.00 (ISBN 0-8191-5163-7); pap. text ed. 9.75 (ISBN 0-8191-5164-5). U Pr of Amer.
Small Business: An Entrepreneur's Plan. Lee A. Eckert et al. 434p. 1985. pap. text ed. 22.00 (ISBN 0-15-581220-3, HC); instr's. manual avail. (ISBN 0-15-581221-1). HarBraceJ.
Small Business: An Information Sourcebook. Ed. by Paul Wasserman & Cynthia Ryans. (Oryx Sourcebook Series in Business & Management). 296p. 1987. 45.00 (ISBN 0-89774-272-9). Oryx Pr.
Small Business & Pattern Bargaining. Walter H. Carpenter, Jr. & Edward Handler. Ed. by Stuart Bruchey & Vincent P. Carosso. LC 78-18953. (Small Business Enterprise in America Ser.). 1979. Repr. of 1961 ed. lib. bdg. 19.00x (ISBN 0-405-11461-3). Ayer Co Pubs.
Small Business & Public Policy. Ed. by William Greenwood et al. 172p. (Orig.). 1985. pap. 8.00 (ISBN 0-918592-83-6). Policy Studies.
Small Business & Public Policy in America. Daljit Singh. 1981. pap. text ed. 12.95x (ISBN 0-89917-347-0). TIS Inc.
Small Business & Venture Capital. Rudolph L. Weissman. Ed. by Stuart Bruchey & Vincent P. Carosso. LC 78-18153. (Small Business Enterprise in America Ser.). 1979. Repr. of 1945 ed. lib. bdg. 14.00x (ISBN 0-405-11510-5). Ayer Co Pubs.
Small Business at the Crossroad. Wilfred Lumer. Ed. by Stuart Bruchey & Vincent P. Carosso. LC 78-18967. (Small Business Enterprise in America Ser.). (Illus.). 1979. Repr. of 1956 ed. lib. bdg. 12.00 (ISBN 0-405-11471-0). Ayer Co Pubs.
Small Business Audit Manual. Larry L. Perry. 344p. 1987. 140.00 (ISBN 0-13-813155-4). P-H.
Small Business Audit Manual Documentation. Larry L. Perry. 176p. 1987. pap. 50.00 (ISBN 0-13-813106-6). P-H.
Small Business, Banks, & SBA Loan Guarantees: Subsidizing the Weak or Bridging a Credit Gap? Elisabeth H. Rhyne. LC 87-36098. 192p. 1988. lib. bdg. 39.95 (ISBN 0-89930-256-4, RSB/, Quorum Bks). Greenwood.
Small Business Bible: The Make-or-Break Factors for Survival & Success. Paul Resnick. 1988. pap. 29.95 (ISBN 0-471-62972-3). Wiley.
Small Business Bible: The Make-or-Break Factors for Survival & Success. Paul Resnik. 1988. pap. 17.95 (ISBN 0-471-62985-5). Wiley.
Small Business Bibliography. University of Pittsburgh, Bureau of Business Research. Ed. by Stuart Bruchey. LC 78-19003. (Small Business Enterprise in America Ser.). 1979. Repr. of 1955 ed. lib. bdg. 25.50x (ISBN 0-405-11507-5). Ayer Co Pubs.
Small Business Breakthrough. Ed. by Peter Lawrence. 140p. 1985. 34.95x (ISBN 0-631-14407-2). Basil Blackwell.
Small Business Case Book. I. A. Fleming. 144p. 1985. text ed. 44.95 (ISBN 0-566-00841-6). Gower Pub Co.
Small Business Communication. (Market Research Reports). 1986. write for info. (ISBN 0-86621-837-8, A1657). Frost & Sullivan.
Small Business Computer Hardware & Software Market in Europe. 450p. 1984. 1950.00 (ISBN 0-86621-569-7, E648). Frost & Sullivan.
Small Business Computer Primer. Robert B. McCaleb. 200p. 1982. pap. 5.95 (ISBN 0-88056-067-3). Weber Systems.
Small Business Computer Systems. Best. pap. 26.67 (ISBN 0-13-814129-0). P-H.
Small Business Computer Today & Tomorrow. William E. Grieb, Jr. 1984. pap. 6.95 (ISBN 0-671-55907-9, Pub. by Baen Bks). PB.
Small Business Computers. (Market Research Reports). 1987. write for info. (ISBN 0-86621-859-9, A1680). Frost & Sullivan.
Small Business Computers: A Guide to Evaluation & Selection. Koichiro Isshiki. (Illus.). 512p. 1982. text ed. 39.33 (ISBN 0-13-814152-5). P-H.
Small Business Counselor. Harry Haynsworth. 1984. 100.00. Callaghan.
Small Business Course for Older Americans. 1983. 35.00 (1046). Am Assn Comm Jr Coll.
Small Business Course Training Tools Directory. 1985. 35.00 (ISBN 0-317-40618-3). Am Assn Comm Jr Coll.
Small Business: Developing the Winning Management Team. George W. Rimler & Neil J. Humphreys. LC 79-54848. pap. 47.50 (ISBN 0-317-26901-1, 2023562). Bks Demand UMI.
Small Business Development. 35.00 (ISBN 0-686-37907-1). Nikmal Pub.
Small Business Development in Brazil: A Study of the UNO Program. Jose G. Schreiber. 64p. (Orig.). 1976. pap. 3.00 (ISBN 0-89192-119-2). Interbk Inc.
Small Business Development: Some Current Issues. Kent O'Neill. 280p. 1987. text ed. 39.00 (ISBN 0-566-05382-9, Pub. by Gower Pub England). Gower Pub Co.
Small Business Enterprise in America Series, 42 bks. Ed. by Stuart Bruchey & Vincent P. Carosso. (Illus.). 1979. lib. bdg. 1049.50x set (ISBN 0-405-11457-5). Ayer Co Pubs.
Small Business Entrepreneurial Services: Suggestions for a Small Business Entrepreneural Service Center. Bibliotheca Press Staff. 20p. 1983. pap. text ed. 3.95 (ISBN 0-939476-95-9, Pub. by Biblio Pr GA). Prosperity & Profits.
Small Business Expense Planner. LaVerne H. Ireland. 49p. (Orig.). 1984. pap. 10.00 (ISBN 0-943932-00-9). Petervin Pr.
Small Business Finance, 2 vols. Ed. by Paul M. Horvitz. (Contemporary Studies in Economic & Financial Analysis Ser.: Vol. 42). 105.00 (ISBN 0-89232-471-6). Jai Pr.
Small Business Financial Problem. Greg Glau. 1988. write for info. (ISBN 0-471-63106-X). Wiley.
Small Business Financing. 68p. 1980. 7.00 (ISBN 0-317-32419-5, 168500); members 5.50 (ISBN 0-317-32420-9). Am Bankers.
Small Business Financing. Ed. by Charlotte Weisman. LC 87-5534. (Special Collection from the Journal of Commercial Bank Lending). 132p. 1987. pap. text ed. 28.00 (ISBN 0-936742-40-2). Robt Morris Assocs.
Small Business Fundamentals. Thomas W. Zimmerer & Norman Scarborough. 480p. 1988. case bound 29.95 (ISBN 0-675-20786-X); supplements avail. Merrill.
Small Business Guide to Borrowing Money. Philip Goldberg & Richard Rubin. (Illus.). 1980. text ed. 36.95 (ISBN 0-07-054198-1). McGraw.
Small Business Guide to Employee Selection. Lin Grensing. 115p. 1986. pap. 6.95 (ISBN 0-88908-638-9, TAB NO. 9551). ISC Pr.
Small Business Guide to Hiring Good People: Selection Interviewing. Barbara A. Schoeneberger. Ed. & illus. by Lynn M. Baber. (Illus.). 38p. (Orig.). 1987. pap. 5.00 (ISBN 0-943725-00-3). Small Busn NE.
Small Business Guide to Successful Advertising. Sandra L. Deaz. 1988. looseleaf 69.95 (ISBN 0-942103-08-4). Enterprise Del.
Small Business Guide to the Commodore 64. Don Vandeventer. Ed. by Paula Vineyard. (Illus.). 200p. (Orig.). 1985. pap. 19.95 (ISBN 0-917525-02-7). Work At Home.
Small Business Handbook. Ed. by Brian Wilson. 250p. 1985. 34.95x (ISBN 0-631-14403-X). Basil Blackwell.
Small Business Handbook: A Comprehensive Guide to Starting & Running Your Own Business. rev. ed. Irving Burstiner. 352p. 1989. pap. 16.95 (ISBN 0-13-814344-7). Prentice Hall Pr.
Small Business Handbook: Comprehensive Guide to Starting & Running Your Own Business. Irving Burstinger. (Illus.). 1979. (Spec); pap. text ed. 15.95 (ISBN 0-13-814194-0). P-H.
Small Business Ideas for Women & How to Get Started. Terri Hilton. LC 75-6859. 32p. 1975. pap. 2.00 (ISBN 0-87576-050-3). Pilot Bks.
Small Business in a Regulated Economy: Issues & Policy Implications. Ed. by Richard J. Judd et al. LC 87-32611. 255p. 1988. lib. bdg. 39.95 (ISBN 0-89930-343-9, JSL/, Quorum Bks). Greenwood.
Small Business in America: The Year 2000 & Beyond. Naisbitt Group. (Illus.). 20p. (Orig.). 1986. pap. 6.00 (ISBN 0-940791-00-5). NFIB Found.
Small Business in American Life. Ed. by Stuart Bruchey. LC 80-10994. 450p. 1980. 40.00x (ISBN 0-231-04872-6). Columbia U Pr.
Small Business in the Third World: Guidelines for Practical Assistance. Malcolm Harper. LC 83-25960. 211p. 1984. 43.95x (ISBN 0-471-90210-1, Pub. by Wiley-Interscience). Wiley.
Small Business Index. Wayne D. Kryszak. LC 78-17540. 228p. 1978. 17.50 (ISBN 0-8108-1150-2). Scarecrow.
Small Business Index, Vol. 2. Wayne D. Kryszak. LC 78-17540. 320p. 1985. 22.50 (ISBN 0-8108-1817-5). Scarecrow.
Small Business Information Source Book. Adrian A. Paradis. LC 87-15925. 136p. (Orig.). 1987. pap. 7.95 (ISBN 0-932620-81-7). Betterway Pubns.
Small Business Investment Companies. Commerce Clearing House, Inc. Ed. by Stuart Bruchey & Vincent P. Carosso. LC 78-18958. (Small Business Enterprise in America Ser.). 1979. Repr. of 1959 ed. lib. bdg. 12.00x (ISBN 0-405-11462-1). Ayer Co Pubs.
Small Business Investment Company Directory & Handbook. 3rd ed. Tyler G. Hicks. 150p. 1987. pap. 15.00 (ISBN 0-934311-10-2). Intl Wealth.
Small Business Investment Company Directory & Handbook. 150p. 1987. 30.00 (ISBN 0-317-55721-1). B Klein Pubns.
Small Business: Its Place & Problems. Abraham D. Kaplan. Ed. by Stuart Bruchey & Vincent P. Carosso. LC 78-18965. (Small Business Enterprise in America Ser.). (Illus.). 1979. Repr. of 1948 ed. lib. bdg. 21.00x (ISBN 0-405-11469-9). Ayer Co Pubs.
Small Business Legal Advisor. William A. Hancock. 272p. 1986. pap. text ed. 10.95 (ISBN 0-07-025999-2). McGraw.
Small Business Legal Handbook. Robert Friedman. 1985. 49.95 (ISBN 0-913864-91-9). Enterprise Del.
Small Business Legal Problem Solver. Goldstein. 1984. 30.95 (ISBN 0-442-22808-2). Van Nos Reinhold.
Small Business Legal Problem-Solver. Arnold S. Goldstein. 240p. 1983. 30.95 (ISBN 0-8436-0890-0); pap. cancelled. Van Nos Reinhold.
Small Business: Look Before You Leap; a Catalog of Sources of Information to Help You Start & Manage Your Own Small Business. 2nd ed. Louis Mucciolo. LC 80-26082. 304p. 1981. pap. 8.95 (ISBN 0-668-05173-6, 5173). Arco.
Small Business Management. Michael D. Ames & Norval L. Wellsfry. (Illus.). 492p. 1983. text ed. 37.00 (ISBN 0-314-69631-8). West Pub.
Small Business Management. 2nd ed. Ralph M. Gaedeke & Dennis H. Tootelian. 1985. text ed. write for info. (ISBN 0-673-16598-1). Scott F.
Small Business Management. 3rd ed. William D. Hailes, Jr. & Raymond T. Hubbard. LC 82-46006. 416p. 1983. pap. text ed. 18.95 (ISBN 0-8273-2108-2); instr's. guide 9.00 (ISBN 0-8273-2109-0). Delmar.
Small-Business Management. 7th ed. Justin G. Longenecker & Carlos W. Moore. LC 86-60502. 1987. text ed. write for info. (ISBN 0-538-07263-6, G26). SW Pub.
Small Business Management. 4th ed. Hal B. Pickle & Royce L. Abrahamson. LC 86-19198. (Production-Operations Management Ser.). 645p. 1986. write for info. (ISBN 0-471-85031-4). Wiley.
Small Business Management: A Guide to Entrepreneurship. 3rd ed. Nicholas C. Siropolis. LC 85-80697. 608p. 1985. text ed. 36.36 (ISBN 0-395-35717-9); instr's manual 3.56 (ISBN 0-395-40046-5); study guide 13.56 (ISBN 0-395-40047-3); enterprise simulation 14.36 (ISBN 0-395-40445-2). HM.
Small Business Management: A Planning Approach. Larry D. Redinbaugh & Clyde W. Neu. (Illus.). 475p. 1980. pap. text ed. 36.75 (ISBN 0-314-52971-3); instr's. manual avail. (ISBN 0-314-52998-5). West Pub.
Small Business Management: A Practical Approach. 2nd ed. Paul Harmon. 272p. 1983. pap. text ed. 21.95 (ISBN 0-8403-3159-2). Kendall-Hunt.
Small Business Management: A Practical Approach. 2nd ed. Daniel J. Sullivan & Joseph F. Lane. 544p. 1983. 34.00 (ISBN 0-205-11558-6, H1558-9); instr's. manual avail. (H1559-7). Allyn.
Small Business Management & Entrepreneurship. Olive D. Church. 544p. 1984. write for info. (ISBN 0-574-20715-5, 13-3715); instr's. guide avail. (ISBN 0-574-20716-3, 13-3716). SRA.
Small Business Management Fundamentals. 3rd ed. Dan Steinhoff. (Management Ser.). 1981. text ed. 29.95x (ISBN 0-07-061146-7). McGraw.
Small Business Management Fundamentals. 4th ed. Dan Steinhoff & J. Burgess. (Management Ser.). 440p. 1986. text ed. 33.95 (ISBN 0-07-061148-3). McGraw.
Small Business Management Fundamentals. 5th ed. Daniel Steinhoff & John Burgess. (Management Ser.). 1988. 30.95 (ISBN 0-07-061150-5). McGraw.
Small Business Management in Australia. 2nd ed. G. Meredith. 352p. 1982. 18.50 (ISBN 0-07-451006-1). McGraw.
Small Business Management: Operation & Profiles. 2nd ed. Ralph M. Gaedeke & Dennis H. Tootelian. 1985. pap. text ed. write for info. (ISBN 0-673-16599-X). Scott F.
Small Business Management Principles. Stanley R. Sondeno. 1985. 33.95x (ISBN 0-256-03168-1). Business Pubns.
Small Business Management Training Tool Directory. 1985. 8.95 (ISBN 0-317-40622-1). Am Assn Comm Jr Coll.

Small Business Marketing: A Selected & Annotated Bibliography. William H. Brannen. LC 78-15082. (American Marketing Association Bibliography Ser.: No. 31). pap. 21.80 (ISBN 0-317-39650-1, 2023352). Bks Demand UMI.

Small Business Matters: Topics, Procedures & Strategies. Mary F. McVicker. LC 87-47977. 320p. 1988. pap. 14.95 (ISBN 0-8019-7813-0). Chilton.

Small Business Meanagement. 4th ed. 416p. 1988. 16.95 (ISBN 0-8273-3128-2). Delmar.

Small Business Opportunities. A. C. Chapman. 348p. 1985. 42.50 (ISBN 0-317-19977-3). Bern Porter.

Small Business or Entrepreneur Related Newsletters & Periodicals: An Updating Directory. Update Publicare Research Staff. 100p. 1983. pap. text ed. 6.95 (ISBN 0-686-39492-5, Pub. by Update Pub Co). Prosperity & Profits.

Small Business Owner's Practical Handbook. Brownstone et al. 1985. write for info. (ISBN 0-471-89864-3). Wiley.

Small Business Problems & Priorities. William J. Dennis, Jr. 117p. (Orig.). 1986. pap. 6.00 (ISBN 0-940791-02-1). NFIB Found.

Small Business Problems in Urban Areas. U. S. House of Representatives, Subcommittee No. 4 on Distribution Problems Affecting Small Business. Ed. by Stuart Bruchey & Vincent P. Carosso. LC 78-18998. (Small Business Enterprise in America Ser.). (Illus.). 1979. Repr. of 1965 ed. lib. bdg. 14.00x (ISBN 0-405-11506-7). Ayer Co Pubs.

Small Business Promotion: Case Studies from Developing Countries. Malcolm Harper & Kavil Ramachandran. 118p. (Orig.). 1984. pap. text ed. 11.50x (ISBN 0-946688-45-1, Pub. by Intermediate Tech England). Intermediate Tech.

Small Business Reference Guide for: Home-Based Business, Small Manufacturers, Self-Publishers, Entrepreneurs, Craftsmen, Retailers, Writers, Artists. Belle M. Biebel. 63p. Date not set. pap. 12.95 (ISBN 0-941825-02-7). Bluechip Bks.

Small Business Research: The Development of Entrepreneurs. Ed. by Terry Webb & Thelma Quince. 228p. 1982. text ed. 34.00x (ISBN 0-566-00381-3). Gower Pub Co.

Small Business Resource Set. Kishel et al. 1986. pap. 40.75 (ISBN 0-471-82909-9). Wiley.

Small Business Safety & Health Manual. 80p. 1984. pap. 14.95 (ISBN 0-87912-120-3, 130.20). Natl Safety Coun.

Small Business Services Suggestions; Poetry, Bk. 1. Alpha Pyramis Research Division Staff. 38p. 1948. pap. text ed. 4.75 (ISBN 0-913597-45-7, Pub. by Alpha Pyramis). Prosperity & Profits.

Small Business Sourcebook, 2 vols. 3rd ed. Ed. by Charity A. Dorgan. 2000p. 1988. 189.00 (ISBN 0-8103-2648-5). Gale.

Small Business Sourcebook. 2nd ed. Ed. by Robert J. Elster. 1837p. 1986. 185.00x (ISBN 0-8103-1597-1). Gale.

Small Business Sourcebook: Supplement. 2nd ed. Ed. by Robert J. Elster. 235p. 1987. pap. 80.00x (ISBN 0-8103-2512-8). Gale.

Small Business Specialists. 63p. 1986. pap. 3.25 (ISBN 0-318-21658-2, S/N 008-000-00462-5). USGPO.

Small Business Start up Manual. John B. Walton. LC 81-50038. (Illus.). 228p. 1981. 19.95 (ISBN 0-939356-00-7). Weybridge.

Small Business Subcontracting Directory. 136p. 1986. pap. 6.50 (S/N 008-040-00190-3). USGPO.

Small Business Success Secrets. Donald Dible. 1981. (Reston); pap. 21.95 (ISBN 0-8359-7010-8). P-H.

Small Business Survival Guide. Bob Coleman. 352p. 1987. pap. 7.95 (ISBN 0-393-30418-3). Norton.

Small Business Survival Guide: A Handbook. Bob Coleman. LC 83-42678. 1984. 18.95 (ISBN 0-393-01768-0). Norton.

Small Business Systems for First-Time Users. I. R. Beaman. 180p. 1982. pap. 20.75 (ISBN 0-471-89427-3). Wiley.

Small Business Tax Advisor: Understanding the New Tax Law. Cliff Roberson. 176p. (Orig.). 1987. pap. 12.95 (ISBN 0-8306-3024-4, 30024, Liberty Hse). Tab Bks.

Small Business: Theory & Policy. Ed. by Cyril Levicki. 152p. (Orig.). 1984. pap. 12.00 (ISBN 0-7099-3327-4, Pub. by Croom Helm Ltd). Routledge Chapman & Hall.

Small Business U. S. A. Small Companies' Role in Sparking America's Economic Transformation. Steven Solomon. 368p. 1986. 19.95 (ISBN 0-517-56240-5). Crown.

Small Businesses that Grow & Grow & Grow. Patricia A. Woy. LC 83-11902. 216p. 1984. pap. 8.95 (ISBN 0-932620-28-0). Betterway Pubns.

Small Busted Women Have Big Hearts. Herbert I. Kavet. 96p. 1984. pap. 3.95 (ISBN 0-8092-5353-4). Contemp Bks.

Small C Compiler: Language, Usage, Theory, & Design. James E. Hendrix. 596p. 1988. 23.95 (ISBN 0-934375-88-7); Book & disk. 38.95 (ISBN 0-934375-97-6). M & T Pub Inc.

Small C Handbook. Hendrix. (Illus.). 1984. pap. 19.95 (ISBN 0-8359-7012-4, Reston). P-H.

Small Canvas: An Introduction to Dreiser's Short Stories. Joseph Griffin. LC 83-49347. 176p. 1985. 24.50 (ISBN 0-8386-3217-3). Fairleigh Dickinson.

Small Carrier Safety Program. 14p. 1982. pap. text ed. 8.00 (ISBN 0-88711-012-6). Am Trucking Assns.

Small Cartoon. Barbara Milton. (Fiction Book Award Winner Ser.). 52p. (Orig.). 1983. pap. 5.95 (ISBN 0-912527-00-5). Word Beat.

Small Catechism in Contemporary English. Martin Luther. LC 15-6732. 1960. pap. 6.50 (ISBN 0-8066-0324-0, 15-6732). Augsburg.

Small Cell Lung Cancer. Ed. by F. Anthony Greco. (Clinical Oncology Monograph). (Illus.). 463p. 1981. 52.50 (ISBN 0-8089-1345-X, 791721). Grune.

Small Cell Lung Cancer. Ed. by S. Seeber. (Recent Results in Cancer Research Ser.: Vol. 97). (Illus.). 210p. 1985. 54.00 (ISBN 0-387-13798-X). Springer-Verlag.

Small Ceremonies. Connie Martin. 1987. 5.50. White Pine.

Small Change. Vassar Miller. Ed. by Joseph F. Lomax & J. Whitebird. LC 77-20728. 1977. signed ed. o.p. 15.00 (ISBN 0-685-87121-5); pap. 3.50 (ISBN 0-930324-00-5). Wings Pr.

Small Change. Francois Truffaut. LC 76-44660. (Illus.). 1977. pap. 1.95 (ISBN 0-394-17921-8, B399, BC). Grove.

Small Change. Francois Truffaut. Tr. by Anselm Hollo from Fr. (Illus.). 192p. (Orig.). 1986. pap. 6.95 (ISBN 0-936839-51-1). Applause Theatre Bk Pubs.

Small Change & Kick for Touch: Two Plays. Peter Gill. 128p. 1985. pap. 8.95 (ISBN 0-7145-2826-9, Dist. by Kampmann & Co). M Boyars Pubs.

Small Change for the Long Haul. Jonathan Greene. 64p. (Orig.). 1984. pap. 4.95 (ISBN 0-88268-009-9). Open Bk Pubns.

Small Change from Big Bucks. Bay Area Committee for Responsive Philanthropy. 1979. pap. 6.00 (ISBN 0-912078-64-2). Volcano Pr.

Small Changes. Marge Piercy. 544p. 1985. pap. 3.95 (ISBN 0-449-21083-9, Crest). Fawcett.

Small Chartist Periodicals. Ed. by William Hill et al. (Chartism, Working-Class Politics in the Industrial Revolution Ser.). 351p. 1987. lib. bdg. 55.00 (ISBN 0-8240-5589-6). Garland Pub.

Small Church Is Different. Lyle E. Schaller. LC 82-1830. 192p. (Orig.). 1982. pap. 7.95 (ISBN 0-687-38717-5). Abingdon.

Small Churches Are the Right Size. David R. Ray. LC 82-11256. 224p. (Orig.). 1982. pap. 7.95 (ISBN 0-8298-0620-2). Pilgrim NY.

Small Cities & Counties: A Guide to Managing Services. Ed. by James M. Banovetz. LC 83-26397. (Municipal Management Ser.). (Illus.). 356p. (Orig.). 1984. pap. text ed. 28.95 (ISBN 0-87326-030-9). Intl City Mgt.

Small Cities & National Development. Ed. by Om Prakash Mathur. 354p. 1982. pap. text ed. 25.00 (ISBN 0-686-46347-1, CRD149, UNCRD). UNIPUB.

Small Cities Community Development Block Grant Program: An Evaluation by the Rural America CDBG Monitoring Project. 55p. 1981. 4.95 (ISBN 0-318-16422-1). Rural America.

Small City & Regional Community: Conference Proceedings, 1986, Vol. VII. Ed. by Robert P. Wolensky & Edward J. Miller. LC 79-644450. viii, 500p. 1987. pap. text ed. 19.00 (ISBN 0-932310-08-7). U of Wis-Stevens Point.

Small City & Regional Community: Proceedings of the 1979 Conference, Vol. II. Ed. by Edward J. Miller & Robert P. Wolensky. (Orig.). 1979. pap. text ed. 16.50 (ISBN 0-932310-01-X). U of Wis-Stevens Point.

Small City & Regional Community: Proceedings of the 1981 Conference, Vol. IV. Ed. by Edward J. Miller & Robert P. Wolensky. LC 79-644450. viii, 550p. (Orig.). 1981. pap. text ed. 16.50 (ISBN 0-932310-03-6). U of Wis-Stevens Point.

Small City & Regional Community: Proceedings of the 1984 Conference, Vol. VI. Ed. by Edward J. Miller & Robert P. Wolensky. LC 79-644450. viii, 450p. (Orig.). 1985. pap. text ed. 16.50 (ISBN 0-932310-06-0). U of Wis-Stevens Point.

Small City & Regional Community: Proceedings of the 1982 Conference, Vol. V. Robert P. Wolensky & Edward J. Miller. LC 79-644450. viii, 450p. 1982. pap. text ed. 16.50 (ISBN 0-932310-04-4). U of Wis-Stevens Point.

Small City & Regional Community: Proceedings of the 1980 Conference, Vol. III. Ed. by Robert P. Wolensky & Edward J. Miller. viii, 450p. (Orig.). 1980. pap. text ed. 16.50 (ISBN 0-932310-02-8). U of Wis-Stevens Point.

Small City Energy Management: Florence, Toledo & Cannon Beach. (Research Monographs). 185p. 1986. 10.00. U OR BGR.

Small Claims. Jill Ciment. LC 86-5643. 208p. 1986. 14.95 (ISBN 1-55584-000-0). Weidenfeld.

Small Claims-Claimkit: A Self-Instructing Guide. James M. Shotwell. Ed. by James Mullin & Robert Ragoni. (Illus.). 372p. (Orig.). 1985. pap. 37.50 (ISBN 0-910531-10-2). Wolcotts.

Small Claims Court. 2nd ed. HALT Staff. (Citizens Legal Manuals Ser.). 64p. 1983. pap. text ed. write for info. (ISBN 0-910073-03-1). HALT DC.

Small Claims Court Collection in New York City: Assessing the Impact of Reform Measures. Francis G. Caro & Suzanne Weis. 66p. (Orig.). 1984. pap. 4.50 (ISBN 0-88156-036-7). Comm Serv Soc Ny.

Small Claims Court Guide for Alberta. 4th ed. Fred Zinkhofer. 122p. 1985. 7.50 (ISBN 0-88908-228-6). ISC Pr.

Small Claims Court Guide for British Columbia. 8th ed. Juhli Anten. 136p. 1983. 6.95 (ISBN 0-88908-185-9). ISC Pr.

Small Claims Court Guide for Ontario. 6th ed. Jennifer Young. 176p. 1986. 7.50 (ISBN 0-88908-356-8). ISC Pr.

Small Claims Court Guide for Washington. Donald D. Stuart. 144p. 1979. 4.50 (ISBN 0-88908-712-1). ISC Pr.

Small Claims Courts: A National Examination. 238p. 1978. pap. 3.00 (ISBN 0-89656-027-9, R-039). Natl Ctr St Courts.

Small Claims Courts: Operations & Prospects. National Center for State Courts Staff. (Research Essay Ser.). 11p. 1978. manuscript 0.66 (E-006). Natl Ctr St Courts.

Small Claims Courts: Records Management & Case Processing. 120p. 1980. pap. 2.50 (ISBN 0-89656-045-7, R-053). Natl Ctr St Courts.

Small Cloud. Ariane. LC 83-14029. (Illus.). 24p. (ps-1). 1984. 10.95 (ISBN 0-525-44085-2). Dutton.

Small Collection of Japanese Lacquer Made. James Crange. 58p. 1910. 640.00x (ISBN 0-317-69449-9, Pub. by Han-Shan Tang Ltd). State Mutual Bk.

Small Comfort: A History of the Minor Tranquilizers. Mickey C. Smith. LC 85-6320. 272p. 1985. 40.95 (ISBN 0-275-91325-2, C1325). Praeger.

Small Comforts: More Comments & Comic Pieces. Tom Bodett. 160p. 1987. 12.95 (ISBN 0-201-13417-9). Addison-Wesley.

Small Comforts: More Comments & Comic Pieces. Tom Bodett. 1988. pap. 7.95 (ISBN 0-201-13689-9). Addison-Wesley.

Small Community Fire Departments: Organization & Operations. LC 82-61905. (Illus.). 75p. 1982. pap. text ed. 9.50 (ISBN 0-686-83431-3, FSP-58). Natl Fire Prot.

Small Community: Foundation of Democratic Life. Arthur E. Morgan. LC 83-73240. 336p. 1984. pap. 10.00 (ISBN 0-910420-28-9). Comm Serv OH.

Small Community, Population & the Economic Order. rev. ed. Griscom Morgan. 1975. pap. 2.00 (ISBN 0-910420-22-X). Comm Serv OH.

Small Community Water Supplies: Technology of Small Water Supply Systems in Developing Countries. E. H. Hofkes. 488p. 1984. 44.95 (ISBN 0-471-90289-6, Pub. by Wiley-Interscience). Wiley.

Small Computer Connection: Telecommunications for the Home & Office. Neil L. Shapiro. (Illus.). 256p. 1983. pap. text ed. 19.95 (ISBN 0-07-056412-4, BYTE Bks). McGraw.

Small Computer Government Market. 310p. 1985. 1600.00 (ISBN 0-86621-340-6, A1423). Frost & Sullivan.

Small Computer Package Software Market. 400p. 1984. 1600.00 (ISBN 0-86621-145-4, A1205). Frost & Sullivan.

Small Computer Small Business. Brian Smith. 1983. pap. 9.95 (ISBN 0-86616-024-8). Greene.

Small Computer Systems & Their Applications in Construction: Conference Proceedings. 135p. 1980. 34.00 (ISBN 0-7277-0106-1, Pub. by T Telford UK). Am Soc Civil Eng.

Small Computer Systems for Solicitors, 2 Pts. C. T. Edge. 152p. (Orig.). 1983. pap. text ed. 38.50x (ISBN 0-566-03442-5). Gower Pub Co.

Small Computer Theory & Applications. D. J. Dailey. (Illus.). 448p. 1987. text ed. 27.95 (ISBN 0-07-050409-1). McGraw.

Small Computers. Fred D'Ignazio. LC 80-85049. (gr. 9 up). 1981. 10.90 (ISBN 0-531-04269-3). Watts.

Small Computers for Business & Industry. Dermot McKeone. 209p. 1979. text ed. 34.25x (ISBN 0-566-02096-3). Gower Pub Co.

Small Computers in Construction: Proceedings of a Symposium Sponsored by the Construction Division. Wayne C. Moore. 89p. 1984. 16.00x (ISBN 0-87262-400-5). Am Soc Civil Eng.

Small Computers in Libraries 1988: Buyer's Guide & Consultant Directory. Ed. by Dana Smith. (Small Computers in Libraries Ser.: Supplement). 48p. 1988. pap. text ed. 29.95 (ISBN 0-88736-242-7). Meckler Corp.

Small Concrete Dams. 50p. 1981. pap. 8.00 (ISBN 0-89312-047-2, EB002W). Portland Cement.

Small Conference. Margaret Mead & Paul Byers. 1968. text ed. 11.20x (ISBN 90-2796-049-6); pap. text ed. 13.75x (ISBN 0-686-22533-3). Mouton.

Small Countries Facing Technological Revolution. Ed. by Chris Freeman & Bengt-Ake Lundvall. 260p. 1988. 37.50 (ISBN 0-86187-978-3, Pub. by Pinter Pubs UK). Columbia U Pr.

Small Countries, Large Issues: Studies in U. S.-Latin American Asymmetries. Mark Falcoff. 126p. 1984. 19.50 (ISBN 0-8447-3562-0); pap. 9.00 (ISBN 0-8447-3563-9). Am Enterprise.

Small Country Houses of Today. Ed. by Lawrence Weaver. (Illus.). 224p. 1983. Repr. of 1911 ed. 49.50 (ISBN 0-907462-34-0). Antique Collect.

Small Craft Handling. (Illus.). 1985. pap. 0.80 (ISBN 0-916682-48-X). Outdoor Empire.

Small Craft Warnings. Tennessee Williams. LC 72-80978. 1972. 5.95 (ISBN 0-8112-0461-8, NDP348). New Directions.

Small Craft Warnings see Theatre of Tennessee Williams.

Small Cruiser Navigation. R. M. Tetley. (Illus.). 144p. 1984. 22.95 (ISBN 0-7153-8520-8). David & Charles.

Small Developing State: Studies in International Political Economy. Dennis J. Gayle. 200p. 1985. text ed. 37.95 (ISBN 0-566-05077-3). Gower Pub Co.

Small Diesel Engine Service Manual. 2nd, rev. ed. Intertec Publishing Corporation Staff. LC 86-81765. (Illus.). 288p. (Orig.). 1987. pap. 12.95 (ISBN 0-87288-238-1). Intertec Pub.

Small Differences: Irish Catholics & Irish Protestants, 1815-1922, An International Perspective. Donald H. Akenson. (Studies in the History of Religion). 256p. 1988. 29.95x (ISBN 0-7735-0636-5). McGill-Queens U Pr.

Small Drainage Structures. (Publications for Developing Countries: Compendium 3). 297p. 1978. 12.00 (ISBN 0-309-02810-8). Transport Res Bd.

Small Ecstasies. Claire M. Owens. LC 83-70658. (Inner Visions Ser.). 192p. 1983. pap. 8.95 (ISBN 0-917086-58-9). A C S Pubns Inc.

Small, Elderly Dragon. Beverly Keller. LC 83-13632. (Illus.). 144p. (gr. 5 up). 1984. 11.75 (ISBN 0-688-02553-6). Lothrop.

Small Endearments: 19th-Century Quilts for Children. Sandi Fox. (Illus.). 160p. 1985. 24.95 (ISBN 0-684-18185-1). Scribner.

Small Energy Sources: Choices That Work. Augusta Goldin. LC 87-167. (Illus.). 176p. (YA) (gr. 7 up). 1988. 17.95 (ISBN 0-15-276215-9, HJ). HarBraceJ.

Small Engine Explained. Bruce Hunter. LC 77-731128. (Orig.). 1977. wkbk. 7.00 (ISBN 0-8064-0163-X, 450); audio visual pkg. 459.00 (ISBN 0-8064-0164-8). Bergwall.

Small Engine Mechanics. 2nd ed. William H. Crouse & Donald L. Anglin. LC 79-4658. (Illus.). 1979. pap. 26.95 (ISBN 0-07-014795-7). McGraw.

Small Engine Mechanics. 3rd ed. William H. Crouse & Donald L. Anglin. 304p. 1986. pap. text ed. 26.95 (ISBN 0-07-014803-1). McGraw.

Small Engine Repair. Jack Rudman. (Occupational Competency Examination Ser.: OCE-32). (Cloth bdg. avail. on request). pap. 13.95 (ISBN 0-8373-5732-2). Natl Learning.

Small Engines. LC 82-10304. (Home Repair & Improvement). (gr. 7 up). lib. bdg. 15.94 (ISBN 0-8094-3511-X, Pub. by Time-Life). Silver.

Small Engines. (Home Repair & Improvement). 1983. 11.95 (ISBN 0-8094-3510-1). Time Life.

Small Engines: Operation & Service. J. Webster. (Illus.). 278p. 1981. 16.48 (ISBN 0-8269-0004-6). Am Technical.

Small Engines: Operation, Maintenance & Repair. Aavim. (Illus.). 288p. (Orig.). 1987. 24.95 (2813P); pap. 14.95 (ISBN 0-8306-2813-4). TAB Bks.

Small Engines Service Manual. 15th ed. Intertec Publishing Corp. LC 86-80559. (Illus.). 368p. (Orig.). 1986. pap. 14.95 (ISBN 0-87288-223-3, SES-15). Intertec Pub.

Small Enterprise & Oligopoly. Harold G. Vatter. Ed. by Stuart Bruchey & Vincent P. Carosso. LC 78-18152. (Small Business Enterprise in America Ser.). 1979. Repr. of 1955 ed. lib. bdg. 12.00x (ISBN 0-405-11508-3). Ayer Co Pubs.

Small Enterprise Development: Economic Issues from African Experience. John M. Page, Jr. & William F. Steel. (Technical Paper: No. 26). 60p. 1984. 5.00 (ISBN 0-8213-0408-9, BK 0408). World Bank.

Small Enterprise Development: Policies & Programmes. rev. 2nd ed. Ed. by Philip A. Neck & Robert E. Nelson. (Management Development Ser.: No. 14). v, 282p. (Orig.). 1987. pap. 24.50 (ISBN 92-2-105699-6). Intl Labour office.

Small Enterprise Development: Policies & Programs. 2nd, rev. ed. Ed. by Philip A. Neck & Robert E. Nelson. (Management Development Ser.: No. 14). 282p. (Orig.). 1987. pap. text ed. 24.50 (ISBN 92-2-105699-6, ILO644, ILO). UNIPUB.

Small Enterprises & Development Policy in the Philippines: A Case Study. Dennis Anderson & Farida Khambata. (Working Paper: No. 468). 239p. 1981. 10.00 (ISBN 0-686-36178-4, WP-0468). World Bank.

Small Enterprises in African Development: A Survey. John M. Page, Jr. (Working Paper: No. 363). ii, 363p. 1981. 10.00 (ISBN 0-686-36186-5, WP-0363). World Bank.

Small Enterprises in Developing Countries: Case Studies & Conclusions. Malcolm Harper & Thiam T. Soon. (Illus.). 115p. (Orig.). 1979. pap. 11.50x (ISBN 0-903031-62-0, Pub. by Intermediate Tech England). Intermediate Tech.

Small Entrepreneurial Firm. G. C. Reid & L. R. Jacobsen. (David Hume Papers). 100p. 1988. pap. write for info. (ISBN 0-08-036577-9, AUP). Pergamon.

Small Escapes under the Sun. John Sinor. 1981. pap. 4.95 (ISBN 0-935572-10-4). Alive Pubns.

Small Faces. Gary Soto. LC 84-72227. 120p. (Orig.). 1986. pap. 8.00 (ISBN 0-934770-49-2). Arte Publico.

Small Factories & Economic Development. Martin Perry. 170p. 1986. text ed. 48.50 (ISBN 0-566-05208-3, Pub. by Gower Pub England). Gower Pub Co.

TITLE INDEX SMALL PAIN.

Small Family Business. Alan Ayckbourn. 90p. (Orig.). 1987. pap. 6.95 (ISBN 0-571-14970-7). Faber & Faber.
Small Family with Rooster. Daniel A. Rose. 224p. 1988. 15.95 (ISBN 0-312-01826-6). St Martin.
Small Farm Development: Understanding & Improving Farming Systems in the Humid Tropics. Richard R. Harwood. LC 79-13169. (IAOS Development-Oriented Literature Ser.). 1979. lib. bdg. 26.50x (ISBN 0-89158-669-5); pap. 14.95x (ISBN 0-89158-699-7). Westview.
Small Farm Grain Storage, Vol. I. Carl Lindblad & Laurel Druben. (Illus.). 204p. 1976. write for info (ISBN 0-86619-052-X). Vols Tech Asst.
Small Farm Grain Storage, Vol. II. Carl Lindblad & Laurel Druben. (Illus.). 170p. 1976. write for info (ISBN 0-86619-053-8). Vols Tech Asst.
Small Farm Grain Storage, Vol. III. Carl Lindblad & Laurel Druben. (Illus.). 148p. 1976. write for info (ISBN 0-86619-054-6). Vols Tech Asst.
Small Farm Grain Storage. Carl Lindblad & Laurel Druben. (Illus.). 331p. 1976. Spanish. write for info. Vols Tech Asst.
Small Farm Implements. H. J. Hopfan & E. Biesalski. (Agricultural Development Papers: No. 32). 79p. (2nd Printing 1978). 1953. pap. 7.50 (ISBN 92-5-100452-8, F1465, FAO). UNIPUB.
Small Farm in Maine. Terry Silber. 1989. pap. 6.95 (ISBN 0-385-26055-5, Anchor Pr). Doubleday.
Small Farm in Maine. Terry Silher. 224p. 1988. 17.95 (ISBN 0-395-37911-3). HM.
Small Farm Mechanization for Developing Countries. Peter Crossley & John Kilgour. LC 83-5935. 253p. 1983. 62.95 (ISBN 0-471-90101-6, Pub. by Wiley-Interscience). Wiley.
Small Farmer Credit: Cultural & Social Factors Affecting Small Farmer Participation in Formal Credit Programs & the Political Economy of Distributing Agricultural Credit & Benefits. Cynthia Gillette et al. (Occasional Paper Ser.: No. 3). 57p. (Orig.). 1973. pap. text ed. 4.85 (ISBN 0-86731-016-2). Cornell CIS RDC.
Small Farmers & Institutional Credit India. S. Gunasekaran. 1985. 16.00x (ISBN 0-317-40616-7, Pub. by Ashish India). South Asia Bks.
Small Farmer's Guide to Raising Livestock & Poultry. Ed. by Alistair Fraser & Katie Thear. (Illus.). 240p. 1981. 14.95 (ISBN 0-668-04687-2). Arco.
Small Farms--Livestock Buildings & Equipment. MWPS Engineers & Northeast Regional Agricultural Engineering Service. LC 83-23697. (Illus.). 1984. pap. 6.00 (ISBN 0-89373-060-2, NRAES-6-MWPS-27). Midwest Plan Serv.
Small Farms Appropriate Technology: Research, Production, Hardware, & Animal Traction. Oleen Hess. 175p. 1985. 20.00 (ISBN 0-318-18269-6). Brandon-Lane Pr.
Small Farms: Livestock Buildings & Equipment. G. D. Wells et al. (Illus.). 100p. 6.00 (ISBN 0-935817-02-6, NRAES-6). NE Agri Engineer.
Small Farms: Persistence with Legitimation. Alessandro Bonanno. (Rural Studies). 224p. 1987. pap. 27.50 (ISBN 0-8133-7341-7). Westview.
Small Fatigue Cracks. Ed. by R. O. Ritchie & J. Lankford. (Illus.). 666p. 1986. 99.00 (ISBN 0-87339-052-0). Metal Soc.
Small Felonies: Fifty Mystery Short Stories. Bill Pronzini. 208p. 1988. 15.95 (ISBN 0-312-02283-2, Pub. by Thomas Dunne Bks). St Martin.
Small Field. Huw Jones. 42p. 1985. 19.00x (ISBN 0-86383-194-X, Pub. by Gomer Pr). State Mutual Bk.
Small Finds from Tell Basta in the Collection of F. G. Hilton Price. Charles C. Van Siclen, III. 140p. 1985. pap. text ed. 25.00x (ISBN 0-933175-03-5). Van Siclen Bks.
Small Firm: An International Survey. Ed. by David J. Storey. LC 83-40075. 274p. 1983. 32.50 (ISBN 0-312-72980-4). St Martin.
Small Firms Growth & Development. Scott et al. 1986. text ed. 41.95 (ISBN 0-566-00811-4, Pub. by Gower Pub England). Gower Pub Co.
Small Firms in Regional Economic Development: Britain, Ireland & the United States. Ed. by D. J. Storey. 256p. 1985. 44.50 (ISBN 0-521-30198-X). Cambridge U Pr.
Small Firms in Singapore. Chew Soon Beng. (Illus.). 280p. 1988. pap. 21.95 (ISBN 0-19-588883-9). Oxford U Pr.
Small Fleet Guide. 2nd ed. LC 80-85327. 96p. 1981. pap. 12.30 (ISBN 0-87912-055-X, 221.20). Natl Safety Coun.
Small Folk: A Celebration of Childhood in America. Sandra Brant & Elissa Cullman. (Illus.). 192p. 1981. 29.95 (ISBN 0-525-93131-7). Dutton.
Small Format Television Production. Compesi & Sherriffs. 1985. 37.00 (ISBN 0-205-08455-9, 488455). Allyn.
Small Fractional Parts of Polynomials. Wolfgang M. Schmidt. LC 77-8028. (Conference Board of the Mathematical Sciences Ser.: No. 32). 41p. 1977. 15.00 (ISBN 0-8218-1682-9, CBMS 32). Am Math.
Small Fragment Set Manual: Technique Recommended by the ASIF Group. 2nd ed. U. Heim & K. M. Pfeiffer. Tr. by R. L. Batten. (Illus.). 400p. 1982. 100.00 (ISBN 0-387-11143-3). Springer-Verlag.
Small Fur. Irina Korschunow. Tr. by James Skofield from Ger. LC 87-45289. (Illus.). 80p. (gr. 1-4). 1988. 11.70i (ISBN 0-06-023247-1); PLB 12.89 (ISBN 0-06-023248-X). HarpJ.
Small Futures: Children, Inequality & the Limits of Liberal Reform. Carnegie Council on Children Staff & Richard DeLone. LC 77-92536. 288p. 1979. 12.95 (ISBN 0-15-183128-9). HarBraceJ.
Small Garden, Bitter Weed: Struggle & Change in Jamaica. George Beckford & Michael Witter. 192p. 1982. 27.50x (ISBN 0-86232-003-8, Pub. by Zed Pr England); pap. 9.95x (ISBN 0-86232-008-9, Pub. by Zed Pr England). Humanities.
Small Garden in the City. Madge Garland. LC 74-76646. (Illus.). 136p. 1974. 12.50 (ISBN 0-8076-0752-5). Braziller.
Small Garden Planner. Graham Rose. (Illus.). 168p. 1988. 19.95 (ISBN 0-671-64709-1). S&S.
Small Gardens for Small Spaces. 1977. 3.95 (ISBN 0-686-22911-8). Bklyn Botanic.
Small Gas Engines. James A. Gray & Richard W. Barrow. 357p. 1976. pap. text ed. 26.00 (ISBN 0-13-813113-9). P-H.
Small Gas Engines. 2nd ed. James A. Gray & Richard W. Barrow. (Illus.). 272p. 1988. text ed. 25.00 (ISBN 0-13-813171-6). P-H.
Small Gas Engines. rev. ed. Alfred C. Roth & Ronald J. Baird. LC 81-6209. (Illus.). 264p. 1985. text ed. 15.60 (ISBN 0-87006-498-3); wkbk 4.60 (ISBN 0-87006-499-1). Goodheart.
Small Gas Engines: How to Repair & Maintain Them. Paul Weissler. LC 87-10136. (Illus.). 288p. (Orig.). 1987. pap. 7.95 (ISBN 0-8069-6588-6). Sterling.
Small Gasoline Engines. 16.95 (ISBN 0-672-23414-9, Audel). Macmillan.
Small Gasoline Engines. 4th ed. George Stephenson. (Illus.). 288p. 1984. pap. text ed. 17.95 (ISBN 0-8273-2242-9); instr's. guide 5.00 (ISBN 0-8273-2243-7). Delmar.
Small Gasoline Engines, Operation & Maintenance. rev. ed. Harry Hoerner & W. Forrest Bear. (Illus.). 136p. 1984. pap. 7.00x (ISBN 0-913163-17-1). Hobar Pubns.
Small Gasoline Engines Student's Workbook. 2nd ed. K. L. MacDonald. 1973. pap. 4.24 scp (ISBN 0-672-97632-3). Bobbs.
Small Georgian Houses in England & Virginia: Origins & Development Through the 1750s. Daniel Reiff. LC 83-40521. (Illus.). 352p. 1986. 65.00x (ISBN 0-87413-254-1). U Delaware Pr.
Small Giant: Sweden Enters the Industrial Era. Carl G. Gustavson. LC 85-25922. 364p. 1986. text ed. 23.95x (ISBN 0-8214-0825-9). Ohio U Pr.
Small Golden Key to the Treasure of the Various Essential Necessities of General & Extraordinary Buddhist Dharma. rev. ed. Thinley Norbu. LC 84-29724. 111p. 1985. pap. 12.00 (ISBN 0-9607000-2-1). Jewel Pub Hse.
Small Golden Shrine from the Tomb of Tutankhamen. M. Eaton-Krauss & E. Graefe. (Illus.). 88p. 1985. text ed. 38.50x (ISBN 0-900416-43-2, Pub. by Aris & Phillips UK). Humanities.
Small Group. Howard L. Nixon. LC 78-13207. (P-H Series in Sociology). (Illus.). 1979. write for info. ref. ed. (ISBN 0-13-814244-0). P-H.
Small Group. 2nd ed. Michael S. Olmsted & A. Paul Hare. 1978. pap. text ed. write for info (ISBN 0-394-32123-5, RanC). Random.
Small Group Communication: A Reader. 5th ed. Robert S. Cathcart & Larry Samovar. 624p. 1988. pap. text ed. write for info. (ISBN 0-697-05187-0). Wm C Brown.
Small Group Communication in Organizations. H. Lloyd Goodall, Jr. 360p. 1984. pap. text ed. write for info. (ISBN 0-697-00233-0). Wm C Brown.
Small-Group Cultures. Tom McFeat. 1974. 29.00 (ISBN 0-08-017073-0); pap. text ed. 16.00 (ISBN 0-08-017770-0). Pergamon.
Small Group Decision Making: Communication & the Group Process. 2nd ed. B. Aubrey Fisher. Ed. by Richard R. Wright. (Illus.). 1979. text ed. 33.95 (ISBN 0-07-021091-8). McGraw.
Small Group Evangelism. rev. ed. Richard Peace. 225p. 1983. pap. 6.95 (ISBN 0-87784-329-5). Inter-Varsity.
Small Group Leaders Handbook. Ron Nicholas. LC 82-68. 156p. (Orig.). 1981. pap. 6.95 (ISBN 0-87784-372-4). Inter-Varsity.
Small Group Problem Solving: An Aid to Organizational Effectiveness. L. Nathanson et al. 1981. pap. write for info. (ISBN 0-201-05203-2). Addison-Wesley.
Small Groups & Foreign Policy Decision-Making. Dean A. Minix. LC 80-8128. (Illus.). 262p. (Orig.). 1982. lib. bdg. 30.75 (ISBN 0-8191-2372-2). U Pr of Amer.
Small Groups & Political Rituals in China. Martin K. Whyte. (Center for Chinese Studies: No. 4). 1974. 40.00x (ISBN 0-520-02499-0); pap. 11.95x (ISBN 0-520-04941-1). U of Cal Pr.
Small Groups & Social Interaction, Vol. 1. Ed. by Herbert H. Blumberg et al. 461p. 1983. 117.00 (ISBN 0-471-10242-3, Pub. by Wiley-Interscience). Wiley.
Small Groups & Social Interactions, Vol. 2. Ed. by Herbert H. Blumberg & A. Paul Hare. 593p. 1983. 137.00 (ISBN 0-471-90091-5, Pub. by Wiley-Interscience). Wiley.
Small Groups: Timber to Build up God's House. Bob Couchman & Win Couchman. LC 82-798. (Carpenter Studyguide). 83p. 1982. pap. 2.95 (ISBN 0-87788-097-2). Shaw Pubs.
Small High School. John Rufi. LC 70-177214. (Columbia University. Teachers College. Contributions to Education: No. 236). Repr. of 1926 ed. 22.50 (ISBN 0-404-55236-6). AMS Pr.
Small Home Plans. 2nd ed. Ed. by L. F. Garlinghouse Co., Staff. (Illus.). 112p. 1986. pap. 2.95 (ISBN 0-938708-16-3). L F Garlinghouse Co.
Small Home Repairs Made Easy. Robert L. Berko. LC 85-71817. write for info. Consumer Ed Res.
Small Homes for Pleasant Living. 35th ed. W. D. Farmer. (Illus.). 40p. (Orig.). 1980. pap. 2.50 (ISBN 0-931518-12-1). W D Farmer.
Small Hotels of California: A Selective Guide to the Best of California's Most Charming Small Hotels & Inns. Bill Gleeson. LC 83-27306. (Illus.). 128p. (Orig.). 1984. pap. 7.95 (ISBN 0-87701-293-8). Chronicle Bks.
Small Hours of the Morning. Margaret Yorke. 224p. 1988. pap. 3.95 (ISBN 0-14-010249-3). Penguin.
Small House: An Artful Guide to Affordable Residential Design. Duo Dickinson. LC 85-23963. (Building Types Ser.). (Illus.). 196p. 1986. text ed. 34.95 (ISBN 0-07-016818-0). McGraw.
Small House at Allington. Anthony Trollope. 1976. Repr. of 1909 ed. 14.95x (ISBN 0-460-00361-5, Evman). Biblio Dist.
Small House at Allington. Anthony Trollope. Ed. by James Kincaid. (World's Classics Paperback Ser.). 1980. pap. 7.95 (ISBN 0-19-281552-0). Oxford U Pr.
Small House in the Sun. Samuel Chamberlain. 1936. pap. 14.95 (ISBN 0-8038-9281-0). Hastings.
Small House in the Sun: The Visage of Rural New England in Photographs. Samuel Chamberlain. 1988. 24.95 (ISBN 0-8038-6704-2). Hastings.
Small Household Appliances. (Illus.). 345p. 1987. spiral bdg. 795.00 (ISBN 0-317-65740-2). Busn Trend.
Small Houses. Jeffrey Weiss & Lila Gault. (Illus.). 96p. 1980. pap. 7.95 (ISBN 0-446-97346-7). Warner Bks.
Small Hydro Power Fluid Machinery. Ed. by D. R. Webb & C. N. Papadakis. 1982. 40.00 (H00233). ASME.
Small Hydro-Power Fluid Machinery. Ed. by D. R. Webb & C. N. Papadakis. 116p. 1980. 18.00 (ISBN 0-317-33613-4, G00180); write for info. (ISBN 0-317-33614-2). ASME.
Small Hydro Power in China: A Survey. Hangzhou Regional Centre (Asia Pacific) for Small Hydro Power. (Illus.). 107p. (Orig.). 1985. pap. 12.50x (ISBN 0-946688-46-X, Pub. by Intermediate Tech England). Intermediate Tech.
Small Hydroelectric Projects for Rural Development: Planning & Management. Ed. by Louis J. Goodman & Ralph N. Love. (Pergamon Policy Studies). 250p. 1981. 30.00 (ISBN 0-08-025966-9). Pergamon.
Small Industry Bulletin for Asia & the Pacific, No. 19. 138p. 15.00 (ISBN 92-1-119222-6, E.84.II.F.17). UN.
Small Industry Bulletin for Asia & the Pacific, No. 20. 17.00 (ISBN 92-1-119411-3, E.85.II.F.22). UN.
Small Industry in Asia's Export-Oriented Growth. Edward K. Chen. 258p. 1986. pap. 23.00 (ISBN 0-317-59556-3, U-APO195, Pub. by APO). UNIPUB-Kraus Intl.
Small Industry in Developing Countries: Some Issues. Dennis Anderson. LC 82-11130. (World Bank Staff Working Papers: No. 518). 57p. (Orig.). 1982. pap. 5.00 (ISBN 0-8213-0006-7, WP0518). World Bank.
Small Industry in the Eighties. Ram K. Vepa. 450p. 1983. text ed. 35.00x (ISBN 0-7069-1964-5, Pub. by Vikas India). Advent NY.
Small Inventions That Make a Big Difference. Ed. by Donald J. Crump. LC 83-23770. (Books for World Explorers, Series 5: No. 2). 104p. (gr. 3-8). 1984. 6.95 (ISBN 0-87044-498-0); PLB 8.50 (ISBN 0-87044-503-0). Natl Geog.
Small Is Beautiful: Economics As If People Mattered. E. F. Schumacher. 304p. 1975. pap. 5.95 (ISBN 0-06-080352-5, P 352, PL). Har-Row.
Small Is Dangerous: Micro States in a Macro World. Sheila Harden. LC 85-2309. 212p. 1985. 25.00 (ISBN 0-312-72981-2). St Martin.
Small Is Politics: Organizational Alternatives in India's Rural Development. 1977. 5.00 (ISBN 0-471-63956-7). Wiley.
Small Is Possible. George McRobie. LC 79-2634. 256p. 1981. 15.00i (ISBN 0-06-013041-5, HarpT). Har-Row.
Small Island Economics: Structure & Performance in the English-Speaking Caribbean Since 1970. DeLisle Worrell. LC 87-12495. 303p. 1987. lib. bdg. 49.95 (ISBN 0-275-92795-4, C2795). Praeger.
Small Junior High School. F. T. Spaulding. (Harvard Studies in Education: Vol. 9). Repr. of 1927 ed. 19.00 (ISBN 0-384-56950-1). Johnson Repr.
Small Kitchens: Making Every Inch Count. Robin Murrell. (Illus.). 168p. 1987. 19.95 (ISBN 0-671-63354-6). S&S.
Small Land. Winifred Rawlins. 1966. 3.00 (ISBN 0-8233-0088-9). Golden Quill.
Small Law Firm Library: Law Office Management & Economics Section. 7.50 (ISBN 0-317-62696-5). DC Bar Assn.
Small Library Cataloging. 2nd ed. Herbert H. Hoffman. LC 86-15504. (Illus.). 226p. 1986. 18.50 (ISBN 0-8108-1910-4). Scarecrow.
Small Library in Family Planning. 4th ed. Compiled by Gloria A. Roberts. 36p. (Orig.). 1988. pap. text ed. 3.00 (ISBN 0-934586-70-5). Plan Parent.
Small Light in the Darkness. Jack Weyland. LC 87-22281. 202p. (YA) (gr. 8-12). 1987. 9.95 (ISBN 0-87579-105-0). Deseret Bk.
Small Local Government & Information Management. Donald F. Morris. 17p. (Orig.). 1984. pap. 2.00 (ISBN 1-55719-078-X). U NE Ctr Applied Urban Rsch.
Small Log Sawmills: Profitable Product Selection, Process Design & Operation. Ed. by Ed M. Williston. LC 80-84893. (Forest Industries Bk.). (Illus.). 368p. 1981. 52.50 (ISBN 0-87930-091-4); pap. 42.50. Miller Freeman.
Small Lots - Big Savings. David Jensen Associates. (Illus.). 25p. (Orig.). 1986. pap. 8.00 (ISBN 0-86718-263-6). Nat Assn H Build.
Small Mac: Users Manual. James E. Hendrix. 100p. 1985. software documentation manual 9.95 (ISBN 0-934375-05-4). M & T Pub Inc.
Small Magellanic Cloud. Paul W. Hodge & Frances W. Wright. LC 76-49159. (Illus.). 80p. 1978. 65.00x (ISBN 0-295-95387-X). U of Wash Pr.
Small Mammals. Ed. by F. B. Golley et al. LC 74-25658. (International Biological Programme Ser.: No. 5). (Illus.). 448p. 1975. 90.00 (ISBN 0-521-20601-4). Cambridge U Pr.
Small Mammals Are Where You Find Them. Helen D. Tee-Van. (Illus.). (gr. 3-7). 1967. lib. bdg. 5.99 (ISBN 0-394-91643-3). Knopf.
Small Manufacturing & Process Industry Seminar Proceedings. LC 85-72347. 460p. 1985. pap. 16.00 (ISBN 0-935406-71-9). Am Prod & Inventory.
Small Manufacturing Enterprises: A Comparative Study of India & Other Economies. Ian M. Little et al. (World Bank Publication). 374p. 1988. 35.00 (ISBN 0-19-520619-3). Oxford U Pr.
Small Manufacturing Reprints. LC 85-47687. 114p. 1985. 13.00 (ISBN 0-935406-64-6). Am Prod & Inventory.
Small Matter of a Horse: The Life of "Nongoloza" Mathebula, 1867-1948. Charles Van Onselen. 72p. 1984. pap. text ed. 8.95x (ISBN 0-86975-239-1, Pub. by Ravan Pr). Ohio U Pr.
Small Meeting Planner. 2nd ed. Leslie E. This. LC 78-72999. 254p. 1979. 19.00x (ISBN 0-87201-806-7). Gulf Pub.
Small Mercies. Elizabeth Weber. (Poetry Ser.). 57p. (Orig.). 1983. Hardbound, sign & Ltd. number ed. of 50 copies 15.00. pap. 5.00 (ISBN 0-937669-10-5) (ISBN 0-937669-09-1). Owl Creek Pr.
Small Michell (Banki) Turbine: A Construction Manual. 58p. 1985. prfct. bnd. 7.65 (ISBN 0-86619-066-X, 11045-BK) (ISBN 0-86619-244-1). Vols Tech Asst.
Small Mines Development in Precious Metals. Intro. by Ta M. Li & Thomas M. Plouf. LC 87-62034. (Illus.). 248p. 1987. pap. 43.50x (ISBN 0-87335-069-3). Soc Mining Eng.
Small Miracles. Warner Troyer & Glenys Moss. LC 86-32832. (Illus.). 204p. Date not set. cancelled (ISBN 0-385-25107-6). Doubleday.
Small Motor Cruises. Nigel Warren. 1979. 22.95 (ISBN 0-8464-0064-2). Beekman Pubs.
Small Motors & Transformers: Design & Construction. Ed. by Edward Molloy. LC 54-32875. pap. 44.00 (ISBN 0-317-10064-5, 2051335). Bks Demand UMI.
Small Museums of the French Riviera. Eloise Danto. (Illus.). 112p. (Orig.). 1985. pap. 9.95 (ISBN 0-9615128-0-6). Eldan Pr.
Small Nations, Giant Firms. Louis W. Goodman. LC 87-42. 181p. 1987. 37.50 (ISBN 0-8419-0996-2); pap. 19.75 (ISBN 0-8419-1112-6). Holmes & Meier.
Small Nuclear Forces & U. S. Security Policy: Threats & Potential Conflicts in the Middle East & South Asia. Ed. by Rodney W. Jones. LC 83-47790. 304p. 1984. 30.00x (ISBN 0-669-06736-9). Lexington Bks.
Small Obligation & Other Stories of Hilo. Susan Nunes. LC 82-72555. 88p. (Orig.). 1982. pap. 5.00 (ISBN 0-910043-00-0). Bamboo Ridge Pr.
Small Office Building Handbook: Design for Reducing First Costs & Utility Costs. Burt, Hill, Kosar, Rittleman Associates Staff. (Illus.). 400p. 1984. 45.95 (ISBN 0-442-21126-0). Van Nos Reinhold.
Small Offset: Preparation & Press. Les Crowhurst & Peter Burton. (Illus.). 172p. 1982. 24.00 (ISBN 0-88362-044-8, 1517). Graphic Arts Tech Found.
Small Offshore Yacht. Tim Thorton. (Illus.). 224p. 1987. 29.95 (ISBN 0-229-11794-5, Pub. by Adlard Coles). Sheridan.
Small Packages. Ernst H. Nussmann. Ed. by Michael L. Sherer. (Orig.). 1987. pap. 6.95 (ISBN 1-55673-027-6, 8812). CSS of Ohio.
Small Pain. rev. ed. Flyin' Thunda Cloud & S. Diane Bogus. 35p. pap. text ed. cancelled (ISBN 0-934172-17-X). WIM Pubns.

Small Paintings of the Masters, 3 vols. Egbert Haverkamp-Begemann et al. Ed. by Leslie Shore. LC 80-51389. (Illus.). 270p. 1980. Set. 3600.00 (ISBN 0-934516-34-0). Vol. 1 (ISBN 0-934516-35-9). Vol. 2 (ISBN 0-934516-36-7). Vol. 3 (ISBN 0-934516-37-5). Shorewood Fine Art.
Small Parrots: Parrakeets. David Seth-Smith. (Illus.). 1979. 14.95 (ISBN 0-87666-978-X, H-1017). TFH Pubns.
Small Part of Time: Essays on Literature, Art & Travel-Henry James, H. G. Wells, Edith Wharton, Max Beerbohm, D. H. Lawrence. Michael Swan. 1957. Repr. 20.00 (ISBN 0-8274-3441-3). R West.
Small Patchwork Projects. Barbara Brondolo. (Illus.). 64p. (Orig.). 1981. pap. 3.95 (ISBN 0-486-24030-4). Dover.
Small Patriot. Betty McPherson. (Pocket Tales Ser.: Bk. 2). (Illus.). 32p. (ps-1). 1987. 8.75 (ISBN 0-918823-01-3). Boyce-Pubns.
Small Pelagic Fishes & Fisheries in African Inland Waters. B. E. Marshall. (CIFA Technical Papers: No. 14). 25p. (Eng. & Fr.). 1985. pap. 7.50 (ISBN 92-5-002152-6, F2716, FAO). UNIPUB.
Small People: How Children Develop & What You Can Do About It. Jean Mercer. LC 78-27345. 165p. 1979. 17.95x (ISBN 0-88229-318-4). Nelson-Hall.
Small People in Colorado Places. Susan Kaye. LC 86-3256. (Illus.). 150p. 1988. pap. 8.95 (ISBN 0-87108-702-2). Pruett.
Small Personal Voice: Essays, Reviews, Interviews. Doris Lessing. 1975. pap. 3.95 (ISBN 0-394-71685-X, Vin). Random.
Small Pets. Hill. Ed. by Barbara Cork. (Illus.). (gr. 3-6). 6.95 (ISBN 0-86020-649-1, 15121); pap. 2.95 (ISBN 0-86020-648-3, 15122); lib. bdg. 11.96 (ISBN 0-88110-087-0). EDC.
Small Piece of Humanity. Pauline L. Browne. 1988. 12.95 (ISBN 0-533-07816-4). Vantage.
Small Pig. Arnold Lobel. LC 69-10213. (Harper I Can Read Bks.). (Illus.). 64p. (gr. k-3). 1969. PLB 9.89 (ISBN 0-06-023932-8). HarpJ.
Small Pig. Arnold Lobel. LC 69-10213. (Trophy I Can Read Bk.). (Illus.). 64p. (gr. k-3). 1988. pap. 3.50 (ISBN 0-06-444120-2, Trophy). HarpJ.
Small Place. Jamaica Kincaid. 96p. 1988. 13.95 (ISBN 0-374-26638-7). FS&G.
Small Place in the Country. Toni Mackenzie. 240p. 1981. pap. 6.95x (ISBN 0-00-216408-6, Pub. by W Collins Australia). Intl Spec Bk.
Small Plays for Special Days. Sue Alexander. LC 76-28424. (Illus.). 64p. (gr. 2-4). 1976. 8.95 (ISBN 0-395-28761-8, Clarion). HM.
Small Plays for Special Days. Sue Alexander. LC 76-28424. (Illus.). 64p. (ps-1). 1988. 4.95 (ISBN 0-89919-798-1, Pub. by Clarion). Ticknor & Fields.
Small Plays for You & a Friend. Sue Alexander. LC 74-4019. (Illus.). 48p. (gr. 1-4). 1974. 6.95 (ISBN 0-395-28762-6, Clarion). HM.
Small Pleasure. C. B. Christiansen. LC 87-19313. 144p. (gr. 7 up). 1988. 12.95 (ISBN 0-689-31369-1, Atheneum Childrens Bks). Macmillan.
Small Poems. Valerie Worth. LC 72-81488. (Illus.). 48p. (gr. 3 up). 1972. 8.95 (ISBN 0-374-37072-9). FS&G.
Small Poems Again. Valerie Worth. LC 85-47513. (Illus.). 48p. (gr. 3 up). 1985. 8.95 (ISBN 0-374-37074-5). FS&G.
Small Potatoes & the Birthday Party. Harriet Ziefert. 64p. (gr. k-6). 1985. pap. 2.25 (ISBN 0-440-48035-3, YB). Dell.
Small Potatoes & the Magic Show. Harriet Ziefert. (Small Potatoes Club Ser.: No. 2). (Illus., Orig.). (gr. k-6). 1984. pap. 2.25 (ISBN 0-440-48114-7, YB). Dell.
Small Potatoes & the Sleep-Over. Harriet Ziefert. (Illus., Orig.). (gr. k-6). 1985. pap. 2.50 (ISBN 0-440-48036-1, YB). Dell.
Small Potatoes & the Snowball Fight. Harriet Ziefert. (Orig.). (gr. k-3). 1986. pap. 2.50 (ISBN 0-440-48115-5, YB). Dell.
Small Potatoes Busy Beach Day. Harriet Ziefert. (gr. k-3). 1986. pap. 2.50 (ISBN 0-440-48045-0, YB). Dell.
Small Potatoes Club & the Small Potatoes & the Magic Show. Harriet Ziefert. (Small Potatoes Club Ser.: No. 1). (Illus.). 64p. (Orig.). (gr. k-6). 1984. pap. 2.50 (ISBN 0-440-48034-5, YB). Dell.
Small Prayers for Small Children. Paul A. Schreivogel. LC 76-135226. (Illus.). 32p. (gr. k-4). 1980. pap. 4.95 (ISBN 0-8066-1804-3, 10-5836). Augsburg.
Small Press Guide to Computers in Publishing. Small Press Magazine Staff. Ed. by Steve Roth. 1987. pap. text ed. 14.95x (ISBN 0-88736-164-1). Meckler Corp.
Small Press Publishers Workbook. Ed. by Bibliotheca Press Research Division Staff. 50p. 1983. wkbk. 8.95 (ISBN 0-939476-77-0, Pub. by Biblio Pr GA). Prosperity & Profits.
Small Press Publishing. Ed. by Frederick M. Finney. LC 78-50210. 1978. 12.00 (ISBN 0-89421-015-7). Challenge Pr.
Small Press Record of Books. 4th ed. 1975. pap. 4.50 (ISBN 0-913218-40-5). Dustbooks.
Small Press Record of Books in Print. 6th ed. Len Fulton. 1977. pap. 8.95 (ISBN 0-913218-03-0). Dustbooks.
Small Press Record of Books in Print. 14th ed. Len Fulton & Ellen Ferber. 1250p. 1985. 29.95 (ISBN 0-913218-07-3). Dustbooks.
Small Press Record of Books in Print. 15th ed. Ed. by Len Fulton. 1100p. 1986. 31.95 (ISBN 0-913218-59-6). Dustbooks.
Small Press Record of Books in Print. 11th ed. Ed. by Len Fulton & Ellen Ferber. 800p. 1982. lib. bdg. 23.95 (ISBN 0-913218-99-5). Dustbooks.
Small Press Record of Books in Print. 9th ed. Ed. by Len Fulton & Ellen Ferber. (Dustbooks Small Press Info. Library). 680p. 1980. 17.95 (ISBN 0-913218-95-2). Dustbooks.
Small Press Record of Books in Print. 8th ed. Ed. by Len Fulton & Ellen Ferber. 1979. 11.95 (ISBN 0-913218-89-8). Dustbooks.
Small Press Record of Books in Print. 12th ed. Ed. by Len Fulton & Ellen Ferber. 950p. 1983. 25.95 (ISBN 0-913218-61-8). Dustbooks.
Small Press Record of Books in Print. 13th ed. Ed. by Len Fulton & Ellen Ferber. 1000p. 1984. 27.95 (ISBN 0-913218-56-1). Dustbooks.
Small Press Record of Books in Print, 1978. 7th ed. Ed. by Len Fulton. (Small Press Information Library). 1978. 10.95 (ISBN 0-913218-60-X). Dustbooks.
Small Press Record of Books in Print, 1987-88. 16th ed. Ed. by Len Fulton. 1200p. 1987. 33.95 (ISBN 0-916685-02-0). Dustbooks.
Small Press Record of Books in Print, 1981-82. 10th ed. Ed. by Len Fulton & Ellen Ferber. 700p. 1981. 21.95 (ISBN 0-913218-69-3). Dustbooks.
Small Printing Houses & Modern Technology. (Monographs on Communication Technology & Utilization: No. 6). (Illus.). 80p. 1981. pap. 5.00 (ISBN 92-3-101637-7, U1145, UNESCO). UNIPUB.
Small Programs for Small Machines: Computers & Education. Jurg Nievergelt & Andrea Ventura. LC 84-28338. 240p. 1985. pap. write for info. (ISBN 0-201-11129-2). Addison-Wesley.
Small Public Libraries & the Planning Process. 58p. 1981. 7.00x (ISBN 0-8389-6512-1); members 6.30x. ALA.
Small Public Library: Design Guide, Site Selection, & Design Case Study. Ann B. Hill. (Publications in Architecture & Urban Planning Ser.: R80-3). (Illus.). 120p. 1980. 12.00 (ISBN 0-938744-13-5). U of Wis Ctr Arch-Urban.
Small Publisher. Audrey Ward & Philip Ward. (Illus.). 1979. 25.00 (ISBN 0-900891-59-9). Oleander Pr.
Small Quilting Projects. Linda Seward. LC 87-15907. (Illus.). 144p. 1988. 19.95 (ISBN 0-8069-6740-4). Sterling.
Small Quilts. Marsha R. McCloskey. (Illus.). 48p. 1982. pap. 6.00 (ISBN 0-943574-15-3). That Patchwork.
Small Railroads You Can Build. 2nd ed. Ed. by Bob Hayden. LC 77-94925. 1978. pap. 4.25 (ISBN 0-89024-535-5). Kalmbach.
Small Rain: A Novel. Madeleine L'Engle. LC 84-47839. 371p. (gr. 7 up). 1984. 14.95 (ISBN 0-374-26637-9); pap. 7.95 (ISBN 0-374-51912-9). FS&G.
Small Residential Structures: Construction Practices & Material Take-off Estimates. Frank J. Gallo & Regis I. Campbell. LC 83-16911. 264p. 1984. 39.95 (ISBN 0-471-88359-X); student manual o.p. 12.95 (ISBN 0-471-86915-5). Wiley.
Small Ring Compounds in Organic Synthesis, I. Ed. by A. De Meijere. (Topics in Current Chemistry Ser.: Vol. 133). (Illus.). 170p. 1986. 59.50 (ISBN 0-387-16307-7). Springer-Verlag.
Small Ring Compounds in Organic Synthesis II. Ed. by A. De Meijere. (Topics in Current Chemistry Ser.: Vol. 135). (Illus.). 160p. 1986. 70.40 (ISBN 0-387-16662-9). Springer-Verlag.
Small Ring Compounds in Organic Sythesis III. Ed. by A. Meijere. (Topics in Current Chemistry Ser.: Vol. 144). (Illus.). 210p. 1987. 89.00 (ISBN 0-387-18368-X). Springer-Verlag.
Small Ring Heterocycles: Oxiranes, Areneoxides, Oxaridines, Dioxetanes, Thietanes, Thietes, Thiazetes, Vol. 42. Ed. by Alfred Hasner. (Chemistry of Heterocyclic Compounds Monographs). 874p. 1985. 215.00 (ISBN 0-471-05624-3). Wiley.
Small Ring Heterocycles, Vol. 42: Aziridines, Azirines, Thiiranes, Thiirenes, Vol. 42. Ed. by Alfred Hassner. LC 82-4790. (Chemistry of Heterocyclic Compounds Ser.). 1983. Pt. 1. 226.00 (ISBN 0-471-05626-X, Pub. by Wiley-Interscience). Wiley.
Small Room. May Sarton. 256p. 1976. pap. 4.95 (ISBN 0-393-00832-0, Norton Lib). Norton.
Small Room with Trouble on My Mind. Mike Henson. (Illus.). 120p. (Orig.). 1983. pap. 5.00 (ISBN 0-931122-31-7). West End.
Small Ruminant Production in the Developing Countries: FAO Animal Production & Health Paper, No. 58. Pref. by H. A. Jasiorowski. (FAO Animal Production & Health Papers). (Illus.). 234p. 1986. pap. text ed. 22.00 (ISBN 92-5-102343-3, F2900, FAO). UNIPUB.
Small Ruminant Production Systems in South & Southeast Asia: Proceedings of a Workshop, Bogor, Indonesia, 6-10 October, 1986. Ed. by C. Devendra. (Proceedings Ser.). (Illus.). 414p. (Orig.). 1987. pap. text ed. 18.00 (ISBN 0-88936-493-1, IDRC256, Pub. by IDRC). UNIPUB.
Small Ruminants in African Agriculture. Ed. by R. T. Wilson & D. Bourzat. 261p. 1985. pap. text ed. 30.00 (ISBN 92-9053-069-3, Pub. by Intl Livestock Africa). Agribookstore.
Small Ruminants in the Near East, 2 vols. A. W. Qureshi & H. A. Fitzhugh. (FAO Animal Production & Health Paper: No. 54). (Orig.). 1987. Vol. 1, 238pp. pap. 14.85 (ISBN 92-5-102516-9, F3084, FAO); Vol. 2, 167pp. pap. 15.75 (ISBN 92-5-102351-4, F3123). UNIPUB.
Small-Rural Community Colleges. Commission on Small Rural Community Colleges Staff. 1988. pap. 15.00 (ISBN 0-87117-177-5). Am Assn Comm Jr Coll.
Small Rural Parish. Bernard Quinn. LC 79-56508. (Orig.). 1980. pap. 3.50x (ISBN 0-914422-11-1). Glenmary Res Ctr.
Small Rural Primary School: A Matter of Quality. Adrian Bell & Alan Sigsworth. 225p. 1987. 38.00x (ISBN 1-85000-155-3, Falmer Pr); pap. 21.00x (ISBN 1-85000-156-1, Falmer Pr). Taylor & Francis.
Small Sacrifices. Ann Rule. 1988. pap. 4.95 (ISBN 0-451-15393-6, Sig). NAL.
Small Sacrifices: A True Story of Passion & Murder. Ann Rule. LC 86-33253. 1987. 18.95 (ISBN 0-453-00540-3). NAL.
Small Salvations. Patricia Dienstfrey. LC 87-14028. (Illus.). 32p. (Orig.). 1987. signed ltd. ed. 35.00 (ISBN 0-317-61606-4); pap. 8.00 (ISBN 0-932716-22-9). Kelsey St Pr.
Small-Sample Reactivity Measurements in Nuclear Reactors. Wesley K. Foell. LC 74-144051. (ANS Monographs). 272p. 1972. 27.00 (ISBN 0-89448-003-0, 300005). Am Nuclear Soc.
Small Scale Accident Investigations. Hendrick. (Occupational Safety & Health Ser.). 544p. 1987. 69.75 (ISBN 0-8247-7510-4). Dekker.
Small Scale Bibliographic Databases. Peter J. Judge & Brenda Gerrie. 1986. 29.95 (ISBN 0-12-391970-3). Acad Pr.
Small-Scale Cane Sugar Processing & Residue Utilization. Issay Isaias. (Agricultural Services Bulletins: No. 19). 61p. 1980. pap. 7.50 (ISBN 92-5-100935-X, F2069, FAO). UNIPUB.
Small-Scale Cash Crop Farming in South Asia: Seminar Proceedings, FAO-DANIDA, Colombo, Sri Lanka, 15-27 Oct. 1979. (Plant Production & Protection Papers: No. 27). 93p. 1981. pap. 7.50 (ISBN 92-5-101050-1, F2191, FAO). UNIPUB.
Small-Scale Enterprises in Korea & Taiwan. Sam P. S. Ho. (Working Paper: No. 384). vi, 151p. 1980. 8.00 (ISBN 0-686-36187-3, WP-0384). World Bank.
Small-Scale Fish Landing & Marketing Facilities. Medina Pizzali. (FAO Fisheries Technical Paper: No. 291). (Illus.). 68p. 1988. pap. 9.00 (ISBN 92-5-102650-5, F3208, FAO). UNIPUB.
Small-Scale Fisheries in Asia: Socioeconomic Analysis & Policy. Theodore Panayotou. 283p. 1986. pap. text ed. 15.00 (ISBN 0-88936-424-9, IDRC229, IDRC). UNIPUB.
Small-Scale Fisheries of San Miguel Bay, Philippines: Biology & Stock Assessment. Ed. by Daniel Pauly & Antonio N. Mines. (ICLARM Technical Reports: No. 7). (Illus.). 124p. (Orig.). 1983. pap. 16.00x (ISBN 0-89955-394-X, Pub. by ICLARM Philippines). Intl Spec Bk.
Small-Scale Fisheries of San Miguel Bay, Philippines: Economics of Production & Marketing. Ed. by Ian R. Smith & Antonio N. Mines. (ICLARM Technical Reports Ser.: No. 8). (Illus.). 143p. (Orig.). 1982. pap. text ed. 25.00x (ISBN 0-89955-395-8, Pub. by ICLARM Philippines). Intl Spec Bk.
Small-Scale Fisheries of San Miguel Bay, Philippines: Occupational & Geographical Mobility. Conner Bailey. (ICLARM Technical Reports: No. 10). (Illus.). 57p. (Orig.). 1983. pap. 11.50x (ISBN 0-89955-396-6, Pub. by ICLARM Philippines). Intl Spec Bk.
Small-Scale Fisheries of San Miguel Bay, Philippines: Social Aspects of Production & Marketing. Ed. by Conner Bailey. (ICLARM Technical Reports Ser.: No. 9). (Illus.). 57p. (Orig.). 1982. pap. text ed. 14.00x (ISBN 0-89955-397-4, Pub. by ICLARM Philippines). Intl Spec Bk.
Small-Scale Fishing with Driftners. L. Karlsen & B. A. Bjarnason. 64p. (Orig.). 1987. pap. text ed. 9.00 (ISBN 92-5-102525-8, F3126, FAO). UNIPUB.
Small Scale Forest-Based Processing Enterprises. (Illus.). 246p. (Orig.). 1987. pap. 24.75 (ISBN 92-5-102570-3, F3130, FAO). UNIPUB.
Small Scale Foundries for Developing Countries: A Guide to Process Selection. J. D. Harper. (Illus.). 66p. (Orig.). 1981. pap. 11.50x (ISBN 0-903031-78-7, Pub. by Intermediate Tech England). Intermediate Tech.
Small Scale Gas Producer Engine Systems. A. Kaupp & J. R. Goss. 290p. 1984. pap. 33.00 (ISBN 3-528-02001-6, Pub. by Vieweg & Sohn Germany). IPS.
Small-Scale Gold Mining: A Manual Based on Experience in Suriname. E. H. Dahlberg. 51p. (Orig.). 1984. pap. 11.25x (ISBN 0-317-46890-1, Pub. by Intermediate Tech England). Intermediate Tech.
Small-Scale Hydroelectric Power Development: Potential Sources of Federal Financial Support for Low-Income Communities. Vanessa C. Cones & Gregory P. Malinowski. (Illus.). 267p. 1980. pressboard binder cover 25.00 (ISBN 0-936130-00-8). Intl Sci Tech.
Small-Scale Industries Promotion in India. Sosthenes Buatsi. (Illus.). 94p. (Orig.). 1987. pap. 15.25x (ISBN 0-946688-24-9, Pub. by Intermed Tech England). Intermediate Tech.
Small Scale Irrigation: A Manual of Low-Cost Water Technology. Peter H. Stern. (Illus.). 152p. (Orig.). 1979. pap. 13.50x (ISBN 0-903031-64-7, Pub. by Intermediate Tech England). Intermediate Tech.
Small Scale Lime-Burning: A Pratical Introduction. Michael Wingate. 185p. (Orig.). 1985. pap. 13.50x (ISBN 0-946688-01-X, Pub. by Intermediate Tech England). Intermediate Tech.
Small Scale Maize Milling. (Technical Memorandum, Technology Ser.: No. 7). xii, 143p. (Orig.). 1984. pap. 12.25 (ISBN 92-2-103640-5). Intl Labour Office.
Small-Scale Maize Milling. (Technology Series: Technical Memorandums: No. 7). 143p. 1985. pap. 12.25 (ISBN 92-2-103640-5, ILO359, ILO). UNIPUB.
Small-Scale Manufacture of Footwear. 3rd ed. (Technical Memorandum, Technology Ser.). 1988. 14.00. Intl Labour Office.
Small-Scale Manufacture of Footwear: Technical Memorandum. (Technology Ser.). 204p. 1984. pap. 14.00 (ISBN 92-2-103079-2, ILO342, ILO). UNIPUB.
Small-Scale Manufacture of Stabilised Soil Blocks. (Technology Ser., Technical Memorandum: No. 12). (Illus.). v, 181p. (Orig.). 1987. pap. 14.00 (ISBN 92-2-105838-7). Intl Labour Office.
Small-Scale Master Builder: Selected Readings on Professional Practice as an Architectural Designer-Builder-Investor at the Personal Scale. Donald P. Grant. LC 83-60946. 198p. (Orig.). 1986. pap. 19.00x (ISBN 0-911215-04-2). Small Master.
Small-Scale Mining: A Review of the Issues. Richard Noetstaller. (Technical Paper: No. 75). 1987. 6.50 (ISBN 0-8213-0980-3, BK0980). World Bank.
Small-Scale Municipal Solid Waste Energy Recovery Systems. Gershman & Brickner. (Illus.). 250p. 1986. 44.95 (ISBN 0-442-22778-7). Van Nos Reinhold.
Small-Scale Oil Extraction From Groundnuts & Copra. Ed. by A. S. Bhalla. (Technology Ser.: No. 5). 111p. (Orig.). 1984. pap. 10.50 (ISBN 92-2-103503-4, ILO292, ILO). UNIPUB.
Small-Scale Oil Extraction from Groundnuts & Copra. 2nd ed. (Technical Memorandum, Technology Ser.: No. 5). 1986. pap. 12.25. Intl Labour Office.
Small-Scale Pig Raising. Dirk Van Loon. LC 78-12938. (Illus.). 272p. 1978. pap. 9.95 (ISBN 0-88266-136-1, Garden Way Pub). Storey Comm Inc.
Small-Scale Poultry Keeping. Ray Feltwell. 176p. 1980. pap. 9.50 (ISBN 0-571-11557-8). Faber & Faber.
Small Scale Power Cogeneration Markets: Update. Business Communications Staff. 139p. 1988. 1750.00 (ISBN 0-89336-623-4, E-043R). BCC.
Small-Scale Processing of Beef. Intro. by A. S. Bhalla. (Technical Memorandum, Technology Ser.: No. 10). iv, 121p. (Orig.). 1985. pap. 14.00 (ISBN 92-2-105050-5). Intl Labour Office.
Small-Scale Processing of Fish. 2nd ed. International Labour Office Staff. (Technical Memorandum, Technology Ser.: No. 3). xi, 118p. (Orig.). 1982. pap. 12.25 (ISBN 92-2-103205-1). Intl Labour Office.
Small-Scale Processing of Pork. Intro. by A. S. Bhalla. (Technical Memorandum, Technology Ser.: No. 9). (Illus.). iv, 129p. (Orig.). 1985. pap. 14.00 (ISBN 92-2-100542-9). Intl Labour Office.
Small-Scale Production of Cementitious Materials. R. J. Spence. (Illus.). 49p. (Orig.). 1980. pap. 7.50x (ISBN 0-903031-74-4, Pub. by Intermediate Tech England). Intermediate Tech.
Small Scale Production of Lime for Building. J. Spiropoulos. (GATE Ser.). (Illus.). 80p. 1985. pap. 11.00 (ISBN 3-528-02016-4, Pub. by Vieweg & Sohn). IPS.
Small-Scale Resource Recovery Systems. Ed. by A. E. Martin. LC 81-18944. (Pollution Technology Review: No. 89). (Illus.). 364p. 1982. 42.00 (ISBN 0-8155-0885-9). Noyes.
Small Scale Retailing in the United Kingdom. David Kirby & John Dawson. 184p. 1979. text ed. 37.00 (ISBN 0-566-00164-0). Gower Pub Co.
Small-Scale Sacred Concertato in the Early Seventeenth Century, 2 vols. Anne Kirwan-Mott. LC 81-13026. (Studies in British Musicology). Vol. 1. pap. 108.50 (ISBN 0-8357-1230-3, 2070260); Vol. 2. pap. 70.50 (2070260). Bks Demand UMI.
Small-Scale Sausage Production. (FAO Animal Production & Health Paper Ser.: No. 52). 123p. 1986. pap. text ed. 12.00 (ISBN 92-5-102187-2, F2848, FAO). UNIPUB.
Small Scale Self-Sufficiency. Richard R. Fuller. 78p. 1982. 25.00x (ISBN 0-901976-60-1, Pub. by United Writers Pubns England). State Mutual Bk.

Smalltown Daily: An Elementary Intermediate Advanced Reader. Ed. by John N. Miller & Raymond C. Clark. LC 84-11649. (InterplayESL Ser.). (Illus.). 96p. (Orig.). 1984. pap. text ed. 7.50x (ISBN 0-86647-005-0). Pro Lingua.
Smara: The Forbidden City. Michel Vieuchange. 276p. 1987. pap. 9.50 (ISBN 0-88001-146-7). Ecco Pr.
Smarre besattelser & Nya bersattelser see **Rose of Jericho & Other Stories.**
Smart Apples: Thirty-One Artificial Intelligence Experiments with the Apple II, II Plus, IIe, IIc, & IIGS. Delton T. Horn. (Illus.). 160p. 1987. 18.95 (ISBN 0-8306-7755-0); pap. 12.95 (ISBN 0-8306-2775-8). TAB Bks.
Smart Attorney's Guide to Accounting Documents for Discovery & Evidence. William N. McNairn. (Illus.). 100p. 1987. pap. text ed. 14.95 (ISBN 0-932621-02-3). Quotamus Pr.
Smart Bargaining: Doing Business with the Japanese. John L. Graham & Yoshihiro Sano. LC 84-404. 184p. 1985. pap. 16.95x (ISBN 0-88730-060-X). Ballinger Pub.
Smart Buildings - Building Automation: A Selected Bibliography of Recent Literature. David K. Ballast. (Architecture Ser.: A 1933). 7p. 1987. 3.00 (ISBN 1-55590-543-9). Vance Biblios.
Smart Buildings & Technology-Enhanced Real Estate, Vols. I & II. Dean Schwanke. 136p. (Orig.). 1985. pap. 56.00 (ISBN 0-87420-640-5). Urban Land.
Smart but Feeling Dumb. Harold N. Levinson. LC 84-40090. 256p. 1984. text ed. 18.50 (ISBN 0-446-51307-5). Warner Bks.
Smart but Feeling Dumb. Harold N. Levinson. 1988. pap. 6.95 (ISBN 0-317-67099-9). Warner Bks.
Smart but Feeling Dumb. Harold N. Levinson. 256p. 1988. 10.95 (ISBN 0-446-38841-6). Warner Bks.
Smart Card. Business Communications Staff. (Illus.). 106p. 1986. pap. 1500.00 (ISBN 0-89336-470-3, G-100). BCC.
Smart Cards: The New Bank Cards. rev. ed. Jerome Svigals. 240p. 1987. Repr. of 1985 ed. 26.95 (ISBN 0-02-948901-6). Macmillan.
Smart Cards: The Ultimate Personal Computer. Jerome Svigals. 208p. 1985. 24.95 (ISBN 0-02-948900-8). Macmillan.
Smart Choices. Victor Craig. LC 81-70755. (Illus.). 112p. 1982. pap. 9.95 (ISBN 0-941156-00-1). Clear View Pubns.
Smart Choices. Nancy J. Kolodny et al. (Illus.). 352p. (gr. 7 up). 1986. 17.95 (ISBN 0-316-50163-8). Little.
Smart Contracting. Richard G. Bak. LC 86-28327. 160p. 1987. pap. 12.95 (ISBN 0-912524-39-1). Busn News.
Smart Cookies Don't Crumble: A Modern Woman's Guide to Living & Loving Her Own Life. Sonya Friedman. 1985. 15.95 (ISBN 0-399-13040-3). Putnam Pub Group.
Smart Cookies Don't Crumble: A Modern Woman's Guide to Living & Loving Her Life. Sonya Friedman. pap. 3.95 (ISBN 0-317-61748-6). PB.
Smart Cookies: Eighty Recipes for Heavenly, Healthful Snacking. Jane Kinderlehrer. LC 85-13913. (Illus.). 176p. (Orig.). 1985. pap. 9.95 (ISBN 0-937858-62-5). Newmarket.
Smart Dithyramb. Susan MacDonald. (Flowering Quince Poetry Ser.: No. 3). 28p. (Orig.). 1979. pap. 7.50 (ISBN 0-940592-04-5). Heyeck Pr.
Smart Enough to Know. Eileen Goudge. (Senior Ser.: No. 2). (Orig.). (gr. 7-12). 1984. pap. 2.25 (ISBN 0-440-98168-9, LFL). Dell.
Smart Eyes. Jamie Marron. Date not set. price not set. Addison-Wesley.
Smart Face: A Dermatologist's Guide to Cosmetics & Skin Care. Thomas Goodman & Stephanie Young. 1988. pap. 9.95 (ISBN 0-13-814377-3). Prentice Hall Pr.
Smart Girl. Sandy Miller. 160p. (YA) (gr. 7 up). 1982. pap. 2.25 (ISBN 0-451-11887-1, Sig Vista). NAL.
Smart Girl. Sandy Miller. 1988. pap. 2.50 (ISBN 0-451-15684-6, Sig). NAL.
Smart Girls, Gifted Women. Barbara A. Kerr. LC 85-29678. 184p. 1986. pap. 13.95 (ISBN 0-910707-07-3). Ohio Psych Pub.
Smart Golf. new ed. Charles F. Kemp. LC 74-82856. (Illus.). 200p. (Orig.). 1974. pap. 3.85 (ISBN 0-87706-057-6). Branch Smith.
Smart Handicapping Made Easy. William Bauman. pap. 5.00 (ISBN 0-87980-270-7). Wilshire.
Smart Homeseller's Sale by Owner Kit. J. R. Paine. 1986. 19.95 (ISBN 0-8187-0065-3). Harlo Pr.
Smart House: The Coming Revolution in Housing. Ralph L. Smith. (Illus.). 120p. 1987. 18.95 (ISBN 0-87683-918-9, A918-9); pap. 11.95 (ISBN 0-87683-919-7, A919-7). GP Pub.
Smart Investing: A Step-by-Step Guide to Financial Security. Andrew J. Senchack. LC 87-1923. 236p. 1987. pap. 14.95 (ISBN 0-87833-575-7). Taylor Pub.
Smart Investor's Guide to Real Estate: Big Profits from Small Investments. 4th ed. Robert Bruss. 15.95 (ISBN 0-517-55854-8). Crown.
Smart Kid Like You. Stella Pevsner. LC 74-19320. 192p. (gr. 4-8). 1975. 10.95 (ISBN 0-395-28876-2, Clarion). HM.
Smart Kid Like You. Stella Pevsner. 234p. (gr. 7 up). 1976. pap. 1.95 (ISBN 0-590-32735-6, Vagabond). Scholastic Inc.
Smart Kids, Stupid Choices. rev. ed. Kevin Leman. Ed. by Kathi Mills. 120p. 1987. pap. 7.95 (ISBN 0-8307-1191-0, 5419026). Regal.
Smart Kids with School Problems. Priscilla Vail. 256p. 1987. 18.95 (ISBN 0-525-24557-X). Dutton.
Smart Kids with School Problems: Things to Know & Ways to Help. Priscilla Vail. 1988. pap. 8.95 (ISBN 0-452-26154-6, Plume). NAL.
Smart Kitchens. David Goldbeck. (Illus.). 100p. (Orig.). 1988. pap. 12.95x (ISBN 0-9606138-1-1). Ceres Pr.
Smart Like Me: High School Age Writers 1966-1988. Dick Lourie & Mark Pawlak. 200p. 1988. casebound 20.00 (ISBN 0-914610-57-0); pap. 10.00. Hanging Loose.
Smart Livermore's Tricks for Stock Market Success. Jesse Livermore. (Recondite Sources of Stock Market Action Library). (Illus.). 132p. 1983. 147.75 (ISBN 0-86654-045-8). Inst Econ Finan.
Smart Love. Jody Hayes & Maureen Redl. 224p. (Orig.). 1989. pap. 9.95 (ISBN 0-87477-472-1). J P Tarcher.
Smart Manager's Guide to Effective CAD Management. CAD Report Staff & Roy L. Wysack. (Smart Manager's Guide Ser.). (Illus.). 384p. 1985. looseleaf 145.00 (ISBN 0-934869-01-4). Cad Cam.
Smart Manager's Guide to Selecting & Purchasing CAD-CAM Systems. CAD Report Staff & L. Stephen Wolfe. (Smart Manager's Guide Ser.). (Illus.). 320p. 1984. looseleaf 125.00 (ISBN 0-934869-00-6). Cad-Cam Pub.
Smart Manufacturing with Artificial Intelligence. Ed. by J. Krakauer. (Manufacturing Update Ser.). 258p. 1987. write for info. (ISBN 0-87263-270-9). SME.
Smart Modems for Personal Computer Communications. William Saffady. 1986. pap. text ed. 29.95x (ISBN 0-88736-081-5). Meckler Corp.
Smart Money. Lia Matera. 208p. (Orig.). 1988. pap. 3.50 (ISBN 0-553-27268-3). Bantam.
Smart Money: How to Be Your Own Financial Adviser. Ken Dolan & Daria Dolan. LC 87-28632. 320p. 1988. 19.95 (ISBN 0-394-56516-9). Random.
Smart Moves. Stuart M. Kaminsky. (A Toby Peters Mystery). 272p. 1987. 15.95 (ISBN 0-312-00190-8, Pub. by Thomas Dunne Bks). St Martin.
Smart Moves for the New Kid on the Block. Gail G. Benson & Jane E. Holston. 75p. (Orig.). (gr. 4-8). 1987. pap. 8.95 (ISBN 0-943385-11-3). Riv Forest Pub.
Smart Moves for the Relocating Family. Gail G. Benson & Jane E. Holston. LC 87-61518. 240p. (Orig.). 1987. pap. 14.95 (ISBN 0-943385-10-5). Riv Forest Pub.
Smart Muffins: Eighty-Three Recipes for Heavenly, Healthful Eating. Jane Kinderlehrer. LC 87-18437. (Illus.). 176p. (Orig.). 1987. pap. 9.95 (ISBN 0-937858-97-8). Newmarket.
Smart Power: Automotive Applications. 1987. 18.00 (ISBN 0-89883-990-4, SP719). Soc Auto* Engineers.
Smart Power Markets & Applications. LC 87-83140. 125.00 (ISBN 0-914405-50-0, 2188). Electronic Trend.
Smart Programming Guide for Sprites. Craig G. Miller. 74p. (Orig.). 1983. pap. 6.95 (ISBN 0-931831-00-8). MG-CA.
Smart Questions. Dorothy Leeds. 240p. 1987. text ed. 15.95 (ISBN 0-07-036996-8). McGraw.
Smart Questions. Dorothy Leeds. 1988. pap. 4.50 (ISBN 0-425-11132-6). Berkley Pub.
Smart Robots: A Handbook of Intelligent Robotic Systems. V. Daniel Hunt. (Illus.). 400p. 1985. 44.00 (ISBN 0-412-00531-X, NO. 9008, Pub. by Chapman & Hall New York). Routledge Chapman & Hall.
Smart Secretary's Guide to Earning More Than Just a Salary. Elaine Kartzman. (Illus.). 1980. 7.95 (ISBN 0-913814-25-3). Nevada Pubns.
Smart Shopping on Florida's Gold Coast. Norma A. Orovitz. LC 85-3725. (Florida Living Ser.). 176p. (Orig.). 1985. pap. 3.95 (ISBN 0-910923-19-1). Pineapple Pr.
Smart Times: A Parent's Guide to Quality Time with Pre-Schoolers. Kent G. Burtt. LC 83-48938. (Illus.). 288p. 1984. 17.45i (ISBN 0-06-015287-7, HarpT). Har-Row.
Smart Tips, Tricks & Traps. Andrew N. Schwartz. LC 87-60015. 450p. (Orig.). 1987. 23.95 (ISBN 0-88022-290-5, 93). Que Corp.
Smart Toys: For Babies from Birth to Two. Kent G. Burtt & Karen Kalkstein. LC 80-8711. (Illus.). 166p. 1981. pap. 10.95 (ISBN 0-06-090860-2, CN860, PL). Har-Row.
Smart Travel: Trade Secrets for Getting There in Style at Little Cost or Effort. Martin Blinder. LC 86-33184. 144p. (Orig.). 1987. pap. 9.95 (ISBN 0-938179-02-0). Mills Sanderson.
Smart Trust Deed Investment in California. 2nd ed. George Coats. LC 87-33370. (Illus.). 292p. (Orig.). 1988. pap. 21.50 (ISBN 0-934581-01-0). Barr-Randol Pub.
Smart Way to Buy a Business: An Entreprenuer's Guide to Questions That Must Be Asked. John C. Kohl, Sr. & Atlee M. Kohl. 1986. 19.95 (ISBN 0-317-53682-6). Woodland Pubs.
Smart Weapons. Business Communications Staff. 1988. 2650.00 (ISBN 0-89336-674-9, GB-115). BCC.
Smart Women. Judy Blume. LC 83-15958. 324p. 1984. 15.95 (ISBN 0-399-12840-9, Putnam). Putnam Pub Group.
Smart Women. Judy Blume. 1985. pap. 3.95 (ISBN 0-671-50268-9). PB.
Smart Women at Work: Twelve Steps to Career Breakthroughs. Terry Ward. 176p. 1987. 15.95 (ISBN 0-8092-4681-3). Contemp Bks.
Smart Women, Foolish Choices. Connell Cowan & Melvyn Kinder. 1986. pap. 4.50 (ISBN 0-451-15257-3, Sig). NAL.
Smart Women, Foolish Choices: Finding the Right Men & Avoiding the Wrong Ones. Connell Cowan & Melvyn Kinder. 224p. 1985. 14.95 (ISBN 0-517-55145-4, C N Potter Bks). Crown.
Smart Women Stupid Books: Stop Reading & Learn to Love Losers. Lisa A. Marsoli & Mel Green. (Illus.). 96p. 1987. pap. 4.95 (ISBN 0-8431-4706-7); bk. & cassette 6.95 (ISBN 0-8431-4707-5). Price Stern.
Smarter Barter. Michael Gershman. 176p. 1986. 16.95 (ISBN 0-670-81273-0). Viking.
Smarter Kids. Lawrence J. Greene. LC 87-15824. 230p. 1987. 16.95 (ISBN 0-89586-547-5). Price Stern.
Smarter Kids. Lawrence J. Greene. 1988. pap. 4.95 (ISBN 0-449-21618-7, Crest). Fawcett.
Smarter Money: An Investment Game Plan for Those Who Made It & Want to Keep It. Frank J. Fabozzi & Stephen Feldman. 228p. 1985. 18.95 (ISBN 0-917253-16-7). Probus Pub Co.
Smarter Not Harder. Conrad Adelman. (Orig.). 1979. pap. 50.00x (ISBN 0-933738-01-3). IBMS Inc.
Smarter Not Harder. 2nd ed. Conrad Adelman. 1981. 50.00x (ISBN 0-686-24979-8). IBMS Inc.
Smarter Not Harder. 3rd ed. Conrad Adelman. 1984. pap. 60.00 (ISBN 0-317-02253-9). IBMS Inc.
Smartest Bear & His Brother Oliver. Alice Bach. LC 74-29348. (Illus.). 48p. (gr. k-4). 1975. PLB 12.89 (ISBN 0-06-020335-8). HarpJ.
Smartype---A Keyboard Program. C. Daiute. 1986. 39.95 (ISBN 0-07-838066-9). McGraw.
Smashed Potatoes: A Kid's Eye View of the Kitchen. Ed. by Jane Martel. LC 74-10947. 96p. (gr. 2 up). 1974. 4.95 (ISBN 0-395-19775-9); pap. 3.50 (ISBN 0-395-19975-1). HM.
Smashing the Communal Pot. Wang Guichen et al. (China Studies). 200p. 1985. pap. 6.95 (ISBN 0-8351-1687-5). China Bks.
Smashing the Gates of Hell in the Last Days. David A. Lewis. LC 86-65887. 1987. pap. 7.95 (ISBN 0-89221-143-1). New Leaf.
Smashing the Idols: A Jewish Inquiry into the Cult Phenomenon. Ed. by Gary Eisenberg. LC 88-10202. 325p. 1988. 30.00 (ISBN 0-87668-974-8). Aronson.
Smashing Times: Irish Women's Campaign for the Vote 1876-1944. Rosemary Owens. 160p. 1984. 17.95 (ISBN 0-946211-07-8, Pub. by Irish Fem Info Ireland); pap. 9.95 (ISBN 0-946211-08-6, Pub. by Irish Fem Info Ireland). Irish Bks Media.
SME Mining Engineering Handbook. LC 72-86922. 1973. 50.00x (ISBN 0-89520-021-X). Soc Mining Eng.
Smear Terror. John T. Flynn. 1982. lib. bdg. 59.95 (ISBN 0-87700-367-X). Revisionist Pr.
Smekh Sil'Nykh: O Khudo Zhnikakh Zhurnala 'Krokodil' I. P. Abramskii. 320p. 1977. 30.00x (ISBN 0-317-14299-2, Pub. by Collets (UK)). State Mutual Bk.
Smell. J. M. Parramon & J. J. Puig. (Child's Guide to the Five Senses Ser.). (Illus.). 32p. (ps). 1985. pap. 3.95 ea. (ISBN 0-8120-3565-8). Span. ed (ISBN 0-8120-3607-7). Barron.
Smell of Burning Starts the Day. Susan Tichy. viii, 72p. 1988. 18.50x (ISBN 0-8195-2153-1); pap. 10.95 (ISBN 0-8195-1154-4). Wesleyan U Pr.
Smell of Earth & Clay: East Greenland Eskimo Songs. Tr. by Lawrence Millman. 1985. pap. 5.00 (ISBN 0-934834-54-7). White Pine.
Smell of Incense the Sound of Silence. John Groff. (Orig.). 1988. pap. 3.85 (ISBN 0-88028-076-X). Forward Movement.
Smell of It & Other Stories. Sonallah Ibrahim. (African Writers Ser.). 1971. pap. text ed. 6.50 (ISBN 0-435-90095-1). Heinemann Ed.
Smell of Matches, Poems. John Stone. 77p. 1988. pap. 6.95 (ISBN 0-8071-1477-4). La State U Pr.
Smelling. Richard Allington. LC 79-27147. (E. G. Beginning to Learn about... Ser.). (Illus.). 32p. (ps-2). 1985. pap. 9.27 (ISBN 0-8172-2488-2). Raintree Pubs.
Smelling. Richard L. Allington & Kathleen Krull. LC 79-27147. (Beginning to Learn about Ser.). (Illus.). 32p. (ps-2). 1980. PLB 15.33 (ISBN 0-8172-1293-0). Raintree Pubs.
Smelling. Henry Pluckrose. (Think About Ser.). 32p. (gr. k-3). 1986. lib. bdg. 10.90 (ISBN 0-531-10172-X). Watts.
Smelling. Kathie B. Smith & Victoria Crenson. LC 87-5887. (Troll Question Bk.). (Illus.). 24p. (gr. k-3). 1987. PLB 8.59 (ISBN 0-8167-1010-4); pap. text ed. 1.95 (ISBN 0-8167-1011-2). Troll Assocs.
Smells in God's World. Kathryn Lutz. Ed. by Patricia H. Lemon. (Graded Press Christian Storybooks). 24p. (Orig.). (ps). 1986. pap. 6.95 packaged with audio cassette (ISBN 0-939697-01-7); audio cassette incl. Graded Pr.
Smells: Things to Do with Them. McPhee Gribble Editorial Staff. (Practical Puffins Ser.). (Illus.). (gr. 2-7). 1978. pap. 2.95 (ISBN 0-14-049148-1, Puffin). Penguin.
Smelly Book. Babette Cole. (Illus.). 40p. (gr. k-5). 1988. 10.95 (ISBN 0-671-65670-8, Little Simon). S&S.
Smelly Jelly Smelly Fish. Michael Rosen. (Illus.). 24p. (ps-4). 1987. 9.95 (ISBN 0-13-814567-9). P-H.
Smelting & Refining Operator's Symposium. 264p. 1985. pap. text ed. 39.00x (ISBN 0-909520-89-5, Pub. by Australian Inst M & M). Brookfield Pub Co.
Smetana. John Clapham. (Master Musicians Ser.). (Illus.). 171p. 1972. 17.95x (ISBN 0-460-03133-3, Pub. by J. M. Dent England). Biblio Dist.
Smetana. Brian Large. LC 84-1825. (Music Reprint Ser.). (Illus.). 524p. 1985. Repr. of 1970 ed. lib. bdg. 52.50 (ISBN 0-306-76243-9). Da Capo.
SMI Handbook of Spring Design. Technology Committee. Ed. by Patricia Williams. (Illus.). 43p. (Orig.). 1981. pap. 5.50 (ISBN 0-9604120-1-8). Spring Manufact.
Smidgen of Honey: A Cookbook. Maxine Wilhelm. LC 86-80962. (Illus.). 86p. 1986. pap. 12.00x (ISBN 0-934188-21-1). Evans Pubns.
Smile! Bil Keane. (Family Circus Ser.). (Illus.). 1984. pap. 2.25 (ISBN 0-449-12806-7, GM). Fawcett.
Smile & Other Poems. Geoffrey Landers. 1986. 5.95 (ISBN 0-533-06583-6). Vantage.
Smile & Say Murder. Carolyn Keene. (Nancy Drew Files Ser.: No. 4). (YA) (gr. 7 up). pap. 2.50 (ISBN 0-671-62557-8). Archway.
Smile & Say Murder. Carolyn Keene. (Nancy Drew Files Ser.). 1988. 9.50 (ISBN 0-942545-26-5); 10.50 (ISBN 0-942545-30-3). Grey Castle.
Smile at the Foot of the Ladder. Henry Miller. LC 58-11829. (Illus.). 64p. 1975. pap. 3.95 (ISBN 0-8112-0556-8, NDP386). New Directions.
Smile Connection: How to Use Humor in Dealing with People. Esther Blumenfeld & Lynne Alpern. Date not set. write for info. S&S.
Smile Connection: How to Use Humor in Dealing with People. Esther Blumenfeld & Lynne Alpers. 300p. 1985. 14.95 (ISBN 0-13-525783-2); pap. 7.95 (ISBN 0-13-525775-1). P-H.
Smile, Ernest & Celestine. Vincent Gabrielle. LC 82-1075. (Illus.). 24p. (ps-3). 1982. 10.75 (ISBN 0-688-01247-7); PLB 10.88 (ISBN 0-688-01249-3). Morrow.
Smile for Auntie. Diane Paterson. LC 76-2285. (Pied Piper Bk.). (Illus.). (gr. k-2). 1976. 7.95 (ISBN 0-8037-8066-4); PLB 7.89 (ISBN 0-8037-8067-2); pap. 3.50 (ISBN 0-8037-7981-X, 0340-100). Dial Bks Young.
Smile from Katie Hattan & Other Natural Wonders. Leon Hale. LC 82-60563. 288p. 1982. 13.95 (ISBN 0-940672-07-3). Shearer Pub.
Smile: How to Cope with Braces. Jeanne Betancourt. LC 81-11800. (Illus.). 96p. (gr. 5 up). 1982. lib. bdg. 8.99 (ISBN 0-394-94732-0); pap. 5.95 (ISBN 0-394-84732-6). Knopf.
Smile in a Mad Dog's I. 2nd ed. Richard Stine. 1977. 6.95 (ISBN 0-916860-02-7). Bean Pub.
Smile in His Lifetime. Joseph Hansen. 304p. (YA) (gr. 7 up). 1985. pap. 6.95 (ISBN 0-452-25675-5, Plume). NAL.
Smile in the Mind's Eye. Lawrence Durrell. LC 81-19864. 96p. 1982. 10.95x (ISBN 0-87663-380-7); pap. 5.95 (ISBN 0-87663-576-1). Universe.
Smile in the Sun. Lee Anderson. (YA) (gr. 7 up). 1983. 9.95 (ISBN 0-8034-8312-0, Avalon). Bouregy.
Smile! Let's Play "Political Dissident" American Style. (Analysis Ser.). 12.50 (ISBN 0-686-45489-8). Inst Analysis.
Smile Like a Plastic Daisy. Sonia Levitin. LC 83-15616. 192p. (gr. 8 up). 1984. 11.95 (ISBN 0-689-31024-2, Atheneum Childrens Bks). Macmillan.
Smile Like a Plastic Daisy. Sonia Levitin. 1986. pap. 2.50 (ISBN 0-449-70120-4, Juniper). Fawcett.
Smile Makes a Lousy Umbrella. Charles M. Schulz. LC 77-71352. (Peanuts Parade Books: No. 17). 1977. pap. 5.25 (ISBN 0-03-021406-8). H Holt & Co.
Smile of Eros: A Novel. John Coriolan. 192p. (Orig.). 1984. pap. 7.95 (ISBN 0-917342-39-9). Gay Sunshine.
Smile of Love. Jean Woodward. (YA) (gr. 7 up). 1981. 9.95 (ISBN 0-686-84706-7, Avalon). Bouregy.
Smile of the Gods: A Thematic Study of Cesare Pavese's Works. Gian-Paolo Biasini. LC 68-9748. 337p. 1968. 20.00x (ISBN 0-915042-19-3). Lib Soc Sci.
Smile... or I'll Kick Your Bed! Tex Goen, Jr. LC 80-20223. (Illus.). 192p. 1981. 12.95 (ISBN 0-393-01433-9). Norton.
Smile, Please! Mathew Price. LC 85-23174. (Surprise Board Bks.). (Illus.). 12p. (ps). 1986. bds. 3.95 (ISBN 0-394-88179-6). Knopf.
Smile, Says Little Crocodile. Jane B. Moncure. (Magic Castle Readers Ser.). (Illus.). 32p. (ps-2). 1987. 11.93 (ISBN 0-516-05723-5). Childrens.
Smile, Says Little Crocodile. Jane B. Moncure. LC 87-13833. (Magic Castle Readers Ser.). (Illus.). 32p. (ps-2). 1987. PLB 7.75 (ISBN 0-89565-401-6). Childs World.

Smoke Control in Fire Safety Design. D. G. Butcher & A. C. Parnell. 1979. 45.00x (ISBN 0-419-11190-5, Pub. by E & FN Spon, NO. 6558). Routledge Chapman & Hall.
Smoke Cookery Cook Book. Georgia Orcutt. (Orig.). 1978. pap. 1.95 (ISBN 0-451-08200-1, J8200, Sig). NAL.
Smoke Detector. Eric Wright. (Nightingale Paperbacks). 1985. pap. 10.95 (ISBN 0-8161-3900-8, Large Print Bks). G K Hall.
Smoke Detectors: A Bibliographical Overview. Coppa & Avery Consultants Staff. (Architecture Ser.: A 1510). 9p. 1985. 2.00 (ISBN 0-89028-660-4). Vance Biblios.
Smoke, Dust & Haze: Fundamentals of Aerosol Behavior. S. K. Friedlander. LC 76-26928. 317p. 1977. 55.00 (ISBN 0-471-01468-0, Pub. by Wiley Interscience). Wiley.
Smoke Eaters: The Story of a Fire Crew. Harvey J. O'Higgins. 19.00 (ISBN 0-8369-4249-3, 6059). Ayer Co Pubs.
Smoke-Free Lodging in California: A Directory of Hotels, Motels, Resorts, & Inns Offering Non-Smoking Accommodations. Ed. by Renee Felciano. 96p. (Orig.). 1986. pap. 11.95 (ISBN 0-9616692-0-9). Pinerolo Pub.
Smoke-Free Workplace. William L. Weis & Bruce W. Miller. LC 85-62780. 196p. 1985. pap. 10.95 (ISBN 0-87975-309-9). Prometheus Bks.
Smoke from the Chimney. Kathy K. Tapp. LC 85-18713. 132p. (gr. 4-7). 1986. 12.95 (ISBN 0-689-50389-X, M K McElderry). Macmillan.
Smoke from the Fires. Michael D. Browne. LC 84-72533. (Poetry Ser.). 80p. 1985. 14.95 (ISBN 0-88748-006-3); pap. 6.95 (ISBN 0-88748-007-1). Carnegie-Mellon.
Smoke in Food Processing. Joseph A. Maga. 176p. 1988. 97.50 (ISBN 0-8493-5155-3, 5155). CRC Pr.
Smoke in the Canyon: My Steam Days in Dunsmuir. Dick Murdock. Ed. by Jayne Murdock. LC 85-90443. (Illus.). 144p. (Orig.). 1986. 25.95 (ISBN 0-932916-11-2); pap. 15.95 (ISBN 0-932916-10-4). May-Murdock.
Smoke: It's Chemistry, Physics & Control by Engineering. 1984. 32.50 (ISBN 0-318-02520-5, 84-9). Society Fire Protect.
Smoke Monster. Wayne Howard. Ed. by Ruth L. Perle. (Alpha Comic Bks.: No. 4). (Illus.). (gr. k-1). 1977. pap. text ed. 0.50 (ISBN 0-89796-858-1). Arista Corp NY.
Smoke on the Mountain: An Interpretation of the Ten Commandments. Joy Davidman. LC 85-7622. 144p. 1985. pap. 7.95 (ISBN 0-664-24680-X). Westminster John Knox.
Smoke over Golan: A Novel of the 1973 Yom Kippur War in Israel. Uriel Ofek. Tr. by Israel I. Taslitt from Hebrew. LC 78-22488. (Illus.). 192p. (gr. 4-7). 1979. PLB 10.89 (ISBN 0-06-024614-6). HarpJ.
Smoke Pollution of Towns. G. V. Sheleikhovskii. 208p. 1961. pap. text ed. 46.50x (ISBN 0-317-46493-0, Pub. by Keter Pub Jerusalem). Coronet Bks.
Smoke Ring. Larry Niven. 1987. 16.95 (ISBN 0-345-30256-7, Del Rey). Ballantine.
Smoke Ring. Larry Niven. 336p. 1988. pap. 4.50 (ISBN 0-345-30257-5, Del Rey). Ballantine.
Smoke Ring: Tobacco, Money & Multinational Politics. rev. ed. Peter Taylor. 1985. pap. 4.95 (ISBN 0-451-62426-2, Ment). NAL.
Smoke Rings. Gladys B. Stern. LC 72-10810. (Short Story Index Reprint Ser.). 1973. Repr. of 1923 ed. 20.00 (ISBN 0-8369-4229-9). Ayer Co Pubs.
Smoke Showin' William F. Noonan. LC 84-80100. (Illus.). 190p. (Orig.). 1984. pap. 19.95 (ISBN 0-9611268-1-7, Pub. by A C Getchell). Quinlan Pr.
Smoke That Thunders. Dominic Mulaisho. LC 79-303379. (African Writers Ser.). 1979. pap. text ed. 7.00 (ISBN 0-435-90204-0). Heinemann Ed.
Smoke That Thunders. Ernest Wilson. (Waterstone Travel Classics Ser.). 254p. 1986. pap. 11.95 (ISBN 0-947752-25-0, Pub. by Waterstone UK). Hippocrene Bks.
Smoke the Burning Body Makes. Steve Schutzman. LC 78-2256. (Illus.). 64p. 1978. pap. 6.00 (ISBN 0-915572-28-1). Panjandrum.
Smoked Glass. Robert H. Newell. LC 70-171060. Repr. of 1868 ed. 29.00 (ISBN 0-404-03663-5). AMS Pr.
Smoked Yankees. Willard B. Gatewood, Jr. LC 86-19352. 344p. 1987. pap. 12.00 (ISBN 0-938626-88-4). U of Ark Pr.
Smoked Yankees & the Struggle for Empire: Letters from Negro Soldiers, 1898-1902. Willard B. Gatewood, Jr. LC 78-146006. pap. 84.80 (ISBN 0-317-27556-9, 2014922). Bks Demand UMI.
SmokeFree - How to Stop Smoking in Nine Easy Steps. Harold H. Dawley, Jr. (Illus.). 127p. (Orig.). 1987. pap. 9.95 (ISBN 0-317-58278-X). Wellness Inst.
SmokeFree - Worksite Smoking Control, Discouragement, & Cessation. Harold H. Dawley, Jr. (Illus.). 90p. (Orig.). 1987. pap. 14.95 (ISBN 0-9617202-1-2). Wellness Inst.
Smokehouse Bear. Gordon Nelson. LC 82-1743. (Illus.). 1982. pap. 6.95 (ISBN 0-88240-227-7). Alaska Northwest.
Smokejumper: A Summer in the American Wilderness. Dale L. Schmaljohn. (Illus.). 163p. (gr. 6-12). 1982. 9.95 (ISBN 0-9608454-0-2); pap. 6.95 (ISBN 0-9608454-1-0). Hyde Park Pr.
Smokeless Coal Fields of West Virginia. W. P. Tams, Jr. LC 63-62525. 1963. 6.00 (ISBN 0-937058-18-1). West Va U Pr.
Smokeless Tobbacco. 1987. pap. 1.00 (ISBN 0-89230-226-7). Do It Now.
Smoker Motivation. A. Wetterer. (Illus.). 175p. 1986. 38.00 (ISBN 0-387-16751-X). Springer-Verlag.
Smoker's Addictionary. Roslyn Schwartz. 1985. pap. 3.95 (ISBN 0-671-54400-4, Linden Pr). S&S.
Smoker's Book of Health: How to Keep Yourself Healthier & Reduce Your Smoking Risks. Tom Ferguson. 224p. 1987. 18.95 (ISBN 0-399-13193-0, Putnam). Putnam Pub Group.
Smoker's Heaven: You Don't Have to Die to Go There. Martin Ehde, Jr. LC 79-57444. (Illus.). 132p. (Orig.). 1980. pap. 4.95 (ISBN 0-936188-01-4). Ehde Pub Co.
Smokers' Humour. Joel Rothman. 78p. 1985. pap. 2.95 (ISBN 0-86051-218-5). Parkwest Pubns.
Smokers, Segars & Stickers. A. D. Faber. (Illus.). 1949. lib. bdg. 10.00. Am Life Foun.
Smoke's Way: Poems from Limited Editions, 1968-1981. William Stafford. LC 82-80525. 112p. 1983. 14.00 (ISBN 0-915308-40-1); pap. 6.00 (ISBN 0-915308-41-X). Graywolf.
Smokescreen. Dick Francis. 224p. 1986. pap. 3.50 (ISBN 0-671-50737-0). PB.
Smokescreen. Anne Mather. (Harlequin Presents Ser.). 192p. 1982. pap. 1.75 (ISBN 0-373-10509-6). Harlequin Bks.
Smokescreens. Jack T. Chick. (Illus.). 93p. 1982. pap. 2.50 (ISBN 0-937958-14-X). Chick Pubns.
Smoketree. Margarita Engle. 20p. 1983. 7.00 (ISBN 0-913719-64-1); pap. 2.00 (ISBN 0-913719-63-3). High-Coo Pr.
Smokey. Bill Peet. (Illus.). (gr. k-3). 1962. PLB 11.95 (ISBN 0-395-15992-X). HM.
Smokey. Bill Peet. (Illus.). 48p. (gr. k-3). 1983. pap. 3.95 (ISBN 0-395-34924-9). HM.
Smokey Bear & the Great Wilderness. Elliott S. Barker. LC 82-19373. (Illus.). 150p. (Orig.). 1982. pap. 12.95 (ISBN 0-86534-017-X). Sunstone Pr.
Smokey Hell Trail. Jon Sharpe. (Trailsman Ser.: No. 79). 176p. 1988. pap. 2.75 (ISBN 0-451-15404-5, Sig). NAL.
Smokey the Fireman. Richard Scarry. LC 86-82366. (Golden Easy Readers Ser.). (Illus.). 40p. (gr. k-2). 1988. 3.95 (ISBN 0-307-11651-4). Western Pub.
Smokey the Shark: And Other Fishy Stories. Charles Keller. (Illus.). (gr. 2-6). 1981. 8.95 (ISBN 0-13-814707-8). P-H.
Smokey the Shark & Other Fishy Tales. Charles Keller. (Illus.). 48p. (gr. 3-7). 1984. pap. 4.95 (ISBN 0-13-814690-X). P-H.
Smokey: The Soul of Motown. Smokey Robinson. (Illus.). 1988. 17.95 (ISBN 0-07-053209-5). McGraw.
Smoking. Robert F. Allen. (Lifegain Program for Changing Our Health Cultures Ser.). 35p. 1981. pap. 5.95 (ISBN 0-318-03838-2). Human Res Inst.
Smoking. rev. ed. Sherry Sonnett. Ed. by Lorna Greenberg. (First Bk.). (Illus.). 72p. (YA) (gr. 7 up). 1988. 9.90 (ISBN 0-531-10489-3). Watts.
Smoking: A Resource to Assist Hospitals in Developing Policies on Smoking. (Resource Package). 65p. 10.00 (ISBN 0-317-36933-4, C-070514). Am Hospital.
Smoking among Young Adults. M. Murray et al. 1988. text ed. 42.00 (ISBN 0-566-05467-1, Pub. by Gower Pub England). Gower Pub Co.
Smoking & Aging. Raymond Bosse & Charles L. Rose. LC 81-48002. 272p. 1984. 37.00x (ISBN 0-669-05230-2). Lexington Bks.
Smoking & Arterial Disease. Ed. by R. M. Greenhalgh. 315p. 1981. text ed. 57.95x (ISBN 0-8464-1215-2). Beekman Pubs.
Smoking & Health. Brian Ward. LC 85-52043. (Life Guides Ser.). (Illus.). 48p. (gr. 4-12). 1986. PLB 12.40 (ISBN 0-531-10180-0). Watts.
Smoking & Its Effects on Health: Report. WHO Expert Committee. Geneva, 1974. (Technical Report Ser.: No. 568). (Also avail. in French & Spanish). 1975. pap. 3.60 (ISBN 92-4-120568-7). World Health.
Smoking & Politics: Policy Making & the Federal Bureaucracy. 3rd ed. A. Lee Fritschler. 208p. 1983. pap. 19.00 (ISBN 0-13-815027-3). P-H.
Smoking & Reproduction: A Comprehensive Bibliography. Ernest L. Abel. LC 82-15660. xviii, 163p. 1982. lib. bdg. 40.95 (ISBN 0-313-23663-1, ASR/). Greenwood.
Smoking & Reproduction: An Annotated Bibliography. Ernest L. Abel. 160p. 1984. 65.00 (ISBN 0-8493-6481-7). CRC Pr.
Smoking & Reproductive Health. Michael J. Rosenberg. 352p. 1987. 35.00 (ISBN 0-88416-549-3). PSG Pub Co.
Smoking & Society: Toward a More Balanced Assessment. Ed. by Robert D. Tollison. 384p. 1985. 37.00x (ISBN 0-669-11603-3). Lexington Bks.
Smoking & the Lung. Ed. by G. Cumming & G. Bonsignore. LC 84-18102. (Ettore Majorana International Science Series, Life Sciences: Vol. 17). 514p. 1985. 89.50x (ISBN 0-306-41828-2, Plenum Pr). Plenum Pub.
Smoking & the State: Social Costs, Rent Seeking & Public Policy. Robert D. Tollison & Richard E. Wagner. LC 87-45981. 144p. 1988. 25.00x (ISBN 0-669-17100-X). Lexington Bks.
Smoking Cigarettes: The Unfiltered Truth: Understanding Why & How to Quit. Janet Benner. LC 87-80270. 144p. (Orig.). 1987. pap. 10.95 (ISBN 0-942723-12-0). Joelle Pub.
Smoking Epidemic: A Matter of Worldwide Concern-Proceedings of the 4th World Conference on Smoking & Health. Ed. by Lars M. Ramstrom. (Illus.). 352p. (Orig.). 1980. pap. text ed. 47.50x (ISBN 0-317-46433-7, Pub. by Almqvist & Wiksell). Coronet Bks.
Smoking: Facilitator's Manual. Sabina M. Dunton & Melody S. Fanning. Ed. by Richard A. McNeely. (Well Aware About Health Risk Reduction Ser.). (Illus.). 186p. (Orig.). 1982. 29.95 (ISBN 0-943562-51-1). Well Aware.
Smoking Flax. Hallie E. Rives. LC 72-2026. (Black Heritage Library Collection Ser.). Repr. of 1897 ed. 17.25 (ISBN 0-8369-9057-9). Ayer Co Pubs.
Smoking Food at Home. Maggie Black. (Illus.). 192p. 1985. 20.95 (ISBN 0-7153-8484-8). David & Charles.
Smoking for Two: Cigarettes & Pregnancy. Peter A. Fried & Harry Oxorn. LC 80-20054. (Illus.). 1980. 10.95 (ISBN 0-02-910720-2). Free Pr.
Smoking Gods: Tobacco in Maya Art, History, & Religion. Francis Robicsek. LC 78-64904. (Illus.). 1978. 39.50 (ISBN 0-8061-1511-4). U of Okla Pr.
Smoking Gun: How the American Tobacco Industry Gets Away with Murder. Elizabeth Whelan. LC 84-50685. 224p. 1984. 15.95 (ISBN 0-89313-039-7). G F Stickley Co.
Smoking Hills. Carter T. Young. LC 86-29060. (Double D Western Ser.). 192p. 1988. 12.95 (ISBN 0-385-24059-7). Doubleday.
Smoking Hills. Carter T. Young. LC 88-20045. 261p. 1988. Repr. of 1988 ed. lib. bdg. 14.95 (ISBN 0-89621-178-9). Thorndike Pr.
Smoking in the Workplace. (ASPA-BNA Survey Ser.: No. 50). 32p. 1986. 30.00 (ISBN 0-87179-976-6). BNA.
Smoking in the Workplace. (ASPA-BNA Survey Ser.: No. 51). 1987. 30.00 (ISBN 0-87179-977-4). BNA.
Smoking-Is It a Sin? Tom McDevitt. 80p. (Orig.). 1981. pap. 1.00 (ISBN 0-933046-03-0). Little Red Hen.
Smoking Leg, & Other Stories. facsimile ed. John Metcalfe. LC 74-152950. (Short Story Index Reprint Ser.). Repr. of 1926 ed. 18.00 (ISBN 0-8369-3828-3). Ayer Co Pubs.
Smoking: Medical Subject Analysis & Research Guide with Bibliography. Jorge S. Reginald. LC 84-45743. 150p. 1987. 34.50 (ISBN 0-88164-270-3); pap. 26.50 (ISBN 0-88164-271-1). ABBE Pubs Assn.
Smoking Not Allowed: The Debate. Gilda Berger. (Impact Ser.). (Illus.). 144p. (YA) (gr. 7-12). 1987. lib. bdg. 12.40 (ISBN 0-531-10420-6). Watts.
Smoking Paradox: Public Regulation in the Cigarette Industry. Gideon Doron. LC 79-50400. 1979. text ed. 20.50 (ISBN 0-89011-531-1). Abt Bks.
Smoking Paradox: Public Regulation in the Cigarette Industry. Gideon Doron. (Illus.). 158p. 1984. Repr. of 1979 ed. lib. bdg. 21.75 (ISBN 0-8191-4089-9). U Pr of Amer.
Smoking Paraphernalia of the East Asia. 26p. 1984. pap. 35.00x (ISBN 0-317-69090-6, Pub. by Han-Shan Tang Ltd). State Mutual Bk.
Smoking: Psychology & Pharmacology. Heather Ashton & Rod Stepney. LC 81-18829. 250p. 1982. (Pub. by Tavistock); pap. 8.95 (ISBN 0-422-77710-2, NO. 3836). Routledge Chapman & Hall.
Smoking Salmon & Trout: Plus Pickling, Salting, Sausaging & Care. Jack Whelan. LC 83-91013. 240p. 1984. pap. 14.95 (ISBN 0-919807-00-3). Pacific Search.
Smoking Technology of the Aborigines of the Iroquois Area of New York State. Edward S. Rutsch. LC 73-92558. 252p. 1972. 25.00 (ISBN 0-8386-7568-9). Fairleigh Dickinson.
Smoking: Third World Alert. Uma R. Nath. (Illus.). 270p. 1986. 22.50. Oxford U Pr.
Smoking: Third World Alert. Uma Ram Nath. (Illus.). 1986. 22.50x (ISBN 0-19-261402-9). Oxford U Pr.
Smoking: Workbook. Sabina M. Dunton & Melody S. Fanning. Ed. by Richard A. McNeely. (Well Aware About Health Risk Reduction Ser.). (Illus.). 109p. (Orig.). 1982. pap. 8.50 (ISBN 0-943562-52-X). Well Aware.
Smoky. Will James. (gr. 7-11). 1926. willow leaf ed. 12.95 (ISBN 0-684-12875-6, ScribT). Scribner.
Smoky God. Willis G. Emerson. (Illus.). 1908. pap. 4.95 (ISBN 0-910122-20-2). Amherst Pr.
Smoky-House. Elizabeth Goudge. 391p. 1983. Repr. lib. bdg. 17.95x (ISBN 0-89966-108-4). Buccaneer Bks.
Smoky Mountain Dreams: The Life Story of Edith Wilson Heston. Brenda P. Russell. 192p. 1987. 11.95 (ISBN 0-8062-3072-X). Carlton.
Smoky Mountain Folks & Their Lore. Joseph S. Hall. (Illus.). 1964. pap. 1.95 (ISBN 0-9600168-0-5). Hall J.
Smoky Mountains. write for info. (ISBN 0-936672-61-7). Aerial Photo.
Smoky Mountains Trout Fishing Guide. Don Kirk. LC 83-61709. (Illus.). 139p. 1985. pap. 8.95 (ISBN 0-89732-036-0). Menasha Ridge.
Smoky the Cow Horse. Will James. (Library of Contemporary Classics). (YA) (gr. 12 up). 1983. pap. 5.95 (ISBN 0-684-17145-7). Scribner.
Smoky the Cow Horse. Will James. LC 87-1129. (Illus.). 324p. (gr. 7 up). 1987. pap. 3.95 (ISBN 0-689-71171-9, Aladdin Bks). Macmillan.
Smoky-Top: The Art & Times of Willie Seaweed. Bill Holm. LC 83-47973. (Thomas Burke Memorial Washington State Museum Monograph: No. 3). (Illus.). 160p. 1983. 24.95 (ISBN 0-295-96038-8). U of Wash Pr.
Smoky Valley. Don Hamilton. 1988. pap. 2.95 (ISBN 0-449-44530-5, GM). Fawcett.
Smolensk: A Guide. M. Dunaev. 102p. 1982. 5.95 (ISBN 0-8285-2320-7, Pub. by Progress Pubs USSR). Imported Pubns.
Smoley's Four Combined Tables. rev. ed. C. K. Smoley. Ed. by E. R. Smoley & N. G. Smoley. 1612p. 1980. fabricoid 47.50 (ISBN 0-911390-00-6). Smoley.
Smoley's Metric Four Combined Tables. C. K. Smoley. Ed. by E. R. Smoley & N. G. Smoley. 1400p. 1976. thumb-indexed 47.50 (ISBN 0-911390-08-1). Smoley.
Smoley's Parallel Tables of Slopes & Rises. E. R. Smoley & N. G. Smoley. 528p. 1980. 32.50 (ISBN 0-911390-03-0). Smoley.
Smoley's Three Combined Tables. rev ed. C. K. Smoley. Ed. by E. R. Smoley & N. G. Smoley. 1112p. 1974. thumb-indexed 42.50 (ISBN 0-911390-01-4). Smoley.
Smollett & the Scottish School: Studies in 18th Century Thought. M. A. Goldberg. 191p. 1985. Repr. of 1959 ed. lib. bdg. 50.00 (ISBN 0-89984-654-8). Century Bookbindery.
Smollett As Poet. Howard S. Buck. 1927. 10.00x (ISBN 0-686-51313-4). Elliots Bks.
Smollett As Poet. Howard S. Buck. LC 74-3310. 1971. Repr. of 1927 ed. lib. bdg. 15.00 (ISBN 0-8414-3120-5). Folcroft.
Smollett: Author of the First Distinction. Ed. by Alan Bold. (Critical Studies). 240p. 1982. text ed. 28.50x (ISBN 0-389-20240-1, 07097). B&N Imports.
Smollett Studies. Claude E. Jones. LC 72-191232. Repr. of 1942 ed. lib. bdg. 20.00 (ISBN 0-8414-5428-0). Folcroft.
Smollett Studies. Claude E. Jones. LC 70-128188. 128p. 1970. Repr. of 1942 ed. 15.00x (ISBN 0-87753-048-3). Phaeton.
Smollett's Hoax: Don Quixote in English. Carmine R. Linsalata. LC 77-181947. (Stanford University. Stanford Studies in Language & Literature: No. 14). Repr. of 1956 ed. 24.00 (ISBN 0-404-51824-9). AMS Pr.
Smollett's Reputation As a Novelist. F. W. Boege. LC 75-96150. 1970. Repr. of 1947 ed. lib. bdg. 18.50x (ISBN 0-374-90741-2, Octagon). Hippocrene Bks.
Smoochy Poochy-Hettie's Apfel Tree. (Book on Amish Ser.). 12.00 (ISBN 0-9609624-2-5). Bookworm Rochester NY.
Smooth As a Baby's Bottom: A Dermatologist's Complete Guide to Your Child's Skin Care. Garry Gewirtzman. Ed. by Kathy Leth. (Illus.). 128p. 1988. 12.95 (ISBN 0-8119-0735-X). Fell.
Smooth As Silk. 2nd ed. Myra Philipps. (Illus.). (gr. 3 up). 1979. 4.95 (ISBN 0-686-10960-0). Basin Pub.
Smooth Compactification of Locally Symmetric Varieties. A. Ash et al. LC 75-38142. (Lie Groups: History, Frontiers & Applications Ser.: No. 4). 340p. 1975. 19.00 (ISBN 0-915692-12-0, 991600061). Math Sci Pr.
Smooth Dynamical Systems. M. Irwin. (Pure & Applied Mathematical Ser.). 1980. 69.00 (ISBN 0-12-374450-4). Acad Pr.
Smooth Face of Evil. Margaret Yorke. 208p. 1985. pap. 2.95 (ISBN 0-445-20033-2, Pub. by Popular Lib). Warner Bks.
Smooth Move. Berniece Rabe. Ed. by Kathleen Tucker. LC 87-2099. (Concept Book Ser.). (Illus.). (gr. 1-4). 1987. PLB 10.75 (ISBN 0-8075-7486-4). A Whitman.
Smooth Muscle: An Assessment of Current Knowledge. Ed. by Edith Bulbring et al. (Illus.). 576p. 1981. text ed. 95.00x (ISBN 0-292-77569-5). U of Tex Pr.
Smooth Muscle Cells in Atherosclerosis. J. C. Geer. Ed. by M. Daria Haust et al. (Monographs on Atherosclerosis: Vol. 2). 1972. 38.00 (ISBN 3-8055-1377-1). S Karger.
Smooth Muscle Contractions. Stephens. 744p. 1984. 89.75 (ISBN 0-8247-1727-9). Dekker.
Smooth Muscle Regeneration: A Review & Experimental Study. J. McGeachie. (Monographs in Developmental Biology: Vol. 9). (Illus.). vii, 90p. 1975. 36.75 (ISBN 3-8055-2058-1). S Karger.
Smooth S-One Manifolds. W. Iberkleid & T. Petrie. (Lecture Notes in Mathematics: Vol. 557). 1976. soft cover 13.00 (ISBN 0-387-08002-3). Springer-Verlag.
Smoothing Techniques for Curve Estimation. Ed. by T. Gasser & M. Rosenblatt. (Lecture Notes in Mathematics: Vol. 757). 1979. pap. 18.00 (ISBN 0-387-09706-6). Springer-Verlag.
Smoothing the Ground: Essays on the Native American Oral Literature. Intro. by Brian Swann. LC 82-16155. 364p. 1983. 37.50x (ISBN 0-520-04902-0); pap. 12.95x (ISBN 0-520-04913-6). U of Cal Pr.
Smoothings of Piecewise Linear Manifolds. Morris W. Hirsch & Barry Mazur. LC 74-2967. (Annals of Mathematics Studies: No. 80). 165p. 1974. 19.50x (ISBN 0-691-08145-X). Princeton U Pr.

Snakes of South-Central Texas. Thomas G. Vermersch & Robert E. Kuntz. (Illus.). 144p. 1987. 12.95 (ISBN 0-89015-584-4). Eakin Pr.

Snakes of Texas. Alan Tennant. Ed. by Barbara Reavis. LC 83-500. (Illus.). 588p. 1983. 60.00 (ISBN 0-932012-65-5). Texas Month Pr.

Snakes of the Catskill Mountains. pap. 1.50 (ISBN 0-686-31390-9). Outdoor Pubns.

Snakes of the Orient: A Checklist. Kenneth R. Welch. LC 86-27298. 192p. 1988. lib. bdg. 22.50 (ISBN 0-89464-203-0). Krieger.

Snakes of the World. Christopher Mattison. (Illus.). 192p. 1986. 21.95 (ISBN 0-8160-1082-X). Facts on File.

Snakes of the World, 2 Vol. Kenneth L. Williams & Van Wallach. LC 88-1. 1988. Vol. 1, 1988 ed., Synopsis of Living & Extinct Species. price not set (ISBN 0-89464-215-4); Vol. 2, 1989 ed., Synopsis of Snake Generic Names. price not set (ISBN 0-89464-216-2). Krieger.

Snakes of the World, 2 vols. Kenneth L. Williams & Van Wallach. 1989. Set. 49.50 (ISBN 0-89464-302-9). Krieger.

Snakes of Virginia. Donald W. Linzey & Michael J. Clifford. LC 81-12951. (Illus.). 159p. 1981. 16.95x (ISBN 0-8139-0826-4). U Pr of Va.

Snake's Spit. Darr Anderson. 325p. 1989. text ed. 17.95. B Deviladog & Co.

Snakes: Their Place in the Sun. Robert M. McClung. LC 79-10238. (Good Earth Ser.). (Illus.). (gr. 2-6). 1979. PLB 7.22 (ISBN 0-8116-6112-1). Garrard.

Snaketrack. Frank Bonham. 176p. 1985. pap. 2.50 (ISBN 0-441-77197-1). Ace Bks.

Snap. Abby Frucht. 358p. 1988. 17.95 (ISBN 0-89919-501-6). Ticknor & Fields.

Snap Box. Paul Gogarty. 1972. 6.00 (ISBN 0-685-29884-1, Pub. by Trigram Pr); signed ed. 12.00 (ISBN 0-685-29885-X); pap. 3.50 (ISBN 0-685-29886-8). Small Pr Dist.

Snap, Crackle & Popular Taste. Jeffrey Schrank. 192p. 1977. pap. 6.95 (ISBN 0-385-28810-7, Delta). Dell.

Snap Judgement. Marilyn Youngblood. (First Love Ser.). 155p. (YA) 1984. pap. 1.95 (ISBN 0-671-53409-2). PB.

Snap! Photography. Miriam Cooper. LC 81-88. (Illus.). 64p. (gr. 3 up). 1981. 8.59 (ISBN 0-671-34021-2). Messner.

Snap Revolution James Fenton in the Philippines: Granta Eighteen. Ed. by Bill Buford. 1986. pap. 6.95 (ISBN 0-14-008596-3). Penguin.

Snap! Snap! Colin Hawkins & Jacqui Hawkins. LC 84-9892. (Illus.). 32p. (ps-3). 1984. 9.95 (ISBN 0-399-21163-2, Putnam); pap. 4.95 (ISBN 0-399-21184-5). Putnam Pub Group.

Snap Your Fingers, Slap Your Face & Wake Up! Bhagwan Shree Rajneesh. Ed. by Ma Deva Sarito. LC 84-43011. (Initiation Talks Ser.). 256p. (Orig.). 1984. pap. 3.95 (ISBN 0-88050-632-6). Chidvilas Inc.

Snapdragon: The Story of John Henry Newman. Joyce Sugg. LC 81-85242. (Illus.). 192p. 1982. pap. 2.00 (ISBN 0-87973-653-4, 653). Our Sunday Visitor.

Snapping. Flo Conway & Jim Siegelman. 272p. 1979. pap. 8.95 (ISBN 0-385-28928-6, Delta). Dell.

Snappy Answers to Stupid Questions, No. 5. Al Jaffee. 1984. pap. 2.25 (ISBN 0-446-30259-7). Warner Bks.

Snappy Bulletin Bits. Paul E. Holdcraft. LC 72-109673. pap. 20.00 (ISBN 0-8357-9027-4, 2016076). Bks Demand UMI.

Snapshooters. Thomas Consilvio. LC 73-81972. (Illus.). 40p. 1974. pap. 4.95 (ISBN 0-913968-00-5). Mouse Pr.

Snapshot Versions of Life. Richard Chalfen. LC 87-70258. (Illus.). 213p. 1987. 22.98 (ISBN 0-87972-387-4); pap. 10.98 (ISBN 0-87972-388-2). Bowling Green Univ.

Snapshot View of Communication Patterns: The New Hampshire Division of Vocational Rehabilitation. Michael Nyhan & Jeff Charles. 67p. 1982. 7.50 (ISBN 0-318-19197-0, R-55). Inst Future.

Snapshots. Marv Bondarowicz. (Illus.). 1977. pap. 5.00 (ISBN 0-89439-000-7). Printed Matter.

Snapshots. Norma Klein. LC 84-7115. (gr. 7 up). 1984. 12.95 (ISBN 0-8037-0129-2, 01258-370). Dial Bks Young.

Snapshots. Norma Klein. 128p. 1986. pap. 2.50 (ISBN 0-449-70157-3, Juniper). Fawcett.

Snapshots. Alain Robbe-Grillet. 72p. 1986. pap. 7.95 (ISBN 0-8101-0728-7). Northwestern U Pr.

Snapshots: A Collection of Readings for Adults. Ed. by Brian Schenk et al. Incl. Reading Level 5. 1984 (ISBN 0-8428-9550-7); Reading Level 6. 1984 (ISBN 0-8428-9551-5); Reading Level 7. 1984 (ISBN 0-8428-9552-3); Reading Level 8. 1984 (ISBN 0-8428-9553-1). 144p. pap. 3.25 ea. Cambridge Bk.

Snapshots: Glimpses of the Other California. Gerald Haslam. LC 85-61449. 130p. (Orig.). 1985. pap. 7.95 (ISBN 0-915685-03-5). Devil Mountain Bks.

Snapshots of a Daughter-In-Law. rev. ed. Adrienne Rich. 1967. pap. 4.95 (ISBN 0-393-04146-8). Norton.

Snapshots: On a Photograph of John McCormack Singing for the Liverpool Dockworkers. William Holland. 1986. pap. 4.95 (ISBN 0-931848-68-7). Dryad Pr.

Snare: A Miss Pink Mystery. Gwen Moffat. 192p. 1988. 14.95 (ISBN 0-312-02284-0). St Martin.

Snare at Sycamore Grove. Juanita T. Osborne. 1986. 9.95 (ISBN 0-8034-8609-X, Avalon). Bouregy.

Snare: Avoiding Emotional & Sexual Entanglements. Lois Mowday. 240p. 1988. 12.95 (ISBN 0-89109-155-6). NavPress.

Snare of the Hunter. Helen MacInnes. 320p. 1985. pap. 3.50 (ISBN 0-449-20862-1, Crest). Fawcett.

Snare of the Hunter. Helen MacInnes. 19.95 (ISBN 0-89190-103-5, Pub. by Am Repr). Amereon Ltd.

Snare of the Trapper. Linda P. Amey. 1985. pap. 3.95 (ISBN 0-87162-414-1, D7250). Warner Pr.

Snared by Snarling S's. Romilda Dilley. (Illus.). 48p. 1982. 20.00 (ISBN 0-88014-048-8). Mosaic Pr OH.

Snares & Swindles in Bridge. Terence Reese & Roger Trezel. 1977. pap. 7.95 (ISBN 0-575-02633-2, Pub. by Gollancz England). David & Charles.

Snares, Deadfalls & Other Traps of the Northern Algonquians & Northern Athapaskans. John M. Cooper. LC 76-43683. (Catholic University of America Anthropological Ser.: No. 5). Repr. of 1938 ed. 17.50 (ISBN 0-404-15516-2). AMS Pr.

Snares of Ibex. Jo Clayton. 1986. pap. 2.95 (ISBN 0-87997-974-7). DAW Bks.

Snares of the Enemy. Pauline King. 208p. 1986. 13.95 (ISBN 0-684-18442-7, ScribT). Scribner.

Snares Without End. Olympe Bhely-Quenum. Ed. by A. J. Arnold & K. Drame. Tr. by Dorothy Blair from Fr. LC 87-7301. (CARAF Bks.). 100p. (Orig.). 1988. 24.95 (ISBN 0-8139-1188-5); pap. 9.95 (ISBN 0-8139-1189-3). U Pr of VA.

Snarfquest: The Book. Larry Elmore. LC 86-51453. 96p. (Orig.). 1987. 9.95; pap. 9.95 (ISBN 0-88038-462-X). TSR Inc.

Snark. William L. DeAndrea. 288p. 1985. 15.95 (ISBN 0-89296-142-2). Mysterious Pr.

Snark. William L. DeAndrea. 304p. 1987. pap. 3.50 (ISBN 0-445-40503-1). Mysterious Pr.

Snarkout Boys & the Avocado of Death. Daniel Pinkwater. LC 81-11737. 160p. (gr. 5 up). 1982. 11.75 (ISBN 0-688-00871-2). Lothrop.

Snarkout Boys & the Avocado of Death. Daniel Pinkwater. Bd. with Avocado of Death. 160p. 1983. pap. 2.25 (ISBN 0-451-12150-3, Sig Vista). NAL.

Snarkout Boys & the Baconburg Horror. Daniel Pinkwater. LC 83-19544. 160p. (gr. 5 up). 1984. 11.75 (ISBN 0-688-02670-2). Lothrop.

Snarkout Boys & the Baconburg Horror. Daniel Pinkwater. 1985. pap. 2.50 (ISBN 0-451-13581-4, Sig Vista). NAL.

Snarling Muse: Verbal & Visual Political Satire from Pope to Churchill. Vincent Carretta. LC 83-6979. (Illus.). 304p. 1983. 29.95x (ISBN 0-8122-7885-2). U of Pa Pr.

Snarly Snuffin. Stephen Cosgrove. (Snuffin Chronicles Ser.). (Illus.). 32p. (Orig.). (ps-3). 1988. pap. 3.95 (ISBN 0-8249-8207-X). Ideals.

Snatch. Bill Pronzini. (Nameless Detective Mystery Ser.). 1984. pap. 4.95 (ISBN 0-88150-021-6, Foul Play). Countryman.

Snatched Before the Storm! Richard Mayhue. 1980. pap. 1.00 (ISBN 0-88469-124-1). BMH Bks.

Snatched by a Killer Wave. Glen Wright. Ed. by Carol Murphy. (Illus.). (gr. 3-6). 1981. PLB 6.95 (ISBN 0-89868-114-6, Read Res); pap. text ed. 4.95 (ISBN 0-89868-121-9, Read Res). ARO Pub.

Snatches. Alec Cairncross. 44p. 5.95 (ISBN 0-86140-051-8). Dufour.

Snatching Men Out of the Fire & Other Series. J. J. Turner. pap. 4.50 (ISBN 0-89315-257-9). Lambert Bk.

SNCC: The New Abolitionists. Howard Zinn. LC 84-27925. x, 286p. 1985. Repr. of 1964 ed. lib. bdg. 38.50 (ISBN 0-313-24801-X, ZIAB). Greenwood.

Sneak It Through. Michael Connor. (Illus.). 112p. (Orig.). 1984. pap. 10.00 (ISBN 0-87364-282-1). Paladin Pr.

Sneak It Through: Security Evasion & Concealment Places. M. Connor. (Criminology Ser.). 1986. lib. bdg. 79.95 (ISBN 0-8490-3561-9). Gordon Pr.

Sneak Peeks: A Hot Shots. Nikki Dewey. LC 81-69907. (Illus.). 64p. 1984. cancelled (ISBN 0-940074-03-6). Family Tree Pony Farm.

Sneakers Meet Your Feet. Vicki Cobb. (How the World Works Science Ser.). (Illus.). 48p. (gr. 4-6). 1985. 11.95 (ISBN 0-316-14896-2). Little.

Sneaking Inmates Down the Alley: Problems & Prospects in Jail Management. David B. Kalinich & John Klofas. (Illus.). 220p. 1986. pap. 27.00 (ISBN 0-398-05264-6). C C Thomas.

Sneaky Tricks to Fool Your Friends. E. Richard Chuchill. LC 86-14448. (Illus.). 128p. (YA) (gr. 6-12). 1987. pap. 3.95 (ISBN 0-8069-4808-6). Sterling.

Sneaky Tricks to Fool Your Friends. Ed. by E. Richard Churchill. LC 86-14448. (Illus.). 128p. (gr. 2-6). 1986. 10.95 (ISBN 0-8069-4806-X); PLB 13.29 (ISBN 0-8069-4807-8). Sterling.

Sneering Desert. Stephen Cosgrove. (Snuffin Chronicles Ser.). (Illus.). (gr. k-6). 1988. pap. 3.95. Ideals.

Sneetches & Other Stories. Dr. Seuss. (Illus.). (gr. k-4). 1961. 8.95 (ISBN 0-394-80089-3, BYR); lib. bdg. 8.99 (ISBN 0-394-90089-8). Random.

Sneeze. David Lloyd. LC 85-46022. (Illus.). 32p. (ps-2). 1986. 7.95 (ISBN 0-694-00135-X, Lipp Jr Bks); PLB 11.89 (ISBN 0-397-32196-1). HarpJ.

Snezhnyi Chas: Stikhi, 1931-35. 2nd ed. Boris I. Poplavskii. Ed. by Simon Karlinsky. (Modern Russian Literature & Culture, Studies & Texts: Vol. 8). 114p. (Rus.). 1980. pap. 7.00 (ISBN 0-933884-13-3). Berkeley Slavic.

SNG Fact Book: Synthetic Pipeline Gas from Coal. 58p. 1978. pap. 2.50 (ISBN 0-318-12700-8, F00683). Am Gas Assn.

Sniff & Tell Riddle Book. Roy McKie. LC 77-90055. (ps-2). 1978. 3.95 (ISBN 0-394-83779-7). Random.

Sniff in Time. Susan Saunders. LC 81-10763. (Illus.). 32p. (ps-3). 1982. 10.95 (ISBN 0-689-30890-6, Atheneum Childrens Bks). Macmillan.

Sniff Shout. John Burningham. LC 83-23551. (Noisy Words Ser.). (Illus.). 24p. (ps). 1984. 4.95 (ISBN 0-670-65349-7, Viking Kestrel). Viking.

Sniff, Sniff Al-er-gee. new ed. Claude A. Frazier. LC 76-27985. (Illus.). (gr. k-3). 1978. 6.75 (ISBN 0-910812-19-5); pap. 3.25 (ISBN 0-910812-24-1). Johnny Reads.

Sniff the Detective. Richard Scarry. LC 86-82365. (Golden Easy Readers Ser.). (Illus.). 40p. (gr. k-2). 1988. 3.95 (ISBN 0-307-11652-2). Western Pub.

Sniffles. Stephen Cosgrove. (Serendipity Bks.). (Illus.). 32p. (gr. k-4). 1988. pap. 2.50 (ISBN 0-8431-2301-X). Price Stern.

Sniffy the Mouse. J. P. Miller. LC 79-66558. (Sniffy Bks.). (Illus.). 24p. (ps). 1980. 3.95 (ISBN 0-394-84397-5, BYR). Random.

Sniggles, Squirrels & Chicken Pox: Forty Original Songs with Activities for Early Childhood. Jackie Weissman. 64p. (ps-5). 1984. pap. 8.95 (ISBN 0-939514-06-0); Vol. I. album 9.95; cassette 9.95; Vol. II. album 9.95; cassette 9.95. Miss Jackie.

Sniglets for Kids. Ed. by Rich Hall et al. (Sniglets Collector Sticker Bks.). (Illus.). 24p. (gr. 3-7). 1985. pap. 1.95 (ISBN 0-89954-397-9). Antioch Pub Co.

Sniglets (Snig'lit)-Any Word That Doesn't Appear in the Dictionary, but Should. Rich Hall. 96p. 1984. pap. 5.95 (ISBN 0-02-012530-5). Macmillan.

Sniper. Anthony V. LaPenta, Jr. LC 75-16563. 1976. 12.95 (ISBN 0-87949-042-X). Ashley Bks.

Snipe's Castle. Roland Mathias. 89p. 1985. 25.00x (ISBN 0-317-54068-8, Pub by Gomer Pr). State Mutual Bk.

Snipe's Index to Economic Geography. 3rd ed. Ronald H. Snipe. Ed. by Elizabeth J. Snipe. 159p. 1980. 19.00 (ISBN 0-938740-01-6). Snipe.

Snipe's Index to Geographical Review. 3rd ed. Ronald H. Snipe. Ed. by Elizabeth J. Snipe. 200p. 1980. 19.00 (ISBN 0-938740-02-4). Snipe.

Snipe's Index to the Annals of the Association of American Geographers. 3rd ed. Ronald H. Snipe. Ed. by Elizabeth J. Snipe. 137p. 1979. 19.00 (ISBN 0-938740-00-8). Snipe.

Sniping: U. S. Marine Corps Manual FM-1-3B. Department of the Navy, U. S. Marine Corps. (Illus.). 270p. 1969. pap. 10.00 (ISBN 0-87364-042-X). Paladin Pr.

Snippets. Mae B. Knight. (Orig.). 1988. pap. 7.00 (ISBN 0-915541-22-X). Star Bks Inc.

Snippy & Snappy. Wanda Gag. (Illus.). (gr. 1-3). 1960. PLB 5.99 (ISBN 0-698-30319-9, Coward). Putnam Pub Group.

Snips & Snails & Walnut Whales. Phyllis Fiarotta. LC 75-9574. (Illus.). 288p. (ps-5). 1975. pap. 8.95 (ISBN 0-911104-49-6, 065). Workman Pub.

Snively Snuffin. Stephen Cosgrove. (Snuffin Chronicles Ser.). (Illus.). 32p. (Orig.). (ps-3). 1988. pap. 3.95 (ISBN 0-8249-8208-8). Ideals.

Snnorri Sagas of Norse Kings. S. Snorri. 390p. 1984. 57.50x (ISBN 82-091-0173-0, N-393). Vanous.

Snobbery with Violence: Crime Stories & Their Audiences. Colin Watson. 1988. pap. 8.95 (ISBN 0-317-67034-4). Mysterious Pr.

Snobissimo. Pierre Daninos. 256p. 1964. 8.95 (ISBN 0-686-55574-0); pap. 3.95 (ISBN 0-686-55575-9). French & Eur.

Snobol Four Primer. Ralph E. Griswold & Madge T. Griswold. (Illus.). 128p. 1973. pap. 25.00 (ISBN 0-13-815381-7). P-H.

SNOBOL Four Programming Language. 2nd ed. Ralph E. Griswold et al. (Automatic Computation Ser). 1971. pap. 28.00 (ISBN 0-13-815373-6). P-H.

SNOBOL Programming for the Humanities. Susan Hockey. 1985. 32.50x (ISBN 0-19-824675-7); pap. 14.95x (ISBN 0-19-824676-5). Oxford U Pr.

Snobs Beware. Marjorie Sharmat. (Sorority Sisters Ser.: No. 2). (Orig.). (gr. 6 up). 1986. pap. 2.50 (ISBN 0-440-98092-5, LFL). Dell.

Snodgrass Site of the Powers Phase of Southeast Missouri. James E. Price & James B. Griffin. (Anthropological Papers Ser.: No. 66). (Illus., Orig.). 1979. pap. 6.00x (ISBN 0-932206-77-8). U Mich Mus Anthro.

SnoDrift Ice Cream Company In-Basket. Richard H. Wirth. (Illus.). 160p. 1983. practice set 10.04 (ISBN 0-07-071145-3). McGraw.

Snohomish County Street Guide & Directory, 1989. Thomas Bros. Maps Staff. (Illus.). 96p. 1988. pap. 12.95 (ISBN 0-88130-298-8). Thomas Bros Maps.

Snoino Mystery. Donna L. Pape. LC 79-17908. (Mystery Ser.). (Illus.). 40p. (gr. 2). 1980. PLB 6.79 (ISBN 0-8116-6410-4). Garrard.

SNOMED Microglossary for Surgical Pathology. 132p. pap. 25.00 (ISBN 0-317-33954-0, NS4). Coll Am Pathol.

Snooker. Ted Lowe. (Sports Ser.). (Illus.). 1977. 6.95 (ISBN 0-7158-0585-1). Charles River Bks.

Snookered. Donald Trelford. 208p. (Orig.). 1986. pap. 11.95 (ISBN 0-571-13640-0). Faber & Faber.

Snoopy & Friends Book 'n' Tape Gift Pack. (Golden Book 'n' Tape Gift Packs Ser.). (Illus.). 24p. (Orig.). (ps-3). 1988. pap. price not set (ISBN 0-307-13820-8). Western Pub.

Snoopy & His Sopwith Camel. Charles M. Schulz. 1979. pap. 1.75 (ISBN 0-449-23799-0, Crest). Fawcett.

Snoopy & His Sopwith Camel. Charles M. Schulz. LC 78-91065. (Illus.). 64p. (gr. 5 up). 1969. 2.95 (ISBN 0-03-083177-6). H Holt & Co.

Snoopy & It Was a Dark & Stormy Night. Charles M. Schulz. 1984. pap. 2.95 (ISBN 0-449-20187-2, Crest). Fawcett.

Snoopy & the Great Pumpkin. Lee Mendelson. (World of Snoopy Ser.). (Illus.). 26p. (ps up). 1986. 12.95 (ISBN 1-55578-006-7). Worlds Wonder.

Snoopy & the Red Baron. Charles M. Schulz. LC 66-22569. (Illus.). 64p. (gr. 5 up). 1966. 2.95 (ISBN 0-03-060560-1). H Holt & Co.

Snoopy at the Dog Show. Lee Mendelson. (World of Snoopy Ser.). (Illus.). 26p. (ps up). 1986. 12.95 (ISBN 1-55578-008-3). Worlds Wonder.

Snoopy Collection. J. C. Suares. pap. 9.95 (ISBN 0-345-30340-7). Ballantine.

Snoopy, Come Home. Charles M. Schulz. (Golden Story Book 'n' Tapes). (Illus.). 24p. (ps-3). 1987. pap. write for info incl. cassette (ISBN 0-307-13990-5, Pub. by Golden Bks). Western Pub.

Snoopy Come Home Movie Book. Charles M. Schulz. 1979. pap. 1.95 (ISBN 0-449-23726-5, Crest). Fawcett.

Snoopy Disguise Kit. Charles M. Schulz. 16p. (gr. 1-4). pap. 1.50 (ISBN 0-590-32475-6). Scholastic Inc.

Snoopy Escritor. Charles M. Schulz. 1.50 (ISBN 0-686-56184-8). French & Eur.

Snoopy Farm Puzzle Book. Charles M. Schulz. 32p. (gr. 1-4). pap. 2.95 (ISBN 0-590-32907-3). Scholastic Inc.

Snoopy Festival. Charles M. Schulz. LC 74-4809. (Peanuts Ser.). 224p. 1980. pap. 7.95 (ISBN 0-03-057503-6). H Holt & Co.

Snoopy Goes Camping. Lee Mendelson. (World of Snoopy Ser.). (Illus.). 26p. (ps up). 1986. 12.95 (ISBN 1-55578-002-4). Worlds Wonder.

Snoopy Hits the Beach. Lee Mendelson. (World of Snoopy Ser.). (Illus.). 26p. (ps up). 1986. 12.95 (ISBN 1-55578-004-0). Worlds Wonder.

Snoopy in Fashion. Connie Boucher. (Illus.). 1988. pap. 14.95 (ISBN 0-87701-574-0). Chronicle Bks.

Snoopy: It's How You Play the Game. Charles M. Schulz. LC 87-83485. (Big Little Golden Bks.). (Illus.). 24p. (gr. k-3). 1988. price not set (ISBN 0-307-10281-5). Western Pub.

Snoopy: My Greatest Adventures. Charles M. Schulz. 48p. (gr. 2 up). 1988. text ed. 7.95 (ISBN 0-88687-377-0, Sparkler Bks). Pharos Bks NY.

Snoopy on Wheels. Charles M. Schulz. (Chunky Book & Doll Packages Ser.). (Illus.). (ps-1). 1985. 5.95 (ISBN 0-394-87531-1). Random.

Snoopy Safari Puzzle Book. Charles M. Schulz. 32p. (gr. 1-4). pap. 2.95 (ISBN 0-590-32908-1). Scholastic Inc.

Snoopy, Spike & the Cat Next Door. Lee Mendelson. (World of Snoopy Ser.). (Illus.). 26p. (ps up). 1986. 12.95 (ISBN 1-55578-010-5). Worlds Wonder.

Snoopy, the World's Greatest Author. Charles M. Schulz. LC 87-83486. (Big Little Golden Bks.). (Illus.). 24p. (gr. k-3). 1988. price not set (ISBN 0-307-10280-7). Western Pub.

Snoopy Top Dog. Charles M. Schulz. 1985. pap. 2.95 (ISBN 0-449-20883-4, Crest). Fawcett.

Snoopy's ABC's. Charles M. Schulz. LC 87-80103. (Golden Books for Beginners). (Illus.). 24p. (gr. 2-4). 1987. 2.95 (ISBN 0-307-10927-5, Pub. by Golden Bks). Western Pub.

Snoopy's America. Lee Mendelson. (World of Snoopy Ser.). (Illus.). 26p. (ps up). 1986. 12.95 (ISBN 1-55578-007-5). Worlds Wonder.

Snoopy's Band. Lee Mendelson. (World of Snoopy Ser.). (Illus.). 26p. (ps up). 1986. 12.95 (ISBN 1-55578-009-1). Worlds Wonder.

Snoopy's Baseball Game. Lee Mendelson. (World of Snoopy Ser.). (Illus.). 26p. (ps up). 1986. 12.95 (ISBN 1-55578-012-1). Worlds Wonder.

Snoopy's Birthday Party. Lee Mendelson. (World of Snoopy Ser.). (Illus.). 26p. (ps up). 1986. 12.95 (ISBN 1-55578-001-6). Worlds Wonder.

Snoopy's Book of Colors. Charles M. Schulz. LC 87-80105. (Golden Books for Beginners). (Illus.). 24p. (gr. 2-4). 1987. 2.95 (ISBN 0-307-10929-1, Pub. by Golden Bks). Western Pub.

Snoopy's Book of Opposites. Charles M. Schulz. LC 87-80107. (Golden Books for Beginners). (Illus.). 24p. (gr. 2-4). 1987. 2.95 (ISBN 0-307-10931-3, Pub. by Golden Bks). Western Pub.

Snoopy's Book of Shapes. Charles M. Schulz. LC 87-80106. (Golden Books for Beginners). (Illus.). 24p. (gr. 2-4). 1987. 2.95 (ISBN 0-307-10930-5, Pub. by Golden Bks). Western Pub.

Snoopy's Facts & Fun Book About Farms. Charles M. Schulz. LC 79-22307. (Snoopy's Facts & Fun Bks.). (Illus.). 40p. (ps-1). 1980. bds. 2.95 (ISBN 0-394-84300-2). Random.

Snow White. (Classic Fairytales Pop-Ups Ser.). (Illus.). (ps-1). 1.98 (ISBN 0-517-39465-0). Outlet Bk Co.

Snow White. (Diamond Series Pop-Ups). (Illus.). (ps-1). 1.29 (ISBN 0-318-12084-4). Outlet Bk Co.

Snow White & Rose Red. Jacob Grimm & Wilhelm K. Grimm. LC 78-18074. (Illus.). 32p. (gr. k-3). 1979. PLB 9.79 (ISBN 0-89375-136-7); pap. 1.95 (ISBN 0-89375-114-6). Troll Assocs.

Snow White & Rose Red. Jacob Grimm & Wilhelm K. Grimm. (Creative's Collection of Fairy Tales). (Illus.). 32p. (gr. 6 up). 1986. 10.45 (ISBN 0-87191-938-9). Creative Ed.

Snow White & Rose Red. Jacob Grimm & Wilhelm K. Grimm. LC 84-4910. (Illus.). 32p. (gr. k-3). 1984. PLB 10.95 (ISBN 0-13-815234-9). P-H.

Snow White & Rose Red. Jacob Grimm & Wilhelm K. Grimm. (Illus.). 32p. (gr. k-3). 1988. 13.95 (ISBN 0-8050-0738-5, North South Bks). H Holt & Co.

Snow White & Rose Red. Ed McBain. 256p. 1986. pap. 3.95 (ISBN 0-445-40513-9). Mysterious Pr.

Snow White & Rose Red. (Illus., Arabic.). (gr. 4-6). 3.50x (ISBN 0-86685-225-5). Intl Bk Ctr.

Snow White & the Dwarfs. Patricia Daniels. LC 79-28431. (Fairy Tales Ser.). (Illus.). 24p. (gr. k-3). 1980. PLB 13.31 (ISBN 0-8393-0251-7). Raintree Pubs.

Snow White & the Dwarfs. Patricia Daniels. LC 79-28431. (Fairy Tale Clippers Ser.). (Illus.). 24p. (gr. k-4). 1980. PLB 27.99 (ISBN 0-8172-1836-X); cassette 14.00. Raintree Pubs.

Snow White & the Little Men. William Springer. 1979. pap. 1.75 (ISBN 0-686-38381-8). Eldridge Pub.

Snow White & the Seven Dwarfs. Margaret Davidson & Carson Davidson. (Make Believe It's You Ser.: No. 2). (Illus.). 80p. (Orig.). (gr. 2-6). 1987. pap. 2.25 (ISBN 0-590-40504-7). Scholastic Inc.

Snow White & the Seven Dwarfs. Walt Disney. (gr. 2 up). 1979. pap. 0.95 (ISBN 0-448-15923-6, G&D). Putnam Pub Group.

Snow White & the Seven Dwarfs. Wanda Gag. (Illus.). (gr. 2-4). 1938. PLB 6.99 (ISBN 0-698-30320-2, Coward). Putnam Pub Group.

Snow White & the Seven Dwarfs. Jacob Grimm & Wilhelm K. Grimm. (Illus., Fr.). (gr. 3-8). 8.95 (ISBN 0-685-11566-6). French & Eur.

Snow-White & the Seven Dwarfs. Jacob Grimm & Wilhelm K. Grimm. Tr. by Randall Jarrell from Ger. LC 28-1489. (Illus.). 32p. (ps up). 1972. 14.95 (ISBN 0-374-37099-0). FS&G.

Snow White & the Seven Dwarfs. Jacob Grimm & Wilhelm K. Grimm. LC 85-12158. (Illus.). 40p. (gr. 1 up). 1985. 13.95 (ISBN 0-88708-012-X). Picture Bk Studio.

Snow-White & the Seven Dwarfs. Jacob Grimm & Wilhelm K. Grimm. Tr. by Randall Jarrell from Ger. (Michael di Capua Bks.). (Illus.). 32p. (ps up). 1987. pap. 5.95 (ISBN 0-374-46868-0, Sunburst). FS&G.

Snow White & the Seven Dwarfs. Marian Jonson. (Children's Theatre Playscript Ser.). (gr. k-12). 1957. pap. 2.25x (ISBN 0-88020-057-X). Coach Hse.

Snow White & the Seven Dwarfs. Judith Kase-Baker. (ps-6). 1984. pap. 3.50 (ISBN 0-87602-256-5). Anchorage.

Snow White & the Seven Dwarfs. Freya Littledale. (Illus.). 48p. (Orig.). (ps-3). 1987. pap. 3.95 (ISBN 0-590-41798-3). Scholastic Inc.

Snow White & the Seven Dwarfs. Illus. by Nicky Marsh. (Children's Classics Ser.). 32p. (gr. k-3). 1988. 5.95 (ISBN 0-8249-8263-0). Ideals.

Snow White & the Seven Dwarfs. Emma Mora. (Illus.). 30p. (ps-1). 1986. 3.95 (ISBN 0-8120-5726-0). Barron.

Snow White & the Seven Dwarfs. (Ladybird Stories Ser.). (Illus., Arabic.). (gr. 1-12). pap. 3.50x (ISBN 0-86685-268-9). Intl Bk Ctr.

Snow White & the Seven Dwarfs. (Derrydale Fairytale Library). (Illus.). (ps-3). 1985. 2.98 (ISBN 0-517-28812-5). Outlet Bk Co.

Snow White & the Seven Dwarfs. 1987. 4.95 (ISBN 0-932715-02-8). Evans FL.

Snow White & the Seven Dwarfs. Suzanne Weyn. (Disney Classics Ser.). (Illus.). 80p. (Orig.). (gr. 4-6). 1987. pap. 2.50 (ISBN 0-590-41170-5). Scholastic Inc.

Snow White & the Seven Little Men: For Those Who Find Great Things in Small Packages. (Faerytales Retold Ser.). (Illus.). 26p. (Orig.). (gr. 1-6). 1984. pap. 3.50 (ISBN 0-916549-01-1). Ariana Prods.

Snow White Finds a Home: A Book about Helping. LC 86-72416. (Disney Classic Value Stories Ser.). (Illus.). 32p. (ps-2). 1987. 3.95 (ISBN 0-307-11671-9, Pub. by Golden Bks). Western Pub.

Snow-White Image: The Hidden Reality of Crime in Switzerland. Flemming Balvig. (Scandinavian Studies in Criminology: Vol. 9). 150p. 1988. 32.50 (ISBN 82-00-07472-2, A Norwegian University Press Publication). Oxford U Pr.

Snow White in New York. Fiona French. 32p. (gr. 1-4). 1987. 9.95 (ISBN 0-19-279808-1). Oxford U Pr.

Snow White in the Enchanted Forest. Jim Razzi. (Disney Choose Your Own Adventure Ser.: No. 1). 48p. (gr. 2). 1985. pap. 4.95 (ISBN 0-553-05401-5). Bantam.

Snow White: Life Almost Lost. Theodor Seifert. Tr. by Boris Matthews from Ger. LC 86-21635. 144p. (Orig.). 1986. 9.95 (ISBN 0-933029-08-X). Chiron Pubns.

Snow White Syndrome: All about Envy. Betsy Cohen. 256p. 1987. 15.95 (ISBN 0-02-526970-4). Macmillan.

Snow White, the Wolf, & the Unicorn. William D. Marsland & Amy L. Marsland. LC 81-81618. 1982. 7.95 (ISBN 0-87212-150-X). Libra.

Snow Woman. David McKee. LC 87-16996. (Illus.). 32p. (gr. 1-3). 1988. 11.95 (ISBN 0-688-07674-2); PLB 12.88 (ISBN 0-688-07675-0). Lothrop.

Snow Woman. David Monobe. 165p. 1984. 7.45 (ISBN 0-89697-167-8). Intl Univ Pr.

Snow World. Kevin Urick. LC 82-51026. 477p. 1983. 16.95 (ISBN 0-917976-16-9, White Ewe Pr). Thunder Baas Pr.

Snowball Express. Joe Claro. (gr. 3-5). 1980. pap. 1.50 (ISBN 0-590-30359-7). Scholastic Inc.

Snowball in Hell. Adam Lassiter. (Dennison's War Ser.: No. 6). 192p. (Orig.). 1986. pap. 2.95 (ISBN 0-553-25456-1). Bantam.

Snowballing. Frank Covino. (Orig.). 1975. pap. 1.50 (ISBN 0-685-54128-2, LB290DK, Leisure Bks). Leisure NY.

Snowbird. Patricia Calvert. 192p. (YA) (gr. 7 up). 1982. pap. 1.95 (ISBN 0-451-13353-6, AE1354, Sig Vista). NAL.

Snowbird Diet: Twelve Days to a Slender Future -- & a Lifetime of Gourmet Dining! Donald S. Robertson & Carol P. Robertson. 1986. pap. 8.95 (ISBN 0-446-38283-3). Warner Bks.

Snowbird Gravy & Dishpan Pie: Mountain People Recall. Patsy M. Ginns. LC 81-16296. (Illus.). xiv, 209p. 1982. 8.95 (ISBN 0-8078-1516-0). U of NC Pr.

Snowblind. Robert Sabbag. 1978. pap. 3.95 (ISBN 0-380-01868-3, 60116-8). Avon.

Snowblind Moon: A Novel of the West. John B. Cooke. 687p. 1985. 19.95 (ISBN 0-671-45089-1). S&S.

Snowblind Moon: Hoop of Nation, Pt. 3. John B. Cooks. 384p. (Orig.). 1986. pap. 3.95 (ISBN 0-8125-8154-7, Dist. by Warner Pub Services & St. Martin's Press). Tor Bks.

Snowblind Moon: The Pipe Carriers, Pt. 2. John B. Cooke. 448p. (Orig.). 1986. pap. 3.95 (ISBN 0-8125-8152-0, Dist. by Warner Pub Services & St. Martin's Press). Tor Bks.

Snowbound Mystery. Gertrude C. Warner. LC 68-9124. (Boxcar Children Mysteries Ser.). (Illus.). (gr. 3-7). 1968. PLB 8.95 (ISBN 0-8075-7517-8). A Whitman.

Snowcastles. Duncan McGeary. (Orig.). 1981. pap. text ed. 1.75 (ISBN 0-505-51625-X, Pub. by Tower Bks). Leisure NY.

Snowcat Poems, Nineteen Eighty to Nineteen Eighty-One: To the Photographs of Robert Frank. Simon Perchik. LC 84-80827. 64p. 1985. lib. bdg. 7.95 (ISBN 0-943512-02-6, 16411). Linwood Pub.

Snowdon Stills. Lord Snowdon. LC 87-62098. (Illus.). 168p. 1987. 29.95 (ISBN 0-8212-1681-3). NYGS.

Snowdonia. William Condry. (Illus.). 200p. 1988. 29.95 (ISBN 0-7153-8734-0). David & Charles.

Snowdrops from a Curate's Garden. rev. ed. Aleister Crowley. Ed. by Martin P. Starr. LC 86-14517. (Illus.). 224p. 1986. 24.95 (ISBN 0-933429-01-0). Teitan Pr.

Snowed In. Alan Gettis. 20p. 1978. 7.00 (ISBN 0-913719-34-X); pap. 2.00 (ISBN 0-913719-33-1). High-Coo Pr.

Snowfire. Jessica Douglass. (Orig.). 1988. pap. 3.95 (ISBN 0-440-20075-X). Dell.

Snowfire. Kimberly Norton. (Orig.). 1983. pap. 1.95 (ISBN 0-317-02743-3, BH095). Holloway.

Snowfire. Kermit Shelby. (Voyager Ser.). (gr. 4-10). 1984. pap. 4.95 (ISBN 0-8010-8253-6). Baker Bk.

Snowflake. Lynne Dennis. (Kitten Kapers Ser.). (Illus.). 24p. (ps). Date not set. 3.95 (ISBN 0-8431-2258-7). Price Stern.

Snowflake Bentley: Man of Science, Man of God. Gloria M. Stoddard. LC 85-71995. (Illus.). 144p. 1985. pap. 6.95 (ISBN 0-933050-31-3). New Eng Pr Vt.

Snowflake in My Hand. Samantha Mooney. LC 82-18328. 100p. 1983. 12.95 (E Friede). Delacorte.

Snowflakes. Joan Sugarman. (Illus.). 48p. (gr. 4-6). 1985. 13.95 (ISBN 0-316-82112-8). Little.

Snowflakes & Snowdrifts: Individualism & Sexuality in America. David Bertelson. 294p. (Orig.). 1986. lib. bdg. 28.25 (ISBN 0-8191-5578-0); pap. text ed. 15.25 (ISBN 0-8191-5579-9). U Pr of Amer.

Snowflakes in the Sun: A How-To Guide to Hawaiian Quilt Making. Charlyne Stewart. LC 85-50143. 96p. 1986. pap. 14.95 (ISBN 0-87069-451-0). Wallace-Homestead.

Snowfoot: White Reindeer of the Arctic. Justin F. Denzel. LC 75-43634. (Famous Animal Stories Ser.). (Illus.). 48p. (gr. 2-5). 1976. PLB 6.89 (ISBN 0-8116-4858-3). Garrard.

Snowharry Takes a Vacation (with Arctic Friends) Sherry C. Miller. (Molly Character - Color Me Ser.: No. 4). (Illus.). 32p. (gr. k-5). 1985. pap. write for info. saddle-stitched (ISBN 0-913379-03-4). Double M Pub.

Snowkill. Ron Faust. 208p. 1981. pap. 2.25 (ISBN 0-686-97418-2, Leisure Bks). Leisure NY.

Snowman. Raymond Briggs. LC 78-55904. (Illus.). 32p. (ps-2). 1986. lib. bdg. 9.99 (ISBN 0-394-93973-5, BYR); pap. 4.95 (ISBN 0-394-88466-3). Random.

Snowman. Raymond Briggs. (Easy Piano Picture Bks.). 1987. 15.95 (ISBN 0-571-10076-7); pap. 7.95 (ISBN 0-571-10074-0). Faber & Faber.

Snowman. Raymond Briggs. LC 78-55904. (Illus.). 32p. (Orig.). (ps-2). 1988. pap. 8.95 book & doll pkg. (ISBN 0-394-81942-X, BYR). Random.

Snowman. Francis H. Wise & Joyce M. Wise. (Learn to Read Ser.: No. 16). (Illus., Dr. Wise Learn to Read Ser.). (gr. 1). 1976. pap. 1.50. Wise Pub.

Snowman Board Books. Raymond Briggs. Incl. Building the Snowman (ISBN 0-316-10813-8); Dressing up (ISBN 0-316-10814-6); Walking in the Air (ISBN 0-316-10815-4); The Party (ISBN 0-316-10816-2). (Illus.). (ps-k). 1985. pap. 3.95 ea. Little.

Snowman for Sale. Donna L. Pape. LC 76-23308. (For Real Ser.). (Illus.). 32p. (gr. k-4). 1977. PLB 6.69 (ISBN 0-8116-4304-2). Garrard.

Snowman Sniffles & Other Verse. N. M. Bodecker. LC 82-13927. (Illus.). 80p. (gr. 4-7). 1983. 9.95 (ISBN 0-689-50263-X, M K McElderry). Macmillan.

Snowman Who Went for a Walk. Mira Lobe. LC 83-27298. (Illus.). 32p. (ps-2). 1984. 10.25 (ISBN 0-688-03865-4, Morrow Junior Books); PLB 10.88 (ISBN 0-688-03866-2). Morrow.

Snowmelt from Yesteryears: Broadside Poem. 1974. vellum ltd. ed. 10.00 (ISBN 0-918704-03-0). Fels & Firn.

Snowmobile Kidnapping. Judy Hughes. (Orig.). 1980. pap. text ed. 1.75 (ISBN 0-505-51566-0, Pub. by Tower Bks). Leisure NY.

Snowmobile Racing. Nicole Puleo. LC 72-5422. (Superwheels & Thrill Sports Bks.). (Illus.). 48p. (gr. 4-9). 1973. PLB 8.95 (ISBN 0-8225-0402-2). Lerner Pubns.

Snowmobile Revolution: Technology & Social Change in the Arctic. Pertti J. Pelto. (Illus.). 225p. 1987. pap. text ed. 8.95x (ISBN 0-88133-287-9). Waveland Pr.

Snowmobile Safety & You. (Illus.). 1982. Student Ed. 1.95 (ISBN 0-916682-33-1); Instr. Ed. 2.95 (ISBN 0-916682-32-3). Outdoor Empire.

Snowmobile Service Manual. 10th, rev. ed. Intertec Publishing Corporation Staff. LC 86-81766. (Illus.). 496p. (Orig.). 1986. pap. 16.95 (ISBN 0-87288-236-5, SMS-10). Intertec Pub.

Snowpack, Cloud-Seeding, & the Colorado River: A Technology Assessment of Weather Modification. Leo Weisbecker. LC 74-15900. 1974. 11.95x (ISBN 0-8061-1225-5); pap. 5.95x (ISBN 0-8061-1226-3). U of Okla Pr.

Snowplow: Clearing Mountain Rails. Gerald Best. LC 66-18290. (Illus.). 1966. 24.95 (ISBN 0-8310-7060-9). Howell-North.

Snows of Kilimanjaro & Other Stories. Ernest Hemingway. 1961. (ScribT); pap. 7.95 (ISBN 0-684-71807-3, SL32, ScribT). Scribner.

Snows of Kilimanjaro & Other Stories. Ernest Hemingway. 160p. 1982. pap. 3.95 rack size (ISBN 0-684-17471-5, ScribT). Scribner.

Snows of Kilimanjaro & Other Stories. Ernest Hemingway. 160p. 1987. pap. 3.95 (ISBN 0-02-051830-7, Collier). Macmillan.

Snows of Nazareth. Judy Vernon. 100p. (Orig.). 1987. pap. 7.95 (ISBN 0-9617776-2-1). J Vernon.

Snow's Secret. Carole Standish. 192p. (Orig.). (gr. 7 up). 1982. pap. 1.95 (ISBN 0-590-32362-8, Windswept). Scholastic Inc.

Snowshoe. Monte Miller. LC 82-83035. (Illus.). 32p. (Orig.). (ps). 1983. pap. 3.95 (ISBN 0-914766-88-0, 0266). Illum Way Pub.

Snowshoe Book. William E. Osgood & Leslie J. Hurley. LC 83-14055. (Illus.). 160p. 1983. pap. 10.95 (ISBN 0-8289-0432-4). Greene.

Snowshoe Trek to Otter River. David Budbill. (Skylark Old Ser.). (Illus.). 96p. (gr. 4-6). 1984. pap. 2.25 (ISBN 0-553-15469-9, Skylark). Bantam.

Snowshoeing. 2nd ed. Gene Prater. LC 80-21452. (Illus.). 176p. (Orig.). 1980. pap. 8.95 (ISBN 0-916890-98-8). Mountaineers.

Snowshoeing. 3rd ed. Gene Prater. (Illus.). 184p. 1988. pap. 9.95 (ISBN 0-89886-178-0). Mountaineers.

Snowskate Goes for Gold. Sherry Miller. (Molly Character - Color Me Ser.: No. 3). (Illus.). 32p. (Orig.). (gr. k-5). 1984. pap. 1.95 saddle-stitched (ISBN 0-913379-02-6). Double M Pub.

Snowstorms in a Hot Climate. Sarah Dunant. LC 88-42665. (Illus.). 256p. 1988. 15.95 (ISBN 0-394-57018-9). Random.

Snowthrower Service Manual. 2nd, rev. ed. Intertec Publishing Corporation Staff. LC 86-81767. (Illus.). 224p. (Orig.). 1987. text ed. 9.95 (ISBN 0-87288-237-3, SSM-2). Intertec Pub.

Snowy Day. Ezra J. Keats. (Illus.). (ps-1). 1962. 11.95 (ISBN 0-670-65400-0). Viking.

Snowy Day. Jack E. Keats. (Picture Puffins Ser.). (Illus.). (ps-k). 1976. pap. 3.95 (ISBN 0-14-050182-7, Puffin). Penguin.

Snowy Day: Stories & Poems. Caroline F. Bauer. LC 85-45858. (Illus.). 80p. (gr. 2-5). 1986. 11.75i (ISBN 0-397-32176-7, Lipp Jr Bks); PLB 11.89 (ISBN 0-397-32177-5). HarpJ.

Snowy Earth Comes Gliding. Evelyn Eaton. 1974. pap. 5.95 (ISBN 0-943404-02-9). Bear Tribe.

Snowy the Rabbit: A Book About Colors. Stephen Hynard. LC 82-22108. (Stories To Learn By Ser.). (Illus.). 32p. (gr. k-3). 1983. PLB 12.33 (ISBN 0-516-08942-0); pap. 2.95 (ISBN 0-516-48942-9). Childrens.

Snowy Torrents: Avalanche Accidents in the United States, 1972-1979. 3rd ed. Knox Williams & Betsy Armstrong. (Illus.). 221p. 1984. pap. 14.95 (ISBN 0-933160-13-5). Teton Bkshop.

Snuff Bottles & Other Stories. Deng Youmei et al. Tr. by Gladys Yang from Chinese. 220p. (Orig.). 1987. pap. 5.95 (ISBN 0-8351-1607-7). China Bks.

Snuffed Out. Myron M. Streeter. 1969. 14.95 (ISBN 0-318-19129-6). SWAC Pr.

Snuffles' House: A Book About Shapes. Daphne Faunce-Brown. LC 82-22116. (Stories to Learn by Ser.). (Illus.). 32p. (gr. k-3). 1983. PLB 12.33 (ISBN 0-516-08943-9); pap. 2.95 (ISBN 0-516-48943-7). Childrens.

Snuffling Hedgehog. Jean T. Fredeking. 1987. pap. 20.00x (ISBN 0-317-59264-5, Pub. by A H Stockwell England). State Mutual Bk.

Snuffs & Butters. Ellen N. La Motte. LC 74-125226. (Short Story Index Reprint Ser). 1925. 17.00 (ISBN 0-8369-3593-4). Ayer Co Pubs.

Snuffy. Dick Bruna. (Dick Bruna Bks.). 1984. 2.95 (ISBN 0-8431-1548-3). Price Stern.

Snuffy & the Fire. Dick Bruna. (Dick Bruna Bks.). 1984. 2.95 (ISBN 0-8431-1549-1). Price Stern.

Snug Harbor. Richard Katrovas. LC 84-20851. 82p. 1986. 17.00x (ISBN 0-8195-5134-1); pap. 8.95 (ISBN 0-8195-6125-8). Wesleyan U Pr.

Snug Little Purchase: How Richard Henderson Bought Kaintuckee from the Cherokees in 1775. Charles Brashers. LC 78-74150. (Illus.). 1979. 7.95 (ISBN 0-933362-01-3); pap. 4.95 (ISBN 0-933362-02-1). Assoc Creative Writers.

Snugg. Stephen Cosgrove. (Bugg Bks.). (Illus.). 32p. (gr. 2-7). 1983. 1.00 (ISBN 0-8431-1204-2). Price Stern.

Snugg. Stephen Cosgrove. (Bugg Bks.). (Orig.). 1984. incl. cassette 3.95 (ISBN 0-8431-1225-5). Price Stern.

Snuggle Book. Lennie Rose. (Illus.). 80p. 1985. pap. 5.95 (ISBN 0-943084-31-8). Turnbull & Willoughby.

Snuggle Bunny. Nancy Jewell. LC 73-183171. (Illus.). 32p. (ps-3). 1972. 11.70i (ISBN 0-06-022833-4). HarpJ.

Snuggle Piggy & the Magic Blanket. Michele Stepto. LC 86-23943. (ps-k). 1987. 9.95 (ISBN 0-525-44308-8). Dutton.

Snuggles' Great Adventure. Paula J. Bussard et al. Ed. by Shirley Wigginton. (Critter County Ser.). (Illus.). 30p. (gr. k-4). 1987. 1.39 (ISBN 0-87403-254-7, 3454). Standard Pub.

Snyder's Letters. Sim O. Wilde. 140p. (Orig.). 1988. pap. write for info. (ISBN 0-9620769-0-2). Wilde & Assocs.

Snyders Mounds & Five Other Mound Groups in Calhoun County, Illinois. David P. Braun et al. LC 82-622498. (University of Michigan, Museum of Anthropology, Technical Reports, Research Reports, No 13. Research Reports in Archaelogy: Contribution: No. 8). pap. 48.00 (2026235). Bks Demand UMI.

Snyder's Walk. Thomas B. Morgan. LC 86-16224. 360p. 1987. pap. 17.95 (ISBN 0-385-23637-9, Dolp). Doubleday.

So Away I Went! William B. Stout. Ed. by James Gilbert. LC 79-7299. (Flight: Its First Seventy-Five Years Ser.). (Illus.). 1979. Repr. of 1951 ed. lib. bdg. 32.50x (ISBN 0-405-12205-5). Ayer Co Pubs.

So Beloved Cousins: The Life & Times of Solon B. Cousins, Jr. Joseph E. Nettles. LC 82-23986. x, 178p. 1983. 12.95x (ISBN 0-86554-070-5, H53). Mercer Univ Pr.

So Bewirbt Man Sich. Wolfgang Manekeller. 160p. (Ger.). 1980. pap. 5.50. Langenscheidt.

So Big. Christopher Carrie. (Crayola Crayons Ser.). (Illus.). 32p. Date not set. 2.70 (ISBN 0-86696-205-0). Binney & Smith.

So Big. Edna Ferber. 1979. pap. 1.95 (ISBN 0-449-23476-2, Crest). Fawcett.

So Big! Harriet Ziefert. LC 86-61785. (Look-at-Me Bks). (Illus.). 14p. (ps). 1987. 2.95 (ISBN 0-394-88555-4, BYR). Random.

So Blue Marble. Dorothy B. Hughes. (Black Dagger Crime Ser.). 160p. 1987. text ed. 14.95x (ISBN 0-86220-709-6, Pub. by Firecrest Pub Ltd). Prescott Pr Nh.

So Busy! Harriet Ziefert. LC 86-61787. (Look-at-Me Books). (Illus.). 14p. (ps). 1987. 2.95 (ISBN 0-394-88557-0, BYR). Random.

So-Called Dollars. E. Kenney. 1984. pap. 6.00 (ISBN 0-942666-26-7). S J Durst.

So-Called Historical Jesus & the Historic Biblical Christ. Martin Kahler. Tr. by Carl E. Braaten from Ger. LC 88-45231. (Texts in Modern Theology Ser.). 160p. 1988. pap. 8.95 (ISBN 0-8006-3206-0). Fortress.

So Can I. Margery Facklam. LC 86-33720. (Illus.). 28p. (gr. 3-5). 1988. 6.95 (ISBN 0-15-200419-X, Gulliver Bks). HarBraceJ.

So Clean! Harriet Ziefert. LC 86-61786. (Look-at-Me Books). (Illus.). 14p. (ps). 1987. 2.95 (ISBN 0-394-88556-2, BYR). Random.

So You Want to Be a Leader. Kenneth O. Gangel. pap. 3.45 (ISBN 0-87509-131-8); leaders guide 2.95 (ISBN 0-87509-298-5). Chr Pubns.

So You Want to Be a Mortgage Banker. 66p. 1986. 25.00 (ISBN 0-929097-27-0, 18283). US League Savi Inst.

So You Want to Be a Profitable Database Publisher. Ed. by Fred S. Rosenau & Leslie R. Chase. LC 83-82192. 1983. pap. 25.00 (ISBN 0-942774-14-0). Info Indus.

So You Want to be a Wizard. Diane Duane. LC 83-5216. 288p. (gr. 7 up). 1983. 14.95 (ISBN 0-385-29305-4). Delacorte.

So You Want to Be a Wizard. Diane Duane. (gr. 5-8). 1986. pap. 2.75 (ISBN 0-440-98252-9, LFL). Dell.

So You Want to Be a Writer. Robert E. Moore. LC 73-90424. 300p. 1974. 15.00x (ISBN 0-87835-046-2). Boyd & Fraser.

So You Want to Be an Executive. Elton T. Reeves. LC 73-138569. pap. 63.50 (ISBN 0-317-09942-6, 2050398). Bks Demand UMI.

So You Want to Be An Information Broker? Ed. by Kelly Warnken & Barbara Felicetti. 100p. 1982. 29.00 (ISBN 0-936288-01-9). Info Alternative.

So You Want to Be an Innkeeper. Mary E. Davies et al. LC 85-13623. (Illus.). 240p. (Orig.). 1985. pap. 10.95 (ISBN 0-89286-252-1, TX9113M275623). One Hund One Prods.

So You Want to Be Happily in Love. Grady Poulard. 92p. 1983. 6.00 (ISBN 0-939296-09-8). Bond Pub Co.

So You Want to Be in Advertising: A Guide to Success in a Fast-Paced Business. Ed. by Ed Caffrey. LC 87-26497. (Illus.). 192p. 1988. 8.95 (ISBN 0-671-64590-0, Fireside). S&S.

So You Want to Be President. Everett Blackman. 88p. 1972. 2.00 (ISBN 0-86690-060-8, 1024-01). Am Fed Astrologers.

So You Want to Build a Live Steam Locomotive. Joseph F. Nelson. LC 74-75879. (Illus.). 164p. 1978. Repr. of 1974 ed. 20.95 (ISBN 0-914104-01-2). Wildwood Pubns MI.

So You Want to Buy a Second-Hand Car? Stephen McClymont. 24p. 1986. 14.00X (ISBN 0-7223-2011-6, Pub. by A H Stockwell England). State Mutual Bk.

So You Want to Do a Science Project! Joel Beller. LC 81-7943. (Illus.). 160p. (gr. 5 up). 1982. PLB 9.95 (ISBN 0-668-04987-1, 4987). Arco.

So You Want to Do Ministry. John Walsh & James DiGiacomo. LC 85-63107. 106p. (Orig.). 1986. pap. 6.95 (ISBN 0-934134-77-4). Sheed & Ward MO.

So You Want to Exercise? Try This! George L. Rafter. (Illus.). 63p. (Orig.). 1987. pap. 4.95 (ISBN 0-9618969-0-6). Reality OH.

So You Want to Fix up an Old House. Peter Hotton. LC 79-14961. (Illus.). 1979. pap. 14.95 (ISBN 0-316-37387-7). Little.

So You Want to Get into the Race. Chuck Klein. 1980. concordance study guide 4.95 (ISBN 0-8423-6082-4). Tyndale.

So You Want to Go Legal? The Legal Secretaries Handbook. 2nd ed. Rosemary K. Small. Ed. by South Carolina Association of Legal Secretaries & Louis S. Amick. 310p. 1981. 3 ring binder 25.00 (ISBN 0-943856-05-1). SC Bar CLE.

So You Want to Go to Law School. John F. Dobbyn. LC 76-19202. 1976. pap. 6.95 (ISBN 0-685-71466-7). West Pub.

So You Want to Grow. Luis Palau. LC 86-80720. 1986. pap. 4.95 (ISBN 0-89081-554-2). Harvest Hse.

So You Want to Have a Long-Range Plan. rev. ed. William W. Simmons. 36p. 1987. pap. 10.00 (ISBN 0-912841-25-7, 02). Planning Forum.

So You Want to Join the Team: A Handbook for Teacher Aides, Volunteers, & Cooperating Teachers & Administrators. Dale L. Brubaker & Molly J. Sloan. 64p. 1980. pap. text ed. 16.95 (ISBN 0-8403-2338-7). Kendall-Hunt.

So You Want to Lead Students. Chuck Klein. 96p. 1982. pap. 4.95 leader's guide (ISBN 0-8423-6084-0). Tyndale.

So You Want to Learn How to Type. rev. ed. J. Robbins Barrett. (Illus.). 23p. 1987. pap. text ed. 5.95 (ISBN 0-9619019-2-6). J R Barrett.

So You Want to Move to the Smokies... 2nd ed. Holly H. Towne. 72p. (Orig.). 1986. pap. 7.95 (ISBN 0-9613947-0-6). H H Towne.

So You Want to Open a Day Care Center: A Basic How to Do It Guide. Patricia C. Gallagher. (Illus.). 100p. (Orig.). 1987. pap. text ed. 12.95 (ISBN 0-943135-07-9). Gallagher Jordon.

So You Want To Open A Restaurant: Making Your Favorite Fantasy Real. Rev. ed. Charles Robbins. Ed. by Susan Suffes. 240p. 1986. 16.95 (ISBN 0-317-55021-7). Beaufort Bks NY.

So You Want to Open a Restaurant: Making Your Favorite Fantasy Real. Charles P. Robbins. 220p. 1982. 13.95 (ISBN 0-936602-37-6); pap. 11.95. Kampmann.

So You Want to Open a Restaurant: The Complete Guide to Owning & Operating Your Business Successfully. Charles Robbins. 1987. pap. 11.95 (ISBN 0-8253-0451-2). Beaufort Bks NY.

So You Want to Own A Horse...? A Guide to the Selection & Care of Your Horse: Including Stories from Forty Years' Practice As a Country Veterinarian. John J. Mettler, Jr. (Illus.). 201p. (Orig.). 1988. pap. cancelled (ISBN 0-9614876-2-3). Golden Hl Pr NY.

So You Want to Quit. Jean Kirkpatrick. 18p. 1983. pap. 1.50 (ISBN 0-318-19527-5). WFS.

So You Want to Raise a Boy? W. Cleon Skousen. LC 61-9555. 1962. pap. 16.95 (ISBN 0-385-02408-8). Doubleday.

So You Want to See a Psychiatrist? Ed. by Bruce L. Danto et al. LC 79-23225. 170p. 1980. lib. bdg. 15.00 (ISBN 0-405-12622-0). Ayer Co Pubs.

So You Want to Set the Pace. Chuck Klein. 96p. 1982. pap. 4.95 (ISBN 0-8423-6083-2). Tyndale.

So You Want To Start a Business! William A. Delaney. 216p. 1984. (Busn); pap. 9.95 (ISBN 0-13-823907-X). P-H.

So You Want to Start a Restaurant? rev. ed. Dewey A. Dyer. 160p. 1983. 19.95 (ISBN 0-8436-2199-0). Van Nos Reinhold.

So You Want to Teach English to Foreigners. C. Leatherdale. 1980. cancelled 10.00 (ISBN 0-85626-192-0, Pub. by Abacus England). IPS.

So You Want to Write a Cookbook. Judy Rehmel. LC 83-61899. (Illus.). 100p. 1983. pap. 6.95 (ISBN 0-915216-88-4). Marathon Intl Pub Co.

So, You Want to Write a Cookbook! Judy Rehmel. (Illus.). 52p. 1982. pap. 5.00x (ISBN 0-913731-04-8). J Rehmel.

So You Want to Write Your Family History. Norma P. Evans. LC 83-82903. (Illus.). 47p. (Orig.). 1983. pap. text ed. 6.50x (ISBN 0-937418-09-9). N P Evans.

So Young, So Fair. Elizabeth Seifert. 1973. Repr. of 1947 ed. lib. bdg. 18.95x (ISBN 0-88411-017-6, Pub. by Aeonian Pr). Amereon Ltd.

So Young, So Fair. Elizabeth Seifert. LC 86-5900. 412p. 1986. Repr. of 1947 ed. 16.95 (ISBN 0-89621-726-4). Thorndike Pr.

So Your Child Has a Learning Problem: Now What? Jane D. Wallbrown & Fred H. Wallbrown. 144p. (Orig.). 1981. pap. 11.95 (ISBN 0-88422-015-X). Clinical Psych.

So You're a Mathematics Supervisor. Ross Taylor. 20p. 1981. pap. 3.00 (ISBN 0-87353-199-X). NCTM.

So You're a Teenage Girl. Jill Renich. (Orig.). (gr. 8 up). pap. 3.95 (ISBN 0-310-31802-5, 10706S). Zondervan.

So You're a Woman. Vynomma Clark. LC 70-180790. 4.95 (ISBN 0-89112-050-5). Abilene Christ U.

So You're Adopted. Fred Powledge. LC 81-23278. 112p. (gr. 7 up). 1982. 11.95 (ISBN 0-684-17347-6, Pub. by Scribner). Macmillan.

So You're Getting Braces. Alvin Silverstein & Virginia Silverstein. LC 77-16488. (Illus.). 128p. (gr. 5 up). 1978. PLB 12.89 (ISBN 0-397-31786-7, Lipp Jr Bks); pap. 3.95 (ISBN 0-397-31787-5). HarpJ.

So You're Getting Married! Carol Benjamin. 1982. pap. 1.25 (ISBN 0-911739-15-7). Abbott Loop.

So You're Getting Married. H. Norman Wright. LC 85-18364. 264p. 1985. write for info. (5418613); 12.95; pap. 7.95. Regal.

So You're Going Abroad: How to Do It. Ann N. Hansen. LC 84-71013. 125p. (Orig.). 1984. pap. 7.95 (ISBN 0-9613491-0-7). At The Sign.

So You're Going to College. Vergilius Ferm. LC 72-85933. (Illus.). 160p. 1972. 6.95 (ISBN 0-8158-0292-7). Chris Mass.

So You're Going to Court: The Law & You. Robert W. Smedley. 302p. 8.00 (ISBN 0-685-41739-5). Fountainhead.

So You're Going to Have a Baby. (Illus.). 1972. pap. 1.50 (ISBN 0-87067-914-7, BH914, Melrose Sq). Holloway.

So You're Going to Have Puppies. Mari Stein. (Illus.). 1973. pap. 3.95 (ISBN 0-918546-03-6). Quarterdeck.

So You're Going To Hearing: Preparing for a Public Law 94-142 Due Process Hearing. Barbara Bateman. (Illus.). 36p. (Orig.). 1980. pap. text ed. 3.95 (ISBN 0-8331-1905-2). Hubbard Sci.

So You're Going to Heaven. M. R. Keith. 1965. 4.95 (ISBN 0-910122-22-9). Amherst Pr.

So! You're Going to the Hospital! James Graham. LC 68-20945. 178p. 1968. 5.00 (ISBN 0-87527-013-1); pap. 3.50 (ISBN 0-87527-038-7). Green.

So You're Having an Operation: A Step-by-Step Guide to Controlling Your Hospital Stay. Karen R. Williams & Janet K. Stensaas. LC 85-6324. 228p. 1986. 19.95 (ISBN 0-13-823949-5). P-H.

So You're Not a Special Educator: A General Handbook for Educating Handicapped Children. Les Sternberg et al. 172p. 1986. pap. 18.50 (ISBN 0-398-05207-7). C C Thomas.

So You're on the Council. National Community Education Association Staff. Ed. by Mary R. Boo. (Illus.). 20p. 1987. wkbk. 2.50 (ISBN 0-932399-02-9). Natl Comm Ed.

So You're on the Council: Facilitator's Guide. Guy Faust. Ed. by Mary R. Boo. 24p. 1987. 5.00 (ISBN 0-932399-03-7). Natl Comm Ed.

So You're on the Hospital Board! 3rd ed. Richard J. Umbdenstock. LC 87-13936. 44p. (Orig.). 1987. pap. 10.00 (ISBN 1-55648-010-5, 196110). AHPI.

So You're the Choir Director: A Handbook for the Choir & Its Director. Leroy E. Hurte. LC 74-29552. 112p. (Orig.). 1985. 6.95x (ISBN 0-931453-01-1); text ed. 10.95x (ISBN 0-931453-00-3); pap. 5.50x (ISBN 0-317-14176-7); pap. text ed. 7.95x (ISBN 0-317-14177-5). Lyric Pub Co.

So You're Thinking about Starting a Business: A Comprehensive Business Start up Manual. Business of Your Own Staff. 240p. 1988. 59.95 (ISBN 0-943267-00-5). Busn Your Own.

So You're Thinking of Going to a Chiropractor. Robert Dryburgh. 160p. 1984. 12.95 (ISBN 0-87983-345-9); pap. 3.95 (ISBN 0-87983-355-6). Keats.

So You've Got a Great Idea. Steve Fiffer. LC 85-26701. 211p. 1986. pap. 8.95 (ISBN 0-201-11536-0). Addison-Wesley.

Soakercise: Exercises for the Hot Tub, Pool & Spa. Sharon R. Hines. (Illus.). 27p. (Orig.). 1981. pap. 3.00 (ISBN 0-941904-03-2). Hot Water Pubs.

Soap & Detergrent Industry. (UNIDO Guides to Information Sources: No. 24). pap. 4.00 (ISBN 92-1-106156-3, ID/181). UN.

Soap & Suds. Diane Paterson. LC 83-9900. (Illus.). 48p. (gr. k up). 1984. lib. bdg. 10.99 (ISBN 0-394-96131-5). Knopf.

Soap Bandit. Dennis Haseley. LC 82-13434. (Illus.). 48p. (gr. 1-4). 1984. 12.95 (ISBN 0-7232-6216-0). Warne.

Soap Box Winners. Ed Radlauer & Ruth Radlauer. LC 82-17867. (Fact & Fiction Bks.). (Illus.). 48p. (gr. 3 up). 1983. PLB 11.93 (ISBN 0-516-07816-X). Childrens.

Soap Bubble Magic. Seymour Simon. LC 84-4432. (Illus.). 48p. (ps-3). 1985. PLB 11.88 (ISBN 0-688-02685-0); 10.25 (ISBN 0-688-02684-2). Lothrop.

Soap Bubbles. 3rd ed. Charles V. Boys. (Illus.). 1959. pap. 3.95 (ISBN 0-486-20542-8). Dover.

Soap Detergents: New Directions. Business Communications Staff. 153p. 1987. 1750.00 (ISBN 0-89336-622-6, C-090). BCC.

Soap: Making It, Enjoying It. 2nd ed. Ann Bramson. LC 75-7286. (Illus.). 120p. 1975. pap. 4.95 (ISBN 0-911104-57-7, 073). Workman Pub.

Soap Opera. Muriel G. Cantor & Suzanne Pingree. (CommText 12 Ser.). 168p. 1983. 19.95 (ISBN 0-8039-2004-0); pap. 9.95 (ISBN 0-8039-2005-9). Sage.

Soap Opera Babylon. Jason Bonderoff. (Illus.). 128p. 1987. pap. 8.95 (ISBN 0-399-51291-8, Perigee). Putnam Pub Group.

Soap Opera Book. Manuela Soares. (Illus.). 1978. 5.98 (ISBN 0-517-53330-8, Harmony); pap. 2.98 o. p. (ISBN 0-517-53331-6). Crown.

Soap Opera Encyclopedia. Christopher Schemering. (Orig.). 1985. pap. 8.95 (ISBN 0-345-32459-5). Ballantine.

Soap Opera Evolution: America's Enduring Romance with Daytime Drama. Marilyn J. Matelski. LC 87-43168. 224p. 1988. lib. bdg. 20.95x (ISBN 0-89950-324-1). McFarland & Co.

Soap Opera Trivia Quiz Book. Anthony Hayward & Penny Wilson. 1987. 29.00x (ISBN 0-317-68316-0, Pub. by Harrap Ltd England). State Mutual Bk.

Soap Opera Trivia Quiz Book, No. 2. 272p. pap. 2.95 (ISBN 0-451-12519-3, Sig). NAL.

Soaps & Detergents. 280p. 1987. 695.00 (ISBN 0-318-02834-4). Busn Trend.

Soaps in the Afternoon. Lavinia Harris. 188p. (Orig.). (gr. 7 up). 1985. pap. 2.25 (ISBN 0-590-33058-6, Point). Scholastic Inc.

Soapy. 2.00 (ISBN 0-686-16134-3). Alaskabks.

Soapy Smith: Bandit of Skagway. Harriet Pullen. (Illus.). 1973. pap. 1.50 (ISBN 0-911803-02-5). Sourdough.

Soapy Smith's Creede. Leland Feitz. pap. 2.50. Little London.

Soar & Surrender. Marlys Wills. (American Romance Ser.: No. 198). 245p. Date not set. pap. 2.50 (ISBN 0-317-63684-7). Harlequin Bks.

Soaring. Carter M. Ayres. LC 85-23667. (Superwheels & Thrill Sports Bks.). (Illus.). 40p. (gr. 4-9). 1986. PLB 8.95 (ISBN 0-8225-0442-1). Lerner Pubns.

Soaring Beyond Problems: Meditations for Difficult Times. Lois B. Swartz. (Illus.). 72p. (Orig.). 1987. pap. 6.95 (ISBN 0-940045-00-1). Walnut Knoll Assocs.

Soaring Cross Country. new ed. Ed Byars & Bill Holbrook. LC 74-78637. (Illus.). 180p. 1974. 9.95 (ISBN 0-914600-00-1). Ridge Soaring.

Soaring on a Grasshopper's Back. Mary Lane. Ed. by Christine Wilson & Austin Wilson. (Illus.). 141p. 1983. 9.95 (ISBN 0-9612144-0-6). Vireo Pr.

Soaring Spirit: Time Frame 600 - 400 B.C. Time-Life Books Editors. (Time Frame Ser.). (Illus.). 1987. 19.93 (ISBN 0-8094-6408-X); lib. bdg. 23.93 (ISBN 0-8094-6409-8). Time-Life.

Soaring: The Diary & Letters of a Denishawn Dancer in the Far East, 1925-1926. Jane Sherman. LC 75-34445. (Illus.). 288p. pap. 74.90 (2029784). Bks Demand UMI.

Soaring to the Top: The Success Manual for Young Adults. Jim Terry & Mary Terry. 300p. (YA) 1989. pap. 7.95 (ISBN 0-931731-07-0). Jimar Prodns.

Soaring: Where Hawks & Eagles Fly. Charles Coombs. LC 87-26588. (Illus.). 144p. (gr. k-6). 1988. 13.95 (ISBN 0-8050-0496-3). H Holt & Co.

Soaring with the Dodo: Essays on Lewis Carroll's Life & Art. Ed. by Edward Guiliano & James R. Kincaid. LC 82-83516. (Illus.). 140p. 1982. 15.00x (ISBN 0-930326-07-5, Pub. by Lewis Carroll Soc). U Pr of Va.

Sob: Etude Geographique D'un Terroir Serer (Senegal) Andre Lericollais. (Atlas Des Structures Agriares Au Sud Du Sahara: No. 7). pap. 22.00x (ISBN 90-2797-195-1). Mouton.

Sobbing at Midnight. Debabrata Rej. 394p. 1984. 10.95 (ISBN 0-89697-136-8). Intl Univ Pr.

Sobek Adventure Vacations. 4th ed. Ed. by Sobek's International Explorers Society Staff. (Illus.). 160p. 1986. lib. bdg. 24.80 (ISBN 0-89471-429-5); pap. 12.95 (ISBN 0-89471-428-7). Running Pr.

Sober Alcoholic: An Organizational Analysis of Alcoholics Anonymous. Irving P. Gellman. 1964. 17.95x (ISBN 0-8084-0279-X). New Coll U Pr.

Sober & Sensual. Kay M. Porterfield. 40p. 1985. pap. 1.95 (ISBN 0-89486-284-7). Hazelden.

Sober Generation: A Topology of Competent Adolescent Coping in Modern Puerto Rico. R. Fernandez Marina et al. 9.35 (ISBN 0-8477-2475-1); pap. 7.50 (ISBN 0-8477-2476-X). U of PR Pr.

Sober Life. John H. Spahr. 112p. 1979. 5.00 (ISBN 0-8059-2626-7). Dorrance.

Sober Living Workbook. Rip O'Keefe. 240p. 1980. pap. 7.95 (ISBN 0-89486-093-3). Hazelden.

Sober Self-Image for Young Adults. 24p. (Orig.). 1985. pap. 0.95 (ISBN 0-89486-312-6). Hazelden.

Sober Spring: One Family's Battle with Addiction. Robert F. Bollendorf. Ed. by Gregory F. Pierce. 100p. (Orig.). 1988. pap. 4.95 (ISBN 0-915388-32-4). Buckley Pubns.

Sobering Up: From Temperance to Prohibition in Antebellum America, Eighteen Hundred to Eighteen Sixty. Ian R. Tyrrell. LC 78-22132. (Contributions in American History: No. 82). 1979. lib. bdg. 35.00x (ISBN 0-313-20822-0, TYT/). Greenwood.

Sobhuza II: Ngwenyama & King of Swaziland. Hilda Kuper. LC 78-2356. 363p. 1978. 55.00 (ISBN 0-8419-0383-2, Africana). Holmes & Meier.

Sobibor: Martyrdom & Revolt. Ed. by Miriam Novitch. (Illus.). 168p. pap. 4.95 (ISBN 0-686-95087-9). ADL.

Sobieski Hours. Ed. by Eleanor P. Spencer. 300.00 (ISBN 0-384-56450-X). Johnson Repr.

Sobolev Spaces. R. A. Adams. (Pure & Applied Mathematics Ser.). 1975. 49.50 (ISBN 0-12-044150-0). Acad Pr.

Sobolev Spaces. V. G. Maz'ja. Tr. by T. O. Saposnikova from Rus. (Springer Series in Soviet Mathematics). (Illus.). 510p. 1985. 59.00 (ISBN 0-387-13589-8). Springer-Verlag.

Sobolev Spaces of Infinite Order & Differential Equations. Ed. by Collet's Holdings, Ltd. Staff. 1986. 42.00x (ISBN 0-317-46723-9, Pub. by Collets (UK)). State Mutual Bk.

Sobolev Spaces of Infinite Order & Differential Equations. Julij A. Dubinskij. 1986. lib. bdg. 48.00 (ISBN 90-277-2147-5, Pub. by Reidel Holland). Kluwer Academic.

Sobotta: Atlas of Human Anatomy, 2 vols. 10th ed. Ed. by Helmut Ferner & Jochen Staubesand. Incl. Vol. 1. Head, Neck, Upper Extremities. (Illus.). 390p (ISBN 0-8067-1710-6); Vol. 2. Thorax, Abdomen, Pelvis, Lower Extremities, Skin. (Illus.). 375p. 1983 (ISBN 0-8067-1720-3). (Illus.). 1983. text ed. 59.50 ea. Urban & S.

Sobotta-Hammersen: Histology-A Color Atlas of Microscopic Anatomy. 3rd ed. Ed. by Frithjof Hammersen. (Illus.). 272p. 1985. text ed. 36.50 (ISBN 0-8067-1743-2). Urban & S.

Sobranie Sochinenii, Vol. 3. Mikhail Bulgakov. 248p. (Rus.). 1983. 25.00 (ISBN 0-88233-698-3). Ardis Pubs.

Sobranie Sochinenii: Complete Works, Vol. 1. Vasily Aksyonov. Ed. by Priscilla Meyer. 250p. (Rus.). 1987. 25.00 (ISBN 0-87501-026-1). Ardis Pubs.

Sobranie Sochinenii V 4 Tomakh, Vol. 1. Evgenii Zamiatin. Ed. by Alexi Tsvetkov. 300p. (Rus.). 1982. cancelled (ISBN 0-88233-767-X). Ardis Pubs.

Sobranie Sochinenii V 5-i Tomakh, Vol 1. Vladislav Khodasevich. Ed. by Robert Hughes & John Malmstad. 330p. (Rus.). 1983. 25.00 (ISBN 0-88233-686-X). Ardis Pubs.

Sobranie Sochinenii: Vol. 1. Mikhail Bulgakov. Tr. by Tom I. Ranniaia. 421p. (Rus.). 1982. 25.00 (ISBN 0-88233-506-5). Ardis Pubs.

Sobranie Sochinenii, Vol. 8: Master i Margarita. Mikhail Bulgakov. Ed. by Ellendea Proffer. (Illus.). 425p. (Rus.). 1988. 25.00 (ISBN 0-88233-345-3). Ardis Pubs.

Sobranie Stikhotvorenii v Dvukh Tomakh, Vol. 1. Boris B. Bozhnev. Ed. by Lazar Fleishman. (Modern Russian Literature & Culture, Studies & Texts: Vol. 23). 177p. (Orig., Rus.). 1987. pap. 9.00 (ISBN 0-933884-53-2). Berkeley Slavic.

Sobranie Stikhov. Vladislav F. Khodasevich. LC 78-65602. 1978. pap. 7.95 (ISBN 0-89830-000-2). Russica Pubs.

Sobranie Stikhov I Pesen V Trekh Tomakh, 3 vols. Vladimir Vysotskii. Ed. by Arkady A. Lvov & Alexander Sumerkin. LC 88-60720. (Illus.). 1000p. (Orig., Rus.). 1988. Set. 129.00 (ISBN 0-89830-115-7); Set. pap. 75.00 (ISBN 0-89830-116-5). Russica Pubs.

Social & Economic History of the Near East in the Middle Ages. E. Ashtor. LC 74-29800. (Near Eastern Center Series, UCLA: No. 13). 1976. 45.00x (ISBN 0-520-02962-3). U of Cal Pr.
Social & Economic History of the Roman Empire, 2 Vols. 2nd ed. Mikhail Rostovtzeff. Ed. by P. M. Frazer. 1957. 115.00x (ISBN 0-19-814231-5). Oxford U Pr.
Social & Economic History of the United States, 2 Vols. Harry J. Carman. 1930-34. 100.00 (ISBN 0-384-07600-9). Johnson Repr.
Social & Economic Impact of Earthquakes on Utility Lifelines: Seismic Considerations in Lifelines Planning, Siting & Design. Ed. by J. Isenberg. LC 80-69153. 250p. 1981. pap. 21.00x (ISBN 0-87262-254-1). Am Soc Civil Eng.
Social & Economic Impact of New Technology: 1978-1984. Ed. by Leslie Grayson. (IFI Data Base Library). 130p. 1984. 85.00x (ISBN 0-306-65209-9, Plenum Pr). Plenum Pub.
Social & Economic Impact of Tourism on Asian Pacific Region. Ed. by Donald E. Hawkins. 316p. 1983. pap. text ed. 21.50 (ISBN 92-833-2004-2, APO131, APO). UNIPUB.
Social & Economic Implications of Cancer in the United States. Thomas A. Hodgson. Ed. by Klaudia Cox. (Ser. 3, No. 20). 50p. 1980. pap. text ed. 1.50 (ISBN 0-8406-0203-0). Natl Ctr Health Stats.
Social & Economic Inequality in the Soviet Union: Six Studies. Murray Yanowitch. LC 77-71634. pap. 53.80 (ISBN 0-317-41979-X, 2026127). Bks Demand UMI.
Social & Economic Inequality in the Soviet Union: Six Studies. Murray Yanowitch. LC 77-71634. pap. 53.80 (2027628). Bks Demand UMI.
Social & Economic Information for Urban Planning. Doris B. Holleb. (Midway Reprint Ser.). 1973. Vol. 1. pap. 4.50x (ISBN 0-226-34958-6); Vol. 2. pap. 7.50x (ISBN 0-226-34959-4). U of Chicago Pr.
Social & Economic Philosophy of John Stuart Mill, 2 vols. John S. Mill. 457p. (Orig.). 1987. 247.65 (ISBN 0-86654-242-6). Inst Econ Finan.
Social & Economic Rights in the Soviet Union & East Europe. Sophia M. Miskiewicz & Aaron Trehub. 256p. 1988. 34.95 (ISBN 0-88738-186-3). Transaction Bks.
Social & Economic Roots of Newton's Principia. B. Hessen. 19.50 (ISBN 0-86527-182-8). Fertig.
Social & Economic Status of College Students. Ora E. Reynolds. LC 71-177189. (Columbia University. Teachers College. Contributions to Education: No. 272). Repr. of 1927 ed. 22.50 (ISBN 0-404-55272-2). AMS Pr.
Social & Economic Structure of the City of New York, 1695-1796. Bruce M. Wilkenfeld. LC 77-14797. (Dissertations in American Economic History Ser.). 1978. 25.50 (ISBN 0-405-11062-6). Ayer Co Pubs.
Social & Educational Issues in Bilingualism & Biculturalism. Ed. by Robert St. Clair et al. LC 80-5700. (Illus.). 174p. (Orig.). 1982. lib. bdg. 27.50 (ISBN 0-8191-1939-3); pap. text ed. 12.25 (ISBN 0-8191-1940-7). U Pr of Amer.
Social & Educational Thought of Harold Rugg. Peter F. Carbone. LC 75-36176. pap. 59.50 (ISBN 0-317-20094-1, 2023374). Bks Demand UMI.
Social & Environmental Aspects of Desertification. 40p. 1980. pap. 7.50 (ISBN 9-2808-0127-9, TUNU085, UNU). UNIPUB.
Social & Environmental Effects of Large Dams. Edward Goldsmith & Nicholas Hildyard. LC 85-2235. (Illus.). 416p. 1986. 29.95 (ISBN 0-87156-848-9, Dist. by Random). Sierra.
Social & Environmental Objectives in Water Resources Planning & Management. 49p. 1984. 12.00x (ISBN 0-87262-404-8). Am Soc Civil Eng.
Social & Environmental Objectives in Water Resourses Planning & Management II. Ed. by Warren Viessman, Jr. & Kyle E. Schilling. (Conference Proceedings Ser.). 336p. 1986. 28.00x (ISBN 0-87262-559-1). Am Soc Civil Eng.
Social & Ethical Interpretations in Mental Development. 2nd ed. James M. Baldwin. LC 73-2960. (Classics in Psychology Ser.). Repr. of 1899 ed. 36.50 (ISBN 0-405-05133-6). Ayer Co Pubs.
Social & Ethnic Dimensions of Matthean Social History: "Go Nowhere among the Gentiles..." (Matt. 10.5b) Amy J. Levine. (Studies in the Bible & Early Christianity: Vol. 14). 350p. 1988. lib. bdg. 59.95 (ISBN 0-88946-614-9). E Mellen.
Social & Foreign Affairs in Iraq. Saddam Hussein. Tr. by Khalid W. Kishtainy. 123p. 1979. 25.00 (ISBN 0-7099-0061-9, Pub. by Croom Helm Ltd). Routledge Chapman & Hall.
Social & Functional Approaches to Language & Thought. Ed. by Maya Hickman. 328p. 1987. 35.00 (ISBN 0-12-347225-3). Acad Pr.
Social & Historical Change: An Islamic Perspective. Ayatullah M. Mutahhari. Ed. by Hamid Algar. Tr. by R. Campbell from Persian. (Contemporary Islamic Thought, Persian Ser.). 156p. 1986. 18.95 (ISBN 0-933782-18-7); pap. 7.95 (ISBN 0-933782-19-5). Mizan Pr.
Social & Human Sciences in Asia & the Pacific. 41p. 1986. pap. 12.50 (ISBN 0-317-46047-1, UB203, UB). UNIPUB.
Social & Industrial Conditions in the North During the Civil War. Emerson D. Fite. LC 74-22742. 328p. 1983. Repr. of 1910 ed. 32.50 (ISBN 0-404-58493-4). AMS Pr.
Social & Industrial Conditions in the North During the Civil War. Emerson D. Fite. 318p. 1976. Repr. of 1910 ed. 20.00 (ISBN 0-87928-070-0). Corner Hse.
Social & Industrial Problems of Shanghai. Eleanor M. Hinder. LC 75-30059. Repr. of 1942 ed. 24.50 (ISBN 0-404-59529-4). AMS Pr.
Social & International Ideals: Being Studies in Patriotism. facs. ed. Bernard Bosanquet. LC 67-23181. (Essay Index Reprint Ser). 1967. Repr. of 1917 ed. 19.00 (ISBN 0-8369-0225-4). Ayer Co Pubs.
Social & International Ideals: Being Studies in Patriotism. Bernard Bosanquet. LC 17-28213. 1968. Repr. of 1917 ed. 31.00 (ISBN 0-527-10042-0). Kraus Repr.
Social & Labor Practices of Multinational Enterprises in the Petroleum Industry. vi, 100p. 1977. pap. 12.25 (ISBN 92-2-101806-7, ILO218, ILO). UNIPUB.
Social & Labour Practices of Multinational Enterprises in Textiles, Clothing & Footwear Industries. (Social & Labour Practices of Multinational Enterprises). (Illus.). 184p. 1985. pap. 12.25 (ISBN 92-2-103882-3, ILO343, ILO). UNIPUB.
Social & Labour Practices of Multinational Enterprises in the Textiles, Clothing & Footwear Industries. xii, 184p. (Orig.). 1984. pap. 12.25 (ISBN 92-2-103882-3). Intl Labour Office.
Social & Labour Practices of Some European-Based Multinationals in the Metal Trades. 2nd ed. 1981. 17.50 (ISBN 92-2-101474-6). Intl Labour Office.
Social & Literary Papers. Charles C. Shackford. LC 72-335. (Essay Index Reprint Ser.). Repr. of 1892 ed. 20.00 (ISBN 0-8369-2825-3). Ayer Co Pubs.
Social & Medical Aspects of Drug Abuse. Ed. by George Serban. 288p. 1984. text ed. 40.00 (ISBN 0-88331-201-8). Luce.
Social & Mental Traits of the Negro. Howard W. Odum. LC 68-56677. (Columbia University. Studies in the Social Sciences: No. 99). Repr. of 1910 ed. 16.50 (ISBN 0-404-51099-X). AMS Pr.
Social & Moral Ideas in the Plays of Galsworthy. Sheo Bhushan Shulka. Ed. by James Hogg. (Poetic Drama & Poetic Theory Ser.). 257p. (Orig.). 1979. pap. 15.00 (ISBN 3-7052-0881-0, Pub. by Salzburg Studies). Longwood Pub Group.
Social & Personality Development. 2nd ed. David R. Shaffer. LC 87-10958. 640p. 1987. casebound 25.50 (ISBN 0-534-08412-5); test items avail. Brooks-Cole.
Social & Personality Development: An Evolutionary Synthesis. K. B. MacDonald. (Perspectives in Developmental Psychology Ser.). (Illus.). 420p. Date not set. price not set (ISBN 0-306-42891-1, Plenum Pr). Plenum Pub.
Social & Personality Development: Essays on the Growth of the Child. William Damon. 504p. 1983. pap. text ed. 14.95x (ISBN 0-393-95307-6). Norton.
Social & Personality Development: From Infancy Through Adolescence. William Damon. (Illus.). 1983. pap. text ed. 15.95x (ISBN 0-393-95248-7). Norton.
Social & Physical Condition of Negroes in Cities, 1897. Conference for the Study of Problems Concerning Negro City Life. (Atlanta Univ. Publ. Ser.: No. 2). (Orig.). Repr. of 1897 ed. 14.00 (ISBN 0-527-03109-7). Kraus Repr.
Social & Political Action: A Buddhist Approach. Ken Jones. (Wisdom East-West Books - Gray Ser.). 328p. (Orig.). 1988. pap. 18.95 (ISBN 0-86171-062-2). Wisdom MA.
Social & Political Conflict in Prussia, 1858-1864. Eugene N. Anderson. 1968. lib. bdg. 31.50x (ISBN 0-374-90266-6, Octagon). Hippocrene Bks.
Social & Political Doctrines of Contemporary Europe. Michael Oakeshott. 241p. 1980. Repr. of 1947 ed. lib. bdg. 35.00 (ISBN 0-89987-625-0). Darby Bks.
Social & Political France. (YFS Ser.: No. 15). 1955. pap. 16.00 (ISBN 0-527-01723-X). Kraus Repr.
Social & Political History of the Jews in Poland, 1919-1939. Joseph Marcus. LC 82-22420. (New Babylon, Studies in the Social Sciences: No. 37). xviii, 569p. 1983. 97.25x (ISBN 90-279-3239-5). Mouton.
Social & Political Ideas of Bipin Chandra Pal. Amalendu P. Mookerjee. LC 75-901635. 1974. 11.00x (ISBN 0-88386-473-8). South Asia Bks.
Social & Political Ideas of Some Great Thinkers of the Renaissance & the Reformation. Ed. by F. J. Hearnshaw. LC 85-7662. 216p. 1985. lib. bdg. 41.50x (ISBN 0-313-23862-6, HREN). Greenwood.
Social & Political Ideas of Some Great Thinkers of the Sixteenth & Seventeenth Centuries. Ed. by Fossey J. Hearnshaw. LC 66-25918. 1967. Repr. of 1926 ed. 21.50x (ISBN 0-8046-0199-2, Pub. by Kennikat). Assoc Faculty Pr.
Social & Political Ideas of Some Representative Thinkers of the Victorian Age: A Series of Lectures Delivered at King's College University of London during the Session 1931-32. Ed. by F. J. Hearnshaw. LC 83-1517. 271p. 1983. Repr. of 1950 ed. lib. bdg. 35.00x (ISBN 0-313-23864-2, HVIC). Greenwood.
Social & Political Ideas of the Muckrakers. facs. ed. David M. Chalmers. LC 70-117765. (Essay Index Reprint Ser). 1964. 14.95 (ISBN 0-8369-1745-6). Ayer Co Pubs.
Social & Political Morality. William Lovett. LC 83-48489. (World of Labour - English Workers 1850-1890 Ser.). 204p. 1984. lib. bdg. 25.00 (ISBN 0-8240-5716-3). Garland Pub.
Social & Political Perspectives in the Thought of Soren Kierkegaard. David B. Fletcher. LC 81-43716. 88p. 1983. lib. bdg. 24.25 (ISBN 0-8191-2689-6); pap. text ed. 8.75 (ISBN 0-8191-2690-X). U Pr of Amer.
Social & Political Perspectives on Energy Policy. Ed. by Karen M. Gentemann. LC 80-21963. 224p. 1981. 36.95 (ISBN 0-275-90631-0, C0631). Praeger.
Social & Political Philosophy. Ed. by Peter A. French et al. (Midwest Studies in Philosophy: Vol. 7). 600p. 1982. 45.00x (ISBN 0-8166-1130-0); pap. 18.95 (ISBN 0-8166-1129-7). U of Minn Pr.
Social & Political Philosophy: Readings from Plato to Gandhi. Ed. by Ronald Santoni & John Somerville. LC 63-18039. 1963. pap. 7.95 (ISBN 0-385-01238-1, Anch). Doubleday.
Social & Political Thought of Bernard Mandeville. Malcolm Jack. Ed. by Maurice Cranston. (Political Theory & Political Philosophy Ser.). 275p. 1987. lib. bdg. 35.00. Garland Pub.
Social & Political Thought of Herbert Spencer. David Wiltshire. (Oxford Historical Monographs). 1978. 29.95x (ISBN 0-19-821873-7). Oxford U Pr.
Social & Political Thought of Karl Marx. Shlomo Avineri. LC 68-12055. (Studies in the History & Theory of Politics). 1971. 47.50 (ISBN 0-521-04071-X); pap. 14.95 (ISBN 0-521-09619-7). Cambridge U Pr.
Social & Political Thought of Leon Trotsky. Baruch Knei-Paz. 1978. pap. 24.95x (ISBN 0-19-827234-0). Oxford U Pr.
Social & Political Thought of Michael Bakunin. Richard B. Saltman. LC 82-9348. (Contributions in Political Science Ser.: No. 88). xiii, 199p. 1983. lib. bdg. 36.95 (ISBN 0-313-23378-0, SPB/). Greenwood.
Social & Private Life at Rome in the Time of Plautus & Terence. Georgia W. Leffingwell. LC 18-17902. (Columbia University. Studies in the Social Sciences: No. 188). Repr. of 1918 ed. 14.50 (ISBN 0-404-51188-0). AMS Pr.
Social & Psychological Aspects of Aging. Ed. by Clark Tibbitts et al. LC 79-8691. (Growing Old Ser.). 1980. Repr. of 1962 ed. lib. bdg. 80.00x (ISBN 0-405-12787-1). Ayer Co Pubs.
Social & Psychological Contexts of Language. Ed. by Robert N. St. Clair & Howard Giles. LC 79-28232. 352p. 1980. text ed. 39.95x (ISBN 0-89859-021-3). L Erlbaum Assocs.
Social & Psychological Correlates of Black Anti-Semitism. Ronald T. Tsukashima. LC 78-63569. 1978. soft cover 11.95 (ISBN 0-88247-536-3). R & E Pubs.
Social & Psychological Distortion of Information. Charles K. West. LC 81-3941. 160p. 1981. text ed. 18.95 (ISBN 0-88229-616-7); pap. text ed. 9.95x (ISBN 0-88229-784-8). Nelson-Hall.
Social & Psychological Origins of the Climacteric Syndrome. John G. Greene. LC 84-13637. 247p. 1984. text ed. 35.50x (ISBN 0-566-00795-9). Gower Pub Co.
Social & Psychological Problems of Women: Prevention & Crisis Intervention. Ed. by Annette U. Rickel et al. LC 83-18423. (Clinical & Community Psychology Ser.). 352p. 1984. text ed. 32.00 (ISBN 0-89116-330-1). Hemisphere Pub.
Social & Psychological Research in Community Settings: Designing & Conducting Programs for Social & Personal Well-Being. Ricardo F. Munoz et al. LC 79-88107. (Social & Behavioral Science Ser.). 1979. text ed. 37.95x (ISBN 0-87589-423-2). Jossey-Bass.
Social & Religious Aspects in Bengal Inscriptions. RK Tripathi. 1987. 40.00x (ISBN 0-8364-2129-9, Pub. by KL Mukhopadhyay). South Asia Bks.
Social & Religious Heretics in Five Centuries. Carl Heath. LC 78-147622. (Library of War & Peace; Non-Resis. & Non-Vio.). 1972. lib. bdg. 46.00 (ISBN 0-8240-0397-7). Garland Pub.
Social & Religious History of the Jews, 18 vols. 2nd, rev. & enl. ed. Salo W. Baron. Incl. Vol. 1. Ancient Times to the Beginning of the Christian Era. 1952 (ISBN 0-231-08838-8); Vol. 2. Ancient Times: Christian Era: the First Five Centuries. 1952 (ISBN 0-231-08839-6); Vol. 3. High Middle Ages: Heirs of Rome & Persia. 1957 (ISBN 0-231-08840-X); Vol. 4. High Middle Ages: Meeting of the East & West. 1957 (ISBN 0-231-08841-8); Vol. 5. High Middle Ages: Religious Controls & Dissensions. 1957 (ISBN 0-231-08842-6); Vol. 6. High Middle Ages: Laws, Homilies & the Bible. 1958 (ISBN 0-231-08843-4); Vol. 7. High Middle Ages: Hebrew Language & Letters. 1958 (ISBN 0-231-08844-2); Vol. 8. High Middle Ages: Philosophy & Science. 1958 (ISBN 0-231-08845-0); Vol. 9. Late Middle Ages & Era of European Expansion, 1200-1650: Under Church & Empire. 1965 (ISBN 0-231-08846-9); Vol. 10. Late Middle Ages & Era of European Expansion, 1200-1650: On the Empire's Periphery. 1965 (ISBN 0-231-08847-7); Vol. 11. Late Middle Ages & Era of European Expansion, 1200-1650: Citizen or Alien Conjurer. 1967 (ISBN 0-231-08848-5); Vol. 12. Late Middle Ages & Era of European Expansion, 1200-1650: Economic Catalyst. 1967 (ISBN 0-231-08849-3); Vol. 13. Late Middle Ages & Era of European Expansion, 1200-1650: Inquisition, Renaissance & Reformation. 1969 (ISBN 0-231-08850-7); Vol. 14. Late Middle Ages & Era of European Expansion, 1200-1650: Catholic Restoration & Wars of Religion. 1969 (ISBN 0-231-08851-5); Vol. 15. Late Middle Ages & Era of European Expansion, 1200-1650: Resettlement & Exploration. 1973 (ISBN 0-231-08852-3); Index. 32.00x. LC 52-404. 45.00x ea. Columbia U Pr.
Social & Religious Life of Italians in the United States. Enrico C. Sartorio. LC 73-13520. 1974. Repr. of 1918 ed. 25.00x (ISBN 0-678-01364-0). Kelley.
Social & Religious Philosophy of Martin Buber: Alienation & the Search for Meaning. Laurence J. Silberstein. Ed. by Robert M. Seltzer. (Reappraisals in Jewish Social & Intellectual History Ser.). 256p. 1988. 35.00x (ISBN 0-8147-7886-0). NYU Pr.
Social & Religious Plays of Strindberg. John Ward. 337p. 1980. 46.50 (ISBN 0-485-11183-7, Pub. by Athlone Pr UK). Humanities.
Social & Religious Themes in English Art, 1840-1860. Lindsay Errington. LC 83-48701. (Theses from the Courtauld Institute of Art Ser.). (Illus.). 584p. 1984. lib. bdg. 70.00 (ISBN 0-8240-5977-8). Garland Pub.
Social & Religious Thought of William Jennings Bryan. Willard H. Smith. 270p. 1975. 10.00x (ISBN 0-87291-076-8). Coronado Pr.
Social & Sexual Revolution: Essays on Marx & Reich. Bertell Ollman. LC 78-71204. 228p. 1979. 20.00 (ISBN 0-89608-081-1); pap. 7.50 (ISBN 0-89608-080-3). South End Pr.
Social & State Structure of the U. S. S. R. Viacheslav A. Karpinsky. Repr. of 1948 ed. lib. bdg. 35.00x (ISBN 0-8371-3116-2, KASU). Greenwood.
Social & Technical Issues in Testing Implications for Test Construction & Usage. Ed. by Barbara S. Plake. (Buros-Nebraska Symposium on Measurement & Testing Ser.: Vol. 1). 192p. 1984. text ed. 24.95x (ISBN 0-89859-299-2). L Erlbaum Assocs.
Social & Technological Interaction with Education. Phillip Hughes. (APEID Occasional Papers: No. 13). 22p. 1985. pap. 5.00 (UB156, UB). UNIPUB.
Social & Vocational Rehabilitation Resources: Africa, Vol. 1. x, 230p. (Orig., Eng. & Fr.). 1984. pap. 14.00 (ISBN 92-2-003776-9). Intl Labour Office.
Social & Vocational Rehabilitation Resources: An International Directory - Asia & the Pacific, Vol. 2. vi, 233p. (Orig.). 1986. pap. text ed. 14.00 (ISBN 92-2-105305-9). Intl Labour Office.
Social Animal. 4th ed. Elliot Aronson. 440p. 1984. pap. text ed. 14.95 (ISBN 0-7167-1606-2). W H Freeman.
Social Animal. 5th ed. Elliot Aronson. 464p. 1988. text ed. 21.95 (ISBN 0-7167-1952-5); pap. text ed. 14.95 (ISBN 0-7167-1955-X). W H Freeman.
Social Anthropology. Edward E. Evans-Pritchard. LC 84-19811. 144p. 1987. lib. bdg. 35.00x (ISBN 0-313-24680-7, EVSA). Greenwood.
Social Anthropology. Edmund Leach. 1982. 24.50x (ISBN 0-19-520371-2). Oxford U Pr.
Social Anthropology. Edmund Leach. Ed. by Frank Kermode. 1982. pap. 9.95 (ISBN 0-19-520428-X). Oxford U Pr.
Social Anthropology: A Natural Science of Society? E. Leach. (Radcliffe-Brown Lectures in Social Anthropology). 1976. pap. 5.50 (ISBN 0-85672-312-6, Pub. by British Acad). Longwood Pub Group.
Social Anthropology & Development Policy. Ed. by Ralph Grillo & Alan Rew. (ASA Monographs). 240p. 1985. 39.95 (ISBN 0-422-79790-1, 9524, Pub. by Tavistock England); pap. 15.95 (ISBN 0-422-79620-4, 9525, Pub. by Tavistock England). Routledge Chapman & Hall.
Social Anthropology & Medicine. Ed. by J. B. Loudon. (Association of Social Anthropologists Monographs). 1976. 82.50 (ISBN 0-12-456350-3). Acad Pr.

Social Change & Education. M. R. Paliwal. 1985. 30.00x (ISBN 0-8364-1255-9, Pub. by Uppal Pub Hse New Delhi). South Asia Bks.

Social Change & Family Processes: Arab Communities in Israel. Majid Al Haj. (Brown University Studies in Population & Development). 200p. 1986. pap. 22.50 (ISBN 0-8133-7325-5). Westview.

Social Change & Fundamental Law: America's Evolving Constitution. Arthur S. Miller. LC 78-66716. (Contributions in American Studies Ser.: No. 41). x, 395p. 1979. lib. bdg. 35.00 (ISBN 0-313-20618-X, MSO/). Greenwood.

Social Change & National Consciousness in Twentieth-Century Ukraine. Bohdan Krawchenko. LC 85-1922. 333p. 1985. 29.95 (ISBN 0-312-73160-4). St Martin.

Social Change & Personality: Essays in Honor of Nevitt Sanford. Ed. by M. B. Freedman. (Recent Research in Psychology Ser.). vii, 231p. 1987. pap. 33.00 (ISBN 0-387-96485-1). Springer-Verlag.

Social Change & Political Development in Weimar Germany. Ed. by Richard Bessel & E. J. Feuchtwanger. LC 80-41179. 298p. 1981. 28.50x (ISBN 0-389-20176-6, 06952). B&N Imports.

Social Change & Political Participation in Turkey. Ergun Ozbudun. LC 76-3013. (Center for International Affairs Ser.). 1976. cloth 34.00x (ISBN 0-691-07580-8). Princeton U Pr.

Social Change & Political Violence in Colonial Nigeria. Bernard Nkemdirim. 160p. 1987. 30.00x (ISBN 0-317-62503-9, Pub. by A H Stockwell England). State Mutual Bk.

Social Change & Prejudice. Bruno Bettelheim & Morris B. Janowitz. LC 64-11214. 1964. 22.95 (ISBN 0-02-903480-9). Free Pr.

Social Change & Rural Development: Intervention or Participation - A Zambian Case Study. M. Nelson-Richards. LC 80-5686. 162p. 1982. lib. bdg. 25.50 (ISBN 0-8191-2291-2); pap. text ed. 10.00 (ISBN 0-8191-2292-0). U Pr of Amer.

Social Change & Scientific Organization: The Royal Instution, 1799-1844. Morris Berman. LC 77-79702. (Illus.). 249p. 1978. 34.95x (ISBN 0-8014-1093-2). Cornell U Pr.

Social Change & the Aged: Recent Trends in the United States. Fred C. Pampel. LC 79-4752. (Illus.). 240p. 1981. 25.00x (ISBN 0-669-02928-9). Lexington Bks.

Social Change & the Chinese in Singapore: A Socio-Economic Geography with Special Reference to Bang Structure. Cheng Lim-Keak. 235p. 1985. text ed. 21.95x (ISBN 9971-69-077-2, Pub. by Singapore U Pr). Ohio U Pr.

Social Change & the Growth of British Power in the Gold Coast: The Fante States Eighteen Hundred & Seven to Eighteen Seventy-Four. Mary McCarthy. LC 83-7019. 208p. (Orig.). 1983. lib. bdg. 27.50 (ISBN 0-8191-3148-2); pap. text ed. 13.25 (ISBN 0-8191-3149-0). U Pr of Amer.

Social Change & the Individual: Japan Before & After Defeat in World War II. Kazuko Tsurumi. 1970. 50.00x (ISBN 0-691-09347-4). Princeton U Pr.

Social Change & the Labouring Poor: Antwerp, 1770-1860. Catharina Lis. LC 85-52070. 224p. 1986. 20.00 (ISBN 0-300-03610-8). Yale U Pr.

Social Change & Training of Educational Personnel. 94p. 1983. pap. text ed. 6.50 (ISBN 0-686-88391-8, UB130, UNESCO Regional Office). UNIPUB.

Social Change & Violence: The Indian Experience. P. R. Rajgopal. 227p. 1987. 35.00x (ISBN 81-85024-27-8, Pub. by Uppal Pub Hse New Delhi). South Asia Bks.

Social Change & Women's Reproductive Health Care: A Guide to Physicians & Their Patients. Nada L. Stotland. 288p. 1988. lib. bdg. 49.95 (ISBN 0-275-92570-6). Praeger.

Social Change As Redefinition of Roles: A Study of Structural & Causal Relationships in the Netherlands of the 'Seventies' I. Gadourek. 532p. 1982. pap. text ed. 32.00 (ISBN 90-232-1898-1, Pub. by Van Gorcum Holland). Longwood Pub Group.

Social Change Environmental Change: EDRA Proceedings: Nineteen Eighty-Five. Ed. by Stephan Klein et al. 450p. 1985. 35.00 (ISBN 0-939922-08-8). EDRA.

Social Change in a Hostile Environment: The Crusaders' Kingdom of Jerusalem. Aharon Ben-Ami. (Princeton Studies on the Near East Ser.). (Illus.). 1969. 28.50x (ISBN 0-691-09344-X). Princeton U Pr.

Social Change in a Late Colonial Metropolis: Manila Nineteen Hundred to Nineteen Forty-One. Daniel F. Doeppers. LC 84-50326. (Monograph Ser.: No. 27). (Illus.). 194p. 1985. pap. 14.00x (ISBN 0-938692-06-2). Yale U SE Asia.

Social Change in a Metropolitan Community. Otis D. Duncan et al. LC 73-76764. 136p. 1973. pap. 7.95x (ISBN 0-87154-216-1). Russell Sage.

Social Change in a Southern Province of Iran. Ali A. Paydarfar. LC 75-15427. (Comparative Urban Studies Monograph Ser: No. 1). (Illus.). 190p. 1974. pap. text ed. 5.50 (ISBN 0-89143-044-X). U NC Inst Res Soc Sci.

Social Change in a Spanish Village. Joseph Aceves. (Illus.). 144p. 1971. pap. 9.95 (ISBN 0-87073-755-4). Schenkman Bks Inc.

Social Change in a Yemeni Highlands Town. Thomas B. Stevenson. (Illus.). 232p. 1985. 22.50x (ISBN 0-87480-112-5). U of Utah Pr.

Social Change in an Industrial Town: Patterns of Progress in Warren, Pennsylvania from Civil War to World War I. Michael P. Weber. LC 75-1634. 1975. 21.50x (ISBN 0-271-01201-3). Pa St U Pr.

Social Change in Brazil, 1945-1985: The Incomplete Transition. Ed. by Edmar L. Bacha & Herbert S. Klein. (Illus.). 368p. (Orig.). Date not set. pap. 22.50x (ISBN 0-8263-1111-3). U of NM Pr.

Social Change in France. Michalina Baughan et al. 1980. 10.95x (ISBN 0-312-73161-2). St Martin.

Social Change in India. B. Kuppuswamy. 1975. 13.50 (ISBN 0-7069-0142-8). Intl Bk Dist.

Social Change in India. 7th ed. B. Kuppuswamy. 440p. 1985. text ed. 30.00x (ISBN 0-7069-2673-0, Pub. by Vikas India). Advent NY.

Social Change in Indian Society. rev. ed. Raghuvir Sinha. 1978. 11.50x (ISBN 0-8364-0182-4). South Asia Bks.

Social Change in Israel: Attitudes & Events, 1967-79. Russell A. Stone. LC 81-17913. 352p. 1982. 42.95 (ISBN 0-275-90910-7, C0910). Praeger.

Social Change in Nigeria. Ed. by Simi Abonja & Tola Pearce. 262p. (Orig.). 1986. pap. text ed. 13.95 (ISBN 0-582-64434-8). Longman.

Social Change in Romania, Eighteen Sixty to Nineteen Forty: A Debate on Development in a European Nation. Ed. by Kenneth Jowitt. LC 78-620022. (Research Ser: No. 36). 1978. pap. 4.50x (ISBN 0-87725-136-3). U of Cal Intl St.

Social Change in Rural England. Howard Newby. LC 79-21703. 272p. 1980. 27.50x (ISBN 0-299-08040-4). U of Wis Pr.

Social Change in Rural Societies: An Introduction to Rural Sociology. 3rd ed. Everett M. Rogers et al. (Illus.). 480p. 1988. text ed. write for info. (ISBN 0-13-815481-3). P-H.

Social Change in Soviet Russia. Alex Inkeles. LC 68-54020. (Russian Research Center Studies: No. 57). 1968. 29.50x (ISBN 0-674-81196-8). Harvard U Pr.

Social Change in the Industrial Revolution. Neil J. Smelser. LC 59-10743. (Illus.). 1959. 20.00x (ISBN 0-226-76311-0). U of Chicago Pr.

Social Change in the Law of Trusts. George W. Keeton. LC 73-9374. 128p. 1974. Repr. of 1958 ed. lib. bdg. 35.00x (ISBN 0-8371-7011-7, KELT). Greenwood.

Social Change in the Modern Era. Daniel Chirot & Robert E. Merton. 330p. 1986. pap. 15.95 (ISBN 0-15-581421-4). HarBraceJ.

Social Change in the Southwest, 1350-1880. Thomas D. Hall. (Studies in Historical Social Change). (Illus.). 320p. 1988. 35.00 (ISBN 0-7006-0374-3). U Pr of Ks.

Social Change in the United States Nineteen Forty-Five to Nineteen Eighty-Three. William Issel. LC 84-16297. 256p. 1985. 24.00 (ISBN 0-8052-3956-1). Schocken.

Social Change in the United States, 1945-1983. William Issel. LC 84-16297. 241p. 1987. pap. 9.95x (ISBN 0-8052-0844-5). Schocken.

Social Change: Modernization & Post-Modernization. Eva Etzioni-Halevy. 280p. 1981. 30.00x (ISBN 0-7100-0767-1); pap. 11.95x (ISBN 0-7100-0768-X). Routledge Chapman & Hall.

Social Change on Mainland China & Taiwan: Nineteen Forty-Nine to Nineteen Eighty. Alan P. Liu. (Occasional Papers-Reprints Series in Contemporary Asian Studies: No. 3). 55p. (Orig.). 1982. pap. 3.00 (ISBN 0-942182-47-2). Occasional Papers.

Social Change: Social Theory & Historical Processes. Anthony D. Smith. LC 75-42477. (Aspects of Modern Sociology: Social Processes Ser.). pap. 48.00 (ISBN 0-317-09554-4, 2019611). Bks Demand UMI.

Social Change, Stress, & Mental Health in the Alps: A Systematic Study of a Village Process. G. Guntern. (Psychiatry Ser.: Vol. 22). (Illus.). 1979. 67.30 (ISBN 0-387-09631-0). Springer-Verlag.

Social Changes During Depression & Recovery. Ed. by William F. Ogburn. LC 72-2381. (FDR & the Era of the New Deal Ser.). 117p. 1974. Repr. of 1935 ed. lib. bdg. 22.50 (ISBN 0-306-70483-8). Da Capo.

Social Changes in England in the Sixteenth-Century As Reflected in Contemporary Literature. Edward P. Cheyney. LC 76-168055. (Illus.). Repr. of 1895 ed. 12.50 (ISBN 0-404-01523-9). AMS Pr.

Social Changes in Indian Society. R. Sinha. 208p. 1978. 16.50. Asia Bk Corp.

Social Characteristics of Cities: A Basis for New Interpretations of the Role of the City in American Life. William F. Ogburn. LC 73-11940. (Metropolitan America Ser.). 80p. 1974. Repr. 16.00 (ISBN 0-405-05409-2). Ayer Co Pubs.

Social Choice. Bernhardt Lieberman. LC 75-132954. (Monographs & Texts in the Behavioral Sciences). (Illus.). 438p. 1971. 88.00 (ISBN 0-677-14770-8). Gordon & Breach.

Social Choice & Democracy. N. J. Schofield. LC 85-17199. (Illus.). 340p. 1985. 60.00 (ISBN 0-387-15604-6). Springer-Verlag.

Social Choice & Individual Values. 2nd ed. Kenneth J. Arrow. (Cowles Foundation Monograph: No. 12). 1970. pap. 6.95 (ISBN 0-300-01364-7, Y233). Yale U Pr.

Social Choice & Multicriterion Decision-Making. Kenneth J. Arrow & Herve Raynaud. (Illus.). 128p. 1986. text ed. 16.50x (ISBN 0-262-01087-9). MIT Pr.

Social Choice & Public Decision-Making: Essays in Honor of Kenneth J. Arrow, Vol. I. Ed. by Walter P. Heller et al. (Illus.). 244p. 1986. 37.50 (ISBN 0-521-30454-7). Cambridge U Pr.

Social Choice & Public Policy. Michael Laver. 208p. 1986. text ed. 39.95x (ISBN 0-631-14693-8); pap. text ed. 15.95x (ISBN 0-631-14694-6). Basil Blackwell.

Social Choice Theory. J. S. Kelly. (Illus.). 190p. 1987. 29.50 (ISBN 0-387-17634-9). Springer-Verlag.

Social Choice Welfare. Ed. by P. K. Pattanaik & M. Salles. (Contribution to Economic Analysis Ser.: Vol. 145). 324p. 1983. 100.00 (ISBN 0-444-86487-3, North-Holland). Elsevier.

Social Cinema of Jean Renoir. Christopher Faulkner. LC 85-43276. 232p. 1986. text ed. 28.00x (ISBN 0-691-06673-6). Princeton U Pr.

Social Class & Church Participation. Erich Goode. Ed. by Harriet Zuckerman & Robert K. Merton. LC 79-9001. (Dissertations on Sociology Ser.). 1980. lib. bdg. 22.00x (ISBN 0-405-12970-X). Ayer Co Pubs.

Social Class & Delinquency. Lynn McDonald. LC 78-5552. 239p. 1969. 25.00 (ISBN 0-208-00835-7, Archon). Shoe String.

Social Class & Educational Opportunity. J. E. Floud et al. LC 73-7195. (Illus.). 152p. 1973. Repr. of 1957 ed. lib. bdg. 35.00x (ISBN 0-8371-6918-6, FLSC). Greenwood.

Social Class & Social Change in Puerto Rico. Melvin M. Tumin & Arnold S. Feldman. LC 70-145756. 1971. 39.50x (ISBN 0-672-61375-1). Irvington.

Social Class & the Divison of Labour. Ed. by Anthony Giddens & Gavin Mackenzie. LC 82-4275. (Illus.). 374p. 1982. 39.50 (ISBN 0-521-24597-4); pap. 14.95 o. p. (ISBN 0-521-28809-6). Cambridge U Pr.

Social Class in Modern Britain. Gordon Marshall et al. 332p. 1988. 39.95 (ISBN 0-87722-585-0). Temple U Pr.

Social Class in Scotland: Past & Present. A. A. MacLaren. 208p. 1982. 39.00x (ISBN 0-85976-013-8, Pub. by Donald Pubs Scotland). State Mutual Bk.

Social Class in the Contemporary United States. Ed. by Gerald Erickson & Harold L. Schwartz. LC 77-92856. (Studies in Marxism: Vol. 2). 101p. 1977. pap. 7.95x (ISBN 0-930656-04-0). MEP Pubns.

Social Class in Urban India: Essays on Cognitions & Structures. Edwin D. Driver & Aloo E. Driver. (Illus.). x, 159p. 1987. pap. 25.50 (ISBN 90-04-08106-2, Pub. by E J Brill). Heinman.

Social Class, Language & Education. Denis Lawton. (International Library of Sociology). 192p. 1968. pap. 9.95x (ISBN 0-7100-6895-6). Routledge Chapman & Hall.

Social Classes in Marxist Theory. Allin Cottress. 330p. 1985. 39.50x (ISBN 0-7100-9906-1). Routledge Chapman & Hall.

Social Clauses & International Trade. Gote Hansson. LC 82-42563. 1983. 25.00 (ISBN 0-312-73162-0). St Martin.

Social Cleavages in Texas. Weston J. McConnell. LC 79-82237. (Columbia University Studies in the Social Sciences: No. 265). Repr. of 1925 ed. 17.50 (ISBN 0-404-51265-8). AMS Pr.

Social Closure: The Theory of Monopolization & Exclusion. Raymond Murphy. 256p. 1988. 52.00 (ISBN 0-19-827268-5). Oxford U Pr.

Social Cognition. Susan T. Fiske & Shelley E. Taylor. (Illus.). 512p. 1984. pap. text ed. write for info (ISBN 0-394-34801-X, RanC). Random.

Social Cognition & Clinical Psychology: A Synthesis. Ed. by Lyn Y. Abramson. 400p. 1988. lib. bdg. 40.00 (ISBN 0-89862-011-2). Guilford Pr.

Social Cognition & Communication. Michael E. Roloff & Charles R. Berger. 352p. 1982. 32.00 (ISBN 0-8039-1898-4); pap. 16.95 (ISBN 0-8039-1899-2). Sage.

Social Cognition & Consumer Behavior. M. Joseph Sirgy. 256p. 1983. 40.95 (ISBN 0-275-91081-4, C1081). Praeger.

Social Cognition & Social Development: A Sociocultural Perspective. Ed. by E. Tory Higgins. LC 82-12897. (Cambridge Studies in Social & Emotional Development). 352p. 1983. o. p. 39.50 (ISBN 0-521-24587-7). Cambridge U Pr.

Social Cognition & Social Development: A Sociocultural Perspective. Ed. by Tory E. Higgins & Willard W. Hartup. (Cambridge Studies in Social & Emotional Development). 415p. 1985. pap. 17.95 (ISBN 0-521-31370-8). Cambridge U Pr.

Social Cognition & the Acquisition of Self. Michael Lewis & Jeanne Brooks-Gunn. LC 79-12070. 316p. 1979. 39.50x (ISBN 0-306-40232-7, Plenum Pr). Plenum Pub.

Social Cognition, Inference, & Attribution. R. S. Wyer & D. E. Carlston. 400p. 1979. 49.95x (ISBN 0-89859-499-5). L Erlbaum Assocs.

Social Cognition: Perspectives on Everyday Understanding. Ed. by Joseph Forgas. LC 81-66400. (European Monographs in Social Psychology: No. 26). 1981. 67.50 (ISBN 0-12-263560-4); pap. 31.50 (ISBN 0-12-263562-0). Acad Pr.

Social Cognition: Studies of the Development of Understanding. George Butterworth & Paul Light. LC 81-24075. 1982. lib. bdg. 20.00x (ISBN 0-226-08609-7). U of Chicago Pr.

Social Cognition: The Ontario Symposium, Vol. 1. Ed. by E. Tory Higgins et al. (Ontario Symposia on Personality and Social Cognition Ser.). 448p. 1981. text ed. 45.00x (ISBN 0-89859-049-3). L Erlbaum Assocs.

Social Cognitive Development: Frontiers & Possible Futures. Ed. by John Flavell & Lee Ross. (Cambridge Studies in Social & Emotional Development). (Illus.). 336p. 1981. o. p. 42.50 (ISBN 0-521-23687-8); pap. 18.95 (ISBN 0-521-28156-3). Cambridge U Pr.

Social-Cognitive Development in Context. Felicisima C. Serafica. LC 82-2913. 283p. 1982. text ed. 35.00 (ISBN 0-89862-623-4, 2623). Guilford Pr.

Social Cohesion: Essays Toward a Sociophysiological Perspective. Ed. by Patricia R. Barchas & Sally P. Mendoza. LC 83-22594. (Contributions in Sociology Ser.: No. 49). (Illus.). xvi, 219p. 1984. lib. bdg. 35.00 (ISBN 0-313-24395-6, BCH/). Greenwood.

Social Communication Among Primates. Ed. by Stuart A. Altman. LC 65-25120. (Midway Reprints Ser.). (Illus.). xiv, 392p. 1982. pap. text ed. 18.00x (ISBN 0-226-01597-1). U of Chicago Pr.

Social Communication & Movement: Studies of Interaction & Expression in Man & Chimpanzee. Ed. by Mario Von Cranach & Ian Vine. (European Monographs in Social Psychology Ser.). 1974. 117.00 (ISBN 0-12-724750-5). Acad Pr.

Social Communication in Advertising: Persons, Products & Images of Well-Being. William Leiss et al. (Illus.). 327p. 1986. pap. 13.95 (ISBN 0-416-01201-9, 9685). Routledge Chapman & Hall.

Social Comparison, Social Justice, & Relative Deprivation. Ed. by John C. Masters & William P. Smith. (Greenwald & Krauss Ser.). 320p. 1987. text ed. 36.00 (ISBN 0-89859-632-7). L Erlbaum Assocs.

Social Competence. Ed. by Jeri D. Wine & Marti D. Smye. LC 81-322. 399p. 1981. 45.00 (ISBN 0-89862-607-2, 2607). Guilford Pr.

Social Competence in Children. Kenneth A. Dodge et al. (Child Development Monograph: No. 213, Vol. 51, No. 2). vi, 88p. 1987. pap. text ed. 9.75x (ISBN 0-226-15506-4). U of Chicago Pr.

Social Competence in Children. Ed. by Martha W. Kent & Jon E. Rolf. LC 78-63587. (Primary Prevention of Psychopathology Ser.: Vol. 3). (Illus.). 351p. 1979. 35.00x (ISBN 0-87451-155-0). U Pr of New Eng.

Social Competence: Interventions for Children & Adults. Ed. by Diana P. Rathjen & John P. Foreyt. LC 80-118. (Pergamon General Psychology Ser.: No. 91). (Illus.). 300p. 1980. text ed. 43.00 (ISBN 0-08-025965-0). Pergamon.

Social Composition of Boards of Education. George S. Counts. LC 79-89167. (American Education: Its Men, Institutions & Ideas, Ser. 1). 1969. Repr. of 1927 ed. 10.00 (ISBN 0-405-01405-8). Ayer Co Pubs.

Social Composition of the Teaching Population. Lotus D. Coffman. LC 72-176657. (Columbia University. Teachers College. Contributions to Education: No. 41). Repr. of 1911 ed. 22.50 (ISBN 0-404-55041-X). AMS Pr.

Social Compulsions of Ideas: Toward a Sociological Analysis of Knowledge. Gerard DeGre. Ed. by Cyril Levitt. 264p. 1984. 39.95 (ISBN 0-88738-003-4). Transaction Bks.

Social Concern & Urban Realism: American Painting of the Nineteen Thirty's. Patricia Hills & Ralph Soyer. (Illus.). 96p. 1983. pap. 10.00 (ISBN 0-87270-052-6, Pub. by Bread & Roses). Pub Ctr Cult Res.

Social Concern & Urban Realism: American Painting of the Nineteen Thirty's. Raphael Soyer. LC 82-74178. (Illus.). 96p. (Orig.). 1983. pap. 10.00 (ISBN 0-917418-72-7). Am Fed Arts.

Social Concern in Calvin's Geneva. William C. Innes. LC 83-23640. (Pittsburgh Theological Monographs: New Series 7). 1983. pap. 22.50 (ISBN 0-915138-33-6). Pickwick.

Social Condition & Education of the People in England & Europe, 2 vols. Joseph Kay. (Development of Industrial Society Ser.). 1200p. 1971. Repr. of 1850 ed. 70.00 set (ISBN 0-7165-1565-2, BBA 03543, Pub. by Irish Academic Pr). Biblio Dist.

Social Condition & Education of the People in England & Europe, 2 Vols. Joseph Kay. LC 72-141318. Repr. of 1850 ed. lib. bdg. 87.50x (ISBN 0-678-00144-8). Kelley.

Social Condition of Humanity. 2nd ed. Irving Zeitlin. 1984. pap. 16.95x (ISBN 0-19-503350-7). Oxford U Pr.

Social Condition of Labor. Elgin R. Gould. LC 78-63816. (Johns Hopkins University. Studies in the Social Sciences. Eleventh Ser. 1893: 1). Repr. of 1893 ed. 11.50 (ISBN 0-404-61079-X). AMS Pr.

Social Condition of Labor. Elgin R. Gould. 1973. pap. 9.00 (ISBN 0-384-19420-6). Johnson Repr.

Social Conditions in an American City. Shelby M. Harrison. LC 75-22821. (America in Two Centuries Ser). (Illus.). 1976. Repr. of 1920 ed. 35.50x (ISBN 0-405-07693-2). Ayer Co Pubs.

Social Criticism of Fenimore Cooper. John F. Ross. LC 73-13848. 1933. lib. bdg. 27.00 (ISBN 0-8414-7226-2). Folcroft.
Social Criticism of Literature. Gertrude Buck. LC 73-472. 1974. Repr. of 1916 ed. lib. bdg. 17.00 (ISBN 0-8414-1496-3). Folcroft.
Social Dance. W. Pillich. (Ballroom Dance Ser.). 1985. lib. bdg. 74.00 (ISBN 0-87700-688-1). Revisionist Pr.
Social Dance. W. Pillich. (Ballroom Dance Ser.). 1986. lib. bdg. 79.95 (ISBN 0-8490-3345-4). Gordon Pr.
Social Dance. Myrna M. Schild. 128p. 1985. pap. text ed. write for info. (ISBN 0-697-00374-4). Wm C Brown.
Social Dance: A Short History. A. H. Franks. (Ballroom Dance Ser.). 1985. lib. bdg. 64.00 (ISBN 0-87700-761-6). Revisionist Pr.
Social Dance: A Short History. A. H. Franks. (Ballroom Dance Ser.). 1986. lib. bdg. 79.95 (ISBN 0-8490-3318-7). Gordon Pr.
Social Dance Rhythms. Alma Heaton. (Ballroom Dance Ser.). 1985. lib. bdg. 79.95 (ISBN 0-8490-3250-4). Gordon Pr.
Social Dancing. Arthur Murray. (Ballroom Dancing Ser.). 1985. lib. bdg. 79.95 (ISBN 0-87700-694-6). Revisionist Pr.
Social Dancing. Arthur Murray. (Ballroom Dance Ser.). 1986. lib. bdg. 79.95 (ISBN 0-8490-3255-5). Gordon Pr.
Social Dancing. A. P. Wright & D. J. Dexter. (Ballroom Dance Ser.). 1985. lib. bdg. 79.00 (ISBN 0-87700-723-3). Revisionist Pr.
Social Dancing. A. P. Wright & D. J. Dexter. (Ballroom Dance Ser.). 1986. lib. bdg. 79.95 (ISBN 0-8490-3388-8). Gordon Pr.
Social Darwinism in American Thought. Richard Hofstadter. 1955. pap. 10.95x (ISBN 0-8070-5461-5, BP16). Beacon Pr.
Social Darwinism in France. Linda L. Clark. LC 82-21795. xi, 261p. 1984. text ed. 28.75 (ISBN 0-8173-0149-6). U of Ala Pr.
Social Darwinism: Science & Myth. rev. ed. Robert C. Bannister. (American Civilization Ser.). 292p. 1988. pap. text ed. 14.95 (ISBN 0-87722-566-4). Temple U Pr.
Social Decay & Eugenical Reform. Ferdinand C. Schiller. Ed. by Charles Rosenberg. LC 83-48657. (History of Hereditarian Thought Ser.). 164p. 1985. Repr. of 1932 ed. lib. bdg. 25.00 (ISBN 0-8240-5827-5). Garland Pub.
Social Defense: The Future of Penal Reform. Marc Ancel. Ed. by Edward P. Wise. LC 86-15458. (Publications of the Comparative Criminal Law Project: No. 16). xxi, 314p. 1987. 47.50x (ISBN 0-8377-0219-4). Rothman.
Social Democracy & After, Socialist Register 1985-1986. Ed. by Ralph Miliband et al. 500p. (Orig.). pap. 12.00 (ISBN 0-85345-709-3, Pub by Merlin England). Monthly Rev.
Social Democracy & Population. Alvan A. Tenney. LC 68-56689. (Columbia University. Studies in the Social Sciences: No. 71). Repr. of 1907 ed. 12.50 (ISBN 0-404-51071-X). AMS Pr.
Social Democracy & Society: Working Class Radicalism in Duesseldorf, Eighteen Ninety to Nineteen Twenty. Mary Nolan. LC 80-29539. (Illus.). 352p. 1981. 44.50 (ISBN 0-521-23473-5). Cambridge U Pr.
Social Democracy & the Rule of Law. Otto Kirchheimer et al. LC 86-32198. 1987. 45.00. Unwin Hyman.
Social Democracy in Post War Europe. W. E. Paterson & T. R. Campbell. LC 73-88177. 64p. 1974. 20.00 (ISBN 0-312-73185-X). St Martin.
Social Democracy Versus Communism. Karl Kautsky. Ed. by David Shub & Joseph Shaplen. (Illus.). 1979. Repr. of 1946 ed. 15.95 (ISBN 0-88355-802-5). Hyperion Conn.
Social Democratic Image of Society: A Study of the Achievements & Origins of Scandinavian Social Democracy in Comparative Perspective. Francis G. Castles. 1978. 21.95x (ISBN 0-7100-8870-1). Routledge Chapman & Hall.
Social Democratic Parties in Europe. Anton Pelinka. 208p. 1983. 35.00 (ISBN 0-275-91057-1, C1057). Praeger.
Social Democratic Parties in Western Europe. William F. Patterson. Ed. by Altsair H. Thomas. LC 77-77314. 1977. 27.50 (ISBN 0-312-73175-2). St Martin.
Social Democrats. Ken Coates. 116p. 60.00x (ISBN 0-85124-357-6, Pub. by Bertrand Russell Hse); pap. 17.50x (ISBN 0-85124-358-4). State Mutual Bk.
Social Democrats -U. S. A. in the Service of Reaction: A Record of Racism, Low Wages, Bureaucracy & Betrayal of Socialism. George Morris. 1976. pap. 0.50 (ISBN 0-87898-119-5). New Outlook.
Social Democrats in Imperial Germany: A Study in Working-Class Isolation & National Integration. Guenther Roth. Ed. by Lewis A. Coser & Walter W. Powell. LC 79-7018. (Perennial Works in Sociology Ser.). 1979. Repr. of 1963 ed. lib. bdg. 26.50x (ISBN 0-405-12117-2). Ayer Co Pubs.
Social-Demokraten & Internationalism: The Copenhagen Social Democratic Newspaper's Coverage of International Labor Affairs, 1871-1958. Gerd Callesen & John Logue. (U. of Gothenburg (Sweden), Research Section Post-War History Publications: No. 8). (Illus.). 73p. 1979. pap. 4.95 (ISBN 0-933522-00-2). Kent Popular.
Social Desirability Variable in Personality Assessment & Research. Allen L. Edwards. LC 81-20141. vii, 108p. 1982. Repr. lib. bdg. 35.00x (ISBN 0-313-23245-8, EDSD). Greenwood.
Social Destiny of Man. Albert Brisbane. LC 68-18217. 1969. Repr. of 1840 ed. 39.50x (ISBN 0-678-00471-4). Kelley.
Social Destiny of Man: Or Association & Reorganization of Industry. Albert Brisbane. LC 68-56752. 1967. Repr. of 1840 ed. 15.00 (ISBN 0-8337-0376-5). B Franklin.
Social Destiny of Mankind. Albert Brisbane. 100.00 (ISBN 0-87968-025-3). Gordon Pr.
Social Development. R. Blunden. (Studies in Developmental Paediatrics). (Illus.). 160p. 1982. text ed. 25.00 (ISBN 0-85200-304-8, Pub. by MTP Pr England). Kluwer Academic.
Social Development. J. E. Grusec & H. Lytton. (Illus.). 500p. 1988. pap. 41.00 (ISBN 0-387-96591-2). Springer-Verlag.
Social Development. David G. Perry & Kay Bussey. (Illus.). 416p. 1984. text ed. write for info (ISBN 0-13-816034-1). P-H.
Social Development & Personality. Ed. by George G. Thompson. LC 77-146673. (Readings in Educational Research Ser.). 1971. 35.50x (ISBN 0-471-86005-0); text ed. 32.50x ten or more copies. McCutchan.
Social Development & Planning in Asia. Ralph Pieries. LC 76-903626. 1976. 17.50x (ISBN 0-88386-820-2). South Asia Bks.
Social Development & Political Violence: A Cross-National Causal Analysis. Chung-si Ahn. (Institute of Social Sciences International Studies Ser.: No. 3). 210p. 1981. text ed. 16.00x (ISBN 0-8248-0941-6). UH Pr.
Social Development: Conceptual, Methodological & Policy Issues. John T. Jones & Rama S. Pandey. 1981. 18.95 (ISBN 0-312-73201-5). St Martin.
Social Development, Cultural Change, & Fertility Decline: A Study of Fertility Change in Kerala. K. Mahadevan & M. Sumangala. 160p. 1988. text ed. 17.95 (ISBN 0-8039-9536-9). Sage.
Social Development in Childhood: Day-Care Programs & Research. Hyman Blumberg Symposium on Research in Early Childhood Education Staff. LC 77-4778. pap. 55.00 (ISBN 0-317-09807-1, 2020543). Bks Demand UMI.
Social Development in Childhood: Day-Care Programs & Research. Ed. by Roger A. Webb. LC 77-4778. (Hyman Blumberg Symposium Ser.: No.4). 224p. 1977. pap. text ed. 6.95x (ISBN 0-8018-1947-4). Johns Hopkins.
Social Development in the Third World: Level of Living Indicators & Social Planning. Ed. by J. G. Hilhorst & M. Klatter. LC 84-23747. 233p. 1985. 34.50 (Pub. by Croom Helm Ltd). Routledge Chapman & Hall.
Social Development in Times of Economic Uncertainty. International Council on Social Welfare Staff. LC 81-3884. 272p. 1981. 34.00x (ISBN 0-231-05326-6). Columbia U Pr.
Social Development in Young Children: A Study of Beginners. Susan S. Isaacs. LC 75-41153. Repr. of 1933 ed. 24.50 (ISBN 0-404-14557-4). AMS Pr.
Social Development in Youth: Structure & Content. Ed. by J. A. Meacham. (Contributions to Human Development Ser.: Vol. 5). (Illus.). xii, 188p. 1981. pap. 48.75 (ISBN 3-8055-2868-X). S Karger.
Social Development Issues: Alternative Approaches to Global Human Needs, Vol. 10, No. 2. Ed. by Wayne G. Johnson & Martin B. Tracy. 1986. pap. 6.00 (ISBN 0-317-58804-4). U of Iowa Sch Soc Wk.
Social Development: Its Nature & Conditions. L. T. Hobhouse. 348p. 1986. Repr. of 1924 ed. lib. bdg. 85.00 (ISBN 0-89984-673-4). Century Bookbindery.
Social Development of Canada. Samuel D. Clark. LC 75-41060. Repr. of 1942 ed. 29.50 (ISBN 0-404-14655-4). AMS Pr.
Social Development of Learning Disabled Persons: Examining the Effects & Treatments of Inadequate Interpersonal Skills. Doreen Kronick. LC 81-81960. (Social & Behavioral Science Ser.). 1981. text ed. 29.95x (ISBN 0-87589-499-2). Jossey-Bass.
Social Development of the Intellect. W. Doise & G. Mugny. Tr. by A. St. James & N. Emler. LC 84-9227. (International Series in Experimental Social Psychology: Vol. 10). 196p. 1984. text ed. 42.00 (ISBN 0-08-030209-2); pap. text ed. 23.00 (ISBN 0-08-030215-7). Pergamon.
Social Development: Psychological Growth & the Parent-Child Relationship. Eleanor E. Maccoby. 436p. 1980. pap. text ed. 16.00 net (ISBN 0-15-581422-2, HC). HarBraceJ.
Social Deviance. 3rd ed. Ronald A. Farrell & Victoria L. Swigert. 420p. 1988. pap. text ed. write for info. (ISBN 0-534-08773-6). Wadsworth Pub.
Social Deviance. S. Giora Shoham. 163p. 1976. 21.50 (ISBN 0-89876-086-0). Gardner Pr.
Social Deviance & the Human Services. Charles Wolfson. 194p. 1984. 24.75 (ISBN 0-398-05005-8). C C Thomas.
Social Deviancy & Adolescent Personality. John C. Ball. LC 72-12308. (Illus.). 119p. 1973. Repr. of 1962 ed. lib. bdg. 35.00x (ISBN 0-8371-6687-X, BASD). Greenwood.
Social Diagnosis. Mary E. Richmond. 512p. 1917. 29.95x (ISBN 0-87154-703-1). Russell Sage.
Social Dialectics: Civilizations & Social Theory. Anouar Abdel-Malek. Tr. by M. Gonzalez from Fr. LC 80-25061. 214p. 1981. 49.50 (ISBN 0-87395-500-5); pap. 19.95x (ISBN 0-87395-502-1). State U NY Pr.
Social Dialectics: Nation & Revolution. Anouar Abdel-Malek. Tr. by M. Gonzalez from Fr. LC 80-25061. 222p. 1981. 49.50 (ISBN 0-87395-501-3); pap. 19.95x (ISBN 0-87395-503-X). State U NY Pr.
Social Differences in Contemporary America. James A. Davis. 196p. 1987. text ed. 11.00 net (ISBN 0-15-581425-7, DAV, HC). HarBraceJ.
Social Differentiation of English in Norwich. P. Trudgill. LC 73-77178. (Cambridge Studies in Liguistics: No. 13). 208p. 1974. 37.50 (ISBN 0-521-20264-7); pap. text ed. 16.95 (ISBN 0-521-29745-1). Cambridge U Pr.
Social Dimension: European Developments in Social Psychology, 2 Vols. Henri Tajfel. (European Studies in Social Psychology). 1984. Vol. 1. 65.00 (ISBN 0-521-23972-9); Vol. 2. 70.00 (ISBN 0-521-23978-8); Vol. 1. pap. 22.95 (ISBN 0-521-28383-3); Vol. 2. pap. 22.95. Cambridge U Pr.
Social Dimension in Medieval & Renaissance Studies see Medievalia et Humanistica.
Social Dimension in Transportation Assessment. Tay Wilson & Charlotte Neff. 356p. 1983. text ed. 38.00x (ISBN 0-566-00630-8). Gower Pub Co.
Social Dimension of Family Treatment. Danuta Mostwin. LC 79-92201. (Illus.). 245p. 1980. pap. 15.95x. Natl Assn Soc Wkrs.
Social Dimensions of AIDS: Method & Theory. Ed. by Douglas Feldman & Thomas M. Johnson. LC 86-9491. 256p. 1986. lib. bdg. 38.95 (ISBN 0-275-92110-7, C2110). Praeger.
Social Dimensions of Development: Social Policy & Planning in the Third World. Margaret Hardiman & James Midgley. LC 81-22006. (Social Development in Third World Ser.). 317p. 1982. 67.95x (ISBN 0-471-10184-2, Pub. by Wiley-Interscience). Wiley.
Social Dimensions of Development: Social Policy & Planning in the Third World. Margaret Hardiman & James Midgley. LC 81-22006. (Social Development in the Third World Ser.). 325p. pap. 84.50 (2029799). Bks Demand UMI.
Social Dimensions of Early Buddhism. Uma Chakravarti. 256p. 1988. 27.50 (ISBN 0-19-562069-0). Oxford U Pr.
Social Dimensions of Law & Justice. Julius Stone. LC 73-168258. 1971. Repr. of 1966 ed. lib. bdg. 75.00x (ISBN 0-912004-01-0). W W Gaunt.
Social Dimensions of Mental Illness, Alcoholism, & Drug Dependence. Don Martindale & Edith Martindale. LC 72-133499. 332p. 1976. lib. bdg. 36.95 (ISBN 0-8371-5175-9, MAM/). Greenwood.
Social Disability: Alcoholism, Drug Addiction, Crime, & Social Disadvantage. Ed. by David Malikin. LC 72-96468. 256p. 1973. 30.00x (ISBN 0-8147-5361-2). NYU Pr.
Social Disease. Paul Rudnick. 1986. 14.45 (ISBN 0-394-55270-9). Knopf.
Social Disease. Paul Rudnick. 1987. pap. 6.95 (ISBN 0-345-33038-2). Ballantine.
Social Doctrine of the Sermon on the Mount. Charles Gore. 59.95 (ISBN 0-8490-1063-2). Gordon Pr.
Social Dynamics: Models & Methods (Monograph) Nancy B. Tuma & Michael T. Hannan. LC 83-25856. (Quantitative Studies Social Relations). 1984. 39.95 (ISBN 0-12-703670-9). Acad Pr.
Social Dynamics, Nursing Coalitions & Infanticide Among Farm Cats, Felis Catus. D. Macdonald. (Advances in Ethology Ser.: Vol. 28). (Illus.). 80p. 1987. pap. text ed. 25.00x (ISBN 3-489-62436-X). Parey Sci Pubs.
Social Dynamics of Financial Markets. Ed. by Patricia A. Adler & Peter Adler. LC 84-4340. (Contemporary Studies in Applied Behavioral Science: Vol. 2). 1984. 52.50 (ISBN 0-89232-435-X). Jai Pr.
Social Dynamics of Gelada Baboons. R. Dunbar & Patsy Dunbar. (Contributions to Primatology Ser.: Vol. 6). (Illus.). 176p. 1975. 59.50 (ISBN 3-8055-2137-5). S Karger.
Social Dynamics of Peace & Conflict. Robert A. Rubinstein & Mary L. Foster. 165p. 1988. 22.00 (ISBN 0-8133-7614-9). Westview.
Social Dynamics of Self-Esteem: Theory to Theory. R. A. Steffenhagen & Jeff D. Burns. LC 87-2421. 258p. 1987. lib. bdg. 39.95 (ISBN 0-275-92325-8, C2325). Praeger.
Social Ecological Psychology & the Psychology of Women see Proceedings of the XXIIIth International Congress of Psychology of the International Union of Psychological Science Acapulo, Mexico, 2-7 September 1984.
Social Ecology, a Critical Analysis. Milla A. Alihan. LC 64-24804. 267p. Repr. of 1938 ed. 20.00x (ISBN 0-8154-0008-X). Cooper Sq.
Social Ecology & Economic Development of Ciudad Juarez. Ed. by Gay Young. (Westview Special Studies on Latin America & the Caribbean). 175p. 1986. pap. 25.00 (ISBN 0-8133-7248-8). Westview.
Social Ecology: Monographs. Mary Vance. (Public Administration Ser.: P 2181). 28p. 1987. 7.50 (ISBN 1-55590-361-4). Vance Biblios.
Social Ecology of Crime. James M. Byrne & Robert J. Sampson. LC 85-27823. (Research in Criminology Ser.). (Illus.). 216p. 1986. 35.00 (ISBN 0-387-96231-X). Springer-Verlag.
Social, Economic, & Environmental Implications in Transportation Planning: Nine Reports. (Transportation Research Record Ser.). 95p. 1976. 4.00 (ISBN 0-309-02497-8). Transport Res Bd.
Social, Economic, Behavioral & Urban Growth Considerations, 9 reports. (Transportation Research Record Ser.). 65p. 1974. 4.20 (ISBN 0-309-02351-3). Transport Res Bd.
Social-Economic Movements: An Historical & Comparative Survey of Socialism. Harry W. Laidler. (Essay Index Reprint Ser.). Repr. of 1944 ed. 44.50 (ISBN 0-518-10149-5). Ayer Co Pubs.
Social Economics. Cedric T. Sandford. 1977. text ed. 27.00x (ISBN 0-435-84780-5); pap. text ed. 11.50x (ISBN 0-435-84781-3). Gower Pub Co.
Social Economics. Friedrich Von Wieser. Tr. by A. F. Hinrichs. LC 67-20930. 1967. Repr. of 1927 ed. 45.00x (ISBN 0-678-00274-6). Kelley.
Social Economy of France. Peter Coffey. LC 73-85269. 160p. 1974. 22.50 (ISBN 0-312-73220-1). St Martin.
Social Economy of West Germany. Graham Hallett. LC 73-85268. 160p. 1974. 22.50 (ISBN 0-312-73255-4). St Martin.
Social Education of Bulgarian Youth. Peter J. Georgeoff. LC 68-22364. pap. 85.30 (ISBN 0-317-39709-5, 2055870). Bks Demand UMI.
Social Education: Principles & Practices. Chris Brown et al. (Contemporary Analysis in Education Ser.: No. 10). 225p. 1986. 38.00x (ISBN 1-85000-112-X, Falmer Pr); pap. 21.00x (ISBN 1-85000-113-8). Taylor & Francis.
Social, Educational, & Religious State of the Manufacturing Districts. Edward Baines. LC 75-5885. (Social History of Education). 1969. Repr. of 1843 ed. 17.50x (ISBN 0-678-08454-8). Kelley.
Social Effects of Inflation. Ed. by Marvin E. Wolfgang & Richard D. Lambert. (Annals of the American Academy of Political & Social Science: No. 456). 250p. 1981. 15.00 (ISBN 0-87761-264-1); pap. 7.95 (ISBN 0-87761-265-X). Am Acad Pol Soc Sci.
Social Effects of Technological Developments in the Food & Drink Industries, Including Those Arising from New Production Methods, & the Need for Training & Retraining: Food & Drink Industries Committee Report II. (Programme of Industrial Activities). 51p. 1985. pap. 7.15 (ISBN 92-2-103821-1, ILO369, ILO). UNIPUB.
Social Effects of Unemployment on Teesside, 1919-39. Kate Nicholas. 254p. 1987. 60.00 (ISBN 0-7190-1772-6, Pub. by Manchester Univ Pr). St Martin.
Social Elements in English Prose Fiction Between 1700 & 1832. C. B. A. Proper. LC 68-1013. 1970. Repr. of 1929 ed. 75.00x (ISBN 0-8383-0612-8). Haskell.
Social Engineering in Family Matters. Burton Mindick. LC 85-6595. 240p. 1985. 38.95 (ISBN 0-275-90040-1, C0040). Praeger.
Social Engineering in Singapore: Educational Policies & Social Change, Eighteen Nineteen to Nineteen Seventy-Two. Harold E. Wilson. 250p. 1978. 20.00x (ISBN 0-8214-0507-1, Pub. by Singapore U Pr); pap. 10.00x (ISBN 0-8214-0525-X). Ohio U Pr.
Social Engineerng in the Philippines: The Aims, Execution & Impact of American Colonial Policy, 1900-1913. Glenn A. May. LC 79-7467. (Contributions in Comparative Colonial Studies: No. 2). 1980. lib. bdg. 36.95 (ISBN 0-313-20978-2, MAE). Greenwood.
Social England Illustrated. Andrew Lang. LC 64-16744. (Arber's an English Garner). 458p. 1964. Repr. of 1890 ed. 24.50x (ISBN 0-8154-0132-9). Cooper Sq.
Social England in the Fifteenth-Century. A. Abram. 1909. Repr. 9.95 (ISBN 0-8274-3443-X). R West.
Social England under the Regency. John Ashton. LC 67-23940. 450p. 1968. Repr. of 1899 ed. 30.00x (ISBN 0-8103-3253-1). Gale.
Social England under the Regency, Vol. I. John Aston. (Illus.). 1976. 25.00x (ISBN 0-7158-1110-X). Charles River Bks.
Social Environment & Health. Stewart Wolf. LC 80-50868. (Jessie & John Danz Lecture Ser.). (Illus.). 112p. 1981. 10.00x (ISBN 0-295-95777-8). U of Wash Pr.
Social Environment of the Schools. Maynard C. Reynolds. LC 80-65498. 104p. (Orig.). 1980. pap. 6.00 (ISBN 0-86586-103-X). Coun Exc Child.
Social Episodes: The Study of Interaction Routines. Joseph Forgas. LC 79-40925. (European Monographs in Social Psychology). 1980. 91.00 (ISBN 0-12-263550-7). Acad Pr.
Social Epistemology. Steve Fuller. LC 87-31056. (Science, Technology, & Society Ser.). 320p. 1988. 27.50 (ISBN 0-253-35227-4). Ind U Pr.

Social Equality. Rudolf Dreikurs. LC 83-72318. 1971. pap. 6.95x (ISBN 0-918560-30-6). A Adler Inst.

Social Equality: The Constitutional Experiment in India. M. Kumar. 264p. 1982. 22.95. Asia Bk Corp.

Social Equality: The Constitutional Experiment in India. Maju Kumar. 1982. text ed. 23.00x. Coronet Bks.

Social, Ergonomic & Stress Aspects of Work with Computers, Vol. 1: Proceedings of the Second International Conference, Honolulu, HI, August 10-14, 1987. Ed. by G. Salvendy et al. (Advances in Human Factors-Ergonomics Ser.: No. 10A). 374p. 1987. 102.50 (ISBN 0-444-42847-X); Set (with Vol. 2) 219.50. Elsevier.

Social-Ethical Significance of Vocabulary. Gladys C. Schwesinger. LC 70-177806. (Columbia University. Teachers College. Contributions to Education: No. 211). Repr. of 1926 ed. 22.50 (ISBN 0-404-55211-0). AMS Pr.

Social Ethics: Morality & Social Policy. 3rd ed. Thomas A. Mappes & Jane S. Zembathy. 528p. 1986. pap. text ed. 24.95 (ISBN 0-07-040125-X). McGraw.

Social Ethics: Morality & Social Policy. 2nd ed. Thomas A. Mappes & Jane S. Zembaty. (Illus.). 448p. 1982. pap. 27.95x (ISBN 0-07-040121-7). McGraw.

Social Evil in Chicago: A Study of Existing Conditions with Recommendations by the Vice Commission of Chicago. Vice Commission Of Chicago. LC 78-112578. (Rise of Urban America). (Illus.). 1970. Repr. of 1911 ed. 31.00 (ISBN 0-405-02479-7). Ayer Co Pubs.

Social Evolution. Benjamin Kidd. 1979. Repr. of 1894 ed. lib. bdg. 30.00 (ISBN 0-8495-3026-1). Arden Lib.

Social Evolution. Robert Trivers. 1985. 28.95 (ISBN 0-8053-8507-X). Benjamin-Cummings.

Social Evolution & Political Theory. Leonard T. Hobhouse. LC 67-27584. 1978. Repr. of 1911 ed. lib. bdg. 15.00 (ISBN 0-89824-004-2). Trillium Pr.

Social Evolution & Sociological Categories. Paul Q. Hirst. LC 76-5413. 140p. 1976. 19.75 (ISBN 0-8419-0257-7). Holmes & Meier.

Social Evolution of Indonesia: The Asiatic Mode of Production & Its Legacy. Fritjov Tichelman. (Studies in Social History: No. 5). 314p. 1980. lib. bdg. 45.00 (ISBN 90-247-2389-2, Pub. by Martinus Nijhoff Netherlands). Kluwer Academic.

Social Exchange: Advances In Theory & Research. Ed. by Kenneth J. Gergen et al. LC 80-18170. 324p. 1980. 39.50x (ISBN 0-306-40395-1, Plenum Pr). Plenum Pub.

Social Exchange, Dramaturgy & Ethnomethodology. J. N. Mitchell. 27.95 (ISBN 0-444-99057-7, MSX, Pub. by Elsevier). Greenwood.

Social Exchange in Developing Relationships. Ed. by Robert L. Burgess & Ted L. Huston. LC 79-6934. 1979. 29.95 (ISBN 0-12-143550-4). Acad Pr.

Social Exchange Theory. Karen S. Cook. LC 86-6613. (Illus.). 224p. 1986. text ed. 29.95 (ISBN 0-8039-2598-0). Sage.

Social Exchange Theory: The Two Traditions. Peter P. Ekeh. LC 74-79403. 256p. 1974. text ed. 17.50x (ISBN 0-674-81201-8). Harvard U Pr.

Social Existence: Metaphysics, Marxism & the Social Sciences. Richard Quinney. (Sage Library of Social Research: Vol. 141). 194p. 1982. 29.95 (ISBN 0-8039-0830-X); pap. 14.95 (ISBN 0-8039-0831-8). Sage.

Social Expectations & Perception: The Case of the Slavic Anthracite Workers. Michael A. Barendse. LC 80-8610. (Penn State Studies: No. 47). (Illus.). 72p. (Orig.). 1981. pap. text ed. 4.95x (ISBN 0-271-00277-8). Pa St U Pr.

Social Expenditure, Nineteen Sixty to Nineteen Ninety: Problems of Growth & Control. OECD. 97p. (Orig.). pap. 15.00x (ISBN 92-64-12656-2). OECD.

Social Experience. James W Vander Zanden. 580p. 1988. text ed. 30.00 (ISBN 0-394-36579-8, RanC); study guide 11.75 (ISBN 0-394-37665-X). Random.

Social Experiment in Program Administration: The Housing Allowance Administrative Agency Experiment. William L. Hamilton. LC 79-87501. 1979. text ed. 33.00 (ISBN 0-89011-533-8). Abt Bks.

Social Experiment in Program Administration: The Housing Allowance Administration Agency Experiment. William L. Hamilton. (Illus.). 318p. 1984. Repr. of 1979 ed. lib. bdg. 34.75 (ISBN 0-8191-4114-3). U Pr of Amer.

Social Experimentation. Jerry A. Hausman & David A. Wise. LC 84-8825. (National Bureau of Economic Research Conference Report Ser.). (Illus.). 288p. 1985. lib. bdg. 33.00x (ISBN 0-226-31940-7). U of Chicago Pr.

Social Experimentation: A Method for Planning & Evaluating Social Intervention. Henry W. Riecken & Robert F. Boruch. 1974. 24.95 (ISBN 0-12-588150-9). Acad Pr.

Social Experimentation & Economic Policy. Robert Ferber & Werner Z. Hirsch. LC 81-6146. (Cambridge Surveys of Economic Literature Ser.). (Illus.). 224p. 1981. 42.50 (ISBN 0-521-24185-5); pap. 15.95 o. p. (ISBN 0-521-28507-0). Cambridge U Pr.

Social Experiments: Methods for Design & Evaluation. Leonard Saxe & Michael Fine. (Sage Library of Social Research: Vol. 131). 304p. 1981. 35.00 (ISBN 0-8039-1710-4); pap. 16.95 (ISBN 0-8039-1711-2). Sage.

Social Experiments with Information Technology & the Challenges of Innovation. Ed. by Lars Qvortrup et al. 1987. lib. bdg. 79.00 (ISBN 90-277-2488-1, Pub. by Reidel Holland). Kluwer Academic.

Social Fabric, 2 vols. Ed. by John H. Cary & Julius Weinberg. 1987. pap. text ed. write for info. (ISBN 0-673-39325-9). Vol. I, American Life from 1607 to the Civil War (ISBN 0-673-39326-7). Vol. II, American Life from Reconstruction to the Present. Scott F.

Social Fabric & Spatial Structure in Colonial Latin America. Ed. by David J. Robinson. LC 79-15744. (Dellplain Latin American Studies Ser.: No. 1). pap. 124.00 (ISBN 0-317-28161-5, 2022589). Bks Demand UMI.

Social Fabric: Dimensions & Issues. Ed. by James F. Short, Jr. (ASA Presidential Series Volume). (Illus.). 275p. 1986. text ed. 35.00 (ISBN 0-8039-2788-6); pap. text ed. 16.95 (ISBN 0-8039-2789-4). Sage.

Social Fabric of the Metropolis Contributions of the Chicago School of Urban Sociology. Ed. by James F. Short, Jr. LC 75-129926. (Heritage of Sociology Ser). 1972. pap. 3.45X (ISBN 0-226-75467-7, P424, Phoen). U of Chicago Pr.

Social Fabric of the Metropolis: Contributions of the Chicago School of Urban Sociology. Ed. by James F. Short, Jr. LC 75-129926. (Heritage of Sociology Ser). 1970. 25.00x (ISBN 0-226-75466-9). U of Chicago Pr.

Social Fabric: South Carolina's Traditional Quilts. Laurel Horton & Lynn R. Myers. (Illus., Orig.). 1987. pap. 10.00 (ISBN 0-317-58571-1). McKissick.

Social Factors Affecting Special Supervision in the Public Schools of the United States. W. A. Jessup. LC 74-176908. (Columbia University. Teachers College. Contributions to Education: No. 43). Repr. of 1911 ed. 22.50 (ISBN 0-404-55043-6). AMS Pr.

Social Factors & Intelligence: A Bibliography, Vol. I. rev. ed. Robert Friis. 27p. 1981. pap. 39.95 (ISBN 0-939552-00-0, 005). Human Behavior.

Social Factors in Medical Progress. Bernhard J. Stern. LC 68-57582. (Columbia University. Studies in the Social Sciences: No. 287). Repr. of 1927 ed. 12.50 (ISBN 0-404-51287-9). AMS Pr.

Social Facts & Fabrications: Customary Law on Kilimanjaro, Eighteen Eighty to Nineteen Eighty. Sally F. Moore. LC 85-7897. 1986. 65.00 (ISBN 0-521-30938-7); pap. 19.95 (ISBN 0-521-31201-9). Cambridge U Pr.

Social Ferment in Vermont, Seventeen Ninety-One to Eighteen Fifty. David M. Ludlum. LC 39-22998. Repr. of 1939 ed. 24.50 (ISBN 0-404-04066-7). AMS Pr.

Social Figures: George Eliot, Social History & Literary Representation. Daniel Cottom. LC 86-19249. (Theory & History of Literature Ser.: Vol. 44). 270p. 1987. 35.00x (ISBN 0-8166-1547-0); pap. 14.95 (ISBN 0-8166-1548-9). U of Minn Pr.

Social Forces & Aging: An Introduction to Social Gerontology. 5th ed. Robert C. Atchley. 527p. 1988. text ed. write for info. (ISBN 0-534-08790-6). Wadsworth Pub.

Social Forces & the Law. 2nd ed. Ronald A. Anderson. 1981. pap. text ed. write for info. (ISBN 0-538-12300-1, L30). SW Pub.

Social Forces & the Manager: Readings & Cases. William R. Allen & Louis K. Bragaw. LC 81-10402. (Management Ser.). 502p. 1982. pap. (ISBN 0-471-08611-8). Wiley.

Social Forces & the Manager: Readings & Cases. William R. Allen & Louis K. Bragaw, Jr. LC 87-3259. 518p. 1987. pap. 31.50 (ISBN 0-89464-225-1). Krieger.

Social Forces in American History. A. M. Simons. 1976. lib. bdg. 59.95 (ISBN 0-8490-2616-4). Gordon Pr.

Social Forces in German Literature. Kuno Francke. 59.95 (ISBN 0-8490-1064-0). Gordon Pr.

Social Forces in German Literature: A Study in the History of Civilization. Kuno Francke. 577p. 1985. Repr. of 1896 ed. lib. bdg. 65.00 (ISBN 0-89987-288-3). Darby Bks.

Social Forces in Modern Literature. Philo M. Buck. 1979. Repr. of 1913 ed. lib. bdg. 37.00 (ISBN 0-8495-0393-0). Arden Lib.

Social Forces in Modern Literature. Philo M. Buck. LC 76-58444. 1913. lib. bdg. 17.00 (ISBN 0-8414-1651-6). Folcroft.

Social Forces in the Middle East. Ed. by Sydney N. Fisher. LC 68-23289. (Illus.). 1968. Repr. of 1955 ed. lib. bdg. 35.00x (ISBN 0-8371-0074-7, FIME). Greenwood.

Social Forecasting Methodology: Suggestions for Research. Doniel P. Harrison. LC 75-41511. (Social Science Frontiers Ser.). 97p. 1976. pap. 6.95x (ISBN 0-87154-376-1). Russell Sage.

Social Forestry for Rural Development. K. M. Tiwari. (Illus.). 108p. 1983. text ed. 21.25x (Pub. by Intl Bk Dist). Intl Spec Bk.

Social Forestry in India: Problems & Prospects. N. D. Bachkheti. 115p. 1987. text ed. 20.00x (ISBN 81-7027-103-7, Pub. by Radiant Pubs India). Advent NY.

Social Formation & Symbolic Landscape. Denis E. Cosgrove. LC 84-21629. (Illus.). 304p. 1985. 28.50x (ISBN 0-389-20540-0, 08102). B&N Imports.

Social Foundations of Contemporary Economics. Georges Sorel. Ed. by John L. Stanley. 270p. 1983. Repr. 39.95 (ISBN 0-87855-482-3). Transaction Bks.

Social Foundations of Education. 2nd ed. Richard D. Van Scotter et al. (Illus.). 432p. 1985. text ed. write for info. (ISBN 0-13-815887-8). P-H.

Social Foundations of German Unification, 1858-1871. Theodore S. Hamerow. Incl. Vol. 1. Ideas & Institutions. 1969. 44.50x (ISBN 0-691-05174-7); pap. 12.50x (ISBN 0-691-00773-X); Vol. II. Struggles & Accomplishments. 1972. LC 75-75241. pap. Princeton U Pr.

Social Foundations of Industrial Powers: A Comparison of France & Germany. Marc Maurice et al. Tr. by Arthur Goldhammer. 400p. 1986. pap. 35.00x (ISBN 0-262-13213-3). MIT Pr.

Social Foundations of Language & Thought. David R. Olson et al. 1980. 19.95 (ISBN 0-393-01303-0). Norton.

Social Foundations of Meaning. E. Von Savigny. 160p. 1988. pap. 29.50 (ISBN 0-387-19006-6). Springer-Verlag.

Social Foundations of Thought & Action: A Social Cognitive Theory. Albert Bandura. (Illus.). 544p. 1986. text ed. 41.00 (ISBN 0-13-815614-X). P-H.

Social Fragmentation & Political Hostility: An Austrian Case Study. G. Bingham Powell, Jr. LC 74-83119. 1970. 22.50x (ISBN 0-8047-0715-4). Stanford U Pr.

Social Framework of Agriculture. Harold H. Mann. Ed. by Daniel Thorner. (Illus.). 501p. 1968. 29.50x (ISBN 0-7146-2333-4, F Cass Co). Biblio Dist.

Social Framework of Agriculture. Harold H. Mann. LC 67-29802. 1967. 45.00x (ISBN 0-678-08007-0). Kelley.

Social France at the Time of Philip Augustus. Achille Luchaire. 1976. lib. bdg. 59.95 (ISBN 0-8490-2617-2). Gordon Pr.

Social France in the XVII Century. Cecile Hugon. 21.75 (ISBN 0-8369-7140-X, 7973). Ayer Co Pubs.

Social Frontier, Nineteen Thirty-Four to Nineteen Forty-Three: A Journal of Educational Criticism & Reconstruction, 5 Vols. Progressive Education Association Staff. LC 70-168564. 1971. Repr. of 1943 ed. 180.00 (ISBN 0-405-03723-6). Ayer Co Pubs.

Social Function of Science. J. D. Bernal. 482p. 1980. Repr. lib. bdg. 40.00 (ISBN 0-8492-3754-8). R West.

Social Function of Social Science. Duncan MacRae, Jr. LC 75-32282. 376p. 1976. 35.00x (ISBN 0-300-01921-1); pap. 9.95x (ISBN 0-300-02670-6). Yale U Pr.

Social Functioning Framework: An Approach to the Human Behavior & Social Environment Sequence. Ruth M. Butler. Date not set. 3.00 (70-320-01). Coun Soc WK Ed.

Social Functioning Patterns in Families of Offspring Receiving Treatment for Drug Abuse. Sharol Cannon. LC 75-42602. 1975. 6.95 (ISBN 0-87212-040-6). Libra.

Social Functions & Economic Aspects of Health Insurance. William A. Rushing. 1987. lib. bdg. 43.95 (ISBN 0-89838-219-X, Pub. by Kluwer-Nijhoff (Netherlands)). Kluwer Academic.

Social Functions of Avoidances & Taboos among the Zulu. Otto F. Raum. (Illus.). 1973. 103.00x (ISBN 3-11-003460-3). De Gruyter.

Social Functions of Iranian Education: An Historical Survey Related to the Current Political Crisis. David C. Woolman. (TWEC World Education Monograph Ser.). 29p. 1979. 2.50. I N Thut World Educ Ctr.

Social Functions of Language in a Mexican-American Community. George C. Barker. LC 70-186238. (Anthropological Papers: No. 22). 56p. 1972. pap. 4.95x (ISBN 0-8165-0317-6). U of Ariz Pr.

Social Functions of the Telephone. Benjamin D. Singer. LC 81-20525. 125p. 1981. perfect bound 9.95. R & E Pubs.

Social Fund. Jo Roll. 1986. 20.00x (ISBN 0-317-57677-1, Pub. by FPSC UK). State Mutual Bk.

Social Future. new rev. ed. Rudolf Steiner. Tr. by Henry B. Monges from Ger. LC 72-87742. 151p. 1972. pap. text ed. 7.95 (ISBN 0-910142-34-3). Anthroposophic.

Social Gardens: Outdoor Spaces for Living & Entertaining. Charlotte M. Frieze. (Illus.). 224p. 1988. 40.00 (ISBN 1-55670-047-4). Stewart Tabori & Chang.

Social Geography in International Perspective. Ed. by John Eyles. LC 85-22997. 304p. 1986. 28.50x (ISBN 0-389-20608-3). B&N Imports.

Social Geography of Great Britain: An Introduction. Hugh D. Clout & Richard J. Dennis. (Pergamon Oxford Geographies). 1980. pap. text ed. 19.25 (ISBN 0-08-021801-6). Pergamon.

Social Geography of the City. David Ley. 449p. 1983. pap. text ed. 22.95 scp (ISBN 0-06-384875-9, HarpC). Har-Row.

Social Geography: Progress & Prospect. Ed. by Michael Pacione. LC 87-506. 328p. 1987. 57.50 (ISBN 0-7099-4026-2, Pub. by Croom Helm UK). Routledge Chapman & Hall.

Social Germany in Luther's Time: Being the Memoirs of Bartholomew Sastrow. Bartholomaus Sastrow. Tr. by Albert D. Vandam. LC 83-45674. Date not set. Repr. of 1902 ed. 39.50 (ISBN 0-404-19863-5). AMS Pr.

Social Gerontology. Hooyman & Kiyak. 1988. text ed. 33.00. Allyn.

Social Gerontology. Ed. by M. B. Kleiman. (Interdisciplinary Topics in Gerontology Ser.: Vol. 17). (Illus.). vi, 206p. 1983. pap. 65.50 (ISBN 3-8055-3649-6). S Karger.

Social Gerontology: New Directions. Ed. by Silvana Di Gregorio. 300p. 1987. lib. bdg. 49.95x (ISBN 0-7099-3894-2, Pub. by Croom Helm UK). Routledge Chapman & Hall.

Social Goals & Educational Reform: American Schools in the Twentieth Century. Ed. by Charles V. Willie & Inabeth Miller. LC 88-217. (Contributions to the Study of Education Ser.: No. 27). 184p. 1988. lib. bdg. 37.95 (ISBN 0-313-24781-1, WIE/). Greenwood.

Social Goals & Social Organization: Essays in Memory of Elisha Pazner. Ed. by Leonid Hurwicz & David Schmeidler. 416p. 1985. 42.50 (ISBN 0-521-26204-6). Cambridge U Pr.

Social Goals, Social Programs & the Aging. Ed. by Carter C. Osterbind. LC 75-44462. (Center for Gerontological Studies & Programs Ser.: No. 24). 1975. pap. 8.00x (ISBN 0-8130-0539-6). U Presses Fla.

Social Gospel for Millions! The Religious Bestsellers of Charles Sheldon, Charles Gordon, & Harold Bell Wright. John Ferre. LC 88-70596. 114p. 1988. text ed. 24.95; pap. text ed. 12.95 (ISBN 0-87972-438-2). Bowling Green Univ.

Social Gospel in the South: The Woman's Home Mission Movement in the Methodist Episcopal Church, South, 1886-1939. John P. McDowell. LC 82-15292. x, 167p. 1982. text ed. 22.50 (ISBN 0-8071-1022-1). La State U Pr.

Social Gospel: Religion & Reform in Changing America. Ronald C. White, Jr. & C. Howard Hopkins. LC 75-34745. (Illus.). 326p. 1975. 29.95 (ISBN 0-87722-083-2); pap. 9.95x (ISBN 0-87722-084-0). Temple U Pr.

Social Graces. Larry Fink. LC 83-72660. (Illus.). 80p. 1984. 17.50 (ISBN 0-89381-135-1); pap. 12.50 (ISBN 0-89381-201-3); ltd. ed. 250.00 (ISBN 0-89381-159-9). Aperture.

Social Group in French Thought. Robert A. Nisbet. Ed. by Harriet Zuckerman & Robert K. Merton. LC 79-9017. (Dissertations on Sociology Ser.). 1980. lib. bdg. 18.00x (ISBN 0-405-12985-8). Ayer Co Pubs.

Social Group Work: A Helping Process. 3rd ed. Gisela Konopka. 256p. 1983. write for info. (ISBN 0-13-815787-1). P-H.

Social Group Work: Competence & Values in Practice. Ed. by Joseph Lassner et al. LC 86-32012. (Social Work with Groups Ser.: Supplement No.2). 226p. 1987. text ed. 34.95 (ISBN 0-86656-643-0). Haworth Pr.

Social Group Work with Older People. National Association of Social Workers. Ed. by Leon Stein. LC 79-8684. (Growing Old Ser.). 1980. Repr. of 1963 ed. lib. bdg. 14.00x. Ayer Co Pubs.

Social Group Work with Older People. Seminar on Social Group Work with Older People Mohonk Lake, NY 1961 & National Association of Social Workers. 16.00 (ISBN 0-405-12801-0). Ayer Co Pubs.

Social Groups & Religious Ideas in the Sixteenth-Century. Ed. by Miriam Chrisman & Otto Grundler. (Studies in Medieval Culture: No. XIII). 1978. pap. 4.95x (ISBN 0-918720-02-8). Medieval Inst.

Social Groupwork & Alcoholism. Ed. by Marjorie Altman & Ruth Crocker. LC 82-2998. (Social Work with Groups Ser.: Vol. 5, No. 1). 92p. 1982. text ed. 22.95 (ISBN 0-917724-94-1, B94); pap. text ed. 14.95 (ISBN 0-86656-439-X). Haworth Pr.

Social Growth Program. Joan Hickmott & Donald Wollman. (Special Education Ser.). (Illus.). 1980. 46.95 (ISBN 0-89568-225-7). Spec Learn Corp.

Social Health Investigator. Jack Rudman. (Career Examination Ser.: C-2970). 1988. pap. 14.00 (ISBN 0-8373-2970-1). Natl Learning.

Social Hierarchies: Essays Toward a Sociophysiological Perspective. Ed. by Patricia R. Barchas. LC 83-22600. (Contributions in Sociology Ser.: No. 47). (Illus.). xvi, 160p. 1984. lib. bdg. 35.00 (ISBN 0-313-23165-6, BSH/). Greenwood.

Social Historians. H. A. Toulmin. 34.95 (ISBN 0-8490-1065-9). Gordon Pr.

Social Histories of the Secondary Curriculum: Subjects for Study. Ivor F. Goodson. Ed. by I. Goodson. (Studies in Curriculum History Ser.: Vol. 1). 250p. 1984. 38.00x (ISBN 1-85000-016-6, Falmer Pr); pap. 22.00x (ISBN 1-85000-015-8, Falmer Pr). Taylor & Francis.

Social History - Twenty Years of Essays from the Journal of Social History. Ed. by Peter N. Stearns. 350p. 1988. 40.00x (ISBN 0-8147-7876-3); pap. 15.00x (ISBN 0-8147-7877-1). NYU Pr.

Social History & Evolution in the Interrelationship of Adat & Islam in Rembau, Negeri Sembilan. Michael G. Peletz. 59p. (Orig.). 1981. pap. text ed. 9.50x (ISBN 9971-902-28-1, Pub. by Inst Southeast Asian Stud). Gower Pub Co.

Social History & Human Experience. Asa Briggs. (Grace A. Tanner Lecture in Human Values Ser.). 22p. 1984. 9.00 (ISBN 0-910153-02-7). E T Woolf.

Social History & Literature. Richard H. Tawney. LC 77-8952. 1977. lib. bdg. 17.00 (ISBN 0-8414-8635-2). Folcroft.

Social History & Social Policy. Ed. by David Rothman & Stanton Wheeler. LC 80-1772. (Studies in Social Discontinuity). 1981. 19.95 (ISBN 0-12-598680-7). Acad Pr.

Social History of American Agriculture. Joseph Schafer. LC 70-99471. (American Scene Ser). 1970. Repr. of 1936 ed. lib. bdg. 37.50 (ISBN 0-306-71857-X). Da Capo.

Social History of American Education. Ed. by B. Edward McClellan & William J. Reese. LC 87-5893. 381p. (Orig.). 1987. 34.95 (ISBN 0-252-01461-8); pap. 11.95 (ISBN 0-252-01462-6). U of Ill Pr.

Social History of American Family Sociology, Eighteen Sixty-Five to Nineteen Forty. Ronald L. Howard. Ed. by John H. Mogey & Louis Th. Van Leeuwen. LC 80-1790. (Contributions in Family Studies Ser.: No. 4). xiii, 150p. 1981. lib. bdg. 35.00 (ISBN 0-313-22767-5, MOA/). Greenwood.

Social History of an Indian Caste: The Kayasths of Hyderabad. Karen I. Leonard. LC 76-52031. (Center for South & Southeast Asian Studies: No. 28). 1978. 34.95x (ISBN 0-520-03431-7). U of Cal Pr.

Social History of Ancient Ireland, 2 vols. Patrick W. Joyce. LC 68-56473. (Illus.). 1968. Repr. of 1913 ed. Set. 55.00 (ISBN 0-405-08677-6, Blom Pubns); 27.50 ea. Vol. 1 (ISBN 0-405-08678-4). Vol. 2 (ISBN 0-405-08679-2). Ayer Co Pubs.

Social History of Art, 4 vols. Arnold Hauser. Incl. Vol. 1. Prehistoric to Middle Ages. 1957. pap. 6.95 (ISBN 0-394-70114-3, V114); Vol. 2. Renaissance to Baroque. 1957. pap. 6.95 (ISBN 0-394-70115-1, V115); Vol. 3. Rococco to Romanticism. 1958. pap. 6.95 (ISBN 0-394-70116-X, V116); Vol. 4. Naturalism of the Film Age. 1958. pap. 5.95 (ISBN 0-394-70117-8, V117). pap. 2.95 ea. (Vin). Random.

Social History of Art, Vol. 1. Arnold Hauser. 1985. pap. 6.95 (Vin). Random.

Social History of Art, Vol. 2. Arnold Hauser. 1985. pap. 6.95 (Vin). Random.

Social History of Art, Vol. 3. Arnold Hauser. 1985. pap. 6.95 (Vin). Random.

Social History of Art, Vol. 4. Arnold Hauser. 1985. pap. 6.95 (Vin). Random.

Social History of Black Slaves & Freedmen in Portugal, 1441-1555. A. C. Saunders. LC 81-7716. (Cambridge Iberian & Latin American Studies). (Illus.). 275p. 1982. 57.50 (ISBN 0-521-23150-7). Cambridge U Pr.

Social History of Bourbon: An Unhurried Account of Our Star-Spangled American Drink. Gerald Carson. LC 84-2216. (Illus.). 312p. 1984. Repr. of 1963 ed. 22.00 (ISBN 0-8131-1509-4). U Pr of KY.

Social History of England. Asa Briggs. 320p. 1986. pap. 9.95 (ISBN 0-14-007492-9). Penguin.

Social History of England, Eighteen Fifty-One to Nineteen Seventy-Five. Francois Bedarida. 448p. 1979. 15.95x (ISBN 0-416-85910-0, NO. 2833); pap. 14.95x (ISBN 0-416-85920-8, NO. 2834). Routledge Chapman & Hall.

Social History of England, 1851-1986. Francois Bedarida. Tr. by A. S. Forster. 448p. 1988. pap. text ed. 17.95 (ISBN 0-317-67351-3). Routledge Chapman & Hall.

Social History of English. Dick Leith. (Language & Society Ser.). 224p. 1983. 24.95x (ISBN 0-7100-9260-1); pap. 10.95x (ISBN 0-7100-9261-X). Routledge Chapman & Hall.

Social History of English Law. A. Harding. 21.25 (ISBN 0-8446-2204-4). Peter Smith.

Social History of English Music. Eric D. Mackerness. LC 75-40994. (Illus.). 307p. 1976. Repr. of 1964 ed. lib. bdg. 29.75x (ISBN 0-8371-8705-2, MAHEM). Greenwood.

Social History of Housing, Eighteen Fifteen to Nineteen Eighty-Five. John Burnett. 384p. 1986. 39.95 (ISBN 0-416-36770-4, 1024). Routledge Chapman & Hall.

Social History of Housing Eighteen Fifteen to Nineteen Seventy. John Burnett. 352p. (Orig.). 1985. pap. 13.95 (ISBN 0-416-73720-X, NO. 9343). Routledge Chapman & Hall.

Social History of Italy, Fifteenth to Seventeenth Centuries. Peter Burke. 1988. text ed. 40.00 (ISBN 0-566-05194-X, Pub. by Gower Pub England). Gower Pub Co.

Social History of Lancashire, 1558-1939. J. K. Walton. LC 88-21659. 406p. 1988. pap. 24.95 (ISBN 0-7190-1701-7, Pub. by Manchester Univ Pr). St Martin.

Social History of Lancashire, 1558-1939. John K. Walton. (Illus.). 288p. 1986. 55.00 (ISBN 0-7190-1820-X, Pub. by Manchester Univ Pr). St Martin.

Social History of Language. Ed. by Peter Burke & Roy Porter. (Cambridge Studies in Oral & Literate Culture 12). (Illus.). 208p. 1987. 34.50 (ISBN 0-521-30158-0); pap. 10.95 (ISBN 0-521-31763-0). Cambridge U Pr.

Social History of Madness: The World Throughout the Eyes of the Insane. Roy Porter. Ed. by Mark Polizzotti. LC 87-33979. 256p. 1988. 18.95 (ISBN 1-55584-185-6). Weidenfeld.

Social History of Mathematics. Ed. by H. Mehrtens. 320p. 1981. 34.50x (ISBN 0-8176-3033-3). Birkhauser.

Social History of Music: From the Middle Ages to Beethoven & Music & Society since 1815. Henry Raynor. LC 78-58318. 1978. pap. 7.95 (ISBN 0-8008-7238-X, Crescendo). Taplinger.

Social History of Nineteenth-Century France. Roger Price. (Illus.). 370p. 1988. 45.00 (ISBN 0-8419-1165-7); pap. 24.50 (ISBN 0-8419-1166-5). Holmes & Meier.

Social History of Occupational Health. Ed. by Paul Weindling. LC 85-21286. 288p. 1985. 31.00 (ISBN 0-7099-3606-0, Pub. by Croom Helm Ltd). Routledge Chapman & Hall.

Social History of Politics: Critical Perspectives in West German Historical Writing since 1945. Ed. by Georg Iggers. LC 85-22349. 256p. 1985. 40.00 (ISBN 0-907582-35-4, Pub. by Berg Pubs); pap. 15.95 (ISBN 0-907582-78-8, Pub. by Berg Pubs). St Martin.

Social History of Puerto Rico. Ed. by Raoul Gordon. 1976. lib. bdg. 59.95 (ISBN 0-8490-1066-7). Gordon Pr.

Social History of Religion in Modern Scotland. Callum Brown. Ed. by Hugh McLeod & Bob Scribner. (Christianity & Society in the Modern World Ser.). 288p. 1987. lib. bdg. 63.50x (ISBN 0-416-36980-4). Routledge Chapman & Hall.

Social History of Rome. Geza Alfoldy. Tr. by John Wood. LC 85-11188. 224p. 1985. 27.50x (ISBN 0-389-20583-4, BNB 08141). B&N Imports.

Social History of Rome. Geza Alfoldy. Tr. by David Braund & Frank Pollock. LC 87-36082. (Ancient Society & History Ser.). 256p. 1988. pap. text ed. 12.95x (ISBN 0-8018-3701-4). Johns Hopkins.

Social History of Scandinavian Immigration, Washington State, 1895-1910. Jorgen Dahlie. LC 80-849. (American Ethnic Groups Ser.). 1981. lib. bdg. 20.00x (ISBN 0-405-13412-6). Ayer Co Pubs.

Social History of the American Family from Colonial Times to the Present. Arthur W. Calhoun. cancelled (ISBN 0-405-03886-0, 13352). Ayer Co Pubs.

Social History of the American Negro. Benjamin G. Brawley. LC 70-37233. Repr. of 1921 ed. 12.50 (ISBN 0-404-00138-6). AMS Pr.

Social History of the Chinese in Singapore & Malaya, 1800-1911. Ching-Hwang Yen. (Illus.). 433p. 1986. 39.95 (ISBN 0-19-582666-3). Oxford U Pr.

Social History of the Fool. Sandra Billington. LC 83-40624. 256p. 1984. 25.00 (ISBN 0-312-73293-7). St Martin.

Social History of the French Revolution. Norman Hampson. LC 64-20652. 1963. pap. 14.95c (ISBN 0-8020-6060-9). U of Toronto Pr.

Social History of the French Revolution. Norman Hampson. 228p. 1987. pap. text ed. 11.95 (ISBN 0-7100-6525-6, Pub. by Routledge UK). Routledge Chapman & Hall.

Social History of the Frontier Nursing Service. Nancy Dammann. (Illus.). 179p. (Orig.). 1982. pap. 5.95 (ISBN 0-9609376-0-9). Soc Change Pr.

Social History of the Machine Gun. John Ellis. LC 74-26204. (Illus.). Repr. of 1975 ed. 46.50 (ISBN 0-8357-9483-0, 2013992). Bks Demand UMI.

Social History of the Machine Gun. John Ellis. 17.00 (ISBN 0-405-14209-9). Ayer Co Pubs.

Social History of the Machine Gun. John Ellis. LC 86-45457. (Illus.). 200p. 1986. pap. 9.95 (ISBN 0-8018-3358-2). Johns Hopkins.

Social History of the Nonconformist Ministry in England & Wales, 1800-1930. Kenneth D. Brown. 256p. 1988. 45.00 (ISBN 0-19-822763-9). Oxford U Pr.

Social History of the Sea Islands, with Special Reference to St. Helena Island, South Carolina. Guion G. Johnson. LC 69-16573. (Illus.). 1969. Repr. of 1930 ed. 35.00 (ISBN 0-8371-1143-9, JOS&). Greenwood.

Social History of the United States: A Guide to Information Sources. Ed. by Donald F. Tingley. LC 78-13196. (American Government & History Information Guide Ser.: Vol. 3). 272p. 1979. 68.00x (ISBN 0-8103-1366-9). Gale.

Social History of the Western World. Harry E. Barnes. 59.95 (ISBN 0-87700-035-2). Revisionist Pr.

Social History of Timbuktu: The Role of Muslim Scholars & Notables, Fourteen Hundred to Nineteen Hundred. Elias Saad. LC 82-14687. (Cambridge Studies in Islamic Civilization). 336p. 1983. 54.50 (ISBN 0-521-24603-2). Cambridge U Pr.

Social History of Traditional Song. Reginald Nettel. LC 70-93274. (Illus.). 1969. Repr. of 1954 ed. 35.00x (ISBN 0-678-07506-9). Kelley.

Social History of Twentieth-Century Urban Riots. James N. Upton. 75p. (Orig.). 1985. pap. 9.95x (ISBN 0-932269-20-6). Wyndham Hall.

Social History of Western Civilization, Vol. I. Richard M. Golden. LC 87-60525. 304p. 1987. pap. text ed. write for info. (ISBN 0-312-00303-X). St Martin.

Social History of Western Civilization, Vol. II. Richard M. Golden. LC 87-60525. 304p. 1987. pap. text ed. write for info. (ISBN 0-312-00431-1). St Martin.

Social History of Western Europe 1450-1720: Tensions & Solidarities among Rural People. Sheldon J. Watts. LC 84-159439. 275p. 1984. pap. 13.00 (ISBN 0-09-156081-0, Pub. by Hutchinson Educ). Longwood Pub Group.

Social Humanities: Toward an Integrative Discipline of Science & Values. Raymond D. Gastil. LC 76-52580. (Jossey-Bass Behavioral Science Ser.). pap. 83.00 (ISBN 0-317-41968-4, 2025673). Bks Demand UMI.

Social Hygiene in Twentieth Century Britain. Greta Jones. (A Volume in the Wellcome Institute Ser.). 192p. 1986. 43.00 (ISBN 0-7099-1481-4, Pub. by Croom Helm UK). Routledge Chapman & Hall.

Social Idealism & Major Utopias in the History of Mankind, 2 vols. O. S. Hertzler. 417p. 1988. Set. 227.45 (ISBN 0-89920-179-2). Am Inst Psych.

Social Idealism & the Problem of Objectivity. Tronn Overend. LC 82-17359. (Scholars' Library). 215p. 1983. text ed. 34.50x (ISBN 0-7022-1712-3). U of Queensland Pr.

Social Ideals in English Letters. Vida D. Scudder. (Belles Lettres in English Ser.). Repr. of 1898 ed. 33.00 (ISBN 0-384-54520-3). Johnson Repr.

Social Ideals in English Letters. Vida D. Scudder. 1973. Repr. of 1923 ed. 20.00 (ISBN 0-8274-1084-0). R West.

Social Ideals in German Literature. Ludwig W. Kahn. LC 75-84876. Repr. of 1938 ed. 12.95 (ISBN 0-404-03626-0). AMS Pr.

Social Ideals of Alfred Tennyson As Related to His Times. William C. Gordon. LC 68-812. (Studies in Tennyson, No. 27). 1969. Repr. of 1906 ed. lib. bdg. 75.00x (ISBN 0-8383-0661-6). Haskell.

Social Ideals of St. Francis. James Meyer. 2.75 (ISBN 0-8199-0296-9, L38825). Franciscan Herald.

Social Ideas of American Educators. Merle Curti. (Quality Paperback Ser.: No. 105). 613p. 1978. pap. 6.95 (ISBN 0-8226-0105-2). Littlefield.

Social Ideas of Religious Leaders, Sixteen Sixty to Sixteen Sixty-Eight. Richard B. Schlatter. LC 77-120663. 1970. Repr. lib. bdg. 18.50x (ISBN 0-374-97102-1, Octagon). Hippocrene Bks.

Social Ideas of the Northern Evangelists, Eighteen Twenty-Six to Eighteen Sixty. Charles C. Cole, Jr. 1966. lib. bdg. 20.50x (ISBN 0-374-91843-0, Octagon). Hippocrene Bks.

Social Identifications: A Social Psychology of Intergroup Relations & Group Processes. Michael Hogg & Dominic Abrams. 200p. 1988. lib. bdg. 60.00 (ISBN 0-415-00694-5). Routledge Chapman & Hall.

Social Identity & Intergroup Relations. Ed. by Henri Tajfel. LC 81-21676. (European Studies in Social Psychology). (Illus.). 608p. 1982. 77.00 (ISBN 0-521-24616-4). Cambridge U Pr.

Social Images & Process in Urban New Guinea: A Study of Port Moresby. Alan Rew. LC 74-17389. (AES Ser). 262p. 1974. text ed. 25.95 (ISBN 0-8299-0024-1). West Pub.

Social Impact Analysis & Development Planning in the Third World. Ed. by William Derman & Scott Whiteford. (Social Impact Assessment Ser.). 250p. 1985. pap. text ed. 29.50x (ISBN 0-86531-786-0). Westview.

Social Impact Assessment: A Cross-Disciplinary Guide to the Literature. Michael J. Carley & Ellan O. Derow. (Social Impact Assessment Ser.). 250p. 1984. 42.50x (ISBN 0-86531-529-9). Westview.

Social Impact Assessment & Management. Larry F. Leistritz et al. LC 83-48219. 300p. 1985. lib. bdg. 49.00 (ISBN 0-8240-9047-0). Garland Pub.

Social Impact Assessment: Experimental Methods & Approaches. Edward J. Soderstrom. LC 81-10632. 154p. 1981. 35.00 (ISBN 0-275-90721-X, C0721). Praeger.

Social Impact Assessment Methods. Ed. by Kurt Finsterbusch et al. 320p. 1983. 29.95 (ISBN 0-8039-2142-X). Sage.

Social Impact Assessment, Monitoring, & Management by the Electric Energy Industry: State-of-the-Practice (AIF-NESP-012) Energy Impact Associates, Inc. Staff. (National Environmental Studies Project: NESP Reports). 150p. 1977. 45.00 (ISBN 0-318-13592-2); to NESP sponsors 15.00 (ISBN 0-318-13593-0). US Coun Energy Awareness.

Social Impact of Bomb Destruction. 1st ed. Fred C. Ikle. LC 58-11611. pap. 70.00 (ISBN 0-317-08300-7, 2005840). Bks Demand UMI.

Social Impact of Energy Development in the West. Ed. by Charles F. Cortese. Date not set. text ed. price not set (ISBN 0-8290-0235-9). Irvington.

Social Impact of Energy Development in the West. Ed. by Charles F. Cortese. Date not set. pap. text ed. price not set (ISBN 0-8290-1083-1). Irvington.

Social Impact of Oil in Scotland. Ron Parsler & Dan Shapiro. 192p. 1980. text ed. 36.50x (ISBN 0-566-00375-9). Gower Pub Co.

Social Impact of Oil: The Case of Peterhead. Robert Moore. 176p. 1982. 27.50x (ISBN 0-7100-0903-8). Routledge Chapman & Hall.

Social Impact of Television: A Research Agenda for the 1980's. W. Russell Neuman. 58p. (Orig.). 1981. pap. text ed. 9.00 (ISBN 0-8191-5851-8, Pub. by Aspen Inst for Humanistic Studies). U Pr of Amer.

Social Impacts of Land Development: An Initial Approach for Estimating Impacts on Neighborhood Usages & Perceptions. Kathleen Christensen. (Land Development Impact Ser.). 144p. 1976. pap. 6.00 (ISBN 0-87766-171-5, 15700). Urban Inst.

Social Implications of Biological Education. Ed. by Arnold B. Grobman. LC 77-131404. 134p. 1971. 5.95 (ISBN 0-87850-000-6). Darwin Pr.

Social Implications of Early Negro Music in the United States: With over 150 of the Songs, Many of Them with Their Music. Bernard Katz. 1979. 18.00 (ISBN 0-405-01875-4, 16393). Ayer Co Pubs.

Social Implications of the Peaceful Uses of Nuclear Energy. Ed. by Otto Klineberg. 169p. (Orig.). 1964. pap. 5.00 (ISBN 92-3-100553-7, U610, UNESCO). UNIPUB.

Social Incentives: A Life-Span Developmental Approach. Joseph Veroff & Joanne B. Veroff. LC 79-8872. 1980. 24.95 (ISBN 0-12-718750-2). Acad Pr.

Social Indicator Models. Ed. by Kenneth C. Land & Seymour Spilerman. LC 74-79447. 412p. 1975. 34.50x (ISBN 0-87154-505-5). Russell Sage.

Social Indicators. Ramkishna Mukherjee. 1975. 9.00x (ISBN 0-333-90090-1). South Asia Bks.

Social Indicators: A Revision of P 1259. Mary Vance. (Public Administration Ser.: P 1840). 52p. 1986. 13.50 (ISBN 0-89028-710-4). Vance Biblios.

Social Indicators: An Aid to Public Policy Evaluation in State Government. C. Kenneth Meyer et al. 1979. 1.00 (ISBN 1-55614-114-9). U of SD Gov Res Bur.

Social Indicators: An Annotated Bibliography of Current Literature. Kevin J. Gilmartin et al. LC 78-67062. (Library of Social Science). 137p. 1979. lib. bdg. 28.00 (ISBN 0-8240-9755-6). Garland Pub.

Social Indicators for Development. Ian Imiles. LC 83-10941. 216p. 1985. 22.50 (ISBN 0-312-73294-5). St Martin.

Social Indicators in Community Research: Proceedings of the Committee of Community Social Researchers, 1976. Community Social Researchers Committee. 1976. 2.00 (ISBN 0-86671-034-5). Comm Coun Great NY.

Social Indicators IV: A Social Report on the U. S. A., 1986. (Illus.). 600p. Date not set. lib. bdg. cancelled (ISBN 0-933937-01-6). Infax Corp.

Social Indicators of Development, 1987. 1987. pap. text ed. 25.00 (ISBN 0-8213-0976-5, WB217, Pub. by Wrld Bank). UNIPUB.

Social Indicators of Well-Being: Americans' Perception of Life Quality. Frank M. Andrews & Stephen B. Withey. LC 76-26179. (Illus.). 476p. 1976. 39.50x (ISBN 0-306-30935-1, Plenum Pr). Plenum Pub.

Social Inequality & Class Radicalism is France & Britain. Duncan Gallie. LC 83-7535. (Illus.). 320p. 1984. 39.50 (ISBN 0-521-25764-6); pap. 16.95 (ISBN 0-521-27700-0). Cambridge U Pr.

Social Inequality & Political Structures: Studies in Class Formation & Interest Articulation in an Indian Coalfield & Its Rural Hinterland. Ed. by John P. Neelsen. 1983. 27.50x (ISBN 0-8364-1071-8, Pub. by Manohar India). South Asia Bks.

Social Inequality: Comparative & Developmental Approaches. Gerald D. Berreman. LC 80-68550. (Studies in Anthropology). 1981. 47.00 (ISBN 0-12-093160-5). Acad Pr.

Social Inequality: Features, Forms & Functions. Pajendra Randey. 317p. 1982. 34.95 (ISBN 0-317-13625-9, Pub. by Anuj Pubns India). Asia Bk Corp.

Social Inequality in a Portuguese Hamlet: Land, Late Marriage, & Bastardy, 1870-1978. Brian J. O'Neill. (Cambridge Studies in Social Anthropology: No. 63). (Illus.). 464p. 1987. 49.50 (ISBN 0-521-32284-7). Cambridge U Pr.

Social Inequality, Stratification, & Mobility. 2nd ed. Judah Matras. (Illus.). 352p. 1984. text ed. write for info (ISBN 0-13-815811-8). P-H.

Social Influence & Social Change. Serge Moscovici. (European Monographs in Social Psychology Ser.). 1977. 55.50 (ISBN 0-12-508450-1). Acad Pr.

Social Influence Process in Counseling & Psychotherapy. Ed. by Fred J. Dorn. (Illus.). 182p. 1986. 27.00x (ISBN 0-398-05256-5). C C Thomas.

Social Influences Affecting the Behavior of Young Children. Ruth P. Koshuk. (SRCD M Ser.). 1941. pap. 15.00 (ISBN 0-527-01518-0). Kraus Repr.

Social Influences on Behavior: Student Booklet. American Psychological Association Staff. (Human Behavior Curriculum Project Ser.). 80p. (Orig.). (gr. 9-12). 1981. pap. text ed. 3.95x (ISBN 0-8077-2619-2). Tchrs Coll.

Social Influences on Behavior: Teachers Handbook. American Psychological Association Staff. (Human Behavior Curriculum Project Ser.). 48p. (Orig.). (gr. 9-12). 1981. pap. 9.95 (ISBN 0-8077-2620-6). Tchrs Coll.

Social Life of Monkey & Apes. S. Zuckerman. 356p. 1981. Repr. of 1932 ed. lib. bdg. 40.00 (ISBN 0-89984-547-9). Century Bookbindery.

Social Life of Monkeys & Apes. 2nd ed. S. Zuckerman. (Illus.). 496p. 1981. 39.95x (ISBN 0-7100-0691-8). Routledge Chapman & Hall.

Social Life of Scotland in the Eighteen-Century, 2 Vol. set. Henry G. Graham. 265p. 1982. Repr. of 1899 ed. lib. bdg. 100.00 (ISBN 0-89984-903-2). Century Bookbindery.

Social Life of Scotland in the Eighteenth-Century. 2nd ed. Henry G. Graham. LC 73-173169. Repr. of 1901 ed. 30.00 (ISBN 0-405-08569-9, Blom Pubns). Ayer Co Pubs.

Social Life of Small Urban Spaces. William H. Whyte. LC 79-56569. (Illus.). 125p. (Orig.). 1980. pap. 9.50 (ISBN 0-89164-057-6). Conservation Foun.

Social Life of the Crow Indians. Robert H. Lowie. LC 74-7987. Repr. of 1912 ed. 11.50 (ISBN 0-404-11875-5). AMS Pr.

Social Life of the Navajo Indians. Gladys A. Reichard. LC 76-82350. (Columbia Univ. Contributions to Anthropology Ser.: Vol. 7). Repr. of 1928 ed. 31.00 (ISBN 0-404-50557-0). AMS Pr.

Social Life of Things: Commodities in Cultural Perspective. Arjun Appadurai. (Illus.). 344p. 1988. pap. 14.95 (ISBN 0-521-35726-8). Cambridge U Pr.

Social Life of Things: Commodities in Cultural Perspective. Ed. by Arjun Appadurai. (Illus.). 384p. 1986. 42.50 (ISBN 0-521-32351-7). Cambridge U Pr.

Social Life of Virginia in the Seventeenth-Century. Philip A. Bruce. 268p. 1968. Repr. of 1907 ed. 18.50 (ISBN 0-87928-002-6). Corner Hse.

Social Limits of Art. John Manfredi. LC 82-8661. (Illus.). 208p. 1982. lib. bdg. 17.50x (ISBN 0-87023-372-6). U of Mass Pr.

Social Limits to Growth. Fred Hirsch. (Twentieth Century Fund Study). 1976. 16.00x (ISBN 0-674-81365-0); pap. 7.95x (ISBN 0-674-81366-9). Harvard U Pr.

Social Living Achievement Activities. Robert L. Doan. (Early Childhood Achievement Unit Ser.). 1979. pap. 6.40x (ISBN 0-87628-286-9). Ctr Appl Res.

Social Logic of Health. Will Wright. 215p. 1982. 22.00x (ISBN 0-8135-0948-3). Rutgers U Pr.

Social Logic of Space. Bill Hillier & Julienne Hanson. LC 83-15004. 320p. 1984. 67.50 (ISBN 0-521-23365-8). Cambridge U Pr.

Social Logics Conversations & Groups in Everyday Life: A Model for the Social Sciences. James H. Parker. LC 85-9111. 208p. (Orig.). 1985. text ed. 26.75 (ISBN 0-8191-4750-8); pap. text ed. 12.50 (ISBN 0-8191-4751-6). U Pr of Amer.

Social, Managerial, & Economic Issues. Jacques Vallee et al. (Group Communication Through Computers: Vol. 4). 222p. 1978. 15.00 (ISBN 0-318-14421-2, R40). Inst Future.

Social Marketing: A New Imperative for Public Health. Richard K. Manoff. LC 84-18279. 304p. 1985. pap. 14.95 (ISBN 0-275-91673-1, B1673). Praeger.

Social Marketing: Perspectives & Viewpoints. Williams Lazer & Eugene J. Kelley. LC 72-92419. (Illus.). pap. 129.50 (ISBN 0-317-09632-X, 2055674). Bks Demand UMI.

Social Maturity Scale for Blind Preschool Children: A Guide to Its Use. Kathryn E. Maxfield & Sandra Bucholz. 49p. 1957. pap. 6.00 (ISBN 0-89128-059-6, PPP059). Am Foun Blind.

Social Meaning of Civic Space: Studying Political Authority Through Architecture. Charles T. Goodsell. LC 87-21466. (Illus.). xviii, 254p. 1988. 25.00x (ISBN 0-7006-0347-6). U Pr of KS.

Social Meaning of Death. Ed. by Renee C. Fox & Richard D. Lambert. LC 79-53669. (Annals of the American Academy of Political & Social Science: No. 447). 1980. 15.00 (ISBN 0-87761-246-3); pap. 7.95 (ISBN 0-87761-247-1). Am Acad Pol Soc Sci.

Social Meaning of Modern Biology: From Social Darwinism to Sociobiology. Howard L. Kaye. LC 85-17953. 224p. 1986. 22.50x (ISBN 0-300-03497-0). Yale U Pr.

Social Meanings of Religious Experiences. George D. Herron. (American Studies Ser.). 1969. Repr. of 1896 ed. 18.00 (ISBN 0-384-22660-4). Johnson Repr.

Social Meanings of Suicide. Jack D. Douglas. 1967. pap. 14.95x (ISBN 0-691-02812-5). Princeton U Pr.

Social Medicine in Eastern Europe: The Organization of Health Services & the Education of the Medical Personnel in Czechoslovakia, Hungary, & Poland. Richard E. Weinerman & Shirley B. Weinerman. LC 72-78525. (Commonwealth Fund Publications Ser). (Illus.). 1969. text ed. 16.00x (ISBN 0-674-81380-4). Harvard U Pr.

Social Medicine of Old Age: Report of an Inquiry in Wolverhampton. J. H. Sheldon. LC 79-8688. (Growing Old Ser.). 1980. Repr. of 1948 ed. lib. bdg. 22.00 (ISBN 0-405-12804-5). Ayer Co Pubs.

Social Medicine: The Advance of Organized Health Services in America. Milton I. Roemer. LC 78-17621. (Health Care & Society Ser.: Vol. 3). 576p. 1978. text ed. 39.50 (ISBN 0-8261-2600-6). Springer Pub.

Social Message of Jesus. Igino Giordani. 1977. 4.50 (ISBN 0-8198-0467-3); pap. 3.50 (ISBN 0-8198-0468-1). Dghtrs St Paul.

Social Message of the Early Church Fathers. Igino Giordani. 1977. 3.95 (ISBN 0-8198-0469-X); pap. 2.95 (ISBN 0-8198-0470-3). Dghtrs St Paul.

Social Message of the Gospels. Ed. by Franz Bockle. LC 68-31249. (Concilium Ser.: Vol. 35). 188p. 7.95 (ISBN 0-8091-0138-6). Paulist Pr.

Social Method & Social Life. Ed. by Michael Brenner. 1981. 47.50 (ISBN 0-12-131550-9). Acad Pr.

Social Methodology for Community Participation in Local Investment: The Experience of Mexico's PIDER Program. Michael Cernea. (Working Paper: No. 598). 147p. 1983. 5.00 (ISBN 0-8213-0205-1, WP 0598). World Bank.

Social Mind: Foundations of Social Philosophy. John E. Boodin. LC 75-3063. (Philosophy in America Ser.). Repr. of 1939 ed. AMS Pr.

Social Ministry. Dieter T. Hessel. LC 82-6960. 228p. 1982. pap. 10.95 (ISBN 0-664-24422-X). Westminster John Knox.

Social Mission of English Criticism, Eighteen Forty-Eight to Nineteen Thirty-Two. Chris Baldick. (Oxford English Monographs). 1983. 45.00x (ISBN 0-19-812821-5). Oxford U Pr.

Social Mission of English Criticism 1848-1932. Chris Baldick. 264p. 1987. pap. 18.95 (ISBN 0-19-812979-3). Oxford U Pr.

Social Mission of Law in India. V. R. Krishna Iyer. 1976. lib. bdg. 10.00 (ISBN 0-88386-733-8); pap. 5.00 (ISBN 0-685-63870-7). South Asia Bks.

Social Mobility & Class Structure in Modern Britain. 2nd ed. John H. Goldthorpe. (Illus.). 398p. 1987. 39.95 (ISBN 0-19-827286-3); pap. 19.95 (ISBN 0-19-827285-5). Oxford U Pr.

Social Mobility & Class Structure in Modern Britain. 2nd ed. John H. Goldthorpe et al. (Illus.). 1982. text ed. write for info.; pap. text ed. write for info. Oxford U Pr.

Social Mobility & Controlled Fertility. H. Y. Tien. 1965. 18.95x (ISBN 0-8084-0280-3). New Coll U Pr.

Social Mobility & Social Structure. Bogdan W. Mach & Wlodzimierz Weslowski. 180p. 1987. text ed. 35.00 (ISBN 0-7100-9982-7, Pub. by Routledge UK). Routledge Chapman & Hall.

Social Mobility in Industrial Society: A Study of Political Sociology. Seymour M. Lipset & Reinhard Bendix. (Institute of Industrial Relations, UC Berkeley). 1959. pap. 5.95 (ISBN 0-520-00756-5). U of Cal Pr.

Social Mobility in Industrial Societies: Women in France & Sweden. Lucienne Portocarero. (Swedish Institute for Social Research: No. 3). 118p. (Orig.). 1987. pap. text ed. 23.50x (ISBN 91-7604-025-9, Pub. by Almqvist & Wiksell). Coronet Bks.

Social Mobility in Industrializing Society. Suresh Kumar. 1986. 24.00 (ISBN 81-7033-015-7, Pub. by Rawat). South Asia Bks.

Social Mobility in Israeli Society. Moshe Lissak. 136p. 1969. 24.95x (ISBN 0-87855-176-X). Transaction Bks.

Social Mobility in the Caste System in India: An Interdisciplinary Symposium. Ed. by James Silverberg. 1968. pap. text ed. 16.80x (ISBN 90-2790-022-1). Mouton.

Social Mobility in the English Bildungsroman: Gissing, Hardy, Bennett, & Lawrence. Patricia Alden. Ed. by A. Walton Litz. LC 86-7050. (Studies in Modern Literature: No. 58). (Illus.). 166p. 1986. 39.95 (ISBN 0-8357-1740-2); pap. write for info. (ISBN 0-8357-1918-9). UMI Res Pr.

Social Mobility in the Nineteenth & Twentieth-Centuries. Hartmut Kaelble. LC 85-13415. 324p. 1986. 32.50 (ISBN 0-312-73448-4). St Martin.

Social Mode of Restoration Comedy. Kathleen M. Lynch. 1965. lib. bdg. 18.50x (ISBN 0-374-95207-8, Octagon). Hippocrene Bks.

Social Movement & Social Change. S. K. Sharma. 219p. 1985. text ed. 40.00x (ISBN 0-86590-398-0, Pub. by B R Pub Corp Delhi). Apt Bks.

Social Movements: An Introduction to Political Sociology. Rudolf Heberle. (Century Sociology Ser.). (Illus.). 1951. 12.95x (ISBN 0-89197-414-8); pap. text ed. 8.95x (ISBN 0-89197-415-6). Irvington.

Social Movements & Political Power: Emerging Forms of Radicalism in the West. Carl Boggs. 304p. 1987. 37.95 (ISBN 0-87722-447-1). Temple U Pr.

Social Movements & Protest in France. Philip G. Cerny. LC 81-21217. 270p. 1982. 25.00x (ISBN 0-312-73310-0). St Martin.

Social Movements & Protest in France. Ed. by Philip G. Cerny. 270p. 1982. pap. 14.00 (ISBN 0-86187-214-2, Pub. by Frances Pinter). Longwood Pub Group.

Social Movements & Social Change. Ed. by Robert H Lauer. LC 76-18747. 320p. 1976. 10.00x (ISBN 0-8093-0771-5). S Ill U Pr.

Social Movements & Social Structure: A Study in the Princely State of Mewar. Pushpendra Surana. 1983. 20.00x (ISBN 0-8364-1003-3, Pub. by Manohar India). South Asia Bks.

Social Movements & Social Transformation. M. S. Rao. 1987. Repr. 27.50x (ISBN 0-8364-2133-7, Pub. by Manohar India). South Asia Bks.

Social Movements & the Legal System: A Theory of Law Reform & Social Change. Joel Handler. (Institute for Research on Poverty Ser.). 1979. 21.00 (ISBN 0-12-322840-9). Acad Pr.

Social Movements for Development. S. K. Srivastava. 1987. 35.00 (ISBN 81-85076-34-0, Pub. by Chugh Pubns India). South Asia Bks.

Social Movements in an Organizational Society: Collected Essays. Mayer N. Zald & John D. McCarthy. 388p. 1986. 29.95 (ISBN 0-88738-119-7). Transaction Bks.

Social Movements in India: Peasant & Backward Classes Movements, Vol. 1. Ed. by M. Rao. 1980. 17.50x (ISBN 0-8364-0199-9). South Asia Bks.

Social Movements in India: Tribal, Sectarian & Women's Movements, Vol. 2. Ed. by Rao Mra. 1981. 17.50x (ISBN 0-8364-0787-3, Pub. by Manoha India). South Asia Bks.

Social Needs Versus Economic Efficiency in China: Sun Yefang's Critique of Socialist Economics. Sun Yefung. Tr. by K. K. Fung. LC 82-10265. 150p. 1982. 40.00 (ISBN 0-87332-209-6). M E Sharpe.

Social Networks: A Developing Paradigm. Ed. by Samuel Leinhardt. 1977. 24.95 (ISBN 0-12-442450-3). Acad Pr.

Social Networks among Biological Scientists. Nicholas C. Mullins. Ed. by Harriet Zuckerman & Robert K. Merton. LC 79-6270. (Dissertations on Sociology Ser.). 1980. lib. bdg. 23.00x (ISBN 0-405-12983-1). Ayer Co Pubs.

Social Networks & Marital Interaction. Charles E. Grantham. Ed. by R. Reed. LC 81-83621. (Illus.). 125p. 1982. pap. 10.00 (ISBN 0-88247-617-3). R & E Pubs.

Social Networks & Mental Health. David E. Biegel et al. 1985. 25.00 (ISBN 0-8039-2420-8). Sage.

Social Networks & Social Support in Community Mental Health. Ed. by Benjamin Gottlieb. (Sage Studies in Community Mental Health: Vol. 4). 300p. 1981. 29.95 (ISBN 0-8039-1669-8); pap. 16.95 (ISBN 0-8039-1670-1). Sage.

Social Networks of Children, Adolescents & College Students. Ed. by Suzanne Salzinger et al. 328p. 1987. text ed. 39.95 (ISBN 0-89859-979-2). L Erlbaum Assocs.

Social New York under the Georges Seventeen Fourteen to Seventeen Seventy-Six, 2 Vols. Esther Singleton. LC 68-58928. (Empire State Historical Publications Ser.: No. 60). (Illus.). 1969. Repr. of 1902 ed. Set. 35.00 (Ira J Friedman). Assoc Faculty Pr.

Social New York under the Georges Seventeen Seventeen to Seventeen Seventy-Six. Esther Singleton. LC 68-26018. (Illus.). 1968. Repr. of 1902 ed. 27.50 (ISBN 0-405-08973-2, Pub. by Blom). Ayer Co Pubs.

Social Norms & the Behavior of College Students. John E. Todd. LC 74-177704. (Columbia University. Teachers College. Contributions to Education: No. 833). Repr. of 1941 ed. 22.50 (ISBN 0-404-55833-X). AMS Pr.

Social Novel at the End of an Era. Warren French. LC 66-10056. (Crosscurrents-Modern Critiques Ser.). 224p. 1966. 7.95x (ISBN 0-8093-0193-8). S Ill U Pr.

Social Nudism in America. Fred Ilfeld, Jr. & Roger Lauer. 1964. pap. 11.95x (ISBN 0-8084-0281-1). New Coll U Pr.

Social Odours in Mammals, 2 vols. Ed. by Richard E. Brown & David W. MacDonald. (Illus.). 1985. Vol. 1. 98.00x (ISBN 0-19-857546-7); Vol. 2. 75.00x (ISBN 0-19-857617-X). Oxford U Pr.

Social Options for Singles: How & Where to Meet People. Jane K. Thompson. 89p. 1983. pap. write for info. (ISBN 0-9613104-1-3). Accent pubns.

Social Orchestra for Flute or Violin: A Collection of Popular Melodies Arranged As Duets, Trios, & Quartets. Stephen Foster. Ed. by H. Wiley Hitchcock. LC 79-169645. (Earlier American Music Ser: Vol. 13). (Illus.). 96p. 1973. Repr. of 1854 ed. lib. bdg. 25.00 (ISBN 0-306-77313-9). Da Capo.

Social Order. 4th ed. Robert Bierstedt. (Illus.). 544p. 1974. text ed. 39.95 (ISBN 0-07-005253-0). McGraw.

Social Order & the General Theory of Strategy. Alexander Atkinson. LC 81-17906. 305p. (Orig.). 1982. pap. 18.95 (ISBN 0-7100-0907-0). Routledge Chapman & Hall.

Social Order & the Limits of Law: A Theoretical Essay. Iredell Jenkins. LC 79-3216. 1980. 44.50x (ISBN 0-691-07241-8); pap. 12.95x (ISBN 0-691-02007-8). Princeton U Pr.

Social Order & the Public Philosophy: An Analysis & Interpretation of the Work of Herbert Blumer. Stanford M. Lyman & Arthur J. Vidich. LC 87-30257. 313p. 1988. 24.00 (ISBN 0-938626-87-6). U of Ark Pr.

Social Order in Child Communication: A Study in Microethnography. Juergen Streeck. (Pragmatics & Beyond: An Interdisciplinary of Language Studies: Vol. IV, No. 8). vii, 130p. (Orig.). 1983. pap. 30.00x (ISBN 0-915027-30-5). Benjamins North Am.

Social Order of a Frontier Community: Jacksonville, Illinois, 1825-70. Don H. Doyle. LC 78-5287. (Illus.). 304p. 1978. 24.95 (ISBN 0-252-00685-2); pap. 9.95 1983 (ISBN 0-252-01036-1). U of Ill Pr.

Social Order of the Slum. Gerald Suttles. (Studies of Urban Society Ser.). 1970. pap. 9.00x (ISBN 0-226-78192-5, P363, Phoen). U of Chicago Pr.

Social Organization. William H. Rivers. LC 76-44785. Repr. of 1924 ed. 22.50 (ISBN 0-404-15968-0). AMS Pr.

Social Organization: A Study of the Larger Mind. Charles H. Cooley. LC 80-15746. (Social Science Classics Ser.). 457p. 1983. pap. 23.95 (ISBN 0-87855-824-1). Transaction Bks.

Social Organization & Behavior of the Acorn Woodpecker in Central Coastal California. Michael H. MacRoberts & Barbara R. MacRoberts. 115p. 1976. 7.50 (ISBN 0-943610-21-4). Am Ornithologists.

Social Organization & Ritualistic Ceremonies of the Blackfoot Indians, 2 parts in 1 vol. Clark Wissler. LC 74-9020. (Anthropological Papers of the American Museum of Natural History: Vol. 7). (Illus.). Repr. of 1912 ed. 24.00 (ISBN 0-404-11917-4). AMS Pr.

Social Organization & Social Usages of the Indians of the Creek Confederacy. John R. Swanton. LC 28-30084. (U. S. Bureau of American Ethnology. Forty Second Annual Report, 1924-25). Repr. of 1928 ed. 37.00 (ISBN 0-384-59040-3). Johnson Repr.

Social Organization & the Applications of Anthropology: Essays in Honor of Lauriston Sharp. Ed. by Robert J. Smith. LC 74-4721. (Illus.). 337p. 1974. 32.50x (ISBN 0-8014-0891-1). Cornell U Pr.

Social Organization: Essays Presented to Raymond Firth. Ed. by Maurice Freedman. 300p. 1967. Repr. of 1898 ed. 32.50x (ISBN 0-7146-1059-3, F Cass Co). Biblio Dist.

Social Organization in Aboriginal Australia. Warren Shapiro. LC 78-32074. 1979. 25.00x (ISBN 0-312-73316-X). St Martin.

Social Organization in South China, Nineteen Eleven to Nineteen Forty-Nine: The Case of the Kuan Lineage in K'ai-P'ing County. Yuen-fong Woon. (Michigan Monographs in Chinese Studies: No. 48). 150p. 1984. 13.00 (ISBN 0-89264-051-0); pap. 8.00 (ISBN 0-89264-048-0). U of Mich Ctr Chinese.

Social Organization of an Urban Grants Economy: A Study of Business Philanthropy & Non-Profit Organizations. Joseph Galaskiewicz. 1985. 59.50 (ISBN 0-12-273860-8). Acad Pr.

Social Organization of an Urban Grants Economy: A Study of Business Philanthropy & Non-Profit Organizations. Joseph Galaskiewicz. 1985. pap. 27.50 (ISBN 0-12-273861-6). Acad Pr.

Social Organization of Disputes & Dispute Processing & Methods for the Investigation of Their Social, Legal & Interactive Properties. Philip Wilkinson. LC 81-196937. 64p. 1980. write for info. (ISBN 0-86226-035-3). Soc Sci Res.

Social Organization of Early Industrial Capitalism. Michael B. Katz et al. LC 81-7044. (Illus.). 464p. 1982. text ed. 42.00x (ISBN 0-674-81445-2). Harvard U Pr.

Social Organization of Gay Males. Joseph Harry & William B. Devall. LC 78-8381. (Praeger Special Studies). 1978. 38.95 (ISBN 0-275-90296-X, C0296). Praeger.

Social Organization of Hamadryas Baboons: A Field Study. Hans Kummer. LC 67-25082. 1968. 16.00x (ISBN 0-226-46171-8). U of Chicago Pr.

Social Organization of Immigration: The Italians in Philadelphia. Richard N. Juliani. Ed. by Francesco Cordasco. LC 80-868. (American Ethnic Groups Ser.). 1981. lib. bdg. 27.50x (ISBN 0-405-13430-4). Ayer Co Pubs.

Social Organization of Law. Donald Black & Maureen Mileski. LC 72-9998. 1973. 29.50 (ISBN 0-12-785057-0). Acad Pr.

Social Organization of Manu'a. rev. ed. Margaret Mead. LC 76-92276. (Bulletin Ser: No. 76). 237p. 1969. pap. 12.00 (ISBN 0-910240-08-6). Bishop Mus.

Social Organization of Manua. Margaret Mead. (BMB Ser.: No. 76). Repr. of 1930 ed. 32.00 (ISBN 0-527-02182-2). Kraus Repr.

Social Organization of Medical Work. Anselm Strauss et al. LC 84-23995. (Illus.). 1985. lib. bdg. 25.00x (ISBN 0-226-77707-3). U of Chicago Pr.

Social Organization of Schools: New Conceptualizations of the Learning Process. Ed. by Maureen T. Hallinan. LC 86-30577. 246p. 1987. 34.50x (ISBN 0-306-42428-2, Plenum Pr). Plenum Pub.

Social Organization of the Manchus: A Study of the Manchu Clan Organization. Sergei M. Shirokogorov. LC 77-38082. Repr. of 1924 ed. 30.00 (ISBN 0-404-56946-3). AMS Pr.

Social Organization of the Northern Tungus. S. M. Shirokogoroff. LC 78-66515. (Classics of Anthropology Ser.: Vol. 28). (Illus.). 1979. lib. bdg. 76.00 (ISBN 0-8240-9620-7). Garland Pub.

Social Organization of the Papago Indians. Ruth M. Underhill. LC 74-82347. (Columbia Univ. Contributions to Anthropology Ser.: Vol. 30). 1969. Repr. of 1939 ed. 32.50 (ISBN 0-404-50580-5). AMS Pr.

Social Organization of the Tewa of New Mexico. Elsie C. Parsons. LC 30-5855. (American Anthro. Association Memoirs). 1929. 34.00 (ISBN 0-527-00535-5). Kraus Repr.

Social Organization of the Western Pueblos. Fred Eggan. LC 50-9388. (Illus.). 1950. 12.50x (ISBN 0-226-19075-7). U of Chicago Pr.

Social Organization of the Western Pueblos. Fred Eggan. LC 50-9388. 1973. pap. 2.95x (ISBN 0-226-19076-5, P557, Phoen). U of Chicago Pr.

Social Organization of Zen Practice: Constructing Transcultural Reality. David L. Preston. (Illus.). 240p. 1988. 37.50 (ISBN 0-521-35000-X). Cambridge U Pr.

Social Organizations. Istvan Szentpeteri. Tr. by J. Decsenyi from Hungarian. 284p. 1986. text ed. 35.00 (ISBN 963-05-4210-2, Pub. by Akademiai Kiado Hungary). Humanities.

Social Origins & Career Lines of Three Generations of American Business Leaders. Suzanne I. Keller. Ed. by Harriet Zuckerman & Robert K. Merton. LC 79-9008. (Dissertations on Sociology Ser.). 1980. lib. bdg. 19.00x (ISBN 0-405-12976-9). Ayer Co Pubs.

Social Origins of a Labor Elite: French Engine-Drivers, 1837-1917. Margot B. Stein. Ed. by William H. McNeill & David H. Pinkney. (Modern European History Ser.). 515p. 1987. lib. bdg. 80.00 (ISBN 0-8240-8043-2). Garland Pub.

Social Origins of Depression: A Study of Psychiatric Disorder in Women. George W. Brown & Tirril Harris. LC 78-3209. 1978. 24.95 (ISBN 0-02-904890-7). Free Pr.

Social Origins of Dictatorship & Democracy. Barrington Moore, Jr. 1966. pap. 12.95 (ISBN 0-8070-5075-X, BP268). Beacon Pr.

Social Origins of Distress & Disease: Depression, Neurasthenia, & Pain in Modern China. Arthur Kleinman. LC 85-29597. 256p. 1986. text ed. 24.00x (ISBN 0-300-03541-1). Yale U Pr.

Social Origins of Distress & Disease: Depression, Neurasthenia, & Pain in Modern China. Arthur Kleinman. LC 85-29597. 256p. 1988. Repr. of 1986 ed. 14.95 (ISBN 0-300-04133-0). Yale U Pr.

Social Origins of Educational Systems. Margaret S. Archer. LC 77-84072. (Illus.). 815p. 1979. 55.00 (ISBN 0-8039-9876-7). Sage.

Social Origins of Political Regionalism: France, 1849-1981. William Brustein. 224p. 1988. 25.00x (ISBN 0-520-06155-1). U of Cal Pr.

Social Origins of the French Revolution. Ralph W. Greenlaw. pap. 7.50 (ISBN 0-669-91116-X). Heath.

Social Origins of the Modern Middle East. Haim Gerber. LC 86-21925. 224p. 1987. lib. bdg. 30.00x (ISBN 0-931477-63-8). Lynne Rienner.

Social Origins of the New South: Alabama, 1860-1885. Jonathan M. Wiener. LC 78-6596. xvi, 250p. 1978. 27.50 (ISBN 0-8071-0397-7); pap. 8.95 (ISBN 0-8071-0888-X). La State U Pr.

Social Participation in a Rural New England Town. J. L. Hypes. LC 77-176894. (Columbia University. Teachers College. Contributions to Education: No. 258). Repr. of 1927 ed. 22.50 (ISBN 0-404-55258-7). AMS Pr.

Social Participation in Urban Society. Ed. by John Edwards & Alan Booth. LC 72-135339. 283p. 1972. pap. text ed. 11.95x (ISBN 0-87073-040-1). Schenkman Bks Inc.

Social Partnership: The Austrian System of Industrial Relations & Social Insurance. Theodor Tomandl & Karl Fuerboeck. LC 85-14344. (Cornell International Industrial & Labor Relations Reports Ser.: No. 12). 176p. 1986. 24.00 (ISBN 0-87546-116-6). ILR Pr.

Social Pathology. Samuel G. Smith. 380p. 1981. Repr. of 1912 ed. lib. bdg. 40.00 (ISBN 0-8495-4950-7). Arden Lib.

Social Patterns in Australian Literature. Tom I. Moore. LC 71-133027. pap. 93.60 (2031441). Bks Demand UMI.

Social Patterns in Normal Aging: Findings from the Duke Longitudinal Studies. Erdman Palmore. LC 81-9800. xii, 137p. 1981. 22.75 (ISBN 0-8223-0458-9). Duke.

Social Pediatrics. Ed. by Robert J. Schlegel. LC 81-80987. (Illus.). 81p. (Orig.). 1981. pap. 12.50 (ISBN 0-934314-03-9). Intl Found Biosocial Dev.

Social Penetration: The Development of Interpersonal Relationships. Irwin Altman & Dalmas A. Taylor. 212p. 1983. pap. text ed. 12.95x (ISBN 0-8290-1046-7). Irvington.

Social Perception in Clinical & Counseling Psychology. J. H. Harvey et al. Ed. by R. P. McGlynn & J. E. Maddux. (Interfaces in Psychology Ser.: No. 2). 185p. 1984. 29.95 (ISBN 0-89672-127-2); pap. 17.95 (ISBN 0-89672-126-4). Tex Tech Univ Pr.

Social Perception in Infants. Ed. by Tiffany Field & Nathan Fox. LC 84-28462. 344p. 1985. text ed. 49.50 (ISBN 0-89391-231-X). Ablex Pub.

Social Perplexities. facs. ed. Allan A. Hunter. LC 68-58797. (Essay Index Reprint Ser). 1932. 15.00 (ISBN 0-8369-0119-3). Ayer Co Pubs.

Social Perspective of Development of Science & Technology in India. Ed. by B. V. Rangarao & N. P. Chaubey. 1983. 22.00x (ISBN 0-8364-0931-0, Pub. by Heritage India). South Asia Bks.

Social Perspectives in the History of Economic Theory. Everett J. Burtt. 1972. pap. write for info. (ISBN 0-312-73325-9). St Martin.

Social Perspectives on Emotion, Vol. 1. Ed. by David D. Franks. 1988. 52.50 (ISBN 0-89232-759-6). Jai Pr.

Social Philosophers. Robert Nisbet. 1983. pap. 5.95 (ISBN 0-671-44048-9). WSP.

Social Philosophy. Joel Feinberg. 1973. pap. write for info. ref. ed. (ISBN 0-13-817254-4). P-H.

Social Philosophy. Hans Fink. 128p. 1981. 19.95x (ISBN 0-416-71990-2, NO. 3476); pap. 7.95x (ISBN 0-416-72000-5, NO. 3475). Routledge Chapman & Hall.

Social Philosophy & Religion of Comte. Edward Caird. LC 11-15832. 1968. Repr. of 1885 ed. 23.00 (ISBN 0-527-14140-2). Kraus Repr.

Social Philosophy of Athletics. Han Lenk. 1979. pap. text ed. 7.60x (ISBN 0-87563-165-7). Stipes.

Social Philosophy of Carlyle & Ruskin. Frederick W. Roe. LC 76-116555. 342p. 1970. Repr. of 1921 ed. 37.50x (ISBN 0-87752-095-X). Gordian.

Social Philosophy of Carlyle & Ruskin. Frederick W. Roe. LC 74-93060. 1969. Repr. of 1921 ed. 26.50x (ISBN 0-8046-0682-X, Pub. by Kennikat). Assoc Faculty Pr.

Social Philosophy of John Taylor of Carolina. Eugene T. Mudge. LC 76-181960. Repr. of 1939 ed. 17.45 (ISBN 0-404-04515-4). AMS Pr.

Social Philosophy of Martin Buber: The Social World as a Human Dimension. John W. Murphy. LC 82-21779. 176p. (Orig.). 1983. lib. bdg. 27.75 (ISBN 0-8191-2940-2); pap. text ed. 12.25 (ISBN 0-8191-2941-0). U Pr of Amer.

Social Philosophy of the St. Louis Hegelians. Frances A. Harmon. LC 75-3159. 1976. Repr. of 1943 ed. 20.00 (ISBN 0-404-59164-7). AMS Pr.

Social Philosophy of William Morris. Anna A. Phelan. 207p. Repr. of 1927 ed. lib. bdg. 32.50 (ISBN 0-8495-4369-X). Arden Lib.

Social Philosophy of William Morris. Anna A. Phelan. LC 76-40079. 1976. lib. bdg. 35.00 (ISBN 0-8414-4703-9). Folcroft.

Social Philosophy of William Morris. Anna A. Von Helmholtz. LC 74-13029. 1974. Repr. of 1927 ed. lib. bdg. 35.00 (ISBN 0-8414-9170-4). Folcroft.

Social Philosophy of Wordsworth. Laura J. Wylie. 1916. lib. bdg. 20.50 (ISBN 0-8414-9330-8). Folcroft.

Social Physics & Cultural Sociology: A Primer of Two Typologies for Masters of Sociological Thought. Alan R. Rowe. LC 81-43803. 42p. (Orig.). 1982. pap. text ed. 6.00 (ISBN 0-8191-2307-2). U Pr of Amer.

Social Physics of Adam Smith. Vernard Foley. LC 76-5710. 282p. 1976. 11.95 (ISBN 0-911198-43-1). Purdue U Pr.

Social Placement of the Portuguese in Hawaii As Indicated by Factors in Assimilation: Thesis. Gerald A. Estep. LC 73-78062. 1974. Repr. of 1941 ed. soft bdg. 10.95 (ISBN 0-88247-271-2). R & E Pubs.

Social Planning: A Strategy for Socialist Welfare. Ed. by Alan Walker. 170p. 1984. 39.95 (ISBN 0-85520-453-2); pap. 14.95x (ISBN 0-85520-454-0). Basil Blackwell.

Social Planning & Human Service Delivery in the Voluntary Sector. Ed. by Gary A. Tobin. LC 84-25307. (Studies in Social Welfare Policies & Programs: No. 1). (Illus.). xxx, 290p. 1985. lib. bdg. 36.95 (ISBN 0-313-23892-8, TOP/). Greenwood.

Social Planning Process: Conceptualization & Methods. Janet Scheff. LC 76-5840. (Planning Ser.: No. S-2). (Illus.). 124p. (Orig.). 1976. pap. 5.00 (ISBN 0-8477-2432-8). U of PR Pr.

Social Plays, 4 Vols. Arthur W. Pinero. Ed. by Clayton Hamilton. LC 79-18169. Repr. of 1922 ed. Set. 150.00 (ISBN 0-404-05080-8); 37.50 ea. Vol. 1 (ISBN 0-404-05081-6). Vol. 2 (ISBN 0-404-05082-4). Vol. 3 (ISBN 0-404-05083-2). Vol. 4 (ISBN 0-404-05084-0). AMS Pr.

Social Poetry of the Georgics. rev. ed. Edward W. Spofford. Ed. by W. R. Connor. LC 80-2668. (Monographs in Classical Studies). 1981. lib. bdg. 12.00 (ISBN 0-405-14051-7). Ayer Co Pubs.

Social Poetry of the Thirties. Ed. by Jack Salzman. LC 78-1617. (American Cultural Heritage Ser.). 1979. 17.95 (ISBN 0-89102-046-2). B Franklin.

Social Policies & Population Growth in Mauritius. Richard M. Titmuss & Brian Abel-Smith. 308p. 1968. Repr. of 1961 ed. 27.50x (ISBN 0-7146-1254-5, F Cass Co). Biblio Dist.

Social Policies in Western Industrial Societies. Charles F. Andrain. LC 85-10840. (Research Ser.: No. 61). (Illus.). xi, 256p. 1985. pap. 12.95x (ISBN 0-87725-161-4). U of Cal Intl St.

Social Policy. 5th ed. T. H. Marshall. Ed. by A. M. Rees. LC 85-8404. 296p. (Orig.). 1985. pap. 10.95 (ISBN 0-09-158021-8, Pub. by Hutchinson Educ). Longwood Pub Group.

Social Policy: A Feminist Analysis. Gillian Pascall. 250p. 1986. text ed. 37.00 (ISBN 0-422-78660-8, 1026, Pub. by Tavistock England); pap. text ed. 14.95 (ISBN 0-317-47502-9, 1043, Pub. by Tavistock England). Routledge Chapman & Hall.

Social Policy & Administration in Britain: A Bibliography. Tessa Blackstone & Peter Vines. 130p. 1975. 17.50x (ISBN 0-87471-811-2). Rowman.

Social Policy & Administration Revised Studies in the Development of Social Services at the Local Level. David Donnison. 1970. 30.00x (ISBN 0-317-05808-8, Pub. by Natl Inst Social Work). State Mutual Bk.

Social Policy & Conflict Resolution. Ed. by Thomas Attig et al. (Studies in Applied Philosophy: Vol. VI). 200p. 1984. 15.00 (ISBN 0-935756-07-8). BGSU Dept Phil.

Social Policy & Social Problems. Stuart Billingham & Robert Blanchard. (Themes & Perspectives in Sociology Ser.). 80p. (Orig.). 1987. pap. text ed. cancelled (ISBN 0-946183-09-0, Pub. by Causeway Pr Ltd England). Sheridan.

Social Policy & Social Programs: A Method for the Practical Public Policy Analyst. Donald E. Chambers. 294p. 1986. text ed. write for info. (ISBN 0-02-320580-6); write for info. tchr's manual. Macmillan.

Social Policy & Social Responsibility: Record of a Study Day, Nineteen Seventy-Nine. 1979. 22.00x (ISBN 0-317-05770-7, Pub. by Natl Inst Social Work). State Mutual Bk.

Social Policy & Social Services. 2nd ed. Alfred J. Kahn. 1979. pap. text ed. write for info (RanC). Random.

Social Policy & Social Welfare. Ed. by Martin Loney et al. 352p. 1983. pap. 19.00x (ISBN 0-335-10408-8, Open Univ Pr). Taylor & Francis.

Social Policy & Social Welfare: Structure & Applications. Thomas M. Meenaghan & Robert O. Washington. LC 79-54669. (Illus.). 1980. text ed. 20.95 (ISBN 0-02-920750-9). Free Pr.

Social Policy & Socialism: The Struggle for Socialist Relations of Welfare. Bob Deacon. 307p. 1983. pap. 10.50 (ISBN 0-86104-721-4, Pub. by Pluto Pr). Longwood Pub Group.

Social Policy & Sociology. Ed. by N. J. Demerath et al. (Studies in Quantitative Relations Ser.). 1975. 33.00 (ISBN 0-12-209450-6). Acad Pr.

Social Policy & the Rural Setting. Julia M. Watkins & Dennis A. Watkins. (Springer Series in Social Work: Vol. 3). 224p. 1984. text ed. 22.95 (ISBN 0-8261-4240-0). Springer Pub.

Social Policy Evaluation: An Economic Perspective. Ed. by Elhanan Helpman. LC 82-22681. (Symposium). 1983. 52.50 (ISBN 0-12-339660-3). Acad Pr.

Social Policy Harmonization in the European Community. John Holloway. 324p. 1981. text ed. 35.50x (ISBN 0-566-00196-9). Gower Pub Co.

Social Policy in a Changing World: The ILO Response: Selected Speeches by Wilfred Jenks, Director-General of the ILO, 1970-1973. 1976. 14.00 (ISBN 92-2-101445-2). Intl Labour Office.

Social Policy in American Society. Robert S. Magill. 250p. 1983. text ed. 34.95 (ISBN 0-89885-138-6). Human Sci Pr.

Social Policy in American Society. Robert S. Magill. 250p. 1984. pap. text ed. 16.95 (ISBN 0-89885-278-1). Human Sci Pr.

Social Policy in Northern Ireland: 1939-1950. John Ditch. 1987. text ed. 37.00x (ISBN 0-566-05309-8, Pub. by Gower Pub England). Gower Pub Co.

Social Policy in the Third World: The Social Dilemmas of Underdevelopment. Stewart MacPherson. LC 82-6837. 220p. 1983. pap. text ed. 9.95x (ISBN 0-86598-090-X, Pub. by Allanheld). Rowman.

Social Policy in the United States in the 1980's: A Bibliography. Ben Silverstein. (Public Administration Ser.: P 2152). 5p. 1987. 3.75 (ISBN 1-55590-292-8). Vance Biblios.

Social Policy in the United States: Material Published 1980-1984. Mary Vance. (Public Administration Ser.: P 1699). 38p. 1985. 6.00 (ISBN 0-89028-449-0). Vance Biblios.

Social Policy in Western Europe & the U. S. A., Nineteen Fifty to Nineteen Eighty: An Assessment. Ed. by Roger Girod et al. LC 84-17747. 128p. 1985. 25.00 (ISBN 0-312-73376-3). St Martin.

Social Policy Issues Affecting the Poor. Georgia L. McMurray. 37p. 1983. pap. text ed. 3.50 (ISBN 0-88156-018-9). Comm Serv Soc NY.

Social Policy: Issues of Choice & Change. Martin Rein. LC 82-19676. 384p. 1983. pap. text ed. 16.95 (ISBN 0-87332-235-5). M E Sharpe.

Social Policy of Nazi Germany. C. W. Guillebaud. LC 71-80553. 1971. Repr. 23.50x (ISBN 0-86527-183-6). Fertig.

Social Policy of the American Welfare State: An Introduction to Policy Analysis. Robert Morris. LC 84-3955. 288p. 1985. pap. text ed. 17.95x (ISBN 0-582-28539-9). Longman.

Social Policy Process in Canada. Dobell & Mansbridge. 111p. 1986. pap. text ed. 8.00x (ISBN 0-88645-030-6, Pub. by Inst Res Pub Canada). Brookfield Pub Co.

Social, Political, & Economic Life in Contemporary Oaxaca. Ed. by Aubrey Williams. (Publications in Anthropology: No. 24). (Illus.). 179p. 1979. 6.95 (ISBN 0-935462-13-9). Vanderbilt Pubns.

Social Politics in the United States. Frederick E. Haynes. LC 70-126648. Repr. of 1924 ed. 28.00 (ISBN 0-404-03168-4). AMS Pr.

Social Power & Influence of Women. Liesa Stamm & Carol D. Ryff. (AAAS Selected Symposium: No. 96). 200p. 1984. lib. bdg. 26.50x (ISBN 0-8133-0000-2). Westview.

Social Power & Political Freedom. Gene Sharp. LC 80-81479. (Extending Horizons Bks). 456p. 1980. 15.95 (ISBN 0-87558-091-2); pap. 8.95 (ISBN 0-87558-093-9). Porter Sargent.

Social Power: Social Psychological Models & Theories. Allen H Henderson. LC 81-15354. (Illus.). 128p. 1981. 35.00 (ISBN 0-275-90644-2, C0644). Praeger.

Social Practice of Symbolization: An Anthropological Analysis. Ivo Strecker. LC 88-707. (London School of Economics Monographs on Social Anthropolgy: No. 60). 240p. 1988. 65.00 (ISBN 0-485-19557-7, Pub. by Athlone Pr UK). Humanities.

Social Preconditions of National Revival in Europe: A Comparative Analysis of the Social Composition of Patriotic Groups among the Smaller European Nations. Miroslav Hroch. 384p. 1985. 47.50 (ISBN 0-521-22891-3). Cambridge U Pr.

Social Pressures in Informal Groups: A Study of Human Factors in Housing. Leon Festinger et al. 1950. 20.00x (ISBN 0-8047-0173-3); pap. 7.95x (ISBN 0-8047-0174-1). Stanford U Pr.

Social Principles & the Democratic State. S. I. Benn & R. S. Peters. 1959. pap. text ed. 17.95x (ISBN 0-04-300028-2). Unwin Hyman.

Social Principles of Jesus. Walter Rauschenbusch. LC 76-50566. 1976. Repr. of 1916 ed. lib. bdg. 35.50 (ISBN 0-8414-7308-0). Folcroft.

Social Problem America: Alienation & Discontinuity. John Wildeman. 291p. 1985. pap. text ed. 19.95x (ISBN 0-8290-1467-5). Irvington.

Social Problems. Michael S. Bassis et al. Ed. by Robert K. Merton. 586p. 1982. text ed. 24.00 net (ISBN 0-15-581430-3, HC); tests avail. (ISBN 0-15-581431-1); study guide net 9.00 (ISBN 0-15-581432-X). HarBraceJ.

Social Problems. 3rd ed. Eitzen. 1985. text ed. 35.00 (ISBN 0-205-08584-9). Allyn.

Social Problems. Amitai Etzioni. (Foundations of Modern Sociology Ser.). 192p. 1976. pap. text ed. write for info (ISBN 0-13-817403-2). P-H.

Social Problems. Henry George. LC 81-11896. 310p. (Avail. in Ger. Span.). 1981. 8.00x (ISBN 0-911312-17-X); pap. 3.00 (ISBN 0-911312-52-8). Schalkenbach.

Social Problems. James M. Henslin & Donald Light, Jr. (Illus.). 656p. 1983. text ed. 34.95 (ISBN 0-07-037836-3). McGraw.

Social Problems. 5th ed. Joseph Julian & William Kornblum. (Illus.). 624p. 1986. text ed. write for info (ISBN 0-13-816851-2). P-H.

Social Problems. Ronald Maris. 1988. 35.00. Dorsey.

Social Problems. McDowell Montero. 525p. 1986. write for info. (ISBN 0-02-382250-3); pap. write for info. instr's manual avail. (ISBN 0-02-382260-0). Macmillan.

Social Problems. Joan W. Moore & Burton M. Moore. (Illus.). 464p. 1982. write for info (ISBN 0-13-817387-7). P-H.

Social Problems. J. John Palen. (Illus.). 1979. text ed. 34.95 (ISBN 0-07-048103-2). McGraw.

Social Problems. Ronald Pavalko. LC 85-61765. 520p. 1986. text ed. 27.95 (ISBN 0-87581-280-5). Peacock Pubs.

Social Problems. 2nd ed. George Ritzer. (Illus.). 608p. 1986. text ed. 20.00 (ISBN 0-394-35427-3, KnopfC). Knopf.

Social Problems. 2nd ed. Ian Robertson & Michael McKee. 494p. 1980. text ed. write for info (ISBN 0-394-32025-5, RanC). Random.

Social Problems. Ronald W. Smith & Andrea Fontana. 1981. text ed. 28.95 (ISBN 0-03-043696-6, HoltC). HR&W.

Social Problems, 3 pts. Incl. Pt. 1. Drunkenness, 4 vols. Set. 449.00x (ISBN 0-7165-1473-7); Pt. 2. Gambling, 2 vols. Set. 178.00x (ISBN 0-7165-1474-5); Pt. 3. Sunday Observance, 3 vols. Set. 307.00x. (British Parliamentary Papers Ser.). 1971 (Pub. by Irish Academic Pr Ireland). Biblio Dist.

Social Problems. Thomas J. Sullivan & Kendrick S. Thompson. 1988. text ed. write for info. (ISBN 0-02-418366-0). Macmillan.

Social Problems - Social Processes: Selected Papers from the Proceedings of the American Sociological Society, 1932. facs. ed. American Sociological Society Staff. Ed. by E. S. Bogardus. LC 67-23173. (Essay Index Reprint Ser). 1933. 17.00 (ISBN 0-8369-0151-7). Ayer Co Pubs.

Social Problems: A Critical Thinking Approach. Paul J. Baker & Louis E. Anderson. 414p. 1987. pap. text ed. write for info. (ISBN 0-534-07428-6). Wadsworth Pub.

Social Problems & Criminal Justice. Emilio Viano & Alvin W. Cohn. LC 73-92238. (Nelson-Hall Law Enforcement Ser.). 288p. 1975. 22.95x (ISBN 0-88229-115-7). Nelson-Hall.

Social Problems & Employment in Hotels, Restaurants & Similar Establishments in Developing Countries: Report II-Third Tripartite Technical Meeting, Geneva 1983. iii, 107p. (Orig.). 1983. pap. 10.50 (ISBN 92-2-103379-1). Intl Labour Office.

Social Problems & Mental Health. Ed. by Jessica Kuper. (Social Science Lexicons). 176p. 1987. pap. text ed. 12.95 (ISBN 0-7102-1170-8, Pub. by Routledge UK). Routledge Chapman & Hall.

Social Problems & Public Policy: Deviance & Liberty. Ed. by Lee Rainwater. 458p. 1974. 34.95x (ISBN 0-202-30263-6); pap. text ed. 21.95x (ISBN 0-202-30264-4). Aldine de Gruyter.

Social Problems & Public Policy: Inequality & Justice. Ed. by Lee Rainwater. LC 72-97244. 464p. 1974. pap. text ed. 21.95x (ISBN 0-202-30247-4). Aldine de Gruyter.

Social Problems & Social Policy Series, 51 vols. Ed. by Gerald N. Grob. (Illus.). 1975. 1799.50x (ISBN 0-405-07474-3). Ayer Co Pubs.

Social Problems & the City: Geographical Perspectives. Ed. by David T. Herbert & David M. Smith. (Illus.). 1979. pap. text ed. 13.95x (ISBN 0-19-874080-8). Oxford U Pr.

Social Problems & the Criminal Justice System: Legal Aspects of Counseling. Barbara L. Smith. 1979. 15.00 (ISBN 0-89421-022-X). Challenge Pr.

Social Problems & the Quality of Life. 3rd ed. Robert H. Lauer. 592p. 1986. pap. text ed. write for info. (ISBN 0-697-00434-1); write for info. instr's. manual-test item file (ISBN 0-697-00841-X). Wm C Brown.

Social Problems & Welfare Ideology. Ed. by N. P. Manning. 238p. 1985. text ed. 38.95x (ISBN 0-566-00938-2). Gower Pub Co.

Social Problems: Causes, Consequences, Interventions. Richard Bourne & Jack Levin. (Illus.). 422p. 1983. text ed. 28.75 (ISBN 0-314-69661-X); tchrs.' manual avail. (ISBN 0-314-71081-7). West Pub.

Social Problems: Christian Perspectives. DeSanto & Polma. 310p. (Orig.). 1985. pap. text ed. 14.95x (ISBN 0-88725-033-5). Hunter Textbks.

Social Problems: Divergent Perspectives. Thomas J. Sullivan et al. LC 79-20676. 728p. 1980. write for info. (ISBN 0-02-418430-6); write for info. study guide (ISBN 0-02-418440-3); write for info. tchr's manual (ISBN 0-02-418460-8). Macmillan.

Social Problems: Focus on Taiwan. Albert O'Hara. 283p. 1980. 7.95 (ISBN 0-89955-176-9, Pub. by Mei Ya China). Intl Spec Bk.

Social Problems in Modern America. 3rd ed. Elbert W. Stewart. (Illus.). 432p. 1983. pap. 27.95 (ISBN 0-07-061427-X). McGraw.

Social Problems in Puerto Rico. Fred K. Fleagle. LC 74-14233. (Puerto Rican Experience Ser). (Illus.). 152p. 1975. Repr. 12.00x (ISBN 0-405-06222-2). Ayer Co Pubs.

Social Problems in the Philosophy of Rousseau. John Charvet. LC 73-88311. (Cambridge Studies in the History & Theory of Politics). pap. 39.50 (ISBN 0-317-26041-3, 2024436). Bks Demand UMI.

Social Problems in the United States. J. Kenneth Morland. LC 74-22542. (Illus.). pap. 160.00 (ISBN 0-317-09589-7, 2012515). Bks Demand UMI.

Social Problems: Issues & Solutions. Charles Zastrow & Lee Bowker. LC 83-19397. (Illus.). 618p. 1984. text ed. 25.95x (ISBN 0-8304-1051-1); instr's. manual avail. (ISBN 0-8304-1111-9); student's study guide 8.95 (ISBN 0-8304-1065-1). Nelson-Hall.

Social Problems of an Industrial Civilization. Elton Mayo. Ed. by Leon Stein. LC 77-70516. (Work Ser.). 1977. Repr. of 1945 ed. lib. bdg. 17.00x (ISBN 0-405-10185-6). Ayer Co Pubs.

Social Problems of Contract, Sub-Contract & Casual Labour in the Petroleum Industry. (Labour-Management Relations Ser.: No. 45). 1974. 7.00 (ISBN 92-2-101103-8). Intl Labour Office.

Social Problems of the Industrial Revolution. Peter Speed. 160p. 1975. pap. 5.90 (ISBN 0-08-018883-4). Pergamon.

Social Problems of the North. C. E. Russell. LC 79-56944. (English Working Class Ser.). 1980. lib. bdg. 26.00 (ISBN 0-8240-0123-0). Garland Pub.

Social Problems of Urban Men. Elmer H. Johnson. LC 72-83996. (Dorsey Series in Anthropology & Sociology). (Illus.). pap. 149.80 (ISBN 0-317-09082-8, 2055672). Bks Demand UMI.

Social Problems: Society in Crisis. Curran & Renzetti. 1987. 30.00 (ISBN 0-205-10482-7); instr's manual avail. (ISBN 0-205-10483-5). Allyn.

Social Problems: The Contemporary Debates. 4th ed. John B. Williamson et al. 1985. pap. text ed. 17.50 (ISBN 0-673-39607-X). Scott F.

Social Problems Through Social Theory: A Selective View. Jerry Jacobs. LC 82-73821. 168p. 1983. pap. text ed. 12.95x (ISBN 0-88105-014-8). Cap & Gown.

Social Process. Charles H. Cooley. LC 65-12395. (Perspectives in Sociology Ser.). 494p. 1966. 10.00x (ISBN 0-8093-0200-4). S Ill U Pr.

Social Process in Maya Prehistory: Studies in Honor of Sir Eric Thompson. Ed. by Norman Hammond. 1978. 136.50 (ISBN 0-12-322050-5). Acad Pr.

Social Process of Scientific Investigation. Ed. by Karin D. Knorr et al. (Sociology of the Sciences Ser.: No. IV). 356p. 1980. lib. bdg. 34.50 (ISBN 90-277-1174-7, Pub. by Reidel Holland); pap. 16.00 (ISBN 90-277-1175-5, Pub. by Reidel Holland). Kluwer Academic.

Social Processes: An Introduction to Sociology. Tamotsu Shibutani. 1986. 40.00x (ISBN 0-520-05050-9); pap. 16.95x (ISBN 0-520-05056-8). U of Cal Pr.

Social Processes & Relationships. Carl J. Couch. LC 87-82055. 350p. (Orig.). 1988. text ed. 30.95 (ISBN 0-930390-88-1); pap. text ed. 15.95 (ISBN 0-930390-87-3). Gen Hall.

Social Processes in Clinical & Counseling Psychology. Ed. by J. E. Maddux et al. (Illus.). 392p. 1987. 35.00 (ISBN 0-387-96533-5). Springer-Verlag.

Social Processes in Early in Number Development. Geoffrey B. Saxe et al. (CDM 216: Vol. 52, No. 2). viii, 162p. 1988. pap. 9.75x (ISBN 0-226-73550-8). U of Chicago Pr.

Social Processes of Scientific Development. Ed. by Richard Whitley. 1974. 24.50x (ISBN 0-7100-7705-X). Routledge Chapman & Hall.

Social Production of Art. Janet Wolff. 208p. 1981. 27.50x (ISBN 0-312-73467-0). St Martin.

Social Production of Art. Janet Wolff. 208p. 1984. pap. 12.50x (ISBN 0-8147-9201-4). NYU Pr.

Social Production of Scientific Knowledge. Ed. by Everett Mendelsohn et al. (Sociology of the Sciences Ser.: Vol. 1). 1977. lib. bdg. 34.00 (ISBN 90-277-0775-8, Pub. by Reidel Holland); pap. 18.50 (ISBN 90-277-0776-6, Pub. by Reidel Holland). Kluwer Academic.

Social Production of Technical Work: The Case of British Engineers. Peter Whalley. LC 85-14813. (Sociology of Work Ser.). 237p. 1986. 34.50x (ISBN 0-88706-252-0). State U NY Pr.

Social Production of Urban Space. M. Gottdiener. 328p. 1985. text ed. 32.50x (ISBN 0-292-77586-5). U of Tex pr.

Social Production of Urban Space. M. Gottdiener. (Illus.). 328p. 1988. pap. 12.95 (ISBN 0-292-77614-4). U of Tex Pr.

Social Profile of Tarakeswar. Prafulla Chakrabarti. 1984. 14.00x (ISBN 0-8364-1244-3, Pub. by Mukhopadhyay India). South Asia Bks.

Social Profile of Working Women. Usha Talwar. 1985. 21.00x (ISBN 0-8364-1387-3, Pub. by Jain Bros). South Asia Bks.

Social Program Implementation. Ed. by Walter Williams & Richard F. Elmore. (Quantitative Studies in Social Relations Ser.). 1976. 24.95 (ISBN 0-12-756850-6). Acad Pr.

Social Programs in Sweden: A Search for Security in a Free Society. Albert H. Rosenthal. LC 67-27098. pap. 53.30 (ISBN 0-317-29497-0, 2055906). Bks Demand UMI.

Social Progress of Nations. Richard J. Estes. 224p. 1984. 27.95 (ISBN 0-275-91151-9, C1151). Praeger.

Social Protection Code: A New Model of Criminal Justice. Tadeusz Grygier. (American Series of Foreign Penal Codes: Vol. 22). xxiv, 96p. 1977. text ed. 15.00x (ISBN 0-8377-0605-X). Rothman.

Social Protest & Popular Culture in Eighteenth-Century Japan. Anne Walthall. LC 85-24647. (Association Asian Studies: No. XLIII). 268p. 1986. 19.95x (ISBN 0-8165-0961-1). U of Ariz Pr.

Social Protest from the Left in Canada Eighteen Seventy to Nineteen Seventy. Peter H. Weinrich. 750p. 1982. 65.00x (ISBN 0-8020-5567-2). U of Toronto Pr.

Social Protest in India: British Protestant Missionaries & Social Reforms, Eighteen Fifty to Nineteen Hundred. G. A. Oddie. 1979. 17.50x (ISBN 0-8364-0195-6). South Asia Bks.

Social Protest in the Eighteenth-Century English Novel. Mona Scheuermann. LC 84-27157. 256p. 1985. 25.00x (ISBN 0-8142-0381-7); pap. 12.95x (ISBN 0-8142-0403-1). Ohio St U Pr.

Social Protest, Violence & Terror in Nineteenth & Twentieth-Century Europe. W. J. Mommsen & Gerhard Hirschfield. LC 81-51615. 320p. 1982. 28.50x (ISBN 0-312-73471-9). St Martin.

Social Psychiatry. Ed. by Vladimir Hudolin. LC 83-4058. 894p. 1984. 115.00 (ISBN 0-306-41342-6, Plenum Pr). Plenum Pub.

Social Psychiatry: Eighteen Essays. Ed. by Ari Kiev. 1970. text ed. 22.95 (ISBN 0-8464-0855-4). Beekman Pubs.

Social-Psychological Analysis of Police Assailants. C. Kenneth Meyer et al. (Criminal Justice Policy & Administration Research Ser.). 1978. 3.00 (ISBN 0-686-04910-1). Univ OK Gov Res.

Social, Psychological & Situational Factors in Wife Abuse. Kathleen H. Hofeller. Ed. by R. Reed. LC 81-83618. (Illus.). 125p. 1982. pap. 13.00 (ISBN 0-88247-620-3). R & E Pubs.

Social Psychological Foundations for School Services. Ed. by Merl E. Bonney et al. 320p. 1986. text ed. 39.95 (ISBN 0-89885-282-X); pap. text ed. 19.95 (ISBN 0-89885-283-8). Human Sci Pr.

Social Psychological Perspectives on Leisure & Recreation. Seppo E. Iso-Ahola. (Illus.). 448p. 1980. 29.50x (ISBN 0-398-03968-2). C C Thomas.

Social Psychological Techniques & the Peaceful Settlement of International Disputes: A Report Based on Proceedings of a Workshop at Lake Mohonk, New York, May 1970. Alex Castles. (UNITAR Research Reports: No. 1). Date not set. price not set. UNITAR.

Social Psychology. 2nd ed. Stan L. Albrecht et al. (Illus.). 480p. 1987. text ed. write for info. (ISBN 0-13-817909-3). P-H.

Social Psychology. Solomon E. Asch. (Illus.). 668p. 1987. pap. 39.95 (ISBN 0-19-852172-3). Oxford U PR.

Social Psychology. Ed. by Kurt W. Back. LC 76-30835. pap. 127.30 (ISBN 0-317-09548-X, 2055188). Bks Demand UMI.

Social Psychology. Andrew Baum et al. 700p. 1984. text ed. write for info (ISBN 0-394-32405-6, RanC). Random.

Social Psychology. John C. Brigham. 1986. text ed. write for info. (ISBN 0-673-39503-0). study guide avail. Scott F.

Social Psychology. 2nd. ed. Roger Brown. 720p. 1986. 27.95x (ISBN 0-02-908300-1). Free Pr.

Social Psychology. George Cvetkovich et al. LC 83-10789. 500p. 1984. text ed. 27.95 (ISBN 0-03-063411-3). HR&W.

Social Psychology. 5th ed. Kay Deaux & Lawrence S. Wrightsman. LC 87-15798. 640p. 1987. casebound 25.00; study guide avail.; instr's. manual avail.; micropac test bank avail. Brooks-Cole.

Social Psychology. Robert S. Feldman. 608p. 1985. text ed. 37.95 (ISBN 0-07-020392-X). McGraw.

Social Psychology. Donelson R. Forsyth. LC 86-17102. (Psychology Ser.). 544p. 1986. text ed. 25.00 pub. net (ISBN 0-534-06744-1). Brooks-Cole.

Social Psychology. Kenneth J. Gergen & Mary M. Gergen. 570p. 1981. text ed. 26.00 net (ISBN 0-15-581562-8, HC); instr's. manual avail. (ISBN 0-15-581563-6); study guide 8.95 (ISBN 0-15-581564-4). HarBraceJ.

Social Psychology. Ed. by H. Hiebsch & H. Branstatter. 250p. 1983. 81.75 (ISBN 0-444-86352-4, North-Holland). Elsevier.

Social Psychology. Arnold S. Kahn. 624p. 1984. text ed. write for info (ISBN 0-697-06658-4); pap. write for info.; test item file avail. (ISBN 0-697-00793-6); instr's manual avail. Wm C Brown.

Social Psychology. 6th ed. Alfred R. Lindesmith et al. (Illus.). 512p. 1988. text ed. price not set (ISBN 0-13-817990-5). P-H.

Social Psychology. H. Andrew Michener et al. 638p. 1986. text ed. 30.95 (ISBN 0-15-581441-9); instr's. manual 8.00 (ISBN 0-15-581442-7). HarBraceJ.

Social Psychology. David Myers. (Illus.). 672p. 1983. text ed. 37.95 (ISBN 0-07-044273-8). McGraw.

Social Psychology. 2nd ed. David Myers. 270p. 1988. text ed. 35.95 (ISBN 0-07-044275-4); pap. text ed. 12.95 study guide, 256p (ISBN 0-07-044277-0). McGraw.

Social Psychology. 2nd ed. Steven Penrod. (Illus.). 560p. 1986. text ed. write for info (ISBN 0-13-817958-1). P-H.

Social Psychology. Daniel Perlman & P. Christopher Cozby. 1983. text ed. 33.95 (ISBN 0-03-053766-5). HR&W.

Social Psychology. 2nd ed. Bertram H. Raven & Jeffrey Z. Rubin. LC 82-23726. 718p. 1983. write for info. (ISBN 0-471-06225-1); tchr's. ed. avail. (ISBN 0-471-87305-5); pap. 12.95 student study guide (ISBN 0-471-87304-7). Wiley.

Social Psychology. Edward A. Ross. LC 73-14178. (Perspectives in Social Inquiry). 394p. 1974. Repr. of 1912 ed. 23.50x (ISBN 0-405-05521-8). Ayer Co Pubs.

Social Psychology. 5th ed. David O. Sears & Jonathan L. Freedman. (Illus.). 640p. 1985. text ed. write for info (ISBN 0-13-817858-5). P-H.

Social Psychology. 6th ed. David O. Sears et al. (Illus.). 576p. Date not set. text ed. price not set (ISBN 0-13-817669-8). P-H.

Social Psychology. Ed. by Bernard Seidenberg. Alvin Snadowsky. LC 75-9236. (Illus.). 1976. text ed. 15.95 (ISBN 0-02-928050-8). Free Pr.

Social Psychology. 1985. 3.00 (ISBN 0-471-63990-7). Wiley.

Social Psychology. 2nd ed. James W. Vander Zanden. 524p. 1981. text ed. write for info (ISBN 0-394-32427-7, RanC). Random.

Social Psychology. 3rd ed. James V. Zanden. 512p. 1983. text ed. write for info (ISBN 0-394-33020-X, RanC). Random.

Social Psychology. 4th ed. James V. Zanden. 576p. 1986. text ed. write for info. (ISBN 0-394-35810-4, RanC). Random.

Social Psychology see Handbook of Cross-Cultural Psychology.

Social Psychology: A Contemporary Approach. Louis Penner. 1978. text ed. 18.95x (ISBN 0-19-502394-3); tchr's. manual avail. (ISBN 0-19-502483-4). Oxford U Pr.

Social Psychology: A Sociological Approach. George McCall. Ed. by J. L. Simmons. 512p. 1982. text ed. 21.00 (ISBN 0-02-920640-5). Free Pr.

Social Psychology: A Sociological Approach Through Interpretive Understanding. Andrew Weigert. 385p. 1983. 22.95 (ISBN 0-268-01708-5). U of Notre Dame Pr.

Social Psychology: A Sociology Perspective. Arthur G. Neal. 544p. 1983. text ed. write for info (ISBN 0-394-34843-5, RanC). Random.

Social Psychology: A Symbolic Interaction Perspective. Jerry D. Cardwell. LC 75-158650. pap. 6.95x (ISBN 0-88295-203-X). Harlan Davidson.

Social Psychology: An Analysis of Human Behavior. Leonard W. Doob. LC 79-136063. 1971. Repr. of 1952 ed. lib. bdg. 35.00x (ISBN 0-8371-5213-5, DOSP). Greenwood.

Social Psychology: An Analysis of Social Behaviour. Kimball Young. 680p. 1984. Repr. of 1930 ed. lib. bdg. 100.00 (ISBN 0-89987-905-5). Darby Bks.

Social Psychology: An Applied Approach. Ronald J. Fisher. LC 81-51855. 712p. 1982. text ed. 20.00 (ISBN 0-312-73473-5); instr's. manual avail.; study guide 6.50 (ISBN 0-312-73475-1). St Martin.

Social Psychology: An Outline & Source Book. Edward A. Ross. 372p. 1982. Repr. of 1920 ed. lib. bdg. 40.00 (ISBN 0-89987-726-5). Darby Bks.

Social Psychology & Behavioral Medicine. J. Richard Eiser. LC 80-42062. 588p. 1982. 68.95x (ISBN 0-471-27994-3). Wiley.

Social Psychology & Developing Countries. Frank Blackler. LC 83-6560. 297p. 1984. 51.95x (ISBN 0-471-90192-X, Pub. by Wiley-Interscience). Wiley.

Social Psychology & Dysfunctional Behavior. M. R. Leary & R. S. Miller. (Springer Series in Social Psychology). (Illus.). 250p. 1986. 37.50 (ISBN 0-387-96325-1). Springer-Verlag.

Social Psychology & Human Values. M. Brewster Smith. 440p. 1988. Repr. of 1969 ed. text ed. 49.50x (ISBN 0-8290-0744-X). Irvington.

Social Psychology & Intergroup Relations. M. Billig. (European Monographs in Social Psychology). 1976. 90.00 (ISBN 0-12-097950-0). Acad Pr.

Social Psychology & Its Applications. Michael J. Saks & Edward Krupat. 592p. 1988. pap. text ed. 35.95 (ISBN 0-06-045698-1, HarpC). Har-Row.

Social Psychology & Medicine. M. Robin DiMatteo & Howard F. Friedman. LC 82-2123. 368p. 1982. text ed. 25.00 (ISBN 0-89946-131-X); 12.95 (ISBN 0-89946-146-8). Oelgeschlager.

Social Psychology & Modern Life. 2nd ed. Patricia N. Middlebrook. 620p. 1980. text ed. 23.00 (ISBN 0-394-31248-1, KnopfC). Knopf.

Social Psychology & Organizational Behaviour. Ed. by Michael Gruneberg & Toby Wall. LC 83-19871. 265p. 1984. text ed. 49.95 (ISBN 0-471-10326-8). Wiley.

Social Psychology at the Crossroads. facsimile ed. Conference On Social Psychology - University Of Oklahoma - 1950. Ed. by John N. Rohrer & Muzafer Sherif. LC 73-111822. (Essay Index Reprint Ser). 1951. 26.00 (ISBN 0-8369-1600-X). Ayer Co Pubs.

Social Psychology: Attitudes, Cognition & Social Behaviour. 2nd ed. J. Richard Eiser. (Illus.). 450p. 1986. 54.50 (ISBN 0-521-32678-8); pap. 17.95 (ISBN 0-521-33934-0). Cambridge U Pr.

Social Psychology: Concepts & Applications. Louis A. Penner. (Illus.). 699p. text ed. 37.75 (ISBN 0-314-93405-7). West Pub.

Social Psychology: Explorations in Understanding. Communications Research Machines, Inc. Staff & Drury Sherrod. (CRM Bks.). 1980. text ed. write for info (ISBN 0-394-32099-9, RanC). Random.

Social Psychology for Social Work. Sheila Feld & Norma Radin. LC 81-17061. 544p. 1982. 24.00x (ISBN 0-231-04190-X). Columbia U Pr.

Social Psychology in Athletics. Bryant J. Cratty. (Illus.). 320p. 1981. text ed. write for info. (ISBN 0-13-817650-7). P-H.

Social Psychology in Court. Michael J. Saks & Reid Hastie. LC 86-10571. 258p. 1986. Repr. of 1979 ed. text ed. 19.50 (ISBN 0-89874-965-4). Krieger.

Social Psychology in the Primary. Kutnick. 1987. pap. text ed. 11.50 (ISBN 0-06-318392-7, Pub. by Har-Row Ltd England). Har-Row.

Social Psychology, Interdependence, Interaction, & Influence. James T. Tedeschi & Svern Lindskold. LC 75-38883. 705p. 1976. 37.50 (ISBN 0-471-85017-9, Pub. by Wiley-Interscience). Wiley.

Social Psychology of Aggression: From Individual Behavior to Social Interaction. Ed. by A. Mummendey. (Springer Series in Social Psychology). (Illus.). 195p. 1984. 34.50 (ISBN 0-387-12443-8). Springer-Verlag.

Social Psychology of Civil Defense. Ronald W. Perry. (Batelle Human Affairs Research Centers Ser.). 144p. 1982. 21.50x (ISBN 0-669-05963-3). Lexington Bks.

Social Psychology of Clothing. Susan B. Kaiser. 544p. 1985. text ed. write for info. (ISBN 0-02-361880-9). Macmillan.

Social Psychology of Creativity. T. M. Amabile. (Springer Series in Social Psychology). (Illus.). 245p. 1983. 35.00 (ISBN 0-387-90830-7). Springer-Verlag.

Social Psychology of Developing Adults. Thomas O. Blank. LC 81-19835. (Personality Processes Ser.). 325p. 1982. 44.95 (ISBN 0-471-08787-4). Wiley.

Social Psychology of Education: Current Research & Theory. Ed. by Robert S. Feldman. (Illus.). 375p. 1986. 42.50 (ISBN 0-521-30620-5). Cambridge U Pr.

Social Psychology of Facial Appearance. R. Bull & N. Rumsey. (Social Psychology Ser.). 400p. 1988. 62.00 (ISBN 0-387-96607-2). Springer-Verlag.

Social Psychology of Female-Male Relations: A Critical Analysis of Central Concepts. Ed. by Richard D. Ashmore & Frances K. Del Boca. 1985. 39.95 (ISBN 0-12-065280-3); pap. 24.95 (ISBN 0-12-065281-1). Acad Pr.

Social Psychology of Groups. John W. Thibaut & Harold H. Kelley. 334p. 1986. pap. text ed. 16.95x (ISBN 0-88738-633-4). Transaction Bks.

Social Psychology of Health & Illness. Ed. by G. S. Sanders & J. Suls. LC 82-1465. (Environment & Health Ser.). 368p. 1982. text ed. 39.95x (ISBN 0-89859-214-3). L Erlbaum Assocs.

Social Psychology of Health: The Claremont Symposium on Applied Social Psychology. Ed. by Shirlynn Spacapan & Stuart Oskamp. 260p. 1988. text ed. 29.95 (ISBN 0-8039-3162-X); pap. text ed. 14.95 (ISBN 0-8039-3163-8). Sage.

Social Psychology of Industry: Human Relations in the Factory. J. A. Brown. 352p. 1987. pap. 6.95 (ISBN 0-14-009109-2). Penguin.

TITLE INDEX SOCIAL ROLE OF THE

Social Psychology of Interaction. Jerold Heiss. (Series in Biology). 400p. 1981. text ed. write for info. (ISBN 0-13-817718-X). P-H.
Social Psychology of Intergroup Conflict. Ed. by W. Stroebe & A. W. Kruglanski. (Springer Ser. in Social Psychology). 240p. 1988. 72.00 (ISBN 0-387-17695-0). Springer Verlag.
Social Psychology of Knowledge. Ed. by Daniel Bar-Tal & Arie W. Kruglanski. (Illus.). 425p. 1988. 54.50 (ISBN 0-521-32114-X). Cambridge U Pr.
Social Psychology of Leisure & Recreation. Seppo E. Iso-Ahola. 350p. 1980. pap. text ed. write for info. (ISBN 0-697-07167-7). Wm C Brown.
Social Psychology of Nonviolent Action: A Study of Three Satyagrahas. Amrot Nakhre. 1982. 15.00x (ISBN 0-8364-0897-7, Pub. by Chanakya). South Asia Bks.
Social Psychology of Organizations. Frederick Glen. (Essential Psychology Ser.). 1976. pap. 4.50x (ISBN 0-416-84050-7, 2735). Routledge Chapman & Hall.
Social Psychology of Organizations. 2nd ed. Daniel Katz & Robert L. Kahn. LC 77-18764. 838p. 1978. write for info. (ISBN 0-471-02355-8). Wiley.
Social Psychology of Organizing. 2nd ed. Karl E. Weick. LC 79-10015. (Topics in Social Psychology Ser.). 294p. 1979. pap. text ed. 13.00 (ISBN 0-394-34827-3, RanC). Random.
Social Psychology of Power. Sik Hung Ng. (European Monographs in Social Psychology). 1981. 58.50 (ISBN 0-12-518180-9). Acad Pr.
Social Psychology of Prejudice. Douglas Bethlehem. LC 85-18423. 256p. 1985. 27.50 (ISBN 0-312-73478-6). St Martin.
Social Psychology of Prejudice: A Systematic Theoretical Review & Propositional Inventory of the American Social Psychological Study of Preujudice. Howard J. Ehrlich. LC 72-10058. pap. 55.50 (ISBN 0-317-10314-8, 2007633). Bks Demand UMI.
Social Psychology of Procedural Justice. Ed. by E. A. Lind & T. R. Tyler. LC 87-38473. (Critical Issues in Social Justice Ser.). (Illus.). 280p. 1988. 32.50x (ISBN 0-306-42726-5, Plenum Pr). Plenum Pub.
Social Psychology of Psychological Research. A. G. Miller. LC 76-143522. 1972. 16.95 (ISBN 0-02-921510-2). Free Pr.
Social Psychology of Religion. Michael Argyle & Benjamin Beit-Hallahmi. 1975. 25.00x (ISBN 0-7100-7997-4); pap. 10.95X (ISBN 0-7100-8043-3). Routledge Chapman & Hall.
Social Psychology of School Learning. Ed. by James H. McMillan. LC 79-6797. (Educational Psychology Ser.). 1980. 24.95 (ISBN 0-12-485750-7). Acad Pr.
Social Psychology of Schooling. Colin Roger. (Routledge Education Bks.). 190p. 1982. 25.00x (ISBN 0-7100-9012-9); pap. 12.95x (ISBN 0-7100-9013-7). Routledge Chapman & Hall.
Social Psychology of Self-Referent Behavior. Howard B. Kaplan. 205p. 1987. 29.50x (ISBN 0-306-42356-1, Plenum Pr). Plenum Pub.
Social Psychology of Sport. Albert V. Carron. 1980. text ed. cancelled (ISBN 0-932392-06-7); pap. 24.95. Mouvement Pubns.
Social Psychology of Telecommunications. John Short et al. LC 75-44335. (Illus.). 205p. pap. 53.30 (2030393). Bks Demand UMI.
Social Psychology of the Epileptic Child. Christopher Bagley. LC 79-142199. (Illus.). 1971. 15.95x (ISBN 0-87024-188-5). U of Miami Pr.
Social Psychology of the Self-Concept. Ed. by Morris Rosenberg & Howard B. Kaplan. (Illus.). 576p. 1982. text ed. 32.50x (ISBN 0-88295-214-5); pap. text ed. 22.50x (ISBN 0-88295-215-3). Harlan Davidson.
Social Psychology of Time: New Perspectives. Ed. by Joseph E. McGrath. (Focus Edition Ser.: Vol. 91). 320p. 1988. text ed. 35.00 (ISBN 0-8039-2766-5); pap. text ed. 16.95 (ISBN 0-8039-2767-3). Sage.
Social Psychology of War & Peace. Mark A. May. 1943. 49.50x (ISBN 0-686-51314-2). Elliots Bks.
Social Psychology: Past & Present: An Integrative Orientation. J. M. Jackson. 176p. Date not set. 22.50 (ISBN 0-89859-916-4); pap. price not set (ISBN 0-89859-917-2). L Erlbaum Assocs.
Social Psychology: People in Groups. Bertran Raven & Jeffrey Rubin. LC 75-32693. 592p. 1976. 29.95 (ISBN 0-471-70970-0). Wiley.
Social Psychology: Science & Application. David L. Watson & Gail DeBortali-Tregerthan. 1984. text ed. write for info. (ISBN 0-673-15638-9); write for info. study guide (ISBN 0-673-15893-4). Scott F.
Social Psychology: Shared, Symboled, Situated Behavior. Glenn M. Vernon & Jerry D. Cardwell. LC 80-5967. (Illus.). 580p. (Orig.). 1981. pap. text ed. 23.50 (ISBN 0-8191-1701-3). U Pr of Amer.
Social Psychology: Society & Self. Jeffrey E. Nash. (Illus.). 425p. 1984. text ed. 34.50 (ISBN 0-314-85281-6). West Pub.
Social Psychology: Sociological Perspectives. Morris Rosenberg & Ralph H. Turner. LC 81-66976. 720p. 1981. pap. text ed. 19.95x (ISBN 0-465-07905-9). Basic.
Social Psychology: Study Guide with Practice Tests. 2nd ed. Terry F. Pettijohn. 320p. 1986. pap. text ed. write for info (ISBN 0-13-817974-3). P-H.
Social Psychology: The Theory & Application of Symbolic Interactionism, 2nd ed. Robert H. Lauer & Warren H. Handel. 400p. 1983. write for info (ISBN 0-13-817841-0). P-H.
Social Psychology Through Symbolic Interaction. 2nd ed. Ed. by Gregory P. Stone & Harvey A. Farberman. LC 80-23770. 544p. 1981. pap. text ed. write for info. (ISBN 0-02-417890-X). Macmillan.
Social Psychology, Understanding Human Interaction. 5th ed. Baron & Byrne. 656p. 1986. 38.00 (ISBN 0-205-10313-8). Allyn.
Social Psychophysiology & Emotion: Theory & Clinical Applications. Ed. by Hugh L. Wagner. LC 87-29435. 336p. 1988. 79.95 (ISBN 0-471-91266-2). Wiley.
Social Psychophysiology: Sourcebook. Ed. by John T. Cacioppo & Richard E. Petty. LC 82-15575. 769p. 1983. text ed. 85.00 (ISBN 0-89862-626-9). Guilford Pr.
Social R & D: Research & Development in the Human Services. J. Rothman. 1980. pap. text ed. write for info. (ISBN 0-13-818112-8). P-H.
Social Realism in the Argentine Narrative. David W. Foster. (Studies in the Romance Languages & Literatures: No. 227). 180p. (Orig.). 1986. pap. 15.00x (ISBN 0-8078-9231-9). U of NC Pr.
Social Realism in the French-Canadian Novel. Ben-Zion Shek. LC 77-379601. pap. 81.50 (ISBN 0-317-30434-8, 2024929). Bks Demand UMI.
Social Realism in Twentieth Century Turkish Literature. 1978. 10.00 (ISBN 0-317-56412-9). UM Ctr NENAS.
Social Realities & Community Psychiatry. H. Warren Dunham. LC 74-10967. 252p. 1976. 34.95 (ISBN 0-87705-215-8). Human Sci Pr.
Social Reality of Death... Kathleeen C. Charmaz. (Sociology Ser.). 1980. text ed. write for info. (ISBN 0-201-01033-X). Addison-Wesley.
Social Reality of Ethnic America. Rudolph Gomez & Clement Cottingham. 1974. pap. text ed. 11.00 (ISBN 0-669-84111-0). Heath.
Social Realty of Death. Kathlene C. Charnaz. 384p. 1980. text ed. write for info (ISBN 0-394-34832-X, RanC). Random.
Social Rebel in American Literature. Ed. by Robert H. Woodward & James J. Clark. LC 68-21801. 404p. (Orig.). 1968. pap. 13.24 scp (ISBN 0-672-63115-6). Odyssey Pr.
Social Reconstruction of the Feminine Character. Sondra Farganis. LC 86-17670. 272p. 1986. 31.50x (ISBN 0-8476-7325-1); pap. 14.95x (ISBN 0-8476-7326-X). Rowman.
Social Reform & Reaction in America: An Annotated Bibliography. Ed. by Carl Degler. LC 82-24294. (Clio Bibliography Ser.: No. 13). 375p. 1984. lib. bdg. 65.50 (ISBN 0-87436-048-X). ABC-Clio.
Social Reform & the Church. John R. Commons. LC 66-21663. (Illus.). 1967. Repr. of 1894 ed. 25.00x (ISBN 0-678-00286-X). Kelley.
Social Reform & the Constitution. Frank J. Goodnow. 1911. 23.50 (ISBN 0-8337-1385-X). B Franklin.
Social Reform & the Reformation. Jacob S. Schapiro. LC 74-127456. (Columbia University Studies in the Social Sciences: No. 90). 1970. Repr. of 1909 ed. 16.50 (ISBN 0-404-51090-6). AMS Pr.
Social Reform in Andhra: Eighteen Forty-Nine to Nineteen Nineteen. V. Ramakrishna. (Illus.). xi, 241p. 1984. text ed. 27.50x (ISBN 0-7069-2349-9, Pub. by Vikas India). Advent NY.
Social Reform in Norway. John E. Nordskog. LC 72-13001. 184p. 1973. Repr. of 1935 ed. lib. bdg. 25.00x (ISBN 0-8371-6736-1, NOSR). Greenwood.
Social Reform in the United States Navy, Seventeen Ninety-Eight to Eighteen Sixty-Two. Harold G. Langley. LC 67-10440. (Illus.). pap. 80.80 (ISBN 0-317-08240-X, 2015037). Bks Demand UMI.
Social Reformers in Urban China: The Chinese Y. M. C. A., Eighteen Ninety-Five to Nineteen Twenty-Six. Shirley Garrett. LC 74-133218. (East Asian Ser.: No. 56). 1970. 17.50x (ISBN 0-674-81220-4). Harvard U Pr.
Social Register: Facsimile Edition of 1887 Books. 300p. 1986. 25.00 (ISBN 0-940281-00-7). Social Reg Assn.
Social Register of Prominent People & Greatest Establishments in the United States see Best of Washington: Its People, Society & Establishments - Hall of Fame.
Social Register, 1979. 1979. 12.95 (ISBN 0-85036-252-0, Pub. by Merlin Pr UK); pap. 6.95 (ISBN 0-85036-253-9, Pub. by Merlin Pr UK). Longwood Pub Group.
Social Register, 1980. Ed. by Ralph Miliband. 1980. 12.95 (Pub. by Merlin Pr UK); pap. 6.95 (ISBN 0-85036-267-9, Pub. by Merlin Pr UK). Longwood Pub Group.
Social Register, 1981. 1981. 12.95 (ISBN 0-85036-279-2, Pub. by Merlin Pr UK); pap. 6.95 (ISBN 0-85036-280-6, Pub. by Merlin Pr UK). Longwood Pub Group.
Social Register: 1988 Edition, 2 vols. 1988. Set. 75.00 (ISBN 0-940281-01-5). Vol. 1, Winter, 1100p. Vol. 2, Summer, 250p. Social Reg Assn.
Social Regulation & the Reagan Revolution: A Tale of Two Agencies. Richard A. Harris & Sidney M. Milkis. 368p. 1989. 32.50 (ISBN 0-19-505732-5); pap. text ed. 12.95 (ISBN 0-19-505733-3). Oxford U Pr.
Social Regulation in Markets for Consumer Goods & Services. David T. Scheffman & Elie Appelbaum. (Ontario Economic Council Research Studies). 200p. 1982. pap. 9.95x (ISBN 0-8020-3384-9). U of Toronto Pr.
Social Regulation: Strategies for Reform. Ed. by Eugene Bardach & Robert A. Kagan. LC 81-85279. 420p. 1982. text ed. 19.95 (ISBN 0-917616-47-2); pap. text ed. 8.95 (ISBN 0-917616-46-4). ICS Pr.
Social Regulatory Policy: Recent Moral Controversies in American Politics. Ed. by Raymond Tatalovich & Byron W. Daynes. 350p. 1988. 40.00 (ISBN 0-8133-0612-4); pap. 16.95. Westview.
Social Relation & Freedom. Benjamin R. Tucker & Thomas Robertson. 1980. lib. bdg. 59.95 (ISBN 0-8490-3084-6). Gordon Pr.
Social Relations & Human Attributes. Paul Hirst & Penny Woolley. 1982. 28.00x (ISBN 0-422-77220-8, NO.3571); pap. 11.95x (ISBN 0-422-77230-5, NO.3570). Routledge Chapman & Hall.
Social Relations & Ideas. Trevor Aston et al. LC 82-9727. (Past & Present Publications). 352p. 1983. 47.50 (ISBN 0-521-25132-X). Cambridge U Pr.
Social Relations & Social Roles. Florian Znaniecki. (Reprints in Sociology Ser). lib. bdg. 39.50 (ISBN 0-697-00219-5); pap. 12.95x (ISBN 0-89197-940-9). Irvington.
Social Relations & Spatial Structures. Ed. by Derek Gregory & John Urry. LC 85-2155. 440p. 1985. 39.95 (ISBN 0-312-73586-3); pap. 14.95 (ISBN 0-312-73484-0). St Martin.
Social Relations in a Philippine Market: Self-Interest & Subjectivity. William G. Davis. LC 71-145783. (Center for South & Southeast Asia Studies, UC Berkeley: No. 15). 1973. 38.50x (ISBN 0-520-01904-0). U of Cal Pr.
Social Relations in a Philippine Town, No. 19. Robert J. Morais. (No. Ill. Univ., Center for SEAsian Studies, Special report). (Illus.). 165p. 1982. pap. 11.00x (ISBN 0-686-35856-2); pap. text ed. 11.00x (ISBN 0-686-37186-0). North Ill U Ctr SE Asian.
Social Relations in Byron's Eastern Tales. Daniel P. Watkins. LC 85-46014. 1987. 24.50 (ISBN 0-8386-3287-4). Fairleigh Dickinson.
Social Relations in Our Southern States. D. R. Hundley. LC 72-11344. (American South Ser.). Repr. of 1860 ed. 21.00 (ISBN 0-405-05060-7). Ayer Co Pubs.
Social Relations in Our Southern States. Daniel R. Hundley. Ed. by William J. Cooper, Jr. LC 78-23811. (Library of Southern Civilization). (Illus.). 1979. pap. text ed. 8.95x (ISBN 0-8071-0559-7). La State U Pr.
Social Relations in the Near East. 2nd, rev. & enl. ed. Stuart C Dodd. LC 75-180333. Repr. of 1940 ed. 62.50 (ISBN 0-404-56239-6). AMS Pr.
Social Relations in the Urban Parish. Joseph H. Fichter. LC 54-11207. pap. 68.00 (ISBN 0-317-07856-9, 2020061). Bks Demand UMI.
Social Relations of Physics, Mysticism & Mathematics. Sal Restivo. 1983. lib. bdg. 49.50 (ISBN 90-277-1536-X, Pub. by Reidel Holland). Kluwer Academic.
Social Relations of Physics, Mysticism & Mathematics. Sal Restivo. (Pallas Paperbacks Ser.). 1985. pap. 14.95 (ISBN 90-277-2084-3, Pub. by Reidel Holland). Kluwer Academic.
Social Relationships & Cognitive Development: A Fyssen Foundation Symposium. Robert A. Hinde. Ed. by Joan Stevenson-Hinde & Anne N. Perret-Clermont. (Illus.). 400p. 1986. 49.95x (ISBN 0-19-852155-3); pap. 29.95x (ISBN 0-19-852167-7). Oxford U Pr.
Social Representations. Ed. by Robert M. Farr & Serge Moscovici. LC 83-18823. (European Studies in Social Psychology). 450p. 1984. 77.50 (ISBN 0-521-24800-0). Cambridge U Pr.
Social Research. J. L. Simmons & George J. McCall. 175p. 1985. text ed. write for info. (ISBN 0-02-410520-1). Macmillan.
Social Research & the Practicing Professions. Robert Merton. 1982. text ed. 31.50 (ISBN 0-89011-569-9); pap. 17.75. Abt Bks.
Social Research & the Practicing Professions. Robert K. Merton. Intro. by Aaron Rosenblatt & Thomas F. Gieryn. 300p. 1984. lib. bdg. 33.25 (ISBN 0-8191-4111-9); pap. text ed. 18.75 (ISBN 0-8191-4129-1). U Pr of Amer.
Social Research Ethics. Ed. by Martin Bulmer. LC 81-4250. 304p. 1982. 45.00 (ISBN 0-8419-0713-7); pap. 17.50 (ISBN 0-8419-0780-3). Holmes & Meier.
Social Research for Consumers. Earl Babbie. 383p. 1982. text ed. write for info. (ISBN 0-534-01125-X). Wadsworth Pub.
Social Research in Developing Countries: Surveys & Censuses in the Third World. Ed. by Martin Bulmer & Donald P. Warwick. LC 83-6970. (Social Development in the Third World Ser.). 383p. 1984. 57.95 (ISBN 0-471-10352-7). Wiley.
Social Research in Puerto Rico: Science, Humanism & Society. Ed. by Ronald J. Duncan & Edward Richardson. LC 83-12635. 255p. 1984. pap. 8.00 (ISBN 0-913480-57-6). Inter Am U Pr.
Social Research in the Judicial Process: Cases, Readings & Text. Wallace D. Loh. LC 84-60263. 832p. 1984. 47.50x (ISBN 0-87154-551-9). Russell Sage.
Social Research Methods. Mark Abrahamson. (Illus.). 400p. 1983. write for info (ISBN 0-13-818088-1). P-H.
Social Research Methods. David Dooley. (Illus.). 400p. 1984. text ed. write for info (ISBN 0-13-818121-7). P-H.
Social Research Methods. D. Forcese & S. Richter. (Illus.). 1973. text ed. 28.95 (ISBN 0-13-818237-X). P-H.
Social Research Methods. Guy et al. 1987. pap. 38.00 (ISBN 0-205-08677-2). Allyn.
Social Research: The Scientific Study of Human Interactions. Morton Hunt. LC 85-60759. 300p. (Orig.). 1985. text ed. 17.50x (ISBN 0-87154-393-1); pap. text ed. 8.95x (ISBN 0-87154-394-X). Russell Sage.
Social Researching: Politics, Problems, Practice. Colin Bell & Helen Roberts. 272p. (Orig.). 1984. pap. 13.95x (ISBN 0-7100-9884-7). Routledge Chapman & Hall.
Social Responses to Handicap. Eda Topliss. LC 81-18602. (Social Policy in Modern Britain Ser.). 198p. pap. 51.50 (2030327). Bks Demand UMI.
Social Responses to Technological Change. Ed. by Augustine Brannigan & Sheldon Goldenberg. LC 84-27934. (Contributions in Sociology Ser.: No. 56). (Illus.). xi, 292p. 1985. lib. bdg. 36.95 (ISBN 0-313-24727-7, BNT/). Greenwood.
Social Responsibilities in Engineering & Science: A Guide for Selecting General Education Courses. Richard H. McCuen & James Wallace. (Illus.). 256p. 1987. pap. text ed. write for info. (ISBN 0-13-818253-1). P-H.
Social Responsibilities of Business. Morrell Heald. 348p. 1988. 34.94 (ISBN 0-88738-231-2). Transaction Bks.
Social Responsibilities of Business: Company & Community, Nineteen Hundred to Nineteen Sixty. Morrell Heald. LC 75-84490. 358p. 1970. 27.50 (ISBN 0-8295-0176-2). UPB.
Social Responsibilities of Business Corporations. LC 76-168378. 1971. pap. 5.00 (ISBN 0-87186-042-2). Comm Econ Dev.
Social Responsibilities of Lawyers: Case Studies. Philip Heymann & Lance Liebman. (University Casebook Ser.). 353p. 1988. pap. text ed. write for info. (ISBN 0-88277-645-2). Foundation Pr.
Social Responsibility: A Selected Bibliography of Articles & Books. Nathan A. Rosen. (Public Administration Ser.: P 1900). 25p. 1986. 6.25 (ISBN 0-89028-820-8). Vance Biblios.
Social Responsibility & Latin America. Ed. by Nancy T. Baden. (Proceedings of the Pacific Coast Council on Latin American Studies: Vol. 8). (Illus.). 190p. (Orig.). 1981. pap. 12.00 (ISBN 0-916304-53-1). SDSU Press.
Social Responsibility & the Business Predicament. Ed. by James D. McKie. LC 74-23967. (Studies in the Regulation of Economic Activity). 361p. 1975. 28.95 (ISBN 0-8157-5608-9); pap. 10.95 (ISBN 0-8157-5607-0). Brookings.
Social Responsibility & the Responsible Society. Bruce Allsopp. 208p. (Orig.). 1985. pap. 19.95x (ISBN 0-85362-220-5, Oriel). Routledge Chapman & Hall.
Social Responsibility in an Age of Revolution. Louis Finkelstein. 1971. 10.00x (ISBN 0-685-31421-9, Pub. by Jewish Theol Seminary). Ktav.
Social Responsibility in Farm Leadership. Walter W. Wilcox. LC 75-33001. 194p. 1976. Repr. of 1956 ed. lib. bdg. 35.00 (ISBN 0-8371-8494-0, WISR). Greenwood.
Social Responsibility in Marketing: A Selected & Annotated Bibliography. Ernest B. Uhr & Lance P. Jarvis. LC 77-5551. (American Marketing Association Bibliography Ser.: No. 27). pap. 20.80 (ISBN 0-317-39652-8, 2023351). Bks Demand UMI.
Social Responsibility of Gynecology & Obstetrics. Ed. by Allan C. Barnes. LC 65-24793. (Illus.). pap. 56.00 (ISBN 0-317-07931-X, 2015431). Bks Demand UMI.
Social Responsibility of the Scientist. Ed. by Martin Brown. LC 75-143503. 1971. pap. text ed. 11.95 (ISBN 0-02-904730-7). Free Pr.
Social Responsiveness of Infants. Ed. by Evelyn B. Thoman & Sharland Trotter. (PRT Ser.: No. 2). 75p. 1978. 9.00 (ISBN 0-931562-01-5). J & J Baby Prod.
Social Revolution in Guatemala: The Carrera Revolt see Applied Enlightenment: Nineteenth Century Liberalism, 1800-1839.
Social Revolution in Mexico. E. Ross. 1976. lib. bdg. 59.95 (ISBN 0-8490-2618-0). Gordon Pr.
Social Role of Art. Richard Cork. 128p. 1981. 30.00x (Pub. by Fraser Bks). State Mutual Bk.
Social Role of Art. Richard Cork. 120p. 1980. 42.00x (ISBN 0-86092-048-8, Pub. by Gordon Fraser). State Mutual Bk.
Social Role of the Executive's Wife. Margaret L. Helfrich. 1965. pap. 3.00x (ISBN 0-87776-123-X, R123). Ohio St U Admin Sci.
Social Role of the Man of Knowledge. Florian Znaniecki. 1965. lib. bdg. 20.00 (ISBN 0-374-98892-7, Octagon). Hippocrene Bks.
Social Role of the Man of Knowledge. Florian Znaniecki. Ed. by John Stanley. (Social Science Classics Ser.). 216p. 1986. pap. text ed. 19.95x (ISBN 0-88738-642-3). Transaction Bks.

Social Roles: A Focus for Social Studies in the Nineteen Eighty's. Douglas P. Superka & Sharryl Hawke. LC 82-5813. (Project SPAN Reports Ser.). 85p. (Orig.). 1982. pap. 11.95 (ISBN 0-89994-274-1). Soc Sci Ed.

Social Roles: Conformity, Conflict, & Creativity. Louis A. Zurcher. (Sociological Observations: Vol. 15). 296p. 1983. 29.95 (ISBN 0-8039-2029-6). Sage.

Social Romanticism in France, Eighteen Thirty to Eighteen Forty-Eight. David O. Evans. LC 77-96180. 1969. Repr. of 1951 ed. lib. bdg. 15.00x (ISBN 0-374-92641-7, Octagon). Hippocrene Bks.

Social Roots of Religion in Ancient India. Ramendra N. Nandi. 218p. 1987. 22.00x (ISBN 81-7074-009-6, Pub. by Bagchi India). South Asia Bks.

Social Scandinavia in the Viking Age. Mary W. Williams. Repr. of 1920 ed. 29.00 (ISBN 0-527-96960-5). Kraus Repr.

Social Science. LC 72-12718. 290p. 1973. 7.00 (ISBN 0-669-85415-8). Amer Bar Assn.

Social Science Activities of Some Eastern European Academies of Science see Cinema & Social Sciences: A Survey of Ethnographic & Sociological Films.

Social Science: An Introduction to the Study of Society. 6th ed. Elgin F. Hunt & David C. Colander. 1194p. 1987. pap. write for info. (ISBN 0-02-358920-5); write for info. study guide. Macmillan.

Social Science & Institutional Change. Robert R. Mayer. LC 81-2705. 202p. 1982. text ed. 24.95 (ISBN 0-87855-432-7). Transaction Bks.

Social Science & National Policy. rev. 2nd. ed. Ed. by Fred R. Harris. LC 72-87663. 152p. 1973. 18.95 (ISBN 0-87855-051-8); pap. text ed. 9.95x (ISBN 0-87855-544-7). Transaction Bks.

Social Science & Natural Hazards. Ed. by James D. Wright & Peter H. Rossi. LC 80-69663. (Illus.). 215p. 1981. text ed. 27.50 (ISBN 0-89011-552-4). Abt Bks.

Social Science & Natural Hazards. Ed. by James D. Wright & Peter H. Rossi. (Illus.). 214p. 1984. Repr. of 1981 ed. lib. bdg. 29.00 (ISBN 0-8191-4078-3). U Pr of Amer.

Social Science & Political Theory. 2nd ed. Walter G. Runciman. LC 69-16286. pap. 52.00 (ISBN 0-317-26386-2, 2024528). Bks Demand UMI.

Social Science & Public Policy: The Roles of Academic Disciplines in Policy Analysis. Ed. by George J. McCall & George H. Weber. LC 83-11832. (Policy Studies Organization Ser.). 200p. 1984. 28.50x (ISBN 0-8046-9330-7). Assoc Faculty Pr.

Social Science & Revolutions. Stan Taylor. LC 82-19431. 192p. 1984. 25.00 (ISBN 0-312-73495-6). St Martin.

Social Science & Social Policy. Martin Bulmer et al. (Contemporary Social Research Ser.: No. 12). 272p. 1987. text ed. 37.95x (ISBN 0-04-312025-3); pap. text ed. 17.95x (ISBN 0-04-312026-1). Unwin Hyman.

Social Science & Social Policy. Ed. by R. Lance Shotland & Melvin M. Mark. 1985. 32.00 (ISBN 0-8039-2160-8). Sage.

Social Science & Social Welfare. Ed. by John M. Romanyshyn. Date not set. 4.50 (74-650-06). Coun Soc WK Ed.

Social Science & the Arts Nineteen Eighty-Four: A State-of-the-Arts Review from the Tenth Annual Conference on Social Theory, Politics & the Arts University of Maryland, College Park, October 12-14, 1984. Ed. by John P. Robinson. (Illus.). 190p. (Orig.). 1986. lib. bdg. 25.75 (ISBN 0-8191-4925-X); pap. text ed. 12.00 (ISBN 0-8191-4926-8). U Pr of Amer.

Social Science & the Challenge of Relativism, 3 Vols. Lawrence E. Hazelrigg. cancelled; Vol. 1, A Wilderness of Mirrors: On Practices in a Gray Age, 06. cancelled; Vol. 2, Claims of Knowledge: On the Labor of Making Found Worlds, 09/1988. cancelled; Vol. 3, Cultures of Nature (in preparation), 06/1988. cancelled. U Presses Fla.

Social Science & the Federal Government. Gene M. Lyons & Richard D. Lambert. LC 76-148005. (Annals of the American Academy of Politcal & Social Science: No. 394). 1971. pap. 7.95 (ISBN 0-87761-136-X). Am Acad Pol Soc Sci.

Social Science Approaches to Business Behavior. Chris Argyris et al. Ed. by Arthur P. Brief. (Continuity in Administrative Science & Ancestral Books in the Management of Organizations). 183p. 1987. lib. bdg. 25.00 (ISBN 0-8240-8201-X). Garland Pub.

Social Science Approaches to Health Services Research. Ed. by Thomas Choi & Jay N. Greenberg. LC 82-23225. 350p. 1983. text ed. 28.00x (ISBN 0-914904-83-3, 0848). Health Admin Pr.

Social Science Approaches to the Judicial Process. J. B. Grossman et al. LC 74-153371. (Symposia on Law & Society Ser). 1971. Repr. of 1966 ed. lib. bdg. 19.50 (ISBN 0-306-70135-9). Da Capo.

Social Science Bibliography on Property, Ownership & Possession: 1580 Citations from Psychology, Anthropology, Sociology, & Related Disciplines. Floyd W. Rudmin et al. (Public Administration Ser.: P 2294). 134p. 1987. 25.00 (ISBN 1-55590-574-9). Vance Biblios.

Social Science Concepts: A Systematic Analysis. Ed. by Giovanni Sartori. 488p. 1985. text ed. 29.95 (ISBN 0-8039-2177-2). Sage.

Social Science Encyclopedia. Ed. by Adam Kuper & Jessica Kuper. 916p. 1986. 75.00 (ISBN 0-7102-0008-0). Routledge Chapman & Hall.

Social Science in America: The First Two Hundred Years. Ed. by Charles M. Bonjean et al. 229p. 1976. 14.95x (ISBN 0-292-77530-X); pap. 7.95 (ISBN 0-292-77531-8). U of Tex Pr.

Social Science in Christian Perspective. Ed. by Paul A. Marshall & Robert E. VanderVennen. (Christian Studies Today). 357p. (Orig.). 1988. lib. bdg. 32.50 (ISBN 0-8191-7103-4, Pub. by Inst Christ Stud); pap. text ed. 17.25 (ISBN 0-8191-7104-2, Pub. by Inst Christ Stud). U Pr of Amer.

Social Science in Court: Mobilizing Experts in the School Desegregation Cases. Mark A. Chesler et al. LC 88-6088. 296p. 1988. text ed. 45.00x (ISBN 0-299-11620-4); pap. text ed. 17.50x (ISBN 0-299-11624-7). U of Wis Pr.

Social Science in Government: Uses & Misuses. Richard P. Nathan. LC 88-47668. 240p. 1988. 18.95 (ISBN 0-465-07911-3). Basic.

Social Science in Law: Cases & Materials. John Monahan & Laurens Walker. LC 84-28620. (University Casebook Ser.). 525p. 1985. 27.00 (ISBN 0-88277-217-1). Foundation Pr.

Social Science in Natural Resource Management Systems. Ed. by Marc L. Miller et al. (Social & Natural Resources Ser.). 279p. 1987. pap. 22.50 (ISBN 0-8133-7485-5). Westview.

Social Science Information & Documentation: Search for Relevance in India. Suren Agrowal. 1987. 30.00x (ISBN 0-8364-2313-5, Pub. by Concept India). South Asia Bks.

Social Science Information & Public Policy Making: The Interaction Between Bureaucratic Politics & the Use of Survey Data. Robert F. Rich. LC 79-92468. (Social & Behavioral Science Ser.). 1981. text ed. 32.95x (ISBN 0-87589-497-6). Jossey-Bass.

Social Science Methods, Decision-Making & Development Planning. Erwin S. Solomon. (Socio-Economic Studies Ser.: No. 8). 103p. 1985. pap. 6.50 (ISBN 92-3-102207-5, U1426, UNESCO). UNIPUB.

Social Science Methods in the Legal Process. Noreen L. Channels. LC 84-11527. (Illus.). 286p. 1985. 39.95x (ISBN 0-86598-013-6, Rowman & Allanheld). Rowman.

Social Science Needs & Priorities in the English-Speaking Caribbean and Surinam: Papers & The Final Report & Recommendations of the UNESCO Expert Meeting, Bridgetown, Barbados, Jan 29-Feb 1, 1980. (Reports & Papers in the Social Sciences: No. 48). 54p. 1982. pap. 5.00 (ISBN 92-3-101962-7, U1248, UNESCO). UNIPUB.

Social Science of Organizations. Ed. by Harold J. Leavitt & Arthur P. Brief. (Continuity in Administrative Science, Ancestral Books in the Management of Organizations). 1987. lib. bdg. 25.00 (ISBN 0-8240-8213-3). Garland Pub.

Social Science of Play, Games & Sport: Learning Experiences. Glyn C. Roberts et al. LC 79-89695. pap. 27.50 (ISBN 0-317-55492-1, 2029532). Bks Demand UMI.

Social Science Organization & Policy, First Series: Belgium, Chile, Egypt, Hungary, Nigeria & Sri Lanka. Intro. by A. B. Cherns. (New Babylon Studies in the Social Sciences: No. 17). 1974. pap. text ed. 16.00x (ISBN 90-2797-290-7). Mouton.

Social Science Practitioner As Expert Witness: A Bibliography. Frederick Frankena. (Public Administration Ser.: P 1825). 8p. 1985. 2.00 (ISBN 0-89028-675-2). Vance Biblios.

Social Science Research: A Handbook. Gerald S. Ferman & Jack Levin. 144p. 1977. pap. 8.95 (ISBN 0-87073-219-6). Schenkman Bks Inc.

Social Science Research: A Skills Handbook. Ed. by Annie S. Barnes. LC 85-51990. 209p. (Orig.). 1985. pap. text ed. 9.95x (ISBN 0-932269-71-0). Wyndham Hall.

Social Science Research & Climate Change. Robert S. Chen & Elise Boulding. 1983. lib. bdg. 43.50 (ISBN 90-277-1490-8, Pub. by Reidel Holland). Kluwer Academic.

Social Science Research & Decision-Making. Carol H. Weiss & Michael J. Bucuvalas. LC 80-12840. 1980. 35.00x. Columbia U Pr.

Social Science Research & Government: Comparative Essays on Britain & the United States. Ed. by Martin Bulmer. (Illus.). 400p. 1987. 49.50 (ISBN 0-521-32350-9). Cambridge U Pr.

Social Science Research & Women in the Arab World. 175p. 1985. pap. 15.75 (ISBN 92-3-102140-0, U1409, UNESCO). UNIPUB.

Social Science Research & Women in the Arab World. UNESCO. LC 84-8941. 175p. 1984. 28.75 (ISBN 0-86187-387-4, Pub. by Frances Pinter). Longwood Pub Group.

Social Science Research Handbook. Ed. by Raymond G. McInnis & James W. Scott. LC 83-49158. (History & Historiography Ser.). 395p. 1985. lib. bdg. 40.00 (ISBN 0-8240-6368-6). Garland Pub.

Social Science Research in Latin America. Ed. by Charles Wagley. LC 65-11971. 1965. 39.00x (ISBN 0-231-02772-9). Columbia U Pr.

Social Science Research in Sarawak. E. R. Leach. pap. 10.00 (ISBN 0-384-31880-0). Johnson Repr.

Social Science Research Methods. Bruce A. Chadwick et al. (Illus.). 448p. 1984. text ed. write for info. (ISBN 0-13-818336-8). P-H.

Social Science Research Methods for Litigation. Donald E. Vinson & Philip K. Anthony. (Contemporary Litigation Ser.). 325p. 1985. 50.00x (ISBN 0-87215-857-8). Michie Co.

Social Science Research on Business: Product & Potential. Ed. by Robert A. Dahl. LC 60-9783. 185p. 1959. pap. 17.00x (ISBN 0-231-02407-X). Columbia U Pr.

Social Science Research on Higher Education & Universities, 3 pts. Wolfgang Nitsch. Ed. by Dietrich Goldschmidt. Incl. Pt. 1. Trend Report. Walter Weller. text ed. 30.40x (ISBN 90-2797-254-0); Pt. 2. Annotated Bibliography. 1970. text ed. 46.00x (ISBN 90-2796-870-5); Pt. 3. Supplement. write for info. (ISBN 0-686-22588-0). 1973. Mouton.

Social Science Skills: Activities for the Secondary Classroom, Grades 9-12, 7 vols. Educational Resources Information Center Staff. Incl. American Government Issues. 11.95x (ISBN 0-8077-2649-4); American Lifestyle Issues. 14.95x (ISBN 0-8077-2648-6); Basic Skills. 11.95x (ISBN 0-8077-2650-8); Economic Issues. 11.95 (ISBN 0-8077-2645-1); Energy - Consumer Issues. 15.95x (ISBN 0-8077-2646-X); World Issues. 17.95x (ISBN 0-8077-2643-5); Population Issues. 14.95x (ISBN 0-8077-2644-3). (Orig.). 1981. (ISBN 0-686-77379-9). Tchrs Coll.

Social Science Trends in Latin America Through Nineteen Fifty. Harold Eugene Davis. LC 50-13154. 136p. 1950. pap. 8.95 (ISBN 0-87419-010-X, U Pr of Wash). Larlin Corp.

Social Science Vocabulary of Swahili. James L. Brain. (Foreign & Comparative Studies Program, African Special Publications: No. 3). (Orig., Swahili.). 1968. pap. text ed. 3.50x (ISBN 0-686-74012-2). Syracuse U Foreign Comp.

Social Sciences. Jack Rudman. (Graduate Record Area Examination Ser.: GRE-44). 27.95 (ISBN 0-8373-5294-0); pap. 15.95 (ISBN 0-8373-5244-4). Natl Learning.

Social Sciences see Comprehensive Dissertation Index 1861-1972: Supplement, 1973.

Social Sciences & African Development Planning. Ed. by Phillips Stevens, Jr. 116p. 1978. pap. 6.00 (ISBN 0-918456-32-0). African Studies Assn.

Social Sciences & Dentistry, Vol. II. Ed. by Lois K. Cohen & Patricia S. Bryant. 429p. 1984. pap. text ed. 50.00x (ISBN 0-317-19760-6). Quint Pub Co.

Social Sciences & Farming Systems Research: Methodological Perspectives on Agricultural Development. Ed. by Jeffrey R. Jones & Ben J. Wallace. 1985. pap. 27.50x (ISBN 0-8133-7136-8). Westview.

Social Sciences & Fieldwork in China: Views from the Field. Ed. by Anne F. Thurston & Burton Pasternak. 175p. 1983. 31.50x (ISBN 0-86531-644-9). Westview.

Social Sciences & History. Jack Rudman. (College-Level Examination Ser.: ATS-9E). (Cloth bdg. avail. on request). pap. 13.95. Natl Learning.

Social Sciences & Humanities see Comprehensive Dissertation Index, 1974: Supplement, 1975.

Social Sciences & Humanities Index, 9 Vols. LC 17-4969. 1965-74. 50.00 (ISBN 0-685-22255-1). Wilson.

Social Sciences & Humanities Index, 18 vols. LC 17-4969. 1907-65. 60.00 (ISBN 0-317-55865-X). Wilson.

Social Sciences & International Agricultural Research: Lessons from the CRSPs. Ed. by Constance M. McCorkle. 300p. 1989. lib. bdg. 35.00. Lynne Rienner.

Social Sciences & Public Policy in the Developing World. Ed. by Laurence D. Stifel et al. LC 81-47748. 384p. 1982. 26.50x (ISBN 0-669-04824-0). Lexington Bks.

Social Sciences & the Church. Ed. by C. L. Mitton. 268p. Date not set. pap. text ed. 7.95 (Pub. by T & T Clark Ltd UK). Fortress.

Social Sciences & the Government: The Asian Scene. Igbal Narain & Yogesh Atal. 1987. 20.00x (ISBN 81-7062-032-5, Pub. by Lancer India). South Asia Bks.

Social Sciences & Their Interrelations. William F. Ogburn & Alexander Goldenweiser. LC 73-14173. (Perspectives in Social Inquiry Ser). 518p. 1974. Repr. 30.00x (ISBN 0-405-05516-1). Ayer Co Pubs.

Social Sciences at Mid-Century. facs. ed. Minnesota University - Graduate School. LC 68-55852. (Essay Index Reprint Ser). 1952. 14.25 (ISBN 0-8369-0710-8). Ayer Co Pubs.

Social Sciences in Agricultural Education: Eight Status Reports from Asia. Ed. by Yogesh Atal. 261p. 1984. pap. 7.50 (UB146, UB). UNIPUB.

Social Sciences in Asia. Ed. by Yogesh Atal. 1974. 14.50 (ISBN 0-88386-552-1). South Asia Bks.

Social Sciences in Asia: Australia, Fiji, Hong Kong, India, Papua New Guinea, Sri Lanka, Vol. 4. (Reports & Papers in the Social Sciences: No. 42). 98p. 1981. pap. 5.00 (ISBN 92-3-101717-9, U1082, UNESCO). UNIPUB.

Social Sciences in Asia: Bangladesh, Iran, Malaysia, Pakistan, Thailand, Vol. 1. (Reports & Papers in the Social Sciences: No. 32). (Illus.). 54p. 1976. pap. 5.00 (ISBN 92-3-101324-6, U616, UNESCO). UNIPUB.

Social Sciences in Asia: Burma, Mongolia, New Zealand, the Philippines, Singapore, Vol. 3. (Reports & Papers in the Social Sciences: No. 35). 1978. pap. 5.00 (ISBN 92-3-101510-9, U777, UNESCO). UNIPUB.

Social Sciences in Educational Studies: A Selective Guide to the Literature. Ed. by Anthony Hartnett. x, 294p. 1982. text ed. 36.00x (ISBN 0-435-80408-1). Heinemann Ed.

Social Sciences in Historical Study. Thomas C. Cochran et al. LC 54-9680. (SSRC Ser.). 1954. pap. 15.00 (ISBN 0-527-03291-3). Kraus Repr.

Social Sciences in Latin America & the Caribbean: Social Science Needs & Priorities, Vol. 1. (Reports & Papers in the Social Sciences: No. 48). 54p. 1982. pap. 5.00 (ISBN 92-3-101962-7, U1248, UNESCO). UNIPUB.

Social Sciences in Professional Education (India) Agriculture, Engineering & Medical. 1976. 13.00x (ISBN 0-88386-882-2). South Asia Bks.

Social Sciences: In Response to Policy Needs. Ed. by K. J. Ratnam. 175p. (Orig.). 1984. pap. 8.75 (UB152, UB). UNIPUB.

Social Sciences in Secondary Schools see Survey on the Ways in Which States Interpret Their International Obligations.

Social Sciences in Soviet Armed Forces. Ed. by David Jones. 1988. 10.50. Academic Intl.

Social Sciences Index. (Sold on service basis). 1974-83. Vols. 19, 1975-80. 110.00; Vols. 10-16, 1980-87. 110.00. Wilson.

Social Sciences, Problems & Orientations: Selected Studies. (Studies in Behavioral Sciences: No. 4). 1968. text ed. 20.80x (ISBN 90-2796-026-7). Mouton.

Social Sciences since the Second World War. Daniel Bell. LC 80-27957. 104p. 1981. 24.95; pap. text ed. 10.95 (ISBN 0-87855-872-1). Transaction Bks.

Social Sciences: Their Nature & Uses. Ed. by William H. Kruskal. LC 81-16263. xvi, 166p. 1986. lib. bdg. 20.00x (ISBN 0-226-45499-1); pap. 9.95 (ISBN 0-226-45500-9). U of Chicago Pr.

Social Sciences Today. Ed. by Robert M. Hutchins & Mortimer J. Adler. LC 75-4299. (The Great Ideas Anthologies Ser.). (Illus.). 618p. 1976. 21.00x (ISBN 0-405-07171-X). Ayer Co Pubs.

Social-Scientific Criticism of the New Testament. Ed. by John H. Elliott. (Semeia Ser.: No. 35). pap. 14.95 (06 20 35). Scholars Pr GA.

Social Scientist as Innovator. Michael Young. 1984. 31.00 (ISBN 0-89011-593-1). Abt Bks.

Social Scientist As Innovator. Michael Young. (Illus.). 282p. 1984. Repr. of 1983 ed. lib. bdg. 32.75 (ISBN 0-8191-4084-8). U Pr of Amer.

Social Scientist in American Industry: Self-Perception of Role, Motivation, & Career. Matthew Radom. LC 76-125193. 1970. 25.00 (ISBN 0-8135-0665-4). Rutgers U Pr.

Social Scientist Investigates Women of the Ancient World. Henry J. Brun. (Illus.). 152p. (gr. 7-12). 1976. PLB 10.97 (ISBN 0-8239-0361-3). Rosen Group.

Social Scientists & Farm Politics in the Age of Roosevelt. Richard S. Kirkendall. 1982. pap. text ed. 14.95x (ISBN 0-8138-1681-5). Iowa St U Pr.

Social Scientists & Politics in Canada: Between Clerisy & Vanguard. Stephen Brooks & Alain G. Gagnon. 152p. 1988. text ed. 22.95x (ISBN 0-7735-0663-2). McGill-Queens U Pr.

Social Scientists & the Physically Handicapped: An Original Anthology. Ed. by William R. Phillips & Janet Rosenberg. LC 79-6011. (Physically Handicapped in Society Ser.). 1980. lib. bdg. 32.50x (ISBN 0-405-13103-8). Ayer Co Pubs.

Social Scientists in Agricultural Research: Lessons from the Mantaro Valley Project, Peru. Douglas Horton. 67p. 1984. pap. 8.00 (ISBN 0-88936-400-1, IDRC219, IDRC). UNIPUB.

Social Secretary. David G. Phillips. (Illus.). 1972. Repr. of 1905 ed. lib. bdg. 29.00 (ISBN 0-8422-8169-X). Irvington.

Social Secretary. David G. Phillips. LC 74-104542. (Illus.). Repr. of 1905 ed. 16.00 (ISBN 0-8398-1567-0). Irvington.

Social Secretary. David G. Phillips. (Illus.). 1982. pap. text ed. 5.95x (ISBN 0-8290-1160-9). Irvington.

Social Security. 3rd ed. Robert J. Myers. LC 84-82489. (McCann Foundation Bks.). 1076p. 32.95x (ISBN 0-256-03307-2). Irwin.

Social Security. Peter G. Peterson. Date not set. 9.45 (ISBN 0-394-53318-6). Random.

Social Security. Ed. by William Robson & F. M. Leventhal. (English Workers & the Coming of the Welfare State Ser., 1918-1945). 55.00 (ISBN 0-8240-7627-3). Garland Pub.

Social Security: A Critique of Radical Reform Proposals. Ed. by Charles W. Meyer. 178p. 1987. 26.00x (ISBN 0-669-14518-1). Lexington Bks.

Social Security Administration & Information Technology, Special Report. LC 86-600567. (OTA-CIT-311 Ser.). (Illus.). 157p. (Orig.). 1986. pap. 8.00 (ISBN 0-318-21559-4, S/N 052-003-01053-4). USGPO.

Social Services Management Trainee. Jack Rudman. (Career Examination Ser.: C-1993). (Cloth bdg. avail. on request). pap. 14.00 (ISBN 0-8373-1993-5). Natl Learning.

Social Services Medical Assistance Specialist. Jack Rudman. (Career Examination Ser.: C-2431). (Cloth bdg. avail. on request). pap. 16.00 (ISBN 0-8373-2431-9). Natl Learning.

Social Services Program Specialist. Jack Rudman. (Career Examination Ser.: C-2235). (Cloth bdg. avail. on request). pap. 16.00 (ISBN 0-8373-2235-9). Natl Learning.

Social Services Systems Manager. Jack Rudman. (Career Examination Ser.: C-2992). (Cloth bdg. avail. on request). 1988. pap. 16.00 (ISBN 0-8373-2992-2). Natl Learning.

Social Services: What Happens to the Clients? Margo Koss et al. 150p. 1979. pap. 7.95x (ISBN 0-87766-272-X, 28400). Urban Inst.

Social Setting of Christian Conversion in South India: The Impact of the Wesleyan Methodists Missionaries. Sudararaj Manickam. 306p. (Orig.). 1977. pap. 34.00x (ISBN 3-515-02639-8, Pub by Franz Steiner). Coronet Bks.

Social Setting of Pauline Christianity: Essays on Corinth. Gerd Theissen. Tr. by John H. Schutz. LC 81-43087. 1982. pap. 8.95 (ISBN 0-8006-2095-X). Fortress.

Social Setting, Stigma & Communicative Competence: Explorations of the Conversational Interactions of Retarded Adults. Sharon Sabsay et al. LC 86-8240. (Pragmatics & Beyond Ser.: VI-6). vi, 137p. (Orig.). 1985. pap. 30.00x (ISBN 0-915027-92-5). Benjamins North Am.

Social Shaping of Science: Institutions, Ideology, & Careers in Science. Roger G. Krohn. LC 75-90792. (Contributions in Sociology: No. 4). (Illus.). 1971. lib. bdg. 35.00 (ISBN 0-8371-1852-2, KRS/). Greenwood.

Social Shaping of Technology. Ed. by Donald Mackenzie & Judy Wajcman. 336p. 1985. 78.00x (ISBN 0-335-15027-6, Open Univ Pr); pap. 29.00x (ISBN 0-335-15026-8). Taylor & Francis.

Social Side of the Reformation in Germany, 3 vols. E. Belfort Bax. Incl. Vol. 1. German Society at the Close of the Middle Ages. LC 67-25997. 276p. 1967. Repr. of 1894 ed. lib. bdg. 29.50x (ISBN 0-678-00312-2); Vol. 2. Peasants' War in Germany 1525-1526. LC 68-57371. 367p. 1968. Repr. of 1899 ed. lib. bdg. 37.50x (ISBN 0-678-00445-5); Vol. 3. Rise & Fall of the Anabaptists. LC 75-101125. 407p. 1970. Repr. of 1903 ed. lib. bdg. 45.00x (ISBN 0-678-00593-1). lib. bdg. 100.00x set (ISBN 0-678-00772-1). Kelley.

Social Significance of Modern Drama. Emma Goldman. 304p. (Orig.). 1987. 18.95 (ISBN 0-936839-62-7); pap. 8.95 (ISBN 0-936839-61-9). Applause Theatre Bk Pubs.

Social Significance of Our Institutions. Henry James, Sr. 47p. 1964. pap. 4.50 (ISBN 0-910120-05-6). Americanist.

Social Significance of Speech. Ed. by S. Platt & H. Platt. (North-Holland Linguistic Ser.: Vol. 23). 194p. 1975. pap. 50.00 (ISBN 0-444-10972-2, North-Holland). Elsevier.

Social Significance of Telematics: An Essay on the Information Society. Lars Qvortrup. Tr. by Philip Edmonds. LC 85-7493. (P&B Ser.: Vol. V, No. 7). xviii, 228p. (Orig.). 1984. pap. 48.00x (ISBN 0-915027-04-6). Benjamins North Am.

Social Significance of the Duel in Seventeenth Century Drama. Norman A. Bennetton. LC 76-137046. 158p. Repr. of 1938 ed. cancelled. Greenwood.

Social Significance of the Duel in Seventh-Century French Drama. Norman A. Bennetton. 1973. Repr. of 1938 ed. 14.00 (ISBN 0-384-03903-0). Johnson Repr.

Social Significance of the Modern Drama. Emma Goldman. 69.95 (ISBN 0-8490-1067-5). Gordon Pr.

Social Silhouettes: Being the Impressions of Mr. Mark Manhattan. fascimile ed. Edgar Fawcett. LC 75-1846. (Leisure Class in America Ser.). 1975. Repr. of 1885 ed. 22.00x (ISBN 0-405-06913-8). Ayer Co Pubs.

Social Situations. M. Argyle et al. (Illus.). 450p. 1981. 59.50 (ISBN 0-521-23260-0); pap. 21.95 (ISBN 0-521-29881-4). Cambridge U Pr.

Social Skills, Vol. 4. W. T. Singleton. (Study of Real Skills). 300p. 1983. lib. bdg. 36.00 (ISBN 0-85200-092-8, Pub. by MTP Pr England). Kluwer Academic.

Social Skills & Personal Problem Solving: A Handbook of Methods. Philip Priestley et al. (Illus.). 1979. 28.00x (ISBN 0-422-76540-6, NO.2394, Pub. by Tavistock England); pap. 15.95x (ISBN 0-422-76550-3, NO.3797). Routledge Chapman & Hall.

Social Skills Assessment & Training with Children: An Empirically Based Handbook. Larry Michelson et al. 276p. 1983. 42.50x (ISBN 0-306-41234-9, Plenum Pr). Plenum Pub.

Social Skills Basis of Psychopathology: Alternatives to Abnormal Psychology. E. Lakin Phillips. (Current Issues in Behavioral Psychology Ser.). 304p. 1979. 42.50 (ISBN 0-8089-1126-0, 793285). Grune.

Social Skills for Nursing Practice. Peter French. (Illus.). 272p. 1983. pap. 17.50 (ISBN 0-7099-1009-6, Pub. by Croom Helm Ltd). Routledge Chapman & Hall.

Social Skills for Severely Retarded Adults: An Inventory & Training Program. Sandra E. McClennen et al. LC 80-51546. 284p. 1980. 3-ring binder 49.95 (ISBN 0-87822-220-0, 2200). Res Press.

Social Skills in Interpersonal Communication. Owen Hargie et al. 290p. 1987. pap. text ed. 19.95 (ISBN 0-914797-41-7, Co-Pub. by Croom Helm Ltd). Brookline Bks.

Social Skills in Prison & the Community: Problem-Solving for Offenders. Philip Priestley et al. 224p. (Orig.). 1984. pap. 14.95x (ISBN 0-7100-9272-5). Routledge Chapman & Hall.

Social Skills in the Classroom. Thomas M. Stephens. 604p. 1982. pap. text ed. 21.50 (ISBN 0-936326-03-4). Cedars Pr.

Social Skills in the Classroom. rev. ed. Thomas M. Stephens. LC 77-13946. 692p. 1984. 21.50 (ISBN 0-936326-04-2). Cedars Pr.

Social Skills Training. Ed. by James Curran & Peter M. Monti. LC 85-32083. 447p. 1986. pap. 16.50x (ISBN 0-8147-1402-1). NYU Pr.

Social Skills Training: A Practical Guide for Interventions. Jeffrey A. Kelly. 272p. 1982. text ed. 21.95 (ISBN 0-8261-3580-3). Springer Pub.

Social Skills Training: A Practical Handbook for Assessment & Treatment. Ed. by James P. Curran & Peter Monti. LC 81-6374. 447p. 1982. 45.00 (ISBN 0-89862-610-2, 2610). Guilford Pr.

Social Skills Training: A Special Issue of Behavioral Counseling Quarterly. Ed. by Craig T. Twentyman. LC 81-84339. 104p. 1982. pap. 12.95 (ISBN 0-89885-125-4). Human Sci Pr.

Social Skills Training & Psychiatric Nursing. Owen Hargie & Patrick J. McCartan. 288p. (Orig.). 1986. pap. 19.00 (ISBN 0-7099-3749-0, Pub. by Croom Helm Ltd). Routledge Chapman & Hall.

Social Skills Training for Children & Youth. Ed. by Craig W. LeCroy. LC 83-228. (Child & Youth Services Ser.: Vol. 5, No. 3 & 4). 152p. 1983. text ed. 29.95 (ISBN 0-86656-184-6, B184). Haworth Pr.

Social Skills Training Manual: Assessment, Programme Design & Management. Jill Wilkinson & Sandra Canter. LC 81-12957. 148p. 1982. (Pub. by Wiley-Interscience); pap. 21.95x (ISBN 0-471-10067-6). Wiley.

Social Skills Training Treatment for Depression. R. E. Becker et al. 128p. 1987. text ed. 22.50 (ISBN 0-08-032818-0, Pub. by PBI); pap. text ed. 12.95 (ISBN 0-08-032817-2, Pub. by PBI). Pergamon.

Social Software of Accounting & Information Systems. Norman B. Macintosh. LC 84-10447. 294p. 1985. 34.95 (ISBN 0-471-90543-7). Wiley.

Social Solidarity among the Japanese in Seattle. S. Frank Miyamoto. LC 84-40328. (Illus.). 100p. 1984. pap. text ed. 7.95 (ISBN 0-295-96151-1). U of Wash Pr.

Social Sources of Adjustment to Blindness. Irving F. Lukoff & Martin Whiteman. LC 73-84034. (Research Ser.: No. 21). 301p. 1970. pap. 7.00 (ISBN 0-89128-060-X, PPR060). Am Foun Blind.

Social Sources of Delinquency: An Appraisal of Analytic Models. Ruth R. Kornhauser. LC 78-3776. (Illus.). 1978. lib. bdg. 22.00x (ISBN 0-226-45113-5). U of Chicago Pr.

Social Sources of Delinquency: An Appraisal of Analytic Models. Ruth R. Kornhauser. LC 78-3776. x, 278p. 1984. pap. 9.00x (ISBN 0-226-45114-3). U of Chicago Pr.

Social Sources of Denominationalism. Richard H. Niebuhr. 1984. 20.00 (ISBN 0-8446-6150-3). Peter Smith.

Social Space for Domestic Animals. Ed. by R. Zayan. (Current Topics in Veterinary Medicine & Animal Science). 1986. lib. bdg. 61.50 (ISBN 0-89838-773-6, Pub. by Martinus Nijhoff Netherlands). Kluwer Academic.

Social Spirit in America. Charles R. Henderson. LC 77-39378. (Select Bibliographies Reprint Ser.). 1972. Repr. of 1897 ed. 18.50 (ISBN 0-8369-9911-8). Ayer Co Pubs.

Social Statics. Herbert Spencer. LC 69-20304. 1969. Repr. of 1851 ed. 39.50x (ISBN 0-678-00484-6). Kelley.

Social Statics. Herbert Spencer. 430p. 1970. Repr. of 1850 ed. 6.00 (ISBN 0-911312-33-1). Schalkenbach.

Social Statics & Social Dynamics. August Comte. (Illus.). 141p. 1986. Repr. 137.45 (ISBN 0-89901-252-3). Found Class Reprints.

Social Statics & Social Dynamics: The Theory of Order & the Theory of Progress. August Comte. (Most Meaningful Classics in World Culture Ser.). (Illus.). 101p. 1983. Repr. of 1899 ed. 137.50 (ISBN 0-89901-103-9). Found Class Reprints.

Social Statics & Social Dynamics: The Theory of Order & the Theory of Progress. August Comte. (Most Meaningful Classics in World Culture Ser.). (Illus.). 123p. 1983. 117.45 (ISBN 0-89266-425-8). Am Classical Coll Pr.

Social Statics, or, the Conditions Essential to Human Happiness Specified, & the First of Them Adopted. Herbert Spencer. 482p. Repr. of 1851 ed. text ed. 49.68x (ISBN 0-576-29167-6, Pub. by Gregg Intl Pubs England). Gregg Intl.

Social Statistics. 2nd ed. Hubert M. Blalock. 1979. text ed. 40.95 (ISBN 0-07-005752-4). McGraw.

Social Statistics & the City: Report of a Conference Held in Washington, D. C., June 22-23, 1967. Ed. by David M. Heer. LC 68-5964. 1968. pap. 3.75x (ISBN 0-674-81465-7). Harvard U Pr.

Social Statistics: Health & Education. Ed. by Ashish Bose et al. 375p. 1982. text ed. 40.00x (ISBN 0-7069-1083-4, Pub. by Vikas India). Advent NY.

Social Statistics in Use. Philip M. Hauser. LC 74-24747. 400p. 1975. 39.95x (ISBN 0-87154-375-3). Russell Sage.

Social Status & Power in Java. L. H. Palmier. (London School of Economics Monographs on Social Anthropology: No. 20). 174p. 1969. pap. 16.95 (ISBN 0-485-19620-4, Pub. by Athlone Pr UK). Humanities.

Social Status & Psychological Disorder: A Casual Inquiry. Bruce P. Dohrenwend & Barbara S. Dohrenwend. LC 72-88310. (Personality Processes Ser). Repr. of 1969 ed. 42.40 (ISBN 0-8357-9978-6, 2012570). Bks Demand UMI.

Social Status in the City. Richard P. Coleman & Bernice L. Neugarten. LC 70-132820. (Jossey-Bass Behavioral Science Ser.). Repr. of 1971 ed. 64.30 (ISBN 0-8357-9348-6, 2013782). Bks Demand UMI.

Social Status of Hindu Women in Northern India: 1206-1707 A. D. Kamala Gupta. 328p. 1987. text ed. 45.00x (ISBN 81-210-0179-X, Pub. by Inter India Pubns N. Delhi). Apt Bks.

Social Status of the Professional Musician from the Middle Ages to the 19th Century. Ed. by Walter Salmen. Tr. by Herbert Kaufman & Barbara Reisner. LC 82-11262. (Sociology of Music Ser.: No. 1). Orig. Title: Sozialstatus des Berufsmusikers vom 17. bis 19. Jahrhundert. (Illus.). 280p. 1983. lib. bdg. 48.00 (ISBN 0-918728-16-9). Pendragon NY.

Social Stigma of Occupations. K. C. Saunders. 244p. 1981. text ed. 35.00 (ISBN 0-566-00334-1). Gower Pub Co.

Social Stigma: The Psychology of Marked Relationships. Edward E. Jones. LC 83-25352. (Illus.). 347p. 1984. 23.95 (ISBN 0-7167-1591-0); pap. 14.95 (ISBN 0-7167-1592-9). W H Freeman.

Social Strategy & Corporate Structure. Chamberlin. 192p. 1982. text ed. 24.95 (ISBN 0-02-905810-4). Free Pr.

Social Stratification: An Annotated Bibliography. LC 86-32024. (Library of Sociology: Vol. 393). 1987. lib. bdg. 55.00 (ISBN 0-8240-9805-6). Garland Pub.

Social Stratification & Career Mobility. Ed. by Walter Mueller & Karl U. Mayer. LC 72-88184. (Sociology Ser.). (Illus.). 1974. text ed. 20.00x (ISBN 90-2797-248-6). Mouton.

Social Stratification & Development in the Mediterranean Basin. Ed. by Mubeccal B. Kiray. LC 72-94477. (Publications of the Institute of Social Studies, Paperback Ser.: No. 9). (Illus.). 288p. (Orig., Eng. & Fr.). 1973. pap. text ed. 17.20x (ISBN 90-2792-406-6). Mouton.

Social Stratification & Inequality: Class Conflict in the United States. Harold R. Kerbo. (Illus.). 576p. 1983. text ed. 32.95 (ISBN 0-07-034176-1). McGraw.

Social Stratification & Mobility in the U. S. S. R. Ed. by Murray Yanowitch & Wesley A. Fisher. LC 72-77202. (Illus.). 402p. 1973. text ed. 30.00 (ISBN 0-87332-008-5). M E Sharpe.

Social Stratification & Occupations. Alexander Stewart et al. Ed. by Ken Prandy & R. M. Blackburn. LC 80-16282. 320p. 1980. 42.50 (ISBN 0-8419-0629-7); pap. 24.50 (ISBN 0-8419-0630-0). Holmes & Meier.

Social Stratification & the Diffusion of Innovations Among the Sukuma of Tanzania. Gertrud Schanne-Raab. (European University Studies: Series 22, Sociology: Vol. 23). 272p. 1977. 29.35 (ISBN 3-261-02134-9). P Lang Pubs.

Social Stratification: Canada. J. Curtis & W. Scott. 1972. write for info. (ISBN 0-13-818625-1). P-H.

Social Stratification: Canada. 2nd ed. J. Curtis & W. Scott. 1979. pap. 16.00 (ISBN 0-13-818633-2). P-H.

Social Stratification in Africa. Arthur Tuden & Leonard Plotnicov. LC 78-91223. 1970. 19.95 (ISBN 0-02-932780-6). Free Pr.

Social Stratification in India. Ed. by K. L. Sharma. 343p. 1986. 34.00x (ISBN 81-85054-15-0, Pub. by Manohor India). South Asia Bks.

Social Stratification in Poland: Eight Empirical Studies. Ed. by Kazimierz M. Slomczynski & Tadeusz K. Krauz. Tr. by Ray Taras from Pol. 371p. 1986. 35.00 (ISBN 0-87332-361-0). M E Sharpe.

Social Stratification in Polynesia. Marshall D. Sahlins. LC 84-45526. (American Ethnological Society Monographs: No. 29). 1988. Repr. of 1958 ed. 34.50 (ISBN 0-404-62928-8). AMS Pr.

Social Stratification in Science. Jonathan R. Cole & Stephen Cole. LC 73-78166. 1973. 20.00x (ISBN 0-226-11338-8); pap. 10.00x (ISBN 0-226-11339-6). U of Chicago Pr.

Social Stratification in the Middle East & North Africa. Ali Banuaziai & Prouchestia Goodarzi. 266p. 1984. 36.00x (ISBN 0-7201-1711-9). Mansell.

Social Stratification: The Forms & Functions of Inequality. 2nd ed. Melvin M. Tumin. (Illus.). 192p. 1985. pap. text ed. write for info. (ISBN 0-13-818659-6). P-H.

Social Stress & Chronic Illness: Mortality Patterns in Industrial Society. David L. Dodge & Walter T. Martin. LC 79-122051. 1970. 19.95x (ISBN 0-268-00435-8). U of Notre Dame Pr.

Social Stress & Family Development. Ed. by David M. Klein & Joan Aldous. 270p. 1988. lib. bdg. 35.00 (ISBN 0-89862-079-1, 2079). Guilford Pr.

Social Stress & the Family: Advances & Developments in Family Stress Theory & Research. Ed. by Hamilton I. McCubbin et al. LC 83-190. (Marriage & Family Review Ser.: Vol. 6, No. 1 & 2). 231p. 1983. text ed. 34.95 (ISBN 0-86656-163-3, B163); pap. text ed. 14.95 (ISBN 0-86656-224-9). Haworth Pr.

Social Stress in the United States: Links to Regional Patterns in Crime & Illness. Arnold S. Linsky & Murray A. Straus. 174p. 1986. 26.00 (ISBN 0-86569-149-5). Auburn Hse.

Social Structure. George P. Murdock. 1965. pap. text ed. 12.95 (ISBN 0-02-922290-7). Free Pr.

Social Structure & Aging: Age Structuring in Comparative Perspective. Ed. by D. Kertzer & K. W. Schaie. 296p. Date not set. 36.00t (ISBN 0-8058-0202-9). L Erlbaum Assocs.

Social Structure & Behavior: Essays in Honor of William Hamilton Sewell. Ed. by Robert Hauser et al. LC 82-3889. (Studies in Population). 1982. 33.00 (ISBN 0-12-333060-2). Acad Pr.

Social Structure & Change among the Tribals: A Study among the Uralies of Idukki District in Kerala. Jacob J. Kattakayam. (Illus.). 192p. 1983. text ed. 27.50x (ISBN 0-86590-128-7). Apt Bks.

Social Structure & Culture Changes in a Lebanese Village. John Gulick. 19.00 (ISBN 0-384-20440-6). Johnson Repr.

Social Structure & Ecology of Elephant-Shrews. G. B. Rathbun. (Advances in Ethology Ser.: Vol. 20). (Illus.). 84p. (Orig.). 1979. pap. text ed. 29.50 (ISBN 3-489-60836-4). Parey Sci Pubs.

Social Structure & Mobility in Economic Development. Ed. by Neil J. Smelser & Seymour M. Lipset. 399p. 1983. Repr. of 1966 ed. text ed. cancelled (ISBN 0-8290-0910-8). Irvington.

Social Structure & Network Analysis. Peter V. Marsden & Nan Lin. (Sage Focus Editions: Vol. 57). (Illus.). 300p. 1982. pap. 16.95 (ISBN 0-8039-1889-5). Sage.

Social Structure & Personality. Talcott Parsons. LC 64-11218. 1964. 19.95 (ISBN 0-02-924850-7); pap. 3.45 (ISBN 0-02-924840-X). Free Pr.

Social Structure & Personality Development: The Individual As a Productive Processor of Reality. Klaus Hurrelmann. (Illus.). 176p. Date not set. price not set (ISBN 0-521-35474-9); pap. price not set (ISBN 0-521-35747-0). Cambridge U Pr.

Social Structure & Social Relations. Ed. by Norman E. Whitten, Jr. (American Ethnologist Ser.: Vol. 11, No. 4). 1984. 12.50 (ISBN 0-317-66329-1). Am Anthro Assn.

Social Structure & the German Reformation. Norman Birnbaum. Ed. by Harriet Zuckerman & Robert K. Merton. LC 79-8976. (Dissertation on Sociology Ser.). 1980. lib. bdg. 40.00x (ISBN 0-405-12952-1). Ayer Co Pubs.

Social Structure in Divided Germany: A Contribution to the Comparative Analysis of Social Systems. Jaroslav Krejci. LC 76-1338. 192p. 1976. 25.00 (ISBN 0-312-73535-9). St Martin.

Social Structure in Farm Animals. G. J. Syme & L. A. Syme. LC 78-26088. (Developments in Animal & Veterinary Sciences Ser.: Vol. 4). 200p. 1979. 73.75 (ISBN 0-444-41769-9). Elsevier.

Social Structure in Southeast Asia. Ed. by George P. Murdock. pap. 19.00 (ISBN 0-384-40650-5). Johnson Repr.

Social Structure of a Cape Coloured Reserve. W. Peter Carstens. LC 75-3985. (Illus.). 264p. 1975. Repr. of 1966 ed. lib. bdg. 35.00x (ISBN 0-8371-7431-7, CACR). Greenwood.

Social Structure of Attention. Ed. by Michael R. Chance & Ray R. Larsen. LC 76-15675. (Illus.). 1976. pap. 87.30 (ISBN 0-317-08030-X, 2017801). Bks Demand UMI.

Social Structure of Modern Britain. 3rd ed. E. A. Johns. 1979. pap. text ed. 16.00 (ISBN 0-08-023342-2). Pergamon.

Social Structure of Revolutionary America. Jackson T. Main. LC 65-17146. pap. 85.00 (ISBN 0-317-08695-2, 2011969). Bks Demand UMI.

Social Structure of the U. S. S. R. Recent Soviet Studies. Ed. by Murray Yanowitch. Tr. by Liv Tudge from Rus. 288p. 1986. 40.00 (ISBN 0-87332-362-9). M E Sharpe.

Social Structures: A Network Approach. Ed. by Barry Wellman & S. D. Berkowitz. (Structural Analysis in the Social Sciences Ser.: No. 2). (Illus.). 528p. 1988. 65.00 (ISBN 0-521-24441-2); pap. 22.95 (ISBN 0-521-28687-5). Cambridge U Pr.

Social Structures & Aging: Psychological Processes. K. Warner Schaie & Carmi Schooler. (Social Structure & Aging Ser.). 296p. 1988. 34.95 (ISBN 0-8058-0093-X). L Erlbaum Assocs.

Social Structures & Alignments: A Study of Rural India. Hetu K. Jha. 1985. 11.00x (ISBN 0-8364-1410-1, Pub. by Usha). South Asia Bks.

Social Thought from Lore to Science, 3 Vols. 3rd ed. Howard Becker & Harry E. Barnes. 16.50 ea. (ISBN 0-8446-1620-6). Peter Smith.
Social Thought in America: The Revolt Against Formalism. Morton White. 1976. pap. 6.95 (ISBN 0-19-519837-9). Oxford U Pr.
Social Thought in Tsarist Russia: The Quest for a General Science of Society, Eighteen Sixty-One to Nineteen Seventeen. Alexander Vucinich. LC 75-12229. 304p. 1976. 24.00x (ISBN 0-226-86624-6). U of Chicago Pr.
Social Thought of Bernard Mandeville: Virtue & Commerce in Early Eighteenth Century England. Thomas A. Horne. LC 77-13573. 1978. 22.50x (ISBN 0-231-04274-4). Columbia U Pr.
Social Thought of J. J. Rousseau. Robert Wokler. Ed. by Maurice Cranston. (Political Theory & Political Philosophy Ser.). 525p. 1987. lib. bdg. 80.00 (ISBN 0-8240-0832-4). Garland Pub.
Social Thought of Jane Addams. Jane Addams. Ed. by Christopher Lasch. LC 82-7135. 300p. 1982. pap. text ed. 15.95x (ISBN 0-8290-0338-X). Irvington.
Social Thought of John Twenty-Third: Mater et Magistra. Jean Y. Calvez. Tr. by George J. McKenzie. LC 75-40992. 1977. Repr. of 1965 ed. lib. bdg. 35.00x (ISBN 0-8371-8711-7, CASCJ). Greenwood.
Social Thought of Saint Bonaventure: A Study in Social Philosophy. Matthew M. DeBenedictis. LC 73-138108. 276p. 1972. Repr. of 1946 ed. lib. bdg. 35.00x (ISBN 0-8371-5684-X, DESB). Greenwood.
Social Thought of the Ancient Civilizations. Joyce O. Hertzler. 250.00 (ISBN 0-87968-383-X). Gordon Pr.
Social Thought of Thomas Merton. David W. Givey. 1983. 9.50 (ISBN 0-8199-0859-2). Franciscan Herald.
Social Thought of W. E. B. Du Bois. Joseph P. De Marco. LC 83-6547. 203p. (Orig.). 1983. lib. bdg. 27.50 (ISBN 0-8191-3235-7); pap. text ed. 13.25 (ISBN 0-8191-3236-5). U Pr of Amer.
Social Thought on Alcoholism. Ed. by Thomas D. Watts. LC 85-23921. 170p. 1986. text ed. 11.50 (ISBN 0-89874-925-5); pap. 9.50. Krieger.
Social Transformation in Rural India. T. K. Oommen. 324p. 1984. text ed. 35.00x (ISBN 0-7069-2476-2, Pub. by Vikas India). Advent NY.
Social Transformation of American Medicine. Paul Starr. LC 81-68412. 514p. 1984. pap. 13.95 (ISBN 0-465-07935-0, CN 5117). Basic.
Social Transformations of the Victorian Age. Thomas H. Escott. LC 73-12848. 1897. lib. bdg. 45.00 (ISBN 0-8414-3908-7). Folcroft.
Social Traps. John Cross & Mel Guyer. (Illus.). 1980. pap. 8.95 (ISBN 0-472-06315-4). U of Mich Pr.
Social Treatment: An Approach to Interpersonal Helping. James K. Whittaker. LC 71-172856. 1974. lib. bdg. 32.95x (ISBN 0-202-36011-3); pap. text ed. 15.95x (ISBN 0-202-36012-1). Aldine de Gruyter.
Social Treatment in Probation & Delinquency. 2nd ed. Pauline V. Young. LC 69-14955. (Criminology, Law Enforcement, & Social Problems Ser.: No. 47). 1969. Repr. of 1952 ed. 24.00x (ISBN 0-87585-047-2). Patterson Smith.
Social Trend. Edward A. Ross. LC 72-117831. (Essay Index Reprint Ser). 1922. 18.00 (ISBN 0-8369-1680-8). Ayer Co Pubs.
Social Trends in the Soviet Union from 1950. Michael Ryan & Richard Prentice. LC 86-33919. 120p. 1987. 39.95 (ISBN 0-312-00543-1). St Martin.
Social Triumph of the Ancient Church. facsimile ed. Shirley J. Case. LC 76-164596. (Select Bibliographies Reprint Ser). Repr. of 1933 ed. 18.00 (ISBN 0-8369-5880-2). Ayer Co Pubs.
Social Typifications & the Elusive Other: Alfred Schutz's Phenomenology & the Sociology of Knowledge. Michael D. Barber. LC 86-73241. 144p. 1988. 26.50x (ISBN 0-8387-5123-7). Bucknell U Pr.
Social Understanding Through Spiritual Scientific Knowledge. 20p. 1982. pap. 2.95 (ISBN 0-88010-075-3). Anthroposophic.
Social Understandings of the Superintendent of Schools. Frederick H. Bair. LC 78-176531. (Columbia University. Teachers College. Contributions to Education: No. 625). Repr. of 1934 ed. 22.50 (ISBN 0-404-55625-6). AMS Pr.
Social Unrest in the Late Middle Ages: Papers of the Fifteenth Annual Conference of the Center for Medieval & Early Renaissance Studies. Ed. by F. X. Newman. LC 85-28420. (Medieval & Renaissance Texts & Studies: Vol. 39). (Illus.). 160p. 1986. 16.00 (ISBN 0-86698-071-7). Medieval & Renaissance NY.
Social Usage. 2nd ed. Anne R. Free. (Illus.). 1969. pap. text ed. write for info. (ISBN 0-13-819607-9). P-H.
Social Use of Information: Ownership & Access. Andrew E. Wessel. LC 76-18211. (Information Sciences Ser.). (Illus.). pap. 66.00 (ISBN 0-317-10572-8, 2022496). Bks Demand UMI.
Social Use of Metaphor: Essays on the Anthropology of Rhetoric. Ed. by J. David Sapir & J. Christopher Crocker. LC 76-53200. 1977. 22.95x (ISBN 0-8122-7725-2). U of Pa Pr.
Social Uses of Social Science. Robert Redfield. Ed. by Margaret P. Redfield. (Papers Ser: Vol. 2). 1963. 12.00x (ISBN 0-226-70636-2). U of Chicago Pr.
Social Value: A Study in Economic Theory Critical & Constructive. Benjamin M. Anderson, Jr. LC 65-26357. 1966. Repr. of 1911 ed. 25.00x (ISBN 0-678-00177-4). Kelley.
Social Value of Property According to St. Thomas Aquinas: A Study in Social Philosophy. William J. McDonald. 59.95 (ISBN 0-8490-1068-3). Gordon Pr.
Social Values & Poetic Acts: The Historical Judgment of Literary Work. Jerome J. McGann. LC 87-14649. 296p. 1988. 27.50x (ISBN 0-674-81495-9). Harvard U Pr.
Social Values & Public Policy. Ed. by William Dunn. (Orig.). 1981. pap. 8.00 (ISBN 0-918592-44-5). Policy Studies.
Social Values & Social Change: Adaptations to Life in America. Ed. by Lynn R. Kahle. LC 83-16074. 346p. 1983. 35.00 (ISBN 0-275-91018-0, C1018). Praeger.
Social Values & the Development of Technology. 17p. 1982. pap. 5.00 (ISBN 92-808-0304-2, TUNU186, UNU). UNIPUB.
Social Values: Index of Modern Information with Bibliography. Duane C. Umbaugh. LC 88-47791. 150p. (Orig.). 1988. 34.50 (ISBN 0-88164-894-9); pap. 26.50 (ISBN 0-88164-895-7). ABBE Pubs Assn.
Social Vision of William Blake. Michael Ferber. LC 85-522. 288p. 1985. text ed. 33.00x (ISBN 0-691-08382-7). Princeton U Pr.
Social Wasps of the Americas Excluding the Vespinae. O. W. Richards. (Illus.). 1978. 99.00x (ISBN 0-565-00785-8, Pub. by Brit Mus Nat Hist). Sabbot-Natural Hist Bks.
Social Web: An Introduction to Sociology. 5th ed. John A. Perry & Erna K. Perry. 405p. 1987. pap. text ed. 24.50 (ISBN 0-06-045123-8, HarpC). Harrow.
Social Welfare. Pathak Shankar. 1981. 15.00x (ISBN 0-8364-0717-2, Pub. by Macmillan India). South Asia Bks.
Social Welfare: A Response to a Human Need. Louise Johnson & Charles Schwartz. 416p. 1988. text ed. 28.50 (ISBN 0-205-10614-5). Allyn.
Social Welfare Abroad: Comparative Data on the Social Insurance & Public Assistance Programs of Selected Industrialized Democracies. Bette K. Fishbein. LC 75-9028. (Illus.). 35p. 1975. pap. 3.00 (ISBN 0-915312-01-8). Inst Socioecon.
Social Welfare Administration: Managing Social Programs in a Developmental Context. Rino J. Patti. (Illus.). 272p. 1983. 28.00 (ISBN 0-13-819458-0). P-H.
Social Welfare & Human Rights. International Council on Social Welfare Staff. LC 31-3460. 398p. 1969. 25.00x (ISBN 0-231-08621-0). Columbia U Pr.
Social Welfare & Social Development. Eugen Pusic. LC 79-189707. (Institute for Social Studies, Paperback Ser.: No. 5). (Illus.). 251p. (Orig.). 1972. pap. text ed. 10.00x (ISBN 90-2791-969-0). Mouton.
Social Welfare & Social Justice. David P. Beverly & Edward A. McSweeney. 208p. 1987. pap. text ed. write for info. (ISBN 0-13-819632-X). P-H.
Social Welfare Examiner. Jack Rudman. (Career Examination Ser.: C-2132). (Cloth bdg. avail. on request). 1988. pap. 12.00 (ISBN 0-8373-2132-8). Natl Learning.
Social Welfare Examiner (Spanish Speaking) Jack Rudman. (Career Examination Ser.: C-2136). (Cloth bdg. avail. on request). 1988. pap. 14.00 (ISBN 0-8373-2136-0). Natl Learning.
Social Welfare for Rural Development: A Case Study. Rash B. Prasad Singh. xix, 254p. 1986. text ed. 37.50x (ISBN 81-210-0041-6, Pub. by Inter India Pubns N Delhi). Apt Bks.
Social Welfare Forum, 1982-1983. National Conference on Social Welfare. 266p. 37.50 (ISBN 0-933597-00-2); pap. 14.95 (ISBN 0-933597-01-0). Natl Conf Soc Welfare.
Social Welfare, Health & Family Planning in India. Pathak Shankar. 1979. 15.00x (ISBN 0-8364-0348-7). South Asia Bks.
Social Welfare: Help or Hindrance. Ed. by Carol Foster et al. (Information Aids Ser.). 72p. 1986. pap. 16.95 (ISBN 0-936474-63-7). Info Plus TX.
Social Welfare in America: An Annotated Bibliography. Ed. by Walter I. Trattner & W. Andrew Achenbaum. LC 83-10855. xxxiii, 324p. 1983. lib. bdg. 36.95 (ISBN 0-313-23002-1, TSW/). Greenwood.
Social Welfare in Asia. Ed. by John Dixon & Hyung S. Kim. LC 85-21279. 432p. 1985. 38.50 (ISBN 0-7099-0853-9, Pub. by Croom Helm Ltd). Routledge Chapman & Hall.
Social Welfare in Britain, Eighteen Eighty-Five to Nineteen Eighty-Five. Ed. by Rex Pope et al. 192p. (Orig.). 1986. 29.00 (ISBN 0-7099-4001-7, Pub. by Croom Helm Ltd); pap. 13.50 (ISBN 0-7099-4035-1). Routledge Chapman & Hall.
Social Welfare in Denmark. Ernst Marcussen et al. Tr. by Geoffrey French from Danish. Ed. by Ritt Bjerregaard. (Danish Information Handbooks: 4th). (Illus.). 192p. 1980. pap. text ed. 10.95x (ISBN 87-7429-039-8, Pub. by Det Danske Selskab Denmark). Nordic Bks.
Social Welfare in Developed Market Countries. John Dixon & Robert Scheurell. (Comparative Social Welfare Ser.). 320p. 1988. lib. bdg. 57.50 (ISBN 0-415-00532-9). Routledge Chapman & Hall.
Social Welfare in Germany & Britain. Gerhard Ritter. Tr. by Kim Traynor from Ger. LC 85-23030. 208p. 1986. 33.95 (ISBN 0-907582-49-4, Pub. by Berg Pubs). St Martin.
Social Welfare in Society. George T. Martin & Mayer N. Zald. LC 81-3837. (Illus.). 576p. 1981. 45.00x (ISBN 0-231-04922-6); pap. 20.00x (ISBN 0-231-04923-4). Columbia U Pr.
Social Welfare in the Middle East. Ed. by John Dixon. 256p. 1986. 43.00 (ISBN 0-7099-4502-7, Pub. by Croom Helm UK). Routledge Chapman & Hall.
Social Welfare in the Nineteen Eighties & Beyond. Eveline M Burns. LC 77-17818. 20p. 1978. pap. 4.00x (ISBN 0-87772-251-X). UCB IGS.
Social Welfare in the South: From Colonial Times to World War I. Elizabeth Wisner. LC 78-123206. viii, 154p. 1970. 20.00 (ISBN 0-8071-0505-8). La State U Pr.
Social Welfare in the Soviet Union. Bernice Q. Madison. 1968. 30.00x (ISBN 0-8047-0654-9). Stanford U Pr.
Social Welfare in Western Society. Gerald Handel. 357p. 1982. text ed. write for info (ISBN 0-394-32213-4, RanC). Random.
Social Welfare Institution: An Introduction. 4th ed. Ronald C. Federico. 1984. text ed. 26.00 (ISBN 0-669-06748-2); instr's manual 2.00 (ISBN 0-669-06749-0). Heath.
Social Welfare Law. David Pearl & Kevin Gray. 308p. 1981. 29.95 (ISBN 0-85664-644-X, Pub. by Croom Helm Ltd); pap. 14.75 (ISBN 0-7099-2004-0). Routledge Chapman & Hall.
Social Welfare of the Aging, Proceedings, Vol. 2. International Association Of Gerontology - 5th Congress. Ed. by Jerome Kaplan & G. J. Aldridge. (Aging Around the World Ser.). 1962. 36.00 (ISBN 0-231-08950-3). Columbia U Pr.
Social Welfare or Social Control? Some Historical Reflections on "Regulating the Poor". Walter I. Trattner. LC 82-15901. 168p. 1983. text ed. 18.95x (ISBN 0-87049-374-4); pap. text ed. 9.95x (ISBN 0-87049-375-2). U of Tenn Pr.
Social Welfare Policy: Analysis & Formulation. 2nd ed. Charles R. Atherton & Charles S. Prigmore. LC 85-60969. 258p. 1986. text ed. 20.50 (ISBN 0-669-06745-8). Heath.
Social Welfare Politics & Public Policy. Diana M. DiNitto & Thomas R. Dye. (Illus.). 352p. 1983. text ed. write for info. (ISBN 0-13-819474-2). P-H.
Social Welfare: Politics & Public Policy. 2nd ed. Diana M. DiNitto & Thomas R. Dye. (Illus.). 272p. 1987. text ed. write for info. (ISBN 0-13-819483-1). P-H.
Social Welfare Spending: Accounting for Changes from Nineteen Fifty to Nineteen Seventy-Eight. Robert J. Lampman. (Institute of Research on Poverty Policy Analysis Ser.). 1984. 32.50 (ISBN 0-12-435260-X). Acad Pr.
Social Will see Johns Hopkins University Psychology Laboratories: Studies.
Social Work: A Rewarding Career. Richard Blake. (Illus.). 136p. 1982. 17.50x (ISBN 0-398-04663-8). C C Thomas.
Social Work Administration: Dynamic Management & Human Relationships. Rex A. Skidmore. (Illus.). 320p. 1983. write for info. (ISBN 0-13-819490-4). P-H.
Social Work Administration in Health Care. Ed. by Abraham Lurie & Gary Rosenberg. LC 84-799. 310p. 1984. text ed. 34.95 (ISBN 0-917724-42-9); pap. 19.95 (ISBN 0-86656-314-8). Haworth Pr.
Social Work Administration in Health Care: A Guide to Professional Practice. Neil F. Bracht. LC 78-7881. 346p. 1978. 29.95 (ISBN 0-917724-04-6, B4); pap. 17.95 (ISBN 0-917724-05-4, B5). Haworth Pr.
Social Work: An Introduction. Mary Macht & Jean Quam. 480p. 1986. text ed. 32.95 (ISBN 0-675-20324-4). Merrill.
Social Work & Alzheimer's Disease: Practice Issues with Victims & Their Families. Ed. by Rose Dobrof. LC 85-220269. (Journal of Gerontological Social Work Ser.: Vol. 9, No. 2). 126p. 1986. text ed. 22.95 (ISBN 0-86656-402-0). Haworth Pr.
Social Work & Child Sexual Abuse. Ed. by Jon R. Conte & David A. Shore. LC 82-11952. (Journal of Social Work & Human Sexuality Ser.: Vol. 1, Nos. 1 & 2). 184p. 1982. text ed. 29.95 (ISBN 0-917724-98-4, B50). Haworth Pr.
Social Work & Criminal Law in Scotland: An Update. George Moore & Chris Wood. (Aberdeen University Press Bks.). 32p. 1987. pap. text ed. 6.50 (ISBN 0-08-035069-0, AUP). Pergamon.
Social Work & Criminal Law in Scotland. George Moore & Chris Wood. 220p. 1982. text ed. 17.50 (ISBN 0-08-025731-3). Pergamon.
Social Work & Dialysis: The Medical & Psychosocial Aspects of Kidney Disease. Carrie L. Fortner-Frazier. LC 78-51754. 224p. 1981. 25.00x (ISBN 0-520-03674-3). U of Cal Pr.
Social Work & Ethnicity. Ed. by Juliet Cheetham. 1982. 33.75x (ISBN 0-317-05807-X, Pub. by Natl Inst Social Work). State Mutual Bk.
Social Work & Genetics: A Guide to Practice. Ed. by Sylvia Schild & Rita B. Black. LC 84-560. (Social Work in Health Care Ser.: Supplement to Vol. 9). 164p. 1984. text ed. 24.95 (ISBN 0-86656-193-5, B193). Haworth Pr.
Social Work & Health Care. Ed. by Rex Taylor. (Research Highlights in Social Work Ser.: No. 19). 144p. 1988. price not set (ISBN 1-85302-016-8, Pub. by J Kingsley Pubs UK). UNIPUB.
Social Work & Health Care Policy. Ed. by Doman Lum. LC 81-68308. (Illus.). 240p. 1982. 28.50x (ISBN 0-86598-065-9, Pub. by Allanheld); pap. text ed. 11.95x (ISBN 0-86598-071-3). Rowman.
Social Work & Health Sciences: Medical Analysis Index with Reference Bibliography. Paula N. Aggerholm. LC 85-47858. 150p. 1987. 34.50 (ISBN 0-88164-392-0); pap. 26.50 (ISBN 0-88164-393-9). ABBE Pubs Assn.
Social Work & Human Problems: Casework, Consultation & Other Topics. Elizabeth E. Irvine. (International Series in Social Work). 1979. 63.00 (ISBN 0-08-023128-4); pap. 25.00 (ISBN 0-08-023127-6). Pergamon.
Social Work & Medical Practice. H. A. Prins & M. B. Whyte. LC 71-184453. 94p. 1972. 23.00 (ISBN 0-08-016847-7). Pergamon.
Social Work & Mental Health. Ed. by James W. Callicutt & Pedro J. Lecca. LC 82-71734. 245p. 1983. 22.95x (ISBN 0-02-905830-9); pap. text ed. 15.95 (ISBN 0-02-905850-3). Free Pr.
Social Work & Primary Health Care. Ed. by A. W. Clare & R. H. Corney. 1983. 52.00 (ISBN 0-12-174740-9). Acad Pr.
Social Work & Psychoanalysis. M. Yelloly. 1980. pap. 24.95 (ISBN 0-442-30167-7). Van Nos Reinhold.
Social Work & Social Living. Bertha C. Reynolds. LC 75-29534. (Classics Ser.). 176p. 1975. pap. 6.95 (ISBN 0-87101-071-2). Natl Assn Soc Wkrs.
Social Work & Social Philosophy: A Guide for Practice. Chris L. Clark & Stewart Asquith. 160p. 1985. 22.95x (ISBN 0-7102-0610-0); pap. 12.95x (ISBN 0-7100-9630-5). Routledge Chapman & Hall.
Social Work & Terminal Care. Ed. by Lee H. Suszycki et al. LC 84-11615. (Foundation of Thanatology Ser.: No. 2). 176p. 1984. 29.95 (ISBN 0-275-91280-9, C1280). Praeger.
Social Work & Thanatology. Ed. by Ben A. Orcutt et al. LC 79-22448. 300p. 1980. lib. bdg. 25.00 (ISBN 0-405-12621-2). Ayer Co Pubs.
Social Work & the Law. 2nd ed. Donald Brieland & John Lemmon. (Illus.). 800p. 1985. 40.75 (ISBN 0-314-77848-9). West Pub.
Social Work & the Unemployed. Katharine H. Briar. 236p. 1988. 16.95 (ISBN 0-87101-153-0). Natl Assn Soc Wkrs.
Social Work as a Profession. 4th ed. Esther L. Brown. LC 75-17207. (Social Problems & Social Policy Ser.). 1976. Repr. of 1942 ed. 18.00x (ISBN 0-405-07479-4). Ayer Co Pubs.
Social Work As Art: Making Sense for Good Practice. Hugh England. 176p. 1986. text ed. 39.95x (ISBN 0-04-360063-8); pap. text ed. 12.95x (ISBN 0-04-360064-6). Unwin Hyman.
Social Work Assistant. Jack Rudman. (Career Examination Ser.: C-796). (Cloth bdg. avail. on request). pap. 12.00 (ISBN 0-8373-0796-1). Natl Learning.
Social Work Day-to-Day: The Experience of Generalist Social Practice. Carolyn W. Konle. LC 81-14303. 224p. 1982. pap. text ed. 15.95 (ISBN 0-582-28345-0). Longman.
Social Work Departments As Organisations. Ed. by J. Lishman. (Research Highlights in Social Work Ser.: No. 4). 112p. 1982. pap. 26.00 (ISBN 1-85302-008-7, JK27, Pub. by J Kingsley Pubs UK). UNIPUB.
Social Work Dictionary. Robert L. Barker. 224p. 1987. 18.95x (ISBN 0-87101-145-X). Natl Assn Soc Wkrs.
Social Work Education. Hong-Chan Li. LC 77-19339. 359p. 1978. lib. bdg. 22.50 (ISBN 0-8108-1108-1). Scarecrow.
Social Work Education, Family Planning, & Population Dynamics. Date not set. 2.75. Coun Soc Wk Ed.
Social Work Education in Conflict. Margaret Richards & Peter Righton. 1979. 25.00x (ISBN 0-317-05763-4, Pub. by Natl Soc Work). State Mutual Bk.
Social Work Education in the United States: The Report of a Study Made for the National Council on Social Work Education. Ernest V. Hollis & Alice L. Taylor. LC 75-136070. (Illus.). 1971. Repr. of 1951 ed. lib. bdg. 25.00x (ISBN 0-8371-5220-8, HOSW). Greenwood.
Social Work: Essays on the Meeting-Ground of Doctor & Social Worker. Richard C. Cabot. LC 76-180561. (Medicine & Society in America Ser). 224p. 1972. Repr. of 1919 ed. 15.00 (ISBN 0-405-03940-9). Ayer Co Pubs.
Social Work Ethics. Charles Levy. LC 75-11007. 266p. 1980. text ed. 34.95 (ISBN 0-87705-254-9); pap. text ed. 16.95 (ISBN 0-87705-493-2). Human Sci Pr.
Social Work Ethics Day to Day: Guidelines for Professional Practice. Carolyn C. Wells & M. Kathleen Masch. LC 85-12890. 1986. pap. 13.95 (ISBN 0-582-28582-8). Longman.

Socialism & Culture: A Collection of Articles. Ed. by Progress Publishers, Moscow. Tr. by V. Khodorousky. 1976. 15.95 (ISBN 0-8464-0856-2). Beekman Pubs.
Socialism & Culture: Problems of the Comtemporary World, No. 112. M. Kim. 158p. 1984. 7.50x (ISBN 0-317-53762-8, Pub. by Collets (UK)). State Mutual Bk.
Socialism & Democracy: A Marxist Look at Socialist Democracy. B. Topornin & E. Machulsky. 221p. 1975. 15.95 (ISBN 0-8464-0857-0). Beekman Pubs.
Socialism & Democracy in Czechoslovakia, 1945-1948. Martin R. Myant. LC 80-41951. (Soviet & East European Studies). pap. 81.20 (2031697). Bks Demand UMI.
Socialism & Energy Resources. I. Kozlov. 198p. 1985. pap. 2.95 (Pub. by Progress Pubs USSR). Imported Pubns.
Socialism & Energy Resources. Igor Kozlov. 198p. 1984. pap. 11.25x (ISBN 0-317-53763-6, Pub. by Collets (UK)). State Mutual Bk.
Socialism & Freedom. Bryan Gould. 135p. 1986. 22.50 (ISBN 0-89341-538-3, Pub. by Longwood Academic); pap. 12.50 (ISBN 0-89341-539-1, Pub. by Longwood Academic). Longwood Pub Group.
Socialism & History: The Political Essays of Henry Pachter. Henry Pachter. Ed. by Stephen E. Bronner. LC 83-18904. (Illus.). 300p. 1984. 34.00x (ISBN 0-231-05660-5). Columbia U Pr.
Socialism & International Economic Order. Elisabeth Tamedly. 302p. 1986. 5.50 (ISBN 0-317-52990-0). Noontide.
Socialism & Labor, & Other Arguments Social, Political & Patriotic. facs. ed. John L. Spalding. LC 67-28768. (Essay Index Reprint Ser). 1902. 17.00 (ISBN 0-8369-0893-7). Ayer Co Pubs.
Socialism & Man. Ernesto C. Guevara. pap. 0.65 (ISBN 0-87348-079-1). Path Pr NY.
Socialism & Nationalism in Contemporary Europe Eighteen Forty-Eight to Nineteen Forty-Five. Ed. by Eric Cahm & Vladimir C. Fisera. 1983. Vol. 1, 116pgs. pap. text ed. 5.95x (ISBN 0-936508-04-3); Vol. 2, 132pgs. pap. 5.95x (ISBN 0-936508-05-1); Vol. 3, 132pgs. pap. 5.95x (ISBN 0-936508-06-X). Barber Pr.
Socialism & Nationalism: Southern Europe: The Experience of Spain & Italy, Vol. III. Eric Cahm & Vladimir C. Fisera. (Studies in Contemporary Europe (1948-1945)). 132p. 50.00x (Pub. By Bertrand Russell Hse); pap. 16.25x (ISBN 0-85124-268-5). State Mutual Bk.
Socialism & Nationalism: Western Europe: Up to the First World War, Vol. II. Eric Cahm & Vladimir C. Fisera. (Studies in Contemporary Europe (1848-1945)). 132p. 50.00x (Pub. by Bertrand Russell Hse); pap. 16.25x (ISBN 0-85124-244-8). State Mutual Bk.
Socialism & Nationalsim: Theories of Revolutionary Socialists & Anarchists Eastern Europe: From Populism to Stalinism, Vol. 1. Eric Cahm & Vladimir C. Fisera. (Studies in Conetemporary Europe (1948-1945)). 116p. 50.00x (Pub. by Bertrand Russell Hse); pap. 16.25x (ISBN 0-85124-226-X). State Mutual Bk.
Socialism & Optimism. S. I. Popov. 288p. 1981. 10.00x (ISBN 0-317-53765-2, Pub. by Collets (UK)). State Mutual Bk.
Socialism & Parliamentary Democracy. Geoff Hodgson. 183p. 40.00x (ISBN 0-85124-207-3, Pub. by Bertrand Russell Hse). State Mutual Bk.
Socialism & Philosophy. Antonio Labriola. LC 79-90007. 223p. 1980. 16.00 (ISBN 0-914386-21-2); pap. 6.50 (ISBN 0-914386-22-0). Telos Pr.
Socialism & Populism in Chile, 1932-52. Paul W. Drake. LC 77-17414. 416p. 1977. 29.95 (ISBN 0-252-00657-7). U of Ill Pr.
Socialism & Private Enterprise in Equatorial Asia. R. A. Freeman. LC 67-31386. (Studies Ser.: No. 20). 1968. 6.95x (ISBN 0-8179-3201-1). Hoover Inst Pr.
Socialism & Saint-Simon (Le Socialisme) Emile Durkheim. Ed. by Alvin W. Gouldner. LC 58-8736. pap. 70.50 (ISBN 0-317-20142-5, 2023199). Bks Demand UMI.
Socialism & Self-Reliance in Tanzania. K. A. Okoko. 200p. 1988. 77.00 (ISBN 0-7103-0269-X, Kegan Paul). Routledge Chapman & Hall.
Socialism & Social Science: Selected Writings of Ervin Szabo. Ervin Szabo. Ed. by Gyorgy Litvan & Janos Bak. 288p. 1982. 28.95x (ISBN 0-7100-9007-2). Routledge Chapman & Hall.
Socialism & Society. 6th ed. J. R. MacDonald. Repr. of 1908 ed. 23.00 (ISBN 0-527-59340-0). Kraus Repr.
Socialism & State. Rudolf Rocker. 59.95 (ISBN 0-8490-1069-1). Gordon Pr.
Socialism & the American Spirit. facsimile ed. Nicholas P. Gilman. LC 70-150183. (Select Bibliographies Reprint Ser). Repr. of 1893 ed. 23.50 (ISBN 0-8369-5696-6). Ayer Co Pubs.
Socialism & the Cities. Ed. by Bruce M. Stave. (National University Publications Interdisciplinary Urban Ser.). 1975. 24.95x (ISBN 0-8046-9133-9, Pub. by Kennikat); pap. 14.95x (ISBN 0-8046-9189-4). Assoc Faculty Pr.
Socialism & the Environment. Ken Coates. 116p. pap. 12.50x (ISBN 0-85124-252-9, Pub by Bertrand Russell Hse). State Mutual Bk.
Socialism & the Freedom of Culture. Gyorgy Aczel. 486p. 1984. 32.50x (ISBN 0-317-53860-8, Pub. by Collets (UK)). State Mutual Bk.
Socialism & the Great State: Essays in Construction. H. G. Wells et al. LC 75-156719. (Essay Index Reprint Ser.). Repr. of 1912 ed. 25.00 (ISBN 0-8369-2863-6). Ayer Co Pubs.
Socialism & the Great War: The Collapse of the Second International. Georges Haupt. 1972. 29.95x (ISBN 0-19-827184-0). Oxford U Pr.
Socialism & the Intelligentsia: 1880-1914. Ed. by Carl Levy. (History Workshop Ser.). 224p. 1988. lib. bdg. 59.95x (ISBN 0-7102-0722-0, Pub. by Routledge Uk); pap. text ed. 19.95x (ISBN 0-7102-1257-7, Pub. by Routledge UK). Routledge Chapman & Hall.
Socialism & the Jews: The Dilemmas of Assimilation in Germany & Austria-Hungary. Robert S. Wistrich. (Littman Library of Jewish Civilization). 1982. 37.50x (ISBN 0-19-710053-8). Oxford U Pr.
Socialism & the Newly Independent Nations: An Account of National Liberation Movements. R. Ulyanovsky. 562p. 1975. 22.95 (ISBN 0-8464-0858-9). Beekman Pubs.
Socialism & the Workers in Massachusetts, 1886-1912. Henry F. Bedford. LC 66-15794. (Illus.). 234p. 1966. 17.50x (ISBN 0-87023-010-7). U of Mass Pr.
Socialism & War. Louis B. Boudin. LC 73-147507. (Library of War & Peace; Labor, Socialism & War). 1972. lib. bdg. 46.00 (ISBN 0-8240-0302-0). Garland Pub.
Socialism & War. Vladimir I. Lenin. 71p. 1977. pap. 0.75 (ISBN 0-8285-1631-6, Pub. by Progress Pubs USSR). Imported Pubns.
Socialism & Wealth: The Creation & Distribution of Socialist Wealth. Y. Lazutkin. 217p. 1975. 17.95 (ISBN 0-8464-0859-7). Beekman Pubs.
Socialism Democracy & Human Rights. Leonid I. Brezhnev. LC 79-42659. 256p. 1981. 28.00 (ISBN 0-08-023605-7). Pergamon.
Socialism, Democracy & Selfmanagement: Political Essays. Michel Raptis. LC 79-56924. 172p. 1980. 26.00 (ISBN 0-312-73653-3). St Martin.
Socialism, Economics & Development. Alec Nove. 280p. 1986. text ed. 37.95x (ISBN 0-04-335054-2); pap. text ed. 14.95x (ISBN 0-04-335055-0). Unwin Hyman.
Socialism for Beginners. Anna Paczuska & Sophie Grillet. (Writers & Readers Documentary Comic Bks). (Illus.). 1986. pap. 6.95 (ISBN 0-906495-92-X). Writers & Readers.
Socialism for Today. Henry N. Brailsford. Ed. by F. M. Leventhal. (English Workers & the Coming of the Welfare State Ser., 1918-1945). 142p. 1985. lib. bdg. 25.00 (ISBN 0-8240-7603-6). Garland Pub.
Socialism: From Utopia to Science. 5th ed. Frederick Engels. Tr. by Edward Aveling. 1974. pap. text ed. 0.75 (ISBN 0-935534-27-X). NY Labor News.
Socialism in a Cold Climate. Ed. by John Griffith. (Counterpoint Ser.). 256p. 1983. pap. 8.95 (ISBN 0-04-335050-X). Unwin Hyman.
Socialism in Cuba. Leo Huberman & Paul M. Sweezy. LC 68-8078. 224p. 1969. pap. 4.50 (ISBN 0-85345-133-8). Monthly Rev.
Socialism in England. Sidney Webb. 154p. 1986. text ed. 41.95 (ISBN 0-566-05144-3, Pub. by Gower Pub England). Gower Pub Co.
Socialism in France: From Jaures to Mitterand. Ed. by Stewart Williams. LC 83-42532. 200p. 1983. 24.95 (ISBN 0-312-73667-3). St Martin.
Socialism in Galicia: The Emergence of Polish Social Democracy & Ukrainian Radicalism, 1860-1890. Himka John-Paul. LC 83-47953. (Harvard Ukrainian Research Institute Monograph). xiii, 253p. (Orig.). 1983. pap. 15.95x (ISBN 0-916458-07-5). Harvard Ukrainian.
Socialism in German American Literature. William F. Kamman. LC 75-328. (Radical Tradition in America Ser.). 124p. 1975. Repr. of 1917 ed. 15.95 (ISBN 0-88355-232-9). Hyperion Conn.
Socialism in Greece. P. Z. Tzannatos. 125p. 1986. text ed. 35.95 (ISBN 0-566-05097-8). Gower Pub Co.
Socialism in India (Rise, Growth & Prospect) Chandrika Singh. xvi, 228p. 1987. text ed. 30.00x (ISBN 81-7018-384-7, Pub. by B R Pub Corp Delhi). Apt Bks.
Socialism in Provence Eighteen Seventy-One to Nineteen Fourteen. T. Judt. LC 78-16419. (Illus.). 1979. pap. 17.95x (ISBN 0-521-29598-X). Cambridge U Pr.
Socialism in Southern Asia. Saul Rose. 1977. Repr. of 1959 ed. lib. bdg. 20.00x (ISBN 0-374-96912-4, Octagon). Hippocrene Bks.
Socialism in Sub-Saharan Africa: A New Assessment. Ed. by Carl G. Rosberg & Thomas M. Callaghy. LC 79-84635. (Research Ser.: No. 38). (Illus.). 1979. pap. 12.95x (ISBN 0-87725-138-X). U of Cal Intl St.
Socialism in the Chinese Countryside. Jurgen Domes. 1980. 35.00x (ISBN 0-7735-0532-6). McGill-Queens U Pr.
Socialism in the Heartland: The Midwestern Experience, Nineteen Hundred to Nineteen Twenty-Five. Ed. by Donald T. Critchlow. LC 85-40602. 224p. 1986. text ed. 21.95x (ISBN 0-268-01719-0). U of Notre Dame Pr.
Socialism in the Heartland: The Midwestern Experience, 1900-1925. Ed. by Donald T. Critchlow. 221p. 1987. pap. text ed. 9.95x (ISBN 0-268-01720-4). U of Notre Dame Pr.
Socialism in the Soviet Union. Jonathan Aurthur. LC 77-5727. 1977. pap. 5.95 (ISBN 0-917348-14-1). Workers Pr.
Socialism in Theological Perspective: A Study of Paul Tillich, Nineteen Eighteen to Nineteen Thirty-Three. John R. Stumme. LC 78-3675. (American Academy of Religion. Dissertation Ser.: No. 21). 1978. pap. 9.95 (ISBN 0-89130-232-8, 010121). Scholars Pr GA.
Socialism in Theory & Practice. Morris Hillquit. 19.25 (ISBN 0-8369-7162-0, 7994). Ayer Co Pubs.
Socialism in Thought & Action. Harry W. Laidler. 546p. 1982. Repr. of 1920 ed. lib. bdg. 50.00 (ISBN 0-8495-3345-7). Arden Lib.
Socialism in Western Europe: The Experience of a Generation. replica ed. Stephen Kramer. 210p. 1984. pap. 24.50x (ISBN 0-86531-861-1). Westview.
Socialism: Institutional, Philosophical & Economic Issues. Ed. by S Prejovich. 1987. lib. bdg. 52.50 (ISBN 90-247-3487-8, Pub. by Reidel Holland). Kluwer Academic.
Socialism, Its Growth & Outcome. William Morris & E. Belfort Bax. LC 83-48493. (World of Labour - English Workers 1850-1890 Ser.). 335p. 1984. lib. bdg. 40.00 (ISBN 0-8240-5720-1). Garland Pub.
Socialism: Its Role in History. Vadim Zagladin. 176p. 1983. 25.00x (ISBN 0-317-42848-9, Pub by Collets (UK)). State Mutual Bk.
Socialism, Liberalism, & Dictatorship in Paraguay. Paul H. Lewis. Ed. by Hoover Institution Pr. & Robert Wesson. (Politics in Latin America, A Hoover Institution Ser.). 170p. 1982. 35.00 (ISBN 0-275-90847-X, C0847). Praeger.
Socialism: New & Old. William Graham. (International Scientific Ser.). 1979. Repr. of 1891 ed. lib. bdg. 40.00 (ISBN 0-8495-2030-4). Arden Lib.
Socialism of a Different Kind: Reshaping the Left in France. Bernard E. Brown. LC 82-6125. (Contributions in Political Science Ser.: No. 85). xiv, 201p. 1982. lib. bdg. 35.00 (ISBN 0-313-23377-2, BFL/). Greenwood.
Socialism of Fools: Georg Ritter Von Schonerer & Austrian Pan-Germanism. Andrew G. Whiteside. 512p. 1975. 44.50x (ISBN 0-520-02434-6). U of Cal Pr.
Socialism of Jaharwalal Nehru. R. C. Dutt. 1981. 18.50x (ISBN 0-8364-0708-3, Pub. by Abhinav India). South Asia Bks.
Socialism of Jawaharlal Nehru. R. C. Dutt. 284p. 1981. 24.95. Asia Bk Corp.
Socialism of My Conception. M. K. Gandhi. Ed. by A. T. Hingorani. 290p. (Orig.). 1981. pap. 6.00 (ISBN 0-934676-29-1). Greenlf Bks.
Socialism of Our Times: A Symposium, Prelude to Depression. Harry W. Laidler & Norman Thomas. LC 76-27725. 1976. Repr. of 1929 ed. lib, bdg. 45.00 (ISBN 0-306-70850-7). Da Capo.
Socialism on Trial. James P. Cannon. LC 73-86630. 1969. 17.00 (ISBN 0-87348-009-0). Path Pr NY.
Socialism on Trial. 2nd ed. James P. Cannon. LC 73-86630. 192p. 1973. pap. 3.95 (ISBN 0-87348-317-0). Path Pr NY.
Socialism, Participation & Agricultural Developement in Post-Revolutionary Ethiopia: A Study of Constraints. Makonen Getu. (Stockholm Studies in Economic History: No. 11). 225p. (Orig.). 1987. pap. 30.00x (ISBN 91-7146-477-8, Pub. by Stockholms Universitet (Stockholm Sweden)). Coronet Bks.
Socialism, Politics & Equality: Hierarchy & Change in Eastern Europe & the U. S. S. R. Walter D. Connor. LC 78-17567. (Illus.). 1979. 40.00x (ISBN 0-231-04318-X); pap. 18.50x (ISBN 0-231-04319-8). Columbia U Pr.
Socialism, Promise or Menace? Morris Hillquit. LC 75-325. (Radical Tradition in America Ser.). 283p. 1975. Repr. of 1914 ed. 23.10 (ISBN 0-88355-228-0). Hyperion Conn.
Socialism: Questions of Theory. R. Kosolapov. 542p. 1979. 14.75x (ISBN 0-317-53769-5, Pub. by Collets (UK)). State Mutual Bk.
Socialism, Radicalism & Nostalgia: Social Criticism in Britain 1775-1830. William Stafford. 250p. 1987. 42.50 (ISBN 0-521-32792-X); pap. 15.95 (ISBN 0-521-33989-8). Cambridge U Pr.
Socialism Re-Examined. Norman Thomas. LC 84-12988. 280p. 1984. Repr. of 1963 ed. lib. bdg. 41.50x (ISBN 0-313-24429-4, THSR). Greenwood.
Socialism: Speeches & Reports. Mikhail S. Gorbachev. 192p. 1988. text ed. 29.95 (ISBN 0-317-65747-X). Humanities.
Socialism: Teacher's Guide. James D. Forman & Nancy E. Gross. 1976. pap. 1.25 (ISBN 0-440-98318-5). Dell.
Socialism: The Active Utopia, Vol. 3. Zygmunt Bauman. LC 75-28243. (Controversies in Sociology Ser.). 148p. 1976. 19.75 (ISBN 0-8419-0240-2). Holmes & Meier.
Socialism: The Grand Delusion. Brian Crozier & Arthur Seldon. LC 84-280. (Illus.). 208p. 1986. text ed. 15.00x (ISBN 0-87663-478-1); pap. text ed. 8.95x (ISBN 0-87663-879-5). Universe.
Socialism: The State & Public in France. Ed. by Philip Cerny & Martin Schain. 220p. (Orig.). 29.95 (ISBN 0-416-01131-4, 9384); pap. 12.95 (ISBN 0-416-01161-6, 9416). Routledge Chapman & Hall.
Socialism Today & Tomorrow. Michael Albert & Robin Hahnel. LC 81-50138. 350p. 1981. 20.00 (ISBN 0-89608-078-1); pap. 9.50 (ISBN 0-89608-077-3). South End Pr.
Socialism, Utopian & Scientific. Frederick Engels. Tr. by Edward Aveling from Ger. 135p. lib. bdg. 22.95; pap. 2.95 (ISBN 0-88286-031-3). C H Kerr.
Socialism: Utopian & Scientific. Frederick Engels. 96p. 1935. pap. 1.50 (ISBN 0-7178-0191-8). Intl Pubs Co.
Socialism: Utopian & Scientific. Frederick Engels. LC 72-92659. 64p. 1972. pap. 1.25 (ISBN 0-87348-264-6). Path Pr NY.
Socialism: Utopian & Scientific-With an Essay on "The Mark". Frederick Engels. Tr. by Edward Aveling from Ger. LC 77-4356. 1977. Repr. of 1935 ed. lib. bdg. 35.00x (ISBN 0-8371-9622-1, ENSO). Greenwood.
Socialism vs. Anarchism. Daniel De Leon. 1970. pap. 0.50 (ISBN 0-935534-39-3). NY Labor News.
Socialisme Au Dix-Huitieme Siecle. Andre Lichtenberger. LC 67-27835. (Fr). 1967. Repr. of 1895 ed. 45.00x (ISBN 0-678-00329-7). Kelley.
Socialisme Britannique et Marxisme Vers la Fin du XIX Siecle see Cahiers de l'Institut de Science Economique Appliquee: Bibliographie Marxologique. Liste Complementaire.
Socialisme D'Etat: L'Industrie et les Classes Industrieeles en France Pendant les Deux Premiers Siecles de L'ere Moderne (1453-1661) Prosper Boissonnade. 380p. (Fr.). Repr. of 1927 ed. lib. bdg. 62.50x. Coronet Bks.
Socialismo Real y Su Significacion Internacional. B. N. Ponomareov. 99p. (Span.). 1979. pap. 1.45 (ISBN 0-8285-1433-X, Pub. by Progress Pubs USSR). Imported Pubns.
Socialism's Dilemmas: State & Society in the Soviet Bloc. Walter D. Connor. 320p. 1988. 32.00x (ISBN 0-231-06606-6). Columbia U Pr.
Socialisms: Theories & Practices. Anthony Wright. 160p. 1986. 22.50x (ISBN 0-19-219188-8). Oxford U Pr.
Socialisms: Theories & Practices. Anthony Wright. 160p. 1987. pap. 10.95 (ISBN 0-19-285199-3). Oxford U Pr.
Socialist Agriculture in Hungary. E. Csizmadia. 180p. 1977. 42.50x (ISBN 0-317-53859-4, Pub. by Collets (UK)). State Mutual Bk.
Socialist Agriculture in Transition: Organizational Response to Failing Performance. Ed. by Josef C. Brada & Karl-Eugen Wadekin. (Special Studies on the Soviet Union & Eastern Europe). 450p. 1987. 58.50 (ISBN 0-8133-7344-1). Westview.
Socialist Agruments. Ed. by David Coates & Gordon Johnston. (Illus.). 248p. 1983. 312.95 (ISBN 0-85520-650-0); pap. 9.95x (ISBN 0-85520-651-9). Basil Blackwell.
Socialist Albania since Nineteen Forty-Four: Domestic & Foreign Developments. Peter R. Prifti. LC 78-1728. (MIT Studies in Communism, Revisionism, & Revolution Ser.: No. 22). 1978. 37.50x (ISBN 0-262-16070-6). MIT Pr.
Socialist Anatomy of Britain. Ed. by David Coates et al. 320p. 1985. 45.00 (ISBN 0-7456-0024-7); pap. 14.95x (ISBN 0-7456-0025-5). Basil Blackwell.
Socialist & Labour Movement in Japan. Arthur M. Young. LC 79-65476. (Studies in Japanese History & Civilization). 145p. 1979. Repr. of 1921 ed. 18.00 (ISBN 0-89093-268-9). U Pubns Amer.
Socialist, Anti-Semite, & Jew: German Social Democracy Confronts the Problem of Anti-Semitism, 1918-1933. Donald L. Niewyk. LC 79-137123. x, 254p. 1971. 30.00 (ISBN 0-8071-0531-7). La State U Pr.
Socialist Authority: The Hungarian Experience. Peter A. Toma. LC 87-11775. 320p. 1988. lib. bdg. 49.95 (ISBN 0-275-92602-8, C2602). Praeger.
Socialist City: Spatial Structure & Urban Policy. Ed. by Richard A. French & F. E. Hamilton. LC 78-16828. pap. 139.80 (ISBN 0-317-55679-7, 2029261). Bks Demand UMI.
Socialist Collective Agreement. L. Nagy. 258p. 1984. 62.50 (Pub. by Collets (UK)). State Mutual BK.
Socialist Construction & Marxist Theory: Bolshevism & Its Critique. Philip Corrigan et al. LC 78-7591. 232p. 1978. 15.00 (ISBN 0-85345-469-8); pap. 7.50 (ISBN 0-85345-580-5). Monthly Rev.
Socialist Corporation & Technocratic Power: The Polish United Workers' Party, Industrial Organization & Workforce Control, 1958-1980. Jean Woodall. (Soviet & East European Studies). (Illus.). 270p. 1982. 44.50 (ISBN 0-521-24269-X). Cambridge U Pr.
Socialist Countries: General Features of Political, Economic, & Cultural Life. 2nd ed. Erwin Marquit. LC 83-9329. (Studies in Marxism: Vol. 3). 228p. 1983. 19.95x (ISBN 0-930656-31-8); pap. 9.95 (ISBN 0-930656-32-6). MEP Pubns.
Socialist Cuba: As Seen by a U. S. Communist Delegation. Joseph North. 1970. pap. 0.60 (ISBN 0-87898-073-3). New Outlook.
Socialist Cuba: Past Interpretations & Future Challenges. Ed. by Sergio G. Roca. (Special Studies on Latin America & the Caribbean). 230p. 1988. pap. 31.00 (ISBN 0-8133-7461-8). Westview.

TITLE INDEX

SOCIALIZATION OF THE INDIAN

Socialist Decision. Paul Tillich. Tr. by Franklin Sherman from Ger. LC 82-21913. 224p. 1983. pap. text ed. 12.00 (ISBN 0-8191-2911-9). U Pr of Amer.

Socialist Democracy. Collets Staff. 64p. 1981. pap. 7.50x (ISBN 0-317-53858-6, Pub. by Collets (UK)). State Mutual Bk.

Socialist Democracy in Czechoslovakia: The Basic Aspects of the Rule of the Working People. Stanislav Matousek. 150p. 1981. pap. 13.75x (ISBN 0-317-53857-8, Pub. by Collets (UK)). State Mutual Bk.

Socialist Development & Public Investment in Tanzania, Nineteen Sixty-Four to Nineteen Seventy-Three. W. Edmund Clark. LC 77-8180. 1978. 35.00x (ISBN 0-8020-5376-9). U of Toronto Pr.

Socialist Economic Integration. J. M. Van Brabant. LC 79-23766. (Soviet & East European Studies). (Illus.). 275p. 1980. 44.50 (ISBN 0-521-23046-2). Cambridge U Pr.

Socialist Economic Policy. Bela Csikos-Nagy. LC 72-90020. 1973. 26.00 (ISBN 0-312-73745-9). St Martin.

Socialist Economy & Economic Policy. Ed. by G. Fink. (Studien uber Wirtschafts- Und Systemvergleiche: Band 13). (Illus.). 279p. pap. 24.20 (ISBN 0-387-81903-7). Springer-Verlag.

Socialist Entrepreneurs: Embourgeoisement in Rural Hungary. Ivan Szelenyi. LC 87-16085. (Illus.). 320p. 1988. text ed. 35.00x (ISBN 0-299-11360-4); pap. text ed. 15.95x (ISBN 0-299-11364-7). U of Wis Pr.

Socialist Feminism: The First Decade 1966-76. 2nd ed. Gloria Martin. LC 85-1621. (Illus.). 223p. (Orig.). 1986. pap. 8.95 (ISBN 0-932323-00-6). Freedom Soc.

Socialist Humanism. Donald C. Hodges. LC 73-96983. 384p. 1974. 19.75 (ISBN 0-87527-042-5). Fireside Bks.

Socialist Humanism: The Outcome of Classical European Morality. Donald C. Hodges. LC 73-96983. 384p. 1974. 19.75. Green.

Socialist in Congress: His Conduct & Responsibilities. 5th ed. Daniel De Leon. 1962. pap. 0.50 (ISBN 0-935534-41-5). NY Labor News.

Socialist Industrial State: Towards a Political Sociology of State Socialism. David Lane. 1977. pap. text ed. 11.95X (ISBN 0-04-320117-2). Unwin Hyman.

Socialist Integration: The Theoretical & Practical Considerations Governing the Economic Relations among Socialist Countries. Mikhail Senin. 284p. 1975. 19.00 (ISBN 0-8464-0860-0). Beekman Pubs.

Socialist International. Nikolai Sibilev. 290p. 1984. 22.50x (ISBN 0-317-53766-0, Pub. by Collets (UK)). State Mutual Bk.

Socialist Iraq: A Study in Iraqi Politics Since 1968. Majid Khadduri. LC 78-51916. 1978. 7.50 (ISBN 0-916808-16-5). Mid East Inst.

Socialist Korea: A Case Study in the Strategy of Economic Development. Ellen Brun & Jacques Hersh. LC 76-1651. (Illus.). 432p. 1977. 16.50 (ISBN 0-85345-386-1). Monthly Rev.

Socialist Labor & Politics in Weimar Germany: The General Federation of German Trade Unions. Gerard Braunthal. LC 77-29131. (Illus.). 253p. 1978. 27.50 (ISBN 0-208-01740-2, Archon). Shoe String.

Socialist Landmarks. 2nd ed. Daniel De Leon. 1977. pap. 1.50 (ISBN 0-935534-29-6). NY Labor News.

Socialist Left & the German Revolution: A History of the German Independent Social Democractic Party, 1917-1922. David W. Morgan. LC 75-5393. 520p. 1975. 49.95x (ISBN 0-8014-0851-2). Cornell U Pr.

Socialist Legalism: Reform & Continuity in Post-Mao People's Republic of China. Ed. by Hungdah Chiu. (Occasional Papers-Reprints Series in Contemporary Asian Studies: No. 1). 35p. (Orig.). 1982. pap. text ed. 2.00 (ISBN 0-942182-45-6). Occasional Papers.

Socialist Life Style & the Family. V. Yazkova. 212p. 1984. pap. 3.95 (ISBN 0-8285-2730-X, Pub. by Progress Pubs USSR). Imported Pubns.

Socialist Life Style & the Family. V. Yazykova. 212p. 1984. 10.00x (ISBN 0-317-53856-X, Pub. by Collets (UK)). State Mutual Bk.

Socialist Literatures: Problems of Development. Dmitry Markov. 324p. 1984. 22.00x (ISBN 0-317-56680-6, Pub. by Collets (UK)). State Mutual Bk.

Socialist Management & Planning: Topics in Comparative Socialist Economics. Nicolas Spulber. LC 73-126220. (International Development Research Center, Studies in Development: No. 2). (Illus.). Repr. of 1971 ed. 48.10 (ISBN 0-8357-9242-0, 2015834). Bks Demand UMI.

Socialist Mathematics Education. Ed. by Frank Swetz. LC 78-68025. 1979. pap. 14.00 (ISBN 0-917574-04-4). Burgundy Pr.

Socialist Movement in Reading, Pennsylvania, Eighteen Thirty-Six to Nineteen Thirty-Six: A Study in Social Change. Henry G. Stetler. LC 73-16306. (Perspectives in American History Ser.: No. 21). (Illus.). viii, 198p. 1974. Repr. of 1943 ed. lib. bdg. 27.50x (ISBN 0-87991-333-9). Porcupine Pr.

Socialist Network. Nesta Webster. 75.00 (ISBN 0-8490-1070-5). Gordon Pr.

Socialist Network. Nesta H. Webster. 163p. 1972. pap. 4.00 (ISBN 0-913022-06-3). Angriff Pr.

Socialist Novel in Britain: Towards the Recovery of a Tradition. H. Gustav Klaus. LC 81-18376. 190p. 1982. 26.50x (ISBN 0-312-73775-0). St Martin.

Socialist Offensive: The Collectivization of Soviet Agriculture, 1929-1930. R. W. Davies. LC 79-15263. (Industrialization of Soviet Russia: Vol. 1). (Illus.). 512p. 1980. text ed. 40.00x (ISBN 0-674-81480-0). Harvard U Pr.

Socialist Opposition in Eastern Europe: The Czechoslovak Example. Jiri Pelikan. LC 76-19161. (Motive Ser.). 1976. 22.50x (ISBN 0-312-73780-7). St Martin.

Socialist-Oriented State: Instrument of Revolutionary Change. V. Y. Chirkin & Y. A. Yudin. 172p. 1978. 15.75x (ISBN 0-317-53767-9, Pub. by Collets (UK)). State Mutual Bk.

Socialist Ownership & Political Systems under Socialism. Wlodzimierz Brus. 256p. 1975. 26.95x (ISBN 0-7100-8247-9). Routledge Chapman & Hall.

Socialist Parties & European Integration: A Comparative History. Kevin Featherstone. LC 87-31400. 384p. 1988. 49.95 (ISBN 0-7190-2673-3, Pub. by Manchester Univ Pr). St Martin.

Socialist Parties in Postwar Japan. Allan Burnett Cole et al. LC 66-21511. (Illus.). pap. 127.00 (ISBN 0-317-09609-5, 2021989). Bks Demand UMI.

Socialist Party of Argentina, 1890-1930. Richard J. Walter. LC 77-620003. (Latin American Monographs: No. 42). 304p. 1977. text ed. 17.50x (ISBN 0-292-77539-3); pap. text ed. 8.95x (ISBN 0-292-77540-7). U of Tex Pr.

Socialist Perspectives, Vol. 1. Phyllis Jacobson & Julius Jacobson. 220p. 1983. 29.95 (ISBN 0-943828-51-1); pap. 9.95 (ISBN 0-943828-52-X). Karz-Cohl Pub.

Socialist Planning. Michael Ellman. LC 78-57757. (Modern Cambridge Economics Ser.). 1979. 52.50 (ISBN 0-521-22229-X); pap. 18.95 (ISBN 0-521-29409-6). Cambridge U Pr.

Socialist Planning. 2nd ed. Michael Ellman. (Modern Cambridge Economics Ser.). 350p. Date not set. price not set (ISBN 0-521-35345-9); pap. 19.95 (ISBN 0-521-35866-3). Cambridge U Pr.

Socialist Population Politics: The Political Implications of Demographic Trends in the U. S. S. R. & Eastern Europe. John Besemeres. LC 80-65260. 320p. 1980. 35.00 (ISBN 0-87332-154-5). M E Sharpe.

Socialist Price Mechanism. Ed. by Alan Abouchar. LC 76-4219. xvi, 297p. 1977. 29.75 (ISBN 0-8223-0366-3). Duke.

Socialist Price Theory & Price Policy. B. Csikos-Nagy. 372p. 1975. 43.75x (Pub. by Collets (UK)). State Mutual Bk.

Socialist Propaganda in the Twentieth-Century British Novel. David Smith. 203p. 1978. 21.50x (ISBN 0-8476-6023-0). Rowman.

Socialist Reconstruction of Society. 20th ed. Daniel De Leon. 1977. pap. 0.50 (ISBN 0-935534-42-3). NY Labor News.

Socialist Register: Annuals: Nineteen Sixty-Eight to Nineteen Seventy-Eight. Ed. by Ralph Milliband & J. Saville. 17.50 ea. (ISBN 0-87556-440-2). Saifer.

Socialist Register, Nineteen Eighty-Seven: Conservatism in Britain & America: Rhetoric & Reality. Ed. by Ralph Miliband et al. 520p. 22.50 (ISBN 0-85036-349-7, Pub. by Merlin UK); pap. 9.75 (ISBN 0-317-58100-7, Pub. by Merlin UK). Longwood Pub Group.

Socialist Register, 1964. Ed. by John Saville & Ralph Miliband. 1964. 12.95 (ISBN 0-85036-075-7, Pub. by Merlin Pr UK). Longwood Pub Group.

Socialist Register, 1968. Ed. by Ralph Miliband. 1968. 12.95 (ISBN 0-85036-079-X, Pub. by Merlin Pr UK). Longwood Pub Group.

Socialist Register, 1972. 1972. 12.95 (ISBN 0-85036-163-X, Pub. by Merlin Pr UK); pap. 6.95 (ISBN 0-85036-162-1, Pub. by Merlin Pr UK). Longwood Pub Group.

Socialist Register, 1973. Ed. by Ralph Miliband. 1973. 12.95 (ISBN 0-85036-179-6, Pub. by Merlin Pr UK); pap. 6.95 (ISBN 0-85036-178-8, Pub. by Merlin Pr UK). Longwood Pub Group.

Socialist Register, 1974. 1974. 12.95 (ISBN 0-85036-187-7, Pub. by Merlin Pr UK). Longwood Pub Group.

Socialist Register, 1976. Ed. by Ralph Miliband. 1976. pap. 6.95 (ISBN 0-85036-218-0, Pub. by Merlin Pr UK). Longwood Pub Group.

Socialist Register, 1977. Ed. by Ralph Miliband. 1977. pap. 6.95 (ISBN 0-85036-225-3, Pub. by Merlin Pr UK). Longwood Pub Group.

Socialist Register: 1977. Ed. by Ralph Miliband & John Saville. 276p. 1977. pap. 5.95 (ISBN 0-85345-435-3, Pub. by Merlin England). Monthly Rev.

Socialist Register, 1978. Ed. by Ralph Miliband. 1978. 12.95 (ISBN 0-85036-234-2, Pub. by Merlin Pr UK). Longwood Pub Group.

Socialist Register: 1978. Ed. by Ralph Miliband & John Saville. 338p. 1978. pap. 5.95 (ISBN 0-85345-453-1, Pub. by Merlin England). Monthly Rev.

Socialist Register: 1982. Martin Eve & David Musson. 1982. 6.50 (ISBN 0-85345-624-0, Pub. by Merlin England). Monthly Rev.

Socialist Register, 1982. Ed. by Martin Eve & David Musson. 1982. 15.95 (ISBN 0-85036-292-X, Pub. by Merlin Pr UK); pap. 6.95 (ISBN 0-85036-293-8, Pub. by Merlin Pr UK). Longwood Pub Group.

Socialist Register, 1983. 1983. 15.95 (ISBN 0-85036-309-8, Pub. by Merlin Pr UK); pap. 8.50 (ISBN 0-85036-310-1, Pub. by Merlin Pr UK). Longwood Pub Group.

Socialist Register 1984: The Uses of Anti-Communism. Ed. by Ralph Miliband et al. 363p. 1984. 20.95 (ISBN 0-85036-325-X, Pub. by Merlin Pr UK). Longwood Pub Group.

Socialist Register 1984: The Uses of Anti-Communism, Vol. 21. Ed. by R. Miliband et al. 300p. 1984. text ed. 25.00x (ISBN 0-85036-324-1, Pub. by Merlin Pr UK). Humanities.

Socialist Register 1985-86. Ed. by Ralph Miliband et al. 1985. 25.00 (ISBN 0-85036-340-3, Pub. by Merlin Pr UK). Longwood Pub Group.

Socialist Register 1985-86: Social Democracy & After. Ed. by Ralph Miliband et al. (Illus.). 504p. 1986. 39.95 (ISBN 0-85036-339-X, Pub. by Merlin Pr UK). Humanities.

Socialist Register, 1987: Conservatism in Britain & America--Rhetoric & Reality. Ed. by Ralph Miliband et al. 532p. 1987. 39.95 (ISBN 0-85036-348-9, Pub. by Merlin Pr UK). Humanities.

Socialist Register, 1988. Ed. by Ralph Miliband et al. 460p. 1988. text ed. 49.95 (ISBN 0-85036-354-3, Pub. by Merlin Pr UK). Humanities.

Socialist Renewal: East & West. Ed. by Ralph Miliband et al. (Socialist Register Ser.). 500p. 1988. pap. 12.00 (ISBN 0-85345-751-4, Pub. by Merlin England). Monthly Rev.

Socialist Republic of Rumania. Stephen Fischer-Galati. LC 69-19468. (Integration & Community Building in Eastern Europe Ser: No. 6). (Illus.). 124p. 1969. 14.50x (ISBN 0-8018-1034-5). Johns Hopkins.

Socialist Review, Vols. 1-7, No. 2. Socialist Party of the United States. 1968. Repr. of 1940 ed. Set. lib. bdg. 94.00x o. p. (ISBN 0-8371-9246-3, S200); Vols. 1 & 2. lib. bdg. 20.00 (ISBN 0-313-21942-7, S201); Vols. 3 & 4. lib. bdg. 20.00 (ISBN 0-313-21943-5, S203); Vol. 5. lib. bdg. 31.00 (ISBN 0-313-21944-3, S205); Vols. 6 & 7. lib. bdg. 30.00 (ISBN 0-313-21945-1, S206). Greenwood.

Socialist Revolution. Karl Marx & Friedrich Engels. 355p. 1978. 4.45 (ISBN 0-8285-0054-1, Pub. by Progress Pubs USSR). Imported Pubns.

Socialist States in the World-System. Christopher K. Chase-Dunn. (Sage Focus Editions: Vol. 58). 320p. 1982. 35.00 (ISBN 0-8039-1878-X). Sage.

Socialist Third World: Urban Development & Territorial Planning. Dean Forbes & Nigel Thrift. 288p. (Orig.). Date not set. text ed. 45.00 (ISBN 0-631-13442-5); pap. text ed. 19.95 (ISBN 0-631-15616-X). Basil Blackwell.

Socialist Thought. Dwight D. Murphey. LC 82-24751. 436p. (Orig.). 1983. lib. bdg. 35.50 (ISBN 0-8191-3025-7); pap. text ed. 18.75 (ISBN 0-8191-3026-5). U Pr of Amer.

Socialist Thought in Imaginative Literature. Stephen Ingle. 211p. 1979. 22.50x (ISBN 0-8476-6129-6). Rowman.

Socialist Thought in Modern India. R. A. Prasad. 1979. 11.00 (ISBN 0-89684-512-5). Orient Bk Dist.

Socialist Thought of Jawaharlal Nehru. Benudhar Pradhan. LC 74-902421. 400p. 1974. 17.50x (ISBN 0-88386-387-1). South Asia Bks.

Socialist Visions. Ed. by Stephen R. Shalom. 350p. 1983. 20.00 (ISBN 0-89608-170-2); pap. 9.00 (ISBN 0-89608-169-9). South End Pr.

Socialist Women: European Socialist Feminism in the Nineteenth & Early Twentieth-Centuries. Ed. by M. J. Boxer & J. H. Quataert. 1978. pap. 19.50 (ISBN 0-444-99050-X). Elsevier.

Socialist Workers Party in World War Two: Writings & Speeches, Nineteen Forty to Nineteen Forty-Three. James P. Cannon. Ed. by George Breitman & Les Evans. LC 75-20719. (Illus.). 48p. 1975. 33.00 (ISBN 0-87348-456-8); pap. 9.95 (ISBN 0-87348-457-6). Path Pr NY.

Socialist World System. G. Pirogov. (Library of Political Knowledge: No. 6). 132p. 1983. 25.00x (ISBN 0-317-39532-7, Pub. by Collets (UK)). State Mutual BK.

Socialist World System. G. Pirogov. (Library of Political Knowledge: No. 6). 132p. 1983. pap. 6.25x (ISBN 0-317-53768-7, Pub. by Collets (UK)). State Mutual Bk.

Socialist Zionism: Theory & Issues in Contemporary Jewish Nationalism. Allon Gal. 225p. 1973. pap. 12.95x (ISBN 0-87073-669-8). Transaction Bks.

Socialistic, Communistic, Mutualistic, & Financial Fragments. William B. Greene. LC 75-319. (Radical Tradition in America Ser.). 271p. 1975. Repr. of 1875 ed. 23.10 (ISBN 0-88355-223-X). Hyperion Conn.

Socialists & Socialism. Thomas E. Watson. (Studies in Populism). 1980. lib. bdg. 69.95 (ISBN 0-87700-324-6). Revisionist Pr.

Socialists & the Ballot Box: An Historical Analysis. Eric T. Chester. LC 85-6475. 192p. 1985. 35.00 (ISBN 0-275-90073-8, C0073). Praeger.

Socialists & the Fight Against Anti-Semitism. Peter Seidman. 32p. 1973. pap. 0.60 (ISBN 0-87348-293-X). Path Pr NY.

Socialists & the Problems of War see American Socialists & the War.

Socialist's Budget (1907) see From Serfdom to Socialism (1907).

Socialist's Faith. Norman Thomas. LC 76-105809. Repr. of 1951 ed. 25.50x (ISBN 0-8046-1436-9, Pub. by kennikat). Assoc Faculty Pr.

Socialists in the Recession: The Search for Solidarity. Giles Radice & Lisanne Radice. LC 86-14265. 200p. 1986. 29.95 (ISBN 0-312-73748-3). St Martin.

Socialists of Rural Andalusia: Unacknowledged Revolutionaries of the Second Republic. George A. Collier. LC 87-9929. (Illus.). 264p. 1987. text ed. 32.50x (ISBN 0-8047-1411-8). Stanford U Pr.

Socialists Register: Annuals: Nineteen Seventy-Nine to Nineteen Eighty-Seven. Ed. by Ralph Milliband & J. Saville. 20.00 ea. Saifer.

Sociality & Sympathy. J. W. Jones. Bd. with The Practice Curve. J. H. Bair. Repr. of 1903 ed; Psychology of Expectations. Clara M. Hitchcock. Repr. of 1903 ed; Motor, Visual & Applied Rhythms. J. B. Miner. Repr. of 1903 ed; Perception of Number. J. F. Messenger. Repr. of 1903 ed; Study of Memory. E. N. Henderson. Repr. of 1903 ed. (Psychology Monographs General & Applied: Vol. 5). pap. 44.00 (ISBN 0-8115-1404-8). Kraus Repr.

Sociality, Ethics, & Social Change: A Critical Appraisal of Reinhold Niebuhr's Ethics in the Light of Rosemary Radford Ruether's Works. annual Judith Vaughan. LC 83-1293. 228p. (Orig.). 1983. text ed. 27.50 (ISBN 0-8191-3100-8); pap. text ed. 13.25 (ISBN 0-8191-3101-6). U Pr of Amer.

Sociality in Preadolescent Boys. Ruth E. Hartley. LC 71-176847. (Columbia University. Teachers College. Contributions to Education: No. 918). Repr. of 1946 ed. 22.50 (ISBN 0-404-55918-2). AMS Pr.

Socialization. Thomas R. Williams. (Illus.). 448p. 1983. write for info. (ISBN 0-13-815597-6). P-H.

Socialization: An Ethnic Study. B. G. Banerjee. xv, 186p. 1986. text ed. 35.00x (ISBN 81-210-0073-4, Pub. by Inter India Pubns N Delhi). Apt Bks.

Socialization & Communication in Primary Groups. Ed. by Thomas R. Williams. (World Anthropology Ser.). (Illus.). xii, 470p. 1975. 43.50 (ISBN 90-279-7730-5). Mouton.

Socialization & Personality Development. 2nd ed. Ed. by Edward F. Zigler & Michael E Lamb. 1982. text ed. 29.95x (ISBN 0-19-503076-1); pap. text ed. 15.95x (ISBN 0-19-503077-X). Oxford U Pr.

Socialization & Schools. Talcott Parsons et al. (Reprint Ser.: No. 1). 604p. 1969. pap. 3.50x (ISBN 0-916690-00-8). Harvard Educ Rev.

Socialization & the Life Cycle. Ed. by Peter I. Rose. LC 78-65243. 1979. pap. text ed. write for info. (ISBN 0-312-73800-5). St Martin.

Socialization as Cultural Communication: Development of a Theme in the Work of Margaret Mead. Ed. by Theodore Schwartz. LC 75-17282. 1976. 26.50x (ISBN 0-520-03061-3); pap. 10.95x (ISBN 0-520-03955-6). U of Cal Pr.

Socialization for Achievement: Essays on the Cultural Psychology of the Japanese. George A. DeVos. LC 78-132420. (Center of Japanese Studies, UC Berkeley: No. 7). 613p. 1973. pap. 15.95x (ISBN 0-520-02893-7). U of Cal Pr.

Socialization Games for Mentally Retarded Adolescents & Adults. David Moxley et al. (Illus.). 130p. 1981. spiral bdg. 14.25 (ISBN 0-398-04546-1). C C Thomas.

Socialization in Drug Abuse. Ed. by Robert Coombs et al. LC 75-37067. 496p. 1976. pap. text ed. 15.95x (ISBN 0-87073-489-X). Schenkman Bks Inc.

Socialization in Physical Education: Learning to Teach. Thomas J. Templin & Paul G. Schempp. (Illus.). 300p. 1988. pap. text ed. 19.95 (ISBN 0-936157-25-9). Benchmark Pr.

Socialization of Affect. Ed. by Sara Harkness & Philip L. Kilbride. (Ethos Ser.: Vol. 11, No. 4). 1983. 10.00 (ISBN 0-317-66365-8). Am Anthro Assn.

Socialization of Emotions. Ed. by Michael Lewis & Carolyn Saarni. (Genesis of Behavior Ser. vol.5). 334p. 1985. 39.50x (ISBN 0-306-41851-7, Plenum Pr). Plenum Pub.

Socialization of Family Size Values: Youth & Family Planning in an Indian Village. Thomas Poffenberger & Kim Sebaly. LC 76-53996. (Michigan Papers on South and Southeast Asia: No. 12). (Illus.). xiv, 159p. (Orig.). 1976. pap. 6.95 (ISBN 0-89148-012-9). Ctr S&SE Asian.

Socialization of Law Students: A Case Study in Three Parts. Wagner P. Thielens, Jr. Ed. by Harriet Zuckerman & Robert K. Merton. LC 79-9034. (Dissertation on Sociology Ser.). 1980. lib. bdg. 42.00x (ISBN 0-405-13001-5). Ayer Co Pubs.

Socialization of Neophyte Nurses. Loretta C. Myers. LC 82-7014. (Studies in Nursing Management: No. 1). (Illus.). 156p. pap. 40.60 (2070022). Bks Demand UMI.

Socialization of the Indian Child. Ed. by Durganand Sinha. 172p. 1981. 17.95 (ISBN 0-940500-07-8, Pub. by Concept Pub India). Asia Bk Corp.

Socialization of the New England Clergy Eighteen Hundred to Eighteen Sixty. Gordon A. Riegler. LC 79-13027. (Perspectives in American History Ser.: No. 37). 187p. 1980. Repr. of 1945 ed. lib. bdg. 25.00x (ISBN 0-87991-361-4). Porcupine Pr.

Socialization, Sexism & Stereotyping: Women's Issues in Nursing. Janet Muff. (Illus.). 434p. 1988. pap. text ed. 17.95x (ISBN 0-88133-372-7). Waveland Pr.

Socialization to Old Age. Irving Rosow. LC 73-78540. 1975. pap. 9.95x (ISBN 0-520-03417-1). U of Cal Pr.

Socialized Agriculture of the U. S. S. R. Plans & Performance. Naum Jasny. 1949. 60.00x (ISBN 0-8047-0401-5). Stanford U Pr.

Socially Responsible Believers: Puritans, Pietists, & Unionists in the History of the United Church of Christ. Lowell H. Zuck. 164p. (Orig.). 1987. pap. 8.95 (ISBN 0-8298-0744-6). Pilgrim NY.

Socially Responsible Investment & Economic Development. Ed. by Jemadari Kamara. (Michigan Business Papers: No. 68). 1987. pap. 6.00 (ISBN 0-87712-253-9). UMI Div Res GSBA.

Socially Responsible Stock Guide (With Supplement Insert, "How to Screen Traditional Investments for Social Factors") Ritchie P. Lowry. 48p. (Orig.). 1985. pap. 2.50 2-wire saddle-stitch bdg. (ISBN 0-933609-01-9). Good Money Pubns.

Socials for All Occasions. Mildred Wade. LC 79-55492. (Orig.). 1980. pap. 4.95 (ISBN 0-8054-7518-4). Broadman.

Sociedad Communista. Karl Marx et al. 172p. 1985. pap. 1.95 (ISBN 0-8285-3354-7, Pub. by Progress Pubs USSR). Imported Pubns.

Sociedad Comunista. Karl Marx et al. 172p. (Span.). 1973. pap. 1.95 (ISBN 0-8285-1485-2, Pub. by Progress Pubs USSR). Imported Pubns.

Sociedad, Derecho y Justicia. Jose T. Monge. LC 84-25862. (Span.). 1985. lib. bdg. 25.00 (ISBN 0-8477-3020-4). U of PR Pr.

Sociedad Espanola: Desde 1500 Hasta Nuestros Dias. Fernando Diaz Plaja. pap. 3.75 (ISBN 0-8477-3117-0). U of PR Pr.

Sociedad Espanola en la Novela de la Postguerra. F. Carenas & Jose Ferrando. 1971. 10.95 (ISBN 0-88303-997-4). E Torres & Sons.

Sociedad y Tipos en las Novelas de Ramon Meza y Suarez Inclan. Manuel A. Gonzales. LC 82-84334. (Coleccion Polymita Ser.). 184p. (Orig., Span.). 1985. pap. 12.95 (ISBN 0-89729-326-6). Ediciones.

Societa Italiana Di Fronte Alle Prime Migrazioni Di Massa: Italian Society at the Beginnings of the Mass Migrations. Ed. by Francesco Cordasco. LC 74-17954. (Italian American Experience Ser). (Illus.). 524p. 1975. Repr. 32.00x (ISBN 0-405-06423-3). Ayer Co Pubs.

Societal Foundations of Education. Jack Rudman. (National Teachers Examination Ser.: NC-2). (Cloth bdg. avail. on request). pap. 13.95 (ISBN 0-8373-8402-8). Natl Learning.

Societal Growth: Processes & Implications. Amos H. Hawley. LC 79-7339. (Illus.). 1979. 19.95 (ISBN 0-02-914200-8). Free Pr.

Societal Issues - Scientific Viewpoints. Margaret A. Strom. LC 87-18822. 256p. 1987. text ed. 41.25 (ISBN 0-88318-537-7); pap. text ed. 31.25 (ISBN 0-317-64885-3). Am Inst Physics.

Societal Learning Approach: A New Approach to Social Welfare Policy & Planning in America. Thomas D. Watts. LC 80-69231. 140p. 1981. perfect bdg. 11.95 (ISBN 0-86548-058-3). R & E Pubs.

Societal Provision for the Long-Term Needs of the Disabled in Britain & Sweden Relative to Decision-Making in Newborn Intensive Care Units. Ernle W. Young. (International Exchange of Experts & Information in Rehabilitation Ser.: No. 25). pap. 3.00 (ISBN 0-939986-38-8). World Rehab Fund.

Societal Responses to Regional Climatic Change: Forecasting by Analogy. Ed. by Michael H. Glantz. (Special Study: No. 35). 275p. 1988. 27.50 (ISBN 0-8133-7639-4). Westview.

Societal Risk Assessment: How Safe Is Safe Enough? Ed. by Richard C. Schwing & Walter A. Albers. LC 80-23833. (General Motors Research Symposia Ser.). 374p. 1980. 70.00x (ISBN 0-306-40554-7, Plenum Pr). Plenum Pub.

Societal Stratification: A Theoretical Analysis. Jonathan Turner. LC 83-7660. 216p. 1984. 35.00x (ISBN 0-231-05740-7, King's Crown Paperbacks); pap. 16.00x (ISBN 0-231-05741-5, King's Crown Paperbacks). Columbia U Pr.

Societal Systems: Methodology, Modeling & Management. Sutherland. (System Science & Engineering Ser.: Vol. 3). 336p. 1978. 57.50 (ISBN 0-444-00239-1, North-Holland). Elsevier.

Societal Utilization of Scientific & Technological Research. (Science Policy Studies & Documents: No. 47). 32p. 1981. pap. 5.00 (ISBN 92-3-101858-2, U1100, UNESCO). UNIPUB.

Societas Ergophthalmologica Internationalis: 5th Symposium, Bordeaux 1974. 6th Symposium, Hamburg 1976. 7th Symposium, Nagoya 1978. Ed. by H. J. Merte. (Problems of Industrial Medicine in Opthamology Ser.: Vol. 5-7). (Illus.). xx, 760p. 1982. pap. 166.00 (ISBN 3-8055-3003-X). S Karger.

Societas et Fraternitas. Karl Schmid & Joachim Wollasch. 40p. 1975. pap. text ed. 5.10x (ISBN 3-11-006580-0). De Gruyter.

Societe & Liberte Chez les Peul Djelgobe De Haute-Volta: Essai D'anthropologie Introspective. Paul Riesman. (Cahiers De L'homme, Nouvelle Serie: No. 14). (Illus.). 1974. pap. 16.80x (ISBN 90-2797-322-9). Mouton.

Societe Anonyme & the Dreier Bequest at Yale University: A Catalogue Raisonne. Ed. by Robert L. Herbert et al. LC 83-3533. (Illus.). 791p. 1984. 140.00x (ISBN 0-300-03040-1). Yale U Pr.

Societe Anonyme, Inc. Selected Publications, 3 vols. (Contemporary Art Ser). (Illus.). 1971. Repr. of 1920 ed. Set. 80.00 (ISBN 0-685-27567-1). Vol. 1 (ISBN 0-405-00770-1). Vol. 2 (ISBN 0-405-00771-X). Vol. 3 (ISBN 0-405-00772-8). Ayer Co Pubs.

Societe Anonyme, the First Museum of Modern Art, 1920-1944: Selected Publications, 3 vols. Societe Anonyme. 80.00 (ISBN 0-405-00798-1, 11379). Ayer Co Pubs.

Societe Belge de Dermatologie et de Syphiligraphie: Belgische Vereniging voor Dermatologie en Syfiligrafie. Ed. by R. Schuppli. (Journal: Dermatologica Ser.: Vol. 158, No. 3). (Illus.). 1979. pap. 22.00 (ISBN 3-8055-3018-8). S Karger.

Societe d'Archeologie Copte, Cairo Bulletin: Vols. 1-22, Cairo, 1935-1973. 919.00 (ISBN 0-8115-3862-1); pap. text ed. 748.00 (ISBN 0-8115-3863-X). Kraus Repr.

Societe Des Anciens Textes Francais Publications, Vols. 1-70 In 125 Vols. Societe Des Anciens Textes Francais. 1875-1925. Set. 3600.00 (ISBN 0-384-56560-3). Johnson Repr.

Societe Des Bronzes De Paris 1909, 2 vols. 96p. Set. pap. 25.00 (ISBN 0-317-54947-2). Apollo.

Societe des Jacobins, 6 Vols. Tr. by Francois V. Aulard. LC 78-161707. (Collection de documents relatifs a l'histoire de Paris pendant la Revolution francaise). Repr. of 1897 ed. Set. 507.00 (ISBN 0-404-52560-1); 84.50 ea. AMS Pr.

Societe Feodale. Joseph L. Calmette. LC 80-1994. Repr. of 1932 ed. 30.00 (ISBN 0-404-18556-8). AMS Pr.

Societe Feodale Allemande et Ses Institutions Du Xe Au XIIe Siecle. Charles E. Perrin. LC 80-2013. Repr. of 1956 ed. 38.50 (ISBN 0-404-18583-5). AMS Pr.

Societe Francaise au Temps de Philippe-Auguste. Achille Luchaire. 462p. (Fr.). Repr. of 1909 ed. lib. bdg. 87.50x. Coronet Bks.

Societe International De Chirurgie Orthopedique et de Traumatology: Fifty Years of Achievement. Ed. by E. Vander Elst. (Illus.). 1979. 18.90 (ISBN 0-387-08968-3). Springer-Verlag.

Societe Rurale Au XIX Siecle: Les Paysans Du Calvados, Eighteen Fifteen to Eighteen Ninty-Five. Gabriel Desert. Ed. by Stuart Bruchey. LC 77-77166. (Dissertations in European Economic History Ser.). (Illus., Fr.). 1977. lib. bdg. 70.50x (ISBN 0-405-10780-3). Ayer Co Pubs.

Societe Suisse de Gynecologie, Bericht ueber die Jahresversammlung, Genf, 1981. Ed. by E. Dreher. (Gynaekologische Rundschau Journal: Vol. 21, Suppl. 3). (Illus.). iv, 88p. 1981. pap. 19.50 (ISBN 3-8055-3479-5). S Karger.

Societes Bantoues du Congo Belge et les Problemes de la Politique Indigene. Georges Van der Kerken. (Fr.). 1920. 44.00 (ISBN 0-8115-3084-1). Kraus Repr.

Societes D'initiation Bambara: Le N'domo, le Kore. Dominique Zahan. (Lemonde D'outre-Mer Passe et Present: Etudes 8). 1960. pap. 21.60x (ISBN 90-2796-165-4). Mouton.

Societies & Languages of the Ancient Near East: Studies in Honour of I. M. Diakonoff. Ed. by M. A. Dandamayev et al. 355p. 1982. pap. 60.00x (Pub. by Aris & Phillips UK) (ISBN 0-85668-205-5). Humanities.

Societies Animals: Animal Societies. Alfred V. Espinas. Ed. by Frank N. Egerton, 3rd. LC 77-74219. (History of Ecology Ser.). 1978. Repr. of 1878 ed. lib. bdg. 34.00 (ISBN 0-405-10390-5). Ayer Co Pubs.

Societies in Upheaval: Insurrections in France, Hungary, & Spain in the Early Eighteenth Century. Linda Frey & Marsha Frey. LC 86-25744. (Contributions to the Study of World History Ser.: No. 6). 154p. 1987. lib. bdg. 29.95 (ISBN 0-313-25592-X, FYU/). Greenwood.

Societies of Borneo: Explorations in the Theory of Cognatic Social Structure. Ed. by G. N. Appell. (Special Publication: No. 6). 1976. pap. 7.50 (ISBN 0-686-36568-2); pap. 5.00 members. Am Anthro Assn.

Societies of the Plains Indians, 13 pts. in 1 vol. Ed. by Clark Wissler. LC 74-9027. (Anthropological Papers of the American Museum of Natural History: Vol. 11). (Illus.). Repr. of 1916 ed. 70.00 (ISBN 0-404-11918-2). AMS Pr.

Societism: The Future Government for the United States of America. Alfred Korn, Jr. LC 76-24512. write for info. (ISBN 0-917498-01-1). Korn.

Society. David Frisby & Derek Sayer. (Key Ideas Ser.). 150p. 1986. 19.95 (ISBN 0-85312-834-0, 9708, Pub. by Tavistock England); pap. 7.50 (ISBN 0-85312-852-9, 9703, Pub. by Tavistock England). Routledge Chapman & Hall.

Society. R. M. MacIver. 596p. 1980. Repr. of 1937 ed. lib. bdg. 75.00 (ISBN 0-89984-338-7). Century Bookbindery.

Society. 1987. write for info. Am Welding.

Society: A Macroscopic View. Maurice N. Richter, Jr. 136p. 1980. pap. text ed. 11.95 (ISBN 0-87073-804-6). Schenkman Bks Inc.

Society: A Textbook of Sociology. R. M. MacIver. 596p. 1982. Repr. of 1937 ed. lib. bdg. 50.00 (ISBN 0-89987-587-4). Darby BKs.

Society Against the State: Essays in Political Anthropology. Pierre Clastres. Tr. by Robert Hurley & Abe Stein. LC 87-50396. 218p. 1987. 18.95 (ISBN 0-942299-00-0). Zone Bks.

Society & Change: The Development of Canadian Sociology Through the Work of S. D. Clark. Harry H. Hiller. 200p. 1982. 25.00x (ISBN 0-8020-5540-0). U of Toronto Pr.

Society & Civilization in Greece & Rome. Victor L. Ehrenberg. LC 64-19580. (Martin Classical Lectures Ser: No. 18). (Illus.). 1964. 8.95t (ISBN 0-674-81510-6). Harvard U Pr.

Society & Community in India. R. K. Mukharjee. 155p. 1979. 12.95. Asia Bk Corp.

Society & Cosmos: Chewong of Peninsular Malaysia. Signe Howell. (Illus.). 294p. 1984. 55.00x (ISBN 0-19-582543-8). Oxford U Pr.

Society & Culture During the Mughal Age. P. N. Chopra. 1987. 74.95. Asia Bk Corp.

Society & Culture in Early Modern France: Eight Essays by Natalie Zemon Davis. Natalie Z. Davis. LC 74-82777. (Illus.). 1975. 32.50x (ISBN 0-8047-0868-1); pap. 16.95 (ISBN 0-8047-0972-6, SP-142). Stanford U Pr.

Society & Culture in Northern India, 1850-1900. Shiva S. Dua. vi, 272p. 1985. 26.50 (ISBN 81-85004-04-8, Pub. by Indian Bibliographies Bureau). Nataraj Bks.

Society & Democracy in Germany. Ralf Dahrendorf. LC 79-15142. 1980. Repr. of 1969 ed. lib. bdg. 41.50x (ISBN 0-313-22027-1, DASO). Greenwood.

Society & Democracy in Germany. Ralf Dahrendorf. 1979. pap. 9.95x (ISBN 0-393-00953-X). Norton.

Society & Development in Contemporary India. Ranjit Tirtha. LC 80-83157. (Illus.). 368p. 1980. 13.50 (ISBN 0-8187-0040-8). Harlo Pr.

Society & Development in Contemporary India: Geographical Perspectives. Ranjit Tirtha. (Illus.). 368p. 1980. 19.50 (ISBN 0-686-27540-3). R Tirtha.

Society & Deviance in Communist Poland: Attitudes Towards Social Control. Jerzy Kwasniewski. Tr. by Margaret Watson. LC 84-6803. 256p. 1984. 27.50 (ISBN 0-312-73803-X). St Martin.

Society & Economics in Islam. Sayyid M. Taleghani. Tr. by R. Campbell from Persian. LC 82-2115. (Contemporary Islamic Thought Ser.). 225p. 1983. 17.95 (ISBN 0-933782-08-X). Mizan Pr.

Society & Economy in Colonial Connecticut. Jackson T. Main. LC 84-42892. 420p. 1985. text ed. 38.00x (ISBN 0-691-04726-X). Princeton U Pr.

Society & Education. 6th ed. Daniel U. Levine & Robert J. Havighurst. 1984. text ed. 39.00 (ISBN 0-205-08084-7, 238084). Allyn.

Society & Education in Japan. Herbert Passin. LC 82-48167. 347p. 1983. pap. 6.25 (ISBN 0-87011-554-5). Kodansha.

Society & Family Strategy: Erie County, New York 1850-1920. Mark J. Stern. LC 86-23121. 160p. 1987. 44.50 (ISBN 0-88706-495-7); pap. 14.95 (ISBN 0-88706-496-5). State U NY Pr.

Society & Freedom: An Introduction to Humanist Sociology. Joseph A. Scimecca. 250p. 1981. text ed. write for info. (ISBN 0-312-73806-4); pap. text ed. write for info. (ISBN 0-312-73807-2). St Martin.

Society & Government in France under Richelieu & Mazarin, 1624-61. Richard Bonney. 304p. 1987. 37.50 (ISBN 0-312-01303-5). St Martin.

Society & Health in a Mountain Community. Harvey L. Smith. 25p. 1961. pap. text ed. 1.50 (ISBN 0-89143-053-9). U NC Inst Res Soc Sci.

Society & Health in Guyana: The Sociology of Health Care in a Developing Nation. Marcel Fredericks et al. LC 84-70752. (Illus.). 189p. (Orig.). 1986. lib. bdg. 22.75 (ISBN 0-89089-295-4). Carolina Acad Pr.

Society & History: Essays by Sylvia L. Thrupp. Ed. by Raymond Grew & Nicholas H. Steneck. LC 75-31056. 352p. 1977. text ed. 18.50x (ISBN 0-472-08880-7). U of Mich Pr.

Society & History: Essays in Honor of Karl August Wittogel. G. L. Ulmen. 1978. 66.50x (ISBN 0-686-26043-0). Mouton.

Society & History in English Renaissance Verse. Lauro Martines. 224p. 1985. 29.95x (ISBN 0-631-14115-4). Basil Blackwell.

Society & History in English Renaissance Verse. Lavro Martines. 200p. (Orig.). Date not set. pap. text ed. 15.95 (ISBN 0-631-15683-6). Basil Blackwell.

Society & Homicide in Thirteenth-Century England. James Buchanan Given. LC 76-23372. 1977. 25.00x (ISBN 0-8047-0939-4). Stanford U Pr.

Society & Identity: Toward a Sociological Psychology. Andrew J. Weigert et al. (ASA Rose Monograph). 176p. 1986. 32.50 (ISBN 0-521-32325-8). Cambridge U Pr.

Society & Ideology: An Inquiry into the Sociology of Knowledge. Gerard DeGre. Ed. by Lewis A. Coser & Walter W. Powell. LC 79-6991. (Perennial Works in Sociology Ser.). 1979. Repr. of 1943 ed. lib. bdg. 15.00x (ISBN 0-405-12091-5). Ayer Co Pubs.

Society & Knowledge. Vere G. Childe. LC 72-10690. 131p. 1973. Repr. of 1956 ed. lib. bdg. 48.50x (ISBN 0-8371-6620-9, CHSK). Greenwood.

Society & Knowledge: Contemporary Perspectives on the Sociology of Knowledge. Ed. by Nico Stehr & Volker Meja. 430p. 1984. 34.95 (ISBN 0-87855-493-9); pap. text ed. 14.95x (ISBN 0-87855-950-7). Transaction Bks.

Society & Legal Change. Alan Watson. 10.00x (ISBN 0-7073-0137-8, Pub. by Scot Acad Pr). Longwood Pub Group.

Society & Literature in America. Perry Miller. LC 77-8170. 1949. lib. bdg. 17.50 (ISBN 0-8414-6198-8). Folcroft.

Society & Literature, Nineteen Forty-Five to Nineteen Seventy. Ed. by Alan Sinfield. LC 83-12844. (Context of English Literature Ser.). 266p. 1983. 29.50 (ISBN 0-8419-0903-2); pap. 16.50 (ISBN 0-8419-0904-0). Holmes & Meier.

Society & Medicine. facs. ed. New York Academy of Medicine. Ed. by Iago Galdston. LC 74-142684. (Essay Index Reprint Ser). 1955. 14.00 (ISBN 0-8369-2124-0). Ayer Co Pubs.

Society & Milieu in the French Geographic Tradition. Anne Buttimer. LC 72-158112. (Monograph: No. 6). 4.95 (ISBN 0-89291-085-2). Assn Am Geographers.

Society & Nature. I. Novik. 301p. 1981. 6.00 (ISBN 0-8285-2049-6, Pub. by Progress Pubs USSR). Imported Pubns.

Society & Nature: A Sociological Inquiry. Hans Kelsen. LC 73-14161. (Perspectives in Social Inquiry Ser.). 404p. 1974. Repr. 23.50x (ISBN 0-405-05507-2). Ayer Co Pubs.

Society & Personality: The Interactionist Approach to Social Psychology. Tamotsu Shibutani. 646p. 1987. pap. 19.95 (ISBN 0-88738-688-1). Transaction Bks.

Society & Politics: An Overview & Reappraisal of Political Sociology. George A. Kourvetaris & Betty A. Dobratz. 176p. 1980. pap. text ed. 10.95 (ISBN 0-8403-2238-0). Kendall-Hunt.

Society & Politics in Ancient Rome: Essays & Sketches. Frank F. Abbott. LC 63-10767. 267p. (gr. 7 up). 1909. 15.00 (ISBN 0-8196-0118-7). Biblo.

Society & Politics in Colonial Trinidad. James Millette. 320p. 1985. 30.95 (ISBN 0-86232-421-1, Pub. by Zed Pr England); pap. 12.25 (ISBN 0-86232-422-X, Pub. by Zed Pr England). Humanities.

Society & Politics in Hong Kong. Siu-kai Lau. x, 205p. 1982. text ed. 24.00x (ISBN 962-201-336-8, Pub. by Chinese U HK). Coronet Bks.

Society & Politics in Hong Kong. Lau Siu-Kai. LC 82-23035. 220p. 1980. 25.00x (ISBN 0-312-73892-7). St Martin.

Society & Politics in Medieval Italy. J. K. Hyde. 1973. write for info. (ISBN 0-312-73920-6). St Martin.

Society & Politics in Revolutionary Bordeaux. Alan Forrest. (Oxford Historical Monographs). 1975. 52.00x (ISBN 0-19-821859-1). Oxford U Pr.

Society & Politics in the Acts of the Apostles. Richard J. Cassidy. 256p. (Orig.). 1987. 19.95 (ISBN 0-88344-568-9); pap. 9.95 (ISBN 0-88344-567-0). Orbis Bks.

Society & Polity in Modern Sri Lanka. K. L. Sharma. 1988. 17.50x (ISBN 81-7003-089-7). South Asia Pubns.

Society & Power: Five New England Towns, 1800-1860. Robert Doherty. LC 77-73477. (Illus.). 128p. 1977. 12.50 (ISBN 0-87023-242-8). U of Mass Pr.

Society & Prisons: With Intro. Added. Thomas M. Osborne. LC 72-172587. (Criminology, Law Enforcement, & Social Problems Ser.: No. 177). 1975. 14.00x (ISBN 0-87585-177-0). Patterson Smith.

Society & Religion During the Age of Industrialization: Christianity in Victorian England. Lee E Grugel. LC 78-65844. (Illus.). 1979. pap. text ed. 10.00 (ISBN 0-8191-0671-2). U Pr of Amer.

Society & Religion in Early Ottoman Egypt. Michael Winter. LC 81-3042. 350p. 1981. 39.95 (ISBN 0-87855-351-7). Transaction Bks.

Society & Religion in Elizabethan England. Richard L. Greaves. LC 81-2530. pap. 160.00 (2056201). Bks Demand UMI.

Society & Religion in Munster. R. Po-chia Hsia. LC 83-14819. (Yale Historical Publications Ser.: No. 131). 320p. 1984. text ed. 30.00t (ISBN 0-300-03005-3). Yale U Pr.

Society & Religion in the Grand Duchy of Lituania: A Reprint of the Seventeen Fifty-Four Nieswiez Edition of Pelnai Pieknej jak ksiezyc lask promieniami swiatu przyswiecajaca. Intro. by Maciej Siekierski. 118p. (Pol.). 1985. pap. 9.50 (ISBN 0-933884-51-6). Berkeley Slavic.

Society & Self in the Novel see English Institute Essays.

Society & Social Change in the Writings of St. Thomas, Ward, Sumner, & Cooley. Mary E. Healy. LC 75-156191. 159p. 1972. Repr. of 1948 ed. lib. bdg. 25.00x (ISBN 0-8371-6140-1, HESC). Greenwood.

Society & State Building in Nepal. R. S. Chauhan. 250p. 1988. text ed. 40.00x (ISBN 81-207-0864-4, Pub. by Sterling Pubs India). Apt Bks.

Society & Technological Change. Rudi Volti. LC 87-60526. 352p. Date not set. pap. write for info. (ISBN 0-312-00311-0). St Martin.

Society & the Dance: The Social Anthropology of Process & Performance. Ed. by Paul Spencer. 208p. 1986. 42.50 (ISBN 0-521-30521-7); pap. 14.95 (ISBN 0-521-31550-6). Cambridge U Pr.

Society & the Environment. Collets Staff. 174p. 1983. 11.25x (ISBN 0-317-53761-X, Pub. by Collets (UK)). State Mutual Bk.

Society & the Environment: A Soviet View. P. Kapitsa et al. 224p. 1977. pap. 3.45 (ISBN 0-8285-0439-3, Pub. by Progress Pubs USSR). Imported Pubns.

Society & the Healthy Homosexual. George Weinberg. 160p. 1983. pap. 5.95 (ISBN 0-312-73851-X). St Martin.

Society & the Holy in Late Antiquity. Peter Brown. LC 80-39862. 350p. 1982. 30.00x (ISBN 0-520-04305-7). U of Cal Pr.

Society & the Homosexual. Gordon Westwood. LC 84-27933. 191p. 1985. Repr. of 1953 ed. lib. bdg. 38.50x (ISBN 0-313-24840-0, SCHO). Greenwood.

Society & the Law: New Meaning for an Old Profession. Floyd J. Davis & Henry H. Foster. LC 78-5643. vi, 488p. 1978. Repr. of 1962 ed. lib. bdg. 38.50x (ISBN 0-313-20445-4, DASL). Greenwood.

Society & the Lyric: A Study of the Song Culture of Eighteenth-Century Scotland. Thomas Crawford. 208p. 1980. 13.50x (ISBN 0-7073-0227-7, Pub. by Scot Acad Pr). Longwood Pub Group.

Society & the New Technology. Kenneth Ruthven. LC 83-7236. (Modern World Issues Ser.). (Illus.). 64p. 1984. pap. 4.95 (ISBN 0-521-27214-9). Cambridge U Pr.

Society & the Sacred: Toward a Theology of Culture in Decline. Langdon Gilkey. LC 81-9775. 225p. 1981. 14.95 (ISBN 0-8245-0089-X). Crossroad NY.

Society & the Sexes in Early Industrial America: Part One of a Bibliographical Guide to the Study of the History of American Women. Jill K. Conway. LC 82-48041. 350p. 1984. lib. bdg. 31.00. Garland Pub.

Society & the Sexes in Medieval Islam. Ed. by A. L. Al-Sayyid-Marsot. LC 79-63268. (Giorgio Levi Della Vida Biennial Conference Ser.: Vol. 6). 149p. 1979. pap. 18.50x (ISBN 0-89003-033-2). Undena Pubns.

Society & Trauma of War. H. Dasberg et al. (Sinai Ser.). (Orig.). 1987. pap. 10.00 (ISBN 90-232-2275-X, Pub. by Van Gorcum Holland). Longwood Pub Group.

Society As Educator in an Age of Transition: Eighty-Sixth Yearbook of the National Society for the Study of Education, Pt. II. Ed. by Kenneth D. Benne & Steven Tozer. xvi, 280p. 1987. lib. bdg. 26.00x (ISBN 0-226-60145-5, Pub. by Natl Soc Stud Educ). U of Chicago Pr.

Society As I Have Found It. facsimile ed. Samuel W. McAllister. LC 75-1855. (Leisure Class in America Ser.). 1975. Repr. of 1890 ed. 31.00x (ISBN 0-405-06921-9). Ayer Co Pubs.

Society As Text: Essays on Rhetoric, Reason & Reality. Richard H. Brown. LC 86-30893. (Illus.). x, 254p. 1987. text ed. 24.95x (ISBN 0-226-07616-4). U of Chicago Pr.

Society As the Patient. Lawrence K. Frank. LC 72-86568. (Essay & General Literature Index Reprint Ser). 1969. Repr. of 1948 ed. 34.50x (ISBN 0-8046-0559-9, Pub. by Kennikat). Assoc Faculty Pr.

Society Based on Work. Anthony P. Carnevale. 102p. 1984. 8.75 (ISBN 0-318-22200-0, IN270). Natl Ctr Res Voc Ed.

Society: Collective Behavior, News & Opinion, Sociology & Modern Society see Collected Papers of Robert Park.

Society, Crime & Criminal Behavior. 5th ed. Don C. Gibbons. LC 86-12204. 576p. 1987. text ed. write for info. (ISBN 0-13-820136-6). P-H.

Society, Culture & Change in the Middle East. Raphael Patai. LC 70-84742. (Illus.). 1971. pap. 16.95x (ISBN 0-8122-1009-3, Pa Paperbks). U of Pa Pr.

Society, Culture & Urbanization. S. N. Eisenstadt & A. Shachar. LC 85-26249. 450p. 1987. text ed. 35.00 (ISBN 0-8039-2478-X). Sage.

Society, Delinquent & Juvenile Court. S. V. Kaldate. 1982. 18.00x (ISBN 0-8364-0911-6, Pub. by Ajanta). South Asia Bks.

Society Finches As Foster Parents. 2nd ed. Robert G. Black. 45p. 1987. pap. 4.95 (ISBN 0-910631-02-6). R G Black.

Society Finches, Breeding. Mervin F. Roberts. (Illus.). 1979. 9.95 (ISBN 0-87666-991-7, KW-030). TFH Pubns.

Society for American Archaeology: Regional Conferences Summary Report. Ed. by Cynthia Irwin-Williams & Don D. Fowler. (SAA Special Publication Ser.). 112p. 1986. 12.50 (ISBN 0-932839-10-X). Soc Am Arch.

Society for Gynecologic Investigation: Proceedings. Scientific Abstracts, 24th Annual Meeting, Tucson, Ariz. March 1977. (Gynecologic Investigation Ser.: Vol. 8, No. 1-2). 1977. 40.00 (ISBN 3-8055-2673-3). S Karger.

Society for International Development: Prospectus Nineteen Eighty-Four. Ed. by Ann Mattis. LC 83-16550. (Duke Press Policy Studies). xxi, 249p. 1983. text ed. 26.50 (ISBN 0-8223-0561-5); pap. text ed. 9.95 (ISBN 0-8223-0562-3). Duke.

Society for Purchasing Books in Wanlockhead. John C. Crawford & Stuart James. 1987. 29.00x (ISBN 0-900649-25-9, Pub. by Scottish Libr Assn). State Mutual Bk.

Society for Pure English, 6 vols, Tracts 1-66. Repr. of 1948 ed. Set. 195.00 (ISBN 0-404-19554-7); 32.50 ea. AMS Pr.

Society for the Propagation of the Faith: Its Foundation, Organization & Success (1822-1922) Edward J. Hickey. LC 73-3557. (Catholic University of America. Studies in American Church History: No. 3). Repr. of 1922 ed. 25.00 (ISBN 0-404-57753-9). AMS Pr.

Society for Vascular Surgery: A History, Nineteen Forty-Five to Nineteen Eighty-Three. Harris B. Shumacker. Ed. by James N. Rogers. LC 83-20450. (Illus.). 450p. 1984. text ed. 15.00 (ISBN 0-9612978-0-8). Society Vascular Surgery.

Society, Freedom & Conscience: The Coming of the Revolution in Virginia, Massachusetts, & New York. Jack P. Greene et al. Ed. by Richard M. Jellison. 1977. pap. text ed. 3.95x (ISBN 0-393-09160-0). Norton.

Society, Government & the Enlightenment: The Experiences of Eighteenth-Century France & Russia. C. B. Behrens. LC 84-48823. 248p. 1985. 19.50i (ISBN 0-06-430386-1, Icon Edns). Har-Row.

Society in America, 3 Vols. Harriet Martineau. LC 1-27890. Repr. of 1837 ed. 145.00 (ISBN 0-404-04260-0). AMS Pr.

Society in America. abr. ed. Harriet Martineau. Intro. by Seymour Lipset. 10.25 (ISBN 0-8446-1302-9). Peter Smith.

Society in America. Harriet Martineau. Ed. by Seymour M. Lipset. LC 80-27647. (Social Science Classics). 357p. 1981. pap. 18.95 (ISBN 0-87855-853-5). Transaction Bks.

Society in Change: Studies in Honor of Bela K. Kiraly. Ed. by Steven B. Vardy. (East European Monograph: No. 132). 680p. 1983. 40.00x (ISBN 0-88033-021-X). East Eur Quarterly.

Society in Colonial North Carolina. Alan D. Watson. (Illus.). x, 93p. 1982. pap. 2.00 (ISBN 0-86526-103-2). NC Archives.

Society in Goa. S. R. Phal. 110p. 1983. text ed. 15.95x (ISBN 0-86590-130-9). Apt Bks.

Society in Imperial Rome: Selections from Juvenal, Martial, Petronius, Seneca, Tacitus & Pliny (Translations from Greek & Roman Authors) Michael Massey. LC 81-15490. 96p. 1982. pap. 6.95 (ISBN 0-521-28036-2). Cambridge U Pr.

Society in Revolutionary North Carolina. Alice E. Mathews. (Illus.). viii, 91p. 1976. pap. 3.00 (ISBN 0-86526-117-2). NC Archives.

Society in the Elizabethan Age. Hubert Hall. 1976. lib. bdg. 59.95 (ISBN 0-8490-2620-2). Gordon Pr.

Society in the Novel. Elizabeth J. Langland. LC 83-23597. xi, 267p. 1984. 26.00x (ISBN 0-8078-1604-3). U of NC Pr.

Society in Transition. 2nd ed. Harry E. Barnes. LC 68-23271. 1968. Repr. of 1952 ed. lib. bdg. 39.25x (ISBN 0-8371-0012-7, BAST). Greenwood.

Society in Transition: Impact on Nursing. Marian M. Pettengill & Lu A. Young. 150p. (Orig.). 1987. pap. 12.50 (ISBN 0-942146-14-X). Midwest Alliance Nursing.

Society in Tribal India. B. B. Sinha. xi, 263p. 1983. text ed. 25.00x (ISBN 0-86590-108-2). Apt Bks.

Society Islands Insects. Pacific Entomological Survey Publications. (BMB). 1935. 21.00 (ISBN 0-527-02219-5). Kraus Repr.

Society, Language & Health. Richard Totman. 1985. 45.00 (ISBN 0-12-696080-1). Acad Pr.

Society, Manners, & Politics in the United States. Michel Chevalier. LC 66-21661. 1966. Repr. of 1839 ed. 45.00x (ISBN 0-678-00195-2). Kelley.

Society, Manners & Politics in the United States: Being a Series of Letters on North America. Michel Chevalier. 1969. Repr. of 1839 ed. 20.50 (ISBN 0-8337-0560-1). B Franklin.

Society, Manners & Politics in the United States: Letters on North America. Michael Chevalier. Ed. by John W. Ward. Tr. by T. G. Bradford. 11.50 (ISBN 0-8446-1111-5). Peter Smith.

Society of American Foresters Ethics Guide. Society of American Foresters. 1985. pap. 4.00 (ISBN 0-939970-29-5). Soc Am Foresters.

Society of American Travel Writers: Membership Directory. 223p. 1988. 50.00. Soc Am Travel Writers.

Society of Anna. Lucile Adler. LC 73-92471. 1974. 12.95 (ISBN 0-89016-001-5); pap. 4.95 (ISBN 0-89016-023-6). Lightning Tree.

Society of Arts & Crafts, Boston Exhibition Record Eighteen-Ninty-Seven to Nineteen Twenty-Seven. Compiled by Karen E. Ulehla. 1981. pap. 10.00. Boston Public Lib.

Society of Biblical Literature Nineteen Eighty-One: Seminar Papers. Ed. by Kent Richards. (SBL Seminar Papers & Abstracts). 1981. pap. 9.00 (ISBN 0-89130-548-3, 06-09-20). Scholars Pr GA.

Society of Biblical Literature: Seminar Papers Nineteen Eighty. Paul J. Achtemeier. (SBL Seminar Papers & Abstracts). 1980. pap. 9.00 (ISBN 0-89130-357-X, 06-09-19). Scholars Pr GA.

Society of Biblical Literature: Seminar Papers Nineteen Eighty-Four. Ed. by Kent H. Richards. 412p. 1984. pap. 15.00 (ISBN 0-89130-810-5, 06 09 23). Scholars Pr GA.

Society of Biblical Literature: Seminar Papers Nineteen Eighty-Three. Ed. by Kent H. Richards. (SBL Seminar Papers). 490p. 1983. pap. 15.00 (ISBN 0-89130-607-2, 06 09 22). Scholars Pr GA.

Society of Captives: A Study of a Maximum Security Prison. Gresham M. Sykes. 1971. 26.50x (ISBN 0-691-09336-9); pap. 8.95x (ISBN 0-691-02814-1). Princeton U Pr.

Society of Critical Care Medicine: Textbook of Critical Care. 2nd ed. William C. Shoemaker et al. (Illus.). 1056p. 1988. 95.00 (ISBN 0-7216-1691-7). Saunders.

Society of Fiber Science & Technology, Japan: ISF '85. 368p. 1986. 115.25 (ISBN 1-85166-013-5, Pub. by Elsevier Applied Sci England). Elsevier.

Society of Friends. Rev. ed. Howard H. Brinton. 1962. pap. 2.50x (ISBN 0-87574-048-0, 048). Pendle Hill.

Society of Illustrators Twenty-Eighth Annual of American Illustration: Illustrators 28. Ed. by Arpi Ermoyan. (Illus.). 440p. 1987. pap. text ed. 49.95 (Dist. by Robert Silver Assocs.). Madison Square.

Society of Independent Artists: The Exhibition Record Nineteen Seventeen to Nineteen Forty-Four. Clark S. Marlor. LC 84-14867. (Illus.). 600p. 1985. 64.00 (ISBN 0-8155-5063-4). Noyes.

Society of Independent Artists: The Exhibition Record 1917-1944. Clark S. Marlor. (Illus.). 600p. 100.00 (ISBN 0-317-54871-9). Apollo.

Society of Industrial & Office Realtors: Industrial Real Estate Market Survey. 230p. 1986. 10.00. Soc Industrial Realtors.

Society of Logistics Engineers Annals. 30.00 (ISBN 0-318-20628-5). Soc Logistics Engrs.

Society of Logistics Engineers Proceedings. Incl. 139p (ISBN 0-318-16585-6); 152p (ISBN 0-318-16586-4); 154p (ISBN 0-318-16587-2); 312p (ISBN 0-318-16588-0). 25.00 ea. Soc Logistics Engrs.

Society of Man. Louis J. Halle. LC 78-31208. 1979. Repr. of 1965 ed. lib. bdg. 35.00x (ISBN 0-313-20942-1, HASM). Greenwood.

Society of Mind. Marvin Minsky. 1987. 22.95 (ISBN 0-671-60740-5). S&S.

Society of Mind. Marvin Minsky. 1988. pap. 9.95 (ISBN 0-671-65713-5, Touchstone Bks). S&S.

Society of Mining Engineers of AIME-RETC Proceedings. LC 76-21404. 1976. 40.00x (ISBN 0-89520-037-6). Soc Mining Eng.

Society of Mutal Backscratchers. Arthur Magill. LC 79-92127. (Illus.). 1980. 10.00 (ISBN 0-8048-1339-6). C E Tuttle.

Society of Naval Architects & Marine Engineers Proceedings. Incl. 372p. 1979. 22.50 (ISBN 0-317-35910-X, SY-10); members 15.00 (ISBN 0-317-35911-8); 318p. 1980. 22.50 (ISBN 0-317-35912-6, SY-11); members 15.00 (ISBN 0-317-35913-4); 314p. 1978. 40.00 (ISBN 0-317-35914-2, SY-8); members 30.00 (ISBN 0-317-35915-0). Soc Naval Arch.

Society of Naval Architects & Marine Engineers: Transactions, Vol. 87. (Illus.). 412p. 1980. 25.00 (ISBN 0-9603048-1-9). Soc Naval Arch.

Society of Naval Architects & Marine Engineers: Transactions, Vol. 88. (Illus.). 450p. 1981. 25.00 (ISBN 0-9603048-2-7). Soc Naval Arch.

Society of Naval Architects & Marine Engineers: Transactions, Vol. 89. (Illus.). 455p. 1982. 25.00 (ISBN 0-9603048-3-5). Soc Naval Arch.

Society of Naval Architects & Marine Engineers: Transactions, Vol. 90. (Illus.). 460p. 1983. write for info. (ISBN 0-9603048-4-3). Soc Naval Arch.

Society of Naval Architects & Marine Engineers: Transactions, Vol. 91. (Illus.). 412p. 1984. 25.00 (ISBN 0-9603048-5-1). Soc Naval Arch.

Society of Naval Architects & Marine Engineers: Transactions, Vol. 92. (Illus.). 392p. 1985. 25.00 (ISBN 0-9603048-6-X). Soc Naval Arch.

Society of Petroleum Engineers Technical Papers, 2 vols. University Microfilms International. LC 80-28727. 1981. Set. 275.00 (ISBN 0-8357-0217-0, Pub. by Collections & Curr). Univ Microfilms.

Society of Petroleum Engineers Technical Papers: Index to the Microfiche Collection, 1980 Supplement. University Microfilms International. 1981. pap. 25.00 (ISBN 0-686-78508-8, Pub. by Collections & Curr). Univ Microfilms.

Society of Publication Designers Twenty Second Publication Design Annual. (Illus.). 256p. 1988. 39.95 (ISBN 0-8230-4887-X). Madison Square.

Society of Renaissance Florence. Ed. by Gene Brucker. 1972. pap. 7.95x (ISBN 0-06-131607-5, TB1607, Torch). Har-Row.

Society of Salty Saints: Story & Prayer from the Street. Micheal Elliott. (Illus.). 128p. 1987. pap. 7.95 (ISBN 0-940989-14-X). Meyer Stone Bks.

Society of Six. Nancy Boas. (Illus.). 224p. 1988. 59.95 (ISBN 0-938491-03-2); pap. 39.95 (ISBN 0-938491-04-0). Bedford Arts Pubs.

Society of Subordinates: Inmate Organization in a Narcotic Hospital. Charles R. Tittle. LC 72-80669. (Indiana University Social Science Ser.: No. 30). pap. 52.00 (ISBN 0-317-09051-8, 2015836). Bks Demand UMI.

Society of the Cincinnati: 1783-1935. William S. Thomas. LC 35-8178. (Illus.). 187p. 1935. 10.00 (ISBN 0-318-16566-X). Anderson Hse Mus.

Society of the Future. Raghavan Iyer. 84. 8.75 (ISBN 0-88695-018-X). Concord Grove.

Society of the Sacred Heart: History of a Spirit 1800-1975. Margaret Williams. 406p. 1978. pap. 12.50 (ISBN 0-232-51395-3). Attic Pr.

Society of the Spectacle. Guy Debord. 1983. 2.50x (ISBN 0-934868-07-7). Black & Red.

Society of Tomorrow. Gustavo De Molinari. 59.95 (ISBN 0-8490-1071-3). Gordon Pr.

Society Organized for War: The Iberian Municipal Militias in the Central Middle Ages, 1000-1284. James F. Powers. 1987. 45.00x (ISBN 0-520-05644-2). U of Cal Pr.

Society, Personality & Culture. Zevedei Barbu. (Blackwell's Sociology Ser.). 183p. 1971. pap. text ed. 9.95 (ISBN 0-8464-1162-8). Beekman Pubs.

Society, Personality & Deviant Behavior: A Study of a Tri-Ethnic Community. Richard Jessor et al. LC 75-20249. 512p. 1975. Repr. of 1968 ed. 26.50 (ISBN 0-88275-339-8). Krieger.

Society, Politics & Culture: Studies in Early Modern England. Mervyn James. (Past & Present Publications). (Illus.). 416p. 1986. 65.00 (ISBN 0-521-25718-2). Cambridge U Pr.

Society, Politics, & Economic Development: A Quantitative Approach. Irma Adelman & Cynthia T. Morris. 336p. 1967. pap. 12.95x (ISBN 0-8018-1301-8). Johns Hopkins.

Society Princess. Barbara Harrison. 1989. pap. 4.50. Zebra.

Society Problems & Method of Study. Ed. by Welford, Argyle, Gless, & Morns. 10.95 (ISBN 0-8022-1848-2). Philos Lib.

Society: Readings for an Introduction to Human Macrosocial Systems. 2nd ed. Ed. by Gladys M. Busch & John A. Busch. LC 85-72578. 358p. 1985. pap. text ed. 17.95 (ISBN 0-935563-01-6). Social Sys Pr.

Society: Revolution & Reform. Ed. by Robert H. Grimm & Alfred F. MacKay. LC 79-99232. (Proceedings of the 1969 Oberlin Colloquium in Philosophy). 1971. 17.50 (ISBN 0-8295-0190-8). UPB.

Society, Schools & Progress in Australia. P. H. Partridge. LC 68-24067. 1968. 29.00 (ISBN 0-08-012919-6); pap. 16.00 (ISBN 0-08-012918-8). Pergamon.

Society, Schools & Progress in England. G. Baron. 1966. pap. text ed. 14.25 (ISBN 0-08-011593-4). Pergamon.

Society, Schools & Progress in Nigeria. L. J. Lewis. 1965. pap. 16.00 (ISBN 0-08-011339-7). Pergamon.

Society, Schools & Progress in Scandinavia. C. W. Dixon. 1965. 38.00 (ISBN 0-08-011405-9); pap. 18.50 (ISBN 0-08-011404-0). Pergamon.

Society, State & Law in Ancient India. A. A. Vigasin & A. M. Samozvantsev. 238p. 1986. text ed. 30.00x (ISBN 0-86590-791-9, Pub. by Sterling Pubs India). Apt Bks.

Society, State, & Schools: A Case for Structural & Confessional Pluralism. Gordon Spykman et al. 224p. (Orig.). 1981. pap. 10.95 (ISBN 0-8028-1880-3). Eerdmans.

Society, State, & Urbanism: Ibn Khaldun's Sociological Thought. Fuad Baali. LC 87-9925. 160p. 1988. 34.50x (ISBN 0-88706-609-7); pap. 12.95x (ISBN 0-88706-610-0). State U NY Pr.

Society, States, & Early Modern Revolution: Agrarian & Urban Rebellions see Rebels & Rulers, Fifteen Hundred to Sixteen-Sixty.

Society, Stress, & Disease: Childhood & Adolescence, Vol. 2. Ed. by Lennart Levi. (Illus.). 1975. 78.00x (ISBN 0-19-264418-1). Oxford U Pr.

Society, Stress, & Disease: The Productive & Reproductive Age, Male-Female Roles & Relationships, Vol. 3. Lennart Levi. (Illus.). 1978. 78.00x (ISBN 0-19-261306-5). Oxford U Pr.

Society, Stress, & Disease: Vol. 5, Old Age. Ed. by Lennart Levi. (Illus.). 410p. 1988. 165.00 (ISBN 0-19-264422-X). Oxford U Pr.

Society, Stress, & Disease: Working Life, Vol. 4. Ed. by Lennart Levi. 1981. text ed. 79.50x (ISBN 0-19-264421-1). Oxford U Pr.

Society Technology & Development. O. N. Wakhlu. 280p. 1984. text ed. 37.50x (ISBN 0-86590-375-1, Pub. by B R Pub Corp Delhi). Apt Bks.

Society, Technology & Risk Assessment. Ed. by J. Conrad. LC 80-40533. 1980. 73.00 (ISBN 0-12-186450-2). Acad Pr.

Society, the City & the Space-Economy of Urbanism. D. Harvey. LC 72-77212. (CCG Resource Papers: No. 18). (Illus.). 1972. pap. text ed. 5.00 (ISBN 0-89291-065-8). Assn Am Geographers.

Society, the Redeemed Form of Man, & the Earnest of God's Omnipotence in Human Nature: Affirmed in Letters to a Friend. Henry James. 1971. Repr. of 1879 ed. 35.00 (ISBN 0-384-26735-1). Johnson Repr.

Society, the Sacred & Scripture in Ancient Judaism. Jack Lightstone. (Studies in Christianity & Judaism). 148p. 1988. pap. text ed. 17.50 (ISBN 0-88920-975-8, Pub. by Wilfrid Laurier Canada). Humanities.

Society, Theory & the French Revolution: Studies in the Revolutionary Imaginary. Brian C. Singer. LC 85-25010. 240p. 1986. 27.50 (ISBN 0-312-73924-9). St Martin.

Society under Siege: A Psychology of Northern Ireland. Rona M. Fields. LC 76-21895. 283p. 1981. 24.95 (ISBN 0-87722-074-3). Temple U Pr.

Society Without Government. LC 74-172235. (Right Wing Individualist Tradition in America Ser). 1972. Repr. of 1971 ed. 15.00 (ISBN 0-405-00440-0). Ayer Co Pubs.

Society Women of Shakespeare's Time. Violet Wilson. 59.95 (ISBN 0-8490-1072-1). Gordon Pr.

Society Women of Shakespeare's Time. Violet A. Wilson. 1979. Repr. of 1924 ed. lib. bdg. 35.00 (ISBN 0-8495-5730-5). Arden Lib.

Society Women of Shakespeare's Time. Violet A. Wilson. LC 73-113370. 1970. Repr. of 1924 ed. 24.00x (ISBN 0-8046-1040-1, Pub. by Kennikat). Assoc Faculty Pr.

Society's Victims-The Police: An Analysis of Job Stress in Policing. 2nd ed. William H. Kroes. (Illus.). 202p. 1985. 21.50x (ISBN 0-398-05120-8). C C Thomas.

Society's Work. Robert Bridges et al. Ed. by Steele Commager. Incl. Nature of Human Speech; English Handwriting; Notes on Relative Clauses; On Some Disputed Points in English Grammar; English Vowel Sounds; Study of American English; English Handwriting; Shakespeare's English; American Pronunciation. (Society for Pure English: Vol. 3). 1979. lib. bdg. 50.00 (ISBN 0-8240-3667-0). Garland Pub.

Socinenija Prinadle-Zascija K Grammatike Votskago Jazyka see First Votyak Grammar.

Socio. Jenaro Prieto et al. 224p. (Span.). 1983. pap. text ed. write for info. (ISBN 0-02-396800-1, Pub. by Scribner). Macmillan.

Socio-Behavioral Approach to Social Work. Date not set. 3.30. Coun Soc Wk Ed.

Socio-Cultural & Psychological Adjustment of the Arab Minority in Israel. Sharif Kanaana. LC 75-36562. 1976. softbound 15.95 (ISBN 0-88247-400-6). R & E Pubs.

Socio-Cultural Approach to Tribal Languages. H. L. Shukla. 100p. 1985. text ed. 20.00x (ISBN 0-86590-703-X, Pub. by B R Pub Corp India). Apt Bks.

Socio-Cultural Creativity in the Converging & Restructuring Process of the New Emerging World. 65p. 1980. pap. 5.00 (ISBN 92-808-0110-4, TUNU079, UNU). UNIPUB.

Socio-Cultural Development Alternatives in a Changing World. 45p. 1979. pap. 6.75 (ISBN 92-808-0007-8, TUNU037, UNU). UNIPUB.

Socio-Cultural Dimensions of Mental Health: A Curriculum & Practice Model. Ed. by Mary W. Day. LC 83-91012. 168p. 1985. 13.95 (ISBN 0-533-06004-4). Vantage.

Socio-Cultural Factors in Modern Family Planning Methods in Tanzania. C. K. Omari. (Studies in African Health & Medicine: Vol. 3). 120p. 1988. lib. bdg. 39.95 (ISBN 0-88946-189-9). E Mellen.

Socio-Cultural Study of 118 Mexican Families Living in a Low-Rent Public Housing Project in San Antonio, Texas. Winifred Murray. Ed. by Carlos E. Cortes. LC 76-1275. (Chicano Heritage Ser.). 1976. Repr. of 1954 ed. lib. bdg. 14.00x (ISBN 0-405-09515-5). Ayer Co Pubs.

Socio-Economic Accounting. Ahmed Belkaoui. LC 83-17682. (Illus.). xii, 324p. 1984. lib. bdg. 40.95 (ISBN 0-89930-065-0, BSE, Quorum). Greenwood.

Socio-Economic Analysis & Planning: Critical Choice of Methodologies. (Socio-Economic Studies: No. 12). (Illus.). 260p. (Orig.). 1987. pap. text ed. 17.00 (ISBN 92-3-102391-8, U1567, UNESCO). UNIPUB.

Socio-Economic & Legal Implications of Urban Land Ceiling & Regulation. Gopal Bhargava. 1983. 12.00x (ISBN 0-8364-1053-X, Pub. by Abhinav India). South Asia Bks.

Socio-Economic & Policy Implications of Energy Price Increases. Armand Pereira et al. Ed. by Wouter Tims. 300p. 1987. text ed. 37.00x (ISBN 0-566-05520-1, Pub. by Gower Pub England). Gower Pub Co.

Socio-Economic Aspects of Blood Transfusion. Ed. by B. P. Moore & R. W. Beal. (Journal: Vox Sanguinis: Vol. 46, Suppl. 1). (Illus.). iv, 108p. 1984. pap. 26.75 (ISBN 3-8055-3880-4). S Karger.

Socio-Economic Aspects of Urban Hydrology: Prepared at a Workshop in Lund, Sweden. R. M. Berthelot. (Studies & Reports in Hydrology: No. 27). (Illus.). 88p. 1979. pap. 5.00 (ISBN 92-3-101702-0, U965, UNESCO). UNIPUB.

Socio Economic Backwardness in Women. Arandita Mukherji. 1987. 9.00x (ISBN 81-7024-096-4, Pub. by Ashish India). South Asia Bks.

Socio-Economic Change in Kerala. K. E. Verghese. 1986. 27.00 (ISBN 0-317-56200-2, Pub. by Ashish India). South Asia Bks.

Socio-Economic Circumstances & Adult Participation in Certain Cultural & Educational Activities. A. A. Kaplan. LC 79-176928. (Columbia University. Teachers College. Contributions to Education: No. 889). Repr. of 1943 ed. 22.50 (ISBN 0-404-55889-5). AMS Pr.

Socio-Economic Correlates of Mortality in Japan & ASEAN. Ed. by Ng Shui Meng. 317p. 1987. pap. text ed. 26.50x (ISBN 9971-988-21-6, Pub. by Gower Pub England). Gower Pub Co.

Socio-Economic Development in a Sean: An International Perspective. Habibullah Khan. 104p. 1986. text ed. 30.00x (ISBN 9971-68-123-4, Pub. by Chopmen Pubs. Singapore); pap. text ed. 15.95x (ISBN 9971-68-124-2, Pub. by Chopmen Pubs. Singapore). Advent NY.

Socio-Economic Development in Tribal Area of Manipur. S. A. Ansari. xix, 106p. 1986. text ed. 20.00x (ISBN 81-7018-295-6, Pub. by B R Pub Corp Delhi). Apt Bks.

Socio-Economic Development of Tribes in India. Devendra Thakur. 1986. 32.50 (ISBN 0-8364-1946-4, Pub. by Deep). South Asia Bks.

Socio-Economic Differentials in Child Mortality in Developing Countries. 319p. 1986. 29.00 (ISBN 92-1-151154-2, E.85.XIII.7). UN.

Socio-Economic Disparities in Israel. Fanny Ginor. 313p. 1979. 24.95 (ISBN 0-87855-332-0); pap. 14.95 (ISBN 965-216-000-8). Transaction Bks.

Socio-Economic Effects & Constraints in Tropical Forest Management. E. G. Hallsworth. LC 82-1090. 233p. 1982. 79.95x (ISBN 0-471-10375-6). Wiley.

Socio-Economic Groups & Income Distribution in Mexico. Wouter Van Ginneken. 1980. 11.95x (ISBN 0-312-73941-9). St Martin.

Socio-Economic History of German Canadians: They, too, Founded Canada. Rudolf A. Helling. Ed. by Bernd Hamm. 156p. (Orig.). 1984. pap. text ed. 28.50x (ISBN 3-515-04014-5, Pub by Franz Steiner). Coronet Bks.

Socio-Economic History of Mughal India. Neelam Chaudhary. 1987. 26.00x (ISBN 0-8364-2314-3, Pub. by Discovery Pub Hse India). South Asia Bks.

Socio-Economic Impact of Microelectronics: International Conference on Socio-Economic Problems & Potentialities of Microelectronics, Sept. 1979, Zandvoort, Netherlands. Ed. by Jan Berting et al. LC 80-49810. (Vienna Centre Ser.). (Illus.). 263p. 1980. 79.00 (ISBN 0-08-026776-9). Pergamon.

Socio-Economic Impact of Sati in Bengal & the Role of Raja Rammohun Roy. Benoy B. Roy. 1987. 31.00x (ISBN 81-85109-70-2, Pub. by Naya Prokash India). South Asia Bks.

Socio-Economic Indicators for Planning: Methodological Aspects & Selected Examples. (Socio-Economic Studies: No. 2). 122p. 1981. pap. 5.00 (ISBN 92-3-101892-2, U1105, UNESCO). UNIPUB.

Socio-Economic Institutions & Cultural Change in Siam, 1851-1910: A Documentary Survey. Ed. by Chatthip Nartsupha & Suthy Prasartset. 86p. (Orig.). 1977. pap. text ed. 12.00 (ISBN 0-566-04012-3, Pub. by Inst Southeast Asian Stud). Gower Pub Co.

Socio-Economic Life of Northern India. Sukla Das. 1980. 22.50 (ISBN 0-8364-0609-5, Abhina India). South Asia Bks.

Socio-Economic Models in Geography. R. J. Chorley & P. Haggett. 468p. 1968. pap. 12.95x (ISBN 0-416-29630-0, NO.2137). Routledge Chapman & Hall.

Socio-Economic Policies for the Elderly. OECD. 168p. (Orig.). 1979. pap. 9.50x (ISBN 92-64-12002-5). OECD.

Socio-Economic Re-Evaluation of the Torts Law of Liability for Personal Injuries. S. M. Hasan. 115p. 1962. pap. 15.00x (ISBN 0-317-54688-0, Pub. by Eastern Bk India). State Mutual Bk.

Socio-Economic Results of Land Reform in Taiwan. Martin M. Yang. 576p. 1970. 20.00x (ISBN 0-8248-0091-5, Eastwest Ctr). UH Pr.

Socio-Economic Status of Indian Women. Murali K. Manohar. 1983. 15.00x (ISBN 0-8364-1059-9, Pub. by Seema India). South Asia Bks.

Socio-Economic Status Trends of the Mexican People Residing in Arizona. Raymond J. Flores. pap. 10.95 (ISBN 0-88247-211-9). R & E Pubs.

Socio-Economic Survey of Recreational Boating & Fishing in the U. S. Virgin Islands. David Olsen. (Illus.). 80p. 1979. 12.00 (ISBN 0-318-14618-5). Isl Resources.

Socio Economic Transformation of Soviet Central Asia. R. G. Gidadhubli. 1988. 30.00x (ISBN 81-7050-050-8, Pub. by Patriot). South Asia Bks.

Socio Economic Transformation of Soviet Central Asia. Ed. by R. G. Gidadhubli. 253p. 1988. text ed. 35.00x (ISBN 81-7050-050-8, Pub. by Patriot Pubs). Advent NY.

Socio-Economie de Proudhon see Cahiers de l'Institut de Science Economique Appliquee.

Socio-Ethical Issues in Nigeria. Nwachukwuike S. Iwe. 270p. 1987. text ed. 33.35 (ISBN 0-8204-0380-6). P Lang Pubs.

Socio Intellectual History of the Isna Ashari Shi'is in India, 7th to 19th Century AD, Vols. 1 & 2. Saiyid A. Rizvi. 1986. Set. 78.50x (ISBN 81-215-0004-4, Munshiram Manoharial India). South Asia Bks.

Socio-Legal Foundations of Civil-Military Relations. James B. Jacobs. 231p. 1986. 24.95 (ISBN 0-88738-033-6). Transaction Bks.

Socio-Medical Inquiries: Recollections, Reflections & Reconsiderations. Irving K. Zola. 340p. 1983. 29.95 (ISBN 0-87722-303-3); pap. 10.95 (ISBN 0-87722-312-2). Temple U Pr.

Socio-Political Aspects of the Palaver in Some African Countries. (Introduction to African Culture: No. 2). 93p. 1979. pap. 5.00 (ISBN 92-3-101641-5, U937, UNESCO). UNIPUB.

Socio-Political Complex. A. Khoshkish. 1979. 72.00 (ISBN 0-08-023391-0); pap. 22.00 (ISBN 0-08-024722-9). Pergamon.

Socio-Political Currents in Bengal: Nineteenth Century Perspective. Bhabani Bhattacharya. 160p. 1980. text ed. 16.50x (ISBN 0-7069-0988-7, Pub. by Vikas India). Advent NY.

Socio Political Study of the Valmiki Ramayana. Ramashraya Sharma. 1971. 22.50 (ISBN 0-89684-319-X). Orient Bk Dist.

Socio-Religious & Cultural Study of the Ancient Indian Coins. Swati Chakraborty. (Illus.). xvi, 394p. 1986. text ed. 50.00x (ISBN 81-7018-316-2, Pub. by B R Pub Corp Delhi). Apt Bks.

Sociobehavioral Studies in Mental Retardation. Ed. by C. Edward Meyers. LC 73-88389. (AAMD Monograph Ser.: No. 1). 1976. 7.15x (ISBN 0-686-16814-3). Am Assn Mental.

Sociobiological Perspectives on Human Development. K. Macdonald. (Illus.). 450p. 1987. 43.00 (ISBN 0-387-96581-5). Springer-Verlag.

Sociobiology & Behavior. 2nd ed. D. P. Barash. 426p. 1982. 52.75 (ISBN 0-444-99091-7); pap. 21.25 (ISBN 0-444-99088-7). Elsevier.

Sociobiology & Epistemology. James S. Fetzer. 1985. lib. bdg. 39.50 (ISBN 90-277-2005-3, Pub. by Reidel Holland); pap. text ed. 14.95 (ISBN 90-277-2006-1). Kluwer Academic.

Sociobiology & Immmigration. Glaister A. Elmer & Evelyn E. Elmer. 43p. 1984. pap. 3.00 (ISBN 0-936247-02-9). Amer Immigration.

Sociobiology & Mental Disorder: A New View. Brant Wenegrat. 1984. pap. write for info. (ISBN 0-201-09686-2, 09686, Hlth-Sci). Addison-Wesley.

Sociobiology & Psychology: Ideas, Issues & Findings. Ed. by Charles Crawford et al. LC 87-6783. 429p. 1987. 55.00 (ISBN 0-89859-580-0). L Erlbaum Assocs.

Sociobiology & the Human Dimension. Georg Breuer. LC 82-1293. 235p. 1983. pap. 17.95 (ISBN 0-521-28778-2). Cambridge U Pr.

Sociobiology & the Law: The Biology of Altruism in the Courtroom of the Future. John H. Beckstrom. LC 84-16415. 160p. 1985. 19.95 (ISBN 0-252-01171-6). U of Ill Pr.

Sociobiology & the Preemption of Social Science. Alexander Rosenberg. LC 80-8091. 240p. 1981. text ed. 25.00x (ISBN 0-8018-2423-0). Johns Hopkins.

Sociobiology Examined. Ed. by Ashley Montagu. 1980. 24.95x (ISBN 0-19-502711-6); pap. 8.95 (ISBN 0-19-502712-4, GB602). Oxford U Pr.

Sociobiology of Ethnocentrism: Evolutionary Dimensions of Xenophobia, Discrimination, Racism & Nationalism. Ed. by Vernon Reynolds. 336p. 1986. 45.00 (ISBN 0-7099-4222-2, Pub. by Croom Helm UK). Routledge Chapman & Hall.

Sociobiology of Ethnocentrism: Evolutionary Dimensions of Xenophobia, Discrimination, Racism, & Nationalism. Ed. by Vernon Reynolds et al. LC 86-19227. 357p. 1987. 40.00x (ISBN 0-8203-0915-X). U of Ga Pr.

Sociobiology of Homo Sapiens. Mark Shapiro. LC 78-60932. 1978. 9.95 (ISBN 0-9601858-0-1). Pinecrest Fund.

Sociobiology of Infant & Adult Male Baboons. David M. Stein. LC 84-338. (Monographs on Infancy: Vol. 5). 208p. 1984. text ed. 39.50 (ISBN 0-89391-265-4). Ablex Pub.

Sociobiology: Sense or Nonsense? Michael Ruse. (Episteme 8 Ser.). 1979. lib. bdg. 29.00 (ISBN 9-0277-0940-8); pap. 9.95 (ISBN 90-277-0943-2). Kluwer Academic.

Sociobiology: Sense or Nonsense. 2nd, rev. ed. Michael Ruse. (Episteme Ser.: No. 8). 248p. 1984. 34.00 (ISBN 90-277-1797-4, Pub. by Reidel Holland); pap. text ed. 14.95 (ISBN 90-277-1798-2). Kluwer Academic.

Sociobiology: The Abridged Edition. Edward O. Wilson. (Illus.). 375p. 1980. 19.50x (ISBN 0-674-81623-4, Beklnap Pr); pap. 12.50 (ISBN 0-674-81624-2). Harvard U Pr.

Sociobiology: The New Synthesis. Edward O. Wilson. LC 74-83910. (Illus.). 416p. 1975. 39.50x (ISBN 0-674-81621-8). Harvard U Pr.

Sociocultural Aspects of Developing Small-Scale Fisheries: Delivering Services to the Poor. Richard B. Pollnac. (Working Paper: No. 490). iii, 61p. 1981. 5.00 (ISBN 0-686-36058-3, WP-0490). World Bank.

Sociocultural Changes in American Jewish Life As Reflected in Selected Jewish Literature. Bernard Cohen. LC 75-146162. 282p. 1972. 24.50 (ISBN 0-8386-7848-3). Fairleigh Dickinson.

Sociocultural Dimensions of Language Change. Ed. by Ben G. Blount & Mary Sanches. 1977. 39.95 (ISBN 0-12-107450-1). Acad Pr.

Sociocultural Dimensions of Language Use. Mary Sanches & Ben G. Blount. (Language, Thought & Culture Ser.). 1975. 29.95 (ISBN 0-12-617850-X). Acad Pr.

Sociocultural Dimensions of Mixtec Ceramics. Michael Lind. Ed. by Ronald Spores & Paula M. McNutt. (Vanderbilt University Publications in Anthropology: No. 33). (Illus.). 120p. (Orig.). 1987. pap. text ed. 13.85 (ISBN 0-935462-24-4). Vanderbilt Pubns.

Sociocultural Roots of Mental Illness: An Epidemiological Survey. J. J. Schwab & M. E. Schwab. LC 78-586. (Topics In General Psychiatry Ser.). (Illus.). 352p. 1978. 49.50x (ISBN 0-306-31089-9, Plenum Pr). Plenum Pub.

Sociocultural Theory in Anthropology. Merwyn S. Garbarino. 114p. 1983. pap. text ed. 7.95x (ISBN 0-88133-056-6). Waveland Pr.

Sociocybernetic Paradoxes: Observation, Control & Evolution of Self-Steering Systems. Ed. by Felix Geyer & Johannes Van Der Zouwen. (Illus.). 248p. (Orig.). 1986. text ed. 45.00 (ISBN 0-8039-9735-3); pap. text ed. 18.95 (ISBN 0-8039-9736-1). Sage.

Sociocybernetics, Vols. 1 & 2. Ed. by R. F. Geyer & J. van der Zouwen. 1978. Vol. 1. pap. 17.00 (ISBN 90-207-0854-6, Pub. by Martinus Nijhoff Netherlands); Vol. 2. pap. 17.00 (ISBN 90-207-0855-4). Kluwer Academic.

Sociocybernetics: Rethinking Social Organization. Ed. by John A. Busch & Gladys M. Busch. (Systems Inquiry Ser.). 139p. 1988. pap. text ed. 16.95x. Intersystems Pubns.

Socioecology & Psychology of Primates. Ed. by Russell H. Tuttle. (World Anthropology Ser.). (Illus.). xvi, 575p. 1975. 52.50 (ISBN 90-279-7709-7). Mouton.

Socioeconomic Adjustments of Tribals: A Case Study of Tripura Jhumias (India) Bani P. Misra. LC 76-903504. 1976. 6.50x (ISBN 0-88386-700-1). South Asia Bks.

Socioeconomic & Political Influences on Industrial Production Decisions in East German Provinces. Robert C. Rickards. (Working Paper Ser.: No. 44). 36p. 1988. 5.00. LBJ Sch Pub Aff.

Socioeconomic Approach to Status Measurement: With a Guide to Occupational & Socioeconomic Status Scores. Charles B. Nam & Mary G. Powers. LC 82-73819. 166p. 1984. text ed. 26.95x (ISBN 0-88105-011-3). Cap & Gown.

Socioeconomic Aspects of Renewable Energy Technologies. Ed. by Ramesh Bhatia et al. LC 87-22890. 226p. 1988. lib. bdg. 49.95 (ISBN 0-275-92851-9, C2851). Praeger.

Socioeconomic Attitudes Toward Population Issues: A Survey of College & University Students. M. Arif Ghayur. LC 84-81429. 159p. 1985. lib. bdg. 21.95x (ISBN 0-930390-67-9). Gen Hall.

Socioeconomic Background & Achievement. Otis D. Duncan et al. LC 72-88537. (Studies in Population Ser). 1972. 19.95 (ISBN 0-12-785174-7). Acad Pr.

Socioeconomic Characteristics & Nutritional Status of Nepalese Children in Chitawan. 81p. 1984. 10.00 (ISBN 0-318-23193-X). Am-Nepal Ed.

Socioeconomic Characteristics of Cardiology Practice. Phillip R. Kletke et al. 69p. (Orig.). 1988. pap. text ed. 250.00 (OP-046). AMA.

Socioeconomic Characteristics of Medical Practice 1987. American Medical Association Staff. 154p. (Orig.). 1987. pap. 45.00 (OP-228/7). AMA.

Socioeconomic Determinants of Fertility in Mexico: Changing Perspectives. Jane R. Rubin-Kurtzman. Tr. by Sandra Del Castillo from Span. (Monograph Ser.: No. 23). iv, 66p. (Orig.). 1987. pap. 9.50 (ISBN 0-935391-73-8). Ctr Mex Studies.

Socioeconomic Evaluation of Drug Therapy. Ed. by W Van Eimeren & B. Horisberger. (Health Systems Research Ser.). (Illus.). xvi, 244p. 1988. 47.90 (ISBN 0-387-18662-X). Springer-Verlag.

Socioeconomic History of Argentina, 1776-1860. Jonathan C. Brown. LC 78-6800. (Cambridge Latin American Studies: No. 35). pap. 82.70 (2031623). Bks Demand UMI.

Socioeconomic Macroregions of Brazil, 1970. Archibald O. Haller. (Working Papers Ser.: No. 83-2). 47p. 1983. pap. text ed. 6.00 (ISBN 0-686-88350-0, CRD156, UNCRD). UNIPUB.

Socioeconomic Profile of South Africa. William R. Duggan. LC 72-91715. (Special Studies in International Economics & Development). 1973. 39.50x (ISBN 0-275-28653-3). Irvington.

Socioeconomic Stress in Rural Families: A Special Issue of Lifestyles: Family & Economic Issues. Dorothy Z. Price & Mari Wilheim. 81p. 1988. pap. 12.95 (ISBN 0-89885-434-2). Human Sci Pr.

Socioeconomic Structure of the Tokyo Metropolitan Complex. Takeo Yazaki. Tr. by Mitsugu Matsuda. (Social Science & Linguistics Institute Special Publications). (Illus.). 401p. 1970. pap. 10.00x (ISBN 0-8248-0240-3). UH Pr.

Socioeconomic Success: A Study of the Effects of Genetic Endowments, Family Environment & Schooling. J. R. Behrman et al. (Contributions to Economic Analysis Ser.: Vol. 128). 276p. 1980. 66.00 (ISBN 0-444-85410-X, North-Holland). Elsevier.

TITLE INDEX SOCIOLOGIE DU DEVELOPPEMENT LATINO-AMERICAIN

Socioeconomics of Surgery. Rutkow. (Illus.). 450p. 1988. text ed. 60.00 (ISBN 0-8016-4306-6). Mosby.
Socioemotional Measures for Preschool & Kindergarten Children: A Handbook. Deborah K. Walker. LC 73-10937. (Jossey-Bass Behavioral Science Ser.). pap. 94.00 (2027772). Bks Demand UMI.
Sociogenesis of Language & Human Conduct. Ed. by Bruce Bain. 580p. 1983. 65.00x (ISBN 0-306-41041-9, Plenum Pr). Plenum Pub.
Sociolegal Status of Women in India. Rama Mehta. 192p. 1987. 24.00x (ISBN 0-8364-2080-2, Pub. by Mittal). South Asia Bks.
Sociolinguistic Aspects of Language Learning & Teaching. Ed. by J. B. Pride. (Illus.). 1979. pap. text ed. 11.95x (ISBN 0-19-437079-8). Oxford U Pr.
Sociolinguistic Attitudes in India: An Historical Reconstruction. Madhav M. Deshpande. (Linguistica Extranea Ser.: Studia 5). 178p. 1979. lib. bdg. 10.50 (ISBN 0-89720-007-1); pap. 7.50 (ISBN 0-89720-008-X). Karoma.
Sociolinguistic Patterns. William Labov. LC 72-80375. (Conduct & Communication Ser.). 360p. 1973. 14.95x (ISBN 0-8122-7657-4); (Pa Paperbks). U of Pa Pr.
Sociolinguistic Perspectives on Soviet National Languages: Their Past, Present & Future. Ed. by Isabelle T. Kreindler. (Contributions to the Sociology of Language Ser.: No. 40). x, 381p. 1985. 91.75 (ISBN 3-11-010211-0). Mouton.
Sociolinguistic Profile of Urban Centers in Cameroon. Ed. by Edna L. Koenig et al. 149p. (Orig.). 1983. pap. 10.00 (ISBN 0-918456-45-2). African Studies Assn.
Sociolinguistic Reflexes of Dialect Interference in West Wirral. Mark Newbrook. (Bamberger Beitrage zur Englischen Sprachwissenschaft Ser.: Bd. 18). 236p. 1986. 28.55 (ISBN 0-317-69897-4). P Lang Pubs.
Sociolinguistic Studies in Language Contact. Ed. by William F. Mackey & Jacob Ornstein. (Trends in Linguistics, Studies & Monographs: No. 6). 1979. text ed. 42.00x (ISBN 90-279-7866-2). Mouton.
Sociolinguistic Variation: A Formal Model. Earl M. Herrick. LC 83-1295. (Illus.). 205p. 1984. text ed. 19.95x (ISBN 0-8173-0173-9). U of Ala Pr.
Sociolinguistics. R. A. Hudson. LC 79-51824. (Cambridge Textbooks in Linguistics Ser.). (Illus.). 1980. 52.50 (ISBN 0-521-22833-6); pap. 15.95x (ISBN 0-521-29668-4). Cambridge U Pr.
Sociolinguistics. Ed. by Janet Pride & Holmes. 1986. pap. 6.95 (ISBN 0-14-022658-3). Penguin.
Sociolinguistics. J. M. Simpson. 160p. 1987. 22.50x (ISBN 0-85224-478-9, Pub. by Edinburgh U Pr Scotland). Columbia U Pr.
Sociolinguistics: An Introduction to Language & Society. rev. ed. Peter Trudgill. 208p. 1983. pap. 6.95 (ISBN 0-14-022479-3, Pelican). Penguin.
Sociolinguistics & Language Acquisition. Nessa Wolfson & Elliot Judd. (Scarcella-Krashen). 344p. 1984. pap. text ed. 18.95 (ISBN 0-88377-269-8). Newbury Hse.
Sociolinguistics & Reading: How Parents Can Contribute to the Development of Children's Language & Reading Ability. Ramona Kruse. LC 81-51218. 30p. 1981. perfect bound 4.50 (ISBN 0-88247-598-3). R & E Pubs.
Sociolinguistics in Hindi Contexts. Raja R. Mehrotra. (Contributions to the Sociology of Language Ser.: No. 38). xii, 153p. 1985. 47.25x (ISBN 0-89925-139-0). Mouton.
Sociolinguistics in the Low Countries. K. Deprez. LC 84-24240. (Studies in the Science of Language Series: No. 5). viii, 359p. (Orig.). 1984. pap. 48.00x (ISBN 90-272-2321-1). Benjamins North Am.
Sociolinguistics of Society. Ralph Fasold. 352p. 1984. 45.00x (ISBN 0-631-13385-2); pap. 14.95x (ISBN 0-631-13462-X). Basil Blackwell.
Sociolinguistics of the Brazilian-Uruguayan Border. Frederik G. Hensey. (Janua Linguarum, Ser. Practica: No. 16). (Illus.). 115p. 1973. pap. text ed. 16.80x (ISBN 90-2792-326-4). Mouton.
Sociolinguistics of Urban Vernaculars: Case Studies & Their Evaluation. Ed. by Norbert Dittmar & Peter Schlobinski. (Soziolinguistik und Sprachkontakt - Sociolinguistics & Language Contact Ser.: Vol. 1). 276p. 1988. lib. bdg. 105.00x (ISBN 0-89925-512-4). De Gruyter.
Sociologia: Curso Introductorio. Roberto Agramonte. LC 77-5905. (Illus.). 1978. pap. 10.00 (ISBN 0-8477-2443-3). U of PR Pr.
Sociologia Industrial Y de la Empresa. Ed. by Jose A. Garmendia et al. (Ciencias Sociales Ser.). (Orig.). 1987. pap. text ed. 33.70 (ISBN 84-0318-288-0). Santillana.
Sociologia y Educacion. 5th ed. Jose A. Caceres. LC 76-10842. 1976. 8.75_o.p (ISBN 0-8477-2735-1); pap. 8.00 (ISBN 0-8477-2736-X). U of PR Pr.
Sociological Abstracts: User's Reference Manual. 3rd ed. Compiled by Miriam Chall. LC 86-63503. v, 118p. 1986. looseleaf 51.50 (ISBN 0-930710-04-5). Soc Abstracts.
Sociological Ambivalence & Other Essays. Robert K. Merton. LC 76-1033. (Illus.). 1976. 13.95 (ISBN 0-02-921120-4). Free Pr.
Sociological & Medical Aspects of Nutrition. Ed. by G. H. Bourne. (World Review of Nutrition & Dietetics Ser.: Vol. 55). (Illus.). xii, 252p. 1988. 154.00 (ISBN 3-8055-4703-X). S Karger.
Sociological Approaches to Health & Medicine. Myfanwy Morgan et al. LC 85-48015. (Social Analysis Ser.). 297p. 1985. 24.50 (ISBN 0-7099-1705-8, Pub. by Croom Helm Ltd); pap. 11.50 (ISBN 0-7099-3514-5). Routledge Chapman & Hall.
Sociological Approaches to Law. Ed. by Adam Podgorecki & Christopher Whelan. 1981. 27.50x (ISBN 0-312-73962-1). St Martin.
Sociological Approaches to the Old Testament. Robert R. Wilson. LC 83-16607. (Guides to Biblical Scholarship). 96p. 1984. pap. 4.50 (ISBN 0-8006-0469-5, 1-469). Fortress.
Sociological Backgrounds of Adult Education. Ed. by R. Burns. (Notes & Essays Ser.: No. 41). 1970. pap. text ed. 2.50 (ISBN 0-685-76690-X, NES 41). Syracuse U Cont Ed.
Sociological Concepts. George V. Zito. (Illus.). 1980. pap. text ed. 5.95x (ISBN 0-8290-0082-8). Irvington.
Sociological Concepts: A Literary Reader. Ronald A. Hardert et al. 102p. 1987. pap. text ed. 6.70 (ISBN 0-9619001-0-5). Prairiend Pr.
Sociological Dilemmas: Toward a Dialectic Paradigm. Piotr Sztompka. LC 79-51686. 1979. 24.95 (ISBN 0-12-681860-6). Acad Pr.
Sociological Domain: The Durkheimians & the Founding of French Sociology. Ed. by Philippe Besnard. LC 82-9485. (Illus.). 336p. 1983. 49.50 (ISBN 0-521-23876-5). Cambridge U Pr.
Sociological Enterprise: A Discussion of Fundamental Concepts. C. C. Harris. LC 79-21637. 1980. 26.00x (ISBN 0-312-73968-0). St Martin.
Sociological Evaluation of the Development of the Sociology of Law. Michael J. Irwin. 1986. 15.95 (ISBN 0-533-06824-X). Vantage.
Sociological Explanation As Translation. Stephen P. Turner. (American Sociological Association Rose Monographs Ser.). 195p. 1980. 24.95 (ISBN 0-521-23030-6); pap. 9.95 (ISBN 0-521-29773-7). Cambridge U Pr.
Sociological Eye: Selected Papers. Everett C. Hughes. 598p. 1984. pap. 24.95 (ISBN 0-87855-959-0). Transaction Bks.
Sociological Footprints: Introductory Readings in Sociology. 4th ed. Ed. by Leonard Cargan & Jeanne H. Ballantine. 482p. 1988. pap. text ed. write for info. (ISBN 0-534-08538-5). Wadsworth Pub.
Sociological Foundations of Education in an Urban Society. John Sikula. 1975. pap. text ed. 6.80x (ISBN 0-87563-085-5). Stipes.
Sociological Health Problems see Individualized Health Incentive Program Modules For Physically Disabled Students.
Sociological Human Ecology: Contemporary Issues & Applications. Ed. by Michael Micklin & Harvey M. Choldin. 448p. 1984. 39.00x (ISBN 0-86531-670-8); pap. 18.95x (ISBN 0-86531-671-6). Westview.
Sociological Ideas: Concepts & Applications. 2nd ed. William C. Levin. 342p. 1988. pap. text ed. write for info. (ISBN 0-534-08892-9). Wadsworth Pub.
Sociological Imagination. C. Wright Mills. 1959. 19.95x (ISBN 0-19-500022-6). Oxford U Pr.
Sociological Imagination. C. Wright Mills. 1967. pap. 7.95 (ISBN 0-19-500751-4). Oxford U Pr.
Sociological Impressionism: A Reassessment of Georg Simmel's Social Theory. David Frisby. xi, 210p. 1981. text ed. 39.00x (ISBN 0-435-82320-5). Gower Pub Co.
Sociological Insights: An Introduction to Non-Obvious Sociology. Randall Collins. 1982. pap. text ed. 5.95x (ISBN 0-19-503037-0). Oxford U Pr.
Sociological Interpretation of Education. David Blackledge & Barry Hunt. LC 85-4145. (Social Analysis Ser.). 353p. 1985. 31.00 (ISBN 0-7099-0647-1, Pub. by Croom Helm Ltd); pap. 15.50 (ISBN 0-7099-0676-5). Routledge Chapman & Hall.
Sociological Lives, Vol. 2: Social Change & the Life Course. Ed. by Matilda W. Riley. (American Sociological Association Presidential Ser.). 192p. 1988. text ed. 29.95 (ISBN 0-8039-3285-5); pap. text ed. 14.95 (ISBN 0-8039-3286-3). Sage.
Sociological Methodology, Nineteen Eighty. Ed. by Karl F. Schuessler. LC 68-54940. pap. 150.00 (ISBN 0-317-26047-2, 2023782). Bks Demand UMI.
Sociological Methodology Nineteen Eighty-Eight, Vol. 18. Ed. by Clifford C. Clogg. 1988. text ed. 40.00 (ISBN 0-912764-25-2). Am Sociological.
Sociological Methodology 1977. Ed. by David R. Heise. LC 76-11879. (Social & Behavioral Science Ser.). (Illus.). 1976. 42.95x (ISBN 0-87589-286-8). Jossey-Bass.
Sociological Methodology 1978. Ed. by Karl F. Schuessler. LC 68-54940. (Social & Behavioral Science Ser). 1977. text ed. 42.95x (ISBN 0-87589-343-0). Jossey-Bass.
Sociological Methodology 1979. Ed. by Karl F. Schuessler. LC 78-62564. (Social & Behavioral Science Ser.). (Illus.). 1978. text ed. 42.95x (ISBN 0-87589-387-2). Jossey-Bass.
Sociological Methodology 1982. Ed. by Samuel Leinhardt. LC 68-54940. (Social & Behavioral Science Ser.). 1982. text ed. 42.95x (ISBN 0-87589-516-6). Jossey-Bass.
Sociological Methodology 1983-1984. Ed. by Samuel Leinhardt. LC 68-54940. (Social & Behavioral Science Ser.). 1983. text ed. 42.95x (ISBN 0-87589-578-6). Jossey-Bass.
Sociological Methodology, 1985. Ed. by Nancy B. Tuma. LC 68-54950. (Social & Behavioral Science Ser.). 1985. text ed. write for info. (ISBN 0-87589-635-9). Jossey-Bass.
Sociological Methods: A Sourcebook. 2nd ed. Norman K. Denzin. 1978. McGraw.
Sociological Outlook. 2nd ed. Reid Luhman. 500p. 1988. pap. text ed. 19.50 (ISBN 0-939693-04-6). Collegiate Pr.
Sociological Paradigms & Organizational Analysis. G. Burrell & G. Morgan. 1979. pap. text ed. 18.50 (ISBN 0-435-82131-8). Heinemann Ed.
Sociological Perspective. 2nd rev. & enl. ed. Ely Chinoy. 11.75 (ISBN 0-8446-1855-1). Peter Smith.
Sociological Perspective. Michael R. Leming et al. 240p. 1988. pap. price not set (ISBN 0-310-21661-3, Pub. by Academic Bks). Zondervan.
Sociological Perspective in Education: A Reader. S. Shukla & K. Kumar. 1986. 27.50x (ISBN 81-7001-007-1, Pub. by Chanakya India). South Asia Bks.
Sociological Perspective of Sport. 3rd ed. Wilbert M. Leonard, II. 802p. 1987. text ed. write for info. (ISBN 0-02-369866-7). Macmillan.
Sociological Perspectives: Basic Concepts & Their Applications. 3rd ed. Ely S. Chinoy & John Hewitt. 1974. pap. text ed. write for info (ISBN 0-394-31869-2, RanC). Random.
Sociological Perspectives in Marriage & the Family. 2nd ed. Ed. by Mildred W. Weil. LC 78-54230. 1979. pap. text ed. 8.95x (ISBN 0-8134-2033-4, 2033). Inter Print Pubs.
Sociological Perspectives on Labor Markets. Ed. by Ivar Berg. LC 81-3656. (Quantitative Studies in Social Relations). 1981. 44.50 (ISBN 0-12-089650-8). Acad Pr.
Sociological Poetics & Aesthetic Theory. Alan Swingewood. LC 86-15633. 1987. 29.95 (ISBN 0-312-00039-1); pap. 11.95 (ISBN 0-312-00040-5). St Martin.
Sociological Practice: The Development of Applied & Clinical Sociology. Ed. by Jan Fritz & Elizabeth Clark. 275p. 1988. text ed. 28.95x (ISBN 0-930390-90-3). Gen Hall.
Sociological Quest: Principles of Sociology. David Orenstein. (Illus.). 415p. 1985. pap. 24.50 (ISBN 0-314-77938-8). West Pub.
Sociological Research: A Philosophy of Science Perspective. E. Kraus. 120p. 1986. pap. 10.00 (ISBN 90-232-2207-5, Pub. by Van Gorcum Holland). Longwood Pub Group.
Sociological Research Methods. 2nd ed. Ed. by Martin Bulmer. 450p. 1984. pap. 14.95 (ISBN 0-333-37346-4). Transaction Bks.
Sociological Review: Cumulative Index 1953-1975 (Volumes 1-23 Second Series) 1983. 20.00 (ISBN 0-317-01052-2). Learned Info.
Sociological Role of the Yoruba Cult-Group. W. R. Bascom. LC 44-47266. (American Anthro. Association Memoirs). Repr. of 1944 ed. 15.00 (ISBN 0-527-00562-2). Kraus Repr.
Sociological Spirit: Critical Essays in a Critical Science. Earl Babbie. 186p. 1988. pap. text ed. write for info. (ISBN 0-534-08982-8). Wadsworth Pub.
Sociological Studies in British University Education. (Sociological Review Monographs: No. 7). pap. 11.00 (ISBN 0-8115-3313-1). Kraus Repr.
Sociological Studies in Child Development, Vol. 1. Peter Adler & Patricia Adler. 1986. 52.50 (ISBN 0-89232-565-8). Jai Pr.
Sociological Studies in Economics & Administration. (Sociological Review Monographs: No. 14). pap. 11.00 (ISBN 0-8115-3319-0). Kraus Repr.
Sociological Studies in the British Penal Services. (Sociological Review Monographs: No. 9). pap. 11.00 (ISBN 0-8115-3315-8). Kraus Repr.
Sociological Studies of Child Development, Vol. 2. Ed. by Peter Adler & Patricia Adler. 56.50 (ISBN 0-89232-760-X). Jai Pr.
Sociological Task. Harold Fallding. LC 68-24428. 1968. 29.50x (ISBN 0-89197-416-4). Irvington.
Sociological Theories of Emile Durkheim. Robert A. Jones. (Masters of Social Theory Ser.: Vol. 2). 1986. 19.95 (ISBN 0-8039-2333-3); pap. 9.95 (ISBN 0-8039-2334-1). Sage.
Sociological Theories of the Economy. Ed. by Barry Hindness. LC 77-11615. 199p. 1978. 36.50 (ISBN 0-8419-0341-7). Holmes & Meier.
Sociological Theories of Today. Pitirim A. Sorokin. Ed. by Lewis A. Coser & Walter W. Powell. LC 79-7022. (Perennial Works in Sociology Ser.). 1979. Repr. of 1966 ed. lib. bdg. 49.50x (ISBN 0-405-12121-0). Ayer Co Pubs.
Sociological Theories, Race & Colonialism. 500p. 1980. pap. 19.00 (ISBN 92-3-101635-0, U1050, UNESCO). UNIPUB.
Sociological Theory. 5th ed. Lewis A. Coser & Bernard Rosenberg. 1982. text ed. write for info. (ISBN 0-02-325220-0). Macmillan.
Sociological Theory. 2nd ed. Mennell. pap. 42.95 (ISBN 0-317-64280-4). Van Nos Reinhold.
Sociological Theory. George Ritzer. 486p. 1982. text ed. 24.00 (ISBN 0-394-32516-8, KnopfC). Knopf.
Sociological Theory. 2nd ed. George Ritzer. 486p. 1988. text ed. 30.00 (ISBN 0-394-35575-X, RanC). Random.
Sociological Theory: An Introduction. Ed. by Walter L. Wallace. LC 68-8162. (Illus.). 1969. text ed. 33.95x (ISBN 0-202-30091-9). Aldine de Gruyter.
Sociological Theory: An Introduction to Concepts, Issues & Research. Mark Abrahamson. (Prentice Hall Series in Sociology). (Illus.). 288p. 1981. text ed. write for info (ISBN 0-13-820803-4). P-H.
Sociological Theory & Medical Sociology. Graham Scambler. 280p. 1988. text ed. 67.50 (ISBN 0-422-60630-8, Pub. by Tavistock England). Routledge Chapman & Hall.
Sociological Theory & Modern Society. Talcott Parsons. LC 67-12517. 1967. 28.50 (ISBN 0-02-924200-2). Free Pr.
Sociological Theory & Philosophical Analysis. Alasdair MacIntyre & Dorothy Emmet. 1970. 6.95 (ISBN 0-02-577460-3). Macmillan.
Sociological Theory & Research: A Critical Appraisal. Ed. by Hubert M. Blalock, Jr. LC 80-754. (Illus.). 1980. 29.95 (ISBN 0-02-903630-5). Free Pr.
Sociological Theory & Social Research. Charles H. Cooley. LC 69-18159. 1969. Repr. of 1930 ed. 37.50x (ISBN 0-678-00477-3). Kelley.
Sociological Theory: Classical Founders & Contemporary Perspectives. Doyle P. Johnson. LC 80-23441. 597p. 1981. 24.00 (ISBN 0-02-360650-9); tchr's ed. 4.00 (ISBN 0-02-360660-6). Macmillan.
Sociological Theory: Classical Statements. David Ashley & David M. Orenstein. 1984. pap. text ed. 30.00 (ISBN 0-205-08249-1, 818249). Allyn.
Sociological Theory: From the Enlightenment to the Present. Calvin J. Larson. LC 86-80124. 247p. (Orig.). 1987. lib. bdg. 28.95x (ISBN 0-930390-72-5); pap. text ed. 14.95x (ISBN 0-930390-71-7). Gen Hall.
Sociological Theory in Transition. Mark Wardell & Stephen Turner. LC 85-18617. 224p. 1986. text ed. 29.95x (ISBN 0-04-301205-1); pap. text ed. 12.95x (ISBN 0-04-301206-X). Unwin Hyman.
Sociological Theory in Use. Ken Menzies. (Illus.). 220p. 1982. 24.95x (ISBN 0-7100-0892-9); pap. 10.95x (ISBN 0-7100-0893-7). Routledge Chapman & Hall.
Sociological Theory of C. Wright Mills. Joseph A. Scimecca. (National University Pubns. Series in American Studies). 1976. 17.95x (ISBN 0-8046-9155-X, Pub. by Kennikat). Assoc Faculty Pr.
Sociological Theory of Law. Niklas Luhmann. Tr. by Elizabeth King-Utz & Martin Albrow. 448p. 1985. 49.50x (ISBN 0-7100-9747-6). Routledge Chapman & Hall.
Sociological Theory 1983. Ed. by Randall Collins. (Social & Behavioral Science Ser.). 1983. text ed. 39.95x (ISBN 0-87589-557-3). Jossey-Bass.
Sociological Theory 1984. Ed. by Randall Collins. (Social & Behavioral Science Ser.). 1984. 39.95x (ISBN 0-87589-587-5). Jossey-Bass.
Sociological Traditions from Generation to Generation: Glimpses of the American Experience. Ed. by Robert K. Merton & Matilda W. Riley. LC 79-26693. (Modern Sociology Ser.). (Illus.). 1980. text ed. 35.00 (ISBN 0-89391-034-1); pap. text ed. 22.50 (ISBN 0-89391-061-9). Ablex Pub.
Sociological Value of Christianity. Georges Chatterton-Hill. LC 83-45605. Date not set. Repr. of 1912 ed. 36.00 (ISBN 0-404-19873-2). AMS Pr.
Sociological View of Sovereignty. John R. Commons. LC 64-17405. Repr. of 1899 ed. 22.50x (ISBN 0-678-00090-5). Kelley.
Sociological Work: Method & Substance. Howard S. Becker. LC 77-115936. 357p. 1976. pap. text ed. 14.95 (ISBN 0-87855-630-3). Transaction Bks.
Sociologie De la Famille: Recueil De Textes Presentes et Commentes. Andree Michel. (Textes De Sciences Sociales: No. 11). 1971. pap. 12.80x (ISBN 0-686-21815-9). Mouton.
Sociologie De Proudhon. Celestin C. Bougle. Ed. by J. P. Mayer. LC 78-67336. (European Political Thought Ser.). (Fr.). 1979. Repr. of 1911 ed. lib. bdg. 25.50x (ISBN 0-405-11681-0). Ayer Co Pubs.
Sociologie Des Communications De Masse: Tendences Actuelles De la Recherche et Bibliographie. Alphons Silbermann. (Current Sociology-la Sociologie Contemporaine: No. 18-3). 1973. pap. 10.00x (ISBN 90-2797-175-7). Mouton.
Sociologie Des Migrations Aux Etats-Unis Societe, Mouvements Sociaux & Ideologies. Rene Duchac. (Premier Serie, Etudes: No. 15). 1974. pap. 25.60 (ISBN 90-2797-191-9). Mouton.
Sociologie Du Developpement Africain: Tendances Actuelles De la Recherche et Bibliographie. Abdelwahab Boudhiba. (Current Sociology: No. 18/2). 1972. pap. 7.20x (ISBN 90-2796-948-5). Mouton.
Sociologie Du Developpement Latino-Americain: Tendances Actuelles De la Recherche et Bibliographie, 2 pts. Ed. by Pablo G. Casanova. Incl. Pt. 1. Etudes Generales. (No. 18). 1971. pap. 7.20x (ISBN 0-686-22179-6); Pt. 2. Etudes Sectorielles. (No. 19). 1973. pap. 12.00x (ISBN 90-2797-218-4). (La Sociologie Contemporaine). pap. Mouton.

Sociologie Du Loisir: Tendances Actuelles De la Recherche & Bibliographie (1945-65) Joffre Dumazedier & Claire Guinchat. (Current Sociology-la Sociologie Contemporaine: No. 16-1). 1969. pap. 9.60x (ISBN 90-2796-576-5). Mouton.
Sociologie du Temps Libre: Problemes et Perspectives. Marie-Charlotte Busch. (Interaction, l'Homme et Son Environment Social Ser.: No. 2). 410p. (Fr.). 1975. pap. text ed. 29.60x (ISBN 90-2797-595-7). Mouton.
Sociologie d'une Revolution. Frantz Fanon. (Petite Coll. Maspero). pap. 9.95 (ISBN 0-685-35635-3). French & Eur.
Sociologie Rurale: Recueil De Textes. Ed. by Placide Rambaud. (Textes De Sciences Sociales: No. 16). (Orig., Fr.). 1976. pap. text ed. 24.80x (ISBN 90-2797-903-0). Mouton.
Sociologische Erkenntnis: Sociological Knowledge: The Positive Philosophy of Social Life. Gustav Ratzenhofer. LC 74-25775. (European Sociology Ser.). 372p. 1975. Repr. 29.00x (ISBN 0-405-06529-9). Ayer Co Pubs.
Sociologism & Existentialism: Two Perspectives on the Individual & Society. Edward A. Tiryakian. Ed. by Lewis A. Coser & Walter W. Powell. LC 79-7026. (Perennial Works in Sociology Ser.). 1979. Repr. of 1962 ed. lib. bdg. 17.00x (ISBN 0-405-12125-3). Ayer Co Pubs.
Sociologist As Consultant. Ed. by Joyce M. Iutcovich & Mark Iutcovich. LC 86-30330. 302p. 1987. lib. bdg. 39.95 (ISBN 0-275-92615-X, C2615). Praeger.
Sociologist Looks at Religion. Joseph H. Fichter. 1988. pap. 15.95 (ISBN 0-89453-637-0). M Glazier.
Sociologists, Economists & Democracy. Brian Barry. LC 78-55039. (Illus.). vi, 202p. 1978. pap. 8.00x (ISBN 0-226-03823-8). U of Chicago Pr.
Sociologists, Economists, & Democracy. Brian Barry. 208p. 1988. pap. 12.95X (ISBN 0-226-03824-6, Midway Reprint). U of Chicago Pr.
Sociologists in Search of Their Intellectual Domain. G. Boalt. 164p. 1979. pap. 25.00x (ISBN 91-22-00268-5, Pub. by Almqvist & Wiksell). Coronet Bks.
Sociologists on Sociology. Ed. by Bob Mullan. LC 87-1828. 288p. 1987. 28.50 (ISBN 0-389-20727-6). B&N Imports.
Sociology. David B. Brinkerhoff & Lynn K. White. (Illus.). 624p. 1985. text ed. 37.00 (ISBN 0-314-85220-4). West Pub.
Sociology. 3rd ed. Ronald C. Federico & Janet Schwartz. LC 82-11375. 592p. 1983. pap. text ed. write for info (ISBN 0-394-34867-2, RanC); write for info (ISBN 0-394-34870-2). Random.
Sociology. 2nd ed. Joseph H. Fichter. LC 70-143688. 1971. text ed. 12.50x (ISBN 0-226-24633-7). U of Chicago Pr.
Sociology. Erich Goode. (Illus.). 608p. 1984. text ed. write for info (ISBN 0-13-820720-8). P-H.
Sociology. Ed. by Robert Hagedorn. 624p. 1983. pap. text ed. write for info.; study guide avail.; instr's. manual avail. Wm C Brown.
Sociology. 5th ed. Paul B. Horton & Chester L. Hunt. (Illus.). 1979. text ed. 33.95 (ISBN 0-07-030430-0). McGraw.
Sociology. 6th ed. Paul B. Horton & Chester L. Hunt. (Illus.). 650p. 1984. text ed. 36.95 (ISBN 0-07-030443-2); study guide 16.95 (ISBN 0-07-030446-7). McGraw.
Sociology. 4th ed. Donald Light, Jr. & Suzanne Keller. 1984. text ed. 24.00 (ISBN 0-394-33738-7, KnopfC); 8.00 (ISBN 0-394-34700-5). Knopf.
Sociology. Albert O'Hara. 160p. 1980. 5.95 (ISBN 0-89955-175-0, Pub. by Mei Ya China). Intl Spec Bk.
Sociology. 6th ed. David Popenoe. (Illus.). 656p. 1986. text ed. write for info (ISBN 0-13-820648-1). P-H.
Sociology. 3rd, rev. ed. Ian Robertson. xvi, 713p. 1987. text ed. 32.95x (ISBN 0-87901-245-5); study guide 8.95 (ISBN 0-87901-246-3); TV study guide 8.95x (ISBN 0-87901-329-X); reader 15.95x (ISBN 0-87901-330-3). Worth.
Sociology. Jack Rudman. (College Proficiency Examination Ser.: CPEP-14). (Cloth bdg. avail. on request). pap. 13.95 (ISBN 0-8373-5414-5). Natl Learning.
Sociology. Jack Rudman. (Graduate Record Examination Ser.: GRE-18). (Cloth bdg. avail. on request). pap. 13.95 (ISBN 0-8373-5218-5). Natl Learning.
Sociology. Jack Rudman. (Undergraduate Program Field Test Ser.: UPFT-23). (Cloth bdg. avail. on request). pap. 13.95 (ISBN 0-8373-6023-4). Natl Learning.
Sociology. 2nd, rev. ed. Richard T. Schaefer. 640p. 1986. text ed. 35.95 (ISBN 0-07-055070-0). McGraw.
Sociology. Richard T. Schaefer & Robert P. Lamm. (Illus.). 608p. 1983. text ed. 34.95 (ISBN 0-07-055065-4). McGraw.
Sociology. 3rd ed. Jon Shepard. LC 86-13224. (Illus.). 624p. 1986. text ed. 37.00 (ISBN 0-314-25181-2); study guide 14.00 (ISBN 0-314-35017-9). West Pub.
Sociology. 2nd ed. Jon M. Shepard. 600p. 1983. text ed. 35.00 (ISBN 0-314-77794-6); instr's. manual, test bank avail. (ISBN 0-314-77795-4); study guide 12.25avail. (ISBN 0-314-77796-2). West Pub.
Sociology. Jon M. Shepard et al. LC 77-4969. (Wiley Self-Teaching Guides). Repr. of 1977 ed. 59.80 (ISBN 0-8357-9979-4, 2011876). Bks Demand UMI.
Sociology. Neil J. Smelser. (Series in Sociology). (Illus.). 640p. 1981. text ed. write for info (ISBN 0-13-820829-8). P-H.
Sociology. Alternate ed. Neil J. Smelser. (Illus.). 448p. 1984. pap. text ed. write for info (ISBN 0-13-820811-5). P-H.
Sociology. 3rd ed. Neil J. Smelser. (Illus.). 464p. 1988. pap. text ed. price not set (ISBN 0-13-821307-0). P-H.
Sociology. 2nd ed. Rodney Stark. 619p. 1987. text ed. write for info. (ISBN 0-534-06834-0). Wadsworth Pub.
Sociology. 3rd ed. Rodney Stark. Date not set. text ed. write for info. (ISBN 0-534-09600-X). Wadsworth Pub.
Sociology. 2nd ed. Wallace & Wallace. 1988. case bound 25.00 (ISBN 0-205-08282-3, 818282); instr's manual avail. (ISBN 0-205-08283-1); test bank avail. (ISBN 0-205-08284-X); study guide avail. (ISBN 0-205-08285-8). Allyn.
Sociology: a Biographical Approach. 2nd ed. Brigitte Berger & Peter L. Berger. LC 74-26580. 1975. 17.95x (ISBN 0-465-07985-7). Basic.
Sociology: A Brief but Critical Introduction. Anthony Giddens. 182p. 1982. pap. text ed. 10.95 (ISBN 0-15-505554-2, HC). HarBraceJ.
Sociology: A Brief But Critical Introduction. 2nd ed. Anthony Giddens. 179p. 1987. pap. text ed. 8.50 (ISBN 0-15-582001-X). HarBraceJ.
Sociology: A Critical Approach to Power, Conflict, & Change. 2nd ed. J. Victor Baldridge. LC 79-22484. 547p. 1980. text ed. write for info. (ISBN 0-02-306720-9); write for info. study guide (ISBN 0-02-306730-6); write for info. tchr's. manual (ISBN 0-02-306750-0); test avail. (ISBN 0-02-306740-3). Macmillan.
Sociology: A Guide to Problems & Literature. 3rd ed. Tom Bottomore. 368p. 1986. text ed. 39.95x (ISBN 0-04-300108-4); pap. text ed. 16.95x (ISBN 0-317-53461-0). Unwin Hyman.
Sociology: A Guide to Reference & Information Sources. Stephen H. Aby. LC 86-27573. (Reference Sources in the Social Sciences Ser.). xvi, 231p. 1987. lib. bdg. 36.00 (ISBN 0-87287-498-2). Libs Unl.
Sociology: A Liberating Perspective. Liazos. 1985. 24.00 (ISBN 0-205-08359-5, 818359). Allyn.
Sociology: A Pragmatic Approach. 2nd ed. Ed. by Julian C. Bridges. (Illus.). 379p. 1982. pap. text ed. 21.95x (ISBN 0-89459-169-X). Hunter Textbks.
Sociology: A Student Handbook. Jonathan H. Turner. 160p. 1984. text ed. 5.00 (ISBN 0-394-33801-4, RanC). Random.
Sociology: An International Bibliography of Serial Literature 1880-1980. Jan Wepsiec. 176p. 1983. 57.00x (ISBN 0-7201-1652-X). Mansell.
Sociology: An Introduction. 2nd ed. Michael S. Bassis et al. 608p. 1984. pap. 15.00 (ISBN 0-394-33825-1). Random.
Sociology: An Introduction. 3rd ed. Michael S. Bassis et al. 508p. 1987. pap. write for info. (ISBN 0-394-36271-3, RanC); write for info. (ISBN 0-394-36308-6). Random.
Sociology: An Introduction. 2nd ed. John E. Conklin. 608p. 1986. text ed. write for info. (ISBN 0-02-324510-7). Macmillan.
Sociology: An Introduction. 2nd ed. Christopher B. Doob. LC 87-3471. (Illus.). 624p. 1988. text ed. 18.75 (ISBN 0-03-012804-8). HR&W.
Sociology: An Introduction. 3rd ed. J. Ross Eshelman et al. 1988. text ed. write for info. (ISBN 0-673-39718-1). Scott F.
Sociology: An Introduction. J. Ross Eshleman & Barbara G. Cashion. 1984. text ed. write for info. (ISBN 0-673-39573-1); tchr's. manual avail.; study guide 12.00 (ISBN 0-673-39574-X); test bank avail. Scott F.
Sociology: An Introduction. 2nd ed. Ed. by Neil J. Smelser. LC 72-11540. Repr. of 1973 ed. 120.00 (ISBN 0-8357-9980-8, 2051232). Bks Demand UMI.
Sociology: An Introduction. Alex Thio. 672p. 1986. text ed. 35.95 scp (ISBN 0-06-046617-0, HarpC). Har-Row.
Sociology: An Introduction. 2nd ed. Alex Thio. 688p. 1988. text ed. 33.95t (ISBN 0-06-046688-X, HarpC). Har-Row.
Sociology: An Introduction for Nurses, Midwives & Health Visitors. Caroline Cox. 224p. 1983. pap. 12.95 (ISBN 0-407-00231-6). Butterworth.
Sociology & Anthropology at DePauw University. Ed. by Clifton J. Phillips. (Sesquicentennial Ser.: No. 5). (Illus.). 32p. (Orig.). 1986. pap. write for info (ISBN 0-936631-04-X). DePauw Univ.
Sociology & Anthropology of Mental Illness: A Reference Guide. rev. ed. Edwin D. Driver. LC 71-103476. 504p. 1972. pap. 25.00x (ISBN 0-87023-062-X). U of Mass Pr.
Sociology & Critical Inquiry. John Walton. 1986. pap. 18.00x (ISBN 0-256-03409-5). Dorsey.
Sociology & Education: An Analysis of the Theories of Spencer & Ward. Elsa P. Kimball. LC 68-58599. (Columbia University. Studies in the Social Sciences: No. 369). Repr. of 1932 ed. 21.50 (ISBN 0-404-51369-7). AMS Pr.
Sociology & Estrangement: Three Sociologists of Imperial Germany. Arthur Mitzman. 370p. 1986. pap. 17.95 (ISBN 0-88738-605-9). Transaction Bks.
Sociology & Everyday Life. David A. Karp & William Yoels. LC 85-62183. 315p. 1986. pap. text ed. 16.95 (ISBN 0-87581-317-8). Peacock Pubs.
Sociology & History. Peter Burke. (Controversies in Sociology Ser.: No. 10). 128p. (Orig.). 1980. pap. text ed. 12.95x (ISBN 0-04-301115-2). Unwin Hyman.
Sociology & Human Destiny: Studies in Sociology, Religion & Society. Ed. by Gregory B. Baum. 224p. 1980. 14.50 (ISBN 0-8164-0110-1, HarpR). Har-Row.
Sociology & Jurisprudence of Leon Petrazycki. Ed. by Jan Gorecki. LC 75-38551. (Office of International Programs & Studies Ser). 156p. 1975. 14.95 (ISBN 0-252-00525-2). U of Ill Pr.
Sociology & Medicine: Studies Within the Framework of the British National Health Service. (Sociological Review Monographs: No. 5). Repr. of 1962 ed. 11.00 (ISBN 0-8115-3311-5). Kraus Repr.
Sociology & Pastoral Work. Francois Houtart. pap. 1.50 (ISBN 0-8199-0133-4, L38828). Franciscan Herald.
Sociology & Philosophy. Emile Durkheim. Tr. by D. F. Pocock. LC 54-2835. 1974. 14.95 (ISBN 0-02-908570-5); pap. 9.95 (ISBN 0-02-908580-2). Free Pr.
Sociology & Political Theory. Harry E. Barnes. LC 74-185842. 1972. Repr. of 1924 ed. lib. bdg. 69.95 (ISBN 0-87700-036-0). Revisionist Pr.
Sociology & Politics of Development: A Theoretical Study. Baidya N. Varma. (International Library of Sociology). 1980. 26.95x (ISBN 0-7100-0428-1). Routledge Chapman & Hall.
Sociology & Politics: The Soviet Case. Vladimir Shlapentokh. Ed. by Ben Armfield. 154p. (Orig.). Date not set. pap. text ed. 35.00 (ISBN 1-55831-043-6). Delphic Associates.
Sociology & School Knowledge. Geoff Whitty. 224p. 1986. pap. 15.95 (ISBN 0-416-36970-7, 9942). Routledge Chapman & Hall.
Sociology & Scientism: The American Quest for Objectivity, 1880-1940. Robert C. Bannister. LC 86-24985. x, 302p. 1987. 29.95x (ISBN 0-8078-1733-3). U of NC Pr.
Sociology & Social Anthropology in Asia & the Pacific. 529p. 1986. pap. 31.50 (ISBN 92-3-102172-9, U1424 6011, UNESCO). UNIPUB.
Sociology & Social Anthropology in Asia & the Pacific. 1985. 20.00 (ISBN 0-471-63992-3). Wiley.
Sociology & Social Change in Korea. Man-Gap Lee. 341p. 1982. text ed. 18.00x (ISBN 0-8248-0937-8). UH Pr.
Sociology & Social Development in Asia: Proceedings of the Symposium. Ed. by Tadashi Fukutake & Kiyomi Morioka. 445p. 1974. 42.50 (ISBN 0-86008-119-2, Pub. by U of Tokyo Japan). Columbia U Pr.
Sociology & Social Practice. N. Yahiel. 1984. text ed. 43.00 (ISBN 0-08-031822-3). Pergamon.
Sociology & Social Progress. Thomas N. Carver. 1905. 17.50 (ISBN 0-686-17694-4). Quality Lib.
Sociology & Social Psychology of Disability & Rehabilitation. Constantina Safilios-Rothschild. LC 81-40787. 348p. 1981. pap. text ed. 13.50 (ISBN 0-8191-1817-6). U Pr of Amer.
Sociology & Social Welfare. Michael Sullivan. 172p. 1987. text ed. 34.95x (ISBN 0-04-301213-2); pap. text ed. 15.95x (ISBN 0-04-301214-0). Unwin Hyman.
Sociology & Socialism. Tom Bottomore. LC 83-22930. 212p. 1984. 25.00 (ISBN 0-312-74004-2); pap. text ed. 11.95 (ISBN 0-312-74005-0). St Martin.
Sociology & Socialism in Contemporary China. Siu-Lun Wong. (International Library of Sociology). 1979. 21.95x (ISBN 0-7100-0089-8). Routledge Chapman & Hall.
Sociology & Society in Contemporary China, 1979-1983: A Special Issue of Chinese Sociology & Anthrology. Ed. by David S. Chu. 224p. 1984. pap. 16.95 (ISBN 0-87332-278-9). M E Sharpe.
Sociology & Teaching: A New Challenge for the Sociology of Education. Ed. by Peter Woods & Andrew Pollard. 256p. 1988. lib. bdg. 55.00x (ISBN 0-7099-3697-4, Pub. by Croom Helm UK). Routledge Chapman & Hall.
Sociology & the Field of Public Health. Edward A. Suchman. LC 63-21228. 182p. 1963. pap. 8.95x (ISBN 0-87154-864-X). Russell Sage.
Sociology & the Human Experience. Donald A. Hobbs. 1985. 18.00 (ISBN 0-02-354790-1); write for info. tchr's. manual (ISBN 0-02-354810-X). Macmillan.
Sociology & the Human Image. David Lyon. LC 83-22644. 220p. 1983. pap. 9.95 (ISBN 0-87784-843-2). Inter-Varsity.
Sociology & the Military Establishment. Morris Janowitz & Roger W. Little. 159p. 1974. 18.95 (ISBN 0-8039-0214-X); pap. 8.95 (ISBN 0-8039-0215-8). Seven Locks Pr.
Sociology & the School: An Interactionist Viewpoint. Peter Woods. 210p. (Orig.). 1983. pap. 10.50x (ISBN 0-7100-9342-X). Routledge Chapman & Hall.
Sociology & the Twilight of Man: Homocentrism & Discourse in Sociological Theory. Charles Lemert. LC 78-17146. (Perspectives in Sociology). 276p. 1979. 17.50x (ISBN 0-8093-0851-7). S Ill U Pr.
Sociology & the Twilight of Man: Homocentrism & Discourse in Sociological Theory. Charles C. Lemert. LC 78-17146. 276p. 1980. pap. 9.95x (ISBN 0-8093-0975-0). S Ill U Pr.
Sociology & Theology. Ed. by David Martin et al. 170p. 1980. 26.00x (ISBN 0-312-74007-7). St Martin.
Sociology As an Art Form. Robert Nisbet. 1976. pap. 6.95x (ISBN 0-19-502103-7). Oxford U Pr.
Sociology as Applied to Medicine. Donald Patrick & Graham Scambler. (Illus.). 256p. 1982. pap. 17.95 (ISBN 0-7216-0825-6, Bailliere-Tindall). Saunders.
Sociology Before Comte. Harry E. Barnes. 59.95 (ISBN 0-87700-202-9). Revisionist Pr.
Sociology by the Discovery Method: Cutting Costs & Teaching More. Gordon D. Morgan. LC 83-62300. 125p. (Orig.). 1985. pap. text ed. 5.95 (ISBN 0-88247-726-9). R & E Pubs.
Sociology: Classification Schedule, Author & Title Listing, Chronological Listing, 2 vols. Harvard University Library Staff. LC 72-83391. (Widener Library Shelflist Ser: No. 45-46). 85.00x set (ISBN 0-674-81625-0). Harvard U Pr.
Sociology: Concepts & Characteristics. 6th ed. Judson R. Landis. 417p. 1986. pap. text ed. write for info. (ISBN 0-534-06438-8). Wadsworth Pub.
Sociology: Concepts & Characteristics. 7th ed. Judson R. Landis. Date not set. pap. text ed. write for info. (ISBN 0-534-10158-5). Wadsworth Pub.
Sociology: Concepts, Issues & Applications. Thomas J. Sullivan & Kenrick S. Thompson. LC 83-21683. 449p. 1984. pap. text ed. write for info. (ISBN 0-02-418480-2); write for info. tchr's. manual (ISBN 0-02-418560-4); write for info. Macmillan.
Sociology: Contemporary Readings. 2nd ed. Ed. by John Stimson & Ardyth Stimson. LC 86-63524. 420p. 1987. pap. 14.95 (ISBN 0-87581-322-4). Peacock Pubs.
Sociology, Education & the Schools: An Introduction to the Sociology of Education. Robert G. Burgess. 208p. 1986. 24.50 (ISBN 0-89397-238-X). Nichols Pub.
Sociology Experiencing a Changing Society. 3rd ed. George Ritzer et al. 608p. 1987. 38.00 (ISBN 0-205-08976-3). Allyn.
Sociology for Canadians: Images of Society. Alexander Himelfarb & C. James Richardson. 512p. 1982. 26.95 (ISBN 0-07-548440-4). McGraw.
Sociology for Community Nurses. Jack. 128p. 1982. 10.00 (ISBN 0-471-25824-5, Wiley Heyden). Wiley.
Sociology for Everyone. Martin Joseph. 368p. 1986. text ed. 34.95 (ISBN 0-7456-0186-3); pap. text ed. 19.95 (ISBN 0-7456-0187-1). Basil Blackwell.
Sociology for Life: Expanding Circles of Social Participation Through Scholarship, Community Service & Teaching. George K. Floro. LC 86-5509. 154p. (Orig.). 1986. lib. bdg. 25.75 (ISBN 0-8191-5327-3); pap. text ed. 13.25 (ISBN 0-8191-5328-1). U Pr of Amer.
Sociology for Nurses. 2nd ed. Christine M. Chapman. (Illus.). 210p. 1982. pap. write for info. (ISBN 0-7216-0900-7, Bailliere-Tindall). Saunders.
Sociology for People. Alfred M. Lee. LC 88-9672. 272p. 1988. text ed. 34.00x (ISBN 0-8156-2442-5). Syracuse U Pr.
Sociology for Whom. 2nd ed. Alfred M. Lee. LC 85-26134. 280p. 1986. pap. text ed. 12.95x (ISBN 0-8156-2355-0). Syracuse U Pr.
Sociology: From Concepts to Practice. Bernard Phillips. (Illus.). 1979. text ed. 40.95 (ISBN 0-07-049787-7). McGraw.
Sociology Full Circle. 4th ed. William Feigelman. 512p. 1985. pap. text ed. 19.95 (ISBN 0-03-063066-5, HoltC). HR&W.
Sociology: Human Society. 4th ed. Melvin L. DeFleur & William D'Antonio. 475p. 1984. text ed. write for info (ISBN 0-394-33742-5, RanC). Random.
Sociology in a Changing World. William Kornblum. 672p. 1987. text ed. write for info. (ISBN 0-03-001419-0); write for info. study guide (ISBN 0-03-020579-4). HR&W.
Sociology in a Different Key: Essays in Non-Linear Sociology. Roy G. Francis. LC 82-72534. 164p. 1983. text ed. 20.95x (ISBN 0-88105-000-8); pap. text ed. 13.95x (ISBN 0-88105-007-5). Cap & Gown.
Sociology in Australia & New Zealand: Theory & Methods. Cora V. Baldock & James Lally. LC 72-778. (Contributions in Sociology: No. 16). (Illus.). 328p. 1975. lib. bdg. 35.00 (ISBN 0-8371-6126-6, BSA/). Greenwood.
Sociology in Bondage: An Introduction to Graduate Study. Harold A. Nelson. LC 80-65605. 145p. 1981. perfect bdg. 9.95 (ISBN 0-86548-051-6). R & E Pubs.
Sociology in India: Retrospect & Prospect. P. K. Nayar. viii, 451p. 1983. text ed. 40.00x (ISBN 0-86590-109-0). Apt Bks.
Sociology in Israel. Leonard Weller. LC 72-849. (Contributions in Sociology: No. 11). 1974. lib. bdg. 35.00 (ISBN 0-8371-6417-6, WES/). Greenwood.

Sociology of Science: An Episodic Memoir. Robert K. Merton. LC 79-9962. (Arcturus Bks Paperbacks). 164p. 1979. pap. 5.95x (ISBN 0-8093-0925-4). S Ill U Pr.

Sociology of Science & Research. Janos Farkas. 504p. 1979. 107.50x (ISBN 0-317-53786-5, Pub. by Collets (UK)). State Mutual Bk.

Sociology of Science & Research. Janos Farkas. 504p. 1979. 117.50x (ISBN 0-317-53855-1, Pub. by Collets (UK)). State Mutual Bk.

Sociology of Science Fiction. Brian M. Stableford. LC 81-21607. (I. O. Evans Studies in the Philosophy & Criticism of Literature: Vol. 4). 189p. 1987. lib. bdg. 19.95x (ISBN 0-89370-165-3); pap. 9.95x (ISBN 0-89370-265-X). Borgo Pr.

Sociology of Science: Theoretical & Empirical Investigations. Robert K. Merton. Ed. by Norman Storer. LC 72-97623. 1979. pap. 15.95x (ISBN 0-226-52092-7, P846, Phoen). U of Chicago Pr.

Sociology of Sciences: An Annotated Bibliography on Invisible Colleges, 1972-1981. Daryl E. Chubin. LC 82-48773. 216p. 1983. lib. bdg. 33.00 (ISBN 0-8240-9223-6). Garland Pub.

Sociology of Secret Societies: Chinese Secret Societies in Singapore & Peninsular Malaysia. Mak Lau Fong. (East Asian Social Science Monographs Ser.). (Illus.). 1981. 34.95x (ISBN 0-19-580471-6). Oxford U Pr.

Sociology of Slavery. Orlando Patterson. LC 70-84198. 310p. 1970. 22.50 (ISBN 0-8386-7469-0). Fairleigh Dickinson.

Sociology of Small Groups. 2nd ed. Theodore M. Mills. (Illus.). 144p. 1984. write for info. (ISBN 0-13-820910-3); pap. write for info (ISBN 0-13-820902-2). P-H.

Sociology of Social Problems. 8th ed. Paul B. Horton et al. (Illus.). 608p. 1985. text ed. write for info (ISBN 0-13-820937-5). P-H.

Sociology of Social Problems. 9th ed. Paul B. Horton et al. (Illus.). 480p. 1988. text ed. write for info. (ISBN 0-13-821687-8). P-H.

Sociology of Sociology. Robert W. Friedrichs. LC 77-91882. 1972. pap. text ed. 13.95 (ISBN 0-02-910880-2). Free Pr.

Sociology of Sociology. (Sociological Review Monographs: No. 16). (Orig.). 1970. 11.00 (ISBN 0-8115-3321-2). Kraus Repr.

Sociology of Southeast Asia: Readings on Social Change & Development. Ed. by Hans-Dieter Evers. (Illus.). 1980. 49.95x (ISBN 0-19-580408-2). Oxford U Pr.

Sociology of Soviet Law. James L. Hildebrand. LC 78-186875. 227p. 1972. Repr. lib. bdg. 38.00 (ISBN 0-930342-83-6). W S Hein.

Sociology of Special Education. Sally Tomlinson. 200p. 1982. pap. 9.95x (ISBN 0-7100-9003-X). Routledge Chapman & Hall.

Sociology of Sport: An Annotated Bibliography. Paul Redekop. (Bibliographies in Sociology Ser.). 169p. 1988. lib. bdg. 23.00 (ISBN 0-8240-8464-0). Garland Pub.

Sociology of Sport: Diverse Perspectives. North American Society for the Study of Sport. Ed. by Susan Greendorfer & Andrew Yiannakis. 191p. 1981. pap. text ed. 17.00x (ISBN 0-88011-002-3, PGRE002). Leisure Pr.

Sociology of Suicide: A Reader. Ed. by Anthony Giddens. 424p. 1971. 32.50x (ISBN 0-7146-2591-4, F Cass Co). Biblio Dist.

Sociology of Talcott Parsons. Francis Bourricaud. Tr. by Arthur Goldhammer. LC 81-1348. xvi, 326p. 1984. pap. 12.50x (ISBN 0-226-06756-4). U of Chicago Pr.

Sociology of Talcott Parsons. Francois Bourricaud. Tr. by Arthur Goldhammer. LC 81-1348. 336p. 1981. lib. bdg. 25.00x (ISBN 0-226-06755-6). U of Chicago Pr.

Sociology of Teaching. Willard Waller. LC 32-20285. pap. 121.00 (ISBN 0-317-09848-9, 2017003). Bks Demand UMI.

Sociology of Teaching. Willard W. Waller. LC 61-13769. (Illus.). 1961. Repr. of 1932 ed. 20.00x (ISBN 0-8462-0292-1). Russell.

Sociology of the African Family. D. Kayonko-Male & P. Onyango. (Illus.). 176p. 1984. pap. text ed. 13.95 (ISBN 0-582-64703-7). Longman.

Sociology of the Arts. Ed. by Mildred Weil & Duncan Hartley. LC 75-7162. 1975. pap. text ed. 4.40x (ISBN 0-8134-1731-7, 1731). Inter Print Pubs.

Sociology of the Bay Colony. Morris Talpalar. LC 75-27960. 396p. 1976. 15.95 (ISBN 0-8022-2176-9). Philos Lib.

Sociology of the Church: Essays in Reconstruction. James B. Jordan. LC 86-80571. 320p. (Orig.). 1986. pap. 9.95 (ISBN 0-939404-12-5). Geneva Ministr.

Sociology of the Family. Richard J. Gelles. 550p. 1989. 25.00 (ISBN 0-8039-2284-1). Sage.

Sociology of the Family. Steven L. Nock. (Illus.). 400p. 1987. text ed. write for info. (ISBN 0-13-821000-4). P-H.

Sociology of the Future. Ed. by Wendell Bell & James Mau. LC 72-158565. 464p. 1971. 40.00x (ISBN 0-87154-106-8). Russell Sage.

Sociology of the Karbis. T. Bhattacharjee. (Illus.). xii, 198p. 1986. text ed. 25.00x (ISBN 81-7018-325-1, Pub. by D K Pub Corp Delhi). Apt Bks.

Sociology of the Kibbutz. Ed. by Ernest Krausz. LC 79-1212. (Studies of Israeli Society: Vol. II). 423p. 1983. 34.95x (ISBN 0-87855-455-6); pap. 14.95x (ISBN 0-87855-902-7). Transaction Bks.

Sociology of the Literature of Politics Edmund Burke, 2 Vols. Sna Rizvi. Ed. by James Hogg. (Romantic Reassessment). 432p. (Orig.). 1982. pap. 30.00 (ISBN 3-7052-0583-8, Pub. by Salzburg Studies). Longwood Pub Group.

Sociology of the Mass Media. David Glover. (Themes & Perspectives in Sociology Ser.). 80p. (Orig.). 1984. pap. text ed. 7.95x (ISBN 0-946183-05-8, Pub. by Causeway Pr Ltd England). Sheridan.

Sociology of the Offbeat: Essays in the Science of Human Social Behavior. Ed. by Robert M. Khoury. LC 81-40726. (Illus.). 418p. (Orig.). 1982. PLB 34.75 (ISBN 0-8191-2457-5); pap. text ed. 17.50 (ISBN 0-8191-2458-3). U Pr of Amer.

Sociology of the Palestinians. K. Nakhleh & E. Zureik. LC 79-12706. 1980. 27.50 (ISBN 0-312-74073-5). St Martin.

Sociology of the Possible. 2nd ed. Richard J. Ofshe. 1977. pap. text ed. write for info (ISBN 0-13-821595-2). P-H.

Sociology of the Professions. Robert Dingwall & Philip Lewis. LC 82-3352. 244p. 1983. 26.50x (ISBN 0-312-74075-1). St Martin.

Sociology of the Renaissance. Alfred W. Von Martin. LC 83-45658. Date not set. Repr. of 1944 ed. 18.50 (ISBN 0-404-19808-2). AMS Pr.

Sociology of the School. Myles W. Rodehaver et al. LC 80-26021. x, 262p. 1981. Repr. of 1957 ed. lib. bdg. 35.00x (ISBN 0-313-22897-3, ROSSC). Greenwood.

Sociology of the School Curriculum. John Eggleston. 1977. pap. 10.95x (ISBN 0-7100-8566-4). Routledge Chapman & Hall.

Sociology of the Social Sciences: A Trend Report & Bibliography. Elisabeth T. Crawford. (Current Sociology-la Sociologie Contemporaine: No. 19-2). 1973. pap. 8.40x (ISBN 90-2797-655-4). Mouton.

Sociology of the Soviet Union. Gary Littlejohn. LC 83-19111. 300p. 1984. 29.95 (ISBN 0-312-74077-8). St Martin.

Sociology of the State. Bertrand Badie & Pierre Birnbaum. Tr. by Arthur Goldhammer from Fr. LC 82-20249. 1983. pap. text ed. 10.95x (ISBN 0-226-03549-2). U of Chicago Pr.

Sociology of Town Planning: A Bibliography, Nos. 1039-1040. James M Simmie et al. 1976. 8.50 (ISBN 0-686-20396-8). CPL Biblios.

Sociology of Tristan da Cunha: Results of the Norwegian Scientific Expedition to Tristan da Cunha, 1937-1938. Peter A. Munch. LC 77-87549. Repr. of 1945 ed. 30.00 (ISBN 0-685-87356-0). AMS Pr.

Sociology of Urban Life. Harry Gold. (Illus.). 416p. 1982. write for info. (ISBN 0-13-821371-2). P-H.

Sociology of Urban Women's Image in African Literature. Kenneth Little. 174p. 1980. 27.50x (ISBN 0-8476-6290-X). Rowman.

Sociology of Virtue: The Political & Social Theories of George Sorel. John L. Stanley. LC 81-40318. 320p. 1981. 42.00x (ISBN 0-520-03790-1). U of Cal Pr.

Sociology of War & Peace. Ed. by Colin Creighton & Martin Shaw. (Explorations in Sociology Ser.: No. 24). 256p. 1986. text ed. 29.95x (ISBN 0-911378-65-0); pap. text ed. 17.95x (ISBN 0-911378-66-9). Sheridan.

Sociology of Welfare: Social Policy, Stratification & Political Order. Graham Room. 1980. 30.00x (ISBN 0-312-74080-8). St Martin.

Sociology of Women: An Introduction. Sara Delamont. 256p. (Orig.). 1980. text ed. 29.95x (ISBN 0-04-301119-5). Unwin Hyman.

Sociology of Work. Theodore Caplow. LC 77-18112. (Illus.). 1978. Repr. of 1954 ed. lib. bdg. 32.00 (ISBN 0-313-20111-0, CASOW). Greenwood.

Sociology of Yiddish: International Journal of the Sociology of Language, No. 24. Ed. by Joshua A. Fishman. 1980. pap. text ed. 19.00x (ISBN 90-279-3058-9). Mouton.

Sociology of Youth. Simon Frith. (Themes & Perspectives in Sociology Ser.). 72p. (Orig.). 1984. pap. text ed. 7.95x (ISBN 0-946183-06-6, Pub. by Causeway Pr Ltd England). Sheridan.

Sociology of Youth. Ragenda Pandey. xviii, 187p. 1985. text ed. 25.00x (ISBN 0-86590-513-4, Pub. by Sterling Pubs India). Apt Bks.

Sociology of Youth Culture & Youth Subcultures. Mike Brake. 1980. pap. 25.00x (ISBN 0-7100-0363-3); pap. 12.95x (ISBN 0-7100-0364-1). Routledge Chapman & Hall.

Sociology; or, the Reconstruction of Society, Government & Property. Lewis Masquerier. 59.95 (ISBN 0-8490-1073-X). Gordon Pr.

Sociology: Or, the Reconstruction of Society, Government, & Property. Lewis Masquerier. Incl. Appendix to Sociology. 31p. Repr. of 1877 ed. LC 76-88504. (Illus.). 213p. 1971. Repr. of 1884 ed. lib. bdg. 35.00x (ISBN 0-8371-4967-3, MASO). Greenwood.

Sociology, Phenomenology & Marxian Analysis: A Critical Discussion of the Theory & Practice of a Science of Society. Barry Smart. (International Library of Sociology). 1976. pap. 12.50 (ISBN 0-7100-8373-4). Routledge Chapman & Hall.

Sociology, Race & Ethnicity: A Critique of American Ideological Intrusions Upon Sociological Theory. H. H. Bash. (Monographs in Sociology). 264p. 1979. 48.00 (ISBN 0-677-05390-8). Gordon & Breach.

Sociology: Readings. John E. Owen. LC 80-39729. 1981. pap. text ed. write for info (ISBN 0-394-33292-X, RanC). Random.

Sociology since Midcentury: Essays in Theory Cumulation. Randall Collins. LC 81-13034. 1981. 29.50 (ISBN 0-12-181340-1). Acad Pr.

Sociology: Social Science & Social Concerns. 3rd ed. Ritchie P. Lowry & Robert P. Rankin. 1977. text ed. 24.50 (ISBN 0-669-99648-3); instr's. manual 2.00 (ISBN 0-669-03186-0); study guide 6.50 (ISBN 0-669-00339-5). Heath.

Sociology: Social Structure & Social Conflict. Harold Kerbo. 1056p. 1989. text ed. price not set (ISBN 0-02-362741-7). Macmillan.

Sociology: Study Guide & Workbook. 6th ed. Faye Barr. 272p. 1986. write for info (ISBN 0-13-820622-8). P-H.

Sociology, Study Guide & Workbook (by Goode) Mark Kassop. 288p. 1984. pap. text ed. write for info (ISBN 0-13-820746-1). P-H.

Sociology: The Basic Concepts. Edward E. Sagarin. LC 76-41969. 1978. pap. 15.95 (ISBN 0-275-50330-5, HoltC). HR&W.

Sociology: The Biological Factor. Michael A. Soroka & George J. Bryjak. 120p. (Orig.). 1985. pap. text ed. 11.95 (ISBN 0-917962-83-4). T H Peek.

Sociology: The Classic Statements. Ed. by Marcello Truzzi. 1971. pap. text ed. write for info (ISBN 0-394-31280-5, RanC). Random.

Sociology: The Core. James V. Zanden. 384p. 1986. pap. text ed. write for info (ISBN 0-394-34109-0, RanC). Random.

Sociology: The Discipline & Its Direction. William J. Chambliss & Thomas E. Ryther. (Illus.). 480p. 1976. pap. text ed. 26.95 (ISBN 0-07-010466-2). McGraw.

Sociology: The Human Science. 2nd, rev. ed. Elbert W. Stewart. 608p. 1981. text ed. 33.95 (ISBN 0-07-061280-3). McGraw.

Sociology: The Science of Human Organization. Jonathan H. Turner et al. LC 84-25368. (Illus.). 504p. 1984. text ed. 28.95x (ISBN 0-8304-1112-7); pap. 9.95 student study guide (ISBN 0-8304-1141-0); instr's. resource manual & test bank avail. (ISBN 0-8304-1142-9). Nelson-Hall.

Sociology: The Study of Society (Canadian) Robert A Stebbins. 592p. 1987. pap. text ed. 24.50 scp (ISBN 0-06-046493-3, HarpC). Har-Row.

Sociology: Themes & Perspectives. F. Haralambos & R. M. Heald. 1982. pap. 49.00x (ISBN 0-7231-0812-9, Pub. by Univ Tutorial Pr Ltd); pap. 29.00x (ISBN 0-7231-0793-9, Pub. by Univ Tutorial Pr Ltd). State Mutual Bk.

Sociology Through Humor. Joseph E. Faulkner. LC 86-26666. 301p. (Orig.). 1986. pap. text ed. 20.00 (ISBN 0-314-28491-5). West Pub.

Sociology Through Literature. 2nd ed. Lewis A. Coser. 544p. 1972. pap. text ed. write for info. (ISBN 0-13-821538-3). P-H.

Sociology Through Science Fiction. Ed. by Martin H. Greenberg et al. 350p. (Orig.). 1974. pap. text ed. write for info. (ISBN 0-312-74165-0). St Martin.

Sociology Tomorrow: An Evaluation of Sociological Theories in Terms of Science. Peter Park. LC 68-27989. 1968. pap. 9.95x (ISBN 0-672-63596-8). Irvington.

Sociology: Understanding Social Behavior. Alan P. Bates & Joseph Julian. (Instructors guide written by Patricia Harvey). 1975. text ed. 34.50 (ISBN 0-395-18652-8); instr's. guide & resource manual 1.90 (ISBN 0-395-18794-X). HM.

Sociology: Understanding Society. Peter Rose et al. (gr. 11-12). 1978. text ed. 24.88 (ISBN 0-13-821322-4). P-H.

Sociology: Windows on Society. Ed. by John Heeren & Marylee Mason. 350p. 1987. pap. text ed. 16.95x (ISBN 0-935732-11-X); instr's. manual avail. Roxbury Pub Co.

Sociology: Women, Men & Society. Elizabeth Almquist et al. (Illus.). 608p. 1978. pap. text ed. 26.75 (ISBN 0-8299-0174-4); instrs.' manual avail. (ISBN 0-8299-0450-6). West Pub.

Sociology, Work & Industry. Tony Watson. 272p. 1980. 30.00x (ISBN 0-7100-0542-3); pap. 12.95x (ISBN 0-7100-0543-1). Routledge Chapman & Hall.

Sociology's Models of Man. W. L. Skidmore. 216p. 1975. 55.00 (ISBN 0-677-04780-0). Gordon & Breach.

Sociomedical Health Indicators. Ed. by Jack Elinson & Athilia E. Siegmann. LC 78-74484. 224p. (Orig.). 1979. pap. 17.95x (ISBN 0-89503-013-6). Baywood Pub.

Sociometric Impact Management. John M. Halstead et al. (Special Study Ser.). 250p. 1984. 42.50x (ISBN 0-86531-724-0). Westview.

Sociometric Research: Data Analysis, Vol. 2. Ed. by Willem E. Saris & Irmtraud N. Gallhofer. LC 86-29834. 250p. 1987. 37.50 (ISBN 0-312-00418-4). St Martin.

Sociometric Research: Data Collection & Scaling, Vol. 1. Ed. by Willem E. Saris & Irmtraud N. Gallhofer. LC 86-2934. 250p. 1987. 37.50 (ISBN 0-312-00419-2). St Martin.

Sociometry, Experimental Method & the Science of Society. J. L. Moreno. 16.00 (ISBN 0-685-06814-5). Beacon Hse.

Sociometry in Group Relations. Helen Jennings. LC 72-9829. (Illus.). 105p. 1973. Repr. of 1959 ed. lib. bdg. 35.00x (ISBN 0-8371-6483-4, JESG). Greenwood.

Sociopath. J. V. Adams. LC 83-82208. 288p. 1983. pap. 3.50 (ISBN 0-9612454-0-9). Jackrabbit.

Sociopathic Personality. Benjamin B. Wolman. LC 86-26363. 170p. 1987. 27.50 (ISBN 0-87630-453-6). Brunner-Mazel.

Sociopathologie du Travail see Cahiers de l'Institut de Science Economique Appliquee.

Sociophobics: The Social Anthropology of Fear. Ed. by David L. Scruton. 175p. 1985. pap. text ed. 24.50x (ISBN 0-8133-7088-4). Westview.

Sociophysiology. Ed. by W. M. Waid. (Springer Series in Social Psychology). (Illus.). 580p. 1984. 39.50 (ISBN 0-387-90861-7). Springer Verlag.

Sociopolitical Structure of Prehistoric Southwestern Societies. Ed. by Steadman Upham & Kent G. Lightfoot. (Investigations in American Archaeology Ser.). 350p. 1988. pap. 37.50 (ISBN 0-8133-7538-X). Westview.

Sociopsychological Aspects of Sexually Transmitted Diseases. Ed. by Margaret Rodway & Marianne Wright. LC 88-638. (Journal of Social Work & Human Sexuality Ser.: Vol. 6, No. 2). (Illus.). 150p. 1988. text ed. 24.95 (ISBN 0-86656-737-2). Haworth Pr.

Sociotechnical Systems: A Sourcebook. Ed. by William A. Pasmore & John J. Sherwood. LC 77-20543. 366p. 1978. pap. 17.95 (ISBN 0-88390-142-0). Univ Assocs.

Sociotechnics: A Trend Report & Bibliography. Ed. by Adam Podgorecki. (La Sociologie Contemporaine: Vol.23, No. 1). 1977. pap. 14.40x (ISBN 90-2797-692-9). Mouton.

Socjologia Amerykanska: Wybor Prac 1950-1960. Ed. by Jerzy Kosinski. 211p. 1962. pap. 6.00 (ISBN 0-940962-41-1). Polish Inst Art & Sci.

Sock Bunnies: Christmas & Spring Edition. Date not set. pap. 4.98 (ISBN 0-317-03192-9). Gick.

Socks. Beverly Cleary. 160p. (gr. k-6). 1980. pap. 3.25 (ISBN 0-440-48256-9, YB). Dell.

Socks. Beverly Cleary. LC 72-10298. (Illus.). 192p. (gr. 3-7). 1973. 10.95 (ISBN 0-688-20067-2); PLB 10.88 (ISBN 0-688-30067-7). Morrow.

Socks. Beverly Cleary. (Illus.). (gr. k-9). 1988. pap. 3.25. Scholastic Inc.

Socks for Supper. Jack Kent. LC 78-6224. (Illus.). 40p. (ps-3). 1978. 5.95 (ISBN 0-8193-0964-8); PLB 5.95 (ISBN 0-8193-0965-6). Parents.

Socks for Supper. Jack Kent. (Illus.). 48p. (ps-2). 1988. pap. 2.95 (ISBN 0-517-57013-0). Crown.

Socks on a Rooster. Richard McCaughan. 1967. 8.95 (ISBN 0-87511-081-9). Claitors.

Socrates. facs. ed. R. Nicol Cross. LC 70-130546. (Select Bibliographies Reprint Ser). 1914. 20.00 (ISBN 0-8369-5519-6). Ayer Co Pubs.

Socrates. J. T. Forbes. 1913. Repr. 39.00 (ISBN 0-8274-3447-2). R West.

Socrates. William K. Guthrie. 1971. pap. 14.95 (ISBN 0-521-09667-7). Cambridge U Pr.

Socrates. Gerasimos X. Santas. (Arguments of the Philosophers Ser.). 1979. 26.95x (ISBN 0-7100-8999-6). Routledge Chapman & Hall.

Socrates. Gerasimos X. Santas. 1982. pap. 10.95 (ISBN 0-7100-9327-6). Routledge Chapman & Hall.

Socrates. A. E. Taylor. LC 73-1436. (Illus.). 192p. 1975. Repr. of 1951 ed. lib. bdg. 22.50x (ISBN 0-8371-6793-0, TASO). Greenwood.

Socrates. Alfred E. Taylor. LC 78-59046. (Illus.). 1986. Repr. of 1951 ed. 19.75 (ISBN 0-88355-718-5). Hyperion Conn.

Socrates & Aristophanes. Leo Strauss. (Midway Reprint Ser.). 1980. pap. text ed. 18.95X (ISBN 0-226-77691-3). U of Chicago Pr.

Socrates & Athens. M. Parker. 88p. 1986. Repr. 11.00 (ISBN 0-86292-185-6, Pub. by Bristol Classical UK). Focus Info Gr.

Socrates & Christ. R. M. Wenley. 1977. 59.95 (ISBN 0-8490-2621-0). Gordon Pr.

Socrates & Legal Obligation. R. E. Allen. 176p. 1981. pap. 8.95x (ISBN 0-8166-0965-9). U of Minn Pr.

Socrates & the Analysand. Nina Fardon. 1985. 10.00x (ISBN 0-317-62164-5, Guild of Pastoral Psych). State Mutual Bk.

Socrates & the Political Community: An Ancient Debate. Mary P. Nichols. LC 86-14421. (SUNY Series in Political Theory: Contemporary Issues). 237p. 1987. 49.50 (ISBN 0-88706-395-0); pap. 16.95 (ISBN 0-88706-396-9). State U NY Pr.

Socrates & the Sophistic Enlightenment: A Commentary on Plato's Protagoras. Patrick Coby. LC 86-47856. 216p. 1987. 27.50 (ISBN 0-8387-5109-1). Bucknell U Pr.

Socrates & the State. Richard Kraut. LC 83-17113. (Illus.). 338p. 1984. 47.50x (ISBN 0-691-07666-9); pap. 10.50 (ISBN 0-691-02241-0). Princeton U Pr.

Socrates & the Three Little Pigs. Tuyosi Mori. LC 85-21564. (Illus.). 44p. (gr. 2 up). 1986. 13.95 (ISBN 0-399-21310-4, G&D). Putnam Pub Group.

Socrates, Buddha, Confucius & Jesus: Taken from Vol. 1 of the Great Philosophers. Karl Jaspers. Tr. by Ralph Manheim. 1966. pap. 3.95 (ISBN 0-15-683580-0, Harv). HarBraceJ.

Soft Words, Hard Words: A Common-Sense Guide to Creative Documentation. Lucia McKay. pap. 14.95 (ISBN 0-912677-13-9). Ashton-Tate Pub.

Soft Workouts. Time-Life Books Editors. (Fitness, Health & Nutrition Ser.). 144p. 1988. 17.27 (ISBN 0-8094-6195-1); lib. bdg. 21.27 (ISBN 0-8094-6196-X). Time-Life.

Soft X-Ray Band Spectra & the Electronic Structures of Metals & Materials. Ed. by Derek J. Fabian. 1969. 99.00 (ISBN 0-12-247450-3). Acad Pr.

Soft X-Ray Optics & Technology. Ed. by Koch & Schmahl. 555p. 1986. 86.00 (ISBN 0-89252-768-4, 733). SPIE.

Softball. Les Palmer & Dewayne J. Johnson. (Illus.). 54p. 1980. pap. text ed. 3.95x (ISBN 0-89641-044-7). American Pr.

Softball. (Scorebooks Ser.). 3.00 (ISBN 0-88314-168-X). AAHPERD.

Softball: A Complete Guide for Coaches & Players. (Illus.). 112p. (Orig.). 1984. pap. 7.95. Athletic Inst.

Softball Concepts for Coaches & Teachers. Billie J. Jones & Mary J. Murray. 224p. 1978. pap. text ed. write for info. (ISBN 0-697-07145-6). Wm C Brown.

Softball, Fast & Slow Pitch. (Illus.). 7.95 (ISBN 0-317-56008-5, AI-617). Athletic Inst.

Softball for Girls. Margaret J. Dobson & Becky L. Sisley. LC 79-24256. 232p. 1980. Repr. of 1971 ed. lib. bdg. 14.00 (ISBN 0-89874-103-3). Krieger.

Softball for Girls & Women. Gladys C. Meyer. (Illus.). 256p. 1982. 15.95 (ISBN 0-684-17458-8, ScribT). Scribner.

Softball for Girls & Women. Gladys C. Meyer. (Illus.). 320p. 1984. pap. 9.95 (ISBN 0-684-18140-1, ScribT). Scribner.

Softball Handbook. Susan Craig & Ken Johnson. LC 84-12253. (Illus.). 160p. (Orig.). 1985. pap. 11.95 (ISBN 0-88011-260-3, PCRA0260). Leisure Pr.

Softball Is for Me. Rosemary G. Washington. LC 81-15562. (Sports for Me Bks.). (Illus.). 48p. (gr. 2-5). 1982. PLB 7.95 (ISBN 0-8225-1130-4). Lerner Pubns.

Softball Rules in Pictures. G. Jacobs McCrory. (Illus.). (gr. 4 up). 1974. pap. 4.95 (ISBN 0-448-11554-9, G&D). Putnam Pub Group.

Softball Rules in Pictures. rev. ed. G. Jacobs McCrory. (Illus.). 80p. 1987. pap. 6.95 (ISBN 0-399-51356-6, Perigee). Putnam Pub Group.

Softball: Slow & Fast Pitch. 4th ed. Marian E. Kneer & Charles L. McCord. 128p. 1987. pap. text ed. write for info. (ISBN 0-697-07242-8). Wm C Brown.

Softcops. Caryl Churchill. 28p. 1984. pap. 4.95 (ISBN 0-413-54910-0, NO. 4106). Heinemann Ed.

Softcover Software: Twenty-Eight Microcomputer Programs for IE's & Managers. Ed. by Gary E. Whitehouse. 1985. 34.95 (ISBN 0-89806-069-9). Inst Indus Eng.

Softener. Melvin Bolton. 1986. 14.95 (ISBN 0-531-15015-1). Watts.

Softening without Liberalization in the Soviet Union: The Case of Juri Kukk. Rein Taagepera. (Illus.). 254p. 1984. lib. bdg. 29.25 (ISBN 0-8191-3800-2); pap. text ed. 14.25 (ISBN 0-8191-3801-0). U Pr of Amer.

Softindex, 1982: Periodical Guide for Computerists Annual. 19.95 (ISBN 0-686-40865-9). Applegate Comp Ent.

Softly in Silver Sandals. Flavia Weedn. (Illus.). 96p. 1986. 9.95 (ISBN 0-913289-11-6). Roserich Ltd.

Software. Network Staff. 1983. 95.00x (ISBN 0-907634-12-5, Pub. by Network Events Ltd). State Mutual Bk.

Software. Ed. by Network Staff. 1982. 69.00x (ISBN 0-904999-41-6, Pub. by Network Events Ltd). State Mutual Bk.

Software. Ed. by Network Staff. 1985. 95.00x (ISBN 0-904999-92-0, Pub. by Network Events Ltd). State Mutual Bk.

Software. Rudy Rucker. 176p. (Orig.). 1982. pap. 2.25 (ISBN 0-441-77408-3). Ace Bks.

Software. Rudy Rucker. 170p. 1987. pap. 2.95 (ISBN 0-380-70177-4). Avon.

Software. Time Life Books Editors. (Understanding Computers Ser.). 128p. 1985. 19.93; lib. bdg. 23.93. Time-Life.

Software Age: A Management Perspective of Cullinet Software. Boar. 1988. price not set (ISBN 0-471-82381-3). Wiley.

Software: An Emerging Industry. OECD Staff. (Information Computer Communications Policy Ser.: No. 9). 203p. (Orig.). 1985. pap. 24.00x (ISBN 92-64-12755-0). OECD.

Software & Advanced Automatic Test Techniques. 1982. 95.00x (ISBN 0-904999-74-2, Pub. by Network Events Ltd). State Mutual Bk.

Software & Bookstores, 1984-85: The Market Develops. Martha Kinney. 85p. 1985. looseleaf binder 295.00x (ISBN 0-88709-001-X). Comm Trends Inc.

Software & Future Developments. Ed. by Network Staff. 1982. 95.00x (ISBN 0-904999-38-6, Pub. by Network Events Ltd). State Mutual Bk.

Software & Hardware Applications of Microcomputers - MIMI '86: Proceedings, ISMM Symposium, Beverly Hills, U. S. A., February 5-7, 1986. Ed. by M. H. Hamza & G. K. Lee. 254p. 1986. 70.00 (ISBN 0-88986-085-8, 097). Acta Pr.

Software & Its Development. Joseph M. Fox. (Illus.). 336p. 1982. text ed. 46.00 (ISBN 0-13-822098-0). P-H.

Software Applications for Libraries. Patrick R. Dewey. (Essential Guide to Apple Computers in Libraries Ser.: Vol. 4). 1987. spiral bdg. 29.95 (ISBN 0-88736-077-7). Meckler Corp.

Software Blueprint & Examples. Yaohan Chu. LC 81-48268. (Computer Science Ser.). (Illus.). 544p. 1982. 43.00x (ISBN 0-669-05329-5). Lexington Bks.

Software Buyer's Guide. Tony Webster. (BYTE Book). (Illus.). 1984. pap. text ed. 19.95 (ISBN 0-07-068967-9). McGraw.

Software Buyer's Guidebook: Strategies for Selecting Business Software. Allan F. Froehlich. (Data Processing Ser.). 200p. 1983. 32.95 (ISBN 0-534-02702-4, Lifetime Learn). Van Nos Reinhold.

Software by Design. Rob Collins. (Illus.). 352p. 1984. pap. cancelled (ISBN 0-88056-310-9). Dilithium Pr.

Software Catalog. Vol. 1. 69.00 (ISBN 0-318-03637-1). ISD.

Software Catalog: Business Software Produced from the International Software Database. 2nd ed. 1985. pap. 58.25 (ISBN 0-444-00986-8). Elsevier.

Software Catalog: Health Professions. International Software Database. 175p. 1984. 37.00 (ISBN 0-444-00952-3). Elsevier.

Software Catalog: Microcomputers. 1000p. 1984. 84.00 (ISBN 0-444-00745-8); incl. update 142.50 (ISBN 0-444-00776-8). Elsevier.

Software Catalog: Microcomputers, 3 vols. 3300p. 1987. Complete set of 3 vols. 135.00 (ISBN 0-444-01154-4). Pt. I (ISBN 0-444-01151-X). Pt. II (ISBN 0-444-01152-8). Pt. III (ISBN 0-444-01153-6). Elsevier.

Software Catalog: Microcomputers. 1987. write for info. Elsevier.

Software Catalog: Microcomputers, Complete Catalog. 1984. 75.00 (ISBN 0-444-00914-0). Elsevier.

Software Catalog: Microcomputers, Summer 1987, 3 vols. 3300p. 1987. Set. 150.00 (ISBN 0-444-01262-1). Elsevier.

Software Catalog: Microcomputers, Summer 1984, Update. International Software Database. 1984. 15.00 (ISBN 0-444-00916-7). Elsevier.

Software Catalog: Microcomputers, Winter 1984-85 Update. International Software Database. 1984. 15.00 (ISBN 0-444-00885-3). Elsevier.

Software Catalog: Minicomputers. 948p. Date not set. price not set. Elsevier.

Software Catalog: Minicomputers, Complete 1984 Edition. International Software Database. 900p. 1984. 115.00 (ISBN 0-444-00913-2). Elsevier.

Software Catalog: Minicomputers, Complete 1984 Update. International Software Database. 1985. 15.00 (ISBN 0-444-00915-9). Elsevier.

Software Catalog: Minicomputers, 1986. 1050p. 1986. 150.00 (ISBN 0-444-01069-6). Elsevier.

Software Catalog of Microcomputers. 1983. write for info. Elsevier.

Software Catalog: Science & Engineering International Software Database. International Software Database Staff. 450p. 1984. pap. 29.00 (ISBN 0-444-00925-6). Elsevier.

Software Catalog: Science & Engineering. 3rd ed. International Software Database Staff. 612p. 1986. pap. 49.50 (ISBN 0-444-01058-0). Elsevier.

Software Catalog: Science & Engineering. 4th ed. MENU Staff. 720p. 1987. 69.00 (ISBN 0-444-01228-1). Elsevier.

Software Catalog: Systems Software Produced from Menu The International Software Database. 750p. 1986. pap. 106.75 (ISBN 0-444-01013-0, North Holland). Elsevier.

Software Challenge. Time-Life Books Editors. (Understanding Computers Ser.). 128p. (YA) (gr. 7 up). 1989. 19.93 (ISBN 0-8094-6058-0); lib. bdg. 23.93 (ISBN 0-8094-6059-9). Time-Life.

Software Communication Skills. Robert L. Glass. (Illus.). 464p. 1988. text ed. 32.00 (ISBN 0-13-821679-7). P-H.

Software Components with Ada: Structures, Tools, & Subsystems. Grady Booch. (Illus.). 640p. 1987. 37.95 (ISBN 0-8053-0610-2). Benjamin-Cummings.

Software Configuration Management. Wayne A. Babich. LC 85-22917. 140p. 1986. pap. text ed. 21.50 (ISBN 0-201-10161-0). Addison-Wesley.

Software Configuration Management. William B Bryan et al. (Tutorial Texts Ser.). 452p. 1980. 25.00 (ISBN 0-8186-0309-7, Q309). IEEE Comp Soc.

Software Configuration Management. J. K. Buckle. (Computer Science Ser.). (Illus.). 168p. 1983. 40.00x (ISBN 0-333-30719-4, Pub. by Macmillan England); pap. 25.00x (ISBN 0-333-33228-8, Pub. by Macmillan England). Scholium Intl.

Software Configuration Management: An Investment in Product Integrity. Edward Bersoff et al. 1980. 48.00 (ISBN 0-13-821769-6). P-H.

Software Configuration Management Documentation. Steve J. Ayer & Frank S. Patrinostro. Ed. by Jack C. Nelson. LC 85-51305. (Software Development Documentation Ser.: Vol. 6). (Illus., Orig.). 1986. pap. 49.50 (ISBN 0-9611694-7-8). Tech Comm Assoc.

Software Configuration Management Manual. Evans. 1989. price not set (ISBN 0-471-61010-0). Wiley.

Software Contract Forms: Nineteen Eighty-Seven Collection. American Bar Association, Science & Technology Staff. 1081p. 1987. pap. 75.00. Amer Bar Assn.

Software Cost Estimating & Life-Cycle Control: Getting the Software Numbers. Lawrence H. Putnam. (Tutorial Texts Ser.). 349p. 1980. 25.00 (ISBN 0-8186-0314-3, Q314). IEEE Comp Soc.

Software Defect Removal. R. Dunn. 368p. 1984. text ed. 37.95 (ISBN 0-07-018313-9). McGraw.

Software Design & Development. Philip Gilbert. 608p. 1983. text ed. write for info. (ISBN 0-574-21430-5, 13-4430); instr's. guide avail. (ISBN 0-574-21431-3, 13-4431). SRA.

Software Design for Electronic Switching Systems. S. Takamura et al. (IEE Telecommunications Ser: No. 8). (Illus.). 256p. 1979. casebound 55.00 (ISBN 0-906048-18-4, TE008). Inst Elect Eng.

Software Design for Microcomputers. Carol A. Ogdin. LC 78-5801. (Illus.). 1978. ref. ed. 32.00 (ISBN 0-13-821744-0). P-H.

Software Design: Methods & Techniques. Lawrence J. Peters. LC 80-50609. 248p. (Orig.). 1981. pap. 27.95 (ISBN 0-917072-19-7, Yourdon). P-H.

Software Design Strategies. 2nd ed. Glen D. Bergland & Ronald D. Gordon. (Tutorial Texts Ser.). 479p. 1981. 30.00 (ISBN 0-8186-0389-5, Q389). IEEE Comp Soc.

Software Design Techniques. 4th ed. Peter Freeman & Anthony I. Wasserman. (Tutorial Texts Ser.). 719p. 1983. 36.00 (ISBN 0-8186-0514-6). IEEE Comp Soc.

Software Development Analysis Documentation. Steve J. Ayer & Frank S. Patrinostro. Ed. by Jack C. Nelson. LC 85-51301. (Software Development Documentation Ser.: Vol. 2). (Illus., Orig.). 1986. pap. 49.50 (ISBN 0-9611694-4-3). Tech Comm Assoc.

Software Development & Management for Microprocessor-Based Systems. Tomlinson G. Rauscher & Linda M. Ott. (Illus.). 256p. 1987. text ed. 32.95 (ISBN 0-317-56706-3). P-H.

Software Development Design Documentation. Steve J. Ayer & Frank S. Patrinostro. Ed. by Jack C. Nelson. LC 85-51302. (Software Development Documentation Ser.: Vol. 3). (Illus., Orig.). 1986. pap. 49.50 (ISBN 0-9611694-3-5). Tech Comm Assoc.

Software Development Documentation, 6 vols. Steve J. Ayer & Frank S. Patrinostro. Ed. by Jack C. Nelson. (Software Development Documentation Ser.). (Illus., Orig.). 1986. Set. pap. 260.00 (ISBN 0-9611694-8-6). Tech Comm Assoc.

Software Development Environments. Anthony I. Wasserman. (Tutorial Texts Ser.). 476p. 1981. 30.00 (ISBN 0-8186-0385-2, Q385). IEEE Comp Soc.

Software Development in Pascal. Sartaj Sahni. 1985. text ed. 39.00 (ISBN 0-942450-01-9). Camelot Pub MN.

Software Development: Manual for the Planning, Realization & Installation of D P Systems. Wolfgang End et al. 345p. 1983. 67.95x (ISBN 0-471-26238-2). Wiley.

Software Development Planning & Management Documents. Steve J. Ayer & Frank S. Patrinostro. Ed. by Jack C. Nelson. LC 85-51300. (Software Development Documentation Ser.: Vol. 1). (Illus., Orig.). 1986. pap. 49.50 (ISBN 0-9611694-2-7). Tech Comm Assoc.

Software Development Process. Ed. by P. J. Wallis. (Computer State of the Art Reports, Series 13: No. 2). (Illus.). 290p. 1985. 350.00 (ISBN 0-08-028595-3, Pub. by PIN). Pergamon.

Software Development Project: Planning & Management. Phillip Bruce & Sam Pederson. LC 81-10457. 210p. 1982. 34.95 (ISBN 0-471-06269-3). Wiley.

Software Development Tools. 1986. lib. bdg. 79.95 (ISBN 0-8490-3745-X). Gordon Pr.

Software Development Tools: A Source Book. Ed. by Stephen J. Andriole. (Illus.). 240p. 1986. text ed. 29.95 (ISBN 0-89433-272-4). Petrocelli.

Software Development Within Limits. John Boddie. (Orig.). 1986. pap. text ed. write for info. (ISBN 0-917072-59-6, Yourdon). P-H.

Software Directory for Molecular Biologists. Christopher J. Rawlings. LC 86-14521. 412p. 1986. 90.00x (ISBN 0-943818-37-0, Stockton Pr). Groves Dict Music.

Software Diversity in Computerized Control Systems. Ed. by U. Voges. (Denpendable Computing & Fault-Tolerant Systems Ser.: Vol. 2). (Illus.). 220p. 1988. 49.50 (ISBN 0-387-82014-0). Springer-Verlag.

Software Engineering. Ed. by F. L. Bauer. 1977. pap. 24.00 (ISBN 0-387-08364-2). Springer-Verlag.

Software Engineering. R. Fairley. 1985. text ed. 46.95 (ISBN 0-07-019902-7). McGraw.

Software Engineering. Ed. by Herbert Freeman & P. M. Lewis, II. 1980. 44.50 (ISBN 0-12-267160-0). Acad Pr.

Software Engineering. Randall W. Jensen & C. Tonies. 1979. 56.00 (ISBN 0-13-822130-8). P-H.

Software Engineering. Ed. by R. H. Perrott. 1978. 54.50 (ISBN 0-12-551450-6). Acad Pr.

Software Engineering. Shari L. Pfleeger. (Illus.). 425p. 1987. write for info (ISBN 0-02-395720-4). Macmillan.

Software Engineering. I. Sommerville. 1982. pap. text ed. write for info. (ISBN 0-201-13795-X). Addison-Wesley.

Software Engineering. 2nd ed. Ian Sommerville. 318p. 1985. pap. text ed. 25.75 (ISBN 0-201-14229-5). Addison-Wesley.

Software Engineering. Marc Thorin. (Illus.). 136p. 1985. pap. text ed. 24.95 (ISBN 0-408-01426-1). Butterworth.

Software Engineering: A Practitioner's Approach. Roger S. Pressman. (Software Engineering & Technology Ser.). 1982. pap. text ed. 48.95 (ISBN 0-07-050781-3). McGraw.

Software Engineering: A Practitioner's Approach. 2nd ed. Roger S. Pressman. (Software Engineering & Technology Ser.). 592p. 1987. text ed. 47.95 (ISBN 0-07-050783-X). McGraw.

Software Engineering: A Programming Approach. Doug Bell & Ian Morrey. 288p. 1987. pap. text ed. 30.00 (ISBN 0-13-821836-6). P-H.

Software Engineering: Analysis & Verification. Theodore G. Lewis. (Illus.). 1982. text ed. 43.00 (ISBN 0-8359-7023-X, Reston). P-H.

Software Engineering & Management. Kenneth D. Shere. (Illus.). 448p. 1988. text ed. 44.00 (ISBN 0-13-822081-6). P-H.

Software Engineering & Modula-2. G. Pomberger. Tr. by Steven Williams. (Illus.). 240p. 1986. text ed. 33.00 (ISBN 0-13-821794-7). P-H.

Software Engineering: Decade of Change. (Computing Ser.). 1986. 50.00 (ISBN 0-86341-083-9, CM008). Inst Elect Eng.

Software Engineering Developments, Series 11. Ed. by P. J. Wallis. (Computer State of the Arts Reports: No. 3). 400p. 1983. 61.00x (ISBN 0-08-028574-0). Pergamon.

Software Engineering Economics. Barry W. Boehm. (Illus.). 768p. 1981. text ed. 59.00 (ISBN 0-13-822122-7). P-H.

Software Engineering Education. Ed. by N. E. Gibbs & R. E. Fairley. (Illus.). 445p. 1986. 32.00 (ISBN 0-387-96469-X). Springer-Verlag.

Software Engineering Education: Needs & Objectives. Interface Workshop. Ed. by A. I. Wasserman & P. Freeman. (Illus.). 1976. pap. 22.00 (ISBN 0-387-90216-3). Springer-Verlag.

Software Engineering Environments. R. N. Charette. 320p. 1986. text ed. 39.95 (ISBN 0-07-010645-2). McGraw.

Software Engineering Environments. Brereton O. Pearl. LC 87-31113. (Information Technology Ser.). 270p. 1988. 59.95 (ISBN 0-470-21022-2). Wiley.

Software Engineering Environments. (Computing Ser.). 1986. 54.00 (ISBN 0-86341-077-4, CM007). Inst Elect Eng.

Software Engineering Environments: Proceedings of the Symposium Held in Lahnstein, West Germany, June 1980. Ed. by H. Hunke. 410p. 1981. 79.00 (ISBN 0-444-86133-5, North-Holland). Elsevier.

Software Engineering for Microprocessor Systems. Ed. by D. Depledge et al. (Digital Electronics, Computing & Software Engineering Ser.). 273p. 1984. casebound 43.00 (ISBN 0-86341-016-2, CM002). Inst Elect Eng.

Software Engineering for Telecommunication Switching Systems. (IEE Conference Publications: No. 259). 265p. 1986. pap. 64.00 (ISBN 0-85296-325-4). Inst Elect Eng.

Software Engineering Handbook. General Electric Company Staff. 224p. 1985. text ed. 64.95 (ISBN 0-07-023165-6). McGraw.

Software Engineering in C. P. E. Margolis & P. Darnell. (Books on Professional Computing). (Illus.). 500p. 1988. pap. 29.95 (ISBN 0-387-96574-2). Springer-Verlag.

Software Engineering Methodology. Ray Turner. 1984. text ed. 34.00 (ISBN 0-8359-7022-1, Reston). P-H.

Software Engineering: Methods & Techniques. J. Blank et al. 241p. 1983. 28.50 (ISBN 0-471-88503-7). Wiley.

Software Engineering Metrics & Models. Samuel D. Conte et al. 500p. 1986. text ed. 45.25 (ISBN 0-8053-2162-4). Benjamin-Cummings.

Software Engineering Nineteen Eighty Six. 117p. 1986. pap. 35.00x (ISBN 0-85825-306-2, Pub. by Inst Engineering Australia). Brookfield Pub Co.

Software Engineering: Planning for Change. David A. Lamb. (Illus.). 256p. 1988. text ed. 47.00 (ISBN 0-13-822982-1). P-H.

Software Engineering Principles. Roger S. Pressman. 256p. 1988. pap. write for info. McGraw.

Software Engineering Project Management. Richard Thayer. (Tutorial Text Ser.). 512p. (Orig.). 1988. pap. 55.00 (ISBN 0-8186-0751-3, EZ751); 55.00 (ISBN 0-8186-4751-5, MICROFICHE). IEEE Comp Soc.

Software Engineering: Reliability, Development & Management. Martin L. Shooman. (Computer Science Ser.). 1983. text ed. 48.95 (ISBN 0-07-057021-3). McGraw.

Software Engineering Risk Analysis & Management. Robert N. Charette. (Illus.). 320p. 1989. 49.95 (ISBN 0-07-010661-4). McGraw.

Software Engineering Standards. 1987. 40.50 (ISBN 0-471-63457-3). Wiley.

Soggy Sneakers Guide to Oregon Rivers. 2nd, rev. ed. Willamette Kayak & Canoe Club. (Illus.). 208p. 1986. pap. 9.00 (ISBN 0-9616257-0-8). Willamette Kayak Canoe Club.

Sogliadatai. Vladimir Nabokov. (Sobranie Rasskazov I Povestei: Vol. 2). (Rus.). 1978. 20.00 (ISBN 0-88233-287-2); pap. 8.00 (ISBN 0-88233-288-0). Ardis Pubs.

Sogo Shosha: The Vanguard of Japanese Economy. Kunio Yoshihara. (Illus.). 1982. pap. 17.95x (ISBN 0-19-582500-4). Oxford U Pr.

Sogoshosha: Engines of Export-Based Growth. Y. Tsurumi. 91p. 1984. pap. text ed. 9.95x (ISBN 0-920380-58-1, Pub. by Inst Res Pub Canada). Brookfield Pub Co.

Sohar: Culture & Society in an Omani Town. Fredrik Barth. LC 82-9925. 304p. 1983. 29.50x (ISBN 0-8018-2840-6). Johns Hopkins.

Soherzo (Hommage A'Prokofieff) Piano Duet. Harold Zabrack. (Orig.). 1979. pap. 3.00 (ISBN 0-934286-14-0). Kenyon.

SoHo. Helene Z. Seeman & Alanna Siegfried. LC 78-22225. (Illus.). 1979. pap. 14.95 (ISBN 0-918212-09-X). Neal-Schuman.

Soho: A Picture Portrait by Carl Glassman. Intro. by John Leonard. LC 84-8507. (Illus.). 96p. 1985. pap. 10.95 (ISBN 0-87663-566-4). Universe.

Soho: Drawings on Drawings. Maris Bishofs. (Illus., Orig.). 1988. pap. 9.95 (ISBN 1-55774-040-2, Dist. by Watts). Adama Pubs Inc.

SoHo: The Artist in the City. Charles R. Simpson. LC 80-27083. 352p. 1981. 20.00x (ISBN 0-226-75937-7). U of Chicago Pr.

Sohrab & Rustem, the Epic Theme of a Combat Between Father & Son: A Study of Its Genesis & Use in Literature & Popular Tradition. Murray A. Potter. LC 75-144527. (Grimm Library: No. 14). Repr. of 1902 ed. 11.50 (ISBN 0-404-53557-7). AMS Pr.

S.O.I. Success Oriented Instruction for Special Education. Beatrice Parnes & Nancy Murto. (Illus.). 88p. 1981. pap. text ed. 7.95 (ISBN 0-914634-86-0). DOK Pubs.

Soie Sauvage. Olga Broumas. 1979. pap. 5.00 (ISBN 0-914742-46-9). Copper Canyon.

Soif et la Faim see Theatre.

Soil. H. V. Jacks. 230p. 1954. 5.95 (ISBN 0-8022-0781-2). Philos Lib.

Soil. Angela Webb. (Talk Abouts Ser.). (Illus.). 32p. (gr. k-3). 1977. PLB 10.90 (ISBN 0-531-10371-4). Watts.

Soil Acidity & Liming. 2nd ed. Ed. by Fred Adams. 1984. 25.00 (ISBN 0-89118-080-X). Am Soc Agron.

Soil Adsorption of Odorant Compounds. P. B. Tarman & H. R. Linden. (Research Bulletin Ser.: No. 33). iv, 28p. 1961. 3.50 (ISBN 0-317-56881-7). Inst Gas Tech.

Soil Aeration & Its Role for Plants. Ed. by J. Glinski & W. Stephiewski. 240p. 1985. 110.00 (ISBN 0-8493-5250-9). CRC Pr.

Soil & Civilization: A Modern Concept of the Soil & the Historical Development of Agriculture. Milton Whitney. LC 72-89088. (Rural America Ser.). 1973. Repr. of 1925 ed. 30.00 (ISBN 0-8420-1503-5). Scholarly Res Inc.

Soil & Fertilizer Nitrogen. F. P. Winteringham. (Technical Reports Ser.: No. 244). 107p. 1985. pap. 29.00 (ISBN 92-0-115184-5, IDC244, IAEA). UNIPUB.

Soil & Freshwater Fish Culture: Simple Methods for Aquaculture. A. G. Coche. (Training Ser.: No. 6). 174p. 1986. pap. 26.25 (ISBN 92-5-101355-1, F2801, FAO). UNIPUB.

Soil & Permafrost Surveys in the Arctic. Kenneth A. Linell & C. F. Tedrow. (Monographs on Soil Survey). (Illus.). 1981. 55.00x (ISBN 0-19-857557-2). Oxford U Pr.

Soil & Rock Hydraulics: Fundamentals, Numerical Methods & Techniques of Electrical Analogs. Fernando O. Franciss. 184p. 1985. text ed. 46.00 (ISBN 90-6191-550-3, Pub. by A A Balkema); pap. text ed. 28.00 (Pub. by A A Balkema). Brookfield Pub Co.

Soil & Rock Mechanics, Culverts, & Compaction, 9 reports. (Transportation Research Record Ser.). 105p. 1975. 4.60 (ISBN 0-309-02453-6). Transport Res Bd.

Soil & Survival: Land Stewardship & the Future of American Agriculture. Joe Paddock et al. LC 86-3988. 228p. 1988. pap. 8.95 (ISBN 0-87156-725-3). Sierra.

Soil & Survival: Land Stewardship & the Future of American Agriculture. Nancy Paddock et al. LC 86-3988. 288p. 1986. 19.95 (ISBN 0-87156-766-0). Sierra.

Soil & Vegetation Systems. Stephen A. Trudgill. (Contemporary Problems in Geography Ser.). (Illus.). 1977. pap. 11.95x (ISBN 0-19-874059-X). Oxford U Pr.

Soil & Vegetation Systems. 2nd ed. Stephen T. Trudgill. (Contemporary Problems in Geography Ser.). (Illus.). 224p. 1988. 58.50 (ISBN 0-19-874139-1); pap. 18.95 (ISBN 0-19-874138-3). Oxford U Pr.

Soil & Water Conservation. (Illus.). 96p. (gr. 6-12). 1968. pap. 1.25x (ISBN 0-8395-3291-1, 3291). BSA.

Soil & Water Conservation. Frederick R. Troeh et al. Ed. by Miriam Troeh. (Illus.). 1980. text ed. 45.00 (ISBN 0-13-822155-3). P-H.

Soil & Water Conservation Engineering. 3rd ed. Glenn O. Schwab et al. LC 80-27961. 525p. 1981. write for info. (ISBN 0-471-03078-3); solutions manual avail. (ISBN 0-471-05018-0). Wiley.

Soil & Water Conservation in Semi-Arid Areas. N. W. Hudson. (FAO Soils Bulletin Ser.: No. 57). 172p. (Orig.). 1987. pap. 21.00 (ISBN 92-5-102606-8, F3174, FAO). UNIPUB.

Soil & Water: Physical Principles & Processes. Daniel Hillel. (Physiological Ecology Ser). 1971. 59.00 (ISBN 0-12-348550-9). Acad Pr.

Soil Bank Community. 117p. pap. 4.00. Hardin Pub Co.

Soil Biochemistry, Vol. 1. Ed. by A. Douglas McLaren & George H. Peterson. LC 66-27705. pap. 130.80 (2027117). Bks Demand UMI.

Soil Biochemistry, Vol. 4. Ed. by E. A. Paul & A. D. McLaren. (Books on Soils & the Environment). 296p. 1975. softcover 75.00 (ISBN 0-8247-7023-4). Dekker.

Soil Biochemistry, Vol. 5. Paul & Ladd. (Books on Soils & the Environment). 504p. 1981. 99.75 (ISBN 0-8247-1131-9). Dekker.

Soil Biochemistry, Vol. 3. Ed. by Eldor A. Paul & A. Douglas McLaren. LC 66-27705. (Books on Soils & the Environment). pap. 88.00 (2027833). Bks Demand UMI.

Soil Biology. rev. ed. Wilhelm Kuhnelt. (Illus.). 483p. 1976. 20.00x (ISBN 0-87013-200-8). Mich St U Pr.

Soil Biology & Conservation of the Biosphere. Szegi. 1977. cancelled 30.00 (ISBN 963-05-1273-4, Pub. by Akademiai Kaido Hungary). IPS.

Soil Biology & Conservation of the Biosphere. J. Szegti. 902p. 1984. 366.00x (ISBN 0-569-08816-X, Pub. by Collets (UK)). State Mutual Bk.

Soil Biology: Reviews of Research. (Natural Resources Research Ser.: No. 9). 240p. 1969. 8.50 (ISBN 92-3-100740-8, U619, UNESCO); pap. 15.00 (U619). UNIPUB.

Soil Biotechnology: Microbiological Factors in Crop Productivity. J. M. Lynch. 202p. 1983. pap. text ed. 30.00x (ISBN 0-632-00952-7, Pub. by Blackwell Sci UK). Blackwell Pubns.

Soil-Borne Plant Pathogens. B. Schippers & W. Gams. 1979. 118.50 (ISBN 0-12-624850-8). Acad Pr.

Soil-Cement Construction Handbook. 45p. 1969. pap. 4.25 (ISBN 0-89312-114-2, EB003S). Portland Cement.

Soil-Cement for Water Control: Laboratory Tests. 27p. 1976. pap. 1.75 (ISBN 0-89312-117-7, IS166W). Portland Cement.

Soil-Cement Inspector's Manual. 64p. 1980. pap. 3.50 (ISBN 0-89312-049-9, PA050S). Portland Cement.

Soil-Cement Laboratory Handbook. 61p. 1971. pap. 5.00 (ISBN 0-89312-116-9, EB052S). Portland Cement.

Soil-Cement Slope Protection for Embankments: Field Inspection & Control. 1976. pap. 3.70 (ISBN 0-89312-155-X, IS168W). Portland Cement.

Soil Chemistry. 2nd ed. Hinrich L. Bohn et al. LC 85-3221. 1985. 29.95 (ISBN 0-471-82217-5). Wiley.

Soil Chemistry, Pt. A: Basic Elements. G. H. Bolt & M. G. Bruggenwert. (Developments in Soil Science Ser.: Vol. 5A). 282p. 1976. 47.50 (ISBN 0-444-41435-5). Elsevier.

Soil Chemistry, Pt. B: Physico-Chemical Models. 2nd, rev. ed. Ed. by G. H. Bolt. (Developments in Soil Science Ser.: Vol. 5B). 538p. 1982. 105.25 (ISBN 0-444-42060-6). Elsevier.

Soil Classification. Ed. by Charles Finkl, Jr. LC 81-6214. (Benchmark Papers in Soil Science: Vol. 1). 416p. 1982. 51.95 (ISBN 0-87933-399-5). Van Nos Reinhold.

Soil Classification for Soil Survey: Monographs on Soil Survey. B. E. Butler. (Illus.). 1980. 35.00x (ISBN 0-19-854510-X): Oxford U Pr.

Soil Compaction & Regeneration: Proceedings of the Workshop on "Soil Compaction: Consequences, Structural Regeneration Processes", Avignon, 17-18 September 1985. Ed. by G. Monnier & M. J. Goss. 160p. 1987. text ed. 33.50 (ISBN 90-6191-780-8, Pub. by A A Balkema). Brookfield Pub Co.

Soil Conditions & Plant Growth. 10th ed. E. W. Russell. LC 74-168964. (Illus.). 867p. 1974. text ed. 39.95x (ISBN 0-582-44048-3). Wiley.

Soil Conservation. Sellers G. Archer. LC 56-6002. (Illus.). 1969. Repr. of 1956 ed. 18.95x (ISBN 0-8061-0346-9). U of Okla Pr.

Soil Conservation. Hugh H. Bennett. LC 74-125731. (American Environmental Studies). 1970. Repr. of 1939 ed. 51.00 (ISBN 0-405-02656-0). Ayer Co Pubs.

Soil Conservation. 2nd ed. Norman Hudson. LC 81-66538. (Paperback Ser.). (Illus.). 324p. 1985. pap. 16.95x (ISBN 0-8014-9343-9). Cornell U Pr.

Soil Conservation & Management in the Humid Tropics. International Conference on Soil Conservation & Management in the Humid Tropics (1975: Ibadan, Nigeria) Staff. Ed. by D. J. Greenland & R. Lal. LC 76-56838. (Illus.). 325p. pap. 84.50 (2029795). Bks Demand UMI.

Soil Conservation: Assessing the National Resources Inventory, Vol. 1. National Research Council. 112p. 1986. pap. text ed. 11.50x (ISBN 0-309-03649-6). Natl Acad Pr.

Soil Conservation: Assessing the National Resources Inventory, Vol. 2. National Research Council. 314p. 1986. pap. text ed. 22.50x (ISBN 0-309-03675-5). Natl Acad Pr.

Soil Conservation for Developing Countries. I. Constantinesco. (Soils Bulletins: No. 30). (Illus.). 104p. (Eng., Fr. & Span., 3rd Printing 1981). 1976. pap. 7.50 (ISBN 92-5-100101-4, F1172, FAO). UNIPUB.

Soil Conservation Policies: An Assessment. Pref. by William C. Moldenhauer. LC 80-406. 154p. (Orig.). 1980. pap. 6.50 (ISBN 0-935734-04-X). Soil & Water Conserv.

Soil Conservation Policies, Institutions, & Incentives. Ed. by Harold G. Halcrow et al. LC 82-699. 330p. 1982. text ed. 6.00 (ISBN 0-935734-06-6). Soil & Water Conserv.

Soil Conservation: Problems & Prospects. Ed. by R. P. Morgan. 576p. 1981. 100.00 (ISBN 0-471-27882-3, Pub. by Wiley-Interscience). Wiley.

Soil Conservationist. Jack Rudman. (Career Examination Ser.: C-1032). (Cloth bdg. avail. on request). pap. 16.00 (ISBN 0-8373-1032-6). Natl Learning.

Soil Cutting & Tillage: Developments in Agricultural Engineering, No. 7. E. McKyes. 218p. 1985. 76.50 (ISBN 0-444-42548-9). Elsevier.

Soil Degradation: Proceedings of the Land Use Seminar on Soil Degradation, Wageningen, 13-15th October 1980. Ed. by D. Boels et al. 286p. 1982. text ed. 56.00 (ISBN 90-6191-220-2, Pub. by A A Balkema). Brookfield Pub Co.

Soil Dynamics. Shamsher Prakash. (Illus.). 432p. 1981. text ed. 47.95 (ISBN 0-07-050658-2). McGraw.

Soil Dynamics. T. H. Wu. LC 79-117987. (Illus.). 1977. Repr. text ed. 25.00x (ISBN 0-918498-01-5). T H Wu.

Soil Dynamics & Earthquake Engineering: Proceedings of the Conference, Southampton, 13-15 July 1982, 2 vols. Ed. by A. S. Cakmak et al. 1017p. 1982. Set. text ed. 145.00 (ISBN 90-6191-253-9, Pub. by A A Balkema). Brookfield Pub Co.

Soil Dynamics & Earthquake Engineering. Ed. by C. A. Brebbia et al. 700p. 1985. 98.00 (ISBN 0-387-15497-3). Springer-Verlag.

Soil Dynamics & Liquefaction. A. S. Cakmak. (Developments in Geotechnical Engineering Ser.: Vol. 42). 1987. 122.00 (ISBN 0-444-98958-7). Elsevier.

Soil Dynamics & Liquefaction. Ed. by A. S. Cakmak. LC 87-70778. 386p. 1987. 112.00 (ISBN 0-931215-57-9). Computational Mech MA.

Soil Dynamics, Deep Stabilization, & Geotechnical Construction. 1985. Repr. 75.00x (ISBN 81-85046-38-7, Pub. by Scientific). State Mutual Bk.

Soil Engineering. 4th ed. Merlin G. Spangler & Richard L. Handy. LC 73-8. 819p. 1982. text ed. 56.50 scp (ISBN 0-7002-2533-1, HarpC). Harrow.

Soil Engineering in Theory & Practice. Alam Singh. 742p. 1981. 62.95. Asia Bk Corp.

Soil Enzymes. Ed. by R. G. Burns. 1978. 96.00 (ISBN 0-12-145850-4). Acad Pr.

Soil Erosion. D. Zachar. (Developments in Soil Science Ser.: Vol. 10). 548p. 1982. 126.50 (ISBN 0-444-99725-3). Elsevier.

Soil Erosion & Conservation. Ed. by S. A. El-Swaify et al. LC 85-2507. 793p. text ed. 35.00 (ISBN 0-935734-11-2). Soil & Water Conserv.

Soil Erosion & Conservation. Royston P. Morgan. 1986. pap. 31.95 (ISBN 0-470-20671-3, Co-Pub. with Longman). Wiley.

Soil Erosion & Conservation in the Tropics. Ed. by W. Kussow & S. A. El-Swaify. (ASA Special Publications Ser.). 149p. 1982. pap. 8.50 (ISBN 0-89118-068-0). Am Soc Agron.

Soil Erosion & Its Control. Quincy C. Ayres. LC 72-2832. (Use & Abuse of America's Natural Resources Ser). (Illus.). 382p. 1972. Repr. of 1936 ed. 30.00 (ISBN 0-405-04501-8). Ayer Co Pubs.

Soil Erosion & Its Control. R. Lal. 500p. 1988. 57.00 (ISBN 0-02-947641-0). Macmillan.

Soil Erosion & Its Control. R. P. Morgan. LC 85-11083. (VNR Soil Science Ser.). (Illus.). 336p. 1985. 46.95x (ISBN 0-442-26441-0). Van Nos Reinhold.

Soil Erosion & Reservoir Sedimentation in Lesotho. Q. K. Chakela. 1981. 29.50 (ISBN 0-8419-9737-3, Africana). Holmes & Meier.

Soil Erosion & Sedimentation in Semi-Arid Tanzania: Studies of Environmental Change & Ecological Imbalance. Carl Christiansson. 208p. 1983. pap. 24.50 (ISBN 0-8419-9743-8, Africana). Holmes & Meier.

Soil Erosion by Water: Some Measures for Its Control on Cultivated Lands. (Agricultural Development Papers: No. 81). 284p. (2nd Printing 1978). 1965. pap. 20.75 (ISBN 92-5-100474-9, F1478, FAO). UNIPUB.

Soil Erosion by Wind & Measures for Its Control on Agriculture Lands. (Agricultural Development Papers: No. 71). 88p. 1960. pap. 7.50 (ISBN 92-5-100473-0, F424, FAO). UNIPUB.

Soil Erosion: Crisis in America's Croplands? Sandra S. Batie. LC 83-1942. (Illus.). 136p. (Orig.). 1983. pap. 8.50 (ISBN 0-89164-068-1). Conservation Foun.

Soil Erosion in European Community--Impact of Changing Agriculture: Proceedings of a Seminar on Land Degradation Due to Hydrological Phenomena in Hilly Areas: Impact of Change of Land Use & Management, Cesena, 9-11 October 1985. Ed. by G. Chisci & R. P. Morgan. 248p. 1986. text ed. 36.00 (ISBN 90-6191-657-7, Pub. by A A Balkema). Brookfield Pub Co.

Soil Erosion: Landscape Systems. Ed. by M. J. Kirkby & R. P. Morgan. (A Series in Geomorphology). 312p. 1981. 104.00x (ISBN 0-471-27802-5, Pub. by Wiley-Interscience). Wiley.

Soil Erosion Management. Ed. by E. T. Craswell et al. 132p. 1986. pap. 19.00x (ISBN 0-949511-12-9, Pub. by Inkata Pr Australia). Intl Spec Bk.

Soil Erosion: Quiet Crisis in the World Economy. Lester Brown. LC 84-62062. (Worldwatch Papers). 1984. pap. 4.00 (ISBN 0-916468-60-7). Worldwatch Inst.

Soil Erosion Research Methods. Pref. by R. Lal. 244p. (Orig.). 1988. pap. text ed. 16.00 (ISBN 0-935734-18-X). Soil & Water Conserv.

Soil Exhaustion As a Factor in the Agricultural History of Virginia & Maryland, 1606-1860. Avery O. Craven. 1926. 11.50 (ISBN 0-8446-1136-0). Peter Smith.

Soil Factors in Crop Production in a Semi-Arid Environment. J. S. Russell & E. L. Greacen. 1978. text ed. 32.00x (ISBN 0-7022-1303-9). U of Queensland Pr.

Soil Fertility. Henry D. Foth & Boyd G. Ellis. 317p. 1988. pap. price not set (ISBN 0-471-82507-7). Wiley.

Soil Fertility & Fertilizers. 4th ed. Samuel L. Tisdale & Werner L. Nelson. 736p. 1985. write for info. (ISBN 0-02-420830-2). Macmillan.

Soil Fertility in the Great Konya Basin, Turkey. (Agricultural Research Reports: No. 15). 1970. pap. 11.75 (ISBN 90-220-0328-0, PDC183, PUDOC). UNIPUB.

Soil Fertility Investigations on Farmers' Fields. G. F. Hauser. (Soils Bulletins: No. 11). 84p. (Eng., Fr. & Span., 2nd Printing 1977). 1970. pap. 7.50 (ISBN 92-5-100383-1, F1322, FAO). UNIPUB.

Soil-Forming Process & Soil Evolution. A. A. Rode. 104p. 1961. 29.00x (ISBN 0-7065-0149-7, Pub. by Keter Pub Jerusalem). Coronet Bks.

Soil Fungi & Soil Fertility. 2nd ed. S. D. Garrett. 1981. pap. text ed. 12.75 (ISBN 0-08-025506-X). Pergamon.

Soil Fungi & Soil Fertility: An Introduction to Soil Mycology. 2nd ed. S. D. Garrett. (Illus.). 150p. 1981. text ed. 25.00 (ISBN 0-08-025507-8). Pergamon.

Soil Fungicides, 2 vols. A. P. Sinha et al. 1988. Vol. I, 224p. 115.00 (ISBN 0-8493-4548-0, 4548); Vol. II, 176p. 99.50 (ISBN 0-8493-4549-9, 4549). CRC Pr.

Soil Genesis & Classification. 2nd ed. S. W. Buol et al. 1980. text ed. 24.95x (ISBN 0-8138-1460-X). Iowa St U Pr.

Soil Geography. James Cruikshank. (Illus.). 265p. pap. 12.95 (ISBN 0-7153-5847-2). David & Charles.

Soil Geography & Land Use. Henry D. Foth & John Schafer. LC 79-27731. 484p. 1980. text ed. write for info. (ISBN 0-471-01710-8). Wiley.

Soil: How the Soil Is Made Up. (Better Farming Ser.: No. 4). (Illus.). 37p. 1976. pap. 6.25 (ISBN 92-5-100143-X, F62, FAO). UNIPUB.

Soil: How to Conserve the Soil. (Better Farming Ser.: No. 5). (Illus.). 29p. 1976. pap. 9.50 (ISBN 92-5-100144-8, F63, FAO). UNIPUB.

Soil: How to Improve the Soil. Rev. ed. (Better Farming Ser.: No. 6). (Illus.). 29p. 1976. pap. 6.25 (ISBN 92-5-100145-6, F64, FAO). UNIPUB.

Soil Improvement: A Ten Year Update. Ed. by Joseph Welsh. 340p. 1987. 30.00x (ISBN 0-87262-598-2). Am Soc Civil Eng.

Soil Improvement by Preloading. Aris C. Stamatopoulos. LC 85-5365. (Geotechnical Engineering Ser.). 261p. 1985. 52.50 (ISBN 0-471-81593-4). Wiley.

Soil Improvement: History, Capabilities, & Outlook: Report by the Committee on Placement & Improvement of Soils of the Geotechnical Engineering Division of the American Society of Civil Engineers. American Society of Civil Engineers Staff. LC 78-104862. (Illus.). pap. 46.50 (ISBN 0-317-08310-4, 2019549). Bks Demand UMI.

Soil Improvement Techniques & Their Evolution. W. F Van Impe. 100p. 1988. text ed. 28.00 (ISBN 90-6191-805-7, Pub. by A A Balkema). Brookfield Pub Co.

Soil Information Systems Technology: Proceedings of the Sixth Meeting of the ISSS Working Group on Soil Information Systems, Bolkesjo, Norway, 28 February - 4 March 1983. Ed. by P. A. Burrough & S. W. Bie. (Illus.). 178p. 1985. pap. 21.00 (ISBN 90-220-0854-1, PDC274, Pudoc). UNIPUB.

Soil Landscape Analysis. Francis D. Hole & James B. Campbell. LC 83-24418. (Illus.). 214p. 1985. 37.95x (ISBN 0-86598-140-X, Rowman & Allanheld). Rowman.

Soil Management. 4th ed. D. B. Davies et al. (Illus.). 287p. 1982. 23.95 (ISBN 0-85236-118-1, Pub. by Farming Pr UK). Diamond Farm Bk.

Soil Management: A World View of Conservation & Production. Ray L. Cook & Boyd G. Ellis. LC 87-17612. 413p. 1987. write for info. (ISBN 0-471-88927-X). Wiley.

Soils & Landforms. John Gerrard. (Illus.). 256p. 1981. text ed. 45.00x (ISBN 0-04-551048-2); pap. text ed. 19.95x (ISBN 0-04-551049-0). Unwin Hyman.
Soils & Quarternary Landscape Evolution. Ed. by John Boardman. LC 84-20994. 391p. 1985. 84.95 (ISBN 0-471-90528-3). Wiley.
Soils & Quaternary Geology: A Handbook for Field Scientists. J. A. Catt. (Monographs on Soil & Resources Survey: No. 11). (Illus.). 300p. 1988. 85.00 (ISBN 0-19-854568-1). Oxford U Pr.
Soils & Quaternary Geology of the Southwestern United States. Ed. by David L. Weide. (Special Paper: No. 203). (Illus.). 158p. 1985. pap. 20.00 (ISBN 0-8137-2203-9). Geol Soc.
Soils & Seeds of Sectarianism. James D. Bales. 1977. pap. 4.50 (ISBN 0-89315-264-1). Lambert Bk.
Soils & Soil Management. 2nd ed. Charles D. Sopher & Jack V. Baird. 1981. text ed. 38.00 (ISBN 0-8359-7031-0, Reston); instr's. manual o.p. avail. (ISBN 0-8359-7032-9). P-H.
Soils & Stratigraphy of Dunes along a Segment of Farm Road, 1731 Bailey County, Texas. Lehand H. Gile. 78p. 1981. 3.00 (ISBN 0-318-17667-X, 81-2). Intl Ctr Arid & Semi-Arid.
Soils & the Environment: A Guide to Their Applications. Gerald W. Olson. 191p. 1982. (Pub by Chapman & Hall England); pap. 18.95x (ISBN 0-412-23760-1, 6587). Routledge Chapman & Hall.
Soils Contaminated by Petroleum: Environmental & Public Health Effects. Ed. by Edward J. Calabrese & Paul T. Kostecki. LC 87-25443. 458p. 1988. 75.00 (ISBN 0-471-85106-X). Wiley.
Soils for Management of Organic Wastes & Waste Waters. Ed. by L. F. Elliott & F. J. Stevenson. (Illus.). 1977. 17.50 (ISBN 0-89118-049-4). Am Soc Agron.
Soils Guide for Growing Plants in the Arizona Desert. Thomas J. Craft. Ed. by Iris L. Craft. LC 87-81562. (Series 1). (Orig.). 1987. pap. text ed. 3.85 (ISBN 0-9619002-0-2). Field Sci.
Soils in Construction. 3rd. ed. W. L. Schroeder. LC 83-14569. 330p. 1984. text ed. 31.95 (ISBN 0-471-86581-8); write for info. solution manual (ISBN 0-471-89140-1). Wiley.
Soils in Relation to Crop Growth. Firman E. Bear. LC 65-23863. 304p. 1977. 23.50 (ISBN 0-88275-927-2). Krieger.
Soils in Waste Treatment & Utilization. Ed. by W. H. Fuller & A. W. Warrick. 1985. Vol. I: Land Treatment, 288p. 95.00 (ISBN 0-8493-5151-0); Vol. II: Pollutant Containment, Monitoring & Closure, 240p. 95.00 (ISBN 0-8493-5152-9). CRC Pr.
Soils Manual. (Illus.). 248p. 1986. 10.00 (ISBN 0-318-13398-9, MS-10). Asphalt Inst.
Soils of Canada, 3 vols. (Illus.). 1978. pap. 35.00 set (ISBN 0-660-00502-6, SSC95, SSC). UNIPUB.
Soils of New Jersey. John C. Tedrow. LC 85-18226. 512p. 1986. text ed. 52.50 (ISBN 0-89874-897-6). Krieger.
Soils of the Arid Zones of Chile. Carlos Diaz Vial & C. Wright. (Soils Bulletins: No. 1). 96p. 1966. pap. 7.50 (ISBN 92-5-101978-9, F2470, FAO). UNIPUB.
Soils of the Desert Southwest. Wallace H. Fuller. LC 74-79390. (Illus.). 102p. 1975. pap. 4.95 (ISBN 0-8165-0441-5). U of Ariz Pr.
Soils of the Great Konya Basin, Turkey. (Agricultural Research Reports: 740). (Illus.). 1970. pap. 28.00 (ISBN 90-220-0304-3, PDC90, PUDOC). UNIPUB.
Soils of the Great Plains: Land Use, Crops, & Grasses. Andrew R. Aandahl. LC 81-7435. (Illus.). xvi, 282p. 1982. 28.50x (ISBN 0-8032-1011-6). U of Nebr Pr.
Soils of the Kilifi Area, Kenya & Separate Appendices. Ed. by H. W. Boxem & T. De Meester. (Agriculture Research Reports: No. 929). (Illus.). 249p. (Orig.). 1987. pap. text ed. 50.00 (ISBN 90-220-0919-X, PDC379, Pub. by PUDOC). UNIPUB.
Soils of the Kucuk Menderes Valley, Turkey. (Agricultural Research Reports: 785). (Illus.). 1972. pap. 40.00 (ISBN 90-220-0421-X, PDC91, PUDOC). UNIPUB.
Soils of the Polar Landscapes. John C. Tedrow. 1977. 80.00x (ISBN 0-8135-0808-8). Rutgers U Pr.
Soils of the World: Soil Families & Soil Types, Vol. 1. M. A. Glazovskaya. Tr. by C. M. Rao from Rus. 224p. 1983. text ed. 33.00 (ISBN 90-6191-419-1, Pub. by A A Balkema). Brookfield Pub Co.
Soils of the World: Soil Geography, Vol. 2. M. A. Glazovskaya. Tr. by C. M. Rao from Rus. 409p. 1984. text ed. 33.00 (ISBN 90-6191-420-5, Pub. by A A Balkema). Brookfield Pub Co.
Soils of Wisconsin. Francis D. Hole. LC 75-12209. (Illus.). 240p. 1976. 40.00x (ISBN 0-299-06830-7). U of Wis Pr.
Soils: Science & Management. Edward Plaster. LC 85-4486. 352p. 1985. text ed. 32.95 (ISBN 0-8273-2406-5); instr's. guide 8.00 (ISBN 0-8273-2407-3). Delmar.
Soils, Their Nature, Classes, Distribution, Uses, & Care. rev. 2nd ed. J. W. Batten & J. Sullivan Gibson. LC 76-40302. (Illus.). 314p. 1977. 14.50 (ISBN 0-8173-2876-9). U of Ala Pr.
Soils under Cyclic & Transient Loading: Proceedings from the International Symposium, Swansea, 7-11th January 1980, 2 vols. Ed. by G. N. Pande & O. C. Zienkiewicz. 894p. 1980. Set. text ed. 145.00 (ISBN 90-6191-076-5, Pub. by A A Balkema). Brookfield Pub Co.
Soirees de l'Orchestre. Hector Berlioz. 436p. 1985. Repr. of 1853 ed. text ed. 62.10x (ISBN 0-576-28420-3, Pub. by Gregg Intl Pubs England). Gregg Intl.
Soiuz Nerushimyi 1922-1982. Ed. by Collet's Holdings, Ltd. Staff. (Illus.). 304p. (Rus.). 1982. 39.00x (ISBN 0-317-40900-X, Pub. by Collets (UK)). State Mutual Bk.
Soixante Ans de Ma Vie Litteraire. Andre Maurois. Incl. Role de l'ecrivain dans le monde d'aujourd'hui. 9.95 (ISBN 0-685-36961-7). French & Eur. French & Eur.
Soji Meihin Ten: Exhibition of Song Ceramics. Japan Ceramic Society. 1955. 100.00x (ISBN 0-317-44208-2, Pub. by Han-Shan Tang Ltd). State Mutual Bk.
Soji: Song Ceramics. Koyama Fukio. 1943. 300.00x (ISBN 0-317-44203-1, Pub. by Han-Shan Tang Ltd). State Mutual Bk.
SoJi-Towakai Soji Tenkan Zufu (Song Ceramics-Catalogue of the Pottery Discussion Society Exhibition. Ed. by Towakai. 1929. 300.00x (Pub. by Han-Shan Tang Ltd). State Mutual Bk.
Sojouner from Puerto Rico. Lisa A. Cardona. LC 86-73094. (Illus.). 172p. Date not set. 35.95 (ISBN 0-914199-03-X); pap. 22.95 (ISBN 0-317-67656-3). Carreta Pr.
Sojourn in America: An Encounter & Reverbration. Som P. Ranchan. 130p. 1985. text ed. 20.00x (ISBN 0-7069-2709-5, Pub. by Vikas India). Advent NY.
Sojourn in Mosaic. Robert A. Elfers. (Orig.). 1979. pap. 2.95 (ISBN 0-377-00089-2). Friendship Pr.
Sojourn on This Sable Earth. Faraz Tyebjee. LC 84-90200. 95p. 1985. 7.95 (ISBN 0-533-06249-7). Vantage.
Sojourn with the Grand Sharif of Makkah. Charles Didier. Tr. by Richard Boulind from Fr. (Arabia Past & Present Ser.: Vol. 18). (Illus.). 176p. 1985. 33.00 (ISBN 0-906672-11-2). Oleander Pr.
Sojourner. Ethel Seese. 1981. 7.00 (ISBN 0-8233-0330-6). Golden Quill.
Sojourner Microcosms: New & Selected Poems, 1959-1977. Anselm Hollo. LC 77-21781. (Selected Works Ser.: No. 2). 1977. 29.95 (ISBN 0-912652-39-X); pap. 12.95 (ISBN 0-912652-38-1); signed & numbered ed. 39.95 (ISBN 0-912652-40-3). Blue Wind.
Sojourner Truth. Peter Krass. (Black Americans of Achievement Ser.). (Illus.). 112p. (gr. 5 up). 1988. lib. bdg. 16.95x (ISBN 1-55546-611-7). Chelsea Hse.
Sojourner Truth. Peter Krass. (Black Americans of Achievement Ser.). (Illus.). 112p. (Orig.). (YA) (gr. 7-12). 1989. pap. 9.95 (ISBN 0-7910-0215-2). Chelsea Hse.
Sojourner Truth. Victoria Ortiz. LC 73-22290. (Illus.). 160p. (YA) (gr. 7 up). 1974. PLB 11.89 (ISBN 0-397-31504-X, Lipp Jr Bks). HarpJ.
Sojourner Truth & the Struggle for Freedom. Edward B. Claflin. LC 87-19325. (Henry Steele Commager's Americans Ser.). (Illus.). 144p. (gr. 3-6). 1987. pap. 4.95 (ISBN 0-8120-3919-X). Barron.
Sojourners & Settlers: Chinese Migrants in Hawaii. Clarence E. Glick. LC 80-13799. 421p. 1980. text ed. 20.00x (ISBN 0-8248-0707-3). UH Pr.
Sojourners & Settlers: The Yemeni Immigrant Experience. Ed. by Jonathan Friedlander. (Illus.). 192p. 1988. 34.95 (ISBN 0-87480-292-X). U of Utah Pr.
Sojourners in Search of Freedom: The Settlement of Liberia by Black Americans. James W. Smith. LC 86-28354. 242p. 1987. lib. bdg. 24.75 (ISBN 0-8191-5787-2). U Pr of Amer.
Sojourners of the Caribbean: Ethnogenesis & Ethnohistory of the Garifuna. Nancie L. Gonzalez. LC 87-6044. (Illus.). 272p. 1988. 29.95 (ISBN 0-252-01453-7). U of Ill Pr.
Sojourns. Cristina P. Hidalgo. 172p. (Orig.). 1984. pap. 10.50x (ISBN 971-10-0166-7, Pub. by New Day Philippines). Cellar.
Sojus-Twenty-Two Erforscht Die Erde. Ed. by Collet's Holdings, Ltd. Staff. 284p. 1980. 46.00x (ISBN 0-317-46724-7, Pub. by Collets (UK)). State Mutual Bk.
Sokagakkai & Mass Society. James W. White. LC 75-93498. 1970. 32.50x (ISBN 0-8047-0728-6). Stanford U Pr.
Sokokis: Native Americans of New Hampshire. Dorothea M. Thompson. (New Hampshire Heroes Ser.). (Illus.). 150p. (Orig.). (gr. 4). 1986. pap. 9.95x (ISBN 0-931947-50-2). Thompson Pr.
Sokolov Investigation into the Mysterious Disappearance of the Russian Imperial Family. Nicolai Sokolov. Tr. by John F. O'Conor. 1968. 12.95 (ISBN 0-8315-0110-3). Speller.
Sol de Arturito. J. Guiulnazarian. 33p. (Span.). 1983. 4.95 (ISBN 0-8285-2596-X, Pub. by Raduga Pubs USSR). Imported Pubns.
Sol de mi Infancia. Luis Salem. 80p. (Orig., Span.). 1980. pap. 3.75 (ISBN 0-89922-166-1). Edit Caribe.
Sol Ecce Surgit Igneus: A Commentary on the Morning & Evening Hymns of Prudentius. Marion M. Van Assendelft. vii, 275p. 1976. 38.00x (ISBN 90-6088-060-9, Pub. by Boumas Boekhuis Netherlands). Benjamins North AM.
Sol-Gel Processes for Ceramic Fuels. (Panel Procceedings Ser.). (Illus.). 179p. 1968. pap. 11.25 (ISBN 92-0-141068-9, ISP207, IAEA). UNIPUB.
Sol LeWitt. Ed. by Alicia Legg. LC 77-15309. (Illus.). 1978. 30.00 (ISBN 0-87070-427-3). Museum Mod Art.
Sol Lewitt: Prints Nineteen Seventy to Nineteen Eighty-Six. Jeremy Lewison. (Illus.). 78p. 1987. pap. 9.95 (ISBN 0-946590-51-6, Pub. by Tate Gall Pubns). Salem Hse Pubs.
Sol Plaatje, South African Nationalist, 1876-1932. Brian Willan. LC 84-2471. (Perspectives on Southern African: No. 36). (Illus.). 430p. 1984. text ed. 42.00x (ISBN 0-520-05274-9); pap. 12.95x (ISBN 0-520-05334-6, CAL 664). U of Cal Pr.
Sol White's Official Baseball Guide. Sol White. LC 83-73430. (Library of Baseball Classics: Vol. 2). (Illus.). 128p. Repr. of 1907 ed. 27.00x (ISBN 0-938100-31-9). Camden Hse.
Sol y Sombra. 3rd ed. Paul Pimsleur et al. (Illus.). 203p. (Orig., Span.). 1983. pap. text ed. 12.00 net (ISBN 0-15-582413-9, HC). HarBraceJ.
Solace of Open Spaces. Gretel Ehrlich. 131p. 1985. 14.95 (ISBN 0-670-80678-1). Viking.
Solace of Open Spaces. Gretel Ehrlich. 148p. 1986. pap. 5.95 (ISBN 0-14-008113-5). Penguin.
Solace Paradigm: An Eclectic Search for Psychological Immunity. Paul C. Horton et al. 1988. text ed. 60.00x (ISBN 0-8236-6210-1). Intl Univs Pr.
Solace: The Missing Dimension in Psychiatry. Paul C. Horton. LC 81-2794. 184p. 1981. 15.00x (ISBN 0-226-35386-9). U of Chicago Pr.
Solace: The Missing Dimension in Psychiatry. Paul C. Horton. LC 81-2794. (Illus.). 176p. 1983. pap. 7.95 (ISBN 0-226-35387-7). U of Chicago Pr.
Solamente Por Gracia. Charles H. Spurgeon. 128p. (Span.). 1982. pap. 3.95 (ISBN 0-8254-1678-7). Kregel.
Solanaceae: Biology & Systematics. Ed. by W. G. D'Arcy. LC 85-17057. (Illus.). 608p. 1986. 72.00x (ISBN 0-231-05780-6). Columbia U Pr.
Solano County Street Atlas: 1988 (Plus the Cities of Woodland, Davis & Napa) Thomas Brothers Maps Staff. (Illus.). 1988. pap. 10.95 (ISBN 0-88130-184-1). Thomas Bros Maps.
Solano County Street Guide & Directory, 1988. Thomas Bros. Maps Staff. (Illus.). 74p. (Orig.). 1988. pap. 10.95 (ISBN 0-88130-281-3). Thomas Bros Maps.
Solano-Sonoma Counties Street Guide & Directory, 1988. Thomas Bros. Maps Staff. (Illus.). 230p. (Orig.). 1988. pap. 18.95 (ISBN 0-88130-287-2). Thomas Bros Maps.
Solar Action: 27 Communities Boost Renewable Energy Use. 1981. pap. 9.00x (ISBN 0-686-84642-7). Am Solar Energy.
Solar Activity & Related Interplanetary & Terrestrial Phenomenon: Proceedings of the European Astronomical Meeting, 1st, Athens, 1972, Vol. 1. European Astronomical Meeting Staff. Ed. by J. Xanthakis. (Illus.). 200p. 1973. 58.50 (ISBN 0-387-06314-5). Springer-Verlag.
Solar-Activity Forecasting. Y. I. Vitinskii. 136p. 1965. text ed. 29.00x (ISBN 0-7065-0385-6, Pub. by Keter Pub Jerusalem). Coronet Bks.
Solar Activity Observations & Predictions, PAAS30. Ed. by Patrick S. McIntosh & Murray Dryer. LC 72-5953. (Illus.). 444p. 1972. 49.50 (ISBN 0-262-13086-6). AIAA.
Solar Air Conditioning: A Bibliography. Mary Vance. (Architecture Ser.: A 1534). 18p. 1986. 5.00 (ISBN 0-89028-704-X). Vance Biblios.
Solar Alcohol: The Fuel Revolution. rev. ed. M. Mandeville & D. Youra. (Illus.). 128p. 1980. pap. 8.95 (ISBN 0-940828-00-6). Olympic Pub.
Solar Alternative: An Economic Perspective. Amy L. Walton & Eugene H. Warren, Jr. (Illus.). 208p. 1982. pap. text ed. 25.00 (ISBN 0-13-822262-2). P-H.
Solar & Aeolian Energy: Proceedings of the International Seminar on Solar & Aeoloan Energy held at Sounion, Greece, Sept. 4-15, 1961. International Seminar on Solar & Aeolian Engery. Ed. by A. G. Spanides & Athan D. Hatzikakidis. LC 62-9965. pap. 125.30 (ISBN 0-317-08517-4, 2019390). Bks Demand UMI.
Solar & Interplanetary Dynamics. Ed. by Murray Dryer & Einar Tandberg-Hanssen. (International Astronomical Union Symposia: No. 91). 570p. 1980. lib. bdg. 66.00 (ISBN 90-277-1162-3, Pub. by Reidel Holland); pap. 29.00 (ISBN 90-277-1163-1, Pub. by Reidel Holland). Kluwer Academic.
Solar & Lunar Returns. Donald A. Bradley. (Illus.). 123p. 1975. pap. 3.95 (ISBN 0-87542-045-1). Llewellyn Pubns.
Solar & Lunar Returns. John Filbey. (Illus.). 336p. (Orig.). 1988. pap. 17.95 (ISBN 0-85030-606-X, Pub. by Aquarian Pr England). Sterling.
Solar & Planetary Longitudes for Years Minus 2500 to Plus 2000 by 10-day Intervals. William D. Stahlman et al. LC 63-10534. pap. 149.00 (ISBN 0-317-07758-9, 2051912). Bks Demand UMI.
Solar & Space Physics. National Research Council. (Space Science in the Twenty-First Century Series: Imperatives for the Decades 1995 to 2015). 149p. 1988. pap. text ed. 12.00x (ISBN 0-309-03848-0). Natl Acad Pr.
Solar & Stellar Physics. Ed. by E. H. Schroeter & M. Schuessler. (Lecture Notes in Physics Ser.: Vol. 292). 231p. pap. 24.20 (ISBN 0-387-18678-6). Springer-Verlag.
Solar & Terrestrial Radiation. Kinsell L. Coulsen. 1975. 44.50 (ISBN 0-12-192950-7). Acad Pr.
Solar & Wind Energy: An Economic Evaluation of Current & Future Technologies. Martin T. Katzman. LC 83-23044. 212p. 1984. 39.95x (ISBN 0-86598-152-3, Rowman & Allanheld). Rowman.
Solar Angular Velocity. Ed. by Bernard R. Durney & Sabatino Sofia. 1987. lib. bdg. 84.00 (ISBN 90-277-2523-3, Pub. by Reidel Holland). Kluwer Academic.
Solar Applications see Alternative Energy Sources V: Energy Research.
Solar Applications in Industry & Commerce. John D. Myers. (Illus.). 432p. 1984. text ed. 43.00 (ISBN 0-13-822404-8). P-H.
Solar Architecture: The Direct Gain Approach. Timothy E. Johnson. (Illus.). 1982. text ed. 34.50 (ISBN 0-07-032598-7). McGraw.
Solar Astrophysics. Foukal. 1988. write for info. (ISBN 0-471-83935-3). Wiley.
Solar Batteries: A Revision of A 599. Mary Vance. (Architecture Ser.: A 1536). 96p. 1986. 22.50 (ISBN 0-89028-706-6). Vance Biblios.
Solar Boat Book. rev. ed. Pat R. Rose. LC 83-70115. (Illus.). 266p. 1983. 14.95 (ISBN 0-89815-089-2); pap. 8.95 (ISBN 0-89815-086-8). Ten Speed Pr.
Solar Business Experience. Ed. by Rick Schwolsky & John Hayes. (Solar Realities Forum: Learning from Experience Ser.). 1982. pap. text ed. 30.00x (ISBN 0-89553-047-3). Am Solar Energy.
Solar Cat Book. enl. ed. James Augustyn. 112p. 1982. pap. 4.95 (ISBN 0-89815-071-X). Ten Speed Pr.
Solar Cell Device Physics. Stephen J. Fonash. LC 81-14934. (Energy Science & Engineering Ser.: Resources, Technology, Management). 1981. 65.00 (ISBN 0-12-261980-3). Acad Pr.
Solar Cells. CNRS Staff. (Illus.). 690p. 1971. 212.00 (ISBN 0-677-50450-0). Gordon & Breach.
Solar Cells & Photodiodes. P. A. Iles & S. I. Soclof. write for info. (ISBN 0-07-031714-3). McGraw.
Solar Cells: From Basic to Advanced Systems. Chenming Hu & Richard M. White. (Series in Electrical Engineering: Power & Energy). (Illus.). 288p. 1983. text ed. 49.95 (ISBN 0-07-030745-8). McGraw.
Solar Cells: Operation Principles Technology & Systems Applications. Martin A. Green. (Illus.). 256p. 1982. 48.00 (ISBN 0-13-822270-3). P-H.
Solar Cells: Their Optics & Metrology. M. M. Koltun. Ed. by N. S. Lidorenko. Tr. by S. Chomet from Rus. LC 88-4570. (Illus.). x, 336p. 1988. 65.00 (ISBN 0-89864-034-2). Allerton Pr.
Solar Cells: Understanding & Using Photovoltaics. T. J. Byers. 256p. (Orig.). 1982. pap. 14.95 (ISBN 0-942412-04-4). Micro Text Pubs.
Solar Chromosphere & Corona: Quiet Sun. R. G. Athay. LC 75-33385. (Astrophysics & Space Science Library: No. 53). 540p. 1975. lib. bdg. 79.00 (ISBN 90-277-0244-6). Kluwer Academic.
Solar Church. Jennifer A. Adams. Ed. by Douglas R. Hoffman. LC 82-11281. 288p. (Orig.). 1982. pap. 9.95 (ISBN 0-8298-0482-X). Pilgrim NY.
Solar Collector Performance Manual. Alwin B. Newton & Stanley H. Gilman. (Illus.). 216p. 1983. pap. text ed. 39.00 (ISBN 0-910110-04-2). Am Heat Ref & Air Eng.
Solar Collectors: A Revision of A-560. Mary Vance. (Architecture Ser.: A 1504). 84p. 1985. 12.75 (ISBN 0-89028-654-X). Vance Biblios.
Solar Collectors in Architecture: Integration of Photovoltaic & Thermal Collectors in New & Old Building Structures. Ed. by W. Palz et al. 320p. 1984. 48.00 (ISBN 90-277-1784-2, Pub. by Reidel Holland). Kluwer Academic.
Solar Collectors: Test Methods & Design Guidelines. W. B. Gillett & J. E. Moon. 1985. lib. bdg. 39.50 (ISBN 90-277-2052-5, Pub. by Reidel Netherlands). Kluwer Academic.
Solar Concentrating Mirrors. P. M. Heggen. (Illus.). 100p. 1988. text ed. 80.00x (ISBN 0-937041-14-9); pap. text ed. 50.00x (ISBN 0-937041-15-7). Systems Co.
Solar Control & Shading Devices. Aladar Olgyay & Victor Olgyay. 1976. pap. 15.50x (ISBN 0-691-02358-1); 47.00x (ISBN 0-691-08186-7). Princeton U Pr.
Solar Controls Book: Fundamentals of Domestic Hot Water & Space Heating Solar Controls, 4 vols. Jon Klima. LC 81-52177. (Illus.). 1982. Set. 39.95 (ISBN 0-940894-04-1); tchr's. guide, solutions manual 5.95 (ISBN 0-940894-05-X). Solar Training.
Solar Controls Book: Fundamentals of Domestic Hot Water & Space Heating Solar Controls: Vol. 1: Basic Electrical Principles for the Solar Installer. Jon Klima. LC 81-52177. (Illus.). 1981. 14.95 (ISBN 0-940894-00-9). Solar Training.

Solar Heated Buildings of North America: 120 Outstanding Examples. William A. Shurcliff. LC 78-57234. (Illus.). 296p. 1978. 14.95 (ISBN 0-931790-01-8). Brick Hse Pub.
Solar Heating: A Bibliography. Mary Vance. (Architecture Ser.: A 1535). 68p. 1986. 16.50 (ISBN 0-89028-705-8). Vance Biblios.
Solar Heating & Cooling: Active & Passive Design. 2nd ed. Jan F. Kreider & Frank Kreith. 496p. 1982. text ed. 44.50 (ISBN 0-07-035486-3). McGraw.
Solar Heating & Cooling: Homeowner's Guide. Sunset Editors. LC 78-53673. (Illus.). 96p. 1978. pap. 5.95 (ISBN 0-376-01524-1, Sunset Bks.). Sunset-Lane.
Solar Heating & Cooling Systems: Design for Australian Conditions. E. Baker et al. (Illus.). 332p. 1984. pap. text ed. 37.00 (ISBN 0-08-029852-4). Pergamon.
Solar Heating Catalogue, No. 2. 1979. pap. 5.00 (ISBN 0-660-10075-4, SSC133, SSC). UNIPUB.
Solar Home Planning: A Bibliography & a Guide. Steven D. Atkinson. LC 87-32341. 353p. 1988. 29.50 (ISBN 0-8108-2098-6). Scarecrow.
Solar Homes & Sun Heating. George Daniels. LC 74-15818. (Illus.). 176p. 1976. 14.45i (ISBN 0-06-010937-8, HarpT). Har-Row.
Solar Houses: A Bibliography. Mary Vance. (Architecture Ser.: A 1505). 31p. 1985. 4.50 (ISBN 0-89028-655-8). Vance Biblios.
Solar Houses in Europe: How They Have Worked. Ed. by W Palz & Tc Steemers. LC 80-49715. (Illus.). 320p. 1981. text ed. 55.00 (ISBN 0-08-026743-2); pap. text ed. 26.00 (ISBN 0-08-026744-0). Pergamon.
Solar Houses: Vol. 17, Facts & Pictures About Authors & Illustrators of Books for Young Peoples. Louis Gropp. LC 78-51802. (Illus.). 1978. 17.95 (ISBN 0-394-50089-X); pap. 9.95 (ISBN 0-394-73543-9). Pantheon.
Solar-Hydrogen Energy Economy: Beyond the Age of Fire. Luther W. Skelton. (Illus.). 224p. 1984. 31.95. Van Nos Reinhold.
Solar-Hydrogen Energy System. E. W. Justi. Tr. by W. Schuh & K. Claus. LC 87-7009. (Illus.). 348p. 1987. 49.50x (ISBN 0-306-42150-X, Plenum Pr). Plenum Pub.
Solar-Hydrogen Energy System: An Authoritative Review of Water-Splitting Systems by Solar Beam & Solar Heat; Hydrogen Production, Storage & Utilization. Ed. by T. Ohta. LC 79-40694. (Illus.). 1979. 73.00 (ISBN 0-08-022713-9). Pergamon.
Solar Insolator-Insulator TM. Richard L. Field. (Solar Energy Ser.: No. 580). (Illus., Orig.). 1978. pap. 3.95 (ISBN 0-931912-11-3). Solpub.
Solar Interiors: Energy Efficient Spaces Designed for Comfort. Katherine Panchyk. (Illus.). 176p. 1984. 31.95 (ISBN 0-442-28786-0). Van Nos Reinhold.
Solar Journal: Oecological Sections. Richard Grossinger. (Illus.). 130p. (Orig.). 1973. pap. 4.50 (ISBN 0-87685-011-5). Black Sparrow.
Solar Kill. Charles Ingrid. (Sand Wars Ser.: Bk. 1). 304p. 1987. pap. 3.50 (ISBN 0-88677-209-5). DAW Bks.
Solar Law. Sandy F. Kraemer. (Environmental Publications). 364p. 1980. text ed. 90.00 (ISBN 0-07-035400-6). Shepards-McGraw.
Solar Livestock Housing Handbook. 1st ed. Midwest Plan Service Staff. LC 82-20889. (Illus.). 88p. (Orig.). 1983. pap. 6.00 (ISBN 0-89373-056-4, MWPS-23). Midwest Plan Serv.
Solar Logos. Coulson Turnbull. 66p. 4.95 (ISBN 0-86690-019-5, 2438-03). Am Fed Astrologers.
Solar Magnetic Fields: Proceedings of the I.A.U. Symposium, No. 43, College de France, Paris, Aug. 31-Sept. 4, 1970. International Astronomical Union Staff. Ed. by R. Howard. LC 78-159656. (I.A.U. Symposia). 361p. 1971. lib. bdg. 76.00 (ISBN 90-277-0201-2, Pub. by Reidel Holland). Kluwer Academic.
Solar Magnetohydrodynamics. E. R. Priest. 1984. lib. bdg. 99.00 (ISBN 90-277-1374-X, Pub. by Reidel Holland); pap. text ed. 34.50 (ISBN 90-277-1833-4, Pub. by Reidel Holland). Kluwer Academic.
Solar Materials Science. Ed. by Lawrence E. Murr. LC 80-18959. 1980. 53.00 (ISBN 0-12-511160-6). Acad Pr.
Solar Maximum Analysis: Proceedings of the SMA-SMY Workshop, Irkutsk, U. S. S. R., June, 1985. Ed. by V. E. Stepanov & V. N. Obdidko. 466p. 1986. lib. bdg. 135.00x (ISBN 90-6764-065-4). Coronet Bks.
Solar Menace. Nick Carter. (Nick Carter Ser.). 224p. (Orig.). 1981. pap. 2.50 (ISBN 0-441-77413-X). Ace Bks.
Solar Neutrinos & Neutrino Astronomy. Ed. by M. L. Cherry & K. Lande. LC 84-63143. (Conference Proceedings Ser.: No. 126). 320p. 1985. lib. bdg. 44.25 (ISBN 0-88318-325-0). Am Inst Physics.
Solar' Nineteen Eighty-Seven: Passive Solar Conference Proceedings, July 11-16, 1987. Ed. by Dennis A. Andrejko & John Hayes. (12th). (Illus.). 574p. 100.00 (ISBN 0-89553-203-4). Am Solar Energy.
Solar' Ninteen Eighty-Seven: Proceedings of the 1987 Annual Meeting, Portland Oregon, July 11-16, 1987. Ed. by John Hayes & Dennis A. Andrejko. (Illus.). 518p. 100.00 (ISBN 0-89553-160-7). Am Solar Energy.
Solar Optical Materials: Applications & Performance of Coatings & Materials in Buildings & Solar Energy Systems - Proceedings of the Conference Held in Oxford, UK, 12-13 April 1988. Ed. by M. G. Hutchins. (Illus.). 180p. 1988. pap. 45.00 (ISBN 0-08-036613-9). Pergamon.
Solar Output & Its Variation. Ed. by O. R. White et al. LC 76-15773. (Illus.). 1977. 25.00x (ISBN 0-87081-071-5). Colo Assoc.
Solar Phenomena in Stars & Stellar Systems. Ed. by R. Bonnet & A. Dupree. 1981. 69.50 (ISBN 90-277-1275-1, Pub. by Reidel Holland). Kluwer Academic.
Solar Plasma, Geomagnetism & Aurora. F. Chapman. (Documents on Modern Physics Ser.). (Illus.). 150p. 1964. 60.00 (ISBN 0-677-00130-4). Gordon & Breach.
Solar Plexus. Theron Dumont. pap. 2.00 (ISBN 0-911662-40-5). Yoga.
Solar Pons Omnibus, 2 Vols. August Derleth. LC 76-17995. (Illus.). 1982. 39.95 set (ISBN 0-87054-006-8, Mycroft & Moran). Arkham.
Solar Potpourri-All Our Shorter Works in One. Richard L. Field. (Solar Energy Ser.: No. 599). (Illus., Orig.). 1977. pap. 9.95 (ISBN 0-931912-03-2). Solpub.
Solar Power. Ed Catherall. LC 81-86269. (Fun with Science Ser.). (Illus.). 12.68 (ISBN 0-382-06627-8). Silver.
Solar Power. Robin McKee. LC 85-70599. (Energy Today Ser.). (Illus.). 31p. (gr. 4-8). 1985. PLB 11.90 (ISBN 0-531-17006-3, Gloucester Pr). Watts.
Solar Power Plants in Almeria: 10 Years of International Cooperation. Gunnar Wettermark. (Illus.). 187p. (Orig.). 1986. pap. text ed. 26.50x (ISBN 91-22-00811-X, Pub. by Almqvist & Wiksell). Coronet Bks.
Solar Products Specifications Guide: A Technical Specifications Guide That Continuously Monitors the Developments of Solar Products. 8th ed. (Illus.). 1983. binder-1 year of update service. 125.00 (ISBN 0-686-65545-1). SolarVision.
Solar Projects for Under Five Hundred Dollars. Mary Twitchell. Ed. by Roger Griffith. LC 83-48971. (Illus.). 306p. (Orig.). 1985. pap. 11.95 (ISBN 0-88266-363-1, Garden Way Pub). Storey Comm Inc.
Solar Prominences. Tandberg-Hanssen. LC 73-88593. (Geophysics & Astrophysics Monographs: Vol. 12). 1974. lib. bdg. 29.00 (ISBN 90-277-0399-X, Pub. by Reidel Holland); pap. text ed. 18.50 (ISBN 90-277-0400-7, Pub. by Reidel Holland). Kluwer Academic.
Solar Radiation Availability on Surfaces in the U. S. as Affected by Season, Orientation, Latitude, Altitude, & Cloudiness. Clarence F. Becker. Ed. by Stuart Bruchey. LC 78-22659. (Energy in the American Economy Ser.). (Illus.). 1979. lib. bdg. 14.00x (ISBN 0-405-11963-1). Ayer Co Pubs.
Solar Radiation-Collection-Storage see Alternative Energy Sources V: Energy Research.
Solar Radiation Data. Ed. by W. Palz. 1982. 24.50 (ISBN 90-277-1387-1, Pub. by Reidel Holland). Kluwer Academic.
Solar Radiation Data from Satellite Images. Ed. by W. Gruter et al. 1986. lib. bdg. 29.95 (ISBN 90-277-2204-8, Pub. by Reidel Holland). Kluwer-Academic.
Solar Radiophysics. Ed. by Donald J. McLean. N. R. Labrun. (Illus.). 550p. 1985. 70.00 (ISBN 0-521-25409-4). Cambridge U Pr.
Solar Remodeling. Ed. by Sunset Editors. LC 82-81372. (Illus.). 96p. (Orig.). 1982. pap. 6.95 (ISBN 0-376-01535-7, Sunset Bks). Sunset-Lane.
Solar Retrofit: Adding Solar to Your Home. Daniel K. Reif. (Illus.). 200p. 1981. pap. 11.95 (ISBN 0-931790-15-8). Brick Hse Pub.
Solar Retrofit: Adding Solar to Your Home. Daniel K. Reif. 199p. 1981. write for info. (ISBN 0-471-87860-X). Wiley.
Solar Return Book of Prediction. Raymond A. Merriman. (Illus.). 132p. 1977. pap. 5.95 perfect bdg. (ISBN 0-930706-00-5). Seek-It Pubns.
Solar Returns. Connie Cummings. LC 80-70673. 110p. 1981. 8.00 (ISBN 0-86690-006-3, 1048-01). Am Fed Astrologers.
Solar Revolution & the Prophet. Pierre Renard. (Testimonials Ser.). (Illus.). 193p. (Orig.). 1980. pap. 11.95 (ISBN 2-85566-135-8, Pub. by Prosveta France). Prosveta USA.
Solar Rising: Proceedings, 2 vols. International Solar Energy Society, American Section, Annual Meeting, Philadelphia, 1981. Ed. by Barbara H. Glenn & Gregroy E. Franta. LC 77-79643. (Illus.). 1982. Set. pap. text ed. 150.00x (ISBN 0-89553-030-9). Am Solar Energy.
Solar Selective Surfaces. O. P. Agnihotri & B. K. Gupta. LC 80-17392. 238p. (Orig.). 1981. 44.95 (ISBN 0-471-06035-6, JW). Krieger.
Solar SNG: The Estimated Availability of Resources for Large-Scale Production of SNG by Anaerobic Digestion of Specially Grown Plant Material. REDEX. 450p. 1979. softcover 15.00 (ISBN 0-318-12701-6, M80779). Am Gas Assn.
Solar Spectrum: Proceedings. Symposium, University of Utrecht, 1963. Ed. by C. De Jager. (Astrophysics & Space Science Library: No. 1). 417p. 1965. lib. bdg. 39.50 (ISBN 90-277-0119-9, Pub. by Reidel Holland). Kluwer Academic.
Solar Still. W. R. Breslin. 36p. 1979. write for info. (ISBN 0-86619-030-9). Vols Tech Asst.
Solar Subdivision Design & Review Manual. (Illus.). 96p. 1983. Tr'ng. Manual. 15.00 (ISBN 0-318-22698-7). Assn Bay Area.
Solar Swimming Pool-Spa Code Review Manual. California Building Officials, Inc. Staff. (Illus.). 1988. 4.00. Intl Conf Bldg Off.
Solar Swimming Pool-Spa Code Review Manual. 4.00 (ISBN 0-318-00056-3). Intl Conf Bldg Off.
Solar System. Susan Becklake. LC 81-51498. (Exploration & Discovery Ser.). (Illus.). 36p. (gr. 5 up). PLB 14.96 (ISBN 0-382-06614-6). Silver.
Solar System. Susan D. Echaore. (Science in Action Ser.). (Illus.). 48p. (gr. 9 up). 1982. pap. text ed. 2.95 (ISBN 0-915510-80-4). Janus Bks.
Solar System. B. W. Jones & Milton Keynes. (Illus.). 400p. 1984. text ed. 55.00 (ISBN 0-08-026496-4); pap. text ed. 26.00 (ISBN 0-08-026495-6). Pergamon.
Solar System. David Lambert. (Planet Earth Ser.). 48p. (gr. 5 up). 1984. lib. bdg. 11.40 (ISBN 0-531-03803-3, A Bookwright Press Bk). Watts.
Solar System. Roman Smoluchowski. LC 83-11661. (Scientific American Library). (Illus.). 192p. 1983. 32.95 (ISBN 0-7167-1492-2). W H Freeman.
Solar System. Kathryn Whyman. (Science Today Ser.). (Illus.). 32p. (gr. 1-6). 1987. lib. bdg. 10.90 (ISBN 0-531-17059-4, Gloucester). Watts.
Solar System. John Wood. 1979. pap. write for info. (ISBN 0-13-822015-8). P-H.
Solar System & Back. Isaac Asimov. 256p. 1972. pap. 1.50 (ISBN 0-380-01444-0, 36012, Discus). Avon.
Solar System Astronomy. George Payne. 1980. text ed. 8.50 wire coil bdg. (ISBN 0-88252-103-9). Paladin Hse.
Solar System: Earth As a Planet, Vol. 2. Gerard P. Kuiper. LC 54-7183. pap. 160.00 (2026779). Bks Demand UMI.
Solar System: From the Renaissance to the Nineteenth Century, Pt. A. Ed. by Curtis Wilson. (General History of Astronomy Ser.: No. 2A). 300p. Date not set. price not set (ISBN 0-521-24254-1). Cambridge U Pr.
Solar System Log. Andrew Wilson. 128p. 1987. pap. 14.95 (ISBN 0-7106-0444-0). Janes Info Group.
Solar System Magnetic Fields. Ed. by E. R. Priest. 1985. lib. bdg. 43.00 (ISBN 90-277-2137-8, Pub. by Reidel Holland). Kluwer Academic.
Solar System: Observations & Interpretations. Margaret G. Kivelson. LC 85-12446. (Illus.). 448p. 1986. text ed. 48.00 (ISBN 0-13-821927-3). P-H.
Solar System: Opposing Viewpoints. Peter Roop & Connie Roop. (Great Mysteries Ser.). (Illus.). 112p. (gr. 3-10). 1987. lib. bdg. 12.95 (ISBN 0-89908-053-7). Greenhaven.
Solar System Photometry Handbook. Ed. by Russell M. Genet. LC 83-21382. (Illus.). 224p. 1983. pap. text ed. 17.95x (ISBN 0-943396-03-4). Willmann-Bell.
Solar Systems. K. Frazier. LC 84-16117. (Planet Earth Ser.). 1985. lib. bdg. 19.94 (ISBN 0-8094-4530-1, Pub. by Time-Life). Silver.
Solar Systems. K. Frazier. (Planet Earth Ser.). (Illus.). 176p. (YA) (gr. 7 up). 1985. 18.60 (ISBN 0-8094-4529-8); lib. bdg. 22.60. Time-Life.
Solar Technology. Donald Hudson & Michael H. Markel. 1984. text ed. 32.00 (ISBN 0-8359-7040-X, Reston). P-H.
Solar-Terrestial Physics: Principles & Theoretical Foundations. Ed. by R. L. Carovillano & J. M. Forbes. 1983. lib. bdg. 115.00 (ISBN 90-277-1632-3, Pub. by Reidel Holland). Kluwer Academic.
Solar-Terrestial Influences on Weather & Climate. Ed. by Billy M. McCormac & Thomas A. Seliga. 1979. lib. bdg. 24.00 (ISBN 90-277-0978-5, Pub. by Reidel Holland). Kluwer Academic.
Solar Terrestrial Physics. J. W. King & W. S. Newman. 1967. 86.00 (ISBN 0-12-407850-8). Acad Pr.
Solar-Terrestrial Physics: Proceedings, 4 vols. International Symposium on Solar-Terrestial Physics, Leningrad, 1970. Ed. by E. R. Dyer. LC 78-170337. (Astrophysics & Space Science Library). 914p. 1972. lib. bdg. 113.00 (ISBN 90-277-0209-8, Pub. by Reidel Holland); in 4 Pts., Pt.1: The Sun, Pt 2: The Interplanetary Medium, Pt. 3: The Magnetosphere, Pt. 4: The Upper Atmosphere avail. Kluwer Academic.
Solar Thermal Central Receiver Systems, 2 pts. Ed. by M. Becker. 900p. 1987. pap. 89.60 (ISBN 0-387-17052-9). Springer-Verlag.
Solar Thermal Energy in Europe. D. Turrent & N. Baker. 1983. lib. bdg. 39.50 (ISBN 90-2771-592-0, Pub. by Reidel Holland). Kluwer Academic.
Solar Thermal Energy Systems: Analysis & Design. John R. Howell et al. 416p. 1982. text ed. 48.95x (ISBN 0-07-030603-6). McGraw.
Solar Thermal Engineering: Space Heating & Hot Water Systems. Peter J. Lunde. LC 79-15389. 612p. 1980. write for info. (ISBN 0-471-03085-6); solution manual avail. (ISBN 0-471-89177-0). Wiley.
Solar Thermal Power Plants: Achievements & Lessons Learned Exemplified by the SSPS Project in Almeria-Spain. F. G. Casal. (Illus.). 160p. 1987. 61.70 (ISBN 0-387-17458-3). Springer-Verlag.
Solar Trek in Haiku. Doris T. Paul. 1987. 5.95 (ISBN 0-533-06708-1). Vantage.
Solar Variability, Weather & Climate. National Research Council Staff. 106p. 1982. pap. text ed. 11.95x (ISBN 0-309-03284-9). Natl Acad Pr.
Solar Voltaic Cells. Wilbur D. Johnston, Jr. (Energy, Power & Environment Ser.: Vol. 7). (Illus.). 224p. 1980. 59.75 (ISBN 0-8247-6992-9). Dekker.
Solar vs. Nuclear: The Solar Nuclear Alternative. Secretariat for Futures Studies, Stockholm. 1980. text ed. 63.00 (ISBN 0-08-024758-X); pap. text ed. 24.00 (ISBN 0-08-024759-8). Pergamon.
Solar Water Heater. 48p. 1988. 7.25 (ISBN 0-86619-025-2). Vols Tech Asst.
Solar Water Heater Handbook: A Guide to Residential Solar Water Heaters. Ed. by Richard Montgomery & Jonathon L. Livingston. LC 85-17801. 335p. 1986. pap. 37.95 (ISBN 0-471-86278-9). Wiley.
Solar Water Heating Systems. H. P. Garg. 1986. lib. bdg. 67.00 (ISBN 90-277-2136-X, Pub. by Reidel Holland). Kluwer Academic.
Solar Water Pumping: A Handbook. Jeff Kenna & Bill Gillet. (Illus.). 123p. (Orig.). 1985. pap. 23.00x (ISBN 0-946688-90-7, Pub. by Intermediate Tech England). Intermediate Tech.
Solar Wind & the Earth. Ed. by S. I. Akasofu & Y. Kamide. 1987. lib. bdg. 99.00 (ISBN 90-277-2471-7, Pub. by Reidel Holland). Kluwer Academic.
Solar Wind: Magnetosphere Coupling ASSL. Ed. by Y. Kamide & J. A. Slavin. (ASSL Ser.: Vol. 126). 1986. lib. bdg. 154.00 (ISBN 90-277-2303-6, Pub. by Reidel Holland). Kluwer Academic.
Solar World Forum, 4 vols. D. O. Hall & J. Morton. 1982. 665.00 (ISBN 0-08-026730-0). Pergamon.
Solar World: Proceedings of the Annual Meeting of the International Solar Energy Society, 3 vols. Ed. by Charles Beach & Edward Fordyce. 1977. Set. pap. text ed. 115.00x (ISBN 0-89553-004-X). Am Solar Energy.
Solaris. Stanislaw Lem. 1987. pap. 4.95 (ISBN 0-15-683750-1, Harv). HarBraceJ.
Solaris Farm: A Story of the Twentieth Century. Milan C. Edson. LC 78-154440. (Utopian Literature Ser). (Illus.). 1971. Repr. of 1900 ed. 31.00 (ISBN 0-405-03523-3). Ayer Co Pubs.
Solarize Your Hot Tub: Be Your Own Solar System & Plumbing Consultant. Sharon R. Hines. (Hot Tub & Spa Workbook Ser.: No. 4). (Illus.). 44p. (Orig.). 1982. pap. 7.50 (ISBN 0-941904-10-5). Hot Water Pubs.
Solarize Your Spa: Be Your Own Solar System & Plumbing Consultant. Sharon R. Hines. (Hot Tub & Spa Workbook Ser.: No. 5). (Illus.). 44p. (Orig.). 1982. pap. 7.50 (ISBN 0-941904-11-3). Hot Water Pubs.
Solarman: The Beginning. David Oliphant & Alison Bellack. (Pendulum Illustrated Originals Ser.). (Illus.). (gr. 4-12). 1979. pap. text ed. 2.45 (ISBN 0-88301-425-4); wkbk. 1.25 (ISBN 0-88301-435-1). Pendulum Pr.
Solcoderm. Ed. by M. Weiner & P. Hafner. (Journal: Dermatologica: Vol. 168, Suppl. 1). (Illus.). iv, 68p. 1984. pap. 21.50 (ISBN 3-8055-3890-1). S Karger.
Sold! Nan Lyons & Ivan Lyons. 1982. 12.95 (ISBN 0-698-11148-6, Coward). Putnam Pub Group.
Sold: A Biography by Legendary Auctioneer. Walter S. Britten & J. DeArman. (Illus.). 200p. 1988. 21.00 (ISBN 0-9619686-0-5). Britten Trust.
Sold by Owner: A Professional Guide for Selling Your Home Successfully. 2nd ed. Alfred E. Wilson. (Illus.). 52p. (Orig.). 1969. pap. text ed. 3.00 (ISBN 0-685-24996-4). Stoney Brook.
Sold by Owner! Secrets of Selling Your House Without a Broker's Fee. Maurice Dubois. (Illus.). 224p. 1988. pap. 12.95 (ISBN 0-8306-9316-5, 30016). TAB Bks.
Sold for a Farthing. Clare Kipps. (Illus.). 1984. 14.50 (ISBN 0-8446-6161-9). Peter Smith.
Sold for Slaughter. (Executioner Ser.: No. 60). 192p. 1983. pap. 2.25 (ISBN 0-373-61060-2, Pub. by Worldwide). Harlequin Bks.
Sold on Sunday School. O. D. Robertson. (Orig.). 1984. pap. text ed. 3.95 (ISBN 0-87148-808-6). Pathway Pr.
Sold: The Rise & Fall of the House of Sotheby. Nicholas Faith. 320p. 1986. 17.95 (ISBN 0-02-536970-9). Macmillan.
Sold to the Lady in the Green Hat. rev. ed. Emma Bailey. 228p. 1969. 8.95 (ISBN 0-914960-01-6). Academy Bks.
Soldeir's Pay: Carbon Typescript. William Faulkner. Ed. by Blotner. (William Faulkner Manuscripts Ser.). 100.00 (ISBN 0-8240-6803-3). Garland Pub.
Soldering Handbook for Printed Circuits & Surface Mounting. H. Manko. 1986. 52.95 (ISBN 0-442-26423-2). Van Nos Reinhold.
Soldering Manual, SM. 2nd ed. American Welding Society Staff. 160p. 1978. 24.00 (ISBN 0-87171-151-6, MJP-P). Am Welding.
Soldering Processes in Printed Circuit. Lambert. (Manufacturing Engineering & Material Processing Ser.). 368p. 1987. 69.75 (ISBN 0-8247-7681-X). Dekker.
Solders & Soldering. 2nd ed. Howard H. Manko. LC 79-9714. (Illus.). 1979. text ed. 48.00 (ISBN 0-07-039897-6). McGraw.
Solders Exercise, 3 bks. Gervase Markham. LC 74-80197. (English Experience Ser.: No. 677). 1974. Repr. of 1639 ed. 45.00 (ISBN 90-221-0677-2). Walter J Johnson.

Sole Proprietorship Service Business Practice Set: Garden Real Estate. Horace R. Brock & Charles E. Palmer. (College Accounting Instructional System Ser.). (Illus.). 232p. 1981. pap. text ed. 15.15 (ISBN 0-07-008104-2). McGraw.

Sole Solution. I. Zelig Josephson. Ed. by Melvin H. Naiman. 1979. 6.00 (ISBN 0-682-49438-0). Exposition-Phoenix.

Sole Spokesman: Jinnah, the Muslim League & the Demand for Pakistan. Ayesha Jalal. (South Asian Studies: No. 31). (Illus.). 336p. 1985. 54.50 (ISBN 0-521-24462-5). Cambridge U Pr.

Sole Survivor. George H. Gay. 15.00 (ISBN 0-938300-08-3). Midway Pubs.

Sole Survivor. Ruthanne L. McCunn. LC 85-71877. (Illus.). 240p. 1985. 14.95 (ISBN 0-932538-61-4); pap. 6.95 (ISBN 0-932538-62-2). Design Ent SF.

Sole Survivor. Warren Murphy & Richard Sapir. (Destroyer Ser.: No. 72). 1988. pap. 3.50 (ISBN 0-451-15359-6, Sig). NAL.

Sole Survivor & the Kynsard Affair. Roy Vickers. 192p. 1982. pap. 3.95 (ISBN 0-486-24433-4). Dover.

Soledad Absoluta: Diario Poetico. Josemilio Gonzales. (UPREX, Poesia: No. 3). pap. 1.85 (ISBN 0-8477-0003-8). U of PR Pr.

Soledad, or Solitudes. rev. ed. R. G. Vliet. LC 85-40826. (Texas Tradition Ser.: No. 6). 270p. 1986. 19.50 (ISBN 0-87565-063-5). Tex Christian.

Soledad or Solitudes. R. G. Vliet. 272p. 1987. pap. 6.95 (ISBN 0-14-008747-8). Penguin.

Soleil Cou Coupe see Cadastre.

Solemn Appeal, Vol. I. Ellen White. 58p. 1988. pap. 8.00 (ISBN 0-914009-83-4). VHI Library.

Solemn Appeal, Vol. II. Ellen White. 65p. 1988. pap. 8.50 (ISBN 0-914009-84-2). VHI Library.

Solemn Review of the Custom of War: Showing That War Is the Effect of Popular Delusion & Proposing a Remedy. Noah Worcester. LC 73-137561. (Peace Movement in America Ser). 1972. Repr. of 1833 ed. lib. bdg. 11.95x (ISBN 0-89198-093-8). Ozer.

Solemnidades. Hamid Galib. (UPREX Poesia Ser.: No. 68). 3.00 (ISBN 0-8477-0068-2). U of PR pr.

Solent Way. Barry Shurlock. 132p. 1987. 30.00x (ISBN 0-905392-40-X, Countryside Bks). State Mutual Bk.

Solent Yachting Scene: In Bygone Years 1890-1938. David Couling. (Illus.). 128p. (Orig.). 1984. pap. 13.95 (ISBN 0-540-07280-X, Stanford Maritime). Sheridan.

Solera Poems. Mary Burritt. LC 79-11408. 55p. 1979. pap. 3.75 (ISBN 0-934332-11-8). L'Epervier Pr.

Soles Emellis. Ed. by Rafael Catala & Roberto Lugo. LC 83-61864. 160p. (Orig., Span.). 1983. pap. text ed. 6.95 (ISBN 0-910235-02-3). Prisma Bks.

Solfege According to the Kodaly Concept, Vol. I. Erzsebet Hegyi. Tr. by Fred Macnicol from Hungarian. LC 75-21981. (Illus.). 429p. 1975. 35.00 (ISBN 0-913932-09-4). Boosey & Hawkes.

Solfege According to the Kodaly Concept, Vol. 2. Erzsebet Hegyi. Tr. by Kata Ittzes from Hungarian. (Illus.). 563p. 1979. 36.00 (ISBN 963-330-274-9, Pub. by Editio Musica Budapest Hungary). Boosey & Hawkes.

Solfege, Ear Training, Rhythm, Dictation, & Music Theory: A Comprehensive Course. Marta A. Ghezzo. LC 78-16047. 272p. 1980. 21.75 (ISBN 0-8173-6403-X). U of Ala Pr.

Solferino: The Birth of a Nation. Patrick Turnbull. 192p. 1985. 24.95x (ISBN 0-7090-2162-3, Pub. by R Hale Ltd UK). State Mutual Bk.

Soli. Ray DiPalma. LC 73-91970. 65p. 1974. 5.95 (ISBN 0-87886-026-6); pap. 2.95 (ISBN 0-87886-027-4). Greenfld Rev Pr.

Solicit, Remake & Resell: The Jeans Recycling Fundraising Project. Recycling Consortium. 1985. pap. text ed. 1.95 (ISBN 0-318-03755-6, Pub. by Recycling Consort). Prosperity & Profits.

Solicit, Remake & Resell: The Panty Hose Recycling Fundraising Project. Recycling Consortium. 1985. pap. text ed. 1.95 (ISBN 0-318-03754-8, Pub. by Recycling Consort). Prosperity & Profits.

Solicitor's Duty in Law & Conduct. P. M. Bird. (Practitioner's Library). 224p. 1988. pap. 25.51 (ISBN 0-08-033073-8, Pub. by Waterlow). Pergamon.

Solid Acids & Bases: Their Catalytic Properties. Kozo Tanabe. 1971. 55.50 (ISBN 0-12-683250-1). Acad Pr.

Solid Analytic Geometry. Abraham A. Albert. pap. 43.50 (ISBN 0-317-09471-8, 2016983). Bks Demand UMI.

Solid & Liquid Lubricants for Extreme Environments: Papers Presented at Symposium Lubricants for Extreme Environments. 79p. 1984. 40.00 (ISBN 0-318-17679-3, SP-15); members 25.00 (ISBN 0-318-17680-7). Soc Tribologists.

Solid & Liquid Wastes: Management, Methods & Socioeconomic Considerations. Ed. by Shyamal K. Majumdar & E. Willard Miller. (Illus.). xxii, 412p. 1984. 35.00 (ISBN 0-9606670-3-2). Penn Science.

Solid Clues: Quantum Physics, Molecular Biology & the Future of Science. Gerald Feinberg. 304p. 1985. 17.95 (ISBN 0-671-45608-3). S&S.

Solid Clues: Quantum Physics, Molecular Biology, & the Future of Science. Gerald Feinberg. 1986. pap. 8.95 (ISBN 0-671-62252-8, Touchstone Bks). S&S.

Solid Earth Geomagnetism. Tsuneji Rikitake & Yoshimori Honkura. 1986. lib. bdg. 74.00 (ISBN 90-277-2120-3, Pub. by Reidel Holland). Kluwer Academic.

Solid Electrolytes. Ed. by S. Geller. LC 77-21873. (Topics in Applied Physics: Vol. 21). (Illus.). 1977. 49.00 (ISBN 0-387-08338-3). Springer-Verlag.

Solid Electrolytes & Their Applications. Ed. by E. C. Subbarao. LC 80-14879. (Illus.). 316p. 1980. 52.50x (ISBN 0-306-40389-7, Plenum Pr). Plenum Pub.

Solid Electrolytes: General Principles, Characterization, Materials, Applications. Ed. by Paul Hagenmuller & W. Van Gool. (Materials Science & Technology Ser.). 1978. 106.50 (ISBN 0-12-313360-2). Acad Pr.

Solid for Mulhooly: A Political Satire. Rufus E. Shapley. LC 76-112572. (Rise of Urban America). (Illus.). 1970. Repr. of 1889 ed. 21.00 (ISBN 0-405-02475-4). Ayer Co Pubs.

Solid for Mulhooly..."I'm Fur 'im" A Sketch of Municipal Politics. Rufus Shavley. LC 76-96894. 179p. Repr. of 1881 ed. lib. bdg. 18.00 (ISBN 0-8398-1855-6). Irvington.

Solid for Mulhooly...I'm Fur 'im: A Sketch of Municipal Politics. Rufus Shavley. 179p. 1986. pap. text ed. 6.95x (ISBN 0-8290-2028-4). Irvington.

Solid Fuel Mineral Deposits: Proceedings of the 27th International Geological Congress, Vol. 14. International Geological Congress Staff. 288p. 1984. lib. bdg. 82.50x (ISBN 90-6764-023-9). Coronet Bks.

Solid-Gas Interface, Vols. 1 & 2. Ed. by E. A. Flood. 1967. Vol. 1. 125.00 (ISBN 0-8247-1200-5); Vol. 2. 125.00 (ISBN 0-8247-1201-3). Dekker.

Solid-Gas Interface: Proceedings of the 2nd International Conference on Surface Activity. International Congress of Surface Activity (2nd: 1957) pap. 89.00 (ISBN 0-317-09040-2, 2051336). Bks Demand UMI.

Solid Geometry. Qazi Zameeruddin & V. K. Khanna. 1985. pap. 15.95x (ISBN 0-7069-2816-4, Pub. by Vikas India). Advent NY.

Solid Gold. (Ultimate Ser.). 320p. 1984. plastic comb 17.95 (ISBN 0-88188-332-8, 00361408); pap. 14.95 (ISBN 0-88188-331-X, 00361409). H Leonard Pub Corp.

Solid Gold Communication Tips & Techniques: From Successful Teachers, Principals & Other Administrators. 1987. 45.00 (ISBN 0-317-59093-6, 418-13986). Natl Sch PR.

Solid Gold Kid. Norma F. Mazer & Harry Mazer. 224p. (YA) (gr. 7 up). 1978. pap. 1.50 (ISBN 0-440-98080-1, LE). Dell.

Solid Gold Mailbox: How to Create Winning Mail Order Campaigns by One Who's Done It All. Walter H. Weintz. 1987. 22.95 (ISBN 0-471-85026-8). Wiley.

Solid Gold Stethoscope. Edgar Berman. 1978. pap. 2.25 (ISBN 0-345-28623-5). Ballantine.

Solid Gold: The Popular Record Industry. R. Serge Denisoff. LC 74-20194. (Cultural & Society Ser). (Illus.). 504p. 1981. pap. 14.95 (ISBN 0-87855-586-2). Transaction Bks.

Solid Ground: Facts of the Faith for Young Christians. David Schroeder. Frwd. by Paul Bubna. 255p. 1982. pap. 4.95 (ISBN 0-87509-323-X); Leader's guide 2.95 (ISBN 0-87509-326-4). Chr Pubns.

Solid Hydrogen: Theory of the Properties of Solid H2, HD, & D2. Jan Van Kranendonk. LC 82-18054. 322p. 1983. 52.50x (ISBN 0-306-41080-X, Plenum Pr). Plenum Pub.

Solid-Liquid Dispersions. Ed. by Th. F. Tadros. 344p. 1987. 49.00 (ISBN 0-12-682178-X). Acad Pr.

Solid-Liquid Equilibrium Data Collection: Binary Systems, Tables, Diagrams & Model Parameters. H. Knapp et al. Intro. by Dieter Behrens & Reiner Eckermann. (Dechema Chemistry Data Ser.: Vol. 8, Pt. 1). (Illus.). 555p. 1987. text ed. 203.00 (ISBN 3-921567-75-0, Pub. by Dechema Germany). Scholium Intl.

Solid-Liquid Flow Abstracts, 3 Vols. Ed. by Gilbert F. Round. 1064p. 1969. Set. 395.00 (ISBN 0-677-40120-5); Vol. 1, 448p. 165.00 (ISBN 0-677-40080-2); Vol. 2, 460p. 180.00 (ISBN 0-677-40090-X); Vol. 3, 156p. 85.00 (ISBN 0-677-40100-0). Gordon & Breach.

Solid-Liquid Flow Slurry Pipeline Transportation. Edward J. Wasp et al. LC 78-75080. 240p. 1979. 47.00x (ISBN 0-87201-809-1). Gulf Pub.

Solid-Liquid Interface. D. P. Woodruff. LC 72-91362. (Cambridge Solid State Science Ser.). (Illus.). 150p. 1973. 34.50 (ISBN 0-521-20123-3). Cambridge U Pr.

Solid-Liquid Interface. D. P. Woodruff. LC 72-91362. (Cambridge Solid State Science Ser.). (Illus.). 182p. 1980. pap. 16.95 (ISBN 0-521-29971-3). Cambridge U Pr.

Solid-Liquid Phase Equilibria. J. Nyvlt. 248p. 1977. 97.50 (ISBN 0-444-99850-0). Elsevier.

Solid-Liquid Separation. J. Gregory. LC 83-22731. 363p. 1984. 104.00 (ISBN 0-470-20021-9). Halsted Pr.

Solid-Liquid Separation. 2nd ed. Ladislav Svarovsky. 1981. text ed. 105.00 (ISBN 0-408-70943-X). Butterworth.

Solid Living in a Shattered World. William H. Hinson. 160p. 1985. 8.95 (ISBN 0-687-39048-6). Abingdon.

Solid Lubricants & Self-Lubricating Solids. Francis J. Clauss. 1972. 73.50 (ISBN 0-12-176150-9). Acad Pr.

Solid Mandala. Patrick White. 1966. 12.95 (ISBN 0-670-65632-1). Viking.

Solid Mandala. Patrick White. 320p. 1983. pap. 6.95 (ISBN 0-14-002975-3). Penguin.

Solid Materials. International Editorial Board Staff. (Structure & Bonding Ser.: Vol. 69). (Illus.). 135p. 1988. 69.50 (ISBN 0-387-18790-1). Springer-Verlag.

Solid Mechanics Research for Quantitative Non-Destructive Evaluation. Ed. by J. D. Achenbach & Y. Rajapakse. 1987. lib. bdg. 122.00 (ISBN 90-247-3428-2, Pub. by Martinus Nijhoff Netherlands). Kluwer Academic.

Solid Modeling: A State-of-the Art Report. 2nd., rev ed. Robert H. Johnson. Ed. by Jonathan Linden. (Illus.). 270p. 1986. 3-ring binder 495.00 (ISBN 0-932007-06-6, SMB). Mgmt Roundtable.

Solid Modeling by Computers: From Theory to Applications. Ed. by Mary S. Pickett & John W. Boyse. (General Motors Research Symposia Ser.). 392p. 1985. 55.00x (ISBN 0-306-41937-8, Plenum Pr). Plenum Pub.

Solid Modeling in Computer Graphics: The Technology, Its Applications, & Supply Sources. (Illus.). 85p. 1984. 129.00 (ISBN 0-914849-02-6). TBC Inc.

Solid: Nine Vital Lessons on Settling, Saving & Solidifying the Black Marriage. Walter A. McCray. 72p. (Orig.). 1981. pap. 3.95 (ISBN 0-933176-05-8). Black Light Fellow.

Solid Organoalkali Metal Reagents. Avery A. Morton. 256p. 1964. 92.00 (ISBN 0-677-00560-1). Gordon & Breach.

Solid Particles in the Solar System. Ed. by Ian Halliday & Bruce A. McIntosh. (International Astronomical Union Symposium: No. 90). 432p. 1980. PLB 50.00 (ISBN 90-277-1164-X, Pub. by Reidel Holland); pap. 26.50 (ISBN 90-277-1165-8). Kluwer Academic.

Solid Pharmaceutics: Mechanical Properties & Rate Phenomena. Jens T. Carstensen. LC 79-6805. 1980. 62.50 (ISBN 0-12-161150-7). Acad Pr.

Solid Phase Biochemistry: Analytical & Synthetic Aspects. Ed. by William H. Scouten. LC 82-21886. (Chemical Analysis: Monographs on Analytical Chemistry & its Application). 779p. 1983. 95.00x (ISBN 0-471-08585-5, Pub. by Wiley-Interscience). Wiley.

Solid Philosophy Asserted Against the Fancies of the Idealists: Or, the Method to Science Farther Illustrated; with Reflexions on Mr. Locke's Essay Concerning Human Understanding. John Sergeant. LC 83-48577. (Philosophy of John Locke Ser.). 496p. 1984. lib. bdg. 60.00 (ISBN 0-8240-5612-4). Garland Pub.

Solid Polyurethane Elastomers. P. Wright & A. P. Cumming. 338p. 1969. 95.00 (ISBN 0-677-61690-2). Gordon & Breach.

Solid Sense of Mathematics, 3 vols. Mary Laycock & Margaret Smart. (Illus.). 64p. (Orig., 64). (gr. 4-9). 1981. pap. text ed. 6.95 ea. (ISBN 0-918932-74-2). Activity Resources.

Solid State AC Motor Controls. Campbell. (Mechanical Engineering Ser.). 240p. 1987. 59.75 (ISBN 0-8247-7728-X). Dekker.

Solid State: An Introduction to the Physics of Crystals. 2nd ed. H. M. Rosenberg. (Physics Ser.). (Illus.). 1978. pap. 12.95x (ISBN 0-19-851845-5); pap. 5.95x solutions manual (ISBN 0-19-851852-8). Oxford U Pr.

Solid State: An Introduction to the Physics of Crystals for Students of Physics, Materials Science, & Engineering. 3rd ed. H. M. Rosenberg. (Physics Ser.: No. 9). (Illus.). 326p. 1988. text ed. 35.00 (ISBN 0-19-851871-4); pap. text ed. 18.95 (ISBN 0-19-851870-6). Oxford U Pr.

Solid-State & Chemical Radiation Dosimetry in Medicine & Biology. (Proceedings Ser.). (Illus.). 471p. 1967. pap. 27.25 (ISBN 92-0-010167-4, ISP138, IAEA). UNIPUB.

Solid-State & Molecular Theory: A Scientific Biography. John C. Slater. LC 74-22367. 357p. 1975. text ed. 36.95x (ISBN 0-471-79681-6, Pub. by Wiley-Interscience). Wiley.

Solid State & Quantum Physics. Ed. by A. D. Boardman. LC 80-40125. (Physics Programs Ser.: Vol. 3). (Illus.). 142p. pap. 37.00 (2030456). Bks Demand UMI.

Solid State & Semiconductor Physics. John P. McKelvey. LC 81-19390. 526p. 1982. Repr. of 1966 ed. 31.50 (ISBN 0-89874-396-6). Krieger.

Solid State Astrophysics. Ed. by Nalin C. Wickramasinghe & D. J. Morgan. LC 75-34355. (Astrophysics & Space Science Library: No. 55). 1975. lib. bdg. 53.00 (ISBN 90-277-0653-0, Pub. by Reidel Holland). Kluwer Academic.

Solid State Batteries. Ed. by C. A. Sequeira & A. Hooper. 1985. lib. bdg. 80.00 (ISBN 90-247-3236-0, Pub. by Martinus Nijhoff Netherlands). Kluwer Academic.

Solid State Cameras. Market Intelligence Research Company Staff. Ed. by W. Hammersley. 150p. (Orig.). 1986. pap. text ed. 995.00x (ISBN 0-916483-12-6, A079). Market Res Co.

Solid State Chemical Sensors. Ed. by Jiri Janata & Robert J. Huber. 1985. 54.00 (ISBN 0-12-380210-5). Acad Pr.

Solid State Chemistry. M. Ardon et al. (Structure & Bonding Ser.: Vol. 65). 160p. 1987. 70.00 (ISBN 0-387-17581-4). Springer-Verlag.

Solid State Chemistry. 1980. 7.20 (ISBN 0-910362-14-9). Chem Educ.

Solid-State Chemistry, Vol. 11. Ed. by M. E. Vol'pin. (Soviet Scientific Reviews Ser.: Section B, Chemistry). 266p. 1988. write for info. (ISBN 3-7186-0410-8). Harwood Academic.

Solid State Chemistry see Physical Chemistry: An Advanced Treatise in Eleven Volumes.

Solid State Chemistry: A Contemporary Overview. Ed. by Smith Holt et al. LC 80-17185. (Advances in Chemistry Ser.: No. 186). 1980. 59.95 (ISBN 0-8412-0472-1). Am Chemical.

Solid State Chemistry & Its Applications. West. 734p. 1988. pap. 39.95 (ISBN 0-471-90874-6). Wiley.

Solid State Chemistry & Its Applications. Anthony West. LC 83-21607. 734p. 1984. 103.00 (ISBN 0-471-90377-9). Wiley.

Solid State Chemistry of Drugs. Stephen Byrn. LC 82-13950. 349p. 1982. 71.00 (ISBN 0-12-148620-6). Acad Pr.

Solid State Chemistry of Energy Conversion & Storage: A Symposium Sponsored by the Division of Inorganic Chemistry at the 71st Meeting of the American Chemical Society. Ed. by John B. Goodenough & M. Stanley Whittingham. LC 77-20011. (Advances in Chemisty Ser.: No. 163). pap. 95.50 (ISBN 0-317-08982-X, 2015231). Bks Demand UMI.

Solid-State Chemistry: Techniques. A. K. Cheetham & Peter Day. (Illus.). 412p. 1987. 70.00 (ISBN 0-19-855165-7). Oxford U Pr.

Solid-State Chemistry: Techniques. Ed. by A. K. Cheetham & Peter Day. (Illus.). 412p. 1988. pap. 35.00 (ISBN 0-19-855286-6). Oxford U Pr.

Solid State Chemistry, 1982. R. Metselaar et al. 852p. 1983. 263.25 (ISBN 0-444-42147-5). Elsevier.

Solid State Circuits. G. J. Pridham. 196p. 1973. 37.00 (ISBN 0-08-016932-5). Pergamon.

Solid State Communications Equipment: Design of Communications Equipment Using Semiconductors. Texas Instruments Inc. (Texas Instruments Electronics Ser.). 1966. text ed. 56.50 (ISBN 0-07-063739-3). McGraw.

Solid State Design for the Radio Amateur. 12.00 (ISBN 0-87259-201-4). Am Radio.

Solid State Devices: A Quantum Physics Approach. D. de De Cogan. 1987. 24.00 (ISBN 0-387-91290-8, Co-pub. by Macmillan Educn Ltd UK). Springer-Verlag.

Solid State Devices & Integrated Circuits. William Cooper & Henry Wiesbecker. 1982. text ed. 40.00 (ISBN 0-8359-7045-0, Reston); solutions manual avail. (ISBN 0-8359-7046-9). P-H.

Solid State Devices 1971: Munich. (Institute of Physics Conference Ser.: No. 12). 1971. cancelled 39.00 (ISBN 0-85498-102-0, Pub. by Inst Physics England). IPS.

Solid State Devices 1972: Lancaster. (Institute of Physics Conference Ser.: No. 15). 1972. cancelled 39.00 (ISBN 0-85498-105-5, Pub. by Inst Physics England). IPS.

Solid State Devices 1973: Munich. (Institute of Physics Conference Ser.: No. 19). 1973. cancelled 39.00 (ISBN 0-85498-109-8, Pub. by Inst Physics England). IPS.

Solid State Devices 1974: Nottingham. (Institute of Physics Conference Ser.: No. 25). 1975. cancelled 39.00 (ISBN 0-85498-115-2, Pub. by Inst Physics England). IPS.

Solid State Devices 1976: Munich. (Institute of Physics Conference Ser.: No. 32). 1977. cancelled 34.00 (ISBN 0-85498-122-5, Pub. by Inst Physics England). IPS.

Solid State Devices 1977: Brighton. (Institute of Physics Conference Ser.: No. 40). 1978. cancelled 39.00 (ISBN 0-85498-131-4, Pub. by Inst Physics England). IPS.

Solid State Devices 1979. Ed. by H. Weiss. (Conference Ser.: No.53). 153p. 1980. cancelled 34.00 (ISBN 0-85498-144-6, Pub. by Inst Physics England). IPS.

Solid State Devices 1980. (Institute of Physics Conference: No. 57). cancelled 55.00 (ISBN 0-85498-148-9, Pub. by Inst Physics England). IPS.

Solid State Devices, 1980: Tenth European Solid State Device Research Conference (ESSDERC) & Fifth Symposium on Solid State Device Technology, York, September 1980. Ed. by J. E. Caroll. (Institute of Physics Conference Ser.: No. 57). (Illus.). 234p. 1981. 66.00 (ISBN 0-317-61522-X, Pub. by A Hilger UK). Taylor & Francis.

Solid State Devices 1982: ESSDERC-SSSDT Meeting at Munich, 13-16 September 1982. Ed. by A. Goetzberger & M. Zerbst. (Illus.). 200p. 1983. 50.00 (ISBN 3-87664-072-5). VCH Pubs.

Solid State Devices, 1983. E. H. Rhoderick. (Institute of Physics Conference Ser.: No. 69). 1984. 79.00x (ISBN 0-85498-160-8, Pub. by A Hilger UK). Taylor & Francis.

Solid State Devices, 1985. Ed. by P. Balk & O. G. Folberth. (Studies in Electrical & Electronic Engineering: No. 23). 242p. 1986. 87.00 (ISBN 0-444-42600-0). Elsevier.

Solid State Devices 1986: 16th European Soild State Device Research Conference, University of Cambridge, September 8-11, 1986. Ed. by D. F. Moore. (Institute of Physics Conference Ser.: No. 82). 264p. 1987. 50.00x (ISBN 0-85498-173-X, Pub. by A Hilger UK). Taylor & Francis.

Solid State Diffusion. J. P. Stark. LC 80-11750. 252p. 1983. Repr. of 1976 ed. lib. bdg. 23.00 (ISBN 0-89874-145-9). Krieger.

Solid State Dosimetry. Ed. by S. Amelinckx et al. 744p. 1970. 182.00 (ISBN 0-677-13470-3). Gordon & Breach.

Solid-State Dosimetry. (Bibliographical Ser.: No. 23). 143p. 1967. pap. 10.00 (ISBN 92-0-114067-3, ISP21 23, IAEA). UNIPUB.

Solid State Electrochemistry & Its Applications to Sensors & Electronic Devices. K. S. Goto. (Materials Science Monographs: Vol. 45). 1987. 129.00 (ISBN 0-444-42912-3). Elsevier.

Solid State Electron Materials. Vetelino. 1988. write for info. (ISBN 0-471-89211-4). Wiley.

Solid State Electronic Amplifiers: An Empirical Approach. Donald P. Beach & Richard A. Lyons. 1984. text ed. 40.00 (ISBN 0-8359-6951-7, Reston). P-H.

Solid-State Electronic Circuits for Engineering Technology. Anthony S. Manera. (Illus.). 672p. 1973. text ed. 39.95 (ISBN 0-07-039871-2). McGraw.

Solid State Electronic Devices. Ben G. Streerman. (Illus.). 550p. 1988. text ed. 48.00 (ISBN 0-13-822941-4). P-H.

Solid State Electronic Devices. 2nd ed. B. Streetman. 1980. 50.67 (ISBN 0-13-822171-5). P-H.

Solid State Electronics. L. Murr. (Electrical Engineering & Electronics Ser.: Vol. 4). 1978. 39.75 (ISBN 0-8247-6676-8). Dekker.

Solid State Electronics. 2nd ed. George B. Ruthkowski. 1980. scp 28.44 (ISBN 0-672-97315-4); scp instructors guide 7.33 (ISBN 0-672-97317-0); scp lab manual 10.28 (ISBN 0-672-97316-2). Bobbs.

Solid State Electronics. George Rutkowski. 512p. 1988. write for info.; write for info. lab manual. Additional materials available. Macmillan.

Solid State Electronics Concepts. J. L. Matthews. 1971. text ed. 39.95 (ISBN 0-07-040960-9). McGraw.

Solid State Electronics: Devices & Circuits. John E. Lackey et al. 784p. 1986. text ed. 34.95 (ISBN 0-03-071882-1, HoltC). HR&W.

Solid-State Electronics Theory with Experiments. M. J. Sanfilippo. (Illus.). 336p. 1987. 25.95 (ISBN 0-8306-0926-1, 2926); pap. 16.95 (ISBN 0-8306-2926-2). TAB Bks.

Solid State Fundamentals for Electricians. G. Rockis. (Illus.). 232p. 1985. 20.96 (ISBN 0-8269-1628-7). Am Technical.

Solid State Gas Sensors. Ed. by P. T. Moseley & B. C. Tofield. 240p. 1987. 95.00x (ISBN 0-85274-514-1, Pub. by A Hilger UK). Taylor & Francis.

Solid State High Frequency Power. Irving M. Gottlieb. 1981. text ed. 38.00 (ISBN 0-8359-7048-5, Reston). P-H.

Solid State Imagers & Their Applications. Ed. by Declerck. 199p. 1985. 43.00 (ISBN 0-89252-626-2, 591). SPIE.

Solid State Imaging Arrays. Ed. by K. N. Prettyjohns & E. L. Dereniak. 223p. 1985. 43.00 (ISBN 0-89252-605-X, 570). SPIE.

Solid State Industrial Electronics. Richard Pearman. 1982. text ed. 43.00 (ISBN 0-8359-7041-8, Reston); instr's. manual avail. (ISBN 0-8359-7042-6). P-H.

Solid-State Microwave Amplifier Design. Tri T. Ha. LC 81-21. 326p. 1981. 47.50x (ISBN 0-471-08971-0). Wiley.

Solid-State Microwave Devices. Thomas S. Laverghetta. 200p. 1987. text ed. 66.00 (ISBN 0-89006-216-1). Artech Hse.

Solid State Motor Control. Richard Hunter. LC 73-254. (Orig.). 1984. wkbk. 8.00 (816); audio visual pkg. 349.00 (ISBN 0-8064-0324-1). Bergwall.

Solid State Nuclear Magnetic Resonance of Fossil Fuels. David E. Axelson. 320p. 1985. text ed. 56.00x (ISBN 0-919868-25-8, Pub. by Multisci Pubns Ltd). Brookfield Pub Co.

Solid State Nuclear Track Detection: Principles, Methods & Applications. S. A. Durrani & R. K Bull. (International Series in Natural Philosophy: Vol. 111). (Illus.). 336p. 1987. text ed. 95.00 (ISBN 0-08-020605-0, PBL). Pergamon.

Solid State Nuclear Track Detectors, 4 vols. S. A. Durrani. (Nuclear Tracts Ser.: No. 286). 1982. Set. 320.00 (ISBN 0-08-029149-X). Pergamon.

Solid State Nuclear Track Detectors: Proceedings. International Conference on Solid State Nuclear Track Detectors, 11th, Bristol, UK, Sept. 1981. Ed. by P. H. Fowler & V. M. Clapham. (Illus.). 958p. 1982. 235.00 (ISBN 0-08-026509-X, C120, C140). Pergamon.

Solid State Nuclear Track Detectors: Proceedings. International Conference on Solid State Nuclear Track Detectors, 10th, Lyon, France, July 1979. Ed. by H. Francois et al. LC 79-41577. (Illus.). 1082p. 1980. 175.00 (ISBN 0-08-025029-7). Pergamon.

Solid State Nuclear Track Detectors: Proceedings, 2 vols. International Conference on Solid State Nuclear Track Detectors, 9th, Neuherberg-Munich, 1976. Ed. by F. Granzer et al. LC 77-30630. (Illus.). 1312p. 1978. Set. 345.00 (ISBN 0-08-021659-5). Pergamon.

Solid State Optical Control Devices, Vol. 464. 1984. 43.00 (ISBN 0-89252-499-5). SPIE.

Solid State Photochemistry. Gerhard M. Schmidt. (Monographs in Modern Chemistry: Vol. 8). (Illus.). 280p. 1976. 55.00 (ISBN 3-527-25671-7). VCH Pubs.

Solid State Physics. Neil W. Ashcroft & N. David Mermin. LC 74-9772. 1976. text ed. 58.00 (ISBN 0-03-083993-9, CBS C). SCP.

Solid-State Physics. G. Bauer et al. (Tracts in Modern Physics Ser.: Vol. 74). (Illus.). v, 153p. 1974. 46.10 (ISBN 0-387-06946-1). Springer-Verlag.

Solid State Physics. 2nd ed. J. S. Blakemore. (Illus.). 506p. Date not set. 27.95 (ISBN 0-521-31391-0). Cambridge U Pr.

Solid State Physics. Gerald Burns. 1985. text ed. 49.95 (ISBN 0-12-146070-3). Acad Pr.

Solid State Physics. Ed. by R. V. Coleman. (Methods of Experimental Physics Ser.: Vol. 11). 1974. 99.00 (ISBN 0-12-475911-4). Acad Pr.

Solid State Physics. H. E. Hall. LC 73-10743. (Manchester Physics Ser.). 351p. 1974. pap. 36.00x (ISBN 0-471-34281-5, Pub. by Wiley-Interscience). Wiley.

Solid State Physics. Stokes. 336p. 1986. 41.00 (ISBN 0-205-10508-4). Allyn.

Solid State Physics, Vol. 38. Ed. by Frederick Seitz et al. (Serial Publication). 1984. 72.00 (ISBN 0-12-607738-X). Acad Pr.

Solid State Physics, Vol. 39. Ed. by Henry Ehrenreich & David Turnbull. 496p. 1986. 72.00 (ISBN 0-12-607739-8). Acad Pr.

Solid State Physics, Vol. 40. Ed. by Henry Ehrenpreich & David Turnbull. 347p. 1987. 69.95 (ISBN 0-12-607740-1). Acad Pr.

Solid State Physics see Methods of Experimental Physics.

Solid State Physics: Advances in Research & Applications. Ed. by H. Ehrenreich. Incl. Vol. 30. 1975. 74.50 (ISBN 0-12-607730-4); Vol. 31. 1976. 74.50 (ISBN 0-12-607731-2). Acad Pr.

Solid State Physics: Advances in Research & Applications. Incl. Vol. 1. 1955 (ISBN 0-12-607701-0); Vol. 2. 1956 (ISBN 0-12-607702-9); Vol. 3. 1956 (ISBN 0-12-607703-7); Vol. 4. 1957 (ISBN 0-12-607704-5); Vol. 5. 1957 (ISBN 0-12-607705-3); Vol. 6. 1958 (ISBN 0-12-607706-1); Vol. 7. 1958 (ISBN 0-12-607707-X); Vol. 8. 1959 (ISBN 0-12-607708-8); Vol. 9. 1959 (ISBN 0-12-607709-6); Vol. 10. 1960 (ISBN 0-12-607710-X); Vol. 11. 1960 (ISBN 0-12-607711-8); Vol. 12. 1961 (ISBN 0-12-607712-6); Vol. 13. 1962 (ISBN 0-12-607713-4); Vol. 14. 1963 (ISBN 0-12-607714-2); Vol. 15. 1963 (ISBN 0-12-607715-0); Vol. 16. 1964 (ISBN 0-12-607716-9); Vol. 17. 1965 (ISBN 0-12-607717-7); Vol 18. 1966 (ISBN 0-12-607718-5); Vol. 19. 1967 (ISBN 0-12-607719-3); Vol. 20. 1968 (ISBN 0-12-607720-7); Vol. 21. 1968 (ISBN 0-12-607721-5); Vol. 22. 1969 (ISBN 0-12-607722-3); Vol. 23. 1970 (ISBN 0-12-607723-1); Vol. 24. 1970 (ISBN 0-12-607724-X); Vol. 25. 1970 (ISBN 0-12-607725-8); Vol. 26. 1971 (ISBN 0-12-607726-6); Vol. 27. 1972 (ISBN 0-12-607727-4); Vol. 28. 1973 (ISBN 0-12-607728-2); Vol. 29. 1974 (ISBN 0-12-607729-0). 74.50 ea. Acad Pr.

Solid State Physics: Advances in Research & Applications, Vol. 35. Ed. by Frederick Seitz et al. LC 55-12200. 1980. 88.50 (ISBN 0-12-607735-5). Acad Pr.

Solid State Physics: Advances in Research & Applications, Vol. 36. Ed. by H. Ehrenreich et al. 1981. 88.50 (ISBN 0-12-607736-3). Acad Pr.

Solid State Physics: Advances in Research & Applications, Vol. 37. H. Ehrebreich. (Serial Publication Ser.). 1982. 88.50 (ISBN 0-12-607737-1). Acad Pr.

Solid State Physics: Liquid Crystals, Supplement No. 14. Ed. by H. Ehrenreich & L. Liebert. 1978. 67.00 (ISBN 0-12-607774-6). Acad Pr.

Solid-State Physics Source Book. (Science Reference Ser.). (Illus.). 500p. Date not set. 45.00 (ISBN 0-07-045503-1). McGraw.

Solid State Physics Supplement, No. 15. Robert M. White & Theodore H. Geballe. 1984. pap. 23.00 (ISBN 0-12-607777-0). Acad Pr.

Solid State Physics under Pressure. Ed. by S. Minomura. 1985. lib. bdg. 69.00 (ISBN 90-277-1897-0, Pub. by Reidel Netherlands). Kluwer Academic.

Solid State Physics, Vol. 41: Advances in Research & Applications. Ed. by Henry Ehrenreich. 321p. 1988. 69.00 (ISBN 0-12-607741-X). Acad Pr.

Solid State Plasmas. M. F. Hoyaux. 1970. 15.95x (ISBN 0-85086-011-3, NO.2914, Pub. by Pion England); pap. 9.50x (ISBN 0-85086-012-1, NO.2907). Routledge Chapman & Hall.

Solid-State Projects You Can Build. Rudolf F. Graf & George J. Whalen. 192p. 1986. pap. 10.95 (ISBN 0-672-22500-X). Sams.

Solid State Protonic Conductors for Fuel Cells & Sensors, Vol. 1. Ed. by Johs. Jensen & Michel Kleitz. 339p. (Orig.). 1982. pap. 47.50x (ISBN 87-7492-364-1, Pub. by Odense Universitets Forlag (Odense Denmark)). Coronet Bks.

Solid State Protonic Conductors for Fuel Cells & Sensors, Vol. 2. Ed. by John B. Goodenough et al. 420p. (Orig.). 1983. pap. 52.50x (ISBN 87-7492-417-6, Pub. by Odense Universitets Forlag (Odense Denmark)). Coronet Bks.

Solid State Protonic Conductors for Fuel Cells & Sensors, Vol. 3. Ed. by John B. Goodenough et al. 284p. (Orig.). 1985. pap. 47.50x (ISBN 87-7492-517-2, Pub. by Odense Universitets Forlag (Odense Denmark)). Coronet Bks.

Solid State Pulse Circuits. 2nd ed. David A. Bell. (Illus.). 432p. 1981. 41.00 (ISBN 0-8359-7057-4, Reston). P-H.

Solid State Pulse Circuits. 3rd ed. David A. Bell. (Illus.). 512p. 1988. text ed. 40.00 (ISBN 0-8359-7052-3). P-H.

Solid-State Radar Transmitters. E. D. Ostroff et al. 272p. 1985. text ed. 66.00 (ISBN 0-89006-169-6). Artech Hse.

Solid State Reactions. 2nd ed. Hermann Schmalzried. (Monographs in Modern Chemistry: Vol. 12). (Illus.). 254p. 1981. 66.00 (ISBN 0-89573-031-6). VCH Pubs.

Solid-State Relay Handbook with Applications. Anthony Bishop. 250p. 1986. pap. 19.95 (ISBN 0-672-22475-5, 22475). Sams.

Solid State Science: Past, Present & Predicted. Ed. by D. L. Weaire & C. G. Windsor. 336p. 1987. 77.00x (ISBN 0-85274-584-2, Pub. by A Hilger UK); pap. 33.00x (ISBN 0-85274-586-9). Taylor & Francis.

Solid-State Sensors & Transducers Markets. Market Intelligence Research Co. Staff. Ed. by Wilmoth Hammersley. 555p. (Orig.). 1987. pap. 995.00x. Market Res Co.

Solid-State Sensors & Transducers Markets, Vol. I. Market Intelligence Research Co. Staff. Ed. by Wilmoth Hammersley. 250p. (Orig.). 1987. pap. 995.00 (ISBN 0-317-58023-X). Market Res Co.

Solid-State Sensors & Transducers Markets, Vol. II. Market Intelligence Research Co. Staff. Ed. by Wilmoth Hammersley. 227p. (Orig.). 1987. pap. 995.00 (ISBN 0-317-58025-6). Market Res Co.

Solid-State Sensors & Transducers Markets, Vol. III. Market Intelligence Research Co. Staff. Ed. by Wilmoth Hammersley. 219p. (Orig.). 1987. pap. 995.00x (ISBN 0-317-58026-4). Market Res Co.

Solid State Theory. Cohen. 1988. write for info. (ISBN 0-471-08761-0). Wiley.

Solid State Theory. Walter A. Harrison. 1980. pap. text ed. 9.95 (ISBN 0-486-63948-7). Dover.

Solid State Transformations. N. N. Sirota. Ed. by F. K. Gorskii. Tr. by Geoffrey D. Archard from Rus. LC 66-18733. pap. 44.80 (ISBN 0-317-08917-X, 2020673). Bks Demand UMI.

Solid State Video Cameras. A. Cristol. (EPO Applied Technology Ser.: Vol. 7). 250p. 1986.*70.00 (ISBN 0-08-030579-2, A130, PBL). Pergamon.

Solid Surface Luminescence Analysis. Robert J. Hurtubise. (Modern Monographs in Analytical Chemistry: Vol. 1). 288p. 1981. 65.00 (ISBN 0-8247-1265-X). Dekker.

Solid Tumor in Childhood. Norman Jaffe. 176p. 1983. 69.00 (ISBN 0-8493-5732-2). CRC Pr.

Solid-Vacuum Interface: Proceedings Symposium on Surface Physics, 3rd, June 26-28, 1974. Ed. by G. A. Bootsma & J. W. Geus. 422p. 1975. Repr. 66.00 (ISBN 0-444-10828-9, North-Holland). Elsevier.

Solid Waste Collection Practice. 1975. 28.00x (ISBN 0-917084-00-4). Am Public Works.

Solid Waste Conversion to Energy. Alter & Dunn. (Pollution Engineering & Technology Ser.: Vol. 11). 184p. 1980. 45.00 (ISBN 0-8247-6917-1). Dekker.

Solid Waste Generation Coefficients: Manufacturing Sectors. Gene Steiker. (Discussion Paper Ser.: No. 70). 1973. pap. 6.50 (ISBN 0-686-32236-3). Regional Sci Res Inst.

Solid Waste Handbook: A Practical Guide. Ed. by William D. Robinson. LC 85-12454. 848p. 1986. 85.00 (ISBN 0-471-87711-5). Wiley.

Solid Waste Management. D. Joseph Hagerty et al. LC 73-10281. (Van Nostrand Reinhold Environmental Engineering Ser.). pap. 79.00 (ISBN 0-317-11224-4, 2014903). Bks Demand UMI.

Solid Waste Management: A Selected & Annotated Bibliography, No. 1295. Marilyn Gehr. 1977. 7.00 (ISBN 0-686-19695-3). CPL Biblios.

Solid Waste Management & the Environment: The Mounting Garbage & Trash Crisis. Homer A. Neal & Jerry R. Schubel. (Illus.). 272p. 1987. text ed. 33.00 (ISBN 0-13-822891-4). P-H.

Solid Waste Management: Selected Topics. Ed. by Michael J. Suess. 210p. 1985. pap. 9.00 (ISBN 92-890-1023-1). World Health.

Solid Waste Management Specialist. (Career Examination Ser.: C-3477). Date not set. pap. 16.00 (ISBN 0-8373-3477-2). Natl Learning.

Solid Waste Research & Development Needs for Emerging Coal Technologies. Compiled by American Society of Civil Engineers Staff. 268p. 1979. pap. 21.50x (ISBN 0-87262-199-5). Am Soc Civil Eng.

Solid Waste-Resource Recovery Management. IRE Research Staff. (Swm-1ser). 1978. 175.00 (ISBN 0-930318-06-4). Intl Res Eval.

Solid Wastes Disposal & Control: Report. WHO Expert Committee. Dubendorf, 1971. (Technical Report Ser.: No. 484). (Also avail. in French & Spanish). 1971. pap. 2.00 (ISBN 92-4-120484-2). World Health.

Solid Wastes: Engineering Principles & Management Issues. George Tchobanoglous et al. (Illus.). 1977. text ed. 58.95 (ISBN 0-07-063235-9). McGraw.

Solid Wastes: Factors Influencing Generation Rates. Douglas B. Cargo. LC 78-16823. (Research Papers Ser.: No. 174). (Illus.). 1977. pap. 12.00 (ISBN 0-89065-081-0). U Chicago Comm Geo.

Solid Wastes from Coal Fired Power Plants: Water Pollution Problems: Part of an IAWPRC International Conference on Coal Fired Power Plants & the Aquatic Environment, 16-18 August 1982, Copenhagen, Vol. 15/11. Ed. by S. H. Jenkins & P. Schjodtz Hansen. LC 83-19445. (Illus.). 258p. 1983. pap. 44.00 (ISBN 0-08-031026-5). Pergamon.

Solidaritaet mit den Leidenden im Judentum. Rachel Rosenzweig. (Studia Judaica: Vol. 10). 1978. 46.40x (ISBN 3-11-005939-8). De Gruyter.

Solidarite de la Famille Dan le Droit Criminel en Grece. Gustave Glotz. LC 72-7891. (Greek History Ser.). (Fr.). Repr. of 1904 ed. 43.00 (ISBN 0-405-04787-8). Ayer Co Pubs.

Solidarity. Anna Sproule. Ed. by Ed MacDonald. (Women History Makers Ser.). (Illus.). 48p. (gr. 4 up). 1988. 11.90 (ISBN 0-531-19503-1, Hampstead Pr). Watts.

Solidarity & Dissent: Union Member Attitudes & the Political Process. Peter Keisler. LC 84-82115. 76p. (Orig.). 1984. pap. 5.75 (ISBN 0-942522-03-6). Free Congr Res.

Solidarity & Fragmentation: Working People & Class Consciousness in Detroit, 1875-1900. Richard Oestreicher. LC 85-1030. (Working Class in American History Ser.). (Illus.). 270p. 1985. 24.95 (ISBN 0-252-01225-9). U of Ill Pr.

Solidarity & Kinship: Essays on American Zionism. Ed. by Nathan M. Kaganoff. (Illus.). 1980. 5.00 (ISBN 0-911934-14-6). Am Jewish Hist Soc.

Solidarity & the Soviet Worker. Elizabeth Teague. 400p. 1988. lib. bdg. 65.00 (ISBN 0-7099-4350-4, Pub. by Croom Helm UK). Routledge Chapman & Hall.

Solidarity Forever: An Oral History of the I. W. W. Stewart Bird et al. LC 84-82491. (Illus.). 256p. 1985. 25.00x (ISBN 0-941702-11-1); pap. 9.95 (ISBN 0-941702-12-X). Lake View Pr.

Solidarity Forever: Rose Schneiderman & the Women's Trade Union League. Gary E. Endelman. 32.00 (ISBN 0-405-14079-7). Ayer Co Pubs.

Solidarity in a Slum. Joseph B. Tamney. 228p. 1975. 18.95 (ISBN 0-87073-406-7). Schenkman Bks Inc.

Solidarity in Poland: Impacts East & West. Ed. by Steve W. Reiquam. LC 87-29537. (Illus.). 72p. (Orig.). 1988. lib. bdg. 16.50 (ISBN 0-943875-05-6); pap. text ed. 6.75 (ISBN 0-943875-02-1). Wilson Ctr Pr.

Solidarity or Survival? American Labor & European Immigrants, 1830-1924. A. T. Lane. LC 86-25735. (Contributions in Labour Studies: No. 21). 242p. 1987. lib. bdg. 35.00 (ISBN 0-313-25544-X, LSV/). Greenwood.

Solidarity: Poland's Independent Trade Union. Denis MacShane. LC 81-165158. 172p. (Orig.). 1982. 30.00 (ISBN 0-85124-319-3); pap. 10.95 (ISBN 0-85124-318-5). Dufour.

Solidarity: Poland's Independent Trade Union. Denis MacShane. 172p. 75.00x (Pub. by Bertrand Russell Hse); pap. 20.00x. State Mutual Bk.

Solidarity Source Book. Ed. by Stan Persky & Henry Flam. 262p. 1982. lib. bdg. 15.95 (ISBN 0-919573-04-5); pap. 7.95 (ISBN 0-919573-05-3). Left Bank.

Solidarity: The Analysis of a Social Movement; Poland 1980-1981. Alain Touraine et al. LC 83-1859. (Illus.). 256p. 1983. 23.95 (ISBN 0-521-25407-8); pap. 12.95 (ISBN 0-521-27595-4). Cambridge U Pr.

Solidarity with the People of Nicaragua. James McGinnis. LC 84-27202. (Illus.). 192p. (Orig.). 1985. pap. 7.95 (ISBN 0-88344-448-8). Orbis Bks.

Solidarity with Victims: Toward a Theology of Social Transformation. Matthew L. Lamb. LC 81-22145. 176p. 1982. 12.95 (ISBN 0-8245-0471-2). Crossroad NY.

Solidarnose z Wolnoscia: Solidarity with Liberty. Ed. by Don C. Lavoie. 233p. (Pol.). 1983. pap. 9.95 (ISBN 0-932790-33-X). Cato Inst.

Solide maligne Tumoren im Kindesalter. Ed. by E. Rossi. (Paediatrische Fortbildungskurse fuer die Praxis: Vol. 39). (Illus.). 100p. 1974. 22.00 (ISBN 3-8055-1691-6). S Karger.

Solidification. A. Ohno. (Illus.). 130p. 1987. pap. 39.00 (ISBN 0-387-18233-0). Springer-Verlag.

Solidification & Cast Structure. I. Minkoff. LC 85-9382. 1986. 64.95 (ISBN 0-471-90798-7). Wiley.

Solidification & Casting of Metals. 574p. 1979. text ed. 72.00x (ISBN 0-904357-16-3, Pub. by Inst Metals). Brookfield Pub Co.

Solidification Characteristics of Some Copper Alloys. University of Stockholm. (INCRA Monograph). 129p. 1982. 30.00 (ISBN 0-943642-08-6). Intl Copper.

Solidification Characteristics of Twelve Commercial Copper-Base Alloys. Swedish Institute for Metal Research. 103p. 1973. 15.45 (ISBN 0-317-34546-X, 165). Intl Copper.

Solidification Processing. Merton Flemings. (Materials Sciences Ser.). (Illus.). 1973. text ed. 52.95 (ISBN 0-07-021283-X). McGraw.

Solidification Processing: Proceedings of International Conference, Ranmoor House, Sheffield, 21-24 Sept. 1987. International Conference Staff. 518p. (Orig.). 1988. pap. 50.00 (ISBN 0-901462-36-5, Pub. by Inst Metals). Brookfield Pub Co.

Solidification Technology in the Foundry & Casthouse. 620p. (Orig.). 1983. 110.00x (ISBN 0-904357-36-8, Pub. by the Metals Society). Brookfield Pub Co.

Solids & Liquids Conveying Systems. Ed. by M. V. Bhatia & Paul N. Cheremisinoff. (Process Equipment Ser.: Vol. 4). 254p. 1982. 29.00 (ISBN 0-87762-310-4). Technomic.

Solids Separation & Mixing. Mahesh V. Bhatia & Paul N. Cheremisinoff. LC 79-63114. (Process Equipment Ser.: Vol. 1). 303p. 1979. 29.00 (ISBN 0-87762-272-8). Technomic.

Solids Separation Processes. Institution of Chemical Engineers. 1982. 79.00 (ISBN 0-08-028757-3). Pergamon.

Solihull As It Was. Hendon Publishing Co., Ltd. Staff. 1986. 16.10x (ISBN 0-317-54178-1, Pub. by Hendon Pub UK). State Mutual Bk.

Soliloquies. William Shakespeare. 1960. 5.95 (ISBN 0-88088-493-2). Peter Pauper.

Soliloquies of a Chalk Giant: Poems. Jeremy Hooker. 1974. wrappers 4.00 (ISBN 0-685-46799-6, Pub. by Enitharmon Pr); 5.00 (ISBN 0-685-46800-3); signed, limited 12.50 (ISBN 0-685-46801-1). Small Pr Dist.

Soliloquies of a Stranger. Donald M. Werkheiser. LC 86-91484. 65p. 1987. 6.95 (ISBN 0-533-07297-2). Vantage.

Soliloquies of Shakespeare: A Study in Technic. Morris L. Arnold. LC 78-58273. Repr. of 1911 ed. 19.50 (ISBN 0-404-00389-3). AMS Pr.

Soliloquy in German Drama. Erwin W. Roessler. LC 15-5583. (Columbia University. Germanic Studies, Old Ser.: No. 19). Repr. of 1915 ed. 19.00 (ISBN 0-404-50419-1). AMS Pr.

Soliloquy in Nineteenth-Century Fiction. Carol H. MacKay. 328p. 1987. 28.50 (ISBN 0-389-20710-1). B&N Imports.

Soliloquy of Satan, & Other Poems. facsimile ed. Elliott B. Henderson. LC 72-37597. (Black Heritage Library Collection). Repr. of 1907 ed. 12.00 (ISBN 0-8369-8973-2). Ayer Co Pubs.

Soliloquy! The Elizabethan & Jacobean Monologues. Ed. & intro. by Carl Keil. (Applause Acting Ser.). 160p. (Orig.). 1987. pap. 6.95 (ISBN 0-936839-92-9). Applause Theatre Bk Pubs.

Soliloquy! The Shakespeare Monologues: Men. Ed. by Michael Earley & Philippa Keil. (Applause Acting Ser.). 192p. (Orig.). 1987. pap. 6.95 (ISBN 0-936839-78-3). Applause Theatre Bk Pubs.

Soliloquy! The Shakespeare Monologues: Women. Ed. by Michael Earley & Philippa Keil. (Applause Acting Ser.). 192p. (Orig.). 1987. pap. 6.95 (ISBN 0-936839-79-1). Applause Theatre Bk Pubs.

Soliman & Perseda. Thomas Kyd. LC 78-133740. (Tudor Facsimilie Texts. Old English Plays: No. 62). Repr. of 1912 ed. 49.50 (ISBN 0-404-53362-0). AMS Pr.

Solimano. David Perez. Ed. by Howard M. Brown. LC 76-20976. (Italian Opera 1640-1770 Ser.). 1979. lib. bdg. 77.00 (ISBN 0-8240-2644-6). Garland Pub.

Solitaire. Lisa Gregory. 448p. (Orig.). 1988. pap. 3.95 (ISBN 0-446-34381-1). Warner Bks.

Solitaire. Eugene Ionesco. (Folio Ser.: No. 827). 200p. 1973. 6.95 (ISBN 0-686-54199-5). Schoenhof.

Solitaire: Aces Up & 399 Other Card Games. David Parlett. (Illus.). 1980. pap. 5.95 (ISBN 0-394-73868-3). Pantheon.

Solitaria. Vasilii V. Rozanov. Tr. by S. S. Koteliansky from Rus. LC 79-13120. 1980. Repr. of 1927 ed. lib. bdg. 35.00x (ISBN 0-313-22004-2, ROSA). Greenwood.

Solitary. Lynn Hall. LC 86-15461. 128p. (gr. 7 up). 1986. 11.95 (ISBN 0-684-18724-8, Pub. by Scribner). Macmillan.

Solitary. Wendall P. Sexton. 176p. 1987. cancelled (ISBN 0-317-60734-0). Carlton.

Solitary, Beneath the Rushing Moon. Jim Johnston. 102p. 1987. pap. 5.95 (ISBN 0-932229-04-2). Falling Water.

Solitary Blue. Cynthia Voigt. LC 83-6007. 204p. (gr. 7 up). 1983. 12.95 (ISBN 0-689-31008-0, Atheneum Childrens Bks). Macmillan.

Solitary Blue. Cynthia Voigt. (Orig.). 1987. pap. 2.95 (ISBN 0-449-70268-5, Juniper). Fawcett.

Solitary Comrade: Jack London & His Work. Joan D. Hedrick. LC 81-2969. xix, 265p. 1982. 25.00x (ISBN 0-8078-1488-1). U of NC Pr.

Solitary Dance. Robert G. Lane. LC 82-81020. (Illus.). 240p. (Orig.). 1983. 12.95 (ISBN 0-943104-82-3); pap. 7.95 (ISBN 0-943104-83-1). Serrell-Simons.

Solitary Horseman. Emilie Loring. Repr. lib. bdg. 15.95 (ISBN 0-88411-379-5, Pub. by Aeonian Pr). Amereon Ltd.

Solitary Man. Jonathan Evans. 448p. (Orig.). 1983. pap. 3.95 (ISBN 0-8125-0279-5, Dist. by Warner Pub Services & Saint Martin's Press). Tor Bks.

Solitary Nodular Lesions of the Lung: Contribution to Its Diagnosis & Management. Rafael A. Gomez et al. (Illus.). 250p. 1987. 32.50 (ISBN 0-87527-245-2). Green.

Solitary Running: A Book of Poetry. Edwin R. Floyd. 1986. 5.95 (ISBN 0-533-06854-1). Vantage.

Solitary Secret. Patricia Hermes. LC 84-22572. 135p. (gr. 6 up). 1985. 11.95 (ISBN 0-15-277190-5, HJ). HarBraceJ.

Solitary Self: Individuality in the Ancrene Wisse. Linda Georgianna. LC 81-2190. 192p. 1981. text ed. 19.50x (ISBN 0-674-81751-6). Harvard U Pr.

Solitary Singer: A Critical Biography of Walt Whitman. Gay W. Allen. LC 84-16462. (Illus.). xx, 616p. 1985. pap. 15.95 (ISBN 0-226-01435-5). U of Chicago Pr.

Solitary Voice: A Collection of Essays on Vardis Fisher. Dorys C. Grover. 1973. 69.95 (ISBN 0-87700-198-7). Revisionist Pr.

Solitary Volcano. Carpenter. Date not set. price not set. HM.

Solitons & Coherent Structures: Dedicated to Martin D. Kruskal on the Occasion of his 60th Birthday. Ed. by K. K. Campbell & A. C. Newell. 490p. 1986. 100.00 (ISBN 0-444-86993-X, North-Holland). Elsevier.

Solitions & Instantions: An Introduction to Solitions & Instantions in Quantum Field Theory. R. Rajaraman. 412p. 1982. 108.00 (ISBN 0-444-86229-3, North-Holland). Elsevier.

Solitons. Ed. by R. K. Bullough & P. J. Caudrey. (Topics in Current Physics: Vol. 17). (Illus.). 400p. 1980. pap. 51.00 (ISBN 0-387-09962-X). Springer-Verlag.

Solitons. P. G. Drazin. LC 83-7170. (London Mathematical Society Lecture Note Ser. No. 85). 136p. 1983. pap. 19.95 (ISBN 0-521-27422-2). Cambridge U Pr.

Solitons. M. Lakshmanan. (Nonlinear Dynamics Ser.). (Illus.). 420p. 1988. 59.50 (ISBN 0-387-18588-7). Springer-Verlag.

Solitons. Ed. by V. L. Pokrovsky et al. (Modern Problems in Condensed Matter Sciences Ser.: Vol. 17). 927p. 1987. 210.75 (ISBN 0-444-87002-4, North Holland). Elsevier.

Solitons: An Introduction. P. G. Drazin & R. S. Johnson. (Cambridge Texts in Applied Mathematics Ser.: No. 3). (Illus.). 230p. Date not set. price not set (ISBN 0-521-33389-X); pap. price not set (ISBN 0-521-33655-4). Cambridge U Pr.

Solitons & Instantons: An Introduction to Solitons & Instantons in Quantum Field Theory. R. Rajaraman. (Personal Library). 410p. 1987. 32.50 (ISBN 0-444-87047-4, North Holland). Elsevier.

Solitons & Instantons, Operator Quantization. Ed. by V. L. Ginzburg. (Proceedings of the Lebedev Physics Institute of the Academy of Sciences of the U. S. S. R. Ser.: Vol. 165). 299p. 1987. text ed. 92.00 (ISBN 0-941743-00-4). Nova Sci Pubs.

Solitons & Linear Wave Equations. Ed. by R. K. Dodd et al. 1984. pap. 32.50 (ISBN 0-12-219122-6). Acad Pr.

Solitons & Nonlinear Equations. R. K. Todd et al. 1983. 73.00 (ISBN 0-12-219120-X). Acad Pr.

Solitons & Particles. Ed. by C. Rebbi & G. Soliani. 836p. 1985. 83.00 (ISBN 9971-966-42-5); pap. 36.00 (ISBN 9971-966-43-3). World Scientific Pub.

Solitons & Polarons in Conducting Polymers. L. Yu. 600p. 1988. 78.00 (ISBN 9971-50-053-1); pap. 37.00 (ISBN 9971-50-054-X). World Scientific Pub.

Solitons & Polarons in Solid State Physics. D. Baeriswyl & A. Bishop. 300p. 1987. 55.00 (ISBN 9971-50-407-3); pap. 30.00 (ISBN 9971-50-408-1). World Scientific Pub.

Solitons & the Inverse Scattering Transform. M. J. Ablowitz & H. Segur. LC 81-50600. (SIAM Studies in Applied Mathematics: No. 4). x, 425p. 1981. Repr. of 1985 ed. text ed. 62.50 (ISBN 0-89871-174-6). Soc Indus-Appl Math.

Solitons in Action. Ed. by Karl Lonngren & Alwyn Scott. 1978. 41.50 (ISBN 0-12-455580-2). Acad Pr.

Solitons in Mathematics & Physics. Alan C. Newell. LC 84-71051. (CBMS-NSF Regional Conference Ser.: No. 48). xvi, 244p. (Orig.). 1985. text ed. 32.00 (ISBN 0-89871-196-7). Soc Indus-Appl Math.

Solitons: Mathematical Methods for Physicists. G. Eilenberger. (Springer Series in Solid-State Sciences: Vol. 19). (Illus.). 192p. 1981. 28.50 (ISBN 0-387-10223-X). Springer-Verlag.

Solitude: A Return to the Self. Anthony Storr. 230p. 1988. 17.95 (ISBN 0-02-931620-0). Free Pr.

Solitude & Privacy: A Study of Social Isolation, Its Causes & Therapy. Paul Halmos. Repr. of 1953 ed. lib. bdg. 35.00x (ISBN 0-8371-2455-7, HASO). Greenwood.

Solitude de la Pitie. Jean Giono. (Folio Ser.: No. 330). 1973. 5.95 (ISBN 0-686-53990-7). Schoenhof.

Solitude de la Pitie see Oeuvres Romanesques.

Solitude in Society: A Sociological Study in French Literature. Robert Sayre. LC 77-16265. 1978. 17.50x (ISBN 0-674-81761-3). Harvard U Pr.

Solitude in the Thought of Thomas Merton. Richard A. Cashen. (Cistercian Studies: No. 40). 208p. 1981. 15.50 (ISBN 0-87907-840-5); pap. 5.50 (ISBN 0-87907-940-1). Cistercian Pubns.

Solitude of Loneliness. John C. Woodward & Janel Queen. 128p. 1988. pap. 9.95 (ISBN 0-669-14505-X). Lexington Bks.

Solitude to Sacrament. Katherine M. Dyckman & L. Patrick Carroll. LC 82-252. 128p. (Orig.). 1982. pap. 2.95 (ISBN 0-8146-1255-5). Liturgical Pr.

Solitudes Crowded with Loneliness. Bob Kaufman. LC 65-15673. (Orig.). 1965. pap. 4.95 (ISBN 0-8112-0076-0, NDP199). New Directions.

Solitudes, Galleries, & Other Poems. Antonio Machado y Ruiz. Tr. by Richard L. Predmore from Span. LC 86-32758. ix, 237p. 1987. lib. bdg. 29.95 (ISBN 0-8223-0713-8). Duke.

Solitude's Lawman. Ray Hogan. LC 87-17111. (Double D Western Ser.). 192p. 1988. pap. 12.95 (ISBN 0-385-24431-2). Doubleday.

Solitude's Lawman. Ray Hogan. 250p. 1988. Repr. of 1988 ed. lib. bdg. 14.95 (ISBN 0-89621-201-7). Thorndike Pr.

Solitudes: Short Stories. Goffredo Parise. Tr. by Isabel Quigly from Ital. LC 84-40551. 173p. (Orig.). 1985. pap. 7.95 (ISBN 0-394-72994-3, Vin). Random.

Sollers Ecrivain see Write Sollers.

Sollicitudo Rei Socialis: On Social Concern. Pope John Paul, II. 104p. 1988. pap. 3.95 (ISBN 1-55586-205-5). US Catholic.

Solo. Jack Higgins. 1983. pap. 4.50 (ISBN 0-440-18078-3). Dell.

Solo: An American Dreamer in Europe, 1933-1934. Wright Morris. 208p. 1984. pap. 6.95 (ISBN 0-14-007131-8). Penguin.

Solo Blues. Paula Gosling. 256p. 1983. pap. 2.50 (ISBN 0-345-30643-0). Ballantine.

Solo Book for Bass Guitar. Arnie Berle. 1983. pap. 5.95 (ISBN 0-8256-2398-7, Amsco Music). Music Sales.

Solo Cooking on a Shoestring. Patricia Carter. 1985. 22.00x (ISBN 0-86025-871-8, Pub. by Ian Henry Pubns England). State Mutual Bk.

Solo Cyclist: How to Train & Race Bicycle Time Trials. Fred Matheny. Ed. by Barbara George. LC 86-50910. (Illus.). 208p. (Orig.). 1986. pap. 14.95 (ISBN 0-941950-10-7). Velo-News.

Solo Faces. James Salter. LC 87-82585. 224p. 1988. pap. 8.95 (ISBN 0-86547-321-8). N Point Pr.

Solo Flight. Elvina T. Pearce. Ed. by Frances Clark & Louise Goss. (gr. 2 up). 1986. pap. text ed. 3.50 (ISBN 0-913277-18-5). New Schl Mus Study.

Solo Forms of Karate, Tai Chi, Aikido & Kung Fu. Bruce Tegner & Alice McGrath. (Illus.). 112p. 1981. pap. 4.95 (ISBN 0-87407-034-1). Thor.

Solo Games: Twelve New Exciting Board Games to Be Played by One Person. H. David Jackson. (Illus.). 75p. (Orig.). 1982. pap. 12.95 (ISBN 0-930256-10-7). Almar.

Solo Guitar Playing, Bk 1. 2nd ed. Frederick M. Noad. LC 76-12833. 1976. pap. 10.95 (ISBN 0-02-871680-9). Schirmer Bks.

Solo Guitar Playing, Bk. 2. Frederick M. Noad. LC 77-2529. (Illus.). 1978. pap. 10.95 (ISBN 0-02-871690-6). Schirmer Bks.

Solo in the City: A Sourcebook for Singles in Metropolitan Denver. Daniel Bradford. 128p. (Orig.). 1985. pap. 6.95 (ISBN 0-9608012-3-5). Metrosource Pubns.

Solo in the New Order: Language & Hierarchy in an Indonesian City. James T. Siegel. 296p. 1987. text ed. 35.00x (ISBN 0-691-09427-6). Princeton U Pr.

Solo La Voz see Only the Voice.

Solo Motets. Ed. by Ernest Warburton. (Johann Christian Bach Ser.). 75.00 (ISBN 0-8240-6067-9). Garland Pub.

Solo: Nanga Parbat. Reinhold Messner. (Illus.). 1980. 29.95 (ISBN 0-19-520196-5). Oxford U Pr.

Solo para Muchachos. Frank H. Richardson. 112p. 1986. pap. 1.95 (ISBN 0-311-46929-9). Casa Bautista.

Solo Parenting: Your Essential Guide. Kathleen McCoy. 1987. pap. 7.95 (ISBN 0-317-56843-4, Plume). NAL.

Solo Parenting: Your Essential Guide. Kathleen McCoy. 288p. 1988. pap. 4.50 (ISBN 0-451-15137-2, Sig). NAL.

Solo Practice. Elizabeth Morgan. 288p. 1984. pap. 3.50 (ISBN 0-425-05971-5). Berkley Pub.

Solo Retirement. Judy Salwen. 180p. 1983. pap. 12.95 (ISBN 0-396-08151-7). Dodd.

Solo Scenes from Great Writers. Sydney Thompson. 80p. 1947. 5.00 (ISBN 0-573-60075-9). French.

Solo Settings to the Poems of Mary Baker Eddy: High Voice Bk, No. 1. Mary Baker Eddy. 116p. (Orig.). pap. 9.50 (ISBN 0-87952-164-3). First Church.

Solo Settings to the Poems of Mary Baker Eddy: High Voice Bk, No. 1. Mary Baker Eddy. 116p. Hign Voice Book 1. pap. 9.50 (ISBN 0-87952-096-5). First Church.

Solo Settings to the Poems of Mary Baker Eddy: High Voice Bk, No. 2. Mary Baker Eddy. 120p. pap. 9.50 (ISBN 0-87952-165-1). First Church.

Solo Settings to the Poems of Mary Baker Eddy: High Voice Bk, No. 2. Mary Baker Eddy. 116p. pap. 9.50 (ISBN 0-87952-097-3). First Church.

Solo Settings to the Poems of Mary Baker Eddy: Low Voice Bk, No. 1. Mary Baker Eddy. 120p. pap. 9.50 (ISBN 0-87952-166-X). First Church.

Solo Settings to the Poems of Mary Baker Eddy: Low Voice Bk, No. 1. Mary Baker Eddy. 116p. pap. 9.50 (ISBN 0-87952-095-7). First Church.

Solo Settings to the Poems of Mary Baker Eddy: Low Voice Bk, No. 2. Mary Baker Eddy. 120p. pap. text ed. 9.50 (ISBN 0-87952-167-8). First Church.

Solo Settings to the Poems of Mary Baker Eddy: Low Voice Bk, No. 2. Mary Baker Eddy. 116p. pap. 9.50 (ISBN 0-87952-094-9). First Church.

Solo Style Contemporary Travis Picking. Mark D. Hanson. 80p. (Orig.). 1988. pap. 17.95; audio cassette incl. Accent Music.

Solo! The Best Monologues of the 80's: Women, Vol. 11. Ed. by Michael Earley & Philippa Keil. (Applause Acting Ser.). 160p. (Orig.). 1987. pap. 5.95 (ISBN 0-936839-66-X). Applause Theatre Bk Pubs.

Solo! The Best Monologues of the 80's: Men, Vol. 1. Michael Earley & Philippa Keil. (Applause Acting Ser.). 160p. (Orig.). 1987. pap. 5.95 (ISBN 0-936839-65-1). Applause Theatre Bk Pubs.

Solo Time U. S. A. Twenty-Three Easy Piano Solos by American Composers. 1948. pap. 4.95 (ISBN 0-8258-0224-5, 04469). Fischer Inc NY.

Solo User's Guide. Jerry Hintze. (Illus.). 373p. (Orig.). 1988. pap. write for info. (ISBN 0-935386-07-6). BMDP Stat.

Sologne: Documents de Litterature Traditionnelle, Vol. 3. Bernard Edeine. (Illus.). 342p. (Fr.). 1975. text ed. 57.60x (ISBN 90-2797-735-6). Mouton.

Sologub's Literary Children: Keys to a Symbolist's Prose. Stanley J. Rabinowitz. (Illus.). 176p. 1980. pap. 11.95 (ISBN 0-89357-069-9). Slavica.

Soloist. Nicholas Christopher. 318p. 1986. 17.95 (ISBN 0-670-80900-4). Viking.

Soloistic Use of the Trombone in Eighteenth-Century Vienna. C. Robert Wigness. LC 74-8189. (Brass Research Ser.: No.2). 1978. pap. text ed. 6.00x (ISBN 0-914282-02-6). Brass Pr.

Solokantanten fuer Alt, Tenor oder Bass mit Instrumenten see Dietrich Buxtehudes Werke.

Solomani: Alien Module 6. Marc W. Miller & John Harshman. (Traveller Ser.). (Illus.). 49p. (Orig.). 1986. pap. 7.00 (ISBN 0-943580-07-2). Game Designers.

Solomon. Rebecca Daniel. (Our Greatest Heritage Ser.). (Illus.). 32p. (gr. 7-12). 1983. wkbk. 4.95 (ISBN 0-86653-139-4, SS 808). Good Apple.

Solomon & Rehoboam. Gordon Lindsay. (Old Testament Ser.). 1.25 (ISBN 0-89985-145-2). Christ Nations.

Solomon & Sheba. Faye Levine. 240p. 1986. pap. 9.95 (ISBN 0-312-74283-5). St Martin.

Solomon & Solomonic Literature. Moncure D. Conway. LC 72-2032. (Studies in Comparative Literature, No. 35). 1972. Repr. of 1899 ed. lib. bdg. 49.95x (ISBN 0-8383-1478-3). Haskell.

Solomon Crow's Christmas Pockets & Other Tales. Ruth Stuart. LC 70-94744. (Short Story Index Reprint Ser.). 1896. 17.00 (ISBN 0-8369-3124-6). Ayer Co Pubs.

Solomon D. Butcher: Photographing the American Dream. John E. Carter. LC 85-5835. (Illus.). x, 142p. 1986. 28.95 (ISBN 0-8032-1404-9). U of Nebr Pr.

Solomon Decision Whose Child Is This? An Adoption Dialogue. Kate Pijanowski. LC 88-71629. 247p. (Orig.). 1989. pap. 9.95 (ISBN 0-934896-48-8). Jan Pubns Inc.

Solomon Grundy. Susan R. Hoguet. LC 85-20453. (Illus.). 32p. (ps-3). 1986. 11.95 (ISBN 0-525-44239-1). Dutton.

Solomon Grundy, Born on Oneday: A Finite Arithmetic Puzzle. Malcolm E. Weiss. LC 76-26560. (Young Math Ser.). (Illus.). (gr. k-3). 1977. PLB 12.89 (ISBN 0-690-01275-6, Crowell Jr Bks). HarpJ.

Solomon Ibn Gabirol: Selected Religious Poems. Solomon Ibn Gabirol. Ed. by Israel Davidson. Tr. by Israel Zangwill. LC 73-2210. (JPS Library of Jewish Classics). 248p. 1974. pap. 3.95 (ISBN 0-8276-0060-7, 360). JPS Phila.

Solomon in All His Glory. Robert Lynd. LC 72-86769. (Essay Index Reprint Ser.). 1923. 19.00 (ISBN 0-8369-1420-1). Ayer Co Pubs.

Solomon Islands. (Let's Visit Places & Peoples - - Nations, Dependencies, & Sovereingties of the World Ser.). (Illus.). (gr. 5 up). 1989. 12.95 (ISBN 0-7910-0163-6). Chelsea Hse.

Solomon Islands: A Travel Survival Kit. David Harcombe. (Illus.). 240p. (Orig.). 1988. pap. 9.95 (ISBN 0-86442-009-9). Lonely Planet.

Solomon Islands Project: A Long-Term Study of Health, Human Biology, & Culture Change. Ed. by Jonathan S. Friedlaender. (Research Monographs on Human Population Biology: No. 4). (Illus.). 422p. 1987. 90.00 (ISBN 0-19-857595-5). Oxford U Pr.

Solomon Leviathan's Nine Hundred Thirty-First Trip Around the World. Ursula K. Le Guin. (Adventures in Kroy Ser.: No. 2). (Illus.). 40p. (YA) (gr. 7 up). 1983. 70.00 (ISBN 0-941826-03-1). Cheap St.

Solomon Leviathan's 931 Trip Around the World. Ursula LeGuin. (gr. k-4). 1988. 13.95 (ISBN 0-399-21491-7, Philomel Bks). Putnam Pub Group.

Solomon Moon. Bill Darrid. 448p. 1985. pap. 3.95 (ISBN 0-345-30356-3). Ballantine.

Solomon on Sex. Joseph C. Dillow. LC 77-1049. 1982. pap. 4.95 (ISBN 0-8407-5813-8). Nelson.

TITLE INDEX SOLUTIONS TO YOUR WRITING

Solomon Papper Festschrift, Vol. 10, No. 3. Ed. by C. A. Vaamonde. (Journal: Mineral & Electroltye Metabolism: Vol. 10, No. 3). (Illus.). vi, 76p. 1984. pap. 47.50 (ISBN 3-8055-3858-8). S Karger.
Solomon Schechter. Norman Bentwich. 1964. 6.00 (ISBN 0-8381-3105-0). United Syn Bk.
Solomon Stone. Mark A. Calde. 384p. 1987. pap. 3.95 (ISBN 0-8041-0219-8). Ballantine.
Solomon System. Phyllis R. Naylor. LC 83-2661. 216p. (gr. 5-9). 1983. 12.95 (ISBN 0-689-30991-0, Atheneum Childrens Bks). Macmillan.
Solomon System. Phyllis R. Naylor. LC 86-21758. 216p. (gr. 5-9). 1987. pap. 3.95 (ISBN 0-689-71128-X, Aladdin Bks). Macmillan.
Solomon the Rusty Nail. William Steig. (Illus.). 32p. (ps up). 1985. 13.95 (ISBN 0-374-37131-8). FS&G.
Solomon the Rusty Nail. William Steig. (Michael di Capua Bks.). (Illus.). 32p. (ps up). 1987. pap. 3.95 (ISBN 0-374-46903-2, Sunburst). FS&G.
Solomon to the Exile: Studies in Kings & Chronicles. John C. Whitcomb, Jr. pap. 5.95 (ISBN 0-88469-054-7). BMH Bks.
Solomons: A Portrait of Traditional & Contemporary Culture in Solomon Islands. Ed. by Julian Maka'a. (Pacific Quarterly Moana Special Issue: Vol. 9, No. 1). (Illus.). 64p. 1985. pap. 12.00 (ISBN 0-317-20178-6, Pub. by Outrigger Pubs New Zealand). Three Continents.
Solomon's Book of Wisdom see Adam Davy's Five Dreams about Edward 2nd.
Solomon's Folly. Leslie Croxford. LC 75-1458. 1978. 12.95 (ISBN 0-8149-0763-6). Vanguard.
Solomon's Folly. Leslie Croxford. LC 83-9199. (Phoenix Fiction Ser.). 208p. 1984. pap. 6.95 (ISBN 0-226-12149-6). U of Chicago Pr.
Solomon's Golden Temple. Penny Frank. (Lion Story Bible Ser.). (Illus.). 24p. (ps-4). 1987. 3.95 (ISBN 0-85648-745-7). Lion USA.
Solomon's New Men. E. W. Heaton. LC 74-13412. (Illus.). 216p. 1975. 15.00x (ISBN 0-87663-714-4, Pica Pr). Universe.
Solomon's Seal. Hammond Innes. 1985. pap. 3.50 (ISBN 0-88184-151-X). Carroll & Graf.
Solomon's Secret see Is This All There Is to Life?.
Solomon's Sword: Clarifying Values in the Church. Robert Meyners & Claire Wooster. LC 77-9391. Repr. of 1977 ed. 27.40 (ISBN 0-8357-9028-2, 2016408). Bks Demand UMI.
Solomon's Wisdom: A Collection of Short Stories. Roberta Kalechofsky. LC 78-62032. 190p. 1978. pap. 6.00x (ISBN 0-916288-05-6). Micah Pubns.
Solomon's Words of Wisdom. Solomon Alter. 48p. 1985. 6.95 (ISBN 0-533-06504-6). Vantage.
Solon & Croesus & Other Greek Essays. facs. ed. Alfred E. Zimmern. LC 67-22130. (Essay Index Reprint Ser). 1928. 16.75 (ISBN 0-8369-1016-8). Ayer Co Pubs.
Solon de l'Automobile see Theatre.
Solon Robinson, Pioneer & Agriculturalist, 2 Vols. Ed. by H. A. Kellar. LC 68-16242. (American Scene Ser). (Illus.). 1968. Repr. of 1936 ed. Set. lib. bdg. 95.00 (ISBN 0-306-71017-X). Da Capo.
Solon Robinson, Pioneer & Agriculturist. Solon Robinson. Ed. by Herbert A. Kellar. LC 74-145268. (Illus.). 1971. Repr. of 1936 ed. 59.00x (ISBN 0-403-01183-3). Scholarly.
Solos. Nubia Kai. 121p. 1988. pap. 8.50 perf. bdg. (ISBN 0-916418-71-5). Lotus.
Solos for the Student Trombonist: An Annotated Bibliography. Vern Kagarice et al. LC 79-17000. (International Trombone Association Ser.: No. 8). 1979. pap. 5.00x (ISBN 0-914282-26-3). Brass Pr.
Solos for Unaccompanied Clarinet: An Annotated Bibliography. James E. Gillespie, Jr. LC 73-87277. (Detroit Studies in Music Bibliography Ser.: No. 28). 1973. 10.00 (ISBN 0-911772-58-8); pap. 6.00 (ISBN 0-89990-010-0). Harmonie Pk Pr.
Solo's Journey. Joy S. Aiken. 256p. 1987. 19.95 (ISBN 0-399-13321-6, Putnam). Putnam Pub Group.
Soloveitchik on Repentance. Joseph D. Soloveitchik. Tr. by Pinchas Peli. 320p. 1984. 11.95 (ISBN 0-8091-2604-4). Paulist Pr.
Soloview, the Character of Old Russia, Vol. 24. Ed. by Alexander V. Muller. 1987. pap. 12.50 (ISBN 0-317-57761-1). Academic Intl.
Solovyev: Prophet of Russian-Western Unity. 1956. 5.95 (ISBN 0-8022-1173-9). Philos Lib.
Solstice. Joyce Carol Oates. 243p. 1985. 15.95 (ISBN 0-525-24293-7). Dutton.
Solstice. Joyce Carol Oates. 1986. pap. 3.95 (ISBN 0-425-09204-6). Berkley Pub.
Solstice. Paul Payack. (Illus.). 16p. 1976. pap. 0.50 (ISBN 0-686-20753-X). Samisdat.
Solstice. Grant Sandres. 44p. 1974. pap. 1.50 (ISBN 0-915242-05-2). Pygmalion Pr.
Solstice D'Ete. Kay Thorpe. (Collection Harlequin Ser.). 192p. 1984. pap. 1.95 (ISBN 0-373-49376-2). Harlequin Bks.
Solstice II. Paul J. Payack. Ed. by Merritt Clifton. (Illus.). 1976. pap. 1.00 (ISBN 0-686-18735-0). Chthon Pr.
Solstice III. Paul J. Payack. Ed. by Merritt Clifton. (Illus.). 1977. 1.00 (ISBN 0-686-19655-4). Chthon Pr.
Solstice, or Star-Tales. Paul J. Payack. Ed. by Merritt Clifton. (Illus.). 1976. pap. 1.00 (ISBN 0-686-16727-9). Chthon Pr.
Solstice Poems. Charles A. Baar. 40p. (Orig.). 1983. pap. 3.00 (ISBN 0-934852-53-7). Lorien Hse.
Solstice Points. Robert Myers. 1988. pap. write for info. (ISBN 0-87500-022-3). RKM Pub Co.
Soltero. Bienvenido M. Noriega, Jr. Tr. by Roland S. Tinio. (Illus.). 159p. (Orig., Tagalog & Eng.). 1985. pap. 10.50 (ISBN 971-10-0252-3, Pub. by New Day Philippines). Cellar.
SOLTI. Paul Robinson. (Art of the Conductor Ser.). (Illus.). 160p. 1979. 11.95 (ISBN 0-8149-0802-0). Vanguard.
Solubilities of Inorganic & Organic Compounds, 3 vols. H. Stephen et al. LC 79-40319. 7300p. 1979. Set. 1285.00 (ISBN 0-08-023599-9). Pergamon.
Solubilities on Inorganic & Organic Compounds, Vol 3. Stephen. 1979. 720.00 (ISBN 0-08-023570-0). Pergamon.
Solubility & PH Calculations. James N. Butler. LC 64-15563. (Chemistry Ser.). (Orig.). (gr. 9 up). 1964. pap. write for info. (ISBN 0-201-00733-9). Addison-Wesley.
Solubility & Related Properties. James. (Drugs & the Pharmaceutical Sciences Ser.). 328p. 1986. 75.00 (ISBN 0-8247-7484-1). Dekker.
Solubility Behavior of Organic Compounds. Grant. 1989. price not set (ISBN 0-471-61314-2). Wiley.
Solubility in Inorganic Two-Component Systems. M. Broul & J. Hyvit. (Physical Sciences Data Ser.: Vol. 6). 574p. 1981. 139.50 (ISBN 0-444-99763-6). Elsevier.
Solubility of Gases & Liquids: A Graphic Approach. W. Gerrard. LC 76-10676. (Illus.). 276p. 1976. 55.00x (ISBN 0-306-30866-5, Plenum Pr). Plenum Pub.
Solubility of Gases & Solids: A Literature Source Book, Pts. A & B. J. Wisniak & M. Herskowitz. (Physical Sciences Data Ser.: Vol. 18). 1984. Set. 416.00 (ISBN 0-444-42300-1). Elsevier.
Solubility of Magnetite in Water & in Aqueous Solutions of Acid & Alkali. G. Bohnsack. 160p. 1988. 87.50 (ISBN 0-89116-831-1). Hemisphere Pub.
Soluble & Nilpotent Linear Groups. D. A. Suprenenko. LC 63-20676. (Translations of Mathematical Monographs: Vol. 9). 1970. Repr. of 1963 ed. 26.00 (ISBN 0-8218-1559-8, MMONO-9). Am Math.
Soluble Silicates. Ed. by James S. Falcone, Jr. LC 82-115114. (ACS Symposium Ser.: No. 194). 1982. 44.95 (ISBN 0-8412-0730-5). Am Chemical.
Solucionario del Libro "Elementos de Matematica Comercial" de Ruperto Vazquez Cruz. Lourdes Correa. pap. 2.50 (ISBN 0-8477-2604-5). U of PR Pr.
Solutations see Theatre.
Solute-Defect Interaction: Theory & Experiment: Proceedings of the International Seminar on Solute-Defect Interacton: Theory & Experiment, Kingston, Ontario, Canada, 5-9 August 1985. Ed. by S. Saimoto et al. LC 86-42542. (Illus.). 488p. 1986. 115.00 (ISBN 0-08-031872-X, A130, A145, C125, Pub. by PPC). Pergamon.
Solute Effects in Very Dilute Ternary Copper Alloys. Stevens Institute of Technology. 22p. 1981. write for info. Intl Copper.
Solute Processes. S. T. Trudgill. LC 85-9557. (Landscape Systems Ser.). 1986. 101.00 (ISBN 0-471-90819-3). Wiley.
Solute-Solvent Interactions, Vol. 2. Johannes Coetzee & Calvin D. Ritchie. 1976. 99.75 (ISBN 0-8247-6416-1). Dekker.
Solute Transport in Plant Cells & Tissues. Ed. by D. A. Baker & J. L. Hall. LC 87-16741. (Monographs & Surveys in the Biosciences). 592p. 1988. 175.00 (ISBN 0-470-20864-3). Wiley.
Solution Behavior of Surfactants: Theoretical & Applied Aspects, 2 vols. Ed. by K. L. Mittal & E. J. Fendler. LC 82-10120. 1982. Vol. 1, 770p. 115.00x (ISBN 0-306-41025-7, Plenum Pr); Vol. 2, 822p. 115.00x (ISBN 0-306-41026-5, Plenum Pr); Set. 185.00x. Plenum Pub.
Solution Chemistry of Surfactants, 2 vols. Ed. by K. L. Mittal. LC 79-15067. 1979. Set. 130.00x (Plenum Pr); 79.50x ea. Vol. 1, 542p (ISBN 0-306-40174-6). Vol. 2, 460p (ISBN 0-306-40175-4). Plenum Pub.
Solution Equilibra. F. R. Hartley et al. 361p. 1985. pap. 29.95 (ISBN 0-470-20280-7). Halsted Pr.
Solution in Asia. Owen Lattimore. LC 72-4439. Repr. of 1945 ed. 19.45 (ISBN 0-404-10635-8). AMS Pr.
Solution Methods for Integral Equations. Ed. by M. A. Goldberg. LC 79-17900. (Mathematical Concepts & Methods in Science & Engineering Ser.: Vol. 18). 360p. 1979. 45.00x (ISBN 0-306-40254-8, Plenum Pr). Plenum Pub.
Solution Mining Symposium, 1974: Proceedings of a Symposium, 103rd AIME Annual Meeting, Dallas, Texas, Feb. 25-27, 1974. Ed. by F. F. Aplan et al. LC 73-94005. pap. 119.80 (ISBN 0-317-29727-9, 2017422). Bks Demand UMI.
Solution of Doctor Resolutus, His Resolutions for Kneeling. David Calderwood. LC 79-84093. (English Experience Ser.: No. 913). 60p. 1979. Repr. of 1619 ed. lib. bdg. 8.00 (ISBN 90-221-0913-5). Walter J Johnson.
Solution of Large Networks by Matrix Methods. 2nd ed. Homer E. Brown. LC 85-5380. 320p. 1985. 44.95 (ISBN 0-471-80074-0). Wiley.
Solution of Non-Linear Systems. S. Vojtasek & K. Janac. Ed. by G. D. Smart. Tr. by Pavel Dolan from Czech. (Illus.). 1970. 14.75 (ISBN 0-8088-3929-2). Davey.
Solution of Nutritional Problems: The Contribution of Producers, Distributors & Nutritionists. Ed. by J. C. Somogyi. (Bibliotheca Nutritio et Dieta: No. 28). (Illus.). 1979. pap. 96.75 (ISBN 3-8055-3025-0). S Karger.
Solution of Partial Differential Equations on Vector & Parallel Computers. James M. Ortega & Robert G. Voigt. LC 85-61387. iii, 96p. (Orig.). 1985. pap. text ed. 13.00 (ISBN 0-89871-055-3). Soc Indus Appl Math.
Solution of Social Problems: Five Perspectives. 2nd ed. Ed. by Martin S. Weinberg et al. 1981. pap. text ed. 9.95x (ISBN 0-19-502787-6). Oxford U Pr.
Solution of the Inverse Problem in Geophysical Interpretation. Ed. by R. Cassinis. LC 81-4067. 392p. 1981. 75.00x (ISBN 0-306-40735-3, Plenum Pr). Plenum Pub.
Solution of the Voynich Manuscript. Leo Levitov. 176p. (Orig.). 1987. lib. bdg. 46.80 (ISBN 0-89412-149-9); pap. 38.80 (ISBN 0-89412-148-0). Aegean Park Pr.
Solution of Variational Inequalities in Mechanics. I. Hlavacek et al. (Applied Mathematical Sciences Ser.: Vol. 66). (Illus.). 325p. 1988. pap. 42.80 (ISBN 0-387-96597-1). Springer-Verlag.
Solution-Oriented Investing: How to Pick the Next High-Flyers. Lawrence Monberg & John Manos. 1985. cancelled (ISBN 0-15-183710-4). HarBraceJ.
Solution Passage: Poems Nineteen Seventy-Eight to Nineteen Eighty-One. Clark Coolidge. 400p. 1986. 18.95 (ISBN 0-940650-55-X); signed ltd. ed. 35.00 (ISBN 0-940650-59-2); pap. 11.95 (ISBN 0-940650-54-1). Sun & Moon CA.
Solution Properties of Polysaccharides. Ed. by David A. Brant. LC 81-236. (ACS Symposium Ser.: No. 150). 1981. 57.95 (ISBN 0-8412-0609-0). Am Chemical.
Solution to the Riddle Dyslexia. H. N. Levinson. (Illus.). 398p. 1980. 36.00 (ISBN 0-387-90515-4). Springer-Verlag.
Solution Training: Overcoming Blocks in Problem Solving. James R. Baugh. LC 79-20717. 256p. 1980. 9.95 (ISBN 0-88289-246-0). Pelican.
Solutions. (Tops Cards Ser.: No. 12). 1978. pap. 10.50 (ISBN 0-941008-12-6). Tops Learning.
Solutions: A Guide to Better Problem Solving. Steven R. Phillips & William H. Bergquist. LC 87-5894. 125p. (Orig.). 1987. pap. text ed. 19.95 (ISBN 0-88390-205-2). Univ Assocs.
Solutions & Condensed Matter Physics: Proceedings. rev. ed. Ed. by A. R. Bishop & T. Schneider. (Series in Solid-State Sciences: Vol. 8). (Illus.). 342p. 1978. 38.50 (ISBN 0-387-09138-6). Springer-Verlag.
Solutions for a Troubled World. Ed. by Mark Macy. LC 87-8859. (Peace Ser.: Vol. I). (Illus.). 314p. (Orig.). 1987. pap. 8.95 (ISBN 0-930705-03-3). M H Macy & Co.
Solutions for Pavement Rehabilitation Problems. Ed. by Sanford P. LaHue, Sr. 1986. 27.00 (ISBN 0-87262-578-8). Am Soc Civil Eng.
Solutions for Practice Set for Introduction to Hospital Accounting. L. Vann Seawell. pap. 8.00 wkbk. (ISBN 0-930228-26-X). Healthcare Fin Mgmt Assn.
Solutions for Technology-Sharing Networks, 1987. Ed. by Public Technology, Inc. 400p. (Orig.). 1987. pap. 40.00 (ISBN 0-317-60094-X). Pub Tech Inc.
Solutions for Technology-Sharing Networks 1986. Ed. by Public Technology, Inc Staff. (Annual Ser.). 436p. (Orig.). 1986. pap. 39.00 (ISBN 1-55657-001-5). Pub Tech Inc.
Solutions for the New Workforce. John J. Sweeney & Karen Nussbaum. (Policies for a New Social Contract Ser.). 160p. 1988. text ed. 14.95 (ISBN 0-932020-62-3); pap. text ed. 9.95 (ISBN 0-932020-63-1). Seven Locks Pr.
Solutions for Today's Sex Problems & Prostitution. 1981. 2.00 (ISBN 0-9600378-5-3). C C Brown Pub.
Solutions in C. Rex Jaeschke. Date not set. price not set. Addison-Wesley.
Solutions in Molecular Systems. A. S. Davydov. 1985. lib. bdg. 54.00 (ISBN 90-277-1854-7, Pub. by Reidel Netherlands). Kluwer Academic.
Solutions in Statistics & Probability. Edward J. Dudewicz. LC 80-68285. (American Sciences Press Ser. in Mathematical & Management Sciences: Vol. 3). 1980. pap. text ed. 34.50 (ISBN 0-935950-00-1). Am Sciences Pr.
Solutions Manual for Chemical Thermodynamics. Peter Rock. (Physical Chem. Ser.). 460p. 1985. text ed. 22.00x (ISBN 0-935702-19-9). Univ Sci Bks.
Solutions Manual for Introduction to Wastewater Treatment Processes. 2nd ed. R. S. Ramalho. 1983. 19.50 (ISBN 0-12-576562-2). Acad Pr.
Solutions Manual for Linear Programming. Vasek Chvatal. 119p. 1984. 8.95 (ISBN 0-7167-1678-X). W H Freeman.
Solutions Manual for Queueing Systems: Theory, Vol. 1. Leonard Kleinrock & Richard Gail. LC 82-80907. 226p. (Orig.). 1982. pap. text ed. 29.50 (ISBN 0-942948-00-9). Tech Trans Inst.
Solutions Manual for Queueing Systems Vol. II: Computer Applications. Leonard Kleinrock & Richard Gail. LC 82-80907. 250p. (Orig.). 1986. pap. text ed. 29.50 (ISBN 0-942948-01-7); Set, Vol. I & II. 55.00. Tech Trans Inst.
Solutions Manual for Statistical Analysis for Business & Economics. 3rd ed. Donald L. Harnett & James L. Murphy. 224p. 1985. write for info. solutions manual (ISBN 0-201-10684-1). Addison-Wesley.
Solutions Manual for the Electrical Engineering Review Manual. Michael R. Lindeburg. (Engineering Review Manual Ser.). 81p. 1983. pap. 9.50 (ISBN 0-932276-41-5). Prof Pubns CA.
Solutions Manual for the Engineer-In-Training Review Manual. Michael R. Lindeburg. (Engineering Review Manual Ser.). 130p. 1982. pap. text ed. 9.50 (ISBN 0-932276-49-0). Prof Pubns CA.
Solutions Manual for the Land Surveyor Reference Manual. Andrew L. Harbin. (Engineering Review Manual Ser.). 129p. 1985. pap. text ed. 16.45 (ISBN 0-932276-48-2). Prof Pubns CA.
Solutions Manual for the Mechanical Engineering Review Manual. Michael R. Lindeburg. (Engineering Review Manual Ser.). 134p. 1984. pap. text ed. 13.95 (ISBN 0-932276-57-1). Prof Pubns CA.
Solutions Manual to Accompany Frank H. Dietrich, II & Thomas J. Kearns Basic Statistics: An Inferential Approach. 2nd ed. Judith A. Stromovsky. 296p. 1986. pap. write for info. (ISBN 0-02-328790-X). Macmillan.
Solutions Manual to Accompany Microprocessor Fundamentals. Halsall et al. 1984. pap. write for info. (ISBN 0-471-88518-5). Wiley.
Solutions Manual to Accompany Petrucci's General Chemistry. 4th ed. Wismer Petrucci & Robert K. Wismer. 420p. 1985. write for info. solutions manual (ISBN 0-02-394540-0). Macmillan.
Solutions Manual to Accompany Transmission Lines Wave Guides & Antennas. Pigott. 1986. pap. write for info. (ISBN 0-471-88511-8). Wiley.
Solutions Manual to Applied Mathematics for Business & Economics, Life Sciences, & Social Sciences. 2nd ed. G. J. Etgen. 719p. 1986. pap. write for info. (ISBN 0-02-305620-7). Macmillan.
Solutions Manual to Environmental Control Principles: A Textbook Supplement to the 1985 Handbook of Fundamentals. 184p. 1985. 45.00 (ISBN 0-317-58598-3, SOL85). Am Heat Ref & Air Eng.
Solutions Manual to the Chemical Engineering Reference Manual. Randall N. Robinson. (Engineer Review Manual Ser.). 56p. 1988. pap. text ed. 13.95 (ISBN 0-932276-78-4). Prof Pubns CA.
Solutions, Minerals & Equilibria. Robert M. Garrels & Charles L. Christ. LC 65-12674. 1982. Repr. of 1965 ed. text ed. 27.50x (ISBN 0-87735-333-6). Freeman Cooper.
Solutions of Einstein's Equations-Techniques & Results: Proceedings of the International Seminar on Exact Solutions of Einstein's Equations, Held in Retzbach Retzbach Germany, November 14-18, 1983. Ed. by C. Hoenselaers et al. (Lecture Notes in Physics Ser.: Vol. 205). vi, 439p. 1984. pap. 29.50 (ISBN 0-387-13366-6). Springer-Verlag.
Solutions of Partial Differential Equations. Dean G. Duffy. (Illus.). 448p. 1986. 25.95 (ISBN 0-8306-0412-X, 2612, TAB-TPR). Tab Bks.
Solutions of Problems in Structures. W. T. Marshall. (Illus.). 1977. pap. text ed. 18.95 (ISBN 0-8464-0862-7). Beekman Pubs.
Solutions: Practical & Effective Antidotes for Sexual & Relationship Problems. rev. ed. Leslie Cameron-Bandler. LC 85-70138. 259p. 1985. pap. 11.95 (ISBN 0-932573-01-0). FuturePace.
Solutions, Relaxation, or Understanding for Tense, Anxious, Depressive, Hostile (Irritated), & Disgusted States & Problems, Set-ST. Russell E. Mason. 1975. pap. 55.00x (ISBN 0-89533-010-5); Tapes only. incl. tape-1a, t-5a, t-11, t-12, t-13, t-14 45.00, Notes, Clinical Applications, rev. ed., 1979, Brief Outlines 3, Substitution Training & Goal Achievement. F I Comm.
Solutions to Boiler & Cooling Water Problems. C. D. Schroeder. LC 85-80320. 250p. 1986. text ed. 44.95 (ISBN 0-88173-010-6). Fairmont Pr.
Solutions to Ethical & Legal Problems in Social Research: Symposium. Ed. by Robert F. Boruch & Joe S. Cecil. LC 83-2697. (Quantitative Studies in Social Relations). 335p. 1983. 38.00 (ISBN 0-12-118680-6). Acad Pr.
Solutions to Problems & Study Aids for Organic Chemistry. Gardner W. Stacy. 176p. 1982. write for info. Kendall-Hunt.
Solutions to Tesla's Secrets & the Soviet Tesla Weapons with Reference Articles for Solutions to Tesla's Secrets, 2 pts. T. E. Bearden. LC 81-85737. (Illus.). 188p. (Orig.). 1982. Set. pap. 14.00 (ISBN 0-9603536-3-1). Tesla Bk Co.
Solutions to Unemployment. David C. Colander. 229p. 1981. pap. text ed. 8.00 net (ISBN 0-15-582456-2, HC). HarBraceJ.
Solutions to Your Writing Problems. Arthur Traiger & Leon Gersten. LC 80-10089. 1980. pap. 6.95 (ISBN 0-8120-0873-1). Barron.

Solvability of Nonlinear Equations & Boundry Value Problems. Svatopluk Fucik. (Mathematics & Its Applications Ser.: No. 4). 400p. 1980. 29.95 (ISBN 90-277-1077-5, Pub. by Reidel Holland). Kluwer Academic.

Solvable Models in Quantum Mechanics. S. A. Albeverio et al. (Text & Monographs in Physics). 480p. 1988. 79.00 (ISBN 0-387-17841-4). Springer-Verlag.

Solvang: Denmark in the U. S. A. rev. ed. Elaine Kuehl. (Illus.). 48p. 1987. pap. 4.95 (ISBN 0-9618144-0-3). Trykkeri Pr.

Solvated Electron in Radiation Chemistry. A. K. Pikaev. 396p. 1971. text ed. 78.00x (ISBN 0-7065-1127-1, Pub. by Keter Pub Jerusalem). Coronet Bks.

Solvation: Ionic & Complex Formation in Non-Aqueous Solvents. K. Burger. (Studies in Analytical Chemistry: Vol. 6). 268p. 1983. 79.00 (ISBN 0-444-99697-4). Elsevier.

Solvation Thermodynamics. Arieh Ben-Naim. LC 87-21738. (Illus.). 260p. 1987. 49.50x (ISBN 0-306-42538-6, Plenum Pr). Plenum Pub.

Solvay Conferences on Physics: Aspects of the Development of Physics Since 1911. J. Mehra. LC 75-28332. 424p. 1976. lib. bdg. 79.00 (ISBN 90-277-0635-2, Pub. by Reidel Holland). Kluwer Academic.

Solve a Mystery: From the Casebook of J. P. Landers, Master Detective, Bk. 1. Marian Lee. LC 82-9712. (Illus.). (gr. 4 up). 1982. PLB 10.60 (ISBN 0-516-01991-0). Childrens.

Solve a Mystery: From the Casebook of J. P. Landers, Master Detective, Bk. 2. Marian Lee. LC 82-9712. (Illus.). (gr. 4 up). 1982. PLB 10.60 (ISBN 0-516-01992-9). Childrens.

Solve a Mystery: From the Casebook of J. P. Landers, Master Detective, Bk. 3. Marian Lee. LC 82-9712. (Illus.). (gr. 4 up). 1982. PLB 10.60 (ISBN 0-516-01993-7). Childrens.

Solve It. James Fixx. 128p. 1983. pap. 2.95 (ISBN 0-446-31080-8). Warner Bks.

Solve Your Child's Sleep Problems. Richard Ferber. 212p. 1985. 16.95 (ISBN 0-671-46027-7). S&S.

Solve Your Child's Sleep Problems. Richard Ferber. 1986. pap. 7.95 (ISBN 0-671-62099-1, Fireside). S&S.

Solve Your Own Business Problems: Staying Sane While Staying Solvent. Wendy M. Greenfield. (Illus.). 1988. 19.95 (ISBN 0-13-823212-1). P-H.

Solved & Unsolved Problems in Number Theory. 3rd, rev. ed. Daniel Shanks. LC 77-13010. vii, 304p. 1985. text ed. 18.95 (ISBN 0-8284-1297-9, 297). Chelsea Pub.

Solved: The Riddle of Heart Attacks. Broda Barnes. 1976. 5.95 (ISBN 0-913730-27-0). Robinson Pr.

Solved: The Riddle of Illness. Stephen Langer. 206p. (Orig.). 1984. 17.95 (ISBN 0-87983-370-X); pap. 9.95 (ISBN 0-87983-357-2). Keats.

Solvency: The Price of Survival. James Chace. LC 82-40159. 128p. 1982. pap. 3.95 (ISBN 0-394-71242-0, Vin). Random.

Solvent Abuse: The Adolescent Epidemic? Joyce M. Watson. 208p. 1986. 31.00 (ISBN 0-7099-3683-4, Pub. by Croom Helm Ltd); pap. 15.50 (ISBN 0-7099-3684-2, Pub. by Croom Helm Ltd). Routledge Chapman & Hall.

Solvent-Dependent Flexibility of Proteins & Principles of Their Function. Alex I. Kaivarainen. 1984. lib. bdg. 58.00 (ISBN 0-318-00436-4, Pub. by Reidel Holland). Kluwer Academic.

Solvent Effects in Organic Chemistry. Christian Reichardt. (Monographs in Modern Chemistry: Vol. 3). (Illus.). 355p. 1979. 69.00 (ISBN 0-89573-011-1). VCH Pubs.

Solvent Extraction Chemistry: Fundamentals & Applications. Tatsuya Sekine & Yuko Hasegawa. LC 75-32474. pap. 160.00 (2027118). Bks Demand UMI.

Solvent Extraction Plants. National Fire Protection Association Staff. 1985. 12.00 (ISBN 0-317-63070-9, 36-85). Natl Fire Prot.

Solvent Extraction Plants. (Thirty Ser). 60p. 1974. pap. 3.00 (ISBN 0-685-44168-7, 36). Natl Fire Prot.

Solvent Extraction: Principles & Applications to Process Metallurgy, Pt. 1. G. M. Ritcey et al. (Process Metallurgy Ser.: Vol. 1, Pt. 1). 362p. 1984. 108.00 (ISBN 0-444-41770-2). Elsevier.

Solvent Extraction: Principles & Applications to Process Metallurgy, Pt. 2. G. M. Ritcey & A. W. Ashbrook. (Process Metallurgy Ser.: Vol. 1, Pt. 2). 738p. 1979. 152.75 (ISBN 0-444-41771-0). Elsevier.

Solvent Extraction Research: Proceedings of the 5th International Conference on Solvent Extraction Chemistry, 1968. Ed. by A. S. Kertes & Y. Marcus. LC 75-99274. pap. 86.50 (ISBN 0-317-10523-X, 2055150). Bks Demand UMI.

Solvent Extraction Reviews, Vol. 1. Ed. by Y. Marcus. 1971. 69.75 (ISBN 0-8247-1438-5). Dekker.

Solvent Problems in Industry: Papers from the 3rd & 4th European Solvents Symposia, Manchester, U. K., 1980 & 1983. Ed. by G. Kakabadse. (Illus.). 251p. 1985. 66.75 (ISBN 0-85334-304-7, Pub. by Elsevier Applied Sci England). Elsevier.

Solvent Properties of Amphiphilic Compounds. Philip A. Winsor. LC 55-2032. pap. 54.30 (ISBN 0-317-09038-0, 2051334). Bks Demand UMI.

Solvent Properties of Surfactant Solutions. Ed. by Keozeo Shinoda. LC 68-1233. (Surfactant Science Ser.: Vol. 2). pap. 93.50 (ISBN 0-317-28559-9, 2055028). Bks Demand UMI.

Solvent Spun Rayon, Modified Cellulose Fibers & Derivatives. Ed. by Albin F. Turbak. LC 77-12220. (ACS Symposium Ser.: No. 58). 1977. 26.95 (ISBN 0-8412-0388-1). Am Chemical.

Solventless & High Solids Industrial Finishes: Recent Developments. Ed. by M. T. Gillies. LC 80-21553. (Chemical Technology Review: No. 179). (Illus.). 342p. 1981. 48.00 (ISBN 0-8155-0828-X). Noyes.

Solvents & Health Sciences: Subject Analysis with Bibliography. Judy P. Payter. LC 87-47635. 160p. 1987. 34.50 (ISBN 0-88164-572-9); pap. 26.50 (ISBN 0-88164-573-7). ABBE Pubs Assn.

Solvents Safety Handbook. Ed. by D. J. De Renzo. LC 86-5208. (Illus.). 696p. 1986. 86.00 (ISBN 0-8155-1074-8). Noyes.

Solving Accounting Problems Using Lotus 1-2-3. John G. Helmkamp et al. 128p. 1986. pap. write for info. (ISBN 0-471-84704-6). Wiley.

Solving Accounting Problems with Lotus 1-2-3 in Introductory Accounting. Donald E. Kieso et al. 183p. 1987. pap. write for info. (ISBN 0-471-62550-7). Wiley.

Solving Business Problems by Simulation. 2nd ed. Jan Szmankiewicz et al. 416p. 1988. 39.95 (ISBN 0-07-084946-3). McGraw.

Solving Business Problems on the Electronic Calculator. 2nd ed. M. K. Polisky & James R. Meehan. 256p. 1983. text ed. 15.56 (ISBN 0-07-041281-2). McGraw.

Solving Business Problems on the Electronic Calculator. 3rd ed. Mildred Polisky. 256p. 1988. pap. 14.68 (ISBN 0-07-041283-9). McGraw.

Solving Child Behavior Problems at Home & at School. Elaine A. Blechman. LC 85-61468. 300p. (Orig.). 1985. pap. 16.95 (ISBN 0-87822-247-2). Res Press.

Solving Cipher Secrets. M. E. Ohaver. 160p. 1983. lib. bdg. 26.80 (ISBN 0-89412-117-0). Aegean Park Pr.

Solving Coaching Problems: Strategies for Successful Team Development. Robert G. Hoehn. 225p. 1983. text ed. write for info. (ISBN 0-205-07818-4, Pub. by Longwood Div). Wm C Brown.

Solving Corrosion Problems in Air Pollution Control Equipment-1984. LC 84-62370. (Illus.). 479p. 1984. 35.00 (ISBN 0-915567-07-5). Natl Corrosion Eng.

Solving Corrosion Problems in Air Pollution Control Equipment-1981. (Illus.). 193p. 1981. 25.00 (ISBN 0-915567-49-0). Natl Corrosion Eng.

Solving Costly Organizational Conflicts: Achieving Intergroup Trust, Cooperation, & Teamwork. Robert R. Blake & Jane S. Mouton. LC 84-47980. (Management Ser.). 1984. 27.95x (ISBN 0-87589-612-X). Jossey-Bass.

Solving Discipline Problems: Strategies for Classroom Teachers. 2nd ed. Charles H. Wolfgang & Carl D. Glickman. 348p. 1986. 31.95 (ISBN 0-205-08630-6, 238630, Pub. by Longwood Div.). Allyn.

Solving Disputes Through Commercial Arbitration. Rodolphe J. De Seife. LC 87-23903. 166p. (Orig.). 1987. pap. 34.95 (ISBN 0-8366-0007-X). Callaghan.

Solving Educational Facility Problems. Theodore J. Kowalski. LC 83-70704. 250p. 1983. 20.95. Accel Devel.

Solving Educational Problems: The Theory & Reality of Innovation in Developing Countries. R. G. Havelock & A. M. Huberman. (IBE Studies & Surveys in Comparative Education). (Illus.). 308p. (A Study prepared for the International Bureau of Education, reprinted 1983. Co-published with OISE, Toronto). 1978. pap. 13.75 (ISBN 92-3-101527-3, U839, UNESCO). UNIPUB.

Solving Educational Problems: The Theory & Reality of Innovation in Developing Countries. Ronald G. Havelock & A. M. Huberman. LC 78-52224. (Praeger Special Studies). 320p. 1978. 35.00 (ISBN 0-275-90298-6, C0298). Praeger.

Solving EEO Problems. 1980. pap. 5.95 (ISBN 0-917386-36-1). Exec Ent Pubns.

Solving Elliptic Problems Using ELLPACK. J. Rice & R. F. Boisvert. (Springer Series in Computational Mathematics: Vol. 2). (Illus.). 350p. 1985. 43.00 (ISBN 0-387-90910-9). Springer Verlag.

Solving Equations in Integers. A. O. Gelfond. 56p. 1981. pap. 2.00 (ISBN 0-8285-2053-4, Pub. by Mir Pubs USSR). Imported Pubns.

Solving Equations: Level Three Texts. rev. ed. (Math Components Ser.). 48p. 1983. 3.50 (ISBN 0-88336-831-5). New Readers.

Solving Equations with Physical Understanding. J. R. Acton & P. T. Squire. (Illus.). 230p. 1985. 80.00x (ISBN 0-85274-757-8, Pub. by A Hilger UK); pap. 41.00x (ISBN 0-85274-799-3, Pub. by A Hilger UK). Taylor & Francis.

Solving Ethical Problems. Murray Friedman. 0.50 (ISBN 0-914131-58-3, I38). Torah Umesorah.

Solving Financial Accounting Problems Using Lotus 1-2-3. Leroy F. Imdieke et al. 1988. write for info. (ISBN 0-471-61226-X); Computerized Practice Set. disk incl. (ISBN 0-471-61947-7); book-disk pack avail. (ISBN 0-471-85588-X). Wiley.

Solving Gap Management. 47p. 1984. 20.00 (ISBN 0-929097-28-9, 16915). US League Savi Inst.

Solving General Chemistry Problems. 5th ed. R. Nelson Smith & Conway Pierce. LC 79-23677. (Illus.). 474p. 1980. pap. text ed. 14.95x (ISBN 0-7167-1117-6); answers to b group avail. W H Freeman.

Solving Geometric Originals. Frank C. Touton. LC 76-177698. (Columbia University. Teachers College. Contributions to Education: No. 146). Repr. of 1924 ed. 22.50 (ISBN 0-404-55146-7). AMS Pr.

Solving German Codes in World War I. William F. Friedman. (Cryptographic Ser.). 1977. pap. 16.80 (ISBN 0-89412-019-0); lib. bdg. 24.80 (ISBN 0-89412-118-9). Aegean Park Pr.

Solving Ground Water Problems with Models, Vols. I & II. 1987. Set. 87.50 (ISBN 0-318-22985-4). Natl Water Well.

Solving Hazardous Waste Problems: Learning from Dioxins. Ed. by Jurgen Exner. LC 87-1389. (Symposium Ser.: No. 338). (Illus.). x, 397p. 1987. 79.95 (ISBN 0-8412-1025-X). Am Chemical.

Solving in Style. John Nunn. 220p. 1985. 16.95 (ISBN 0-04-794020-4). Unwin Hyman.

Solving Inexact Search Problems. M. M. Botvinnik. Tr. by A. A. Brown. (Symbolic Computation). (Illus.). 255p. 1984. 31.00 (ISBN 0-387-90869-2). Springer-Verlag.

Solving Learning & Behavior Problems of Children: A Planning System to Integrate Assessment & Treatment. Mark N. Ozer. LC 79-28316. (Social & Behavioral Science Ser.). 1980. text ed. 32.95x (ISBN 0-87589-445-3). Jossey-Bass.

Solving Least Squares Problems. Charles L. Lawson & Richard J. Hanson. (Illus.). 384p. 1974. 58.00 (ISBN 0-13-822585-0). P-H.

Solving Life Problems. Incl. Community Resources Level I. Marie Talbot. 1980. pap. text ed. 5.95 (ISBN 0-07-062643-X); Community Resources Level II. Keiselbach. 1980. pap. text ed. 5.95 (ISBN 0-07-033471-4); Community Resources Level III. Donna Blitzer. 1980. pap. text ed. 5.95 (ISBN 0-07-005901-2); Consumer Economics, Level I. Lorre Sintetos. 1980. pap. text ed. 5.95 (ISBN 0-07-057681-5); Consumer Economics, Level II. Donna Blitzer et al. 1980; Consumer Economics Level III. Theodore Silveira. 1980. pap. text ed. 5.95 (ISBN 0-07-057455-3); Government and Law Level I. Catherine Boxer. 1980. pap. text ed. 5.95 (ISBN 0-07-006851-8); Government and Law Level II. Jones & Clark. 1980. pap. text ed. 5.95 (ISBN 0-07-032783-1); Government and Law Level III. Lee Stolmack. 1980. pap. text ed. 5.95 (ISBN 0-07-061670-1); Health, Level I. Robert H. London & Janet London. 1980; Health, Level II. Robert H. London & Janet London. 1980; Health, Level III. Diane Joyce. 1980; Occupational Knowledge, Level I. Mary J. Cook. 1980. pap. text ed. 5.95 (ISBN 0-07-012485-X); Occupational Knowledge, Level II. Joan Jones. 1980. pap. text ed. 5.95 (ISBN 0-07-032778-5); Occupational Knowledge, Level III. Joan Jones. 1980. pap. text ed. 5.95 (ISBN 0-07-032779-3). (McGraw-Hill Paperbacks). 1980. pap. McGraw.

Solving Life's Problems. Paul Y. Cho. LC 80-62782. 142p. (Orig.). 1980. pap. 5.95 (ISBN 0-88270-450-8). Bridge Pub.

Solving Local Government Problems: Practical Applications of Operations Research in Cities & Regions. Charles E. Pinkus & Anne Dixson. (Illus.). 304p. 1981. pap. text ed. 29.95x (ISBN 0-04-658233-9). Unwin Hyman.

Solving Managerial Problems Using Lotus 1-2-3. Groomer. 1987. pap. write for info. (ISBN 0-471-85593-6). Wiley.

Solving Marriage Problems. Jay E. Adams. LC 83-17653. 132p. 1983. pap. 4.50 (ISBN 0-87552-081-2). Presby & Reformed.

Solving Marriage Problems: Biblical Solutions for Christian Counselors. Jay E. Adams. (Jay Adams Library). 144p. 1986. pap. 4.95 (ISBN 0-310-51081-3, 12120P). Zondervan.

Solving Math Word Problems for Students & Adults. Harold Schneider. 1965. 5.75 (ISBN 0-911642-01-3). Word-Fraction.

Solving Noise & Transmission Problems in Telephone Loop Plant. Roger F. Tokarz. (Illus.). 1983. 10.00 (ISBN 0-317-06293-X). Intertec IL.

Solving of Problem-Situations by Preschool Children. Augusta Alpert. LC 74-176514. (Columbia University. Teachers College. Contributions to Education: No. 323). Repr. of 1928 ed. 22.50 (ISBN 0-404-55323-0). AMS Pr.

Solving Offset Ink Problems. Nelson R. Eldred. LC 86-83038. 96p. 1987. 28.00 (ISBN 0-88362-090-1, 1310). Graphic Arts Tech Found.

Solving Ordinary Differential Equations I. E. Hairer et al. (Springer Series in Computational Mathematics: Vol. 8). (Illus.). xiv, 480p. 1986. 69.00 (ISBN 0-387-17145-2). Springer-Verlag.

Solving Plant Problems: Design, Operation, Maintenance. Ed. by William O'Keefe & Thomas C. Elliott. LC 84-12605. (Illus.). 272p. 1985. text ed. 34.50 (ISBN 0-07-050585-3). McGraw.

Solving Polynomial Systems Using Continuation for Engineering & Science Problems. Alexander Morgan. (Illus.). 384p. 1987. text ed. 54.00 (ISBN 0-13-822313-0). P-H.

Solving Problems in Algebra & Trigonometry. V. Litvinenko & A. Mordkovich. 312p. 1987. 8.95 (ISBN 0-8285-3763-1, Pub. by Mir Pubs USSR). Imported Pubns.

Solving Problems in Analytical Chemistry. Stephen Brewer. LC 79-17164. 538p. 1980. pap. text ed. write for info. (ISBN 0-471-04098-3). Wiley.

Solving Problems in Chemistry. Gary K. Himes et al. Ed. by Ellen Lappa. (Illus.). (gr. 10-12). 1983. pap. text ed. 7.60 (ISBN 0-675-06399-X). Merrill.

Solving Problems in Electrical Power & Power Electronics. Harold F. Gwyther. (Solving Problems Ser.). 272p. 1988. pap. 31.95 (ISBN 0-470-21053-2). Wiley.

Solving Problems in Fluid Mechanics, 2 vols. John F. Douglas. 1986. Vol. 1. pap. 18.95 (ISBN 0-470-20775-2); Vol. 2. pap. 18.95 (ISBN 0-470-20776-0). Wiley.

Solving Problems in Meetings. James D. Jorgensen et al. LC 79-21782. 112p. 1981. 16.95x (ISBN 0-88229-521-7). Nelson-Hall.

Solving Problems in Soil Mechanics. Benjamin H. Sutton. (Solving Problems Ser.). 234p. 1986. pap. 24.95 (ISBN 0-470-20691-8, Co-Pub. with Longman). Wiley.

Solving Problems in Solid Mechanics, 2 vols. S. A. Urry & P. J. Turner. (Solving Problems Ser.). 1986. Vol. 1. pap. 24.95 (ISBN 0-470-20686-1, Co-Pub. with Longman); Vol. 2. pap. 24.95 (ISBN 0-470-20687-X, Co-Pub. with Longman). Wiley.

Solving Problems in Structures, Vol. 1. P. C. Croxton & L. H. Martin. LC 87-2667. (Solving Problems Ser.). 319p. 1987. pap. 28.95 (ISBN 0-470-20797-3, Co-Pub. with Longman). Wiley.

Solving Problems in Technical Writing. LynnDianne Beene & Peter White. (Illus.). 272p. 1988. 29.95 (ISBN 0-19-505330-3); pap. text ed. 11.95 (ISBN 0-19-505331-1). Oxford U Pr.

Solving Problems in Vibrations. J. S. Anderson & M. Bratos-Anderson. 222p. 1987. pap. 23.95 (ISBN 0-470-20774-4, Co-Pub. with Longman). Wiley.

Solving Problems Kids Care About. Randall Souviney. (Illus.). 1981. pap. 11.95 (ISBN 0-673-16534-5). Scott F.

Solving Problems on Concurrent Processors, Vol. I: General Techniques & Regular Problems. G. Fox et al. (Illus.). 432p. 1988. text ed. 48.00 (ISBN 0-13-823022-6). P-H.

Solving Problems Together. Hogie Wyckoff. LC 80-1003. 272p. 1980. pap. 7.95 (ISBN 0-394-17739-8, E 767, Ever). Grove.

Solving Production-Management. (Problems Ser. 1965-1967). 45p. 50.00 (ISBN 0-318-19671-9). Clothing Mfrs.

Solving Psychic Problems. Manly P. Hall. pap. 2.50 (ISBN 0-89314-354-5). Philos Res.

Solving Rebar Corrosion Problems in Concrete: Proceedings. (Illus.). 147p. 1983. pap. 25.00 (ISBN 0-915567-99-7, 52165). Natl Corrosion Eng.

Solving Sheetfed Offset Press Problems. 2nd ed. Lloyd DeJidas et al. LC 86-830391. 140p. 1987. 37.00 (ISBN 0-88362-089-8). Graphic Arts Tech Found.

Solving Somebody Else's Blues: A Study of Police Mediation Activities. Paul E. Lawson. LC 81-40881. (Illus.). 246p. (Orig.). 1982. lib. bdg. 29.25 (ISBN 0-8191-2173-8); pap. text ed. 13.25 (ISBN 0-8191-2174-6). U Pr of Amer.

Solving Statue of Limitations Problems. Adolph J. Levy. LC 87-32509. (Kluwer Litigation Library). 831p. 1987. text ed. 80.00 (ISBN 0-930273-65-6). Kluwer Law Bk.

Solving the Literacy Mystery. Raymond E. Laurita. 287p. (Orig.). 1983. pap. 14.95 (ISBN 0-914051-01-6). Leonardo Pr.

Solving the Ministry's Toughest Problems, 2 vols. Ed. by Stephen Strang et al. 432p. 1984. Vol. I. 24.95 (ISBN 0-930525-00-0); Vol. II. write for info. (ISBN 0-930525-01-9). Strang Comms Co.

Solving the Mystery of the Miracle Money. Robert Tilton. 74p. 1987. pap. 6.95 (ISBN 0-914307-66-5). Word Faith.

Solving the Problem of Medicare. Peter Ferrara et al. 1984. 10.00 (ISBN 0-943802-11-3). Natl Ctr Pol.

Solving the Puzzle of Your Hard to Raise Child. William G. Crook & Laura J. Stevens. LC 87-9652. (Illus.). 352p. 1987. 17.95 (ISBN 0-394-56054-X). Random.

Solving the Riddle of the Shakespeare Sphinx. Marie B. Hall. Date not set. pap. 18.50 (ISBN 0-938760-09-2). Veritat Found.

Solving the U. S. Energy Problem. Ernest J. Oppenheimer. 50p. (Orig.). 1984. pap. 5.00 (ISBN 0-9603982-4-4). Pen & Podium.

Solving Urban Location Problems: Human Intuition Versus the Computer. Jerry B. Schneider. (Discussion Paper Ser.: No. 40). 1970. pap. 6.50 (ISBN 0-686-32209-6). Regional Sci Res Inst.

Solving Word Problems in Algebra: A Systematic Method. Lionel J. Soracco, Jr. Ed. by William Leschensky. (Illus.). 71p. (gr. 8-12). 1981. duplicating masters, manual & 16 cassettes 284.50 (ISBN 0-917792-07-6). Math Hse.

Solving Word Problems in the Primary Grades: Addition & Subtraction. Miriam M. Feinberg. LC 88-9964. (Illus.). 40p. 1988. pap. 7.00 (ISBN 0-87353-255-4). NCTM.

Solving World Hunger: The U. S. Stake. E. Boyd Wennergren et al. (Illus.). 112p. 1986. pap. 7.95 (ISBN 0-932020-42-9). Seven Locks Pr.

Some Aspects of Indonesian Politics under the Japanese Occupation: 1944-1945. Benedict R. Anderson. LC 61-66733. (Cornell University Modern Indosnesia Project Interim Reports Ser.). pap. 34.00 (ISBN 0-317-11172-8, 2010810). Bks Demand UMI.

Some Aspects of Industrial Finance in India. George Rosen. LC 62-11761. 1962. 6.00 (ISBN 0-02-926910-5). Free Pr.

Some Aspects of Instinctive Life. E. L. Grant-Watson. 1985. 10.00x (ISBN 0-317-62167-X, Guild of Pastoral Psych). State Mutual Bk.

Some Aspects of International Library Cooperation. Ernest C. Richardson. 1977. lib. bdg. 75.00. Gordon Pr.

Some Aspects of Irish Emigration from Ireland to the North American Colonies Between 1660-1775. Audrey Lockhart. LC 76-6351. (Irish Americans Ser.). 1976. 20.00 (ISBN 0-405-09345-4). Ayer Co Pubs.

Some Aspects of Islamic Culture. 3.00 (ISBN 0-686-83584-0). Kazi Pubns.

Some Aspects of Italian Economic Affairs 1940-1943, with Particular Reference to Italian Relations with Germany. Angela Raspin. (Outstanding Theses from the London School of Economics Ser.). 475p. 1987. lib. bdg. 75.00 (ISBN 0-8240-1929-6). Garland Pub.

Some Aspects of Italian Immigration to the United States. Antonio Stella. LC 74-17956. (Italian American Experience Ser). 178p. 1975. Repr. 16.00x (ISBN 0-405-06425-X). Ayer Co Pubs.

Some Aspects of Kipling's Verse. A. Rutherford. (Chatterton Lectures on an English Poet). 1965. pap. 2.25 (ISBN 0-85672-259-6, Pub. by British Acad). Longwood Pub Group.

Some Aspects of Labor Mobility in Bombay City. P. Ramachandran. 1974. 9.50 (ISBN 0-89684-508-7). Orient Bk Dist.

Some Aspects of Medical Geography. L. Dudley Stamp. (Heath Clark Lectures, 1962). (Illus.). 103p. 1964. 29.50 (ISBN 0-485-26315-7, Pub. by Athlone Pr UK). Humanities.

Some Aspects of Mughal Architecture. R. Nath. LC 76-902803. 1976. 38.50x (ISBN 0-88386-825-3). South Asia Bks.

Some Aspects of Orthodox Spirituality. pap. 0.25 (ISBN 0-686-02578-4). Eastern Orthodox.

Some Aspects of Pediatric Anaesthesia. Ed. by D. J. Steward. (Monographs in Anaesthesiology: Vol. 10). 370p. 1982. 148.00 (ISBN 0-444-80327-0, Biomedical Pr). Elsevier.

Some Aspects of Planning Control see Business Management: 1.

Some Aspects of Population Growth, Trade & Factor Mobility. Andre Sapir. (Working Paper: No. 694). 56p. 1985. 5.00 (ISBN 0-8213-0476-3, 0694). World Bank.

Some Aspects of Portuguese Colonization & Sea Trade in West Africa in the 15th & 16th Centuries. A. Teixeira Da Mota. (Hans Wolff Memorial Lecture Ser.). 29p. (Orig.). 1978. pap. text ed. 2.50 (ISBN 0-941934-22-5). Indiana Africa.

Some Aspects of Professional Freedom of Teachers: An International Pilot Inquiry. Ben Morris. (Monographs on Education: No. 9). 213p. 1977. pap. 6.00 (ISBN 92-3-101424-2, U781, UNESCO). UNIPUB.

Some Aspects of Prophet Muhammad's Life. Ed. by M. Tariq Quaraishi. LC 83-71409. 89p. (Orig.). 1985. pap. 4.50 (ISBN 0-89259-045-9). Am Trust Pubns.

Some Aspects of Relative Poverty in Sri Lanka 1969-70. Pravin Visaria. (World Bank Staff Working Paper: No. 461). xii, 242p. 1981. 15.00 (ISBN 0-686-39733-9, WP-0461). World Bank.

Some Aspects of Self-Insight As Found in Students of a Two-Year Normal School. Robert W. Shaw. LC 70-178811. (Columbia University. Teachers College. Contributions to Education: No. 448). Repr. of 1931 ed. 22.50 (ISBN 0-404-55448-2). AMS Pr.

Some Aspects of Shakespeare's Sonnets. S. P. Sengupta. 1966. text ed. 20.00. Coronet Bks.

Some Aspects of Socio-Economic & Community Factors in Planning Urban Freeway. Kwame P. Annor. 27p. (Orig.). 1970. pap. 2.50 (ISBN 1-55719-047-X). U NE Ctr Applied Urban Rsch.

Some Aspects of Text Grammars: A Study in Theoretical Linguistics & Poetics. Teun A. Van Dijk. (Janua Linguarum, Ser. Major: No. 63). 375p. 1972. text ed. 40.80x (ISBN 0-686-22546-5). Mouton.

Some Aspects of Thackeray. Lewis Melville. 1911. Repr. 25.00 (ISBN 0-8274-3449-9). R West.

Some Aspects of the American Short Stories. W. E. Allen. (Sarah Tryphena Phillips Lectures in American Literature & History). 1973. pap. 5.50 (ISBN 0-85672-085-2, Pub. by British Acad). Longwood Pub Group.

Some Aspects of the Diction of English Poetry. Henry C. Wyld. LC 73-12461. 1933. lib. bdg. 20.50 (ISBN 0-8414-9404-5). Folcroft.

Some Aspects of the Economics of Zakah. AMSS Staff. 1984. 3.50 (ISBN 0-89259-019-X). Am Trust Pubns.

Some Aspects of the Effect of the Dominant American Culture Upon Children of Italian-Born Parents. Joseph W. Tait. LC 77-177729. (Columbia University. Teachers College. Contributions to Education: No. 866). Repr. of 1942 ed. 22.50 (ISBN 0-404-55866-6). AMS Pr.

Some Aspects of the Effect of the Dominant American Culture Upon Children of Italian-Born Parents. Joseph W. Tait. LC 72-81351. (Illus.). 1972. Repr. of 1942 ed. lib. bdg. 15.00x (ISBN 0-678-00919-8). Kelley.

Some Aspects of the Foundations of General Equilibrium Theory: The Posthumous Papers of Peter J. Kalman. Ed. by J. R. Green. LC 78-14520. (Lecture Notes in Economics & Mathematical Systems: Vol. 159). 1978. pap. 14.00 (ISBN 0-387-08918-7). Springer-Verlag.

Some Aspects of the Genius of Giovanni Boccaccio. Edward Hutton. 1977. lib. bdg. 59.95 (ISBN 0-8490-2625-3). Gordon Pr.

Some Aspects of the Genius of Giovanni Boccaccio. Edward Hutton. 1922. 10.00 (ISBN 0-8274-3450-2). R West.

Some Aspects of the Geography of Manipur. S. A. Ansari. (Illus.). 131p. 1985. text ed. 25.00x (ISBN 0-86590-583-5, Pub. by B R Pub Corp Delhi). Apt Bks.

Some Aspects of the Greek Genius. S. H. Butcher. 1975. Repr. of 1891 ed. 14.50 (ISBN 0-8274-4044-8). R West.

Some Aspects of the Greek Genius. Samuel H. Butcher. LC 79-101552. 1969. Repr. of 1891 ed. 28.50x (ISBN 0-8046-0721-4, Pub. by Kennikat). Assoc Faculty Pr.

Some Aspects of the Islamic Economy. M. N. Siddiqui. pap. 2.00 (ISBN 0-686-18378-9). Kazi Pubns.

Some Aspects of the Lexical Structure of a Mazatec Historical Text. George M. Cowan. (Publications in Linguistics & Related Fields Ser.: No. 11). 146p. 1965. pap. 1.95 (ISBN 0-88312-011-9); microfiche (2) 4.00 (ISBN 0-88312-411-4). Summer Inst Ling.

Some Aspects of the Life & Works of James Augustine Joyce. Peter Allt. 1978. Repr. lib. bdg. 15.50 (ISBN 0-8495-0111-3). Arden Lib.

Some Aspects of the Life & Works of James Augustine Joyce. Peter Allt. 50p. 1980. Repr. of 1942 ed. lib. bdg. 15.00 (ISBN 0-89987-026-0). Darby Bks.

Some Aspects of the Life & Works of James Augustine Joyce. Peter Allt. LC 74-2083. 1952. lib. bdg. 15.00 (ISBN 0-8414-2962-6). Folcroft.

Some Aspects of the Multinational Corporation's Exposure to the Exchange Rate Risk. Hassanand T. Jadwani. Ed. by Stuart Bruchey. LC 80-576. (Multinational Corporations Ser.). (Illus.). 1980. lib. bdg. 21.00x (ISBN 0-405-13369-3). Ayer Co Pubs.

Some Aspects of the Optimal Control of Distributed Parameter Systems. J. L. Lions. (CBMS-NSF Regional Conference Ser.: No. 6). vi, 92p. (Orig.). 1972. pap. text ed. 11.50 (ISBN 0-89871-004-9). Soc Indus-Appl Math.

Some Aspects of the Problem of Small Enterprise As Seen in Four Selected Industries. Harold G. Vatter. LC 77-14789. (Dissertations in American Economic History Ser.). 1978. 53.00 (ISBN 0-405-11060-X). Ayer Co Pubs.

Some Aspects of the Religious Music of the United States Negro. George R. Ricks. Ed. by Richard M. Dorson. LC 77-70621. (International Folklore Ser.). 1977. Repr. of 1977 ed. lib. bdg. 36.50x (ISBN 0-405-10123-6). Ayer Co Pubs.

Some Aspects of the Tariff Question. 3rd ed. Frank W. Taussig. LC 68-58025. 1972. Repr. of 1931 ed. lib. bdg. 45.00x (ISBN 0-678-00734-9). Kelley.

Some Aspects of the Tariff Question: An Examination of the Development of American Industries Under Protection. Frank W. Taussig. LC 72-137297. Repr. of 1931 ed. 13.00 (ISBN 0-404-06348-9). AMS Pr.

Some Aspects of the Technique of Japanese Painting. Charles Holme. 1901. 112.00x (ISBN 0-317-69095-7, Pub. by Han-Shan Tang Ltd). State Mutual Bk.

Some Aspects of the Victorian Age. H. H. Asquith. LC 74-13333. 1918. lib. bdg. 15.00 (ISBN 0-8414-2997-9). Folcroft.

Some Aspects of Vacuum Ultraviolet Radiation Physics. Boris Vodar & J. Romand. LC 73-20163. 1974. 71.00 (ISBN 0-08-016984-8). Pergamon.

Some Aspects of Vedanta Philosophy. Swami Siddheswarananda. Tr. by Krishna Bhakti & K. Narayana Marar. 318p. (Orig.). 1976. pap. 4.50 (ISBN 0-87481-471-5). Vedanta Pr.

Some Aspects of Wheat & Rice Price Policy in India. Raj Krishna & G. S. Raychaudhuri. (Working Paper: No. 381). 62p. 1980. 5.00 (ISBN 0-686-36078-6, WP-0381); pap. 3.00 o. p. (ISBN 0-686-39646-4, WP-0381). World Bank.

Some Australian Poets. facsimile ed. Archie J. Coombes. LC 76-107688. (Essay Index Reprint Ser). 1938. 12.00 (ISBN 0-8369-1492-9). Ayer Co Pubs.

Some Authors. facs. ed. Walter A. Raleigh. LC 68-55855. (Essay Index Reprint Ser). 1923. 20.00 (ISBN 0-8369-0807-4). Ayer Co Pubs.

Some Baha'is to Remember. O. Z. Whitehead. (Illus.). 304p. 18.50 (ISBN 0-85398-147-7); pap. 10.50 (ISBN 0-85398-148-5). G Ronald Pub.

Some Ballad Folks. Thomas G. Burton. LC 78-56937. 1978. pap. 5.00 (ISBN 0-913239-22-4); with cassette 7.00 (ISBN 0-913239-23-2). Appalach Consortium.

Some Basic Concepts in Mathematics for the Non-Math Major. Norman E. Cromack. 216p. 1986. pap. text ed. 17.95 (ISBN 0-8403-4187-3). Kendall-Hunt.

Some Basic Hypergeometric Orthogonal Polynomials that Generalize Jacobi Polynomials. R. Askey & J. Wilson. LC 84-28117. (Memoirs of the AMS Ser.: No. 319). 56p. 1985. pap. text ed. 12.00. Am Math.

Some Basic Rights of Soviet Citizens. Franklin Folsom. 166p. 1983. 16.25x (ISBN 0-317-53854-3, Pub. by Collets (UK)). State Mutual Bk.

Some Basic Theory for Statistical Inference. E. J. Pitman. LC 78-11921. (Monographs on Applied Probability & Statistics). 105p. 1979. 21.00x (ISBN 0-412-21720-1, 6221, Pub. by Chapman & Hall England). Routledge Chapman & Hall.

Some Beekeepers & Associates, Pt. I. Joseph O. Moffett. (Illus.). 140p. lib. bdg. 19.90 (ISBN 0-686-31814-5); pap. 9.90 (ISBN 0-686-28741-X). Moffett.

Some Bibliographical Notes on the Novels of George Bernard Shaw. Maurice Holmes. LC 77-4041. lib. bdg. 15.50 (ISBN 0-8414-4921-X). Folcroft.

Some Birds Have Funny Names. Diana H. Cross. LC 80-28168. (Illus.). (gr. k-3). 1981. lib. bdg. 7.95 (ISBN 0-517-54005-3). Crown.

Some Blood: Joint Poems. C. Mehrl Bennett & John M. Bennett. 16p. 1982. signed & lettered ed. 8.00 (ISBN 0-935350-08-X); pap. 3.00 (ISBN 0-935350-07-1). Luna Bisonte.

Some Book-Hunting Adventures. R. S. Garnett. 1973. Repr. of 1931 ed. 30.00 (ISBN 0-8274-0197-3). R West.

Some Book-Hunting Adventures: Diversion (Shakespeare, Shelley) R. S. Garnett. 1978. Repr. of 1931 ed. lib. bdg. 25.00 (ISBN 0-8495-1942-X). Arden Lib.

Some Boone Descendants & Kindred of the St. Charles district. Lilian H. Oliver. LC 84-70107. 442p. 1984. pap. 33.00 (ISBN 0-939052-02-4). Dean Pubns.

Some British Pioneers of Social Medicine. Major Greenwood. LC 71-126320. (Biography Index Reprint Ser.: London University Heath Clark Lectures, 1946). Repr. of 1948 ed. 14.00 (ISBN 0-8369-8026-3). Ayer Co Pubs.

Some Buried Caesar. Rex Stout. 15.95 (ISBN 0-89190-340-2, Pub. by Am REpr). Amereon Ltd.

Some Business Recently Transacted in the White World. Edward Dorn. 83p. (Orig.). 1971. pap. 2.00 (ISBN 0-686-05069-X). Frontier Press Calif.

Some Call It Heresy. Martin Weber. Ed. by Raymond Woolsey. 128p. (Orig.). 1985. pap. 6.95 (ISBN 0-8280-0248-7). Review & Herald.

Some Call It Perjury. Linda DuBreuil. 1979. pap. 1.75 (ISBN 0-8439-0633-2, Leisure Bks). Leisure NY.

Some Cambridge Controversies in the Theory of Capital. Geoffrey Harcourt. LC 71-161294. pap. 70.50 (ISBN 0-317-20586-2, 2024469). Bks Demand UMI.

Some Catholic Novelists. facs. ed. Patrick Braybrooke. LC 67-22078. (Essay Index Reprint Ser.). 1931. 19.00 (ISBN 0-8369-1323-X). Ayer Co Pubs.

Some Catholic Novelists: Their Art & Outlook. P. Braybrooke. 59.95 (ISBN 0-8490-1075-6). Gordon Pr.

Some Celebrities in Verse. Patrick Braybrooke. Repr. 15.00 (ISBN 0-8274-3451-0). R West.

Some Cemetery Records of Abbeville County, South Carolina. South Carolina, WPA. LC 82-82909. 105p. 1982. pap. 7.50 (ISBN 0-8063-0997-0). Genealog Pub.

Some Ceramic Wares Reportedly Excavated Near Changsha. Isaac Newton. 1953. 20.00x (ISBN 0-317-45246-0, Pub. by Han-Shan Tang Ltd). State Mutual Bk.

Some Champions: Previously Uncollected Autobiographical Sketches & Fiction. Ring Lardner. Intro. by Matthew J. Bruccoli & Richard Layman. 208p. 1976. pap. 3.95 (ISBN 0-684-15065-4, ScribT). Scribner.

Some Chapters on Money. Fred M. Taylor. LC 79-1594. 1981. Repr. of 1906 ed. 25.75 (ISBN 0-88355-899-8). Hyperion Conn.

Some Characteristics of Poverty-U. S. A. 1985. pap. 2.35x (ISBN 0-8395-3632-1, 3632). BSA.

Some Characteristics of Scots Literature. James C. Smith. 1973. lib. bdg. 22.00 (ISBN 0-8414-1537-4). Folcroft.

Some Characteristics of Scott's Poetry in Our Early Female Novelists. A. M. Williams. 1973. Repr. of 1904 ed. 20.00 (ISBN 0-8274-0564-2). R West.

Some Chatham Neighbors of Yesterday. Ruth H. Foley. (Illus.). 76p. 1984. pap. 4.95 (ISBN 0-9613694-0-X). Thompson Forbes Co.

Some Chemicals Used in Plastics & Elastomers. (IARC Monographs on the Evaluation of the Carcinogenic Risk of Chemicals to Humans: Vol. 39). 403p. 1986. pap. 36.00 (ISBN 92-832-1239-8). World Health.

Some Chinese Ghosts. Lafcadio Hearn. 1972. Repr. of 1887 ed. lib. bdg. 29.95 (ISBN 0-8422-8074-X). Irvington.

Some Chinese Ghosts. Lafcadio Hearn. 203p. 1907. 140.00x (ISBN 0-317-69099-X, Pub. by Han-Shan Tang Ltd). State Mutual Bk.

Some Chinese Porcelain Services Ordered by the Swedish Count in the 18th Century. 10.00x (ISBN 0-317-45249-5, Pub. by Han-Shan Tang Ltd). State Mutual Bk.

Some Choose Hell. (S.O.B. Ser.: No. 9). Date not set. pap. 2.50 (Pub. by Worldwide). Harlequin Bks.

Some Christian Convictions: A Practical Restatement in Terms of Present-Day Thinking. Henry S. Coffin. LC 79-167328. (Essay Index Reprint Ser.). Repr. of 1915 ed. 17.00 (ISBN 0-8369-2763-X). Ayer Co Pubs.

Some Classes of Singular Equations. Prossdorf. (Mathematical Library: Vol. 17). 418p. 1978. 110.75 (ISBN 0-7204-0501-7, North-Holland). Elsevier.

Some Code Controls of School Building Construction in American Cities: An Evaluation of Certain Building Code Requirements. John W. Sahlstrom. LC 70-177222. (Columbia University. Teachers College. Contributions to Education: No. 581). Repr. of 1933 ed. 22.50 (ISBN 0-404-55581-0). AMS Pr.

Some Collected Writings. Tom Hendricks. (Illus.). 355p. 1986. 50.00 (ISBN 0-933987-09-9). T M H Pub Co.

Some Colonial Dames of Royal Descent: Pedigrees Showing Lineal Descent from Kings of Some Members of the National Society of the Colonial Dames of America, & of the Order of the Crown. Charles H. Browning. LC 76-81187. 360p. 1969. Repr. of 1900 ed. 20.00 (ISBN 0-8063-0057-4). Genealog Pub.

Some Communications of Broad Reference. Laura R. Jackson. 50p. 1983. limited signed 75.00 (ISBN 0-935716-22-X). Lord John.

Some Comparative Aspects of Irish Law. Alfred G. Donaldson. LC 57-8815. (Duke University. Commonwealth-Studies Center. Publication: No. 3). pap. 76.80 (ISBN 0-317-41731-2, 2023376). Bks Demand UMI.

Some Comparative Aspects of Law Relating to Sale of Goods. (International & Comparative Law Quarterly Supplement Publication Ser.: No. 9). pap. 11.00 (ISBN 0-8115-3230-5). Kraus Repr.

Some Composers of Opera. facsimile ed. Dyneley Hussey. LC 79-167360. (Essay Index Reprint Ser). Repr. of 1952 ed. 12.00 (ISBN 0-8369-2654-4). Ayer Co Pubs.

Some Concepts & Consequences of the Theory of Government & Binding. Noam Chomsky. (Linguistic Inquiry Monographs). 96p. 1982. 25.00x (ISBN 0-262-03090-X); pap. text ed. 8.95x (ISBN 0-262-53042-2). MIT Pr.

Some Concepts of Indian Culture. N. A. Nikam. 212p. 1980. 15.95. Asia Bk Corp.

Some Consideration upon Clandestine Marriages. Henry Gally. LC 83-48583. (Marrige, Sex & the Family in England Ser.). 265p. 1984. lib. bdg. 30.00 (ISBN 0-8240-5904-2). Garland Pub.

Some Considerations for the Management of Coastal Lagoon & Estuarine Fisheries. James M. Kapetsky. (Fisheries Technical Papers: No. 218). 54p. (Eng., Fr. & Span.). 1981. pap. 7.50 (ISBN 92-5-101136-2, F2260, FAO). UNIPUB.

Some Considerations on the Keeping of Negroes. John Woolman. LC 77-82231. (Anti-Slavery Crusade in America Ser). 1969. Repr. of 1800 ed. 11.50 (ISBN 0-405-00670-5). Ayer Co Pubs.

Some Contemporary American Poets. John G. Fletcher. 1978. Repr. of 1920 ed. lib. bdg. 15.00 (ISBN 0-8495-1620-X). Arden Lib.

Some Contemporary American Poets. John G. Fletcher. LC 75-1170. 1973. lib. bdg. 15.00 (ISBN 0-8414-4223-1). Folcroft.

Some Contemporary Americans. Percy H. Boynton. LC 66-23516. 1924. 15.00 (ISBN 0-8196-0181-0). Biblo.

Some Contemporary Dramatists. Graham Sutton. LC 67-27655. Repr. of 1925 ed. 24.50x (ISBN 0-8046-0452-5, Pub. by Kennikat). Assoc Faculty Pr.

Some Contemporary Dramatists. Graham Sutton. 1973. Repr. of 1925 ed. 11.00 (ISBN 0-8274-1300-9). R West.

Some Contemporary Elements in Classical Chinese Art. Tseng Yu-Ho. LC 63-17008. (Illus.). 102p. (Orig.). 1963. pap. 4.95 (ISBN 0-87022-812-9). UH Pr.

Some Contemporary Letters see Portuguese Expedition to Abyssinia in 1541-1543.

Some Contemporary Novelists: Women. facs. ed. Reginald B. Johnson. LC 67-26751. (Essay Index Reprint Ser). 1920. 17.00 (ISBN 0-8369-0575-X). Ayer Co Pubs.

Some Contemporary Poets. Harold Monro. LC 76-40456. 1973. Repr. of 1920 ed. lib. bdg. 25.50 (ISBN 0-8414-0137-3). Folcroft.

Some Conventions of Standard Written English. 3rd ed. William H. Pixton. 1979. pap. text ed. 7.95 (ISBN 0-8403-2643-2). Kendall-Hunt.

Some Copper Country Names & Places. (Copper Country Local History Ser.: Vol. 5). (Illus.). 54p. 1975. 2.00 (ISBN 0-942363-04-3). C J Monette.

Some Followers of Domenico Ghirlandajo. Everett Fahy. LC 75-23790. (Outstanding Dissertations in the Fine Arts - 15th Century). (Illus.). 1976. lib. bdg. 50.00 (ISBN 0-8240-1986-5). Garland Pub.

Some Food Colours, Emulsifiers, Stabilizers, Anti-Caking Agents, & Certain Other Substances: Thirteenth Report - Rome, 1969 see Specifications for the Identity & Purity of Food Additives & Their Toxicological Evaluation.

Some Footnotes for the Future. Bob Heman. (Illus.). 24p. (Orig.). 1986. pap. 3.00 (ISBN 0-935350-15-2). Luna Bisonte.

Some Forerunners of Italian Opera. facsimile ed. William J. Henderson. LC 70-160976. (Select Bibliographies Reprint Ser). Repr. of 1911 ed. 19.00 (ISBN 0-8369-5843-8). Ayer Co Pubs.

Some Forerunners of the Newspaper in England, 1476-1622. Matthias A. Shaaber. 1966. lib. bdg. 27.50x (ISBN 0-374-97296-6, Octagon). Hippocrene Bks.

Some Fossil Plant Types of Illinois. Raymond E. Janssen. (Scientific Papers Ser.: Vol. I). (Illus.). 124p. 1940. 3.00x (ISBN 0-89792-094-5); pap. 2.00x (ISBN 0-89792-000-7). Ill St Museum.

Some Founders of Physiology: Contributors to the Growth of Functional Biology. Chauncey D. Leake. LC 58-622. pap. 33.00 (2026395). Bks Demand UMI.

Some Founding Papers of the University of Illinois. Compiled by Richard A. Hatch. LC 66-21365. Repr. of 1967 ed. 27.60 (ISBN 0-8357-9697-3, 2019018). Bks Demand UMI.

Some French Contemporary Opinions of the Russian Revolution of 1905. Encarnacion Alzona. LC 70-158244. (Columbia University Studies in the Social Sciences: No. 228). Repr. of 1921 ed. 12.50 (ISBN 0-404-51228-3). AMS Pr.

Some French Writers. facsimile ed. Edward Delille. LC 78-37526. (Essay Index Reprint Ser). Repr. of 1893 ed. 18.00 (ISBN 0-8369-2543-2). Ayer Co Pubs.

Some Friend! Carol Carrick. LC 79-11490. (Illus.). 112p. (gr. 6 up). 1979. 8.95 (ISBN 0-395-28966-1, Clarion). HM.

Some Friend. Carol Carrick. LC 79-11490. 112p. (gr. 3-6). 1987. pap. 3.95 (ISBN 0-89919-525-3, Pub. by Clarion). Ticknor & Fields.

Some Friends. Pritish Nandy. 104p. 1983. pap. 6.00 (ISBN 0-86578-238-5). Ind-US Inc.

Some Friends of Doctor Johnson. Frederick M. Smith. LC 74-11157. 1974. Repr. of 1931 ed. lib. bdg. 29.00 (ISBN 0-8414-7507-5). Folcroft.

Some Friends of Walt Whitman: A Study in Sex-Psychology. Edward Carpenter. lib. bdg. 25.00 (ISBN 0-8414-3467-0). Folcroft.

Some Functions of Sound-Repetition in 'Les Fleurs du Mal' G. Chesters. (Occasional Papers in Modern Languages: No. 11). 91p. 1975. pap. text ed. 6.95x (ISBN 0-85958-403-8, Pub. by U of Hull UK). Humanities.

Some Fundamental Approaches in Skin Research. Ed. by J. W. Mali. (Current Problems in Dermatology Ser.: Vol. 9). (Illus.). viii, 152p. 1981. pap. 65.50 (ISBN 3-8055-3080-3). S Karger.

Some Fundamental Problems in Indian Philosophy. 2nd ed. C. Kunhan Raja. 1974. 10.50 (ISBN 0-8426-0735-8). Orient Bk Dist.

Some Fundamentals of Analytical Chemistry: A Symposium Presented at the Seventy-Sixth Annual Meeting, American Societyfor Testing & Materials. American Society for Testing & Materials Committee E-3 on Chemical Analysis of Metals Special Publication. LC 74-81159. (American Society for Testing & Materials Ser.: No. 564). (Illus.). pap. 21.80 (ISBN 0-317-09329-0, 2015507). Bks Demand UMI.

Some Gangster Pain. Gillian Conoley. LC 86-70209. (Poetry Ser.). 80p. 1987. 14.95 (ISBN 0-88748-026-8); pap. 7.95 (ISBN 0-88748-027-6). Carnegie-Mellon.

Some Gentle Moving Thing. 2nd ed. James C. Floyd. LC 82-60198. (Illus.). 70p. (gr. 7-9). 1982. 5.95 (ISBN 0-938232-11-8). Winston-Derek.

Some Geographic Factors That Influenced the Ancient Populations of the Chaco Canyon, New Mexico. Reginald G. Fisher. LC 34-27678. 24p. 1982. lib. bdg. 19.95x (ISBN 0-89370-734-1). Borgo Pr.

Some Geographical Aspects of Western African Development. R. J. Church. LC 72-634680. (Papers in International Studies: Africa Ser.: No. 10). (Illus.). 1971. pap. 3.50x (ISBN 0-89680-043-1, Ohio U Ctr Intl). Ohio U Pr.

Some Geometric Beauty Found: Poems, 1920's-1950's. Laurence Hartmus. 58p. 1986. pap. text ed. 8.75 (ISBN 0-915868-04-0). Hartmus Pr.

Some George Eliot Notebooks: An Edition of the Carl H. Pforzheimer Library's George Eliot Holograph Notebooks, MS. 707 (Volume 1) William Baker. Ed. by James Hogg. (Romantic Reassessment Ser.). 332p. (Orig.). 1976. pap. 15.00 (ISBN 0-317-40100-9, Pub. by Salzburg Studies). Longwood Pub Group.

Some George Eliot Notebooks: An Edition of the Carl H. Pforzheimer Library's George Eliot Holograph Notebooks, MS. 708-710 (Volume 2) William Baker. Ed. by James Hogg. (Romantic Reassessment Ser.). (Orig.). 1984. pap. 15.00 (ISBN 0-317-40101-7, Pub. by Salzburg Studies). Longwood Pub Group.

Some George Eliot Notebooks: An Edition of the Carl H. Pforzheimer Library's George Eliot Holograph Notebooks, MS. 711, Vol. 3. William Baker. Ed. by James Hogg. (Romantic Reassessment Ser.). 267p. (Orig.). 1980. pap. 15.00 (ISBN 3-7052-0500-5, Pub. by Salzburg Studies). Longwood Pub Group.

Some George Eliot Notebooks: An Edition of the Carl H. Pforzheimer Library's George Eliot Holohgraph Notebooks, MS, Vol.4. William Baker. Ed. by James Hogg. (Romantic Reassessment Ser.). (Orig.). 1986. pap. 15.00 (ISBN 3-7052-0501-3, Pub. by Salzburg Studies). Longwood Pub Group.

Some Georgia County Records, Vol. 1. Silas E. Lucas, Jr. 432p. 1981. Repr. of 1977 ed. 37.50 (ISBN 0-89308-044-6). Southern Hist Pr.

Some Georgia County Records, Vol. 2. Silas E. Lucas, Jr. 488p. 1981. Repr. of 1977 ed. 37.50 (ISBN 0-89308-057-8). Southern Hist Pr.

Some Georgists & the Money Question. Laurance Labadie. (Men & Movements in the History & Philosophy of Anarchism Ser.). 1979. lib. bdg. 59.95 (ISBN 0-685-96416-7). Revisionist Pr.

Some Gectechnical & Geophysical Systems & their Applications to the Planning of Fishery Harbour Development Programmes in Developing Countries. (Fisheries Technical Papers: No. 91). 28p. 1969. pap. 7.50 (ISBN 0-686-92743-5, F1742, FAO). UNIPUB.

Some Ghost Stories. A. M. Burrage. 1981. 8.50 (ISBN 0-686-69311-6). Bookfinger.

Some Girls Do & Some Don't: Sheet Music Covers. Tony Locantro. (Illus.). 100p. (Orig.). 1986. pap. 25.00 (ISBN 0-7043-3456-9, Pub. by Quartet Bks). Salem Hse Pubs.

Some Glad Morning. Faye Gibbons. LC 81-22549. 240p. (gr. 4-6). 1982. 11.75 (ISBN 0-688-01068-7). Morrow.

Some Glittering Aspects of Islamic Civilization. M. Sibai. 1988. 9.50. Kazi Pubns.

Some Goddesses of the Pen. facs. ed. Patrick Braybrooke. LC 67-22079. (Essay Index Reprint Ser.). 1928. 17.00 (ISBN 0-8369-1324-8). Ayer Co Pubs.

Some Gorgeous Accident. James Kennaway. 200p. 1986. 29.75x (ISBN 0-906391-13-X, Pub. by Mainstream). State Mutual Bk.

Some Great English Novels. Orlo Williams. LC 76-23209. 1926. lib. bdg. 20.00 (ISBN 0-8414-9538-6). Folcroft.

Some Great English Novels. Orlo Williams. 1979. 42.50 (ISBN 0-685-94348-8). Bern Porter.

Some Great English Novels. Orlo Williams. LC 70-131858. 1971. Repr. of 1926 ed. 9.00x (ISBN 0-403-00745-3). Scholarly.

Some Great Leaders in the World Movement. facs. ed. Robert E. Speer. LC 67-26786. (Essay Index Reprint Ser). 1911. 18.00 (ISBN 0-8369-0895-3). Ayer Co Pubs.

Some Great Men of Queen's. facs. ed. Ed. by Robert C. Wallace. LC 79-86792. (Essay Index Reprint Ser). 1941. 14.00 (ISBN 0-8369-1200-4). Ayer Co Pubs.

Some Great Political Idealists of the Christian Era. Fossey J. Hearnshaw. LC 78-107711. (Essay Index Reprint Ser.). 1937. 18.00 (ISBN 0-8369-1513-5). Ayer Co Pubs.

Some Greek Masterpieces in Dramatic & Burolic Poetry. William Stebbing. 1919. 25.00 (ISBN 0-8274-3979-2). R West.

Some Guidelines on Africa for the Next President. Helen Kitchen. (Significant Issues Ser.: Vol. 10, No. 4). 48p. (Orig.). 1988. pap. 7.95 (ISBN 0-89206-114-6). CSI Studies.

Some Habits & Customs of the Working Classes by Journeyman Engineer. Thomas Wright. LC 67-19960. 1961. Repr. of 1867 ed. 35.00x (ISBN 0-678-00268-1). Kelley.

Some Half Hidden Aspects of Indian Social Justice. V. R. Iyer. 139p. 1980. 135.00x (ISBN 0-317-54656-2, Pub. by Eastern Bk India). State Mutual Bk.

Some Halogenate Hydrocarbon & Pesticide Exposures. (IARC Monographs on the Evaluation of the Carcinogenic Risk of Chemicals to Humans: Vol. 41). 434p. 1987. pap. 39.00 (ISBN 92-832-1241-X). World Health.

Some Halogenated Hydrocarbons & Pesticide Exposures. (IARC Monographs on the Evaluation of the Carcinogenic Risk of Chemicals to Humans: Vol. 41). 434p. 1987. pap. 39.00 (ISBN 9-2832-1241-X). World Health.

Some Hard-to-Locate Sources of Information on Current Affairs see Spectrum: A Guide to the Independent Press & Informative Organizations.

Some Hawaiian Oribatoidea. A. P. Jacot. (BMB). Repr. of 1934 ed. 15.00 (ISBN 0-527-02227-6). Kraus Repr.

Some Hellenistic Elements in Primitive Christianity. W. L. Knox. (British Academy, London, Schweich Lectures on Biblical Archaeology Series, 1942). pap. 19.00 (ISBN 0-8115-1284-3). Kraus Repr.

Some Henry True Descendants in Texas. Ed. by Charles W. True, Jr. (Illus.). 300p. 1984. lib. bdg. 40.00 (ISBN 0-9613360-0-5). True Ent.

Some Henry True Descendants on the Frontier. Ed. by Charles W. True, Jr. 361p. 1984. lib. bdg. 32.00 (ISBN 0-9613360-1-3). True Ent.

Some Heretics of Yesterday. Samuel E. Herrick. LC 83-45614. Date not set. Repr. of 1885 ed. 37.50 (ISBN 0-404-19832-5). AMS Pr.

Some Historical Account of Guinea. A. Benezet. 131p. 1968. Repr. of 1788 ed. 29.50x (ISBN 0-7146-1888-8, F Cass Co). Biblio Dist.

Some Homosexual Men. David Sonenschein. 225p. 1983. pap. 8.95 (ISBN 0-915289-07-5). D Sonenschein.

Some Huguenot & Other Early Settlers on the Kennebec in the Present Town of Dresden (ME) 31p. 1986. pap. 4.25 (ISBN 0-935207-39-2). DanBury Hse Bks.

Some Hyphomycetes That Prey on Free-Living Terricolous Nematodes. Charles Drechsler. (Mycologia Ser.: No. 29). (Illus.). 103p. 1937. pap. text ed. 12.00x (ISBN 0-945345-05-4). Lubrecht & Cramer.

Some Imaginal Factors Influencing Verbal Expression see Psychology of Clothing.

Some Imagist Poets, an Anthology, 3 vols in one. 1915-1917. 23.00 (ISBN 0-527-84700-3). Kraus Repr.

Some Implications of Social Psychology. O. H. Harland. 104p. 1982. Repr. of 1928 ed. lib. bdg. 30.00 (ISBN 0-89987-392-8). Darby Bks.

Some Impressions of the United States. facs. ed. Edward A. Freeman. LC 76-117875. (Select Bibliographies Reprint Ser). 1883. 21.50 (ISBN 0-8369-5328-2). Ayer Co Pubs.

Some Indian Saints. Gopinath Talwalker. (Illus.). 64p. (Orig.). (gr. 5 up). 1980. pap. 2.50 (ISBN 0-89744-208-3, Pub. by Natl Bk Trust India). Auromere.

Some Influences in Modern Philosophic Thought. Arthur T. Hadley. LC 67-27604. 1968. Repr. of 1913 ed. 15.00x (ISBN 0-8046-0188-7, Pub. by Kennikat). Assoc Faculty Pr.

Some Influences of the Requirements & Examinations of the College Entrance Examination Board on Mathematics in Secondary Schools in the United States. Leslie H. Whitcraft. LC 70-177640. (Columbia University. Teachers College. Contributions to Education: No. 557). Repr. of 1933 ed. 22.50 (ISBN 0-404-55557-8). AMS Pr.

Some Information Respecting America. Thomas Cooper. LC 67-29498. (Illus.). 1969. Repr. of 1794 ed. 35.00x (ISBN 0-678-00570-2). Kelley.

Some Ingredients for Growth: Edward Shann Memorial Lectures in Economics. H. C. Coombs. 1963. pap. 3.00x (ISBN 0-85564-033-2, Pub. by U of W Austral Pr). Intl Spec Bk.

Some Inscriptions of the Safaitic Bedouin. Willard B. Oxtoby. (American Oriental Ser.: Vol. 50). (Illus.). 1968. pap. 8.00x (ISBN 0-940490-50-1). Am Orient Soc.

Some Instructions to My Wife. Stanley Crawford. 176p. 1985. 20.00 (ISBN 0-916583-14-7); pap. 4.50 (ISBN 0-916583-15-5). Dalkey Arch.

Some Intellectual Consequences of the English Revolution. Christopher Hill. LC 79-5408. (Curti Lecture Ser.). 1980. 19.50x (ISBN 0-299-08140-0); pap. 8.95x (ISBN 0-299-08144-3). U of Wis Pr.

Some Issues Important in Developing Basic Radiation Protection Recommendations: Proceedings of the Twentieth Annual Meeting of the National Council on Radiation Protection & Measurements. LC 84-25504. 325p. (Orig.). 1985. text ed. 19.00. NCRP Pubns.

Some Issues in Development Administration. Ed. by P. Ramachandran & M. A. Oommen. 223p. 1987. 18.00x (Pub. by Oxford IBH). South Asia Bks.

Some Issues in Joint Union-Management Quality of Worklife Improvement Efforts. Paul D. Greenberg & Edward M. Glaser. LC 80-14044. 85p. 1980. pap. 4.95 (ISBN 0-911558-70-5). W E Upjohn.

Some Japanese Hanging Scrolls. W. Jose De Gruyter. 1949. 1225.00x (ISBN 0-317-69102-3, Pub. by Han-Shan Tang Ltd). State Mutual Bk.

Some Japanese Portraits. Donald Keene. LC 76-39679. 228p. 1979. 15.50 (ISBN 0-87011-298-8). Kodansha.

Some Japanese Portraits. Donald Keene. LC 76-39679. 228p. 1983. pap. 5.95 (ISBN 0-87011-575-8). Kodansha.

Some Just Clap Their Hands: Raising a Handicapped Child. Margaret Mantle. LC 85-15026. 264p. 1985. 16.95 (ISBN 0-915361-24-8, 097331, Dist. by Watts); pap. 12.95. Adama Pubs Inc.

Some Kannada Poems. Ed. by A. K. Ramanujan & M. G. Krishnamurthi. 1975. 8.00 (ISBN 0-88253-636-2); pap. text ed. cancelled (ISBN 0-88253-635-4). Ind-US Inc.

Some Key Issues for the World Periphery: Selected Essays. Miguel S. Wionczek. 480p. 1981. 110.00 (ISBN 0-08-025783-6). Pergamon.

Some Kind of Hero. James Kirkwood. 1976. pap. 2.95 (ISBN 0-451-11576-7, AE1576, Sig). NAL.

Some Kind of Hero. Max Layton. 1988. 19.95 (Pub. by Mosaic Pr Canada); pap. 10.95 (ISBN 0-88962-387-2, Pub. by Mosaic Pr Canada). Riverrun NY.

Some Kind of Paradise: The Emergence of American Science Fiction. Thomas D. Clareson. LC 84-29060. (Contribution to the Study of Science Fiction & Fantasy: No. 16). xiv, 248p. 1985. lib. bdg. 35.00 (ISBN 0-313-23167-2, CSK/). Greenwood.

Some Kind of Power: Navajo Children's Skinwalker Narratives. Margaret K. Brady. 224p. 1984. 14.95 (ISBN 0-87480-238-5). U of Utah Pr.

Some Kind of Wonderful. Adrienne Edwards. (Second Chance at Love Ser.: No. 449). 1988. pap. 2.50 (ISBN 0-425-10987-9). Berkley Pub.

Some Kind of Wonderful: Movie Tie-In. David Bischoff. (YA) (gr. 9 up). 1987. pap. 2.50 (ISBN 0-440-98042-9). Dell.

Some Ksatriya Tribes of Ancient India. Bimala C. Law. LC 78-72468. Date not set. Repr. of 1924 ed. 42.00 (ISBN 0-404-17338-1). AMS Pr.

Some Lamb. Stan Rice. 1975. signed 10.00 (ISBN 0-685-78914-4); perfect bound in wrappers 4.00 (ISBN 0-685-78915-2). Figures.

Some Lamb & Browning Letters to Leigh Hunt. Luther A. Brewer. LC 72-196923. 1924. lib. bdg. 8.50 (ISBN 0-8414-2541-8). Folcroft.

Some Late Cenozoic Echinoidea from Cabo Blanco, Venezuela see Bulletins of American Paleontology.

Some Late Cenozoic Stony Corals from Northern Venezuela see Bulletins of American Paleontology.

Some Late Pleistocene Diatoms of the Kenai Peninsula, Alaska. R. B. McLaughlin & J. L. Stone. (Nova Hedwigia, Beiheft 82). (Illus.). 150p. 1986. pap. 60.00x (ISBN 3-443-51002-7). Lubrecht & Cramer.

Some Leading Principles of Political Economy Newly Expounded. John E. Cairnes. LC 66-22617. 1967. Repr. of 1874 ed. 39.50x (ISBN 0-678-00205-3). Kelley.

Some Legal Phases of Corporate Financing, Reorganization & Regulation. Francis L. Stetson. LC 87-81957. (Business Enterprises Reprint Ser.). x, 387p. 1987. Repr. of 1927 ed. lib. bdg. 38.50 (ISBN 0-89941-582-2). W S Hein.

Some Lessons from Our Legal History. William S. Holdsworth. viii, 198p. 1983. Repr. of 1928 ed. lib. bdg. 22.50x (ISBN 0-8377-0709-9). Rothman.

Some Lessons from Our Legal History. William S. Holdsworth. Ed. by Bernard D. Reams, Jr. LC 28-9876. (Historical Reprints in Jurisprudence & Classical Legal Literature Ser.). viii, 198p. 1983-84. Repr. of 1928 ed. lib. bdg. 38.00 (ISBN 0-89941-252-1). W S Hein.

Some Lessons in Mathematics. T. J. Fletcher. pap. 12.95x (ISBN 0-521-09248-5). Cambridge U Pr.

Some Lessons in Metaphysics. Jose Ortega Y Gasset. LC 76-80025. pap. 5.95x (ISBN 0-393-00514-3, Norton Lib.). Norton.

Some Letters & Miscellanea of Charles Brown, the Friend of John Keats & Thomas Richards. M. Buxton Forman. LC 76-26940. 1937. lib. bdg. 18.00 (ISBN 0-8414-4205-3). Folcroft.

Some Letters of William Vaughn Moody. William V. Moody. Ed. by D. G. Mason. LC 76-94471. Repr. of 1913 ed. 16.00 (ISBN 0-404-04359-3). AMS Pr.

Some Lichens of Tropical Africa IV: Dermatocarpaceae to Pertusariaceae. C. W. Dodge. 1964. pap. 48.00x (ISBN 3-7682-5412-7). Lubrecht & Cramer.

Some Lichens of Tropical Africa V: Lecanoraceae to Physiaceae. C. W. Dodge. 1971. pap. 60.00x (ISBN 3-7682-5438-0). Lubrecht & Cramer.

Some Life. Jack Grapes. 24p. (Orig.). 1986. pap. 3.00 (ISBN 0-941017-03-6). Bombshelter Pr.

Some Light on Christian Education. Ed. by James W. Deuink. (Illus.). 195p. (Orig.). 1984. pap. 5.23 (ISBN 0-89084-262-0). Bob Jones Univ Pr.

Some Light Remarks. Thomas Dickman. LC 79-92087. 1980. 7.95 (ISBN 0-87212-120-8). Libra.

Some Like It Dark. Kipp Washington. 1985. pap. 2.50 (ISBN 0-87067-268-1, BH268). Holloway.

Some Limit Theorems in Statistics. R. R. Bahadur. (CBMS-NSF Regional Conference Ser.: No. 4). v, 42p. 1971. pap. text ed. 10.00 (ISBN 0-89871-175-4). Soc Indus-Appl Math.

Some Literary Associations of East Anglia: George Borrow, George Crabbe, John Evelyn, Edward Fitzgerald, Charles Lamb, Lord Tennyson & William Wordsworth. William A. Dutt. 1978. Repr. of 1907 ed. 35.00 (ISBN 0-8492-0689-8). R West.

Some Literary Eccentrics. John Fyvie. 1973. Repr. of 1906 ed. 30.00 (ISBN 0-8274-0193-0). R West.

Some Living Masters of the Pulpit: Studies in Religious Personality. facsimile ed. Joseph F. Newton. LC 71-152203. (Essay Index Reprint Ser). Repr. of 1923 ed. 18.00 (ISBN 0-8369-2287-5). Ayer Co Pubs.

Some Longer Elizabethan Poems. A. H. Bullen. LC 64-16751. (Arber's an English Garner Ser.). 1964. Repr. of 1890 ed. 23.50x (ISBN 0-8154-0040-3). Cooper Sq.

Some Loves of the Seraphic Saint. Father Augustine. 1979. 5.95 (ISBN 0-8199-0776-6). Franciscan Herald.

Some Machiavellian Moments in English Renaissance Drama. Richard Corballis. Ed. by James Hogg. (Elizabethan & Renaissance Studies). 134p. (Orig.). 1978. pap. 15.00 (ISBN 3-7052-0714-8, Pub. by Salzburg Studies). Longwood Pub Group.

Some MacLean Poets of the Seventeenth & Early Eighteenth Centuries. Colm O'Baoill. 416p. 1980. 20.00x (ISBN 0-7073-0271-4, Pub. by Scot Acad Pr). Longwood Pub Group.

Some Makers of American Law. Bernard Schwartz. 182p. 1985. lib. bdg. 30.00 (ISBN 0-379-20688-9). Oceana.

Some of the Ancestors & Descendants of James & George Ashford Jr. of Fairfield County, South Carolina. Charlie R. Ashford, Sr. LC 85-71620. 123p. Repr. of 1956 ed. 60.00 (ISBN 0-916497-23-2); microfiche 6.00 (ISBN 0-916497-22-4). Burnett Micro.

Some of the Best from C & H News - Views, Vol. I. (Copper Country Local History Ser.: Vol. 24). (Illus.). 108p. 1985. 2.50 (ISBN 0-942363-23-X). C J Monette.

Some of the Best from C & H News & Views, Vol. II. Clarence J. Monette. (Copper Country Local History Ser.: No. 30). (Illus.). 120p. (Orig.). 1987. pap. 2.50 (ISBN 0-942363-29-9). C J Monette.

Some of the Best Houses in Nevada. 1981. pap. 6.00x (ISBN 0-933990-04-9). Canterbury Pr.

Some of the Cat Poems. Artie Gold. (Illus.). 1978. pap. 2.00 (ISBN 0-916696-08-1). Cross Country.

Some of the Days of Everett Anderson. Lucille Clifton. LC 78-98922. (gr. k-2). 10.95 (ISBN 0-8050-0290-1); pap. 3.95 (ISBN 0-8050-0289-8). H Holt & Co.

Some of the English. Oliver M. Hueffer. 1930. 30.00 (ISBN 0-8274-3461-8). R West.

Some of the Hardest Glosses in Old English. Herbert D. Meritt. 1968. 15.00x (ISBN 0-8047-0620-4). Stanford U Pr.

Some of the Interactive Processes in Reading & Their Role in Reading Skill. Charles A. Perfetti & Steven Roth. 50p. 1980. 1.00 (ISBN 0-318-14738-6). Learn Res Dev.

Some of the Things I Did Not Do: Stories. Janet B. Shaw. LC 83-18319. (Illinois Short Fiction Ser.). 144p. 1984. 11.95 (ISBN 0-252-01109-0). U of Ill Pr.

Some of the Usages & Abuses in the Management of Our Manufacturing Corporations. James C. Ayer. LC 75-126399. (Research & Source Works Ser.: No. 435). 1971. Repr. of 1863 ed. wrappers 11.00 (ISBN 0-8337-0140-1). B Franklin.

Some of Us Survived: The Story of an Armenian Boy. Kerop Bedoukian. LC 79-10601. 186p. (gr. 6 up). 1979. 9.95 (ISBN 0-374-37132-6). FS&G.

Some Official Correspondence, 1812-1827, 2 Vols. in 1. G. Canning. Ed. by E. J. Stapleton. Repr. of 1887 ed. 36.00 (ISBN 0-527-14811-3). Kraus Repr.

Some Old Flemish Towns. G. W. Edwards. 59.95 (ISBN 0-8490-1078-0). Gordon Pr.

Some Old Love Stories. T. P. O'Connor. 1979. Repr. of 1895 ed. lib. bdg. 35.00 (ISBN 0-8495-4208-1). Arden Lib.

Some Old Portraits. Booth Tarkington. LC 78-93382. (Essay Index Reprint Ser.). 1939. 27.50 (ISBN 0-8369-1315-9). Ayer Co Pubs.

Some-One Died! What Is Life? David L. Riley, Sr. (Illus.). 200p. (Orig.). 1988. pap. 12.00 (ISBN 0-9618976-1-9). D L Riley.

Some Other Aspects of Judaism. Robert Chernoff. LC 86-90273. 113p. 1987. 8.95 (ISBN 0-533-07207-7). Vantage.

Some Other Country: New Zealand's Best Short Stories. Ed. by Marion McLeod & Bill Manhire. 256p. 1985. pap. text ed. 11.95x (ISBN 0-86861-633-8). Unwin Hyman.

Some Other Folks. Sarah P. Greene. LC 74-98570. (Short Story Index Reprint Ser.). 1884. 18.00 (ISBN 0-8369-3144-0). Ayer Co Pubs.

Some Other Place: The Right Place. Donald Harrington. 474p. 1988. pap. 10.95 (ISBN 0-15-683801-X). HarBraceJ.

Some Other Summer. C. S. Adler. (gr. 3-7). 1988. pap. 2.50 (Camelot). Avon.

Some Outstanding Clocks over Seven Hundred Years 1250-1950: 1250-1950. H. Alan Lloyd. (Illus.). 216p. 1981. ltd. ed. 69.50 (ISBN 0-907462-04-9). Antique Collect.

Some Parent-Child Relationships As Shown in Clinical Case Studies. Marian J. Fitz-Simons. LC 71-176776. (Columbia University. Teachers College. Contributions to Education: No. 643). Repr. of 1935 ed. 22.50 (ISBN 0-404-55643-4). AMS Pr.

Some Part of Myself. J. Frank Dobie. 1967. 15.95 (ISBN 0-316-18790-9). Little.

Some Part of Myself. J. Frank Dobie. LC 79-67708. (Illus.). 292p. 1980. pap. 9.95 (ISBN 0-292-77558-X). U of Tex Pr.

Some Particulars. Thomas A. Clark. 1971. pap. 7.50 (ISBN 0-912330-12-0, Dist. by Inland Bk). Jargon Soc.

Some Passages in the Life & Death of John Earl of Rochester. Gilbert Burnet. LC 73-12355. 1787. lib. bdg. 25.00 (ISBN 0-8414-3202-3). Folcroft.

Some People. Harold Nicholson. 1978. Repr. lib. bdg. 20.00 (ISBN 0-8495-4009-7). Arden Lib.

Some People Are Indians. Ed. by George A. Boyce. LC 75-190224. (Illus.). (gr. 4-6). 1974. 6.95 (ISBN 0-8149-0714-8). Vanguard.

Some People Are Throwing You into Confusion. (Mennonite Faith Ser.). 1988. 1.95. Herald Pr.

Some People Are Throwing You Into Confusion. Pierre Widmer. LC 83-82879. (Mennonite Faith Ser.: No. 14). 80p. 1984. pap. 1.50 (ISBN 0-8361-3358-7). Herald Pr.

Some People, Places, & Things That Will Not Appear in My Next Novel. John Cheever. LC 79-116947. (Short Story Index Reprint Ser.). 1961. 15.00 (ISBN 0-8369-3449-0). Ayer Co Pubs.

Some People Think We Don't Learn Anything in This School. Colleen McNally et al. LC 77-71871. (Illus.). 1977. pap. 4.95 (ISBN 0-915492-03-2). Ash Lad Pr.

Some Perpectives of the Major Biochemical Cycles. Ed. by Gene E. Likens. LC 80-42017. (SCOPE Ser.: Report 17). 175p. 1981. 48.95x (ISBN 0-471-27989-7). Wiley.

Some Persistent Questions on Beginning Reading. Ed. by Robert C. Aukerman. LC 73-190454. pap. 45.80 (ISBN 0-317-55490-5, 2029595). Bks Demand UMI.

Some Personal Experiences with Popularizing Mathematical Methods in China. L. Hua & F. Wang. (Mathematical Modeling Ser.: No. 2). 250p. 1988. 35.00t (ISBN 0-8176-3372-3). Birkhauser.

Some Personal Letters of Herman Melville & a Bibliography. facs. ed. Meade Minnigerode. LC 78-75511. (Select Bibliographies Reprint Ser.). 1922. 15.00 (ISBN 0-8369-5013-5). Ayer Co Pubs.

Some Personal Recollections of George Gissing. Ellen Gissing. 1929. lib. bdg. 15.00 (ISBN 0-8414-4652-0). Folcroft.

Some Personality Determinants of the Effects of Participation. Victor H. Vroom. Ed. by Arthur P. Brief. (Continuity in Administrative Science & Ancestral Books in the Management of Organizations). 91p. 1987. lib. bdg. 25.00 (ISBN 0-8240-8225-7). Garland Pub.

Some Perspectives on Fundamental Nuclear & High Energy Research. Ed. by M. Conversi et al. 350p. 1983. pap. text ed. 50.00x (ISBN 0-911767-10-X). Hadronic Pr Inc.

Some Philosophers on Education: Papers Concerning the Doctrines of Augustine, Aristole, Aquinas & Dewey. 2nd ed. Ed. by Donald A. Gallagher. 1961. 6.95 (ISBN 0-87462-403-7). Marquette.

Some Philosophical Aspects of Poetry. Stopford A. Brooke. LC 74-8074. 1872. lib. bdg. 15.00 (ISBN 0-8414-3188-4). Folcroft.

Some Phoenix Blood. Horatio Colony. LC 69-11622. 1969. 12.00 (ISBN 0-8283-1008-4). Branden Pub Co.

Some Physical, Dosimetry & Biomedical Aspects of Californium. (Panel Proceedings Ser.). (Illus.). 278p. 1977. pap. 31.50 (ISBN 92-0-111476-1, ISP418, IAEA). UNIPUB.

Some Pictures from My Life: A Diary. Marcia S. Rizzi. LC 72-87034. (Illus.). 64p. (Orig.). 1972. pap. 2.95 (ISBN 0-87810-022-9). Times Change.

Some Pioneer Families of Wisconsin, Vol 2. Ed. by Betty Patterson. 139p. 1988. pap. 8.00 (ISBN 0-910255-49-0). Wisconsin Gen.

Some Plant Galls of Illinois. Glen S. Winterringer. (Story of Illinois Ser.: No. 12). (Illus.). 51p. 1961. pap. 1.00x (ISBN 0-89792-022-8). Ill St Museum.

Some Plants Have Funny Names. Diana Harding. LC 82-23438. (Illus.). 48p. (gr. k-3). 1983. 8.95 (ISBN 0-517-54840-2). Crown.

Some Poems. Richard Burns. 1977. 9.50 (ISBN 0-685-90001-0, Pub. by Enitharmon Pr). Small Pr Dist.

Some Poems - Poets. Samuel Charters. 1971. 5.95 (ISBN 0-685-04674-5); pap. 2.95 (ISBN 0-685-04675-3). Oyez.

Some Poems & a Devotion of John Donne. John Donne. LC 76-21761. 1976. Repr. of 1941 ed. lib. bdg. 25.00 (ISBN 0-8414-3732-7). Folcroft.

Some Poems & Some Talk about Poetry. Frank Manley & Flyod C. Watkins. LC 84-13061. 1985. 12.50x (ISBN 0-87805-230-5). U Pr of Miss.

Some Poems, My Friends. Norman A. Kirk. (Illus.). 64p. 1981. 25.00 (ISBN 0-939622-12-2); pap. 5.00 (ISBN 0-939622-11-4). Four Zoas Night.

Some Poems on My Day Off. John Sjoberg. (Morning Coffee Chapbook Ser.). (Illus.). 24p. (Orig.). 1984. pap. 7.50 (ISBN 0-915124-94-7). Coffee Hse.

Some Points to Consider When You Discuss Merit Pay. Luann Van Loozen. 40p. (Orig.). 1983. pap. 4.50 (ISBN 0-87652-071-9, 021-00116); videotape 195.00 (ISBN 0-87652-086-7). Am Assn Sch Admin.

Some Policy Considerations for Sign Legislation. R. J. Claus. 1973. pap. 3.00 (ISBN 0-911380-31-0). Signs of Times.

Some Political & Social Ideas of English Dissent, 1763-1800. Anthony Lincoln. LC 72-120642. 1970. Repr. lib. bdg. 20.50x (ISBN 0-374-95012-1, Octagon). Hippocrene Bks.

Some Political Ideas & Persons. John Bailey. 1973. Repr. of 1921 ed. 10.00 (ISBN 0-8274-1488-9). R West.

Some Political Issues in the Background of World War II. Francis Neilson. (Revisionist Historiography Ser.). 1979. lib. bdg. 39.95 (ISBN 0-685-96637-2). Revisionist Pr.

Some Political Writings of James Otis, 2 vols. in 1. James Otis. LC 75-31099. Repr. of 1929 ed. 16.50 (ISBN 0-404-13516-1). AMS Pr.

Some Portraits of the Lake Poets & Their Homes. Ashley P. Abraham. 1978. Repr. of 1914 ed. lib. bdg. 30.50 (ISBN 0-8495-0129-6). Arden Lib.

Some Portraits of the Lake Poets, & Their Homes. Ashley P. Abraham. LC 75-28026. 1975. Repr. of 1914 ed. lib. bdg. 32.50 (ISBN 0-8414-2874-3). Folcroft.

Some Post-Independence Bengali Poems. Tr. by Pradeep Banerjee. (Translated from Bengali). 8.00 (ISBN 0-89253-606-3). Ind-US Inc.

Some Practical Laws of Learning. B. R. Bugelski. LC 77-84042. (Fastback Ser.: No. 96). 1977. pap. 0.90 (ISBN 0-87367-096-5). Phi Delta Kappa.

Some Practical Suggestions on the Conduct of a Rescue Home: Including Life of Dr. Kate Waller Barrett. facsimile ed. Kate W. Barrett. LC 74-3928. (Women in America Ser.). Orig. Title: Fifty Years Work with Girls. 186p. 1974. Repr. of 1903 ed. 20.00x (ISBN 0-405-06075-0). Ayer Co Pubs.

Some Preachers Do. Bertie C. Bay. 93p. 1975. pap. 1.95 (ISBN 0-89114-072-7). Baptist Pub Hse.

Some Predators Are Male. Miles Tripp. 192p. 1985. 12.95 (ISBN 0-312-74348-3). St Martin.

Some Prefer Nettles. Junichiro Tanizaki. Tr. by Edward G. Seidensticker from Japanese. (Perigee Japanese Library). 224p. 1981. pap. 8.95 (ISBN 0-399-50521-0, Perigee). Putnam Pub Group.

Some Preliminary Conclusions Regarding Factors which Affect Army Recruiting Success in the Midwestern Regional Recruiting Command. David W. Hinton & Jason Chen. 12p. (Orig.). 1976. pap. 1.00 (ISBN 1-55719-068-2). U NE Ctr Applied Urban Rsch.

Some Present Aspects of the Work of Teachers' Voluntary Associations in the United States. Carter Alexander. (Columbia University. Teachers College. Contributions to Education: No. 36). Repr. of 1910 ed. 22.50 (ISBN 0-404-55036-3). AMS Pr.

Some Presidential Interpretations of the Presidency. Norman J. Small. LC 78-64145. (Johns Hopkins University. Studies in the Social Sciences. Fiftieth Ser. 1932: 2). Repr. of 1932 ed. 18.50 (ISBN 0-404-61256-3). AMS Pr.

Some Presidential Interpretations of the Presidency. Norman J. Small. LC 71-87353. (Politics & Law Ser). 1970. Repr. of 1932 ed. lib. bdg. 29.50 (ISBN 0-306-71663-1). Da Capo.

Some Presidents: Wilson to Nixon. William A. Williams. 1972. pap. 1.95 (70227). Random.

Some "Prime" Comparisons. Stephen I. Brown. LC 78-12339. (Illus.). 106p. 1978. pap. 7.00 (ISBN 0-87353-131-0). NCTM.

Some Principles of Elizabethan Staging. G. F. Reynolds. LC 78-130233. Repr. of 1905 ed. 5.00 (ISBN 0-404-05286-X). AMS Pr.

Some Principles of Elizabethan Staging. George F. Reynolds. LC 72-193209. Repr. of 1905 ed. lib. bdg. 17.00 (ISBN 0-8414-7423-0). Folcroft.

Some Principles of Fiction. Robert Liddell. LC 73-433. 162p. 1974. Repr. of 1954 ed. lib. bdg. 9.50x (ISBN 0-8371-6764-7, LIPF). Greenwood.

Some Principles of Good Writing. rev. ed. Dorothy E. Bradbury. Bd. with Library Search in the Social Sciences. Helen E. Klein et al. 32p. 1980. 2.95 (ISBN 0-87101-620-6). Natl Assn Soc Wkrs.

Some Principles of Literary Criticism. Caleb T. Winchester. 1973. lib. bdg. 30.00 (ISBN 0-8414-9723-0). Folcroft.

Some Principles of Maritime Strategy. Julian Corbett. Ed. by John P. Hattendorf & Wayne P. Hughes, Jr. (Classics of Sea Power Ser.). 416p. 1988. 23.95 (ISBN 0-87021-880-8). Naval Inst Pr.

Some Principles of Maritime Strategy. Julian Corbett. (Illus.). 351p. 1988. 35.00 (ISBN 0-08-036693-7, Pub. by Pergamon-Brasseys). Pergamon.

Some Principles of Maritime Strategy. Julian S. Corbett. LC 76-154122. (BCL Ser. II). Repr. of 1911 ed. 24.50 (ISBN 0-404-09227-6). AMS Pr.

Some Problems about Time. P. T. Geach. (Philosophical Lectures (Henriette Hertz Trust)). 1965. pap. 5.50 (ISBN 0-85672-305-3, Pub. by British Acad). Longwood Pub Group.

Some Problems & Alternatives in Developing Federal Block Grants: To States for Public Welfare Purposes. E. A. Lutz. LC 77-74945. (American Federalism-the Urban Dimension). (Illus.). 1978. lib. bdg. 30.00x (ISBN 0-405-10493-6). Ayer Co Pubs.

Some Problems in Chemical Kinetics & Reactivity, Vol. 2. Nikolai N. Semenov. Tr. by Michel Boudart. LC 57-10321. (Illus.). pap. 85.80 (ISBN 0-317-09946-9). Bks Demand UMI.

Some Problems in Market Distribution: Illustrating the Application of a Basic Philosophy of Business. Arch W. Shaw. LC 15-19535. (Illus.). 1915. 8.95x (ISBN 0-674-81960-8). Harvard U Pr.

Some Problems in Medieval Historiography. G. G. Coulton. 1974. lib. bdg. 59.95 (ISBN 0-8490-1079-9). Gordon Pr.

Some Problems in the Provision of Professional Education for College Teachers. H. M. Byram. LC 79-176621. (Columbia University. Teachers College. Contributions to Education: No. 576). Repr. of 1933 ed. 22.50 (ISBN 0-404-55576-4). AMS Pr.

Some Problems of Co-Operative Organization. Rob Paton. 81p. 1978. 21.25x (ISBN 0-317-54697-X, Pub. by Plunkett Foundation). State Mutual Bk.

Some Problems of Development Financing: A Case Study of the Turkish First Five-Year Plan 1963-1967. M. Durdag. LC 72-77873. 297p. 1973. lib. bdg. 42.00 (ISBN 90-277-0267-5, Pub. by Reidel Holland). Kluwer Academic.

Some Problems of India's Economic Policy. Ed. by Dharan D. Wadhva. 1978. 14.00x (ISBN 0-8364-0263-4). South Asia Bks.

Some Problems of Marx's Theory of History. Ashok Rudra. (R C Dutt Lectures). 76p. 1988. pap. 7.95x (ISBN 0-86131-754-8, Pub. by Orient Longman LTD India). Apt Bks.

Some Problems of Mathematics & Physics. L. V. Ahlfors et al. LC 76-4884. (Translations Ser.: No. 2, Vol. 104). 1976. 61.00 (ISBN 0-8218-3054-6, TRANS 2-104). Am Math.

Some Problems of Philosophy. William James. (Works of William James Ser.). 1979. text ed. 30.00x (ISBN 0-674-82035-5). Harvard U Pr.

Some Problems of Philosophy see Writings Nineteen Two to Nineteen Ten.

Some Problems of Philosophy: A Beginning of an Introduction to Philosophy. William James. 1968. Repr. of 1911 ed. lib. bdg. 35.00x (ISBN 0-8371-4464-7, JAPP). Greenwood.

Some Problems of Rotor Dynamics. Ales Tondl. Ed. by Jan Gonda. Tr. by Pavel Dolan from Czech. LC 66-72920. pap. 108.50 (ISBN 0-317-26203-3, 2052128). Bks Demand UMI.

Some Problems of Sanskrit Poetics. S. K. De. 1981. 12.00x (ISBN 0-8364-0733-4, Pub. by Mukhopadhyay). South Asia Bks.

Some Problems of Self-Reference in John Buridan. A. N. Prior. (Dawes Hicks Lectures on Philosophy). 1962. pap. 5.50 (ISBN 0-85672-026-7, Pub. by British Acad). Longwood Pub Group.

Some Problems of Shakespeare's Henry the Fourth. A. E. Morgan. LC 73-13542. 1924. Repr. lib. bdg. 17.50 (ISBN 0-8414-6010-8). Folcroft.

Some Problems of Sylow Type in Locally Finite Groups. M. Curzio. 1981. 36.00 (ISBN 0-12-363605-1). Acad Pr.

Some Problems of the Management of Shared Stocks. J. A. Gulland. (Fisheries Technical Papers: No. 206). 29p. (Eng. & Fr., 2nd Printing 1981). 1980. pap. 7.50 (ISBN 92-5-101022-6, F2149, FAO). UNIPUB.

Some Problems of Wages & Their Regulation in Great Britain Since 1918. Allan G. Fisher. LC 66-21672. 1966. Repr. of 1926 ed. 35.00x (ISBN 0-678-00183-9). Kelley.

Some Productive Consequences of Engel's Law. W. F. Gossling. 1974. 70.00x (ISBN 0-904870-04-9, Pub. by Input-Output UK). State Mutual Bk.

Some Prominent Muslim Hindu Poets. Sansar Chandra. 132p. 1986. 13.00X (ISBN 81-7043-000-3, Pub. by Macmillan India). South Asia Bks.

Some Prominent Virginia Families, 4 vols. in 2. Louise Pecquet Du Bellet. LC 76-13286. (Illus.). 1715p. 1976. Repr. of 1907 ed. 72.50 set (ISBN 0-8063-0722-6). Genealog Pub.

Some Properties of Differentiable Varieties & Transformations: With Special Reference to the Analytic & Algebraic Cases. 2nd ed. Beniamino Segre. LC 72-137498. (Ergebnisse der Mathematik und Ihrer Grenzgebiete: Vol. 13). 1971. pap. 34.00 (ISBN 0-387-05085-X). Springer-Verlag.

Some Properties of the Bank Model. G. P. Dunn et al. (Bank of England, Discussion Papers, Technical Ser.: No. 9). pap. 28.80 (ISBN 0-317-26529-6, 2023978). Bks Demand UMI.

Some Prose Writings. W. Carew Hazlitt. 1906. 45.00 (ISBN 0-8274-3462-6). R West.

Some Qualities Associated with Success in the Christian Ministry. Mary E. Moxcey. LC 76-177095. (Columbia University. Teachers College. Contributions to Education: No. 122). Repr. of 1922 ed. 22.50 (ISBN 0-404-55122-X). AMS Pr.

Some Queer People. Landbroke Black. 1979. Repr. lib. bdg. 30.00 (ISBN 0-8414-9842-3). Folcroft.

Some Queer People: Margaret Fuller, Poe, Beddoes. Landbroke Black. 1973. 35.00 (ISBN 0-8274-1477-3). R West.

Some Questions About Language. Mortimer Adler. LC 75-1221. 203p. 1976. 19.95 (ISBN 0-87548-320-8). Open Court.

Some Questions in Constructive Functional Analysis: Proceedings. Steklov Institute of Mathematics, Academy of Sciences, U.S.S.R., No. 114. LC 73-21929. (No. 114). 238p. 1974. 75.00 (ISBN 0-8218-3014-7, STEKLO-114). Am Math.

Some Questions in the Theory of Moments. N. I. Ahiezer & M. G. Krein. LC 63-22077. (Translations of Mathematical Monographs: Vol. 2). 1974. Repr. of 1962 ed. 33.00 (ISBN 0-8218-1552-0, MMONO-2). Am Math.

Some Rain. James E. Luczak. (Illus.). 60p. (Orig.). 1983. pap. 4.00 (ISBN 0-88145-001-4). Broadway Play.

Some Rain Must Fall. Elizabeth Spalding McFadden. LC 65-16848. (Dest Ser.). 1984. pap. 2.99 (ISBN 0-317-28324-3). Pacific Pr Pub Assn.

Some Random Reminiscences: The Autobiography of Harold C. Holmes. limited ed. Harold C. Holmes. (Illus.). 10.00 (ISBN 0-910740-01-1). Holmes.

Some Random Series of Functions. Jean-Pierre Kahane. (Cambridge Studies in Advanced Mathematics: No. 5). 250p. 1985. 54.50 (ISBN 0-521-24966-X). Cambridge U Pr.

Some Reasons Against Woman Suffrage. Francis Parkman. Ed. by Norman E. Tanis. (Northridge Facsimile Ser.: Pt. VIII). 1977. pap. 10.00 (ISBN 0-937048-07-0). CSUN.

Some Thermodynamic Aspects of Inorganic Chemistry. 2nd ed. D. A. Johnson. LC 81-10146. (Cambridge Texts in Chemistry & Biochemistry). 275p. 1982. 47.50 (ISBN 0-521-24204-5); pap. 18.95 (ISBN 0-521-28521-6). Cambridge U Pr.
Some Things Are Different, Some Things Are the Same. Marya Dantzer-Rosenthal. Ed. by Kathleen Tucker. (Albert Whitman Concept Bks.). (Illus.). 32p. (ps-2). 1986. 11.95 (ISBN 0-8075-7535-6). A Whitman.
Some Things Are Never Discounted. Fran Sciacca & Jill Sciacca. (Lifelines Ser.). (YA) (gr. 7 up). 1988. pap. 3.95 (ISBN 0-89066-114-6). World Wide Pubs.
Some Things Dark & Dangerous. Ed. by Joan Kahn. 224p. 1982. pap. 2.25 (ISBN 0-380-01556-0, 61168-6, Flare). Avon.
Some Things Fierce & Fatal. Ed. by Joan Kahn. 176p. 1982. pap. 2.25 (ISBN 0-380-00388-0, 61176-7, Flare). Avon.
Some Things Go Together. Charlotte Zolotow. LC 82-48694. (Illus.). 24p. (ps-3). 1983. 11.95i (ISBN 0-690-04327-9, Crowell Jr Bks); PLB 11.89 (ISBN 0-690-04328-7). HarpJ.
Some Things Go Together. Charlotte Zolotow. LC 82-48694. (Trophy Picture Bks.). (Illus.). 32p. (ps-3). 1987. pap. 3.95 (ISBN 0-06-443133-9, Trophy). HarpJ.
Some Things I Did. Roxy L. Gordon. (Illus.). 160p. 1971. 12.50 (ISBN 0-88426-012-7). Encino Pr.
Some Things Remembered. Hillier Krieghbaum. LC 81-20097. 9.75 (ISBN 0-916346-44-7). Harbor Hill Bks.
Some Things Strange & Sinister. Ed. by Joan Kahn. LC 72-9871. 256p. (YA) (gr. 7 up). 1973. 14.70i (ISBN 0-06-023086-X); PLB 13.89 (ISBN 0-06-023087-8). HarpJ.
Some Things That Fly There Be see Poetry Unfolding.
Some Things That Matter. facsimile ed. George A. Riddell. LC 74-37793. (Essay Index Reprint Ser). Repr. of 1922 ed. 18.00 (ISBN 0-8369-2620-X). Ayer Co Pubs.
Some Things Worth Knowing. facsimile ed. Stuart Chase. LC 76-90622. (Essay Index Reprint Ser.). 1958. 21.50 (ISBN 0-8369-1557-7). Ayer Co Pubs.
Some Things You Just Can't Do by Yourself. (ps-3). 1973. 3.50 (ISBN 0-938678-00-0). New Seed.
Some Thoughts About Verse. T. S. Omond. 1923. 10.00 (ISBN 0-8274-3464-2). R West.
Some Thoughts Concerning the Several Causes & Occasions of Atheism, Especially in the Present Age. John Edwards. LC 80-48568. (Philosophy of John Locke Ser.). 268p. 1984. lib. bdg. 35.00 (ISBN 0-8240-5603-5). Garland Pub.
Some Thoughts for My Friends. rev. ed. Mari Stein. (Illus.). 1977. pap. 4.95 (ISBN 0-918546-02-8). Quarterdeck.
Some Thoughts on Beethoven's Choral Symphony, with Writings on Other Musical Subjects. Ralph Vaughan-Williams. LC 81-2079. (Illus.). 172p. 1981. Repr. of 1953 ed. lib. bdg. 35.00x (ISBN 0-313-23049-8, VWST). Greenwood.
Some Thoughts on Beethoven's Choral Symphony with Writings on other Musical Subjects. Richard Vaughan Williams. 172p. Repr. of 1957 ed. lib. bdg. 39.00 (Pub. by Am Repr Serv). Am Biog Serv.
Some Thoughts on Byzantine Military Strategy. Walter E. Kaegi, Jr. 18p. 1983. pap. 2.00 (ISBN 0-916586-95-2). Holy Cross Orthodox.
Some Thoughts on Canada-United States Sectoral Free Trade. Michael Hart. 1984. pap. text ed. 7.00x (ISBN 0-88645-014-4, Pub. by Inst Res Pub Canada). Brookfield Pub Co.
Some Thoughts on Higher Education. Soedjatmoko. (Occasional Paper: No. 15). 1975. pap. 1.00 (ISBN 0-89192-155-9, Pub. by ICED). Interbk Inc.
Some Thoughts on Hilaire Belloc: Ten Studies. Patrick Braybrook. 1973. 17.50 (ISBN 0-8274-1717-9). R West.
Some Thoughts on Hilaire Belloc: Ten Studies. Patrick Braybrooke. LC 68-1140. (Studies in Irish Literature, No. 16). 1969. Repr. lib. bdg. 48.95x (ISBN 0-8383-0649-7). Haskell.
Some Thoughts on Marriage. Margaret Ruhe. 36p. 1982. pap. 1.95 (ISBN 0-933770-23-5). Kalimat.
Some Thoughts on the Gita. 162p. 1983. pap. 5.95 (ISBN 0-912181-08-7). East School Pr.
Some Thoughts on the Interest of Money in General, & Particularly in the Publick Funds. Repr. of 1738 ed. 26.00 (ISBN 0-384-56610-3). Johnson Repr.
Some Thoughts on the Mayor of Casterbridge. W. H. Gardner. LC 74-16131. 1930. lib. bdg. 15.00 (ISBN 0-8414-4554-0). Folcroft.
Some Thoughts on the Mayor of Casterbridge. W. H. Gardner. 52p. 1980. Repr. of 1930 ed. lib. bdg. 10.00 (ISBN 0-8492-4959-7). R West.
Some Thoughts That Seem Important. Ollie Goldsmith. (Illus.). 1983. 9.90 (ISBN 0-911843-00-0). Myriad.
Some Thoughts to Live By Philosophy of Fleet Admiral Chester W. Nimitz of Fredericksburg, Texas. 1971. pap. 1.00 (ISBN 0-934841-02-0). Adm Nimitz Foun.
Some Three Hundred Fresh Allusions to Shakeapeare from 1594 to 1694. F. J. Furnivall. (New Shakespeare Soc., London, Ser. 4: No. 3). pap. 37.00 (ISBN 0-8115-0240-6). Kraus Repr.
Some Time in the Sun: The Hollywood Years of F. Scott Fitzgerald, William Faulkner, Nathanael West, Aldous Huxley, & James Agee. Tom Dardis. (Illus.). 312p. 1988. pap. 12.95 (ISBN 0-87910-116-4, Dist. by Longwood Publishing Group). Limelight Edns.
Some Topics in Graph Theory. H. Y. Yap. (London Mathematical Society Lecture Note Ser.: No. 108). (Illus.). 230p. 1986. pap. 24.95 (ISBN 0-521-33944-8). Cambridge U Pr.
Some Topics in Nonlinear Function Analysis. M. C. Joshi & R. K. Bose. 311p. 1985. 19.95 (ISBN 0-470-20024-3). Halsted Pr.
Some Topics on Inverse Problems: Proceedings of the Fourteenth Workshop on Interdisciplinary Study of Inverse Problems, Montpellier, France, Nov 30-Dec 4, 1987. Ed. by Pierre C. Sabatier. 420p. 1988. 58.00 (ISBN 9971-50-647-5, ZB0642PP). World Scientific Pub.
Some Topological & Geometrical Structures in Banach Spaces. Ghoussoub et al. (MEMO Ser.: Vol. 378). 124p. 1987. pap. text ed. 15.00 (ISBN 0-8218-2441-4). Am Math.
Some Traces of the Pre-Olympian World in Greek Literature & Myth. E. A Butterworth. LC 85-21959. (Illus.). 1966. 44.25x (ISBN 3-11-005010-2). De Gruyter.
Some Traditional Sri Lankan Medical Techniques Related to Acupuncture. 98p. 1981. pap. 5.00 (ISBN 92-808-0236-4, TUNU160, UNU). UNIPUB.
Some Trees. John Ashbery. LC 56-5946. (American Poetry Ser: No. 14). 1978. pap. 4.95 (ISBN 0-912946-47-4). Ecco Pr.
Some Trends in the Evolution of Science Curriculum Centres in Asia. (APEID Occasional Papers: No. 12). 49p. 1983. pap. 5.00 (ISBN 0-686-44036-6, UB128, UNESCO Regional Office). UNIPUB.
Some Tribal Origins, Laws & Customs of the Balkans. Mary E. Durham. LC 76-44710. (Illus.). Repr. of 1928 ed. 37.50 (ISBN 0-404-15856-0). AMS Pr.
Some Trust in Chariots. Donald Eidson. 69p. 1984. text ed. 9.95 (ISBN 0-89390-055-9). Resource Pubns.
Some Turns of Thought in Modern Philosophy: Five Essays. facs. ed. George Santayana. LC 67-23268. (Essay Index Reprint Ser). 1933. 11.00 (ISBN 0-8369-0849-X). Ayer Co Pubs.
Some Types of Attention see Report.
Some Unease & Angels. Elaine Feinstein. LC 77-11250. pap. 5.00 (ISBN 0-940580-05-5). Green River.
Some Unknown Facts of American History. Julian G. Hearne, Jr. 244p. 1987. 17.00 (ISBN 0-9618158-0-9). McClain.
Some Unpublished Letters of Henry D. & Sophia E. Thoreau: A Chapter in the History of a Still-Born Book. Henry David Thoreau. Ed. by Samuel A. Jones. LC 80-2684. (Thoreau Ser.). (Illus.). 136p. Repr. of 1899 ed. 18.00 (ISBN 0-404-19078-2). AMS Pr.
Some Unpublished Letters of Horace Walpole. Spencer Walpole. 1974. Repr. of 1902 ed. lib. bdg. 25.00 (ISBN 0-8414-9438-X). Folcroft.
Some Unpublished Letters of Lord Chesterfield. Lord Chesterfield. 1937. 32.50 (ISBN 0-8274-3465-0). R West.
Some Unpublished Letters of Lord Chesterfield. Sidney L. Gulick. Repr. of 1937 ed. lib. bdg. 17.00 (ISBN 0-8414-4590-7). Folcroft.
Some Unpublished Letters of Sir Walter Scott: From the Collection in the Brotherton Library. Walter Scott. Ed. by J. Alexander Symington. LC 73-11308. 1974. Repr. of 1932 ed. lib. bdg. 30.00 (ISBN 0-8414-7577-6). Folcroft.
Some Unseen Power: Diary of a Ghost Hunter. Philip Paul. 208p. 1988. 39.00x (ISBN 0-7090-2384-7, Pub. by R Hale Ltd UK). State Mutual Bk.
Some Uses of Life Insurance in Estate Planning. John J. Creedon. 95p. 1974. pap. 2.00 (ISBN 0-317-30857-2, B300). Am Law Inst.
Some Values Derived from Extensive Reading of General Science. Francis D. Curtis. LC 75-177601. (Columbia University. Teachers College. Contributions to Education: No. 163). Repr. of 1924 ed. 22.50 (ISBN 0-404-55163-7). AMS Pr.
Some Vanity of Mine Art: The Masque in English Renaissance Drama, 2 vols. Catherine M. Shaw. Ed. by James Hogg. (Jacobean Drama Studies). 580p. (Orig.). 1979. pap. 30.00 (ISBN 3-7052-0372-X, Salzburg Studies). Longwood Pub Group.
Some Verdicts of History Reviewed: Abraham Cowley, Matthew Prior, Benjamin Franklin, William Cobbett. William Stebbing. 1978. Repr. of 1887 ed. lib. bdg. 50.00 (ISBN 0-8495-4882-9). Arden Lib.
Some Verdicts of History Reviewed: Essay Index Reprint Ser. William Stebbing. LC 72-8545. 1972. Repr. of 1887 ed. 24.50 (ISBN 0-8369-7327-5). Ayer Co Pubs.
Some Versions of Pastoral. William Empson. LC 52-1182. 1960. pap. 8.95 (ISBN 0-8112-0038-8, NDP92). New Directions.
Some Victorian & Georgian Catholics. facs. ed. Patrick Braybrooke. LC 67-22080. (Essay Index Reprint Ser.). 1932. 18.00 (ISBN 0-8369-1325-6). Ayer Co Pubs.
Some Victorian Portraits & Others. Hilda Martindale. LC 76-126324. (Biography Index Reprint Ser.). Repr. of 1948 ed. 14.00 (ISBN 0-8369-8030-1). Ayer Co Pubs.
Some Victorian Portraits & Others. Hilda Martindale. 106p. 1980. Repr. lib. bdg. 25.00 (ISBN 0-89984-332-8). Century Bookbindery.
Some Victorian Portraits & Others. Hilda Martindale. 1977. Repr. of 1948 ed. lib. bdg. 29.50 (ISBN 0-8414-6224-0). Folcroft.
Some Views from the Campus. Ed. by Fredrick C. Mosher & Kenneth W. Thompson. LC 87-8193. (Papers on Presidential Transitions & Foreign Policy: Vol. IV). 128p. (Orig.). 1987. lib. bdg. 19.75 (ISBN 0-8191-6331-7, Co-pub. by White Miller Center); pap. text ed. 8.75 (ISBN 0-8191-6332-5, Co-pub. by White Miller Center). U Pr of Amer.
Some Vistas of Modern Mathematics: Dynamic Programming, Invariant Imbedding, & the Mathematical Biosciences. Richard E. Bellman. LC 68-12974. pap. 37.80 (ISBN 0-317-08655-3, 2004315). Bks Demand UMI.
Some Welsh Legends & Other Poems. Ed. by John H. Davies. LC 77-94572. 1979. Repr. of 1893 ed. lib. bdg. 35.00 (ISBN 0-89341-181-7). Longwood Pub Group.
Some Winded, Wild Beast. Christina V. Pacosz. 1985. pap. 2.50x. Black & Red.
Some Women of France. Paul B. Watson. LC 73-90691. (Essay Index Reprint Ser.). 1936. 21.50 (ISBN 0-8369-1433-3). Ayer Co Pubs.
Some Wood Properties of Pinus Patula from Uganda & Techniques Developed. R. A. Plumptre. 1978. 30.00x (ISBN 0-85074-032-0, Pub. by For Lib Comm England). State Mutual Bk.
Some Words Have Wings. Leon Knight. LC 85-70303. 60p. (Orig.). 1985. pap. 4.50 (ISBN 0-940248-24-7). Guild Pr.
Some Words Help, Some Words Hurt. Elspeth C. Murphy. LC 87-31474. (Proverbs to Grow on Ser.). 24p. (ps-2). 1988. pap. 2.95 (ISBN 1-55513-164-6, Chariot Bks). Cook.
Some Words of Jane Austen. Stuart M. Tave. LC 73-78670. xii, 288p. 1976. pap. 3.95X (ISBN 0-226-79017-7, P676, Phoen). U of Chicago Pr.
Some Words on Allegory in England. Frederick Y. Powell. LC 72-193088. 1910. lib. bdg. 22.00 (ISBN 0-8414-9267-0). Folcroft.
Some Wordsworth Finds. James Medborough. LC 73-628. 1974. Repr. of 1895 ed. lib. bdg. 17.50 (ISBN 0-8414-1443-2). Folcroft.
Some Working-Class Movements of the Nineteenth Century. R. F. Wearmouth. 1977. lib. bdg. 59.95 (ISBN 0-8490-2630-X). Gordon Pr.
Some Yellow Flowers. Mara Smith & Ray Smith. (Orig.). 1978. pap. 2.00 (ISBN 0-686-02397-8). Kirk Pr.
Somebody Come & Play. Clare McNally. 320p. (Orig.). 1987. pap. 3.95 (ISBN 0-8125-2164-1, Dist. by St Martin's Pr & Warner Pub Servs). Tor Bks.
Somebody Else's Kids. Torey L. Hayden. 336p. 1982. pap. 3.95 (ISBN 0-380-59949-X). Avon.
Somebody Else's Life. Morris Philipson. 1988. pap. 7.95 (ISBN 0-317-70133-9, PL). Har-Row.
Somebody in Boots. Nelson Algren. (Classic Reprint Ser.). 250p. 1987. pap. 8.95 (ISBN 0-938410-40-7). Thunder's Mouth.
Somebody Killed Reddy Fox. Susan K. Sibley. Ed. by Ronald H. Bayes. (Illus.). 64p. (Orig.). 1980. pap. 5.00 (ISBN 0-932662-33-1). St Andrews NC.
Somebody Killed the Messenger. Clarissa Watson. 224p. 1988. 16.95 (ISBN 0-689-11963-1). Atheneum.
Somebody Lives Inside: The Holy Spirit. Sharon L. Roberts. (Concept Books for Children). (Illus.). 24p. (Orig.). (gr. k-4). 1986. pap. 3.95 saddlestitched (ISBN 0-570-08530-6, 56-1557). Concordia.
Somebody Loves You. Helen S. Rice. 128p. 1976. 13.95 (ISBN 0-8007-0818-0); large-print ed. 10.95 (ISBN 0-8007-1120-3). Revell.
Somebody-Nothing. Ed. by Lisl Beer. (Silver Series of Puppet Plays). pap. 1.50 (ISBN 0-8283-1253-2). Branden Pub Co.
Somebody Please Love Me. Aviva Hellman. 1985. pap. 3.95 (ISBN 0-8217-1604-2). Zebra.
Somebody Real. Compiled by Nicholas Duva. (Illus.). 192p. (Orig.). (gr. 5-12). 1973. 6.95 (ISBN 0-912834-01-3); pap. 3.95 (ISBN 0-912834-04-8). Am Faculty Pr.
Somebody Special to Love. Marilyn Donahue. LC 88-14809. (Quick Fox Line Ser.). (gr. 3-7). 1988. pap. 3.95 (ISBN 0-89191-360-2, Chariot Bks). Cook.
Somebody Talks A Lot. Paul Hoover. LC 82-20217. 1982. pap. 3.50 (ISBN 0-916328-17-1). Yellow Pr.
Somebody to Kill. Richard Reinsmith. (Bodyguard Ser.). 240p. 1984. pap. 2.50 (ISBN 0-8439-2072-6, Leisure Bks). Leisure NY.
Somebody's Brother. Carla Eugster. 1983. pap. 6.00 (ISBN 0-686-89395-6). Samisdat.
Somebody's Brother: A History of the Salvation Army Men's Social Service Department 1891-1985. E. H. McKinley. LC 86-8604. (Studies in American Religion: Vol. 21). 264p. 1986. lib. bdg. 59.95x (ISBN 0-88946-048-5). E Mellen.
Somebody's Calling My Name. Wyatt T. Walker. LC 79-14155. 1979. 8.95 (ISBN 0-8170-0849-7). Judson.
Somebody's Darling. Larry McMurtry. 352p. 1987. pap. 6.95 (ISBN 0-317-56596-6, Touchstone Bks). S&S.
Somebody's Darling. Larry McMurtry. 416p. 1988. pap. 4.50 (ISBN 0-671-66014-4). PB.
Somebody's Daughter, Somebody's Wife. Lorinda Hagen. (Orig.). 1980. pap. 2.50 (ISBN 0-8439-8000-1, Tiara Bks). Leisure NY.
Somebody's Else's Life. Morris Philipson. LC 86-45680. 288p. 1987. 16.45i (ISBN 0-06-015668-6, HarpT). Har-Row.
Somebody's Else's Life. Morris Philipson. LC 86-45680. 288p. 1988. pap. 7.95 (ISBN 0-06-091454-8, PL-1454, PL). Har-Row.
Somebody's Hero. Bluth Brothers Staff. (Buddies Ser.). (Illus.). 48p. (gr. k-6). 1984. 5.95 (ISBN 0-8249-8063-8). Ideals.
Somebody's Horse. Dorothy N. Morrison. LC 86-3648. 224p. (gr. 4-8). 1986. 13.95 (ISBN 0-689-31290-3, Atheneum Childrens Bks). Macmillan.
Somebody's Horse. Dorothy N. Morrison. (gr. 4-8). 1987. pap. 2.95 (ISBN 0-8167-1046-5). Troll Assocs.
Somebody's Husband, Somebody's Son: The Story of the Yorkshire Ripper. Gordon Burn. 288p. 1985. 16.95 (ISBN 0-670-80328-6). Viking.
Somebody's Husband, Somebody's Son: The Story of the Yorkshire Ripper. Gordon Burn. 288p. 1986. pap. 3.95 (ISBN 0-14-009614-0). Penguin.
Somebody's Mother. Adele Gordon. 48p. 1983. 6.95 (ISBN 0-89962-325-5). Todd & Honeywell.
Somebody's Mother. Susan F. Kepner. LC 87-18003. (Illus.). 64p. (Orig.). 1987. pap. 4.95 (ISBN 0-89407-088-6). Strawberry Hill.
Somebody's Neighbors. Rose Cooke. 1972. Repr. of 1881 ed. lib. bdg. 46.00 (ISBN 0-8422-8028-6). Irvington.
Somebody's Wish. Fred Hopper. 80p. 1988. 8.95 (ISBN 0-89962-633-5). Todd & Honeywell.
Someday. Charlotte Zolotow. LC 64-16654. (Illus.). (gr. k-3). 1965. PLB 11.89 (ISBN 0-06-027016-0). HarpJ.
Someday Angeline. Louis Sachar. (Illus.). 156p. (Orig.). (gr. 3-7). 1983. pap. 2.75 (ISBN 0-380-83444-8, Camelot). Avon.
Someday I'll Travel. Peter S. Gilchrist. LC 80-85057. (Illus.). 200p. 1980. text ed. 20.00 (ISBN 0-917122-02-X). Gilchem Corp.
Someday It'll All Be Yours...Or Will It? How to Survive-& Enjoy Succession in a Family Business. Donald J. Jonovic. LC 83-26823. 205p. 1984. 24.95x (ISBN 0-915607-00-X). Jamieson Pr.
Someday Syndrome. Rod Parsley. 37p. 1986. pap. 2.95 (ISBN 0-88144-069-8). Christian Pub.
Someday the Rabbi Will Leave. Harry Kemelman. 288p. 1986. pap. 3.50 (ISBN 0-449-20945-8, Crest). Fawcett.
Someday with My Father. Helen E. Buckley. LC 85-42637. (Illus.). 32p. (ps-3). 1985. 12.70i (ISBN 0-06-020877-5); PLB 12.89g (ISBN 0-06-020878-3). HarpJ.
Someday You'll Find Her, Charlie Brown. Charles M. Schulz. LC 82-3666. (Charlie Brown TV Specials Ser.). (Illus.). 48p. (gr. 1-6). 1982. lib. bdg. 6.99 (ISBN 0-394-95429-7). Random.
Somedays It Feels Like It Wants to Rain. David Zaslow. LC 76-46244. (Illus.). (gr. 2-6). 1976. pap. 3.95 (ISBN 0-89411-001-2). Kids Matter.
Somehow Tenderness Survives: Stories of Southern Africa. Ed. by Hazel Rochman. LC 88-916. (Charlotte Zolotow Book Ser.). 160p. (YA) (gr. 7 up). 1988. 12.75 (ISBN 0-06-025022-4); PLB 12.95 (ISBN 0-06-025023-2). HarpJ.
Somehow We Survive. Ed. by Sterling Plumpp. (Illus.). 160p. 1982. 10.95 (ISBN 0-938410-02-4); pap. 6.95 (ISBN 0-938410-01-6). Thunder's Mouth.
Someone. Robert Pinget. Tr. by Barbara Wright from Fr. LC 83-63101. 253p. 1984. 12.95 (ISBN 0-87376-043-3). Red Dust.
Someone Cares: The Collected Poems of Helen Steiner Rice. Helen S. Rice. 128p. 1972. 13.95 (ISBN 0-8007-0524-6); large-print ed. o.p. 12.95 (ISBN 0-8007-0959-4). Revell.
Someone Close Drinks too Much. 16p. 1983. 0.75 (ISBN 0-89486-183-2). Hazelden.
Someone Else to Love. Susan P. Schutz. LC 75-37143. (Illus.). 95p. (Orig.). 1976. pap. 4.95 (ISBN 0-88396-014-1). Blue Mtn Pr CO.
Someone Else's Dreams. John Yamrus. LC 80-70611. (Illus.). 60p. (Orig.). 1981. pap. 4.95 (ISBN 0-930090-12-8); pap. 10.00 special ltd. ed. (ISBN 0-686-69666-2). Applezaba.
Someone Else's Grave. Alison Smith. 192p. 1984. 11.95 (ISBN 0-312-74400-5, J Kahn). St Martin.
Someone for Sara. Judith Enderle. (Caprice Romance Ser.: No. 10). 192p. 1984. pap. 2.25 (ISBN 0-441-77461-X, Pub. by Tempo). Ace Bks.
Someone Heard... A Comprehensive Educator's Handbook for Child Abuse & Neglect Recognition & Prevention. Lucy D. Braun. Ed. by Toni M. Strollo. vi, 63p. (Orig., Designed to accompany the book, "Death from Child Abuse... & No One Heard". PRoduct is sold only as part of a set, including the book). 1988. wkbk. 10.00 (ISBN 0-930507-07-X). Currier-Davis.
Someone I Love Died. Christine Tangvald. (Please Help Me God Ser.). 24p. (ps-2). 1988. 5.95 (ISBN 1-55513-490-4, Chariot Bks). Cook.

Something Iridescent. Roger Pfingston. LC 85-72587. 98p. (Orig.). 1987. pap. 7.95 (ISBN 0-935306-37-4). Barnwood Pr.

Something Is Going to Happen. Charlotte Zolotow. LC 87-26661. (Illus.). 32p. (ps-3). 1988. 12.95i (ISBN 0-06-027028-4); PLB 12.89 (ISBN 0-06-027029-2). HarpJ.

Something Is Happening Here. Ramon Hernandez. LC 82-61182. 300p. (Orig.). 1983. pap. 15.00 (ISBN 0-89295-025-0). Society Sp & Sp-Am.

Something Is Stirring in World Orthodoxy. S. Harakas. 1978. pap. 3.25 (ISBN 0-937032-04-2). Light&Life Pub Co MN.

Something Is Wrong at My House. Diane Davis. LC 84-62129. (Illus.). 40p. (Orig.). (gr. 1-6). 1985. PLB 9.95 (ISBN 0-943990-11-4); pap. 3.50 (ISBN 0-943990-10-6). Parenting Pr.

Something I've Been Meaning to Tell You. Alice Munro. 208p. 1983. pap. 2.95 (ISBN 0-451-14343-4, Sig). NAL.

Something I've Been Meaning to Tell You: Thirteen Stories. Alice Munro. 256p. 1984. pap. 8.95 (ISBN 0-452-26021-3, Plume). NAL.

Something Left to Lose. Robin Brancato. LC 75-30699. (Illus.). 192p. (gr. 7 up). 1976. 6.95 (ISBN 0-394-83183-7). Knopf.

Something Like a Poem. Neil Paterson. 32p. 1986. 20.00X (ISBN 0-7223-1988-6, Pub. by A H Stockwell England). State Mutual Bk.

Something Like an Autobiography. Akira Kurosawa. Tr. by Audie Bock. LC 81-48100. 224p. 1982. 14.50 (ISBN 0-394-50938-2). Knopf.

Something Like an Autobiography. Akira Kurosawa. Tr. by Audie E. Bock from Japanese. LC 82-48900. 240p. 1983. pap. 8.95 (ISBN 0-394-71439-3, Vin). Random.

Something Like Horace: Studies in the Art & Allusion of Pope's Horatian Satires. John M. Aden. LC 71-83208. 1969. 7.95x (ISBN 0-8265-1138-4). Vanderbilt U Pr.

Something Meaningful for God. Ed. by C. J. Dyck. LC 80-10975. (MCC Story Ser.: Vol. 4). 408p. (Orig.). 1981. pap. 7.95x (ISBN 0-8361-1244-X). Herald Pr.

Something Meaningful for God. LC 80-10975. 408p. 1981. pap. 7.95 (ISBN 0-317-64800-4). Herald Pr.

Something Medieval. J. K. Randall. LC 80-80808. (Illus.). 41p. Date not set. 12.95 (ISBN 0-939044-24-2). Lingua Pr.

Something More. Catherine Marshall. 1976. pap. 3.50 (ISBN 0-380-00601-4, 60104-4). Avon.

Something More Than Force: Poems for Guatemala, 1971-1981. Zoe Anglesey. 48p. 1982. signed & numbered ed. 20.00x (ISBN 0-938566-13-X). Adastra Pr.

Something More than Force: Poems for Guatemala, 1971-1982. 2nd ed. Zoe Anglesey. 48p. 1984. pap. 3.50 (ISBN 0-938566-21-0). Adastra Pr.

Something More Than Human: Biographies of Leaders in American Methodist Higher Education. Ed. by Charles E. Cole. LC 85-51267. (Illus.). 256p. 1986. 7.95 (ISBN 0-938162-04-7). United Meth Educ.

Something More Than Love...the X Factors in a Good Marriage. rev. ed. Harold J. Sala. LC 77-94646. 1983. pap. 8.95 (ISBN 0-89636-103-9). Accent Bks.

Something More Than Night: The Case of Raymond Chandler. Peter Wolfe. LC 84-71588. 242p. 1985. 21.95 (ISBN 0-87972-293-2); pap. 10.95 (ISBN 0-87972-294-0). Bowling Green Univ.

Something New. M. E. Cooper. (Couples Ser.: No. 24). 208p. (Orig.). (gr. 7 up). 1987. pap. 2.50 (ISBN 0-590-40794-5). Scholastic Inc.

Something New Begins. Lilian Moore. LC 81-1723. (Illus.). 128p. (gr. 3 up). 1982. 10.95 (ISBN 0-689-30818-3, Atheneum Childrens Bks). Macmillan.

Something New to Do. Ski Michaels. LC 85-14021. (Illus.). 48p. (Orig.). (gr. 1-3). 1986. PLB 9.49 (ISBN 0-8167-0634-4); pap. text ed. 1.95 (ISBN 0-8167-0635-2). Troll Assocs.

Something New under the Sun, Building Connecticut's First Solar Home. Ruth F. Frank. LC 79-22222. (Illus.). 1980. 8.95 (ISBN 0-931790-03-4). Brick Hse Pub.

Something Nice to Look At. (gr. k-2). 4.25 (ISBN 0-87497-103-9, 18355). Merrimack.

Something of Men I Have Known with Some Papers of a General Nature, Political, Historical & Retrospective. Adlai E Stevenson. 31.00 (ISBN 0-8369-6992-8, 7869). Ayer Co Pubs.

Something of the Night. Mary McMullen. 160p. 1986. pap. 2.95 (ISBN 0-515-08752-1). Jove Pubns.

Something of the Wonderful. John M. Scott. 1986. 4.50 (ISBN 0-8198-6867-1); pap. 3.50 (ISBN 0-8198-6868-X). Dghtrs St Paul.

Something of Value. Donna F. Crow. 192p. 1988. pap. 5.95 (ISBN 0-89693-354-7). SP Pubns.

Something Old, Something New. Lillian Africano. 384p. 1983. pap. 3.50 (ISBN 0-515-05865-3). Jove Pubns.

Something Old, Something New. Emily Chase. (Girls of Canby Hall Ser.). 224p. (Orig.). (gr. 5-10). 1986. pap. 2.50 (ISBN 0-590-40391-5). Scholastic Inc.

Something Old, Something New: Ethnic Weddings in America. Gail F. Stern et al. LC 87-71305. (Illus.). 34p. (Orig.). 1987. pap. 5.00 (ISBN 0-937437-02-6). Balch IES Pr.

Something Olde, Something New, Something Borrowed - Ever True. Judith D. Meade. 48p. (Orig.). 1988. pap. 4.95 (ISBN 0-945785-01-1). LFL Creations.

Something on My Mind. Nikki Grimes. LC 77-86266. (Pied Piper Bk.). (Illus.). 32p. (gr. k up). 1986. pap. 3.95 (ISBN 0-8037-0273-6, 0383-120). Dial Bks Young.

Something Out There. Leslie Davis. (Moonstone Mystery Romance Ser.: No. 5). (gr. 5 up). pap. 2.50 (ISBN 0-671-62856-9). Archway.

Something Out There. Nadine Gordimer. 1984. 15.95 (ISBN 0-670-65660-7). Viking.

Something Out There. Nadine Gordimer. (Fiction Ser.). 208p. 1986. pap. 5.95 (ISBN 0-14-007711-1). Penguin.

Something Precious Surrounds Me. Dee Hedenland. 1987. 5.95 (ISBN 0-533-07089-9). Vantage.

Something Queer at the Ball Park. Elizabeth Levy. (Something Queer Ser.). (Illus.). 48p. (gr. 1-4). 1984. pap. 2.50 (ISBN 0-440-48116-3, YB). Dell.

Something Queer at the Ball Park. Elizabeth Levy. 12.75 (ISBN 0-317-60064-8). Peter Smith.

Something Queer at the Haunted School. Elizabeth Levy. LC 81-1940. (Something Queer Ser.). (Illus.). 48p. (gr. 1-3). 1982. 8.95 (ISBN 0-440-08349-4); PLB 8.89 (ISBN 0-440-08355-9). Delacorte.

Something Queer at the Haunted School. Elizabeth Levy. (Something Queer Ser.). (Illus.). 48p. (gr. 1-4). 1983. pap. 2.50 (ISBN 0-440-48461-8, YB). Dell.

Something Queer at the Haunted School. Elizabeth Levy. LC 81-1940. (Illus.). 48p. (ps-3). 1982. pap. 9.95 (ISBN 0-385-28992-8). Delacorte.

Something Queer at the Lemonade Stand. Elizabeth Levy. Tr. by Mordicai Gerstein. LC 81-69666. (Something Queer Ser.). (Illus.). 48p. (gr. 1-3). 1982. 7.95 (ISBN 0-440-07859-8); PLB 7.89 (ISBN 0-440-07878-4). Delacorte.

Something Queer at the Lemonade Stand. Elizabeth Levy. (Something Queer Ser.). (Illus.). 48p. (gr. k-6). 1983. pap. 2.50 (ISBN 0-440-48495-2, YB). Dell.

Something Queer at the Lemonade Stand. Elizabeth Levy. LC 81-69666. (Illus.). 48p. (ps-3). 1982. pap. 10.95 (ISBN 0-385-28901-4). Delacorte.

Something Queer at the Library. Elizabeth Levy. (Something Queer Ser.). (Illus.). 48p. (gr. 1-4). 1984. pap. 2.50 (ISBN 0-440-48120-1, YB). Dell.

Something Queer in Rock N' Roll. Elizabeth Levy. LC 86-19772. 48p. (gr. k-3). 1987. pap. 12.95 (ISBN 0-385-29547-2). Delacorte.

Something Queer Is Going On. Elizabeth Levy. (Something Queer Ser.). (Illus.). 48p. (gr. 1-4). 1982. pap. 2.50 (ISBN 0-440-47974-6, YB). Dell.

Something Queer Is Going On. Elizabeth Levy. 13.00 (ISBN 0-8446-6257-7). Peter Smith.

Something Queer on Vacation. Elizabeth Levy. LC 78-72858. (Something Queer Ser.). (Illus.). (gr. 1-3). 1980. 10.95 (ISBN 0-440-08346-X); PLB 10.89 (ISBN 0-440-08347-8). Delacorte.

Something Queer on Vacation. Elizabeth Levy. (Something Queer Ser.). (Illus.). 48p. (gr. 1-4). 1982. pap. 2.50 (ISBN 0-440-47968-1, YB). Dell.

Something Queer on Vacation. Elizabeth Levy. LC 78-72858. (Illus.). 48p. (ps-3). 1980. pap. 6.95 (ISBN 0-385-28987-1). Delacorte.

Something Said: Essays. Gilbert Sorrentino. LC 84-60690. 288p. (Orig.). 1984. pap. 15.50 (ISBN 0-86547-177-0). N Point Pr.

Something Shady. Sarah Dreher. 272p. 1986. pap. 8.95 (ISBN 0-934678-07-3). New victoria Pubs.

Something Sleeping in the Hall. Karla Kuskin. LC 82-47721. (Charlotte Zolotow Bks.). (Illus.). 64p. (gr. k-3). 1985. 9.70i (ISBN 0-06-023633-7); PLB 10.89g (ISBN 0-06-023634-5). HarpJ.

Something Special. Associated Women's Organization, Mars Hill Bible School. Ed. by Peggy Simpson & Linda Stanley. 1977. pap. 4.95 (ISBN 0-89137-408-6). Quality Pubns.

Something Special. Imogene Forte et al. (Illus.). 200p. (ps-3). 1982. pap. text ed. 9.95 (ISBN 0-86530-001-1, IP-011). Incentive Pubns.

Something Special. David McPhail. (Illus.). 32p. (ps-3). 1988. 10.95 (ISBN 0-316-56324-2, Joy St Bks). Little.

Something Special for Me. Vera B. Williams. LC 82-11884. (Illus.). 32p. (gr. k-3). 1983. 11.75 (ISBN 0-688-01806-8); PLB 11.88 (ISBN 0-688-01807-6). Greenwillow.

Something Special for Me. Vera B. Williams. (Illus.). (ps-3). 1987. 3.95 (ISBN 0-688-06526-0, Mulberry Bks). Morrow.

Something Special Horse. Lynn Hall. LC 84-23636. (Illus.). 112p. (gr. 5-7). 1985. 11.95 (ISBN 0-684-18343-9, Pub. by Scribner). Macmillan.

Something Special Within. 2nd ed. Betts Richter. (Illus.). 48p. (ps-5). 1982. pap. 5.50 (ISBN 0-87516-488-9). DeVorss.

Something Supernatural. Janet McReynolds. 103p. 1986. pap. 3.95 (ISBN 0-88144-038-8). Christian Pub.

Something Suspicious. Kathryn O. Galbraith. LC 85-4003. 168p. (gr. 3-7). 1985. 11.95 (ISBN 0-689-50322-9, M K McElderry). Macmillan.

Something Suspicious. Kathryn O. Galbraith. 128p. (gr. 3 up). 1987. pap. 2.50 (ISBN 0-380-70253-3, Camelot). Avon.

Something the Cat Dragged In. Charlotte MacLeod. 208p. (Orig.). 1988. pap. 3.50 (ISBN 0-380-69096-9). Avon.

Something to Be Desired. Thomas McGuane. LC 83-43198. 224p. 1984. 14.45 (ISBN 0-394-52873-5). Random.

Something to Be Desired. Thomas McGuane. (Vintage Contemporaries Ser.). 1985. pap. 4.95 (ISBN 0-394-73156-5, Vin). Random.

Something to Believe in. Robert L. Short. LC 75-36754. (Illus.). 1977. pap. 5.95i (ISBN 0-06-067381-8, RD 169, HarpR). Har-Row.

Something to Cheer About: Legends from the Golden Age of Sports. Jack McDonald. 240p. (Orig.). 1986. pap. 6.95 (ISBN 0-15-683804-4, Harv). HarBraceJ.

Something to Count On. Emily Moore. LC 79-23277. 112p. (gr. 5 up). 1980. 9.95 (ISBN 0-525-39595-4). Dutton.

Something to Keep You Warm: The Roland Freeman Collection of Black American Quilts from the Mississippi Heartland. Ed. by Patti C. Black & Roland L. Freeman. (Illus.). 46p. (Orig.). 1981. pap. 6.00 (ISBN 0-938896-31-8). Mississippi Archives.

Something to Live For. Lissa H. Johnson. 1986. 5.95 (ISBN 0-8007-5228-7). Revell.

Something to Love: Barbara Pym's Novels. Diana T. Benet. LC 85-20976. (Literary Frontiers: No. 27). 144p. 1986. pap. 8.95 (ISBN 0-8262-0493-7). U of Mo Pr.

Something to Play. Geoffrey Brace. (Resources of Music Ser.). 5.95 (ISBN 0-521-07753-2). Cambridge U Pr.

Something to Quack About, Vol. 1. Sherry Gunter. (Illus.). 32p. (Orig.). 1987. pap. 6.95 (ISBN 0-941284-46-8). Deco Design Studio.

Something to Read to Someone: Sixteen Drawings. Spencer Holst & Beate Wheeler. 32p. 1980. ltd., signed ed. 15.00 (ISBN 0-930794-24-9); pap. 3.50 (ISBN 0-930794-34-6). Station Hill Pr.

Something to Say: William Carlos Williams on Younger Poets. William Carlos Williams. Intro. by James E. Breslin. LC 85-8890. 256p. 1985. 23.95 (ISBN 0-8112-0955-5). New Directions.

Something to Sing about, for Young Voices. Sally E. Schott & Lois B. Land. (Illus.). 352p. (gr. 7-9). 1984. pap. text ed. 25.95 (ISBN 0-911320-05-9); wkbk. for levels 1-3 2.95 (ISBN 0-911320-06-7). Schirmer Bks.

Something to Think about. Hennie Bristow. pap. 2.50 (ISBN 0-89315-292-7). Lambert Bk.

Something to Write Home About. Rachel Ingalls. LC 88-3029. 320p. 1988. 15.95 (ISBN 0-916782-98-0). Harvard Common Pr.

Something under the Bed Is Drooling: A Calvin & Hobbes Collection. Bill Watterson. 1988. pap. 6.95 (ISBN 0-8362-1825-6). Andrews & McMeel.

Something Upstairs: A Tale of Ghosts. Avi. LC 88-60094. 128p. (gr. 5-7). 1988. 11.95 (ISBN 0-531-05782-8); PLB 11.99 (ISBN 0-531-08382-9). Orchard Bks Watts.

Something Wicked. Carolyn G. Hart. 208p. (Orig.). 1988. pap. 3.50 (ISBN 0-553-27222-5). Bantam.

Something Wicked This Way Comes. Ray Bradbury. (gr. 6-12). 1983. pap. 3.50 (ISBN 0-553-25774-9). Bantam.

Something Wicked This Way Comes. Ray Bradbury. LC 82-48732. 1983. 18.45 (ISBN 0-394-53041-1). Knopf.

Something Wonderful. Judith McNaught. 432p. 1988. pap. 3.95 (ISBN 0-317-67375-0). PB.

Something Wonderful Right Away. Jeffrey Sweet. 432p. 1986. pap. 3.95 (ISBN 0-380-01884-5, 79707-0, Discus). Avon.

Something Wonderful Right Away. Jeffrey Sweet. LC 86-27319. (Illus.). 432p. 1987. pap. 14.95 (ISBN 0-87910-073-7). Limelight Edns.

Something Worth Saving. Myrna Marshall. (Living Bks). 192p. (Orig.). 1987. 3.50 (ISBN 0-8423-6068-9). Tyndale.

Something You Do in the Dark. Daniel Curzon. LC 77-150260. 1979. pap. 12.95 (ISBN 0-87949-138-8). Ashley Bks.

Something's Fishy. Sindy McKay. (Muppet Magic Ser.). (Illus.). 26p. (ps up). 1986. 12.95 (ISBN 1-55578-610-3). Worlds Wonder.

Something's Fishy in the Adirondacks. Francis Betters. 1985. 9.95 (ISBN 0-318-20255-7). Adirondack S P.

Something's Fishy! Jokes about Sea Creatures. Rick Walton & Ann Walton. (Make Me Laugh! Joke Bks.). (Illus.). 32p. (gr. 1-4). 1987. PLB 5.95 (ISBN 0-8225-0993-8); pap. 2.95. Lerner Pubns.

Something's Got to Help-& Yoga Can. Joy F. Herrick & Nancy Schraffenberger. LC 73-80177. (Illus.). 128p. 1974. 5.95 (ISBN 0-87131-126-7). M Evans.

Somethings It's O.K. to Tell Secrets. (gr. k-9). 1988. pap. 3.95. Scholastic Inc.

Something's Wrong in My House. Katherine Leiner. Ed. by M. Kline. (Illus.). 64p. (gr. k-6). 1988. 10.90 (ISBN 0-531-10506-7). Watts.

Something's Wrong with My Child: A Parent's Handbook about Children with Learning Disabilities. Milton Brutten et al. LC 79-10285. 284p. 1979. pap. 6.95 (ISBN 0-15-683805-2, Harv). HarBraceJ.

Something's Wrong with My Child! A Straightforward Presentation to Help Professionals & Parents to Better Understand Themselves in Dealing with the Emotionally-Charged Subject of Disabled Children. Harriet W. Rose. 210p. 1987. 26.75x (ISBN 0-398-05325-1). C C Thomas.

Somethin's Cookin' in the Mountains: A Cookbook Guidebook to Northeast Georgia. Rev. ed. Ed. by Jay Bucek & Cathy Bucek. (Illus.). 304p. 1986. casebnd. 9.95 (ISBN 0-9608770-4-5). Soque.

Somethin's Cookin' in the Mountains: A Cookbook Guidebook to Northeast Georgia. rev. ed. Ed. by Jay Bucek & Kathy Bucek. (Illus.). 304p. 1986. spiral bnd. 9.95 (ISBN 0-9608770-5-3). Soque.

Sometime. Robert Herrick. (Collected Works of Robert Herrick). 1988. Repr. of 1933 ed. lib. bdg. 59.00x. Am Biog Serv.

Sometime see Collected Works.

Sometime after the Equinox. Jorj Bent. (Orig.). 1981. pap. 2.25 (ISBN 0-505-51695-0, Pub. by Tower Bks). Leisure NY.

Sometime Before the Dawn. Richard M. Cromie. 111p. (Orig.). 1982. 10.00 (ISBN 0-914733-07-9); pap. 5.95 (ISBN 0-914733-08-7). Desert Mn.

Sometime King. Compiled by Kate Ftizsimons. (Illus.). 35.00x (ISBN 0-317-20301-0, Pub. by Minimax Bks UK). State Mutual Bk.

Sometime the Cow Kick Your Head: Light Year '88-9. Ed. by Robert Wallace. (Illus.). 260p. 1988. 15.95 (ISBN 0-933248-11-3). Bits Pr.

Sometimes. John Yau. LC 79-67780. 66p. 1980. 9.95 (ISBN 0-935296-02-6); pap. 4.95 (ISBN 0-935296-03-4). Sheep Meadow.

Sometimes a Family Has to Move. Jane W. Watson et al. (Read Together Books for Parents & Children). (Illus.). 32p. (ps-1). 1988. pap. 3.95 (ISBN 0-517-56593-5). Crown.

Sometimes a Family Has to Split Up. Jane W. Watson et al. (Read Together Books for Parents & Children). (Illus.). 32p. (ps-1). 1988. pap. 3.95 (ISBN 0-517-56811-X). Crown.

Sometimes a Great Notion. Ken Kesey. 640p. 1977. pap. 8.95 (ISBN 0-14-004529-5). Penguin.

Sometimes a Shining Moment. Eliot Wigginton. LC 85-19967. (Illus.). 456p. 1986. (Anchor Pr); pap. 10.95 (ISBN 0-385-13359-6, Anchor Pr). Doubleday.

Sometimes Everything Feels Just Right. Elspeth C. Murphy. (David & I Talk to God Ser.). (Illus.). (gr. k-2). 1987. pap. 2.95 (ISBN 1-55513-038-0, Chariot Bks). Cook.

Sometimes Giant. Claud C. Crawford. 96p. (Orig.). 1984. pap. 6.95 (ISBN 0-933697-03-1). Claud Crawford.

Sometimes I Cry. Christine A. Burda. 48p. 1987. 6.95 (ISBN 0-8062-3131-9). Carlton.

Sometimes I Dance When I Walk. Britt Boswell. LC 85-72098. (Illus.). 92p. 1985. pap. 11.95 (ISBN 0-914546-60-0). Rose Pub.

Sometimes I Don't Like School. Paula Z. Hogan. LC 79-24055. (Life & Living from a Child's Point of View Ser.). (Illus.). 32p. (gr. k-5). 1980. PLB 15.33 (ISBN 0-8172-1357-0). Raintree Pubs.

Sometimes I Don't Love My Mother. Hila Colman. 188p. (gr. 7 up). 1979. pap. 2.25 (ISBN 0-590-33736-X, Vagabond). Scholastic Inc.

Sometimes I Dream Horses. Jeanne W. Peterson. LC 83-47710. (Illus.). 32p. (ps-3). 1987. 10.95i (ISBN 0-06-024712-6); PLB 10.89 (ISBN 0-06-024713-4). HarpJ.

Sometimes I Feel. Rochelle Barsuhn. LC 85-10351. (Illus.). 32p. (gr. 1-2). 1985. PLB 4.95 (ISBN 0-89693-228-1). Dandelion Hse.

Sometimes I Get Angry. Jane W. Watson et al. (Read-Together Books for Parents & Children). (Illus.). 32p. (ps up). 1986. pap. 2.95 (ISBN 0-517-56088-7). Crown.

Sometimes I Get Lonely. Elspeth Murphy. LC 80-70251. (David & I Talk to God Ser.). (Illus.). 24p. (gr. k-2). 1981. pap. 2.95 (ISBN 0-89191-367-X, 53678). Cook.

Sometimes I Get Mad. Elspeth C. Murphy. (David & I Talk to God Ser.). (gr. k-2). 1981. pap. 2.95 (ISBN 0-89191-493-5, 54932). Cook.

Sometimes I Get Scared. Elspeth Murphy. (David & I Talk to God Ser.). (Illus.). (gr. k-2). 1980. pap. 2.95 (ISBN 0-89191-275-4). Cook.

Sometimes I Get So Mad. Paula Z. Hogan. LC 79-24057. (Life & Living from a Child's Point of View Ser.). (Illus.). 32p. (gr. k-5). 1980. PLB 15.33 (ISBN 0-8172-1359-7). Raintree Pubs.

Sometimes I Hate Myself. Katie Tonn. (Uplook Ser.). 1978. pap. 0.99 (ISBN 0-8163-0386-X, 19422-5). Pacific Pr Pub Assn.

Sometimes I Have To. David Ridyard. LC 85-17356. (Growing Up Bks.). (Illus.). 32p. (gr. 2-3). 1985. PLB 10.95 (ISBN 0-918831-16-4). Stevens Inc.

Sometimes I Have to Cry. Elspeth C. Murphy. (David & I Talk to God Ser.). (Illus.). (gr. k-2). 1981. pap. 2.95 (ISBN 0-89191-494-3, 54940). Cook.

Sometimes I Hurt: Reflections on the Book of Job. Mildred Tengbom. 192p. (Orig.). 1986. pap. 6.50 (ISBN 0-570-03981-9, 12-2897). Concordia.

Sometimes I Like to Cry. Elizabeth Stanton & Henry Stanton. Ed. by Caroline Rubin. LC 77-19131. (Albert Whitman Concept Bks.). (Illus.). 32p. (ps-2). 1978. PLB 11.95 (ISBN 0-8075-7537-2). A Whitman.

Son of Poop. Gerald Locklin. 1973. 3.50 (ISBN 0-917554-14-0). Maelstrom.
Son of Porthos. Alexandre Dumas. 287p. 1983. Repr. lib. bdg. 19.95x (ISBN 0-89966-316-8). Buccaneer Bks.
Son of Promise. Paula FitzGerald & Edward FitzGerald. (Son of Man Trilogy Ser.: Pt. 1). 122p. (Orig.). 1988. pap. 7.50 (ISBN 0-935915-00-1). Corinth Pub.
Son of Prophecy: Henry Tudor's Road to Bosworth. David Rees. (Illus.). 176p. 1985. 13.95 (ISBN 0-85159-004-7, Pub. by Black Raven Pr); pap. 6.95 (ISBN 0-85159-005-5). Longwood Pub Group.
Son of Singapore. Kok Seng Tan. (Writing in Asia Ser.). 1972. pap. text ed. 5.00x (ISBN 0-686-65342-4, 00220). Heinemann Ed.
Son of Someone Famous. M. E. Kerr. LC 73-14338. 176p. (YA) (gr. 7 up). 1974. PLB 12.89 (ISBN 0-06-023147-5). HarpJ.
Son of Someone Famous. M. E. Kerr. 160p. (gr. 7 up). 1983. pap. 2.50 (ISBN 0-451-13722-1, Sig Vista). NAL.
Son of Tarzan. Edgar Rice Burroughs. (Tarzan Ser.: No. 4). 224p. 1975. pap. 2.50 (ISBN 0-345-33556-2). Ballantine.
Son of Tecun Uman: A Maya Indian Tells His Life Story. Ed. by James D. Sexton. LC 81-11702. 250p. 1981. pap. 12.95x (ISBN 0-8165-0751-1). U of Ariz Pr.
Son of the Alhambra: Diego Hurtado de Mendoza, 1504-1575. Erika Spivakovsky. (Illus.). 466p. 1970. 25.00x (ISBN 0-292-70093-8). U of Tex Pr.
Son of the Black Stallion. Elizabeth Enright. 288p. (gr. 4-6). pap. 2.25 (ISBN 0-590-30387-2). Scholastic Inc.
Son of the Black Stallion. Walter Farley. (Illus.). (gr. 4-6). 1963. (BYR); lib. bdg. 10.99 (ISBN 0-394-90603-9); pap. 2.95 (ISBN 0-394-83612-X). Random.
Son of the Bowery: The Life Story of an East Side American. facsimile ed. Charles Stelzle. LC 74-179540. (Select Bibliographies Reprint Ser.). Repr. of 1926 ed. 21.00 (ISBN 0-8369-6669-4). Ayer Co Pubs.
Son of the Carolinas: A Story of the Hurricane Upon the Sea Islands. Elizabeth C. Satterthuait. LC 72-2064. (Black Heritage Library Collection Ser.). Repr. of 1898 ed. 16.00 (ISBN 0-8369-9062-5). Ayer Co Pubs.
Son of the Day & the Daughter of the Night. George MacDonald. LC 84-145155. (Illus.). 40p. (YA) (gr. 7-9). pap. 12.95 (ISBN 0-914676-45-8). Green Tiger Pr.
Son of the Dine' J. Walter Wood. (Indian Culture Ser.). (gr. 5-9). 1972. 1.95 (ISBN 0-89992-023-3). Coun India Ed.
Son of the Endless Night. John Farris. 512p. 1986. pap. 4.50 (ISBN 0-8125-8266-7, Dist. by Warner Pub Service & St. Martin's Press). Tor Bks.
Son of the Gamblin' Man: The Youth of an Artist. Mari Sandoz. LC 76-17066. x, 333p. 1976. 27.50x (ISBN 0-8032-0895-2); pap. 8.95 (ISBN 0-8032-5833-X, BB 626, Bison). U of Nebr Pr.
Son of the Male Muse: New Gay Poetry Anthology. Ed. by Ian Young. LC 83-15041. (Illus.). 192p. (Orig.). 1983. pap. 8.95 (ISBN 0-89594-118-X). Crossing Pr.
Son of the Middle Border. Hamlin Garland. LC 78-26593. xxvi, 467p. 1979. o. p. 29.95x (ISBN 0-8032-2102-9); pap. 6.95 (ISBN 0-8032-7000-3, BB 694, Bison). U of Nebr Pr.
Son of the Middle Border. Hamlin Garland. 467p. 1985. Repr. of 1917 ed. lib. bdg. 49.00 (ISBN 0-8414-4326-2). Folcroft.
Son of the Middle Border. Hamlin Garland. 467p. 1985. Repr. of 1922 ed. lib. bdg. 42.50 (ISBN 0-89987-327-8). Darby Bks.
Son of the Middle Border. Hamlin Garland. (Collected Works of Hamlin Garland). 1988. Repr. of 1917 ed. lib. bdg. 59.00x. Am Biog Serv.
Son of the Middle Border see Collected Works.
Son of the Morning. Joyce Carol Oates. 1979. pap. 2.75 (ISBN 0-449-24073-8, Crest). Fawcett.
Son of the Morning. Joyce Carol Oates. LC 78-56428. 1978. 17.95 (ISBN 0-8149-0800-4). Vanguard.
Son of the Morning. E. J. O'Brien. 1973. Repr. of 1932 ed. 20.00 (ISBN 0-8274-1204-5). R West.
Son of the Morning & Other Stories. Phyllis Gotlieb. 240p. 1983. pap. 2.95 (ISBN 0-441-77221-8, Pub. by Ace Science Fiction). Ace Bks.
Son of the Morning Star: Custer & the Little Bighorn. Evan S. Connell. LC 84-60681. 464p. 1984. 20.00 (ISBN 0-86547-160-6). N Point Pr.
Son of the Morning Star: Custer & the Little Bighorn. Evan S. Connell. LC 85-42560. (Illus.). 448p. 1988. pap. 9.95 (ISBN 0-06-097003-0, PL-7161, PL). Har-Row.
Son of the Passion. Godfrey Poage. 1977. 3.50 (ISBN 0-8198-0458-4). Dghtrs St Paul.
Son of the Revolution. Liang Heng & Judith Shapiro. LC 82-18704. (Illus.). 364p. 1983. 14.50 (ISBN 0-394-52568-X). Knopf.
Son of the Revolution. Liang Heng & Judith Shapiro. 1984. pap. 6.95 (ISBN 0-394-72274-4, Vin). Random.
Son of the Sioux. Gerald D. Adams. (Orig.). 1981. pap. 1.95 (ISBN 0-505-51703-5, Pub. by Tower Bks). Leisure NY.
Son of the Slime That Ate Cleveland. Marjorie Sharmat. (Illus.). 108p. (Orig.). (gr. k-6). 1985. pap. 2.50 (ISBN 0-440-48086-8, YB). Dell.
Son of the Soil. Wilson Katiyo. 147p. 1976. cased 12.00 (ISBN 0-86036-002-4, Pub. by R Collins UK). Three Continents.
Son of the Sun. Moyra Caldecott. 192p. 1986. 14.95 (ISBN 0-85031-647-2, Pub. by Allison & Busby England). Schocken.
Son of the Sun see Captain David Grief.
Son of the Sun: The Life & Philosophy of Akhnaton, King of Egypt. 4th ed. Savitri Devi. LC 80-54808. (Illus.). 323p. 1981. Repr. of 1946 ed. 11.95 (ISBN 0-912057-17-3, G-534). AMORC.
Son of the White Wolf. Robert E. Howard. LC 77-73604. 1977. 12.95x (ISBN 0-913960-09-8). Fax Collect.
Son of the White Wolf. Robert E. Howard. 192p. 1987. pap. 2.95 (ISBN 0-441-77521-7, Pub. by Charter Bks). Ace Bks.
Son of the Wilderness: The Life of John Muir. Linnie M. Wolfe. LC 78-53294. (Illus.). 398p. 1978. 29.50x (ISBN 0-299-07730-6); pap. 10.95 (ISBN 0-299-07734-9). U of Wis Pr.
Son of the Wind. 159p. 1985. pap. 3.50 (ISBN 0-317-19599-9). Rebel Mont Tem.
Son of the Wolf. Jack London. Repr. lib. bdg. 19.95 (ISBN 0-89190-654-1, Pub. by River City Pr). Amereon Ltd.
Son of the Wolf. Jack London. 1900. 39.00x (ISBN 0-403-08613-2). Somerset Pub.
Son of the Wolf. Jack London. (Illus.). 256p. 1980. pap. 5.95 (ISBN 0-932458-02-5). Star Rover.
Son of Thunder: Patrick Henry & the American Republic. Henry Mayer. 320p. 1986. 22.50 (ISBN 0-531-15009-7). Watts.
Son of Zelman. Oscar Pinkus. 176p. 1982. 19.95 (ISBN 0-87073-548-9); pap. 11.95 (ISBN 0-87073-549-7). Schenkman Bks Inc.
Son-Ripened Fruit: Living Out the Fruit of the Spirit. (Orig.). 1986. pap. 1.95 (ISBN 0-8024-2551-8). Moody.
Son-Rise. Barry N. Kaufman. (Illus.). 1977. pap. 3.95 (ISBN 0-446-32794-8). Warner Bks.
Son Songs for Christian Folk, 2 vols. Gary L. Johnson. Incl. Vol. I. pap. 1.95 (ISBN 0-87123-509-9, 280509); Vol. II. pap. 1.95 (ISBN 0-87123-532-3, 280532). 1975. pap. Bethany Hse.
Son to Susanna: The Private Life of John Wesley. G. Elsie Harrison. 1937. Repr. 35.00 (ISBN 0-8274-3468-5). R West.
Son Who Said He Wouldn't. Louise Ulmer. (Arch Bks.). (gr. k-4). 1981. pap. 1.29 (ISBN 0-570-06145-8, 59-1262). Concordia.
Son Who Was Older Than His Father. 2nd ed. Joseph H. Hughes, Jr. LC 77-926281. 1977. signed 10.00 (ISBN 0-686-22889-8); pap. 3.95 (ISBN 0-686-22890-1). Aaron-Jenkins.
Sonahchi. Pat Carr. LC 88-70067. 75p. (Orig.). 1988. pap. 8.95 (ISBN 0-938317-06-7). Cinco Puntos.
Sonali's Friend. Alaka Shankar. (Illus.). 16p. (Orig.). (gr. k-3). 1980. pap. 2.50 (ISBN 0-89744-218-0, Pub. by Children's Bk Trust India). Auromere.
Sonar Bangla. Asif Currimbhoy. 1972. pap. text ed. 4.80 (ISBN 0-88253-764-4). Ind-US Inc.
Sonar Images. Harold E. Edgerton. (Illus.). 224p. 1986. pap. text ed. write for info (ISBN 0-13-822644-X). P-H.
Sonar Images. Harold E. Edgerton. (Illus.). 304p. 1986. text ed. 47.00 (ISBN 0-13-822651-2). P-H.
Sonar y Hacer. Rafael Arrillaga Torrens. LC 76-56437. (Coleccion Mente y Palabra). 1977. 6.25 (ISBN 0-8477-0546-3); pap. 5.00 (ISBN 0-8477-0547-1). U of PR Pr.
Sonata. Rosamond T. Albert. LC 84-90297. 214p. 1986. 13.95 (ISBN 0-533-06342-6). Vantage.
Sonata. F. Helena Marks. text ed. 13.00 (ISBN 0-8369-8188-X). Ayer Co Pubs.
Sonata for Trombone & Piano. Helen Stanley. (Orig.). 1983. pap. 5.00 (ISBN 0-317-14724-2). Kenyon.
Sonata for Viola (or Clarinet) & Piano. Marion Bauer. (Women Composers Ser.: No. 18). 50p. 1986. Repr. of 1951 ed. lib. bdg. 23.50 (ISBN 0-306-76249-8). Da Capo.
Sonata for Viola (or Violincello) & Piano. Rebecca Clarke. (Women Composers Ser.: No. 20). 65p. 1986. Repr. of 1921 ed. lib. bdg. 29.50 (ISBN 0-306-76251-X). Da Capo.
Sonata for Violin & Piano: Op. 34, No. 19. Amy Beach. (Women Composers Ser.: No. 19). 46p. 1986. Repr. of 1899 ed. lib. bdg. 23.50 (ISBN 0-306-76250-1). Da Capo.
Sonata Form. William H. Hadow. LC 74-24101. Repr. 19.50 (ISBN 0-404-12943-9). AMS Pr.
Sonata Forms. Charles Rosen. (Illus.). 1980. 18.95x (ISBN 0-393-01203-4). Norton.
Sonata Forms. rev. ed. Charles Rosen. (Illus.). 352p. 1988. 19.95; pap. 10.95. Norton.
Sonata in C Minor, Opus 21 see Three Piano Works.
Sonata in the Baroque Era. 4th ed. William S. Newman. 1983. 18.95x (ISBN 0-393-95275-4). Norton.
Sonata in the Classic Era. 3rd ed. William S. Newman. 1983. 22.50x (ISBN 0-393-95286-X). Norton.
Sonata, Its Form & Meaning As Exemplified in the Piano Sonatas by Mozart: A Descriptive Analysis with Musical Examples. F. Helena Marks. LC 78-66911. (Encore Music Editions Ser.). (Illus.). 1980. Repr. of 1921 ed. 21.50 (ISBN 0-88355-751-7). Hyperion Conn.
Sonata of Icarus. Jurgis Gliauda. Tr. by Raphael Sealey. (Illus.). 1968. 5.00 (ISBN 0-87141-024-9). Manyland.
Sonata since Beethoven. William S. Newman. xxvi, 854p. 1969. 39.95x (ISBN 0-8078-1121-1). U of NC Pr.
Sonataos in Fugos. M. K. Ciulionis. 1980. 32.00x (ISBN 0-317-14318-2, Pub. by Collets (UK)). State Mutual Bk.
Sonatas & Other Multi-Movement Works Unpublished in Bach's Lifetime. Carl P. Bach. Ed. by Dorrell Berg. (Carl Bach (1714 to 1788): The Collected Works for Solo Keyboard Ser.). 285p. 1986. lib. bdg. 75.00 (ISBN 0-8240-6453-4). Garland Pub.
Sonatas for Two Pianos, (Seventeen Seventy-Five to Eighteen Fifteen) Ed. by Nicholas Temperley. (London Pianoforte School Ser., 1770-1860). 120p. 1986. lib. bdg. 75.00 (ISBN 0-8240-6169-1). Garland Pub.
Sonatas of Beethoven, As He Played & Taught Them. Kenneth Drake. LC 80-8608. 220p. pap. 57.20 (2056420). Bks Demand UMI.
Sonate (12) D'intavolatura per L'organo E' L'cemba see Monuments of Music & Music Literature in Facsimile: Series One.
Soncino Books of the Bible, 14 vols. Incl. Chumash. 22.50 (ISBN 0-900689-24-2); Daniel. 12.95; Hoshua & Judges. 12.95x (ISBN 0-900689-25-0); Samuel I-II. 12.95; Chronicles. 12.95; King I-II. 12.95; Isaiah. 12.95; Jeremiah. 12.95; Ezekiel. 12.95; Twelve Prophets. 12.95; Psalms. 12.95; Proverbs. 12.95; Job. 12.95; Five Meeillah. 14.95; Nedarim. 22.95x; Shebu'oth. 22.95 (ISBN 0-900689-96-X). Set. 165.00x (ISBN 0-900689-23-4). Bloch.
Soncino Chumash. A. Cohen. 1203p. 1947. 22.50. Soncino Pr.
Soncino Haggadah. Cecil Roth. 4.95x (ISBN 0-685-01039-2). Bloch.
Soncino Hebrew-English Talmud. Incl. Tractate Berakoth. 22.95x (ISBN 0-685-23064-3); Tractate Baba Mezia. 22.95x (ISBN 0-685-23065-1); Tractate Gittin. 22.95x (ISBN 0-685-23066-X); Tractate Baba Kamma. 22.95x (ISBN 0-685-23067-8); Tractate Kiddushin. 22.95x (ISBN 0-685-23068-6); Tractate Pesahim. 22.95x (ISBN 0-685-23069-4); Tractate Sanhedrin. 22.95x (ISBN 0-685-23070-8); Tractate Kethuboth. 22.95x (ISBN 0-685-23071-6); Tractate Shabbath, 2 vols. Set. 45.95x (ISBN 0-685-23072-4); Tractate Yoma. 22.95x (ISBN 0-685-23073-2); Baba Bathra, 2 vols. 45.95x (ISBN 0-686-85719-4); Hullin. 22.95x (ISBN 0-686-85720-8). Bloch.
Soncino Talmud, 18 Vols. (Eng.). Set. 375.00x (ISBN 0-900689-22-6). Bloch.
Sondheim & Co. Craig Zadan. LC 86-45165. (Illus.). 384p. 1986. 27.95i (ISBN 0-06-015649-X, HarpT). Har-Row.
Sondheim & Co. 2nd, rev. & updated ed. Graig Zadan. LC 86-45165. (Illus.). 408p. 1988. pap. 16.95 (ISBN 0-06-091400-9, PL/1400, PL). Har-Row.
Sone Que la Nieve Ardia. Antonio Skarmeta. 242p. (Span.). 1981. pap. 8.00 (ISBN 84-85594-03-7, 3003). Ediciones Norte.
Sonetos. Luis De Gongora. Ed. by Birute Ciplijauskaite. 691p. 1981. 35.00x (ISBN 0-942260-17-1). Hispanic Seminary.
Sonetos 'Al Italico Modo' de Inigo Lopez de Mendoza, Marques de Santillana. Ed. by Maxim P. Kerkhof & Dirk Tuin. (Spanish Ser.: No. 18). 120p. 1985. 10.00x (ISBN 0-942260-47-3). Hispanic Seminary.
Sonetos de Calderon en Sus Obras Dramaticas: Estudio y Edicion. Rafael Osuna. (Studies in the Romance Languages & Literatures: No. 148). 1974. pap. 10.50x (ISBN 0-8078-9148-7). U of NC Pr.
Sonfield on Securities: Public & Private Offerings. Sonfield. 1988. price not set (ISBN 0-471-60601-4). Wiley.
Song. Calvin Miller. (Illus.). 1977. pap. 6.95 (ISBN 0-87784-785-1). Inter-Varsity.
Song. Charlotte Zolotow. LC 81-6357. (Illus.). 24p. (ps-3). 1982. PLB 11.88 (ISBN 0-688-00817-8). Greenwillow.
Song & Action: The Victory Odes of Pindar. Kevin Crotty. 176p. 1982. text ed. 22.50x (ISBN 0-8018-2746-9). Johns Hopkins.
Song & Counter-Song: Sceve's Delie & Petrarch's Rime. JoAnn DellaNeva. LC 83-81597. (French Forum Monographs: 49). 128p. (Orig.). 1983. pap. 10.95x (ISBN 0-917058-49-6). French Forum.
Song & Dance Activies for Elementary Children. Harriet R. Reeves. LC 85-12029. 241p. 1985. pap. 17.95x tchr's ed. (ISBN 0-13-822677-6, Busn). P-H.
Song & Dance Activities for Elementary Children's. Harriet R. Reeves. 1984. 17.95x (ISBN 0-13-260613-5, Parker). P-H.
Song & Dance Man. Karen Ackerman. LC 87-3200. (Illus.). 32p. (ps-2). 1988. 11.95 (ISBN 0-394-89330-1); lib. bdg. 11.99 (ISBN 0-394-99330-6). Knopf.
Song & Dance Man: The Films of Gene Kelly. Tony Thomas. LC 73-90949. (Illus.). 256p. 1974. 12.00 (ISBN 0-8065-0400-5, Pub. by Citadel Pr). Lyle Stuart.
Song & Democratic Culture in Britain. Ian Watson. LC 83-4591. 190p. 1983. 25.00 (ISBN 0-312-74473-0). St Martin.
Song & the Seed. Marie Gilbert. (Illus.). 1983. 10.00 (ISBN 0-940580-27-6); pap. 5.00 (ISBN 0-940580-28-4). Green River.
Song & the Story. George M. Bass. LC 83-73126. 1984. 7.00 (ISBN 0-89536-652-5, 1970). CSS of Ohio.
Song Anthology One. 3rd, rev. ed. Anne Leyerle & William D. Leyerle. LC 79-90829. 159p. (gr. 9 up). 1985. pap. 10.95 plastic comb (ISBN 0-9602296-3-9). Leyerle Pubns.
Song Anthology Two. Ed. by Anne L. Leyerle & William D. Leyerle. 159p. (YA) (gr. 9 up). 1984. pap. 10.95 plastic comb. (ISBN 0-9602296-4-7). Leyerle Pubns.
Song at the Scaffold. rev. ed. Gertrud Von Le Fort. Ed. by Martin McMurtrey & Robert Knopp. (Illus., Orig.). 1954. pap. text ed. 3.95 (ISBN 0-910334-24-2). Cath Authors.
Song Between Two Stars. Gaston Puel. (Translated from French). 6.75 (ISBN 0-89253-770-1); flexible cloth 4.80 (ISBN 0-89253-771-X). Ind-US Inc.
Song Bird Patterns. William Veasey. LC 82-62972. (Blue Ribbon Pattern Series: Bk. IV). (Illus.). 64p. 1983. pap. 14.95 (ISBN 0-916838-79-X). Schiffer.
Song Book. Tom Lehrer. 11.95 (ISBN 0-89190-092-6, Pub. by Am Repr). Amereon Ltd.
Song Book 'n' Tape Gift Pack. (Golden Story Book 'n' Tape Gift Packs Ser.). (Illus.). 24p. (Orig.). (ps-3). 1988. pap. price not set (ISBN 0-307-13806-2). Western Pub.
Song Book of Israel. D. Rayford Bell. LC 80-67409. 303p. 1983. 6.95 (ISBN 0-9604820-3-2); pap. 4.95 (ISBN 0-9604820-2-4). D R Bell.
Song Called Hope. Arthur Gordon. 48p. 1985. 6.95 (ISBN 0-8378-5081-9). Gibson.
Song Catcher in Southern Mountains. Dorothy Scarborough. LC 37-4992. Repr. of 1937 ed. 18.50 (ISBN 0-404-05569-9). AMS Pr.
Song Celestial. Edwin Arnold. 1971. pap. 1.50 (ISBN 0-8356-0418-7, Quest). Theos Pub Hse.
Song Celestial: Bhagavad-Gita. Tr. by Edwin Arnold from Sanskrit. 176p. 1985. Repr. 3.50 (ISBN 0-87612-210-1). Self Realization.
Song Celestial or Bhaggvad-Gita: From the Mahabharata, Being a Discourse Between Arjuna, Prince of India, & the Supreme Being under the Form of Krishna. Tr. by Edwin Arnold. 1967. pap. 5.00 (ISBN 0-7100-6268-0). Routledge Chapman & Hall.
Song Ceramics. Mary Tregear. 1982. 210.00x (ISBN 0-317-45253-3, Pub. by Han-Shan Tang Ltd). State Mutual Bk.
Song Ceramics. Mary Tregear. (Illus.). 262p. 50.00 (ISBN 0-317-55045-4). Apollo.
Song Crafters Tool Kit, the Basic, Vol. I. Ed. by Adel Meisenheimer. (YA) (gr. 9 up). 1987. Multi-media print/cassette. 39.95 (ISBN 0-944582-02-8). Song Crafters.
Song Crafters Tool Kit: The Basics, Special Gospel Music Edition, Vol. I. Adel Meisenheimer. (YA) (gr. 9 up). 1987. Multi-media print/cassette. 39.95 (ISBN 0-944582-00-1). Song Crafters.
Song Cycle. Joan N. Burstyn. LC 76-552177. 1976. 3.75x (ISBN 0-915176-16-5). Woods Hole Pr.
Song, Dance, & Customs of Peasant Poland. Sula Benet. LC 76-44690. Repr. of 1951 ed. 26.00 (ISBN 0-404-15906-0). AMS Pr.
Song, Dance & Storytelling: Aspects of the Performing Arts in Japan. Frank Hoff. LC 78-101975. (East Asia Papers: No. 15). 229p. 1978. 6.00 (ISBN 0-939657-15-5). Cornell East Asia Pgm.
Song-Dynastie (960 - Bis 1279. Dieter Kuhn. 528p. 1987. 455.00x (Pub. by Han-Shan Tang Ltd). State Mutual Bk.
Song Dynasty Poems. John Knoepfle & Wang Shouyi. 73p. (Chinese & Eng.). 1986. 11.95 (ISBN 0-933180-85-3); pap. 4.95 (ISBN 0-933180-82-9). Spoon Riv Poetry.
Song for a New Generation. Gertrude M. Lutz. LC 78-155239. 92p. 1971. 4.00 (ISBN 0-8233-0161-3). Golden Quill.
Song for All Seasons. Libby Stopple. Ed. by R. H. Dromgoole & Alison Heinemann. LC 77-89399. (Illus.). 1977. 7.95 (ISBN 0-913632-15-5); pap. 5.95 (ISBN 0-913632-13-9). Am Univ Artforms.
Song for an Equinox. St.-John Perse. Tr. by Richard Howard. (Bollinger Ser.: Vol. 69). 1977. 14.50x (ISBN 0-691-09938-3). Princeton U Pr.
Song for Anninho. Gayl Jones. LC 80-85231. 88p. 1981. pap. 4.50x perfect bd. (ISBN 0-916418-26-X). Lotus.
Song for Avalokita. Henri Wasser. 80p. 1979. 3.95 (ISBN 0-8059-2656-9). Dorrance.
Song for Joseph: Luke 2: 1-20, the Christmas Story. Bd. with Little Shepherd & the First Christmas: Luke 2: 8-20, the First Christmas. (ps-3). bk. & cassette 5.95 (ISBN 0-317-60402-3, 59-2146). Concordia.
Song for Linda, No. 122. Dan Daley. (Sweet Dreams Ser.). 144p. (Orig.). (YA) (gr. 7-12). 1987. pap. 2.50 (ISBN 0-553-26419-2). Bantam.

Song for Lovers. S. Craig Glickman. LC 75-21454. 204p. (Orig.). 1976. pap. 6.95 (ISBN 0-87784-768-1). Inter-Varsity.

Song for Mumu. Lindsay Barrett. LC 73-99065. 1974. 8.95 (ISBN 0-88258-006-X). Howard U Pr.

Song for One or Two: Music & the Concept of Art in Early China. Kenneth J. DeWoskin. LC 81-19519. (Michigan Monographs in Chinese Studies: No. 42). (Illus.). 216p. (Orig.). 1982. pap. 7.00 (ISBN 0-89264-042-1). U of Mich Ctr Chinese.

Song for Sarah: A Young Mother's Journey Through Grief, & Beyond. Paula D'Arcy. LC 79-14684. 124p. 1979. 5.95 (ISBN 0-87788-778-0). Shaw Pubs.

Song for Satawal. Kenneth Brower. 224p. 1984. pap. 6.95 (ISBN 0-14-007041-9). Penguin.

Song for the Prince. Lisa Latella. (Illus.). 36p. (Orig.). (gr. k up). 1984. pap. write for info. (ISBN 0-9608592-1-7). Gallery Arts.

Song for Three Voices. Curt Johnson. LC 84-11345. 276p. (Orig.). 1985. pap. 8.95 (ISBN 0-914140-13-2). Carpenter Pr.

Song from the Starting Tree. Adam C. Moore. 48p. 1986. 9.00x (ISBN 0-7223-2034-5, Pub. by A H Stockwell England). State Mutual Bk.

Song Games from Trinidad & Tobago. J. D. Elder. LC 64-25264. (American Folklore Society Bibliographical & Special Ser.: No. 16). 119p. 1965. pap. 5.95x (ISBN 0-292-73508-1). U of Tex Pr.

Song Heard in a Strange Land: Narcissa Her Story, Bk. 1. Marje Blood. LC 85-81462. 220p. 1985. p. 13.95o. (ISBN 0-9615233-0-1); pap. 9.95 (ISBN 0-9615233-1-X). Image Imprints.

Song Hits from the Turn of the Century. Paul Charosh & Robert Fremont. LC 74-20444. 296p. 1975. pap. 5.95 (ISBN 0-486-23158-5). Dover.

Song I Sang to You: A Selection of Poems. Myra C. Livingston. LC 84-4585. (Illus.). 96p. (ps-3). 1984. 12.95 (ISBN 0-15-277105-0, HJ). HarBraceJ.

Song: I Want a Witness. Michael S. Harper. LC 72-81793. (Pitt Poetry Ser). 1972. pap. 8.95 (ISBN 0-8229-5231-9). U of Pittsburgh Pr.

Song in a Strange Land. Diana Hamilton. (Harlequin Presents Ser.: No. 993). 192p. Date not set. pap. 1.95 (ISBN 0-317-63734-7). Harlequin Bks.

Song in a Strange Land. George Keithley. LC 73-88043. 1974. 5.95 (ISBN 0-8076-0728-2). Braziller.

Song in a Weary Throat: An American Pilgrimage. Pauli Murray. LC 86-45674. 496p. 1987. 24.45i (ISBN 0-06-015704-6, HarpT). Har-Row.

Song in My Head & Other Poems. Felice Holman. LC 84-23573. (Illus.). 64p. (gr. 5-7). 1985. 11.95 (ISBN 0-684-18295-5, Pub. by Scribner). Macmillan.

Song in Stone. Ed. by Lee B. Hopkins. LC 82-45589. (Illus.). 48p. (gr. 2-6). 1983. 11.70i (ISBN 0-690-04269-8, Crowell Jr Bks); PLB 11.89 (ISBN 0-690-04270-1). HarpJ.

Song in the Forest. Peter Hoper. (Time & the Forest Trilogy Ser.: Bk. 1). 218p. 1979. pap. 14.95 (ISBN 0-86868-025-7, Pub. by J McIndoe Ltd New Zealand). Intl Spec Bk.

Song in the Ground. Jacqueline Mehrabi. (Illus.). 48p. (Orig.). (gr. k-4). 1986. pap. text ed. 4.00 (ISBN 0-85398-225-2). G Ronald Pub.

Song in the Morning. Gerald Seymour. 1987. 16.95 (ISBN 0-393-02409-1). Norton.

Song in the Walnut Grove. David Kherdian. LC 82-6596. (Illus.). 112p. (gr. 3-7). 1982. 8.95 (ISBN 0-394-85519-1); lib. bdg. 8.99 (ISBN 0-394-95519-6). Knopf.

Song Is a Rainbow: Movement, Music, & Rhythm Instruments in the Nursery School & Kindergarten. Patty Zeitlin. 1982. pap. 15.95 (ISBN 0-673-16460-8). Scott F.

Song-Lines of a Day. Narendra Sethi. 8.00 (ISBN 0-89253-737-X); flexible cloth 4.80 (ISBN 0-89253-738-8). Ind-US Inc.

Song List: A Guide to Contemporary Music from Classical Sources. Ed. by James L. Limbacher. LC 73-78293. 1973. 16.50 (ISBN 0-87650-041-6). Pierian.

Song Lyrics of Simple Love. 2nd ed. Harry J. Vassilion. 1981. write for info. Vassilion.

Song Made Out of a Pale Smoke. Bruce Renner. LC 81-15617. 51p. text ed. 9.95 (ISBN 0-934332-37-1); pap. text ed. 4.95 (ISBN 0-934332-36-3). L'Epervier Pr.

Song Ming Zhixiu. 14p. 1983. 84.00x (Pub. by Han-Shan Tang Ltd). State Mutual Bk.

Song of a Soldier's Wife. Dang Tran Con & Phan Huy Ich. Tr. by Huynh Sanh Thong. LC 85-73465. (Lac-Viet Ser.: No. 3). (Illus.). 118p. 1986. pap. 7.00 (ISBN 0-938692-24-0). Yale U SE Asia.

Song of a Soul. Alban M. Emley. 96p. 1973. pap. 4.95 (ISBN 0-911336-76-1). Sci of Mind.

Song of Abraham. Ellen G. Traylor. 1981. pap. 4.95 (ISBN 0-8423-6071-9). Tyndale.

Song of Africa. Ronald Wheatley. LC 83-22311. 1989. 19.95 (ISBN 0-87949-239-2). Ashley Bks.

Song of Ariran: A Korean Communist in the Chinese Revolution. Nym Wales & Kim San. LC 72-75808. (Illus.). 346p. 1973. pap. 6.95 (ISBN 0-87867-022-X). Ramparts.

Song of Ascents: A Spiritual Autobiography. E. Stanley Jones. LC 68-17451. (Festival Bks). 1979. pap. 2.25 (ISBN 0-687-39100-8). Abingdon.

Song of Bernadette. Franz Werfel. Tr. by Ludwig Lewisohn. Repr. lib. bdg. 27.95x (ISBN 0-88411-720-0, Pub. by Aeonian Pr). Amereon Ltd.

Song of Creation. Helmut Hirnschall. (Illus.). 80p. 17.95 (ISBN 0-920882-06-4). Hancock House.

Song of Creation. Cyril A. Reilly. 64p. 1983. pap. 9.95 (ISBN 0-86683-710-8, HarpR). Har-Row.

Song of Creation: Selections from the First Article. H. Boone Porter. LC 86-6285. 120p. (Orig.). 1986. pap. 6.95 (ISBN 0-936384-34-4). Cowley Pubns.

Song of Deborah. Bette M. Ross. 256p. 1981. pap. 7.95 (ISBN 0-8007-5217-1). Revell.

Song of Deeds: A Study of the Anathemata of David Jones. Neil Corcoran. 120p. 1982. text ed. 22.50x (ISBN 0-7083-0806-6, Pub. by U of Wales). Humanities.

Song of Degree. Stephen Kaung. Tr. by Carl Fang from Eng. (Chinese.). 1983. pap. write for info. (ISBN 0-941598-12-8). Living Spring Pubns.

Song of Desire. Rosalind Carson. (Superromances Ser.). 384p. 1982. pap. 2.50 (ISBN 0-373-70040-7, Pub. by Worldwide). Harlequin Bks.

Song of Eden. Lucy Snow. (Superromances Ser.). 384p. 1983. pap. 2.95 (ISBN 0-373-70083-0, Pub. by Worldwide). Harlequin Bks.

Song of Enlightenment. Ch'an Master Yung Chia. Tr. by Buddhist Text Translation Society Staff. (Illus.). 85p. (Orig.). 1983. pap. 5.00 (ISBN 0-88139-100-X). Buddhist Text.

Song of Erne. Robert Harbinson. 1987. pap. 6.95 (ISBN 0-85640-394-6, Pub. by Blackstaff Ireland). Irish Bks Media.

Song of Eve. June Strong. Ed. by Gerald Wheeler. 160p. 1987. 2.50 (ISBN 0-8280-0388-2). Review & Herald.

Song of God. Bhagavad-Gita. Tr. by Swami Prabhavananda & Christopher Isherwood. pap. 2.95 (ISBN 0-451-62576-5, Ment). NAL.

Song of God. Eugene E. Whitworth. 101p. Date not set. pap. 4.00. Grt Western Univ.

Song of God: A Summary Study of Bhagavad-Gita. Swami Bhaktipada. LC 84-45783. (Illus.). 304p. 1987. 11.95 (ISBN 0-932215-09-2); pap. 7.95 (ISBN 0-932215-00-9). Palace Pub.

Song of Heyoehkah. Hyemeyohsts Storm. 320p. 1983. pap. 12.95 (ISBN 0-345-30731-3). Ballantine.

Song of Hiawatha. Henry Wadsworth Longfellow. (Dent's Illustrated Children's Classics Ser.). (Illus.). 222p. (gr. 6 up). 1975. pap. 11.00x (ISBN 0-460-05046-X, BKA 01610, Pub. by J M Dent England). Biblio Dist.

Song of Homana. Jennifer Roberson. (Chronicles of the Cheysoli: Bk. 2). 324p. 1987. pap. 3.95 (ISBN 0-88677-195-1). DAW Bks.

Song of Hope: The Green Revolution in a Panjab Village. Murray J. Leaf. 304p. 1984. text ed. 32.00 (ISBN 0-8135-1025-2). Rutgers U Pr.

Song of Jesus. Ron O'Grady. (Illus.). 80p. (Orig.). 1984. pap. 10.95 (ISBN 0-85819-470-8, Pub. by JBCE). ANZ Religious Pubns.

Song of Joy. Elaine L. Schulte. 224p. 1987. pap. 5.95 (ISBN 0-310-47281-4, 15574P). Zondervan.

Song of Joy & Other Poems. Byron H. Reece. LC 85-22355. 128p. 1985. Repr. of 1952 ed. 13.95 (ISBN 0-87797-105-6). Cherokee.

Song of Jubilee. James Forman. LC 74-149224. 192p. (gr. 7 up). 1971. 10.95 (ISBN 0-374-37142-3). FS&G.

Song of Kali. Dan Simmons. 352p. 1985. 15.95 (ISBN 0-312-94408-X, Dist. by St. Martin). Bluejay Bks.

Song of Kali. Dan Simmons. 1986. pap. 3.95 (ISBN 0-8125-2566-3). Tor Bks.

Song of Krsna. Ed. by Deben Bhattacharya. (Illus.). 1978. cloth 12.50 (ISBN 0-87728-421-0); pap. 5.95 (ISBN 0-87728-422-9). Weiser.

Song of Lawino & Song of Ocol. Okot P'Bitek. (African Writers Ser.: No. 266). (Illus.). 151p. 1984. pap. text ed. 7.50 (ISBN 0-435-90266-0). Heinemann Ed.

Song of Life. new ed. Sushil K. Gupta. (Illus.). 1979. 25.00 (ISBN 0-686-77178-8); pap. 15.00 (ISBN 0-685-91450-X). Sverge-Haus.

Song of Life. Charles Johnston. 69p. 1983. pap. 3.95 (ISBN 0-912181-00-1). East School Pr.

Song of Love. Joan W. Anglund. 1987. 6.95 (ISBN 0-684-18836-8). Scribner.

Song of Love. Evo Findlow. 1985. 24.95x (ISBN 0-7090-1849-5, Pub. by R Hale Ltd UK). State Mutual Bk.

Song of Love. Betty Headapohl. (Living Books). 224p. 1985. pap. 3.50 (ISBN 0-8423-6072-7). Tyndale.

Song of Love. Tr. by George Keyt. Orig. Title: Gita Govinda. 123p. 1969. pap. 2.00 (ISBN 0-88253-048-8). Ind-US Inc.

Song of Love. Evelyn Wray. 1986. 9.95 (ISBN 0-8034-8621-9, Avalon). Bouregy.

Song of Love & Death: The Meaning of Opera. Peter Conrad. LC 87-10352. 416p. 1987. 19.95 (ISBN 0-671-64353-3, Poseidon Pr). PB.

Song of Love & Death: The Meaning of Opera. Peter Conrad. 416p. 1988. 9.95 (ISBN 0-671-67263-0, Poseidon Pr). PB.

Song of Madness & Other Poems. Francisco Matos Paoli. Ed. by Yvette E. Miller. Tr. by Frances Aparicio. LC 85-11. 160p. (Span. & Eng.). 1985. pap. 13.95 (ISBN 0-935480-18-8). Lat Am Lit Rev Pr.

Song of Man. Aaron Nissenson. 1964. 14.95x (ISBN 0-8084-0046-0). New Coll U Pr.

Song of Mavin Manyshaped. Sheri S. Tepper. 192p. 1985. pap. 2.75 (ISBN 0-441-77523-3, Pub. by Ace Science Fiction). Ace Bks.

Song of Meditation. T. S. Innocenti. (Illus.). 70p. (Orig.). 1988. pap. 10.95 (ISBN 0-929287-00-2). Flax Pr.

Song of Miriam: And Other Stories, Vol. 1. Marie Corelli. LC 71-37263. (Short Story Index Reprint Ser). Repr. of 1898 ed. 15.00 (ISBN 0-8369-4074-1). Ayer Co Pubs.

Song of Moses. David Ward-Steinman. 1968. pap. 6.50x (ISBN 0-916304-04-3, JW). SDSU Press.

Song of Motley: Being the Reminiscences of a Hungry Tenor. Leo Slezak. Ed. by Andrew Farkas. LC 76-29968. (Opera Biographies). (Illus.). 1977. Repr. of 1938 ed. lib. bdg. 24.50x (ISBN 0-405-09707-7). Ayer Co Pubs.

Song of Napalm: Poems. Bruce Weigl. Ed. by Ann Godoff. 96p. 1988. 13.95t (ISBN 0-87113-241-9). Atlantic Monthly.

Song of Nightingale: An Anthology of Modern Soviet Short Stories. Margrita A. Belai et al. Tr. by Y. C. Bhatnagar. 214p. 1987. 17.50x (ISBN 81-202-0189-2, Pub. by Ajanta). South Asia Bks.

Song of Our Syrian Guest. Knight. 3.50. Pilgrim NY.

Song of Pentecost. W. J. Corbett. (Illus.). 224p. (gr. 5 up). 1983. 10.95 (ISBN 0-525-44051-8). Dutton.

Song of Roland. Ed. by Leonard Bacon. 1919. 20.00 (ISBN 0-8274-3469-3). R West.

Song of Roland. Isabel Butler. LC 76-40196. 1904. Repr. 15.00 (ISBN 0-8414-1794-6). Folcroft.

Song of Roland. rev. ed. Tr. by Jessie Crosland. LC 66-30609. (Medieval Library). 1970. Repr. of 1926 ed. 16.50x (ISBN 0-8154-0057-8). Cooper Sq.

Song of Roland. Tr. by Frederick Goldin. 1978. pap. 5.95x (ISBN 0-393-09008-6). Norton.

Song of Roland. Tr. by Robert Harrison. 1970. pap. 2.95 (ISBN 0-451-62343-6, ME2343, Ment). NAL.

Song of Roland. Roland. Tr. by C. Scott Moncrieff. 150p. 1959. pap. 4.95 (ISBN 0-472-06032-5, 32, AA). U of Mich Pr.

Song of Roland. Tr. by Dorothy L. Sayers. (Classics Ser.). (Orig.). (YA) (gr. 9 up). 1957. pap. 2.95 (ISBN 0-14-044075-5). Penguin.

Song of Roland. Tr. by C. H. Sisson. 135p. 1983. 14.50 (ISBN 0-85635-421-X). Carcanet.

Song of Roland. Tr. by Patricia Terry. LC 65-26528. (Orig.). 1965. pap. 7.87 scp (ISBN 0-672-60476-0, LLA221). Bobbs.

Song of Roland. Marny Worden. 1974. pap. 3.00 (ISBN 0-913072-11-7). Natl Assn Deaf.

Song of Roland: A Generative Study of the Formulaic Language in the Single Combat. Ashby G. Beach. (Faux Titre Ser.: No. 20). 190p. 1985. pap. text ed. 32.50x (ISBN 90-6203-526-4, Pub. by Rodopi Holland). Humanities.

Song of Roland: An Analytical Edition, 2 vols. Ed. by Gerard J. Brault. Tr. by Gerard Brault. (Illus.). 1978. Vol. 1. Introduction & Commentary 32.00x (ISBN 0-271-00516-5); Vol. 2. Oxford text & English Translation 25.00x (ISBN 0-271-00204-2). Pa St U Pr.

Song of Roland: Formulaic Style & Poetic Craft. Joseph J. Duggan. LC 75-186101. (Center for Medieval & Renaissance Studies, UCLA: Publications: No. 6). 1973. 30.00x (ISBN 0-520-02201-7). U of Cal Pr.

Song of Roland Terry. Patricia Terry. 1965. pap. text ed. write for info. (ISBN 0-02-419780-7). Macmillan.

Song of Sixpence. A. J. Cronin. 16.95 (ISBN 0-89190-218-X, Pub. by Am Repr). Amereon Ltd.

Song of Solomon. G. Lloyd Carr & D. J. Wiseman. LC 83-22651. (Tyndale Old Testament Commentaries Ser.). 240p. 1984. 14.95 (ISBN 0-87784-918-8); pap. 8.95 (ISBN 0-87784-268-X). Inter-Varsity.

Song of Solomon. James Durham. (Geneva Ser.). 460p. 1982. Repr. of 1840 ed. 14.95 (ISBN 0-85151-352-2). Banner of Truth.

Song of Solomon. E. C. Hadley. pap. 3.95 (ISBN 0-88172-080-1). Believers Bkshelf.

Song of Solomon. Toni Morrison. 352p. (RL 7). 1978. pap. 4.50 (ISBN 0-451-12933-4, AE2933, Sig). NAL.

Song of Solomon. Toni Morrison. 1977. 14.45 (ISBN 0-394-49784-8). Knopf.

Song of Solomon. Toni Morrison. LC 87-5809. 320p. 1987. pap. 7.95 (ISBN 0-452-26011-6, Pub. by Plume). NAL.

Song of Solomon. Toni Morrison. 352p. 1988. pap. 4.50 (ISBN 0-451-15261-1, Sig). NAL.

Song of Solomon. Paige Patterson. (Everyman's Bible Commentary Ser.). (Orig.). 1986. pap. 5.95 (ISBN 0-8024-2057-5). Moody.

Song of Solomon: Make Full My Joy. Don Andersen. (Kingfisher Ser.). (Orig.). 1987. pap. 6.95 (ISBN 0-87213-002-9). Loizeaux.

Song of Songs. Intro. by Harold Bloom. (Modern Critical Interpretations Ser.). 184p. 1988. lib. bdg. 24.50 (ISBN 0-87754-917-6). Chelsea Hse.

Song of Songs. Ed Curtis. (Bible Study Commentary). 128p. (Orig.). 1988. pap. 6.95 (ISBN 0-310-36871-5, 18288P). Zondervan.

Song of Songs. Jeanne Guyon. 1983. pap. 6.95 (ISBN 0-940232-16-2). Christian Bks.

Song of Songs. Dan T. Muse. pap. 5.95 (ISBN 0-911866-78-7). Advocate.

Song of Songs. Watchman Nee. 1967. pap. 4.95 (ISBN 0-87508-420-6). Chr Lit.

Song of Songs. Tr. by Marvin H. Pope. LC 72-79417. (Anchor Bible Ser.: Vol. 7C). (Illus.). 1977. pap. 22.00 (ISBN 0-385-00569-5, Anchor Pr). Doubleday.

Song of Songs & Lamentations: A Commentary & Translation. Robert Gordis. 1974. 25.00x (ISBN 0-87068-256-3). Ktav.

Song of Songs & the Ancient Egyptian Love Songs. Michael V. Fox. LC 84-40494. (Illus.). 544p. 1985. text ed. 32.50x (ISBN 0-299-10090-1). U of Wis Pr.

Song of Songs, Ruth, Lamentations, Ecclesiastes, Esther. James A. Fischer. (Collegeville Bible Commentary Ser.). 112p. 1986. pap. 2.95 (ISBN 0-8146-1480-9). Liturgical pr.

Song of Symptoms. Patersimilias. 1980. 1.75x (ISBN 0-85032-186-7, Pub. by Daniel Co England). State Mutual Bk.

Song of the Axe. Paul O. Williams. 256p. 1984. pap. 2.95 (ISBN 0-345-31658-4, Del Ray). Ballantine.

Song of the Bird. Anthony DeMello. LC 84-10105. (Illus.). 192p. 1984. pap. 7.95 (ISBN 0-385-19615-6, Im). Doubleday.

Song of the Birds: Sayings, Stories & Impressions of Pablo Casals. Julian L. Webber. 120p. 1987. 14.95 (ISBN 0-86051-305-X). Parkwest Pubns.

Song of the Blood. Jared Smith. 1983. 4.00. Horizon.

Song of the Blood. Jared Smith. 48p. Date not set. pap. 3.50 (ISBN 0-912292-73-3). The Smith.

Song of the Boat. Lorenz Graham. LC 74-5183. (Illus.). (gr. 2-5). 1975. 11.70 (ISBN 0-690-75231-8, Crowell Jr Bks); PLB 11.89 (ISBN 0-690-75232-6). HarpJ.

Song of the Brush: Japanese Paintings from the Sanso Collection. Ed. by John M. Rosenfield. (Illus.). 87p. 1979. text ed. 35.00 (ISBN 0-932216-02-1); pap. text ed. 22.50 (ISBN 0-932216-03-X). Seattle Art.

Song of the Brush: Japanese Paintings from the Sanso Collection. Ed. by John M. Rosenfield. LC 79-19922. (Seattle Art Museum Ser.). (Illus.). 172p. 1979. 35.00x (ISBN 0-295-95867-7). U of Wash Pr.

Song of the Cardinal. Gene Stratton-Porter. Repr. lib. bdg. 16.95x (ISBN 0-89190-945-1, Pub. by River City Pr). Amereon Ltd.

Song of the Cheyenne. Jory Sherman. 192p. 1989. pap. 2.95 (ISBN 0-8125-8873-8). Tor Bks.

Song of the Cosmos. Devarakunda B. Tilak. (Translated from Telugu). 8.00 (ISBN 0-89253-613-6); flexible cloth 4.80 (ISBN 0-89253-614-4). Ind-US Inc.

Song of the Coyote: Freeing the Imagination Through the Arts. Phyllis L. Sawyers & Frances L. Henry. (Illus.). 302p. (Orig.). 1980. pap. text ed. 19.95x (ISBN 0-89641-036-6). American Pr.

Song of the Dark Druid. Josepha Sherman. LC 86-91555. (Endless Quest Bks.: No. 36). 160p. (Orig.). (gr. 3-8). 1987. pap. 2.25 (ISBN 0-88038-442-5). TSR Inc.

Song of the Earth & Other Poems. M. G. Adiga. Tr. by A. K. Ramanujan from Kannada. (Writers Workshop Redbird Ser.). 1975. 8.00 (ISBN 0-88253-640-0); pap. text ed. 4.00 (ISBN 0-88253-639-7). Ind-US Inc.

Song of the Evening. Nandini Satpathi. Tr. by J. B. Mohanty from Oriya. 110p. (Orig.). 1975. pap. 1.50 (ISBN 0-88253-770-9). Ind-US Inc.

Song of the Forest. Colin Mackay. 240p. (Orig.). 1987. pap. text ed. 5.95 (ISBN 0-345-34647-5, Pub. by Available Pr). Ballantine.

Song of the Free Self: The Song of Who I Am. Tisziji Munoz. 43p. (Orig.). pap. text ed. 10.00 (ISBN 0-945174-03-9). Illum Soc Pubns.

Song of the God Body. James Broughton. 1978. pap. 20.00 signed (ISBN 0-686-23064-7). Man-Root.

Song of the Iron Hoop. Theodora Lloyd. 77p. 1985. 16.00x (ISBN 0-85088-400-4, Pub. by Gomer Pr). State Mutual Bk.

Song of the Lark. Willa Cather. 1983. pap. 8.95 (ISBN 0-395-34530-8). HM.

Song of the Lark. Willa Cather. 29.95 (ISBN 0-88411-288-8, Pub. by Aeonian Pr). Amereon Ltd.

Song of the Lark. Willa Cather. 480p. 1988. pap. 8.95 (ISBN 0-395-33111-0). HM.

Song of the Lark see Early Novels & Stories.

Song of the Loom: New Traditions in Navajo Weaving. Frederick J. Dockstader. LC 86-27610. (Illus.). 132p. 1987. 35.00 (ISBN 0-933920-87-3, Dist. by Rizzoli); Museum distribution only. pap. 25.00 (ISBN 0-933920-88-1). Hudson Hills.

Song of the Lord. David K. Blomgren. 70p. 1986. pap. 6.95 (ISBN 0-317-56988-0). Bible Temple.

Song of the Meadowlark. John A. Sanford. LC 85-45443. 352p. 1986. 16.45 (ISBN 0-06-015546-9, HarpT). Har-Row.

Song of the Meadowlark. John A. Stanford. 320p. 1987. pap. 3.95 (ISBN 0-8125-8843-6, Dist. by St Martin's Pr & Warner Pub Servs). Tor Bks.

Song of the Moon. Judith Harris. LC 83-82014. 16p. 1983. pap. 3.50 (ISBN 0-914061-00-3). Orchises Pr.

Song of the Nibelungs: A Verse Translation from the Middle High German Nibelungenlied. Tr. by Frank G. Ryder. LC 82-17432. (Waynebooks Ser: No. 15). 435p. 1962. text ed. 25.00x (ISBN 0-8143-1191-1); pap. text ed. 8.95x (ISBN 0-8143-1192-X, WB15). Wayne St U Pr.

Song of the North Wind: A Story of the Snow Goose. Paul A. Johnsgard. LC 79-13939. (Illus.). xii, 150p. 1979. 14.50x (ISBN 0-8032-2556-3); pap. 6.95 (ISBN 0-8032-7552-8, BB 719, Bison). U of Nebr Pr.

Song of the Outriggers. Ralph R. Whitaker. LC 68-20946. 311p. 1968. 8.95 (ISBN 0-87527-087-5). Fireside Bks.

Song of the Outriggers: Big Game Fishing on the Ocean Surface. Ralph R. Whitaker. LC 68-20946. (Illus.). 311p. 1968. 8.95. Green.

Song of the Paddle: An Illustrated Guide to Wilderness Camping. Bill Mason. (Illus.). 208p. 1988. 24.95 (ISBN 0-942802-83-7); pap. 19.95 (ISBN 0-942802-84-5). Northword.

Song of the Paddle: An Illustrated Guide to Wilderness Camping. Bill Mason. (Illus.). 208p. 1988. 29.95 (ISBN 1-55013-079-X, Pub. by Key Porter Canada); pap. 19.95 (ISBN 1-55013-082-X, Pub. by Key Porter Canada). U of Toronto Pr.

Song of the Plains. Audrey H. Winkler. LC 78-66206. 1978. 7.95x (ISBN 0-9603312-0-4). Wynaud Pr.

Song of the Sea. David A. Wilson. 40p. (Orig.). 1970. pap. 2.00 (ISBN 0-934852-04-9). Lorien Hse.

Song of the Sea Otter. Edith T. Hurd. LC 83-4675. (Sierra Club Bks.). (Illus.). 48p. (gr. 2-7). 1983. (Pant Bks Young); PLB 9.95 (ISBN 0-394-86191-4). Pantheon.

Song of the Seasons. Robert Welber. (Illus.). (ps-2). 1973. Pantheon.

Song of the Self Supreme: Astavakra Gita. Tr. by Radhakamal Mukerjee. LC 74-24308. 293p. 1981. 9.95 (ISBN 0-913922-14-5). Dawn Horse Pr.

Song of the Seven Herbs. Stan Padilla. LC 87-10234. (Illus.). 72p. (Orig.). 1987. pap. 9.95 (ISBN 0-913990-56-6). Book Pub Co.

Song of the Seven Herbs. Walking Night Bear. LC 83-80087. (Illus.). 60p. (gr. 2up). 1983. pap. 8.95 (ISBN 0-943986-21-4). Gold Circle.

Song of the Shaggy Canary. Phyllis A. Wood. LC 73-14785. (Hiway Book: A High Interest - Low Reading Level Book). 156p. (gr. 6 up). 1974. 8.95 (ISBN 0-664-32543-2). Westminster John Knox.

Song of the Silent Snow. Hubert Selby, Jr. LC 85-14940. 244p. 1986. 16.95 (ISBN 0-7145-2840-4, Dist. by Kampmann & Co). M Boyars Pubs.

Song of the Silent Snow & Other Stories. Hubert Selby, Jr. 224p. 1987. pap. 6.95 (ISBN 0-8021-3008-9, Ever). Grove.

Song of the Siren. Philippa Carr. 352p. 1985. pap. 3.50 (ISBN 0-449-20772-2, Crest). Fawcett.

Song of the Sky: Versions of Native American Songs & Poems. Tr. by Brian Swann. 200p. (YA) 1981. 25.00 (ISBN 0-939622-26-2); pap. 12.50 (ISBN 0-939622-25-4). Four Zoas Night.

Song of the Soul: An Introduction to the Namokar Mantra & the Science of Sound. Acharya S. Kumar. 104p. (Orig.). 1987. 5.00 (ISBN 0-943207-00-2). Siddhachalam.

Song of the Soul: In Celebration of Korea. Lenore Beechman. LC 83-15536. (Illus.). 38p. (Orig.). 1984. pap. 4.95 (ISBN 0-377-00137-6). Friendship Pr.

Song of the Soul Set Free. Caroline Gilroy. 103p. (Orig.). 1986. pap. 3.95 (ISBN 0-8341-1138-1). Beacon Hill.

Song of the Sparrow: Meditations & Poems to Pray by. Murray Bodo. (Illus.). 187p. (Orig.). 1976. pap. 3.95 (ISBN 0-912228-26-1). St Anthony Mess Pr.

Song of the Spirit. Herbert L. Beierle. 1978. 20.00 (ISBN 0-940480-01-8). U of Healing.

Song of the Swallows. Leo Politi. (Illus.). 32p. (gr. k-3). 1986. pap. 4.95 (Aladdin). Macmillan.

Song of the Swallows. Leo Politi. (Illus.). 32p. (ps-3). 1987. 12.95 (ISBN 0-684-18831-7, Pub. by Scribner); pap. 4.95 (ISBN 0-689-71140-9). Macmillan.

Song of the Trees. Mildred Taylor. LC 74-18598. (Illus.). 56p. (gr. 2-5). 1975. 7.95 (ISBN 0-8037-5452-3); PLB 7.89 (ISBN 0-8037-5453-1). Dial Bks Young.

Song of the Trees. Mildred D. Taylor. 64p. 1984. pap. 2.25 (ISBN 0-553-26756-6). Bantam.

Song of the Undersea. Ronald Kirkbride. 1967. 10.95 (ISBN 0-8392-1163-5). Astor-Honor.

Song of the Vineyard: A Guide Through the Old Testament. rev. ed. Davie Napier. LC 78-14672. 360p. 1981. pap. 5.95 (ISBN 0-8006-1352-X, 1-1352). Fortress.

Song of the Virgin. Spiros Zodhiates. LC 82-71643. (Illus.). 1974. pap. 3.95 (ISBN 0-89957-510-2). AMG Pubs.

Song of the Wave & Other Poems. facsimile ed. George C. Lodge. LC 70-104517. 135p. Repr. of 1898 ed. lib. bdg. 19.00 (ISBN 0-8398-1168-3). Irvington.

Song of the Wave & Other Poems. George C. Lodge. 135p. 1986. pap. text ed. 5.95x (ISBN 0-8290-2030-6). Irvington.

Song of the West: Selected Poems. Georg Trakl. Tr. by Robert Firmage from Ger. LC 88-61179. 128p. 1988. 19.95 (ISBN 0-86547-352-8); pap. 9.95 (ISBN 0-86547-353-6). N Point Pr.

Song of the Whip. Evan Evans, pseud. 261p. 1975. Repr. of 1936 ed. lib. bdg. 15.95 (ISBN 0-89190-210-4, Pub. by River City Pr). Amereon Ltd.

Song of the Whip. Evan Evans, pseud. 192p. 1986. pap. 2.75 (ISBN 0-515-08885-4). Jove Pubns.

Song of the White-Throat. Edward J. Danforth. LC 77-70657. (Illus.). 1977. pap. 5.95 (ISBN 0-9601174-1-5). E J Danforth.

Song of the Wild. Allan W. Eckert. 252p. 1980. 14.95 (ISBN 0-316-20877-9). Little.

Song of the Wind. Madge Swindells. (Orig.). 1986. pap. 4.50 (ISBN 0-451-14248-9, Sig). NAL.

Song of the Wolf. Scott C. Stone. 1987. pap. 3.95 (ISBN 0-451-14775-8, Sig). NAL.

Song of the World. Jean Giono. Tr. by Henri Fluchere & Geoffrey Myers. LC 80-28523. (Giono Novels Ser.). 320p. 1981. pap. 11.00 (ISBN 0-86547-038-3). N Point Pr.

Song of Three Friends & the Song of Hugh Glass. John G. Neihardt. 335p. 1982. Repr. of 1941 ed. lib. bdg. 25.00 (ISBN 0-89984-360-3). Century Bookbindery.

Song of Truth & Semblance. Cees Nooteboom. Tr. by Adrienne Dixon from Dutch. LC 84-848. Orig. Title: Een Liedvan schijn en wezen. 83p. 1984. 12.95 (ISBN 0-8071-1176-7). La State U Pr.

Song of Years. Bess S. Aldrich. 490p. 1975. Repr. of 1937 ed. lib. bdg. 25.95x (ISBN 0-88411-251-9, Pub. by Aeonian Pr). Amereon Ltd.

Song of Years. Bess S. Aldrich. 1985. pap. 2.95 (ISBN 0-451-13925-9, Sig Vista). NAL.

Song Offerings by Rabindranath Tagore. Rabindranath Tagore. (Illus.). 117p. 1987. 117.50 (ISBN 0-89901-329-5). Found Class Reprints.

Song on Record Two. Ed. by Alan Blyth. 300p. 1988. 39.50 (ISBN 0-521-33155-2). Cambridge U Pr.

Song on Record, Vol. 1: Lieder. Ed. by Alan Blyth. 364p. 1986. 42.50 (ISBN 0-521-26844-3). Cambridge U Pr.

Song Out of Harlem. Antar S. Mberi. LC 80-12500. (Vox Humana Ser.). 96p. 1980. 8.95 (ISBN 0-89603-018-0); pap. 3.50 (ISBN 0-89603-021-0). Humana.

Song Painting, Nos. 1-4. 770.00x (ISBN 0-317-69104-X, Pub. by Han-Shan Tang Ltd). State Mutual Bk.

Song Pentecost. W. J. Corbett. (gr. k-6). 1985. pap. 3.25 (ISBN 0-440-48092-2, YB). Dell.

Song Presentation for Popular Singers: Book II. Al Berkman. 1984. 10.00 (ISBN 0-934972-02-8). Melrose Bk Co.

Song Presentation for Popular Singers: Book I. Al Berkman. 1979. 10.00 (ISBN 0-934972-01-X). Melrose Bk Co.

Song Spectrum, Vol. 1. (Ultimate Ser.). 304p. 1984. plastic comb 17.95 (ISBN 0-88188-277-1, 00361412); pap. 14.95 (ISBN 0-88188-276-3, 00361413). H Leonard Pub Corp.

Song Spectrum, Vol. 2. (Ultimate Ser.). 320p. 1984. plastic comb 17.95 (ISBN 0-88188-279-8, 00361414); pap. 14.95 (ISBN 0-317-38349-3, 00361415). H Leonard Pub Corp.

Song Stories of Hawaii. Carol Roes. (Illus.). 24p. (gr. 1-8). 1959. pap. 5.50 (ISBN 0-930932-17-X). M Loke.

Song: Teddy Horsley Sings the Song of Creation. Leslie J. Francis & Nicola Slee. (Teddy Horsley Books for Young Christians). (Illus.). 24p. (ps-2). 1986. pap. 1.25 (ISBN 0-00-599782-8, Collins Liturgical). HarpR.

Song to Creation: A Dialogue with a Text. E. Mihaly. (Jewish Perspectives Ser.: Vol. 1). 7.50x (ISBN 0-87820-500-4, HUC Pr). Ktav.

Song to Creation: A Dialogue with a Text. Eugene Mihaly. LC 75-35761. pap. 27.00 (ISBN 0-317-42034-8, 2025694). Bks Demand UMI.

Song to Demeter. Cynthia Birrer & William Birrer. LC 86-20895. (Illus.). 32p. (ps-3). 1987. 11.75 (ISBN 0-688-04040-3); PLB 11.88 (ISBN 0-688-04041-1). Lothrop.

Song Tradition of Tristan Da Cunha. Peter A. Munch. (Folklore Monographs Ser: Vol. 22). 1970. pap. text ed. 19.95 (ISBN 0-391-02076-5). Res Ctr Lang Semiotic.

Song Twice over. Brenda Jagger. LC 85-15586. 504p. 1986. 18.95 (ISBN 0-688-06169-9). Morrow.

Song Twice Over. Brenda Jagger. 544p. 1987. pap. 4.50 (ISBN 0-449-21040-5, Crest). Fawcett.

Song Without Music: Chinese Tz'u Poetry. Ed. by Stephen C. Soong. LC 81-670049. (Renditions Ser). (Illus.). 288p. 1981. 25.00x (ISBN 0-295-95811-1, Pub. by Chinese Univ Hong Kong). U of Wash Pr.

Song Yuan Ciqi Tezhan Mulu: Catalogue of the Special Exhibition of Song & Yuan Porcelains. National Palace Museum Staff. 160p. 1971. 30.00x (ISBN 0-317-45256-8, Pub. by Han-Shan Tang Ltd). State Mutual Bk.

Songbird. Linda Shaw. 1987. pap. 3.95 (ISBN 0-671-45474-9). PB.

Songbird Carving. Roslyn L. Daisey & Patricia S. Kurman. (Illus.). 256p. 1986. 45.00 (ISBN 0-88740-057-4). Schiffer.

Songbird Carving, Vol. II. Roslyn L. Daisey & Patricia S. Kurman. (Illus.). 1988. 45.00 (ISBN 0-88740-119-8). Schiffer.

Songbird Carving with Ernest Muehlmatt: World-Class Ribbon Winner Teaches You How to Carve & Paint 10 Favorite Songbirds. Ernest Muehlmatt & Roger Schroeder. (Illus.). 288p. 1987. 39.95 (ISBN 0-8117-1817-4). Stackpole.

Songbirds. Ed. by Lynn Hughes. LC 81-40509. (Illus.). 56p. 1981. 4.95 (ISBN 0-89480-189-9, 341). Workman Pub.

Songbirds in Your Garden. 1988. incl. audiocassette 21.95 (ISBN 0-87857-773-4). Rodale Pr Inc.

Songbirds in Your Garden. John K. Terres. LC 86-45701. (Illus.). 288p. 1987. pap. 10.95 (ISBN 0-06-091377-0, PL1377, PL). Har-Row.

Songbook: Down with Ronald Reagan, Chieftain of Capitalist Reaction & Other Songs of Revolutionary Struggle & Socialism. Marxist-Leninist Party, U. S. A. (Illus.). 84p. 1982. pap. 1.00 (ISBN 0-86714-024-0). Marxist-Leninist.

Songbook of Absences. Miguel Hernandez. Tr. by Tom Jones. LC 72-91778. 1980. 7.50 (ISBN 0-910350-06-X). Charioteer.

Songbook of the American Revolution. Carolyn Rabson. 1974. pap. 4.00 (ISBN 0-911014-18-7). Neo Pr.

Songci Tezhan Mulu: Special Exhibition of Song Ceramics. National Palace Museum Staff. 103p. 1978. 30.00x (ISBN 0-317-45259-2, Pub. by Han-Shan Tang Ltd). State Mutual Bk.

Songdai Beifang Minjian Ciqi. Chen Wanli. 1955. 100.00x (ISBN 0-317-43946-4, Pub. by Han-Shan Tang Ltd.). State Mutual Bk.

Songdai Minjian Taoci Wenyang-Cizhou Yaoxing: Designs on Song Period Folk Ceramics-the Cizhou Moulds. 1960. 300.00x (ISBN 0-317-43955-3, Pub. by Han-Shan Tang Ltd.). State Mutual Bk.

Songe. Henry De Montherlant. (Folio Ser.: No. 1458). pap. 8.95 (ISBN 0-685-36987-0). Schoenhof.

Songes et Mensonges De L'astrologie see Dreams & Illusions of Astrology.

Songlines. Bruce Chatwin. 1987. 18.95 (ISBN 0-670-80605-6). Viking.

Songlines. Bruce Chatwin. 304p. 1988. pap. 7.95 (ISBN 0-14-009429-6). Penguin.

Songmaster. Orson S. Card. 384p. 1987. pap. 3.95 (ISBN 0-8125-3255-4, Dist. by St Martin's Pr & Warner Pub Servs). Tor Bks.

Songprints: The Musical Experience of Five Shoshone Women. Judith Vander. LC 87-24488. (Music in American Life). 336p. 1988. 29.95 (ISBN 0-252-01531-2); incl. cass. 35.95 (ISBN 0-252-01532-0); 60 min. cassette 9.95. U of Ill Pr.

Songs. Nadia Boulanger. (Women Composers Ser.: No. 16). 85p. 1985. Repr. of 1922 ed. lib. bdg. 27.50 (ISBN 0-306-76233-1). Da Capo.

Songs. Charley J. Greasybear. Ed. by Tom Trusky & Judson Crews. LC 78-58484. (Modern & Contemporary Poets of the West). (Orig.). 1979. pap. 4.50 (ISBN 0-916272-10-9). Ahsahta Pr.

Songs. Christopher Logue. 1960. 10.95 (ISBN 0-8392-1106-6). Astor-Honor.

Songs about Animals & Others. (Golden Song Book 'n' Tapes). (Illus.). (ps-3). pap. write for info. incl. cassette (ISBN 0-307-13975-1, Golden Bks). Western Pub.

Songs after Lincoln. Paul Horgan. 74p. 1965. 4.95 (ISBN 0-374-26664-6). FS&G.

Songs Alive. 56p. Date not set. incl. 1 cassette 19.50 (ISBN 0-88432-193-2, S32521). J Norton Pubs.

Songs along the Mahantonga: Pennsylvania Dutch Folksongs. Walter E. Boyer et al. 232p. 1964. Repr. of 1951 ed. 35.00x (ISBN 0-8103-5002-5). Gale.

Songs America Voted By. Irwin Silber. Date not set. price not set. Stackpole.

Songs & Ballads, Chiefly of the Reign of Philip & Mary. Ed. by Thomas Wright. LC 78-122836. 1970. Repr. of 1860 ed. 25.50 (ISBN 0-8337-3896-8). B Franklin.

Songs & Ballads from over the Sea. facsimile ed. Ed. by E. A. Helps. LC 78-168783. (Granger Index Reprint Ser.). Repr. of 1912 ed. 21.00 (ISBN 0-8369-6303-2). Ayer Co Pubs.

Songs & Ballads of Dundee. N. Gatherer. (Illus.). 176p. 1985. pap. text ed. 15.00x (ISBN 0-85976-146-0, Pub. by John Donald Pub UK). Humanities.

Songs & Ballads of Greater Britain. facsimile ed. Ed. by E. A. Helps. LC 70-37016. (Granger Index Reprint Ser.). Repr. of 1913 ed. 21.00 (ISBN 0-8369-6315-6). Ayer Co Pubs.

Songs & Ballads of Northern England. John Stokoe. 1978. Repr. of 1889 ed. lib. bdg. 39.50 (ISBN 0-8492-8046-X). R West.

Songs & Ballads of the American Revolution. Ed. by Frank Moore & Peter Decker. LC 79-76562. (Eyewitness Accounts of the American Revolution Ser., No. 2). (Illus.). 1969. Repr. of 1856 ed. 23.50 (ISBN 0-405-01164-4). Ayer Co Pubs.

Songs & Ballads of the Maine Lumberjacks. Ed. by Roland P. Gray. LC 73-75944. 216p. 1969. Repr. of 1924 ed. 35.00x (ISBN 0-8103-3835-1). Gale.

Songs & Ballads of the Southern People, 1861-65. Frank Moore. LC 79-147834. (Research & Source Works Ser.: No. 767). 1971. Repr. of 1886 ed. lib. bdg. 22.50 (ISBN 0-8337-2451-7). B Franklin.

Songs & Ballads, with Other Short Poems, Chiefly of the Reign of Philip & Mary. Thomas Wright. 214p. 1980. Repr. of 1860 ed. lib. bdg. 45.00 (ISBN 0-8495-5827-1). Arden Lib.

Songs & Dances. Philip M. Royster. LC 80-85233. 61p. 1981. pap. 3.50x perfect bd. (ISBN 0-916418-28-6). Lotus.

Songs & Dances of Native America. rev. ed. Lynn Huenemann. (Songs from Singing Cultures Ser.: Vol. 3). (Illus.). Date not set. (ISBN 0-937203-09-2); pap. (ISBN 0-937203-10-6); Spiral ed. (ISBN 0-937203-11-4); Cassette. (ISBN 0-937203-12-2). World Music Pr.

Songs & Folklore of Puerto Rico. Monserrate Deliz. (Puerto Rico Ser.). 1979. lib. bdg. 59.95 (ISBN 0-8490-3007-2). Gordon Pr.

Songs & Hymns for Primary Children. Ed. by W. Lawrence Curry. (gr. 1-3). 1978. softcover 3.95 (ISBN 0-664-10117-8). Westminster John Knox.

Songs & Lyrics from the English Masques & Light Operas. Ed. by Frederick Boas. 175p. 1949. Repr. 15.00x (ISBN 0-403-03693-3). Scholarly.

Songs & Lyrics from the English Playbooks. Ed. by Frederick S. Boas. Repr. of 1945 ed. 15.00x (ISBN 0-403-04290-9). Somerset Pub.

Songs & Lyrics from the English Playbooks. Repr. of 1945 ed. lib. bdg. 20.50 (ISBN 0-8414-1623-0). Folcroft.

Songs & Lyrics from the Plays of Beaumont & Fletcher. Beaumont & Fletcher. Ed. by E. H. Fellows. LC 79-180038. Repr. of 1928 ed. 24.50 (ISBN 0-405-08249-5, Blom Pubns). Ayer Co Pubs.

Songs & Masques: With Observations in the Art of English Poesy. Thomas Campion. Ed. by A. H. Bullen. 1973. Repr. of 1889 ed. lib. bdg. 35.00 (ISBN 0-8414-0150-0). Folcroft.

Songs & Poems. Alexander Galich. Tr. by Gerry Smith from Rus. 188p. 1983. 25.00 (ISBN 0-88233-784-X). Ardis Pubs.

Songs & Poems of Robert Burns. Ed. by Ralph Knight. 1959. 16.95x (ISBN 0-8084-0384-2). New Coll U Pr.

Songs & Prayers of Victory. Basilea Schlink. 1978. pap. 1.50 (ISBN 3-87209-652-4). Evang Sisterhood Mary.

Songs & Sayings of an Ulster Childhood. Alice Kane. Ed. by Edith Fowke. 256p. 10.95 (ISBN 0-86327-005-0, Pub. by Wolfhound Pr Ireland). Irish Bks Media.

Songs & Sayings of Walther Von der Vogelweide. Ed. by Frank Betts. 69.95 (ISBN 0-8490-2631-8). Gordon Pr.

Songs & Sayings of Walther von der Vogelweide, Minnesanger. Walther von der Vogelweide. Tr. by Frank Betts. LC 75-41287. Repr. of 1917 ed. 11.50 (ISBN 0-404-14752-6). AMS Pr.

Songs & Song Writers. Henry T. Finck. 59.95 (ISBN 0-8490-1083-7). Gordon Pr.

Songs & Song Writers. Henry T. Finck. LC 78-31290. 1979. Repr. of 1902 ed. lib. bdg. 25.00 (ISBN 0-89341-439-5). Longwood Pub Group.

Songs & Song Writers. Henry T. Finck. 14.25 (ISBN 0-8369-7135-3, 7968). Ayer Co Pubs.

Songs & Sonnets from Laura's Lifetime. Francis Petrarch. Tr. by Nicholas Kilmer from Ital. LC 80-28300. 144p. 1981. pap. 7.50 (ISBN 0-86547-028-6). N Point Pr.

Songs & Sonnets of Pierre De Ronsard. Pierre De Ronsard. Tr. by Curtis H. Page from Fr. LC 76-48455. (Library of World Literature Ser.). 1985. Repr. of 1924 ed. 19.95 (ISBN 0-88355-604-9). Hyperion Conn.

Songs & Stories from Tennessee. John T. Moore. LC 70-94739. (Short Story Index Reprint Ser.). 1902. 20.00 (ISBN 0-8369-3119-X). Ayer Co Pubs.

Songs & Stories from Uganda. W. Moses Serwadda. Ed. by Hewitt Pantaleoni. LC 87-18904. (Illus.). 96p. 1987. Set. pap. 17.95 (ISBN 0-937203-17-3); pap. 12.95 (ISBN 0-937203-15-7); cassette 5.95 (ISBN 0-937203-16-5). World Music Pr.

Songs & Stories, Selected & Annotated. Edwin Markham. 29.00 (ISBN 0-8369-4268-X, 6066). Ayer Co Pubs.

Songs, Ballads & Instrumental Pieces Composed by King Henry the VIII. Henry VII. Ed. by Mary Trefusis. LC 74-26054. Repr. of 1912 ed. 32.50 (ISBN 0-404-12962-5). AMS Pr.

Songs, Ballads, & Stories. William Allingham. LC 75-148743. Repr. of 1877 ed. 24.00 (ISBN 0-404-00347-8). AMS Pr.

Songs: Bulat Okudzhava, Vol. II. Bulat Okudzhava. Ed. by Vladimir Frumkin. Tr. by Tanya Wolfson et al. 117p. (Rus. & Eng.). 1986. text ed. 30.00 (ISBN 0-87501-021-0); pap. text ed. 10.00 (ISBN 0-87501-022-9). Ardis Pubs.

Songs by Thirty Americans for High Voice. Ed. by Rupert Hughes. LC 77-1942. (Music Reprint Series). 1976. Repr. of 1904 ed. lib. bdg. 32.50 (ISBN 0-306-70824-8). Da Capo.

Songs, Carols & Other Miscellaneous Poems, from the Balliol Ms. Richard Hill. Ed. by Roman Dyboski. (EETS, ES Ser.: No. 101). Repr. of 1907 ed. 35.00 (ISBN 0-527-00305-0). Kraus Repr.

Songs Divine. Abhendananda. Tr. by P. S. Aiyer from Sanskrit. 69p. 1985. 6.95 (ISBN 0-87481-653-X, Pub. by Ramakrishna Math Madras India). Vedanta Pr.

Songs, Eighteen Eighty to Nineteen Hundred & Four. Claude Debussy. Ed. by Rita Benson. (Orig.). 1981. pap. 7.95 (ISBN 0-486-24131-9). Dover.

Songs Every Child Should Know: A Selection of the Best Songs of All Nations for Young People. Ed. by Dolores M. Bacon. 221p. 1986. Repr. of 1906 ed. lib. bdg. 35.00 (ISBN 0-8492-9624-2). R West.

Songs for a Hometown Boy. Mark Vinz. 1977. 5.25 (ISBN 0-941490-14-9). Solo Pr.

Songs for a Son. Robert L. Peters. (Orig.). 1967. pap. 2.75 (ISBN 0-393-04288-X). Norton.

Songs for Awakening. Heng Yin et al. (Illus.). 112p. (Orig.). 1979. pap. 8.00 (ISBN 0-917512-63-4). Buddhist Text.

Songs for Camps & Reunions. Roger Revell. 1986. pap. 4.00 (ISBN 0-8309-0447-6). Herald Hse.

Songs for Children of the World. Ed. by Roberta McKinney. 16p. (Orig.). (gr. 1-8). 1984. pap. 12.95 set of 10 (ISBN 0-87487-740-7, Suzuki Method). Birch Tree Gr.

Songs for Choirs: A Collection for Mixed Voices. Ed. by William Appleby & Frederick Fowler. 1972. pap. 6.00 (ISBN 0-19-330158-X). Oxford U Pr.

Songs for Early Childhood. 1958. 3.25 ea. (ISBN 0-664-10058-9). Westminster John Knox.

Songs for Gail Guidry's Guitar. John Knoepfle. 1969. sewn in wrappers 3.00 (ISBN 0-912284-02-1). New Rivers Pr.

Songs for Isadora. Linda W. Wagner. (Dialogues on Dance Ser.: No.1). 32p. 1981. pap. 6.00 (ISBN 0-317-06435-5). Ommation Pr.

Songs for Jadina. Alan C. Lau. LC 80-66984. 94p. (Orig.). 1981. pap. 4.95 (ISBN 0-912678-46-1). Greenfld Rev Pr.

Songs for Language Learning. Sandra J. Shanin. 40p. (Orig.). 1984. pap. text ed. 49.95 (ISBN 0-88450-899-4, 4633-B). Communication Skill.

Songs for My Fathers. Gary Smith. LC 83-82775. 78p. 1984. pap. 5.00 perf. bnd. (ISBN 0-916418-55-3). Lotus.

Songs for Patricia. Norman Rosten. Ed. by Barbara Paturick. (Illus.). 48p. (Orig.). 1988. pap. 6.95 (ISBN 0-939602-04-0). Blue Star.

Songs for Preschool Children. Ed. by Marian Bennett. LC 80-25091. 96p. (Orig.). 1981. pap. 7.95 (ISBN 0-87239-429-8, 5754). Standard Pub.

Songs for Seers. Pol Ndu. LC 73-91413. 35p. 1974. pap. 2.95 (ISBN 0-88357-036-X). Nok Pubs.

Songs for the Bride: Wedding Rites of Rural India. William G. Archer. Ed. by Barbara S. Miller & Mildred Archer. (Studies in Oriental Culture). 224p. 1985. 22.50x (ISBN 0-317-18769-4). Brooklyn Coll Pr.

Songs for the Journey. Mary Christopher. (Illus.). 158p. (Orig.). 1988. pap. 7.98 (ISBN 0-943699-00-2). Entheo Bks.

Songs for the Joy of Living. Illus. by Children at Sunrise Ranch. (Illus.). 50p. (gr. 1-10). 1985. ring-bound 11.95 (ISBN 0-932869-01-7). Emissaries Divine.

Songs for the Revolution. Hunce Voelcker. (Illus.). 3.00 (ISBN 0-917996-03-8). Panjandrum.

Songs for Wanderers. Sheila Moon. 1978. 5.00 (ISBN 0-8233-0287-3). Golden Quill.

Songs for Well-Behaved Children. Barry L. Polisar. (gr. k-6). 1979. incl. cassette 9.95 (ISBN 0-317-56150-2). Rainbow Morn.

Songs for Well Behaved Children. Barry L. Polisar. (gr. k-6). Repr. of 1979 ed. 9.95 (ISBN 0-9615696-6-2); audio cassette avail. Rainbow Morn.

Songs for Young Children. LC 75-40910. (Illus.). (gr. k-3). 1976. spiral bdg. 4.95 (ISBN 0-916406-31-8). Accent Bks.

Songs from a Colonial Tavern. Tayler Vrooman. LC 64-8087. (Illus.). 48p. (Orig.). 1964. pap. 4.95 (ISBN 0-910412-46-4). Williamsburg.

Songs from a Spanish Sierra. Marky Daniel. (Illus.). 1984. pap. 5.00 (ISBN 0-911287-04-3). Blue Begonia.

Songs from Alice. Lewis Carroll & Don Harper. LC 79-11314. (Illus.). 48p. (gr. k-3). 1979. reinforced bdg. 8.95 (ISBN 0-8234-0358-0); cassette 9.95 (ISBN 0-8234-0421-8). Holiday.

Songs from an Island. Marjorie Johnson. LC 74-33876. 112p. 1975. 6.00 (ISBN 0-8233-0220-2). Golden Quill.

Songs from Green Pastures. Edith Schaeffer. 64p. 1988. 12.95 (ISBN 0-310-54630-3, Pub. by Daybreak). Zondervan.

Songs from Hollywood Musical Comedies, 1927 to the Present: A Dictionary. Allen L. Woll. LC 75-24089. (Reference Library of the Humanities: Vol. 44). 300p. 1976. lib. bdg. 37.00 (ISBN 0-8240-9958-3). Garland Pub.

Songs from Mother Goose. (Illus.). (ps-3). pap. write for info. incl. cassette (ISBN 0-307-13974-3, Golden Bks). Western Pub.

Songs from My Father's Pockets. Llewellyn I. Giles. (Illus.). 64p. 1983. pap. 4.50 perf. bound (ISBN 0-937724-01-7). Shadow Pr.

Songs from My Heart: Poems & Photographs. Daisaku Ikeda. LC 78-3560. (Illus.). 112p. 1978. 12.50 (ISBN 0-8348-0133-7). Weatherhill.

Songs from the Baltic Coast. A. Luur et al. 88p. 1987. 20.00 (ISBN 0-8285-3775-5, Pub. by Perioodika Tallinn). Imported Pubns.

Songs From the British Drama. Ed. by Edward B. Reed. 1925. 65.00x (ISBN 0-686-83775-4). Elliots Bks.

Songs from the Center of the Well. rev. ed. Chetanananda. 96p. 1985. pap. 6.95 (ISBN 0-915801-03-5). Rudra Pr.

Songs from the Dramatists. Ed. by Robert Bell. 268p. 1981. Repr. lib. bdg. 45.00 (ISBN 0-8495-0484-8). Arden Lib.

Songs from the Drowned Lands. Eileen Kernaghan. 1983. pap. 2.50 (ISBN 0-441-77242-0, Ace Science Fiction). Ace Bks.

Songs from the Ghetto. facsimile ed. Morris Rosenfeld. LC 76-104556. 123p. Repr. of 1898 ed. lib. bdg. 19.00 (ISBN 0-8398-1766-5). Irvington.

Songs from the Heart. Steven A. Seager. 64p. 1987. 7.95 (ISBN 0-8062-3137-8). Carlton.

Songs from the House of Pilgrimage. Stephen Isaac. LC 77-169595. 1971. 9.50 (ISBN 0-8283-1334-2). Christward.

Songs from the Land of Dawn. facs. ed. Tr. by Lois J. Erickson. LC 68-58828. (Granger Index Reprint Ser). 1949. 14.00 (ISBN 0-8369-6014-9). Ayer Co Pubs.

Songs from the Novels of Thomas Love Peacock. Thomas L. Peacock. 1972. Repr. lib. bdg. 20.00 (ISBN 0-8414-9209-3). Folcroft.

Songs from the Pursuit of a No Strings Vision. Gloria George. LC 87-70420. 69p. 1987. 12.95 (ISBN 0-942275-00-4). Cedar Pr.

Songs from the Restoration Theatre. Willard Thorp. LC 76-102003. (Music Reprint Ser.). 1970. Repr. of 1934 ed. lib. bdg. 25.00 (ISBN 0-306-71867-7). Da Capo.

Songs from the Seashell Archives, No. 2. Elizabeth A. Scarborough. (Specta Ser.). (Orig.). 1988. pap. 4.95 (ISBN 0-553-27009-5). Bantam.

Songs from the Williamsburg Theatre. abr. ed. John W. Molnar. LC 78-165363. (Illus.). 48p. (Orig.). 1974. pap. 3.95 (ISBN 0-87935-011-3). Williamsburg.

Songs from This Earth on Turtle's Back: An Anthology of Poetry by American Indian Writers. Intro. by Joseph Bruchac. LC 82-82420. 300p. (Orig.). 1983. pap. 9.95 (ISBN 0-912678-58-5). Greenfld Rev Pr.

Songs from Unsung Worlds. Ed. by Bonnie B. Gordon. 260p. 1985. casebound 14.95 (ISBN 0-317-59882-1); pap. 9.95. AAAS.

Songs from Unsung Worlds: Science In Poetry. Ed. by Bonnie Gordon. 250p. 1985. pap. 11.95 (ISBN 0-8176-3296-4). Birkhauser.

Songs from Vagabondia. Bliss Carman & Richard Hovey. 59.95 (ISBN 0-87968-314-7). Gordon Pr.

Songs from Vagabondia. Bliss Carman & Richard Hovey. (American Studies). (Illus.). 1969. Repr. of 1907 ed. lib. bdg. 12.00 (ISBN 0-384-07590-8). Johnson Repr.

Songs from Xanadu: Studies in Mongrol-Dynasty Song-Poetry (San-ch'u) J. I. Crump. LC 83-7809. (Michigan Monographs in Chinese Studies: No. 47). (Illus.). xi, 232p. (Orig.). 1983. pap. 10.00 (ISBN 0-89264-047-2). U of Mich Ctr Chinese.

Songs I-XXX. Robert Kelly. 100p. 1968. 6.00 (ISBN 0-913219-03-7). Pym-Rand Pr.

Songs in a Time of War. Ken Saro-Wiwa. 44p. (Orig.). 1985. pap. 6.00 (Pub. by Saros Intl Pubs UK). Three Continents.

Songs in Action. 2nd ed. R. Phyllis Gelineau. 304p. 1988. pap. 26.95 (Parker Publishing Co). P-H.

Songs in Collections: An Index. Desiree De Charms & Paul Breed. 1966. 38.00 (ISBN 0-911772-53-7). Harmonie Pk Pr.

Songs in Signed English. Harry Bornstein. (Signed English Ser.). 44p. 1973. pap. 9.00 incl. record (ISBN 0-913580-12-0, Clerc Bks). Gallaudet Univ Pr.

Songs in the Night, S.C. Dennis Saylor. 8.00 (ISBN 0-686-71747-3). Palos Verdes.

Songs in the Plays of Lope de Vega: A Study of Their Dramatic Function. Gustavo Umpierre. (Serie A: Monagrafias, XLVI). 110p. (Orig.). 1975. pap. 14.50 (ISBN 0-900411-97-X, Pub. by Tamesis Bks Ltd). Longwood Pub Group.

Songs My Dead Mother Sang Me. 1983. spiral bound 11.95 (ISBN 0-89556-039-9). Gateways Bks & Tapes.

Songs, Odes, Glees & Ballads: A Bibliography of American Presidential Campaign Songsters. William Miles. 200p. 1989. lib. bdg. 42.50x (ISBN 0-88736-230-3). Meckler Corp.

Songs of a Black Bird. Carolyn Rodgers. 1969. pap. 1.50 (ISBN 0-88378-003-8). Third World.

Songs of a Bridge Builder. D. B. Steinman. 12.00 (ISBN 0-88253-762-8); flexible cloth 4.80 (ISBN 0-88253-761-X). Ind-US Inc.

Songs of a Native Son. L. Charles Merrill. 1979. 5.00 (ISBN 0-8233-0297-0). Golden Quill.

Songs of a Returning Soul. Elizabeth Libbey. LC 81-71587. 1981. pap. 6.95 (ISBN 0-915604-67-1). Carnegie-Mellon.

Songs of a Worker. Arthur O'Shaughnessy. Ed. by Ian Fletcher & John Stokes. LC 76-20159. (Decadent Consciousness Ser.). 1978. lib. bdg. 46.00 (ISBN 0-8240-2782-5). Garland Pub.

Songs of America: A Cavalcade of Popular Songs with Commentaries. Ed. by David Ewen. LC 77-26155. (Illus.). 1978. Repr. of 1947 ed. lib. bdg. 35.00 (ISBN 0-313-20166-8, EWSA). Greenwood.

Songs of American Folks. facsimile ed. Ed. by Satis N. Coleman & Adolph Bregman. LC 68-57060. (Granger Index Reprint Ser). 1942. 13.00 (ISBN 0-8369-6011-4). Ayer Co Pubs.

Songs of American Labor, Industrialization & the Urban Work Experience: A Discography. Richard A. Reuss. Ed. by Yvonne Lockwood. (Program on Workers Culture Ser.). (Illus.). 109p. 1983. pap. 4.75 (ISBN 0-87736-344-7). U of Mich Inst Labor.

Songs of an Immigrant: Poems. Samuel Hinton. LC 86-91214. 56p. 1987. 5.00 (ISBN 0-941607-00-3); pap. 3.50 (ISBN 0-941607-01-1). Pensar Educ Pr.

Songs of Autumn: Bilingual Edition. Sigitas Geda. Tr. by Jonas Zdanys from Lithuanian. LC 78-26139. 1979. signed ed. o.s.i. 10.00x (ISBN 0-918366-16-X); pap. 3.00 (ISBN 0-918366-11-9). Slow Loris.

Songs of Belfast. Ed. by David Hammond. 92p. 1986. pap. 7.95 (ISBN 0-85342-776-3, Pub. by Mercier Pr Ireland). Irish Bks Media.

Songs of Bilitis. Pierre Louys. (Illus.). 192p. 1988. pap. 4.95 (ISBN 0-486-25670-7). Dover.

Songs of Bloody Harlan. Lee Pennington. Intro. by John E. Westburg. 1975. pap. 5.00 (ISBN 0-87423-017-9). Westburg.

Songs of Bob Dylan, Nineteen Sixty-Six to Nineteen Seveny-Five. Bob Dylan. 1976. slip cased, spiral bound 19.95 (ISBN 0-394-40888-8); pap. 12.95 (ISBN 0-394-73523-4). Knopf.

Songs of Brother Nemo. Charles A. Stratton, III. 128p. 1988. 9.95 (ISBN 0-89962-672-6). Todd & Honeywell.

Songs of Cathay. Tr. by T. Z. Koo. 1984. pap. text ed. 15.00 (ISBN 0-87556-384-8). Saifer.

Songs of Cheer. Ed. by Carol Ferntheil. (Illus.). 16p. (Orig.). 1979. pap. 0.85 (ISBN 0-87239-345-3, 7948). Standard Pub.

Songs of Childhood. Reginald De Koven. 59.95 (ISBN 0-8490-1084-5). Gordon Pr.

Songs of Childhood. Walter De La Mare. 106p. (gr. 3 up). pap. 3.50 (ISBN 0-486-21972-0). Dover.

Songs of Childhood. Walter De La Mare. 13.50 (ISBN 0-8446-1966-3). Peter Smith.

Songs of Childhood. Walter Ramal, pseud. (Poetry Library). 184p. 1985. Repr. of 1902 ed. 19.75x (ISBN 0-89609-257-7). Roth Pub Inc.

Songs of Cifar & the Sweet Sea. Pablo A. Cuadra. Tr. by Grace Schulman & Ann M. De Zavala. LC 79-4115. (A Center for Inter-American Relations Book). 144p. 1979. 25.00x (ISBN 0-231-04772-X); pap. 14.00x (ISBN 0-231-04773-8). Columbia U Pr.

Songs of Cornwall. Kenneth Pelmear. 1985. 8.00x (ISBN 0-317-58060-4, Pub. by Dyllansow & Truran). State Mutual Bk.

Songs of Death: Performance, Interpretation, & the Text of "Richard III". R. Chris Hassel, Jr. LC 86-14659. (Illus.). x, 196p. 1987. 21.95x (ISBN 0-8032-2341-2). U of Nebr Pr.

Songs of Degrees. Stephen Kaung. Ed. by Herbert L. Fader. 1970. 4.00 (ISBN 0-935008-32-2); pap. 2.75 (ISBN 0-935008-33-0). Christian Fellow Pubs.

Songs of Deliverance. Flower A. Newhouse. LC 72-94582. 250p. 1972. 9.50 (ISBN 0-910378-08-8). Christward.

Songs of Distant Earth. Arthur C. Clarke. 1986. 17.95 (ISBN 0-345-33219-9, Del Rey). Ballantine.

Songs of Distant Earth. Arthur C. Clarke. 336p. 1987. pap. 4.95 (ISBN 0-345-32240-1, Del Rey). Ballantine.

Songs of Duncan MacIntyre. Angus MacLeod. 1978. 25.00x (ISBN 0-7073-0040-1, Pub. by Scot Acad Pr). Longwood Pub Group.

Songs of Eastern Birds. Donald J. Borror. pap. 7.95 booklet with record (ISBN 0-486-22378-7). Dover.

Songs of Eastern Birds. Donald J. Borror. 64p. 1984. pap. 7.95 incl. cassette (ISBN 0-486-99912-2). Dover.

Songs of England, Ireland, & Scotland: A Bonnie Bunch of Roses. Dan Milner & Paul Kaplan. 1983. pap. 12.95 (ISBN 0-8256-0256-4, Pub. by Oak). Music Sales.

Songs of Eternal Faith: Artistic Piano Arrangements of Best-Loved Hymns. Lynn S. Lund. LC 81-80954. 56p. (Orig.). 1982. pap. 6.95 (ISBN 0-88290-184-2, 2901). Horizon Utah.

Songs of Eternity: A Collection of Philosophical Poems. Prem Kirpal. 91p. 1987. pap. text ed. 7.95x (ISBN 0-7069-3287-0, Pub. by Vikas India). Advent NY.

Songs of Experience. William Blake. (Fine Arts). 48p. 1984. pap. 3.50 (ISBN 0-486-24636-1). Dover.

Songs of Experience: The Poetics of Tamil Devotion. Norman J. Cutler. (Religion in Asia & Africa Ser.). 1987. 27.50x (ISBN 0-253-35334-3). Ind U Pr.

Songs of Flight & Song of the Lute. Maria Illo. (Illus.). 79p. (Orig.). 1983. pap. 5.95 (ISBN 0-9613159-0-3). Emerald Forest.

Songs of Flying Dragons. Peter H. Lee. LC 73-92866. (Harvard-Yenching Institute Monographs Ser: No. 22). 352p. 1975. text ed. 22.50x (ISBN 0-674-82075-4). Harvard U Pr.

Songs of Freedom. Sarah C. Reese. LC 82-83859. 67p. 1983. pap. 5.00 perf. bnd. (ISBN 0-916418-47-2). Lotus.

Songs of Freedom: The Psalter As a School of Prayer. Charles Cummings. 1986. pap. 6.95 (ISBN 0-87193-245-8). Dimension Bks.

Songs of Fun & Faith by "Fish & Chip". Kenneth L. Pike & Stephen B. Pike. LC 79-115755. (Edward Sapir Monograph in Language, Culture, & Cognition: No. 1). viii, 48p. (Orig.). 1977. pap. 2.50x (ISBN 0-933104-00-6). Jupiter Pr.

Songs of Glory: Medieval Art from 900-1500. David Mickenberg et al. 400p. (Orig.). 1985. pap. text ed. 20.00 (ISBN 0-911919-01-5). Okla Mus Art.

Songs of Glory: The Romanesque Facades of Aquitaine. Linda Seidel. LC 81-3342. (Illus.). 1981. lib. bdg. 25.00x (ISBN 0-226-74513-9). U of Chicago Pr.

Songs of Glory: The Romanesque Facads of Aquitaine. Linda Seidel. LC 81-3342. (Illus.). x, 220p. 1981. 14.95 (ISBN 0-226-74514-7). U of Chicago Pr.

Songs of God. Joseph Murphy. LC 79-52353. (Orig.). 1979. pap. 6.00 (ISBN 0-87516-379-3). DeVorss.

Songs of God's Grace. M. R. Bawa Muhaiyaddeen. LC 73-91016. (Illus.). 154p. 1974. pap. 4.95 (ISBN 0-914390-02-3). Fellowship Pr PA.

Songs of Gods, Songs of Humans: The Epic Tradition of the Ainu. Tr. by Donald Philippi from Ainu. LC 81-83970. 432p. 1982. pap. 16.75 (ISBN 0-86547-063-4). N Point Pr.

Songs of Gods, Songs of Humans: The Epic Tradition of the Ainu. Donald L. Philippi. LC 78-18002. 1979. 45.50x (ISBN 0-691-06384-2). Princeton U Pr.

Songs of Gold Mountains: Cantonese Rhymes from San Francisco Chinatown. Marion K. Horn. 1987. 35.00x (ISBN 0-520-05607-8). U of Cal Pr.

Songs of Hawaii & Spirituals. Carol Roes. LC 81-771212. (Illus.). 1978. 14.95 (ISBN 0-930932-02-1). M Loke.

Songs of Heaven. Robert E. Coleman. 160p. 1982. pap. 5.95 (ISBN 0-8007-5097-7, Power Bks). Revell.

Songs of Home (Canciones de Hogar) Cesar Vallejo. Tr. by Richard Schaaf & Kathleen Ross. 24p. 1981. pap. 3.25 (ISBN 0-917488-05-9). Ziesing Bros.

Songs of Homer. Geoffrey S. Kirk. 1962. 62.50 (ISBN 0-521-05890-2). Cambridge U Pr.

Songs of Homer, Il see Homer & the Epic.

Songs of Hope. Ed. by Holland Boring. 1979. pap. 2.75 (ISBN 0-88027-059-4). Firm Foun Pub.

Songs of Hope & Peace. Chavez-Melo. 7.95 (ISBN 0-8298-0710-1). Pilgrim NY.

Songs of Hugo Wolf. Eric Sams. (Eulenburg Music Bks.). xii, 402p. 1983. lib. bdg. 35.00 (ISBN 0-903873-32-X). Da Capo.

Songs of Idaho. Ed. by Glen Lockery. 94p. 1988. 19.95 (ISBN 0-9619700-0-6); pap. 12.95 (ISBN 0-9619700-1-4). Univ ID Alumni Assn.

Songs of Innocence. William Blake. LC 70-165396. 1971. pap. 3.50 (ISBN 0-486-22764-2). Dover.

Songs of Innocence & Experience, 2 bks. William Blake. 112p. 1986. Set. pap. 7.00 (ISBN 0-486-25264-7). Dover.

Songs of Innocence & of Experience. William Blake. Ed. by Ruthven Todd. LC 72-14319. 1794. lib. bdg. 25.00 (ISBN 0-8414-2525-6). Folcroft.

Songs of Innocence & of Experience. William Blake. (Illus.). 1977. pap. 10.95 (ISBN 0-19-281089-8). Oxford U Pr.

Songs of Inspiration: Artistic Piano Arrangements of New Latter-day Saint Hymns. Lynn S. Lund. 40p. 1986. pap. text ed. 7.95 (ISBN 0-88290-276-8). Horizon Utah.

Songs of Ireland. J. L. Hatton & J. L. Molly. 220p. 1983. Repr. of 1983 ed. lib. bdg. 65.00 (ISBN 0-89987-423-1). Darby Bks.

Songs of Irish Rebellion: Political Street Ballads & Rebel Songs, 1780-1900. Georges D. Zimmermann. LC 67-21410. 344p. Repr. of 1967 ed. 35.00x (ISBN 0-8103-5025-4). Gale.

Songs of Jim Reeves. Jim Reeves. (P-V-G Personality Folio Ser.). (Illus.). 80p. 1985. pap. 8.95 (ISBN 0-88188-340-9, 00358033). H Leonard Pub Corp.

Songs of John MacDonald, Bard of Keppoch. A. MacKenzie. 1973. 20.00x (ISBN 0-7073-0046-0, Pub. by Scot Acad Pr). Longwood Pub Group.

Songs of Joyful Praise. Ed. by Frank Roberts. 1975. pap. 2.00x (ISBN 0-88027-060-8). Firm Foun Pub.

Songs of Kabir. Tr. by Rabindranath Tagore. LC 74-82318. 1974. pap. 7.95 (ISBN 0-87728-271-4). Weiser.

Songs of Life. facsimile ed. George R. Margetson. LC 76-39095. (Black Heritage Library Collection). Repr. of 1910 ed. 12.00 (ISBN 0-8369-9033-1). Ayer Co Pubs.

Songs of Living. Eithne Strong. LC 62-41413. pap. 20.00 (ISBN 0-317-26740-X, 2024356). Bks Demand UMI.

Songs of Love. Jan Renfrow. (Illus.). 32p. (Orig.). 1987. pap. 8.00 (ISBN 0-9613072-2-6). J Renfrow.

Songs of Marriage - Songs of Love. Lois Lowenstein & Alison Alpert. 1988. incl. cass. 24.95 (ISBN 1-55774-032-1, Dist. by Watts); ltd. ed. hand bd. 90.00 (ISBN 1-55774-046-1, Dist. by Watts). Adama Pubs Inc.

Songs of Meera: Lyrics in Ecstasy. Tr. by Baldoon Dhingra. 136p. 1977. pap. 2.50 (ISBN 0-86578-093-5). Ind-US Inc.

Songs of Meleager: Made into English with Designs by Frederich Baron Corvo. Frederich B. Corvo. LC 82-49103. (Degeneration & Regeneration Ser.). 150p. 1984. lib. bdg. 25.00 (ISBN 0-8240-5566-7). Garland Pub.

Songs of Mririda. Mririda. Tr. by Daniel Halpern & Paula Paley. LC 74-82761. (Keepsake Ser: Vol. 6). (Illus.). 52p. 1974. 10.00 (ISBN 0-87775-062-9). Unicorn Pr.

Songs of My People. facsimile ed. Charles B. Johnson. LC 76-161263. (Black Heritage Library Collection). Repr. of 1918 ed. 11.25 (ISBN 0-8369-8822-1). Ayer Co Pubs.

Songs of Nature. facsimile ed. Ed. by John Burroughs. LC 79-98077. (Granger Index Reprint Ser). 1901. 19.00 (ISBN 0-8369-6070-X). Ayer Co Pubs.

Songs of Nepal: An Anthology of Nevar Folk-Songs & Hymns. Ed. by Siegfried Lienhard. (Asian Studies at Hawaii: No. 30). 232p. 1984. pap. text ed. 17.00x (ISBN 0-8248-0680-8). UH Pr.

Songs of Oberlin. Ed. by Carolyn Rabson. LC 83-8152. (Illus.). 120p. 1983. 8.50 (ISBN 0-9611434-0-1); pap. 5.00 (ISBN 0-9611434-1-X). Oberlin Con Lib.

Songs of Oscar Hammerstein II. Oscar Hammerstein. LC 74-21637. (Illus.). 1975. 14.95 (ISBN 0-02-871020-7); pap. 9.95 (ISBN 0-02-871010-X). Schirmer Bks.

Songs of Ourselves. Rose B. Green. LC 81-67779. 64p. 1982. 9.95 (ISBN 0-8453-4737-3, Cornwall Bks). Assoc Univ Prs.

Songs of Percy French. James N. Healy. 80p. 1983. pap. 7.95 (ISBN 0-85342-394-6, Pub. by Mercier Pr Ireland). Irish Bks Media.
Songs of Peter Rabbit: Music by Dudley Glass. Beatrix Potter. (Illus.). 1951. pap. 3.95 (ISBN 0-7232-1035-7). Warne.
Songs of Power. Jean Starr. Ed. by Ana Takseena. 24p. (Orig.). 1987. pap. text ed. 3.00 (ISBN 0-944667-00-7). Little Sister Pubns.
Songs of Praise. Percy Dearmer. Ed. by Ralph Vaughan Williams & Martin Shaw. Incl. Music Ed. rev. & enl. ed. 1932. 19.95x (ISBN 0-19-231207-3). Oxford U Pr.
Songs of Praise. Selected by Kathleen Krull. 32p. 1988. 15.95 (ISBN 0-15-277108-5). HarBraceJ.
Songs of Praise. Georgiana L. Lahr. 1988. 8.95 (ISBN 0-533-07844-X). Vantage.
Songs of Robert Burns. Robert Burns. Ed. by James C. Dick. LC 79-144552. Repr. of 1903 ed. 37.50 (ISBN 0-404-08511-3). AMS Pr.
Songs of Robert Schumann. Eric Sams. (Eulenburg Music Ser.). (Illus.). 256p. 1982. pap. text ed. 18.50 (ISBN 0-903873-18-4). Da Capo.
Songs of Rod McKuen. Rod McKuen. 1960. 5.95 (ISBN 0-318-00972-2). Cheval Bks.
Songs of Sacramento. Poets of Little Sister Publications Staff. Ed. by Ana Takseena. (Illus.). 43p. (Orig.). 1987. pap. text ed. 4.00 (ISBN 0-944667-01-5). Little Sister Pubns.
Songs of Scandinavia. G. Borrow. 59.95 (ISBN 0-8490-1085-3). Gordon Pr.
Songs of Scotland, Ancient & Modern, 4 vols. Allan Cunningham. LC 75-144551. Repr. of 1825 ed. Set. 135.00 (ISBN 0-404-08640-3); 33.75 ea. Vol. 1 (ISBN 0-404-08641-1). Vol. 2 (ISBN 0-404-08642-X). Vol. 3 (ISBN 0-404-08643-8). Vol. 4 (ISBN 0-404-08644-6). AMS Pr.
Songs of Scotland Prior to Burns. Ed. by Robert Chambers. LC 73-144548. Repr. of 1862 ed. 27.50 (ISBN 0-404-08627-6). AMS Pr.
Songs of Self-Esteem. Minnie O'Leary et al. (Illus.). 23p. 1981. pap. 4.95 (ISBN 0-9603656-2-1); cassette 4.95 (ISBN 0-686-79639-X); bk. & cassette 8.95 (ISBN 0-686-79640-3). Whitenwife Pubns.
Songs of Sesame Street in Poems & Pictures. Jeffrey Moss & David Axelrod. LC 83-3329. (Illus.). 48p. (ps-3). 1983. lib. bdg. 6.99 (ISBN 0-394-95245-6). Random.
Songs of Seventy Six: A Folksinger's History of the Revolution. Oscar Brand. LC 72-83733. (Illus.). 176p. 1972. 10.00 (ISBN 0-87131-092-9); pap. 4.95 (ISBN 0-87131-170-4). M Evans.
Songs of Seydou Camara, Vol. 1: Kambili. Charles Bird & Mamadou Koita. (Occasional Papers in Mande Studies). 120p. (Orig.). 1974. pap. text ed. 5.00 (ISBN 0-941934-12-8). Indiana Africa.
Songs of Sixpence: Rhymes for Reading Readiness. Arnold Cheyney & Jeanne Cheyney. 1988. pap. 6.95 (ISBN 0-673-18865-5). Scott F.
Songs of Solitude, No. I. Michael Wrenn. (Songs Ser.). (Illus.). 64p. 1984. 12.50 (ISBN 0-9612012-0-7). Pathfinders Pubns MS.
Songs of Something Else: Selected Poems of Gunnar Ekelof. Tr. by Leonard Nathan & James Larson. LC 81-47915. (Lockert Library of Poetry in Translation (Bilingual Edition)). 344p. 1982. cloth 27.50x (ISBN 0-691-06511-X); pap. 11.95 (ISBN 0-691-01389-6). Princeton U Pr.
Songs of South Street--Street of Ships. Eric P. Russell & Mark Lovewell. (Illus.). 1978. pap. text ed. 4.00 (ISBN 0-9601250-0-0). Chanteyman.
Songs of Spiritual Change see Selected Works of the Dalai Lama VII: Songs of Spiritual Change.
Songs of Struggle & Protest. Ed. by John McDonnell. 136p. (Orig.). 1986. pap. 7.95 (ISBN 0-85342-775-5, Pub. by Mercier Pr Ireland). Irish Bks Media.
Songs of Submission: On the Practice of Subud. Hurbert Bissing. 180p. (Orig.). 1982. pap. 11.50 (ISBN 0-227-67852-4, Pub. by J Clarke UK). Attic Pr.
Songs of Suffering. Nathan R. Kollar. 160p. (Orig.). 1982. pap. 7.95 (ISBN 0-86683-672-1, HarpR). Har-Row.
Songs of Thanksgiving. Bettye D. Little. 1987. 6.95 (ISBN 0-533-06796-0). Vantage.
Songs of the Ages (Psalms) Leader's Guide. (New Horizons Bible Study). 48p. (Orig.). 1984. pap. 1.95 (ISBN 0-89367-091-X). Light & Life.
Songs of the Ages (Psalms) Student Guide. (New Horizon Bible Study). 68p. (Orig.). 1984. pap. 2.50 (ISBN 0-89367-090-1). Light & Life.
Songs of the American West. Ed. by Richard E. Lingenfelter & Richard A. Dwyer. (Illus.). 1968. 40.00x (ISBN 0-520-00753-0). U of Cal Pr.
Songs of the Bards of Bengal. Tr. & intro. by Deben Bhattacharya. 1970. pap. 4.95 (ISBN 0-394-17385-6, E543, Ever). Grove.
Songs of the Blue Angel. Leilah Wendell. LC 86-51081. 121p. 1987. 6.95 (ISBN 1-55523-055-5). Winston-Derek.
Songs of the Cowboys. Compiled by N. Howard Thorp. LC 84-11872. xxii, 184p. 1984. 17.95x (ISBN 0-8032-4410-X); pap. 5.95 (ISBN 0-8032-9403-4, BB 876, Bison). U of Nebr Pr.
Songs of the Famine Immigrants: Words & Music. 96p. 1986. Repr. of 1854 ed. cancelled (ISBN 0-940134-42-X). Irish Genealog.
Songs of the Fog Maiden. Tomie De Paola. LC 78-12822. (Illus.). 32p. (ps-3). 1979. reinforced bdg. 8.95 (ISBN 0-8234-0341-6). Holiday.
Songs of the Free. facsimile ed. Compiled by Maria W. Chapman. LC 71-170693. (Black Heritage Library Collection). Repr. of 1836 ed. 17.50 (ISBN 0-8369-8883-3). Ayer Co Pubs.
Songs of the Good Earth. Margaret Phillips. LC 79-10731. 62p. 1980. pap. 4.95 (ISBN 0-88289-221-5). Pelican.
Songs of the Harp: Twenty Songs about Harps & Harpers. Sylvia Woods. 48p. 1983. pap. 5.95 (ISBN 0-9602990-1-7). Woods Mus Bks Pub.
Songs of the Incarnation. 1987. 20.00x (ISBN 0-9501351-8-6, Pub. by Wild Goose Pubns Scotland). State Mutual Bk.
Songs of the Industrial North. Gordon Tyrrall. 1986. 32.00x (ISBN 0-317-54392-X, Pub. by Hesketh UK). State Mutual Bk.
Songs of the Irish. Ed. by Donal O'Sullivan. 200p. 1981. pap. 17.95 (ISBN 0-85342-653-8, Pub. by Mercier Pr Ireland). Irish Bks Media.
Songs of the Maggodee. Keith D. Holmes. (Illus.). 95p. (Orig.). 1982. pap. text ed. 5.00x (ISBN 0-9608250-0-2). Educ Serv Pub.
Songs of the Martyrs: Hassidic Melodies of Maramures. Max Eisikovits. LC 79-67624. 1980. pap. 7.95 (ISBN 0-87203-089-X). Hermon.
Songs of the Michigan Lumberjacks. Earl C. Beck. (University of Michigan Studies & Publications). pap. 76.80 (ISBN 0-317-29151-3, 2055620). Bks Demand UMI.
Songs of the Musconetcong: 1968. 2nd ed. A. M. Sullivan. LC 74-157815. 1973. 10.00 (ISBN 0-916344-01-0); sight & sound ed. incl. 2 cassettes & bk. 25.00 (ISBN 0-916344-02-9); sound ed. incl. 2 cassettes 20.00 (ISBN 0-916344-03-7); cassette I 12.00 (ISBN 0-916344-04-5); cassette II 12.00 (ISBN 0-916344-05-3). Guinea Hollow.
Songs of the Nativity. William H. Husk. 205p. 1980. Repr. of 1868 ed. lib. bdg. 40.50 (ISBN 0-8414-2094-7). Folcroft.
Songs of the North. Sigurd Olson. 1988. 16.25 (ISBN 0-8446-6300-X). Peter Smith.
Songs of the North: A Sigurd Olson Reader. Ed. by Howard F. Mosher. 320p. 1987. pap. 7.95 (ISBN 0-14-017007-3). Penguin.
Songs of the People of God: The Companion to the Australian Hymn Book. rev. ed. Wesley Milgate. 352p. 1986. pap. 15.95 (ISBN 0-00-599806-9, Collins Liturgical). HarpR.
Songs of the Russian People: As Illustrative of Slavonic Mythology & Russian Social Life. W. R. Ralston. LC 77-132444. (Studies in Music, No. 42). 1970. Repr. of 1872 ed. lib. bdg. 69.95x (ISBN 0-8383-1224-1). Haskell.
Songs of the Sabbath Sacrifice: Edition, Translation, & Commentary. Carol Newsom. (Harvard Semitic Museum Ser.). 1985. 34.95 (ISBN 0-89130-837-7, 04-04-27). Scholars Pr GA.
Songs of the Sage. Curley Fletcher. (Illus.). 80p. 1986. pap. 9.95 (ISBN 0-87905-257-0, Peregrine Smith). Gibbs Smith Pub.
Songs of the Sage. Mae Urbanek. (Illus.). 242p. 3.50x (ISBN 0-940514-07-9). Urbanek.
Songs of the Sailor & Lumberman. rev ed. William M. Doeflinger. Orig. Title: Shantymen & Shantyboys. (Illus.). 397p. pap. write for info. (ISBN 0-916638-40-5). Meyerbooks.
Songs of the Saints of India. John S. Hawley & Mark Juergensmeyer. (Illus.). 256p. 1988. 32.50 (ISBN 0-19-505220-X); pap. text ed. 9.95 (ISBN 0-19-505221-8). Oxford U Pr.
Songs of the Sea & Sailor's Chanteys. Ed. by Robert Frothingham. LC 70-99029. (Granger Index Reprint Ser). 1924. 18.00 (ISBN 0-8369-6103-X). Ayer Co Pubs.
Songs of the Shore. Robert L. Malone. (Illus.). 72p. 1981. 8.95 (ISBN 0-9606234-0-X). Ark & Arbor.
Songs of the Sierras. Joaquin Miller. LC 71-104528. 309p. Repr. of 1871 ed. lib. bdg. 36.50 (ISBN 0-8398-1260-4). Irvington.
Songs of the Soil. Fenton Johnson. LC 73-18583. Repr. of 1916 ed. 11.50 (ISBN 0-404-11394-X). AMS Pr.
Songs of the Soul. Sri Chinmoy. 96p. (Orig.). 1983. pap. 5.00 (ISBN 0-88497-738-2). Aum Pubns.
Songs of the Soul. Paramahansa Yogananda. LC 83-60701. (Illus.). 200p. 1983. 6.50 (ISBN 0-87612-025-7). Self-Realization.
Songs of the Soul. Paramhansa Yogananda. LC 80-69786. 1980. pap. 10.95 (ISBN 0-937134-02-3). Amrita Found.
Songs of the South. Jennie T. Clarke. 1896. 25.00 (ISBN 0-686-17676-6). Quaker City.
Songs of the South: An Ancient Chinese Anthology of Poems. Qu Yuan et al. Tr. by David Hawkes. (Penguin Classics Ser.). 352p. 1986. pap. 5.95 (ISBN 0-14-044375-4). Penguin.
Songs of the South & West see Ozark Folksongs.
Songs of the Spirit. Aleister Crowley. 1973. lib. bdg. 79.95 (ISBN 0-87968-220-5). Krishna Pr.
Songs of the Synagogue of Florence, 2 vols. Ed. by Fernando D. Belgrado. Incl. Vol. 1. The Three Festivals (ISBN 0-87203-108-X); Vol. 2. The High Holy Days. 0p (ISBN 0-87203-109-8). (Illus.). 60p. 1982. 32.95 ea. Hermon.
Songs of the Teton Sioux. Harry W. Paige. (Great West & Indian Ser: Vol. 39). (Illus.). 1969. 9.50 (ISBN 0-87026-019-7). Westernlore.
Songs of the Tewa. Herbert J. Spinden. (Illus.). 1976. 12.95 (ISBN 0-913270-55-5). Sunstone Pr.
Songs of the Tewa. Ed. & tr. by Herbert J. Spinden. LC 74-9023. (Eng.). Repr. of 1933 ed. 15.00 (ISBN 0-404-11901-8). AMS Pr.
Songs of the Theater: A Definitive Index to the Songs of the Musical Stage. Richard Lewine & Alfred Simon. LC 84-13068. 916p. 1984. 78.00 (ISBN 0-8242-0706-8). Wilson.
Songs of the Vaisnava Acaryas. Ed. by Swami Acyutananda. 1979. pap. 6.95 (ISBN 0-912776-56-0). Bhaktivedanta.
Songs of Thomas D'Urfey. Thomas D'Urfey. Ed. by Cyrus L. Day. (Harvard Studies in English). 1969. Repr. of 1933 ed. 23.00 (ISBN 0-384-11020-7). Johnson Repr.
Songs of Three Centuries. fasc. rev. & enl. ed. Ed. by John Greenleaf Whittier. LC 72-38606. (Granger Index Reprint Ser.). Repr. of 1890 ed. 21.00 (ISBN 0-8369-6338-5). Ayer Co Pubs.
Songs of Triumph. Georgiana L. Lahr. 1987. 8.95 (ISBN 0-533-07209-3). Vantage.
Songs of Urea & Futuna. E. G. Burrows. (BMB). Repr. of 1945 ed. 23.00 (ISBN 0-527-02291-8). Kraus Repr.
Songs of Western Birds. Donald J. Borror. 64p. 1984. pap. 7.95 incl. cassette (ISBN 0-486-99913-0). Dover.
Songs of Work & Protest. Edith Fowke & Joe Glazer. 290p. 1973. Repr. of 1960 ed. 8.50 (ISBN 0-486-22899-1). Dover.
Songs of Zion. Ed. by Verolga Nix & Jefferson Cleveland. LC 81-8039. 352p. (Orig.). 1981. pap. 7.95 accompanist ed. (ISBN 0-687-39121-0); pap. 7.95 (ISBN 0-687-39120-2). Abingdon.
Songs Sacred & Serious: For Two-Part Choir. 65p. pap. 3.50 (ISBN 0-318-13638-4). Board Jewish Educ.
Songs, Set Two: A Short Count. Edward Dorn. 28p. (Orig.). 1970. pap. 1.00 (ISBN 0-686-05052-5). Frontier Press Calif.
Songs That Children Sing. new ed. Eleanor Chroman. LC 79-93961. (Orig.). (gr. k-6). 1970. pap. 6.95 (ISBN 0-8256-0011-1, Oak). Music Sales.
Songs That Every Child Should Know. M. Bacon. (ps-6). 59.95 (ISBN 0-8490-1086-1). Gordon Pr.
Songs to Brighten Your Day: For Teachers of Young Children. Dee Gibson & Joe Scruggs. (Illus., Orig.). 1984. pap. 9.95 audio tape and bk. package (ISBN 0-916123-00-6). Ed Graphics Pr.
Songs to Her God: Spirituality of Ann Griffiths. A. M. Allchin. LC 87-22155. 132p. (Orig.). 1987. pap. 7.95 (ISBN 0-936384-53-0). Cowley Pubns.
Songs to Krishna. Subramania Bharati. Tr. by David Bunce from Tamil. (Writers Workshop Saffronbird Ser.). 1975. 14.00 (ISBN 0-88253-642-7). Ind-US Inc.
Songs to Play. (gr. k-3). 1987. 12.95 (ISBN 0-8054-4704-0). Broadman.
Songs to Seven Strings: Russian Guitar Poetry & Soviet "Mass Song". Gerald S. Smith. LC 83-49453. (Soviet History, Politics, Society & Thought Ser.). (Illus.). 288p. 1985. 25.00x (ISBN 0-253-35391-2). Ind U Pr.
Songs to Share. Rose B. Goldstein. (Illus.). 64p. (Eng. & Hebrew.). (ps-5). 2.95x (ISBN 0-8381-0720-6, 10-720). United Syn Bk.
Songs to Sing with Babies: Songs & Games to Develop Skills in Young Children 0-6 Yrs. Jackie Weissman. 64p. 1983. pap. 8.95 (ISBN 0-939514-05-2). Miss Jackie.
Songs Unsung. Lewis Morris. 1979. Repr. of 1883 ed. lib. bdg. 15.00 (ISBN 0-8495-3843-2). Arden Lib.
Songs Visions Traditions of Northwest Indian Tribes. Paul Martin. 3.00 (ISBN 0-686-15297-2). Great Raven Pr.
Songs We Sing. Harry Coopersmith. (Illus.). 1950. 22.50x (ISBN 0-8381-0723-0). United Syn Bk.
Songs Without Music. Alexander S. Justice & Mary B. Justice. 31p. (Orig.). 1985. pap. 35.00 (ISBN 0-935313-05-2). Space Travel.
Songsters & Saints: Vocal Traditions on Race Records. Paul Oliver. (Illus.). 339p. 1984. 29.95 (ISBN 0-521-24827-2); pap. 11.95 (ISBN 0-521-26942-3). Cambridge U Pr.
Songwriter-Publisher Contract. Robert A. Livingston. 1985. 15.00 (ISBN 0-932303-04-8). GLGLC Music.
Songwriter's & Musician's Guide to Making Great Demos. Harvey Rachlin. 192p. 1988. pap. 12.95 (ISBN 0-89879-305-X). Writers Digest.
Songwriter's Demo Manual & Success Guide. George J. Williams, III. Ed. by Bill Dalton. LC 82-50166. (Illus.). 200p. (Orig.). 1984. lib. bdg. 24.95 (ISBN 0-935174-10-9, Mus Business Books); pap. 12.95 (ISBN 0-935174-05-2). Tree by River.
Songwriter's Guide to Collaboration. Walter Carter. 178p. (Orig.). 1988. pap. 12.95 (ISBN 0-89879-322-X). Writers Digest.
Songwriter's Handbook. rev. ed. Tom T. Hall. LC 87-9468. (Illus.). 160p. 1987. Repr. of 1976 ed. 14.95 (ISBN 0-934395-40-3). Rutledge Hill Pr.
Songwriter's Handbook. Harvey Rachlin. LC 77-2946. (Illus.). 1977. 15.95 (ISBN 0-308-10321-1). T Y Crowell.
Songwriter's Market '89. Ed. by Julie Whaley. (Illus.). 512p. 1988. 17.95 (ISBN 0-89879-333-5). Writers Digest.
Songwriter's Rhyming Dictionary. Sammy Cahn. 208p. 1984. pap. 8.95 (ISBN 0-452-00678-3, Mer). NAL.
Songwriters Rhyming Dictionary. Jane Whitfield. 1974. pap. 7.00 (ISBN 0-87980-293-6). Wilshire.
Songwriters' Success Manual. Lee Pincus. LC 77-352498. (Illus.). 1976. pap. 9.95 (ISBN 0-918318-01-7). Music Pr.
Songwriters' Success Manual. 2nd ed. LC 78-60263. 1978. pap. 9.95 (ISBN 0-918318-02-5). Music Pr.
Songwriting: A Structured Approach. Robert A. Berger. LC 83-70101. (Illus.). 108p. (Orig.). 1983. pap. 8.95 (ISBN 0-911999-00-0). Beer Flat.
Sonia Begonia. Joanne Rocklin. LC 85-23120. (Illus.). 96p. (gr. 3-7). 1986. 11.95 (ISBN 0-02-777310-8). Macmillan.
Sonia Begonia. Joanne Rocklin. 112p. (gr. 3-7). 1987. pap. 2.50 (ISBN 0-380-70307-6, Camelot). Avon.
Sonia Delaunay. Text by Arthur A. Cohen. (Illus.). 206p. 1988. 65.00 (ISBN 0-8109-0292-3). Abrams.
Sonia Delaunay: A Retrospective. Ed. by Robert T. Buck et al. LC 79-57450. (Illus.). 236p. 1980. pap. 27.50 (ISBN 0-914782-32-0, Dist. by Univ. of Washington Press). Buffalo Acad.
Sonia Delaunay: Art into Fashion. Sonia Delaunay. 112p. 1986. pap. 14.95 (ISBN 0-8076-1166-2). Braziller.
Sonia Delaunay's Alphabet. Sonia Delaunay. LC 72-172414. (Illus.). (ps-3). 1972. 12.70 (ISBN 0-690-75258-X, Crowell Jr Bks). HarpJ.
Sonia ou le Dictionnaire des maux Courants. Pierre Daninos. 352p. (Fr.). 1962. 8.95 (ISBN 0-686-55576-7). French & Eur.
Sonia: Survival in War & Peace. Sonia Milner. LC 83-50758. 1983. pap. 4.95 (ISBN 0-88400-102-4). Shengold.
Sonic Design: The Nature of Sound & Music. Robert Cogan & Pozzi Escot. (Illus.). 544p. 1976. 24.95. P-H.
Sonic Scotia. N. R. Baljian-Gara. (Contemporary Poets of Dorrance Ser.). 53p. 1980. 3.50 (ISBN 0-8059-2751-4). Dorrance.
Sonja. Marian Lokvam et al. Ed. by Emily Lovas & Rhoda-Gale Pollack. LC 81-82156. (Illus.). 100p. 1981. 12.95 (ISBN 0-940316-00-5). E J Hill & Co Inc.
Sonjo of Tanganyika. Robert F. Gray. LC 73-13319. (Illus.). 181p. 1974. Repr. of 1963 ed. lib. bdg. 35.00x (ISBN 0-8371-7119-9, GRST). Greenwood.
Sonnenberg Gardens: A Splendid Collection of Gardens. Lynn L. Monroe. (Illus.). 32p. (Orig.). 1985. pap. 4.98 (ISBN 0-9615125-0-4). L L Monroe.
Sonnenfest Der Braminen: Vienna, 1790. Wenzel Muller. Ed. by Thomas Bauman. (German Opera Ser.). 500p. 1986. lib. bdg. 125.00 (ISBN 0-8240-8865-4). Garland Pub.
Sonnentempel. Herge. (Illus.). 62p. (Ger.). pap. 15.95 (ISBN 0-686-54317-3). French & Eur.
Sonnet. John Fuller. (Critical Idiom Ser.). 1972. pap. 5.50x (ISBN 0-416-65690-0, NO.2205). Routledge Chapman & Hall.
Sonnet Adoration of the Avatar: The Splendor of the Sathya Sai. Benito F. Reyes. (Illus.). 300p. 1985. 45.00 (ISBN 0-939375-08-7); pap. 25.00 (ISBN 0-939375-06-0). World Univ Amer.
Sonnet: An Anthology. Ed. by Robert M. Bender & Charles L. Squier. 1987. pap. 5.95 (ISBN 0-671-63732-0). PB.
Sonnet Eighteen see Poetry Unfolding.
Sonnet En Italie et En France Au Seizieme Siecle, 2 Vols. Hugues Vaganay. 1962. Repr. of 1903 ed. 40.50 (ISBN 0-8337-3608-6). B Franklin.
Sonnet in England & America: A Bibliography of Criticism. Compiled by Herbert S. Donow. LC 82-929. xxii, 477p. 1982. lib. bdg. 50.95 (ISBN 0-313-21336-4, DSE/). Greenwood.
Sonnet in England & Other Essays. James Noble. LC 74-23638. 1974. Repr. of 1893 ed. lib. bdg. 30.50 (ISBN 0-8414-6257-7). Folcroft.
Sonnet Is Forever: Forms Yesterday & Today. Raymond McCarty. 128p. Date not set. price not set (ISBN 0-938310-06-2); pap. price not set (ISBN 0-938310-08-9). Volunteer Pubns.
Sonnet: Its Origin, Structure & Place in Poetry. C. Tomlinson. 59.95 (ISBN 0-8490-1087-X). Gordon Pr.
Sonnet: Its Origin, Structure & Place in Poetry. Charles Tomlinson. LC 72-192912. 1874. lib. bdg. 25.50 (ISBN 0-8414-8428-7). Folcroft.
Sonnet-No Me Mueve, Mi Dios-Its Theme in Spanish Tradition. Sr. M. Cyria Huff. LC 73-94177. (Catholic University of America Studies in Romance Languages & Literatures Ser: No. 33). Repr. of 1948 ed. 20.00 (ISBN 0-404-50333-0). AMS Pr.
Sonnet over Time: A Study in the Sonnets of Petrarch, Shakespeare, & Baudelaire. Sandra L. Bermann. LC 87-87220. (Studies in Comparative Literature: No. 63). 180p. 1988. 25.00x (ISBN 0-8078-7063-3). U of NC Pr.
Sonnet Theory & Practice in Nineteenth-Century France. D. Scott. (Occasional Papers in Modern Languages Ser.: No. 12). 97p. 1977. pap. text ed. 6.95x (ISBN 0-85958-408-9, Pub. by U of Hull UK). Humanities.
Sonnet Variations. Peyton Houston. LC 62-16775. 1962. pap. 6.00 (ISBN 0-317-02754-9, Dist. by Inland Bk). Jargon Soc.
Sonnets. William Alabaster. Ed. by G. M. Story & Helen Gardner. LC 83-45405. Repr. of 1959 ed. 20.00 (ISBN 0-404-20004-4). AMS Pr.

Sons of the Mountains: Ethnohistory of the Vietnamese Central Highlands to 1954, Vol. 1. Gerald C. Hickey. LC 80-21819. (Illus.). 512p. 1982. 55.00x (ISBN 0-300-02453-3). Yale U Pr.

Sons of the Old Country. Waldemar Ager. Tr. by Trygve M. Ager from Nor. LC 82-17484. Orig. Title: Gamlelandets Sonner. xvi, 255p. 1984. 25.00x (ISBN 0-8032-1016-7); pap. 6.95 (ISBN 0-8032-5905-0, BB 871, Bison). U of Nebr Pr.

Sons of the Prophets: Leaders in Protestantism from Princeton Seminary. Ed. by Hugh T. Kerr. 1963. 29.50x (ISBN 0-691-07136-5). Princeton U Pr.

Sons of the Shaking Earth. Eric Wolf. LC 59-12290. (Illus.). 1959. (Phoen); pap. 8.00X (ISBN 0-226-90500-4, P90, Phoen). U of Chicago Pr.

Sons of the Sheik. E. M. Hull. 1976. Repr. of 1925 ed. lib. bdg. 20.95 (ISBN 0-89190-735-1, Pub. by River City Pr). Amereon Ltd.

Sons of the Sheik. E. M. Hull. (Barbara Cartland's Library of Love: No. 11). 213p. 1980. 12.95 (ISBN 0-7156-1472-X, Pub. by Duckworth London). Longwood Pub Group.

Sons of the Soil: Migration & Ethnic Conflict in India. M. Weiner. LC 78-51202. 1978. 47.00x (ISBN 0-691-09379-2). Princeton U Pr.

Sons of the South. Clayton Rand. LC 61-8069. (Illus.). 212p. 1961. 7.95 (ISBN 0-911116-76-1). Pelican.

Sons of the Utah Pioneers Ancestor Album. Ed. by Heritage Publishers Services Staff. 250p. 1987. 49.95 (ISBN 0-939379-01-5). Herit Pubs Servs.

Sons of the Wave. Warren Murphy & Molly Corchran. 1988. 17.95 (ISBN 0-453-00632-9). NAL.

Sons of the White Wolf. Robert E. Howard. 1987. pap. 2.95 (ISBN 0-317-63414-3, Pub. by Ace Science Fiction). Ace Bks.

Sons of the Wild Jackass. Ray T. Tucker & Frederick R. Barkley. LC 70-99727. (Essay Index Reprint Ser). 1932. 26.50 (ISBN 0-8369-1385-X). Ayer Co Pubs.

Sons of the Wilderness. Charles Thompson. 1988. Repr. of 1937 ed. 9.95 (ISBN 0-9617367-6-3). Guild Pr IN.

Sons of the Wind: The Sacred Stories of the Lakota. Ed. by D. M. Dooling. 168p. (Orig.). 1984. pap. text ed. 8.95 (ISBN 0-930407-00-8). Parabola Mag.

Sons of the Wind: The Search for Identity in Spanish American Indian Literature. Braulio Munoz. 321p. (Orig.). 1982. 35.00 (ISBN 0-8135-0973-4); pap. 14.00 (ISBN 0-8135-0972-6). Rutgers U Pr.

Sons of Thunder. Barbara F. Vroman. LC 81-81756. 395p. 1981. smythe sewn 14.95 (ISBN 0-9606240-1-5). Pearl-Win.

Sons of Vernon Hill. Franz Walthe. LC 81-90165. 1987. 15.95 (ISBN 0-533-05078-2). Vantage.

Sons, Slaves, & Freedman in Roman Commerce. Aaron Kirshenbaum. LC 87-1506. 1987. 29.95x (ISBN 0-8132-0644-8, Magnes Pr). Cath U Pr.

Sonya Begonia & the Eleventh Birthday Blues. Susan Smith. (Best Friends Ser.: No. 1). 96p. (gr. 4-5). 1988. pap. 2.50 (ISBN 0-671-64040-2, Minstrel Bks). S&S.

Sonya Begonia & the Eleventh Birthday Blues. Susan Smith. (Best Friends Ser.). (gr. 3-7). 1988. pap. 2.50 (ISBN 0-317-69590-8). PB.

Sonya: The Life of Countess Tolstoy. Anne Edwards. 528p. 1983. pap. 8.95 (ISBN 0-88184-050-5). Carroll & Graf.

Sonya's Mommy Works. Arlene Alda. Ed. by Kate Klimo. (Illus.). 48p. (ps-3). 1982. 7.95 (ISBN 0-671-45157-X, Little Simon). S&S.

Sonya's Mommy Works. Arlene Alda. LC 82-6550. (Illus.). 48p. (gr. k-3). 1982. 9.29 (ISBN 0-671-46167-2). Messner.

Soo-Scenes in & about Sault Ste. Marie Michigan in 1887. Chase Osborn. (Illus.). 46p. 1983. pap. 5.00 (ISBN 0-912382-30-9). Black Letter.

Sooch! Joe Soucheray. LC 81-11322. (Illus.). 270p. 1984. 8.95 (ISBN 0-932272-07-X). Minneapolis Tribune.

Soochow & the 4th Marines. William R. Evans. LC 87-71954. (Illus.). 160p. (Orig.). 1988. pap. 9.00 (ISBN 0-9617585-1-1). Atwood Pub Co.

Soochow University Political Science Series see Shaping of British Policy During the Nationalist Revolution in China.

Soohrab, a Poem see Suhrab & Rustam: A Poem from the Shah Namah of Firdausi.

Soon Coming World Emperor. Kenneth Hannah. 48p. (Orig.). pap. 2.95 (CPS-012). Christian Pub.

Soon-Hee in America. Schi-Zhin Rhie. LC 77-81780. (Illus.). 36p. (gr. k-3). 1977. PLB 6.50x (ISBN 0-930878-00-0). Hollym Intl.

Soon Jack November. Sharon Thie. (Illus.). 44p. (Orig.). 1984. pap. 3.00 (ISBN 0-88680-215-6). I E Clark.

Soon She Must Die. Anna Clarke. (Nightingale Paperbacks Ser.). 1984. pap. 9.95 (ISBN 0-8161-3703-X, Large Print Bks). G K Hall.

Soon She Must Die. Anna Clarke. 1985. 24.95x (ISBN 0-7090-1687-5, Pub. by R Hale Ltd UK). State Mutual Bk.

Soon to Be a Major Motion Picture. Eddie Cope. 52p. 1976. pap. 2.50 (ISBN 0-88680-179-6); royalty 35.25 (ISBN 0-317-03589-4). I E Clark.

Sooner or Later. Bruce Hart & Carol Hart. (YA) (gr. 7 up). 1978. pap. 2.50 (ISBN 0-380-42978-0, Flare). Avon.

Sooner or Later. Bruce Hart & Carole Hart. (YA) (gr. 7 up). pap. 2.50 (ISBN 0-380-64717-6, 64717-6, Flare). Avon.

Sooner or Later. Bruce Hart & Carole Hart. (gr. k-9). 1988. pap. 2.50. Scholastic Inc.

Sooner or Later. Millie R. Hynes. (Illus.). 106p. (Orig.). 1982. pap. 4.95 (ISBN 0-939688-07-7). Directed Media.

Sooner or Later: The Timing of Parenthood in Adult Lives. Pamela Daniels & Kathy Weingarten. 384p. 1983. pap. 6.95 (ISBN 0-393-30132-X). Norton.

Sooner Than You Think. Patricia B. Huntzicker. 1985. pap. 3.95 (ISBN 0-930584-04-X). J Grauer.

Sooners: A Story of Oklahoma Football. Rev. & enl. ed. Jim Weeks. LC 74-84330. (College Sports Ser.). Orig. Title: Oklahoma Football. 1982. 10.95 (ISBN 0-87397-238-4). Strode.

Soong Dynasty. Sterling Seagrave. LC 83-48802. (Illus.). 640p. 1985. 22.00i (ISBN 0-06-015308-3, HarpT). Har-Row.

Soong Dynasty. Sterling Seagrave. LC 83-48802. (Illus.). 544p. 1986. pap. 9.95 (ISBN 0-06-091318-5, PL 1318, PL). Har-Row.

Soong Sisters. Emily Hahn. Repr. of 1941 ed. lib. bdg. 22.50x (ISBN 0-8371-4429-9, HASI). Greenwood.

Soong Sisters. Emily Hahn. 349p. 1943. 140.00x (ISBN 0-317-69105-8, Pub. by Han-Shan Tang Ltd). State Mutual Bk.

Soot in Combustion Systems & Its Toxic Properties. Ed. by J. Lahaye & G. Prado. (NATO Conference Series IV, Materials Science: Vol. 7). 430p. 1983. 69.50x (ISBN 0-306-41245-4, Plenum Press). Plenum Pub.

Sootblowers, Lancers, & Rods. Center for Occupational Research & Development Staff. (EUTEC Power Plant Operator Curriculum Ser.). (Illus.). 32p. 1985. pap. text ed. write for info. (ISBN 1-55502-215-4). Ctr Res & Dev.

Soothsayer. Rene De Goscinny. (Asterix Ser.). (Illus.). 1976. 5.95x (ISBN 0-340-19525-8). Intl Learn Syst.

Soothsayer. Margaret Dobson. (Jane Bailey Ser.: No. 3). (Orig.). 1987. pap. 2.95 (ISBN 0-440-18149-6). Dell.

Soothsayer. R. Goscinny & M. Uderzo. (Illus.). 15.95 (ISBN 0-686-56212-7). French & Eur.

Soothsayers & Omens. Jay Wright. LC 76-45852. 1976. 4.25 (ISBN 0-913282-10-3). Seven Woods Pr.

Soothsayers, the Omens see Florentine Codex, General History of the Things of New Spain.

Soothsayings of Bakis: Goethe's Tragi-Comic Observations on Life, Time, & History. Johann Wolfgang Von Goethe. Ed. by Harold Jantz. LC 66-25527. pap. 24.00 (ISBN 0-317-08237-X, 2003864). Bks Demand UMI.

Soper's Scrap Book Recitation, First Series. facsimile ed. LC 72-84354. (Granger Index Reprint Ser). 1879. 10.00 (ISBN 0-8369-6063-7). Ayer Co Pubs.

Soper's Scrap Book Recitation, Fourth Series. facsimile ed. LC 72-84354. (Granger Index Reprint Ser). 1885. 10.00 (ISBN 0-8369-6091-2). Ayer Co Pubs.

Soper's Scrap Book Recitation, Sixth Series. facsimile ed. LC 72-84354. (Granger Index Reprint Ser). 1888. 10.00 (ISBN 0-8369-6131-5). Ayer Co Pubs.

Soper's Scrap Book Recitation, Third Series. facsimile ed. LC 72-84354. (Granger Index Reprint Ser). 1882. 10.00 (ISBN 0-8369-6090-4). Ayer Co Pubs.

Sophardic Haggadah. Marc D. Angel. 128p. (Orig.). 1988. pap. price not set (ISBN 0-88125-145-3). Ktav.

SOPHE Heritage Collection of Health Education Monographs, 3 vols. Society for Public Health Education Staff. LC 81-51486. 1000p. 1982. Set. text ed. 60.00x (ISBN 0-89914-008-4); pap. text ed. 40.00x (ISBN 0-89914-009-2). Third Party Pub.

Sophia & Praxis: The Boundaries of Politics. Ed. by J. M. Porter. LC 84-12154. 160p. (Orig.). 1984. pap. text ed. 14.95x (ISBN 0-934540-19-5). Chatham Hse Pubs.

Sophia of the Bible: The Spirit of Wisdom. Aurora Terrenus. 89p. (Orig.). Date not set. pap. 4.95 (ISBN 0-945717-89-X). Celestial Comns.

Sophia: The Future of Feminist Spirituality. Susan A. Cady et al. 120p. 1986. 14.95 (ISBN 0-06-254200-1, HarpR). Har-Row.

Sophiatown: Coming of Age in South Africa. Don Mattera. LC 88-47885. 192p. 1989. 14.95 (ISBN 0-8070-0206-2). Beacon Pr.

Sophic Hydrolith. Johann A. Siebmacher. Tr. by A. E. Waite from Lat. 1987. pap. 6.95 (ISBN 0-916411-59-1). Alchemical Pr.

Sophie. Geoffrey Wagner. 320p. 1982. pap. 2.95 (ISBN 0-505-51795-7, Pub. by Tower Bks). Leisure NY.

Sophie & Gussie. Marjorie W. Sharmat. LC 72-85188. (Ready-to-Read Ser). (Illus.). 64p. (gr. 1-3). 1973. 6.95 (ISBN 0-02-782310-5). Macmillan.

Sophie & Jack. Judy Taylor. (Illus.). 32p. (ps-2). 1983. PLB 9.95 (ISBN 0-399-20947-6, Philomel). Putnam Pub Group.

Sophie & Jack Help Out. Judy Taylor. LC 83-13302. (Illus.). 32p. (gr. k-2). 1984. 8.95 (ISBN 0-399-21059-8, Philomel). Putnam Pub Group.

Sophie & Simon. Marie-France Mangin. Tr. by Didi Charney from Fr. (Aladdin Storybooks). (Illus.). 36p. (Orig.). (gr. 1-3). 1988. pap. 2.95 (ISBN 0-689-71193-X, Aladdin Bks). Macmillan.

Sophie Canetang: Jemima Puddle-Duck. Beatrix Potter. (Fr.). (gr. 3-7). 1981. bds. 5.00 (ISBN 0-7232-0653-8). Warne.

Sophie Du Pont: A Young Lady in America: Sketches, Diaries, & Letters 1823-1833. Betty-Bright Low & Jacqueline Hinsley. (Illus.). 192p. 1987. 35.00 (ISBN 0-8109-1136-1). Abrams.

Sophie Horowitz Story. Sarah Schulman. 208p. (Orig.). 1984. pap. 7.95 (ISBN 0-930044-54-1). Naiad Pr.

Sophie Kay's Microwave. Sophie K. Petros. (Illus.). 80p. (Orig.). 1984. pap. 4.95 (ISBN 0-8249-3022-3). Ideals.

Sophie Taeuber-Arp. Carolyn Lanchner. (Illus.). 56p. 1981. pap. 4.95 (ISBN 0-87070-598-9). Museum Mod Art.

Sophie the Rag Picker. Tilde Michels. (Illus.). (gr. k-1). 1962. 10.95 (ISBN 0-8392-3036-2). Astor-Honor.

Sophie's Bucket. Catherine Stock. LC 84-15461. (Illus.). 32p. (gr. k up). 1985. 13.00 (ISBN 0-688-04224-4); PLB 12.88 (ISBN 0-688-04225-2). Lothrop.

Sophie's Choice. William Styron. 640p. 1982. pap. 4.95 (ISBN 0-553-25960-1). Bantam.

Sophie's Choice. William Styron. 1980. 15.95 (ISBN 0-394-46109-6). Random.

Sophie's Choice Chili or How to Cure Your Frigidity. Compiled by Madeleine S. Gary. 96p. (Orig.). 1985. pap. 4.50 (ISBN 0-913459-02-X). New Writers Guild.

Sophie's Knapsack. Catherine Stock. LC 87-3103. (Illus.). (ps-2). 1988. 11.95 (ISBN 0-688-06457-4); 11.88 (ISBN 0-688-06458-2). Lothrop.

Sophie's Surprise. 2nd ed. Lee Richardson. (Illus.). 28p. (gr. 3-8). 1984. 16.95 (ISBN 0-9613476-0-0). Shirlee.

Sophist. Charles Bernstein. 171p. 1987. 16.95 (ISBN 0-940650-78-9); pap. 11.95 (ISBN 0-940650-79-7); (signed edition) 30.00 (ISBN 0-940650-80-0). Sun & Moon CA.

Sophistes & Politicus of Plato. Plato. Rev. by Lewis Campbell. LC 72-9286. (Philosophy of Plato & Aristotle Ser.). Repr. of 1867 ed. 28.00 (ISBN 0-405-04836-X). Ayer Co Pubs.

Sophistic Movement. G. B. Kerferd. LC 80-41934. 200p. 1981. 37.50 (ISBN 0-521-23936-2); pap. 14.95 (ISBN 0-521-28357-4). Cambridge U Pr.

Sophisticated Estate Planning after the Tax Reform Act of 1986. American Bar Association, Section of Real Property-Probate & Trust Law. LC 87-100297. 289p. 1986. pap. 44.95 (ISBN 0-89707-275-8). Amer Bar Assn.

Sophisticated Leisure: Nineteen Eighty-Seven Travel Directory. Bruce Coville et al. (Illus.). 348p. 1986. pap. 8.95 (ISBN 0-9614965-5-X). Schueler Comm.

Sophisticated Leisure Travel Directory, 1986. Bruce Coville et al. (Illus.). 348p. 1986. pap. 8.95 (ISBN 0-9614965-4-1). Schueler Comm.

Sophisticated Rebels: The Political Culture of European Dissent, 1968-1987. H. Stuart Hughes. (Studies in Cultural History). 192p. 1988. 20.00 (ISBN 0-674-82130-0). Harvard U Pr.

Sophisticated Silhouettes: The Shape of Fashion, 1910-1960. Beverly Birks. (Illus.). 24p. 1986. 8.00 (ISBN 0-915171-06-6). Katonah Gal.

Sophisticated Tax Planning for Real Estate Transactions. Sanford C. Presant & Leslie H. Loffman. 605p. 1988. pap. 45.00 (N4-4491). PLI.

Sophisticated Traveler: Beloved Cities. Ed. by A. M. Rosenthal & Arthur Gelb. 1984. 14.45 (ISBN 0-394-53645-2, Pub. by Villard Bks). Random.

Sophisticated Traveler: Beloved Cities: Europe. Ed. by A. M. Rosenthal & Arthur Gelb. (Nonfiction Ser.). 496p. 1985. pap. 8.95 (ISBN 0-14-008147-X). Penguin.

Sophisticated Traveler: Winter: Love It or Leave It. Ed. by A. M. Rosenthal & Arthur Gelb. 1985. pap. 8.95 (ISBN 0-14-008148-8). Penguin.

Sophisticated Traveler: Winter: Love It or Leave It. Ed. by A. M. Rosenthal & Arthur Gelb. 560p. 1985. pap. 8.95 (ISBN 0-317-46920-7). Penguin.

Sophisticated Traveler's Pocket Guide to Airport Facilities & Ground Services, 1987. G. H. Gizinski. LC 86-63679. (Illus.). 116p. 1986. pap. 14.95 (ISBN 0-941521-00-1). Mkt Dynam Consults.

Sophisticated Traveler's Pocket Guide to Airport Facilities & Ground Services, 1988. G. H. Gizinski. (Illus.). 150p. 1987. pap. 14.95 (ISBN 0-941521-01-X). Mkt Dynam Consults.

Sophisticate's Guide to Living Alone Successfully. Edan Schappert. LC 88-19377. (Illus.). 208p. (Orig.). 1988. pap. 9.95 (ISBN 1-55870-107-9). Betterway Pubns.

Sophisticates Primer of Relativity. 2nd ed. P. W. Bridgman. 1982. 20.00x (ISBN 0-8195-5077-9); pap. 9.95 (ISBN 0-8195-6078-2). Wesleyan U Pr.

Sophists. William K. Guthrie. 1971. pap. 17.95 (ISBN 0-521-09666-9). Cambridge U Pr.

Sophists & Their Legacy: Proceedings of the Fourth International Colloquium on Ancient Philosophy, Homburg, 1979. Ed. by George B. Kerferd. 148p. (Orig.). 1981. pap. text ed. 48.50x (ISBN 3-515-03427-7, Pub. by Franz Steiner). Coronet Bks.

Sophists: Rhetoric, Democracy, & Plato's Idea of Sophistry. Harold Barrett. LC 87-21051. 96p. (Orig.). 1988. pap. text ed. 6.95 (ISBN 0-88316-557-0). Chandler & Sharp.

Sophists, Socratics & Cynics. H. D. Rankin. LC 83-12206. 264p. 1983. 28.50x (ISBN 0-389-20421-8). B&N Imports.

Sophoclean Chorus: A Study of Character & Function. Cynthia P. Gardiner. LC 86-16008. 216p. 1986. text ed. 22.50x (ISBN 0-87745-155-9). U of Iowa Pr.

Sophocles. Siegfried Melchinger. Tr. by David Scrase. LC 72-79931. (Literature & Life Ser.). (Illus.). 1974. 16.95x (ISBN 0-8044-2617-1). Ungar.

Sophocles: A Study of Heroic Humanism. Cedric H. Whitman. LC 51-10794. 1951. 24.50x (ISBN 0-674-82140-8). Harvard U Pr.

Sophocles: Ajax. W. B. Stanford. 376p. 1981. Repr. of 1963 ed. 24.00 (ISBN 0-86292-009-4, Pub. by Bristol Classical UK). Focus Info Gr.

Sophocles: Antigone. Ed. by Andrew Brown & Andrew Brown. (Classical Texts-Greek Texts Ser.). 204p. (Eng., Gr.). 1987. text ed. 49.95 (ISBN 0-85668-266-7, Pub. by Aris & Phillips); pap. text ed. 16.50 (ISBN 0-85668-267-5). Humanities.

Sophocles' Antigone. Nicolas P. Gross. (Greek Commentaries Ser.). 111p. (Orig.). 1988. pap. text ed. 5.00. Bryn Mawr Commentaries.

Sophocles: Antigone. Ed. by Wolff & Martin L. D'ooge. (College Series of Greek Authors). 196p. (Eng. & Gr.). Repr. of 1887 ed. 12.95x (ISBN 0-935005-81-1). Ibis Pub VA.

Sophocles: Antigone & Oedipus the King. J. Wilkins & M. Macleod. 116p. 1987. 11.00 (ISBN 0-86292-240-2, Pub. by Bristol Classical UK). Focus Info Gr.

Sophocles Oedipus at Colonus. Gilbert P. Rose. (Greek Commentaries Ser.). 132p. (Orig.). 1988. pap. text ed. 6.00. Bryn Mawr Commentaries.

Sophocles: Oedipus Tyrannus. R. C. Jebb. 208p. 1981. Repr. of 1885 ed. 15.25 (ISBN 0-86292-002-7, Pub. by Bristol Classical UK). Focus Info Gr.

Sophocles, Oedipus Tyrannus. Intro. by John A. Symonds. 132p. 1970. pap. 2.50x (ISBN 0-87291-009-1). Coronado Pr.

Sophocles One. Sophocles. Incl. Oedipus the King. Tr. by David Grene; Oedipus at Colonus. Tr. by Robert Fitzgerald; Antigone. Tr. by Elizabeth Wycoff. (Complete Greek Tragedies Ser). 55p. 1954. pap. 6.50x (ISBN 0-226-30785-9, P313, Phoen). U of Chicago Pr.

Sophocles: The Dramatist. Arthur Waldock. pap. 61.00 (ISBN 0-317-26367-6, 2024565). Bks Demand UMI.

Sophocles the Dramatist. Arthur J. Waldock. pap. 9.95 (ISBN 0-521-09374-0). Cambridge U Pr.

Sophocles, the Plays & Fragments, 1892-1900, 7 Vols. Richard C. Jebb. 1892-1900. Set. 325.00 (ISBN 0-403-00289-3). Scholarly.

Sophocles: The Theban Plays. Tr. & intro. by Don Taylor. 320p. 1986. pap. 6.95 (ISBN 0-413-42460-X, 9997): Routledge Chapman & Hall.

Sophocles: Three Theban Plays. C. A. Trypanis. 160p. 1986. pap. text ed. 16.50 (ISBN 0-85668-375-2, Pub. by Aris & Phillips UK). Humanities.

Sophocles Two. Sophocles. Ed. by David Greene & Richmond Lattimore. Incl. Ajax. John Moore; Women of Trachis. Michael Jameson; Electra. David Grene; Philoctetes. David Grene. LC 54-10731. (Complete Greek Tragedies Ser: No. 4). 70p. 1957. pap. 6.50x (ISBN 0-226-30786-7, P314, Phoen). U of Chicago Pr.

Sophocles's Oedipus Rex. Intro. by Harold Bloom. (Modern Critical Interpretations Ser.). 1987. 24.50 (ISBN 0-87754-918-4). Chelsea Hse.

Sophomore. Linda A. Cooney. (Class of '88 Ser.). 224p. (Orig.). (gr. 7 up). 1987. pap. 2.50 (ISBN 0-590-40349-4). Scholastic Inc.

Sophomore: Class of Eighty-Nine. Linda A. Cooney. 224p. (YA) (gr. 7 up). 1988. pap. 2.50 (ISBN 0-590-41675-8). Scholastic Inc.

Sophronia; or, Letters to the Ladies. Ed. by Michael F. Shugrue. (Flowering of the Novel Ser.: 1740-1775). 1974. Repr. of 1761 ed. lib. bdg. 61.00 (ISBN 0-8240-1158-9). Garland Pub.

Sophus K. Winther. Barbara H. Meldrum. LC 82-74094. (Western Writers Ser.: No. 60). (Illus., Orig.). 1983. pap. 2.95x (ISBN 0-88430-034-X). Boise St Univ.

Sophus Lie's Eighteen Eighty Transformation Group Paper. M. Ackerman & Robert Hermann. LC 75-17416. (Lie Groups: History, Frontiers on Applications Ser.: No. 1). 1975. 55.00 (ISBN 0-915692-10-4). Math Sci Pr.

Sophus Lie's 1884 Differential Invariants Paper. Robert Hermann & M. Ackerman. LC 75-43189. (Lie Groups: History Frontiers & Applications Ser.: No. 3). 273p. 1975. 36.00 (ISBN 0-915692-13-9, 991600053). Math Sci Pr.

Sopianae. F. Fulep. (Archaeologia Hungarica: Vol. 50). 391p. 1984. text ed. 60.00x (ISBN 963-05-3017-1, Pub. by Akademia Kiado Hungary). Humanities.

Sopianae: The History of Pecs During the Roman Era & the Problem of the Continuity of the Late Roman Population. Ferenc Fulep. 392p. 1984. 138.00x (ISBN 0-569-08819-4, Pub. by Collets (UK)). State Mutual Bk.

Sopping Thursday. Edward Gorey. (Illus.). 72p. (Orig.). 1971. pap. 4.95 (ISBN 0-88496-176-1). Capra Pr.

Sopping Thursday. Edward Gorey. (Illus.). 72p. 1988. Repr. lib. bdg. 19.95x (ISBN 0-8095-4022-3). Borgo Pr.

Soppliment Musicali. Gioseffo Zarlino. (Monuments of Music & Literature in Facsimile, Ser. II: Vol. 15). (Illus.). 1979. Repr. of 1588 ed. 52.50x. Broude.

Sopranino. Patrick Ellam & Colin Mudie. 224p. 1986. pap. 12.95 (ISBN 0-246-12943-3). Sheridan.

Soprano on Her Head: Right-side-up Reflections on Life-& Other Performances. Eloise Ristad. LC 81-23369. 201p. (Orig.). 1982. 10.00 (ISBN 0-911226-20-6); pap. 7.50 (ISBN 0-911226-21-4). Real People.

Soprano Recorder Songbook for Children. Rhoda B. Weber & Bob Margolis. (Illus., Orig.). 1985. pap. 3.50 (ISBN 0-931329-00-0, SRS-1); pap. 9.95 tchr's. manual (ISBN 0-931329-01-9, TMSRS-1). Manhattan Beach.

Soprano Voice. Anthony Frissell. 1971. 10.00 (ISBN 0-8283-1388-1). Branden Pub Co.

Sopwith Fighters. J. M. Bruce. (Vintage Warbirds Ser.: No. 5). (Illus.). 64p. (Orig.). 1986. pap. 9.95 (ISBN 0-85368-790-0, Pub. by Arms & Armour). Sterling.

Sor Juana & Other Plays. Estela Portillo Trambley. LC 82-73752. ii, 195p. 1983. pap. 12.00x (ISBN 0-916950-33-6). Biling Rev-Pr.

Sor Juana Anthology. Tr. by Alan S. Trueblood. 272p. 1988. text ed. 29.50 (ISBN 0-674-82120-3). Harvard U Pr.

Sor Juana Ines de la Cruz. Gerard Flynn. LC 75-120482. (World Authors Ser.). 1971. lib. bdg. 17.95 (ISBN 0-8057-2256-4). Irvington.

Sor Juana Ines de la Cruz o las Trampas de la Fe. Octavio Paz. 658p. (Span.). 1982. 12.50 (ISBN 968-16-1211-6, 3008). Ediciones Norte.

Sor Juana Ines de la Cruz: Poems. Ed. by Margaret Sayers Peden. LC 85-71537. 144p. (Eng. & Span.). 1985. pap. text ed. 10.00x (ISBN 0-916950-60-3). Biling Rev-Pr.

Sor Juana: Or, the Traps of Faith. Octavio Paz. Tr. by Margaret S. Peden from Span. LC 88-3002. (Illus.). 560p. 1988. 29.95 (ISBN 0-674-82105-X). Harvard U Pr.

Sor Juana's Dream. Luis Harss. Tr. by Luis Harss from Span. (Orig.). 1987. pap. 9.95 (ISBN 0-930829-07-7). Lumen Inc.

S.O.R. Losers. Avi. LC 84-11022. 104p. (gr. 5-7). 1984. 9.95 (ISBN 0-02-793410-1). Bradbury Pr.

S.O.R. Losers. Avi. (gr. k-9). 1988. pap. 2.50. Scholastic Inc.

Sorbets! Jim Tarantino. (Crossing Press Specialty Cookbook Ser.). 150p. (Orig.). 1988. 20.95 (ISBN 0-89594-270-4); pap. 8.95 (ISBN 0-89594-269-0). Crossing Pr.

Sorby Centennial Symposium on the History of Metallurgy, Cleveland, Ohio, October 22-23, 1963. Ed. by Cyril S. Smith. LC 65-17635. (Metallurgical Society Conference: Vol. 27). pap. 145.00 (ISBN 0-317-10418-7, 2001515). Bks Demand UMI.

Sorby on Geology, Vol. III. Ed. by Charles H. Summerson. (Geological Milestones Ser.). (Illus.). 241p. 1978. 8.50 (ISBN 0-932981-28-3). Univ Miami CSL.

Sorby on Sedimentology, Vol. I. Ed. by Charles H. Summerson. (Geological Milestones Ser.). (Illus.). 226p. 1976. 8.50 (ISBN 0-932981-27-5). Univ Miami CSL.

Sorcerer. Anne E. Crompton. LC 82-61042. 176p. 1982. Repr. of 1971 ed. 16.95 (ISBN 0-933256-36-1). Second Chance.

Sorcerer. Anne E. Crompton. LC 82-61042. 176p. 1983. pap. 9.95 (ISBN 0-933256-37-X). Second Chance.

Sorcerer. Mark Manley. 320p. (Orig.). Date not set. pap. 3.95 (ISBN 0-445-20524-5, Pub. by Popular Lib). Warner Bks.

Sorcerer & His Apprentice. R. A. Gilbert. 222p. Date not set. pap. 11.95 (ISBN 0-85030-374-5, Pub. by Thorsons UK). Weiser.

Sorcerer & Witch in Melanesia. Ed. by Michele Stephen. 208p. 1987. text ed. 35.00 (ISBN 0-8135-1227-1). Rutgers U Pr.

Sorcerers! Ed. by Jack Dann & Gardner Dozois. 256p. 1986. pap. 2.95 (ISBN 0-441-77532-2, Pub. by Ace Science Fiction). Ace Bks.

Sorcerers. Jacob Needleman. LC 86-8733. 235p. 1986. 16.95 (ISBN 0-916515-10-9). Mercury Hse Inc.

Sorcerers: A Laotian Tale. Knute Skinner. (Illus.). 1973. pap. 1.50 (ISBN 0-686-05613-2). Goliards Pr.

Sorcerer's Apprentice. David Eastman. LC 87-13767. (Illus.). 32p. (gr. k-4). 1987. PLB 9.79 (ISBN 0-8167-1067-8); pap. text ed. 1.95 (ISBN 0-8167-1068-6). Troll Assocs.

Sorcerer's Apprentice. Wanda Gag & Margot Tomes. LC 78-23990. (Illus.). (gr. k-3). 1979. 6.95 (ISBN 0-698-20481-6, Coward). Putnam Pub Group.

Sorcerer's Apprentice. Charles Johnson. LC 85-47776. 256p. 1986. 9.95 (ISBN 0-689-11653-5). Atheneum.

Sorcerer's Apprentice. Robin Muller. LC 86-61415. (Illus.). 30p. (gr. 2-4). 1986. 11.95 (ISBN 0-382-09382-8). Silver.

Sorcerer's Apprentice. As told by Felicity Trotman. (Stories Clippers Ser.). (Illus.). 32p. (gr. k-5). 1985. PLB 15.33 (ISBN 0-8172-2505-6); pap. 9.27 (ISBN 0-8172-2513-7). Raintree Pubs.

Sorcerer's Apprentice. Walt Disney Productions. LC 73-9891. (Illus.). 48p. (ps-2). 1974. 5.95 (ISBN 0-394-82551-9, BYR); lib. bdg. 4.99 (ISBN 0-394-92551-3). Random.

Sorcerer's Apprentice: A Journey Through East Africa. Elspeth Huxley. LC 73-13327. 1975. Repr. of 1948 ed. lib. bdg. 35.00x (ISBN 0-8371-7126-1, HUSO). Greenwood.

Sorcerer's Apprentice: An Anthropology of Public Policy. Cyril S. Belshaw. 360p. 1976. pap. text ed. 22.00 (ISBN 0-08-018312-3). Pergamon.

Sorcerer's Apprentice: Tales & Conjurations. Charles Johnson. 180p. 1987. pap. 5.95 (ISBN 0-14-009865-8). Penguin.

Sorcerer's Apprentice: Tales of the Modern Hospital. S. Tisdale. 192p. 1986. text ed. 15.95 (ISBN 0-07-064784-4). McGraw.

Sorcerer's Apprentice: Tales of the Modern Hospital. Sallie Tisdale. (Owl Bks.). 1988. pap. 9.95 (ISBN 0-8050-0578-1). H Holt & Co.

Sorcerer's Apprentice: The French Scientist's Image of German Science, 1840-1919. Harry W. Paul. LC 77-178986. (University of Florida Social Sciences Monographs: No. 44). 86p. 1972. pap. 6.00x (ISBN 0-8130-0347-4). U Presses Fla.

Sorcerer's Apprentices. Nicholas S. Gray. (gr. 3-7). 1987. Repr. 6.95 (ISBN 0-312-57282-4). St Martin.

Sorcerer's Handbook. Wade Baskin. (Illus.). 640p. 1974. pap. 4.95 (ISBN 0-8065-0399-8, Pub. by Citadel Pr). Lyle Stuart.

Sorcerer's Heir. Paula Volsky. 1988. pap. 3.50 (ISBN 0-441-77231-5). Ace Bks.

Sorcerer's Lady. Paula Volsky. 256p. 1987. pap. 2.95 (ISBN 0-441-77533-0, Pub. by Ace Science Fiction). Ace Bks.

Sorcerers of Dobu: The Social Anthropology of the Dobu Islanders of the Western Pacific. R. F. Fortune. 1979. Repr. of 1932 ed. lib. bdg. 25.00 (ISBN 0-8495-1736-2). Arden Lib.

Sorcerer's Samplecase: Selected Poems in a Jugular Vein. Ed. by Stanley McNail. (Illus.). 26p. (Orig.). (YA) (gr. 7 up). 1986. pap. 3.00 (ISBN 0-940945-00-2). Embassy Hall Edns.

Sorcerer's Scrapbook. Michael Berenstain. LC 80-5754. (Illus.). 64p. (gr. 3-7). 1981. Random.

Sorcerer's Shadow. David C. Smith. 1982. pap. 2.50 (ISBN 0-686-97453-0). Zebra.

Sorcerers Skull. Robert E. Vardeman. 224p. 1984. pap. 2.75 (ISBN 0-441-77542-X). Ace Bks.

Sorceress. John Jakes. (Brak Ser.: No. 3). 1981. pap. 2.25 (ISBN 0-505-51709-4, Pub. by Tower Bks). Leisure NY.

Sorceress & the Book of Spells. Anne Schraff. Ed. by Rick Nayer. (Narnia Solo Adventures Ser.). 192p. (Orig.). 1988. pap. 2.95 (ISBN 0-425-11029-X). Berkley Pub.

Sorceress of the Witch World. Andre Norton. (Witch World Ser.: No. 6). 288p. 1986. pap. 3.50 (ISBN 0-441-77558-6, Pub. by Ace Science Fiction). Ace Bks.

Sorcery. J. Finley Hurley. 256p. 1985. 25.00x (ISBN 0-7102-0292-X). Routledge Chapman & Hall.

Sorcery & Cecelia. Patricia C. Wrede & Caroline Stevermer. 1988. pap. 2.95 (ISBN 0-441-77559-4). Ace Bks.

Sorcery Club. Elliot O'Donnell. Ed. by R. Reginald & Douglas Menville. LC 75-46295. (Supernatural & Occult Fiction Ser.). (Illus.). 1976. Repr. of 1912 ed. lib. bdg. 26.50 (ISBN 0-405-08156-1). Ayer Co Pubs.

Sorcery Four: The Crown of Kings. Steve Jackson. (Penguin Fiction Ser.). 240p. (Orig.). 1985. pap. 4.95 (ISBN 0-14-007209-8). Penguin.

Sorcery in America Series. Gordon Lindsay. (Sorcery & Spirit World Ser.: Vol. 2). 1.25 ea. (ISBN 0-89985-951-8). Christ Nations.

Sorcery One: The Shamutanti Hills. Steve Jackson. 160p. 1984. pap. 3.95 (ISBN 0-14-006794-9). Penguin.

Sorcery Spell Book. Steve Jackson. 112p. 1984. pap. 3.95 (ISBN 0-14-006793-0). Penguin.

Sorcery Three: The Seven Serpents. Steve Jackson. (Penguin Fiction Ser.). 240p. 1984. pap. 3.95 (ISBN 0-14-007208-X). Penguin.

Sorcery Two: Khare-Cityport of Traps. Steve Jackson. (Illus.). 192p. (gr. 8). 1984. pap. 3.95 (ISBN 0-14-006801-5). Penguin.

Sordello's Story, Retold in Prose. Annie R. Wall. LC 76-47474. 1976. lib. bdg. 27.50 (ISBN 0-8414-9607-2). Folcroft.

Sore Throat-The Danger Within. David J. Gerrick. (Illus.). 1978. 20.00 (ISBN 0-685-89681-1). Dayton Labs.

Sore Throats & Sonnets of Love & Opposition. Howard Brenton. 47p. 1979. pap. 4.95 (ISBN 0-413-46580-2, 3012). Routledge Chapman & Hall.

Sorely Trying Day. Russell Hoban. LC 64-11836. (Illus.). (gr. k-3). 1964. PLB 12.89 (ISBN 0-06-022421-5). HarpJ.

Soren Kierkegaard. Elmer H. Duncan. Ed. by Bob E. Patterson. LC 76-2862. (Markers of the Modern Theological Mind Ser.). 1976. 8.95 (ISBN 0-87680-463-6, 80463). Word Bks.

Soren Kierkegaard. Johannes Hohlenberg. 1978. Repr. of 1954 ed. lib. bdg. 23.00x (ISBN 0-374-93923-3, Octagon). Hippocrene Bks.

Soren Kierkegaard & His Critics: An International Bibliography of Criticism. Compiled by Francois H. Lapointe. LC 80-783. viii, 430p. 1980. lib. bdg. 46.95 (ISBN 0-313-22333-5, LKI/). Greenwood.

Soren Kierkegaard: Modern Philosopher & Existentialist. Alan L. Paley. LC 72-81903. (Outstanding Personalities Ser.: No. 40). 32p. 1972. lib. bdg. 3.75 incl. catalog cards (ISBN 0-87157-550-7); pap. 2.50 vinyl laminated covers (ISBN 0-87157-050-5). SamHar Pr.

Soren Kierkegaard's Journals & Papers, 7 vols. Soren Kierkegaard. Ed. by Howard V. Hong & Edna H. Hong. Tr. by Howard V. Hong & Edna H. Hong. Incl. Vol. 1. A-E. LC 67-13025. 572p. 1967. 40.00x (ISBN 0-253-18240-9); Vol. 2. F-K. 640p. 1970. 47.50x (ISBN 0-253-18241-7); Vol. 3. L-R. 944p. 1976. 60.00x (ISBN 0-253-18242-5); Vol. 4. S-Z. 800p. 1976. 50.00x (ISBN 0-253-18243-3); Vol. 5. Autobiographical, Part One, 1829-1848. 576p. 1978. 47.50x (ISBN 0-253-18244-1); Vol. 6. Autobiographical, Part Two, 1848-1855. 648p. 1978. 50.00x (ISBN 0-253-18245-X); Vol. 7. Index & Composite Collation. 160p. 1978. 30.00x (ISBN 0-253-18246-8). Ind U Pr.

Sorghum & Pearl Millet Disease Identification Handbook. R. J. Williams et al. 88p. (Orig.). 1978. pap. text ed. 8.90x (ISBN 92-9066-011-2, Pub. by ICRISAT (India)). Agribookstore.

Sorghum & the Millets: Their Composition & Nutritive Value. Joseph Hulse et al. LC 79-40871. 1980. 278.50 (ISBN 0-12-361350-7). Acad Pr.

Sorghum for Acid Soils: Proceedings of a Workshop on Evaluating Sorghum for Tolerance to Al-Toxic Soils in Latin America. Ed. by Lynn M. Gourley & Jose G. Salinas. 337p. (Orig.). 1987. pap. text ed. 24.00 (ISBN 84-89206-64-3, Pub. by CIAT Colombia). Agribookstore.

Sorley MacLean: Critical Essays. Ed. by Raymond J. Ross & Joy M. Hendry. (Illus.). 240p. 1987. 25.50 (ISBN 0-7073-0426-1, Pub. by Scot Acad Pr). Longwood Pub Group.

Sorley Maclean Poems 1932-82. Sorley Maclean et al. Ed. by Daniel Gillis. Tr. by Sorley Maclean from Scots Gaelic. LC 87-2755. (Columban Celtic Ser.: Vol. 2). 180p. (Orig.). 1986. 12.95 (ISBN 0-941638-01-4); pap. 8.95 (ISBN 0-941638-02-2). Iona Phila.

Soroban (Abacus) to Silicon Chip. Floyd T. Waterman. 49p. (Orig.). 1984. pap. 3.50 (ISBN 1-55719-061-5). U NE Ctr Applied Urban Rsch.

Sorority. Sheila Schwartz. 464p. (Orig.). 1987. pap. 3.95 (ISBN 0-445-20165-7, Pub. by Popular Lib). Warner Bks.

Sorority Girls, No. 4. 208p. (Orig.). 1986. pap. 2.50 (ISBN 0-449-13003-7, Pub by Girls Only). Ballantine.

Sorority Girls, No. 5. Anne H. Lowell. 224p. 1986. pap. 2.50 (ISBN 0-449-13006-1, Pub. by Girls Only). Ballantine.

Sorority Girls, No. 10. Anne H. Lowell. (Orig.). 1987. pap. 2.50 (ISBN 0-449-13218-8). Fawcett.

Sorority Girls, No. 12. Anne H. Lowell. (Orig.). 1987. pap. 2.50 (ISBN 0-449-13221-8, Juniper). Fawcett.

Sorority Girl's No. 2: Nowhere to Run. Anne H. Lowell. 160p. (Orig.). 1986. pap. 2.50 (ISBN 0-449-12883-0). Ballantine.

Sorority Girls No. 3: Starting Over. Anne H. Lowell. (Orig.). 1986. pap. 2.50 (ISBN 0-449-13001-0, Pub. by Girls Only). Ballantine.

Sorpresivamente. Andres Rivero. LC 1-67366. (Short Stories in Spanish Ser.). 80p. 1981. pap. 4.00 (ISBN 0-933648-03-0). Cruzada Span Pubns.

Sorption Isotherms & Water Activity of Food Materials. Ed. by W. Wolf et al. 236p. 1985. 42.00 (ISBN 0-444-00997-3). Elsevier.

Sorrat: A History of the Neihardt Psychokinesis Experiments, 1961-1981. John T. Richards. LC 81-18312. 356p. 1982. 21.00 (ISBN 0-8108-1491-9). Scarecrow.

Sorraya in a Coma. Esmail Fassih. 304p. 1985. 14.95x (ISBN 0-86232-525-0, Pub. by Zed Pr England); pap. 7.95 (ISBN 0-86232-526-9, Pub. by Zed Pr England). Humanities.

Sorrel Horse. Ruth N. Moore. LC 82-3136. 144p. (Orig.). (gr. 5-10). 1982. pap. 3.95 (ISBN 0-8361-3303-X). Herald Pr.

Sorrell & Son. Warwick Deeping. 416p. 1987. pap. 5.95 (ISBN 0-14-010129-2). Penguin.

Sorrow Beyond Dreams. Peter Handke. Tr. by Ralph Manheim from Ger. 70p. 1975. 6.95 (ISBN 0-374-26680-8). FS&G.

Sorrow Child. Shara Herington. 1983. 3.50 (ISBN 0-318-04448-X). Pudding Hse Pubns.

Sorrow, Grief & God. Salvatore Cipparone. 4.95 (ISBN 0-686-20577-4). Ivory Scroll.

Sorrow of Architecture. Liam Rector. LC 83-20685. 75p. 1984. 14.00 (ISBN 0-937872-16-4); pap. 6.00 (ISBN 0-937872-17-2). Dragon Gate.

Sorrow of the Lonely & the Burning of the Dancers. Edward L. Schieffelin. LC 75-10999. (Illus.). 256p. 1975. pap. text ed. write for info. (ISBN 0-312-74550-8). St Martin.

Sorrow of the Snows. Upendranath Askh. Tr. by Jai Ratan. (Translated from Hindi). 9.00 (ISBN 0-89253-639-X); flexible cloth 6.75 (ISBN 0-89253-640-3). Ind-US Inc.

Sorrow Speaks. Mary L. Williams. 1968. pap. 2.95 (ISBN 0-8272-3405-8). CBP.

Sorrowful & Immaculate Heart of Mary: Message of Berthe Petit, Franciscan Tertiary (1870-1943) Pref. by T. Cadoux. 110p. 1966. pap. 3.00 (ISBN 0-913382-02-7, 101-2). Prow Bks-Franciscan.

Sorrowful & Immaculate Heart of Mary. Duffner. 47p. 0.90 (ISBN 0-911988-24-6). AMI Pr.

Sorrowful City. Harry Morris. LC 65-29103. 1965. 6.00 (ISBN 0-8130-0164-1). U Presses Fla.

Sorrows & Celebrations. Scott M. Thornton. LC 83-51615. (Illus.). 80p. (Orig.). 1984. pap. 5.95 (ISBN 0-9613117-8-9). Tavistock Poetry.

Sorrows of Frederick & Holy Ghosts. Romulus Linney. LC 76-47904. 1977. pap. 3.95 (ISBN 0-15-683848-6, Harv). HarBraceJ.

Sorrows of Han: A Chinese Tragedy. Ma Chi-Yuan. Tr. by J. F. Davis. (Oriental Translation Fund Ser: No. 4). 1969. pap. 7.00 (ISBN 0-384-34820-3). Johnson Repr.

Sorrows of Priapus: The Poetic Truths of Mind & Body in Myth & Experience. Edward Dahlberg. (Illus.). 120p. 1988. pap. 10.95 (ISBN 0-7145-0670-2, Dist. by Kampmann & Co). M Boyars Pubs.

Sorrows of Satan. Marie Corelli. (Illus.). pap. 5.95 (ISBN 0-910122-06-7). Amherst Pr.

Sorrows of the Young Werther. W. J. Goethe. (Illus.). 131p. 1984. 117.75 (ISBN 0-89266-481-9). Am Classical Coll Pr.

Sorrows of Werther: Elective Affinities & Tales see Goethe's Popular Works.

Sorrows of Young Werther. Johann Wolfgang von Goethe. Tr. by Elizabeth Mayer et al. Bd. with Novella. 1973. pap. 3.96 (ISBN 0-394-71958-1, Vin). Random.

Sorrows of Young Werther & Novella. Johann W. Von Goethe. Tr. by Elizabeth Mayer et al. LC 84-4592. 201p. 1984. 7.95 (ISBN 0-394-60509-8). Modern Lib.

Sorrows of Young Werther & Selected Writings. Johann Wolfgang von Goethe. Tr. by Catherine Hutter. (Orig.). 1962. pap. 3.50 (ISBN 0-451-52154-4, Sig Classics). NAL.

Sorry. Laura Alden. LC 82-9660. (What Does it Mean? Ser.). (Illus.). 32p. (gr. 1-2). 1982. PLB 5.95 (ISBN 0-89565-236-6, 4897, Pub. by Childs World). Standard Pub.

Sorry. Sue Riley. LC 77-16811. (What Does It Mean? Ser.). (Illus.). (ps-2). 1978. PLB 6.75 (ISBN 0-89565-013-4). Childs World.

Sorry. Sue Riley. LC 77-16811. (What Does it Mean? Ser.). (Illus.). 32p. (ps-2). 1978. 10.33 (ISBN 0-516-06145-3). Childrens.

Sorry. Illus. by Tony Tallarico. (Mind Your Manners Ser.). (Illus.). (ps-1). 1985. text ed. 3.95 (ISBN 0-89828-152-0, 81520). Tuffy Bks.

Sorry about the Explosion: A Humorous Guide to Computers. David D. Busch. (P-H Personal Computing Ser.). (Illus.). 128p. 1985. pap. text ed. 7.95 (ISBN 0-13-822834-5). P-H.

Sorry, Dad. Edward Blishen. 217p. 1984. pap. 5.95 (ISBN 0-8052-8209-2, Pub. by Allison & Busby, England). Schocken.

Sorry I Stirred It. Bill Vaughan. 1964. 3.95 (ISBN 0-671-68090-0). S&S.

Sorry I'm Late. My Hair Won't Start. Cathy Guisewite. 1985. pap. 2.95 (ISBN 0-449-20925-3, Crest). Fawcett.

Sorry, Miss Folio! Jo Furtado. (Illus.). 32p. (ps-3). 1988. 10.95 (ISBN 0-916291-18-9). Kane-Miller Bk.

Sorry! No Hard Feelings? David Hayes. (Irish Play Ser.). 1978. pap. 2.50x (ISBN 0-912262-44-3). Proscenium.

Sorry! Wrong Planet! Maria Ensio. 64p. 1988. 6.95 (ISBN 0-8062-3239-0). Carlton.

Sort of Columbus: The American Voyages of Saul Bellow's Fiction. Jeanne Braham. LC 83-10539. 151p. 1984. 17.00x (ISBN 0-8203-0690-8). U of Ga Pr.

Sort of Life, Vol. 1. Graham Greene. 1982. pap. 2.95 (ISBN 0-671-45198-7). WSP.

Sort of Peace. Margaret T. Davis. (Breadmakers Trilogy Ser.). 224p. 1983. 13.95 (ISBN 0-8052-8153-3, Pub. by Allison & Busby England). Schocken.

Sort of Samurai. James Melville. 208p. 1985. pap. 2.95 (ISBN 0-449-20821-4, Crest). Fawcett.

Sort of Tragedy. Philip Lauben. 24.95x (ISBN 0-7090-1821-5, Pub. by R Hale Ltd UK). State Mutual Bk.

Sort of Utopia: Scarsdale, Eighteen Ninety-One to Nineteen Eighty-One. Carol A. O'Connor. LC 82-5855. (Illus.). 283p. 1983. 52.50 (ISBN 0-87395-659-1); pap. 17.95 (ISBN 0-87395-660-5). State U NY Pr.

Sorties. James Dickey. LC 83-24421. 227p. 1984. pap. 9.95 (ISBN 0-8071-1140-6). La State U Pr.

Sortilege. Abdiasdo Nasciemento. 1980. pap. 2.95 (ISBN 0-88378-086-0). Third World.

Sortileges. Michel De Ghelderode. 279p. 1966. 9.95 (ISBN 0-686-56046-9). French & Eur.

Sortilegios. Maria R. Jaen. (Span.). 1984. pap. 10.00 (ISBN 84-398-148-52). Society Sp & Sp-Am.

Sorting. Henry Pluckrose. Ed. by FS Staff. (Knowabouts Ser.). (Illus.). 32p. 1988. 10.40 (ISBN 0-531-10548-2). Watts.

Sorting & Sequencing. Dana McMillan. 64p. (gr. k-2). 1985. 8.95 (ISBN 0-912107-34-0). Monday Morning Bks.

Sorting & Sort Systems. Harold Lorin. (Illus.). 480p. 1975. write for info. (ISBN 0-201-14453-0). Addison-Wesley.
Sorting It Out. Anne S. Perlman. LC 82-70744. 1982. 14.95 (ISBN 0-915604-72-8); pap. 6.95 (ISBN 0-915604-73-6). Carnegie-Mellon.
Sorting It Out with God. Jim Auer. 64p. 1982. pap. 1.95 (ISBN 0-89243-163-6). Liguori Pubns.
Sorting Life Out. Purgraski. LC 60-9573. 1978. 24.00x (ISBN 0-930004-00-0); free student packet, 36 pgs. C E M Comp.
Sorting Metaphors. Ricardo Pau-Llosa. 1983. pap. 6.95 (ISBN 0-938078-15-1). Anhinga Pr.
Sorting of Household Waste & Thermal Treatment of Waste. Ed. by M. P. Ferranti & G. L. Ferrero. (Illus.). xiv, 521p. 1985. 81.00 (ISBN 0-85334-382-9, Pub. by Elsevier Applied Sci England). Elsevier.
Sorting Out Buttons. T. Toomet. 48p. 1985. pap. 2.99 (ISBN 0-8285-3146-3, Pub. by Perioodika Tallinn). Imported Pubns.
Sorting Out Money Values & Student Packet of Ready-to-Be-Duplicated Worksheets. rev. ed. Carolyn B. Purgraski et al. LC 59-4503. (Sorting Life Out Ser.). 292p. 1981. tchr's. ed. 25.00 (ISBN 0-930004-02-7); P. 68. student packet avail. C E M Comp.
Sorting Out the Ownership Rights in Intellectual Property: A Guide to Practcal Counseling & Legal Representation. 214p. 1980. pap. 20.00 (ISBN 0-686-47988-2). Amer Bar Assn.
Sorts, Ontology, & Metaphor: The Semantics of Sortal Structure. Shalom Lappin. (Foundations of Communication Ser.). 173p. 1981. 38.00x (ISBN 3-11-008309-4). De Gruyter.
SOS at Midnight. Tompkins. 1985. 5.00 (ISBN 0-87259-034-8). Am Radio.
SOS for Teachers: Strategies of Self-Improvement. James D. Long & Robert L. Williams. LC 81-84078. (Illus.). 250p. 1982. pap. text ed. 12.95 (ISBN 0-916622-23-1). Princeton Bk Co.
SOS! Help for Parents. Lynn Clark. LC 85-16950. (Illus.). 240p. (Orig.). 1985. pap. 9.95 (ISBN 0-935111-16-6). Parents Pr Ky.
SOS: Save on Shopping Directory. 9th rev. ed. Iris Ellis. 1985. pap. 8.95 (ISBN 0-394-72809-2, Pub. by Villard Bks). Random.
SOS: Social Options for Singles How & Where to Meet People. Jane K. Thompson. 90p. 1983. 5.95. S O S.
Soslasno li c Evangelijem Dejstvoval i uchil Ljuter? N. I. Florinsky. 166p. 1975. pap. text ed. 6.00 (ISBN 0-317-30257-4). Holy Trinity.
Sosoki. Izumishi Kubosai Kinen Bijutsukan. (Illus.). 116p. 1986. 105.00x (ISBN 0-317-69200-3, Pub. by Han-Shan Tang Ltd). State Mutual Bk.
Sostoianie Sna. Alexei Tsvetkov. 115p. (Rus.). 1981. 18.50 (ISBN 0-88233-710-6); pap. 4.00 (ISBN 0-88233-711-4). Ardis Pubs.
Sot-Weed Factor. John Barth. LC 87-1399. 768p. 1987. pap. 9.95 (ISBN 0-385-24088-0, Anchor Pr). Doubleday.
Sotadic Zone. Richard F. Burton. LC 77-90796. 1977. Repr. lib. bdg. 12.50 (ISBN 0-89341-466-2). Longwood Pub Group.
Sotah, 1 vol. (Hebrew & Eng.). 15.00 (ISBN 0-910218-70-6). Bennet Pub.
Sotai: Balance & Health Through Natural Movement. Keizo Hashimoto & Yoshizaki Kawakami. (Illus.). 240p. 1983. pap. 12.95 (ISBN 0-87040-534-9). Japan Pubns USA.
Sotai Natural Exercise. Keizo Hashimoto. Tr. by Herman Aihara. (Illus.). 120p. (Orig.). 1981. pap. 8.50 (ISBN 0-918860-33-4). G Ohsawa.
Sotana de Juan Ruiz-Elementos Eclesiasticos en el Libro de Buen Amor. Julian A. Bueno. LC 81-84295. 166p. 1983. 17.00x (ISBN 0-938972-02-2). Spanish Lit Pubns.
Sotheby's Directory of Silver, 1600-1940. Vanessa Brett. LC 85-50360. (Illus.). 432p. 1986. 57.50 (ISBN 0-85667-193-2, Pub. by P Wilson Pubs). Sotheby Pubns.
Sotheby's International Price Guide: Antiques & Collectibles, 1985-1986. Ed. by John L. Marion. LC 85-15730. (Illus.). 688p. 1985. 25.00 (ISBN 0-86565-055-1); pap. 18.95 (ISBN 0-86565-060-8). Vendome.
Sotheby's International Price Guide: Antiques & Collectibles 1987-88. Ed. by John Marion. (Illus.). 700p. 1987. 35.00. Vendome.
Sotheby's International Price Guide: Antiques & Collectibles 1988-89. Ed. by John Marion. (Illus.). 700p. 1988. 35.00. Apollo.
Sotheby's International Price Guide, Vol. 4: 1988-89 Edition. Ed. by John L. Marion. LC 88-60430. (Illus.). 736p. 1988. 35.00 (ISBN 0-85667-359-5, Pub. by P Wilson Pubs). Sotheby Pubns.
Sotheby's International Price Guide 1986-87. Ed. by John Marion. 736p. 1986. pap. 22.95 (ISBN 0-86565-066-7); 35.00 (ISBN 0-86565-065-9). Vendome.
Sotheby's International Price Guide, 1987-88. Ed. by John Marion. (Illus.). 736p. 1987. pap. 25.00 (ISBN 0-317-66281-3). Vendome.
Sotheby's Price Guide: Antiques & Collectibles 1987-88. Ed. by John Marion. (Illus.). 688p. 35.00 (ISBN 0-317-55012-8). Apollo.
Sotheby's World Wine Encyclopedia: A Comprehensive Reference Guide to the Wines of the World. Tom Stevenson. (Illus.). 1988. 40.00 (ISBN 0-8212-1690-2). NYGS.
Sotira. Porphyrios Dikaois et al. (University Museum Monographs: No. 23). (Illus.). xiii, 252p. 1961. text ed. 30.00 (ISBN 0-934718-15-6). Univ Mus of U PA.
Soto. Marcel Joray & Jesus R. Soto. (Illus.). 276p. (Span. & Eng.). 1985. 145.00 (ISBN 0-8390-0341-2). Abner Schram Ltd.
Sots Art. Margarita Tupitsyn & John E. Bowlt. LC 86-42517. (Illus.). 60p. (Orig.). 1986. pap. 10.00 (ISBN 0-915557-54-1). New Mus Contemp Art.
Sotsass Associates. Ettore Sottsass et al. LC 87-27881. (Illus.). 256p. 1988. 45.00 (ISBN 0-8478-0892-0); pap. 29.95 (ISBN 0-8478-0893-9). Rizzoli Intl.
Sotsgorod: The Problem of Building Socialist Cities. Nikolai A. Miliutin. Tr. by Arthur Sprague from Rus. LC 73-13429. (Illus.). 143p. 1974. 37.50x (ISBN 0-262-13089-0). MIT Pr.
Sotto Voce (Poetry) Paul Tanaquil. 1923. 29.50x (ISBN 0-686-83777-0). Elliots Bks.
Souches et Racines. Julien Olivier. (Illus.). 175p. (Fr.). 1981. pap. text ed. 4.50 (ISBN 0-911409-09-2). Natl Mat Dev.
Soucie's Field Guide of Fishing Facts. Gary Soucie. (Illus.). 160p. 1988. pap. 8.95 (ISBN 0-671-66645-2, Fireside). S&S.
Soudan Francais. C. Monteil. LC 78-20138. (Collection de contes et de chansons populaires: Vol. 28). Repr. of 1905 ed. 21.50 (ISBN 0-404-60378-5). AMS Pr.
Soudan Francais: Contes Soudanaises. Charles Monteil. (Fr.). 1905. 20.00 (ISBN 0-8115-3048-5). Kraus Repr.
Souffle see Comedies et Actes Divers.
Souffles, Quiches, Mousses & the Random Egg. George Bradshaw. LC 78-156508. 1971. 11.45i (ISBN 0-06-010451-1, HarpT). Har-Row.
Souffrances et Bonheur du Chretien. Francois Mauriac. pap. 9.50 (ISBN 0-685-34305-7). French & Eur.
Souhern Ocean Atlas. A. L. Gordon et al. 291p. 1986. text ed. 195.00 (ISBN 90-6191-630-5, Pub. by A A Balkema). Brookfield Pub Co.
Soul Afire: Revelations of the Mystics. H. A. Reinhold. 1977. Repr. of 1944 ed. 30.00. Century Bookbindery.
Soul Aflame. Barbara Wood. 1988. pap. 4.95 (Onyx). NAL.
Soul After Death: Contemporary "After-Death" Experiences in the Light of the Orthodox Teaching on the Afterlife. 2nd, rev. ed. Hieromonk S. Rose. 287p. 1987. pap. 5.00 (ISBN 0-938635-04-2). St Herman AK.
Soul & Body. C. A. Meier. Ed. by Julia Butterfield et al. LC 85-50669. 351p. 1986. 29.95 (ISBN 0-932499-00-7); pap. 15.95 (ISBN 0-932499-01-5). Lapis Pr.
Soul & Body in Husserlian Phenomenology. Anna-Teresa Tymieniecka. 1983. lib. bdg. 59.00 (ISBN 90-277-1518-1, Pub. by Reidel Holland). Kluwer Academic.
Soul & Death. Erastus Evans. 1985. 10.00x (ISBN 0-317-62174-2, Guild of Pastoral Psych). State Mutual Bk.
Soul & Heritage of Japan Pictorial Encyclopedia. Gakken Staff. LC 87-80647. (Illus.). 136p. 1987. 29.95 (ISBN 0-87040-752-X). Japan Pubns USA.
Soul & Its Mechanism. Alice A. Bailey. 1971. 15.00 (ISBN 0-85330-015-1); pap. 7.00 1987 (ISBN 0-85330-115-8). Lucis.
Soul & Its Vestures. C. W. Leadbeater. 24p. 1983. pap. 1.50 (ISBN 0-918980-12-7). St Alban Pr.
Soul & Money. Hillman et al. LC 81-84495. 89p. (Orig.). 1982. pap. 9.50 (ISBN 0-88214-318-2). Spring Pubns.
Soul & Spirit. Jessie Penn-Lewis. 1962. pap. 3.50 (ISBN 0-87508-953-4). Chr Lit.
Soul & the Body. Martial Gueroult. Tr. by Roger Ariew from Fr. LC 83-14025. (Descartes' Philosophy Interpreted According to the Order of Reason Ser.: Vol. 2). 352p. (Orig.). 1985. 35.00x (ISBN 0-8166-1257-9); pap. 15.95 (ISBN 0-8166-1258-7). U of Minn Pr.
Soul & the Ethic. Ann R. Colton. 262p. 1965. 7.95 (ISBN 0-917187-07-5). A R C Pub.
Soul & the Structure of Being in Late Neoplatonism-Syrianus, Proclus & Simplicius. Ed. by H. J. Blumenthal & A. C. Lloyd. 104p. 1982. pap. text ed. 12.50x (ISBN 0-85323-404-3, Pub. by Liverpool U Pr). Humanities.
Soul As a Function of Relationship in Psychology & Religion. Faye Pye & B. A. Cantab. 1985. 10.00x (ISBN 0-317-62178-5, Guild of Pastoral Psych). State Mutual Bk.
Soul Brothers & Sister Lou. Kristin Hunter. (YA) (gr. 7 up). 1975. pap. 2.25 (ISBN 0-380-00686-3, 59717-9, Flare). Avon.
Soul Building Sermon Outlines. Russell E. Spray. (Dollar Sermon Library). 1977. pap. 2.50 (ISBN 0-8010-8118-1). Baker Bk.
Soul Butter & Hog Wash & Other Essays on the American West. Ed. by Thomas G. Alexander. LC 77-89974. (Charles Redd Monographs in Western History Ser.: No. 8). 1978. pap. 4.95 (ISBN 0-8425-1232-2). Brigham.
Soul Catcher. Frank Herbert. 256p. 1984. pap. 3.50 (ISBN 0-425-09141-4). Berkley Pub.
Soul Claiming. Jody Aliesan. LC 75-23822. (Haystack Ser). (Illus.). 76p. 1975. 6.00 (ISBN 0-913142-16-6); pap. 3.50 (ISBN 0-913142-15-8). Mulch Pr.
Soul Clap Hands & Sing. Paule Marshall. (Library of Contemporary Literature). 208p. 1988. pap. 7.95 (ISBN 0-88258-155-4). Howard U Pr.
Soul Clap Its Hands & Sing. Natalie Petesch. 200p. 1981. 20.00 (ISBN 0-89608-120-6); pap. 6.50 (ISBN 0-89608-119-2). South End Pr.
Soul Concepts of the Navaho. Berard Haile. 1964. pap. 6.50 (ISBN 0-686-32654-7). St Michaels.
Soul Consciousness. R. Swinburne Clymer. 1955. 6.95 (ISBN 0-686-00830-8). Philos Pub.
Soul Eater. K. W. Jeter. 320p. (Orig.). 1983. pap. 3.50 (ISBN 0-8125-2005-X, Dist. by Warner Pub Services & Saint Martin's Press). Tor Bks.
Soul Economy & Waldorf Education. Rudolf Steiner. 320p. (Orig.). pap. 20.00; 30.00 (ISBN 0-88010-139-3). Anthroposophic.
Soul Flame. Barbara Wood. LC 86-3893. 384p. 1987. 18.95 (ISBN 0-394-55571-6). Random.
Soul Flame. Barbara Wood. 1988. pap. 4.95 (ISBN 0-451-40066-6, Onyx). NAL.
Soul Flight. Emily Powell. LC 86-62447. 72p. 1986. pap. 7.95 (ISBN 0-938875-02-7). Pittenbruach Pr.
Soul Food. Tr. by Kenneth N. Taylor. 1973. pap. 5.95 (ISBN 0-8423-6100-6). Tyndale.
Soul Friend: The Practice of Christian Spirituality. Kenneth Leech. LC 79-2994. 272p. 1980. 15.45 (ISBN 0-06-065225-X, HarpR). Har-Row.
Soul Gallery. Albert Huffstickler. Ed. by Richard A. Spiegel. (Illus.). 38p. (Orig.). 1987. pap. 3.50 (ISBN 0-934776-06-7). Bard Pr.
Soul Game. John B. Gerald. 204p. (Orig.). 1980. pap. 10.00 (ISBN 0-941917-01-0). Gerald & Maas.
Soul Hunters. George Markstein. Ed. by Jonathan Gillett. 320p. 1987. 15.95 (ISBN 0-531-15033-X). Watts.
Soul Hunters. George Markstein. 416p. 1988. pap. 3.95 (ISBN 1-55817-062-6). Windsor NY.
Soul in Egyptian Metaphysics. Manly P. Hall. pap. 2.50 (ISBN 0-89314-355-3). Philos Res.
Soul in Exile: Lives of a Palestinian Revolutionary. Fawaz Turki. 288p. 1987. 26.00 (ISBN 0-85345-746-8); pap. 10.00 (ISBN 0-85345-747-6). Monthly Rev.
Soul in Paraphrase: Prayer & the Religious Affections. Don E. Saliers. 160p. 1980. 8.95 (ISBN 0-8164-0121-7, HarpR). Har-Row.
Soul in the Opera House. W. Calvin McCain. LC 82-229693. 80p. 1982. pap. 5.00 (ISBN 0-931680-02-6). Dunbar Pub.
Soul Making: The Desert Way of Spirituality. Alan Jones. LC 84-48222. 192p. 1985. 15.95 (ISBN 0-06-064182-7, HarpR). Har-Row.
Soul Mates. Tomval-Valtom. 96p. (Orig.). 1985. pap. 5.95 (ISBN 0-9615048-0-3). St Thomas Pub.
Soul Mates: An Illustrated Satire. Josh Volk. LC 88-90143. (Illus.). 224p. (Orig.). 1988. pap. 14.95 (ISBN 0-9620303-1-7). J Volk.
Soul Mates: The Facts & the Fallacies. Robert E. Birdsong. (Aquarian Academy Supplementary Lecture Ser.: No. 9). 22p. (Orig.). 1980. pap. 1.25 (ISBN 0-917108-32-9). Sirius Bks.
Soul Mending: Letters to Friends in Crisis. Joseph P. Bishop. 160p. 1986. pap. 8.95 (ISBN 0-8192-1379-9). Morehouse.
Soul Murder Case: A Confession of the Victim. Robert D. Pharr. 1975. pap. 3.45 (ISBN 0-380-00404-6, Equinox). Avon.
Soul Music. Bruce Culp. 48p. 1989. 7.95 (ISBN 0-89962-801-X). Todd & Honeywell.
Soul Music: Birth of a Sound in Black America. Michael Haralambos. (Quality Paperbacks Ser.). (Illus.). 188p. 1985. pap. 7.95 (ISBN 0-306-80246-5). Da Capo.
Soul of a Child. Edwin Bjorkman. LC 79-144883. (Literature Ser). 322p. 1972. Repr. of 1922 ed. 39.00x (ISBN 0-403-00869-7). Scholarly.
Soul of a New Machine. Tracy Kidder. 1981. 16.95 (ISBN 0-316-49170-5, Pub. by Atlantic Monthly Pr). Little.
Soul of a New Machine. Tracy Kidder. 304p. 1982. pap. 4.50 (ISBN 0-380-59931-7). Avon.
Soul of a People. 4th ed. Harold Fielding-Hall. LC 78-72436. Repr. of 1903 ed. 33.50 (ISBN 0-404-17295-4). AMS Pr.
Soul of a Tree. George Nakashima. 223p. 1981. 326.00x (ISBN 0-317-69108-2, Pub. by Han-Shan Tang Ltd). State Mutual Bk.
Soul of a Tree: A Woodworker's Reflections. George Nakashima. LC 81-80655. (Illus.). 221p. 1981. 65.00 (ISBN 0-87011-482-4). Kodansha.
Soul of a Tree: A Woodworker's Reflections. George Nakashima. 224p. 1988. pap. 34.95 (ISBN 0-87011-903-6). Kodansha.
Soul of Ambiguity: The Tiger in Southeast Asia. Robert Wessing. (Special Report Series, Center for Southeast Asian Studies, Northern Illinois Univ.: No. 24). vi, 148p. (Orig.). 1987. pap. 9.50x (ISBN 0-318-22372-4, Ctr SE Asian Stud). Cellar.
Soul of an Immigrant. Constantine M. Panunzio. LC 69-18787. (American Immigration Collection Ser., No. 1). 1969. Repr. of 1928 ed. 13.00 (ISBN 0-405-00535-0). Ayer Co Pubs.
Soul of Ancient Mexico. Edmond B. Szekely. (Illus.). 136p. 1968. pap. 7.50 (ISBN 0-89564-027-9). IBS Intl.
Soul of Christmas. Helen King. (Illus.). 32p. (gr. k-4). 1972. 4.50 (ISBN 0-87485-057-6). Johnson Chi.
Soul of CP-M: How to Use the Hidden Power of Your CP-M System. Michael Waite & Lafore. LC 83-61059. 400p. 1983. pap. 19.95 (ISBN 0-672-22030-X, 22030). Sams.
Soul of Denmark. S. Desmond. 1977. lib. bdg. 59.95 (ISBN 0-8490-2632-6). Gordon Pr.
Soul of Dickens. Walter Crotch. LC 73-21705. (Studies in Dickens, No. 52). 1974. lib. bdg. 49.95x (ISBN 0-8383-1763-4). Haskell.
Soul of Dickens. Walter W. Crotch. 1973. Repr. of 1916 ed. 25.00 (ISBN 0-8274-0057-8). R West.
Soul of Fire. John Uhlmann & Peggy Heinrich. 170p. 1987. text ed. 19.95 (ISBN 0-317-58721-8). Exposition-Phoenix.
Soul of Fire: A Biography of Mary McSwiney. Charlotte H. Fallon. 200p. 1986. pap. 15.95 (ISBN 0-85342-797-6, Pub. by Mercier Pr Ireland). Irish Bks Media.
Soul of India. Satyavrata R. Patel. LC 74-901610. 232p. 1974. 13.25 (ISBN 0-89684-453-6). Orient Bk Dist.
Soul of Japan. Elie Faure. lib. bdg. 59.95 (ISBN 0-8490-1089-6). Gordon Pr.
Soul of John Brown. Stephen Graham. LC 70-109915. Repr. of 1920 ed. 25.00 (ISBN 0-404-00162-9). AMS Pr.
Soul of Liberty: The Universal Ethic of Freedom & Human Rights. Fred E. Foldvary. LC 79-56782. (Illus.). 330p. 1980. pap. 6.75 (ISBN 0-9603872-1-8). Gutenberg.
Soul of Lilith. Marie Corelli. (Illus.). pap. 4.95 (ISBN 0-910122-05-9). Amherst Pr.
Soul of London. Ford Madox Ford. LC 72-91. (English Literature Ser.: No. 33). 1972. Repr. of 1911 ed. lib. bdg. 39.95x (ISBN 0-8383-1407-4). Haskell.
Soul of Man. Paul Carus. 59.95 (ISBN 0-8490-1090-X). Gordon Pr.
Soul of Man under Socialism. Oscar Wilde. (Illus.). 64p. lib. bdg. 22.95 (ISBN 0-88286-057-7); pap. 3.95 (ISBN 0-88286-056-9). C H Kerr.
Soul of Man under Socialism. Oscar Wilde. (Orig.). 1985. pap. 1.50 (ISBN 0-88211-012-8, Pub. by Journeyman Pr England). Riverrun NY.
Soul of Mbira: Music & Traditions of the Shona People of Zimbabwe. Paul F. Berliner. LC 76-24578. (Perspectives on Southern Africa Ser.: No. 26). 1978. 36.50x (ISBN 0-520-03315-9); pap. 8.95x (ISBN 0-520-04268-9). U of Cal Pr.
Soul of Modern Economic Man: Ideas of Self-Interest, Thomas Hobbes to Adam Smith. Milton L. Myers. LC 82-23790. 160p. 1983. lib. bdg. 17.50x (ISBN 0-226-55448-1). U of Chicago Pr.
Soul of Modern Economic Man: Ideas of Self-Interest, Thomas Hobbes to Adam Smith. Milton L. Myers. LC 82-23790. x, 148p. 1985. pap. 6.95x (ISBN 0-226-55450-3). U of Chicago Pr.
Soul of Modern Poetry. R. H. Strachan. LC 70-113348. 1970. Repr. of 1922 ed. 23.00x (ISBN 0-8046-1054-1, Pub. by Kennikat). Assoc Faculty Pr.
Soul of My Soul: Reflections from a Life of Prayer. Catherine De Hueck Doherty. LC 85-72771. 128p. (Orig.). 1985. pap. 4.95 (ISBN 0-87793-298-0). Ave Maria.
Soul of Nigeria. Isaac O. Delano. LC 74-15026. (Illus.). Repr. of 1937 ed. 35.00 (ISBN 0-404-12024-5). AMS Pr.
Soul of Nigeria. Isaac O. Delano. 1937. 26.00 (ISBN 0-8115-3063-9). Kraus Repr.
Soul of Osiris. Aleister Crowley. 1973. lib. bdg. 79.95 (ISBN 0-87968-177-2). Krishna Pr.
Soul of Samuel Pepys. Gamaliel Bradford. LC 75-85993. 1969. Repr. of 1924 ed. 23.50x (ISBN 0-8046-0603-X, Pub. by Kennikat). Assoc Faculty Pr.
Soul of Soil: A Guide to Ecological Soil Management. 2nd ed. Grace Gershuny & Joseph Smillie. (Illus.). 125p. (Orig.). 1986. pap. 6.50 (ISBN 0-9616496-0-7). GAIA Services.
Soul of the Anthology. William C. Lawton. 1973. Repr. of 1923 ed. 25.00 (ISBN 0-8274-0152-3). R West.
Soul of the Apostolate. Jean-Baptiste Chautard. 1977. pap. 6.00 (ISBN 0-89555-031-8). TAN Bks Pubs.
Soul of the Black Preacher. Johnson. 4.95. Pilgrim NY.
Soul of the Desert. Aleister Crowley. LC 74-10890. 1976. 9.00 (ISBN 0-913576-08-5, Dist. by Teitan Pr). Thelema Pubns.
Soul of the Far East. Percival Lowell. 1973. Repr. of 1888 ed. 35.00 (ISBN 0-8274-1046-8). R West.
Soul of the Ghost Moth: Paths of a Naturalist. Philip S. Callahan. (Illus.). 1980. 10.00 (ISBN 0-8159-6840-X). Devin.
Soul of the Indian: An Interpretation. Charles A. Eastman. LC 79-26355. xvi, 170p. 1980. pap. 5.95 (ISBN 0-8032-6701-0, BB 735, Bison). U of Nebr Pr.
Soul of the Macintosh. The Waite Group. Date not set. write for info. S&S.
Soul of the Night: An Astronomical Pilgrimage. Chet Raymo. LC 85-6480. (Illus.). 208p. 1985. 15.95 (ISBN 0-13-822883-3). P-H.
Soul of the Night: An Astronomical Pilgrimage. Chet Raymo. Date not set. write for info. S&S.
Soul of the Tiger: Searching for Nature's Answers in Exotic Southeast Asia. Jeffrey A McNeely & Paul S. Wachtel. LC 87-13687. (Illus.). 336p. 1988. pap. 19.95 (ISBN 0-385-24225-5). Doubleday.

Sound Engineer Home Study Course: Basic. Sherman Keene. 1986. 145.00 (ISBN 0-942080-09-2). SKE Pub.

Sound Engineer Home Study Course: Intermediate. Sherman Keene. 1986. 145.00 (ISBN 0-942080-10-6). SKE Pub.

Sound Eternal, 2 vols. Richard Pugsley & Betty C. Pugsley. 1987. Set. pap. 21.95 (ISBN 0-941478-92-0); Vol. 1. pap. 9.95 (ISBN 0-941478-50-5); Vol. 2. pap. 12.95 (ISBN 0-941478-91-2). Paraclete Pr.

Sound Evidence. June Thomson. 295p. 1986. pap. 10.95x (ISBN 0-8161-3986-5, Large Print Bks). G K Hall.

Sound Experiments. Ray Broekel. LC 82-17869. (New True Bks.). (Illus.). 48p. (gr. k-4). 1983. PLB 12.60 (ISBN 0-516-01686-5); pap. 3.95 (ISBN 0-516-41686-3). Childrens.

Sound Friendships: The Story of Willa & Her Hearing Ear Dog. Elizabeth Yates. LC 86-29110. 96p. 1987. 12.95 (ISBN 0-88150-080-1). Countryman.

Sound Friendships: The Story of Willa & Her Hearing Ear Dog. 2nd ed. Elizabeth Yates. 96p. (YA) (gr. 8 up). 1988. pap. 7.95 (ISBN 0-88150-081-X). Countryman.

Sound Health: Music & Sounds That Make Us Whole. Steven Halpern & Savary Louis. LC 84-48219. 192p. (Orig.). 1985. pap. 9.95 (ISBN 0-06-063671-8, HarpR). Har-Row.

Sound Heritage: Voices from British Columbia. Saeko Usukawa. (Illus.). 276p. 1987. 16.95 (ISBN 0-88894-443-8, Pub. by Douglas & McIntyre-Grounwood). Salem Hse Pubs.

Sound Ideas: Automated Accounting for the Microcomputer. 2nd ed. Dale H. Klooster & Warren W. Allen. 1987. write for info. (ISBN 0-538-01373-7, A36). SW Pub.

Sound in the Theatre. rev. ed. Harold Burris-Meyer et al. LC 78-66064. 1979. 14.95 (ISBN 0-87830-157-7). Theatre Arts.

Sound Investment. Sonia Sanchez. LC 74-75591. 1980. pap. 2.95. Third World.

Sound It Out. Bernetta Gresko. (Illus.). 75p. (gr. 2-8). 1985. pap. 8.95 (ISBN 0-939755-10-6). Sunset Prods.

Sound Judgment. J. P. Swain. (Illus.). 1987. pap. 15.00 (ISBN 0-317-66567-7). San Francisco Pr.

Sound Ladder Game. Genevieve Arnold. 1973. text ed. 3.00 (ISBN 0-686-09404-2). Expression.

Sound Language & Awareness Psychology. J. Jones. LC 85-90320. (Illus.). 236p. (Orig.). 1985. pap. 12.50 (ISBN 0-9615111-1-7). Sandbird Pub.

Sound-Learning in the First Two Years see Speech Development of a Bilingual Child.

Sound: Magnetic Sound Recording for Motion Pictures. Ed. by Eastman Kodak Company. LC 77-87984. (Illus.). 1977. pap. text ed. 6.25 (ISBN 0-87985-202-X, S-75). Eastman Kodak.

Sound, Man & Building. L. H. Schaudinischky. (Illus.). xv, 413p. 1976. 77.50 (ISBN 0-85334-655-0, Pub. by Elsevier Applied Sci England). Elsevier.

Sound Medicine: Healing with Music, Voice, & Song. Laeh M. Garfield. 192p. 1987. 8.95 (ISBN 0-89087-483-2). Celestial Arts.

Sound Mind: Or Contributions to the Natural History & Physiology of the Human Intellect. John Haslam. LC 78-72797. Repr. of 1819 ed. 21.50 (ISBN 0-404-60860-4). AMS Pr.

Sound, Noise & Vibration Control. 2nd ed. Lyle F. Yerges. LC 83-11303. 272p. 1983. Repr. of 1978 ed. text ed. 21.00 (ISBN 0-89874-654-X). Krieger.

Sound of American Literature a Century Ago. C. Bode. (Sarah Tryphena Phillips Lectures in American Literature & History). 1961. pap. 5.50 (ISBN 0-902732-22-6, Pub. by British Acad). Longwood Pub Group.

Sound of Bells: The Episcopal Church in South Florida, 1892-1969. Joseph D. Cushman, Jr. LC 75-30946. (Illus.). 1976. 15.00 (ISBN 0-8130-0518-3). U Presses Fla.

Sound of Breathing. Adelaide Blomfield. 1977. 6.25 (ISBN 0-941490-15-7). Solo Pr.

Sound of Chariots. Mollie Hunter. LC 72-76523. 256p. (gr. 7 up). 1972. PLB 12.89 (ISBN 0-06-022669-2); 12.70i (ISBN 0-06-022668-4). HarpJ.

Sound of Chariots. Mollie Hunter. LC 72-76523. (Trophy Bk.). 256p. (gr. 5-9). 1988. pap. 3.95 (ISBN 0-06-440235-5, Trophy). HarpJ.

Sound of Coaches. Leon Garfield. (Illus.). 240p. (gr. 7 up). 1985. pap. 2.95 (ISBN 0-14-030961-6, Puffin). Penguin.

Sound of Detection: Ellery Queen's Adventures in Radio. Francis M. Nevins, Jr. & Ray Stanich. (Illus.). viii, 109p. (Orig.). 1983. pap. 6.95 (ISBN 0-941028-01-1). Brownstone Bks.

Sound of Detection: Ellery Queen's Adventures in Radio. Francis M. Nevins, Jr. & Ray Stanich. LC 85-25462. 109p. 1985. Repr. of 1983 ed. lib. bdg. 19.95x (ISBN 0-89370-556-X). Borgo Pr.

Sound of Drums. Spencer B. King. LC 84-6631. xii, 544p. 1984. 32.95 (ISBN 0-86554-107-8, MUP/H112). Mercer Univ Pr.

Sound of English: A Bibliography of Language Recordings. Michael D. Linn & Maarit-Hannele Zuber. 84p. (Orig.). 1984. pap. 7.00 (ISBN 0-8141-4570-1). NCTE.

Sound of Greek: Studies in the Greek Theory & Practice of Euphony. W. B. Stanford. (Sather Classical Lectures: No. 38). (YA) (gr. 9 up). 1967. incl. 7" record 42.00x (ISBN 0-520-01204-6). U of Cal Pr.

Sound of Gunfire. Frank Bonham. 192p. 1984. pap. 2.25 (ISBN 0-441-77596-9). Ace Bks.

Sound of History: Songs & Social Comment. Roy Palmer. (Illus.). 376p. 1988. 39.95 (ISBN 0-19-215890-2). Oxford U Pr.

Sound of Horns. David Lyon. LC 82-24968. 63p. 1984. pap. 4.95 (ISBN 0-934332-38-X). L'Epervier Pr.

Sound of Leadership: Presidential Communication in the Modern Age. Roderick P. Hart. LC 87-5863. (Illus.). 296p. 1987. 39.95x (ISBN 0-226-31812-5); pap. 14.95 (ISBN 0-226-31813-3). U of Chicago Pr.

Sound of Light. Irina Starr. LC 69-20335. 1977. pap. 3.50 (ISBN 0-87516-220-7). DeVorss.

Sound of Loneliness Is Painful Like a Dark Corner. 2nd ed. Eileen A. Loos et al. (Illus.). 206p. Date not set. pap. 5.95 (ISBN 0-9616160-2-4). Bench Pr NY.

Sound of Midnight. Charles L. Grant. 256p. 1987. pap. 3.95 (ISBN 0-8125-1864-0, Dist. by St Martin's Pr & Warner Pub Servs). Tor Bks.

Sound of Mountain Water. Wallace Stegner. LC 85-8568. 286p. 1985. pap. 7.50 (ISBN 0-8032-9158-2, BB 946, Bison). U of Nebr Pr.

Sound of Music. Rodgers & Hammerstein. 1960. 12.95 (ISBN 0-394-40724-5). Random.

Sound of One Hand Clapping. Bhagwan Shree Rajneesh. Ed. by Ma Yoga Pratima. (Initiation Talks Ser.). (Illus.). 632p. (Orig.). 1981. pap. 8.95 (ISBN 0-88050-633-4). Chidvilas Inc.

Sound of One Mind Thinking. Eugene M. Schwartz. LC 80-27128. (Illus., Orig.). 1981. pap. 6.95 (ISBN 0-89407-040-1). Strawberry Hill.

Sound of Our Own Voices: Women's Study Clubs, 1860-1900. Theodora P. Martin. LC 87-47535. (Illus.). 256p. 1987. 25.00 (ISBN 0-8070-6710-5). Beacon Pr.

Sound of Our Own Voices: Women's Study Clubs, 1860-1910. Theodora P. Martin. LC 87-47535. (Illus.). 272p. 1989. pap. 10.95 (ISBN 0-8070-6749-0). Beacon Pr.

Sound of Running Feet. Josephine Lawrence. LC 74-22791. Repr. of 1937 ed. 22.50 (ISBN 0-404-58445-4). AMS Pr.

Sound of Running Water. Bhagwan Shree Rajneesh. Ed. by Ma Prem Asha. LC 83-180798. (Photobiography Ser.). (Illus.). 564p. 1980. 100.00 (ISBN 0-88050-134-0). Chidvilas Inc.

Sound of Shadows. Elma W. Foster. LC 71-179822. (New Poetry Ser.). Repr. of 1960 ed. 16.00 (ISBN 0-404-56022-9). AMS Pr.

Sound of Silence: Moving with T'ai Chi. Carol R. Murphy. LC 75-41548. (Orig.). 1976. pap. 2.50x (ISBN 0-87574-205-X, 205). Pendle Hill.

Sound of Solitude. Rod McKuen. LC 83-47554. (Illus.). 192p. 1983. 10.95i (ISBN 0-06-015199-4, HarpT). Har-Row.

Sound of Solitude. Date not set. price not set (ISBN 0-937571-09-1). Trudco Pub.

Sound of Strangers: Musical Culture, Acculturation, & the Post-Civil War Ethnic American. Nicholas Tawa. LC 81-21235. 318p. 1982. 24.00 (ISBN 0-8108-1504-4). Scarecrow.

Sound of Surprise. Whitney Balliett. LC 77-17852. (Roots of Jazz Ser.). 1978. Repr. of 1961 ed. lib. bdg. 29.50 (ISBN 0-306-77543-3). Da Capo.

Sound of the Bell. Penny S. Anderson. LC 83-7453. (Illus.). 32p. (gr. 3-4). 1983. PLB 4.95 (ISBN 0-89693-217-6). Dandelion Hse.

Sound of the City: Rise of Rock and Roll. rev. ed. Charlie Gillett. LC 84-42671. 528p. 1984. pap. 7.95 (ISBN 0-394-72638-3). Pantheon.

Sound of the Flute: The Cuban Impact. Raoul J. Fajardo. (Illus.). 216p. (Orig.). 1981. pap. 5.00x (ISBN 0-940774-00-3). Pulsante Assn News.

Sound of the Fortepiano: A Discography of Music on Early Pianos. Ann P. Basart. LC 85-1660. (Fallen Leaf Reference Books In Music: No. 2). xiv, 472p. (Orig.). 1986. pap. 29.95 (ISBN 0-914913-01-8). Fallen Leaf.

Sound of the Mountain. Yasunari Kawabata. Tr. by Edward G. Seidensticker from Japanese. (Perigee Japanese Library). 288p. 1981. pap. 5.95 (ISBN 0-399-50527-X, Perigee). Putnam Pub Group.

Sound of the Trumpet. Grace L. Hill. (Grace Livingston Hill Classic Ser.). 216p. 1984. Repr. of 1943 ed. 8.95 (ISBN 0-8007-1212-9). Revell.

Sound of the Trumpets. George Reid. (Horizon Ser.). 224p. 1981. 10.95 (ISBN 0-8127-0328-6); pap. write for info. (ISBN 0-8127-0321-9). Review & Herald.

Sound of the Week. Sally Barrett. (gr. k-4). 1980. 9.95 (ISBN 0-916456-63-3, GA 184). Good Apple.

Sound of Two Hands Clapping. Kenneth Tynan. LC 81-22148. (Quality Paperbacks Ser.). 256p. 1982. pap. 7.95 (ISBN 0-306-80164-7). Da Capo.

Sound of Waves. Yukio Mishima. 1956. 11.45 (ISBN 0-394-44629-1). Knopf.

Sound of Waves. Yukio Mishima. Tr. by Meredith Weatherby. (The Perigee Japanese Library). 192p. 1981. pap. 6.95 (ISBN 0-399-50487-7, Perigee). Putnam Pub Group.

Sound of Wings. Spencer Dunmore. 352p. 1988. pap. 3.95 (ISBN 0-8125-1714-8, Dist. by St Martin's Pr & Warner Pub Servs). Tor Bks.

Sound of Wonder: Interviews from "The Science Fiction Radio Show", 2 vols. Daryl Lane. Ed. by Daryl Lane & William Vernon. LC 84-42818. (Illus.). 1985. pap. 20.00 ea. Vol. 1, 216pgs (ISBN 0-89774-175-7). Vol. 2, 208pgs (ISBN 0-89774-233-8). Oryx Pr.

Sound Off! American Military Women Speak Out. Dorothy Schneider & Carl J. Schneider. 260p. 1988. 18.95 (ISBN 0-525-24589-8). Dutton.

Sound Pattern of Hungarian. Robert M. Vago. 150p. 1980. pap. text ed. 8.95 (ISBN 0-87840-177-6). Georgetown U Pr.

Sound Pattern of Russian: A Linguistic & Acoustical Investigation. Morris Halle. (D a C S R Ser: No. 1). 1971. Repr. of 1959 ed. text ed. 30.50x (ISBN 0-686-22395-0). Mouton.

Sound Patterns in Second Language Acquisition. Ed. by A. James & J. Leather. (Studies on Language Acquisition). iv, 250p. 1987. pap. write for info. (ISBN 90-6765-307-1). Foris Pubns.

Sound Pleasure: A Prelude to Active Listening. Donald Ivey. LC 75-30287. (Illus., Orig.). 1977. pap. text ed. 15.00 (ISBN 0-02-870900-4); record package 15.00 (ISBN 0-02-870870-9). Schirmer Bks.

Sound Pleasure: A Prelude to Active Listening. 2nd ed. Donald Ivey. 490p. 1985. pap. 18.95 (ISBN 0-02-872270-1). Macmillan.

Sound Production- Technical Notes for the Non-Technician. Michael Roberts. (Monographs on Communication Technology & Utilization). (Illus.). 178p. 1986. 9.75 (ISBN 92-3-102299-7, U1505, UNESCO). UNIPUB.

Sound Propagation in Stratified Fluids. C. H. Wilcox. (Applied Mathematical Sciences Ser.: Vol. 50). ix, 198p. 1984. pap. 24.00 (ISBN 0-387-90986-9). Springer-Verlag.

Sound Propagation in the Sea. R. J Urick. LC 82-81923. 272p. 1982. 28.95 (ISBN 0-932146-08-2). Peninsula CA.

Sound Recording & Reproduction. Glyn Alkin. LC 80-41481. (Illus.). 216p. 1987. pap. 16.50 (ISBN 0-240-51273-1). Focal Pr.

Sound Recording Practice: A Handbook Compiled by The Association of Professional Recording Studios. 3rd ed. Ed. by John Borwick. (Illus.). 576p. 1987. 65.00 (ISBN 0-19-311927-7). Oxford U Pr.

Sound Scriptural Outlines, No. 3. Wade H. Horton. 1977. 7.25 (ISBN 0-87148-781-0); pap. 6.25 (ISBN 0-87148-780-2). Pathway Pr.

Sound Scriptural Sermon Outlines, No. 4. Wade H. Horton. 1979. 7.95 (ISBN 0-87148-783-7); pap. 6.95 (ISBN 0-87148-784-5). Pathway Pr.

Sound Scriptural Sermon Outlines, No. 5. Wade H. Horton. 1982. text ed. 7.95 (ISBN 0-87148-799-3); pap. 6.95 (ISBN 0-87148-800-0). Pathway Pr.

Sound Scriptural Sermon Outlines, No. 6. Wade H. Horton. 1984. text ed. 7.95 (ISBN 0-87148-806-X); pap. text ed. 6.95 (ISBN 0-87148-807-8). Pathway Pr.

Sound Scriptural Sermon Outlines, No. 2. Wade H. Horton. 1974. 7.25 (ISBN 0-87148-769-1); pap. 6.25 (ISBN 0-87148-770-5). Pathway Pr.

Sound Sex & the Aging Heart: Sex in the Mid & Later Years with Special Reference to Cardiac Problems. Lee Scheingold & Nathaniel N. Wagner. LC 74-662. (Illus.). 168p. 1974. 26.95 (ISBN 0-87705-155-0). Human Sci Pr.

Sound-Shadows of the New World. Ved Mehta. LC 85-5045. 1986. 17.95 (ISBN 0-393-02225-0). Norton.

Sound-Shadows of the New World. Ved Mehta. 1987. pap. 8.95 (ISBN 0-393-30437-X). Norton.

Sound Shape of Language. Roman Jakobson & Linda Waugh. LC 78-19552. pap. 80.00 (ISBN 0-317-27826-6, 2056041). Bks Demand UMI.

Sound, Sign & Meaning: Quinquagenary of the Prague Linguistic Circle. Ed. by Ladislav Matejka. (Michigan Slavic Contributions Ser.: No. 6). 1978. 25.00 (ISBN 0-930042-26-3). Mich Slavic Pubns.

Sound Skill Builder: Use with Sure Steps to Reading & Spelling, 3 bks. Florence W. Blank & Carolyn W. Guertin. Incl. Bk. 1. price not set (ISBN 0-916720-04-7); Bk. 2. price not set (ISBN 0-916720-05-5); Bk. 3. price not set (ISBN 0-916720-06-3). (gr. 1-7). Date not set. Weiss Pub.

Sound Sleeping in the Neighborhood. Jerry Van Amerongen. 1988. pap. 7.95 (ISBN 0-8362-1802-7). Andrews & McMeel.

Sound: Space. Bernhard Leitner. LC 77-93954. 109p. 1978. pap. 25.00x usa (ISBN 0-8147-4983-6). NYU Pr.

Sound Structure in Music. Robert Erickson. LC 72-9352. (Illus.). 1975. 35.00x (ISBN 0-520-02376-5). U of Cal Pr.

Sound, Structures, & Their Interactions. 2nd ed. Miguel C. Junger & David Feit. (Illus.). 493p. 1986. text ed. 45.00x (ISBN 0-262-10034-7). MIT Pr.

Sound Structures: Studies for Antonie Cohen. Ed. by M. Van der Broecke & V. J. Van Heuven. (Publications in Language Sciences). xxvi, 318p. 1983. write for info. (ISBN 90-70176-18-1); pap. write for info. (ISBN 90-70176-93-9). Foris Pubns.

Sound Studios: An Introductory Bibliography. Mary Vance. (Architecture Ser.: A 1649). 7p. 1986. 3.00 (ISBN 0-89028-979-4). Vance Biblios.

Sound System Engineering. 2nd ed. Davis & Davis. 688p. 1986. 39.95 (ISBN 0-672-21857-7). Sams.

Sound System of French. Jean Casagrande. 256p. 1984. lexotone 19.95 (ISBN 0-87840-085-0). Georgetown U Pr.

Sound Systems. Donald Aldous. 1984. lib. bdg. 10.90 (ISBN 0-531-09224-0, Warwick). Watts.

Sound the Charge. Richard Weingardt. LC 78-59321. (Illus.). 184p. (gr. 6-12). 9.95 (ISBN 0-932446-00-0); pap. 4.95 (ISBN 0-932446-01-9). Jacqueline Enter.

Sound the Retreat. Simon Raven. 224p. 1986. 14.95 (ISBN 0-8253-0343-5). Beaufort Bks NY.

Sound the Shofar: The Story & Meaning of Rosh HaShanah & Yom Kippur. Miriam Chaikin. LC 86-2651. (Illus.). 96p. (gr. 3-7). 1986. 13.95 (ISBN 0-89919-373-0, Pub. by Clarion); pap. 4.95 (ISBN 0-89919-427-3, Pub. by Clarion). Ticknor & Fields.

Sound Thinking - Basic Learning, the Making & Sharing of Music. Catherine H. Kiernan. 1987. 9.95 (ISBN 0-8062-2238-7). Carlton.

Sound Transmission Through a Fluctuating Ocean. Ed. by S. M. Flatte. LC 77-88676. (Cambridge Monographs on Mechanics & Applied Mathematics). (Illus.). 1979. 67.50 (ISBN 0-521-21940-X). Cambridge U Pr.

Sound Waves. David Colley. 240p. 1985. 14.95 (ISBN 0-312-74607-5). St Martin.

Sound Waves in Solids. H. F. Pollard. 1977. 33.00x (ISBN 0-85086-053-9, NO.2933, Pub. by Pion England). Routledge Chapman & Hall.

Sounder. William H. Armstrong. LC 70-85030. (Illus.). 128p. (YA) (gr. 6 up). 1969. 12.70 (ISBN 0-06-020143-6); PLB 12.89 (ISBN 0-06-020144-4). HarpJ.

Sounder. William H. Armstrong. 1969. pap. 3.95 (ISBN 0-06-080379-7, P379, PL). Har-Row.

Sounder. William H. Armstrong. LC 70-85030. (Trophy I Can Read Bks.). (Illus.). 116p. (gr. 6 up). 1972. pap. 2.95 (ISBN 0-06-440020-4, Trophy). HarpJ.

Sounder. William H. Armstrong. (Illus.). 99p. (gr. 2-6). 1987. Repr. of 1969 ed. lib. bdg. 12.95 (ISBN 1-55736-003-0). ABC-Clio.

Sounder. William H. Armstrong. 116p. (YA) (gr. 7 up). pap. 2.50 (ISBN 0-590-40212-9); Teaching Guide. 1.25 (ISBN 0-590-40905-0). Scholastic Inc.

Sounding. Hank Searls. LC 81-69190. 369p. 1982. 13.00 (ISBN 0-394-52471-3). Random.

Sounding. Hank Searls. 288p. (Orig.). 1985. pap. 3.50 (ISBN 0-345-32526-5). Ballantine.

Sounding of Storytellers. John R. Townsend. LC 79-2418. 1979. 15.25 (ISBN 0-397-31882-0). Har-Row.

Sounding of the Trumpet. Frances J. Roberts. 1966. 2.95 (ISBN 0-932814-24-7). Kings Farspan.

Sounding Right. Robbins Burling. 160p. 1982. pap. text ed. 14.50 (ISBN 0-88377-216-7). Newbury Hse.

Sounding Rocket Conference, 4th: Proceedings, 1982. 1982. 50.00 (ISBN 0-317-06667-6). AIAA.

Sounding Rockets, Balloons, & Related Space Systems Confrence 7th Proceedings. American Institute of Aeronautics & Astronautics Staff. 1986. 60.00 (ISBN 0-317-55304-6). AIAA.

Sounding the Territory. Laurel Goldman. LC 81-12409. 320p. 1982. 13.00 (ISBN 0-394-51935-3). Knopf.

Sounding Words with Roy & Joy. Betty Donatelli. (Happy Learning Ser.). (Illus.). 11p. (Orig.). (gr. k-2). 1984. pap. 1.00 (ISBN 0-912981-06-7). Hse Bon Giovanni.

Soundings. Ed. by Carol Spelius. 240p. 1985. pap. 7.95 (ISBN 0-317-60866-5). Lake Shore Pub.

Soundings. Quincy Troupe. 1988. 14.95 (ISBN 0-86316-002-6); pap. 8.95 (ISBN 0-86316-102-2). Writers & Readers.

Soundings: A Thematic Guide for Daily Scripture Prayer. rev. ed. Chris Aridas. 200p. 1988. pap. 4.95 (ISBN 0-914544-71-3). Living Flame Pr.

Soundings at Tell Fakhariyah. Calvin W. McEwan et al. LC 57-11216. (Oriental Institute Pubns. Ser: No. 79). (Illus.). 1958. 40.00x (ISBN 0-226-62180-4, OIP79). U of Chicago Pr.

Soundings in Tibetan Civilization. Barbara N. Aziz & M. Kapstein. 1986. 32.00x (ISBN 0-8364-1587-6, Pub. by Manohar India). South Asia Bks.

Soundings: Music in the Twentieth Century. Glenn Watkins. (Illus.). 728p. 1987. 26.00 (ISBN 0-317-66989-3). Schirmer Bks.

Soundings: Psychohistorical & Psycholiterary. Rudolph Binion. 164p. 1981. 19.95 (ISBN 0-914434-16-0); pap. 9.95 (ISBN 0-914434-17-9). Psychohistory Pr.

Soundless Music of Life. Thomas Hora. (Discourses in Metapsychiatry Ser.). 48p. 1983. pap. 3.95 (ISBN 0-913105-04-X). PAGL Pr.

Soundpieces: Interviews with American Composers. Cole Gagne & Tracy Caras. LC 81-13520. (Illus.). 436p. 1982. 32.50 (ISBN 0-8108-1474-9). Scarecrow.

Sounds. Wassily Kandinsky. Tr. by Elizabeth R. Napier from Ger. LC 80-6211. (Illus.). 144p. 39.00t (ISBN 0-300-02510-6); pap. 14.95 (ISBN 0-300-02664-1). Yale U Pr.

Sounds! J. Douglas Lee. LC 85-25197. (Bright Idea Bks.). (Illus.). 48p. (gr. 1-3). 1985. PLB 10.95 (ISBN 0-918831-73-3). Stevens Inc.

Sounds All Around. Joy T. Friedman. LC 80-83935. Orig. Title: Look Around & Listen. (Illus.). 80p. (gr. k-2). 1981. PLB 10.15 (ISBN 0-448-13945-6, G&D); pap. 3.95 (ISBN 0-448-14755-6). Putnam Pub Group.

Sounds All Around, No. 26-32. Jane B. Moncure. LC 82-4516. (Five Senses Ser.). (Illus.). 32p. (ps-3). 1982. PLB 11.93 (ISBN 0-516-03252-6); pap. 2.95 (ISBN 0-516-43252-4). Childrens.

Sounds & Alphabet of Czech with Notes. D. J. Hunns. 1986. 49.00x (Pub. by Drake Educ Assocs). State Mutual Bk.

Sounds & Alphabet of Polish with Notes. D. J. Hunns. 1986. 49.00x (Pub. by Drake Educ Assocs). State Mutual Bk.

Sounds & Alphabet of Serbo-Croatian with Notes. D. J. Hunns. 1986. 49.00x (Pub. by Drake Educ Assocs). State Mutual Bk.

Sounds & History of the German Language. E. Prokosch. 1979. Repr. of 1916 ed. lib. bdg. 30.00 (ISBN 0-8495-4352-5). Arden Lib.

Sounds & Language: A Work-Play Aproach. Barbara Frimmer. 224p. 1986. pap. text ed. 12.95x (ISBN 0-8134-2535-2). Inter Print Pubs.

Sounds & Letters. Linda Hayward. (Illus.). 96p. (ps-2). 1986. pap. 5.95 (ISBN 0-448-18991-7, G&D). Putnam Pub Group.

Sounds & Letters see Reading Readiness Program.

Sounds & Phonemes of Wulfila's Gothic. James W. Marchand. (Janua Linguarum Ser. Practica: No. 25). 1973. pap. text ed. 23.60x (ISBN 90-2792-432-5). Mouton.

Sounds & Scores. Henry Mancini. 244p. 1973. Repr. 19.95 (ISBN 0-89524-060-2, 4001). Cherry Lane.

Sounds Around Us. Seth H. Wittner. (Illus.). 32p. (Orig.). (ps). 1988. Incl. audio-cassette. pap. 9.95 (ISBN 0-9619269-8-8). Sound World Record.

Sounds Easy! Sharron Bassano. (Sounds Easy Ser.). (Illus.). 57p. 1980. pap. text ed. 4.25x (ISBN 0-88084-040-4); cassette 10.95x (ISBN 0-88084-041-2). Alemany Pr.

Sounds, Feelings, Thoughts: Seventy Poems by Wislawa Szymborska. Wislawa Szymborska. Tr. by Magnus J. Krynski & Robert A. Maguire. LC 80-8579. (Lockert Library of Poetry in Translation). 261p. 1981. 27.00x (ISBN 0-691-06469-5); pap. 10.80x (ISBN 0-691-01380-2). Princeton U Pr.

Sounds for Little Folks. Clara B. Stoddard. 1973. text ed. 6.00 (ISBN 0-686-09395-X). Expression.

Sounds from the Bullpen. Howard Munce. 80p. 1983. pap. 9.95 (ISBN 0-942604-01-6). Madison Square.

Sounds from the Unknown: A Collection of Japanese-American Tanka. Tr. by Lucille M. Nixon & Tomoe Tana. LC 64-16108. 133p. (Orig.). 1963. 9.95 (ISBN 0-8040-0278-9, Pub. by Swallow); pap. 4.95 (ISBN 0-8040-0279-7, Pub. by Swallow). Ohio U Pr.

Sounds Interesting: Resource Material for Teachers. Alan Maley & Alan Duff. 36p. 1975. 6.50 (ISBN 0-521-20758-4); cassette 13.95 (ISBN 0-521-20757-6). Cambridge U Pr.

Sounds Intriguing: Resource Material for Teachers. Alan Maley & Alan Duff. 73p. 1979. 6.95 (ISBN 0-521-22138-2); cassette 13.95 (ISBN 0-521-22135-8). Cambridge U Pr.

Sounds Magnificent: The Story of the Symphony. Herbert Chappell. (Illus.). 172p. 1986. 24.95 (ISBN 0-88186-380-7). Parkwest Pubns.

Sounds of American English. Thomas D. Houchin. (Orig.). 1976. pap. text ed. 8.33 (ISBN 0-87720-974-X). AMSCO Sch.

Sounds of American English: A Handbook for English as a Foreign Language, English-Vietnamese Edition. Virginia F. Allen & Cao Quan. 49p. 1986. tchrs ed. 8.00 (ISBN 0-940723-04-2). SIIS.

Sounds of Children. F. Williams et al. (Illus.). 1977. pap. text ed. write for info (ISBN 0-13-823062-5). P-H.

Sounds of English. Keith D. Holmes. Set. tchrs guide 25.00 (ISBN 0-9608250-4-5); per set, 4 disc recordings 25.00 (ISBN 0-9608250-3-7). Educ Serv Pub.

Sounds of English & Dutch. Beverley Collins & Inger Mees. 293p. 1982. 39.50 (ISBN 90-6021-477-3, Pub. by Martinus Nijhoff Netherlands). Kluwer Academic.

Sounds of English & German. William G. Moulton. LC 62-20024. (Orig.). 1962. pap. 9.50x (ISBN 0-226-54309-9). U of Chicago Pr.

Sounds of English & Spanish. Robert P. Stockwell & J. Donald Bowen. LC 65-17302. (Orig.). 1965. pap. 6.00x (ISBN 0-226-77503-8). U of Chicago Pr.

Sounds of French: An Introduction. Bernard Tranel. (Illus.). 256p. 1987. 39.50 (ISBN 0-521-30443-1); pap. 14.95 (ISBN 0-521-31510-7); cassette 13.95 (ISBN 0-521-35002-6). Cambridge U Pr.

Sounds of Jazz, Bk. 1. Tony Caramia. Ed. by Louise Goss & Sam Holland. 16p. 1983. pap. text ed. 2.95 (ISBN 0-913277-01-0). New Schl Mus Study.

Sounds of Jazz, Bk.2. Tony Caramia. Ed. by Louise Goss & Sam Holland. 12p. 1983. pap. text ed. 2.95 (ISBN 0-913277-02-9). New Schl Mus Study.

Sounds of Joy & Praise: Accompaniment. write for info. (ISBN 0-8198-6873-6). Dghtrs St Paul.

Sounds of Joy & Praise: Singers Edition. 0.50 (ISBN 0-8198-6872-8). Dghtrs St Paul.

Sounds of Language: An Inquiry into the Role of Genetic Factors in the Development of Sound Systems. Leonard F. Brosnahan. LC 82-975. 250p. 1982. Repr. of 1961 ed. lib. bdg. 35.00x (ISBN 0-313-23353-5, BRSOL). Greenwood.

Sounds of Latin. Roland G. Kent. (Language Monographs: Vol. 12). 1932. 29.00 (ISBN 0-527-00816-8). Kraus Repr.

Sounds of My Soul. Willadeene & Joan. (Illus.). 64p. 1981. pap. 4.00 (ISBN 0-682-49811-4). Exposition-Phoenix.

Sounds of People & Places: Readings in the Geography of American Folk & Popular Music. Ed. by George O. Carney. LC 87-10481. (Illus.). 362p. (Orig.). 1987. pap. text ed. 17.25 (ISBN 0-8191-6414-3). U Pr of Amer.

Sounds of Silence: Japanese Women. John R. Terry. 176p. 1988. pap. 9.95 (ISBN 0-933704-69-0). Dawn Pr.

Sounds of Speech Communications. J. M. Pickett. LC 79-21729. (Perspectives in Audiology). (Illus.). 256p. 1980. text ed. 23.00x (ISBN 0-89079-119-8, 1316). Pro Ed.

Sounds of Speed: The Automotive Record Collector's Price Guide. Tim Goebel. (Illus.). 200p. (Orig.). 1988. pap. 17.95 (ISBN 0-9619489-0-6). Burnin Rubber.

Sounds of Stillness. Allen J. Weenink. 1984. 3.95 (ISBN 0-89536-686-X, 4862). CSS of Ohio.

Sounds of the Breath. David J. Gerrick. (Illus.). 1978. 20.00 (ISBN 0-916750-54-X). Dayton Labs.

Sounds of the Diseased Heart. Aldo A. Luisada. LC 74-176171. (Illus.). 416p. 1973. text ed. 32.50 (ISBN 0-87527-113-8). Green.

Sounds of the Earth. I. Sokolov-Mikitov. 80p. 1985. 6.95 (ISBN 0-8285-3417-9, Pub. by Malysh Pubs USSR). Imported Pubns.

Sounds of the Heart. David J. Gerrick. (Illus.). 1978. 20.00 (ISBN 0-916750-55-8). Dayton Labs.

Sounds of the Normal Heart. Aldo A. Luisada. LC 78-176172. (Illus.). 280p. 1972. 32.50 (ISBN 0-87527-051-4). Green.

Sounds of the Passion. Wallace H. Kirby. 1984. 4.25 (ISBN 0-89536-647-9, 1944). CSS of Ohio.

Sounds of the Passion: Meditations on Jesus' Journey to the Cross. David M. Owen. LC 87-28996. 112p. (Orig.). 1975. pap. 5.95 (ISBN 0-8066-2298-9, 10-5950). Augsburg.

Sounds of the River Naranjana. Armand Schwerner. LC 82-16910. 128p. 1983. ltd., signed ed. 30.00 (ISBN 0-88268-032-3); pap. 6.95 (ISBN 0-930794-60-5); 15.95 (ISBN 0-930794-59-1). Station Hill Pr.

Sounds of Valley Streams: Enlightenment in Dogen's Zen. Francis H. Cook. Ed. by Kenneth Inada. (Buddhist Studies). 144p. 1988. text ed. 34.50 (ISBN 0-88706-922-3); pap. text ed. 10.95 (ISBN 0-88706-924-X). State U NY Pr.

Sounds of Yourself. Theta Burke. LC 76-48010. 1977. pap. 5.95 (ISBN 0-916872-02-5). Delafield Pr.

Sounds Real: Radio in Everyday Life. C. S. Higgins & P. D. Moss. LC 81-21808. (Illus.). 237p. 1983. text ed. 27.50 (ISBN 0-7022-1900-2); pap. 14.95 (ISBN 0-7022-1910-X). U of Queensland Pr.

Sounds So Good to Me: The Bluesman's Story. Barry L. Pearson. LC 83-14764. (Illus.). 208p. 1984. 16.95 (ISBN 0-8122-1171-5). U of Pa Pr.

Sounds, Sounds, All Around. Jean Watson. (Illus.). 16p. 1983. pap. 0.99 (ISBN 0-86683-706-X, AY8299, HarpR). Har-Row.

Soundscape with Humans. Tony Perez. (Orig.). 1974. pap. 1.50 (ISBN 0-915242-02-8). Pygmalion Pr.

Soundtrack: The Music of the Movies. Mark Evans. (Paperback Ser.). 1979. pap. 9.95 (ISBN 0-306-80099-3). Da Capo.

Soup. Robert N. Peck. (gr. 3 up). 1979. pap. 2.75 (ISBN 0-440-48186-4, YB). Dell.

Soup. Robert N. Peck. LC 73-15117. (Illus.). 104p. (gr. 3 up). 1974. lib. bdg. 9.99 (ISBN 0-394-92700-1). Knopf.

Soup & Me. Robert N. Peck. 128p. (gr. 3 up). 1979. pap. 2.75 (ISBN 0-440-48187-2, YB). Dell.

Soup & Me. Robert N. Peck. LC 75-9514. (Illus.). 112p. (gr. 3-6). 1975. lib. bdg. 9.99 (ISBN 0-394-93157-2). Knopf.

Soup & Salad Bars. Rest Business staff. 1983. 23.95 (ISBN 0-8436-2220-2). Van Nos Reinhold.

Soup & Salad Bars. Restaurant Business Magazine Editors. 64p. 1981. 22.95 (ISBN 0-8436-2208-3). Van Nos Reinhold.

Soup, Beautiful Soup. Felipe Rojas-Lombardi. (Illus.). 1984. 17.95 (ISBN 0-394-53886-2). Random.

Soup Book. Louis P. De Gouy. LC 73-88332. 428p. 1974. pap. 5.95 (ISBN 0-486-22998-X). Dover.

Soup for All Seasons. Brad McCrorie. LC 87-13385. 192p. 1987. pap. 10.95 (ISBN 0-385-25136-X). Doubleday.

Soup for President. Robert N. Peck. LC 77-3548. (Illus.). (gr. 6 up). 1978. lib. bdg. 9.99 (ISBN 0-394-93675-2). Knopf.

Soup for President. Robert N. Peck. (gr. 3-6). 1986. pap. 2.50 (ISBN 0-440-48188-0, YB). Dell.

Soup for Supper. Phyllis Root. LC 85-45273. (Illus.). 32p. (ps-2). 1986. 11.25i (ISBN 0-06-025070-4); PLB 10.89 (ISBN 0-06-025071-2). HarpJ.

Soup in the Saddle. Robert N. Peck. LC 82-14010. (Illus.). 96p. (gr. 3-6). 1983. 9.95 (ISBN 0-394-85294-X); lib. bdg. 9.99 (ISBN 0-394-95294-4). Knopf.

Soup in the Saddle. Robert N. Peck. (gr. k-6). 1988. pap. 2.75 (ISBN 0-440-48104-X, YB). Dell.

Soup on Fire. Robert N. Peck. LC 87-5261. (Illus.). 112p. (gr. 4-7). 1987. pap. 13.95 (ISBN 0-385-29580-4). Delacorte.

Soup on Ice. Robert N. Peck. LC 85-218. (Illus.). 128p. (gr. 3-7). 1985. 10.95 (ISBN 0-394-87613-X); lib. bdg. 9.99 (ISBN 0-394-97613-4). Knopf.

Soup on Ice. Robert N. Peck. (gr. k-6). 1988. pap. price not set (ISBN 0-440-40115-1, YB). Dell.

Soup on Wheels. Robert N. Peck. LC 80-17661. (Illus.). 128p. (gr. 3 up). 1981. lib. bdg. 9.99 (ISBN 0-394-94581-6). Knopf.

Soup on Wheels. Robert N. Peck. (gr. 3-7). 1986. pap. 2.75 (ISBN 0-440-48190-2, YB). Dell.

Soup Pot. Ethel Marbach. (Envelope Library). (Illus.). 12p. (Orig.). (YA) (gr. 7-9). 1982. pap. 2.50 (ISBN 0-914676-49-0). Green Tiger Pr.

Soup, Salad, & Pasta Innovations. Karen Lee & Alexandra Branyon. LC 86-13573. (Illus.). 256p. 1987. pap. 10.95 (ISBN 0-385-19864-7). Doubleday.

Soup, Salad, Sandwich Cookbook. Naomi Arbit & June Turner. (Illus.). 64p. (Orig.). 1981. pap. 3.95 (ISBN 0-8249-3001-0). Ideals.

Soup Stone. Iris VanRynbach. LC 86-31830. (Illus.). 32p. (ps-3). 1988. 11.95 (ISBN 0-688-07254-2); lib. bdg. 11.88 (ISBN 0-688-07255-0). Greenwillow.

Soup-to-Dessert High Fiber Cookbook. Betty Wason. pap. 2.50 (ISBN 0-451-09991-5, E9991, Sig). NAL.

Soup Wisdom. rev. ed. Freida Arkin & Consumer Reports Book Editors. 144p. pap. 6.95 (ISBN 0-89043-018-7). Consumer Reports.

Soupcon I: Seasonal Samplings from the Junior League of Chicago. rev. ed. (Illus.). 391p. 1974. spiral bdg. 11.95 (ISBN 0-9611622-0-1). JLC Inc.

Soupcon II: More Seasonal Samplings from the Junior League of Chicago. LC 81-81137. (Illus.). 387p. 1981. spiral bdg. 11.95 (ISBN 0-9611622-1-X). JLC Inc.

Souped up Recipes from Lipton. Thomas J. Lipton Kitchens. LC 78-66988. pap. write for info. (ISBN 0-87502-063-1). Benjamin Co.

Soups. Jeannette Seaver. 214p. 1983. 13.95 (ISBN 0-86579-031-0). Seaver Bks.

Soups. LC 79-17129. (Good Cook Ser.). (Illus.). 1979. lib. bdg. 22.60 (ISBN 0-8094-2867-9, Pub. by Time-Life). Silver.

Soups. Ed. by Time-Life Books. (Good Cook Ser.). 1980. 13.95 (ISBN 0-8094-2866-0). Time-Life.

Soups. Hannah Wright. 304p. 1985. pap. 19.00x (ISBN 0-7090-2054-6, Pub. by R Hale Ltd UK). State Mutual Bk.

Soups & Salads. Bon Appetit Magazine Editors. LC 82-23295. (Cooking with Bon Appetit Ser.). (Illus.). 144p. 1984. 12.95 (ISBN 0-89535-116-1). Knapp Pr.

Soups & Salads. Sandi Cooper. Ed. by Betsy Lawrence. LC 81-70441. (Great American Cooking Schools Ser.). (Illus.). 84p. 1982. pap. 5.95 (ISBN 0-941034-13-5). I Chalmers.

Soups & Salads see Cooking with Bon Appetit.

Soups & Sandwiches. Sue Deeming & Bill Deeming. LC 83-80967. (Illus.). 160p. 1983. pap. 6.95 (ISBN 0-89586-216-6). Price Stern.

Soups & Stews. Aaron. (Easy Cooking Ser.). 1983. 5.95 (ISBN 0-8120-5533-0). Barron.

Soups & Stews. Barbara Grunes. (Illus.). 64p. (Orig.). pap. 3.95 (ISBN 0-8249-3043-6). Ideals.

Soups & Stews. Cynthia Scheer. Ed. by Karin Shakery. LC 85-73032. (California Culinary Academy Ser.). (Illus.). 128p. (Orig.). 1986. pap. 7.95 (ISBN 0-89721-048-4). Ortho.

Soups, Chowders & Stews. Georgia Orcutt. Ed. by Sandra Taylor. LC 80-53728. (Flavor of New England Ser.). 144p. 1981. pap. 8.95 (ISBN 0-911658-17-3). Yankee Bks.

Soup's Drum. Robert N. Peck. LC 79-17982. (Illus.). 128p. (gr. 3-6). 1980. lib. bdg. 9.99 (ISBN 0-394-94251-5). Knopf.

Soup's Drum. Robert N. Peck. (gr. k-6). 1988. pap. 2.95 (ISBN 0-440-40003-1). Dell.

Soups for the Professional Chef. Terence Janericco. (Illus.). 192p. 1988. 24.95 (ISBN 0-442-24398-7). Van Nos Reinhold.

Soups: From Amish & Mennonite Kitchens. Ed. by Phyllis P. Good & Rachel T. Pellman. (Pennsylvania Dutch Cookbooks Ser.). (Illus., Orig.). 1982. pap. 2.50 (ISBN 0-934672-08-3). Good Bks PA.

Soup's Goat. Robert N. Peck. LC 83-16245. (Illus.). 112p. (gr. 4-6). 1984. lib. bdg. 9.99 (ISBN 0-394-96322-9); pap. 9.95 (ISBN 0-394-86322-4). Knopf.

Soup's Goat. Robert N. Peck. (gr. k-6). 1989. pap. price not set (ISBN 0-440-40130-5, YB). Dell.

Soups of Hakafri Restaurant: Kosher Edition. Rena Franklin. LC 81-16011. (Illus.). 144p. 1981. 12.95 (ISBN 0-937404-13-6). Triad Pub FL.

Soups of Hakafri Restaurant: Original Version. Rena Franklin. LC 82-2678. (Illus.). 144p. 1982. 12.95 (ISBN 0-937404-12-8). Triad Pub FL.

Soups on the Piano. Mary M. Bitting. 64p. 1984. 6.95 (ISBN 0-89962-341-7). Todd & Honeywell.

Soups, Salads, Sandwiches, Snacks Cookbook. Carolyn Schlemme. LC 86-51112. (Great American Ser.). 154p. 1987. pap. 5.95x (ISBN 0-89914-022-X). Third Party Pub.

Soup's Uncle. Robert N. Peck. (Illus.). (gr. 4-7). 1988. 13.95 (ISBN 0-440-50062-1). Delacorte.

Soupsongs & Webster's Ark. Roy Blount, Jr. Date not set. 12.95 (ISBN 0-317-67391-2). HM.

Soupsongs-Webster's Art. Roy Blount, Jr. (Illus.). 128p. 1987. 12.95 (ISBN 0-395-43007-0). HM.

Soupy Sales' Greatest Jokes Ever Told. Soupy Sales. 160p. 1987. pap. 4.95 (ISBN 0-02-040590-1). Macmillan.

Sour Grapes. Jon Elster. (Studies in the Subversion of Rationality). 220p. 1985. pap. 13.95 (ISBN 0-521-31368-6). Cambridge U Pr.

Sour Grapes: Studies in the Subversion of Rationality. Jon Elster. LC 82-22034. 220p. 1983. 42.50 (ISBN 0-521-25230-X). Cambridge U Pr.

Sour Land. William H. Armstrong. LC 70-135783. (YA) (gr. 7 up). 1971. 12.89 (ISBN 0-06-020141-X); PLB 11.89 (ISBN 0-06-020142-8). HarpJ.

Sour Land. William H. Armstrong. LC 70-135783. (Trophy I Can Read Bks.). 128p. (YA) (gr. 7 up). 1976. pap. 2.95 (ISBN 0-06-440074-3, Trophy). HarpJ.

Sour Lemon Score. Richard Stark. 160p. 1985. 13.95 (ISBN 0-8052-8241-6, Pub. by Allison & Busby England). Schocken.

Sour Prince. Ed Flesch. 24p. 1972. pap. 2.00 (ISBN 0-88680-180-X); 20.00 (ISBN 0-317-03629-7). I E Clark.

Sour Prince. Ed Flesch. 20p. (Piano-Vocal Score by Ed Flesch). 1972. pap. 5.00 (ISBN 0-88680-181-8). I E Clark.

Sour Sweet. Timothy Mo. LC 84-40702. (Aventura Ser.). (Orig.). 1985. pap. 8.95 (ISBN 0-394-73680-X, Vin). Random.

Source. James Michener. 1988. pap. 5.95 (ISBN 0-449-44525-9, Crest). Fawcett.

Source. James A. Michener. 1965. 24.95 (ISBN 0-394-44630-5). Random.

Source, Vol. 1. Steven J. Barta. 78p. 1986. pap. text ed. 8.95 (ISBN 0-88188-996-2). H Leonard Pub Corp.

Source see History of Roman Private Law.

Source: A Guidebook of American Genealogy. Ed. by Arlene H. Eakle & Johni Cerny. LC 84-70206. 786p. 1984. 39.95 (ISBN 0-916489-00-0). Ancestry.

Source: A Reference Guide to Information & Resources. 3rd ed. Randall L. Voight & Ronald Olson. LC 78-51744. (Illus.). 1986. 12.00x (ISBN 0-930318-03-X); pap. 7.95x (ISBN 0-930318-04-8). Intl Res Eval.

Source & Meaning in Spenser's Allegory: A Study of the Faerie Queene. John E. Hankins. 1972. 49.95x (ISBN 0-19-812013-3). Oxford U Pr.

Source & Sink During the Reproductive Period of Wheat Development & Its Regulation with Special Reference to Cytokinins. Helmut Herzog. (Advances in Agronomy & Crop Science Ser.: No. 8). (Illus.). 104p. (Orig.). 1987. pap. text ed. 32.00x (ISBN 3-489-61310-4). Parey Sci Pubs.

Source Book & Bibliographical Guide to American Church History. Peter G. Mode. 1964. Repr. of 1921 ed. 17.50x (ISBN 0-910324-06-9). Canner.

Source Book for African Anthropology, Pts. 1-2. W. D. Hambly. (Field Museum of Natural History). (Illus.). 1937. Set. 61.00 (ISBN 0-527-01886-4). Kraus Repr.

Source Book for Electrophotography. Technical Association of the Pulp & Paper Industry. LC 72-190595. (Technical Association of the Pulp & Paper Industry CA Report Ser.: No. 42). pap. 21.00 (ISBN 0-317-29315-X, 2022364). Bks Demand UMI.

Source Book for Energy Auditors, 2 vols. Ed. by M. D. Lyberg. 694p. (Orig.). 1987. Set. pap. 125.00x. Coronet Bks.

Source Book for Linguistics. William Cowan & Jeromira Rakusan. LC 85-26862. (Paperbacks Ser.: No. 5). xxvi, 338p. 1985. pap. 15.95x (ISBN 0-915027-82-8). Benjamins North Am.

Source Book for Linkage in Man. Bronya J. Keats et al. LC 78-21207. 1979. 47.50x (ISBN 0-8018-2188-6). Johns Hopkins.

Source Book for Medieval Economic History. Roy C. Cave & Herbert H. Coulson. LC 64-25840. 1936. 15.00 (ISBN 0-8196-0145-4). Biblo.

Source Book for Medieval History. Oliver J. Thatcher & E. H. McNeal. LC 70-149676. Repr. of 1905 ed. 37.50 (ISBN 0-404-06363-2). AMS Pr.

Source Book for Older Americans-Income, Rights & Benefits see Social Security, Medicare & Pensions: A Sourcebook for Older Americans.

Source Book for Russian History from Early Times to 1917, 3 vols. Ed. by George Vernadsky et al. Incl. Vol. 1. Early Times to Late 17th Century. 66.70; Vol. 3. Alexander Second to the February Revolution. 65.00. LC 70-115369. Repr. of 1972 ed. (2016776). Bks Demand UMI.

Source Book for Social Psychology. Kimball Young. 1977. Repr. of 1928 ed. lib. bdg. 45.00 (ISBN 0-8492-3102-7). R West.

Source Book for Sociology. Kimball Young. 639p. 1980. Repr. of 1935 ed. lib. bdg. 45.00 (ISBN 0-8495-6105-1). Arden Lib.

Source Book for Teaching English Overseas. Michael Lewis & Jimmie Hill. (Orig.). 1981. pap. text ed. 15.00x (ISBN 0-435-28992-6). Heinemann Ed.

Source Book for the Study of Thomas Harriot. John W. Shirley. Ed. by I. Bernard Cohen. LC 80-2111. (Development of Science Ser.). (Illus.). 1981. lib. bdg. 50.00x (ISBN 0-405-13831-8). Ayer Co Pubs.

Source Book in Ancient Philosophy. rev. ed. Charles Bakewell. LC 75-148613. 439p. 1973. Repr. of 1939 ed. 45.00x (ISBN 0-87752-139-5). Gordian.

Source Book in Animal Biology. Thomas S. Hall. LC 74-120317. (Source Books in the History of the Sciences Ser). 1971. 47.00x (ISBN 0-674-82141-6). Harvard U Pr.

Source Book in Anthropology. rev. ed. Ed. by Alfred L. Kroeber & T. T. Waterman. (Illus.). Repr. of 1931 ed. 24.00 (ISBN 0-384-30475-3). Johnson Repr.

Source Book in APL: Papers by Adin D. Falkoff & Kenneth E. Iverson. Ed. by Eugene E. McDonnell. 144p. (Orig.). 1981. pap. 15.00 (ISBN 0-917326-10-5). APL Pr.

Source Book in Astronomy & Astrophysics, 1900-1975. Ed. by Kenneth R. Lang & Owen Gingerich. LC 78-9463. (Source Bks. in the History of the Sciences). 1979. 70.00x (ISBN 0-674-82200-5). Harvard U Pr.

Source Book in Chemistry, Nineteen Hundred to Nineteen Fifty. Henry Leicester. (Source Books in History of Science). text ed. 20.00x (ISBN 0-674-82231-5). Harvard U Pr.

Source Book in Chinese Philosophy. W. Chan. 1963. 67.50x (ISBN 0-691-07137-3); pap. 13.50x (ISBN 0-691-01964-9). Princeton U Pr.

Source Book in Classical Analysis. Garrett Birkhoff. LC 72-85144. (Source Books in the History of the Sciences Ser). 488p. 1973. text ed. 29.50x (ISBN 0-674-82245-5). Harvard U Pr.

Source Book in Failure Analysis: A Discriminative Selection of Outstanding Articles & Case Histories from the Periodical Literature. American Society for Metals Staff. Ed. by American Society for Metals Staff, the Periodical Publication Department. LC 74-22347. (ASM Engineering Bookshelf Ser.). (Illus.). pap. 103.50 (ISBN 0-317-09642-7, 2019492). Bks Demand UMI.

Source Book in Geography. Ed. by George Kish. LC 77-25972. (Source Books in the History of the Sciences). 1978. 37.00x (ISBN 0-674-82270-6). Harvard U Pr.

Source Book in Geology, Fourteen Hundred to Nineteen Hundred. Shirley L. Mason. Ed. by Kirtley F. Mather. (Source Books in the History of the Sciences Ser). (Illus.). 1970. text ed. 40.00x (ISBN 0-674-82277-3). Harvard U Pr.

Source Book in Mathematics. David E. Smith. 701p. 1984. pap. 13.95 (ISBN 0-486-64690-4). Dover.

Source Book in Mathematics, 1200-1800. Dirk J. Struik. LC 68-21986. (Source Books in the History of the Sciences Ser.). pap. 110.80 (ISBN 0-317-09449-1, 2017753). Bks Demand UMI.

Source Book in Matroid Theory. Joseph Kung. 512p. 1986. 65.00 (ISBN 0-8176-3173-9). Birkhauser.

Source Book in Medieval Science. Edward Grant. LC 70-183977. (Source Books in the History of Science Ser). 896p. 1974. text ed. 49.50x (ISBN 0-674-82360-5). Harvard U Pr.

Source Book in the History of Psychology. Ed. by Richard J. Herrnstein & Edwin G. Boring. (Source Books in the History of the Sciences Ser). (Illus.). 1965. 32.50x (ISBN 0-674-82410-5); pap. 12.95x (ISBN 0-674-82411-3). Harvard U Pr.

Source Book in Theatrical History. Alois M. Nagler. Orig. Title: Sources of Theatrical History. (Illus.). 1952. pap. 9.95 (ISBN 0-486-20515-0). Dover.

Source Book in Theatrical History. Alois M. Nagler. (Illus.). 16.75 (ISBN 0-8446-2638-4). Peter Smith.

Source Book: Kodak Ektagraphic Slide Projectors. Ed. by Eastman Kodak Company & A. L. Price. LC 81-69536. (Illus.). 164p. 1984. pap. 11.95 (ISBN 0-87985-335-2, S-74). Eastman-Kodak.

Source Book of Advaita Vedeanta. Eliot Deutsch & J. A. Van Buitenen. LC 75-148944. pap. 65.60 (ISBN 0-317-12996-1, 2017216). Bks Demand UMI.

Source Book of Agricultural Chemistry. Charles A. Browne. Ed. by Frank N. Egerton, 3rd. LC 77-74205. (History of Ecology Ser.). 1978. Repr. of 1944 ed. lib. bdg. 23.50x (ISBN 0-405-10375-1). Ayer Co Pubs.

Source Book of American State Legislation, 1985-1986. American Legislative Exchange Council Staff & James Butcher. LC 82-642083. 1985. 10.00 (ISBN 0-317-37050-2). Am Legislative.

Source Book of Ancient History. George W. Botsford. 1929. 40.00 (ISBN 0-8274-3934-2). R West.

Source Book of Antiques & Jewelry Designs. Compiled by C. P. Hornung. (Quality Paperbacks Ser.). (Illus.). 1977. pap. 6.95 (ISBN 0-306-80070-5). Da Capo.

Source-Book of Biological Names & Terms. 3rd ed. Edmund C. Jaeger. (Illus.). 360p. 1978. 40.00x (ISBN 0-398-00916-3). C C Thomas.

Source Book of Educational Materials for Medical Radiographers. 1986. lib. bdg. 79.95 (ISBN 0-8490-3806-5). Gordon Pr.

Source Book of Flavors. Henry B. Heath. (Illus.). 1981. 97.95 (ISBN 0-87055-370-4). AVI.

Source Book of Franchise Opportunities. Robert E. Bond. LC 84-71569. 250p. 1984. 19.95 (ISBN 0-87094-475-4). Dow Jones-Irwin.

Source Book of Franchise Opportunities, 1988. Robert S. Bond. 500p. 1988. pap. 24.95 (ISBN 1-55623-090-7). Dow Jones-Irwin.

Source Book of Geriatric Assessment, 2 vols, Vol. 2. Liliane Israel et al. (Limited Volume Ser.). xxviii, 668p. Set. bound 249.50 (ISBN 3-8055-3832-4). S Karger.

Source Book of Indian Archaeology. Ed. by F. R. Allchin & D. K. Chakrabarti. (Illus.). 366p. 1979. text ed. 30.00x. Coronet Bks.

Source Book of Medical History. Logan Clendening. 1942. pap. 11.95 (ISBN 0-486-20621-1). Dover.

Source Book of Medical History. Ed. by Logan Clendening. 15.50 (ISBN 0-8446-1871-3). Peter Smith.

Source Book of Modern Hinduism. Glyn Richards. 222p. 1988. 50.00x (ISBN 0-7007-0173-7, Pub. by Curzon Pr Ltd UK). State Mutual Bk.

Source Book of Proposed Music Notation Reforms. Gardner Read. LC 86-14315. (Music Reference Collection Ser.: No. 11). 489p. 1987. lib. bdg. 45.00 (ISBN 0-313-25446-X, RHN/). Greenwood.

Source Book of the Genus Phytophtora. O. K. Ribeiro. (Illus.). 1978. lib. bdg. 32.00x (ISBN 3-7682-1200-9). Lubrecht & Cramer.

Source Book of the History of Education for the Greek & Roman Period. Paul Monroe. 515p. 1982. Repr. of 1948 ed. lib. bdg. 65.00 (ISBN 0-8495-3940-4). Arden Lib.

Source Book of World War Two Aircraft. John M. Emory. (Illus.). 160p. 1987. 39.95 (ISBN 0-7137-1722-X, Pub. by Blandford Pr England). Sterling.

Source Book on Applications of the Laser in Metalworking. E. Metzbower. 1981. 55.00 (ISBN 0-87170-117-0). ASM.

Source Book on Astronomy & Astrophysics. Ed. by K. Lang & O. Gingerich. 922p. 1980. 41.95 (ISBN 0-318-13544-2, B0163). Harvard U Pr.

Source Book on Brazing & Brazing Technology: A Comprehensive Collection of Outstanding Articles from the Periodical & Reference Literature. American Society for Metals Staff. Compiled by Melvin M. Schwartz. LC 80-17457. pap. 110.00 (2027050). Bks Demand UMI.

Source Book on Brazing & Brazing Technology. M. M. Schwartz. 1980. 55.00 (ISBN 0-87170-099-9). ASM.

Source Book on Brazing and Brazing Technology, SBB. 428p. 1980. 48.00 (SBB). Am Welding.

Source Book on Cold Forming: A Discriminative Selection of Outstanding Articles from the Periodical Literature. American Society for Metals Staff. LC 75-6855. (American Society for Metals. Engineering Bookshelf Ser.). (Illus.). pap. 93.80 (ISBN 0-317-11151-5, 2019501). Bks Demand UMI.

Source Book on Copper & Copper Alloys: A Comprehensive Collection of Outstanding Articles from the Periodical & Reference Literature. American Society for Metals Staff. LC 79-21667. pap. 106.00 (2027045). Bks Demand UMI.

Source Book on Ductile Iron: A Discriminative Selection of Outstanding Articles from the Periodical & Reference Literature. American Society for Metals Staff. Ed. by A. H. Rauch. LC 77-9278. (ASM Engineering Bookshelf Ser.). pap. 100.00 (ISBN 0-317-27679-4, 2019500). Bks Demand UMI.

Source Book on Electron Beam & Laser Welding. M. M. Schwartz. 1981. 55.00 (ISBN 0-87170-104-9). ASM.

Source Book on Environmental & Safety Considerations for Planning & Design of LNG Marine Terminals. 46p. 1976. pap. 7.00x (ISBN 0-87262-158-8). Am Soc Civil Eng.

Source Book on Forming of Steel Sheet: A Discriminative Selection of Outstanding Articles from the Periodical & Reference Literature. Ed. by John R. Newby. LC 76-28176. (American Society for Metals. Engineering Bookshelf Ser.). (Illus.). pap. 99.80 (ISBN 0-317-11148-5, 2019498). Bks Demand UMI.

Source-Book on French Law: System, Methods, Outlines of Contract. 2nd ed. Otto Kahn-Freund et al. 1979. pap. 38.00x (ISBN 0-19-825349-4). Oxford U Pr.

Source Book on Gear Design, Technology & Performance. Maurice A. Hawes. 1979. 55.00 (ISBN 0-87170-092-1). ASM.

Source Book on Heat Treating: A Discriminative Selection of Outstanding Articles from the Literature Periodicals. American Society for Metals Staff. LC 75-25598. (ASM Engineering Bookshelf Ser.: Vol. 1: Materials & Processes). (Illus.). pap. 99.50 (ISBN 0-317-09661-3, 2051904). Bks Demand UMI.

Source Book on Industrial Alloy & Engineering Data: A Comprehensive Collection of Alloy & Engineering Data in Tabular & Graphical Form. American Society for Metals Staff. LC 77-28985. pap. 120.80 (ISBN 0-317-26761-2, 2024347). Bks Demand UMI.

Source Book on Innovative Welding Processes. M. M. Schwarta. 1981. 55.00 (ISBN 0-87170-105-7). ASM.

Source Book on Maraging Steels: A Comprehensive Collection of Outstanding Articles from the Periodical & Reference Literature. American Society for Metals Staff. Compiled by Raymond F. Decker. LC 79-13743. (AMS Engineering Bookshelf Ser.). (Illus.). pap. 100.00 (ISBN 0-317-09610-9, 2019493). Bks Demand UMI.

Source Book on Materials Selection: A Discriminative Selection of Outstanding Articles from the Periodical & Reference Literature. American Society for Metals Staff. Ed. by Russell B. Gunie. LC 77-1347. pap. 121.80 (2027047). Bks Demand UMI.

Source Book on Nitriding: A Discriminative Selection of Outstanding Articles from the Periodical & Reference Literature. American Society for Metals Staff. LC 77-23934. pap. 82.00 (2027048). Bks Demand UMI.

Source Book on Powder Metallurgy: A Comprehensive Collection of Oustanding Articles from the Periodical & Reference Literature. American Society for Metals Staff. Ed. by Samuel Bradbury. LC 78-24466. pap. 109.80 (ISBN 0-317-26758-2, 2024348). Bks Demand UMI.

Source Book on Selection & Fabrication of Aluminum Alloys: A Comprehensive Collection of Outstanding Articles from the Industrial & Reference Literature. American Society for Metals Staff. LC 78-18869. pap. 120.00 (2027044). Bks Demand UMI.

Source Book on Stainless Steels: A Discriminative Selection of Outstanding Articles from the Periodical & Reference Literature. American Society for Metals Staff. Compiled by American Society for Metals Staff, Periodical Publication Department Staff. LC 76-867. (ASM Engineering Bookshelf Ser.). (Illus.). pap. 104.00 (ISBN 0-317-09622-2, 2019497). Bks Demand UMI.

Source Book on the Early History of Cuthbert & Randolph County, Georgia. Annette M. Suarez. Ed. by William B. Williford. LC 82-72108. (Illus.). 520p. 1982. 25.00 (ISBN 0-87797-061-0). Cherokee.

Source Book on the Teaching of Psychology: Including Supplement. Ed. by Paul J. Woods. 278p. 1973. looseleaf bdg 29.95 (ISBN 0-914044-01-X). Scholars Pr Ltd.

Source Book on Wear Control Technology: A Comprehensive Collection of Outstanding Articles from the Periodical & Reference Literature. American Society for Metals Staff. Ed. by David A. Rigney & W. A. Glaeser. LC 78-12162. (ASM Engineering Bookshelf Ser.). pap. 116.00 (ISBN 0-317-26756-6, 2024349). Bks Demand UMI.

Source Book Profiles, 1988. The Foundation Center. Ed. by Francine Jones. LC 77-79015. (Annual Publication). 1376p. 1988. pap. text ed. 295.00 (ISBN 0-87954-235-7). Foundation Ctr.

Source Book: Social & Health Services for the Greater New York Area, 1984-1985. 1062p. 1983. 40.00 (ISBN 0-89059-029-X, UPB128, UPB); pap. 29.00 (ISBN 0-89059-030-3, UPB127). UNIPUB.

Source Book 1989-90: Social & Health Services in the Greater New York Area. United Way of New York City & Human Resources Administration, City of New York. 1504p. 1988. pap. 38.50 (ISBN 0-89774-543-4). Oryx Pr.

Source Books for Japanese Craftsmen; Netsuke. Jack Hillier. (Illus.). 43p. 1979. pap. 20.00 (ISBN 0-87556-749-5). Saifer.

Source Catalog: Communications. LC 79-176088. (Source Catalog Ser.). 1972. Vol. 1. pap. 4.75x (ISBN 0-8040-0557-5, Pub. by Swallow); Vol. 2, Communities-Housing. pap. 11.95x (ISBN 0-8040-0601-6, Pub. by Swallow). Ohio U Pr.

Source Data Automation. Automated Education Center Staff. LC 72-125996. 1969. 29.00 (ISBN 0-403-04479-0). Scholarly.

Source Directory: Assistance to Third World Broadcasters. Ed. by Miriam Williford. LC 79-3610. 200p. 1979. loose leaf 6.50 (ISBN 0-916584-14-3). Ford Found.

Source Directory of Camera Restoration Materials. 3.95 (ISBN 0-89816-041-3). Embee Pr.

Source Document in Schizophrenia, Whoever Had Most Fish Would Be Lord & Master. Julius Laffal. LC 74-82625. 340p. 1979. 19.95 (ISBN 0-913622-02-8). Gallery Pr.

Source: Getting Back. Richlore Foundation Staff. LC 76-47214. (Illus., Orig.). 1989. pap. 7.95 (ISBN 0-89407-003-7). Strawberry Hill.

Source Materials on the Government & Politics of Germany. James K. Pollock. 1964. 12.50x (ISBN 0-685-21805-8). Wahr.

Source Music in Motion Pictures. Irene K. Atkins. LC 81-65338. (Illus.). 192p. 1983. 22.50 (ISBN 0-8386-3076-6). Fairleigh Dickinson.

Source of African Philosophy: The Ethiopian Philosophy of Man. Claude Summer. 153p. 1986. text ed. 62.50x (ISBN 3-515-04438-8, Pub by Franz Steiner). Coronet Bks.

Source of Human Good. Henry N. Wieman. LC 63-2226. (Arcturus Books Paperbacks). 318p. 1964. pap. 10.95x (ISBN 0-8093-0117-2). S Ill U Pr.

Source of Life: The Eucharist & Christian Living. Rene Voillaume. Tr. by Dinah Livingstone from Fr. 1977. pap. 2.95 (ISBN 0-914544-17-9). Living Flame Pr.

Source of Magic. Piers Anthony. 1979. pap. 4.95 (ISBN 0-345-35058-8, Del Rey Bks). Ballantine.

Source of Measures: Key to the Hebrew Egyptian Mystery. J. Ralston Skinner. LC 72-84846. (Secret Doctrine Reference Ser). (Illus.). 500p. (Repr. of 1894 ed. with new index added). 1982. 27.00 (ISBN 0-913510-47-5). Wizards.

Source of Poetry. Fredric D. Ramey. LC 82-91155. (Illus.). 68p. 1984. pap. 15.00 (ISBN 0-910889-01-5). F D Ramey.

Source of Precious Life. Leonard J. Cirino. 60p. (Orig.). 1988. 15.00 (ISBN 0-944550-03-7); pap. 6.00 (ISBN 0-318-24015-7). Pygmy Forest Pr.

Source of Supply. 4th ed. Global Engineering Documents Staff. Ed. by Carla J. Hook. 712p. 1988. write for info. perfect bdg. (ISBN 0-912702-42-7). Global Eng.

Source of Supply (SOS) 3rd, rev. ed. Global Engineering Documents Staff. Ed. by Carla J. Hook. 588p. 1987. write for info. perfect bdg. (ISBN 0-912702-41-9). Global Eng.

Source of "The Ancient Mariner". Ivor James. LC 72-196916. 1890. Repr. lib. bdg. 30.00 (ISBN 0-8414-5367-5). Folcroft.

Source: Poems. Fred Chappell. 57p. 1985. pap. 6.95 (ISBN 0-8071-1277-1). La State U Pr.

Source Readings in Music Education. Michael L. Mark. 1982. text ed. 19.95x (ISBN 0-02-871910-7). Schirmer Bks.

Source Readings in Music History, 5 vols. Ed. by Oliver Strunk. Incl. Vol. 1. Antiquity & the Middle Ages. pap. 7.95x (ISBN 0-393-09680-7); Vol. 2. The Renaissance Era. pap. 5.95x (ISBN 0-393-09681-5); Vol. 3. Baroque Era. pap. 9.95x (ISBN 0-393-09682-3); Vol. 4. Classic Era. pap. 5.95x (ISBN 0-393-09683-1); Vol. 5. Romantic Era. pap. 6.95x (ISBN 0-393-09684-X). (Illus.). 1950. Repr. one vol. ed 24.95x (ISBN 0-393-09742-0, NortonC). Norton.

Source Region of the Solar Wind. Ed. by W. K. Schmidt & H. Grunwaldt. 1982. lib. bdg. 49.50 (ISBN 90-277-1537-8, Pub. by Reidel Holland). Kluwer Academic.

Source, Sanction & Salvation: Patterns in Judaic Christian Ethics. John P. Reeder. 176p. 1988. pap. text ed. price not set (ISBN 0-13-823436-1). P-H.

Source Studies in American Colonial Education. Robert F. Seybolt. LC 71-165731. (American Education, Ser. 2). 1971. Repr. of 1925 ed. 16.00 (ISBN 0-405-03720-1). Ayer Co Pubs.

Source Term Evaluation for Accident Conditions: Proceedings of a Symposium Columbus, Ohio 28 Oct-Nov, 1985. (Proceedings Ser.). (Illus.). 777p. (Orig.). 1986. pap. text ed. 155.00 (ISBN 92-0-020086-9, ISP700, IAEA). UNIPUB.

Source: What the Bible Says about the Problems of Contemporary Life. John L. McKenzie. (Basics of Christian Thought Ser.). 228p. 1984. 14.95 (ISBN 0-88347-172-8). Thomas More.

Sourcebook. 2nd ed. Kirk Hershey. Date not set. pap. 19.95 (ISBN 1-55835-007-1, R724). Am Inst Arch.

Sourcebook: Federal Agency Use of Alternative Means of Dispute Resolution. Marguerite S. Millhauser & Charles Pou, Jr. (Illus.). 1065p. (Orig.). 1987. pap. 31.00 (ISBN 0-318-22951-X, S/N 052-003-01070-4). USGPO.

Sourcebook for Aphasia: A Guide to Family Activities & Community Resources. Susan H. Brubaker. LC 81-23099. 206p. 1982. pap. 14.00x (ISBN 0-8143-1697-2). Wayne St U Pr.

Sourcebook for Basic Writing Teachers. Theresa Enos. 676p. 1987. text ed. write for info. (ISBN 0-394-35193-2, RanC). Random.

Sourcebook for Child Abuse & Neglect: Intervention, Treatment, & Prevention Through Crisis Programs. Ed. by Oliver C. Tzeng & Jamia J. Jacobsen. (Illus.). 452p. 1988. text ed. 59.75x (ISBN 0-398-05419-3). C C Thomas.

Sourcebook for Elementary Science. 2nd ed. Elizabeth B. Hone et al. (Teaching Science Ser.). 475p. 1971. text ed. 24.00 net (ISBN 0-15-582855-X, HC). HarBraceJ.

Sourcebook for English Papers: 1001 Ideas for Term Papers, Projects, Reports, & Speeches. Walter J. Miller. (Education & Guidance Ser.). 288p. (Orig.). 1987. pap. 6.95 (ISBN 0-668-06609-1). Arco.

Sourcebook for Environmental Studies. Ed. by Peter S. Berry. 1975. pap. text ed. 14.00 (ISBN 0-8464-0865-1). Beekman Pubs.

Sourcebook for Hispanic Literature & Language: A Selected Annotated Guide to Spanish, Spanish-American & Chicano Bibliography, Literature, Linguistics, Journals, & Other Source Materials. 2nd ed. Donald W. Bleznick. LC 83-3060. xii, 304p. 1983. 21.50 (ISBN 0-8108-1616-4). Scarecrow.

Sourcebook for Innovative Drug Delivery: Manufactures of Devices & Pharmaceuticals, Suppliers of Products & Services, Sources of Information. 152p. 1987. 75.00 (ISBN 0-9618649-0-7). Canon Comns.

Sourcebook for Modern Catechetics. Ed. by Michael Warren. LC 83-50246. 493p. (Orig.). 1983. pap. 15.95 (ISBN 0-88489-152-6). St Mary's.

Sourcebook for Programmable Calculators. Texas Instruments. 1979. text ed. 44.50 (ISBN 0-07-063746-6). McGraw.

Sourcebook for Remediating Language. Ann J. Glaser et al. 200p. 1987. pap. text ed. 18.95 (ISBN 0-88450-972-9). Communication Skill.

Sourcebook for Research in Law & Medicine. Salvatore F. Fiscina et al. LC 84-62877. 330p. 1985. text ed. 45.00 (ISBN 0-932500-24-2). Natl Hlth Pub.

Sources of African & Middle-Eastern Economic Information, 2 vols. Ed. by Euan Blauvelt & Jennifer Durlacher. LC 81-4125. 1982. Vol. 1. lib. bdg. 150.00 (ISBN 0-313-23059-5, BAF/01); Vol. 2. lib. bdg. 150.00 (ISBN 0-313-23060-9, BAF/02). Greenwood.

Sources of American Independence: Selected Manuscripts from the Collection of the William L. Clements Library, 2 vols. Howard H. Peckham. LC 77-25964. (Clements Library Bicentennial Studies). 1978. Set. lib. bdg. 40.00x (ISBN 0-226-65321-8). U of Chicago Pr.

Sources of Ancient & Primitive Law. Compiled by Albert Kocourek & John H. Wigmore. (Evolution of Law: Select Readings on the Origin & Development of Legal Institutions Ser.: Vol. 1). xvii, 702p. 1979. Repr. of 1915 ed. lib. bdg. 38.50x (ISBN 0-8377-2328-0). Rothman.

Sources of Anti-Slavery Constitutionalism in America, 1760-1848. William M. Wiecek. LC 77-6169. (Illus.). 272p. 1977. 32.50x (ISBN 0-8014-1089-4). Cornell U Pr.

Sources of Art Noveau. Stephan T. Madsen. LC 75-26819. (Quality Paperbacks Ser.). (Illus.). 1976. pap. 10.95 (ISBN 0-306-80024-1). Da Capo.

Sources of Art Noveau. Stephan T. Madsen. Tr. by Ragnar Christopherson. LC 74-34464. (Architecture & Decorative Arts Ser.). (Illus.). 488p. 1975. Repr. of 1956 ed. lib. bdg. 59.50 (ISBN 0-306-70733-0). Da Capo.

Sources of Asian Pacific Economic Information, 2 vols. Ed. by Euan Blauvelt & Jennifer Durlacher. LC 80-28645. 1981. Set. lib. bdg. 150.00 (ISBN 0-313-22963-5, BLS/); Vol. 1. lib. bdg. 75.00 (ISBN 0-313-22964-3, BLS/1); Vol. 2. lib. bdg. 75.00 (ISBN 0-313-22965-1, BLS/2). Greenwood.

Sources of Birth, Marriage, Death. Arlene H. Eakle. 83p. 1974. pap. 6.00 (ISBN 0-940764-09-1). Genealog Inst.

Sources of British Chronicle History in Spenser's Faerie Queene. Carrie A. Harper. LC 65-15868. (Studies in Spenser, No. 26). 1969. Repr. of 1910 ed. lib. bdg. 49.95x (ISBN 0-8383-0565-2). Haskell.

Sources of Charlotte Bronte's Novels: Persons and Places. Herbert E. Wroot. LC 68-1923. 1970. Repr. of 1935 ed. 75.00x (ISBN 0-8383-0688-8). Haskell.

Sources of Chinese Tradition, 2 Vols. Ed. by William T. De Bary. LC 60-9911. (Records of Civilization, Sources & Studies & Introduction to Oriental Classics Ser.). 1960. 1 vol. ed. o.p 30.00x (ISBN 0-231-02255-7); Vol. 1, 578 P. pap. 16.00x (ISBN 0-231-08602-4); Vol. 2, 322 P. pap. 14.00x (ISBN 0-231-08603-2). Columbia U Pr.

Sources of Classicism: Five Centuries of Architectural Books from the Collections of the Humanities Research Center. Drury B. Alexander. (Illus.). 1978. pap. 5.00 (ISBN 0-87959-084-X). U of Tex H Ransom Ctr.

Sources of Compiled Legislative Histories: Bibliography of Government Documents, Periodical Articles & Books, 1st Congress - 96th Congress. Nancy P. Johnson. (AALL Publications Ser.: No. 14). iv, 146p. 1979. loose-leaf in vinyl, 3-ring binder 35.00x (ISBN 0-8377-0112-0); 1981 suppl. incl. Rothman.

Sources of Connecticut Law. Shirley Bysiewicz. 1987. 65.00 (ISBN 0-88063-157-0). Butterworth Legal Pubs.

Sources of Construction Information: An Annotated Guide to Reports, Books, Periodicals, Standards, & Codes. Jules B. Godel. LC 77-4671. 673p. 1977. 45.00 (ISBN 0-8108-1030-1). Scarecrow.

Sources of Contemporary Philosophical Realism in America. Herbert W. Schneider. LC 62-16954. 1964. pap. text ed. 6.95x (ISBN 0-672-60282-2). Irvington.

Sources of Economic & Social Statistics of India. Ed. by Moonis Raza et al. 1979. 24.00x (ISBN 0-8364-0536-6, Pub. by Eureka India). South Asia Bks.

Sources of Economic Growth in the U. S. & the Alternatives Before Us. Edward F. Dennison. 279p. 1962. pap. 6.00 (ISBN 0-87186-213-1). Comm Econ Dev.

Sources of English Constitutional History, 2 vols. rev. ed. Carl Stephenson & F. G. Marcham. 1972. Vol. 1. pap. text ed. 26.95 scp (ISBN 0-06-044202-6, HarpC); (HarpC). Har-Row.

Sources of English Legal History: Private Law to 1750. J. H. Baker. 698p. 1987. pap. 28.00. Butterworth Legal Pubs.

Sources of English Literature: A Guide for Students, Sanders Lecture, 1926. Arundell J. Esdaile. LC 75-102863. (Bibliography & Reference Works: No. 293). 1970. Repr. of 1928 ed. 17.00 (ISBN 0-8337-1069-9). B Franklin.

Sources of Federal Funding for Biological Research. Ed. by Peter C. Escherich & Roger E. McManus. 1983. pap. 8.00 (ISBN 0-942924-04-5). Assn Syst Coll.

Sources of Four Plays Ascribed to Shakespeare. G. Harold Metz. LC 88-4793. 448p. 1988. text ed. 48.00 (ISBN 0-8262-0690-5). U of Mo Pr.

Sources of Genealogical Material in Wales. Peggy Magee. 1983. pap. 2.50 (ISBN 0-937267-02-3). Magee Pubns.

Sources of Gravitational Radiation. Larry Smarr. LC 79-50177. (Illus.). 1979. 39.50 (ISBN 0-521-22778-X). Cambridge U Pr.

Sources of Indian Tradition, 2 vols. 2nd ed. Rev. by Ainslie T. Embree & Stephen Hay. (Introduction to Oriental Civilizations Ser.). 1988. Vol. I, 560p. 42.50x (ISBN 0-231-06650-3); Vol. I. pap. 17.00x (ISBN 0-231-06651-1); Vol. II, 464p. 42.50x (ISBN 0-231-06414-4); Vol. II. pap. 16.00x (ISBN 0-231-06415-2). Columbia U Pr.

Sources of India's Strength: Foundation Course - 1. Ed. by S. C. Datt et al. 344p. 1986. pap. text ed. 14.95x (ISBN 0-7069-2829-6, Pub. by Vikas India). Advent NY.

Sources of Industrial Growth & Structural Change: The Case of Turkey. Merih Celasun. (Working Paper: No. 614). 188p. 1983. 8.00 (ISBN 0-8213-0258-2, WP 0614). World Bank.

Sources of Inequality in Earnings. P. J. Taubman. LC 75-23117. (Contributions to Economic Analysis: Vol. 96). 274p. 1976. 73.75 (ISBN 0-444-10965-X, North-Holland). Elsevier.

Sources of Information in Librarianship & Information Science. R. J. Prytherch. 208p. 1983. 26.00x (ISBN 0-566-03436-0, 06087-9, Pub. by Gower Pub Co England). Lexington Bks.

Sources of Information in Librarianship & Information Science. 2nd ed. Ray Prytherch. 190p. 1987. text ed. 37.00x (ISBN 0-566-05509-0, Pub. by Gower Pub England). Gower Pub Co.

Sources of Information in Librarianship & Information Science: A Grafton Book. Ray Prytherch. 212p. 1983. 26.00x (ISBN 0-317-03078-7, 06087-9). Lexington Bks.

Sources of Information in the Social Sciences. 3rd ed. Ed. by William H. Webb. LC 84-20494. 832p. 1986. 75.00x (ISBN 0-8389-0405-X). ALA.

Sources of Information in Transportation: Part 1, General Transportation. 3rd ed. Mary J. Burke et al. (Public Administration Ser.: Bibliography P-1599). 71p. 1985. pap. 10.50 (ISBN 0-89028-249-8). Vance Biblios.

Sources of Information in Transportation: Part 2, Air Transportation. 3rd ed. Jane M. Janiak & Marty H. Lovelock. (Public Administration Ser.: Bibliography P-1600). 40p. 1985. pap. 6.00 (ISBN 0-89028-250-1). Vance Biblios.

Sources of Information in Transportation: Part 3, Shipping. 3rd ed. George J. Billy et al. (Public Administration Ser.: Bibliography P-1601). 49p. 1985. pap. 7.50 (ISBN 0-89028-251-X). Vance Biblios.

Sources of Information in Transportation: Part 4, Railroads. 3rd ed. Gilda Martinello. (Public Administration Ser.: Bibliography P-1602). 20p. 1985. pap. 3.00 (ISBN 0-89028-252-8). Vance Biblios.

Sources of Information in Transportation: Part 5, Trucking. 3rd ed. Linda Rothbart et al. (Public Administration Ser.: Bibliography P-1603). 67p. 1985. pap. 9.75 (ISBN 0-89028-253-6). Vance Biblios.

Sources of Information in Transportation: Part 6, Inland Water Transportation. 3rd ed. Mary L. Roy. (Public Administration Ser.: Bibliography P-1604). 39p. 1985. pap. 6.00 (ISBN 0-89028-254-4). Vance Biblios.

Sources of Information in Transportation: Part 7, Pipelines. 3rd ed. Marie Tilson & Jane Law. (Public Administration Ser.: Bibliography P-1605). 34p. 1985. pap. 5.25 (ISBN 0-89028-255-2). Vance Biblios.

Sources of Information in Transportation: Part 8, Highways. 3rd ed. Daniel C. Krummes et al. (Public Administration Ser.: Bibliography P-1606). 68p. 1985. pap. 10.50 (ISBN 0-89028-256-0). Vance Biblios.

Sources of Information in Transportation: Part 9, Urban Transportation. 3rd ed. Michael C. Kleiber & Sylvie Hetu. (Public Administration Ser.: Bibliography P-1607). 23p. 1985. pap. 3.75 (ISBN 0-89028-257-9). Vance Biblios.

Sources of Information in Water Resources. Gerald J. Giefer. LC 75-20953. 312p. 1976. 30.00 (ISBN 0-912394-15-3). Water Info.

Sources of Information on Alternative Energy Technologies Held at the Science Reference & Information Service. P. M. Dunning. 1986. pap. 22.50 (ISBN 0-7123-0732-X, Pub. by British Lib). Longwood Pub Group.

Sources of Innovation. Eric A. Von Hippel. 232p. 1988. 27.00 (ISBN 0-19-504085-6). Oxford U Pr.

Sources of Instinctive Life. Rosario Palmeri. LC 65-27461. 66p. 1966. 6.95 (ISBN 0-8022-1260-3). Philos Lib.

Sources of Inter-State Conflict. Robert Litwak. LC 80-28448. (Security in the Persian Gulf Ser.: Vol. 2). 100p. 1981. pap. text ed. 12.50x (ISBN 0-86598-045-4, Pub. by Allanheld). Rowman.

Sources of International Comparative Advantage: Theory & Evidence. Edward E. Leamer. (Illus.). 384p. 1985. pap. 13.50x (ISBN 0-262-62051-0). MIT Pr.

Sources of "Jane Eyre". Florence S. Dry. LC 73-3188. 1973. lib. bdg. 16.50 (ISBN 0-8414-1859-4). Folcroft.

Sources of Japanese Tradition, 2 Vols. Ed. by William T. De Bary. LC 58-7167. (Records of Civilizations, Sources & Studies). 1958. 65.00 (ISBN 0-231-02254-9); Vol. 1. pap. 16.00 (ISBN 0-231-08604-0); Vol. 2. pap. 15.00 (ISBN 0-231-08605-9). Columbia U Pr.

Sources of John Dryden's Comedies. Ned B. Allen. LC 67-21718. 1967. Repr. of 1935 ed. 35.00x (ISBN 0-87752-002-X). Gordian.

Sources of John Dryden's Comedies. Ned B. Allen. LC 77-9975. 1978. Repr. of 1935 ed. lib. bdg. 30.50 (ISBN 0-8492-0016-4). R West.

Sources of Keyboard Music in England. Charles V. Borren. Tr. by James E. Matthew. LC 78-106714. 1970. Repr. of 1914 ed. lib. bdg. 35.00x (ISBN 0-8371-3444-7, BOKM). Greenwood.

Sources of Keyboard Music in England. Charles Van Den Borren. Tr. by J. E. Matthew. LC 77-75227. 1977. Repr. of 1914 ed. lib. bdg. 20.00 (ISBN 0-89341-131-0). Longwood Pub Group.

Sources of Law. Helen Silving. LC 68-54165. viii, 404p. 1968. lib. bdg. 40.00 (ISBN 0-930342-22-4). W S Hein.

Sources of Law: A Comparative Empirical Study National Systems of Sources of Law. Chantal Kourlisky. 376p. 1982. 100.00x (ISBN 0-569-08734-1, Pub. by Collets (UK)). State Mutual Bk.

Sources of Law, Legal Change & Ambiguity. Alan Watson. LC 83-21783. 164p. 1984. 28.95 (ISBN 0-8122-7919-0). U of Pa Pr.

Sources of Light: Contemporary American Luminism. Harvey West & Chris Bruce. (Illus.). 84p. (Orig.). 1985. pap. 22.50 (ISBN 0-935558-13-6). Henry Art.

Sources of Masonic Symbolism. Alex Horne. (Illus.). 98p. 1982. Repr. text ed. 11.95 (ISBN 0-88053-074-X, M-064). Macoy Pub.

Sources of Meaning in Motion Pictures & Television. Calvin Pryluck. Ed. by Garth S. Lowett. LC 75-21434. (Dissertations on Film Ser.). 1976. lib. bdg. 20.00 (ISBN 0-405-07535-9). Ayer Co Pubs.

Sources of Military Doctrine: France, Britain & Germany Between the World Wars. Barry R. Posen. LC 84-7610. (Cornell Studies in Security Affairs). 288p. 1984. 35.00x (ISBN 0-8014-1633-7). Cornell U Pr.

Sources of Military Doctrine: France, Britain & Germany Between the World Wars. Barry R. Posen. LC 84-7610. (Cornell Studies in Security Affairs). 288p. 1986. pap. 11.95x (ISBN 0-8014-9427-3). Cornell U Pr.

Sources of Modern Architecture & Design. Nikolaus Pevsner. (World of Art Ser.). (Illus.). 216p. 1985. pap. 11.95 (ISBN 0-500-20072-6). Thames Hudson.

Sources of Modern Atheism: One Hundred Years of Debate over God. Marcel Neusch. LC 82-60596. 1983. pap. 9.95 (ISBN 0-8091-2488-2). Paulist Pr.

Sources of Modern Eclecticism. Demetri Porphyrios. (Academy Architecture Ser.). (Illus.). 128p. 1982. 19.95 (ISBN 0-312-74673-3). St Martin.

Sources of Modern International Law. George A. Finch. ix, 124p. Repr. of 1937 ed. 19.00 (ISBN 0-384-15685-1). Johnson Repr.

Sources of Modern Painting. Ed. by James S. Plaut. LC 79-91372. (Contemporary Art Ser). Repr. of 1939 ed. 17.00 (ISBN 0-405-00734-5). Ayer Co Pubs.

Sources of Modern Photography Series, 51 bks. Ed. by Peter C. Bunnell & Robert A. Sobieszek. (Illus.). 1979. Vols. 1-25. lib. bdg. 559.00x (ISBN 0-405-09597-X); Vols. 26-51. lib. bdg. 1393.00x (ISBN 0-405-18980-X). Ayer Co Pubs.

Sources of Mortality Changes in Italy Since Unification. Elizabeth Hoffman. Ed. by Stuart Bruchey. LC 80-2811. (Dissertations in European Economic History II). (Illus.). 1981. lib. bdg. 27.50x (ISBN 0-405-13995-0). Ayer Co Pubs.

Sources of Much Ado About Nothing. Charles T. Prouty. Bd. with Ariodanto & Ieneura. Peter Beverly. LC 76-128893. (Select Bibliographies Reprint Ser). Repr. of 1950 ed. 17.00 (ISBN 0-8369-5513-7). Ayer Co Pubs.

Sources of Municipal Revenue in Illinois. Lent D. Upson. (Illus.). Repr. of 1912 ed. 12.00 (ISBN 0-384-63300-5). Johnson Repr.

Sources of Organizational & Personal Power in the U. S. Senate: A Test of Alternative Models. Samuel A. Kirkpatrick & Lawrence K. Pettit. (Legislative Research Ser: No. 7). 29p. 1973. pap. 1.50 (ISBN 0-686-20793-9). Univ OK Gov Res.

Sources of our Liberties: With a Postscript 1978; Bibliographical Note by Stanley N. Katz. Deluxe Rev. ed. American Bar Associtation Staff. 488p. 1978. 50.00 (ISBN 0-910058-91-1); pap. 7.50 (ISBN 0-910058-90-3). Amer Bar Assn.

Sources of Power of the Apostolic Witness. Robert Shank. 125p. 1982. pap. 3.95 (ISBN 0-911620-05-2). Westcott.

Sources of Property Market Information: A Bibliography of Practice-Based Market Research & Indices. Douglas Scarrett. 60p. 1988. text ed. 50.00 (ISBN 0-566-05663-1, Pub. by Gower Pub England). Gower Pub Co.

Sources of Published & Unpublished Administrative Opinions in New York State. Robert A. Carter. 12p. 1985. 5.00 (ISBN 0-318-22976-5). NYS Library.

Sources of Quantum Mechanics. Ed. by B. L. Van Der Waerden. pap. text ed. 8.50 (ISBN 0-486-61881-1). Dover.

Sources of Religious Insight. Josiah Royce. LC 76-56454. 1977. Repr. lib. bdg. 20.00x (ISBN 0-374-96989-2, Octagon). Hippocrene Bks.

Sources of Renewal: The Fulfillment of Vatican II. Pope John Paul II. LC 79-1780. 448p. 1980. 15.00 (ISBN 0-06-064188-6, HarpR). Har-Row.

Sources of Secession. Gerrit J. Ten Zythoff. (Historical Series of the Reformed Church in America: Vol. 17). 216p. (Orig.). 1987. pap. 12.95 (ISBN 0-8028-0328-8). Eerdmans.

Sources of Self Evaluation: A Formal Theory of Significant Others & Social Influence. Murray Webster, Jr. & Barbara Sobieszek. LC 74-5066. pap. 53.30 (ISBN 0-8357-9981-6, 2016473). Bks Demand UMI.

Sources of Shang History. David N. Keightley. 281p. 1978. 175.00x (Pub. by Han-Shan Tang Ltd). State Mutual Bk.

Sources of Shang History: The Oracle-Bone Inscriptions of Bronze Age China. David N. Keightley. LC 74-29806. 1979. 57.00x (ISBN 0-520-02969-0); pap. 22.50x (ISBN 0-520-05455-5). U of Cal Pr.

Sources of Social Power: A History of Power from the Beginning to AD 1760, Vol. 1. Michael Mann. (Illus.). 608p. 1986. 62.50 (ISBN 0-521-30851-8); pap. 19.95 (ISBN 0-521-31349-X). Cambridge U Pr.

Sources of Spenser's Classical Mythology. Alice E. Randall. LC 72-115364. Repr. of 1896 ed. 6.00 (ISBN 0-404-05223-1). AMS Pr.

Sources of Spenser's Classical Mythology. Alice E. Randall. 35.00 (ISBN 0-8490-1092-6). Gordon Pr.

Sources of Spenser's Classical Mythology. Alice E. Randall. 1896. Repr. 17.50 (ISBN 0-8274-3476-6). R West.

Sources of Spenser's Classical Mythology. Alice E. Sawtelle. LC 77-6714. 1896. lib. bdg. 19.50 (ISBN 0-8414-7592-X). Folcroft.

Sources of Stones Used in Prehistoric Mesoamerican Sites. Ed. by Robert F. Heizer et al. (Illus.). 1976. pap. 7.95 (ISBN 0-87919-060-4). Ballena Pr.

Sources of Swiss Anabaptism. Ed. by Leland Harder. LC 85-5520. (Classics of the Radical Reformation: No. 4). 816p. 1985. 69.00x (ISBN 0-8361-1251-2). Herald Pr.

Sources of Synge. Adelaide Estill. LC 74-10977. 1939. lib. bdg. 19.00 (ISBN 0-8414-3954-0). Folcroft.

Sources of Synge. Adelaide Estill. 1978. 42.50 (ISBN 0-685-89414-2). Bern Porter.

Sources of the African Past. David Robinson & Douglas Smith. LC 79-5399. 203p. 1979. 44.50 (ISBN 0-8419-0337-9, Africana); pap. 18.50 (ISBN 0-8419-0338-7). Holmes & Meier.

Sources of the American Republic: A Documentary History of Politics, Society, & Thought, Vol. 1. 2nd. ed. Marvin Meyers et al. 1967. pap. write for info. (ISBN 0-673-05342-3). Scott F.

Sources of the American Republic: A Documentary History of Politics, Society & Thought, Vol. 2. 2nd. ed. Marvin Meyers et al. 1969. pap. write for info. (ISBN 0-673-05762-3). Scott F.

Sources of the American Social Tradition, 2 vols. Ed. by David J. Rothman & Shiela Rothman. LC 74-78474. 1975. 1 vol. ed. o.p. 18.50x (ISBN 0-465-08083-9); Vol. 1. pap. 12.95x (ISBN 0-465-08084-7); Vol. 2. pap. 12.95x (ISBN 0-465-08085-5). Basic.

Sources of the Constitution of the United States Considered in Relation to Colonial & English History. 2nd, rev., enl. ed. C. Ellis Stevens. xviii, 313p. 1987. Repr. of 1894 ed. lib. bdg. 30.00x (ISBN 0-8377-2616-6). Rothman.

Sources of the Court of Sapience. Curt F. Buhler. 1932. pap. 8.00 (ISBN 0-384-06235-0). Johnson Repr.

Sources of the Faust Tradition. Philip M. Palmer & Robert P. More. LC 65-29231. (Studies in Comparative Literature, No. 35). 1969. Repr. of 1936 ed. lib. bdg. 49.95x (ISBN 0-8383-0608-X). Haskell.

Sources of the Faust Tradition. Philip M. Palmer & Robert P. More. 1966. lib. bdg. 20.00x (ISBN 0-374-96194-8, Octagon). Hippocrene Bks.

Sources of the History of Latin America, Africa, Asia, Australia & Oceania in Hungaria. Ed. by National Archives of Hungary. (Guide to the Sources for the History of Nations Ser. 3: Vol. 9). 520p. 1988. lib. bdg. 82.00 (ISBN 3-598-21485-5). K G Saur.

Sources of the History of North Africa, Asia & Oceania in Scandinavia: Sources of the History of North Africa, Asia & Oceania in Denmark, Pt. 1. Ed. by Danish National Archives Staff. (Guide to the Sources for History of Nations 3rd Ser.: North Africa, Asia & Oceania: Vol. 3, Pt. 1). 842p. 1980. lib. bdg. 110.00 (ISBN 3-598-21474-X). K G Saur.

Sources of the History of North Africa, Asia & Oceania in Scandinavia, Vol. 3: Sources of the History of North Africa, Asia & Oceania in Finland, Norway, Sweden, Pt. 2. Ed. by National Archives of Finland, Norway & Sweden Staff. (Guide to the Sources for the History of Nations 3rd Ser.: North Africa, Asia & Oceania: Vol. 3, Pt. 1). 224p. 1981. lib. bdg. 95.00 (ISBN 3-598-21475-8). K G Saur.

Sources of the Morning. Alan F. Hilfiker. LC 77-85211. 1978. 5.00 (ISBN 0-8233-0265-2). Golden Quill.

Sources of the Parson's Tale. Kate O. Petersen. LC 72-954. Repr. of 1901 ed. 11.00 (ISBN 0-404-04997-4). AMS Pr.

Sources of the Polish Tradition, 3 vols. Raymond Cwieka. Bd. with Vol. 1. Great Polish Walking Dance: Polonaise. pap. 15.00 (ISBN 0-317-13909-6); Vol. 2. Elegant Running-Sliding Dance: Mazur, Maqurka. 1983; Vol. 3. Dance Figures: Historical Contemporary (A Choreographer's Handbook) 1984. Complete 3 vols. set. pap. 35.00 (ISBN 0-317-13907-X); Vols. II & III Bound as a Set. pap. 25.00 (ISBN 0-317-13908-8). R Cwieka.

Sources of the Quaker Peace Testimony. Howard H. Brinton. 1944. pap. 2.50x (ISBN 0-87574-027-8, 027). Pendle Hill.

Sources of the Religious Element in Flaubert's Salammbo. A. Hamilton. (Elliott Monographs: Vol. 4). 1917. 12.00 (ISBN 0-527-02608-5). Kraus Repr.

Sources of the Roman de Brut of Wace. Margaret Houck. LC 74-6013. 1941. Repr. lib. bdg. 49.00 (ISBN 0-8414-4817-5). Folcroft.

Sources of the Synoptic Gospels. Carl S. Patton. 263p. 1980. Repr. of 1915 ed. lib. bdg. 50.00 (ISBN 0-89984-385-9). Century Bookbindery.

Sources of the Western Tradition. Marvin Perry et al. LC 86-81593. 1987. Vol. 1 From Ancient Times to the Enlightenment. pap. text ed. 17.96 (ISBN 0-395-35031-X); Vol. 2 From the Scientific Revolution to the Present. pap. text ed. 17.96. HM.

Sources of the White Devil. G. Boklund. (Essays & Studies on English Language & Literature: Vol. 17). pap. 24.00 (ISBN 0-8115-0215-5). Kraus Repr.

Sources of the White Devil, John Webster. Gunnar Boklund. LC 68-1396. (Studies in Comparative Literature, No. 35). 1969. Repr. of 1957 ed. lib. bdg. 75.00x (ISBN 0-8383-0648-9). Haskell.

Sources of Theatrical History see Source Book in Theatrical History.

Sources of Thermodynamic Data on Mesogens: A Special Issue of the Journal of Molecular Crystals & Liquid Crystals. A. Beguin et al. 340p. 1984. pap. text ed. 94.00 (ISBN 0-677-16575-7). Gordon & Breach.

Sources of Tritium & Its Behavior upon Release to the Environment. D. G. Jacobs. LC 68-67209. (AEC Critical Review Ser.). 90p. 1968. 10.25 (ISBN 0-87079-345-4, TID-24635); microfiche 6.50 (ISBN 0-87079-346-2, TID-24635). DOE.

Sources of Unity in Ben Jonson's Comedy. Mary C. Williams. Ed. by James Hogg. (Jacobean Drama Studies). 230p. (Orig.). 1972. pap. 15.00 (ISBN 3-7052-0320-7, Pub. by Salzburg Studies). Longwood Pub Group.

Sources of Unofficial U. K. Statistics. David Mort & Leona Siddall. 480p. 1986. text ed. 89.95X (ISBN 0-566-02620-1, Pub. by Gower Pub England). Gower Pub Co.

Sources of Value. Stephen C. Pepper. 1958. 43.00x (ISBN 0-520-01798-6). U of Cal Pr.

Sources of Vitality in American Church Life. Ed. by Robert L. Moore. LC 78-71065. (Studies in Ministry & Parish Life). 1978. text ed. 13.95x (ISBN 0-913552-14-3). Exploration Pr.

Sources of Western Literacy: The Middle Eastern Civilizations. Felix Reichmann. LC 79-8292. (Contributions in Librarianship & Information Science: No. 29). 274p. 1980. lib. bdg. 35.00 (ISBN 0-313-20948-0, RWL/). Greenwood.

Sources of Western Morality: From Primitive Society Through the Beginning of Christianity. Georgia E. Harkness. LC 72-10723. Repr. of 1954 ed. 21.50 (ISBN 0-404-10643-9). AMS Pr.

Sources of World Financial & Banking Information. Ed. by G. R. Dicks. LC 80-28654. 720p. 1981. lib. bdg. 125.00 (ISBN 0-313-22966-X, DSW/). Greenwood.

Sources of Wuthering Heights. Florence Dry. LC 73-22134. 1937. lib. bdg. 16.50 (ISBN 0-8414-3715-7). Folcroft.

Sources on National Movement, Vol. 1: January 1919-Septemer 1920, Protest, Disturbance & Defiance. Ed. by V. N. Datta & S. C. Mittal. 1985. 24.00x (ISBN 0-8364-1499-3, Pub. by Allied India). South Asia Bks.

Sources on Punjab History. W. Eric Gustafson & Kenneth Jones. LC 75-903111. 1975. 16.00 (ISBN 0-88386-584-X). South Asia Bks.

Sources, Processes & Methods in Coleridge's Biographia Literaria. Kathleen Wheeler. LC 79-41683. 240p. 1980. 44.50 (ISBN 0-521-22690-2). Cambridge U Pr.

Sources: Synchronicity Readings for Dealing with Life's Issues. Strephon Kaplan-Williams. 80p. pap. 3.95 (ISBN 0-918572-41-X). Journey Pr.

Sourdough Breads & Coffee Cakes from Lane Farm: Worth 104 Recipes. Ada Lou Roberts. (Cookery, Wine, Nutrition). 192p. 1983. pap. 3.95 (ISBN 0-486-24529-2). Dover.

Sourdough Cookery. Rita Davenport. LC 77-71168. (Illus.). 1977. pap. 8.95 (ISBN 0-89586-155-0). Price Stern.

Sourdough Cookin' Dean Tucker. 1976. 3.95 (ISBN 0-89036-071-5). Hawkes Pub Inc.

Sourdough Expedition: Stories of Pioneer Alaskans Who Climbed Mount McKinley in 1910. Ed. by Terrence Cole. LC 85-13402. (Northern History Library). (Illus.). 64p. (Orig.). 1985. pap. 6.95 (ISBN 0-88240-305-2). Alaska Northwest.

Sourdough Jim Pitcher: The Autobiography of a Pioneer Alaskan. James S. Pitcher. LC 85-22857. (Northern History Library). (Illus.). 64p. (Orig.). 1985. pap. 6.95 (ISBN 0-88240-308-7). Alaska Northwest.

Sourdough Rye & Other Good Breads. Sue A. Gross. 1974. pap. 2.50 (ISBN 0-917234-00-6). Kitchen Harvest.

Souriciere. Marie Cardinal. (French Easy Readers, C Ser.). 96p. 1986. pap. text ed. 5.95 (ISBN 0-88436-914-5, 40296). EMC.

Sourire de L'aube. Betty Roland. (Collection Colombine Ser.). 192p. 1983. pap. 1.95 (ISBN 0-373-48069-5). Harlequin Bks.

Sourires Pinces see Oeuvres.

Sourvenirs due triangle d'or see Recollections of the Golden Triangle.

Sous-Caste de L'Inde du Sud: Organisation Sociale et Religion des Pramalai Kallar. Louis Dumont. (Le Monde D'outre Mer Passe et Present Etudes: No. 1). (Fr.). 1957. pap. text ed. 21.60x (ISBN 0-686-22530-9). Mouton.

Sous la Lune des Tropiques. Robyn Donald. (Collection Harlequin). 192p. 1983. pap. 1.95 (ISBN 0-373-49323-1). Harlequin Bks.

Sous la Revolution, le Consulat, l'Empire see Histoire de la Presse Francaise.

Sous le Signe de la Licorne. Robyn Anzelon. (Harlequin Seduction Ser.). 332p. 1984. pap. 3.25 (ISBN 0-373-45036-2). Harlequin Bks.

Sous le Signe du Dragon. Paul Claudel. 232p. 1958. 8.95 (ISBN 0-686-54436-6). French & Eur.

Sous le Soleil de Satan. Georges Bernanos. 1957. 11.95 (ISBN 0-685-11569-0). French and Eur.

Sous les Rois Tres Chretiens (Du XIIIe au XVIIIe Siecle) see Histoire du Catholicisme en France.

Sousa's Great Marches in Piano Transcription. John P. Sousa. LC 74-93543. 111p. (Orig.). 1975. pap. 5.95 (ISBN 0-486-23132-1). Dover.

Souslin Problem. K. J. Devlin & H. Johnsbraten. (Lecture Notes in Mathematics Ser.: Vol. 405). vii, 132p. 1974. pap. 18.00 (ISBN 0-387-06860-0). Springer-Verlag.

Souslinoid & Analytic Sets in a General Setting. Arthur Kruse. LC 52-42839. (Memoirs: No. 86). 127p. 1969. pap. 11.00 (ISBN 0-8218-1286-6, MEMO-86). Am Math.

South. Photos by Bill Weems. LC 87-81210. (Illus.). 128p. (Text by John Egerton). 1987. 34.95 (ISBN 0-932575-32-3). Gr Arts Ctr Pub.

South - South Economic Cooperation: Problems & Prospects. Govind R. Agrawal & Mitre Kolisevski. (Research & Information System for Nonaligned & Other Developing Countries Ser.). xii, 263p. 1987. text ed. 27.50x (ISBN 81-7027-102-9, Pub. by Radiant Pubs India). Advent NY.

South: A Central Theme. Ed. by Monroe L. Billington. LC 76-23223. (American Problem Studies). 122p. 1976. pap. text ed. 6.95 (ISBN 0-88275-410-6). Krieger.

South: A Tour of Its Battle Fields & Ruined Cities. J. T. Trowbridge. LC 69-18549. (American Negro: His History & Literature Ser., No. 2). 1969. Repr. of 1866 ed. 23.50 (ISBN 0-405-01898-3). Ayer Co Pubs.

South Africa. Don Brothers. (Places & Peoples of the World Ser.). (Illus.). 120p. 1989. lib. bdg. 12.95x (ISBN 1-55546-790-3). Chelsea Hse.

South Africa. A. J. Christopher. LC 81-8254. (World's Landscapes Ser.). (Illus.). 256p. (Orig.). 1982. pap. text ed. 15.95x (ISBN 0-582-49001-4). Wiley.

South Africa. Mike Evans. (Issues Ser.). (Illus.). 32p. (gr. 4-9). Date not set. lib. bdg. 10.90 (ISBN 0-531-17056-X, Gloucester Pr). Watts.

South Africa, 2 Pts. Leo Kuper & Hilda Kuper. Incl. Pt. 1-Human Rights & Genocide; Pt. 2-Biography As Interpretation. (Hans Wolff Memorial Lecture Ser.). 63p. (Orig.). 1981. pap. text ed. 5.00 (ISBN 0-941934-33-0). Indiana Africa.

South Africa. Don Lawson. LC 85-22469. (First Books Ser.). (Illus.). 72p. (gr. 4-9). 1986. lib. bdg. 10.40 (ISBN 0-531-10128-2). Watts.

South Africa. Reuben Musiker. (World Bibliographical Ser.: No. 7). 194p. 1979. 25.25 (ISBN 0-903450-16-X). ABC-Clio.

South Africa. Charles K. Robertson. 128p. 1986. pap. 3.95 (ISBN 0-88144-072-8). Christian Pub.

South Africa. Ed. by Robert Schuettinger. (JSPES Monograph: No. 1). 1977. pap. 20.00 (ISBN 0-930690-02-8). Coun Soc Econ.

South Africa. rev. ed. (Illus.). 156p. (Orig.). 1988. pap. 8.95 (ISBN 3-88989-032-6). Hunter Pub NY.

South Africa. R. Conrad Stein. LC 86-9651. (Enchantment of the World Ser.). (Illus.). 128p. (gr. 5-9). 1986. PLB 22.60 (ISBN 0-516-02784-0). Childrens.

South Africa. Anthony Trollope. 1987. pap. 5.95 ea. Part I (ISBN 0-87052-434-8, 0108). Part II (ISBN 0-87052-391-0, 0124). Hippocrene Bks.

South Africa a Century Ago. Anne Barnard. Ed. by W. H. Wilkins. LC 71-116271. x, 316p. 1972. Repr. of 1901 ed. 29.00 (ISBN 0-403-00461-6). Scholarly.

South Africa a Century Ago: Letters Written from the Cape of Good Hope, 1797-1801. Anne L. Barnard. Ed. by W. H. Wilkins. Repr. of 1901 ed. 29.00 (ISBN 0-527-05300-7). Kraus Repr.

South Africa: A Different Kind of War. Julie Frederikse. LC 86-47875. (Illus.). 192p. 1987. pap. 12.95 (ISBN 0-8070-0203-8, BP 755). Beacon Pr.

South Africa: A Glance at Current Conditions. John H. Browne. LC 70-76494. 1969. Repr. 35.00 (ISBN 0-8371-1091-2, BRS&). Greenwood.

South Africa: A Modern History. 3rd ed. T. H. Davenport. 1987. 45.00 (ISBN 0-317-52356-2); pap. 19.95 (ISBN 0-8020-6574-0). U of Toronto Pr.

South Africa: A Modern History. T. R. Davenport. 1977. pap. 14.95c (ISBN 0-8020-6312-8). U of Toronto Pr.

South Africa: A Modern History. T. R. Davenport. LC 77-375725. pap. 111.80 (2056136). Bks Demand UMI.

South Africa: A Plural Society in Transition. Ed. by D. J. Van Vuuren et al. (Illus.). 510p. 1986. text ed. 37.95 (ISBN 0-409-11083-3). Butterworth.

South Africa: A Study in Conflict. Pierre Van den Berghe. 1967. pap. 11.95x (ISBN 0-520-01294-1, CAMPUS 159). U of Cal Pr.

South Africa: A Study in Conflict. Pierre L. Van Den Berghe. LC 79-27899. (Illus.). x, 371p. 1980. Repr. of 1965 ed. lib. bdg. 35.00x (ISBN 0-313-22349-1, VASA). Greenwood.

South Africa & Its Neighbors: Regional Security & Self-Interest. Ed. by Robert I. Rotberg et al. LC 84-48006. 192p. 1985. 25.00x (ISBN 0-669-09025-5). Lexington Bks.

South Africa & Its Neighbours. Dennis Austin. (Chatham House Papers). 296p. 1985. pap. 10.95x (ISBN 0-7102-0620-8). Routledge Chapman & Hall.

South Africa & Nuclear Proliferation. J. D. Moore. 260p. 1987. 32.50 (ISBN 0-312-74698-9). St Martin.

South Africa & the Anthropologist. Adam Kuper. 256p. 1987. text ed. write for info. (ISBN 0-7102-0982-7, 09872, Kegan Paul). Routledge Chapman & Hall.

South Africa & the Bomb: Responsibility & Deterrence. Ronald W. Walters. 192p. 1986. 27.00x (ISBN 0-669-14197-6). Lexington Bks.

South Africa & the United States: The Erosion of an Influence Relationship. Richard E. Bissell. LC 81-22663. (Studies of Influence in International Relations). 172p. 1982. 35.00 (ISBN 0-275-90764-3, C0764). Praeger.

South Africa & the World: The Foreign Policy of Apartheid. Amry Vandenbosch. LC 76-111516. (Illus.). 312p. 1970. 25.00 (ISBN 0-8131-1223-0). U Pr of Ky.

South Africa: Apartheid & After. John S. Saul. Date not set. 28.00 (ISBN 0-8133-0126-2); pap. 14.50 (ISBN 0-8133-0127-0). Westview.

South Africa As a European-American Issue. Ed. by Gregory F. Treverton. 190p. 1988. pap. 6.95 (ISBN 0-87609-030-7). Coun Foreign.

South Africa at War: White Power & the Crisis in Southern Africa. Richard Leonard & Lawrence Hill. 280p. 1983. 8.95 (ISBN 0-317-36642-4). Africa Fund.

South Africa at War: White Power & the Crisis in Southern Africa. Richard W. Leonard. LC 82-23405. 288p. (Orig.). 1983. 19.95 (ISBN 0-88208-108-X); pap. 9.95 (ISBN 0-88208-109-8). Chicago Review.

South Africa: Cape Colony, Natal, Orange Free State South African Republic, Rhodesia, & All Other Territories South of the Zambesi. 6th ed. George M. Theal. LC 69-18999. (Illus.). 1969. Repr. of 1894 ed. 35.00 (ISBN 0-8371-0904-3, THS&). Greenwood.

South Africa: Challenge & Hope. rev. ed. American Friends Service Committee Staff. Ed. by Lyle Tatum. 1987. 15.95 (ISBN 0-8090-8750-2); pap. 7.95 (ISBN 0-8090-1530-7). Hill & Wang.

South Africa: Coming of Age under Apartheid. Jason Laure & Ettagale Laure. LC 79-23109. (Illus.). 192p. 1980. 15.95. FS&G.

South Africa: Economic & Political Aspects. Hector M. Robertson. LC 57-8817. (Duke University, Commonwealth-Studies Center Publication Ser.: No. 2). pap. 51.00 (ISBN 0-317-20422-X, 2023442). Bks Demand UMI.

South Africa: Foreign Investment & Apartheid. Lawrence Litvak et al. Ed. by Helen Hopps. 100p. 1979. pap. 4.95 (ISBN 0-89758-009-5). Inst Policy Stud.

South Africa: from Soweto to Uitenhage: Essays on the Struggle for National Liberation. Bernard Magubane. LC 86-73223. 225p. 1988. 29.95 (ISBN 0-86543-050-0); pap. 9.95 (ISBN 0-86543-051-9). Africa World.

South Africa from the Great Trek to the Union. Frank R. Cana. LC 70-97398. Repr. of 1909 ed. 35.00x (ISBN 0-8371-2652-5, CSA&). Greenwood.

South Africa: Human Rights & the Rule of Law. International Commission of Jurists, Geneva. 250p. 1988. 37.50x (ISBN 0-86187-979-1, Pub. by Pinter Pubs UK). Columbia U Pr.

South Africa in Crisis. Ed. by Jesmond Blumenfeld. 312p. 1987. lib. bdg. 45.00x (ISBN 0-7099-4252-4, A0408, Pub. by Croom Helm UK). Routledge Chapman & Hall.

South Africa in Namibia. Robert S. Jaster. (Illus.). 122p. (Orig.). 1985. lib. bdg. 23.25 (ISBN 0-8191-4683-8, Co-Pub. by Ctr Int'l Affairs Harvard Univ); pap. 8.25 (ISBN 0-8191-4684-6). U Pr of Amer.

South Africa in Pictures. Department of Geography, Lerner Publications. (Visual Geography Ser.). (Illus.). 64p. (gr. 5 up). 1988. PLB 9.95 (ISBN 0-8225-1835-X). Lerner Pubns.

South Africa in Southern Africa: The Intensifying Vortex of Violence. Ed. by Thomas M. Callaghy. 432p. 1983. 56.95 (ISBN 0-275-90956-5, C0956). Praeger.

South Africa in the Nineteen Eighties: State of Emergency. CIIR Staff. 104p. 1986. 20.00x (ISBN 0-946848-39-4, Pub. by CIIR). State Mutual Bk.

South Africa: In Transition to What? Ed. by Helen Kitchen. (Washington Papers: No. 132). 206p. 1988. lib. bdg. 35.95 (ISBN 0-275-92974-4, C2975); pap. 12.95 (ISBN 0-275-92975-2, B2974). Praeger.

South Africa Inc. The Oppenheimer Empire. David Pallister et al. 1988. 25.00 (ISBN 0-300-04251-5). Yale U Pr.

South Africa into the Nineteen Eighties. Ed. by Richard E. Bissell & Chester A. Crocker. (Special Studies on Africa). 1979. lib. bdg. 41.50 (ISBN 0-89158-373-4). Westview.

South Africa: Morality & Action: Quaker Efforts in a Difficult Environment. Henrik Van Der Merwe. (Studies in Quakerism: No. 7). 64p. (Orig.). 1981. pap. 3.00 (ISBN 0-89670-007-0). Progresiv Pub.

South Africa: Myths & Realities of Divestiture. Ed. by Linda Griffin. (International Economics Seminar Ser.). (Illus.). 36p. (Orig.). 1985. pap. 5.95 (ISBN 0-87641-250-9). Carnegie Ethics & Intl Affairs.

South Africa: No Easy Path to Peace. Graham Leach. (Illus.). 312p. 1987. pap. 7.95 (ISBN 0-413-15330-4, A0168). Routledge Chapman & Hall.

South Africa Review Service Company Reports. 20p. 1984. 25.00 ea. IRRC Inc DC.

South Africa: The Cordoned Heart. Francis Wilson. Ed. by Omar Badsha. LC 85-31015. 1986. 25.00 (ISBN 0-393-02341-9); pap. 14.95 (ISBN 0-393-30335-7). Norton.

South Africa: The Prospects of Peaceful Change. Theodor Hanf et al. LC 81-47583. 512p. 1981. 35.00x (ISBN 0-253-35394-7). Ind U Pr.

South Africa: The Struggle Against White Racist Rule. Ed. by David Mermelstein. 1986. write for info. Grove.

South Africa: Time Running Out. Study Commission on U. S. Policy Toward Southern Africa. LC 81-2742. (Perspectives on Southern Africa: No. 29). (Illus.). 1981. 27.50x (ISBN 0-520-04504-1); pap. 12.95 (ISBN 0-520-04547-5). U of Cal Pr.

South Africa Today: No Easy Path to Peace. Graham Leach. 256p. 1986. text ed. 24.95 (ISBN 0-7102-0848-0). Routledge Chapman & Hall.

South Africa Travel Guide. (Berlitz Travel Guides). (Illus.). 1982. pap. 6.95 (ISBN 0-02-969880-4, Berlitz). Macmillan.

South Africa: Troubled Land. Elaine Pascoe. (Illus.). 128p. (YA) (gr. 7-12). 1987. lib. bdg. 12.90 (ISBN 0-531-10432-X). Watts.

South Africa Will Be Free. Mary Harris-Robinson. 15p. 1988. 5.95 (ISBN 0-533-07400-2). Vantage.

South Africa Without Apartheid: Dismantling Racial Domination. Heribert Adam & Kogila Moodley. (Perspectives on Southern Africa Ser.: No. 39). 300p. 1986. 22.50X (ISBN 0-520-05769-4); pap. 9.95 (ISBN 0-520-05770-8). U of Cal Pr.

South African Anti-Terrorist Operations Manual. 1986. lib. bdg. 79.95 (ISBN 0-8490-3860-X). Gordon Pr.

South African Bibliography to the Year 1925: A Revision & Continuation of Sidney Mendelssohn's South African Bibliography (1910, 4 vols. 3152p. 1979. Set. 424.00x (ISBN 0-7201-0556-0). Mansell.

South African Butterflies. Ed. by Clare Abbott & Stephen Henning. (Illus.). 100p. 12.95 (ISBN 0-86954-211-7, Pub. by Macmillan S Africa). Intl Spec Bk.

South African Churches in a Revolutionary Situation. Marjorie Hope & James Young. LC 81-9584. 288p. (Orig.). 1981. pap. 9.95 (ISBN 0-88344-466-6). Orbis Bks.

South African Communists Speak, 1915-1980. Y. M. Dadoo et al. 474p. 1981. pap. 25.00x (ISBN 0-686-83901-3, Pub. by Inkuleko). Imported Pubns.

South African Disease. Cedric De Beer. 96p. 1986. 24.00x (ISBN 0-946848-13-0, Pub. by CIIR). State Mutual Bk.

South African Disease: Apartheid Health & Health Services. Cedric De Beer. LC 86-70877. 240p. 1986. 19.95 (ISBN 0-86543-038-1); pap. 7.95 (ISBN 0-86543-039-X). Africa World.

South African Dispatches. Donald Woods. LC 86-11934. 224p. 1987. 16.95 (ISBN 0-8050-0143-3). H Holt & Co.

South African Dispatches: Letters to My Countrymen. Donald Woods. LC 86-11934. (Owl Bks.). 1988. pap. 7.95 (ISBN 0-8050-0783-0). H Holt & Co.

South African Economy. 4th ed. D. Hobart Houghton. 1976. 26.00x (ISBN 0-19-570080-5). Oxford U Pr.

South African Folk-Tales. James A. Honeij. LC 78-67717. (Folktale). Repr. of 1910 ed. 19.00 (ISBN 0-404-16094-8). AMS Pr.

South African Food & Agriculture in World War II. J. M. Tinley. (Illus.). 1954. 15.00x (ISBN 0-8047-0457-0). Stanford U Pr.

South African Fossil Ape-Man: The "Australopithecinae". Robert Broom & G. W. Schepers. LC 76-44698. Repr. of 1946 ed. 49.50 (ISBN 0-404-15910-9). AMS Pr.
South African Freedom Reader, Vol. I. Ed. by South African Scholars Center Staff. (Illus.). 1988. 20.95 (ISBN 0-939074-11-7). Harvest Pubns.
South African Game: Sport & Racism. Robert Archer & Antoine Bouillon. 368p. 1982. 29.95x (ISBN 0-86232-066-6, Pub. by Zed Pr England); pap. 9.95 (ISBN 0-86232-082-8, Pub. by Zed Pr England). Humanities.
South African Geology. Ernest H. Schwarz. 22.00 (ISBN 0-8369-9194-X, 9063). Ayer Co Pubs.
South African Geotechnical Conference, 1980: A Supplement to the Proceedings of the Regional Conference for Africa on Soil Mechanics & Foundation Engineering Held in Accra, 7th, in June 1980. Ed. by A. A. Williams. 120p. 1985. text ed. 48.50 (ISBN 90-6191-592-9, Pub. by A A Balkema). Brookfield Pub Co.
South African History: A Bibliographical Guide with Special Reference to Territorial Expansion & Colonization. Naomi Musiker & Reuben Musiker. Ed. by James A. Casada. LC 82-49171. (Themes in European Expansion Ser.: Vol. 5). 297p. 1984. lib. bdg. 54.00 (ISBN 0-8240-9174-4). Garland Pub.
South African Jewish Voices. Ed. by Roberta Kalechofsky. LC 81-83903. (Echad 2: a Global Anthology Ser.). 280p. 1982. pap. text ed. 10.00 (ISBN 0-916288-10-2). Micah Pubns.
South African Literature (Dokumente Texte Und Tendenzen) Liberation & the Art of Writing. 120p. (Orig.). 1987. pap. 13.00 (0170-5881, Pub. by Evangelische Akademie Bad Boll BRD). Three Continents.
South African Novel in English: Essays in Criticism & Society. Ed. by Kenneth Parker. LC 78-18343. 202p. 1979. 39.50 (ISBN 0-8419-0425-1, Africana). Holmes & Meier.
South African Novel in English Since 1950: An Information & Resource Guide. G. E. Gorman. 1978. 40.50 (ISBN 0-8161-8178-0, Hall Reference). G K Hall.
South African Passage: Diaries of the Wilderness Leadership School. Ian Player. (Illus.). 250p. 1987. 13.95 (ISBN 1-55591-009-2). Fulcrum Inc.
South African Perspective on the New Testament: Essays by South African New Testament Scholars Presented to Bruce Manning Metzger During His Vist to South Africa in 1985. J. H. Petzer & P. J. Hartin. (Illus.). xii, 274p. 1986. 41.75 (ISBN 90-04-07720-0, Pub. by E J Brill). Heinman.
South African Pocket Oxford Dictionary. rev. ed. William Branford. 1988. 18.95 (ISBN 0-19-570503-3). Oxford U Pr.
South African Politics. Leonard Thompson & Andrew Prior. LC 81-14635. 288p. 1982. text ed. 35.50t (ISBN 0-300-02767-2); pap. 8.95x (ISBN 0-300-02779-6, Y-424). Yale U Pr.
South African Quagmire: In Search of a Peaceful Path to Democratic Pluralism. Ed. by S. Prakash Sethi. LC 86-28754. 504p. 1987. prof. ref. 32.00x (ISBN 0-88730-191-6). Ballinger Pub.
South African Quirt. Walter D. Edmonds. 192p. 1985. 14.95 (ISBN 0-316-21153-2). Little.
South African Review, No. 3. Ed. by South African Research Service Editors. 300p. 1986. pap. 24.95x (ISBN 0-86975-289-8, Pub. by Ravan Pr). Ohio U Pr.
South African Review, No. 4. Ed. by Glenn Moss & Ingrid Obery. 599p. (Orig.). 1988. pap. text ed. 25.95x (Pub. by Ravan Pr). Ohio U Pr.
South African Scenery, a Textbook of Geomorphology. 3rd rev. ed. Lester C. King. (Illus.). 1967. 17.95x (ISBN 0-02-847900-9). Hafner.
South African Society: Realities & Future Prospects. Human Sciences Research Council Staff. LC 86-27107. (Contributions in Ethnic Studies: No. 21). (Illus.). 232p. 1987. lib. bdg. 29.95 (ISBN 0-313-25724-8, MSB/). Greenwood.
South African Sugar Art. Margie Smuts. Ed. by Jackie Athey. LC 79-52244. (Continental's Creative Cake Ser.). (Illus.). 64p. (Orig.). 1979. pap. 4.95x (ISBN 0-916096-21-1). Books Bakers.
South African Supercook: One Hundred Creative Menus. Pat Kossuth. (Illus.). 167p. 14.95 (ISBN 0-86954-232-X, Pub. by Macmillan S Africa). Intl Spec Bk.
South African Testament: From Personal Encounter to Theological Challenge. H. Paul Santmire. 266p. (Orig.). 1987. pap. 7.95 (ISBN 0-8028-0266-4). Eerdmans.
South African War Casualty Rolls: Natal Field Force, 20th October, 1899-26th October, 1900. Ed. by Picton Publishing Staff. 237p. 1987. 133.00x (Pub. by Picton UK). State Mutual Bk.
South African Wine Dictionary. 2nd ed. Eric H. Bolsmann. 206p. 1984. pap. text ed. 16.50 (ISBN 0-86961-143-7, Pub. by A A Balkema). Brookfield Pub Co.
South African Women on the Move. CIIR Staff. 280p. 1985. 36.00 (ISBN 0-946848-80-7, Pub. by CIIR). State Mutual Bk.
South African Women on the Move. Vukani Makhosikazi. (Illus.). 272p. 1985. text ed. 25.00 (ISBN 0-86232-620-6, Pub. by Zed Pr UK); pap. text ed. 12.50 (ISBN 0-86232-621-4, Pub. by Zed Pr UK). Humanities.
South African Women Speak. Ed. by Jane Barrett et al. LC 86-45005. 268p. 1986. pap. 11.95 (ISBN 0-394-62201-4, Ever). Grove.
South Africa's City of Diamonds. Worger. LC 86-26675. 352p. 1987. text ed. 30.00 (ISBN 0-300-03716-3). Yale U Pr.
South Africa's Defense Posture: Coping with Vulnerability. Chester A. Crocker. (Washington Papers: Vol. IX, No. 84). 104p. (Orig.). 1981. pap. text ed. 7.95 (ISBN 0-8191-6028-8, Pub. by CSIS). U Pr of Amer.
South Africa's Impact on Britain's Return to Gold, 1925. Bruce R. Dalgaard. Ed. by Stuart Bruchey. LC 80-2801. (Dissertations in European Economic History II). (Illus.). 1981. lib. bdg. 20.00x (ISBN 0-405-13985-3). Ayer Co Pubs.
South Africa's Military Capabilities. W. F. Gutteridge. (Illus.). 200p. 1988. 20.01 (ISBN 0-08-031173-3, Pub. by BDP); pap. text ed. 11.01 (ISBN 0-08-031174-1). Pergamon.
South Africa's Moment of Truth. Edgar Lockwood. 196p. 1988. pap. 5.95 (ISBN 0-377-00180-5). Friendship Pr.
South Africa's National Bibliography, 1983. cancelled. Intl Pubns Serv.
South Africa's Options. F. Van Zyl Slabbert & David Welsh. 1979. 20.00x (ISBN 0-312-74696-2). St Martin.
South Africa's Outward Strategy: A Foreign Policy Dilemma for the United States. Larry W. Bowman. LC 72-183388. (Papers in International Studies: Africa Ser.: No. 13). (Illus.). 32p. 1971. pap. 3.25x (ISBN 0-89680-046-6, Ohio U Ctr Intl). Ohio U Pr.
South Africa's Outward Strategy: A Foreign Policy Dilemma for the United States. Larry W. Bowman. LC 72-183388. (Papers in International Studies. Africa Ser.: No. 13). pap. 20.00 (ISBN 0-317-11331-3, 2007421). Bks Demand UMI.
South Africa's Past in Stone & Paint. Miles C. Burkitt. LC 76-44700. Repr. of 1928 ed. 23.50 (ISBN 0-404-15912-5). AMS Pr.
South Africa's Plan & Capability in Nuclear Field. (Disarmament Studies: No. 2). 40p. 5.00x (ISBN 0-8002-3315-8). Intl Pubns Serv.
South Africa's Security Dilemmas. Christopher Coker. LC 87-2437. (Washington Papers: No. 127). 125p. 1987. lib. bdg. 29.95 (ISBN 0-275-92771-7, C2771); pap. 9.95 (ISBN 0-275-92772-5, B2772). Praeger.
South Africa's Transkei, the Politics of Domestic Colonialism. Gwendolyn Carter & Thomas Karis. LC 67-15937. 208p. pap. 53.50 (ISBN 0-317-27594-1, 2014773). Bks Demand UMI.
South After Gettysburg: Letters of Cornelia Hancock from the Army of the Potomac, 1863-1865. facsimile ed. Cornelia Hancock. Ed. by Henrietta S. Jaquette. LC 77-160975. (Select Bibliographies Reprint Ser). Repr. of 1937 ed. 21.00 (ISBN 0-8369-5845-4). Ayer Co Pubs.
South America. rev. ed. William E. Carter. (First Bks.). (Illus.). 72p. (gr. 4 up). 1983. PLB 10.40 (ISBN 0-531-04531-5). Watts.
South America. D. V. Georges. LC 86-9584. (New True Bks.). (Illus.). 48p. (gr. k-4). 1986. PLB 12.60 (ISBN 0-516-01296-7); pap. 3.95 (ISBN 0-516-41296-5). Childrens.
South America. 3rd ed. Arthur Morris. (Illus.). 320p. 1987. pap. 24.95 (ISBN 0-389-20744-6). B&N Imports.
South America. 2nd ed. Arthur S. Morris. LC 79-13729. (Illus.). 288p. 1982. pap. 23.50x (ISBN 0-389-20243-6, 07042). B&N Imports.
South America. Francene Sabin. LC 84-8586. (Illus.). 32p. (gr. 3-6). 1985. PLB 8.45 (ISBN 0-8167-0292-6); pap. text ed. 1.95 (ISBN 0-8167-0293-4). Troll Assocs.
South America. Marion Sichel. (National Costume Reference Ser.). (Illus.). 80p. (YA) (gr. 7-12). 1986. 12.95 (ISBN 1-55546-158-1). Chelsea Hse.
South America. (Michael's Guides Ser.). (Illus.). 750p. (Orig.). 1988. pap. text ed. 14.95 (ISBN 965-288-009-4). Hunter Pub NY.
South America: An Economic & Regional Geography. Edward W. Shanahan. 1976. lib. bdg. 59.95 (ISBN 0-8490-2633-4). Gordon Pr.
South America & the First World War: The Impact of the War on Brazil, Argentina, Peru, & Chile. Bill Albert. (Cambridge Latin American Studies Ser.: No. 65). (Illus.). 388p. 1988. 42.50 (ISBN 0-521-34650-9). Cambridge U Pr.
South America, Central America & the Caribbean, 1988. 425p. 1987. 140.00x (ISBN 0-946653-39-9, Pub. by Europa England). Gale.
South America, Central America & the Caribbean, 1986. 90.00x (ISBN 0-317-44262-7, Pub. by Europa). Intl Pubns Serv.
South America into the Nineteen Nineties: Evolving International Relationships in a New Era. Ed. by G. Pope Atkins. 1988. write for info. CSI Studies.
South America into the 1990s: Evolving International Relationships in a New Era. Ed. by G. Pope Atkins. (Special Studies on Latin America & the Caribbean). 230p. 1988. 36.50 (ISBN 0-8133-7515-0). Westview.
South America Looks at the United States. Clarence H. Haring. LC 72-111716. (American Imperialism: Viewpoints of United States Foreign Policy, 1898-1941). 1970. Repr. of 1928 ed. 17.00 (ISBN 0-405-02025-2). Ayer Co Pubs.
South America: Observations & Impressions. James Bryce. (Latin America in the 20th Century Ser.). 1977. Repr. of 1912 ed. lib. bdg. 69.50 (ISBN 0-306-70835-3). Da Capo.
South America of the Poets. Selden Rodman. (Arcturus Books Paperbacks). (Illus.). 286p. 1972. pap. 2.95x (ISBN 0-8093-0573-9). S Ill U Pr.
South America on a Shoestring. 3rd ed. Geoff Crowther. 752p. (Orig.). 1986. pap. 14.95 (ISBN 0-908086-75-X). Lonely Planet.
South America on Thirty Dollars a Day: Frommer's Thirty Dollars-A-Day Guides. rev. ed. Arnold Greenberg & Harriet Greenberg. 432p. 1987. pap. 12.95 (ISBN 0-671-62457-1). P-H.
South America on Twenty-Five Dollars a Day. Arnold Greenberg. 432p. 1985. pap. 9.95 (ISBN 0-671-53156-5). Prentice Hall Pr.
South America: Problems & Prospects. Ed. by Irwin Isenberg. (Reference Shelf Ser: Vol. 47, No. 2). 1975. 10.00 (ISBN 0-8242-0570-7). Wilson.
South America River Trips, Vol. I. George Bradt. LC 80-69523. (Illus.). 108p. (Orig.). 1981. pap. 7.95 (ISBN 0-933982-13-5). Bradt Ent.
South America River Trips, Vol. III. Tanis Jordan & Martin Jordan. (Illus.). 144p. (Orig.). Date not set. pap. cancelled (ISBN 0-933982-31-3). Bradt Ent.
South America Travel Digest. 16th ed. Charles Jacobs & Babette Jacobs. (Illus.). 168p. 1986. pap. 9.95 (ISBN 0-912640-39-1). Travel Digests.
South America, 1987. Steve Birnbaum. (Illus.). 784p. 1986. pap. 11.95 (ISBN 0-395-42335-X). HM.
South America, 1989. Stephen Birnbaum. (Birnbaum's Travel Guides Ser.). 800p. 1988. pap. 12.95 (ISBN 0-395-48263-1). HM.
South American Cook Book; Including Central America, Mexico & the West Indies. Bob Brown et al. LC 72-166427. 1971. pap. 6.95 (ISBN 0-486-20190-2). Dover.
South American Development: A Geographical Introduction. 2nd ed. Rosemary Bromley & Ray Bromley. LC 82-1171. (Cambridge Topics in Geography Ser.: No. 2). (Illus.). 112p. 1982. 14.95 (ISBN 0-521-23496-4); pap. 9.95 (ISBN 0-521-28008-7). Cambridge U Pr.
South American Economic Handbook. (Economic Handbook Ser.). 325p. 1986. 80.00X (ISBN 0-86338-125-1, Pub. by Euromonitor Pubns). Gale.
South American Handbook, 1986. 62nd ed. 1985. cancelled 41.00 (ISBN 0-900751-24-X). Intl Pubns Serv.
South American Handbook, 1989. Ed. by John Brooks. 1350p. 1989. pap. 29.95 (ISBN 0-13-823717-4). Prentice Hall Pr.
South American Herpetofauna: Its Origin, Evolution & Dispersal. Ed. by William E. Duellman et al. (U of KS Museum of Nat. Hist. Monograph: No. 7). (Illus.). 485p. 1979. pap. 15.00 (ISBN 0-89338-008-3). U of KS Mus Nat Hist.
South American Indian Languages: Retrospect & Prospect. Ed. by Harriet E. Klein & Louisa R. Stark. (Texas Linguistics Ser.). 869p. 1985. text ed. 32.50x (ISBN 0-292-77592-X). U of Tex Pr.
South American Indian Narrative Theoretical & Analytical Approaches: An Annotated Bibliography. Susan A. Niles. LC 80-9020. 205p. 1985. lib. bdg. 31.00 (ISBN 0-8240-9308-9). Garland Pub.
South American Indians: A Case Study in Evolution. Francisco M. Salzano & Sidia M. Callegari-Jacques. (Research Monographs on Human Population Biology Ser.). 272p. 1988. 75.00 (ISBN 0-19-857635-8). Oxford U Pr.
South American Kinship: Eight Kinship Systems from Brazil & Colombia. Ed. by William R. Merrifield. LC 85-80410. (International Museum of Cultures Publications: No. 18). (Illus.). 132p. (Orig.). 1985. pap. 12.00x (ISBN 0-88312-173-5); microfiche (2) 4.00 (ISBN 0-88312-255-3). Summer Inst Ling.
South American Land Birds: A Photographic Aid to Identification. John S. Dunning. Ed. by Robert S. Ridgely. LC 82-9351. (Illus.). 400p. 1982. 39.50 (ISBN 0-915180-21-9); pap. 39.50 (ISBN 0-915180-22-7). Harrowood Bks.
South American Mythology. Harold Osborne. LC 85-28567. (Library of the World's Myths & Legends). (Illus.). 144p. 1986. 18.95 (ISBN 0-87226-043-7). P Bedrick Bks.
South American Republics, 2 Vols. Thomas C. Dawson. Repr. of 1903 ed. Set. 45.00 (ISBN 0-404-02011-9). AMS Pr.
South American Romances: The Purple Lane; Green Mansions; el Ombu. W. H. Hudson. 823p. 1981. Repr. of 1930 ed. lib. bdg. 40.00 (ISBN 0-89987-368-5). Darby Bks.
South American Sketches of R. B. Cunninghame Graham. R. B. Cunninghame Graham. Ed. by John Walker. LC 77-18604. 1978. 18.95 (ISBN 0-8061-1468-1). U of Okla Pr.
South American Sociologists, A Directory. Gunter W. Remmling. (Guides & Bibliographies Ser.). pap. 20.00 (2027326). Bks Demand UMI.
South American Trade of Baltimore. F. R. Rutter. pap. 10.00 (ISBN 0-384-52643-8). Johnson Repr.
South American Trade of Baltimore. Frank R. Rutter. LC 78-68359. (Johns Hopkins University. Studies in the Social Sciences. Fifteenth Ser. 1897: 9). Repr. of 1897 ed. 11.50 (ISBN 0-404-61115-X). AMS Pr.
South American Trilogy: Osman Lins, Felisberto Hernandez & Luis Fernando Vidal. Trilingual ed. Ed. by Luis A. Ramos-Garcia. (Span., Eng. & Port.). 1982. 5.95 (ISBN 0-934840-04-0). Studia Hispanica.
South Americans. Alan Cullison. (Peoples of North America Ser.). (Illus.). 112p. (gr. 5 up). Date not set. lib. bdg. 16.95x (ISBN 0-87754-863-3). Chelsea Hse.
South & Central America. John Pimlott. Ed. by Franklin Watts Ltd. (Conflict in 20th Century Ser.). (Illus.). 64p. (gr. k-12). 1988. 12.90 (ISBN 0-531-10540-7). Watts.
South & Central America (Including Caribbean & Bermuda; see Supplement to the World Trade Annual 1983: Trade of the Industrial Nations with Eastern Europe & the Developing Nations.
South & Faulkner's Yoknapatawpha: The Actual & the Apocryphal. Ed. by Evans Harrington & Ann J. Abadie. LC 77-8741. 1977. 10.95x (ISBN 0-87805-035-3); pap. 5.95 (ISBN 0-87805-037-X). U Pr of Miss.
South & North & Other Poems. Lyall Wilkes. 48p. 1984. 8.95 (ISBN 0-85362-208-6, Oriel). Routledge Chapman & Hall.
South & South East Asia. B. N. Pandey. LC 79-26753. 1980. 25.00 (ISBN 0-312-74710-1). St Martin.
South & Southeast Asia: Doctoral Dissertations & Masters' Theses Completed at the University of California at Berkeley, 1906-1973. rev. ed. Ed. by Richard J. Kozicki & Peter Ananda. (Occasional Papers: No. 11). 58p. 1983. pap. text ed. 8.25 (ISBN 0-8191-3121-0, Co-pub. by Ctr S SE Asia). U Pr of Amer.
South & Southeast Asia: Enduring Scholarship Selected from the Far Eastern Quarterly, the Journal of Asian Studies 1941-1971. Ed. by John A. Harrison. LC 72-83465. (Thirtieth Anniversary Commemorative Ser: Vol. 3). 246p. 1972. pap. 3.75x (ISBN 0-8165-0364-8). U of Ariz Pr.
South & Southeast Asia Studies, 55 titles in 57 vols. (AMS Press Reprint Ser.). Repr. of 1954 ed. Set. write for info. (ISBN 0-404-54800-8). AMS Pr.
South & Southeast England. (AA Regional Touring Guides). (Illus.). 176p. 1988. pap. 19.95 (ISBN 0-86145-500-2, Pub. by British Tour). Salem Hse Pubs.
South & Southwest: Literary Essays & Reminiscences. Jay B. Hubbell. LC 65-26839. xi, 369p. 1965. 27.95 (ISBN 0-8223-0090-7). Duke.
South & the Concurrent Majority. David M. Potter. Ed. by Don E. Fehrenbacher & Carl N. Degler. LC 72-84123. (Walter Lynwood Fleming Lectures). viii, 90p. 1972. 7.95x (ISBN 0-8071-0229-6). La State U Pr.
South & the Nation. E. P. Lawton. LC 63-16251. 1963. 6.95 (ISBN 0-87208-002-1); pap. 2.50 (ISBN 0-87208-003-X). Island Pr Pubs.
South & the North in American Religion. Samuel S. Hill. LC 80-234. (Mercer University Lamar Memorial Lecture Ser.: No. 23). 168p. 1980. 14.00x (ISBN 0-8203-0516-2). U of Ga Pr.
South & the North: Poems of a Tragic Hemisphere. Gary E. Erb. 32p. (Orig.). 1987. pap. 3.00 (ISBN 0-939634-05-8). Laughing Waters.
South & the Politics of Slavery, 1828-1856. William J. Cooper, Jr. LC 78-751. 456p. 1978. 40.00 (ISBN 0-8071-0385-3); pap. 9.95 (ISBN 0-8071-0775-1). La State U Pr.
South & the Presidency: From Reconstruction to Carter. Henry Paolucci. 1978. pap. 3.00 (ISBN 0-918680-07-7). Griffon Hse.
South & the Sectional Conflict. David M. Potter. LC 68-8941. xvi, 322p. 1968. pap. text ed. 10.95 (ISBN 0-8071-0201-6). La State U Pr.
South & Three Sectional Crises. Don E. Fehrenbacher. LC 79-18143. (Walter Linwood Fleming Lectures). viii, 88p. 1980. text ed. 10.95 (ISBN 0-8071-0671-2). La State U Pr.
South & West Wales. Peter Gibson. (Vistor's Guide Ser.). 1986. pap. 8.95 (ISBN 0-935161-41-4). Hunter Pub NY.
South Arabian Hunt. R. B. Serjeant. 150p. 1976. 45.00x (ISBN 0-317-39155-0, Pub. by Luzac & Co Ltd). State Mutual Bk.
South As It Is: 1865-1866. John R. Dennett. Ed. by Henry M. Christman. LC 86-7095. 383p. 1986. pap. 12.50x (ISBN 0-8203-0887-0). U of GA Pr.
South Asia. 2nd ed. B. L. Johnson. 1981. text ed. 22.50x (ISBN 0-435-35488-4). Heinemann Ed.
South Asia. Angus Maude. LC 66-18564. 1966. 10.95 (ISBN 0-8023-1076-1). Dufour.
South Asia: A Short History of the Subcontinent. 2nd ed. Milton W. Meyer. (Quality Paperback: No. 34). 268p. (Orig.). 1976. pap. 3.95 (ISBN 0-8226-0034-X). Littlefield.
South Asia & Burma Retrospective Bibliograhpy, Stage 1: 1556-1800. Ed. by Graham Shaw. 1987. 30.00 (ISBN 0-7123-0119-4, Pub. by British Lib). Longwood Pub Group.
South Asia in International Politics. P. K. Mishra. 498p. 1986. 49.95x (ISBN 0-317-39867-9, Pub. by UDH Pubs India). Asia Bk Corp.

South Asia in the World Today. Henry Brodie et al. Ed. by Phillips Talbot. LC 78-161774. (BCL Ser. I). Repr. of 1950 ed. 22.50 (ISBN 0-404-09042-7). AMS Pr.

South Asia in Transition: Conflicts & Tensions. Ed. by Kalim Bahadur. 1986. 21.00 (ISBN 81-7050-023-0, Pub. by Patriot). South Asia Bks.

South Asia in Transition: Conflicts & Tensions. Ed. by Kalim Bahadur. 320p. 1986. 15.00 (ISBN 0-318-23245-6, Pub. by Patriot Pubs). Nataraj Bks.

South Asia-Pacific Region: Emerging Trends. K. P. Misra & V. D. Chopra. 1988. 27.00x (Pub. by Patriot). South Asia Bks.

South Asian Archaeology. Ed. by Norman Hammond. LC 73-76367. (Illus.). 320p. 1974. 20.00 (ISBN 0-8155-5021-9, NP). Noyes.

South Asian Archaeology 1981: Proceedings. International Conference of the Association of South Asian Archaeologists in Western Europe, 6th. Ed. by Bridget Allchin et al. LC 83-14377. (University of Cambridge Oriental Publications Ser.: No. 34). (Illus.). 300p. 1984. 75.00 (ISBN 0-521-25599-6). Cambridge U Pr.

South Asian Civilizations: A Bibliographic Synthesis. Maureen L. Patterson. LC 81-52518. (Illus.). 900p. 1982. 70.00x (ISBN 0-226-64910-5). U of Chicago Pr.

South Asian Insecurity & the Great Powers. Barry G. Buzan & Gowher Rizvi. LC 86-1820. 256p. 1986. 32.50 (ISBN 0-312-74714-4). St Martin.

South Asian Intellectuals & Social Change. Yogendra Malik. 1982. 24.00x (ISBN 0-8364-0825-X); 15.00x (ISBN 0-686-81181-X). South Asia Bks.

South Asian Languages: A Handbook. Ed. by C. Shackle. 1986. pap. 9.00x (ISBN 0-8364-1629-5). South Asia Bks.

South Asian Languages: Structure, Convergence & Diglossia. B. Krishnamurti et al. 1986. 38.00X (ISBN 81-208-0033-8, Pub. by Motilal Banarsidass). South Asia Bks.

South Asian Microform Project (SAMP) Catalog: 1980 Cumulative Education. 246p. 12.50 (ISBN 0-932486-33-9). Ctr Res Lib.

South Asian Religion & Society. Ed. by Asko Parpola & Bent S. Hansen. (Studies on Asian Topics (Scandinavian Institute of Asian Studies): No. 11). 262p. 1986. pap. 25.00 (ISBN 0-913215-16-3). Riverdale Co.

South Asian Sculpture: The Harold P. & Jane F. Ullman Collection. Ronald Y. Otsuka & Mary C. Lanius. LC 74-30854. (Illus.). 1975. pap. 3.50 (ISBN 0-914738-06-2). Denver Art Mus.

South Asian Security: Problems & Prospects. B. M. Jain. 220p. 1985. text ed. 25.00x (ISBN 81-7027-085-5, Pub. by Radiant Pub India). Humanities.

South Asian Security: Problems & Prospects. B. M. Jain. 201p. 1985. 24.95. Asia Bk Corp.

South Asian Societies: A Study of Values & Social Controls. Christoph Von Furer-Haimendorf. 240p. 1982. 41.00x (ISBN 0-85692-031-2, Pub. by E-W Pubns England). State Mutual Bk.

South Asians in North America: An Annotated & Selected Bibliography. Ed. by Jane Singh et al. LC 87-73457. (Occasional Paper Ser.: No. 14). 200p. (Orig.). 1988. pap. write for info. (ISBN 0-944613-03-9). UC Berkeley Ctr SE Asia.

South Atlantic Palaeoceanography. Ed. by Kenneth J. Hsu & Helmut J. Weissert. (Illus.). 368p. 1985. 70.00 (ISBN 0-521-26609-2). Cambridge U Pr.

South Atlantic Studies for Sturgis E. Leavitt. facsimile ed. South Atlantic Modern Language Association. Ed. by Thomas B. Stroup & Sterling A. Stoudemire. LC 77-37941. (Essay Index Reprint Ser). Repr. of 1953 ed. 19.00 (ISBN 0-8369-2628-5). Ayer Co Pubs.

South Bay Trails: Outdoor Adventures Around the Santa Clara Valley. Francis Spangle & Jean Rusmore. LC 82-62813. (Illus.). 224p. (Orig.). 1984. pap. 11.95 (ISBN 0-89997-022-2). Wilderness Pr.

South Biscay Pilot. 3rd, rev. ed. Robin Brandon. (Illus.). 388p. 1987. 75.00 (ISBN 0-229-11680-9, Pub. by Adlar Coles). Sheridan.

South Biscay Pilot: The Gironde Estuary to La Coruna. Robin Brandon. (Illus.). 388p. 1977. 59.95x (ISBN 0-8464-1273-X). Beekman Pubs.

South by Java Head. Alistair Maclean. 1976. Repr. of 1958 ed. lib. bdg. 18.95 (ISBN 0-89190-173-6, Pub. by River City Pr). Amereon Ltd.

South by Java Head. Alistair MacLean. 1984. pap. 2.95 (ISBN 0-449-20577-0, Crest). Fawcett.

South by Southeast: Paintings by Ray Ellis; Text by Walter Cronkite. LC 83-60427. (Illus.). 128p. 1983. 50.00 (ISBN 0-8487-0539-4). Oxmoor Hse.

South by Southwest: 24 Stories from Modern Texas. Ed. by Don Graham. 300p. (Orig.). 1986. 22.50 (ISBN 0-292-77600-4); pap. 9.95 (ISBN 0-292-77601-2). U of Tex Pr.

South by West: A Galaxy of Southwestern & Western Scenes & Portraits. Everett A. Gillis. 48p. (Orig.). 1981. pap. 5.00 (ISBN 0-938328-00-X). Pisces Pr TX.

South Caribbean Travel Guide. Berlitz Editors. (Travel Guides for English Speakers Ser.). 1981. pap. 6.95 (ISBN 0-02-969810-3, Berlitz). Macmillan.

South Carolina. Allan Carpenter. LC 79-11453. (New Enchantment of America State Bks.). (Illus.). 96p. (gr. 4 up). 1979. PLB 15.93 (ISBN 0-516-04140-1). Childrens.

South Carolina. Turner Educational Services, Inc. Staff & James I. Clark. (Portrait of America Library). 48p. (gr. 4 up). 1986. PLB 15.33 (ISBN 0-86514-475-3); pap. text ed. 9.27 (ISBN 0-86514-550-4); Beta Video 113.33 (ISBN 0-86514-107-X); VHS Video 113.33 (ISBN 0-86514-182-7); 3-4" Video 136.00 (ISBN 0-86514-257-2); tchr. study guide 13.27 (ISBN 0-86514-332-3); student activity bk. 6.60 (ISBN 0-86514-407-9); Index 13.27. Raintree Pubs.

South Carolina. Louis B. Wright. (States & the Nation). (Illus.). 225p. 1976. 14.95 (ISBN 0-393-05560-4, Co-Pub by AASLH). Norton.

South Carolina. Louis B. Wright. (Illus.). 1977. pap. 1.95 (ISBN 0-393-05640-6). Norton.

South Carolina: A Geography. Charles F. Kovacik & John J. Winberry. (Westview Geographies of the U. S. Ser.). 230p. 1986. 45.00 (ISBN 0-89158-987-2). Westview.

South Carolina: A Guide to the Palmetto State. Federal Writers' Project Staff. (American Guidebook Ser.). 514p. 1941. Repr. 69.00x (ISBN 0-403-02189-8). Somerset Pub.

South Carolina: A Journalist & His State. Eugene B. Sloan. LC 74-20533. (Illus.). 1974. text ed. 39.95x (ISBN 0-915114-01-1). Lewis-Sloan.

South Carolina: A Scenic Discovery. Clyde H. Smith. Ed. by James B. Patrick. (Scenic Discovery Ser.). (Illus.). 128p. 1984. 30.00 (ISBN 0-89909-048-6). Yankee Bks.

South Carolina: A Short History, 1520-1948. David D. Wallace. LC 61-15974. (Illus.). 1984. Repr. of 1951 ed. 24.95x (ISBN 0-87249-079-3). U of SC Pr.

South Carolina: An Illustrated History of the Palmetto State. Ernest M. Lander, Jr. Ed. by Amy Adelstein. (Illus.). 208p. (YA) (gr. 7 up). 1988. 32.95 (ISBN 0-89781-262-X). Windsor Pubns Inc.

South Carolina Architecture, 1670-1970. LC 75-117158. 5.00 (ISBN 0-910326-08-8). Carolina Art.

South Carolina As a Royal Province, Seventeen Nineteen to Seventeen Seventy-Six. facsimile ed. William R. Smith. LC 75-114897. (Select Bibliographies Reprint Ser). 1903. 27.50 (ISBN 0-8369-5301-0). Ayer Co Pubs.

South Carolina Automotive Directory. Ed. by T. L. Spelman. 1985. 24.95 (ISBN 1-55527-029-8). Auto Contact Inc.

South Carolina Ballads. facsimile ed. Ed. by Reed Smith. LC 74-38025. (Black Heritage Library Collection). Repr. of 1928 ed. 16.00 (ISBN 0-8369-8991-0). Ayer Co Pubs.

South Carolina Ballads with a Study of the Traditional Ballad Today. Reed Smith. LC 74-187374. 186p. 1972. Repr. of 1928 ed. 20.00 (ISBN 0-87152-102-4). Reprint.

South Carolina Baptists: 1670-1805. Leah Townsend. LC 74-6312. (Illus.). 391p. 1978. Repr. of 1935 ed. 20.00 (ISBN 0-8063-0621-1). Genealog Pub.

South Carolina Census Index, 1790. Ronald V. Jackson. (Illus.). lib. bdg. 22.00 (ISBN 0-317-17067-8). Accelerated Index.

South Carolina Census Index, 1800. Ronald V. Jackson. (Illus.). lib. bdg. 30.00 (ISBN 0-317-17068-6). Accelerated Index.

South Carolina Census Index, 1810. Ronald V. Jackson & Gary R. Teeples. LC 77-86086. (Illus.). lib. bdg. 29.00 (ISBN 0-89593-128-1). Accelerated Index.

South Carolina Census Index, 1820. Ronald V. Jackson. LC 77-86087. (Illus.). lib. bdg. 32.00 (ISBN 0-89593-129-X). Accelerated Index.

South Carolina Census Index, 1830. Ronald V. Jackson. LC 77-86088. (Illus.). lib. bdg. 35.00 (ISBN 0-89593-130-3). Accelerated Index.

South Carolina Census Index, 1840. Ronald V. Jackson. LC 77-86078. (Illus.). lib. bdg. 40.00 (ISBN 0-89593-131-1). Accelerated Index.

South Carolina Census Index, 1850. Ronald V. Jackson & Gary R. Teeples. LC 77-86079. (Illus.). lib. bdg. 55.00 (ISBN 0-89593-132-X). Accelerated Index.

South Carolina Census Index, 1860: An Every-Name Index, 2 vols. Compiled by Bryan L. Dilts. LC 84-9149. 1985. lib. bdg. 199.00x (ISBN 0-914311-52-2); microfiche 99.00x (ISBN 0-914311-53-0). Index Pub.

South Carolina Census Index, 1890: Union Veterans. Ronald V. Jackson. (Illus.). lib. bdg. 15.00 (ISBN 0-317-17069-4). Accelerated Index.

South Carolina Chronology & Factbook, Vol. 40. Robert I. Vexler. LC 78-26305. (Chronologies & Documentary Handbook of the States). 147p. 1978. 8.50 (ISBN 0-379-16165-6). Oceana.

South Carolina Chronology, 1497-1970. George C. Rogers, Jr. LC 72-13365. (Tricentennial Booklets: No. 11). 64p. 1973. pap. text ed. 4.95 (ISBN 0-87249-234-6). U of SC Pr.

South Carolina Colonial Land Policies. Robert K. Ackerman. LC 74-16184. (Tricentennial Studies: No. 9). 1977. 19.95x (ISBN 0-87249-254-0). U of SC Pr.

South Carolina Condominium Law Manual. MacGregor. 80.00 (ISBN 0-409-26510-1). D & S Pub.

South Carolina Consumer Credit Law & Regulations. Harry J. Haynsworth, IV. (Consumer Law & Practice in South Carolina Ser.). 515p. 1984. 3 ring binder 50.00 (ISBN 0-318-04040-9). SC Bar CLE.

South Carolina Cook Book. rev. ed. Ed. by South Carolina Extension Homemakers Council & Clemson Extension Home Economics Staff. LC 54-4697. (Illus.). 426p. 1984. pap. 8.95 (ISBN 0-87249-354-7). U of SC Pr.

South Carolina Cookbook. 2.85 (ISBN 0-936672-28-5). Aerial Photo.

South Carolina County Maps. rev. ed. Ed. by C. J. Puetz. (Illus.). 128p. Date not set. pap. 11.90 (ISBN 0-916514-14-5). Cnty Maps.

South Carolina Deed Abstracts, 1719-1772. Clara B. Langley. Incl. Vol. 1. 1719-1740, Books A-T. 392p (ISBN 0-89308-271-6); Vol. 2. 1740-1755, Books V-PP. 370p (ISBN 0-89308-272-4); Vol. 3. 1755-1768, Books QQ-HHH. 386p (ISBN 0-89308-273-2); Vol. 4. 1768-1772, Books III-ZZZ. 400p (ISBN 0-89308-317-8). 1983. 37.50 ea. Southern Hist Pr.

South Carolina: Economic & Social Conditions in 1944. W. H. Callcott. LC 74-34437. 248p. 1975. Repr. of 1945 ed. 16.50 (ISBN 0-87152-189-X). Reprint.

South Carolina Folk Tales. Writer's Program. LC 76-28225. 1976. Repr. of 1941 ed. lib. bdg. 35.00 (ISBN 0-8414-7821-X). Folcroft.

South Carolina Folktales. Federal Writers' Project, South Carolina. LC 73-3651. (American Guide Ser). Repr. of 1941 ed. 10.00 (ISBN 0-404-57951-5). AMS Pr.

South Carolina: From the Highlands to the Lowlands. 32p. (ps-12). 2.75 (ISBN 0-936672-66-8). Aerial Photo.

South Carolina Genealogical Research. 192p. 1985. pap. 9.00 (ISBN 0-913857-08-4). Genealog Sources.

South Carolina Genealogies: Articles from the South Carolina Historical & Geneological Magazine, Vols. I-V. LC 82-20497. 1983. Set. 125.00 (ISBN 0-87152-368-X); Vol. I, 456p. 25.00 ea. (ISBN 0-87152-369-8). Vol. II, 472 (ISBN 0-87152-370-1). Vol. III, 480 (ISBN 0-87152-371-X). Vol. IV, 464 (ISBN 0-87152-372-8). Vol. V, 208 (ISBN 0-87152-373-6). Reprint.

South Carolina Ghost Tales. Nell S. Graydon. 12.95 (ISBN 0-910206-06-6). Beaufort SC.

South Carolina Ghosts: From the Mountains to the Coast. Nancy Roberts. (Illus.). 152p. 1983. 12.95 (ISBN 0-87249-428-4); pap. 7.95 (ISBN 0-87249-429-2). U of SC Pr.

South Carolina Highway Department, 1917-1987. John H. Moore. 350p. 1987. text ed. 9.95x (ISBN 0-87249-528-0). U of SC Pr.

South Carolina Hiking Trails. Allen DeHart. LC 83-49035. (Illus.). 288p. 1984. pap. 8.95 (ISBN 0-87742-009-5). Globe Pequot.

South Carolina Historical & Biographical Index, Vol. 1. Ronald Vern Jackson. LC 78-53716. (Illus.). 1984. lib. bdg. 30.00 (ISBN 0-89593-199-0). Accelerated Index.

South Carolina Historical Magazine Index 71-81, 1970-1980, with Additions & Corrections 1-53, 1900-1952. rev ed. Ed. by Harlan Greene & Frank Q. O'Neill. LC 5-32201. 384p. 1981. pap. 25.00 (ISBN 0-87152-356-6). Reprint.

South Carolina Imprints, 1731-1800: A Descriptive Bibliography. Christopher Gould & Richard P. Morgan. LC 84-21662. 325p. 1985. lib. bdg. 75.00 (ISBN 0-87436-415-9). ABC-Clio.

South Carolina in the Confederation. Charles G. Singer. LC 76-49490. (Perspectives in American History Ser.: No. 39). (Illus.). vii, 183p. 1977. Repr. of 1941 ed. lib. bdg. 27.50x (ISBN 0-87991-363-0). Porcupine Pr.

South Carolina in the Eighteen Eighties: A Gazetteer. John H. Moore. Date not set. price not set (ISBN 0-87844-069-0). Sandlapper Pub Co.

South Carolina: In Words & Pictures. Dennis Fradin. LC 79-22550. (Young People's Stories of Our States Ser.). (Illus.). 48p. (gr. 2-5). 1980. PLB 13.27 (ISBN 0-516-03940-7). Childrens.

South Carolina Industrial Directory, 1988. 600p. 1988. pap. 60.00 (ISBN 0-318-02870-0). Manufacturers.

South Carolina Jockey Club. John B. Irving. LC 75-1143. (Illus.). 262p. 1975. Repr. of 1857 ed. 16.50 (ISBN 0-87152-194-6). Reprint.

South Carolina Jography: A Fun Run Through the Palmetto State. Carole Marsh. (Carole Marsh Bks.). (Illus.). 50p. (Orig.). (gr. 3-9). 1986. pap. 7.95 (ISBN 0-935326-96-0). Gallopade Pub Group.

South Carolina Journals & Journalists. Ed. by James B. Meriwether. LC 75-22200. 364p. 1975. 15.00 (ISBN 0-87152-212-8). Reprint.

South Carolina Legal History. Ed. by Herbert A. Johnson. LC 79-24275. 1980. 16.50 (ISBN 0-87152-312-4). Reprint.

South Carolina Legal Research Handbook. Robin K. Mills & Jon S. Schultz. LC 75-21933. vi, 115p. 1976. lib. bdg. 28.00 (ISBN 0-930342-16-X). W S Hein.

South Carolina Life & Health. 5th ed. 1985. write for info. (ISBN 0-930868-24-2). Merritt Co.

South Carolina Living: History, Geography, Government, Today (3rd grade Social Studies text) Kathleen L. Sloan. 1987. pap. 25.00x (ISBN 0-915114-05-4). Lewis-Sloan.

South Carolina Logging Railroads. Thomas Fetters. 1988. write for info. (ISBN 0-911581-09-X). Heimburger Hse Pub.

South Carolina Loyalists in the American Revolution. Robert S. Lambert. 480p. 1987. text ed. 29.95x (ISBN 0-87249-506-X). U of SC Pr.

South Carolina Marriages, 1688-1799. Brent H. Holcomb. LC 80-80449. 349p. 1983. Repr. of 1980 ed. 20.00 (ISBN 0-8063-0891-5). Genealog Pub.

South Carolina Marriages, 1800-1820. Brent H. Holcomb. LC 81-80885. 171p. 1981. 15.00 (ISBN 0-8063-0939-3). Genealog Pub.

South Carolina Naturalizations, 1783-1850. Brent H. Holcomb. LC 84-81863. 255p. 1985. 20.00 (ISBN 0-8063-1101-0). Genealog Pub.

South Carolina Negro Legislators: A Glorious Success. Lawrence C. Bryant. 1974. 15.00 (ISBN 0-686-05553-5); pap. 10.00 (ISBN 0-686-05554-3). L C Bryant.

South Carolina Negroes, 1877-1900. George B. Tindall. LC 52-14558. (Illus.). 1970. Repr. of 1952 ed. lib. bdg. 24.95 (ISBN 0-87249-042-4). U of SC Pr.

South Carolina: One of the Fifty States. Lewis P. Jones. LC 85-1882. (Illus.). 720p. (gr. 8). 1985. text ed. 29.95x (ISBN 0-87844-062-3); tchr's. manual avail. (ISBN 0-87844-063-1). Sandlapper Pub Co.

South Carolina Property & Casualty. 5th ed. 310p. 1987. write for info. (ISBN 0-930868-25-0). Merritt Co.

South Carolina Provincial Troops. Alexander S. Salley, Jr. LC 76-57909. 234p. 1977. Repr. of 1902 ed. 15.00 (ISBN 0-8063-0757-9). Genealog Pub.

South Carolina: Resources & Population, Institutions & Industries. LC 78-187375. (Illus.). 768p. 1972. Repr. of 1883 ed. 28.25 (ISBN 0-87152-103-2). Reprint.

South Carolina Rules of Court, 1986 Edition. 850p. 1985. pap. 25.00 (ISBN 0-314-99743-1). West Pub.

South Carolina Silly Trivia. Carole Marsh. (Carole Marsh Bks.). (Illus.). 60p. (Orig.). (gr. 3-12). 1986. pap. 7.95 (ISBN 0-935326-95-2). Gallopade Pub Group.

South Carolina Statutes at Large of South Carolina, 12 vols. LC 74-19726. Repr. of 1841 ed. Set. 648.00 (ISBN 0-404-12500-X); 54.00 ea. AMS Pr.

South Carolina Story. Anne R. Osborne. (Illus.). 240p. Date not set. price not set (ISBN 0-87844-023-2). Sandlapper Pub Co.

South Carolina Survival. Betty L. Hall & Hunter Draper. 160p. (Orig.). (gr. 10-12). 1979. pap. text ed. 5.84 (ISBN 0-03-055521-3). Westwood Pr.

South Carolina: Synoptic History for Laymen. 3nd, rev. ed. Lewis P. Jones. LC 72-143040. (Illus.). 300p. (Orig.). 1979. pap. text ed. 8.95 (ISBN 0-87844-004-6). Sandlapper Pub Co.

South Carolina Tax List 1733-1742. Tony Draine & John Skinner. LC 86-72105. 98p. 1987. pap. 16.00 (ISBN 0-938599-01-1). Congaree Pubns.

South Carolina Tax List 1760-1774. Tony Draine & John Skinner. 250p. 1987. pap. 25.00 (ISBN 0-938599-02-X). Congaree Pubns.

South Carolina: The WPA Guide to the Palmetto State. Federal Works Agency, Work Projects Administration, Federal Writers' Project Staff. (American Guide Ser.). (Illus.). 514p. 1988. text ed. 29.95x (ISBN 0-87249-602-3); pap. 14.95 (ISBN 0-87249-603-1). U of SC Pr.

South Carolina: Trusts. 8.50 (ISBN 0-686-90895-3); suppl. 6.00 (ISBN 0-686-90896-1). Am Law Inst.

South Carolina Upcountry, Fifteen Forty to Nineteen Eighty: Historical & Biographical Sketches, Vol. II. E. D. Herd, Jr. 294p. (Orig.). 1982. pap. 9.95 (ISBN 0-87921-067-2). Attic Pr.

South Carolina Water Ways. Mariam Cropper. LC 77-86081. lib. bdg. 10.00 (ISBN 0-89593-133-8). Accelerated Index.

South Carolina Water Ways. Ronald V. Jackson. (Illus.). lib. bdg. 20.00 (ISBN 0-317-17045-7). Accelerated Index.

South Carolina Women: They Dared to Lead. Idella Bodie. LC 78-64858. (Illus.). 160p. 1978. Clothbound 9.95 (ISBN 0-87844-044-5). Sandlapper Pub Co.

South Carolina Women Writers. LC 78-31300. 1979. 15.00 (ISBN 0-87152-292-6). Reprint.

South Carolina's Civil War of 1775. Lewis Jones. LC 75-32396. 1975. pap. 2.95 (ISBN 0-87844-027-5). Sandlapper Pub Co.

South Carolina's Historic Restaurants & Their Recipes. Dawn O'Brien & Karen Mulford. LC 84-18556. (Illus.). 205p. 1984. 12.95 (ISBN 0-89587-041-X). Blair.

South Carolina's Low Country: A Past Preserved. Catherine C. Messmer. (Illus.). 1988. 35.95 (ISBN 0-87844-070-4). Sandlapper Pub Co.

South Carolinians in the Revolution. Sara S. Ervin. LC 65-24109. (Illus.). 217p. 1981. Repr. of 1949 ed. 15.00. Genealog Pub.

South Central California Counties Public Schools, 1986, Vol. 3. Lillian S. Clancy. (California Public Schools Ser.: How Are They Doing?). 400p. (Orig.). 1985. pap. 24.95 (ISBN 0-939580-30-6). Sindowilf Ltd.

South Central California Counties Public Schools, 1987, Vol. 3. Lillian S. Clancy. (California Public Schools: How Are They Doing? Ser.). 400p. (Orig.). 1987. pap. 24.95 (ISBN 0-939580-39-X). Sindowilf Ltd.

South Central California Counties Public Schools, 1988, Vol. 3. Lillian S. Clancy. (California Public Schools: How Are They Doing? Ser.). 400p. (Orig.). 1988. pap. 25.95 (ISBN 0-939580-47-0). Sindowilf Ltd.

South Central Frontiers. Paul Erb. LC 74-12108. (Studies in Anabaptist & Mennonite History, No. 17). (Illus.). 448p. 1974. 19.95x (ISBN 0-8361-1196-6). Herald Pr.

South Central Juvenile Care Center: Evaluation Project. National Center for State Courts Staff. 55p. 1978. manuscript 3.30 (NCRO-023). Natl Ctr St Courts.

South Central (Louisiana, Arkansas, Missouri, Kansas, Oklahoma) Thomas G. Aylesworth & Virginia L. Aylesworth. (Let's Discover the States Ser.). (Illus.). 66p. (gr. 5 up). 1988. lib. bdg. 14.95x (ISBN 1-55546-561-7). Chelsea Hse.

South-Central Section Field Guide. Ed. by O. T. Hayward. (DNAG Centennial Field Guide Ser.: No. 4). (Illus.). 1988. 43.50. Geol Soc.

South Central States. Geraldine Woods & Harold Woods. (First Book Ser.). 72p. (gr. 4up). 1984. lib. bdg. 10.40 (ISBN 0-531-04737-7). Watts.

South China in the Sixteenth Century: Being the Narratives of Galeote Pereira, Fr. Gasporda Cruz, O.P., Fr. Martin de Rada, O.E.S.A. (1550-1575) Ed. by C. R. Boxer. (Hakluyt Society Works Ser.: No. 2, Vol. 106). (Illus.). Repr. of 1953 ed. 60.00 (ISBN 0-8115-0398-4). Kraus Repr.

South China Sea Basin: Geo-Strategy, the Regional Balance, & Patterns of the Future. Joo-Jock Lim. 140p. 1979. 13.00x (ISBN 0-8214-0513-6, Pub. by Singapore U Pr). Ohio U Pr.

South China Sea Oil: Two Problems of Ownership & Production Development. Roderick O'Brien. 78p. (Orig.). 1977. pap. text ed. 9.50x (ISBN 0-566-04013-1, Pub. by Inst Southeast Asian Stud). Gower Pub Co.

South China Silk District: Local Historical Transformation & World-System Theory. Alvin Y. So. LC 86-14575. 206p. 1986. 52.50 (ISBN 0-88706-321-7); pap. 17.95 (ISBN 0-88706-322-5). State U NY Pr.

South Clyde Estuary: An Illustrated Architectural Guide. Frank Walker. (RIAS Guides to Scotland Ser.: No. 5). (Illus.). 152p. 1987. pap. 7.25 (ISBN 0-7073-0476-8, Pub. by Scot Acad Pr). Longwood Pub Group.

South Corner of Time: Hopi, Navaio, Papago, Yaqui Tribal Literature. Ed. by Larry Evers. LC 76-617570. (Sun Tracks Ser.: No. 6). 240p. 1981. pap. 17.50 (ISBN 0-8165-0731-7). U of Ariz Pr.

South Country. Edward Thomas. (Illus.). 304p. 1984. pap. 5.95x (ISBN 0-460-11370-4, DEL-05074, Pub. by Evman England). Biblio Dist.

South County Studies: Of Some Eighteenth Century Persons, Places & Conditions. in That Portion of Rhode Island Called Narragansett. facsimile ed. Esther B. Carpenter. LC 75-160961. (Select Bibliographies Reprint Ser). Repr. of 1924 ed. 21.00 (ISBN 0-8369-5829-2). Ayer Co Pubs.

South Dakota. new ed. Allan Carpenter. LC 78-3385. (New Enchantment of America State Bks.). (Illus.). 96p. (gr. 4 up). 1978. PLB 15.93 (ISBN 0-516-04141-X). Childrens.

South Dakota. John R. Milton. (States & the Nation Ser.). (Illus.). 1977. 14.95 (ISBN 0-393-05627-9, Co-Pub by AASLH). Norton.

South Dakota. Turner Educational Services, Inc. Staff et al. (Portrait of America Library). 48p. (gr. 4 up). 1986. PLB 15.33 (ISBN 0-86514-458-3); pap. text ed. 9.27 (ISBN 0-86514-533-4); Beta Video 113.33 (ISBN 0-86514-083-9); VHS Video 113.33 (ISBN 0-86514-158-4); 3-4" Video 136.00 (ISBN 0-86514-233-5); tchr. study guide 13.27 (ISBN 0-86514-308-0); student activity bk. 6.60 (ISBN 0-86514-383-8); Index 13.27. Raintree Pubs.

South Dakota: A Guide to the State. Federal Writers' Project Staff. (American Guidebook Ser.). 421p. 1938. Repr. 69.00x (ISBN 0-403-02190-1). Somerset Pub.

South Dakota Activity Book. Pat Bartholow. 1986. pap. 1.50 (ISBN 0-317-67935-X). Dakota Kids.

South Dakota Budgetary Developments: Process & Trends, 1967-1983. Loren M. Carlson. 1984. 1.00 (ISBN 1-55614-116-5). U of SD Gov Res Bur.

South Dakota Business Directory, 1988-1989. rev. ed. American Directory Publishing Co., Inc. Staff. 368p. 1988. pap. 65.00 (ISBN 0-944316-34-4). Amer Directory.

South Dakota Census Index 1885. Ronald V. Jackson. (Illus.). lib. bdg. 38.00 (ISBN 0-317-17070-8). Accelerated Index.

South Dakota Census Index, 1890: Union Veterans. Ronald V. Jackson. (Illus.). lib. bdg. 15.00 (ISBN 0-317-17071-6). Accelerated Index.

South Dakota Chronology & Factbook, Vol. 41. Robert I. Vexler. LC 78-26887. (Chronologies & Documentary Handbook of the States). 148p. 1978. 8.50 (ISBN 0-379-16166-4). Oceana.

South Dakota: Conflict of Laws. 8.50 (ISBN 0-686-90897-X); suppl. 6.00 (ISBN 0-686-90898-8). Am Law Inst.

South Dakota: Contracts. 9.50 (ISBN 0-686-90899-6); suppl. 7.00 (ISBN 0-686-90900-3). Am Law Inst.

South Dakota Geographic Names. new ed. Ed. by Virginia D. Sneve. LC 73-80523. 639p. 1973. 19.95 (ISBN 0-88498-008-1). Brevet Pr.

South Dakota in Washington: Profile of a Congressional Delegation. Charles O. Jones. 1966. 1.00 (ISBN 1-55614-117-3). U of SD Gov Res Bur.

South Dakota: In Words & Pictures. Dennis Fradin. LC 80-25349. (Young People's Stories of Our States Ser.). (Illus.). 48p. (gr. 2-5). 1981. PLB 13.27 (ISBN 0-516-03941-5). Childrens.

South Dakota Jails: Current Conditions & Proposed Directions. Donald C. Dahlin. 1971. 5.00 (ISBN 1-55614-000-2). U of SD Gov Res Bur.

South Dakota: Land of Shining Gold. Francie M. Berg. LC 81-67726. (Old West Region Ser.: Vol. 2). (Illus.). 176p. 1982. 16.95 (ISBN 0-918532-07-8); pap. 10.95 (ISBN 0-918532-08-6). Flying Diamond Bks.

South Dakota Legal Research Guide. Delores Jorgensen. 198p. 1988. lib. bdg. 25.00 (ISBN 0-89941-633-0). W S Hein.

South Dakota Life & Health Supplement. 1988. write for info. (ISBN 0-930868-22-6). Merritt Co.

South Dakota Manufacturers & Processors Directory, 1987-88. 256p. 1987. 30.00 (ISBN 0-318-02871-9). Manufacturers.

South Dakota Poll: A Critical Analysis. Kenneth A. Bode. 1970. 1.00 (ISBN 1-55614-001-0). U of SD Gov Res Bur.

South Dakota Recreation Guide. Lynn D. Soli & Barbara McCaig. LC 85-51898. (Illus.). 82p. (Orig.). 1985. pap. 9.95 (ISBN 0-9610130-3-6). Melius Peterson Pub.

South Dakota State Court Administrator: Filing System Report & Manual. National Center for State Courts Staff. 18p. (On loan through the NCSC Library). 1975. write for info. (MAB-145). Natl Ctr St Courts.

South Dakota State Finance. 1951. 5.00 (ISBN 1-55614-002-9). U of SD Gov Res Bur.

South Dakota Studies Program: Activity Manual. David D. Laudenschlager. Ed. by Eunice A. Combs. (Illus.). 135p. (gr. 4). 1982. Duplication Masters 49.00 (ISBN 0-943068-64-9); Teacher's Guide 5.00 (ISBN 0-943068-63-0). Graphic Learning.

South Dakota: Torts, Vols. 1-2. Set. 8.50 (ISBN 0-686-90901-1); suppl. 6.00 (ISBN 0-686-90902-X). Am Law Inst.

South Dakota: Trusts. 8.50 (ISBN 0-686-90903-8); suppl. 6.00. Am Law Inst.

South Dakota Votes for Governor: Eighteen Eighty-Nine to Nineteen Seventy-Eight. Kenneth Meyer et al. 1981. cancelled. U of SD Gov Res Bur.

South Dakota's Congressional Staffs. Alan L. Clem. 1981. 1.00 (ISBN 1-55614-003-7). U of SD Gov Res Bur.

South Dakota's Nineteen Sixty-Five Legislative Session. George M. Platt. 1965. 1.00 (ISBN 1-55614-004-5). U of SD Gov Res Bur.

South Devon: Combe, Tor & Seascape. Anne Born. (Illus.). 192p. 1985. 24.95 (ISBN 0-575-03249-9, Pub. by Gollancz England). David & Charles.

South Downs. (AA-OS Leisure Guides). (Illus.). 112p. 1988. pap. 19.95 (ISBN 0-86145-657-2, Pub. by British Tour). Salem Hse Pubs.

South During Reconstruction 1865-1877. E. Merton Coulter. LC 48-5161. (History of the South Ser.: Vol. 8). (Illus.). 1947. 30.00x (ISBN 0-8071-0008-0). La State U Pr.

South-East Africa, Fourteen Eighty Eight-Fifteen Thirty. E. V. Axelson. Repr. of 1940 ed. 22.00 (ISBN 0-527-03950-0). Kraus Repr.

South East & East Anglia. (AA Road Map Ser.). (Illus.). 1988. pap. 8.95 (ISBN 0-86145-521-5, Pub. by British Tour). Salem Hse Pubs.

South-East Asia. 2nd ed. Charles Fisher. 1966. 69.95x (ISBN 0-416-42480-5, NO.2200). Routledge Chapman & Hall.

South East Asia. rev. ed. Milton Osborne. 208p. (Orig.). 1983. pap. text ed. 9.95x (ISBN 0-86861-269-3). Unwin Hyman.

South-East Asia Handbook. Stefan Loose & Renate Ramb. (Travellers Handbook Ser.). 558p. 1985. pap. 12.95 (ISBN 3-922025-12-9). Riverdale Co.

South-East Asia in Indian Foreign Policy. Asis K. Majumdar. 1983. 22.50 (ISBN 0-8364-0932-9, Pub. by Naya Prokash India). South Asia Bks.

South-East Asia on a Shoestring. 5th ed. Tony Wheeler. 574p. (Orig.). 1985. pap. 9.95 (ISBN 0-908086-67-9). Lonely Planet.

South-East Asia: Race, Culture, & Nation. Guy Hunter. (Institute of Race Relations Ser.). (Orig.). 1966. pap. 5.95x (ISBN 0-19-500334-9). Oxford U Pr.

South East Asia 1930-1970: The Legacy of Colonialism & Nationalism. Fred R. Von Der Mehden, pseud. (Library of World Civilization Ser). (Illus.). 144p. 1974. 9.95x (ISBN 0-393-05513-2); pap. 7.95x (ISBN 0-393-09320-4). Norton.

South East Asian Pottery: Thai in Particular. J. C. Watt. 1971. 10.00x (ISBN 0-317-45264-9, Pub. by Han-Shan Tang Ltd). State Mutual Bk.

South-East Asian Seas: Oil under Troubled Waters: Hydrocarbon Potential, Jurisdictional Issues, & International Relations. Mark J. Valencia. (Natural Resources of South-East Asia Ser.). (Illus.). 125p. 1986. 24.95x (ISBN 0-19-582645-0). Oxford U Pr.

South-Eastern Europe. 2nd rev. ed. Royal Institute of International Affairs. Repr. of 1939 ed. 28.00 (ISBN 0-384-56750-9). Johnson Repr.

South-Eastern Europe: A Political & Economic Survey. Royal Institute of International Affairs. LC 81-7168. xvi, 203p. 1981. Repr. of 1939 ed. lib. bdg. 35.00x (ISBN 0-313-23195-8, ROSU). Greenwood.

South-Eastern Europe after Tito: A Powder-Keg for the 1980s? Ed. by David Carlton & Carlo Schaerf. LC 82-7352. 250p. 1983. 22.50x (ISBN 0-312-74730-6). St Martin.

South England Pilot, Vol. I: North Foreland to Selsey Bill. Robin Brandon. 1984. 60.00x (ISBN 0-317-14446-4, Pub. by Imray Laurie Norie & Wilson UK). State Mutual Bk.

South England Pilot, Vol. II: Selsey Bill to Hengistbury Head & the Isle of Wight. Robin Brandon. 1984. 60.00x (ISBN 0-317-14448-0, Pub. by Imray Laurie Norie & Wilson UK). State Mutual Bk.

South England Pilot, Vol. III: Hengistbury Head to Start Point. Robin Brandon. 1983. 60.00x (ISBN 0-85288-080-4, Pub. by Imray Laurie Norie & Wilson UK). State Mutual Bk.

South England Pilot, Vol. IV: Start Point to Land's End. Robin Brandon. 160p. 1979. 60.00x (ISBN 0-85288-067-7, Pub. by Imray Laurie Norie & Wilson UK). State Mutual Bk.

South English Legendary. Ed. by Carl Horstmann. (EETS, OS Ser.: No. 87). Repr. of 1887 ed. 65.00 (ISBN 0-527-00084-1). Kraus Repr.

South Florida Bay & Coastal Fishing. Mike Fuery. LC 76-360969. (Illus., Orig.). 1987. pap. 6.95 (ISBN 0-944295-00-2). Sanibel Sanddollar Pubns.

South Florida Benthic Marine Algae. W. J. Woekerling. (Sedimenta V). (Illus.). 150p. 1976. pap. 7.00 (ISBN 0-932981-04-6). Univ Miami CSL.

South Florida Carbonate Sediments. R. N. Ginsburg et al. (Sedimenta II). (Illus.). 71p. (Orig.). 1972. pap. 6.00 (ISBN 0-932981-02-X). Univ Miami CSL.

South Florida Cookery. Alex D. Hawkes. 1964. 5.00 (ISBN 0-87482-018-9). Wake-Brook.

South Florida's Vanished People: Travels in the Homeland of Ancient Calusa. Byron D. Voegelin. LC 72-94649. (Illus.). 1977. 6.95 (ISBN 0-87208-038-2); pap. 4.95 (ISBN 0-87208-106-0). Island Pr Pubs.

South Fork of the American River: From Chili Bar Dam to Salmon Falls Road. Keith Robinson & Fred Lehman. (Whitewater Ser.). (Illus.). 1982. pap. 3.95 (ISBN 0-941838-00-5). Lore Unlim.

South France Pilot, Chapter I: Introduction & Information. Robin Brandon. 640p. 1983. 50.00x (ISBN 0-85288-088-X, Pub. by Imray Laurie Norie & Wilson UK). State Mutual Bk.

South France Pilot, Chapter II: Languedoc-Roussillon. Robin Brandon. 640p. 1984. 50.00x (ISBN 0-317-14450-2, Pub. by Imray Laurie Norie & Wilson UK). State Mutual Bk.

South France Pilot, Chapter III: West Cote d'Azur. Robin Brandon. 640p. 1984. 50.00x (ISBN 0-317-14451-0, Pub. by Imray Laurie Norie & Wilson UK). State Mutual Bk.

South France Pilot, Chapter IV: East Cote d'Azur. Robin Brandon. 640p. 1982. 50.00x (ISBN 0-85288-077-4, Pub. by Imray Laurie Norie & Wilson UK). State Mutual Bk.

South France Pilot, Chapter V: The Riviera. Robin Brandon. 640p. 1982. 50.00x (ISBN 0-85288-078-2, Pub. by Imray Laurie Norie & Wilson UK). State Mutual Bk.

South France Pilot, Chapter VI: Corsica. Robin Brandon. 640p. 1983. 75.00x (ISBN 0-85288-054-5, Pub. by Imray Laurie Norie & Wilson UK). State Mutual Bk.

South from Granada. Gerald Brenan. LC 80-40376. (Illus.). 282p. 1980. pap. 12.95 (ISBN 0-521-28029-X). Cambridge U Pr.

South from Granada. Gerald Brenan. 282p. 1976. Repr. of 1957 ed. lib. bdg. 20.50x (ISBN 0-374-90978-4, Octagon). Hippocrene Bks.

South from Hell-fer-Sartin: Kentucky Mountain Folk Tales. Leonard W. Roberts. 296p. 22.00 (ISBN 0-8131-1637-6); pap. 10.00 (ISBN 0-8131-0175-1). U Pr of Ky.

South Group Ball Court: Structures R-11-a & R-11-b, with a Preliminary Note on the West Group Ball Court (Structures K-6-a & K-6-b) Linton Satterthwaite. (Piedras Negras Preliminary Papers: No. 2). pap. 20.00 (ISBN 0-317-26208-4, 2052123). Bks Demand UMI.

South in American Literature, 1607-1900. Jay B. Hubbell. LC 54-9434. pap. 160.00 (ISBN 0-317-26775-2, 2023404). Bks Demand UMI.

South in Architecture. Lewis Mumford. LC 67-27462. (Architecture & Decorative Art Ser.). 1967. Repr. of 1941 ed. lib. bdg. 25.00 (ISBN 0-306-70972-4). Da Capo.

South in Contemporary Literature. Addison Hibbard. LC 73-7753. 1930. Repr. lib. bdg. 16.00 (ISBN 0-8414-4702-0). Folcroft.

South in History & Literature. Mildred L. Rutherford. 59.95 (ISBN 0-8490-1093-4). Gordon Pr.

South in Northern Eyes. Howard R. Floan. LC 72-6774. (American History & Americana Ser., No. 47). 1972. Repr. of 1958 ed. lib. bdg. 42.95x (ISBN 0-8383-1647-6). Haskell.

South in the New Nation, 1789-1819. Thomas P. Abernethy. LC 61-15488. (History of the South Ser.: Vol. 4). (Illus.). xvi, 530p. 1961. 30.00x (ISBN 0-8071-0004-8); pap. 12.95x (ISBN 0-8071-0014-5). La State U Pr.

South in the Revolution, 1763-1789. John R. Alden. LC 57-12096. (History of the South Ser.: Vol. 3). (Illus.). xvi, 442p. 1957. 30.00x (ISBN 0-8071-0003-X); pap. 9.95x (ISBN 0-8071-0013-7). La State U Pr.

South India: Political Institutions & Political Change, 1880-1940. C. J. Baker & D. A. Washbrook. 1975. 35.00x (ISBN 0-8419-5016-4). Holmes & Meier.

South Indian Agaricales, Preliminary Study of Some Dark Spored Species. K. Natarajan & N. Raman. (Bibliotheca Mycologica: No. 89). (Illus.). 204p. 1983. text ed. 60.00x (ISBN 3-7682-1344-7). Lubrecht & Cramer.

South Indian Coins. Sri T. Desikachari. (Illus.). 210p. 1986. 18.00X (ISBN 0-8364-1724-0, Pub. by Chanakya India). South Asia Bks.

South Indian Cookery. Mary L. Skelton & G. Gopal Rao. 115p. 1975. pap. 3.00 (ISBN 0-89253-030-8). Ind-US Inc.

South Indian Customs. P. V. Ayyar. 182p. 1986. Repr. 18.00X (ISBN 0-8364-1723-2, Pub. by Usha). South Asia Bks.

South Indian Festivities. P. V. Ayyar. (Illus.). 212p. 1986. 32.00X (ISBN 0-8364-1722-4, Pub. by Usha). South Asia Bks.

South Indian History & Society: Studies from Inscriptions, A.D. 850-1800. Noboru Karashima. 1984. 29.95x (ISBN 0-19-561586-7). Oxford U Pr.

South Indian Images of Gods & Goddesses. H. Krishna Sastri. 308p. 1986. Repr. 37.50X (ISBN 0-8364-1710-0, Pub. by Chanakya India). South Asia Bks.

South Indian Inscriptions, 3 vols. E. Hultzsch. 1988. Repr. of 1913 ed. Vol. 1. 42.50x (ISBN 81-7013-009-3, Pub. by Navrang); Vol II, Pts. 1-2. 64.00x (ISBN 0-8364-2284-8, Pub. by Navrang); Vol. II, Pts 3-5. 70.00x (ISBN 0-8364-2285-6, Pub. by Navrang). South Asia Bks.

South Indian Megalithic Burials: The Pandukal Complex. Lawrence S. Leshnik. (Illus.). 321p. 1974. text ed. 97.50x (ISBN 3-515-01955-3, Pub by Franz Steiner). Coronet bks.

South Indian Shrines. P. V. Ayyar. 648p. 1986. Repr. 14.00X (ISBN 0-8364-1721-6, Pub. by Usha). South Asia Bks.

South Is Another Land: Essays on the Twentieth-Century South. Ed. by Bruce L. Clayton & John A. Salmond. LC 86-29625. (Contributions in American History Ser.: No. 124). 230p. 1987. lib. bdg. 35.00 (ISBN 0-313-25556-3, CMR/). Greenwood.

South Island. (Mobil New Zealand Guides). 423p. (Orig.). 1988. pap. 14.95 (ISBN 0-474-00130-X). Hunter Pub NY.

South Italian Folkways in Europe & America. Phyllis H. Williams. LC 69-16768. (Illus.). 1969. Repr. of 1938 ed. 8.50x (ISBN 0-8462-1322-2). Russell.

South, Its Economic-Geographic Development. Almon E. Parkins. Repr. of 1938 ed. lib. bdg. 35.00x (ISBN 0-8371-2904-4, PATS). Greenwood.

South Jersey Dining Guide. Ed Hitzel. (South Jersey Dining Ser.: IV). (Illus., Orig.). 1986. pap. 4.95 (ISBN 0-9612852-2-2). S Jersey Dining.

South Jersey Dining Guide. 1987 ed. 1986. 4.95 (ISBN 0-9612852-3-0). S Jersey Dining.

South Jersey Towns: History & Legend. William McMahon. LC 78-163961. (Illus.). 384p. 1973. pap. 8.95 (ISBN 0-8135-0718-9). Rutgers U Pr.

South Korea. Patricia M. Bartz. (Illus.). 1972. 49.95x (ISBN 0-19-874008-5). Oxford U Pr.

South Korea. (Let's Visit Places & Peoples - - Nations, Dependencies, & Sovereignties of the World Ser.). (Illus.). (gr. 5 up). 1988. 12.95 (ISBN 0-7910-0118-0). Chelsea Hse.

South Korea see Business Opportunity Report Series.

South Korea & the U. S. A. Mutual Security & Economic Cooperation, 1945-1968. Hyun-Dong Kim. 1987. 95.00x (ISBN 0-904404-64-1, Pub. by P Norbury Pubns Ltd). State Mutual Bk.

South Korea: Education, Culture & Economy. Georgie D. Hyde. LC 87-34908. 320p. 1988. 49.95 (ISBN 0-312-01666-2). St Martin.

South Korea Handbook. Robert Nilsen. Ed. by Mark Morris. (Illus.). 600p. (Orig.). 1988. pap. 14.95 (ISBN 0-918373-20-4). Moon Pubns CA.

South Korea in the Wake of the Oil Price Rise. Nancy L. Happe. LC 80-8624. (Outstanding Dissertation in Economics Ser.). 300p. 1984. 36.00 (ISBN 0-8240-4181-X). Garland Pub.

South Korea: The Politicization of Trade Policy. Adrienne A. Kearney et al. 170p. Date not set. pap. text ed. 50.00 (ISBN 1-55813-017-9, HI-3836-P). Hudson Inst.

South Korea: Violations of Human Rights. Amnesty International Staff. 109p. (Orig.). 1986. pap. 5.00 (ISBN 0-939994-21-6, Pub. by Amnesty Intl Pubns UK). Amnesty Intl USA.

Southeast & Southern England. David K. C. Jones. (Geomorphology of the British Isles Ser.). 1980. 25.00x (ISBN 0-416-84550-9, NO.6506). Routledge Chapman & Hall.

Southeast Asia. Drew Middleton & Gene Brown. (Great Contemporary Issues Ser.). 35.00 (ISBN 0-405-13399-5). Ayer Co Pubs.

Southeast Asia. 3rd ed. Milton Osborne. (Illus.). 236p. 1985. pap. text ed. 11.95x (ISBN 0-86861-668-0). Unwin Hyman.

Southeast Asia. (Economist Business Traveller's Guides). (Illus.). 1988. 17.95 (ISBN 0-13-227513-9). Prentice Hall Pr.

Southeast Asia. Z. Michael Szaz. (JSPES Monograph: No. 12). 1984. pap. 15.00 (ISBN 0-318-03037-3). Coun Soc Econ.

Southeast Asia. Time-Life Books Editors. (Library of Nations). (Illus.). 160p. 1987. 14.95 (ISBN 0-8094-5160-3); lib. bdg. write for info. (ISBN 0-8094-5161-1). Time-Life.

Southeast Asia. Time-Life Books Editors. (Library of Nations). (Illus.). 160p. (YA) (gr. 7 up). 1987. lib. bdg. 23.93 (ISBN 0-8094-5318-5). Time-Life.

Southeast Asia. rev. ed. Ed. by W. A. Withington. LC 78-54259. (World Cultures Ser.). (Illus.). (gr. 6 up). 1988. text ed. 16.95; text ed. 13.95 (ISBN 0-934291-32-2); tchr's. guide 9.95 (ISBN 0-934291-33-0). Gateway Pr MI.

Southeast Asia see Learning about People & Cultures.

Southeast Asia: A Critical Bibliography. Kennedy G. Tregonning. LC 68-9845. pap. 29.90 (2031486). Bks Demand UMI.

Southeast Asia: A Cultural Study Through Celebration. Phil Scanlon, Jr. (Northern Illinois Univ., Centre for Southeast Asian Studies, Special Report, Occas. Paper: No. 23). (Illus.). xvii, 185p. (Orig.). 1985. pap. 14.00x (ISBN 0-318-18414-1, Ctr SE Asian Stud). Cellar.

Southeast Asia: A History. Lea E. Williams. LC 75-32358. (Illus.). 316p. 1976. pap. 11.95x (ISBN 0-19-502000-6). Oxford U Pr.

Southeast Asia & the Enemy Beyond: ASEAN Perceptions of External Threats. Robert O. Tilman. (Special Studies on South & Southeast Asia). 194p. 1987. pap. 25.00 (ISBN 0-8133-7130-9). Westview.

Southeast Asia & the Law of the Sea: Some Preliminary Observations on the Political Geography of Southeast Asian Seas. Yong L. Lee. 50p. 1978. pap. 4.00x (ISBN 0-8214-0466-0, Pub. by Singapore U Pr). Ohio U Pr.

Southeast Asia Divided: The ASEAN-Indochina Crises. Ed. by Donald E. Weatherbee. (Westview Replica Ser.). 120p. 1985. pap. 22.50x (ISBN 0-86531-895-6). Westview.

Southeast Asia Emerges. rev. ed. Steven Warshaw et al. LC 73-93982. (Asia Emerges Ser.). (Illus.). 356p. (Orig.). 1987. pap. 9.95 (ISBN 0-87297-021-3); tchr's. guide 2.95. Diablo.

Southeast Asia: Essays in the Political Economy of Structural Change. Ed. by Richard Robison & Richard Higgott. 320p. 1985. 39.95x (ISBN 0-7102-0325-X); pap. 18.95x (ISBN 0-7102-0471-X). Routledge Chapman & Hall.

Southeast Asia Field Trip for the Library of Congress, Nineteen Seventy to Nineteen Seventy-One. Cecil Hobbs. 94p. 1971. pap. 3.50 (ISBN 0-87727-085-6, DP 85). Cornell SE Asia.

Southeast Asia From 1945. Ian Beckett. (Conflict in the 20th Century Ser.). (Illus.). 64p. (gr. 4-12). 1987. lib. bdg. 12.90 (ISBN 0-531-10322-6). Watts.

Southeast Asia in International Politics, 1941-1956. Evelyn Colbert. LC 76-28008. 384p. 1977. 45.00x (ISBN 0-8014-0971-3). Cornell U Pr.

Southeast Asia in the Age of Commerce 1450-1680: The Lands below the Winds, Vol. 1. Anthony Reid. LC 87-20749. 272p. 1988. 25.00x (ISBN 0-300-03921-2). Yale U Pr.

Southeast Asia in the Coming World. facsimile ed. Ed. by Philip W. Thayer. LC 70-167426. (Essay Index Reprint Ser). Repr. of 1953 ed. 20.00 (ISBN 0-8369-2444-4). Ayer Co Pubs.

Southeast Asia in the Eyes of Europe: The Sixteenth Century. Donald F. Lach. LC 64-19848. 1968. pap. 1.95x (ISBN 0-226-46746-5, P294, Phoen). U of Chicago Pr.

Southeast Asia in the Ninth to Fourteenth Centuries. Ed. by David G. Marr & A. C. Milner. 416p. 1986. text ed. 28.00x (ISBN 9971-988-40-2, Pub. by Inst Southeast Asian Stud). Gower Pub Co.

Southeast Asia: Nature, Society, & Development. Ed. by Shinichi Ichimura. LC 77-777. (Center for Southeast Asian Studies, Kyoto University). 373p. 1976. text ed. 17.50x (ISBN 0-8248-0543-7); pap. text ed. 10.00x (ISBN 0-8248-0554-2). UH Pr.

Southeast Asia on a Shoestring. 6th ed. Tony Wheeler. (Illus.). 620p. 1989. pap. 14.95 (ISBN 0-86442-056-0). Lonely Planet.

Southeast Asia: Past & Present. 2nd ed. D. R. Sar Desai. 448p. 1988. 33.00 (ISBN 0-8133-0445-8); pap. 18.95 (ISBN 0-8133-0446-6). Westview.

Southeast Asia Politics: Malayasia & Indonesia. G. P. Bhattacharjee. 1977. 11.00x (ISBN 0-88386-841-5). South Asia Bks.

Southeast Asia: Problems & Prospects a Conference Report. Ed. by Ray S. Cline et al. 125p. (Orig.). 1985. pap. 10.00 (ISBN 0-318-12024-0). World Power Prog.

Southeast Asia: Realm of Contrasts. 3rd rev. ed. Ashok K. Dutt. 275p. 1985. 37.50x (ISBN 0-86531-561-2); pap. text ed. 19.95x (ISBN 0-86531-562-0). Westview.

Southeast Asia Travel Guide. 3rd ed. Sunset Editors. LC 81-82867. 160p. 1982. pap. 9.95 (ISBN 0-376-06764-0, Sunset Bks). Sunset-Lane.

Southeast Asia Under Japanese Occupation: Transition & Transformation. Ed. by Alfred W. McCoy. LC 80-610. (Monograph Ser.: No. 22). (Illus.). 250p. 1980. pap. 14.00x (ISBN 0-938692-08-9). Yale U SE Asia.

Southeast Asian Affairs Nineteen Eighty-Seven. Ed. by Mohammed Ayoob. 363p. 1987. text ed. 23.00 (Pub. by Inst of Southeast Asian Stud). Gower Pub Co.

Southeast Asian Affairs, 1983. (Southeast Asian Affairs Ser.). 336p. 1983. text ed. 39.00 (ISBN 0-566-00691-X, Pub. by Inst Southeast Asian Stud). Gower Pub Co.

Southeast Asian Affairs, 1984. Ed. by Pushpa Thambipillai. 384p. 1985. text ed. 45.00 (ISBN 0-566-00875-0). Gower Pub Co.

Southeast Asian Affairs, 1985. Ed. by Lim Joo-Jock. 374p. 1986. text ed. 41.50 (ISBN 0-566-05136-2, Pub. by Gower Pub England). Gower Pub Co.

Southeast Asian Affairs, 1986. Ed. by Institute of Southeast Asian Studies Staff. 373p. 1987. text ed. 41.50x (ISBN 0-566-05414-0, Pub. by Gower Pub England). Gower Pub Co.

Southeast Asian Affairs, 1987. Ed. by Mohammed Ayoob. 363p. 1987. text ed. 23.00 (Pub. by Inst Southeast Asian Stud). Gower Pub Co.

Southeast Asian Archipelagic States: Concept, Evolution & Current Practice. Phiphat Tangsubkul. LC 83-25487. (East-West Environment & Policy Institute Research Report Ser.: No. 15). vi, 90p. 1984. pap. text ed. 3.00. EW Ctr HI.

Southeast Asian Birth Customs: Three Studies in Human Reproduction. Donn V. Hart et al. LC 65-18348. (Monographs). 315p. 1965. pap. 12.00x (ISBN 0-87536-318-0). HRAFP.

Southeast Asian Ceramic Society. Southeast Asian Ceramic Society Staff. 1979. 100.00x (ISBN 0-317-68643-7, Pub. by Han-Shan Tang Ltd). State Mutual Bk.

Southeast Asian Ceramics. Robert Moes. (Illus.). 16p. 1975. pap. 1.00 (ISBN 0-87273-051-4). Bklyn Mus.

Southeast Asian Ceramics: Ninth Through Seventeenth Centuries. Dean F. Frasche. LC 76-20204. (Illus.). 144p. 1976. 25.00 (ISBN 0-87848-047-1). Asia Soc.

Southeast Asian Conference on Logic: Proceedings of the Logic Conference Singapore, 1981. Ed. by C. T. Chong & M. J. Wicks. (Studies in Logic & the Foundations of Mathematics: No. 111). xiv, 210p. 1983. 63.25 (ISBN 0-444-86706-6, I-250-83, North-Holland). Elsevier.

Southeast Asian Cooking. Jay Harlow. Ed. by Sandra Gary. LC 87-70192. (California Culinary Academy Ser.). (Illus.). 128p. (Orig.). 1987. pap. 7.95 (ISBN 0-89721-098-0). Ortho.

Southeast Asian History & Historiography: Essays Presented to D. G. E. Hall. Ed. by C. D. Cowan & O. W. Wolters. LC 75-18726. (Illus.). 448p. 1976. 42.50x (ISBN 0-8014-0841-5). Cornell U Pr.

Southeast Asian References in the British Parliamentary Papers, 1801-1972-73: An Index. Compiled by Thomas F. Willer. LC 77-620034. (Papers in International Studies: Southeast Asia Ser.: No. 48). 1977. pap. 8.50x (ISBN 0-89680-033-4, Ohio U Ctr Intl). Ohio U Pr.

Southeast Asian Seas: Frontiers for Development. L. S. Chia & C. MacAndrews. 1982. 36.50 (ISBN 0-07-099247-9). McGraw.

Southeast Asian Studies: Options for the Future. Report of a Conference at the Wilson Center March 1984. Ed. by Ronald A. Morse. 192p. (Orig.). 1985. lib. bdg. 31.00 (ISBN 0-8191-4317-0, Pub. by Woodrow Wilson Intl Ctr); pap. text ed. 14.00 (ISBN 0-8191-4318-9). U Pr of Amer.

Southeast Asian Textile Designs. Caren Caraway. (International Design Library). (Illus.). 48p. (Orig.). 1983. pap. 5.95 (ISBN 0-88045-034-7). Stemmer Hse.

Southeast Asian Transitions: Approaches Through Social History. Ed. by Ruth T. McVey & Adrienne Suddard. LC 78-4171. (Southeast Asian Studies Ser.: No. 8). 1978. 30.00x (ISBN 0-300-02184-4). Yale U Pr.

Southeast Asian World. John F. Cady. LC 76-53353. (World of Asia Ser). (Illus.). 1977. pap. text ed. 5.95x (ISBN 0-88273-502-0). Forum Pr IL.

Southeast Asians: A New Beginning in Lowell. James Higgins & Joan Ross. LC 86-62068. (Illus.). 132p. (Orig., Khmer, Laotian & Vietnamese.). 1986. pap. 14.95 (ISBN 0-914613-04-9). Mill Town Graph.

Southeast Building, the Twin Basilicas, the Mosaic House. Saul S. Weinberg. LC 75-25699. (Corinth Ser: Vol. 1, Pt. 5). (Illus.). 1971. Repr. of 1960 ed. 25.00x (ISBN 0-87661-015-7). Am Sch Athens.

Southeast Classic Maya Zone: Symposium at Dumbarton Oaks. Ed. by Elizabeth H. Boone et al. LC 87-22290. (Illus.). 420p. 1988. pap. 40.00X (ISBN 0-88402-170-X). Dumbarton Oaks.

Southeast Coast. Photos by Art Carter. LC 85-71193. (Illus.). 160p. (Text by George Reiger). 1985. 29.50 (ISBN 0-912856-95-5). Gr Arts Ctr Pub.

Southeast England. (AA Beautiful Britain Ser.). 160p. 1988. 24.95 (ISBN 0-86145-518-5, Pub. by British Tour). Salem Hse Pubs.

Southeast England & East Anglia. Roger Bigham. (Ward Lock Regional Guides Ser.). 160p. (Orig.). 1984. pap. 9.95 (ISBN 0-7063-6226-8, Pub. by Automobile Assn Brit). Salem Hse Pubs.

Southeast Europe Axis: Armies Handbook. 172p. 1982. 13.95 (ISBN 0-941052-62-1, 62); pap. 9.95 (ISBN 0-941052-10-9, 12). Valor Pub.

Southeast Europe Axis: Army Order of Battle. 172p. 1982. 13.95 (ISBN 0-941052-61-3, 61); pap. 9.95 (ISBN 0-941052-09-5, 11). Valor Pub.

Southeast Exporting: Profiles, Typology, & the Role of Technology in Selected U. S. Firms. Cedric L. Suzman et al. (Research Monograph: No. 90). 1981. spiral bdg. 25.00 (ISBN 0-88406-146-9). GA St U Busn Pub.

Southeast Frontier of New Spain. Peter Gerhard. LC 78-70295. (Illus.). 1979. 31.00x (ISBN 0-691-05273-5). Princeton U Pr.

Southeast Indians: An Educational Coloring Book. Spizzirri Publishing, Inc. Staff & Linda Spizzirri. (Illus.). 32p. (gr. k-5). 1985. pap. 1.49 (ISBN 0-86545-065-X). Spizzirri.

Southeast (Kentucky, Tennessee, Georgia) Thomas G. Aylesworth & Virginia L. Aylesworth. (Let's Discover the States Ser.). (Illus.). 66p. 1987. lib. bdg. 14.95x (ISBN 1-55546-557-9). Chelsea Hse.

Southeast Litigation Guide, 12 vols. Bill Colson & Sidney O. Smith, Jr. 1981. Set, updates avail. looseleaf 720.00 (ISBN 0-317-09801-2, 633); Updates 1985 185.00; 1986 230.00. Bender.

Southeast Maya Periphery. Ed. by Patricia A. Urban & Edward M. Schortman. (Illus.). 407p. 1986. 37.50x (ISBN 0-292-77589-X). U of Tex Pr.

Southeast States. Gilda Beeger. (First Book Ser.). 96p. (gr. 4 up). 1984. lib. bdg. 10.40 (ISBN 0-531-04738-5). Watts.

Southeastern Broadsides Before 1877: A Bibliography. Ed. by Ray O. Hummel, Jr. LC 71-634933. (Publications Ser: No. 33). 1971. 15.00 (ISBN 0-88490-064-9). VA State Lib.

Southeastern Broadsides Before 1877: A Bibliography. Ed. by Ray O. Hummel, Jr. LC 71-634933. (Virginia State Library Publications Ser.: No. 33). pap. 128.80 (ISBN 0-317-29836-4, 2017496). Bks Demand UMI.

Southeastern Ceremonial Complex & Its Interpretation. James H. Howard & Carl H. Chapman. (Memoir Ser.: No. 6). (Illus.). 169p. (Orig.). 1968. pap. 4.00 (ISBN 0-943414-21-0). MO Arch Soc.

Southeastern Check Stamped Pottery Tradition: A View from Louisiana. Ian W. Brown. LC 82-10101. (MCJA Special Papers Ser.: Vol. 4). (Illus.). 112p. 1982. pap. text ed. 6.25x (ISBN 0-87338-272-2). Kent St U Pr.

Southeastern Connecticut: Sixty-Five Natural Color Views a Pictorial Guide. John Urwiller. (Illus.). 1980. pap. 3.00 (ISBN 0-910258-11-2). Book & Tackle.

Southeastern Europe: A Guide to Basic Publications. Paul L. Horecky. LC 73-110336. 1970. 50.00x (ISBN 0-226-35190-4). U of Chicago Pr.

Southeastern Europe Under Ottoman Rule, 1354-1804. Peter F. Sugar. LC 76-7799. (History of East Central Europe Ser.: Vol. 5). 384p. 1977. pap. 12.95x (ISBN 0-295-96033-7). U of Wash Pr.

Southeastern Frontiers: Europeans, Africans, & American Indians, 1513-1840: A Critical Bibliography. James H. O'Donnell, III. LC 81-48086. (Newberry Library D'Arcy McNickle Center for the History of the American Indian Bibliographical Ser.). 136p. 1982. pap. 4.95x (ISBN 0-253-35398-X). Ind U Pr.

Southeastern Indians. Charles Hudson. LC 75-30729. (Illus.). 592p. 1976. 29.95x (ISBN 0-87049-187-3); pap. 12.95 (ISBN 0-87049-248-9). U of Tenn Pr.

Southeastern Indians since the Removal Era. Ed. by Walter L. Williams. LC 78-10490. (Illus.). 272p. 1979. pap. 12.00x (ISBN 0-8203-0483-2). U of Ga Pr.

Southeastern Nigeria in the Nineteenth Century. C. C. Ifemesia. LC 78-95186. 1978. 12.95x (ISBN 0-88357-066-1); pap. 4.95 (ISBN 0-88357-091-2). NOK Pubs.

Southeastern Organized Baseball. Robert P. Dews. 272p. 1988. pap. 6.00. R P Dews.

Southeastern Organized Baseball: Nineteen Ten to Nineteen Fifty. R. L. Tant. Ed. by Robert P. Dews. 272p. 1988. pap. 10.00 (ISBN 0-317-70112-6). R P Dews.

Southeastern Pomo Ceremonials: The Kuksu Cult & Its Successors. Abraham M. Halpern. (Publications in Anthropological Records: Vol. 29). (Orig.). 1988. pap. 20.00 (ISBN 0-520-09731-9). U of Cal Pr.

Southeastern Section Field Guide. Ed. by T. L. Neathery. (DNAG Centennial Field Guides Ser.: No. 6). (Illus.). 1986. 40.50 (ISBN 0-8137-5406-2). Geol Soc.

Southeastern States. Harold W. Rickett. (Wild Flowers of the United States Ser.: Vol. 2). 1976. text ed. 74.00x (ISBN 0-89327-277-9). NY Botanical.

Southeastern States. (Mobile Travel Guides Ser.). 1988. pap. 9.95 (ISBN 0-13-586892-0). Prentice Hall Pr.

Southeastern Studies: Toward A.D. 2000. Ed. by John I. Durham. LC 77-80400. (Emerging Directions in Christian Ministry Ser.: Vol. 1). viii, 146p. 1981. 8.95 (ISBN 0-86554-026-8, MUP-H004). Mercer Univ Pr.

Southeastern Symposium on System Theory, 20th, 1988: Proceedings. IEEE Staff. LC 74-642491. 699p. 1988. lib. bdg. 90.00 (ISBN 0-8186-8847-5, 847); pap. 90.00 (ISBN 0-8186-0847-1, 847); microfiche 90.00 (ISBN 0-8186-4847-3, 847). IEEE Comp Soc.

Southeastern Woodland Indian Designs. Caren Caraway. (International Design Library). (Illus.). 48p. (Orig.). 1985. pap. 5.95 (ISBN 0-88045-072-X). Stemmer Hse.

Southeastern Zip Code Directory. 8th, rev. ed. Kelly King. 288p. pap. 10.95 (ISBN 0-943983-04-5). Natl Direct.

Southern: A Motive Power Pictorial 1968-1982. Paul K. Withers & Tom L. Sink. LC 87-90068. 238p. 1987. 32.95 (ISBN 0-9618503-0-2). Paul K Withers.

Southern, a Narrow Gauge Odyessey. 2nd ed. Richard L. Dorman. (Illus.). 156p. 1988. 29.95 (ISBN 0-9616656-3-7). Rd Pubns.

Southern Accents Historic Houses of the South. Southern Accents Press Editors. 208p. 1984. 35.00. S&S.

Southern Africa. A. J. Christopher. LC 76-21207. (Studies in Historical Geography Ser.). (Illus.). 294p. 1976. 29.50 (ISBN 0-208-01620-1, Archon). Shoe String.

Southern Africa. David J. Cranmer & Valerie A. Woolston. LC 80-14066. (World Education Ser.). (Illus.). 256p. (Orig.). 1980. pap. text ed. 6.00 (ISBN 0-910054-58-4). Am Assn Coll Registrars.

Southern Africa. Francis Fleming. 1981. Repr. lib. bdg. 19.00x (ISBN 0-403-00408-X). Scholarly.

Southern Africa see From Dependence to Statehood in Commonwealth Africa: Selected Documents, World War I to Independence.

Southern Africa after Zimbabwe. Alex Callinicos. 192p. pap. 7.50 (ISBN 0-86104-336-7, Pub. by Pluto Pr). Longwood Pub Group.

Southern Africa: An American Enigma. R. Ali. LC 85-31254. 239p. 1987. lib. bdg. 37.95 (ISBN 0-275-92380-0, C2380). Praeger.

Southern Africa & the United States. Ed. by William A. Hance et al. LC 68-18147. 1968. 25.00x (ISBN 0-231-03117-3). Columbia U Pr.

Southern Africa & Western Security. Robert J. Hanks. LC 83-48628. (Foreign Policy Report Ser.). 71p. 1984. 7.50 (ISBN 0-89549-055-2). Inst Foreign Policy Anal.

Southern Africa in Conflict: Implications for U. S. Policy in the 1980's. Robert S. Jaster. 1982. pap. 6.00 (ISBN 0-8447-1098-9). Am Enterprise.

Southern Africa in Crisis. Ed. by Gwendolyn M. Carter & Patrick O'Meara. LC 76-48534. pap. 69.80 (ISBN 0-317-27939-4, 2056027). Bks Demand UMI.

Southern Africa in Crisis: Regional & International Responses. (Report Ser.: No. 28). 1988. price not set. Intl Peace.

Southern Africa in the 1980s. Ed. by Olajide Aluko & Timothy M. Shaw. 320p. 1985. text ed. 39.95x (ISBN 0-04-320169-5). Unwin Hyman.

Southern Africa: Prospects for Peace & Security: International Conference of Peace & Security in Southern, 2nd, Dar es Salaam, March 2-6, 1986. (Report Ser.: No. 25). 186p. 1987. 12.00 (ISBN 0-89838-921-6, Pub. by Kluwer-Nijhoff (Netherlands)). Kluwer Academic.

Southern Africa: Regional Security Problems & Prospects. Ed. by Robert Jaster. LC 85-2031. (Adelphi Library). 170p. 1985. 27.50 (ISBN 0-312-74684-9). St Martin.

Southern Africa Since the Portuguese Coup. Ed. by John Seiler. (Westview Special Studies on Africa). (Illus.). 272p. 1980. 36.50x (ISBN 0-89158-767-5). Westview.

Southern Africa since 1800. 2nd ed. Donald Denoon & Balaam Nyeko. 256p. 1984. pap. text ed. 16.95 (ISBN 0-582-72707-3). Longman.

Southern Africa: Toward Economic Liberation. Ed. by Amon J. Nsekela. (Illus.). 294p. 1981. text ed. 31.50x (ISBN 0-8476-4741-2). Rowman.

Southern Africa: Toward Economic Liberation. Ed. by Amon J. Nskela. 274p. 1981. 35.00x (ISBN 0-86036-154-3). State Mutual Bk.

Southern Africa: Year of the Whirlwind. Colin Legum. LC 77-6264. (Current Affairs Ser.). 72p. 1977. pap. 8.50x (ISBN 0-8419-0318-2, Africana). Holmes & Meier.

Southern African Catholic Bishops' Statements. 1977. 2.00x (ISBN 0-904393-19-4, Pub. by CIIR). State Mutual Bk.

Southern African Epiphytic Orchids. John S. Ball. Ed. by Jane Browning & Peter Ashton. (Illus.). 247p. 1978. lib. bdg. 37.50x (ISBN 0-86875-001-8). Lubrecht & Cramer.

Southern African History Before 1900: A Select Bibliography of Articles. Leonard Thompson et al. LC 70-143322. (Bibliographical Ser.: No. 49). 1971. 9.95x (ISBN 0-8179-2491-4). Hoover Inst Pr.

Southern African Literature: An Introduction. Stephen Gray. LC 79-53358. (Illus.). 209p. 1979. text ed. 28.50x (ISBN 0-06-492530-7). B&N Imports.

Southern African Prehistory & Paleoenvironments. Ed. by R. G. Klein. 352p. 1983. lib. bdg. 43.50 (ISBN 90-6191-097-8, Pub. by Balkema RSA). IPS.

Southern African Prehistory & Paleoenvironments. Ed. by Richard G. Klein. 416p. 1984. text ed. 43.50 (ISBN 0-317-65001-7, Pub. by A A Balkema). Brookfield Pub Co.

Southern Agrarians. Paul K. Conkin. LC 87-22496. (Illus.). 240p. 1988. lib. bdg. 24.95x (ISBN 0-87049-560-7); pap. 12.95 (ISBN 0-87049-561-5). U of Tenn Pr.

Southern Agriculture Since the Civil War. Ed. by Robson. cancelled (ISBN 0-87461-031-1). McNally & Loftin.

Southern Anglicanism: The Church of England in Colonial South Carolina. Charles S. Bolton. LC 81-6669. (Contributions to the Study of Religion: No. 5). (Illus.). 248p. 1982. lib. bdg. 35.00 (ISBN 0-313-23090-0, BOS/). Greenwood.

Southern Appalachian Reader. Thomas Wolfe et al. Ed. by Nellie McNeil et al. (Illus.). 300p. (YA) (gr. 10-12). 1988. pap. text ed. 12.95 (ISBN 0-913239-50-X). Appalach Consortium.

Southern Arizona Folk Arts. James S. Griffith. LC 88-17471. 270p. (Orig.). 1988. 29.95 (ISBN 0-8165-1001-6); pap. 14.95 (ISBN 0-8165-1084-9). U of Ariz Pr.

Southern Ark: Zoological Discovery in New Zealand. J. R. Andrews. (Illus.). 238p. 1987. 70.00 (ISBN 0-7126-1620-9, Pub. by Century Hutchinson). David & Charles.

Southern Ark: Zoological Discovery in New Zealand, 1769-1900. J. H. R. Andrews. LC 88-10701. (Illus.). 238p. 1988. text ed. 39.00x (ISBN 0-8248-1192-5). UH Pr.

Southern Asia Accessions List 1952-1960, 9 Vols. in 6. Cecil Hobbs et al. LC 71-151056. (Library of Congress Publications in Reprint Ser). 1971. Repr. of 1952 ed. Set. 197.50 (ISBN 0-405-03423-7); Vol. 1. ACC 1-3 33.00 (ISBN 0-405-03437-7); Vol. 2. ACC 4-5 32.00 (ISBN 0-405-03438-5); Vol. 3. ACC 6 32.00 (ISBN 0-405-03439-3); Vol. 4. ACC 7 32.00 (ISBN 0-405-03440-7); Vol. 5. ACC 8 36.50 (ISBN 0-405-03441-5); Vol. 6. ACC 9 32.00 (ISBN 0-405-03442-3). Ayer Co Pubs.

Southern Asia: Classified, Alphabetical, & Chronological Listings. Harvard University Library Staff. LC 68-15927. (Widener Library Shelflist Ser: No. 19). 1968. 25.00x (ISBN 0-674-82500-4). Harvard U Pr.

Southern Athapaskan Migration: A. D. 200-1750. LC 85-60644. 128p. 1987. 18.80 (ISBN 0-912586-60-5). Navajo Coll Pr.

Southern Bald Eagles: Proceedings of International Days, 1985. Ed. by Terrence N. Ingram. 250p. (Orig.). 1986. pap. 20.00 (ISBN 0-318-04606-7). Eagle Foun.

Southern Baptist Convention & Its People. Robert A. Baker. 18.95 (ISBN 0-8054-6516-2). Broadman.

Southern Baptist Holy War. Joe E. Barnhart. LC 86-5988. 256p. 1986. pap. 16.95 (ISBN 0-87719-037-2). Texas Month Pr.

Southern Baptist Preaching Today. R. Earl Allen & Joel Gregory. 1987. pap. 11.95 (ISBN 0-8054-5714-3). Broadman.

Southern Barbarians. Michael Cooper. 216p. 1971. 525.00x (ISBN 0-317-68590-2, Pub. by Han-Shan Tang Ltd). State Mutual Bk.

Southern Baroque Art: A Study of Painting, Architecture & Music in Italy & Spain of the 17th & 18th Centuries. facsimile ed. Sacheverell Sitwell. LC 70-179539. (Select Bibliographies Reprint Ser.). Repr. of 1924 ed. 22.00 (ISBN 0-8369-6668-6). Ayer Co Pubs.

Southern Bed & Breakfast Book. rev. ed. Corinne M. Ross. LC 85-45690. (Illus.). 192p. 1986. pap. 8.95 (ISBN 0-88742-062-1). Globe Pequot.

Southern Belle in the American Novel. Kathryn L. Seidel. LC 85-8519. 220p. 1985. 22.50x (ISBN 0-8130-0811-5); pap. 10.00 (ISBN 0-8130-0835-2). U Presses Fla.

Southern Black Creative Writers, 1829-1953: Biobibliographies. Compiled by M. Marie Foster. LC 88-5595. (Bibliographies & Indexes in Afro-American & African Studies: No. 22). 132p. 1988. lib. bdg. 29.95 (ISBN 0-313-26207-1, FSW/). Greenwood.

Southern Black Leaders of the Reconstruction Era. Ed. by Howard N. Rabinowitz. LC 81-11372. (Blacks in the New World Ser.). (Illus.). 448p. 1982. 27.50 (ISBN 0-252-00929-0); pap. 10.95 (ISBN 0-252-00972-X). U of Ill Pr.

Southern Black, Slave & Free: A Bibliography of Anti- & Pro-Slavery Books & Pamphlets of Social & Economic Conditions in the Southern States from the Beginnings to 1950. Lawrence Thompson. LC 74-97478. 1970. 15.00x (ISBN 0-87875-004-5). Whitston Pub.

Southern Black Utterances Today. Ed. by Toni C. Bambara & Leah Wise. (Southern Exposure Ser.). (Illus.). 120p. (Orig.). 1975. pap. 2.50 (ISBN 0-943810-04-3). Inst Southern Studies.

Southern Businessmen & Desegregation. Ed. by Elizabeth Jacoway & David R. Colburn. LC 81-19362. xii, 332p. 1982. text ed. 32.50 (ISBN 0-8071-0893-6). La State U Pr.

Southern Caddo: An Anthology. Ed. by H. F. Gregory & David H. Thomas. LC 83-47626. (North American Indian Ser.). 550p. 1986. 75.00 (ISBN 0-8240-5886-0). Garland Pub.

Southern Cal Football see Trojans: A Story of Southern California Football.

Southern California. Insight Guides Staff. 384p. 1984. pap. 15.95 (ISBN 0-13-823600-3). P-H.

Southern California. 1988. 12.95 (ISBN 0-933692-17-X). A R Collings.

Southern California. (Michael's Guides Ser.). (Illus.). 192p. (Orig.). 1987. pap. 7.95 (ISBN 965-288-017-5). Hunter Pub NY.

Southern California. Kathy Strong. (Off the Beaten Path Ser.). (Illus.). 1989. pap. price not set (ISBN 0-87106-623-8). Globe Pequot.

Southern California - One Hundred Years Go. Compiled by Skip Whitson. (Sun Historical Ser). (Illus., Orig.). 1976. pap. 3.50 ea.; Vol. 1. pap. (ISBN 0-89540-033-2, SB-033); Vol. 2. pap. (ISBN 0-89540-034-0, SB-034). Sun Pub.

Southern California: An Island on the Land. Carey McWilliams. LC 73-77787. 415p. 1973. pap. 8.95 (ISBN 0-87905-007-1, Peregrine Smith). Gibbs Smith Pub.

Southern California Anthology. Ed. by McLaughlin & Westphal. 1985. pap. 9.95 (ISBN 0-915520-81-8). Ross-Erikson.

Southern California Anthology, Vol. V. Ed. by Andrew Ragan & Cherilyn Cummings. 144p. (Orig.). 1987. pap. 5.95 (ISBN 0-9615108-2-X). USC MPWP.

Southern California Atlas & Gazetteer. DeLorme Mapping Staff. (Atlas & Gazetteer Ser.). 128p. (Orig.). 1986. pap. 12.95 (ISBN 0-89933-205-6, 205-6). DeLorme Map.

Southern California Business Directory & Buyer's Guide. Ed. by M. F. O'Hora. 1986. 95.00 (ISBN 0-937628-05-0, Pub. by Civic Data). Times Mirror.

Southern California Business Directory, 1988-89. Stoerck. 1500p. 1988. 133.00 (ISBN 0-911510-96-6). TMP Pub.

Southern California Counties Public Schools, 1986, Vol. I. Lillian S. Clancy. (California Public Schools Ser.: How Are They Doing?). 400p. (Orig.). 1985. pap. 24.95 (ISBN 0-939580-28-4). Sindowilf Ltd.

Southern California Counties Public Schools, 1987, Vol. 1. Lillian S. Clancy. (California Public Counties Public Schools: How Are They Doing? Ser.). 400p. (Orig.). 1987. pap. 24.95 (ISBN 0-939580-37-3). Sindowilf Ltd.

Southern California Counties Public Schools, 1988, Vol. 1. Lillian S. Clancy. (California Public Schools: How Are They Doing? Ser.). 400p. (Orig.). 1987. pap. 25.95 (ISBN 0-939580-45-4). Sindowilf Ltd.

Southern California Country: An Island on the Land. Carey McWilliams. LC 76-111847. (Essay Index Reprint Ser). 1946. 26.50 (ISBN 0-8369-1674-3). Ayer Co Pubs.

Southern California Job Bank: A Comprehensive Guide to Major Local Employers. 2nd ed. Ed. by J. Michael Fiedler et al. (Job Bank Ser.). 300p. (Orig.). 1985. 9.95 (ISBN 0-937860-21-2). Adams Inc Ma.

Southern California Ordinal Scales of Development. Ashurst Doanld et al. (Series In Six Ser.). 638p. 1985. Set. 117.00 (ISBN 0-943292-16-6). Foreworks.

Southern California Peaks. Walt Wheelock. (Illus.). 1973. wrappers 1.95 (ISBN 0-910856-32-X). La Siesta.

Southern California Tennis Champions Centennial 1887-1987. Patricia H. Yeomans. LC 87-61603. (Illus.). 320p. 1987. 10.00. S CA Committee.

Southern California Travel Guide. 5th ed. Sunset Editors. LC 78-70269. (Illus.). 128p. 1979. pap. 8.95 (ISBN 0-376-06759-4, Sunset Bks). Sunset-Lane.

Southern California Women Writers & Artists. Ed. by Aleida Rodriguez & Jacqueline De Angelis. (Anthology Ser.). (Illus.). 178p. 1984. pap. 8.00 (ISBN 0-9613060-1-7). Bks Of A Feather.

Southern California's Deteriorating Marine Environment: An Evaluation of the Health of the Benthic Marine Biota of Ventura, Los Angeles & Orange Counties. Rimmon C. Fay. LC 72-83453. (Environmental Studies Ser: No. 2). (Illus.). 76p. 1972. pap. 4.50x (ISBN 0-912102-06-3). Cal Inst Public.

Southern California's Seacoast: Then & Now. Howard Gregory. 1982. 19.95 (ISBN 0-9607086-1-8); pap. 10.95 (ISBN 0-9607086-0-X). H Gregory.

Southern Capitalism: The Political Economy of North Carolina, 1880-1980. Phillip Wood. LC 86-11469. (Illus.). xiii, 272p. 1986. text ed. 37.50 (ISBN 0-8223-0673-5); pap. 12.95 (ISBN 0-8223-0746-4). Duke.

Southern Capitalists: The Ideological Leadership of an Elite, 1832-1885. Laurence Shore. LC 86-1395. (Fred W. Morrison Series in Southern Studies). xii, 282p. 1986. 25.00x (ISBN 0-8078-1702-3). U of NC Pr.

Southern Celebration: Charleston & Savannah Proclaimed. Jane Sobel et al. (Illus.). 1985. 17.95 (ISBN 0-19-540623-0). Skyline Press.

Southern Cemetery of Matricia. Judit Topal. 106p. 1981. 90.00x (ISBN 0-569-08702-3, Pub. by Collets (UK)). State Mutual Bk.

Southern Cheyennes. Donald J. Berthrong. LC 63-8990. (Civilization of the American Indian Ser.: No. 66). (Illus.). 456p. 1981. pap. 14.95 (ISBN 0-8061-1199-2). U of Okla Pr.

Southern Chivalry. facsimile ed. LC 71-178482. (Black Heritage Library Collection). Repr. of 1861 ed. 10.00 (ISBN 0-8369-8931-7). Ayer Co Pubs.

Southern Civil Religions in Conflict: Black & White Baptists & Civil Rights, 1947-1957. Andrew M. Manis. LC 86-25028. 176p. 1987. 22.00x (ISBN 0-8203-0931-1). U of Ga Pr.

Southern Claims Commission. Frank W. Klingberg. 1978. Repr. of 1955 ed. lib. bdg. 19.50x (ISBN 0-374-94594-2, Octagon). Hippocrene Bks.

Southern Colonies in the Seventeenth Century, 1607-1689. Wesley F. Craven. LC 49-3595. (History of the South Ser.: Vol. 1). (Illus.). xvi, 452p. 1949. 30.00x (ISBN 0-8071-0001-3); pap. text ed. 9.95x (ISBN 0-8071-0011-0). La State U Pr.

Southern Commercial Conventions, 1837-1859. Herbert Wender. LC 78-64138. (Johns Hopkins University. Studies in the Social Sciences. Forty-Eighth Ser. 1930: 4). Repr. of 1930 ed. 24.50 (ISBN 0-404-61250-4). AMS Pr.

Southern Common People: Studies in Nineteenth-Century Social History. Edward Magdol & Jon L. Wakelyn. LC 79-7724. (Contributions in American History Ser.: No. 86). (Illus.). xii, 386p. 1982. lib. bdg. 36.95 (ISBN 0-313-21403-4, MLL/). Greenwood.

Southern Community in Crisis: Harrison County, Texas, 1850-1880. Randolph B. Campbell. LC 83-50844. 460p. 1983. 24.95 (ISBN 0-87611-061-8); ltd. ed. 65.00. Tex St Hist Assn.

Southern Cone Nations. William F. Sater. LC 84-5920. (World of Latin America Ser.). (Illus.). 112p. 1984. pap. text ed. 6.95x (ISBN 0-88273-606-X). Forum Pr IL.

Southern Cone: Realities of the Authoritarian State in South America. Cesar Caviedes. LC 83-17842. 222p. 1984. text ed. 36.50x (ISBN 0-86598-109-4, Rowman & Allanheld). Rowman.

Southern Cooking. Columbia Sailing Club Ladies Auxilary Staff. LC 75-32400. (Illus.). 215p. 1975. pap. 5.95 index, spiral bound (ISBN 0-87844-030-5). Sandlapper Pub Co.

Southern Cooking. Henrietta Dull. (Illus.). 352p. 1987. Repr. of 1928 ed. 14.95 (ISBN 0-87797-151-X). Cherokee.

Southern Cooking from Mary Mac's Tea Room. Margaret Lupo. (Orig.). 1988. pap. 9.95 (ISBN 0-440-50076-1, Dell Trade Pbks). Dell.

Southern Cooking from Mary Mac's Tea Room. Margaret Lupo & Susan H. Smith. 176p. 1983. pap. 8.95 (ISBN 0-939944-37-5); spiral 8.95 (ISBN 0-03-004438-3). Marmac Pub.

Southern Cooking to Remember. Kathryn T. Windham. LC 76-19963. 1978. 9.95 (ISBN 0-87397-098-5). Strode.

Southern Critics. Louise S. Cowan. 1971. 3.95x (ISBN 0-918306-01-9). U of Dallas Pr.

Southern Cross. Terry Coleman. 480p. 1980. pap. 2.75 (ISBN 0-345-28365-1). Ballantine.

Southern Cross. Jack McKinney. (Robotech Ser.: No. 7). 224p. (Orig.). 1987. pap. 2.95 (ISBN 0-345-34140-6, Del Re). Ballantine.

Southern Cross: Poems. Charles Wright. 1981. 10.00 (ISBN 0-394-52148-X); pap. 5.95 (ISBN 0-394-74888-3). Random.

Southern Cross to Pole Star. A. F. Tschiffely. (Library of Travel Classics). (Illus., Orig.). 1983. pap. 9.95 (ISBN 0-87477-282-6). J P Tarcher.

Southern Cult Motifs from the Utz Oneota Site, Saline County, Missouri. Robert T. Bray. (Missouri Archaeologist Ser.: Vol. 25). (Illus.). 164p. (Orig.). 1963. pap. 3.00 (ISBN 0-943414-41-5). MO Arch Soc.

Southern Decoys of Virginia & the Carolinas. Henry A. Fleckenstein, Jr. LC 83-61650. (Illus.). 232p. 1983. 39.50 (ISBN 0-916838-86-2). Schiffer.

Southern Delights. Dave Smith. LC 83-7732. (Illus.). 80p. 1984. 10.95 (ISBN 0-912348-11-9). Croissant & Co.

Southern Derringers of the Mississippi Valley. Turner Kirkland. 2.00 (ISBN 0-913150-00-2). Pioneer Pr.

Southern Discomfort. Rita Mae Brown. 1983. pap. 4.50 (ISBN 0-553-23108-1). Bantam.

Southern Dreams & Trojan Women. Leo Snow. 400p. 1986. pap. 4.50 (ISBN 0-380-70149-9). Avon.

Southern Echoes. Louise Pike. LC 72-1519. (Black Heritage Library Collection Ser.). Repr. of 1900 ed. 12.75 (ISBN 0-8369-9046-3). Ayer Co Pubs.

Southern Economic Journal: Cumulative Index, Volume 1-49, 1933 to 1983. Ed. by Vincent J. Tarascio. 1985. 95.00 (ISBN 0-89232-455-4). Jai Pr.

Southern Editorials on Secession. Ed. by Dwight L. Dumond. 1964. 16.50 (ISBN 0-8446-1162-X). Peter Smith.

Southern Elections: County & Precinct Data, 1950-1972. Numan V. Bartley & Hugh D. Graham. LC 78-5525. 416p. 1978. 40.00 (ISBN 0-8071-0278-4). La State U Pr.

Southern Emancipator: Moncure Conway: The American Years, 1832-1865. John D'Entremont. 304p. 1987. 29.95 (ISBN 0-19-504264-6). Oxford U Pr.

Southern Encounters: Southerners of Note in Ralph McGill's South. Ralph McGill. Ed. by Calvin M Logue. LC 83-953. 344p. 1982. 23.50 (ISBN 0-86554-050-0, MUP-H48). Mercer Univ Pr.

Southern England: An Archaeological Guide. James Dyer. LC 73-76369. (Illus.). 380p. 1974. 16.00 (ISBN 0-8155-5016-2, NP). Noyes.

Southern Enigma: Essays on Race, Class, & Folk Culture. Ed. by Walter J. Fraser, Jr. & Winfred B. Moore, Jr. LC 82-20966. (Contributions in American History Ser.: No. 105). (Illus.). x, 240p. 1983. lib. bdg. 36.95 (ISBN 0-313-23640-2, FSE/). Greenwood.

Southern Enterprize: The Work of National Evangelical Societies in the Antebellum South. John W. Kuykendall. LC 81-23723. (Contributions to the Study of Religion Ser.: No. 7). xv, 188p. 1982. lib. bdg. 35.00 (ISBN 0-313-23212-1, KSE/). Greenwood.

Southern Essays of Richard M. Weaver. Richard M. Weaver. Ed. & pref. by George M. Curtis, III. LC 87-2624. xxii, 288p. 1987. 10.00 (ISBN 0-86597-057-2); pap. 4.50 (ISBN 0-86597-058-0). Liberty Fund.

Southern Europe: A Systematic Geographical Study. Monica Beckinsale & Robert Beckinsale. LC 74-14940. (Illus.). 352p. 1975. 55.00 (ISBN 0-8419-0178-3). Holmes & Meier.

Southern Europe Transformed. Alun Williams. 1984. pap. text ed. 13.50 (ISBN 0-06-318281-5). Har-Row.

Southern Evangelicals & the Social Order, 1800-1860. Anne C. Loveland. LC 80-11200. xiv, 354p. 1980. 35.00 (ISBN 0-8071-0690-9); pap. 9.95x (ISBN 0-8071-0783-2). La State U Pr.

Southern Excursions: Essays on Mark Twain & Others. Lewis Leary. LC 79-154269. (Southern Literary Studies). xviii, 230p. 1971. 27.50 (ISBN 0-8071-0938-X). La State U Pr.

Southern Exposure. (Illus.). 128p. 3.00 (ISBN 0-317-35967-3). Southern Exposure.

Southern Exposure. Peter M. Wilson. 1979. write for info (ISBN 0-8495-5732-1). Arden Lib.

Southern Exposure: Canadian Promoters in Latin America & the Caribbean, 1896-1930. Christopher Armstrong & H. V. Nelles. (Illus.). 432p. Date not set. 35.00x (ISBN 0-8020-2660-5). U of Toronto Pr.

Southern Exposure: Not a Regional Exhibition. Alternative Museum Staff. LC 85-71155. (Illus.). 56p. (Orig.). 1985. pap. text ed. 7.00 (ISBN 0-932075-02-9). Alternative Mus.

Southern Family. Gail Godwin. Ed. by Harvey Ginsberg. LC 87-12381. 540p. 1987. 18.95 (ISBN 0-688-06530-9). Morrow.

Southern Family. Gail Godwin. 604p. 1988. pap. 4.95 (ISBN 0-380-70313-0). Avon.

Southern Federalists, 1800-1816. James H. Broussard. LC 78-2374. 488p. 1978. 40.00 (ISBN 0-8071-0288-1). La State U Pr.

Southern Fiction Prior to 1860: An Attempt at First-Hand Bibliography. James G. Johnson. 1909. 12.00 (ISBN 0-384-27680-6). Johnson Repr.

Southern Fish & Seafood Cookbook. 3rd ed. Jon Wongrey. (Illus.). 141p. 1975. pap. 7.95 (ISBN 0-87844-026-7). Sandlapper Pub Co.

Southern Flower Gardening. William D. Adams. LC 79-29715. (Illus.). 96p. (Orig.). 1980. pap. 6.95x (ISBN 0-88415-291-X, Pub. by Pacesetter Pr). Gulf Pub.

Southern Folk Art. Cynthia E. Rubin. LC 84-61210. (Illus.). 264p. 1985. 35.00 (ISBN 0-8487-0645-5). Oxmoor Hse.

Southern Folk Ballads, Vol. I. W. K. McNeil. LC 87-751904. (American Folklore Ser.). 220p. 1987. 19.95 (ISBN 0-87483-038-9); pap. 9.95 (ISBN 0-87483-039-7). August Hse.

Southern Folk Ballads, Vol. II. W. K. McNeil. (American Folklore Ser.). 1988. 19.95 (ISBN 0-87483-046-X); pap. 9.95 (ISBN 0-87483-047-8). August Hse.

Southern Folk Dance. (American Folklore Ser.). 1989. 19.95 (ISBN 0-317-59657-8); pap. 9.95 (ISBN 0-317-59658-6). August Hse.

Southern Folk, Plain & Fancy: Native White Social Types. John S. Reed. LC 86-1479. (Mercer University Lamar Memorial Lecture: No. 29). 136p. 1986. 13.95 (ISBN 0-8203-0862-5). U of GA Pr.

Southern Folk, Plain & Fancy: Native White Social Types. John S. Reed. LC 86-1479. (Illus.). 136p. 1988. pap. 7.95 (ISBN 0-8203-1023-9). U of Ga Pr.

Southern Food: At Home, on the Road, in History. John Egerton. LC 86-46007. 24.95 (ISBN 0-394-54494-3). Knopf.

Southern Fried. William P. Fox, Jr. LC 83-46019. (Classics of Modern American Humor Ser.). Date not set. Repr. of 1962 ed. 24.00 (ISBN 0-404-19931-3). AMS Pr.

Southern Fried Rat & Other Gruesome Tales. Daniel Cohen. LC 82-25120. (Illus.). 128p. (gr. 7 up). 1983. 9.95 (ISBN 0-87131-400-2). M Evans.

Southern Frontier, Vols. 1-6. 1970. Repr. 39.00x (ISBN 0-8371-1260-5, SOF&, Pub. by Negro U Pr). Greenwood.

Southern Frontier, Sixteen Seventy to Seventeen Thirty-Two. Verner Crane. LC 76-54227. 1977. Repr. of 1956 ed. lib. bdg. 22.50x (ISBN 0-8371-9336-2, CRSF). Greenwood.

Southern Frontier, 1670-1732. Verner W. Crane. 384p. 1982. pap. text ed. 7.95x (ISBN 0-393-00948-3). Norton.
Southern Galaxy Catalogue: A Catalogue of 5481 Galaxies South of Declination-17 Degress Found on 1.2m U. K. Schmidt IIIa-J Plates. Harold G. Corwin et al. LC 85-50556. (University of Texas Monographs in Astronomy: No. 4). 342p. (Orig.). 1985. pap. write for info. (ISBN 0-9603796-3-0). U of Tex Dept Astron.
Southern Garden: A Handbook for the Middle South. rev. ed. Elizabeth Lawrence. LC 67-30978. (Illus.). xxx, 257p. 1984. pap. 9.95 (ISBN 0-8078-4100-5). U of NC Pr.
Southern Gardener's Soil Handbook. William Peavy. LC 78-58245. (Illus.). 96p. (Orig.). 1979. pap. 6.95x (ISBN 0-88415-817-9, Pub. by Pacesetter Pr). Gulf Pub.
Southern Gardens, Southern Gardening. William L. Hunt. LC 81-69425. (Illus.). xv, 191p. 1982. 16.95 (ISBN 0-8223-0463-5). Duke.
Southern Gates of Arabia. Freya Stark. LC 83-613. (Library of Travel Classics). (Illus.). 352p. 1983. 9.95 (ISBN 0-87477-265-6). J P Tarcher.
Southern Gates of Arabia: A Journey to the Hadhramaut. Freya Stark. 1972. 28.50 (ISBN 0-7195-2425-3). Transatl Arts.
Southern Georgia Canoeing. Bob Sehlinger & Don Otey. LC 84-115744. (Illus.). 312p. 1980. pap. 10.95 (ISBN 0-89732-007-7). Menasha Ridge.
Southern Ghosts. Nancy Roberts. LC 85-14901. (Illus.). 80p. 1985. Repr. of 1979 ed. 12.95 (ISBN 0-87797-098-X). Cherokee.
Southern Ghosts. Nancy Roberts. (Illus.). 72p. (gr. 5 up). 1987. pap. 5.95 (ISBN 0-87844-075-5). Sandlapper Pub Co.
Southern Gourmet. Virginia Robbins. 8.95 (ISBN 0-918544-94-7). Wimmer Bks.
Southern Governors & Civil Rights: Racial Segregation As a Campaign Issue in the Second Reconstruction. Earl Black. 384p. 1976. 29.50x (ISBN 0-674-82510-1). Harvard U Pr.
Southern Harmony & Musical Companion. WIlliam Walker. Ed. by Glenn C. Wilcox. LC 87-752491. 392p. 1987. Repr. of 1835 ed. 20.00 (ISBN 0-8131-1626-0). U Pr of Ky.
Southern Harvest: A Collection of Stories. Renato E. Madrid. viii, 187p. (Orig.). 1987. pap. 9.50x (ISBN 971-10-0297-3, Pub. by New Day Philippines). Cellar.
Southern Herb Growing. Madalene Hill & Gwen Barclay. Ed. by Jean Hardy. (Illus.). 288p. 1987. 29.95 (ISBN 0-940672-41-3). Shearer Pub.
Southern Heritage All Pork Cookbook. LC 84-60634. (Illus.). 144p. 1985. 9.95 (ISBN 0-8487-0611-0). Oxmoor Hse.
Southern Heritage Beef, Veal & Lamb Cookbook. LC 83-61838. (Southern Heritage Cookbook Library). (Illus.). 143p. 1984. 9.95 (ISBN 0-8487-0608-0). Oxmoor Hse.
Southern Heritage Breads Cookbook. LC 82-62139. (Southern Heritage Cookbook Library). (Illus.). 144p. 1983. 9.95 (ISBN 0-8487-0602-1). Oxmoor Hse.
Southern Heritage Breakfast & Brunch Cookbook. (Southern Heritage Cookbook Library). (Illus.). 144p. 1985. 9.95 (ISBN 0-8487-0613-7). Oxmoor Hse.
Southern Heritage Cakes Cookbook. LC 82-62141. (Southern Heritage Cookbook Library). (Illus.). 143p. 1983. 9.95 (ISBN 0-8487-0601-3). Oxmoor Hse.
Southern Heritage Celebrations Cookbook. LC 83-60430. (Southern Heritage Cookbook Library). (Illus.). 143p. 1983. 9.95 (ISBN 0-8487-0607-2). Oxmoor Hse.
Southern Heritage Company's Coming Cookbook. LC 82-62140. (Southern Heritage Cookbook Library). (Illus.). 144p. 1983. 9.95 (ISBN 0-8487-0603-X). Oxmoor Hse.
Southern Heritage Cookie Jar Cookbook. (Southern Heritage Cookbook Library). (Illus.). 144p. 1985. 9.95 (ISBN 0-8487-0616-1). Oxmoor Hse.
Southern Heritage Family Gatherings Cookbook. LC 83-62574. (Southern Heritage Cookbook Library). (Illus.). 144p. 1984. 9.95 (ISBN 0-8487-0610-2). Oxmoor Hse.
Southern Heritage Gift Receipts Cookbook. (Southern Heritage Cookbook Library). (Illus.). 144p. 1986. 9.95 (ISBN 0-8487-0615-3). Oxmoor Hse.
Southern Heritage Just Desserts Cookbook. LC 83-82156. (Illus.). 144p. 1985. 9.95 (ISBN 0-8487-0606-4). Oxmoor Hse.
Southern Heritage Pies & Pastries Cookbook. LC 83-62573. (Southern Heritage Cookbook Library). (Illus.). 144p. 1984. 9.95 (ISBN 0-8487-0609-9). Oxmoor Hse.
Southern Heritage Plain & Fancy Poultry. LC 82-62142. (Southern Heritage Cookbook Library). (Illus.). 144p. 1983. 9.95 (ISBN 0-8487-0604-8). Oxmoor Hse.
Southern Heritage Sea & Stream Cookbook. LC 84-61240. (The Southern Heritage Cookbook Library). (Illus.). 144p. 1985. 9.95 (ISBN 0-8487-0612-9). Oxmoor Hse.
Southern Heritage Socials & Soirees Cookbook. (Southern Heritage Cookbook Library). (Illus.). 144p. 1985. 9.95 (ISBN 0-8487-0617-X). Oxmoor Hse.
Southern Heritage Soups & Stews Cookbook. (Southern Heritage Cookbook Library). (Illus.). 144p. 1985. 9.95 (ISBN 0-8487-0614-5). Oxmoor Hse.
Southern Heritage Sporting Scene Cookbook. (Southern Heritage Cookbook Library). (Illus.). 144p. 1986. 9.95 (ISBN 0-8487-0618-8). Oxmoor Hse.
Southern Heritage Vegetables Cookbook. LC 83-60429. (The Southern Heritage Cookbook Library Ser.). (Illus.). 144p. 1984. 9.95 (ISBN 0-8487-0605-6). Oxmoor Hse.
Southern Highlander & His Homeland. John C. Campbell. LC 79-15028. (Illus.). 508p. 1969. pap. 13.00x (ISBN 0-8131-0121-2). U Pr of Ky.
Southern History of the War. Confederate States of America, War Department Staff. Repr. of 1863 ed. 47.00 (ISBN 0-527-18950-2). Kraus Repr.
Southern History of the War, 2 vols. Edward A. Pollard. Incl. Vol. 1. The First Year of the War; Vol. 2. The Second Year of the War. LC 79-95075. (Select Bibliography Reprint Ser.). Repr. of 1863 ed. 66.00 set (ISBN 0-8369-5075-5). Ayer Co Pubs.
Southern Home Landscaping. Ken Smith. LC 81-86376. (Illus.). 192p. (Orig.). 1982. pap. 12.95 (ISBN 0-89586-063-5). Price Stern.
Southern Honor: Ethics & Behavior in the Old South. Bertram Wyatt-Brown. 1982. pap. 12.95 (ISBN 0-19-503310-8). Oxford U Pr.
Southern Honor: Ethics & Behavior in the Old South. Bertram Wyatt-Brown. 1982. text ed. 35.00x (ISBN 0-19-503119-9). Oxford U Pr.
Southern Horizons. facsimile ed. Williams Haynes. LC 78-152174. (Essay Index Reprint Ser). Repr. of 1946 ed. 22.00 (ISBN 0-8369-2366-9). Ayer Co Pubs.
Southern Hunting Tales. Martin Greenberg et al. 1989. pap. price not set. August Hse.
Southern Idaho Ghost Towns. Wayne Sparling. LC 73-156484. (Illus., Orig.). 1974. pap. 5.95 (ISBN 0-87004-229-7). Caxton.
Southern Indian Boy. Caroline Dormon. (Illus.). 1967. 3.95 (ISBN 0-87511-027-4). Claitors.
Southern Indian Myths & Legends. Ed. by Virginia P. Brown & Laurella Owens. (Illus.). 160p. 1985. 15.95 (ISBN 0-912221-02-X). Beechwood.
Southern Indiana. Jean Alley & Hartley Alley. LC 65-11797. (Illus.). 128p. 1965. pap. 6.95x (ISBN 0-253-18291-3). Ind U Pr.
Southern Indians & Benjamin Hawkins, 1796-1816. Florette Henri. LC 85-40945. (Illus.). 392p. 1986. 24.95 (ISBN 0-8061-1968-3). U of Okla Pr.
Southern Indians in the American Revolution. James H. O'Donnell. LC 76-146662. pap. 46.30 (ISBN 0-317-28845-8, 2020630). Bks Demand UMI.
Southern Indians: The Story of the Civilized Tribes Before Removal. R. S. Cotterill. LC 54-5931. (Civilization of the American Indian Ser.: Vol. 38). 259p. 1954. pap. 9.95 (ISBN 0-8061-1171-2). U of Okla Pr.
Southern Institutes: Or, an Inquiry into the Origin & Early Prevalence of Slavery & the Slave Trade. facs. ed. George S. Sawyer. LC 78-83877. (Black Heritage Library Collection Ser). 1858. 18.00 (ISBN 0-8369-8648-2). Ayer Co Pubs.
Southern Interiors. Nena Griffith. 1988. 35.00 (ISBN 0-8487-0740-0). Oxmoor Hse.
Southern Is. Mary N. Kratt. LC 84-60340. (Illus.). 64p. 1985. 5.95 (ISBN 0-931948-68-1). Peachtree Pubs.
Southern Italy: An Archaeological Guide. Margaret Guido. Ed. by Glyn Daniel. LC 72-85245. (Illus.). 1973. 16.00 (ISBN 0-8155-5011-1, NP). Noyes.
Southern Italy: From Rome to Calabria. 6th ed. Paul Blanchard. (Blue Guides Ser.). 1986. pap. 16.95 (ISBN 0-393-30079-X). Norton.
Southern Junior League Cookbook. Ed. by Ann Seranne. (Illus.). 1977. 12.95 (ISBN 0-679-50769-8). McKay.
Southern Junior League Cookbook. Ed. by Anne Seranne. 640p. 1981. pap. 12.95 (ISBN 0-345-33899-5). Ballantine.
Southern Kensington: Brompton. Ed. by F. H. Sheppard. (Survey of London Ser.: Vol. XLI). 110.00 (ISBN 0-485-48241-X, Pub. by Athlone Pr UK). Humanities.
Southern Kensington: Kensington's Square to Earl's Court. Hermione Hobhouse. (Survey of London Ser.: Vol. XLII). (Illus.). 475p. 1986. 110.00 (ISBN 0-485-48242-8, Pub. by Athlone Pr UK). Humanities.
Southern Kikuyu Before 1903, 3 vols. L. S. Leakey et al. Ed. by J. Ensminger & G. S. B. Beecher. 1978. Vol. 1. 99.00 (ISBN 0-12-439901-0); Vol. 2. 99.00 (ISBN 0-12-439902-9); Vol. 3. 99.00 (ISBN 0-12-439903-7). Acad Pr.
Southern King Arthur Family. O. S. Nock. LC 76-2885. (Illus.). 96p. 1976. 19.95 (ISBN 0-7153-7156-8). David & Charles.
Southern Ladies & Gentlemen. Florence King. 256p. 1976. pap. 3.50 (ISBN 0-553-25302-6). Bantam.
Southern Lady: From Pedestal to Politics 1830-1930. Anne F. Scott. LC 73-123750. xvi, 248p. 1972. pap. 8.95 (ISBN 0-226-74347-0, P479, Phoen). U of Chicago Pr.
Southern Landscape & Garden Design. J. Carroll Kell. LC 80-473. (Illus.). 116p. (Orig.). 1980. pap. 6.95x (ISBN 0-88415-811-X, Pub. by Pacesetter Pr). Gulf Pub.
Southern Landscape Tradition in Texas. John B. Jackson. LC 80-65249. (Anne Burnett Tandy Lectures in Amercian Civilization Ser.: No. 1). 37p. 1980. pap. 9.50 (ISBN 0-88360-035-8, Dist. by Univ. of Texas Pr). Amon Carter.
Southern Lau, Fiji: An Ethnography. L. Thompson. (BMB). Repr. of 1940 ed. 34.00 (ISBN 0-527-02270-5). Kraus Repr.
Southern Lawns & Groundcovers. Richard Duble & J. Carroll Kell. LC 77-73533. (Illus.). 96p. (Orig.). 1977. pap. 6.95x (ISBN 0-88415-426-2, Pub. by Pacesetter Pr). Gulf Pub.
Southern Lawyer: Fifty Years at the Bar. Aubrey L. Brooks. viii, 214p. 1950. 16.95x (ISBN 0-8078-0600-5). U of NC Pr.
Southern Legacies. Nancy P. Walker. Ed. by Nancy W. Stone & William E. Stone. (Illus.). 256p. 1982. pap. 12.95 (ISBN 0-939114-75-5). Wimmer Bks.
Southern Legislative Dictionary. Richard Allin. (Illus.). 36p. 1983. pap. 3.95 (ISBN 0-914546-50-3). Rose Pub.
Southern Letters. Noble L. Prentis. text ed. 13.50 (ISBN 0-8369-9232-6, 9086). Ayer Co Pubs.
Southern Liberal Journalists & the Issue of Race, 1920-1944. John T. Kneebone. LC 85-1104. (Fred W. Morrison Series in Southern Studies). xx, 312p. 1985. 27.50x (ISBN 0-8078-1660-4). U of NC Pr.
Southern Life, Vol. 1. James A. Lewis. (Illus.). 68p. 1987. pap. 10.00 (ISBN 0-9617322-4-5). Flat Surface.
Southern Light. J. R. Salamanca. LC 85-45674. 688p. 1986. 19.45 (ISBN 0-394-48252-2). Knopf.
Southern Lights & Shadows. facs. ed. Ed. by William D. Howells & Henry M. Alden. LC 75-83907. (Black Heritage Library Collection Ser). 1907. 15.25 (ISBN 0-8369-8606-7). Ayer Co Pubs.
Southern Literary Cookbook. Audrey Cash. 1978. 6.95 (ISBN 0-685-39051-9). New Hope FL.
Southern Literary Culture: A Bibliography of Masters' & Doctors' Theses. Ed. by O. B. Emerson & Marion C. Michael. LC 78-10771. 400p. 1979. 25.00 (ISBN 0-8173-9514-8). U of Ala Pr.
Southern Literary Journal & Monthly Magazine. Incl. Vol. 1-3. Old Series. Repr. of 1837 ed; Vol. 1-4. New Series, 3 vols. Repr. of 1838 ed. Set. lib. bdg. 430.00 (ISBN 0-404-19555-5). AMS Pr.
Southern Literary Messenger, Vol. 1-36. (Vols. 35 & 36 misnumbered in the originals as vols. 37 & 38). Repr. of 1864 ed. Set. lib. bdg. 2745.00 (ISBN 0-404-19556-3); lib. bdg. 37.50 ea. AMS Pr.
Southern Literary Studies. C. A. Smith. LC 67-27651. Repr. of 1927 ed. 21.50x (ISBN 0-8046-0426-6, Pub. by Kennikat). Assoc Faculty Pr.
Southern Literary Study: Problems & Possibilities. Ed. by Louis D. Rubin, Jr. & C. Hugh Holman. LC 75-11553. xiii, 235p. 1975. 22.50x (ISBN 0-8078-1252-8). U of NC Pr.
Southern Literature from 1579-1895. Louise Manly. Repr. of 1895 ed. lib. bdg. 30.50 (ISBN 0-8414-6476-6). Folcroft.
Southern Literature in Transition: Heritage & Promise. Philip Castille & William Osborne. 176p. 1984. pap. text ed. 12.50x (ISBN 0-87870-209-1). Memphis St Univ.
Southern Living Annual Recipes, 1986. (Illus.). 384p. 1986. 19.95 (ISBN 0-8487-0686-2). Oxmoor Hse.
Southern Living Annual Recipes, 1987. (Illus.). 384p. 1987. 19.95 (ISBN 0-8487-0717-6). Oxmoor Hse.
Southern Living Annual Recipes, 1988. (Illus.). 1988. 19.95 (ISBN 0-8487-0733-8). Oxmoor Hse.
Southern Living Cookbook. Ed. by Foods Editor of Southern Living. (Illus.). 448p. 1987. 24.95 (ISBN 0-8487-0709-5). Oxmoor Hse.
Southern Living Growing Vegetables & Herbs. Ed. by John A. Floyd, Jr. LC 83-60426. (Illus.). 272p. 1984. 19.95 (ISBN 0-8487-0542-4). Oxmoor Hse.
Southern Living Microwave Cookbook. Margaret C. Agnew. (Illus.). 1988. 19.95 (ISBN 0-8487-0725-7). Oxmoor Hse.
Southern Mail. Antoine De Saint-Exupery. Tr. by Curtis Cate. LC 79-182749. 120p. 1972. pap. 2.95 (ISBN 0-15-683901-6, Harv). HarBraceJ.
Southern Mandarins: Letters of Caroline Gordon to Sally Wood, 1924-1937. Caroline Gordon. Ed. by Sally Wood. LC 83-16229. (Southern Literary Studies). xx, 218p. 1984. text ed. 25.00x (ISBN 0-8071-1137-6). La State U Pr.
Southern Marches of Imperial Ethiopia: Essays in History & Social Anthropology. Ed. by Donald Donham & Wendy James. (African Studies: No. 51). (Illus.). 336p. 1986. 44.50 (ISBN 0-521-32237-5). Cambridge U Pr.
Southern-Mesic Forest of Southeastern Wisconsin: Species, Composition & Community Structure. James B. Levenson. (Contributions in Biology & Geology Ser.: No. 41). (Illus.). 246p. 1981. 12.50 (ISBN 0-89326-068-1). Milwaukee Pub Mus.
Southern Methodist Football: Mustang Mania. Temple Pouncey. LC 80-53025. (College Sports Ser.). (Illus.). 1980. 10.95 (ISBN 0-87397-176-0). Strode.
Southern Methodist University Bankruptcy Law Institute, No. 679. Ed. by L. King et al. 85.00 (ISBN 0-317-67057-3). Bender.
Southern Methodist University: Founding & Early Years. Mary M. Thomas. LC 74-80248. (Illus.). 240p. 1974. 15.00 (ISBN 0-87074-138-1). SMU Press.
Southern Methodist University Institute on International Finance: World Trade & Trade Fianace. Ed. by Joseph J. Norton. 1985. 85.00 (624). Bender.
Southern Methodist University Products Liability Institute: Case (Sixth Annual Symposium. Ed. by Vincent S. Walkowiak. LC 85-122235. New proceedings avail annually. 90.00 (423). Bender.
Southern Ming, Sixteen Forty-Four to Sixteen Sixty-Two. Lynn Struve. LC 83-23341. (Illus.). 312p. 1984. 34.00x (ISBN 0-300-03057-6). Yale U Pr.
Southern Miscellany: Essays in Honor of Glover Moore. Ed. by Frank A. Dennis. LC 80-20373. 202p. 1981. 6.95 (ISBN 0-87805-129-5). U Pr of Miss.
Southern Music - American Music. Bill C. Malone. LC 79-4005. (New Perspectives on the South Ser.). (Illus.). 224p. (General Editor, Charles P. Roland). 1979. 18.00 (ISBN 0-8131-0300-2). U Pr of Ky.
Southern Mystique: Technology & Human Values in a Changing Region. Ed. by W. David Lewis & B. Eugene Griessman. LC 76-55011. 177p. 1977. 11.95 (ISBN 0-8173-5317-8). U of Ala Pr.
Southern Negro Agricultural Worker: 1850-1870. Charles E. Seagrave. LC 75-2596. (Dissertations in American Economic History). (Illus.). 1975. 18.00x (ISBN 0-405-07217-1). Ayer Co Pubs.
Southern New England. Henry Wiencek. Ed. by Roger G. Kennedy. (Smithsonian Guide to Historic America Ser.). (Illus.). 400p. (Orig.). 1989. 24.95 (ISBN 1-55670-059-8); pap. text ed. 16.95 (ISBN 1-55670-051-2). Stewart Tabori & Chang.
Southern New England, Connecticut, Massachusetts, Rhode Island. Thomas G. Aylesworth & Virginia L. Aylesworth. LC 87-17880. (Let's Discover the States Ser.). (Illus.). 66p. (gr. 5 up). 1988. lib. bdg. 14.95x (ISBN 1-55546-552-8). Chelsea Hse.
Southern New Hebrides: An Ethnological Record. Clarence B. Humphreys. LC 75-35123. Repr. of 1926 ed. 24.00 (ISBN 0-404-14139-0). AMS Pr.
Southern Nigeria in Transition, 1885-1906. J. C. Anene. 1966. 34.50 (ISBN 0-521-04033-7). Cambridge U Pr.
Southern Nights. Elizabeth Moore. 1987. pap. 3.95 (ISBN 0-671-61908-X). PB.
Southern Nights. Felicia Woods. (Orig.). 1984. pap. 1.95 (ISBN 0-87067-231-2, BH231). Holloway.
Southern Nights & City Lights. Ron Hudspeth. LC 82-61870. 179p. 1982. 1.98 (ISBN 0-931948-41-X). Peachtree Pubs.
Southern Nilotic History: Linguistic Approaches to the Study of the Past. Christopher Ehret. LC 70-116611. Repr. of 1971 ed. 40.70 (ISBN 0-8357-9472-5, 2015430). Bks Demand UMI.
Southern Ocean - CCAMLR: Convention Area, Fishing Areas 48, 58 & 88, Vol. I. Ed. by W. Fischer & J. C. Hureau. (FAO Species Identification Sheets for Fishery Purposes Ser.). (Illus.). 232p. (Orig.). 1986. pap. text ed. 45.00 (ISBN 92-5-102357-3, F2934, FAO). UNIPUB.
Southern Ocean, CCAMLR Convention Area, Fighting Areas 48, 58 & 88, Vol. II. Ed. by W. Fischer & J. C. Hureau. (FAO Species Identificaion Sheets for Fishery Purposes Ser.). (Illus.). 470p. (Orig.). 1986. pap. text ed. 45.00 (ISBN 92-5-102358-1, F2935, FAO). UNIPUB.
Southern Odyssey - Travelers in the Antebellum North. John Hope Franklin. LC 74-27190. (Walter Linwood Fleming Lectures). (Illus.). 320p. 1976. 30.00 (ISBN 0-8071-0161-3); pap. 9.95 (ISBN 0-8071-0351-9). La State U Pr.
Southern of the Western States see Report on the Social Statistics of Cities.
Southern Oregon Cross Country Ski Trails. John W. Lund. (Illus.). 222p. (Orig.). 1987. pap. 9.95 (ISBN 0-9619389-1-9). J W Lund.
Southern Oregon: Short Trips into History. Marjorie L. O'Harra. (Illus.). 200p. 1985. pap. 11.95 (ISBN 0-943388-06-6). South Oregon.
Southern Oregon Wilderness Areas. Donna Aitkenhead. Ed. by Oral Bullard. (Illus.). 112p. (Orig.). 1988. pap. 9.95 (ISBN 0-911518-78-9). Touchstone Oregon.
Southern Overland Route: Cyclists' Guide to a Major Scenic & Historic Route Through the Southwest. Lowell Lindsay & Diana Lindsay. (Illus.). 168p. (Orig.). 1985. pap. 7.95 (ISBN 0-932653-00-6). Sunbelt Pubns.
Southern Pacific Bay Area Steam. Harre W. Demoro. LC 78-72990. (Illus.). 144p. 1979. 35.00 (ISBN 0-89685-037-4). Chatham Pub CA.
Southern Pacific Country. Donald Sims. (Illus.). 192p. 1988. 39.95 (ISBN 0-87046-082-X). Interurban.
Southern Pacific Motive Power Annual, 1967-68. (Illus.). 15.00 (ISBN 0-89685-002-1). Chatham Pub CA.
Southern Pacific Motive Power Annual, 1970. (Illus.). 25.00 (ISBN 0-89685-004-8). Chatham Pub CA.
Southern Pacific Motive Power Annual, 1971. (Illus.). 1971. 15.00 (ISBN 0-89685-005-6). Chatham Pub CA.
Southern Pacific Motive Power Annual, 1973. (Illus.). 1974. 25.00 (ISBN 0-89685-007-2). Chatham Pub CA.
Southern Pacific of Mexico: And the West Coast Route. John R. Signon & John A. Virchner. LC 86-31883. (Illus.). 168p. 39.95 (ISBN 0-317-55966-4). Gldn West Bks.

Southwest American Indian Designs. Caren Caraway. (International Design Library). (Illus.). 48p. (Orig.). 1983. pap. 5.95 (ISBN 0-88045-035-5). Stemmer Hse.

Southwest & by West of Cape Cod. Llewellyn Howland. Ed. by Mark Alvarez. LC 87-2094. 192p. 1987. 12.95 (ISBN 0-89909-142-3). Yankee Bks.

Southwest & South Central Area. (Mobil Travel Guide Ser.). 1988. pap. 9.95 (ISBN 0-13-586900-5). Prentice Hall Pr.

Southwest Arizona Ghost Towns. Stanley W. Paher. (Illus.). pap. 2.95 (ISBN 0-913814-32-6). Nevada Pubns.

Southwest Art Review. Karen Kodner. (Illus.). 224p. 1983. 19.95 (ISBN 0-913765-00-7); pap. 14.95 (ISBN 0-913765-02-3). Krantz Co.

Southwest Borderlands: Veins of Silver & Gold. Robert H. Perez. (Illus.). 160p. (YA) (gr. 10-12). 1982. pap. text ed. 7.50 (ISBN 0-940870-13-4); tchr's man. 2.50 (ISBN 0-940870-14-2). U of AZ Ed Mat.

Southwest China off the Beaten Track. 1988. 12.95 (ISBN 0-8442-9804-2). Natl Textbk.

Southwest Conference on Optics, '85. Ed. by S. C. Stotlar. 667p. 1985. 75.00 (ISBN 0-89252-575-4, 540). SPIE.

Southwest Cook Book. Sunset Books & Sunset Magazine Editors. LC 87-80953. 96p. (Orig.). 1987. pap. text ed. 6.95 (ISBN 0-376-02632-4). Sunset-Lane.

Southwest Energy Complex: A Policy Evaluation. Malcolm F. Baldwin. LC 73-79429. pap. 20.00 (ISBN 0-317-11229-5, 2015787). Bks Demand UMI.

Southwest Gardening. rev. ed. Rosalie Doolittle & Harriet Tiedebohl. LC 52-11535. (Illus.). 237p. 1967. pap. 8.95 (ISBN 0-8263-0027-8). U of NM Pr.

Southwest Graduate Symposium of Spanish & Portuguese, Literature & Language at the University of Texas. Ed. by Luis A. Ramos-Garcia. 1980. 5.00 (ISBN 0-934840-03-2). Studia Hispanica.

Southwest: Handbook of North American Indians, Vol. 10. Ed. by Alfonso Ortiz. LC 77-17162. (Illus.). 868p. 1983. 25.00 (ISBN 0-87474-190-4). Smithsonian.

Southwest Indian Arts & Crafts. 2nd, rev. ed. Mark Bahti. LC 82-83654. (Illus.). 48p. 1983. lib. bdg. 8.95 (ISBN 0-916122-92-1); pap. 4.50 (ISBN 0-916122-91-3). KC Pubns.

Southwest Indian Craft Arts. Clara L. Tanner. LC 66-24299. (Illus.). 206p. 1968. 27.50 (ISBN 0-8165-0083-5). U of Ariz Pr.

Southwest Indian Painting: A Changing Art. rev. ed. Clara L. Tanner. LC 74-160812. (Illus.). 477p. 1980. 50.00 (ISBN 0-8165-0309-5). U of Ariz Pr.

Southwest Indian Silver from the Doneghy Collection. Ed. by Louise Lincoln. (Illus.). 189p. 1982. text ed. 29.95x (ISBN 0-292-72440-3); pap. 15.95 (ISBN 0-292-72441-1). U of Tex Pr.

Southwest Indians: An Educational Coloring Book. Spizzirri Publishing Co. Staff. Ed. by Linda Spizzirri. (Illus.). 32p. (gr. 1-8). 1986. pap. 1.49 (ISBN 0-86545-075-7). Spizzirri.

Southwest Journals of Adolph F. Bandelier, 1889-1892. Ed. by Charles H. Lange et al. LC 65-17862. (Illus.). 806p. 1984. 47.50x (ISBN 0-8263-0734-5). U of NM Pr.

Southwest Louisiana. W. H. Perrin. 1971. 22.50 (ISBN 0-87511-094-0). Claitors.

Southwest Memories. Raymond W. Baland. 1986. 8.95 (ISBN 0-533-06792-8). Vantage.

Southwest of England. Martyn F. Wakelin. LC 86-8315. (Varieties of English Around the World Text Ser.: Series T5). xii, 231p. (Orig.). 1986. pap. 36.00x (ISBN 90-272-4713-7). Benjamins North Am.

Southwest: Old & New. W. Eugene Hollon. LC 61-9232. (Illus.). xxii, 533p. 1968. pap. 9.95x (ISBN 0-8032-5091-6, BB 353, Bison). U of Nebr Pr.

Southwest Pacific & the War. LC 44-2703. 1944. text ed. 3.00x (ISBN 0-911090-25-8); pap. text ed. 2.00x (ISBN 0-911090-26-6). Pacific Bk Supply.

Southwest Review Reader. Ed. by Margaret L. Hartley. LC 74-28267. (Illus.). 256p. 1974. 12.95 (ISBN 0-87074-147-0). SMU Press.

Southwest Saga: How It Really Was. William C. McGaw. (Illus.). 160p. (Orig.). 1988. pap. 5.00 (ISBN 0-914846-35-3). Golden West Pub.

Southwest: South or West? Frank E. Vandiver. LC 75-16448. (Illus.). 48p. 1975. 4.00 (ISBN 0-89096-003-8). Tex A&M Univ Pr.

Southwest Tales: A Contemporary Collection. Ed. by Alurista & Xelina. LC 85-61180. 176p. 1986. pap. 8.00 (ISBN 0-939558-09-2). Maize Pr.

Southwest Tastes: From the PBS Television Series 'Great Chefs of the West' Ellen Brown. 208p. 1988. 19.95 (ISBN 0-89586-578-5). Price Stern.

Southwest (Texas, New Mexico, Colorado) Thomas G. Aylesworth & Virginia L. Aylesworth. (Let's Discover the States Ser.). (Illus.). 66p. (gr. 5 up). 1988. lib. bdg. 14.95x (ISBN 1-55546-562-5). Chelsea Hse.

Southwest: Three Peoples in Geographical Change, 1600-1970. D. W. Meinig. (Historical Geography of North America Ser). (Orig.). 1971. pap. text ed. 10.95x (ISBN 0-19-501289-5). Oxford U Pr.

Southwest U. S. A. Gerd Kittel. LC 86-50495. (Illus.). 104p. 1986. 40.00 (ISBN 0-500-54121-3). Thames Hudson.

Southwest under Stress: National Resource Development Issues in a Regional Setting. Allen V. Kneese & F. Lee Brown. 268p. 1981. pap. 14.95 (ISBN 0-8018-2708-6). Resources Future.

Southwest Virginia & the Valley. Intro. by A. D. Smith & Co. Staff. (Illus.). 527p. 1987. pap. 30.00 (ISBN 1-55613-083-X). Heritage Bk.

Southwestern American Literature: A Bibliography. Ed. by John Q. Anderson et al. LC 76-3121. 445p. 1980. 25.00 (ISBN 0-8040-0683-0, Swallow). Ohio U Pr.

Southwestern Archaeology. 2nd ed. John C. McGregor. LC 65-10079. (Illus.). 518p. 1982. pap. 16.95 (ISBN 0-252-00989-4). U of Ill Pr.

Southwestern Archaeology: A Bibliography. Frank G. Anderson. 1982. lib. bdg. 91.00 (ISBN 0-8240-9554-5). Garland Pub.

Southwestern Arts & Crafts Projects. Rev. ed. Patricia Byrnes & Nancy Krenz. LC 77-18988. (Illus.). (gr. 1-8). 1979. pap. 9.95 (ISBN 0-913270-62-8). Sunstone Pr.

Southwestern Book Trails. Lawrence C. Powell. LC 82-82399. 1982. lib. bdg. 15.00x (ISBN 0-88307-657-8); pap. 4.95 (ISBN 0-88307-656-X). Gannon.

Southwestern Ceramics: A Comparative Review: A School of American Research Advanced Seminar. Ed. by Albert H. Schroder. (Arizona Archaeologist Ser.: No. 15). (Illus.). 317p. (Orig.). 1988. pap. 10.00 (ISBN 0-939071-10-X). AZ Archaeol.

Southwestern Colonial Ironwork. Marc Simmons & Frank Turley. LC 79-66181. (Series in Southwestern Culture: No. 2). (Illus.). 1981. 26.95 (ISBN 0-89013-127-9); pap. 16.95 (ISBN 0-89013-128-7). Museum NM Pr.

Southwestern Cookery: Indian & Spanish Influences. Franklin H. Giddings & John B Clark. 14.00 (ISBN 0-405-05054-2). Ayer Co Pubs.

Southwestern Cooking: New & Old. Ronald Johnson. LC 84-19603. 296p. 1985. Repr. of 1968 ed. 17.50 (ISBN 0-8263-0788-4). U of NM Pr.

Southwestern Expedition of Zebulon M. Pike. facs. ed. Ed. by Milo M. Quaife. LC 70-124252. (Select Bibliographies Reprint Ser). 1925. 16.00 (ISBN 0-8369-5440-8). Ayer Co Pubs.

Southwestern Fiction Nineteen Sixty to Nineteen Eighty: A Classified Bibliography. Mary L. Morris. LC 85-24578. 114p. 1986. pap. 9.95x (ISBN 0-8263-0866-X). U of NM Pr.

Southwestern Indian Ceremonials. Tom Bahti. LC 79-136004. (Illus.). 64p. 1982. 8.95 (ISBN 0-916122-27-1); pap. 4.50 (ISBN 0-916122-02-6). KC Pubns.

Southwestern Indian Drypainting. Leland C. Wyman. LC 82-23891. (School of American Research Southwest Indian Art Ser.). (Illus.). 343p. 1983. 55.00x (ISBN 0-8263-0640-3). U of NM Pr.

Southwestern Indian Recipe Book. Zora G. Hesse. (Wild & Woolly West Ser, No. 23). (Illus.). 60p. (Orig.). 1973. 8.00 (ISBN 0-910584-32-X); pap. 2.00 (ISBN 0-910584-89-3). Filter.

Southwestern Indian Tribes. Tom Bahti. LC 68-31188. (Illus.). 72p. 1968. 8.95 (ISBN 0-916122-26-3); pap. 4.50 (ISBN 0-916122-01-8). KC Pubns.

Southwestern Indians see West on Wood: Antique Wood Engravings of the Old West.

Southwestern Journal of Adolph F. Bandelier, 1883-1884. Adolph F. Bandelier. Ed. by Charles H. Lange & Carroll L. Riley. LC 65-17862. pap. 140.50 (ISBN 0-317-26629-2, 2025431). Bks Demand UMI.

Southwestern Journals of Adolf F. Bandelier, 1880-1882. Adolph F. Bandelier. Ed. by Charles H. Lange & Carroll L. Riley. LC 65-17862. pap. 125.50 (ISBN 0-317-26625-X, 2025430). Bks Demand UMI.

Southwestern Journals of Adolph F. Bandelier, 1885-1888. Adolph F. Bandelier. Ed. by Charles H. Lange & Carroll L. Riley. LC 65-17862. pap. 160.00 (ISBN 0-317-26630-6, 2025432). Bks Demand UMI.

Southwestern Landscaping with Native Plants. Judith Phillips. (Illus.). 160p. 1987. 27.95 (ISBN 0-89013-165-1); pap. 17.95 (ISBN 0-89013-166-X). Museum NM Pr.

Southwestern Livestock Show & Rodeo. Nora Ramirez. (Southwestern Studies Ser.: No. 32). 1972. pap. 5.00 (ISBN 0-87404-140-6). Tex Western.

Southwestern Lore. Ed. by J. Frank Dobie. LC 33-1134. (Texas Folklore Society Publications: No. 9). (Illus.). 208p. 1965. Repr. of 1931 ed. 12.95 (ISBN 0-87074-042-3). SMU Press.

Southwestern Medical Dictionary: Spanish-English & English-Spanish. Margarita Kay. LC 76-54591. 217p. (Span. & Eng.). 1977. pap. 8.50 (ISBN 0-8165-0529-2). U of Ariz Pr.

Southwestern: Ornamentation & Design the Architecture of John Gaw Meem. Anne Taylor. LC 85-2785. (Illus.). 105p. 1988. pap. 16.95 (ISBN 0-86534-069-2). Sunstone Pr.

Southwestern Sampler. Barbara Grunes & Phyllis Magida. (Illus.). 192p. 1987. pap. 7.95 (ISBN 0-8092-4722-4). Contemp Bks.

Southwestern Soap. Ella Salmi. (Reading Books for College Students, or Adult School Students in Grade levels: Bks. 1 & 2). (Illus.). 50p. 1983. pap. text ed. 4.00 (ISBN 0-686-38860-7); tchr's. guide 7.50 (ISBN 0-686-38861-5). Mentors.

Southwestern States. Harold W. Rickett. (Wild Flowers of the United States Ser.: Vol. 4). 1970. text ed. 81.00x (ISBN 0-89327-280-9). NY Botanical.

Southwestern United States Under Mexico: Rare Imprints Concerning California, Arizona, New Mexico & Texas, 1821-1846. Ed. & intro. by David J. Weber. LC 76-7344. (Chicano Heritage Ser.). (Illus.). 1976. 36.00x (ISBN 0-405-09543-0). Ayer Co Pubs.

Southwestern University Law Review: Los Angeles, 1916-1986, 16 vols. Bound set. 532.50x (ISBN 0-686-90042-1). microfilm avail. Rothman.

Southwestern Vocabulary: The Words They Used. Corneleus C. Smith, Jr. LC 83-72230. (Illus.). 168p. 1984. 19.50 (ISBN 0-87062-150-5). A H Clark.

Southwold Diary of James Maggs: Vol. I 1818-1848. Ed. by Alan Bottomley. (Suffolk Records Society Ser.: No. XXV). (Illus.). 160p. 1985. 19.95 (ISBN 0-85115-185-X, Pub. by Boydell & Brewer). Longwood Pub Group.

Southwold Diary of James Maggs, Vol. II: 1848-1876. Ed. by Alan Bottomley. (Suffolk Records Society Ser.: No. XXVI). (Illus.). 160p. 1985. 22.00 (ISBN 0-85115-411-5, Pub. by Boydell & Brewer). Longwood Pub Group.

Soutien De Famille. Alphonse Daudet. 460p. 1898. 8.95 (ISBN 0-686-55599-6). French & Eur.

Soutine. Raymond Cogniat. (Q L P Art Ser.). (Illus.). 96p. 1974. 14.95 (ISBN 0-517-51136-3). Crown.

Soutine. Alfred Werner. (Masters of Art Ser.). (Illus.). 128p. 1986. 19.95 (ISBN 0-8109-1500-6). Abrams.

Soutine. Monroe Wheeler. LC 66-26125. (Museum of Modern Art Publications in Reprint Ser). Repr. of 1950 ed. 12.00 (ISBN 0-405-01523-2). Ayer Co Pubs.

Souvenir. David A. Kaufelt. 1983. 14.95 (ISBN 0-453-00445-8). NAL.

Souvenir. David A. Kaufelt. 1985. pap. 3.95 (ISBN 0-451-13324-2, Sig). NAL.

Souvenir Album of Topeka. Ed. by Robert W. Richmond. (Illus.). 56p. 2.45 (ISBN 0-686-79885-6, 64). Shawnee County Hist.

Souvenir Book of the Ephrata Cloister: Complete History from Its Settlement in 1728 to the Present Time. Samuel G. Zerfass. LC 72-2960. Repr. of 1921 ed. 24.00 (ISBN 0-404-10724-9). AMS Pr.

Souvenir Buildings: A Collection of Identified Miniatures, 2 vols. Dort F. Brown. (Illus.). 203p. (Orig., Vol. 1, 1977, Vol. 2, 1979). pap. 6.95 set (ISBN 0-9603420-0-1). D E Brown.

Souvenir de Deux Existences. Jean Giraudoux. 1975. 9.95 (ISBN 0-686-54012-3). French & Eur.

Souvenir of the City of Riverside. The Riverside Fire Department et al. (Illus.). 127p. 1987. Repr. of 1906 ed. 10.00 (ISBN 0-935661-16-6). Riverside Mus Pr.

Souvenir Programs of Five Great World Series - 1914, 1917, 1919, 1926, 1934. Ed. by Bert R. Sugar. 16.50 (ISBN 0-8446-5822-7). Peter Smith.

Souvenir Programs of Twelve Classics Movies, 1927-1941. Ed. by Miles Kreuger. 16.50 (ISBN 0-8446-5595-3). Peter Smith.

Souvenirs. Jean-Baptiste Nampere de Champagny. 211p. Repr. of 1846 ed. lib. bdg. 46.50x. Coronet Bks.

Souvenirs. Charles Peguy. pap. 1.95 (ISBN 0-685-37041-0). French & Eur.

Souvenirs & Prophecies: The Young Wallace Stevens. Holly Stevens. 1977. 15.00 (ISBN 0-394-49138-6). Knopf.

Souvenirs De Guerre see Memoirs of War, 1914-15.

Souvenirs de la Cour d'Assises. Andre Gide. 120p. 1914. 8.95 (ISBN 0-686-56057-4). French & Eur.

Souvenirs de la Vie du Paradis. Georges Duhamel. 204p. 9.95 (ISBN 0-686-55196-6). French & Eur.

Souvenirs de 1848. facsimile ed. George Sand. 202p. 1976. 25.00 (ISBN 0-686-54946-5). French & Eur.

Souvenirs d'Egotisme. Stendhal, pseud. (Folio Ser.: No. 1430). 7.95 (ISBN 0-685-35022-3). Schoenhof.

Souvenirs d'Enfance, 3 tomes. Marcel Pagnol. Incl. Tome I. Gloire de mon Pere. 14.95 (ISBN 0-685-37010-0); Tome II. Chateau de ma Mere. 15.50 (ISBN 0-685-37011-9); Tome III. Temps des Secrets. 15.95 (ISBN 0-685-37012-7). French & Eur.

Souvenirs d'Enfance: Le Temps des Amours, Vol. 4. Marcel Pagnol. 329p. 1977. 15.95 (ISBN 0-686-54844-2). French & Eur.

Souvenirs D'un Vieil Amateur D'Art de l'Extreme-Orient. Ed. by Raymond Koechlin. 112p. 1930. 200.00x (Pub. by Han-Shan Tang Ltd). State Mutual Bk.

Souvenirs, Eighteen Ninety-Five to Nineteen Eighteen: My Life with Maeterlinck. Georgette Leblanc. Tr. by Janet Flanner from Fr. LC 76-22154. (Music Reprint Ser.). 352p. 1976. Repr. of 1932 ed. lib. bdg. 39.50 (ISBN 0-306-70841-8). Da Capo.

Souvenirs, Eighteen Seventy-Eight to Eighteen Ninety-Three. Charles L. De Freycinet. LC 73-258. (Europe 1815-1945 Ser.). 524p. 1973. Repr. of 1913 ed. lib. bdg. 65.00 (ISBN 0-306-70560-5). Da Capo.

Souvenirs Fresh & Rancid. Alfred Adler. LC 83-81147. 224p. 1982. 14.95 (ISBN 0-394-53218-X, GP868). Grove.

Souvenirs Fresh & Rancid. Alfred Adler. 224p. 1982. pap. 6.95 (ISBN 0-394-62467-X, Ever). Grove.

Souvenirs: Les Casques, La Mort d'Ivan Illitch, Maitre et Serviteur, etc. Leo Tolstoy. 1620p. 41.50 (ISBN 0-686-56587-8). French & Eur.

Souvenirs, Notes et Pensees Intimes. Gustave Flaubert. 109p. 1965. 8.95 (ISBN 0-686-55990-8). French & Eur.

Souvenirs Personnels, 1848-1851. Victor Hugo. 328p. 1952. 5.95 (ISBN 0-686-54042-5). French & Eur.

Souvenirs Poetiques. Paul Valery. pap. 3.95 (ISBN 0-685-36626-X). French & Eur.

Souviens-Toi Que je T'Aime. Sally Wentworth. (Harlequin Romantique Ser.). 192p. 1983. pap. 1.95 (ISBN 0-373-41219-3). Harlequin Bks.

Sou'west in Wanderer IV. Eric Hiscock. (Illus.). 224p. (Orig.). 1986. pap. 12.95 (ISBN 0-911378-60-X). Sheridan.

Sou'west in Wanderer 4. Eric C. Hiscock. (Illus.). 1973. 22.50 (ISBN 0-19-217528-9). Oxford U Pr.

Sovereign Adventure: The Grail of Mankind. Anna Morduch. 196p. 1970. 13.50 (ISBN 0-227-67754-4). Attic Pr.

Sovereign Council of New France: A Study in Canadian Constitutional History. Raymond D. Cahall. LC 15-13350. (Columbia University Studies in the Social Sciences: No. 156). Repr. of 1915 ed. 21.00 (ISBN 0-404-51156-2). AMS Pr.

Sovereign Debt. 35.00 (ISBN 0-317-29539-X, #CO1929, Law & Business). HarBraceJ.

Sovereign Entrepreneur: Oil Policies in Advanced & Less Developed Capitalist Countries. Merrie G. Klapp. LC 86-19909. (Cornell Studies in Political Economy). 256p. 1987. 27.50x (ISBN 0-8014-1997-2). Cornell U Pr.

Sovereign Ghost: Studies in Imagination. Denis Donoghue. LC 75-27923. 1977. 25.00x (ISBN 0-520-03134-2). U of Cal Pr.

Sovereign God. James M. Boice. LC 77-14879. (Foundations of the Christian Faith: Vol. 1). 1978. pap. 7.95 (ISBN 0-87784-743-6). Inter-Varsity.

Sovereign Immunity: The Tort Liability of Government & Its Officials. 102p. 1979. 5.00 (ISBN 0-318-15228-2). Natl Attys General.

Sovereign Individuals of Capitalism. Nicholas Abercrombie et al. 224p. 1986. 39.95x (ISBN 0-04-301230-2); pap. text ed. 14.95x (ISBN 0-04-301231-0). Unwin Hyman.

Sovereign Lending: Managing Legal Risk. Ed. by Michael Gruson & Ralph Reisner. (Euromoney Ser.). 272p. (Orig.). 1984. pap. 115.00 (ISBN 0-903121-61-1, Pub. by Woodhead-Faulkner). Longwood Pub Group.

Sovereign People or Sovereign Governments. H. C. Kroeker. 168p. 1981. pap. text ed. 12.95x (ISBN 0-920380-34-4, Pub. by Inst Res Pub Canada). Brookfield Pub Co.

Sovereign Rescheduling: Risk & Portfolio Management. Ronald Solberg. (Illus.). 220p. 1988. text ed. 50.00x (ISBN 0-04-332122-4). Unwin Hyman.

Sovereign Risk Analysis. Shelagh A. Heffernan. 200p. 1986. text ed. 24.95x (ISBN 0-04-332119-4). Unwin Hyman.

Sovereign Spirit: Discerning His Gifts. Martyn Lloyd-Jones. 160p. 1986. pap. 7.95 (ISBN 0-87788-697-0). Shaw Pubs.

Sovereign State of Boogedy Boogedy & Other Plays. Lonnie Carter. LC 86-18503. (Illus.). 205p. (Orig.). 1986. pap. text ed. 11.95 (ISBN 0-933951-04-3). Locust Hill Pr.

Sovereign Statehood: The Basis of International Society. Alan James. LC 85-26707. (Key Concepts in International Relations Ser.: No. 2). 1986. text ed. 39.95x (ISBN 0-04-320190-3); pap. text ed. 14.95x (ISBN 0-04-320191-1). Unwin Hyman.

Sovereign States in an Age of Uncertainty. Ed. by Ronald Hoffman & Peter J. Albert. LC 81-19660. (U. S. Capitol Historical Society, Perspectives on the American Revolution Ser.). 288p. 1982. 25.00x (ISBN 0-8139-0926-0). U Pr of Va.

Sovereign Sun: Selected Poems. Odysseus Elytis. Tr. by Kimon Friar from Gr. 200p. 1979. pap. 9.95 (ISBN 0-87722-113-8). Temple U Pr.

Sovereignity of the Sea. Thomas W. Fulton. LC 11-7247. 1976. Repr. of 1911 ed. 58.00 (ISBN 0-527-31860-4). Kraus Repr.

Sovereigns of Industry. Edwin M. Chamberlin. LC 75-308. (Radical Tradition in America Ser). 165p. 1975. Repr. of 1875 ed. 18.70 (ISBN 0-88355-212-4). Hyperion Conn.

Sovereignty: An Inquiry into the Political Good. Bertrand De Jouvenel. Tr. by J. F. Huntington. LC 57-9548. 1957. 20.00x (ISBN 0-226-14161-6). U of Chicago Pr.

Sovereignty & an Empty Purse: Banks & Politics in the Civil War. Bray Hammond. LC 79-113003. 1970. 44.50x (ISBN 0-691-04601-8). Princeton U Pr.

Sovereignty & Coinage in Classical Greece. Thomas R. Martin. LC 84-26292. (Illus.). 300p. 1985. text ed. 36.00x (ISBN 0-691-03580-6). Princeton U Pr.

Sovereignty & Freedom: A Struggle for Balance. Ed. by Freeman Barton. 92p. (Orig.). 1978. pap. 2.50 (ISBN 0-913439-00-2). Henceforth.

Sovereignty & Intervention. Richard N. Gardner & Andre Glucksmann. write for info. Trilateral Comm.

Soviet Calculus of Nuclear War. Roman Kolkowicz & Ellen Mickiewicz. LC 85-45344. 288p. 1986. 35.00x (ISBN 0-669-11566-5); pap. 16.95x (ISBN 0-669-12580-6). Lexington Bks.
Soviet Censorship. Ed. by Martin Dewhirst & Robert Farrell. LC 73-9844. 177p. 1973. 20.00 (ISBN 0-8108-0674-6). Scarecrow.
Soviet Central Asia in Ferment. Ann Sheehy. (CSIS Washington Papers). 1988. write for info. Praeger.
Soviet Character. A. Tolstoy et al. 253p. 1986. 10.95 (ISBN 0-8285-3436-5, Pub. by Raduga Pubs USSR). Imported Pubns.
Soviet Character: Painting by Soviet Artists 1960s-1980s. Vladimir Leniashin. 1986. 210.00x (ISBN 0-317-61393-6, Pub. by Collets (UK)). State Mutual Bk.
Soviet Charismatics: The Pentecostals in the U. S. S. R. William c. Fletcher. (American University Studies VII (Theology & Religion): Vol. 9). 287p. 1985. text ed. 25.15 (ISBN 0-8204-0226-5). P Lang Pubs.
Soviet Chess. Ed. by R. G. Wade. 1976. pap. 3.00 (ISBN 0-87980-311-8). Wilshire.
Soviet Chess School. A. Kotov & M. Yudovich. 192p. 1985. 6.95 (ISBN 0-8285-2901-9, Pub. by Raduga Pubs USSR). Imported Pubns.
Soviet-Chinese Relations, Nineteen Fourty-Five to Nineteen Hundred Seventy. Oleg B. Borisov & B. T. Koloskov. Ed. by Vladimir Petrov. LC 74-31443. pap. 95.50 (2056219). Bks Demand UMI.
Soviet Cinema. Thorold Dickinson & Catherine De La Roche. Ed. by Roger Manvell. LC 77-169327. (National Cinema Series). (Illus.). 140p. 1972. Repr. of 1948 ed. 18.00 (ISBN 0-405-03891-7). Ayer Co Pubs.
Soviet Cinema: Directors & Films. Alexander S. Birkos. LC 76-7082. (Illus.). x, 344p. (Orig.). 1976. 32.50 (ISBN 0-208-01581-7, Archon). Shoe String.
Soviet Cinema in the Silent Era, 1919-1934. Denise J. Youngblood. Ed. by Diane Kirkpatrick. LC 85-2772. (Studies in Cinema: No. 35). 352p. 1985. 44.95 (ISBN 0-8357-1659-7). UMI Res Pr.
Soviet Civil Law. Olimpiad S. Ioffe. 1988. lib. bdg. 112.00 (ISBN 90-247-3676-5, Pub. by Martinus Nijhoff Netherlands). Kluwer Academic.
Soviet Civil Law. O. N. Sadikov. Intro. by William B. Simons. LC 87-4518. 500p. 1987. 75.00 (ISBN 0-87332-429-3). M E Sharpe.
Soviet Codes of Law. William B. Simons. (Law in Eastern Europe Ser.: No. 23). 1288p. 1980. 92.50x (ISBN 90-286-0810-9, Pub. by Sijthoff & Noordhoff). Kluwer Academic.
Soviet Collective Farm: 1929-1930. R. W. Davies. LC 79-15273. (Industrialization of Soviet Russia: Vol. 2). 256p. 1980. text ed. 21.00x (ISBN 0-674-82600-0). Harvard U Pr.
Soviet Colossus. Michael Kort. 318p. 1985. pap. text ed. write for info. (ISBN 0-02-366160-7, Pub. by Scribner). Macmillan.
Soviet Comes of Age. facs. ed. LC 68-20337. (Essay Index Reprint Ser). 1938. 21.50 (ISBN 0-8369-0892-9). Ayer Co Pubs.
Soviet Commercial Design of the Twenties. Mikhail Anikst. (Illus.). 144p. 1987. 37.50 (ISBN 0-89659-766-0). Abbeville Pr.
Soviet Communism: The Socialist Vision. Ed. by Julius Jacobson. LC 73-164981. (New Politics Ser.). 372p. 1972. 24.95 (ISBN 0-87855-005-4); pap. text ed. 12.95x (ISBN 0-87855-505-6). Transaction Bks.
Soviet Communist Party. 3rd ed. Ed. by Ronald Hill & Peter Frank. 172p. 1986. pap. text ed. 10.95x (ISBN 0-04-497024-2). Unwin Hyman.
Soviet Communist Party. 2nd ed. Ronald J Hill & Peter Frank. 176p. 1983. pap. text ed. 8.95x (ISBN 0-04-324009-7). Unwin Hyman.
Soviet Communists in Power: A Study Moscow During the Civil War 1918-21. Richard Sakwa. LC 87-24167. 324p. 1988. 55.00 (ISBN 0-312-01582-8). St Martin.
Soviet Concepts of Peace, Peaceful Coexistence & Detente. Ronald R. Nelson & Peter Schweizer. LC 87-34520. 198p. (Orig.). 1988. lib. bdg. 27.50 (ISBN 0-8191-6832-7, Pub. by Natl Forum Foun); pap. text ed. 14.50 (ISBN 0-8191-6833-5, Pub. by Natl Forum Foun). U Pr of Amer.
Soviet Conference on Charged Particle Accelerators, Moscow, 1968, 2 vols. A. A. Vasil'ev. 1436p. 1971. Set. 275.00x (ISBN 0-7065-1204-9, Pub. by Keter Pub Jerusalem). Coronet Bks.
Soviet Constitution & the Myths of Sovietologists. A. Lukyanov. 246p. 1984. 11.25x (ISBN 0-317-53788-1, Pub. by Collets (UK)). State Mutual Bk.
Soviet Construction Materials Industry. Genrikh Bukhsbaum. Ed. by Andreas Tamberg. (Orig.). Date not set. pap. text ed. 35.00 (ISBN 1-55831-004-5). Delphic Associates.
Soviet Contributions to the Sociology of Language. P. Luelsdorff. 1977. pap. text ed. 22.80x (ISBN 90-279-7613-9). Mouton.
Soviet Control Structure: Capabilities for Wartime Survival. William F. Scott & Harriet F. Scott. LC 83-2004. (Strategy Paper Ser.: No. 39). 150p. 1983. pap. 12.00x (ISBN 0-8448-1452-0, Pub. by Crane Russak & Co). Taylor & Francis.
Soviet Cosmonaut Team: A Comprehensive Guide to Men & Women of the Soviet Manned Space Programme, 1986. Gordon R. Hooper. 330p. 1986. pap. text ed. 25.00x (ISBN 0-9511312-0-6, Pub GRH Publications, England). Univelt Inc.
Soviet Cost-Accounting in the Machine-Building & Metal-Working Industry (Theory & Practice) Selected Papers with Analysis. Ehiel Ash et al. Ed. by Erika D. Nobel. Tr. by Vladimir Talmy from Rus. (Illus.). 200p. (Orig.). Date not set. pap. text ed. 45.00. Delphic Associates.
Soviet Cost-Accounting Practices. Ed. by Erika Nobel. (Orig.). Date not set. pap. text ed. 42.50 (ISBN 1-55831-071-1). Delphic Associates.
Soviet Court & Human Rights. 21p. 1975. pap. 3.00 (ISBN 0-317-30696-0). Amer Bar Assn.
Soviet Court: Guide to the Constitutional Principles of the Administration of Justice in the U. S. S. R. Vladimir Terebilov. 182p. 1973. 15.95 (ISBN 0-8464-0866-X). Beekman Pubs.
Soviet Criminologists & Criminal Policy. Peter H. Solomon, Jr. LC 77-3357. (Studies of the Russian Institute Ser.). 1978. 30.00 (ISBN 0-231-04316-3). Columbia U Pr.
Soviet Critique of Neopositivism: The History & Structure of the Critique of Logical Positivism & Related Doctrines by Soviet Philosophers in the Years 1947-1967. Wolfhard Von Boeselager. Tr. by T. J. Blakeley from Ger. LC 74-81935. (Sovietica Ser: No. 35). 180p. 1975. lib. bdg. 31.50 (ISBN 90-277-0508-9, Pub. by Reidel Holland). Kluwer Academic.
Soviet Cultural Offensive. Frederick G. Barghoorn. LC 75-18397. 353p. 1976. Repr. of 1960 ed. lib. bdg. 38.50x (ISBN 0-8371-8334-0, BASCO). Greenwood.
Soviet Cultural Offensive: The Role of Cultural Diplomacy in Soviet Foreign Policy. Frederick C. Barghoorn. LC 60-12227. pap. 90.30 (ISBN 0-317-09488-2, 2000893). Bks Demand UMI.
Soviet Cybernetic Technology: A Timeline Researcher's Data Base & Guide to Professional Literature from Early First Generation Through Third Generation, Volume II, 2 vols. Ed. by George M. Weinberger. 342p. (Orig.). 1985. lib. bdg. 31.00 ea. Vol. I (ISBN 0-8191-4821-0). Vol. II (ISBN 0-8191-4823-7). pap. text ed. 15.50 ea. Vol. I (ISBN 0-8191-4822-9). Vol. II (ISBN 0-8191-4824-5). U Pr of Amer.
Soviet C3. Ed. by Stephen J. Cimbala. (AFCEA Signal Magazine C3I Ser.). (Illus.). 472p. 1987. text ed. 39.95 (ISBN 0-916159-15-9). AFCEA Intl Pr.
Soviet Decipherment of the Indus Valley Script: Translation & Critique. Ed. by A. R. K. Zide & K. V. Zvelebil. 1976. pap. text ed. 20.80x (ISBN 90-2793-104-6). Mouton.
Soviet Decision Making for National Security. Ed. by Jiri Valenta & W. C. Potter. 400p. 1984. text ed. 40.00x (ISBN 0-04-351063-9); pap. text ed. 19.95x (ISBN 0-04-351065-5). Unwin Hyman.
Soviet Decision Making in Practice: The U. S. S. R. & Israel, 1947-1954. Yaacov Ro'i. LC 79-64857. 540p. 1980. 34.95 (ISBN 0-87855-267-7). Transaction Bks.
Soviet Decorative Art, Nineteen Seventeen to Nineteen Forty-Five. V. M. Vasilenko. 256p. 1984. 97.00x (ISBN 0-317-61396-0, Pub. by Collets (UK)). State Mutual Bk.
Soviet Defectors: The KGB Most Wanted List. Victor Krasnov. LC 85-17661. (Publication Ser.: No. 323). 330p. 1986. lib. bdg. 16.95x (ISBN 0-8179-8231-0). Hoover Inst Pr.
Soviet Defectors: The KGB Wanted List. Vladimir Krasnov. 1987. pap. 9.95 (ISBN 0-317-57948-7). Hoover Inst Pr.
Soviet Defence Enigma: Estimating Costs & Burden. Ed. by Carl G. Jacobsen. (SIPRI Ser.). (Illus.). 224p. 1987. 47.00 (ISBN 0-19-829118-3). Oxford U Pr.
Soviet Deterrence Doctrine. Young-Hoon Kang. (Institute of Social Sciences International Studies Ser.: No. 2). 136p. 1981. text ed. 14.00x (ISBN 0-8248-0940-8). UH Pr.
Soviet Developmental Psychology: An Anthology. Michael Cole. LC 77-85709. 1977. pap. 160.00 (ISBN 0-317-08144-6, 2021854). Bks Demand UMI.
Soviet Dissent: Contemporary Movements for National, Religious & Human Rights. Ludmilla Alexeyeva. Tr. by John Glad & Carol Pearce. LC 84-11811. xxii, 522p. 1985. 35.00 (ISBN 0-8195-5124-4, Dist. by Harper); pap. 15.95. Wesleyan U Pr.
Soviet Dissent: Contemporary Movements for National, Religious, & Human Rights. Ludmilla Alexeyeva. (Illus.). xxii, 522p. 1986. pap. 14.95 (ISBN 0-8195-6176-2). Wesleyan U Pr.
Soviet Dissent in Historical Perspective. Marshall S. Shatz. LC 80-13318. 240p. 1981. 37.50 (ISBN 0-521-23172-8). Cambridge U Pr.
Soviet Dissident Literature: A Critical Guide. Josephine Woll & Vladimir Treml. 304p. 1983. lib. bdg. 29.00 (ISBN 0-8161-8626-X, Hall Reference). G K Hall.
Soviet Dissidents: Their Struggle for Human Rights. rev. ed. Joshua Rubenstein. LC 85-47523. 335p. 1985. pap. 10.95 (ISBN 0-8070-3215-8, BP 704). Beacon Pr.
Soviet Documents on Foreign Policy, Vols. I-III. Ed. by Jane Degras. 1978. Repr. of 1953 ed. lib. bdg. 115.00x set (ISBN 0-374-92096-6, Octagon). Hippocrene Bks.
Soviet-East European Dialogue: Relations of a New Type? Nish Jamgotch, Jr. LC 68-29991. (Studies: No. 21). 1968. 8.95x (ISBN 0-8179-3211-9); pap. 5.95 (ISBN 0-8179-3212-7). Hoover Inst Pr.
Soviet-East European Dilemmas. Ed. by Karen Dawisha & Philip Hanson. LC 80-28573. 226p. 1981. 32.50 (ISBN 0-8419-0697-1); pap. 14.95 (ISBN 0-8419-0698-X). Holmes & Meier.
Soviet-East European Relations As a Problem for Western Policy. Richard D. Vine. 272p. 1987. lib. bdg. 65.00x (ISBN 0-7099-5113-2, Pub. by Croom Helm UK). Routledge Chapman & Hall.
Soviet-East European Relations: Consolidation & Conflict, 1968-1980. Robert L. Hutchings. LC 83-47761. 336p. 1984. text ed. 27.50x (ISBN 0-299-09310-7); pap. 12.50x (ISBN 0-299-09314-X). U of Wis Pr.
Soviet-East European Survey, 1983-1984: Selected Research & Analysis from Radio Free Europe Radio Liberty. Ed. by Vojtech Mastny. (Policy Studies). xvi, 436p. 1985. 49.50 (ISBN 0-8223-0643-3); pap. 16.50 (ISBN 0-8223-0650-6). Duke.
Soviet-East European Survey, 1984-1985: Selected Research & Analysis from Radio Free Europe-Radio Liberty. Ed. by Vojtech Mastny. LC 85-10281. xii, 400p. (Orig.). 1986. text ed. 59.50 (ISBN 0-8223-0656-5); pap. text ed. 19.95 (ISBN 0-8223-0699-9). Duke.
Soviet-East European Survey, 1985-1986: Selected Research & Analysis from Radio Free Europe-Radio Liberty. Ed. by Vojtech Mastny. x, 451p. 1987. 52.50 (ISBN 0-8223-0721-9); pap. 19.95 (ISBN 0-8223-0765-0). Duke.
Soviet-East European Survey, 1986-1987: Selected Research & Analysis from Radio Free Europe-Radio Liberty. Ed. by Vojtech Mastny. 364p. 1987. pap. 29.85 (ISBN 0-8133-7477-4). Westview.
Soviet Ecomomy: Past, Present & Future. Franklyn D. Holzman. LC 82-84003. (Headline Ser.: 260). (Illus.). 64p. 1982. pap. 4.00 (ISBN 0-87124-078-5). Foreign Policy.
Soviet Economic Assistance to the Less Developed Countries: A Statistical Analysis. Quintin V. Bach. (Illus.). 200p. 1988. 55.00 (ISBN 0-19-828572-8). Oxford U Pr.
Soviet Economic Development. 2nd ed. Raymond Hutchings. 368p. 1983. 35.00x (ISBN 0-8147-3419-7); pap. 13.50x (ISBN 0-8147-3420-0). NYU Pr.
Soviet Economic Facts: 1917-1981. Clark & Matko. LC 81-23299. 200p. 1983. 27.50x (ISBN 0-312-74758-6). St Martin.
Soviet Economic Growth: A Comparison with the United States. U. S. Library Of Congress - Legislative Reference Service. LC 69-10165. 1969. Repr. of 1957 ed. lib. bdg. 35.00x (ISBN 0-8371-0722-9, ULSE). Greenwood.
Soviet Economic Planning: Theory & Practice. Edward Tesler. Ed. by Andrew Michta & Andreas Tamberg. (Orig.). Date not set. pap. text ed. 35.00 (ISBN 1-55831-050-9). Delphic Associates.
Soviet Economic Statistics. Ed. by Vladimir G. Treml & John P. Hardt. LC 74-184790. xii, 455p. 1972. 42.00 (ISBN 0-8223-0251-9). Duke.
Soviet Economic Structure & Performance. 3rd ed. Paul R. Gregory & Robert C. Stuart. 1986. text ed. 33.95 scp (ISBN 0-06-042507-5, HarpC). Har-Row.
Soviet Economic System. 2nd ed. Alec Nove. 404p. 1981. pap. text ed. 13.50x (ISBN 0-04-335042-9). Unwin Hyman.
Soviet Economic System. 3rd ed. Alec Nove. 420p. 1986. pap. text ed. 17.95x (ISBN 0-04-497025-0). Unwin Hyman.
Soviet Economic System: A Legal Analysis. Olimpiad S. Ioffe & Peter B. Maggs. (Special Studies on the Soviet Union & Eastern Europe). 326p. 1987. 48.50 (ISBN 0-8133-7222-4). Westview.
Soviet Economic Warfare. Robert L. Allen. 1960. 12.00 (ISBN 0-8183-0209-7). Pub Aff Pr.
Soviet Economy. David A. Dyker. (Illus.). 173p. 1976. 19.95 (ISBN 0-8464-1138-5). Beekman Pubs.
Soviet Economy: A Collection of Western & Soviet Views. 2nd ed. Ed. by Harry G. Shaffer. LC 69-16223. (Illus., Orig.). 1969. pap. text ed. 16.95x (ISBN 0-89197-420-2). Irvington.
Soviet Economy & Society. David Lane. 384p. 1985. 45.00x (ISBN 0-8147-5015-X); pap. 20.00x (ISBN 0-8147-5016-8). NYU Pr.
Soviet Economy: Continuity & Change. Ed. by Morris Bornstein. LC 80-21159. 381p. (Orig.). 1981. pap. text ed. 19.95x (ISBN 0-89158-959-7). Westview.
Soviet Economy: Development of Azerbaijan. Vinod Mehta. (Illus.). vi, 116p. 1984. text ed. 15.00x (ISBN 0-86590-416-2, Pub. by Sterling Pubs India). Apt Bks.
Soviet Economy Forges Ahead: A Look at the Five-Year Plan Ending 1975. F. I. Kotov et al. 235p. 1975. 15.95 (ISBN 0-8464-0868-6). Beekman Pubs.
Soviet Economy: New Economic Strategy. Vinod Mehta. 210p. 1987. text ed. 27.50x (ISBN 81-207-0670-6, Pub. by Sterling Pubs). Apt Bks.
Soviet Economy: Problems & Prospects. Padma Desai. 336p. 1987. text ed. 39.95 (ISBN 0-631-15227-X). Basil Blackwell.
Soviet Economy Today: With Guidelines for the Economic & Social Development of the U. S. S. R. for 1981 to 1985 & for the Period Ending in 1990. LC 81-1121. (Contributions in Economics & Economic History Ser.: No. 41). 220p. 1981. lib. bdg. 56.95 (ISBN 0-313-21414-X, NSE/). Greenwood.
Soviet Economy Towards the Year 2000. Ed. by Abram Bergson & Herbert S. Levine. 496p. 1983. text ed. 49.95x (ISBN 0-04-335045-3). Unwin Hyman.
Soviet Economy: Towards the Year 2000. Ed. by Abram Bergson & Herbert S. Levine. 496p. (Orig.). 1985. pap. text ed. 19.95x (ISBN 0-04-335053-4). Unwin Hyman.
Soviet Education. 4th, rev ed. Nigel Grant. 1979. pap. 6.95 (ISBN 0-14-020660-4, Pelican). Penguin.
Soviet Education: An Annotated Bibliography & Readers' Guide to Works in English, 1893-1978. Compiled by Yushin Yoo. LC 79-54058. xvi, 408p. 1980. lib. bdg. 85.00 (ISBN 0-313-22085-9, YSE/). Greenwood.
Soviet Education: Anton Makarenko & the Years of Experiment. James Bowen. 244p. 1965. pap. 8.50x (ISBN 0-299-02644-2). U of Wis Pr.
Soviet Education for Science & Technology. Alexander G. Korol. LC 73-9212. 513p. 1974. Repr. of 1957 ed. lib. bdg. 48.50x (ISBN 0-8371-6978-X, KOSE). Greenwood.
Soviet Education: The Gifted & the Handicapped. Ed. by J. Riordan. 240p. 1988. lib. bdg. 55.00 (ISBN 0-415-00574-4). Routledge Chapman & Hall.
Soviet-Egyptian Relations, 1945-85. Mohrez M. El Hussini. LC 86-13748. 562p. 1987. 49.95 (ISBN 0-312-74781-0). St Martin.
Soviet Emigre Artist: Life & Work in the U. S. S. R. & the United States. Marilyn Rueschemeyer & Igor Golomshtok. LC 84-23558. (Illus.). 150p. 1985. pap. 27.50 (ISBN 0-87332-296-7). M E Sharpe.
Soviet Energy & Western Europe. A. Stent. 1982. pap. 9.95 (ISBN 0-275-91554-9, B1554). Praeger.
Soviet Energy System: Resource Use & Policies. Leslie Dienes & Theodore Shabad. LC 78-20814. (Scripta Series in Geography). 298p. 1979. 24.95x (ISBN 0-470-26629-5). Halsted Pr.
Soviet Energy Technologies: Planning, Policy, Research & Development. Robert W. Campbell. LC 80-7562. 288p. 1980. 25.00x (ISBN 0-253-15965-2). Ind U Pr.
Soviet Estimate: U. S. Intelligence Analysis & Soviet Strategic Forces. John Prados. LC 85-43379. 384p. 1986. text ed. 36.50x (ISBN 0-691-07685-5); pap. 10.50x (ISBN 0-691-02235-6). Princeton U Pr.
Soviet Ethnology & Anthropology Today. Ed. by Yu Bromley. (Studies in Anthropology Ser.: No. 1). 401p. 1974. pap. text ed. 58.00x (ISBN 90-2792-725-1). Mouton.
Soviet Evangelicals: Since World War II. Walter Sawatsky. LC 81-94121. 560p. 1981. 19.95x (ISBN 0-8361-1238-5); pap. 14.95x (ISBN 0-8361-1239-3). Herald Pr.
Soviet Evidence in North American Courts: An Analysis of Problems & Concerns with Reliance on Communist Source Evidence in Alleged War Criminal Trials. S. Paul Zumbakis. LC 86-70027. ii, 168p. Date not set. price not set. Amer Due Process.
Soviet Expansion in the Third World: Afghanistan, A Case Study. Nasir Shansab. LC 86-51372. (Illus.). 214p. 1987. 15.95 (ISBN 0-910155-07-0). Bartleby Pr.
Soviet Experience in Transfer of Technology to Industrially Less Developed Countries. (UNITAR Research Reports). pap. 7.00 (ISBN 92-1-157051-4, E.75.XV.RR/15). UN.
Soviet Family Law. Yuri I. Luryi. LC 80-83797. vi, 93p. 1980. lib. bdg. 32.00 (ISBN 0-89941-062-6). W S Hein.
Soviet Family of Nations: A Latvian Journey. Darshan Singh. 110p. 1984. text ed. 13.95x (ISBN 0-86590-212-7, Pub. by Sterling Pubs India). Apt Bks.
Soviet Far East & Central Asia. William Mandel. LC 75-30111. (Institute of Pacific Relations). Repr. of 1944 ed. 16.50 (ISBN 0-404-59545-6). AMS Pr.
Soviet Far East Military Buildup: Nuclear Dilemma & Asian Security. Ed. by Richard A. Solomon & Masataka Kosaka. 250p. 1986. 29.95x (ISBN 0-86569-140-1); pap. 16.95 (ISBN 0-86569-148-7). Auburn Hse.
Soviet Far Eastern Policy, 1931-1945. Harriet L. Moore. 25.00x (ISBN 0-86527-187-9). Fertig.
Soviet Fiction since Stalin: Science, Politics & Literature. Rosalind J. Marsh. LC 85-30610. 348p. 1986. 28.50x (ISBN 0-389-20609-1). B&N Imports.
Soviet Fine Arts, Nineteen Seventeen to Nineteen Forty-One: Paintings, Sculpture, Graphic Arts, Stage-Sets. Ed. by B. Veimann & O. Sopotsinsky. 212p. 1977. 90.00x (ISBN 0-317-14319-0, Pub. by Collets (UK)). State Mutual Bk.
Soviet First Strike Threat: The U. S. Perspective. Jack H. Nunn. LC 82-344. 304p. 1982. 42.95 (ISBN 0-275-90871-2, C0871). Praeger.
Soviet Forces in Space. Baker. (Soviet Military Power Ser.). (Illus.). 48p. (gr. 3-8). Date not set. PLB 15.93 (ISBN 0-86625-335-1). Rourke Corp.
Soviet Foreign Policy, Vol. 36, No. 4. Ed. by Robbin Laird. LC 87-71980. 1987. 12.95. Acad Poli Sci.

Soviet Legal System. 3rd ed. J. N. Hazard. LC 77-24349. 621p. 1977. 20.00. Oceana.
Soviet Legal System & Arms Inspection: A Case Study in Policy Implementation. Zigurds L. Zile et al. LC 71-151963. (Special Studies in International Politics & Government). 1972. 28.75x (ISBN 0-275-28211-2). Irvington.
Soviet Legal System: Selected Contemporary Legislation & Documents. William E. Butler. LC 78-2419. (Parker School Studies in Foreign & Comparative Law). 733p. 1978. 45.00 (ISBN 0-379-00791-6). Oceana.
Soviet Legal System: The Law in the 1980's. John N. Hazard & William E. Butler. LC 84-1106. (Parker School Studies in Foreign & Comparative Law). 424p. 1984. lib. bdg. 45.00 (ISBN 0-379-20141-0). Oceana.
Soviet Legislation of Women's Rights: A Collection of Normative Acts. Vladimir Barnashov. 216p. 1978. 15.00x (ISBN 0-317-56545-1, Pub. by Collets (UK)). State Mutual Bk.
Soviet Legislation on Children's Rights. V. Tolkunova & E. G. Azarova. 192p. 1982. 4.95 (ISBN 0-8285-2510-2, 330396, Pub. by Progress Pubs USSR). Imported Pubns.
Soviet Legislation on Women's Rights. 215p. 1978. 6.45 (ISBN 0-8285-3362-8, 133627, Pub. by Progress Pubs USSR). Imported Pubns.
Soviet Lexicon: Important Concepts, Terms, & Phrases. Roy D. Laird & Betty A. Laird. 224p. 1987. 27.00x (ISBN 0-669-16738-X); pap. text ed. 12.95x (ISBN 0-669-16739-8). Lexington Bks.
Soviet Literary Structuralism: Background Debate Issues. Peter Seyffert. 378p. (Orig.). 1985. pap. 17.95 (ISBN 0-89357-140-7). Slavica.
Soviet Literary Theory & Practice During the First Five-Year Plan, 1928-1932. Harriet Borland. LC 69-13833. 1969. Repr. of 1950 ed. lib. bdg. 35.00 (ISBN 0-8371-1075-0, BOSL). Greenwood.
Soviet Literature Yesterday, Today & Tomorrow. Yuri Kuzmenko. 328p. 1983. 25.00x (ISBN 0-317-39535-1, Pub. by Collets (UK)). State Mutual Bk.
Soviet Local & Republic Elections. Max E. Mote. LC 65-26268. (Studies: No. 10). 123p. 1965. pap. 6.95x (ISBN 0-8179-3102-3). Hoover Inst Pr.
Soviet Man & His World. Klaus Mehnert. Tr. by Maurice Rosenbaum. LC 76-14778. 1976. Repr. of 1962 ed. lib. bdg. 38.50x (ISBN 0-8371-8567-X, MESOM). Greenwood.
Soviet Management & Labor Relations. Bruno Grancelli. 272p. 1987. text ed. 39.95x (ISBN 0-04-497040-4). Unwin Hyman.
Soviet Manned Space Program. Phillip Clark. (Illus.). 1988. 24.95 (ISBN 0-517-56954-X, Orion Bks). Crown.
Soviet Marketing & Economic Development. Roger Skurski. LC 82-792. 256p. 1984. 27.50x (ISBN 0-312-74842-6). St Martin.
Soviet Marriage Market: Mate Selection in Russia & the U. S. S. R. Wesley A. Fisher. LC 78-19737. 320p. 1980. 46.95 (ISBN 0-275-90483-0, C0483). Praeger.
Soviet Marxism: A Critical Analysis. Herbert Marcuse. LC 57-10943. 271p. 1985. pap. 14.00 (ISBN 0-231-08379-3). Columbia U Pr.
Soviet Marxism & Nuclear War: An International Debate. Ed. by John Somerville. LC 80-25820. (Contributions in Philosophy: No. 18). 176p. 1981. lib. bdg. 56.95 (ISBN 0-313-22531-1, SSM/). Greenwood.
Soviet Marxism & Social Science. William M. Mandell. 1984. pap. 3.00 (ISBN 0-87867-097-1). Ramparts.
Soviet Media & Their Message. 47p. 1977. pap. 1.00 (ISBN 0-317-30748-7). Amer Bar Assn.
Soviet Men of Science. John Turkevich. Ed. by J. Blanshei et al. LC 75-19267. 441p. 1975. Repr. of 1963 ed. lib. bdg. 48.50x (ISBN 0-8371-8246-8, TUSM). Greenwood.
Soviet Metal-Fabricating & Economic Development: Practice Versus Policy. David Granick. 382p. 1967. 30.00x (ISBN 0-299-04290-1). U of Wis Pr.
Soviet Military Aircraft. Bill Sweetman. (Concise Guide Ser.). (Illus.). 208p. 1981. 12.95 (ISBN 0-89141-135-6, Pub. by Hamlyn Pub England). Presidio Pr.
Soviet Military Aircraft World Weapon Database, Vol. II. Ed. by Neta Crawford et al. (World Weapon Database Ser.). 1088p. 1987. 95.00x (ISBN 0-669-14887-3). Lexington Bks.
Soviet Military Buildup & U. S. Defense Spending. Barry M. Blechman et al. LC 77-86492. (Brookings Institution Studies in Defense Policy Ser.). pap. 20.00 (ISBN 0-317-30181-0, 2025363). Bks Demand UMI.
Soviet Military Doctrine: Continuity, Formulation, & Dissemination. Harriet F. Scott & William F. Scott. 320p. 1988. 44.50 (ISBN 0-8133-0656-6). Westview.
Soviet Military Doctrine, 1960 to the Present. Alfred L. Monks. LC 82-15273. 357p. 1984. text ed. 39.50x (ISBN 0-8290-0726-1). Irvington.
Soviet Military Interventions since Nineteen Forty-Five. Alex Schmid. 200p. 1985. 34.95 (ISBN 0-88738-063-8). Transaction Bks.
Soviet Military Medicine: Research Subject Index with Bibliography. Russell Manedov. LC 88-47621. 150p. 1988. 34.50 (ISBN 0-88164-722-5); pap. 26.50 (ISBN 0-88164-723-3). ABBE Pubs Assn.
Soviet Military Missions in the Third World. Mark Katz. (CSIS Significant Issues Ser.). 1988. write for info. CSI Studies.
Soviet Military Policy since World War II. William Lee & Richard F. Staar. 263p. (Orig.). 1986. pap. text ed. 10.95x (ISBN 0-8179-8302-3). Hoover Inst Pr.
Soviet Military: Political Education, Training & Morale. E. S. Williams. LC 86-6556. 256p. 1986. 29.95 (ISBN 0-312-74835-3). St Martin.
Soviet-Military Power. Tom Gervasi. 176p. 1988. 14.95 (ISBN 0-394-75715-7, Vin). Random.
Soviet Military Power. Tom Gervasi. Date not set. price not set (Vin). Random.
Soviet Military Power. U. S. Department of the Army - Army Library Staff. Repr. of 1959 ed. lib. bdg. 35.00x (ISBN 0-8371-2502-2, SOMP). Greenwood.
Soviet Military Power: An Assessment of the Threat, 1988. 7th ed. (Illus.). 175p. 1988. 10.00 (S/N 008-000-00488-9). USGPO.
Soviet Military Power & Performance. John Erickson & E. J. Feuchtwanger. LC 78-26158. ix, 219p. 1979. 25.00 (ISBN 0-208-01779-8, Archon). Shoe String.
Soviet Military Power, 1985. (Illus.). 143p. (Orig.). 1985. pap. 6.00 (S/N 008-000-00410-2). USGPO.
Soviet Military Power, 1986. (Illus.). 156p. (Orig.). 1986. pap. 7.50 (ISBN 0-318-20147-X, S/N 008-000-00437-4). USGPO.
Soviet Military Psychiatry: The Theory & Practice of Coping with Battle Stress. Richard A. Gabriel. LC 85-24795. (Contributions in Military Studies: No. 53). (Illus.). 186p. 1986. lib. bdg. 36.95 (ISBN 0-313-25225-4, GSM/). Greenwood.
Soviet Military Strategy. 3rd ed. V. D. Sokolovskiy. Tr. by Harriet F. Scott from Rus. LC 73-94042. (Illus.). 580p. 1975. (Pub. by Crane Russak & Co); pap. 48.00x (ISBN 0-8448-1382-6). Taylor & Francis.
Soviet Military Strategy in Space. Nicholas L. Johnson. 320p. 1987. 34.95 (ISBN 0-7106-0449-1). Janes Info Group.
Soviet Military Strategy in Western Europe in the Nineteen Seventies. Stuart K. Schwartzman. 191p. (Orig.). 1979. pap. text ed. 19.00x (ISBN 0-89126-078-1). MA-AH Pub.
Soviet Military Thinking. Ed. by Derek Leebaert. 304p. 1981. pap. text ed. 15.95x (ISBN 0-04-355016-9). Unwin Hyman.
Soviet Military Trends: Implications for U. S. Security. William R. Kintner & Robert L. Pfaltzgraff, Jr. LC 71-170291. (American Enterprise Institute for Public Policy Research Special Analysis Ser.: No. 6). pap. 20.00 (ISBN 0-317-29840-2, 2017445). Bks Demand UMI.
Soviet Military: 1980-1982, 3 vols. Myron J. Smith, Jr. Set. 29.00 (ISBN 0-87436-408-6). Regina Bks.
Soviet Missiles. Barton Wright. LC 85-45506. (World Weapons Data Base Ser.). (Illus.). 720p. 1986. 75.00x (ISBN 0-669-11798-6). Lexington Bks.
Soviet Multinational State. Ed. by Martha B. Olcott & Lubomyr Hajda. 225p. 1987. text ed. 35.00 (ISBN 0-87332-389-0). M E Sharpe.
Soviet National Income & Product in 1937. Abram Bergson. LC 75-104222. 1970. Repr. of 1953 ed. lib. bdg. 35.00x (ISBN 0-8371-3332-7, BESO). Greenwood.
Soviet National Income, Nineteen Fifty-Eight to Nineteen Sixty-Four: National Accounts of the U. S. S. R. in the Seven Year Plan Period. Abraham S. Becker. LC 70-77483. 626p. pap. 160.00 (2029944). Bks Demand UMI.
Soviet Nationalities in Strategic Perspective. Enders Wimbush. LC 84-40374. 256p. 1985. 27.95 (ISBN 0-312-74847-7). St Martin.
Soviet Nationality Policies & Practices. Ed. by Jeremy R. Azrael. LC 77-83478. 408p. 1978. 54.95 (ISBN 0-275-90283-8, C0283). Praeger.
Soviet Nationality Problems. Ed. by Edward Allworth. LC 77-166211. (Illus.). 296p. 1971. 35.00x (ISBN 0-231-03493-8). Columbia U Pr.
Soviet Natural Resources in the World Economy. Ed. by Robert G. Jensen & Theodore Shabad. LC 82-17317. 700p. 1983. lib. bdg. 100.00x (ISBN 0-226-39831-5). U of Chicago Pr.
Soviet Naval Architecture Theory & Application of Hydrodynamics. Ephraim Juhir. Ed. by Patra McSharry. 128p. (Orig.). Date not set. pap. text ed. 35.00 (ISBN 1-55831-047-9). Delphic Associates.
Soviet Naval Developments. United States Navy Office of Information & Norman Polmar. 16.50 (ISBN 0-405-13276-X). Ayer Co Pubs.
Soviet Naval Diplomacy. rev. ed. Newton B. Dismukes, Jr. & James M. McConnall. (Pergamon Policy Studies). (Illus.). 450p. 1979. pap. text ed. 26.00 (ISBN 0-08-023905-6). Pergamon.
Soviet Naval Forces & Nuclear Warfare: Weapons, Employment, & Policy. James J. Tritten. (Studies in Military Affairs). 282p. 1986. pap. 33.00 (ISBN 0-8133-7206-2). Westview.
Soviet Naval Influence: Domestic & Foreign Dimensions. Ed. by Michael McGwire & John McDonnell. LC 75-23982. (Special Studies). 698p. 1977. text ed. 70.95 (ISBN 0-275-90271-4, C0271). Praeger.
Soviet Naval Threat to Europe: Military & Political Dimensions. Bruce W. Watson & Susan M. Watson. (Special Studies on the Soviet Union & Eastern Europe). 368p. 1988. pap. 39.50 (ISBN 0-8133-7664-5). Westview.
Soviet Naval Trends. Norman Friedman. 52p. 1980. 15.00 (ISBN 0-318-14355-0, HI3201DP). Hudson Inst.
Soviet Navy. Miller. (Soviet Military Power Ser.). (Illus.). 48p. (gr. 3-8). Date not set. PLB 15.93 (ISBN 0-86625-336-X). Rourke Corp.
Soviet Navy: Strengths & Liabilities. Ed. by Bruce W. Watson & Susan M. Watson. (Special Studies on the Soviet Union & Eastern Europe). 384p. 1985. softcover 38.50x (ISBN 0-86531-767-4). Westview.
Soviet Navy Today. Milan Vego. (Warships Illustrated Ser.: No. 6). (Illus.). 68p. (Orig.). 1986. pap. 9.95 (ISBN 0-85368-763-3, Pub. by Arms & Armour). Sterling.
Soviet Novel: History As Ritual. Katerina Clark. LC 80-18758. xvi, 302p. 1985. pap. 11.95x (ISBN 0-226-10767-1). U of Chicago Pr.
Soviet Nuclear Power Plants: Reactor Types, Water, & Chemical Control Systems, Turbines. David Katsman. Ed. by Walter Guntharp. Tr. by Vladimir Talmy from Rus. (Orig.). Date not set. pap. text ed. 35.00 (ISBN 1-55831-020-7). Delphic Associates.
Soviet Nuclear Weapons Policy: A Research Guide. William C. Green. 250p. 35.00x (ISBN 0-86531-817-4). Westview.
Soviet Odyssey. Suzanne Rosenberg. (Illus.). 228p. 1988. 19.95 (ISBN 0-19-540654-0). Oxford U Pr.
Soviet of Justice: Figures & Policy. P. Van den Berg. 1985. lib. bdg. 71.50 (ISBN 90-247-3086-4, Pub. by Martinus Nijhoff Netherlands). Kluwer Academic.
Soviet Oil & Gas Exports to the West: Commercial Transaction or Security Threat? Jonathan Stern. (Energy Policy Studies). 250p. 1986. text ed. 41.95 (ISBN 0-566-05124-9, Pub. by Gower England). Gower Pub Co.
Soviet Oil & Gas to 1990. David Wilson & Geoffrey Drayton. (Economist Intelligence Unit Special Ser.). (Illus.). 208p. 1982. text ed. 25.00 (ISBN 0-89011-581-8). Abt Bks.
Soviet Oil & Gas to 1990. David Wilson & Geoffrey Drayton. (Economist Intelligence Ser.). 248p. 1982. 29.95x. Ballinger Pub.
Soviet Oil & Natural Gas Industries: Problems of Reserve Estimation. Alexei Mahmoudov. Ed. by John Williams. (Orig.). Date not set. pap. text ed. 35.00 (ISBN 1-55831-029-0). Delphic Associates.
Soviet Oil & Security Interests in the Barents Sea. Helge O. Bergesen et al. LC 86-29773. 159p. 1987. 29.95 (ISBN 0-312-00491-5). St Martin.
Soviet Oil: The Move Offshore. Stephen Lewarne. (Special Study on the Soviet Union & Eastern Europe: No. 32). 170p. 1988. 25.00 (ISBN 0-8133-7641-6). Westview.
Soviet Olympic Death Rate, National Discrimination & the Ukrainian issue. LC 84-52118. 158p. 1984. 15.00. Smoloskyp.
Soviet Opposition to Stalin, a Case Study in World War Two. George Fischer. LC 70-97344. Repr. of 1952 ed. lib. bdg. 35.00x (ISBN 0-8371-3098-0, FISO). Greenwood.
Soviet Painting in the Tretyakov Gallery. A. Lebedev. 136p. 1976. 50.00x (ISBN 0-569-08318-4, Pub. by Collets UK). State Mutual Bk.
Soviet Paintings in the Tretyakov Gallery. A. Lebedev. 1976. 39.00x (ISBN 0-317-14320-4, Pub. by Collets (UK)). State Mutual Bk.
Soviet Paradox: External Expansion & Internal Decline. Seweryn Bialer. 1986. 22.95 (ISBN 0-394-54095-6). Knopf.
Soviet Paradox: External Expansion, Internal Decline. Seweryn Bialer. 1987. 9.95 (ISBN 0-394-75288-0, Vin). Random.
Soviet Partisans in World War Two. Ed. by John A. Armstrong. (Illus.). 812p. 1964. 45.00x (ISBN 0-299-03060-1). U of Wis Pr.
Soviet Party-State: Aspects of Ideocratic Despotism. Carl A. Linden. LC 83-13984. 144p. 1983. 37.95 (ISBN 0-275-91037-7, C1037). Praeger.
Soviet Peace Programme in Action. Vadim Zagladin. 158p. 1984. 6.25x (ISBN 0-317-53822-5, Pub. by Collets (UK)). State Mutual Bk.
Soviet Peasants, or: The Peasants' Art of Starving. Lev Timofeev. Tr. by Jean Alexander & Alexander Zaslavsky. 160p. 1985. 15.00 (ISBN 0-914386-12-3). Telos Pr.
Soviet Penal Policy. Ivo Lapenna. LC 80-15755. (Background Bk.). 148p. 1980. Repr. of 1968 ed. lib. bdg. 35.00x (ISBN 0-313-22570-2, LASP). Greenwood.
Soviet Penetration of Afghanistan: 1950-1979. Patrick J. Garrity. (Occasional Paper of the Study of Statesmanship & Political Philosophy: No. 4). 34p. (Orig.). 1982. pap. text ed. 2.00 (ISBN 0-930783-10-7). Claremont Inst.
Soviet Perceptions of East-West Relationships. 43p. 1977. pap. 1.00 (ISBN 0-317-30753-3). Amer Bar Assn.
Soviet Perceptions of Military Doctrine & Military Power: The Interaction of Theory & Practice. John J. Dziak. LC 81-3260. (NSIC Strategy Paper Ser.: No. 36). 80p. 1981. pap. text ed. 9.50x (ISBN 0-8448-1389-3, Pub. by Crane Russak & Co). Taylor & Francis.
Soviet Perceptions of the Developing World During the 1980s: The Ideological Basis. Daniel S. Papp. LC 84-40812. 192p. 1985. 29.00x (ISBN 0-669-10166-4). Lexington Bks.
Soviet Perceptions of the Oil Factor in U. S. Foreign Policy: The Middle East-Gulf Region. Herbert L. Sawyer. (Replica Edition Ser.). 160p. 1983. pap. 24.00x (ISBN 0-86531-982-0). Westview.
Soviet Perceptions of the U. S. Congress: The Impact on Superpower Relations. Robert T. Huber. (Special Study on the Soviet Union & Eastern Europe). 224p. 1988. 35.00 (ISBN 0-8133-7603-3). Westview.
Soviet Perceptions of the United States. Morton Schwartz. LC 76-7767. 1978. 26.50x (ISBN 0-520-03234-9); pap. 8.95x (ISBN 0-520-04094-5). U of Cal Pr.
Soviet Perceptions of the World Order. Ed. by Stephen H. Millett. 1982. cancelled. Westview.
Soviet Perceptions of U. S. Foreign Policy. John Lenczowski. LC 81-70713. 312p. 1982. 31.50x (ISBN 0-8014-1451-2). Cornell U Pr.
Soviet Perceptions of War & Peace. Ed. by Graham D. Vernon. 201p. (Orig.). 1981. pap. 6.00 (ISBN 0-318-20148-8, S/N 008-020-00862-1). USGPO.
Soviet Perspective on the Strategic Defense Initiative. D. Mikheyev. LC 87-2313. (IFPA Foreign Policy Reports). 84p. 1987. pap. 9.95 (ISBN 0-08-035748-2, PDP). Pergamon.
Soviet Perspective on the Strategic Defense Initiative. Dimitry Mikheyev. LC 87-2323. (Foreign Policy Report Ser.). xii, 95p. 9.95 (ISBN 0-317-65162-5). Inst Foreign Policy Anal.
Soviet Perspectives on African Socialism. Arthur J. Klinghoffer. LC 68-26304. 276p. 1969. 24.50 (ISBN 0-8386-6907-7). Fairleigh Dickinson.
Soviet Philosophy: A General Introduction to Contemporary Soviet Thought. T. J. Blakeley. (Sovietica Ser.: No. 18). 81p. 1964. lib. bdg. 18.50 (ISBN 90-277-0038-9, Pub. by Reidel Holland). Kluwer Academic.
Soviet Philosphy Revisited. Adelmann. (Boston College Studies in Philosophy: No. 5). 1977. 31.50 (ISBN 90-247-1977-1, Pub. by Martins Nijhoff Netherlands). Kluwer Academic.
Soviet Planned Economic Order. William H. Chamberlin. LC 70-107342. (BCL Ser.: No. I). 1970. Repr. of 1931 ed. 11.50 (ISBN 0-404-00595-0). AMS Pr.
Soviet Planning & Spatial Efficiency: The Prewar Cement Industry. Alan Abouchar. LC 70-126203. (Indiana University Russian & East European Ser.: Vol. 39). (Illus.). pap. 27.40 (ISBN 0-317-08589-1, 2015812). Bks Demand UMI.
Soviet Planning: Essays in Honour of Naum Jasny. Ed. by Jane Degras. LC 81-19072. (Illus.). xi, 225p. 1982. Repr. of 1964 ed. lib. bdg. 35.00x (ISBN 0-313-23203-2, DESP). Greenwood.
Soviet Planning: Evolution in 1965-1980. Fyodor I. Kushnirsky. (Orig.). Date not set. pap. text ed. 35.00 (ISBN 1-55831-000-2). Delphic Associates.
Soviet Planning in Peace & War, Nineteen Thirty-Eight to Nineteen Forty-Five. Mark Harrison. (Soviet & East European Studies). 320p. 1985. 47.50 (ISBN 0-521-30371-0). Cambridge U Pr.
Soviet Planning Today, Proposals for an Optimally Functioning Economic System. Michael Ellman. LC 72-145613. (Department of Applied Economics, Occasional Papers: No. 25). (Illus.). 1971. o. p. 23.95 (ISBN 0-521-08156-4); pap. 11.95x o. p. (ISBN 0-521-09648-0). Cambridge U Pr.
Soviet Poetry, 1950s-1970s: Russian Reader. Ed. by V. Kovsky. 287p. 1987. pap. 6.95 (ISBN 0-8285-3478-0, Pub. by Rus Lang Pubs USSR). Imported Pubns.
Soviet Poets & Poetry. facs. ed. Alexander S. Kaun. LC 68-14906. (Essay Index Reprint Ser). 1943. 13.00 (ISBN 0-8369-0586-5). Ayer Co Pubs.
Soviet Policies in China, 1917-1924. Allen S. Whiting. 1954. 35.00x (ISBN 0-8047-0612-3); pap. 11.95 (ISBN 0-8047-0613-1, SP77). Stanford U Pr.
Soviet Policies in the Eighties. Rakesh Gupta. 188p. 1988. text ed. 25.00x (Pub. by Patriot Pubs). Advent NY.
Soviet Policies in the Eighties. Rakesh Gupta. 1988. 20.00x (ISBN 81-7050-060-5, Pub. by Patriot). South Asia Bks.
Soviet Policies Toward the Nordic Countries. Orjan Berner. LC 86-9087. 206p. (Orig.). 1986. lib. bdg. 24.75 (ISBN 0-8191-5381-8, Pub. by Ctr Qutl Affairs Harvard); pap. 12.50 (ISBN 0-8191-5382-6, Pub by Ctr Qutl Affairs Havard). U Pr of Amer.
Soviet Policy & Practice Towards Third-World Conflicts. Steven T. Hosmer & Thomas W. Wolfe. 336p. 1982. 35.00x (ISBN 0-669-06054-2). Lexington Bks.
Soviet Policy & the Chinese Communists, 1931-1946. Charles B. McLane. LC 73-37861. (Select Bibliographies Reprint Ser). 1972. Repr. of 1958 ed. 16.00 (ISBN 0-8369-9964-9). Ayer Co Pubs.
Soviet Policy for the 1980s. Ed. by Archie Brown & Michael Kaser. LC 82-48593. 296p. 1983. 22.50x (ISBN 0-253-35412-9). Ind U Pr.
Soviet Policy in Developing Countries. 2nd ed. Ed. by Raymond W. Duncan. LC 78-20847. 262p. 1981. 16.50 (ISBN 0-88275-846-2). Krieger.

Soviet Semiotics: An Anthology. Ed. by Daniel P. Lucid. LC 77-4543. (Illus.). 1978. text ed. 28.50x (ISBN 0-8018-1980-6). Johns Hopkins.

Soviet Semiotics: An Anthology. Ed. by Daniel P. Lucid. LC 77-4543. 272p. 1988. pap. text ed. 12.95x (ISBN 0-8018-3656-5). Johns Hopkins.

Soviet Short Stories. Avrahm Yarmolinsky. Repr. of 1960 ed. 25.00. Darby Bks.

Soviet Sisterhood. Ed. by Barbara Holland. LC 84-43196. (Illus.). 272p. 1985. 25.00x (ISBN 0-253-35420-X); pap. 10.95x (ISBN 0-253-28790-1). Ind U Pr.

Soviet Social Experiments, 1965-1977. Ed. by Lynn Visson. Tr. by Boris Rabbot. 1982. cancelled. Westview.

Soviet Social Scientists Talking: An Official Debate about Women. Ed. by Mary Buckley. 182p. 1986. text ed. 39.50x (ISBN 0-333-42806-4, Pub. by Macmillan London); pap. text ed. 19.50x (ISBN 0-333-42807-2, Pub. by Macmillan London). Sheridan.

Soviet Society & Culture: Essays in Honor of Vera Dunham. Ed. by Terry L. Thompson & Richard Sheldon. 304p. 1988. 24.50 (ISBN 0-8133-0500-4). Westview.

Soviet Society & the Communist Party. Ed. by Karl W. Ryavec. LC 78-53179. 240p. 1978. 17.50x (ISBN 0-87023-258-4). U of Mass Pr.

Soviet Society under Gorbachev: Current Trends & the Prospects for Change. Ed. by Maurice Friedberg & Heyward Isham. 228p. Date not set. 28.50 (ISBN 0-87332-442-0); pap. 12.95 (ISBN 0-87332-443-9). M E Sharpe.

Soviet Sociology: Lost Illusions. Ilya Zemtsov. 1986. pap. 13.95 (ISBN 0-915979-14-4). Hero Books.

Soviet Soldier. V. Drozdov & A. Korkeshkin. 180p. 1980. pap. 4.45 (ISBN 0-8285-1666-9, Pub. by Progress Pubs USSR). Imported Pubns.

Soviet Sources of Military Doctrine & Strategy. William F. Scott. LC 75-18537. (Strategy Paper Ser.: No. 26). 72p. 1975. 12.00x (ISBN 0-8448-0709-5, Pub. by Crane Russak & Co). Taylor & Francis.

Soviet Space Challenge. (Illus.). 24p. 1987. pap. 2.00 (ISBN 0-318-23845-4, 008-000-00487-1). USGPO.

Soviet Space Programs 1980-1985. Nicholas L. Johnson. LC 57-43769. (Science & Technology Ser.: Vol. 66). (Illus.). 298p. 1987. lib. bdg. 55.00x (ISBN 0-87703-291-2, Pub. by Am Astro Soc); pap. 45.00x (ISBN 0-87703-292-0, Pub. by Am Astro Soc). Univelt Inc.

Soviet Space Threat. Thomas H. Krebs. 1984. write for info (ISBN 0-943802-09-1). Natl Ctr Pol.

Soviet State. E. Permyak. 159p. 1981. 7.95 (ISBN 0-8285-2112-3, Pub. by Progress Pubs USSR). Imported Pubns.

Soviet State: The Domestic Roots of Soviet Foreign Policy. Ed. by Curtis Keeble. 256p. 1984. 49.00x (ISBN 0-8133-0159-9); pap. text ed. 17.95x (ISBN 0-8133-0158-0). Westview.

Soviet Statistics of Physical Output of Industrial Commodities: Their Compilation & Quality. Gregory Grossman. LC 85-8016. (National Bureau of Economic Research: No. 69). xvi, 151p. 1985. Repr. of 1960 ed. lib. bdg. 38.50x (ISBN 0-313-24623-8, GSOS). Greenwood.

Soviet Steam Generator Technology (Fossil Fuel & Nuclear Power Plants) Joseph Rosengaus. Ed. by Andreas Tamberg. (Illus., Orig.). Date not set. pap. text ed. 35.00 (ISBN 1-55831-042-8). Delphic Associates.

Soviet Strategic Deception. Ed. by Brian D. Dailey & Patrick J. Parker. 560p. 1986. 49.00x (ISBN 0-669-13208-X). Lexington Bks.

Soviet Strategic Forces: Requirements & Responses. Robert P. Berman & John C. Baker. LC 82-70889. (Studies in Defense Policy). 171p. 1982. 26.95 (ISBN 0-8157-0926-9); pap. 9.95 (ISBN 0-8157-0925-0). Brookings.

Soviet Strategic Initiatives: Challenge & Response. C. J. Jacobsen. LC 79-89850. 183p. 1979. 36.95 (ISBN 0-275-90369-9, C0369). Praeger.

Soviet Strategy in Latin America. Robert S. Leiken. (Washington Papers: No. 93). 144p. 1982. 9.95 (ISBN 0-275-91543-3, B1543). Praeger.

Soviet Strategy in the Nuclear Age. Raymond L. Garthoff. LC 74-10015. 283p. 1974. Repr. of 1958 ed. lib. bdg. 66.50x (ISBN 0-8371-7658-1, GASS). Greenwood.

Soviet Strategy of Terror. Samuel Francis. 100p. 1985. pap. 6.95 (ISBN 0-89195-218-7). Heritage Found.

Soviet Strategy Toward Western Europe. Ed. by Edwina Moreton & Gerald Segal. 304p. 1984. pap. text ed. 15.95x (ISBN 0-04-330346-3). Unwin Hyman.

Soviet Structural Folkloristics: Texts by Meletinsky, Nekludov, Novik, & Segal, with Tests of the Approach by Jilek & Jilek-Aall, Reid, & Layton, Vol. 1. Ed. by Pierre Maranda. LC 73-79892. (Approaches to Semiotics Ser.: No. 42). 194p. 1974. 24.80x (ISBN 90-2792-683-2). Mouton.

Soviet Studies in Language & Language Behavior. Ed. by J. Prucha. (Linguistics Ser.: Vol. 24). 240p. 1976. pap. 58.00 (ISBN 0-444-10990-0, North-Holland). Elsevier.

Soviet Studies in the Psychology of Learning & Teaching Mathematics. Incl. Bk. 1. The Learning of Math Concepts. 216p (ISBN 0-87353-148-5); Bk. 2. The Structure of Mathematical Abilities. 128p (ISBN 0-87353-149-3); Bk. 3. Problem Solving in Arithmetic & Algebra. 183p (ISBN 0-87353-150-7); Bk. 4. Problem Solving in Geometry. 154p (ISBN 0-87353-151-5); Bk. 5. Development of of Spatial Abilities. 168p (ISBN 0-87353-152-3); Bk. 6. Instruction in Problem Solving. 136p (ISBN 0-87353-153-1); Bk. 7. Children's Capacity for Learning Mathematics. 261p (ISBN 0-87353-154-X); Bk. 8. Methods of Teaching Mathematics. 271p (ISBN 0-87353-155-8); Bk. 9. Problem-Solving Processes of Mentally Retarded Children. 170p (ISBN 0-87353-156-6); Bk. 10. Teaching Mathematics to Mentally Retarded Children. 224p (ISBN 0-87353-157-4); Bk. 11. Analysis & Synthesis As Problem-Solving Methods. 171p (ISBN 0-87353-158-2); Bk. 12. Problems of Instruction. 172p (ISBN 0-87353-159-0); Bk. 13. Analysis of Reasoning Processes. 231p. 1975 (ISBN 0-87353-160-4); Bk. 14. Teaching Arithmetic in the Elementary School. 202p (ISBN 0-87353-161-2). 1969. pap. 7.00 ea; pap. 33.00 set, vol. 7-14 (ISBN 0-87353-147-7). NCTM.

Soviet Studies of Premodern China: Assessments of Recent Scholarship. Ed. by Gilbert Rozman. (Michigan Monographs in Chinese Studies: No. 50). 300p. 1985. 17.50t (ISBN 0-89264-052-9); pap. 9.00t (ISBN 0-89264-053-7). U of Mich Ctr Chinese.

Soviet Studies on the Church & the Believer's Response to Atheism. Dimitry V. Pospielovsky. Date not set. price not set. St Martin.

Soviet Study of International Relations. Allen Lynch. (Soviet & East European Studies). 212p. 1987. 34.50 (ISBN 0-521-33055-6). Cambridge U Pr.

Soviet Style in Management. Nathan Leites. 128p. 1985. pap. 12.00x (ISBN 0-8448-1490-3, Pub. by Crane Russak & Co). Taylor & Francis.

Soviet Style in War. Nathan Leites. LC 81-19433. 423p. 1982. 42.00x (ISBN 0-8448-1415-6, Pub. by Crane Russak & Co). Taylor & Francis.

Soviet Submarine Operations in Swedish Waters 1980-1986. Milton Leitenberg. LC 87-13216. (Washington Papers: No. 128). 208p. 1987. lib. bdg. 32.95 (ISBN 0-275-92841-1, C2841); pap. 9.95 (ISBN 0-275-92842-X, B2842). Praeger.

Soviet Submarines. Miller. (Soviet Military Power Ser.). (Illus.). 48p. (gr. 3-8). Date not set. PLB 15.93 (ISBN 0-86625-332-7). Rourke Corp.

Soviet Subsidization of Trade with Eastern Europe: A Soviet Perspective. Michael Marrese & Jan Vanous. LC 83-192. (Research Ser.: No. 52). (Illus.). xxvi, 250p. 1983. pap. 14.50x (ISBN 0-87725-152-5). U of Cal Intl St.

Soviet Succession: Leadership in Transition. Dimitri K. Simes. (Washington Papers: Vol. VI, No. 59). 80p. (Orig.). 1978. pap. text ed. 7.95 (ISBN 0-8191-6008-3, Pub. by CSIS). U Pr of Amer.

Soviet Succession Struggles: Kremlinology & the Russian Question from Lenin to Gorbachev. Anthony D'Agonstino. 384p. 1987. text ed. 45.00x (ISBN 0-04-497043-9). Unwin Hyman.

Soviet Superpower: The Soviet Union, 1945-1980. Peter J. Mooney. 210p. (Orig.). 1982. pap. text ed. 12.50x (ISBN 0-435-31601-X). Heinemann Ed.

Soviet System in Theory & Practice. Ed. by Harry G. Shaffer. write for info. Pergamon.

Soviet System in Theory & Practice: Western & Soviet Views. 2nd ed. Ed. by Harry G. Shaffer. 475p. (Orig.). 1984. 24.95x (ISBN 0-8044-1828-4); pap. 12.95 (ISBN 0-8044-6857-5). Ungar.

Soviet System of Government. 5th ed. John N. Hazard. LC 79-16827. 1980. lib. bdg. 23.00x (ISBN 0-226-32193-2); pap. text ed. 12.95x (ISBN 0-226-32194-0). U of Chicago Pr.

Soviet Tanks & Combat Vehicles: Nineteen Forty-Six to the Present. Steven J. Zaloga & James W. Loop. (Illus.). 288p. 1987. 39.95 (ISBN 0-85368-743-9, Pub. by Arms & Armour). Sterling.

Soviet Theatre. Pavel A. Markov. LC 78-12536. (New Soviet Library: No. 3). 1979. Repr. of 1934 ed. lib. bdg. 35.00x (ISBN 0-313-20647-3, MASTH). Greenwood.

Soviet Theatrical Poster. A. Borovsky. (Illus.). 1977. 40.00x (ISBN 0-569-08416-4, Pub. by Collets (UK)). State Mutual Bk.

Soviet Theory of Development: India & the Third World in Marxist-Leninist Scholarship. Stephen Clarkson. LC 78-1771. pap. 84.00 (2026430). Bks Demand UMI.

Soviet Theory of International Relations. Margot Light. 384p. 1988. pap. 15.95 (ISBN 0-312-01891-6). St Martin.

Soviet Theory of Knowledge. T. J. Blakeley. (Sovietica Ser.: No. 16). 203p. 1964. lib. bdg. 21.00 (ISBN 90-277-0040-0, Pub. by Reidel Holland). Kluwer Academic.

Soviet Theory, Technique & Training for Running & Hurdling. Michael Yessis. Ed. by Fred Wilt. 92p. (Orig.). 1984. pap. 8.95 (ISBN 0-89279-069-5). Championship Bks.

Soviet Thin Film Technology: From Research to Production. Aleksey Lusnikov. Ed. by Erika D. Nobel. (Illus., Orig.). Date not set. pap. text ed. 35.00. Delphic Associates.

Soviet-Third World Relations. Carol R. Saivetz & Sylvia W. Edgington. 150p. 1985. 42.50x (ISBN 0-86531-647-3); pap. 16.95x (ISBN 0-86531-648-1). Westview.

Soviet-Third World Relations: Vol. 1: Soviet-Middle East Relations, Vol. 1. Charles B. McLane. 126p. 1973. 28.50 (ISBN 0-903424-06-1). Columbia U Pr.

Soviet-Third World Relations: Vol. 2: Soviet-Asian Relations. Charles B. McLane. 1974. 28.50 (ISBN 0-903424-07-X). Columbia U Pr.

Soviet-Third World Relations: Vol. 3: Soviet-African Relations, Vol. 3. Charles B. McLane. 190p. 1975. 31.50 (ISBN 0-903424-08-8). Columbia U Pr.

Soviet Threat, Vol. 33, No. 1. LC 78-56914. 1978. 6.50 (ISBN 0-318-01782-2). Acad Poli Sci.

Soviet Threat in NATO's Northern Flank. Marian Leighton. 95p. 1979. pap. 5.95 (ISBN 0-87855-803-9). Transaction Bks.

Soviet Trade from the Pacific to the Levant: With an Economic Study of the Soviet Far Eastern Region. Violet Conolly. LC 79-5206. (Illus.). 238p. 1980. Repr. of 1935 ed. 23.50 (ISBN 0-8305-0066-9). Hyperion Conn.

Soviet Trade Unions & Labor Relations. Emily C. Brown. LC 66-21332. pap. 101.50 (ISBN 0-317-29769-4, 2017260). Bks Demand UMI.

Soviet Trade Unions: Their Development in the 1970's. Blair A. Ruble. LC 80-29646. (Soviet & East European Studies). (Illus.). 160p. 1981. 37.50 (ISBN 0-521-23704-1). Cambridge U Pr.

Soviet Trade Unions: Their Place in Soviet Labour Policy. Isaac Deutscher. LC 73-837. (Russian Studies: Perspectives on the Revolution Ser.). 156p. 1984. Repr. of 1950 ed. 26.00 (ISBN 0-88355-033-4). Hyperion Conn.

Soviet-Type Economic Systems: A Guide to Information Sources. Z. Edward O'Relley. LC 73-17583. (Economics Information Guide Ser.: Vol. 12). 240p. 1978. 68.00x (ISBN 0-8103-1306-5). Gale.

Soviet Ukraine. Ed. by Collet's Holdings, Ltd. Staff. 1984. 20.00x (ISBN 0-317-42832-2, Pub by Collets (UK)). State Mutual Bk.

Soviet Ukrainian Art: Painting, Sculpture, Graphic Arts. Platon Biletsy. 118p. 1979. 30.00x (Pub. by Collets (UK)). State Mutual Bk.

Soviet Ukrainian Dissent: A Study of Political Alienation. Jaroslaw Bilocerkowycz. (Westview Special Studies on the Soviet Union & Eastern Europe). 280p. 1986. pap. 27.50 (ISBN 0-8133-7240-2). Westview.

Soviet Union. Ed. by Neal Bernards et al. (Opposing Viewpoints Ser.). (Illus.). 1987. lib. bdg. 13.95 (ISBN 0-89908-429-X); pap. 6.95 (ISBN 0-89908-404-4). Greenhaven.

Soviet Union. 2nd ed. Congressional Quarterly, Inc. Staff. 383p. 1986. pap. 15.95 (ISBN 0-87187-383-4). Congr Quarterly.

Soviet Union. Ed. by R. W. Davies. (Illus.). 1978. pap. text ed. 12.95x (ISBN 0-04-947023-X). Unwin Hyman.

Soviet Union. rev. ed. Ed. by W. A. Jackson. (Global Community Ser.). (Illus.). 176p. (YA) (gr. 6 up). 1988. text ed. 16.95 (ISBN 0-934291-34-9); tchr's. guide 9.95 (ISBN 0-934291-35-7). Gateway Pr MI.

Soviet Union. 3rd ed. Vadim Medish. 368p. 1987. pap. text ed. 24.00 (ISBN 0-13-823634-8). P-H.

Soviet Union. 2nd ed. W. H. Parker. LC 82-20360. (World's Landscapes Ser.). (Illus.). 224p. 1983. 14.95 (ISBN 0-582-30111-4). Wiley.

Soviet Union. 2nd ed. W. H. Parker. (World's Landscapes Ser.). 218p. 1986. pap. 29.95 (ISBN 0-470-20556-3, Co-Pub. with Longman). Wiley.

Soviet Union. James Riordan. (Countries Ser.). (Illus.). 48p. (gr. 5 up). 1987. pap. 6.95 (ISBN 0-317-62433-4); lib. bdg. 14.96 (ISBN 0-317-62434-2). Silver.

Soviet Union. LC 85-40575. (Library of Nations). 1985. lib. bdg. 18.60 (Pub. by Time-Life). Silver.

Soviet Union. (Library of nations). 1985. 14.95 (ISBN 0-8094-5327-4); lib. bdg. write for info. Time-Life.

Soviet Union. Time-Life Books Editors. (Library of Nations). (Illus.). 160p. (YA) (gr. 7 up). 1984. lib. bdg. 23.93 (ISBN 0-8094-5302-9). Time-Life.

Soviet Union. Time-Life Books Editors. (Library of Nations). (Illus.). 160p. (YA) (gr. 7 up). 1986. lib. bdg. 23.93. Time-Life.

Soviet Union see Learning about People & Cultures.

Soviet Union: A Geographical Study. 2nd ed. G. Melvyn Howe. (Illus.). 501p. 1987. pap. 29.95 (ISBN 0-470-20674-8). Halsted Pr.

Soviet Union: A Half-Century of Communism. Ed. by Kurt London. LC 68-28873. 493p. 1968. 49.50x (ISBN 0-8018-0388-8). Johns Hopkins.

Soviet Union: A Systematic Geography. Leslie Symons et al. LC 82-6683. (Illus.). 278p. 1983. text ed. 32.50x (ISBN 0-389-20309-2); pap. text ed. 24.50x (ISBN 0-389-20310-6). B&N Imports.

Soviet Union after Brezhnev. Ed. by Martin McCauley. LC 83-12956. (Illus.). 160p. 1983. 17.50 (ISBN 0-8419-0918-0); pap. 12.50 (ISBN 0-8419-0919-9). Holmes & Meier.

Soviet Union & Africa. V. Lopatov. 192p. 1987. pap. 3.95 (ISBN 0-8285-3546-9, Pub. by Progress USSR). Imported Pubns.

Soviet Union & Africa: The History of the Involvement. Milene Charles. LC 80-67227. 250p. 1980. lib. bdg. 26.25 (ISBN 0-8191-1255-0); pap. text ed. 12.25 (ISBN 0-8191-1256-9). U Pr of Amer.

Soviet Union & Arab Nationalism. Seyyed H. Nasr. 320p. 1987. text ed. 39.95 (ISBN 0-7103-0213-4, Kegan Paul). Routledge Chapman & Hall.

Soviet Union & Asia. Harish Kapur. 220p. 1988. 35.00 (ISBN 0-86187-956-2, Pub. by Pinter Pubs UK). Columbia U Pr.

Soviet Union & Ballistic Missile Defense. Bruce Parrott. (SAIS Papers in International Affairs). 124p. 1987. pap. 17.95 (ISBN 0-8133-7429-4). Westview.

Soviet Union & Black Africa. Christopher Stevens. LC 75-38653. 276p. 1976. 35.00 (ISBN 0-8419-0251-8). Holmes & Meier.

Soviet Union & Central Europe in the Post-War Era: A Study in Precarious Security. Kristian Gerner. 236p. 1985. 32.50 (ISBN 0-312-74905-8). St Martin.

Soviet Union & Cuba. Peter Shearman. LC 87-4689. (Chatham House Papers: No. 38). 103p. 1988. pap. 12.95 (ISBN 0-7102-1229-1, Pub. by Routledge UK). Routledge Chapman & Hall.

Soviet Union & Cuba: Interests & Influences. W. Raymond Duncan. Ed. by Alvin Rubinstein. LC 84-26296. 240p. 1985. 35.00 (ISBN 0-275-90088-6, C0088); pap. 15.95 (ISBN 0-275-91662-6, B1662). Praeger.

Soviet Union & East Asia in the 1980's. Ed. by Jae K Park & Joseph M. Ha. 284p. 1983. pap. 14.95x (ISBN 0-86531-655-4, Pub by Kyungnam U Korea). Westview.

Soviet Union & Eastern Europe. Ed. by George Schopflin. (Handbooks to the Modern World Ser.). 638p. 1986. 45.00x (ISBN 0-8160-1260-1). Facts On File.

Soviet Union & Eastern Europe: A Bibliographic Guide of Recommended Books for Small & Medium-Sized Libraries & School Media Centers. Stephan M. Horak. LC 84-25053. 387p. 1985. lib. bdg. 27.50 (ISBN 0-87287-469-9). Libs Unl.

Soviet Union & Eastern Europe, 1988. 19th, rev. ed. M. Wesley Shoemaker. LC 73-103333. (World Today Ser.). (Illus.). 146p. 1988. pap. 6.50 (ISBN 0-943448-44-1). Stryker-Post.

Soviet Union & European Security. L. C. Kumar. LC 86-73079. 1987. text ed. 25.00x (ISBN 0-89891-011-0). Advent NY.

Soviet Union & European Security. Y. Nalin & A. Nikolayev. 141p. 1975. 14.75 (ISBN 0-8464-0875-9). Beekman Pubs.

Soviet Union & India. Peter Duncan. (Chatham House Papers). 96p. 1988. pap. text ed. 12.95 (ISBN 0-415-00212-5). Routledge Chapman & Hall.

Soviet Union & International Law: A Study Based on the Legislation, Treaties & Foreign Relations of the Union of Socialist Soviet Republics. T. A. Taracouzio. Repr. of 1935 ed. 40.00 (ISBN 0-527-88900-8). Kraus Repr.

Soviet Union & International Politics. Klaus Von Beyme. LC 87-1550. 255p. 1987. 27.50 (ISBN 0-312-00436-2). St Martin.

Soviet Union & Iran, No. 8. Miron Rezun. (Collection De Relations Internationales Ser.). 425p. 1981. 39.50x (ISBN 90-286-2621-2, Pub. by Sijthoff & Noordhoff). Kluwer Academic.

Soviet Union & Iran: Soviet Policy in Iran from the Beginnings of the Pahlavi Dynasty until the Soviet Invasion in 1941. Miron Rezun. (Encore Edition Ser.: No. 44). 425p. 1988. 43.00 (ISBN 0-8133-7616-5). Westview.

Soviet Union & Iranian Azerbaijan: The Use of Nationalism for Political Penetration. David B. Nissman. (Westview Special Studies on the Soviet Union & Eastern Europe). 156p. 1986. pap. 18.95 (ISBN 0-8133-7318-2). Westview.

Soviet Union & National Liberation Movements in the Third World. Galia Golin. 368p. 1988. text ed. 49.95 (ISBN 0-04-445111-3). Unwin Hyman.

Soviet Union & Northern Waters. Ed. by Clive Archer. 288p. 1988. lib. bdg. 49.95 (ISBN 0-415-00489-6). Routledge Chapman & Hall.

Soviet Union & Revolutionary Iran. Aryeh Yodfat. LC 83-3130. 163p. 1984. 29.95x (ISBN 0-312-74911-2). St Martin.

Soviet Union & Revolutionary Warfare. Richard H. Shultz. (Series P-371). 283p. 1988. text ed. 25.95 (ISBN 0-8179-8711-8); pap. text ed. 16.95 (ISBN 0-8179-8712-6). Hoover Inst Pr.

Soviet Union & SALT. Samuel Burbon Payne, Jr. 224p. 1980. text ed. 30.00x (ISBN 0-262-16077-3). MIT Pr.

Soviet Union & Social Science Theory. Jerry F. Hough. (Russian Research Center Studies: No. 77). 1977. 24.50x (ISBN 0-674-82980-8). Harvard U Pr.

Soviet Union & Strategic Arms. Robbin Laird & Dale Herspring. (Special Study). 170p. 1984. 28.50x (ISBN 0-8133-0054-1); pap. text ed. 18.95x (ISBN 0-8133-0151-3). Westview.

Soviet Union & Terrorism. Roberta Goren. Ed. by Jillian Becker. LC 84-12366. (Illus.). 280p. 1984. text ed. 31.95 (ISBN 0-04-327073-5); pap. text ed. 14.95 (ISBN 0-04-327074-3). Unwin Hyman.

Soweto: Black Revolt - White Reaction. John Kane-Berman. 268p. 1981. pap. text ed. 13.95x (ISBN 0-86975-090-9, Pub. by Ravan Pr). Ohio U Pr.

Soweto Country Club: A Photographic Essay. Nigel Dickinson. 224p. 1986. pap. 10.95 (ISBN 0-8052-8265-3, Pub. by Allison & Busby England). Schocken.

Soweto Legacy. Lorry Lutz. 288p. 1988. pap. 4.50 (ISBN 0-8423-5826-9). Tyndale.

Soweto, My Love: A Testimony to Black Life in South. Molapatence C. Ramusi. LC 88-12262. 1988. 22.95 (ISBN 0-8050-0263-4). H Holt & Co.

Soweto Remembered: Conversations with Freedom Fighters. Paddy Colligan. (Illus.). xiv, 115p. (Orig.). 1981. pap. 3.25 (ISBN 0-89567-050-X). World View Forum.

Soweto: The Fruit of Fear: A School Children's Revolt That Ignited a Nation. Peter Magubane. LC 86-71992. 125p. 1987. 29.95 (ISBN 0-86543-041-1, Copub. by William B. Eerdmans Pub.); pap. 14.95 (ISBN 0-86543-040-3). Africa World.

Soweto's Children: The Development of Attitudes. Beryl Geber & Stanton Newman. (European Monographs in Social Psychology: No. 20). 1980. 64.50 (ISBN 0-12-278750-1). Acad Pr.

SOWHAT - Spelling Only Without A Test. Julia Alarie & Elizabeth Conlon. Ed. by Ellen Sussman. (Creative Assignments in Spelling Ser.). (Illus.). (gr. 3-6). 1980. pap. text ed. 5.95 (ISBN 0-933606-06-0, MS-605). Monkey Sisters.

Sowing: An Autobiography of the Years 1880 to 1904. Leonard Woolf. LC 75-12870. (Illus.). 206p. (Volume I in 5-volume autobiography). 1975. pap. 2.95 (ISBN 0-15-683945-8, HB319, Harv). HarBraceJ.

Sowing & Reaping. Lilian Hance. 1981. 14.00x (ISBN 0-7223-1418-3, Pub. by A H Stockwell England). State Mutual Bk.

Sowing & Reaping. facsimile ed. Booker T. Washington. LC 70-161275. (Black Heritage Library Collection). Repr. of 1900 ed. 10.75 (ISBN 0-8369-8834-5). Ayer Co Pubs.

Sowing & the Reaping. George Stewart. LC 71-109540. 1970. pap. 2.50 (ISBN 0-87004-200-9). Caxton.

Sowing in Famine. Jerry Savelle. 32p. (Orig.). 1982. pap. 1.50 (ISBN 0-686-83911-0). Harrison Hse.

Sowing the Body: Psychoanalysis & Ancient Representations of Women. Page DuBois. (Women in Culture & Society Ser.). (Illus.). xvi, 228p. 1988. 29.95x (ISBN 0-226-16757-7). U of Chicago Pr.

Sowing the Spring. facs. ed. James G. Southworth. LC 68-54372. (Essay Index Reprint Ser). 1940. 17.00 (ISBN 0-8369-0891-0). Ayer Co Pubs.

Sowing the Wind & Other Stories. facs. ed. Timothy S. Arthur. LC 77-137721. (American Fiction Reprint Ser). Repr. of 1864 ed. 17.00 (ISBN 0-8369-7020-9). Ayer Co Pubs.

Sowjetische Erkenntnismetaphysik und ihr Verhaeltnis zu Hegel. K. G. Ballestrem. (Sovetica Ser.: No. 27). 189p. (Ger.). 1968. lib. bdg. 26.00 (ISBN 90-277-0037-0, Pub. by Reidel Holland). Kluwer Academic.

Sowjetische Staatsbuergerschaft. Tatjana Kowal-Wolk. (European University Studies: No. 2, Vol. 297). 199p. (Ger.). 1982. 24.20 (ISBN 3-8204-7132-4). P Lang Pubs.

Sow's Head & Other Poems. Robert Peters. LC 68-24447. (Illus.). 1968. 4.95 (ISBN 0-685-79046-0). Small Pr Dist.

Sow's Head & Other Poems. Robert Peters. LC 68-24447. Repr. of 1968 ed. 22.80 (2027600). Bks Demand UMI.

Soy Protein & Human Nutrition. Ed. by Harold L. Wilcke et al. LC 78-25585. 1979. 45.50 (ISBN 0-12-751450-3). Acad Pr.

Soy Protein & National Food Policy. Ed. by F. H. Schwarz. 350p. 1988. 38.50 (ISBN 0-8133-7632-7). Westview.

Soy Protein in the Preventin of Artherosclerosis. Ed. by G. Descovisch. (Illus.). 150p. 1982. text ed. 29.00 (ISBN 0-85200-450-8, Pub. by MTP Pr England). Kluwer Academic.

Soy Source. John Downes. 200p. 1987. pap. 8.95 (ISBN 1-85327-001-6, Pub. by Prism Pr). Avery Pub.

Soya Foods Cookery. Leah Leneman. (Illus.). 128p. 1988. pap. 9.95 (ISBN 0-7102-1028-0, Pub. by Kegan Paul). Routledge Chapman & Hall.

Soybean. Snyder. 1987. 52.95 (ISBN 0-442-28216-8). Van Nos Reinhold.

Soybean Cookbook. Mildred Lager & Dorothea Van Gundy Jones. LC 63-21327. 1968. pap. 2.50 (ISBN 0-668-01770-8). Arco.

Soybean Cookery. Virg Lemley & Jo Lemley. 1975. pap. 3.75 (ISBN 0-931798-04-3). Wilderness Hse.

Soybean Diseases of the North Central Region. Ed. by T. D. Wyllie & D. H. Scott. LC 88-70266. (Illus.). 149p. 1988. 19.00x (ISBN 0-89054-087-X). Am Phytopathol Soc.

Soybean Granule Recipes. Alan Briscoe. 24p. 1974. pap. 1.95 (ISBN 0-88290-040-4). Horizon Utah.

Soybean in Tropical & Subtropical Cropping Systems. rev. ed. Ed. by S. Shanmugasundaram et al. 485p. (Orig.). 1986. pap. text ed. 25.00 (ISBN 0-318-23636-2, Pub. by Asian Veg Res Taiwan). Agribookstore.

Soybean Physiology, Agronomy, & Utilization. Ed. by Geoffrey A. Norman. 1978. 47.00 (ISBN 0-12-521160-0). Acad Pr.

Soybean Rust. Ed. by K. R. Bromfield. (APS Monograph Ser.). 65p. 1984. 13.50 (ISBN 0-89054-062-4). Am Phytopathol Soc.

Soybean Utilization. Harry E. Snyder & T. W. Kwon. 1987. 42.95 (ISBN 0-317-58961-X). AVI.

Soybeans & Their Products: Markets, Models & Policy. James P. Houck et al. LC 72-79099. (Illus.). 278p. 1972. 16.95x (ISBN 0-8166-0659-5). U of Minn Pr.

Soybeans & Their Uses with Recipe Ingredient Replacements. Center for Self-Sufficiency, Research Division Staff. LC 83-90709. 50p. 1985. pap. text ed. 3.95 (ISBN 0-910811-03-2, Pub. by Center Self Suff). Prosperity & Profits.

Soybeans for the Tropics: Research, Production & Utilization. Ed. by S. R. Singh et al. LC 87-16137. 1988. 49.95 (ISBN 0-471-91419-3). Wiley.

Soybeans: Improvement, Production & Uses. Ed. by B. E. Caldwell. (Illus.). 1973. 14.50 (ISBN 0-89118-017-6). Am Soc Agron.

Soybeans in Family Meals. 1986. lib. bdg. 69.95 (ISBN 0-8490-3792-1). Gordon Pr.

Soyfoods Industry & Market: Directory & Databook 1985. William Shurtleff & Akiko Aoyagi. (Soyfoods Market Studies). (Illus.). 222p. (Orig.). 1985. pap. text ed. 135.00 (ISBN 0-933332-20-3). Soyfoods Center.

Soymilk Industry & Market: Worldwide & Country-by-Country Analysis. 2nd ed. William Shurtleff & Akiko Aoyagi. (Soyfoods Market Studies). 220p. (Orig.). 1987. spiral bdg. 350.00 (ISBN 0-933332-27-0). Soyfoods Center.

Sozaboy. Ken Saro-Wiwa. 186p. (Orig.). 1986. 16.00 (ISBN 978-2460-01-X, Pub. by Saros Intl Pubs UK); pap. 8.00 (ISBN 978-2460-02-8, Pub. by Saros Intl Pubs UK). Three Continents.

Soziale Herkunft Der Neuzeitlichen Dialektliteratur Englands. Ernst F. Hoevel. 1929. pap. 9.00 (ISBN 0-384-23900-5). Johnson Repr.

Soziale Herkunft Der Schweizer Taufer in Der Feformationszeit. Ed. by Paul Peachey. 157p. (Orig., Ger.). 1954. pap. 5.95x (ISBN 0-8361-1160-5). Herald Pr.

Soziale Lage Alleinstehender Aelterer Frauen In Grossstaedten Aus Drei Westeuropaischen Laendern. Gerhard Naegele. 168p. (Ger.). 1982. write for info. (ISBN 3-8204-5806-9). P Lang Pubs.

Soziale Lyrik in England, 1880-1914. Eva Walraf. pap. 8.00 (ISBN 0-384-65630-7). Johnson Repr.

Sozialismus in Theorie & Praxis: Festschrift Fuer Richard Loewenthal Zum 70. Geburtstag Am 15. April 1978. Ed. by Horn et al. 1978. 55.20 (ISBN 3-11-007221-1). De Gruyter.

Sozialismus und Religion. Franz Linden. Repr. of 1932 ed. 16.00 (ISBN 0-384-32740-0). Johnson Repr.

Sozialistisches Zivilrecht. Valentin Petev. (Sammlung Goeschen Ser.: No. 2851). 246p. 1975. 7.90x (ISBN 3-11-004697-0). De Gruyter.

Sozialstatus des Berufsmusikers vom 17. bis 19. Jahrhundert see Social Status of the Professional Musician from the Middle Ages to the 19th Century.

Sozialstrategien der Deutschen Arbeitsfront (Social Strategies of the German Labor Front) Yearbooks of the Institute of Labor Science, 6 vols, Pt. A. Ed. by Foundation for 20th-Century Social History. 5250p. (Ger.). 1987. Set. lib. bdg. 1100.00 (ISBN 3-598-31572-4). K G Saur.

Sozialverischerungsprinzip und Staatszuschuesse in der Gesetzlichen Rentenversicherung. Richard Koessler. (Finanzwissenschaftliche Schriften: Vol. 18). 241p. (Ger.). 1982. 28.95 (ISBN 3-8204-5749-6). P Lang Pubs.

Sozio-Genese des chronischen Alkoholismus. P. Wuethrich. (Sozialmedizinische und paedagogische Jugendkunde: Band 10). (Illus.). 200p. 1974. 26.75 (ISBN 3-8055-1695-9). S Karger.

Soziologie der Angestellten: Sociology of the White Collar. Fritz Croner. LC 74-25744. (European Sociology Ser.). 312p. 1975. Repr. 23.50x (ISBN 0-405-06499-3). Ayer Co Pubs.

Soziologie Des Krieges: Sociology of War. 2nd ed. Sebald R. Steinmetz. LC 74-25789. 720p. 1975. Repr. 53.00x (ISBN 0-405-06541-8). Ayer Co Pubs.

Soziologischer Almanach. Elke Ballerstedt & Wolfgang Glatzer. 616p. (Ger.). 1982. text ed. 34.50x (ISBN 3-593-32419-9). Irvington.

Soziologisches Woerterbuch. H. Schoeck. 400p. (Ger.). 1975. 24.95 (ISBN 0-686-56468-5, M-7622, Pub. by Herder). French & Eur.

Sozo What It Means to Be Saved. David Pacetti. 62p. 1985. pap. 2.95 (ISBN 0-88144-041-8). Christian Pub.

SO2, NO, & NO2 Oxidation Mechanisms: Atmospheric Considerations. Ed. by Jack G. Calvert & John I. Teasley. (Acid Precipitation Ser.: Vol. 3). 272p. 1984. text ed. 39.95 (ISBN 0-250-40568-7). Butterworth.

Spa Book: A Guide to the Top 101 Resorts in America. Judith B. Hirsch. (Illus.). 288p. (Orig.). 1988. pap. 10.95 (ISBN 0-399-51491-0, Perigee Bks). Putnam Pub Group.

Spa Book: A Guided, Personal Tour of Health Resorts & Beauty Spas for Men & Women. Judy Babcock & Judy Kennedy. LC 82-18249. (Illus.). 288p. 1983. 14.95 (ISBN 0-517-54950-6). Crown.

Spa Cuisine: Delicious Dishes from America's Great Spas. Health Travel International Staff. 288p. 1985. 16.95 (ISBN 0-312-74927-9). St Martin.

Spa Finder. Joseph Jeffrey. (Illus.). 100p. (Orig.). 1987. pap. text ed. 4.00 (ISBN 0-9619967-0-6). Spa Finders Travel.

Spa Food: Menus & Recipes from the Sonoma Mission Inn. Edward Safdie & Judy Knipe. (Illus.). 174p. 1985. 19.95 (ISBN 0-517-55654-5, C N Potter Bks). Crown.

Spa Guide: For Men & Women, Health Spas for Every Budget. Ed Colbert & Judy Colbert. 224p. 1988. pap. 10.95 (ISBN 0-87106-677-7). Globe Pequot.

Spa Plumbing: Be Your Own Consultant. Sharon R. Hines. (Hot Tub & Spa Workbook Ser.: No. 3). (Illus.). 36p. (Orig.). 1982. pap. 4.95 (ISBN 0-941904-09-1). Hot Water Pubs.

Spa Specialities: From the Kitchen of Lake Austin Resort. Deborah Hart. (Illus.). 422p. (Orig.). 1987. 17.95 (ISBN 0-9619476-0-8). Lake Austin Resort.

Space. Illus. by Lesley Boney. (Tracing Mix & Match Ser.). (Illus.). 48p. (gr. k-5). 1988. pap. 2.95 (ISBN 0-8431-2247-1). Price Stern.

Space. Nancy L. Dehnbostel & Mary E. Hartman. (P.E.P.P.E.R. Ser.). (Illus.). 44p. (gr. 1-6). 1982. 5.95 (ISBN 0-88047-010-0, 8205). DOK Pubs.

Space. Anthony Feldman. (Illus.). 336p. 1980. 24.95 (ISBN 0-87196-416-3). Facts on File.

Space. Tim Furniss. LC 85-51185. (Modern Technology Ser.). (Illus.). 32p. (gr. 4-9). 1985. PLB 11.90 (ISBN 0-531-10087-1). Watts.

Space. James A. Michener. (Illus.). 640p. 1982. 17.95 (ISBN 0-394-50555-7); signed, ltd. ed. o.p. 50.00 (ISBN 0-394-52764-X). Random.

Space. Ann Packard & Shirley Stafford. (Learning Experience for Young Children Ser.). 58p. (ps-3). 1981. write for info. (ISBN 0-9607580-2-X). S Stafford.

Space. Illa Podendorf. LC 82-4507. (New True Bks.). (gr. k-4). 1982. 12.60 (ISBN 0-516-01650-4); pap. 3.95 (ISBN 0-516-41650-2). Childrens.

Space. Ian Ridpath. LC 83-50389. (Silver Burdett Color Library). 48p. (gr. 4 up). 1983. 14.96 (ISBN 0-382-06726-6). Silver.

Space. rev. ed. James Seevers. LC 87-20801. (Read About Science Ser.). (Illus.). 48p. (gr. 3). 1987. PLB 15.33 (ISBN 0-8172-3260-5). Raintree Pubs.

Space. James A. Michener. 1983. pap. 4.95 (ISBN 0-449-20379-4, Crest). Fawcett.

Space. (How & Why Activity Bks.). (Illus.). 32p. (ps up). 1986. 1.95 (ISBN 0-8431-4285-5). Price Stern.

Space. Ed. by Time-Life Books Staff. (Understanding Computers Ser.). 1987. 12.95 (ISBN 0-8094-5716-4); lib. bdg. write for info. (ISBN 0-8094-5717-2). Time Life.

Space - Gagarin & After. K. P. Prakasan. 1987. text ed. 25.00x (ISBN 81-207-0584-X, Pub. by Sterling Pubs India). Apt Bks.

Space: A Design Element. Gerald F. Brommer. LC 74-82680. (Concepts of Design Ser). (Illus.). 80p. (gr. 7up). 1974. ref. ed. 10.95 (ISBN 0-87192-062-X). Davis Mass.

Space: A Developing Role for Europe, 18th European Space Symposium. Ed. by L. J. Carter & Peter M. Bainum. (Science & Technology Ser.: Vol. 56). (Illus.). 278p. 1984. lib. bdg. 45.00x (ISBN 0-87703-193-2, Pub. by Am Astro Soc); pap. text ed. 35.00x (ISBN 0-87703-194-0); fiche suppl. 20.00x (ISBN 0-87703-195-9). Univelt Inc.

Space: A Postcard Book. (Illus.). 64p. 1988. pap. 6.95 (ISBN 0-89471-615-8). Running Pr.

Space Activities of the United Nations & International Organizations. 271p. 1986. 27.00 (ISBN 92-1-100287-7, E.86.I.2). UN.

Space Adrift: Landmark Preservation & the Marketplace. John J. Costonis. LC 73-5405. (Illus.). 229p. 1974. 22.95 (ISBN 0-252-00402-7). U of Ill Pr.

Space Adventures in Your Home. F. Rabiza. Tr. by Aoezander Repyev. 192p. 1987. 8.95 (ISBN 0-8285-2785-7, Pub. by Mir Pubs USSR). Imported Pubns.

Space Age. Y. Shkolenko. 231p. 1987. pap. 3.95 (ISBN 0-8285-3547-7, Pub. by Progress USSR). Imported Pubns.

Space Age Facilities Conference: Second Aero Space Transport Division Specialty Conference, April 24-26, 1968, Los Angeles, California. Space Age Facilities Conference. LC 74-15643. pap. 115.30 (ISBN 0-317-10926-X, 2007869). Bks Demand UMI.

Space Age Facilities: Papers, Specialty Conference, Cocoa Beach, Fl., November 17-19, 1965. American Society of Civil Engineers, Aero-Space Transport Division Staff. LC 68-23. pap. 99.50 (ISBN 0-317-10983-9, 2004908). BKs Demand UMI.

Space Age in Fiscal Year 2001: Proceedings of the Goddard Memorial Symposium, Washington, D.C., 1961. Ed. by E. Konecci et al. (Science & Technology Ser.: Vol. 10). 1967. 35.00x (ISBN 0-87703-038-3, Pub. by Am Astronaut). Univelt Inc.

Space Age Laws of Success. George S. Lewis. LC 87-6009. (Orig.). 1987. text ed. 15.95x (ISBN 0-937771-14-7); pap. text ed. 10.95x (ISBN 0-937771-15-5). Spencers Intl.

Space Age Marriage Techniques. George S. Lewis. LC 87-60010. (Orig.). 1987. text ed. 15.95x (ISBN 0-937771-13-9); pap. text ed. 12.95x (ISBN 0-937771-12-0). Spencers Intl.

Space Age Mazes. Dave Phillips. (gr. 2 up). 1988. pap. 2.95 (ISBN 0-486-25659-6). Dover.

Space Age Predictions. George S. Lewis. LC 86-90555. 71p. 1986. lib. bdg. 10.95 (ISBN 0-937771-00-7); pap. text ed. 10.95 (ISBN 0-937771-02-3). Spencers Intl.

Space Age Science. 2nd ed. Edward F. Hills. (Illus.). 50p. pap. 1.50 (ISBN 0-915923-02-5). Christian Res Pr.

Space-Age Solar System. Joseph F. Baugher. LC 87-6255. 464p. 1988. pap. write for info. (ISBN 0-471-85034-9). Wiley.

Space Age Terrors! Hilary Milton. Ed. by Betty Schwartz. (Plot Your Own Horror Stories Ser.: No. 3). (Illus.). 128p. (Orig.). 1983. pap. 2.95 (ISBN 0-671-49248-9). Wanderer Bks.

Space Aircraft. 1985. 47.00 (ISBN 0-89883-907-6, SP 636). Soc Auto Engineers.

Space Analysis for Management. 1986. 20.00 (ISBN 0-317-56081-6). Greene Co.

Space & Beyond. Raymond A. Montgomery. (Choose Your Own Adventure Ser.). 117p. (gr. 2-7). 1987. Repr. of 1979 ed. 8.95 (ISBN 0-942545-11-7); lib. bdg. 9.95 (ISBN 0-942545-16-8). Grey Castle.

Space & Beyond. D. Terman. (Choose Your Own Adventure Ser.: No. 4). (ps-7). 1987. pap. 2.25 (ISBN 0-553-25921-0). Bantam.

Space & Development: Proceedings of Vikram Sarabhi Symposium of the Twenty-Second Plenary Meeting of the Committee on Space Research, Bangalore, India, 29 May -9 June 1979. Ed. by Yash Pal. LC 79-41358. (Illus.). 100p. 1980. 25.00 (ISBN 0-08-024441-6). Pergamon.

Space & Energy. L. G. Napolitano. 1977. 110.00 (ISBN 0-08-021053-8). Pergamon.

Space & Environment: An Annotated Bibliography, No. 954. David R. Unruh. 5.00 (ISBN 0-686-20382-8). CPL Biblios.

Space & Equipment Guidelines for Student Publications. Campbell & Kennedy. 1.50 (ISBN 0-318-19223-3). Quill & Scroll.

Space & Geometry. Ernst Mach. 148p. 1984. pap. 5.95 (ISBN 0-87548-177-9). Open Court.

Space & Illusion in the Japanese Garden. Teiji Itoh. (Illus.). 232p. 1980. pap. 14.95 (ISBN 0-8348-1522-2). Weatherhill.

Space & National Security. Paul B. Stares. LC 87-14694. 219p. 1987. 28.95 (ISBN 0-8157-8110-5); pap. 10.95t (ISBN 0-8157-8109-1). Brookings.

Space & Place: The Perspective of Experience. Yi-Fu Tuan. (Illus., LC 77-072910). 1977. pap. 10.95 (ISBN 0-8166-0884-9). U of Minn Pr.

Space & Science Fiction Plays for Young People. Ed. by Sylvia E. Kamerman. 1981. 13.95 (ISBN 0-8238-0252-3). Plays.

Space & Society. Ed. by Howard J. Taubenfeld. LC 64-21185. 196p. 1964. 12.50 (ISBN 0-379-00210-8). Oceana.

Space & Society: Challenges & Choices. Ed. by Paul Anaejionu et al. (Science & Technology Ser.: Vol. 59). (Illus.). 442p. (Orig.). 1984. lib. bdg. 55.00x (ISBN 0-87703-204-1, Pub. by Am Astro Soc); pap. text ed. 35.00x (ISBN 0-87703-205-X). Univelt Inc.

Space & Spacecraft. Caroline Pitcher. (Make It Yourself Ser.). (Illus.). 32p. (gr. k-3). PLB 11.90 (ISBN 0-531-04659-1). Watts.

Space & Spirit in Modern Japan. Barrie B. Greenbie. LC 87-32041. 1988. 29.95 (ISBN 0-300-04122-5). Yale U Pr.

Space & Storage. Ed. by Time Life Books. LC 75-34852. (Home Repair & Improvement Ser.). (Illus.). (gr. 7 up). 1976. lib. bdg. 15.94 (ISBN 0-8094-2351-0, Pub. by Time-Life). Silver.

Space & the Doctrine of Maya. G. De Purucker. (Esoteric Teachings Ser.: Vol. III). 118p. 1987. pap. 7.00 lexitone cover (ISBN 0-913004-54-5). Point Loma Pub.

Space & Time. Arno Peters. (Orig.). 1984. pap. 4.95 (ISBN 0-377-00149-X). Friendship Pr.

Space & Time in Geomorphology. Ed. by Colin E. Thorn. (Binghamton' Symposia in Geomorphology, International Ser.: No. 12). (Illus.). 350p. 1982. text ed. 60.00x (ISBN 0-04-551056-3). Unwin Hyman.

Space & Time in Homer. rev. ed. Geoffrey C. Horrocks. Ed. by W. R. Connor. LC 80-2655. (Monographs in Classical Studies). 1981. lib. bdg. 35.00 (ISBN 0-405-14042-8). Ayer Co Pubs.

Space & Time In Landscape Architectural History. William Mann. 290p. 1981. 15.00 (ISBN 0-318-17832-X). Landscape Architecture.

Space & Time in the Microworld. D. I. Blokhintsev. Tr. by Z. Smith from Rus. LC 72-77871. Orig. Title: Prostranstuo I Uremja V Micromire. 330p. 1973. lib. bdg. 60.50 (ISBN 90-277-0240-3, Pub. by Reidel Holland). Kluwer Academic.

Space Angel. John M. Roberts. 192p. 1983. pap. 1.95 (Del Rey). Ballantine.

Space Applications of the Crossroads. Ed. by John H. McElroy & Larry E. Heacock. (Science & Technology Ser.: Vol. 55). (Illus.). 308p. 1983. lib. bdg. 45.00x (ISBN 0-87703-186-X, Pub. by Am Astronaut); 35.00x (ISBN 0-87703-187-8). Univelt Inc.

Space: New Opportunities for International Ventures. Ed. by William C. Hayes, Jr. (Science & Technology Ser.: Vol. 49). 300p. 1980. lib. bdg. 35.00x (ISBN 0-87703-124-X, Pub. by Am Astronaut); pap. text ed. 25.00 (ISBN 0-87703-125-8). Univelt Inc.

Space Nuclear Power. Joseph A. Angelo, Jr. LC 84-16701. 304p. 1985. 49.50. Orbit Bk Co.

Space Nuclear Power. Joseph A. Angelo, Jr. & David Buden. LC 84-16701. 304p. 1985. lib. bdg. 49.50 (ISBN 0-89464-000-3, Pub. by Orbit Book Co). Krieger.

Space Nuclear Power Systems: The Proceedings on the First Symposium on Space Nuclear Power Systems, 2 Vols. Ed. by Mohamed S. El-Genk & Mark D. Hoover. LC 84-16634. 610p. 1985. 110.00 (ISBN 0-89464-004-6). Orbit Bk Co.

Space Nuclear Power Systems, 1985, 2 vols. Mohamed S. El-Genk & Mark D. Hoover. LC 86-23815. 404p. 1987. lib. bdg. 110.00. Orbit Bk Co.

Space Nuclear Power Systems 1985: The Proceeding of the Second Symposium on Space Nuclear Power Systems, 1985, 2 vols. Mohamed S. El-Genk & Mark D. Hoover. LC 86-23815. 404p. 1987. lib. bdg. 110.00 (ISBN 0-89464-008-9). Orbit Bk Co.

Space Nuclear Power Systems (1986, Vol. 5. Ed. by Mohamed S. El-Genk & Mark D. Hoover. LC 87-18551. 1988. 110.00 (ISBN 0-89464-017-8). Orbit Bk Co.

Space Odysseys of Arthur C. Clarke. George E. Slusser. LC 77-24438. (Milford Ser: Popular Writers of Today: Vol. 8). 64p. 1977. lib. bdg. 16.95x (ISBN 0-89370-112-2); pap. 7.95x (ISBN 0-89370-212-9). Borgo Pr.

Space Of. David Jaffin. 1978. 20.00 (ISBN 0-686-26668-4); pap. 8.00 (ISBN 0-686-26669-2). Elizabeth Pr.

Space of Death. Michel Ragon. Tr. by Alan Sheridan. LC 83-5958. (Illus.). 328p. 1983. 24.95 (ISBN 0-8139-0995-3). U Pr of Va.

Space of Half an Hour. Keith Waldrop. (Poetry Ser.). 80p. 1983. 15.00 (ISBN 0-930901-19-3); pap. 4.00 (ISBN 0-930901-20-7). Burning Deck.

Space of Literature: A Translation of "L'Espace Litteraire". Maurice Blanchot. Tr. by Ann Smock from Fr. LC 82-2062. xviii, 276p. 1982. 23.50x (ISBN 0-8032-1166-X). U of Nebr Pr.

Space on Earth: Architecture: People & Buildings. Charles Knevitt. 232p. 1986. pap. 19.95 (ISBN 0-423-01440-4, 1027). Routledge Chapman & Hall.

Space Operational Analysis. Manuel Marti, Jr. LC 80-81340. (Illus.). 216p. 1981. 19.95 (ISBN 0-914886-11-8). PDA Pubs.

Space Optics for Astrophysics & Earth & Planetary Remote Sensing. LC 88-60868. (Nineteen Eighty-Eight Technical Digest Ser.: Vol. 10). 250p. (Orig.). 1988. lib. bdg. write for info. postconference ed. (ISBN 1-55752-049-6); pap. write for info. conference ed. (ISBN 1-55752-048-8). Optical Soc.

Space, Our Next Frontier. Ed. by John C. Goodman. 1985. write for info. (ISBN 0-943802-14-8). Natl Ctr Pol.

Space Out: Jokes about Outer Space. Peter Roop et al. LC 84-5650. (Make Me Laugh! Joke Bks.). (Illus.). 32p. (gr. 1-4). 1984. PLB 5.95 (ISBN 0-8225-0984-9). Lerner Pubns.

Space Outside. Guy Russell. LC 75-35693. 1975. pap. 15.00 (ISBN 0-916348-07-5). Sigga Pr.

Space Panorama. P. D. Lowman, Jr. (Illus.). 1968. 50.00. Heinman.

Space Patrol, No. 22. Julius Goodman. (Choose Your Own Adventure Ser.). (Illus.). 128p. 1983. pap. 2.25 (ISBN 0-553-26259-9). Bantam.

Space Patrol Comics. Frances Linke. (Space Patrol Ser.: No. 2). 70p. (Orig.). 1977. pap. 15.00 (ISBN 0-933276-05-2). Nin-Ra Ent.

Space Patrol III. Frances Linke. (Space Patrol Ser.: No. 3). 205p. 30.00 (ISBN 0-933276-06-0). Nin-Ra Ent.

Space Patrol III. Frances Linke. Ed. by Ray Linke. (Space Patrol Ser.: No. 3). (Illus.). 205p. 1980. lib. bdg. 40.00x (ISBN 0-933276-07-9). Nin-Ra Ent.

Space Patrol Memories, by Tonga. Frances Linke, pseud. Ed. by Ted Wahle. (Space Patrol Ser.: No. 1). (Illus.). 173p. (Orig.). 1976. 35.00 (ISBN 0-933276-00-1); lib. bdg. 40.00x (ISBN 0-933276-01-X); pap. 30.00 (ISBN 0-933276-03-6). Nin-Ra Ent.

Space-Perception & the Philosophy of Science. Patrick A. Heelan. LC 82-4842. (Illus.). 300p. 1982. 35.00x (ISBN 0-520-04611-0). U of Cal Pr.

Space Physics. R. S. White. 332p. 1970. 114.00 (ISBN 0-677-02020-1). Gordon & Breach.

Space Physics & Space Astronomy. Michael D. Papagiannis. LC 72-179021. (Illus.). 308p. 1972. 80.00 (ISBN 0-677-04000-8). Gordon & Breach.

Space Physiology & Medicine. 2nd ed. Ed. by Arnauld E. Nicogossian et al. (Illus.). 300p. 1989. price not set (ISBN 0-8121-1162-1). Lea & Febiger.

Space Pirates. Laurence Swinburne. 64p. 1984. text ed. 2.60 (ISBN 0-07-025752-3). McGraw.

Space Place. Barry Asmus. Ed. by Helen Graves. LC 87-42903. 140p. 8.95 (ISBN 1-55523-115-2). Winston-Derek.

Space Plasma Simulations. Ed. by Maha Ashour-Abdalla & Daryl A. Dutton. 1985. Repr. 69.00 (ISBN 90-277-2108-4, Pub. by Reidel Holland). Kluwer Academic.

Space Power. G. Harry Stine. 256p. (Orig.). 1981. pap. 2.50 (ISBN 0-441-77744-9). Ace Bks.

Space Power Systems Engineering, PAAS16. Ed. by G. C. Szego & J. E. Taylor. LC 66-16539. (Illus.). 1302p. 1966. 94.50 (ISBN 0-317-36822-2). AIAA.

Space Program Quiz & Fact Book. Timothy Benford & Brian Wilkes. LC 84-48816. (Illus.). 240p. (Orig.). 1985. pap. 9.95 (ISBN 0-06-096005-1, PL6005, PL). Har-Row.

Space Program Quiz & Fact Book. Timothy Benford & Brian Wilkes. LC 84-48816. 240p. 1985. 15.45 (ISBN 0-06-015454-3, HarpT). Har-Row.

Space Race. Jon Trux. 160p. 1986. 35.95 (ISBN 0-450-06046-2, New Eng Lib). David & Charles.

Space Race. Pearce Wright. (Issues Ser.). (Illus.). 32p. (gr. 4-8). 1987. lib. bdg. 11.90 (ISBN 0-531-17041-1, Gloucester Pr). Watts.

Space Radiation Effects. American Society for Testing & Materials Staff. LC 64-14650. (American Society for Testing & Materials Ser.: Special Technical Publication, No. 363). pap. 41.30 (ISBN 0-317-11242-2, 2000753). Bks Demand UMI.

Space Radiation Effects on Materials. Radioisotopes & Radiation Effects Committee E-10. LC 62-20905. (American Society for Testing & Materials. Special Technical Publication Ser.: No. 330). pap. 20.00 (ISBN 0-317-09203-0, 2000123). Bks Demand UMI.

Space Raiders & the Planet of Doom. Stephen Mooser. (Which Way Bks.). (Illus., Orig.). (gr. 4-6). 1983. pap. 1.95 (ISBN 0-671-46732-8). Archway.

Space Raiders & the Planet of Doom see Sugarcane Island.

Space Remote Sensing System: An Introduction. H. S. Chen. 1985. 70.00 (ISBN 0-12-170880-2); pap. 43.00 (ISBN 0-12-170881-0). Acad Pr.

Space Rendezvous, Rescue, Recovery, 2 Vols. Ed. by N. V. Petersen. (Advances in the Astronautical Sciences Ser.: Vol. 16). 1963. Pt. 1. 45.00x (ISBN 0-87703-017-0, Pub. by Am Astronaut); Pt. 2. 30.00x (ISBN 0-87703-018-9). Univelt Inc.

Space Rescue & Safety 1974. Ed. by Philip H. Bolger. (Science & Technology Ser.: Vol. 37). (Illus.). 294p. 1975. lib. bdg. 25.00x (ISBN 0-87703-073-1, Pub. by Am Astronaut). Univelt Inc.

Space Rescue & Safety, 1975. New ed. Ed. by Philip H. Bolger. (Science & Technology Ser: Vol. 41). (Illus.). 1976. lib. bdg. 25.00x (ISBN 0-87703-077-4, Pub. by Am Astronaut). Univelt Inc.

Space Research, Vols. 13-19. Ed. by Michael J. Rycroft. 1979. Vol. 13, 1977. 115.00 (ISBN 0-08-021787-7); Vol. 14, 1977. 140.00 (ISBN 0-08-021788-5); Vol. 15, 1977. 115.00 (ISBN 0-08-021789-3); Vol. 16, 1977. 115.00 (ISBN 0-08-021795-8); Vol. 17, 1977. 115.00 (ISBN 0-08-021636-6); Vol. 18, 1978. 140.00 (ISBN 0-08-022021-5); Vol. 19, 1979. 140.00 (ISBN 0-08-023417-8). Pergamon.

Space Research--Physical & Technical Principles. M. G. Kroshkin. 316p. 64.00x (ISBN 0-7065-1169-7, Pub. by Keter Pub Jerusalem). Coronet Bks.

Space Research & Technology. Ed. by G. V. Thompson. 224p. 1962. 84.00 (ISBN 0-677-11910-0). Gordon & Breach.

Space Research: Directions for the Future. Space Science Board. 1966. pap. 8.75x (ISBN 0-309-01403-4). Natl Acad Pr.

Space Research, Vol. 20: Proceedings of the Open Meetings of the Working Groups on Physical Sciences of the Twenty-Second Plenary Meeting of the Committee on Space Research, Bangalore, India, 29 May- 9 June 1979. M. J. Rycroft. LC 79-41359. (Illus.). 294p. 1980. 70.00 (ISBN 0-08-024437-8). Pergamon.

Space Resources: Breaking the Bonds of the Earth. John S. Lewis & Ruth A. Lewis. LC 86-32677. (Illus.). 384p. 1987. 30.00x (ISBN 0-231-06498-5). Columbia U Pr.

Space Rock. Ed. by Susan Schade. LC 87-12762. (Step into Reading Bks.). (Illus.). 48p. (Orig.). (gr. 2-3). 1988. PLB 6.99 (ISBN 0-394-99384-5, BYR); pap. 2.95 (ISBN 0-394-89384-0, BYR). Random.

Space Rocket. Tim Furniss. Ed. by FS-Aladdin Staff. (Engineers at Work Ser.). (Illus.). 32p. (gr. 4-9). 1988. 10.90 (ISBN 0-531-17099-3, Gloucester Pr). Watts.

Space Safety & Rescue Nineteen Eighty-Two to Nineteen Eighty-Three. Ed. by Gloria W. Heath. (Science & Technology Ser.: Vol. 58). (Illus.). 378p. (Orig.). 1984. lib. bdg. 50.00x (ISBN 0-87703-202-5, Pub. by Am Astro Soc); pap. text ed. 40.00x (ISBN 0-87703-203-3). Univelt Inc.

Space Safety & Rescue: 1979-1981, Vol. 54. Jeri W. Brown. (Science & Technology Ser.). (Illus.). 456p. 1983. lib. bdg. 45.00x (ISBN 0-87703-177-0, Pub. by Am Astronaut); pap. text ed. 35.00x (ISBN 0-87703-178-9). Univelt Inc.

Space Satellites. Gregory Vogt. (Space Library). (Illus.). 32p. (gr. 4-9). 1987. PLB 11.90 (ISBN 0-531-10141-X). Watts.

Space Science & Applications. Ed. by John H. McElroy et al. LC 85-23817. 260p. 1986. 55.65 (ISBN 0-87942-195-9). Inst Electrical.

Space Science & Technology: Directory of Courses. 104p. (Orig.). 1987. pap. 17.00 (ISBN 0-11-513989-3, HM1719, Pub. by Her Maj Station Ofc). UNIPUB.

Space Science Comes of Age: Perspectives in the History of the Space Sciences. Ed. by Paul A. Hanle & Von Del Chamberlain. LC 80-28966. (Illus.). 194p. 1981. 24.95x (ISBN 0-87474-508-X, HASS); pap. 14.95x (ISBN 0-87474-507-1, HASSP). Smithsonian.

Space Science in the Twenty-First Century: Imperatives for the Decades 1995 to 2015, 7 vols. National Research Council. 1988. Set. pap. text ed. 67.00x (ISBN 0-309-03899-5). Natl Acad Pr.

Space Science Projects for Young Scientists. David W. McKay & Bruce G. Smith. LC 86-7745. (Projects for Young Scientists Ser.). (Illus.). 128p. (YA) (gr. 7-12). 1986. PLB 12.90 (ISBN 0-531-10244-0). Watts.

Space Sciences. Christopher Lampton. (Reference First Bk.). (Illus.). 96p. (gr. 4 up). 1983. PLB 10.40 (ISBN 0-531-04539-0). Watts.

Space Settler Personality Test. Alexander S. Justice & Mary B. Justice. (Orig.). 1985. pap. 15.00 (ISBN 0-935313-01-X). Space Travel.

Space Shots, Shuttles & Satellites. Melvin Berger. LC 83-19279. (Illus.). 80p. (gr. 4-6). 1984. 7.99 (ISBN 0-399-61210-6, Putnam). Putnam Pub Group.

Space Shuttle. N. S. Barrett. LC 84-52003. (Picture Library). (Illus.). 32p. (gr. 1-6). 1985. PLB 10.90 (ISBN 0-531-04949-3). Watts.

Space Shuttle. Wilbur Cross. LC 84-7702. (Science & Technology Ser.). (Illus.). 100p. (gr. 5-12). 1985. lib. bdg. 17.27 (ISBN 0-516-00513-8); pap. 4.95 (ISBN 0-516-40513-6). Childrens.

Space Shuttle. George S. Fichter. (First Bks.). (Illus.). 72p. (gr. 4 up). 1981. lib. bdg. 10.40 (ISBN 0-531-04354-1). Watts.

Space Shuttle. Nigel Hawkes. LC 82-50855. (Inside Story Ser.). (Illus.). 40p. (gr. 4 up). 1983. PLB 12.40 (ISBN 0-531-04583-8). Watts.

Space Shuttle. Michael Jay. (Easy-Read Fact Books Ser.). (Illus.). 32p. (gr. 2-4). 1984. lib. bdg. 10.90 (ISBN 0-531-04708-3). Watts.

Space Shuttle. Kate Petty. (First Library Ser.). (Illus.). 32p. (ps-3). 1984. PLB 10.90 (ISBN 0-531-04812-8). Watts.

Space Shuttle. L. B. Taylor, Jr. LC 78-4777. (Illus.). (gr. 6 up). 1979. 12.70i (ISBN 0-690-03897-6, Crowell Jr Bks). HarpJ.

Space Shuttle: A Quantum Leap. George Torres. (Illus.). 1984. cancelled (ISBN 0-8283-1976-6). Branden Pub Co.

Space Shuttle: A Quantum Leap. George J. Torres. (Illus.). 144p. 1986. 12.95 (ISBN 0-89141-253-0). Presidio Pr.

Space Shuttle: A Triumph in Manufacturing. Ed. by R. Vaughn. 230p. 1985. 35.00 (ISBN 0-87263-171-0). SME.

Space Shuttle Action Book. Patrick Moore. LC 82-62927. (Pop-up Bks.). (Illus.). 12p. (gr. 3-8). 1983. 11.95 (ISBN 0-394-85602-3). Random.

Space Shuttle & Spacelab Utilization: Near-Term & Long-Term Benefits for Mankind, Vol. 37. Ed. by G. W. Morgenthaler & M. Hollstein. LC 57-43769. (Advances in the Astronautical Sciences Ser.). 1978. Pt. I, 400p. lib. bdg. 40.00x (ISBN 0-87703-096-0, Pub. by Am Astronaut); Pt. II, 465p. lib. bdg. 45.00x (ISBN 0-87703-097-9). Univelt Inc.

Space Shuttle: Dawn of an Era. Ed. by William F. Rector, III & Paul A. Penzo. (Advances in the Astronautical Sciences Ser.: Vol. 41). 1980. Part 1, 452pp. lib. bdg. 45.00x (ISBN 0-87703-111-8, Pub. by Am Astronaut); pap. 35.00x (ISBN 0-87703-112-6, Pub. by Am Astronaut); Part 2, 528pp. lib. bdg. 55.00x (ISBN 0-87703-113-4); pap. 40.00x (ISBN 0-87703-114-2); microfiche suppl. 5.00x (ISBN 0-87703-136-3). Univelt Inc.

Space Shuttle Disaster. James McCarter. Ed. by Janet Caulkins. (Great Disasters Ser.). (Illus.). 32p. (gr. 1-6). 1988. 10.90 (ISBN 0-531-18164-2, Pub. by Bookwright Pr). Watts.

Space Shuttle Environment. Ed. by Thomas D. Wilkerson et al. LC 85-81606. 460p. 1985. 25.00 (ISBN 0-939204-28-2, 84-20). Eng Found.

Space Shuttle: Its Story & How to Make a Flying Paper Model. Frank Ross, Jr. LC 79-12155. (Illus.). (gr. 5 up). 1979. 10.25 (ISBN 0-688-41882-1). Lothrop.

Space Shuttle Log. Tim Furniss. 1986. pap. 14.95 (ISBN 0-7106-0360-6). Janes Info Group.

Space Shuttle Log: The First 25 Flights. Gene Gurney & Jeff Forte. (Illus.). 240p. 1987. (TAB-Aero); pap. 18.95 (ISBN 0-8306-8390-9). TAB Bks.

Space Shuttle Missions of the 80's. Ed. by W. J. Bursnall et al. LC 57-43769. (Advances in the Astronautical Sciences Ser.: Vol. 32, Pts. 1 & 2). (Illus.). 1977. lib. bdg. 95.00x set (ISBN 0-87703-120-7, Pub. by Am Astronaut); Pt. 1. lib. bdg. 40.00x (ISBN 0-87703-078-2); Pt. 2. lib. bdg. 55.00x (ISBN 0-87703-087-1); microfiche suppl. 65.00x (ISBN 0-87703-133-9). Univelt Inc.

Space Shuttle Operators' Manual. Kerry M. Joels & David Larkin. Designed by Gregory P. Kennedy. (Orig.). 1982. pap. 12.95 (ISBN 0-345-33103-6). Ballantine.

Space Shuttle Operator's Manual. Rev. ed. Kerry M. Joels et al. (Orig.). Date not set. pap. 14.95 (ISBN 0-345-34181-3). Ballantine.

Space Shuttle Payloads. Ed. by G. W. Morgenthaler. (Science & Technology Ser.: Vol. 30). 530p. 1973. lib. bdg. 40.00x (ISBN 0-87703-063-4, Pub. by Am Astronaut). Univelt Inc.

Space Shuttle Story. Luke Begarnie. (Illus.). 48p. (gr. 4-7). pap. 3.95 (ISBN 0-590-40211-0). Scholastic Inc.

Space Shuttles. Isaac Asimov et al. (Asimov Science Fiction Ser.: No. 7). 352p. 1987. pap. 3.95 (ISBN 0-451-15017-1, Sig). NAL.

Space Shuttles. Margaret Friskey. LC 81-16648. (New True Bks.). (Illus.). 48p. (gr. k-4). 1982. PLB 12.60 (ISBN 0-516-01655-5); pap. 3.95 (ISBN 0-516-41655-3). Childrens.

Space Shuttles & Interplanetary Missions: Proceeding. Sixteenth Annual Meeting, Anaheim, California, 1970. (Advances in the Astronautical Sciences Ser.: Vol. 28). 1970. 35.00x (ISBN 0-87703-055-3, Pub. by Am Astronaut). Univelt Inc.

Space Shuttles: Projects for Young Scientists. Gregory Vogt. (Illus.). 128p. (gr. 9up). PLB 12.90 (ISBN 0-531-04669-9). Watts.

Space Simulation Conference, 12th, 1982: Shuttle Plus One-A New View of Space. 363p. 15.00 (ISBN 0-317-36272-0); members 12.00 (ISBN 0-317-36273-9). Inst Environ Sci.

Space Simulation Conference, 3rd, 1968: Proceedings. 226p. 8.00 (ISBN 0-317-36285-2). Inst Environ Sci.

Space Skimmer. David Gerrold. 1976. Repr. of 1972 ed. lib. bdg. 17.95x (ISBN 0-88411-192-X, Pub. by Aeonian Pr). Amereon Ltd.

Space Skimmer. David Gerrold. 1981. pap. 2.50 (ISBN 0-345-29851-9, Del Rey). Ballantine.

Space Songs. Myra C. Livingston. LC 87-19628. (Illus.). 32p. (gr. 1-4). 1988. PLB 14.95 (ISBN 0-8234-0675-X). Holiday.

Space Spotter's Guide. Isaac Asimov. (Isaac Asimov's Library of the Universe). (Illus.). (gr. 4-6). 1988. PLB 10.95 (ISBN 0-317-66518-9). Stevens Inc.

Space Stamps. 88p. 1984. 11.00 (ISBN 0-318-13310-5). Am Topical Assn.

Space Station. Necia H. Apfel. (First Book Ser.). (Illus.). 72p. (gr. 4-9). 1987. PLB 9.90 (ISBN 0-531-10394-3). Watts.

Space Station: A Personal Journey. Hans Mark. LC 86-32892. (Illus.). viii, 264p. 1987. 24.95x (ISBN 0-8223-0727-8). Duke.

Space Station: An Idea Whose Time Has Come. T. R. Simpson. LC 84-21253. 320p. 1985. 22.20 (ISBN 0-87942-182-7, PC01768). Inst Electrical.

Space Station Automation, No. II. Ed. by Chiou. 275p. 1986. 50.00 (ISBN 0-89252-764-1, 729). SPIE.

Space Station Automation, No. III. Ed. by Chiou. 192p. 1987. 50.00 (ISBN 0-89252-886-9, 851). SPIE.

Space Station Automation, No. I. Ed. by W. C. Chiou. 106p. 1985. 36.00 (ISBN 0-89252-615-7, 580). SPIE.

Space Station Beyond IOC. Ed. by M. Jack Friedenthal. LC 57-43769. (Advances in Astronautical Sciences Ser.: Vol. 59). (Illus.). 1986. lib. bdg. 40.00x (ISBN 0-87703-252-1, Pub. by Am Astro Soc); pap. text ed. 30.00x (ISBN 0-87703-253-X, Pub by Am Astro Soc). Univelt Inc.

Space Station Director. Ed. by Andrew Lawler & James Vedda. 180p. 1988. pap. text ed. 147.00 (ISBN 0-935453-16-4). Pasha Pubns.

Space Station Friendship: A Visit with the Crew in 2007. Dick Lattimer. 240p. 1988. 14.95 (ISBN 0-8117-1683-X). Stackpole.

Space Station Operations Task Force Summary Report, Final Report, & Charts. (Illus.). 229p. (Orig.). 1987. pap. 15.00 (S/N 033-000-01015-0). USGPO.

Space Station Program: Description, Applications & Opportunities. Space Station Task Force National Aeronautics & Space Administration. LC 85-4963. (Illus.). 754p. 1985. 67.00 (ISBN 0-8155-1024-1). Noyes.

Space Station Seventh Grade. Jerry Spinelli. LC 82-47915. 192p. (gr. 7 up). 1982. 14.95 (ISBN 0-316-80709-5). Little.

Space Station Seventh Grade. Jerry Spinelli. (gr. 7-12). 1984. pap. 2.95 (ISBN 0-440-96165-3, LFL). Dell.

Space Stations. Gregory Vogt. Ed. by Frank Sloan. (Space Library). (Illus.). 32p. (YA) (gr. 7-9). 1988. 11.90 (ISBN 0-531-10460-5). Watts.

Space Stations & Platforms. Gordon R. Woodcock. LC 84-25442. 232p. 1986. text ed. 43.50 (ISBN 0-89464-001-1). Orbit Bk Co.

Space Stations & Space Platforms: Concepts, Design, Infrastructure, & Uses, PAAS 99. Ed. by Ivan Bekey & Daniel Herman. LC 85-19972. 392p. 1986. 59.50 (ISBN 0-930403-01-0). AIAA.

Space Stations: Proceeding. Sixteenth Annual Meeting, Anaheim, California, 1970. (Advances in the Astronautical Sciences Ser.: Vol. 27). 1970. 45.00x (ISBN 0-87703-054-5, Pub. by Am Astronaut). Univelt Inc.

Space Story. Karla Kuskin. LC 76-24312. (Illus.). (ps-3). 1978. PLB 11.89 (ISBN 0-06-023542-X). HarpJ.

Space Structures. Ed. by C. Avram & D. Anastasescu. (Developments in Civil Engineering Ser.: Vol. 9). 378p. 1984. 105.25 (ISBN 0-444-99639-7, I-394-83). Elsevier.

Space Structures for Sports Buildings: Proceedings of the International Colloquium, Beijing, China, 27-30 October 1987. Ed. by T. T. Lan & Y. Zhilian. 662p. 1988. 117.00 (ISBN 1-85166-183-2). Elsevier.

Spaceship Returns to the Apple Tree. Louis Slobodkin. LC 58-11080. (Illus.). 128p. (gr. 3-5). 1972. 2.95 (ISBN 0-02-045010-9, Collier). Macmillan.

Spaceships. Gregory Vogt. (Space Library). (Illus.). 32p. (gr. 4-6). 1987. PLB 10.90 (ISBN 0-531-10405-2). Watts.

Spaceships. Gregory Vogt. (Space Library). (Illus.). 32p. (gr. 1). 1988. 10.90. Watts.

Spaceships & Spells. Ed. by Jane Yolen et al. LC 87-175. 224p. (YA) (gr. 7 up). 1987. 12.95i (ISBN 0-06-026796-8); PLB 12.89 (ISBN 0-06-026797-6). HarpJ.

Spaceships in Pre-History. Peter Kolosimo. (Illus.). 380p. 1982. pap. text ed. 7.95 (ISBN 0-8065-0731-4, Pub. by Citadel Pr). Lyle Stuart.

Spaceships of the Ancients. Bernice W. Foley. LC 78-59116. (Illus.). (gr. 3-6). 1978. 6.95 (ISBN 0-915964-04-X). Veritie Pr.

Spaceshots: The Beauty of Nature Beyond Earth. Timothy Ferris. LC 84-42705. (Illus.). 143p. 1984. 15.95 (ISBN 0-394-53890-0). Pantheon.

Spacetime & Geometry: The Alfred Schild Lectures. Ed. by Richard A. Matzner & L. C. Shepley. 199p. 1982. text ed. 37.50x (ISBN 0-292-77567-9). U of Tex Pr.

Spacetime & Singularities: An Introduction. Gregory L. Naber. (London Mathematical Society Student Texts Ser.: No. 10). (Illus.). 176p. Date not set. price not set (ISBN 0-521-33327-X); pap. price not set (ISBN 0-521-33612-0). Cambridge U Pr.

Spacetime Donuts. Rudy Rucker. 224p. (Orig.). 1981. pap. 2.50 (ISBN 0-441-77775-9). Ace Bks.

Spacetime Physics. Edwin F. Taylor & John A. Wheeler. LC 65-13566. (Physics Ser.). (Illus.). 208p. 1966. pap. text ed. 16.95x (ISBN 0-7167-0336-X); answer book avail. W H Freeman.

SpaceTime: Science-Fiction Roleplaying in a Future That's Too Close for Comfort. Greg Porter. (Illus.). 128p. (Orig.). 1988. pap. 14.95 (ISBN 0-943891-03-5). Blacksburg Tactical.

Spacewar. David Ritchie. LC 81-69153. (Illus.). 256p. 1982. 14.95 (ISBN 0-689-11264-5). Atheneum.

Spacewar. David Ritchie. (Illus.). 1983. pap. 6.95 (ISBN 0-452-25461-2, Plume). NAL.

Spacialist. Michael Blitz. 50p. 1986. 12.50 (ISBN 0-916258-15-7, Woodbine Press); pap. 7.50 (ISBN 0-916258-16-5). Mercury Print.

Spacing of Bridging for Open Web Steel Joists. (Technical Digest Ser.: No. 2). 2.00 (ISBN 0-318-04226-6). Steel Joist Inst.

Spacings--of Reason & Imagination in Texts of Kant, Fichte, Hegel. John Sallis. LC 86-11417. 194p. 1987. text ed. 25.00x (ISBN 0-226-73440-4); pap. 10.95x (ISBN 0-226-73441-2). U of Chicago Pr.

Spacion. Evan Adar. LC 85-51325. 226p. 1986. 18.95 (ISBN 0-912159-03-0). Caravan Pr.

Spacion: The Ultimate Reality: A New Vista of Space, Mind & Human Potential. Evan Adar. LC 85-51325. 228p. (Orig.). 1986. 18.95 (ISBN 0-934669-00-7, 421); pap. 16.95 (ISBN 0-934669-01-5). USP Inc LA.

Spacious Days & Other Essays. F. C. Owlett. 1973. Repr. of 1937 ed. 15.00 (ISBN 0-8274-1138-3). R West.

Spacious Past: Historians & Others. Pardon E. Tillinghast. Ed. by Robin W. Wicks. LC 83-49148. (History & Historiography Ser.). 193p. 1985. lib. bdg. 20.00 (ISBN 0-8240-6379-1). Garland Pub.

Spacks Street: New & Selected Poems. Barry Spacks. LC 82-15377. (JHU Poetry & Fiction Ser.). 128p. 1982. text ed. 14.00x (ISBN 0-8018-2890-2); pap. 6.95 (ISBN 0-8018-2892-9). Johns Hopkins.

Spada: The Bandit Who Lived for Love & revenge. Paplo Corsaro. Tr. by Nancy C. Bellantoni from Ital. 350p. 1988. 15.95 (ISBN 0-944957-26-9). Rivercross Pub.

Spadacrene Anglica: Or, the English Spaw-Fountaine in Yorkshire. Edmund Deane. LC 74-80172. (English Experience Ser.: No. 651). 32p. 1974. Repr. of 1626 ed. 5.00 (ISBN 90-221-0651-9). Walter J Johnson.

Spadafore Diagnostic Reading Test Manual. Gerald J. Spadafore. 80p. 1983. pap. 15.00 (ISBN 0-87879-342-9); test plates 18.00 (ISBN 0-87879-343-7); test booklets 15.00 (ISBN 0-87879-344-5). Acad Therapy.

Spade Coin Types of the Chou Dynasty. Arthur B. Coole. LC 76-86803. (Encyclopedia of Chinese Coins Ser.: Vol. 3). (Illus.). 1973. 35.00x (ISBN 0-88000-011-2). Quarterman.

Spade Sage. Annette Beven. (Jataka Tales Ser.). (Illus.). 24p. (gr. 1-5). 1984. pap. 5.95 (ISBN 0-913546-71-2). Dharma Pub.

Spadeful of Spacetime. Ed. by Fred Saberhagen. 224p. (Orig.). 1981. pap. 2.25 (ISBN 0-441-77766-X). Ace Bks.

Spadina Avenue. Rosemary Donegan. (Illus.). 192p. 1986. 24.95 (ISBN 0-88894-472-1, Pub. by Douglas & McIntyre-Grounwood). Salem Hse Pubs.

Spaetantike Bildschmuck des Konstantinsbogen: Text Vol. & Vol. with Plates. Hans P. L'Orange & Arnim Von Gerkan. (Studien zur spaetantiken Kunstgeschichte, Vol. 10). (Illus.). 238p. 1978. Repr. of 1939 ed. 240.00x (ISBN 3-11-002249-4). De Gruyter.

Spaetantike Kaiserportraits. Richard Delbrueck. (Studien zur spaetantiken Kunstgeschichte, Vol. 8). (Illus.). xx, 252p. 1978. Repr. of 1933 ed. 170.00x (ISBN 3-11-005700-X). De Gruyter.

Spaetbronzezeitliche Seevoelkersturm: Ein Forschungsueberblick mit Folgerungen zur biblischen Exodusthematik. August Strobel. (Beiheft 145 Zur Zeitschrift fuer die Alttestamentliche Wissenschaft Ser). 1976. 61.00x (ISBN 3-11-006761-7). De Gruyter.

Spaeten Almanach-Erzaehlungen: E.T.A. Hoffmanns. Hans Toggenburger. (European University Studies: No. 1, Vol. 658). 261p. (Ger.). 1983. 30.45 (ISBN 3-261-03263-4). P Lang Pubs.

SPAG: Standard Products Application Guide. 1984. 50.00 (ISBN 0-318-01729-6). Milford Null.

Spaghetti. David A. Wilson & Liana D. Wilson. 12p. (Orig.). 1985. pap. 1.50 (ISBN 0-934852-28-6). Lorien Hse.

Spaghetti Again? A Beginning Reader in English. Jean W. Bodman & Judith B. McKoy. 111p. 1987. pap. write for info. (ISBN 0-02-311590-4). Macmillan.

Spaghetti from the Chandelier: And Other Humorous Adventures of a Minister's Family. Ruth Truman. 160p. 1984. pap. 7.95 (ISBN 0-687-39146-6). Abingdon.

Spaghetti Westerns: Cowboys & Europeans from Karl May to Sergio Leone. Christopher Frayling. LC 80-40822. (Cinema & Society Ser.). (Illus.). 304p. 1981. pap. 13.95 (ISBN 0-7100-0504-0). Routledge Chapman & Hall.

Spagnolo Senza Sforzo. Albert O. Cherel. 24.95 (ISBN 0-685-11571-2); Three cassettes. 125.00. French & Eur.

Spagyric Quest of Beroaldus Cosmopolita. Arthur Machen. (Illus.). 24p. 1976. pap. 4.00 (ISBN 0-9603300-1-1). Purple Mouth.

Spain, 2 vols. A. Calvert. 1976. Set. lib. bdg. 250.00 (ISBN 0-8490-2634-2). Gordon Pr.

Spain. G. W. Edwards. 59.95 (ISBN 0-8490-1095-0). Gordon Pr.

Spain. Dana Facaros & Michael Pauls. (Cadogan Guides Ser.). (Illus.). 350p. (Orig.). 1987. pap. 12.95 (ISBN 0-87106-833-8). Globe Pequot.

Spain. Dana Facaros & Michael Pauls. (Cadogan Guides). (Illus.). 1989. pap. price not set (ISBN 0-87106-642-4). Globe Pequot.

Spain. J. Harrison. 1976. lib. bdg. 59.95 (ISBN 0-8490-2635-0). Gordon Pr.

Spain. John Howard. (Countries Ser.). (Illus.). 48p. (gr. 5-10). 1987. PLB 14.96 (ISBN 0-382-09470-0); pap. 6.95 (ISBN 0-382-09477-8). Silver.

Spain. Carmen Irizarry. LC 75-44868. (Silver Burdett Countries Ser.). (Illus.). (gr. 6 up). 1976. PLB 14.96 (ISBN 0-382-06100-4). Silver.

Spain. John Lomas. (Illus.). 283p. 1981. Repr. of 1925 ed. lib. bdg. 30.00 (ISBN 0-89984-323-9). Century Bookbindery.

Spain. Arthur Miller. (Places & Peoples of the World Ser.). (Illus.). 96p. (gr. 5 up). 1989. lib. bdg. 12.95x (ISBN 1-55546-795-4). Chelsea Hse.

Spain. Jan Morris. (Illus.). 1979. 16.95 (ISBN 0-19-520169-8). Oxford U Pr.

Spain. Jan Morris. (Illus.). 1988. 24.95 (ISBN 0-13-824152-X). Prentice Hall Pr.

Spain. Graham J. Shields. (World Bibliographical Ser.: No. 60). 340p. 1985. 55.00 (ISBN 1-85109-003-7). ABC-Clio.

Spain. (Panorama Bks.). (Illus., Fr.). 3.95 (ISBN 0-685-11572-0). French & Eur.

Spain. LC 86-61769. (Library of Nations Ser.). (YA) (gr. 7 up). 1986. lib. bdg. 18.60 (ISBN 0-8094-5314-2, Pub. by Time-Life). Silver.

Spain. (Library of Nations). 160p. 1987. 14.95 (ISBN 0-8094-5181-6). Time Life.

Spain. Time-Life Books Editors. (Library of Nations). (Illus.). 160p. (YA) (gr. 7 up). 1986. lib. bdg. 23.93. Time-Life.

Spain. R. Tyler. 1976. lib. bdg. 134.95 (ISBN 0-8490-2636-9). Gordon Pr.

Spain, Pt. 1. Julian G. Plante. (Checklist of Manuscripts Microfilmed for the Hill Monastic Manuscript Library Ser.: Vol. II). vi, 295p. (Orig.). 1978. pap. 15.75 (ISBN 0-8357-0366-5). Hill Monastic.

Spain: A Companion to Spanish Studies. Ed. by P. E. Russell. (Illus.). 608p. 1983. pap. 22.00 (ISBN 0-416-84110-4, NO. 3908). Routledge Chapman & Hall.

Spain: A Country Study. Ed. by Eugene K. Keefe. LC 76-9820. (Area Handbook Ser.: DA Pam 550-179). (Illus.). 442p. 1976. 13.00 (ISBN 0-318-21891-7, S/N 008-020-00611-4). USGPO.

Spain: A Guide to Political & Economic Institutions. P. J. Donaghy & M. T. Newton. (Illus.). 248p. 1988. 39.50 (ISBN 0-521-30032-0); pap. 11.95 (ISBN 0-521-31734-7). Cambridge U Pr.

Spain: A Hugo Phrase Book. (Hugo's Language Courses Ser.: No. 567). 96p. 1970. pap. 3.25 (ISBN 0-8226-0567-8). Littlefield.

Spain: A Nation Comes of Age. Robert Graham. 327p. 1984. 14.95 (ISBN 0-312-74958-9). St Martin.

Spain: A Phaidon Cultural Guide. Phaidon Press Limited Staff. (Illus.). 600p. 1985. 16.95 (ISBN 0-13-824145-7). P-H.

Spain: A Shining New Democracy. Geraldine Woods. LC 86-30935. (Discovering Our Heritage Ser.). (Illus.). 128p. (gr. 5 up). 1987. PLB 12.95 (ISBN 0-87518-363-8). Dillon.

Spain: A Short History of its Politics, Literature, & Art from the Earliest Times to the Present. Henry D. Sedgwick. 400p. 1985. Repr. of 1925 ed. 50.00 (ISBN 0-8495-5076-9). Arden Lib.

Spain after Franco: The Making of a Competitive Party System. Richard Gunther et al. LC 84-16172. 416p. 1986. pap. 14.95x (ISBN 0-520-06336-8). U of Cal Pr.

Spain Again. Alvah Bessie. LC 74-28742. (Illus.). 242p. 1975. pap. 5.95 (ISBN 0-88316-516-3). Chandler & Sharp.

Spain: An Interpretation. Angel Ganivet. LC 75-41109. 1976. Repr. of 1946 ed. 15.50 (ISBN 0-404-14755-0). AMS Pr.

Spain & Africa. Archer M. Huntington. 1943. 3.50 (ISBN 0-87535-054-2). Hispanic Soc.

Spain & Britain Seventeen Fifteen to Seventeen Nineteen: The Jacobite Issue. Bart Smith. (Outstanding Theses from the London School of Economics & Political Science Ser.). 375p. 1987. lib. bdg. 60.00 (ISBN 0-8240-1932-6). Garland Pub.

Spain & Her People. J. Zimmerman. 1976. lib. bdg. 59.95 (ISBN 0-8490-2637-7). Gordon Pr.

Spain & Her Rivals on the Gulf Coast. (Gulf Coast History & Humanities Conference Publications Ser.). 15.00 (ISBN 0-940836-02-5); pap. 10.00 (ISBN 0-940836-03-3). U of W Fla.

Spain & Morocco on Forty Dollars a Day. rev. ed. (Frommer's Dollar-A-Day Guides Ser.). (Illus.). 1989. pap. 12.95 (ISBN 0-13-824277-1). Prentice Hall Pr.

Spain & Morocco (Plus the Canary Islands) on Twenty-Five Dollars a Day. Darwin Porter. 504p. 1985. pap. 9.95 (ISBN 0-671-52436-4). Prentice Hall Pr.

Spain & Portugal, 2 vols. Graeme M. Adam. 1980. Set. lib. bdg. 199.00 (ISBN 0-8490-3183-4). Gordon Pr.

Spain & Portugal. Graeme M. Adam. 1976. lib. bdg. 59.95 (ISBN 0-8490-2638-5). Gordon Pr.

Spain & Portugal. (Michelin Red Guides). 19.95 (ISBN 0-686-56383-2). French & Eur.

Spain & Portugal: Democratic Beginnings. Ed. by Grant S. McClellan. (Reference Shelf Ser.: Vol. 50, No. 5). 1978. 10.00 (ISBN 0-8242-0626-6). Wilson.

Spain & Portugal in the New World, 1492-1700. Lyle N. McAlister. LC 83-21745. (Europe & the World in the Age of Expansion Ser.: Vol. 3). (Illus.). 600p. 1984. 35.00x (ISBN 0-8166-1216-1); pap. 15.95 (ISBN 0-8166-1218-8). U of Minn Pr.

Spain & Portugal in Twenty-Two Days. rev. ed. Rick Steves. (Twenty-Two Days Ser.). (Illus.). 136p. 1987. pap. 6.95 (ISBN 0-912528-63-X). John Muir.

Spain & Portugal, 1986. Pat Brooks & Lester Brooks. Date not set. price not set. NAL.

Spain & Spanish America in the Libraries of the University of California, 2 vols. California University Library Staff. LC 68-56591. (Bibliography & Reference Ser.: No. 115). 1968. Repr. of 1928 ed. Set. 80.50 (ISBN 0-8337-4020-2). B Franklin.

Spain & the American Civil War: Relations at Mid-Century, 1855 to 1868, Vol. 70, Pt. 4. James W. Cortada. (Transactions Ser.: Vol. 70, pt. 4.). 1980. 10.00 (ISBN 0-87169-704-1). Am Philos.

Spain & the Empire: 1519-1643. Bohdan Chudoba. LC 71-84177. 1969. Repr. of 1952 ed. lib. bdg. 23.00x (ISBN 0-374-91559-8, Octagon). Hippocrene Bks.

Spain & the Great Powers, Nineteen Thirty-Six to Nineteen Forty-One. Dante A Puzzo. LC 72-3101. (Select Bibliographies Reprint Ser). 1972. Repr. of 1962 ed. 21.00 (ISBN 0-8369-6868-9). Ayer Co Pubs.

Spain & the Loss of America. Timothy E. Anna. LC 82-11118. xxiv, 343p. 1983. 27.50x (ISBN 0-8032-1014-0). U of Nebr Pr.

Spain & the Roanoke Voyages. Paul E. Hoffman. (America's 400th Anniversary Ser.). (Illus.). xiii, 74p. (Orig.). 1987. pap. 5.00 (ISBN 0-86526-209-8). NC Archives.

Spain & the Spaniards, 2 vols. E. De Amicis. 1976. lib. bdg. 250.00 (ISBN 0-8490-2639-3). Gordon Pr.

Spain & the Spanish. Wardell Villiers. 1976. lib. bdg. 59.95 (ISBN 0-8490-2640-7). Gordon Pr.

Spain & the Tragic Week in May. A. Souchy. 59.95 (ISBN 0-8490-1096-9). Gordon Pr.

Spain & the United States: Since World War II. Richard R. Rubottom & J. C. Murphy. LC 83-19247. 176p. 1984. 35.00 (ISBN 0-275-91259-0, C1259). Praeger.

Spain & the Western Tradition: The Castilian Mind in Literature from "El Cid" to Calderon, Vols. 1-4. Otis H. Green. pap. 9.95x ea.; Vol. 1, 1963. (ISBN 0-299-02954-9); Vol. 2, 1964. (ISBN 0-299-03294-9); Vol. 3, 1965. (ISBN 0-299-03794-0); Vol. 4, 1966. (ISBN 0-299-04084-4). U of Wis Pr.

Spain & the Western Tradition: The Castilian Mind in Literature from El Cid to Calderon, Vols. 2-4. Otis H. Green. 20.00x ea.; Vol. 2, 1964. (ISBN 0-299-03290-6); Vol. 3, 1965. (ISBN 0-299-03790-8); Vol. 4, 1966. (ISBN 0-299-04080-1). U of Wis Pr.

Spain at Its Best. Robert S. Kane. (World at Its Best Travel Ser.). (Illus.). 304p. 1985. pap. 9.95 (ISBN 0-8442-9556-6, Passport Bks.). Natl Textbk.

Spain at the Dawn of History: Iberians, Phoenicians, & Greeks. Richard J. Harrison. LC 88-51688. (Ancient Peoples & Places Ser.). (Illus.). 176p. 1988. 27.50 (ISBN 0-500-02111-2). Thames Hudson.

Spain at the Polls, Nineteen Seventy-Seven, Nineteen Seventy-Nine & Nineteen Eighty-Two: A Study of the National Elections. Ed. by Howard R. Penniman & Eusebio M. Mujal-Leon. LC 85-20523. (At the Polls Ser.). xviii, 372p. 1985. 42.50 (ISBN 0-8223-0663-8); pap. text ed. 14.95 (ISBN 0-8223-0695-6). Duke.

Spain: Conditional Democracy. Ed. by Christopher Abel & Nissa Torrents. LC 83-40172. 224p. 1984. 24.50 (ISBN 0-312-74959-7). St Martin.

Spain: Dictatorship to Democracy. 2nd ed. Raymond Carr & Juan P. Fusi. 304p. 1981. pap. text ed. 14.95x (ISBN 0-04-946014-5). Unwin Hyman.

Spain: Eighteen Hundred Eight to Nineteen Seventy-Five. 2nd ed. Raymond Carr. (Oxford History of Modern Europe Ser.). 1982. pap. 19.95x (ISBN 0-19-822128-2). Oxford U Pr.

Spain (Eighteen Thirty-Four to Eighteen Forty-Four) A New Society. Carlos Marichal. (Serie A: Monografias, LXXII). 232p. 1977. 27.00 (ISBN 84-399-7339-X, Pub. by Tamesis Bks Ltd). Longwood Pub Group.

Spain: English Edition-Country, City & Regional Guides. (Michelin Green Guides). pap. 10.95 (ISBN 0-686-56389-1). French & Eur.

Spain, Fourteen Sixty-Nine to Seventeen Fourteen: A Society of Conflict. Henry Kamen. (Illus.). 320p. 1983. pap. text ed. 15.95 (ISBN 0-582-49226-2). Longman.

Spain from the South. J. Trend. 1976. lib. bdg. 34.95 (ISBN 0-8490-2641-5). Gordon Pr.

Spain from the South. J. B. Trend. 304p. 1988. 200.00x (ISBN 1-85077-182-0, Pub. by Darf Pubs Ltd). State Mutual Bk.

Spain in America. Charles Gibson. (New American Nation Ser.). 1968. pap. 7.95x (ISBN 0-06-133077-9, TB3077, Torch). Har-Row.

Spain in Conflict: Problems of Spanish Democracy, 1931-1939. Ed. by Martin Blinkhorn. 304p. 1986. text ed. 45.00 (ISBN 0-8039-9745-0). Sage.

Spain in Revolt. H. Gannes. 59.95 (ISBN 0-8490-1097-7). Gordon Pr.

Spain in Revolt, 1814-1931. Joseph McCabe. 1976. lib. bdg. 59.95 (ISBN 0-8490-2642-3). Gordon Pr.

Spain in the Twentieth-Century World: Essays on Spanish Diplomacy, 1898-1978. Ed. by James W. Cortada. LC 78-75257. (Contributions in Political Science: No. 30). 1980. lib. bdg. 46.95 (ISBN 0-313-21326-7, CST/). Greenwood.

Spain in the 19th Century. E. Latimer. 1976. lib. bdg. 59.95 (ISBN 0-8490-2643-1). Gordon Pr.

Spain in the 1980s: The Democratic Transition & a New International Role. Ed. by Robert Clark & Michael Haltzel. LC 87-1304. (Wilson Center Series on International Security Studies). 224p. 1987. 29.95x (ISBN 0-88730-231-9); pap. 14.95x (ISBN 0-88730-269-6). Ballinger Pub.

Spain in Transition: Franco's Regime. Arnold Hottinger. (Washington Papers: Vol. II, No. 18). 68p. (Orig.). 1974. pap. text ed. 7.95 (ISBN 0-8191-5975-1, Pub. by CSIS). U Pr of Amer.

Spain in Transition: Prospects & Policies. Arnold Hottinger. (Washington Papers: Vol. I, No. 19). 72p. (Orig.). 1974. pap. text ed. 7.95 (ISBN 0-8191-5976-X, Pub. by CSIS). U Pr of Amer.

Spain, Let This Cup Pass from Me. Cesar Vallejo. Tr. by Alvaro Cardona-Hine from Span. LC 72-88550. 1972-78. pap. 4.00 (ISBN 0-88031-049-9). Invisible-Red Hill.

Spain Overseas. Bernard Moses. 1929. 12.00 (ISBN 0-527-65410-8). Kraus Repr.

Spain, Portugal & Morocco, 1988. The Harvard Student Agencies, Inc. Staff. (Let's Go Ser.). (Illus.). 592p. 1988. pap. 10.95x (ISBN 0-312-01463-5). St Martin.

Spain: Studies in Political Security. Ed. by Joyce Lasky Schub & Raymond Carr. (Washington Papers: No. 117). 125p. 1985. 35.00 (ISBN 0-275-90192-0, C0192); pap. 9.95 (ISBN 0-275-91666-9, B1666). Praeger.

Spain, the EEC & NATO. Paul Preston et al. LC 83-26949. (Chatham House Papers: No. 22). 1984. 10.95x (ISBN 0-7100-9559-7). Routledge Chapman & Hall.

Spain, the Jews & Franco. Haim Avni. Tr. by Emanuel Shimoni from Hebrew. LC 80-39777. 320p. 1981. 19.95 (ISBN 0-8276-0188-3, 469). JPS Phila.

Spain: The Mainland. Ian Robertson. (Blue Guides Ser.). (Illus.). pap. 17.95 (ISBN 0-393-30006-4). Norton.

Spain, the Monarchy & the Atlantic Community. David C. Jordan. LC 79-65887. (Foreign Policy Reports Ser.). 55p. 1979. 5.00 (ISBN 0-89549-010-2). Inst Foreign Policy Anal.

Spain: The Question of Torture. Amnesty International Staff. 59p. (Orig.). 1985. pap. 3.50 (ISBN 0-939994-13-5, Pub. by Amnesty Intl Pubns UK). Amnesty Intl USA.

Spain: The Root & the Flower: An Interpretation of Spain, the Spanish People. 3rd, expanded, & updated ed. John A. Crow. LC 84-8652. 1985. 35.00x (ISBN 0-520-05123-8); pap. 12.95x (ISBN 0-520-05133-5). U of Cal Pr.

Spain: The Unfinished Revolution. Arthur H. Landis. LC 72-83435. 452p. 1975. pap. 2.95 (ISBN 0-7178-0443-7). Intl Pubs Co.

Spain to Nineteen Ninety. Brinsley Best. (Euromoney Ser.). 242p. (Orig.). 1984. pap. 175.00 (ISBN 0-903121-52-2, Pub. by Woodhead-Faulkner). Longwood Pub Group.

Spain: Tragedy & Truth. Rudolf Rocker. 59.95 (ISBN 0-8490-1098-5). Gordon Pr.

Spain under the Bourbons, 1700-1833: A Collection of Documents. Ed. & tr. by W. N. Hargreaves-Mawdsley. LC 72-12666. (History in Depth Ser.). xl, 269p. 1973. pap. 12.95 (ISBN 0-87249-290-7). U of SC Pr.

Spain under the Habsburgs, 2 vols. 2nd, rev. ed. John Lynch. 1984. Set. pap. 28.00x set (ISBN 0-8147-5011-7); Vol. 1, Empire & Absolutism, 1516-1598, 400p. pap. 15.00x (ISBN 0-8147-5009-5); Vol. 2, Spain & America 1598-1700, 328p. pap. 15.00x (ISBN 0-8147-5010-9). NYU Pr.

Spain, 1985. Pat Brooks & Lester Brooks. Ed. by Robert C. Fisher. (Fisher Annotated Travel Guides Ser.). 384p. 1984. 12.95 (ISBN 0-8116-0063-7). NAL.

Spain's Colonial Outpost. John A. Schutz. Ed. by Norris Hundley, Jr. (Golden State Ser.). 135p. (Orig.). 1984. pap. 6.95x (ISBN 0-87835-150-7). Boyd & Fraser.

Spain's Colonial Outpost. John A. Schutz. Ed. by Norris Hundley, Jr. (Golden State Ser.). (Illus.). 138p. 1985. pap. 7.50. MTL.

Spain's Declining Power in South America 1730-1806. Bernard Moses. LC 65-21911. Repr. of 1919 ed. 25.00x (ISBN 0-8154-0158-2). Cooper Sq.

Spain's Empire in the New World. Colin M. MacLachlan. Date not set. cancelled (ISBN 0-520-05697-3). U of Cal Pr.

Spain's Entry into NATO: Conflicting Political & Strategic Perspectives. Ed. by Federico G. Gil & Joseph S. Tulchin. 150p. 1988. lib. bdg. 19.95 (ISBN 1-55587-117-8). Lynne Rienner.

Spain's Transition to Democracy: The Politics of Constitution-Making. Andrea R. Bonime-Blanc. LC 85-31541. (Studies of the Research Institute on International Change, Columbia University). 1986. 24.50 (ISBN 0-8133-7147-3). Westview.

Spallation Nuclear Reactions & Their Applications. new ed. Ed. by Benjamin S. Shen & Milton Merker. (Astrophysics & Space Science Library: No. 59). 1976. lib. bdg. 39.50 (ISBN 90-277-0746-4, Pub. by Reidel Holland). Kluwer Academic.

Spalona Rzeka: Burned River. Leszek Zielinski. Ed. by Milada Zapolnik. LC 84-90253. (Illus.). 60p. (Orig., Pol.). 1984. pap. 6.00 (ISBN 0-930401-00-X). Artex Pr.

Span of the Year. Vera F. Panova. Tr. by Vera Traill from Rus. LC 75-39007. (Soviet Literature in English Translation Ser.). 282p. 1977. Repr. of 1957 ed. 20.60 (ISBN 0-88355-410-0). Hyperion-Conn.

Spandau: The Secret Diaries. Albert Speer. 1981. pap. 3.95 (ISBN 0-671-42447-5). PB.

Spandrel Beam Behavior & Design. (PCI Journal Reprints Ser.). 70p. pap. 13.00 (ISBN 0-318-19816-9, JR304). Prestressed Concrete.

Spanende Werkzeugmaschinen, Deutsch-Englische Begriffserlauterungen und Kommentare. Henry G. Freeman. 617p. (Ger. & Eng., Machine Tools, German-English Explanations and Comments). 1973. 150.00 (ISBN 3-7736-5082-5, M-7624, Pub. by Verlag W. Girardet). French & Eur.

Spangle. Gary Jennings. LC 86-47687. 800p. 1987. 21.95 (ISBN 0-689-11723-X). Atheneum.

Spangled Unicorn. Noel Coward. LC 82-83582. (Illus.). 101p. 1982. Repr. of 1932 ed. 8.95 (ISBN 0-910638-00-4). Frisch H.

Spaniard in Elizabethan England: The Correspondence of Antonio Perez's Exile Volume I. Gustav Ungerer. (Serie A: Monagrafias, XXVII). 505p. (Orig.). 1974. pap. 36.00 (ISBN 0-900411-84-8, Pub. by Tamesis Bks Ltd). Longwood Pub Group.

Spaniard in Elizabethan England: The Correspondence of Antonio Perez's Exile Volume II. Gustav Ungerer. (Serie A: Monografias, LIV). 450p. (Orig.). 1976. pap. 36.00 (ISBN 0-7293-0021-8, Pub. by Tamesis Bks Ltd). Longwood Pub Group.

Spaniard in the Portuguese Indies: The Narrative of Martin Fernandez De Figueroa. Martin Fernandez De Figueroa. Ed. by James B. McKenna. LC 67-27089. (Studies in Romance Languages: No. 31). 1967. 17.50x (ISBN 0-674-83085-7). Harvard U Pr.

Spaniards: A Portrait of the New Spain. John Hooper. 288p. 1987. pap. 6.95 (ISBN 0-14-009808-9). Penguin.

Spaniards: An Introduction to Their History. Americo Castro. Tr. by Willard F. King & Selma Margaretten. LC 67-14000. 638p. 1980. 45.00x (ISBN 0-520-05469-5). U of Cal Pr.

Spaniards & Indians in Southeastern Mesoamerica: Essays on the History of Ethnic Relations. Ed. by Murdo J. MacLeod & Robert Wasserstrom. LC 82-23725. (Latin American Studies Ser.). (Illus.). xviii, 291p. 1983. 26.50 (ISBN 0-8032-3082-6). U of Nebr Pr.

Spaniels. Gerald Bishop. (Illus.). 176p. 1984. 20.95 (ISBN 0-7153-8483-X). David & Charles.

Spaniels. H. J. Ullman & E. Ullman. (Barron's Pet Care Ser.). (Illus.). (gr. k-12). 1982. pap. 3.95 (ISBN 0-8120-2424-9). Barron.

Spanisch-Islamische Systeme Sich Kreuzender Boegen. Christian Ewert. (Madrider Forschungen Ser: Vol. 12, Pt. 1). 1978. 180.00x (ISBN 3-11-006967-9). De Gruyter.

Spanischer Sprachhumor. Werner Beinhauer. pap. 10.00 (ISBN 0-384-03785-2). Johnson Repr.

Spanisches Supplement Zu Medizinisches Woerterbuch. E. Veillon & A. Nobel. (Ger.). 1971. 48.00 (ISBN 3-456-00271-8, M-7623, Pub. by H. Huber Vlg.). French & Eur.

Spanish. Christopher Kendris. (Master the Basics Ser.). 256p. 1987. pap. 6.95 (ISBN 0-8120-3763-4). Barron.

Spanish. Jack Rudman. (National Teachers Examination Ser.: NT-14). (Cloth bdg. avail. on request). pap. 13.95 (ISBN 0-8373-8424-9). Natl Learning.

Spanish. Jack Rudman. (Undergraduate Program Field Test Ser.: UPFT-24). (Cloth bdg. avail. on request). pap. 13.95 (ISBN 0-8373-6024-2). Natl Learning.

Spanish. Jack Rudman. (College Level Examination Ser.: CLEP-46). 1988. 25.95 (ISBN 0-8373-5396-3); pap. 13.95 (ISBN 0-8373-5346-7). Natl Learning.

Spanish. (Graduate Record Examination Ser.: GRE-19). (Cloth bdg. avail. on request). pap. 13.95 (ISBN 0-8373-5219-3). Natl Learning.

Spanish. (Hugo's Phrasebooks). 128p. (Orig.). 1988. pap. 3.25 (ISBN 0-85285-084-0). Hunter Pub NY.

Spanish. (Original Berlitz Express Language Courses Ser.). 1988. pap. 24.95 (ISBN 0-02-960190-8, Berlitz); 2 cassettes incl. Macmillan.

Spanish see Cassell's Colloquials.

Spanish: A Modular Approach, 3 vols. 2nd ed. Katherine J. Hampares & Nelly E. Santos. Incl. Bk. 1. Grammar & Dialogs. 427p. pap. text ed. 21.95 scp (ISBN 0-06-042595-4); Bk. 2. Programmed Workbook. 400p. pap. text ed. 10.50 scp (ISBN 0-06-042596-2); Bk. 3. Reading. 156p. pap. text ed. 7.50 scp (ISBN 0-06-042597-0); scp tapes 229.00 (ISBN 0-06-047448-3); instr's manual avail. (ISBN 0-06-362627-6). 1982. pap. (HarpC). Har-Row.

Spanish: A Modular Approach, Bk. 2. 2nd ed. Katherine J. Hampares & Nelly E. Santos. LC 80-23538. Repr. of 1982 ed. 103.50 (2027612). Bks Demand UMI.

Spanish: A Short Course. 3rd ed. Zenia S. Da Silva. 374p. 1985. text ed. 32.50 scp (ISBN 0-06-041513-4, HarpC). Har-Row.

Spanish ABC's. Barbara Salinas-Norman. (Illus.). 64p. (ps-2). cancelled (ISBN 0-934925-07-0). Pinata Pubns.

Spanish Alive! Spanish for Young Children: Songbook & Cassette. Lonnie G. Daizovi. (Spanish for Young Children Ser.). (Illus.). 32p. (Orig., Span. & Eng.). (ps-3). 1986. pap. text ed. 11.95 songbook & cassette (ISBN 0-935301-50-X); wkbk. 4.25; wkbk. & cassette 8.95 (ISBN 0-935301-56-9); tchr's. manual 23.95 (ISBN 0-935301-53-4); storybook & cassette 11.95 (ISBN 0-935301-54-2). Vibrante Pr.

Spanish America after Independence, c. 1820-c 1870. Ed. by Leslie Bethell. 448p. 1987. 49.50 (ISBN 0-521-34128-0); pap. 14.95 (ISBN 0-521-34926-5). Cambridge U Pr.

Spanish America in Song & Story. H. A. Holmes. 59.95 (ISBN 0-8490-1099-3). Gordon Pr.

Spanish-American Blanketry: Its Relationship to Aboriginal Weaving in the Southwest. H. P. Mera. LC 87-12715. (Illus.). 96p. (Orig.). 1987. 29.95 (ISBN 0-933452-21-7); pap. 14.95 (ISBN 0-933452-22-5). Schol Am Res.

Spanish-American Blanketry: Its Relationship to Aboriginal Weaving in the Southwest. H. P. Mera. (Illus.). 96p. 1988. 29.95 (ISBN 0-295-96614-9); pap. 14.95 (ISBN 0-295-96615-7). U of Wash Pr.

Spanish American Cookbook. L. Mendoza. 1974. lib. bdg. 69.95 (ISBN 0-685-51363-7). Revisionist Pr.

Spanish-American Diplomatic Relations Preceding the War of 1898. Horace E. Flack. LC 78-63912. (Johns Hopkins University, Studies in the Social Sciences. Twenty-Fourth Ser. 1906: 1-2). Repr. of 1906 ed. 14.50 (ISBN 0-404-61164-8). AMS Pr.

Spanish-American Folk-Songs. Ed. by Eleanor Hague. LC 18-7996. (AFS M). Repr. 16.00 (ISBN 0-527-01062-6). Kraus Repr.

Spanish-American Frontier, 1783-1795: The Westward Movement & the Spanish Retreat in the Mississippi Valley. Arthur P. Whitaker. LC 27-23368. (Illus.). xiv, 296p. 1969. pap. 6.50x (ISBN 0-8032-5216-1, BB 398, Bison). U of Nebr Pr.

Spanish-American Independence Movement. Jay Kinsbruner. LC 76-15260. (Berkshire Studies Ser.). 158p. 1976. pap. text ed. 6.50 (ISBN 0-88275-428-9). Krieger.

Spanish American Literature: A History. 2nd rev. & enl. ed. Enrique Anderson-Imbert. LC 70-75087. (Waynebooks Ser: Vols. 28-29). pap. Vol. 2, 1910-1963, 345 p. pap. 8.95x (ISBN 0-8143-1388-4). Wayne St U Pr.

Spanish-American Literature in Translation, 2 vols. Ed. by Willis K. Jones. Incl. Vol. 1. A Selection of Prose, Poetry, & Drama Before 1888. LC 65-28798. xv, 356p; Vol. 2. A Selection of Poetry, Fiction, & Drama Since 1888. LC 63-181511. xxi, 469p. pap. 6.50x (ISBN 0-8044-6319-0). Set. write for info. (ISBN 0-8044-2434-9). Ungar.

Spanish American Modernism: A Selected Bibliography. Robert Anderson. LC 73-82616. pap. 47.80 (ISBN 0-317-26809-0, 2024315). Bks Demand UMI.

Spanish-American Revolutions 1808-1826. 2nd ed. John Lynch. 1986. 24.95 (ISBN 0-393-02349-4); pap. text ed. 9.95x (ISBN 0-393-95537-0). Norton.

Spanish American Short Story: A Critical Anthology. Seymour Menton. LC 76-7765. (Latin American Studies Center, UCLA: No. 49). 1980. 40.00x (ISBN 0-520-03232-2); pap. 11.95x (ISBN 0-520-04641-2). U of Cal Pr.

Spanish-American Song & Game Book. Writers Program. New Mexico. LC 73-3642. Repr. of 1942 ed. 18.50 (ISBN 0-404-57941-8). AMS Pr.

Spanish-American War. R. A. Alger. 1976. lib. bdg. 59.95 (ISBN 0-8490-2644-X). Gordon Pr.

Spanish-American War. facsimile ed. Russell A. Alger. LC 78-146850. (Select Bibliographies Reprint Ser). Repr. of 1901 ed. 33.00 (ISBN 0-8369-5617-6). Ayer Co Pubs.

Spanish-American War. Preece. 1985. lib. bdg. 56.00 (ISBN 0-8240-8947-2). Garland Pub.

Spanish-American War & President McKinley. Lewis L. Gould. LC 82-13672. (Illus.). x, 166p. 1982. pap. 7.95x (ISBN 0-7006-0227-5). U Pr of KS.

Spanish-American War Volunteer. 2nd rev. enl. facsimile ed. William H. Coston. LC 75-164384. (Black Heritage Library Collection). Repr. of 1899 ed. 26.50 (ISBN 0-8369-8843-4). Ayer Co Pubs.

Spanish-American Women Writers: A Bibliographical Research Checklist. Lynn E. Cortina. LC 82-48281. 304p. 1983. lib. bdg. 39.00 (ISBN 0-8240-9247-3). Garland Pub.

Spanish American Writing since Nineteen Fourty-One. George R. McMurray. 240p. 1987. text ed. 19.95x (ISBN 0-8044-2623-6). Ungar.

Spanish-Americans As a Political Factor in New Mexico, 1912-1950. E. B. Fincher. LC 73-14202. (Mexican American Ser.). 332p. 1974. 23.00x (ISBN 0-405-05676-1). Ayer Co Pubs.

Spanish & English, English & Spanish Dictionary - Self Pronouncing. rev. ed. Ed. by Velazquez et al. LC 72-94281. (Span. & Eng.). 1973. thumb-indexed 23.95 (ISBN 0-13-615534-0). P-H.

Spanish & English Literature of the 16th & 17th Centuries. Edward M. Wilson. Ed. by Don Cruickshank. LC 79-53063. (Illus.). 352p. 1980. 42.50 (ISBN 0-521-22844-1). Cambridge U Pr.

Spanish & English Literature of the 16th & 17th Centuries: Studies in Discretion, Illusion, & Mutability. Edward M. Wison. Ed. by D. W. Cruickshank. LC 79-41612. pap. 75.30 (2027255). Bks Demand UMI.

Spanish & French Rivalry in the Gulf Region of the U. S., 1678-1702: The Beginnings of Texas & Pensacola. facsimile ed. William E. Dunn. (Select Bibliographies Reprint Ser). Repr. of 1917 ed. 18.00 (ISBN 0-8369-5792-X). Ayer Co Pubs.

Spanish & Hispanic Presence in Florida from the Discovery to the Bicentennial. Jose A. Cubenas. 1979. pap. 4.00 (ISBN 84-499-2888-5). Edit Mensaje.

Spanish & Indian Place Names of California: Their Meaning & Their Romance. Nellie Sanchez. Ed. by Carlos E. Cortes. LC 76-1573. (Chicano Heritage Ser.). (Illus.). 1976. Repr. of 1930 ed. 23.00x (ISBN 0-405-09523-6). Ayer Co Pubs.

Spanish & Mexican Land Grants. Ed. by Carlos E. Cortes. LC 73-14216. (Mexican American Ser.). (Illus.). 1974. Repr. 30.00x (ISBN 0-405-05690-7). Ayer Co Pubs.

Spanish & Mexican Land Grants in California. Rose H. Avina. Ed. by Carlos E. Cortes. LC 76-1231. (Chicano Heritage Ser.). (Illus.). 1976. 16.00x (ISBN 0-405-09483-3). Ayer Co Pubs.

Spanish & Mexican Land Grants in New Mexico & Colorado. Ed. by John R. Van Ness & Christine M. Van Ness. (Illus.). 116p. 1980. pap. text ed. 9.95x (ISBN 0-89745-012-4). Sunflower U Pr.

Spanish & Mexican Land Grants in New Mexico & Colorado. Ed. by John R. Van Ness & Christine M. Van Ness. (Illus.). 119p. (Orig.). 1980. pap. 9.95x (ISBN 0-317-47102-3). Sunflower U Pr.

Spanish & Mexican Records of the American Southwest: A Bibliographical Guide to Archive & Manuscript Sources. Henry P. Beers. LC 79-4313. 493p. 1979. 24.95x (ISBN 0-8165-0673-6). U of Ariz Pr.

Spanish & Portugese Languages in the United States: An Original Anthology. Ed. by Carlos E. Cortes. LC 79-6234. (Hispanics in the United States Ser.). 1981. lib. bdg. 33.50x (ISBN 0-405-13181-X). Ayer Co Pubs.

Spanish & Portuguese Gardens. R. Nichols. 1976. 59.95 (ISBN 0-8490-2646-6). Gordon Pr.

Spanish & Portuguese in Social Context. Ed. by John J. Bergen & Garland D. Bills. LC 83-9076. 124p. (Orig.). 1983. pap. 9.95 (ISBN 0-87840-087-7). Georgetown U Pr.

Spanish & Portuguese Romances of Chivalry. Henry Thomas. 1920. 29.00 (ISBN 0-527-89700-0). Kraus Repr.

Spanish & Portuguese South America, 2 vols. Robert G. Watson. LC 76-177856. Repr. of 1884 ed. Set. 60.00 (ISBN 0-404-06874-X). AMS Pr.

Spanish & Portuguese South America During the Colonial Period, 2 vols. Robert G. Watson. 200.00 (ISBN 0-8490-1100-0). Gordon Pr.

Spanish & Spanish-American Literature: An Annotated Guide to Selected Bibliographies. Hensley C. Woodbridge. LC 82-23958. (Selected Bibliographies in Language & Literature: 4). 74p. 1983. 14.50x (ISBN 0-87352-954-5); pap. 7.50x (ISBN 0-87352-955-3). Modern Lang.

Spanish Anthology: A Collection of Lyrics from the Thirteenth Century to the Present Time. Ed. by J. D. Ford. 1977. lib. bdg. 59.95. Gordon Pr.

Spanish Approach to Pensacola 1689-1693. Ed. by Irving A. Leonard. LC 67-24720. (Quivira Society Publications: Vol. 9). 1967. Repr. of 1939 ed. 17.00 (ISBN 0-405-00083-9). Ayer Co Pubs.

Spanish Arcadia. Nellie Sanchez. Ed. by Carlos E. Cortes. LC 76-1579. (Chicano Heritage Ser.). (Illus.). 1976. Repr. of 1929 ed. 26.50x (ISBN 0-405-09524-4). Ayer Co Pubs.

Spanish Archives of New Mexico, 2 vols. Ralph E. Twitchell. Ed. by Carlos E. Cortes. LC 76-1607. (Chicano Heritage Ser.). (Illus.). 1976. Repr. of 1914 ed. Set. 81.50x (ISBN 0-405-09529-5); Vol. 1. 37.50x (ISBN 0-405-09544-9); Vol. 2. 44.00x (ISBN 0-405-09549-X). Ayer Co Pubs.

Spanish Armada. David Anderson. Ed. by Ed MacDonald. (Armada Ser.). (Illus.). 48p. (gr. 4-8). 1988. 11.40 (ISBN 0-531-19505-8, Hampstead Pr). Watts.

Spanish Armada. James A. Froude. 76p. 1972. pap. 1.00x (ISBN 0-87291-036-9). Coronado Pr.

Spanish Armada. David McDowall. (Living Through History Ser.). (Illus.). 68p. (YA) (gr. 7-9). 1988. 17.95 (ISBN 0-7134-5671-X, Pub. by Batsford England). David & Charles.

Spanish Armada. Colin Martin & Geoffrey Parker. (Illus.). 1988. 27.50 (ISBN 0-393-02607-8). Norton.

Spanish Armada: The Experience of War in 1588. Felipe Fernandez-Armesto. (Illus.). 320p. 1988. 24.95 (ISBN 0-19-822926-7). Oxford U Pr.

Spanish Art Tomorrow. Luis Gonzales-Robles. (Illus.). 72p. 1983. pap. 12.00 (ISBN 0-89062-157-8). Pub Ctr Cult Res.

Spanish at a Glance. Wald. (Phrase Book-Dictionaries for Travelers Ser.). 1984. pap. 5.95 (ISBN 0-8120-2711-6). Barron.

Spanish at Sight. Clark Stillman & Alexander Gode. LC 61-16867. (Illus.). 1961. pap. 5.95x (ISBN 0-8044-6874-5). Ungar.

Spanish Background of American Literature, 2 vols. Stanley T. Williams. (Illus.). 874p. 1968. Repr. of 1955 ed. Set. 59.50 (ISBN 0-208-00356-8, Archon). Shoe String.

Spanish Ballads. Ed. by S. G. Morley. 1977. lib. bdg. 59.95 (ISBN 0-8490-2647-4). Gordon Pr.

Spanish Ballads. Ed. by Sylvanus G. Morley. LC 78-137068. 1977. Repr. of 1911 ed. lib. bdg. 35.00x (ISBN 0-8371-5531-2, MOSB). Greenwood.

Spanish Ballads. Ed. by C. Colin Smith. 1964. text ed. 8.75 (ISBN 0-08-010914-4); pap. text ed. 6.95 (ISBN 0-08-010913-6). Pergamon.

Spanish Ballads with English Verse Translations. Roger Wright. (Hispanic Classics--Medieval Ser.). (Eng. & Span.). 1987. text ed. 49.95 (ISBN 0-85668-339-6, Pub. by Aris & Phillips UK); pap. text ed. 16.50 (ISBN 0-85668-340-X, Pub. by Aris & Phillips UK). Humanities.

Spanish Baroque Art. Sacheverell Sitwell. LC 71-175874. (Illus.). Repr. of 1931 ed. 15.00 (ISBN 0-405-08979-1). Ayer Co Pubs.

Spanish Bayonet. Stephen V. Benet. LC 77-131621. 1926. Repr. 29.00 (ISBN 0-685-27275-3). Scholarly.

Spanish Bayonet. Stephen Vincent Benet. 268p. 1985. Repr. of 1926 ed. lib. bdg. 45.00 (ISBN 0-8492-3600-2). R West.

Spanish Bilingual Dictionary: A Beginners Guide in Words & Pictures. Gladys Lipton & Olivia Munoz. LC 74-26654. (Span. & Eng.). (gr. 7-12). 1975. pap. text ed. 7.95 (ISBN 0-8120-0468-X). Barron.

Spanish Bilingual Dictionary: Compact Guide. rev. ed. Gladys Lipton & Olivia Munoz. LC 78-27770. (Illus., Span. & Eng.). (gr. 7-12). 1982. pap. 4.95 (ISBN 0-8120-2008-1). Barron.

Spanish Borderlands see Chronicles of America.

Spanish Borderlands Frontier, 1513-1821. John F. Bannon. LC 74-110887. (Histories of the American Frontier Series). (Illus.). 320p. 1974. pap. 12.95x (ISBN 0-8263-0309-9). U of NM Pr.

Spanish Brabanter: A Seventeenth-Century Dutch Social Satire in Five Acts. G. A. Bredero. Tr. & intro. by H. David Brumble, III. LC 81-19004. (Medieval & Renaissance Texts & Studies: Vol. 11). (Illus.). 150p. 1982. 15.00 (ISBN 0-86698-018-0). Medieval & Renaissance NY.

Spanish Bride. Georgette Heyer. 1984. pap. 2.95 (ISBN 0-451-13276-9, Sig). NAL.

Spanish Bureaucratic-Patrimonialism in America. Magali Sarfatti. (Politics of Modernization Ser.: No. 1). 1966. pap. 2.00x (ISBN 0-87725-201-7). U of Cal Intl St.

Spanish Business Law. Bernardo Maria Cremades. LC 85-5619. 1985. 121.00 (ISBN 9-06-544220-0, Pub. by Kluwer Law & Taxation). Kluwer Academic.

Spanish Businessmate. 192p. Date not set. pap. 5.95 (ISBN 0-8442-9650-3, Passport Bks). Natl Textbk.
Spanish Cape Mystery. Ellery Queen. 354p. 1976. lib. bdg. 17.95x (ISBN 0-89966-146-7). Buccaneer Bks.
Spanish Captives in North Africa in the Early Modern Age. Ellen G. Friedman. LC 83-47759. 320p. 1983. text ed. 29.50x (ISBN 0-299-09380-8). U of Wis Pr.
Spanish Cathedral Music in the Golden Age. Robert Stevenson. LC 76-1013. (Illus.). 523p. 1976. Repr. of 1961 ed. lib. bdg. 41.50x (ISBN 0-8371-8744-3, STSP). Greenwood.
Spanish Catholicism: An Historical Overview. Stanley G. Payne. LC 83-25946. 280p. 1984. text ed. 27.50x (ISBN 0-299-09800-1). U of Wis Pr.
Spanish Censuses of Pensacola, Seventeen Eighty-Four to Eighteen Twenty, Vol. 3. Ed. by William S. Coker & G. Douglas Inglis. LC 80-26615. (Spanish Borderlands Ser.). (Illus.). 198p. 1980. pap. 20.00 (ISBN 0-933776-04-7). Perdido Bay.
Spanish Central America: A Socioeconomic History, 1520-1720. Murdo J. MacLeod. LC 70-174456. 1985. lib. bdg. 40.00x (ISBN 0-520-05356-7). U of Cal Pr.
Spanish Ceramic Designs. Anita Benarde. (International Design Library). (Illus.). 48p. (Orig.). 1984. pap. 5.95 (ISBN 0-88045-059-2). Stemmer Hse.
Spanish Chapel. Dorothy Daniels. (Inflation Fighters Ser.). 192p. 1982. pap. 1.50 (ISBN 0-8439-1066-6, Leisure Bks). Leisure NY.
Spanish Chapel. Dorothy Daniels. 1977. pap. text ed. 1.25 (ISBN 0-505-51165-7, BT51165, Pub. by Tower Bks). Leisure NY.
Spanish Character & Other Essays: With a Bibliography of His Publications & an Index to His Collected Works. Irving Babbitt. Ed. by Frederick Manchester et al. LC 83-45695. Repr. of 1940 ed. 29.50 (ISBN 0-404-20013-3). AMS Pr.
Spanish Character: Attitudes & Mentalities from the Sixteenth to the Nineteenth Century. Bartholome Bennassar. Tr. by Benjamin Keen. LC 76-55563. 1979. 38.00x (ISBN 0-520-03401-5). U of Cal Pr.
Spanish Christian Cabala: The Works of Luis de Leon, Santa Teresa de Jesus, & San Juan de la Cruz. Catherine Swietlicki. LC 86-7018. (Illus.). 216p. 1986. text ed. 25.00 (ISBN 0-8262-0608-5). U of Mo Pr.
Spanish City Planning in North America. Dora P. Crouch & Daniel J. Garr. (Illus.). 304p. 1982. 47.50x (ISBN 0-262-03081-0). MIT Pr.
Spanish Civil War. Alan Paley. Ed. by Sigurd C. Rahmas. (Events of Our Times Ser.: No. 23). 32p. (Orig.). 1982. 3.75 (ISBN 0-87157-724-0); pap. text ed. 2.50 (ISBN 0-87157-224-9). SamHar Pr.
Spanish Civil War. rev. ed. Hugh Thomas. LC 76-5531. (Illus.). 1977. 40.00i (ISBN 0-06-014278-2, HarpT). Har-Row.
Spanish Civil War: A History in Pictures. Ed. by Raymond Carr. 1986. 29.95 (ISBN 0-393-02337-0). Norton.
Spanish Civil War: A History in Pictures. Intro. by Raymond Carr. (Illus.). 1988. pap. 12.95 (ISBN 0-393-30499-X). Norton.
Spanish Civil War: An Exhibit. Compiled by Paul P. Rogers. (Illus.). 1978. pap. 5.00 (ISBN 0-87959-083-1). U of Tex H Ransom Ctr.
Spanish Civil War: An Illustrated Chronicle 1936-1939. Preston. (Orig.). 1988. pap. text ed. 12.00 (ISBN 0-256-06275-7). Dorsey.
Spanish Civil War As a Religious Tragedy. Jose M. Sanchez. LC 86-40581. 272p. 1987. text ed. 22.95x (ISBN 0-268-01726-3). U of Notre Dame Pr.
Spanish Civil War: Guide to the Microfilm Collection. (Illus.). 1988. text ed. 150.00 (ISBN 0-89235-128-4). Res Pubns CT.
Spanish Civil War in American & European Films. Marjorie A. Valleau. LC 82-1944. (Studies in Cinema: No. 18). (Illus.). pap. 57.50 (2070211). Bks Demand UMI.
Spanish Civil War: 1936-1939. Paul Preston. (Illus.). 192p. 1986. 20.00 (ISBN 0-394-55565-1). Grove.
Spanish Civil War, 1936-1939: American Hemispheric Perspectives. Ed. by Mark Falcoff & Fredrick B. Pike. LC 81-14644. xxiv, 357p. 1982. 31.00x (ISBN 0-8032-1961-X). U of Nebr Pr.
Spanish Cockpit. Franz Borkenau. Ed. by Peter Ayrton. 320p. 1986. pap. 9.50 (ISBN 0-7453-0188-6, Pub. by Pluto Pr). Longwood Pub Group.
Spanish Colonial Administration, 1782-1810: The Intendant System in the Viceroyalty of the Rio De la Plata. John Lynch. LC 69-13979. 1969. Repr. of 1958 ed. lib. bdg. 35.00x (ISBN 0-8371-0546-3, LYSC). Greenwood.
Spanish Colonial Art & Architecture of Mexico & the U. S. Southwest. Mary Grizzard. (Illus.). 180p. (Orig.). 1986. lib. bdg. 30.00 (ISBN 0-8191-5632-9); pap. text ed. 17.75 (ISBN 0-8191-5633-7). U Pr of Amer.
Spanish Colonial Silver. Leona D. Boylan. (Illus.). 216p. 1975. pap. 13.95 (ISBN 0-89013-066-3). Museum NM Pr.
Spanish Colonial Tucson: A Demographic History. Henry F. Dobyns. LC 75-10344. 246p. 1976. 14.95x (ISBN 0-8165-0546-2); pap. 8.95 (ISBN 0-8165-0438-5). U of Ariz Pr.
Spanish Colonie, or Briefe Chronicle of the Acts & Gestes of the Spaniardes in the West Indies. Bartholome De Las Casas. LC 77-6866. (English Experience Ser.: No. 859). 1977. Repr. of 1583 ed. lib. bdg. 27.50 (ISBN 90-221-0859-7). Walter J Johnson.
Spanish Colonization in the Southwest. F. Blackmar. 1976. lib. bdg. 59.95 (ISBN 0-8490-2648-2). Gordon Pr.
Spanish Colonization in the Southwest. F. W. Blackmar. pap. 9.00 (ISBN 0-685-92932-9). Johnson Repr.
Spanish Colonization in the Southwest. Frank W. Blackmar. LC 78-63794. (Johns Hopkins University. Studies in the Social Sciences. Eighth Ser. 1890: 4). Repr. of 1890 ed. 11.50 (ISBN 0-404-61059-5). AMS Pr.
Spanish Company Handbook. 128p. 1988. 43.00 • (ISBN 84-7695-033-0). Addor.
Spanish Composition Through Literature. Candido Ayllon & Paul Smith. 1968. text ed. 29.95 (ISBN 0-13-824052-3). P-H.
Spanish Conquerors. Irving B. Richman. 1919. 19.50x (ISBN 0-686-83782-7). Elliots Bks.
Spanish Conquerors see Chronicles of America.
Spanish Conquest. Thomas Campanella. 59.95 (ISBN 0-8490-1101-9). Gordon Pr.
Spanish Conquest in America & Its Relation to the History of Slavery & to the Government of Colonies, 4 Vols. new ed. Arthur Helps. Ed. by M. Oppenheim. LC 72-15297. Repr. of 1904 ed. 125.00 (ISBN 0-404-03270-2). AMS Pr.
Spanish Contact Vernaculars in the Philippine Islands. Keith Whinnom. LC 57-18812. pap. 36.00 (ISBN 0-317-28809-1, 2020772). Bks Demand UMI.
Spanish Conversation & Composition. Thomas O. Bente. 1976. text ed. 23.95 (ISBN 0-07-004808-8). McGraw.
Spanish Cooking. Ediciones Danae. (Golden Cooking Card Bks.). (Illus.). 42p. (Orig.). 1973. pap. 3.95 (ISBN 4-07-973636-3, Pub. by Shufunmoto Co Ltd Japan). C E Tuttle.
Spanish Costume: Extremadura. Ruth M. Anderson. (Illus.). 1951. 11.00 (ISBN 0-87535-067-4). Hispanic Soc.
Spanish Costume: Extremadura. Ruth M. Anderson. (Illus.). 342p. 1951. 11.00 (ISBN 0-317-00618-5, Pub. by Hispanic Soc). Interbk Inc.
Spanish Country Inns & Paradors. Karen Brown. 1988. pap. 12.95 (ISBN 0-446-38813-0, Pub. by Travel Pr). Warner Bks.
Spanish Crown & the Defense of the Caribbean, 1535-1585: Precedent, Patrimonialism, & Royal Parsimony. Paul E. Hoffman. LC 79-16864. xxii, 354p. 1980. 37.50 (ISBN 0-8071-0583-X). La State U Pr.
Spanish Cultural Reader. Emilio Gonzalez et al. 1969. text ed. 18.00x (ISBN 0-669-49841-6). Heath.
Spanish Dancing. Robert Harrold & Helen Wingrave. 64p. 1986. pap. 10.00x (ISBN 0-85936-000-8, Pub. by Spellmount Ltd Pubs). State Mutual Bk.
Spanish Dancing. Lalagia. Ed. by Ana Ivanova. (Illus.). 168p. (Orig.). 1986. pap. 16.95 (ISBN 0-903102-88-9, Pub. by Dance Bks England). Princeton Bk Co.
Spanish Dancing. Harrold Wingrave. (Ballroom Dance Ser.). 1985. lib. bdg. 79.95 (ISBN 0-87700-861-2). Revisionist Pr.
Spanish Dancing. Harrold Wingrave. (Ballroom Dance Ser.). 1986. lib. bdg. 79.95 (ISBN 0-8490-3301-2). Gordon Pr.
Spanish Dictionary. G. H. Calvert. (Routledge Pocket Dictionaries Ser.). 560p. 1980. pap. 7.95 (ISBN 0-7100-0558-X). Routledge Chapman & Hall.
Spanish Dishes from the Old Clay Pot. rev. ed. Elinor Burt. (Cookery Ser.). (Illus.). 280p. 1979. cancelled (ISBN 0-89496-002-4); pap. 6.95 (ISBN 0-89496-001-6). Ross Bks.
Spanish Doctor. Matt Cohen. LC 84-6426. 352p. 1985. 16.95 (ISBN 0-8253-0227-7). Beaufort Bks NY.
Spanish Dollars & Silver Tokens: Of England. E. M. Kelly. 1977. 25.00 (ISBN 0-685-51517-6, Pub by Spink & Son England). S J Durst.
Spanish Drama: Lope De Vaga & Calderon. George H. Lewes. 1980. lib. bdg. 59.95 (ISBN 0-8490-3201-6). Gordon Pr.
Spanish Drama of the Golden Age. Ed. by Raymond R. MacCurdy. (Span.). 1985. 49.50 (ISBN 0-89197-985-9); pap. text ed. 24.95x (ISBN 0-89197-986-7). Irvington.
Spanish Drama of the Golden Age, Vols. 1-2. Regueiro & Riechenberger. cloth 85.00 (ISBN 0-87535-137-9). Hispanic Soc.
Spanish Drama of the Golden Age: A Catalogue of the Comedia Collection in the University of Pennsylvania Libraries. Jose M. Regeiro. LC 75-172289. 106p. 1971. 55.00 (ISBN 0-89235-009-1). Res Pubns CT.
Spanish Drawings, Fifteenth to Nineteenth Centuries. Jose Gomez Sicre. Ed. by Tana G. Losada. LC 83-45771. Repr. of 1950 ed. 45.00 (ISBN 0-404-20110-5). AMS Pr.
Spanish Economy: An Introduction. Ramon Tamames. LC 86-6501. 304p. 1986. 35.00 (ISBN 0-312-74987-2). St Martin.
Spanish Economy in the Twentieth Century. Joseph Harrison. LC 84-16115. 240p. 1985. 32.50 (ISBN 0-312-74988-0). St Martin.
Spanish Economy, 1959-1976. Alison Wright. LC 77-3022. 195p. 1977. 37.50 (ISBN 0-8419-0290-9). Holmes & Meier.
Spanish Empire in America. C. H. Haring. 11.25 (ISBN 0-8446-4021-2). Peter Smith.
Spanish Empire in America. Clarence H. Haring. LC 47-1142. 1963. pap. 7.95 (ISBN 0-15-684701-9, Harv). HarBraceJ.
Spanish-English & English-Spanish Dictionary. (Span. & Eng.). pap. 2.30 (ISBN 0-686-00482-5). Dennison.
Spanish-English Comparative Dictionary of Cognates: Diccionario Comparativo de Cognados en Espanol e Ingles. Elizabeth R. Donn. Ed. by Isabel Camacho de Rodas & Jean K. Lyle. LC 85-90321. (Illus.). 212p. (Orig., Eng. & Span.). 1985. pap. 12.95 (ISBN 0-932058-02-7). RoDonn Pub.
Spanish-English Dictionary. Ed. by R. F. Brown. (Span. & Eng.). 24.50 (ISBN 0-87559-033-0). Shalom.
Spanish-English Dictionary. Carlos Castillo & Otto F. Bond. (Span. & Eng.). 1983. pap. 3.95 (ISBN 0-671-50853-9). PB.
Spanish-English Dictionary. 24.50 (ISBN 0-685-00817-7, 076-3). Saphrograph.
Spanish-English: Dictionary for Chiropractors. Dorothy H. Mills. LC 84-60237. (Illus.). 250p. (Orig.). Date not set. pap. text ed. 15.00 (ISBN 0-935356-07-X). Mills Pub Co.
Spanish-English, English-Spanish Chemical Vocabulary. J. R. Barcelo. (Span. & Eng.). pap. 7.50 (ISBN 84-205-0696-6). Heinman.
Spanish-English, English-Spanish Commercial Dictionary. C. R. Orozco. (Span. & Eng.). 1969. pap. 14.50 (ISBN 0-08-006380-2). Pergamon.
Spanish-English, English-Spanish Commercial Dictionary: "The Secretary". rev. & enl. ed. A. Frias-Sucre Giraud. (Eng. & Span.). 12.50 (ISBN 8-4261-1223-4). Heinman.
Spanish-English, English-Spanish Crossword Puzzle Book. Lily Powell-Froissard. (Span. & Eng.). 1979. pap. 2.95 (ISBN 0-8065-0676-8, Pub. by Citadel Pr). Lyle Stuart.
Spanish-English English-Spanish Dictionary. Ottenheimer Publishers. 288p. 1987. pap. 2.95 (ISBN 0-06-461003-9, DI/3, B&N Bks). Har-Row.
Spanish-English, English-Spanish Dictionary New Comprehensive, 2 Vols. U. Benedetto. (Span. & Eng.). Set. 70.00; Spanish-English. 35.00; English-Spanish. 35.00. Heinman.
Spanish-English, English-Spanish Dictionary of Aeronautics. Ed. by Sumaas Editorial Staff. 55.00 (ISBN 84-7309-012-8). Heinman.
Spanish-English, English-Spanish Dictionary of Chemistry & Chemical Products. 2nd, Rev. ed. G. G. Hawley. 110.00 (ISBN 84-282-0418-7). Heinman.
Spanish-English, English-Spanish Dictionary of Medical Terms. 5th, rev., enl. ed. F. Ruiz-Torres. 50.00. Heinman.
Spanish-English, English-Spanish Medical Guide. Howard H. Hirschhorn. (gr. 11 up). 1968. pap. text ed. 3.50 (ISBN 0-88345-157-3, 17429). Prentice ESL.
Spanish-English, English-Spanish Naval Dictionary. 3rd, rev. & enl. ed. L. Leal Y Leal. pap. 12.50 (ISBN 84-283-1089-0). Heinman.
Spanish-English, English-Spanish New Practical Dictionary. Arthur S. Butterfield. 1985. pap. 10.00 (ISBN 84-7640-026-8). Heinman.
Spanish-English, English-Spanish Technical Dictionary, 2 Vols. G. Malgorn. Tr. by M. R. Rodriguez & P. Armisen. 1985. Set. pap. 35.00; Span.-Eng., 3rd ed. 17.50 (ISBN 84-283-1354-7); Eng.-Span. 17.50 (ISBN 84-283-0923-X). Heinman.
Spanish-English, English-Spanish Thematic Dictionary. J. Merino. 1977. pap. 10.00 (ISBN 84-283-0918-3). Heinman.
Spanish-English Handbook. rev. ed. Grace Howell & Jesus Perez Y Sabido. 158p. 1977. pap. 19.95 (ISBN 0-87489-073-X). Med Economics.
Spanish-English Housekeeping. Ruth M. Dietz. (Illus.). 156p. (Eng. & Span.). 1983. pap. 7.95 (ISBN 0-89015-379-5). Eakin Pr.
Spanish-English Technical Dictionary. R. L. Guinle. 37.50 (ISBN 0-87559-187-6). Shalom.
Spanish Explorations in the Strait of Juan De Fuca. Henry R. Wagner. LC 70-137275. Repr. of 1933 ed. 26.50 (ISBN 0-404-06801-4). AMS Pr.
Spanish Explorers in the Southern United States, 1528-1543. Ed. by Frederick W. Hodge & Theodore H. Lewis. (Original Narratives). (Illus.). 411p. 1977. Repr. of 1907 ed. 21.50x (ISBN 0-06-480372-4). B&N Imports.
Spanish Explorers in the Southern United States, 1528-1543. LC 84-80799. (Illus.). 411p. 1984. ltd. ed. 60.00 (ISBN 0-87611-071-5); pap. 9.95 (ISBN 0-87611-067-7). Tex St Hist Assn.
Spanish Fascism in the Franco Era: Falange Espanola de las JONS, 1936-76. Sheelagh M. Ellwood. LC 86-29665. 224p. 1987. 32.50 (ISBN 0-312-00540-7). St Martin.
Spanish Film Directors (1950-1985) Ronald Schwartz. LC 85-8287. 267p. 1986. 20.00 (ISBN 0-8108-1818-3). Scarecrow.
Spanish Film under Franco. Virginia Higginbotham. (Illus.). 176p. 1987. text ed. 20.00x (ISBN 0-292-77591-1); pap. 9.95 (ISBN 0-292-77603-9). U of Tex Pr.
Spanish Folk Architecture, Vol. 1. L. Feduchi. (Illus.). 389p. 1982. 59.95 (ISBN 84-7031-017-8, Pub. by Editorial Blume Spain). Intl Spec Bk.
Spanish Folk Ceramics. J. Llorens Artigas & J. Corredor-Matheos. (Illus.). 235p. 1982. 35.00 (ISBN 84-7031-362-2, Pub. by Editorial Blume Spain). Intl Spec Bk.
Spanish Folk-Tales from New Mexico. Jose M. Espinosa. LC 38-9815. (AFS M). Repr. of 1937 ed. 23.00 (ISBN 0-527-01082-0). Kraus Repr.
Spanish Food & Drink. Maria E. Pellicer. Ed. by Janet Caulkins. (Food & Drink Ser.). (Illus.). 48p. (gr. k-6). 1988. 11.90 (ISBN 0-531-18173-1, Pub. by Bookwright Pr). Watts.
Spanish for Beginners. Charles Duff. (Orig.). 1958. pap. 6.95 (ISBN 0-06-463271-7, EH 271, B&N Bks). Har-Row.
Spanish for Bus-Finance see Basic Spanish Grammar.
Spanish for Business (Beginning) Juan Kattan-Ibarra & Tim Connell. 164p. 1984. pap. text ed. 8.95 (ISBN 0-8219-0140-0, 70280); tchr's guide 2.00 (ISBN 0-8219-0142-7, 70817). EMC.
Spanish for Business (Intermediate) Juan Kattan-Ibarra & Tim Connell. 176p. 1984. pap. text ed. 8.95 (ISBN 0-8219-0141-9, 70281); tchr's guide 2.00 (ISBN 0-8219-0143-5, 70818). EMC.
Spanish for Business: Intermediate Level. Albert C. Eyde & Beatriz P. Zeller. 162p. (Orig.). 1984. pap. 110.00x incl. 6, 1 hour audio cassettes (ISBN 0-88432-129-0, S24300). J Norton Pubs.
Spanish for Communication, Level 1. William E. Bull et al. 1972. Pt. A. text ed. 17.28 (ISBN 0-395-12449-2); Pt. B. text ed. 17.28 (ISBN 0-395-12450-6); Combined Ed. text ed. 21.20 (ISBN 0-395-19942-5); write for info. Additional Ancellaries available. (ISBN 0-395-19944-1). HM.
Spanish for Communication see Basic Spanish Grammar.
Spanish for Conversation. 4th ed. John K. Leslie. LC 75-3774. 423p. 1976. text ed. write for info. (ISBN 0-471-52810-2); tchr's. manual avail. (ISBN 0-471-01417-6); wkbk. avail. (ISBN 0-471-52811-0); tapes 3.00 (ISBN 0-471-01841-4). Wiley.
Spanish for Law Enforcement see Basic Spanish Grammar.
Spanish for Law Enforcement Officers, 2 vols. Mariano Garcia. 1972. Vol. 1. pap. text ed. 7.95 (ISBN 0-8325-9626-4); Vol. 2. pap. text ed. 8.95 (ISBN 0-8325-9628-0); instructor's guide 4.95 (ISBN 0-8325-9625-6); wkbk. 1 6.95 (ISBN 0-8325-9627-2); wkbk. 2 6.95 (ISBN 0-8325-9629-9). Natl Textbk.
Spanish For Med-Personnel see Basic Spanish Grammar.
Spanish for Medical Personnel. Ed. by Janet E. Meizel. LC 80-14791. (Prog. Bk.). 1980. incls. text & cassettes 55.00 (ISBN 0-88416-329-6); text ed. 13.00 text only; cassettes only 42.00. PSG Pub Co.
Spanish for Oral & Written Review. 3rd ed. Mario Iglesias & Walter Meiden. 464p. 1986. pap. text ed. 21.95 (ISBN 0-03-001767-X, HoltC). HR&W.
Spanish for School Nurses: English-Spanish. Barbara Thuro. LC 85-70256. (Orig.). Date not set. pap. 9.95 (ISBN 0-932825-02-8). Ammie Enter.
Spanish for Social Services see Basic Spanish Grammar.
Spanish for Social Workers. Alicia E. Portuondo & Greta L. Singer. LC 80-53983. (Senda Didactica). 96p. (Orig.). 1981. pap. 8.50 (ISBN 0-918454-25-5). Senda Nueva.
Spanish for Teachers see Basic Spanish Grammar.
Spanish for Teachers: Applied Linguistics. William E. Bull. LC 84-12529. 314p. 1984. Repr. of 1965 ed. lib. bdg. 24.50 (ISBN 0-89874-776-7). Krieger.
Spanish for the Health Professional. 39p. 75.00x (S24200); 4 cassettes incl. J Norton Pubs.
Spanish for the Professions. Jorge A. Santana. 256p. 1981. pap. text ed. write for info (ISBN 0-394-32652-0, RanC). Random.
Spanish Front: Writers on the Civil War. Ed. by Valentine Cunningham. 320p. 1986. 24.95x (ISBN 0-19-212258-4); pap. 7.95 (ISBN 0-19-282006-0). Oxford U Pr.
Spanish Gambit. Stephen Hunter. LC 85-459. 1985. 15.95 (ISBN 0-517-55731-2). Crown.
Spanish Gambit. Stephen Hunter. 352p. 1986. pap. 3.95 (ISBN 0-441-77776-7, Pub. by Charter Bks). Ace Bks.
Spanish Gambits. Leonid Shamkovich & Eric Schiller. (Macmillan Chess Library). (Illus.). 96p. 1986. pap. 8.95 (ISBN 0-02-029020-9, Collier). Macmillan.
Spanish Gardens. Marquesa De Casa Valdes. (Illus.). 300p. 1987. 69.50 (ISBN 1-85149-064-7). Antique Collect.
Spanish Gardens & Patios. M. Byne. 1976. lib. bdg. 75.00 (ISBN 0-8490-2649-0). Gordon Pr.
Spanish Genre Painting in the Seventeenth Century. M. Haraszti. 283p. 1983. 70.00x (ISBN 963-05-2818-5, Pub. by Akademiai Kiado Hungary). Humanities.
Spanish Genre Painting in the Seventeenth Century. Mariana Haraszti-Takacs. 284p. 1983. 182.00x (Pub. by Collets UK). State Mutual Bk.
Spanish Gipsy Paso Doble Flamenco Style. (Ballroom Dance Ser.). 1986. lib. bdg. 79.95 (ISBN 0-8490-3422-1). Gordon Pr.
Spanish Glass. Alice W. Frothingham. (Illus.). 1964. 12.50 (ISBN 0-87535-127-1). Hispanic Soc.

Spanish Rose. Shirlee Busbee. 460p. 1986. 3.95 (ISBN 0-380-89833-0). Avon.
Spanish Rule of Trade to the West-Indies. Jose de Veitia Linaje. Tr. by John Stevens. LC 72-177863. Repr. of 1702 ed. 24.50 (ISBN 0-404-06759-X). AMS Pr.
Spanish (Ruy Lopez) Chigorin. Anatoly Bikhovsky. (Illus.). 128p. 1983. pap. 20.95 (ISBN 0-7134-3626-3, Pub. by Batsford England). David & Charles.
Spanish (Ruy Lopez) Marshall. T. D. Harding. 1977. pap. 22.95 (ISBN 0-7134-0252-0, Pub. by Batsford England). David & Charles.
Spanish St. Augustine: The Archaeology of a Colonial Creole Community (Monographs) Ed. by Kathleen Deagan. (Studies in Historical Archaeology). 1983. 35.00 (ISBN 0-12-207880-2). Acad Pr.
Spanish Salt: A Collection of All the Proverbs Which Are to Be Found in Don Quixote. Ulick R. Burke. LC 73-21636. 1877. lib. bdg. 32.50 (ISBN 0-8414-9902-0). Folcroft.
Spanish Scientists in the New World: The Eighteenth-Century Expeditions. Iris W. Engstrand. LC 80-50863. (Illus.). 234p. 1981. 27.50x (ISBN 0-295-95764-6). U of Wash Pr.
Spanish Sea: The Gulf of Mexico in North American Discovery, 1500-1685. Robert S. Weddle. LC 84-40554. (Illus.). 456p. 1985. 43.50x (ISBN 0-89096-211-1). Tex A&M Univ Pr.
Spanish Seaborne Empire. John H. Parry. (History of Human Society Ser). (Illus.). 1966. 15.95 (ISBN 0-394-44650-X). Knopf.
Spanish Sentimental Romance 1440-1550: A Critical Bibliography. Keith Whinnom. (Research Bibliographies & Checklists Ser.: No. 41). 85p. (Orig.). 1983. pap. 9.95 (ISBN 0-7293-0144-3, Pub. by Grant & Cutler). Longwood Pub Group.
Spanish Short Stories. Ed. by Jean Franco. (YA) (gr. 9 up). 1966. pap. 5.95 (ISBN 0-14-002500-6). Penguin.
Spanish Short Stories & Poems. Fernando Rubio-Boitel. 1979. pap. 1.50 (ISBN 0-686-23892-3). Rubio-Boitel.
Spanish Sleuth: The Detective in Spanish Fiction. Patricia Hart. LC 85-45932. 256p. 1987. 29.50x (ISBN 0-8386-3278-5). Fairleigh Dickinson.
Spanish Smile. Scott O'Dell. (gr. 7 up). 1982. 12.95 (ISBN 0-395-32867-5). HM.
Spanish Smile. Scott O'Dell. 1983. pap. 2.25 (ISBN 0-449-70094-1, Juniper). Fawcett.
Spanish Socialist Party: A History of Factionalism. Richard Gillespie. (Illus.). 528p. 1989. 72.00 (ISBN 0-19-822798-1). Oxford U Pr.
Spanish Southwest Fifteen Forty-Two to Seventeen Ninety-Four, 2 Vols. Henry R. Wagner. LC 66-30073. (Quivira Society Publications, Vol. 7, 2 Pts). 1968. Repr. of 1937 ed. Set. 59.50 (ISBN 0-405-00079-0). Ayer Co Pubs.
Spanish-Speaking Children of the Southwest: Their Education & the Public Welfare. Herschel T. Manuel. 236p. 1965. pap. text ed. 6.95x (ISBN 0-292-70097-0). U of Tex Pr.
Spanish-Speaking Groups in the United States. John H. Burma. LC 73-81471. 214p. (New preface by author). 1974. Repr. of 1954 ed. 15.00 (ISBN 0-87917-024-7). Ethridge.
Spanish-Speaking People in the United States: American Ethnological Society Proceedings, 1968. Ed. by June Helm. LC 84-45504. 1988. pap. 25.00 (ISBN 0-404-62662-9). AMS Pr.
Spanish, Sr. High School. Jack Rudman. (Teachers License Examination Ser.: T-57). (Cloth bdg. avail. on request). pap. 13.95 (ISBN 0-8373-8057-X). Natl Learning.
Spanish Step-by-Step. Charles Berlitz. LC 78-73610. 1979. 15.95 (ISBN 0-89696-029-3, Everest House Bk.). Dodd.
Spanish Step-by-Step. Charles Berlitz. 1985. pap. 9.95 (ISBN 0-396-08595-4). Dodd.
Spanish Still Life: In the Golden Age, 1600-1650. William B. Jordan. (Illus.). 252p. 1986. 45.00 (ISBN 0-8109-1508-1). Abrams.
Spanish Still Life in the Golden Age: 1600-1650. William B. Jordan & Sarah Schroth. LC 85-50356. (Illus.). 250p. 1985. 45.00 (ISBN 0-912804-19-X, Dist. by Harry N. Abrams Inc). Kimbell Art.
Spanish Stories - Cuentos Espanoles: A Dual-Language Book. Ed. by Angel Flores. 352p. (Eng. & Span.). 1987. pap. 6.95 (ISBN 0-486-25399-6). Dover.
Spanish Story: Franco & the Nations at War. Herbert Feis. LC 86-25772. 298p. 1987. Repr. of 1966 ed. lib. bdg. 47.50x (ISBN 0-313-25208-4, FESS). Greenwood.
Spanish Story of the Armada & Other Essays. James A. Froude. LC 71-144613. Repr. of 1892 ed. 24.50 (ISBN 0-404-02628-1). AMS Pr.
Spanish Study Aid. Gerard R. Wolfe. 1978. pap. 2.75 (ISBN 0-87738-033-3). Youth Ed.
Spanish Sunshine. E. Elsner. 1976. lib. bdg. 59.95 (ISBN 0-8490-2653-9). Gordon Pr.
Spanish Surname Recent Migrant Families: Life Cycle, Family, Socioeconomics & Housing Status. T. John Alexander. LC 78-68462. 1979. perfect bdg. 9.95 (ISBN 0-88247-555-X). R & E Pubs.
Spanish-Swedish-Spanish Dictionary. 340p. (Span. & Swedish.). 1968. pap. 14.95 (ISBN 0-686-92501-7, S-37811). French & Eur.
Spanish Tapestry: Town & Country in Castile. Michael Kenny. 12.00 (ISBN 0-8446-0736-3). Peter Smith.
Spanish Terror: Spanish Imperialism in the Sixteenth Century. Maurice Rowdon. LC 74-196578. pap. 85.80 (ISBN 0-317-28441-X, 2051265). Bks Demand UMI.
Spanish Texas, Fifteen Nineteen to Nineteen Ten. David M. Vigness. (Texas History Ser.). (Illus.). 52p. 1983. pap. text ed. 2.95x (ISBN 0-89641-128-1). American Pr.
Spanish Texas Pilgrimage: The Old Franciscan Missions & Other Spanish Settlements of Texas, 1632-1821. Marion A. Habig. Date not set. write for info. (ISBN 0-8199-0883-5). Franciscan Herald.
Spanish Texas: Yesterday & Today. Gerald Ashford. LC 72-157044. (Illus.). 1971. 12.50 (ISBN 0-8363-0090-4). Jenkins.
Spanish Textile Tradition of New Mexico & Colorado. Museum of International Folk Art Staff. (Southwestern Culture Ser.). 1979. pap. 24.95 (ISBN 0-89013-113-9). Museum Nm Pr.
Spanish the Easy Way, Bk. 1. (Easy Way Ser.). 1982. 8.95 (ISBN 0-8120-2504-0). Barron.
Spanish the Easy Way, Bk. 2. Christopher Kendris. (Easy Way Ser.). 160p. 1983. pap. 8.95 (ISBN 0-8120-2636-5). Barron.
Spanish Theory of Empire in the Sixteenth Century. John H. Parry. LC 73-447. 1940. lib. bdg. 26.50 (ISBN 0-8414-1471-8). Folcroft.
Spanish Thread on Indian Looms: Mexican Folk Costumes. Frances F. Berdan & Russell J. Barber. Tr. by Rafael E. Correa. (Illus.). 112p. (Eng. & Span.). 1988. pap. 8.00 (ISBN 0-945486-04-9). CSU SBAG.
Spanish Three Years Workbook. Nassi & Levy. 1988. 14.00 (ISBN 0-87720-536-1). Amsco Sch.
Spanish Through Reading. Hirsch Hootkins. 1950. 6.50x (ISBN 0-685-21806-6). Wahr.
Spanish to Portugese. Foreign Service Institute Staff. 91p. 1980. 2 cassettes incl. 35.00x (ISBN 0-88432-059-6, SP500). J Norton Pubs.
Spanish Traditional Lyric. J. G. Cummins. LC 76-1222. 1977. pap. text ed. 12.50 (ISBN 0-08-018116-3). Pergamon.
Spanish Tragedy. Thomas Kyd. Ed. by Charles T. Prouty. LC 52-409. (Crofts Classics Ser.). 1951. pap. text ed. 3.95x (ISBN 0-88295-051-7). Harlan Davidson.
Spanish Tragedy. Thomas Kyd. Ed. by J. R. Mulryne. (New Mermaids Ser.). 1974. pap. 2.95x (ISBN 0-393-90017-7). Norton.
Spanish Tragedy. Thomas Kyd. Ed. by Philip Edwards. (Revels Plays Ser.). 153p. 1981. pap. 11.00 (ISBN 0-7190-1609-6, Pub. by Manchester Univ Pr). St Martin.
Spanish Tragedy. Thomas Kyd. Ed. by Frederick Boas. LC 82-45786. (Malone Society Reprint Ser.: No. 88). Repr. of 1948 ed. 40.00 (ISBN 0-404-63056-1). AMS Pr.
Spanish Translations of Selected 1976 Journal Articles. (AWWA Handbooks - General). (Illus.). 88p. 1977. pap. text ed. 12.00 (ISBN 0-89867-018-7). Am Water Wks Assn.
Spanish Travel Aide. Victoria Macaulay. (Illus.). 176p. 1975. pap. 3.95 (ISBN 0-8323-0366-6). Binford-Metropolitan.
Spanish Travel Pack. Hugo. 748p. 1986. 12.95 (ISBN 0-935161-09-0); one-hour cassette incl. Hunter Pub NY.
Spanish-Tudor House Plans. Ed. by National Plan Service, Inc. Staff. (Illus.). 32p. Date not set. pap. 3.95 (ISBN 0-934039-20-8, A33). Natl Plan Serv.
Spanish Tudor: The Life of Bloody Mary. Hilda F. Prescott. LC 77-112942. Repr. of 1940 ed. 32.50 (ISBN 0-404-05133-2). AMS Pr.
Spanish Twenty-Four Hundred: A Programmed Review of Spanish Grammar. 2nd ed. Katherine J. Hampares. 1980. pap. text ed. 23.50 scp (ISBN 0-06-042603-9, HarpC). Har-Row.
Spanish Ulcer: A Hisotry of the Peninsular War. David Gates. LC 85-13807. (Illus.). 557p. 1986. 29.95 (ISBN 0-393-02281-1). Norton.
Spanish Underground Drama. George E. Wellwarth. LC 76-39288. (Illus.). 188p. 1972. 21.50x (ISBN 0-271-01154-8). Pa St U Pr.
Spanish Verb Drills. Pauline Baker. 136p. 1983. pap. 5.95 (ISBN 0-8442-7032-6, Passport Bks). Natl Textbk.
Spanish Verb Finder, Vol. I. Ed. by Kenneth P. Theda. 560p. 1983. pap. write for info (ISBN 0-88107-009-2). Curtis Media.
Spanish Verb Wheel. Stuart Cuthbertson & Lulu L. Cuthbertson. 1935. 5.00 (ISBN 0-669-31427-7). Heath.
Spanish Verbs. (Hugo's Verbs Simplified Ser.). 96p. 1988. 3.95 (ISBN 0-85285-100-6). Hunter Pub NY.
Spanish Verbs & Essentials of Grammar. Ina W. Ramboz. 136p. 1983. pap. 6.95 (ISBN 0-8442-7214-0, Passport Bks.). Natl Textbk.
Spanish Verse of the Sixteenth Age. Ed. by P. D. Tettenborn. 1977. lib. bdg. 59.95 (ISBN 0-8490-2654-7). Gordon Pr.
Spanish Villanciocos of the 18th Century: The Music of Juan Frances de Iribarren. Marta Sanchez. Ed. by Yvette E. Miller. (Explorations Ser.). 320p. 1987. pap. text ed. 16.95 (ISBN 0-935480-26-9). Lat Am Lit Rev Pr.
Spanish Vocabulary & Structure for the Health Professional, Bk. 1. 2nd ed. Dorothy H. Mills et al. LC 80-54900. (Illus.). 157p. (Eng. & Span.). 1981. pap. text ed. 15.00 (ISBN 0-935356-02-9). Mills Pub Co.
Spanish Vocabulary of Four Native Spanish-Speaking Pre-First-Grade Children. Loyd S. Tireman. LC 48-45159. 64p. 1982. lib. bdg. 22.95x (ISBN 0-89370-737-6). Borgo Pr.
Spanish Voyage to Vancouver & the North-West Coast of America. Jose Espinosa y Tello. Tr. by Cecil Jane. LC 70-136389. (Illus.). Repr. of 1930 ed. 10.00 (ISBN 0-404-02356-8). AMS Pr.
Spanish War: An American Epic 1898. G. J. O'Toole. (Illus.). 440p. 1984. 19.95 (ISBN 0-393-01839-3). Norton.
Spanish War: An American Epic 1898. G. J. O'Toole. (Illus.). 448p. 1986. pap. 7.95 (ISBN 0-393-30304-7). Norton.
Spanish West. W. W. Johnson. LC 76-1423. (Old West Ser.). (Illus.). (gr. 7 up). 1976. 19.94 (ISBN 0-8094-1535-6, Pub. by Time-Life). Silver.
Spanish West. William W. Johnson. (Old West Ser.). (Illus.). 1976. 14.95 (ISBN 0-8094-1533-X). Time-Life.
Spanish WithCase. Albert O. Cherel. 24.95 (ISBN 0-685-11574-7); Four cassettes. 125.00. French & Eur.
Spanish... Without A6. Mikhail Yudovich. (Macmillan Chess Library). (Illus.). 128p. 1986. pap. 8.95 (ISBN 0-02-029060-8, Collier). Macmillan.
Spanish Word Machine Book I & II. Virgilio Moya et al. Tr. by Maria Ramirez. (Spanish Word Machine Bks.). 26p. (gr. 4-7). 1980. PLB 3.95 ea. (ISBN 0-931218-24-1, 1040). Joybug.
Spanish Word Machine: Book 1. Virgilio Moya et al. LC 79-92122. (Spanish Word Machine Bks.). (Illus., Orig.). (gr. 4-7). 1982. pap. 3.95 (ISBN 0-931218-09-8, 1041). Joybug.
Spanish Word Machine: Book 2. Virgilio Moya et al. LC 79-92122. (Spanish Word Machine Bks.). 26p. (Orig.). (gr. 4-7). 1982. pap. 3.95 (ISBN 0-931218-10-1, 1042). Joybug.
Spanish Workbook 1. Robert J. Nassi & Bernard Bernstein. 1976. pap. text ed. 9.00 wkbk. (ISBN 0-87720-987-1). AMSCO Sch.
Spanish Workbook 2. Robert Nassi & Bernard Bernstein. 1977. wkbk. 9.16 (ISBN 0-87720-988-X). AMSCO Sch.
Spanish Writers in Exile. Ed. by Angel Flores. 1977. 42.50 (ISBN 0-685-74168-0). Bern Porter.
Spanish Writers of Nineteen Thirty-Six: Crisis & Commitment in the Poetry of the Thirties & Forties. Ed. by Jaime Ferran & Daniel Testa. (Serie A: Monagrafias, XXXI). 141p. (Orig.). 1973. pap. 14.50 (ISBN 0-900411-71-6, Pub. by Tamesis Bks Ltd). Longwood Pub Group.
Spanking Girls. Carter Brown. 1979. pap. 1.50 (ISBN 0-505-51383-8, Pub. by Tower Bks). Leisure NY.
Spanking the Maid. Robert Coover. 1981. 55.00 (ISBN 0-89723-023-X); specially bound manuscript ed. 125.00 (ISBN 0-89723-024-8). Bruccoli.
Spanking the Maid. Robert Coover. LC 81-48546. 256p. 1982. 10.95 (ISBN 0-394-52561-2, GP-850). Grove.
Spanking the Maid. Robert Coover. 256p. 1981. pap. 4.95 (ISBN 0-394-17971-4, E804, Ever). Grove.
Spanking: Why? When? How? Roy Lessin. LC 79-54028. 96p. 1979. pap. 3.50 (ISBN 0-87123-494-7, 200494). Bethany Hse.
Spanning Niagara: The International Bridges, 1848-1962. Ralph Greenhill. LC 85-149504. (Illus.). 48p. (Orig.). 1985. pap. 10.00 (ISBN 0-295-96235-6). U of Wash Pr.
Spanning the Gate: Building the Golden Gate Bridge. rev. ed. Stephen Cassady. LC 77-83284. (Illus.). 144p. 1986. 24.95 (ISBN 0-916290-35-2). Squarebooks.
Spanning the Gate: Building the Golden Gate Bridge. rev. ed. Stephen Cassady. 144p. 1986. pap. 14.95 (ISBN 0-916290-36-0). Squarebooks.
Spanning Two Centuries: Historic Bridges of Australia. Colin O'Connor. 1986. 39.50 (ISBN 0-317-46038-2). U of Queensland Pr.
Spanos: Eine Byzantinische Satire Als Parodie, Einleitung, Kritischer Text, Kommentar und Glossar. Ed. by Hans Eideneier. 1977. 84.00x (ISBN 3-11-006606-8). De Gruyter.
Spansk-Norsk Ordbok. S. Loennecken. 411p. (Span. & Norwegian.). 1980. 39.95 (ISBN 0-686-92543-2, S-37620). French & Eur.
SPAR Membership Directory. (Orig.). pap. 20.00 (ISBN 0-318-11806-8). SPAR.
Sparda by the Bitter Sea: Imperial Interaction in Western Anatolia. Jack Balcer. (Brown Judaic Studies: No. 52). 616p. 1985. 39.95 (ISBN 0-89130-657-9, 14 00 52); pap. 29.95 (ISBN 0-89130-818-0). Scholars Pr GA.
Spare Chancellor: The Life of Walter Bagehot. Alastair Buchan. 1960. 5.00 (ISBN 0-87013-051-X). Mich St U Pr.
Spare Days. Marvin Barrett. LC 87-33329. 170p. 1988. 16.95 (ISBN 1-55710-006-3, Arbor Hse). Morrow.
Spare Mad. Mad Magazine Editors. (Mad Ser.: No. 77). 1988. pap. 2.95 (ISBN 0-446-34944-5). Warner Bks.
Spare Me! The Insanity of Bowling. Dawson Taylor. (Illus.). 96p. (Orig.). 1986. pap. 6.95 (ISBN 0-8092-5017-9). Contemp Bks.
Spare No Exertions: One Hundred Seventy-Five Years of the Reformed Presbyterian Theological Seminary. Robert M. Copeland. LC 86-60501. (Illus.). 144p. 1986. 4.95x (ISBN 0-9616417-0-3). Ref Presby Theo.
Spare Parts for People. Margery Facklam & Howard Facklam. (Illus.). 128p. (YA) (gr. 9-12). 1987. 14.95 (ISBN 0-15-277410-6, HJ). HarBraceJ.
Spare Parts Inc. James A. Cran. LC 85-50729. 153p. 1986. 19.95 (ISBN 0-913495-02-6); pap. 9.95 (ISBN 0-913495-03-4). Taurus Pub Co.
Spare Parts List for Fordson Tractors: 1917-1945. Trent Valley Publications Staff. (Illus.). 128p. 1988. Repr. 50.00x (ISBN 1-870253-05-1, Pub. by Trent Valley UK). State Mutual Bk.
Spare the Couch: Self-Change for Self Improvement. Donald L. Tasto & Eric K. Skjei. (Illus.). 1979. 11.95 (ISBN 0-13-824466-9, Spec). P-H.
Spare the Rod?! A Resource Guide: Alternatives to Corporal Punishment. 1987. 13.50 (ISBN 0-317-66230-9). Natl Assn Soc Wkrs.
Spare the Rod: Breaking the Cycle of Child Abuse. Phil E. Quinn. 192p. 1988. 11.95 (ISBN 0-687-39145-8). Abingdon.
Spare Time at Sea. 2nd ed. Ronald Hope. (Illus.). 231p. 1974. 14.95 (ISBN 0-8464-0878-3). Beekman Pubs.
Spare Your People! Richard Swanson. LC 85-73213. 230p. 1986. pap. 3.95 (ISBN 0-88270-596-2). Bridge Pub.
Sparire, 2 vols. Enzo Cucchi. Tr. by Meg Shore & Catherine Schelbert. (Illus.). 30p. (Orig., Ital., Eng. & Ger.). 1987. Set. pap. 22.00 letterpress (ISBN 0-935875-05-0). Blumarts Inc.
Spark. Davie Elspeth. 288p. (Orig.). 1983. pap. 7.95 (ISBN 0-7145-0538-2). Riverrun NY.
Spark: A Handbook of Classroom Ideas to Motivate the Teaching of Primary Social Studies. (Spice Ser). 1977. 8.95 (ISBN 0-89273-104-4). Educ Serv.
Spark Duplicating Masters: Social Studies, 2 Vols. (Spice Ser.). (gr. k-4). 1978. Vol. 1, Gr. K-2. 8.95 (ISBN 0-89273-553-8); Vol. 2, Gr. 2-4. 8.95 (ISBN 0-89273-554-6). Educ Serv.
Spark from Heaven: The Mystery of the Madonna of Medjugorje. Mary Craig. 248p. (Orig.). 1988. pap. 7.95 (ISBN 0-87793-386-3). Ave Maria.
Spark Is Struck! Jack Hall & the ILWU in Hawaii. Sanford Zalburg. LC 79-91284. (Illus.). 664p. 1980. pap. 5.95 (ISBN 0-8248-0672-7). UH Pr.
Spark of Enterprise: A History of Dixie Foundry - Magic Chef, Inc. John C. Longwith. LC 87-91291. (Illus.). 192p. 1988. 16.95 (ISBN 0-944897-00-2). Magic Chef.
Spark of Genius, the World's First Prenatal Teaching Book. Joseph L. Susedik. Ed. by Paul Younkers. LC 30-15964. (Susedik Method Ser.). (Illus.). 148p. (Orig.). 1985. pap. 14.95 (ISBN 0-914717-07-3). Susedik Meth.
Spark of Goodness. Charles Brady. LC 82-11949. 372p. 1983. 14.95 (ISBN 0-395-31257-4). HM.
Spark Your Social Science. pap. 4.95 tchr's study guide (ISBN 0-686-19379-2). E V Salitore.
Sparke Towards the Kindling of Sorrow for Zion. Thomas Gataker. LC 76-57382. (English Experience Ser.: No. 800). 1977. Repr. of 1621 ed. lib. bdg. 7.00 (ISBN 90-221-0800-7). Walter J Johnson.
Sparkerpolice Guidebook: How to Play Sparkerpolice. Swedish Intelligence Editors & Jim Morrison. Tr. by Per Rundqvist. Orig. Title: Swedish. (Illus.). (YA) (gr. 11-12). Date not set. 35.00 (ISBN 0-915628-17-1). Zeppelin.
Sparking the Rain. Frank Rossini. Ed. by Rodger Moody & Randall Roorda. (Illus.). 28p. 1979. pap. 3.00 (ISBN 0-9610508-1-0). Silverfish Rev Pr.
Sparkle: PR for Library Staff. Virginia Baeckler. LC 80-50566. (Illus.). 80p. (Orig.). 1980. pap. 5.00x (ISBN 0-9603232-1-X). Sources.
Sparkling Devotions for Women's Groups. Mary A. Vandermey. 144p. 1985. pap. 4.95 (ISBN 0-8010-9300-7). Baker Bk.
Sparkling Object Sermons for Children. C. W. Bess. (Object Lesson Ser.). 120p. (Orig.). 1982. pap. 4.95 (ISBN 0-8010-0824-7). Baker Bk.
Sparkling Plug Collectors Guide, Vol. 1. Cornelius Bergbower. (Illus.). 96p. (Orig.). 1986. pap. 9.95 (ISBN 0-9616653-0-0). C Bergbower.
Sparkling Words. Ruth K. Carlson. 1979. 10.00 (ISBN 0-88252-009-1). Paladin Hse.
Sparks. Elizabeth Fritch. (Richmond Ser.: Vol. 4). (Orig.). 1982. pap. 3.50 (ISBN 0-89083-962-X). Zebra.
Sparks. Richard Stine. (Illus.). 112p. (Orig.). 1987. pap. 6.95 (ISBN 0-9617782-0-2). Pal Pr Ojai.
Sparks. Meg Wolitzer. 294p. 1985. 15.95. HM.
Sparks, Flames & Cinders. Irma H. Cervantes. (Illus.). 96p. 1982. 9.95x (ISBN 0-9609600-0-7). Five Windmills.
Sparks Fly Upward. Glen Haley. (Illus.). 264p. (Orig.). 1988. pap. 9.95 (ISBN 0-9608764-8-0). Wayfinder Pr.
Sparks from Rainbows. Julia A. Blodgett. 48p. 1987. 7.50 (ISBN 0-8062-3086-X). Carlton.
Sparks from Synergy's Fire. 2nd ed. Mary K. Cox. LC 83-50644. (Illus.). 80p. 1983. pap. 1.95 (ISBN 0-910217-02-5). Synergetics WV.
Sparks in the Night. Beth Batlle. LC 87-5563. 158p. 1987. 13.75 (ISBN 0-930950-11-9); pap. 7.75 (ISBN 0-930950-12-7). Nopoly Pr.

Spatial Geography. Robert O. Whyte. (Illus., Orig.). 1982. 26.00x (ISBN 0-19-561163-2). Oxford U Pr.
Spatial Hearing: The Psychophysics of Human Sound Localization. Jens Blauert. 1983. 47.50x (ISBN 0-262-02190-0). MIT Pr.
Spatial Impact of Technological Change. Ed. by John Brotchie et al. LC 87-11460. 480p. 1987. text ed. 37.95 (ISBN 0-389-20753-5). B&N Imports.
Spatial Impact of Technological Change. Ed. by John Brotchie et al. 336p. 1987. lib. bdg. 55.00x (ISBN 0-7099-5006-3, Pub. by Croom Helm UK). Routledge Chapman & Hall.
Spatial Inequalities & Regional Development. Hendrik Folmer & Jan Oosterhaven. 1979. lib. bdg. 34.50 (ISBN 0-89838-006-5, Pub. by Martins Nijhoff Netherlands). Kluwer Academic.
Spatial Interaction Modelling & Residential Choice Analysis. Wal Van Lierop. 300p. 1985. text ed. 45.00x (ISBN 0-317-40027-4, Pub. by Gower Pub England). Gower Pub Co.
Spatial Interaction Theory & Planning Models. A. Karlqvist et al. (Studies in Regional & Urban Economics: Vol. 3). 388p. 1978. 73.75 (ISBN 0-444-85182-8, North-Holland). Elsevier.
Spatial Kinematics Chains: Analysis - Synthesis - Optimization. J. Angeles. (Illus.). 369p. 1982. 49.00 (ISBN 0-387-11398-3). Springer-Verlag.
Spatial Learning Strategies: Techniques, Applications & Related Issues. Charles D. Holley & Charles F. Dansereau. LC 83-15715. (Educational Psycholoy Ser.). 1984. 44.00 (ISBN 0-12-352620-5). Acad Pr.
Spatial Light Modulators & Applications, No. II. Ed. by Efron. 1988. 43.00 (ISBN 0-89252-860-5, 825). SPIE.
Spatial Light Modulators & Applications. LC 88-60863. (Nineteen Eighty-Eight Technical Digest Ser.: Vol. 8). 175p. (Orig.). 1988. lib. bdg. write for info. postconference ed. (ISBN 1-55752-051-8); pap. write for info. conference ed. (ISBN 1-55752-050-X). Optical Soc.
Spatial Models of Election Competition. Steven J. Brams. 87p. 1983. pap. 6.95 (ISBN 0-912843-01-2). COMAP Inc.
Spatial Models of Electoral Choice: An Empirical Analysis. George B. Rabinowitz. (Working Papers in Methodology: No. 7). 192p. 1973. pap. text ed. 5.00 (ISBN 0-89143-031-8). U NC Inst Res Soc Sci.
Spatial Objective Analysis. T. J. Thiebaux. 300p. 1987. 63.00 (ISBN 0-12-686930-8). Acad Pr.
Spatial Organisation of Culture. Ed. by Ian Hodder. LC 78-1354. 1978. 29.95x (ISBN 0-8229-1134-5). U of Pittsburgh Pr.
Spatial Organization & Exchange: Archaeological Survey on Northern Black Mesa. Ed. by Stephen Plog & Shirley Powell. (Illus.). 400p. 1985. text ed. 30.00x (ISBN 0-8093-1214-X). S Ill U Pr.
Spatial Organization of Cerebral Processes. M. N. Livanov. 178p. 1975. text ed. 38.00x (ISBN 0-7065-1514-5, Pub. by Keter Pub Jerusalem). Coronet Bks.
Spatial Organization of Multinational Corporations. Ian M. Clarke. LC 85-2265. 288p. 1985. 35.00x (ISBN 0-312-75028-5). St Martin.
Spatial Organization of New Land Settlement in Latin America. Jacob Maos. (Dellplain Latin American Studies: Vol.15). 170p. 1984. lib. bdg. 32.50x (ISBN 0-86531-626-0). Westview.
Spatial Orientation. Hermann Schone. Tr. by Camilla Strausfeld. LC 84-42561. (Princeton Series in Neurobiology & Behavior). (Illus.). 368p. 1984. text ed. 61.00x (ISBN 0-691-08363-0); pap. 16.50x (ISBN 0-691-08364-9). Princeton U Pr.
Spatial Orientation: Theory, Research, & Application. Ed. by Herbert L. Pick & Linda P. Acredolo. 398p. 1983. 65.00x (ISBN 0-306-41255-1, Plenum Pr). Plenum Pub.
Spatial Patterns & Statistical Distributions see Statistical Ecology.
Spatial Perspectives on Industrial Organization & Decision-Making. Ed. by F. E. Hamilton. LC 73-14379. 533p. 1974. 83.95 (ISBN 0-471-34715-9, Pub. by Wiley-Interscience). Wiley.
Spatial Perspectives on Industrial Organization & Decision Making. Ed. by F. E. Hamilton. LC 73-14379. pap. 144.90 (2031757). Bks Demand UMI.
Spatial Perspectives on School Desegregation & Busing. J. Dennis Lord. Ed. by Salvatore J. Natoli. LC 76-57034. (Resource Papers for College Geography Ser.). (Illus.). 1977. pap. text ed. 5.00 (ISBN 0-89291-124-7). Assn Am Geographers.
Spatial Planning for Urban Development in Bangladesh. Charles L. Choguill. (Working Papers Ser.: No. 82-3). 27p. 1982. pap. 6.00 (ISBN 0-686-95384-3, CRD135, UNCRD). UNIPUB.
Spatial Policy Problems of the British Economy. Ed. by M. Chisholm & G. Manners. LC 70-160090. (Illus.). 1971. 39.50 (ISBN 0-521-08235-8). Cambridge U Pr.
Spatial Price Equilibrium: Advances in Theory, Computation & Application. P. T. Harker. (Lecture Notes in Economics & Mathematical Systems Ser.: Vol. 249). (Illus.). vii, 277p. 1985. pap. 22.50 (ISBN 0-387-15681-X). Springer-Verlag.
Spatial Price Theory of Imperfect Competition. Hiroshi Ohta. LC 87-22333. (Economic Ser.: No. 8). (Illus.). 254p. 1988. PLB 34.50x (ISBN 0-89096-372-X). Tex A&M Univ Pr.
Spatial Pricing & Differentiated Markets. George Norman. 185p. 1987. pap. text ed. 24.95 (ISBN 0-85086-121-7, 1161, Pub. by Pion England). Routledge Chapman & Hall.
Spatial Processes: Models & Applications. A. D. Cliff & J. K. Ord. 1980. 30.00x (ISBN 0-85086-081-4, NO.2225, Pub. by Pion). Routledge Chapman & Hall.
Spatial Regional & Population Economics. Ed. by Mark Perlman et al. 412p. 1972. 115.00 (ISBN 0-677-15020-2). Gordon & Breach.
Spatial Relationships. Fred Justus. (Early Education Ser.). 24p. (gr. k-1). 1981. wkbk. 5.00 (ISBN 0-8209-0221-7, K-23). ESP.
Spatial Representation & Behavior: Application & Theory Across the Life Span. Ed. by Lynn S. Liben et al. (Developmental Psychology Ser.). 1980. 39.95 (ISBN 0-12-447980-4). Acad Pr.
Spatial Representation & Spatial Interaction. I. Masser & P. J. B. Brown. (Studies in Applied Regional Science: Vol. 10). 1978. pap. 18.00 (ISBN 90-207-0717-5, Pub. by Martins Nijhoff Netherlands). Kluwer Academic.
Spatial Search: Applications to Planning Problems in the Public Sector. B. H. Massam. (Urban & Regional Planning Ser.: Vol. 23). 1983. pap. text ed. 29.00 (ISBN 0-08-030823-6). Pergamon.
Spatial Sector Programming Models in Agriculture. Earl O. Heady & Uma K. Srivastava. (Illus.). 484p. 1975. text ed. 17.95x (ISBN 0-8138-1575-4). Iowa St U Pr.
Spatial Statistics. Brian D. Ripley. LC 80-26104. (Probability & Mathematical Statistics Ser.). 252p. 1981. 41.95 (ISBN 0-471-08367-4). Wiley.
Spatial Statistics & Models. Gary L. Gaile & Cort J. Willmott. 1984. lib. bdg. 69.00 (ISBN 90-277-1618-8, Pub. by Reidel Holland). Kluwer Academic.
Spatial Strategies in Retailing. Risto Laulajainen. 1987. lib. bdg. 69.00 (ISBN 90-277-2595-0, Pub. by Reidel Holland). Kluwer Academic.
Spatial Structure & the Microcomputer: Selected Mathematical Techniques. A. N. Barrett & A. L. Mackay. (Computer Science Ser.). 218p. 1987. pap. 24.50x (ISBN 0-333-39284-1, Pub. by Macmillan England). Scholium Intl.
Spatial Structure of Administrative Systems. B. H. Massam. LC 75-185557. (CCG Resource Papers Ser.: No. 12). (Illus.). 1972. pap. text ed. 5.00 (ISBN 0-89291-059-3). Assn Am Geographers.
Spatial Structure of the Medical Care Process. Jerry B. Schneider. (Discussion Paper Ser.: No. 14). 1967. pap. 6.50 (ISBN 0-686-32183-9). Regional Sci Res Inst.
Spatial Structure of the Metropolitan Regions of Brazil. Yoon J. Lee. (Working Paper: No. 722). 40p. 1985. 3.50 (ISBN 0-8213-0509-3, WP 0722). World Bank.
Spatial Synthesis in Computer-Aided Building Design. Ed. by C. N. Eastman. (Illus.). 333p. 1975. 61.00 (ISBN 0-85334-611-9, Pub. by Elsevier Applied Sci England). Elsevier.
Spatial Theory of Voting: An Introduction. James M. Enelow & Melvin J. Hinich. LC 83-7758. 334p. 1984. 44.50 (ISBN 0-521-25507-4); pap. 15.95 (ISBN 0-521-27515-6). Cambridge U Pr.
Spatial Time Series Analysis-Forecasting-Control. R. J. Bennett. 674p. 1979. 87.50x (ISBN 0-85086-069-5, NO.2935, Pub. by Pion England). Routledge Chapman & Hall.
Spatial Urban Pattern & Growth of Urbanisation. Narayan Singh Vashistha. xix, 284p. 1986. text ed. 45.00x (ISBN 81-210-0035-1, Pub. by Inter India Pubns N Delhi). Apt Bks.
Spatial Variation. 2nd ed. B. Matern. (Lecture Notes in Statistics: Vol. 36). (Illus.). 155p. 1986. pap. 18.30 (ISBN 0-387-96365-0). Springer-Verlag.
Spatial Variation of Black Urban Households. David R. Meyer. LC 72-128466. (Research Papers Ser.: No. 129). 127p. 1970. pap. 12.00 (ISBN 0-89065-036-5). U Chicago Comm Geo.
Spatial Vision. Russell De Valois & Karen K. De Valois. (Oxford Psychology Ser.: Vol. 14). (Illus.). 412p. 1988. 69.00 (ISBN 0-19-505019-3). Oxford U Pr.
Spatiality of the Novel. Joseph A. Kestner. LC 78-14377. 230p. 1979. 22.50x (ISBN 0-8143-1612-3). Wayne St U Pr.
Spatially Oriented Behavior. Ed. by A. Hein & M. Jeanherod. (Illus.). 365p. 1983. 41.00 (ISBN 0-387-90789-0). Springer-Verlag.
Spatio-Temporal Coherence & Chaos in Physical Systems: Proceedings of a Workshop, Los Alamos Center for Nonlinear Studies, Los Alamos, NM, January 21-24, 1986. Ed. by A. R. Bishop et al. 500p. 1987. text ed. 58.00 (ISBN 0-444-87044-X, North Holland). Elsevier.
Spatiotemporal Consciousness in English & German Romanticism. Amala M. Hanke. (European University Studies: Series 18, Comparative Literature Vol. 25). 212p. 1981. pap. 21.60 (ISBN 3-261-04863-8). P Lang Pubs.
Spatmittelalterliche Geistliche Literatur in der Nationalsprache, Vol. 1. Ed. by James Hogg. (Analecta Cartusiana Ser.: No. 106/1). 236p. (Orig.). 1983. pap. 25.00 (ISBN 0-317-42595-1, Pub. by Salzburg Studies). Longwood Pub Group.
Spatmittelalterliche Geistliche Literatur in der Nationalsprache, Vol. 2. Ed. by James Hogg. (Analecta Cartusiana Ser.: No. 106/2). 190p. (Orig.). 1984. pap. 25.00 (ISBN 0-317-42596-X, Pub. by Salzburg Studies). Longwood Pub Group.
Spawn. Shaun Hutson. 368p. 1988. pap. 3.95 (ISBN 0-8439-2622-8, Pub. by Leisure Bks CT). Leisure NY.
Spawn of Dragonspear. Steve Perrin. LC 87-51259. (Advanced Dungeons & Dragons Gamebook Ser.: No. 17). (Illus.). 192p. (Orig.). (YA) (gr. 7-12). 1988. pap. 2.95 (ISBN 0-88038-570-7). TSR Inc.
Spawn of Hell. William Schoell. 400p. 1987. pap. 3.95 (ISBN 0-8439-2483-7, Leisure Bks). Leisure NY.
Spawning. Fritzen Ravenswood. (Orig.). 1981. pap. 2.95 (ISBN 0-89083-866-6). Zebra.
Spaziergange durch Cambridge. Frank A. Reeve. (Cambridge Town, Gown & County Ser.: Vol. 27). (Illus., Ger.). 1978. pap. 4.00 (ISBN 0-900891-44-0). Oleander Pr.
SPC Primer: Programmed Introduction to Statistical Process Control Techniques. Thomas Pyzdek. Orig. Title: Applied Industrial Statistics. (Orig.). 1985. pap. text ed. 14.95 (ISBN 0-930011-00-7). Quality Am.
SPC Simplified. Robert T. Amsden et al. (Illus.). 300p. 1986. pap. 16.95 (ISBN 0-317-59597-0, 12862-UPB140). UNIPUB-Kraus Intl.
SPE: Society of Petroleum Engineers Technical Papers, 2 Vols. Jean Hoornstra. 950p. 1986. 100.00 (ISBN 0-8357-0710-5, Pub. by Collections & Curr). Univ Microfilms.
Business Law: Bibliography of Books in the Harold F. Lusk Collection, Indiana University Business/SPEA Library. John D. Donnell. 40p. 1986. pap. 10.00 (ISBN 0-89028-760-0). Vance Biblios.
Speak & Get Results: Complete Guide to Presentations & Speeches That Work in Any Business Situation. Sandy Linver. 256p. 1983. 14.95 (ISBN 0-671-44204-X). Summit Bks.
Speak & Listen. Robert Bostrum. pap. text ed. write for info. Burgess MN Intl.
Speak Arabic: Script Version. Tim Francis. (Access to Arabic Ser.). Date not set. Incl. 2 tapes & video. 99.95x (ISBN 0-86685-427-4). Intl Bk Ctr.
Speak Arabic: Transliterated Version. Tim Francis. (Access to Arabic Ser.). Date not set. Incl. 2 tapes & video. 99.95x (ISBN 0-86685-428-2). Intl Bk Ctr.
Speak Cantonese, Bk. 1. rev. ed. Po-Fei Huang & Gerard P. Kok. 11.95 (ISBN 0-88710-094-5); tapes avail. (ISBN 0-88710-095-3). Yale Far Eastern Pubns.
Speak Cantonese, Bk. 2. Po-fei Huang. 11.95 (ISBN 0-88710-096-1); tapes avail. (ISBN 0-88710-097-X). Yale Far Eastern Pubns.
Speak Cantonese, Bk. 3. rev. ed. Po-Fei Huang. 10.95 (ISBN 0-88710-098-8); tapes avail. (ISBN 0-88710-099-6). Yale Far Eastern Pubns.
Speak Chinese. M. Gardner Tewksbury. 7.95 (ISBN 0-88710-100-3); tapes avail. (ISBN 0-88710-101-1). Yale Far Eastern Pubns.
Speak Chinese: Selections for Memorization. Linda Hsia & Y. C. Wang. 1.95 (ISBN 0-88710-102-X); tapes avail. (ISBN 0-88710-103-8). Yale Far Eastern Pubns.
Speak Chinese: Translation Exercises. 2.95 (ISBN 0-88710-106-2). Yale Far Eastern Pubns.
Speak Easy. 2nd ed ed. Brent D. Peterson et al. (Illus.). 280p. 1984. pap. text ed. 22.75 (ISBN 0-314-77783-0); instrs.' manual avail. (ISBN 0-314-77784-9). West Pub.
Speak Easy. Sarah Silverson & Jan Smith. 1982. with 3-4 inch Umatic Videocassettes 395.00x (ISBN 0-88432-113-4, V71109); with Betamax Videocassette 380.00x (ISBN 0-88432-114-2, V71110); with VHS videocassette 380.00x (ISBN 0-88432-115-0, V71111); tchr's. manual 3.50x (ISBN 0-88432-085-5). J Norton Pubs.
Speak Easy. Sarah K. Silverson et al. (Video Course Through Mime Sketches Ser.). (Orig.). 1984. pap. text ed. 7.95 (ISBN 0-582-79857-4); tchrs. ed. 4.95 (ISBN 0-582-79891-4); VHS Video 179.00 (ISBN 0-582-79836-1); Beta o.p. 380.00 (ISBN 0-582-79838-8); UMATIC o.p. 395.00 (ISBN 0-582-79837-X); cass. 34.95 (ISBN 0-582-79871-X). Longman.
Speak Easy: How to Talk Your Way to the Top. Sandy Linver. LC 78-10612. 222p. 1979. 8.95 (ISBN 0-671-40020-7). Summit Bks.
Speak Easy: How to Talk Your Way to the Top. Sandy Linver. 224p. 1988. pap. 7.95 (ISBN 0-671-67224-X). Summit Bks.
Speak Easy Phrase Guide. Carolyn M. Heard. pap. 4.95 (ISBN 0-686-45241-0). S&S.
Speak Easy: 101 Ways to Think on Your Feet Without Falling on Your Face. Charles Osgood. LC 87-28244. 128p. 1988. 14.95 (ISBN 0-688-06713-1). Morrow.
Speak English, Text 1. Joseph M. Coyle & Mary A. Corley. (Speak Eng. Ser.). (Illus.). 80p. (Orig.). 1980. pap. text ed. 4.95 (ISBN 0-8325-0501-3). Natl Textbk.
Speak English, Wkbk 1. Barbara Weitz. (Speak Eng. Ser.). (Illus.). 64p. (Orig.). 1980. wkbk. 4.95 (ISBN 0-8325-0502-1). Natl Textbk.
Speak English, Text 2. Mary Ann Corley & Betty Smallwood. (Speak English Ser.). (Illus.). 96p. (Orig.). 1981. pap. 4.95 (ISBN 0-8325-0506-4). Natl Textbk.
Speak English, Workbook 2. Mary Ann Corley & Betty Smallwood. (Speak English Ser.). (Illus.). 72p. (Orig.). 1981. pap. 4.95 (ISBN 0-8325-0507-2). Natl Textbk.
Speak English, Text 3. Mary Ann Corley & Charles Hancock. (Speak English Ser.). (Illus.). 80p. (Orig.). 1981. pap. text ed. 4.95 (ISBN 0-8325-0510-2). Natl Textbk.
Speak English, Workbook 3. Charles Hancock. (Speak English Ser.). (Illus.). 64p. (Orig.). 1981. pap. text ed. 4.95 (ISBN 0-8325-0511-0). Natl Textbk.
Speak English, Text 4. Barbara Izzo & Marie Keefe. (Speak English Ser.). (Illus.). 80p. (Orig.). 1983. pap. text ed. 4.95 (ISBN 0-8325-0514-5). Natl Textbk.
Speak English, Wkbk. 4. Lowry L. Taylor. (Speak English Ser.). (Illus.). 64p. (Orig.). 1983. pap. text ed. 4.95 (ISBN 0-8325-0515-3). Natl Textbk.
Speak English: A Practical Course for Foreign Students. Marie Durel. (Orig.). 1972. pap. 6.95 (ISBN 0-06-463320-9, EH 320, B&N Bks). Har-Row.
Speak English from the Heart. John R. Terry. (Special Advanced Course Ser.). 200p. 1982. pap. 7.50 (ISBN 0-933704-03-8). Dawn Pr.
Speak English from the Heart. 2nd ed. John R. Terry. (Intermediate Course Ser.). 220p. 1979. pap. 7.50 (ISBN 0-933704-13-5). Dawn Pr.
Speak English from the Heart. 3rd ed. John R. Terry. (Advanced Course Ser.). 250p. 1981. pap. 7.50 (ISBN 0-933704-17-8). Dawn Pr.
Speak English from the Heart. 7th ed. John R. Terry. (Elementary Course Ser.). 214p. 1979. pap. 7.50 (ISBN 0-933704-18-6). Dawn Pr.
Speak English from the Heart. 8th ed. John R. Terry. (Elementary Course Ser.). 216p. 1984. pap. 7.50 (ISBN 0-933704-49-6). Dawn Pr.
Speak English from the Heart. 4th ed. John R. Terry. (Intermediate Course Ser.). 220p. 1987. pap. 7.50 (ISBN 0-933704-62-3). Dawn Pr.
Speak for Success. Eugene Ehrlich. 288p. 1984. pap. 4.50 (ISBN 0-553-26494-X). Bantam.
Speak for the Dead. Margaret Yorke. 1988. 16.95 (ISBN 0-670-82403-8). Viking.
Speak for Yourself. 2nd ed. James H. Byrns. 329p. 1985. pap. text ed. write for info (ISBN 0-394-34099-X, RanC). Random.
Speak for Yourself. rev. ed. Jessica S. Driver. LC 55-11267. (Essentials of Speaking & Reading Aloud Ser.: No. 193-96). (Illus.). 245p. pap. 11.95 (ISBN 0-9614864-0-6). Speak Yourself.
Speak for Yourself, Bk. I. Ed. by Elizabeth A. Fein. 1985. pap. text ed. 10.95 (ISBN 0-88377-460-7); Bk. II. pap. text ed. 10.95 (ISBN 0-88377-282-5). Newbury Hse.
Speak for Yourself. Marilyn W. Wrasman & Diana B. Haag. Tr. by Constance Ring. (Illus.). 106p. pap. text ed. cancelled (ISBN 0-914296-57-4). Ed Activities.
Speak for Yourself: An Integrated Method of Voice & Speech Training. Julia Cummings-Wing. LC 83-26862. (Illus.). 272p. 1984. lib. bdg. 24.95x (ISBN 0-8304-1024-4); pap. text ed. 11.95x (ISBN 0-88229-827-5). Nelson-Hall.
Speak for Yourself-with Confidence. Elayne Snyder & Jane Field. (Illus.). 224p. 1983. pap. 7.95 (ISBN 0-452-25457-4, Plume). NAL.
Speak Freely: Conversational American English. Elliot Glass & Paul Arcario. 346p. 1985. pap. text ed. 10.00 net (ISBN 0-15-583171-2, HC). HarBraceJ.
Speak French to Your Baby. Therese Pirz. (Illus.). 1983. 14.95 (ISBN 0-9606140-0-1); pap. 11.95 (ISBN 0-9606140-1-X). Chou-Chou.
Speak into the Mirror: A Story of Linguistic Anthropology. John Doe. LC 88-236. 320p. (Orig.). 1988. lib. bdg. 29.50 (ISBN 0-8191-6943-9); pap. text ed. 16.50 (ISBN 0-8191-6944-7). U Pr of Amer.
Speak Italian to Your Baby. 152p. 1984. 14.95 (ISBN 0-9606140-4-4); pap. 11.95 (ISBN 0-9606140-5-2). Chou-Chou.
Speak Like a Pro: In Business & Public Speaking. Margaret Bedrosian. LC 86-15880. 212p. 1987. 19.95 (ISBN 0-471-84466-7); pap. 12.95 (ISBN 0-471-84467-5). Wiley.
Speak Like Rain. Frances Ottesen. 50p. (Orig.). 1986. pap. 6.00x (ISBN 0-9605220-1-8). Otafra.
Speak Lord; I Hear. 1988. pap. 4.95 (ISBN 0-914544-69-1). Living Flame Pr.
Speak Lord! Reflections on the Ordination Rite for Deacons. Steve Landregan. 52p. (Orig.). 1987. pap. 2.95 (ISBN 1-55586-150-4). US Catholic.
Speak, Lord, Your Servant Is Listening. rev., ed. David E. Rosage. 112p. 1987. pap. 3.50 (ISBN 0-89283-371-8). Servant.
Speak Mandarin. Henry Fenn et al. Ed. by M. Gardner Tewksbury. 238p. 1979. 145.00x (ISBN 0-88432-027-8, M201); cassettes incl. J Norton Pubs.
Speak Mandarin. Henry C. Fenn & M. Gardner Tewksbury. (Yale Linguistic Ser). 1967. pap. text ed. 15.95 (ISBN 0-300-00084-7); wkbk. 23.00x (ISBN 0-300-00454-0); 13.95x (ISBN 0-300-00085-5); teacher's manual, text ed. o.p. 10.00x (ISBN 0-300-00455-9). Yale U Pr.

Speaking Korean, Bk. I. Francis Y. Park. LC 84-80023. 489p. 1984. text ed. 34.50x (ISBN 0-930878-50-7). Hollym Intl.

Speaking Korean, Bk. II. Francis Y. Park. LC 84-80023. 559p. text ed. 34.50x (ISBN 0-930878-51-5). Hollym Intl.

Speaking Mexicano: The Dynamics of Syncretic Language in Central Mexico. Jane H. Hill & Kenneth C. Hill. LC 86-1370. 493p. 1986. 40.00x (ISBN 0-8165-0898-4). U of Ariz Pr.

Speaking Naturally: Communication Skills in American English. Ed. by Bruce Tillitt & Mary N. Bruder. (Illus.). 115p. 1985. pap. 6.95 (ISBN 0-521-27130-4); cassette 13.95 (ISBN 0-521-25007-2). Cambridge U Pr.

Speaking of Abraham Lincoln: The Man & His Meaning for Our Times. Richard N. Current. LC 83-3568. 208p. 1983. 17.50 (ISBN 0-252-01056-6). U of Ill Pr.

Speaking of Alternative Medicine: Accupuncture, the Needle That Heals All Ailments. Nilesh Baxi & C. H. Asrani. (Health & Cure Ser.). 1985. text ed. 17.95x (ISBN 0-86590-612-2, Pub. by Sterling Pubs India). Apt Bks.

Speaking of Apes: A Critical Anthology of Two-Way Communication with Man. Ed. by Thomas A. Sebeok & D. J. Umiker-Sebeok. LC 79-17714. (Illus.). 500p. 1980. 55.00x (ISBN 0-306-40279-3, Plenum Pr). Plenum Pub.

Speaking of Arts: A Giriama Impression. David Parkin. LC 82-70267. (First Annual Alan P. Merriam Lecture). 1982. pap. text ed. 5.00 (ISBN 0-941934-37-3). Indiana Africa.

Speaking Of: Ayurvedic Remedies for Common Diseases. T. L. Devaraj. 145p. 1985. 17.95. Asia Bk Corp.

Speaking of Ayurvedic Remedies for Common Diseases: Simple Remedies Based on Herbal Medicines. T. L. Devaraj. (Health & Cure Ser.). 1985. text ed. 17.95x (ISBN 0-317-19697-9, Pub. by Sterling Pubs India). Apt Bks.

Speaking of Cardinals. facs. ed. Thomas B. Morgan. LC 70-134119. (Essay Index Reprint Ser). 1946. 18.00 (ISBN 0-8369-2002-3). Ayer Co Pubs.

Speaking of Change: A Selection of Speeches & Articles. facsimile ed. Edward A. Filene. LC 76-156640. (Essay Index Reprint Ser). Repr. of 1939 ed. 22.00 (ISBN 0-8369-2355-3). Ayer Co Pubs.

Speaking of Chaucer. E. Talbert Donaldson. 190p. 1983. pap. 8.95x (ISBN 0-939464-15-2). Labyrinth Pr.

Speaking of Chinese. Raymond Chang & Margaret S. Chang. (Illus.). 1978. 12.95 (ISBN 0-393-04503-X). Norton.

Speaking of Chinese. Raymond Chang & Margaret S. Chang. (Illus.). 208p. 1983. pap. 6.95 (ISBN 0-393-30061-7). Norton.

Speaking of Employment: A Symposium Report on Disabled People in the Workplace. 9.00 (ISBN 0-318-17533-9); cass. 9.00. Mainstream DC.

Speaking of Ethnography. Michael H. Agar. (Qualitative Research Methods Ser.: Vol. 2). 96p. (Orig.). 1985. 12.50 (ISBN 0-8039-2561-1); pap. text ed. 6.00 (ISBN 0-8039-2492-5). Sage.

Speaking of Faith. Ed. by Diane Eck. 1986. 28.50X (ISBN 0-8364-1873-5, Pub. by Minerva India). South Asia Bks.

Speaking of Faith: Global Perspectives on Women, Religion & Social Change. Diana L. Eck & Devaki Jain. 288p. 1987. 29.95 (ISBN 0-86571-100-3); pap. 12.95 (ISBN 0-86571-101-1). New Soc Pubs.

Speaking of Finance. Kristy. 1987. write for info. (ISBN 0-471-09858-2). Wiley.

Speaking of Friends: The Variety of Man-to-Man Friendships. James Maas. (Illus.). 143p. (Orig.). 1985. pap. 7.95 (ISBN 0-915288-50-8). Shameless Hussy.

Speaking of Friendship: Middle-Class Women & Their Friends. Helen Gouldner. LC 86-29407. (Contributions in Women's Studies: No. 80). 196p. 1987. lib. bdg. 29.95 (ISBN 0-313-25068-5, GSF/). Greenwood.

Speaking of Gender. Ed. by Elaine Showalter. 256p. 1988. 29.95 (ISBN 0-415-90026-3); pap. 12.95 (ISBN 0-415-90027-1). Routledge Chapman & Hall.

Speaking of Home. facs. ed. Lillian W. Tryon. LC 77-86789. (Essay Index Reprint Ser). 1916. 14.00 (ISBN 0-8369-1198-9). Ayer Co Pubs.

Speaking Of: Homoeopathy. H. L. Chitkara. 72p. 1987. text ed. 17.95x (ISBN 81-207-0606-4, Pub. by Sterling Pubs India). Apt Bks.

Speaking of Horror: Interviews with Writers of Weird & Supernatural Literature. Darrell Schweitzer. LC 84-357. (Milford Series: Popular Writers of Today: Vol. 48, No. 2). 144p. (Orig.). 1989. lib. bdg. 16.95x (ISBN 0-89370-177-7); pap. text ed. 7.95x (ISBN 0-89370-277-3). Borgo Pr.

Speaking of Inalienable Rights, Amy. G. B. Trudeau. LC 75-29722. 1976. pap. 4.95 (ISBN 0-03-017221-7). H Holt & Co.

Speaking of Indians: With an Accent on the Southwest. Bernice Johnston. LC 72-134776. pap. 28.00 (ISBN 0-317-28049-X, 2025554). Bks Demand UMI.

Speaking of Jesus: Finding the Words for Witness. Richard Lischer. LC 81-70556. 144p. 1982. pap. 1.95 (ISBN 0-8006-1631-6, 1-1631). Fortress.

Speaking of Literature & Society. Lionel Trilling. Ed. by Diana Trilling. LC 80-7944. 448p. 1980. 17.95 (ISBN 0-15-184710-X). HarBraceJ.

Speaking of Love: Kierkegaard's Plan for Faith. C. Edward Deyton. LC 86-13187. 122p. (Orig.). 1986. lib. bdg. 20.75 (ISBN 0-8191-5503-9); pap. text ed. 9.25 (ISBN 0-8191-5504-7). U Pr of Amer.

Speaking of Maine: A Selection from the Writings of Virginia Chase. Virginia Chase. Ed. by Margaret Shea. (Illus.). 128p. (Orig.). 1983. pap. 8.95 (ISBN 0-89272-170-7). Down East.

Speaking of Man. Abraham Myerson. Ed. by Gerald N. Grob. LC 78-22577. (Historical Issues in Mental Health Ser.). 1979. Repr. of 1950 ed. lib. bdg. 21.00x (ISBN 0-405-11929-1). Ayer Co Pubs.

Speaking of My Life. Far West Editions Staff. 149p. 1979. pap. 4.95 (ISBN 0-686-47084-2). Far West Edns.

Speaking Of: Nature Cure. K. Lakshmana Sarma & S. Swaminathan. 230p. 1987. text ed. 27.95x (ISBN 81-207-0614-5, Pub. by Sterling Pubs India). Apt Bks.

Speaking of Numbers: Skillbuilding in English & Arithmetic Worktext 1. Daniel Rusthoi. (Illus.). (gr. 9-12). 1979. pap. text ed. 7.95 (ISBN 0-8325-0468-8); ans. key 2.00 (ISBN 0-8325-0469-6). Natl Textbk.

Speaking of Operations. Irvin S. Cobb. LC 71-92422. 65p. 1928. Repr. 19.00x (ISBN 0-403-00556-6). Scholarly.

Speaking of Pets. H. Miller. LC 58-13603. 9.95 (ISBN 0-8303-0031-7). Fleet.

Speaking of Pianists. 3rd ed. Abram Chasins. (Quality Paperback Ser.). x, 330p. 1982. pap. 9.95 (ISBN 0-306-80168-X). Da Capo.

Speaking of Science Fiction. Ed. by Paul Walker. (Illus.). 1978. 18.75x (ISBN 0-930346-02-5); pap. 6.95 (ISBN 0-930346-01-7). Luna Pubns.

Speaking of Science: Proceedings of the Royal Institution, Vol. 51. 176p. 1979. pap. 34.00x (ISBN 0-85066-186-2). Taylor & Francis.

Speaking of Science Seventy-Seven: Proceedings of the Royal Institution, Vol. 50. 300p. 1978. 32.00x (ISBN 0-85066-135-8). Taylor & Francis.

Speaking of Sex: Mothers & Daughters. Carol Kleiman & Catherine E. Kleiman. 230p. (YA) 1987. 14.95 (ISBN 0-933893-35-3). Bonus Books.

Speaking of Silence: Christians & Buddhists on the Contemplative Way. Ed. by Susan Walker. 336p. 1987. pap. 12.95 (ISBN 0-8091-2880-2). Paulist Pr.

Speaking of Siva. Tr. by A. K. Ramanujan. (Classics Ser.). 200p. 1973. pap. 5.95 (ISBN 0-14-044270-7). Penguin.

Speaking Of: Skin Care: Look Younger Be More Beautiful. Parvesh Handa. (Health & Cure Ser.). 1985. text ed. 17.95x (ISBN 0-86590-614-9, Pub. by Sterling Pubs India). Apt Bks.

Speaking of Snapdragons. Sheila Hayes. 144p. (gr. 5-9). 1982. 13.95 (ISBN 0-525-66785-7, 01063-320). Lodestar Bks.

Speaking of Soap Operas. Robert C. Allen. LC 84-21894. x, 246p. 1985. 27.50x (ISBN 0-8078-1643-4); pap. 9.95x (ISBN 0-8078-4129-3). U of NC Pr.

Speaking of Success. Ed. by Mary A. Warner. LC 87-63104. (Illus.). 64p. 1988. 5.95 (ISBN 0-88088-504-1). Peter Pauper.

Speaking of Survival. Daniel B. Freeman. (Illus.). 1982. pap. 6.95x (ISBN 0-19-503110-5); cassette 12.00x (ISBN 0-19-434105-4). Oxford U Pr.

Speaking of the Girls... Frances Weaver. 1986. pap. 5.95 (ISBN 0-9617930-1-5). Midlife Musings.

Speaking of the Middle Ages. Paul Zumthor. Tr. by Sarah White from Fr. LC 85-16545. (Regents Studies in Medieval Culture). xii, 102p. 1986. 13.50x (ISBN 0-8032-4907-1). U of Nebr Pr.

Speaking of Words: A Language Reader. 3rd ed. James MacKillop & Donna W. Cross. LC 81-6734. 336p. 1986. pap. text ed. 15.95 (ISBN 0-03-003953-3). HR&W.

Speaking on Issues. Ellen W. Echeverria. 240p. 1987. pap. text ed. write for info. (ISBN 0-03-003433-7). HR&W.

Speaking Out, Fighting Back: Personal Experiences of Women Who Survived Childhood Sexual Abuse in the Home. Vera Gallagher & William F. Dodds. LC 85-15491. 240p. (Orig.). 1987. pap. 8.95 (ISBN 0-88089-022-3). Madrona Pubs.

Speaking Out, Fighting Back: Personal Experiences of Women Who Survived Childhood Sexual Abuse in the Home. Sr. Vera Gallagher & William F. Dodds. LC 85-15491. 240p. 1985. 14.95 (ISBN 0-88089-010-X). Madrona Pubs.

Speaking Out for America's Children. Milton J. Senn. LC 76-49756. (Fastback Ser.: No. 17). 1977. 27.00x (ISBN 0-300-02107-0); pap. 9.95x (ISBN 0-300-02113-5). Yale U Pr.

Speaking Out for Psychiatry: A Handbook for Involvement with the Mass Media. Group for the Advancement of Psychiatry. LC 87-24229. (Gap Report Ser.: No. 124). 124p. 1987. 20.00 (ISBN 0-87630-488-9); pap. 13.95 (ISBN 0-87630-487-0). Brunner-Mazel.

Speaking Out on Health: An Anthology. Ed. by Literacy Volunteers of New York City Staff. (New Writers' Voices Ser.). 64p. (Orig.). 1988. pap. text ed. 2.95 (ISBN 0-929631-05-6). Lit Vols NYC.

Speaking Out: The Reagan Presidency from Inside the White House. Larry Speakes & Robert Pack. LC 88-3247. (Illus.). 320p. 1988. 19.95 (ISBN 0-684-18929-1). Scribner.

Speaking Personally: Quizzes & Questionnaires for Fluency Practice. Gillian P. Ladousse. 113p. 1983. pap. 6.95 (ISBN 0-521-28869-X). Cambridge U Pr.

Speaking Poetry. Geoffrey H. Crump. LC 76-23449. 1976. Repr. of 1953 ed. lib. bdg. 25.00 (ISBN 0-8414-3596-0). Folcroft.

Speaking, Relating & Learning. Stephen T. Boggs. LC 85-7388. 216p. 1986. text ed. 32.50 (ISBN 0-89391-330-8). Ablex Pub.

Speaking, Singing & Teaching: A Multidisciplinary Approach to Language Variation (Swallow VIII) Ed. by F. Barkin & E. Brandt. (No. 20). (Illus.). vi, 482p. 1980. 10.00. AZ Univ ARP.

Speaking the Gospel Through the Ages: A History of Evangelism. Milton L. Rudnick. 1984. 24.95 (ISBN 0-570-04204-6, 15-2172). Concordia.

Speaking the Gospel Today: A Theology for Evangelism. Robert A. Kolb. 1984. 16.95 (ISBN 0-570-04205-4, 15-2173). Concordia.

Speaking the Speech. 2nd ed. Edwin Cohen. 1983. pap. text ed. 15.95 (ISBN 0-03-062006-6). HR&W.

Speaking the Truth: Ecumenism, Liberation, & Black Theology. James H. Cone. 176p. (Orig.). 1986. pap. 8.95 (ISBN 0-8028-0226-5). Eerdmans.

Speaking to an Audience. Jerome Zolten & Gerald M. Phillips. 1985. pap. text ed. write for info. (ISBN 0-02-432020-X). Macmillan.

Speaking to an Audience: A Practical Method of Preparing & Performing. Jerome Zolten & Gerald M. Phillips. 352p. (Orig.). 1985. pap. text ed. 11.96 scp (ISBN 0-672-61626-2); scp instr's. guide 3.67 (ISBN 0-672-61627-0). Bobbs.

Speaking to Clio. Alberto Savinio. Tr. by John Shepley from Ital. LC 86-63743. 140p. 1987. 14.95 (ISBN 0-910395-22-5). Marlboro Pr.

Speaking to Clio. Alberto Savinio. Tr. by John Shepley from Ital. 140p. 1987. pap. 9.00 (ISBN 0-910395-23-3). Marlboro Pr.

Speaking to Communicate: An Introduction to Speech. Raymond L. Fischer. 145p. 1981. pap. text ed. 8.95x (ISBN 0-917974-77-8). Waveland Pr.

Speaking to Strangers. J. Day Mason. (Illus.). 105p. 1987. 40.00 (ISBN 0-933858-22-1). Kennebec River.

Speaking to Succeed in Business Industry Professions. Leon Fletcher. 368p. 1988. pap. text ed. 20.95 (ISBN 0-06-042099-5, HarpC). Har-Row.

Speaking to the Third World. Peter L. Berger & Michael Novak. 1985. pap. 7.00 (ISBN 0-8447-3581-7). Am Enterprise.

Speaking Tree: A Study of Indian Culture & Society. Richard Lannoy. 1971. 32.50x (ISBN 0-19-501469-3). Oxford U Pr.

Speaking Tree: A Study of Indian Culture & Society. Richard Lannoy. LC 74-158205. (Illus.). 1974. pap. 12.95 (ISBN 0-19-519754-2). Oxford U Pr.

Speaking Truth to Power. Aaron Wildavsky. 464p. 1987. pap. 19.95 (ISBN 0-88738-697-0). Transaction Bks.

Speaking Up. Bernard Levin. 1982. 32.00x (ISBN 0-686-44533-3, Pub. by Jonathan Cape). State Mutual Bk.

Speaking Up. Janet Stone & Jane Bachner. 1978. pap. text ed. 6.95 (ISBN 0-07-061674-4). McGraw.

Speaking up at Work. Catherine Robinson & Jenise Rowekamp. (Illus.). 180p. 1985. pap. 5.95x (ISBN 0-19-434196-8); tchr's. manual 2.95x (ISBN 0-19-434197-6). Oxford U Pr.

Speaking Well. 4th ed. Loren Reid. (Illus.). 448p. 1982. pap. 24.95x (ISBN 0-07-051784-3). McGraw.

Speaking Well of God. Edward Vick. LC 79-9336. (Anvil Ser.). 1979. pap. 8.95 (ISBN 0-8127-0245-X). Review & Herald.

Speaking with a Purpose. Arthur Koch. 176p. 1988. pap. text ed. price not set (ISBN 0-13-825878-3). P-H.

Speaking with an Audience. 2nd ed. John J. Makay. 128p. 1984. pap. text ed. 10.95 (ISBN 0-8403-2230-5). Kendall-Hunt.

Speaking with an Audience: Communicating Ideas & Attitudes. 3rd ed. John J. Makay. 144p. 1983. pap. text ed. 11.95 (ISBN 0-8403-3208-4, 40320801). Kendall-Hunt.

Speaking with Confidence & Skill. Lynne Kelly & Arden K. Watson. 224p. 1986. pap. text ed. 13.50 scp (ISBN 0-06-043627-1, HarpC). Har-Row.

Speaking with Deaf-Blind Children. Judy Katz-Levine. (Illus.). 20p. (Orig.). 1983. pap. 4.25 (ISBN 0-930707-00-1). Free Begin Pr.

Speaking with Style: The Socio-Linguistic Skills of Children. Elaine S. Andersen. 250p. 1985. 43.00 (ISBN 0-7099-0559-9, Pub. by Croom Helm Ltd). Routledge Chapman & Hall.

Speaking with Tongues: Historically & Psychologically Considered. George B. Cutten. 1927. 42.50x (ISBN 0-685-69805-X). Elliots Bks.

Speaking with Your Hands. Martin Sternberg & Lily Corbett. 1977. pap. 4.50 (ISBN 0-913072-29-X). Natl Assn Deaf.

Spear. James Herbert. (Orig.). 1980. pap. 2.50 (ISBN 0-451-09060-8, E9060, Sig). NAL.

Spear-Birds. Bernard Evslin. (Monsters of Mythology Ser.). (Illus.). 104p. Date not set. lib. bdg. 19.95x (ISBN 1-55546-259-5). Chelsea Hse.

Spear of Azzurra. Megan Stine & H. William Stine. Ed. by Stephanie Spinner. LC 85-19571. (Thundercats Thriller Series). (Illus.). 64p. (gr. 2-6). 1986. pap. 1.95 (ISBN 0-394-87879-5). Random.

Spear of Destiny. Leo Rutman. LC 87-46268. 272p. 1988. 17.95 (ISBN 1-55611-084-7). D I Fine.

Spear of Destiny: The Occult Power Behind the Spear Which Pierced the Side of Christ... & How Hitler Inverted the Force in a Bid to Conquer the World. Trevor Ravenscroft. LC 82-60165. 384p. 1982. pap. 9.95 (ISBN 0-87728-547-0). Weiser.

Spear of Mars. Reginald Bretnor. (Future at War Ser.: Vol. II). 320p. (Orig.). 1988. pap. 3.50 (ISBN 0-671-65423-3). Baen Bks.

Spearhead: A Novel. Peter Driscoll. 304p. 1989. 17.95 (ISBN 0-316-19341-0). Little.

Spearhead Governatore: Remembrances of the Campaign in Italy. William A. Lessa. LC 85-50821. (Illus.). 272p. 1985. 25.00x (ISBN 0-89003-163-0). Undena Pubns.

Spearhead: The World War History of the 5th Marine Division. 11th ed. Howard M. Conner. (Elite Unit Ser.). 325p. 1987. Repr. of 1950 ed. 35.00 (ISBN 0-89839-103-2). Battery Pr.

Spearheaders: A Personal History of Darby's Rangers. James Altieri. LC 79-18951. Repr. of 1960 ed. 19.95 (ISBN 0-89201-061-4). Zenger Pub.

Spearheads for Reform: The Social Settlements & the Progressive Movement, 1890 to 1914. Allen F. Davis. 340p. 1985. 27.00 (ISBN 0-8135-1072-4); pap. 12.00 (ISBN 0-8135-1073-2). Rutgers U Pr.

Spearless Leader: Senator Borah & the Progressive Movement in the 1920s. Leroy Ashby. LC 74-170963. 84.00 (ISBN 0-8357-9698-1, 2011733). Bks Demand UMI.

Spearmen of Arn. Del DowDell. 1978. pap. 1.75 (ISBN 0-505-51326-9, Pub. by Tower Bks). Leisure NY.

Spearplay. David Huey. LC 85-52271. 180p. (Orig.). 1986. pap. 7.95 (ISBN 0-86568-073-6, 220). Unique Pubns.

Spec Builder's Guide. Jack P. Jones. LC 84-1697. (Illus.). 448p. (Orig.). 1984. pap. 24.00 (ISBN 0-910460-38-8). Craftsman.

Spec Guide: The World's Largest Catalog of Renewable Energy & Building Energy Products. 9th ed. (Illus.). 1986. 49.50 (ISBN 0-317-57802-2). SolarVision.

Special Agent (FBI) Jack Rudman. (Career Examination Ser.: C-1060). (Cloth bdg. avail. on request). pap. 15.00 (ISBN 0-8373-1060-1). Natl Learning.

Special Agent (Wildlife) Jack Rudman. (Career Examination Ser.: C-2221). (Cloth bdg. avail. on request). pap. 14.00 (ISBN 0-8373-2221-9). Natl Learning.

Special & Medically Compromised Patients in Dentistry. John B. Thornton & John T. Wright. (Illus.). 320p. 1988. pap. write for info. (ISBN 0-88416-572-8). PSG Pub Co.

Special & Spurious Solutions of X(T) equals -aF(X(T-1), Vol. 310. Roger Nussbaum & Heinz O. Peitgen. LC 84-14568. (Memoirs of the American Mathematical Society: No. 310). 131p. 1984. pap. 15.00 (ISBN 0-8218-2311-6). Am Math.

Special Anniversary Issue: Highlights from the Past. (Special Issues of the Anthropology & Education Quarterly Ser.: Vol. 15, No. 1). 1984. 7.50 (ISBN 0-317-66343-7). Am Anthro Assn.

Special Applications in Piping Dynamic Analysis. Ed. by E. Van Stijgeren. (PVP Ser.: Vol. 67). 80p. 1982. 20.00 (H00224). ASME.

Special Artist's Handbook: Art Activities & Adaptive Aids for Handicapped Children. Susan Rodriguez. LC 84-4704. (Illus.). 288p. (Orig.). 1984. pap. 17.95x (ISBN 0-13-826355-8). P-H.

Special Assessments: A Study in Municipal Finance. Victor Rosewater. LC 68-56686. (Columbia University. Studies in the Social Sciences: No. 7). Repr. of 1898 ed. 16.50 (ISBN 0-404-51007-8). AMS Pr.

Special Assessments Procedures for Cities & Villages. Michigan Municipal League. (Ordinance Analysis: No. 11). 1986. write for info. MI Municipal.

Special Baby. Illus. by Carolyn Bracken. (Tuck-A-Toy Ser.). (Illus.). 7p. (ps). 1985. 3.95 (ISBN 0-8407-6665-3). Nelson.

Special Baby. (Baker Flip & Find Bks.). (Illus.). (ps-2). 1986. 2.95 (ISBN 0-8010-3531-7). Baker Bk.

Special Bibliography in Monetary Economics & Finance. J. Cohen. 214p. 1976. 108.00 (ISBN 0-677-00690-X). Gordon & Breach.

Special Branch: The Spy Novel from 1890 to 1980. LeRoy Panek. LC 81-80214. 21.95 (ISBN 0-87972-178-2); pap. 11.95 (ISBN 0-87972-179-0). Bowling Green.

Special Breed of Man. Ed Edell. (Illus.). 233p. 1984. pap. 3.95 (ISBN 0-934588-08-2). Ranger Assocs.

Special Care: Medical Decisions at the Beginning of Life. Fred M. Frohock. LC 85-31806. xiv, 264p. 1986. 19.95 (ISBN 0-226-26581-1). U of Chicago Pr.

Special Caste? Tamil Women of Sri Lanka. Else Skjonsberg. 160p. 1983. pap. 8.75 (ISBN 0-86232-071-2, Pub. by Zed Pr England). Humanities.

Special Forces Handbook: Guerilla Tactics, Demolition Techniques, Improvised Incendiaries, Air Ops, Unconventional Warfare, Survival Skills, Weapons & Communications. 1986. lib. bdg. 79.95 (ISBN 0-8490-3672-0). Gordon Pr.
Special Forces Operational Techniques, Dept of the Army Field Manual 31-20. (Illus.). 533p. 1965. pap. 16.95 (ISBN 0-87364-047-0). Paladin Pr.
Special Forces Operational Techniques: Unconventional Warfare, Counter Insurgency, Improvised Weapons, Intelligence, Logistics, Infiltration. 1986. lib. bdg. 79.95 (ISBN 0-8490-3673-9). Gordon Pr.
Special Foster Care: A History & Rationale. Bradford A. Bryant. (Orig.). 1980. pap. text ed. 4.50 (ISBN 0-9604068-0-8). People Places.
Special Friends. Peter Enns. (Stories That Live Ser.: No. II, Bk. II). (Illus.). 24p. (ps-5). 4.95 (ISBN 0-936215-22-4); cassette incl. STL Intl.
Special Friends of Jesus: New Testament Stories. Francine M. O'Connor. 64p. (ps-5). 1986. pap. 3.95 (ISBN 0-89243-255-1). Liguori Pubns.
Special Functions. Earl D. Rainville. LC 70-173380. (Illus.). xii, 365p. 1972. Repr. of 1960 ed. text ed. 19.95 (ISBN 0-8284-0258-2). Chelsea Pub.
Special Functions. Z. X. Wang & D. R. Guo. 800p. 1988. 92.00 (ISBN 9971-50-659-9); pap. 46.00 (ISBN 9971-50-667-X). World Scientific Pub.
Special Functions & Linear Representations of Lie Groups. Jean Dieudonne. LC 79-22180. (CBMS Regional Conference Ser. in Mathematics: No. 42). 59p. 1982. pap. 13.00 (ISBN 0-8218-1692-6, CBMS-42). Am Math.
Special Functions & the Theory of Group Representations. Rev. ed. N. Ja. Vilenkin. LC 68-19438. (Translations of Mathematical Monographs: Vol. 22). 613p. 1983. pap. 59.00 (ISBN 0-8218-1572-5, MMONO-22). Am Math.
Special Functions & Their Applications. rev. ed. N. N. Lebedev. Tr. by Richard A. Silverman from Rus. LC 72-86228. 320p. 1972. pap. 6.95 (ISBN 0-486-60624-4). Dover.
Special Functions & Their Approximations, 2 Vols. Yudell L. Luke. LC 68-23498. (Mathematics in Science & Engineering Ser.,: Vol. 53). 1969. Vol. 1. 79.50 (ISBN 0-12-459901-X); Vol. 2. 89.50 (ISBN 0-12-459902-8). Acad Pr.
Special Functions: Group Theoretical Aspects & Applications. Ed. by R. A. Askey et al. 1984. lib. bdg. 49.50 (ISBN 90-277-1822-9, Pub. by Reidel Holland). Kluwer Academic.
Special Functions in Queuing Theory: & Related Stochastic Processes. H. M. Srivastava & B. R. Kashyap. LC 81-17683. 1982. 51.00 (ISBN 0-12-660650-1). Acad Pr.
Special Functions of Applied Mathematics. Ed. by B. C. Carlson. 1977. 39.00 (ISBN 0-12-160150-1). Acad Pr.
Special Functions of Mathematical Physics. A. Nikiforov & V. Uvarov. 500p. 1987. 119.00 (ISBN 0-8176-3183-6). Birkhauser.
Special Functions, Probability Semigroups, & Hamiltonian Flows. P. J. Feinsilver. (Lecture Notes in Mathematics Ser.: Vol. 696). 1978. pap. 14.00 (ISBN 0-387-09100-9). Springer-Verlag.
Special Gift. Steve McKinstry. (Illus.). 32p. 1981. 6.95 (ISBN 0-910079-01-3). Lucy & Co.
Special Graduating Opportunities. Ed. by Alex Sandri-White. 8.50x (ISBN 0-685-22756-1). Aurea.
Special Guest Cookbook: Elegant Menus & Recipes for Those Who Are Allergic to Certain Foods, Bland Dieters, Calorie Counters, Cholesterol Conscious, Diabetic, Hypoglycemic, Kosher, Milk Sensitive, Pritikin Porselytes, Salt-Avoiding, Strictly Vegetarian. Arlene Eisenberg et al. LC 81-17106. 400p. 1982. 19.95 (ISBN 0-8253-0090-8). Beaufort Bks NY.
Special Guest for Mr. & Mrs. Bumba. Pearl A. Howard. (Mr. Bumba Bks.). 32p. (gr. k-3). 1983. Repr. of 1971 ed. 3.95 (ISBN 0-8225-0123-6). Lerner Pubns.
Special Holidays Handbook. Sandi Veranos et al. LC 85-24317. (Holiday Handbooks Ser.). (Illus.). 96p. 1986. lib. bdg. 12.95 (ISBN 0-89565-307-9). Childs World.
Special Horoscope Dimensions. Noel Tyl. LC 73-19924. (Principles & Practice of Astrology Ser.: Vol. 9). (Illus.). 206p. (Orig.). 1976. pap. 3.95 (ISBN 0-87542-808-8). Llewellyn Pubns.
Special Illumination: The Sufi Use of Humour. Idries Shah. 64p. 1977. 11.95 (ISBN 0-900860-57-X, Pub. by Octagon Pr England). Ins Study Human.
Special Index One: Annual Lists & General Index of the Parliamentary Papers Relating to the East Indies 1801-1907. (Bibliography on Parliamentary Papers Ser.). 248p. Repr. of 1909 ed. 91.00x (ISBN 0-7165-0411-1, BBA 03098, Pub. by Irish Academic Pr Ireland). Biblio Dist.
Special Infant: An Interdisciplinary Approach to the Optimal Development of Infants. Ed. by Jack M. Stack. LC 81-4478. 351p. 1982. 39.95x (ISBN 0-89885-028-2). Human Sci Pr.
Special Interest Groups in American Politics. Stephen Miller. LC 83-4691. 160p. 1983. 22.95 (ISBN 0-87855-485-8). Transaction Bks.
Special Interests & Policymaking: Agricultural Policies & Politics in Britain & The United States of America, 1956-70. Graham K. Wilson. LC 77-684. pap. 53.50 (ISBN 0-317-09612-5, 2022407). Bks Demand UMI.
Special Investigations Inspector. Jack Rudman. (Career Examination Ser.: C-748). (Cloth bdg. avail. on request). 14.00 (ISBN 0-8373-0748-1). Natl Learning.
Special Investigator. Jack Rudman. (Career Examination Ser.: C-1588). (Cloth bdg. avail. on request). pap. 14.00 (ISBN 0-8373-1588-3). Natl Learning.
Special Issue on the Centenary Perspective. 80p. 1977. 2.00 (ISBN 0-317-33902-8, 48-8). Central Conf.
Special Issue on the Liturgical Needs of Our Time. 133p. 2.00 (ISBN 0-317-33903-6, 65-8). Central Conf.
Special Issue on Universalism-Particularism. 136p. 1977. 2.75 (ISBN 0-317-33904-4, 51-8). Central Conf.
Special Issues in Nutrition. Ed. by Lucille S. Hurley. 96p. (Orig.). 1987. pap. 17.50 (ISBN 0-943029-00-7). Am Inst Nutrition.
Special Issues Index: Specialized Contents of Business, Industrial, & Consumer Journals. Compiled by Robert Sicignano & Doris Prichard. LC 82-11725. ix, 309p. 1982. lib. bdg. 39.95 (ISBN 0-313-23278-4, SII/). Greenwood.
Special Kind of Freedom. Fay D. Lindsay. (Illus.). 99p. (Orig.). 1982. pap. 7.00 (ISBN 0-943980-01-1). AIGA Pubns.
Special Kind of Love: Care for the Dying Child. Robert W. Buckingham. LC 82-22073. 192p. 1983. 12.95 (ISBN 0-8264-0229-1). Continuum.
Special Kind of Marrying. LC 80-67686. 120p. 1980. pap. 3.50 (ISBN 0-915388-09-X). Buckley Pubns.
Special Kind of Parenting: Meeting the Needs of Handicapped Children. Julia P. Good & Joyce G. Reis. LC 85-80903. (Illus.). 172p. 1985. pap. 8.95 (ISBN 0-912500-27-1). La Leche.
Special Kind of Woman. D. R. Franklin. 1985. 24.95x (ISBN 0-7090-2202-6, Pub. by R Hale Ltd UK). State Mutual Bk.
Special Lectures. International Congress of Phonetic Sciences, 9th, Copenhagen, 1979. Ed. by Fischer-Jorgensen. (Journal: Phonetica: Vol. 37, No. 1-2). (Illus.). 108p. 1980. pap. 22.00 (ISBN 3-8055-1414-X). S Karger.
Special Legacy: An Oral History of Soviet Jewish Emigres in the United States. Sylvia Rothchild. 1985. 17.95 (ISBN 0-671-47325-5). S&S.
Special Legacy: An Oral History of Soviet Jewish Emigres in the United States. Sylvia Rothchild. 336p. 1986. pap. 8.95 (ISBN 0-671-62817-8, Touchstone). S&S.
Special Legislation Affecting Public Schools. Uhlman S. Alexander. LC 78-176507. (Columbia University. Teachers College. Contributions to Education: No. 353). Repr. of 1929 ed. 22.50 (ISBN 0-404-55353-2). AMS Pr.
Special Librarian As a Supervisor or Middle Manager. 2nd ed. Martha J. Bailey. LC 86-3782. 176p. 1986. pap. text ed. 18.95 (ISBN 0-87111-315-5). SLA.
Special Librarianship: A New Reader. Ed. by Eugene B. Jackson. LC 80-11530. pap. 160.00 (ISBN 0-317-52031-8, 2027493). Bks Demand UMI.
Special Libraries: A Cumulative Index, 1971-1980. Compiled by Ron Coplen. 94p. 1982. pap. 18.75 (ISBN 0-87111-314-7). SLA.
Special Libraries: A Cumulative Index, 1981-1986. Compiled by Joyce Post. 40p. 1987. pap. 20.00 (ISBN 0-87111-327-9). SLA.
Special Libraries: A Guide for Management. 2nd, rev. ed. Janet L. Ahrensfeld et al. LC 86-1847. 85p. 1986. pap. text ed. 15.50 (ISBN 0-87111-318-X). SLA.
Special Libraries & Information Centers: An Introductory Text. Ellis Mount. LC 83-571. 200p. 1983. pap. text ed. 25.00 (ISBN 0-87111-282-5). SLA.
Special Libraries at Work. Elizabeth Ferguson & Emily R. Mobley. LC 83-25533. ix, 206p. 1984. 25.00 (ISBN 0-208-01939-1, Lib Prof Pubns); pap. 19.50x (ISBN 0-208-01938-3, Lib Prof Pubns). Shoe String.
Special Library Role in Networks: A Conference Held at the General Motors Research Laboratories, Warren, Michigan, May 5-6, 1980. Special Libraries Association. Ed. by Robert W. Gibson, Jr. LC 81-140531. pap. 76.50 (ISBN 0-317-30408-9, 2024959). Bks Demand UMI.
Special Lines. Patricia R. Herring. 37p. (Orig.). 1986. pap. 5.95 (ISBN 0-9616484-0-6). Santos Santos Pubns.
Special Love. Harriette S. Abels. 192p. 1987. pap. 2.50 (ISBN 0-425-10036-7, Pub. by Berkley-Pacer). Berkley Pub.
Special Magic: Computers, Classroom Strategies, & Exceptional Children. Mary Male. 304p. 1988. pap. text ed. 22.95 (ISBN 0-87484-761-3). Mayfield Pub.
Special Management Needs of Alpine Ecosystems. Ed. by D. Johnson. 100p. 4.50 (ISBN 0-318-16603-8). Soc Range Mgmt.
Special Materials. Ed. by H. H. Hausner et al. LC 66-5483. (Modern Developments in Powder Metallurgy: Vol. 14). 624p. 1981. 50.00 (ISBN 0-918404-53-3). Metal Powder.
Special Matrices & Their Applications in Numerical Mathematics. Miroslav Fiedler. 1986. lib. bdg. 84.00 (ISBN 90-247-2957-2, Pub. by Martinus Nijhoff Netherlands). Kluwer Academic.
Special Meditations for Health, Wealth, Love. Joseph Murphy. pap. 2.50 (ISBN 0-87516-336-X). DeVorss.
Special Messenger. Ruth A. LaVigne. 1978. 3.50 (ISBN 0-8198-0555-6); pap. 2.50 (ISBN 0-8198-0556-4). Dghtrs St Paul.
Special Methods in Light Microscopy, Vol. 17. Robert B. McLaughlin. LC 77-86749. (Illus.). 1977. 28.00 (ISBN 0-904962-06-7). Microscope Pubns.
Special Mexican Dishes. Amalia R. Clark. pap. 8.95x (ISBN 0-89741-010-6). Roadrunner Tech.
Special Ministers of the Eucharist. William J. Belford. 1979. pap. 1.95 (ISBN 0-916134-39-3). Pueblo Pub Co.
Special Ministries for Caring Churches. Compiled by Robert E. Korth. 128p. 1986. pap. 5.95 (ISBN 0-87403-145-1, 3183). Standard Pub.
Special Museums of the Northeast: A Guide to Uncommon Collections from Maine to Washington, DC. Nancy Frazier. LC 85-8027. (Illus.). 288p. (Orig.). 1985. pap. 9.95 (ISBN 0-87106-869-9). Globe Pequot.
Special National Procedures Concerning Non-Discrimination in Employment with Particular Reference to the Private Sector: A Practical Guide. 2nd ed. 1981. 10.50 (ISBN 92-2-100199-7). Intl Labour Office.
Special Needs & Services. Ed. by Stevanne Auerbach. LC 74-28029. (A Comprehensive Guide Child Care Guide Ser.: Vol. IV). 256p. 1979. text ed. 29.95 (ISBN 0-87705-349-9). Human Sci Pr.
Special Needs: Bridging the Curriculum Gap. Jonathan Solity & Shirley Bull. 272p. 1987. 65.00x (ISBN 0-335-10282-4, Open Univ Pr.); pap. 24.00x (ISBN 0-335-10281-6). Taylor & Francis.
Special Needs in Ordinary Schools: A Teacher's Guide. Neville J. Jones. 1988. 29.50 (ISBN 0-7130-0182-8, Pub. by Woburn Pr England). Biblio Dist.
Special Needs in Technology Education. Martin Kimeldorf. LC 83-71907. (Illus.). 279p. 1984. text ed. 11.95. Davis Mass.
Special Needs: Special Answers. Lillie Pope et al. (Illus.). (gr. k-6). 1979. 15.95 (ISBN 0-87594-181-8). Book-Lab.
Special Needs Student in Vocational Education: Selected Readings. Ed. by Stanley J. Urban. 1974. text ed. 9.50x (ISBN 0-8422-5155-3); pap. text ed. 7.50x (ISBN 0-8422-0378-8). Irvington.
Special Occasion Cake Decorating. Vi Wittington. (Illus.). 80p. (Orig.). 1984. pap. 4.95 (ISBN 0-8249-3028-2). Ideals.
Special Occasion Desserts. Bon Appetit Magazine Editors. LC 85-14659. (Bon Appetit Ser.). (Illus.). 144p. 12.95 (ISBN 0-89535-170-6). Knapp Pr.
Special Occasions. Teresa Nelson. (Illus.). 28p. 1985. pap. 4.95 (ISBN 0-933491-02-6). Hot Off Pr.
Special Occasions: Holiday Entertaining All Year Round. John Hadamuscin. 1988. 22.50 (ISBN 0-517-57005-X, Harmony). Crown.
Special Offer. Jerry Bumpus. LC 80-20671. 1981. pap. 5.95x (ISBN 0-914140-08-6). Carpenter Pr.
Special Officer. Jack Rudman. (Career Examination Ser.: C-749). (Cloth bdg. avail. on request). pap. 12.00 (ISBN 0-8373-0749-X). Natl Learning.
Special Officer-Senior Special Officer-Bridge & Tunnel Officer. 3rd ed. Ed. by Hy Hammer. LC 83-3701. (Illus.). 192p. (Orig.). 1983. pap. 8.00 (ISBN 0-668-05614-2, 5614). Arco.
Special Olympics. Ed. by Robert Cipriano. (Special Education Ser.). (Illus., Orig.). 1980. pap. 16.00 (ISBN 0-89568-111-0). Spec Learn Corp.
Special Operations: AAF Aid to European Resistance Movements 1943-45. Harris G. Warren. 269p. 1947. pap. text ed. 27.00x (ISBN 0-89126-020-X). MA-AH Pub.
Special Operations in United States Strategy. Ed. by Frank R. Barnett et al. LC 84-601134. 329p. 1984. pap. 4.25 (ISBN 0-318-20149-6, S/N 008-020-01011-1). USGPO.
Special Optical Effects. Zoran Perisic. LC 80-41005. (Illus.). 1981. text ed. 42.95 (ISBN 0-240-51007-0). Focal Pr.
Special Paper Number Three. 319p. 1970. 24.00. Mineralogical Soc.
Special Parents: Birth & Early Years. Barbara Furneaux. (Children with Special Needs Ser.). 1988. 52.00x (ISBN 0-335-15123-X, Open Univ Pr); pap. 19.00x (ISBN 0-335-15122-1, Open Univ Pr). Taylor & Francis.
Special People. Burt Hirschfeld. Date not set. price not set. Maxim Bks.
Special People... Getting to Know Them: Resources in Mental Retardation. 1.00 (ISBN 0-686-70272-7). Boston Public Lib.
Special Physical Education. 5th ed. Hollis Fait & John M. Dunn. 576p. 1984. text ed. write for info. (ISBN 0-697-05987-1). Wm C Brown.
Special Picture Cookbook. Freida R. Steed. 108p. 1977. pap. 16.00x (ISBN 0-89079-010-8, 1056). Pro Ed.
Special Place: A Child's Story about Entering Counseling for Children Ages 4 Through 6. Diana L. McCoy. (Illus.). 24p. (Orig.). (ps-1). 1988. pap. 5.50 (ISBN 0-9619250-2-7). Magic Lantrn.
Special Place: A Child's Story about Entering Counseling for Children Ages 7 Through 10. Diana L. McCoy. (Illus.). 32p. (gr. 2-5). 1988. pap. text ed. 5.50 (ISBN 0-9619250-3-5). Magic Lantrn.
Special Places: In Northern California, Oregon, Washington, British Columbia, Idaho & Montana. 3rd ed. Fred Nystrom & Mardi Murvin. LC 87-82767. (Illus.). 240p. 1988. 13.95 (ISBN 0-932575-61-7). GR Arts Ctr Pub.
Special Plays for Holidays. Helen L. Miller. LC 86-9332. (Orig.). (gr. 1-6). 1986. pap. 10.95 (ISBN 0-8238-0275-2). Plays.
Special Prayers. A. Dellinger & S. Fletcher. (ps-3). pap. 0.59 (ISBN 0-570-08315-X, 56HH1447). Concordia.
Special Problems. 1978. 2.00. Am Law Inst.
Special Problems in Child & Adolescent Behavior: A Social & Behavioral Approach. Ed. by Larry E. Beutler & Richard Greene. LC 78-56115. 1978. 14.95 (ISBN 0-87762-253-1). Technomic.
Special Problems in Prosecution see Roles & Functions of the Prosecutor.
Special Problems in the Study of Sufi Ideas. Idries Shah. 45p. 1978. pap. 5.95 (ISBN 0-900860-21-9, Pub by Octagon Pr England). Ins Study Human.
Special Problems of Multiemployer Plans. Paul S. Berger & Stephen L. Hester. (Kinds of Qualified Plans). 45p. 1978. pap. 2.00 (ISBN 0-317-31072-0, B333). Am Law Inst.
Special Problems of Negro Education. Doxey A. Wilkerson. LC 76-82097. (Illus.). Repr. of 1939 ed. 35.00x (ISBN 0-8371-3210-X, WIN&, Pub. by Negro U Pr). Greenwood.
Special Procedures for Testing Soil & Rock for Engineering Purposes. 5th ed. American Society for Testing & Materials Staff. LC 70-114701. (ASTM Special Technical Publication Ser.: No. 479). pap. 160.00 (ISBN 0-317-55525-1, 2056329). Bks Demand UMI.
Special Procedures for Testing Soil & Rock for Engineering Purposes- STP 479. 630p. 1970. 15.75 (ISBN 0-8031-0051-5, 04-479000-38). ASTM.
Special Procedures in Chest Radiology. Stuart S. Sagel. LC 75-19855. (Saunders Monographs in Clinical Radiology: Vol. 8). pap. 44.70 (ISBN 0-317-08662-6, 2016680). Bks Demand UMI.
Special Processing: Mapcon IV Multiprocessor & Array Processor Conference. Ed. by Howard L. Johnson. (Illus.). 136p. (Orig.). 1988. pap. 28.00x (ISBN 0-911801-31-6). Soc Computer Sim.
Special Projects Coordinator. Jack Rudman. (Career Examination Ser.: C-2933). (Cloth bdg. avail. on request). pap. 16.00 (ISBN 0-8373-2933-7). Natl Learning.
Special Purpose Computers. Ed. by Berni J. Alder. (Computational Techniques Ser.). 200p. 1988. price not set (ISBN 0-12-049260-1). Acad Pr.
Special Purpose Rooms. LC 80-19808. (Home Repair & Improvement Ser.). (gr. 7 up). lib. bdg. 15.94 (ISBN 0-8094-3459-8, Pub. by Time-Life). Silver.
Special Purpose Rooms. Time-Life Books Editors. (Home Repair & Improvement Ser.). (Illus.). 128p. 1981. 11.95 (ISBN 0-8094-3458-X). Time-Life.
Special-Purpose Steam Turbines for Refinery Services. 3rd ed. 1987. 25.00. Am Petroleum.
Special Reading Problems: Some Helps Training Module-Trainer's Guide. rev. ed. Susanne Miller. 32p. 1983. 140 slides, cassette tapes 132.00 (ISBN 0-930713-47-8). Lit Vol Am.
Special Reading Problems Some Helps Tutor Notes. Susanne Miller. 9p. 1983. 2.00 (ISBN 0-930713-25-7). Lit Vol Am.
Special Readings in Conservation. (Conservation Guides: No. 4). 112p. (Eng., Fr. & Span.). 1978. pap. 8.50 (ISBN 92-5-100615-6, F1508, FAO). UNIPUB.
Special Recipes for Special People. David Lurio. LC 82-60769. (Illus.). 70p. 1982. 9.95 (ISBN 0-910423-00-8). Skylight.
Special Recreation: Persons with Disabilities. Dan Kennedy et al. 381p. 1987. text ed. write for info. (ISBN 0-697-06142-6). Wm C Brown.
Special Recreational Services Therapeutic & Adapted. Jay S. Shivers & Hollis F. Fait. LC 84-14329. (Illus.). 354p. 1985. text ed. 24.00 (ISBN 0-8121-0964-3). Lea & Febiger.
Special Relationship. David Gentleman. (Illus.). 64p. 1987. pap. 10.95 (ISBN 0-571-14992-8). Faber & Faber.
Special Relationship: Anglo-American Relations since 1945. Ed. by W. Roger Louis & Hedley Bull. LC 86-8472. 408p. 1987. 59.00 (ISBN 0-19-822925-9). Oxford U Pr.
Special Relationship Between W. Germany & Israel. Lily G. Feldman. 352p. 1984. text ed. 39.95x (ISBN 0-04-327068-9). Unwin Hyman.
Special Relationships: A Foreign Correspondent's Memoirs from Roosevelt to Reagan. Henry Brandon. (Illus.). 432p. 1988. 19.95 (ISBN 0-689-11588-1). Atheneum.
Special Relativity. W. G. Dixon. LC 77-83991. (Illus.). 1978. 57.50 (ISBN 0-521-21871-3). Cambridge U Pr.
Special Relativity. French. 1971. pap. 33.95 (ISBN 0-442-30782-9). Van Nos Reinhold.
Special Relativity. Anthony P. French. (M. I. T. Introductory Physics Ser). 1968. pap. 10.95x (ISBN 0-393-09793-5). Norton.
Special Relativity for Physicists. G. Stephenson & C. W. Kilmister. (Illus.). 108p. 1987. pap. text ed. 3.95 (ISBN 0-486-65519-9). Dover.

Special Relativity: The Foundation of Macroscopic Physics. W. G. Dixon. LC 77-83991. (Illus.). 261p. 1982. pap. 24.95 (ISBN 0-521-27241-6). Cambridge U Pr.

Special Report: California School Adminstrators Facts & Myths. Association of California School Adminstrators. 1987. pap. text ed. 3.50 (ISBN 0-943397-03-0). Assn Calif Sch Admin.

Special Report Collection, Nineteen Seventy-Nine to Date. Robert R. Prechter, Jr. 98p. 1987. 39.00 (ISBN 0-932750-09-5). New Classics Lib.

Special Report Financial & Economic Data of the Men's & Boys' Clothing Industry. 25p. 1975. 7.00 (ISBN 0-318-19682-4). Clothing Mfrs.

Special Report of the Director-General on the Application of the Declaration Concerning the Policy of Apartheid in South Africa. ILO International Labour Conference, 71st Session, 1985. 209p. 1985. pap. 19.25 (ISBN 92-2-103721-5, ILO459, ILO). UNIPUB.

Special Report of the Director-General on the Application of the Declaration Concerning the Policy of Apartheid in South Africa: International Labour Conference, 72nd Session, 1986. ILO Staff. iv, 186p. (Orig.). 1986. pap. 17.50 (ISBN 92-2-105167-6). Intl Labour Office.

Special Report on Financial & Economic Data of the Men's & Boys' Clothing Industry. 24p. 1977. 7.00 (ISBN 0-318-19686-7). Clothing Mfrs.

Special Report on Financial & Economic Data of the Men's Clothings Industry. 24p. 1979. 7.00 (ISBN 0-318-19695-6). Clothing Mfrs.

Special Report on Financial & Economic Data of the Men's & Boys' Clothing Industry. 18p. 1980. 7.00 (ISBN 0-318-19696-4). Clothing Mfrs.

Special Report on Florida Law: Independent Contractor vs. Employee. James R. Urquhart, III. 26p. (Orig.). 1987. pap. text ed. 14.95 (ISBN 0-942496-05-1). Fidelity Pub.

Special Report on New York State Law: Independent Contractor vs. Employee. James R. Urquhart. 30p. (Orig.). 1987. pap. text ed. 14.95 (ISBN 0-942496-07-8). Fidelity Pub.

Special Report on Spouse Abuse in Texas. James S. Stachura & Raymond H. Teske, Jr. 18p. 1979. 2.00 (ISBN 0-318-02508-6). S Houston Employ.

Special Report on Surnames in Ireland, Together with Varieties & Synonymes of Surnames & Christian Names in Ireland, 2 vols. in 1. Robert E. Matheson. 172p. 1988. Repr. of 1909 ed. 15.00 (3830). Genealog Pub.

Special Report on Surnames in Ireland: Varieties & Synonymes of Surnames & Christian Names in Ireland, 2 Vols. in 1. Robert E. Matheson. LC 68-54684. 172p. 1982. Repr. of 1901 ed. 14.00 (ISBN 0-8063-0187-2). Genealog Pub.

Special Report on the Pollution of River Waters. James P. Kirkwood. LC 75-125750. (American Environmental Studies). (Illus.). 1970. Repr. of 1876 ed. 24.00 (ISBN 0-405-02676-5). Ayer Co Pubs.

Special Reports on American Broadcasting, 1932-1947. Ed. by Christopher H. Sterling. LC 74-7682. (Telecommunications Ser). 1974. Repr. of 1974 ed. 52.00x (ISBN 0-405-06059-9). Ayer Co Pubs.

Special Reports on Educational Subjects, 28 vols. Office of Special Inquiries & Reports. (Incl. 2 suppls.). Repr. of 1914 ed. Set. 1850.00 (ISBN 0-384-57015-1). Johnson Repr.

Special Research Methods for Gerontology. Ed. by M. P. Lawton & A. R. Herzog. (Society & Aging Ser.: Vol. 2). Date not set. price not set (ISBN 0-89503-053-5). Baywood Pub.

Special Rigger. Jack Rudman. (Career Examination Ser.: C-750). (Cloth bdg. avail. on request). pap. 14.00 (ISBN 0-8373-0750-3). Natl Learning.

Special Santas. Mary A. Farmer. (Illus.). 14p. 1981. pap. 4.00 (ISBN 0-943574-08-0). That Patchwork.

Special Sections & Promotions. Arold A. DeLuca. (Illus.). 48p. 1981. pap. 5.00 (ISBN 0-317-17222-0). Dynamo Inc.

Special Senses. 2nd ed. George J. McKenzie et al. (Penguin Library of Nursing Ser.). (Illus.). 215p. (Orig.). 1986. pap. text ed. 17.00 (ISBN 0-443-03081-2). Churchill.

Special Senses see Anatomy & Physiology: A Programmed Approach.

Special Sermons by George Sweeting. George Sweeting. 1985. pap. 14.95 (ISBN 0-8024-8211-2). Moody.

Special Services in Hospitals: Monographs. Mary Vance. (Public Administration Ser.: P 1678). 17p. 1985. 2.25 (ISBN 0-89028-408-3). Vance Biblios.

Special Services Manager. Jack Rudman. (Career Examination Ser.: C-2147). (Cloth bdg. avail. on request). 1988. pap. 16.00 (ISBN 0-8373-2147-6). Natl Learning.

Special Session on New & Promising Developments in the Entire Field of Irrigation, Drainage and Flood Control: Proceedings, Special Session, New Delhi, 6 papers. 96p. 1966. 6.50 (ISBN 0-318-16975-4); members 2.50 (ISBN 0-318-16976-2). US Comm Irrigation.

Special Sessions Convened in February 1892 (for 1893) & Convened in June 1893 see Laws of the Choctaw Nation Passed at the Regular Session of the General Council Convened at Tushka Humma, October 1892 & Adjourned November 4, 1892.

Special Sign Hanger. Jack Rudman. (Career Examination Ser.: C-751). (Cloth bdg. avail. on request). pap. 14.00 (ISBN 0-8373-0751-1). Natl Learning.

Special Signs of Grace: The Seven Sacraments & Sacramentals. Joseph Champlin. (Illus.). 160p. 1986. pap. 6.95 (ISBN 0-8146-1466-3). Liturgical Pr.

Special Sisters: Woman in the European Middle Ages. 4th ed. Arthur F. Ide. LC 82-23352. (Woman in History Ser.: Vol. 12b). (Illus.). 115p. 1983. lib. bdg. 10.95 (ISBN 0-86663-097-X); pap. text ed. 2.95 (ISBN 0-86663-096-1). Ide Hse.

Special Statistical Report on Profit, Sales & Production Trends for the Men's & Boys' Tailored Clothing Industry. 12p. 1982. 15.00 (ISBN 0-318-19697-2). Clothing Mfrs.

Special Statistical Report on Profit, Sales, Production & Marketing Trends for the Men's & Boys' Tailored Clothing Industry. 15p. 1983. 15.00 (ISBN 0-318-19698-0). Clothing Mfrs.

Special Strengths. Gail Radley. (Illus.). 64p. (gr. 2-6). 1984. pap. 5.95 (ISBN 0-87743-702-5, Pub. by Bellwood Pr). Baha'i.

Special Study of Securities Markets: Report, Pts. 1-6. U. S. Securities & Exchange Commission. LC 63-61766. 1982. Repr. of 1963 ed. Set. lib. bdg. 175.00 (ISBN 0-89941-227-0). W S Hein.

Special Study of the Incidence of Retardation. L. B. Blan. LC 79-176569. (Columbia University. Teachers College. Contributions to Education: No. 40). Repr. of 1911 ed. 22.50 (ISBN 0-404-55040-1). AMS Pr.

Special Subunit. Vadim Kozhenikov. Tr. by Jan Butler. 493p. 1983. pap. 4.00 (ISBN 0-8285-2577-3, Pub. by Raduga Pubs USSR). Imported Pubns.

Special Survey Report: Child Care Assistance Programs. 16p. 1987. 30.00 (ISBN 0-87179-978-2). BNA.

Special Survey Report: Employee Expense Reimbursement Rates. 1988. 30.00 (ISBN 0-87179-979-0). BNA.

Special Survey Report: Nineteen Eighty-Seven Year-End Holiday Practices. 1987. 30.00. BNA.

Special Teachers-Special Boys. Peter Fisher & Marc Rubin. LC 78-19417. 1979. pap. 4.95 (ISBN 0-312-75152-4). St Martin.

Special Teams: Raiders-Cowboys. Ken Rappoport. 192p. 1982. pap. 2.25. Ace Bks.

Special Techniques in Internal Fixation. C. F. Brunner & B. G. Waber. (Illus.). 198p. 1981. 84.00 (ISBN 0-387-11056-9). Springer-Verlag.

Special Techniques of Applied Kinesiology. Clifford S. Garner. (Illus.). viii, 55p. (Orig.). 1983. pap. 11.95 (ISBN 0-9612808-0-8). C S Garner.

Special Tests of Visual Function. Ed. by E. Zrenner. (Developments in Ophthalmology Ser.: Vol. 9). (Illus.). xii, 240p. 1984. 99.50 (ISBN 3-8055-3885-5). S Karger.

Special Theory of Relativity. J. Aharoni. (Physics Ser.). 331p. 1985. pap. 8.00 (ISBN 0-486-64870-2). Dover.

Special Theory of Relativity. V. A. Ugarov. 406p. 1979. 11.25 (Pub. by Mir Pubs USSR). Imported Pubns.

Special Theory of Relativity: It"s Origin, Meanings, & Implications. D. Bohm. 1979. text ed. write for info. (ISBN 0-8053-1001-0, Adv Bk Prog MSP). Addison-Wesley.

Special Things for Special Days. Pat Short & Billie Davidson. 1980. pap. 10.95 (ISBN 0-673-16432-2). Scott F.

Special Ticketing. Barbara A. Krygel. (Ticketing Ser.: No. 2). (Illus.). 50p. 1983. pap. text ed. 12.95x (ISBN 0-917063-01-5); of 3 bks. 24.95x set. Travel Text.

Special Times for Parents & Kids Together. Lisa L. Durkin. 176p. (Orig.). 1987. pap. 8.95 (ISBN 0-446-38680-4). Warner Bks.

Special Times with God. David Shibley & Naomi Shibley. LC 81-14116. 160p. (ps). 1981. 5.95 (ISBN 0-8407-5780-8). Nelson.

Special Topics in Carcinogenesis. Ed. by E. Grundmann. LC 73-11951. (Recent Results in Cancer Research: Vol. 44). (Illus.). 220p. 1974. 44.00 (ISBN 0-387-06460-5). Springer-Verlag.

Special Topics in Electrochemistry. P. A. Rock. 224p. 1977. 89.50 (ISBN 0-444-41627-7). Elsevier.

Special Topics in Endocrinology & Metabolism, Vol. 1. Ed. by Margo P. Cohen & Piero P. Foa. 154p. 1979. 25.00x (ISBN 0-8451-0700-3). A R Liss.

Special Topics in Endocrinology & Metabolism, Vol. 2. Ed. by Margo P. Cohen & Piero P. Foa. 174p. 1981. 27.00 (ISBN 0-8451-0701-1). A R Liss.

Special Topics in Endocrinology & Metabolism, Vol. 3. Ed. by Margo P Cohen & Piero P. Foa. (Special Topics in Endocrinology & Metabolism Ser.). 142p. 1982. 31.00 (ISBN 0-8451-0702-X). A R Liss.

Special Topics in Endocrinology & Metabolism, Vol. 4. Ed. by Margo P. Cohen & Piero P. Foa. (Special Topics in Endocrinology & Metabolism). 270p. 1982. 42.00 (ISBN 0-8451-0703-8). A R Liss.

Special Topics in Endocrinology & Metabolism, Vol. 5. Ed. by Margo P. Cohen & Piero P. Foa. 310p. 1983. 53.00 (ISBN 0-8451-0704-6, 0704). A R Liss.

Special Topics in Endocrinology & Metabolism, Vol. 6. Margo P. Cohen & Piero P. Foa. 274p. 1984. 64.00 (ISBN 0-8451-0705-4). A R Liss.

Special Topics in Endocrinology & Metabolism, Vol. 7. Margo P. Cohen & Piero P. Foa. 298p. 1985. 56.00 (ISBN 0-8451-0706-2). A R Liss.

Special Topics in Fluid Dynamics. K. O. Friedrichs. (Notes on Mathematics & Its Applications Ser.). 190p. 1966. pap. 36.00 (ISBN 0-677-01005-2). Gordon & Breach.

Special Topics in Foundations. Ed. by Braja M. Das. (Sessions Proceedings Ser.). 136p. 1988. 16.00 (ISBN 0-87262-645-8). Am Soc Civil Eng.

Special Topics in Heterocyclic Chemistry. Ed. by Arnold Weissberger & Edward Taylor. LC 76-10672. (Chemistry of Heterocyclic Compounds Ser.: Vol. 30). 616p. 1977. 85.00 (ISBN 0-471-67253-X, JW). Krieger.

Special Topics in Statistics for the Behavioral Sciences. Randy Wilcox. 416p. 1987. 36.00 (ISBN 0-89859-936-9). L Erlbaum Assocs.

Special Topics in Topological Algebras. A. Guichardet. (Notes on Mathematics & Its Applications Ser.). 202p. (Orig.). 1968. 50.00 (ISBN 0-677-30010-7). Gordon & Breach.

Special Topics of Applied Mathematics: Functional Analysis, Numerical Analysis & Optimization. J. Frehse & D. Pallaschke. 248p. 1980. 89.50 (ISBN 0-444-86035-5, North-Holland). Elsevier.

Special Topics of Elementary Mathematics see History of Mathematics.

Special Trade. Sally Wittman. LC 77-25673. (Illus.). (ps-3). 1978. 10.70i (ISBN 0-06-026553-1); PLB 10.89 (ISBN 0-06-026554-X). HarpJ.

Special Trade. Sally Wittman. LC 77-25673. (Trophy Picture Bks.). (Illus.). 32p. (ps-2). 1985. pap. 3.95 (ISBN 0-06-443071-5, Trophy). HarpJ.

Special Trade Release! The Gauntlet Malice. Deberah T. Harris. 1988. pap. 7.95 (ISBN 0-8125-3952-4, Dist. by St Martin's Pr & Warner Pub Servs). Tor Bks.

Special Transport Services for Elderly & Disabled People. J. M. Bailey & A. D. Layzell. 360p. 1983. text ed. 44.00x (ISBN 0-566-00615-4). Gower Pub Co.

Special Treatment: The Untold Story of the Survival of Thousands of Jews in Hitler's Third Reich. Alan Abrams. (Illus.). 261p. 1985. 14.95 (ISBN 0-8184-0364-0). Lyle-Stuart.

Special Trick. Mercer Mayer. LC 69-18220. (Pied Piper Bk.). (Illus.). (gr. k-3). 1976. pap. 3.95 (ISBN 0-8037-8103-2, 0383-120). Dial Bks Young.

Special Trigonometric Series in K Dimensions. Stephen Wainger. LC 52-42839. (Memoirs: No. 59). 102p. 1965. pap. 11.00 (ISBN 0-8218-1259-9, MEMO-59). Am Math.

Special Unit, Barlinnie Prison: Its Evolution Through Its Art. Ed. by Christopher Carroll & Joyce Laing. 1982. 40.00x (ISBN 0-906474-18-3, Pub. by Third Eye Centre); pap. 30.00x (ISBN 0-906474-15-9). State Mutual Bk.

Special Update: 1986 Immigration & Nationality Acts. National Lawyers Guild. 1987. pap. 35.00 (ISBN 0-87632-542-8). Clark Boardman.

Special Use & Conditional Use Districts: A Way to Impose More Specific Zoning Controls. Stephen E. Davenport & Philip P. Green. LC 83-621940. 1980. pap. 3.50 (ISBN 0-318-01109-3). U of NC Inst Gov.

Special Valor: The U. S. Marines & the Pacific War. Richard Wheeler. 480p. 1985. pap. 10.95 (ISBN 0-452-00737-2, Mer). NAL.

Special Values of Dirichlet Series, Monodromy, & the Periods of Automorphic Forms. Peter Stiller. LC 84-3060. (Memoirs of the American Mathematical Society: No. 299). 120p. 1984. pap. 13.00 (ISBN 0-8218-2300-0). Am Math.

Special Way to Care: A Guide for Neighbors, Friends, & Community in their Efforts to Provide Financial & Emotional Support for Terminally & Catastrophically Ill Children. Sheila Petersen. 180p. (Orig.). 1988. pap. write for info. (ISBN 0-9619785-0-3). Friends Karen.

Special Ways with Ordinary Days. Sharon Meisenheimer. (gr. k-3). 1988. pap. 10.95 (ISBN 0-8224-6347-4). D S Lake Pubs.

Special Welding Processes-Terms in 16 Languages see Terms for Welding & Allied-Processes in Different Languages (11W): WT.

Special You. (Benziger Family Life Program Ser.). 6p. 1978. 2.45 (ISBN 0-02-651750-7); tchrs. ed. 4.00 (ISBN 0-02-651760-4); family handbook 1.00 (ISBN 0-02-651790-6). Benziger Pub Co.

Specialisation & Cooperation of the Socialist Economies. Yu. Kormov. 217p. 1980. 7.95 (ISBN 0-8285-1869-6, Pub. by Progress Pubs USSR). Imported Pubns.

Specialist. Gayle Rivers. 304p. 1986. pap. 3.95 (ISBN 0-441-77812-7, Pub. by Charter Bks). Ace Bks.

Specialist. Chic Sale. 1985. Repr. of 1929 ed. 5.00 (ISBN 0-911416-00-5, 911416). Specialist.

Specialist Care of the Competition Horse. British Horse Society Staff. (British Horse Society Manual of Stable Management Ser.: Bk. 5). (Illus.). 160p. 1988. pap. 12.95 (ISBN 0-939481-13-8). Half Halt Pr.

Specialist: Full Moon in Dendera. Roberto Raviola. Ed. by Bernd Metz. Tr. by Tom Leighton. (Illus.). 48p. 1987. pap. 8.95 (ISBN 0-87416-044-8). Catalan Communs.

Specialist: His Philosophy, His Disease, His Cure. Archie J. Bahm. LC 76-16883. 126p. 1977. 7.50 (ISBN 0-911714-08-1, World Bks). Bahm.

Specialist in Crime. E. Millen. 1986. 15.00X (ISBN 0-245-50507-5, Pub. by Harrap Ltd England). State Mutual Bk.

Specialist in Education. Jack Rudman. (Career Examination Ser.: C-752). (Cloth bdg. avail. on request). pap. 16.00 (ISBN 0-8373-0752-X). Natl Learning.

Specialist Techniques in Engineering Mathematics. A. C. Bajpai et al. LC 80-41274. 401p. 1980. 97.95 (ISBN 0-471-27907-2, Pub. by Wiley-Interscience); pap. 48.95 (ISBN 0-471-27908-0). Wiley.

Specialists. Lawrence Block. 160p. 1985. pap. 4.95 (ISBN 0-88150-043-7). Countryman.

Specialist's Guide to Bureau Print Precancels. 3rd. ed. (Illus.). 1980. 30.00 (ISBN 0-686-74110-2). G W Noble.

Speciality Care Products for Your Home Entertainment Center. Thomas J. Zarecki. (Illus.). 100p. Date not set. 2.00 (ISBN 0-936503-02-5). TJ Enter IL.

Speciality Modeling. Tori Hartman & Carolyn Strauss. 128p. 1988. pap. 10.95 (ISBN 0-525-48356-X). Dutton.

Specialization Bulletin, No. 8. 70p. 1982. pap. 5.00 (ISBN 0-686-48281-6). Amer Bar Assn.

Specialization Bulletin, No. 9. Standing Committee on Specialization. 70p. 1982. 5.00. Amer Bar Assn.

Specialization, Exchange & Complex Societies. Ed. by Elizabeth M. Brumfiel & Timothy Earle. (New Directions in Archaeology Ser.). (Illus.). 160p. 1987. 39.50 (ISBN 0-521-32118-2). Cambridge U Pr.

Specialization of Medicine with Particular Reference to Opthalmology. George Rosen. LC 79-180586. (Medicine & Society in America Ser). 106p. 1972. Repr. of 1944 ed. 11.00 (ISBN 0-405-03966-2). Ayer Co Pubs.

Specialization of Verbal Facility at the College Entrance Level. Warren G. Findley. LC 70-176770. (Columbia University. Teachers College. Contributions to Education: No. 567). Repr. of 1933 ed. 22.50 (ISBN 0-404-55567-5, CE567). AMS Pr.

Specialized Agencies & the United Nations. Douglas Williams. 272p. 1987. 29.95 (ISBN 0-312-00486-9). St Martin.

Specialized Catalogue of the Postal Issues of the Ryulyu Islands (Issued Under United States Administration: The Nansei Shoto Provisional Postage Stamps, Pt. 3. 2nd rev. ed. Melvin H. Schoberlin & Arthur L. F. Askins. viii, 148p. 1983. 22.50 (ISBN 0-318-17071-X). Ryukyu Philatelic.

Specialized Cleaning, Finishing & Coating Processes: Proceedings of a Conference Held February 5-6, 1980, Los Angeles, California. American Society for Metals Staff. LC 81-2755. (Materials-Metalworking Technology Ser.). pap. 106.00 (ISBN 0-317-26754-X, 2024350). Bks Demand UMI.

Specialized Course Outline for Gerontology Social Work Education. Date not set. 12.05. Coun Soc Wk Ed.

Specialized Courts Dealing with Sex Delinquency, a Study of the Procedure in Chicago, Boston, Philadelphia, & New York. George E. Worthington & Ruth Topping. LC 69-14954. (Criminology, Law Enforcement, & Social Problems Ser.: No. 50). 1969. Repr. of 1925 ed. 18.00x (ISBN 0-87585-050-2). Patterson Smith.

Specialized Curing Methods for Coatings & Plastics-Recent Advances. M. W. Ranney. LC 77-71928. (Chemical Technology Review Ser.: No. 88). (Illus.). 1977. 39.00 (ISBN 0-8155-0660-0). Noyes.

Specialized Information Service. Incl. Cocaine. 1987. pap. 3.50 (ISBN 0-89230-172-4); Heroin. 1987. pap. 3.50 (ISBN 0-89230-176-7); Inhalants. pap. 3.50 (ISBN 0-89230-174-0); LSD. 1984. pap. 3.50 (ISBN 0-89230-173-2); Methaqualone. 1987. pap. 3.50 (ISBN 0-89230-175-9). Do it Now.

Specialized Legal Research. Ed. by Leah F. Chanin. 432p. 1987. 60.00. Little.

Specialized Studies in Polynesian Anthropology. K. Luomala et al. (BMB Ser.). Repr. of 1947 ed. 15.00 (ISBN 0-527-02301-9). Kraus Repr.

Specialized Study Options U. S. A, Vol. 1: Technical Programs. Ed. by Edrice Howard. 350p. (Orig.). pap. text ed. 19.95 (ISBN 0-87206-140-X). Inst Intl Educ.

Specialized Study Options U. S. A., 1986-88: Vol. 2, Professional Development. Ed. by Edrice Howard. (Orig.). pap. text ed. 19.95 (ISBN 0-317-57394-2). Inst Intl Educ.

Specially for Christmas. Pauline Smith. 32p. 1985. pap. 1.50 (ISBN 0-908175-82-5, Pub. by Boolarong Pubn Australia). Intl Spec Bk.

Specially Selected. Edward V. Lucas. LC 77-117891. (Essay Index Reprint Ser). 1920. 17.00 (ISBN 0-8369-1673-5). Ayer Co Pubs.

Specialties of the House. Compiled by Our Lady of Grace Montessori School of Manhasset. 486p. 10.00 (ISBN 0-918544-96-3). Wimmer Bks.

Specialties of the House: Great Recipes from Great Chicago Restaurants. Frwd. by Jeff Smith. (Illus.). 1988. spiral bound 9.95 (ISBN 1-55652-026-3). Chicago Review.

Specialty Adhesives (A1647) (Marketing Research Reports). 1986. write for info. (ISBN 0-86621-828-9). Frost & Sullivan.

Specialty Ag Chems: Update. Business Communications Staff. 140p. 1987. pap. 1950.00 (ISBN 0-89336-543-2, GA-035N). BCC.
Specialty & Hi Performance Fiber: Update. Business Communications Staff. 311p. 1987. pap. 1950.00 (ISBN 0-89336-526-2, GB-069R). BCC.
Specialty Biocides Market. Frost & Sullivan, Inc. Staff. 240p. 1986. 1875.00 (ISBN 0-86621-763-0, A1580). Frost & Sullivan.
Specialty Board Review: Anesthesiology. 2nd ed. Thomas P. Beach. LC 78-1942. (Illus.). 1984. pap. 19.95 (ISBN 0-8385-8625-2). Appleton & Lange.
Specialty Board Review: Family Practice, ARCO. 3rd ed. Ernest Y. Yen & V. Bhushan Bhardwaj. 224p. 1986. pap. text ed. 19.95 (ISBN 0-317-60736-7, A8628-8). Appleton & Lange.
Specialty Board Review: General Surgery. 3rd ed. Charles G. Rob & J. Raymond Hinshaw. (Specialty Board Review Ser.). 192p. 1986. pap. 18.95 (ISBN 0-8385-8630-9). Appleton & Lange.
Specialty Board Review: Internal Medicine. Robert E. Pieroni. (Illus.). 128p. (Orig.). 1986. 18.95. Appleton & Lange.
Specialty Board Review: Internal Medicine, ARCO. 2nd ed. Robert E. Pieroni. (Illus.). 121p. 1986. pap. text ed. 18.95 (ISBN 0-317-60698-0, A8632-0). Appleton & Lange.
Specialty Board Review: Obstetrics & Gynecology. 3rd ed. Preston P. Williams & Thomas M. Julian. 257p. 1986. pap. 18.95 (ISBN 0-8385-8634-1, A8634-6). Appleton & Lange.
Specialty Booksellers Directory. Ed. by John Kremer et al. LC 87-15510. 200p. (Orig.). 1987. pap. 19.95 (ISBN 0-912411-16-3). Ad-Lib.
Specialty Chemicals Handbook. 2nd ed. 325p. 1987. 120.00x (ISBN 0-8002-4170-3, Pub. by Japan Chemical Week). Taylor & Francis.
Specialty Items Used Today (Sheet Metal) Including Methods of Design & Fabrication & Important Trade Topics. 3rd ed. Richard S. Budzik. LC 74-79537. (Illus.). 1987. 54.95 (ISBN 0-912914-30-0). Practical Pubns.
Specialty Nursing Courses: OR. 78p. 1976. 5.00 (ISBN 0-939583-18-6). Assn Oper Rm Nurses.
Specialty of the House. Stanley Ellin. 268p. Repr. of 1956 ed. lib. bdg. 17.95x (ISBN 0-88411-147-4). Amereon Ltd.
Specialty of the House & Other Stories: The Complete Mystery Tales, 1948-1978. Stanley Ellin. LC 79-67149. 557p. 1979. 15.00 (ISBN 0-89296-049-3). Mysterious Pr.
Specialty Plastics In New Military Applications. Business Communications Staff. 275p. 1986. pap. 2250.00 (ISBN 0-89336-540-8, P-093). BCC.
Specialty Polymers. Ed. by H. J. Cantow et al. (Advances in Polymer Science Ser.: Vol. 41). (Illus.). 186p. 1981. 58.00 (ISBN 0-387-10554-9). Springer-Verlag.
Specialty Positions. (SPEC Kit & Flyer Ser.: No. 80). 133p. 1982. Kit & Flyer. 20.00 (ISBN 0-318-16112-5, 80); ARL members 10.00. OMS.
Specialty Retailing: Markets & Strategies for the 1990s. Ed. by Peter Allen. 250p. 1987. 995.00 (ISBN 0-941285-15-4). FIND-SVP.
Specialty Software for Large Manufacturers. Frost & Sullivan, Inc. Staff. 194p. 1986. 1800.00 (ISBN 0-86621-498-4, A1571). Frost & Sullivan.
Specialty Store & Its Advertising. 12.00 (ISBN 0-87102-056-4, 60-6657); instr's. manual 4.00. Natl Ret Merch.
Specialty Water Treatment Chemicals. Business Communications Staff. 155p. 1985. pap. 1750.00 (ISBN 0-89336-433-9, C-002N). BCC.
SpecialWare Directory: A Guide to Software Sources for Special Education 1985. 2nd ed. Ed. by LINC Associates, Inc. Staff. LC 85-23880. 168p. pap. 22.50 (ISBN 0-89774-192-7). Oryx Pr.
Speciation of Fission & Activation Products in the Environment. Ed. by R. S. Bulman & J. R. Cooper. 434p. 1986. 92.00 (ISBN 0-85334-422-1, Pub. by Elsevier Applied Sci England). Elsevier.
Speciation of Metals in Water, Sediment & Soil Systems. (Lecture Notes in Earth Sciences: Vol. 11). vii, 190p. 1987. pap. 21.70 (ISBN 0-387-18071-0). Springer Verlag.
Species Algarum. F. T. Kuetzing. 1970. Repr. of 1849 ed. 65.00x (ISBN 90-6123-084-5). Lubrecht & Cramer.
Species Algarum Rite Cognitae Cum Symonymus, Differentis Specificis et Descriptionibus Succinctis, 2 vols. C. A. Agardh. 1970. Repr. of 1828 ed. 56.50x (ISBN 90-6123-001-2). Lubrecht & Cramer.
Species at Risk: Research in Australia. Ed. by R. H. Groves & W. D. Ride. 250p. 1982. 40.00 (ISBN 0-387-11416-5). Springer-Verlag.
Species Concept Hymenomycetes: Proceedings. Symposium Lausanne, Switzerland Aug. 16 to 20 1976. Ed. by H. Clemencon. (Bibliotheca Mycologica: No. 61). (Illus.). 1978. pap. text ed. 74.00x (ISBN 3-7682-1173-8). Lubrecht & Cramer.
Species Conservation Priorities in the Tropical Forests of Southeast Asia. Ed. by Russell A. Mittermeier & William R. Konstant. 58p. 1982. pap. 10.00 (ISBN 0-942635-02-7). Wrld Wldlife Fund.
Species Filicum, 5 vols. W. J. Hooker. 1970. Repr. of 1864 ed. 300.00x (ISBN 3-7682-0690-4). Lubrecht & Cramer.
Species Graminum Iconibus et Descriptionbus Illustravit, 3 vols. in 1. K. B. Trinius. (Illus.). 1970. Repr. of 1836 ed. 180.00x (ISBN 3-7682-0669-6). Lubrecht & Cramer.
Species Groups of South American Frogs of the Genus Eleutherodactylus: (Leptodactylidae) John D. Lynch. (Occasional Papers: No. 61). 24p. 1976. 1.50 (ISBN 0-317-04878-3). U of KS Mus Nat Hist.
Species-Index to Schmidt-Hustedt: Atlas Zur Diatomaceen Kunde. G. Dallas Hanna. (Illus.). 1969. pap. 24.00x (ISBN 3-7682-0611-4). Lubrecht & Cramer.
Species Muscorum Frondosorum. J. Hedwig. (Illus.). 1960. Repr. of 1801 ed. 48.00x (ISBN 3-7682-7055-6). Lubrecht & Cramer.
Species of Aphytis of the World (Hymenoptera: Aphelinidae) Rosen. (Entomologica Ser.: No. 17). 1979. lib. bdg. 137.00 (ISBN 90-6193-127-4, Pub. by Junk Pubs Netherlands). Kluwer Academic.
Species of Artocarpus Indigenous to the British India: And the Indo-Malayan Species of Quercus & Castnopsis, 2 pts, Vol. II. The Royal Botanic Garden, Calcutta, Annals of & George King. (Illus.). 107p. 1979. Repr. of 1899 ed. 80.00 (ISBN 0-88065-010-9, Pub. by Messers Today & Tomorrows Printers & Publishers India). Scholarly Pubns.
Species of Asellotes (Isopoda: Paraselloidea) from Anvers Island, Antarctica: Paper 1 in Antarctic Biology of the Antarctic Seas VI. George A. Schultz. Ed. by David L. Pawson. (Antarctic Research Ser.: Vol. 26). 36p. 1976. pap. 14.95 (ISBN 0-87590-129-8). Am Geophysical.
Species of Dalbargia of South Eastern Asia. Royal Botanic Garden, Calcutta, Annals of & D. Prain. (Annals of Royal Botanic Garden, Calcutta Ser.: Vol. X, Pt. 1). (Illus.). 114p. 1979. Repr. of 1904 ed. 100.00 (ISBN 0-88065-013-3, Pub. by Messers Today & Tomorrows Printers & Publishers India). Scholarly Pubns.
Species of Ficus of the Indo-Malayan & Chinese Countries. G. King. (Illus.). 1969. Repr. 300.00x (ISBN 3-7682-0609-2). Lubrecht & Cramer.
Species of Intoxication. Michael Gizzi. (Burning Deck Poetry Ser.). 68p. 1983. 15.00 (ISBN 0-930901-10-X); pap. 4.00 (ISBN 0-930901-11-8). Burning Deck.
Species of Selenophoma on North American Grasses. Roderick Sprague & A. G. Johnson. (Studies in Botany: No. 10). (Illus.). 44p. 1950. pap. 4.95x (ISBN 0-87071-020-6). Oreg St U Pr.
Species of Special Concern in Pennsylvania. Ed. by Hugh H. Genoways & Fred J. Brenner. LC 84-73248. (Special Publications: No. 11, CMNH). (Illus.). 436p. 1985. 30.00 (ISBN 0-935868-11-9). Carnegie Mus.
Species of the Genus SCHWAGERINA & Their Stratigraphic Significance. J. W. Beede & H. T. Kniker. (Bull Ser.: 2433). (Illus.). 96p. 1924. 1.00 (ISBN 0-686-29344-4). Bur Econ Geology.
Species Problem. Ed. by Ernst Mayr. LC 73-17831. (Natural Sciences in America Ser.). (Illus.). 410p. 1974. Repr. 26.00x (ISBN 0-405-05749-0). Ayer Co Pubs.
Species Relationships in the Avian Genus Aimophila. Larry L. Wolf. 220p. 1977. 12.00 (ISBN 0-943610-23-0). Am Ornithologists.
Species Taxa of North American Birds: A Contribution to Comparative Systematics. Ernst Mayr & Lester L. Short. (Illus.). 127p. 1970. 7.00 (ISBN 0-686-35797-3, 9). Nuttall Ornith.
Specific Contribution of the Chemical Industries to the Vocational Training & Advanced Training of Manpower in Developing Countries: Report 2. Chemical Industries Committee, Ninth Session, Geneva September 21-30, 1982. iv, 82p. 1982. 10.50 (ISBN 92-2-103055-5). Intl Labour Office.
Specific Distinctness & Adaptive Differences in Southwestern Meadowlarks. Sievert Rohwer. (Occasional Papers: No. 44). 14p. 1976. pap. 1.25 (ISBN 0-317-04634-9). U of KS Mus Nat Hist.
Specific Gravity of Fine & Coarse Aggregates. (Training Aids Ser.: No. 8). 1974. Package: instr's. manual, student wkbk, slides. tape. 400.00 (ISBN 0-317-58414-6); Instr's. manual, 26 pg. 12.00 (ISBN 0-317-58415-4); Student wkbk., 21 pg. 8.00 (ISBN 0-317-58416-2). Natl Asphalt Pavement.
Specific Heart Muscle Disease. C. Symons et al. (Illus.). 160p. 1983. 34.00 (ISBN 0-7236-0641-2). PSG Pub Co.
Specific Heat of Solids. Ed. by Ared Cezairliyan. (CINDAS Data Series on Material Properties). 500p. 1988. 98.00. Hemisphere Pub.
Specific Learning Disabilities-Nature & Needs. Saroj D. Sutaria. (Illus.). 488p. 1985. 32.75 (ISBN 0-398-05035-X). C C Thomas.
Specific Pathogen Free Swine: Development, Application, Consequences. Norman R. Underdahl. LC 73-77749. (Illus.). xiv, 157p. 1974. 16.50x (ISBN 0-8032-0833-2). U of Nebr Pr.
Specific Reading Disability: Advances in Theory & Method. Ed. by Dirk J. Bakker & Paul Satz. (Modern Approaches to the Diagnosis & Instruction of Multi-Handicapped Children: Vol. 3). 166p. 1970. text ed. 25.00 (ISBN 90-237-4103-X, Pub. by Swets & Zeitlinger Netherlands). Hogrefe Intl.
Specific Receptors of Antibodies, Antigens & Cells: Proceedings. International Convocation on Immunology, 3rd, Buffalo, 1972. Ed. by N. R. Rose. 300p. 1973. 102.75 (ISBN 3-8055-1372-0). S Karger.
Specific Skill Reading Series: 1982. Richard A. Boning. Incl. Detecting the Sequence, 14 bks. (gr. 1-12); Drawing Conclusions, 14 bks. (gr. 1-12); Following Directions, 14 bks. (gr. 1-12); Getting the Facts, 14 bks. (gr. 1-12); Getting the Main Idea, 14 bks. (gr. 1-12); Locating the Answer, 14 bks. (gr. 1-12); Using the Context, 14 bks. (gr. 1-12); Working with Sounds, 14 bks. (gr. 1-12); Identifying Inferences, 10 bks. (gr. 1-5). 2.70 ea.; tchr's manuals 4.10 ea.; Spirit Masters Set. 9.50 (ISBN 0-87965-798-7); Elementary Set. 196.00 (ISBN 0-87965-824-X); Midway Set (4-9) 148.60 (ISBN 0-87965-826-6); Secondary Set (7-12) 138.25 (ISBN 0-87965-825-8). B Loft.
Specific Test in English for Everyday International Use: SEVI One. B. J. Carroll. 40p. 1983. Complete Kit. 45.00 (ISBN 0-08-030340-4, Dist. by Alemany Pr); Instr's. manual & marking card. 3.50 (ISBN 0-08-030338-2); Twenty magazine booklets. 27.00 (ISBN 0-08-030337-4); Twenty answer booklets. 18.00 (ISBN 0-08-030336-6); Cassette. 10.60 (ISBN 0-08-030339-0). Alemany Pr.
Specification Analysis in the Linear Model. Ed. by Maxwell King & David Giles. (International Library of Economics). 416p. 1987. text ed. 42.50 (ISBN 0-7102-0614-3). Routledge Chapman & Hall.
Specification & Estimation Problems in Models of Spatial Dependence. Robert Haining. (Studies in Geography: No. 24). 1977. pap. 10.95 (ISBN 0-8101-0521-7). Northwestern U Pr.
Specification & Uses of Econometric Models. T. Merritt Brown. LC 70-88172. 1970. 27.50 (ISBN 0-312-75110-9). St Martin.
Specification Case Studies. Ian Hayes. (Illus.). 336p. 1987. text ed. 33.00 (ISBN 0-13-826579-8). P-H.
Specification Clauses for Rehabilitation & Conversion Work. Levitt Bernstein & Anthony Richardson. (Illus.). 128p. 1982. 27.50 (ISBN 0-85139-582-1). Nichols Pub.
Specification, Estimation, & Analysis of Macroeconomic Models. Ray C. Fair. (Illus.). 384p. 1984. text ed. 35.00x (ISBN 0-674-83180-2). Harvard U Pr.
Specification: Fittings. Ed. by Engineering Equipment & Materials Users Assoc. Staff. Date not set. 175.00x (Pub. by EEMUA). State Mutual Bk.
Specification: Flanges - Composite & Solid. Engineering Equipment & Materials Users Assoc. Staff. Date not set. 175.00x (Pub. by EEMUA). State Mutual Bk.
Specification for Qualification of Welding Procedures & Welders for Piping & Tubing, D10.9. 60p. 1980. 27.00 (ISBN 0-87171-210-5). Am Welding.
Specification for Rotating Elements of Equipment D14.6. 69p. 1981. 22.00 (ISBN 0-87171-217-2). Am Welding.
Specification for Standardized Protein Solution (Bovine Serum Albumin) Approved Standard. 2nd ed. National Committee for Clinical Laboratory Standards. 1979. 20.00 (ISBN 0-318-19368-X, C1-A2). Natl Comm Clin Lab Stds.
Specification for Structural Joints Using ASTM A325 or A490 Bolts. 48p. 1985. 4.00 (ISBN 0-318-22850-5, S329). Am Inst Steel Construct.
Specification for the Design, Fabrication & Erection of Structural Steel for Buildings. 168p. 1978. 10.00 (ISBN 0-318-12811-X, S326). Am Inst Steel Construct.
Specification for the Design, Fabrication & Erection of Steel Safety-Related Structures for Nuclear Facilities: AISC-ANSI N690. 288p. 1984. 10.00 (ISBN 0-318-17777-3, S327). Am Inst Steel Construct.
Specification for Underwater Welding: D3.6. 51p. 1983. 20.00 (ISBN 0-87171-222-9). Am Welding.
Specification for Welding Earthmoving & Construction Equipment: D14.3-82. (Illus.). 80p. 1982. pap. 26.00; member 19.50. Am Welding.
Specification for Welding of Presses & Press Components: D14.5. 83p. 1980. 22.00 (ISBN 0-87171-187-7). Am Welding.
Specification for Welding of Sheet Metal: D9.1-84. 1984. 20.00 (ISBN 0-87171-240-7). Am Welding.
Specification Forms for Process Measurement & Control Instruments, Primary Elements & Control Valves: ISA Standard S20. 72p. 1981. pap. text ed. 24.00x (ISBN 0-87664-347-0). Instru Soc.
Specification, Management & Ownership of ATE. Ed. by Network Staff. 1982. 95.00x (ISBN 0-904999-72-6, Pub. by Network Events Ltd). State Mutual Bk.
Specification of a CAD One: Neutral File of CAD Geometry. 2nd, rev. ed. Ed. by E. G. Schlechtendahl. (Research Reports Esprit Project 322-CAD 1: Vol. 1). xv, 255p. 1988. pap. 27.10 (ISBN 0-387-18397-3). Springer-Verlag.
Specification of Chipboard for furniture. 1981. 60.00x (ISBN 0-317-43704-6, Pub. by F I R A). State Mutual Bk.
Specification of Complex Systems. B. Cohen et al. 160p. 1986. text ed. write for info. (ISBN 0-201-14400-X). Addison-Wesley.
Specification of Computer Programs. Wladyslaw M. Turski & Thomas S. Maibum. 300p. 1987. text ed. 27.95x (ISBN 0-201-14226-0). Addison-Wesley.
Specification of Gamma - Ray Brachytherapy Sources. LC 73-94306. (NCRP Reports Ser.: No. 41). 1974. 10.00 (ISBN 0-913392-23-5). NCRP Pubns.
Specification of High Activity Gamma-Ray Sources, No. 18. International Commission on Radiation Units & Measurements. LC 72-131967. 1970. 9.00 (ISBN 0-913394-36-X). Intl Comm Rad Meas.
Specification Searches: Ad Hoc Inference with Nonexperimental Data. E. E. Leamer. LC 77-26855. (Probability & Mathematical Statistics Ser.). 370p. 1978. 54.95x (ISBN 0-471-01520-2, Pub. by Wiley-Interscience). Wiley.
Specification Tested Products Guide. 64p. 10.00 (ISBN 0-318-18037-5); insureds 5.00. Factory Mutual.
Specification Tests Building Materials Guide. 64p. cancelled (ISBN 0-318-14060-8, P8016). Factory Mutual.
Specification: Tubes - Seamless & Welded. Engineering Equipment & Materials Users Assoc. Staff. Date not set. 150.00x (Pub. by EEMUA). State Mutual Bk.
Specification Writer's Handbook. H. Leslie Simmons. LC 84-29179. 1985. Professional ed., 375p. 49.95 (ISBN 0-471-88615-7); College ed., 387p. pap. 27.95 (ISBN 0-471-81579-9). Wiley.
Specification Writing: An Introduction. John J. Scott. 1984. pap. text ed. 32.95 (ISBN 0-408-01370-2). Butterworth.
Specification Writing: For Architects & Surveyors. 8th ed. Arthur Willis & Christopher Willis. 120p. 1983. 22.50x (ISBN 0-246-12228-5, Pub. by Granada England). Sheridan.
Specifications & Criteria for Biochemical Compounds. 3rd ed. Division of Chemistry & Chemical Technology. 224p. 1972. 22.25x (ISBN 0-309-01917-6). Natl Acad Pr.
Specifications for Adhesives. International Plastics Selector, Inc. 55.00 (ISBN 0-686-48216-6, 0308). T-C Pubns CA.
Specifications for Architecture Engineering & Construction. 2nd ed. Chesley Ayers. 1984. text ed. 47.50 (ISBN 0-07-002642-4). McGraw.
Specifications for Carbon & Alloy-Steel Plates for Pressure Vessels. American Society for Testing & Materials Staff. pap. 46.50 (ISBN 0-317-28482-7, 2019125). Bks Demand UMI.
Specifications for Commercial Interiors: Professional Liabilities, Regulations, & Performance Criteria. S. C. Reznikoff. (Illus.). 304p. 1979. 37.50 (ISBN 0-8230-7353-X, Whitney Lib). Watson-Guptill.
Specifications for Electric Overhead Traveling Cranes, No. 70. rev. ed. 84p. 1988. 10.00 (ISBN 0-318-17123-6, III-11). Material Handling.
Specifications for Identity & Purity & Toxicological Evaluation of Food Colours, Dec 17, 1964. (Nutrition Meetings Reports: No. 38B). pap. 17.00 (F1208, FAO). UNIPUB.
Specifications for Identity & Purity of Buffering Agents, Salts, Emulsifers, Thickening Agents, Stabilizers, Flavouring Agents, Food Colours, Sweetening Agents & Miscellaneous Food Additives: Prepared by the 26th Session of the Joint FAO-WHO Expert Committee on Food Additives, Rome, April 19-28, 1982. (Food & Nutrition Papers: No. 25). 1982. pap. 18.25 (ISBN 92-5-101239-3, F2351, FAO). UNIPUB.
Specifications for Identity & Purity of Certain Food Additives. (Food & Nutrition Papers: No. 34). (Illus.). 236p. (Orig.). 1987. pap. text ed. 24.75 (ISBN 92-5-102428-6, F3001, FAO). UNIPUB.
Specifications for Identity & Purity of Certain Food Additives. (FAO Food & Nutrition Paper: No. 37). (Illus.). 151p. (Orig.). 1987. pap. text ed. 13.75 (ISBN 92-5-102499-5, F3037, FAO). UNIPUB.
Specifications for Identity & Purity of Food Additives. (Food & Nutrition Papers: No. 31/2). 138p. 1985. pap. 11.25 (ISBN 92-5-102128-7, F2690, FAO). UNIPUB.
Specifications for Identity & Purity of Food Colours. (Food & Nutrition Papers: No. 31/1). 195p. 1985. pap. 14.00 (ISBN 92-5-102127-9, F2689, FAO). UNIPUB.
Specifications for Identity & Purity. (Food & Nutrition Papers: No. 28). 145p. (Eng. & Fr.). 1983. pap. text ed. 11.25 (ISBN 92-5-101389-6, F2525, FAO). UNIPUB.
Specifications for Paving & Industrial Asphalts. 56p. 5.00 (ISBN 0-318-13399-7, SS-2). Asphalt Inst.
Specifications for Pesticides Used in Public Health: Insecticides - Molluscicides - Repellants - Methods. 6th ed. 384p. 1985. pap. 28.80 (ISBN 92-4-156084-3). World Health.
Specifications for Pesticides Used in Public Health: Insecticides, Rodenticides, Molluscicides, Repellents, Methods. 4th ed. (Also avail. in French & Spanish). 1973. 16.00 (ISBN 92-4-154022-2). World Health.
Specifications for Plant Protection Products Nicotine Sulphate. (Specifications for Plant Protection Products). 1979. pap. 7.50 (ISBN 92-5-100552-4, F1468, FAO). UNIPUB.
Specifications for Reagents Mentioned in the International Pharmacopoeia. (Also avail. in French). 1963. 8.00 (ISBN 92-4-154002-8). World Health.

Spectator, 5 vols. Ed. by Donald F. Bond. 1987. Vol. 1. 110.00 (ISBN 0-19-818610-X); Vol. 2. 110.00 (ISBN 0-19-818611-8); Vol. 3. 110.00 (ISBN 0-317-66428-X); Vol. 4. 110.00 (ISBN 0-317-66429-8); Vol. 5. 110.00 (ISBN 0-317-66430-1). Oxford U Pr.

Spectator. Ed. by Rachel Salazar. LC 86-4477. 128p. 1986. 14.95 (ISBN 0-932511-04-X); pap. 6.95 (ISBN 0-932511-05-8). Fiction Coll.

Spectator. 1988. 5.00. Inkblot Pubns.

Spectator, a Digest-Index. William Wheeler. LC 72-191656. 1892. lib. bdg. 32.00 (ISBN 0-8414-9670-6). Folcroft.

Spectator & the Landscape in the Art Criticism of Diderot & His Contemporaries. Ian Lochhead. LC 82-4770. (Studies in the Fine Arts: Criticism: No. 14). pap. 34.60 (2070027). Bks Demand UMI.

Spectator Bird. Wallace Stegner. LC 78-26789. 214p. 1979. pap. 5.95 (ISBN 0-8032-9107-8, BB 705, Bison). U of Nebr Pr.

Spectator Harvest. Spectator Magazine. LC 79-105038. (Essay Index Reprint Ser.). 1935. 20.00 (ISBN 0-8369-1481-3). Ayer Co Pubs.

Spectator Reader. Ed. & intro. by Michael McFee. LC 85-61379. (Illus.). 224p. (Orig.). 1985. pap. 7.95 (ISBN 0-9614785-1-9). Spectator Publ.

Spectator Society: The Philippines under Martial Rule. Benjamin N. Muego. (CIS Southeast Asia Ser.: No. 77). 201p. 1986. pap. text ed. 12.50x (ISBN 0-89680-138-1, Ohio U Ctr Intl). Ohio U Pr.

Spectators on the Paris Stage in the Seventeenth & Eighteenth Centuries. Barbara G. Mittman. Ed. by Oscar Brockett. LC 84-16339. (Theater & Dramatic Studies: No. 25). 170p. 1984. 42.95 (ISBN 0-8357-1610-4). UMI Res Pr.

Specter. Joan L. Nixon. LC 82-70322. 160p. (gr. 7 up). 1982. pap. 12.95 (ISBN 0-385-28948-0). Delacorte.

Specter of the Absurd: Sources & Criticisms of Modern Nihilism. Donald A. Crosby. (SUNY Series in Philosophy). 416p. 1988. 49.50 (ISBN 0-88706-719-0); pap. 19.95 (ISBN 0-88706-720-4). State U NY Pr.

Specter or Delusion? The Supernatural in Gothic Fiction. Margaret L. Carter. Ed. by Robert Scholes. LC 87-6055. (Studies in Speculative Fiction: No. 15). (Illus.). 131p. 1987. 34.95 (ISBN 0-8357-1822-0). UMI Res Pr.

Specters. Jeff Gelf. 256p. (Orig.). 1988. pap. 3.75 (ISBN 1-55785-015-1). Bart Books.

Spectra. Judith E. Edwards. (Illus.). 32p. (Orig.). 1982. pap. 3.00 (ISBN 0-932662-41-2). St Andrews NC.

Spectra & Chemical Interactions. P. S. Braterman et al. LC 67-11280. (Structure & Bonding: Vol. 26). 1976. 36.00 (ISBN 0-387-07591-7). Springer-Verlag.

Spectra & Energy Levels of Rare Earth Ions in Crystals. Gerhard H. Dieke. Ed. by H. M. Crosswhite & Hannah Crosswhite. LC 67-29453. pap. 103.30 (ISBN 0-317-09061-5, 2011960). Bks Demand UMI.

Spectra & Structures of Simple Free Radicals: An Introduction to Molecular Spectroscopy. Gerhard Herzberg. LC 70-124722. (George Fisher Baker Non-Resident Lectureships in Chemistry Ser.). 240p. 1971. 35.00x (ISBN 0-8014-0584-X). Cornell U Pr.

Spectra & Structures of Simple Free Radicals: An Introduction to Molecular Spectroscopy. Gerhard Herzberg. 240p. 1988. pap. 7.95 (ISBN 0-486-65821-X). Dover.

Spectra & the Steenrod Algebra. H. A. Margolis. (Mathematical Library: Vol. 29). 500p. 1984. 100.00 (ISBN 0-444-86516-0, North-Holland). Elsevier.

Spectra of Graphs: Theory & Applications. Ed. by Dragos Cvetlovic et al. LC 79-50490. (Pure & Applied Mathematics Ser.). 1980. 74.50 (ISBN 0-12-195150-2). Acad Pr.

Spectral Analysis & Its Applications. Gwilym M. Jenkins & Donald G. Watts. LC 67-13840. 1968. 52.95x (ISBN 0-8162-4464-2). Holden-Day.

Spectral Analysis & the Time Series, 2 Vols. in 1, Vol. 1 & Vol.2. Ed. by M. B. Priestley. (Probability & Mathematical Statistics Ser.). 1983. 43.50 (ISBN 0-12-564922-3). Acad Pr.

Spectral Analysis & Time Series: Vol. 1, Univariate Series. M. B. Priestly. (Probability & Mathematical Statistics Ser.). 1981. 122.00 (ISBN 0-12-564901-0). Acad Pr.

Spectral Analysis & Time Series: Vol. 2, Multivariate Series, Prediction & Control. M. B. Priestly. LC 80-40235. (Probability & Mathematical Statistics Ser.). 1981. 67.50 (ISBN 0-12-564902-9). Acad Pr.

Spectral Analysis in Geophysics. M. Bath. (Developments in Solid Earth Geophysics: Vol. 7). 563p. 1974. Repr. of 1974 ed. 139.50 (ISBN 0-444-41222-0). Elsevier.

Spectral Analysis: Methods & Techniques. Ed. by James A. Blackburn. 304p. 1970. 79.75 (ISBN 0-8247-1045-2). Dekker.

Spectral Analysis of Economic Time Series. C. W. Granger & M. Hatanaka. (Princeton Studies in Mathematical Economics Ser.: Vol. 1). 1964. 41.00x (ISBN 0-691-04177-6). Princeton U Pr.

Spectral Analysis of Time Series. L. H. Koopmans. 1974. 58.50 (ISBN 0-12-419250-5). Acad Pr.

Spectral Analysis of Time Series. I. G. Zurbenko. (North-Holland Series in Statistics & Probability: No. 2). 248p. 1986. 105.25 (ISBN 0-444-87607-3, North Holland). Elsevier.

Spectral & Chemical Characterization of Organic Compounds: A Laboratory Handbook. 2nd ed. W. J. Criddle & G. P. Ellis. LC 80-40497. 115p. 1980. 84.95x (ISBN 0-471-27813-0, Pub. by Wiley-Interscience); pap. 31.95 (ISBN 0-471-27812-2). Wiley.

Spectral Approximation of Linear Operators. Francoise Chatelin. (Computer Science & Applied Mathematics Ser.). 1983. 69.50 (ISBN 0-12-170620-6). Acad Pr.

Spectral Atlas of Nitrogen Dioxide: 5530a to 6480a. Donald K. Hsu et al. 1978. 69.00 (ISBN 0-12-357950-3). Acad Pr.

Spectral Atlas of Polcyclic Aromatic Compounds: Including Data on Occurence & Biological Activity. Ed. by W. Karcher et al. 1985. lib. bdg. 94.00 (ISBN 90-277-1652-8, Pub. by Reidel Holland). KLuwer Academic.

Spectral Boy. Donald Petersen. LC 64-13611. (Wesleyan Poetry Program: Vol. 22). (Orig.). 1964. 17.00x (ISBN 0-8195-2022-5); pap. 8.95 (ISBN 0-8195-1022-X). Wesleyan U Pr.

Spectral Classification & Multicolor Photometry: Proceedings. International Astronomical Union Symposium No. 50, Villa Carlos Paz, Argentina, Oct. 18-24, 1971. Ed. by Ch. Fehrenbach & B. E. Westerlund. LC 72-87471. 314p. 1973. lib. bdg. 53.00 (ISBN 90-277-0280-2, Pub. by Reidel Holland); pap. text ed. 37.00 (ISBN 90-277-0363-9). Kluwer Academic.

Spectral Decompositions on Banach Spaces. I. Erdelyi & R. Lange. LC 77-26174. (Lecture Notes in Mathematics: Vol. 623). 1977. pap. 14.00 (ISBN 0-387-08525-4). Springer-Verlag.

Spectral Emanations: New & Selected Poems. John Hollander. LC 77-20645. 1978. pap. 7.95 (ISBN 0-689-10878-8). Atheneum.

Spectral Evolution of Galaxies. Ed. by Cesare Chiosi & Alvio Renzini. (Astrophysics & Space Science Library). 1986. lib. bdg. 78.00 (ISBN 0-318-18944-5, Pub. by Reidel Holland). Kluwer Academic.

Spectral Geometry: Direct & Inverse Problems. P. H. Berard. (Lecture Notes in Mathematics Ser.: Vol. 1207). xiv, 272p. 1986. pap. 23.40 (ISBN 0-387-16788-9). Springer-Verlag.

Spectral Line Broadening by Plasmas. Hans R. Griem. (Pure & Applied Physics: A Series of Monographs & Textbooks, Vol. 39). 1974. 99.50 (ISBN 0-12-302850-7). Acad Pr.

Spectral Line Shapes. Ed. by Burkhard Wende. 1981. 149.00 (ISBN 3-11-008150-4). De Gruyter.

Spectral Line Shapes, Vol. 4. Ed. by Reginald J. Exton. LC 81-1328. (Illus.). 646p. 1987. 59.00 (ISBN 0-937194-09-3). A Deepak Pub.

Spectral Line Shapes: Proceedings, 6th International Conference, Boulder, CO, July, 1982, Vol. 2. Ed. by Keith Burnett. 1057p. 1983. 239.00 (ISBN 3-11-008846-0). De Gruyter.

Spectral Line Shapes, Vol. 3: Proceedings, Seventh International Congress Aussois, France, June 11-15, 1984. Ed. by Francois Rostas. (Illus.). xx, 769p. 1985. 220.00 (ISBN 3-11-010119-X). De Gruyter.

Spectral Methods for Partial Differential Equations. Ed. by Robert G. Voigt et al. LC 84-50634. (Proceedings Ser.). (Illus.). vii, 267p. 1984. text ed. 30.00 (ISBN 0-89871-195-9). Soc Indus-Appl Math.

Spectral Methods in Econometrics. George S. Fishman. LC 72-78517. (Rand Corporation Research Studies). 1969. text ed. 16.00x (ISBN 0-674-83191-8). Harvard U Pr.

Spectral Methods in Fluid Dynamics. C. Canuto et al. (Computational Physics Ser.). (Illus.). 600p. 1987. 86.00 (ISBN 0-387-17371-4). Springer-Verlag.

Spectral Methods in Linear Transport Theory. Ed. by H. G. Kaper & C. J. Lekkerkerker. (Operator Theory, Advances & Applications Ser.: Vol. 5). 360p. 1982. text ed. 31.95 (ISBN 0-8176-1372-2). Birkhauser.

Spectral of Partial Differential Operators. M. Schechter. (North-Holland Series in Applied Mathematics & Mechanics: No. 14). 310p. 1986. 49.00 (ISBN 0-444-87822-X, North-Holland). Elsevier.

Spectral Problems in Organic Chemistry. R. Davis & C. H. J. Wells. (Illus.). 200p. 1984. pap. text ed. 10.95 (ISBN 0-412-00561-1, 9019, Pub. by Chapman & Hall England). Routledge Chapman & Hall.

Spectral Representations of Schroedinger Operators with Long-Range Potentials. Satto. (Lecture Notes in Mathematics: Vol. 727). 1979. pap. 14.00 (ISBN 0-387-09514-4). Springer-Verlag.

Spectral Sequence Constructors in Algebra & Topology. D. Barnes. LC 84-14622. (Memoirs of the AMS Ser.: No. 317). 174p. 1985. pap. text ed. 20.00 (ISBN 0-8218-2319-1). Am Math.

Spectral, Spatial, & Temporal Properties of Lasers. A. M. Ratner. LC 76-167677. (Optical Physics & Engineering Ser.). 220p. 1972. 49.50x (ISBN 0-306-30542-9, Plenum Pr). Plenum Pub.

Spectral Techniques & Fault Detection. Mark G. Karpovsky. 1985. 49.50 (ISBN 0-12-400060-6). Acad Pr.

Spectral Techniques in Digital Logic. Stanley L. Hurst et al. (Microelectric Signal Processing Techniques Ser.). 1985. 98.50 (ISBN 0-12-362680-3). Acad Pr.

Spectral Theorem. H. Helson. (Lecture Notes in Mathematics Ser.: Vol. 1227). vi, 104p. 1986. pap. 12.80 (ISBN 0-387-17197-5). Springer-Verlag.

Spectral Theory. Ed. by M. Birman. LC 78-93768. (Topics in Mathematical Physics: Vol. 3). pap. 24.80 (ISBN 0-317-12984-8, 2020693). Bks Demand UMI.

Spectral Theory. Edgar R. Lorch. LC 62-9824. (University Texts in the Mathematical Sciences Ser.). pap. 42.50 (ISBN 0-317-08657-X, 2051947). Bks Demand UMI.

Spectral Theory & Differential Operators. Ed. by D. E. Edmunds & W. D. Evans. (Oxford Mathematical Monographs Ser.). (Illus.). 592p. 1987. 115.00 (ISBN 0-19-853542-2). Oxford U Pr.

Spectral Theory & Wave Operators for the Schrodinger Equation. A. M. Berthier. (Themes in Resource Management Ser.). 320p. 1986. pap. 35.95 (ISBN 0-470-20417-6, Co-Pub. with Longman). Wiley.

Spectral Theory of Automorphic Functions: Proceedings of the Steklov Institute of Mathematics, No. 153. A. B. Venkov. LC 83-2694. (No. 153). 1983. 74.00 (ISBN 0-8218-3078-3). Am Math.

Spectral Theory of Banach Space Operators. S. Kantorovitz. (Lecture Notes in Mathematics: Vol. 1012). 179p. 1983. pap. 12.00 (ISBN 0-387-12673-2). Springer Verlag.

Spectral Theory of Differential Operators. Ed. by E. W. Knowles & R. T. Lewis. (Mathematics Studies: Vol. 55). 384p. 1981. 84.25 (ISBN 0-444-86277-3, North-Holland). Elsevier.

Spectral Theory of Functions & Operators, II: 1983. Ed. by N. K. Nikol'skii. LC 80-11102. (Proceedings of the Steklov Institute of Mathematics: Vol. 155). 176p. 1983. pap. text ed. 61.00 (ISBN 0-8218-3072-4, STEKLOV 155). Am Math.

Spectral Theory of Functions & Operators, 1 pt. Ed. by N. K. Nikol'skii. LC 80-1102. (Proceedings of the Steklov Institute of Mathematics: No. 130). 1980. 56.00 (ISBN 0-8218-3030-9, STEKLO-130). Am Math.

Spectral Theory of Geometrically Periodic Hyperbolic 3-Manifolds. Charles L. Epstein. LC 85-21443. (Memoirs of the AMS Ser.: No. 335). x, 161p. 1985. pap. 17.00 (ISBN 0-8218-2336-1). Am Math.

Spectral Theory of Hyponormal Operators. Daoxing Xia. (Operator Theory, Advances & Applications: Vol. 10). 256p. 1983. text ed. 43.95 (ISBN 3-7643-1541-5). Birkhauser.

Spectral Theory of Linear Operators. H. R. Dowson. 1978. 108.00 (ISBN 0-12-220950-8). Acad Pr.

Spectral Theory of Linear Operators & Related Topics. H. Helson et al. (Operator Theory Series: Advances & Applications: No. 14). 308p. 1985. text ed. 49.95x (ISBN 0-8176-1642-X). Birkhauser.

Spectral Theory of Matrices. Friedland. (Pure & Applied Mathematics Ser.). 1988. write for info. (ISBN 0-471-09252-5). Wiley.

Spectral Theory of Ordinary Differential Operators. Erich Muller-Pfeiffer. LC 80-42097. (Mathematics & Its Application Ser.). 246p. 1981. 74.95 (ISBN 0-470-27103-5). Halsted Pr.

Spectral Theory of Ordinary Differential Operators. J. Weidmann. (Lecture Notes in Mathematics Ser.: Vol. 1258). vi, 303p. 1987. pap. 28.60 (ISBN 0-387-17902-X). Springer-Verlag.

Spectral Theory of Random Fields. M. I. Yadrenko. Ed. by A. V. Balakrishnan. LC 82-60934. (Translations Series in Mathematics & Engineering). 267p. 1983. pap. text ed. 25.00 (ISBN 0-911575-00-6). Optimization Soft.

Spectral Theory of Random Fields. Mikhail I. Yadrenko. Ed. by A. V. Balakrishnan. (Translation Series in Mathematics & Engineering). 272p. 1983. pap. 31.50 (ISBN 0-387-90823-4). Springer-Verlag.

Spectral Theory of Self-Adjoint Operators in Hilbert Space. M. S. Birman & M. Z. Solomjak. 1987. lib. bdg. 98.00 (ISBN 90-277-2179-3, Pub. by Reidel Netherlands). Kluwer Academic.

Spectral Theory of Toeplitz Operators. Louis B. Boutet De Monvel & Victor Guillemin. LC 80-8538. (Annals of Mathematics Studies: No. 99). 222p. 1981. 23.00x (ISBN 0-691-08284-7); pap. 11.00x (ISBN 0-691-08279-0). Princeton U Pr.

Spectral Transform & Solutions: Tools to Solve & Investigate Evolution Equations. F. Calogero & A. Degasperis. (Studies in Math & Its Applications: Vol. 13). 516p. 1982. 137.00 (ISBN 0-444-86368-0, North Holland). Elsevier.

Spectre. Stephen Laws. 288p. 1987. pap. 3.95 (ISBN 0-8125-2102-1, Dist. by St Martin's Pr & Warner Pub Servs). Tor Bks.

Spectre. Robert Tyler. 100p. (Orig.). (YA) 1987. pap. 4.95 (ISBN 0-943449-03-0). Excel Pub.

Spectre Bridegroom & Other Horrors: Original Anthology. Ed. by R. Reginald. LC 75-46305. (Supernatural & Occult Fiction Ser.). (Illus.). 1976. lib. bdg. 23.50x (ISBN 0-405-08165-0). Ayer Co Pubs.

Spectres De Vibration et Symetrie des Cristaux. H. Poulet & J. P. Mathieu. 452p. (Fr.). 1970. 115.00 (ISBN 0-677-50180-3). Gordon & Breach.

Spectrochemical Analysis. James D. Ingle, Jr. & Stanley R. Crouch. (Illus.). 608p. 1988. text ed. 47.33 (ISBN 0-13-826876-2). P-H.

Spectrochemical Analysis by Atomic Absorption. W. J. Price. 392p. 1979. casebound 100.00 (ISBN 0-471-25967-5, Wiley Heyden). Wiley.

Spectrochemical Analysis by Atomic Absorption. William J. Price. pap. 101.00 (2026682). Bks Demand UMI.

Spectrochemical Analysis by X-Ray Fluorescence. Rudolf O. Muller. LC 70-107540. 350p. 1972. 55.00x (ISBN 0-306-30436-8, Plenum Pr). Plenum Pub.

Spectroelectrochemistry: Theory & Practice. Ed. by R. J. Gale. (Illus.). 452p. 1988. 85.00x (ISBN 0-306-42855-5, Plenum Pr). Plenum Pub.

Spectrometric Identification of Organic Compounds. 4th ed. Robert M. Silverstein et al. LC 80-20548. 442p. 1981. write for info. (ISBN 0-471-02990-4); answers avail. (ISBN 0-471-86355-6). Wiley.

Spectrometric Techniques. Ed. by G. A. Vanasse. 1977. Vol. 1. 78.00 (ISBN 0-12-710401-1); Vol. 2, 1981. 61.50 (ISBN 0-12-710402-X). Acad Pr.

Spectrometric Techniques, Vol. IV. Ed. by George Vanasse. 1985. 85.00 (ISBN 0-12-710404-6). Acad Pr.

Spectrometric Techniques, Vol. 3. Ed. by George Vanasse. LC 76-13949. 1984. 68.00 (ISBN 0-12-710403-8). Acad Pr.

Spectrophotometry of Haemoglobin Derivatives. O. W. Van Assendelft. 174p. 1970. text ed. 34.00x (ISBN 90-232-0560-X, Pub. by Van Gorcum Holland). Coronet Bks.

Spectrophysics. Anne P. Thorne. 380p. (Orig.). 1988. pap. text ed. 35.00 (ISBN 0-412-27470-1). Routledge Chapman & Hall.

Spectroscopic & Chromatographic Analysis of Mineral Oil. S. H. Kagler. 560p. 1973. text ed. 105.00x (ISBN 0-7065-1118-2, Pub. by Keter Pub Jerusalem). Coronet Bks.

Spectroscopic & Photometric Classification of Population II Stars. Ed. by A. Davis Philip. 114p. 1986. 26.00 (ISBN 0-933485-05-0); pap. 17.00 (ISBN 0-933485-04-2). L Davis Pr.

Spectroscopic Characterization Techniques for Semiconductor Technology, No. III. Ed. by Gelembocki et al. 1988. 43.00 (ISBN 0-89252-981-4, 946). SPIE.

Spectroscopic Characterization Techniques for Semiconductor Technology, No. II. Ed. by F. H. Pollak & R. Tsu. 175p. 1985. 43.00 (ISBN 0-89252-559-2, 524). SPIE.

Spectroscopic Membrane Probes. Ed. by Leslie M. Loew. 1988. 125.00 ea. Vol. I, 240 pgs (ISBN 0-8493-4535-9, 4535). Vol. II, 208 pgs (ISBN 0-8493-4536-7, 4536). Vol. III, 240 pgs (ISBN 0-8493-4537-5, 4537). CRC Pr.

Spectroscopic Methods in Organic Chemistry. 3rd ed. D. H. Williams & I. Fleming. (Illus.). 1980. pap. 39.95 (ISBN 0-07-084108-X). McGraw.

Spectroscopic Properties of Inorganic & Organometallic Compounds, Vols. 1-11. Ed. by E. A. Ebsworth. Incl. Vol. 1. 1967 Literature. 1968. 32.00 (ISBN 0-85186-003-6); Vol. 2. 1968 Literature. 1969. 36.00 (ISBN 0-85186-013-3); Vol. 3. 1969 Literature. 1970. 37.00 (ISBN 0-85186-023-0); Vol. 4. 1970 Literature. 1971. 41.00 (ISBN 0-85186-033-8); Vol. 5. 1971 Literature. 1972. 43.00 (ISBN 0-85186-043-5); Vol. 6. 1972 Literature. 1973. 47.00 (ISBN 0-85186-053-2); Vol. 7. 1973 Literature. 1974. 61.00 (ISBN 0-85186-063-X); Vol. 8. 1974 Literature. 1975. 65.00 (ISBN 0-85186-073-7); Vol. 9. 1975 Literature. 1976. 72.00 (ISBN 0-85186-083-4); Vol. 10. 1976 Literature. 1977. 82.00 (ISBN 0-685-55715-4, Pub. by Royal Soc Chem London); Vol. 11. 1977 Literature. 1978. 82.00 (ISBN 0-85186-103-2). LC 76-6662. Am Chemical.

Spectroscopic Properties of Inorganic & Organometallic Compounds, Vol. 13. 428p. 1980. 131.00 (ISBN 0-85186-113-X). Am Chemical.

Spectroscopic Properties of Inorganic & Organometallic Compounds, Vol. 20. Ed. by G. Davidson & E. A. Ebsworth. (Royal Society of Chemistry Specialist Periodical Reports). (Illus.). 510p. 1987. text ed. 216.00x (ISBN 0-85186-183-0, Pub. by Royal Soc Chem). Scholium Intl.

Spectroscopic Techniques for Organic Chemists. James W. Cooper. LC 79-23952. 376p. 1980. 34.50x (ISBN 0-471-05166-7). Wiley.

Spectroscopy. (Topics in Current Chemistry: Vol. 86). (Illus.). 1979. 85.00 (ISBN 0-387-09462-8). Springer-Verlag.

Spectroscopy & Excitation Dynamics of Condensed Molecular Systems. Ed. by V. M. Agranovitch & R. M. Hochstrasser. (Modern Problems in Condensed Matter Sciences Ser.: Vol. 4). xii, 702p. 1983. 218.50 (ISBN 0-444-86313-3). Elsevier.

Spectroscopy & Kinetics. Ed. by J. Mattson et al. (Computers in Chemistry & Instrumentation Ser: Vol. 3). 352p. 1973. 79.75 (ISBN 0-8247-6058-1). Dekker.

Spectroscopy & the Dynamics of Molecular Biological Systems. Peter M. Bayley & Robert E. Dale. 1985. 52.00 (ISBN 0-12-083240-2). Acad Pr.

Spectroscopy in Biochemistry, 2 vols. Ed. by J. Ellis Bell. 336p. Vol. 1, May 1981. 95.00 (ISBN 0-8493-5551-6); Vol. 2, April, 1981. 95.00 (ISBN 0-8493-5552-4). CRC Pr.

Spectroscopy in Biology & Chemistry: Neutron, X-Ray, Laser. Ed. by Sow-Hsin Chen & Sidney Yip. 1974. 65.50 (ISBN 0-12-170850-0). Acad Pr.

Spectroscopy in Chemistry & Physics: Modern Trends. Ed. by F. J. Comes & A. Muller. (Studies in Physical & Theoretical Chemistry: Vol. 8). 342p. 1980. 105.25 (ISBN 0-444-41856-3). Elsevier.

Spectroscopy in Heterogeneous Catalysis. William Delgass et al. LC 78-27885. 1979. 65.00 (ISBN 0-12-210150-2). Acad Pr.

Spectroscopy in Inorganic Chemistry. C. N. Rao & J. R. Ferraro. 1970-1971. Vol. 1. 79.00 (ISBN 0-12-580201-3); Vol. 2. 85.00 (ISBN 0-12-580202-1). Acad Pr.

Spectroscopy in the Biomedical Science. Ed. by R. Michael Gendreau. 240p. 1986. 99.00 (ISBN 0-8493-5740-3). CRC Pr.

Spectroscopy, Luminescence & Radiation Centers in Minerals. A. S. Marfunin. Tr. by W. W. Schiffer from Rus. (Illus.). 1979. 62.50 (ISBN 0-387-09070-3). Springer-Verlag.

Spectroscopy: NMR, Fluorescence, FT-IR. C. W. Frank et al. (Advances in Polymer Science Ser.: Vol. 54). (Illus.). 170p. 1984. 49.00 (ISBN 0-387-12591-4). Springer-Verlag.

Spectroscopy of Astrophysical Plasmas. Ed. by A. Dalgarno & D. Layzer. (Illus.). 320p. 1987. 59.50 (ISBN 0-521-26315-8); pap. 19.95 (ISBN 0-521-26927-X). Cambridge U Pr.

Spectroscopy of Biological Molecules: Proceedings of the First European Conference on the Spectroscopy of Biological Molecules, Reims, France, 1985. Alain J. Alix et al. LC 85-17771. 465p. 1985. 74.95 (ISBN 0-471-90883-5). Wiley.

Spectroscopy of Biological Molecules, Theory & Applications: Chemistry, Physics, Biology & Medicine. Ed. by Camille Sandorfy. (NATO Advanced Science Institutes Series C: Mathematical & Physical Sciences). 1984. lib. bdg. 89.00 (ISBN 90-277-1849-0, Pub. by Reidel Holland). Kluwer Academic.

Spectroscopy of Biological Systems. Ed. by R. J. Clark & R. E. Hester. (Advances in Spectroscopy Ser.). 547p. 1986. 179.95 (ISBN 0-471-90978-5). Wiley.

Spectroscopy of Condensed Media: Dynamics of Molecular Interactions. C. H. Wang. 1985. 84.00 (ISBN 0-12-734780-1). Acad Pr.

Spectroscopy of Flames. 2nd ed. A. G. Gaydon. 1974. 49.95x (ISBN 0-412-12870-5, 6120, Pub. by Chapman & Hall). Routledge Chapman & Hall.

Spectroscopy of Inorganic-Based Materials. Ed. by R. J. Clark & R. E. Hester. (Advances in Laser Spectroscopy Ser.). 1987. write for info. (ISBN 0-471-91483-5). Wiley.

Spectroscopy of Molecular Excitons. V. L. Broude et al. (Springer Series in Chemical Physics: Vol. 16). (Illus.). 290p. 1985. 53.00 (ISBN 0-387-12409-8). Springer-Verlag.

Spectroscopy of Molecular Ions. Ed. by A. Carrington & B. A. Thrush. (Series A, Vol. 324, 1988). (Illus.). 220p. 1988. text ed. 110.00x (ISBN 0-85403-340-8, Pub. by Royal Soc London). SCholium Intl.

Spectroscopy of Solid-State Laser-Type Materials. Ed. by B. Di Bartolo. LC 87-15271. (Ettore Majorana International Science Series, Physical Sciences: Vol. 30). (Illus.). 618p. 1987. 115.00x (ISBN 0-306-42617-X, Plenum Pr). Plenum Pub.

Spectroscopy of Solids Containing Rare Earth Ions. A. A. Kaplyanski & R. M. Macfarlene. (Modern Problems in Condensed Matter Sciences Ser.: Vol. 21). 1987. 200.00 (ISBN 0-444-87051-2). Elsevier.

Spectroscopy of Surfaces. Ed. by R. J. Clark & R. E. Hester. (Advances in Spectroscopy Ser.). 400p. 1988. write for info. (ISBN 0-471-91895-4). Wiley.

Spectroscopy One see Encyclopedia of Physics.

Spectroscopy Source Book. McGraw-Hill Editors. (Science Reference Ser.). (Illus.). 300p. 1988. text ed. 40.00 (ISBN 0-07-045505-8). McGraw.

Spectroscopy Two see Encyclopedia of Physics.

Spectroscopy with Polarized Light: Solute Alignment by Photoselection, in Liquid Crystals, Polymers & Membranes. J. Michl & E. W. Thulstrup. 573p. 1987. lib. bdg. 130.00 (ISBN 0-89573-346-3). VCH Pubs.

Spectrovision Inc. A Business Communication Simulation. Robert J. Ackley & Laura B. Greer. (Business Communications Ser.: 1-321). 183p. 1984. pap. text ed. write for info. (ISBN 0-471-86276-2, Pub by Wiley); tchr's. manual avail. (ISBN 0-471-87996-7). Wiley.

Spectrum. Vivienne Christensen. LC 86-50604. (Illus.). 140p. 1987. 9.95 (ISBN 1-55523-031-8). Winston-Derek.

Spectrum. S. M. Dobson. 32p. 1986. 20.00X (ISBN 0-7223-2010-8, Pub. by A H Stockwell England). State Mutual Bk.

Spectrum: A Guide to the Independent Press & Informative Organizations. 17th, rev. ed. Compiled by Bayliss Corbett. LC 81-642893. 81p. 1987. pap. 15.00x (ISBN 0-933152-09-4). Bayliss Corbett.

Spectrum: A Guide to the Independent Press & Informative Organizations. 18th, rev. ed. Compiled by Bayliss Corbett. LC 81-642893. Orig. Title: Some Hard-to-Locate Sources of Information on Current Affairs. 81p. 1988. pap. 15.00 (ISBN 0-933152-10-8). Bayliss Corbett.

Spectrum: A Reader. Hans A. Ostrom et al. 552p. 1987. pap. text ed. 13.00 (ISBN 0-15-583186-0); instr's. manual avail. (ISBN 0-15-583187-9). HarBraceJ.

Spectrum: A Science Fiction Anthology. Ed. by Kingsley Amis & Robert Conquest. 15.95 (ISBN 0-8488-0105-9, Pub. by Amereon Hse). Amereon Ltd.

Spectrum Add-On Guide. Allan Scott. (Illus.). 160p. (Orig.). 1984. pap. 11.95 (ISBN 0-246-12563-2, Pub. by Granada England). Sheridan.

Spectrum Analyzer Theory & Applications. Morris Engelson & Fred Telewski. LC 73-81244. (Modern Frontiers in Applied Science Ser.). pap. 71.80 (ISBN 0-317-30035-0, 2025050). Bks Demand UMI.

Spectrum Anthology of Short Classics, 2 Vols. Ed. by Charles Bangs. LC 86-60606. (Orig.). Set. pap. write for info. complete set (ISBN 0-938555-02-2). Vol. 1, 226 pgs (ISBN 0-938555-00-6). Vol. 2, 219 pgs (ISBN 0-938555-01-4). Spectrum Music.

Spectrum Four. 1984. pap. text ed. 6.75 (ISBN 0-13-826660-3). Prentice ESL.

Spectrum Gamesmaster. Kay Ewbank & Mike James. (Illus.). 160p. (Orig.). 1984. pap. 13.95 (ISBN 0-246-12515-2, Pub. by Granada England). Sheridan.

Spectrum Graphics LOGO. C. J. Leigh. 1984. 90.00x (ISBN 0-317-43597-3, Pub. by Sigma Pr). State Mutual Bk.

Spectrum in Chemistry. J. E. Crooks. 1978. pap. 35.00 (ISBN 0-12-195552-4). Acad Pr.

Spectrum Management Engineering. Ed. by L. Matos. LC 85-10721. (Reprint Ser.). 1985. 75.10 (ISBN 0-87942-189-4, PC01834). Inst Electrical.

Spectrum Management Techniques. Donald M. Jansky. Ed. by Donald R. White. LC 76-52508. (Illus.). 187p. 1977. text ed. 32.00 (ISBN 0-932263-11-9). White Consult.

Spectrum of Atomic Hydrogen: Advances. 500p. 1988. 78.00 (ISBN 9971-50-261-5); pap. 37.00 (ISBN 9971-50-287-9, Pub. by World Sci Singapore). World Scientific pub.

Spectrum of Consciousness. Ken Wilber. LC 76-39690. (Illus.). 1977. 12.00 (ISBN 0-8356-0495-0). Theos Pub Hse.

Spectrum of English. Incl. Orange. (gr. k). pap. text ed. 2.20 (ISBN 0-02-645510-2); tchr's ed. 3.20 (ISBN 0-02-645520-X); Red. (gr. 1). pap. text ed. 2.64 (ISBN 0-02-645530-7); tchr's ed. 3.32 (ISBN 0-02-645540-4); Blue. (gr. 2). pap. text ed. 2.88 (ISBN 0-02-645550-1); tchr's ed. 3.32 (ISBN 0-02-645560-9); Yellow. (gr. 3). pap. text ed. 7.68 (ISBN 0-02-645570-6); spiral bound tchr's ed. 10.00 (ISBN 0-02-645580-3); student activity bk. 2.40 (ISBN 0-02-643560-8); activity bk. tchr's ed. 2.80 (ISBN 0-02-643570-5); tchr's guide 2.00 (ISBN 0-02-643170-X); test prog. 1.88, profile chart. 68 (ISBN 0-685-60080-7) (ISBN 0-02-645860-8). 1978. Benziger Pub Co.

Spectrum of English: Gold. (gr. 6). 6.30 (ISBN 0-02-645660-5); tchr's annotated ed. spiralbound 7.50 (ISBN 0-686-67308-5); tchr's annotated ed. hardcover 7.50 (ISBN 0-02-645670-2); activity bk. gold 1.65 (ISBN 0-02-643620-5); activity bk. tchr's ed. 2.10 (ISBN 0-02-643630-2); testing program gold 1.20 (ISBN 0-02-643220-X); tchr's guide for testing program 1.50 (ISBN 0-02-643230-7); student profile chart gold 0.42 (ISBN 0-02-645890-X). Benziger Pub Co.

Spectrum of English: Green. (gr. 5). 6.30 (ISBN 0-02-645630-3); tchr's annotated ed spiralbound 7.50 (ISBN 0-02-645640-0); tchr's annotated ed. hardcover 7.50 (ISBN 0-02-643720-1); activity bk. green 1.65 (ISBN 0-02-643600-0); activity bk. tchr's ed. 2.10 (ISBN 0-02-643610-8, 64361); testing program green 1.20 (ISBN 0-02-643200-5); tchr's guide for testing program 1.50 (ISBN 0-02-643210-2); student profile chart green 0.42 (ISBN 0-02-645880-2). Benziger Pub Co.

Spectrum of English: Purple. (gr. 4). 5.76 (ISBN 0-02-645600-1); tchr's annotated ed. spiralbound 7.50 (ISBN 0-02-645610-9); tchr's annotated ed. hardcover 7.50 (ISBN 0-02-643710-4); activity bk. purple 1.65 (ISBN 0-02-643580-2); activity bk. tchr's ed. 2.10 (ISBN 0-02-643590-X); testing program purple 1.20 (ISBN 0-02-643180-7); tchr's guide for testing program 1.50 (ISBN 0-02-643190-4); student profile chart purple 0.42 (ISBN 0-02-645870-5). Benziger Pub Co.

Spectrum of Lexicography: Papers from AILA Brussels 1984. Ed. by Robert Ilson. LC 87-18414. ix, 158p. 1987. 26.00x (ISBN 1-55619-033-6). Benjamins North Am.

Spectrum of Love. rev. ed. Walter Rinder. LC 72-96369. (Illus.). 64p. 1984. pap. 4.95 (ISBN 0-912310-19-7). Celestial Arts.

Spectrum of Political Engagement: Mounier, Benda, Nizan, Brasillach, Sartre. David Schalk. LC 78-70318. 1979. 28.00x (ISBN 0-691-05275-1). Princeton U Pr.

Spectrum of Psychiatric Research. Ed. by Michael Shepherd. 256p. 1985. 32.50 (ISBN 0-521-26585-1). Cambridge U Pr.

Spectrum of Rhetoric. Dorothy Guinn & Danie Marder. 1987. pap. text ed. write for info. (ISBN 0-316-33132-5). Little.

Spectrum of Ritual: A Biogenetic Structural Analysis. Eugene G. D'Aquili et al. LC 78-19015. 408p. 1979. 37.00x (ISBN 0-231-04514-X). Columbia U Pr.

Spectrum of Social Time. G. Gurvitch. Ed. by Myrtle Korenbaum. Tr. by Phillip Bosserman from Fr. (Synthese Library). 152p. 1964. lib. bdg. 21.00 (ISBN 90-277-0006-0, Pub. by Reidel Holland). Kluwer Academic.

Spectrum of the Fantastic: Selected Essays from the Sixth International Conference on the Fantastic in the Arts. Ed. by Donald Palumbo. LC 87-25216. (Contributions ot the Study of Science Fiction & Fantasy Ser.: No. 31). (Illus.). 288p. 1988. lib. bdg. 45.00 (ISBN 0-313-25502-4, PPF/). Greenwood.

Spectrum of UFO Research: Proceedings of the 1981 CUFOS Conference. Ed. by Mimi Hynek. (Illus.). 232p. 1988. pap. 11.00. J A Hynek Ctr UFO.

Spectrum of Visual Arts for Young Children. Anne G. Blond & Leslye Janusz. Ed. by Jessica Radin. LC 76-3044. (Illus.). 114p. 1976. pap. 4.95 (ISBN 0-916634-00-0). Double M Pr.

Spectrum One: Teacher's Edition. Dye & Frankfort. (Spectrum Ser.). 158p. 1982. pap. text ed. 12.50 (ISBN 0-13-826751-0, 20103). Prentice ESL.

Spectrum One: Textbook. Diane Warshawsky. (Spectrum Ser.). (Illus.). 136p. (gr. 7-12). 1982. pap. text ed. 6.75 (ISBN 0-13-826637-9, 20088). Prentice ESL.

Spectrum One: Workbook. Abrams & Rein. (Spectrum Ser.). (Illus.). 92p. (gr. 7-12). 1982. pap. text ed. 4.25 (ISBN 0-13-826694-8, 20090). Prentice ESL.

Spectrum Three. Warshawsky & Constinett. Incl. Joan Dye & Nancy Frankfort. 208p. 1983. pap. text ed. 12.50 tchr's ed. (ISBN 0-13-826777-4, 20280); Abrams et al. pap. text ed. 4.25 wkbk. (ISBN 0-13-826710-3, 20278). 144p. 1983. pap. text ed. 6.75 (ISBN 0-13-826652-2, 20127); cassettes 45.00 (ISBN 0-13-826835-5). Prentice ESL.

Spectrum Two: Teacher's Edition. Dye & Frankfort. (Spectrum Ser.). 1983. pap. text ed. 12.50 (ISBN 0-13-826769-3, 20266). Prentice ESL.

Spectrum Two: Textbook. Sandra Costinett. (Spectrum Ser.). (gr. 7-12). 1982. pap. text ed. 6.75 (ISBN 0-13-826645-X, 20115). Prentice ESL.

Spectrum Two: Workbook. Abrams & Byrd. (Spectrum Ser.). 96p. (gr. 7-12). 1982. pap. text ed. 4.25 (ISBN 0-13-826702-2, 20254). Prentice ESL.

Speculation & Revelation. Lev Shestov. Tr. by Bernard Martin from Rus. LC 81-38425. x, 312p. 1982. lib. bdg. 32.95x (ISBN 0-8214-0422-9). Ohio U Pr.

Speculation As a Fine Art & Thoughts on Life. Dickson G. Watts. 1979. Repr. of 1965 ed. 5.00 (ISBN 0-87034-056-5). Fraser Pub Co.

Speculation in Commodity Contracts & Options. 2nd ed. L. Dee Belveal. 250p. 1985. 40.00 (ISBN 0-87094-672-2). Dow Jones-Irwin.

Speculation in Gold & Silver. Kenneth E. Carpenter. LC 74-367. (Vol. 14). 1974. gold 13.00x (ISBN 0-405-05928-0). Ayer Co Pubs.

Speculation in Murder. Joan P. Mitchell. (Private Library Collection). 1986. mini-bound 6.95 (ISBN 0-938422-28-6). SOS Pubns CA.

Speculation on the New York Stock Exchange, September, 1904-March, 1907. Algernon A. Osborne. (Columbia University. Studies in the Social Sciences: No. 137). Repr. of 1913 ed. 16.50 (ISBN 0-404-51137-6). AMS Pr.

Speculation on the Stock & Produce Exchanges of the United States. Henry C. Emery. LC 70-76663. (Columbia University, Studies in the Social Sciences Ser.: No. 18). Repr. of 1896 ed. 12.50 (ISBN 0-404-51018-3). AMS Pr.

Speculations, 1 Vol. J. H. Hacsi. 205p. (Orig.). 1983. pap. text ed. 9.95 (ISBN 0-9612146-0-0). Champagne Pr.

Speculations. Thomas E. Hulme. LC 78-64034. (Des Imagistes: Literature of the Imagist Movement). Repr. of 1924 ed. 24.00 (ISBN 0-404-17115-X). AMS Pr.

Speculations About Jakob. Uwe Johnson. Tr. by Ursule Molinaro. LC 62-17528. 240p. 1972. pap. 4.95 (ISBN 0-15-684719-1, HB236, Harv). HarBraceJ.

Speculations on American History. Morton Borden & Otis L. Graham. 1977. pap. text ed. 11.50 (ISBN 0-669-00488-X). Heath.

Speculations on the Fourth Dimension: Selected Writings of C. H. Hinton. Charles H. Hinton. Ed. by Rudolf V. Rucker. (Illus.). 1980. pap. 4.95 (ISBN 0-486-23916-0). Dover.

Speculative Dialogues. Lascell Abercrombie. 1988. Repr. of 1971 ed. lib. bdg. 49.00x. Am Biog Serv.

Speculative Dialogues. Lascelles Abercrombie. 1971. Repr. of 1913 ed. 39.00 (ISBN 0-403-00799-2). Scholarly.

Speculative Freemasonary. John Yarker. 1987. pap. 3.95 (ISBN 0-916411-66-4, Pub. by Sure Fire). Holmes Pub.

Speculative Grammar, Universal Grammar, Philosophical Analysis: Papers in the Philosophy of Language. Ed. by Dino Buzzetti & Maurizio Ferriani. LC 87-8081. (Studies in the History of the Language Sciences: No. 42). x, 268p. 1988. 36.00x (ISBN 90-272-4525-8). Benjamins North Am.

Speculative Grammars of the Middle Ages: The Doctrine of Partes Orationis of the Modistae. G. L. Bursill-Hall. LC 70-151246. (Approaches to Semiotics Ser: No. 11). 424p. 1971. text ed. 44.80x (ISBN 90-2791-913-5). Mouton.

Speculative High-Rise Dilemma: Fully Sprinklered or Hydraulic Fire Alarm. David R. Baker. 4.35 (ISBN 0-318-03823-4, TR84-6). Society Fire Protect.

Speculative Markets. Sarkis J. Khoury. 480p. 1984. text ed. write for info. (ISBN 0-02-362850-2). Macmillan.

Speculative Markets. Robert Strong. 1988. 34.95 (ISBN 0-88462-165-0). Longman Finan.

Speculative Masonry Its Mission, Its Evolution & Its Landmarks. A. S. Macbride. 264p. 1971. Repr. of 1924 ed. text ed. 6.00 (ISBN 0-88053-040-5, M-89). Macoy Pub.

Speculative Notes & Notes on Speculation, Ideal & Real. D. Morier Evans. 1968. Repr. of 1864 ed. 16.00 (ISBN 0-8337-1089-3). B Franklin.

Speculative Notes & Notes on Speculation: Ideal & Real. D. Morier Evans. LC 73-85788. 1969. Repr. of 1864 ed. 39.50x (ISBN 0-678-00560-5). Kelley.

Speculative Pragmatism. Sandra B. Rosenthal. LC 85-31813. 224p. 1986. lib. bdg. 25.00X (ISBN 0-87023-526-5). U of Mass Pr.

Speculator: Bernard M. Baruch in Washington, 1917-1965. Jordan A. Schwarz. LC 80-17386. (Illus.). xvii, 679p. 1981. 32.50x (ISBN 0-8078-1396-6). U of NC Pr.

Speculators & Patriots: Essays in Business Biography. Ed. by R. P. Davenport-Hines. 224p. 1986. 32.50x (ISBN 0-7146-3301-1, F Cass Co). Biblio Dist.

Speculi Britanniae Pars. John Norden. Ed. by Henry Ellis. (Camden Socitety, London. Publications, First Ser.: No. 9). Repr. of 1840 ed. 19.00 (ISBN 0-404-50109-5). AMS Pr.

Speculi Britanniae Pars: An Historical & Chorographical Description of the County of Essex. John Norden. Repr. of 1840 ed. 19.00 (ISBN 0-384-41925-9). Johnson Repr.

Speculi Britanniae; the Description of Hartfordshire. John Norden. LC 74-171778. (English Experience Ser.: No. 403). 38p. 1971. Repr. of 1598 ed. 20.00 (ISBN 90-221-0403-6). Walter J Johnson.

Speculum Amantis: Love Poems. Arthur H. Bullen. 1902. 25.00 (ISBN 0-89984-035-3). Century Bookbindery.

Speculum Amantis: Love Poems from Rare Song-Books & Miscellanies of the Seventeenth Century see Collections of Lyrics & Poems: Sixteenth & Seventeenth Centuries.

Speculum Britanniae: The First Parte, a Description of Middlesex. John Norden. LC 70-171777. (English Experience Ser.: No. 402). 58p. 1971. Repr. of 1593 ed. 20.00 (ISBN 90-221-0402-8). Walter J Johnson.

Speculum Caritatis see Mirror of Charity.

Speculum Christiani: A Middle English Religious Treatise of the 14th Century. (EETS OS: No. 182). Repr. of 1933 ed. 65.00 (ISBN 0-527-00179-1). Kraus Repr.

Speculum Devotorum of an Anonymous Carhusian of Sheen: From the manuscripts Cambridge University Library (Gg. I.6 & Foyle Vol.2) James Hogg. (Analecta Carusiana Ser.: No. 12). 173p. (Orig., English, Middle.). 1973. pap. 25.00 (ISBN 3-7052-0013-5, Pub by Salzburg Studies). Longwood Pub Group.

Speculum Devotorum of an Anonymous Carhusian of Sheen: From the Manuscripts Cambridge University Library (Gg. I.6 & Foyle Vol.3, Pt. 2) Ed. by james Hogg. (Analecta Carusiana Ser.: No. 13). 174p. (Orig., English, Middle.). 1974. pap. 25.00 (ISBN 3-7052-0014-3, Pub by Salzburg Studies). Longwood Pub Group.

Speculum Devotorum of an Anonymous Carthusian of Sheen: Introduction. James Hogg. (Analceta Cartusiana Ser.: No. 11). (Orig.). 1985. pap. 25.00 (ISBN 3-7052-0012-7, Pub by Salzburg Studies). Longwood Pub Group.

Speculum Duorum: Or a Mirror of Two Men. G. Cambrensis. Ed. by I. Lefevre & R. B. Huygens. (History & Law Ser.: No. 27). 298p. 1974. text ed. 22.50x (ISBN 0-7083-0544-X, Pub. by U of Wales). Humanities.

Speculum Guidonis de Warewyke. Ed. by Georgiana L. Morrill. (EETS, ES Ser.: No. 75). Repr. of 1898 ed. 42.00 (ISBN 0-527-00277-1). Kraus Repr.

'Speculum Inclusorum' MS. British Library London Harley 2372: A Critical Edition, Vol. 1. James Hogg. (Analecta Cartusiana Ser.: No. 59-1). (Orig.). 1985. pap. 25.00 (ISBN 3-7052-0086-0, Pub. by Salzburg Studies). Longwood Pub Group.

'Speculum Incusorum' MS. British Library London Harley 2372. James Hogg. (Analecta Cartusiana Ser.: No. 59-2). 139p. (Orig., Lat.). 1981. pap. 25.00 (ISBN 3-7052-0087-9, Pub. by Salzburg Studies). Longwood Pub Group.

Speculum Mentis: The Map of Knowledge. Robin G. Collingwood. LC 82-15552. 327p. 1982. Repr. of 1924 ed. lib. bdg. 41.50x (ISBN 0-313-23701-8, COSM). Greenwood.

Speculum Musicae. Jacobi Leodiensis, III & F. Joseph Smith. (Wissenschaftliche Abhanlungen: Musicological Studies: Vol. 43). 140p. 1983. lib. bdg. 38.00 (ISBN 0-931902-37-1). Inst Mediaeval Mus.

Speculum Musicae of Jacobus Leodiensis II. F. Joseph Smith. (Wissenschaftliche Abhandlungen-Musicological Studies Ser.: Vol. 22). 160p. 1971. lib. bdg. 50.00 (ISBN 0-912024-95-X). Inst Mediaeval Mus.

Speculum Musicae of Jacobus Leodiensis I. F. Joseph Smith. (Wissenschaftliche Abhandlugen-Musicological Studies: Vol. 13). 72p. 1967. lib. bdg. 12.00 (ISBN 0-912024-83-6). Inst Mediaeval Mus.

Speculum Nauticum: A Looking Glasse, for Sea-Men. John Aspley. LC 77-6849. (English Experience Ser: No. 844). 1977. Repr. of 1624 ed. lib. bdg. 17.50 (ISBN 90-221-0844-9). Walter J Johnson.

Speculum of the Other Woman. Luce Irigaray. Tr. by Gillian C. Gill from Fr. LC 84-45151. 416p. 1985. 44.50x (ISBN 0-8014-1663-9); pap. 16.95x (ISBN 0-8014-9330-7). Cornell U Pr.

Speculum Sacerdotale. (EETS, OS Ser.: No. 200). Repr. of 1936 ed. 45.00 (ISBN 0-527-00200-3). Kraus Repr.

Speculum Speculationum. Alexander Nequam. Ed. by Rodney M. Thomson. (Auctores Britannici Medii Aevi XI Ser.: No. XI). 550p. 1988. 96.00 (ISBN 0-19-726067-5). Oxford U Pr.

Speculum Topographicum: Or, the Topographicall Glasse. Arthur Hopton. LC 74-80189. (English Experience Ser.: No. 669). (Illus.). 203p. 1974. Repr. of 1611 ed. 45.00 (ISBN 90-221-0669-1). Walter J Johnson.

Speculum Vitae. John Smeltz. Ed. by James Hogg. (Elizabeth & Renaissance Studies). (Orig.). 1984. pap. 15.00 (ISBN 3-7052-0752-0, Pub. by Salzburg Studies). Longwood Pub Group.

Speech - Language Treatment of the Aphasias: An Integrated Clinical Approach. Rehabilitation Institute of Chicago Staff. Ed. by Martha Burns & Anita Halper. 1988. 44.00 (ISBN 0-87189-891-8). Aspen Pub.

Speech: A Basic Text. 3rd ed. Robert Jeffrey & Owen Peterson. 384p. 1988. pap. text ed. 18.95t (ISBN 0-06-043282-9, HarpC). Har-Row.

Speech: A Basic Text. 2nd ed. Robert C. Jeffrey & Owen Peterson. 412p. 1982. pap. text ed. 22.50 scp (ISBN 0-06-043279-9, HarpC). Har-Row.

Speech Acoustics & Perception. Arthur Boothroyd. Ed. by Harvey Halpern. LC 86-3236. (Studies in Communicative Disorders). (Illus.). 48p. 1986. pap. text ed. 7.00x (ISBN 0-89079-079-5, 1368). Pro Ed.

Speech Act Phenomenology. Lanigan. 1977. pap. 24.00 (ISBN 90-247-1920-8, Pub. by Martins Nijhoff Netherlands). Kluwer Academic.

Speech Act Theory & Pragmatics. Ed. by John R. Searle et al. (Synthese Language Library: No. 10). xii, 312p. 1980. lib. bdg. 39.50 (ISBN 90-277-1043-0, Pub. by Reidel Holland); pap. 19.50 (ISBN 90-277-1045-7). Kluwer Academic.

Speech Acts. John R. Searle. LC 68-24484. 1970. 39.50 (ISBN 0-521-07184-4); pap. 11.95x (ISBN 0-521-09626-X). Cambridge U Pr.

Speech Acts: Hints & Samples. Carroll Britch et al. 112p. (Orig.). 1983. pap. text ed. 8.95x (ISBN 0-88133-016-7). Waveland Pr.

Speech Acts in Argumentative Discussions: A Theoretical Model for the Analysis of Discussions Directed Towards Solving Conflicts of Opinion. F. H. Van Eemeren & R. Grootendorst. (PDA Ser.). vi, 215p. 1984. write for info. (ISBN 90-6765-018-8). Foris Pubns.

Speech Acts, Speakers & Hearers Reference & Referential Strategies in Spanish. Henk Haverkate. LC 84-24200. (Pragmatics & Beyond Ser.: Vol. V, No. 4). xi, 142p. (Orig.). 1984. pap. 34.00x (ISBN 0-915027-42-9). Benjamins North Am.

Speech Acts Taxonomy As a Tool for Ethnographic Description: An Analysis Based on Videotapes of Continuous Behavior in Two New York Households. Nira Reiss. LC 86-8207. (Pragmatics & Beyond Ser.: VI-7). x, 153p. (Orig.). 1985. pap. 36.00x (ISBN 0-915027-93-3). Benjamins North Am.

Speech After Laryngectomy. Louis M. DiCarlo et al. (Special Education & Rehabilitation Monograph: No. 1). (Illus.). 1955. 8.95x (ISBN 0-8156-2016-0). Syracuse U Pr.

Speech After Stroke. 2nd ed. S. Stryker. (Illus.). 442p. 1981. spiral lexotone 28.75 (ISBN 0-398-04122-9). C C Thomas.

Speech Analysis. Ed. by Ronald W. Schafer & John D. Markel. LC 78-65706. 480p. 1979. 52.05 (ISBN 0-87942-119-3, PC01123). Inst Electrical.

Speech Analysis, Synthesis & Perception. 2nd rev. ed. J. L. Flanagan. LC 70-172068. (Communications & Cybernetics: Vol. 3). (Illus.). 440p. 1972. 42.00 (ISBN 0-387-05561-4). Springer-Verlag.

Speech & Brain Mechanisms. Wilder Penfield & Lamar Roberts. LC 59-5602. (Illus.). 304p. 1959. 41.00x (ISBN 0-691-08039-9); pap. 11.50x (ISBN 0-691-02366-2). Princeton U Pr.

Speech & Deafness. rev. ed. Donald R. Calvert & S. Richard Silverman. 304p. 1983. pap. text ed. 16.95 (ISBN 0-88200-070-5). Alexander Graham.

Speech & Drama. 2nd ed. Rudolf Steiner. 417p. 1985. pap. 19.00 (ISBN 0-88010-142-3). Anthroposophic.

Speech & Drama Club Activities. Gerald L. Ratcliff. (Theatre Student Ser.). 108p. 1982. lib. bdg. 14.95 (ISBN 0-8239-0565-9). Rosen Group.

Speech & Facsimile Scrambling & Decoding: Basic Text on Speech Scrambling. (Cryptographic Ser.). 1981. lib. bdg. 30.80 (ISBN 0-89412-119-7); pap. 22.80 (ISBN 0-89412-046-8). Aegean Park Pr.

Speech & Hearing. Ed. by Dale C. Garell & Solomon H. Snyder. (Encyclopedia of Health Ser.). (Illus.). (YA) (gr. 7-12). 1989. 17.95 (ISBN 0-7910-0029-X). Chelsea Hse.

Speech & Hearing Problems in the Classroom. Phyllis P. Phillips. LC 74-78838. (Speech & Hearing Ser.). (Illus.). 159p. (Orig.). 1984. pap. text ed. 5.95 (ISBN 0-8220-1807-1). Cliffs.

Speech & Hearing Science: Anatomy & Physiology. 2nd ed. W. R. Zemlin. (Illus.). 704p. 1981. text ed. 42.00 (ISBN 0-13-827378-2). P-H.

Speech & Hearing Science: Selected Readings. Ed. by Norman J. Lass. 382p. 1974. text ed. 49.50x (ISBN 0-8422-5154-5); pap. text ed. 14.50x (ISBN 0-8422-0377-X). Irvington.

Speech & Hearing Therapist. Jack Rudman. (Career Examination Ser.: C-754). (Cloth bdg. avail. on request). pap. 14.00 (ISBN 0-8373-0754-6). Natl Learning.

Speech & Language. Doreen Kimura. (Readings from the Encyclopedia of Neuroscience Ser.). 110p. 1988. 24.50 (ISBN 0-8176-3400-2). Birkhauser.

Speech & Language. 1981. 2.50 (ISBN 0-939418-39-8). Ferguson-Florissant.

Speech & Language: Advances in Basic Research & Practice. Ed. by Norman J. Lass. (Serial Publication: Vol. 9). 1983. 65.00 (ISBN 0-12-608609-5). Acad Pr.

Speech & Language: Advances in Basic Research & Practice, Vol. 1. Ed. by Norman J. Lass. (Serial Publication). 1979. 65.00 (ISBN 0-12-608601-X). Acad Pr.

Speech & Language: Advances in Basic Research & Practice, Vol. 3. Ed. by Norman J. Lass. (Serial Publication). 1980. 65.00 (ISBN 0-12-608603-6). Acad Pr.

Speech & Language: Advances in Basic Research & Practice, Vol. 4. Ed. by Norman J. Lass. 1980. 65.00 (ISBN 0-12-608604-4). Acad Pr.

Speech & Language: Advances in Basic Research & Practice, Vol. 5. Ed. by Norman J. Lass. (Serial Publication). 1981. 65.00 (ISBN 0-12-608605-2). Acad Pr.

Speech & Language: Advances in Basic Research & Practice, Vol. 6. Ed. by Norman J. Lass. (Serial Publication). 496p. 1982. 65.00 (ISBN 0-12-608606-0). Acad Pr.

Speech & Language: Advances in Basic Research & Practice, Vol. 7. Norman J. Lass. (Serial Publication Ser.). 1982. 65.00 (ISBN 0-12-608607-9). Acad Pr.

Speech & Language: Advances in Basic Research & Practice, Vol. 8. Ed. by Norman J. Lass. (Serial Publication Ser.). 1982. 65.00 (ISBN 0-12-608608-7). Acad Pr.

Speech & Language: Advances in Basic Research & Practice, Vol. 10. Norman J. Lass. (Serial Publication). 1984. 65.00 (ISBN 0-12-608610-9). Acad Pr.

Speech & Language: Advances in Basic Research & Practice, Vol. 2. Ed. by Norman J. Lass. (Serial Publication). 1979. 65.00 (ISBN 0-12-608602-8). Acad Pr.

Speech & Language Assessment for the Bilingual Handicapped. Larry J. Mattes & Donald R. Omark. LC 84-9601. (Illus.). 174p. 1984. pap. 20.50 (ISBN 0-316-55089-2). College-Hill.

Speech & Language Based Interaction with Machines. Waterworth. LC 87-27558. 170p. 1988. 44.95 (ISBN 0-470-21033-8). Wiley.

Speech & Language Disorders. Gilda Berger. LC 80-85052. (Impact Bks.). (YA) (gr. 7 up). 1981. PLB 12.90 (ISBN 0-531-04263-4). Watts.

Speech & Language Evaluation in Neurology: Adult Disorders. Ed. by John Darby, Jr. 460p. 1985. 79.50 (ISBN 0-8089-1719-6, 790976). Grune.

Speech & Language Evaluation in Neurology: Childhood Disorders. Ed. by John Darby, Jr. 304p. 1985. 57.50 (ISBN 0-8089-1720-X, 790979). Grune.

Speech & Language in Psychoanalysis. Jacques Lacan. Tr. by Anthony Wilden from Fr. LC 68-15446. 368p. 1981. pap. 10.95x (ISBN 0-8018-2617-9). Johns Hopkins.

Speech & Language in the Laboratory, School & Clinic. Ed. by James F. Kavanagh & Winifred Strange. 1978. 45.00x (ISBN 0-262-11065-2). MIT Pr.

Speech & Language Pathology. Jack Rudman. (National Teachers Examination Ser.: NT-33). (Cloth bdg. avail. on request). pap. 13.95 (ISBN 0-8373-8443-5). Natl Learning.

Speech & Language: Principles & Processes of Behavior Change. C. Woodruff Starweather. (Illus.). 448p. 1983. write for info. (ISBN 0-13-832501-4). P-H.

Speech & Language Rehabilitation: A Workbook for the Neurologically Impaired & Language Delayed, Vol. 1. 3rd ed. Robert L. Keith. (Illus.). 300p. 1987. pap. text ed. 12.95x (ISBN 0-8134-2691-X). Inter Print Pubs.

Speech & Language Rehabilitation: A Workbook for the Neurologically Impaired, Vol. 2. 2nd ed. Robert Keith. 1984. pap. 12.95x (ISBN 0-8134-2339-2). Inter Print Pubs.

Speech & Language: Vol. 11: Advances in Basic Research & Theory. Ed. by Norman J. Lass. (Serial Publication). 1984. 65.00 (ISBN 0-12-608611-7). Acad Pr.

Speech & Law in a Free Society. Franklyn S. Haiman. LC 81-7546. x, 500p. 1981. lib. bdg. 30.00x (ISBN 0-226-31213-5); pap. 15.00 (ISBN 0-226-31214-3). U of Chicago Pr.

Speech & Lipreading Instructional Program. Mary A. Shurina. 1977. pap. text ed. 10.95 (ISBN 0-8134-1840-2, 1840); instructor's booklet 1.00x (ISBN 0-8134-1839-9, 1839). Inter Print Pubs.

Speech & Music. Ed. by Herbert Eimert & Karlheinz Stockhausen. Tr. by Margaret Shenfield & Ruth Koenig. (Reihe: No. 6). 1964. pap. 4.75 (ISBN 0-900938-14-5, UE26106E). Eur-Am Music.

Speech & Phenomena: And Other Essays on Husserl's Theory of Signs. Jacques Derrida. Tr. by David B. Allison from Ger. LC 72-80565. (Studies in Phenomenology & Existential Philosophy). 1973. text ed. 23.95x (ISBN 0-8101-0397-4); pap. 11.95 (ISBN 0-8101-0590-X). Northwestern U Pr.

Speech & Reality. Eugen Rosenstock-Huessy. 1969. pap. 10.00 (ISBN 0-912148-02-0). Argo Bks.

Speech & Reason: Language Disorder in Mental Disease & a Translation of Philipp Wegener's The Life of Speech. D. Wilfred Abse. LC 72-163981. 1971. 30.00x (ISBN 0-8139-0344-0). U Pr of Va.

Speech & Society: The Christian Linguistic Social Philsophy of Eugen Rosenstock-Huessy. George A. Morgan. 192p. 1987. 25.00x (ISBN 0-8130-0852-2). U Presses Fla.

Speech & Speaker Recognition. Ed. by Manfred R. Schroeder. (Bibliotheca Phonetica Ser.: No. 12). (Illus.). viii, 204p. 1985. 92.75 (ISBN 3-8055-4012-4). S Karger.

Speech & Speech Disorders in Western Thought Before 1600. Ynez V. O'Neill. LC 79-7361. (Contributions in Medical History: No. 3). 1980. lib. bdg. 35.00 (ISBN 0-313-21058-6, OSD/). Greenwood.

Speech & the Hearing Impaired Child: Theory & Practice. Daniel Ling. LC 76-21920. (Illus.). 1976. text ed. 20.95 (ISBN 0-88200-074-8, A0669). Alexander Graham.

Speech & Voice Characteristics of the Deaf. Joanne D. Subtelny et al. 1981. incl. 5 cassettes, student handbook, & administration manual 50.00 (ISBN 0-88200-142-6, A0235). Alexander Graham.

Speech Art Classification. T. Ballmer & W. Brennenstuhl. (Springer Series in Language & Communication: Vol. 8). (Illus.). 274p. 1980. 31.50 (ISBN 0-387-10294-9). Springer-Verlag.

Speech As an Art. H. D. Flowers, II. 240p. 1978. pap. text ed. 18.95 (ISBN 0-8403-1939-8). Kendall-Hunt.

Speech As Instruction. H. Shands. 1977. 41.00x (ISBN 90-279-7725-9). Mouton.

Speech Assessment & Speech Improvement for the Hearing Impaired. Ed. by Joanne D. Subtelny. 420p. 1980. pap. text ed. 19.95 (ISBN 0-88200-138-8, A0138). Alexander Graham.

Speech Audiologist. Jack Rudman. (Career Examination Ser.: C-753). (Cloth bdg. avail. on request). pap. 14.00 (ISBN 0-8373-0753-8). Natl Learning.

Speech Audiometry. Ed. by Michael Martin. 300p. 1987. 66.00x (ISBN 0-85066-641-4); pap. 33.00x (ISBN 0-85066-638-4). Taylor & Francis.

Speech Bingo, Set 1. Kathleen M. Morrissey. (Illus.). 1980. pap. 7.95x (ISBN 0-8134-2144-6). Inter Print Pubs.

Speech Can Change Your Life. Dorothy Sarnoff. 367p. 1971. pap. 4.50 (ISBN 0-440-18199-2, Dell Pbks). Dell.

Speech Chain: The Physics & Biology of Spoken Language. Peter B. Denes & Elliot N. Pinson. LC 74-180069. 192p. 1973. pap. 4.50 (ISBN 0-385-04238-8, Anch). Doubleday.

Speech Chairman - Sr. H.S. Jack Rudman. (Teachers License Examination Ser.: CH-27). (Cloth bdg. avail. on request). pap. 15.95 (ISBN 0-8373-8177-0). Natl Learning.

Speech Chief. Jane O. James. (Illus.). 64p. 1980. pap. 2.95x (ISBN 0-8134-2108-X). Inter Print Pubs.

Speech Choir. Marjorie Gullan. LC 71-116405. (Granger Index Reprint Ser). 1937. 19.00 (ISBN 0-8369-6146-3). Ayer Co Pubs.

Speech Class Goes Home. Carolyn S. Tavzel. (Illus.). 80p. 1985. text ed. 11.95x (ISBN 0-8134-2484-4, 2484). Inter Print Pubs.

Speech Communication. 5th ed. William D. Brooks & Robert W. Heath. 400p. 1985. pap. text ed. write for info. (ISBN 0-697-00461-9); student wkbk. avail. (ISBN 0-697-00521-6); instr's. manual avail. (ISBN 0-697-00520-8). Wm C Brown.

Speech-Communication. Kathleen M. Galvin & Cassandra Book. 1972. pap. text ed. 11.95 (ISBN 0-8442-5127-5). Natl Textbk.

Speech Communication. Saundra Hybels & Richard Weaver. 352p. 1986. pap. text ed. write for info (ISBN 0-394-33931-2, RanC). Random.

Speech Communication. Jack Rudman. (National Teachers Examination Ser.: NT-35). (Cloth bdg. avail. on request). pap. 13.95 (ISBN 0-8373-8445-1). Natl Learning.

Speech Communication: A Basic Approach. 4th ed. Ernest G. Bormann & Nancy C. Bormann. 280p. 1985. pap. text ed. 16.95 (ISBN 0-06-040867-7, HarpC). Har-Row.

Speech Communication: A Career Education Approach. 2nd ed. Ray E. Nadeau & John M. Muchmore. 276p. 1979. text ed. 14.00 (ISBN 0-394-34978-4, RanC). Random.

Speech Communication: A Contemporary Introduction. 3rd ed. Gordon I. Zimmerman et al. (Illus.). 288p. 1986. pap. text ed. 26.00 (ISBN 0-314-93529-0). West Pub.

Speech Communication: A Reader. Richard Weaver, 2nd. 1975. text ed. 10.95 (ISBN 0-88429-014-X). Best Bks Pub.

Speech Communication & Human Interaction. 2nd ed. Thomas M. Scheidel. 1976. text ed. write for info. (ISBN 0-673-15005-4). Scott F.

Speech Communication: Expanding a Practical Approach. Barbara Tucker & Donna E. Tallman. 288p. 1985. pap. text ed. 17.95 (ISBN 0-8403-3795-7). Kendall-Hunt.

Speech Communication for International Students. Paulette Dale & James C. Wolf. (Illus.). 160p. 1988. pap. text ed. price not set (ISBN 0-13-827312-X). P-H.

Speech Communication for the Classroom Teacher. 3rd ed. Pamela J. Cooper. 1988. pap. text ed. 21.00. Gorsuch Scarisbrick.

Speech Communication: Fundamentals & Practice. 7th ed. Raymond S. Ross. (Illus.). 416p. 1986. text ed. write for info (ISBN 0-13-827536-X). P H.

Speech Communication in Society. 2nd ed. Charles R. Gruner et al. 1977. text ed. 24.67 (ISBN 0-205-05732-2, 4857321); instr's. manual avail. (ISBN 0-205-05733-0). Allyn.

Speech Communication Reader. Marcus L. Ambrester & Faye D. Julian. 217p. (Orig.). 1983. pap. text ed. 10.95x (ISBN 0-88133-013-2). Waveland Pr.

Speech Communication Readings. Malcolm McAvoy. 168p. (gr. 10-12). 1983. pap. 12.95 (ISBN 0-8403-3134-7). Kendall-Hunt.

Speech Communication: Theory & Practice. Albert Tepper. 1978. pap. text ed. 7.95 (ISBN 0-8403-1931-2). Kendall-Hunt.

Speech Communication with Computers. Ed. by Leonhard Bolc. 1978. pap. cancelled (ISBN 3-4461-2650-3). Adlers Foreign Bks.

Speech Communication Workbook: Exercises & Activities. Ellen A. Hay. LC 87-9564. (Illus.). 303p. 1988. pap. text ed. 12.95x (ISBN 0-935732-09-8); instr's. manual avail. Roxbury Pub Co.

Speech Communications. Douglas O'Shaughnessy. (Electrical & Computer Engineering Ser.). (Illus.). 600p. 1986. text ed. write for info. (ISBN 0-201-16520-1). Addison-Wesley.

Speech: Content & Communication. 5th ed. Charles S. Mudd & Malcolm O. Sillars. 352p. 1985. pap. 20.50 scp (ISBN 0-06-044661-7, HarpC). Har-Row.

Speech Correction: An Introduction to Speech Pathology & Audiology. Charles Van Riper & Lon L. Emerick. LC 83-13905. (Illus.). 512p. 1984. write for info. (ISBN 0-13-829531-X). P-H.

Speech Correction Through Story-Telling Units. Elizabeth M. Nemoy. 1973. text ed. 6.00 (ISBN 0-686-09399-2). Expression.

Speech Criticism. 2nd ed. Lester Thonssen et al. LC 80-20234. 592p. 1981. Repr. of 1970 ed. text ed. 34.50 (ISBN 0-89874-247-1). Krieger.

Speech Delivered in the Starr-Chamber, at the Censure of J. Bastwick. William Laud. LC 79-171771. (English Experience Ser.: No. 396). 92p. 1971. Repr. of 1637 ed. 20.00 (ISBN 90-221-0396-X). Walter J Johnson.

Speech Development of a Bilingual Child, 4 vols. Werner F. Leopold. Incl. Vol. 6. Vocabulary Growth in the First Two Years. Repr. of 1954 ed (ISBN 0-404-50706-9); Vol. 11. Sound-Learning in the First Two Years. Repr. of 1947 ed (ISBN 0-404-50711-5); Vol. 18. Grammar & General Problems in the First Two Years. Repr. of 1949 ed (ISBN 0-404-50718-2); Vol. 19. Diary from Age Two. Repr. of 1949 ed (ISBN 0-404-50719-0). (Northwestern University. Humanities Ser). Set. 90.00 (ISBN 0-404-50749-2); 22.50 ea. AMS Pr.

Speech Disorders: Aphasia, Apraxie & Agnosia. Walter R. Brain. LC 63-5076. (Illus.). pap. 50.00 (ISBN 0-317-41727-4, 2025730). Bks Demand UMI.

Speech Disorders: Clinical Evaluation & Diagnosis. Ed. by E. Jeffrey Metter. LC 84-23794. (Neurologic Illness: Diagnosis & Treatment Ser.). 256p. 1985. text ed. 40.00 (ISBN 0-89335-223-3); cassette tape 12.95; Set. 49.95. PMA Pub Corp.

Speech Disorders in Adults: Recent Advances. Ed. by Janis M. Costello. LC 84-29199. (Illus.). 250p. 1985. 31.00 (ISBN 0-316-15767-8). College-Hill.

Speech Disorders in Children: Recent Advances. Ed. by Janis M. Costello. LC 83-23141. (Illus.). 374p. 1984. 31.00 (ISBN 0-316-15768-6). College-Hill.

Speech Drills for Children in Form of Play. Barrows & Case. 1973. text ed. 2.00 (ISBN 0-686-09392-5). Expression.

Speech: Dynamic Communication. 3rd ed. Milton Dickens. 400p. 1974. text ed. 15.00 net (ISBN 0-15-583193-3, HC); instr's. manual avail. (ISBN 0-15-583194-1). HarBraceJ.

Speech-Ease Screening Inventory. Speach-Ease Staff. 1985. 34.95x (ISBN 0-8134-2475-5, 2475). Inter Print Pubs.

Speech Enhancement. Joe S. Lim. (Illus.). 384p. 1983. 51.00 (ISBN 0-13-829705-3). P-H.

Speeches for Socialism. James P. Cannon. Ed. by George L. Weissman. LC 70-156380. 1971. 33.00 (ISBN 0-87348-196-8); pap. 10.95 (ISBN 0-87348-198-4). Path Pr NY.
Speeches in Congress. Joshua R. Giddings. LC 68-55887. Repr. of 1853 ed. cancelled (ISBN 0-8371-0444-0, GIS&, Pub. by Negro U Pr). Greenwood.
Speeches in the House of Commons, 3 vols. W. Pitt. Repr. of 1817 ed. Set. 102.00 (ISBN 0-527-71506-9). Kraus Repr.
Speeches in Vergil's Aeneid. Gilbert Hida. LC 73-39787. 368p. 1972. 41.00x (ISBN 0-691-06234-X). Princeton U Pr.
Speeches, Lectures & Letters: Second Series. Wendell Phillips. LC 79-82210. (Anti-Slavery Crusade in America Ser). 1969. Repr. of 1891 ed. 21.00 (ISBN 0-405-00649-7). Ayer Co Pubs.
Speeches of Adolf Hitler. Adolf Hitler. 1975. lib. bdg. 250.00 (ISBN 0-8490-1107-8). Gordon Pr.
Speeches of Andrew Johnson, President of the United States. Andrew Johnson. 1968. Repr. of 1865 ed. 32.00 (ISBN 0-8337-1855-X). B Franklin.
Speeches of Benjamin Harrison. Benjamin Harrison. Ed. by Charles Hedges. LC 74-137915. (American History & Culture in the Nineteenth Century Ser). 1971. Repr. of 1892 ed. 41.50x (ISBN 0-8046-1494-6, Pub. by Kennikat). Assoc Faculty Pr.
Speeches of Charles Dickens. Ed. by K. J. Fielding. 466p. 1988. text ed. 90.00 (ISBN 0-391-03588-6, Co-Pub. by Harvester Pr UK). Humanities.
Speeches of Isaeus. Isaeus. Ed. by W. R. Connor. LC 78-18614. (Greek Texts & Commentaries Ser.). (Illus.). 1979. Repr. of 1904 ed. lib. bdg. 57.50x (ISBN 0-405-11453-2). Ayer Co Pubs.
Speeches of Jesus. Wilhelm Wyse. 735p. Repr. of 1904 ed. lib. bdg. 110.00x (Pub. by G Olms BRD). Coronet Bks.
Speeches of Juan Domingo Peron. new ed. Juan D. Peron. 698p. 1973. 75.00 (ISBN 0-8490-1108-6). Gordon Pr.
Speeches of the American Presidents. Compiled by Janet Podell & Steven Anzovin. 600p. 1988. 60.00 (ISBN 0-8242-0761-0). Wilson.
Speeches of the Earl of Shaftesbury. A. A. Cooper. 456p. 1971. Repr. of 1868 ed. 37.50x (ISBN 0-7165-1765-5, BBA 03100, Pub. by Irish Academic Pr). Biblio Dist.
Speeches of the Governors of Massachusetts from 1765 to 1775. Alden Bradford. LC 71-119048. (Era of the American Revolution Ser). 1971. Repr. of 1818 ed. 59.50 (ISBN 0-306-71947-9). Da Capo.
Speeches of Thucydides. H. F. Harding. 1973. 15.00x (ISBN 0-87291-060-1); pap. 7.50x. Coronado Pr.
Speeches on Foreign Policy, 1934-1939. facsimile ed. Edward F. Halifax. Ed. by H. H. Craster. LC 72-156658. (Essay Index Reprint Ser). Repr. of 1940 ed. 20.00 (ISBN 0-8369-2401-0). Ayer Co Pubs.
Speeches on Peace, Financial Reform, Colonial Reform, & Other Subjects. rev. ed. R. Cobden. Repr. of 1849 ed. 23.00 (ISBN 0-527-18210-9). Kraus Repr.
Speeches on Questions of Public Policy, 2 Vols. 2nd ed. J. Bright. Ed. by J. Rogers. Repr. of 1868 ed. Set. 48.00 (ISBN 0-527-10920-7). Kraus Repr.
Speeches on Questions of Public Policy, 2 Vols. in 1. 3rd ed. R. Cobden. Repr. of 1908 ed. 50.00 (ISBN 0-527-18220-6). Kraus Repr.
Speeches on the American Question. J. Bright. 1865. 23.00 (ISBN 0-527-10930-4). Kraus Repr.
Speeches on the American War & Letters to the Sheriffs of Bristol. Edmund Burke. LC 72-8666. (American Revolutionary Ser.). 272p. Repr. of 1898 ed. lib. bdg. 34.50 (ISBN 0-8398-0191-2). Irvington.
Speeches on the Passage of the Bill for the Removal of the Indians. U. S. 21st Congress, 1st Session, 1829-1830. Repr. of 1830 ed. 29.00 (ISBN 0-527-91840-7). Kraus Repr.
Speeches to the Party. James P. Cannon. LC 73-86189. 352p. 1973. 27.00 (ISBN 0-87348-320-0); pap. 10.95 (ISBN 0-87348-321-9). Path Pr NY.
Speechless Dialect: Shakespeare's Open Silences. Philip C. McGuire. LC 84-24115. 1985. 32.50x (ISBN 0-520-05373-7). U of Cal Pr.
Speechmaking: What Can (& Usually Does) Go Wrong & How to Prevent It. Robert Reilly. 64p. pap. text ed. cancelled (ISBN 0-931368-20-0). Ragan Comm.
Speechphone Spoken Word List. Hazel Brown. (Speechphone Ser.). 125p. 1980. Repr. of 1959 ed. incl. 3 tapes 39.50x (ISBN 0-88432-064-2, S23713, Speechphone). J Norton Pubs.
Speechreading: An Aid to Understanding. Harriet Kaplan et al. LC 85-6913. xiv, 138p. 1985. pap. text ed. 14.95x (ISBN 0-913580-98-8, Clerc Bks). Gallaudet Univ Pr.
Speechreading (Lipreading) Janet Jeffers & Margaret Barley. (Illus.). 408p. 1980. 43.75x (ISBN 0-398-02185-6). C C Thomas.
Speechwriting: A Handbook for All Occasions. Joseph J. Kelley, Jr. 224p. 1981. pap. 6.95 (ISBN 0-452-25299-7, Z5299, Plume). NAL.
Speed. William S. Burroughs, Jr. LC 83-42919. 192p. 1984. 14.95 (ISBN 0-87951-192-3). Overlook Pr.
Speed. William S. Burroughs, Jr. 192p. 1988. pap. 8.95 (ISBN 0-87951-314-4). Overlook Pr.
Speed. R. R. Knudson. (Skinny Bks.). (Illus.). 80p. (gr. 2 up). 1983. 8.95 (ISBN 0-525-44052-6). Dutton.
Speed & Power. (Understanding Computers Ser.). 1987. 12.95 (ISBN 0-8094-5704-0). Time Life.
Speed & the Quarter Horse: A Payload of Sprinters. Nelson C. Nye. LC 73-140120. (Illus.). 1973. 17.95 (ISBN 0-87004-220-3). Caxton.
Speed Cleaning. The Clean Team & Jeff Campbell. (Orig.). 1987. pap. 5.95 (ISBN 0-440-58015-3, LE). Dell.
Speed Culture: Amphetamine Use & Abuse in America. Lester Grinspoon & Peter Hedblom. LC 74-27257. 368p. 1975. 24.50x (ISBN 0-674-83192-6); pap. 8.95 (ISBN 0-674-83194-2). Harvard U Pr.
Speed Dictation with Previews in Gregg Shorthand. Charles E. Zoubek. (Diamond Jubilee Ser.). 1963. text ed. 28.95 (ISBN 0-07-073041-5). McGraw.
Speed Hypnosis. Harry Arons. pap. 3.00 (ISBN 0-87505-299-1). Borden.
Speed in Animals, Their Specialization for Running & Leaping. Alfred B. Howell. (Illus.). 1965. Repr. of 1944 ed. 17.95x (ISBN 0-02-846110-X). Hafner.
Speed in the Air: A History of Aviation. David W. Wragg. (Illus.). 192p. 1974. 15.95x (ISBN 0-8464-0879-1). Beekman Pubs.
Speed Master: The Speed Calculator & Converter for Obtaining Final Times of Thoroughbred Race Horses. Anthony R. Cipolla, Jr. (Illus.). 27p. (Orig.). 1987. pap. 22.00 information & instruction manual (ISBN 0-9619200-0-9). Speed Master.
Speed of Darkness. Rodney Morales. Ed. by Eric Chock & Darrell Lum. 200p. (Orig.). 1988. pap. 8.00 (ISBN 0-910043-16-7). Bamboo Ridge Pr.
Speed of Information-Processing & Intelligence. Ed. by Philip A. Vernon. LC 87-14532. 400p. 1987. text ed. 49.50 inst. (ISBN 0-89391-427-4); text ed. 29.50 pers. Ablex Pub.
Speed of Love: An Exploration of Christian Faithfulness in a Technological World. David P. Young. 150p. (Orig.). 1986. pap. 6.95 (ISBN 0-377-00159-7). Friendship Pr.
Speed of Slow Component & Duration in Caloric Nystagmus. N. G. Henriksson. 1956. 12.00 (ISBN 0-384-22370-2). Johnson Repr.
Speed Reading. Tony Buzan. (Illus.). 171p. 1984. pap. 7.95 (ISBN 0-525-48076-5). Dutton.
Speed Reading. rev. ed. Tony Buzan. Ed. by Leslie Wells. (Illus.). 208p. 1988. pap. 8.95 (ISBN 0-525-48439-6). Dutton.
Speed Reading. Luther Misenheimer, III. (Language Arts Ser.). 24p. (gr. 6-10). 1979. wkbk. 5.00 (ISBN 0-8209-0324-8, LA-10). ESP.
Speed Reading. Robert L. Zorn. LC 79-2744. (Everyday Handbook Ser.: EH 502). 128p. (Orig.). 1980. pap. 6.95 (ISBN 0-06-463502-3, EH 502, B&N Bks). Har-Row.
Speed Reading Made Easy. Arlyne F. Real. 224p. 1985. pap. 10.95 (ISBN 0-317-69295-X). Beautiful Mind.
Speed Reading Made Easy. rev. ed. Arlyne F. Rial. LC 85-6725. (Illus.). 224p. 1985. pap. 10.95 (ISBN 0-385-19835-3). Doubleday.
Speed Reading Made Easy. Nila B. Smith. 288p. 1982. pap. 3.50 (ISBN 0-446-31442-0). Warner Bks.
Speed Reading Made Easy see Reference Collection Boxed Set.
Speed Reading Naturally. Lillian P. Wenick. (Illus.). 288p. 1983. pap. 16.95 (ISBN 0-13-833905-8). P-H.
Speed Reading Self Taught: A Blank Book. Kelly Choda. 64p. (Orig.). 1983. pap. 1.50 (ISBN 0-86541-023-2). Filter.
Speed Reading Simplified & Self-Taught. Joseph A. Quattrini. 160p. 1985. pap. 6.95 (ISBN 0-668-06253-3). Arco.
Speed Reading: The Computer Course, Apple IIC. Bureau of Business Practice Staff. Date not set. price not set. P-H.
Speed Sailing. Gary Jobson & Mike Toppa. LC 84-10947. (Illus.). 336p. 1984. 22.95 (ISBN 0-688-03974-X, Pub. by Hearst Marine Bks). Morrow.
Speed Tailoring. Mary A. Roehr. (Illus.). 60p. (Orig.). 1987. pap. 12.95 (ISBN 0-9619229-3-1). M Roehr Cust Tailor.
Speed: The Biography of Charles W. Holman. 2nd ed. Noel E. Allard. (Illus.). 94p. 1986. pap. 13.95 (ISBN 0-911139-01-X). Flying Bks.
Speed-the-Plow. David Mamet. 1988. pap. 7.95 (ISBN 0-8021-3046-1); 12.95 (ISBN 0-8021-1028-2). Grove.
Speed Train Your Own Retriever: The Quick Efficient, Proven System for Training a Finished Dog. Larry Mueller. (Illus.). 192p. (Orig.). 1987. pap. 16.95 (ISBN 0-8117-2201-5). Stackpole.
Speedbikes. Mick Woollett. LC 83-11952. (Illus.). 64p. (Orig.). 1984. pap. 3.95 (ISBN 0-668-05961-3). Arco.
Speedboat. Renata Adler. (Vintage Contemporaries Ser.). 192p. Date not set. pap. 5.95 (ISBN 0-394-72753-3, Vin). Random.
Speedboat. Renata Adler. LC 87-45591. 192p. 1988. pap. 7.95 (ISBN 0-06-097143-6, PL-7143, PL). Har-Row.
Speedboat. James Marshall. LC 75-40349. (Illus.). 48p. (gr. 1-4). 1976. PLB 13.95 (ISBN 0-395-24384-X). HM.
Speedboat Kings. J. Lee Barrett. (Michigan Heritage Library: Vol. IV). 145p. 1986. Repr. of 1939 ed. 15.00 (ISBN 0-915056-21-6, Co-Pub Historical Soc MI). Hardscrabble Bks.
Speedbuilding for Court Reporting, Vol. 1. Dot Mathias & Sally Floyd. Ed. by Beverly L. Ritter. 322p. 1986. pap. 25.00 (ISBN 0-938643-03-7). Stenotype Educ.
Speedbuilding for Court Reporting, Vol. 2. Sally Floyd & Dot Mathias. Ed. by Beverly L. Ritter. 326p. 1986. pap. 25.00 (ISBN 0-938643-04-5). Stenotype Educ.
Speeding into Lost Landscapes. Jeannette G. Maino. (Orig.). 1982. pap. 5.50 (ISBN 0-941885-00-3). Dry Creeks Bks.
Speeding up Shakespeare. William J. Lawrence. LC 68-20235. 1968. Repr. of 1937 ed. 18.00 (ISBN 0-405-08739-X). Ayer Co Pubs.
Speeding up Shakespeare. William J. Lawrence. 1973. 12.25 (ISBN 0-8274-0320-8). R West.
Speedreading: The How-to Book for Every Busy Manager, Executive & Professional. Diane D. Fink et al. LC 81-10373. (Wiley Self Teaching Guide Ser.). 195p. 1982. pap. 9.95 (ISBN 0-471-08407-7, Pub. by Wiley Pr). Wiley.
SpeedScript: The Word Processor for Apple Personal Computers. Charles Brannon & Kevin Martin. Ed. by Compute! Publications, Inc. Staff. 91p. (Orig.). 1985. pap. 10.95 (ISBN 0-87455-000-9). Compute Pubns.
SpeedScript: The Word Processor for the Commodore 64 & VIC-20. Charles Brannon. Ed. by Compute! Publications, Inc. Staff. 160p. (Orig.). 1985. pap. 9.95 (ISBN 0-942386-94-9). Compute Pubns.
SpeedScript: The Word Processor for the Commondore 64 & VIC-20. Charles Brannon. 139p. 1988. incl. disk 19.95 (ISBN 0-87455-055-6). Compute Pubns.
SpeedScript: The Word Processor for the Atari. Charles Brannon. Ed. by Compute! Publications, Inc. Staff. (Orig.). 1985. pap. 9.95 (ISBN 0-87455-003-3). Compute Pubns.
Speedway. Ruth L. Schechter. LC 83-7408. (Orig.). 1983. pap. 5.95 (ISBN 0-941608-03-4). Chantry Pr.
Speedwriting Dictation & Transcription: College Edition. LC 76-41046. 1977. pap. text ed. 18.08 scp (ISBN 0-672-98051-7); scp tchr's manual 3.67 (ISBN 0-672-98052-5). Bobbs.
Speedwriting Dictionary: College Edition. LC 76-41047. (Landmark Ser.). 1977. text ed. 17.55 scp (ISBN 0-672-98095-9). Bobbs.
Speedwriting for the Legal Secretary. Berniece Craft et al. LC 78-10833. 1979. pap. 17.55 scp (ISBN 0-672-97013-9); tchr's. manual o.p. 3.33 (ISBN 0-672-97014-7). Bobbs.
Speedwriting Legal Dictionary. Berniece R. Craft. 170p. 1972. pap. 5.99 scp (ISBN 0-672-96142-3). Bobbs.
Speedwriting Medical Dictation Course. Goodwin W. Gilson & Rose Palmer. 266p. 1960. text ed. 24.80 scp (ISBN 0-672-96153-9); scp tchr's manual 7.33 (ISBN 0-672-96154-7); scp cassette tapes 232.92 (ISBN 0-672-97884-9). Bobbs.
Speedwriting Shorthand Abridged Dictionary: Regency Edition. Joe M. Pullis & Cheryl Pullis. (Speedwriting Shorthand Ser.). 192p. (gr. 10-12). 1984. text ed. 6.55 scp (ISBN 0-672-98504-7). Bobbs.
Speedwriting Shorthand Dictation & Transcription: Regency Edition. Joe M. Pullis et al. (Speedwriting Shorthand Ser.). 352p. (gr. 10-12). 1984. text ed. 23.40 scp (ISBN 0-672-98506-3); scp instr's. guide 3.67 (ISBN 0-317-00348-8). Bobbs.
Speedwriting Shorthand Training System. 1982. scp complete pkg. Resource manual, Student manuals, Dictionaries & tapes 500.00 (ISBN 0-672-90022-X). Bobbs.
Speedy. Max Brand. 1988. 30.00x (ISBN 0-86025-234-5, Pub. by Ian Henry Pubns England). State Mutual Bk.
Speedy Delivery. Fred Rogers. LC 73-15437. (I Am, I Can, I Will Ser.). (Illus.). 44p. (ps-4). 1979. pap. 4.95 (ISBN 0-8331-0037-8). Hubbard Sci.
Speedy Extinction of Evil & Misery: Selected Prose of James Thomson (B. V.) James Thomson. Ed. by William D. Schaefer. LC 67-11799. 359p. pap. 93.40 (2029961). Bks Demand UMI.
Speedy French: To Get You There & Back. Babe Hart. (Speedy Language Ser.). 24p. (Orig., Fr.). 1976. pap. 2.95 (ISBN 0-9602838-1-1). Baja Bks.
Speedy German: To Get You There & Back. Babe Hart. Ed. & tr. by Babe Hart. (Speedy Language Ser.). (Illus.). 24p. (Ital.). 1977. pap. 2.95 (ISBN 0-9602838-3-8). Baja Bks.
Speedy Gourmet. C. Norman Shealy. (Illus.). 216p. 1984. 12.95 (ISBN 0-89804-900-8, Pub. by Brindabella Books); pap. 6.95 (ISBN 0-89804-901-6). Ariel OH.
Speedy Greek. Babe Hart. Ed. & illus. by Babe Hart. (Speedy Language Ser.). (Illus.). 24p. (Orig.). 1983. pap. 2.95 (ISBN 0-9602838-8-9). Baja Bks.
Speedy Ingles. Babe Hart. (Speedy Language Ser.). 24p. (Orig.). 1982. pap. 2.50 (ISBN 0-9602838-7-0). Baja Bks.
Speedy Italian: To Get You There & Back. Babe Hart. Ed. & tr. by Babe Hart. (Speedy Language Ser.). (Illus.). 24p. 1977. pap. 2.50 (ISBN 0-9602838-2-X). Baja Bks.
Speedy Japanese: To Get You There & Back. Babe Hart. (Speedy Language Ser.). (Illus.). 24p. (Orig., Japanese.). 1979. pap. 2.95 (ISBN 0-9602838-4-6). Baja Bks.
Speedy O'Hare's Sun Valley Race. Gene Kay. (Illus.). 36p. (ps-7). 1987. pap. 8.95 (ISBN 0-945222-24-6). Gazelle Prodns.
Speedy Russian: To Get You There & Back. Babe Hart. (Speedy Language Ser.). 24p. (Orig., Rus.). 1979. pap. 2.95 (ISBN 0-9602838-5-4). Baja Bks.
Speedy Spanish for Medical Personnel. T. L. Hart. Ed. by T. L. Hart & Babe Hart. Tr. by Babe Hart. (Speedy Language Ser.). (Illus.). 24p. (Orig., Span.). 1980. pap. 2.95 (ISBN 0-9602838-6-2). Baja Bks.
Speedy Spanish for Physical Therapists. T. L. Hart. (Speedy Language Ser.). 24p. 1987. pap. 2.95 (ISBN 0-9615829-3-6). Baja Bks.
Speedy Spanish: To Get You There & Back. Babe Hart. (Speedy Language Ser.). 24p. (Orig., Span.). 1975. pap. 2.95 (ISBN 0-9602838-0-3). Baja Bks.
Speedy Trial: Federal & State Practice. Robert L. Misner. 828p. 1983. 50.00x (ISBN 0-87215-621-4); 1984 supplement 15.00x (ISBN 0-87215-824-1). Michie Co.
Speedy Trial: Practice & Procedure. Robert K. Calhoun & Richard Zimmer. 150p. 1985. 35.00 (CR-33410); June '82 supp. 14.00; September '85 supp. 15.00. Cal Cont Ed Bar.
Speedy Wheels. William Bumble. 32p. (gr. 4up). 1988. 3.95 (ISBN 0-590-41996-X). Scholastic Inc.
Speenhamland County: Poverty & the Poor Law in Berkshire, 1782-1834. Mark Neuman. Ed. by Peter Stansky & Leslie Hume. LC 81-48364. (Modern British History Ser.). 225p. 1982. lib. bdg. 40.00 (ISBN 0-8240-5160-2). Garland Pub.
Speer's Colorado Advanced Technology Directory. R. D. Speer Associates. 300p. 1985. ringbound 95.00 (ISBN 0-915669-51-X). Strategic Assessments.
Speer's Colorado Advanced Technology Directory. R. D. Speer Associates Staff. 300p. 1984. ringbound 95.00 (ISBN 0-915669-50-1). Strategic Assessments.
Speer's Digest of Toxic Substances State Law: 1984 to '85 Trends, Summaries & Forecasts. 2nd ed. R. D. Speer. (Speer's Digest Series of Policy & Law). (Illus.). 300p. (Orig.). 1985. lib. bdg. 95.00x (ISBN 0-915669-02-1); pap. 80.00x (ISBN 0-915669-03-X). Strategic Assessments.
Speer's Digest of Toxic Substances State Law 1983-1984: Trends, Summaries, & Forecasts. Ed. by R. D. Speer & Gerard A. Bulanowski. (Speer's Digest Series of Policy & Law). (Illus.). 372p. 1983. 100.00 (ISBN 0-915669-01-3); pap. 85.00 perfect bdg. (ISBN 0-915669-00-5). Strategic Assessments.
Spel Is a Four-Letter Word. J. Richard Gentry. LC 86-33526. 56p. (Orig.). 1987. pap. text ed. 6.00x (ISBN 0-435-08440-2). Heinemann Ed.
Speleology: The Study of Caves. George W. Moore & G. Nicholas Sullivan. LC 77-18176. (Illus.). pap. text ed. 5.95 (ISBN 0-939748-00-2). Cave Bks MO.
Spell. Hermann Broch. Tr. by H. F. Broch de Rotherman. 1986. 22.50 (ISBN 0-374-26761-8). FS&G.
Spell: An Extraveganza. Charlotte Bronte. 1979. Repr. of 1931 ed. lib. bdg. 32.50 (ISBN 0-8495-0511-9). Arden Lib.
Spell Bound, Vol. 5. Jennifer Rabin. (Avon Young Adult Ser.). 192p. (YA) (gr. 5-9). 1987. pap. 2.50 (ISBN 0-380-75132-1). Avon.
Spell by Writing. Wendy Bean & Christine Bouffler. 92p. (Orig.). 1987. pap. 10.00x (ISBN 0-909955-69-7). Heinemann Ed.
Spell: Extravanganza. Charlotte Bronte. Ed. by George E Maclean. LC 72-191958. 1931. lib. bdg. 27.00 (ISBN 0-8414-0804-1). Folcroft.
Spell for Chameleon. Piers Anthony. LC 77-1666. 1977. pap. 3.95 (ISBN 0-345-34753-6). Ballantine.
Spell for Old Bones. Eric Linklater. Ed. by R. Reginald & Douglas Melvill. LC 77-84250. (Lost Race & Adult Fantasy Ser.). 1978. Repr. of 1950 ed. lib. bdg. 20.00x (ISBN 0-405-10996-2). Ayer Co Pubs.
Spell It Fast. Robert C. Gilboy. pap. 5.95 (ISBN 0-87491-071-4). Acropolis.
Spell It Right! Ray C. Meyers & Dale Goodban. 1979. pap. text ed. 11.95x (ISBN 0-917962-61-3). T H Peek.
Spell It Right! 3rd ed. Harry Shaw. LC 85-45920. 149p. 1986. pap. 5.95 (ISBN 0-06-097048-0, PL 7048, PL). Har-Row.
Spell Law. Peter C. Fenlon & S. Coleman Charlton. (Illus.). 112p. 1984. 12.00 (ISBN 0-915795-01-9). Iron Crown Ent Inc.
Spell: Now I Can... Pink Book. Ronald Ridout. (Now I Can Ser.). (Illus.). 24p. (ps-1). 1988. pap. 2.95 (ISBN 0-8249-8238-X). Ideals.
Spell: Now I Can... Red Book. Ronald Ridout. (Now I Can Ser.). (Illus.). 24p. (gr. k-1). 1988. pap. 2.95 (ISBN 0-8249-8239-8). Ideals.
Spell of Algeria & Tunisia. F. Miltoun. 554p. 1985. 300.00x (ISBN 1-85077-060-3, Pub. by Darf Pubs Ltd). State Mutual Bk.
Spell of Hawaii. Ed. by A. Grove Day & Carl Stroven. LC 69-11908. 346p. 1985. pap. 3.95 (ISBN 0-935180-13-3). Mutual Pub Hi.
Spell of Music: An Attempt to Analyse the Enjoyment of Music. John A. Fuller-Maitland. LC 76-102239. (Select Bibliographies Reprint Ser). 1926. 15.00 (ISBN 0-8369-5124-7). Ayer Co Pubs.
Spell of New Mexico. Ed. by Tony Hillerman. LC 76-21523. 1984. pap. 9.95 (ISBN 0-8263-0776-0). U of NM Pr.

Spell of Plato see Open Society & Its Enemies.

Spell of the Black Raven. R. G. Austin. (Which Way Bks.: No. 3). (Illus.). (gr. 3-6). 1982. pap. 1.95 (ISBN 0-671-45757-8). Archway.

Spell of the Sorcerer's Skull. John Bellairs. LC 84-7114. (gr. 5 up). 1984. 11.95 (ISBN 0-8037-0120-9, 01160-350); PLB 11.89 (ISBN 0-8037-0122-5). Dial Bks Young.

Spell of the Sorcerer's Skull. John Bellairs. 176p. 1985. pap. 2.75 (ISBN 0-553-15357-9, Skylark). Bantam.

Spell of the Witch World. Andre Norton. (Science Fiction Ser.). 224p. (Orig.). 1987. pap. 3.50 (ISBN 0-88677-242-7). DAW Bks.

Spell of the Yukon. Robert Service. 12.95 (ISBN 0-89190-929-X, Pub. by Am Repr). Amereon Ltd.

Spell of Words. Lina Eckenstein. 59.95 (ISBN 0-8490-1109-4). Gordon Pr.

Spell of Words: Studies in Language Bearing on Custom. Lina Eckenstein. LC 68-23153. 312p. 1969. Repr. of 1932 ed. 30.00x (ISBN 0-8103-3892-0). Gale.

Spell of Words: Studies in Language Bearing on Custom. Lina Eckenstein. 1932. 8.25 (ISBN 0-8274-3491-X). R West.

Spell Singers. Alan B. Newcomer. 1988. pap. 3.50 (ISBN 0-88677-314-8). DAW Bks.

Spell Sword: A Darkover Novel. Marion Zimmer Bradley. (Science Fiction Ser.). 1987. pap. 3.95 (ISBN 0-88677-237-0). DAW Bks.

Spell Well. Bobbe D'Ambrosio et al. (Makemaster Bk.). (gr. 1-6). 1980. pap. 10.95 (ISBN 0-8224-6455-1). D S Lake Pubs.

Spellbinder. Seth Kohlhaas. 240p. (Orig.). 1982. pap. 2.75 (ISBN 0-8439-1024-0, Leisure Bks). Leisure NY.

Spellbinder. Harold Robbins. 1985. pap. 4.95 (ISBN 0-671-55859-5). PB.

Spellbinder, No. 221. Iris Johansen. 192p. 1987. pap. 2.50 (ISBN 0-553-21855-7, Loveswept). Bantam.

Spellbinders. Margaret C. Banning. 1976. lib. bdg. 14.35x (ISBN 0-89968-008-9). Lightyear.

Spellbinders: Charismatic Political Leadership. Ann R. Willner. LC 83-5914. 232p. 1984. 25.00x (ISBN 0-300-02809-1). Yale U Pr.

Spellbinders: Charismatic Political Leadership. Ann R. Willner. LC 83-5914. 232p. 1985. pap. 9.95x (ISBN 0-300-03405-9, Y-528). Yale U Pr.

Spellbinding: Skills to Create Win-Win Relationships. Gene Z. Laborde. (Communication Ser.). (Illus.). 170p. 1987. 14.95 (ISBN 0-9613172-9-9). Syntony Inc Pub.

Spellbound. Francis Beeding. (Movie Mystery Greats Ser.). 320p. 1987. pap. 3.50 (ISBN 0-8217-2002-3). Zebra.

Spellbound. Christopher Pike. 224p. (Orig.). (YA) (gr. 8 up). 1988. pap. 2.75 (ISBN 0-671-64979-5). Archway.

Spellbound. Megan Stine & William H. Stine. (Micro Adventure Ser.: No. 10). 128p. (Orig.). (gr. 7 up). 1985. pap. 1.95 (ISBN 0-590-33385-2). Scholastic Inc.

Spellbound. Margaret Way. (Harlequin Romances Ser.). 192p. 1983. pap. 1.75 (ISBN 0-373-02537-8). Harlequin Bks.

Spellbound: Growing up in God's Country. David McKain. LC 88-4721. 272p. 1988. 18.95 (ISBN 0-8203-1048-4). U of Ga Pr.

Spellbound: Studies on Mesmerism & Literature. Maria M. Tatar. LC 78-51199. 1978. 38.00x (ISBN 0-691-06377-X). Princeton U Pr.

Spellcaster. Katy Brown. (Twistaplot Ser.: No. 15). (Illus.). 96p. (Orig.). (gr. 4 up). 1985. pap. 1.95 (ISBN 0-590-33232-5). Scholastic Inc.

Spellcraft, Hexcraft & Witchcraft. Anna Riva. (Illus.). 64p. 1977. pap. 3.95 (ISBN 0-943832-00-4). Intl Imports.

Spellfire. Ed Greenwood. LC 88-50056. (Forgotten Realms Novel Ser.). 392p. (Orig.). 1988. pap. 3.95 (ISBN 0-88038-587-1). TSR Inc.

Spelling. Cambridge Book Editors. (Illus.). pap. text ed. 4.75 (ISBN 0-8428-0076-X); key 2.00 (ISBN 0-8428-0027-1). Cambridge Bk.

Spelling. Kathy Sweeney et al. 64p. (gr. 2-4). 1985. 6.95 (ISBN 0-912107-38-3). Monday Morning Bks.

Spelling. Mary L. Wallace. Ed. by Alton L. Raygor. (Communication Skills Ser.). 288p. 1981. pap. 19.95 (ISBN 0-07-067901-0). McGraw.

Spelling: A Mnemonics Approach. 2nd ed. Alvin R. Brown. 1985. write for info. wkbk. (ISBN 0-538-14190-5, N19). SW Pub.

Spelling Ability: Its Measurement & Distribution. B. R. Buckingham. LC 78-176610. (Columbia University. Teachers College. Contributions to Education: No. 59). Repr. of 1913 ed. 22.50 (ISBN 0-404-55059-2). AMS Pr.

Spelling & Vocabulary Simplified & Self-Taught. Veronica F. Towers. LC 84-6326. 144p. 1984. pap. 5.95 (ISBN 0-668-05539-1). Arco.

Spelling As a Secondary Learning: The Extension of Spelling Vocabularies with Different Methods of Organizing & Teaching the Social Studies. I. Keith Tyler. LC 79-177688. (Columbia University. Teachers College. Contributions to Education: No. 781). Repr. of 1939 ed. 22.50 (ISBN 0-404-55781-3). AMS Pr.

Spelling: Basic Skills for Effective Communication. Ed. by Walter B. Barbe et al. 1982. 14.95 (ISBN 0-88309-118-6). Zaner-Bloser.

Spelling Bee. Sharon Gordon. LC 81-4648. (Illus.). 32p. (gr. k-2). 1981. PLB 9.89 (ISBN 0-89375-535-4); pap. 2.95 (ISBN 0-89375-536-2). Troll Assocs.

Spelling Bee Speller, 3 vols. S. H. Chang. LC 81-90754. (Orig.). (gr. 4-8). 1984. Set. pap. 19.95 (ISBN 0-942462-22-X). Hondale.

Spelling Bee Speller: The Final Rounds, Vol. 3. S. H. Chang. LC 81-90754. (Spelling Bee Speller Ser.). 240p. (Orig.). (gr. 4-8). 1984. pap. 7.95 (ISBN 0-942462-03-3). Hondale.

Spelling Bee Speller: The First Round, Vol. 1. S. H. Chang. LC 81-90754. (Spelling Bee Speller Ser.). 240p. (Orig.). (gr. 4-8). 1984. pap. 7.95 (ISBN 0-942462-01-7). Hondale.

Spelling Bee Speller: The Middle Rounds, Vol. 2. S. H. Chang. LC 81-90754. (Spelling Bee Speller Ser.). 240p. (Orig.). (gr. 4-8). 1984. pap. 7.95 (ISBN 0-942462-02-5). Hondale.

Spelling Beehive Activity Book. Joan Lamport et al. (Tool Box Ser.). (Illus.). (gr. 2-3). 0.75 (ISBN 0-89796-846-8, XTW 06). Arista Corp NY.

Spelling Book of Greek Roots. Raymond E. Laurita. 150p. (Orig.). 1988. pap. text ed. 14.95 (ISBN 0-914051-10-5). Leonardo Pr.

Spelling by Principles. Genevie L. Smith. 1966. text ed. write for info. (ISBN 0-13-834242-3). P-H.

Spelling by Sound & Structure. Rachel Siegrist. (gr. 2-6). 1979. write for info. (ISBN 0-686-25261-6); tchr's. ed. avail. (ISBN 0-686-25262-4). Rod & Staff.

Spelling: Caught or Taught? A New Look. Margaret Peters. 144p. (Orig.). 1985. pap. 9.95x (ISBN 0-7102-0359-4). Routledge Chapman & Hall.

Spelling Corner. Arnold B. Cheyney. 1985. pap. 8.95 (ISBN 0-673-15960-4). Scott F.

Spelling Drills & Exercises: Programmed for the Typewriter. 3rd ed. LeRoy A. Brendel & Doris Near. (Illus.). 1979. pap. 12.88 (ISBN 0-07-007491-7). McGraw.

Spelling Fifteen Hundred. 3rd ed. J. N. Hook. 294p. 1986. pap. text ed. 14.00 net (ISBN 0-15-583212-3, Pub. by HC). HarBraceJ.

Spelling for Fun, Bk. 1. Cynthia Brown & Herb Kohl. (Illus.). 48p. (gr. 5-9). wkbk 3.00 (ISBN 0-939408-00-7). Continuity Pr.

Spelling for Fun, Bk. 2. Cynthia Brown & Herb Kohl. (Illus.). 48p. (gr. 4-9). wkbk. 3.00 (ISBN 0-939408-01-5). Continuity Pr.

Spelling for Law Enforcement. David Sanderlin. 60p. 1987. pap. 6.95 (ISBN 0-940309-02-5). Innovat Eureka.

Spelling Games & Puzzles for Junior High. Robert D. Miller. (Makemaster Bk.). (gr. 6-8). 1976. pap. 8.95 (ISBN 0-8224-6460-8). D S Lake Pubs.

Spelling Improvement. 3rd ed. Patricia M. Fergus. 1977. pap. text ed. 14.95 (ISBN 0-07-020456-X, C). McGraw.

Spelling Improvement: A Program for Self-Improvement. 4th ed. Patricia M. Fergus. 256p. 1983. pap. 19.95 (ISBN 0-07-020476-4). McGraw.

Spelling Is Special. Jerry J. Mallett. 1984. pap. 9.95 (ISBN 0-673-15951-5). Scott F.

Spelling Made Easy. Lester D. Basch & Milton Finkelstein. 1974. pap. 3.00 (ISBN 0-87980-288-X). Wilshire.

Spelling Made Easy. Visual Education Corporation Staff. (Illus.). 168p. (gr. 9 up). 1984. wkbk. 9.24 (ISBN 0-07-039661-2). McGraw.

Spelling Made Simple. rev. ed. Stephen V. Ross. LC 80-2624. (Made Simple Ser.). (Illus.). 192p. 1981. pap. 6.95 (ISBN 0-385-17482-9). Doubleday.

Spelling Mistakes see Italian Straw Hat.

Spelling One-Two, 2 bks. (gr. k-3). 1979. Bk. 2. pap. 0.99 (ISBN 0-440-08246-3); Bk. 1. pap. text ed. 1.29 (ISBN 0-440-08214-5). Dell.

Spelling: Patterns of Sound. Odette P. Sims. 128p. 1974. pap. text ed. 22.95 wktxt. (ISBN 0-07-057500-2). McGraw.

Spelling Power: A Spelling Workbook with Comprehension Drills. Burton Goodman. 224p. (Orig.). 1987. pap. text ed. 8.00 (ISBN 0-89061-449-0). Jamestown Pubs.

Spelling Program: Diagnostic & Prescriptive, 3 bks. (gr. 2 up). 1980. Set of 30 Bks. (10 Ea. of 3 Levels) 88.25 (ISBN 0-87965-072-9); pap. 2.95 test booklet (ISBN 0-87965-050-8). B Loft.

Spelling Puzzles: Grade 1. Jean Syswerda. Ed. by Joan Hoffman. (I Know It! Bks.). (Illus.). 32p. (gr. 1). 1980. pap. 1.95 wkbk. (ISBN 0-938256-16-5). Sch Zone Pub Co.

Spelling Puzzles: Grade 2. Jean Syswerda. Ed. by Joan Hoffman. (I Know It! Bks.). (Illus.). 32p. (gr. 2). 1979. wkbk. 1.95 (ISBN 0-938256-17-3). Sch Zone Pub Co.

Spelling Puzzles: Grade 3. Jean Syswerda. Ed. by Joan Hoffman. (I Know It! Bks.). (Illus.). 32p. (gr. 3). 1979. wkbk. 1.95 (ISBN 0-938256-18-1). Sch Zone Pub Co.

Spelling Puzzles: Grade 4. Jean Syswerda. Ed. by Joan Hoffman. (I Know It! Bks.). (Illus.). 32p. (gr. 4). 1979. wkbk. 1.95 (ISBN 0-938256-19-X). Sch Zone Pub Co.

Spelling Simplified. Judi Kesselman-Turkel & Franklynn Peterson. 176p. (Orig.). 1983. pap. 5.95 (ISBN 0-8092-5510-3). Contemp Bks.

Spelling Skillbuilder. Bernard Percy. 1984. write for info. wkbk. (ISBN 0-538-14030-5, N03). SW Pub.

Spelling Speedway. Linda Schwartz. (Language Arts Ser.). 32p. (gr. 4-7). 1979. 3.95 (ISBN 0-88160-069-5, LW 802). Learning Wks.

Spelling: Structure & Strategies. Paul R. Hanna & Richard E. Hodges. LC 82-40222. (Illus.). 304p. 1982. pap. text ed. 13.00 (ISBN 0-8191-2460-5). U Pr of Amer.

Spelling: Syllabus. 2nd ed. Delpha Hurlburt. (gr. 7-12). 1980. pap. text ed. 7.65 student syllabus (ISBN 0-89420-053-4, 187898); cassette recordings 134.10 (ISBN 0-89420-185-9, 187900). Natl Book.

Spelling Test Form. Boder. 1982. 12.50 (ISBN 0-8089-1447-2, 790636). Grune.

Spelling Tests: Grade 3. Marie Shaw. Incl. Grade 4. wkbk. 5.00 (ISBN 0-8209-0169-5, ST-4); Grade 5. wkbk. 5.00 (ISBN 0-8209-0170-9, ST-5); Grade 6. wkbk. 5.00 (ISBN 0-8209-0171-7, ST-6). (Spelling Ser.). 24p. 1979. wkbk. 5.00 (ISBN 0-8209-0168-7, ST-3). ESP.

Spelling the Easy Way. 2nd ed. Joseph Marsand & Francis Griffith. (Easy Way Ser.). 320p. 1988. pap. 9.95 (ISBN 0-8120-3346-9). Barron.

Spelling the Easy Way. (Easy Way Ser.). 1982. 8.95 (ISBN 0-8120-2502-4). Barron.

Spelling the Word: George Herbert & the Bible. Chana Bloch. 1985. 37.50x (ISBN 0-520-05121-1). U of Cal Pr.

Spelling the Written Word, Bk. A. Mildred Middleton. 262p. 1985. pap. text ed. 10.00 (ISBN 0-8403-3190-8). Kendall Hunt.

Spelling the Written Word, Bk. C. Mildred Middleton & Eddie Tsang. (Administrators Guide SD100). 232p. 1984. shrink wrapped 10.00 (ISBN 0-8403-3192-4). Kendall Hunt.

Spelling the Written Word, Bk. D. Student ed. Mildred Middleton & Eddie Tsang. (SD100). 176p. (gr. 10). 1983. pap. text ed. 3.85 (ISBN 0-8403-3198-3). Kendall Hunt.

Spelling the Written Word, Bk. B. student ed. Mildred L. Middleton. (Sd100). 176p. (gr. 9). 1984. pap. text ed. 3.85 (ISBN 0-8403-3196-7). Kendall Hunt.

Spelling the Written Word, Bk. B. Tsang Middleton. (Administratores Guide SD 100). 232p. shrink-wrapped 10.00 (ISBN 0-8403-3191-6). Kendall Hunt.

Spelling the Written Word: Administrators Guide, Bk. D. Tsang Middleton. (SD100). 232p. 1984. shrink wrapped 7.50 (ISBN 0-8403-3193-2). Kendall Hunt.

Spelling the Written Word: Student Edition, Bk. A. Middleton. 140p. 1984. pap. text ed. 2.70 (ISBN 0-8403-3195-9). Kendall-Hunt.

Spelling Thinkercises. Becky Daniel. 64p. (gr. 4-8). 1988. wkbk. 6.95 (ISBN 0-86653-423-7, GA1035). Good Apple.

Spelling Trends, Contest, & Methods. Ruel A. Allred. (What Research Says to the Teacher Ser.). 2.95 (ISBN 0-8106-1062-0). NEA.

Spelling Trouble. 1982. 15.00x (ISBN 0-903653-32-X, Pub. by New Playwrights Network). State Mutual Bk.

Spelling Your Way to Success. rev. ed. Joseph Mersand & Francis Griffith. LC 73-16791. (gr. 9 up). 1982. pap. text ed. 6.95 (ISBN 0-8120-2339-0). Barron.

Spellkey. Ann Downer. LC 86-28709. 224p. (YA) (gr. 7 up). 1987. 13.95 (ISBN 0-689-31329-2, Atheneum Childrens Bks). Macmillan.

Spello: Life Today in Ancient Umbria. John Hartcup & Adeline Hartcup. 176p. 1985. 13.95 (ISBN 0-8052-8222-X, Pub. by Allison & Busby England). Schocken.

Spells. Isaac Asimov et al. (Issac Asimov's Ser.: No. 4). 352p. 1985. pap. 3.95 (ISBN 0-451-13578-4, Sig). NAL.

Spells & Bindings. Time-Life Books Editors. (Enchanted World Ser.). (Illus.). 144p. (YA) (gr. 7 up). 1985. 19.93; lib. bdg. 23.93. Time-Life.

Spells of Mortal Weaving. Esther M. Friesner. (Twelve Kingdom Ser.). 224p. 1986. pap. 2.95 (ISBN 0-380-75001-5). Avon.

Spellsinger. Alan D. Foster. 352p. pap. 2.95 (ISBN 0-446-90352-3). Warner Bks.

Spellsinger II: The Hour of the Gate. Alan D. Foster. 304p. pap. 3.50 (ISBN 0-446-32609-7). Warner Bks.

Spellsinger III: The Day of the Dissonance. Alan D. Foster. 304p. (Orig.). 1984. pap. 2.95 (ISBN 0-446-32133-8). Warner Bks.

Spellsinger IV: The Moment of the Magician. Alan D. Foster. 320p. (Orig.). 1985. pap. 3.50 (ISBN 0-446-32326-8). Warner Bks.

Spellsinger V: The Paths of the Perambulator. Alan D. Foster. 288p. 1986. pap. 3.95 (ISBN 0-446-32679-8). Warner Bks.

Spellsinger VI: The Time of the Transference. Alan D. Foster. 288p. 1987. pap. 3.50 (ISBN 0-446-30009-8). Warner Bks.

Spelunking. Van K. Brock. 1978. 1.50 (ISBN 0-936814-04-7). New Collage.

Spence & Lila. Bobbie Ann Mason. LC 87-46155. (Illus.). 96p. 1988. 12.95 (ISBN 0-06-015911-1, HarpT). Har-Row.

Spence & the Mean Old Bear. Christa Chevalier. Ed. by Abby Levine. LC 86-1570. (Spence Bks.). (Illus.). 32p. (ps-1). 1986. 10.50 (ISBN 0-8075-7572-0). A Whitman.

Spence & the Sleepytime Monster. Christa Chevalier. Ed. by Kathleen Tucker. LC 83-25988. (Just for Fun Bks.). (Illus.). 32p. (ps-1). 1984. PLB 10.50 (ISBN 0-8075-7574-7). A Whitman.

Spence at the Blue Bazaar. Michael Allen. 1981. pap. 0.35 (ISBN 0-440-18308-1). Dell.

Spence Is Small. Christa Chevalier. Ed. by Abby Levine. LC 87-2054. (Illus.). (ps-3). 1987. PLB 10.50 (ISBN 0-8075-7567-4). A Whitman.

Spence Isn't Spence Anymore. Christa Chevalier. Ed. by Abby Levine. (Illus.). 32p. (ps-1). 1985. 10.50 (ISBN 0-8075-7565-8). A Whitman.

Spencer Brade, M.D. Frank G. Slaughter. 375p. 1975. Repr. of 1942 ed. lib. bdg. 21.95 (ISBN 0-89190-287-2, Pub. by River City Pr). Amereon Ltd.

Spencer Butte Pioneers: One Hundred Years on the Sunny Side of the Butte 1850-1950. Lois Barton. Ed. by Northwest Matrix Staff & Charlotte Mills. LC 82-61837. (Illus.). 144p. 1982. pap. 11.95x (ISBN 0-9609420-0-9). S Butte Pr.

Spencer Fullerton Baird & the U. S. Fish Commission: A Study in the History of American Science. new ed. Dean C. Allard, Jr. Ed. by Keir B. Sterling. LC 77-81128. (Biologists & Their World Ser.). 1978. lib. bdg. 33.00x (ISBN 0-405-10738-2). Ayer Co Pubs.

Spencer Holst Stories. Spencer Holst. 128p. 1976. 6.95. Horizon.

Spencer, New York History: Tales of Trails & Crossroads Days Before Yesterday. Edison Signor & Emogene Signor. 248p. (Orig.). 1985. text ed. 37.50x (ISBN 0-943240-21-2); pap. text ed. 30.00x. UHLS Pub.

Spencer Roane: Judicial Advocate of Jeffersonian Principles. Margaret E. Horsnell. LC 86-9911. (American Legal & Constitutional History Ser.). 1986. 30.00 (ISBN 0-8240-8272-9). Garland Pub.

Spencer Tracy. Romano Tozzi. LC 74-33234. (Film Stars Ser.). (Illus.). 5.95 (ISBN 0-88365-289-7). Brown Bk.

Spencer Tracy: Tragic Idol. Bill Davidson. (Illus.). 1988. 17.95 (ISBN 0-525-24631-2). Dutton.

Spencer's Computer Dictionary for Everyone. 3rd ed. Donald D. Spencer. (Illus.). 288p. 1985. 17.95 (ISBN 0-684-18250-5, ScribT); pap. 8.95 (ISBN 0-684-18251-3). Scribner.

Spencer's Computer Dictionary for Everyone. 3rd ed. Donald D. Spencer. LC 84-22131. 290p. (YA) (gr. 9 up). 1985. 18.95 (NO. 2001); pap. 10.95 (NO. 2002). Camelot Pub.

Spencer's 'Fierce Warres & Faithful Loves' Martial & Chivalric Symbolism in 'The Faerie Queene' Michael Leslie. (Illus.). 216p. 1984. 45.00 (ISBN 0-85991-150-0, Pub. by Boydell & Brewer). Longwood Pub Group.

Spencer's Last Journey, Being the Journal of an Expedition to Tierra Del Fuego. Baldwin Spencer. LC 76-44790. Repr. of 1931 ed. 34.50 (ISBN 0-404-15972-9). AMS Pr.

Spencers of Amberson Avenue: A Turn-of-the-Century Memoir. Ethel Spencer. LC 83-47827. (Illus.). 170p. 1983. pap. 8.95 (ISBN 0-8229-5356-0). U of Pittsburgh Pr.

Spencer's Scientific Correspondence with Sir J. G. Frazer & Others. Baldwin Spencer. Ed. by R. R. Marett & T. K. Penniman. LC 76-44792. Repr. of 1932 ed. 19.50 (ISBN 0-404-15973-7). AMS Pr.

Spend All Your Kisses, Mr. Smith. Jack Smith. 1979. pap. text ed. 2.95 (ISBN 0-07-058988-7). McGraw.

Spend Game. Jonathan Gash. (Crime Monthly Ser.). 204p. 1982. pap. 3.95 (ISBN 0-14-006190-8). Penguin.

Spend It or Save It? Pension Lump-Sum Distributions & Tax Reform. G. L. Atkins. (Illus.). 104p. 1986. pap. text ed. 10.50 (ISBN 0-8191-5541-1, Pub. by Employee Benefit Rsch Inst). U Pr of Amer.

Spend It or Save It? Pension Lump-Sum Distributions & Tax Reform. G. Lawrence Atkins. LC 86-6413. 85p. 1986. 10.00 (ISBN 0-86643-046-6). Employee Benefit.

Spend Sad Sundays Singing Songs to Sassy Sisters. Chester Fuller. 1974. pap. 1.50 (ISBN 0-88378-037-2). Third World.

Spend Your Life in Slender. Emmett Miller. 1988. 8.95 (ISBN 1-55525-206-0). Nightingale-Conant.

Spending Advertising Money. 2nd ed. Simon Broadbent. 1976. 34.95 (ISBN 0-8464-0880-5); pap. 22.95 (ISBN 0-686-77120-6). Beekman Pubs.

Spending Advertising Money. 4th ed. Simon Broadbent & Brian Jacobs. 424p. 1984. pap. text ed. 26.95x (ISBN 0-09-155971-5, Pub. by Busn Bks England). Brookfield Pub Co.

Spending Less & Enjoying It More: How to Get Control of Your Money. H. Roehm. 1984. pap. text ed. 8.95 (ISBN 0-07-053417-9). McGraw.

Spending Time Alone with God. Barry St. Clair. 144p. 1984. pap. 4.95 (ISBN 0-88207-302-8). Victor Bks.

Spendthrift Miser see Comedies of Goldoni.

Spendthrifts. Benito P. Galdos. 1978. Repr. of 1952 ed. lib. bdg. 35.00 (ISBN 0-8495-1919-5). Arden Lib.

Spengler im Dritten Reich see Hour of Decision.

Spenser. Richard W. Church. Ed. by John Morley. LC 68-58372. (English Men of Letters). Repr. of 1887 ed. lib. bdg. 12.50 (ISBN 0-404-51703-X). AMS Pr.

Spenser. Richard W. Church. 1973. lib. bdg. 15.00 (ISBN 0-8414-3029-2). Folcroft.

Spenser. Emile Legouis. Repr. of 1926 ed. lib. bdg. 17.50 (ISBN 0-8414-5680-1). Folcroft.

Spenser. Simon Shepherd. (Harvester New Readings). 128p. 1989. text ed. 35.00 (ISBN 0-391-03475-8). Humanities.

Spenser. Tuckwell Spenser. 85p. Repr. of 1906 ed. lib. bdg. 17.50 (ISBN 0-8495-5219-2). Arden Lib.
Spenser. W. Tuckwell. LC 72-191658. 1906. lib. bdg. 18.00 (ISBN 0-8414-8410-4). Folcroft.
Spenser & His Poetry, 3 vols. in 1. rev. ed. George L. Craik. LC 74-99247. Repr. of 1871 ed. 46.00 (ISBN 0-404-01826-2). AMS Pr.
Spenser & His Poetry. S. E. Winbolt. 1912. lib. bdg. 27.50 (ISBN 0-8414-9722-2). Folcroft.
Spenser & His Poetry. Samuel E. Winbolt. LC 70-120978. (Poetry & Life Series). Repr. of 1912 ed. 7.25 (ISBN 0-404-52534-2). AMS Pr.
Spenser & Literary Pictorialism. John B. Bender. LC 71-166361. 224p. 1972. 28.00x (ISBN 0-691-06211-0). Princeton U Pr.
Spenser & the Allegorists. J. F. Kermode. (Warton Lectures on English Poetry Ser.). 1962. pap. 5.50 (ISBN 0-902732-62-5, Pub. by British Acad). Longwood Pub Group.
Spenser & the Enchanted Glass. Charles G. Osgood. LC 76-11837. 1930. lib. bdg. 16.50 (ISBN 0-8414-2406-3). Folcroft.
Spenser & the Motives of Metaphor. A. L. DeNeef. LC 82-14737. vii, 197p. 1983. 31.75 (ISBN 0-8223-0487-2). Duke.
Spenser & the System of Courtly Love. Earle B. Fowler. LC 72-194882. 1934. lib. bdg. 15.00 (ISBN 0-8414-4276-2). Folcroft.
Spenser & the System of Courtly Love. Earle B. Fowler. LC 67-30903. 91p. 1967. Repr. of 1934 ed. 15.00x (ISBN 0-87753-016-5). Phaeton.
Spenser & the Table Round. Charles B. Millican. 1967. Repr. lib. bdg. 16.50x (ISBN 0-374-95719-3, Octagon). Hippocrene Bks.
Spenser & the Table Round: A Study in the Contemporaneous Background for Spenser's Use of the Arthurian Legend. Charles B. Milligan. 1977. lib. bdg. 59.95 (ISBN 0-8490-2656-3). Gordon Pr.
Spenser As a Fabulist. Louis S. Friedland. (Studies in Spenser, No. 26). 1970. pap. 39.95x (ISBN 0-8383-0031-6). Haskell.
Spenser in Ireland. Pauline Henley. LC 72-191233. 1972. lib. bdg. 19.00 (ISBN 0-8414-5041-2). Folcroft.
Spenser in Ireland. Pauline Henley. LC 70-131741. 1970. Repr. of 1928 ed. 7.00 (ISBN 0-403-00628-7). Scholarly.
Spenser in Southern Ireland. Alexander C. Judson. LC 77-4018. 1933. lib. bdg. 32.50 (ISBN 0-8414-5276-8). Folcroft.
Spenser, Marvell, & Renaissance Pastoral. Patrick Cullen. LC 76-123566. pap. 42.60 (2014653). Bks Demand UMI.
Spenser, Milton, & Renaissance Pastoral. Richard Mallette. LC 78-73154. 224p. 1980. 20.00 (ISBN 0-8387-2412-4). Bucknell U Pr.
Spenser of His Age Being Selected Works of Phineas Fletcher. Phineas Fletcher. 1979. Repr. of 1905 ed. lib. bdg. 40.00 (ISBN 0-8495-1629-3). Arden Lib.
Spenser: Selected Poetry. Edmund Spenser. Ed. by A. Kent Hieatt & Constance Hieatt. LC 76-91402. (Crofts Classics Ser). 1970. pap. text ed. 1.95x (ISBN 0-88295-095-9). Harlan Davidson.
Spenser: Selections, with Essays by Hazlitt, Coleridge & Leigh Hunt. Edmund Spenser. LC 76-29399. 1977. Repr. of 1923 ed. 19.50 (ISBN 0-404-15358-5). AMS Pr.
Spenser Studies: A Renaissance Poetry Annual, Vol. 7. Ed. by Patrick Cullen & Thomas Roche, Jr. 45.00 (ISBN 0-404-19207-6). AMS Pr.
Spenser Studies, Vol. VII: A Renaissance Poetry Annual. Ed. by Patrick Cullen & Thomas P. Roche, Jr. 45.00 (ISBN 0-404-19200-9). AMS Pr.
Spenser: The Faerie Queene. Ed. by A. C. Hamilton. LC 77-2738. (Longman Annotated English Poets Ser.). 1978. text ed. pap. text ed. 27.95 (ISBN 0-582-49705-1). Longman.
Spenserian Poetics: Idolatry, Iconoclasm & Magic. Kenneth Gross. LC 85-47701. 256p. 1985. 26.95x (ISBN 0-8014-1805-4). Cornell U Pr.
Spenser's Allegory: The Anatomy of Imagination. Isabel G. MacCaffrey. 1976. 55.00x (ISBN 0-691-06306-0); pap. 18.50x (ISBN 0-691-10043-8). Princeton U Pr.
Spenser's Anatomy of Heroism: A Commentary on the Faerie Quenne. Maurice Evans. LC 74-96087. 1970. 47.50 (ISBN 0-521-07662-5). Cambridge U Pr.
Spenser's Art: A Companion to Book One of "The Faerie Queene". Mark Rose. LC 74-21229. 160p. 1975. text ed. 11.00x (ISBN 0-674-83193-4). Harvard U Pr.
Spenser's Cosmic Philosophy of Religion. E. M. Albright. LC 72-100730. 1970. Repr. of 1929 ed. 39.95x (ISBN 0-8383-0001-4). Haskell.
Spenser's Defense of Lord Grey. Harry S. Jones. LC 73-170822. Repr. of 1919 ed. 8.50 (ISBN 0-404-03599-X). AMS Pr.
Spenser's Defense of Lord Grey. Harry S. Jones. 1919. pap. 8.00 (ISBN 0-384-27770-5). Johnson Repr.
Spenser's English Rivers. Charles G. Osgood. LC 77-22473. 1920. lib. bdg. 16.50 (ISBN 0-8414-6542-8). Folcroft.
Spenser's "Faerie Queene" & the Cult of Elizabeth. Robin H. Wells. LC 82-11568. 192p. 1983. text ed. 28.50x (ISBN 0-389-20324-6). B&N Imports.
Spenser's "Fierce Warres & Faithfull Loves" Martial & Chivalric Symbolism in "The Faerie Queene". Michael Leslie. LC 83-14929. (Illus.). 224p. 1983. 45.00x (ISBN 0-389-20465-X, 08026). B&N Imports.
Spenser's Images of Life. Clive S. Lewis. Ed. by A. Fowler. 1967. pap. 9.95, 1978 (ISBN 0-521-29284-0). Cambridge U Pr.
Spenser's Pastorals: The Shepheardes Calender & "Colin Clout". Nancy J. Hoffman. LC 77-4540. 1978. text ed. 18.50x (ISBN 0-8018-1984-9). Johns Hopkins.
Spenser's Proverb Lore: With Special Reference to His Use of the "Sententiae" of Leonard Culman & Publilius Syrus. Charles G. Smith. LC 78-85078. 1970. text ed. 27.00x (ISBN 0-674-83200-0). Harvard U Pr.
Spenser's Shepheardes Calender: A Study in Elizabethian Allegory. Paul McLane. LC 61-14876. 1969. pap. 9.95x (ISBN 0-268-00262-2). U of Notre Dame Pr.
Spenser's Shepherd's Calendar in Relation to Contemporary Affairs. James J. Higginson. LC 73-11428. 1912. Repr. lib. bdg. 30.50 (ISBN 0-8414-4724-1). Folcroft.
Spenser's Theory of Friendship. Charles G. Smith. Repr. of 1935 ed. 11.50 (ISBN 0-404-06119-2). AMS Pr.
Spenser's Theory of Friendship. Charles G. Smith. 1939. lib. bdg. 17.00 (ISBN 0-8414-1579-X). Folcroft.
Spenser's Use of Ariosto for Allegory. Susannah J. McMurphy. LC 77-539. 1924. lib. bdg. 17.00 (ISBN 0-8414-5992-4). Folcroft.
Spenser's World of Glass: A Reading of The Faerie Queen. Kathleen Williams. (California Library Reprint Series: No. 34). 1973. 32.50x (ISBN 0-520-02369-2). U of Cal Pr.
Spent Arrow. Inez Evans. Ed. by Robley Evans & Bob Evans. 306p. (YA) (gr. 7-12). 1987. 15.95 (ISBN 0-934188-24-6). Evans Pubns.
Spent Fuel Policy & Its Implications: Proceedings, American Nuclear Society Executive Conference. 276p. softcover 28.00 (ISBN 0-317-33078-0, 650006). Am Nuclear Soc.
Spent Nuclear Fuel Heat Transfer; Fuel Casks & Transfer Operations: Proceedings of AMSE, Annual Winter Meeting, December 1971. AMSE Staff. Ed. by D. J. Groetch & N. Todreas. LC 79-180673. (American Society of Mechanical Engineers, Heat Transfer Division Ser.: Vol. 2). pap. 20.00 (ISBN 0-317-09924-8, 2016901). Bks Demand UMI.
Speranza: A Biography of Lady Wilde. Horace Wyndham. LC 79-8088. Repr. of 1951 ed. 26.50 (ISBN 0-404-18396-4). AMS Pr.
Sperber und Verwandte Mhd: Novellen. Heinrich Niewohner. (Ger). pap. 13.00 (ISBN 0-685-02115-7). Johnson Repr.
Sperling. Jane T. Clement. 154p. 1986. pap. 6.00 (ISBN 3-922819-36-2). Plough.
Sperm Action: Proceedings. International Seminar on Reproductive Physiology & Sexual Endocrinology, 5th, Brussels, May, 1975. Ed. by P. O. Hubinont. 1976. 65.50 (ISBN 3-8055-2244-4). S Karger.
Sperm Cell. Ed. by Jean Andre. 1983. 71.75 (ISBN 90-247-2784-7, Pub. by Martinus Nijhoff Netherlands). Kluwer Academic.
Sperm Competition & the Evolution of Animal Mating Systems. Robert L. Smith. 1984. 49.00 (ISBN 0-12-652570-6). Acad Pr.
Sperm Whale. A. A. Berzin. 400p. 1972. text ed. 82.00x (ISBN 0-7065-1262-6, Pub. by Keter Pub Jerusalem). Coronet Bks.
Sperm Whale. 54p. 5.00 (ISBN 0-318-13866-2). Ctr Action Endangered.
Spermatogenesis, Genetic Aspects. W. Hennig. (Results & Problems in Cell Differentiation Ser.: Vol. 15). (Illus.). 200p. 1987. 59.50 (ISBN 0-387-17959-3). Springer-Verlag.
Spermatophores: Development, Structure, Biochemical Attributes & Role in the Transfer of Spermatozoa. T. Mann. (Zoophysiology Ser.: Vol. 15). (Illus.). 240p. 1984. 73.00 (ISBN 0-387-13583-9). Springer-Verlag.
Spero Divorce Folio. 3rd ed. Keith E. Spero. 16p. 1966. pap. 3.35 (ISBN 0-88450-109-4, 6103). Lawyers & Judges.
Spes--Diccionario Abreviado Latino-Espanol, Espanol-Latino. 9th ed. 316p. (Lat. & Span.). 1978. leatherette 14.95 (ISBN 84-7153-221-2, S-12409). French & Eur.
Spes--Diccionario Ilustrado Latino-Espanol, Espanol-Latino. 12th ed. 800p. (Lat. & Span.). 1979. leatherette 24.95 (ISBN 84-7153-197-6, S-17540). French & Eur.
Speyside Railways: Exploring the Remains of the Great North of Scotland Railway & Its Environs. R. Burgess & R. Kinghorn. (Illus.). 128p. 1988. pap. 11.75 (ISBN 0-08-036411-X, AUP). Pergamon.
Spezialwoerterbuch Maschinenwesen. Henry G. Freeman. 207p. (Ger. & Eng., Dictionary of Mechanical Engineering). 1971. 95.00 (M-7625, Pub. by Verlag W. Girardet). French & Eur.
Spezielle Plastische Chirurgie see Handbuch der Plastischen Chirurigie.
Spezifitaet und Variabilitaet im Zygaenapurpuralis-Komples (Lepidoptera Zyganenidae) C. M. Naumann et al. (Theses Zoologicae: No. 2). (Illus.). 264p. 1983. text ed. 60.00x (ISBN 3-7682-1339-0). Lubrecht & Cramer.
Sphagnophyta. H. A. Crum. (North American Flora Series II: Pt. II). 1984. 25.00x (ISBN 0-89327-252-3). NY Botanical.
Sphecid Wasps of the World: A Generic Revision. R. M. Bohart & A. S. Menke. 1976. 90.00x (ISBN 0-520-02318-8). U of Cal Pr.
Sphere. Michael Crichton. LC 86-46321. 1987. 17.95 (ISBN 0-394-56110-4). Knopf.
Sphere. Michael Crichton. 1988. pap. 4.95. Ballantine.
Sphere & Ash: History of Baseball. J. C. Morse. LC 84-72178. (Camden House Library of Baseball Classics: Vol. 3). (Illus.). 88p. 1984. Repr. of 1888 ed. 27.00x (ISBN 0-938100-35-1). Camden Hse.
Sphere & the Labryinth: Avant-Gardes & Architecture from Piranesi to the 1970's. Manfredo Tafuri. Tr. by Pellegrino D'Acierno & Robert Connolly. (Illus.). 400p. 1987. 39.95 (ISBN 0-262-20061-9). MIT Pr.
Sphere of Light. Roberta E. Berke. (Illus.). 1972. 10.00 (ISBN 0-685-29890-6, Pub. by Trigram Pr); signed ed. 18.00 (ISBN 0-685-29891-4). Small Pr Dist.
Sphere Packings, Lattices, & Groups. J. C. Conway & N. J. Sloane. (Grundlehren der Mathematischen Wissenschaften Ser.: Vol. 290). (Illus.). 550p. 1987. 87.00 (ISBN 0-387-96617-X). Springer-Verlag.
Sphereland. Dionys Burger. Tr. by Cornelie J. Rheinboldt from Fr. (Illus.). 224p. 1983. pap. 6.95 (ISBN 0-06-463574-0, EH 574, B&N Bks). Har-Row.
Spheres of Existence. C. L. James. LC 81-80431. (Selected Writings Ser.: Vol. 2). 272p. 1981. pap. 7.95 (ISBN 0-88208-128-4). Chicago Review.
Spheres of Influence. Corneliu Bogdan & Eugen Preda. (Social Science Monographs). 160p. 1988. 24.00 (ISBN 0-88033-961-6). East Eur Quarterly.
Spheres of Influence. facs. ed. Sydney Morrell. LC 70-142672. (Essay Index Reprint Ser). 1946. 20.00 (ISBN 0-8369-2197-6). Ayer Co Pubs.
Spheres of Justice: A Defense of Pluralism & Equality. Michael Walzer. LC 82-72408. 356p. 1983. 19.95 (ISBN 0-465-08190-8). Basic.
Spheres of Justice: A Defense of Pluralism & Equality. Michael Walzer. LC 82-72409. 345p. 1984. pap. 13.95x (ISBN 0-465-08189-4, TB-5111). Basic.
Spheres of Liberty: Changing Perceptions of Liberty in American Culture. Michael Kammen. LC 86-40052. 208p. 1986. 19.50 (ISBN 0-299-10840-6). U of Wis Pr.
Spherical & Ellipsoidal Harmonics. Ernest W. Hobson. LC 55-233. xi, 500p. 1955. 19.95 (ISBN 0-8284-0104-7). Chelsea Pub.
Spherical Astronomy. Robin Green. 480p. 1985. 80.00 (ISBN 0-521-23988-5); pap. 29.95 (ISBN 0-521-31779-7). Cambridge U Pr.
Spherical Astronomy for Astrologers. George Noonan. 64p. 1974. 3.00 (ISBN 0-86690-134-5, 1357-01). Am Fed Astrologers.
Spherical Harmonics. C. Mueller. (Lecture Notes in Mathematics: Vol. 17). 1966. pap. 10.70 (ISBN 0-387-03600-8). Springer-Verlag.
Spherical Harmonics & Tensors for Classical Field Theory. M. N. Jones. LC 85-2419. (Applied & Engineering Mathematical Ser.). 230p. 1985. 74.95 (ISBN 0-471-90766-9). Wiley.
Spherical Models. Magnus J. Wenninger. LC 78-58806. 1979. pap. 15.95 (ISBN 0-521-29432-0). Cambridge U Pr.
Spherical Near-Field Antenna Measurements: Theory & Practice. J. E. Hansen et al. Ed. by J. R. Wait et al. (Electromagnetic Waves Ser.). 1988. 95.00 (ISBN 0-86341-110-X). Inst Elect Eng.
Spheroids in Cancer Research. Ed. by H. Acker et al. (Recent Results in Cancer Research Ser.: Vol. 95). (Illus.). 210p. 1984. 54.00 (ISBN 0-387-13691-6). Springer-Verlag.
Sphincter of Oddi: Proceedings of the Gastroenterological Symposium, 3rd. Gastroenterological Symposium Staff. Ed. by J. Delmont. (Illus.). 1977. 41.50 (ISBN 3-8055-2623-7). S Karger.
Sphingolipid Biochemistry. Julian N. Kanfer & Sen-itiroh Hakomori. (Handbook of Lipid Research Ser.: Vol. 3). 500p. 1983. 69.50x (ISBN 0-306-41092-3, Plenum Pr). Plenum Pub.
Sphinx. Robin Cook. 1980. pap. 4.50 (ISBN 0-451-14871-1, AE3147, Sig). NAL.
Sphinx. Bernard Evslin. (Monsters of Mythology Ser.). (Illus.). 104p. Date not set. lib. bdg. 19.95x (ISBN 1-55546-260-X). Chelsea Hse.
Sphinx. David Lindsay. (Supernatural Fictions Ser.). 320p. 1988. 17.95 (ISBN 0-88184-416-0). Carroll & Graf.
Sphinx. D. M. Thomas. 256p. 1987. 17.95 (ISBN 0-670-81415-6). Viking.
Sphinx. D. M. Thomas. 1988. pap. 4.95 (ISBN 0-671-64158-1). WSP.
Sphinx & the Rainbow: Brain, Mind, & Future Vision. David Loye. LC 83-42803. (New Science Library). (Illus.). 256p. (Orig.). 1983. pap. 17.95 (ISBN 0-87773-241-8); pap. 8.95 (ISBN 0-87773-242-6). Shambhala Pubns.
Sphinx & the Rainbow: Brain, Mind & Future Vision. David Loye. pap. 8.95 (ISBN 0-394-72187-X). Shambhala Pubns.
Sphinx at Dawn: Two Stories. Madeleine L'Engle. (Illus.). 48p. 1982. 7.95 (ISBN 0-8164-0527-1, HarpR). Har-Row.
Sphinx des Glaces. Jules Verne. 8.95 (ISBN 0-686-55951-7). French & Eur.
Sphinx Ranch Date Recipes. R. I. Heetland. 120p. (Orig.). 1986. pap. 5.00 (ISBN 0-914846-28-0). Golden West Pub.
Sphinx Rouge. Alexandre Dumas. 533p. 1966. 8.95 (ISBN 0-686-55205-9). French & Eur.
Sphinx Smiles Twice. Antigone Maroudis. 1976. 8.00x (ISBN 0-686-19992-8); pap. 6.75x (ISBN 0-686-19993-6). Intl Learn Syst.
Sphota Theory of Language. Harold G. Coward. 1981. 12.00x (ISBN 0-8364-0692-3). South Asia Bks.
Sphota Theory of Language: A Philosophical Analysis. Harold G. Coward. xx, 158p. 1986. 14.00x (ISBN 81-208-0181-4, Pub. by Motilal Banarsidass). South Asia Bks.
Sphota Theory of Language: A Philosophical Analysis. Harold G. Coward. 158p. 1986. 14.00 (ISBN 0-317-70027-8, Pub. by Motilal Banarsidas). Orient Bk Dist.
Sphygmomanometers: Electronic or Automated. Cancelled 35.00 (SP9). Assn Adv Med Instrn.
SPI Handbook of Technology & Engineering of Reinforced Plastics-Composites. 2nd ed. Gilbert J. Mohr et al. LC 80-26338. 416p. 1981. Repr. of 1973 ed. 29.50 (ISBN 0-89874-295-1). Krieger.
SPI-SPE Plastics Show & Conference - East: Conference Proceedings, Philadelphia Civic Center, Philadelphia, PA, June 21-23, 1984. The SPI-SPE Connection- An Industry First. Society of Plastics Engineers. pap. 86.00 (ISBN 0-317-30376-7, 2024725). Bks Demand UMI.
Spice: A Handbook of Classroom Ideas to Motivate the Teaching of Primary Language Arts. (Spice Ser). 1973. 8.95 (ISBN 0-89273-101-X). Educ Serv.
Spice & Diet Cookbooklet. 13p. pap. 1.00 (ISBN 0-318-19109-1). Am Spice Trade.
Spice & Magic. Betty Beath. 143p. 1985. pap. 7.50 (ISBN 0-908175-68-X, Pub. by Boolarong Pubn Australia). Intl Spec Bk.
Spice & Spirit of Kosher-Jewish Cooking. Ed. by Esther Blau. LC 77-72116. (Illus.). 1977. 18.95 (ISBN 0-8197-0455-5). Bloch.
Spice & Spirit of Kosher-Jewish Cooking. Lubavitch Womens Organization. Ed. by Esther Blau. LC 77-72116. (Illus.). 1977. 16.95 (ISBN 0-930178-01-7). Lubavitch Women.
Spice & Spirit of Kosher-Passover Cooking. Ed. by Esther Blau & Cyrel Deitsch. LC 77-72116. (Lubavitch Women's Organization Ser.). 1981. 7.95 (ISBN 0-317-14690-4). Lubavitch Women.
Spice Box. Grace L. Hill. (Grace Livingston Hill Classic Ser.). 228p. 1985. 8.95 (ISBN 0-8007-1432-6). Revell.
Spice Box: A Vegetarian Indian Cookbook. Manju S. Singh. LC 81-3179. (Illus.). 224p. 1981. 21.95 (ISBN 0-89594-052-3); pap. 8.95 (ISBN 0-89594-053-1). Crossing Pr.
Spice Duplicating Masters, 2 vols. (Spice Duplicating Masters Ser). 1973. Vol. 1, Grades K-2. 8.95 (ISBN 0-89273-501-5); Vol. 2, Grades 2-4. 8.95 (ISBN 0-89273-502-3). Educ Serv.
Spice for Life. Walt Schmidt. 48p. 1985. 6.95 (ISBN 0-8378-5075-4). Gibson.
Spice of America. June Swanson. LC 83-5298. (Good Time Library). (Illus.). 96p. (gr. 2-6). 1983. PLB 8.95 (ISBN 0-87614-252-8). Carolrhoda Bks.
Spice of America. June Swanson. (Illus.). 96p. (ps-3). 1987. pap. 4.95 (ISBN 0-87614-479-2, First Ave Edns). Lerner Pubns.
Spice of Life. Sheldon Greenberg & Elisabeth L. Ortiz. LC 84-70582. (Illus.). 192p. 1984. 17.95 (ISBN 0-943276-04-7). Amaryllis Pr.
Spice of Life. James M. Hendrickson & Angela LaBarca. 180p. 1979. pap. text ed. 10.00 net (ISBN 0-15-583251-4, HC). HarBraceJ.
Spicer & Oppenheim Guide to Securities Markets Around the World. Financial Services Group, Spicer & Oppenheim Staff. 1988. pap. 19.95 (ISBN 0-471-61162-X). Wiley.
Spicer & Oppenheim Guide to Securities Markets Around the World. The Spicer & Oppenheim Financial Services Group. 1988. 39.95 (ISBN 0-471-61289-8); pap. 14.95 (ISBN 0-317-66882-X). Wiley.
Spicer Edition. Hollander Publishing Company Inc. (Truck Interchange Ser.). 420p. 1975. 39.50 (ISBN 0-943032-05-9). Hollander Co.
Spicer: Leader with the Common Touch. Godfrey T. Anderson. Ed. by Gerald Wheeler. LC 83-3279. (Illus.). 128p. (Orig.). 1983. pap. 5.95 (ISBN 0-8280-0150-2). Review & Herald.
Spices, 2 vols. Purseglove et al. (Tropical Agriculture Ser.). (Illus.). 1981. Vol. 1. text ed. 50.00x (ISBN 0-582-46811-6); Vol. 2. text ed. 50.00x (ISBN 0-582-46342-4). Wiley.
Spices, Vol. 1. J. W. Perseglove et al. 450p. 1981. 54.95 (ISBN 0-470-20565-2, Co-Pub. with Longman). Wiley.
Spices, Vol. 2. J. W. Purseglove et al. 368p. 1981. 54.95 (ISBN 0-470-20566-0, Co-Pub. with Longman). Wiley.

Spin Glasses & Biology. Ed. by D. Stein. (DLMP Ser.). 450p. 1988. 78.00 (ISBN 9971-50-537-1); pap. 46.00 (ISBN 9971-50-538-X). World Scientific Pub.

Spin Glasses & Other Frustrated Systems. D. Chowdhury. 200p. 1986. 28.00 (ISBN 9971-50-029-9, Z0233P-B). World Scientific Pub.

Spin Glasses & Other Frustrated Systems. Debashish Chowdhury. (Physics Ser.). (Illus.). 388p. 1987. pap. 29.95 (ISBN 0-691-08461-0). Princeton U Pr.

Spin Labeling in Pharmacology. Jordan L. Holtzman. 1984. 44.00 (ISBN 0-12-354050-X). Acad Pr.

Spin Labeling Methods in Molecular Biology. Gerktis Likhtenshtefin. LC 76-16500. pap. 67.80 (ISBN 0-317-28454-1, 2055151). Bks Demand UMI.

Spin Labeling: Theory & Applications. Ed. by Lawrence J. Berliner. (Molecular Biology Ser.: Vol. 1). 1976. 70.00 (ISBN 0-12-092350-5). Acad Pr.

Spin Labeling Two: Theory & Applications. Ed. by L. J. Berliner. LC 75-3587. (Molecular Biology Ser.). 1979. 70.00 (ISBN 0-12-092352-1). Acad Pr.

Spin Off. Catharine T. Herford. 60p. 1984. 15.00x (ISBN 0-7212-0690-5, Pub. by Regency Pr). State Mutual Bk.

Spin-off Products & Services: The Commercialization of Internally Supported Resources. E. Patrick McGuire. (Report Ser.: No. 695). 32p. 1976. pap. 30.00 (ISBN 0-8237-0129-8). Conference Bd.

Spin-Orbit Coupling in Molecules. W. G. Richards & D. L. Cooper. (International Series of Monographs on Chemistry). 1981. 39.95x (ISBN 0-19-855614-4). Oxford U Pr.

Spin Out. Martyn Godfrey. (Encounters Sre.). 96p. 1985. pap. text ed. 3.95 (ISBN 0-8219-0166-4, 35356); wkbk 1.20 (ISBN 0-8219-0167-2, 35715). EMC.

Spin Polarizarion & Magnetic Effects in Radical Reactions. Yu N. Molin. (Studies in Physical & Theoretical Chemistry: Vol. 22). 1984. 123.75 (ISBN 0-444-99677-X). Elsevier.

S.P.I.N. Selling. Neil Rackham. 224p. 1988. text ed. 19.95 (ISBN 0-07-051113-6). McGraw.

Spin Span Spun: Fact & Folklore for Spinners. B. Hochberg. LC 79-89003. (Illus., Orig.). 1979. pap. 5.95 (ISBN 0-9600990-3-4). B Hochberg.

Spin Temperature & Nuclear Spin Relaxation in Matter: Basic Principles & Applications. Dieter Wolf. (International Series of Monographs on Physics). (Illus.). 1979. text ed. 49.95x (ISBN 0-19-851295-3). Oxford U Pr.

Spin the Spin. S. Tomonaya. 300p. 1988. 44.00 (ISBN 9971-50-330-1). World Scientific Pub.

Spin Waves & Magnetic Excitations. Ed. by A. S. Borovik-Romanov & S. K. Sinha. (Modern Problems in Condensed Matter Sciences Ser.: Vol. 22). 960p. 1988. Part 1. 131.50 (ISBN 0-444-87068-7); Part 2. 131.50 (ISBN 0-444-87078-4, North Holland). Elsevier.

Spin Your Wheels. Sally Hamilton. (Learning Works Creative Writing Ser.). 48p. (gr. 4-6). 1982. 4.95 (ISBN 0-88160-051-2, LW 237). Learning Wks.

Spina Bifida: A Multidisciplinary Approach. Ed. by Robert L. McLaurin et al. LC 86-8184. 509p. 1986. lib. bdg. 67.95 (ISBN 0-275-92100-X, C2100). Praeger.

Spina Bifida for the Clinician. Ed. by Gordon Brocklehurst. (Clinics in Developmental Medicine Ser.: Vol. 57). 300p. 1976. text ed. 27.50 (ISBN 0-433-04410-1, Pub. by Spastics Intl England). Lippincott.

Spina Bifida-Neural Tube Defects: Basic Research, Interdisciplinary Diagnostics & Treatment, Results & Prognosis. Ed. by D. Voth et al. (Illus.). xi, 320p. 1986. 95.50 (ISBN 3-11-010768-6). De Gruyter.

Spina Bifida Occulta. C. C. James & L. P. Lassman. LC 81-80964. 230p. 1981. 59.50 (ISBN 0-8089-1383-2, 792162). Grune.

Spinal Afferent Processing. Ed. by Tony L. Yaksh. 540p. 1986. 79.50x (ISBN 0-306-42046-5, Plenum Pr). Plenum Pub.

Spinal & Supraspinal Mechanisms of Voluntary Motor Control & Locomotion. Ed. by J. E. Desmedt. (Progress in Clinical Neurophysiology Ser.: Vol. 8). (Illus.). x, 374p. 1980. 92.00 (ISBN 3-8055-0022-X). S Karger.

Spinal Chord Dysfunction: Assessment. L. S. Illis. (Illus.). 280p. 1988. 82.00 (ISBN 0-19-261624-2). Oxford U Pr.

Spinal Cord. 3rd ed. George Austin. LC 82-15523. (Illus.). 848p. 1983. monograph 91.00 (ISBN 0-89640-079-4). Igaku-Shoin.

Spinal Cord & It's Reaction to Traumatic Injury. Windle. (Modern Pharmacology-Toxicology Ser.: Vol. 18). 448p. 1980. 69.75 (ISBN 0-8247-6688-1). Dekker.

Spinal Cord Injuries. Daniel Ruge. (Illus.). 236p. 1969. 25.25 (ISBN 0-398-01630-5). C C Thomas.

Spinal Cord Injuries in Children. Ed. by James E. Wilberger. (Illus.). 304p. 1986. monograph 39.50 (ISBN 0-87993-264-3). Futura Pub.

Spinal Cord Injuries: Psychological, Social, & Vocational Rehabilitation. 2nd ed. Roberta B. Trieschmann. LC 87-71320. 350p. 1988. 39.50 (ISBN 0-939957-08-6). Demos Pubns Inc.

Spinal Cord Injury. Ed. by Hazel Adkins. (Clinics in Physical Therapy Ser.: Vol. 6). (Illus.). 288p. 1985. text ed. 35.00 (ISBN 0-443-08360-6). Churchill.

Spinal Cord Injury. Ed. by N. E. Naftchi. LC 81-8573. (Illus.). 306p. 1982. text ed. 45.00 (ISBN 0-88331-202-6). Luce.

Spinal Cord Injury: A Guide for Patient & Family. Lynn Phillips et al. 320p. 1987. text ed. 29.00 (ISBN 0-88167-274-2); pap. text ed. 14.00 (ISBN 0-88167-275-0). Raven.

Spinal Cord Injury: A Guide to Functional Outcomes in Occupational Therapy. Ed. by Judy P. Hill. 257p. 1987. 46.00 (ISBN 0-87189-604-4). Aspen Pub.

Spinal Cord Injury: A Guide to Functional Outcomes in Physical Therapy Management. A Rehabilitation Institute of Chicago Procedure Manual. LC 84-18474. (Illus.). 233p. 1984. 44.00 (ISBN 0-89443-552-3). Aspen Pub.

Spinal Cord Injury: A Treatment Guide for Occupational Therapists. rev. ed. Dorothy Wilson et al. LC 74-75685. 76p. 1984. text ed. 21.95 (ISBN 0-317-61281-6). Slack Inc.

Spinal Cord Injury: An Illustrated Guide for Health Care Professionals. Marcia Hanak & Ann Scott. 176p. 1983. text ed. 16.95 (ISBN 0-8261-4171-4). Springer Pub.

Spinal Cord Injury Medical Engineering. Ed. by D. N. Ghista. (Illus.). 592p. 1986. 93.50x (ISBN 0-398-05167-4). C C Thomas.

Spinal Cord Monitoring. Ed. by J. Schramm & S. J. Jones. (Illus.). 352p. 1985. 84.00 (ISBN 0-387-15774-3). Springer-Verlag.

Spinal Cord Reconstruction. Ed. by Carl C. Kao et al. (Illus.). 510p. 1983. text ed. 122.00 (ISBN 0-89004-538-0). Raven.

Spinal Cord Sensation: Sensory Processing in the Dorsal Horn. Ed. by A. G. Brown. 357p. 1981. 32.50x (ISBN 0-7073-0295-1, Pub. by Scot Acad Pr). Longwood Pub Group.

Spinal Cord (Spinal Medulla) C. R. Noback & J. K. Harting. Ed. by H. Hofer et al. (Primatologia Ser.: Vol. 2, Pt. 2). (Illus.). 1971. pap. 30.00 (ISBN 3-8055-1205-8). S Karger.

Spinal Cord Tumors: Experimental Neurosurgery Neurosurgical Intensive Care. Ed. by R. Wenkwe et al. (Advances in Neurosurgery Ser.: Vol. 14). (Illus.). 400p. 1986. pap. 66.00 (ISBN 0-387-16360-3). Springer-Verlag.

Spinal Deformities & Neurological Dysfunction. Ed. by Shelley N. Chou & Edward L. Seljeskog. LC 76-5665. (Seminars in Neurological Surgery). 300p. 1978. 60.50 (ISBN 0-89004-183-0). Raven.

Spinal Deformity. Pierre Stagnara. Tr. by John Dove from Fr. (Illus.). 1988. text ed. 125.00 (ISBN 0-407-00427-0, Pub. by Masson Paris). Butterworth.

Spinal Degenerative Diseases. R. S. Maurice-Williams. (Illus.). 356p. 1981. 45.00 (ISBN 0-7236-0583-1). PSG Pub Co.

Spinal Engine. S. Gracovetsky. (Illus.). 450p. 1988. 49.00 (ISBN 0-387-82030-2). Springer-Verlag.

Spinal Fitness Class. Raymond K. Woltz. Ed. by T. Bruce Henderson. (Illus.). 92p. 1983. pap. 14.95 (ISBN 0-9613447-0-9). R K Woltz.

Spinal Injury. 2nd. ed. David Yashon. (Illus.). 395p. 1986. 74.50 (ISBN 0-8385-8636-8). Appleton & Lange.

Spinal Manipulation. 4th ed. J. S. Bourdillon. (Illus.). 1987. text ed. 39.95 (ISBN 0-8385-8642-2, A8642-9). Appleton & Lange.

Spinal Network. Sam Maddox. LC 87-12812. (Illus.). 372p. (Orig.). 1987. pap. 24.95 (ISBN 0-943489-00-8). Spinal Network.

Spinal Opiate Analgesia: Experimental & Clinical Studies. Ed. by T. L. Yaksh & H. Mueller. (Anaesthesiology & Intensive Care Medicine Ser.: Vol. 144). (Illus.). 164p. 1982. pap. 34.00 (ISBN 0-387-11036-4). Springer-Verlag.

Spinal Phlebography: Lumbar & Cervical Techniques. Ed. by J. Theron & J. Moret. (Illus.). 1978. 83.00 (ISBN 0-387-08867-9). Springer-Verlag.

Spinal Specialist's Guide to Exercise, Fitness & Health. F. Michael Blair. LC 85-1234. (Illus.). 188p. 1985. pap. 12.95 (ISBN 0-932620-41-8). Betterway Pubns.

Spindle Dynamics & Chromosome Movements see International Review of Cytology: Supplements.

Spindle Stage: Principles & Practice. Donald F. Bloss. LC 80-21488. (Illus.). 416p. 1981. 80.00 (ISBN 0-521-23292-9). Cambridge U Pr.

Spindletop. Michel Halbouty & James Clark. LC 52-7149. 306p. 1980. Repr. of 1952 ed. 23.00x (ISBN 0-87201-791-5). Gulf Pub.

Spindletop. Sibyl Hancock. (Stories for Young Americans Ser.). (Illus.). (gr. 4-7). 1981. 7.95 (ISBN 0-89015-265-9). Eakin Pr.

Spindrift. Phyllis A. Whitney. 320p. 1981. pap. 2.95 (ISBN 0-449-22746-4, Crest). Fawcett.

Spine. Karen Hanson. LC 73-161968. 69p. 1971. 2.95 (ISBN 0-87886-009-6). Greenfld Rev Pr.

Spine, 2 vols. 2nd ed. Ed. by Richard H. Rothman & Frederick A. Simeone. LC 74-4584. (Illus.). 922p. 1982. Vol. 1. 89.00 (ISBN 0-7216-7719-3); Vol. 2. 94.00 (ISBN 0-7216-7720-7); Set. 175.00 (ISBN 0-7216-7718-5). Saunders.

Spine. Michael Spence. (Illus.). 76p. (Orig.). 1987. pap. 5.75 (ISBN 0-911198-89-X). Purdue U Pr.

Spine Chillers. John Galsworthy et al. Ed. by A. G. Eyre. (Longman Simplified English Ser.). 82p. 1980. pap. 3.95 (ISBN 0-582-52672-8). Longman.

Spine of Software: Designing Provably Correct Software-Theory & Practice. Robert L. Baber. LC 86-32483. 300p. 1988. 51.95 (ISBN 0-471-91474-6). Wiley.

Spinifex & Hessian: Women in Northwest Australia 1860-1900. Susan Hunt. 168p. 1987. pap. 22.95 (ISBN 0-85564-242-4, Pub. by U of W Austrail Pr). Intl Spec Bk.

Spinks Catalog of British Commemorative Medals (1558 to Present) D. Fearon. (Illus.). 1984. lib. bdg. 30.00 (ISBN 0-86350-029-3, Pub. by Spink & Son England). S J Durst.

Spink's Catalogue of British Commentorative Medals. Daniel Fearson. 1985. 22.95 (ISBN 0-03-004214-3, Pub. by Webb & Bower). H Holt & Co.

Spink's Complete Catalogue of British Commonwealth Orders, Decorations & Medals. E. C. Joslin. 192p. 1983. 25.95 (ISBN 0-03-063263-3). H Holt & Co.

Spinky Sulks. William Steig. (Michael di Capua Books). (Illus.). 32p. (ps up). 1988. 13.95 (ISBN 0-317-69888-5). FS&G.

Spinner Fishing for Steelhead, Salmon & Trout. Jed Davis. (Illus.). 97p. 1985. 24.95 (ISBN 0-936608-41-2); pap. 12.95 (ISBN 0-936608-40-4). F Amato Pubns.

Spinner in the Sun. Myrtle Reed. 1976. lib. bdg. 17.25x (ISBN 0-89968-111-5). Lightyear.

Spinner: People & Culture in Southeastern Massachusetts. Joseph D. Thomas & Donna Huse. (Illus.). 200p. (Orig.). 1981. Set. write for info. (ISBN 0-932027-00-8); Set. pap. write for info. (ISBN 0-932027-01-6). Spinner Pubns.

Spinner: People & Culture in Southeastern Massachusetts. Joseph D. Thomas & Donna Huse. (Vol. I). (Illus.). 128p. (Orig.). 1981. 17.95 (ISBN 0-932027-02-4); pap. 3.50 (ISBN 0-932027-03-2). Spinner Pubns.

Spinner: People & Culture in Southeastern Massachusetts. Joseph D. Thomas & Donna Huse. (Vol. II). (Illus.). 136p. (Orig.). 1982. 19.95 (ISBN 0-932027-04-0); pap. 7.95 (ISBN 0-932027-05-9). Spinner Pubns.

Spinner: People & Culture in Southeastern Massachusetts. Joseph D. Thomas & Donna Huse. (Vol. III). (Illus.). 208p. (Orig.). 1984. 24.95 (ISBN 0-932027-06-7); pap. 9.95 (ISBN 0-932027-07-5). Spinner Pubns.

Spinneret. Timothy Zahn. 352p. 1985. 15.95 (ISBN 0-312-94411-X). Bluejay Bks.

Spinneret. Timothy Zahn. 1986. 3.50 (ISBN 0-671-65598-1). Baen Bks.

Spinners & Weavers of Auffay: Rural Industry & the Sexual Division of Labor in a French Village, 1750-1850. Gay L. Gullickson. (Illus.). 288p. 1986. 34.50 (ISBN 0-521-32280-4). Cambridge U Pr.

Spinner's Christmas Gift. Elaine M. Ward. (Story Tree Ser.). (Illus.). 64p. (Orig.). (ps). 1982. pap. 1.95 (ISBN 0-89505-072-2). Tabor Pub.

Spinner's Encyclopedia. Enid Anderson. (Illus.). 240p. 1988. 24.95 (ISBN 0-7153-8794-4, Pub. by David & Charles Pub England). Sterling.

Spinner's Wharf. Iris Gower. 384p. 1986. 16.95 (ISBN 0-312-75237-7). St Martin.

Spinner's Wharf. Iris Gower. 1988. pap. 3.95 (ISBN 1-55547-215-X). Critics Choice Paper.

Spinnin' How to Score a Hit As a Mobile DJ for Fun & Profit. Robert A. Lindquist. Ed. by David Warner & Clare Dygert. (Illus.). 110p. 1987. pap. 15.00 (ISBN 0-943047-00-5). TNT Prodns.

Spinning. 50.00x (ISBN 0-85083-009-5, Pub. by Engineering Ind). State Mutual Bk.

Spinning a Sacred Yarn: Women Speak from the Pulpit. LC 82-569. 230p. (Orig.). 1982. pap. 8.95 (ISBN 0-8298-0604-0). Pilgrim NY.

Spinning & Plug Fishing: An Illustrated Textbook. Barrie Rickards & Ken Whitehead. (Illus.). 27.00 (ISBN 0-85115-462-X, Pub. by Boydell & Brewer). Longwood Pub Group.

Spinning & Weaving: A Practical Guide. Eileen Hobden. (Illus.). 114p. 1987. 13.95 (ISBN 0-317-64165-4, Pub. by Bishopsgate Pr London); pap. 9.95 (ISBN 0-317-64166-2). Intl Spec Bk.

Spinning & Weaving with Wool. Paula Simmons. LC 77-76137. (Illus.). 224p. 1977. pap. 14.95 (ISBN 0-914718-23-1). Globe Pequot.

Spinning Designer Yarns. Diane Varney. LC 87-80523. (Illus.). 96p. (Orig.). 1987. pap. 12.00 (ISBN 0-934026-29-7). Interweave.

Spinning for Trout. Bob Gooch. (Illus.). 192p. 1984. pap. 7.95 (ISBN 0-684-18076-6, ScribT). Scribner.

Spinning Gold. Tom Gardner. (Illus.). 250p. (Orig.). 1987. pap. 19.95 (ISBN 0-938889-02-8). Time Warp Pub.

Spinning Inward: Using Guided Imagery with Children. rev., expanded ed. Maureen Murdock. LC 87-9740. (Illus.). 158p. 1987. pap. 15.95 (ISBN 0-87773-422-4). Shambhala Pubns.

Spinning Straw into Gold. C. C. Cribb. LC 79-84880. (If God Has It I Want It! Ser.). pap. 2.95 (ISBN 0-932046-15-0). Manhattan Ltd NC.

Spinning Tops & Gyroscopic Motion. Harold Crabtree. LC 66-23755. (Illus.). 1977. text ed. 18.95 (ISBN 0-8284-0204-3). Chelsea Pub.

Spinning Wheel's Complete Book of Dolls, Vol. II. Ed. by Spinning Wheel Staff. (Illus.). 290p. Date not set. 24.95 (ISBN 0-912823-00-3). Gold Horse.

Spinning Wheels, Spinners & Spinning. new ed. Patricia Baines. pap. 12.95 (ISBN 0-686-37658-7). Robin & Russ.

Spinning Wire from Molten Metal. LC 78-24515. 116p. 1978. pap. 22.00 (ISBN 0-8169-0109-0, S-180). Am Inst Chem Eng.

Spinoff, Nineteen Eighty-Six. 130p. 1986. pap. 6.50 (ISBN 0-318-21374-5, S/N 033-000-00989-5). USGPO.

Spinoff, 1987. (Illus.). 130p. 1987. pap. 7.00 (ISBN 0-318-23846-2, 033-000-01008-7). USGPO.

Spinor & Non-Euclidean Tensor Calculus with Applications. I. Beju. (Illus.). 275p. 1983. 35.00 (ISBN 0-85626-334-6). Abacus Pr.

Spinorial Chessboard. P. Budinich & A. Trautman. (Trieste Notes in Physics Ser.). 130p. 1988. pap. 27.50 (ISBN 0-387-19078-3). Springer-Verlag.

Spinors & Space-Time: Spinor & Twistor Methods in Space-Time Geometry, Vol. 2. Roger Penrose & Wolfgang Rindler. (Cambridge Monographs on Mathematical Physics). (Illus.). 500p. 1986. 89.50 (ISBN 0-521-25267-9). Cambridge U Pr.

Spinors & Space-Time: Two-Spinor Calculus & Relativistic Fields, Vol. I. Roger Penrose & Wolfgang Rindler. (Cambridge Monographs on Mathematics). 450p. 1987. pap. 29.95 (ISBN 0-521-33707-0). Cambridge U Pr.

Spinors & Space Time, Vol. 1: Two-Spinor Calculus & Relativistic Fields. Roger Penrose & Wolfgang Rindler. 480p. 1984. 97.50 (ISBN 0-521-24527-3). Cambridge U Pr.

Spinors & Space-Time, Vol. 2: Spinor & Twistor Methods in Space-Time Geometry. Roger Penrose & Wolfgang Rindler. (Cambridge Monographs on Mathematical Physics). (Illus.). 512p. 1988. pap. 34.50 (ISBN 0-521-34786-6). Cambridge U Pr.

Spinors, Clifford, & Cayley Algebras. Robert Hermann. (Interdisciplinary Mathematics Ser.: Vol. 7). 276p. 1974. 25.00 (ISBN 0-915692-06-6, 991600215). Math Sci Pr.

Spinors in Hilbert Space. P. A. Dirac. LC 74-18371. 92p. 1974. 25.00x (ISBN 0-306-30798-7, Plenum Pr). Plenum Pub.

Spinosaurus. D. White. (Dinosaur Library). (Illus.). 24p. (gr. 3 up). Date not set. PLB 13.27 (ISBN 0-86592-517-8). Rourke Corp.

Spinoza. facsimile ed. John Caird. LC 75-164593. (Select Bibliographies Reprint Ser). Repr. of 1888 ed. 21.00 (ISBN 0-8369-5877-2). Ayer Co Pubs.

Spinoza. R. J. Delahunty. (Arguments of the Philosophers Ser.). 352p. 1985. 49.95x (ISBN 0-7102-0375-6). Routledge Chapman & Hall.

Spinoza. Stuart Hampshire. (Orig.). 1952. pap. 4.95 (ISBN 0-14-020253-6, Pelican). Penguin.

Spinoza. Stuart Hampshire. 192p. pap. 6.95 (ISBN 0-14-022778-4). Penguin.

Spinoza. Karl Jaspers. Ed. by Hannah Arendt. Tr. by Ralph Manheim from Ger. LC 74-4336. (From the Great Philosophers Ser.). 120p. 1974. pap. 2.95 (ISBN 0-15-684730-2, Harv). HarBraceJ.

Spinoza. Frederick Pollock. 59.95 (ISBN 0-8490-1110-8). Gordon Pr.

Spinoza. Leon Roth. LC 78-14139. 1986. Repr. of 1954 ed. 23.75 (ISBN 0-88355-813-0). Hyperion Conn.

Spinoza. Roger Scruton. 140p. 1987. 15.95 (ISBN 0-19-287631-7); pap. 4.95 (ISBN 0-19-287630-9). Oxford U Pr.

Spinoza: A Collection of Critical Essays. Ed. by Marjorie Grene. LC 78-62973. (Modern Studies in Philosophy). 1979. text ed. 18.95x (ISBN 0-268-01692-5); pap. text ed. 9.95x (ISBN 0-268-01693-3). U of Notre Dame Pr.

Spinoza & Grammatical Tradition. A. J. Klijnsmit. (Mededeingen vanwege het Spinozahuis Ser.: No. 49). 16p. 1986. 4.25 (ISBN 90-04-08095-3, Pub. by E J Brill). Heinman.

Spinoza & Moral Freedom. S. Paul Kashap. LC 86-30210. (SUNY Series in Philosophy). 130p. 1987. 34.50 (ISBN 0-88706-529-5); pap. 12.95 (ISBN 0-88706-530-9). State U NY Pr.

Spinoza & the Rise of Liberalism. Lewis S. Feuer. LC 83-18508. x, 323p. 1983. Repr. of 1958 ed. lib. bdg. 41.50x (ISBN 0-313-24250-X, FESR). Greenwood.

Spinoza & the Rise of Liberalism. Lewis S. Feuer. 344p. 1987. pap. 19.95 (ISBN 0-88738-701-2). Transaction Bks.

Spinoza & the Sciences. Ed. by Nails Grene. 1986. lib. bdg. 54.50 (ISBN 90-277-1976-4, Pub. by Reidel Holland). Kluwer-Academic.

Spinoza As Educator. William L. Rabenort. LC 70-177175. (Columbia University. Teachers College. Contributions to Education: No. 38). Repr. of 1911 ed. 22.50 (ISBN 0-404-55038-X). AMS Pr.

Spinoza: Essays in Interpretation. Ed. by Eugene Freeman & Maurice Mandelbaum. LC 72-84079. (Monist Library of Philosophy Ser.). 329p. 1975. pap. 9.95 (ISBN 0-87548-196-5). Open Court.

Spinoza-Hegel Paradox: A Study of the Choice Between Traditional Idealism & Systematic Pluralism. Henry A. Myers. Repr. of 1944 ed. 15.00 (ISBN 0-8337-4914-5). B Franklin.

Spinoza: His Life & Philosophy. Frederick Pollock. (Reprints in Philosophy Ser.). (Illus.). Repr. of 1880 ed. lib. bdg. 47.00x (ISBN 0-697-00055-9). Irvington.

Spinoza: His Life, Correspondence & Ethics. R. Willis. 1977. lib. bdg. 76.95 (ISBN 0-8490-2657-1). Gordon Pr.

Spinoza in Germany from 1670. David Bell. (Bithell Series of Dissertations: Vol. 7). 192p. 1984. pap. text ed. 29.95x (ISBN 0-85457-117-5, Pub. by Inst Germanic UK). Humanities.

Spinoza: New Perspectives. Ed. by Robert W. Shahan & J. I. Biro. LC 77-18541. 1980. 17.95 (ISBN 0-8061-1459-2); pap. text ed. 8.95x (ISBN 0-8061-1647-1). U of Okla Pr.

Spinoza of Market Street & Other Stories. Isaac Bashevis Singer. Tr. by Elaine Gottleib et al from Yiddish. 214p. 1961. 8.95 (ISBN 0-374-26776-6); pap. 4.95 (ISBN 0-374-50256-0). FS&G.

Spinoza on Knowing, Being, & Freedom: Proceedings of the Spinoza Symposium at the International School of Philosophy, Leusden 1973. Ed. by J. G. Van der Bend. 196p. 1974. text ed. 38.50x (ISBN 90-232-1150-2, Pub. by Van Gorcum Holland). Coronet Bks.

Spinoza on Nature. Ed. by James Collins. 360p. 1984. 32.50x (ISBN 0-8093-1160-7). S Ill U Pr.

Spinoza: Practical Philosophy. Gilles Deleuze. Tr. by Robert Hurley from Fr. 160p. (Orig.). Date not set. 21.95 (ISBN 0-87286-220-8); pap. 9.95 (ISBN 0-87286-218-6). City Lights.

Spinoza's Critique of Religion. Leo Strauss. Tr. by E. M. Sinclair from Ger. LC 65-10948. 364p. 1982. pap. 8.50 (ISBN 0-8052-0704-X). Schocken.

Spinoza's Earliest Publication? Ed. by Richard H. Popkin & Michael Signer. 100p. 1987. 17.50 (ISBN 90-232-2223-7, Pub. by Van Gorcum Holland). Longwood Pub Group.

Spinoza's Metaphysics: Essays in Critical Appreciation. James B. Wilbur. (Philosophia Spinozae Perennis Ser.: No. 1). 170p. 1976. pap. text ed. 19.00 (ISBN 90-232-1361-0, Pub. by Van Gorcum Holland). Longwood Pub Group.

Spinoza's Methodology. 2nd ed. H. G. Hubbeling. 167p. 1968. pap. text ed. 32.50x (ISBN 90-232-0519-7, Pub. by Van Gorcum Holland). Coronet Bks.

Spinoza's Philosophy of Law. Gail Belaief. LC 78-118275. (Studies in Philosophy: No. 24). (Illus.). 151p. (Orig.). 1971. pap. text ed. 12.00x (ISBN 90-2791-851-1). Mouton.

Spinoza's Political & Ethical Philosophy. Robert A. Duff. LC 71-108858. 1920. Repr. of 1903 ed. lib. bdg. 45.00x (ISBN 0-678-00615-6). Kelley.

Spinoza's Political & Ethical Philosophy. Robert A. Duff. 1973. Repr. of 1903 ed. 14.00 (ISBN 0-8274-1391-2). R West.

Spinoza's Theory of Truth. Thomas C. Mark. LC 72-3721. pap. 37.80 (ISBN 0-317-09237-5, 2006117). Bks Demand UMI.

Spinrad's Encyclopedia Treasury for Speakers. Leonard Spinrad & Thelma Spinrad. LC 86-4946. 322p. 1986. 29.95 (ISBN 0-13-834706-9, Pub. by Busn Pro Bks). P-H.

Spins in Chemistry. R. McWeeny. (Current Chemical Concepts Ser). 1970. 47.00 (ISBN 0-12-486750-2). Acad Pr.

Spinster. Sylvia Ashton-Warner. 256p. 1986. pap. 7.95 (ISBN 0-671-61767-2, Touchstone). S&S.

Spinster & Her Enemies: Feminism & Sexuality, 1880 to 1930. Sheila Jeffreys. 252p. (Orig.). 1986. pap. 9.95 (ISBN 0-86358-050-5, Pandora Pr). Routledge Chapman & Hall.

Spinsters in Jeopardy. Ngaio Marsh. 1976. Repr. of 1953 ed. lib. bdg. 18.95x (ISBN 0-88411-495-3, Pub. by Aeonian Pr). Amereon Ltd.

Spinsters in Jeopardy. Ngaio Marsh. 256p. 1986. pap. 2.95 (ISBN 0-515-08718-1). Jove Pubns.

Spinsters in Jeopardy. Ngaio Marsh. (Portway Ser.). 400p. 1987. lib. bdg. 17.50 (ISBN 0-7451-7075-7, Pub. by Chivers Pr UK). G K Hall.

Spiny, the Alaska King Crab. Richard Nickerson & Michael Anderson. (Illus.). 1987. write for info. (ISBN 0-9607358-6-0). Fathom Pub.

Spionidae: Invertebrates of the San Francisco Bay Estuary System, Vol. 1. William J. Light. Ed. by Welton L. Lee. (Illus.). 1978. text ed. 12.50x (ISBN 0-910286-58-2). Boxwood.

Spiral. David L. Lindsey. LC 86-47655. 320p. (Orig.). 1986. 16.95 (ISBN 0-689-11625-X). Atheneum.

Spiral. David L. Lindsey. 416p. 1988. pap. 4.50 (ISBN 0-317-67379-3). PB.

Spiral Dance: Rebirth of the Ancient Religion of the Goddess. Starhawk. (Orig.). 1979. pap. 11.95 (ISBN 0-06-067535-7, RD 301, HarpR). Har-Row.

Spiral Flame: A Study in the Meaning of D. H. Lawrence. David Boadella. Ed. by Arthur Efron & Dennis Hoerner. (Illus.). 1977. pap. 6.00 (ISBN 0-9602478-2-3). Paunch.

Spiral of Artificiality. Paul Laster & Renee Riccardo. Ed. by Deborah Bershad. (Illus.). 24p. (Orig.). 1987. pap. write for info. (ISBN 0-936739-09-6). Hallwalls Inc.

Spiral of Conflict: Berkeley, 1964. Max Heirich. LC 73-125073. (Illus.). 502p. 1973. pap. 18.50x (ISBN 0-231-08325-4). Columbia U Pr.

Spiral of Fire. Deborah T. Harris. 320p. 1989. pap. price not set. Tor Bks.

Spiral of Life: Unlocking Your Potential with Astrology. Rev. ed. Joanne Wickenburg & Virginia Meyer. LC 87-6567. 180p. (Orig.). 1987. pap. 7.95 (ISBN 0-916360-00-8). CRCS Pubns CA.

Spiral of Silence: Public Opinion - Our Social Skin. Elisabeth Noelle-Neumann. LC 83-18204. (Illus.). 212p. 1986. pap. 8.95 (ISBN 0-226-58933-1); lib. bdg. 20.00x (ISBN 0-226-58932-3). U of Chicago Pr.

Spiral Path: A Gay Contribution to Human Survival. David Fernbach. 240p. (Orig.). 1981. pap. 6.95 (ISBN 0-932870-12-0). Alyson Pubns.

Spiral Path: Essays and Interviews on Women's Spirituality. Ed. by Theresa K. O'Brien. LC 87-50282. 438p. 1988. pap. 13.95 (ISBN 0-936663-01-4). Yes Intl.

Spiral Road. Jan De Hartog. 24.95 (ISBN 0-88411-071-0, Pub. by Aeonian Pr). Amereon Ltd.

Spiral Road: Change in a Chinese Village Through the Eyes of a Communist Party Leader. Huang Shu-Min. (Development, Conflict, & Social Change Ser.: No. 120). 165p. 1988. 17.95 (ISBN 0-8133-7637-8). Westview.

Spiral Structure of Our Galaxy: Proceedings of the I.A.U. Symposium, No. 38, Basel, Swetzerland, 1969. International Astronomical Union Staff. Ed. by W. Becker & G. Contopoulos. LC 75-115886. (I.A.U. Symposia). 478p. 1970. lib. bdg. 45.00 (ISBN 90-277-0109-1, Pub. by Reidel Holland). Kluwer Academic.

Spirals. Douglas MacDonald. (Offset Offshoot Ser.: No.4). 34p. 1979. pap. 10.00 (ISBN 0-317-06440-1). Ommation Pr.

Spirals: A Woman's Journey Through Family Life. Joan Gould. LC 87-28352. 320p. 1988. 18.95 (ISBN 0-394-55705-0). Random.

Spirals of Growth. Dwight Johnson. LC 83-70691. 168p. (Orig.). 1983. pap. 6.50 (ISBN 0-8356-0580-9, Quest). Theos Pub Hse.

Spire. William G. Golding. LC 63-15314. 1965. pap. 3.95 (ISBN 0-15-684741-8, Harv). HarBraceJ.

Spires & Poplars. Alfred R. Bellinger. LC 72-144711. (Yale Younger Poets Ser.: No. 4). Repr. of 1920 ed. 18.00 (ISBN 0-404-53804-5). AMS Pr.

Spires of Form: A Study of Emerson's Aesthetic Theory. Vivian C. Hopkins. LC 80-2537. Repr. of 1951 ed. 33.50 (ISBN 0-404-19263-7). AMS Pr.

Spires of Form: Glimpses of Evolution. Victor B. Scheffer. LC 84-22374. (Illus.). 178p. 1985. pap. 7.95 (ISBN 0-15-684744-2, Harv). HarBraceJ.

Spiridon. George Sand. 270p. 1976. 27.50 (ISBN 0-686-54947-3). French & Eur.

Spiridonova, Revolutionary Terrorist. facs. ed. Isaac Steinberg. LC 72-150201. (Select Bibliographies Reprint Ser). 1935. 24.50 (ISBN 0-8369-5714-8). Ayer Co Pubs.

Spirit. Arthur Kornhaber. 304p. 1988. 17.95 (ISBN 0-312-02286-7, Pub. by Thomas Dunne Bks). St Martin.

Spirit Above the Dust: A Study of Herman Melville. Ronald Mason. 269p. Repr. of 1951 ed. 12.00x (ISBN 0-911858-19-9). Appel.

Spirit Aflame: Luis Palau's Mission to London. Susan Holton & David L. Jones. 258p. 1985. 7.95 (ISBN 0-8010-4293-3). Baker Bk.

Spirit & Ancestor: A Century of Northwest Coast Indian Art at the Burke Museum. Bill Holm. (Illus.). 256p. 1987. 50.00 (ISBN 0-295-96509-6); pap. 24.95 (ISBN 0-295-96510-X). U of Wash Pr.

Spirit & Gospel in Mark. Robert M. Mansfield. 208p. 9.95 (ISBN 0-913573-43-4). Hendrickson Ma.

Spirit & Influence of Chivalry. J. Batty. 1976. lib. bdg. 59.95 (ISBN 0-8490-2658-X). Gordon Pr.

Spirit & Intellect: Thomas Upham's Holiness Theology. Darius L. Salter. LC 86-10048. (Studies in Evangelicalism: No. 7). 283p. 1986. 27.50 (ISBN 0-8108-1899-X). Scarecrow.

Spirit & Its Letter: Traces of Rhetoric in Hegel's Philosophy of Bildung. John H. Smith. LC 87-47960. 320p. 1988. 32.50x (ISBN 0-8014-2048-2). Cornell U Pr.

Spirit & Life, Book of the Sun. Ed. by Daniel H. Shubin. Tr. by John W. Volkov from Rus. 768p. 1984. 40.00 (ISBN 0-318-20027-9). D H Shubin.

Spirit & Purpose of Planning. 2nd ed. Ed. by M. J. Bruton. (Built Envionment Ser.). (Illus.). 208p. 1984. pap. 14.95 (ISBN 0-09-153401-1, Pub. by Hutchinson Educ). Longwood Pub Group.

Spirit & Spirituality. 2nd ed. J. D. Thomas. LC 81-68342. (Way of Life Ser.). 1982. pap. 3.95 (ISBN 0-89112-121-8). Abilene Christ U.

Spirit & Structure of German Fascism. Robert A. Brady. 1971. pap. 3.95 (ISBN 0-8065-0239-8, Pub. by Citadel Pr). Lyle Stuart.

Spirit & Structure of German Fascism. Robert A. Brady. LC 68-9629. 1970. Repr. of 1937 ed. 40.00x (ISBN 0-86527-189-5). Fertig.

Spirit & Struggle in Southern Asia. Ed. by Barbara H. Chase & Martha L. Man. 105p. (Orig.). 1986. pap. 5.95 (ISBN 0-377-00157-0). Friendship Pr.

Spirit & the Bride Say, "Come!" Mary's Role in the New Pentecost. George W. Kosicki & Gerald J. Farrell. 112p. pap. 3.95 (ISBN 0-911988-41-6). AMI Pr.

Spirit & the Congregation: Studies in I Corinthians 12-15. Ralph P. Martin. 160p. (Orig.). 1984. 11.95 (ISBN 0-8028-3608-9). Eerdmans.

Spirit & the Drum: A Memoir of Africa. Edith Turner. LC 86-30825. 165p. 1987. 18.95 (ISBN 0-8165-1009-1). U of Ariz Pr.

Spirit & the Flesh: Sex in Utopian Communities. Robert H. Lauer & Jeanette C. Lauer. LC 83-7444. 256p. 1983. 17.50 (ISBN 0-8108-1635-0). Scarecrow.

Spirit & the Flesh: Sexual Diversity in American Indian Culture. Walter L. Williams. LC 86-47505. 312p. 1986. 21.95 (ISBN 0-8070-4602-7). Beacon Pr.

Spirit & the Flesh: Sexual Diversity in American Indian Culture. Walter L. Williams. LC 86-47505. (Illus.). 364p. 1988. pap. 9.95 (ISBN 0-8070-4611-6, BP 803). Beacon Pr.

Spirit & the Forms of Love. Daniel D. Williams. LC 81-40368. 316p. 1981. lib. bdg. 29.25 (ISBN 0-8191-1691-2); pap. text ed. 13.00 (ISBN 0-8191-1692-0). U Pr of Amer.

Spirit & the Future of Islam, 2 vols. Abdullah Ali. 155p. 1983. Set. 187.50x (ISBN 0-86722-051-1). Inst Econ Pol.

Spirit & the Mind. Samuel H. Sandweiss. 1985. pap. 6.30 (ISBN 0-9600958-9-6). Birth Day.

Spirit as Lord. Philip Rosato. 240p. 1981. 29.95 (ISBN 0-567-09305-0, Pub. by T&T Clark Ltd UK). Fortress.

Spirit Baptism: A Biblical Investigation. Howard M. Ervin. 208p. 1987. pap. 9.95 (ISBN 0-317-65914-6). Hendrickson MA.

Spirit, Being & Self. P. T. Raju. (Studies in Indian & Western Philosophy). 285p. 1982. 29.95 (ISBN 0-940500-98-1, Pub. by S. Asian Pubs India). Asia Bk Corp.

Spirit, Being & Self: Studies in Indian & Western Philosophy. P. T. Raju. 284p. 1986. 20.00X (ISBN 0-8364-1853-0, Pub. by South Asia Pubs). South Asia Bks.

Spirit, Being, & Self: Studies in Indian & Western Philosophy. P. T. Raju. 285p. 1982. 29.95. Asia Bk Corp.

Spirit Bible. Compiled by Eugene S. Geissler. LC 73-88004. 272p. 1973. pap. 2.25 (ISBN 0-87793-062-7). Ave Maria.

Spirit Builder. Clinton White. 214p. 1985. pap. 7.00 (ISBN 0-934109-02-8). Banquet Hse.

Spirit Capable: The Story of Commonwealth Edison. John Hogan. LC 86-61287. (Illus.). 464p. 1986. 24.95 (ISBN 0-916371-04-2). Mobium Pr.

Spirit-Centered Wholeness: Beyond the Psychology of Self. Ed. by H. Newton Malony. LC 87-23028. (Studies in the Psychology of Religion: Vol. 2). 256p. 1987. lib. bdg. 49.95 (ISBN 0-88946-246-1). E Mellen.

Spirit Channeling: Evaluating the Latest in New Age Spiritism. Brooks Alexander. (Viewpoint Pamphlet Ser.). 32p. (YA) (gr. 7 up). 1988. pap. 1.95 (ISBN 0-8308-1105-2). Inter-Varsity.

Spirit Child. Tr. by John Bierhorst. LC 84-720. (Illus.). 32p. (ps-3). 1984. 12.00 (ISBN 0-688-02609-5); PLB 11.88 (ISBN 0-688-02610-9). Morrow.

Spirit Christology: Recovering the Biblical Paradigm of Christian Faith. Paul W. Newman. LC 87-10390. 258p. (Orig.). 1987. lib. bdg. 27.25 (ISBN 0-8191-6375-9); pap. text ed. 14.75 (ISBN 0-8191-6376-7). U Pr of Amer.

Spirit Color Album. Will Eisner. Ed. by Jens P. Agger. (Spirit Color Album Ser.: Vol. II). (Illus.). 110p. 1983. Repr. 5.95 (ISBN 0-87816-010-8). Kitchen Sink.

Spirit Color Album. Will Eisner. Ed. by Jens P. Agger. (Spirit Color Album Ser.: Vol. III). (Illus.). 100p. 1983. 5.95 (ISBN 0-87816-011-6). Kitchen Sink.

Spirit-Controlled Family Living. Tim LaHaye & Beverly LaHaye. 224p. pap. 6.95 (ISBN 0-8007-5026-8, Power Bks). Revell.

Spirit-Controlled Woman. Beverly LaHaye. LC 76-5562. 1976. pap. 5.95 (ISBN 0-89081-020-6, 0206). Harvest Hse.

Spirit-Filled. Jack Hayford. 112p. (Orig.). 1987. mass 2.95, (ISBN 0-8423-6407-2). Tyndale.

Spirit-Filled: Anointed by Christ the King. Jack W. Hayford. LC 84-80747. (Orig.). 1984. pap. 2.95 (ISBN 0-916847-04-7). Living Way.

Spirit-Filled Church. John Lancaster. LC 75-22584. 112p. 1975. pap. 1.25 (ISBN 0-88243-601-5, 02-0601). Gospel Pub.

Spirit Filled Church in Action. A. B. Simpson. 112p. 1975. 3.45 (ISBN 0-87509-037-0). Chr Pubns.

Spirit-Filled Life. Verla A. Mooth. 1978. 6.00 (ISBN 0-682-49113-6). Exposition-Phoenix.

Spirit-Filled Pastor's Guide. Ralph M. Riggs. 296p. 1948. pap. 6.95 (ISBN 0-88243-588-4, 02-0588). Gospel Pub.

Spirit Fruit. rev. ed. John M. Drescher. LC 73-21660. 352p. 1978. pap. 8.95 (ISBN 0-8361-1867-7). Herald Pr.

Spirit Fruit: A Gentle Utopia. H. Roger Grant. (Illus.). 203p. 1988. 22.50 (ISBN 0-87580-137-4). N Ill U Pr.

Spirit Fruit & Voice. 2nd ed. Jacob Beilhart. (Illus.). 176p. 1986. pap. 6.95 (ISBN 0-918588-08-1). Barksdale Foun.

Spirit Guides: We Are Not Alone. Iris Belhayes. (Inner Visions Ser.). (Orig.). 1986. pap. 12.95 (ISBN 0-917086-80-5). A C S Pubns Inc.

Spirit Hand. Robert Stern. LC 78-11247. (Illus.). 1978. cloth 20.00 (ISBN 0-916906-14-0); signed ed 50.00 (ISBN 0-916906-15-9); pap. 12.00 (ISBN 0-916906-13-2). Konglomerati.

Spirit Himself. rev. ed. Ralph M. Riggs. 210p. 1977. 5.50 (ISBN 0-88243-590-6, 02-0590). Gospel Pub.

Spirit Horses. Lou Cameron. 192p. 1986. pap. 2.50 (ISBN 0-441-77809-7, Pub. by Charter Bks). Ace Bks.

Spirit, Hurry: Poems by Rolly Kent. Rolly Kent. Ed. by James Hepworth. 64p. 1985. 14.95 (ISBN 0-917652-51-7); pap. 7.95 (ISBN 0-917652-50-9). Confluence Pr.

Spirit in a Cage. John T. Richard. 1984. pap. 5.95 (ISBN 0-89896-131-9). Larksdale.

Spirit in Ashes: Hegel, Heidegger & Man-Made Mass Death. Edith Wyschogrod. LC 84-26932. 296p. 1985. 25.00x (ISBN 0-300-03322-2). Yale U Pr.

Spirit in Galatia: Paul's Interpretation of Pneuma As Divine Power. David J. Lull. LC 79-26094. (Society of Biblical Literature Dissertation: No. 49). 1980. 15.95 (ISBN 0-89130-367-7, 06-01-49); pap. 10.95 (ISBN 0-89130-368-5). Scholars Pr GA.

Spirit in Matter: A Scientist's Answer to the Bishop Queries. cancelled (ISBN 0-906492-16-5, Pub. by Kolisko Archives). St George Bk Serv.

Spirit in My Life. James Alberione. 1977. pap. 0.95 (ISBN 0-8198-0460-6). Dghtrs St Paul.

Spirit in the Church. Megan McKenna & Darryl Ducote. LC 78-71531. (Followers of the Way Ser.: Vol. 4). (gr. 9-12). 1979. 22.50; cassette 7.50 (ISBN 0-8091-7669-6). Paulist Pr.

Spirit in the Church. Karl Rahner. 1979. pap. 3.95 (ISBN 0-8245-0399-6). Crossroad NY.

Spirit in the Flesh. Joel Gross. 1986. 16.95 (ISBN 0-525-24418-2). Dutton.

Spirit in the Flesh. Joel Gross. 1988. pap. 4.95 (ISBN 0-451-15308-1, Sig). NAL.

Spirit in the Land: Beyond Time & Space with America's Channelers. Mark C. Vaz. 1988. pap. 3.95 (ISBN 0-451-15717-6, Sig). NAL.

Spirit Journey: Stories & Paintings of Bali. Madi Kertonegoro. Ed. by Stephanie T. Fried. Tr. by Judy Marentetee from Indonesian. (Illus.). 136p. (Orig.). 1988. pap. 13.95 (ISBN 0-931125-06-5). Wild Trees Press.

Spirit Knife. Donald C. Porter. (White Indian Ser.: No. 15). 320p. 1988. pap. 3.95 (ISBN 0-553-27161-X). Bantam.

Spirit Lake People: Memories of Mount St. Helens. G. Alan Guggenheim. Ed. by James Mortland. (Illus.). 180p. Date not set. 24.95 (ISBN 0-910377-06-5); lib. bdg. 24.95 (ISBN 0-910377-07-3); pap. 14.95 (ISBN 0-910377-08-1). Guggenheim.

Spirit Lamp: An Aesthetic, Literary & Critical Magazine, Vols. 1-4, No. 2. LC 79-8081. (Clothbound in 1 vol.). Repr. of 1892 ed. write for info. (ISBN 0-404-18390-5). AMS Pr.

Spirit Life. D. Stuart Briscoe. 160p. 1983. pap. 5.95 (ISBN 0-8007-5185-X). Revell.

Spirit Lost. Nancy Thayer. 1988. 16.95 (ISBN 0-684-18950-X). Scribner.

Spirit Manifestations & "the Gift of Tongues". Robert Anderson. pap. 1.50 (ISBN 0-87213-015-0). Loizeaux.

Spirit Master. John Shea. (Basics of Christian Thought Ser.). 1987. 14.95 (ISBN 0-88347-206-6). Thomas More.

Spirit Matters: The Worldwide Impact of Religion on Contemporary Politics. Ed. by Richard L. Rubenstein. LC 86-25172. 384p. 1987. 21.95 (ISBN 0-88702-203-0, Pub. by Wash Inst DC); pap. 12.95 (ISBN 0-88702-211-1, Pub.by Wash Inst DC). Paragon Hse.

Spirit Meadow. 192p. 1987. 15.95 (ISBN 0-8027-0970-2). Walker & Co.

Spirit Mediumship & Society in Africa. John Beattie & John Middleton. LC 70-80849. 310p. 1969. 44.50 (ISBN 0-8419-0009-4, Africana). Holmes & Meier.

Spirit Mound Township Revisited: A Rural View of the 1972 Campaign. Alan L. Clem. 1973. 1.00 (ISBN 1-55614-005-3). U of SD Gov Res Bur.

Spirit Mountain: An Anthology of Yuman Story & Song. Ed. by Leanne Hinton & Lucille Watahomigie. LC 84-112. (Sun Tracks Ser.: No. 10). 344p. 1984. 45.00x (ISBN 0-8165-0843-7); pap. 19.95 (ISBN 0-8165-0817-8). U of Ariz Pr.

Spirit Moves: A Handbook of Dance & Prayer. Carla De Sola. LC 77-89743. (Illus.). 1977. pap. 9.95 (ISBN 0-918208-04-1). Liturgical Conf.

Spirit Moves: A Handbook of Dance & Prayer. Carla De Sola. Ed. & intro. by Doug Adams. LC 77-89743. (Illus.). 152p. 1986. pap. 9.95 (ISBN 0-941500-38-1). Sharing Co.

Spirit Moves: Dance & Prayer. De Sola. 169p. 1977. 9.95 (ISBN 0-318-16446-9). Sacred Dance Guild.

Spirit of Aikido. Kisshomaru Ueshiba. Tr. by Taitetsu Unno from Japanese. (Illus.). 144p. 1984. 15.95 (ISBN 0-87011-600-2). Kodansha.

Spirit of Aikido. Kisshomaru Ueshiba. Tr. by Taitetsu Unno. LC 83-48881. (Illus.). 128p. 1988. pap. 4.95 (ISBN 0-87011-850-1). Kodansha.

Spirit of Akikido. Uyeshiba. 14.95x. Wehman.

Spirit of Allah. Amir Taheri. (Illus.). 349p. 1988. pap. cancelled (ISBN 0-917561-54-6). Adler & Adler.

Spirit of Allah: Khomeini & the Islamic Revolution. Amir Taheri. LC 85-18715. 349p. 1986. 18.95 (ISBN 0-917561-04-X). Adler & Adler.

Spirit of America Day. Ed. by America's Foundation Staff. 8p. 1984. 1.00 (ISBN 0-686-39642-1). Spirit Am Day.

Spirit of America: The Biographies of Forty Living Congressional Medal of Honor Recipients. Hugh F. Kayser. LC 81-12533. 1982. 16.95. ETC Pubns.

Spirit of American Government. James A. Smith. Ed. by Seward C. Strout. LC 65-13854. (John Harvard Library). 1965. 32.00x (ISBN 0-674-83220-5). Harvard U Pr.

Spirit of American Literature. rev. ed. John Macy. (American Studies). Repr. of 1913 ed. 35.00 (ISBN 0-384-34940-4). Johnson Repr.

Spirit of American Literature. Darshan S. Maini. 300p. 1988. text ed. 35.00x (ISBN 0-938719-27-0). Envoy Press.

Spirit of American Philosophy. John E. Smith. LC 82-5612. (SUNY Series in Philosophy). 253p. 1983. 39.50x (ISBN 0-87395-650-8); pap. 10.95x (ISBN 0-87395-651-6). State U NY Pr.

Spirit of Anglicanism: Hooker - Temple. William J. Wolf et al. 1979. pap. 7.95 (ISBN 0-8192-1263-6). Morehouse.

Spirit of Australia: The Crime Fiction of Arthur W. Upfield. Ray B. Browne. LC 87-71998. (Illus.). 292p. 1988. 30.95 (ISBN 0-87972-402-1); pap. 15.95 (ISBN 0-87972-403-X). Bowling Green Univ.

Spirit of Bambatse. H. Rider Haggard. LC 79-15278. (Forgotten Fantasy Library: Vol. 22). 1979. pap. 5.95 (ISBN 0-87877-121-2). Newcastle Pub.

Spirit of Bambatse: A Romance. H. Rider Haggard. Ed. by R. Reginald & Douglas Menville. LC 80-19674. (Newcastle Forgotten Fantasy Library Ser.: Vol. 22). 329p. 1980. Repr. of 1979 ed. lib. bdg. 19.95x (ISBN 0-89370-521-7). Borgo Pr.

Spirit of Buddhism. Hari S. Gour. LC 78-72432. Repr. of 1929 ed. 57.50 (ISBN 0-404-17299-7). AMS Pr.

Spirit of Buddhism Today. Koin Takada. Tr. by Philip Yampolsky. (Illus.). 1973. 9.95 (ISBN 0-89346-095-8); pap. 2.95 (ISBN 0-89346-043-5). Heian Intl.

Spirit of "C" An Introduction to Modern Programming. Henry Mullish & Herbert Cooper. 527p. 1987. pap. text ed. 35.50 (ISBN 0-314-28500-8); instr's. manual avail. (ISBN 0-314-35228-7). West Pub.

Spirit of Calvary. J. C. Metcalfe. 1970. pap. 3.25 (ISBN 0-87508-921-6). Chr Lit.

Spirit of Canoe Camping. Harry Drabik. (Illus.). 126p. 1981. pap. 5.95 (ISBN 0-931714-11-7). Nodin Pr.

Spirit of Catalonia. J. Trueta. 1976. lib. bdg. 34.95 (ISBN 0-8490-2659-8). Gordon Pr.

Spirit of Catholicism. Karl Adam. Tr. by Dom J. McCann from Ger. 237p. 1981. Repr. of 1929 ed. lib. bdg. 30.00. Darby Bks.

Spirit of Champions. Del Hessel. 56p. (Orig.). 1984. pap. write for info. (ISBN 0-89279-066-0). Championship Bks.

Spirit of Chinese Philanthropy: A Study in Mutual Aid. Tsu Yu-Yue. LC 68-56690. (Columbia University. Studies in the Social Sciences: No. 125). Repr. of 1911 ed. 14.50 (ISBN 0-404-51125-2). AMS Pr.

Spirit of Christ. rev. ed. Andrew Murray. LC 79-51335. 288p. 1983. pap. 4.95 (ISBN 0-87123-589-7, 210589). Bethany Hse.

Spirit of Christ. Andrew Murray. 1970. pap. 4.95 (ISBN 0-87508-395-1). Chr Lit.

Spirit of Christ. 2nd ed. Andrew Murray. 240p. 1984. pap. 3.50 (ISBN 0-88368-126-9). Whitaker Hse.

Spirit of Christmas. Henry Van Dyke. LC 84-19389. (Illus.). 64p. 1984. pap. 3.95 (ISBN 0-89783-033-4). Larlin Corp.

Spirit of Christmas. Henry Van Dyke. LC 87-72760. 200p. (Orig.). 1988. pap. cancelled (ISBN 0-88270-643-8). Bridge Pub.

Spirit of Color: The Art of Karl Gerstner. Karl Gerstner. Ed. by Henri Stierlin. (Illus.). 220p. 1981. 45.00 (ISBN 0-262-07084-7). MIT Pr.

Spirit of D. H. Lawrence: Centenary Studies. Ed. by Gamini Salgado & G. K. Das. LC 86-17385. 272p. 1986. 27.50x (ISBN 0-389-20665-2). B&N Imports.

Spirit of Delight. facs. ed. George M. Harper. LC 78-76902. (Essay Index Reprint Ser). 1928. 18.00 (ISBN 0-8369-0016-2). Ayer Co Pubs.

Spirit of Democratic Capitalism. Michael Novak. 433p. 1982. 19.95 (ISBN 0-671-43154-4). S&S.

Spirit of Dissension: Economics, Politics, & the Revolution in Maryland. Ronald Hoffman. LC 73-8127. (Maryland Bicentennial Studies). (Illus.). 294p. 1974. 32.50x (ISBN 0-8018-1521-5). Johns Hopkins.

Spirit of Dorsai. Gordon R. Dickson. 1985. pap. 3.50 (ISBN 0-441-77806-2). Ace Bks.

Spirit of England. Arthur Bryant. 236p. Date not set. cancelled (ISBN 0-88186-379-3). Parkwest Pubns.

Spirit of Enterprise. George Gilder. 1984. 17.95 (ISBN 0-671-45482-X). S&S.

Spirit of Enterprise Nineteen Eighty-Seven Rolex Awards. D. Reed. 1987. 36.95 (ISBN 0-7476-0003-1). Van Nos Reinhold.

Spirit of Enterprise: 1987 Rolex Awards. D. Reed. 34.95 (ISBN 0-317-64284-7). Van Nos Reinhold.

Spirit of Flame. L. Ukrainka. Tr. by Percival Cundy from Slavic. LC 76-147225. (Illus.). 1970. Repr. of 1950 ed. lib. bdg. 38.50x (ISBN 0-8371-5990-3, UKSF). Greenwood.

Spirit of Flame. L. Ukrainka. Tr. by Percival Cundy. 320p. 1950. 10.00 (ISBN 0-317-36113-9). UNWLA.

Spirit of Flame: A Study of St. John of the Cross. Edgar A. Peers. LC 76-40107. 1976. Repr. of 1943 ed. lib. bdg. 30.00 (ISBN 0-8414-6784-6). Folcroft.

Spirit of Fog Island. Margaret Sutton. (Judy Bolton Mysteries). 1976. Repr. of 1951 ed. lib. bdg. 15.95x (ISBN 0-88411-713-8, Pub. by Aeonian Pr). Amereon Ltd.

Spirit of French Canada: A Study of the Literature. Ian F. Fraser. LC 70-168135. Repr. of 1939 ed. 17.50 (ISBN 0-404-02548-X). AMS Pr.

Spirit of French Letters. Mabell Smith. 1973. Repr. of 1912 ed. 22.50 (ISBN 0-8274-0891-9). R West.

Spirit of Gardening. Jeff Cox. (Illus.). 224p. 1986. 16.95 (ISBN 0-87857-638-X). Rodale Pr Inc.

Spirit of H. H. Richardson on the Midland Prairies. Paul C. Larson. (Great Plains Environmental Design Ser.). (Illus.). 174p. 1988. pap. 24.95x (ISBN 0-8138-0017-X). Iowa St U Pr.

Spirit of H. H. Richardson on the Midland Prairies. Paul C. Larson et al. (Illus.). 176p. 1988. pap. 24.95 (ISBN 0-938713-02-7). Univ MN Art Mus.

Spirit of Hebrew Poetry, 2 vols in one. Johann G. Herder. Tr. by James Marsh. LC 70-131583. (Sources in the History of Interpretation: No. 1). 1971. 35.00x (ISBN 0-8401-1065-0). A R Allenson.

Spirit of Hebrew Poetry. Isaac Taylor. LC 74-30247. (Studies in Poetry, No. 38). 1974. lib. bdg. 56.95x (ISBN 0-8383-1988-2). Haskell.

Spirit of Himalaya: The Story of a Truth Seeker. Swami Amar Jyoti. LC 78-73995. (Illus.). 1979. 7.95 (ISBN 0-933572-00-X). Truth Consciousness.

Spirit of Himalaya: The Story of a Truth Seeker. 2nd rev. ed. Swami Amar Jyoti. LC 85-50206. (Illus.). 128p. 1985. pap. 5.95 (ISBN 0-933572-06-9). Truth Consciousness.

Spirit of Indian Culture: Saints of India. Vivek Bhattacharya. 622p. 1980. 32.95 (ISBN 0-940500-40-X). Asia Bk Corp.

Spirit of Inquiry: The Graduate Library School at Chicago, 1921-51. John Richardson. 254p. 1982. 35.00x (ISBN 0-8389-3273-8, 82-11582). ALA.

Spirit of Iron. Janice J. Shefelman. Ed. by Edwin M. Eakin. (Mina Jordan Ser.: No. 3). 136p. (gr. 4-7). 1987. 8.95 (ISBN 0-89015-636-0). Eakin Pr.

Spirit of Islam. S. Ali. 512p. 1987. 300.00x (ISBN 1-85077-179-0, Pub. by Darf Pubs Ltd). State Mutual Bk.

Spirit of Islam. S. A. Ali. 22.50 (ISBN 0-317-60638-7). Kazi Pubns.

Spirit of Islam. Afif Tabbarah. 20.00x (ISBN 0-86685-029-5). Intl Bk Ctr.

Spirit of Jesus. Vincent M. Walsh. 1984. pap. 5.00 (ISBN 0-943374-10-3). Key of David.

Spirit of Jewish Law. George Horowitz. LC 53-7535. 1979. Repr. of 1953 ed. text ed. 65.00x (ISBN 0-87632-167-8). Bloch.

Spirit of Judaism. facsimile ed. Josephine Lazarus. LC 77-38031. (Essay Index Reprint Ser). Repr. of 1895 ed. 16.00 (ISBN 0-8369-2602-1). Ayer Co Pubs.

Spirit of Judgment. Watchman Nee. Ed. by Herbert L. Fader et al. Tr. by Stephen Kaung from Chinese. 158p. (Orig.). 1984. pap. 3.25 (ISBN 0-935008-63-2). Christian Fellow Pubs.

Spirit of Karate-Doh. 2nd ed. Hiroshi Hamada. 110p. 1982. pap. text ed. 15.95 (ISBN 0-8403-2693-9). Kendall-Hunt.

Spirit of Language in Civilization. Karl Vossler. Tr. by Oscar Oeser. LC 75-41285. Repr. of 1932 ed. 17.00 (ISBN 0-404-14625-2). AMS Pr.

Spirit of Laws, 2 vols. Baron De Montesquieu. Tr. by Thomas Nugent from Fr. 684p. 1986. Repr. of 1900 ed. lib. bdg. 100.00 (ISBN 0-8495-1149-6). Arden Lib.

Spirit of Liberalism. Harvey C. Mansfield, Jr. LC 78-7809. 1978. 16.00x (ISBN 0-674-83312-0). Harvard U Pr.

Spirit of Liberty. Tsing-Fang Chen. (Illus.). 100p. (Orig.). 1986. write for info. (ISBN 0-9616961-1-7); pap. write for info. (ISBN 0-9616961-0-9). Lucia Gallery.

Spirit of Liberty. 3rd enl ed. Learned Hand. Ed. by Irving Dilliard. 1977. pap. 4.95x (ISBN 0-226-31544-4, P712, Phoen). U of Chicago Pr.

Spirit of Literature. Powell Spring. 1945. Repr. 10.00 (ISBN 0-8274-3494-4). R West.

Spirit of London's River. L. M. Bates. 200p. 1984. 40.00x (ISBN 0-905418-43-3, Pub. by Gresham England). State Mutual Bk.

Spirit of Man. facs. ed. Ed. by Whit Burnett. LC 68-58775. (Essay Index Reprint Ser). 1958. 22.00 (ISBN 0-8369-0036-7). Ayer Co Pubs.

Spirit of Man: An Anthology in English & French. Robert Bridges. 1983. Repr. of 1934 ed. lib. bdg. 40.00. Century Bookbindery.

Spirit of Manufacturing Excellence: An Executive's Guide to the New Mind Set. Ernest C. Huge & Alan D. Anderson. (APICS Ser.). 132p. 1987. 30.00 (ISBN 0-87094-989-6). Dow Jones-Irwin.

Spirit of Masonry. rev. ed. Foster Bailey. 1979. pap. 6.00 (ISBN 0-85330-135-2). Lucis.

Spirit of Masonry. William Hutchinson. (Illus.). 234p. (Orig.). 1988. pap. 14.95 (ISBN 0-85030-531-4, Pub. by Aquarian Pr England). Sterling.

Spirit of May. Jean-Jacques Servan-Schreiber. 1969. pap. text ed. 4.95 (ISBN 0-07-056315-2). McGraw.

Spirit of Mediterranean Places. Michel Butor. Tr. by Lydia Davis from Fr. LC 85-63763. 160p. 1987. pap. 9.00 (ISBN 0-910395-17-9). Marlboro Pr.

Spirit of Might. Jerry Savelle. 77p. (Orig.). 1982. pap. 2.50 (ISBN 0-89274-242-9, HH-242). Harrison Hse.

Spirit of Modern Philosophy. Josiah Royce. 519p. 1983. pap. 8.95 (ISBN 0-486-24432-6). Dover.

Spirit of Modern Philosophy: An Essay in the Form of Lectures. Josiah Royce. 1977. Repr. of 1892 ed. lib. bdg. 30.00 (ISBN 0-8492-2315-6). R West.

Spirit of Modern Republicanism: The Moral Vision of the American Founders & the Philosophy of Locke. Thomas L. Pangle. 352p. 1988. 22.50 (ISBN 0-226-64540-1). U of Chicago Pr.

Spirit of Music. Alexander Blok. Tr. by I. Freiman from Rus. LC 72-14050. (Soviet Literature in English Translation Ser.). (Illus.). 70p. 1973. Repr. of 1946 ed. 10.00 (ISBN 0-88355-001-6). Hyperion Conn.

Spirit of Music. Edward Dickinson. 59.95 (ISBN 0-8490-1111-6). Gordon Pr.

Spirit of Music: How to Find It & How to Share It. Edward Dickinson. (Select Bibliographies Reprint Ser.). Repr. of 1925 ed. 18.00 (ISBN 0-8369-6683-X). Ayer Co Pubs.

Spirit of Music: How to Find It & How to Share It. Edward Dickinson. 218p. 1982. Repr. of 1927 ed. lib. bdg. 25.00 (ISBN 0-8495-1142-9). Arden Lib.

Spirit of Nature & the Philosophical Conception of Science, 2 vols. E. A. Burtt. 336p. 1986. 187.45 (ISBN 0-89266-567-X). Am Classical Coll Pr.

Spirit of One Earth: Reflection on Teilhard de Chardin & Global Spirituality. Ed. by Ursula King. 208p. 1988. pap. 12.95 (ISBN 0-913757-93-4). Paragon Hse.

Spirit of Place, & Other Essays. Alice Meynell. 1979. lib. bdg. 35.00 (ISBN 0-8495-3762-2). Arden Lib.

Spirit of Place in Keats: Sketches of Persons & Places Known by Him, & His Reaction to Them. Guy Murchie. 1979. Repr. of 1955 ed. lib. bdg. 37.50 (ISBN 0-8495-3779-7). Arden Lib.

Spirit of Place in Keats: Sketches of Persons & Places Known by Him, & His Reaction to Them. Guy Murchie. LC 78-11851. 1978. Repr. of 1955 ed. lib. bdg. 52.50 (ISBN 0-8414-6327-1). Folcroft.

Spirit of Place in Keats: Sketches of Persons & Places Known by Him, & His Reaction to Them. Guy Murchie. (Illus.). 274p. 1986. Repr. of 1955 ed. lib. bdg. 30.00 (ISBN 0-89984-772-2). Century Bookbindery.

Spirit of Place: Japanese Paintings of the Sixteenth through Nineteenth Centuries. Louisa Cunningham. Ed. by Peter Neill. (Illus.). 80p. (Orig.). 1984. pap. 6.95x (ISBN 0-89467-030-1). Yale Art Gallery.

Spirit of Place: Letters & Essays on Travel. Lawrence Durrell. Ed. by Alan G. Thomas. 432p. 1984. pap. 8.95 (ISBN 0-918172-17-9). Leetes Isl.

Spirit of Place: Lucy Maud Montgomery & Prince Edward Island. Francis W. Bolger et al. (Illus.). 1983. 14.95 (ISBN 0-19-540389-4). Oxford U Pr.

Spirit of Poland: A Photographic Meditation. Roger J. Radlowski & John Kirvan. (Illus.). 60p. (Orig.). 1980. pap. 6.95 (ISBN 0-03-056666-5, HarpR). Har-Row.

Spirit of Prayer & Spirit of Love. William Law. Ed. by Sydney Spencer. 301p. 1969. 22.00 (ISBN 0-227-67720-X). Attic Pr.

Spirit of Prayer: From the Works of Hannah More. Hannah More. 144p. 1986. pap. 6.95 (ISBN 0-310-43641-9, 10272P). Zondervan.

Spirit of Prophecy, Vol. I. large print ed. Ed. by Charline Brians. 27p. 1984. pap. 5.00 (ISBN 0-9608650-3-9). VHI Library.

Spirit of Protest in Old French Literature. Mary M. Wood. LC 17-30250. (Columbia University. Studies in Romance Philology & Literature: No. 21). Repr. of 1917 ed. 19.00 (ISBN 0-404-50621-6). AMS Pr.

Spirit of Protestantism. Robert M. Brown. (YA) (gr. 9 up). 1961. pap. 8.95 (ISBN 0-19-500724-7). Oxford U Pr.

Spirit of Reform: British Literature & Politics, 1832-1867. Patrick Brantlinger. 1977. 20.00x (ISBN 0-674-83315-5). Harvard U Pr.

Spirit of Revelation. Joseph F. McConkie. LC 84-1705. 144p. 1984. 6.95 (ISBN 0-87747-990-9). Deseret Bk.

Spirit of Revolt: Anarchism & the Cult of Authority. Richard K. Fenn. LC 86-15430. 192p. 1986. 27.95x (ISBN 0-8476-7522-X). Rowman.

Spirit of Romance. Ezra Pound. LC 53-5860. 1968. pap. 7.75 (ISBN 0-8112-0163-5, NDP266). New Directions.

Spirit of Ryan. Ev Cassagneres. (Illus.). 256p. 1982. pap. 11.95 (ISBN 0-8306-2333-7, 2333). TAB Bks.

Spirit of Sail: On Board the World's Great Sailing Ships. John Dyson. (Illus.). 168p. 1987. 35.00 (ISBN 0-8050-0566-8). H Holt & Co.

Spirit of St. Louis. Hudson River ed. Charles A. Lindbergh. (Illus.). 1953. lib. rep. ed. 25.00x (ISBN 0-684-14421-2, ScribT); (ScribT). Scribner.

Spirit of St. Louis. Charles A. Lindbergh. 544p. 1985. pap. 5.95 (ISBN 0-380-69855-2, Discus). Avon.

Spirit of Scott. Judi Sturge. 1977. 5.95 (ISBN 0-686-10956-2). J Sturge.

Spirit of Seventeen Eighty-Seven. Milton Lomask. 1987. pap. 2.50 (ISBN 0-317-57107-9, Juniper). Fawcett.

Spirit of Seventeen Eighty-Seven: The Making of Our Constitution. Milton Lomask. LC 80-14654. 224p. (gr. 7 up). 10.95 (ISBN 0-374-37149-0). FS&G.

Spirit of Seventy-Six & Other Essays. Carl Becker et al. (Brookings Institution Reprint Ser). Repr. of 1927 ed. lib. bdg. 27.00x (ISBN 0-697-00150-4). Irvington.

Spirit of Seventy-Six: The Growth of American Patriotism Before Independence. Carl Bridenbaugh. 1975. 16.95x (ISBN 0-19-501931-8). Oxford U Pr.

Spirit of Seventy-Six: The Growth of American Patriotism Before Independence, 1607-1776. Carl Bridenbaugh. LC 75-4323. 1975. pap. 5.95 (ISBN 0-19-502179-7). Oxford U Pr.

Spirit of Shady Side: Peninsula Life 1664-1984. Virginia W. Fitz. LC 84-52251. (Illus.). 122p. 1984. pap. 9.50 (ISBN 0-9614295-0-X). Shady Side Pen.

Spirit of Social Work. Edward T. Devine. LC 75-17216. (Social Problems & Social Policy Ser.). 1976. Repr. of 1911 ed. 19.00x (ISBN 0-405-07487-5). Ayer Co Pubs.

Spirit of Solitude: Conventions & Continuities in Late Romance. Jay Macpherson. LC 81-11462. (Illus.). 364p. 1982. 32.00x (ISBN 0-300-02632-3). Yale U Pr.

Spirit of Sport: Essays about Sport & Values. Ed. by John W. Molloy, Jr. & Richard C. Adams. LC 87-50692. 150p. 1987. text ed. 24.95x (ISBN 0-317-67979-1); pap. text ed. 14.95x (ISBN 1-55605-012-7). Wyndham Hall.

Spirit of Student Council. Earl Reum. Ed. by C. Bruce. (gr. 7-9). 1981. pap. 5.00 (ISBN 0-88210-117-X). Natl Assn Principals.

Spirit of Surrealism. Edward B. Henning. LC 79-63387. (Illus.). 228p. 1979. 29.95x (ISBN 0-910386-52-8, Pub. by Cleveland Mus Art). Ind U Pr.

Spirit of Surrealism. Edward B. Henning. LC 79-63387. (Illus.). pap. 49.00 (ISBN 0-317-10524-8, 2022658). Bks Demand UMI.

Spirit of Survival. Gail Sheehy. LC 86-2424. 342p. 1986. 17.95 (ISBN 0-688-05878-7). Morrow.

Spirit of Survival. Gail Sheehy. 464p. 1987. pap. 4.95 (ISBN 0-553-26573-3). Bantam.

Spirit of Survival. Gail Sheehy. 570p. 1987. lib. bdg. 21.95x (ISBN 0-8161-4271-8, Large Print Bks). G K Hall.

Spirit of Sweetwater. Hamlin Garland. (Collected Works of Hamlin Garland). 1988. Repr. of 1898 ed. lib. bdg. 59.00x. Am Biog Serv.

Spirit of Sweetwater see Collected Works.

Spirit of System: Lamarck & Evolutionary Biology. Richard W. Burkhardt, Jr. 1977. 20.00x (ISBN 0-674-83317-1). Harvard U Pr.

Spirit of the Age or Contemporary Portraits: Coleridge, Scott, Byron, Wordsworth. William Hazlitt. 271p. 1983. Repr. of 1904 ed. lib. bdg. 35.00 (ISBN 0-89987-477-0). Darby Bks.

Spirit of the Age or Contemporary Portraits. Tr. by William Hazlitt. 271p. 1979. Repr. lib. bdg. 25.00 (ISBN 0-89987-353-7). Darby Bks.

Spirit of the Age: The Story of "Old Bushmills". Alf McCreary. (Illus.). 232p. 1983. 19.50 (ISBN 0-9509083-0-4, Pub. by Blackstaff Pr). Longwood Pub Group.

Spirit of the Alberta Indian Treaties. Richard Price. 202p. 1979. pap. text ed. 8.95x (ISBN 0-920380-23-9, Pub. by Inst Res Pub Canada). Brookfield Pub Co.

Spirit of the Alberta Indian Treaties. Ed. by Richard Price. xx, 202p. 1987. pap. 14.95x (ISBN 0-88864-123-0, Pub. by Univ of Alta Pr Canada). U of Nebr Pr.

Spirit of the American Revolution, As Revealed in the Poetry of the Period: A Study of American Patriotic Verse from Seventeen Sixty to Seventeen Eighty-Three. Samuel W. Patterson. 1979. Repr. of 1915 ed. lib. bdg. 30.00 (ISBN 0-8492-2184-6). R West.

Spirit of the Andes. Jose S. Chocano. Tr. by E. W. Underwood. 1977. lib. bdg. 59.95 (ISBN 0-8490-2660-1). Gordon Pr.

Spirit of the Border. Zane Grey. 1976. Repr. of 1904 ed. lib. bdg. 19.95 (ISBN 0-89190-755-6, Pub. by River City Pr). Amereon Ltd.

Spirit of the Border. Zane Grey. 256p. (Orig.). 1981. pap. 2.25 (ISBN 0-505-51739-6, Pub. by Tower Bks). Leisure NY.

Spirit of the Border. Zane Grey. 256p. (Orig.). 1987. pap. 2.95 (ISBN 0-8439-2564-7). Leisure NY.

Spirit of the Capitalistic System. Werner Sombart. (Illus.). 133p. 1985. 127.50 (ISBN 0-86654-155-1). Inst Econ Finan.

Spirit of the Chinese Revolution. Arthur N. Holcombe. LC 73-876. (China Studies: from Confucius to Mao Ser.). vi, 185p. 1973. Repr. of 1930 ed. 18.00 (ISBN 0-88355-070-9). Hyperion Conn.

Spirit of the Church: Antiquity. Stanley M. Burgess. 228p. 1984. pap. 9.95 (ISBN 0-913573-10-8). Hendrickson MA.

Spirit of the Common Law. Roscoe Pound. (gr. 11-12). text ed. 8.00x (ISBN 0-8338-0056-6). M Jones.

Spirit of the Cotswolds. Susan Hill. (Illus.). 208p. Date not set. 22.95 (ISBN 0-7181-2905-9, Pub. by Michael Joseph). Viking.

Spirit of the Counter-Reformation. H. Outram Evennett. LC 68-11282. 1970. pap. 5.95x (ISBN 0-268-00425-0). U of Notre Dame Pr.

Spirit of the Court: Selected Proceedings of the Fourth Congress of the International Courtly Literature Society, Toronto 1983. Ed. by Glynn S. Burgess & Robert A. Taylor. 408p. 1985. 72.00 (ISBN 0-85991-176-4, Pub. by Boydell & Brewer). Longwood Pub Group.

Spirit of the Disciplines: Understanding How God Changes Lives. Dallas Willard. LC 86-45033. 224p. 1988. 14.95 (ISBN 0-06-069441-6, HarpR). Har-Row.

Spirit of the Earth. John Hart. 1984. pap. 8.95 (ISBN 0-8091-2581-1). Paulist Pr.

TITLE INDEX SPIRITUAL AWAKENING: CLASSIC WRITINGS

Spirit of the Empty Hand. Stan Schmidt. Ed. by Randall G. Hassell & Dale F. Poertner. 251p. (Orig.). 1984. pap. 9.95 (ISBN 0-911921-02-8). Focus Pubns Mo.

Spirit of the Ghetto. facsimile ed. Hutchins Hapgood. Ed. by Moses Rischin. LC 67-12099. (John Harvard Library). (Illus.). 1967. 27.00x (ISBN 0-674-83265-5). Harvard U Pr.

Spirit of the Ghetto. Hutchins Hapgood. Ed. by Moses Rischin. (Illus.). 360p. 1983. pap. 7.95 (ISBN 0-674-83266-3, Belknap Pr). Harvard U Pr.

Spirit of the Gospel. Watchman Nee. Ed. by Herbert L. Fader. Tr. by Stephen Kaung from Chinese. 100p. (Orig.). 1986. pap. 3.50 (ISBN 0-935008-67-5). Christian Fellow Pubs.

Spirit of the Guard. Richard E. Bauer. 122p. 1981. pap. 7.95 (ISBN 0-89279-071-7). R E Bauer.

Spirit of the Hawk. Rose Estes. 224p. (Orig.). 1988. pap. 3.95 (ISBN 0-553-27408-2, Spectra). Bantam.

Spirit of the Hills. Dan O'Brien. (Illus.). 256p. 1988. 17.95 (ISBN 0-517-56727-X). Crown.

Spirit of the Huckleberry: Sensuousness in Henry Thoreau. Victor C. Friesen. xxii, 145p. 1984. 21.00x (ISBN 0-88864-043-9, Pub. by Univ of Alta Pr Canada). U of Nebr Pr.

Spirit of the Korean Tiger, 3 vols. Zozayong. (Fr.). Set. 175.00 (ISBN 0-89581-227-4, M-6210). French & Eur.

Spirit of the Laws. Baron de Montesquieu. 1969. pap. 13.95x (ISBN 0-317-30542-5). Free Pr.

Spirit of the Laws. C. de Montesquieu. (Library of Classic: No. 9). pap. text ed. 9.95x (ISBN 0-02-849270-6). Hafner.

Spirit of the Laws: A Compendium of the First English Editon with an English Translation of "An Essay on Causes Affecting Mind & Characters", 1737-1743. Montesquieu. Ed. by David W. Carrithers. 1978. 48.50x (ISBN 0-520-02566-0); pap. 12.95x (ISBN 0-520-03455-4). U of Cal Pr.

Spirit of the Legal Profession. Robert N. Wilkin. viii, 178p. 1981. Repr. of 1938 ed. lib. bdg. 18.50x (ISBN 0-8377-1308-0). Rothman.

Spirit of the Letter: Essays in European Literature. Renato Poggioli. LC 65-22064. 1965. 24.50x (ISBN 0-674-83310-4). Harvard U Pr.

Spirit of the Mountains. Emma B. Miles. LC 75-19222. (Tennesseana Editions Ser.). (Illus.). 256p. 1975. 14.95x (ISBN 0-87049-181-4); pap. 6.95x (ISBN 0-87049-465-1). U of Tenn Pr.

Spirit of the Nation: Ballads & Songs with Ancient & Original Music. LC 81-81466. 1981. 35.00x (ISBN 0-89453-260-X). M Glazier.

Spirit of the New England Tribes: Indian History & Folklore, 1620-1984. William S. Simmons. LC 85-40936. 343p. (Orig.). 1986. 30.00x (ISBN 0-87451-370-7); pap. 14.95 (ISBN 0-87451-372-3). U Pr of New Eng.

Spirit of the Oxford Movement. Christopher H. Dawson. LC 75-30020. Repr. of 1934 ed. 29.50 (ISBN 0-404-14025-4). AMS Pr.

Spirit of the Public Journals or, Beauties of the American Newspapers. Ed. by George Bourne. LC 74-125679. (American Journalists Ser.). 1970. Repr. of 1806 ed. 18.00 (ISBN 0-405-01654-9). Ayer Co Pubs.

Spirit of the Revolution. John C. Fitzpatrick. LC 71-120875. (American Bicentennial Ser). 1970. Repr. of 1924 ed. 24.50x (ISBN 0-8046-1268-4, Pub. by Kennikat). Assoc Faculty Pr.

Spirit of the Sikhs, 3 vols. Puran Singh. 1984. Repr. of 1920 ed. Pt.1. 7.50x (ISBN 0-8364-1115-3, Pub. by Punjabi); Pt.2, v.1. 7.50x (ISBN 0-8364-1116-1); Pt.2, Vol.2. 7.50x (ISBN 0-8364-1117-X). South Asia Bks.

Spirit of the Sixties see Singing Soldiers: A History of the Civil War in Song.

Spirit of the South Shore. William A. Raia. Ed. by Donald J. Heimburger. LC 84-51673. (Illus.). 80p. 1984. 22.95 (ISBN 0-911581-03-0); pap. 11.95. Heimburger Hse Pub.

Spirit of the Stone Thrown to the Bottom of a Lake. Stephen Petroff. 144p. (Orig.). 1987. pap. 9.95 (ISBN 0-937966-23-1). Dog Ear.

Spirit of the Upanishads. Yogi Ramacharaka. 6.00 (ISBN 0-911662-11-1). Yoga.

Spirit of the Wind: The Horse in Saudi Arabia. Keith Collie. (Illus.). 111p. cancelled (ISBN 0-88072-092-1). Longwood Pub Group.

Spirit of Truth: Ecumenical Perspectives on the Holy Spirit. Ed. by Theodore Stylianopoulos & S. Mark Heim. 197p. 1986. pap. 10.95 (ISBN 0-917651-39-1). Holy Cross Orthodox.

Spirit of Uppsala. Ed. by Atle Grahl-Madsen & Jiri Toman. xviii, 601p. 1984. 128.00 (ISBN 3-11-008822-3). De Gruyter.

Spirit of Vengeance: Nativism & Louisiana Justice, 1921-1924. John V. Baiamonte, Jr. LC 85-19143. (Illus.). 257p. 1986. 25.00 (ISBN 0-8071-1279-8). La State U Pr.

Spirit of Versailles: Business of Environmental Management. International Chamber of Commerce. 435p. (Orig.). 1986. pap. 35.00 (ISBN 92-842-1022-4). ICC Pub.

Spirit of Voltaire. Norman L. Torrey. LC 68-10948. (Illus.). 1968. Repr. of 1938 ed. 11.00x (ISBN 0-8462-1114-9). Russell.

Spirit of Walt Whitman. L. Conrad Hartley. LC 73-538. 1973. lib. bdg. 25.00 (ISBN 0-8414-1595-1). Folcroft.

Spirit of Winter Camping. Harry Drabik. (Illus.). 104p. (Orig.). 1985. pap. 5.95 (ISBN 0-931714-24-9). Nodin Pr.

Spirit of Wisdom & Revelation. Watchman Nee. Tr. by Stephen Kaung. 1980. pap. 3.25 (ISBN 0-935008-48-9). Christian Fellow Pubs.

Spirit of Wit: Reconsideration of Rochester. Ed. by Jeremy Treglown. 199p. 1982. 25.00 (ISBN 0-208-02012-8, Archon Bks). Shoe String.

Spirit of Your Marriage. David Ludwig. LC 79-50088. 1979. pap. 7.95 (ISBN 0-8066-1721-7, 10-5890). Augsburg.

Spirit of Youth & the City Streets. Jane Addams. LC 72-76862. 192p. 1972. 19.95 (ISBN 0-252-00276-8). U of Ill Pr.

Spirit of Zen: A Way of Life, Work & Art in the Far East. Alan W. Watts. 1958. pap. 7.95 (ISBN 0-394-17418-6, E219, Ever). Grove.

Spirit of Zen: A Way of Life, Work & Art in the Far East. rev. ed. Alan W. Watts. (Illus.). 136p. Date not set. pap. 7.95 (ISBN 0-8021-3056-9). Grove.

Spirit of '76 in Rhode Island. Benjamin Cowell. LC 72-10847. 560p. 1973. Repr. of 1850 ed. 25.00 (ISBN 0-8063-0542-8). Genealog Pub.

Spirit on the Wall. Ann O. Garcia. LC 81-85094. 192p. (YA) (gr. 7 up). 1982. 9.95 (ISBN 0-8234-0447-1). Holiday.

Spirit Playmates. Don Trifiletti. (Illus.). 48p. 1988. 6.95 (ISBN 0-89962-667-X). Todd & Honeywell.

Spirit Possession & Mediumship in Africa & Afro-America: An Annotated Bibliography. Irving I. Zaretsky & Cynthia L. Shambaugh. LC 78-4181. (Reference Library of Social Science: Vol. 56). 470p. 1978. lib. bdg. 48.00 (ISBN 0-8240-9823-4). Garland Pub.

Spirit Possession & Popular Religion: From the Camisards to the Shakers. Clarke Garrett. LC 86-46284. 288p. 1987. text ed. 29.50x (ISBN 0-8018-3486-4). Johns Hopkins.

Spirit River to Angels' Roost: Religions I Have Loved & Left. Patricia Joudry. LC 76-22996. 1977. 12.95 (ISBN 0-912766-46-8). Tundra Bks.

Spirit Run. Houston A. Baker, Jr. LC 81-82664. 38p. 1982. pap. 3.00x (ISBN 0-916418-38-3). Lotus.

Spirit, Saints & Immortality. Patrick Sherry. LC 83-519. 102p. 1984. 39.50x (ISBN 0-87395-755-5); pap. 14.95x (ISBN 0-87395-756-3). State U NY Pr.

Spirit Seizures. Melissa Pritchard. LC 87-5932. (Winner of the Flannery O'Connor Award for Short Fiction Ser.). 136p. 1987. 13.95 (ISBN 0-8203-0959-1). U of Ga Pr.

Spirit Shadows. Silvester Brito. 4.50 (ISBN 0-317-52048-2). Jelm Mtn.

Spirit Soars. Tom Pinkston. 34p. pap. 3.00 (ISBN 0-942494-47-4). Coleman Pub.

Spirit Song. Mary Summer Rain. Ed. by Robert Friedman. LC 85-15894. 200p. (Orig.). 1985. pap. 7.95 (ISBN 0-89865-405-X, Unilaw). Donning Co.

Spirit Speaks in Us. John Sheets. 210p. 1986. 8.95 (ISBN 0-87193-250-4). Dimension Bks.

Spirit Spirit: Shaman Songs. rev. enl. ed. David Cloutier. (Illus.). 100p. 1980. pap. 4.50 (ISBN 0-914278-30-4). Copper Beech.

Spirit, Spirits & Spirituality. A. E. Knoch. 157p. 1977. pap. text ed. 4.00 (ISBN 0-910424-69-1). Concordant.

Spirit Summonings. Time-Life Books Editors. (Mystery of Unknown Ser.). 160p. 1989. 17.27 (ISBN 0-8094-6344-X); lib. bdg. 21.27 (ISBN 0-8094-6345-8). Time-Life.

Spirit Teachings Through the Mediumship of William Stainton Moses. William S. Moses. LC 75-36910. (Occult Ser.). 1976. Repr. of 1924 ed. 24.50x (ISBN 0-405-07968-0). Ayer Co Pubs.

Spirit That Moves Us Reader: Seventh Anniversary Anthology. Ed. by Morty Sklar. LC 82-10685. (Contemporary Anthology Ser.: No. 4). (Illus.). 208p. 1982. 12.00 (ISBN 0-930370-13-9); pap. 6.00 perfectbound (ISBN 0-930370-14-7); signed cloth A-Z 25.00x (ISBN 0-930370-12-0). Spirit That Moves.

Spirit: The First Ninety-Three Dailies. Will Eisner. (U. S. Classics Ser.). (Illus.). 32p. (Orig.). 1980. pap. 3.95 (ISBN 0-912277-15-7). K Pierce Inc.

Spirit: The Last Two Hundred Forty-Five Dailies. Will Eisner. (U. S. Classics Ser.). (Illus.). 72p. 1980. pap. 6.95 (ISBN 0-912277-18-1). K Pierce Inc.

Spirit to Ride the Whirlwind. Athena V. Lord. LC 81-3775. 228p. (YA) (gr. 7 up). 1981. 10.95 (ISBN 0-02-761410-7). Macmillan.

Spirit Touching Spirit, A Contemporary Hymnal. Handt Hanson. 240p. 1986. 11.95 (ISBN 0-933173-01-6). Prince Peace Pub.

Spirit-Transformation & Development in Organizations. Harrison Owen. LC 87-70469. 248p. (Orig.). 1987. pap. text ed. 20.95 (ISBN 0-9618205-0-0). Abbott Pub.

Spirit-Traps. Daniel Hughes. LC 85-4708. 48p. (Orig.). 1985. pap. 5.00 (ISBN 0-914278-45-2). Copper Beech.

Spirit: Two Hundred Dailies. Will Eisner. (U. S. Classics Ser.). (Illus.). 64p. 1978. pap. 5.95 (ISBN 0-912277-16-5). K Pierce Inc.

Spirit: Two Hundred More Dailies. Will Eisner. (U. S. Classics Ser.). (Illus.). 64p. 1980. pap. 5.95 (ISBN 0-912277-17-3). K Pierce Inc.

Spirit within Structure: Essays in Honor of George Jonhston on the Occasion of His Seventieth Birthday. Ed. by E. J. Furcha. LC 82-24614. (Pittsburgh Theological Monographs: New Ser.: No. 3). xvi, 194p. 1983. pap. 12.50 (ISBN 0-915138-53-0). Pickwick.

Spirit Wolf. Gary D. Svee. 1987. 15.95 (ISBN 0-8027-0941-9). Walker & Co.

Spirit Wood. Robert Masello. 1987. pap. 3.50 (ISBN 0-671-63572-7). PB.

Spirit World: Pattern in the Expressive Folk Culture of Afro-American New Orleans. Michael P. Smith. LC 83-63336. (Illus.). 120p. (Orig.). 1984. pap. 14.00 (ISBN 0-9613133-0-7). New Orleans Urban.

Spirit Wrestler. James Houston. LC 79-1829. 320p. 1980. 12.50 (ISBN 0-15-184755-X). HarBraceJ.

Spirite. Theophile Gautier. Ed. by R. Reginald & Douglas Menville. Tr. by Arthur D. Hall. LC 76-1433. (Supernatural & Occult Fiction Ser.). (Illus.). 1976. Repr. of 1890 ed. lib. bdg. 24.50x (ISBN 0-405-08419-6). Ayer Co Pubs.

Spirite: Avec: La Morte Amoureuse. Theophile Gautier. 240p. 1972. 10.95 (ISBN 0-686-55912-6). French & Eur.

Spirited Affairs. 1982. 15.00x (ISBN 0-903653-91-5, Pub. by New Playwrights Network). State Mutual Bk.

Spirited Life: Bertha Mahony Miller & Children's Books. Eulalie S. Ross. LC 73-84132. (Illus.). 247p. 1973. 12.95 (ISBN 0-87675-057-9). Horn Bk.

Spirited Women Heroes of the Goethezeit. Julie D. Prandi. LC 83-48708. (American University Studies I: Vol. 22). 140p. 1983. pap. text ed. 15.25 (ISBN 0-8204-0033-5). P Lang Pubs.

Spirited Years: A History of the Antebellum Naval Academy. Charles Todorich. (Illus.). 192p. 1984. 19.95 (ISBN 0-87021-520-5). Naval Inst Pr.

Spiritfruit. Cecilia M. WAtson. (Anchor Ser.). 80p. 1986. pap. 5.95 (ISBN 0-8163-0628-1). Pacific Pr Pub Assn.

Spiritism & Religion. Johan Liljencrants. 1926. 19.50 (ISBN 0-8159-6820-5). Devin.

Spiritism & the Dead. Theodore J. Sutherland. (Intimate Life of Man Library Bk.). (Illus.). 127p. 1983. Repr. of 1889 ed. 117.75 (ISBN 0-89901-090-3). Found Class Reprints.

Spiritism & the Extension of Man into Worlds Unknown. A. T. Schofield. (Illus.). 137p. 1983. 127.75. Found Class Reprints.

Spiritism & the World After Death. A. T. Schofield. (Illus.). 137p. 1980. Repr. of 1920 ed. deluxe ed. 117.75 (ISBN 0-89901-014-8). Found Class Reprints.

Spiritism in Ghana: A Study of New Religious Movements. Robert W. Wyllie. Ed. by Conrad Cherry. LC 79-20486. (Studies in Religion: No. 21). 139p. 1980. 14.00 (ISBN 0-89130-355-3, 01-00-21); pap. 9.95 (ISBN 0-89130-356-1). Scholars Pr GA.

Spirits. Daniel M. Epstein. LC 86-31214. 64p. 1987. 16.95 (ISBN 0-87951-273-3). Overlook Pr.

Spirits. Daniel M. Epstein. 64p. 1988. pap. 8.95 (ISBN 0-87951-274-1). Overlook Pr.

Spirits & Demons at Work: Alcohol & Other Drugs on the Job. 2nd ed. Harrison M. Trice & Paul M. Roman. LC 78-23804. 294p. 1979. pap. 10.00 (ISBN 0-87546-072-0). ILR Pr.

Spirits & Liqueurs. 2nd ed. Peter A. Hallgarten. (Books on Wine). 192p. 1983. pap. 8.95 (ISBN 0-571-13057-7). Faber & Faber.

Spirits & Other Stories. Richard Bausch. 1987. 15.95 (ISBN 0-671-63875-0, Linden Pr). S&S.

Spirits & Other Stories. Richard Bausch. 240p. 1988. pap. 6.95 (ISBN 0-14-010963-3). Penguin.

Spirits & Power: An Analysis of Shona Cosmology. Hubert Bucher. (Illus.). 1980. 29.95x (ISBN 0-19-570176-3). Oxford U Pr.

Spirits & Seasons. Mary A. Napoleone & E. Jane Johanson. (Illus.). 83p. 1982. pap. 3.95 (ISBN 0-9610038-0-4). Heatherdown Pr.

Spirits' Book. rev. ed. Allan Kardec. Tr. by Anna Blackwell from Fr. 431p. 1982. pap. 6.95 (ISBN 0-931941-00-8). Starlite.

Spirits, Heroes & Hunters from North American Indian Mythology. Marion Wood. LC 81-14572. (World Mythologies Ser.). (Illus.). 156p. 1982. 16.95 (ISBN 0-8052-3792-5). Schocken.

Spirits in Bondage: A Cycle of Lyrics. C. S. Lewis. 1984. pap. 3.95 (ISBN 0-15-684748-5, Harv). HarBraceJ.

Spirits in Rebellion: The Rise & Development of New Thought. Charles S. Braden. LC 63-13245. 584p. 1984. pap. 15.95x (ISBN 0-87074-025-3). SMU Press.

Spirits of Cavern & Hearth. M. Coleman Easton. 288p. 1988. 16.95 (ISBN 0-312-02287-5). St Martin.

Spirits of Frederick. Alyce T. Weinberg. LC 79-54039. (Illus.). 73p. (Orig.). 1979. pap. 3.95x (ISBN 0-9604552-0-5). A T Weinberg.

Spirits of London: A Psychobiography for Travelers. Curtis Wilson Smith. LC 87-91611. 108p. (Orig.). (YA) (gr. 11 up). 1988. pap. 4.95 (ISBN 0-944208-00-2). Seventh Wing Pubns.

Spirits of Protest: Spirit-Mediums & the Articulation of Consensus among the Zezuru of Southern Rhodesia (Zimbabwe) Peter Fry. LC 75-20832. (Cambridge Studies in Social Anthropology: No. 14). pap. 39.80 (2031654). Bks Demand UMI.

Spirits of Resistance & Capitalist Discipline: Factory Women in Malaysia. Aihwa Ong. LC 86-22980. (Anthropology of Work Ser.). 256p. 1987. 49.50 (ISBN 0-88706-380-2); pap. 14.95x (ISBN 0-88706-381-0). State U NY Pr.

Spirits of Seventy-Six: A Catholic Inquiry. Donald D'Elia. 182p. (Orig.). pap. 6.95 (ISBN 0-931888-10-7). Christendom Coll Pr.

Spirits of the Place. Tony Connor. 88p. 1986. 16.95 (ISBN 0-85646-164-4, Pub. by Anvil Pr Poetry); pap. 8.95 (ISBN 0-85646-165-2). Longwood Pub Group.

Spirit's Pilgrimage. Mirabehn. LC 84-6071. (Illus.). 336p. 1984. 16.95 (ISBN 0-915556-12-X); pap. 9.95 sewn (ISBN 0-915556-13-8). Great Ocean.

Spirits Rebellious. Kahlil Gibran. Ed. by Martin L. Wolf. Tr. by Anthony R. Ferris from Arabic. 128p. 1973. pap. 3.95 (ISBN 0-8065-0364-5, Pub. by Citadel Pr). Lyle Stuart.

Spirits Rebellious. Kahlil Gibran. (Illus.). 1948. 10.45 (ISBN 0-394-44668-2). Knopf.

Spirits, Shamans, & Stars: Perspectives from South America. Ed. by David L. Browman. Ronald A. Scwartz. (World Anthropology Ser.). (Illus.). xiv, 276p. 1979. text ed. 35.25 (ISBN 90-279-7890-5). Mouton.

Spirits, Spooks, & Other Sinister Creatures. Ed. by Helen Hoke. (Terrific Triple Title Ser.). (gr. 7 up). 1984. lib. bdg. 12.90 (ISBN 0-531-04769-5). Watts.

Spirits, Stars, & Spells: The Profits & Perils of Magic. L. Sprague De Camp & Catherine C. De Camp. LC 65-25470. (Illus.). 348p. 1980. 17.00 (ISBN 0-913896-17-9). Owlswick Pr.

Spirit's Sword: God's Infallible Book. B. E. Underwood. 1969. 3.95 (ISBN 0-911866-50-7); pap. 2.95 (ISBN 0-911866-91-4). Advocate.

Spiritual Aerobics. Linda Schott. 89p. 1987. pap. 4.95 (ISBN 0-89225-298-7). Gospel Advocate.

Spiritual Aids for Those in Renew: Ponderings, Poems & Promises. Robert F. Morneau. LC 84-12299. 111p. (Orig.). 1984. pap. 4.50 (ISBN 0-8189-0473-9). Alba.

Spiritual Alchemy. rev. ed. Omraam M. Aivanhov. (Complete Works: Vol. 2). (Illus.). 205p. 1986. pap. 11.95 (ISBN 2-85566-371-7, Pub. by Prosveta France). Prosveta USA.

Spiritual Alchemy: Course III, Lessons 49-53. (Illus.). 1976. pap. 7.85 (ISBN 0-87887-359-7). Church of Light.

Spiritual Almanac: Guidelines for Better Living Each Month of the Year. Don Jennings. 240p. 1984. pap. 5.95 (ISBN 0-13-834748-4). P-H.

Spiritual & Anabaptist Writers. Ed. by George H. Williams & Angel M. Mergal. LC 57-5003. (Library of Christian Classics). 418p. 1977. pap. 11.95 (ISBN 0-664-24150-6). Westminster John Knox.

Spiritual Approach to Astrology: A Complete Textbook of Astrology. Myrna Lofthus. LC 78-62936. (Illus.). 428p. 1983. 12.95 (ISBN 0-916360-10-5). CRCS Pubns CA.

Spiritual Approach to Male-Female Relations. Scott Miners. LC 83-40326. 220p. (Orig.). 1984. pap. 6.50 (ISBN 0-8356-0583-3, Quest). Theos Pub Hse.

Spiritual Aspects of Indian Music. Simon R. Leopold. 1985. 22.50x (ISBN 0-8364-1258-3, Pub. by Sundeep). South Asia Bks.

Spiritual Aspects of the Healing Art. Compiled by Dora Kunz. LC 85-40410. 294p. (Orig.). 1985. pap. 6.50 (ISBN 0-8356-0601-5, Quest). Theos Pub Hse.

Spiritual Aspects of the New Poetry. facs. ed. Amos N. Wilder. LC 68-16988. (Essay Index Reprint Ser). 1940. 16.25 (ISBN 0-8369-0995-X). Ayer Co Pubs.

Spiritual Astrology: A Layperson's Guide to Self Unfoldment. Jan Spiller. 122p. 1984. perfect bdg. 5.95 (ISBN 0-930706-16-1). Seek-It Pubns.

Spiritual Astrology: Course VII, Lessons 71-83. (Illus.). pap. 12.75 (ISBN 0-87887-360-0). Church of Light.

Spiritual Astrology: Your Personal Path to Self-Fulfillment. Jan Spiller & Karen McCoy. 448p. 1988. pap. 9.95 (ISBN 0-671-66041-1, Fireside). S&S.

Spiritual Authority. Watchman Nee. Tr. by Stephen Kaung. 1972. 4.75 (ISBN 0-935008-34-9); pap. 3.75 (ISBN 0-935008-35-7). Christian Fellow Pubs.

Spiritual Authority & Temporal Power in the Indian Theory of Government. Ananda K. Coomaraswamy. (Amer Oriental Soc Ser.). 1942. pap. 16.00 (ISBN 0-527-02696-4). Kraus Repr.

Spiritual Autobiography in Early America. Daniel B. Shea, Jr. LC 87-40375. (Wisconsin Series on American Autobiography). 304p. 1988. text ed. 35.00x (ISBN 0-299-11650-6); pap. text ed. 12.95x (ISBN 0-299-11654-9). U of Wis Pr.

Spiritual Automobile. James W. Cuffee. Ed. by Charles Knickerbocker. 44p. 1980. 4.75 (ISBN 0-682-48997-2). Exposition-Phoenix.

Spiritual Awakening. Darshan Singh. LC 81-50726. (Illus.). 338p. (Orig.). 1982. pap. 7.50 (ISBN 0-918224-11-X). Sawan Kirpal Pubns.

Spiritual Awakening: Classic Writings of the Eighteenth Century to Inspire the Twentieth Century Reader. Ed. by Sherwood E. Wirt. LC 86-70283. 256p. (Orig.). 1986. pap. 8.95 (ISBN 0-89107-394-9, Crossway Bks). Good News.

Spiritual Basics: New Life in Christ. Lyman Coleman. (Free University - Lay Academy in Christian Discipleship Ser.). (Orig.). 1981. pap. 1.25 student's bk. (ISBN 0-687-37355-7); pap. 4.95 tchr's bk. (ISBN 0-687-37354-9). Abingdon.

Spiritual Being in the Heavenly Bodies & in the Kingdoms of Nature. Rudolf Steiner. 210p. (Ger.). 1981. pap. 9.95 (ISBN 0-919924-14-X, Pub. by Steiner Book Centre Canada). Anthroposophic.

Spiritual Body & Celestial Earth: From Mazdean Iran to Shi Ite Iran. Henry Corbin. Tr. by Nancy Pearson. (Bollingen Ser: No. 91). 1977. text ed. 44.50x (ISBN 0-691-09937-5). Princeton U Pr.

Spiritual Breakthrough to the Next Millennium. Max Kappeler. LC 85-82058. 75p. 1986. pap. 7.00 (ISBN 0-942958-12-8). Kappeler Inst Pub.

Spiritual Burnout. Malcolm Smith. 354p. 1988. 14.95 (ISBN 0-89274-517-7). Harrison Hse.

Spiritual Cannibalism. Swami Rudrananda. 192p. (Orig.). 1987. pap. 10.94 (ISBN 0-915801-07-8). Rudra Pr.

Spiritual Care. Dietrich Bonhoeffer. Tr. by Jay C. Rochelle. LC 85-47711. 128p. 1985. pap. 4.95 (ISBN 0-8006-1874-2). Fortress.

Spiritual Care. 3rd ed. Judith A. Shelly & Sharon Fish. LC 88-871. (Spiritual Perspectives in Nursing Ser.). (Illus.). 252p. 1988. pap. 9.95 incl. wkbk. (ISBN 0-8308-1254-7). Inter-Varsity.

Spiritual Care of Puerto Rican Migrants. Ed. by Ivan Illich et al. LC 79-6206. (Hispanics in the United States Ser.). 1981. Repr. of 1970 ed. lib. bdg. 23.00x (ISBN 0-405-13156-9). Ayer Co Pubs.

Spiritual Centers in Man. Manly P. Hall. Orig. Title: Operative Occutism. pap. 2.50 (ISBN 0-89314-383-9). Philos Res.

Spiritual Choices: The Problem of Recognizing Authentic Paths to Inner Transformation. Ed. by Dick Anthony et al. LC 86-5027. 375p. 1986. 24.95 (ISBN 0-913729-14-0); pap. 12.95 (ISBN 0-913729-19-1). Paragon Hse.

Spiritual Cleansing. Draja Mickaharic. LC 81-70348. 128p. 1982. pap. 5.95 (ISBN 0-87728-531-4). Weiser.

Spiritual Cleansing. Draja Mickaharic. pap. 5.95 (ISBN 0-942272-09-9). Original Pubns.

Spiritual Combat. Lawrence Scupoli. LC 78-61668. (Spiritual Masters Ser.). 256p. 1978. pap. 4.95 (ISBN 0-8091-2158-1). Paulist Pr.

Spiritual Conferences. Frederick W. Faber. LC 78-66304. 1978. pap. 11.00 (ISBN 0-89555-079-2). TAN Bks Pubs.

Spiritual Conferences. John Tauler. Tr. by Eric Colledge & M. Jane. LC 78-74568. 1979. pap. 9.00 (ISBN 0-89555-082-2). TAN Bks Pubs.

Spiritual Conquest of Mexico: An Essay on the Apostolate & the Evangelizing Methods of the Mendicant Orders in New Spain, 1523-1572. Robert Ricard. Tr. by Lesley B. Simpson from Span. (Illus.). 435p. 1974. pap. 10.95x (ISBN 0-520-04784-2). U of Cal Pr.

Spiritual Considerations in the Preventive Treatment & Cure of Disease. Jane H. Thompson. 128p. 1984. cancelled (ISBN 0-85362-211-6, Oriel). Routledge Chapman & Hall.

Spiritual Counsels of Father John of Kronstadt. W. Jardine Grisbrooke. 230p. (Orig.). 1982. pap. 9.95 (ISBN 0-913836-92-3). St Vladimirs.

Spiritual Counsels of Father John of Kronstadt: Select Passages from "My Life in Christ". Ed. by Jardine W. Grisbrooke. 256p. 1983. pap. 13.95 (ISBN 0-227-67856-7, Pub. by J Clarke UK). Attic Pr.

Spiritual Crisis of Man. rev ed. Paul Brunton. LC 83-60829. 224p. 1984. pap. 7.95 (ISBN 0-87728-593-4). Weiser.

Spiritual Crisis of the Gilded Age. Paul A. Carter. LC 72-156938. (Illus.). 295p. 1971. 16.00 (ISBN 0-87580-026-2). N Ill U Pr.

Spiritual Dancing: Yesterday, Today & Tomorrow. Samuel L. Lewis. Ed. by Saadi Klotz. 120p. (Orig.). Date not set. pap. 9.50 (ISBN 0-915424-11-8). Sufi Islamia-Prophecy.

Spiritual Depression: Its Causes & Cure. D. Martyn Lloyd-Jones. 1965. pap. 7.95 (ISBN 0-8028-1387-9). Eerdmans.

Spiritual Depths. Martha I. Brown. 104p. 1986. pap. 5.00 (ISBN 0-9618538-0-8). Martha I Brown.

Spiritual Development: An Interdisciplinary Study. Daniel A. Helminiak. 256p. 1987. 15.95 (ISBN 0-8294-0530-5). Loyola.

Spiritual Diary. Ed. by Douglas Baker. 1987. 90.00x (ISBN 0-9505502-7-2, Pub. by Claregate Coll UK). State Mutual Bk.

Spiritual Diary. 1962. 5.50 (ISBN 0-8198-6823-X); pap. 4.50. Dghtrs St Paul.

Spiritual Diary. 375p. (Orig.). pap. 7.95 (ISBN 0-89389-073-1). Himalayan Pubs.

Spiritual Diary. 380p. 1982. 3.50 (ISBN 0-87612-021-4). Self Realization.

Spiritual Diary, 5 Vols. Emanuel Swedenborg. LC 77-93540. Complete Set. 30.00 (ISBN 0-87785-081-X); Vol. 1. 10.00 (ISBN 0-87785-079-8); Vols. 2-5. 25.00 (ISBN 0-87785-080-1). Swedenborg.

Spiritual Diary of Emanuel Swedenborg, 6 vols. Emanuel Swedenborg. lib. bdg. 700.00 (ISBN 0-87968-560-3). Krishna Pr.

Spiritual Dilemma of the Jewish People. Arthur W. Kac. 5.95 (ISBN 0-8010-5456-7). Baker Bk.

Spiritual Dimension of Green Politics. Charlene Spretnak. LC 86-70255. 96p. (Orig.). 1986. pap. 4.95 (ISBN 0-939680-29-7). Bear & Co.

Spiritual Dimensions of Healing Addictions. Donna Cunningham & Andrew Ramer. 184p. 1988. 9.95 (ISBN 0-9615875-5-5). Cassandra Pr.

Spiritual Dimensions of Mental Health. Judith A. Shelley & Sandra D. John. LC 83-12769. 168p. 1983. pap. 8.95 (ISBN 0-87784-876-9). Inter-Varsity.

Spiritual Dimensions of Nursing Practice. Carson. 400p. 1988. price not set. Saunders.

Spiritual Dimensions of Pastoral Care: Witness to the Ministry of Wayne E. Oates. Ed. by Gerald L. Borchert & Andrew D. Lester. LC 84-19581. 152p. (Orig.). 1985. pap. 11.95 (ISBN 0-664-24562-5). Westminster John Knox.

Spiritual Dimensions of Psychology. Hazrat I. Khan. 256p. 1988. pap. 12.95 (ISBN 0-930872-36-3). Omega Pr NY.

Spiritual Direction. Martin Thornton. LC 83-73658. 145p. 1984. pap. 6.95 (ISBN 0-936384-17-4). Cowley Pubns.

Spiritual Direction: An Invitation to Abundant Life. Francis W. Vanderwall. LC 81-83185. 128p. (Orig.). 1982. pap. 4.95 (ISBN 0-8091-2399-1). Paulist Pr.

Spiritual Direction & Mid-Life Development. Raymond Studzinski. 1985. 12.95 (ISBN 0-8294-0480-5). Loyola.

Spiritual Direction: Contemporary Readings. Intro. by Kevin Cullingan. 237p. (Orig.). 1983. pap. 5.95 (ISBN 0-914544-43-8). Living Flame Pr.

Spiritual Direction: Letters of Starets Macarius of Optina Monastery. pap. 2.95 (ISBN 0-686-00254-7). Eastern Orthodox.

Spiritual Director. Damien Isabel. (Synthesis Ser.). 1976. pap. 2.00 (ISBN 0-8199-0712-X). Franciscan Herald.

Spiritual Directory of St. Francis de Sales. 3.50 (ISBN 0-8198-6860-4); 2.25 (ISBN 0-8198-6861-2). Dghtrs St Paul.

Spiritual Discernment & Politics: Guidelines for Religious Communities. J. B. Libanio. Tr. by Theodore Morrow from Port. LC 82-2257. Orig. Title: Discernment E politica. 144p. (Orig.). 1982. pap. 1.74 (ISBN 0-88344-463-1). Orbis Bks.

Spiritual Discipline in Hinduism, Buddhism, & the West. Harry M. Buck. LC 81-12812. (Focus on Hinduism & Buddhism Ser.). 64p. 1981. pap. 5.95x (ISBN 0-89012-022-6). Anima Pubns.

Spiritual Disciplines for Everyday Living. Ronald V. Wells. (Illus.). 260p. 1987. pap. 9.95 (ISBN 0-9618701-0-9). RDC Bks.

Spiritual Disciplines: Growth Through the Practice of Prayer, Fasting, Dialogue, & Worship. rev. ed. James E. Massey. Ed. by Joseph D. Allison. 112p. 1985. pap. 6.95 (ISBN 0-310-37151-1, 12410P). Zondervan.

Spiritual Discourses. Ayatollah Morteza Motahhari. Ed. by M. Salman Tawhidi. Tr. by Aluddin Pazargadi. 139p. (Orig.). 1986. pap. 4.95 (ISBN 0-9616897-0-6). MSA Inc.

Spiritual Doctrine of Blessed Elizabeth of the Trinity: Apostolic Contemplative. Luigi Borriello. Tr. by Jordan Aumann from Span. 154p. (Orig.). 1986. pap. 7.95 (ISBN 0-8189-0500-X). Alba.

Spiritual Drama in the Life of Thackeray. M. Stephenson. 59.95 (ISBN 0-8490-1112-4). Gordon Pr.

Spiritual Drama in the Life of Thackeray. M. F. Stephenson. 1974. lib. bdg. 29.00 (ISBN 0-8414-7962-3). Folcroft.

Spiritual Dryness. Walter Trobisch. pap. 0.75 (ISBN 0-87784-138-1). Inter-Varsity.

Spiritual Dynamics. G. Raymond Carlson. LC 76-5633. (Radiant Life Ser.). 128p. 1976. pap. 2.50 (ISBN 0-88243-894-8, 02-0894); teacher's guide 3.95 (ISBN 0-88243-168-4, 32-0168). Gospel Pub.

Spiritual Dynamics of Howard Thurman's Theology. Mozella G. Mitchell. LC 85-1227. 225p. (Orig.). 1985. pap. 14.95x (ISBN 0-932269-42-7). Wyndham Hall.

Spiritual Economics--the Prosperity Process. Eric Butterworth. 220p. 1983. 5.95 (ISBN 0-87159-142-1). Unity School.

Spiritual Empowerment in Afro-American Literature: Frederick Douglass, Rebecca Jackson, Booker T. Washington, Richard Wright, Toni Morrison. James H. Evans, Jr. LC 87-14196. (Studies in Art & Religious Interpretation). 192p. 1987. lib. bdg. 39.95x (ISBN 0-88946-560-6). E Mellen.

Spiritual Encounter with the Holy One. Jean Koberlein. LC 84-8938. (Mellen Lives Ser.: Vol. 2). 200p. 1984. pap. 9.95x (ISBN 0-88946-012-4). E Mellen.

Spiritual Exercise for New Parents. Elwyn A. Smith. LC 85-47714. 64p. 1985. pap. 1.00 (ISBN 0-8006-1863-7, 1-1863). Fortress.

Spiritual Exercise for the Grieving. Elwyn A. Smith. LC 84-47935. 64p. 1984. pap. 3.50 (ISBN 0-8006-1807-6, 1-1807). Fortress.

Spiritual Exercise for the Sick. Elwyn A. Smith. LC 83-48141. 64p. 1983. pap. 3.50 (ISBN 0-8006-1751-7, 1-1751). Fortress.

Spiritual Exercises. Robert Kelly. LC 81-10038. 164p. (Orig.). 1981. signed ed. 25.00 (ISBN 0-87685-508-7); pap. 7.50 (ISBN 0-87685-507-9). Black Sparrow.

Spiritual Exercises According to Saint Bonaventure. Dominic Faccin. Tr. by Owen A. Colligan. (Spirit & Life Ser). 1955. 3.00 (ISBN 0-686-11568-6). Franciscan Inst.

Spiritual Exercises & the Ignatian Mystical Horizon. Harvey D. Egan. LC 76-5742. (Study Aids on Jesuit Topics, Series 4: No. 5). xii, 216p. 1976. smyth sewn 7.00 (ISBN 0-912422-18-1); pap. 6.00 (ISBN 0-912422-14-9). Inst Jesuit.

Spiritual Exercises of St. Ignatius: A Literal Translation & a Contemporary Reading. David L. Fleming. Ed. by George E. Ganss. LC 77-93429. (Study Aids on Jesuit Topics Ser.: No. 7). 290p. 1978. smyth sewn 9.00 (ISBN 0-912422-31-9). Inst Jesuit.

Spiritual Exercises of St. Ignatius Based on Studies in the Language of the Autograph. Louis J. Puhl. (Request Reprint). 1968. pap. 4.00 (ISBN 0-8294-0065-6). Loyola.

Spiritual Exercises of St. Ignatius Loyola: Resources in Religion, No. 3. Tr. by Elisabeth M. Tetlow. LC 87-8296. 162p. (Orig.). 1987. lib. bdg. 23.50 (ISBN 0-8191-6379-1, Pub. by College Theology Society); pap. text ed. 10.75 (ISBN 0-8191-6380-5, Pub. by College Theology Society). U Pr of Amer.

Spiritual Exercises of St. Ignatius. St. Ignatius. Tr. by Anthony Mottola. 1964. pap. 4.95 (ISBN 0-385-02436-3, D170, Im). Doubleday.

Spiritual Exercises of St. Ignatius of Loyola. St. Ignatius. Tr. by Lewis Delmage. 1978. 4.00 (ISBN 0-8198-0557-2); pap. 2.25 (ISBN 0-8198-0558-0). Dghtrs St Paul.

Spiritual Family. John-Roger. 1976. pap. 5.00 (ISBN 0-914829-21-1, 978-5). Mandeville LA.

Spiritual First Aid from A to Z. Robert S. Mazeroni. 176p. (Orig.). 1987. pap. 2.95 (ISBN 0-345-33824-3, Pub. by Ballantine Epiphany). Ballantine.

Spiritual Folk-Songs of Early America. Ed. by George P. Jackson. 11.25 (ISBN 0-8446-2297-4). Peter Smith.

Spiritual Food Gleanings. Ed. by James C. Yu. Tr. by Ming-Tao Wang from Eng. 128p. (Orig., Chinese.). 1987. pap. text ed. 2.50. Evangel Lit.

Spiritual Formation in the Catholic Seminary. 64p. 1984. pap. 4.95 (ISBN 1-55586-920-3). US Catholic.

Spiritual Foundation of Morality. Rudolf Steiner. Tr. by Mabel Cotterell. 90p. 1979. pap. 4.75 (ISBN 0-919924-09-3, Pub. by Steiner Book Centre Canada). Anthroposophic.

Spiritual Foundations for Social Action. Polly Edgar et al. (Studies in Quakerism: No. 14). 52p. 1987. pap. 4.00 (ISBN 0-89670-017-8). Progresiv Pub.

Spiritual Foundations of Society: An Introduction to Social Philosophy. S. L. Frank. Ed. & tr. by Boris Jakim. 196p. 1986. text ed. 22.95x (ISBN 0-8214-0848-8). Ohio U Pr.

Spiritual Franciscans. D. S. Muzzey. 59.95 (ISBN 0-8490-1113-2). Gordon Pr.

Spiritual Friend: Reclaiming the Gift of Spiritual Direction. Tilden Edwards. LC 79-91408. 272p. 1980. pap. 9.95 (ISBN 0-8091-2288-X). Paulist Pr.

Spiritual Friendship. Aelred of Rievaulx. (Cistercian Fathers Ser.: No. 5). 144p. pap. 5.00 (ISBN 0-87907-705-0). Cistercian Pubns.

Spiritual Gifts. John MacArthur, Jr. (John MacArthur's Bible Studies). 1985. pap. 5.95 (ISBN 0-8024-5121-7). Moody.

Spiritual Gifts. George Shalm. 131p. 1983. pap. 4.95 (ISBN 0-912315-04-0). Word Aflame.

Spiritual Gifts & Their Operation. Howard Carter. 96p. 1968. pap. 1.95 (ISBN 0-88243-593-0, 02-0593). Gospel Pub.

Spiritual Gifts: Empowering the New Testament Church. Kenneth S. Hemphill. LC 88-6913. (Orig.). 1988. pap. 6.95 (ISBN 0-8054-5918-9). Broadman.

Spiritual Gifts for Christians Today. Knofel Staton. 118p. (Orig.). 1973. pap. 3.95 (ISBN 0-89900-134-3). College Pr Pub.

Spiritual Gifts in the Local Church. David Pytches. 288p. (Orig.). 1987. pap. 6.95 (ISBN 0-87123-984-1). Bethany Hse.

Spiritual Gifts Inventory. Ralph W. Neighbour, Jr. (Illus.). 32p. 1987. pap. 3.95 (ISBN 0-937931-29-2). Global TN.

Spiritual Gifts-Ministries & Manifestations. B. E. Underwood. pap. 6.95 (ISBN 0-911866-03-5). Advocate.

Spiritual Gifts: Ministries & Manifestations. B. E. Underwood. pap. 3.95 student wkbk. (ISBN 0-911866-04-3); pap. 6.95 tchr's. guide (ISBN 0-911866-05-1). Advocate.

Spiritual Gifts: Your Portion of Christ's Bounty. 4th ed. Robert D. Noble. 42p. (Orig.). 1985. pap. 4.00 (ISBN 0-944687-01-6). Gather Family Inst.

Spiritual Gospel. Jim Lewis. LC 82-51231. 145p. (Orig.). 1982. pap. 8.95 (ISBN 0-942482-05-0). Unity Church Denver.

Spiritual Greatness: Studies in Exodus. Tom Julien. (Orig.). 1979. pap. 4.95 (ISBN 0-88469-121-7). BMH Bks.

Spiritual Growth. Don Clowers. 164p. (Orig.). 1984. pap. text ed. 9.95 (ISBN 0-914307-28-2). Word Faith.

Spiritual Growth: Being Your Higher Self. Saraya Roman. Ed. by Elaine Ratner. (Earth Life Ser.). 216p. 1988. pap. 9.95 (ISBN 0-915811-12-X). H J Kramer Inc.

Spiritual Growth: I Am the Way, the Truth, & the Life. rev. ed. Joan Jungerman. 1.50 (ISBN 0-8091-9314-0). Paulist Pr.

Spiritual Growth in the Congregation. Robert H. Boyte & Kelly Boyte-Peters. Ed. by Herbert Lambert. 112p. (Orig.). 1988. pap. 7.95 (ISBN 0-8272-3428-7). CBP.

Spiritual Growth in Youth Ministry. J. David Stone. LC 85-12623. 216p. 1985. 12.95 (ISBN 0-931529-04-2). Group Bks.

Spiritual Growth Through Creative Drama. Pam Barragar. 128p. 1981. pap. 5.95 (ISBN 0-8170-0923-X). Judson.

Spiritual Guidance. Josef Sudbrack. 1984. pap. 3.95 (ISBN 0-8091-2571-4). Paulist Pr.

Spiritual Guidance for the Separated & Divorced. Medard Laz. 64p. 1982. pap. 1.95 (ISBN 0-89243-158-X). Liguori Pubns.

Spiritual Guidance of Man. Rudolf Steiner. 1983. pap. 5.95 (ISBN 0-910142-35-1). Anthroposophic.

Spiritual Guide. Michael Molinos. Ed. by Gene Edwards. 110p. pap. 6.95 (ISBN 0-940232-08-1). Christian Bks.

Spiritual Guide to Eternal Life. Alex La Perchia. LC 77-75258. 89p. 1977. 6.95 (ISBN 0-8022-2203-X). Philos Lib.

Spiritual Handbook for Women. Dandi D. Knorr. 192p. 1984. 13.95 (ISBN 0-13-834796-4, Spec); pap. 6.95 (ISBN 0-13-834788-3). P-H.

Spiritual Harvest: Reflections on the Fruits of the Spirit. Mary L. Carney. 112p. 1987. pap. 6.95 (ISBN 0-687-39231-4). Abingdon.

Spiritual Healing. Ed. by Willis H. Kinnear. 110p. (Orig.). 1973. pap. 4.95 (ISBN 0-911336-50-8). Sci of Mind.

Spiritual Healing. 4th ed. Swami Paramananda. 1975. pap. 3.50 (ISBN 0-911564-10-1). Vedanta Ctr.

Spiritual Healing. Nelson White & Anne White. LC 85-50745. (Illus.). 65p. (Orig.). 1985. pap. text ed. 12.00 (ISBN 0-939856-42-5). Tech Group.

Spiritual Healing for Today. Raymond C. Barker. LC 88-70091. 136p. (Orig.). 1988. pap. 5.95 (ISBN 0-87516-607-5). DeVorss.

Spiritual Healing in a Scientific Age. Robert Peel. LC 86-43015. 288p. 1987. 19.95 (ISBN 0-06-066484-3, HarpR). Har-Row.

Spiritual Healing: Miracle or Mirage? Alan Young. LC 81-82932. 280p. (Orig.). 1982. pap. 7.95 (ISBN 0-87516-460-9). DeVorss.

Spiritual Heritage of India. Swami Prabhavananda. LC 63-10517. 1979. pap. 8.95 (ISBN 0-87481-035-3). Vedanta Pr.

Spiritual Heritage of Islam Quantal. Ed. by Muhseen A. Shaeer. (Books Of Oral Tradition). (Orig.). 1988. pap. 10.50. Quantal.

Spiritual Heritage of Tyagaraja. Tyagaraja. Tr. by C. Ramanujachari. (Sanskrit, Telegu & Eng.). 14.95 (ISBN 0-87481-440-5). Vedanta Pr.

Spiritual Hierarchies & Their Reflection in the Physical World: Zodiac, Planets, Cosmos. Rudolf Steiner. Tr. by Rene M. Querido. LC 75-114688. 140p. (Ger.). 1983. pap. 8.95 (ISBN 0-88010-061-3). Anthroposophic.

Spiritual High Treason. Jimmy Swaggart. 1987. 12.95 (ISBN 0-935113-07-X). Swaggart Ministries.

Spiritual Hunger. Gordon Lindsay. 2.50 (ISBN 0-89985-020-0). Christ Nations.

Spiritual Hunger of the Modern Child. J. G. Bennett & Mario Montessori. Ed. by Wendy Addison. LC 87-71204. 220p. 1985. pap. 8.95 (ISBN 0-934254-06-0). Claymont Comm.

Spiritual Ideals for Modern Man. Swami Vivididshanando. 198p. 1980. o. p. (ISBN 0-87481-566-5). Vedanta Pr.

Spiritual Image in Modern Art. Compiled by Kathleen J. Regier. LC 87-40127. (Illus.). 215p. (Orig.). 1987. pap. 9.95 (ISBN 0-8356-0621-X, Quest). Theos Pub Hse.

Spiritual Import of Society. John S. Connor. LC 85-91374. 208p. 1987. 10.95 (ISBN 0-533-06881-9). Vantage.

Spiritual in Art: Abstract Painting 1890-1985. Maurice Tuchman et al. (Illus.). 436p. 1986. 55.00 (ISBN 0-89659-669-9, Co-Pub & Dist by Abbeville Press); pap. 24.95 (ISBN 0-87587-130-5). LA Co Art Mus.

Spiritual Insights for Daily Living: A Daybook of Reflections on Ancient Spiritual Truths of Relevance for Our Contemporary Lives. Ed. by Elizabeth W. Fenske. (Illus.). 416p. (Orig.). pap. 7.50 (ISBN 0-914071-09-2). Spirit Front Fellow.

Spiritual Interpretation of History. Shailer Mathews. 1977. lib. bdg. 59.95 (ISBN 0-8490-2661-X). Gordon Pr.

Spiritual Interpretation of Scripture. Joel S. Goldsmith. pap. 6.95 (ISBN 0-87516-310-6). DeVorss.

Spiritual Intimidation. Nelson White & Anne White. LC 84-51476. 65p. (Orig.). 1984. pap. 15.00 (ISBN 0-939856-39-5). Tech Group.

Spiritual Journey. Francis K. Nemeck & Marie T. Coombs. LC 85-45664. (Orig.). 1986. pap. 10.95 (ISBN 0-89453-546-3). M Glazier.

Spiritual Journey: The Monastic Way. Jean-Marie Howe. (Orig.). 1988. pap. price not set (ISBN 0-932506-68-2). St Bedes Pubns.

Spiritual Journeys. Ed. by Robert Baram. 442p. 1987. 11.95 (ISBN 0-8198-6877-9, Pub. by St Paul Editions); pap. 9.95 (ISBN 0-8198-6876-0, Pub. by St Paul Editions). Dghtrs St Paul.

Spiritualitat Heute und Gestern, Vol. 4. Ed. by James Hogg. (Analecta Cartusiana Ser.: No. 35). (Illus.). 131p. (Orig., Fr., Ital., Ger. & Eng.). 1984. pap. 25.00 (ISBN 3-7052-0040-2, Pub by Salzburg Studies). Longwood Pub Group.

Spiritualitat Heute und Gestern, Vol. 5. Ed. by James Hogg. (Analecta Cartusiana Ser.: No. 35). (Orig.). 1984. pap. 25.00 (ISBN 3-7052-0041-0, Pub by Salzburg Studies). Longwood Pub Group.

Spiritualite de l'Heresie: le Catharisme. Rene Nelli. LC 78-63189. (Heresies of the Early Christian & Medieval Era: Second Ser.). Repr. of 1953 ed. 31.00 (ISBN 0-404-16226-6). AMS Pr.

Spirituality & Administration: The Role of the Bishop in Twelfth-Century Auxerre. Constance B. Bouchard. LC 78-55889. 1979. 11.00x (ISBN 0-910956-79-0, SAM5); pap. 5.00x (ISBN 0-910956-67-7). Medieval Acad.

Spirituality & Analogia Entis According to Erich Przywara, S. J. Metaphysics & Religious Experience, the Ignation Exercises, the Balance in 'Similarity' & 'Greater Dissimilarity' According to Lateran IV. James V. Zeitz. LC 82-17588. 358p. (Orig.). 1983. lib. bdg. 34.75 (ISBN 0-8191-2783-3); pap. text ed. 16.75 (ISBN 0-8191-2784-1). U Pr of Amer.

Spirituality & Chemical Dependency: Guidelines for Treatment. Kitty Joachim. Ed. by Virginia Biegun. 29p. (Orig.). 1988. pap. text ed. 4.00 (ISBN 0-944335-00-4). Oxford Inst.

Spirituality & Human Emotion. Robert C. Roberts. 134p. 1983. pap. 6.95 (ISBN 0-8028-1939-7). Eerdmans.

Spirituality & Justice. Donal Dorr. 264p. (Orig.). 1985. pap. 10.95 (ISBN 0-88344-449-6). Orbis Bks.

Spirituality & Liberation: Overcoming the Great Fallacy. Robert McAfee Brown. LC 87-29425. (Illus.). 160p. (Orig.). 1988. pap. 9.95 (ISBN 0-664-25002-5). Westminster John Knox.

Spirituality & Pastoral Care. Nelson S. Thayer. LC 84-48716. (Theology & Pastoral Care Ser.). 128p. 1985. pap. 3.50 (ISBN 0-8006-1734-7, 1-1734). Fortress.

Spirituality & Prayer, Jewish & Christian Understandings (Stimulus Bk.) Ed. by Gabe Huck & Leon Klenicki. LC 82-62966. 200p. (Orig.). 1983. pap. 7.95 (ISBN 0-8091-2538-2). Paulist Pr.

Spirituality & Society: Postmodern Visions. Ed. by David R. Griffin. (Constructive Postmodern Thought Ser.). 1988. 39.50 (ISBN 0-88706-853-7); pap. 12.95 (ISBN 0-88706-854-5). State U NY Pr.

Spirituality & the Desert Experience. Charles Cummings. 1976. cancelled (ISBN 0-87193-166-4). Dimension Bks.

Spirituality & the Gentle Life. Adrian Van Kaam. 8.95 (ISBN 0-87193-037-4). Dimension Bks.

Spirituality & Total Health. Ishwar C. Puri. Ed. by Edward D. Scott. 29p. (Orig.). 1986. pap. 2.00 (ISBN 0-937067-08-3). Inst Study Hum Aware.

Spirituality for an Anxious Age. Patrick Brennan. 151p. 1985. pap. 7.95 (ISBN 0-88347-194-9). Thomas More.

Spirituality for Ministry. Urban T. Holmes, III. LC 81-47839. 244p. 1982. 15.45 (ISBN 0-06-064008-1, HarpR). Har-Row.

Spirituality in Church & World. Ed. by Christian Duquoc. LC 65-28868. (Concilium Ser.: Vol. 9). 174p. 7.95 (ISBN 0-8091-0139-4). Paulist Pr.

Spirituality in Conflict: Saint Francis & Giotto's Bardi Chapel. Rona Goffen. (Illus.). 220p. 1988. lib. bdg. 42.50x (ISBN 0-271-00621-8). Pa St U Pr.

Spirituality in the Secular City. Ed. by Christian Duquoc. LC 66-30386. (Concilium Ser.: Vol. 19). 192p. 7.95 (ISBN 0-8091-0140-8). Paulist Pr.

Spirituality Named Compassion, & the Healing of the Global Village, Humpty Dumpty, & Us. Matthew Fox. 1979. pap. 7.95 (ISBN 0-86683-751-5, HarpR). Har-Row.

Spirituality of Compassion. Joan Puls. LC 87-51633. 160p. 1988. pap. 7.95 (ISBN 0-89622-352-3). Twenty Third.

Spirituality of Connelly. Caritas McCarthy. LC 86-21718. (Studies in Women & Religion: Vol. 19). 280p. 1986. lib. bdg. 59.95 (ISBN 0-88946-530-4). E Mellen.

Spirituality of Gentleness. Judith Lechman. 192p. 1987. 14.45 (ISBN 0-06-065221-7, HarpR). Har-Row.

Spirituality of Liberation: Toward Political Holiness. Jon Sobrino. Tr. by Robert R. Barr from Span. 224p. 1988. 23.95 (ISBN 0-88344-617-0); pap. 11.95 (ISBN 0-88344-616-2). Orbis Bks.

Spirituality of Parenting. Maureen Gallagher. (Illus.). 32p. 1985. pap. 2.00 (ISBN 0-934134-18-9). Sheed & Ward MO.

Spirituality of Paul. Thomas H. Tobin. (Message Biblical Spirituality Ser.: Vol. 12). 1988. 12.95 (ISBN 0-89453-562-5); pap. 9.95 (ISBN 0-89453-578-1). M Glazier.

Spirituality of St. Ignatius Loyola: An Account of Its Historical Development. Hugo Rahner. Tr. by Francis J. Smith. LC 53-5586. (Request Reprint). 1968. 3.50 (ISBN 0-8294-0066-4). Loyola.

Spirituality of St. Teresa of Avila. A. Haneman. 1988. write for info. (ISBN 0-8198-6843-4, SP0712); pap. 3.95 (ISBN 0-8198-6844-2). Dghtrs St Paul.

Spirituality of Teilhard de Chardin. Robert S. Faricy. 128p. (Orig.). 1981. pap. 5.95 (ISBN 0-86683-608-X, HarpR). Har-Row.

Spirituality of the American Transcendentalists: Selected Writings of Ralph Waldo Emerson, Amos Bronson Alcott, Theodore Parker, & Henry David Thoreau. Ed. by Catherine L Albanese. LC 87-34730. 480p. 1988. 59.95 (ISBN 0-86554-258-9, MUP-H220). Mercer Univ Pr.

Spirituality of the Beatitudes: Matthew's Challenge for First World Christians. Michael H. Crosby. LC 80-24755. 254p. (Orig.). 1981. pap. 9.95 (ISBN 0-88344-465-8). Orbis Bks.

Spirituality of the Catholic Church. William A. Kaschmitter. 980p. 1982. 20.00 (ISBN 0-912414-33-2). Lumen Christi.

Spirituality of the Christian East: A Systematic Handbook. Tomas Spidlik. Tr. by Anthony P. Gythiel from Fr. (Cistercian Studies Ser.: No. 79). 1986. 48.95 (ISBN 0-87907-879-0); pap. 17.00 (ISBN 0-87907-979-7). Cistercian Pubns.

Spirituality of the Future: A Search Apropos of R. C. Zaehner's Study in Sri-Aurobindo & Teilhard de Chardin. K. D. Sethna. LC 76-14764. 320p. 1981. 32.50 (ISBN 0-8386-2028-0). Fairleigh Dickinson.

Spirituality of the Later English Puritans: An Anthology. Ed. by Dewey D. Wallace, Jr. LC 87-24692. 320p. 1988. 39.95 (ISBN 0-86554-275-9, MUP-H238). Mercer Univ Pr.

Spirituality of the Middle Ages. Jean LeClercq et al. (History of Christian Spirituality Ser.: Vol. 2). 616p. 1982. pap. 14.95 (ISBN 0-8164-2373-3, HarpR). Har-Row.

Spirituality of the New Testament & the Fathers. Louis Bouyer. (History of Christian Spirituality Ser.: Vol. 1). 560p. 1982. pap. 13.95 (ISBN 0-8164-2372-5, HarpR). Har-Row.

Spirituality of the Religious Educator. Ed. by James M. Lee. LC 85-2250. 209p. (Orig.). 1985. pap. 12.95 (ISBN 0-89135-045-4). Religious Educ.

Spirituality of the Road. David J. Bosch. LC 79-10856. (Mennonite Missionary Fellowship: No. 6). 104p. 1979. pap. 4.95 (ISBN 0-8361-1889-8). Herald Pr.

Spirituality of Western Christendom. Ed. by E. Rozanne Elder. LC 76-22615. (Cistercian Studies Ser.: No. 30). (Illus.). 1976. pap. 6.95 (ISBN 0-87907-987-8). Cistercian Pubns.

Spirituality of Western Christendom II: The Roots of Modern Christian Spirituality. Ed. by Rozanne E. Elder. (Cistercian Studies: Nbr. 55). pap. write for info. Cistercian Pubns.

Spirituality of Wholeness: The New Look at Grace. Bill Huebsch. LC 87-51566. 160p. 1988. pap. 7.95 (ISBN 0-89622-355-8). Twenty Third.

Spirituality Recharted. Hubert Van Zeller. 1985. pap. 4.95 (ISBN 0-932506-39-9). St Bedes Pubns.

Spirituality: What It Is. 3rd ed. Kirpal Singh. LC 81-52000. (Illus.). 112p. 1982. pap. 5.50 (ISBN 0-918224-16-0). Sawan Kirpal Pubns.

Spiritualizing Dietetics. Johnny Lovewisdom. lib. bdg. cancelled (ISBN 0-933278-09-8). Twen Fir Cent.

Spiritualizing Everyday Life & Worship of the Spirit by the Spirit. 2nd ed. Swami Ashokananda. 70p. 1987. pap. 4.00x (ISBN 0-9612388-0-1). Vedanta Soc N Cal.

Spiritually Single. Marcia Mitchell. LC 83-15754. 112p. 1983. pap. 3.95 (ISBN 0-87123-591-9, 210591). Bethany Hse.

Spiritually Yours: Applying Gospel Principles for Personal Progression. S. Brent Farley. LC 81-82054. 160p. 1982. 6.95 (ISBN 0-88290-192-3, 1068). Horizon Utah.

Spirituals. Bruce Beasley. (New Poets Ser.). viii, 56p. 1988. 17.00x (ISBN 0-8195-2135-3); pap. 8.95 (ISBN 0-8195-1136-6). Wesleyan U Pr.

Spirituals & the Blues. James H. Cone. pap. 5.95 (ISBN 0-8164-2073-4, SP74, HarpR). Har-Row.

Spirituals Reborn: Melody. M. Paget. LC 74-76574. 96p. (gr. 9-12). 1976. Pt. 1. pap. text ed. 5.95 (ISBN 0-521-08714-7); Pt. 2. pap. text ed. 5.95 (ISBN 0-521-21332-0); choral o.p. 13.95 (ISBN 0-521-08713-9). Cambridge U Pr.

Spirituelle Aufzeichnungen. Paul Twitchel. Tr. by Institutue Lanfranco et al. 256p. (Orig., Ger.). 1980. pap. 3.95 (ISBN 0-914766-53-8, 0528). Illum Way Pub.

Spiritus Mundi: Essays on Literature, Myth, & Society. Northrop Frye. LC 76-12364. (Midland Bks: NO. 289). 320p. 1976. 20.00x (ISBN 0-253-35432-3); pap. 7.95x (ISBN 0-253-20289-2). Ind U Pr.

Spiro Agnew: Controversial Vice-President of the Nixon Administration. Gerald Kurland. Ed. by D. Steve Rahmas. LC 72-190234. (Outstanding Personalities Ser: No. 16). 32p. (Orig.). (gr. 7-12). 1972. PLB 3.75 incl. catalog cards (ISBN 0-87157-516-7); pap. 2.50 vinyl laminated covers (ISBN 0-87157-016-5). SamHar Pr.

Spiro Mound, Vol. 14. Henry W. Hamilton & Charles C. Willoughby. Ed. by Carl H. Chapman. (Missouri Archaeologist). (Illus.). 276p. 1981. pap. 10.00 (ISBN 0-943414-06-7). MO Arch Soc.

Spiro Mound Copper. Henry Hamilton et al. Ed. by Carl H. Chapman. LC 74-31740. (Memoir Ser.: No. 11). (Illus.). 212p. (Orig.). 1974. pap. 5.00 (ISBN 0-943414-27-X). MO Arch Soc.

Spirtual Dimensions of Healing Addictions. Donna Cunningham & Andrew Ramer. Date not set. price not set. Cassandra Pr.

Spirulina. Jack J. Challem. (Good Health Guide Ser.). 1982. pap. 1.95 (ISBN 0-87983-262-2). Keats.

Spirulina Cookbook: Recipes for Rejuvenating the Body. Sonia Beasley. LC 81-40027. (Illus.). 192p. (Orig.). 1981. pap. 6.95 (ISBN 0-916438-39-2). Univ of Trees.

Spirulina Diet. Saundra Howard. 192p. 1982. 12.00 (ISBN 0-8184-0335-7). Lyle Stuart.

Spirulina: Food for a Hungry World; A Pioneer's Story in Aquaculture. Hiroshi Nakamura. Ed. by Christopher Hills. Tr. by Robert Wargo from Japanese. LC 82-4816. (Illus.). 224p. (Orig.). 1982. pap. 10.95 (ISBN 0-916438-47-3). Univ of Trees.

Spit Bug Who Couldn't Spit. Penny Pollock. (Illus.). 48p. 1982. PLB 6.99 (ISBN 0-399-61152-5, Putnam). Putnam Pub Group.

Spit in the Ocean: A Jake Samson Mystery. Shelley Singer. 208p. 1987. 14.95 (ISBN 0-312-00685-3). St Martin.

Spit Nolan. Bill Naughton. (Classic Short Stories Ser.). 1987. lib. bdg. 10.45 (ISBN 0-88682-122-3). Creative Ed.

Spit-Shine Syndrome: Organizational Irrationality in the American Field Army. Christopher Bassford. LC 87-37551. (Contributions in Military Studies: No. 76). 192p. 1988. lib. bdg. 37.95 (ISBN 0-313-26215-2, BFP/). Greenwood.

Spitalfields Acts, 1818-28. LC 72-2544. (British Labour Struggles Before 1850 Ser). (7 pamphlets). 1972. 24.50 (ISBN 0-405-04436-4). Ayer Co Pubs.

Spitalfields & Mile End New Town. P. A. Bezodis. LC 74-6547. (London County Council. Survey of London: No. 27). Repr. of 1957 ed. 74.50 (ISBN 0-404-51677-7). AMS Pr.

Spitfire. Barbara Phillips. (Orig.). 1981. pap. 1.95 (ISBN 0-8439-8044-3, Tiara Bks). Leisure NY.

Spitfire: A Documentary History. Alfred Price. (Illus.). 1979. 5.95 (ISBN 0-684-16060-9, ScribT). Scribner.

Spitfire: A Living Legend. J. Flack. (Color Library Ser.). (Illus.). 128p. 1985. pap. 12.95 (ISBN 0-85045-619-3, Pub. by Osprey England). Motorbooks Intl.

Spitfire: A Test Pilot's Story. Jeffrey Quill. (Illus.). 332p. 1984. 19.95 (ISBN 0-295-96152-X). U of Wash Pr.

Spitfire in Action. Jerry Scutts. (Aircraft in Action Ser.). (Illus.). 1984. pap. 5.95 (ISBN 0-89747-092-3, 1039). Squad Sig Pubns.

Spits Bars. Schwartz. 63.95 (ISBN 0-317-64285-5). Van Nos Reinhold.

Spitting Images. Sean Kelly. (Spitting Image Productions Ser.). (Illus.). 1987. 14.95 (ISBN 0-15-184768-1, Harv); pap. 9.95 (ISBN 0-15-684819-8). HarBraceJ.

Splanchnologia - Organa sensuum et integumentum commune - Cor et lien see Atlas of Systematic Human Anatomy.

Splash. Teddy Teller. 1983. pap. 1.75 (ISBN 0-912963-00-X). Eldridge Pub.

Splash! All about Baths. Susan K. Buxbaum & Rita G. Gelman. (Illus.). 32p. (ps-3). 1987. 14.95 (ISBN 0-316-30726-2). Little.

Splash & Trickle. Ivah Green. LC 68-56818. (Illus.). 32p. (gr. 2-3). 1968. PLB 9.95 (ISBN 0-87783-037-1); pap. 3.94 deluxe ed. (ISBN 0-87783-109-2); cassette o.s.i. 7.94x (ISBN 0-87783-226-9). Oddo.

Splash & Trickle. Ivah Green. (Illus.). (gr. 2-3). 1978. pap. 1.25 (ISBN 0-89508-062-1). Rainbow Bks.

Splash of Fall. Susanne Glover & Georgeann Grewe. (Illus.). 128p. (gr. 2-5). 1987. pap. 8.95 (ISBN 0-86653-410-5). Good Apple.

Splash of Red. Antonia Fraser. 1984. pap. 3.50 (ISBN 0-393-30213-X). Norton.

Splash of Spring. Susanne Glover & Georgeann Grewe. (Illus.). 128p. (gr. 2-5). 1987. pap. 8.95 (ISBN 0-86653-412-1). Good Apple.

Splash of Winter. Suzanne Glover & Georgeann Grewe. (Illus.). 128p. (gr. 2-5). 1987. pap. 8.95 (ISBN 0-86653-411-3). Good Apple.

Splash, Splash. Arthur Dorros. LC 87-47541. (Illus.). 12p. (ps-1). 1987. 2.95 (ISBN 0-694-00188-0, Crowell Jr Bks). HarpJ.

Splash the Dolphin. Cynthia Overbeck. Tr. by Dyan Hammarberg from Fr. LC 76-1218. (Animal Friends Bks). (Illus.). 24p. (gr. k-4). 1976. PLB 5.95 (ISBN 0-87614-061-4). Carolrhoda Bks.

Splash: YMCA Progressive Swimming. Ed. by YMCA of the U. S. A. Staff. (Illus., Orig.). (gr. 1-5). 1986. pap. text ed. 5.00x (ISBN 0-87322-058-7, LYMC4733). Human Kinetics.

Splashman. Lydia Weaver. 1985. pap. 2.50 (ISBN 0-451-14020-6, Sig Vista). NAL.

Splatter Times Anthology. Donald Farmer. 176p. (Orig.). Date not set. pap. 14.95 (ISBN 0-938782-09-6). Fantaco.

Spleen: Structure, Function, Pathology, Clinical Aspects, Therapy. Ed. by K. Lennert & D. Harms. (Illus.). 1970. 103.30 (ISBN 0-387-04969-X). Springer-Verlag.

Splendeur Divine: Introduction a L'etude De la Mentalite Mesopotamienne. Elena Cassin. (Civilisations et Societes: No. 8). pap. 18.40x (ISBN 90-2796-077-1). Mouton.

Splendeurs et Miseres des Courtisanes. Honore De Balzac. (Coll. GF). pap. 9.95 (ISBN 0-685-34094-5). French & Eur.

Splendid Art of Decorating Eggs. Rosemary Disney. 192p. 1986. pap. 5.95 (ISBN 0-486-25030-X). Dover.

Splendid Art of Opera: A Concise History. Ethan Mordden. (Illus.). 448p. 1980. 19.95 (ISBN 0-416-00731-7, NO.0152). Routledge Chapman & Hall.

Splendid Century. W. H. Lewis. LC 53-9235. 1954. pap. 9.95 (ISBN 0-688-06009-9). Morrow.

Splendid Ceremonies: State Entries & Royal Funerals in the Low Countries, 1515-1791--A Bibliography. John Landwehr. (Illus.). 350p. 1971. text ed. 87.50x (ISBN 0-317-55881-1, Pub. by B De Graaf Netherlands). Coronet Bks.

Splendid Chaos. John Shirley. LC 87-30796. 368p. 1988. 17.95 (ISBN 0-531-15065-8). Watts.

Splendid Encounters: The Thought & Conduct of Diplomacy. Dorothy V. Jones. LC 84-180. (Illus.). x, 132p. 1984. pap. 10.00 (ISBN 0-226-40618-0). U of Chicago Pr.

Splendid Executioner. Timothy Downey. 1987. 17.95 (ISBN 0-525-24486-7). Dutton.

Splendid Executioner. Timothy Downey. Date not set. pap. 2.95 (ISBN 0-317-67706-3, Ivy Bks). Ballantine.

Splendid Failure: Hart Crane & the Making of The Bridge. Edward J. Brunner. LC 84-2690. 296p. 1985. 22.95 (ISBN 0-252-01094-9). U of Ill Pr.

Splendid Folly. Margaret Pedler. 1976. lib. bdg. 13.75x (ISBN 0-89968-218-9). Lightyear.

Splendid Hotel. Gilbert Sorrentino. LC 73-78786. 64p. 1973. signed, ltd. ed 25.00 (ISBN 0-8112-0514-2). New Directions.

Splendid Idle Forties. Gertrude F. Atherton. LC 68-20004. (Americans in Fiction Ser.). (Illus.). lib. bdg. 19.50 (ISBN 0-8398-0069-X); pap. text ed. 7.95x (ISBN 0-89197-947-6). Irvington.

Splendid Indiscretion. Elizabeth Mansfield. 1987. pap. 2.50 (ISBN 0-515-09263-0). Jove Pubns.

Splendid Innovations: The World of French Design 1650-1785. Henry Joyce. 48p. 1986. pap. text ed. 5.00 (ISBN 0-9606718-3-8). Hyde Collect.

Splendid Isolation: The Curious History of South American Mammals. George G. Simpson. LC 79-17630. (Illus.). 275p. 1983. pap. 11.95x (ISBN 0-300-03094-0, Y-472). Yale U Pr.

Splendid Outcast: Beryl Markham's African Stories. Beryl Markham. LC 87-60876. 160p. 1987. 14.95 (ISBN 0-86547-301-3). N Point Pr.

Splendid Outcast: Beryl Markham's African Stories. Beryl Markham. 1988. pap. 7.50 (ISBN 0-440-50030-3, LE). Dell.

Splendid Risk. Bernard Mullahy. LC 81-40445. 256p. 1982. text ed. 12.95 (ISBN 0-268-01705-0). U of Notre Dame Pr.

Splendid Soft Toy Book. rev. ed. Erna Rath. Ed. by Charlotte de la Bedoyere. (Illus.). 128p. 1984. 16.94 (ISBN 0-85532-537-2). Pathway Bk Serv.

Splendid Spur. Arthur T. Quiller-Couch. 304p. 1983. pap. 7.50 (ISBN 0-907746-25-X, Pub. by A Mott Ltd). Longwood Pub Group.

Splendid Vista. Esther L. Vogt. 184p. 1989. pap. 5.95 (ISBN 0-8361-3485-0). Herald Pr.

Splendid Voyage: An Introduction to New Sciences & New Technologies. Pangratios Papacosta. (Frontiers of Science Ser.). (Illus.). 256p. 1987. pap. 10.95 (ISBN 0-13-835380-8). P-H.

Splendid Wayfaring: The Exploits & Adventures of Jedediah Smith & the Ashley-Henry Men, 1822-1831. John G. Neihardt. LC 71-116054. (Illus.). xii, 290p. 1970. pap. 5.25 (ISBN 0-8032-5723-6, BB 525, Bison). U of Nebr Pr.

Splendid Yearning. Myra Rowe. 432p. (Orig.). Date not set. pap. 3.95 (ISBN 0-446-35166-0). Warner Bks.

Splendide-Hotel. Gilbert Sorrentino. LC 84-3228. 64p. 1984. 12.00 (ISBN 0-916583-00-7); pap. 3.95 (ISBN 0-916583-01-5). Dalkey Arch.

Splendini of the Apes. Scott Pinzon. 208p. 1984. pap. 5.95 (ISBN 0-310-45611-8, 18356P). Zondervan.

Splendor of Egypt. Ed. by Dickran Kouymjian & Angele Kouymjian. LC 75-2270. (Illus.). 230p. 1977. deluxe ed. 500.00x (ISBN 0-88206-008-2). Caravan Bks.

Splendor of God. Honore W. Morrow. 21.95 (ISBN 0-89190-310-0, Pub. by Am Repr). Amereon Ltd.

Splendor of His Way. Stephen Kaung. Tr. by Lily Hsu from Eng. (Chinese.). 1984. pap. write for info. (ISBN 0-941598-14-4). Living Spring Pubns.

Splendor of His Ways. Stephen Kaung. Ed. by Herbert L. Fader. 1974. 5.00 (ISBN 0-935008-42-X); pap. 3.25 (ISBN 0-935008-43-8). Christian Fellow Pubs.

Splendor of Lebanon. Ed. by Marwan R. Buheiry & Leila G. Buheiry. LC 77-13169. 1977. deluxe ed. 500.00x (ISBN 0-88206-018-X). Caravan Bks.

Splendor of Life. Faye R. Trent. LC 85-51411. 90p. 1985. 5.95 (ISBN 0-938232-79-7, Dist. by Baker & Taylor Co.). Winston-Derek.

Splendor of Longing in the Tale of Genji. Norma Field. 304p. 1987. text ed. 45.00 (ISBN 0-691-06691-4); pap. text ed. 12.50 (ISBN 0-691-01436-1). Princeton U Pr.

Splendor of Persian Carpets. Erwin Gans-Ruedin. LC 78-57908. (Illus.). 552p. 1978. 100.00 (ISBN 0-8478-0179-9). Rizzoli Intl.

Splendor of the Church. De Lubac Henri. LC 86-82080. 382p. 1986. pap. 12.95 (ISBN 0-89870-120-1). Ignatius Pr.

Splendor of the Faith: Meditations on the Credo of the People of God. Anton Morgenroth. 206p. (Orig.). 1983. pap. 7.95 (ISBN 0-931888-14-X). Christendom Coll Pr.

Splendor of the Holy Land. Ed. by Marwan Buhiery. LC 77-5503. 1979. deluxe ed. 500.00x (ISBN 0-88206-019-8). Caravan Bks.

Splendor of the Psalms: A Photographic Meditation. Herb Montgomery & Mary Montgomery. LC 77-78261. (Books to Encourage & Inspire). (Illus.). 1977. pap. 6.95 (ISBN 0-03-022956-1, HarpR). Har-Row.

Splendor of Turkish Weaving: An Exhibition of Silks & Carpets of the 13th-18th Centuries. Louise W. Mackie. (Illus.). 86p. 1973. 8.00 (ISBN 0-87405-002-2). Textile Mus.

Splendor Solis: A.D. 1582. Solomon Trismosin. (Illus.). 104p. 1976. 12.50 (ISBN 0-911662-57-X). Yoga.

Splendora. Edward Swift. 264p. 1988. pap. 6.95 (ISBN 0-8216-2001-0). Lyle Stuart.

Splendors of the Past: Lost Cities of the Ancient World. LC 80-7827. (Illus.). 296p. 1981. 19.95 (ISBN 0-87044-358-5). Natl Geog.

Splendour of Tipharet. rev. ed. Omraam M. Aivanhov. (Complete Works: Vol. 10). (Illus.). 253p. (Orig.). 1988. pap. 12.95 (ISBN 2-85566-421-7, Prosveta France). Prosveta USA.

Splendours of Kerala. Ronald Bernier et al. LC 80-901927. (Illus.). 148p. 1979. 32.50 (ISBN 0-89684-456-0). Orient Bk Dist.

Splendours of Tamilnadu. 1981. 35.00x (ISBN 0-8364-0762-8, Pub. by Marg India). South Asia Bks.

Splendours of the Gonzaga. David Chambers & Jane Martineau. (Illus.). 360p. (Orig.). 1984. pap. 25.00 (ISBN 0-317-30092-X, Pub. by Victoria & Albert Mus UK). Faber & Faber.

Splendours of the Raj: British Architecture in India 1660-1947. Philip Davies. (Illus.). 272p. 1988. pap. 10.95 (ISBN 0-14-009247-1). Penguin.

Splendours of the Vijayanagara. 1981. 30.00x (ISBN 0-8364-0792-X, Pub. by Marg India). South Asia Bks.

Splicing Handbook. Barbara Merry. (Illus.). 112p. 1987. pap. 9.95 (ISBN 0-87742-952-9). Intl Marine.

Splicing of Precast Prestressed Concrete Piles: Pt. 1-Review & Performance of Splices, Pt. 2-Tests & Analysis of Cement-Dowel Splice. (PCI Journal Reprints Ser.). 56p. pap. 8.00 (ISBN 0-686-40067-4, JR149). Prestressed Concrete.

Splicing Wire & Fiber Rope. Raoul Graumont & John Hensel. LC 45-3379. (Illus.). 128p. 1945. pap. 6.00 (ISBN 0-87033-118-3). Cornell Maritime.

Spline Functions. Ed. by K. Bohmer et al. (Lectures in Mathematics: Vol. 501). 1976. pap. 23.00 (ISBN 0-387-07543-7). Springer-Verlag.

Spline Functions & Approximation Theory. Ed. by A. Meir. A. Sharma. (International Series of Numerical Mathematics: No. 21). 386p. 1973. 54.95x (ISBN 0-8176-0670-X). Birkhauser.

Spline Functions: Basic Theory. Larry L. Schumaker. LC 80-14448. (Pure & Applied Mathematics Ser.). 553p. 1981. 62.95x (ISBN 0-471-76475-2, Pub. by Wiley Interscience). Wiley.

Spline Smoothing & Nonparametric Regressions. Eubank. (Statistical Textbooks Monographs). 456p. 1987. 89.75 (ISBN 0-8247-7869-3). Dekker.

Splines & Variational Methods. P. M. Prenter. LC 75-4689. (Pure & Applied Mathematics Ser.). 323p. 1975. 46.00x (ISBN 0-471-69660-9, Pub. by Wiley-Interscience). Wiley.

Splint Woven Basketry. Robin T. Daugherty. LC 86-80913. (Illus.). 168p. 1986. pap. 15.00 (ISBN 0-934026-22-X). Interweave.

Splinter of the Mind's Eye. Alan D. Foster. pap. 2.50 (ISBN 0-345-32023-9, Del Rey). Ballantine.

Splintered Eye. Beth S. Patric. LC 87-12192. 1987. 15.95 (ISBN 0-88282-031-1). New Horizon NJ.

Splintered Light: Logos & Language in Tolkien's World. Verlyn Flieger. LC 83-14204. Repr. of 1983 ed. 47.30 (2027542). Bks Demand UMI.

Splintered Party: National Liberalism in Hessen & the Reich, 1867-1918. Dan S. White. LC 75-23213. 445p. 1976. 24.50x (ISBN 0-674-83320-1). Harvard U Pr.

Splinters & Other Shortness Bids. Max Hardy. 1987. pap. 6.95 (ISBN 0-939460-34-3). M Hardy.

Splinters from the Past: Discovering History in Old Houses. Alex D. Fowler. Ed. by Lucy Meyer & Anne Adams. (Illus.). 208p. 1984. 15.00 (ISBN 0-910301-08-5). M C H S.

Splinters of Bone. Tr. by B. M. Bennani. LC 74-25797. Orig. Title: Darweesh. 1974. 2.95 (ISBN 0-912678-17-8). Greenfld Rev Pr.

Splinters of Light. Eric Auer. LC 75-46407. 56p. 1977. pap. 5.00x (ISBN 0-940580-00-4). Green River.

Splinters on the Wind. Rodney Reinhart. (Illus.). 1985. 3.00 (ISBN 0-931081-01-7). Operation DOME.

Splinting in Hand Therapy. Erik Moberg & Carl-Goren Hagert. (Illus.). 88p. 1984. pap. text ed. 29.95 (ISBN 0-86577-106-5). Thieme Med Pubs.

Splinting of Burn Patients. photocopy ed. K. Von Prince & M. H. Yeakel. (Illus.). 136p. 1974. 23.00 (ISBN 0-398-03198-3). C C Thomas.

Splinting the Burn Patient. Carol Walters. 1987. 18.50 (ISBN 0-943596-08-4). Ramsco Pub.

Splish, Splash! Yvonne Hooker. (Poke-&-Look Books). (Illus.). (ps-1). 1983. 6.95 (ISBN 0-448-01454-8, G&D). Putnam Pub Group.

Split. Richard Stark. (Parker Mysteries Ser.). 160p. 1985. 13.95 (ISBN 0-8052-8229-7, Pub. by Allison & Busby England). Schocken.

Split & Dalmatia. Berlitz Editors. (Travel Guides Ser.). 1977. pap. 4.95 (ISBN 0-317-12275-4, Berlitz). Macmillan.

Split Ends. Jill E. Stevens. LC 81-65120. (Illus.). 1982. 9.50 (ISBN 0-9605818-1-2); pap. 5.95 (ISBN 0-9605818-0-4). John Alden Bks.

Split Image. (Executioner Ser.: No. 102). Date not set. pap. 2.25 (ISBN 0-317-63970-6, Pub. by Worldwide). Harlequin Bks.

Split Image: Male & Female after God's Likeness. Anne Atkins. 256p. (Orig.). 1987. pap. 8.95 (ISBN 0-8028-0250-8). Eerdmans.

Split Images. Elmore Leonard. 288p. 1983. pap. 3.95 (ISBN 0-380-63107-5). Avon.

Split Images. Elmore Leonard. (Large Print Bks (General Ser.)). 362p. 1986. lib. bdg. 16.95 (ISBN 0-8161-3949-0). G K Hall.

Split in a Predominate Party: The Indian National Congress in 1969. Mahendra P. Singh. 1981. 24.00x (ISBN 0-8364-0721-0, Pub. by Abhinav India). South Asia Bks.

Split in Two. Michael Daniels. 8.00 (ISBN 0-89253-680-2). Ind-US Inc.

Split Infinitive see Metaphor.

Split Infinitive & a System of Clauses see Doughty's English.

Split Infinity. Piers Anthony. 368p. 1981. pap. 3.95 (ISBN 0-345-35491-5, Del Rey). Ballantine.

Split Minds - Split Brains. Ed. by Jacques Quen. LC 86-12532. 224p. 1986. 38.00x (ISBN 0-8147-6951-9). NYU Pr.

Split Pedigree Book. Russell Meerdink Company, Ltd. Research Staff. 140p. 1987. looseleaf 16.00 (ISBN 0-929346-01-7). R Meerdink Co Ltd.

Split Pedigree Book. Repr. write for info. (ISBN 0-85131-259-4, NL51, Pub. by J A Allen U K). S R Smith Sporting Bks.

Split-Ply Twining. Virginia Harvey. LC 75-4651. (Threads in Action Monographs: No. 1). (Illus.). 44p. (gr. 7 up). 1976. pap. 7.95 (ISBN 0-916658-32-5). Shuttle Craft.

Split Rock: Epoch of a Lighthouse. Stephen P. Hall. LC 77-26287. (Minn. Historic Sites Pamphlet Ser.: No. 15). (Illus.). 24p. 1978. pap. 2.95x (ISBN 0-87351-122-0). Minn Hist.

Split Second. Garry Kilworth. 240p. 1985. pap. 2.95 (ISBN 0-445-20114-2, Pub. by Popular Lib). Warner Bks.

Split Second: A Lennox Kemp Mystery. M. R. Meek. 170p. 1987. 13.95 (ISBN 0-684-18734-5). Scribner.

Split Second: The World of High-Speed Photography. Stephen Dalton. (Illus.). 144p. 1985. 21.95 (ISBN 0-88162-063-7). Salem Hse Pubs.

Split Seconds: A Remembrance. Tamara Geva. LC 83-27509. 368p. 1984. pap. 8.95 (ISBN 0-87910-006-0). Limelight Edns.

Split Self from Goethe to Broch. Peter B. Waldeck. LC 77-92576. 190p. 1979. 20.00 (ISBN 0-8387-2214-8). Bucknell U Pr.

Split Signals: Television & Politics in the Soviet Union. Ellen Mickie Wicz. (Communications & Society Ser.). 304p. 1988. 24.95 (ISBN 0-19-505463-6). Oxford U Pr.

Split Sisters. C. S. Adler. LC 85-15411. (Illus.). 161p. (gr. 4-8). 1986. 10.95 (ISBN 0-02-700380-9). Macmillan.

Split Time. Charles Crawford. LC 87-184. (Charlotte Zolotow Bks.). 224p. (YA) (gr. 7 up). 1987. 12.95i (ISBN 0-06-021324-8); PLB 12.89 (ISBN 0-06-021380-9). HarpJ.

Split Vision: Arab Portrayal in the American Media. Ed. by Edmund Ghareeb. LC 77-90775. 171p. 1977. pap. 8.00 (ISBN 0-934484-11-2). Inst Mid East & North Africa.

Split Vision: The Portrayal of Arabs in the American Media. rev & exp. ed. Ed. by Edmund Ghareeb. LC 83-71909. 397p. 1983. 12.95 (ISBN 0-943182-00-X); pap. 6.95 (ISBN 0-943182-01-8). Am-Arab Affairs.

Splitting. Jennifer Sarasin. (Cheerleaders Ser.: No. 6). 192p. (Orig.). (gr. 7 up). 1985. pap. 2.50 (ISBN 0-590-40840-2). Scholastic Inc.

Splitting & Projective Identification. James S. Grotstein. LC 84-45724. 256p. 1985. 27.50x (ISBN 0-87668-756-7). Aronson.

Splitting Firewood. David Tresemer. (Illus.). 160p. (Orig.). 1981. pap. 6.95 (ISBN 0-938670-01-8). By Hand & Foot.

Splitting in Topological Groups. Karl H. Hofmann & Paul S. Mostert. LC 52-42839. (Memoirs: No. 43). 82p. 1972. pap. 14.00 (ISBN 0-8218-1243-2, MEMO-43). Am Math.

Splitting of a Stone. Ronald Montgomery. 72p. 1988. 7.95 (ISBN 0-8062-3195-5). Carlton.

Splitting of Terms in Crystals. Hans A. Bethe. LC 58-2296. (Translated from Annals of Physics Ser.: Vol. 3). (Illus.). pap. 20.00 (ISBN 0-317-09920-5, 2003370). Bks Demand UMI.

Splitting the Mind: An Experimental Study of Normal Men see Influence of Intuition in the Acquisition of Skill.

Splitting Up. Kate Petty. Ed. by FS-Aladdin Staff. (First Timers Ser.). (Illus.). 24p. (gr. 1-3). 1988. 9.90 (ISBN 0-531-17105-1, Gloucester Pr). Watts.

Splitting Up: When Your Friend Gets a Divorce. Dandi D. Knorr. (Heart & Hand Ser.). 144p. (Orig.). 1988. pap. 7.95 (ISBN 0-87788-769-1). Shaw Pubs.

Splurge. Paul Violi. LC 81-8911. 81p. (Orig.). 1982. pap. 7.00 (ISBN 0-915342-35-9). SUN.

Spock Must Die. James Blish. (Star Trek Ser.). 128p. 1985. pap. 2.95 (ISBN 0-553-24634-8). Bantam.

Spohady Memoirs. Petro Grigorenko. Ed. by Michael Smyk. Tr. by Dmytro Kyslycia from Rus. LC 84-51852. Orig. Title: Ukranian. 751p. 1984. 30.00 (ISBN 0-912601-01-9). Ukrainian News.

Spoil of Office. Hamlin Garland. 1988. Repr. lib. bdg. 75.00x. Am Biog Serv.

Spoil of Office see Collected Works.

Spoilage of Tropical Fish & Product Development. A. Reilly. (FAO Fisheries Report: No. 317). 474p. 1986. pap. text ed. 35.00 (ISBN 92-5-102339-5, F2877, FAO). UNIPUB.

Spoiled System: A Call For Civil Service Reform. Robert G. Vaughn. 360p. 1975. 12.95 (ISBN 0-686-36544-5). Ctr Responsive Law.

Spoiler. Domenic Stansberry. Ed. by Joyce Johnson & Upton B Brady. 288p. 1987. 15.95 (ISBN 0-87113-075-0). Atlantic Monthly.

Spoilers. Rex E. Beach. LC 71-96874. (Illus.). 324p. Repr. of 1906 ed. lib. bdg. 9.25 (ISBN 0-8398-0157-2). Irvington.

Spoilers. Rex E. Beach. LC 76-144869. (Illus.). 323p. Repr. of 1905 ed. 10.00x (ISBN 0-403-00856-5). Scholarly.

Spoilers. Matt Braun. 224p. (Orig.). 1981. pap. 1.95 (ISBN 0-671-82034-6). PB.

Spoilers. David Hooks. Ed. by Jim Connor. 400p. 1988. pap. 3.95 (ISBN 0-7701-0872-5). Paperjacks US.

Spoilers of the Sea. facsimile ed. John P. Cranwell. LC 78-93331. (Essay Index Reprint Ser.). 1941. 27.50 (ISBN 0-8369-1563-1). Ayer Co Pubs.

Spoils of August. Barbara L. Greenberg. LC 73-15012. (Wesleyan Poetry Program: No. 71). 72p. 1974. 17.00x (ISBN 0-8195-2071-3); pap. 8.95 (ISBN 0-8195-1071-8). Wesleyan U Pr.

Spoils of Poynton. Henry James. Bd. with London Life; Chaperon. LC 78-158789. (Novels & Tales of Henry James: Vol. 10). xxi, 499p. Repr. of 1908 ed. 37.50x (ISBN 0-678-02810-9). Kelley.

Spoils of Poynton. Henry James. 1977. pap. 3.95 (ISBN 0-14-001922-7). Penguin.

Spoils of Poynton. Henry James. Ed. by Bernard Richards. (World's Classics Ser.). 1982. pap. 3.95 (ISBN 0-19-281605-5). Oxford U Pr.

Spoils of Poynton. Henry James. Ed. & intro. by David Lodge. 254p. 1988. pap. 3.95 (ISBN 0-14-043288-4). Penguin.

Spoils of War. Thomas Fleming. LC 84-18270. 528p. 1985. 18.95 (ISBN 0-399-12968-5, Putnam). Putnam Pub Group.

Spoils of War. Thomas Fleming. 640p. 1986. pap. 4.50 (ISBN 0-380-70065-4). Avon.

Spoils of War. Peter McCurtin. (Soldier of Fortune Ser.: No. 3). 192p. 1982. pap. 2.25 (ISBN 0-505-51779-5, Pub. by Tower Bks). Leisure NY.

Spoils System in New York. LC 73-19191. (Politics & People Ser.). 187p. 1974. Repr. 12.00x (ISBN 0-405-05900-0). Ayer Co Pubs.

Spokane Country Homestead. Henry L. Reimers. 110p. 1981. pap. 5.95 (ISBN 0-87770-244-6). Ye Galleon.

Spokane Falls Illustrated. Harry H. Hook & Francis J. Maguire. (Illus.). 62p. 1984. 4.95. Ye Galleon.

Spokane Indians: Children of the Sun. Robert H. Ruby & John A. Brown. LC 79-108797. (Civilization of the American Indian Ser.: Vol. 104). (Illus.). 346p. 1982. pap. 11.95 (ISBN 0-8061-1757-5). U of Okla Pr.

Spokane Light Cookbook. Daniel J. Petek. (Illus.). 144p. (Orig.). 1987. pap. 5.95 (ISBN 0-9615201-4-0). BCG Ltd.

Spokane Sketchbook. Roland Colliander et al. LC 73-22207. (Illus.). 96p. 1974. 12.95 (ISBN 0-295-95326-8). U of Wash Pr.

Spokane Style Cookbook. Daniel J. Petek. (Illus.). 72p. (Orig.). 1985. pap. 4.95 (ISBN 0-9615201-0-8). BCG Ltd.

Spokane: The City & the People. Mike Schmeltzer. (Illus., Orig.). 1988. pap. 13.95 (ISBN 0-938314-53-X). Am Geog Pub.

Spokane Too! Cookbook. Daniel J. Petek. (Illus.). 120p. (Orig.). 1986. pap. 4.95 (ISBN 0-9615201-3-2). BCG Ltd.

Spokane's Street Railways: An Illustrated History. Charles V. Mutschler & Clyde L Parent. 208p. (Orig.). 1987. 30.00 (ISBN 0-943181-01-1). IERHS.

Spoke. Hannah Weiner. LC 83-40580. 115p. (Orig.). 1984. 6.95 (ISBN 0-940650-26-6). Sun & Moon CA.

Spoken Albanian. Leonard Newmark et al. LC 79-56549. 348p. 1980. pap. 10.00x (ISBN 0-87950-005-0); 6 dual track cassettes 65.00x (ISBN 0-87950-007-7); Bk. & cassettes 70.00x (ISBN 0-87950-008-5). Spoken Lang Serv.

Spoken Amharic, Bk. 1, Units 1-50. S. Obolensky et al. 500p. (Amharic.). 1980. Bk. 1 & cassette 1 155.00x (ISBN 0-87950-654-7). Spoken Lang Serv.

Spoken Amharic, Book 2, Units Fifty-One to Sixty. S. Obolensky et al. (Spoken Language Ser.). 500p. (Amharic.). 1980. Sold only with cassettes. pap. text ed. 15.00x (ISBN 0-87950-651-2); cassettes 5 dual track 60.00x (ISBN 0-87950-653-9); book 2 & cassettes 2 75.00x (ISBN 0-87950-655-5); books 1 & 2 & cassettes 1 & 2 230.00x (ISBN 0-87950-656-3). Spoken Lang Serv.

Spoken Amoy Hokkien: Vocabulary Units 1-30. Nicholas C. Bodman. (Spoken Language Ser.). 630p. 1987. pap. text ed. 40.00x (ISBN 0-87950-450-1); cassettes, 16 dual track 120.00x (ISBN 0-87950-451-X); bk. & cassettes combined 160.00x (ISBN 0-87950-452-8). Spoken Lang Serv.

Spoken & Written Hindi. Gordon H. Fairbanks & Bal G. Misra. 504p. 1966. 29.50x (ISBN 0-8014-0123-2). Cornell U Pr.

Spoken & Written Language. Deborah Tannen. Ed. by Roy O. Freedle. LC 81-12865. (Advances in Discourse Processes Ser.: Vol. 9). 300p. (Orig.). 1982. text ed. 49.50x (ISBN 0-89391-094-5); pap. 29.50 (ISBN 0-89391-099-6). Ablex Pub.

Spoken Arabic (Iraqi) Merrill Y. Van Wagoner. LC 75-11338. (Spoken Language Ser.). 294p. (Prog. Bk.). 1975. pap. 10.00x (ISBN 0-87950-010-7). cassettes six dual track 65.00x (ISBN 0-87950-016-6); cassettes with course-bk. 75.00x (ISBN 0-87950-017-4). Spoken Lang Serv.

Spoken Arabic of Cairo. Maurice Salib. 1985. pap. 25.00x (ISBN 977-424-054-5, Pub. by Am Univ Cairo Pr). Columbia U Pr.

Spoken Arabic of the Arabian Gulf. Librarie Du Liban. 1976. pap. 4.50x (ISBN 0-86685-042-2). Intl Bk Ctr.

Spoken Arabic (Saudi) Merrill Y. Van Wagoner et al. LC 76-17389. (Spoken Language Ser.). 160p. (Prog. Bk.). 1979. pap. 8.00x (ISBN 0-87950-410-2); cassettes 5 dual track 60.00x (ISBN 0-87950-411-0); cassettes with course-bk 65.00x (ISBN 0-87950-412-9). Spoken Lang Serv.

Spoken Arabic-Self Taught. A. M. Ashiurakis. 118p. 1985. pap. 35.00x (ISBN 1-85077-090-5, Pub. by Darf Pubs Ltd). State Mutual Bk.

Spoken Arabic: The Conversational Language of the Near East. Emile Karam. 130p. 1982. 10.00x (ISBN 0-686-47156-3); book & cassette 20.00 (ISBN 0-86685-327-8). Intl Bk Ctr.

Spoken Arabic: The Language of Lebanon. Emile Karam. LC 82-5513. 1982. pap. 8.95 (ISBN 0-932506-18-6); pap. 16.50 with cassette (90 min.). St Bedes Pubns.

Spoken Bengali: Standard, East Bengal. Jack A. Dabbs. LC 66-63243. 1966. 5.00 (ISBN 0-911494-03-0). Dabbs.

Spoken Bulgarian. Carleton T. Hodge. 493p. 1980. pap. text ed. 15.00x (ISBN 0-87950-658-X); cassettes 19 dual track 120.00x (ISBN 0-87950-660-1); book & cassettes 135.00x (ISBN 0-87950-662-8). Spoken Lang Serv.

Spoken Burmese. William S. Cornyn. (Spoken Language Ser.). 165p. 1979. pap. 10.00x Bk. 1, Units 1-12 (ISBN 0-87950-020-4); 6 dual track cassettes for bk. 1 65.00x (ISBN 0-87950-025-5); cassettes & bk. 1 75.00x (ISBN 0-87950-026-3); pap. 10.00x Bk. 2, Units 13-30 (ISBN 0-87950-021-2). Spoken Lang Serv.

Spoken by the Spirit. Ralph W. Harris. LC 73-87106. 128p. 1973. pap. 2.50 (ISBN 0-88243-725-9, 02-0725). Gospel Pub.

Spoken Cambodian. F. E. Huffman. (Spoken Lang. Ser.). 464p. 1985. pap. 20.00x (ISBN 0-317-27409-0); 14 cassettes 95.00x; book & cassettes 115.00x (ISBN 0-87950-473-0). Spoken Lang Serv.

Spoken Cantonese, Bk I. Elisabeth L. Boyle & Pauline N. Delbridge. 410p. 1980. pap. 20.00x (ISBN 0-87950-675-X); cassettes I 15 dual track 100.00x (ISBN 0-87950-677-6); book I & cassettes I 115.00x (ISBN 0-87950-679-2). Spoken Lang Serv.

Spoken Cantonese, Bk. II. Elisabeth L. Boyle & Pauline N. Delbridge. 410p. 1980. pap. 15.00x (ISBN 0-87950-676-8); cassettes II 15 dual track 100.00x (ISBN 0-87950-678-4); bk. II & cassettes II 115.00x; bks. I & II & cassettes I & II 230.00x (ISBN 0-87950-681-4). Spoken Lang Serv.

Spoken Chamorro: With Gramatical Notes & Glossary. 2nd ed. Donald Topping. LC 80-14596. (PALI Language Texts: Micronesia). 376p. (Orig.). 1980. pap. text ed. 11.00x (ISBN 0-8248-0417-1). UH Pr.

Spoken Chinese. Charles F. Hockett. LC 76-767. (Spoken Language Ser.). 1976. pap. 10.00x Bk. 1, Units 1-12, 268 p. (ISBN 0-87950-031-X); 6 12-inch LP records 50.00x (ISBN 0-87950-034-4); bk. 1 & records 60.00x (ISBN 0-87950-035-2); cassettes six dual track 65.00x (ISBN 0-87950-036-0); bk. 1 & cassettes 75.00x (ISBN 0-87950-037-9); pap. 15.00x Bk. 2, Units 13-30, 393 p. (ISBN 0-87950-032-8). Spoken Lang Serv.

Spoken Chinese Nine Hundred, 2 bks. Date not set. Set. incl. 2 tapes 49.95 (SPCHNI). China Bks.

Spoken Cree: West Coast of James Bay. C. Douglas Ellis. vi, 715p. 1983. pap. 21.00x (ISBN 0-88864-044-7, Pub. by Univ of Alta Pr Canada). U of Nebr Pr.

Spoken Danish. Jeannette Dearden & Karin Stig-Nielsen. bk. I, units 1-12, 1976 341p. 10.00x (ISBN 0-87950-044-1); bk. II, units 13-30, 1980 567 p. 15.00x (ISBN 0-87950-045-X); bk. I & cassettes 75.00x (ISBN 0-87950-051-4); cassettes, 6 dual track 65.00x (ISBN 0-87950-050-6). Spoken Lang Serv.

Spoken Dutch. Leonard Bloomfield. LC 75-15107. (Spoken Language Ser.). 266p. (Prog. Bk.). 1975. pap. 10.00x (ISBN 0-87950-054-9); cassettes 5 dual track 65.00x (ISBN 0-87950-060-3); cassettes with course-bk. 75.00x (ISBN 0-87950-061-1). Spoken Lang Serv.

Spoken East Armenian. Gordon H. Fairbanks & Earl W. Stevick. LC 75-15932. (Spoken Language Ser). 428p. (Prog. Bk.). 1975. pap. 15.00x (ISBN 0-87950-420-X). cassettes, six dual track 65.00x (ISBN 0-87950-421-8); course bk. with cassettes 75.00x (ISBN 0-87950-422-6). Spoken Lang Serv.

Spoken Egyptian Arabic. Samia Mehrez. 250p. (Orig.). 1985. pap. 165.00x plus 12, 1 hour audio cassettes (ISBN 0-88432-131-2, A400). J Norton Pubs.

Spoken English As a Foreign Language. William E. Welmers. 31p. 1979. pap. 2.50x (ISBN 0-87950-289-4). Spoken Lang Serv.

Spoken Essays (Shakespeare-the Naturalistic Theory of Hamlet) J. M. Robertson. LC 74-13254. 1973. lib. bdg. 29.00 (ISBN 0-8414-7333-1). Folcroft.

Spoken Fijian: An Intensive Course in Bauan Fijian, with Grammatical Notes & Glossary. Albert J. Schutz & Rusiate T. Komaitai. LC 76-157881. (PALI Language Texts: Melanesia Ser.). pap. 79.10 (ISBN 0-317-58205-4, 2029724). Bks Demand UMI.

Spoken Finnish. Thomas A. Sebeok. LC 74-164345. (Spoken Language Ser.). 502p. 1977. pap. 15.00x Units 1-30 (ISBN 0-87950-070-0); 3 dual track cassettes 50.00x (ISBN 0-87950-075-1); bk. & cassettes 65.00x (ISBN 0-87950-076-X). Spoken Lang Serv.

Spoken French. Francois Denoeu & R. A. Hall, Jr. LC 74-152740. (Spoken Language Ser.). 230p. 1973. pap. 10.00x Units 1-12 (ISBN 0-87950-080-8); 6 dual track cassettes 65.00x (ISBN 0-87950-085-9); bk. & cassettes 75.00x (ISBN 0-87950-086-7). Spoken Lang Serv.

Spoken French for Students & Travelers. 2nd ed. Bernard F. Uzan & Charles E. Kany. 1978. pap. text ed. 12.50 (ISBN 0-669-00878-8). Heath.

Spoken German. Renate Hiller. 1980. pap. text ed. 12.00 (ISBN 0-669-03022-8). Heath.

Spoken German. William G. Moulton & Jenni K. Moulton. LC 76-416. (Spoken Language Ser.). 290p. 1971. pap. 10.00x Units 1-12 (ISBN 0-87950-091-3); 6 dual track cassettes 65.00x (ISBN 0-87950-096-4); bk. & cassttes 75.00x (ISBN 0-87950-097-2). Spoken Lang Serv.

Spoken Greek. Henry Kahanes et al. LC 74-150404. (Spoken Language Ser.). 1976. pap. 10.00x Units 1-12, 305p. (ISBN 0-87950-100-6); 6 dual track cassttes for bk. 1 65.00x (ISBN 0-87950-105-7); pap. 20.00x Bk. 2, Units 13-30, 650p. Sold only with cassettes for bk. 2 (ISBN 0-87950-101-4); 6 dual track cassettes for bk. 2 65.00x (ISBN 0-87950-107-3); bk. 1 & cassettes 75.00x (ISBN 0-87950-106-5). bk. 2 & cassettes 85.00x (ISBN 0-87950-108-1); combined bk. 1 & 2 plus cassettes 1 & 2 160.00x (ISBN 0-87950-109-X). Spoken Lang Serv.

Spoken Hausa. J. Ronayne Cowan & Russell G. Schuh. LC 75-15184. (Spoken Language Ser). 350p. (Programmed book). 1976. pap. text ed. 10.00x (ISBN 0-87950-401-3); cassetes for units 1-12, six dual track 65.00x (ISBN 0-87950-402-1); book & cassettes for units 1-12 75.00x (ISBN 0-87950-403-X); cassettes for units 13-25 (14 hours) 100.00x (ISBN 0-87950-404-8). Spoken Lang Serv.

Spoken Hawaiian. Samuel H. Elbert. LC 77-98134. (Illus.). 266p. (Orig.). 1970. pap. text ed. 8.00x (ISBN 0-87022-216-3). UH Pr.

Spoken Hindustani. Henry Hoenigswald. LC 74-175966. (Spoken Language Ser.). 270p. (gr. 9-12). 1976. pap. 10.00x Bk. 1, Units 1-12 (1971) (ISBN 0-87950-110-3); 6 dual track cassettes 65.00x (ISBN 0-87950-115-4); bk. & cassettes 75.00x (ISBN 0-87950-116-2). Spoken Lang Serv.

Spoken History. George E. Evans. 256p. 1987. 15.95 (ISBN 0-571-14982-0). Faber & Faber.

Spoken Hungarian. Thomas A. Sebeok. LC 74-176085. (Spoken Language Ser.). 230p. (gr. 9-12). 1983. pap. 10.00x Units 1-12 (ISBN 0-87950-120-0); 6 dual track cassettes 65.00x (ISBN 0-87950-126-X); bk. & cassettes 75.00x (ISBN 0-87950-127-8). Spoken Lang Serv.

Spoken into the Void: Collected Essays by Adolf Loos, 1897-1900. Adolf Loos. Tr. by Jane O. Newman & John H. Smith. 160p. 1987. pap. 12.50 (ISBN 0-262-62057-X). MIT Pr.

Spoken Italian. Vincenzo Cioffari. LC 75-15151. (Spoken Language Ser.). 220p. (Prog. Bk.). 1976. pap. 10.00x (ISBN 0-87950-130-8). cassettes six dual track 65.00x (ISBN 0-87950-135-9); cassettes with course-bk. 75.00x (ISBN 0-87950-136-7). Spoken Lang Serv.

Spoken Italian for Students & Travelers. 2nd ed. Charles Speroni & Charles K. Kany. 1978. pap. text ed. 12.00 (ISBN 0-669-00577-0). Heath.

Spoken Japanese. Bernard Bloch & Eleanor H. Jorden. LC 74-150406. (Spoken Language Ser.). 387p. (gr. 9-12). 1975. pap. 10.00x Units 1-12 (ISBN 0-87950-140-5); 6 12-inch LP records 50.00x (ISBN 0-87950-143-X); bk. & records 60.00x (ISBN 0-87950-144-8); 6 dual track cassettes 65.00x (ISBN 0-87950-145-6); bk. & cassettes 75.00x (ISBN 0-87950-146-4). Spoken Lang Serv.

Spoken Korean. Fred Lukoff. LC 73-17223. (Spoken Language Ser.). 370p. (gr. 9-12). 1975. pap. 10.00x Bk. 1, Units 1-12 (ISBN 0-87950-150-2); pap. 15.00x Bk. 2, 305p. Units 13-30 (ISBN 0-87950-151-0); 6 dual track cassettes for bk. 1 65.00x (ISBN 0-87950-155-3); Bk. 1 & cassettes 75.00x (ISBN 0-87950-156-1). Spoken Lang Serv.

Spoken Language Tests see Language Classroom.

Spoken Malay. Isidore Dyen. Incl. Units 1-12. v, 192p. pap. 10.00x (ISBN 0-87950-160-X); Bk. 2, Units 13-30. 324p. pap. 10.00x (ISBN 0-87950-161-8); Cassettes, Six Dual Track. 65.00x (ISBN 0-87950-165-0); Cassette Course - Bk. 1 & Cassettes. pap. 75.00x (ISBN 0-87950-166-9). LC 74-176207. (Spoken Language Ser.). 192p. (Prog. Bk.). 1974. pap. 10.00x. Spoken Lang Serv.

Spoken Marshallese. Byron W. Bender. (PALI Language Texts: Micronesian). 463p. (Orig.). 1969. pap. text ed. 13.00x (ISBN 0-87022-070-5). UH Pr.

Spoken Ministry among Friends: Three Centuries of Progress & Development. Seth B. Hinshaw. (Illus.). 160p. (Orig.). 1987. pap. 7.50 (ISBN 0-942585-14-3). NC Frnds Hist Soc.

Spoken Modern Hebrew. Joseph A. Reif & Hanna Levinson. (Spoken Language Ser.). 590p. 1980. pap. 15.00x (ISBN 0-87950-683-0); cassettes, 31 dual track 180.00x (ISBN 0-87950-684-9); text & cassettes 195.00x (ISBN 0-87950-685-7). Spoken Lang Serv.

Spoken Norwegian. Einar Haugen. LC 75-15152. (Spoken Language Ser.). 312p. (gr. 9-12). 1976. pap. 10.00x Bk. 1, Units 1-12 (ISBN 0-87950-170-7); pap. 15.00x Bk. 2, 1978, Units 13-30 (ISBN 0-87950-171-5); 6 dual track cassettes for bk. 1 65.00x (ISBN 0-87950-175-8); bk. 1 & cassettes 75.00x (ISBN 0-87950-176-6). Spoken Lang Serv.

Spoken Norwegian. 3rd ed. Einar Haugen & Kenneth Chapman. 450p. 1982. text ed. 26.95 (ISBN 0-03-060013-8). HR&W.

Spoken Pangasinan. Richard A. Benton. LC 79-152457. (University of Hawaii, Honolulu. Pacific & Asian Linguistics Institute). pap. 160.00 (ISBN 0-317-10118-8, 2017214). Bks Demand UMI.

Spoken Persian. Serge Obolinsky et al. Incl. Book, Units 1-12. 401p. pap. 10.00x (ISBN 0-87950-295-9); Cassettes, Five Dual Track. 90.00x (ISBN 0-87950-297-5); Cassette Course, Bk. & Cassettes. pap. 105.00x (ISBN 0-87950-299-1). LC 73-15155. (Spoken Language Ser). (Prog. Bk.). 1973. Spoken Lang Serv.

Spoken Polish. Alexander M. Schenker. (Spoken Language Ser.). 487p. 1981. pap. 25.00x (ISBN 0-87950-040-9); cassettes, 19 dual track 120.00x (ISBN 0-87950-041-7); cassettes & bk. 135.00x (ISBN 0-87950-042-5). Spoken Lang Serv.

Spoken Portuguese. Margarida F. Reno et al. bk. I, units 1-12, 1978 218p. 10.00x (ISBN 0-87950-180-4); bk. II, units 13-30, 1978 307p. 10.00x (ISBN 0-87950-181-2); bk. I & cassettes 75.00 (ISBN 0-87950-186-3); cassettes for bk. I, 6 dual track 65.00x (ISBN 0-87950-185-5). Spoken Lang Serv.

Spoken Romanian. F. B Agard. LC 74-1000. (Spoken Language Ser.). 342p. (gr. 9-12). 1976. pap. 15.00x Units 1-30 (ISBN 0-87950-315-7); 6 dual track cassettes 65.00x (ISBN 0-87950-317-3); bk. & cassettes 80.00x (ISBN 0-87950-314-9). Spoken Lang Serv.

Spoken Russian. Leonard Bloomfield et al. bk.I, units 1-12, 1971 481p. 10.00x (ISBN 0-87950-190-1); bk. II, units 13-30, 1971 398p. 15.00x (ISBN 0-87950-191-X); bk.I & cassettes I 75.00x (ISBN 0-87950-197-9); bk.I & cassettes IE 110.00x (ISBN 0-87950-202-9); bk.II & cassettes IIE 110.00x (ISBN 0-87950-203-7); bks.I & II, cassettes IE & IIE 220.00x (ISBN 0-87950-204-5); cassettes I for Bk.I, 6 dual track 65.00x (ISBN 0-87950-196-0); cassettes IE for bk.I, 15 dual track 100.00x (ISBN 0-87950-200-2); cassettes IIE for bk.II, 11 dual track 95.00x (ISBN 0-87950-201-0). Spoken Lang Serv.

Spoken Russian: A Practical Course. S. C. Boyanus. Ed. by N. B. Jopson. 366p. 1980. lib. bdg. 35.00 (ISBN 0-89987-055-4). Darby Bks.

Spoken Seen: Film & the Romantic Imagination. Frank D. McConnell. LC 75-11342. pap. 53.50 (ISBN 0-317-42067-4, 2025886). Bks Demand UMI.

Spoken Serbo-Croatian. Carleton Hodge. LC 74-150403. (Spoken Language Ser.). 276p. (gr. 9-12). 1973. pap. 10.00x Bk. 1, Units 1-12 (ISBN 0-87950-210-X); pap. 10.00x Bk. 2, 432p. Units 13-30 (ISBN 0-87950-211-8); 6 dual track cassettes 65.00x (ISBN 0-87950-215-0); bk. 1 & cassettes 75.00x (ISBN 0-87950-216-9). Spoken Lang Serv.

Spoken Sinhalese, Bk. I & Cassettes I. G. H. Fairbanks et al. (Spoken Language Ser.). 1980. Set. 140.00x (ISBN 0-87950-444-7). Spoken Lang Serv.

Spoken Sinhalese, Bk. II & Cassettes II. G. H. Fairbanks et al. (Spoken Language Ser.). 1980. Set. 125.00x (ISBN 0-87950-445-5). Spoken Lang Serv.

Spoken Sinhalese, Bks. I, II & Cassettes I, II. G. H. Fairbanks et al. (Spoken Language Ser.). 1980. 265.00x (ISBN 0-87950-446-3). Spoken Lang Serv.

Spoken Sinhalese. G. H. Fairbanks et al. (Spoken Languages Ser.). (Prog. Bk.). 1979. Bk. I, Lessons 1-24, 415 p. pap. 15.00x (ISBN 0-87950-440-4); Bk. II Lessons 25-36, 260 p. pap. 15.00x (ISBN 0-87950-442-0); cassettes I for bk. I (21 dual track) 125.00x (ISBN 0-87950-441-2); cassettes II for bk. II (13 dual track) 110.00x (ISBN 0-87950-443-9). Spoken Lang Serv.

Spoken Spanish. S. N. Trevino. LC 75-15933. (Spoken Language Ser.). (Prog. Bk.). 1975. Book, Units 1-12, 276 p. pap. 10.00x (ISBN 0-87950-220-7). cassettes 6 dual track 65.00x (ISBN 0-87950-225-8); cassettes with course-bk. 75.00x (ISBN 0-87950-226-6). Spoken Lang Serv.

Spoken Spanish for Students & Travelers. 3rd ed. Manuel Duran et al. 1978. pap. text ed. 12.00 (ISBN 0-669-00879-6). Heath.

Spoken Standard Chinese, Vol. 1. Hugh M. Stimson & Parker Po-Fei Huang. 10.95 (ISBN 0-88710-107-0); tapes avail. (ISBN 0-88710-108-9). Yale Far Eastern Pubns.

Spoken Standard Chinese, Vol. 2. Hugh M. Stimson & Parker Po-Fei Huang 1976. 10.95 (ISBN 0-88710-110-0); tapes avail. (ISBN 0-88710-111-9). Yale Far Eastern Pubns.

Spoken Standard Chinese Workbook, Vol. I. Vivien Wong-Quincey Lu & Hugh M. Stimson. (Standard Chinese Ser.). 136p. (Chinese.). 1982. 6.95 (ISBN 0-88710-109-7). Yale Far Eastern Pubns.

Spoken Standard Chinese Workbook, Vol. II. Vivien Wong-Quincey Lu & Hugh M. Stimson. (Standard Chinese Ser.). 114p. 1982. 7.95 (ISBN 0-88710-112-7). Yale Far Eastern Pubns.

Spoken Swahili. Anthony J. Vitale. LC 79-92846. 310p. 1979. Bk. & Cassettes. pap. 75.00x (ISBN 0-87950-365-3); pap. 10.00x bk. only (ISBN 0-87950-363-7); six dual track cassettes 65.00x (ISBN 0-87950-364-5). Spoken Lang Serv.

Spoken Swedish. Fritz Frauchiger & William R. Van Buskirk. 261p. 1980. pap. text ed. 10.00x (ISBN 0-87950-704-7); cassettes 24 dual track 140.00x (ISBN 0-87950-705-5); bk. & cassettes 150.00x (ISBN 0-87950-706-3). Spoken Lang Serv.

Spoken Tagalog. J. Donald Bowen. LC 65-25321. (Spoken Language Ser.). 551p. (Orig.). 1982. pap. text ed. 30.00x (ISBN 0-87950-465-X); Cassettes I, Units 1-12. 6 dual track cassettes 90.00x (ISBN 0-87950-466-8); bk. & cassettes 120.00x; Cassettes II, Exercise Tests. 18 dual cassettes 100.00x (ISBN 0-87950-468-4); Book & Cassette I & II. 220.00x (ISBN 0-87950-469-2). Spoken Lang Serv.

Spoken Taiwanese. N. C. Bodman & Wu Su-Chu. (Spoken Language Ser.). 208p. (Chinese.). 1980. pap. 10.00x (ISBN 0-87950-460-9); cassettes 9 dual track 100.00x (ISBN 0-87950-461-7); text & cassettes 110.00x (ISBN 0-87950-462-5). Spoken Lang Serv.

Spoken Telugu. Leigh Lisker. LC 63-12992. (Spoken Language Ser.). xxvii, 345p. (gr. 9-12). 1976. pap. 10.00x Bk. 1, Units 1-30 (ISBN 0-87950-376-9); 6 dual track cassettes for Units 1-12 90.00x (ISBN 0-87950-377-7); book & cassettes I 100.00x (ISBN 0-87950-378-5); cassettes II for units 13-20, 5 dual track 50.00x (ISBN 0-87950-379-3). Spoken Lang Serv.

Spoken Thai. Mary R. Haas & Heng R. Subhanka. LC 74-166349. (Spoken Language Ser.). 307p. (gr. 9-12). 1978. pap. 10.00x (ISBN 0-87950-229-0); 6 dual track cassettes 65.00x (ISBN 0-87950-235-5); bk. & cassettes 75.00x (ISBN 0-87950-236-3); bk. 2, 410p. 15.00x (ISBN 0-87950-230-4). Spoken Lang Serv.

Spoken Turkish. Norman A. McQuown. LC 74-152747. (Spoken Language Ser.). 378p. (gr. 9-12). 1971. pap. 10.00x Bk. 1, Units 1-12 (ISBN 0-87950-240-1); pap. 15.00x Bk. 2, Units 13-30 (ISBN 0-87950-241-X); 6 dual track cassettes 65.00x (ISBN 0-87950-245-2); Bk. 1 & cassettes 75.00x (ISBN 0-87950-246-0). Spoken Lang Serv.

Spoken Urdu. Muhammad Barker. LC 75-15183. (Spoken Language Ser.). 530p. (gr. 9-12). 1975. pap. 10.00x Bk. 1 (ISBN 0-87950-340-8); pap. 15.00x Bk. 2, 576p. (ISBN 0-87950-341-6); pap. 15.00x Bk. 3, 230p. (ISBN 0-87950-342-4); 3 bk. set 40.00x (ISBN 0-87950-343-2); 6 dual track cassettes for bk. 1 90.00x (ISBN 0-87950-344-0); 1 & cassette 105.00xbk. (ISBN 0-87950-347-5); 6 dual track cassettes for bk. 2 75.00x (ISBN 0-87950-345-9); bk. 2 & cassettes 90.00x (ISBN 0-87950-348-3); Bks. 1-2 & cassettes 1 & 2 195.00x (ISBN 0-87950-349-1). Spoken Lang Serv.

Spoken Urdu, Vol. I. Muhammad Barker & Hamdani. 497p. 1975. with 9 cassettes 135.00x (ISBN 0-88432-106-1, U200). J Norton Pubs.

Spoken Urdu, Vol. II. Muhammad Barker & Hamdani. 568p. 1976. 95.00x (ISBN 0-88432-107-X, U250); cassettes incl. J Norton Pubs.

Spoken Vietnamese. Robert B. Jones & Huynh S. Thong. LC 79-3165. (Spoken Language Ser.). xiii, 295p. (gr. 9-12). 1976. pap. 10.00x (ISBN 0-87950-371-8); 6 dual track cassettes 65.00x (ISBN 0-87950-372-6); bk. & cassettes 75.00x (ISBN 0-87950-373-4). Spoken Lang Serv.

Spoken Welsh I, 2 texts. 329p. Set. 95.00x (ISBN 0-88432-209-2); 6 cassettes incl. J Norton Pubs.

Spoken Welsh II. 183p. 40.00x (ISBN 0-907551-01-7); 2 cassettes incl. J Norton Pubs.

Spoken Word. Harry H. Schanker. Ed. by John A. Rothermich. LC 80-24143. (Illus.). 384p. 1981. text ed. 21.08 (ISBN 0-07-055135-9). McGraw.

Spoken Word. Sheldon Tostengard. LC 88-45229. (Resources for Preaching Ser.). 112p. 1989. pap. 5.95 (ISBN 0-8006-1149-7). Fortress.

Spoken Word: A BBC Guide. Robert Burchfield. 1982. pap. 3.95 (ISBN 0-19-520380-1). Oxford U Pr.

Spoken Word & the Work of Interpretation. Dennis Tedlock. LC 82-40489. (Illus.). 400p. 1983. 17.95x (ISBN 0-8122-7880-1). U of Pa Pr.

Spoken Word Recognition. Ed. by Uli H. Frauenfelder & Lorraine K. Tyler. (Cognition Special Issues Ser.). 224p. 1987. pap. text ed. 17.50x (ISBN 0-262-56039-9, Pub. by Bradford Pr). MIT Pr.

Spoken Words: Effects of Situation & Social Group on Oral Word Usage & Frequency. William S. Hall et al. (Psychology of Reading & Reading Instruction Ser.). 504p. 1984. pap. 45.00 (ISBN 0-89859-387-5). L Erlbaum Assocs.

Spoken Words of Love. Ruth Wingard. 1986. 6.95 (ISBN 0-533-06768-5). Vantage.

Spoken Yoruba. E. W. Stevick & Odaleye Aremu. (Spoken Language Ser.). 381p. 1980. pap. 15.00x (ISBN 0-87950-708-X); cassettes, 34 dual track 185.00x (ISBN 0-87950-710-1); text & cassettes 200.00x (ISBN 0-87950-712-8). Spoken Lang Serv.

Spokesman for the Devil. Albert F. Fugett. (Illus.). 165p. 1985. 14.95 (ISBN 0-9614870-0-3). Triple Seven.

Spokesman for the Minority: A Bibliography of Sidney Lanier, William Vaughn Moody, Henry Timrod, Frederick Goddard Tuckerman, & Jones Very, with Selective Annotations. Jeanetta Boswell. LC 86-24828. x, 296p. 1987. 29.50 (ISBN 0-8108-1944-9). Scarecrow.

Spokesmen. facs. ed. Thomas K. Whipple. LC 70-142711. (Essay Index Reprint Ser). 1928. 19.00 (ISBN 0-8369-2179-8). Ayer Co Pubs.

Spokesperson: A Public Appearance Primer. 2nd ed. Ken W. Huskey. (Illus.). 150p. 1986. pap. 10.00 (ISBN 0-9604840-1-9). K W Huskey.

Spomenica Palih Srba Vazduhoplovaca. Milos Acin-Kosta. 300p. (Serbo-Croatian.). 1975. pap. 10.00 (ISBN 0-931931-10-X). Ravnogorski.

Spondylarthropathies: Involvement of the Gut: Proceedings of the First Conference, Ghent, September 10-13, 1986. Ed. by H. Mielants & E. M. Veys. (International Congress Ser.: No. 720). 456p. 1987. 141.00 (ISBN 0-444-80894-9). Elsevier.

Spondyloarthropathies. Ed. by Andrei Calin. 432p. 1984. 69.50 (ISBN 0-8089-1613-0, 790763). Grune.

Spondyloarthropathies. Ed. by Morris Ziff & Stanley B. Cohen. (Advances in Inflammation Research Ser.: Vol. 9). (Illus.). 288p. 1985. text ed. 73.00 (ISBN 0-88167-089-8). Raven.

Sponge Gray. Grawin N. Betts. LC 79-93426. 1980. 6.95 (ISBN 0-87212-133-X). Libra.

Spongee Sponge. Bob Reese. LC 82-23608. (Critterland Ocean Adventures Ser.). (Illus.). 24p. (ps-2). 1983. PLB 9.27 (ISBN 0-516-02315-2); pap. 1.95 (ISBN 0-516-42315-0). Childrens.

Sponges. Patricia R. Bergquist. LC 77-93644. 1978. 44.50x (ISBN 0-520-03658-1). U of Cal Pr.

Sponges & Spongiomorphs: Notes for a Short Course Organized by J. K. Rigby & C. W. Stearn. Ed. by T. W. Broadhead. (University of Tennessee Studies in Geology). (Illus.). 220p. 1983. pap. 12.00 (ISBN 0-910249-06-7). U of Tenn Geo.

Spon's International Construction Costs Handbook. Ed. by Davis et al. 300p. 1988. lib. bdg. 85.00 (ISBN 0-419-14210-X, Pub. by E FN Spon England). Routledge Chapman & Hall.

Sponsor: Notes on a Modern Potentate. Erik Barnouw. (Illus.). 1978. pap. 8.95 (ISBN 0-19-502614-4). Oxford U Pr.

Sponsored Research in the History of Art, Vol. 5: 1980-1986, A Cumulative Record. National Gallery of Art Staff. 849p. 1986. pap. 29.95 (ISBN 0-89774-547-7). Oryx Pr.

Sponsored Research in the History of Art, Vol. 6: 1985-1986 & 1986-1987. National Gallery of Art Staff. 530p. 1987. pap. 29.95 (ISBN 0-89774-548-5). Oryx Pr.

Sponsored Research in the History of Art, Vol. 7: 1987-1988. National Gallery of Art Staff. 428p. 1988. pap. 29.95 (ISBN 0-89774-549-3). Oryx Pr.

Sponsors: A Guide for Video & Filmmakers. 45p. 1987. 6.00 (ISBN 0-935654-10-0). Ctr for Arts Info.

Sponsorship. Steve Sleight. (Illus.). 256p. 1989. 24.95 (ISBN 0-07-707084-4). McGraw.

Sponsorship. 20p. (Orig.). 1986. pap. 0.85 (ISBN 0-89486-371-1). Hazelden.

Sponsorship-Endorsement-Publicity. IAA Global Products-Services Commission & Keith V. Monk. 9p. 1985. 5.00 (ISBN 0-318-22255-8). Intl Advertising Assn.

Sponsorship in Sports Arts & Leisure. 1987. 200.00x (Pub. by ESC Ltd UK). State Mutual Bk.

Sponsorship: The Newest Marketing Skill. Victor Head. 128p. (Orig.). 1983. 28.95 (ISBN 0-85941-151-6, Pub. by Woodhead-Faulkner). Longwood Pub Group.

Spontaneite Revolutionnaire Dans Une Revolution Populaire see Cahiers de l'Institut de Science Economique Appliquee.

Sport in Society: Issues & Controversies. 3rd ed. Coakley. 1985. pap. 23.95 (ISBN 0-8016-1234-9). Mosby.
Sport in Soviet Society. J. Riordan. LC 76-9729. (Soviet & East European Studies). (Illus.). 1977. 57.50 (ISBN 0-521-21284-7); pap. 19.95 (ISBN 0-521-28023-0). Cambridge U Pr.
Sport in the Market. Peter J. Sloane. (Institute of Economic Affairs, Hobart Papers Ser.: No. 85). pap. 5.95 technical (ISBN 0-255-36130-0). Transatl Arts.
Sport in the Modern World-Chances & Problems, Papers, Results, Materials: Proceedings. Scientific Congress Munich, Aug 21-25, 1972. Ed. by O. Grupe. 630p. 1974. 56.10 (ISBN 0-387-06607-1). Springer-Verlag.
Sport in the Socio-Cultural Process. 3rd ed. Marie Hart & Susan Birrell. 521p. 1981. pap. text ed. write for info. (ISBN 0-697-07099-9). Wm C Brown.
Sport in the West. Ed. by Donald J. Mrozek. (Illus.). 71p. (Orig.). 1983. pap. text ed. 9.95x (ISBN 0-89745-041-8). Sunflower U Pr.
Sport Inside Out: Readings in Literature & Philosophy. Ed. by David L. Vanderwerken & Spencer K. Wertz. LC 84-23951. 782p. 1985. text ed. 34.50x (ISBN 0-87565-003-1); pap. text ed. 14.95x (ISBN 0-87565-006-6). Tex Christian.
Sport Law Study Guide. Stephen C. Jefferies. 1985. 3-ring notebook 18.00x, (ISBN 0-931250-95-1, ACEP0200). Human Kinetics.
Sport Marketing Encyclopedia. David Wilkinson. 1984. 54.95x (ISBN 0-87322-063-3, BWIL0063). Human Kinetics.
Sport Medicine: Incidence & Treatment of Athletic Injuries. E. C. Percy et al. LC 73-10382. (Sport Medicine Ser.: Vol. 1). 1973. 29.00x (ISBN 0-8422-7142-2). Irvington.
Sport Medicine: Pathology. Olof Ringertz et al. LC 73-10369. (Sport Medicine Ser.: Vol. 3). 1973. 29.00x (ISBN 0-8422-7141-4). Irvington.
Sport Medicine: Physiology. Kenneth D. Rose et al. LC 73-11032. (Sport Medicine Ser.: Vol. 4). 202p. 1974. text ed. 29.00x (ISBN 0-8422-7139-2). Irvington.
Sport Medicine: Protection, Treatment & Nutrition. Russel M. Lane et al. LC 73-10420. (Sport Medicine Ser.: Vol. 2). 1974. 29.00x (ISBN 0-8422-7140-6). Irvington.
Sport of Crime. Ed. by Carol-Lynn R. Waugh & Martin H. Greenberg. (Orig.). 1989. pap. 3.50 mass mrkt. (ISBN 1-55802-248-1). Lynx Bks.
Sport of Judo. K. Kobayashi. 7.50x (ISBN 0-685-38453-5). Wehman.
Sport of Judo. Kiyoshi Kobayashi & Harold E. Sharp. LC 57-75. (Illus.). (gr. 9 up). 1957. pap. 7.95 (ISBN 0-8048-0542-3). C E Tuttle.
Sport of Nature. Nadine Gordimer. 1987. 18.95 (ISBN 0-394-54802-7). Knopf.
Sport of Nature. Nadine Gordimer. 352p. 1988. pap. 7.95 (ISBN 0-14-008470-3). Penguin.
Sport of Queens. Dick Francis. 272p. 1986. pap. 3.95. Warner Bks.
Sport of Queens: The Autobiography of Dick Francis. Dick Francis. 272p. 1988. pap. 3.95 (ISBN 0-445-40206-7). Mysterious Pr.
Sport of Skin Diving. Charles F. Cicciarella. (Illus.). 68p. (Orig.). 1982. pap. text ed. 3.95x (ISBN 0-89641-100-1). American Pr.
Sport of the Gods. Paul L. Dunbar. LC 69-18588. (American Negro: His History & Literature Ser., No. 2). 1969. Repr. of 1902 ed. 21.00 (ISBN 0-405-01859-2). Ayer Co Pubs.
Sport of the Gods. Paul L. Dunbar. pap. 7.00x (ISBN 0-685-16798-4, N266P). Mnemosyne.
Sport Pedagogy. Ed. by Maurice Pieron & George Graham. LC 85-18113. 222p. 1986. text ed. 27.50x (ISBN 0-87322-013-7, BPIE0013). Human Kinetics.
Sport Physiology Study Guide: A Manual to Accompany the Coaches Guide to Sport Physiology. Stephen C. Jefferies. 1986. 3-ring binder 18.00x (ISBN 0-87322-061-7, ACE0202). Human Kinetics.
Sport, Power & Culture: A Social & Historical Analysis of Popular Sports in Britain. John Hargreaves. LC 86-15503. 288p. 1986. 35.00 (ISBN 0-312-75324-1). St Martin.
Sport Psychology: An Analysis of Athlete Behavior. 2nd ed. Ed. by William F. Straub. 1980. pap. 24.95 (ISBN 0-932392-03-2); text ed. cancelled. Mouvement Pubns.
Sport Psychology: Psychological Consideration in Maximizing Sport Psychology. Ed. by L. K. Bunker & R. J. Rotella. 1985. 24.95 (ISBN 0-932392-20-2). Mouvement Pubns.
Sport Psychology: The Coach's Perspective. Robert A. Mechikoff & Bill Kozar. 132p. 1983. 18.50 (ISBN 0-398-04889-4). C C Thomas.
Sport Psychology: The Psychological Health of the Athlete. Ed. by Jerry R. May & Michael J. Asken. LC 87-787361. 1987. 35.00 (ISBN 0-89335-304-3). PMA Pub Corp.
Sport Record. Ed. by Richard Wyszynski. 120p. 1974. 75.00 (ISBN 0-318-13787-9). Consol Athletic Comm.
Sport, Recreation & Leisure Pack. Liz Jackson. 182p. 1987. 175.00x (ISBN 1-85008-011-9, Pub. by Framework UK). State Mutual Bk.
Sport Science Perspectives for Women. Ed. by Jacqueline Puhl & C. Harmon Brown. LC 87-4023. 248p. 1987. text ed. 28.00x (ISBN 0-87322-110-9, BPUH0110). Human Kinetics.
Sport Scuba Diving in Depth: An Introduction to Basic Scuba Instruction & Beyond. Tom Griffiths. LC 83-6310. (Illus.). 1984. pap. text ed. 14.50 (ISBN 0-916622-32-0). Princeton Bk Co.
Sport Shoes & Playing Surfaces: Biomechanical Properties. Ed. by E. C. Frederick. LC 83-83166. 208p. 1984. text ed. 27.00x (ISBN 0-931250-51-X, BFRE0051). Human Kinetics.
Sport Signs. Harley Hamilton & Nancy K. Jones. Incl. Signs & Printed Words, General Vocabulary. 64p. pap. 6.00 (ISBN 0-317-42767-9); Football. 48p. pap. 5.00 (ISBN 0-317-42768-7); Basketball. 48p. pap. 5.00 (ISBN 0-317-42769-5); Baseball-Softball. 48p. pap. 5.00 (ISBN 0-317-42770-9); Track & Field. 40p. pap. 4.00 (ISBN 0-317-42771-7); Volley Ball. 28p. pap. 3.00 (ISBN 0-317-42772-5). (Six Book Series in Sign Language). 1985. pap. 28.00 set (ISBN 0-317-42766-0). Modern Signs.
Sport-Source. Ed. by Bob Anderson. LC 75-16003. (Illus.). 430p. (Orig.). 1975. 18.95 (ISBN 0-89037-061-3). Anderson World.
Sport und Rekord. Maria Kloeren. Repr. of 1935 ed. 24.00 (ISBN 0-384-29860-5). Johnson Repr.
Sport under Communism. rev. ed. Ed. by James Riordan. 200p. 1982. pap. 15.95c (ISBN 0-7735-0533-4). McGill Queen's U Pr.
Sport Under Communism: A Comparative Study. Ed. by James Riordan. 1978. 24.95x (ISBN 0-7735-0505-9). McGill-Queens U Pr.
Sport with Terriers. Patricia A. Lent. LC 73-85940. (Illus.). 1973. 13.95 (ISBN 0-914124-01-3). Arner Pubns.
Sportin' News. Terry Strokes. LC 85-3472. 96p. (Orig.). 1985. pap. 8.95 (ISBN 0-918518-44-X). Ion Books.
Sporting & Athletic Equipment. 400p. 1987. 795.00 (ISBN 0-318-00538-7). Busn Trend.
Sporting & Athletic Equipment Market. 400p. 1987. 795.00. Busn Trend.
Sporting & Leisure Goods Market. 359p. 1984. 1550.00 (ISBN 0-86621-562-X, E641). Frost & Sullivan.
Sporting Art & English Society. Stephen Deuchar. LC 88-165. 1988. text ed. 45.00t (ISBN 0-300-04116-0). Yale U Pr.
Sporting Body, Sporting Mind: An Athlete's Guide to Mental Training. John Syer & Christopher Connolly. (Illus.). 160p. 1984. Cambridge U Pr.
Sporting Body, Sporting Mind: An Athlete's Guide to Mental Training. John Syer & Christopher Connolly. (Illus.). 160p. 1988. pap. 14.95 (ISBN 0-13-835539-8). P-H.
Sporting Club. Thomas McGuane. 220p. 1974. 8.95 (ISBN 0-374-26796-0). FS&G.
Sporting Club. Thomas McGuane. 1979. pap. 3.95 (ISBN 0-14-005275-5). Penguin.
Sporting Club. Thomas McGuane. 224p. 1987. pap. 5.95 (ISBN 0-14-009909-3). Penguin.
Sporting Days. John T. Foote. LC 72-121544. (Short Story Index Reprint Ser). (Illus.). 1937. 14.50 (ISBN 0-8369-3500-4). Ayer Co Pubs.
Sporting Fords: Capris. Jeremy Walton. (Collector's Guide Ser.). (Illus.). 128p. 1983. 29.95 (ISBN 0-900549-72-6, Pub. by Motor Racing Pubns England). Motorbooks Intl.
Sporting Fords: Cortinas. Graham Robson. (Collector's Guide Ser.). (Illus.). 130p. 1982. 29.95 (ISBN 0-900549-68-8, Pub. by Motor Racing England). Motorbooks Intl.
Sporting Fords: Escorts. Graham Robson. (Collector's Guide Ser.). (Illus.). 130p. 1982. 29.95 (ISBN 0-900549-71-8, 65-06422, Pub. by Motor Racing England). Motorbooks Intl.
Sporting Goods. 1985. write for info. (ISBN 0-86621-356-2, A1440). Frost & Sullivan.
Sporting Gun. James Douglas. (Illus.). 240p. 1983. 29.95 (ISBN 0-7153-8324-8). David & Charles.
Sporting Image: Readings in American Sport History. Ed. by Paul J. Zingg. 384p. (Orig.). 1988. lib. bdg. 32.50 (ISBN 0-8191-6817-3); pap. text ed. 14.25 (ISBN 0-8191-6818-1). U Pr of Amer.
Sporting Injuries. 2nd ed. Peter Dornan & Richard Dunn. (Illus.). 256p. 1988. pap. text ed. 12.95x (ISBN 0-7022-2064-7). U of Queensland Pr.
Sporting Life Gourmet. Kathleen Krenzel & Robyn Heckendorf. (Illus.). 74p. (Orig.). 1980. 9.95x (ISBN 0-9605410-0-4). R Louis Pub.
Sporting Myth & the American Experience: Studies in Contemporary Fiction. Wiley L. Umphlett. LC 73-8306. 205p. 1975. 20.00 (ISBN 0-8387-1363-7). Bucknell U Pr.
Sporting News Baseball Trivia Book. (Illus.). 286p. 1983. pap. 9.95 (ISBN 0-89204-103-X). Sporting News.
Sporting News Baseball Trivia II. 286p. 1987. pap. 10.95 (ISBN 0-89204-242-7). Sporting News.
Sporting News Complete Baseball Record Book, 1988. 304p. 1988. pap. 12.95 (ISBN 0-89204-266-4). Sporting News.
Sporting News Football Register, 1988. 480p. 1988. pap. 10.95 (ISBN 0-89204-286-9). Sporting News.
Sporting News Football Trivia Book. 320p. 1985. pap. 9.95 (ISBN 0-89204-201-X). Sporting News.
Sporting News Hockey Guide, 1988-89. 240p. 1988. pap. 10.95 (ISBN 0-89204-290-7). Sporting News.
Sporting News Hockey Register, 1988-89. 1988. 10.95 (ISBN 0-89204-291-5). Sporting News.
Sporting News Official Baseball Guide, 1988. 528p. 1988. pap. cancelled (ISBN 0-89204-264-8). Sporting News.
Sporting News Official Baseball Register. 576p. 1988. pap. 10.95 (ISBN 0-89204-265-6). Sporting News.
Sporting News Official NBA Guide, 1988-89. 498p. 1988. pap. 10.95 (ISBN 0-89204-288-5). Sporting News.
Sporting News Official NBA Register, 1988-89. 368p. 1988. pap. 10.95 (ISBN 0-89204-289-3). Sporting News.
Sporting News Pro Football Guide, 1988. 400p. 1988. pap. 10.95 (ISBN 0-89204-285-0). Sporting News.
Sporting News Selects Baseball's 25 Greatest Pennant Races. Lowell Reidenbaugh. LC 87-61058. (Illus.). 256p. 1987. 19.95 (ISBN 0-89204-256-7). Sporting News.
Sporting News Selects Baseball's 25 Greatest Teams. Lowell Reidenbaugh. Ed. by Steve Zesch. LC 88-42860. (Greatest Ser.). (Illus.). 256p. 1988. 19.95 (ISBN 0-89204-280-X). Sporting News.
Sporting News Selects Baseball's 50 Greatest Games. Lowell Reidenbaugh. 288p. 1988. pap. 12.95 (ISBN 0-89204-278-8). Sporting News.
Sporting News Selects College Football's 25 Greatest Teams. LC 88-42855. (Greatest Ser.). (Illus.). 1988. pap. 14.95 (ISBN 0-89204-281-8). Sporting News.
Sporting News Super Bowl Book, 1988. 368p. 1988. pap. 10.95 (ISBN 0-89204-287-7). Sporting News.
Sporting News: The First Hundred Years, Eighteen Eighty-Six to Nineteen Eighty-Six. Lowell Reidenbaugh. 272p. 1985. 24.95 (ISBN 0-89204-204-4). Sporting News.
Sporting News: The Game for All America. 256p. 1988. 35.00 (ISBN 0-89204-279-6). Sporting News.
Sporting News: The Series. 336p. 1988. pap. 12.95 (ISBN 0-89204-272-9). Sporting News.
Sporting Scots of Nineteenth-Century Canada. Gerald Redmond. LC 80-67124. (Illus.). 352p. 1982. 40.00 (ISBN 0-8386-3069-3). Fairleigh Dickinson.
Sporting Set: An Original Anthology. Ed. by Leon Stein. LC 75-1877. (Leisure Class in America Ser.). (Illus.). 1975. 20.00x (ISBN 0-405-06941-3). Ayer Co Pubs.
Sporting Spirit: Athletes in Literature & Life. Robert J. Higgs & Neil D. Isaacs. LC 76-16435. 304p. 1977. pap. text ed. 13.00 net (ISBN 0-15-583351-0, HC). HarBraceJ.
Sporting Time: New York City & the Rise of Modern Athletics, 1820-1870. Melvin L. Adelman. LC 85-13967. (Sports in Society Ser.). (Illus.). 408p. 1986. 24.95 (ISBN 0-252-01250-X). U of Ill Pr.
Sporting Use of the Handgun. Mason Williams. (Illus.). 288p. 1979. 16.25 (ISBN 0-398-03850-3). C C Thomas.
Sporting Way to Reading Comprehension. Katherine Oana. Ed. by William H. Cooper. LC 84-51195. (Illus.). 68p. (Orig.). (gr. 3-8). 1984. 3.95 (ISBN 0-914127-17-9). Univ Class.
Sporting Wife: A Guide to Game & Fish Cooking. Ed. by Barbara Hargreaves. (Illus.). 336p. 1988. pap. 15.95 (ISBN 0-85493-121-X, Pub. by Gollancz England). David & Charles.
Sporting Woman. Mary A. Boutilier & Lucinda F. SanGiovanni. LC 82-83147. 306p. 1983. text ed. 24.00x (ISBN 0-931250-35-8, BBOU0035). Human Kinetics.
Sporting World of R. S. Surtees. John Welcome. (Illus.). 1982. 22.50x (ISBN 0-19-211766-1). Oxford U Pr.
Sportplane Builder. rev. ed. Tony Bingelis. Ed. by David A. Rivers. (Illus.). 320p. 1987. pap. 17.95x (ISBN 0-911721-84-3, Pub. by Bingelis). Aviation.
Sportplane Construction Techniques. Tony Bingelis. (Illus.). 368p. 1987. pap. 20.95 (ISBN 0-317-67367-X, Pub. by Bingelis). Aviation.
Sports. Melvin Berger. (Reference First Bk.). (Illus.). 96p. (gr. 4 up). 1983. PLB 10.40 (ISBN 0-531-04540-4). Watts.
Sports. Leonard E. Fisher. LC 80-16467. (Nineteenth Century America Ser.). (Illus.). 64p. (gr. 5 up). 1980. reinforced bdg. 7.95 (ISBN 0-8234-0419-6). Holiday.
Sports. Tim Hammond. LC 88-1573. (Eyewitness Bks.). (Illus.). 64p. (gr. 5 up). 1988. 12.95 (ISBN 0-394-89616-5); lib. bdg. 13.99 (ISBN 0-394-99616-X). Knopf.
Sports. Joan Nichols & Larry Nichols. (Math Is Everywhere Ser.). (Illus., Orig.). (gr. 1-9). 1974. pap. 6.95 (ISBN 0-918932-41-6). Activity Resources.
Sports. (Illus.). 72p. (gr. 6-12). 1972. pap. 1.25x (ISBN 0-8395-3255-5, 3255). BSA.
Sports, Vol. 1 (incl. 1978-1980 Supplements) Ed. by Eleanor C. Goldstein. (Social Issues Resources Ser.). 1981. 75.00 (ISBN 0-89777-023-4). Soc Issues.
Sports, Vol. 2 (incl. 1981-1985 Supplements) Ed. by Eleanor C. Goldstein. 1986. 75.00 (ISBN 0-89777-055-2). Soc Issues.
Sports: A Multimedia Guide for Children & Young Adults. Calvin Blickle & Frances Corcoran. LC 80-13519. (Selection Guide Ser.: No. 6). 245p. 1980. 27.95 (ISBN 0-87436-283-0). Neal-Schuman.
Sports: A Reference Guide. Robert J. Higgs. LC 81-20320. (American Popular Culture Ser.). xi, 317p. 1982. lib. bdg. 36.95 (ISBN 0-313-21361-5, HSR/). Greenwood.
Sports: A Social Perspective. Timothy Curry & Robert Jiobu. (Illus.). 288p. 1984. write for info. (ISBN 0-13-837823-1). P-H.
Sports Address Book. Ed. by Scott Callis. 288p. 1988. 7.95 (ISBN 0-671-64771-7). PB.
Sports after Fifty: Fit Yourself into Fun Sports. Ted Overton. (Illus.). 224p. 1988. 17.95 (ISBN 0-913179-20-5). Azimuth Pr.
Sports & Anabolic Steroids: Index of Modern Information. Hugo H. Bronsen. LC 88-47866. 150p. 1988. 34.50 (ISBN 0-88164-924-4); pap. 26.50 (ISBN 0-88164-925-2). ABBE Pubs Assn.
Sports & Athletic Injuries: Medical Subject Analysis & Research Index with Bibliography. Hugo H. Bronsen. LC 83-71667. 120p. 1985. 34.50 (ISBN 0-88164-052-2); pap. 26.50 (ISBN 0-88164-053-0). ABBE Pubs Assn.
Sports & Athletics: Philosophy in Action. Joseph C. Mihalich. LC 81-20837. (Quality Paperback Ser.: No. 371). 236p. (Orig.). 1982. pap. text ed. 7.95 (ISBN 0-8226-0371-3). Littlefield.
Sports & Blood Pressure: Medical Subject Index with Bibliography. Jerry B. Holtz. LC 88-47625. 150p. 1988. 34.50 (ISBN 0-88164-664-4); pap. 26.50 (ISBN 0-88164-665-2). ABBE Pubs Assn.
Sports & Fitness: An Information Guide. Ray Prytherch. 200p. 1988. text ed. 30.00x (ISBN 0-566-03569-3, Pub. by Gower Pub England). Gower Pub Co.
Sports & Freedom: The Rise of Big-Time College Athletics. Ronald A. Smith. (Sports History & Society Ser.). (Illus.). 320p. 1988. 26.95 (ISBN 0-19-505314-1). Oxford U Pr.
Sports & Games in Verse & Rhyme. Ed. by Allan D. Jacobs & Leland B. Jacobs. LC 74-18274. (Garrard Poetry Ser.). (Illus.). 64p. (gr. 2-5). 1975. PLB 6.69 (ISBN 0-8116-4118-X). Garrard.
Sports & Games the Indians Gave Us. Alex Whitney. (gr. 7 up). 1977. 7.95 (ISBN 0-679-20391-5). McKay.
Sports & Heart Rate: Medical Subject Index with Bibliography. Alfred H. Irving. LC 88-47626. 150p. 1988. 34.50 (ISBN 0-88164-666-0); pap. 26.50 (ISBN 0-88164-667-9). ABBE Pubs Assn.
Sports & Law: Contemporary Issues. Ed. by Herb Appenzeller. 295p. 1985. 25.00x (ISBN 0-87215-929-9). Michie Co.
Sports & Pastimes of the Middle Ages. John M. Carter. LC 87-34593. (Illus.). 80p. (Orig.). 1988. pap. text ed. 8.25 (ISBN 0-8191-6842-4). U Pr of Amer.
Sports & Pastimes of the People of England: Including Rural & Domestic Recreations. Joseph Strutt. LC 67-23901. (Social History Reference Ser.). (Illus.). 386p. 1968. Repr. of 1903 ed. 42.00x (ISBN 0-8103-3260-4). Gale.
Sports & Pastimes: Scenes from Persian, Turkish & Moghul Art. Norah M. Titley. (Illus.). 36p. (Orig.). 1979. pap. 2.95 (ISBN 0-904654-10-9, Pub. by British Lib). Longwood Pub Group.
Sports & Physical Education: A Guide to the Reference Resources. Compiled by Bonnie Gratch et al. LC 82-24159. xxi, 198p. 1983. lib. bdg. 36.95 (ISBN 0-313-23433-7, GED/). Greenwood.
Sports & Recreation. (Children's Encyclopedia Ser.). (Illus.). 96p. (gr. 3 up). 1987. PLB 240.00 (ISBN 0-317-64441-6); pap. 13.27 (ISBN 0-8172-3061-0). Raintree Pubs.
Sports & Recreation for the Disabled: A Resource Handbook of Activities & Adapted Equipment for the Physically & Mentally Impaired. Michael J. Paciorek & Jeffery A. Jones. (Illus.). 250p. (Orig.). 1988. pap. text ed. 14.95 (ISBN 0-936157-31-3). Benchmark Pr.
Sports & Recreational Activities for Men & Women. 9th ed. Mood et al. 1986. 25.95 (ISBN 0-8016-3463-6). Mosby.
Sports & Recreational Injuries. Jeffey K. Riffer. 623p. 1986. text ed. 90.00 (ISBN 0-07-052828-4). Shepards-McGraw.
Sports & Recreational Programs for the Child & Young Adult with Physical Disability: Proceedings of Winter Park Seminar. 101p. 1984. 10.00 (ISBN 0-89203-001-1, 4000025). Amer Acad Ortho Surg.
Sports & Social Values. Robert L. Simon. (Illus.). 192p. 1985. pap. text ed. write for info. (ISBN 0-13-837881-9). P-H.
Sports & Society. Ed. by Dwight W. Hoover & John T. Koumoulides. (Conspectus of History Ser.). (Orig.). 1983. pap. 5.95 (ISBN 0-937994-03-0). Ball State Univ.
Sports & Society. Robert Lipsyte & Gene Brown. (Great Contemporary Issues Ser.). 35.00 (ISBN 0-405-13143-7). Ayer Co Pubs.
Sports & the Courts. Herb Appenzeller & Thomas Appenzeller. 423p. 1980. 19.50x (ISBN 0-87215-243-X). Michie Co.
Sports & the Humanities: A Symposium. Ed. by William J. Baker & James A. Rog. LC 83-50027. 126p. (Orig.). 1983. pap. 8.95 (ISBN 0-89101-055-6). U Maine Orono.
Sports & the Law. Herb Appenzeller et al. (Illus.). 200p. 1984. pap. text ed. 12.25 (ISBN 0-314-79386-0). West Pub.
Sports & the Macho Male. 2nd ed. John Mitzel. 1976. pap. 2.50 (ISBN 0-915480-06-9). Fag Rag.

TITLE INDEX

SPORTS PAGES.

Sports & the Spirit of Play in American Fiction: Hawthorne to Faulkner. Christian Messenger. LC 81-4843. 352p. 1982. 35.00x (ISBN 0-231-05168-9); pap. 14.00x (ISBN 0-231-05169-7). Columbia U Pr.

Sports: As Reported by the New York Times. new ed. Ed. by Gene Brown & Arleen Keylin. LC 76-2450. (Illus.). 1976. 12.98 (ISBN 0-405-06689-9). Ayer Co Pubs.

Sports Babylon: Sex, Drugs, & Other Dirty Dealings in the World of Sports. Mark Sabljak & Martin H. Greenberg. (Illus.). 308p. 1988. 6.98 (ISBN 0-517-66717-7, Pub. by Bell Publishing Co). Crown.

Sports Betting: A Winner's Handbook. Jerry L. Patterson & Jack Painter. 224p. (Orig.). 1985. pap. 8.95 (ISBN 0-399-51130-X, Perigee). Putnam Pub Group.

Sports Birthdays: The Fan's Daybook. Eugene Lesser. LC 85-71054. 400p. pap. 9.95 (ISBN 0-916804-03-8). Ed Buryn Pub.

Sports Bloopers: Weird, Wacky & Unexpected Moments in Sports. Phyllis Hollander & Zander Hollander. (Illus.). 64p. (Orig.). (gr. 4 up). 1985. pap. 2.50 (ISBN 0-590-41947-1). Scholastic Inc.

Sports Books for Children: An Annotated Bibliography. Barbara K. Harrah. LC 78-18510. 540p. 1978. 30.00 (ISBN 0-8108-1154-5). Scarecrow.

Sports Buildings. Konya. 1987. 37.95 (ISBN 0-442-24630-7). Van Nos Reinhold.

Sports Car & Competition Driving. Paul Frere. LC 63-5821. 1963. 14.95 (ISBN 0-8376-0034-0). Bentley.

Sports Car: Its Design & Performance. 4th ed. Colin Campbell. LC 77-94089. (Illus.). 306p. 1979. 14.95 (ISBN 0-8376-0158-4). Bentley.

Sports Classics: American Writers Choose Their Best. Ed. by Howard Siner. 320p. 1983. 16.95 (ISBN 0-698-11248-2, Coward). Putnam Pub Group.

Sports Collector's Bible. 4th rev. ed. Bert R. Sugar. LC 82-45889. 578p. 1983. pap. 12.95 (ISBN 0-672-52741-3). Bobbs.

Sports Collectors' Digest Baseball Cards Price Guide. Dan Albaugh & Bob Lemke. LC 87-80033. (Illus.). 500p. 1987. pap. 10.95 (ISBN 0-87341-094-7). Krause Pubns.

Sports Collectors Digest Baseball Price Card Guide. 2nd ed. Dan Albaugh & Bob Lemke. LC 87-80033. 1988. pap. text ed. 12.95 (ISBN 0-87341-105-6). Krause Pubns.

Sports Conditioning & Weight Training. 2nd ed. William J. Stone & William Kroll. 249p. 1986. pap. text ed. write for info. (ISBN 0-697-06817-X). Wm C Brown.

Sports-Confident Child: A Parents' Guide to Helping Children. Chris Hopper. LC 87-46064. (Illus.). 256p. 1988. pap. 9.95 (ISBN 0-679-73951-3). Pantheon.

Sports, Culture, & Personality. Donald W. Calhoun. LC 80-84355. (Illus.). 320p. (Orig.). 1981. pap. text ed. 14.95x (ISBN 0-918438-68-3, PCAL0068). Leisure Pr.

Sports Date Book. Harvey Frommer. (Orig.). (gr. 5 up). 1981. pap. 2.50 (ISBN 0-448-17214-3, Pub. by Tempo). Ace Bks.

Sports Day. (Tales from Fern Hollow Ser.). (Illus.). 22p. (ps-1). 1985. 1.98 (ISBN 0-517-42789-3). Outlet Bk Co.

Sports Encyclopedia: Baseball. 8th ed. David S. Neft & Richard Cohen. LC 85-1833. 610p. 1988. 29.95. St Martin.

Sports Encyclopedia: Baseball. 6th, rev. ed. David S. Neft & Richard M. Cohen. 544p. 1985. 27.50 (ISBN 0-312-75337-3, Pub. by Marek); pap. 14.95 (ISBN 0-312-75336-5, Pub. by Marek). St Martin.

Sports Encyclopedia: Baseball. 7th ed. David S. Neft & Richard M. Cohen. LC 85-1833. 608p. 1987. 29.95 (ISBN 0-312-00750-7). St Martin.

Sports Encyclopedia: Baseball. 8th ed. David S. Neft & Richard M. Cohen. 608p. 1988. 29.95. St Martin.

Sports Encyclopedia: Baseball. 7th ed. Ed. by David S. Neft & Richard M. Cohen. 608p. 1987. pap. 14.95 (ISBN 0-312-00686-1). St Martin.

Sports Encyclopedia: Baseball. rev. ed. David S. Neft et al. LC 73-15137. 544p. 1982. pap. 12.95 (ISBN 0-448-14047-0, G&D). Putnam Pub Group.

Sports Encyclopedia Baseball, 1988. David Neft & Richard M. Cohen. 624p. 1988. pap. 15.95 (ISBN 0-312-01828-2). St Martin.

Sports Encyclopedia North America, 50 vols, Vols. 1-2. Ed. by John D. Windhausen. 1987. 32.00 ea. (ISBN 0-317-56137-5). Academic Intl.

Sports Encyclopedia: Pro Football. 5th ed. David S. Neft et al. 592p. 1987. 24.95 (ISBN 0-312-01351-5). St Martin.

Sports Encyclopedia: Pro Football: The Modern Era, 1960 to the Present. 5th, rev. ed. David S. Neft & Richard M. Cohen. 640p. 1988. pap. 15.95 (ISBN 0-312-02289-1). St Martin.

Sports Encyclopedia: The Modern Era, 1960 to the Present. 5th ed. David S. Neft et al. 592p. 1987. pap. 15.95 (ISBN 0-312-01094-X). St Martin.

Sports Equipment. 1985. 125.00x (ISBN 0-686-71957-3, Pub. by Euromonitor). State Mutual Bk.

Sports Equipment Book. Michael Emberley. (Illus.). 32p. (gr. 3 up). 1982. 12.95 (ISBN 0-316-23405-2). Little.

Sports Fiction for Adults: An Annotated Bibliography of Novels, Plays, Short Stories & Poetry with Sporting Settings. Suzanne Wise. LC 84-45368. (Library of the Humanities Ser.). 222p. 1985. lib. bdg. 33.00 (ISBN 0-8240-8820-4). Garland Pub.

Sports Films: A Complete Reference. Compiled by Harvey M. Zucker & Lawrence J. Babich. LC 85-43601. 622p. 1987. lib. bdg. 39.95x (ISBN 0-89950-227-X). McFarland & Co.

Sports, Fitness & Leisure Markets. 3rd ed. Fairchild Market Research Division Staff. (Fairchild Fact Files). (Illus.). 50p. 1986. pap. 17.50 (ISBN 0-87005-552-6). Fairchild.

Sports Fitness & Training. Peter Jokl et al. LC 86-12185. 432p. 1987. 27.95 (ISBN 0-394-54972-4). Pantheon.

Sports Fitness for Women. Elizabeth Day & Ken Day. (Illus.). 120p. 1986. 18.95 (ISBN 0-7134-4692-7, Pub. by Batsford England). David & Charles.

Sports-Fitness-Leisure Markets. 4th ed. Fairchild Market Research Division Staff. (Fact File Ser.). 60p. (Orig.). 1988. pap. 17.50 (ISBN 0-87005-639-5). Fairchild.

Sports for Sale: Television, Money, & the Fans. David A. Klatell & Norman Marcus. (Illus.). 272p. 1988. 18.95. Oxford U Pr.

Sports for the Handicapped. Anne Allen. (gr. 6 up). 1981. lib. bdg. 10.85 (ISBN 0-8027-6437-1). Walker & Co.

Sports for the Leg Amputee. Bernice Kegel. 72p. 1986. pap. 3.50 (ISBN 0-934230-14-5). Medic Pub.

Sports, Games, & Play. 2nd ed. Jeffrey H. Goldstein. 392p. 1988. text ed. 36.00 (ISBN 0-89859-875-3). L Erlbaum Assocs.

Sports, Games, & Play: Social & Psychological Viewpoints. Ed. by J. H. Goldstein. 480p. 1979. 39.95 (ISBN 0-89859-467-7). L Erlbaum Assocs.

Sport's Golden Age, a Closeup of the Fabulous Twenties. facs. ed. Ed. by Allison Danzig & Peter Brandwein. LC 68-58784. (Essay Index Reprint Ser). 1948. 22.00 (ISBN 0-8369-0013-8). Ayer Co Pubs.

Sports Great Magic Johnson. James Haskins. 64p. (YA) (gr. 4-12). 1989. lib. bdg. 12.95 (ISBN 0-89490-160-5). Enslow Pubs.

Sports: Guidebook for Reference & Research. Hugo H. Bronsen. LC 88-47627. 150p. 1988. 34.50 (ISBN 0-88164-652-0); pap. 26.50 (ISBN 0-88164-653-9). ABBE Pubs Assn.

Sports Hall of Fame. Bruce Nash & Allan Zullo. 1987. write for info. PB.

Sports Hall of Oblivion. Chuck Hershberger. LC 86-159616. 111p. (Orig.). 1985. pap. 3.95 (ISBN 0-938455-00-1). Sports Hall Oblivion.

Sports Hall of Shame. Bruce Nash & Allan Zullo. 1987. pap. 8.95 (ISBN 0-671-63387-2). PB.

Sports Health: The Complete Book of Athletic Injuries. Marshall Hoffman & William Southmayd. (Illus.). 464p. 1981. pap. 16.95 (ISBN 0-399-51107-5, Pedigree). Putnam Pub Group.

Sports Illustrated Baseball: Playing the Winning Way. Jerry Kindall. (Winner's Circle Bks.). 1988. 9.95 (ISBN 0-452-26100-7). NAL.

Sports Illustrated Baseball's Record Breakers. Bill Gutman. (Illus.). 144p. (gr. 5 up). 1988. pap. 2.50 (ISBN 0-671-64481-5). Archway.

Sports Illustrated Basketball: The Keys to Excellence. Neil D. Isaacs & Dick Motta. (Illus.). 112p. 1988. pap. 9.95 (ISBN 0-452-26207-0). NAL.

Sports Illustrated Bowling: Styling Your Game for Success. Herm Weiskopf & Chuck Pezzano. (Winner's Circle Bks.). 144p. 1988. 9.95 (ISBN 0-452-26038-8). NAL.

Sports Illustrated Canoeing: Skills for the Serious Paddler. Dave Harrison. (Winner's Circle Bks.). 1988. 9.95 (ISBN 0-452-26109-0). NAL.

Sports Illustrated Competitive Swimming: Techniques for Champions. Mark Schubert. (Illus.). 256p. (Orig.). 1988. pap. 9.95 (ISBN 0-452-26106-6). NAL.

Sports Illustrated Cross-Country Skiing: A Complete Guide. Casey Sheahan. (Illus.). 224p. 1988. pap. 9.95 (ISBN 0-452-26208-9). NAL.

Sports Illustrated Figure Skating: Championship Techniques. John M. Petkevich. (Illus.). 192p. 1988. pap. 9.95 (ISBN 0-452-26209-7). NAL.

Sports Illustrated Fly Fishing: Learn from a Master. Bill Mason. (Winner's Circle Bks.). (Illus.). 256p. (Orig.). 1988. pap. 11.95 (ISBN 0-452-26097-3). NAL.

Sports Illustrated Football: Winning Defense. Bud Wilkinson. (Illus.). 176p. 1987. pap. 9.95 (ISBN 0-452-26036-1). NAL.

Sports Illustrated Football Winning Offense. Bud Wilkinson. (Illus.). 208p. (Orig.). 1987. pap. 9.95 (ISBN 0-452-26035-3). NAL.

Sports Illustrated Golf: Play Like a Pro. Mark Mulvoy. (Winner's Circle Bks.). 1988. 9.95 (ISBN 0-452-26098-1). NAL.

Sports Illustrated Great Moments in Baseball. Bill Gutman. (gr. 5 up). 1987. pap. 2.50 (ISBN 0-671-63126-8). Archway.

Sports Illustrated Great Moments in Pro Football. Bill Gutman. (Illus.). (gr. 4 up). 1987. pap. 2.50 (ISBN 0-671-63015-6). Archway.

Sports Illustrated Hockey: Learn to Play the Modern Way. Jack Falla. (Illus.). 256p. 1987. pap. 9.95 (ISBN 0-452-26042-6). NAL.

Sports Illustrated Lacrosse: Fundamentals & Strategies for Winning. David Urick. (Winner's Circle Bks.). (Illus.). 256p. (Orig.). 1988. pap. 9.95 (ISBN 0-452-26102-3). NAL.

Sports Illustrated Pitching: The Keys to Excellence. Pat Jordan. (Winner's Circle Bks.). 1988. 9.95 (ISBN 0-452-26101-5). NAL.

Sports Illustrated Pro Football's Record Breakers. Bill Gutman. (gr. 5 up). 1987. pap. 2.50 (ISBN 0-671-64375-4). Archway.

Sports Illustrated Racquetball: Strategies for Winning. Victor I. Spear. (Winner's Circle Bks.). 176p. 1988. 9.95 (ISBN 0-452-26043-4). NAL.

Sports Illustrated Scuba Diving. Hank Ketels & Jack McDowell. 1979. pap. 5.95xi (ISBN 0-397-01305-1, LP-136). Har-Row.

Sports Illustrated Scuba Diving: Underwater Adventuring for Everyone. Hank Ketels & Jack McDowell. (Winner's Circle Bks.). 1988. 9.95 (ISBN 0-452-26108-2). NAL.

Sports Illustrated Skiing: Six Ways to Reach Your Skiing Potential. Tim Petrick. (Illus.). 192p. 1987. pap. 9.95 (ISBN 0-452-26039-6). NAL.

Sports Illustrated Soccer: The Complete Player. Dan Herbst. (Illus.). 192p. 1988. pap. 9.95 (ISBN 0-452-26206-2). NAL.

Sports Illustrated Strange & Amazing Football Stories. Bill Gutman. (Illus.). (gr. 4 up). 1987. pap. 2.50 (ISBN 0-671-61133-X). Archway.

Sports Illustrated Strange & Amazing Baseball. Bill Gutman. (gr. 5 up). 1987. pap. 2.50. Archway.

Sports Illustrated Strength Training: Add Stength & Power to Your Total Fitness Program. John Garhammer. (Illus.). 208p. 1987. pap. 9.95 (ISBN 0-452-26041-8). NAL.

Sports Illustrated Tennis: Strokes for Success. Doug MacCurdy & Shawn Tully. (Winner's Circle Bks.). 1988. 9.95 (ISBN 0-452-26103-1). NAL.

Sports Illustrated Track: Championship Running. Mel Rosen & Karen Rosen. (Winner's Circle Bks.). 1988. 9.95 (ISBN 0-452-26105-8). NAL.

Sports in America. James A. Michener. 1987. pap. 4.95 (ISBN 0-449-21450-8, Crest). Fawcett.

Sports in America. James A. Michener. LC 75-40549. (YA) (gr. 7-12). 1976. 15.95 (ISBN 0-394-40646-X). Random.

Sports in America. Ed. by Janet Podell. LC 85-22656. (Reference Shelf Ser.: Vol. 57 No. 5). 160p. 1986. pap. 10.00 (ISBN 0-8242-0713-0). Wilson.

Sports in American Culture, 1980: Proceedings. Sports in American Culture Conference, University of South Florida, May 8-9 1980. Ed. by Don Harkness. (Illus.). 50p. (Orig.). 1980. pap. 3.25 (ISBN 0-934996-09-1). American Studies Pr.

Sports in American Life. Frederick W. Cozens & Florence S. Stumpf. LC 75-22810. (America in Two Centuries Ser). 1976. Repr. of 1953 ed. 29.00x (ISBN 0-405-07681-9). Ayer Co Pubs.

Sports in Modern America. William J. Baker & John M. Carroll. Ed. by Bob Broeg. LC 81-51300. (Illus.). 192p. (Orig.). 1981. pap. text ed. 11.00 (ISBN 0-933150-30-X). River City MO.

Sports in the Western World. William J. Baker. LC 82-3669. (Illus.). 368p. 1982. pap. 14.50x (ISBN 0-8476-7194-1). Rowman.

Sports in the Western World. rev. ed. William J. Baker. (Sport & Society Ser.). (Illus.). 1988. pap. 14.95 (ISBN 0-252-06042-3). U of Ill Pr.

Sports Industry & Collective Bargaining. Paul D. Staudohar. LC 86-7160. 204p. (Orig.). 1986. 22.50 (ISBN 0-87546-117-4); pap. 9.95 (ISBN 0-87546-118-2). ILR Pr.

Sports Injuries. Hans Kraus. (Illus.). 160p. (Orig.). 1983. pap. 4.95 (ISBN 0-399-50861-9, G&D). Putnam Pub Group.

Sports Injuries. Lars Peterson. (Illus.). 488p. 1986. pap. text ed. 35.50 (ISBN 0-8151-6678-8). Year Bk Med.

Sports Injuries. 2nd ed. Paul F. Vinger & Earl F. Horner. (Illus.). 474p. 1986. 48.00 (ISBN 0-88416-498-5). PSG Pub Co.

Sports Injuries: A Unique Self-Diagnosis & Treatment Guide. Malcolm Read & Paul Wade. LC 83-16555. (Illus.). 160p. 1985. 12.95 (ISBN 0-668-06049-2); pap. 7.95 (ISBN 0-668-06051-4). Arco.

Sports Injuries & Their Treatment. Ed. by Basil Helal et al. (Illus.). 520p. 1986. text ed. 79.50x (ISBN 0-412-23950-7, Pub. by Chapman & Hall UK). Sheridan Med Bks.

Sports Injuries: Mechanisms, Treatment, & Prevention. Richard C. Schneider & John C. Kennedy. (Illus.). 8809p. 1985. 99.95 (ISBN 0-683-07609-4). Williams & Wilkins.

Sports Injury Handbook. Hans Kraus. (Illus.). 160p. 1987. pap. 9.95 (ISBN 0-941130-26-6). N Lyons Bks.

Sports Injury Management Series, 4 vols. Ed. by Terry Malone. 1988. 24.95 ea. (ISBN 0-683-07864-X); 50.00 set. No. 1: Evaluation of Isokinetic Equipment. No. 2: Muscle Injury & Rehabilitation. No. 3: Shoulder Injuries. No. 4: Basketball Injuries & Treatment. Williams & Wilkins.

Sports Junkies Rejoice! The Birth of ESPN. Bill Rasmussen. 256p. 1983. 14.95 (ISBN 0-318-00106-3). QV Pub.

Sports Law. George W. Schubert et al. 395p. 1986. text ed. 20.95 (ISBN 0-314-99967-1). West Pub.

Sports Law: Cases & Materials. Ray Yasser. 660p. 1985. lib. bdg. 49.50 (ISBN 0-8191-4827-X); pap. text ed. 26.00 (ISBN 0-8191-4828-8). U Pr of Amer.

Sports Law for Educational Institutions. Steven C. Wade & Robert D. Hay. 1988. 37.85 (ISBN 0-89930-335-8, HSL/, Quorum Bks). Greenwood.

Sports Literature. Ed. by John Brady & James Hall. (Patterns in Literary Art Ser.). 276p. (gr. 9-12). 1974. pap. 13.80 (ISBN 0-07-007085-7). McGraw.

Sports Market Place. Ed. by Richard A. Lipsey. 600p. 1988. pap. 125.00. Sportsguide.

Sports Medicine. Melvin Berger. LC 81-43891. (Scientists at Work Ser.). (Illus.). 128p. (gr. 5 up). 1982. 12.70i (ISBN 0-690-04209-4, Crowell Jr Bks); PLB 12.89 (ISBN 0-690-04210-8). HarpJ.

Sports Medicine. Edward Edelson. (Healthy Body Ser.). (Illus.). 108p. (gr. 5 up). 1988. lib. bdg. 17.95x (ISBN 0-7910-0030-3). Chelsea Hse.

Sports Medicine. Ed. by Dale C. Garell & Solomon H. Snyder. (Encyclopedia of Health Ser.). (Illus.). (YA) (gr. 7-12). 1989. 17.95. Chelsea Hse.

Sports Medicine. Allan J. Ryan & Fred L. Allman. 1974. 88.00 (ISBN 0-12-605060-0). Acad Pr.

Sports Medicine. Nathan J. Smith. (Blue Bk.). (Illus.). 238p. 1987. pap. 19.95 (ISBN 0-7216-1167-2). Saunders.

Sports Medicine. Richard H. Strauss. (Illus.). 576p. 1984. 68.00 (ISBN 0-7216-8611-7). Saunders.

Sports Medicine & Athletic Injuries. Alfred F. Morris. 400p. 1984. pap. text ed. write for info (ISBN 0-697-00087-7). Wm C Brown.

Sports Medicine & Medical Ethics. Hoerner. cancelled (ISBN 0-88416-542-6). PSG Pub Co.

Sports Medicine: Facts for the 80's. Ed. by Susan Tellem et al. 128p. (Orig.). 1984. pap. 8.95 (ISBN 0-9608846-3-7). PM Inc.

Sports Medicine Fitness Course. David C. Nieman. LC 86-12912. (Illus.). 500p. (Orig.). 1986. pap. 22.95 (ISBN 0-915950-76-6). Bull Pub.

Sports Medicine: Fitness, Training, Injuries. 3rd ed. Otto Appenzeller. 512p. 1988. text ed. 49.50 (ISBN 0-8067-0143-9); pap. text ed. 37.50 (ISBN 0-8067-0133-1). Urban & S.

Sports Medicine for the Athletic Female. Ed. by Christine E. Haycock. LC 83-23838. 424p. 1984. pap. 10.95 (ISBN 0-399-51007-9, G&D). Putnam Pub Group.

Sports Medicine for the Primary Care Physician. Richard Birrer. (Illus.). 347p. 1983. 37.95 (ISBN 0-8385-8651-1). Appleton & Lange.

Sports Medicine for the Primary Care Physician. Ed. by Richard B. Birrer. 347p. 1984. 34.95. Soc Tchrs Fam Med.

Sports Medicine: Health Care for the Young Athlete. Sports Medicine Committee. LC 82-73444. 326p. 1983. pap. 20.00 (ISBN 0-910761-02-7). Am Acad Pediat.

Sports Medicine in Primary Care. Robert C. Cantu. LC 81-70166. 240p. 1982. 24.95 (ISBN 0-669-04593-4, Collamore); pap. 16.95 (ISBN 0-669-05429-1, Collamore). Heath.

Sports Medicine: International Survey with Research Subject Index & Bibliography. Hugo H. Bronsen. LC 82-72013. 158p. 1983. 34.50 (ISBN 0-941864-42-1); pap. 26.50 (ISBN 0-941864-43-X). ABBE Pubs Assn.

Sports Medicine Prevention Evaluation Management & Rehabilitation. Steven P. Roy & Richard F. Irvin. (Illus.). 560p. 1983. text ed. 39.33 (ISBN 0-13-837807-X). P-H.

Sports Medicine Research Today. 1988. looseleaf binder 120.00. BIOSIS.

Sports Medicine, Sports Science: Bridging the Gap. Robert C. Cantu & W. Jay Gillespie. LC 81-70165. 252p. 1982. 18.95 (ISBN 0-669-05226-4, Collamore). Heath.

Sports Memorabilia. 2nd ed. John A. Douglas. LC 87-51418. (Illus.). 256p. 1988. pap. 19.95 (ISBN 0-87069-509-6). Wallace-Homestead.

Sports Nutrition. Joyce Sorenson & Nancy Murray. (Menus for Better Health Ser.). 36p. (Orig.). 1982. pap. 1.95 (ISBN 0-911638-13-X). Witkower.

Sports Nutrition: A Guide for the Professional Working with Active People. Sports & Cardiovascular Nutritionists Dietetic Practice Group Staff & The American Dietetic Association Staff. (Illus.). 164p. (Orig.). 1986. pap. text ed. 23.95 (ISBN 0-88091-025-9). Am Dietetic Assn.

Sports of the Times: Great Moments in Sports History. Gene Brown. Ed. by Arleen Keylin & Daniel Lundy. 14.98 (ISBN 0-405-14225-0, 19816). Ayer Co Pubs.

Sports Officiating: A Legal Guide. Alan S. Goldberger. LC 82-83925. (Illus.). 160p. (Orig.). 1984. pap. 11.95 (ISBN 0-88011-092-9, PGOL0092). Leisure Pr.

Sports Ophthalmology. Ed. by Louis D. Pizzarello & Barrett G. Haik. (Illus.). 216p. 1987. 29.75x (ISBN 0-398-05309-X). C C Thomas.

Sports Page. Stanley Woodward. LC 68-55638. (Illus.). 1968. Repr. of 1949 ed. lib. bdg. 35.00 (ISBN 0-8371-0762-8, WOSP). Greenwood.

Sports Pages. Arnold Adoff. LC 85-45169. (Illus.). 80p. (gr. 3-7). 1986. 11.25i (ISBN 0-397-32102-3, Lipp Jr Bks); PLB 10.89g (ISBN 0-397-32103-1). HarpJ.

Sports Pages: A Critical Bibliography of Twentieth-Century American Novels & Stories Featuring Baseball, Basketball, Football & Other Pursuits. Grant Burns. LC 86-31388. 284p. 1987. 25.00 (ISBN 0-8108-1966-X). Scarecrow.
Sports People. Date not set. price not set. Abrams.
Sports Performance Factors. William Southmayd & James Rippe. 1986. pap. 10.95 (ISBN 0-399-51188-1, Perigee). Putnam Pub Group.
Sports Photography. Bill Hurter. LC 78-70044. (Photography How-to Ser.). (Illus.). 1978. pap. 3.95 (ISBN 0-8227-4026-5). Petersen Pub.
Sports Physical Therapy. Ed. by Donna B. Bernhardt. (Clinics in Physical Therapy Ser.: Vol. 10). (Illus.). 223p. 1986. text ed. 30.00 (ISBN 0-443-08444-0). Churchill.
Sports Physiology. 2nd ed. Edward L. Fox. 418p. 1984. text ed. write for info. (ISBN 0-697-05994-4). Wm C Brown.
Sports Pool Draft Book. rev. ed. Challenger Progress Press Staff. Ed. by Nancy D. Dominitz. (Illus.). 68p. 1986. pap. cancelled (ISBN 0-914629-08-5, Dist. by St. Martin). Prima Pub Comm.
Sports Psyching: Playing Your Best Game All of the Time. Thomas A. Tutko & Umberto Tosi. LC 75-27975. 229p. 1976. pap. 7.95 (ISBN 0-87477-136-6). J P Tarcher.
Sports Psychology: Concepts & Applications. Richard H. Cox. 400p. 1985. pap. text ed. write for info. (ISBN 0-697-00141-5). Wm C Brown.
Sports Quotations: Maxims, Quips & Pronouncements for Writers & Fans. Andrew J. Maikovich. LC 83-20005. 174p. 1984. lib. bdg. 18.95x (ISBN 0-89950-100-1). McFarland & Co.
Sports Reporting. Bruce Garrison & Mark Sabljak. (Illus.). 252p. 1985. text ed. 24.95x (ISBN 0-8138-1691-2). Iowa St U Pr.
Sports: Research & Medical Guidebook with Bibliography. Riley N. Wiseman. LC 87-47660. 150p. 1987. 34.50 (ISBN 0-88164-678-4); pap. 26.50 (ISBN 0-88164-679-2). Abbe Pubs Assn.
Sports Riddles. Joseph Rosenbloom. LC 81-7232. (Illus.). 64p. (gr. 6 up). 1982. 8.95 (ISBN 0-15-277994-9, HJ). HarBraceJ.
Sports, Sex, Drugs...& Other American Pastimes. Judd Biasiotto. (Illus.). 175p. (Orig.). 1988. pap. 10.00 (ISBN 0-933079-09-5). World Class Enterprises.
Sports Skills for Boys & Girls. J. H. Humphrey & J. N. Humphrey. (Illus.). 128p. 1980. pap. 13.50 (ISBN 0-398-04027-3). C C Thomas.
Sports Spectators. Allen Guttmann. LC 86-8268. 224p. 1986. 24.95 (ISBN 0-231-06400-4). Columbia U Pr.
Sports Spectators. Allen Guttmann. 236p. 1988. pap. 12.50x (ISBN 0-231-06401-2). Columbia U Pr.
Sports Splash: A Handbook of Reading Activities for Use With Children. Ed. by Carol H. Thomas. (Fun with Reading Bk.). (Illus.). 120p. (Orig.). 1983. pap. 15.00x (ISBN 0-89774-000-9). Oryx Pr.
Sports Star: Carl Lewis. S. H. Burchard. (Sports Star Ser.). (Illus.). (gr. 1-5). cancelled (ISBN 0-15-278054-8, HJ). HarBraceJ.
Sports Star: Fernando Valenzuela. S. H. Burchard. LC 82-47932. (Sports Star Ser.). (Illus.). 64p. (ps-3). 1982. pap. 2.95 (ISBN 0-15-278045-9, VoyB). HarBraceJ.
Sports Star: Fernando Valenzuela. S. H. Burchard. LC 82-47932. (Sports Star Ser.). (Illus.). 64p. (ps-3). 1982. 8.95 (ISBN 0-15-278044-0, HJ). HarBraceJ.
Sports Star: George Brett. S. H. Burchard. LC 81-13293. (Sports Star Ser.). (Illus.). 64p. (gr. 1-5). 1982. pap. 2.95 (ISBN 0-15-278041-6, VoyB). HarBraceJ.
Sports Star: Herschel Walker. S. H. Burchard. LC 83-22674. (Sports Star Ser.). (Illus.). 64p. (gr. 1-5). 1984. pap. 5.95 (ISBN 0-15-278053-X, VoyB). HarBraceJ.
Sports Star: Sugar Ray Leonard. S. H. Burchard. LC 82-48764. (Sports Star Ser.). 64p. (gr. 1-5). 1983. PLB 11.95 (ISBN 0-15-278048-3, HJ). HarBraceJ.
Sports Star: Sugar Ray Leonard. S. H. Burchard. LC 82-48764. (Sports Star Ser.). (Illus.). 64p. (gr. 1-5). 1983. pap. 4.95 (ISBN 0-15-278049-1, VoyB). HarBraceJ.
Sports Star: The Book of Baseball Greats. S. H. Burchard. LC 82-48763. (Sports Star Ser.). 64p. (gr. 1-5). 1983. PLB 10.95 (ISBN 0-15-278060-2, HJ). HarBraceJ.
Sports Star: Tracy Austin. S. H. Burchard. LC 81-84215. (Sports Star Ser.). (Illus.). 64p. (gr. 1-5). 1982. pap. 2.95 (ISBN 0-15-278043-2, VoyB). HarBraceJ.
Sports Star: Wayne Gretzky. S. H. Burchard. LC 82-47931. (Sports Star Ser.). (Illus.). 64p. (ps-3). 1982. pap. 2.95 (ISBN 0-15-278047-5, VoyB). HarBraceJ.
Sports Stars Cookbook. Harvey Shapiro. (Illus.). 1976. plastic bdg. 5.95 (ISBN 0-915088-11-8). C Hungness.
Sports Success Book: The Athlete's Guide to Sports Achievement. Karl M. Woods. LC 84-19832. (Illus.). 256p. (Orig.). (YA) 1985. 17.95 (ISBN 0-933857-00-4); pap. 12.95 (ISBN 0-933857-01-2). Copperfield Pr.
Sports Success Book: The Young Athlete's Guide to Sports Achievement. Karl M. Woods. (Illus.). 224p. 1985. cancelled (ISBN 0-89651-709-8); pap. 9.95 (ISBN 0-89651-710-1). B L Pub.
Sports Success Workout Book. Karl M. Woods. (Illus.). 208p. pap. cancelled (ISBN 0-89651-711-X). B L Pub.
Sports Teasers: A Book of Games & Puzzles. Zander Hollander. (Sports Library). (Illus.). 160p. (gr. 6-9). 1982. pap. 1.95 (ISBN 0-394-85014-9). Random.
Sports Trip. Lee Mountain. (Attention Span Stories Ser). (Illus.). 48p. (Orig., Reading level gr. 2-3, Interest level gr. 6-9). 1978. pap. text ed. 4.80x (ISBN 0-89061-147-5, 583). Jamestown Pubs.
Sports Violence. Ed. by J. H. Goldstein. (Springer Series in Social Psychology). (Illus.). 250p. 1983. 32.00 (ISBN 0-387-90828-5). Springer-Verlag.
Sports, Vol. 3 (incl. 1986-1987 Supplements) Ed. by Eleanor C. Goldstein. 1987. 30.00 (ISBN 0-89777-087-0). Soc Issues.
Sports with Dogs. Ellie Milon. (Illus.). 160p. 1988. price not set (ISBN 0-931866-33-2). Alpine Pubns.
Sports Women. Ed. by M. J. Adrian. (Medicine & Sport Science Ser.: Vol. 24). (Illus.). viii, 160p. 1987. 98.75 (ISBN 3-8055-4501-0). S Karger.
Sports Writing Handbook. Thomas Fensch. (Communications Textbook Ser.). 224p. 1988. pap. 14.95 (ISBN 0-8058-0263-0) (ISBN 0-8058-0396-3). L Erlbaum Assocs.
Sportsathon Puzzles, Jokes, Facts & Games. Vic Braden & Louis Phillips. (Puffin Activity Bks.). (Illus.). (ps-k). 1986. pap. 4.95 (ISBN 0-14-032028-8, Puffin). Penguin.
Sportscape. John R. Gleeson, III. LC 84-52105. (Illus.). 176p. (Orig.). 1984. pap. 12.95 (ISBN 0-912661-04-6). Woodsong Graph.
Sportscasting: A Practical Guide to Success. John Hitchcock. 1987. pap. 15.00 (ISBN 0-943987-00-8). Origin Co.
Sportscience: Physical Laws & Optimum Performance. Peter J. Brancazio. LC 83-20152. 400p. 1984. 18.95 (ISBN 0-671-45584-2). S&S.
Sportset: A Math Practice Set. Jerry Funk. 100p. 1981. pap. text ed. 11.00 (ISBN 0-205-07670-X, 177670); instr's manual avail. (ISBN 0-205-07671-8). Allyn.
Sportsfitness for Women. Sandra Rosenzweig. LC 81-48048. (Illus.). 448p. 1982. (HarpT). Har-Row.
Sportshots. Wally Neibart & Mickey Charles. (Illus.). 120p. 1982. pap. 4.95 (ISBN 0-943588-00-6). Baron-Scott Enterp.
Sportsmanlike Driving. 7th ed. American Automobile Association Staff. 1977. text ed. 23.56 (ISBN 0-07-001292-X, W). McGraw.
Sportsmanlike Driving. rev. ed. American Automobile Association Staff. Ed. by Carolyn E. Cranford. (Illus.). (gr. 10-12). 1980. text ed. 21.08 (ISBN 0-07-001330-6); pap. text ed. 13.80 (ISBN 0-07-001331-4). McGraw.
Sportsmanlike Driving. 9th ed. American Automobile Association Staff. 352p. (gr. 9-12). 1987. text ed. 20.68 (ISBN 0-07-001338-1); pap. text ed. 13.52 (ISBN 0-07-001339-X). McGraw.
Sportsmans Book of U. S. Records. Joseph Glogan. (Illus.). 96p. (Orig.). 1980. pap. text ed. 4.95 (ISBN 0-937328-00-6). NY Outdoor Guide.
Sportsmans Book of U. S. Records. 2nd ed. Joseph Glogan. (Illus.). 122p. 1981. pap. text ed. 4.95 (ISBN 0-937328-01-4). NY Outdoor Guide.
Sportsmans Book of U. S. Records. 3rd ed. Joseph Glogan. (Illus.). 144p. 1982. pap. text ed. 4.95 (ISBN 0-937328-02-2). NY Outdoor Guide.
Sportsmans Book of U. S. Records. 4th ed. Joseph Glogan. (Illus.). 168p. 1983. pap. text ed. 4.95 (ISBN 0-937328-03-0, Dist. by Caroline House, Inc.). NY Outdoor Guide.
Sportsmans Book of U. S. Records. 5th ed. Joseph Glogan. (Illus.). 104p. pap. text ed. 3.95 (ISBN 0-937328-04-9). NY Outdoor Guide.
Sportsman's Dictionary of Fishing & Hunting Lingo. Vin T. Sparano. (Illus.). 1987. 12.45 (ISBN 0-679-51360-4). McKay.
Sportsman's Notebook. Ivan S. Turgenev. Tr. by Charles Hepburn & Natasha Hepburn. 398p. 1986. pap. 10.50 (ISBN 0-88001-119-X). Ecco Pr.
Sportsman's Pocket Companion. Peter Hawker. 1982. pap. 195.00x (ISBN 0-904475-26-3, Pub. by A Atha Pubs Ltd). State Mutual Bk.
Sportsmedicine Book. Gabe Mirkin & Marshall Hoffman. LC 78-14908. 1978. 24.45i (ISBN 0-316-57434-1); pap. 14.95 (ISBN 0-316-57436-8). Little.
Sportsmen in a Landscape. facs. ed. Aubrey Noakes. LC 72-134122. (Essay Index Reprint Ser). 1954. 24.00 (ISBN 0-8369-2005-8). Ayer Co Pubs.
Sportsmen under Stress. Angela Patmore. (Illus.). 272p. 1987. 24.95 (ISBN 0-09-166070-X, Pub. by Century Hutchinson). David & Charles.
Sportspeed. George B. Dintiman & Robert D. Ward. LC 88-4193. (Illus.). 172p. (Orig.). 1988. pap. 11.95 (ISBN 0-88011-325-1). Leisure Pr.
SportsTalent. Robert Arnot & Charles Gaines. 320p. 1986. pap. 8.95 (ISBN 0-14-007790-1). Penguin.
Sportswear, Casual Wear, Separates, Jeans: Women's, Misses', Juniors' 6th ed. Fairchild Market Research Division Staff. (Fairchild Fact Files Ser.). (Illus.). 50p. 1986. pap. 17.50 (ISBN 0-87005-555-0). Fairchild.
Sportswear, Casual Wear, Separates: (Women's, Misses & Juniors) 10th ed. Fairchild Market Research Division Staff. (Fact File Ser.). 45p. 1988. pap. 17.50 (ISBN 0-87005-642-5). Fairchild.
Sportswear in Vogue since 1910. Christina Probert. LC 83-26574. (Accessories in Vogue Ser.). (Illus.). 96p. 1984. pap. 12.95 (ISBN 0-89659-499-8). Abbeville Pr.
Sportswit. Lee Green. LC 83-48840. 270p. 1984. 15.45i (ISBN 0-06-015272-9, HarpT). Har-Row.
Sportswit. Lee Green. 544p. 1986. pap. 4.50 (ISBN 0-449-20948-2). Fawcett.
Sportswriter. Richard Ford. LC 85-40537. (Vintage Contemporaries Ser.). 432p. 1986. pap. 6.95 (ISBN 0-394-74325-3, Vin). Random.
Sporty Blank Reproducible Worksheets. Patti Carson & Janet Dellosa. (Stick-Out-Your-Neck Ser.). (Illus.). 96p. (gr. 1-6). pap. 6.95 (ISBN 0-88724-031-3, 0919). Carson-Dellos.
Sporty Game. John Newhouse. LC 81-48123. 1982. 22.45 (ISBN 0-394-51447-5). Knopf.
Spot & Scot. Ruth Kraft. (Illus.). (gr. 1-2). 1970. pap. 1.50 (ISBN 0-912472-03-0). Miller Bks.
Spot at Play. Eric Hill. LC 84-17848. (Little Spot Board Bks.). (Illus.). 14p. (ps-1). 1985. bds. 3.50 (ISBN 0-399-21228-0, Putnam). Putnam Pub Group.
Spot at the Fair. Eric Hill. LC 84-17849. (Little Spot Board Bks.). (Illus.). 14p. (ps-1). 1985. bds. 3.50 (ISBN 0-399-21229-9, Putnam). Putnam Pub Group.
Spot Drills. Rayner Markley. (Illus.). 142p. 1983. Bk. 1. pap. text ed. 6.50x (ISBN 0-19-434125-9); Bk. 2. pap. text ed. 6.95x (ISBN 0-19-434126-7); Bk. 3. pap. text ed. 6.95x (ISBN 0-19-503156-3): Oxford U Pr.
Spot Goes Splash! Eric Hill. (Soft Spot Ser.). (Illus.). 8p. (gr. k-1). 1984. vinyl foam-filled 2.95 (ISBN 0-399-21068-7, Putnam). Putnam Pub Group.
Spot Goes to School. Eric Hill. LC 84-42695. (Soft Spots Ser.). (Illus.). 22p. (ps-2). 1984. 9.95 (ISBN 0-399-21073-3, Putnam). Putnam Pub Group.
Spot Goes to School. Ed. by Eric Hill. (Lift-the-Flap Ser.). (Illus.). 22p. (Arabic & Eng.). (ps-2). 1988. 10.95 (ISBN 0-940793-06-7, Pub. by Crocodile Bks.). Interlink Pub.
Spot Goes to the Beach. Eric Hill. LC 84-18291. (Illus.). 22p. (gr. k). 1985. 9.95 (ISBN 0-399-21247-7, Putnam). Putnam Pub Group.
Spot Goes to the Circus. Eric Hill. LC 85-24471. (Spot Lift-the-Flap Bks.). (Illus.). 22p. (ps). 1986. 10.95 (ISBN 0-399-21317-1, Putnam). Putnam Pub Group.
Spot Goes to the Farm. Eric Hill. (ps-1). 1987. 10.95 (ISBN 0-399-21434-8). Putnam Pub Group.
Spot Learns to Count. Eric Hill. (Spot's Color-a-Story Bks.). (Illus.). (ps-2). 1983. pap. 1.95 (ISBN 0-399-20985-9, Putnam). Putnam Pub Group.
Spot Looks at Colors. Eric Hill. (Little Spot Board Bks.). (Illus.). 14p. (ps-k). 1986. 3.50 (ISBN 0-399-21349-X, Putnam). Putnam Pub Group.
Spot Looks at Shapes. Eric Hill. (Little Spot Board Bks.). (Illus.). 14p. (ps-1). 1986. 3.50 (ISBN 0-399-21350-3, Putnam). Putnam Pub Group.
Spot of Purple Is Deaf. Ed. by Van K. Brock & Francis Poole. pap. 3.50 (ISBN 0-938078-01-1). Anhinga Pr.
Spot on the Farm. Eric Hill. LC 84-17850. (Little Spot Baord Bks.). (Illus.). 14p. (ps-1). 1985. bds. 3.50 (ISBN 0-399-21230-2, Putnam). Putnam Pub Group.
Spot Reducing Diet. Hermien Lee & Linda Lane. (Illus.). 288p. 1984. 15.95 (ISBN 0-698-11243-1, Coward). Putnam Pub Group.
Spot Tells the Time. Eric Hill. (Spot's Color-a-Story Bks.). (Illus.). (ps-2). 1983. pap. 1.95 (ISBN 0-399-20986-7, Putnam). Putnam Pub Group.
Spot Test Analysis: Clinical,Environmental, Forensic & Geochemical Applications. Ervin Jungreis. LC 84-15176. (Chemical Analysis: A Series of Monographs on Analytical Chemistry & Its Applications: No. 1-075). 368p. 1985. text ed. 60.00x (ISBN 0-471-86524-9, Pub. by Wiley-Interscience). Wiley.
Spot Tests in Inorganic Analysis. 6th ed. F. Feigl & Y. Anger. 669p. 1972. 158.00 (ISBN 0-444-40929-7). Elsevier.
Spot Tests in Organic Analysis. 7th ed. Fritz Feigl & Y. Anger. 772p. 1966. 158.00 (ISBN 0-444-40209-8). Elsevier.
Spot: The Rise of Political Advertising on Television. Rev. ed. Edwin Diamond & Stephen Bates. 404p. (Orig.). 1988. text ed. 25.00x (ISBN 0-262-04095-6); pap. 10.95x (ISBN 0-262-54049-5). MIT Pr.
Spot the Warships. 3rd ed. James Goss. 56p. 1987. 25.00x (ISBN 0-85937-294-4, Pub. by K Mason Pubns Ltd UK). State Mutual Bk.
Spot Va a la Escuela (Spot Goes to School) (Span.). (gr. 3-7). 11.95 (ISBN 0-399-21223-X, Pub. by Putnam). Putnam Pub Group.
Spot Va a la Granja. Eric Hill. (Illus.). 22p. (Span.). (ps-1). 1987. 11.95 (ISBN 0-399-21463-1). Putnam Pub Group.
Spot Va a la Playa (Spot Goes to the Beach) (Span.). (ps-1). 1986. 9.95 (ISBN 0-399-21259-0). Putnam Pub Group.
Spot Va al Circo. Eric Hill. (Spot Lift-the-Flap Bks.). (Illus.). 22p. (Span.). (ps). 1986. 9.95 (ISBN 0-399-21318-X, Putnam). Putnam Pub Group.
Spot Visits the Hospital. (Spot Storybk.). (ps-2). 1987. 4.95 (ISBN 0-399-21397-X, Putnam). Putnam Pub Group.
Spotlessly Leopard. Winifred B. Newman. LC 82-24423. (Illus.). 48p. (Orig.). (gr. 2-6). 1983. pap. 4.95 (ISBN 0-87743-700-9, Pub. by Bellwood Pr). Baha'i.
Spotlight. Peter Chilver. 207p. 1987. pap. text ed. 14.95 (ISBN 0-85950-567-7, Pub. by S Thornes). Dufour.
Spotlight. Patricia Wentworth. 17.95 (Pub. by Aeonian Pr). Amereon LTD.
Spotlight on Card Play: A New Approach to the Practical Analysis of Bridge Hands. Robert Darvas & Paul Lukacs. (Master Bridge Ser.). (Illus.). 160p. 1982. pap. 9.95 (ISBN 0-575-03078-X, Pub. by Gollancz England). David & Charles.
Spotlight on Computer Literacy. Ellen Richman. (gr. 6-8). 1984. pap. 13.20 (ISBN 0-676-39623-2). Random.
Spotlight on Construction Productivity. Louis E. Alfeld. Date not set. 98.00 (ISBN 0-317-59584-9). Constr Ind Pr.
Spotlight on Films. S. Larsen. 1976. lib. bdg. 69.95 (ISBN 0-8490-2662-8). Gordon Pr.
Spotlight on Love. Julie Cahn. (Dream Your Own Romance Ser.: No. 3). (gr. 2-7). 1984. 2.95 (ISBN 0-671-52625-1). Wanderer Bks.
Spotlight on Possums. Rupert Russell. (Illus.). 91p. 1980. 18.00x (ISBN 0-7022-1478-7). U of Queensland Pr.
Spotlight on Stress: Study Guide. Gary Collins. 32p. 1983. 1.50 (ISBN 0-88449-100-5, A424650). Vision Hse.
Spotlight on the Bilderbergers. 63p. Date not set. 5.00 (ISBN 0-317-53253-7). Noontide.
Spotlight on the Child: Studies in the History of American Children's Theatre. Ed. by Roger L. Bedard & C. John Tolch. (Contributions in Drama & Theatre Studies: No. 28). 1989. price not set (ISBN 0-313-25793-0, BDT/). Greenwood.
Spotlight on the Family: Public Policy & Private Responsibility. Steven Bayne & David Biale. LC 88-70021. 60p. (Orig.). 1988. pap. 7.00 (ISBN 0-87495-098-8). Am Jewish Comm.
Spotlight to Fame. Patti Beckman. (Silhouette Romances Ser.). 1984. lib. bdg. 8.95 (ISBN 0-8398-2804-7, Gregg). G K Hall.
Spot's Alphabet. Eric Hill. (Spot's Color-a-Story Bks.). (Illus.). (ps-2). 1983. pap. 1.95 (ISBN 0-399-20984-0, Putnam). Putnam Pub Group.
Spots & Splashes & a Million Butterflies see Magga Birds of Ranatan.
Spot's Big Book of Words. Eric Hill. 1988. 9.95 (ISBN 0-399-21644-8). Putnam Pub Group.
Spot's Big Book of Words. Eric Hill. (gr. 2 up). 1988. 9.95 (ISBN 0-399-21563-8, Putnam). Putnam Pub Group.
Spot's Birthday Party. Eric Hill. (Illus.). (ps-k). 1982. 10.95 (ISBN 0-399-20903-4, Putnam). Putnam Pub Group.
Spot's Busy Year. Eric Hill. (Spot's Color-a-Story Bks.). (Illus.). (ps-2). 1983. pap. 1.95 (ISBN 0-399-20987-5, Putnam). Putnam Pub Group.
Spot's Doghouse. Eric Hill. (Illus.). (ps-1). 1986. pap. 15.95 (ISBN 0-399-21366-X, Putnam). Putnam Pub Group.
Spots, Feathers, & Curly Tails. Nancy Tafuri. LC 87-15638. (Illus.). 32p. (ps-1). 1988. 11.95 (ISBN 0-688-07536-3); lib. bdg. 11.88 (ISBN 0-688-07537-1). Greenwillow.
Spot's First Christmas. Eric Hill. LC 82-23073. (Illus.). (ps-2). 1983. 9.95 (ISBN 0-399-20963-8, Putnam). Putnam Pub Group.
Spot's First Easter. Eric Hill. (ps-1). 1988. 10.95 (ISBN 0-399-21435-6). Putnam Pub Group.
Spot's First Picnic. Eric Hill. (Spot Storybk.). (ps-2). 1987. 4.95 (ISBN 0-399-21398-8, Putnam). Putnam Pub Group.
Spot's First Walk. Eric Hill. (Lift the Flap Bk.). (Illus.). (ps). 1981. 10.95 (ISBN 0-399-20838-0). Putnam Pub Group.
Spot's First Walk. Ed. by Eric Hill. (Lift-the-Flap Ser.). (Illus.). 22p. (Arabic & Eng.). (ps-2). 1988. 10.95 (ISBN 0-940793-05-9, Pub. by Crocodile Bks). Interlink Pub.
Spot's First Walk see Primer Paseo de Spot.
Spot's First Words. Eric Hill. (Little Spot Board Bks.). (Illus.). 14p. 1986. 3.50 (ISBN 0-399-21348-1, Putnam). Putnam Pub Group.
Spot's Friends. Eric Hill. (Soft Spots Ser.). (Illus.). 8p. (gr. k-1). 1984. vinyl foam-filled 2.95 (ISBN 0-399-21066-0, Putnam). Putnam Pub Group.
Spot's Toys. Eric Hill. (Soft Spots Ser.). (Illus.). 8p. (gr. k-1). 1984. 2.95 (ISBN 0-399-21067-9, Putnam). Putnam Pub Group.
Spotted Boy & Commanches. Mabel Earp Cason. LC 63-21050. (Dest Ser.). 1984. pap. 6.95 (ISBN 0-317-28327-8). Pacific Pr Pub Assn.
Spotted Cow. Schomer Lichtner. LC 81-81117. (Illus.). 48p. (Orig.). 1969. pap. 4.50 (ISBN 0-941074-01-3). Lichtner.
Spotted Hemlock. Gladys Mitchell. 240p. 1986. pap. 2.95 (ISBN 0-7701-0483-5). Paperjacks US.
Spotted Hemlock: A Murder Mystery. Gladys Mitchell. 240p. 1985. 14.95 (ISBN 0-312-75350-0). St Martin.
Spotted Horse. Henry Tall Bull & Tom Weist. (Indian Culture Ser.). (gr. 2-10). 1970. 1.95 (ISBN 0-89992-002-0). Coun India Ed.

Spotted Hyena: A Study of Predation & Social Behavior. Hans Kruuk. LC 70-175304. (Wildlife Behavior & Ecology Ser). 368p. 1972. 27.50x (ISBN 0-226-45507-6). U of Chicago Pr.

Spotted Hyena: A Study of Predation & Social Behavior. Hans Kruuk. LC 70-175304. (Wildlife Behavior & Ecology Ser.). 1979. pap. 8.95x (ISBN 0-226-45508-4, P854, Phoen). U of Chicago Pr.

Spotted Pony & the Manitou. Jim Burris. (Illus.). 32p. (gr. 3-6). 1985. 5.95 (ISBN 0-89962-446-4). Todd & Honeywell.

Spotted Sphinx. Joy Adamson. LC 77-85008. (Helen & Kurt Wolff Bk.). (Illus.). 313p. 1969. 9.50 (ISBN 0-15-184795-9). HarBraceJ.

Spotted Tail's Folk: A History of the Brule Sioux. rev. ed. George E. Hyde. LC 61-6497. (Civilization of the American Indian Ser.: Vol. 57). (Illus.). 361p. 1979. pap. 12.95 (ISBN 0-8061-1380-4). U of Okla Pr.

Spotter's Guide to Cats. (Illus.). pap. 2.50 (ISBN 0-8317-7957-8). Smith Pubs.

Spotter's Guide to Dinosaurs & Other Prehistoric Animals. (Illus.). pap. 2.50 (ISBN 0-8317-7960-8). Smith Pubs.

Spotter's Guide to Dogs. (Illus.). pap. 2.50 (ISBN 0-8317-7958-6). Smith Pubs.

Spotter's Handbook to Wildflowers, Trees & Birds of North America. LC 79-10397. (Spotter's Guides Ser.). (Illus.). 1980. 5.95 (ISBN 0-8317-7953-5, Mayflower Bks); pap. 3.95 (ISBN 0-8317-7954-3). Smith Pubs.

Spotting the Fakes-Counterfeits & Forgeries. Eugene Baker. LC 80-15998. (Junior Detective Ser.). (Illus.). 32p. (gr. 2-5). 1980. PLB 6.95 (ISBN 0-89565-153-X). Childs World.

Spotty the Goat see There's a Skunk in My Trunk.

Spotz vs. GCM, Inc. James H. Seckinger. 198p. 1983. 13.95 (ISBN 1-55681-083-0); tchr's. manual 5.00 (ISBN 1-55681-084-9). Natl Inst Trial Ad.

Spousage of a Virgin to Christ. John Alcock. LC 74-80158. (English Experience Ser.: No. 638). (Illus.). 19p. 1974. Repr. of 1496 ed. 3.50 (ISBN 90-221-0638-1). Walter J Johnson.

Spouse Abuse: A Treatment Program for Couples. Peter H. Neidig & Dale H. Friedman. LC 84-61187. 256p. (Orig.). 1984. pap. text ed. 15.95 (ISBN 0-87822-234-0, 2340). Res Press.

Spouse Abuse: An Annotated Bibliography of Violence Between Mates. Eugene A. Engeldinger. LC 85-14546. 331p. 1986. 27.50 (ISBN 0-8108-1838-8). Scarecrow.

Spouse, Parent Worker. Faye J. Crosby. LC 86-26695. 256p. 1987. 25.00 (ISBN 0-300-03843-7). Yale U Pr.

Spouse Spats. Joy Kerley. (Illus.). 87p. (Orig.). 1984. pap. text ed. 8.00 (ISBN 0-9614268-0-2). Teen Round Up.

Spout Spring: A Black Community. Peter Kunkel & Sara S. Kennard. Ed. by George Spindler & Louise Spindler. (Case Studies in Cultural Anthropology). (Illus.). 112p. 1983. pap. text ed. cancelled (ISBN 0-8290-0275-8). Irvington.

Spouted Beds. K. B. Mathur & N. Epstein. 1974. 59.00 (ISBN 0-12-480050-5). Acad Pr.

Spoyle of Antwerpe Faithfully Reported by a True Englishman. George Gascoigne. LC 74-25952. (English Experience Ser.: No. 180). 52p. 1969. Repr. of 1576 ed. 8.00 (ISBN 90-221-0180-0). Walter J Johnson.

Spraakkunst Van Het Marind. P. Drabbe. 1955. 28.00 (ISBN 0-384-12595-6). Johnson Repr.

Sprachdenken. Franz Rosenzweig & Rafael Rosenzweig. 1983. lib. bdg. 50.00 (ISBN 90-247-2695-6, Pub. by Martinus Nijhoff Netherlands). Kluwer Academic.

Sprache Caxtons. Helmut Wiencke. 16.00 (ISBN 0-384-68340-1). Johnson Repr.

Sprache der Guang in Togo und auf der Goldkuste und Funf Andere Togosprachen. Diedrich Westermann. (Ger.). 1922. 21.00 (ISBN 0-8115-3093-0). Kraus Repr.

Sprache des Anderen. Internationales Kolloquium, 9th, Hannover, Sept. 1975. Ed. by G. Hofer. (Bibliotheca Psychiatrica Ser.: No. 154). 200p. 1976. 56.00 (ISBN 3-8055-2346-7). S Karger.

Sprache Huldrych Zwinglis im Kontrast zur Sprache Luthers. Walter Schenker. (Studia Linguistica Germanica: Vol. 14). (Illus.). 1977. 66.00x (ISBN 3-11-006605-X). De Gruyter.

Sprache Ohne Worte: Idee Einer Allgemeinen Wissenschaft der Sprache. Rudolph Kleinpaul. (Approaches to Semiotics Ser: No. 19). 456p. 1972. Repr. of 1888 ed. text ed. 47.20x (ISBN 0-686-22540-6). Mouton.

Sprache und Literatur bis zum Ende des see Aufstieg und Niedergang der romischen Welt: Section 1, von den Anfangen Roms bis zum Ausgang der Republik.

Sprache und Literatur 1 see Aufstieg und Niedergang der romischen Welt: Section 1, von den Anfangen Roms bis zum Ausgang der Republik.

Sprache und Politik: Untersuchungen zum Sprachgebrauch der "Paulskirche". Horst Gruenert. LC 74-80634. (Studia Linguistica Germanica: Vol. 10). 1974. 35.60x (ISBN 3-11-003609-6). De Gruyter.

Sprache Und Schrift Der Jucen. Wilhelm Grube. 147p. 1941. Repr. of 1926 ed. 60.00x (ISBN 0-317-69456-1, Pub. by Han-Shan Tang Ltd). State Mutual Bk.

Sprache und Stil in Waelschen Gast Des Thomasin Von Circlaria. Friedrich Ranke. (Ger). 18.00; pap. 13.00 (ISBN 0-685-02141-6). Johnson Repr.

Sprachen der Logik und Die Logik der Sprache. M. J. Cresswell. (Grundlagen der Kommunikation De Gruyter Studienbuch). 1979. 14.40x (ISBN 3-11-004923-6). De Gruyter.

Sprachen Europas in Systematischer Uebersicht (Bonn; 1850) Linguistische Untersuchungen. August Schleicher. (Amsterdam Classics in Linguistics: 4). viii, 270p. 1983. 48.00x (ISBN 90-272-0875-1). Benjamins North Am.

Sprachforschung der Aufklaerung Im Spiegel der Grossen Franzoesischen Enzyklopaedie. Irene Monreal-Wickert. 210p. (Ger.). 1977. 59.95 (ISBN 3-87808-403-X, M-7054). French & Eur.

Sprachfuehrer Fuer die Krankenpflege. Deutsche Schwestergemeinschaft. 253p. (Elementary Guide of Nursing). 1968. pap. 19.95 (ISBN 3-8047-0338-0, M-7627, Pub. by Wissenschaftliche Vlg.). French & Eur.

Sprachgeschichte: Ein Handbuch zur Geschichte der Deutschen Sprache und Ihrer Erforschung, 2 pts. Ed. by Werner Besch & Eskar Reichmann. (Handbuecher zur Sprach und Kommunikations Wissenschaft). (Illus.). xxxiiii, 948p. (Ger.). 1984. 216.00x (ISBN 3-11-007396-X). De Gruyter.

Sprachherkunftsforschung, Vol. I: Einleitung & Phonogenese. Ed. by Gyula Decsy. (Bibliotheca Nostratica: Vol 2). 87p. 1977. 22.00 (ISBN 3-447-01861-5). Eurolingua.

Sprachherkunftsforschung, Vol. II: Semogenese-Palaosemiotik. Ed. by Gyula Decsy. (Bibliotheca Nostratica: Vol. 2). 78p. 1981. 22.00 (ISBN 0-931922-06-2). Eurolingua.

Sprachkunst und Uebersetzung. Ed. by Hans-Albrecht Koch. 203p. (Ger.). 1983. 24.20 (ISBN 3-261-03331-2). P Lang Pubs.

Sprachliche Rhythmus in Den Buhnenstucken John Millington Synges. Uwe Stork. Ed. by James Hogg. (Poetic Drama & Poetic Theory). 103p. (Orig.). 1980. pap. 15.00 (ISBN 3-7052-0888-8, Pub. by Salzburg Studies). Longwood Pub Group.

Sprachphilosophie Des Hl, Thomas Von Aquin. F. Manthey. (Philosophy Reprints Ser.). (Ger.). Repr. of 1937 ed. lib. bdg. 45.00x (ISBN 0-697-00042-7). Irvington.

Sprachphilosophie in Antike und Mittelalter: Bochumer Kolloquim, 2-4, June 1982. Burkhard Mojsisch. (Bochum Studies in Philosophy: No. 3). 448p. (Ger.). 1986. 47.00x (ISBN 90-6032-233-9, Pub. by B R Gruner Netherlands). Benjamins North Am.

Sprachschatze der Angelsachsischen Dichter. Christian W. Grein. 100.00 (ISBN 0-8490-1118-3). Gordon Pr.

Sprachthematik In der Prosa Ingeborg Bachmanns. Andreas Hapkemeyer. (European University Studies: No. 1, Vol. 496). 131p. (Ger.). 1982. 17.35 (ISBN 3-8204-5771-2). P Lang Pubs.

Sprachwandel: Reader Zur diachronischen Sprachwissenschaft. Ed. by Dieter Cherubim. (Grundlagen der Kommunikation). x, 362p. 1979. pap. 14.40x (ISBN 3-11-004330-0). De Gruyter.

Sprang: Language & Techniques. 2nd ed. Jules Kliot. 16p. 1974. pap. 2.95 (ISBN 0-916896-03-X). Lacis Pubns.

Spravvochnik Lichni'ch Imen Narodov RSFSR: (Dictionary of Russian Personal Names) Ed. by A. B. Superanskoi. 655p. (Rus.). 1987. 10.95 (ISBN 0-8285-3580-9, Pub. by Rus Lang Pubns USSR). Imported Pubns.

Spray Application Using Flammable & Combustible Liquids. (Thirty Ser.). 56p. 1973. pap. 2.00 (ISBN 0-685-44167-9, 33). Natl Fire Prot.

Spray Application Using Flammable & Combustible Materials. National Fire Protection Association Staff. 26p. 1985. 12.00 (ISBN 0-317-63067-9, 33-85). Natl Fire Prot.

Spray Drying Handbook. 4th ed. K. Masters. LC 84-28999. 1985. 99.95 (ISBN 0-470-20151-7). Halsted Pr.

Spray Hitter. Mary G. Bonner. (Illus.). (gr. 4-7). 1956. PLB 6.19 (ISBN 0-8313-0011-6). Lantern.

Spray It Loud. Jill Posener. (Illus.). 96p. 1987. pap. 9.95 (ISBN 0-86358-100-5, 81005, Pub. by Pandora Pr). Routledge Chapman & Hall.

Spraycan Art. Henry Chalfant & James Prigoff. LC 87-50389. (Illus.). 96p. (Orig.). 1987. pap. 14.95 (ISBN 0-500-27469-X). Thames Hudson.

Spraying under the Bed for Wolves. Anne George. (Illus.). 40p. (Orig.). 1985. pap. 5.00 (ISBN 0-945301-02-2). Druid Pr.

Spread a Little Christmas Cheer. Berta Poorman & Sonja Poorman. 1982. pap. 4.95 (ISBN 0-686-38388-5). Eldridge Pub.

Spread a Little Happiness: The First Hundred Years of the British Musical. Sheridan Morley. 1987. 29.95 (ISBN 0-500-01398-5). Thames Hudson.

Spread Mooring Systems. Ed. by Celina Henderson. Tr. by Marcela Rossman from Eng. (Rotary Drilling Ser.: Unit V, Lesson 2). (Illus.). 53p. (Orig., Span.). 1982. pap. text ed. 5.95 (ISBN 0-88698-045-3, 2.50212). PETEX.

Spread Mooring Systems. (Rotary Drilling Ser.: Unit V, Lesson 2). (Illus.). 47p. (Orig.). 1976. pap. text ed. 5.95 (ISBN 0-88698-070-4, 2.50210). PETEX.

Spread of Machinery, 1793-1806. LC 72-2545. (British Labour Struggles Before 1850 Ser). (5 pamphlets). 1972. 23.50 (ISBN 0-405-04437-2). Ayer Co Pubs.

Spread of Terror: Plus Lots of Cartoons We Could Have Put on the Cover but Didn't. P. S. Mueller. 1986. pap. 5.95 (ISBN 0-933893-15-9). Bonus Books.

Spread of Tumors in the Human Body. 3rd ed. Rupert A. Willis. LC 75-312789. (Illus.). pap. 107.30 (ISBN 0-317-41709-6, 2025722). Bks Demand UMI.

Spread-Spectrum Communications. Ed. by C. E. Cook et al. F. W. Ellersick. 286p. 1983. 39.95x (ISBN 0-471-87886-3, Pub. by Wiley Interscience). Wiley.

Spread-Spectrum Communications. Ed. by C. E. Cook et al. LC 83-12665. 296p. 1983. 44.45 (ISBN 0-87942-170-3, PC01636). Inst Electrical.

Spread Spectrum Communications, 3 vols. Marvin K. Simon et al. LC 84-4959. (Electrical Engineering, Telecommunications, & Signal Processing Ser.). 1985. Set. text ed. 139.85 (ISBN 0-88175-017-4, Computer Sci Pr); Vol. I, 402p. text ed. 49.95 (ISBN 0-88175-012-3); Vol. II, 358p. text ed. 49.95 (ISBN 0-88175-014-X); Vol. III, 423p. text ed. 49.95 (ISBN 0-88175-015-8). W H Freeman.

Spread Spectrum in Communication. Ed. by R. Skaug & J. F. Hjelmstad. 218p. 1985. casebound 74.00 (ISBN 0-86341-034-0, TE012). Inst Elect Eng.

Spread Spectrum Signal Design: LPE & AJ Systems. David L. Nicholson. 304p. 1988. 44.95 (ISBN 0-7167-8150-6). W H Freeman.

Spread Spectrum Systems. 2nd ed. Robert C. Dixon. 422p. 1984. text ed. 43.95x (ISBN 0-471-88309-3, Wiley-Interscience). Wiley.

Spreading Deserts: The Hand of Man. Erik Eckholm & Lester R. Brown. LC 77-81479. (Institute Papers). 1977. pap. 4.00 (ISBN 0-916468-12-7). Worldwatch Inst.

Spreading Flame: The Stories of the Churches of Troy Annual Conference. Charles D. Schwartz & Ouida D. Schwartz. LC 85-70363. (Illus.). 360p. 1986. text ed. 25.00x (ISBN 0-914960-57-1); pap. text ed. 18.00X (ISBN 0-914960-61-X). Academy Bks.

Spreading Light: Religious Education for Special Children. Antonia Malone. 144p. 1986. pap. 8.95 (ISBN 0-8091-2798-9). Paulist Pr.

Spreading Resistance Symposium: Proceedings of a Symposium Held At the National Bureau of Standards, Gaithersburg, Md., June 13-14, 1974. Spreading Resistance Symposium (1974: Gaitherburg, MD) Ed. by James R. Ehrstein. LC 75-600857. (Semiconductor Measurement Technology Ser., Special Technical Paper: No. 572). pap. 73.30 (ISBN 0-317-29813-5, 2016595). Bks Demand UMI.

Spreading the American Dream: American Economic & Cultural Expansion 1890-1945. Emily Rosenberg. (American Century Ser.). 269p. 1982. 12.95 (ISBN 0-8090-8798-7); pap. 6.95 (ISBN 0-8090-0146-2). Hill & Wang.

Spreading the Gospel. Bernard R. Youngman. (Background to the Bible Ser.). (gr. 8-12). pap. 9.95 (ISBN 0-7175-0420-4). Dufour.

Spreading the Word: Groundings in the Philosophy of Language. Simon Blackburn. (Illus.). 1984. pap. 12.50x (ISBN 0-19-824651-X). Oxford U Pr.

Spreading Truth. Joe Dennis. 64p. 1979. pap. text ed. 1.95 (ISBN 0-89114-086-7); P. 78. tchrs. ed. 1.95 (ISBN 0-89114-087-5). Baptist Pub Hse.

Spreading Your Wings: A Young Woman's Introduction to Life. Linda Bairstow. LC 87-92072. 1988. 8.95 (ISBN 0-87212-210-7). Libra.

Spreadsheet Applications in Accounting Information Systems: Includes SuperCalc 3 Educational Version. J. Monroe. 1985. 24.95 (ISBN 0-471-82255-8). Wiley.

Spreadsheet Applications in Business Statistics: Includes SuperCalc Registered 3, Educational Version. Jeffrey Mock. 1986. incl. disk 24.95 (ISBN 0-471-82375-9). Wiley.

Spreadsheet Applications in Financial Analysis. Jerome S. Osteryoung & Richard S. Lamothe. 1985. incl. disk 24.95 (ISBN 0-471-82498-4). Wiley.

Spreadsheet Applications in Managerial Accounting. Angelo E. DiAntonio. 1985. pap. text ed. write for info. (ISBN 0-8359-6962-2, Reston). P-H.

Spreadsheet Dilemma. Peter Mackie & Phyllis Mackie. 160p. 1984. pap. 5.95 (ISBN 0-88056-140-8). Weber Systems.

Spreadsheet Software for Farm Business Management. Dick Landis & Edward Schmisseur. 1985. text ed. 27.00 (ISBN 0-8359-6956-8, Reston); pap. text ed. 22.00 (ISBN 0-8359-6955-X). P-H.

Spreadsheet Software! Using Quattro. James Shuman. 320p. 1989. pap. text ed. price not set (ISBN 0-394-39529-8). Knopf.

Spreadsheet Templates & Applications in the Management of Operations. 3rd ed. Jack R. Meredith. Ed. by Scott M. Shafer. 148p. 1987. pap. write for info. (ISBN 0-471-85582-0). Wiley.

Spreadsheeting on the TRS-80 Color Computer. Harry Anbarlian. (Personal Computing Ser.). 320p. 1983. 28.95 (ISBN 0-07-001595-3, BYTE Bks); text ed. 50.00 incl. cassettes (ISBN 0-07-079110-4). McGraw.

Spreadsheeting 101. Donna A. Driscoll. 350p. 1986. software diskette & books 29.95 (ISBN 0-317-52449-6). Simp Soft Computer.

Spreadsheets for Beginners. Elayne E. Schulman & Richard R. Page. LC 86-10967. (Computer Literacy Skills Ser.). (Illus.). 112p. (gr. 7-12). 1987. PLB 11.90 (ISBN 0-531-10232-7). Watts.

Spreadsheets for the IBM: A Librarian's Guide. Patricia Swersey. (Essential Guide to the Library IBM PC Ser: Vol. 6). 1987. spiral bdg. 29.95 (ISBN 0-88736-047-5). Meckler Corp.

Spreadsheets Go to School: Applications for Administrators. Edward Caffarella. 1985. 26.00 (ISBN 0-8359-7060-4, Reston). P-H.

Spreadsheets on the IBM PC. Tom Simondi. 128p. 1984. pap. 4.95 (ISBN 0-912003-24-3). Bk Co.

Spreadsheets: Principles & Applications Using VisiCalc - Apple Version. Kenneth S. Close & Eugene Hite. 1985. write for info. wkbk. & template diskette (ISBN 0-538-10200-4, J20). SW Pub.

Spreadsheets: Principles & Applications Using Visicalc - IBM Version. Kenneth S. Close & Eugene Hite. 1985. write for info. wkbk. & template diskette (ISBN 0-538-10210-1, J21). SW Pub.

Sprechbewegung und Sprachstruktur: Morphographisch-Strukturelle Ableitungs Herarchie Eines Modell-Universume der Sprechdewegung und Sprachstruktur. Reinhold Solle. (Janua Linguarum, Ser. Maior: No. 94). 296p. (Orig.). 1975. text ed. 44.00x (ISBN 90-2793-297-2). Mouton.

Sprechen Wir Daruber: German Conversation - A Functional Approach. Werner Haas & Heimy Taylor. LC 83-19793. 181p. 1984. pap. write for info. (ISBN 0-471-87125-7). Wiley.

Spree. Max A. Collins. 320p. 1987. 15.95 (ISBN 0-312-93029-1, Dist. by Warner Pub Servs & St Martin Pr). Tor Bks.

Spree. Max A. Collins. 320p. 1988. pap. 3.95 (ISBN 0-8125-0165-9, Dist. by St Martin's Pr & Warner Pub Servs). Tor Bks.

Spree et le Mincio see Cahiers de l'Institut de Science Economique Appliquee.

Sprich Deutsch! 2nd ed. Philip Grundlehner. (Ger.). 1983. pap. text ed. 19.95 (ISBN 0-03-060616-0). HR&W.

Sprichwoertersammlungen, 2 vols. Johannes Agricola. Ed. by Sander L. Gilman. (Ausgaben Deutscher Literatur des XV. Bis XVIII Jahrhunderts). 989p. 1971. 154.00x (ISBN 3-11-003710-6). De Gruyter.

Sprichworter und Lieder Aus der Gegend Von Turfan. Albert V. Le Coq. Repr. of 1911 ed. 16.00 (ISBN 0-384-32000-7). Johnson Repr.

Spridgets. (Illus.). 256p. 29.95 (ISBN 0-902280-96-1, P996, Pub. by Oxford Ill Pr). Haynes Pubns.

Spriditis: A Children's Musical Play. Anna Brigadere. Tr. by Vilnis Baumanis from Latvian. 60p. (Orig.). 1984. pap. 3.50x (ISBN 0-88020-109-6); pap. text ed. 25.00x incl. piano score by Andrejs Jansons. Coach Hse.

Sprig Muslin. Georgette Heyer. 340p. 1983. Repr. lib. bdg. 16.95x (ISBN 0-89966-128-9). Buccaneer Bks.

Sprig Muslin. Georgette Heyer. 256p. 1988. pap. 2.95 (ISBN 0-425-10718-3). Berkley Pub.

Sprig of Holly. new ed. Halford E. Luccock. Ed. & intro. by Charles S. Hartman. LC 78-17096. 64p. 1978. text ed. 3.50 (ISBN 0-8298-0354-8). Pilgrim NY.

Sprig of Hope. Robert T. Young. LC 79-20946. 1980. pap. 6.50 (ISBN 0-687-39260-8). Abingdon.

Sprig the Tree Frog. Margaret S. Pursell. Tr. by Dyan Hammarberg from Fr. LC 76-1224. (Animal Friends Bks.). (Illus.). 24p. (gr. k-4). 1976. PLB 5.95 (ISBN 0-87614-064-9). Carolrhoda Bks.

Sprigs of Truth. Marian F. Winkelman. 1983. 6.50 (ISBN 0-533-05372-2). Vantage.

Spring. Richard Allington. Kathleen Krull. LC 80-25093. (E. G. Beginning to Learn about... Ser.). (Illus.). 32p. (ps-2). 1985. pap. 9.27 (ISBN 0-8172-2489-0). Raintree Pubs.

Spring. Richard L. Allington & Kathleen Krull. LC 80-25093. (Beginning to Learn About Ser.). (Illus.). 32p. (ps-2). 1981. PLB 15.33 (ISBN 0-8172-1342-2). Raintree Pubs.

Spring. A. Balzola & J. M. Parramon. (Exploring the Seasons Ser.). (Illus.). 32p. (ps-3). 1981. 11.93 (ISBN 0-516-02381-0). Childrens.

Spring. Robert Highsmith. (Illus.). 26p. (ps). 1986. 2.95 (ISBN 0-02-747930-7). Macmillan.

Spring. David Lambert. (Seasons Ser.). (Illus.). 48p. (gr. 4-6). 1987. lib. bdg. 12.90 (ISBN 0-531-18105-7, Pub. by Bookwright Pr). Watts.

Spring. Bela Liscinszky. (Foods for All Seasons Ser.). (Illus.). 112p. 1985. 9.95 (ISBN 963-13-1982-2, Pub. by Corvina Kiado Hungary). Intl Spec Bk.

Spring. Colin McNaughton. LC 83-45233. (Very First Bks.). (Illus.). 10p. (ps-k). 1983. bds. 4.95 (ISBN 0-8037-0044-X, 0481-140). Dial Bks Young.

Spring. Sean O'Leary. (Busy Fingers Ser.). (Illus.). 16p. (gr. 1-4). 1987. pap. 3.95 (ISBN 0-86278-128-0, Pub. by O'Brien Pr Ireland). Irish Bks Media.

Spring. Louis Santrey. LC 82-19381. (Discovering the Seasons Ser.). (Illus.). 32p. (gr. 4-7). 1982. lib. bdg. 10.79 (ISBN 0-89375-909-0); pap. text ed. 2.50 (ISBN 0-89375-910-4). Troll Assocs.

Spring. Alana Willoughby. Ed. by Alton Jordan. (Elephant Ser.). (Illus.). (gr. k-3). 1975. PLB 3.95 (ISBN 0-89868-019-0, Read Res); pap. text ed. 1.75 (ISBN 0-89868-052-2). ARO Pub.

Spring Activity Book. Elaine R. Cohen. (Stick-Out-Your Neck Ser.). (Illus.). 32p. (gr. 4 up). 1984. pap. 1.98 (ISBN 0-88724-068-2, CD-8052). Carson-Dellos.

Spring Activity Book. Susan Vesey. (Illus.). 32p. (gr. 1 up). 1987. pap. 3.95 (ISBN 0-7459-1015-7). Lion USA.

Spring & May. Nancy M. Davis et al. (Davis Teaching Units Ser.: Vol. 1, No. 9). (Illus.). 46p. (Orig.). (ps-4). 1986. pap. 5.95 (ISBN 0-937103-11-X). DaNa Pubns.

Spring & Summer in N.C. Forests. Rosa K. Mullet. 238p. 1982. pap. 5.95 (ISBN 0-686-35755-8). Rod & Staff.

Spring & the Spectacle. Margaret Chatterjee. 4.80 (ISBN 0-89253-555-5); flexible cloth 4.00 (ISBN 0-89253-556-3). Ind-US Inc.

Spring Awakening. Frank Wedekind. Tr. by Tom Osborn from Ger. (Orig.). 1979. pap. 4.95 (ISBN 0-7145-0634-6). Riverrun NY.

Spring Awakening: A Play. Frank Wedekind. Tr. by Edward Bond. 96p. 1981. pap. 6.95 (ISBN 0-413-47620-0, NO.2120). Heinemann Ed.

Spring Break for Love. Ruth Burnett. 1985. 9.95 (ISBN 0-8034-8527-1, Avalon). Bouregy.

Spring Break Nineteen Eighty-Six. Starlog Editors. 1986. pap. 3.95 (ISBN 0-317-40172-6, Sig). NAL.

Spring Bulletin Boards. Imogene Forte. (Easy-To-Make-&-Use Ser.). 64p. (gr. k-6). 1987. pap. text ed. 5.95 (ISBN 0-86530-169-7, IP-113-0). Incentive Pubns.

Spring Came on Forever. Bess S. Aldrich. 333p. Repr. of 1935 ed. lib. bdg. 20.95x (ISBN 0-88411-261-6, Pub. by Aeonian Pr). Amereon Ltd.

Spring Came on Forever. Bess S. Aldrich. LC 84-19671. viii, 333p. 1985. pap. 8.95 (ISBN 0-8032-5907-7, BB 904, Bison). U of Nebr Pr.

Spring Cleaning: Household Poisons. Jacquie Milligan. (Child Safety Ser.). (Illus.). 48p. 1986. stitched 4.95 (ISBN 0-513-01829-8). Denison.

Spring Comes Again to Arnet. Patrick W. Gray. Ed. by John M. Gogol & Robert A. Davies. (Poetry Chapbook Ser.). (Illus.). 38p. (Orig.). 1987. pap. 3.95 (ISBN 0-932191-08-8). Mr Cogito Pr.

Spring Designers Handbook. Carlson. (Mechanical Engineering Ser.: Vol. 1). 1978. 59.75 (ISBN 0-8247-6623-7). Dekker.

Spring Embrace. Joyce Lezan. (Orig.). 1983. pap. 1.95 (ISBN 0-317-02741-7, BH213). Holloway.

Spring Family. G. T. Ridlon. LC 76-138078. (Saco Valley Settlements Ser). 1970. pap. 2.00 (ISBN 0-8048-0835-X). C E Tuttle.

Spring Fever. Kerry Allyne. (Harlequin Romances Ser.). 192p. 1983. pap. 1.50 (ISBN 0-373-02527-0). Harlequin Bks.

Spring Fever. Diane Hoh. (Cheerleaders Ser.: No. 27). 288p. (YA) (gr. 7-10). 1987. pap. 2.95 (ISBN 0-590-40505-5). Scholastic Inc.

Spring Fever. Tom Smario. 64p. (Orig.). 1985. pap. 6.00 (ISBN 0-940584-09-3). Gull Bks.

Spring Fever: Spring Super Edition, No. 2. Francine Pascal. (Sweet Valley High Ser.). 240p. (Orig.). (YA) (gr. 7-12). 1987. pap. 2.95 (ISBN 0-553-26420-6). Bantam.

Spring Fires. Cynthia Wright. 432p. (Orig.). 1983. pap. 3.50 (ISBN 0-345-27514-4). Ballantine.

Spring Flora of Virginia. A. M. Harvill, Jr. (Illus.). 1970. 8.50 (ISBN 0-87012-046-8). McClain.

Spring Flora of Wisconsin. 4th ed. Norman C. Fassett. LC 74-27307. (Illus.). 430p. 1976. 18.50x (ISBN 0-299-06750-5); pap. 9.95 (ISBN 0-299-06754-8). U of Wis Pr.

Spring Follows Winter: My Experience with the Death of My Husband. Lynn Yarbrough. (Illus.). 64p. (Orig.). 1987. pap. 3.95 (ISBN 0-936625-09-0). Womans Mission Union.

Spring Forward-Fall Back. Sheila O. Taylor. 288p. 1985. pap. 7.95 (ISBN 0-930044-70-3). Naiad Pr.

Spring Fun Book. Patti Carson & Janet Dellosa. (Stick-Out-Your-Neck Ser.). (Illus.). 32p. (ps-2). 1984. pap. 1.59 (ISBN 0-88724-059-3, CD-8047). Carson-Dellos.

Spring Garden. Perla Meyers. (Burpee's American Harvest Cookbooks Ser.). (Illus.). 128p. 1987. pap. 8.95 (ISBN 0-671-63362-7, Fireside). S&S.

Spring Green. Valrie M. Selkowe. LC 84-11202. (Illus.). 32p. (ps-1). 1985. 11.75 (ISBN 0-688-04055-1); PLB 11.88 (ISBN 0-688-04056-X). Lothrop.

Spring Harvest. Gladys Taber. 17.95 (ISBN 0-89190-599-5, Pub. by Am Repr). Amereon Ltd.

Spring Hill Resprung. 2nd ed. Jack Murphy. 64p. 1985. 12.50 (ISBN 0-908175-13-2, Pub. by Boolarong Pubn Australia). Intl spec bk.

Spring Holiday Poems: Source Material for Programs. Nona K. Duffy. LC 86-71208. (Illus.). 76p. (Orig.). 1986. pap. 4.95 (ISBN 1-55618-001-2). Brunswick Pub.

Spring Holidays. Samuel Epstein & Beryl Epstein. LC 64-12340. (Holiday Bks.). (gr. 2-5). 1964. PLB 7.56 (ISBN 0-8116-6553-4). Garrard.

Spring in October: The Story of the Polish Revolution 1956. Konrad Syrop. LC 75-35032. (Illus.). 207p. 1976. Repr. of 1958 ed. lib. bdg. 22.50x (ISBN 0-8371-8574-2, SYSO). Greenwood.

Spring in the Enchanted Forest. (Enchanted Forest Ser.). (Illus.). (ps-1). 1985. 2.98 (ISBN 0-517-46980-4). Outlet Bk Co.

Spring in This World of Poor Mutts. Joseph Ceravolo. LC 68-56371. (Frank O'Hara Award Ser.). 1978. 17.95 (ISBN 0-916190-20-X); pap. 6.00 (ISBN 0-916190-21-8). Full Court NY.

Spring in Washington. Louis J. Halle. LC 87-46315. (Illus.). 248p. 1988. 18.95x (ISBN 0-8018-3688-3); pap. 7.95 (ISBN 0-8018-3652-2). Johns Hopkins.

Spring Is a New Beginning. Joan W. Anglund. LC 63-7892. (Illus.). (gr. k-3). 1963. 7.95 (ISBN 0-15-278161-7, HJ). HarBraceJ.

Spring Is Green. Harry Bornstein. (Signed English Ser.). 52p. 1973. pap. 6.50 (ISBN 0-913580-17-1, Clerc Bks). Gallaudet Univ Pr.

Spring Is Here! Jane B. Moncure. LC 75-14202. (Illus.). (ps-2). 1975. 7.95 (ISBN 0-913778-11-7). Childs World.

Spring Is Here! Jane B. Moncure. LC 75-14202. (Seasons Awareness Bks.). 24p. (ps-2). 1975. PLB 11.93 (ISBN 0-516-05857-6). Childrens.

Spring Jaunts: Some Walks, Excursions, & Personal Explorations of City, Country, & Seashore. Anthony Bailey. LC 86-80347. 256p. 1986. 16.95 (ISBN 0-374-26799-5). FS&G.

Spring Journal: Poems. Edwin Honig. LC 68-27540. (Wesleyan Poetry Program Ser.: Vol. 41). 1968. 17.00x (ISBN 0-8195-2041-1); pap. 8.95 (ISBN 0-8195-1041-6). Wesleyan U Pr.

Spring Laughter. Christina Rainsford. LC 80-66877. 103p. 1980. 5.50 (ISBN 0-8233-0316-0). Golden Quill.

Spring Love. Jennifer Sarasin. 240p. (Orig.). (gr. 7 up). 1984. pap. 2.25 (ISBN 0-590-40345-1, Wildfire). Scholastic Inc.

Spring Manufacturing Handbook. Carlson. (Mechanical Engineering Ser.). 344p. 1982. 69.75 (ISBN 0-8247-1678-7). Dekker.

Spring Meeting, Detroit, 1985: Proceedings. Industrial Relations Research Association Staff. 3.00 (ISBN 0-913447-29-3). Indus Relations Res.

Spring Meeting, Proceedings, 1984, Cleveland. write for info. Indus Relations Res.

Spring Meeting, 1988, Cincinnati: Proceedings. 1988. 4.00 (ISBN 0-913447-40-4). Indus Relations Res.

Spring Moon. Bette B. Lord. 1982. pap. 4.95 (ISBN 0-380-59923-6, 59923-6). Avon.

Spring Motivators: Positive Reinforcement Activities & Awards for March, April, & May. Ed. by Marlene Canter et al. (Illus.). 32p. (Orig.). 1987. wkbk. 4.95. Canter & Assoc.

Spring of Butterflies: And Other Chinese Folk Tales. He Liyi. Ed. by Neil Philips. LC 85-12887. (Illus.). 160p. 1985. 13.00 (ISBN 0-688-06192-3). Lothrop.

Spring of Prosperity. Torkom Saraydarian. LC 80-67685. 1982. pap. 5.00 (ISBN 0-911794-13-1). Aqua Educ.

Spring of the Ram. Dorothy Dunnett. LC 87-46045. 480p. 1988. 19.95 (ISBN 0-394-56437-5). Knopf.

Spring of the Tiger. Victoria Holt. 384p. 1985. pap. 3.95 (ISBN 0-449-20845-1, Crest). Fawcett.

Spring of Youth. Tr. by Mark C. Setton from Korean. Bd. with Three-Year Hill. (Korean Folk Tales Ser.: No. 14). (Illus.). 32p. (Eng. & Korean.). (gr. 1-8). 1986. PLB write for info. (ISBN 0-87296-013-7, Pub. by Si-sa-yong-o-sa- Korea); bilingual cassette incl. Si-sa-yong-o-sa.

Spring Onions & Cornbread. Bettie M. Sellers. 80p. 1986. pap. text ed. 6.95 (ISBN 0-935265-11-2). Agee Pub.

Spring Pools. Robert Frost. (Illus.). 64p. 1983. boxed portfolio 295.00 (ISBN 0-317-31386-X). Lime Rock Pr.

Spring Preschool-K Practice. Patti Carson & Janet Dellosa. (Stick-Out-Your-Neck Ser.). (Illus.). 32p. (ps-k). 1984. pap. 1.98 (ISBN 0-88724-019-4, CD-8034). Carson-Dellos.

Spring Primary Reading & Art Activities. Patti Carson & Janet Dellosa. (Stick-Out-Your-Neck Ser.). (Illus.). 32p. (gr. 1-3). 1984. pap. 1.98 (ISBN 0-88724-066-6, CD-8046). Carson-Dellos.

Spring Puppets & Plays. Nancy Ludwig. (Stick-Out-Your-Neck Ser.). (Illus.). 31p. (ps-4). 1984. pap. 1.98 (ISBN 0-88724-157-3, CD-8059). Carson-Dellos.

Spring Remembered: A Scottish Jewish Childhood. Evelyn Cowan. LC 78-66450. 1979. 8.50 (ISBN 0-8008-7367-X). Taplinger.

Spring Seminar Proceedings, 1986. Ed. by American Production & Inventory Control Society Staff. 300p. 1986. pap. 15.00 (ISBN 0-935406-76-X). Am Prod & Inventory.

Spring Shade: Poems 1931-1970. Robert Fitzgerald. LC 74-145931. 1971. 6.50 (ISBN 0-8112-0280-1); pap. 2.75 (ISBN 0-8112-0052-3, NDP311). New Directions.

Spring Silkworms & Other Stories. 2nd ed. Mao Dun. 1980. 9.95 (ISBN 0-8351-0615-2). China Bks.

Spring Silkworms & Other Stories. 2nd ed. Dun Mao Tun. Tr. by Sidney Shapiro from Chinese. 237p. 1979. 9.95 (ISBN 0-917056-90-6, Pub. by Foreign Lang Pr China). Cheng & Tsui.

Spring Silkworms & Other Stories. Yen-Ping Shen, pseud. Tr. by Sidney Shapiro. LC 75-36238. Repr. of 1956 ed. 24.50 (ISBN 0-404-14486-1). AMS Pr.

Spring Sketches. Harriet L. Smith et al. (Humor Ser.). (Illus.). 50p. (Orig.). 1973. pap. 3.00x (ISBN 0-913626-01-5). S S S Pub Co.

Spring Snow. Yukio Mishima. 1972. 13.45 (ISBN 0-394-44239-3). Knopf.

Spring Snow. Yukio Mishima. (Sea of Fertility Tetralogy Ser.). 384p. (gr. 12). 1975. pap. 4.95 (ISBN 0-671-54062-9). WSP.

Spring Sonata. Bernice Rubens. 224p. 1986. pap. 4.50 (ISBN 0-446-32896-0). Warner Bks.

Spring Sowing. Liam O'Flaherty. LC 72-10748. (Short Story Index Reprint Ser). 1973. Repr. of 1924 ed. 19.00 (ISBN 0-8369-4221-3). Ayer Co Pubs.

Spring Story. Jill Barklem. LC 80-15300. (Brambly Hedge Bks.). (Illus.). 32p. (gr. 1 up). 1986. pap. 8.95 (ISBN 0-399-20746-5, Philomel); PLB 6.99 (ISBN 0-399-61156-8). Putnam Pub Group.

Spring Street Boys Hit the Road. Mel Cebulash. 108p. (YA) (gr. 7 up). pap. 1.95 (ISBN 0-590-32291-5). Scholastic Inc.

Spring Street Boys Settle a Score. Mel Cebulash. (gr. 7 up). pap. 1.95 (ISBN 0-590-32290-7). Scholastic Inc.

Spring Street Boys Team Up. Mel Cebulash. 96p. (YA) (gr. 7 up). pap. 1.95 (ISBN 0-590-32289-3). Scholastic Inc.

Spring Surprises. Toni Bauman & June Zinkgraf. (gr. k-6). 1979. 13.95 (ISBN 0-916456-54-4, GA109). Good Apple.

Spring Symphony Poetry Anthology. Mary Bibb. LC 85-70796. 120p. (Orig.). 1985. pap. 5.00x (ISBN 0-9608778-1-9). M Bibb.

Spring Thunder & After: The Maoist & Ultra-Leftist Movements in India, 1962-75. Asish K. Roy. LC 76-18729. 1976. 13.50x (ISBN 0-88386-536-X). South Asia Bks.

Spring Tide. Mary Ray. (Illus.). 174p. (gr. 5-9). 1979. pap. 2.95 (ISBN 0-571-11331-1). Faber & Faber.

Spring Tides. Jacques Poulin. Tr. by Sheila Fischman. (Anansi Fiction Ser.: No. 51). 160p. (Orig., Fr.). 1986. pap. 9.95 (ISBN 0-88784-149-X, Pub. by Hse Anansi Pr Canada). U of Toronto Pr.

Spring-Time with the Poets. Frances Martin. Repr. of 1891 ed. 15.00 (ISBN 0-686-19870-0). Ridgeway Bks.

Spring Torrents. Ivan S. Turgenev. Tr. by Leonard Shapiro from Rus. (Classics Ser.). 1980. pap. 4.95 (ISBN 0-14-044369-X). Penguin.

Spring Training. Henry Horenstein. LC 87-34842. 48p. (gr. 3 up). 1988. PLB 15.95 (ISBN 0-02-744440-6). Macmillan.

Spring Trances in the Control Emerald Night. Christopher Dewdney. 1978. Repr. perfect bound in wrappers 5.00 (ISBN 0-685-04174-3); signed ed. 7.50 (ISBN 0-686-66326-8). Figures.

Spring Turkey Hunting: The Serious Hunter's Guide. John M. McDaniel. (Illus.). 224p. 1986. 21.95 (ISBN 0-8117-1688-0). Stackpole.

Spring Valley's Spotted Champion. Gary C. Vezzoli. 104p. 1988. 6.95 (ISBN 0-8059-3030-2). Dorrance.

Spring Wild Flowers of West Virginia. Earl L. Core. LC 81-50933. 1981. 4.00 (ISBN 0-937058-02-5). West Va U Pr.

Spring Wildflowers of New England. Dwelley. (Illus.). 1973. 10.95 (ISBN 0-89272-008-5). Down East.

Spring Wildflowers of New Mexico. William C. Martin & Charles R. Hutchins. LC 83-25954. (New Mexico Natural History Ser.). (Illus.). 257p. 1984. 24.95x (ISBN 0-8263-0742-6); pap. 12.95 (ISBN 0-8263-0743-4). U of NM Pr.

Spring Wildflowers of the San Francisco Bay Region. Helen K. Sharsmith. (California Natural History Guides: No. 11). (Illus.). 1965. pap. 6.95 (ISBN 0-520-01168-6). U of Cal Pr.

Spring Will Come. Sherry Deborde. 384p. pap. 3.95 (ISBN 0-373-97046-3, Pub by Worldwide). Harlequin Bks.

Spring Wind of the Silent Administrator. Myrna L Etheridge. 80p. (Orig.). 1987. pap. 4.00 (ISBN 0-937417-02-5). Etheridge Minist.

Spring 1975: An Annual of Archetypal Psychology & Jungian Thought. annual Ed. by James Hillman. 220p. (Orig.). 1975. pap. 15.00 (ISBN 0-88214-010-8). Spring Pubns.

Spring 1976: An Annual of Archetypal Psychology & Jungian Thought. Ed. by James Hillman. 214p. (Orig.). 1976. pap. 15.00 (ISBN 0-88214-011-6). Spring Pubns.

Spring 1977: An Annual of Archetypal Psychology & Jungian Thought. Ed. by James Hillman. 222p. (Orig.). 1977. 15.00 (ISBN 0-88214-012-4). Spring Pubns.

Spring 1978: An Annual of Archetypal Psychology & Jungian Thought. Ed. by James Hillman. 206p. (Orig.). 1978. pap. 15.00 (ISBN 0-88214-013-2). Spring Pubns.

Spring 1979: An Annual of Archetypal Psychology & Jungian Thought. Ed. by James Hillman. 231p. (Orig.). 1979. pap. 15.00 (ISBN 0-88214-014-0). Spring Pubns.

Spring 1980: An Annual of Archetypal Psychology & Jungian Thought. Ed. by James Hillman. 173p. (Orig.). 1980. pap. 15.00 (ISBN 0-88214-015-9). Spring Pubns.

Spring 1982: An Annual of Archetypal Psychology & Jungian Thought. Ed. by James Hillman. 316p. (Orig.). 1982. pap. 15.00 (ISBN 0-88214-017-5). Spring Pubns.

Spring 1983: An Annual of Archetypal Psychology & Jungian Thought. Ed. by James Hillman. 211p. (Orig.). 1983. pap. 15.00 (ISBN 0-88214-019-1). Spring Pubns.

Spring, 1984: A Choice of Futures. Arthur C. Clarke. 272p. 1984. pap. 3.50 (ISBN 0-345-31358-5). Fawcett.

Spring 1986: An Annual of Archetypal Psychology & Jungian Thought. Ed. by James Hillman. 189p. (Orig.). 1986. pap. 15.00 (ISBN 0-88214-022-1). Spring Pubns.

Spring 1987: An Annual of Archetypal Psychology & Jugian Thought. Ed. by James Hillman. (Annual Journal Ser.). 172p. (Orig.). 1987. pap. 15.00 (ISBN 0-88214-023-X). Spring Pubns.

Springboard. Joan McNichols & Gerri Purkiss. (Illus., Orig.). (gr. k-8). 1973. pap. 7.95 (ISBN 0-918932-42-4). Activity Resources.

Springboard for Overlord, Hampshire & the D-Day Landings. Anthony Kemp. (Down Memory Lane, Old Hampshire Ser.). (Illus.). 70p. (Orig.). 1987. pap. 4.95 (ISBN 0-903852-42-X, Pub. by Milestone Pubns UK). Seven Hills Bks.

Springboard to French. The Language School of Seattle, Washington. 40p. 1985. 19.95x (ISBN 0-88432-142-8); 2 cassettes incl. J Norton Pubs.

Springboard to German. The Language School of Seattle, Washinton. 40p. 1985. 19.95x (ISBN 0-88432-143-6); 2 cassettes incl. J Norton Pubs.

Springboard to Journalism. 4th ed. Ed. by James F. Paschal. (Illus.). 72p. 1985. pap. text ed. 9.95x (ISBN 0-916082-02-4). Columbia Scholastic.

Springboard to Spanish. The Language School of Seattle, Washington. 40p. 1985. 19.95x (ISBN 0-88432-144-4); 2 casettes incl. J Norton Pubs.

Springboard to the Future-Yearbook Compendium. 140p. 1987. pap. 3.25 (ISBN 0-86544-041-7). Salv Army Suppl South.

Springboards: A College Reader. James Schiavone. 1977. pap. text ed. 11.00 (ISBN 0-87720-955-3). AMSCO Sch.

Springboards for Writing. Brenda McNeal. (gr. 8-12). 1979. pap. text ed. 8.00x (ISBN 0-87879-222-8). Acad Therapy.

Springboards to Creative Thinking. Patricia T. Muncy. LC 85-11389. 237p. 1985. pap. 17.50x (ISBN 0-87628-775-5). Ctr Appl Res.

Springer Spaniel. Dorothy M. Hooper. (Popular Dog Ser.). (Illus.). 244p. 1988. 24.95 (ISBN 0-09-158140-0, Pub. by Century Hutchinson). David & Charles.

Springer Tracts in Modern Physics, Vol. 36. Ed. by G. Hoehler. (Illus.). iv, 242p. (Eng. & Ger.). 1964. 34.90 (ISBN 0-387-03215-0). Springer-Verlag.

Springer Tracts in Modern Physics, Vol. 38. Ed. by G. Hoehler. (Illus.). iv, 188p. (Eng. & Ger.). 1965. 34.30 (ISBN 0-387-03405-6). Springer-Verlag.

Springer Tracts in Modern Physics, Vol. 40. Ed. by G. Hoehler. (Illus., Eng. & Ger.). 1966. 34.30 (ISBN 0-387-03669-5). Springer-Verlag.

Springer Tracts in Modern Physics, Vol. 46. Ed. by G. Hoehler. (Illus.). iv, 132p. (Eng. & Ger.). 1968. 34.90 (ISBN 0-387-04340-3). Springer-Verlag.

Springer Tracts in Modern Physics, Vol. 47. Ed. by G. Hoehler. (Illus.). v, 225p. (Eng. & Ger.). 1968. 50.80 (ISBN 0-387-04341-1). Springer-Verlag.

Springer Tracts in Modern Physics, Vol. 49. Ed. by G. Hoehler. (Illus.). iii, 146p. 1969. 34.30 (ISBN 0-387-04712-3). Springer-Verlag.

Springer Tracts in Modern Physics, Vol. 51. Ed. by G. Hoehler. LC 25-9130. (Illus.). 1969. 29.00 (ISBN 0-387-04714-X). Springer-Verlag.

Springer Tracts in Modern Physics, Vol. 53. Ed. by G. Hoehler. (Illus.). 1970. 29.00 (ISBN 0-387-05016-7). Springer-Verlag.

Springer Tracts in Modern Physics, Vol. 54. Ed. by G. Hoehler. LC 25-9130. (Illus.). 1970. 43.70 (ISBN 0-387-05017-5). Springer-Verlag.

Springer Tracts in Modern Physics, Vol. 58. Ed. by G. Hoehler. (Illus.). 1971. 56.70 (ISBN 0-387-05383-2). Springer-Verlag.

Springer Tracts in Modern Physics, Vol. 60. Ed. by G. Hoehler. LC 25-9130. (Illus.). iv, 233p. 1971. 56.70 (ISBN 0-387-05653-X). Springer-Verlag.

Springer Tracts in Modern Physics, Vol. 61. E. A. Niekisch. Ed. by G. Hoehler. LC 25-9130. (Illus.). 200p. 1972. 44.30 (ISBN 0-387-05739-0). Springer-Verlag.

Springer Tracts in Modern Physics, Vol. 65. Ed. by G. Hoehler. LC 25-9130. (Illus.). 148p. 1972. 37.80 (ISBN 0-387-05876-1). Springer-Verlag.

Springfellow's Parade see Bunny's Nutshell Library.

Springfield Carbine on the Western Frontier. Kenneth Hammer. (Illus.). 1970. pap. 2.00 (ISBN 0-88342-214-X). Old Army.

Springfield Nineteen Hundred & Three Rifles. William S. Brophy. (Illus.). 624p. 1985. 49.95 (ISBN 0-8117-0872-1). Stackpole.

Springfield Saga: The Thompsons of Fort Thompson on New River Pulaski County, Virginia. Patricia G. Johnson. (Illus.). 74p. (Orig.). 1985. pap. 11.00 (ISBN 0-9614765-0-8). Pat G Johnson.

Springhouse Drug Reference. Ed. by Donna Hilton. 1280p. 1988. pap. 29.95 (ISBN 0-87434-107-8). Springhouse Pub.

Springhouse: Poems. Norman Dubie. 1986. 14.95 (ISBN 0-393-02302-8); pap. 6.95 (ISBN 0-393-30323-3). Norton.

Springing the Time Trap: Time Management for Today's Busy Homemaker. Deniece Schofield. LC 87-16278. 1987. pap. 8.95 (ISBN 0-87579-100-X, Shadow Mountain). Deseret Bk.

Sputnik Psalomtschika-odnogolosnij obikhod. 624p. 1959. pap. 30.00 (ISBN 0-317-30389-9). Holy Trinity.

Sputnik, Scientists, & Eisenhower: A Memoir of the First Special Assistant to the President for Science & Technology. James R. Killian, Jr. LC 77-21560. 1977. 32.50x (ISBN 0-262-11066-0); pap. 9.95x (1982) (ISBN 0-262-61035-3). MIT Pr.

Sputnik to Space Shuttle: The Complete Story of Space Flight. Iain Nicolson. (Illus.). 224p. 1985. pap. 9.95 (ISBN 0-396-08231-9). Dodd.

Sputtering by Particle Bombardment II. Ed. by R. Behrisch. (Topics in Applied Physics Ser.: Vol. 52). (Illus.). 385p. 1983. 54.50 (ISBN 0-387-12593-0). Springer Verlag.

Sputtering by Particle Bombardment I: Physics & Applications. Ed. by R. Behrisch. (Topics in Applied Physics Ser.: Vol. 47). (Illus.). 1981. 46.80 (ISBN 0-387-10521-2). Springer-Verlag.

Spy. James Fenimore Cooper. Ed. by James H. Pickering. (Masterworks of Literature Ser.). 1971. pap. 10.95x (ISBN 0-8084-0027-4). New Coll U Pr.

Spy. James Fenimore Cooper. 1976. lib. bdg. 19.95 (ISBN 0-89968-161-1). Lightyear.

Spy. Norman Garbo. 288p. 1984. pap. 3.50 (ISBN 0-449-20514-2, Crest). Fawcett.

Spy at the Gate. Valerie Gray. 304p. 1987. 16.95 (ISBN 0-312-00191-6). St Martin.

Spy at the Gate. Valerin Gray. 1986. 55.00x (Pub. by Book Guild Ltd). State Mutual Bk.

Spy at Villa Miranda. Elsie Lee. 272p. 1987. pap. 2.95 (ISBN 0-8217-2096-1). Zebra.

Spy-Counterspy: An Encyclopedia of Espionage. Vincent Buranelli & Nan Buranelli. 352p. 1982. text ed. 35.95 (ISBN 0-07-008915-9). McGraw.

Spy Development, 1985. Ed. & tr. by Robert C. Sandness. (Orig.). 1984. write for info. (ISBN 0-9614076-2-X); pap. 8.50 (ISBN 0-9614076-0-3). Sandness.

Spy: Dr. Bancroft, America's First Double Agent. Arthur Mullin. 400p. 1987. 18.95 (ISBN 0-88496-268-7). Capra Pr.

Spy Factory & Secret Intelligence. Ed. by John Mendelsohn. (Covert Warfare Ser.). 400p. (YA) 1987. lib. bdg. 70.00 (ISBN 0-8240-7951-5). Garland Pub.

Spy for Freedom: The Story of Sarah Aaronsohn. Ida Cowen & Irene Gunther. LC 84-10193. (Jewish Biography Ser.). (Illus.). 176p. (gr. 5 up). 1984. 14.95 (ISBN 0-525-67150-1, 01451-440). Lodestar Bks.

Spy for George Washington. Jay Leibold. (Choose Your Own Adventure Ser.: No. 48). 128p. (gr. 4). 1985. pap. 2.25 (ISBN 0-553-25497-9). Bantam.

Spy Game. John McNeil. 1982. pap. 2.95 (ISBN 0-686-97470-0). Zebra.

Spy Hook: A Novel. Len Deighton. LC 88-45443. 304p. 1988. 18.95 (ISBN 0-394-55178-8). Knopf.

Spy in Chancery. Kenneth Benton. (Black Dagger Crime Ser.). 256p. 1987. text ed. 14.95x (ISBN 0-86220-712-6, Pub. by Firecrest Pub Ltd). Prescott Pr Nh.

Spy in Question. Tim Sebastian. 336p. 1988. pap. 17.95 (ISBN 0-385-29655-X). Delacorte.

Spy in the Deuce Court. Frank Deford. LC 85-28200. 256p. 1986. 17.95 (ISBN 0-399-13134-5). Putnam Pub Group.

Spy in the Deuce Court. Frank Deford. 320p. 1987. pap. 2.95 (ISBN 0-8041-0138-8, Pub. by Ivy). Ballantine.

Spy in the House of Love. Anais Nin. LC 66-6833. 140p. 1959. pap. 5.95 (ISBN 0-8040-0280-0, Pub. by Swallow). Ohio U Pr.

Spy in the House of Love. Anais Nin. 1986. pap. 3.95 (ISBN 0-553-26391-9, Windstone). Bantam.

Spy in the House of Love see Cities of the Interior.

Spy in the House of Medicine. George A. Silver. LC 76-2184. 320p. 1976. 53.95 (ISBN 0-912862-18-1). Aspen Pub.

Spy in the Neighborhood. Marjorie W. Sharmat. LC 73-129754. (Illus.). 128p. (gr. 3-6). 1974. pap. 0.95 (ISBN 0-02-045130-X, Aladdin Bks). Macmillan.

Spy in the Vatican. Branko Bokun. 224p. (Orig.). 1988. pap. 9.95 (ISBN 0-9510525-2-7). Riverrun NY.

Spy in Winter. Michael Hastings. 320p. 1985. pap. 3.95 (ISBN 0-8125-8350-7, Dist. by Warner Pub Services & Saint Martin's Press). Tor Bks.

Spy is Dead. Charles Russell. (Crime Club Ser.). 1989. 12.95 (ISBN 0-385-24614-5). Doubleday.

Spy on Spider. John N. Chance. (Lythway Ser.). 176p. 1988. lib. bdg. 17.50x (ISBN 0-7451-0713-3, Pub. by Chivers Pr UK). G K Hall.

Spy on Third Base. Matt Christopher. (Springboard Bks.). (Illus.). (gr. 2-4). 1988. 9.95 (ISBN 0-316-13996-3). Little.

Spy Overhead: The Story of Industrial Espionage. Clinch Calkins. LC 70-156408. (American Labor Ser., No. 2). 1971. Repr. of 1937 ed. 32.00 (ISBN 0-405-02917-9). Ayer Co Pubs.

Spy Paramount. E. Phillips Oppenheim. Repr. lib. bdg. 18.95x (ISBN 0-89190-414-X, Pub. by River City Pr). Amereon Ltd.

Spy Planes. David Baker. (Military Aircraft Library). (Illus.). 48p. (gr. 3-8). 1987. PLB 75.96 6 bk. set (ISBN 0-317-60506-2); PLB 12.66 (ISBN 0-317-60507-0). Rourke Corp.

Spy, Steal & Smuggle: Israel's Special Relationship with the United States. Claudia Wright. LC 86-22215. (AAUG Special Report Ser.: No. 5). 33p. (Orig.). 1986. pap. 4.50 (ISBN 0-937694-76-2). Assn Arab-Amer U Grads.

Spy Story. John G. Cawelti & Bruce A. Rosenberg. LC 86-30716. x, 260p. 1987. 22.50 (ISBN 0-226-09868-0). U of Chicago Pr.

Spy Story. Len Deighton. 1983. pap. 3.50 (ISBN 0-671-47164-3, 80058). PB.

Spy Story. Len Deighton. 272p. 1985. pap. 3.95 (ISBN 0-345-31569-3). Ballantine.

Spy-Tech. G. Yost. 1986. 54.75X (ISBN 0-245-54335-X, Pub. by Harrap Ltd England). State Mutual Bk.

Spy-Tech: An Intriguing Look into the World of Espionage & Intelligence. Graham Yost. (Illus.). 288p. 1984. 17.95 (ISBN 0-8160-1115-X); pap. 12.95 (ISBN 0-8160-1677-1). Facts on File.

Spy Unmasked: Or, the Memoirs of Enoch Crosby, Alias Harvey Birch, the Hero of James Fenimore Cooper's "the Spy". facsimile ed. H. L. Barnum. LC 75-29452. (Illus.). 264p. 1975. Repr. of 1828 ed. 11.50 (ISBN 0-916346-15-3). Harbor Hill Bks.

Spy vs. Spy Follow-up File. Antonio Prohias. (Illus.). 192p. 1975. pap. 2.50 (ISBN 0-446-32823-5). Warner Bks.

Spy vs. Spy Follow up File. Antonio Prohias. 192p. 1987. pap. 2.95 (ISBN 0-446-34543-1). Warner Bks.

Spy vs. Spy: Stalking Soviet Spies in America. Ronald Kessler. (Illus.). 320p. 1988. 19.95 (ISBN 0-684-18945-3). Scribner.

Spy Wednesday. William Hood. 50p. 1987. pap. 3.95 (ISBN 0-425-09747-1). Berkley Pub.

Spy Wednesday: A Novel. William Hood. 1986. 14.95 (ISBN 0-393-02250-1). Norton.

Spy Wednesday's Kind. Francis Sullivan. LC 79-65678. (Orig.). 1979. pap. 4.00 (ISBN 0-912292-60-1). The Smith.

Spy Who Came in from the Cold. John Le Carre. 224p. 1984. pap. 4.50 (ISBN 0-553-26442-7). Bantam.

Spy Who Drank Blood. Gordon Linzner. LC 84-14127. 144p. (Orig.). 1984. pap. 5.95 (ISBN 0-917053-01-X). Space And.

Spy Who Fell off the Back of the Bus. Marc Lovell. (Crime Club Ser.). 1989. 12.95 (ISBN 0-385-24608-0). Doubleday.

Spy Who Got Away: The Inside Story of Edward Lee Howard, the CIA Agent Who Betrayed His Country's Secrets & Escaped to Moscow. David Wise. LC 87-43229. (Illus.). 1988. 18.45 (ISBN 0-394-56281-X). Random.

Spy Who Loved Me. Ian Fleming. pap. 9.95 Fr. ed (ISBN 0-685-11575-5). French & Eur.

Spy Who Loved Me. Ian Fleming. 192p. 1986. pap. 3.50 (ISBN 0-425-08681-X). Berkley Pub.

Spy Who Played Jazz. William J. Moody. (Private Library Collection). 1986. 6.95 (ISBN 0-938422-40-5). SOS Pubns CA.

Spy Who Sat & Waited. R. Wright Campbell. (gr. 11 up). 1979. pap. 2.50 (ISBN 0-671-82111-3). PB.

Spy Wore Red. Aline. 1988. pap. 4.95 (ISBN 1-55773-034-2, Charter Bks). Berkley Pub.

Spy Wore Red: My Adventures As an Undercover Agent in World War II. Aline. LC 86-29644. 288p. 1987. 18.95 (ISBN 0-394-55665-8). Random.

Spycatcher. Peter Wright & Paul Greengrass. 1988. pap. 4.95 (ISBN 0-440-20132-2). Dell.

Spycatcher Affair. Chapman Pincher. 288p. 1988. 19.95 (ISBN 0-312-02290-5). St Martin.

Spycatcher: The Candid Autobiography of a Senior Intelligence Officer. Peter Wright. 1987. 19.95 (ISBN 0-670-82055-5). Viking.

Spying Heart: More Thoughts on Reading & Writing Books for Children. Katherine Paterson. 196p. 1988. 14.95 (ISBN 0-525-67267-2). Lodestar Bks.

Spylane: The Secret World of Aerial Intelligence Gathering. David Donald. (Illus.). 128p. 1987. 14.95 (ISBN 0-87938-258-9). Motorbooks Intl.

Spymaster's Handbook. Michael Kurland. (Illus.). 192p. 1988. 17.95 (ISBN 0-8160-1314-4). Facts on File.

Spymaster's Odyssey: The Secret Service of Allen Dulles. Richard H. Smith. (Illus.). cancelled (ISBN 0-698-10703-9, Coward). Putnam Pub Group.

Spymasters of Israel. Stewart Steven. (Espionage-Intelligence Library: No. 12). 432p. 1986. pap. 4.95 (ISBN 0-345-33927-4). Ballantine.

Spy's Bedside Book. Graham Greene & Hugh Greene. 256p. 1985. pap. 7.95 (ISBN 0-88184-188-9). Carroll & Graf.

Spy's Wife. Reginald Hill. 1985. pap. 2.95 (ISBN 0-445-20030-8, Pub. by Popular Lib). Warner Bks.

Spyship. Tom Keene & Brian Haynes. 384p. 1985. pap. 3.95 (ISBN 0-8125-0585-9, Dist. by Warner Pub Services & St. Martin's Press). Tor Bks.

SQL Programming for the IBM PC. Richard Finklestein. (Illus.). 300p. (Orig.). 1988. pap. 29.95 (ISBN 0-672-48418-8). Sams.

SQL: The Structured Query Language. Carolyn J. Hursch & Jack L. Hursch. (Illus.). 260p. 1988. 24.95 (ISBN 0-8306-9016-6, 3016); pap. 16.95 (ISBN 0-8306-3016-3). TAB Bks.

Squad Helps Dog Bite Victim & Other Flubs from the Nation's Press. Columbia Journalism Review Editors. LC 79-8553. (Illus.). 128p. 1980. pap. 5.95 (ISBN 0-385-15828-9, Dolp). Doubleday.

Squadron Ninety-Five. Harold Buckley. LC 78-169409. (Literature & History of Aviation Ser). 1971. Repr. of 1933 ed. 19.00 (ISBN 0-405-03754-6). Ayer Co Pubs.

Squalid Splendor: Touring India with "Gandhi". Moral Quest. (Illus.). 295p. (Orig.). 1987. pap. 9.95 (ISBN 0-940341-00-X). Metamyth.

Squall Across the Atlantic: American Civil War Prize Cases & Diplomacy. Stuart L. Bernath. LC 76-79042. pap. 62.20 (2031425). Bks Demand UMI.

Squall Line. James Magorian. LC 85-73614. 52p. 1986. pap. 3.00 (ISBN 0-930674-19-7). Black Oak.

Squandering Eden: Africa at the Edge. Mort Rosenblum & Doug Williamson. 1987. 19.95 (ISBN 0-15-184860-2). HarbraceJ.

Squanicook Eclogues. Melissa Green. 1987. 13.95 (ISBN 0-393-02455-5). Norton.

Squanicook Eclogues. Melissa Green. 1988. pap. 7.95 (ISBN 0-393-30495-7). Norton.

Squanto. Feenie Ziner. (gr. 7 up). Date not set. 17.50 (Linnet). Shoe string.

Squanto & the First Thanksgiving. Joyce K. Kessel. LC 82-10313. (Carolrhoda On My Own Bks). (Illus.). 48p. (gr. k-3). 1983. PLB 8.95 (ISBN 0-87614-199-8). Carolrhoda Bks.

Squanto & the First Thanksgiving. Joyce K. Kessel. (Illus.). 48p. (ps-4). Date not set. pap. 3.95 (ISBN 0-87614-452-0, First Ave Edns). Lerner Pubns.

Squanto: Friend of the Pilgrims. Clyde Bulla. (gr. 2-3). 1971. pap. 2.50 (ISBN 0-590-33937-0, Schol Pap). Scholastic Inc.

Squanto, Friend of the Pilgrims. Clyde R. Bulla. LC 54-9145. (Illus.). (gr. 2-5). 1954. 12.70i (ISBN 0-690-76642-4, Crowell Jr Bks). HarpJ.

Squanto, Friend of the Pilgrims. Clyde R. Bulla. 112p. (gr. 2-5). 1988. pap. 2.50 (ISBN 0-590-40465-2). Scholastic Inc.

Squanto: Indian Adventurer. Stewart Graff & Polly A. Graff. LC 65-10158. (Indians Ser.). (Illus.). 80p. (gr. 2-5). 1965. PLB 6.69 (ISBN 0-8116-6601-8). Garrard.

Squanto, the Pilgrim Adventure. new ed. Kate Jassem. LC 78-18042. (Illus.). 48p. (gr. 4-6). 1979. PLB 9.59 (ISBN 0-89375-161-8); pap. 1.95 (ISBN 0-89375-151-0). Troll Assocs.

Square. Choi-n-hoon. 160p. 1985. 35.00x (ISBN 0-907349-85-4, Pub by Spindlewood); pap. 25.00x (ISBN 0-907349-56-0). State Mutual Bk.

Square. Marguerite Duras. (Blanche Ser.). 160p. 1955. 10.95 (ISBN 0-686-55851-0). Schoenhof.

Square. Marguerite Duras. Ed. by Claude M. Begue. (Fr). 1965. pap. text ed. 2.50x (ISBN 0-685-16005-X). Macmillan.

Square see Four Novels.

Square & Folk Dancing. Hank Greene. (Illus.). 416p. 1984. 18.45i (ISBN 0-06-015325-3, HarpT). Har-Row.

Square Bear & Other Riddle Rhymes. William Cole. (Illus.). 48p. (gr. k-3). pap. 1.50 (ISBN 0-590-10320-2). Scholastic Inc.

Square Ben Drew see Circle Sarah Drew.

Square Dance. Alan Hines. LC 83-48814. 304p. 1984. 14.45i (ISBN 0-06-015297-4, HarpT). Har-Row.

Square Dance. Alan Hines. LC 83-48814. 298p. 1987. pap. 5.95 (ISBN 0-06-091394-0, PL1394, PL). Har-Row.

Square Dances of Today, & How to Teach & Call Them. Richard G. Kraus. LC 50-10717. pap. 33.50 (ISBN 0-317-28453-3, 2055152). Bks Demand UMI.

Square Dancing Everyone. Schild. 120p. (Orig.). 1987. pap. text ed. 9.95x (ISBN 0-88725-079-3). Hunter Textbks.

Square Dancing in the Ice Age. Abbie Hoffman. 288p. 1984. pap. 8.00 (ISBN 0-89608-194-X). South End Pr.

Square Dancing in the Ice Age: Underground Writings. Abbie Hoffman. 242p. 1982. pap. 5.95 (ISBN 0-399-50739-6, Perigee). Putnam Pub Group.

Square Dancing Is for Me. Mildred Hammond. LC 82-17134. (Sports For Me Bks.). (Illus.). 48p. (gr. 2-5). 1983. PLB 7.95 (ISBN 0-8225-1138-X). Lerner Pubns.

Square Foot Gardening: A New Way to Garden in Less Space with Less Work. Mel Bartholomew. Ed. by Anne Halpin. (Illus.). 352p. 1981. 17.95 (ISBN 0-87857-340-2); pap. 11.95 (ISBN 0-87857-341-0). Rodale Pr Inc.

Square John: The Story of Ex-Con Tony McGilvary & the HELP Program. Marlene Webber & Tony McGilvary. 1988. 14.95 (ISBN 0-8020-6687-9). U of Toronto Pr.

Square Jungle. J. Jason Grant. (Orig.). 1979. pap. 1.95 (ISBN 0-87067-632-6, BH632). Holloway.

Square Meals. Jane Stern & Michael Stern. LC 84-47527. (Illus.). 360p. 1985. pap. 8.95 (ISBN 0-394-74162-5). Knopf.

Square Meals: Taste Thrills of Only Yesterday-From Mom's Best Pot Roast & Tuna Noodle Casserole to the Perfect Tea Time Chocolate Bread. Jane Stern & Michael Stern. LC 84-47527. (Illus.). 1984. 17.95 (ISBN 0-394-53112-4). Knopf.

Square Mile: The City of London in Color. Terence Coen & Alec Forshaw. (Illus.). 96p. 1987. 29.95 (ISBN 0-7134-5400-8, Pub. by Batsford England). David & Charles.

Square Moon. Gerard Dogger. 1986. 49.00x (ISBN 0-86332-052-X, Pub. by Book Guild Ltd). State Mutual Bk.

Square One. Arnold Forster. 1988. price not set. D I Fine.

Square One. Lucy C. LeGros. 41p. (gr. k-2). 1988. tchr's ed. 4.95 (ISBN 0-937306-08-8); 16.95 (ISBN 0-937306-09-6). Creat Res NC.

Square Pegs & Round Holes. Candace Brown-Nixon. 107p. (Orig.). 1986. pap. text ed. 16.95x (ISBN 0-944549-00-4). EES Pubns.

Square Pegs & Round Holes: How to Match the Personality to the Job. Lee Elston. LC 84-73007. 72p. (Orig.). 1984. pap. 8.95 (ISBN 0-9614220-0-9). First Step Ent.

Square Pegs, Round Holes: The Learning-Disabled Child in the Classroom & at Home. Harold B. Levy. LC 73-3422. (Illus.). 288p. 1973. pap. 9.95 (ISBN 0-316-52233-3). Little.

Square Shooter. Walt Coburn. 1978. pap. 1.25 (ISBN 0-505-51228-9, Pub. by Tower Bks). Leisure NY.

Square Shooter. William M. Raine. 1976. Repr. of 1935 ed. lib. bdg. 18.95x (ISBN 0-88411-555-0, Pub. by Aeonian Pr). Amereon Ltd.

Square Sun Square Moon: A Collection of Prose Essays. Paul Reps. LC 67-14277. (Illus., Orig.). 1967. pap. 6.50 (ISBN 0-8048-0544-X). C E Tuttle.

Square That Hat. Arthur T. Armstrong. 1987. 8.95 (ISBN 0-533-07259-X). Vantage.

Square-to-Square Golf Swing. Golf Digest Editors & Dick Aultman. 1975. pap. 9.95 (ISBN 0-671-21947-2, Fireside). S&S.

Square Trap. Irving Shulman. Ed. by Carlos E. Cortes. LC 76-1585. (Chicano Heritage Ser.). 1976. Repr. of 1953 ed. 23.50x (ISBN 0-405-09525-2). Ayer Co Pubs.

Squarerigging. Frank Brookesmith. (Illus.). 270p. 1981. 12.95 (ISBN 0-89182-038-8); pap. 7.95 (ISBN 0-89182-039-6). Charles River Bks.

Squares. Graham Percy. (Shape Ser.). 16p. (ps). 1986. bds. 3.95 (ISBN 0-915391-16-3, Pub. by Mad Hatter Bks). Slawson Comm.

Squares & Rectangles see Key to Geometry Series.

Squares of the Natural Numbers in Radiation Protection. Herbert M. Parker. (Taylor Lecture Ser.: No. 1). 1977. 8.00 (ISBN 0-686-30847-6). NCRP Pubns.

Squaring the Circle: Poland Nineteen Eighty to Nineteen Eighty-One. Tom Stoppard. LC 84-28732. 179p. 1985. 14.95 (ISBN 0-571-12537-9); pap. 5.95 (ISBN 0-571-12538-7). Faber & Faber.

Squaring the Waves. Geoffrey F. Dutton. 60p. 1986. pap. 9.95 (ISBN 1-85224-007-5, Pub. by Bloodaxe Bks). Dufour.

Squash: A Player's History. Rex Bellamy. (Illus.). 236p. 1988. 24.95 (ISBN 0-434-98073-0, Pub. by W Heinemann Ltd). David & Charles.

Squash Family Cookbook. Marjorie B. Zucker. (Illus.). 1977. pap. 4.50 (ISBN 0-686-23105-8). M B Zucker.

Squash Rackets. Tony Swift. (EP Sports Ser.). (Illus.). 1974. 6.95 (ISBN 0-7158-0584-3). Charles River Bks.

Squash Racquets. Margaret V. Bloss & Norman Bramall. (Physical Education Activities Ser.). 80p. 1967. pap. text ed. write for info. (ISBN 0-697-07027-1). Wm C Brown.

Squash Racquets: The Khan Game. Hashim Khan & Richard E. Randall. LC 68-12250. (Illus.). 170p. 1972. pap. 7.95 (ISBN 0-8143-1469-4). Wayne St U Pr.

Squash: The Ambitious Player's Guide. Alan Colburn. 112p. 1984. pap. 9.95 (ISBN 0-571-13361-4). Faber & Faber.

Squatter Settlements: Monographs. Mary Vance. (Public Administration Ser.: P 1765). 13p. 1985. 2.00 (ISBN 0-89028-565-9). Vance Biblios.

Squatters & Oligarchs: Authoritarian Rule & Policy Change in Peru. David Collier. LC 75-34112. (Illus.). 200p. 1976. 22.50x (ISBN 0-8018-1748-X). Johns Hopkins.

Squatters & the Roots of Mau-Mau 1905-1963. Tabitha Kanogo. LC 87-11201. 206p. 1987. text ed. 25.95x (ISBN 0-8214-0873-9); pap. text ed. 12.95x (ISBN 0-8214-0874-7). Ohio U Pr.

Squaw Man. Edwin M. Doyle & Julie O. Faversham. 1988. pap. text ed. 7.95 (ISBN 0-8290-2142-6). Irvington.

Squaw Man. Edwin M. Royle & Julie O. Faversham. LC 77-104559. 294p. Repr. of 1906 ed. lib. bdg. 28.00 (ISBN 0-8398-1769-X). Irvington.

Squaw Mountain Massacre. Doyle Trent. 1985. pap. 2.50 (ISBN 0-8217-1635-2). Zebra.

Squaw Tree: Ghost, Miracles & Mysteries of New Mexico. Alice Bullock. LC 77-86728. 1978. 12.00 (ISBN 0-89016-041-4); pap. 7.95 (ISBN 0-89016-040-6). Lightning Tree.

Squaw Winter. Virginia L. Long. Ed. by Micheal Hathaway. (Illus.). 64p. (Orig.). 1987. pap. 4.00 (ISBN 0-943795-00-1). Kindred Pr.

Squawk to the Moon, Little Goose. Edna M. Preston. LC 84-22296. (Illus.). 32p. (ps-1). 1985. pap. 3.95 (ISBN 0-14-050546-6, Puffin). Penguin.

Squeak Saves the Day & Other Tooley Tales. Zilpha K. Snyder. (Illus.). 192p. (gr. 2-5). 1988. pap. 14.95 (ISBN 0-385-29661-4). Delacorte.

Squeak the Dinosaur. Marcus Donnely. (Illus.). 32p. (ps-2). 1987. 8.00 (ISBN 0-938715-02-X). Toy Works Pr.

Squeakers. Stephen Cosgrove. (Serendipity Bks.). (Illus.). 32p. (Orig.). (gr. 1-4). 1985. pap. 2.50 (ISBN 0-8431-1442-8). Price Stern.

Sri Pancaratra-Raksha of Vedanta Desika. 2nd ed. Pandit M. Duraiswami. 1967. 6.00 (ISBN 0-8356-7482-7, ALS 36). Theos Pub Hse.

Sri Ramakrishna in the Eyes of Brahma & Christian Admirers. Ed. by Nanda Mookerjee. LC 76-904430. 1976. 6.50x (ISBN 0-88386-791-5). South Asia Bks.

Sri Ramakrishna's Life & Message in the Present Age: With the Author's Reminiscences of Holy Mother & Some Direct Disciples. Swami Satprakashananda. LC 75-46386. 208p. 1976. 7.95 (ISBN 0-916356-54-X). Vedanta Soc St Louis.

SRI Robot Handbook. Stanford Research Institute Staff. 368p. 1988. text ed. 42.50 (ISBN 0-07-060777-X). McGraw.

Sri Sankara Vijayam. Ramachandran. 1977. pap. 2.95 (ISBN 0-89744-123-0, Pub. by Ganesh & Co. India). Auromere.

Sri Sarada Devi: Consort of Sri Ramakrishna. Ed. by Nanda Mookerjee. 1978. 6.00x (ISBN 0-8364-0173-5). South Asia Bks.

Sri Sarasvati in Indian Art & Literature. Niranjan Ghosh. (Sri Garib Das Oriental Ser.: No. 11). (Illus.). 160p. 1984. 35.00 (ISBN 81-7030-057-6, Pub. by Sri Satguru Pubns India). Orient Bk Dist.

Sri Sarasvati Puja: Goddess of Knowledge & Education. Panduranga Malyala. (Illus.). 28p. 1982. 2.00 (ISBN 0-938924-10-9). Sri Shirdi Sai.

Sri Satyanarayana Katha see Model Building of Solar Systems.

Sri Shirdi Sai Baba. Date not set. 5.00 (ISBN 0-938924-34-6). Sri Shirdi Sai.

Sri Sumarah & Other Stories. Umar Kayam. Tr. by Harry Aveling. (Writing in Asia Ser.). 1981. pap. text ed. 7.00x (ISBN 0-686-77689-5, 00211). Heinemann Ed.

Sri Swami Satchidananda: Apostle of Peace. Sita Bordow et al. LC 86-10533. (Illus.). 454p. (Orig.). 1986. pap. 12.95 (ISBN 0-932040-31-4). Integral Yoga Pubns.

SRI: The Founding Years, Vol. 1. Weldon B. Gibson. 1980. 27.50x (ISBN 0-913232-80-7). W Kaufmann.

Sri: The Take-off Days, Vol. 2. Weldon Gibson. Ed. by Wilbur Ashworth. 216p. 1986. 27.50x (ISBN 0-86576-103-5). W Kaufmann.

Sri Vishnu Sahasranamam. Swami Tapasyananda. 4.50 (ISBN 0-317-69971-7). Orient Bk Dist.

Sri Visnu-Sahara-Nama-Stotra: A Thousand Names of Lord Visnu with the Commentary of Srila Baladeva Vidyabhusana. Vyasadeva & Baladeva Vidyabhusana. Tr. by Kusakratha Dasa from Sanskrit. (Krsna Library: Vol. 15). 178p. (Orig.). 1988. pap. text ed. 6.00 (ISBN 0-944833-25-X). Krsna Inst.

Sriharicarita Mahakavya of Srihari Padmanabhasastrin. Ed. by T. Venkatacharaya. 11.50 (ISBN 0-8356-7322-7). Theos Pub Hse.

Srila Baladea Vidyabhusana's Sri Prameya-Ratnavali: The Jewel Necklace of Truths. Kusakratha Dasa. Tr. by Baladeva Vidyabhusana from Sanskrit. (Krsna Library: Vol. 21). 107p. (Orig.). 1988. pap. text ed. 6.00 (ISBN 0-944833-14-4). Krsna Inst.

Srila Baladeva Vidyabhusana's Sri Aisvarya-kadambini: The Monsoon of Lord Krsna's Opulence. Baladeva Vidyabhusana. Tr. by Kusakratha Dasa from Sanskrit. (Krsna Library: Vol. 5). 110p. (Orig.). 1987. pap. text ed. 6.00 (ISBN 0-944833-04-7). Krsna Inst.

Srila Bhaktivinoda Thakura's Srila Gaurana-Smarana-Mangala-Stotra. Bhaktivinoda Thakura. Tr. by Kusakratha Dasa from Sanskrit. (Krsna Library: Vol. 16). 64p. (Orig.). 1988. pap. text ed. 6.00 (ISBN 0-944833-26-8). Krsna Inst.

Srila Jiva Gosvamis Sri Tattva-Sandarbha: An Essay on Truth. Jiva Gosvami. Tr. by Kusakratha dasa from Sanskrit. (Krsna Library: Vol. 6). 257p. 1987. pap. text ed. 10.00 (ISBN 0-944833-06-3). Krsna Inst.

Srila Kavi-Karnapura's Sri Caitanya-Sahasa-Nama-Stotra: A Thousand Names of Lord Caitanya. Kavi-karnapura. Tr. by Kusakratha Dasa from Sanskrit. (Krsna Library: Vol. 12). 65p. (Orig.). 1988. pap. 6.00 (ISBN 0-944833-11-X). Krsna Inst.

Srila Kavi-Karnapura's: Sri Gaura-ganoddesa-dipika. Kavi-karnapura. Tr. by Kusakratha Dasa from Sanskrit. (Krsna Library: Vol. 11). 126p. (Orig.). 1987. pap. 6.00 (ISBN 0-944833-10-1). Krsna Inst.

Srila Madhvacarya's Sri Tattva-Mukaval or Mayavada-Sata-Dusan: The Pearl Necklace of Truths, or 100 Refutations of the Mayavada Fallacy. Madhvacarya. Tr. by Kusakratha dasa from Sanskrit. (Krsna Library: Vol. 13). 110p. (Orig.). 1988. pap. 6.00 (ISBN 0-944833-12-8). Krsna Inst.

Srila Prabodhananda Sarasvati's Sri Caitanya-candramrta: The Nectar Moon of Sri Caitanya. Probodhananda Sarasvati. Tr. by Kusakratha Dasa from Sanskrit. (Krsna Library: Vol. 2). 156p. 1987. pap. text ed. 6.00 (ISBN 0-944833-07-1). Krsna Inst.

Srila Prabodhananda Sarasvati's Sri Vrndavana-Mahimamrta: The Nectar Glory of Sri Vrndavana, Vol. 1. Prabodhananda Sarasvati. Tr. by Kusakratha Dasa from Sanskrit. (Krsna Library: Vol. 17). 166p. (Orig.). 1988. pap. text ed. 6.00 (ISBN 0-944833-16-0). Krsna Inst.

Srila Prabodhananda Sarasvati's Sri Vrndavana-Mahimamtra: The Nectar Glory of Sri Vrndavana, Vol. 2. Prabodhananda Sarasvati. Tr. by Kusakratha Dasa from Sanskrit. (Krsna Library: Vol. 18). 166p. (Orig.). 1988. pap. text ed. 6.00 (ISBN 0-944833-17-9). Krsna Inst.

Srila Prabodhananda Sarasvati's Sri Vrndavana-Mahimamrta: The Nectar of Glory Sri Vrndavana, Vol. 3. Prabodhananda Sarasvati. Tr. by Kusakratha Dasa from Sanskrit. (Krsna Library: Vol. 19). 150p. (Orig.). 1988. pap. text ed. 6.00 (ISBN 0-944833-18-7). Krsna Inst.

Srila Raghunatha dasa Gosvami's Sri Vraja-vilasa-stava: Prayers Glorifying the Lord's Pastimes in Vraja. Raghunatha Gsvami. Tr. by Kusakratha Dasa from Sanskrit. (Krsna Library: Vol. 4). 97p. (Orig.). 1987. pap. text ed. 6.00 (ISBN 0-944833-03-9). Krsna Inst.

Srila Rupa Gosvami's Sri Astadasa-cchandah-stava: Eighteen Chandah Prayers. Rupa Gosvami. Tr. by Kusakratha dasa from Sanskrit. (Krsna Library: Vol. 9). 121p. (Orig.). 1987. pap. text ed. 6.00 (ISBN 0-944833-00-4). Krsna Inst.

Srila Rupa Gosvami's Sri Govinda-virudavali: Calling Out to Lord Krsna. Rupa Gosvami. Tr. by Kusakratha Dasa from Sanskrit. (Krsna Library: Vol. 8). 123p. 1987. pap. text ed. 6.00 (ISBN 0-944833-08-X). Krsna Inst.

Srila Rupa Gosvami's Sri Sri Radha-Krsna-gaoddesa-dipka: A Lamp to See the Associates of Sri Sri Radha Krsna. Rupa Gosvami. Tr. by Kusakratha dasa. (Krsna Library: Vol. 7). 304p. 1987. pap. text ed. 10.00 (ISBN 0-944833-05-5). Krsna Inst.

Srimad-Bhagavad-Gita. 7th ed. Swami Paramananda. Orig. Title: Bhagavad-Gita, Srimad. 1981. 5.75 (ISBN 0-911564-03-9); lexitone bdg. 3.50. Vedanta Ctr.

Srimad Bhagavad Gita: Pocket Book Edition. Swami Jyotir Maya Nanda. (Illus.). 384p. 1986. pap. 3.00 (ISBN 0-934664-44-7). Yoga Res Foun.

Srimad Bhagavatam: Eighth Canto, 3 vols. Swami A. C. Bhaktivedanta. LC 73-169353. (Illus.). 1976. 12.95 ea. Vol. 1 (ISBN 0-912776-90-0). Vol. 2 (ISBN 0-912776-91-9). Vol. 3 (ISBN 0-912776-92-7). Bhaktivedanta.

Srimad Bhagavatam: Eleventh Canto, 4 Vols. Bhakivedanta Swami. (Illus.). 416p. 1983. 12.95 ea. (ISBN 0-89213-125-X). Bhaktivedanta.

Srimad-Bhagavatam: Eleventh Canto, Vol. 1. Hridayananda dasa Goswami Acaryadeva. (Illus.). 450p. 1982. 12.95 (ISBN 0-89213-112-8); text ed. 9.95 (ISBN 0-686-98021-2). Bhaktivedanta.

Srimad Bhagavatam: Fifth Canto, 2 vols. Swami A. C. Bhaktivedanta. LC 73-169353. (Illus.). 1976. 12.95 ea. (ISBN 0-686-85716-X). Vol. 1 (ISBN 0-912776-78-1). Vol. 2 (ISBN 0-912776-79-X). Bhaktivedanta.

Srimad Bhagavatam: First Canto, 3 vols. Swami A. C. Bhaktivedanta. LC 73-169353. (Illus.). 1972. 12.95 ea. Vol. 1 (ISBN 0-912776-27-7). Vol. 2 (ISBN 0-912776-29-3). Vol. 3 (ISBN 0-912776-34-X). Bhaktivedanta.

Srimad Bhagavatam: Fourth Canto, 4 vols. Swami A. C. Bhaktivedanta. LC 73-169353. (Illus.). 1974. 12.95 ea. Vol. 1 (ISBN 0-912776-38-2). Vol. 2 (ISBN 0-912776-47-1). Vol. 3 (ISBN 0-912776-48-X). Vol. 4 (ISBN 0-912776-49-8). Bhaktivedanta.

Srimad Bhagavatam: Ninth Canto, 3 vols. Swami A. C. Bhaktivedanta. LC 73-169353. (Illus., Sanskrit & Eng.). 1977. 12.95 ea. Vol. 1 (ISBN 0-912776-94-3). Vol. 2 (ISBN 0-912776-95-1). Vol. 3 (ISBN 0-912776-96-X). Bhaktivedanta.

Srimad Bhagavatam: Second Canto, 2 vols. Swami A. C. Bhaktivedanta. LC 73-169353. (Illus.). 1972. 12.95 ea. Vol. 1 (ISBN 0-912776-28-5). Vol. 2 (ISBN 0-912776-35-8). Bhaktivedanta.

Srimad Bhagavatam: Seventh Canto, 3 vols. Swami A. C. Bhaktivedanta. LC 73-169353. (Illus.). 1976. 12.95 ea. Vol. 1 (ISBN 0-912776-86-2). Vol. 2 (ISBN 0-912776-87-0). Vol. 3 (ISBN 0-912776-89-7). Bhaktivedanta.

Srimad Bhagavatam: Sixth Canto, 3 vols. Swami A. C. Bhaktivedanta. LC 73-169353. (Illus.). 1976. 12.95 ea. Vol. 1 (ISBN 0-912776-81-1). Vol. 2 (ISBN 0-912776-82-X). Vol. 3 (ISBN 0-912776-83-8). Bhaktivedanta.

Srimad-Bhagavatam: Tenth Canto, Vol 1. Swami Prabhupada A. C. Bhaktivedanta. LC 73-169353. 1977. 12.95 (ISBN 0-912776-97-8). Bhaktivedanta.

Srimad-Bhagavatam: Tenth Canto, Vol 2. Swami Prabhupada A. C. Bhaktivedanta. 1977. 12.95 (ISBN 0-912776-98-6). Bhaktivedanta.

Srimad-Bhagavatam: Tenth Canto, Vol. 3. Swami Prabhupada A. C. Bhaktivedanta. (Illus.). 112p. 1980. 12.95 (ISBN 0-89213-107-1). Bhaktivedanta.

Srimad Bhagavatam: Third Canto, 4 vols. Swami A. C. Bhaktivedanta. LC 73-169353. (Illus.). 1974. 12.95 ea. Vol. 1 (ISBN 0-912776-37-4). Vol. 2 (ISBN 0-912776-44-7). Vol. 3 (ISBN 0-912776-46-3). Vol. 4 (ISBN 0-912776-75-7). Bhaktivedanta.

Srimad Bhagavatam: 11th Canto, Vol. 5. Bhaktivedanta Swami. 1985. 12.95 (ISBN 0-89213-126-8). Bhaktivedanta.

Srimad Bhagavatam: 12th Canto, Vol. 1. Bhaktivedanta Swami & Hridayananda Das Goswami. 1985. 12.95 (ISBN 0-89213-129-2). Bhaktivedanta.

Srimad Bhagavatam: 12th Canto, Vol. 2. Bhaktivedanta Swami. 1985. 12.95 (ISBN 0-89213-130-6). Bhaktivedanta.

Srimad Devi Bhagawatam, Pts. I & II. Tr. by Swami Vijnanananda from Sanskrit. LC 75-985029. 1977. 55.00x (ISBN 0-89684-455-2). Orient Bk Dist.

Srimadbhagavatam: A Concise Narrative. Gunada C. Sen. 1987. 26.00x (ISBN 81-215-0036-2, Munshiram Manoharial India). South Asia Bks.

Srinagar Workshop on High Temperature Superconductivity. Ed. by A. K. Gupta et al. 450p. 1988. 58.00 (ISBN 9971-50-703-X). World Scientific Pub.

Srngara-Prakasa of Bhoja, 2 vols. Bhoja. Ed. by V. Raghavan. LC 87-33908. (Oriental Ser.). 1888p. (Sanskrit.). 1988. Set. text ed. 90.00 (ISBN 0-674-83340-6). Harvard U Pr.

SRS-A & Leukotrienes: Proceedings of the Annual Symposium of Basic Medical Sciences, 10th. Basic Medical Sciences, Annual Symposium Staff. Ed. by Priscilla J. Piper. LC 80-41758. (Prostaglandins Research Studies Ser.). 282p. 1981. 107.00x (ISBN 0-471-27959-5, Pub. by Wiley-Interscience). Wiley.

Sruti Gita: The Song of the Srutis. Tr. by Gambhirananda from Sanskrit. 99p. 1982. pap. 4.95 (ISBN 0-87481-510-X). Vedanta Pr.

SS. (Third Reich Ser.). (Illus.). 1989. price not set (ISBN 0-8094-6950-2); lib. bdg. price not set (ISBN 0-8094-6951-0). Time-Life.

SS Armor. (Illus.). 1986. pap. 7.95 (ISBN 0-89747-066-4, 6014). Squad Sig Pubns.

SS-GB. Len Deighton. 1984. pap. 3.95 (ISBN 0-345-31809-9). Ballantine.

SS-GB. Len Deighton. 1980. pap. 3.95. Ballantine.

SS-GB. Len Deighton. 1979. 10.95 (ISBN 0-394-50409-7). Knopf.

Ssabier und der Ssabismus, 2 Vols. D. Chwolsohn. 1856. 85.00 (ISBN 0-384-09053-2). Johnson Repr.

Ssquestres D'Altona et la Tragioque Moderne see Cahiers de l'Institut de Science Economique Appliquee.

SSS Newsletter, 11 vols. Ed. by Rado L. Lencek et al. 238p. 1973-78. write for info. Soc Slovene Studies.

Sta Oni Nazivaju Demokratijom? Milos Acin-Kosta. 210p. (Orig., Serbo-Croatian.). 1953. pap. 1.00 (ISBN 0-317-61884-9). Ravnogorski.

Staal en Arbeid, 2 pts. M. C. Van Elteren. (Illus.). 1100p. 1986. pap. 68.25 (ISBN 90-04-07816-9, Pub. by E J Brill). Heinman.

Staat Im Wachstum Versucheiner Finanzwirthschaftlichen Analyse der Preussischen Haushaltsrechungen, 1871-1913, 2 vols. Peter-Michael Prochnow. Ed. by Stuart Bruchey. LC 80-2825. (Dissertations in European Economic History II). (Illus.). 1981. lib. bdg. 32.00x (ISBN 0-405-14009-6). Ayer Co Pubs.

Staat und Gesellschaft der Griechen und Romer. Von Ulrich & B. Niese Wiliamovitz-Moellendorff. Ed. by J. P. Mayer. LC 78-67398. (European Political Thought Ser.). (Ger.). 1979. Repr. of 1923 ed. lib. bdg. 19.00x (ISBN 0-405-11750-7). Ayer Co Pubs.

Staat und Manufaktur im Romischen Reiche. Axel W. Persson. Ed. by Moses Finley. LC 79-4998. (Ancient Economic History Ser.). (Ger.). 1980. Repr. of 1923 ed. lib. bdg. 12.00x (ISBN 0-405-12387-6). Ayer Co Pubs.

Staatliche Regulierung Sozialer Innovation in der Bundesrepublik und in Frankreich. Gabriele Gottelmann. (European University Studies: No. 31, Vol. 35). 313p. (Ger.). 1983. 36.30 (ISBN 3-8204-7760-8). P Lang Pubs.

Staatsburgerin: Organ fur die Interessen der Arbeiterinnen. Ed. by Erlautert von Ulla Wischermann & Hartwig Gebhardt. 200p. 1987. lib. bdg. 60.00 (ISBN 3-598-10694-7). K G Saur.

Staatslehre des Franz Suarez, S. J. Heinrich Rommen. Ed. by J. P. Mayer. LC 78-67381. (European Political Thought Ser.). (Ger.). 1979. Repr. of 1926 ed. lib. bdg. 27.50x (ISBN 0-405-11731-0). Ayer Co Pubs.

Staatsphilosophie des Englischen Idealismus. Klaus Dockhorn. 1937. pap. 20.00 (ISBN 0-384-12065-2). Johnson Repr.

Staatsverwaltung der Beserzten Gebiete, Erster Band, Belgien. Ludwig Von Kohler. (Wirtschafts-Und Sozialgeschichte des Weltkrieges (Deutsche Serie)). (Ger.). 1927. 70.00x (ISBN 0-317-27587-9). Elliots Bks.

Stab. Robert Alley. 224p. 1982. pap. 2.50 (ISBN 0-345-30689-9). Ballantine.

Stab in the Dark. Lawrence Block. 192p. 1985. pap. 2.95 (ISBN 0-515-08635-5). Jove Pubns.

Stabat Mater: Noble Icon of the Outcast & the Poor. Peter Daino. LC 87-30633. 80p. 1988. pap. 4.95 (ISBN 0-8189-0526-3). Alba.

Stabbing of George Harry Storrs. Jonathan Goodman. LC 83-8267. (Illus.). 254p. 1983. 17.50 (ISBN 0-8142-0349-3). Ohio St U Pr.

Stabilisation: An Economic Policy for Producers & Consumers. E. M. Lloyd. Ed. by F. M. Leventhal. (English Workers & the Coming of the Welfare State Ser., 1918-1945). 128p. 1985. lib. bdg. 28.00 (ISBN 0-8240-7617-6). Garland Pub.

Stabilisation, Disinfection & Odour Control in Sewage Sludge Treatment: An Annotated Bibliography Covering the Period 1950-1983. Ed. by A. M. Bruce & E. S. Connor. 200p. 1984. text ed. 63.95x (ISBN 0-470-20033-2). Halsted Pr.

Stability Analysis of Earth Slopes. Yang Huang. 1983. 37.95 (ISBN 0-442-23689-1). Van Nos Reinhold.

Stability & Change in American Politics: The Coming of Age of the Generation of the 1960's. Michael X. Delli Carpini. 304p. 1986. 45.00x (ISBN 0-8147-1780-2). NYU Pr.

Stability & Change in American Politics: The Coming of Age of the Generation of the 1960's. Michael X. Delli Carpini. 396p. (Orig.). 1986. pap. text ed. 15.00 (ISBN 0-8147-1784-5). NYU Pr.

Stability & Change in Australian Politics. Don Aitkin. LC 76-56692. 1977. 26.00x (ISBN 0-312-75478-7). St Martin.

Stability & Change in Congress. 4th ed. Barbara Hinckley. 370p. 1987. 19.50 (ISBN 0-06-042849-X, HarpC). Har-Row.

Stability & Change in Highland Chiapas, Mexico. Henning Siverts. (Bergen Studies in Social Anthropology: No. 4). 152p. (Orig.). 1985. pap. text ed. 9.95x (ISBN 0-936508-51-5, Pub. by Dept Soc Anthropology, University of Bergen, Norway). Barber Pr.

Stability & Change in Literacy Learning. Don Holdaway. LC 83-22636. 72p. 1984. pap. text ed. 6.50x (ISBN 0-435-08209-4). Heinemann Ed.

Stability & Change: Innovation In an Educational Context. S. Rosenblum & K. S. Louis. LC 80-28291. (Environment, Development, Public Policy & Social Services Ser.). 370p. 1981. 39.50x (ISBN 0-306-40665-9, Plenum Pr). Plenum Pub.

Stability & Complexity in Model Ecosystems. Robert M. May. (Population Biology Monographs: No. 6). 150p. 1973. 30.50x (ISBN 0-691-08125-5); pap. 11.95 (ISBN 0-691-08130-1). Princeton U Pr.

Stability & Constancy in Visual Perception: Mechanisms & Processes. Ed. by William Epstein. LC 76-28769. (Wiley Series in Behavior). pap. 118.50 (ISBN 0-317-55551-0, 2056335). Bks Demand UMI.

Stability & Control. Donald Layton & Dimitrios Pouliezos. 200p. 1988. text ed. 39.95 (ISBN 0-938862-56-1). Weber Systems.

Stability & Control of Discrete Processes. J. P. Lasalle. (Applied Mathematical Sciences: Vol. 62). (Illus.). 610p. 1986. pap. 22.00 (ISBN 0-387-96411-8). Springer-Verlag.

Stability & Dynamic Systems. M. I. Al'muhamedov et al. (Translations Ser.: No. 1, Vol. 5). 1962. 30.00 (ISBN 0-8218-1605-5, TRANS 1-5). Am Math.

Stability & Flexibility: An Analysis of Natural Systems. N. D. Cook. (Systems Science & World Order Library). (Illus.). 246p. 1982. 32.00 (ISBN 0-317-66881-1); pap. 15.75 (ISBN 0-08-028135-4). Pergamon.

Stability & Flexibility: An Analysis of Natural Systems. 1980. 34.00 (ISBN 0-08-024683-4). Pergamon.

Stability & Inflation: Essays in Memory of A. W. Phillips. Ed. by A. R. Bergstrom et al. LC 77-4420. 323p. 1978. 110.00xcloth (ISBN 0-471-99522-3, Pub. by Wiley-Interscience). Wiley.

Stability & Perfection of Nash Equilibria. E. Van Damme. (Illus.). 370p. 1987. 99.00 (ISBN 0-387-17101-0). Springer-Verlag.

Stability & Periodic Solutions of Ordinary & Functional Differential Equations. Monograph ed. T. A. Burton. 1985. 70.00 (ISBN 0-12-147360-0); pap. 48.50 (ISBN 0-12-147361-9). Acad Pr.

Stability & Progress in the World Economy. Ed. by Douglas Hague. LC 84-22545. xvi, 267p. 1985. Repr. of 1958 ed. lib. bdg. 41.50 (ISBN 0-313-24683-1, IESP). Greenwood.

Stability & Robustness of Multivariable Feedback Systems. Michael George Safonov. (Signal Processing, Optimization & Control Ser.). 171p. 1980. 40.00x (ISBN 0-262-19180-6). MIT Pr.

Stability & Seismic Resistance of Buttress Dams. N. S. Motsonelidze. Tr. by V. S. Kothekar from Rus. 293p. 1987. text ed. 48.50 (ISBN 90-6191-490-6, Pub. by A A Balkema). Brookfield Pub Co.

Stability & Seismic Resistance of Buttress Dams. N. S. Motsonelidze. 278p. 1987. 30.00x (ISBN 81-204-0207-3, Pub. by Oxford IBH). South Asia Bks.

Stability & Strife: England 1714-1760. W. A. Speck. (New History of England Ser.). pap. text ed. 9.95x (ISBN 0-674-83350-3). Harvard U Pr.

Stability & Strife: England 1714-1760. W. A. Speck. (New History of England Ser.). 1977. 16.00x (ISBN 0-674-83347-3). Harvard U Pr.

Stability & Switching in Cellular Differentiation. Ed. by R. M. Clayton & D. E. Truman. LC 83-18053. (Advances In Experimental Medicine & Biology Ser.: Vol. 158). 496p. 1982. 85.00x (ISBN 0-306-41181-4, Plenum Pr). Plenum Pub.

Stability & the Industrial Elite in China & the Soviet Union. Constance S. Meaney. LC 87-83158. (China Research Monographs: No. 34). 160p. (Orig.). 1988. pap. 15.00x (ISBN 0-912966-98-X). IEAS.

Stability & Trim for the Ship's Officer. 3rd, rev. ed. William E. George. LC 82-74137. (Illus.). 359p. 1983. text ed. 16.00x (ISBN 0-87033-297-X). Cornell Maritime.

Stability & Trim of Fishing Vessels & Other Small Ships. 2nd ed. J. Anthony Hind. (Illus.). 132p. 1982. 19.00 (ISBN 0-85238-121-2, FN97, FNB). UNIPUB.

Stability & Trim of Fishing Vessels. J. Anthony Hind. 1978. 40.00 (Pub. by Fishing News England). State Mutual Bk.

Stacions of Rome. F. J. Furnivall. (EETS, OS Ser.: No. 25). Repr. of 1867 ed. 20.00 (ISBN 0-527-00025-6). Kraus Repr.

Stack A Dollar. Elroy Walters. 1985. pap. 2.50 (ISBN 0-317-39980-2). Holloway.

Stack Management: A Practical Guide to Shelving & Maintaining Collections. William Hubbard. LC 80-28468. 110p. 1981. pap. 8.00x (ISBN 0-8389-0319-3). ALA.

Stack the Deck. rev. ed. Robert B. Cahill & Herbert J. Hrebic. (Illus.). 1980. pap. 6.00 (ISBN 0-933282-00-1). Stack the Deck.

Stack the Deck. Robert B. Cahill & Herbert J. Hrebic. (Writing Program Ser.). (gr. 9-12). 1973. text ed. 9.00 (ISBN 0-933282-11-7); pap. text ed. 9.10. Stack the Deck.

Stackelberg Differential Games in Economic Models. A. Bagchi. (Lecture Notes in Control & Information Sciences Ser.: Vol. 64). viii, 203p. 1984. pap. 17.00 (ISBN 0-387-13587-1). Springer-Verlag.

Stacking Blending Reclaiming of Bulk Materials. Ed. by Reinhard H. Wohlbier. (Series on Bulk Materials Handling: Vol. 1, No. 5). 780p. 1977. 60.00x (ISBN 0-87849-018-3, Trans Tech Germany). Trans Tech.

Stacking the Chips. Ed. by John Bessant & Sam Cole. 260p. cancelled (ISBN 0-86187-359-9, Pub. by Frances Pinter). Longwood Pub Group.

Stacking the Chips: Information Technology & the Distribution of Income. John Bessant & Sam Cole. LC 85-11883. 300p. 1985. 26.95x (ISBN 0-8476-7461-4, Rowman & Allanheld). Rowman.

Stacking the Deck: A Social Skills Game for Retarded Adults. Richard M. Foxx & Martin J. McMorrow. 24p. (Orig.). 1983. pap. text ed. 19.95 (ISBN 0-87822-231-6). Res Press.

Stackpole Family. G. T. Ridlon. LC 70-138079. (Saco Valley Settlements Ser). 1970. pap. 1.50 (ISBN 0-8048-0836-8). C E Tuttle.

STACS 84: Symposium of Theoretical Aspects of Computer Science Paris, April 11-13, 1984. Ed. by M. Fontet & K. Mehlhorn. (Lecture Notes in Computers Science: Vol. 166). vi, 338p. (Eng. & Fr.). 1984. pap. 19.00 (ISBN 0-387-12920-0). Springer Verlag.

STACS 85. Ed. by K. Mehlhorn. (Lecture Notes in Computer Science Ser.: Vol. 182). vii, 374p. 1985. pap. 20.00 (ISBN 0-387-13912-5). Springer-Verlag.

Stacs 86. Ed. by B. Monien & G. Vidal-Naquet. (Lecture Notes in Computer Science Ser.: Vol. 210). ix, 368p. 1986. pap. 23.00 (ISBN 0-387-16078-7). Springer-Verlag.

STACS 87: Annual Symposium on Theoretical Aspects of Computer Science, Passau, FRG, 4th, February, 19-21, 1987. Ed. by F. J. Brandenburg et al. (Lecture Notes in Computer Science Ser.: Vol. 247). x, 484p. 1987. pap. 33.60 (ISBN 0-387-17219-X). Springer-Verlag.

STACS 88. Ed. by R. Cori & M. Wirsing. (Lecture Notes in Computer Science Ser.: Vol. 294). ix, 404p. 1988. pap. 33.30 (ISBN 0-387-18834-7). Springer-Verlag.

Stacy. Kim Townsend. 1977. pap. 1.95 (ISBN 0-8439-0507-7, Leisure Bks). Leisure NY.

Stadium: Microcomputer Word Processing Program. D. Gioffre. 272p. 1987. pap. text ed. 8.96 (ISBN 0-07-023328-4). McGraw.

Stadt und Eidgenossenschaft im Alten Testament: Eine Auseinandersetzung mit Max Webers Studie "Das Antike Judentum". Christa Schaefer-Lichtenberger. 485p. (Ger.). 1983. 43.20 (ISBN 3-11-008591-7). De Gruyter.

Stadt und Verkehr: Theorie und Praxis der Stadtischen Verkehrsplanung. Kurt Leibbrand. 404p. (Ger.). 1980. 75.95x (ISBN 0-8176-1072-3). Birkhauser.

Stadtmauer von Resafa in Syrien. Walter Karnapp. (Denkmaeler Antiker Architektur: Vol. 11). (Illus.). 1976. 78.00x (ISBN 3-11-006535-5). De Gruyter.

Stadtrechtsbuch von Sillein: Einleitung Edition und Glossar. Ilpo T. Piirainen. (Quellen und Forschungen zur Sprach und Kulturgeschichte der Germanischen Voelker 46). 1972. 33.60x (ISBN 3-11-003543-X). De Gruyter.

Staedtekonferenz Ueber Abfallbeseitigung: Conference on Urban Waste Disposal. Ed. by Giulio Milazzo. 700p. (Eng., Fr., Ger. & Ital.). 1983. write for info (ISBN 0-8176-1282-3). Birkhauser.

Staff Analyst. Jack Rudman. (Career Examination Ser.: C-1551). (Cloth bdg. avail. on request). pap. 16.00 (ISBN 0-8373-1551-4). Natl Learning.

Staff Analyst-Associate Staff Analyst. Hugh E. O'Neill. LC 82-11411. 192p. (Orig.). 1983. pap. 10.00 (ISBN 0-668-05522-7, 5522). Arco.

Staff & Student Supervision: A Task-Centered Approach. Dorothy E. Pettes. 1979. 30.00x (ISBN 0-317-05776-6, Pub. by Natl Soc Work). State Mutual Bk.

Staff Burnout: Job Stress in the Human Services. Cary Cherniss. LC 80-19408. (Sage Studies in Community Mental Health: Vol. 2). (Illus.). 200p. 1980. pap. 16.95 (ISBN 0-8039-1339-7). Sage.

Staff Development, Pt. II. Ed. by Gary A. Griffin. LC 82-62382. (National Society for the Study of Education Ser.: Bk. 82). 275p. 1984. pap. text ed. 10.00x (ISBN 0-226-60093-9). U of Chicago Pr.

Staff Development, Vol. 1. Ed. by Journal of Nursing Administration Staff. LC 75-3506. 91p. 1975. pap. text ed. 25.25 (ISBN 0-913654-08-6). Aspen Pub.

Staff Development, Vol. 2. Ed. by Journal of Nursing Administration Staff. LC 77-85308. 61p. 1977. pap. 25.25 (ISBN 0-913654-40-X). Aspen Pub.

Staff Development, No. 955. (Journal Reprint Ser.). 8.75 (ISBN 0-317-57161-3). Inst Real Estate.

Staff Development: A Humanistic Approach. Russell Dobson et al. LC 80-67254. 175p. 1980. pap. text ed. 11.00 (ISBN 0-8191-1131-7). U Pr of Amer.

Staff Development & Educational Change. Ed. by Houston & Pankratz. 1980. 5.00 (ISBN 0-686-38077-0). Assn Tchr Ed.

Staff Development & Organization Development: ASCD 1981 Yearbook. Ed. by Betty Dillon-Peterson. LC 80-70653. 149p. 1981. pap. text ed. 9.75 (ISBN 0-87120-104-6, 610-81232). Assn Supervision.

Staff Development Coordinator. Jack Rudman. (Career Examination Ser.: C-2171). (Cloth bdg. avail. on request). 1988. pap. 14.00 (ISBN 0-8373-2171-9). Natl Learning.

Staff Development for School Improvement: A Focus on the Teacher. Ed. by Marvin F. Wideen & Ian Andrews. 250p. 1987. 38.00x (ISBN 1-85000-171-5, Falmer Pr.); pap. 19.00x (ISBN 1-85000-172-3). Taylor & Francis.

Staff Development for the Social Studies Teacher. Elizabeth Dillon-Peterson & G. Dale Greenawald. LC 80-11118. 102p. 1980. 9.95 (ISBN 0-89994-243-1). Soc Sci Ed.

Staff Development in Action, Vol. 2. Sue Carroll et al. 172p. 1987. 170.00x (ISBN 1-85008-050-X, Pub. by Framework UK). State Mutual Bk.

Staff Development in Human Service Organizations. Harvey J. Bertcher. (Illus.). 256p. 1988. text ed. write for info. (ISBN 0-13-840273-6). P-H.

Staff Development in Libraries: Bibliography. 49p. 1983. 7.50 (ISBN 0-8389-6758-2). Library Admin.

Staff Development in Mental Retardation Services: A Practical Manual. James F. Gardner & Michael S. Chapman. LC 85-5650. 334p. (Orig.). 1985. pap. text ed. 21.00 (ISBN 0-933716-48-6, 486). P H Brookes.

Staff Development in the Secondary School: Management Perspectives. Chris Day & Roger Morre. 320p. 1986. 39.00 (ISBN 0-7099-0895-4, Pub. by Croom Helm Ltd); pap. 17.00 (ISBN 0-7099-4539-6). Routledge Chapman & Hall.

Staff Development: New Demands, New Realities, New Perspectives. Ann Lieberman & Lynn Miller. LC 78-27453. 1979. 16.95x (ISBN 0-8077-2512-9). Tchrs Coll.

Staff Development: Problems & Solutions. American Associations of School Administrators Staff. 82p. (Orig.). 1987. pap. text ed. 13.95 (ISBN 0-87652-110-3, 021-00164). Am Assn Sch Admin.

Staff Development Series II: Orientation-Or. (Modular Independent Learning System Ser.). 94p. 1986. 7.00 (ISBN 0-317-65182-X). Assn Oper Rm Nurses.

Staff Development Series 1980-1981, 2 pts. (Modular Independent Learning System Ser.). Pt. I: Inservice Education OR. 7.00 (ISBN 0-939583-19-4). Pt. 2: Orientation OR. Assn Oper Rm Nurses.

Staff Development Specialist. Jack Rudman. (Career Examination Ser.: C-2489). (Cloth bdg. avail. on request). pap. 14.00 (ISBN 0-8373-2489-0). Natl Learning.

Staff Development: Staff Liberation. Ed. by Charles W. Beegle & Roy A. Edelfelt. LC 77-5187. 124p. 1977. 6.50 (ISBN 0-87120-083-X, 611-77106). Assn Supervision.

Staff Dismissal. Shirley B. Neill. (Critical Issues Reports: No. 3). 1978. pap. 8.95 (ISBN 0-686-02455-9, 02100512). Am Assn Sch Admin.

Staff for the President: The Executive Office, 1921-1952. Alfred D. Sander. (Contributions in Political Science Ser.: No. 229). 1989. price not set (ISBN 0-313-26526-7, SRJ/). Greenwood.

Staff Handbook for a High School Student Newspaper. Scott Sprain. 129p. 1981. 7.75 (ISBN 0-8141-4674-0). NCTE.

Staff Management in Library & Information Work. Noragh Jones & Peter Jordan. 250p. 1986. text ed. 50.50 (ISBN 0-566-03563-4, Pub. by Gower Pub England). Gower Pub Co.

Staff Management: Material for Management Training in Agricultural Cooperatives (MATCOM, Vienna) 133p. 1981. 24.50 (ISBN 92-2-102939-5). Intl Labour Office.

Staff Nurse. Jack Rudman. (Career Examination Ser.: C-756). (Cloth bdg. avail. on request). pap. 14.00 (ISBN 0-8373-0756-2). Natl Learning.

Staff Orientation in Early Childhood Programs. Barbara O'Sullivan. Ed. by Jill Hix. (Illus.). 172p. (Orig.). (ps). 1987. pap. 21.95 (ISBN 0-934140-44-8). Toys 'n Things.

Staff Personality Problems in the Library Automation Process: A Case in Point. Jay E. Daily. 157p. 1985. 28.50 (ISBN 0-87287-505-9). Libs Unl.

Staff Physician. Jack Rudman. (Career Examination Ser.: C-1493). (Cloth bdg. avail. on request). pap. 23.95 (ISBN 0-8373-1493-3). Natl Learning.

Staff Recognition: Unlocking the Potential for Success. 1985. 42.00 (ISBN 0-87545-035-0, 418-13978). Natl Sch Pr.

Staff Relations in the Civil Service: The Canadian Experience. Saul J. Frankel. LC 63-4271. pap. 86.00 (ISBN 0-317-20715-6, 2023829). Bks Demand UMI.

Staff Report Readings for Credit Executives. 153p. 1982. 40.00 (ISBN 0-939050-35-8). Credit Res NYS.

Staff-Resident Interaction Chronograph: Observational Assessment Instrumentation for Service & Research. Ed. by Gordon L. Paul et al. Mark H. Licht & Marco J. Mariotto. (Assessment in Residential Treatment Settings Ser.: No. 3). 280p. Date not set. pap. text ed. price not set (ISBN 0-87822-277-4). Res Press.

Staff Studies for the World Economic Outlook. International Monetary Fund Staff. (World Economic & Financial Surveys Ser.). 206p. 1987. pap. 15.00 (ISBN 0-939934-86-8). Intl Monetary.

Staff Studies for the World Economic. Outlook IMF Research Dept. (World Economic & Financial Surveys Ser.). xi, 195p. 1986. pap. 15.00 (ISBN 0-939934-73-6). Intl Monetary.

Staff Supervision in the Probation Service: Keeping Pace with Change. Michael Davies. 220p. 1988. text ed. 44.40 (ISBN 0-566-05623-2, Pub. by Gower Pub England). Gower Pub Co.

Staff Support & Staff Training. T. Collins & T. Bruce. (Residential Social Work Ser.). 168p. 1984. pap. 11.95 (ISBN 0-422-76920-7, 4003, Pub. by Tavistock England). Routledge Chapman & Hall.

Staff Training for Automation: Kit & Flyer No. 109. 116p. 1984. 20.00 (ISBN 0-318-18194-0). OMS.

Staff Training in Mental Handicap. Ed. by James Hogg. 224p. 1986. 27.50 (ISBN 0-7099-3728-8, Pub. by Croom Helm UK). Routledge Chapman & Hall.

Staff Training in Mental Handicap. Ed. by James Hogg & Peter Mittler. 1987. text ed. 29.95 (ISBN 0-914797-35-2, Co-Pub. by Croom Helm Ltd). Brookline Bks.

Staffing, Vol. II. Journal of Nursing Administration Staff. LC 75-1675. 47p. 1975. pap. 25.25 (ISBN 0-913654-06-X). Aspen Pub.

Staffing, Vol. III. Journal of Nursing Administration Staff. LC 75-43268. 43p. 1976. pap. 25.25 (ISBN 0-913654-21-3). Aspen Pub.

Staffing A Small Business: Hiring, Compensating & Evaluating. Anita E. Worthington & E. Robert Worthington. Ed. by Emmett Ramey. (Successful Business Library). 225p. 1987. 3-ring binder 33.95 (ISBN 0-916378-49-7, Oasis). PSI Res.

Staffing a Small Business: Hiring, Compensating & Evaluating. Anita E. Worthington & E. Robert Worthington. (Successful Business Library). 239p. 1987. pap. 18.95 (ISBN 1-55571-018-2, Oasis). PSI Res.

Staffing for DRGs: A Unit-Specific Approach for Nurse Managers. Elaine Deines. LC 83-81646. (Help Series of Management Guides). 130p. 1983. pap. 15.95 (ISBN 0-933036-20-5). Ganong W L Co.

Staffing for DRGs-Part II: Nursing Care Strategies for DRG-Specific Staffing. Elaine Deines. LC 83-81646. (HELP Series of Management Guides). 128p. 1985. pap. 15.95 (ISBN 0-933036-21-3). Ganong W L Co.

Staffing for Foreign Affairs: Personnel Systems for the 1980's & 1990's. William I. Bacchus. LC 83-42546. 272p. 1983. 29.50x (ISBN 0-691-07660-X). Princeton U Pr.

Staffing for Optimum Performance. Victoria L. Sears. LC 85-80707. 200p. (Orig.). 1986. pap. 49.95 (ISBN 0-88057-403-8). Exec Ent Pubns.

Staffing of Congress: A Selected Bibliography. Jamie W. Coniglio. (Public Administration Ser.: P 1749). 5p. 1985. 2.00 (ISBN 0-89028-529-2). Vance Biblios.

Staffing of Nuclear Power Plants & the Recruitment, Training & Authorization of Operating Personnel. (Safety Ser.: No. 50-Sg-01). 32p. pap. 7.00 (ISBN 92-0-123379-5, ISP514, IAEA). UNIPUB.

Staffing Organizations. Benjamin Schneider. Ed. by Lyman W. Porter. LC 75-20584. (Management & Organizations Ser.). (Illus.). 200p. 1976. pap. text ed. write for info. (ISBN 0-673-16147-1). Scott F.

Staffing Organizations. 2nd ed. Benjamin Schneider & Neal Schmitt. LC 82-5594. (Organizational Behavior & Human Resources Ser.). 1986. text ed. write for info. (ISBN 0-673-16655-4). Scott F.

Staffing Policies & Strategies: ASPA Handbook of Personnel & Industrial Relations, Vol. I. 2nd, rev. ed. Ed. by Dale Yoder & Herbert G. Heneman, Jr. (Illus.). 306p. pap. text ed. 15.00 (ISBN 0-87179-318-0, 0318). BNA.

Staffing the Commercial Credit Department. LC 85-25843. (Illus.). 52p. (Orig.). 1985. pap. text ed. 30.00 (ISBN 0-936742-26-7). Robt Morris Assocs.

Staffing the Contemporary Organization: A Guide to Planning, Recruiting, & Selecting for Human Resource Professionals. Donald L. Caruth et al. LC 87-13092. 323p. 1988. lib. bdg. 45.00 (ISBN 0-89930-236-X, CFG/, Quorum Bks). Greenwood.

Stafford As It Was. Hendon Publishing Co., Ltd. Staff. 1986. 16.10x (ISBN 0-317-54180-3, Pub. by Hendon Pub UK). State Mutual Bk.

Stafford Cripps' Mission to Moscow, 1940-42. Gabriel Gorodetsky. (Illus.). 377p. 1985. 49.50 (ISBN 0-521-23866-8). Cambridge U Pr.

Staffords, Earls of Stafford & Dukes of Buckingham 1394-1521. Carole Rawcliffe. LC 77-71425. (Studies in Medieval Life & Thought: No. 11). (Illus.). 1978. 44.50 (ISBN 0-521-21663-X). Cambridge U Pr.

Staffordshire, Vol. VI. Ed. by M. W. Greenslade. (Victoria History of the Counties of England Ser.). (Illus.). 1979. 129.00x (ISBN 0-19-722733-3). Oxford U Pr.

Staffordshire. Arthur Mee. (King's England Ser.). cancelled (ISBN 0-340-15030-0). Intl Pubns Serv.

Staffordshire Bull Terrier Champions, 1975-1986. Camino E. E. & B. Co. (Illus.). 128p. 1988. pap. 29.95 (ISBN 0-940808-72-2). Camino E E & B.

Staffordshire Bull Terrier in America. Eltinge et al. Ed. by Steve Eltinge. 140p. (gr. 4 up). 1986. pap. 24.95 (ISBN 0-9617204-0-9). MIP Pub.

Staffordshire Portrait Figures. P. D. Pugh. (Illus.). 1987. 89.50 (ISBN 1-85149-010-8). Antique Collect.

Staffordshire Pottery: The Tribal Art of England. Anthony Oliver. (Illus.). 192p. 1980. 65.00 (ISBN 0-434-54392-6, Pub. by W Heinemann Ltd). David & Charles.

Staffordshire Romantic Transfer Patterns: Cup Plates & Early Victorian China. Petra Williams. LC 78-55047. (Illus.). 763p. 1978. 25.00x (ISBN 0-914736-05-1). Fountain Hse East.

Staffordshire Romantic Transfer Patterns II: Cup Plates, & Early Victorian China. Petra Williams & Marguerite Weber. LC 78-55047. (Illus.). 700p. 1986. 32.50x (ISBN 0-914736-09-4). Fountain Hse East.

Stafne's Oral Radiographic Diagnosis. 5th ed. Contrib. by Joseph A. Gibilisco. (Illus.). 535p. 1985. 49.00 (ISBN 0-7216-4114-8). Saunders.

Stage: A Handbook of Classroom Ideas to Motivate the Teaching of Elementary Dramatics. (Spice Ser). 1968. 8.95 (ISBN 0-89273-107-9). Educ Serv.

Stage & Drama in the plays of Christopher Marlowe. David H. Zucker. Ed. by James Hogg. (Elizabethan & Renaissance Studies). 188p. (Orig.). 1972. pap. 15.00 (ISBN 3-7052-0656-7, Pub. by Salzburg Studies). Longwood Pub Group.

Stage & Set Design. Rodolfo Di Giammarco. (Illus.). 24p. Date not set. 5.00 (ISBN 0-930209-04-4). Otis Art.

Stage & Structure. Iris Levin. Ed. by Sidney Strauss. LC 85-15624. (Human Development Ser.: Vol. 1). 336p. 1986. text ed. 49.50 inst. ed. (ISBN 0-89391-224-7); text ed. 32.50 pers. ed. Ablex Pub.

Stage & the Licensing Act, 1729-1739. Ed. by Vincent J. Liesenfeld & P. R. Backscheider. LC 78-66661. (Eighteenth Century English Drama Ser.). lib. bdg. 73.00 (ISBN 0-8240-3576-3). Garland Pub.

Stage & the Page: London's "Whole Show" in the Eighteenth Century Theatre. Ed. by George W. Stone, Jr. LC 80-19027. (Clark Library Professorship, UCLA: No. 6). 1981. 25.00x (ISBN 0-520-04201-8). U of Cal Pr.

Stage & the School. 5th ed. K. A. Ommanney & Harry H. Schanker. 1982. text ed. 27.04 (ISBN 0-07-047671-3). McGraw.

Stage & the School. 4th ed. K. A. Ommanney & Harry H. Schanker. 1971. text ed. 29.88 (ISBN 0-07-047657-8, W). McGraw.

Stage & Theatre, 3 vols. (British Parliamentary Papers Ser.). 1971. Set. 272.00x (ISBN 0-7165-1431-1, Pub. by Irish Academic Pr Ireland). Biblio Dist.

Stage Attacked. Northbrooke & Gosson: A Treatise Against Dicing, Dancing, Plays & Interludes. Bd. with School of Abuse: A Pleasant Invective Against Poets, Pipers, Players, Jesters, Etc. (Shakespeare Society of London Publications: Vol. 15). pap. 21.00 (ISBN 0-8115-0177-9). Kraus Repr.

Stage Business in Shakespeare's Plays. Arthur C. Sprague. LC 77-10647. 1954. lib. bdg. 17.00 (ISBN 0-8414-7791-4). Folcroft.

Stage-Coach & Tavern Days. A. M. Earle. LC 68-26351. (American History & Americana Ser., No. 47). (Illus.). 1969. Repr. of 1900 ed. lib. bdg. 58.95x (ISBN 0-8383-0280-7). Haskell.

Stage Coach & Tavern Days. Alice M. Earle. LC 70-81558. (Illus.). Repr. of 1900 ed. 25.00 (ISBN 0-405-08476-5, Blom Pubns). Ayer Co Pubs.

Stage Coach & Tavern Tales of the Old Northwest. Harry E. Cole. Ed. by Louise P. Kellogg. LC 77-137353. 376p. 1972. Repr. of 1930 ed. 46.00x (ISBN 0-8103-3073-3). Gale.

Stage Combat. William Hobbs. (Illus.). 96p. 1981. 10.95 (ISBN 0-312-75493-0). St Martin.

Stage Condemn'd. George Ridpath. LC 79-170443. (English Stage Ser.: Vol. 29). 1973. lib. bdg. 61.00 (ISBN 0-8240-0612-7). Garland Pub.

Stage Controversy in France from Corneille to Rousseau. Moses Barras. LC 78-159116. 365p. 1973. Repr. of 1933 ed. text ed. 40.00x (ISBN 0-87753-051-3). Phaeton.

Stage Costume Design: Theory, Technique & Style. 2nd ed. Douglas Russell. (Illus.). 512p. 1985. text ed. 40.00 (ISBN 0-13-840349-X). P-H.

Stage Costume Handbook. Berneice Prisk. LC 78-27695. 1979. Repr. of 1966 ed. lib. bdg. 52.50x (ISBN 0-313-20912-X, PRSC). Greenwood.

Stage Costume Techniques. Joy S. Emery. (Theatre & Drama Ser.). (Illus.). 368p. 1981. write for info. (ISBN 0-13-840330-9). P-H.

Stagnation in the West? Jimmy Wheeler. 56p. 1979. 12.00 (ISBN 0-318-14356-9, HI-3027-2-P). Hudson Inst.

Stag's Hornbook: Convivial & Merry Verse. John McClure. 1979. Repr. of 1920 ed. lib. bdg. 25.00 (ISBN 0-8492-1726-1). R West.

Stain. Rikki Ducornet. LC 84-48117. 192p. 1984. 12.95 (ISBN 0-394-54284-3, GP-955). Grove.

Stained Glass. William F. Buckley, Jr. 352p. 1981. pap. 3.95 (ISBN 0-380-54791-0). Avon.

Stained Glass: A Beginner's Guide to Creating Beautiful Home Decorations. William R. C. Shedenhelm. (Illus.). 112p. (Orig.). 1987. pap. 9.95 (ISBN 0-8306-2796-0). TAB Bks.

Stained Glass: A Guide to Information Sources. Ed. by Darlene Brady & William Serban. LC 79-23712. (Art & Architecture Information Guide Ser.: Vol. 10). 586p. 1980. 68.00x (ISBN 0-8103-1445-2). Gale.

Stained Glass Before Seventeen Hundred in American Collections: New England & New York State. Ed. by Jane Hayward & Madeline H. Caviness. (Studies in the History of Art: No. 15). (Illus.). 220p. (Orig.). 1985. pap. 25.00 (ISBN 0-89468-078-1, Dist. by U Pr of New Eng). Natl Gallery Art.

Stained Glass Before 1540: An Annotated Bibliography. Madeline H. Caviness & Evelyn R. Staudinger. 1983. lib. bdg. 54.00 (ISBN 0-8161-8332-5, Hall Reference). G K Hall.

Stained Glass Before 1700 in American Collections, Vol. II. Ed. by Madeline H. Caviness et al. LC 84-22794. (Studies in the History of Art: No. 23). (Illus.). 1987. pap. 27.50x (ISBN 0-317-56158-8). U Pr of New Eng.

Stained Glass Cook Book. Helena Kedda. (Illus.). 56p. (Orig.). 1982. pap. 4.95x (ISBN 0-9608958-0-9). Paw-Print.

Stained Glass Craft. J. A. Divine & G. Blachford. 115p. 1972. pap. 2.95 (ISBN 0-486-22812-6). Dover.

Stained Glass Craft. J. A. Divine & G. Blachford. (Illus.). 14.00 (ISBN 0-8446-4539-7). Peter Smith.

Stained Glass Craft Made Simple: Step-by-Step Instructions Using the Modern Copper-Foil Method. James McDonell. 32p. 1985. pap. 2.95 (ISBN 0-486-24963-8). Dover.

Stained Glass Crafts. Romilda Dilley. (Illus.). 24p. (gr. 4-12). 1986. pap. 2.95 wkbk. (ISBN 0-87239-990-7, 2155). Standard Pub.

Stained Glass Elegies. Shusaku Endo. Tr. by Van C. Gessel. 176p. 1987. pap. 7.95 (ISBN 0-396-09147-4). Dodd.

Stained Glass Elegies: Stories. Shusaku Endo. Tr. by Van C. Gessel. 166p. 1985. 13.95 (ISBN 0-396-08643-8). Dodd.

Stained Glass for Everyone. Carolyn Kyle. (Illus.). 104p. 1986. pap. 8.95 (ISBN 0-317-37884-8). Putnam Pub Group.

Stained Glass for Everyone. Carolyn Kyle. (Illus.). 96p. 1984. pap. 8.95 (ISBN 0-935133-00-3). CKE Pubns.

Stained Glass Frames for Plants & Mirrors. Carolyn Kyle. (Illus.). 34p. Date not set. pap. 6.95 (ISBN 0-935133-05-4). CKE Pubns.

Stained Glass from Mind to Light: An Inquiry into the Nature of the Medium. Narcissus Quagliata. LC 76-10019. (Orig.). 1976. 25.00x (ISBN 0-916854-00-0). Mattole Pr.

Stained Glass Gift Shoppe. Terra Parma. Ed. by Stained Glass Images Inc. Staff. (Illus.). 1988. 9.95 (ISBN 0-936459-08-5). Stained Glass.

Stained Glass Hours: Modern Pilgrimage. Tom Davies & John Hodder. (Illus.). 161p. 1985. 30.95 (ISBN 0-450-06053-5, New Eng Lib). David & Charles.

Stained Glass in Australia. Jenny Zimmer. (Illus.). 188p. 1985. 69.00x (ISBN 0-19-554369-6). Oxford U Pr.

Stained Glass in England 1180-1540. Sarah Crewe. 86p. 1987. pap. 18.95 (ISBN 0-11-300015-4, HM1174, Pub. by Her Maj Station Ofc). UNIPUB.

Stained Glass in Thirteenth-Century Burgundy. Virginia C. Raguin. LC 81-47946. (Illus.). 263p. 1982. 56.50x (ISBN 0-691-03987-9). Princeton U Pr.

Stained Glass Magic: Mix & Match Patterns & Projects. Kay Weiner. LC 78-21827. (Chilton's Arts & Crafts Ser.). (Illus.). 224p. 1979. pap. 12.50 (ISBN 0-8019-6726-0). Chilton.

Stained Glass: Music for the Eye. Robert Hill & Jill Hill. LC 79-65725. (Illus.). 108p. (Orig.). 1979. pap. 12.95 (ISBN 0-295-95699-2). U of Wash Pr.

Stained Glass New Designs. Christopher Martin & Jackie Estes. (Illus.). 97p. Date not set. pap. 8.95 (ISBN 0-935133-04-6). CKE Pubns.

Stained Glass of Saint-Pere de Chartres. Meredith P. Lillich. LC 77-13926. (Illus.). 1978. 50.00x (ISBN 0-8195-5023-X). Wesleyan U Pr.

Stained Glass of the Collegiate Church of the Holy Trinity, Tattershall (LINCS) Richard Marks. LC 83-48698. (Theses from the Courtauld Institute of Art Ser.). (Illus.). 450p. 1984. lib. bdg. 55.00 (ISBN 0-8240-5980-8). Garland Pub.

Stained Glass of the Middle Ages in England & France. Hugh Arnold. LC 83-45692. (Illus.). Repr. of 1939 ed. 84.50 (ISBN 0-404-20008-7). AMS Pr.

Stained Glass of William Morris & His Circle: A Catalogue, Vol. 2. A. Charles Sewter. LC 72-91307. (Studies in British Art Ser.). 344p. 1975. 170.00x (ISBN 0-300-01836-3). Yale U Pr.

Stained Glass of William Morris & His Circle, Vol. 1. A. Charles Sewter. LC 72-91307. (Studies in British Art Ser.). (Illus.). 384p. 1974. 140.00x (ISBN 0-300-01471-6). Yale U Pr.

Stained Glass Pattern Book: Eighty-Eight Designs for Workable Projects. Ed Sibbett, Jr. LC 76-15447. (Pictorial Archive Ser). (Illus., Orig.). 1976. pap. 3.95 (ISBN 0-486-23360-X). Dover.

Stained Glass Pattern Book: Eighty-Eight Designs for Workable Projects. Ed Sibbett, Jr. 13.25 (ISBN 0-8446-5522-8). Peter Smith.

Stained Glass: Poems. William Mills. LC 78-11893. 1979. 13.95x (ISBN 0-8071-0488-4); pap. 6.95 (ISBN 0-8071-0489-2). La State U Pr.

Stained Glass Primer, Vol. 1. Peter Mollica. 1971. pap. 4.95 (ISBN 0-9601306-1-6). Mollica Stained Glass.

Stained Glass Primer, Vol. 2. rev ed. Peter Mollica. 1978. pap. 4.95 (ISBN 0-9601306-3-2). Mollica Stained Glass.

Stained Glass Primer, (Japanese Version) Peter Mollica. Ed. by Norm Fogel. Tr. by Eisuke Sasagawa. (Illus.). 87p. (Orig.). 1981. pap. 4.95 (ISBN 0-9601306-4-0). Mollica Stained Glass.

Stained Glass Quilting Technique. Roberta M. Horton. (Illus.). 20p. 1984. pap. 6.95 (ISBN 0-914881-02-7). C & T Pub.

Stained Glass Shades for Small Lamps: With Full-Size Templates. Ed Sibbett, Jr. (Illus.). 64p. (Orig.). 1988. pap. 4.95 (ISBN 0-486-25628-6). Dover.

Stained Glass State Birds & Flowers. Carolyn Kyle. (Illus.). 136p. Date not set. pap. 9.95 (ISBN 0-935133-03-8). CKE Pubns.

Stained Glass Treasures. Donna Schulze. (Illus.). 48p. (Orig.). 1985. pap. 6.50 (ISBN 0-940353-00-8). Papillon Texas.

Stained Glass Window. Charlotte M. Stein. LC 88-70883. (Illus.). 150p. (Orig.). 1988. pap. 10.95 (ISBN 0-916634-12-4). Double M Pr.

Staining for Electron Microscopy. Hayat. 1988. price not set (ISBN 0-471-83025-9). Wiley.

Stainless Steel. R. A. Lula. 240p. 1985. 54.00 (ISBN 0-87170-208-8). ASM.

Stainless Steel Castings - STP 756. Ed. by Behal & Melilli. 454p. 1982. 45.00 (ISBN 0-8031-0740-4, 04-756000-01). ASTM.

Stainless Steel Rat. Harry Harrison. 192p. 1986. pap. 2.95 (ISBN 0-441-77924-7, Pub. by Ace Science Fiction). Ace Bks.

Stainless Steel Rat for President. Harry Harrison. 192p. 1982. pap. 3.50 (ISBN 0-553-25661-0, Spectra). Bantam.

Stainless Steel Rat Gets Drafted. Harry Harrison. LC 87-47566. 240p. 1987. pap. 14.95 (ISBN 0-553-05220-9, Spectra). Bantam.

Stainless Steel Rat Is Born. Harry Harrison. 224p. (Orig.). 1985. pap. 3.50 (ISBN 0-553-24708-5, Spectra). Bantam.

Stainless Steel Rat Saves the World. Harry Harrison. 192p. 1987. pap. 2.95x (ISBN 0-441-77913-1, Pub. by Charter Bks). Ace Bks.

Stainless Steel Rat Wants You! Harry Harrison. 1979. pap. 3.50 (ISBN 0-553-25395-6, Spectra). Bantam.

Stainless Steel Rat's Revenge. Harry Harrison. 192p. 1986. pap. 2.95 (ISBN 0-441-77912-3, Pub. by Ace Science Fiction). Ace Bks.

Stainless Steel Rule. Jean Ferris. LC 85-45731. 192p. (gr. 7 up). 1986. 12.95 (ISBN 0-374-37212-8). FS&G.

Stainless Steels '84. 587p. 1985. pap. text ed. 62.00x (ISBN 0-904357-68-6, Pub. by Inst Metals). Brookfield Pub Co.

Stainless Steels '87: Proceedings of Conference, University of York, 14-16 September '87. 392p. 1988. text ed. 90.00 (ISBN 0-901462-42-X, Pub. by Inst Metals). Brookfield Pub Co.

Stainslavski's Encounter with Shakespeare: The Evolution of a Method. Joyce V. Morgan. Ed. by Bernard Beckerman. LC 83-17979. (Theater & Dramatic Studies: No. 14). 186p. 1984. 42.95 (ISBN 0-8357-1485-3). UMI Res Pr.

Stair Builders Handbook. T. W. Love. LC 74-4298. (Illus.). 1974. pap. 13.75 (ISBN 0-910460-07-8). Craftsman.

Stair Layout. S. Badzinski, Jr. (Illus.). 72p. 1971. pap. 10.24 (ISBN 0-8269-0700-8). Am Technical.

Staircase for Silence. Alan Ecclestone. 158p. 1977. pap. 6.50 (ISBN 0-232-51364-3). Attic Pr.

Staircase Seventeen. Gauri Pant. (Writers Workshop Redbird Ser.). 1975. 8.00 (ISBN 0-88253-644-3); pap. text ed. 4.00 (ISBN 0-88253-643-5). Ind-US Inc.

Staircase to Writing & Reading. 3rd ed. Alan Casty & Donald J. Tighe. (Illus.). 1979. write for info. (ISBN 0-13-840579-4). P-H.

Stairomastix see Poetaster.

Stairway C. Elvire Murail. Tr. by M. L. Linden. 192p. 1986. pap. 3.95 (ISBN 0-380-89678-8, Bard). Avon.

Stairway to Destiny. Miriam MacGregor. (Romances Ser.: No. 2849). 192p. Date not set. pap. 1.95 (ISBN 0-317-63906-4). Harlequin Bks.

Stairway to Doom: A Miss Mallard Mystery. Robert Quackenbush. LC 82-21484. (Illus.). 48p. (ps-5). 1983. PLB 9.95 (ISBN 0-13-804595-X). P-H.

Stairway to Down. Robert Quackenbush. (Illus.). 48p. (gr. 1-5). 1986. pap. 5.95 (ISBN 0-13-840604-9). P-H.

Stairway to Forever. Robert Adams. 272p. (Orig.). 1988. pap. 3.50 (ISBN 0-671-65434-9). Baen Bks.

Stairway to Heaven. Zecharia Sitchin. 336p. 1983. pap. 4.95 (ISBN 0-380-63339-6). Avon.

Stairway to Heaven: Religion in Rock. Davin Seay & Mary Neely. 384p. 1986. pap. 9.95 (ISBN 0-345-33022-6, Pub. by Ballantine Epiphany). Ballantine.

Stairway Walks in San Francisco. Adah Bakalinsky. LC 82-81462. (Illus.). 128p. (Orig.). 1984. pap. 6.95 (ISBN 0-938530-10-0, 10-0). Lexikos.

Stairways of My Mind & Other Journeys. A. B. Feuer. 48p. 1984. 5.95 (ISBN 0-89962-398-0). Todd & Honeywell.

Stake in the Land see Americanization Studies: The Acculturation of Immigrant Groups into American Society.

Stake Your Claim. Emmet Fox. LC 52-11683. 1952. 8.95 (ISBN 0-06-062970-3, HarpR). Har-Row.

Staked Goat. Jeremiah Healy. LC 85-45034. 224p. 1986. 14.45i (ISBN 0-06-015515-9, HarpT). Har-Row.

Staked Goat. Jeremiah Healy. 320p. 1987. pap. 3.95 (ISBN 0-671-63677-4). PB.

Staked Plain. Frank X. Tolbert. LC 87-9754. (Southwest Life & Letters Ser.). 292p. 1987. 22.50x (ISBN 0-87074-252-3); pap. 10.95 (ISBN 0-87074-253-1). SMU Press.

Staked Plains Rendezvous. Roe Richmond. (Lashtrow Ser.: No. 7). 208p. (Orig.). 1981. pap. 1.95 (ISBN 0-8439-1019-4, Leisure Bks). Leisure NY.

Stakeholders of the Organizational Mind: Toward a New View of Organizational Policy Making. Ian I. Mitroff. LC 83-48161. (Management Ser.). 1983. text ed. 24.95x (ISBN 0-87589-580-8). Jossey-Bass.

Stakes of Power: 1845-1877. rev. ed. Roy F. Nichols & Eugene H. Berwanger. (Making of America Ser.). 258p. 1982. pap. 7.95 (ISBN 0-8090-0151-9). Hill & Wang.

Stakes of the Warrior. Georges Dumezil. Ed. by Jaan Puhvel. Tr. by David Weeks from Fr. LC 82-13384. 128p. 1983. text ed. 27.00x (ISBN 0-520-04834-2). U of Cal Pr.

Stakes Winners of 1981. Ed. by Blood-Horse, Inc. Staff. (Annual Supplement Ser.). 800p. 1982. lib. bdg. 30.00 (ISBN 0-936032-48-0); pap. 20.00 (ISBN 0-936032-49-9). Blood-Horse.

Stakes Winners of 1983: Annual Supplement to The Blood Horse. 900p. (Orig.). 1984. 30.00 (ISBN 0-936032-69-3); pap. 21.50 (ISBN 0-936032-70-7). Blood Horse.

Stakes Winners of 1984: Annual Supplement. 900p. 1985. 30.00 (ISBN 0-936032-85-5); pap. 21.50 (ISBN 0-936032-81-2). Blood-Horse.

Stakes Winners of 1985. 900p. 1986. 40.00 (ISBN 0-936032-90-1); pap. 31.50 (ISBN 0-936032-91-X). Blood-Horse.

Stakes Winners of 1986. The Blood Horse Staff. 900p. 1987. 40.00 (ISBN 0-939049-04-X); pap. 31.50 (ISBN 0-939049-09-0). Blood Horse.

Stakes Winners of 1987. pap. 31.50 (ISBN 0-939049-19-8). Blood Horse.

Stakhanovism & the Politics of Productivity in the USSR, 1935-1941. Lewis H. Siegelbaum. (Soviet & East European Studies). (Illus.). 275p. 1988. 34.50 (ISBN 0-521-34548-0). Cambridge U Pr.

Staking Claims. Page Edwards, Jr. LC 79-66572. 160p. 1980. 11.95 (ISBN 0-7145-2689-4, Dist by Scribner); pap. 7.95 (ISBN 0-7145-2774-2). M Boyars Pubs.

Staking out the Terrain: Power Differentials among Natural Resource Management Agencies. Jeanne N. Clarke & Daniel McCool. LC 85-12663. (Environmental Public Policy Ser.). 189p. 1985. 54.50 (ISBN 0-88706-020-X); pap. 17.95x (ISBN 0-88706-021-8). State U NY Pr.

Staking Your Claim on Healing. C. C. Cribb. LC 79-83919. (If God Has It I Want It!). 1979. pap. 2.95 (ISBN 0-932046-14-2). Manhattan Ltd NC.

Stalag Luft III: The Secret Story. Arthur A. Durand. LC 87-33871. (Illus.). 456p. 1988. 29.95 (ISBN 0-8071-1352-2). La State U Pr.

Stalagmen. Donald Edgar. 1984. 30.00x (ISBN 0-906549-27-2, Pub. by J Clare Bks); pap. 18.00x (ISBN 0-906549-29-9, Pub. by J Clare Bks). State Mutual Bk.

Stale Food vs. Fresh Food: Cause & Cure of Choked Arteries. 6th ed. Robert S. Ford. 48p. 1977. pap. 7.00 (ISBN 0-686-09051-9). Magnolia Lab.

Stalemate. Icchokas Meras. Orig. Title: Lygiosios Trunka Akimirka. 172p. 1980. 8.95 (ISBN 0-8184-0296-2). Lyle Stuart.

Stalemate: A Police Collective Bargaining Game. University of Oklahoma Bureau of Government Research Staff. 67p. 1981. 4.50 (ISBN 0-686-32072-7). Univ OK Gov Res.

Stalemate at Panmunjon. Wilbert L. Walker. LC 79-90648. 158p. 1980. 9.00 (ISBN 0-935428-00-3). Heritage Pr.

Stalemate: Political Economic Origins of Supply-Side Policy. Howard A. Winant. LC 87-15157. 224p. 1988. lib. bdg. 39.95 (ISBN 0-275-92806-3, C2806). Praeger.

Stalemates: The Truth about Extra Marital Affairs. Marcella B. Weiner & Bernard D. Starr. 275p. 1988. 17.95 (ISBN 0-88282-036-2). New Horizon NJ.

Stalin. Alex De Jonge. LC 86-30688. (Illus.). 544p. 1987. pap. 12.95 (ISBN 0-688-07291-7, Quill). Morrow.

Stalin. Stephen Graham. LC 73-112803. 1970. Repr. of 1931 ed. 19.50x (ISBN 0-8046-1070-3, Pub. by Kennikat). Assoc Faculty Pr.

Stalin. David Killingray et al. Ed. by Malcolm Yapp et al. (World History Ser.). (Illus.). 32p. (gr. 6-11). 1980. lib. bdg. 6.95 (ISBN 0-89908-126-6); pap. text ed. 2.45 (ISBN 0-89908-101-0). Greenhaven.

Stalin: A Critical Survey of Bolshevism. Boris Souvarine. LC 72-4300. (World Affairs Ser.: National & International Viewpoints). 704p. 1972. Repr. of 1939 ed. 40.00 (ISBN 0-405-04591-3). Ayer Co Pubs.

Stalin: A Political Biography. 2nd ed. Isaac Deutscher. pap. 16.95 (ISBN 0-19-500273-3). Oxford U Pr.

Stalin & Co. the Politburo: The Men Who Run Russia. Walter Duranty. 1979. Repr. of 1949 ed. lib. bdg. 20.00 (ISBN 0-8495-1107-0). Arden Lib.

Stalin & German Communism: A Study in the Orgins of the State Party. Ruth Fischer. LC 81-3418. (Social Science Classics). 700p. 1982. pap. 23.95 (ISBN 0-87855-822-5). Transaction Bks.

Stalin & His Generals: Soviet Military Memoirs of World War II. Ed. by Seweryn Bialer. (Encore Edition Ser.). 650p. 1984. softcover 55.00x (ISBN 0-86531-610-4). Westview.

Stalin & His Times. Arthur E. Adams. (Illus.). 243p. 1986. pap. text ed. 8.95x (ISBN 0-88133-250-X). Waveland Pr.

Stalin & the Expansion of Soviet Power. Mary-Anne Pernoud. pap. 1.50 (ISBN 0-940604-05-1). Intl Inst Adv Stud.

Stalin & the Kirov Murder. Robert Conquest. 176p. 1988. 16.95 (ISBN 0-19-505579-9). Oxford U Pr.

Stalin & the Poles: An Indictment of the Soviet Leaders. Bronislaw Kusnierz. LC 79-2909. 317p. 1980. Repr. of 1949 ed. 26.00 (ISBN 0-8305-0079-0). Hyperion Conn.

Stalin: And the Shaping of the Soviet Union. Alex De Jonge. LC 85-21554. (Illus.). 576p. 1986. 19.95 (ISBN 0-688-04730-0). Morrow.

Stalin As Revolutionary, Eighteen Seventy-Nine to Nineteen Twenty-Nine: A Study in History & Personality. Robert C. Tucker. (Illus.). 1973. 12.95 (ISBN 0-393-05487-X); pap. 11.95 (ISBN 0-393-00738-3). Norton.

Stalin Embattled, Nineteen Forty-Three to Nineteen Forty-Eight. William O. McCagg. LC 77-28286. pap. 110.30 (2032034). Bks Demand UMI.

Stalin File. Martin McCauley. (World Leaders Ser.). 1979. 17.95 (ISBN 0-7134-1918-0, Pub. by Batsford England). David & Charles.

Stalin, Hitler & Europe, 2 vols. James E. McSherry. Incl. Origins of World War Two, 1933-1939. Vol. 1. 30.00x (ISBN 0-912162-03-1); Imbalance of Power, 1939-1941. (Illus.). Vol. 2. 33.00x (ISBN 0-912162-04-X). LC 72-79473. 1968-70 (ISBN 0-912162-02-3). Open Door.

Stalin in October: The Man Who Missed the Revolution. Robert M. Slusser. LC 87-3666. 304p. 1987. text ed. 28.50x (ISBN 0-8018-3457-0). Johns Hopkins.

Stalin in the Bronx & Other Stories. Suzanne Ruta. 144p. 1987. 16.95 (ISBN 0-8021-0018-X). Grove.

Stalin: Man & Ruler. Robert H. McNeal. LC 88-15525. (Illus.). 400p. 1988. 34.95 (ISBN 0-8147-5443-0). NYU Pr.

Stalin: Man of Steel. Albert Marrin. (YA) (gr. 7 up). 1988. 13.95 (ISBN 0-670-82102-0, Viking Kestrel). Viking.

Stalin on China: A Collection of Five Writings on the Chinese Question. Joseph V. Stalin. LC 75-39037. (China Studies: from Confucius to Mao Ser.). 106p. 1977. Repr. of 1951 ed. 15.00 (ISBN 0-88355-392-9). Hyperion Conn.

Stalin Revolution: Foundations of Soviet Totalitarianism. 2nd ed. Ed. by Robert V. Daniels. (Problems in European Civilization Ser.). 1972. pap. 8.00 (ISBN 0-669-82495-X). Heath.

Stalin School of Falsification. Leon Trotsky. Tr. by George Saunders. (Illus.). 1980. lib. bdg. 27.00 (ISBN 0-87348-215-8); pap. 8.95 (ISBN 0-87348-216-6). Path Pr NY.

Stalin: The History of a Dictator. H. Montgomery Hyde. (Quality Paperback Ser.). (Illus.). 679p. 1982. pap. 10.95 (ISBN 0-306-80167-1). Da Capo.

Stalin: The Iron Fisted Dictator of Russia. Alan L. Paley. Ed. by D. Steve Rahmas. LC 76-185663. (Outstanding Personalities Ser.: No. 7). 32p. 1972. lib. bdg. 3.75 incl. catalog cards (ISBN 0-87157-507-8); pap. 2.50 vinyl laminated covers (ISBN 0-87157-007-6). SamHar Pr.

Stalin: The Man & His Era. Adam Ulam. LC 87-47529. 760p. 1987. pap. 15.95 (ISBN 0-8070-7001-7, BP 764). Beacon Pr.

Stalin und der Aufstieg Hitlers: Die Deutschlandpolitik der Kommunistischen Internationale, 1929-1934. Thomas Weingartner. (Beitrage zur Auswaertigen und International Politik, No. 4). (Ger.). 1970. 19.00x (ISBN 3-11-002702-X). De Gruyter.

Stand High & Soar. Felia Matias. 144p. 1985. pap. 8.95 (ISBN 0-89962-441-3). Todd & Honeywell.
Stand in the Door. Charles H. Doyle & Terrell Stewart. Ed. by James M. Phillips. LC 79-13509. (Illus.). 430p. 1988. 29.95x (ISBN 0-932572-09-X). Phillips Pubns.
Stand in the Door. W. Darryl Goldman. LC 80-65309. 176p. 1980. pap. 2.95 (ISBN 0-88243-599-X, 02-0599). Gospel Pub.
Stand in the Gap for Your Children. Norvel Hayes. 31p. (Orig.). 1982. pap. 1.95 (ISBN 0-89274-257-7). Harrison Hse.
Stand in the Mountains. Peter Taylor. LC 85-70509. 113p. 24.95 (ISBN 0-913720-60-7). Beil.
Stand in the Wind. Jean Little. LC 73-5486. (Illus.). 256p. (gr. 4-6). 1975. PLB 12.89 (ISBN 0-06-023904-2). HarpJ.
Stand Letters for Building Construction. Chappell. 1987. 39.95 (ISBN 0-85139-979-7). Van Nos Reinhold.
Stand Letters in Architectural Practices. Chappell. 1987. 39.95 (ISBN 0-85139-977-0). Van Nos Reinhold.
Stand on Zanzibar. John Brunner. 1976. pap. 2.50. Ballantine.
Stand on Zanzibar. John Brunner. LC 79-19062. 1979. Repr. of 1968 ed. lib. bdg. 16.50x (ISBN 0-8376-0438-9). Bentley.
Stand on Zanzibar. John Brunner. 1988. pap. 3.95 (ISBN 0-345-34787-0, Del Rey). Ballantine.
Stand Perfect in Wisdom: Colossians & Ephesians. Robert G. Gromacki. 1981. pap. 5.95 (ISBN 0-8010-3767-0). Baker Bk.
Stand Still Like the Hummingbird. Henry Miller. LC 62-10408. 1967. pap. 6.95 (ISBN 0-8112-0322-0, NDP236). New Directions.
Stand Still Summer. Betty K. Thomae. 1985. 8.95 (ISBN 0-8158-0431-8). Chris Mass.
Stand Tall. P. C. Erickson. (Illus., Orig.). (gr. 4-8). 1978. pap. 2.95 (ISBN 0-89036-111-8). Hawkes Pub Inc.
Stand Tall! Every Woman's Guide to Preventing Osteoporosis. Morris Notelovitz & Marsha Ware. 208p. 1985. pap. 7.95 (ISBN 0-553-34143-X). Bantam.
Stand Tall! The Informed Woman's Guide to Preventing Osteoporosis. Morris Notelowitz & Marsha Ware. (Illus.). 208p. 1982. 12.95 (ISBN 0-937404-15-2). Triad Pub FL.
Stand the Storm: A History of the Atlantic Slave Trade. Edward Reynolds. 192p. 1984. 14.95 (ISBN 0-8052-8191-6, Pub. by Allison & Busby, England); pap. 8.95 (ISBN 0-8052-8192-4). Schocken.
Stand Tough. Powell. 1983. 4.50 (ISBN 0-88207-592-6). Victor Bks.
Stand up & Be Counted: Calling for Public Confession of Faith. R. T. Kendall. 128p. (Orig.). 1985. pap. 3.95 (ISBN 0-310-38351-X, 9281P). Zondervan.
Stand Up but Don't Get Off. Louis A. Warner. LC 72-85218. 306p. (Orig.). 1972. pap. 2.75 (ISBN 0-913502-08-1). NELF Pr.
Stand Up, Friend, with Me. Edward Field. 1964. pap. 3.95 (ISBN 0-394-17336-8, E671, Ever). Grove.
Stand Up, Shake Hands, "Say How Do You Do?". Marjabelle Young & Ann Buchwald. LC 77-80159. (Illus.). 1977. 12.95 (ISBN 0-88331-100-3). Luce.
Stand Up. Speak Out: An Introduction to Public Speaking. 2nd ed. Estelle Zannes & Gerald M. Goldhaber. 304p. 1983. pap. text ed. write for info (ISBN 0-394-34996-2, RanC). Random.
Stand Up, Speak Out, Talk Back! R. E. Alberti & M. L. Emmons. 1984. pap. 3.50 (ISBN 0-671-54758-5). PB.
Stand Up-Speak Up-or Shut Up: A Practical Guide to Public Speaking. L. Perry Wilbur. LC 81-4387. 192p. 1981. 12.95 (ISBN 0-934878-05-6). Dembner Bks.
Stand Watie & the Agony of the Cherokee Nation. Kenny A. Franks. LC 79-124380. 1979. 14.95x (ISBN 0-87870-063-3). Memphis St Univ.
Standalone Text Processors Market. 360p. 1984. 1900.00 (ISBN 0-86621-681-2, E753). Frost & Sullivan.
Standard, Vols. 11-26. Ed. by Frank S. Murray. Incl. Vol. 11, o.s.i; Vol. 12; Vol. 13. 1961; Vol. 14. 1962 (ISBN 0-910840-62-8); Vol. 15. 1963 (ISBN 0-910840-63-6); Vol. 16. 1964 (ISBN 0-910840-64-4); Vol. 17. 1965 (ISBN 0-910840-65-2); Vol. 18. 1966 (ISBN 0-910840-66-0); Vol. 19. 1967 (ISBN 0-910840-67-9); Vol. 20. 1968 (ISBN 0-910840-68-7); Vol. 21. 1969 (ISBN 0-910840-69-5); Vol. 22. 1970 (ISBN 0-910840-70-9); Vol. 23. 1971 (ISBN 0-910840-71-7); Vol. 24. 1972 (ISBN 0-910840-72-5); Vol.25. 1973 (ISBN 0-910840-73-3); Vol. 26. 1974 (ISBN 0-910840-74-1). 3.00x ea. Kingdom.
Standard, Vol. 27. Ed. by Frank S. Murray. 1975. 3.00x (ISBN 0-910840-75-X). Kingdom.
Standard, Vol. 28. Ed. by Frank S. Murray. 1976. 3.00x (ISBN 0-910840-76-8). Kingdom.
Standard, Vol. 29. Ed. by Frank S. Murray. 1977. 3.00x (ISBN 0-910840-77-6). Kingdom.
Standard, Vol. 30. Ed. by Frank S. Murray. 1978. 3.00x (ISBN 0-910840-78-4). Kingdom.
Standard Accounting Manual for Savings Institutions. 276p. 1988. 185.00 (ISBN 0-929097-00-9, 12955). US League Savi Inst.
Standard Accounting Manual Supplement. 89p. cancelled (ISBN 0-317-67618-0, 16618). US League Savi Inst.
Standard Accounting System for Lutheran Congregations. Neal D. Meitler & Linda M. La Porte. 1981. 4.95 (ISBN 0-8100-0129-2, 21N2001). Northwest Pub.
Standard Achievement Recording System: (STARS) Donald E. Smith & Judith M. Smith. 1976. pap. text ed. 41.85x (ISBN 0-914004-47-6). Ulrich.
Standard Aircraft Handbook. 4th ed. Ed. by Larry Reithmaier. (Illus.). 240p. 1987. vinyl 9.95 (ISBN 0-8306-8812-9, 28512V, TAB-Aero). TAB Bks.
Standard Aircraft Workers' Manual. Fletcher Aircraft Company Staff. 190p. 1985. spiral bdg. 7.50x (ISBN 0-911721-29-0, Pub. by Fletcher). Aviation.
Standard Albanian: A Reference Grammar for Students. Leonard D. Newmark et al. LC 81-52125. 368p. 1982. 47.50x (ISBN 0-8047-1129-1). Stanford U Pr.
Standard Alphabet for Reducing Unwritten Languages & Foreign Graphic Systems to a Uniform Orthography in European Letters. 2nd ed. Richard Lepsius. Ed. by J. Alan Kemp. (Amsterdam Classics in Linguistics Ser.: Vol. 5). xvii, 336p. 1981. 54.00x (ISBN 90-272-0876-X). Benjamins North Am.
Standard American Bridge Updated. Norma Sands. pap. 5.95 (ISBN 0-9605648-0-2). Rocky Mtn Bks.
Standard American Foxtrot. (Ballroom Dance Ser.). 1985. lib. bdg. 72.00 (ISBN 0-87700-740-3). Revisionist Pr.
Standard American Waltz. (Ballroom Dance Ser.). 1985. lib. bdg. 64.50 (ISBN 0-87700-813-2). Revisionist Pr.
Standard American Waltz. (Ballroom Dance Ser.). 1986. lib. bdg. 79.95 (ISBN 0-8490-3414-0). Gordon Pr.
Standard & Poor's 500. Carol Mull. LC 83-72385. 100p. 1984. 30.00 (ISBN 0-86690-261-9, 2400-01). Am Fed Astrologers.
Standard & Protocols for Communications Network. James W. Conrad. 397p. 1982. 59.95 (ISBN 0-935506-03-9). Carnegie Pr.
Standard Application of Electrical Details. Jerome F. Mueller. 1984. text ed. 46.50 (ISBN 0-07-043961-3). McGraw.
Standard Application of Mechanical Details. Jerome F. Mueller. 352p. 1985. text ed. 46.00 (ISBN 0-07-043962-1). McGraw.
Standard Aviation Maintenance Handbook. rev. ed. (Illus.). 235p. 1985. pap. text ed. 7.95 (ISBN 0-89100-282-0, EA-282-0). IAP.
Standard Baseball Card Price Guide. Gene Florence. (Illus.). 320p. 1988. pap. 9.95 (ISBN 0-89145-385-7). Collector Bks.
Standard BASIC Dictionary for Programming. John P. Steiner. LC 84-11436. 256p. 1983. 23.95 (ISBN 0-13-841560-9, Busn); pap. 19.95 (ISBN 0-13-841552-8). P-H.
Standard BASIC Programming: For Business & Management Applications. James S. Quasney & John Maniotes. LC 80-65168. (Illus.). 428p. 1980. pap. text ed. 18.75x (ISBN 0-87835-081-0). Boyd & Fraser.
Standard BASIC Programming with True BASIC. Avery Catlin. (Illus.). 400p. 1987. pap. text ed. 26.00 (ISBN 0-13-841578-1). P-H.
Standard Bearer. Efraim Sevela. Tr. by Donald Arthur & Richard Lourie. 1983. 14.95 (ISBN 0-89651-701-2); pap. 8.95 (ISBN 0-89651-703-9). B L Pub.
Standard-Bearer: A Novel. Edilberto K. Tiempo. 210p. (Orig.). 1985. pap. 10.75x (ISBN 971-10-0237-X, Pub. by New Day Philippines). Cellar.
Standard Bearer: A Story of Army Life in the Time of Caesar. Albert C. Whitehead. (Illus.). (gr. 7-11). 1943. 15.00 (ISBN 0-8196-0116-0). Biblo.
Standard Bible Atlas. Orrin Root. (Illus.). 32p. 1973. pap. 3.50 (ISBN 0-87239-251-1, 3169). Standard Pub.
Standard Biphasic-Contrast Examination of the Stomach & Duodenum: Method Results & Radiological Atlas. J. Odo Op den Orth. 182p. 1979. 56.60 (ISBN 90-247-2159-8, Pub. by Martinus Nijhoff Netherlands). Kluwer Academic.
Standard Boiler Room Questions & Answers. 3rd ed. Stephen M. Elonka & Alex Higgins. (Illus.). 384p. 1982. text ed. 42.50 (ISBN 0-07-019301-0). McGraw.
Standard Book of British & American Verse: Preface by Christopher Morley. facsimile ed. Ed. by Nella Braddy. LC 72-38594. (Granger Index Reprint Ser.). Repr. of 1932 ed. 34.00 (ISBN 0-8369-6326-1). Ayer Co Pubs.
Standard Book of Dog Breeding. Alvin Grossman. LC 83-7315. (Other Dog Bks.). (Illus.). 1983. 16.95 (ISBN 0-87714-054-5). Denlingers.
Standard Book of Dog Grooming. rev. ed. Diane Fenger & Arlene F. Steinle. LC 81-67721. (Other Dog Books). (Illus.). 1983. pap. 29.95 (ISBN 0-87714-089-8). Denlingers.
Standard Book of Quilt-Making & Collecting. Marguerite Ickis. (Illus.). 14.75 (ISBN 0-8446-0720-7). Peter Smith.
Standard Book of Quiltmaking & Collecting. Marguerite Ickis. (Illus.). 1949. pap. 6.50 (ISBN 0-486-20582-7). Dover.
Standard California Codes: Uniform Commercial Code. Bender's Editorial Staff. 1963. Updates avail. 32.50 (686). Bender.
Standard California Codes: 5-in-1. 1974. Updates avail. annually. 50.00 (700). Bender.
Standard California Penal Code & Selected Penal Provisions of Other Codes. 1961. Annual replacement vol. 25.50 (698); 25.50. Bender.
Standard Cantilever Retaining Walls. Morton Newman. LC 81-14248. 670p. 1981. Repr. of 1976 ed. lib. bdg. 46.50 (ISBN 0-89874-389-3). Krieger.
Standard Carnival Glass Price Guide. 5th ed. Bill Edwards. (Illus.). 64p. 1986. pap. 5.95 (ISBN 0-89145-315-6). Collector Bks.
Standard Carnival Glass Price Guide. 6th ed. Bill Edwards. (Illus.). 64p. 1988. pap. 7.95 (ISBN 0-89145-361-X, 1830). Collector Bks.
Standard Carnival Price Guide. 4th ed. Bill Edwards. 64p. 1984. pap. 4.95 (ISBN 0-89145-260-5). Collector Bks.
Standard Catalog of American Cars, 1805-1942. 2nd ed. Beverly R. Kimes. LC 85-50390. 1536p. (Orig.). 1985. pap. 29.95 (ISBN 0-87341-045-9). Krause Pubns.
Standard Catalog of American Cars: 1946-1975. 2nd ed. (Illus.). 800p. 1987. 24.95 (ISBN 0-87341-096-3, TC-045838). Motorbooks Intl.
Standard Catalog of American Light Duty Trucks. Krause Publications Staff. Ed. by John Gunnell. LC 86-83144. (Illus.). 800p. 1987. pap. 24.95 (ISBN 0-87341-091-2). Krause Pubns.
Standard Catalog of Baseball Cards. Bob Lemke & Dan Albaugh. (Illus.). 800p. 1988. pap. 24.95 (ISBN 0-87341-110-2). Krause Pubns.
Standard Catalog of British Coins. H. A. Seaby. 1987. lib. bdg. 20.00 (ISBN 0-686-45259-3, Pub. by B A Seaby England). S J Durst.
Standard Catalog of British Colonial & Commonwealth Coins. Andre R. DeClermont & John Wheeler. Ed. by Colin R. Bruce, II. LC 85-50753. (Illus.). 704p. 1986. 40.00 (ISBN 0-87341-076-9). Krause Pubns.
Standard Catalog of Broken Bank Notes of the United States, 4 vol. Barbara Bellin & James Haxby. LC 85-5043. (Illus.). 2559p. 1988. Set. price not set (ISBN 0-87341-043-2). Krause Pubns.
Standard Catalog of Depression Script of U. S. Ralph Mitchell & Neil Shafer. LC 85-52834. (Illus.). 320p. 1985. pap. 27.50 (ISBN 0-87341-047-5). Krause Pubns.
Standard Catalog of Provincial Banks & Banknotes. G. L. Grant. 1978. 30.00 (ISBN 0-686-52192-7, Pub by Spink & Son England). S J Durst.
Standard Catalog of United States Altered & Counterfeit Coins. Virgil Hancock & Larry Spanbauer. (Illus.). 1979. deluxe ed. 37.50 (ISBN 0-685-91296-5); lib. bdg. 30.00 (ISBN 0-915262-26-6). S J Durst.
Standard Catalog of United States Paper Money. 7 ed ed. Chester Krause & Robert Lemke. Ed. by Robert Wilhite. LC 81-81876. (Illus.). 192p. 1988. 19.95 (ISBN 0-87341-112-9). Krause Pubns.
Standard Catalog of U. S. Paper Money. 5th, rev. ed. Chester L. Krause & Robert F. Lemke. LC 81-81876. (Illus.). 1985. pap. 18.95 (ISBN 0-87341-078-5). Krause Pubns.
Standard Catalog of United States Paper Money. 6th ed. Robert Lemke & Cheste Krause. Ed. by Bob Wilhite. LC 81-81876. (Illus.). 192p. 18.95 (ISBN 0-87341-102-1). Krause Pubns.
Standard Catalog of World Coins. 13th ed. Chester Krause & Clifford Mishler. LC 79-640940. (Illus.). 1536p. 1986. pap. 29.95 (ISBN 0-87341-086-6). Krause-Pubns.
Standard Catalog of World Coins. 15th ed. Chester Krause & Clifford Mishler. Ed. by Colin Bruce, III. LC 79-640940. (Illus.). 1792p. 1988. pap. 33.95 (ISBN 0-87341-107-2). Krause Pubns.
Standard Catalog of World Gold Coins. Chester Krause & Clifford Mishle. LC 85-61548. (Illus.). 704p. 1985. pap. 39.95 (ISBN 0-87341-031-9). Krause Pubns.
Standard Catalog of World Paper Money: General Issues, Vol. 2. 5th ed. Albert Pick & Colin Bruce. (Illus.). 1000p. 1986. 45.00 (ISBN 0-317-47031-0). Krause Pubns.
Standard Catalog of World Paper Money: Specialized Issues, Vol. 1. 4th ed. Albert Pick. Ed. by Colin Bruce & Neil Shafer. LC 80-81510. (Illus.). 684p. 1984. cancelled (ISBN 0-87341-032-7). Krause Pubns.
Standard Catalog of World Paper Money: Specialized, Vol. 1. 5th ed. Albert Pick. Ed. by Colin Bruce & Neil Shafer. (Illus.). 100p. 1986. 45.00 (ISBN 0-317-47019-1). Krause Pubns.
Standard Catalog World Coins. 14th ed. Chester Krause & Clifford Mishler. LC 79-640940. (Illus.). 1600p. 1987. pap. 29.95 (ISBN 0-87341-095-5). Krause Pubns.
Standard Catalog World Gold Coins. 2nd ed. Chester Krause & Clifford Mishler. Ed. by Colin Bruce. LC 85-61548. (Illus.). 700p. 1987. pap. 45.00 (ISBN 0-87341-099-8). Krause Pubns.
Standard Catalogue of British Orders, Decorations & Medals. E. C. Joslin. 1984. 30.00 (ISBN 0-685-51506-0, Pub by Spink & Son England). S J Durst.
Standard Catalolgue of British Coins: Coins of England & the United Kingdom, 1987, Vol. 1. 23nd, rev. ed. Ed. by Stephen Mitchell & Brian Reeds. (Coins of Scotland, Ireland & the Islands Ser.: Vol. 2). (Illus.). 336p. 1986. 20.00 ea. (ISBN 0-900652-96-9, Pub. by Seaby UK). Numismatic Fine Arts.
Standard Christmas Program Book, No. 45. Ed. by Judith Sparks. 48p. 1984. pap. 1.95 (ISBN 0-87239-749-1, 8645). Standard Pub.
Standard Christmas Program Book, No. 46. Laurie Hoard. 48p. 1985. pap. 1.95 (ISBN 0-87239-850-1, 8646). Standard Pub.
Standard Christmas Program Book, No. 47. 48p. 1986. pap. 1.95 (ISBN 0-87239-935-4, 8647). Standard Pub.
Standard Christmas Program Book, No. 48. Compiled by Pat Fittro. 48p. 1987. pap. 2.25 (ISBN 0-87403-208-3, 8648). Standard Pub.
Standard Christmas Program Book, No. 49. Compiled by Pat Fittro. 48p. 1988. pap. 2.25 (ISBN 0-87403-370-5, 8649). Standard Pub.
Standard Clauses in a Licensing Agreement. 47p. (Orig.). 1981. pap. text ed. 12.50x (ISBN 0-911378-36-7). Sheridan.
Standard COBOL. 2nd ed. Mike Murach. LC 74-34184. (Illus.). 400p. 1975. pap. text ed. 20.95 (ISBN 0-574-18401-5, 13-4010); instr's guide avail. (ISBN 0-574-18402-3, 13-4011). SRA.
Standard COBOL: A Problem-Solving Approach. Marilyn Z. Smith. 308p. 1974. pap. text ed. 26.95 (ISBN 0-395-17091-5). HM.
Standard Code of Parliamentary Procedure. 3rd, rev. ed. Alice F. Sturgis. 1988. text ed. 15.95 (ISBN 0-07-062399-6). McGraw.
Standard Codes Formats Protocols & Common Commands for Use with - Standard 488.2 1987. (IEEE Standards Publications). 1988. pap. 52.00 (ISBN 0-471-61871-3). Wiley.
Standard Costs & Variance Analysis. 146p. 15.95 (ISBN 0-86641-015-5, 7463). Natl Assn Accts.
Standard Costs for Asphalt Paving. (Management Ser.: No. 2). 16p. 1972. 20.00 (ISBN 0-317-58417-0). Natl Asphalt Pavement.
Standard Country or Area Codes for Statistical Use. (Statistical Papers Ser.: No. 49). pap. 4.00 (ISBN 92-1-161202-0, E.82.XVII.8). UN.
Standard Cut Glass Value Guide. Jo Evers. (Illus.). 155p. 1981. pap. 8.95 (ISBN 0-89145-002-5). Collector Bks.
Standard Data Encryption Algorithm. Harry Katzan, Jr. LC 77-13582. (Illus.). 1977. text ed. 14.00 (ISBN 0-89433-016-0). Petrocelli.
Standard Data for Arc Welding: SDAW. 126p. 1975. 39.00 (ISBN 0-317-37077-4). Am Welding.
Standard Descriptions of Printed Books see Bibliographical Study of Shakespeare.
Standard Dialogues. facsimile ed. Ed. by Alexander Clark. LC 77-109137. (Granger Index Reprint Ser). 1898. 15.00 (ISBN 0-8369-6121-8). Ayer Co Pubs.
Standard Dictionary of Librarianship: Standardworterbuch fur das Bibliothekwesen, Volume 1: English - German. Ed. by Eberhard Sauppe. 800p. (Eng. & Ger.). 1988. lib. bdg. 65.00 (ISBN 3-598-10619-X). K G Saur.
Standard Dictionary of Librarianship: Standardworterbuch Fur das Bibliotheksweñ, 2 vols, Vol. 1 & 2. Ed. by Eberhard Sauppe. 1600p. (Ger. & Eng.). Set. lib. bdg. 125.00 (ISBN 3-598-10618-1). Vol. 1, 12/1986. Vol. 2, 06/1987. K G Saur.
Standard Dictionary of Librarianship: Standardworterbuch fur das Bibliothekswen, Vol. 2. Ed. by Eberhard Sauppe. 800p. (Ger. & Eng.). 1989. lib. bdg. 65.00 (ISBN 3-598-10620-3). K G Saur.
Standard Dictionary of the Social Sciences English-German. Wolfgang J. Koschnik. 664p. 1984. lib. bdg. 50.00 (ISBN 3-598-10526-6). K G Saur.
Standard Dictionary of the Social Sciences: German-English, Vol. 2. Wolfgang J. Koschnick. x, 680p. 1988. lib. bdg. 55.00 (ISBN 3-598-10527-4). K G Saur.
Standard Directory of Advertisers: Classified Edition. National Register Publishing Co. Staff. LC 5-21147. 1984. 263.00 (ISBN 0-87217-000-4). Natl Register.
Standard Directory of Advertisers: Geographical Edition. National Register Publishing Co. Staff. LC 15-21147. 1984. 263.00. Natl Register.
Standard Directory of Advertising Agencies, 3 vols. National Register Publishing Co. Staff. LC 66-6149. 1983. 144.00 ea.; 327.00 set (ISBN 0-87217-003-9). Natl Register.
Standard Directory of Proof Marks. Gerhard Wirnsberger. Tr. by R. A. Steindler from Ger. LC 75-11048. (Illus.). 1976. pap. 9.95 (ISBN 0-89149-006-X). Jolex.
Standard Directory of Worldwide Marketing. National Register Publishing Co. Staff. LC 84-62414. 1987. 177.00 (ISBN 0-87217-075-6). Natl Register.
Standard Documentary Credit Forms. rev. ed. International Chamber of Commerce Staff. 88p. 1986. pap. 21.00 (ISBN 92-842-1027-5). ICC Pub.
Standard Easter Program Book, No. 35. Ed. by Laurie Hoard. 48p. (Orig.). 1984. pap. 1.95 (ISBN 0-87239-768-8, 8705). Standard Pub.
Standard Easter Program Book, No. 36. Compiled by Laurie Hoard. 48p. 1985. pap. 1.95 (ISBN 0-87239-870-6, 8706). Standard Pub.
Standard Easter Program Book, No. 37. Compiled by Pat Fittro. (Standard Easter Program Bks.). 48p. 1986. pap. 1.95 (ISBN 0-87403-083-8, 8707). Standard Pub.

Standard of Excellence: Andrew W. Mellon Founds the National Gallery of Art at Washington, D. C. David E. Finley. LC 73-5676. (Illus.). 200p. 1975. 12.50x (ISBN 0-87474-132-7, FISE). Smithsonian.
Standard of Living. Mildred B. Young. 1941. pap. 2.50x (ISBN 0-87574-012-X, 012). Pendle Hill.
Standard of Living Among Workingmen's Families in New York City. Robert C. Chapin. LC 72-137159. (Poverty U. S. A. Historical Record Ser.). 1971. Repr. of 1909 ed. 32.00 (ISBN 0-405-03097-5). Ayer Co Pubs.
Standard of Living in Japan. Kokichi Morimoto. LC 78-63963. (Johns Hopkins University Studies in the Social Sciences, Thirty-Sixth Series 1918: No. 2). Repr. of 1918 ed. 17.50 (ISBN 0-404-61210-5). AMS Pr.
Standard of Living in 1860. Edgar W. Martin. Repr. of 1942 ed. 26.00 (ISBN 0-384-35588-9). Johnson Repr.
Standard of Living of German Labor under Nazi Rule. Hilde Oppenheimer-Bluhm. (Social Research Supplement Ser.: No. 5). 1943. pap. 10.00 (ISBN 0-527-00865-6). Kraus Repr.
Standard of Living: Tanner Lectures, Clare Hall, Cambridge 1985. Amartya Sen. Ed. by Geoffrey Hawthorn. 150p. 1987. 24.95 (ISBN 0-521-32101-8). Cambridge U Pr.
Standard of Living: Tanner Lectures, Clare Hall, Cambridge 1985. Amartya Sen. Ed. by Geoffrey Hawthorn. 125p. Date not set. pap. price not set (ISBN 0-521-36840-5). Cambridge U Pr.
Standard of Perfection. 206p. 10.00. Am Rabbit Breeders.
Standard of Pronunciation in English. Thomas Lounsbury. 1904. 25.00 (ISBN 0-8274-3503-7). R West.
Standard of Usage in English. Thomas R. Lounsbury. 1979. Repr. of 1908 ed. lib. bdg. 27.00 (ISBN 0-8414-5757-3). Folcroft.
Standard Oil Company (Indiana) Oil Pioneer of the Middle West. Paul H. Giddens. LC 75-41757. (Companies & Men Ser.: Business Enterprises in America). (Illus.). 1976. Repr. of 1955 ed. 64.00x (ISBN 0-405-08073-5). Ayer Co Pubs.
Standard Old Bottle Price Guide. Carlo Sellari & Dot Sellari. (Illus.). 256p. 1988. pap. 14.95 (ISBN 0-89145-383-0). Collector Bks.
Standard on Aircraft Maintenance. 84p. 3.75 (ISBN 0-686-68288-2). Natl Fire Prot.
Standard on Assessment-Ratio Studies. 23p. 1980. pap. 8.00 (ISBN 0-88329-107-X). IAAO.
Standard on Certification of Assessing Officers & Valuation Personnel. 3p. 1979. pap. 8.00 (ISBN 0-88329-105-3). IAAO.
Standard on Contracting for Assessment Services. 9p. 1986. pap. 8.00 (ISBN 0-88329-060-X). IAAO.
Standard on Live Fire Training Evolutions in Structures. National Fire Protection Association Staff. 1986. 10.50 (ISBN 0-317-63545-X, 1403-86). Natl Fire Prot.
Standard on Pre-Entry Education of Assessing Officers & Valuation Personnel. 13p. 1978. pap. 8.00 (ISBN 0-88329-104-5). IAAO.
Standard on Property Use Codes. 3p. 1980. pap. 8.00 (ISBN 0-88329-106-1). IAAO.
Standard on Public Relations. 9p. 1977. pap. 8.00 (ISBN 0-88329-102-9). IAAO.
Standard on the Application of the Three Approaches to Value in Mass Appraisal. 23p. 1983. pap. 8.00 (ISBN 0-88329-149-5). IAAO.
Standard on Training of Assessing Officers & Valuation Personnel. 5p. 1978. pap. 8.00 (ISBN 0-88329-103-7). IAAO.
Standard on Urban Land Valuation. 5p. 1987. pap. 8.00 (ISBN 0-88329-063-4). IAAO.
Standard on Valuation of Personal Property. 9p. 1985. pap. 8.00 (ISBN 0-88329-139-8). IAAO.
Standard Operas: Their Plots, Their Music, Their Composers, a Handbook. George P. Upton. 1980. lib. bdg. 72.95 (ISBN 0-8490-3173-7). Gordon Pr.
Standard Operating Procedures, Aircraft Rescue & Fire Fighting. (Four Hundred Ser.). 140p. 1973. pap. 2.00 (ISBN 0-685-44137-7, 402). Natl Fire Prot.
Standard Operations Manual for the Marine Transportation Sector of the Offshore Mineral & Oil Industry. Ed. by Richard A. Block & Charles B. Collins. 61p. (Orig.). 1979. pap. text ed. 5.00 (ISBN 0-934114-09-9, BK-116). Marine Educ.
Standard or Head-Dress? Zelia Nuttall. (HU PMP Ser.). 1888. 13.00 (ISBN 0-527-01183-5). Kraus Repr.
Standard Orthopaedic Operations: A Guide for the Junior Surgeon. 3rd ed. J. Crawford Adams. LC 84-19976. (Illus.). 463p. 1985. text ed. 98.00 (ISBN 0-443-03232-7). Churchill.
Standard Pascal: An Introduction to Structured Software Design: Workbook. Victor J. Law & Johnette Hassell. (Illus.). 576p. 1986. pap. write for info. (ISBN 0-697-00080-X). instr's. manual avail. (ISBN 0-697-00121-0); wkbk. avail. (ISBN 0-697-00274-8). Wm C Brown.
Standard Pascal User Reference Manual. Doug Cooper. 1983. pap. 13.95 (ISBN 0-393-30121-4). Norton.
Standard Pennsylvania Practice, 30 Vols. LC 80-84968. write for info. Lawyers Co-Op.
Standard Periodical Directory: 1988. 11th, rev. ed. Ed. by Patricia Hagood. LC 64-7598. 1600p. 1988. 325.00 (ISBN 0-917460-18-9). Oxbridge Comm.
Standard Plant Operators Manual. 3rd ed. Stephen M. Elonka. LC 79-22089. (Illus.). 416p. 1980. text ed. 49.50 (ISBN 0-07-019298-7). McGraw.
Standard Plant Operator's Questions & Answers, 2 vols. 2nd ed. Stephen M. Elonka & Joseph R. Robinson. 1981. Set. text ed. 64.00 (ISBN 0-07-079191-0); Vol. 1. text ed. 35.00 (ISBN 0-07-019315-0); Vol. 2. text ed. 35.00 (ISBN 0-07-019316-9). McGraw.
Standard Plumbing Engineering Design. 2nd ed. Louis S. Nielsen. LC 81-2451. (Illus.). 384p. 1982. text ed. 45.00 (ISBN 0-07-046541-X). McGraw.
Standard Postcard Catalog. 2nd ed. James L. Lowe. LC 82-70056. (Illus.). 288p. (Orig.). 1982. pap. text ed. 21.95 (ISBN 0-913782-10-6). Deltiologists Am.
Standard Pseudoisochromatic Plates: For Acquired Color Vision Defects, Part II. Hiroshi Ichikawa & Kaitiro Hukami. (Illus.). 1983. spiral bound monograph 46.00 (ISBN 0-89640-081-6). Igaku-Shoin.
Standard Pseusoisochromatic Plates: For Congenital Color Vision Defects, Pt. 1. Hiroshi Ichikawa et al. (Illus.). 1978. spiral bdg. 49.50 (ISBN 0-89640-030-1). Igaku-Shoin.
Standard Ptolemaic Silver. Edward T. Newell. LC 80-70056. (Illus.). 1981. pap. 6.00 (ISBN 0-915262-49-5); supplement incl. S J Durst.
Standard Radio Communications Manual: With Instrumentation & Testing Techniques. R. Harold Kinley. 415p. 1985. 29.95 (ISBN 0-13-842394-6, Busn). P-H.
Standard Radio Communications Manual: With Instrumentation & Testing Techniques. R. Harold Kinley. 432p. 1988. pap. 16.95 (ISBN 0-13-842386-5). P-H.
Standard Rate in American Trade Unions. David A. McCabe. LC 78-63941. (Johns Hopkins University Studies in the Social Sciences. Thirtieth Series 1912: No. 2). Repr. of 1912 ed. 24.50 (ISBN 0-404-61190-7). AMS Pr.
Standard Rate in American Trade Unions. David A. McCabe. LC 70-156435. (American Labor Ser., No. 2). 1971. Repr. of 1912 ed. 17.00 (ISBN 0-405-02932-2). Ayer Co Pubs.
Standard Rebus Glossary. Charlotte Clark & Cornelia Oakes Davies. 95p. 1974. pap. text ed. 8.50 (ISBN 0-913476-41-2). Am Guidance.
Standard Reference Tables for Metric Conversion of Transporation Tariffs. rev. ed. ANMC Tariff Task Group Staff. 90p. 1982. 19.00 (ISBN 0-686-47622-0). Am Natl.
Standard Refrigeration & Air Conditioning Questions & Answers. 3rd ed. Stephen M. Elonka & Quaid W. Minich. (Illus.). 416p. 1983. text ed. 45.50 (ISBN 0-07-019317-7). McGraw.
Standard Research Test Method for Determining Smoke Generation of Solid Materials. National Fire Protection Association Staff. 20p. 1987. 12.00 (ISBN 0-317-63373-2, 258-87). Natl Fire Prot.
Standard Selections. facsimile ed. Ed. by Robert I. Fulton et al. LC 79-152150. (Granger Index Reprint Ser.). Repr. of 1907 ed. 24.00 (ISBN 0-8369-6253-2). Ayer Co Pubs.
Standard Speaker: Containing Exercises in Prose & Poetry. facsimile ed. Epes Sargent. LC 75-37020. (Granger Index Reprint Ser.). Repr. of 1852 ed. 25.00 (ISBN 0-8369-6319-9). Ayer Co Pubs.
Standard Specifications for Movable Highway Bridges. 1979. pap. 5.00 (ISBN 0-686-27096-7, MHB-70). AASHTO.
Standard Specifications for Structural Supports for Highway Signs, Luminaires & Traffic Signals. 1975. pap. 3.00 (ISBN 0-686-20956-7, LTS-1). AASHTO.
Standard Specifications for Transportation Materials & Methods of Sampling & Testing, 2 vols. 14th ed. 1986. Set. 65.00 set (ISBN 0-686-20936-2, HM-14). AASHTO.
Standard Specifications for Welding. 1977. pap. 5.00 (ISBN 0-686-23281-X, WBS-2). AASHTO.
Standard Structural Details for Building Construction. Morton Newman. 1967. text ed. 60.00 (ISBN 0-07-046345-X). McGraw.
Standard Swahili-English Dictionary. Ed. by Frederick Johnson. (Swahili & Eng.). 1939. 37.00x (ISBN 0-19-864403-5). Oxford U Pr.
Standard Symbols for Fire Fighting Operations. National Fire Protection Association Staff. 1986. 10.50 (ISBN 0-317-63328-7, 178-86). Natl Fire Prot.
Standard Symbols for Welding Brazing & Nondestructive Examination (A2.4-86) rev. ed. American Welding Society Staff. (Illus.). 80p. 1986. pap. write for info. (ISBN 0-87171-266-0). Am Welding.
Standard System for the Evaluation of Bean Germplasm. Ed. by Aart Van Schoonhoven & Marcial A. Pastor-Coorales. 53p. (Orig.). 1987. pap. text ed. 6.00 (ISBN 84-89206-69-4, Pub. by CIAT Colombia). Agribookstore.
Standard Terms of Energy Economy: Ruttley. World Energy Conference Staff. 1978. 120.00 (ISBN 0-08-022445-8). Pergamon.
Standard Test Method for Measuring the Smoke Generated by Solid Materials. 1974. pap. 2.50 (ISBN 0-685-58190-X, 258-T). Natl Fire Prot.
Standard Test Method for Potential Heat of Building Materials. National Fire Protection Association Staff. 1987. 10.50 (ISBN 0-317-63377-5, 259-87). Natl Fire Prot.
Standard Tests in the Elementary School, Nursery School to Sixth Grade. L. W. Webb & Anna M. Shatwell. 532p. 1984. Repr. of 1932 ed. lib. bdg. 45.00 (ISBN 0-89987-882-2). Darby Bks.
Standard Textbook for Professional Estheticians. Joel Gerson & Bobbi R. Madry. Ed. by Israel Rubinstein. (Illus.). 1986. 25.25 (ISBN 0-87350-147-0). Milady Pub.
Standard Textbook of Cosmetology. rev. ed. Constance V. Kibbe. (Illus.). 1985. 20.70 (ISBN 0-87350-403-8). Milady Pub.
Standard Textbook of Professional Barber Styling. Milady Barber Textbook Committee Staff. 1983. text ed. 21.35 (ISBN 0-87350-140-3). Milady Pub.
Standard Trade Index of Japan: 1987-88. 31st ed. 1445p. 1987. 227.00 (ISBN 0-8002-4096-0). Intl Pubns Serv.
Standard Turns: Cross Turns, Spot Turns, Pivots, Twinkles. (Ballroom Dance Ser.). 1986. lib. bdg. 79.95 (ISBN 0-8490-3401-9). Gordon Pr.
Standard Types of Building Construction: 1979. National Fire Protection Association Staff. 1979. 8.00 (ISBN 0-317-07387-7, NFPA 220). Natl Fire Prot.
Standard Types of Building Construction. National Fire Protection Association Staff. 1985. 10.50 (ISBN 0-317-63334-1, 220-85). Natl Fire Prot.
Standard Types of Building Construction. (Two Hundred Ser.). 1961. pap. 2.00 (ISBN 0-685-58037-7, 220). Natl Fire Prot.
Standard-Vacuum Oil Company & United States East Asian Policy, 1933-1941. Irvine H. Anderson. 280p. 1975. 32.00x (ISBN 0-691-04629-8). Princeton U Pr.
Standard Vocal Repertoire, Bk. 2: For High Voice. Ed. by Richard D. Row. (Illus.). 80p. 1963. pap. 8.50 (ISBN 0-8258-0253-9, RB-71). Fischer Inc NY.
Standard Wine Cookbook. Anne Director. (Culinary Arts Ser.). (Illus.). 192p. 1979. cancelled (ISBN 0-89496-014-8); pap. 6.95 (ISBN 0-686-77351-9). Ross Bks.
Standard Woerterbuch fuer Werbung, Massenmedien und Marketing. Deutsch-English-Standard Dictionary of Advertising, Mass Media & Marketing. German-English. Wolfgang J. Koschnick. Orig. Title: Standardwoerterbuch fuer Werbung, Massenmedien und Marking, Deutsch-English. x, 592p. (Ger. & Eng.). 1987. lib. bdg. 87.50 (ISBN 0-89925-293-1). De Gruyter.
Standard 1982. Ed. by Frank S. Murray. (Sermons Ser.). 192p. 1982. 3.00x (ISBN 0-910840-82-2). Kingdom.
Standard 1983 Termination. Ed. by Frank S. Murray. (Sermons Ser.). 192p. 1983. 3.00x (ISBN 0-910840-83-0). Kingdom.
Standardisation of Manifolds for Refrigerated Liquefield Gas Carriers. LNG Staff & OCIMF Staff. 1979. 36.00x (ISBN 0-317-61480-0, Pub. by Witherby & Co England). State Mutual Bk.
Standardization: A New Discipline. Lal C. Verman. LC 72-8370. (Illus.). pap. 120.30 (ISBN 0-317-10688-0, 2015419). Bks Demand UMI.
Standardization & Control of Biologicals Produced by Recombinant DNA Technology. Ed. by F. T. Perkins & W. Hennessen. (Developments in Biological Standardization Ser.: Vol. 59). (Illus.). viii, 216p. 1985. pap. 46.75 (ISBN 3-8055-4027-2). S Karger.
Standardization in Blood Fractionation including Coagulation Factors: Joint IABS-CSL Symposium, Melbourne, May 1986. Ed. by P. Schiff & W. Hennessen. (Developments in Biological Standardization Ser.: Vol. 67). (Illus.). viii, 388p. 1987. pap. 133.50 (ISBN 3-8055-4607-6). S Karger.
Standardization: Mathematical Methods in Assortment Determination. C. Bongers. 265p. 1980. lib. bdg. 24.00 (ISBN 0-89838-029-4, Pub. by Martinus Nijhoff Netherlands). Kluwer Academic.
Standardization of Air Material, Nineteen Thirty-Nine to Nineteen Forty-Four: Controls, Policies, Procedures. Martin P. Claussen. (USAF Historical Studies: No. 67). 81p. 1951. pap. text ed. 10.00x (ISBN 0-317-20158-1). MA-AH Pub.
Standardization of Albumin, Plasa Substitutes & Plasmapheresis. Ed. by W. Hennessen. (Developments in Biological Standardization Ser.: Vol. 48). (Illus.). viii, 326p. 1981. pap. 50.00 (ISBN 3-8055-2496-X). S Karger.
Standardization of Biometric & Observation Methods for Cupeidae (Especially Sardina Pilchardus) Used in Fisheries Biology. (GFCM Studies & Reviews: No. 1). 44p. (Eng., Fr. & Span., 2nd Printing 1965). 1957. pap. 7.50 (ISBN 92-5-101919-3, F1767, FAO). UNIPUB.
Standardization of Cell Substrates for the Production of Virus Vaccines: Proceedings. Joint WHO-IABS, Geneva, 1976. Ed. by International Association of Biological Standardization & R. H. Regamey. (Developments in Biological Standardization Ser.: Vol. 37). (Illus.). 1977. 29.50 (ISBN 3-8055-2784-5). S Karger.
Standardization of Host Suitability Studies & Reporting of Resistance to the Root-Knot Nematodes. J. N. Sasser et al. 1984. pap. text ed. write for info. (ISBN 0-931901-03-0). NCSU Plant Pathol.
Standardization of Liberian Ethnic Nomenclature. Svend Holsoe. (Liberian Research Working Papers: No. 6). 1979. 4.00 (ISBN 0-686-33171-0). Liberian Studies.
Standardization of Nomenclature: International Journal of the Sociology of Language, No. 23. Ed. by J. C. Sager. 1980. pap. text ed. 14.40x (ISBN 90-279-3028-7). Mouton.
Standardization of PpH Measurements. 2nd ed. Yung C. Wu et al. (Standard Reference Materials, National Bureau of Standards, Special Publication Ser.: No. 260-53). 55p. 1988. pap. 2.75 (S/N 003-003-02850-9). USGPO.
Standardization of Procedures for the Study of Glucose-6-Phosphate Dehydrogenase: A Report. WHO Scientific Group, Geneva, 1966. (Technical Report Ser: No. 366). 53p. (Eng., Fr., Rus. & Span.). 1967. pap. 2.00 (ISBN 92-4-120366-8). World Health.
Standardization of Radiation Dosimetry in the Soviet Union, France, the United Kingdom, the Federal Republic of Germany & Czechoslavakia. (Illus.). 101p. (Orig.). 1973. pap. 9.25 (ISBN 92-0-117073-4, ISTR4, IAEA). UNIPUB.
Standardization of Radioactive Waste Categories. (Technical Reports Ser.: No. 101). (Illus., Orig.). 1970. pap. 9.00 (ISBN 92-0-125070-3, IDC101, IAEA). UNIPUB.
Standardization of Radionuclides. (Proceedings Ser.). (Illus.). 744p. 1967. pap. 53.00 (ISBN 92-0-030067-7, ISP139, IAEA). UNIPUB.
Standardization of Selected Management Concepts. Arthur G. Beden. Ed. by Stuart Bruchey. (American Business History Ser.). 385p. 1986. lib. bdg. 45.00 (ISBN 0-8240-8351-2). Garland Pub.
Standardization of Technical Terminology: Principles & Practices - STP 806. Ed. by C. G. Interrante & F. J. Heymann. LC 82-73769. 146p. 1983. text ed. 24.00 (ISBN 0-8031-0247-X, 04-806000-42). ASTM.
Standardization of Tests for Defective Children see On the Function of the Cerebrum.
Standardized Accountancy in Germany with A New Appendix. H. W. Singer. LC 82-48372. (Accountancy in Transition Ser.). 94p. 1982. lib. bdg. 20.00 (ISBN 0-8240-5329-X). Garland Pub.
Standardized Accounting for Architects. 3rd ed. Robert F. Mattox. (Illus.). 188p. 1982. 22.75 (ISBN 0-913962-48-1); members 16.00. Am Inst Arch.
Standardized Chord Symbol Notation: A Uniform System for the Music Profession. 2nd ed. Carl Brandt & Clinton Roemer. 45p. 1976. pap. text ed. 5.95 (ISBN 0-9612684-2-5). Roerick Music.
Standardized Designs for Grain Stores in Hot Dry Climates. (Agricultural Services Bulletins Ser.: No. 62). 135p. 1985. pap. 22.50 (ISBN 92-5-102193-7, F2748, FAO). UNIPUB.
Standardized Development of Computer Software: Part 1, Methods. Robert C. Tausworthe. 1977. Pt. 2, Standards. 44.00 (ISBN 0-13-842195-1); 44.00 (ISBN 0-13-842203-6); comb. set (pts 1&2) o.p. 57.67 (ISBN 0-13-842211-7). P-H.
Standardized Input-Output Tables of ECE Countries for Years around 1970. Conference of European Statisticians. 198p. 1983. pap. text ed. 16.50 (ISBN 92-1-116281-5, E.82.II.E.23). UN.
Standardized Input-Output Tables of ECE Countries for Years Around 1975. 192p. 1983. pap. text ed. 17.50 (ISBN 92-1-116283-1, E.82.II.E.24). UN.
Standardized Nursing Care Plans for Emergency Departments. Bourg et al. 1986. spiral bdg. 26.95 (ISBN 0-8016-1257-8). Mosby.
Standardized Pilot Milk Plants. W. S. Hall. (Animal Production & Health Papers: No. 3). (Illus.). 104p. 1976. pap. 12.50 (ISBN 92-5-100089-1, F440, FAO). UNIPUB.
Standardized Quantity Recipe File for Quality & Cost Control. Institution Management Department - Iowa State University. 1971. 29.95x (ISBN 0-8138-1565-7). Iowa St U Pr.
Standardized Reasoning Tests in Arithmetic & How to Utilize Them. 2nd, rev. & enl. ed. Cliff W. Stone. LC 70-177817. (Columbia University. Teachers College. Contributions to Education: No. 83). Repr. of 1921 ed. 22.50 (ISBN 0-404-55083-5). AMS Pr.
Standardized System for Evaluating Hazardous Waste Sites. Date not set. 15.00 (ISBN 0-318-23012-7). Natl Water Well.
Standardized System for Evaluating Waste Disposal Sites. Harry LeGrand. 42p. 15.00 (ISBN 0-318-02530-2). Natl Water Well.
Standardizing Behavioral Measurements Across Cultures, Nations & Time. Richard H. Pfau. (World Education Monographs). 1984. 3.50. I N Thut World Educ Ctr.
Standardizing Biomechanical Testing in Sport. Ed. by David A. Dainty & Robert W. Norman. LC 86-15391. 160p. 1987. text ed. 23.00x (ISBN 0-87322-074-9, BDAI0074). Human Kinetics.
Standardizing Methods of Assessing Causality of Adverse Drug Reactions. Ed. by J. Venulet et al. 1982. 43.50 (ISBN 0-12-717350-1). Acad Pr.

Standardizing Properties & Analytical Methods Related to Animal Waste Research. 355p. 1975. 15.00 (ISBN 0-317-33231-7, CO275). Am Soc Ag Eng.

Standards: A Chronicle of Books for Our Time. Stanley E. Hyman. 1966. 6.75 (ISBN 0-8180-1112-2). Horizon.

Standards & Colors of the American Revolution. Edward W. Richardson. (Illus.). 350p. 1982. 33.95 (ISBN 0-8122-7839-9). U of Pa Pr.

Standards & Guidelines for Electroplated Plastics. 3rd ed. American Society of Electroplated Plastics Staff. (Illus.). 160p. 1984. 51.00 (ISBN 0-13-842310-5). P-H.

Standards & Guidelines for the Field of Volunteerism. Ed. by Ann Jacobson. 190p. 1979. 7.95 (ISBN 0-318-17173-2, C39). VTNC Arlington.

Standards & Practices for the IBM System 34-36. David Greenblatt. (Illus.). 245p. 1985. 99.00 (ISBN 0-930941-02-0). D G C Assocs Inc.

Standards & Practices for the IBM System-38. David Greenblatt. (Illus.). 162p. 1985. 495.00 (ISBN 0-930941-03-9). D G C Assocs Inc.

Standards & Procedures for Systems Documentation. Andrew W. Poschmann. LC 83-45207. 288p. 1984. pap. 55.00x comb bdg. (ISBN 0-8144-7015-7). AMACOM.

Standards & Specifications for Local Building Materials: The Report of the ARSO-CSC-UNCHS Workshop, 16-24 March, 1987. (Illus.). 60p. (Orig.). 1987. pap. 15.25x (ISBN 0-946688-79-6, Pub. by Intermed Tech England). Intermediate Tech.

Standards & Specifications Information Sources. Ed. by Erasmus J. Struglia. LC 65-24659. (Management Information Guide Ser.: No. 6). 190p. 1973. 68.00x (ISBN 0-8103-0806-1). Gale.

Standards & Standardization. Sullivan. 136p. 1983. 28.75 (ISBN 0-8247-1919-0). Dekker.

Standards Compliance Analyst. Jack Rudman. (Career Examination Ser.: C-3109). 1988. pap. 14.00 (ISBN 0-8373-3109-9). Natl Learning.

Standards Development in the Private Sector: Thoughts on Interest Representation & Procedural Fairness. Robert G. Dixon, Jr. Ed. by Amy E. Dean. LC 78-50058. 1978. pap. text ed. 3.00 (ISBN 0-87765-118-3, STD-CSS). Natl Fire Prot.

Standards Engineering Society Annual Conference Proceedings, 36th. Ed. by Donald A. Elinski. 206p. 1987. pap. text ed. 35.00 (ISBN 0-9616825-1-5). Standards Eng.

Standards for Adult Community Residential Services. 2nd ed. 65p. 1980. pap. 7.50 (ISBN 0-942974-27-1). Am Correctional.

Standards for Adult Correctional Institutions. 2nd ed. 163p. 1981. pap. 15.00 (ISBN 0-942974-25-5). Am Correctional.

Standards for Adult Local Detention Facilities. 2nd ed. 142p. 1981. pap. 15.00 (ISBN 0-942974-26-3). Am Correctional.

Standards for Adult Parole Authorities. 2nd ed. 53p. 1980. pap. 7.50 (ISBN 0-942974-28-X). Am Correctional.

Standards for Adult Probation & Parole Field Services. 2nd ed. 65p. 1981. pap. 7.50 (ISBN 0-942974-29-8). Am Correctional.

Standards for Approval If Law Schools & Interpretations. ABA, Legal Education & Admissions to the Bar Section. 315p. 1987. pap. 4.25. Amer Bar Assn.

Standards for Art Libraries & Fine Arts Slide Collections. (Occasional Papers: No. 2). 48p. (Orig.). 1983. pap. 10.00 (ISBN 0-942740-01-7). Art Libs Soc.

Standards for Blood Banks & Transfusion Services. Ed. by Paul Holland. 1987. pap. 10.00 (ISBN 0-915355-35-3). Am Assn Blood.

Standards for Carpentry & Woodworking. (DIN Standards Ser.). write for info 439.00 (ISBN 0-686-31843-9, 11295-3/80). IPS.

Standards for Central Heating & Central Raw Water Heating Systems. (DIN Standards Ser.). write for info (ISBN 0-686-31844-7, 11350-1/84). IPS.

Standards for Child-Support Payments: Intra-Family Transfers. Judith Cassetty. LC 81-47441. write for info. (ISBN 0-669-04592-6). Lexington Bks.

Standards for Church & Synagogue Libraries. LC 77-6634. (Guide Ser.: No. 6). 20p. 1977. pap. 4.95x (ISBN 0-915324-12-1); pap. 3.95 members. CSLA.

Standards for Clamping Devices 2: Workpiece Holders, Clamping & Other Devices. (DIN Standards Ser.). write for info (ISBN 0-686-31853-6, 11354-2/151). IPS.

Standards for Clinical Education in Physical Therapy. Jean Barr et al. 1981. pap. 6.00 (ISBN 0-912452-33-1). Am Phys Therapy Assn.

Standards for Concrete & Reinforced Concrete Works. (DIN Standards Ser.). for info 468.00_write (ISBN 0-686-31839-0, 11294-3/78). IPS.

Standards for Critical Care. 3rd ed. Johanson et al. (Illus.). 704p. 1988. pap. text ed. 29.95 (ISBN 0-8016-2569-6). Mosby.

Standards for Drawing Practice II: Recording of Dimensions & Tolerances, Lettering, Information on Surfaces, Welding & Threads. (DIN Standards Ser.). write for info (ISBN 0-686-31852-8, 11302-3/148). IPS.

Standards for Educational & Psychological Testing. Ed. by AERA, APA, & NCME. LC 85-71493. 108p. (Orig.). 1985. pap. 23.00 (ISBN 0-912704-95-0, 4260010); members 16.00. Am Psychol.

Standards for Employee Assistance Programs. ALMACA Staff. pap. 0.50 (ISBN 0-318-22967-6). ALMACA.

Standards for Epoxies Used in Microelectronics. NASA Staff & MSFC Staff. 115p. 1983. pap. 58.00 (ISBN 0-938648-17-9). T-C Pubns CA.

Standards for Equipment Employed in the Mooring & Ships at Single Point Moorings. OCIMF Staff. 1978. 36.00x (ISBN 0-317-61485-1, Pub. by Witherby & Co England). State Mutual Bk.

Standards for Evaluation Practice. Ed. by Peter H. Rossi. LC 81-48579. (Program Evaluation Ser.: No. 15). 1982. pap. text ed. 14.95x (ISBN 0-87589-917-X). Jossey-Bass.

Standards for Evaluations of Educational Programs, Projects & Materials. Joint Committee on Standards for Educational Evaluation. LC 80-12192. 224p. 1980. text ed. 11.95 (ISBN 0-07-032725-4). McGraw.

Standards for Fats & Oils, Vol. 5. Lawson. 22.95 (ISBN 0-317-64286-3). Van Nos Reinhold.

Standards for Fire Tests of Window Assemblies. (Two Hundred Ser.). 1970. pap. 2.00 (ISBN 0-685-58055-5, 257). Natl Fire Prot.

Standards for Health Services in Correctional Institutions. 2nd ed. American Public Health Association, Jails & Prisons Task Force Staff. Ed. by Nancy N. Dubler. LC 86-14078. 137p. 1986. 15.00 (ISBN 0-87553-143-1). Am Pub Health.

Standards for Imposing Lawyer Sanctions. ABA, Center for Professional Responsibility. 63p. 1986. pap. 5.95. Amer Bar Assn.

Standards for Juvenile Community Residential Facilities. 2nd ed. 63p. 1983. pap. 10.00 (ISBN 0-942974-44-1). Am Correctional.

Standards for Juvenile Detention Facilities. 2nd ed. 133p. 1983. pap. 15.00 (ISBN 0-942974-43-3). Am Correctional.

Standards for Juvenile Probation & Aftercare Services. 2nd ed. 69p. 1983. pap. 10.00 (ISBN 0-942974-45-X). Am Correctional.

Standards for Juvenile Training Schools. 2nd ed. 129p. 1983. pap. 15.00 (ISBN 0-942974-42-5). Am Correctional.

Standards for Library Functions at the State Level. 3rd ed. Ed. by Association of Specialized & Cooperative Library Agencies, Subcommittee on Standards for Library Functions at the State Level. LC 85-1372. 48p. 1985. pap. 6.75x (ISBN 0-8389-3317-3). ALA.

Standards for Library Services in Health Care Institutions. Association of Hospital & Institution Libraries, Hospital Library Standards Committee. LC 74-124576. pap. 20.00 (ISBN 0-317-27838-X, 2024220). Bks Demand UMI.

Standards for Living. Larry L. Benz. LC 77-70791. 1977. pap. 1.99 (ISBN 0-87148-779-9). Pathway Pr.

Standards for Local Area Networks: Carrier Sense Multiple Access with Collision Detection (CSMA-CD) Access Method & Physical Layer Specifications - Standards 802.3. (IEEE Standards Publications). 1985. 25.00 (ISBN 0-471-82749-5). Wiley.

Standards for Local Area Networks: Token-Passing Bus Access Method & Physical Layer Specifications - Standard 802.4. (IEEE Standards Publications). 238p. 1985. 29.00 (ISBN 0-471-82750-9). Wiley.

Standards for Measuring Shoreline Changes. Ed. by William F. Tanner. 87p. 1978. pap. 5.00 (ISBN 0-686-36732-4). FSU Geology.

Standards for Natural Stone Works & Concrete Stone Works. (DIN Standards Ser.). write for info (ISBN 0-686-31842-0, 1348-2/79). IPS.

Standards for Obstetric, Gynecologic & Neonatal Nursing. 3rd ed. 55p. 1986. 20.00. Am Coll Obstetric.

Standards for Obstetric-Gynecologic Services. 6th ed. 109p. 1985. 25.00 (ISBN 0-317-40735-X). Am Coll Obstetric.

Standards for Oil Tanker Manifolds & Associated Equipment. 3rd ed. OCIMF Staff. 1981. 36.00x (ISBN 0-317-61489-4, Pub. by Witherby & Co England). State Mutual Bk.

Standards for Open System Interconnection: A Solution to Incompatibility. Keith G. Knightson et al. 400p. 1987. text ed. 39.95 (ISBN 0-07-035119-8). McGraw.

Standards for Petroleum & Its Products, Pt. 1: Methods for Analysis & Testing. 41st ed. Institute of Petroleum Staff. 359p. 1982. 210.00 (ISBN 0-471-26146-7, Pub. by Wiley Heden). Wiley.

Standards for Plumbing Works. (DIN Standards Ser.). write for info (ISBN 0-686-31845-5, 11352-3-86). IPS.

Standards for Publication of Judicial Opinions: A Report of the Committee on Use of Appellate Court Energies of the Advisory Council for Appellate Justice. National Center for State Courts Staff. 46p. 1973. manuscript 2.76 (MAB-111). Natl Ctr St Courts.

Standards for Publicity Programs in State Supported Colleges & Universities Derived from the Institutions Responsibility for Reporting to Its Constituents. Melvin W. Hyde. LC 73-176893. (Columbia University Teachers College Contributions to Education Ser.: No. 506). Repr. of 1931 ed. 22.50 (ISBN 0-404-55506-3). AMS Pr.

Standards for Pump Makers & Users. 1973. pap. 25.00x (ISBN 0-685-85163-X, Dist. by Air Science Co.). BHRA Fluid.

Standards for School Buses & Operations: 1985 Edition. 130p. 11.00 (ISBN 0-87912-052-5, 294.39). Natl Safety Coun.

Standards for Selected Prestressed Units, 5 units. Incl. Standard Prestressed Concrete Beams for Highway Bridge Spans 30 to 140 Ft. 7p (STD 101-68); Standard Prestressed Box Beams for Highway Bridge Spans to 103 Ft. 7p (STD-107-59); Standard Prestressed Concrete Slabs for Highway Bridge Spans to 55 Ft. 7p (STD-108-59); Standard Prestressed Concrete Piles, Square, Octagonal & Cylinder. 7p (STD-112-81); Prestressed Concrete Channel Slabs for Short Span Bridges. 7p (STD-114-62). 1985. Set. 8.00 (ISBN 0-318-19729-4, STD-1). Prestressed Concrete.

Standards for Selection of Truck Fleet Personnel: A Guide for Hiring Professional Drivers & Other Employees in the Trucking Industry. rev. ed. American Trucking Associations Department of Safety. 40p. 1985. pap. text ed. 3.50 (ISBN 0-88711-086-X). Am Trucking Assns.

Standards for Specialized Courts Dealing with Children. United States Children's Bureau Staff. LC 78-10186. (Children's Bureau Publication: 546). vi, 99p. 1978. Repr. of 1954 ed. lib. bdg. 22.50 (ISBN 0-313-20678-3, CBSS). Greenwood.

Standards for Suicide Prevention & Crisis Centers. Jerome A. Motto et al. LC 73-17029. 114p. 1974. text ed. 26.95 (ISBN 0-87705-105-4). Human Sci Pr.

Standards for the Accreditation of Home Care. 60p. 1988. pap. 30.00 (ISBN 0-86688-147-6). Joint Comm Hlthcare.

Standards for Tools: Tools for Stamping Practice, Pt. V. write for info (ISBN 0-686-28184-5, 11079-1/46). IPS.

Standards for Traffic Justice. 12p. 1975. pap. write for info. Amer Bar Assn.

Standards for Ventilation Systems. (DIN Standards Ser.). write for info (ISBN 0-686-31840-4, 11351-3/85). IPS.

Standards for Vocational Automotive Service Instruction. 118p. 1979. write for info. (ISBN 0-943350-07-7). Motor Veh Man.

Standards for Vocational Truck-Tractor-Trailer Service Instruction. 84p. 1982. write for info. (ISBN 0-943350-06-9). Motor Veh Man.

Standards for Youth Services in Public Libraries in New York State. 42p. 1984. 6.00 (ISBN 0-931658-06-3). NY Lib Assn.

Standards in Absorption Spectrometry. C. Burgess & A. Knowles. (Techniques in Visible & Ultraviolet Spectrometry Ser.). 1981. 29.95x (ISBN 0-412-22470-4, 2230, Pub. by Chapman & Hall). Routledge Chapman & Hall.

Standards in Fluorescence Spectrometry. Ed. by J. N. Miller & M. A. West. 160p. 1981. 29.95x (ISBN 0-412-22500-X, NO.6400, Pub by Chapman & Hall England). Routledge Chapman & Hall.

Standards in Information Technology & Industrial Control: Contributions from IFIP Working Group 5.4 1988. Ed. by N. E. Malagardis & T. J. Williams. 294p. 1988. 71.00 (ISBN 0-444-70403-5, North Holland). Elsevier.

Standards in Laboratory Animal Management, 2 vols. 1983. 75.00x (ISBN 0-317-43813-1, Pub. by Univ Federation Animal). State Mutual Bk.

Standards in Pediatric Orthopedics: Tables, Charts, & Graphs Illustrating Growth. Robert N. Hensinger. (Illus.). 416p. 1986. text ed. 66.00 (ISBN 0-88167-183-5). Raven.

Standards in Programming. G. Longworth. 206p. 1981. pap. 109.25 (ISBN 0-471-89428-1). Wiley.

Standards, Interpretation & Audit Criteria for Performance of Occupational Health Programs. 208p. 50.00 (ISBN 0-932627-15-3). Am Indus Hygiene.

Standards of American Legislation. rev. ed. Ernst Freund. LC 65-17289. 1965. pap. 2.45x (ISBN 0-226-26271-5, P182, Phoen). U of Chicago Pr.

Standards of Bibliographical Description. Curt F. Buhler. LC 73-1431. 120p. 1973. Repr. of 1949 ed. lib. bdg. 35.00x (ISBN 0-8371-6796-5, BUBD). Greenwood.

Standards of Care for the Health Care Professional. Meredith B. Cox. (Legal Aspects of Medical & Health Records Ser.). (Illus.). xiii, 130p. 1984. pap. 25.00 (ISBN 0-912665-05-X). Cox Pubns.

Standards of Care in Emergency Medicine. Herbert Wigder & Mark S. Grotefeld. 1989. write for info. Little.

Standards of Child & Adolescent: Psychiatric & Mental Health Nursing Practice. American Nurses' Association Staff. (Orig.). 1985. pap. 2.75 (ISBN 0-317-60340-X, PMH-7). ANA.

Standards of Child Welfare: A Report of the Children's Bureau Conferences, May & June, 1919. Ed. by William L. Chenery & Ella A. Merrit. LC 74-1672. (Children & Youth Ser.: Vol. 6). 464p. 1974. Repr. of 1919 ed. 33.00x (ISBN 0-405-05952-3). Ayer Co Pubs.

Standards of College Health Nursing Practice. American Nurses' Association Staff. 21p. (Orig.). 1986. pap. 2.75 (ISBN 0-317-60342-6, CH-15). ANA.

Standards of Community Health Nursing Practice. American Nurses' Association Staff. 20p. (Orig.). 1986. pap. 2.75 (ISBN 0-317-61935-7, CH-2). ANA.

Standards of Emergency Nursing Practice. Emergency Department Nurse Association. 1983. pap. 17.95 (ISBN 0-8016-1616-6). Mosby.

Standards of Emergency Nursing Practice. 109p. 17.95 (ISBN 0-318-17557-6). Emerg Nurses IL.

Standards of Home Health Nursing Practice. American Nurses' Association Staff. 22p. (Orig.). 1986. pap. 2.75 (ISBN 0-317-60343-4, CH-14). ANA.

Standards of Judicial Administration, 3 vols. 1974-77. Set. pap. 9.00 (ISBN 0-317-63243-4). Amer Bar Assn.

Standards of Maternal & Child Health Nursing Practice. American Nurses' Association Staff. 27p. 1983. pap. 2.75 (ISBN 0-317-60345-0, MCH-3). ANA.

Standards of Nursing Care: A Guide for Evaluation. 2nd ed. Joan H. Carter et al. LC 72-75096. 304p. 1976. pap. text ed. 16.95 (ISBN 0-8261-1362-1). Springer Pub.

Standards of Nursing Care of the Critically Ill. American Association of Critical Care Nurses Staff. (Illus.). 368p. 1980. pap. text ed. 16.95 (ISBN 0-8359-7061-2). Appleton & Lange.

Standards of Nursing Practice. American Nurses' Association Staff. 6p. (Orig.). 1973. pap. 1.75 (ISBN 0-317-60346-9, NP-41). ANA.

Standards of Nursing Practice in Correctional Facilities. American Nurses' Association Staff. 26p. (Orig.). 1985. pap. 2.75 (ISBN 0-317-60348-5, CH-11). ANA.

Standards of Oncology Nursing Practice. Mary H. Brown et al. LC 86-11102. 622p. 1986. pap. 28.95 (ISBN 0-471-84283-4). Wiley.

Standards of Patentability for European Inventions. Hans Ullrich. (IIC Studies: Vol. 1). 116p. 1977. pap. 37.00 (ISBN 3-527-25695-4). VCH Pubs.

Standards of Practice for the Primary Health Care Nurse Practitioner. American Nurses' Association Staff. 16p. (Orig.). 1987. pap. 2.75 (ISBN 0-317-60349-3, NP-71). ANA.

Standards of Practice Handbook. 3rd ed. Ed. by Financial Analysts Federation & Institute of Chartered Financial Analysts. 150p. 1986. pap. text ed. 10.00 (ISBN 0-938367-03-X). Finan Analysts.

Standards of Professional Conduct for Lawyers & Judges. Norman Redlich. 1984. pap. text ed. 14.00 (ISBN 0-316-73658-9). Little.

Standards of Psychiatric-Mental Health Nursing Practice. (No. PMH-1). 22p. 1982. 2.00 (ISBN 0-686-40483-1); pap. 2.75. ANA.

Standards of Public Morality. Arthur T. Hadley. LC 73-2509. (Big Business; Economic Power in a Free Society Ser.). Repr. of 1907 ed. 13.00 (ISBN 0-405-05090-9). Ayer Co Pubs.

Standards of Reasonableness in Local Freight Discriminations. John M. Clark. LC 68-56651. (Columbia University. Studies in the Social Sciences: No. 97). Repr. of 1910 ed. 16.50 (ISBN 0-404-51097-3). AMS Pr.

Standards of Rehabilitation Nursing Practice. American Nurses' Association Staff & Rehabilitation Nurses Association Staff. 16p. (Orig.). 1986. pap. 2.75 (ISBN 0-317-60350-7, MS-15). ANA.

Standards of School Nursing Practice. 1983. 3.00. Am Sch Health.

Standards of Success. Teresina R. Havens. 1983. pap. 2.50x (ISBN 0-87574-043-X, 043). Pendle Hill.

Standards of the Expansion Joint Manufacturers Association. 5th ed. Expansion Joint Manufacturers Association Staff. 152p. 1980. 40.00 (ISBN 0-318-16766-2). Tubular Exch.

Standards of the Tubular Exchange Manufacturers Association. 6th ed. 242p. 1978. 75.00 (ISBN 0-318-16767-0); 1982 addenda incl. Tubular Exch.

Standards of Wage Determination. Paul Bullock. 99p. 1960. 2.00 (ISBN 0-89215-024-6). U Cal LA Indus Rel.

Standards on Fumigation. 1973. pap. 2.00 (ISBN 0-685-58082-2, 57). Natl Fire Prot.

Standards: One Hundred All-Time Favorites, Vol. 1. (Ultimate Ser.). 256p. 1982. plastic comb 17.95 (ISBN 0-88188-131-7, 00361425); pap. 14.95 (ISBN 0-88188-161-9, 00361421). H Leonard Pub Corp.

Standards: One Hundred All-Time Favorites, Vol. 3. (Ultimate Ser.). 256p. 1982. plastic comb 17.95 (ISBN 0-88188-133-3, 00361427); pap. 14.95 (ISBN 0-88188-163-5, 00361423). H Leonard Pub Corp.

Standards, Principles & Techniques in Quality Food Production. 3rd. ed. Lendal Kotschevar. 1983. 29.95 (ISBN 0-8436-0583-9). Van Nos Reinhold.

Standards, Principles & Techniques in Quantity Food Production. 4th ed. Lendal Kotschevar. (Illus.). 512p. 1988. text ed. 34.95 (ISBN 0-442-25662-0). Van Nos Reinhold.
Standards Relating to Appellate Courts. 111p. 1977. pap. 3.00 (ISBN 0-317-30667-7). Amer Bar Assn.
Standards Relating to Court Delay. 1976. pap. write for info. Amer Bar Assn.
Standards Relating to Court Delay Reduction. National Conference of State Trial Judges. 22p. 1985. pap. write for info. (ISBN 0-89707-181-6, 484-0002-01). Amer Bar Assn.
Standards Relating to Court Organization. 120p. 1974. pap. 3.00 (ISBN 0-686-47860-6). Amer Bar Assn.
Standards Relating to Juror Use & Management. 208p. 1983. pap. 17.00 (ISBN 0-317-63128-4, 523-0015-01). Amer Bar Assn.
Standards Relating to Juror Use & Management: Tentative Draft. ABA, Committee on Jury Standards & Judicial Administration Division Staff. 208p. 1982. pap. 10.00 (ISBN 0-89656-063-5, R-069). Natl Ctr St Courts.
Standards Relating to Trial Courts. 141p. 1976. pap. 3.00 (ISBN 0-317-63272-8, 685-0002-01). Amer Bar Assn.
Standardwoerterbuch fuer Werbung, Massenmedien und Marking, Deutsch-English see Standard Woerterbuch fuer Werbung, Massenmedien und Marketing. Deutsch-English-Standard Dictionary of Advertising, Mass Media & Marketing. German-English.
Standin' Tall Cleanliness. Janeen Brady. (Illus.). 22p. (Orig.). (ps-6). 1984. pap. text ed. 1.50 activity bk. (ISBN 0-944803-54-7); cassette & bk. 8.95 (ISBN 0-944803-55-5). Brite Music Inc.
Standin' Tall Courage. Janeen Brady. (Illus.). 22p. (Orig.). (ps-6). 1982. pap. text ed. 1.50 activity bk. (ISBN 0-944803-43-1); cassette & bk. 8.95 (ISBN 0-944803-45-8). Brite Music Inc.
Standin' Tall Dependability. Janeen Brady & Diane Woolley. (Illus.). 22p. (Orig.). (ps-6). 1984. pap. text ed. 1.50 activity bk. (ISBN 0-944803-59-8); cassette & bk. 8.95 (ISBN 0-944803-60-1). Brite Music Inc.
Standin' Tall Forgiveness. Janeen Brady. (Illus.). 22p. (Orig.). (ps-6). 1981. pap. text ed. 1.50 activity bk. (ISBN 0-944803-39-3); cassette & bk. 8.95 (ISBN 0-944803-40-7). Brite Music Inc.
Standin' Tall Gratitude. Janeen Brady & Diane Woolley. (Illus.). 22p. (Orig.). (ps-6). 1982. pap. text ed. 1.50 activity bk. (ISBN 0-944803-48-2); cassette & bk. 8.95 (ISBN 0-944803-49-0). Brite Music Inc.
Standin' Tall Happiness. Janeen Brady & Diane Woolley. (Illus.). 22p. (Orig.). (ps-6). 1982. pap. text ed. 1.50 activity bk. (ISBN 0-944803-46-6); cassette & bk. 8.95 (ISBN 0-944803-47-4). Brite Music Inc.
Standin' Tall Honesty. Janeen Brady. (Illus.). 22p. (Orig.). (ps-6). 1981. pap. text ed. 1.50 activity bk. (ISBN 0-944803-37-7); cassette & bk. 8.95 (ISBN 0-944803-38-5). Brite Music Inc.
Standin' Tall Love. Janeen Brady & Diane Woolley. (Illus.). 22p. (Orig.). (ps-6). 1982. pap. text ed. 1.50 activity bk. (ISBN 0-944803-50-4); cassette & bk. 8.95 (ISBN 0-944803-51-2). Brite Music Inc.
Standin' Tall Obedience. Janeen Brady. (Illus.). 22p. (Orig.). (ps-6). 1981. pap. text ed. 1.50 activity bk. (ISBN 0-944803-35-0); cassette & bk. 8.95 (ISBN 0-944803-36-9). Brite Music Inc.
Standin' Tall Self-Esteem. Janeen Brady & Diane Woolley. (Illus.). 22p. (Orig.). (ps-6). 1984. pap. text ed. 1.50 activity bk. (ISBN 0-944803-56-3); cassette & bk. 8.95 (ISBN 0-944803-57-1). Brite Music Inc.
Standin' Tall Service. Janeen Brady & Diane Woolley. (Illus.). 22p. (Orig.). (ps-6). 1984. pap. text ed. 1.50 activity bk. (ISBN 0-944803-52-0); cassette & bk. 8.95 (ISBN 0-944803-53-9). Brite Music Inc.
Standin' Tall Work. Janeen Brady. (Illus.). 22p. (Orig.). (ps-6). 1981. pap. text ed. 1.50 activity bk. (ISBN 0-944803-41-5); cassette & bk. 8.95 (ISBN 0-944803-42-3). Brite Music Inc.
Standing & Understanding: A Re-Appraisal of the Christian Faith. Stanley B. Frost. LC 68-59095. pap. 46.80 (ISBN 0-317-26033-2, 2023834). Bks Demand UMI.
Standing at Armageddon: The United States, 1877-1919. Nell I. Painter. LC 86-33111. 1987. 25.00 (ISBN 0-393-02405-9). Norton.
Standing at the Crossroads: Southern Life in the Twentieth Century. Pete Daniel. Ed. by Eric Foner. 256p. 18.95 (ISBN 0-8090-8821-5); pap. 7.95 (ISBN 0-8090-0167-5). Hill & Wang.
Standing Before God: Studies on Prayer in Scripture & in Essays in Honor of John M. Oesterreicher. Asher Finkel & Lawrence Frizzell. 1981. 39.50x (ISBN 0-87068-708-5). Ktav.
Standing By. Terry Miller. 312p. (Orig.). 1984. 14.95 (ISBN 0-9604724-7-9); pap. 8.95 (ISBN 0-9604724-6-0). Gay Pr NY.
Standing By. Juanita Ryan. LC 83-51593. 192p. (Orig.). 1984. pap. 6.95 (ISBN 0-8423-6601-6). Tyndale.
Standing by Words: Essays. Wendell Berry. LC 83-61390. 224p. (Orig.). 1983. pap. 10.50 (ISBN 0-86547-122-3). N Point Pr.
Standing Commissions of the Supreme Soviet: Effective Co-optation. Robert W. Siegler. LC 81-19925. 304p. 1982. 40.95 (ISBN 0-275-90902-6, C0902). Praeger.
Standing Committee on Federal Judiciary: What it is & How it Works. 3rd ed. 14p. 1983. pap. write for info. (ISBN 0-89707-072-0). Amer Bar Assn.
Standing Conference on Library Materials on Africa: Theses on Africa. 74p. 1964. pap. 25.00x (ISBN 0-7146-2991-X, F Cass Co). Biblio Dist.
Standing Fast: The Autobiography of Roy Wilkins. (Illus.). 464p. 1984. pap. 7.95 (ISBN 0-14-007373-6). Penguin.
Standing Female Nude. Carol A. Duffy. 64p. (Orig.). 1985. pap. 8.95 (ISBN 0-85646-150-4, Pub. by Anvil Pr Poetry). Longwood Pub Group.
Standing Firm When You'd Rather Retreat. Gene A. Getz. LC 86-429. (Biblical Renewal Ser.). 168p. (Orig.). 1986. pap. 6.95 (ISBN 0-8307-1093-0, 5418594). Regal.
Standing for Their Faith. William Woodson. 1979. 8.95 (ISBN 0-317-39803-2). Gospel Advocate.
Standing Guard: Protecting Foreign Capital in the 19th & 20th Centuries. Charles Lipson. LC 83-24260. (Studies in International Political Economy: Vol. 11). 330p. 1985. 37.00x (ISBN 0-520-03468-6); pap. 11.95x (ISBN 0-520-05327-3). U of Cal Pr.
Standing Hills. Caroline Stickland. 208p. 1987. 13.95 (ISBN 0-312-00193-2). St Martin.
Standing in the Open Space of Being. Jordan L. Flint. LC 86-51343. 59p. 1987. 6.95 (ISBN 1-55523-067-9). Winston Derek.
Standing of Psychoanalysis. B. A. Farrell. (Oxford Paperback University Ser.). 1981. text ed. 18.95x (ISBN 0-19-219133-0); pap. 9.95x (ISBN 0-19-289120-0). Oxford U Pr.
Standing Off: My Life in Rugby. Gareth Davies. 192p. 1986. 23.50x (ISBN 0-356-12157-7, Pub. by MacD & Co). Trans-Atl Phila.
Standing on the Outside. Lindsay Armstrong. (Harlequin Presents Ser.: No. 983). 192p. Date not set. pap. 1.95 (ISBN 0-317-63717-7). Harlequin Bks.
Standing Orders. John Hooker. 384p. 1987. 17.95 (ISBN 0-670-81339-7). Viking.
Standing Ovation: How to Be an Effective Speaker & Communicator. James Humes. LC 87-45058. 304p. 1988. 16.95 (ISBN 0-06-015809-3). Har-Row.
Standing Ovations. 4th ed. Junior Board of the Tri-City Symphony Orchestra. Ed. by Rose Ann Hass & Junior Board of the Tri-City Symphony. (Illus.). 308p. Repr. of 1979 ed. plastic spiral 9.50. Jr Bd Tri-City Symph.
Standing Ovations. Tri-City Symphony Orchestra Board Editors. (Illus.). 308p. Repr. of 1979 ed. spiral bdg. 9.50. Bawden Bros.
Standing Room Only? Edward A. Ross. Ed. by Gerald Grob. LC 76-46101. (Anti-Movements in America Ser.). 1977. Repr. of 1927 ed. lib. bdg. 29.00x (ISBN 0-405-09972-X). Ayer Co Pubs.
Standing Room Only: The World's Exploding Population. Karl Sax. LC 83-1757. Orig. Title: Challenge of Overpopulation, 1955 edition. xviii, 206p. 1983. Repr. of 1960 ed. lib. bdg. 35.00x (ISBN 0-313-23968-1, SAST). Greenwood.
Standing Room, Stories. Hollis Summers. LC 84-10004. 104p. 1984. text ed. 15.95x (ISBN 0-8071-1191-0); pap. 9.95 (ISBN 0-8071-1200-3). La State U Pr.
Standing Still & Walking in New York. Frank O'Hara. Ed. by Donald Allen. LC 74-75455. 192p. 1983. pap. 6.95 (ISBN 0-912516-12-7). Grey Fox.
Standing Still While Traffic Moved about Me. Robert Hutchinson. LC 79-165697. 1971. 5.95x (ISBN 0-87130-028-1); pap. 2.95 (ISBN 0-87130-029-X). Eakins.
Standing Stones: And Other Monuments of Early Ireland. 2nd ed. Kenneth McNally. (Illus.). 128p. 1988. pap. 16.95 (ISBN 0-86281-201-1, Pub. by Appletree Pr). Irish Bks Media.
Standing Strong: Notes from Joseph's Journal. Sandy Larsen. (Bible Discovery Guides for Teen Campers Ser.). (Illus.). 32p. (Orig.). 1986. pap. 1.50 camper (ISBN 0-87788-784-5); pap. 3.50 counselor (ISBN 0-87788-785-3). Shaw Pubs.
Standing Tall in Credit Management. William H. Bryan. (New Horizons Ser.: No. 6). 45p. 1977. pap. 3.25 (ISBN 0-934914-28-1). NACM.
Standing up for America: A Biography of Lee Iacocca. Patricia Haddock. LC 86-32965. (People in Focus Ser.). (Illus.). 128p. (gr. 6 up). 1987. PLB 11.95 (ISBN 0-87518-362-X). Dillon.
Standing Up for Jesus. Wesley T. Runk. (gr. k-4). 1985. 4.50 (ISBN 0-89536-725-4, 5809). CSS of Ohio.
Standing Up to Preach. Alan Walker. LC 83-72736. 84p. (Orig.). 1983. pap. 3.95 (ISBN 0-88177-005-1, DR005B). Discipleship Res.
Standing Watch. Christopher Bursk. (New Poetry Ser.). 1978. 8.95 (ISBN 0-395-27118-5); pap. 4.50 (ISBN 0-395-27199-1). HM.
Standish O'Grady. Phillip L. Marcus. LC 74-124647. (Irish Writers Ser.). 92p. 1971. 4.50 (ISBN 0-8387-7751-1); pap. 1.95 (ISBN 0-8387-7660-4). Bucknell U Pr.
Standoff at the Border: A Failure of Micro-Diplomacy. Thomas J. Price. (Southwestern Studies: No. 87). (Orig.). 1988. 10.00 (ISBN 0-87404-174-0); pap. 5.00 (ISBN 0-87404-173-2). Tex Western.
Standortgemasse Verbesserung und Bewirtschaftung Von Alpenweiden. Walter Dietl. (Tierhaltung Ser.: No. 7). (Illus.). 67p. (Ger.). 1979. pap. 15.95x (ISBN 0-8176-1028-6). Birkhauser.
Standpipe & Hose Systems. National Fire Protection Association Staff. 1986. 10.50 (ISBN 0-317-63051-2, 14-86). Natl Fire Prot.
Standpipes & Hose Systems. (Ten Ser). 1981. pap. 6.00 (ISBN 0-685-58128-4, 14). Natl Fire Prot.
Standpunt: Over Onderwijs, Democratie En Wetenschap. Adriaan D. De Groot. 1971. 11.60x (ISBN 90-2796-917-5). Mouton.
Stands a Calder Man. Janet Dailey. (Orig.). 1983. pap. 4.50 (ISBN 0-671-47398-0). PB.
Stands A Calder Man. Janet Dailey. Incl. This Calder Range; This Caldor Sky; Calder Born, Calder Bred. boxed set 15.80 (ISBN 0-671-90082-X). PB.
Stands a Calder Man. Janet Dailey. 432p. 1987. pap. 4.50 (ISBN 0-671-63785-1). PB.
Stanfield Place. Rita D. Perrier. 272p. 1985. 14.95 (ISBN 0-8059-2976-2). Dorrance.
Stanford Bank Game: Version 9. George G. Parker. Orig. Title: Stanford Bank Management Simulator v. 9. 72p. 1986. pap. text ed. 15.00 (ISBN 0-89426-085-5). Scientific Pr.
Stanford Bank Management Simulator v. 9 see Stanford Bank Game: Version 9.
Stanford Binet: Form L-M, Compilation. John R. Whitworth & Dorothy L. Sutton. 256p. 1982. pap. 35.00 binder (ISBN 0-87879-324-0). Acad Therapy.
Stanford-Binet Intelligence Scale. 1972 norms ed. L. M. Terman & M. A. Merrill. 1973. kit 189.00 (ISBN 0-395-15925-3); record bklet & manual 20.88 (ISBN 0-395-09542-5); manual 21.93 (ISBN 0-395-15936-9). HM.
Stanford Companion to Victorian Fiction. LC 88-61462. 695p. 1988. text ed. 60.00 (ISBN 0-8047-1528-9). Stanford U Pr.
Stanford Environmental Law Annual, 1984: Animal Rights. Ed. by Woods. 150p. cancelled (ISBN 0-318-04414-5). Stanford Enviro.
Stanford Environmental Law Annual 1979: Coastal Futures - Legal Issues Affecting the Development of the California Coast. 203p. (Orig.). 1979. pap. 5.00 (ISBN 0-318-11822-X). Stanford Enviro.
Stanford Environmental Law Annual 1983: Energy Development & the Environment. 225p. (Orig.). 1983. pap. 10.00 (ISBN 0-318-11833-5). Stanford Enviro.
Stanford Environmental Law Annual 1982: Land Use Regulation on the San Francisco Peninsula. 182p. (Orig.). 1982. pap. 7.50 (ISBN 0-318-11831-9). Stanford Enviro.
Stanford Environmental Law Annual 1980-81: California Water Law. 140p. (Orig.). 1981. pap. 7.50 (ISBN 0-318-11827-0). Stanford Enviro.
Stanford Environmental Law Journal, 1986-87: Superfund Hazardous Wastes. Ed. by Dunn & Semeraro. 330p. 1987. 15.00 (ISBN 0-942007-32-8). Stanford Enviro.
Stanford Intramural Law Review, 1 Vol. 1948. bound 30.00x (ISBN 0-686-90043-X). Rothman.
Stanford Journal of International Law: 1966-1986, 22 vols. Bound set. 612.50x (ISBN 0-686-90045-6). Rothman.
Stanford Law Review: 1948-1986, 38 vols. Bound set. 1580.00x (ISBN 0-686-90046-4). microfilm & microfiche avail. Rothman.
Stanford Mathematics Problem Book: With Hints & Solutions. George Polya et al. LC 73-86270. pap. 20.00 (ISBN 0-317-09309-6, 2019663). Bks Demand UMI.
Stanford Short Stories. Ed. by Wallace Stegner & Richard Scowcroft. Incl. 1962. 174p. 15.00x (ISBN 0-8047-0392-2); 1964. 168p. 15.00x (ISBN 0-8047-0393-0); 1968. 170p. 15.00x (ISBN 0-8047-0396-5). Stanford U Pr.
Stanford Stories: Tales of a Young University. Charles K. Field & William H. Irwin. LC 71-121541. (Short Story Index Reprint Ser). 1900. 20.00 (ISBN 0-8369-3497-0). Ayer Co Pubs.
Stanford Studies in History, Economics & Political Science, 18 vols. Stanford University. Repr. Set. write for info. (ISBN 0-404-50960-6). AMS Pr.
Stanford Studies in Language & Literature. Ed. by Hardin Craig. LC 76-25581. 1942. lib. bdg. 44.00 (ISBN 0-8414-3389-5). Folcroft.
Stanford Studies in Language & Literature, 34 vols. in 30. Stanford University Staff. Repr. of 1961 ed. Set. 755.00 (ISBN 0-404-51800-1). AMS Pr.
Stanford Studies in Language & Literature 1941: Fiftieth Anniversary of the Founding of Stanford University. facs. ed. Stanford University, School of Letters Staff. Ed. by H. Craig. LC 67-30232. (Essay Index Reprint Ser). 1941. 27.50 (ISBN 0-8369-0901-1). Ayer Co Pubs.
Stanford University, Nineteen Sixteen to Forty-One. John P. Mitchell. LC 58-59714. pap. 30.00 (ISBN 0-317-30440-2, 2024927). Bks Demand UMI.
Stanford University: The First Twenty-Five Years. Orrin L. Elliott. Ed. by Walter P. Metzger. LC 76-55191. (Academic Profession Ser.). (Illus.). 1977. Repr. of 1937 ed. lib. bdg. 49.50x (ISBN 0-405-10013-2). Ayer Co Pubs.
Stanford White. Charles C. Baldwin. LC 78-150512. (Architecture & Decorative Art Ser.: Vol. 39). 1971. Repr. of 1931 ed. lib. bdg. 49.50 (ISBN 0-306-70138-3). Da Capo.
Stanford White. Charles C. Baldwin. LC 75-31800. (Architectural & Decorative Art Ser.). 1976. pap. 6.95 (ISBN 0-306-80031-4). Da Capo.
Stanford Wong's Blackjack Newsletters, Vol. 5. Stanford Wong. (Illus.). 216p. (Orig.). 1983. pap. 25.00 (ISBN 0-935926-08-9). Pi Yee Pr.
Stanford Wong's Blackjack Newsletters, Vol. 4: 1982. Stanford Wong. (Illus.). 214p. (Orig.). 1982. pap. 25.00 (ISBN 0-935926-07-0). Pi Yee Pr.
Stanford Wong's Blackjack Newsletters, 1981, Vol. 3. Stanford Wong. (Illus.). 222p. (Orig.). 1981. pap. 25.00 (ISBN 0-935926-06-2). Pi Yee Pr.
Stanford Wong's Blackjack Newsletters 1984, Vol. 6. Stanford Wong. (Illus.). 91p. (Orig.). 1984. pap. 15.00 (ISBN 0-935926-09-7). Pi Yee Pr.
Stanford's Sailing Companion: With 1975 Tide Tables. F. S. Campbell & R. J. Riley. (Illus.). 228p. 1973. 19.95 (ISBN 0-8464-0882-1). Beekman Pubs.
Stanger's Partnership Sponsor Directory, 1985. Ed. by Robert A. Stanger & Co Staff. 328p. 1985. 75.00 (ISBN 0-943570-08-5). R A Stanger.
Stanislaus County: An Illustrated History. Kathleen M. Gooch. Ed. by Nora Perren. (Illus.). 176p. (YA) (gr. 7 up). 1988. 27.95 (ISBN 0-89781-245-X). Windsor Pubns Inc.
Stanislaus Mouse Learns How to Fly. Joe Gornall. (Storybook Special Ser.). (Illus.). 32p. (ps-2). Date not set. 8.95 (ISBN 0-8431-2224-2). Price Stern.
Stanislaus River: From Camp Nine to Parrots Ferry. Keith Robinson & Fred Lehman. (Whitewater Ser.). (Illus.). 1982. pap. 3.95 (ISBN 0-941838-01-3). Lore Unlim.
Stanislaus: The Struggle for a River. Tim Palmer. LC 81-43692. (Illus.). 280p. 1982. 24.95x (ISBN 0-520-04605-6); pap. 9.95 (ISBN 0-520-05225-0). U of Cal Pr.
Stanislavski: A Life. Jean Benedetti. (Illus.). 320p. 1988. 25.00 (ISBN 0-87830-984-5). Routledge Chapman & Hall.
Stanislavski: An Introduction. Jean Benedetti. 1982. pap. 5.95 (ISBN 0-87830-578-5). Theatre Arts.
Stanislavski in Rehearsal: The Final Years. V. O. Toporkov. Tr. by Christine Edwards. 1979. 14.95 (ISBN 0-87830-162-3). Theatre Arts.
Stanislavski on Opera. Constantin Stanislavski & P. I. Rumyantsev. Tr. by Elizabeth R. Hapgood. LC 72-87119. (Illus.). 1975. pap. 14.95 (ISBN 0-87830-552-1). Theatre Arts.
Stanislavski Produces Othello. Constantin Stanislavski. Tr. by Helen Nowak. 1984. pap. 12.95 (ISBN 0-87830-589-0). Theatre Arts.
Stanislavski System: The Professional Training of an Actor. 2nd, rev. ed. Sonia Moore. 144p. 1984. pap. 4.95 (ISBN 0-14-046660-6). Penguin.
Stanislavski's Legacy. rev. ed. Constantin Stanislavski. Tr. by Elizabeth R. Hapgood. LC 68-16450. (Orig.). 1968. pap. 6.95 (ISBN 0-87830-504-1). Theatre Arts.
Stanislavsky: A Life. David Magarshack. 432p. 1985. pap. 12.95 (ISBN 0-571-13791-1). Faber & Faber.
Stanislavsky Directs. Nikolai Gorchakov. Tr. by Marina Goldina. LC 85-18214. 416p. 1985. pap. 10.95 (ISBN 0-87910-051-6). Limelight Edns.
Stanislavsky Directs. Nikolai M. Gorchakov. Tr. by Miriam Goldina. LC 73-15243. 402p. 1974. Repr. of 1954 ed. lib. bdg. 45.00x (ISBN 0-8371-7164-4, GOSD). Greenwood.
Stanislavsky, Konstantin: Selected Works. Compiled by Oksana Korneva. 310p. 1984. 35.00x (ISBN 0-317-42834-9, Pub by Collets (UK)). State Mutual BK.
Stanislavsky on the Art of the Stage. Konstantin Stanislavsky. 316p. 1967. pap. 11.95 (ISBN 0-571-08172-X). Faber & Faber.
Stanislavsky on the Art of the Stage. Konstantin Stanislavsky. Tr. & intro. by David Magarshack. 1986. pap. 9.95 (ISBN 0-8090-0532-8). FS&G.
Stanislavsky on the Art of the Stage. Konstantin Stanislavsky. Tr. & intro. by David Magarshack. 1988. pap. 11.95. Faber & Faber.
Stanislavsky Technique: America. Mel Gordon. (Acting Ser.). 296p. (Orig.). 1989. pap. 8.95 (ISBN 0-936839-10-4). Applause Theatre Bk Pubs.
Stanislavsky Technique: Russia. Mel Gordon. (Applause Acting Ser.). 220p. 1988. 18.95 (ISBN 0-936839-09-0); pap. 8.95 (ISBN 0-936839-08-2). Applause Theatre Bk Pubs.
Stanislaw Ignacy Witkiewicz: A Reader. Ed. & tr. by Daniel Gerould. 1988. 20.95 (ISBN 1-55554-015-5). Paj Pubns.
Stanislaw Lem. J. Madison Davis. (Starmont Reader's Guide Ser.: No. 32). 144p. 1989. lib. bdg. 17.95x (ISBN 0-89370-959-X). Borgo Pr.
Stanislaw Lem. J. Madison Davis. Ed. by Roger C. Schlobin. (Reader's Guides to Contemporary Science Fiction & Fantasy Authors Ser.: Vol. 32). (Illus., Orig.). 1988. 17.95x (ISBN 0-930261-21-6); pap. 9.95x (ISBN 0-930261-20-8). Starmont Hse.
Stanislaw Lem. Ed. by Joseph D. Olander & Martin H. Greenberg. LC 78-56276. (Writers of the 21st Century Ser.). cancelled (ISBN 0-8008-7373-6); pap. cancelled (ISBN 0-8008-7373-4). Taplinger.
Stanislaw Lem. Richard E. Ziegfeld. (Recognitions Ser.). 200p. (Orig.). 1986. 16.95x (ISBN 0-8044-2994-4); pap. 8.95 (ISBN 0-8044-6992-X). Ungar.

Star-Gate Diary of Discovery. Richard Geer. 80p. 1985. pap. 5.95 spiral wire bdg. (ISBN 0-911167-06-4). Star-Gate.

Star Gates. Corinne Heline. (Illus.). 204p. 1986. pap. text ed. 7.95 (ISBN 0-933963-09-2). New Age Bible.

Star Gazing, Comet Tracking & Sky Mapping. Melvin Berger. LC 84-8302. (Illus.). 64p. (gr. 5 up). 1985. PLB 7.99 (ISBN 0-399-61211-4). Putnam Pub Group.

Star Gazing Through Binoculars: A Complete Guide to Binocular Astronomy. Stephen Mensing. (Illus.). 208p. 1986. pap. 14.95 (ISBN 0-8306-2703-0, NO. 2703). TAB Bks.

Star Giant. Dorothy Skinkle. 1978. pap. 1.50 (ISBN 0-505-51267-X, Pub. by Tower Bks). Leisure NY.

Star Girl. Henry Winterfield. (gr. 2-7). 1976. pap. 1.25 (ISBN 0-380-00659-6, 28506, Camelot). Avon.

Star God. Allen L. Wold. 224p. (Orig.). 1988. pap. 3.50 (ISBN 1-55785-065-8). Bart Books.

Star Guard. Andre Norton. 224p. 1984. pap. 2.50 (ISBN 0-345-35036-7, Del Rey). Ballantine.

Star Guide. Franklyn M. Branley. LC 82-45928. (Voyage into Space Bks.). (Illus.). 64p. (gr. 3-6). 1987. 11.95i (ISBN 0-690-04350-3, Crowell Jr Bks); PLB 11.89 (ISBN 0-690-04351-1). HarpJ.

Star Guide: A Unique System for Identifying the Brightest Stars in the Night Sky. Steven L. Beyer. LC 85-13039. (Illus.). 404p. 1986. 22.95 (ISBN 0-316-09267-3); pap. 12.95 (ISBN 0-316-09268-1). Little.

Star Guide (Nineteen Eighty-Eight to Nineteen Eighty-Nine) Where to Reach Movie Stars, TV Stars, Rock Stars, Sports Stars, & Other Famous Celebrities. Terry Robinson. 191p. 1987. pap. 9.95 (ISBN 0-943213-00-2). Axiom Info Res.

Star Healer: A Sector General. James White. 224p. (Orig.). 1985. pap. 2.75 (ISBN 0-345-32089-1). Fawcett.

Star Hunter see Voodoo Planet.

Star Hunters. Jo Clayton. (Science Fiction Ser.). 1987. pap. 2.95 (ISBN 0-88677-219-2). DAW Bks.

Star in the Pail. David McCord. (Illus.). 48p. (gr. k-3). 1986. 6.95 (ISBN 0-316-55521-5). Little.

Star in the Pasture. Katherine Zwers & John Tobin. Tr. by Carol Heyer. 32p. (ps-2). 1988. 7.95 (ISBN 0-8249-8273-8). Ideals.

Star in the West: A Humble Attempt to Discover the Long Lost Ten Tribes of Israel. facs. ed. Elias Boudinot. LC 79-121499. (Select Bibliographies Reprint Ser). 1816. 17.00 (ISBN 0-8369-5457-2). Ayer Co Pubs.

Star Is Born. Dale Bringman. (Orig.). 1987. pap. 3.95 (ISBN 0-89536-881-1, 7867). CSS of Ohio.

Star Is Born. Ronald Haver. LC 88-45214. (Illus.). 320p. 1988. 24.95 (ISBN 0-394-53714-9). Knopf.

Star Is Born: An Album & Diary for Baby's First Year. Faye Hammel. (Illus.). 32p. 1983. 4.00 (ISBN 0-89345-951-8, Biograf Pubns). Garber Comm.

Star Is Torn. Robyn Archer & Diana Simmonds. (Illus.). 208p. 1987. pap. 12.95 (ISBN 0-525-48346-2). Dutton.

Star Ka'ats & the Winged Warriors. Andre Norton & Dorothy Madlee. (Star Ka'ats Ser.). (Illus.). (gr. 3-5). 1983. pap. 1.95 (ISBN 0-671-45289-4). Archway.

Star King. Jack Vance. (Demon Prince Ser.: Bk. 1). 224p. 1983. Repr. of 1964 ed. 15.95. Underwood-Miller.

Star King. Jack Vance. 320p. 1989. pap. price not set. Tor Bks.

Star Lake Archaeological Project: Anthropology of a Headwaters Area of Chaco Wash, New Mexico. Ed. by Walter K. Wait & Ben A. Nelson. LC 81-13596. (Publications in Archaeology). (Illus.). 480p. 1983. 24.95x (ISBN 0-8093-0949-1). S Ill U Pr.

Star League. (Free Worlds League Ser.). (Illus.). 192p. 1988. pap. 15.00 (ISBN 1-55560-070-0). FASA Corp.

Star Light, Star Bright. Marian Wells. 200p. (Orig.). 1986. pap. 5.95 (ISBN 0-87123-883-7, 210883). Bethany Hse.

Star Lord. Louise Lawrence. LC 77-25674. (YA) (gr. 7 up). 1978. PLB 12.89 (ISBN 0-06-023777-5). HarpJ.

Star Lord. Louise Lawrence. LC 77-25674. 176p. (YA) (gr. 7 up). 1988. pap. 2.75 (ISBN 0-694-05620-0, Starwanderer). HarpJ.

Star Maiden: An Ojibway Tale. Barbara J. Esbensen. (ps-3). 1988. 14.95 (ISBN 0-316-24951-3). Little.

Star Maker. Olaf Stapledon. 256p. 1987. pap. 8.95 (ISBN 0-87477-435-7). J P Tarcher.

Star Maker see Last & First Men.

Star-Making Machinery: Inside the Business of Rock & Roll. Geoffrey Stokes. 1977. pap. 4.95 (ISBN 0-394-72432-1, Vin). Random.

Star Man's Son. Andre Norton. 224p. 1985. pap. 2.95 (ISBN 0-345-32588-5, Del Rey). Ballantine.

Star Maps. William R. Fix. (Octopus Bk.). (Illus.). 1979. 14.95 (ISBN 0-7064-1066-1, Mayflower Bks); pap. 8.95 (ISBN 0-7064-1085-8). Smith Pubs.

Star Maps for Beginners. I. M. Levitt & Roy K. Marshall. pap. 8.95 (ISBN 0-671-68810-3, Fireside). S&S.

Star Maps for Beginners. I. M. Levitt & Roy K. Marshall. (Illus.). 64p. 1983. 7.95 (ISBN 0-671-47258-5, Fireside). S&S.

Star Maps for Beginners. J. M. Levitt & Roy K. Marshall. 64p. 1987. pap. 7.95 (ISBN 0-671-63676-6, Fireside). S&S.

Star Mother's Youngest Child. Louise Moeri. (Illus.). 48p. (ps-2). 1975. 10.95 (ISBN 0-395-21406-8, Sandpiper); pap. 4.95 (ISBN 0-395-29929-2). HM.

Star Myths & Stories: From Andromeda to Virgo. Percy M. Proctor. (Illus.). 1972. 8.50 (ISBN 0-682-47470-3, Banner). Exposition-Phoenix.

Star Myths: Show-Business Biographies on Film. Robert M. Miller. LC 83-14292. 416p. 1983. 29.50 (ISBN 0-8108-1643-1). Scarecrow.

Star-Names & Their Meanings see Star Names: Their Lore & Meaning.

Star Names: Their Lore & Meaning. rev. ed. Richard H. Allen. 1963. pap. 7.95 (ISBN 0-486-21079-0). Dover.

Star Names: Their Lore & Meaning. Richard H. Allen. Orig. Title: Star-Names & Their Meanings. 16.00 (ISBN 0-8446-1527-7). Peter Smith.

Star of Bethlehem. Frank E. Stranges. 20p. (Orig.). 1985. pap. text ed. 2.00 (ISBN 0-933470-06-1). Intl Evang.

Star of Danger. Marion Zimmer Bradley. 224p. 1988. pap. 2.95 (ISBN 0-441-77958-1). Ace Bks.

Star of Gettysburg. Joseph A. Altsheler. 1976. Repr. of 1915 ed. lib. bdg. 21.95x (ISBN 0-88411-945-9, Pub. by Aeonian Pr). Amereon Ltd.

Star of Gypsies. Robert Silverberg. LC 86-81477. 1986. 18.95 (ISBN 0-917657-92-6). D I Fine.

Star of Gypsies. Robert Silverberg. 480p. 1988. pap. 3.95 (ISBN 0-445-20618-7, Pub. by Popular Lib). Warner Bks.

Star of Lancaster. Jean Plaidy. (Plantagenet Saga Ser.). 320p. 1982. 12.95 (ISBN 0-399-12758-5, Putnam). Putnam Pub Group.

Star of Light. Patricia St. John. (gr. 5-8). 1953. pap. 4.50 (ISBN 0-8024-0004-3). Moody.

Star of Melvin. Nathan Zimelman. LC 86-171. (Illus.). 32p. (ps-2). 1987. PLB 12.95 (ISBN 0-02-793750-X). Macmillan.

Star of Peace. Jan de Hartog. LC 83-47552. (Cornelia & Michael Bessie Ser.). 400p. 1984. 16.45i (ISBN 0-06-039029-8, HarpT). Har-Row.

Star of Redemption. Franz Rosenzweig. Tr. by William W. Hallo from Ger. LC 84-40833. 464p. 1985. text ed. 30.00 (ISBN 0-268-01717-4); pap. text ed. 12.95 (ISBN 0-268-01718-2). U of Notre Dame Pr.

Star of Song: The Life of Christina Nilsson. Guy Charnace. LC 80-2264. 1981. Repr. of 1870 ed. 14.50 (ISBN 0-404-18817-6). AMS Pr.

Star of the West. Cordia Byers. 536p. (Orig.). 1987. pap. 3.95 (ISBN 0-449-13143-2, GM). Fawcett.

Star of the West, 8 vols. (Illus.). 544p. Set. 155.00x (ISBN 0-85398-078-0). G Ronald Pub.

Star of Wonder. Daniel M. Epstein. LC 86-16301. 144p. 1986. 15.95 (ISBN 0-87951-257-1). Overlook Pr.

Star on Many a Battlefield: Brevet Brigadier General Joseph Karge in the Civil War. Francis C. Kajencki. LC 77-89781. 1979. 25.00 (ISBN 0-8386-2149-X). Fairleigh Dickinson.

Star on the Door. Maggie Teyte. Ed. by Andrew Farkas. LC 76-29971. (Opera Biographies Ser.). (Illus.). 1977. Repr. of 1958 ed. lib. bdg. 17.00x (ISBN 0-405-09710-7). Ayer Co Pubs.

Star over Adobe. Dorothy L. Pillsbury. LC 63-21376. 208p. 1983. 16.95 (ISBN 0-89016-074-0); pap. 8.95 (ISBN 0-89016-068-6). Lightning Tree.

Star Over Gobi (Mildred Cable) Cecil Northcott. 1960. 3.50 (ISBN 0-87508-624-1). Chr Lit.

Star Papers: Experience of Art & Nature. Henry W. Beecher. (Works of Henry Ward Beecher). vi, 359p. Repr. of 1855 ed. lib. bdg. 49.00 (ISBN 0-932051-01-4, Pub. by Am Repr Serv). Am Biog Serv.

Star Papers: Or, Experiences of Art & Nature. Henry W. Beecher. LC 75-39679. (Essay Index Reprint Ser.). Repr. of 1855 ed. 24.50 (ISBN 0-8369-2745-1). Ayer Co Pubs.

Star Particle Theory: An Introductory Survey. James S. Hughes, Jr. (Illus.). 16p. 1974. 15.00 (ISBN 0-915386-00-3). Arctinurus Co.

Star Patrol: The Adventures Begin. Herbert R. Simmons & Lester L. Boyice. (Illus.). 56p. (ps-7). 1987. lib. bdg. 8.95 (ISBN 0-930355-05-9). ELRAMCO Enter.

Star Peace: Assured Survival. Ben Bova. 384p. 1986. pap. 7.95 (ISBN 0-8125-9406-1, Dist. by Warner Publisher Services & St. Martin's Press). Tor Bks.

Star People. Brad Steiger & Francie Steiger. (Orig.). pap. 2.95 (ISBN 0-425-08157-5). Berkley Pub.

Star Photo Album. (Photo Bks.). 12p. 1983. bds. 4.95 (ISBN 0-89531-030-9). Sharon Pubns.

Star Pilots: Omni Ser. Laura J. Mixon. (No. 1). 192p. (Orig.). (YA) (gr. 7 up). 1987. pap. 2.50 (ISBN 0-590-40277-3). Scholastic Inc.

Star Pits see Tango Charlie & Foxtrot Romeo.

Star Poems & Other Poems. Clifford Davidson. LC 76-27932. (Illus.). 1976. pap. 5.00 (ISBN 0-87423-021-7). Westburg.

Star Point Series & Ceremonies. rev. & enl. ed. Brunke. 96p. 1984. pap. 6.50 (ISBN 0-88053-362-5, S-307). Macoy Pub.

Star Profile: Social Training Achievement Record. C. Williams. 35p. 1985. instr's manual 10.00x (ISBN 0-906054-39-7, Pub. by British Inst Mental); record sheets 9.00x (ISBN 0-317-39025-2, Pub. by British Inst Mental). State Mutual Bk.

Star Quality: The Collected Stories of Noel Coward. Noel Coward. 1987. pap. 10.95 (ISBN 0-525-48313-6, 01063-320, Obelisk). Dutton.

Star Quest. Robert E. Mills. (Star Quest Ser.: No. 1). 1978. pap. 1.75 (ISBN 0-505-51259-9, Pub. by Tower Bks). Leisure NY.

Star Quest for Quilters. Betty Boyink. 80p. (Orig.). 1986. pap. 12.50 (ISBN 0-9612608-7-4). B Boyink.

Star Quilt. Roberta H. Whiteman. LC 83-80591. (Illus.). 96p. (Orig.). 1984. 13.00 (ISBN 0-930100-16-6); pap. 6.95 (ISBN 0-930100-17-4). Holy Cow.

Star Raft: China's Encounters with Africa. Philip Snow. LC 88-189. (Illus.). 256p. 1988. 18.95 (ISBN 1-55584-184-8). Weidenfeld.

Star Rangers. Andre Norton. 1980. pap. 1.95 (ISBN 0-449-24076-2, Crest). Fawcett.

Star Rangers. Andre Norton. 224p. 1985. pap. 2.50 (ISBN 0-345-32308-4, Dey Rey). Ballantine.

Star Rangers & the Spy. Jean Blashfield. LC 83-91422. (Fantasy Forest Adventures Ser.). 80p. (gr. 2-5). 1984. pap. 1.95 (ISBN 0-394-72457-7). Random.

Star Rangers Meet the Solar Robot. Bev Charette & Mario Macari, Jr. LC 84-50624. (Fantasy Forest Adventures Ser.). 80p. (gr. 2-5). 1984. pap. 1.95 (ISBN 0-394-72783-5, Pub. by BYR). Random.

Star Rebel. F. M. Busby. 208p. (Orig.). 1984. pap. 2.75 (ISBN 0-553-25054-X). Bantam.

Star Rhythms. 2nd ed. William Lonsdale. (Io Ser.: No. 27). (Illus.). 180p. 1982. pap. 8.95 (ISBN 0-938190-00-8). North Atlantic.

Star Rider. Carole Carreck. (Starlight Adventure Ser.). (Illus.). 356p. (gr. 5-8). 1985. pap. 2.95 (ISBN 0-14-031840-2, Puffin). Penguin.

Star Riders of Ren. Calvin Miller. LC 82-48408. (Singreale Chronicles Ser.: Vol. 2). (Illus.). 224p. (Orig.). 1983. pap. 7.95 (ISBN 0-06-250576-9, CN-4050, HarpT). Har-Row.

Star Rising. Jess Carr. (Orig.). 1980. pap. 3.50 (ISBN 0-505-51575-X, Pub. by Tower Bks). Leisure NY.

Star Rocker. Joseph Slate. LC 81-47854. (Illus.). 32p. (ps-1). 1982. PLB 7.89g (ISBN 0-06-025749-0). HarpJ.

Star Rover. Jack London. 348p. 1983. pap. 8.95 (ISBN 0-911842-31-4). Valley Sun.

Star Running Backs of the NFL. Bill Libby. (NFL Punt, Pass & Kick Library: No. 15). (Illus.). (gr. 5-9). 1971. (BYR). Random.

Star Sapphire. Rebecca Danton. 1980. pap. 1.75 (ISBN 0-449-50058-6, Coventry). Fawcett.

Star Scorers of AVAA. Dennis DeNure. (Illus.). 125p. 1984. 19.95 (ISBN 0-915659-01-8). Video Athlete.

Star Seed. Mary A. Fontenot. (Illus.). 32p. (gr. k-4). 1986. Repr. 6.95 (ISBN 0-88289-628-8). Pelican.

Star Shine. Constance C. Greene. LC 85-40458. (Viking Kestrel Novels). 144p. (gr. 5-9). 1985. 11.95 (ISBN 0-670-80772-9, Viking Kestrel). Viking.

Star Shine. Constance C. Greene. (gr. k-6). 1987. pap. 2.75 (ISBN 0-440-47920-7, YB). Dell.

Star Showers. Jean Low. 64p. 1982. 5.00 (ISBN 0-682-49817-3). Exposition-Phoenix.

Star Sight Reduction Tables for 42 Stars: Assumed Altitude Method; (for 1986-1992) 2nd ed. Thomas D. Davies. LC 86-47714. 440p. 1986. pap. text ed. 28.50x (ISBN 0-87033-355-0). Cornell Maritime.

Star Signs. Leonard E. Fisher. LC 83-305. (Illus.). 32p. (gr. 1-4). 1983. reinforced bdg. 13.95 (ISBN 0-8234-0491-9). Holiday.

Star Signs for Lovers. Robert Worth. LC 78-57049. 208p. 1978. pap. 2.45 (ISBN 0-87754-075-6). Chelsea Hse.

Star Smash. Sumner Hayward. (Illus.). 268p. 1986. 14.95 (ISBN 0-935659-00-5). Oboe Bks.

Star Snatchers. Linda Lowery. LC 85-51053. (Dungeons & Dragons Ser.). (Illus.). 80p. (gr. 2-5). 1985. pap. 2.25 (ISBN 0-394-74244-3). Random.

Star Soldier. Steve Tymon. LC 84-52308. (Illus.). 128p. (Orig.). 1985. 7.95 (ISBN 0-931683-03-3); pap. 3.95 (ISBN 0-931683-01-7). Sci Fict & Fant Prodns.

Star Songs: A Book of Inspired Astrology. Velma Swann. LC 87-80999. (Illus.). 64p. (Orig.). 1987. pap. 5.50 (ISBN 0-9615149-8-1). Fenton Valley Pr.

Star-Spangled Banana: And Other Revolutionary Riddles. Compiled by Charles Keller & Richard Baker. Tomie De Paola. (Illus.). 62p. (gr. 2 up). 1974. 3.95 (ISBN 0-13-842971-5, Pub. by Treehouse). P-H.

Star-Spangled Banner. Oscar G. Sonneck. LC 68-16245. (Music Reprint Ser.). (Illus.). 1969. Repr. of 1914 ed. lib. bdg. 29.50 (ISBN 0-306-71108-7). Da Capo.

Star-Spangled Banner. Peter Spier. LC 73-79112. (Illus.). 48p. (gr. 1 up). 1973. 12.95 (ISBN 0-385-09458-2); pap. 11.95 (ISBN 0-385-07746-7). Doubleday.

Star-Spangled Banner. Peter Spier. LC 73-79112. (Illus.). 48p. (gr. 1 up). 1986. pap. 5.95 (ISBN 0-385-23401-5, Pub. by Zephyr-BFYR). Doubleday.

Star-Spangled Banner: Words & Music Issued Between 1814-1864. Joseph Muller. LC 79-169653. (Music Ser.). (Illus.). 1973. Repr. of 1935 ed. lib. bdg. 35.00 (ISBN 0-306-70263-0). Da Capo.

Star Spangled Beer: A Guide to America's New Microbreweries & Brewpubs. Jack Erickson. (Illus.). 156p. (Orig.). 1987. pap. 13.95 (ISBN 0-941397-00-9). Redbrick Pr.

Star-Spangled Books: Books, Sheet Music, Newspapers, Manuscripts & Persons Associated with the Star-Spangled Banner. P. W. Filby & Edward G. Howard. LC 70-187215. (Illus.). 200p. 1972. 17.50 (ISBN 0-938420-17-8). Md Hist.

Star Spangled Love. J. Alex Bordeleau. 226p. 1984. 8.68 (ISBN 0-89697-203-8). Intl Univ Pr.

Star-Spangled Puzzles. Mary L. Maloney. (Pocketful of Puzzles Ser.). (Illus., Orig.). 1977. pap. 8.40x (ISBN 0-87628-650-3, C-6503-1). Ctr Appl Res.

Star Spangled Screen: The American World War II Film. Bernard F. Dick. LC 85-9205. 304p. 1985. 26.00 (ISBN 0-8131-1531-0). U Pr of Ky.

Star: Statistical Analysis Routines. Hadi Salavitabar. 1987. Program & Data Diskettes with User's Guide. software & wkbk. 37.95 (ISBN 0-06-045702-3). Har-Row.

Star Struck. Rob John. (Club Hollywood Ser.: No. 2). 160p. (YA) (gr. 7-12). 1987. pap. 2.50 (ISBN 0-451-14938-6, Sig Vista). NAL.

Star-Studded Classroom. Fred Eichelman. (Illus.). 50p. 1981. pap. text ed. 5.95 (ISBN 0-934750-28-9). Jalamap.

Star Surgeon. Alan E. Nourse. 160p. 1986. pap. 2.95 (ISBN 0-441-78343-0, Pub. by Ace Science Fiction). Ace Bks.

Star Surgeon. James White. 160p. (Orig.). 1981. pap. 1.95 (ISBN 0-345-29169-7, Del Rey). Ballantine.

Star System Tenopia, No. 4. Richard Brightfield. 144p. (Orig.). 1986. pap. 2.50 (ISBN 0-553-25637-8). Bantam.

Star Tales: North American Indian Stories about the Stars. Gretchen Mayo. 96p. (gr. 5 up). 1987. 12.85 (ISBN 0-8027-6672-2); PLB 12.85 (ISBN 0-8027-6673-0). Walker & Co.

Star Thrower. Loren Eiseley. LC 79-10406. 319p. 1979. pap. 6.95 (ISBN 0-15-684909-7, Harv). HarBraceJ.

Star to Guide Us. Don C. McGlothlin. LC 82-61488. (Illus.). 304p. 1982. pap. 4.95 (ISBN 0-9610002-0-1). President Pubs.

Star to Steer Her By: A Self-Teaching Guide to Offshore Navigation. Edward J. Bergin. LC 83-71313. 216p. 1983. pap. 16.50 (ISBN 0-87033-309-7). Cornell Maritime.

Star Too Far. Don Fearheiley. (Orig.). 1957. pap. 1.95 (ISBN 0-8054-9701-3). Broadman.

Star Trails: Reproducible Carryover Worksheets for R, S, L, TH, SH, CH. rev. & Combined ed. Valeda Blockcolsky & Joan M. Frazer. 258p. (gr. k-8). 1983. pap. 19.95 (ISBN 0-88450-862-5, 7029-B). Communication Skill.

Star Trap. Simon Brett. 1986. pap. 3.50 (ISBN 0-440-18300-6). Dell.

Star Travel. Gatland & Jeffries. (World of the Future Ser.). (gr. 5-9). 1979. (Usborne-Hayes); PLB 12.96 (ISBN 0-88110-005-6); pap. 4.95 (ISBN 0-86020-243-7). EDC.

Star Treasure. Keith Laumer. 1986. 2.95 (ISBN 0-671-65596-5). Baen Bks.

Star Trek. James Blish. 13.95 (ISBN 0-8488-0431-7). Amereon Ltd.

Star Trek. James A. Lely. (TV & Movie Tie-Ins Ser.). (Illus.). (gr. 4 up). 1979. PLB 8.95 (ISBN 0-87191-718-1). Creative Ed.

Star Trek. Jeff Rovin. (Orig.). Date not set. pap. 1.95 (ISBN 0-425-04442-4). Berkley Pub.

Star Trek - The Next Generation: Encounter at Farpoint. David Gerrold. pap. 3.95 (ISBN 0-317-64615-X). PB.

Star Trek - The Next Generation: Officer's Manual. (Illus.). 128p. 1988. pap. 15.00 (ISBN 1-55560-079-4). FASA Corp.

Star Trek - The Next Generation: Ship Recognition Manual - Yachts. 48p. 1988. pap. 8.00 (ISBN 1-55560-064-6). FASA Corp.

Star Trek - The Next Generation: Star Fleet Ground Forces Manual. 144p. 1988. pap. 15.00 (ISBN 0-931787-09-2). FASA Corp.

Star Trek Compendium. Asherman. pap. 9.95 (ISBN 0-671-62726-0). PB.

Star Trek: Crisis on Centaurus, No. 28. Brad Ferguson. (Orig.). 1986. pap. 3.50 (ISBN 0-671-61115-1). PB.

Star Trek: Dreadnought. Diane Carey. pap. 3.50 (ISBN 0-671-61873-3). PB.

Star Trek Guide. J. Ed Clauss. 1976. pap. 7.95x (ISBN 0-88411-079-6, Pub. by Aeonian Pr). Amereon Ltd.

Star Trek II: Biographies. William Rotsler & Wendy Barish. 160p. (gr. 3-7). 1982. pap. 3.80 (ISBN 0-671-46391-8). Wanderer Bks.

Star Trek II Gift Set, 3 vols. William Rotsler. Boxed Set. pap. 9.50 (ISBN 0-317-12429-3). Wanderer Bks.

Star Trek II: Short Stories. William Rotsler & Wendy Barish. LC 82-17558. 160p. (gr. 3-7). 1982. pap. 2.95 (ISBN 0-671-46390-X). Wanderer Bks.

Star Trek II: The Wrath of Khan. Vonda N. McIntyre. 1982. pap. 3.50 (ISBN 0-671-63494-1). PB.

Star Trek III: Plot-It-Yourself Adventure Stories, the Vulcan Treasure. William Rotsler. Ed. by Wendy Barish. 128p. (Orig.). (gr. 3 up). 1984. pap. 3.95 (ISBN 0-671-50138-0). Wanderer Bks.

Star Trek III Short Stories. William Rotsler. Ed. by Wendy Barish. 160p. (Orig.). (gr. 3 up). 1984. pap. 3.85 (ISBN 0-671-50139-9). Wanderer Bks.

Starlight. David Lyon. 400p. cancelled (ISBN 0-943828-60-0). Karz-Cohl Pub.
Starlight Express. (Illus.). 88p. 1987. pap. 12.95 (ISBN 0-88188-578-9). H Leonard Pub Corp.
Starlight Miracle. Renate Chapman. 1986. 9.95 (ISBN 0-8034-8608-1, Avalon). Bouregy.
Starlight Nights. Leslie C. Peltier. LC 65-20992. (Illus.). 236p. 1980. pap. 8.95 (ISBN 0-933346-02-6, 6026). Sky Pub.
Starlight Over Tunis. Barbara Cartland. (Camfield Ser.: No. 50). 176p. 1987. pap. 2.75 (ISBN 0-515-09213-4). Jove Pubns.
Starlight Ranch & Other Stories of Army Life on the Frontier. Charles King. LC 73-94737. (Short Story Index Reprint Ser.). 1890. 17.00 (ISBN 0-8369-3117-3). Ayer Co Pubs.
Starlight Rider. Ernest Haycox. (Large Print Books (General Ser.)). 343p. 1985. lib. bdg. 15.95 (ISBN 0-8161-3883-4). G K Hall.
Starlight, Star Bright. Frances West. (Second Chance at Love Ser.: No. 441). 1988. pap. 2.50 (ISBN 0-425-10837-6). Berkley Pub.
Starlight, Starbright. Iris Johansen. (Loveswept Ser.: No. 232). 192p. (Orig.). 1988. pap. 2.50 (ISBN 0-553-21861-1, Loveswept). Bantam.
Starling. Christopher Feare. (Illus.). 1984. 29.95x (ISBN 0-19-217705-2). Oxford U Pr.
Starlit Surrender. Judith Cuevas. 448p. 1988. pap. 3.75 (ISBN 0-8217-2270-0). Zebra.
Starlord: The Conquest of Earth. Stuart D. Waymire. (Illus.). 1988. 17.95. Thundblt Pr NV.
Starluck. Donald Wismer. LC 81-43375. 186p. (YA) 1982. 15.00 (ISBN 0-317-54349-0). Ultramarine Pub.
Starmaker. Wilfred McCormick. 1963. 5.95 (ISBN 0-8315-0109-X). Speller.
Starmakers Ablaze I: Log Cabin Triangles. Kaye Wood. (Illus., Orig.). 1988. pap. 19.95 (ISBN 0-944588-01-8). K Wood Pub.
Starmakers Ablaze II: Quilting Log Cabin Diamonds. Kaye Wood. (Illus.). 96p. (Orig.). 1987. pap. 19.95 (ISBN 0-944588-00-X, STR2). K Wood Pub.
Starmakers & Svengalis: The Inside Story of British Pop Music Management from 1955 to the present. Johnny Rogan. (Illus.). 288p. 1988. 27.50x (ISBN 0-356-15138-7, Pub. by Mcdonald & Jone's England). Hippocrene Bks.
Starman. Alan D. Foster. (Orig.). 1984. pap. 2.95 (ISBN 0-446-32598-8). Warner Bks.
Starman Jones. Robert A. Heinlein. Ed. by Judy-Lynn Del Rey. 256p. 1975. pap. 2.50 (ISBN 0-345-32811-6). Ballantine.
Starmen of Llyrdis. Leigh Brackett. 176p. 1976. pap. 1.95 (ISBN 0-345-28483-6). Ballantine.
Starmont Index to Argosy, 1930-1943. Compiled by Fred Cook. (Magazine Index Ser.: No. 1). Date not set. 29.95; pap. 19.95. Starmont Hse.
Starmont Index to Argosy, 1930-43. Fred Cook. (Starmont Magazine Index Ser.: No. 1). 300p. 1989. lib. bdg. 29.95x (ISBN 0-8095-5350-3). Borgo Pr.
Starmont Index to Argosy, 1930-43. Compiled by Fred Cook. (Starmont Magazine Index Ser.: Vol. 1). Date not set. 29.95x (ISBN 1-55742-019-X); pap. 19.95x (ISBN 1-55742-018-1). Starmont Hse.
Starmont Index to the Character Pulps. Fred Cook. (Starmont Magazine Index Ser.: No. 2). 300p. 1989. lib. bdg. 29.95x (ISBN 0-8095-5351-1). Borgo Pr.
Starmont Index to the Character Pulps. Compiled by Fred Cook. (Starmont Magazine Index Ser.: Vol. 2). (Illus., Orig.). 1989. 29.95x (ISBN 1-55742-023-8); pap. 19.95x (ISBN 1-55742-022-X). Starmont Hse.
Staroamer's Fate. Chuck Rotham. (Orig.). 1986. pap. 2.95 (ISBN 0-445-20102-9, Pub. by Popular Lib). Warner Bks.
Starpirate's Brain. Ron Goulart. 1987. pap. 2.95 (ISBN 0-312-90053-8). St Martin.
Starpol Hunter, No. 3, 6 bks. John Tully. (Starpol Ser.). (Illus.). 144p. (gr. 3-8). 1987. Set. pap. text ed. 29.70 (ISBN 1-55624-915-2, WG9152). Wright Group.
Starpower. Garry Shirts. 1969. 59.00 (ISBN 0-318-00397-X). Simile II.
Starquake. Robert L. Forward. LC 85-6183. 1986. pap. 3.95 (ISBN 0-345-31233-3, Dey Rey). Ballantine.
Starr of Wyoming. W. F. Bragg. 1981. pap. 2.25 (ISBN 0-8439-0860-2, Leisure Bks). Leisure NY.
Starr: The Story of My Life in Football. Bart Starr & Murray Olderman. LC 87-19847. (Illus.). 320p. 1987. 17.95 (ISBN 0-688-06752-2). Morrow.
Starr-Weiner Report on Sex & Sexuality in the Mature Years. B. D. Starr & M. B. Weiner. 312p. 1982. pap. text ed. 5.95 (ISBN 0-07-060878-4). McGraw.
Starred Reprint of Cases on Torts. 7th ed. Prosser et al. 29.50 (ISBN 0-317-06412-6, 9766). Foundation Pr.
Starrigger. John DeChancie. 272p. 1987. pap. 2.95 (ISBN 0-441-78305-8, Pub. by Charter Bks). Ace Bks.
Starrigger. John DeChancie. 1987. pap. 2.95 (ISBN 0-317-63307-4, Pub. by Ace Science Fiction). Ace Bks.
Starring First Grade. Miriam Cohen. LC 84-5929. (Illus.). 32p. (gr. k-3). 1985. 11.75 (ISBN 0-688-04029-2); PLB 11.88 (ISBN 0-688-04030-6). Greenwillow.
Starring First Grade. Miriam Cohen. (gr. k-6). 1987. pap. 2.50 (ISBN 0-440-48250-X, YB). Dell.
Starring Francine & Dave: Three One-Act Plays. Ruth Young. LC 88-60093. (Illus.). 32p. (ps-2). 1988. 13.95 (ISBN 0-531-05781-X); PLB 13.99 (ISBN 0-531-08381-0). Orchard Bks Watts.
Starring Miss Barbara Stanwyck. Ella Smith. 384p. 1985. 19.95 (ISBN 0-517-55695-2). Crown.
Starring Mothers: Thirty Portraits of Accomplished Women. Barbra Walz & Jill Barber. LC 86-29160. (Illus.). 160p. 1987. (Dolp); pap. 12.95 (ISBN 0-385-23118-0, Dolp). Doubleday.
Starring Peter & Leigh. Susan B. Pfeffer. LC 78-72855. 1978. 7.95 (ISBN 0-440-08226-9). Delacorte.
Starring Punky Brewster. Ann Matthews. (Punky Brewster Ser.). (Illus.). (gr. 2-5). 1987. pap. 2.50 (ISBN 0-671-62728-7, Minstrel Bks). S&S.
Starring Quincy Rumpel. Betty Waterton. 94p. (Orig.). (YA) (gr. 7 up). 1987. pap. 4.95 (ISBN 0-88899-048-0, Pub. by Douglas & McIntyre-Grounwood). Salem Hse Pubs.
Starring Sally J. Freedman. (gr. 4 up). 1978. pap. 3.25 (ISBN 0-440-98239-1). Dell.
Starring Sally J. Freedman As Herself. Judy Blume. LC 76-57805. 96p. (gr. 4-7). 1977. 12.95 (ISBN 0-02-711070-2). Bradbury Pr.
Starring Sally J. Freedman As Herself. Judy Blume. 240p. (gr. 4 up). 1986. pap. 3.25 (ISBN 0-440-48253-4, LFL). Dell.
Starring Sally J. Freedman As Herself see Judy Blume Collection.
Starring Stephanie. Susan Saunders. (Sleepover Friends: No. 2). (Illus.). 96p. (Orig.). (gr. 4-6). 1987. pap. 2.50 (ISBN 0-590-40642-6). Scholastic Inc.
Starring Your Love Life. Jonathan Sternfield. (Love Life Guides Ser.: No. 1). 192p. (Orig.). 1988. pap. 2.95 (ISBN 1-55802-041-1). Lynx Bks.
Starr's Guide to the John Muir Trail & the High Sierra Region. 12th rev. ed. Walter A. Starr, Jr. Ed. by Douglas Robinson. LC 67-25840. (Totebook Ser.). (Illus.). 224p. 1974. pap. 8.95 (ISBN 0-87156-172-7); map 1.95 (ISBN 0-87156-173-5). Sierra.
Starry Place Between the Antlers: Why I Live in South Carolina. James Dickey. 1981. 2.00 (ISBN 0-89723-030-2); limited signed ed. 25.00 (ISBN 0-89723-031-0). Bruccoli.
Starry Rift. James Tiptree, Jr. 256p. 1986. 14.95 (ISBN 0-312-93744-X, Dist. by St. Martin's Press). Tor Bks.
Starry Rift. James Tiptree, Jr. 256p. 1989. pap. price not set (ISBN 0-8125-5627-5). Tor Bks.
Starry Room: Naked Eye Astronomy in the Intimate Universe. Fred Schaaf. (Illus.). 19.95 (ISBN 0-471-62088-2). Wiley.
Starry Sky to Starry Sky: Poems by Mary Jane White with Translations from Marina Tsvetaeva. Mary J. White. LC 87-80785. 96p. (Orig.). 1988. 15.00 (ISBN 0-930100-26-3); pap. 7.95 (ISBN 0-930100-25-5). Holy Cow.
Starry Starry Night. 2nd ed. Paul Burton. 30p. 1988. pap. text ed. 3.00 (ISBN 0-941470-09-1). Hilltop Pr CA.
Stars. Heather Couper. (Space Scientist Ser.). 32p. (gr. 4-9). 1986. lib. bdg. 11.90 (ISBN 0-531-10054-5). Watts.
Stars. Phoebe Crosby. LC 60-9233. (Junior Science Ser.). (Illus.). (gr. 2-5). 1960. PLB 6.69 (ISBN 0-8116-6153-9). Garrard.
Stars! Daphne Davis. LC 83-590. (Illus.). 280p. 1983. 29.95 (ISBN 0-941434-34-6). Stewart Tabori & Chang.
Stars. Daphne Davis. 280p. 1984. pap. 14.95 (ISBN 0-671-53083-6, Fireside). S&S.
Stars! Daphne Davis. 1985. 14.98 (ISBN 0-517-47980-X). Outlet Bk Co.
Stars. Richard Dyer. (British Film Institute Bks.). (Illus.). 204p. 1979. pap. 13.50 (ISBN 0-85170-085-3, Pub. by British Film Ins England). U of Ill Pr.
Stars. George Forbes. 1928. 15.00 (ISBN 0-686-17423-2). Ridgeway Bks.
Stars. George Forbes. 1928. 15.00 (ISBN 0-932062-58-X). Sharon Hill.
Stars. Louis Sabin. LC 84-2605. (Illus.). 32p. (gr. 3-6). 1985. PLB 8.45 (ISBN 0-8167-0152-0); pap. text ed. 1.95 (ISBN 0-8167-0153-9). Troll Assocs.
Stars. Seymour Simon. LC 85-32012. (Illus.). 32p. (ps-3). 1986. 13.95 (ISBN 0-688-05855-8, Morrow Junior Books); lib. bdg. 12.88 (ISBN 0-688-05856-6). Morrow.
Stars. Ed. by Time-Life Books Inc. Staff. (Voyage Through the Universe Ser.). 144p. 1989. price not set (ISBN 0-8094-6858-1); lib. bdg. price not set (ISBN 0-8094-6859-X). Time-Life.
Stars. Roy Wandelmaier. LC 84-8642. (Now I Know Ser.). (Illus.). 32p. (gr. k-2). 1985. PLB 9.89 (ISBN 0-8167-0339-6); pap. text ed. 2.95 (ISBN 0-8167-0442-2). Troll Assocs.
Stars. rev. ed. Herbert S. Zim & Robert H. Baker. (Golden Guide Ser.). (Illus.). (gr. 6 up). 1985. pap. 3.95 (ISBN 0-307-24493-8, Golden Pr). Western Pub.
Stars: A New Way to See Them. 3rd ed. H. A. Rey. (Illus.). (gr. 8 up). 1967. 11.95 (ISBN 0-395-08121-1). HM.
Stars: A New Way to See Them. H. A. Rey. (gr. 4 up). 1976. pap. 8.95 (ISBN 0-395-24830-2). HM.
Stars Above, Stars Below. Margaret Hasse. 1985. pap. 4.50 (ISBN 0-89823-056-X). New Rivers Pr.
Stars & Bars. William Boyd. LC 84-27368. 288p. 1985. 16.95 (ISBN 0-688-02599-4). Morrow.
Stars & Bars. William Boyd. 336p. 1986. pap. 6.95 (ISBN 0-14-008889-X). Penguin.
Stars & Clusters. Cecilia Payne-Gasposchkin. LC 79-4472. (Books on Astronomy). (Illus.). 1979. 27.00x (ISBN 0-674-83440-2). Harvard U Pr.
Stars & Featured Players of Paramount of 1930-1931. Ed. by R. Gordon. 1976. lib. bdg. 80.00 (ISBN 0-8490-2663-6). Gordon Pr.
Stars & Films of 1937 & 1938, 2 vols. Ed. by Stephen Watts. 1976. lib. bdg. 200.00 (ISBN 0-8490-2664-4). Gordon Pr.
Stars & Garters: Twenty Extraordinary Vintage American Postcards to Tear Out & Send. Ed. by Hal Morgan & Andreas Brown. (Illus.). 16p. (Orig.). 1983. pap. 4.95 (ISBN 0-942820-05-3). Steam Pr MA.
Stars & Nebulas. William J. Kaufmann, III. LC 78-17544. (Illus.). 204p. 1978. pap. text ed. 12.95 (ISBN 0-7167-0085-9). W H Freeman.
Stars & Other Korean Short Stories. Sun-won Hwang. Tr. by Edward W. Poitrass. (Writing in Asia Ser.). 227p. (Orig., Korean.). 1980. pap. text ed. 9.00x (ISBN 0-686-98153-7). Heinemann Ed.
Stars & Outer Space Made Easy. Carlos S. Mundt. LC 74-6491. (Illus.). 95p. (gr. 4 up). 1963. 11.95 (ISBN 0-911010-71-8); pap. 5.95 (ISBN 0-911010-70-X). Naturegraph.
Stars & Planets. Robin Kerrod. (Illus.). 125p. 1984. pap. 6.95 (ISBN 0-668-06263-0). Arco.
Stars & Planets. James Muirden. (Do You Know Ser.). (Illus.). 32p. (gr. k-6). 1987. lib. bdg. 11.90 (ISBN 0-531-19023-4, Warwick). Watts.
Stars & Planets: A Useful & Entertaining Tool to Guide Youngsters into the Twenty-First Century. Christopher Lampton. (Illus.). 48p. (gr. 1-7). 1988. 9.95 (ISBN 0-385-23786-3); pap. 9.95 (ISBN 0-385-23785-5). Doubleday.
Stars & Star Handlers. Whitney Stine. LC 84-60759. (Illus.). 404p. 1985. 17.95 (ISBN 0-915677-08-3). Roundtable Pub.
Stars & Star Systems. Ed. by Bengt E. Westerlund. (Astrophysics & Space Science Library: No. 75). 1979. lib. bdg. 34.00 (ISBN 90-277-0983-1, Pub. by Reidel Holland). Kluwer Academic.
Stars & Strikes: Unionization of Hollywood. Murray Ross. LC 41-24783. Repr. of 1941 ed. 17.00 (ISBN 0-404-05408-0). AMS Pr.
Stars & Stripes: A Celebration of the American Flag by Ninety-Six International Designers & Artists. Kit Hinrichs. (Illus.). 144p. (Orig.). 1987. pap. 16.95 (ISBN 0-87701-436-1). Chronicle Bks.
Stars & Stripes: Doughboy Journalism in World War I. Alfred E. Cornebise. LC 83-12863. (Contributions in Military History Ser.: No. 37). (Illus.). xiii, 221p. 1984. lib. bdg. 35.00 (ISBN 0-313-24230-5, COS/). Greenwood.
Stars & Stripes Forever. Elliot H. Paul. LC 74-22802. Repr. of 1939 ed. 24.00 (ISBN 0-404-58459-4). AMS Pr.
Stars & Stripes: The Early Years. Ken Zumwalt. 1988. 16.95 (ISBN 0-89015-658-1). Eakin Pr.
Stars & Stripes: The Official Newspaper of the A E F, Vols. 1-2. U. S. Army A E F 1917-1920. (No. 19). 1971. Repr. of 1918 ed. 200.00 (ISBN 0-405-00290-4, 19521). Ayer Co Pubs.
Stars & Tears. Chiara Lubich. LC 85-72399. 153p. 1986. pap. 5.25 (ISBN 0-911782-54-0). New City.
Stars & Telescopes for the Beginner. Roy Worvill. LC 79-14034. (Illus.). 1980. 7.95 (ISBN 0-8008-4464-5). Taplinger.
Stars & the Land. Grace B. Freeman. 16p. (Orig.). 1983. pap. 4.95 (ISBN 0-9607730-7-X). Johns Pr.
Stars & the Milky Way System: Proceedings of the European Astronomical Meeting, 1st, Athens, 1972, Vol. 2. European Astronomical Meeting Staff. Ed. by L. N. Mavridis. LC 73-9108. (Illus.). 300p. 1974. 85.00 (ISBN 0-387-06383-8). Springer-Verlag.
Stars & the Mind: A Study of the Impact of Astronomical Development on Human Thought. M. Davidson. 59.95 (ISBN 0-8490-1121-3). Gordon Pr.
Stars & the Stripes. Boleslaw Mastai & Marie-Louise D'Otrange. (Illus.). 1973. 25.00 (ISBN 0-394-47217-9). Knopf.
Stars & Your Baby. Michael Colmer. (Illus.). 256p. (Orig.). 1987. pap. 7.95 (ISBN 0-7137-1946-X, Pub. by Javelin England). Sterling.
Stars Are Ours. Andre Norton. 192p. 1983. pap. 2.50 (ISBN 0-441-78435-6). Ace Bks.
Stars Are the Styx. Theodore Sturgeon. 1979. pap. 2.75 (ISBN 0-440-18006-6). Dell.
Stars Are the Styx. Theodore Sturgeon. LC 83-27870. 382p. 1984. pap. 6.95 (ISBN 0-312-94419-5). Bluejay Bks.
Stars at Noon. Jacqueline Cochran & Floyd Odlum. Ed. by James Gilbert. LC 79-7241. (Flight: Its First Seventy-Five Years Ser.). (Illus.). 1979. Repr. of 1954 ed. lib. bdg. 24.50x (ISBN 0-405-12156-3). Ayer Co Pubs.
Stars at Noon. Denis Johnson. LC 86-45274. 192p. 1986. 15.95 (ISBN 0-394-53840-4). Knopf.
Stars at Noon. Denis Johnson. LC 87-40094. (Vintage Contemporaries Ser.). 192p. 1988. pap. 5.95 (ISBN 0-394-75427-1, Vin). Random.
Stars Candles Windflowers. Mona L. Banos. 1987. 5.95 (ISBN 0-533-07284-0). Vantage.
Stars' End. Glen Cook. 352p. (Orig.). 1982. pap. 2.95 (ISBN 0-446-30156-6). Warner Bks.
Stars Fell on Alabama. Carl Carmer. LC 85-8107. (Library of Alabama Claasics Ser.). xxii, 294p. (Orig.). 1985. 22.50 (ISBN 0-8173-0236-0); pap. 10.95 (ISBN 0-8173-0235-2). U of Ala Pr.
Stars for Lincoln, Doctors & Dogs. J. Benbow Bullock. LC 80-66936. (Illus.). 100p. (Orig.). 1981. pap. 4.95 (ISBN 0-937024-00-7). Gourmet Guides.
Stars for Your Sky. Leonard W. Mann. 1982. pap. 4.95 (ISBN 0-89536-520-0, 1901). CSS of Ohio.
Stars: From Birth to Black Hole. David J. Darling. LC 84-23067. (Discovering Our Universe Ser.). (Illus.). 64p. (gr. 4 up). 1985. PLB 10.95 (ISBN 0-87518-284-4). Dillon.
Stars, Galaxies, Cosmos. William R. Corliss. LC 87-60007. (Catalog of Astronomical Anomalies Ser.). (Illus.). 246p. 1987. 17.95 (ISBN 0-915554-21-6). Sourcebook.
Stars, Gates & Kings. Lorna Madsen & Theodore W. Clymer. (Chapman Puzzle Bks.). (Orig.). (gr. k-2). 1985. pap. 2.00 (ISBN 0-930687-22-1). Chapman Brook.
Stars in Flight: A Study in Air Force Character & Leadership. Edgar F. Puryear, Jr. LC 80-28631. (Illus.). 312p. 1981. 14.95 (ISBN 0-89141-127-5); pap. 8.95 (ISBN 0-89141-128-3). Presidio Pr.
Stars In Her Eyes. Elizabeth Bernard. (Satin Slippers Ser.: No. 3). 160p. 1987. pap. 2.95 (ISBN 0-449-13302-8). Fawcett.
Stars in My Eyes. Edward Field. LC 77-95137. (Illus.). 91p. 1978. pap. 7.95 (ISBN 0-8180-1537-3). Sheep Meadow.
Stars in My Pocket Like Grains of Sands. Samuel R. Delany. LC 84-45180. 384p. 1984. 16.95 (ISBN 0-553-05053-2). Bantam.
Stars in Shroud. Gregory Benford. 352p. (Orig.). 1984. pap. 2.95 (ISBN 0-8125-3181-7, Dist. by Warner Pub Services & Saint Martin's Press). Tor Bks.
Stars in Space. Patrick Moore. (Junior Reference Ser). (Illus.). (gr. 7 up). 1966. 13.95 (ISBN 0-7136-1299-1). Dufour.
Stars in the Night. Don Summers. 1971. pap. 1.25 (ISBN 0-915374-33-1, 33-1). Rapids Christian.
Stars in the Sky. Joseph Jacobs. LC 78-11718. (Illus.). 32p. (ps up). 1979. 6.95 (ISBN 0-374-37229-2). FS&G.
Stars in Your Eyes. Emilie Loring. 1976. Repr. of 1941 ed. lib. bdg. 17.95x (ISBN 0-88411-362-0, 362, Pub. by Aeonian Pr). Amereon Ltd.
Stars in Your Eyes: A Guide to the Northern Skies. Upper Willamette Valley Project Office Staff. (Illus.). 23p. 1985. pap. 1.50 (ISBN 0-318-23528-5, S/N 008-022-00155-7). USGPO.
Stars in Your Hands. Beverly C. Jaegers. (Illus.). 90p. 1975. pap. text ed. 5.00. Aries Prod.
Stars, Moons & Planets. Donald D. Wolf & Margot L. Wolf. LC 82-80878. (Matter-of-Fact Bks.). (Illus.). 64p. (gr. 3-8). 1982. pap. 3.95 (ISBN 0-448-04089-1, G&D). Putnam Pub Group.
Stars My Destination. Alfred Bester. 1987. 15.95 (ISBN 0-531-15050-X). Watts.
Stars, Nebulae & the Interstellar Medium: Observational Physics & Astrophysics. C. R. Kichin. 400p. 1987. 77.00 (ISBN 0-85274-580-X, Pub. by A Hilger UK); pap. 33.00 (ISBN 0-85274-581-8). Taylor & Francis.
S.T.A.R.S. No Sweat Diet. Alexander S. Justice & Mary B. Justice. (Orig.). 1985. pap. 15.00 (ISBN 0-935313-02-8). Space Travel.
Stars of Childsland. Larry D. Templeton. (Illus.). 22p. (gr. k-3). 1982. pap. 1.98 (ISBN 0-9608914-0-4). Templeton.
Stars of Country Music: Uncle Dave Macon to Johnny Rodriguez. Ed. by Bill C. Malone & Judith McCullough. LC 75-15848. (Music in American Life Ser.). 488p. 1975. 22.50 (ISBN 0-252-00527-9). U of Ill Pr.
Stars of Destiny: The Ancient Science of Astrology & How to Make Use of it Today. Katherine T. Craig. 312p. 1981. pap. 17.50 (ISBN 0-89540-115-0, SB-115). Sun Pub.
Stars of Fortune. Cynthia Harnett. LC 83-24836. (Cynthia Harnett's Adventure Novels Ser.). (Illus.). 288p. (gr. 5 up). 1984. 9.95 (ISBN 0-8225-0892-3). Lerner Pubns.
Stars of Jade. Julius D. Staal. LC 84-50263. (Chinese Astronomy Ser.). (Illus.). 225p. (Orig.). 1984. pap. text ed. 19.95 (ISBN 0-914653-00-8). Writ Pr.
Stars of Jonestown. K. Ramlogan. 80p. 1987. 7.95 (ISBN 0-8062-3138-6). Carlton.
Stars of Obron: Chambo Returns. Alta M. Rymer. (Tales of Planet Artembo Ser.: Bk. 3). (Illus.). 48p. (Orig.). (gr. 4-6). 1987. pap. text ed. 12.50 (ISBN 0-9600792-3-8). Rymer Bks.
Stars of the American Ballet Theatre in Performance Photographs. Fred Fehl. 144p. 1984. pap. 8.95 (ISBN 0-486-24755-4). Dover.
Stars of the American Musical Theater in Historic Photographs. Ed. by Stanley Applebaum & James Camner. 1983. 16.50 (ISBN 0-8446-5933-9). Peter Smith.
Stars of the American Musical Theater in Historic Photographs: 361 Portraits from the 1860s to 1950. Stanley Appelbaum & James Camner. (Illus.). 176p. 1981. pap. 9.95 (ISBN 0-486-24209-9). Dover.

Stars of the Ballet & Dance in Performance Photographs. Fred Fehl. (Illus.). 144p. (Orig.). (gr. 6 up). 1983. pap. 9.95 (ISBN 0-486-24492-X). Dover.
Stars of the Broadway Stage, 1940-1970. Fred Fehl. (Illus.). 144p. (Orig.). pap. 8.95 (ISBN 0-486-24398-2). Dover.
Stars of the Contemporary Ballet: 106 Full-Page Photographs. Daniel S. Sorine. (Performing Arts: Drama, Film & Dance Ser.). 112p. (Orig.). 1984. pap. 6.95 (ISBN 0-486-24568-3). Dover.
Stars of the Major Leagues. Dave Klein. LC 73-18739. (Illus.). 160p. (YA) (gr. 7-12). 1974. lib. bdg. 3.69 (ISBN 0-394-92762-1, BYR). Random.
Stars of the Opera, 1950-1985, in Photographs. Ed. by James Camner. 128p. 1986. pap. 9.95 (ISBN 0-486-25240-X). Dover.
Stars of the Screen 1931. Cedric O. Bermingham. 1976. lib. bdg. 75.00 (ISBN 0-8490-3065-X). Gordon Pr.
Stars of the Silents. Edward Wagenknecht. LC 87-4508. (Filmmakers Ser.: No. 19). (Illus.). 180p. 1987. 20.00 (ISBN 0-8108-1992-9). Scarecrow.
Stars of the Twilight. Mada Scott. LC 84-51156. 161p. 1984. pap. 4.95 (ISBN 0-931117-00-3). Univ Pub.
Stars Over Hawaii. Edwin H. Bryan, Jr. (Illus.). 1977. pap. 5.95 (ISBN 0-912180-30-7). Petroglyph.
Stars over Texas. rev. ed. Carolyn Adams. (Illus.). 128p. (gr. 1-6). 1983. 8.95 (ISBN 0-89015-411-2). Eakin Pr.
Stars, Planets & Galaxies. Sune Engelbrekston. (Knowledge Through Color Ser.: No. 54). 160p. 1975. pap. 4.95 (ISBN 0-553-26441-9). Bantam.
Stars: Poems. C. G. Hanzlicek. LC 77-270. (Breakthrough Bks). 80p. 1977. 6.95 (ISBN 0-8262-0226-8). U of Mo Pr.
Stars Principal. J. D. McClatchy. 80p. 1986. 16.95 (ISBN 0-02-582960-2, Collier); pap. 9.95 (ISBN 0-02-070030-X, Collier). Macmillan.
Stars Speak: Astronomy in the Bible. Stewart Custer. (Illus.). 203p. (Orig.). 1977. pap. 7.34 (ISBN 0-89084-059-8). Bob Jones Univ Pr.
Stars, Spells, Secrets & Sorcery. Barbara Haislip. 288p. (YA) (gr. 9 up). 1978. pap. 1.75 (ISBN 0-440-98454-8, LFL). Dell.
Stars, Spells, Secrets & Sorcery: A Do It Yourself Guide to the Occult. Barbara Haislip. (Illus.). 320p. (gr. 5 up). 1976. 14.95 (ISBN 0-316-33820-6). Little.
Stars, States & Historic Dates: Activities, Research & Readings in American History. Hilda K. Weisburg & Ruth Toor. 1987. 12.95 (ISBN 0-931315-03-4). Lib Learn Res.
Stars: Their Structure & Evolution. Rev. ed. R. J. Tayler. (Wykeham Science Ser.: No. 10). 220p. 1981. pap. cancelled (ISBN 0-85109-110-5). Taylor & Francis.
Stars: Their Structure & Evolution. R. J. Tayler & A. S. Everest. (Wykeham Science Ser.: No. 10). 220p. 1974. Repr. 18.00x (ISBN 0-8448-1112-2, Pub. by Crane Russak & Co). Taylor & Francis.
Stars Through the Mist, Winter of Change & Three for a Wedding. Betty Neels. (Harlequin Romances Ser.: 3 Vols. in 1). 576p. 1983. pap. 3.95 (ISBN 0-373-20073-0). Harlequin Bks.
Stars Unite. (Zodiac Club Ser.). 1984. pap. 1.95 (ISBN 0-399-21106-3). Putnam Pub Group.
Stars Upstream: Life Along an Ozark River. Leonard Hall. LC 59-5772. (Illus.). 272p. 1983. pap. 9.95 (ISBN 0-8262-0074-5). U of Mo Pr.
Stars Were Ours: Essays on Science Fiction Publishing from Paperback Quarterly. R. Reginald & Billy C. Lee. (Starmont Popular Culture Studies: No. 4). 96p. Date not set. lib. bdg. 19.95x (ISBN 0-89370-997-2). Borgo Pr.
Stars Were Ours: The Best from Paperback Quarterly I. Ed. by R. Reginald & Billy Lee. (Starmont Popular Culture Studies: No. 4). (Illus., Orig.). 1988. 19.95x (ISBN 0-930261-83-6); pap. text ed. 9.95x (ISBN 0-930261-82-8). Starmont Hse.
Stars Which See: Stars Which Do Not See. Marvin Bell. LC 76-39922. 1977. pap. 4.95 (ISBN 0-689-10779-X). Atheneum.
Stars Will Speak. George Zebrowski. LC 85-42638. 224p. (YA) (gr. 7 up). 1985. 11.70i (ISBN 0-06-026886-7); PLB 11.89g (ISBN 0-06-026887-5). HarpJ.
Stars Will Speak. George Zebrowski. LC 85-42638. 224p. (YA) (gr. 7 up). 1987. pap. 2.95 (ISBN 0-694-05618-9, Starwanderer). HarpJ.
Starsailing: Solar Sails & Interstellar Space Travel. Louis Friedman. LC 87-14229. (Illus.). 144p. 1988. pap. 9.95 (ISBN 0-471-62593-0). Wiley.
Starship. Poul Anderson. 2.95 (ISBN 0-8125-3061-6, Dist. by Warner Pub Services & Saint Martin's Press). Tor Bks.
Starship & the Canoe. Kenneth Brower. LC 82-48519. 256p. 1983. pap. 7.95 (ISBN 0-06-091030-5, CN 1030, PL). Har-Row.
Starship Death. Randall Garrett. 240p. 1982. pap. 2.50 (ISBN 0-8439-1074-7, Leisure Bks). Leisure NY.
Starship Troopers. Robert A. Heinlein. 1987. pap. 3.95 (ISBN 0-441-78358-9, Pub. by Ace Science Fiction). Ace Bks.
Starship Warrior see Sugarcane Island.
Starships: Stories Beyond the Boundaries of the Universe. Ed. by Isaac Asimov et al. 352p. (Orig.). 1983. pap. 3.50 (ISBN 0-449-20126-0, Crest). Fawcett.
Starsilk. Sydney J. Van Scyoc. 256p. 1984. pap. 2.95 (ISBN 0-425-08077-3). Berkley Pub.
Starsilk. Sydney J. Van Scyoc. 1987. pap. 5.95 (ISBN 0-425-07207-X). Berkley Pub.
Starskimmer. John G. Betancourt. LC 85-50155. (Amazing Stories Ser.: Bk. 5). 222p. (Orig.). 1986. pap. 2.95 (ISBN 0-88038-262-7). TSR Inc.
Starslammers. Walt Simonson. (Marvel Graphic Novel Ser.: No. 6). 5.95 (ISBN 0-939766-21-3). Marvel Comics.
Starsong. Dan Parkinson. LC 87-51261. (Illus.). 352p. (Orig.). 1988. pap. 3.95. TSR Inc.
StarSpeak: Hollywood on Everything. Doug McClelland. LC 86-29877. (Illus.). 225p. (Orig.). 1987. pap. 14.95 (ISBN 0-571-12981-1). Faber & Faber.
Starspinner. Dale Aycock. 240p. 1981. pap. 2.25 (ISBN 0-8439-0973-0, Leisure Bks). Leisure NY.
Starstruck. Cynthia Blair. (gr. 6 up). 1987. pap. 2.50 (ISBN 0-317-57100-1, Juniper). Fawcett.
Starstruck. Marisa Gioffre. 144p. (Orig.). (gr. 5-8). 1985. pap. 2.25 (ISBN 0-590-33797-1, Apple Paperbacks). Scholastic Inc.
Starstruck. Elaine Lee & M. W. Kaluta. (Marvel Graphic Novel Ser.: No. 13). 6.95 (ISBN 0-87135-001-7). Marvel Comics.
Starswarmer. Gregory Benford. 320p. 1988. 17.95 (ISBN 0-553-05322-1). Bantam.
Start Again, Britain. Charles Villiers. (Illus.). 280p. 1985. 22.95 (ISBN 0-7043-2480-6, Pub. by Quartet Bks). Salem Hse Pubs.
Start & Run a Profitable Beauty Salon: A Complete Step-by-Step Business Plan. Paul Poque. 158p. (Orig.). 1983. pap. 14.95 (ISBN 0-88908-568-4, 9521). ISC Pr.
Start & Run a Profitable Consulting Business: A Step-by-Step Business Plan. Douglas Gray. 232p. 1987. pap. 12.95 (ISBN 0-88908-648-6). ISC Pr.
Start & Run a Profitable Consulting Business. Douglas Gray. pap. 12.95 (ISBN 0-88908-598-6, 9532). TAB Bks.
Start & Run a Profitable Craft Business. William G. Hynes. 154p. (Orig.). 1984. pap. 10.95 (ISBN 0-88908-579-X, 9526). TAB Bks.
Start & Run a Profitable Craft Business. William G. Hynes. 106p. 1987. pap. 10.95 (ISBN 0-88908-644-3). ISC Pr.
Start & Run a Profitable Home Typing Business. Barbara Aliaga. 94p. 1984. pap. 9.95 (ISBN 0-88908-585-4). ISC Pr.
Start & Run a Profitable Restaurant: A Complete Step-by-Step Business Plan. Michael M. Coltman. (Illus.). 168p. (Orig.). 1983. pap. 10.95 (ISBN 0-88908-567-6, 9523). ISC Pr.
Start & Run a Profitable Retail Business: A Complete Step-by-Step Business Plan. Michael M. Coltman. 160p. (Orig.). 1983. pap. 11.95 (ISBN 0-88908-570-6, 9520). ISC Pr.
Start & Run a Profitable Video Stores: A Complete Step-by-Step Business Plan. Stan Loh. 168p. (Orig.). 1983. pap. 10.95 (ISBN 0-88908-571-4, 9522). ISC Pr.
Start at the Piano. Ernest Lubin. LC 78-110975. (Orig.). (gr. 5-8). 1977. pap. 8.95 (ISBN 0-8256-2636-6, Amsco Music). Music Sales.
Start at the Top. Burton Morgan. (Illus.). 136p. 1986. 16.95 (ISBN 0-9609734-6-X). Worthprinting.
Start at the Top. Burton D. Morgan. (Illus.). 131p. 1982. 14.95 (ISBN 0-9609310-0-7). Ohio-Summit Pub.
Start Bridge the Easy Way. Hugh Kelsey. (Master Bridge Ser.). 96p. 1983. pap. 7.95 (ISBN 0-575-03254-5, Pub. by Gollancz England). David & Charles.
Start Collecting Fossils. (Start Collecting Ser.). (Illus.). 128p. (Orig.). 1988. pap. 8.95 (ISBN 0-89471-671-9). Running Pr.
Start Collecting Stamps. Ed. by Running Press Staff. (Start Collecting Ser.). (Illus.). 128p. (Orig.). 1988. pap. 8.95 (ISBN 0-89471-670-0). Running Pr.
Start Digging! Dan Herr. 1987. 9.95 (ISBN 0-88347-204-X). Thomas More.
Start Dressmaking. Ann Ladbury. (Illus.). 120p. 1987. 18.95 (ISBN 0-85219-683-0, Pub. by Batsford England). David & Charles.
Start Early for an Early Start: You & the Young Child. Ed. by Ferne Johnson. LC 76-44237. pap. 47.80 (ISBN 0-317-26575-X, 2023956). Bks Demand UMI.
Start English for Science. G. D. Nogas & A. R. Bolitho. 29p. (Orig.). 1982. pap. text ed. 6.95 (ISBN 0-582-74819-4); tchrs. ed. 4.50 (ISBN 0-582-74820-8). Longman.
Start in Life. Florence Dyer. 1985. 5.00x (ISBN 0-9506431-1-4, Pub. by Dyllansow & Truran). State Mutual Bk.
Start Living Every Day of Your Life: How to Use the Science of Mind. Margaret R. Stortz. 96p. 1981. pap. 4.50 (ISBN 0-911336-87-7). Sci of Mind.
Start Me Up: The Music Biz Meets the Personal Computer. Rod Firestone & Benjamin Krepack. (Illus.). 190p. (Orig.). 1986. pap. 12.95 (ISBN 0-9616446-0-5). Mediac Pr.
Start of International Development Cooperation in the United States 1945-1952. Jaap Van Soest. 232p. 1978. pap. text ed. 15.00 (ISBN 90-232-1589-3, Pub. by Van Gorcum Holland). Longwood Pub Group.
Start of the Trail. Louise D. Rich. 16.95 (ISBN 0-89190-726-2, Pub. by Am Repr). Amereon Ltd.
Start Over. Bill Berkson. (Desert Island Chapbook Ser.). 32p. 1983. pap. 3.50 (ISBN 0-939180-24-3). Tombouctou.
Start Reading for Adults. M. C. Vincent. (Reading for Adults Ser.). (Illus.). 96p. (Orig.). 1984. pap. text ed. 7.95 (ISBN 0-582-52637-X). Longman.
Start Right with Goldfish. Robert Gannon. (Orig.). pap. 2.95 (ISBN 0-87666-081-2, M-504). TFH Pubns.
Start Right with Tropical Fish. (Illus.). pap. 2.95 (ISBN 0-87666-160-6, M-510). TFH Pubns.
Start Supervising. 3rd ed. Ed. by Howard F. Shout. 160p. 1984. pap. 17.00 (ISBN 0-87179-441-1, 0441). BNA.
Start the Fire. Lee Roberson. 385p. 1986. pap. 7.95 (ISBN 0-931117-04-6). Univ Pub.
Start to Navigate. Conrad Dixon. (Illus.). 120p. 1977. 9.95x (ISBN 0-8464-1139-3). Beekman Pubs.
Start to Navigate. 2nd ed. Conrad Dixon. (Illus.). 128p. (Orig.). 1983. pap. 9.95 (ISBN 0-229-11706-6, Pub. by Adlard Coles). Sheridan.
Start to Read. Lillian Lieberman et al. (TAB & LIL Reading Ser.). 64p. (gr. k-2). 1986. 6.95. Monday Morning Bks.
Start to Win. 2nd ed. Eric Twiname. Ed. by Gerald Sambrooke-Sturgess. (Illus.). 220p. 1983. 24.95 (ISBN 0-229-11688-4, Pub. by Adlard Coles). Sheridan.
Start Trek: The Romulan Way, No. 35. Diane Duane & Peter Morwood. 1987. pap. 3.50 (ISBN 0-317-62587-X). PB.
Start Up - Survival Success of Your Small Business, Vols. I & II. Max Fallek. 1986. looseleaf 3-ring binder 135.00 (ISBN 0-939069-16-4). Amer Inst Small Bus.
Start-up & Shutdown Procedures: Subcritical Units. Center for Occupational Research & Development Staff. (EUTEC Power Plant Operator Curriculum Ser.). (Illus.). 32p. 1985. pap. text ed. write for info. (ISBN 1-55502-253-7). Ctr Res & Dev.
Start-up & Shutdown Procedures: Supercritical Units. Center for Occupational Research & Development Staff. (EUTEC Power Plant Operator Curriculum Ser.). (Illus.). 28p. 1985. pap. text ed. write for info. (ISBN 1-55502-254-5). Ctr Res & Dev.
Start-Up Companies: Planning, Financing, & Operating the Successful Business. Ed. by Richard Harroch. 1200p. looseleaf 80.00 (ISBN 0-318-20273-5, 00592). NY Law Pub.
Start Up Companies: Planning, Financing & Organizing the Successful Business. Richard D. Harroch. 1200p. 1985. 80.00 (ISBN 0-318-12055-0). NY Law Pub.
Start-up Entrepreneur: How You Can Succeed in Building Your Own Company into a Major Enterprise Starting from Scratch. James R. Cook. LC 86-45650. 320p. 1987. pap. 9.95 (ISBN 0-06-097070-7, PL 7070, PL). Har-Row.
Start-Up Money: How to Finance Your New Small Business. 2nd, rev. ed. Michael McKeever. LC 84-61578. (Illus.). 220p. 1986. pap. 12.95 (ISBN 0-87337-023-6). Nolo Pr.
Start-Up Telemarketing: How to Launch a Profitable Sales Operation. Stanley Fidel. (Business Strategy Ser.). 287p. 1987. 24.95 (ISBN 0-471-01064-2); pap. 12.95 (ISBN 0-471-62945-6). Wiley.
Start with a Hull. Loris Goring. (Illus.). 223p. 1986. 39.95 (ISBN 0-7153-8744-8). David & Charles.
Start with a Number. (Let's Draw Ser.). (Illus.). 24p. (gr. k up). 1988. pap. 2.95 (ISBN 0-8249-8201-0). Ideals.
Start with Listening. Pat Dunkel & Christine Gorder. 256p. 1987. pap. text ed. 10.50 (ISBN 0-06-632132-8); tapescript & cassettes avail. Newbury Hse.
Start with the Sun: Studies in the Whitman Traditon. James E. Miller, Jr. et al. LC 60-5493. viii, 261p. 1963. pap. 5.50x (ISBN 0-8032-5135-1, BB 165, Bison). U of Nebr Pr.
Start Writing. Franklin I. Bacheller. (Illus.). 144p. 1988. pap. text ed. price not set (ISBN 0-13-843012-8). P-H.
Start Your Engines: Racing the Championship Trail. Jay Denan. LC 79-64702. (Illus.). 32p. (gr. 4-9). 1980. PLB 9.79 (ISBN 0-89375-260-6); pap. 2.50 (ISBN 0-89375-261-4). Troll Assocs.
Start Your Own At-Home Child Care Business. Patricia Gallagher. 1989. 18.95 (ISBN 0-385-24896-2); pap. 7.95 (ISBN 0-385-24582-3). Doubleday.
Start Your Own Bed & Breakast Business: Earn Extra Cash from Your Extra Room. Date not set. pap. 5.95 (ISBN 0-671-60037-0). PB.
Start Your Own Construction & Land Development Business. Adam Starchild. LC 83-2366. 232p. 1983. lib. bdg. 23.95x (ISBN 0-8304-1013-9). Nelson-Hall.
Start Your Own Private School-Legally, 2 vols. Dorie A. Erickson. LC 80-51385. 65p. (Orig.). 1980. pap. 11.95x set (ISBN 0-937242-00-4). Scandia Pubs.
Start-Your-Own Sticker Club Kit. Pat Brigandi. (Illus.). 24p. (gr. k up). 1987. pap. 3.95 (ISBN 0-590-40551-9). Scholastic Inc.
Start Your Own Store: Managing, Merchandising & Evaluating. Sidney Packard & Alan J. Carron. (Illus.). 272p. 1982. text ed. 29.00 (ISBN 0-13-842948-0). P-H.
Starter Blueprint Workbook for Pre-Job Training. Ed. by Joseph R. Todd. 104p. (Orig.). 1981. pap. 8.95 (ISBN 0-910399-31-X). Natl Tool & Mach.
Starter Kit. 30p. 8.50 (ISBN 0-317-40066-5). Cable TV Info Ctr.
Starter Math for Pre-job Training. Ed. by Joseph R. Todd. 114p. (Orig.). 1981. pap. 8.95 (ISBN 0-910399-29-8). Natl Tool & Mach.
Starter One Hundred One, Bk. 8. Ruth A. O'Keefe. Ed. by AEVAC, Inc. (Structured Beginning Reading Program). 96p. wkbk. 3.50 (ISBN 0-913356-14-X). AEVAC.
Starter Series: Instructor's Guide & Answer Book. 67p. (Orig.). 1981. pap. 9.95 (ISBN 0-910399-32-8). Natl Tool & Mach.
Starter Shop Practics for Pre-job Training. Ed. by Joseph R. Todd. 112p. (Orig.). 1981. pap. 8.95 (ISBN 0-910399-30-1). Natl Tool & Mach.
Starter Tennis. rev. ed. 1985. 5.00 (ISBN 0-938822-67-5). USTA-CERT.
Starters. Terence C. Stygall. 1982. 15.00x (ISBN 0-86319-011-1, Pub. by New Playwrights Network). State Mutual BK.
Startide Rising. David Brin. 352p. 1983. pap. 4.50 (ISBN 0-553-25603-3). Bantam.
Startide Rising. David Brin. 18.00 (ISBN 0-932096-38-7). Phantasia Pr.
Starting a Business After Fifty. rev. ed. Samuel Small. LC 74-6251. 46p. 1977. pap. 2.50 (ISBN 0-87576-008-2). Pilot Bks.
Starting a Business in Pittsburgh. Neil F. Fogarty. (Orig.). 1988. pap. 7.95 (ISBN 0-929260-01-5). Cricklewood Pr.
Starting a Business Kit. Allan Smith. 90p. 1988. write for info. (ISBN 0-931113-20-2). Success Publ.
Starting a Business to Sell Your Artwork. Business of Your Own Staff. 240p. 1988. 59.95 (ISBN 0-943267-11-0). Busn Your Own.
Starting a Business to Sell Your Craft Items. Business of Your Own Staff. 230p. 1988. 59.95 (ISBN 0-943267-08-0). Busn Your Own.
Starting a Clothing Boutique. Business of Your Own Staff. 230p. 1988. 59.95 (ISBN 0-943267-07-2). Busn Your Own.
Starting a Day Care Center. Business of Your Own Staff. 240p. 1988. 59.95 (ISBN 0-943267-06-4). Busn Your Own.
Starting a Flower Shop. Business of Your Own Staff. 240p. 1988. 59.95 (ISBN 0-943267-05-6). Busn Your Own.
Starting a Franchise. Business of Your Own Staff. 240p. 1988. 59.95 (ISBN 0-943267-09-9). Busn Your Own.
Starting a Gift Shop. Business of Your Own Staff. 240p. 1988. 59.95 (ISBN 0-943267-01-3). Busn Your Own.
Starting a Hitech Company & Securing Multi-Round Financing. LC 87-83137. 985.00 (ISBN 0-914405-24-1, 2188). Electronic Trend.
Starting a Home Based Business. Business of Your Own Staff. 240p. 1988. 59.95 (ISBN 0-943267-03-X). Busn Your Own.
Starting a Job. Richard H. Turner. (Follet Success Skills Ser.). 64p. pap. 3.75 (ISBN 0-8428-2273-9). Cambridge Bk.
Starting a Mail Order Business. Business of Your Own Staff. 240p. 1988. 59.95 (ISBN 0-943267-10-2). Busn Your Own.
Starting a Marine Aquarium. Craig Barker. 1972. 4.95 (ISBN 0-87666-751-5, PS-305). TFH Pubns.
Starting a Mini-Business: A Guidebook for Seniors. rev. ed. Nancy Olsen. Orig. Title: Starting a Mini-Business: A Guidebook for Seniors & Others Who Dream of Having Their Own Part-Time, Home-Based Business. (Illus.). 144p. 1988. pap. 8.95 (ISBN 0-933271-02-6). Fair Oaks CA.
Starting a Mini-Business: A Guidebook for Seniors & Others Who Dream of Having Their Own Part-Time, Home-Based Business see Starting a Mini-Business: A Guidebook for Seniors.
Starting a New Job. John J. McHugh, Jr. LC 81-7819. (Practical Job Skills Ser.). (gr. 9-12). 1982. pap. text ed. 3.95 (ISBN 0-88436-789-4, 25255); wkbk. 3.75 (ISBN 0-88436-790-8, 25655). EMC.
Starting a Public Relations Firm. Ed. by Ruth Q. Smith. 240p. 1988. 59.95 (ISBN 0-943267-04-8). Busn Your Own.
Starting a Secretarial Service. Business of Your Own Staff. Ed. by Emily Miller. 230p. 1988. 59.95 (ISBN 0-943267-12-9). Busn Your Own.
Starting a Self Sufficiency Library: A Workbook. Center for Self-Sufficiency, Research Division Staff. 25p. 1983. pap. text ed. 7.95 (ISBN 0-910811-32-6, Pub. by Center Self Suff). Prosperity & Profits.
Starting a Small Business. Charles L. Martin. Ed. by Michael G. Crisp. LC 87-73184. (Fifty-Minute Ser.). (Illus.). 96p. (Orig.). 1988. pap. 7.95 (ISBN 0-931961-44-0). Crisp Pubns.
Starting a Small Business. Woodrow Smith. 152p. 1984. pap. text ed. 13.95 (ISBN 0-8403-3369-2). Kendall-Hunt.
Starting a Small Business: A Simulation Game. Shiv K. Gupta & Ray T. Hamman. (Illus.). 64p. 1974. P-H.

Starting a Small Restaurant: A Guide to Excellence in the Purveying of Public Victuals. 2nd, Rev. ed. Daniel Miller. LC 83-6188. 224p. (Orig.). 1983. 13.95 (ISBN 0-916782-38-7); pap. 9.95 (ISBN 0-916782-37-9). Harvard Common Pr.

Starting a Successful Business in Canada. 9th ed. Jack D. James. 192p. 1987. 12.95 (ISBN 0-88908-640-0). ISC Pr.

Starting a Successul Business on the West Coast. 2nd ed. Douglas L. Clark. 194p. 1987. pap. 12.95 (ISBN 0-88908-921-3). ISC Pr.

Starting a Youth Ministry. Larry Keefauver. LC 84-80321. 80p. (Orig.). 1984. pap. 5.95 (ISBN 0-936664-19-3). Group Bks.

Starting an Antique Shop. Business of Your Own Staff. 240p. 1988. 59.95 (ISBN 0-943267-02-1). Busn Your Own.

Starting an Unemployment Benefits Clinic: A How to Guide. 15.00. Natl Lawyers Guild.

Starting & Building Your Own Accounting Business. Jack Fox. LC 84-7336. (National Association of Accounts Ser.: 1-700). 257p. 1984. text ed. 42.50x (ISBN 0-471-80053-8). Wiley.

Starting & Managing a Business from Your Home. Lynne Wayman. (Starting & Managing Ser.: Vol. 2). 54p. 1986. pap. 2.00 (S/N 045-000-00232-2). USGPO.

Starting & Managing a Small Business of Your Own. 4th ed. Wendell O. Metcalf. 84p. 1982. pap. 4.75 (ISBN 0-318-11832-7, S/N 045-000-00212-8). USGPO.

Starting & Managing a Small Business of Your Own. 1984. lib. bdg. 79.95 (ISBN 0-87700-528-1). Revisionist Pr.

Starting & Managing a Small Service Business, Vol. 101. Robert A. Schaefer. (Starting & Managing Ser.). 63p. 1986. pap. 2.00 (ISBN 0-318-21664-7, S/N 045-000-00238-1). USGPO.

Starting & Managing the Small Business. Arthur H. Kuriloff & John M. Hemphill, Jr. (Illus.). 608p. 1983. text ed. 34.95 (ISBN 0-07-035662-9). McGraw.

Starting & Managing the Small Business. 2nd ed. Arthur H. Kuriloff & John M. Hemphill. 688p. 1987. text ed. 33.95 (ISBN 0-07-035665-3). McGraw.

Starting & Managing Your Practice: A Guide Book for Physicians. Center for Research in Ambulatory Health Care Administration Staff & James G. Lawson. LC 82-2253. 288p. 1983. text ed. 30.00 (ISBN 0-89946-091-7). Oelgeschlager.

Starting & Operating a Business in Alaska. Michael D. Jenkins & General Business Services (GBS) (Successful Business Library). 275p. 1988. (3-ring binder) 29.95 (ISBN 1-55571-026-3, Oasis). PSI Res.

Starting & Operating a Business in Alabama. Young, Arthur & Co. Staff & Michael D. Jenkins. (Successful Business Library). 275p. 1986. 3-ring binder 29.95 (ISBN 0-916378-75-6, Oasis). PSI Res.

Starting & Operating a Business in Arizona. Young, Arthur & Co. Staff & Michael D. Jenkins. (Successful Business Library). 275p. 1986. 3-ring binder 29.95 (ISBN 0-916378-76-4, Oasis). PSI Res.

Starting & Operating a Business in Arkansas. Young, Arthur & Co. Staff & Michael D. Jenkins. (Successful Business Library). 275p. 1986. 3-ring binder 29.95 (ISBN 0-916378-35-7, Oasis). PSI Res.

Starting & Operating a Business in California. 7th ed. Michael D. Jenkins. (Successful Business Library). 300p. 1986. 3-ring binder 29.95 (ISBN 1-55571-001-8, Oasis). PSI Res.

Starting & Operating a Business in Colorado. Michael D. Jenkins et al. (Successful Business Library). 278p. 1986. 3-ring binder 29.95 (ISBN 0-916378-52-7, Oasis). PSI Res.

Starting & Operating a Business in Connecticut. Young, Arthur & Co. Staff & Michael D. Jenkins. (Successful Business Library). 275p. 1986. 3-ring binder 29.95 (ISBN 0-916378-77-2, Oasis). PSI Res.

Starting & Operating a Business in Delaware. General Business Services Staff & Michael D. Jenkins. (Successful Business Library). 275p. 1988. 3-ring binder 29.95 (ISBN 1-55571-011-5, Oasis). PSI Res.

Starting & Operating a Business in Florida. Michael D. Jenkins & Jonathan H. Warner. (Successful Business Library Ser.). 295p. 1983. 3-ring binder 29.95 (ISBN 0-916378-25-X, Oasis). PSI Res.

Starting & Operating a Business in Georgia. Michael D. Jenkins et al. (Successful Business Library). 250p. 1985. 3-ring binder 29.95 (ISBN 0-916378-37-3, Oasis). PSI Res.

Starting & Operating a Business in Hawaii. Michael D. Jenkins. (Successful Business Library). 275p. 1988. 3 ring binder 29.95 (ISBN 1-55571-019-0, Oasis). Psi Res.

Starting & Operating a Business in Idaho. Michael D. Jenkins & General Business Services (GBS) (Successful Business Library). 275p. 1988. 29.95 (ISBN 1-55571-027-1, Oasis). PSI Res.

Starting & Operating a Business in Illinois. Young, Arthur & Co. Staff & Michael D. Jenkins. (Successful Business Library). 290p. 1985. 3-ring binder 29.95 (ISBN 0-916378-38-1, Oasis). PSI Res.

Starting & Operating a Business in Illinois. 2nd ed. Young, Arthur, & Co. Staff & Michael D. Jenkins. (Successful Business Library). 275p. 1988. 29.95 (ISBN 1-55571-024-7); 3-ring binder 29.95 (ISBN 1-55571-044-1). PSI Res.

Starting & Operating a Business in Indiana. Young, Arthur & Co. Staff & Michael D. Jenkins. (Successful Business Library). 290p. 1985. 3-ring binder 29.95 (ISBN 0-916378-39-X, Oasis). PSI Res.

Starting & Operating a Business in Iowa. Young, Arthur & Co. Staff & Michael D. Jenkins. (Successful Business Library). 275p. 1987. 3-ring binder 29.95 (ISBN 0-916378-78-0, Oasis). PSI Res.

Starting & Operating a Business in Japan. Helene Thian. 1988. pap. 12.95 (ISBN 0-8048-1544-5). C E Tuttle.

Starting & Operating a Business in Kansas. Michael D. Jenkins & David L. Dahl. (Successful Business Library). 200p. 1983. 29.95 (ISBN 0-916378-31-4, Oasis). PSI Res.

Starting & Operating a Business in Kentucky. Young, Arthur & Co. Staff & Michael D. Jenkins. (Successful Business Library). 275p. 1987. 3-ring binder 29.95 (ISBN 0-916378-79-9, Oasis). PSI Res.

Starting & Operating a Business in Louisiana. Michael D. Jenkins & David J. Ramm. (Successful Business Library). 250p. 1985. 3-ring binder 29.95 (ISBN 0-916378-56-X, Oasis). PSI Res.

Starting & Operating a Business in Maryland. Young, Arthur & Co. Staff & Michael D. Jenkins. (Successful Business Library). 275p. 1986. 3-ring binder 29.95 (ISBN 0-916378-80-2, Oasis). PSI Res.

Starting & Operating a Business in Michigan. Young, Arthur & Co. Staff & Michael D. Jenkins. (Successful Business Library). 275p. 1986. 3-ring binder 29.95 (ISBN 0-916378-65-9, Oasis). PSI Res.

Starting & Operating a Business in Minnesota. Michael D. Jenkins et al. (Successful Business Library). 275p. 1987. 3-ring binder 29.95 (ISBN 0-916378-70-5, Oasis). PSI Res.

Starting & Operating a Business in Mississippi. Michael D. Jenkins & General Business Services (GBS) (Successful Business Library). 275p. 1988. (3-ring binder) 29.95 (ISBN 1-55571-025-5, Oasis). PSI Res.

Starting & Operating a Business in Missouri. Michael D. Jenkins & Rodney V. Hipp. (Successful Business Library). 250p. 1986. 3-ring binder 29.95 (ISBN 0-916378-36-5, Oasis). PSI Res.

Starting & Operating a Business in Montana. Michael D. Jenkins & General Business Services (GBS) (Successful Business Library). 275p. 1989. (3-ring binder) 29.95 (ISBN 1-55571-028-X, Oasis). PSI Res.

Starting & Operating a Business in Nebraska. Michael D. Jenkins & Franklin Forbes. Ed. by Rosanno Alejandro. (Successful Business Library). 275p. 1988. three-ring binder 29.95 (ISBN 1-55571-023-9, Oasis). PSI Res.

Starting & Operating a Business in Nevada. Young, Arthur & Co. Staff et al. (Successful Business Library). 275p. 1987. 3-ring binder 29.95 (ISBN 0-916378-81-0, Oasis). PSI Res.

Starting & Operating a Business in New Mexico. Michael D. Jenkins. (Successful Business Library). 275p. 1988. 3-ring binder 29.95 (ISBN 0-916378-73-X, Oasis). PSI Res.

Starting & Operating a Business in New York. Young, Arthur & Co. Staff & Michael D. Jenkins. (Successful Business Library). 275p. 1985. 3-ring binder 29.95 (ISBN 0-916378-62-4, Oasis). PSI Res.

Starting & Operating a Business in New Jersey. Young, Arthur & Co. Staff & Michael D. Jenkins. (Successful Business Library). 275p. 1985. 3-ring binder 29.95 (ISBN 0-916378-61-6, Oasis). PSI Res.

Starting & Operating a Business in North Dakota. Michael D. Jenkins & General Business Services (GBS) (Successful Business Library). 275p. 1989. (3-ring binder) 29.95 (ISBN 1-55571-029-8, Oasis). PSI Res.

Starting & Operating a Business in Ohio. Young, Arthur & Co. Staff & Michael D. Jenkins. (Successful Business Library). 275p. 1985. 3-ring binder 29.95 (ISBN 0-916378-64-0, Oasis). PSI Res.

Starting & Operating a Business in Oklahoma. Young, Arthur & Co. Staff & Michael D. Jenkins. (Successful Business Library). 275p. 1985. 3-ring binder 29.95 (ISBN 0-916378-40-3, Oasis). PSI Res.

Starting & Operating a Business in Oregon. Young, Arthur & Co. Staff & Michael D. Jenkins. (Successful Business Library Ser.). 275p. 1987. 3-ring binder 29.95 (ISBN 1-55571-013-1, Oasis). PSI Res.

Starting & Operating a Business in Pennsylvania. Young, Arthur & Co. Staff & Michael D. Jenkins. (Successful Business Library). 275p. 1985. 3-ring binder 29.95 (ISBN 0-916378-54-3, Oasis). PSI Res.

Starting & Operating a Business in South Dakota. Michael D. Jenkins & General Business Services (GBS) (Successful Business Library). 275p. 1989. (3-ring binder) 29.95 (ISBN 1-55571-030-1, Oasis). PSI Res.

Starting & Operating a Business in Tennessee. Young, Arthur & Co. Staff & Michael D. Jenkins. (Successful Business Library). 275p. 1987. 3-ring binder 29.95 (ISBN 0-916378-68-3, Oasis). PSI Res.

Starting & Operating a Business in Texas. Michael D. Jenkins & Donald L. Sexton. (Successful Business Library). 275p. 1983. 3-ring binder 29.95 (ISBN 0-916378-24-1, Oasis). PSI Res.

Starting & Operating a Business in Utah. Young, Arthur & Co. Staff & Michael D. Jenkins. (Successful Business Library). 275p. 1987. 3-ring binder 29.95 (ISBN 1-55571-003-4, Oasis). PSI Res.

Starting & Operating a Business in Virginia. Young, Arthur & Co. Staff et al. (Successful Business Library). 275p. 1986. 3-ring binder 29.95 (ISBN 0-916378-21-7, Oasis). PSI Res.

Starting & Operating a Business in Washington. Young, Arthur & Co. Staff & Michael D. Jenkins. (Successful Business Library). 275p. 1985. 3-ring binder 29.95 (ISBN 0-916378-63-2, Oasis). PSI Res.

Starting & Operating a Business in Wisconsin. Young, Arthur & Co. Staff & Michael D. Jenkins. (Successful Business Library). 275p. 1987. 3-ring binder 29.95 (ISBN 0-916378-74-8, Oasis). PSI Res.

Starting & Operating a Business in Wyoming. Michael D. Jenkins & Daniel J. Herron. Ed. by Rosemari A. Griego. (Successful Business Library). 275p. 1988. 3-ring binder 29.95 (ISBN 1-55571-016-6, Oasis). PSI Res.

Starting & Operating a Business in District of Columbia. Michael D. Jenkins & General Business Services (GBS) (Successful Business Library). 275p. 1989. (3-ring binder) 29.95 (ISBN 1-55571-031-X, Oasis). PSI Res.

Starting & Operating a Business in Massachusetts. Young, Arthur & Co. Staff & Michael D. Jenkins. (Successful Business Library). 275p. 1985. 3-ring binder 29.95 (ISBN 0-916378-59-4, Oasis). PSI Res.

Starting & Operating a Business in North Carolina. Young, Arthur & Co. Staff & Michael D. Jenkins. (Successful Business Library). 275p. 1987. 3-ring binder 29.95 (ISBN 0-916378-66-7, Oasis). PSI Res.

Starting & Operating a Business in New Hampshire. Young, Arthur & Co. Staff & Michael D. Jenkins. (Successful Business Library). 275p. 1987. 3-ring binder 29.95 (ISBN 1-55571-012-3, Oasis). PSI Res.

Starting & Operating a Business in South Carolina. Young, Arthur & Co. Staff & Michael D. Jenkins. (Successful Business Library). 275p. 1987. 3-ring binder 29.95 (ISBN 0-916378-55-1, Oasis). PSI Res.

Starting & Operating a Business in West Virginia. Michael D. Jenkins & Steven Ferguson. (Successful Business Library). 275p. 1986. 3-ring binder 29.95 (ISBN 0-916378-72-1, Oasis). PSI RES.

Starting & Operating a Clipping Service. rev. ed. Demaris C. Smith. LC 80-10477. 54p. 1987. pap. 3.95 (ISBN 0-87576-133-X). Pilot Bks.

Starting & Operating a Microcomputer Support Center: National Bureau of Standards Special Publication 500-128. Ted Landberg & Stanley Winkler. LC 85-600595. (Computer Science & Technology Ser.). 40p. (Orig.). 1985. pap. 1.75 (ISBN 0-318-21576-4, S/N 003-003-02683-2). USGPO.

Starting & Operating a Playgroup for Profit. Susan Chidakel. LC 75-44029. 47p. 1985. pap. 3.95 (ISBN 0-87576-055-4). Pilot Bks.

Starting & Operating a Vintage Clothing Shop. Rose F. Whitis. LC 83-8170. 46p. 1983. pap. 3.50 (ISBN 0-87576-104-6). Pilot Bks.

Starting & Operating a Word Processing Service. Jean W. Murray. LC 83-2229. 32p. 1983. pap. 3.50 (ISBN 0-87576-102-X). Pilot Bks.

Starting & Operating Your Own FM Radio Station: From License Application to Program Management. Peter Hunn. (Illus.). 160p. 1988. pap. 12.95 (ISBN 0-8306-2933-5, 2933). TAB Bks.

Starting & Running a Money-Making Bar. Bruce Fier. (Illus.). 240p. 1986. pap. 14.95 (ISBN 0-8306-2661-1, 2661P). TAB Bks.

Starting & Running a Money-Making Bar. Bruce Fier. 230p. 1988. 14.95 (119). Am Bartenders.

Starting & Running a Nonprofit Organization. Joan Hummel. LC 80-15210. 160p. 1980. 20.00x (ISBN 0-8166-0986-1); pap. 11.95 (ISBN 0-8166-0989-6). U of Minn Pr.

Starting & Succeeding in Your Own Photography Business. Jeanne C. Thwaites. LC 84-2336. 343p. 1984. 19.95 (ISBN 0-89879-112-X). Writers Digest.

Starting Anew after Seventy: The Story of Ida Ella Jones, Primitive Artist. Ida J. Williams. (Illus.). 1980. 5.50 (ISBN 0-682-49544-1). Exposition-Phoenix.

Starting Blocks. Terry Raburn. (Radiant Life Ser.). 128p. 1988. pap. price not set (ISBN 0-88243-860-3, 02-0860). Gospel Pub.

Starting Bluegrass Banjo from Scratch. Wayne Erbsen. (Illus.). 80p. (Orig.). 1978. pap. 7.95 (ISBN 0-8258-0001-3, PCB 104). Fischer Inc NY.

Starting Business Operations in Germany. Harald Jung & Joachim Gres. 1984. pap. 18.00 (ISBN 90-6544-179-4, Pub. by Kluwer Law Netherlands). Kluwer Academic.

Starting Chess. Tony Gillam. 1978. pap. 9.95 (ISBN 0-7134-1478-2, Pub. by Batsford England). David & Charles.

Starting English. Joanna Gray et al. 125p. 1984. pap. text ed. 11.95 (ISBN 0-03-062992-6). HR&W.

Starting Even: An Equal-Opportunity Program to Combat the Nation's New Poverty - A Twentieth-Century Fund Report. Robert Haveman. 320p. 1988. 19.95 (ISBN 0-671-66762-9). S&S.

Starting Forth. 2nd ed. Leo Brodie et al. (Illus.). 272p. 1986. text ed. 30.00 (ISBN 0-13-843087-X). P-H.

Starting FORTH: An Introduction to the FORTH Language & Operating System for Beginners & Professionals. 2nd ed. Leo Brodie. (Illus.). 304p. 1986. pap. 23.95 (ISBN 0-13-843079-9). P-H.

Starting Fresh: How to Plan for a Simpler, Happier & More Fulfilling New Life in the Country. John F. Edwards. Ed. by Ben Dominitz. 180p. (Orig.). 1988. pap. 8.95 (ISBN 0-914629-62-X). Prima Pub Comm.

Starting from Ellis Island. Frank Higgins. LC 79-7740. 1979. 3.25 (ISBN 0-933532-01-6). BkMk.

Starting from Home: A Writer's Beginnings. Milton Meltzer. 144p. (gr. 7 up). Date not set. 13.95 (ISBN 0-670-81604-3, Viking Kestrel). Viking.

Starting from San Francisco. enl. & rev. ed. Lawrence Ferlinghetti. LC 67-23492. 1967. pap. 1.00 (ISBN 0-8112-0046-9, NDP220). New Directions.

Starting from Scratch: A Different Kind of Writer's Manual. Rita Mae Brown. 272p. 1988. 16.95 (ISBN 0-553-05246-2). Bantam.

Starting from Scratch: Our Island for Ocelots. Jeanette Travers. LC 75-37390. (Illus.). (YA) (gr. 9 up). 1976. 8.95 (ISBN 0-8008-7369-6). Taplinger.

Starting from Scratch: 500 Profitable Business Opportunities. Joe S. Gould. 320p. 1987. 19.95 (ISBN 0-471-85024-1); pap. 14.95 (ISBN 0-471-01190-8). Wiley.

Starting from Troy. Rachel Hadas. LC 74-25957. (Chapbook Series Two). 1975. 5.00 (ISBN 0-87923-119-X). Godine.

Starting From Zero. Barbara Crooker. 28p. 1987. pap. 3.50 (ISBN 0-9613465-8-2). Great Elm.

Starting in Business. Terence Lundberg. 192p. 1985. pap. 9.95 (ISBN 0-85941-295-4, Pub. by Woodhead-Faulkner). Longwood Pub Group.

Starting in Medical Pracrtice. Morton Walker & John P. Trowbridge. 192p. (Orig.). 1987. pap. 25.95 (ISBN 0-87489-473-5, 473-5). Med Economics.

Starting Life Drawing. Michael Woods. (Illus.). 96p. 1988. 22.95 (ISBN 0-85219-690-3, Pub. by Batsford England). David & Charles.

Starting, Lighting, Ignition & Generating Systems. 10th ed. 1987. 8.00. IBMA Pubns.

Starting Millionaire Success Kit. 3rd ed. Tyler G. Hicks. 361p. 1987. pap. 99.50 (ISBN 0-934311-01-3). Intl Wealth.

Starting Off: An Update of Orientation & Member Development Programs. Jan Carpenter. (State Legislative Reports: Vol. 11, No. 15). 14p. 1986. pap. 5.00 (ISBN 1-55516-171-5). Natl Conf State Legis.

Starting on a Shoestring: Building a Business Without a Bank Roll. Arnold S. Goldstein. LC 83-23379. (Small Business Management Ser.: 1-471). 286p. 1984. 12.95 (ISBN 0-471-88439-1, Ronald Pr); pap. 12.95. Wiley.

Starting on Monday: Christian Living in the Workplace. Christopher Carstens & William P. Mahedy. 176p. 1987. 11.95 (ISBN 0-345-32910-4). Ballantine.

Starting Out. Ed. by P. I. Lomakin. 191p. 1985. pap. 2.95 (ISBN 0-8285-3023-8, Pub. by Rus Lang Pubs USSR). Imported Pubns.

Starting Out: Class & Community in the Lives of Working-Class Youth. Victoria A. Steinitz & Ellen R. Solomon. 296p. 1986. 29.95 (ISBN 0-87722-430-7). Temple U Pr.

Starting Out for the Difficult World. Robert Dana. LC 87-203. 80p. 1987. 16.45i (ISBN 0-06-055094-5, HarpT). Har-Row.

Starting Out for the Difficult World. Robert Dana. LC 87-203. 80p. 1987. pap. 8.95 (ISBN 0-06-096197-X, PL6197, PL). Har-Row.

Starting Out in Stained Glass. Mount Tom Studio Artisans. LC 82-18438. (Illus.). 160p. 1983. lib. bdg. 14.95 (ISBN 0-668-05984-2); pap. 8.95 (ISBN 0-668-05577-4). Arco.

Starting Out in the Thirties. Alfred Kazin. LC 79-22491. 1980. pap. 4.95 (ISBN 0-394-74336-9, Vin). Random.

Starting Out Right: Choosng Books About Black People for Young Children. Ed. by Bettye I. Latimer. 96p. pap. 3.25 (ISBN 0-936746-07-6, W50). Day Care Coun.

Starting Out Right: Guidelines for Organizing a New Retail Cooperative. Jesse Singerman. 1986. pap. 5.00 (ISBN 0-9608298-0-6). NCBA.

Starting Out Right: Guidelines for Organizing a New Retail Cooperative. rev. ed. Jesse Singerman. 1986. pap. 5.00 (ISBN 0-317-55257-0). Blooming.

State & American Foreign Economic Policy. Ed. by G. John Ikenberry et al. LC 88-47736. (Studies in Political Economy). 256p. 1988. 29.95x (ISBN 0-8014-2229-9); pap. 9.95x (ISBN 0-8014-9524-5). Cornell U Pr.

State & Business in India: A Historical Perspective. Dwijendra Tripathi. 1987. 26.00x (ISBN 81-85054-26-6, Pub. by Manohar India). South Asia Bks.

State & Campus: State Regulation of Religiously Affiliated Higher Education. Fernand N. Dutile & Edward M. Gaffney. LC 83-27366. 526p. 1984. pap. 19.95 (ISBN 0-268-01712-3). U of Notre Dame Pr.

State & Capital: A Marxist Debate. Ed. by John Holloway & Sol Picciotto. LC 78-65361. 226p. 1979. text ed. 18.95x (ISBN 0-292-77551-2). U of Tex Pr.

State & Capital Accumulation in Latin America: Brazil, Chile, Mexico. Ed. by Christian Anglade & Carlos Fortin. LC 84-12015. (Pitt Latin American Ser.). (Illus.). 269p. 1985. 29.95x (ISBN 0-8229-1144-2). U of Pittsburgh Pr.

State & City Atlas. 352p. 1988. spiral bdg. 14.95 (ISBN 0-376-09017-0). Sunset-Lane.

State & City Guide Books, 61 vols. Federal Writers' Project Staff. (American Guidebook Ser.). Repr. of 1942 ed. Set. lib. bdg. 3598.00x (ISBN 0-403-02249-5). Somerset Pub.

State & Civil Society: Studies in Hegel's Political Philosophy. Ed. by Z. Pelczynski. LC 84-3144. 300p. 1984. 57.50 (ISBN 0-521-24793-4). Cambridge U Pr.

State & Class: A Sociology of International Affairs. Ralph Pettman. 1980. 27.50 (ISBN 0-312-75602-X). St Martin.

State & Class in Africa. Ed. by Nelson Kasfir. 132p. 1984. 29.50x (ISBN 0-7146-3239-2, BHA-03239, F Cass Co). Biblio Dist.

State & Community Governments in the Federal System. Charles Press & Kenneth VerBerg. LC 78-22064. 1979. text ed. 21.95x (ISBN 0-471-02725-1); tchrs.' manual 6.00 (ISBN 0-471-04909-3). Wiley.

State & Community Governments in the Federal System. 2nd ed. Charles Press & Kenneth VerBurg. LC 82-21864. 596p. 1983. text ed. write for info. (ISBN 0-02-396550-9); tchr's. ed. avail. (ISBN 0-02-396560-6). Macmillan.

State & Conflict in the Middle East. Gabriel Ben-Dor. 200p. 1986. text ed. 32.50x (ISBN 0-7146-3224-4, F Cass Co). Biblio Dist.

State & Cosmos in the Art of Tenochtitlan. Richard F. Townsend. LC 79-63726. (Studies in Pre-Columbian Art & Archaeology: No. 20). (Illus.). 78p. 1979. pap. 8.00x (ISBN 0-88402-083-5). Dumbarton Oaks.

State & Countryside: Development Policy & Agrarian Politics in Latin America. Merilee S. Grindle. LC 85-8081. (Studies in Development). 272p. 1986. text ed. 27.50x (ISBN 0-8018-3278-0); pap. text ed. 11.95x (ISBN 0-8018-2935-6). Johns Hopkins.

State & Culture in Medieval India. Khaliq A. Nizami. 336p. 1986. 37.50X (ISBN 0-8364-1637-6, Pub. by Adam Pubs). South Asia Bks.

State & Democracy: Revitalizing America's Government. Marc V. Levine et al. (Alternative Policies for America Ser.). 256p. 1988. text ed. 49.95 (ISBN 0-415-90045-X); pap. text ed. 17.95 (ISBN 0-415-90076-X). Routledge Chapman & Hall.

State & Development in the Third World: A World Politics Reader, 2 pts. Ed. by Atul Kohli. 288p. 1986. Part I: Conceptual Issues. text ed. 32.50x (ISBN 0-691-07699-5); Part II: Empirical Cases. pap. text ed. 8.95x (ISBN 0-691-02245-3). Princeton U Pr.

State & Development of Display Techniques. Ed. by Network Staff. 1985. 95.00x (ISBN 0-907634-22-2, Pub. by Network Events Ltd). State Mutual Bk.

State & Diplomacy in Early Modern Japan: Asia in the Development of the Tokugawa Bakufu. Ronald P. Toby. LC 83-42582. (Illus.). 309p. 1984. 35.50x (ISBN 0-691-05401-0). Princeton U Pr.

State & Diplomatic Immunity. Charles Lewis. 272p. 1985. 85.00 (ISBN 1-85044-047-6). Lloyds London Pr.

State & Economic Development: Peru Since 1968. E. V. Fitzgerald. LC 75-30443. (Department of Applied Economics, Occasional Papers Ser.: No. 49). (Illus.). 140p. 1976. pap. 13.95x o. p. (ISBN 0-521-29054-6). Cambridge U Pr.

State & Economic Distribution in Malaysia. Tan Loong-Hoe. 96p. (Orig.). 1982. pap. text ed. 7.50x (ISBN 9971-902-44-3, Pub. by Inst Southeast Asian Stud). Gower Pub Co.

State & Economic Enterprise in Japan. Ed. by William W. Lockwood. LC 65-15386. (Studies in the Modernization of Japan). Repr. of 1965 ed. 120.00 (ISBN 0-8357-9514-4, 2015225). Bks Demand UMI.

State & Economics in the Middle East. Alfred Bonne. LC 72-11325. (Illus.). 452p. 1973. Repr. of 1955 ed. lib. bdg. 38.50x (ISBN 0-8371-6661-6, BOSE). Greenwood.

State & Economy in Australia. Brian Head. (Illus.). 1983. 37.50x (ISBN 0-19-554354-8). Oxford U Pr.

State & Enterprise: Canadian Manufacturing & the Federal Government, 1917-1931. Tom Traves. (State & Economic Life Ser.). 1979. pap. 9.95c (ISBN 0-8020-6353-5). U of Toronto Pr.

State & Family in Singapore: Restructuring an Industrial Society. Janet W. Salaff. LC 87-47962. (Anthropology of Contemporary Issues Ser.). (Illus.). 320p. 1988. 37.50x (ISBN 0-8014-2140-3). Cornell U Pr.

State & Federal Corrupt-Practices Legislation. Earl R. Sikes. Repr. of 1928 ed. 12.50 (ISBN 0-404-06004-8). AMS Pr.

State & Federal Exploratory Wells & Core Holes Drilled off the West Coast of Continental U. S. A. Prior to 1974. 1975. 40.00 (ISBN 0-686-28277-9). Munger Oil.

State & Federal Government in Switzerland. John M. Vincent. LC 78-64253. (Johns Hopkins University. Studies in the Social Sciences. Extra Volumes: 9). Repr. of 1891 ed. 23.00 (ISBN 0-404-61357-8). AMS Pr.

State & Federal Grants-In-Aid. Henry J. Bittermann. Repr. of 1938 ed. 37.00 (ISBN 0-384-04511-1). Johnson Repr.

State & Federal Programs for Special Student Population. 72p. 1982. 4.00 (ISBN 0-318-18002-2, F-82-2). Ed Comm States.

State & Government Employee Unions in France. Frederic Meyers. LC 73-634398. (Comparative Studies in Public Employment Labor Relations Ser.). 1971. 10.00x (ISBN 0-87736-007-3); pap. 5.00x (ISBN 0-87736-008-1). U of Mich Inst Labor.

State & Government in Ancient India. A. S. Altekar. 1977. 15.00 (ISBN 0-89684-321-1). Orient Bk Dist.

State & Government in Medieval Islam: An Introduction to the Study of Islamic Political Theory; the Jurists. Ann K. Lambton. (London Oriental Ser.: Vol. 36). 1981. 49.95x (ISBN 0-19-713600-1). Oxford U Pr.

State & Government in the Federal Republic of Germany: The Executive at Work. N. Johnson. (Governments of Western Europe Ser.). 240p. 1983. text ed. 48.00 (ISBN 0-08-030188-6); pap. text ed. 17.75 (ISBN 0-08-030190-8). Pergamon.

State & Human Services: Organizational Change in a Political Context. Laurence E. Lynn, Jr. 1980. text ed. 27.50x (ISBN 0-262-12084-4). MIT Pr.

State & I: Hypotheses on Juridical & Technocratic Humanism. Grahame Lock. xvi, 268p. 1981. 39.00 (ISBN 90-6021-491-9, Pub. by Martinus Nijhoff Netherlands). Kluwer Academic.

State & Ideology in the Middle East & Pakistan. Ed. by Fred Halliday & Hamza Alavi. 320p. 1988. 27.00; pap. 11.00 (ISBN 0-85345-735-2). Monthly Rev.

State & Labor in Modern Japan. Sheldon Garon. LC 86-30890. 326p. 1987. 35.00x (ISBN 0-520-05983-2). U of Cal Pr.

State & Local Administration of School Transportation. Roe L. Johns. LC 76-176911. (Columbia University Teachers College. Contributions to Education Ser.: No. 330). Repr. of 1928 ed. 17.50 (ISBN 0-404-55330-3). AMS Pr.

State & Local Finance. Ed. by William E. Mitchell & Ingo Walter. LC 77-110554. pap. 95.00 (ISBN 0-317-09323-1, 2012396). Bks Demand UMI.

State & Local Finance: The Pressures of the 80's. Committee on Taxation, Resources & Economic Development & George F. Break. LC 83-47757. 1984. 25.00x (ISBN 0-299-09340-9). U of Wis Pr.

State & Local Government. Laurence Santrey. LC 84-8440. (Illus.). 32p. (gr. 3-6). 1985. PLB 8.45 (ISBN 0-8167-0270-5); pap. text ed. 1.95 (ISBN 0-8167-0271-3). Troll Assocs.

State & Local Government. 3rd ed. Murray S. Stedman. 1982. pap. text ed. write for info. (ISBN 0-673-39483-2). Scott F.

State & Local Government. 3rd ed. Bruce Stinebrickner. (Annual Editions Ser.). (Illus.). 288p. 1987. pap. text ed. 9.95 (ISBN 0-87967-686-8). Dushkin Pub.

State & Local Government Administration. Dodd Rabin. (Public Administration & Public Policy-A Comprehensive Publication Program Ser.). 544p. 1985. 39.75 (ISBN 0-8247-7355-1). Dekker.

State & Local Government Civil Rights Liability. Ivan E. Bodensteiner & Rosalie B. Levinson. 1987. Two-volume set 160.00. Callaghan.

State & Local Government Debt Financing. M. David Gelfand & Robert S. Amdursky. LC 85-25550. 1986. 140.00. Callaghan.

State & Local Government Finance & Financial Management: A Compendium of Current Research. Municipal Finance Officers Association Government Finance Research Center. LC 78-70328. 690p. 1978. 18.00 (ISBN 0-686-84363-0). Municipal.

State & Local Government Finance: A Selectively Annotated Bibliography, No. 783. Ed. by James J. Brown. 1975. 5.50 (ISBN 0-686-20351-8). CPL Biblios.

State & Local Government Finance: Institutions, Theory, Policy. Ronald C. Fisher. 1988. text ed. price not set (ISBN 0-673-18155-3). Scott F.

State & Local Government Fiscal Almanac 1982-MFOA Membership Directory. Municipal Finance Officers Association. 400p. 1982. pap. 50.00 (ISBN 0-686-84339-8); pap. 35.00 members (ISBN 0-686-84340-1). Municipal.

State & Local Government in a Federal System. 2nd ed. Daniel R. Mandelker & Dawn Clark Netsch. (Contemporary Legal Education Ser.). 871p. 1983. 30.00x (ISBN 0-87215-663-X). Michie Co.

State & Local Government in America. 5th ed. Daniel Grant & Lloyd Omdahl. 576p. 1987. write for info. (ISBN 0-205-08720-5); instr's. manual avail. (ISBN 0-697-06803-X). Wm C Brown.

State & Local Government in an Urban Society. Richard D. Bingham. 448p. 1986. text ed. write for info (ISBN 0-394-33206-7, RanC). Random.

State & Local Government in Idaho & the Nation. Sydney Duncombe & Robert Weisel. LC 84-50973. 157p. (Orig.). 1984. pap. text ed. 9.95 (ISBN 0-89301-099-5). U of Idaho Pr.

State & Local Government in New Mexico. F. Chris Garcia et al. LC 79-2189. (Illus.). 1979. pap. 8.95x (ISBN 0-8263-0511-3). U of NM Pr.

State & Local Government Political Dictionary. Jeffrey M. Elliot & Sheikh R. Ali. LC 87-18722. (Clio Dictionaries in Political Science Ser.: No. 12). 325p. 1987. lib. bdg. 37.50 (ISBN 0-87436-417-5); pap. 17.00 (ISBN 0-87436-512-0). ABC-Clio.

State & Local Government: Politics & Public Policies. 2nd ed. David C. Saffell. (Political Science Ser.). 384p. 1981. pap. text ed. write for info. (ISBN 0-201-06568-1). Addison-Wesley.

State & Local Government: Politics & Public Policies. 2nd ed. David C. Saffell. 480p. 1982. text ed. write for info (ISBN 0-394-34938-5, RanC). Random.

State & Local Government: Politics & Public Policies. 3rd ed. David C. Saffell. 304p. 1986. pap. text ed. write for info. (ISBN 0-394-35808-2, RanC). Random.

State & Local Government Procurement: Developments in Legislation & Litigation. Louis F. DelDuca & Patrick J. Falvey. LC 87-108173. 67p. Date not set. price not set (ISBN 0-89707-253-7). Amer Bar Assn.

State & Local Government Purchasing. 2nd ed. Ed. by Council of State Governments Staff. 298p. (Orig.). 1983. pap. 21.00 (ISBN 0-87292-033-X, C-3). Coun State Govts.

State & Local Government Responsibilities to Provide Medical Care for Indigents. Michael Dowell. (Illus.). 384p. (Orig.). 1985. pap. 25.00 (ISBN 0-941077-02-0, 40,275). NCLS Inc.

State & Local Government: The New Battleground. Gerald L. Houseman. (Illus.). 352p. 1986. pap. text ed. write for info. (ISBN 0-13-843368-2). P-H.

State & Local Government: The Third Century of Federalism. Richard H. Leach & Timothy G. O'Rourke. (Illus.). 400p. 1988. text ed. price not set (ISBN 0-13-843251-1). P-H.

State & Local Governmental Units. (American Institute of CPAs Audit Guides Ser.). 1986. pap. 16.50 (ISBN 0-87051-033-9). Am Inst CPA.

State & Local Industrial Policy Question. Harvey A. Goldstein. LC 86-72373. (Illus.). 300p. (Orig.). pap. 31.95 (ISBN 0-918286-46-8); lib. bdg. 45.95. Planners Pr.

State & Local Politics. 5th ed. David R. Berman. 400p. 1986. write for info. (ISBN 0-205-10459-2); Test Item File avail. (ISBN 0-697-06791-2). Wm C Brown.

State & Local Politics & Policy: Change & Reform. Michael J. Ross. (Illus.). 352p. 1987. pap. text ed. write for info. (ISBN 0-13-843384-4). P-H.

State & Local Politics: Fundamentals & Perspectives. Michael Engel. LC 84-51678. 352p. 1985. text ed. write for info. (ISBN 0-312-75615-1); instr's. manual avail. St Martin.

State & Local Politics: The Great Entanglement. 2nd ed. Robert S. Lorch. (Illus.). 464p. 1986. text ed. write for info (ISBN 0-13-843467-0). P-H.

State & Local Roles in Regulating Pit Bulls. (Policy & Practice Reports). 10p. 1986. 2.50. U OR BGR.

State & Local Tax Performance Nineteen Seventy-Eight. rev. ed. Kenneth E. Quindry & Niles Schoening. 1980. pap. 3.00 (ISBN 0-686-29037-2). S Regional Ed.

State & Local Tax Revolt: New Directions for the 80's. Dean Tipps & Lee Webb. 380p. 1980. 5.95 (ISBN 0-89788-010-2). NCPA Washington.

State & Local Tax Service. Prentice-Hall Editorial Staff. LC 41-8277. Date not set. price not set. P-H.

State & Local Taxation & Finance in a Nutshell. M. David Gelfand & Peter W. Salsich, Jr. LC 85-20283. (Nutshell Ser.). 315p. 1985. pap. text ed. 9.95 (ISBN 0-314-95571-2). West Pub.

State & Local Taxation Cases & Materials. 4th ed. Jerome R. Hellerstein & Walter Hellerstein. LC 78-2418. (American Casebook Ser.). 1041p. 1978. Includes 1982 supplement. text ed. 32.95 (ISBN 0-8299-2000-5); tchr's. manual avail. West Pub.

State & Local Taxation, Cases & Materials. 5th ed. Jerome R. Hellerstein & Walter Hellerstein. (American Casebook Ser.). 1060p. 1988. text ed. write for info. (ISBN 0-314-39782-5). West Pub.

State & Local Taxation of Natural Resources in the Federal System: Legal, Economic & Political Perspectives. LC 85-52446. 406p. 1986. 79.00 (ISBN 0-89707-216-2, 547-0088-01). Amer Bar Assn.

State & Local Taxes. (Information Services Ser.). Date not set. price not set ring bound looseleaf. P-H.

State & Metropolitan Area Data Book, 1986: A Statistical Abstract Supplement. 751p. 1986. 28.00 (S/N 003-024-06334-4). USGPO.

State & Movement of Water in Living Organisms. Society for Experimental Biology (Great Britain) LC 65-27550. (Symposia of the Society for Experimental Biology Ser.: No. 19). pap. 112.00 (2014957). Bks Demand UMI.

State & Municipal Construction Law. 132p. 1976. spiral bdg. 20.00 (ISBN 0-686-47819-3). Amer Bar Assn.

State & Nation Building. Rajni Kothari. 336p. 1976. 16.95. Asia Bk Corp.

State & Nation in the Third World: The Western State & African Nationalism. Anthony D. Smith. LC 82-10672. 180p. 1983. 26.50x (ISBN 0-312-75605-4). St Martin.

State & National Parks: Lodges, Cabins & Resorts, 1985-1986. 2nd ed. John Thaxton. (Compleat Traveler Ser.). (Illus.). 640p. (Orig.). 1985. pap. 8.95 (ISBN 0-89102-318-6). B Franklin.

State & Nations in the U. S. S. R. V. S. Shevtsov. 208p. 1982. 6.45 (ISBN 0-8285-2419-X, Pub. by Progress Pubs USSR). Imported Pubns.

State & Nuclear Power: Conflict & Control in the Western World. Joseph A. Camilleri. LC 83-19824. 366p. 1984. 25.00x (ISBN 0-295-96094-9). U of Wash Pr.

State & Opposition in Military Brazil. Maria H. Alves. (Latin American Monographs: No. 63). 368p. 1985. 22.50x (ISBN 0-292-77598-9). U of Tex Pr.

State & Opposition in Military Brazil. Maria H. Alves. (Latin American Monographs). (Illus.). 368p. 1988. pap. 12.95 (ISBN 0-292-77617-9). U of Tex Pr.

State & Peasant Politics in Sri Lanka. Mick Moore. (Cambridge South Asian Studies: No. 34). 250p. 1985. 49.50 (ISBN 0-521-26550-9). Cambridge U Pr.

State & Political Theory. Martin Carnoy. LC 83-43064. 304p. 1984. 30.50x (ISBN 0-691-07669-3); pap. 9.95x (ISBN 0-691-02226-7). Princeton U Pr.

State & Politics in Contemporary India. Moin Shakir. 209p. 1986. 18.50X (ISBN 81-202-0157-4, Pub. by Ajanta). South Asia Bks.

State & Politics in the U. S. S. R. David Lane. 418p. 1985. 45.00x (ISBN 0-8147-5013-3); pap. 20.00x (ISBN 0-8147-5014-1). NYU Pr.

State & Poverty in India: The Politics of Reform. Atul Kohli. LC 85-25554. (Cambridge South Asian Studies: No. 37). (Illus.). 220p. 1987. 39.50 (ISBN 0-521-32008-9). Cambridge U Pr.

State & Province Vital Records Guide. Mike Burgess & Mary W. Burgess. LC 87-6312. (Borgo Reference Library: Vol. 16). 64p. 1988. lib. bdg. 19.95x (ISBN 0-89370-815-1); pap. 7.95x (ISBN 0-89370-915-8). Borgo Pr.

State & Public Bureaucracies: A Comparative Perspective. Ed. by Metin Heper. LC 87-15059. (Contributions in Political Science Ser.: No. 193). 232p. 1987. lib. bdg. 37.95 (ISBN 0-313-25438-9, HSK/). Greenwood.

State & Public Welfare in Nineteenth-Century America: Five Investigations, 1833-1877. Gerald N. Grob. LC 75-17244. (Social Problems & Social Policy Ser.). (Illus.). 1976. 46.50x (ISBN 0-405-07515-4). Ayer Co Pubs.

State & Regional Patterns in American Manufacturing, 1860-1900. Albert W. Niemi, Jr. LC 73-13289. (Contributions in Economics Ser., No. 10). 209p. 1974. lib. bdg. 56.95 (ISBN 0-8371-7148-2, NAM). Greenwood.

State & Revolution. Vladimir I. Lenin. 1965. pap. 2.50 (ISBN 0-8351-0372-2). China Bks.

State & Revolution. Vladimir I. Lenin. 103p. 1932. pap. 2.00 (ISBN 0-7178-0196-9). Intl Pubs Co.

State & Revolution in Algeria. Rachid Tlemcani. 256p. 1986. 30.00 (ISBN 0-8133-0439-3). Westview.

State & Revolution in East Africa. John Saul. LC 79-11458. 454p. 1980. 16.00 (ISBN 0-85345-487-6); pap. 6.95 (ISBN 0-85345-508-2). Monthly Rev.

State & Revolution in Finland. Risto Alapuro. 320p. 1988. 30.00x (ISBN 0-520-05813-5). U of Cal Pr.

State & Revolution in Iran: 1962-1982. Hossein Bashiriyeh. LC 83-19218. 203p. 1984. 27.50 (ISBN 0-312-75612-7). St Martin.

State & Rural Class Formation in Ghana: A Comparative Analysis. Piet Konings. (Monographs from the African Studies Centre). 420p. 1986. PLB 75.00 (ISBN 0-7103-0117-0, Kegan Paul). Routledge Chapman & Hall.

State & Scholars in T'ang China. D. L. McMullen. 380p. 1987. 210.00x (Pub. by Han-Shan Tang Ltd). State Mutual Bk.

State & Scholars in T'ang China. D. L. McMullen. (Cambridge Studies in Chinese History, Literature & Institutions). 448p. 1988. 49.50 (ISBN 0-521-32991-4). Cambridge U Pr.

State & Social Revolution in Iran: A Theoretical Perspective. Farrokh Moshiri. LC 84-48103. (American University Studies X (Political Science): Vol. 5). 252p. 1985. text ed. 28.85 (ISBN 0-8204-0149-8). P Lang Pubs.

State & Social Transformation in Tunisia & Libya, 1830-1980. Lisa Anderson. LC 85-43266. (Princeton Studies on the Near East). (Illus.). 320p. 1986. text ed. 37.00 (ISBN 0-691-05462-2); pap. 10.50 (ISBN 0-691-00819-1). Princeton U Pr.

State Control of Private Incorporated Institutions of Higher Education As Defined in Decisions of the U. S. Supreme Court: Laws of the States Governing the Incorporation of Institutions of Higher Education, & Charters of Selected Private Colleges & Universities. Lester W. Bartlett. LC 73-176538. (Columbia University Teachers College. Contributions to Education Ser.: No. 207). Repr. of 1926 ed. 22.50 (ISBN 0-404-55207-2). AMS Pr.

State Control of Textbooks with Special Reference to Florida. Clyde J. Tidwell. LC 77-177710. (Columbia University Teachers College. Contributions to Education Ser.: No. 299). Repr. of 1928 ed. 22.50 (ISBN 0-404-55299-4). AMS Pr.

State Controlled Substances Scheduling Authorities. 6p. 1984. 5.00 (ISBN 0-317-45883-3, C-28). Coun State Govts.

State Corporate Income Tax. Ed. by Charles McLure. 550p. 1984. 59.95x (ISBN 0-8179-7881-X). Hoover Inst Pr.

State Court Administrative Offices. 2nd ed. Robert G. Nieland & Rachel N. Doan. LC 82-82912. 1982. pap. 6.95 (ISBN 0-938870-28-9). Am Judicature.

State Court Caseload Statistics: Annual Report 1976. National Center for State Courts Staff & National Court Statistics Project Staff. 440p. 1980. pap. 12.50 (ISBN 0-89656-044-9, R-052). Natl Ctr St Courts.

State Court Caseload Statistics: Annual Report 1977. National Center for State Courts Staff. 461p. 1982. pap. 12.50 (R-078). Natl Ctr St Courts.

State Court Caseload Statistics: Annual Report 1978. National Center for State Courts Staff. 473p. 1983. pap. 12.50 (R-080). Natl Ctr St Courts.

State Court Caseload Statistics: Annual Report 1979. National Center for State Courts Staff. 496p. 1983. pap. 12.50 (R-090). Natl Ctr St Courts.

State Court Caseload Statistics: Annual Report 1980. National Center for State Courts Staff. 494p. 1984. pap. 18.00 (ISBN 0-89656-078-3, R-092). Natl Ctr St Courts.

State Court Caseload Statistics: Annual Report 1981. National Center for State Courts Staff. (On loan from NCSC Library). 1985. pap. write for info. (ISBN 0-89656-079-1, R-093). Natl Ctr St Courts.

State Court Caseload Statistics: Annual Report 1984. 276p. 1986. pap. 12.50 (ISBN 0-89656-081-3, R-098). Natl Ctr St Courts.

State Court Caseload Statistics: Annual Report 1985. 311p. 1987. pap. 15.00 (R-103). Natl Ctr St Courts.

State Court Information Systems: Court Technology & Management, Vol. 3. (On loan from NCSC Library). 1982. write for info. Natl Ctr St Courts.

State Court Information Systems: State of the Art, Vol. I. National Center for State Courts Staff. (On loan from NCSC Library). 1980. write for info. Natl Ctr St Courts.

State Court Information Systems: Technology Transfer Guides & Selected Modules, Vol. 2. (On loan through the NCSC Library). 1981. write for info. Natl Ctr St Courts.

State Court Model Annual Report. National Center for State Courts Staff. (On loan through the NCSC Library). 1980. write for info. (ISBN 0-89656-042-2, R-050). Natl Ctr St Courts.

State Court Perspective on Case Management in the U. S. Tax Court. National Center for State Courts Staff. 26p. 1985. manuscript 2.00 (WRO-056). Natl Ctr St Courts.

State Court Records Retention Study. National Center for State Courts Staff. 224p. 1985. manuscript 14.00 (SERO-009). Natl Ctr St Courts.

State Courts: A Blueprint for the Future. National Center for State Courts Staff. 360p. 1978. 3.00 (R-038). Natl Ctr St Courts.

State Courts & the Death Penalty After Furman v. Georgia. National Center for State Courts Staff. 30p. (On loan through the NCSC Library). 1973. pap. write for info. (R-004). Natl Ctr St Courts.

State Courts: Options for the Future. Victoria S. Cashman & Theodore J. Fetter. 58p. 1980. 4.00. Natl Ctr St Courts.

State Courts: Options for the Future. (On Loan Through NCSC Library). 68p. 1980. pap. write for info. (ISBN 0-89656-037-6, R-045). Natl Ctr St Courts.

State Credentialing of the Behavioral Science Professions: Counselors, Psychologists, & Social Workers. 1986. 25.00 (ISBN 0-317-45885-X, C-41). Coun State Govts.

State Credentialing of the Health Occupations & Professions. 1986. 25.00 (ISBN 0-317-45889-2, C-40). Coun State Govts.

State Debt & Public Liability in Oklahoma. Ed. by Bureau of Government Research Staff. 22p. 1982. 2.00 (ISBN 0-318-01378-9). Univ OK Gov Res.

State Deferred Compensation Programs: Their Status in 36 States. 80p. 1983. 4.50 (ISBN 0-317-45865-5, C-17). Coun State Govts.

State Deficit Management Strategies: LFP, No. 60. Corina L. Eckl. 1987. pap. 6.25 (ISBN 1-55516-060-3). Natl Conf State Legis.

State, Democracy & Legality in the U. S. S. R. Victor Chkhikvadze. 371p. 1975. 17.95 (ISBN 0-8464-0883-X). Beekman Pubs.

State, Democracy, & the Military: Turkey in the 1980s. Ed. by Metin Heper & Ahmet Evin. 265p. 1988. lib. bdg. 49.95x (ISBN 0-89925-454-3). De Gruyter.

State Demographics: Population Profiles of the 50 States. Ed. by American Demographics Magazine Staff. LC 83-70909. 300p. 1984. 59.50 (ISBN 0-87094-451-7). Dow Jones-Irwin.

State Department Policy Planning Staff Papers. George F. Kennan. Ed. by Anna K. Nelson. LC 83-14212. 976p. 1983. lib. bdg. 138.00 (ISBN 0-8240-5500-4). Garland Pub.

State Desegregation Initiatives in a Period of Transition. 73p. 1983. 5.00 (ISBN 0-318-17963-6, LEC-83-12). Ed Comm States.

State Divided: Opposition in Pennsylvania to the American Revolution. Anne M. Ousterhout. LC 86-29573. (Contributions in American History Ser.: No. 123). 358p. 1987. lib. bdg. 39.95 (ISBN 0-313-25728-0, OUS/). Greenwood.

State Documents on Federal Relations. Ed. by Herman V. Ames. LC 78-77697. (American Constitutional & Legal History Ser). 1970. Repr. of 1900 ed. lib. bdg. 42.50 (ISBN 0-306-71335-7). Da Capo.

State Economic Development: Wisconsin's Planning Methods & Potentials. Richard B. Andrews. LC 68-9014. (Land Economics Monographs, No. 2). (Illus.). 116p. 1968. pap. 7.00x (ISBN 0-299-95023-9). U of Wis Pr.

State Economic Policies of the Ch'ing Government: 1840-1895. Jerome Chen. LC 78-24797. (Modern Chinese Economy Ser.: Vol. 2). 250p. 1980. lib. bdg. 33.00 (ISBN 0-8240-4251-4). Garland Pub.

State, Economy & Society in Western Europe, 1815-1975: A Data Handbook, 2 vols. Peter Flora et al. Incl. Vol. 1. The Growth of Mass Democracies & Welfare States. 1983 (ISBN 0-912289-00-7); Vol. 2. The Growth of Industrial Societies & Capitalist Economies. 1986. (Illus.). 650p. lib. bdg. 72.50x ea. St James Pr.

State, Education, & Social Class in Mexico, 1880-1928. Mary K. Vaughan. LC 81-18733. (Origins of Modern Mexico Ser.). 316p. 25.00 (ISBN 0-87580-079-3). N Ill U Pr.

State Education Reforms & Emerging Issues: What Legislatures Did in 1985 & Where They Are Going in 1986. The National Conference of State Legislatures Staff. (State Legislative Report: Vol. 11, No. 3). pap. 5.00 (ISBN 1-55516-159-6). Natl Conf State Legis.

State Education Reforms & Emerging Issues: What Legislatures Did in 1986 & Where They Are Going in 1987. Peggy Siegel. (State Legislative Reports: Vol. 12, No. 6). 1987. pap. 5.00 (ISBN 1-55516-179-0). Natl Conf State Legis.

State Efforts at Health Care Cost Containment: 1986 Update. rev. ed. Michelle Polchow. pap. 15.00 (ISBN 1-55516-672-5). Natl Conf State Legis.

State Efforts to Assess Excellence. 28p. 1985. 4.00 (ISBN 0-318-22541-7, E-85-1). Ed Comm States.

State Elections in India, Vol. 4: The North: Data Handbook on Vidhan Sabha Elections, 1952-1985. V. B. Singh & Shankar Bose. (Elections in India Ser.). 728p. 1988. text ed. 75.00 (ISBN 0-8039-9549-0). Sage.

State Elections in India, Vol. 5: The South: Data Handbook on Vidhan Sabhan Sabha Elections, 1952-1985. V. B. Singh & Shankar Bose. (Elections in India Ser.). 750p. 1988. text ed. 75.00 (ISBN 0-8039-9558-X). Sage.

State Elective Officials & the Legislatures, 1987-88. The Council of State Governments Staff. Ed. by Deborah Gona. 160p. (Orig.). 1987. pap. 30.00 (ISBN 0-87292-071-2). Coun State Govts.

State Elective Officials & the Legislatures, 1983-84. (Orig.). 1983. pap. 15.00 (ISBN 0-87292-034-8). Coun State Govts.

State Elective Officials & the Legislatures (1985-86) Supplement One to "The Book of the States". L. E. Purcell. (Orig.). 1985. pap. 17.50 (ISBN 0-87292-055-0). Coun State Govts.

State Emblems. Compiled by Ethel M. Ramsey & William H. Ramsey, Jr. 1983. pap. 3.50 (ISBN 0-686-40183-2). Basin Pub.

State Emergency Medical Services Communications Systems & Level of Preparedness for Disasters. 25p. 1986. 20.00 (ISBN 0-317-45909-0, C-35). Coun State Govts.

State Emergency Medical Services Facilities & Regulatory Control. 27p. 1986. 20.00 (ISBN 0-317-45910-4, C-36). Coun State Govts.

State Emergency Medical Services Public Information & Education Systems. 23p. 1986. 20.00 (ISBN 0-317-45913-9, C-38). Coun State Govts.

State Employee Labor Relations. 64p. 1977. 3.50 (ISBN 0-317-34027-1, RM624). Coun State Govts.

State Employment Policy in Hard Times. Ed. by Michael Barker. LC 83-5674. (Duke Press Policy Studies). xxix, 252p. 1983. 32.50 (ISBN 0-8223-0538-0). Duke.

State Energy Policy: Current Issues, Future Directions. Ed. by Stephen W. Sawyer & John R. Armstrong. (Special Studies in Natural Resources & Energy Management). 250p. 1985. pap. 31.00x (ISBN 0-8133-7027-2). Westview.

State Estimates of Disability & Utilization of Medical Services, 1969-1971 Derived from the United States Health Interview Survey. National Center for Health Statistics Staff. (Series 10: No. 108). 55p. 1976. pap. 1.50 (ISBN 0-8406-0076-3). Natl. Ctr Health Stats.

State Executions: Omnibus Title. Incl. The Hangmen of England. Horace Bleackley. LC 77-2187. (No. 170). 1977. Repr. of 1929 ed; The Dramaturgy of State Executions. John Lofland. 1977. (Criminology, Law Enforcement & Social Problems Ser.: Publication No. 170). 1984. 20.00x (ISBN 0-87585-170-3). Patterson Smith.

State Executive Reorganization since 1940: A Selected Bibliography. Alva W. Stewart. (Public Administration Ser.: P 1683). 12p. 1985. 2.00 (ISBN 0-89028-413-X). Vance Biblios.

State Export Programs: A Resource Guide. 179p. 1987. 60.00 (ISBN 0-87179-932-4). BNA.

State Fair Blue Ribbon Cookbook. Opal M. Hayes. LC 76-7358. (Illus.). 1976. 9.95 (ISBN 0-88280-046-9). ETC Pubns.

State Fair Book. Jack Pierce. LC 79-91308. (Carolrhoda Photo Bks.). (Illus.). (ps-3). 1980. PLB 9.95 (ISBN 0-87614-124-6). Carolrhoda Bks.

State, Finance & Industry: A Comparative Analysis of Post-War Trends in Six Advanced Industrial Economies. Ed. by Andrew Cox. LC 86-1747. 352p. 1986. 35.00 (ISBN 0-312-75618-6). St Martin.

State Fire Marshals Conference Report. Ed. by Amy E. Dean. LC 77-87129. 1977. pap. text ed. 7.50 (ISBN 0-87765-110-8). Natl Fire Prot.

State Fiscal Conditions. Steven D. Gold. (Legislative Finance Papers: No. 55). 32p. 1987. pap. 6.25 (ISBN 1-55516-055-7). Natl Conf State Legis.

State Fiscal Conditions Entering 1984. (Legislative Finance Papers Ser.). 28p. 1984. 15.00 (ISBN 1-55516-042-5). Natl Conf State Legis.

State Fiscal Indicators. Steven Gold. (Legislative Finance Paper Ser.). 107p. 1982. 10.00 (ISBN 1-55516-534-6). Natl Conf State Legis.

State Fiscal Issues in 1988. Corina Eckl. (State Legislative Reports: Vol. 13, No. 1). 1988. pap. 5.00 (ISBN 1-55516-186-3). Natl Conf State Legis.

State Fiscal Policies for Child Care & Early Childhood Education, Vol. 12, No. 7. Terry Gnezda. Ed. by Karn Hansen. 7p. 1987. pap. 5.00 (ISBN 1-55516-180-4). Natl Conf State Legis.

State Flowers. Reissue. ed. Anne O. Dowden. LC 78-41927. (Illus.). 96p. (gr. 5 up). 1987. 13.70i (ISBN 0-690-01339-6, Crowell Jr Bks); PLB 13.95 (ISBN 0-690-03884-4). HarpJ.

State Forestry for the Axe. Robert Miller. (Institute of Economic Affairs, Hobart Papers Ser.: No. 91). pap. 5.95 technical (ISBN 0-255-36145-9). Transatl Arts.

State Formation & Political Legitimacy. Ed. by Myron J. Aronoff et al. (Political Anthropology: Vol. 6). 340p. 1987. 24.95 (ISBN 0-88738-161-8). Transaction Bks.

State Formation in Eastern Africa. Ed. by Ahmed I. Salim. LC 84-15103. 260p. 1986. 29.95 (ISBN 0-312-75614-3). St Martin.

State, France, & the Sixteenth Century. Howell Lloyd. (Early Modern Europe Today Ser.). 256p. 1983. text ed. 34.95x (ISBN 0-04-940066-5). Unwin Hyman.

State Fuel Use Taxes: A Guide for Motor Carriers. American Trucking Associations, Inc., State Laws Department Staff. 124p. 1987. pap. text ed. 35.00 (ISBN 0-88711-075-4). Am Trucking Assns.

State Futures Commissions. Keon Chi. Ed. by L. Edward Purcell. 32p. (Orig.). pap. 12.00 (ISBN 0-87292-039-9, RM 722). Coun State Govts.

State Governance of Education. 48p. 1883. 6.00 (ISBN 0-318-17957-1, EG-83-1). Ed Comm States.

State Government & Economic Development. Gerald D. Nash. Ed. by Stuart Bruchey. LC 78-56676. (Management of Public Lands in the U. S. Ser.). 1979. Repr. of 1964 ed. lib. bdg. 28.50x (ISBN 0-405-11346-3). Ayer Co Pubs.

State Government & Politics: Jammu & Kashmir. M. K. Teng. vi, 167p. 1985. text ed. 20.00x (ISBN 0-86590-592-4, Pub. by Sterling Pubs India). Apt Bks.

State Government & Politics: Sikkim. N. Sengupta. 308p. 1985. text ed. 35.00x (ISBN 0-86590-694-7, Pub. by Sterling Pubs India). Apt Bks.

State Government Associations: A Reconnaissance. R. Leo Penne et al. LC 86-146573. (National League of Cities State-Local Backgrounder Ser.). (Illus.). 1986. write for info. (ISBN 0-933729-07-3). Natl League Cities.

State Government: CQ's Guide to Current Issues & Activities 1985-1986. Congressional Quarterly, Inc. Staff & Thad L. Beyle. 218p. 1985. pap. 8.95 (ISBN 0-87187-353-2). Congr Quarterly.

State Government Export Promotion: An Exporter's Guide. Alan R. Posner. LC 84-1999. x, 192p. 1984. lib. bdg. 36.95 (ISBN 0-89930-042-1, PGE/, Quorum). Greenwood.

State Government in Georgia. 2nd ed. Lawrence R. Hepburn. LC 86-29433. 200p. (YA) 1986. pap. 10.95 (ISBN 0-89854-114-X). U of GA Inst Govt.

State Government in Iowa. Institute of Public Affairs Staff. 1985. pap. 3.50 (ISBN 0-318-04358-0). U Iowa IPA.

State Government in Maryland, 1777-1781. Beverly W. Bond. LC 78-63907. (Johns Hopkins University. Studies in the Social Sciences. Twenty-Third Ser. 1905: 3-4). Repr. of 1905 ed. 15.50 (ISBN 0-404-61159-1). AMS Pr.

State Government Influence in U. S. International Economic Policy. John M. Kline. LC 82-48473. 288p. 1983. 33.00x (ISBN 0-669-06141-7). Lexington Bks.

State Government Organization: A Preliminary Compilation. 1979. incl. update 20.00 (ISBN 0-317-34028-X, R M678); state officials 14.00 (ISBN 0-317-34029-8). Coun State Govts.

State Government Policy. Dennis Judd et al. (Orig.). 1981. pap. 8.00 (ISBN 0-918592-49-6). Policy Studies.

State Government: Politics in Wyoming. 2nd ed. Tim R. Miller. 192p. 1985. pap. text ed. 12.95 (ISBN 0-8403-3616-0). Kendall-Hunt.

State Government Research Directory. 1st ed. Kay Gill & Susan E. Tufts. 349p. 1986. 175.00x (ISBN 0-8103-1591-2). Gale.

State Government: The Political Process. David C. Saffell. 352p. 1984. text ed. write for info (ISBN 0-394-34935-0, RanC). Random.

State Government 1986-87: CQs Guide to Current Issues & Activities. Congressional Quarterly, Inc. Staff & Thad Beyle. 204p. 1986. pap. 9.95 (ISBN 0-87187-390-7). Congr Quarterly.

State Government, 1987-88. Thad L. Beyle. 221p. 1987. pap. 9.95 (ISBN 0-87187-423-7). Congr Quarterly.

State Government, 1988-89. Thad Beyle. 200p. 1988. 9.95 (ISBN 0-87187-467-9). Congr Quarterly.

State Governments in India. Maheshwari. 1980. 17.00x (ISBN 0-8364-0587-0, Pub. by Macmillan India). South Asia Bks.

State Greats. Carole Marsh. (gr. 4-9). Date not set. pap. 14.95. Gallopade Pub Group.

State Guide for RV Manufacturers. 101p. 1985. 41.50. RV Indus Assn.

State, Hegemonic Classes, & Working Class Power: An Overview. (Unip-311 Ser.). 28p. 1982. pap. 5.00 (ISBN 92-808-0311-5, TUNU188, UNU). UNIPUB.

State Hermitage: Proceedings, Vol. 22. Collet's Staff. 1982. 42.00x (ISBN 0-317-57355-1, Pub. by Collets UK). State Mutual Bk.

State Hospitals in the Depression. National Committee for Mental Health. Ed. by Gerald N. Grob. LC 78-22579. (Historical Issues in Mental Health Ser.). 1979. Repr. of 1934 ed. lib. bdg. 14.00x (ISBN 0-405-11931-3). Ayer Co Pubs.

State Immunity. Gamal M. Badr. 1984. pap. text ed. 46.00 (ISBN 90-247-2880-0, Pub. by Martinus Nijhoff Netherlands). Kluwer Academic.

State in Burma. Robert H. Taylor. LC 87-16200. 400p. 1988. text ed. 32.00x (ISBN 0-8248-1141-0). UH Pr.

State in Capitalist Europe: A Casebook. Ed. by Stephen Bornstein et al. (Casebook Series on European Politics & Society: No. 3). Date not set. pap. text ed. 19.95x (ISBN 0-04-350059-5). Unwin Hyman.

State in Capitalist Society: An Analysis of the Western System of Power. Ralph Miliband. LC 78-93689. 1978. o.s.i 10.00x (ISBN 0-465-08197-5); pap. 12.95x (ISBN 0-465-09734-0, TB-5050). Basic.

State in Catholic Thought: A Treatise in Political Philosophy. Heinrich A. Rommen. Repr. of 1945 ed. lib. bdg. 35.00x (ISBN 0-8371-2437-9, ROCT). Greenwood.

State in Constitutional & International Law. Robert T. Crane. LC 78-63921. (Johns Hopkins University. Studies in the Social Sciences. Twenty-Fifth Ser. 1907: 6-7). Repr. of 1907 ed. 13.50 (ISBN 0-404-61172-9). AMS Pr.

State in Disarray: Conditions of Chad's Survival. Michael P. Kelley. (Special Studies on Africa). 222p. 1986. pap. 34.00 (ISBN 0-8133-0362-1). Westview.

State in Its Relations with the Church. William E. Gladstone. 1196p. Repr. of 1841 ed. text ed. 62.10x (ISBN 0-576-02192-X, Pub. by Gregg Intl Pubs England). Gregg Intl.

State in Modern Society: New Directions in Political Sociology. Roger King. LC 86-23320. 271p. 1987. 25.00 (ISBN 0-934540-61-6); pap. 12.95x (ISBN 0-934540-60-8). Chatham Hse Pubs.

State in Northern Ireland: Political Forces & Social Classes. Paul Bow et al. LC 79-13020. 1980. 9.95 (ISBN 0-312-75608-9). St Martin.

State in Relation to Labour. 4th ed. William S. Jevons. Ed. by Francis Hirst. LC 67-16344. 1968. Repr. of 1910 ed. 27.50x (ISBN 0-678-00434-X). Kelley.

State in Socialist Society. Ed. by Neil Harding. LC 83-15339. 316p. 1984. 44.50x (ISBN 0-87395-838-1); pap. 16.95x (ISBN 0-87395-839-X). State U NY Pr.

State in the Making. David Horowitz. Tr. by Julian Meltzer from Hebrew. LC 81-6649. viii, 349p. 1981. Repr. of 1953 ed. lib. bdg. 35.00x (ISBN 0-313-23011-0, HOSI). Greenwood.

State in Western Europe. Richard Scase. LC 80-10364. 113p. 1980. 30.00 (ISBN 0-312-75610-0). St Martin.

State of Food & Agriculture. annual Incl. 1957. pap. 5.25 (ISBN 0-685-48263-4, F441). UNIPUB; 1963. 227p. pap. 13.75 (ISBN 92-5-101500-7, F1479, FAO). UNIPUB; 1969. pap. 17.00 (ISBN 92-5-101500-7, F442). UNIPUB; 1970. pap. 22.25, o. p. (F443). UNIPUB; 1971. 23p. pap. 23.75 (ISBN 92-5-101507-4, F444). UNIPUB; 1974. 196p. 1975. pap. 27.00 (ISBN 92-5-101509-0, F446). UNIPUB; 1975. 150p. 1976. pap. 22.50 (ISBN 92-5-101510-4, F447). UNIPUB; 1976. (No. 4). (Illus.). 157p. 1978. (FAO). UNIPUB; 1977. 224p. 1979. UNIPUB; 1978. (No. 9). 162p. 1980. pap. 17.00, o. p. (ISBN 92-5-100737-3, F1850). UNIPUB; 1979. (No. 10). 214p. 1981. pap. 20.75 (ISBN 92-5-100897-3, F2113, FAO). UNIPUB; 1980. (No. 12). 181p. 1982. pap. 19.50 (ISBN 92-5-101043-9, F2214). UNIPUB; 1981. (No. 14). 177p. 1983. pap. 30.75 (ISBN 92-5-101201-6, F2266, FAO). UNIPUB; 1984 World Review: The Ten Years Since the World Food Conference - Urbanization, Agriculture & Food Systems. 185p. 1986. pap. 30.00 (ISBN 92-5-102227-5, F2814). UNIPUB. (Agricultural Ser.). (Illus., Orig., FAO). UNIPUB.

State of Food & Agriculture: World Review Livestock Production: A World Perspective 1982. (Agricultural Ser.: No. 15). 203p. 1983. pap. text ed. 30.75 (ISBN 92-5-101341-1, F2317, FAO). UNIPUB.

State of Food & Agriculture, 1984: World Review: Ten Years Since the World Food Conference Urbanization, Agriculture & Food Systems. (FAO Agricultural Ser.: No. 18). 185p. 1986. pap. text ed. 30.00 (ISBN 92-5-102227-5, F2814, FAO). UNIPUB.

State of Food & Agriculture, 1985: Mid-Decade Review of Food & Agriculture. (Illus.). 189p. 1987. pap. text ed. 24.00 (ISBN 92-5-102390-5, F3029, FAO). UNIPUB.

State of Grace. Joy Williams. (Signature Editions Ser.). 264p. 1986. pap. 6.95 (ISBN 0-684-18645-4). Scribner.

State of Graduate Education. Ed. by Bruce L. R. Smith. LC 85-72214. (Dialogue on Public Policy Ser.). 193p. 1985. pap. 11.95 (ISBN 0-8157-7995-X). Brookings.

State of Hispanic America, Vols. I-IV. Jeff Casey-Gaspar et al. (Orig.). pap. text ed. 14.00 ea. Natl His Univ.

State of Independece. Caryl Phillips. 1988. pap. 6.95 (ISBN 0-02-015080-6, Collier). Macmillan.

State of Independence. Caryl Phillips. 158p. 1986. 13.95 (ISBN 0-374-26976-9). FS&G.

State of Ireland: A Novella & Seventeen Short Stories. Benedict Kiely. LC 79-92210. (Illus.). 400p. 1980. 16.95 (ISBN 0-87923-320-6). Godine.

State of Ireland: A Novella & Seventeen Stories. Benedict Kiely. 1982. pap. 6.95 (ISBN 0-14-006083-9). Penguin.

State of Israel. Israel T. Naamani. LC 79-12757. (Illus.). 1980. pap. 7.95x (ISBN 0-87441-278-1). Behrman.

State of Jefferson & Other Yarns. Thomas K. Worcester. (Illus.). 80p. (Orig.). 1982. pap. 7.95 (ISBN 0-911518-65-7). Touchstone Oregon.

State of Marine Pollution in the Mediterranean Legislative Controls. (GFCM Studies & Reviews: No. 51). 72p. (Eng. & Fr., 2nd Printing 1973). 1972. pap. 7.50 (ISBN 92-5-101970-3, F921, FAO). UNIPUB.

State of Maryland Court Clerks' Association: Procedural Manual for Court Clerks. National Center for State Courts Staff. 328p. 1977. manuscript 19.68 (MARO-003). Natl Ctr St Courts.

State of Medicine. John W. Todd. 1981. lib. bdg. 18.00 (ISBN 0-85200-384-6, Pub. by MTP Pr England). Kluwer Academic.

State of Mind. Ed. by Robert N. Linscott. LC 72-8483. (Essay Index Reprint Ser.). 1972. Repr. of 1948 ed. 25.50 (ISBN 0-8369-7321-6). Ayer Co Pubs.

State of Mind, My Story: Ramtha: The Adventure Begins. J. Z. Knight. 448p. 1987. 18.95 (ISBN 0-446-51405-5). Warner Bks.

State of Mind of Mrs. Sherwood. Naomi R. Smith. 1973. Repr. of 1946 ed. 25.00 (ISBN 0-8274-0887-0). R West.

State of Mind: Ramtha, the Adventure Begins. J. Z. Knight. 1987. 17.95. Warner Bks.

State of Ming Coin Knives & Minor Knife Coins. Arthur B. Coole. LC 72-86802. (Encyclopedia of Chinese Coins Ser.: Vol. 6). (Illus.). 1977. 35.00x (ISBN 0-88000-013-9). Quarterman.

State of Mississippi's Procurement Policies & Minority Business Enterprises. Richard A. Hudlin & K. Farouk Brimah. 1981. 1.00 (ISBN 0-686-38010-X). Voter Ed Proj.

State of Monetary Economics: Proceedings. Conference of the Universities. LC 75-19702. (National Bureau of Economic Research Ser.). (Illus.). 1975. Repr. of 1963 ed. 17.00x (ISBN 0-405-07582-0). Ayer Co Pubs.

State of Nature & the Structure & Goals of Our Political Societies, 2 vols. John Locke. (Illus.). 185p. 1984. Repr. of 1937 ed. Set. 165.00 (ISBN 0-89901-173-X). Found Class Reprints.

State of Nebraska State Court Organization Profile. National Center for State Courts Staff. 166p. 1977. manuscript 9.96 (MAB-113). Natl Ctr St Courts.

State of New York Law Revision Committee Reports, 1954-1956, 6 vols. Joel V. Burstein. LC 79-90809. 1980. Repr. of 1954 ed. Set. lib. bdg. 220.00 (ISBN 0-89941-030-8). W S Hein.

State of North Carolina vs Christian Liberty. Kent Kelly. 112p. (Orig.). 1978. pap. 2.95 (ISBN 0-9604138-3-9). Calvary Pr.

State of North Carolina's Procurement Policies & Minority Business Enterprises. Richard A. Hudlin & Brimah K. Farouk. 1981. 1.00 (ISBN 0-686-38011-8). Voter Ed Proj.

State of North Carolina's Procurement Policies & Minority Business Enterprises. Michael Langley. 1980. 1.00 (ISBN 0-686-38008-8). Voter Ed Proj.

State of North Dakota District Court Benchbook. National Center for State Courts Staff. 128p. 1982. manuscript 7.68 (NCRO-051). Natl Ctr St Courts.

State of Nutrition in the Arab Middle East. Vinayak N. Patwardhan & William J. Darby. LC 73-123036. (Illus.). 1972. 15.00x (ISBN 0-8265-1162-7). Vanderbilt U Pr.

State of Particle Accelerators & High Energy Physics (Fermilab Summer School, 1981) Ed. by R. A. Carrigan, Jr. & F. R. Huson. LC 82-73861. (AIP Conference Proceedings Ser.: No. 92). 337p. 1982. lib. bdg. 33.75 (ISBN 0-88318-191-6). Am Inst Physics.

State of Peace: The Women Speak. Ed. by Elaine Starkman et al. 88p. 1987. pap. 8.00 (ISBN 0-940584-12-3). Gull Bks.

State of Population Theory. Ed. by David Coleman & Roger Schofield. 320p. 1985. 45.00x (ISBN 0-631-13975-3). Basil Blackwell.

State of Prisons & of Child-Saving Institutions in the Civilized World. Enoch C. Wines. LC 68-55784. (Criminology, Law Enforcement, & Social Problems Ser.: No. 24). 1968. Repr. of 1880 ed. 20.00x (ISBN 0-87585-024-3). Patterson Smith.

State of Prisons in England & Wales. 4th ed. John Howard. LC 74-129312. 1973. Repr. of 1792 ed. write for info. Patterson Smith.

State of Prisons in England & Wales see Prisons & Lazarettos.

State of Public Library Services to Teenagers in Britain 1981. Margaret R. Marshall. LC 83-108898. (LIR Report 5). (Illus.). 84p. (Orig.). 1982. pap. 12.75 (ISBN 0-7123-3006-2, Pub. by British Lib). Longwood Pub Group.

State of Russia Under the Present Czar. John Perry. (Russian Through European Eyes Ser). 1968. Repr. of 1716 ed. lib. bdg. 45.00 (ISBN 0-306-77021-0). Da Capo.

State of Science & Research: Some New Indicators. Ed. by Nestor E. Terleckyj. (Illus.). 200p. 1977. 22.00 (ISBN 0-89158-124-3). Natl Planning.

State of Selected Stocks of Tuna & Billfish in the Pacific & Indian Oceans: Summary Report of the Workshop on the Assessment of Selected Tunas & Billfish Stocks in the Pacific & Indian Oceans, Shimizu, Japan, 13-22 June 1979. (Fisheries Technical Papers: No. 200). 95p. 1980. pap. 9.50 (ISBN 92-5-101003-X, F2030, FAO). UNIPUB.

State of Sequoyah: An Impressionistic Look at Eastern Oklahoma. Jerald C. Walker. (Illus.). 116p. 1985. 25.00 (ISBN 0-913504-95-5). Lowell Pr.

State of Siege. Eric Ambler. 160p. 1985. pap. 2.95 (ISBN 0-425-06768-8). Berkley Pub.

State of Siege. Janet Frame. LC 66-20188. 1981. pap. 4.95 (ISBN 0-8076-0986-2). Braziller.

State of Siege: Ukraine's National Predicament. Yuriy Badzyo. Ed. by Roman Senkus. LC 81-67209. (Illus.). 130p. (Orig.). 1981. 9.95 (ISBN 0-86725-001-1); pap. 3.75 (ISBN 0-86725-000-3). ERUHG.

State of Small Business: A Report of the President, Transmitted to Congress, 1987. 363p. 1987. pap. 10.00 (ISBN 0-318-23761-X, 045-000-00246-2). USGPO.

State of Sociology: Problems & Prospects. James F. Short, Jr. 320p. 1981. 29.95 (ISBN 0-8039-1657-4); pap. 14.00 (ISBN 0-8039-1658-2). Sage.

State of South Carolina's Procurement's Policies & Minority Business Enterprises. Michael Langley. 1980. write for info. Voter Ed Proj.

State of Stony Lonesome. Jessamyn West. 256p. 1984. 12.95 (ISBN 0-15-184903-X). HarBraceJ.

State of Taxation. A. R. Prest. (Institute of Economic Affairs, Readings Ser.: No. 16). pap. 7.50 techical (ISBN 0-255-36093-2). Transatl Arts.

State of the Alliance 1986-1987: North Atlantic Assembly Reports. John Cartwright et al. (Special Studies in International Relations). 364p. 1987. pap. 33.50 (ISBN 0-8133-7404-9). Westview.

State of the Alliance, 1987-1988: North Atlantic Assembly Reports. Gianfranco Astori et al. (Special Studies in International Relations). 350p. 1987. pap. 25.00 (ISBN 0-8133-7527-4). Westview.

State of the Ark: An Atlas of Conservation in Action. Lee Durrell. LC 86-11500. (Illus.). 224p. 1986. pap. 14.95 (ISBN 0-385-23668-9). Doubleday.

State of the Art. Arthur C. Danto. (Illus.). 240p. 1987. 19.95 (ISBN 0-13-770868-8). P-H.

State of the Art. Pauline Kael. LC 85-10368. 400p. 1985. (Pub. by W Abrahams Bk); pap. 12.95 (ISBN 0-525-48186-9, Pub. by W Abrahams Bk). Dutton.

State of the Art. 1988. pap. 18.00. Norton.

State of the Art: A Photographic History of the Integrated Circuit. Stan Augarten. LC 83-669. (Illus.). 90p. 1983. pap. 9.95 (ISBN 0-89919-195-9). Ticknor & Fields.

State of the Art Extracorporeal Shock Wave Lithotripsy. Ed. by Lawrence Kandel & Lloyd H. Harrison. David L. McCullough. (Illus.). 400p. 1987. 55.00 (ISBN 0-87993-309-7). Futura Pub.

State-of-the-Art in Community-Based Education in American Community College. Kenneth B. McGuire. 1988. pap. 15.00 (ISBN 0-87117-180-5). Am Assn Comm Jr Coll.

State of the Art in Decision Support Systems. Gerald W. Hopple. (Decision Support Systems Ser.). 128p. 1988. 29.95 (ISBN 0-89435-247-4). QED Info Sci.

State of the Art in Family Therapy Research: Controversies & Recommendations. Ed. by Lyman C. Wynne. 1987. text ed. 30.00 (ISBN 0-9615519-2-5). Family Process.

State of the Art in Family Therapy Research: Controversies & Recommendations. Intro. by Lyman C. Wynne. LC 87-951. 312p. (Orig.). 1988. pap. 18.00 (ISBN 0-9615519-3-3). Family Process.

State of the Art in Hospital Advertising-1987. Ned Barnett et al. Ed. by Pamela Taulbee. 60p. (Orig.). 1987. pap. 39.95 (ISBN 0-937925-33-0). Capitol VA.

State of the Art in Numerical: An Analysis. Ed. by D. A. Jacobs. (Mathematics & Its Application Ser.). 1977. 134.00 (ISBN 0-12-378650-9). Acad Pr.

State of the Art in Numerical Analysis. Ed. by A. Iserles & M. J. Powell. (Institute of Mathematics & its Applications Conference Ser.: No. 9). (Illus.). 734p. 1987. 98.00 (ISBN 0-19-853614-3). Oxford U Pr.

State of the Art in Quantitative Coronary Arteriography. Ed. by J. H. Reiber & P. W. Serruys. (Developments in Cardiovascular Medicine Ser.). 1986. lib. bdg. 96.50 (ISBN 0-89838-804-X, Pub. by Martinus Nijhoff Netherlands). Kluwer Academic.

State of the Art in Underground Development & Construction. Ed. by Eric D. Storr. 250p. 1984. pap. text ed. 30.00x (ISBN 0-85825-202-3, Pub. by Inst Engineers Australia). Brookfield Pub Co.

State of the Art: Irrigation Drainage & Flood Control, Nos. 1-3. No. 1, 676p, 1978. 36.00 (ISBN 0-318-16938-X); No. 2, 264p, 1981. 39.00 (ISBN 81-85068-02-X); No. 3, 1984. 39.00 (ISBN 81-85068-08-9). US Comm Irrigation.

State-of-the-Art: Irrigation, Drainage & Flood Control, No.2. Ed. by K. K. Framji. 264p. 1981. 36.00 (ISBN 81-85068-02-X). US Comm Irrigation.

State of the Art of Computer Aided Environmental Design. Kaiman Lee. LC 76-358975. (Illus.). 309p. 1975. 50.00x (ISBN 0-915250-14-4). Environ Design.

State of the Art of Ecological Modelling: Proceedings of the Conference on Ecological Modelling, Copenhagen, 28 August 2, September 1978. S. E. Jorgensen. LC 78-41208. (Environmental Sciences & Applications Ser.: Vol. 7). 1979. pap. 195.00 (ISBN 0-08-023443-7). Pergamon.

State of the Art of Precast Prestressed Concrete Tank Construction. 50p. 10.00 (ISBN 0-318-17393-X, JR283). Prestressed Concrete.

State of the Art of Surgery, Nineteen Seventy-Nine to Nineteen Eighty. Ed. by M. Allgower & F. Arder. 116p. 1980. pap. 7.10 (ISBN 0-387-10136-5). Springer-Verlag.

State of the Art on Design & Performance of Power Cylinder Components. 130p. 1983. 30.00 (ISBN 0-89883-323-X, SP552). Soc Auto Engineers.

State-of-the-Art Report. Center for Occupational Research & Development Staff. (Robotics-Automated Systems Technology Ser.). 100p. 1984. pap. text ed. 20.00 (ISBN 1-55502-149-2). Ctr Res & Dev.

State-of-the-Art Report on Air-Supported Structures. American Society of Civil Engineers Staff. LC 79-125997. (Illus.). pap. 25.80 (ISBN 0-317-10911-1, 2019556). Bks Demand UMI.

State-of-the-Art Report on Composite or Mixed Steel Concrete Construction for Buildings. H. S. Iyengar. pap. 40.00 (ISBN 0-317-42235-9, 2026069). Bks Demand UMI.

State-of-the-Art Report on Prestressed Concrete Ties for North American Railroads. (PCI Journal Reprints Ser.). 16p. 1985. pap. 6.00 (ISBN 0-318-19778-2, JR213). Prestressed Concrete.

State of the Art Report on Seismic Resistance of Prestressed & Precast Concrete Structures. (PCI Journal Reprints Ser.). 52p. pap. 7.00 (JR194). Prestressed Concrete.

State of the Art Reports 1986, 8 vols. Infotech Staff. (Infotech Ser.: No. 14). 3043p. 1987. Set. 2625.00 (ISBN 0-08-034099-7). Pergamon.

State of the Art: Small Scale (to 50 kw) Gas Producer Engine Systems. A. Kaupp & J. R. Goss. (Illus.). 278p. (Orig.). 1983. 40.00x (ISBN 0-942914-03-1); pap. 20.00x (ISBN 0-942914-02-3). Tipi Wkshp Bks.

State of the Art Survey of Dispute Resolution Programs Involving Juveniles. Special Committee on Dispute Resolution Staff. 54p. 1982. pap. 1.50 (ISBN 0-317-30567-0). Amer Bar Assn.

State of the Art Symposium: Polymer Chemistry. Symposium on State of the Art Chemical Educators III (Polymer Chemistry 1981: Atlanta) pap. 30.00 (ISBN 0-317-26617-9, 2025425). Bks Demand UMI.

State of the Black Economy. Lloyd Hogan. LC 80-53746. 128p. (Orig.). 1980. pap. 14.95 (ISBN 0-87855-816-0). Transaction Bks.

State of the Child. Mark Testa & Fred Wulczyn. LC 80-70497. (Research Reports on Children in Illinois Ser.: Vol. 1). xiv, 111p. (Orig.). 1980. pap. text ed. 10.00 (ISBN 0-932132-33-2). NORC.

State of the Child, 1985. Mark Testa & Edward Lawlor. 120p. 1986. pap. text ed. 15.00 (ISBN 0-932132-35-9). NORC.

State of the Church. Andrew Murray. 1983. pap. 2.95 (ISBN 0-87508-407-9). Chr Lit.

State of the Discipline, Nineteen Seventies - Nineteen Eighties. Ed. by Jasper P. Neel. 106p. 1979. pap. 12.00x (ISBN 0-87352-089-0, J156). Modern Lang.

State of the Environment. Essam El-Hinnawi & Manzur H. Hashmi. (Illus.). 192p. 1987. 85.00 (ISBN 0-408-02183-7). Butterworth.

State of the Environment: A View Toward the Nineties. Conservation Foundation Staff. LC 87-15193. (Illus.). 614p. 1987. 19.95 (ISBN 0-89164-098-3). Conservation Foun.

State of the Environment: An Assessment at Mid-Decade. Conservation Foundation Staff. LC 84-12651. (Illus.). 586p. (Orig.). 1984. pap. 16.00 (ISBN 0-89164-084-3). Conservation Foun.

State of the Environment in OECD Member Countries. 177p. 1979. 10.00x (ISBN 92-64-11946-9). OECD.

State of the Environment Report for Canada. P. M. Bird & D. J. Rapport. 263p. 1986. pap. text ed. 30.00 (ISBN 0-317-66572-3, SSC227, SSC). UNIPUB.

State of the Environment Report for Canada. Peter M. Bird & David J. Rapport. (Illus.). 263p. (Orig.). 1986. pap. text ed. 5.00 (ISBN 0-660-12050-X, SSC27, Pub. by State Canada). UNIPUB.

State of the Environment 1982. Conservation Foundation Staff. LC 82-8257. (Illus.). 439p. (Orig.). 1982. pap. 15.00 (ISBN 0-89164-070-3). Conservation Foun.

State of the Expedition from Canada, As Laid Before the House of Commons. John Burgoyne. LC 70-77104. (Eyewitness Accounts of the American Revolution Ser., No. 2). 1969. Repr. of 1780 ed. 21.00 (ISBN 0-405-01146-6). Ayer Co Pubs.

State of the Language. Ed. by Leonard Michaels & Christopher Ricks. (Published with the English-Speaking Union, San Francisco Branch)). 1979. 30.00x (ISBN 0-520-03763-4); pap. 14.95 (ISBN 0-520-04400-2). U of Cal Pr.

State of the Language: English Observed. Philip Howard. 1985. 18.95 (ISBN 0-19-520467-0). Oxford U Pr.

State of the Masses. Richard F. Hamilton & James D. Wright. LC 85-20127. (Social Institutions & Social Change Ser.). (Illus.). 482p. (Orig.). 1986. lib. bdg. 42.95 (ISBN 0-202-30324-1); pap. text ed. 19.95 (ISBN 0-202-30325-X). Aldine de Gruyter.

State of the Nation. John Dos Passos. LC 73-718. (Illus.). 333p. 1973. Repr. of 1944 ed. lib. bdg. 35.00x (ISBN 0-8371-6782-5, DOSN). Greenwood.

State of the Nation. rev. ed. Desmond Fennell. 146p. 1984. pap. 5.95 (ISBN 0-907085-61-X, Pub. by Ward River Pr Ireland). Irish Bks Media.

State of the Nation: A Conference of the Committee for the Free World. Ed. by Steven C. Munson. LC 84-23444. 126p. (Orig.). 1985. lib. bdg. 15.00 (ISBN 0-8191-4390-1, Comm for the Free World); pap. text ed. 5.00 (ISBN 0-8191-4391-X). U Pr of Amer.

State of the Nation & the Agenda for Higher Education. Howard R. Bowen. LC 81-20746. (Higher Education Ser.). 1982. text ed. 23.95x (ISBN 0-87589-515-8). Jossey-Bass.

State of the Nation: Presidential Addresses to Parliament from Dr. Rajendra Prasad to Neelam Sanjiva Reddy. R. L. Handa. 1983. text ed. 35.00x (ISBN 0-86590-162-7, Pub. by Sterling India). Apt Bks.

State of the Nations: Constraints on Development in Independent Africa. Ed. by Michael F. Lofchie. (African Studies Center, UCLA: No. 2). 1971. 35.00x (ISBN 0-520-01740-4). U of Cal Pr.

State of the Novel: Dying Art or New Science. Walker Percy. (Illus.). 20p. 1988. 50.00 (ISBN 0-917905-05-9); deluxe ed. 125.00 (ISBN 0-317-66751-3). Faust Pub Co.

State of the Police. Phil Scraton. 184p. (Orig.). 1985. pap. 9.50 (ISBN 0-7453-0100-2, Pub. by Pluto Pr). Longwood Pub Group.

State of the Poor. Frederick M. Eden. Ed. by A. G. Rogers. LC 68-56502. 1969. Repr. of 1928 ed. 24.50 (ISBN 0-405-08485-4, Blom Pubns). Ayer Co Pubs.

State of the Presidency. 2nd ed. Thomas E. Cronin. 1980. pap. text ed. write for info. (ISBN 0-673-39429-8). Scott F.

State of the Rio Grande-Rio Bravo: A Study of Water Resource Issues Along the Texas-Mexico Border. David J. Eaton. LC 87-10748. (PROFMEX Ser.). 336p. 1986. 24.95x (ISBN 0-8165-0990-5). U of Ariz Pr.

State Socialism & Anarchism & Other Essays: Including the Attitude of Anarchism Toward Industrial Combinations & Why I Am an Anarchist. Benjamin R. Tucker. LC 72-77201. (Libertarian Broadsides Ser.: No. 4). 40p. 1985. pap. 2.15 (ISBN 0-87926-015-7). R Myles.

State, Society & Economy in Saudi Arabia. Ed. by Tim Niblock. 1981. 29.95x (ISBN 0-312-75617-8). St Martin.

State, Society & University in Germany, Seventeen Hundred to Nineteen Fourteen. Charles McClelland. LC 79-13575. 1980. 57.50 (ISBN 0-521-22742-9). Cambridge U Pr.

State-Society Struggle: Zaire in Comparative Perspective. Thomas M. Callaghy. LC 84-5865. 515p. 1984. 50.00 (ISBN 0-231-05720-2); pap. 21.50x (ISBN 0-231-05721-0). Columbia U Pr.

State-Space & Frequency Domain Methods in the Control of Distributed Parameter Systems. S. P. Banks. (Topics in Control Ser.). 125p. 1983. pap. 29.00 (ISBN 0-86341-000-6, TC003). Inst Elect Eng.

State Space & Input-Output Linear Systems. D. F. Delchamps. (Illus.). 425p. 48.00 (ISBN 0-387-96659-5). Springer-Verlag.

State Space & Linear Systems. Donald M. Wiberg. (Schaum Outline Ser). 1971. pap. text ed. 10.95 (ISBN 0-07-070096-6). McGraw.

State-Space Methods for Control Systems. Csaki. 1976. cancelled 46.00 (ISBN 963-05-0862-1, Pub. by Akademiai Kaido Hungary). IPS.

State Space Modeling of Time Series. M. Aoki. (Universitext Ser.). (Illus.). xi, 314p. 1987. pap. 25.00 (ISBN 0-387-17257-2). Springer-Verlag.

State Space Modelling of Time Series. M. Aoki. (Illus.). 330p. 1986. 67.00 (ISBN 0-387-17256-4). Springer-Verlag.

State Space Theory of Discrete Linear Control. Vladimir Strejc. LC 79-991. 426p. 1981. 75.00x (ISBN 0-471-27594-8, Pub. by Wiley-Interscience). Wiley.

State Standards & Local Planning Regulation for Farmland Preservation in Oregon. Robert E. Coughlin. Ed. by Benjamin H. Stevens. (Discussion Paper Ser.: No. 124). 67p. (Orig.). 1981. pap. 6.50 (ISBN 1-55869-001-8). Regional Sci Res Inst.

State Statistical & Economic Abstract Series: Minnesota. (Illus.). 141p. (Orig.). 1987. pap. 12.00 (S/N 003-000-00653-1). USGPO.

State Statutes on School District Collective Bargaining. 261p. 1987. notebook 100.00 (ISBN 0-88364-125-9). Natl Sch Boards.

State Succession Relating to Unequal Treaties. Lung-Fong Chen. LC 74-9820. xiii, 324p. 1974. 31.00 (ISBN 0-208-01433-0, Archon). Shoe String.

State Superlatives: A Galaxy from AL to WY. Jerry Orr. LC 85-81061. (Illus.). 224p. (Orig.). pap. cancelled (ISBN 0-917125-08-8). Home Run Pr.

State Supervision & Regulation of Budgetary Procedure in Public School Systems: An Evaluation of State Provisions for Budget-Making in Local School Systems. R. G. Campbell. LC 73-176625. (Columbia University Teachers College. Contributions to Education Ser.: No. 637). Repr. of 1935 ed. 22.50 (ISBN 0-404-55637-X). AMS Pr.

State Supervision of Local Finance: Proceedings of a Conference, December 4, 5, 6, 1941. Municipal Finance Officers Association of the United States & Canada & United States. Bureau of the Census. LC 84-221045. 127p. write for info. Municipal.

State Supreme Court Litigants & Their Disputes: The Impact of Socioeconomic Development from 1870 to 1970. James W. Meeker. Ed. by Harold Hyman & Stuart Bruchey. (American Legal & Constitutional History Ser.). 180p. 1986. lib. bdg. 25.00 (ISBN 0-8240-8287-7). Garland Pub.

State Supreme Courts in Nation & State. G. Alan Tarr & Mary C. Porter. LC 87-2303. 288p. 1988. 28.50x (ISBN 0-300-03912-3). Yale U Pr.

State Supreme Courts: Policymakers in the Federal System. Ed. by Mary P. Cornelia & G. Alan Tarr. LC 81-13431. (Contributions in Legal Studies Ser.: No. 24). (Illus.). xxvii, 221p. 1982. lib. bdg. 36.95 (ISBN 0-313-22942-2, PSC/). Greenwood.

State Takeover Statutes & Poison Pills. Robert H. Winter & Robert D. Rosenbaum. 85.00. P-H.

State Tax Commissions in the United States. J. W. Chapman, Jr. 1973. Repr. of 1897 ed. 13.00 (ISBN 0-384-08507-5). Johnson Repr.

State Tax Commissions in the United States. James W. Chapman, Jr. LC 78-63860. (Johns Hopkins University. Studies in the Social Sciences. Fifteenth Series 1897: Nos. 10-11). Repr. of 1897 ed. 11.50 (ISBN 0-404-61116-8). AMS Pr.

State Tax Expenditure Review Mechanisms. (Legislative Finance Papers). 30p. 1985. 6.25 (ISBN 1-55516-047-6). Natl Conf State Legis.

State Tax Handbook: As of January 1, 1985. Clark. 232p. 1984. 13.00 (ISBN 0-317-44582-0). Commerce.

State Tax Handbook: As of October 1, 1985. Clark. 248p. 1985. 13.00 (ISBN 0-317-47516-9, 5491). Commerce.

State Tax Handbook As of October 1, 1987. 256p. (Orig.). 1987. pap. 15.00 (5290). Commerce.

State Tax Policies & Senior Citizens: A Legislator's Guide. 155p. 1985. 10.00 (ISBN 1-55516-536-2). Natl Conf State Legis.

State Tax Policy & the Development of Small & New Business. Roger Vaughan. LC 83-179310. 144p. 1983. pap. 10.00 (ISBN 0-914193-01-5). Coalition NE Govn.

State Tax Policy: Evaluating the Issues. Andrew Reschovsky et al. (Illus.). 300p. 1983. pap. 15.00 (ISBN 0-943142-04-0). St Local Inter.

State Tax Relief for the Poor: A Legislator's Guide. Steven D. Gold. (Orig.). 1987. pap. 12.00 (ISBN 1-55516-540-0). Natl Conf State Legis.

State Tax Study Commissions: An Overview of Four Approaches. (Legislative Finance Papers Ser.). 68p. 1985. 6.25 (ISBN 1-55516-048-4). Natl Conf State Legis.

State Taxation. 35.00 (ISBN 0-317-29639-6, #CO2216, Law & Business). HarBraceJ.

State Taxation: A Revision of P 793. Mary Vance. (Public Administration Ser.: P 1931). 56p. 1986. 14.50 (ISBN 0-89028-851-8). Vance Biblios.

State Taxation & Economic Development. 158p. 1979. 10.95. NCPA Washington.

State Taxation & Economic Development. Roger J. Vaughan. Ed. by Michael Barker. LC 79-54265. (Studies in State Development Policy: Vol. 1). 159p. 1979. pap. 11.95 (ISBN 0-934842-00-0). CSPA.

State Taxation: Corporate Income & Franchise Taxes, Pt. I. Jerome R. Hellerstein. 1983. Cumulative Suppls., annual. 97.50 (ISBN 0-88262-748-1, ST); Suppl., 1984. 40.25. Warren Gorham & Lamont.

State Taxation of Banks & Thrift Institutions. 2nd ed. Taxation Section Members. 450p. 1983. looseleaf bdg. 80.00 (ISBN 0-317-16895-9). Amer Bar Assn.

State Taxation of Foreign Source Income. Ernest S. Christian, Jr. LC 81-70922. 61p. 1982. 5.00 (ISBN 0-910586-44-6). Finan Exec.

State Taxation of Forest & Land Resources: Symposium Proceedings. (Lincoln Institute Monograph: No. 80-6). 149p. 1980. pap. text ed. 12.00 (ISBN 0-686-29507-2). Lincoln Inst Land.

State Taxation of Geothermal Resources Compared with State Taxation of Other Energy Minerals. Sharon C. Wagner. (Special Report Ser.: No. 4). (Illus.). 86p. (Orig.). 1979. pap. 4.00 (ISBN 0-934412-04-9). Geothermal.

State Taxation of Interstate Commerce. Paul J. Hartman. LC 53-11622. xi, 323p. 1953. lib. bdg. 35.00 (ISBN 0-89941-358-7). W S Hein.

State Taxation of Multi-National Corporations after Container Corporation: Corporate Strategies to Deal with Worldwide Unitary Tax. Law & Business Inc. Staff et al. LC 83-234944. (Illus.). v, 203p. Date not set. price not set (Law & Business). HarBraceJ.

State Taxation of Personal Incomes. Alzada Comstock. LC 74-78007. (Columbia University Studies in the Social Sciences: No. 229). Repr. of 1921 ed. 20.00 (ISBN 0-404-51229-1). AMS Pr.

State Taxation Policy & Economic Growth. Ed. by Michael Barker. LC 83-1551. (Duke Press Policy Studies). xix, 284p. 1983. 31.75 (ISBN 0-8223-0535-6). Duke.

State, the Family, & Education. Miriam E. David. (Radical Social Policy Ser.). 304p. (Orig.). 1980. pap. 17.50x (ISBN 0-7100-0601-2). Routledge Chapman & Hall.

State, the Investor, & the Railroad: The Boston & Albany, 1825-1867. Stephen Salsbury. LC 67-20881. (Center for the Study of the History of Liberty in America Ser). (Illus.). 1967. 29.50x (ISBN 0-674-83580-8). Harvard U Pr.

State, the Law & the Family: Critical Perspectives. Michael Freeman. 328p. (Orig.). 1985. pap. 16.95 (ISBN 0-422-79080-X, 9332, Pub. by Tavistock England). Routledge Chapman & Hall.

State Theory of Money. Georg F. Knapp. Tr. by H. M. Lucas & James Bonar. LC 75-140544. 1973. Repr. of 1924 ed. lib. bdg. 35.00x (ISBN 0-678-00831-0). Kelley.

State-to-State Chemistry. Ed. by Philip R. Brooks & Edward F. Hayes. LC 77-14164. (ACS Symposium Ser.: No. 56). 1977. 31.95 (ISBN 0-8412-0386-5). Am Chemical.

State Tourism Offices: A Selected Bibliography. Anthony G. White. (Public Administration Ser.: P 2059). 9p. 1986. 3.00 (ISBN 1-55590-119-0). Vance Biblios.

State Tracts: Being a Further Collection of Several Choice Treatises Relating to the Government from the Year 1660 to 1689. Ed. by Gerald M. Straka. LC 72-83171. (English Studies Ser.). 1972. Repr. of 1692 ed. lib. bdg. 54.00 (ISBN 0-8420-1428-4). Scholarly Res Inc.

State Trademark & Unfair Competition Law. United States Trademark Association Staff. LC 87-17637. 1987. looseleaf 115.00 (ISBN 0-87632-556-8, T7). Clark Boardman.

State Trademark Statutes. U. S. Trademark Association Staff. LC 66-29726. (Incl. periodic suppls). 1974. looseleaf 95.00 (ISBN 0-88238-029-X); 1983 supplement 23.00 (ISBN 0-88238-064-8). Law-Arts.

State Trading & Development. Ed. by Praxy Fernandes. 277p. 1982. pap. 20.00x (ISBN 92-9038-070-5, Pub. by Intl Ctr Pub Yugoslavia). Kumarian Pr.

State Trading in International Markets: Theory & Practice of Industrialized & Developing Countries. M. M. Kostecki. 1982. 35.00x (ISBN 0-312-75693-3). St Martin.

State Tradition in Western Europe: A Study of Idea & Institution. Kenneth H. Dyson. 1980. 27.00x (ISBN 0-19-520209-0). Oxford U Pr.

State Transportation Issues & Actions. (Special Report Ser.). 109p. 1980. 10.00 (ISBN 0-317-36105-8). Transport Res Bd.

State Tretyakov Gallery. E. N. Atsarkina & V. M. Volodarskii. (Illus.). 720p. (Rus.). 1984. 63.00x (ISBN 0-317-57452-3, Pub. by Collets UK). State Mutual Bk.

State Tretyakov Gallery: History & Collections. V. Ia. Bruk. 446p. 1986. 315.00x (ISBN 0-317-61402-9, Pub. by Collets (UK)). State Mutual Bk.

State Trials of the United States During the Administration of Washington & Adams with References Historical & Professional & Preliminary Notes on the Politics of the Times. Francis Wharton. LC 72-121595. (Bibliography & Reference Ser.: No. 352). 1970. Repr. of 1849 ed. lib. bdg. 40.50 (ISBN 0-8337-3760-0). B Franklin.

State Trials Political & Social, 4 Vols. in 2. H. Stephen. Repr. of 1902 ed. Set. 50.00 (ISBN 0-527-86300-9). Kraus Repr.

State Trooper. Jack Rudman. (Career Examination Ser.: C-757). (Cloth bdg. avail. on request). pap. 15.00 (ISBN 0-8373-0757-0). Natl Learning.

State Trooper. 8th ed. LC 83-15906. 160p. (Orig.). 1983. pap. 8.95 (ISBN 0-668-05765-3, 5765). Arco.

State Trooper Highway Patrol Officer State Traffic Officer. 9th ed. Hy Hammer & Edward Scheinkman. (ARCO Civil Service). 224p. 1988. 10.95 (ISBN 0-13-843624-X). Prentice Hall Pr.

State Universities & Democracy. Allan Nevins. LC 77-9308. 1977. Repr. of 1962 ed. lib. bdg. 35.00x (ISBN 0-8371-9705-8, NESU). Greenwood.

State University Surveys the Humanities. University of North Carolina Division of the Humanities. Ed. by L. C. MacKinney. LC 72-3386. (Essay Index Reprint Ser.). Repr. of 1945 ed. 19.00 (ISBN 0-8369-2916-0). Ayer Co Pubs.

State Variable Methods in Automatic Control. Katsuhisa Furuta & Akira Sano. LC 87-35481. 200p. 1988. write for info. (ISBN 0-471-91877-6). Wiley.

State Variables for Engineers. P. M. DeRusso et al. LC 65-21443. 608p. 1965. 59.95 (ISBN 0-471-20380-7). Krieger.

State Variations of Commercial Law. National Association of Credit Management Staff. Ed. by Lester Nelson. 1984. 2 bdrs. looseleaf 200.00. Oceana.

State Venture Capital Initiatives. National Conference of State Legislatures Staff. (State Legislative Report: Vol. 11, No. 2). 22p. pap. 5.00 (ISBN 1-55516-158-8). Natl Conf State Legis.

State Verdict Survey. 25.00. Jury Verdict.

State Veterans' Laws: Digests of State Laws Regarding Rights, Benefits, & Privileges of Veterans & Their Dependents (Revised to February 1, 1984) 324p. 1984. 8.00 (ISBN 0-318-23087-9, 052-070-05914-1). USGPO.

State vs. Elinor Norton. Mary R. Rinehart. 288p. 1988. pap. 3.50 (ISBN 0-8217-2412-6). Zebra.

State, War & Peace. J. A. Fernandez-Santamaria. LC 76-27903. (Studies in Early Modern History). 1977. 52.50 (ISBN 0-521-21438-6). Cambridge U Pr.

State Water Quality Planning Issues. 64p. (Orig.). 1982. pap. 8.00 (ISBN 0-87292-031-3, RM 719). Coun State Govts.

State We're in Washington: A Citizen's Handbook. League of Women Voters of Washington Staff. 80p. 1984. pap. text ed. 5.75 (ISBN 0-8403-3507-5). Kendall-Hunt.

State-Wide Dialect Collecting see Oil Refinery Terms in Oklahoma.

State Without Stakes: Religious Toleration in Reformation Poland. Janusz Tazbir. Tr. by A. T. Jordan. (Library of Polish Studies: Vol. 3). text ed. 4.00 (ISBN 0-917004-05-1). Kosciuszko.

State Your Claim! (Consumer Redress) Marilyn Thypin & Lynne Glasner. LC 79-9559. (Consumer Education Ser.: No. 2). (Orig.). (gr. 9-12). 1980. pap. text ed. 3.95 (ISBN 0-88436-517-4, 30258). EMC.

Statecraft. William Sanderson. 59.95 (ISBN 0-8490-1123-X). Gordon Pr.

Statecraft & Agriculture in Mexico, 1980-1982: Domestic & Foreign Policy Considerations in the Making of Mexican Agricultural Policy. John J. Bailey & John E. Link. (Research Report Ser.: No. 23). 40p. (Orig.). 1981. pap. 5.50 (ISBN 0-935391-22-3, RR-23). Ctr Mex Studies.

Statecraft As Soulcraft: What Government Does. George F. Will. 192p. 1983. 13.50 (ISBN 0-671-42733-4). S&S.

Statecraft As Soulcraft: What Government Does. George F. Will. 1984. pap. 7.95 (ISBN 0-671-42734-2, Touchstone). S&S.

Statecraft, Domestic Politics & Foreign Policy Making: The El Chamizal Dispute. Alan C. Lamborn & Stephen P. Mumme. (Special Studies in International Relations). 211p. 1988. pap. 29.50 (ISBN 0-8133-7291-7). Westview.

Statecraft in the Dark: Israel's Practice of Quiet Diplomacy. Aharon Klieman. (Publications of JCSS: No. 142). 140p. 1988. 18.00 (ISBN 0-8133-0717-1). Westview.

Statehood & Union: A History of the Northwest Ordinance. Peter S. Onuf. LC 86-43046. (Midwestern History & Culture Ser.). (Illus.). 224p. 1987. 27.50x (ISBN 0-253-35482-X). Ind U Pr.

Stateless in Gaza. Paul Cossali & Clive Robson. (Illus.). 172p. 1986. text ed. 29.95x (ISBN 0-86232-508-0, Pub. by Zed Pr); pap. 12.50 (ISBN 0-86232-509-9). Humanities.

Statelessness: With Special Reference to the United States (Study in Nationality & Conflict of Laws) C. Seckler-Hudson. Repr. of 1934 ed. 31.00 (ISBN 0-527-81000-2). Kraus Repr.

Stately Gardens of Britain. Thomas Hinde. (Illus.). 1983. 29.95 (ISBN 0-393-01763-X). Norton.

Stately Ghosts of England. Diana Norman. (Dorset Press Reprints Ser.). (Illus.). 191p. 1988. 16.95 (ISBN 0-88029-208-3). Hippocrene Bks.

Stately Homicide. S. T. Haymon. 256p. 1986. pap. 3.50 (ISBN 0-445-20161-4, Pub. by Popular Lib). Warner Bks.

Stately Picturesque Dream: Scenes of Florida, Cuba & Mexico in 1880. University Gallery, University of Florida, Staff. (Illus.). 64p. (Orig.). 1984. pap. 9.50 (ISBN 0-8130-0795-X). U Presses Fla.

Statemaking & Social Movements: Essays in History & Theory. Ed. by Charles C. Bright & Susan F. Harding. LC 84-7430. 404p. 1984. text ed. 22.95 (ISBN 0-472-10050-5). U of Mich Pr.

Stateman's Year-Book Historical Companion. Ed. by John Paxton. 700p. 1988. 39.95 (ISBN 0-312-00047-2). St Martin.

Stateman's Year-Book, 1976-1977. Ed. by John Paxton. LC 4-3776. 1976. 19.95 (ISBN 0-312-76055-8). St Martin.

Stateman's Year-Book, 1988-89. 125th ed. Ed. by John Paxton. 1700p. 1988. 59.95 (ISBN 0-312-02094-5). St Martin.

Statement & Inference: With Other Philosophical Papers. John C. Wilson. 1926. 109.00x (ISBN 0-19-824336-7). Oxford U Pr.

Statement before the House Committee on the Judiciary Subcommittee on Civil & Constitutional Rights, April 3, 1985. Jules Lobel & Barbara Wolvovitz. 3.50. Natl Lawyers Guild.

Statement of Accounting Principles. Thomas H. Sanders et al. 138p. 6.00 (ISBN 0-86539-009-6). Am Accounting.

Statement of Basic Accounting Theory. Basic Accounting Theory Committee. 100p. 6.00 (ISBN 0-86539-008-8). Am Accounting.

Statement of Basic Auditing Concepts, Vol. 6. Basic Auditing Concepts Committee. (Studies in Accounting Research). 58p. 1973. 6.00 (ISBN 0-86539-018-5). Am Accounting.

Statement of Editorial Principles & Procedures: A Working Manual for Editing Nineteenth-Century American Texts. rev. ed. Center for Editions of American Authors Staff. x, 25p. (Orig.). 1972. pap. 7.50x (ISBN 0-87352-008-4, S62). Modern Lang.

Statement of Financial Accounting Standards No. 5: Impact on Corporate Risk & Insurance Management. Robert C. Goshay. LC 78-65314. (Financial Accounting Standards Board Research Report). (Illus.). 68p. (Orig.). 1978. pap. 2.50 (ISBN 0-910065-05-5). Finan Acct Found.

Statement of Guidance on Advertising, Publicity & Solicitation. (International Ethics Guidelines Ser.). 1982. pap. 3.50 (ISBN 0-317-01700-4). Am Inst Cpa.

Statement of Guidance on Professional Competence. (International Ethics Guidelines Ser.). 1982. pap. 3.50 (ISBN 0-317-01704-7). Am Inst Cpa.

Statement of Loans, Statement of Development Credits Subscription. World Bank Staff. 1987. 100.00 (IB0941). World Bank.

Statement of Principle & Standards for Internal Auditing the Banking Industry. Bank Administration Institute. 24p. 1977. 18.00 (217). Bank Admin Inst.

Statement of Some New Principles on the Subject of Political Economy. John Rae. LC 65-10366. 45.00x (ISBN 0-678-00065-4). Kelley.

Statement of the Arts & Manufactures of the U. S. for the Year 1810 see American Industry & Manufactures in the Nineteenth Century.

Statement of the Laws of Argentina in Matters Affecting Business. Carlos Alurralde. 1976. lib. bdg. 134.95 (ISBN 0-8490-2666-0). Gordon Pr.

Statement of the Laws of Honduras in Matters Affecting Business. 4th ed. OAS General Secretariat for Legal Affairs. 292p. 1981. pap. text ed. 10.00 (ISBN 0-8270-1421-X). OAS.

Statement on Accounting Theory & Theory Acceptance. Concepts & Standards for External Financial Reports Committee. 61p. 6.00 (ISBN 0-86539-010-X). Am Accounting.

Statement on Central America. rev. ed. United States Catholic Conference. (Orig., Eng. & Span.). 1987. pap. 2.95 (ISBN 1-55586-192-X). US Catholic.

Statement on Conditions for Acceptance of an Appointment when Another Accountant in Public Practice is Already Carrying Our Work for the Same Client. (International Ethics Guidelines Ser.). 1983. 3.50 (ISBN 0-317-01711-X). Am Inst Cpa.

Static Electrification: London 1975. (Institute of Physics Conference Ser.: No. 27). 1975. cancelled 49.00 (ISBN 0-85498-117-9, Pub. by Inst Physics England). IPS.

Static Element: Selected Poems of Natan Zach. Tr. by Natan Zach & Shulamit Yasny-Starkman. LC 82-71257. 72p. 1982. 12.95 (ISBN 0-689-11318-8); pap. 7.95 (ISBN 0-689-11319-6). Atheneum.

Static Microeconomic Model of Pure Competition. C. Klein. (Lecture Notes in Economics & Mathematical Systems Ser.: Vol. 306). 139p. 1988. pap. 19.40 (ISBN 0-387-19358-8). Springer-Verlag.

Static of the Spheres. Eric Kraft. 96p. 1986. pap. 4.95 (ISBN 0-446-38356-2). Warner Bks.

Static Position of Classifying Alcoholism & Drug Addiction As Identical Illnesses. Virgil R. Adkins. 91p. 1986. 4.25 (ISBN 0-89697-276-3). Intl Univ Pr.

Static Power Frequency Changers: Theory, Performance & Application. L. Gyugyi & B. R. Pelly. LC 76-6088. 442p. 1976. 69.95x (ISBN 0-471-67800-7, Pub. by Wiley-Interscience). Wiley.

Static Quadrupole Effects in Disordered Cubic Solids. O. Kanert & M. Mehring. Ed. by P. Diehl. Bd. with Nuclear Magnetic Relaxation Spectroscopy. F. Noack. (NMR-Basic Principles & Progress: Vol. 3). (Illus.). 130p. 1971. 32.00 (ISBN 0-387-05392-1). Springer-Verlag.

Static Test Methods for Composites. M. Tarnopolski. 300p. 1985. 49.00. T-C Pubns CA.

Static Test Methods for Composites. Yu M. Tarnopolskii & T. Ya Kintsis. Ed. by George Lubin. (Illus.). 288p. 1984. 48.95 (ISBN 0-442-28281-8). Van Nos Reinhold.

Statical & Geomechanical Models. E. Fumagalli. (Illus.). xv, 182p. 1973. 62.00 (ISBN 0-387-81096-X). Springer-Verlag.

Statically Indeterminate Structures. Wang Chu-Kia. (Illus.). 1953. text ed. 45.95 (ISBN 0-07-068130-9). McGraw.

Statically Indeterminate Structures: Their Analysis & Design. Paul Andersen. LC 52-11520. (Illus.). pap. 81.50 (ISBN 0-317-10804-2, 2012568). Bks Demand UMI.

Statics. 2nd ed. James L. Meriam. LC 71-136719. (Illus.). pap. 98.50 (ISBN 0-317-08359-7, 2019288). Bks Demand UMI.

Statics see Applied Mechanics.

Statics see Engineering Mechanics.

Statics & Dynamics: Dynamics. 2nd ed. Jerry H. Ginsberg & Joseph Genin. 608p. 1984. text ed. write for info. (ISBN 0-471-06495-5). Wiley.

Statics & Dynamics of Nonlinear Systems. Ed. by G. Benedek et al. (Springer Series in Solid-State Sciences: Vol. 47). (Illus.). 311p. 1983. 43.00 (ISBN 0-387-12841-7). Springer Verlag.

Statics & Dynamics: Statics. Jerry H. Ginsberg & Joseph Genin. LC 83-10426. 432p. 1984. 39.95 (ISBN 0-471-06494-7). Wiley.

Statics & Mechanics of Materials. Braja M. Das & Paul C. Hassler. (Illus.). 560p. 1988. text ed. 42.67 (ISBN 0-13-844655-5). P-H.

Statics & Strength of Materials. 4th ed. Milton G. Bassin. 496p. 1988. text ed. 39.95 (ISBN 0-07-004023-0). McGraw.

Statics & Strength of Materials. 3rd ed. Milton G. Bassin et al. (Illus.). 1979. text ed. 39.95 (ISBN 0-07-004030-3). McGraw.

Statics & Strength of Materials. Fa-Hwa Cheng. 500p. 1987. text ed. write for info. (ISBN 0-02-322300-6). Macmillan.

Statics & Strength of Materials. Irving Granet. 1983. text ed. 31.95 (ISBN 0-03-060309-9). HR&W.

Statics & Strength of Materials. 3rd ed. Alfred E. Jensen & Harry H. Chenoweth. LC 75-8820. (Illus.). 608p. 1975. text ed. 42.95 (ISBN 0-07-032472-7). McGraw.

Statics & Strength of Materials. Irving J. Levinson. 1970. 39.00 (ISBN 0-13-844506-0). P-H.

Statics & Strength of Materials. Karl K. Stevens. (Illus.). 1979. write for info (ISBN 0-13-844688-1). P-H.

Statics & Strength of Materials: A Parallel Approach. Lawrence Wolf. 512p. 1988. case bound 34.95 (ISBN 0-675-20622-7); supplements avail. Merrill.

Statics & Strength of Materials for Technology. 2nd ed. Don A. Halperin. LC 79-26256. 287p. 1981. text ed. 28.95 (ISBN 0-471-06042-9); solutions manual avail. Wiley.

Statics & Strength of Structures. Mario Salvadori. LC 70-138821. 1971. 50.00. P-H.

Statics & Strengths of Materials. 4th ed. Alfred E. Jensen & Harry H. Chenoweth. LC 82-12642. 1983. text ed. 42.95 (ISBN 0-07-032494-8). McGraw.

Statics & Strengths of Materials. George Kraut. 1984. text ed. write for info. (ISBN 0-8359-7112-0, Reston); instr's. manual avail. (ISBN 0-8359-7113-9). P-H.

Statics & Strengths of Materials. Harold W. Morrow. (Illus.). 512p. 1981. text ed. write for info (ISBN 0-13-844720-9). P-H.

Statics Exam File. Ed. by Charles E. Smith. LC 84-21141. (Exam File Ser.). 346p. (Orig.). 1985. pap. 9.95 (ISBN 0-910554-47-1). Engineering.

Statics for Architecture. Jafar Vossoughi. (Illus.). 1986. 31.95 (ISBN 0-442-29111-6). Van Nos Reinhold.

Statics, Formfinding & Dynamics of Air-Supported Membrane Structures. Vladimir Firt. 1983. lib. bdg. 83.00 (ISBN 90-247-2672-7, Pub. by Martinus Nijhoff Netherlands). Kluwer Academic.

Statics of Structural Components: Understanding the Basics of Structural Design. Giuseppe DeCampoli. LC 82-20122. 296p. 1983. 29.95 (ISBN 0-471-87169-9, Pub. by Wiley-Interscience). Wiley.

Statics: SI Version. 2nd ed. J. L. Meriam. 381p. 1975. write for info. (ISBN 0-471-59604-3); study guide 123pp 14.95 (ISBN 0-471-86458-7). Wiley.

Statics, Structure & Stress: A Teaching Text for Problem-Solving in Theory of Structures & Strength of Materials. W. Fisher Cassie. LC 74-158981. (Longman Text Ser.). pap. 141.30 (ISBN 0-317-09285-5, 2016309). Bks Demand UMI.

Stating Objectives for Classroom Instruction. 3rd ed. Norman E. Gronlund. 80p. 1985. text ed. write for info. (ISBN 0-02-348000-9). Macmillan.

Stating Your Case-How to Interview for a Job As a Lawyer. Joseph Ryan. LC 82-10996. 250p. 1982. pap. text ed. 9.95 (ISBN 0-314-67111-0). West Pub.

Station Champbaudet. Eugene Labiche. 9.95 (ISBN 0-686-54251-7); pap. 4.95 (ISBN 0-686-54252-5). French & Eur.

Station Gehenna. Andrew Weiner. (Isaac Asimov Presents Ser.). 192p. 1987. 15.95 (ISBN 0-86553-191-9). Congdon & Weed.

Station Gehenna. Andrew Weiner. 256p. 1988. pap. 3.95 (ISBN 0-373-30306-8, Pub. by Worldwide). Harlequin Bks.

Station in the Delta. John Cassidy. 320p. 1981. pap. 2.95 (ISBN 0-345-30849-2). Ballantine.

Station Installation & Maintenance, Vol. II. Frank E. Lee. 1986. 11.95 (ISBN 0-686-98058-1). Telecom Lib.

Station Island. Seamus Heaney. LC 84-21067. 123p. 1985. 11.95 (ISBN 0-374-26978-5). FS&G.

Station Island. Seamus Heaney. 1985. pap. 6.95 (ISBN 0-374-51935-8). FS&G.

Station J: An American Play. Richard France. LC 82-14936. 170p. (Orig.). 1983. pap. 9.95 (ISBN 0-8290-0538-2). Irvington.

Station KBOE. 3rd ed. O. Church. 240p. 1984. text ed. 7.44 (ISBN 0-07-010837-4). McGraw.

Station Life in New Zealand. Mary A. Barker. LC 87-47528. (Virago-Beacon Traveler Ser.). 256p. 1987. pap. 9.95 (ISBN 0-8070-7029-7, BP 765). Beacon Pr.

Station Master on the Underground Railroad: The Life & Letters of Thomas Garrett. James McGowan. LC 77-84816. (Illus.). 181p. 1977. 7.95 (ISBN 0-916178-00-5). Whimsie Pr.

Station No. 21: Fargo. Hank Mitchum. (Stagecoach Ser.). 192p. (Orig.). 1985. pap. 2.75 (ISBN 0-553-25290-9). Bantam.

Station No. 23: El Paso. Hank Mitchum. (Stagecoach Ser.). 192p. (Orig.). 1986. pap. 2.75 (ISBN 0-553-25549-5). Bantam.

Station, No. 24: Mesa Verde. Hank Mitchum. (Stagecoach Ser.). 208p. (Orig.). 1986. pap. 2.75 (ISBN 0-553-25808-7). Bantam.

Station, No. 25: San Antonio. Hank Mitchum. (Stagecoach Ser.). 192p. (Orig.). 1986. pap. 2.75 (ISBN 0-553-26180-0). Bantam.

Station, No. 27: Pecos. Hank Mitchum. (Stagecoach Ser.). 192p. (Orig.). 1987. pap. 2.75 (ISBN 0-553-26193-2). Bantam.

Station Stop: A Collection of Haiku & Related Forms. Richard Tice. LC 85-90484. (Illus.). 87p. 1986. 7.95 (ISBN 0-935961-00-3). Middlewood Pr.

Station Supervisor. Jack Rudman. (Career Examination Ser.: C-2105). (Cloth bdg. avail. on request). 1988. pap. 12.00 (ISBN 0-8373-2105-0). Natl Learning.

Station Wagon in Spain. Frances P. Keyes. 256p. 1977. pap. 1.50 (ISBN 0-449-23193-3, Crest). Fawcett.

Station Wagon Set. Faith Baldwin. 1976. Repr. of 1939 ed. lib. bdg. 22.95x (ISBN 0-88411-604-2, Pub. by Aeonian Pr). Amereon Ltd.

Station-Work Uniforms for Fire Fighters. National Fire Protection Association Staff. 1985. 10.50 (ISBN 0-317-63572-7, 1975-85). Natl Fire Prot.

Stationary Ark. Gerald Durrell. 1984. pap. 6.95 (ISBN 0-671-50758-3, Touchstone). S&S.

Stationary Bicycles. Michael T. Cannell & Judith Zimmer. Ed. by Susan Wallach. LC 84-40600. (At Home Gym Ser.). 64p. 1985. pap. 2.95 (ISBN 0-394-72973-0, Pub. by Villard Bks). Random.

Stationary Combustion Engines & Gas Turbines. National Fire Protection Association Staff. 1984. 10.50 (ISBN 0-317-63071-7, 37-84). Natl Fire Prot.

Stationary Combustion Engines & Gas Turbines. (Thirty Ser). 1970. pap. 2.00 (ISBN 0-685-58106-3, 37). Natl Fire Prot.

Stationary Engineer. Jack Rudman. (Career Examination Ser.: C-758). (Cloth bdg. avail. on request). pap. 14.00 (ISBN 0-8373-0758-9). Natl Learning.

Stationary Engineer (Electric) Jack Rudman. (Career Examination Ser.: C-759). (Cloth bdg. avail. on request). pap. 14.00 (ISBN 0-8373-0759-7). Natl Learning.

Stationary Engineer, High Pressure Boiler Operating Engineer, High Pressure Plant Tender. Harry Mahler. 1986. pap. 9.00 (ISBN 0-668-06075-1). P-H.

Stationary Engineer 1. Jack Rudman. (Career Examination Ser.: C-1903). (Cloth bdg. avail. on request). pap. 14.00 (ISBN 0-8373-1903-X). Natl Learning.

Stationary Engineer 2. Jack Rudman. (Career Examination Ser.: C-1904). (Cloth bdg. avail. on request). pap. 16.00 (ISBN 0-8373-1904-8). Natl Learning.

Stationary Fireman. Jack Rudman. (Career Examination Ser.: C-760). (Cloth bdg. avail. on request). pap. 12.00 (ISBN 0-8373-0760-0). Natl Learning.

Stationary Gas Turbine Alternative Fuels - STP 809. Ed. by J. S. Clark & S. M. De Corso. LC 82-73767. 360p. 1983. 43.00 (04-809000-13). ASTM.

Stationary Phases in Gas Chromatography. G. E. Baiulescu & A. V. Ilie. 1975. 85.00 (ISBN 0-08-018075-2). Pergamon.

Stationary Random Processes Associated with Point Processses. T. Rolski. (Lecture Notes in Statistics Ser.: Vol. 5). 152p. 1982. pap. 18.50 (ISBN 0-387-90575-8). Springer-Verlag.

Stationary Semiconductor Device Equations. P. A. Markowich. (Computational Microelectronics Ser.). (Illus.). 210p. 1985. 45.00 (ISBN 0-387-81892-8). Springer-Verlag.

Stationary Sequences & Random Fields. Murray Rosenblatt. 288p. 1985. 34.95x (ISBN 0-8176-3264-6). Birkhauser.

Stationary States. Alan Holden. (Illus., Orig.). 1971. pap. text ed. 4.95x (ISBN 0-19-501497-9). Oxford U Pr.

Stationary Stochastic Processes. T. Hida. (Mathematical Notes Ser.: No. 8). 1970. 21.50x (ISBN 0-691-08074-7). Princeton U Pr.

Stationers' Company: A History, 1403-1959. Cyprian Blagden. LC 76-48000. 1960. 30.00x (ISBN 0-8047-0935-1). Stanford U Pr.

Stationer's Company: Extracts, 2 vols in 1, Vols. 1-2. J. P. Collier. (Shakespeare Society of London Ser.: Vol. 12). pap. 42.00 (ISBN 0-8115-0174-4). Kraus Repr.

Stationing & Stability of Semi-Submersibles. Ed. by Society for Underwater Technology (SUT) Staff. 1988. lib. bdg. 79.00 (ISBN 0-86010-831-7, Pub. by Graham & Trotman). Kluwer Academic.

Stations. Keith Bosley. 112p. (Orig.). 1979. pap. 6.95 (ISBN 0-85646-055-9, Pub. by Anvil Pr Poetry). Longwood Pub Group.

Stations of the Cross. J. B. Mulligan. 1979. pap. 1.00 (ISBN 0-686-25264-0). Samisdat.

Stations of the Cross. Laurel Rooney. (gr. 1-3). 1984. 9.95 (ISBN 0-89837-094-9, Pub. by Pflaum Press). Pflaum Pr.

Stations of the Cross of Our Lord & Master Jesus Christ. Ermenegildo Panciatichi. (Illus.). 156p. 1987. 177.50 (ISBN 0-86650-211-4). Gloucester Art.

Stations of the Lost: The Treatment of Skid Row Alcoholics. Jacqueline P. Wiseman. LC 79-13632. 1979. pap. 9.95X (ISBN 0-226-90307-9, P853). U of Chicago Pr.

Stations of the Mind: New Directions for Reality Therapy. William Glasser & William T. Powers. LC 80-8205. (Illus.). 288p. 1981. 15.95i (ISBN 0-06-011478-9, HarpT). Har-Row.

Stations of the Nightmare. Philip Jose Farmer. 256p. 1988. pap. 3.95 (ISBN 0-8125-3773-4). Tor Bks.

Statira by Pietro Ottoboni & Alessandro Scarlatti: The Textual Sources, with a Documentary Postscript. William Holmes. LC 82-12357. (Monographs in Musicology: No. 2). 120p. 1983. lib. bdg. 18.00 (ISBN 0-918728-18-5). Pendragon NY.

Statism & Anarchy. Mikhail Bakunin. Ed. by J. Frank Harrison. 74. lib. bdg. 79.95 (ISBN 0-87700-219-3). Revisionist Pr.

Statist & Statistician. Ed. by Victor L. Hilts & I. Bernard Cohen. LC 80-2091. (Development of Science Ser.). (Illus.). 1981. lib. bdg. 55.00x (ISBN 0-405-13856-3). Ayer Co Pubs.

Statistic: Art or Science? V. V. Shvyrkov. LC 82-61951. (Illus.). 105p. (Orig.). 1982. text ed. 13.40 (ISBN 0-942004-05-1). Throwkoff Pr.

Statistic Europe. 5th ed. Ed. by Joan M. Harvey. 320p. 1987. 130.00x (ISBN 0-900246-48-0, Pub. by CBD Res Ltd). Gale.

Statistic of World Trade in Steel 1986. 73p. (Eng., Fr. & Rus.). 1987. pap. 16.00 (ISBN 92-1-016207-2, E/F/R.87.II.E.12). UN.

Statistical Abstract of Colorado, 1976-77. Compiled by Thomas G. Tyler. (Illus.). 1977. 15.75x (ISBN 0-918370-01-9). Transrep.

Statistical Abstract of Colorado, 1987. Gerald L. Allen. 771p. 1987. pap. 45.00 (ISBN 0-89478-097-2). U CO Busn Res Div.

Statistical Abstract of Latin America, Vol. 22. Ed. by James W. Wilkie & Stephen Haber. LC 56-63569. (Statistical Abstract of Latin America Ser.). 1983. lib. bdg. 75.00x (ISBN 0-87903-241-3). UCLA Lat Am Ctr.

Statistical Abstract of Latin America, Vol. 23. Ed. by James W. Wilkie & Adam Perkal. LC 56-63569. 1984. lib. bdg. 100.00x (ISBN 0-87903-244-8). UCLA Lat Am Ctr.

Statistical Abstract of Latin America, Vol. 24. Ed. by James W. Wilkie & Adam Perkal. LC 56-63569. 700p. 1986. lib. bdg. 127.00x (ISBN 0-87903-245-6). UCLA Lat Am Ctr.

Statistical Abstract of Latin America, 1981, Vol. 21. Ed. by James W. Wilkie. LC 56-63569. 1981. lib. bdg. 50.00x (ISBN 0-87903-239-1). UCLA Lat Am Ctr.

Statistical Abstract of Oklahoma, 1984. 511p. 1986. pap. 20.00x (ISBN 0-931880-01-7). U OK Ctr Econ.

Statistical Abstract of the United States-Mexico Borderlands. Peter L. Reich. (Statistical Abstract of Latin America Supplement Ser.: Vol. 9). 204p. 1984. lib. bdg. 45.00x (ISBN 0-87903-243-X). UCLA Lat Am Ctr.

Statistical Abstract of the United States, 1988: National Data Book & Guide to Sources. 108th ed. (Illus.). 973p. 1987. 30.00 (S/N 003-024-06708-1). USGPO.

Statistical Abstract of Utah - 1987. 10th ed. Ed. by University of Utah, Bureau of Economic & Business Research Staff. 1987. lib. bdg. 25.00 (ISBN 0-942486-05-6); pap. 40.00 (ISBN 0-317-59225-4). Univ Utah.

Statistical Abstract, 1985. 27th ed. Department of Commerce Staff. (Illus.). 261p. (Orig.). 1985. pap. text ed. 11.20 (ISBN 0-8182-0069-3). Commonweal PA.

Statistical Account of the Parish of St. Just-in-Penwith. John Butler. 1985. 40.00x (ISBN 0-907566-61-8, Pub. by Dyllansow & Truran). State Mutual Bk.

Statistical Account of Upper Canada, 2 Vols. Robert F. Gourlay. 1967. Repr. of 1822 ed. 60.00 set (ISBN 0-384-19475-3). Johnson Repr.

Statistical Adjustment of Data. William E. Deming. 261p. 1984. pap. 7.95 (ISBN 0-486-64685-8). Dover.

Statistical Analysis: A Computer Oriented Approach. 2nd ed. A. A. Afifi & Stanley P. Azen. 1979. 44.95 (ISBN 0-12-044460-7). Acad Pr.

Statistical Analysis: A Decision Making Approach. 2nd ed. Robert Parsons. 1978. text ed. 39.50 scp (ISBN 0-06-045016-9, HarpC). Har-Row.

Statistical Analysis: An Interdisciplinary Introduction to Univariate & Multivariate Methods. Sam K. Kachigan. LC 85-61811. (Illus.). 589p. 1986. text ed. 35.95x (ISBN 0-942154-99-1). Radius Pr.

Statistical Analysis & Mathematical Modelling of AIDS. J. C. Jager & E. J. Ruitenberg. (Illus.). 160p. 1988. 56.50 (ISBN 0-19-261745-1). Oxford U Pr.

Statistical Analysis for Business Decisions. new ed. Paul Jedamus et al. (Illus.). 1976. text ed. 38.95 (ISBN 0-07-032302-X). McGraw.

Statistical Analysis for Business Decisions. Gary E. Meek & Stephen J. Turner. 768p. 1983. text ed. 36.95 (ISBN 0-395-32274-X); instr's. manual 2.00 (ISBN 0-395-32825-X). HM.

Statistical Analysis for Decision Making. 4th ed. Morris Hamburg. 701p. 1987. text ed. 35.95 (ISBN 0-15-583453-3); study guide 9.50; solutions manual (121p.) 3.95 (ISBN 0-317-56198-7); test book 3.50 (ISBN 0-15-583456-8); Easystat - a guide. write for info. spiral bdg. (ISBN 0-15-583458-4); disk 7.00 (ISBN 0-15-583457-6). HarBraceJ.

Statistical Analysis for Decision Making. Charles A. Nickerson & Ingeborg A. Nickerson. (Illus.). 1979. text ed. 25.00 (ISBN 0-89433-001-2). Petrocelli.

Statistical Analysis for Engineers: A Computer-Based Approach. J. Wesley Barnes. 512p. 1988. text ed. 59.00 (ISBN 0-13-844788-8). P-H.

Statistical Analysis for Microcomputers. William Deaton. (Illus.). 96p. 1984. incl. disk 49.95 (ISBN 0-88056-217-X). Dilithium Pr.

Statistical Analysis in Business. Stephen A. Book & Marc J. Epstein. 1982. text ed. write for info. (ISBN 0-673-16002-5). Scott F.

Statistical Analysis in Chemistry & the Chemical Industry. Carl A. Bennett et al. LC 54-11428. (Wiley Publications in Statistics). pap. 160.00 (ISBN 0-317-09349-5, 2055153). Bks Demand UMI.

Statistical Analysis in Psychology & Education. 5th, rev. ed. George A. Ferguson. LC 80-19584. (Psychology Ser.). (Illus.). 560p. 1980. text ed. 36.95x (ISBN 0-07-020482-9). McGraw.

Statistical Analysis in Psychology & Education. 6th ed. George A. Ferguson. (Illus.). 576p. 1988. 38.95 (ISBN 0-07-020485-3). McGraw.

Statistical Analysis of American Divorce. Alfred Cahen. LC 68-58553. (Columbia University Studies in the Social Sciences: No. 360). Repr. of 1932 ed. 14.50 (ISBN 0-404-51360-3). AMS Pr.

Statistical Analysis of Compositional Data. J. Aitchison. (Monographs on Statistics & Applied Probability). 400p. 1986. text ed. 49.95 (ISBN 0-412-28060-4, 9864, Pub. by Chapman & Hall England). Routledge Chapman & Hall.

Statistical Analysis of Counting Processes. M. Jacobson. (Lecture Notes in Statistics Ser.: Vol. 12). 226p. 1982. pap. 21.00 (ISBN 0-387-90769-6). Springer-Verlag.

Statistical Analysis of Data. T. W. Anderson & S. L. Sclove. 628p. 1986. text ed. 35.00 (ISBN 0-89426-071-5). Scientific Pr.

Statistical Analysis of Data-Set Quality. V. Shvyrkov. LC 85-20211. (Illus.). 190p. (Orig.). 1985. pap. text ed. 33.10 (ISBN 0-942004-13-2). Throwkoff Pr.

Statistical Handbook of U. K. Agriculture. Denis K. Britton et al. 20.00x (ISBN 0-686-79165-7, Pub. by Dominican Ireland). State Mutual Bk.

Statistical Handbook on Aging Americans. Ed. by Frank L. Schick. LC 85-43607. (Illus.). 312p. 1986. lib. bdg. 39.50 (ISBN 0-89774-259-1). Oryx Pr.

Statistical History of Acting Editions of Shakespeare: Supplement to Shakespeare as Spoken, Vol. 13. William P. Halstead. LC 82-20232. 628p. 1983. lib. bdg. 46.25 (ISBN 0-8191-2854-6). U Pr of Amer.

Statistical History of Acting Editions of Shakespeare: Supplement to Shakespeare as Spoken, Vol. 14. William P. Halstead. LC 82-20232. 654p. 1983. lib. bdg. 46.25 (ISBN 0-8191-2855-4). U Pr of Amer.

Statistical History of the American Presidential Elections: With Supplementary Tables Covering 1968 to 1980. Svend Petersen. LC 81-6348. xxiii, 275p. 1981. Repr. of 1963 ed. lib. bdg. 41.50x (ISBN 0-313-22952-X, PESH). Greenwood.

Statistical Image Processing & Graphics. Wegman & DePriest. (Statistics: Monographs Ser.). 320p. 1986. 74.75 (ISBN 0-8247-7600-3). Dekker.

Statistical Independence in Probability Analysis & Number Theory. Mark Kac. (Carus Monograph: No. 12). 93p. 1969. pap. 12.50 (ISBN 0-88385-012-5). Math Assn.

Statistical Indicators for Asia & the Pacific, Vol. XVI, No. I. 84p. 1986. 9.50 (ISBN 92-1-119420-2, E.86.II.F.12). UN.

Statistical Indicators for Asia & the Pacific, Vol. XV, No. 2. 84p. 1985. 9.50 (ISBN 92-1-119277-3, E.85.11.F.17). UN.

Statistical Indicators for Asia & the Pacific, Vol. XV, No. 3. 84p. 1985. 11.50 (ISBN 92-1-119284-6, E.85.11.F.20). UN.

Statistical Indicators for Asia & the Pacific, June 1986, Vol. XVI, No. 2. 84p. 1987. 9.50 (ISBN 92-1-119424-5, E.86.II.F.15). UN.

Statistical Indicators for Asia & the Pacific, 12 1985, Vol. XVII, No. 4. 84p. 1985. 9.50 (ISBN 92-1-119417-2, E.86.II.F.7). UN.

Statistical Indicators for the Planning & Evaluation of Public Health Programmes: Report. WHO Expert Committee on Health Statistics. Geneva, 1970, 14th. (Also avail. in Spanish). 1971. pap. 2.00 (ISBN 92-4-120472-9). World Health.

Statistical Indicators on Youth. 202p. 1986. 15.50 (ISBN 92-1-061099-7, E.85.XVII.12). UN.

Statistical Indices of Family Health: Report. WHO Study Group. (Technical Report Ser.: No. 587). (Also avail. in French & Spanish). 1976. pap. 3.20 (ISBN 92-4-120587-3). World Health.

Statistical Inference. Vijay K. Rohatgi. LC 83-21848. (Probability & Mathematical Statistics Ser.). 940p. 1984. 47.95x (ISBN 0-471-87126-5, 1-346, Pub. by Wiley-Interscience). Wiley.

Statistical Inference. S. D. Silvey. (Monographs on Statistics & Applied Probability). 1975. 15.95 (ISBN 0-412-13820-4, 6248, Pub. by Chapman & Hall). Routledge Chapman & Hall.

Statistical Inference: A Commentary for the Social & Behavioural Sciences. Michael Oakes. LC 85-17933. 1986. 41.95 (ISBN 0-471-10443-4). Wiley.

Statistical Inference Based on Ranks. Thomas P. Hettmansperger. LC 83-23519. (Probability & Mathematical Statistics Applied Probability & Statictics Sections Ser.). 323p. 1984. 44.95x (ISBN 0-471-88474-X, 1-345, Pub. by Wiley-Interscience). Wiley.

Statistical Inference for Markov Processes. Patrick Billingsley. LC 61-8646. (Midway Reprint Ser.). 84p. 1975. pap. text ed. 5.50x (ISBN 0-226-05077-7). U of Chicago Pr.

Statistical Inference for Spatial Processes. B. D. Ripley. (Illus.). 160p. Date not set. price not set (ISBN 0-521-35234-7). Cambridge U Pr.

Statistical Inference in Linear Models, Vol. 1. Ed. by Helga Bunke & Olaf Bunke. (Probability & Mathematical Statistics Ser.: 1-345). 614p. 1986. 100.00 (ISBN 0-471-10334-9). Wiley.

Statistical Inference under Order Restrictions: The Theory & Application of Isotonic Regression. Richard E. Barlow et al. LC 74-39231. (Wiley Series in Probability & Mathematical Statistics: No. 8). pap. 100.00 (2026680). Bks Demand UMI.

Statistical Interference for Stochastic Processes. Ed. by Ishwar Basawa & Prakasa Rao. LC 79-50533. (Probability & Mathematical Statistics Ser.). 1980. 96.00 (ISBN 0-12-080250-3). Acad Pr.

Statistical Linguistic Analysis of American English. A. Hood Roberts. (Janua Linguarum, Series Practica: No. 8). 1965. text ed. 46.40x (ISBN 90-2790-627-0). Mouton.

Statistical Manual of the AOAC. W. J. Youden & E. H. Steiner. (Illus.). 96p. 1975. 19.50 (ISBN 0-935584-15-3); 21.50. Assoc Official.

Statistical Measures of Corporate Bond Financing Since 1900. Walter B. Hickman & Elizabeth T. Simpson. (Financial Research Program V, Studies in Corporate Bond Financing: No. 3). 612p. 1960. 44.00 (Dist. by Princeton U Pr). Natl Bur Econ Res.

Statistical Mechanical Theory of the Electrolytic Transport of Non-Electrolytes. R. F. Snipes. (Lecture Notes in Physics Ser.: Vol. 24). 210p. 1973. pap. 14.70 (ISBN 0-387-06566-0). Springer-Verlag.

Statistical Mechanics. Ed. by Ryuzo Abe. Tr. by Yasushi Takahashi. 178p. 1974. 20.00 (ISBN 0-86008-118-4, Pub. by U of Tokyo Japan). Columbia U Pr.

Statistical Mechanics. Aggarwal. 400p. 1987. 29.95 (ISBN 0-470-20866-X). Halsted Pr.

Statistical Mechanics, 2 pts. Ed. by Bruce J. Berne. Incl. Pt. 1, Equilibrium Techniques. LC 76-46977. 242p. 59.50x (ISBN 0-306-33505-0); Pt. 2, Time-Dependent Processes. 362p. 69.50x (ISBN 0-306-33506-9). LC 76-46977. (Modern Theoretical Chemistry Ser.: Vols. 5 & 6). (Illus.). 1977 (Plenum Pr). Plenum Pub.

Statistical Mechanics. rev., 2nd ed. Ralph H. Fowler. (Illus.). 875p. 1980. 110.00 (ISBN 0-521-05025-1); pap. 44.50 (ISBN 0-521-09377-5). Cambridge U Pr.

Statistical Mechanics. 2nd ed. Kerson Huang. LC 86-32466. 576p. 1987. 45.80 (ISBN 0-471-81518-7). Wiley.

Statistical Mechanics. R. Kubo. 426p. 1971. text ed. 53.25 (ISBN 0-7204-0090-2, North-Holland). Elsevier.

Statistical Mechanics. R. Kubo. Ed. by H. Ichimura et al. 426p. 1988. pap. 32.50 (ISBN 0-444-87103-9, North Holland). Elsevier.

Statistical Mechanics. Shang-Keng Ma. 576p. 1985. 74.00 (ISBN 9971-966-06-9); pap. 33.00 (ISBN 9971-966-07-7). World Scientific Pub.

Statistical Mechanics. Donald A. McQuarrie. (Chemistry Ser.). 640p. 1976. text ed. 60.95 scp (ISBN 0-06-044366-9, HarpC). Har-Row.

Statistical Mechanics, Vols. 1-2. K. Singer. LC 72-95106. Vol. 1 1973. 1972 literature 32.00 (ISBN 0-85186-750-2, Pub. by Royal Soc Chem London); Vol. 2 1975. 1974 literature 45.00 (ISBN 0-85186-760-X). Am Chemical.

Statistical Mechanics see Physical Chemistry: An Advanced Treatise in Eleven Volumes.

Statistical Mechanics: A Set of Lectures. R. P. Feynman. 1987. pap. 37.75 (ISBN 0-8053-2509-3, Adv Bk Prog MSP). Addison-Wesley.

Statistical Mechanics & Dynamics. 2nd ed. Henry Eyring et al. LC 81-1125. 785p. 1982. 46.95 (ISBN 0-471-37042-8). Wiley.

Statistical Mechanics & Field Theory: Mathematical Aspects. Ed. by T. C. Dorlas et al. (Lecture Notes in Physics Ser.: Vol. 257). vii, 328p. 1986. 32.50 (ISBN 0-387-16777-3). Springer-Verlag.

Statistical Mechanics & Field Theory. Ed. by R. N. Sen & C. Weil. 250p. 1971. 63.00x (ISBN 0-7065-1263-4, Pub. by Keter Pub Jerusalem). Coronet Bks.

Statistical Mechanics & Manybody Problems. rev ed. K. M. Khanna. (Illus.). 450p. 1986. 45.00 (ISBN 1-55528-067-6, Pub. by Messers Today & Tomorrow Printers & Publishers). Scholarly Pubns.

Statistical Mechanics: Methods & Applications. Franz Mohling. 608p. 1982. text ed. 65.95x (ISBN 0-470-27340-2). Halsted Pr.

Statistical Mechanics: New Concepts, New Problems, New Applications. Ed. by Stuart A. Rice & Karl F. Freed. LC 72-85434. pap. 108.50 (ISBN 0-317-08081-4, 2019965). Bks Demand UMI.

Statistical Mechanics of Chain Molecules. Paul J. Flory. 432p. 1988. write for info. (ISBN 0-19-520756-4). Oxford U Pr.

Statistical Mechanics of Elasticity. Jerome H. Weiner. LC 82-20056. 454p. 1983. 59.95 (ISBN 0-471-09773-X, Pub. by Wiley-Interscience). Krieger.

Statistical Mechanics of Irreversible Change: Proceedings of the 6th IUPAP Conference on Statistical Mechanics, 1971. IUPAP Conference. LC 55-8426. pap. 35.00 (ISBN 0-317-08501-8, 2010184). Bks Demand UMI.

Statistical Mechanics of Magnetically Ordered Systems. Y. A. Izyumov & Y. N. Skryabin. Tr. by Roger Cooke from Rus. (Illus.). 296p. Date not set. price not set (ISBN 0-306-11015-6, Consultants). Plenum Pub.

Statistical Mechanics of Periodic Frustrated Ising Systems. R. Liebmann. (Lecture Notes in Physics Ser.: Vol. 251). vii, 142p. 1986. 12.70 (ISBN 0-387-16473-1). Springer-Verlag.

Statistical Mechanics of Quarks & Hadrons: Proceedings of the International Symposium, University of Bieleveld, France, Aug., 1980. Ed. by H. Satz. 480p. 1981. 108.00 (ISBN 0-444-86227-7, North-Holland). Elsevier.

Statistical Mechanics of the Liquid Surface. Clive A. Croxton. LC 79-40819. (Illus.). 367p. pap. 95.50 (2030376). Bks Demand UMI.

Statistical Mechanics: Principles & Selected Applications. Terrell L. Hill. 448p. 1987. pap. text ed. 9.95 (ISBN 0-486-65390-0). Dover.

Statistical Mechanics: Proceedings of the 10th Annual Open University Conference on Statistical Mechanics. Ed. by Allan I. Solomon. 160p. 1988. 28.00 (ISBN 9971-50-554-1). World Scientific Pub.

Statistical Mechanics: Rigorous Results. David Ruelle. 1988. write for info. (ISBN 0-201-09416-9). Addison-Wesley.

Statistical Method from the Viewpoint of Quality Control. Walter A. Shewhart. 192p. 1986. pap. text ed. 6.00 (ISBN 0-486-65232-7). Dover.

Statistical Method in Biological Assay. 3rd ed. David J. Finney. LC 78-64339. 60.00x (ISBN 0-02-844640-2). Hafner.

Statistical Method in Biological Assay: The Biomathematics of Disease. D. J. Finney. (Charles Griffin Series-Mathematics in Medicine). (Illus.). 522p. 1987. 60.00 (ISBN 0-19-520567-7). Oxford U Pr.

Statistical Methodologies for Analyzing for a Complex Sample Survey: United States 1980, No. 7. James M. Lepkowski et al. Ed. by Mary Olmsted. 204p. Date not set. pap. text ed. 4.50 (ISBN 0-8406-0355-X). Natl Ctr Health Stats.

Statistical Methodology for Analyzing Data from a Complex Survey: The First National Health & Nutrition Examination Survey. J. Richard Landis & Stephen A. Eklund. Ed. by Klaudia Cox. (No. 92). 50p. 1982. pap. 4.75 (ISBN 0-686-81990-X). Natl Ctr Health Stats.

Statistical Methods. 5th ed. Herbert Arkin & Raymond R. Colton. 344p. (Orig.). 1971. pap. 6.95 (ISBN 0-06-460027-0, CO 27, B&N Bks). Har-Row.

Statistical Methods. 7th ed. William G. Cochran & George W. Snedecor. (Illus.). 508p. 1980. text ed. 31.95x (ISBN 0-8138-1560-6). Iowa St U Pr.

Statistical Methods. 3rd ed. Pfaffenberger & Patterson. 1987. 39.95 (ISBN 0-256-03664-0); student wkbk. 14.50 (ISBN 0-256-03665-9). Irwin.

Statistical Methods. 7th ed. Snedecor & Cochran. 593p. 22.50 (ISBN 0-318-13250-8, P227). Am Soc QC.

Statistical Methods & Scientific Inference. rev. ed. Ronald A. Fisher. 1973. 14.95x (ISBN 0-02-844740-9). Hafner.

Statistical Methods & Systems for Safety Analysis. Sanathanan. (Probability & Mathematical Statistics Ser.). 1988. write for info. (ISBN 0-471-85443-3). Wiley.

Statistical Methods & the Geographer. 4th ed. S. Gregory. LC 77-7025. (Geographies for Advanced Study Ser). (Illus.). 1978. pap. text ed. 14.95x (ISBN 0-582-48186-4). Wiley.

Statistical Methods & the Geographer. 4th ed. S. Gregory. 256p. 1978. pap. 15.95 (ISBN 0-470-20483-4, Co-Pub. with Longman). Wiley.

Statistical Methods & the Improvement of Data Quality. Tommy Wright. 1983. 32.00 (ISBN 0-12-765480-1). Acad Pr.

Statistical Methods: Concepts, Application & Computation. Y. P. Agarwal. 1986. text ed. 37.50x (ISBN 81-207-0157-7, Pub. by Sterling Pubs India). Apt Bks.

Statistical Methods for Agricultural Sciences. Reza A. Hoshmand. 410p. 1988. 29.95x (ISBN 0-88192-096-7). Timber.

Statistical Methods for Building Price Data. D. T. Beeston. 1983. 38.00x (ISBN 0-419-12270-2, NO. 6795, Pub. by E & FN Spon); pap. 21.00 (NO. 6794, Pub. by Chapman & Hall). Routledge Chapman & Hall.

Statistical Methods for Cancer Studies. Cornell. (Statistics: Textbooks & Monographs). 344p. 1984. Repr. of 1972 ed. 65.00 (ISBN 0-8247-7169-9). Dekker.

Statistical Methods for Comparative Studies: Techniques for Bias Reduction. Sharon Anderson et al. LC 79-27220. (Series in Probability & Mathematical Statistics: Applied Probability & Statistics). 289p. 1980. 40.95 (ISBN 0-471-04838-0, Pub. by Wiley-Interscience). Wiley.

Statistical Methods for Engineers. Richard H. McCuen. (Illus.). 400p. 1985. text ed. 51.00 (ISBN 0-13-844903-1). P-H.

Statistical Methods for Environmental Pollution Monitoring. Richard Gilbert. (Professional Books Ser.). (Illus.). 384p. 1987. 42.95 (ISBN 0-442-23050-8). Van Nos Reinhold.

Statistical Methods for Forecasting. Bovas Abraham & Johannes Ledolter. LC 83-7006. (Probability & Mathematics Statistics Ser.). 480p. 1983. 44.95x (ISBN 0-471-86764-0, 1-346). Wiley.

Statistical Methods for Geographers. W. A. Clark & P. L. Hosking. LC 85-20309. 518p. 1986. write for info. (ISBN 0-471-81807-0). Wiley.

Statistical Methods for Health Care Research. Barbara H. Munro et al. LC 64-4438. (Illus.). 352p. 1986. pap. text ed. 22.50 (ISBN 0-397-54503-7, Lippincott Medical). Lippincott.

Statistical Methods for Librarians. Ray L. Carpenter. LC 78-3476. 134p. 1978. 15.00x (ISBN 0-8389-0256-1). ALA.

Statistical Methods for Managers & Administrators. Isabel S. Patchett. 336p. 1982. 33.95 (ISBN 0-442-23124-5). Van Nos Reinhold.

Statistical Methods for Meta-Analysis. Larry V. Hedges & Ingram Olkin. 1985. 51.50 (ISBN 0-12-336380-2). Acad Pr.

Statistical Methods for Motor Efficiency Data. 1978p. 2.00 (ISBN 0-318-17070-1). Natl Elec Mfrs.

Statistical Methods for Planners. Thomas R. Willemain. (Illus.). 352p. 1980. 24.95x (ISBN 0-262-23101-8). MIT Pr.

Statistical Methods for Planning Pharmaceutical Research. Bergman & Gittins. (Statistics-Textbook & Monographs Ser.). 280p. 1985. 59.50 (ISBN 0-8247-7146-X). Dekker.

Statistical Methods for Psychology. 2nd ed. Howell. 1987. text ed. 31.00 (ISBN 0-87150-068-X, 36G0140, Duxbury Pr). PWS Kent Pub.

Statistical Methods for Quality Control. Ryan. 1987. write for info. (ISBN 0-471-84337-7). Wiley.

Statistical Methods for Quality Improvement. Ed. by Hitoshi Kume. 231p. 1985. pap. 26.50 (ISBN 4-906224-34-2, Pub. by Assoc for Overseas Technical Scholarship). UNIPUB-Kraus Intl.

Statistical Methods for Rates & Proportions. 2nd ed. Joseph L. Fleiss. LC 80-26382. (Probability & Mathematical Statistics Ser.). 321p. 1981. 41.00x (ISBN 0-471-06428-9). Wiley.

Statistical Methods for Research Workers. 14th ed. Ronald A. Fisher. (Illus.). 1973. 19.95x (ISBN 0-02-844730-1). Hafner.

Statistical Methods for Social Scientists. Eric Hanushek & John Jackson. (Quantitative Studies in Social Relations Ser.). 374p. 1977. 29.95 (ISBN 0-12-324350-5). Acad Pr.

Statistical Methods for Survival Data Analysis. E. Lee. 38.95 (ISBN 0-317-64289-8). Van Nos Reinhold.

Statistical Methods for Survival Data Analysis. Elisa T. Lee. LC 80-24720. 557p. 1980. 37.00 (ISBN 0-534-97987-4, Lifetime Learn); solutions manual 5.95 (ISBN 0-534-97972-6). Van Nos Reinhold.

Statistical Methods for Survival Data Analysis Solution Manual. E. Lee. pap. 6.95 (ISBN 0-317-64287-1). Van Nos Reinhold.

Statistical Methods for Textile Technologists. T. Murphy et al. 107p. 1979. 40.00x (ISBN 0-686-63797-6). State Mutual Bk.

Statistical Methods for the Analysis of Biomedical Data. Robert F. Woolson. LC 87-6069. (Probability & Mathematical Statistics Ser.). 656p. 1987. 49.95 (ISBN 0-471-80615-3). Wiley.

Statistical Methods for the Earth Scientist: An Introduction. Roger Till. LC 73-22704. 154p. 1978. pap. 28.95x (ISBN 0-470-26340-7). Halsted Pr.

Statistical Methods for the Evaluation of Computer Systems Performance. Ed. by Walter Freiberger et al. 1972. 81.00 (ISBN 0-12-266950-9). Acad Pr.

Statistical Methods for the Social & Behavioral Sciences. Ronald C. Serlin & Leonard A. Marascuilo. (Psychology Ser.). (Illus.). 720p. 1987. text ed. 44.95 (ISBN 0-7167-1824-3). W H Freeman.

Statistical Methods for the Social Sciences. Alan Agresti & Barbara F. Agresti. (Illus.). 554p. 1979. text ed. 25.95x (ISBN 0-02-301100-9). Dellen Pub.

Statistical Methods in Agriculture & Experimental Biology. R. Mead & R. N. Curnow. 300p. 1983. 55.00 (ISBN 0-412-24230-3, NO. 6767); pap. 27.00 (ISBN 0-412-24240-0, NO. 6768). Routledge Chapman & Hall.

Statistical Methods in Biology. 2nd ed. Ed. by Norman T. J. Bailey. LC 80-15774. (Biological Science Text Ser.). 216p. 1981. pap. 16.95x (ISBN 0-470-27006-3). Halsted Pr.

Statistical Methods in Cancer Research, Vol. 1. N. E. Breslow & N. E. Day. (International Agency for Research on Cancer Ser. (IARC)). (Illus.). 1980. text ed. 30.00x (ISBN 0-19-723032-6). Oxford U Pr.

Statistical Methods in Cancer Research, Vol. II: The Design & Analysis of Cohort Studies. Ed. by N. E. Breslow & N. E. Day. (IARC Scientific Publications: No. 82). (Illus.). 400p. 1988. 45.00 (ISBN 92-832-1182-0). Oxford U Pr.

Statistical Methods in Cancer Research: Vol. III The Design & Analysis of Long-Term Animal Experiments. Ed. by J. J. Gart et al. (IARC Scientific Ser.: No. 79). 240p. 1987. 45.00 (ISBN 92-832-1179-0). Oxford U Pr.

Statistical Methods in Discrimination Litigation. D. H. Kaye & Mikel Aickin. 1986. 49.75 (ISBN 0-8247-7514-7). Dekker.

Statistical Methods in Econometrics. 3rd, rev. ed. A. Malinvaud. (Studies in Mathematical & Managerial Economics Ser.: Vol. 6). 770p. 1980. 68.50 (ISBN 0-444-85473-8, North-Holland). Elsevier.

Statistical Methods in Education. Harvey J. Goehring, Jr. LC 80-84066. (Illus.). viii, 337p. 1981. text ed. 27.50 (ISBN 0-87815-033-1). Info Resources.

Statistical Methods in Education & Psychology. 2nd ed. Gene V. Glass & Kenneth D. Hopkins. (Illus.). 608p. 1984. text ed. write for info. (ISBN 0-13-844944-9). P-H.

Statistical Methods in Education & Psychology. A. K. Kurtz & S. T. Mayo. 1979. 22.00 (ISBN 0-387-90265-1). Springer-Verlag.

Statistical Methods in Engineering & Quality Control: An Introduction. John. (Probability & Mathematical Statistics Ser.). 1987. write for info. (ISBN 0-471-82986-2). Wiley.

Statistical Methods in Experimental Physics. Eadie. 1984. Repr. 42.50 (ISBN 0-317-11385-2). Elsevier.

Statistical Methods in Experimental Physics. W. T. Eadie et al. LC 75-157034. 296p. 1972. 42.50 (ISBN 0-444-10117-9, North-Holland). Elsevier.

Statistical Methods in Food & Consumer Research. Maximo C. Gacula, Jr. & Jagbir Singh. (Food Science & Technology Ser.). 1984. 98.00 (ISBN 0-12-272050-4). Acad Pr.

Statistical Methods in Geology: For Field & Lab Decisions. R. F. Cheeney. (Illus.). 192p. 1983. pap. text ed. 15.95x (ISBN 0-04-550030-4). Unwin Hyman.

Statistical Methods in Hydrology. C. T. Haan. 1977. text ed. 21.95x (ISBN 0-8138-1510-X). Iowa St U Pr.

Statistical Study of Literary Vocabulary. G. Udny Yule. LC 68-8027. viii, 306p. 1968. Repr. of 1944 ed. 29.50 (ISBN 0-208-00689-3, Archon). Shoe String.

Statistical Summary Report of the 1979 University of California Union Catalog Data Base. Blanche Grosswald. (Working Paper: No. 10). 1980. 5.00 (ISBN 0-686-87251-7). UCDLA.

Statistical Survey of Museums in the United States & Canada. American Association of Museums Staff. LC 75-21957. (America in Two Centuries Ser). 1976. Repr. of 1965 ed. 13.00x (ISBN 0-405-07735-1). Ayer Co Pubs.

Statistical Survey Techniques. Raymond J. Jessen. LC 77-21476. (Probability & Mathematical Statistics Applied Probablity & Statistics Section). 520p. 1978. 50.95x (ISBN 0-471-44260-7, Pub. by Wiley-Interscience). Wiley.

Statistical Tables. 2nd ed. F. James Rohlf & Robert R. Sokal. LC 81-2576. (Illus.). 219p. 1981. pap. text ed. 13.95 (ISBN 0-7167-1258-X). W H Freeman.

Statistical Tables for Multivariate Analysis: A Handbook with References to Applications. H. Kres. Tr. by P. Wadsack. (Springer Series in Statistics). (Illus.). 530p. 1983. 69.50 (ISBN 0-387-90909-5). Springer Verlag.

Statistical Tables for the Social, Biological & Physical Sciences. F. C. Powell. LC 80-42241. (Illus.). 96p. 1982. 17.95 (ISBN 0-521-24141-3); pap. 6.95 (ISBN 0-521-28473-2). Cambridge U Pr.

Statistical Techniques for Analytical Review in Auditing. Kenneth W. Stringer & Trevor R. Stewart. LC 85-17874. 301p. 1986. 45.00 (ISBN 0-471-86076-X). Wiley.

Statistical Techniques for Manpower Planning. David J. Bartholomew & Andrew F. Forbes. LC 78-8604. (Probability & Mathematical Statistics: Applied Section Ser.). 288p. 1979. 84.95x (ISBN 0-471-99670-X, Pub. by Wiley-Interscience). Wiley.

Statistical Techniques for Social Research. Anthony A. Hickey. 362p. 1985. text ed. write for info (ISBN 0-394-32843-4, RanC). Random.

Statistical Techniques in Business & Economics. 6th ed. Robert D. Mason. 1986. 37.95x (ISBN 0-256-03383-8); study guide 12.95x (ISBN 0-256-03384-6). Irwin.

Statistical Techniques in Simulation, Pt. 1. J. P. Kleijnen. (Statistics: Textbooks & Monographs: Vol. 9). 304p. 1974. 59.75 (ISBN 0-8247-7220-2). Dekker.

Statistical Techniques in Simulation, Pt. 2. Jack P. Kleijnen. LC 74-79920. (Statistics, Textbooks & Monographs: No. 9). pap. 132.40 (2030866). Bks Demand UMI.

Statistical Testing of Business-Cycle Theories. Jan Tinbergen. LC 68-16357. 254p. 1968. Repr. of 1939 ed. 20.00x (ISBN 0-87586-009-5). Agathon.

Statistical Tests & Experimental Design: A Guidebook. David Sheskin. 325p. 1984. 26.50 (ISBN 0-89876-094-1). Gardner Pr.

Statistical Theories of Turbulence. Chia-Ch'iao Lin. (Princeton Aeronautical Paperbacks Ser: No. 10). pap. 20.00 (ISBN 0-317-09284-7, 2001133). Bks Demand UMI.

Statistical Theory. rev. ed. Lancelot Hogben. (Illus.). 1968. 15.00x (ISBN 0-393-06305-4). Norton.

Statistical Theory. 3rd ed. Bernard W. Lindgren. (Illus.). 576p. 1976. text ed. write for info. (ISBN 0-02-370830-1). Macmillan.

Statistical Theory: An Introduction. Delmar Crabill. 296p. (Orig.). 1984. pap. text ed. 13.00 (ISBN 0-8191-3796-0). U Pr of Amer.

Statistical Theory & Data Analysis: Proceedings of the Pacific Area Statistical Conference, 1985. Ed. by K. Matusita. 812p. 1985. 168.50 (ISBN 0-444-87665-0, North-Holland). Elsevier.

Statistical Theory & Data Analysis: Proceedings of the 2nd Pacific Area Statistical Conference, Tokyo, Japan, 10-12 December, 1986, Vol. II. Ed. by K. Matusita. 566p. 1988. 152.75 (ISBN 0-444-70387-X, North Holland). Elsevier.

Statistical Theory & Inference in Research. Bancroft & Chein-Pai Han. (Statistics: Textbooks & Monographs Ser.: Vol. 40). 432p. 1981. 59.75 (ISBN 0-8247-1400-8). Dekker.

Statistical Theory & Methodlogy of Trace Analysis. C. Liteanu & I. Rica. (Ellis Horwood Series in Analytical Chemistry). 446p. 1980. 116.95x (ISBN 0-470-26797-6). Halsted Pr.

Statistical Theory & Methodology: In Science & Engineering. 2nd. ed. K. A. Brownlee. LC 84-3941. 608p. 1984. Repr. of 1965 ed. lib. bdg. 52.50 (ISBN 0-89874-748-1). Krieger.

Statistical Theory & Random Matrices. Carmeli. (Pure & Applied Mathematics Ser.). 184p. 1983. 49.75 (ISBN 0-8247-1779-1). Dekker.

Statistical Theory of Extended Radar Targets. F. A. Basalov & R. V. Ostrovityanov. Tr. by William F. Barton & David K. Barton. Orig. Title: Statisticheskaya Teoriya Radiolokatsii Protyazhennyz Tselei. 364p. 1985. text ed. 65.00 (ISBN 0-89006-144-0). Artech Hse.

Statistical Theory of Linear Systems. E. J. Hannan & M. Deistler. LC 87-19863. (Probability & Mathematical Statistics Ser.). 380p. 1988. 42.95 (ISBN 0-471-80777-X). Wiley.

Statistical Theory of Liquids. Iosif Z. Fisher. Tr. by Theodore M. Switz. LC 64-22249. pap. 86.80 suppl. (ISBN 0-317-08823-8, 2020284). Bks Demand UMI.

Statistical Theory of Non-Equilibrium Processes in a Plasma. Yu L. Klimontovich. 1967. 63.00 (ISBN 0-08-011966-2). Pergamon.

Statistical Theory of Nuclear Fission. Peter Fong. (Documents on Modern Physics Ser.). 228p. (Orig.). 1969. 94.00 (ISBN 0-677-01850-9). Gordon & Breach.

Statistical Theory of Reliability. Ed. by Marvin Zelen. LC 63-9061. (U. S. Army. Mathematical Research Center. Madison, Wis.: No. 9). pap. 46.00 (ISBN 0-317-09139-5, 2015375). Bks Demand UMI.

Statistical Theory of Reliability & Life Testing: Probability Models. Richard Barlow & Frank Proschan. LC 81-51480. 1981. Repr. of 1975 ed. text ed. 30.00 (ISBN 0-9606764-0-6). To Begin With.

Statistical Theory of Sampling Inspection by Attributes. A. Hald. (Probability & Mathematical Statistics Ser.). 1981. 106.00 (ISBN 0-12-318350-2). Acad Pr.

Statistical Theory of the Analysis of Experimental Designs. Junjiro Ogawa. LC 73-90769. (Statistics, Textbooks & Monographs: Vol. 8). pap. 118.80 (2027339). Bks Demand UMI.

Statistical Thermodynamics. M. C. Gupta. 450p. 1988. 24.95 (ISBN 0-470-21151-2). Wiley.

Statistical Thermodynamics. H. G. Hayman. 1967. 31.75 (ISBN 0-444-40272-1). Elsevier.

Statistical Thermodynamics. Donald A. McQuarrie. 343p. 1985. pap. text ed. 29.50x (ISBN 0-935702-18-0). Univ Sci Bks.

Statistical Thermodynamics, 2 vols. A. Munster. Vol. 1, 1969. 72.00 (ISBN 0-12-510901-6); Vol. 2, 1974. 90.00 (ISBN 0-12-510902-4). Acad Pr.

Statistical Thermodynamics. Rev. ed. Chang L. Tieu & John H. Lienhard. LC 84-27910. (Illus.). 397p. 1985. text ed. 45.00 (ISBN 0-89116-048-5). Hemisphere Pub.

Statistical Thermodynamics: A Version of Statistical Mechanics for Students of Physics & Chemistry. Ralph H. Fowler & E. A. Guggenheim. pap. 160.00 (ISBN 0-317-08661-8, 2051495). Bks Demand UMI.

Statistical Thermodynamics of Alloys. N. A. Gokcen. 320p. 1986. 49.50x (ISBN 0-306-42177-1, Plenum Pr). Plenum Pub.

Statistical Thermodynamics of Nonequilibrium Processes. J. Keizer. (Illus.). 520p. 1987. 49.00 (ISBN 0-387-96501-7). Springer-Verlag.

Statistical Thermodynamics of Simple Liquids & Their Mixtures. Boublik et al. (Studies in Physical & Chemistry: Vol. 2). 146p. 1980. 73.75 (ISBN 0-444-99784-9). Elsevier.

Statistical Thinking: A Structural Approach. 2nd ed. John L. Phillips, Jr. LC 81-17368. (Illus.). 181p. 1982. pap. text ed. 11.95x (ISBN 0-7167-1380-2). W H Freeman.

Statistical Thinking for Behavioral Scientists. Hildebrand. 1986. text ed. 30.50 (ISBN 0-87150-949-0, 36G8370, Duxbury Pr). PWS Kent Pub.

Statistical Thinking for Managers. 2nd ed. Ott & Hildebrand. 1987. text ed. write for info. (ISBN 0-87150-036-1, 36G0180, Duxbury Pr). PWS Kent Pub.

Statistical Thinking for Managers. Lyman Ott & David Hildebrand. 840p. 1982. text ed. 31.00 (ISBN 0-87150-401-4, 6090, Duxbury Pr). PWS Kent Pub.

Statistical Tolerance Regions: Classical & Bayesian. I. Guttman. (Griffin's Statistical Monographs: No. 26). 150p. 1970. pap. text ed. 17.95X (ISBN 0-85264-172-9). Lubrecht & Cramer.

Statistical Tools for Simulation Practioners. Kleinjen. (Statistics: Textbooks & Monographs). 520p. 1986. 69.75 (ISBN 0-8247-7333-0). Dekker.

Statistical Treatment of Environmental Isotope Data in Precipitation. (Technical Reports Ser.: No. 206). (Illus.). 276p. 1981. pap. 35.00 (ISBN 92-0-145081-8, IDC206, IAEA). UNIPUB.

Statistical Treatment of Experimental Data. rev. ed. J. R. Green & D. Margerison. (Physical Sciences Data Ser.: Vol. 2). 1978. 73.75 (ISBN 0-444-41725-7). Elsevier.

Statistical Treatment of Experimental Data. Hugh D. Young. 1962. pap. text ed. 6.95 (ISBN 0-07-072646-9). McGraw.

Statistical Treatment of Fatigue Experiments. L. G. Johnson. 116p. 1964. 47.50 (ISBN 0-444-40322-1). Elsevier.

Statistical Trends in Transport, 1965-1984. OECD. (EMCT Ser.). 136p. (Orig.). 1987. pap. 24.00x (ISBN 92-821-0114-2). OECD.

Statistical Trends in Transport, 1965-1983. OECD Staff. (ECMT Ser.). 112p. (Orig.). 1986. pap. 19.00x (ISBN 92-821-0130-4). OECD.

Statistical View of the Commerce of the United States of America. Timothy Pitkin. Repr. of 1835 ed. 24.00 (ISBN 0-384-46625-7). Johnson Repr.

Statistical View of the Commerce of the United States of America. Timothy Pitkin. LC 65-26374. 1967. Repr. of 1816 ed. 45.00x (ISBN 0-678-00219-3). Kelley.

Statistical View of the Trusts: A Manual of Large American Industrial & Mining Corporations Active Around 1900. David Bunting. LC 72-9824. (Contributions in Economics & Economic History Ser.: No. 9). 311p. 1974. lib. bdg. 56.95 (ISBN 0-8371-6624-1, BOM/). Greenwood.

Statistical View of the United States. J. B. Debow. (Demographic Monographs). 408p. 1970. 80.00 (ISBN 0-677-02200-X). Gordon & Breach.

Statistical Work of the National Government. Laurence F. Schmeckebier. (Brookings Institution Reprint Ser). Repr. of 1925 ed. lib. bdg. 39.00 (ISBN 0-697-00167-9). Irvington.

Statistical Yearbook. 1981. 65.00 (ISBN 92-1-061001-6, EF.83.XVII.1); pap. 55.00 (ISBN 92-1-061000-8, EF.83.XVII.1). UN.

Statistical Yearbook. (Eng. & Fr.). 1985. 85.00 (ISBN 92-1-061105-5, EF86.XVII.1). UN.

Statistical Yearbook: Czechoslovakia. (Yearly). text ed. 35.00x (ISBN 0-89918-193-7, C193). Vanous.

Statistical Yearbook for Asia & the Pacific, 1982. LC 84-46787. 575p. 1982. 52.00 (ISBN 92-1-019003-3, EF.84.II.F.8). UN.

Statistical Yearbook for Asia & the Pacific, 1983. 629p. 54.00 (EF.84.II.F.10). UN.

Statistical Yearbook for Asia & the Pacific 1982. 550p. (Orig.). 1981. 52.00 (ISBN 92-1-019003-3, EF.84.11.F.8). UN.

Statistical Yearbook for Asia & the Pacific, 1984. 630p. 1986. 54.00 (ISBN 92-1-119414-8, E/F.85.11.F.21). UN.

Statistical Yearbook for Latin America & the Caribbean: 1985. (Eng., Span.). 1986. 27.00 (ISBN 92-1-021023-9, E/S.86.II.G.1). UN.

Statistical Yearbook for Latin America & the Caribbean 1986. 782p. (Eng. & Span.). 1988. pap. 65.00 (ISBN 92-1-021024-7, E.S.87.II.G.1). UN.

Statistical Yearbook for Latin America, 1983. 749p. 1983. 40.00 (ISBN 92-1-021003-4, E/S.84.II.G.2). UN.

Statistical Yearbook for Latin America, 1984. 765p. 1986. 40.00 (ISBN 92-1-021022-0, E/S.85.II.G.1). UN.

Statistical Yearbook for Latin America, 1984. 40.00 (ISBN 92-1-021022-0). Intl Pubns Serv.

Statistical Yearbook, Hungarian. (Yearly). pap. 34.50x (ISBN 0-89918-288-7, H288). Vanous.

Statistical Yearbook of China, 1985. State Statistical Bureau Staff of the People's Republic of China. 674p. 1986. 69.00x (ISBN 0-19-828558-2). Oxford U Pr.

Statistical Yearbook of China 1986. 776p. 1987. 84.00 (ISBN 0-19-828563-9). Oxford U Pr.

Statistical Yearbook of Community, Technical, & Junior Colleges: 1988 Edition. Ed. by Jim Palmer. 1988. pap. 35.00 (ISBN 0-87117-176-7, 1110). Am Assn Comm Jr Coll.

Statistical Yearbook: Poland. (Yearly). text ed. 22.50x (ISBN 0-89918-485-5, P485). Vanous.

Statistical Yearbook: Yugoslavia. (Yearly). text ed. 46.00x (ISBN 0-89918-671-8, Y671). Vanous.

Statistical Yearbook: 1982. (Eng. & Fr.). 1984. 70.00 (ISBN 92-1-061042-3, EF.84.XVII.I); pap. 60.00 (ISBN 0-317-66533-2). UN.

Statistical Yearbook, 1983-1984. 34th ed. LC 50-2746. 1070p. 1986. 70.00x (ISBN 0-8002-3156-2); pap. 60.00x (ISBN 0-8002-3157-0). Intl Pubns Serv.

Statistical Yearbook 1983-1984: ST-ESA-STAT-SER.S-10. 1137p. 70.00 (ISBN 92-1-061103-9, E/F.85.XVII.1); pap. 60.00 (ISBN 0-317-56363-7). UN.

Statistical Yearbook 1984. 1097p. (Eng., Fr & Span.). 1985. 63.00 (ISBN 92-3-002259-4, U1405, UNESCO). UNIPUB.

Statistical Yearbooks: An Annotated Bibliography of the General Statistical Yearbooks of Major Political Subdivisions of the World. United States Library of Congress. LC 78-10213. 1978. Repr. lib. bdg. 35.00x (ISBN 0-313-20676-7, CAST). Greenwood.

Statisticheskaya Teoriya Radiolokatsii Protyazhennyz Tselei see Statistical Theory of Extended Radar Targets.

Statistician. Jack Rudman. (Career Examination Ser.: C-761). (Cloth bdg. avail. on request). pap. 14.00 (ISBN 0-8373-0761-9). Natl Learning.

Statistics. Norman H. Crowhurst. 110p. (Orig.). 1981. pap. text ed. 10.45 (ISBN 0-89420-111-5, 413040); cassette recordings 103.95 (ISBN 0-89420-202-2, 413000). Natl Book.

Statistics. David Freedman et al. (Illus.). 608p. 1978. text ed. 34.95x (ISBN 0-393-09076-0); instr's. manual 6.95x (ISBN 0-393-09041-8). Norton.

Statistics. 5th ed. W. M. Harper. 400p. (Orig.). 1987. pap. text ed. 23.50x (ISBN 0-7121-1995-7, Pub. by Pitman Pub Ltd London). Trans-Atl Phila.

Statistics. Allan G. Johnson. 433p. 1988. text ed. 18.00 (ISBN 0-15-583542-4, HC); net study guide 8.00 (ISBN 0-15-583544-0); instr's manual 2.75 (ISBN 0-15-583543-2). HarBraceJ.

Statistics. S. Letchford. 1981. pap. 14.95 (ISBN 0-85258-189-0). Van Nos Reinhold.

Statistics. 2nd ed. James T. McClave & Frank H. Dietrich, II. LC 81-17434. (Illus.). 766p. 1982. text ed. 27.50 (ISBN 0-89517-034-5). Dellen Pub.

Statistics. 4th ed. James T. McClave & Frank H. Dietrich, II. 1988. write for info. (ISBN 0-02-379260-4). Macmillan.

Statistics. Jack Rudman. (College Level Examination Ser.: CLEP-26). (Cloth bdg. avail. on request). pap. 13.95 (ISBN 0-8373-5326-2). Natl Learning.

Statistics. Jack Rudman. (College Proficiency Examination Ser.: CPEP-15). 25.95 (ISBN 0-8373-5465-X); pap. 13.95 (ISBN 0-8373-5415-3). Natl Learning.

Statistics. Jack Rudman. (ACT Proficiency Examination Program Ser.: PEP-57). 1988. 25.95 (ISBN 0-8373-5957-0); pap. 13.95 (ISBN 0-8373-5907-4). Natl Learning.

Statistics. William C. Schefler. 520p. 1988. text ed. 29.95 (ISBN 0-8053-8780-3). instr's guide avail. (ISBN 0-8053-8781-1); workdisk software avail. (ISBN 0-8053-8783-8). Benjamin-Cummings.

Statistics. Murray R. Spiegel. 1961. pap. text ed. 10.95 (ISBN 0-07-060227-1). McGraw.

Statistics. Jane J. Srivastava. LC 72-7559. (Young Math Ser.). (Illus.). (gr. 1-5). 1973. PLB 12.89 (ISBN 0-690-77300-5, Crowell Jr Bks). HarpJ.

Statistics. 2nd ed. Robert S. Witte. 448p. 1985. text ed. 28.95 (ISBN 0-03-063593-4, HoltC). HR&W.

Statistics--Asia & Australasia: Sources for Market Research. 2nd ed. Ed. by Joan M. Harvey. 240p. 1984. 145.00x (ISBN 0-900246-41-3, Pub. by CBD Res Ltd). Gale.

Statistics: A Biomedical Introduction. Byron W. Brown, Jr. & Myles Hollander. LC 77-396. (Probability & Mathematical Statistics Ser.). 456p. 1977. 40.50 (ISBN 0-471-11240-2). Wiley.

Statistics: A Computer Integrated Approach. Alan H. Kvanli. 935p. 1988. text ed. 35.00 (ISBN 0-314-60541-X). West Pub.

Statistics: A Conceptual Approach. K. Laurence Weldon. (Illus.). 528p. 1986. text ed. write for info. (ISBN 0-13-845819-7). P-H.

Statistics: A First Course. 4th ed. John E. Freund. (Illus.). 496p. 1986. text ed. write for info. (ISBN 0-13-845975-4). P-H.

Statistics: A First Course. 4th ed. Richard M. Smith. (Illus.). 220p. 1986. write for info. study guide & wkbk. (ISBN 0-13-845991-6). P-H.

Statistics: A Fresh Approach. 3rd ed. Donald H. Sanders et al. 448p. 1985. text ed. 38.95 (ISBN 0-07-054678-9). McGraw.

Statistics: A Guide to Biological & Health Sciences. Ed. by J. M. Tanur et al. LC 76-50856. 1977. pap. text ed. 8.95x (ISBN 0-8162-8564-0). Holden-Day.

Statistics: A Guide to Political & Social Issues. Ed. by Judith M. Tanur et al. LC 76-50852. 1977. pap. text ed. 8.95x (ISBN 0-8162-8574-8). Holden-Day.

Statistics: A New Approach. W. Allen Wallis & Harry V. Roberts. 1956. text ed. 12.95 (ISBN 0-02-933720-8). Free Pr.

Statistics: A Second Course in Statistics. 2nd ed. Robert Loveday. LC 74-96095. (Illus.). 1969. text ed. 11.95x (ISBN 0-521-07234-4). Cambridge U Pr.

Statistics: A Self-Teaching Guide. 3rd ed. Donald J. Koosis. LC 85-6292. 282p. 1985. pap. 10.95 (ISBN 0-471-82720-7). Wiley.

Statistics: A Spectator Sport. Richard Jaeger. LC 83-17740. 350p. 1983. 29.95 (ISBN 0-8039-2171-3); pap. 16.50 (ISBN 0-8039-2172-1). Sage.

Statistics: A Tool for Social Research. Joseph F. Healey. 351p. 1984. text ed. write for info. (ISBN 0-534-02985-X). Wadsworth Pub.

Statistics: A Tool for the Social Sciences. 4th ed. Larson et al. 1987. text ed. 27.50 (ISBN 0-87150-034-5, 36G0170, Duxbury Pr). PWS Kent Pub.

Statistics: A Tool for the Social Sciences. 3rd ed. Lyman Ott et al. 512p. 1983. text ed. 26.50 (ISBN 0-87150-400-6, 6084, Duxbury Pr). PWS Kent Pub.

Statistics: A Tutorial Workbook. Robert Pisani. 1985. pap. text ed. 8.95x (ISBN 0-393-95457-9); Apple IIe 19.95x (ISBN 0-393-99140-7); IBM PC 19.95x (ISBN 0-393-99135-0). Norton.

Statistics, Africa: Sources for Social, Economic, & Market Research. 2nd ed. Ed. by Joan M. Harvey. 1978. 80.00x (ISBN 0-900246-26-X, Pub. by CBD Research Ltd.). Gale.

Statistics America: Sources for Social, Economic, & Marketing Research. 2nd ed. Joan M. Harvey. 300p. 1980. 185.00x (ISBN 0-900246-16-2, Pub. by CBD Res Ltd.). Gale.

Statistics: An Applied Approach. Neil R. Ullman. LC 77-171918. Repr. of 1972 ed. 118.60 (ISBN 0-8357-9982-4, 2055154). Bks Demand UMI.

Statistics: An Appraisal. Ed. by Herbert A. David & Herbert T. David. 664p. 1984. text ed. 34.50x (ISBN 0-8138-1721-8). Iowa St U Pr.

Statistics: An Introduction. Robert Goldman & Joel Weinberg. (Illus.). 672p. 1985. text ed. write for info. (ISBN 0-13-845918-5). P-H.

Statistics: An Introduction. Harold J. Larson. LC 83-8414. 428p. 1983. Repr. of 1975 ed. 29.50 (ISBN 0-89874-639-6). Krieger.

Statistics: An Introduction. A. D. Rickmers & H. N. Todd. 1967. text ed. 45.95 (ISBN 0-07-052616-8). McGraw.

Statistics: An Introduction to Numerical Reasoning. Ray A. Waller. LC 78-60357. (Pilot ed). 1979. pap. text ed. 19.95x (ISBN 0-8162-9314-7). Holden-Day.

Statistics: An Introduction to Quantitative Economic Research. rev. ed. Daniel B. Suits. LC 63-8246. (Illus.). xix, 288p. 1985. pap. text ed. 15.00 (ISBN 0-916717-01-1). Halyburton.

Statistics in Language Studies. Anthony Woods et al. (Cambridge Textbooks in Linguistics). (Illus.). 350p. 1986. 39.50 (ISBN 0-521-25326-8); pap. 17.95 (ISBN 0-521-27312-9). Cambridge U Pr.
Statistics in Linguistics. Christopher Butler. 224p. 1985. 39.95x (ISBN 0-631-14264-9); pap. 14.95x (ISBN 0-631-14265-7). Basil Blackwell.
Statistics in Litigation: Practical Applications for Lawyers. Richard A. Wehmhoefer. 531p. 1985. text ed. 90.00 (ISBN 0-07-017857-7). Shepards McGraw.
Statistics in Medical Research: Methods & Issues with Applications in Cancer Research. Ed. by Valerie Mike & Kenneth E. Stanley. LC 82-10871. (Probability & Mathematics Statistics Ser.). 551p. 1983. 46.95x (ISBN 0-471-86911-2). Wiley.
Statistics in Medicine. Theodore Colton. LC 73-1413. 400p. 1975. pap. 26.00 (ISBN 0-316-15250-1). Little.
Statistics in Medicine. 1987. write for info. Wiley.
Statistics in Ornithology. Ed. by B. J. Morgan & P. M. North. LC 85-10052. (Lecture Notes in Statistics Ser.: Vol. 29). xxv, 418p. 1985. pap. 33.00 (ISBN 0-387-96189-5). Springer-Verlag.
Statistics in Plain English. Harvey J. Brightman. 1986. write for info. wkbk. (ISBN 0-538-13210-8, M21). SW Pub.
Statistics in Political & Behavioral Science. 2nd ed. Dennis J. Palumbo. LC 76-15572. 469p. 1977. 35.00x (ISBN 0-231-04010-5). Columbia U Pr.
Statistics in Practice. Sheila M. Gore & Douglas G. Altman. 100p. 1982. pap. 19.00x (ISBN 0-7279-0085-4, Pub. by British Med Assoc UK). Taylor & Francis.
Statistics in Psychology & Education. Henry E. Garrett. LC 82-15599. xii, 491p. 1982. Repr. of 1966 ed. lib. bdg. 59.50x (ISBN 0-313-23653-4, GAST). Greenwood.
Statistics in Research & Development. Roland Caulcutt. 352p. 1982. 49.95 (ISBN 0-412-23720-2, NO. 6784, Pub. by Chapman & Hall). Routledge Chapman & Hall.
Statistics in Research: Basic Concepts & Techniques for Research Workers. 4th ed. Bernard Ostle & Linda C. Malone. 664p. 1987. text ed. 44.95x (ISBN 0-8138-1569-X); solutions manual 6.00. Iowa St U Pr.
Statistics in Small Doses. rev. 2nd ed. Winifred M. Castle. LC 76-8430. (Illus.). 1977. pap. text ed. 19.00 (ISBN 0-443-01491-4). Churchill.
Statistics in the Environmental Sciences - STP 845. ASTM Committee D-19 on Water. Ed. by Steven M. Gertz & M. D. London. LC 83-73439. 115p. 1984. pap. 24.00 (ISBN 0-8031-0206-2, 04-845000-16). ASTM.
Statistics in the Labor Market. Trewin. (Lecture Notes in the Statistics Ser.). 256p. 1983. 39.75 (ISBN 0-8247-1912-3). Dekker.
Statistics in the Making. Mary L. Mark. (Illus.). 1958. 6.00 (ISBN 0-87776-092-6, R92). Ohio St U Admin Sci.
Statistics in the Pharmaceutical Industry. Buncher & Tsay. (Statistics; Textbooks & Monographs Ser.: Vol. 36). 544p. 1981. 75.00 (ISBN 0-8247-1163-7). Dekker.
Statistics Inference for Branching Processes. Guttorp. (Probability & Mathematical Ser.). 1987. write for info. (ISBN 0-471-82291-4). Wiley.
Statistics Made Simple. H. T. Hayslett, Jr. LC 67-10414. (Made Simple Ser.). 1968. pap. 6.95 (ISBN 0-385-02355-3). Doubleday.
Statistics: Making Sense of Data. Olson. 800p. 1986. text ed. write for info. (ISBN 0-205-08790-6). Wm C Brown.
Statistics Manual. Edwin L. Crow et al. (Illus.). 1955. pap. 6.00 (ISBN 0-486-60599-X). Dover.
Statistics: Meaning & Method. 2nd ed. Lawrence L. Lapin. 543p. 1980. text ed. 27.00 net (ISBN 0-15-583769-9, HC); instr's. manual avail. (ISBN 0-15-583778-8); study guide 8.95 (ISBN 0-15-583770-2). HarBraceJ.
Statistics Modeling Techniques. Shapiro & Gross. (Statistics: Textbooks & Monographs: Vol. 39). 416p. 1981. 39.75 (ISBN 0-8247-1387-7). Dekker.
Statistics Needed for National Policies Related to Fertility. National Center for Health Statistics Staff. (Series 4). 1976. pap. 1.95 (ISBN 0-8406-0080-1). Natl Ctr Health Stats.
Statistics Needed to Ascertain the Effects of the Environment on Health. Ed. by Taloria Stevenson. (Series 4: No. 20). 1977. pap. 1.95 (ISBN 0-8406-0093-3). Natl Ctr Health Stats.
Statistics of Agricultural Co-Operatives in the U. K. 1982-1983. T. F. Riordan. 38p. 1984. 49.00x (ISBN 0-85042-062-8, Pub. by Plunkett Foundation). State Mutual Bk.
Statistics of Agricultural Co-Operatives in the U. K., 1983-1984. Compiled by T. F. Riordan. 44p. 1985. 24.00x (ISBN 0-317-54646-5, Pub. by Plunkett Foundation). State Mutual Bk.
Statistics of Agricultural Co-Operatives in the U. K., 1984-85. Compiled by T. F. Riordan. 44p. 1986. 24.00x (ISBN 0-85042-074-1, Pub. by Plunkett Foundation). State Mutual Bk.
Statistics of Crop Responses to Fertilizers. (Orig.). 1966. pap. 6.75 (ISBN 0-685-09408-1, F449, FAO). UNIPUB.
Statistics of Deadly Quarrels. Lewis F. Richardson. Ed. by Quincy Wright & C. C. Lienau. (Illus.). 1960. 45.00x (ISBN 0-910286-10-8). Boxwood.
Statistics of Extremes. Emil J. Gumbel. LC 57-10160. 1958. 45.00x (ISBN 0-231-02190-9). Columbia U Pr.
Statistics of Health Services & of Their Activities: Report. WHO Expert Committee on Health Statistics. Geneva, 1968, 13th. (Technical Report Ser.: No. 429). (Also avail. in French & Spanish). 1969. pap. 2.00 (ISBN 92-4-120429-X). World Health.
Statistics of Indian Tribes, Agencies & Schools. U. S. Office of Indian Affairs. 1976. Repr. of 1903 ed. 24.00 (ISBN 0-527-92020-7). Kraus Repr.
Statistics of Insanity see On the Different Forms of Insanity in Relation to Jurisprudence.
Statistics of Natural Selection. Brian F. Manly. (Population & Community Biology Ser.). 450p. 1985. text ed. 55.00 (ISBN 0-412-25630-4, 9673, Pub. by Chapman & Hall England). Routledge Chapman & Hall.
Statistics of Natural Selection. Bryan F. Manly. 500p. 1988. pap. text ed. 37.50 (ISBN 0-412-30700-6, Pub. by Chapman & Hall England). Routledge Chapman & Hall.
Statistics of Random Processes I: General Theory. R. S. Liptser & A. N. Shiryayev. Tr. by A. B. Aries. (Applications of Mathematics Ser.: Vol. 5). 1977. 58.00 (ISBN 0-387-90226-0). Springer-Verlag.
Statistics of Road Traffic Accidents in Europe, Vol. XXXI. 104p. 1986. 12.50 (ISBN 92-1-016176-9, E/F/R.85.II.E.12, Vol. XXXI). UN.
Statistics of Road Traffic Accidents in Europe, Vol. XXXII. 102p. 1987. 18.00 (ISBN 92-1-016194-7, E-F-R.86.II.E.11). UN.
Statistics of Road Traffic Accidents in Europe, 1983. 108p. (Eng., Fr. & Rus.). 1985. pap. 13.50 (ISBN 92-1-016181-5, E.84.II.E.32). UN.
Statistics of Spatial Data. Cressie. (Probability & Mathematical Statistics Ser.). 1987. write for info. (ISBN 0-471-84336-9). Wiley.
Statistics of Students Abroad: 1974-1978. Office of Statistics, Division of Statistics on Education Staff. (Statistical Reports & Studies: No. 27). (Illus.). 275p. (Eng & Fr.). 1982. pap. 6.75 (ISBN 92-3-002050-8, U1253, UNESCO). UNIPUB.
Statistics of the Foreign & Domestic Commerce of the United States. United States Treasury Department Staff. LC 6-17305. Repr. of 1846 ed. 21.00 (ISBN 0-384-63120-7). Johnson Repr.
Statistics of the United States. U.S. Census Office, 1860. LC 75-22852. (America in Two Centuries Ser). 1976. Repr. of 1866 ed. 48.50x (ISBN 0-405-07719-X). Ayer Co Pubs.
Statistics of World Trade in Steel, 1983. 71p. 1985. 8.50 (ISBN 92-1-016163-7, E/F/R.84.II.E.20). UN.
Statistics of World Trade in Steel, 1984. 73p. 1986. 8.50 (ISBN 92-1-016174-2, E/F/R.85.II.E.10). UN.
Statistics on American Business Abroad, 1950-1975: An Original Anthology. U. S. Department of Commerce Staff. Ed. by Stuart Bruchey & Eleanor Bruchey. LC 76-5035. (American Business Abroad Ser.). (Illus.). 1976. 28.00x (ISBN 0-405-09301-2). Ayer Co Pubs.
Statistics on Film & Cinema: 1955-1977. (Statistical Reports & Studies: No. 25). (Illus.). 99p. 1981. pap. 5.00 (ISBN 92-3-101961-9, U1156, UNESCO). UNIPUB.
Statistics on Narcotic Drugs for 1984: Furnished by Governments in Accordance with the International Treaties & Maximum Levels of Opium Stocks in 1984. 106p. 1986. 15.00 (ISBN 92-1-048034-1, E.85.XI.3). UN.
Statistics on Narcotic Drugs for 1983. 106p. (Eng., Fr. & Span.). 1985. pap. 12.50 (ISBN 92-1-048032-5, EFS.84.XI.6). UN.
Statistics on Narcotic Drugs for 1986. 106p. (Eng., Fr. & Span.). 1987. pap. 17.00 (ISBN 92-1-048040-6, E/F/S.87.XI.1). UN.
Statistics on Narcotic Drugs Furnished by Governments in Accordance with the International Treaties & Maximum Levels on Opium Stock. (Eng., Fr. & Span.). 1986. pap. 13.50 (ISBN 92-1-048038-4, EFS.86.XI.1). UN.
Statistics on Outdoor Recreation, Pts. 1 & 2. Ed. by Marion Clawson & Carlton S. Van Doren. 368p. 1984. 16.50. Part 1, The Record Through 1956. Part 2, The Record Since 1956. Resources Future.
Statistics on Psychotropic Substances for 1986 Furnished by the Government in Accordance with the Convention of 1971 on Psychotropic Substances, Resolution I of the United Nations Conference for the Adoption of a Protocol on Psychotropic Substances & Resolution 1576(L) of the Economic & Social Council. 108p. (Eng., Fr. & Span.). 1987. pap. 17.50 (ISBN 92-1-048041-4, E/F/S.87.XI.2). UN.
Statistics on Psychotropic Substances for 1984. 1986. 12.50 (ISBN 92-1-048036-8, E.85.XI.4). UN.
Statistics on Radio & Television 1960-1976. UNESCO, Division of Statistics on Culture & Communication Staff. (Statistical Reports & Studies: No. 23). (Illus.). 124p. 1979. pap. 5.00 (ISBN 92-3-101681-4, U929, UNESCO). UNIPUB.
Statistics on Social Work Education in the United States: 1984. Allen Rubin. Date not set. 7.50 (85-410-02). Coun Soc WK Ed.
Statistics on Social Work in the United States, 1986. 10.00. Coun Soc Wk Ed.
Statistics Primer for Managers: How to Ask the Right Questions About Forecasting, Control & Investment. John J. Clark & Margaret T. Clark. (Illus.). 272p. 19.95. Macmillan.
Statistics Primer for Managers: How to Read a Statistical Report or a Computer Printout & Get the Right Answer. John J. Clark & Margaret T. Clark. (Illus.). 258p. 1983. 20.00. Free Pr.
Statistics: Principles & Methods. rev. ed. Johnson. 520p. 1987. 31.50 (ISBN 0-471-85075-6). Wiley.
Statistics: Probability, Inference & Decision. 2nd ed. Robert L. Winkler & William L. Hays. 986p. 1975. 40.95x (ISBN 0-03-014011-0). Dryden Pr.
Statistics Problem Solver. rev. ed. Research & Education Association Staff. LC 78-64581. (Illus.). 1056p. 1986. pap. text ed. 19.85 (ISBN 0-87891-515-X). Res & Educ.
Statistics Simplified & Self Taught. Stanley H. Stern. LC 83-25762. 128p. (Orig.). 1984. pap. 6.95 (ISBN 0-668-05813-7). Arco.
Statistics Sources. 11th ed. Ed. by Steven Wasserman & Jacqueline W. O'Brien. 1550p. 1987. 280.00 (ISBN 0-8103-4398-3). Gale.
Statistics Sources, 1989. 12th ed. Ed. by Steven Wasserman. 1988. 290.00 (ISBN 0-8103-2586-1). Gale.
Statistics: Statistical Modules Reflecting Groupings of Categories Such As Book Budgets for Small, Medium & Large Law Libraries. Bardie Wolfe. (Law Library Information Reports Ser.: vol. 11). 1988. pap. 100.00 (ISBN 0-87802-086-1). Glanville.
Statistics: Step-by-Step. Howard B. Christensen. LC 76-10903. (Illus.). 1977. text ed. 40.76 (ISBN 0-395-24527-3); instr's. manual with solutions 4.36 (ISBN 0-395-24528-1). HM.
Statistics Subject Indexed from Mathematical Reviews, 1980-84, 1973-79, 1959-72, 1940-58, 2 vols. (Probability of Statistics Cumulative Index Ser.: No. 40-84). 508p. 1987. pap. text ed. 67.00 (ISBN 0-8218-0107-4). Am Math.
Statistics Tables. H. R. Neave. 1977. pap. text ed. 6.95x (ISBN 0-04-001001-5). Unwin Hyman.
Statistics the Easy Way. D. Downing & J. Clark. (Easy Way Ser.). 368p. 1983. pap. 8.95 (ISBN 0-8120-2666-7). Barron.
Statistics: The Essentials for Research. 2nd ed. Henry E. Klugh. LC 73-16182. 426p. 1974. text ed. 37.95x (ISBN 0-471-49372-4). Wiley.
Statistics: The Essentials for Research. Henry E. Klugh. LC 73-16182. 442p. 1974. 37.95. Krieger.
Statistics: The Exploration & Analysis of Data. Jay Devore & Roxy Peck. (Illus.). 699p. text ed. 41.50 (ISBN 0-314-93172-4). West Pub.
Statistics Theory & Practice: Selected Papers. Maurice Kendall. Ed. by Alan Stuart. (Charles Griffin Book). 268p. 1987. 45.00 (ISBN 0-19-520588-X). Oxford U Pr.
Statistics Through Problem Solving. 2nd ed. DeSanto et al. Ed. by Frank Avenoso & Philip Cheifetz. LC 73-77244. (gr. 9-12). 1978. pap. text ed. 18.50 (ISBN 0-916060-04-7). Math Alternatives.
Statistics Today: A Comprehensive Introduction. D. R. Byrkit. 1987. 33.95 (ISBN 0-8053-0740-0); study guide 9.95 (ISBN 0-8053-0741-9); instr's guide free to adopters (ISBN 0-8053-0743-5). Benjamin-Cummings.
Statistics: Tool of the Behavioral Sciences. Margaret H. Johnson & Robert M. Liebert. 1977. write for info (ISBN 0-13-844704-7). P-H.
Statistics Two Hundred Ninety-One Supplements. A. L. France. 152p. 1984. pap. text ed. 12.95 (ISBN 0-89917-427-2, Pub. by College Town Pr). Tichenor Pub.
Statistics Using Ranks: A Unified Approach. Ray Meddis. 448p. 1984. pap. 24.95x (ISBN 0-631-13788-2). Basil Blackwell.
Statistics with Applications to the Biological & Health Sciences. 2nd ed. Richard Remington & M. Anthony Schork. (Illus.). 432p. 1985. text ed. write for info. (ISBN 0-13-846171-6). P-H.
Statistics with Vague Data. Rudolf Kruse & Klaus D. Meyer. 1987. lib. bdg. 59.00 (ISBN 90-277-2562-4, Pub. by Reidel Holland). Kluwer Academic.
Statistics Without Tears: A Primer for Non-Mathematicians. Derek Rowntree. LC 82-3157. (Illus.). 200p. 1982. (ScribT); pap. 7.95 (ISBN 0-684-17502-9). Scribner.
Statistics Without Tears: A Primer for Non-Mathematician. Derek Rowntree. 199p. 1981. pap. text ed. write for info. (ISBN 0-02-404090-8, Pub. by Scribner). Macmillan.
Statistics Workbook. S. Letchford. pap. 16.95 (ISBN 0-85258-220-X). Van Nos Reinhold.
Statistics Workbook for Social Science Students. M. F. Fuller & D. A. Lury. 250p. 1977. text ed. 29.95x (ISBN 0-86003-016-4, Pub. by Philip Allan UK); pap. text ed. 15.00x (ISBN 0-86003-117-9). Humanities.
Statistik Analyse System, Vol. 1. F. Faulbaum & U. Hanning. 268p. (Ger.). 1983. pap. text ed. 25.20x (ISBN 3-437-40124-6). Lubrecht & Cramer.
Statistik-Software Three: Konferenz Ueber die Wissenschaffliche Anwendung von Statistik-Software, 1985. Ed. by W. Lehmacher & A. Hoermann. 393p. (Ger.). 1986. pap. 34.80x (ISBN 3-437-40170-X). Lubrecht & Cramer.
Statistique Bibliographie De la France Sous la Monarchie Au XVIIIE Siecle. Robert Estivals. (Livre & Societes: No. 2). 1965. pap. 34.40x (ISBN 90-2796-138-7). Mouton.
Statistische Analysen. V. Nollau. (Lehr und Hadbucher der Ingenieurwissenschaften: No. 37). 378p. 1978. 27.95x (ISBN 0-8176-1019-7). Birkhauser.
Statistische Methoden. A. Linder. (Mathematische Reihe Ser.: No. 3). (Illus.). 484p. 1976. 66.95 (ISBN 0-8176-0833-8). Birkhauser.
Statius Achilled. Ed. by W. R. Connor & O. A. Dilke. LC 78-67127. (Latin Texts & Commentaries Ser.). (Lat. & Eng.). 1979. Repr. of 1954 ed. lib. bdg. 14.00x (ISBN 0-405-11598-9). Ayer Co Pubs.
Statius & the Silvae: Poets, Patrons & Epideixis in the Graeco-Roman World. Alex Hardie. (ARCA Classical & Medieval Texts, Papers, & Monographs: No. 9). 261p. 1983. text ed. 40.00 (ISBN 0-905205-13-8, Pub. by F Cairns). Longwood Pub Group.
Statius Silvae. Stephen Newmyer. (Latin Commentaries Ser.). 117p. (Orig.). 1987. pap. text ed. 8.00. Bryn Mawr Commentaries.
Statius: Silvae IV. Ed. by K. M. Coleman. Statius. (Illus.). 320p. 1988. 64.00 (ISBN 0-19-814031-2). Oxford U Pr.
Statlab. J. L. Hodges et al. (Illus.). 384p. 1975. text ed. 42.95 (ISBN 0-07-029134-9). McGraw.
Statler Brothers Songbook. cancelled (ISBN 0-89524-044-0). Cherry Lane.
Statlib: A Statistical Computing Library. William M. Brelsford & Daniel A. Relles. 448p. 1981. pap. text ed. 48.00 (ISBN 0-13-846220-8). P-H.
Statlib Primer: The Forecasting Process. H. Levenbach. 1983. pap. 19.95 (ISBN 0-317-64290-1). Van Nos Reinhold.
Statlib Primer: The Forecasting Process Through Statistical Computing. Hans Levenbach et al. (Research Methods Ser.). (Illus.). 180p. 1983. pap. 18.95 (ISBN 0-534-97936-X, Lifetime Learn). Van Nos Reinhold.
Statmaster: Exploring & Computing Statistics. C. Michael Levy & William J. Froming. 1983. write for info. (ISBN 0-673-39522-7); IBM demonstration package (ISBN 0-673-49245-1); Apple demonstration package (ISBN 0-673-49246-X); write for info. IBM instr's. disc (ISBN 0-673-49243-5); write for info. Apple instr's. disc (ISBN 0-673-49244-3). Scott F.
Statmaster for Business & Economics. Michael Levy et al. 1986. write for info. (ISBN 0-673-39523-5); Apple instr's disk. write for info (ISBN 0-673-49249-4); IBM instr's disk. write for info (ISBN 0-673-49250-8); IBM demo. package. write for info (ISBN 0-673-49252-4); Apple demo. package. write for info (ISBN 0-673-49251-6). Scott F.
Statokinetic Reflexes in Equilibrium & Movement. Tadashi Fukuda. Tr. by Hitoshi Okhubo & Shinya Ushio. 311p. 1984. 64.50 (ISBN 0-86008-343-8, Pub. by U of Tokyo Japan). Columbia U Pr.
Statpak. N. Crockett et al. 254p. 1988. pap. 34.95 (ISBN 0-471-33435-9). Wiley.
STATS for Those in the Know! Susie McAuley. LC 88-90536. 76p. (Orig.). (ps-5). 1988. pap. text ed. price not set (ISBN 0-9619964-0-4). S McAuley.
Statuatory Supplement to Labor Law: Collective Bargaining in a Free Society. 3rd ed. Walter E. Oberer et al. (American Casebook Ser.). 165p. 1986. pap. 9.95 (ISBN 0-314-25469-2). West Pub.
Statue. Arnold Bennett. LC 74-17141. (Collected Works of Arnold Bennett: Vol. 75). 1976. Repr. of 1911 ed. 19.25 (ISBN 0-518-19156-7). Ayer Co Pubs.
Statue in Search of a Pedestal: A Biography of the Marquis de Lafayette. Noel B. Gerson. 17.95 (ISBN 0-88411-640-9, Pub. by Aeonian Pr). Amereon Ltd.
Statue in the Harbor: A Story of Two Apprentices. Jeffrey Eger. LC 85-61511. (Illus.). 96p. (gr. 4-8). 1985. PLB 8.96 (ISBN 0-382-09145-0); pap. 4.75 (ISBN 0-382-09146-9). Silver.
Statue of America: The First 100 Years of the Statue of Liberty. LC 85-42808. (Illus.). 224p. (gr. 7 up). 1985. 14.95 (ISBN 0-317-66372-0, Four Winds). Macmillan.
Statue of Liberty. Leonard E. Fisher. LC 85-42878. (Illus.). 64p. (gr. 3-7). 1985. reinforced bdg. 12.95 (ISBN 0-8234-0586-9). Holiday.
Statue of Liberty. Mary V. Fox. LC 85-15421. (Illus.). 64p. (gr. 3 up). 1985. 9.79 (ISBN 0-671-60482-1); pap. 6.95 (ISBN 0-671-60481-3). Messner.
Statue of Liberty. Michael George. (Illus.). 56p. (Orig.). 1985. pap. 14.95 (ISBN 0-8109-2294-0). Abrams.
Statue of Liberty. Charles Mercer. LC 78-21305. (Illus.). (gr. 5 up). 1979. 12.95 (ISBN 0-399-20670-1). Putnam Pub Group.
Statue of Liberty. Charles Mercer. LC 84-26574. (Illus.). 96p. (gr. 4 up). 1985. pap. 7.95 (ISBN 0-399-21231-0, Putnam). Putnam Pub Group.
Statue of Liberty. William E. Shapiro. (First BK.). (Illus.). 72p. (gr. 4-8). 1985. PLB 10.40 (ISBN 0-531-10047-2). Watts.
Statue of Liberty. Marvin Trachtenberg. (Illus.). 224p. 1986. pap. 12.95 (ISBN 0-14-008493-2). Penguin.

Statute & Rules of Procedure: International Civil Service Commission. 1988. pap. 4.00 (ISBN 92-1-100321-0, E.87.I.19). UN.
Statute of Limitations in American Conflicts of Law. Alejo De Cervera. LC 65-23494. 5.00 (ISBN 0-8477-3001-8). U of PR Pr.
Statute of Limitations on Malpractice. Alexander Kahapea. (Illus.). 320p. 1983. 25.00 (ISBN 0-89962-295-X). Todd & Honeywell.
Statute of the International Law Commission. 1982. 1.00 (ISBN 92-1-133250-8, E.82.V.8). UN.
Statute of York & the Interest of the Commons. George L. Haskins. LC 77-4920. 1977. Repr. of 1935 ed. lib. bdg. 35.00x (ISBN 0-8371-9610-8, HASY); microfiche avail. (ISBN 0-8371-9612-4). Greenwood.
Statutes & Rules Supplement for Use with Cases & Material on Admiralty. 3rd ed. Lucas. 252p. 1986. pap. 7.95 (ISBN 0-88277-520-0). Foundation Pr.
Statutes & Their Interpretation in the First Half of the 14th Century. Theodore F. Plucknett. LC 85-81796. (Cambridge Studies in English Legal History). 1986. Repr. of 1922 ed. 47.50x. W W Gaunt.
Statutes at Large, Being a Collection of All the Laws of Virginia from the First Session of the Legislature in the Year 1619, 13 Vols. facsim. ed. Ed. by William W. Hening. LC 69-18889. (Jamestown Foundation of the Commonwealth of Va). 1969. 300.00x set (ISBN 0-8139-0254-1); 40.00x ea. U Pr of Va.
Statutes at Large of Pennsylvania from 1682-1801, 17 vols. Compiled by James T. Mitchell. LC 74-19615. Repr. of 1915 ed. Set. 875.00 (ISBN 0-404-12413-5); 51.50 ea. AMS Pr.
Statutes at Large of the Provisional Government of the Confederate States of America. James Matthews. LC 87-83739. 922p. 1988. Repr. of 1864 ed. lib. bdg. 75.00 (ISBN 0-89941-629-2). W S Hein.
Statutes at Large of Virginia from October Session 1792, to December Session 1806, 3 Vols. Ed. by Samuel Shepherd. LC 79-119153. Repr. of 1835 ed. Set. lib. bdg. 95.00 (ISBN 0-404-06010-2). AMS Pr.
Statutes-at-Large of Virginia Sixteen Nineteen to Seventeen Ninety-Two, 13 vols. Ed. by William W. Hening. Repr. of 1819 ed. Set. 390.00 (ISBN 0-686-74545-0). AMS Pr.
Statutes of Limitations. Monroe Engel. LC 87-46078. 1988. 16.95 (ISBN 0-394-57040-5). Knopf.
Statutes of Limitations in American Conflicts of Law. Alejo De Cervera. LC 65-23494. 189p. 1966. 12.50 (ISBN 0-379-00259-0). Oceana.
Statutes of the Urban & Regional Communities of Montreal, Quebec & Outaousais. write for info. (162). Commerce.
Statutes on Slavery: The Pamphlet Literature, 2 vols. Ed. by Paul Finkelman. (Slavery, Race & the American Legal System, 1700-1872 Ser.). 709p. 1988. lib. bdg. 150.00 (ISBN 0-8240-6724-X). Garland Pub.
Statutes, Rules & Examples. Alastair I. McAdam & Tom M. Smith. LC 85-238078. 1985. 38.00 (ISBN 0-409-49423-2). Butterworth Legal Pubs.
Statutory Definitions of Nursing Practice & Their Conformity to Certain ANA Principles. 51p. 1983. 5.00 (ISBN 0-318-17545-2, D-81). ANA.
Statutory Exclusion of Crimes from Juvenile Court: 1981 Statutes Analysis. John L. Hutzler. 8p. 1981. 2.00. Natl Juv & Family Ct Judges.
Statutory Obligation of an Employer to Furnish Information to a Union. 2nd. ed. Bertram Gottlieb & Charles Werner. 1985. pap. 11.00 (ISBN 0-89806-019-2, NO. 111). Inst Indus Eng.
Statutory Requirements for Licensure of Nurses. Clare LaBar. LC 86-122065. 1985. 15.00. ANA.
Statutory Supplement to Cases & Materials on Labor Law, 1987. Douglas L. Leslie. 1987. pap. 12.95 (ISBN 0-316-52153-1). Little.
Statutory Supplement to Labor Law: Cases, Materials & Problems. Bernard D. Meltzer & Stanley D. Henderson. LC 84-81751. 1985. pap. text ed. 8.95 (ISBN 0-316-56648-9). Little.
Statutory Time Limitations: Washington State. rev. ed. Butterworths Staff. LC 80-70623. 470p. 1988. looseleaf 55.00 (ISBN 0-409-20203-7). Butterworth WA.
Staubach Corp. James Benjamin & Stanley Kratchman. 1988. pap. 7.95 (ISBN 0-256-06496-2). Irwin.
Staunton's Chess Tournament: London 1815. Howard Staunton. (Classic Chess Ser.). (Illus.). 480p. 1986. 35.95 (ISBN 0-7134-5059-2, Pub. by Batsford England). David & Charles.
Staupitz Und Luther. Ernst Wolf. (Ger). pap. 28.00 (ISBN 0-384-69018-1). Johnson Repr.
Stave Churches in Norway. G. Bugge. 84p. (Orig.). 1983. pap. 22.00x (N609). Vanous.
Stave Churches in Norway. Roggenkamp. 24.00 (ISBN 0-85440-205-5). Anthroposophic.
Stavelot Triptych, Mosan Art, & the Legend of the True Cross. The Pierpont Morgan Library. (Illus.). 1980. text ed. 29.95x (ISBN 0-19-520225-2). Oxford U Pr.
Stavelot Triptych: Mosan Art & the Legend of the True Cross. William Voelke. LC 80-8970. (Illus.). 80p. 1980. pap. 5.00 (ISBN 0-87598-071-6). Pierpont Morgan.
Staves Calends Legends. Thomas Meyer. 1979. 17.50 (ISBN 0-912330-36-8, Dist. by Inland Bk); pap. 10.00 (ISBN 0-912330-37-6, Dist. by Inland Bk). Jargon Soc.
Staves for Louisville. William Carigan. LC 81-81067. 1981. 10.95 (ISBN 0-9605986-0-X). Juniper Pubs.
Stavrogin's Confession & the Plan of the Life of a Great Sinner. Fyodor Dostoyevsky. LC 72-2556. (Studies in Fiction: No. 34). 1972. Repr. of 1922 ed. lib. bdg. 48.95x (ISBN 0-8383-1494-5). Haskell.
Stavronikita Monastery: History-Icons-Embroideries. Christos Patrinelis et al. (Illus.). 241p. 1974. 75.00 (ISBN 0-89241-076-0). Caratzas.
Stay Alive & Other Stories. Jane Anderson et al. (Follet Adult Basic Reading Comprehension Program Ser.). 64p. pap. 2.95 (ISBN 0-8428-2253-4). Cambridge Bk.
Stay Alive, My Son. Pin Yathay & John Man. (Illus.). 264p. 1988. pap. 6.95 (ISBN 0-671-66394-1, Touchstone Bks). S&S.
Stay Alive, My Son. Pin Yathy & John Man. 256p. 1987. 19.95 (ISBN 0-02-935861-2). Free Pr.
Stay Away from Simon. Carol Carrick. LC 84-14289. (Illus.). 64p. (gr. 2-5). 1985. pap. 10.95 (ISBN 0-89919-343-9, Clarion). Ticknor & Fields.
Stay Away from the Junkyard! Tricia Tusa. LC 87-15274. (Illus.). 32p. (gr. k-3). 1988. PLB 14.95 (ISBN 0-02-789541-6). Macmillan.
Stay Away, Joe. Dan Cushman. LC 52-12887. 1968. pap. 14.95 (ISBN 0-911436-01-4). Stay Away.
Stay by the River. Susan Engberg. 256p. 1985. 15.95 (ISBN 0-670-80620-X). Viking.
Stay by the River. Susan Engberg. 224p. 1986. pap. 6.95 (ISBN 0-14-007989-0). Penguin.
Stay Fit & Healthy until You're Dead. Dave Barry. Ed. by Roger Yepsen. (Illus.). 96p. 1985. pap. 5.95 (ISBN 0-87857-570-7). Rodale Pr Inc.
Stay Home & Make Money. Russ Von Hoelscher. 120p. 1981. pap. 9.95 (ISBN 0-686-32128-6). Profit Ideas.
Stay Home & Mind Your Own Business: How to Manage Your Time, Space, Personal Obligations, Money, Business, & Yourself While Working at Home. Jo Frohbieter-Mueller. LC 87-15922. (Illus.). 280p. (Orig.). 1987. pap. 9.95 (ISBN 0-932620-83-3). Betterway Pubns.
Stay Hungry. Charles Gaines. 256p. 1985. pap. 3.50 (ISBN 0-345-31966-4). Ballantine.
Stay on Your Toes, Maggie Adams! Karen S. Dean. LC 85-91176. 153p. (YA) (gr. 6-8). 1986. pap. 2.50 (ISBN 0-380-89711-3, Flare). Avon.
Stay Out of the Shower! Twenty-Five Years of Shockers Beginning with Pyscho. William Schoell. LC 85-4477. (Illus.). 1985. pap. 14.95 (ISBN 0-934878-61-7). Dembner Bks.
Stay Put, Robbie McAmis. Frances G. Tunbo. LC 87-18123. (Chaparral Bks.). (Illus.). (gr. 4 up). 1988. PLB 15.95 (ISBN 0-87565-025-2). Tex Christian.
Stay Safe. Bea Mandel & Byron Mandel. 1987. pap. cancelled. Prima Pub Comm.
Stay Tuned: A Concise History of American Broadcasting. Christopher H. Sterling & John M. Kittross. 562p. 1978. text ed. write for info. (ISBN 0-534-00514-4). Wadsworth Pub.
Stay Tuned: An Inside Look at the Making of Prime Time Television. Richard Levinson & William Link. 1981. 11.95 (ISBN 0-312-76136-8). St Martin.
Stay Tuned-Behind the Screens at Channel 5: How a Television Station Really Works. Peggy Lamson. LC 86-46245. (Illus.). 224p. 1987. 17.95 (ISBN 0-87923-681-7). Godine.
Stay Tuned for Danger. Carolyn Keene. (Nancy Drew Files Ser.: No. 17). 160p. (Orig.). (YA) (gr. 7 up). 1987. pap. 2.75 (ISBN 0-671-64141-7). Archway.
Stay up Late. David Byrne. LC 87-10399. (Illus.). (ps up). 1987. 14.95 (ISBN 0-670-81895-X, Viking Kestrel). Viking.
Stay Well: A Nationally Acclaimed Family Doctor Tells You How. Robert T. Johnson. LC 85-60510. 1985. 15.95. Horizon Utah.
Stay with It Snoopy: Selected Cartoons from, Summers Fly, Winters Walk, Vol. III. Charles M. Schulz. 128p. 1982. pap. 1.95 (ISBN 0-449-24310-9, Crest). Fawcett.
Stay Young at Heart. John D. Cantwell. LC 75-25958. (Illus.). 213p. 1975. 17.95 (ISBN 0-88229-247-1). Nelson-Hall.
Stay Young, Reduce Your Rate of Aging. John K. Beddow. 101p. (Orig.). 1986. pap. 4.20 (ISBN 0-9617531-0-2). Shape Tech Ltd.
Stayed on Freedom. Ed. by Pat Bryant. (Southern Exposure Ser.). (Illus.). 128p. (Orig.). 1981. pap. 4.50 (ISBN 0-943810-10-8). Inst Southern Studies.
Staying Afloat. Muriel Spanier. 1985. 17.45 (ISBN 0-394-54652-0). Random.
Staying Afloat. Muriel Spanier. 1986. pap. 3.95 (ISBN 0-449-20881-8, Pub. by Crest). Fawcett.
Staying Alive. Leonore Fleischer. (Illus., Orig.). 1983. pap. 2.95 (ISBN 0-671-47786-2). PB.
Staying Alive. Robin Morris. 288p. 1989. pap. price not set. Tor Bks.
Staying Alive: A Writer's Guide. Norman Spinrad. Ed. by Hank Stine. LC 82-14736. 162p. 1983. pap. 5.95 (ISBN 0-89865-259-6). Donning Co.
Staying Alive in Alaska's Wild. Andy Nault. Ed. by Tee Loftin. (Illus.). 224p. (Orig.). (gr. 5 up). 1980. pap. 8.75 (ISBN 0-934812-01-2). Tee Loftin.
Staying Alive: The Psychology of Human Survival. Roger Walsh. LC 84-5482. (New Science Library). 125p. (Orig.). 1984. pap. 12.95 (ISBN 0-87773-293-0, 72690-1). Shambhala Pubns.
Staying Alive: The Psychology of Human Survival. Roger Walsh. pap. 12.95 (ISBN 0-394-72690-1). Shambhala Pubns.
Staying Alive... Wait until You're Dead before You Die. Michael P. McKinley. 84p. 1983. pap. 5.00x (ISBN 0-9610370-1-6). Thinking Pubns.
Staying at the Top. Sonny Kleinfield. 304p. 1987. pap. 4.50 (ISBN 0-451-14977-7, Sig). NAL.
Staying at the Top. Evelyn Rothstein et al. Ed. by Joan Ostacher. LC 86-80111. (Illus.). 175p. 1986. 9.95 (ISBN 0-913935-42-5). ERA-CCR.
Staying at the Top: The Life of a CEO. Sonny Kleinfield. 288p. 1986. 17.95 (ISBN 0-453-00521-7). NAL.
Staying Awake: More Fun Than Sleeping. Leroy Bradford. LC 81-90342. 54p. (Orig.). 1981. 10.00 (ISBN 0-9616758-0-2); pap. 9.00x (ISBN 0-686-36897-5). Ms Leroy Pr.
Staying Back. Janice Hobby. (Illus.). (gr. k-6). 1982. 10.95 (ISBN 0-937404-00-4); pap. 6.95 (ISBN 0-937404-16-0). Triad Pub FL.
Staying Beautiful: Beauty Tips & Attitudes from My 40 Years As a Model. Carmen Lewis & Alfred A. Lewis. LC 84-48142. (Illus.). 224p. 1985. 19.95i (ISBN 0-06-015386-5, HarpT). Har-Row.
Staying Employed: The Work Manual for the Eighties...& Beyond. William Homolka. LC 84-60968. 100p. (Orig.). 1984. pap. 9.95 (ISBN 0-917601-00-9). New World NY.
Staying Flexible. Time-Life Books Editors. (Fitness, Health & Nutrition Ser.). 144p. 1987. 17.27 (ISBN 0-8094-6167-6); lib. bdg. 21.27 (ISBN 0-8094-6168-4). Time-Life.
Staying Found: The Complete Map & Compass Handbook. June Fleming. LC 81-52429. (Illus.). 192p. (Orig.). 1982. pap. 7.95 (ISBN 0-394-75152-3, Vin). Random.
Staying Hard. Charles Gaines & George Butler. (Orig.). 1980. pap. 10.95 (ISBN 0-671-41265-5). S&S.
Staying Healthy: A Bibliography of Health Promotion Materials. 1984. lib. bdg. 79.95 (ISBN 0-87700-550-8). Revisionist Pr.
Staying Healthy: A Bibliography of Health Promotion Materials. lib. bdg. 79.95 (ISBN 0-8490-3807-3). Gordon Pr.
Staying Healthy in Asia, Africa & Latin America: Your Complete Health Guide to Traveling & Living in Less-Developed Regions of the World. rev. ed. Dirk G. Schroeder. (Illus.). 208p. 1987. pap. 7.95 (ISBN 0-917704-19-3). Volunteers Asia Pr.
Staying Healthy-Nutrition, Lifestyle & Medicine. Research Reports Editors. LC 83-15292. 203p. 1984. pap. 9.95 (ISBN 0-87187-278-1). Congr Quarterly.
Staying Healthy with Diabetes: A Program of Individualized Care. Gary Arsham & Ernest Lowe. 220p. (Orig.). 1988. pap. 10.95 (ISBN 0-937721-51-4). Diabetes Ctr MN.
Staying Healthy with the Seasons. Elson Haas. LC 80-69469. (Illus.). 192p. (Orig.). 1981. pap. 9.95 (ISBN 0-89087-306-2). Celestial Arts.
Staying Healthy Without Medicine: A Manual of Home Prevention & Treatment. Daniel P. Marshall & J. Gregory Rabold. LC 83-2297. (Illus.). 312p. 1983. lib. bdg. 28.95x (ISBN 0-88229-635-3). Nelson-Hall.
Staying Home Instead: How to Quit the Working-Mom Rat Race & Survive Financially. Christine Davidson. LC 85-45298. 192p. 1986. 25.00x (ISBN 0-669-11266-6); pap. 12.95 (ISBN 0-669-12878-3). Lexington Bks.
Staying in... John E. Biegert. (Looking Up Ser.). 1985. pap. 1.25 (ISBN 0-8298-0567-2). Pilgrim NY.
Staying in Love. William J. Diehm. LC 85-28681. 128p. (Orig.). 1986. pap. 6.95 (ISBN 0-8066-2191-5, 10-5996). Augsburg.
Staying in Love. Norton F. Kristy. 1985. pap. 7.00 (ISBN 0-87980-419-9). Wilshire.
Staying in Shape: An Insider's View of the Great Spas. Carleton Varney. LC 83-3794. (Illus.). 224p. 1983. 19.95 (ISBN 0-672-52722-7). Bobbs.
Staying Is Nowhere: An Anthology of Kondh & Paraja Poetry. Sitakant Mahapatra. (Saffronbird Bk.). 1976. lib. bdg. 12.00 (ISBN 0-89253-126-6); flexible bdg. 6.75 (ISBN 0-89253-142-8). Ind-US Inc.
Staying Married Is the Best Revenge. Michael Moore. 96p. Date not set. 3.95 (ISBN 1-55601-006-0). Solson Pubns.
Staying Nine. Pam Conrad. LC 87-45862. (Illus.). 80p. (gr. 2-5). 1988. 11.95i (ISBN 0-06-021319-1); PLB 11.89 (ISBN 0-06-021320-5). HarpJ.
Staying Off the Beaten Track. 1987. pap. 12.95 (ISBN 0-317-66325-9). Salem Hse Pubs.
Staying OK. Amy B. Harris & Thomas A. Harris. 272p. 1986. 4.50 (ISBN 0-380-70130-8). Avon.
Staying OK: How to Maximize Good Feelings & Minimize Bad Ones. Amy Harris & Thomas A. Harris. LC 84-48164. (Illus.). 288p. 1985. 15.45i (ISBN 0-06-015315-6, HarpT). Har-Row.
Staying on Alone: Letters of Alice B. Toklas. rev. ed. Alice B. Toklas. Ed. by Edward Burns. 1973. 11.95 (ISBN 0-87140-569-5); pap. 8.95 (ISBN 0-87140-131-2). Liveright.
Staying on Top When Things Go Wrong. Linda R. Wright. 120p. 1983. pap. 2.95 (ISBN 0-8423-6623-7). Tyndale.
Staying Out of Court: A Manager's Guide to Employment Law. Cliff Roberson. LC 84-48799. 192p. 1985. 29.00x (ISBN 0-669-09769-1). Lexington Bks.
Staying Out of Hell. James A. Thom. 1985. pap. 3.95 (ISBN 0-345-30665-1). Ballantine.
Staying Out of Hock. Harry S. Dahlstrom. (Illus.). 50p. (Orig.). 1987. pap. 3.79 (ISBN 0-940712-54-7). Dahlstrom & Co.
Staying Overnight. Mercer Mayer. LC 87-83014. (Golden Easy Readers Ser.). (Illus.). 40p. (gr. k-2). 1988. 3.95 (ISBN 0-307-11662-X). Western Pub.
Staying Overnight. Kate Petty. Ed. by FS-Aladdin Staff. (First Timers Ser.). (Illus.). 24p. 1988. 9.90 (ISBN 0-531-17106-X, Gloucester Pr). Watts.
Staying Positive in a Negative World. Roger Campbell. 132p. 1984. pap. 5.50 (ISBN 0-89693-377-6). Victor Bks.
Staying Power. P. Fryer. 595p. 1984. text ed. 39.95x (ISBN 0-391-03167-8). Humanities.
Staying Power. Anne Ortlund & Ray Ortlund. LC 86-5192. 192p. 1986. 10.95 (ISBN 0-8407-9055-4). Oliver-Nelson.
Staying Power: How You Can Win in Life's Tough Situations. Anne Ortlund & Ray Ortlund. 192p. 1986. 10.95. Nelson Comm.
Staying Safe: How to Protect Yourself Against Sexual Assault. Elizabeth M. Ozer & Nkenge Toure. (Illus.). 23p. (Orig.). (gr. 2-6). pap. text ed. 3.00 (ISBN 0-318-04650-4). Rape Crisis Ctr.
Staying Sober. Terence T. Gorski. 227p. 1986. pap. 10.95 (ISBN 0-317-56689-X). Ind Pr MO.
Staying Sober. Terence T. Gorski & Merlene Miller. 1986. pap. 10.95 (ISBN 0-8309-0459-X). Herald Hse.
Staying Sober. Judy Myers & Maribeth Mellin. 1988. pap. 7.95 (ISBN 0-671-66125-6). PB.
Staying Sober: The Complete Nutrition & Exercise Program for the Recovering Alcoholic. Judy Myers & Maribeth Mellin. (Illus.). 192p. 1987. 15.95 (ISBN 0-86553-172-2). Congdon & Weed.
Staying Straight: Adolescent Recovery. Mary Montagne. 40p. (Orig.). 1987. pap. 2.95 (ISBN 0-9613416-6-1). Comm Intervention.
Staying Supple. John Jerome. (New Age Ser.). 140p. (Orig.). 1987. pap. 8.95 (ISBN 0-553-34429-3). Bantam.
Staying the Course. Alice M. Silver. LC 81-82697. 94p. 1982. 12.95 (ISBN 0-8022-2390-7). Philos Lib.
Staying the Course: Henry M. Jackson & National Security. Ed. by Dorothy Fosdick. LC 87-2015. (Illus.). 206p. 1987. 20.00 (ISBN 0-295-96498-7); pap. 9.95 (ISBN 0-295-96501-0). U of Wash Pr.
Staying Thin. Robert Linn. 1982. pap. 2.95 (ISBN 0-89083-916-6). Zebra.
Staying Thin Cookbook. Eric Perkins. LC 87-63417. 200p. 1988. 16.95 (ISBN 0-935055-38-X). Nautilus Inc.
Staying Thin for Kids: The Family Guide to Health & Fitness. Eric Perkins. 1988. 16.95 (ISBN 0-935055-39-8). Nautilus Inc.
Staying Thin: The Model's Health & Fitness Regimen. Eric Perkins. LC 87-61224. (Illus.). 136p. 1987. 14.95 (ISBN 0-935055-37-1). Nautilus Inc.
Staying Together. Diane Hoh. (Cheerleaders Ser.: No. 12). 176p. (Orig.). (gr. 7 up). 1985. pap. 2.25 (ISBN 0-590-33928-1). Scholastic Inc.
Staying Together: A Practical Way to Make Your Relationship Succeed & Grow. Reginald Beech. 1985. pap. 20.30 (ISBN 0-471-90809-6). Wiley.
Staying Together: Forty Ways to Make your Marriage Work. Tom Owen-Towle. (Illus.). 108p. (Orig.). 1987. pap. 7.95x (ISBN 0-931104-21-1). Sunflower Ink.
Staying Up. Robert Swindells. 160p. (YA) (gr. 7 up). 1988. 13.95 (ISBN 0-19-271546-1). Oxford U Pr.
Staying Well. Richard E. Ecker. LC 84-4664. 132p. (Orig.). 1984. pap. 4.95 (ISBN 0-87784-967-6). Inter-Varsity.
Staying with It. John Jerome. 213p. 1984. 14.95 (ISBN 0-670-66876-1). Viking.
Staying with It. John Jerome. (Nonfiction Ser.). 240p. 1985. pap. 6.95 (ISBN 0-14-008270-0). Penguin.
Staying with Relations. Rose Macaulay. 320p. 1987. pap. 9.50 (ISBN 0-88001-148-3). Ecco Pr.
Staying Young. Thomas Hager & Lauren Kessler. 1987. 17.95 (ISBN 0-8160-1303-9). Facts on File.
Staying Young. Liz Renay. 192p. 11.95 (ISBN 0-8184-0329-2). Lyle Stuart.
Staying Young: How to Look Good, Feel Better & Live Longer. Frances S. Goulart. (Illus.). 228p. 1987. 16.95 (ISBN 0-13-846213-5); pap. 9.95 (ISBN 0-13-846205-4). P-H.
Stazwoerterbuch des Buch und Verlagswesens. Ulrich Stiehl. 1000p. (Ger. & Eng., Dictionary of Book Publishing). 1977. 175.00 (ISBN 3-7940-4147-X, M-7619, Pub. by Saur). French & Eur.
STD: Sexually Transmitted Diseases. Stephen Zinner. 1985. 16.45 (ISBN 0-671-49957-2). Summit Bks.
Stead. Cid Corman. 1966. pap. 6.00 (ISBN 0-685-00990-4). Elizabeth Pr.
Steadfast Heart. Dorothy Mack. 1988. pap. 2.95 (ISBN 0-451-15601-3, Sig). NAL.

Steaming Through Kent. Peter Hay. 1986. 34.75x (ISBN 0-906520-13-4, Pub. by Middleton Pr UK). State Mutual Bk.
Steaming to Bamboola: The World of a Tramp Freighter. Christopher Buckley. 224p. 1987. pap. 6.95 (ISBN 0-14-009922-0). Penguin.
Steaming Up! Samuel M. Vauclain. LC 73-6837. (Illus.). 1973. 15.95 (ISBN 0-87095-044-4). Gldn West Bks.
Steamship Accounting. Phillip C. Cheng. LC 70-80637. 192p. 1969. 11.00x (ISBN 0-87033-117-5). Cornell Maritime.
Steamship Conquest of the World, 1812-1912. Frederick Talbot. 1977. lib. bdg. 59.95 (ISBN 0-8490-2668-7). Gordon Pr.
Stecheson Classified Song Directory: With Supplement Thru 1978. Anne Stecheson & Anthony Stecheson. 1961. 40.00 (ISBN 0-910468-08-7). Criterion Mus.
Stedman Pocket Dictionary. 822p. 1987. pap. text ed. 16.95 (ISBN 0-683-07921-2). Williams & Wilkins.
Stedman's Medical Dictionary. 22nd ed. Stedman. 1586p. 1972. 9.95 (ISBN 0-683-07919-0, Pub. by Williams & Wilkins). Krieger.
Stedman's Medical Dictionary. 24th ed. (Illus.). 1750p. 1981. lib. bdg. 35.95 (ISBN 0-683-07915-8). Williams & Wilkins.
Steel & Carbide Booklet. 52p. 0.50 (ISBN 0-318-13875-1); 0.50. Cutting Tool Mfg.
Steel & Iron Dimensional Standards. 5th ed. (Din Handbook: No. 28). write for info. (ISBN 0-686-39808-4, 11125-1, Pub. by DIN Germany). IPS.
Steel & Iron-Quality Standards One. (Din Handbook: No. 4). write for info. (ISBN 0-686-39806-8, 11441-1, Pub. by DIN Germany). IPS.
Steel & Iron Quality Standards Two. (Din Handbook: No. 155). write for info. (ISBN 0-686-39807-6, 11441-1, Pub. by DIN Germany). IPS.
Steel & Its Heat Treatment. 2nd ed. Kark-Erik Thelning. (Illus.). 680p. 1984. text ed. 115.00 (ISBN 0-408-01424-5). Butterworth.
Steel & Metal Workers-It Takes a Fight to Win! 2nd ed. Gus Hall. (Illus.). 64p. 1972. pap. 0.25 (ISBN 0-87898-094-6). New Outlook.
Steel & Steelworkers: The Sons of Vulcan. Charles Docherty. (Illus.). x, 247p. 1983. text ed. 32.00x (ISBN 0-435-82196-2). Gower Pub Co.
Steel & Style: The Story of Alessi Household Ware. Patrizia Scarzella. 187p. 45.00 (ISBN 0-317-66854-4). Princeton Arch.
Steel & the State. Thomas R. Howell et al. (Economic Competition Among Nations Ser.). 640p. 1988. pap. 44.50 (ISBN 0-8133-7676-9). Westview.
Steel Assembly Weight Determination. Practical Engineering Applications Software. 1984. IBM-PC Version. incl. disk 125.00 (ISBN 0-471-80293-X); Apple Version. incl. disk 125.00 (ISBN 0-471-88428-6). Wiley.
Steel Band. John Bartholomew. (Topics in Music Ser.). 48p. 1986. pap. 7.95x (ISBN 0-19-321329-X). Oxford U Pr.
Steel Bars, Chain, & Springs, Bearing Steel, Steel Forgings (116 Standards) see ASTM Annual Book of Standards, 1986.
Steel-Belted Grimm. Mike Peters. 128p. 1988. pap. 5.95 (ISBN 0-88687-366-5, Topper Bks.). Pharos Bks NY.
Steel Boatbuilding, Vol. 2. Thomas Colvin. (Illus.). 208p. 1986. 30.00 (ISBN 0-87742-203-6). Intl Marine.
Steel Boatbuilding, Vol. 1. Thomas Colvin. LC 84-48520. (Illus.). 276p. 1985. 32.50 (ISBN 0-87742-189-7). Intl Marine.
Steel Box Girder Bridges: Conference Proceedings. 319p. 1973. 52.75 (ISBN 0-901948-76-4, Pub. by T Telford UK). Am Soc Civil Eng.
Steel Brother. Gordon R. Dickson. 256p. (Orig.). 1985. pap. 2.95 (ISBN 0-8125-3552-9, Dist. by Warner Pub Services & St. Martin's Press). Tor Bks.
Steel Buildings: Analysis & Design. 3rd ed. Stanley W. Crawley & Robert M. Dillon. 672p. 1984. text ed. write for info. (ISBN 0-471-86414-5); solution manual avail. (ISBN 0-471-89130-4). Wiley.
Steel Casting Handbook Supplements. Incl. Supplement 1. Design Rules & Data. 2.00 (ISBN 0-686-44966-5); Supplement 3. Tolerances. 2.00 (ISBN 0-686-44967-3); Supplement 4. Drafting Practices for Castings. 2.00 (ISBN 0-686-44968-1); Supplement 5. General Properties of Steel Castings. 2.00 (ISBN 0-686-44969-X); Supplement 6. Repair Welding & Fabrication Welding of Steel Castings. 5.00 (ISBN 0-686-44970-3); Supplement 7. Welding of High Alloy Castings. 5.00 (ISBN 0-686-44971-1); Supplement 8. High Alloy Data Sheets, Corrosion Series. 5.00 (ISBN 0-686-44972-X); Supplement 9. High Alloy Data Sheets, Heat Series. 5.00 (ISBN 0-686-44973-8); Supplement 10. A Glossary of Foundry Terms. 2.00 (ISBN 0-686-44974-6); Supplement 11. Hardenability & Heat Treatment. 2.00 (ISBN 0-686-44975-4). 20.00 (ISBN 0-686-44963-0); Set. 35.00 (ISBN 0-686-44964-9); 3-Ring Binder 4.00 (ISBN 0-686-44965-7). Steel Founders.
Steel Castings Handbook. 5th ed. 450p. 1980. 35.00 (ISBN 0-317-59786-8, OS8100). Am Foundrymen.
Steel Castings Handbook. 5th ed. Ed. by Peter F. Wieser. (Illus.). 536p. 1980. 35.00 (ISBN 0-9604674-0-8). Steel Founders.
Steel City: Hamilton & Region. Ed. by M. J. Dear et al. 308p. 1987. 35.00x (ISBN 0-8020-2563-3); pap. 15.95 (ISBN 0-8020-6582-1). U of Toronto Pr.
Steel City: Urban & Ethnic Patterns in Gary, Indiana, 1906-1950. Raymond A. Mohl & Neil Betten. (Illus.). 227p. 1986. 32.50 (ISBN 0-8419-1010-3); pap. 23.50 (ISBN 0-8419-1077-4). Holmes & Meier.
Steel Coffin at Forty Fathoms. James I. Clark. LC 79-21052. (Quest, Adventure, Survival Ser.). (Illus.). 48p. (gr. 4-8). 1980. PLB 15.33 (ISBN 0-8172-1567-0). Raintree Pubs.
Steel Coffin at Forty Fathoms. James I. Clark. LC 79-21052. (Quest, Adventure, Survival Ser.). (Illus.). 48p. (gr. 4-9). 1982. pap. 9.27 (ISBN 0-8172-2071-2). Raintree Pubs.
Steel-Concrete Composite Beams for Building. C. Davies. LC 75-1080. 125p. 1975. 21.50 (ISBN 0-470-19876-1, JW). Krieger.
Steel-Concrete Composite Structures: Stability & Strength. Ed. by R. Narayanan. 347p. 1988. 93.75 (ISBN 1-85166-134-4). Elsevier.
Steel Construction: A Bibliography. Mary Vance. (Architecture Ser.: A 1447). 31p. 1985. 4.50 (ISBN 0-89028-537-3). Vance Biblios.
Steel Construction Inspector. Jack Rudman. (Career Examination Ser.: C-765). (Cloth bdg. avail. on request). pap. 16.00 (ISBN 0-8373-0765-1). Natl Learning.
Steel Crisis: The Economics & Politics of a Declining Industry. William Scheuerman. LC 85-28100. 235p. 1986. lib. bdg. 38.95 (ISBN 0-275-92124-7, C2124). Praeger.
Steel Crocodile. D. G. Compton. (Orig.). 1980. pap. 2.25 (ISBN 0-671-83078-3, Timescape). PB.
Steel Decisions & the National Economy. Henry W. Broude. LC 63-13958. (Yale Studies in Economics: No. 16). pap. 86.80 (ISBN 0-317-29591-8, 2021983). Bks Demand UMI.
Steel Design for Engineers & Architects. Rene Amon et al. 432p. 1982. 44.95 (ISBN 0-442-20297-0). Van Nos Reinhold.
Steel Design for Structural Engineers. Nicholas Willems & B. O. Kuzmanovic. (Illus.). 640p. 1983. 48.00 (ISBN 0-13-846287-9). P-H.
Steel Designer's Manual. 4th. Rev. ed. (Illus.). 1089p. (Orig.). 1983. pap. text ed. 39.50x (ISBN 0-00-383202-3, Pub. by Collins England). Sheridan.
Steel Detailers' Manual. Alan Hayward. 128p. 1988. pap. write for info (ISBN 0-00-383062-4, Pub. by Collins England). Sheridan.
Steel: Diary of a Furnace Worker. Charles R. Walker. Ed. by Leon Stein. LC 77-70544. (Work Ser.). 1977. Repr. of 1922 ed. lib. bdg. 17.00x (ISBN 0-405-10213-5). Ayer Co Pubs.
Steel Doll, 1986. Lee F. Reese. (Illus.). 323p. 1986. pap. 25.00 (ISBN 0-9604372-5-8). Lex Bk Co CA.
Steel Drug: Cocaine in Perspective. Patricia G. Erickson et al. Ed. by Reginald G. Smart. 192p. 1986. 29.00x (ISBN 0-669-14572-6); pap. 12.95 (ISBN 0-669-14669-2). Lexington Bks.
Steel Engravings in Nineteenth Century British Topographical Books. Merlyn Holloway. viii, 205p. 1977. 50.00 (ISBN 0-900470-79-8). Oak Knoll.
Steel Erection Safety. Center for Occupational Research & Development Staff. (Job Safety & Health Instructional Materials Ser.). (Illus.). 44p. 1981. pap. text ed. 3.50 (ISBN 1-55502-141-7). Ctr Res & Dev.
Steel Eye. Chet Gottfried. LC 84-5444. 160p. (Orig.). 1984. pap. 5.95 (ISBN 0-917053-00-1). Space And.
Steel Eye. Chet Gottfried. LC 84-14467. 151p. 1984. Repr. lib. bdg. 19.95x (ISBN 0-89370-855-0). Borgo Pr.
Steel Fabrication Safety Manual. 120p. 1981. 6.00 (ISBN 0-318-12802-0, F502). Am Inst Steel Construct.
Steel Fiber Concrete: Proceedings, U. S.-Sweden Joint Seminar (NSF-STU), Stockholm, Sweden, June 2-5, 1985. Ed. by S. P. Shah & A. Skarendahl. 532p. 1986. 82.50 (ISBN 1-85166-043-7, Pub. by Elsevier Applied Sci England). Elsevier.
Steel Fiber Concrete: U. S.-Sweden Joint Seminar. Ed. by Surendra P. Shah & Ake Skarendahl. (Illus.). 520p. (Orig.). 1985. pap. text ed. 62.50x (ISBN 91-970408-4-3). Coronet Bks.
Steel for Line Pipe & Pipeline Fittings. 372p. (Orig.). 1983. pap. text ed. 90.00x (ISBN 0-904357-45-7, Pub. by the Metals Society). Brookfield Pub Co.
Steel Forgings: STP 903. Ed. by E. G. Nisbett & Albert S. Melilli. LC 86-14066. (Illus.). 610p. 1986. text ed. 59.00 (ISBN 0-8031-0465-0, 04-903000-02). ASTM.
Steel Foundry Melting Practice. 1973. 30.00 (ISBN 0-686-44984-3). Steel Founders.
Steel Foundry Workplace Improvement Guidebooks. Incl. Section I. General Engineering Principles. 10.00 (ISBN 0-686-44980-0); Section V. Cleaning & Finishing. 10.00 (ISBN 0-686-44981-9); Appendices. 10.00 (ISBN 0-686-44982-7). 10.00 (ISBN 0-686-44978-9); 3-Ring Binder 4.00 (ISBN 0-686-44979-7). Steel Founders.
Steel-Framed Structures: Stability & Strength. Ed. by R. Narayanan. 352p. 1985. 90.00 (ISBN 0-85334-329-2, Pub. by Elsevier Applied Sci England). Elsevier.
Steel Hawk & Other Stories. Bhabani Bhattacharya. 143p. 1968. pap. 2.95 (ISBN 0-88253-020-8). Ind-US Inc.
Steel Homes. Carl Giles & Barbara Giles. (Illus.). 320p. (Orig.). 1984. 21.95 (ISBN 0-8306-0641-6, 1641); pap. 16.95 (ISBN 0-8306-1641-1, 1641P). TAB Bks.
Steel in Marine Structures. Ed. by C. Noordhoek & J. De Back. 954p. 1987. 268.50 (ISBN 0-444-42805-4). Elsevier.
Steel in the Eighties. 280p. 1980. 22.50x (ISBN 92-64-12081-5). OECD.
Steel Industry in Brief: Canada. Ed. by R. L. Deily & W. E. Pietrucha. 45p. 15.00 (ISBN 0-317-40468-7). Iron & Steel.
Steel Industry in Brief: Continunous Casting Installations World-Wide. 114p. 1982. 75.00 (ISBN 0-317-40459-8). Iron & Steel.
Steel Industry in Brief: Databook U. S. A. Ed. by R. L. Deily & W. E. Pietrucla. 202p. 1983. pap. 75.00 (ISBN 0-317-34775-6). Iron & Steel.
Steel Industry in Brief: Japan. Ed. by R. L. Deily. 156p. 1977. pap. 75.00 (ISBN 0-317-34776-4). Iron & Steel.
Steel Industry in Brief: Mexico. Ed. by R. L. Deily & W. E. Pietrucha. 45p. 15.00 (ISBN 0-317-40466-0). Iron & Steel.
Steel Industry in Communist China. Yuan-li Wu. LC 64-8250. (Publications Ser.: No. 36). 334p. 1965. 13.95x (ISBN 0-8179-1361-0). Hoover Inst Pr.
Steel Industry in the Eighties. 176p. 1980. text ed. 60.00x (ISBN 0-904357-31-7, Pub. by Inst Metals). Brookfield Pub Co.
Steel Industry of India. William A. Johnson. LC 66-23471. (Rand Corporation Research Studies). 1966. 25.00x (ISBN 0-674-83715-0). Harvard U Pr.
Steel Industry Wage Structure: A Study of the Joint Union-Management Job Evaluation Program in the Basic Steel Industry. Jack Steiber. LC 59-12977. (Wertheim Publications in Industrial Relations). (Illus.). 1959. 27.50x (ISBN 0-674-83760-6). Harvard U Pr.
Steel Market in Nineteen Eighty-Five & Outlook for Nineteen Eighty-Six. OECD Staff. 38p. (Orig.). 1986. pap. 9.00x (ISBN 9-2641-2849-2). OECD.
Steel Market in Nineteen Eighty-Four & the Outlook for 1985. OECD. 36p. (Orig.). 1985. pap. 9.00x (ISBN 92-64-12752-6). OECD.
Steel Market in Nineteen Eighty-Six & Outlook for Nineteen Eighty-Seven. OECD. 39p. (Orig.). 1987. pap. 9.00x (ISBN 92-64-12990-1). OECD.
Steel Market in Nineteen Eighty-Three & the Outlook for Nineteen Eighty-Four. OECD. 38p. (Orig.). 1984. pap. 9.00x (ISBN 92-64-12598-1). OECD.
Steel Market in Nineteen Eighty-Two & the Outlook for Nineteen Eighty-Three. OECD. 38p. 1983. pap. 9.00x (ISBN 92-64-12481-0). OECD.
Steel Market in 1983. 1984. pap. 16.50 (ISBN 92-1-116314-5, E.84.II.E.14). UN.
Steel Market in 1984. 1985. pap. 16.50 (E.85.II.E.28). UN.
Steel Market in 1985. 1986. pap. 19.00 (ISBN 92-1-116375-7, E.86.II.E.24). UN.
Steel Market in 1986. 180p. 1988. pap. 28.00 (ISBN 92-1-116407-9, E.87.II.E.32). UN.
Steel Markets & Mini-Mills: Market Research Study. Milos Markovic. (Illus.). 260p. 1988. 2500.00 (ISBN 0-945235-02-X). Lead Edge Reports.
Steel Mill Lubrication. 150p. 1984. 25.00 (ISBN 0-318-17685-8, SP-18). Soc Tribologists.
Steel Mill or Treadmill? How to Stop the Big Steel Steal. Communist Party Steel & Metal Workers Commission. 1971. pap. 0.15 (ISBN 0-87898-069-5). New Outlook.
Steel on Immigration Law. Richard D. Steel. LC 84-80827. 1985. 85.00 (ISBN 0-318-04268-1); Suppl. 1987. 33.50. Lawyers Co-Op.
Steel Pipe: Design & Installation - M11. (AWWA Manuals). (Illus.). 260p. 1964. pap. text ed. 23.40 (ISBN 0-89867-069-1, M11). Am Water Wks Assn.
Steel Pipelines 2: Standards for Design & Constructions. (DIN Standards Ser.). write for info (ISBN 0-686-31849-8, 11201-3/141). IPS.
Steel Pipelines 3: Standards for Accessories & Testing. (DIN Standards Ser.). write for info (ISBN 0-686-31850-1, 11202-3/142). IPS.
Steel Piping, Tubing, & Fittings (115 Standards) see ASTM Annual Book of Standards, 1986.
Steel Plate, Sheet, Strip, & Wire (145 Standards) Metallic Coated Products see ASTM Annual Book of Standards, 1986.
Steel Players' Handbook. Stephen P. Shelton. LC 86-80902. (Illus.). 112p. (Orig.). 1986. 16.96 (ISBN 0-318-20174-7); pap. 14.95 (ISBN 0-937555-24-X). Kelby Pub.
Steel Producers. Ed. by ICC Information Group Ltd. Staff. 1987. 695.00x (ISBN 1-85319-045-4, ICC Info Group Ltd UK). State Mutual Bk.
Steel Production: Processes, Products, & Residuals. Clifford S. Russell & William J. Vaughan. LC 75-36945. (Resources for the Future Ser). 350p. 1976. 26.50x. Johns Hopkins.
Steel Production, Processes, Products, & Residuals. Clifford S. Russell & William J. Vaughan. 348p. 1976. 26.50 (ISBN 0-8018-1824-9). Resources Future.
Steel Products Manual - Strip Steel. Work for Hire Staff. 88p. (Orig.). Date not set. pap. 30.00 (ISBN 0-932897-34-7). Iron & Steel.
Steel Products Manual: Tool Steel. 80p. 1988. pap. 9.00 (ISBN 0-932897-31-2). Iron & Steel.
Steel Selection: A Guide for Improving Performance & Profits. Roy F. Kern & Manfred E. Suess. LC 78-13610. 460p. 1979. 54.50 (ISBN 0-471-04287-0, JW). Krieger.
Steel Shark. Bruno Krauss. (Sea Wolf Ser.: No. 1). 1981. pap. 2.25 (ISBN 0-89083-755-4). Zebra.
Steel Skeleton, Vol. 2: Plastic Behaviour & Design. John F. Baker et al. LC 54-3769. pap. 111.80 (ISBN 0-317-26067-7, 2024427). Bks Demand UMI.
Steel Square. H. H. Siegele. LC 79-63089. (Home Craftsman Bk.). (Illus.). 1979. pap. 8.95 (ISBN 0-8069-8854-1). Sterling.
Steel Square. 2nd ed. G. Townsend. (Illus.). 172p. 1947. pap. 8.24 (ISBN 0-8269-0685-0). Am Technical.
Steel Steeds Christie: A Memoir of J. Walter Christie. J. Edward Christie. (Illus.). 86p. 1985. pap. text ed. 16.00x (ISBN 0-89745-059-0). Sunflower U Pr.
Steel String Guitar: Construction & Repair. David R. Young. (Bold Strummer Guitar Ser.). (Illus.). 188p. (Orig.). 1988. 24.95 (ISBN 0-933224-11-7); pap. 15.95 (ISBN 0-933224-08-7). Bold Strummer Ltd.
Steel String Guitar: Its History & Construction. 2nd rev ed. Donald Brosnac. (Illus.). 112p. 1976. pap. 7.95 (ISBN 0-915572-26-5). Panjandrum.
Steel Structures. William McGuire. 1968. text ed. 59.00 (ISBN 0-13-846493-6). P-H.
Steel Structures-Advances, Design & Construction: Proceedings of the International Conference on Steel & Aluminum Structures, Cardiff, U. K., 8-10 July, 1987. Ed. by R. Narayanan. 860p. 1987. 153.00 (ISBN 1-85166-120-4, Pub. by Elsevier Applied Sci England). Elsevier.
Steel Structures: Design & Behavior. 2rd ed. Charles G. Salmon & John E. Johnson. (Illus.). 1007p. 1980. text ed. 59.50 scp (ISBN 0-06-045694-9, HarpC). Har-Row.
Steel Structures Painting Manual, 2 vols. Ed. by John D. Keane. Incl. Vol. 1. Good Painting Practices. 2nd ed. 580p. 1982; Vol. 2. Systems & Specifications. 4th ed. (Illus.). 400p. 1985. (Illus.). text ed. 120.00 set (ISBN 0-938477-02-1). SSPC.
Steel Structures Painting Manual, Vol. 1: "Good Painting Practice". 2nd ed. Ed. by John D. Keane et al. (Illus.). 580p. 1982. 70.00 (ISBN 0-938477-00-5); incl. Vol. 2 120.00. SSPC.
Steel Structures Painting Manual, Vol. 2: Systems & Specifications. 4th ed. Ed. by John D. Keane et al. 1985. 70.00 (ISBN 0-938477-01-3); incl. Vol. 1 120.00. SSPC.
Steel Structures: Practical Design Studies. T. J. MacGinley. 300p. 1981. 39.95x (ISBN 0-419-12560-4, NO. 6631, E & FN Spon England); pap. 17.95x (ISBN 0-419-11710-5, NO. 6598). Routledge Chapman & Hall.
Steel Structures: Recent Research Advances & Their Applications to Design. Ed. by M. N. Pavlovic. 604p. 1986. 144.00 (ISBN 1-85166-046-1). Elsevier.
Steel Summers. William F. Keefe. Ed. by Keith Irvine. (Illus.). 140p. (Orig.). 1986. pap. 5.95 (ISBN 0-917256-31-X). Ref Pubns.
Steel, the Mist & the Blazing Sun. Christopher Anvil. 288p. 1986. pap. 2.95 (ISBN 0-441-78572-7, Pub. by Ace Science Fiction). Ace Bks.
Steel Titan: The Life of Charles M. Schwab. Robert Hessen. (Illus.). 1975. 32.95x (ISBN 0-19-501937-7). Oxford U Pr.
Steel Wire & Wire Products Industry: An Analysis of Current Markets & Prospects for Future Growth. 290p. 1986. 695.00 (ISBN 0-317-55179-5). Busn Trend.
Steel Worker. John A. Fitch. LC 70-89757. (American Labor, from Conspiracy to Collective Bargaining Ser., No. 1). 393p. 1969. Repr. of 1910 ed. 21.00 (ISBN 0-405-02121-6). Ayer Co Pubs.
Steel Workers Rank & File. Philip Nyden. 192p. 1984. 35.00 (ISBN 0-275-91236-1, C1236). Praeger.
Steeldust. J. P. Brown. 192p. 1986. 14.95 (ISBN 0-8027-4065-0). Walker & Co.
Steeldust II: The Flight. 208p. 1987. 15.95 (ISBN 0-8027-0944-3). Walker & Co.
Steele Family. G. T. Ridlon. LC 76-142769. (Saco Valley Settlements Ser). 1970. pap. 1.50 (ISBN 0-8048-0839-2). C E Tuttle.
Steele Rudd Selection: The Best Dad & Dave Stories with Other Rudd Classics. Steele Rudd. Ed. by Frank Moorhouse. LC 86-975. (Illus.). 240p. (Orig.). 1987. pap. 9.95 (ISBN 0-7022-1978-9). U of Queensland Pr.
Steeled in Adversity. Salo W. Baron. (Texts & Studies). (Hebrew.). 1977. 15.00 (ISBN 0-911934-15-4). Am Jewish Hist Soc.
Steeleglas, Fifteen Seventy-Five & the Complaynte of Philomene Fifteen Seventy-Six. George Gascoigne. Ed. by EDward Arber. 1983. pap. 12.50 (ISBN 0-87556-496-8). Saifer.
Steele's Answers. D. Steele. 6.95 (ISBN 0-686-27781-3). Schmul Pub Co.
Steelhead. Mel Marshall. LC 72-96089. (Illus.). 186p. 1973. 15.95 (ISBN 0-8329-0932-7, Pub. by Winchester Pr). New Century.
Steelhead Drift Fishing. Bill Luch. (Illus.). 94p. (Orig.). 1976. pap. 6.95 (ISBN 0-936608-00-5). F Amato Pubns.

Steelhead Fly Fishing & Flies. Trey Combs. (Illus.). 118p. (Orig.). 1976. pap. 15.95 (ISBN 0-936608-03-X). F Amato Pubns.

Steelhead Fly Tying Manual. Tom Light & Neal Humphrey. (Illus.). 100p. (Orig.). 1979. pap. 11.95 (ISBN 0-936608-20-X). F Amato Pubns.

Steelheading for the Simple-Minded. Bob Ellsberg. (Illus.). 96p. (Orig.). 1987. pap. 7.95 (ISBN 0-944294-00-6). Outdoor Enterprises.

Steelmaking Before Bessemer, 2 vols. Barraclugh. 681p. 1984. Set. text ed. 89.00x (ISBN 0-318-21258-7, Pub. by Inst Metals). Vol.II (ISBN 0-904357-64-3). Brookfield Pub Co.

Steelmaking Conference: Proceedings of the 66th Conference. LC 83-111773. 650p. 1983. 60.00 (ISBN 0-89520-155-0). Iron & Steel.

Steelmaking Conference: Proceedings of the 68th Conference. 510p. 1985. 60.00 (ISBN 0-932897-02-9). Iron & Steel.

Steelmaking Conference Proceedings, 65th, Pittsburgh Meeting, March 28-31, 1982, Sponsored by the Steelmaking Division, the Iron & Steel Society of Aime. Iron & Steel Society of AIME. pap. 97.00 (ISBN 0-317-26839-2, 2023494). Bks Demand UMI.

Steelmasters & Labor Reform, 1886-1923. Gerald G. Eggert. LC 81-50636. 229p. 1981. 24.95x (ISBN 0-8229-3801-4). U of Pittsburgh Pr.

Steels: Microstructure & Properties. Robert W. Honeycombe. LC 81-17681. (Metallurgy & Materials Science Ser.). pap. 64.00 (2027039). Bks Demand UMI.

Steeltech. Portcullis Press, Ltd. Staff. 72p. 1986. 80.00x (ISBN 0-317-54377-6, Pub. by Portcullis Pr UK). State Mutual Bk.

Steeltown: An Industrial Case History of the Conflict Between Progress & Security. Charles R. Walker. LC 78-81489. (Illus.). 1970. Repr. of 1950 ed. 12.00x (ISBN 0-8462-1398-2). Russell.

Steelwork. Gilbert Sorrentino. LC 79-119484. 1970. 12.00 (ISBN 0-685-46841-0). Small Pr Dist.

Steelworkers in America: The Non-Union Era. David Brody. 1970. pap. 7.95x (ISBN 0-06-131485-4, TB1485, Torch). Har-Row.

Steelworkers in America: The Non-Union Era. David Brody. LC 76-83855. (Illus.). 1970. Repr. of 1960 ed. 13.00x (ISBN 0-8462-1406-7). Russell.

Steelworkers Rank & File: The Political Economy of a Union Reform Movement. Philip Nyden. (Illus.). 176p. 1984. text ed. 27.95x (ISBN 0-03-063370-2). Bergin & Garvey.

Steely Blue. Dennis Smith. 256p. 1984. 15.95 (ISBN 0-671-44019-5). S&S.

Steely Blue. Dennis Smith. 336p. 1987. pap. 3.95x (ISBN 0-441-78581-6, Pub. by Charter Bks). Ace Bks.

Steelyard Blues: New Structures in Steel. (Report on the Americas Ser.: Vol. XIII, No. 1). 52p. 2.50 (ISBN 0-317-34966-X). NA Cong Lat Am.

Steenburgen Diagnostic-Prescriptive Math Program. Fran S. Gelb. 1978. Level I (gr. 1-3); Level II (gr. 4-6) complete program 30.00 (ISBN 0-87879-209-0). Acad Therapy.

Steenrod Algebra & Its Applications: Proceedings. Ed. by F. P. Peterson. (Lecture Notes in Mathematics Ser.: Vol. 168). 1970. 18.00 (ISBN 0-387-05300-X). Springer-Verlag.

Steenrod Connections & Connectivity in H Spaces. J. Lin. (MEMO Ser.: No. 369). 96p. 1987. pap. text ed. write for info. (ISBN 0-8218-2431-7). Am Math.

Steen's Mountain in Oregon's High Desert Country. E. R. Jackman & John Scharff. LC 67-24205. (Illus.). 1967. 39.95 (ISBN 0-87004-028-6). Caxton.

Steens Mt. Scrapbook. Janice P. Gutenberg. LC 23-939860. 1982. 24.95 (ISBN 0-939860-05-8). Tremaine Graph & Pub.

Steep Holm: Case History in the Study of Evolution. John Fowley. 228p. 40.00x (ISBN 0-686-75653-3, Pub. by Dorset). State Mutual Bk.

Steepe & the Sown see Corridors of Time: New Haven & London, 1927-1956.

Steeple People & the World: Planning for Mission Through the Church. John Killinger. (Orig.). 1977. pap. 2.50 (ISBN 0-377-00059-0). Friendship Pr.

Steeplechasing. John Hislop. (Illus.). 24.00 (ISBN 0-85131-045-1, BL6684, Pub. by J A Allen U K). S R Smith Sporting Bks.

Steeple's Shadow: On the Myths & Realities of Secularization. David Lyon. 176p. (Orig.). 1987. pap. 9.95 (ISBN 0-8028-0261-3). Eerdmans.

Steer Your Own Career: A Practical Guide to Effective & Satisfying Career Change. Bob Bisdee. 150p. 1988. pap. 12.95 (ISBN 0-89397-307-6). Nichols Pub.

Steerage & Ten Other Stories. Jose R. Migueis. Frwd. by George Monteiro. LC 82-84530. (Illus.). 224p. (Orig.). 1983. pap. 6.00 (ISBN 0-943722-06-3). Gavea-Brown.

Steering & Suspension. 2nd ed. John Remling. (Automotive Ser.). 422p. 1983. write for info. (ISBN 0-471-87614-3). Wiley.

Steering Gear: Test Routines & Check List Card. ICS Staff. 1978. 7.00x (ISBN 0-317-61493-2, Pub. by Witherby & Co). State Mutual Bk.

Steering the Economy: The British Experiment. Samuel Brittan. LC 71-152814. 505p. 1971. 22.95 (ISBN 0-912050-05-5, Library Pr). Open Court.

Steering the Elephant: How Washington Works. Ed. by Robert Rector & Michael Sanera. LC 86-40225. 384p. 1987. 24.95 (ISBN 0-87663-499-4). Universe.

Steering the Polity: Communication & Politics in Israel. Itzhak Galnoor. (Illus.). 384p. 1982. 29.95 (ISBN 0-8039-1340-0). Sage.

Stefan Grossman's Annual Fingerpicking Guitar. Stefan Grossman. 68p. 1986. pap. text ed. cancelled (ISBN 0-931759-14-5). Centerstream Pub.

Stefan Problem. L. I. Rubenstein. LC 75-168253. (Translations of Mathematical Monographs: Vol. 27). 1971. 62.00 (ISBN 0-8218-1577-6, MMONO-27). Am Math.

Stefan Zweig-Heute. Ed. by Mark H. Gelber. (New Yorker Studien zur Neueren Deutschen Literaturgeschichte: Band 7). 226p. (Ger.). 1987. text ed. 45.00 (ISBN 0-8204-0378-4). P Lang Pubs.

Stefanesti: Portrait of a Romanian Shtetl. G. Sternberg. (Illus.). 320p. 1984. text ed. 41.00 (ISBN 0-08-030840-6). Pergamon.

Stefanie Powers: Superlife! Stephanie Powers & Judith B. Quine. 224p. 1985. 17.95 (ISBN 0-671-50616-1). S&S.

Stefano Delle Chiaie: Portrait of a Black Terrorist. Stuart Christie. (Black Papers: No. 1). 182p. (Orig.). 1988. pap. 9.95 (ISBN 0-946222-09-6). Left Bank.

Stefansson: Ambassador of the North. Donat M. Le Bourdais. LC 63-17243. (Emulation Bk.). pap. 51.50 (ISBN 0-317-28425-8, 2022307). Bks Demand UMI.

Stefansson & the Canadian Arctic. Richard J. Diubaldo. (Illus.). 1978. 32.95 (ISBN 0-7735-0324-2). McGill-Queens U Pr.

Stefansson-Anderson Arctic Expedition: Preliminary Ethnological Report. Vilhjalmur Stefansson. LC 74-5880. (Anthropological Papers of the American Museum of Natural History: Vol. 14.). Repr. of 1919 ed. 42.50 (ISBN 0-404-11688-4). AMS Pr.

Steffi Graf. Judy Monroe. Ed. by Carnival Enterprises Staff. LC 87-30115. (Sports Close-Ups Ser.). (Illus.). 48p. (gr. 5-6). 1988. PLB 10.95 (ISBN 0-89686-368-9). Crestwood Hse.

Steffie Can't Come Out to Play. Fran Arrick. 160p. (gr. 7 up). 1979. pap. 2.50 (ISBN 0-440-97635-9, LFL). Dell.

Stegel Movement Activities. new ed. Jack Evans. Ed. by Frank Alexander. (Illus.). 1978. 4.95 (ISBN 0-915256-05-3). Front Row.

Steggie Makes a Friend: A Tiny Dinos Story about Shyness. Guy Gilchrist. LC 88-40027. (Tiny Dinos Ser.). (Illus.). 24p. (ps-2). 1988. bds. 4.95 (ISBN 1-55782-100-3). Warner Bks.

Stegosaurus. Janet Riehecky. LC 88-15347. (Dinosaurs Ser.). (Illus.). 32p. (gr. k-4). 1988. lib. bdg. 8.95 (ISBN 0-89565-385-0). Childs World.

Stegosaurus: The Dinosaur with the Smallest Brain. Elizabeth Sandell. Ed. by Marjorie Oelerich & Howard Schroeder. LC 88-995. (Dinosaur Discovery Era Ser.). (Illus.). 32p. (gr. k-5). 1988. PLB 9.95 (ISBN 0-944280-02-1); pap. 4.95 (ISBN 0-944280-08-0). BSP Pub Inc.

Stehekin: A Valley in Time. Grant McConnell. 200p. 1988. 14.95 (ISBN 0-89886-181-0). Mountaineers.

Stehekin: The Enchanted Valley. Fred T. Darvill, Jr. LC 80-16628. (Illus.). 128p. (Orig.). 1981. pap. 6.95 (ISBN 0-913140-42-2). Signpost Bk Pub.

Steichen: A Life in Photography. Edward Steichen. 1985. pap. 12.95 (ISBN 0-517-55696-0). Crown.

Steidlmayer on Markets: A New Approach to Trading. J. Peter Steidlmayer. (Illus.). 1989. 34.95 (ISBN 0-471-62115-3). Wiley.

Steiff Teddy Bears, Dolls & Toys with Prices. Shirley Conway & Jean Wilson. LC 82-50485. 152p. pap. 14.95 (ISBN 0-87069-415-4). Wallace-Homestead.

Stein on Probate. Robert A. Stein. 225.00 (ISBN 0-86678-537-X). Butterworth Legal Pubs.

Stein on Probate, 2 vols. 2nd ed. Robert A. Stein. 1986. Set. looseleaf 225.00. Butterworth MN.

Stein: The Era of Reform in Prussia, 1807-1815. Guy S. Ford. 1922. 11.25 (ISBN 0-8446-1189-1). Peter Smith.

Steinbeck. F. Watt. (Writers & Critics Ser.). 117p. 1978. 24.50 (ISBN 0-912378-06-9). Chips.

Steinbeck: A Biography. Jack J. Delaney. LC 84-26323. (Illus.). Date not set. price not set (ISBN 0-8022-2476-8). Philos Lib.

Steinbeck: A Life in Letters. Ed. by Elaine Steinbeck & Robert Wallsten. LC 75-15756. 906p. 1975. 22.50 (ISBN 0-670-66961-X). Viking.

Steinbeck: A Life in Letters. John Steinbeck. Ed. by Elaine Steinbeck & Robert Wallsten. 1976. pap. 9.95 (ISBN 0-14-004288-1). Penguin.

Steinbeck & Covici: The Story of a Friendship. Thomas Fensch. LC 78-26594. 1979. 12.95 (ISBN 0-8397-7888-0); pap. 9.95 (ISBN 0-8397-7889-9). Eriksson.

Steinbeck & Hemingway: Dissertation Abstracts & Research Opportunities. Ed. by Tetsumaro Hayashi. LC 80-15540. 242p. 1980. 17.50 (ISBN 0-8108-1321-1). Scarecrow.

Steinbeck & His Critics: A Record of 25 Years: An Anthology. Ernest W. Tedlock & C. V. Wickev. LC 56-12746. pap. 88.00 (2026752). Bks Demand UMI.

Steinbeck Bibliographies: An Annotated Guide. Robert B. Harmon. LC 86-33830. 145p. 1987. 15.00 (ISBN 0-8108-1963-5). Scarecrow.

Steinbeck Country. Steve Crouch. LC 72-95690. (Images of America Ser.). (Illus.). 192p. 1975. 18.50 (ISBN 0-517-52715-4); pap. 9.95 o. p. (ISBN 0-517-52716-2). Crown.

Steinbeck Country Narrow Gauge. Horace W. Fabing & Rick Hamman. LC 85-16776. (Illus.). 236p. 1985. 29.95 (ISBN 0-87108-693-X). Pruett.

Steinbeck House Cookbook. Valley Guild Staff. Ed. by Kay Hillyard. LC 84-50259. (Illus.). 224p. 1984. 16.95 (ISBN 0-9612742-0-4). Valley Guild.

Steinbeck: The Man & His Work. Ed. by Richard Astro & Tetsumaro Hayashi. LC 76-632182. (Illus.). 194p. 1971. pap. text ed. 11.95x (ISBN 0-87071-443-0). Oreg St U Pr.

Steinbeck's Literary Dimension: A Guide to Comparative Studies. Tetsumaro Hayashi. LC 72-7457. 191p. 1973. 17.50 (ISBN 0-8108-0550-2). Scarecrow.

Steinbeck's Reading: A Catalogue of Books Owned & Borrowed. Robert DeMott. LC 80-8516. 1983. lib. bdg. 52.00 (ISBN 0-8240-9468-9). Garland Pub.

Steinbeck's "The Red Pony" Essays in Criticism. Ed. by Tetsumaro Hayashi & Thomas J. Moore. (Steinbeck Monograph Ser.: No. 13). 1988. 25.00 (ISBN 0-317-67415-3). Steinbeck Society.

Steinbeck's World War II Fiction, "The Moon is Down" Three Explications. Ed. by Tetsumaro Hayashi. (Steinbeck's World War II Fiction). 50p. 1986. pap. 20.00 (ISBN 0-317-44819-6). Steinbeck Society.

Steinbrenner's Yankees: An Inside Account. Ed Linn. LC 82-1002. 322p. 1982. 14.95 (ISBN 0-03-060416-8). H Holt & Co.

Steiner: The Lyran Commonwealth. (Battletech Ser.). 80p. (Orig.). 1988. pap. 15.00 (ISBN 1-55560-033-6). FASA Corp.

Steiner's Theosophy: Notes on the Book "Theosophy". Carl Unger. 1982. Repr. 5.95 (ISBN 0-916786-64-1). St George Bk Serv.

Steinlen Cats. Theophile-Alexandre Steinlen. (Illus.). 48p. 1980. pap. 3.50 (ISBN 0-486-23950-0). Dover.

Steinlen: The Graphic Work. E. De Crauzat. (Illus.). 248p. (Fr.). 1983. Repr. of 1913 ed. 95.00 (ISBN 0-915346-71-0). A Wofsy Fine Arts.

Steinlen's Lithographs: One Hundred Twenty-One Plates from "Gil Blas Illustre". Theophile-Alexandre Steinlen. (Illus.). 128p. 1980. pap. 7.95 (ISBN 0-486-23943-8). Dover.

Steinman's Bergerman & Roth, New York Real Estate Property Forms: Annotated, 5 vols. 2nd ed. Irving I. Steinman. 1948. looseleaf set 395.80 (140); Updates avail. 1985 245.00; 1986 308.50. Bender.

Steinmetz: The Philosopher. P. L. Alger. 194p. 1965. 59.00 (ISBN 0-677-65170-8). Gordon & Breach.

Steinzeug Fifteen Bis Nineteen Jahrundert. Josef Horschik. 496p. (Ger.). 1978. 270.00x (ISBN 0-317-57362-4, Pub. by Collets UK). State Mutual Bk.

Steklov Seminar, 1984: Statistics & Control of Stochastic Processes. Ed. by N. V. Krylov et al. xiii, 507p. 1985. 59.50 (ISBN 0-387-96101-1). Springer-Verlag.

Stelae. Victor Segalen. Tr. by Nathaniel Tarn. 1969. perfect bound in wrappers 2.50 (ISBN 0-685-79039-8). Small Pr Dist.

Steles. Victor Segalen. Ed. by Michael Taylor. LC 87-80272. (Illus.). 144p. 1987. pap. 12.50 (ISBN 0-932499-21-X). Lapis Pr.

Stella Adler on Acting. Stella Adler. LC 88-47514. (Illus.). 144p. 1988. 14.95 (ISBN 0-553-05299-3). Bantam.

Stella: One Woman's Victory over Cancer. Stella Andres & Brad Steiger. 160p. 1986. 14.95 (ISBN 0-86700-015-5, Synergy Books). P Walsh Pr.

Stella: The Brooklyn Bridge. (Let's Get Lost in a Painting Ser.). 1983. write for info. Garrard.

Stellar Almanac: A History & Tour Guide of the Infernal Kingdom of Hades. P. Scott Hollander. LC 73-94036. 1974. 7.95 (ISBN 0-87707-137-3). Infernal Artists.

Stellar & Planetary Magnetism. A. M. Soward. (Fluid Mechanics of Astrophysics & Geophysics Ser.: Vol. 2). 392p. 1983. 88.00 (ISBN 0-677-16430-0). Gordon & Breach.

Stellar Astronomy, 2 Vols. Chiu Hone-Yee et al. 756p. 1969. Vol. 1,388. 150.00 (ISBN 0-677-13790-7); Vol. 2,368. 120.00 (ISBN 0-677-13800-8); Set. 235.00 (ISBN 0-677-12980-7). Gordon & Breach.

Stellar Atmospheres. Ed. by Jesse L. Greenstein. LC 61-9045. (Stars & Stellar Systems Ser: Vol. 6). (Illus.). 1961. 50.00x (ISBN 0-226-45958-6). U of Chicago Pr.

Stellar Evolution. Ed. by Hong-Yee Chiu & Amador Muriel. 827p. 1972. 60.00x. MIT Pr.

Stellar Evolution. 2nd ed. A. J. Meadows. 1978. pap. text ed. 9.50 (ISBN 0-08-021669-2). Pergamon.

Stellar Evolution. Otto Struve. 1950. 37.00x (ISBN 0-691-08043-7). Princeton U Pr.

Stellar Evolution & Nucleosynthesis. Hubert Reeves. (Documents on Modern Physics Ser.). 114p. (Orig.). 1968. 39.00 (ISBN 0-677-30150-2). Gordon & Breach.

Stellar Formation. V. C. Reddish. 225p. 1978. 69.00 (ISBN 0-08-018062-0); pap. 28.00 (ISBN 0-08-023053-9). Pergamon.

Stellar Healing: Course XVI, Lessons 197-208. (Illus.). 1976. pap. 11.25 (ISBN 0-87887-355-4). Church of Light.

Stellar Instability & Evolution: Proceedings. Symposium of the International Astronomical Union, No. 59, Mount Stromlo, Canberra, Australia, Aug. 16-18, 1973. Ed. by P. Ledoux et al. LC 74-80520. 200p. 1974. lib. bdg. 37.00 (ISBN 90-277-0479-1, Pub. by Reidel Holland); pap. text ed. 26.00 (ISBN 90-277-0480-5). Kluwer Academic.

Stellar Interiors. Schatzman. (Monographs & Texts in Physics & Astronomy). 1988. write for info. (ISBN 0-471-08324-0). Wiley.

Stellar Man. John Baines. Ed. by Judith Hipskind. LC 84-48085. (Hermetic Science Ser.). (Illus.). 384p. (Orig.). 1985. pap. 9.95 (ISBN 0-87542-026-5, L-026). Llewellyn Pubns.

Stellar Missiles. Repp. 5.00 (ISBN 0-686-00483-3); pap. 2.00 (ISBN 0-686-00484-1). Fantasy Pub Co.

Stellar Nucleosynthesis. Ed. by Cesare Chiosi & Alvio Renzini. 1984. lib. bdg. 55.00 (ISBN 90-277-1729-X, Pub. by Reidel Holland). Kluwer Academic.

Stellar Paths: Photographic Astrometry with Long-Focus Instruments. Peter Van de Kamp. xix, 149p. 1981. 34.95 (ISBN 90-277-1256-5, Pub. by Reidel Holland). Kluwer Academic.

Stellar Populations. Ed. by C. A. Norman et al. (Space Telescope Science Institute Symposium Ser.: No. 1). 270p. 1987. 32.50 (ISBN 0-521-33380-6). Cambridge U Pr.

Stellar Pulsation. Ed. by A. N. Cox & W. M. Sparks. (Lecture Notes in Physics Ser.: Vol. 274). xii, 422p. 1987. 40.60 (ISBN 0-387-17668-3). Springer-Verlag.

Stellar Radial Velocities. Ed. by A. G. Davis Philip & D. W. Latham. 1985. pap. 32.00 (ISBN 0-933485-00-X). L Davis Pr.

Stellar Rotation. A. Slettebak. 372p. 1970. 127.00 (ISBN 0-677-60170-0). Gordon & Breach.

Stellar Rotation: Proceedings of the I.A.U. Symposium, Ohio State University, Columbus, 1969, International Astronomical Union Staff. Ed. by A. Slettebak. LC 76-118131. 355p. 1970. lib. bdg. 45.00 (ISBN 90-277-0156-3, Pub. by Reidel Holland). Kluwer Academic.

Stellar Structures. Midway rep. ed. Ed. by Lawrence H. Aller & Dean B. McLaughlin. LC 63-16723. (Stars & Stellar Systems Ser.: Vol. 8). (Illus.). 1981. pap. 35.00x (ISBN 0-226-45969-1). U of Chicago Pr.

Stellar Turbulence: Proceedings of Colloquium 51 of the International Astronomical Union, Held at the University of Western Ontario, London, Ontario, Canada, August 27-30, 1979. Ed. by D. F. Gray. (Lecture Notes in Physics Ser.: Vol. 114). 308p. 1980. pap. 26.00 (ISBN 3-540-09737-6). Springer-Verlag.

Stellarian. Alice Morrey-Bailey. LC 86-81777. 158p. 1986. 8.95 (ISBN 0-88290-279-2). Horizon Utah.

Stellman's Way. Greg Tobin. 1985. pap. 2.50 (ISBN 0-345-31704-1). Ballantine.

Stello. Alfred De Vigny. Ed. by Germain. Bd. with Consultations du Docteur Noir; Daphne. (Class. Garnier). pap. 22.95 (ISBN 0-685-37142-5). French & Eur.

Stello: A Session with Doctor Noir. Alfred De Vigny. Tr. by Irving Massey. LC 68-48328. pap. 54.00 (ISBN 0-317-20719-9, 2023828). Bks Demand UMI.

Stellung der Pygmaenvolker in der Entwicklungs-Geschichte des Menschen. Wilhelm Schmidt. (Classics of Anthropology Ser.). 120.00 (ISBN 0-8240-9636-3). Garland Pub.

Stellung Des Verbums in der Alteren Althoch-Deutschen Prosa. Paul Diels. 1906. pap. 22.00 (ISBN 0-384-11746-5). Johnson Repr.

Stem. David Giannini. 1982. 3.00 (ISBN 0-934834-29-6). White Pine.

Stem Cells & Tissue Homeostasis. Ed. by B. I. Lord & C. S. Potten. LC 77-80844. (British Society for Cell Biology Symposium Ser.). (Illus.). 1978. 85.00 (ISBN 0-521-21799-7). Cambridge U Pr.

Stem Cells & Tissue Homeostasis. Ed. by Brian I. Lord et al. LC 77-80844. (Symposium of the British Society for Cell Biology Ser.: No. 2). pap. 94.00 (2027336). Bks Demand UMI.

Stem Dictionary of the English Language. John Kennedy. LC 78-142547. 284p. 1971. Repr. of 1870 ed. 51.00x (ISBN 0-8103-3377-5). Gale.

Stem Dictionary of the English Language. John Kennedy. 1890. 30.00 (ISBN 0-8274-3506-1). R West.

Stem Vocabulary of the Navaho Language, 2 vols. Berard Haile. LC 73-15403. (Navaho.). Repr. of 1951 ed. Set. 64.50 (ISBN 0-404-11241-2). AMS Pr.

Stemming the Tide: Arms Control in the Johnson Years. Glenn T. Seaborg & Benjamin S. Loeb. (Illus.). 528p. 1987. 24.95 (ISBN 0-669-13105-9). Lexington Bks.

Sten. Alan Cole & Chris Bunch. 1988. pap. 2.95 (ISBN 0-345-00692-5, Del Rey). Ballantine.

Sten. Allan Cole & Chris Bunch. 288p. 1984. pap. 2.95 (ISBN 0-345-32460-9, Del Rey). Ballantine.

Stencil Book of Christmas. Illus. by Tony Tallarico. (Learning Bks). (Illus.). 24p. (ps-5). 1987. bds. 6.95 (ISBN 0-89828-283-7, 82837). Tuffy Bks.
Stencil Book of Dinosaurs. Illus. by Tony Tallarico. (Learning Bks). (Illus.). 24p. (ps-5). 1987. bds. 6.95 (ISBN 0-89828-282-9, 82829). Tuffy Bks.
Stencil Book of Fairy Tales. Illus. by Tony Tallarico. (Learning Bks). (Illus.). 24p. (ps-5). 1987. bds. 6.95 (ISBN 0-89828-281-0, 82810). Tuffy Bks.
Stencil Book of Numbers. Illus. by Tony Tallarico. (Learning Bks). (Illus.). 24p. (ps-5). 1987. bds. 6.95 (ISBN 0-89828-276-4, 82764). Tuffy Bks.
Stencil Book of Objects. Illus. by Tony Tallarico. (Learning Bks). (Illus.). 24p. (ps-5). 1987. bds. 6.95 (ISBN 0-89828-278-0, 82780). Tuffy Bks.
Stencil Patch. Nancy J. Martin. (Illus.). 54p. 1984. pap. 6.00 (ISBN 0-943574-24-2). That Patchwork.
Stenciled House: An Inspirational & Practical Guide to Transforming Your Home. Lyn Le Grice. 1989. 24.95 (ISBN 0-671-66670-3). S&S.
Stenciled Quilt. Marie Sturmer. Ed. by Cathryn Baskin. LC 86-50090. (Illus.). 160p. 1986. pap. 15.95 (ISBN 0-89909-103-2). Yankee Bks.
Stenciled Strawberry Cookbook: Patterns for Fine Dining. Junior League of Albany, N. Y., Inc. Staff. (Illus.). 320p. 1985. 14.95 (ISBN 0-9614012-0-6). Jr League Albany Pubns.
Stencilled Ornament & Illustration. Compiled by Dorothy Abbe. pap. 15.00 (ISBN 0-89073-064-4). Boston Public Lib.
Stencilling. Helen Barnett & Susy Smith. (Illus.). 80p. 1987. 14.95 (ISBN 0-88162-304-0). Salem Hse Pubs.
Stencilling: A Design & Source Book. Bridget H. Fraser. (Illus.). 192p. 1987. 24.95 (ISBN 0-8050-0108-5). H Holt & Co.
Stencilwork on Floors, Walls, & Ceilings: A Bibliography. Mary E. Huls. (Architecture Ser.: A 1921). 5p. 1987. 3.00 (ISBN 1-55590-511-0). Vance Biblios.
Stendal Raid. Al Dempsey. 352p. 1988. pap. 3.95 (ISBN 0-8125-8186-5, Dist. by St Martin's Pr & Warner Pub Servs). Tor Bks.
Stendal's Paper Mirror: Patterns of Self-Consciousness in His Novels. James T. Day. LC 86-27328. (American University Studies II: Romance Languages & Literature: Vol. 20). 236p. 1987. text ed. 32.90 (ISBN 0-8204-0184-6). P Lang Pubs.
Stendhal. Ed. & intro. by Harold Bloom. (Modern Critical Views Ser.). 256p. 1987. lib. bdg. 24.50x (ISBN 1-55546-311-8). Chelsea Hse.
Stendhal. Andrew Paton. 59.95 (ISBN 0-8490-1124-8). Gordon Pr.
Stendhal & Romantic Esthetics. Ed. by Emile J. Talbot. LC 85-80420. (French Forum Monographs: No. 61). 181p. (Orig.). 1985. pap. 12.95x (ISBN 0-917058-62-3). French Forum.
Stendhal & the Age of Napoleon: An Interpretive Biography. Gita May. LC 77-8379. 332p. 1977. 35.00x (ISBN 0-231-04344-9). Columbia U Pr.
Stendhal Et L'Angleterre. Ed. by Keith G. McWatters & Christopher W. Thompson. 306p. 1986. text ed. 39.95x (ISBN 0-85323-045-5, Pub. by Liverpool U Pr). Humanities.
Stendhal Fichier, 3 Vols. Compiled by Francois Michel. 1964. Set. 298.00 (ISBN 0-8161-0583-9, Hall Library). G K Hall.
Stendhal: Fiction & the Themes of Freedom. Victor Brombert. LC 75-37057. vi, 210p. 1986. pap. 15.00x (ISBN 0-226-07548-6). U of Chicago Pr.
Stendhal: Henri Beyle. Paul Hazard. Tr. by Eleanor Hard. 1979. Repr. of 1929 ed. lib. bdg. 20.00 (ISBN 0-8495-2284-6). Arden Lib.
Stendhal: Memoirs of an Egotist. Stendhal. Tr. by David Ellis from Fr. 1975. 6.95 (ISBN 0-8180-0224-7). Horizon.
Stendhal: The Education of a Novelist. Geoffrey Strickland. 276p. 1974. pap. 12.95x (ISBN 0-521-09837-8). Cambridge U Pr.
Stendhal: The Promise of Happiness. David Wakefield. 208p. 1984. 95.00 (ISBN 0-85390-027-2, Pub. by Gordon Fraser). State Mutual Bk.
Stendhal the Romantic Rationalist. William H. Fineshriber. LC 72-187169. 1932. lib. bdg. 17.00 (ISBN 0-8414-4254-1). Folcroft.
Stendhal und die Musik: Forschungsbericht und Kritische Bibliographie, 1900-1980. Helmut C. Jacobs. (Bonner Romanistischen Arbeiten: Vol. 17). 262p. (Ger.). 1983. 31.05 (ISBN 3-8204-7772-1). P Lang Pubs.
Stendhal's the Red & the Black. Intro. by Harold Bloom. (Modern Critical Interpretations Ser.). 1987. 19.95 (ISBN 1-55546-076-3). Chelsea Hse.
Stendhal's Violin: A Novelist & His Reader. Roger Pearson. 320p. 1988. 65.00 (ISBN 0-19-815851-3). Oxford U Pr.
Stengel: His Life & Times. Robert W. Creamer. (Illus.). 336p. 1984. 16.95 (ISBN 0-671-22489-1). S&S.
Stengel: His Life & Times. Robert W. Creamer. 352p. 1985. pap. 8.95 (ISBN 0-440-57829-9, Dell Trade Pbks). Dell.
Stenographer. Jack Rudman. (Career Examination Ser.: C-766). (Cloth bdg. avail. on request). pap. 12.00 (ISBN 0-8373-0766-X). Natl Learning.
Stenographer (Law) Jack Rudman. (Career Examination Ser.: C-1036). (Cloth bdg. avail. on request). pap. 14.00 (ISBN 0-8373-1036-9). Natl Learning.
Stenographer-Secretary. Jack Rudman. (Career Examination Ser.: C-2559). (Cloth bdg. avail. on request). pap. 14.00 (ISBN 0-8373-2559-5). Natl Learning.
Stenographer-Typist. Jack Rudman. (Career Examination Ser.: C-1966). (Cloth bdg. avail. on request). pap. 12.00 (ISBN 0-8373-1966-8). Natl Learning.
Stenographer-Typist GS1-4. Jack Rudman. (Career Examination Ser.: C-767). (Cloth bdg. avail. on request). pap. 12.00 (ISBN 0-8373-0767-8). Natl Learning.
Stenographer-Typist GS5-7. Jack Rudman. (Career Examination Ser.: C-768). (Cloth bdg. avail. on request). pap. 12.00 (ISBN 0-8373-0768-6). Natl Learning.
Stenographer-Typist: U. S. Government Positions GS2 & GS7. 8th ed. Ed. by Hy Hammer. LC 81-17675. (Illus.). 224p. (Orig.). 1983. pap. 8.00 (ISBN 0-668-05412-3). Arco.
Stenographic-Secretarial Associate. Jack Rudman. (Career Examination Ser.: C-2452). (Cloth bdg. avail. on request). pap. 14.00 (ISBN 0-8373-2452-1). Natl Learning.
Stenographic Secretary. Jack Rudman. (Career Examination Ser.: C-1653). (Cloth bdg. avail. on request). 1988. Repr. of 1977 ed. 14.00 (ISBN 0-8373-1653-7). Natl Learning.
Stenographic Specialist. Jack Rudman. (Career Examination Ser.: C-2453). (Cloth bdg. avail. on request). pap. 14.00 (ISBN 0-8373-2453-X). Natl Learning.
Stenography & Typewriting (Gregg & Pitman) Chairman - Sr. H.S. Jack Rudman. (Teachers License Examination Ser.: CH-28). (Cloth bdg. avail. on request). pap. 15.95 (ISBN 0-8373-8178-9). Natl Learning.
Stenography & Typewriting (Gregg & Pitman) Sr. H.S. Jack Rudman. (Teachers License Examination Ser.: T-60). (Cloth bdg. avail. on request). pap. 13.95 (ISBN 0-8373-8060-X). Natl Learning.
Stenoscript ABC Shorthand - SRA Edition. 1968. text ed. write for info. (ISBN 0-574-15001-3, 15-1001); tchr's. handbook avail. (ISBN 0-574-15003-X, 15-1003); write for info. student wkbk. (ISBN 0-574-15002-1, 15-1002); write for info. tapes-cassettes (ISBN 0-574-15020-X, 15-1020); answer key avail. (ISBN 0-574-15030-7, 15-1030). SRA.
Stenospeed: A Complete Shorthand Program. Frances Greer. (Stenospeed Ser.). (Illus.). 236p. 1976. text ed. write for info (ISBN 0-574-20800-3, 13-3800); write for info tchr's guide (13-3801); write for info dictation cassettes (ISBN 0-574-20805-4, 13-3805). SRA.
Stenospeed for the Legal Secretary. SRA. 353p. 1981. pap. text ed. write for info. (ISBN 0-574-20880-1, 13-3880). SRA.
Stenospeed for the Medical Secretary. SRA. 418p. 1981. pap. text ed. write for info. (ISBN 0-574-20885-2, 13-3885). SRA.
Stenospeed Shorthand. Frances A. Greer. 300p. 1974. 8.75 (ISBN 0-911744-31-2). Intl Educ Systems.
Stenospeed Shorthand Twenty-five Thousand Word Dictionary. Frances Greer & Frances Greer. (Illus.). 384p. 1971. 8.50 (ISBN 0-911744-26-6). Intl Educ Systems.
Stenospeed Workbook. Frances A. Greer. 150p. 1974. pap. 3.45 (ISBN 0-911744-32-0). Intl Educ Systems.
Step Backwards. Patricia Lake. (Harlequin Presents Ser.). 192p. 1983. pap. 1.75 (ISBN 0-373-10570-3). Harlequin Bks.
Step by Step. Ed. by Douglas Dowd & Mary Nichols. (Illus.). 1965. pap. 1.45 (ISBN 0-393-00317-5, Norton Lib). Norton.
Step by Step. A. S. Larmour. 211p. 1986. 45.00x (ISBN 0-7212-0736-7, Pub. by Regency Pr). State Mutual Bk.
Step by Step. Bruce McMillan. LC 87-4195. (Illus.). 32p. (ps-2). 1987. 11.75 (ISBN 0-688-07233-X); PLB 11.88 (ISBN 0-688-07234-8). Lothrop.
Step by Step. Rick C. White. (Illus., Orig.). 1981. pap. 3.50 (ISBN 0-935648-08-9). Halldin Pub.
Step By Step - Sixteen Steps Toward Legally Sound Sexual Abuse Investigations. 1987 ed. Jan Hindman. 44p. pap. 7.50 (ISBN 0-9611034-3-4). AlexAndria OR.
Step-by-Step: A Cathechetical Handbook for the RCIA. Mary T. Malone. 1986. pap. 19.95 (ISBN 0-697-02204-8). Wm C Brown.
Step by Step: A Complete Movement Education Curriculum from Pre-School to 6th Grade. Sheila Kogan. Ed. by Frank Alexander. (Illus.). 240p. 1982. 15.95 (ISBN 0-915256-10-X). Front Row.
Step-by-Step Basic Carpentry. Better Homes & Gardens Editors. (Step-by-Step Home Repair Ser.). (Illus.). 96p. 1981. pap. 6.95 (ISBN 0-696-01185-9). BH&G.
Step-by-Step Basic Plumbing. (Step by Step Home Repair Ser.). (Illus.). 96p. 1981. pap. 6.95 (ISBN 0-696-01405-X). BH&G.
Step-by-Step Basic Wiring. (Step by Step Home Repair Ser.). 1980. pap. 6.95 (ISBN 0-696-01090-9). BH&G.
Step-by-Step Basketball Fundamentals for the Player & Coach. John Scott. (Illus.). 200p. 1988. pap. 12.95 (ISBN 0-13-846668-8). P-H.
Step-by-Step Book about Budgerigars. G. Radtke. (Step by Step Book About). (Illus.). 63p. (Orig.). 1987. pap. 3.95 (ISBN 0-86622-463-7, SK-002). TFH Pubns.
Step by Step Book about Canaries. A. Barrie. (Step by Step Book about Ser.). (Illus.). 64p. 1987. 3.95 (ISBN 0-86622-461-0, SK-004). TFH Pubns.
Step by Step Book about Chinchillas. H. Kuhnder. (Step by Step Book about Ser.). (Illus.). 64p. (Orig.). 1987. pap. 3.95 (ISBN 0-86622-452-1, SK-006). TFH Pubns.
Step-by-Step Book about Chinchillas. Horst Kuhner. (Step-by-Step Book about Ser.). (Illus.). 64p. 1987. lib. bdg. 9.95 (ISBN 0-86622-920-5, 3K-006X). TFH Pubns.
Step by Step Book about Cockatiels. A. Barrie. (Step by Step Book about Ser.). (Illus.). 64p. (Orig.). 1987. pap. 3.95 (ISBN 0-86622-453-X, SK-007). TFH Pubns.
Step by Step Book about Discus. G. Keller. (Step by Step Book about Ser.). (Illus.). 64p. 1987. 3.95 (ISBN 0-86622-465-3, SK-008). TFH Pubns.
Step by Step Book about Ferrets. J. Field & M. Field. (Step by Step Book about Ser.). (Illus.). 64p. 1987. 3.95 (ISBN 0-86622-462-9, SK-009). TFH Pubns.
Step-by-Step Book about Finches. E. Radford. (Step by Step Book About). 64p. 1987. pap. 3.95 (ISBN 0-86622-466-1, SK-010). TFH Pubns.
Step-by-Step Book about Gerbils. Patrick Bradley & Heather Pence. (Step by Step Book About). (Illus.). 64p. (Orig.). 1987. pap. 3.95 (ISBN 0-86622-467-X, SK-011). TFH Pubns.
Step by Step Book about Goldfish. J. C. Harris. (Step by Step Book about Ser.). (Illus.). 64p. (Orig.). 1987. pap. 3.95 (ISBN 0-86622-457-2, SK-012). TFH Pubns.
Step by Step Book about Guinea Pigs. A. Barrie. (Step by Step Book about Ser.). (Illus.). 64p. (Orig.). 1987. pap. 3.95 (ISBN 0-86622-450-5, SK-013). TFH Pubns.
Step by Step Book about Hamsters. A. Barrie. (Step by Step Book about Ser.). (Illus.). 64p. 1987. pap. 3.95 (ISBN 0-86622-458-0, SK-014). TFH Pubns.
Step by Step Book about Housebreaking & Training Your Puppy. J. C. Harris. (Step by Step Book about Ser.). (Illus.). 64p. 1987. 3.95 (ISBN 0-86622-478-5, SK025). TFH Pubns.
Step by Step Book about Iguana. J. C. Harris. (Step by Step Book about Ser.). (Illus.). 64p. 1987. 3.95 (ISBN 0-86622-459-9, SK-015). TFH Pubns.
Step by Step Book about Lovebirds. A. Weston. (Step by Step Book about Ser.). (Illus.). 64p. 1987. 3.95 (ISBN 0-86622-456-4, SK-016). TFH Pubns.
Step-by-Step Book about Our First Aquarium. Anmarie Barrie. (Step-by-Step Book Ser.). (Illus.). 64p. 1987. 3.95 (ISBN 0-86622-454-8, SK003). TFH Pubns.
Step-by-Step Book about Our First Aquarium. Anmarie Barrie. (Step-by-Step Book about Ser.). (Illus.). 64p. 1987. lib. bdg. 9.95 (ISBN 0-86622-923-X, SK-005K). TFH Pubns.
Step by Step Book about Parrots. L. Softer. (Step by Step Book about Ser.). (Illus.). 64p. 1987. 3.95 (ISBN 0-86622-484-X, SK031). TFH Pubns.
Step-by-Step Book about Rabbits. A. Barrie. (Step by Step Book About). (Illus.). 64p. 1987. 3.95 (ISBN 0-86622-475-0, SK-001); lib. bdg. 9.95 (ISBN 0-86622-924-8, SK-001K). TFH Pubns.
Step-by-Step Book about Rottweilers. Heinrich V. Beine. (Step-by Step Book about Ser.). (Illus.). 64p. 1987. lib. bdg. 9.95 (ISBN 0-86622-921-3). TFH Pubns.
Step by Step Book about Rottweilers. H. Von Beine. (Step by Step Book about Ser.). (Illus.). 64p. 1987. 3.95 (ISBN 0-86622-455-6, SK-005). TFH Pubns.
Step by Step Book about Setting up an Aquarium. C. W. Emmens. (Step by Step Book about Ser.). (Illus.). 64p. 1987. 3.95 (ISBN 0-86622-486-6, SK033). TFH Pubns.
Step by Step Book about Snakes. R. Anderson. (Step by Step Book about Ser.). (Illus.). 64p. 1987. pap. 3.95 (ISBN 0-86622-460-2, SK-017). TFH Pubns.
Step-By-Step Book about Snakes. Robert Anderson. (Illus.). 64p. 1987. 9.95 (ISBN 0-86622-914-0, SK-017X). TFH Pubns.
Step-By-Step Book about Tortoises. Christine Adrian. (A Step-By-Step Book about Ser.). (Illus.). 63p. (Orig.). 1987. pap. 3.95 (ISBN 0-86622-487-4, SK-034). TFH Pubns.
Step by Step Book about Tropical Fish. C. W. Emmens. (Step by Step Book about Ser.). (Illus.). 64p. 1987. pap. 3.95 (ISBN 0-86622-471-8, SK-018). TFH Pubns.
Step by Step Book about Turtles. J. Jahn. (Step by Step Book about Ser.). (Illus.). 64p. (Orig.). 1987. pap. 3.95 (ISBN 0-86622-451-3, SK-019). TFH Pubns.
Step-by-Step Bookkeeping. rev. ed. Robert Ragan. LC 74-7814. (Illus.). 1979. pap. 6.95 (ISBN 0-8069-8690-5). Sterling.
Step by Step Books, 3 vols. Intro. by Sunny Widell. 618p. 1988. Set. pap. 23.85 (ISBN 0-9619770-4-3). Pearl Publishing.
Step by Step: College Writing. 3rd ed. Randy DeVillez. 328p. 1984. pap. text ed. 15.95 (ISBN 0-8403-3306-4, 40330601). Kendall-Hunt.
Step-By-Step Guide For Making Busts & Masks (Cold-Cast Bronze or Plaster-Hydrocal) 2nd ed. Donna Brice. LC 82-15703. (Illus.). 52p. 1983. 18.95 (ISBN 0-910733-00-7); pap. 10.95 (ISBN 0-910733-01-5). ICTL Pubns.
Step by Step Guide to Chinese Cooking. Kenneth Lo. 1976. 7.50 (ISBN 0-600-38090-4). Transatl Arts.
Step-by-Step Guide to Correct English. 2nd ed. Mary A. Pulaski. LC 81-4657. 160p. 1982. pap. 5.95 (ISBN 0-668-05277-5, 5277). Arco.
Step-by-Step Guide to Developing a Profitable Marketing Plan. Robert F. Stennholz & Lyn M. Stennholz. 80p. 1986. pap. 12.95 (ISBN 0-317-64326-6). AgriData.
Step by Step Guide to Engine Blueprinting. R. Voeglin. (How to Ser.). (Illus.). 128p. 1985. pap. 12.95 (ISBN 0-931472-21-0, S-A Design Pub Co). Motorbooks Intl.
Step-by-Step Guide to Getting Government Contracts. William Reed. 96p. 1987. pap. 9.95 (ISBN 0-941157-04-0). Pride & Co.
Step-by-Step Guide to Landscaping & Gardening. Leo L. Bailey. LC 74-84421. (Illus.). 1974. 12.50 (ISBN 0-682-48084-3, Banner). Exposition-Phoenix.
Step-by-Step Guide to Personal Management for Blind Persons. 2nd ed. LC 74-76827. 135p. 1974. pap. 6.50 spiral bdg. (ISBN 0-89128-061-8, PRP061). Am Foun Blind.
Step-By-Step Guide to Photo-Offset Lithography. Robert M. Swerdlow. (Illus.). 400p. 1982. write for info. (ISBN 0-13-846584-3). P-H.
Step-by-Step Guide to Photography. Michael Langford. LC 78-54894. (Illus.). 1978. 24.95 (ISBN 0-394-41604-X). Knopf.
Step by Step Guide to Photography. Michael Langford. LC 78-54894. 1979. pap. text ed. 14.50 (ISBN 0-394-32373-4, KnopfC). Knopf.
Step-by-Step Guide to Plant Propagation. Phillip M. Browse. 1979. pap. 9.95 (ISBN 0-671-24832-4, Fireside). S&S.
Step-by-Step Guide to Pruning. Christopher Brickell. 1979. pap. 9.95 (ISBN 0-671-24831-6, Fireside). S&S.
Step-By-Step Guide to Screen-Process Printing. Robert M. Swerdlow Education Group. 1986. pap. 19.95 (ISBN 0-317-40348-6). P-H.
Step-by-Step Guide to Screen Process Printing. Robert M. Swerdlow. (Illus.). 192p. 1985. pap. 19.95 (ISBN 0-13-846956-3). P-H.
Step-by-Step Guide to the Job Search Process. National Association of Social Workers, Massachusetts Chapter & Boston College Child Welfare Career Advisement Program. 50p. 1983. 3.00 (ISBN 0-317-67645-8). Natl Assn Soc Wkrs.
Step-by-Step Household Repairs. Better Homes & Gardens Editors. (Step-by-Step Home Repair Ser.). (Illus.). 96p. 1982. pap. 6.95 (ISBN 0-696-00775-4). BH&G.
Step by Step: How to Actively Ensure the Best Possible Care for Your Aging Relative. Ted Rossi. Date not set. pap. 9.95 (ISBN 0-446-38427-5). Warner Bks.
Step by Step in Esperanto. 8th ed. Montagu C. Butler. 281p. 1979. 6.95x (ISBN 0-85230-071-9, 1019). Esperanto League North Am.
Step by Step in the Jewish Religion. Isadore Epstein. 143p. 1958. pap. 4.95 (ISBN 0-900689-12-9). Soncino Pr.
Step by Step in the Jewish Religion. Isidore Epstein. PLB 4.95x. Bloch.
Step-by-step Indian Cooking. Sharda Gopal. (Illus.). 192p. 1987. 19.95 (ISBN 0-8120-5829-1). Barron.
Step-by-Step Japanese Cooking. Lesley Downer & Minoru Yoneda. 192p. 1986. 24.95 (ISBN 0-8120-5688-4). Barron.
Step-by-Step Keyboarding for the Personal Computer. Steven Radlauer. 368p. 1984. pap. 9.95 (ISBN 0-8120-2628-4); For IBM-PC, IBM-PCjr. 34.95 (ISBN 0-8120-7200-6); For Commodore 64. 34.95 (ISBN 0-8120-7198-0); For Apple IIe, Apple II, Apple II Plus. 34.95 (ISBN 0-8120-7199-9). Barron.
Step-by-Step Knifemaking. David Boye. LC 77-22383. 1977. pap. 10.95 (ISBN 0-87857-181-7). Rodale Pr Inc.
Step-by-Step Learning Guide for Older Retarded Children. Vicki M. Johnson & Roberta A. Werner. 1977. pap. 10.95x (ISBN 0-8156-2181-7). Syracuse U Pr.
Step-by-Step Learning Guide for Retarded Infants & Children. Vicki M. Johnson & Roberta A. Werner. LC 75-22172. (Illus.). 208p. 1975. pap. 12.95x (ISBN 0-8156-2174-4). Syracuse U Pr.
Step by Step: Management of the Volunteer Program in Agencies. Marie MacBride. 54p. 1979. pap. 5.95 (ISBN 0-318-17158-9, C37). VTNC Arlington.
Step-by-Step Masonry & Concrete. Better Homes & Gardens Editors. (Step-by-Step Home Repair Ser.). (Illus.). 96p. 1982. pap. 6.95 (ISBN 0-696-00685-5). BH&G.
Step-by-Step Microwave Cookbook. Better Homes & Gardens Editors. 1987. 24.95 (ISBN 0-696-01500-5). BH&G.
Step by Step Microwave Cooking for Boys & Girls. Bonnie Aeschliman. (Illus.). 64p. (Orig.). (gr. k-7). 1985. pap. 3.95 (ISBN 0-8249-3049-5). Ideals.
Step-by-Step Microwave Cooking for Boys & Girls. Bonnie Aeschliman. (Illus.). 64p. (gr. 3-6). 1986. PLB 13.27 (ISBN 0-516-09165-4). Childrens.

TITLE INDEX STEPHEN DECATUR.

Step by Step, Nineteen Thirty-Six to Nineteen Thirty-Nine. facsimile ed. Winston Churchill. LC 72-156631. (Essay Index Reprint Ser). Repr. of 1939 ed. 19.00 (ISBN 0-8369-2310-3). Ayer Co Pubs.

Step-by-Step Perspective Drawing for Architects, Draftsmen, & Designers. rev. ed. Claudius Coulin. 1984. pap. 17.95 (ISBN 0-442-21752-8). Van Nos Reinhold.

Step by Step Success, Bks 1-4. Eleanor D. Griffin. 1970. prepaid 1.00 ea. Bk. 1 (ISBN 0-913692-05-0). Bk.2 (ISBN 0-913692-06-9). Bk. 3 (ISBN 0-913692-07-7). Bk.4 (ISBN 0-913692-08-5). Learning Inc.

Step-by-Step Telephone Installation & Repair. Joe G. Pena. (Illus.). 192p. (Orig.). 1986. pap. 10.95 (ISBN 0-8306-1984-4). Tab Bks.

Step by Step Theater. Gregory Thompson. (gr. 1-4). 1989. pap. 8.95 (ISBN 0-8224-6348-2). D S Lake Pubs.

Step-by-Step Through LOGO Turtle Graphics. Robert Williams. 1984. pap. write for info (ISBN 0-13-846635-1). P-H.

Step-by-Step Through the Bible: Puzzles, Quizzes & Writing Experiences for Teaching Important Biblical Passages. J. Louise Gustafson & Christine L. Poziemski. (Learning Connections Ser.). 160p. (Orig.). 1984. pap. 9.95 (ISBN 0-86683-835-X, 8442, HarpR). Har-Row.

Step by Step to Ballroom Dancing. A. S. Villacorta. (Ballroom Dance Ser.). 1985. lib. bdg. 79.00 (ISBN 0-87700-706-3). Revisionist Pr.

Step by Step to Ballroom Dancing. A. S. Villacorta. (Ballroom Dance Ser.). 1986. lib. bdg. 79.95 (ISBN 0-8490-3376-4). Gordon Pr.

Step by Step to Ballroom Dancing. Aurora S. Villacorta. LC 74-17704. 1974. pap. text ed. 9.95x (ISBN 0-8134-1686-8, 1686). Inter Print Pubs.

Step by Step to Better Crochet. (Illus.). 144p. 1984. 14.95 (ISBN 0-668-06058-1, 6058); pap. 9.95 (ISBN 0-668-06063-8, 6063). Arco.

Step by Step to Better Knitting. (Illus.). 144p. 1984. lib. bdg. 14.95 (ISBN 0-668-06055-7); pap. 9.95 (ISBN 0-668-06060-3). Arco.

Step by Step to Better Knitting & Crochet. Ed. by Marshall Cavendish. LC 81-67434. (Illus.). 288p. 1982. 19.95 (ISBN 0-668-05343-7, 5343). Arco.

Step by Step to College Success. A. Jerome Jewler & John N. Gardner. 202p. 1987. pap. text ed. write for info. (ISBN 0-534-07998-9). Wadsworth Pub.

Step by Step to Great Retreats. Darlene Huffa. Ed. by Theresa Hayes. LC 87-32937. (Illus.). 64p. 1988. 4.95 (ISBN 0-87403-474-4, 18-03177). Standard Pub.

Step by Step to Jerusalem. Hersh Goldman. 45p. 1978. pap. 2.95 (ISBN 0-88482-760-7). Hebrew Pub.

Step-by-Step to Natural Food. Diane Campbell. 224p. comb bdg. 7.95 (ISBN 0-9603766-0-7). C C Pubs.

Step by Step We Climb, Vol. 1. Intro. by Sunny Widell. LC 77-79377. (Step by Step Bks.). 218p. 1988. pap. 7.95 (ISBN 0-9619770-1-9). Pearl Publishing.

Step by Step We Climb to Freedom, Vol. 2. Intro. by Sunny Widell. LC 81-11299. (Step by Step Bks.). 192p. 1988. pap. 7.95 (ISBN 0-9619770-2-7). Pearl Publishing.

Step by Step We Climb to Freedom & Victory, Vol. 3. Pearl Dorris. Intro. by Sunny Widell. LC 83-799. (Step by Step Bks.). 208p. 1988. pap. 7.95 (ISBN 0-9619770-3-5). Pearl Publishing.

Step-by-Stepparenting: A Guide to Successful Living with a Blended Family. James D. Eckler. LC 88-4276. 204p. (Orig.). 1988. pap. 7.95 (ISBN 0-932620-93-0). Betterway Pubns.

Step Carefully in Night Grass. Susan L. Bartels. LC 74-75750. 55p. 1974. 5.95 (ISBN 0-910244-76-6). Blair.

Step Eight: Getting Honest. 16p. (Orig.). 1983. pap. 1.15 (ISBN 0-89486-175-1). Hazelden.

Step Eight: Restoring Relationships. Pat M. 20p. 1982. pap. 0.85 (ISBN 0-89486-135-2). Hazelden.

Step Eleven: Centering Ourselves. 16p. (Orig.). 1983. pap. 1.15 (ISBN 0-89486-179-4). Hazelden.

Step Eleven: Maintaining the New Way of Life. Mel B. 16p. (Orig.). 1982. pap. 0.75 (ISBN 0-89486-160-3). Hazelden.

Step Farther Out. Jerry Pournelle. 416p. 1983. pap. 3.50 (ISBN 0-441-78583-2). Ace Bks.

Step Farther Out. Jerry Pournelle. 1987. pap. 6.95 (ISBN 0-441-78584-0, Pub. by Ace Science Fiction). Ace Bks.

Step Five: And the Truth Will Set You Free. 16p. (Orig.). 1983. pap. 0.95 (ISBN 0-89486-165-4). Hazelden.

Step Four: Face to Face with Yourself. 24p. (Orig.). 1983. pap. 0.95 (ISBN 0-89486-164-6). Hazelden.

Step Four for Young Adults. Paul E. Bjorklund. 44p. 1981. pap. 1.50 (ISBN 0-89486-118-2). Hazelden.

Step Four for Young Adults. rev. ed. Paul E. Bjorklund. (Step Pamphlets for Young Adults Ser.). 24p. 1981. pap. 1.50 (ISBN 0-317-46559-7). Hazelden.

Step Further. 2nd ed. Joni Eareckson & Steve Estes. (Illus.). 192p. 1980. pap. 7.95 (ISBN 0-310-23971-0, 12007P). Zondervan.

Step Further. Joni Eareckson & Steve Estes. 176p. 1987. pap. 2.95 (ISBN 0-553-26274-2). Bantam.

Step-Growth Polymerizations. Ed. by David H. Solomon. LC 75-182216. (Kinetics & Mechanics of Polymerization Ser.: Vol. 3). (Illus.). pap. 77.40 (ISBN 0-317-07874-7, 2055002). Bks Demand UMI.

Step I Have Taken. E. Dennett. Ed. by R. P. Daniel. 53p. pap. 3.50 (ISBN 0-88172-140-9). Believers Bkshelf.

Step in the Right Direction: Getting a Better View on Life. Bill Cosby et al. Ed. by Charlie W. Shedd. (Illus.). 104p. (Orig.). (YA) (gr. 6-9). 1981. pap. text ed. 7.32 (ISBN 0-933419-02-3). Quest Intl.

Step into China. Neil Johnson. LC 87-20266. (Illus.). 32p. (YA) (gr. 3-6). 1988. 9.79 (ISBN 0-671-64338-X); pap. 5.95 (ISBN 0-671-65852-2). Messner.

Step into Heaven, Here & Now: The Acrobatics of Soul. Ron Kurz. 48p. (Orig.). 1986. pap. 4.95 (ISBN 0-939829-00-2). R Kurz.

Step into Skiing Discoveries. Jul Kingery. LC 77-91906. (Skiing Your Way Ser.). (Illus.). 1978. pap. 7.97 (ISBN 0-9604574-0-2). Alpine-Tahoe.

Step into the Night. Joanne Ryder. LC 88-37982. (Illus.). 32p. (ps-3). 1988. 13.95 (ISBN 0-02-777951-3, Four Winds). Macmillan.

Step It Down: Games, Plays, Songs, & Stories from the Afro-American Heritage. Bessie Jones & Bess L. Hawes. LC 87-5945. (Brown Thrasher Bk.). 264p. 1987. pap. 10.95 (ISBN 0-8203-0960-5). U of Ga Pr.

Step Nine: Building Bridges. 16p. (Orig.). 1983. pap. 1.15 (ISBN 0-89486-176-X). Hazelden.

Step on a Crack: You Break Your Father's Back. Pamela Camille. LC 88-80654. 320p. (Orig.). 1988. pap. 12.95 (ISBN 0-945985-00-2). Freedom Lights Pr.

Step on It. Russell Epprecht. (New York Quartet Ser.: Vol. III). 200p. (Orig.). Date not set. pap. 8.95 cancelled (ISBN 0-912195-12-6). Domesday Bks.

Step One for Family & Friends. Nancy G. Timmerman. 24p. (Orig.). 1985. pap. 0.95 (ISBN 0-89486-300-2). Hazelden.

Step One for Young Adults. Della Van Dyke & Jane Nakken. (Step Pamphlets for Young Adults Ser.). 24p. (Orig.). 1985. pap. 1.50 (ISBN 0-89486-304-5). Hazelden.

Step One: The Foundation of Recovery. William Springborn. 24p. (Orig.). 1977. pap. 0.95 (ISBN 0-89486-017-8). Hazelden.

Step One: The Gospel & the Ghetto. Harv Oostdyk. 342p. 1983. pap. 8.95 (ISBN 0-89221-094-X). New Leaf.

Step One: When Will Power Is Not Enough. 24p. 1982. pap. 1.15 (ISBN 0-89486-151-4). Hazelden.

Step out in Ministry! Carol Crook. LC 86-71831. 203p. (Orig.). 1986. pap. 9.95 (ISBN 0-939399-07-5). Bks of Truth.

Step-Parent Adoptions: A Self-Help Guide to Legally Adopting Your Step-Children. Nerys Blown. (Orig.). pap. 12.95 (ISBN 0-88908-660-5). ISC Pr.

Step-Parenting: Understanding the Emotional Problems & Stresses. Christine Atkinson. 128p. (Orig.). 1986. pap. 8.95 (ISBN 0-7225-1264-3, Pub. by Thorsons (England)). Sterling.

Step Seven: Let Go & Let God. 16p. (Orig.). 1983. pap. 1.15 (ISBN 0-89486-169-7). Hazelden.

Step Six: Getting Ready to Let Go. 16p. (Orig.). 1983. pap. 1.15 (ISBN 0-89486-168-9). Hazelden.

Step Ten: A Good Tenth Step. Mel B. 20p. (Orig.). 1982. pap. 0.85 (ISBN 0-89486-153-0). Hazelden.

Step Ten: Accepting Ourselves. 16p. (Orig.). 1983. pap. 1.15 (ISBN 0-89486-178-6). Hazelden.

Step Three for Young Adults. Della Van Dyke. (Step Pamphlets for Young Adults Ser.). 20p. (Orig.). 1986. pap. 1.50 (ISBN 0-89486-352-5). Hazelden.

Step Three: Giving Up the Game. 24p. 1982. pap. 1.15 (ISBN 0-89486-152-2). Hazelden.

Step Three: Turning It Over. James G. Jensen. 12p. 1980. pap. 0.70 (ISBN 0-89486-107-7). Hazelden.

Step to an Ecology of Mind. Gregory Bateson. 1975. pap. 4.95 (ISBN 0-345-33291-1). Ballantine.

Step to Energy Independence: Gasohol. Ed. by T. P. Lyons. LC 81-68334. (Illus.). 346p. 1982. 45.00x (ISBN 0-412-00241-8, NO. 6710, Pub. by Chapman & Hall). Routledge Chapman & Hall.

Step to the Music. Phyllis A. Whitney. 240p. 1985. pap. 2.50 (ISBN 0-449-70058-5, Juniper). Fawcett.

Step Toward Freedom. Linda G. Maddox. (Orig.). (YA) (gr. 12). 1989. pap. 5.95 (ISBN 0-8054-5070-X). Broadman.

Step Twelve: Living the Program. 16p. (Orig.). 1983. pap. 1.15 (ISBN 0-89486-194-8). Hazelden.

Step Twelve: The Language of the Heart. Peter McDonald. 24p. (Orig.). 1983. pap. 0.95 (ISBN 0-89486-167-0). Hazelden.

Step Two: A Promise of Hope. James G. Jensen. 16p. 1980. pap. 0.75 (ISBN 0-89486-106-9). Hazelden.

Step Two for Family & Friends. Nancy G. Timmerman. 12p. (Orig.). 1985. pap. 0.70 (ISBN 0-89486-301-0). Hazelden.

Step Two for Young Adults. Jane Nakken. (Step Pamphlets for Young Adults Ser.). 20p. (Orig.). 1986. pap. 1.50 (ISBN 0-89486-351-7). Hazelden.

Step Two: You Are Not Alone. 24p. 1982. pap. 1.15 (ISBN 0-89486-150-6). Hazelden.

Stepchildren of Music. facs. ed. Eric Blom. LC 67-28731. (Essay Index Reprint Ser). 1926. 18.00 (ISBN 0-8369-0217-3). Ayer Co Pubs.

Stepchildren of Progress: The Political Economy of Development in an Indonesian Mining Town. Kathryn M. Robinson. LC 86-5847. (Anthropology of Work Ser.). 315p. (Orig.). 1986. 59.50 (ISBN 0-88706-119-2); pap. 17.95 (ISBN 0-88706-120-6). State U NY Pr.

Stepdaughter. Caroline Blackwood. 109p. 1988. pap. 5.95 (ISBN 0-14-006923-2). Penguin.

Stepfamilies: A Catholic Guide. Paul J. Cullen. LC 88-60925. 160p. 1988. pap. 4.95 (ISBN 0-87973-508-2, 508). Our Sunday Visitor.

Stepfamilies: A Guide to Working with Stepparents & Stepchildren. Emily B. Visher & John S. Visher. LC 78-25857. 1979. 27.50 (ISBN 0-87630-190-1). Brunner-Mazel.

Stepfamilies: Making Them Work. Erna Paris. 240p. 1985. pap. 2.95 (ISBN 0-380-89670-2). Avon.

Stepfamilies: Myths & Realities. Emily B. Visher & John S. Visher. 1980. pap. 7.95 (ISBN 0-8065-0743-8, Pub. by Citadel Pr). Lyle Stuart.

Stepfamilies: New Patterns of Harmony. Linda Craven. LC 82-60652. (Teen Survival Library). (Illus.). 192p. (gr. 7 up). 1982. 9.79 (ISBN 0-671-44080-2); pap. 4.95 (ISBN 0-671-49486-4). Messner.

Stepfamily. Anne Emery. LC 79-26908. 140p. (gr. 5-7). 1980. 9.50 (ISBN 0-664-32660-9). Westminster John Knox.

Stepfamily: Living, Loving & Learning. Elizabeth Einstein. LC 84-23635. 214p. 1985. pap. 8.95 (ISBN 0-87773-313-9, 73524-2). Shambhala Pubns.

Stepfamily: Living, Loving & Learning. Elizabeth Einstein. pap. 8.95 (ISBN 0-394-73524-2). Shambhala Pubns.

Stepfather. 2nd ed. Tony Gorman. LC 83-90199. (Orig.). 1985. pap. 9.95 (ISBN 0-9610894-0-7). Gentle Touch.

Stepfather Bank. D. C. Poyer. 288p. 1987. 16.95 (ISBN 0-312-00687-X). St Martin.

Stepfathering. Michael Chandler. 1984. 3.50 (ISBN 0-318-04449-8). Pudding Hse Pubns.

Stepfathering. Mark B. Rosin. 1988. pap. 6.95 (ISBN 0-345-35408-7). Ballantine.

Stepfathering: Stepfathers' Advice on Creating a New Family. Mark B. Rosin. 1987. 18.95 (ISBN 0-671-54697-X). S&S.

Stepford Wives. Ira Levin. 192p. 1979. pap. 2.25 (ISBN 0-440-18294-8). Dell.

Stephane Grappelli. Raymond Horricks. (Quality Paperbacks Ser.). (Illus.). 134p. 1985. pap. 8.95 (ISBN 0-306-80257-0). Da Capo.

Stephane Mallarme. Harold Bloom. (Modern Critical Views Ser.). 256p. 1987. lib. bdg. 24.50x (ISBN 1-55546-289-8). Chelsea Hse.

Stephane Mallarme. Arthur Ellis. LC 77-790. 1977. Repr. of 1927 ed. lib. bdg. 20.00 (ISBN 0-8414-3982-6). Folcroft.

Stephane Mallarme. Stephane Mallarme. 159p. 1980. Repr. of 1927 ed. lib. bdg. 20.00 (ISBN 0-8492-6835-4). R West.

Stephane Mallarme Eighteen Forty-Two to Eighteen Ninety-Eight. Grange Woolley. LC 77-11499. (Illus.). 264p. Repr. of 1942 ed. 31.50 (ISBN 0-404-16358-0). AMS Pr.

Stephane Mallarme in English Verse. Arthur Ellis. 1927. Repr. 27.00 (ISBN 0-8274-3886-9). R West.

Stephane Mallarme, Twentieth-Century Criticism, 1901-1971. rev. ed. D. Hampton Morris. LC 77-708. (Romance Monographs: No. 25). 1977. 22.00x (ISBN 84-399-6423-4). Romance.

Stephania - Middle & Late Bronze-Age Cemetery in Cyprus. J. B. Hennessy. (Colt Archaeological Institute Ser.). 56p. 1963. text ed. 17.50x (ISBN 0-85668-069-9, Pub. by Aris & Phillips UK). Humanities.

Stephanie & the Coyote. 3rd, rev. ed. Jack L. Crowder & Faith Hill. Tr. by William Morgan. (Illus.). 32p. (Eng. & Navajo.). (gr. 3 up). Date not set. pap. 4.95 (ISBN 0-9616589-0-8). Upper Strata.

Stephanie Strikes Back. Susan Saunders. (Sleepover Friends Ser.: No. 7). 96p. (gr. 3-7). 1988. pap. 2.50 (ISBN 0-590-41694-4, Pub. by Apple Paperbacks). Scholastic Inc.

Stephans' Railroad Directory Vol. 2: Railroad Magazine 1929-1987, Railroad Model Craftmans 1932-1987. Earl Stephans. Ed. by Earl Stephans & Karen Stephans. (Stephans' Railroad Directory Ser.). (Illus.). 600p. 1988. pap. 27.75 (ISBN 0-9616890-1-3). Tioga Pubns.

Stephen A. Douglas. Robert W. Johannsen. (Illus.). 1973. 45.00x (ISBN 0-19-501620-3). Oxford U Pr.

Stephen A. Douglas: A Study in American Politics. Allen Johnson. LC 77-98690. (American Scene Ser). 1970. Repr. of 1908 ed. lib. bdg. 55.00 (ISBN 0-306-71836-7). Da Capo.

Stephen: A Singular Saint. Martin N. Scharkemann. 207p. 1968. write for info. Concordia Schl Grad Studies.

Stephen & Arnold As Critics of Wordsworth. John D. Wilson. 1982. 42.50 (ISBN 0-686-81922-5). Bern Porter.

Stephen & Bloom at Life's Feast: Alimentary Symbolism & the Creative Process in James Joyce's "Ulysses". Lindsay Tucker. LC 84-2342. 187p. 1984. 20.00 (ISBN 0-8142-0361-2). Ohio St U Pr.

Stephen & Matilda. David Birt. (Resource Units: Middles Ages, 1066-1485 Ser.). (Illus.). 24p. 1974. pap. text ed. 12.95 10 copies & tchr's guide (ISBN 0-582-39375-2). Longman.

Stephen Antonakos: Neons & Works on Paper. Sally Yard. LC 84-81111. (Illus.). 48p. (Orig.). 1984. pap. 10.00 (ISBN 0-934418-21-7). La Jolla Mus Contemp Art.

Stephen Archer, & Other Tales. facsimile ed. George Macdonald. LC 79-152946. (Short Story Index Reprint Ser.). Repr. of 1883 ed. 20.00 (ISBN 0-8369-3805-4). Ayer Co Pubs.

Stephen Batman's the Doome Warnein All Men to Judgement. Facsimilie ed. Ed. by Jonathan Crewe. (Renaissance Imagination Ser.). Repr. of 1581 ed. 66.00 (ISBN 0-8240-5461-X). Garland Pub.

Stephen Collins Forster: A Guide to Research. Ed. by Calvin Elliker. (Reference Library of Humanities). 210p. 1988. lib. bdg. 30.00 (ISBN 0-8240-6640-5). Garland Pub.

Stephen Collins Foster. H. V. Milligan. 69.95 (ISBN 0-87968-313-9). Gordon Pr.

Stephen Cox. Michael Compton. (Illus.). 24p. (Orig.). Date not set. pap. 6.95 (ISBN 0-946590-47-8, Pub. by Tate Gall Pubns). Salem Hse Pubs.

Stephen Crane. Thomas Beer. LC 72-4407. 248p. 1972. Repr. of 1923 ed. lib. bdg. 20.50x (ISBN 0-374-90519-3, Octagon). Hippocrene Bks.

Stephen Crane. Intro. by Harold Bloom. (Modern Critical Views Ser.). 167p. 1987. 24.50 (ISBN 0-87754-694-0). Chelsea Hse.

Stephen Crane. Jean Cazemajou. (Pamphlets on American Writers Ser: No. 76). (Orig.). 1969. pap. 1.25x (ISBN 0-8166-0526-2, MPAW76). U of Minn Pr.

Stephen Crane. James B. Colvert. LC 84-3805. (Album Biographies Ser.). (Illus.). 352p. 1984. pap. 12.95 (ISBN 0-15-684946-1, Harv). HarBraceJ.

Stephen Crane. Bettina L. Knapp. (Literature & Life Ser.). 208p. 1987. 16.95x (ISBN 0-8044-2468-3). Ungar.

Stephen Crane. Thomas L. Raymond. LC 73-495. 1912. lib. bdg. 20.50 (ISBN 0-8414-1484-X). Folcroft.

Stephen Crane: A Bibliography. Ames W. Williams. LC 79-102866. (Bibliography & Reference Ser.: No. 298). 1970. Repr. of 1948 ed. text ed. 20.50 (ISBN 0-8337-3807-0). B Franklin.

Stephen Crane: A Collection of Critical Essays. Ed. by M. Bassan. 1967. 12.95 (ISBN 0-13-188888-9, Spec). P-H.

Stephen Crane: A Critical Bibliography. R. W. Stallman. LC 79-103837. (Illus.). 1972. 26.00x (ISBN 0-8138-0357-8). Iowa St U Pr.

Stephen Crane: A Critical Biography. John Berryman. 365p. 1982. pap. 9.25 (ISBN 0-374-51732-0). FS&G.

Stephen Crane: A List of His Writings & Articles. B. J. Stolper. 1930. lib. bdg. 25.50 (ISBN 0-8414-8002-8). Folcroft.

Stephen Crane: An Exhibition of His Writings Held at the Columbia University Libraries: 1871-1900. Stephen Crane. (Illus.). 1956. 5.00x (ISBN 0-686-00800-6). O'Brien.

Stephen Crane: An Omnibus. Stephen Crane. Ed. by Robert W. Stallman. 1952. 12.95 (ISBN 0-394-42070-5). Knopf.

Stephen Crane & Literary Impressionism. James Nagel. LC 80-16051. 200p. 1980. 22.50x (ISBN 0-271-00267-0). Pa St U Pr.

Stephen Crane at Brede: An Anglo-American Literary Circle of the Eighteen Nineties. Gordon Milne. LC 80-8126. 69p. 1980. lib. bdg. 19.75 (ISBN 0-8191-1139-2); pap. text ed. 8.25 (ISBN 0-8191-1140-6). U Pr of Amer.

Stephen Crane: In Memoriam. Alfred E. Keet. LC 77-4112. lib. bdg. 17.50 (ISBN 0-8414-5540-6). Folcroft.

Stephen Crane in Transition: Centenary Essays. Ed. & intro. by Joseph Katz. LC 72-1390. (Illus.). 247p. 1972. 15.00 (ISBN 0-87580-032-7). N Ill U Pr.

Stephen Crane: Sullivan County Tales & Sketches. facsimile ed. R. W. Stallman. (Illus.). 1968. pap. 8.90x (ISBN 0-8138-2310-2). Iowa St U Pr.

Stephen Crane: The Critical Heritage. Ed. by Richard Weatherford. (Critical Heritage Ser.). 1984. pap. 15.00 (ISBN 0-7102-0397-7). Routledge Chapman & Hall.

Stephen Crane: The Critical Heritage. Ed. by Richard M. Weatherford. (Critical Heritage Ser.). 362p. 1973. 30.00x (ISBN 0-7100-7636-3). Routledge Chapman & Hall.

Stephen Crane's Artistry. Frank Bergon. LC 75-19159. 174p. 1975. 23.50x (ISBN 0-231-03905-0). Columbia U Pr.

Stephen Crane's Artistry. Frank Bergon. LC 75-19159. 190p. pap. 49.40 (2029824). Bks Demand UMI.

Stephen Crane's Love Letters to Nellie Crouse. Ed. by Edwin H. Cady & Lester G. Wells. 1954. 19.95x (ISBN 0-8156-2014-4). Syracuse U Pr.

Stephen Crane'sthe Red Badge of Courage. Intro. by Harold Bloom. (Modern Critical Interpretations Ser.). 1987. 24.50 (ISBN 1-55546-004-6). Chelsea Hse.

Stephen De Staebler: The Figure. Donald Kuspit. LC 87-27659. (Illus.). 1988. 35.00 (ISBN 0-87701-508-2); pap. 19.95 (ISBN 0-87701-496-5). Chronicle Bks.

Stephen Decatur. Cyrus T. Brady. 1978. Repr. of 1900 ed. lib. bdg. 17.50 (ISBN 0-8492-3713-0). R West.

Stephen Dodson Ramseur: Lee's Gallant General. Gary w. Gallagher. LC 84-13035. (Illus.). xiv, 232p. 1985. 19.95 (ISBN 0-8078-1627-2). U of NC Pr.

Stephen Donaldson. Melissa Barth. (Starmont Reader's Guide Ser.: No. 46). 144p. 1989. lib. bdg. 17.95x (ISBN 0-89370-973-5). Borgo Pr.

Stephen Donaldson. Melissa Barth. Ed. by Roger C. Schlobin. (Reader's Guides to Contemporary Science Fiction & Fantasy Authors Ser.: Vol. 46). (Orig.). Date not set. 17.95x (ISBN 1-55742-029-7); pap. 9.95x (ISBN 1-55742-028-9). Starmont Hse.

Stephen F. Austin: The Father of Texas. Jean Flynn. (Stories for Young Americans Ser.). (Illus.). 64p. (gr. 4-7). 1981. 6.95 (ISBN 0-89015-285-3). Eakin Pr.

Stephen Foster, America's Troubadour. John Tasker Howard. 445p. 1982. Repr. of 1943 ed. lib. bdg. 50.00 (ISBN 0-8495-2436-9). Arden Lib.

Stephen Foster Song Book. Stephen Foster. 224p. (Orig.). 1974. pap. 7.50 (ISBN 0-486-23048-1). Dover.

Stephen Gardiner & the Tudor Reaction. James A. Muller. LC 69-16755. 1969. Repr. lib. bdg. 29.50x (ISBN 0-374-96004-6, Octagon). Hippocrene Bks.

Stephen Gosson. William A. Ringler. 1971. lib. bdg. 16.50x (ISBN 0-374-96814-4, Octagon). Hippocrene Bks.

Stephen Hales: Scientist & Philanthropist. D. G. Allan & R. E. Schofield. 1980. 50.00 (ISBN 0-85967-482-7). Scolar.

Stephen Hawking's Universe. John Boslough. LC 84-4673. (Illus.). 160p. 1984. 12.95 (ISBN 0-688-03530-2); 7.95. Morrow.

Stephen Hawking's Universe: An Introduction to the Most Remarkable Scientist of Our Time. John Boslough. 1987. pap. 7.95 (ISBN 0-688-06270-9, Quill). Morrow.

Stephen Hero. rev. ed. James Joyce. LC 63-14454. (Illus.). 1969. pap. 6.95 (ISBN 0-8112-0074-4, NDP133). New Directions.

Stephen J. Field: Craftsman of the Law. Carl B. Swisher. (Brookings Institution Reprint Ser). (Illus.). lib. bdg. 39.00 (ISBN 0-697-00171-7). Irvington.

Stephen J. Field: Craftsman of the Law. Carl B. Swisher. (Court & the Constitution Ser). 1969. pap. 2.95X (ISBN 0-226-78747-8, P345, Phoen). U of Chicago Pr.

Stephen King. Stephen King. (Classics Ser.). 992p. 1986. deluxe ed. write for info. (ISBN 1-55580-013-0). Octopus Bks.

Stephen King As Richard Bachman. Michael R. Collings. LC 85-21336. (Starmont Studies in Literary Criticism: No. 10). 168p. 1985. Repr. lib. bdg. 17.95x (ISBN 0-89370-982-4). Borgo Pr.

Stephen King As Richard Bachman. Michael R. Collings. LC 85-2832. (Studies in Literary Criticism: No. 10). (Illus.). 176p. (Orig.). 1985. 17.95x (ISBN 0-930261-01-1); pap. 9.95x (ISBN 0-930261-00-3). Starmont Hse.

Stephen King Goes to Hollywood. Chuck Miller & Tim Underwood. 1987. 19.95 (ISBN 0-453-00552-7). NAL.

Stephen King Goes to Hollywood. Ed. by Tim Underwood & Chuck Miller. 1987. pap. 9.95 (ISBN 0-452-25937-1, Plume). NAL.

Stephen King Phenomenon. Michael R. Collings. (Studies in Literary Criticism: No. 14). (Illus., Orig.). 1987. 17.95x (ISBN 0-930261-13-5); pap. 9.95x (ISBN 0-930261-12-7). Starmont Hse.

Stephen King Phenomenon. Michael R. Collings. LC 87-32577. (Starmont Studies in Literary Criticism: No. 14). 144p. 1987. Repr. of 1985 ed. lib. bdg. 17.95X (ISBN 0-89370-986-7). Borgo Pr.

Stephen King: The Art of Darkness. Rev. ed. Douglas Winter. 1986. pap. 7.95 (ISBN 0-452-25804-9, Plume). NAL.

Stephen King: The Art of Darkness. Douglas E. Winter. 1984. 14.95 (ISBN 0-453-00476-8). NAL.

Stephen King: The Art of Darkness. Douglas E. Winter. 352p. 1986. pap. 4.50 (ISBN 0-451-14612-3, Sig). NAL.

Stephen King: The First Decade, Carrie to Pet Sematary. Joseph Reino. (United States Authors Ser.). 176p. 1988. 17.95 (ISBN 0-8057-7512-9, Twayne). G K Hall.

Stephen Korner: Philosphical Analysis & Reconstruction. Ed. by J. Srzednicki. 1987. lib. bdg. 49.50 (ISBN 90-247-3543-2, Pub. by Martinus Nijhoff Netherlands). Kluwer Academic.

Stephen Langton. Maurice Powicke. 227p. 1965. 17.00 (ISBN 0-85036-085-4, Pub. by Merlin Pr UK). Longwood Pub Group.

Stephen Leacock. Gerhard R. Lomer. 1954. Repr. lib. bdg. 27.00 (ISBN 0-8414-5881-2). Folcroft.

Stephen Leacock. Peter McArthur. LC 74-19412. 1974. Repr. of 1923 ed. lib. bdg. 20.50 (ISBN 0-8414-5926-6). Folcroft.

Stephen Leacock: A Check-List & Index of His Writings. Gerhard R. Lomer. 1978. Repr. of 1954 ed. lib. bdg. 25.00 (ISBN 0-8492-1596-X). R West.

Stephen Leacock: Humour & Humanity. Gerald Lynch. 216p. 1988. text ed. 24.95x (ISBN 0-7735-0652-7). McGill-Queens U Pr.

Stephen Long & America Frontier Expedition. Roger Nichols & Patrick L. Halley. LC 78-68878. (Illus.). 280p. 1980. 25.00 (ISBN 0-87413-149-9). U Delaware Pr.

Stephen Mallory White. Kenneth M. Johnson. (Los Angeles Miscellany Ser.: No. 11). 33p. 1980. 15.00 (ISBN 0-87093-311-6). Dawsons.

Stephen Morris. Nevil Shute. 1980. 23.95 (ISBN 0-434-69932-2, Pub. by W Heinemann Ltd). David & Charles.

Stephen of Sawley: Treatises. Ed. by Bede K. Lackner. Tr. by Jeremiah F. O'Sullivan. 1984. 24.95 (ISBN 0-87907-636-4). Cistercian Pubns.

Stephen R. Deane: Early Maine Folk Calligrapher. Marius B. Peladeau. Ed. by Jean Howells. (Illus.). 128p. 1987. 15.95 (ISBN 0-933858-03-5); ltd. ed. 67.50 (ISBN 0-933858-04-3). Kennebec River.

Stephen Remarx: The Story of a Venture into Ethics, 1893. James G. Adderly. Ed. by Robert L. Wolff. Bd. with Christian. Thomas H. Caine. Repr. of 1897 ed. LC 75-485. (Victorian Fiction Ser). 1976. lib. bdg. 73.00 (ISBN 0-8240-1562-2). Garland Pub.

Stephen Roskill, Nineteen Three to Nineteen Eighty-Two. John Ehrman. (Memoirs of the Fellows of the British Academy). (Illus.). 1985. pap. 5.50 (ISBN 0-85672-504-8, Pub. by British Acad). Longwood Pub Group.

Stephen S. Townsend. Dorothy C. Remick. (Illus.). 160p. 1981. 12.50 (ISBN 0-89962-050-7). Todd & Honeywell.

Stephen S. Wise: Servant of the People. Ed. by Carl H. Voss. LC 69-13549. (Illus.). 1969. 5.50 (ISBN 0-8276-0161-1, 233). JPS Phila.

Stephen Sayre: American Revolutionary Adventurer. John Alden. LC 83-771. (Illus.). 219p. 1983. 30.00x (ISBN 0-8071-1067-1). La State U Pr.

Stephen Shore Photographs. Michael Auping. LC 81-83669. (Illus.). 20p. 1981. pap. 0.25 (ISBN 0-916758-07-9). Ringling Mus Art.

Stephen Spender: A Study in Poetic Growth. Surya Nath Pandey. Ed. by James Hogg. (Poetic Drama & Poetic Theory). 230p. (Orig.). 1982. pap. 15.00 (ISBN 3-7052-0889-6, Pub. by Salzburg Studies). Longwood Pub Group.

Stephen Spender & the Thirties. A. K. Weatherhead. LC 73-2891. 241p. 1975. 22.50. Bucknell U Pr.

Stephen the Black. Caroline H. Pemberton. LC 72-1520. (Black Heritage Library Collection). Repr. of 1899 ed. 16.00 (ISBN 0-8369-9044-7). Ayer Co Pubs.

Stephen, the First Martyr. Hodges. (Arch Bks.). 24p. (Orig.). (gr. k-4). 1985. pap. 1.29 (ISBN 0-570-06194-6, 59-1295). Concordia.

Stephen Thomas Riley: The Years of Stewardship. Ed. by Malcolm Freiberg. (Illus.). 121p. 1976. pap. 10.00 (ISBN 0-934909-16-4). Mass Hist Soc.

Stephen Vincent Benet. W. R. Benet. 1979. 42.50 (ISBN 0-685-94349-6). Bern Porter.

Stephen Vincent Benet. William R. Benet. LC 76-52937. 1977. Repr. of 1943 ed. lib. bdg. 15.00 (ISBN 0-8414-1773-3). Folcroft.

Stephen Vincent Benet. Parry Stroud. (Twayne's United States Authors Ser). 1962. pap. 8.95x (ISBN 0-8084-0285-4, T27, Twayne). New Coll U Pr.

Stephen Yan Seafood Wokbook. Stephen Yan. (Illus.). 176p. Date not set. spiral bdg. 9.95 (ISBN 0-919493-87-4, Pub. by Key Porter Canada). U of Toronto Pr.

Stephen's Bag. Ellen Singerman. Ed. by Patricia McKissack & Fredrick McKissack. (Reading Well Ser.). (Illus.). 30p. (Orig.). (gr. 1-3). 1987. pap. 9.95 (ISBN 0-88335-729-1); pap. text ed. 4.95 (ISBN 0-88335-749-6). Milliken Pub Co.

Stephen's Defense & Martyrdom. Gordon Lindsay. (Acts in Action Ser.: Vol. 2). pap. 1.25 (ISBN 0-89985-963-1). Christ Nations.

Stephen's Green Revisited. Richard Weber. LC 68-54471. 1968. 11.95 (ISBN 0-85105-140-5). Dufour.

Stephen's Passion. 2nd ed. Roberta Kalechofsky. LC 75-30158. (Dover Pictorial Archives Ser.). (Illus.). 107p. (Orig.). 1975. pap. 6.00x (ISBN 0-916288-01-3). Micah Pubns.

Stephensons' Britain. Derrick Beckett. (Illus.). 240p. 1984. 24.95 (ISBN 0-7153-8269-1). David & Charles.

Stepkids: A Survival Guide for Teenagers in Stepfamilies. Ann Getzoff & Carolyn McClenahan. LC 83-21779. 192p. 1984. 13.95 (ISBN 0-8027-0757-2). Walker & Co.

Stepkids: A Survival Guide for Teenagers in Stepfamilies...& for Stepparents Doubtful of Their Own Survival. Ann Getzoff & Carolyn McClenahan. 171p. (YA) (gr. 5 up). 1985. pap. 8.95 (ISBN 0-8027-7236-6). Walker & Co.

Stepmatricial Generative Phonology of German. James E. Copeland. 1970. pap. text ed. 11.20x (ISBN 0-686-22396-9). Mouton.

Stepmotherhood: How to Survive Without Feeling Frustrated, Left Out, or Wicked. Cherie Burns. LC 85-40271. 256p. 1985. 14.45 (ISBN 0-8129-1145-8). Times Bks.

Stepmotherhood: How to Survive Without Feeling Frustrated, Left Out or Wicked. Cherle Burns. LC 86-45083. 240p. 1986. pap. 6.95 (ISBN 0-06-097064-2, PL/7064, PL). Har-Row.

Stepmothers Try Harder. Penny Humphrey. (Illus.). 1987. pap. 4.95 (ISBN 0-87131-525-4). M Evans.

Stepmothers Try Harder. Penny Humphrey. (Illus.). 64p. 1987. pap. 4.95 (ISBN 0-317-62752-X). H Holt & Co.

Stepparenting. Jeanette Lofas & Dawn E. Sova. 256p. 1987. pap. 2.95 (ISBN 0-8217-1683-2). Zebra.

Stepparenting. Veryl Rosenbaum & Jean Rosenbaum. LC 77-22070. 160p. 1977. 7.95 (ISBN 0-88316-530-9). Chandler & Sharp.

Steppe. Piers Anthony. 256p. (Orig.). 1985. 13.95 (ISBN 0-312-93748-2, Dist. by St. Martin's Press). Tor Bks.

Steppe. Piers Anthony. 256p. 1986. pap. 3.50 (ISBN 0-8125-3120-5, Dist. by Warner Pub. Services & St. Martin's Press). Tor Bks.

Steppe & Other Stories. facsimile ed. Anton P. Chekhov. Tr. by Adeline L. Kaye. LC 70-106263. (Short Story Index Reprint Ser.). 1915. 16.00 (ISBN 0-8369-3300-1). Ayer Co Pubs.

Steppe & the Sown. H. J. Fleure & Harold Peake. (Corridors of Time Ser.: No.5). 1928. 39.50x (ISBN 0-686-83785-1). Elliots Bks.

Steppenwolf. Hermann Hesse. 1983. pap. 3.95 (ISBN 0-553-25533-9). Bantam.

Steppenwolf. Hermann Hesse. 190p. 1983. Repr. lib. bdg. 18.95x (ISBN 0-89966-448-2). Buccaneer Bks.

Steppenwolf & Siddhartha. Hesse. (Book Notes Ser.). 1985. pap. 2.50 (ISBN 0-8120-3542-9). Barron.

Steppenwolf & Siddhartha Notes. Carolyn R. Welch. 81p. (Orig.). 1973. pap. text ed. 3.95 (ISBN 0-8220-1224-3). Cliffs.

Steppin' Out: New York Nightlife & the Transformation of American Culture, 1890-1930. Lewis A. Erenberg. LC 80-930. (Contributions in American Studies Ser.: No. 50). (Illus.). xix, 291p. 1981. lib. bdg. 35.00 (ISBN 0-313-21342-9, EUN/). Greenwood.

Steppin' Out: New York Nightlife & the Transformation of American Culture, 1890-1930. Lewis A. Erenberg. LC 84-2770. (Illus.). xx, 292p. 1984. pap. 11.95 (ISBN 0-226-21515-6). U of Chicago Pr.

Stepping from the Shadows. Patricia A. McKillip. 224p. 1984. pap. 2.95 (ISBN 0-425-07107-3). Berkley Pub.

Stepping Heavenward. Elizabeth Prentiss. pap. 7.95 (ISBN 0-685-99369-8). Reiner.

Stepping Heavenward. 1967. 0.50 (ISBN 0-686-05837-2). Crusade Pubs.

Stepping into CAD. Mark Merickel. LC 86-61229. (Illus.). 242p. (Orig.). 1986. pap. 24.95 wkbk. (ISBN 0-934035-05-9); instr's. guide, 242 pg. 24.95 (ISBN 0-934035-06-7). New Riders Pubn.

Stepping into CAD Professional Edition. Mark Merickel. (Illus.). 308p. 1987. pap. 29.95 (ISBN 0-934035-14-8); Drafting Macro Disk 14.95 (ISBN 0-934035-41-5); instr's. guide 24.95 (ISBN 0-934035-07-5). New Riders Pub.

Stepping into College English. Frederick C. Arnold. 264p. 1984. pap. 9.50 (ISBN 0-933704-48-8). Dawn Pr.

Stepping into College English. 4th ed. Frederick C. Arnold. 264p. 1988. pap. 9.50 (ISBN 0-933704-63-1). Dawn Pr.

Stepping into Stepparenting: A Practical Guide. Larry C. Jensen & Janet M. Jensen. LC 81-85479. 150p. 1981. perfect bound 9.95 (ISBN 0-88247-597-5). R & E Pubs.

Stepping into the Bible. Beverly E. Kostich. (ps-6). 1988. pap. 3.95 (ISBN 0-317-68086-2). Abingdon.

Stepping into Yourself, Grades Three to Six. Sindy Rosenbaum. 1988. pap. 8.95 (ISBN 0-673-38244-3). Scott F.

Stepping Lightly: An A to Z Guide for Stepparents. Cynthia Lewis-Steere. LC 81-15224. (Illus.). 213p. (Orig.). 1981. pap. 7.95 (ISBN 0-89638-051-3). CompCare.

Stepping Motors & Their Microprocessor Control. Takashi Kenjo. (Monographs in Electrical & Electronic Engineering). (Illus.). 1984. 49.50x (ISBN 0-19-859326-0); pap. 19.95x (ISBN 0-19-859339-2). Oxford U Pr.

Stepping Off the Pedestal: Academic Women in the South. Ed. by Patricia A. Stringer & Irene Thompson. LC 81-14115. ix, 181p. 1982. 32.00 (ISBN 0-87352-331-8, B13C); pap. 17.50x (ISBN 0-87352-332-6, B13P). Modern Lang.

Stepping Out. Carolyn Stoloff. LC 70-168608. 1971. 5.00 (ISBN 0-87775-085-8); pap. 2.00 (ISBN 0-87775-026-2). Unicorn Pr.

Stepping Out: An Introduction to the Arts. Ada Long & Robert Yowell. 128p. 1985. pap. text ed. 16.95 (ISBN 0-8403-3639-X). Kendall Hunt.

Stepping Out of the Plane under the Protection of the Army. Sal Salasin. 88p. (Orig.). 1988. pap. 8.95 (ISBN 0-9614644-6-1). Another Chicago Pr.

Stepping out on Faith: The Story of Colombian Missionaries, George & Helen Constance. Helen Constance. LC 88-70986. (Illus.). 175p. (Orig.). 1988. pap. write for info. (ISBN 0-87509-409-0). Chr Pubns.

Stepping Out, Sharing Christ in Everyday Circumstances. Margaret Rockwell. LC 84-47804. 134p. 1984. pap. 5.95 (ISBN 0-89840-072-4). Heres Life.

Stepping Out: Short Stories on Friendships Between Women. Ed. by Ann Oosthuizen. (Pandora Fiction Ser.). 192p. 1986. pap. 8.95 (ISBN 0-86358-048-3, 80483). Routledge Chapman & Hall.

Stepping over Stones: True-to-Life Stories for Young Teens. Marian Bray. (Illus.). 112p. (Orig.). (YA) (gr. 7-10). Date not set. pap. 4.50 (ISBN 0-8066-2360-8, 10-5999). Augsburg.

Stepping Stones. Mollie Chappell. 1985. 24.95x (ISBN 0-7090-1824-X, Pub. by R Hale Ltd UK). State Mutual Bk.

Stepping Stones. Dorothy E. Watts. Ed. by Raymond Woolsey. (Morning Watch Ser.). 384p. (gr. 1 up). 1987. text ed. 8.50 (ISBN 0-8280-0384-X). Review & Herald.

Stepping Stones. Sharon O. Zeller. (Illus.). 115p. (Orig.). Date not set. pap. price not set (ISBN 0-9617700-0-7). S Zeller.

Stepping Stones: A Collection of Modern Poetry. Ed. by Louisa Persing. (Illus.). 1977. 5.95 (ISBN 0-686-20028-4). Palomar.

Stepping Stones: A Journal. 128p. 1985. 4.95 (ISBN 0-89638-095-5). CompCare.

Stepping Stones for Boys & Girls. Margaret M. Stevens. (Illus.). (gr. 5 up). 1977. pap. 4.00 (ISBN 0-87516-248-7). DeVorss.

Stepping Stones for Little Feet. Margaret M. Stevens. (Illus.). 31p. (gr. 4-6). 1975. pap. 4.00 (ISBN 0-87516-202-9). DeVorss.

Stepping Stones: Meditations in a Garden. Lillian Marshall. (Illus.). 64p. 1984. 5.95 (ISBN 0-88088-506-8). Peter Pauper.

Stepping Stones: Memoirs of Colonial Nigeria, 1907-1960. Sylvia Leith-Ross. 191p. 1983. 21.00 (ISBN 0-7206-0600-4, Pub. by P Owen Ltd). Dufour.

Stepping Stones of Faith. rev. ed. Donald R. Gilmore. LC 86-91881. 88p. 1987. write for info. (ISBN 0-9617810-0-9). D R Gilmore.

Stepping Stones: Seventeen Powerful Stories of Growing Up. Ed. by Robert S. Gold. 320p. (YA) (gr. 7 up). 1981. pap. 3.25 (ISBN 0-440-98269-3, LFL). Dell.

Stepping Stones: The Pilgrims' Own Story. Compiled by Adelia W. Notson & Robert C. Notson. LC 86-72939. (Illus.). 232p. 1987. 19.95 (ISBN 0-8323-0453-0). Binford-Metropolitan.

Stepping Stones Three. Margaret M. Stevens. (Illus.). 32p. (gr. 1-8). 1983. pap. 4.00 (ISBN 0-87516-518-4). DeVorss.

Stepping Stones to Further Jewish-Christian Relations: An Unabridged Collection of Christian Documents. Helga Croner. 157p. pap. 10.00 (ISBN 0-686-95183-2). ADL.

Stepping Stones to Go. Shigemi Kishikawa. LC 65-13411. (Illus.). 1965. pap. 7.95 (ISBN 0-8048-0547-4). C E Tuttle.

Stepping Stones to Grief Recovery. rev. ed. Deborah Roth. 160p. 1988. pap. 8.95 (ISBN 0-9616605-2-X). IBS Press.

Stepping Stones to Grief Recovery. Deborah Roth. 160p. 1988. Repr. lib. bdg. 22.95x (ISBN 0-8095-6553-6). Borgo Pr.

Stepping Stones to Sobriety. William Pittman. 210p. pap. 8.95 (ISBN 0-934125-04-X). Glen Abbey Bks.

Stepping Stones to the Library. 1972. pap. 7.95 (ISBN 0-913308-04-8). Fordham Pub.

Stepping Stones to Women's Liberty: Feminist Ideas in the Women's Suffrage Movement, 1900-1918. Les Garner. LC 83-25360. 144p. 1984. 24.50 (ISBN 0-8386-3223-8). Fairleigh Dickinson.

Stepping Stones Toward an Ethics for Fellow Existers. Herbert Spiegelberg. 1984. lib. bdg. 57.00 (ISBN 90-247-2963-7, Pub. by Martinus Nijhoff Netherlands). Kluwer Academic.

Stepping Stool. Sarah C. Clements. (Illus.). 44p. (Orig.). 1988. pap. 4.95 (ISBN 0-9619736-0-9). Woodmede Farm Pr.

Stepping Up in Faith. Jack W. Hayford. LC 84-80748. (Orig.). 1984. pap. 2.95 (ISBN 0-916847-02-0). Living Way.

Stepping up to Supervisor. Marion E. Haynes. LC 82-18068. (Illus.). 182p. 1986. pap. 13.95 (ISBN 0-941021-00-9). Exec Roundtable.

Steppingstones. James A. Scarborough. 256p. 1987. 15.00 (ISBN 0-9618823-0-1). Merigold Spirit Ctr.

Steppingstones One: Student Edition. J. Johnston. 1981. pap. write for info. (ISBN 0-201-04654-7, World Language Div); write for info. tchr.'s guide (ISBN 0-201-04655-5); write for info. cassette (ISBN 0-201-04656-3). Addison-Wesley.

Steppingstones Two: Student Edition. J. Johnston. 1981. pap. write for info. (ISBN 0-201-04657-1, World Lanuage Div); write for info. (ISBN 0-201-04658-X); write for info. cassette (ISBN 0-201-04659-8). Addison-Wesley.

Steps. Jerzy Kosinski. LC 87-40279. 152p. 1988. pap. 5.95 (ISBN 0-394-75716-5, Vin). Random.

Steps. Jerzy N. Kosinski. LC 83-42697. 1968. 7.95 (ISBN 0-394-60209-9). Modern Lib.

Steps along the Way: A Governor's Scrapbook. Lamar Alexander. LC 86-18184. 160p. 1986. 19.95 (ISBN 0-8407-4215-0). Nelson.

Steps & Steeples: Cork at the Turn of the Century. Colm Lincoln. (Illus.). 148p. 1981. 18.95 (ISBN 0-905140-82-6, Pub. by O'Brien Pr Ireland). Irish Bks Media.

Steps Going Down. Joseph Hansen. LC 85-17134. 320p. 1985. 14.95 (ISBN 0-88150-054-2, Foul Play). Countryman.

Steps Going Down. Joseph Hansen. 320p. 1986. pap. 3.50 (ISBN 0-14-008810-5). Penguin.

Steps Heavenward. R. L. Berry. 123p. pap. 1.00 (ISBN 0-686-29142-5). Faith Pub Hse.

Steps in Clothing Skills. Draper & Bailey. (gr. 7-9). 1978. text ed. 20.80 (ISBN 0-02-665710-4); tchr's guide 2.00 (ISBN 0-02-665720-1). Bennett IL.

Steps in Composition. 3rd ed. Lynn Q. Troyka & Jerrold Nudelman. (Illus.). 480p. 1982. pap. text ed. write for info (ISBN 0-13-846329-8). P-H.

Stereotypes, Distortions & Omissions in U. S. History Textbooks: A Content Analysis Instrument for Detecting Racism & Sexism. Council on Interracial Books for Children, Inc. Staff. 143p. (gr. 11-12). 1977. pap. 8.95x (ISBN 0-930040-03-1). CIBC.

Stereotypes in English Literature: Shylock & Fagin; The Jews in the Middle Ages. 54p. 0.50 (ISBN 0-88464-040-X). ADL.

Stereotyping of Women: Its Effects on Mental Health. Violet Franks & Esther D. Rothblum. (Springer Series-Focus on Women: No. 5). 288p. 1983. 23.95 (ISBN 0-8261-3820-9); student ed. 18.95. Springer Pub.

Steric Aspects of Biomolecular Interactions. Ed. by G. Naray-Szabo & K. Simon. 386p. 1987. 150.00 (ISBN 0-8493-6840-5). CRC Pr.

Steric Effects in Biomolecules: Proceedings International Symposium, Eger, Hungary, October 5-8, 1981. G. Naray-Szabo. (Studies in Physical Theoretical Chemistry: Vol. 18). 418p. 1982. 126.50 (ISBN 0-444-99693-1). Elsevier.

Steric Effects in Drug Design. Ed. by M. Charton & I. Motoc. (Topics in Current Chemistry Ser.: Vol. 114). (Illus.). 172p. 1983. 38.00 (ISBN 0-387-12398-9). Springer-Verlag.

Steric Exclusion Liquid Chromatography of Polymers. Janca. (Chromatography Science Ser.). 456p. 1984. 65.00 (ISBN 0-8247-7065-X). Dekker.

Steric Fit in Quantitative Structure-Activity Relations. Ed. by A. T. Balaban et al. (Lecture Notes in Chemistry: Vol. 15). (Illus.). 178p. 1980. pap. 21.00 (ISBN 0-387-09755-4). Springer-Verlag.

Sterile Cuckoo. John Nichols. (Shoreline Bks.). 1987. pap. 7.95 (ISBN 0-393-30472-8, Shoreline Bks). Norton.

Sterile Dosage Forms: Their Preparation & Clinical Application. 3rd ed. Salvatore Turco & Robert E. King. LC 86-21470. (Illus.). 409p. 1987. text ed. 35.00 (ISBN 0-8121-1067-6). Lea & Febiger.

Sterile-Insect Technique & Its Field Application. (Panel Proceedings Ser.). (Illus.). 138p. (Orig.). 1974. pap. 12.75 (ISBN 92-0-111374-9, ISP364, IAEA). UNIPUB.

Sterile Insect Technique & Radiation in Insect Control: Proceedings of a Symposium, Neuherberg, 29 June - 3 July 1981, Jointly Organized by IAEA & FAO. (Proceedings Ser.). (Illus.). 494p. 1982. pap. 80.00 (ISBN 92-0-010082-1, ISP595, IAEA). UNIPUB.

Sterile-Male Technique for Control of Fruit Flies. (Panel Proceedings Ser.). (Illus., Orig.). 1970. pap. 14.50 (ISBN 92-0-111570-9, ISP276, IAEA). UNIPUB.

Sterile-Male Technique for Eradication or Control of Harmful Insects. (Panel Proceedings Ser.). 1969. pap. 9.75 (ISBN 92-0-111369-2, ISP224, IAEA). UNIPUB.

Sterile Pharmaceutical Packaging: Compatibility & Stability. (Technical Report Ser.: No. 5). 125p. avail. PDA.

Sterility Principle for Insect Control or Eradication, 1970. (Proceedings). 1970. pap. 38.50 (ISBN 92-0-010171-2, ISP265, IAEA). UNIPUB.

Sterility Principle for Insect Control: 1974. (Proceedings Ser.). (Illus.). 622p. 1975. pap. 62.00 (ISBN 92-0-010275-1, ISP377, IAEA). UNIPUB.

Sterilization & Disinfection see D.A.E Project: Instructional Materials for Dental Health Professions.

Sterilization & Disinfection Index of Modern Information: Index for Medicine & Research with Bibliography. Stanley B. Gessler. LC 88-47628. 150p. 1988. 34.50 (ISBN 0-88164-650-4); pap. 26.50 (ISBN 0-88164-651-2). ABBE Pubs Assn.

Sterilization & Preservation of Biological Tissues by Ionizing Radiation. (Panel Proceedings Ser.). (Illus.). 127p. (Orig.). 1970. pap. 9.75 (ISBN 92-0-111370-6, ISP247, IAEA). UNIPUB.

Sterilization for Human Betterment. E. S. Gosney & Paul Popenoe. Ed. by Gerald N. Grob. LC 78-22561. (Historical Issues in Mental Health Ser.). 1979. Repr. of 1929 ed. lib. bdg. 16.00x (ISBN 0-405-11915-1). Ayer Co Pubs.

Sterilization of Carrie Buck: Was She Feebleminded - Or Society's Pawn? J. David Smith. Date not set. price not set. New Horizon NJ.

Sterkfontein Ape-Man Plesianthropus. Robert Broom et al. LC 76-44699. Repr. of 1949 ed. 24.50 (ISBN 0-404-15909-5). AMS Pr.

Sterling A. Brown: Building the Black Aesthetic Tradition. Joanne V. Gabbin. LC 84-19777. (Contributions in Afro-American & African Studies Ser.: No. 86). (Illus.). xvi, 248p. 1985. lib. bdg. 36.95 (ISBN 0-313-23720-4, GSB/). Greenwood.

Sterling & the Tariff, Nineteen Twenty-Nine to Nineteen Twenty-Two. Barry J. Eichengreen. LC 81-6673. (Princeton Studies in International Finance: No. 48). 1981. pap. text ed. 6.50x (ISBN 0-88165-219-9). Princeton U Int Finan Econ.

Sterling Apparel Company: An Experimental Exercise. William R. Thomas. 160p. 1981. pap. text ed. 12.95 (ISBN 0-8403-2456-1). Kendall-Hunt.

Sterling Dialogues. facsimile ed. Ed. by William M. Clark. LC 76-103086. (Granger Index Reprint Ser). 1898. 17.00 (ISBN 0-8369-6101-3). Ayer Co Pubs.

Sterling-Dollar Diplomacy in Current Perspective: The Origins & the Prospects of Our International Economic Order. Richard N. Gardner. LC 79-26572. 1980. 45.00x (ISBN 0-231-04944-7); pap. 16.00x (ISBN 0-231-04945-5). Columbia U Pr.

Sterling Flatware Pattern Index. 3rd rev. ed. Ed. by Donald S. McNeil. LC 83-6136. 188p. binder 49.95 (ISBN 0-931744-05-9). Jewelers Bk Club.

Sterling in Decline. Alec Cairncross & Barry Eichengreen. 270p. 1985. 45.00x (ISBN 0-631-13368-2); pap. 12.95x (ISBN 0-631-13938-9). Basil Blackwell.

Sterling: Its Meaning in World Finance. Judd Polk. Ed. by Mira Wilkins. LC 78-3945. (International Finance Ser.). (Illus.). 1978. Repr. of 1956 ed. lib. bdg. 26.50x (ISBN 0-405-11245-9). Ayer Co Pubs.

Sterling Legend: Story of Lost Dutchman Mine. 1987. 4.95 (ISBN 0-935182-05-5). Gembooks.

Sterling Partnership. Ed. by Doug Woolfolk & Ruth Newcomer. (Illus.). 112p. 1980. 12.50 (ISBN 0-86518-012-1). Moran Pub Corp.

Sterling's Managed Float: The Operations of the Exchange Equalisation Account, 1932-39. Susan Howson. LC 80-23197. (Princeton Studies in International Finance Ser.: No. 46). 1980. pap. text ed. 6.50x (ISBN 0-88165-217-2). Princeton U Int Finan Econ.

Stern. Bruce J. Friedman. 1989. pap. 7.95 (ISBN 0-87113-262-1). Atlantic Monthly.

Stern der Erlosung. Rozenzweig. 1976. lib. bdg. 63.00 (ISBN 90-247-1766-3, Pub. by Martinus Nijhoff Netherlands). Kluwer Academic.

Stern Gear, Shafting & Propellers see IMAS Seventy-Three: Proceedings.

Stern Ohne Himmel see Star Without a Sky.

Stern Trawler. Peter Hjul. 1978. 50.00 (ISBN 0-685-63457-4). State Mutual Bk.

Stern-Wheelers Up Columbia: A Century of Steamboating in the Oregon Country. Randall V. Mills. LC 77-7161. (Illus.). xii, 212p. 1977. 18.95x (ISBN 0-8032-0937-1); pap. 3.75 (ISBN 0-8032-5874-7, BB 650, Bison). U of Nebr Pr.

Sternberg. Ed. by Peter Baxter. (Britsh Film Institute Bks.). (Illus.). 144p. 1980. 15.95 (ISBN 0-85170-098-5, Pub. by British Film Inst England); pap. 8.95 (ISBN 0-85170-099-3, Pub. by British Film Inst England). U of Ill Pr.

Sterne. H. D. Traill. Ed. by John Morley. LC 68-58403. (English Men of Letters Ser.). Repr. of 1889 ed. lib. bdg. 12.50 (ISBN 0-404-51734-X). AMS Pr.

Sterne: A Study. Walter Sichel. 1973. lib. bdg. 25.75 (ISBN 0-8414-8078-8). Folcroft.

Sterne: A Study. Walter S. Sichel. LC 78-163500. (English Literature Ser., No. 33). 1971. Repr. of 1910 ed. lib. bdg. 57.95x (ISBN 0-8383-1310-8). Haskell.

Sterne: The Critical Heritage. Ed. by Alan B. Howes. (Critical Heritage Ser). 1974. 40.00x (ISBN 0-7100-7788-2). Routledge Chapman & Hall.

Sterne: Tristram Shandy. Wolfgang Iser. (Landmarks in World Literature Ser.). 128p. 1988. 19.95 (ISBN 0-521-32807-1); pap. 5.95 (ISBN 0-521-31263-9). Cambridge U Pr.

Sternenhimmel see Astro-Dome Book: 3-D Map of the Night Sky.

Sterner Plan for Italian Unity. Raymond Grew. 1963. 56.50x (ISBN 0-691-05155-0). Princeton U Pr.

Sternheim Plays: Volume I: the Bloomers, the Snob, Paul Schippel, 1913 & the Fossil. Carl Sternheim. Tr. by M. A. Brown et al from Ger. (German Expressionist Ser.). (Orig.). 1980. pap. 6.95 (ISBN 0-7145-0027-5). Riverrun NY.

Stern's Guide to the Cruise Vacation. Steven B. Stern. 222p. 1988. 10.95 (ISBN 0-88289-693-8). Pelican.

Stern's Guide to the Greatest Resorts of the World. Steven B. Stern. Ed. by Cathy Hainer. 250p. 1987. pap. 14.95 (ISBN 0-89865-534-X). Donning Co.

Sterochemistry. O. Bertrand Ramsay. 1982. 48.95 (ISBN 0-471-26103-3, Wiley Heyden). Wiley.

Steroid Analysis by HPLC. Kautsky. (Chromatographic Science Ser.: Vol. 16). 424p. 1981. 79.75 (ISBN 0-8247-1324-9). Dekker.

Steroid & Sterol Hormone Action. Ed. by T. C. Spelsberg & R. Kumar. 1987. lib. bdg. 78.50 (ISBN 0-89838-894-5, Pub. by Kluwer-Nijhoff (Netherlands)). Kluwer Academic.

Steroid Biochemistry. E. Heftmann. 1969. 60.50 (ISBN 0-12-336650-X). Acad Pr.

Steroid Converting Enzymes & Diseases. Ed. by K. Fotherby & S. B. Pal. LC 84-17034. (Illus.). ix, 261p. 1984. 82.00x (ISBN 3-11-009556-4). De Gruyter.

Steroid Hormone Action. Ringold. 1988. write for info. (ISBN 0-471-61266-9). Wiley.

Steroid Hormone Action. Ed. by Gordon Ringold. LC 88-6783. (UCLA Symposia on Cellular & Molecular Biology, New Ser.: Vol. 75). 304p. 1988. 96.00 (ISBN 0-8451-2674-1, 2674). A R Liss.

Steroid Hormone Analysis, Vol. 1. Ed. by Hans Carstensen. LC 67-17002. pap. 126.80 (2027121). Bks Demand UMI.

Steroid Hormone Receptors: Structure & Function. H. Eriksson & J. A. Gustafsson. 1984. 96.25 (ISBN 0-444-80559-1, I-070-84). Elsevier.

Steroid Hormone Receptors: Their Intracellular Localization. Ed. by C. R. Clark. (Ellis Horwood Series in Biomedicine: No. 3). 277p. 1987. lib. bdg. 82.00 (ISBN 0-89573-498-2). VCH Pubs.

Steroid Hormone Regulation of the Brain: Proceedings of an International Symposium, 27-28 October 1980, Wenner-Gren Center, Stockholm, Sweden. K. Fuxe et al. (Wenner-Gren Ser.: Vol. 34). (Illus.). 428p. 1981. 105.00 (ISBN 0-08-026864-1). Pergamon.

Steroid Hormone Resistance: Mechanisms & Clinical Aspects. Ed. by George P. Chrousos et al. LC 85-23250. (Advances in Experimental Medicine & Biology Ser.: Vol. 196). 454p. 1986. 69.50x (ISBN 0-306-42229-8, Plenum Pr). Plenum Pub.

Steroid Hormones: A Practical Approach. Ed. by B. Green & R. E. Leake. 264p. 1987. 47.00 (ISBN 0-947946-65-9); pap. 29.00 (ISBN 0-947946-53-5). IRL Pr US.

Steroid Hormones in Saliva. Ed. by D. B. Ferguson. (Frontiers of Oral Physiology Ser.: Vol. 5). (Illus.). x, 162p. 1984. 76.75 (ISBN 3-8055-3848-0). S Karger.

Steroid Induced Utherine Proteins: Proceedings Symposium, Marburg, September 27-29, 1979. Ed. by M. Beato. (Developments in Endocrinology Ser.: Vol. 8). 1980. 84.25 (ISBN 0-444-80203-7). Elsevier.

Steroid Microbiology. Pinhas Z. Margalith. (Illus.). 286p. 1986. 38.25x (ISBN 0-398-05187-9). C C Thomas.

Steroid-Protein Interactions, No. II. U. F. Westphal. (Monographs on Endocrinology: Vol. 27). (Illus.). 620p. 1985. 110.00 (ISBN 0-387-15321-7). Springer-Verlag.

Steroid Receptors & Disease: Cancer, Autoimmune, Bone & Circulatory Disorders. Sheridan et al. 600p. 1988. 125.00 (ISBN 0-8247-7954-1). Dekker.

Steroid Receptors & the Management of Cancer, 2 vols. E. Brad Thompson & Marc E. Lippman. 1979. Vol. 1, 272p. 95.00 (ISBN 0-8493-5477-3); Vol. 2, 176p. 65.00 (ISBN 0-8493-5478-1). CRC Pr.

Steroid Receptors in Health & Disease. Ed. by V. K. Moudgil. (Serono Symposia, U. S. A. Ser.). (Illus.). 326p. Date not set. 75.00x (ISBN 0-306-42987-X, Plenum Pr). Plenum Pub.

Steroid Receptors, Metabolism & Prostate Cancer. Ed. by F. H. Schroeders & H. J. De Voogt. (International Congress Ser.: Vol. 494). 278p. 1980. 76.00 (ISBN 0-444-90119-1, Excerpta Medica). Elsevier.

Steroid Therapy. Daniel L. Azarnoff. LC 74-24511. pap. 88.00 (ISBN 0-317-29812-7, 2016651). Bks Demand UMI.

Steroids see Rodd's Chemistry of Carbon Compounds.

Steroids & Brain Edema. Ed. by K. Schuermann & H. J. Reulen. LC 72-91334. (Illus.). 350p. 1972. pap. 32.00 (ISBN 0-387-05958-X). Springer-Verlag.

Steroids & Peptides: Selected Chemical Aspects for Biology, Biochemistry & Medicine. Joseph B. Dence. LC 79-21236. 432p. 1980. 74.95 (ISBN 0-471-04700-7, Pub. by Wiley-Interscience). Krieger.

Steroids & Terpenoids see Methods in Enzymology.

Steroids in Human Skin. M. Gulesz. 121p. 1971. 37.00x (ISBN 0-569-06763-4, Pub. by Collets (UK)). State Mutual Bk.

Sterol Biosynthesis Inhibitors & Anti-Feeding Compounds. (Chemistry of Plants Protection Ser.: Vol. 1). (Illus.). 160p. 1985. 44.50 (ISBN 0-387-13487-5). Springer-Verlag.

Sterol Biosynthesis Inhibitors: Pharmaceutical & Agrochemical Aspects. D. Berg & M. Plempel. (Ellis Horwood Series in Biomedicine). 515p. 1988. lib. bdg. write for info. (ISBN 0-89573-671-3, Pub. by Gustav Fischer Verlag). VCH Pubs.

Sterols & Bile Acids: New Comprehensive Biochemistry, Vol. 12. Ed. by H. Danielsson & J. Sjovall. 447p. 1986. 109.00 (ISBN 0-444-80670-9). Elsevier.

Strerope: The Veiled Pleiad. facsimile ed. William H. Acklan. LC 78-38637. (Black Heritage Library Collection). Repr. of 1892 ed. 19.25 (ISBN 0-8369-8963-5). Ayer Co Pubs.

Sterospecific Polymerization of Isoprene. E. Ceausescu. (Illus.). 300p. 1983. 80.00 (ISBN 0-08-029987-3). Pergamon.

Sterrekinderen see Star Children: Morris & Emma Schaver Publications Fund.

Stet! Tricks of the Trade for Writers & Editors. Ed. by Bruce O. Boston. LC 85-82111. 310p. 1986. pap. 15.95 (ISBN 0-935012-07-9). Edit Experts.

Stetson Law Review: 1970-1986, 15 vols. Bound set. 465.00x (ISBN 0-686-90048-0). microfilm avail. Rothman.

Steuben Glass. M. J. Madigan. (Illus.). 340p. 55.00 (ISBN 0-317-55006-3). Apollo.

Steuben Glass: A Monograph. 3rd rev. ed. James Plaut. LC 72-78376. (Illus.). 111p. 1972. pap. 6.95 (ISBN 0-486-22892-4). Dover.

Steuben Glass: An American Tradition in Crystal. Mary J. Madigan. LC 81-22907. (Illus.). 340p. 1982. 65.00 (ISBN 0-8109-1642-8). Abrams.

Steuben Village & Mounds: A Multicomponent Late Hopewell Site in Illinois. Dan F. Morse. LC 64-7124. (Anthropological Papers Ser.: No. 21). (Illus.). Repr. of 1963 ed. 44.00 (ISBN 0-8357-9613-2, 2011182). Bks Demand UMI.

Steve Biko. Hilda Bernstein. 149p. 1978. 3.50 (ISBN 0-317-36653-X, 46). Africa Fund.

Steve Birnbaum Brings You the Best of Walt Disney World. Steve Birnbaum. 192p. 1985. pap. 7.95 (ISBN 0-395-39404-X). HM.

Steve Caney's Toybook. Steven Caney. LC 75-8814. (Illus.). 176p. (ps-6). 1972. 8.95 (ISBN 0-911104-15-1, 022); pap. 6.95 (ISBN 0-911104-17-8, 023). Workman Pub.

Steve Canyon: Fortieth Anniversary Collection: 19th in a Series of Steve Canyon Reprints. Milton Caniff. Ed. by Peter Poplaski. (Illus.). 144p. 1987. 39.95 (ISBN 0-87816-032-9); pap. 7.95 (ISBN 0-317-65618-X). Kitchen Sink.

Steve Carlton: Baseball's Silent Strongman. Nathan Aaseng. LC 83-17516. (Lerner Achievers Ser.). (Illus.). 64p. (gr. 4-9). 1984. PLB 7.95 (ISBN 0-8225-0491-X). Lerner Pubns.

Steve Garvey's Hitting System: Raise Your Batting Average, Hit in Game Situations, & Solve All Your Hitting Problems. Steve Garvey & Bob Gluck. (Illus.). 176p. (Orig.). 1987. pap. 9.95 (ISBN 0-8092-4788-7). Contemp Bks.

Steve Jobs: The Journey Is the Reward. Jeffrey S. Young. 1987. pap. 18.95 (ISBN 0-673-18864-7). Scott F.

Steve Jobs: The Journey Is the Reward. Jeffrey S. Young. 448p. 1988. pap. 4.95 (ISBN 1-55802-378-X). Lynx Bks.

Steve McQueen: The Final Chapter. Grady Ragsdale. LC 83-14681. 1983. 13.95 (ISBN 0-88449-105-6, A524534). Vision Hse.

Steve Mizerak's Pocket Billiards Tips & Trick Shots. Steve Mizerak & Joel Cohen. (Illus.). 192p. 1982. pap. 8.95 (ISBN 0-8092-5779-3). Contemp Bks.

Steve Mizerak's Winning Pocket Billiards. Steve Mizerak & Joel Cohen. (Illus.). 192p. (Orig.). 1984. pap. 7.95 (ISBN 0-8092-5777-7). Contemp Bks.

Steve Nelson, American Radical. Steve Nelson et al. LC 80-26528. 475p. 1981. 29.95x (ISBN 0-8229-3441-8). U of Pittsburgh Pr.

Steve Paxon: Can't Lose for Winning. Ethel Barrett. LC 84-26238. 1985. pap. 4.95 (ISBN 0-8307-1022-1, 5418424). Regal.

Steve Reeves: One of Kind. Milton T. Moore, Jr. LC 82-90099. 192p. (Orig.). 1983. pap. 14.95x (ISBN 0-9608138-0-2). M T Moore.

Steve Train's Ordeal. Max Brand. 1980. pap. 1.75 (ISBN 0-671-41489-5). PB.

Steve Yeager. William M. Raine. 1976. Repr. of 1915 ed. lib. bdg. 18.95x (ISBN 0-88411-556-9, Pub. by Aeonian Pr). Amereon Ltd.

Stevedores & Dockers: A Study of Trade Unionism in the Port of London, 1870-1914. John C. Lovell. LC 74-99263. (Illus.). 1969. 35.00x (ISBN 0-678-07003-2). Kelley.

Steven & the Green Turtle. William J. Cromie. LC 77-85040. (Science I Can Read Bks.). (Illus.). 64p. (gr. k-3). 1970. PLB 10.89 (ISBN 0-06-021374-4). HarpJ.

Steven Caney's Invention Book. Steven Caney. LC 84-40679. (Illus.). 208p. 1985. pap. 7.95 (ISBN 0-89480-076-0, 406). Workman Pub.

Steven Caney's Kids' America. Steven Caney. LC 77-27465. (Illus.). 416p. (gr. k-9). 1978. pap. 11.95 (ISBN 0-911104-80-1, IBM 1147). Workman Pub.

Steven Caney's Playbook. Steven Caney. LC 75-9816. (Illus.). 240p. (ps-5). 1975. pap. 8.95 (ISBN 0-911104-38-0, 050). Workman Pub.

Steven Raichlen's Guide to Boston Restaurants: Including Cape Cod, Suburbs & Surrounding Areas. Steven Raichlen. LC 83-19534. 176p. 1984. pap. 7.95 (ISBN 0-86616-031-0). Greene.

Steven Spiegberg's Amazing Stories II. Steven Bauer. 1987. pap. 3.50 (ISBN 0-317-63431-3, Charter Pub). Berkley Pub.

Steven Spielberg. D. L. Mabery. (Entertainment World Ser.). (Illus.). 40p. (gr. 4-9). 1986. PLB 8.95 (ISBN 0-8225-1612-8). Lerner Pubns.

Steven Spielberg. Donald R. Mott & Cheryl M. Saunders. (Twayne Filmmakers Ser.). 220p. 1986. lib. bdg. 18.95x (ISBN 0-8057-9307-0, Twayne, Twayne). G K Hall.

Steven Spielberg: Creator of E. T. Tom Collins. LC 83-21068. (Taking Part Ser.). (Illus.). 48p. (gr. 3 up). 1983. PLB 9.95 (ISBN 0-87518-249-6). Dillon.

Steven Spielberg's Amazing Stories. Steven Bauer. 240p. 1986. pap. 3.50 (ISBN 0-441-01906-4, Pub. by Charter Bks). Ace Bks.

Stevenage: A Sociological Study of a New Town. Harold Orlans. LC 71-139142. 1971. Repr. of 1952 ed. lib. bdg. 35.00x (ISBN 0-8371-5758-7, ORST). Greenwood.

Stevenage, Nineteen Forty-Six to Nineteen Eighty-Six: Images of the First New Town. Ed. by Timothy Collings. 170p. 1986. 49.00x (ISBN 0-907590-18-7, Pub. by S P A Bks Ltd). State Mutual Bk.

Stevens & Simile: A Theory of Language. Jacqueline V. Brogan. 260p. 1986. text ed. 28.50x (ISBN 0-691-06689-2). Princeton U Pr.

Stevens Arms Catalogues, Eighteen Seventy-Seven to Eighteen Niney-Nine. 1st ed. Bill West. LC 76-143774. (West Arms Library). (Illus.). 1971. 10.00x (ISBN 0-911614-11-7). B West.

Stevens' Handbook of Experimental Psychology. 2nd ed. Ed. by Richard C. Atkinson et al. 1988. 150.00 (ISBN 0-471-61625-7). Wiley.

Stevens' Handbook of Experimental Psychology: Learning & Cognition, Vol. 2. 2nd ed. Ed. by Richard C. Atkinson et al. 1988. 95.00 (ISBN 0-471-04207-2). Wiley.

Stevens' Handbook of Experimental Psychology: Perception & Motivation, Vol. 1. 2nd ed. Ed. by Richard C. Atkinson et al. LC 87-31637. 1988. 85.00 (ISBN 0-471-04203-X). Wiley.
Stevens' Poetry of Thought. Frank Doggett. 240p. (Orig.). 1966. pap. 8.95x (ISBN 0-8018-0174-5). Johns Hopkins.
Stevenson & Edinburgh. M. McLaren. LC 73-21775. (English Biography Ser., No. 31). 1974. lib. bdg. 48.95x (ISBN 0-8383-1831-2). Haskell.
Stevenson & Edinburgh. Moray McLaren. 1973. Repr. of 1950 ed. 20.00 (ISBN 0-8274-1013-1). R West.
Stevenson & Edinburgh: A Centenary Study. Moray Mc Laren. LC 73-8356. 1950. lib. bdg. 18.00 (ISBN 0-8414-6136-8). Folcroft.
Stevenson & the Art of Fiction. David Daiches. 1980. Repr. of 1951 ed. lib. bdg. 15.00 (ISBN 0-89987-155-0). Darby Bks.
Stevenson & the Art of Fiction. David Daiches. LC 73-1140. 1951. lib. bdg. 15.00 (ISBN 0-8414-1856-X). Folcroft.
Stevenson & Victorian England. Jenni Calder. 141p. 1981. 16.00x (ISBN 0-85224-399-5, Pub. by Edinburgh U Pr Scotland). Columbia U Pr.
Stevenson at Manasquan. Charlotte Eaton. LC 76-42995. 1976. lib. bdg. 15.00 (ISBN 0-8414-3919-2). Folcroft.
Stevenson Bibliography. J. Herbert Slater. LC 73-21753. (English Biography Ser., No. 31). 1974. lib. bdg. 75.00x (ISBN 0-8383-1832-0). Haskell.
Stevenson: How to Know Him. Richard A. Rice. 1916. Repr. lib. bdg. 35.00 (ISBN 0-8414-7429-X). Folcroft.
Stevenson in Hawaii. Martha M. McGaw, Sr. LC 77-13757. (Illus.). 1978. Repr. of 1950 ed. lib. bdg. 35.00x (ISBN 0-8371-9864-X, MCSH). Greenwood.
Stevenson Study, Treasure Island. David Barnett. LC 73-16347. 1924. lib. bdg. 15.00 (ISBN 0-8414-3339-9). Folcroft.
Stevensoniana. J. A. Hammerton. 1973. Repr. of 1907 ed. 25.00 (ISBN 0-8274-0393-3). R West.
Stevensoniana: Being a Reprint of Various Literary & Pictorial Miscellany Associated with Robert Louis Stevenson, the Man & His Work. 94p. Repr. of 1900 ed. lib. bdg. 85.00 (ISBN 0-918377-60-9). Russell Pr.
Stevenson's Attitude to Life. Franklin Genung. LC 73-12550. 1901. lib. bdg. 15.00 (ISBN 0-8414-4414-5). Folcroft.
Stevenson's Essential Grammar. Nancy Stevenson. 131p. 9.95 (ISBN 0-941112-21-7); wkbk. 3.95 (ISBN 0-941112-22-5). Stevenson Lang Skills.
Stevenson's Germany: The Case Against Germany in the Pacific. C. Brunsdon Fletcher. LC 78-111755. (American Imperialism: Viewpoints of United States Foreign Policy, 1898-1941). 1970. Repr. of 1920 ed. 17.00 (ISBN 0-405-02018-X). Ayer Co Pubs.
Stevenson's Germany: The Case Against Germany in the Pacific. C. Brunsdon Fletcher. 1973. Repr. of 1920 ed. 25.00 (ISBN 0-8274-0407-7). R West.
Stevenson's Shrine. Laura Stubbs. 1973. Repr. of 1903 ed. 25.00 (ISBN 0-8274-0422-0). R West.
Stevie. Jack Barbera & William McBrien. (Illus.). 384p. 1988. pap. 9.95 (ISBN 0-19-505657-4). Oxford U Pr.
Stevie. John Steptoe. LC 69-16700. (Illus.). (ps-3). 1969. 11.70i (ISBN 0-06-025763-6); PLB 12.89 (ISBN 0-06-025764-4). HarpJ.
Stevie. John Steptoe. LC 69-16700. (Trophy Picture Bks.). (Illus.). 32p. (ps-3). 1986. pap. 3.95 (ISBN 0-06-443122-3, Trophy). HarpJ.
Stevie. John Steptoe. (Illus.). (gr. 1-4). 1987. incl. cassette 19.95 (ISBN 0-87499-050-5); pap. 12.95 incl. cassette (ISBN 0-87499-049-1); 4 paperbacks, cassette & guide 27.95 (ISBN 0-87499-051-3). Live Oak Media.
Stevie Has His Heart Examined. Sue Sauer et al. Ed. by Nancy Goldstein. (Illus.). (ps-7). 1983. pap. text ed. 4.25 (ISBN 0-937423-00-9). U M H & C.
Stevie Has His Heart Repaired. Sue Sauer et al. Ed. by Nancy Goldstein. (Illus.). (ps-7). 1979. pap. text ed. 4.25 (ISBN 0-937423-01-7). U M H & C.
Stevie Nicks. Ethlie A. Vare & Ed Ochs. 1985. pap. 2.95 (ISBN 0-345-32238-X). Ballantine.
Stevie Smith: A Bibliography. Jack Barbera et al. (Twentieth Century Literary Bibliographies Ser.). 1987. lib. bdg. 47.50x (ISBN 0-88736-101-3). Meckler Corp.
Stevie Smith: A Bibliography. Jack Barbera et al. 288p. 1986. 66.00 (ISBN 0-7201-1837-9). Mansell.
Stevie Smith: A Biography. Jack Barbera & William McBrien. (Illus.). 384p. 1987. 24.95 (ISBN 0-19-520549-9). Oxford U Pr.
Stevie Smith: A Selection. Pref. by Hermione Lee. (Illus.). 224p. 1985. 16.95 (ISBN 0-571-13029-1); pap. 6.95 (ISBN 0-571-13030-5). Faber & Faber.
Stevie Wonder. Carl R. Green & William R. Sanford. Ed. by Howard Schroeder. LC 86-16713. (Center Stage Ser.). (Illus.). 32p. (gr. 4-5). PLB 9.95 (ISBN 0-89686-296-8). Crestwood Hse.
Stevie Wonder. Ruuth. (Illus.). 96p. 1980. pap. 1.25 (ISBN 0-87067-315-7, BH315). Holloway.
Stevie Wonder. John Swenson. LC 86-45167. (Illus.). 176p. (Orig.). 1986. pap. 12.95 (ISBN 0-06-097067-7, PL-7067, PL). Har-Row.
Stevie Wonder: The Illustrated Discography. 96p. 1985. pap. 7.95 (ISBN 0-7119-0616-5). Cherry Lane.
Steward: A Biblical Symbol Come of Age. Douglas J. Hall. 1982. pap. 7.95 (ISBN 0-377-00133-3). Friendship Pr.
Steward-ship Adventure: Christianomics for Kids Grades 3-6 Leader's Guide. James W. Jackson & AnnaMarie Jackson. (Christianomics Ser.). 40p. (Orig.). 1988. tchr's. ed. 5.95 (ISBN 1-55513-839-X, 68395). Cook.
Steward-ship Adventure: Christianomics for Kids. James W. Jackson. (Christianomics Ser.). (Illus.). 24p. (Orig.). (gr. 3-6). 1988. wkbk. 2.95 (ISBN 1-55513-840-3, 68403). Cook.
Stewards of Creation. Jerry Schmalenberger. (Orig.). 1987. pap. 4.50 (ISBN 0-89536-894-3, 7880). CSS of Ohio.
Stewards of Excellence: Studies in Modern English & American Poets. A. Alvarez. LC 70-159035. 191p. 1971. Repr. of 1958 ed. 25.00x (ISBN 0-87752-152-2). Gordian.
Stewards of God. Edward J. Higgins. 1984. 3.25 (ISBN 0-86544-022-0). Salv Army Suppl South.
Stewards of God's Grace. Siegfried Grossman. 192p. (Orig.). 1981. pap. text ed. 14.95 (ISBN 0-85364-287-7). Attic Pr.
Stewards of the Land: The American Farm School & Modern Greece. Brenda L. Marder. (East European Monographs: No. 59). 234p. 1979. 24.00x (ISBN 0-914710-52-4). East Eur Quarterly.
Stewards of the Mysteries of God: Group Leader's Guide. Michael L. Sherer. 1985. 2.50 (ISBN 0-89536-780-7, 5831). CSS of Ohio.
Stewards of the Mysteries of God: Master Planning Guide. Michael L. Sherer. 1985. 1.75 (ISBN 0-89536-779-3, 5830). CSS of Ohio.
Stewards of the Mysteries of God: Worship Resources. Michael L. Sherer. 1985. 2.75 (ISBN 0-89536-781-5, 5832). CSS of Ohio.
Stewards of the State: The Governor of Michigan. George Weeks. (Illus.). 208p. 1987. 20.95 (ISBN 0-9614344-2-2). Historical Soc MI.
Stewardship: An Adventure in Christian Living. Daniel Mueller. 1987. pap. 6.95 (ISBN 0-937172-69-3). JLJ Pubs.
Stewardship Enlistment & Commitment. Raymond B. Knudsen. 130p. 1985. pap. 8.95 (ISBN 0-8192-1371-3). Morehouse.
Stewardship: Lessons from the Bible. Gerald Oliver. LC 84-62421. write for info. (ISBN 0-9614316-0-1). Natl Inst Phil.
Stewardship of Creation: Basic Resource Guide. 96p. pap. 6.75 (ISBN 0-664-24489-0). Westminster John Knox.
Stewardship of Creation: Guide for Older Youth. 32p. Pack of 10. pap. 31.50 (ISBN 0-664-24492-0). Westminster John Knox.
Stewardship of Creation: Guide for Older Children. 30p. 1984. Pack of ten. pap. 31.50 (ISBN 0-664-24490-4). Westminster John Knox.
Stewardship of Creation: Guide for Younger Youth. 32p. Pack of 10. pap. 31.50 (ISBN 0-664-24491-2). Westminster John Knox.
Stewardship of Creation: Introductory Kit. Set of Four Guides. pap. 14.50 (ISBN 0-664-24560-9). Westminster John Knox.
Stewardship of Creation: Resource Packets for Older Children. 24p. 1987. pap. 15.95 (ISBN 0-317-70007-3). Westminster John Knox.
Stewardship of Creation: Resource Packets for Older Youth. 24p. 1987. pap. 15.95 (ISBN 0-664-24169-7). Westminster John Knox.
Stewardship of Creation: Resource Packets for Younger Youth. 24p. 1987. pap. 15.95 (ISBN 0-664-24168-9). Westminster John Knox.
Stewardship of Wealth. Kingdon W. Swayne. LC 85-60034. 32p. (Orig.). 1985. pap. 2.50x (ISBN 0-87574-259-9). Pendle Hill.
Stewardship Preaching. Mark Gravrock. (Ser. B). 56p. (Orig.). 1984. pap. 5.95 (ISBN 0-8066-2076-5, 10-6002). Augsburg.
Stewardship Preaching. Stephen O. Swanson. (Series A). 56p. 1983. pap. 5.95 (ISBN 0-8066-2029-3, 10-6001). Augsburg.
Stewardship Preaching: Series C. Richard H. Foege. 56p. (Orig.). 1985. pap. 5.95 (ISBN 0-8066-2152-4, 10-6003). Augsburg.
Stewardship Source Book. Robert Shannon & Michael Shannon. 160p. 1987. pap. 5.95 (ISBN 0-87403-250-4, 3180). Standard Pub.
Stewardship: Taking Care of God's World. Sarah Fletcher. (Illus.). (gr. k-4). 1984. pap. 3.95 (ISBN 0-570-04106-6, 56-1498). Concordia.
Stewardship Talks & Resources. Leila T. Ammerman. (Pulpit Library Ser.). 68p. 1988. pap. 3.95 (ISBN 0-8010-0214-1). Baker Bk.
Stewardship, the Divine Order. Genieve DeHoyos. LC 81-82055. 200p. 1982. 6.95 (ISBN 0-88290-191-5, 1065). Horizon Utah.
Stewardship: Total Life Commitment. R. Leonard Carroll. 144p. 1967. pap. 4.25 (ISBN 0-87148-755-1). Pathway Pr.
Stewart Edward White. Judy Alter. LC 75-7011. (Western Writers Ser.: No. 18). (Illus., Orig.). 1975. pap. 2.95x (ISBN 0-88430-017-X). Boise St Univ.
Stewart White Returns. Robert R. Leichtman. (From Heaven to Earth Ser.). (Illus.). 96p. (Orig.). 1980. pap. 3.50 (ISBN 0-89804-062-0). Ariel OH.
Stews & Ragouts: Simple & Hearty One-Dish Meals. Kay S. Nelson. 1978. pap. 4.50 (ISBN 0-486-23662-5). Dover.
Stews & Ragouts: Simple & Hearty One-Dish Meals. Kay S. Nelson. 10.25 (ISBN 0-8446-5680-1). Peter Smith.
STFM Fellowship Directory. Compiled by STFM. 30p. cancelled. Soc Tchrs Fam Med.
STFM Membership Directory 1988-89. Compiled by STFM. 246p. 1986. 25.00 (ISBN 0-942295-13-7). Soc Tchrs Fam Med.
STI Review, No. 1: Autumn 1986. OECD. (Science, Technology & Industry Ser.). 130p. (Orig.). 1987. pap. 16.00x (ISBN 0-318-22337-6). OECD.
Stichus. Plautus. Bd. with Three Bob Day; Truculentus; Tale of a Traveling Bag; Fragments. (Loeb Classical Library: No. 328). 13.95x (ISBN 0-674-99362-4). Harvard U Pr.
Stick. Elmore Leonard. 304p. 1984. pap. 3.95 (ISBN 0-380-67652-4). Avon.
Stick. Elmore Leonard. 1985. lib. bdg. 15.95 (ISBN 0-8161-3908-3, Large Print Bks). G K Hall.
Stick & Rudder. Wolfgang Langewiesche. (Illus.). 1944. text ed. 16.95 (ISBN 0-07-036240-8). McGraw.
Stick Exercises. Cherie Phillips. (Illus.). 250p. 1987. pap. write for info. (ISBN 0-9616287-0-7). Spectrum Pubns.
Stick Fighting. M. Hatsumi & Q. Chambers. 9.95x (ISBN 0-685-38454-3). Wehman.
Stick Fighting for Combat. Michael D. Echanis. LC 78-65738. (Specialties Ser.). (Illus.). 1978. pap. 9.95 (ISBN 0-89750-059-8, 130). Ohara Pubns.
Stick Fighting: Self-Defense. Bruce Tegner. LC 70-109225. (Illus.). 128p. 1972. pap. 5.95 (ISBN 0-87407-020-1, T-20). Thor.
Stick-Fighting: Sport Forms. Bruce Tegner. (Illus.). 127p. 1982. pap. 4.95 (ISBN 0-87407-043-0, T-21). Thor.
Stick Fighting: Techniques of Self-Defense. Masaaki Hatsumi & Quintin Chambers. LC 79-158643. (Illus.). 147p. pap. 12.95 (ISBN 0-87011-475-1). Kodansha.
Stick It, Stitch It & Stuff It Toybook. Penelope Frith. LC 74-32476. (Illus.). 114p. 1975. 5.95 (ISBN 0-87131-178-X). M Evans.
Stick Out Your Tongue! Jokes about Doctors & Patients. Peter Roop & Connie Roop. (Make Me Laugh! Joke Bks.). (Illus.). 32p. (gr. 1-4). 1986. PLB 5.95 (ISBN 0-8225-0990-3). Lerner Pubns.
Stick Stories. Margie Brown. (Illus., Orig.). 1982. pap. 7.95 (ISBN 0-89390-035-4). Resource Pubns.
Stickeen. John Muir. 90p. 1981. pap. 3.95 (ISBN 0-930588-05-3). Heyday Bks.
Stickeen. John Muir. 1977. Repr. of 1916 ed. lib. bdg. 30.00 (ISBN 0-8274-4325-0). R West.
Stickeen: An Adventure with a Dog & a Glacier. John Muir. Pref. by William R. Jones. (Illus.). 1978. pap. 2.95 (ISBN 0-89646-032-0). Outbooks.
Stickeen: Story of a Dog. John Muir. 48p. 1988. Repr. 7.95 (ISBN 0-317-65871-9). Applewood.
Stickers Forever. Linda W. Aber & Hal Aber. (Stuck on Stickers Ser.: No. 4). (Illus.). 24p. pap. 2.95 (ISBN 0-590-33611-8). Scholastic Inc.
Stickfighting: A Practical Guide for Self-Protection. Evan S. Baltazzi. LC 83-70808. (Illus.). 224p. 1983. 22.50 (ISBN 0-8048-1450-3). C E Tuttle.
Stickhandling & Passing. Paul J. Deegan. LC 76-8444. (Sports Instruction Ser.). (Illus.). (gr. 4 up). 1976. PLB 8.95 (ISBN 0-87191-520-0); pap. 3.95 (ISBN 0-686-67437-5). Creative Ed.
Sticking Together: Friendships for Life. Sandy Larsen. (Bible Discovery Guides for Teen Campers Ser.). 32p. (Orig.). 1987. pap. 1.50 camper (ISBN 0-87788-787-X); pap. 3.50 counselor (ISBN 0-87788-788-8). Shaw Pubs.
Stickit Minister, & Some Common Men. facsimile 2nd ed. Samuel R. Crockett. LC 72-163023. (Short Story Index Reprint Ser.). Repr. of 1893 ed. 18.00 (ISBN 0-8369-3937-9). Ayer Co Pubs.
Stickleback Fish. Kathleen Pohl. (Nature Close-Ups Ser.). (Illus.). 32p. (gr. 3-4). 1986. PLB 15.33 (ISBN 0-8172-2722-9); pap. text ed. 9.27 (ISBN 0-8172-2740-7). Raintree Pubs.
Sticklewort & Feverfew. Robert D. Sutherland. LC 79-92898. (Illus.). 360p. (gr. 2 up). 1980. 16.00 (ISBN 0-936044-00-4); pap. 9.00 (ISBN 0-936044-01-2). Pikestaff Pr.
Stickley Craftsman Furniture Catalogs. Gustav Stickley et al. 192p. 1979. pap. 7.95 (ISBN 0-486-23838-5). Dover.
Stickley Craftsman Furniture Catalogs: Unabridged Reprints of Two Mission Furniture Catalogs-"Craftsman Furniture Made by Gustav Stickley" & "the Work of L. & J. G. Stickley". Gustav Stickley. (Illus.). 16.75 (ISBN 0-8446-5821-9). Peter Smith.
Stickley Craftsman Furniture Catalogs: Unabridged Reprints of Two Mission Furniture Catalogs. Gustav Stickley. (Illus.). 193p. Repr. of 1910 ed. 20.00 (ISBN 0-317-54992-8). Apollo.
Stickman. Seth Pfefferle. 288p. 1987. pap. 3.95 (ISBN 0-8125-2417-9, Dist. by St Martin's Pr & Warner Pub Servs). Tor Bks.
Sticks & Stones. rev. ed. Lewis Mumford. (Illus.). 1955. pap. 3.95 (ISBN 0-486-20202-X). Dover.
Sticks & Stones: A Leaflet for the Left Hand. Jon Racherbaumer. 52p. (Orig.). 1978. pap. 5.00 (ISBN 0-915926-40-7). Magic Ltd.
Sticks & Stones & Ice Cream Cones. Phyllis Fiarotta. LC 74-160843. (Illus.). 322p. (gr. k-5). 1973. pap. 8.95 (ISBN 0-911104-30-5). Workman Pub.
Sticks & Stones Book. Elizabeth Pieper. 1976. 4.50 (ISBN 0-937540-06-4, HPP-8). Human Policy Pr.
Sticks & Straw: Comparative house forms in Southern Sudan & Northern Kenya. Jonathan E. Arensen. LC 81-50907. (International Museum of Cultures Ser.: No. 13). (Illus.). 140p. (Orig.). 1983. pap. 12.00 (ISBN 0-88312-164-6); microfiche (2) 4.00 (ISBN 0-88312-249-9). Summer Inst Ling.
Sticks that Kill: A Novel. Trevor Shearston. LC 83-10394. (Illus.). 592p. 1984. 14.95 (ISBN 0-7022-1763-8). U of Queensland Pr.
Sticky Fingers: A Close Look at America's Fastest-growing Crime. W. W. McCullough. LC 80-69696. pap. 39.50 (ISBN 0-317-26942-9, 2023591). Bks Demand UMI.
Sticky Icky Movement Activities: Children Have Great Fun Performing Creative Movement Activities to Imaginative Challenges You Read Aloud. Ryerson Johnson. Ed. by Frank Alexander. (Illus.). 14p. (Orig.). 1985. pap. 2.95 (ISBN 0-915256-17-7). Front Row.
Stickybeak. Hazel Edwards. Ed. by Rhoda Sherwood. LC 88-42915. (Illus.). 32p. (ps-1). 1988. PLB 11.25 (ISBN 1-55532-932-2). Stevens Inc.
Stickybear Book of Weather. Richard Hefter. LC 83-2191. (Stickybear Bks.). (Illus.). 32p. (ps-1). 1983. 5.95 (ISBN 0-911787-01-1). Optimum Res Inc.
Stickybear's Scary Night. Richard Hefter. (Stickybear Bks.). (Illus.). 29p. (ps-1). 1984. 1.95 (ISBN 0-911787-41-0). Optimum Res Inc.
Stieglitz: A Memoir-Biography. Sue D. Lowe. (Illus.). 419p. 1983. 25.50 (ISBN 0-374-26990-4); pap. 14.95 (ISBN 0-374-51827-0). FS&G.
Stiff Computation. Richard C. Aiken. (Illus.). 1984. 75.00x (ISBN 0-19-503453-8). Oxford U Pr.
Stiff Upper Lip. Lawrence Durrell. (Illus.). 94p. (Orig.). 1983. pap. 3.95 (ISBN 0-571-06722-0). Faber & Faber.
Stiff Upper Lip, Jeeves. P. G. Wodehouse. LC 83-47592. 192p. 1983. pap. 3.95 (ISBN 0-06-080668-0, P668, PL). Har-Row.
Stiffest of the Corpse: An Exquisite Corpse Reader, 1983-1988. Ed. by Andrei Codrescu. 256p. (Orig.). 1988. pap. 10.95 (ISBN 0-87286-213-5). City Lights.
Stifter: Bunte Steine. Eve Mason. Ed. by Martin Swales. (Critical Guides to German Texts: No. 5). 91p. 1986. pap. 4.95 (ISBN 0-7293-0246-6, Pub. by Grant & Cutler). Longwood Pub Group.
Stiftungen-Buch der Cistercienser-Klosters Zwetl. Zwetl, Austria (Cistercian Monastery) xvi, 736p. Repr. of 1851 ed. 62.00 (ISBN 0-384-71300-9). Johnson Repr.
Stigma. Charles Bernstein. 1981. pap. 3.00 (ISBN 0-930794-49-4). Station Hill Pr.
Stigma. Bill Clendenen. 224p. (Orig.). 1988. pap. 3.50 (ISBN 0-553-27077-X). Bantam.
Stigma. Robert M. Page. (Concepts in Social Policy Ser.). 156p. (Orig.). 1984. pap. 13.95x (ISBN 0-7100-9786-7). Routledge Chapman & Hall.
Stigma: A Social Psychological Analysis. Irwin Katz. LC 80-20765. 160p. 1981. text ed. 19.95x (ISBN 0-89859-078-7). L Erlbaum Assocs.
Stigma & Social Welfare. Paul Spiker. LC 83-40194. 240p. 1984. 22.50 (ISBN 0-312-76200-3). St Martin.
Stigma: Notes on the Management of Spoiled Identity. Erving Goffman. 1986. pap. 6.95 (ISBN 0-671-62244-7, Touchstone Bks). S&S.
Stigma: Notes on the Management of Spoiled Identity. Irving Goffman. (Orig.). 1963. pap. 5.95 (ISBN 0-13-846626-2, Spec). P-H.
Stigma of Poverty: A Critique of Poverty Theories & Policies. 2nd ed. Chaim I. Waxman. LC 77-5760. 1983. text ed. 30.00 (ISBN 0-08-029408-1); pap. text ed. 12.95 (ISBN 0-08-029407-3). Pergamon.
Stigmata & Modern Science. Charles M. Carty. 31p. 1974. pap. 0.75 (ISBN 0-89555-104-7). TAN Bks Pubs.
Stihotvoreniya 1962 & Pornografska Poema 1968. Atanas Slavov. Ed. by Christo Ognjanoff. 74p. (Bulgarian.). 1980. pap. 7.00 (ISBN 0-937785-00-8). Slabhair.
Stikhi: Nineteen Twenty-One to Nineteen Eighty-Three. Nina Berberova. LC 84-60081. (Russica Poetry Ser.: No. 4). 120p. (Orig., Rus.). 1984. pap. 7.95 (ISBN 0-89830-072-X). Russica Pubs.
Stikhi o Terrore. Maksimilian A. Voloshin. 69p. (Rus.). 1983. pap. 4.00 (ISBN 0-933884-38-9). Berkeley Slavic.
Stikhi, Poems, Poemes. Irina Ratushinskaya. Tr. by Meery Devergnas et al. LC 84-12974. 134p. (Rus., Eng. & Fr.). 1984. pap. text ed. 8.50 (ISBN 0-938920-54-5). Hermitage.
Stikhotvoreniia. Osip E. Mandelshtam. 194p. (Rus.). 1984. pap. 6.50 (ISBN 0-933884-39-7). Berkeley Slavic.
Stikhotvoreniia: Na Opushke Sna. Inna Lisnianskaia. 101p. (Rus.). 1984. pap. 4.50 (ISBN 0-88233-991-5). Ardis Pubs.
Stikhotvoreniya. Mikhail Eremin. Ed. & afterword by Lev Losev. LC 86-14317. (Rus.). 1986. pap. 8.50. Hermitage.
Stikine River. Ed. by Alaska Geographic Staff. LC 79-20674. (Alaska Geographic Ser.: Vol. 6, No. 4). (Illus.). 1979. pap. 9.95 (ISBN 0-88240-133-5). Alaska Northwest.
Stil' Prozy Lermontova. V. V. Vinogradov. 128p. 1986. Repr. 23.50 (ISBN 0-88233-964-8). Ardis Pubs.

Stile Floreale: The Cult of Nature in Italian Design. Gabriel P. Weisberg. 1988. 45.00 (ISBN 0-295-96671-8); pap. 24.95 (ISBN 0-295-96670-X). U of Wash Pr.
Stiletto. Roger Aplon. 1976. 12.00 (ISBN 0-931848-13-X); pap. 4.50 (ISBN 0-931848-14-8). Dryad Pr.
Stiletto. Harold Robbins. 1978. pap. 4.50 (ISBN 0-440-18284-0). Dell.
Stilistik: Sprachpragmatische Grundlegung der Stilbeschreibung. Barbara Sandig. (Grundlagen der Kommunikation De Gruyter Studienbuch). 1978. 16.80x (ISBN 3-11-007374-9). De Gruyter.
Still. B. P. Nichol. 73p. (Orig.). 1983. pap. 5.00 (ISBN 0-88978-146-X). Left Bank.
Still a Dream: The Changing Status of Blacks Since 1960. Sar A. Levitan et al. LC 74-16539. 1975. pap. 9.95x (ISBN 0-674-83856-4). Harvard U Pr.
Still a Few Bugs in the System. G. B. Trudeau. LC 70-182752. 1972. pap. 5.25 (ISBN 0-03-091356-X). H Holt & Co.
Still Another Day. Pablo Neruda. Tr. by William O'Daly. LC 84-70299. 80p. (Span. & Eng.). 1984. ltd. Eng. ed. 75.00x (ISBN 0-914742-78-7); pap. 9.00 (ISBN 0-914742-77-9). Copper Canyon.
Still Another Pelican in the Breadbox. Kenneth Patchen. Ed. by Richard Morgan. LC 82-82905. 96p. 1981. pap. 5.95 (ISBN 0-917530-14-4). Pig Iron Pr.
Still Barred from Prison. Claire Culhane. 196p. 1985. 34.95 (ISBN 0-920057-32-2); pap. 14.95 (ISBN 0-920057-33-0). Black Rose Bks.
Still Close to the Island. Cyril Dabydeen. 111p. 1980. pap. 8.00 (ISBN 0-88970-036-2, Pub. by Commoner's Pub Canada). Three Continents.
Still Cove Journal. Gladys Taber. Intro. by Constance T. Colby. LC 80-8220. (Illus.). 192p. 1981. 13.45i (ISBN 0-06-014227-8, HarpT). Har-Row.
Still Forest Pool. Jack Kornfield & Paul Breiter. LC 85-40411. (Illus.). 225p. (Orig.). 1985. pap. 6.50 (ISBN 0-8356-0597-3, Quest). Theos Pub Hse.
Still Forms on Foxfield. Joan Slonczewski. 224p. 1988. pap. 2.95 (ISBN 0-380-75328-6). Avon.
Still Full of Sap, Still Green. Alfred H. Deutsch. LC 79-21558. 130p. 1979. pap. 2.50 (ISBN 0-8146-1051-X). Liturgical Pr.
Still Glides the Stream. D. E. Stevenson. 278p. 1976. lib. bdg. 19.95x (ISBN 0-89966-158-0). Buccaneer Bks.
Still Glides the Stream. Flora Thompson. (Illus.). 1981. 16.95x (ISBN 0-19-217414-2); pap. 5.95x (ISBN 0-19-281192-4). Oxford U Pr.
Still Going Bananas. Charles Keller. 1980. 8.95 (ISBN 0-13-846832-X). P-H.
Still Going Bananas. Charles Keller. (Illus.). 48p. (gr. 3-7). 1982. pap. 3.95 (ISBN 0-13-846840-0, Pub. by Treehouse). P-H.
Still Grow the Stars. Harriette De Jarnette. 432p. (Orig.). 1986. pap. 3.95 (ISBN 0-8439-2332-6, Leisure Bks). Leisure NY.
Still Higher for His Highest. Oswald Chambers. 192p. 1970. 6.95 (ISBN 0-87508-142-8). Chr Lit.
Still Higher for His Highest. Oswald Chambers. LC 75-120048. 1970. Repr. of 1970 ed. 10.95 (ISBN 0-310-22410-1, 6494); large print o.p. 6.95 (ISBN 0-310-22417-9, 12565L). Zondervan.
Still Hour. Austin Phelps. 1979. pap. 3.95 (ISBN 0-85151-202-X). Banner of Truth.
Still House of Time. Carl S. Criswell. 1980. 5.50 (ISBN 0-8233-0325-X). Golden Quill.
Still-Hunter. Theodore S. Van Dyke. (Illus.). 390p. 1987. Repr. of 1882 ed. 21.95 (ISBN 0-936075-13-9). Gunnerman Pr.
Still Image in Keat's Poetry. R. S. Swaminathan. Ed. by James Hogg. (Romantic Reassessment ser.). 406p. (Orig.). 1981. pap. 15.00 (ISBN 3-7052-0570-6, Pub. by Salzburg Studies). Longwood Pub Group.
Still in the Image: Essays in Biblical Theology & Anthrpology. Waldemar Janzen. LC 82-83886. (Institute of Mennonite Studies: No.6). 226p. (Orig.). 1982. pap. 10.95 (ISBN 0-87303-076-1). Faith & Life.
Still Life. Miriam Borgenicht. 272p. 1986. 14.95 (ISBN 0-312-76201-1). St Martin.
Still Life. Antonia Byatt. 376p. 1986. 16.95 (ISBN 0-684-18577-6, ScribT). Scribner.
Still Life. John Byrne. (Paisley Patterns Trilogy Ser.). 44p. 1983. pap. 5.95 (ISBN 0-907540-22-8, NO.3984). Routledge Chapman & Hall.
Still Life. Richard Cobb. 9.95 (ISBN 0-318-01620-6). Salem Hse Pubs.
Still Life. Catherine Harnett. LC 83-50967. (Series Eight). 60p. 1983. pap. 4.00 (ISBN 0-931846-25-0). Wash Writers Pub.
Still Life. Diane Keaton & Marvin Heiferman. 1985. 14.95 (Fireside). S&S.
Still Life. Peter Nadin. 96p. (Orig.). 1983. pap. 5.95 (ISBN 0-934378-36-3). Tanam Pr.
Still Life. Martin J. Rosenblum. LC 82-83128. 40p. (Orig.). 1987. Limited edition. 10.00 (ISBN 0-89018-010-5); pap. 7.00 (ISBN 0-89018-009-1). Lionhead Pub.
Still Life. Susan Sanders. 32p. 1973. pap. 2.50 (ISBN 0-914946-51-X). Cleveland St Univ Poetry Ctr.
Still Life & Other Poems. Sanford Pinsker. 1975. 2.00 (ISBN 0-912678-16-X). Greenfld Rev Pr.
Still Life of the Middle Temple with Some of Its Table Talk Preceeded by Fifty Years' Reminiscences. William G. Thorpe. Ed. by Roy M. Mersky & J. Myron Jacobstein. LC 73-85733. (Classics in Legal History Reprint Ser.: Vol. 21). 392p. 1973. Repr. of 1892 ed. lib. bdg. 40.00 (ISBN 0-89941-020-0). W S Hein.
Still Life Painting. Charles Sterling. 1982. pap. 18.95 (ISBN 0-06-430096-X, IN-096). Har-Row.
Still-Life Painting from Antiquity to the Present. rev. ed. Charles Sterling. LC 78-24827. (Icon Editions Ser.). (Illus.). 320p. 1981. 27.50i (ISBN 0-06-438530-2, HarpT). Har-Row.
Still Life Painting Techniques. Adrian Ryan. 1978. 24.95 (ISBN 0-7134-0635-6, Pub. by Batsford England). David & Charles.
Still Life Painting Techniques. Ed. by Mary Suffudy. (Illus.). 144p. 1985. pap. 16.95 (ISBN 0-8230-4986-8). Watson-Guptill.
Still Life with Menu Cookbook. Mollie Katzen. (Illus.). 304p. 1988. 34.95 (ISBN 0-89815-256-9); pap. 24.95 (ISBN 0-89815-236-4). Ten Speed Pr.
Still Life with Woodpecker. Tom Robbins. 288p. (Orig.). 1981. pap. 4.50 (ISBN 0-553-25851-6). Bantam.
Still-Lifes & Nature Studies from the George J. McDonald Collection. J. J. White & G. J. McDonald. (Illus.). 20p. (Orig.). 1984. pap. 3.00 (ISBN 0-913196-45-2). Hunt Inst Botanical.
Still Modern After All These Years. Brooks Johnson & Thomas Styron. LC 82-83632. (Illus.). 48p. (Orig.). 1982. pap. 6.00 (ISBN 0-940744-40-6). Chrysler Museum.
Still Moment: Essays on the Art of Eudora Welty. Ed. by John F. Desmond. LC 78-3719. 1978. 17.50 (ISBN 0-8108-1129-4). Scarecrow.
Still More Antonyms: Together & Apart & Other Words That Are As Different in Meaning As Rise & Fall. Joan Hanson. LC 76-22421. (Joan Hanson Word Bks.). (Illus.). (gr. k-3). 1976. PLB 4.95 (ISBN 0-8225-1106-1). Lerner Pubns.
Still More Children's Liturgies. Ed. by Robert Hamma. 1988. pap. 14.95 (ISBN 0-8091-2888-8). Paulist Pr.
Still More Funny Laws. Earle Harvey & Jim Harvey. 128p. 1987. pap. 1.95 (ISBN 0-451-14720-0, Sig). NAL.
Still More Homonyms: Night & Knight & Other Words That Sound the Same but Look As Different As Ball & Bawl. Joan Hanson. LC 76-22427. (Joan Hanson Word Bks.). (Illus.). (ps-3). PLB 4.95 (ISBN 0-8225-1107-X). Lerner Pubns.
Still More Jokes. J. Michael Shannon. LC 85-27971. (Laughing Matters Ser.). (Illus.). 48p. (gr. 3-6). 1986. lib. bdg. 10.60 (ISBN 0-516-01867-1); pap. 2.95 (ISBN 0-516-41867-X). Childrens.
Still More Knock-Knocks, Limericks, & Other Silly Sayings. Laura Alden. LC 85-27975. (Laughing Matters Ser.). (Illus.). 48p. (gr. 3-6). 1986. lib. bdg. 10.60 (ISBN 0-516-01868-X). Childrens.
Still More of the World's Best Dirty Jokes. Mr. J. (Illus.). 120p. 1983. pap. 3.95 (ISBN 0-8065-0834-5, Pub. by Citadel Pr). Lyle Stuart.
Still More of the World's Best Dirty Jokes. Mr. J. pap. 2.95 (ISBN 0-345-32622-9). Ballantine.
Still More of the World's Best Dirty Jokes. (Illus.). 144p. 1981. 8.95 (ISBN 0-8065-0780-2, Pub. by Citadel Pr). Lyle Stuart.
Still More Poetry Hunter. Ed. by Barbara Fisher & Richard Spiegel. (Illus.). 36p. (Orig.). (gr. k-6). 1981. pap. 2.00 (ISBN 0-934830-24-X). Ten Penny.
Still More Prejudice. facsimile ed. Arthur B. Walkley. LC 72-111870. (Essay Index Reprint Ser). 1925. 18.00 (ISBN 0-8369-1633-6). Ayer Co Pubs.
Still More Riddles. J. Michael Shannon. LC 85-29065. (Laughing Matters Ser.). (Illus.). 48p. (gr. 3-6). 1986. lib. bdg. 10.60 (ISBN 0-516-01869-8); pap. 2.95 (ISBN 0-516-41869-6). Childrens.
Still More Seasonings for Sermons, Vol. 3. Phil Barnhart. 1986. 7.50 (ISBN 0-89536-787-4, 6805). CSS of Ohio.
Still More Single Shot Rifles. James J. Grant. 1979. 17.50 (ISBN 0-913150-41-X). Pioneer Pr.
Still More Small Poems. Valerie Worth. LC 78-11739. (Illus.). 48p. (gr. 3 up). 1978. 8.95 (ISBN 0-374-37258-6). FS&G.
Still More Snappy Answers to Stupid Questions. Al Jaffee. (Illus.). 192p. 1988. pap. 2.95 (ISBN 0-446-35068-0). Warner Bks.
Still More Stories from Grandma's Attic. Arleta Richardson. (gr. 1-7). 1980. pap. 3.50 (ISBN 0-89191-252-5). Cook.
Still More Tell Me Why. Arkady Leokum. (Illus.). (gr. k-6). 1968. 9.95 (ISBN 0-448-04458-7, G&D). Putnam Pub Group.
Still More to Tell Me. (Illus.). 480p. 9.95 (ISBN 0-317-31372-X). Putnam Pub Group.
Still More Two-Minute Mysteries. Donald J. Sobol. 128p. (gr. 6 up). 1986. pap. 2.50 (ISBN 0-590-41137-3, Apple Paperbacks). Scholastic Inc.
Still of the Night. Robert Alley. 224p. (Orig.). 1982. pap. 2.50. Ballantine.
Still Philadelphia: A Photographic History, 1890-1940. Fredric M. Miller & Morris J. Vogel. LC 82-19227. 312p. 1983. 24.95 (ISBN 0-87722-306-8). Temple U Pr.
Still Photography: The Problematic Model. Ed. by Lew Thomas & Peter D'Agostino. LC 80-85053. 1981. pap. 19.95 (ISBN 0-917986-16-4). NFS Pr.
Still Pictures. LaMond F. Beatty. Ed. by James E. Duane. LC 80-21448. (Instructional Media Library: Vol. 14). (Illus.). 112p. 1981. 23.95 (ISBN 0-87778-174-5). Educ Tech Pubns.
Still Point. Raymond Roseliep. 1979. pap. 2.50 (ISBN 0-930600-12-6). Uzzano Pr.
Still Point: Reflections on Zen & Christian Mysticism. William Johnston. LC 75-95713. 1986. pap. 9.00 (ISBN 0-8232-0861-3). Fordham.
Still Proclaiming Your Wonders: Homilies for the Eighties. Walter J. Burghardt. 256p. (Orig.). 1984. pap. 9.95 (ISBN 0-8091-2632-X). Paulist Pr.
Still River. Hal Clement. LC 86-26603. 1987. 16.95 (ISBN 0-345-32916-3). Ballantine.
Still Searching... Alfred Chalk. Ed. by Barbara Holley. Orig. Title: Rose Also Fades. (Illus.). 80p. pap. 4.50 (ISBN 0-933494-22-X). Earthwise Pubns.
Still Seeing Things. John M. Brown. LC 79-156176. 1971. Repr. of 1950 ed. lib. bdg. 25.00x (ISBN 0-8371-6119-3, BRSS). Greenwood.
Still Small Voice. Robert W. Crary. LC 86-72563. (Illus.). 180p. (Orig.). 1987. pap. 8.95 (ISBN 0-87516-584-2). DeVorss.
Still Small Voices: The Real Heroes of the Arab-Israeli Conflict. John Wallach & Janet Wallach. 192p. 1988. 16.95 (ISBN 0-15-184970-6). HarBraceJ.
Still Storm. Francoise Sagan. 208p. 1987. lib. bdg. 16.95x (ISBN 0-8161-4199-1, Large Print Bks). G K Hall.
Still Stripping the Law on Coal. C. Johnson & E. Hildebrandt. 120p. 1984. 12.00 (ISBN 0-318-20483-5); non-profit organizations 6.00 (ISBN 0-318-20484-3). Natl Resources Defense Coun.
Still Struggling: A Portrait of Low-Income Women in the 1980's. Barbara A. Stolz. LC 85-40235. 224p. 1985. 27.00x (ISBN 0-669-10930-4). Lexington Bks.
Still the Best Fringe, Profit Sharing & Pension Plans. (Special Report Ser.: No. 3). 94p. 1988. pap. 24.00 (ISBN 0-916181-02-2). Blackman Kallick Bartelstein.
Still the Dawn Calls. Peter Quinones. 176p. 1986. 12.95 (ISBN 0-317-38506-2). Todd & Honeywell.
Still the Frame Holds: Women Poets & Writers. Sheila Roberts. LC 87-823. (I. O. Evans Studies in the Philosophy & Criticism of Literature: No. 10). 128p. Date not set. lib. bdg. 19.95x (ISBN 0-89370-304-4); pap. text ed. 9.95x (ISBN 0-89370-404-0). Borgo Pr.
Still the Golden Door: The Third World Comes to America. David M. Reimers. LC 84-29273. 320p. 1985. 27.50x (ISBN 0-231-05770-9). Columbia U Pr.
Still the Golden Door: The Third World Comes to America. Ed. by David M. Reimers. 319p. 1987. pap. text ed. 14.50 (ISBN 0-231-05771-7). Columbia U Pr.
Still! The Only Investment Guide You'll Ever Need. Andrew Tobias. Date not set. write for info. S&S.
Still Time to Die. Jack Belden. (China in the 20th Century Ser). xi, 322p. 1975. Repr. of 1944 ed. lib. bdg. 32.50 (ISBN 0-306-70735-7). Da Capo.
Still to Be Born. Pat Schwiebert & Paul Kirk. 112p. 3.25 (ISBN 0-9615197-2-X). Perinatal Loss.
Still under the Thumb. Brian Burch. 1988. pap. 1.00. Samisdat.
Still Waters. Kathleen Creighton. (Loveswept Ser.: No. 176). 192p. (Orig.). 1987. pap. 2.50 (ISBN 0-553-21781-X). Bantam.
Still Waters. Phillip Keller. 160p. 1986. pap. 4.95 (ISBN 0-8499-4173-3). Word Bks.
Still Waters By. Merilu Tiemich. 120p. (Orig.). 1986. pap. 5.00 (ISBN 0-937953-01-6). Tiptoe Pub.
Still Waters: Mystery Tales of the Canals. Margaret Cornish. 192p. 1988. 39.00x (ISBN 0-7091-9625-3, Pub. by R Hale Ltd UK). State Mutual Bk.
Still Waters of the Air: Poems by Three Modern Spanish Poets. Ed. by Richard Lewis. (Illus.). 111p. 1970. 7.50 (ISBN 0-89062-122-5, Pub. by Touchstone). Pub Ctr Cult Res.
Still Worlds Collide: Philip Wylie & the End of the American Dream. Clifford P. Bendau. LC 80-10756. (Milford Ser.: Popular Writers of Today: Vol. 30). 63p. 1980. lib. bdg. 16.95x (ISBN 0-89370-144-0); pap. 7.95x (ISBN 0-89370-244-7). Borgo Pr.
Stillborn Education: A Critique of the American Research University. Paul Von Blum. (Illus.). 222p. (Orig.). 1986. lib. bdg. 25.75 (ISBN 0-8191-5509-8); pap. text ed. 13.50 (ISBN 0-8191-5510-1). U Pr of Amer.
Stillborn Republic: Social Coalitions & Parties Strategies in Greece, 1922-1936. George T. Mavrogordatos. LC 82-2781. 416p. 1983. text ed. 45.00x (ISBN 0-520-04358-8). U of Cal Pr.
Stillborn Revolution. Werner T. Angress. pap. 132.30 (ISBN 0-317-09317-7, 2000030). Bks Demand UMI.
Stillborn: The Invisible Death. John DeFrain et al. LC 85-45340. 247p. 1986. 22.00x (ISBN 0-669-11352-2); pap. 10.95 (ISBN 0-669-11354-9). Lexington Bks.
Stillman: American Consul in a Cretan War. rev. ed. G. G. Arnakis. 146p. 1966. 10.00 (ISBN 0-318-12222-7); pap. 8.00 (ISBN 0-318-12223-5). Ad Council.
Stillman: Articles & Despatches from Crete. Ed. by G. G. Arnakis. LC 76-9149. 138p. 1976. 10.00 (ISBN 0-317-34064-6); pap. 7.00 (ISBN 0-317-34065-4). Ctr Neo Hellenic.
Stillmeadow & Sugarbridge. Gladys Taber & Barbara Webster. 21.95 (ISBN 0-89190-589-8, Pub. by Am Repr). Amereon Ltd.
Stillmeadow Cook Book. Gladys Taber. 336p. 1983. pap. 9.95 (ISBN 0-940160-18-8). Parnassus Imprints.
Stillmeadow Daybook. Gladys Taber. 18.95 (ISBN 0-89190-598-7, Pub. by Am Repr). Amereon Ltd.
Stillmeadow Daybook. Gladys Taber. LC 86-45152. 288p. 1986. 14.95i (ISBN 0-06-015641-4, HarpT). Har-Row.
Stillmeadow Road. Gladys Taber. LC 83-48388. (Illus.). 288p. 1984. 15.95i (ISBN 0-06-015241-9, HarpT). Har-Row.
Stillmeadow Sampler. Gladys Taber. 288p. 1981. pap. 7.95 (ISBN 0-940160-11-0). Parnassus Imprints.
Stillmeadow Sampler. Gladys Taber. 18.95 (ISBN 0-89190-597-9, Pub. by Am Repr). Amereon Ltd.
Stillmeadow Seasons. Gladys Taber. Repr. lib. bdg. 18.95x (ISBN 0-89190-594-4, Pub. by River City Pr). Amereon Ltd.
Stillness & Shadows. John Gardner. LC 85-45592. 448p. 1986. 18.45 (ISBN 0-394-54402-1). Knopf.
Stillness at Appomattox. Bruce Catton. 512p. 1970. pap. 5.95 (ISBN 0-671-53143-3). WSP.
Stillness Heard Round the World: The End of the Great War, November 1918. Stanley Weintraub. (Illus.). 488p. 1987. pap. 9.95 (ISBN 0-19-505208-0). Oxford U Pr.
Stillness of the World Before Bach: New Selected Poems. Lars Gustafsson. Ed. by Christopher Middleton. Tr. by Yvonne L. Sandstroem & Harriet Watts. LC 87-316690. 128p. 1988. 18.95 (ISBN 0-8112-1057-X); pap. 9.95 (ISBN 0-8112-1058-8, NDP656). New Directions.
Stillness, the Dancing. Linda Bierds. 1988. 9.95 (ISBN 0-8050-0766-0). H Holt & Co.
Stillness Without Shadows. Joseph J. Juknialis. LC 86-60167. 75p. 1986. pap. 7.95 (ISBN 0-89390-081-8). Resource Pubns.
Stillroom Cookery: The Art of Preserving Foods Naturally, with Recipes, Menus & Metric Measures. Grace Firth. LC 76-28240. (Illus.). 1977. 4.95 (ISBN 0-914440-13-6). EPM Pubns.
Still's Disease: Juvenile Chronic Polyarthritis. Ed. by Malcoln Jayson. 1976. 67.50 (ISBN 0-12-381250-X). Acad Pr.
Stills from a Moving Picture. Lyle Glazier. (Paunch Ser.: No. 39). 1974. pap. 4.00 (ISBN 0-9602478-3-1). Paunch.
Stillstand des Herzens see Heartstop.
Stillwatch. Mary H. Clark. 1984. 14.95 (ISBN 0-671-46952-5). S&S.
Stillwatch. Mary Higgins Clark. 1986. pap. 4.95 (ISBN 0-440-18305-7). Dell.
Stillwater Coarse Fishing. Melvyn Russ. (Illus.). 112p. 1986. 8.95 (ISBN 0-946284-83-0, Pub. by Crowood Pr). Longwood Pub Group.
Stillwater, Minnesota's Birthplace. Patricia C. Johnston. LC 82-80726. (Illus.). 96p. 1982. 25.00 (ISBN 0-942934-01-6); pap. 9.95 (ISBN 0-942934-00-8). Johnston Pub.
Stillwater Through the Years. Robert E. Cunningham. LC 79-89768. (Illus.). 1980. Repr. of 1974 ed. text ed. 14.95x (ISBN 0-934188-05-X). Evans Pubns.
Stillwater Tragedy. Thomas B. Aldrich. LC 68-20001. (Americans in Fiction Ser.). 333p. lib. bdg. 29.00 (ISBN 0-8398-0055-X); pap. text ed. 5.95x (ISBN 0-89197-949-2). Irvington.
Stillwater Trout. John Merwin. 232p. (Orig.). 1988. pap. 13.95 (ISBN 0-317-68260-1). N Lyons Bks.
Stillwater Valley. Sue Snorf. LC 84-73410. 112p. 1985. 7.50 (ISBN 0-8233-0405-1). Golden Quill.
Stillwater Where Oklahoma Began. Robert E. Cunningham. LC 79-89767. (Illus.). 1979. Repr. of 1969 ed. text ed. 14.95x (ISBN 0-934188-04-1). Evans Pubns.
Stilt Jack. John Thompson. (House of Anansi Poetry Ser.: No. 36). 48p. (Orig.). 1978. pap. 6.95 (ISBN 0-88784-055-8, Pub. by Hse Anansi Pr Canada). U of Toronto Pr.
Stiltwalk. Joe Bowen. LC 81-90324. (Illus.). 157p. 1981. 10.95 (ISBN 0-9606834-0-2); pap. 6.95 (ISBN 0-9606834-1-0). JMB Pubns.
Stilus Artifex. C. Stace & P. V. Jones. LC 78-164453. 1971. text ed. 5.95x (ISBN 0-521-08143-2). Cambridge U Pr.
Stilwell & the American Experience in China 1911-1945. Barbara W. Tuchman. (Illus.). 1984. pap. 6.95 (ISBN 0-553-25798-6). Bantam.
Stilwell & the American Experience in China, 1911-1945. Barbara W. Tuchman. LC 77-135647. (Illus.). 1971. 21.95 (ISBN 0-02-620290-5). Macmillan.
Stilwell Papers. Joseph W. Stilwell. Ed. by Theodore H. White. LC 83-45889. Repr. of 1948 ed. 44.50 (ISBN 0-404-20247-0, D811). AMS Pr.
Stimulants & Narcotics: Medically, Philosophically, & Morally Considered. George M. Beard. Ed. by Gerald N. Grob. LC 80-1213. (Addiction in America Ser.). 1981. Repr. of 1871 ed. lib. bdg. 15.00x (ISBN 0-405-13569-6). Ayer Co Pubs.

Stochastic Differential Systems, Bad Honnef, FRG 1982: Proceedings. Ed. by M. Kohlmann & N. Christopeit. (Lecture Notes in Control & Information Sciences Ser.: Vol. 43). 377p. 1982. pap. 21.30 (ISBN 0-387-12061-0). Springer-Verlag.
Stochastic Differential Systems; Filtering & Control: Proceedings. Ed. by B. Crigelionis. (Lecture Notes in Control & Information Sciences Ser.: Vol. 25). 362p. 1981. pap. 29.00 (ISBN 0-387-10498-4). Springer-Verlag.
Stochastic Differential Systems: Proceedings. Ed. by M. Arato et al. (Lecture Notes in Control & Information Sciences Ser.: Vol. 36). 230p. 1981. pap. 19.50 (ISBN 0-387-11038-0). Springer-Verlag.
Stochastic Differential Systems, Stochastic Control Theory & Applications. Ed. by W. Fleming & P. L. Lions. (IMA Volumes in Mathematics & its Applications: Vol. 10). (Illus.). xiii, 609p. 1988. 49.80 (ISBN 0-387-96641-2). Springer-Verlag.
Stochastic Dynamic Properties of Linear Econometric Models. J. Wolters. (Lecture Notes in Economics & Mathematical Systems: Vol. 182). (Illus.). 154p. 1980. pap. 18.00 (ISBN 0-387-10240-X). Springer Verlag.
Stochastic Economics: With Applications of Stochastic Processes, Control & Programming. Gerhard Tintner & Jati K. Sengupta. 1972. 66.00 (ISBN 0-12-691650-0). Acad Pr.
Stochastic Equations for Complex Systems. A. V. Skorohod. 1987. lib. bdg. 69.00 (ISBN 90-277-2408-3, Pub. by Reidel Holland). Kluwer Academic.
Stochastic Field Theory of Behavior. K. Rainio. (Commen. Scientarum Socialium Ser.: No. 34). 250p. (Orig.). 1986. pap. 43.50x (ISBN 951-653-142-3). Coronet Bks.
Stochastic Filtering Theory. G. Kallianpur. (Applications of Mathematics Ser.: Vol. 13). 350p. 1980. 46.00 (ISBN 0-387-90445-X). Springer-Verlag.
Stochastic Functional Differential Equations. S. E. Mohammed. 256p. 1984. pap. 24.95 (ISBN 0-470-20546-6, Co-Pub. with Longman). Wiley.
Stochastic Geometry. Ed. by E. F. Harding & D. G. Kendall. LC 72-8603. (Series in Probability & Mathematical Statistics). 416p. 1974. 84.95x (ISBN 0-471-35141-5). Wiley.
Stochastic Geometry, Geometric Statistics, Stereology. Ed. by Collet's Holdings, Ltd. Staff. 1985. 63.00x (ISBN 0-317-46734-4, Pub. by Collets (UK)). State Mutual Bk.
Stochastic Integration. Michel Metivier & J. Pellaumail. LC 79-23096. (Probability & Mathematical Statistics Ser.). 1980. 44.50 (ISBN 0-12-491450-0). Acad Pr.
Stochastic Integration & Stochastic Differential Equations. K. Bichteler. (North-Holland Mathematics Studies). 1984. write for info. (North-Holland). Elsevier.
Stochastic Linear Programming. P. Kall. (Econometrics & Operations Research: Vol. 21). 120p. 1976. 26.00 (ISBN 0-387-07491-0). Springer-Verlag.
Stochastic Man. Robert Silverberg. 240p. 1981. pap. 2.25 (ISBN 0-449-13570-5, GM). Fawcett.
Stochastic Man. Robert Silverberg. 240p. 1987. pap. 3.95 (ISBN 0-446-34507-5). Warner Bks.
Stochastic Maximum Principle for Optimal Control of Diffusions. U. G. Haussmann. (Research Notes in Mathematics). 160p. 1986. pap. 31.95 (ISBN 0-470-20786-8). Wiley.
Stochastic Methods & Computer Techniques in Quantum Dynamics. Ed. by H. Mitter & L. Pittner. (Acta Physica Austriaca Ser.: Supplementum 26). (Illus.). vi, 452p. 1984. 61.00 (ISBN 0-387-81835-9). Springer-Verlag.
Stochastic Methods in Biology. Ed. by M. Kimura & G. Kallianpur. (Lecture Notes in Biomathematics Ser.: Vol. 70). vi, 229p. 1987. pap. 22.80 (ISBN 0-387-17648-9). Springer-Verlag.
Stochastic Methods in Economics & Finance. T. G. Malliaris. (Advanced Textbooks in Economics: Vol. 17). 304p. 1982. 58.00 (ISBN 0-444-86201-3, North-Holland). Elsevier.
Stochastic Methods in Mathematics & Physics: Proceedings of the Twenty-Fourth Karpacz Winter School, Karpacz, Poland, Jan 13-27, 1988. Ed. by R. Gielerak & W. Karwowski. 650p. 1988. 78.00 (ISBN 9971-50-648-3, ZB0643MP). World Scientific Pub.
Stochastic Methods in Quantum Mechanics. Gudder. (Probability & Applied Mathematics Ser.: Vol. 1). 220p. 1979. 49.75 (ISBN 0-444-00299-5, North Holland). Elsevier.
Stochastic Methods in Structural Dynamics. Ed. by G. I. Schueller & M. Shinozuke. 1988. lib. bdg. 76.50 (ISBN 90-247-3611-0, Pub. by Martinus Nijhoff). Kluwer Academic.
Stochastic Methods of Operations Research. Jurg Kohlas. LC 81-21574. 160p. 1982. 39.50 (ISBN 0-521-23899-4); pap. 16.95 (ISBN 0-521-28292-6). Cambridge U Pr.
Stochastic Model for Immunological Feedback in Carcinogenesis: Analysis & Approximations. N. Dubin. (Lecture Notes in Biomathematics Ser.: Vol. 9). 1976. pap. 14.00 (ISBN 0-387-07786-3). Springer-Verlag.
Stochastic Modeling & Analysis: A Computational Approach. Henk C. Tijms. LC 85-22696. 1986. 42.95 (ISBN 0-471-90911-4). Wiley.
Stochastic Modeling of Elementary Psychological Processes. James T. Townsend & F. Gregory Ashby. LC 82-9613. (Illus.). 560p. 1984. 77.50 (ISBN 0-521-24181-2); pap. 34.50 (ISBN 0-521-27433-8). Cambridge U Pr.
Stochastic Modeling of Ocean Dynamics. I. E. Timchenko. 320p. 1984. text ed. 135.00 (ISBN 3-7186-0231-8). Harwood Academic.
Stochastic Modeling of Ocean Fisheries Resource Management. Tracy R. Lewis. LC 81-51282. (Illus.). 118p. 1983. 30.00x (ISBN 0-295-95838-3). U of Wash Pr.
Stochastic Modelling & Control. Mark H. Davis & Richard Vinter. (Monographs on Statistics & Applied Probability). 350p. 1985. 39.95x (ISBN 0-317-17595-5, 6874, Pub. by Chapman & Hall England). Routledge Chapman & Hall.
Stochastic Modelling & Filtering: Proceedings of the IFIP-WG 7-1 Working Conference, Rome, Italy, December 10-14, 1984. Ed. by A. Germani. (Lecture Notes in Control & Information Sciences: Vol. 91). iv, 218p. 1987. pap. 35.60 (ISBN 0-387-17575-X). Springer-Verlag.
Stochastic Modelling of Social Processes. Ed. by Andreas Dickman & Peter Mitter. 1984. 39.50 (ISBN 0-12-215490-8). Acad Pr.
Stochastic Models, Estimation & Control Vol. 1. Peter S. Maybeck. LC 78-8836. (Mathematics in Science & Engineering Ser.). 1979. 39.50 (ISBN 0-12-480701-1). Acad Pr.
Stochastic Models, Estimation & Control, Vol. 2. Peter S. Maybeck. (Mathematics in Science & Engineering Ser.). 289p. 1982. 46.50 (ISBN 0-12-480702-X). Acad Pr.
Stochastic Models, Estimation & Control, Vol. 3. Peter S. Maybeck. (Mathematics in Science & Engineering Ser.). 270p. 1982. 46.50 (ISBN 0-12-480703-8). Acad Pr.
Stochastic Models for Social Processes. 3rd ed. D. J. Bartholomew. (Probability & Mathematical Statistics Ser.). 365p. 1982. 71.95x (ISBN 0-471-28040-2, Pub. by Wiley-Interscience). Wiley.
Stochastic Models for Social Processes. 2nd ed. D. J. Bartholomew. LC 73-2776. (Probability & Mathematical Statistics Ser.: Applied Probability & Statistic Section). 408p. 1974. 68.95 (ISBN 0-471-05451-8, Pub. by Wiley-Interscience). Wiley.
Stochastic Models for Spike Trains of Single Neurons. S. K. Srinivasan & G. Sampath. (Lecture Notes in Biomathematics Ser.: Vol. 16). 1977. 14.00 (ISBN 0-387-08257-3). Springer-Verlag.
Stochastic Models in Biology. Narendra Goel & Nira Richter-Dyn. 1974. 62.50 (ISBN 0-12-287460-9). Acad Pr.
Stochastic Models in Medicine & Biology: Proceedings of a Symposium Conducted by the Mathematics Research Center, 1963. John Gurland. LC 64-14509. (U. S. Army Mathematics Research Center Ser.: No. 10). pap. 102.50 (ISBN 0-317-12991-0, 2021134). Bks Demand UMI.
Stochastic Models in Operations Research: Stochastic Optimization, Vol. 2. D. P. Heyman & M. J. Sobel. 1984. text ed. 52.95 (ISBN 0-07-028632-9). McGraw.
Stochastic Models in Operations Research, Vol. 1: Stochastic Processes & Operating Characteristics. D. P. Heyman & M. J. Sobel. 1982. text ed. 52.95x (ISBN 0-07-028631-0). McGraw.
Stochastic Models in Population Genetics. Ed. by Wen-Hsiung Li. (Benchmark Papers in Genetics: Vol. 7). 1977. 76.50 (ISBN 0-12-786955-7). Acad Pr.
Stochastic Models in Reliability Theory. Ed. by S. Oskai & Y. Hatoyama. (Lecture Notes in Economics & Mathematical Systems Ser.: Vol. 235). vii, 212p. 1985. pap. 19.00 (ISBN 0-387-13888-9). Springer-Verlag.
Stochastic Models of Air Pollutant Concentration. J. Grandell. (Lecture Notes in Statistics Ser.: Vol. 30). v, 110p. 1985. pap. 13.00 (ISBN 0-387-96197-6). Springer-Verlag.
Stochastic Models of Buying Behavior. William F. Massy et al. 1970. 35.00x (ISBN 0-262-13039-4); pap. 9.95x (ISBN 0-262-63052-4). MIT Pr.
Stochastic Models of Control & Economic Dynamics. V. I. Arkin & J. V. Evstigneev. 208p. 1987. 62.00 (ISBN 0-12-062080-4); pap. cancelled (ISBN 0-12-062081-2). Acad Pr.
Stochastic Models of Migration. S. Ginsburg. Date not set. price not set. Elsevier.
Stochastic Monotonicity & Queuing Applications of Birth-Death Processes. E. A. Van Doorn. (Lecture Notes in Statistics Ser.: Vol. 4). 118p. 1981. pap. 15.00 (ISBN 0-387-90547-2). Springer-Verlag.
Stochastic Nonlinear Systems in Physics, Chemistry, & Biology. Ed. by L. Arnold & R. Lefever. (Springer Series in Synergetics: Vol. 8). (Illus.). viii, 237p. 1985. 33.00 (ISBN 0-387-10713-4). Springer-Verlag.
Stochastic Optimal Control: The Discrete Time Case. Dimitri P. Bertsekas & Steven E. Shreve. (Mathematics in Science & Engineering Ser.). 1978. 73.50 (ISBN 0-12-093260-1). Acad Pr.
Stochastic Optimal Control: Theory & Application. Robert F. Stengel. LC 86-9096. 638p. 1986. 54.95 (ISBN 0-471-86462-5). Wiley.
Stochastic Optimization. Ed. by V. I. Arkin et al. (Lecture Notes in Control & Information Sciences Ser.: Vol. 81). (Illus.). 770p. 1986. pap. 70.50 (ISBN 0-387-16659-9). Springer-Verlag.
Stochastic Optimization & Economic Models. Jati K. Sengupta. 1986. lib. bdg. 79.50 (ISBN 90-277-2301-X, Pub. by Reidel Holland). Kluwer Academic.
Stochastic Optimization Models in Finance. W. T. Ziemba. 1975. 77.00 (ISBN 0-12-780850-7). Acad Pr.
Stochastic Parameter Regression Models. Paul Newbold & Theodore Bos. (University Papers: No. 51). 1985. 6.50 (ISBN 0-8039-2425-9). Sage.
Stochastic Partial Differential Equations & Applications. Ed. by G. Da Prato & L. Turvato. (Lecture Notes in Mathematics Ser.: Vol. 1236). v, 257p. 1987. pap. 23.60 (ISBN 0-387-17211-4). Springer-Verlag.
Stochastic Phenomena & Chaotic Behavior im Complex Systems: Proceedings. UNESCO Working Group on Systems Analysis, 4th, Flattnitz, Karnten, Austria June 6-10, 1983. Ed. by P. Schuster. (Synergetics Ser.: Vol. 21). (Illus.). 270p. 1984. 45.00 (ISBN 0-387-13194-9). Springer-Verlag.
Stochastic Point Processes. S. K. Srinivasan. (Charles Griffin Series Griffins Statistical Monographs: No. 34). (Illus.). 186p. 1987. pap. 19.95 (ISBN 0-19-520587-1). Oxford U Pr.
Stochastic Point Processes & Their Applications. S. K. Srinivasan. LC 73-84664. (Griffin Statistical Monograph Ser.: No. 34). (Orig.). 1973. pap. 15.25x (ISBN 0-02-852660-0). Hafner.
Stochastic Population Models in Ecology & Epidemology. M. S. Bartlett. (Monographs in Applied Probability & Statistics). 1960. 10.95x (ISBN 0-416-52330-7, NO.6429). Routledge Chapman & Hall.
Stochastic Population Theories. D. Ludwig. (Lecture Notes in Biomathematics Ser.: Vol. 3). 1978. pap. 16.00 (ISBN 0-387-07010-9). Springer-Verlag.
Stochastic Problems in Control. American Society of Mechanical Engineers Staff. LC 68-8579. pap. 31.00 (ISBN 0-317-08716-9, 2016484). Bks Demand UMI.
Stochastic Problems in Population Genetics. T. Maruyama. LC 77-24644. (Lecture Notes in Biomathematics Ser.: Vol. 17). (Illus.). 1977. pap. text ed. 18.00 (ISBN 0-387-08349-9). Springer-Verlag.
Stochastic Process in Demography & Applications. Biswas. 350p. 1988. 24.95 (ISBN 0-470-21048-6). Wiley.
Stochastic Process: Problems & Solutions. L. Takacs. 1966. pap. 10.95x (ISBN 0-412-20340-5, 6284, Pub. by Chapman & Hall). Routledge Chapman & Hall.
Stochastic Processes. J. L. Doob. LC 52-11857. (Wiley Series in Probability & Mathematical Statistics - Probability & Mathematical Statistics Section). 654p. 1953. 60.95x (ISBN 0-471-21813-8, Pub. by Wiley-Interscience). Wiley.
Stochastic Processes. Emanuel Parzen. LC 62-9243. (Illus.). 1962. pap. 26.95x (ISBN 0-8162-6664-6). Holden-Day.
Stochastic Processes. Sheldon M. Ross. LC 82-8619. (Probability & Mathematical Statistics Ser.). 309p. 1982. text ed. 42.95 (ISBN 0-471-09942-2); solutions manual avail. (ISBN 0-471-87236-9). Wiley.
Stochastic Processes: A Survey of the Mathematical Theory. J. Lamperti. LC 77-24321. (Applied Mathematical Sciences Ser.: Vol. 23). 1977. pap. 32.50 (ISBN 0-387-90275-9). Springer-Verlag.
Stochastic Processes & Application in Biology & Medicine, Pt. 1: Theory. M. Iosifescu & P. Tautu. LC 73-77733. (Biomathematics, Ser.: Vol. 3). 331p. 1973. 42.00 (ISBN 0-387-06270-X). Springer-Verlag.
Stochastic Processes & Estimation Theory with Applications. Touraj Assefi. LC 79-17872. 304p. 1979. 37.50 (ISBN 0-471-06454-8, (JW)). Krieger.
Stochastic Processes & Filtering Theory. A. H. Jazwinski. (Mathematics in Science & Engineering Ser.: Vol. 64). 1970. 77.00 (ISBN 0-12-381550-9). Acad Pr.
Stochastic Processes & Integration. M. M. Rao. 467p. 1981. 55.00x (ISBN 90-286-0438-3, Pub. by Sijthoff & Noordhoff). Kluwer Academic.
Stochastic Processes & the Wiener Integral. LC 72-91439. (Pure & Applied Mathematics Ser.: No. 13). pap. 139.80 (ISBN 0-317-07837-2, 2055026). Bks Demand UMI.
Stochastic Processes & Their Applications. Ed. by K. Ito & T. Hida. (Lecture Notes in Mathematics Ser.: Vol. 1203). vi, 222p. pap. 18.50 (ISBN 0-387-16773-0). Springer-Verlag.
Stochastic Processes Applied to Physics & Other Related Topics: Proceeding of the Conferencein Cali, Colombia, June21-July 9, 1982. Ed. by B. Gomez et al. (ACIF Ser.: Vol. 1). xxvi, 782p. 1983. 83.00 (ISBN 9971-950-56-1). World Scientific Pub.
Stochastic Processes Formalism & Applications. Ed. by G. S. Agarwal & S. Dattagupta. (Lecture Notes in Physics Ser.: Vol. 184). 324p. 1983. pap. 21.00 (ISBN 0-387-12326-1). Springer-Verlag.
Stochastic Processes in Chemical Physics: The Master Equation. Irwin Oppenheim et al. LC 76-27843. 1977. text ed. 47.50x (ISBN 0-262-15017-4). MIT Pr.
Stochastic Processes in Classical & Quantum Systems. Ed. by S. Albeverio et al. (Lecture Notes in Physics: Vol. 262). xi, 551p. 1986. 53.90 (ISBN 0-387-17166-5). Springer-Verlag.
Stochastic Processes in Demography & Their Computer Implementation. C. J. Mode. (Biomathematics Ser.: Vol. 14). (Illus.). 430p. 1985. 90.00 (ISBN 0-387-13622-3). Springer-Verlag.
Stochastic Processes in Dynamical Problems. American Society of Mechnical Engineers Staff. LC 71-105935. pap. 30.30 (ISBN 0-317-27786-3, 2024180). Bks Demand UMI.
Stochastic Processes in Engineering Systems. 2nd ed. E. Wong & B. Hajek. (Texts in Electrical Engineering Ser.). 240p. 1985. 36.00 (ISBN 0-387-96061-9). Springer-Verlag.
Stochastic Processes in Hydrology. Vujica Yevjevich. LC 78-168495. 25.00 (ISBN 0-918334-01-2). WRP.
Stochastic Processes in Mathematical Physics & Engineering: Proceedings. Symposium in Applied Mathematics, New York, 1963. Ed. by R. Bellman. LC 64-18128. (Proceedings of Symposia in Applied Mathematics Ser.: Vol. 16). 318p. 1980. pap. 38.00 (ISBN 0-8218-1316-1, PSAPM-16). Am Math.
Stochastic Processes in Physics & Chemistry. N. G. Van Kampen. 420p. 1982. 76.75 (ISBN 0-444-86200-5, North-Holland); pap. 29.75 (ISBN 0-444-86650-7). Elsevier.
Stochastic Processes in Physics & Engineering. Ed. by S. Albeverio et al. 1988. lib. bdg. 89.00 (ISBN 90-277-2659-0, Pub. by Reidel Holland). Kluwer Academic.
Stochastic Processes in Quantum Theory & Statistical Physics: Proceedings, Marseille, France, 1981. Ed. by S. Albeverio et al. (Lecture Notes in Physics Ser.: Vol. 173). 337p. 1982. pap. 21.00 (ISBN 0-387-11956-6). Springer-Verlag.
Stochastic Processes in Queueing Theory. A. A. Borovkov. LC 75-43242. (Applications of Math Ser.: Vol. 4). (Illus.). 1976. pap. 56.00 (ISBN 0-387-90161-2). Springer-Verlag.
Stochastic Processes in Underwater Acoustics. Ed. by C. R. Baker. (Lecture Notes in Control & Information Sciences: Vol. 85). v, 205p. 1986. pap. 22.60 (ISBN 0-387-16869-9). Springer-Verlag.
Stochastic Processes-Mathematics & Physics. Ed. by S. Albeverio & P. Blanchard. (Lecture Notes in Mathematics Ser.: Vol. 1250). vi, 359p. 1987. pap. 32.90 (ISBN 0-387-17797-3). Springer-Verlag.
Stochastic Processes: Mathematics & Physics. Ed. by S. Albeverio et al. (Lecture Notes in Mathematics Ser.: Vol. 1158). vi, 257p. 1986. pap. 21.30 (ISBN 0-387-15998-3). Springer-Verlag.
Stochastic Processes with Learning Properties. Ed. by International Center for Mechanical Sciences. (CISM Pubns. Ser: Vol. 84). 151p. 1976. pap. 19.50 (ISBN 0-387-81337-3). Springer-Verlag.
Stochastic Programming. Ed. by F. Archetti et al. (Lecture Notes in Control & Information Sciences Ser.: Vol. 76). v, 285p. 1985. pap. 22.00 (ISBN 0-387-16044-2). Springer-Verlag.
Stochastic Programming. Ed. by M. A. Dempster. LC 77-92826. (Institute of Mathematics & Its Applications Conference Ser.). 1980. 4.00 (ISBN 0-12-208250-8). Acad Pr.
Stochastic Programming. Vyacheslav V. Kolbin. Tr. by Igor P. Grigoryev. (Theory & Decision Library: No. 14). 1977. lib. bdg. 34.00 (ISBN 90-277-0750-2, Pub. by Reidel Holland). Kluwer Academic.
Stochastic Programming with Multiple Objective Functions. I. M. Stancu-Minasian. 1985. lib. bdg. 59.00 (ISBN 90-277-1714-1, Pub. by Reidel Holland). Kluwer Academic.
Stochastic Programming '84, 2 Vols, Parts I & II. Ed. by R. J. Wets & A. Prekopa. (Mathematical Programming Studies: Vols. 27 & 28). 400p. 1986. Set. pap. 63.50 (ISBN 0-444-87993-5). Elsevier.
Stochastic Quantization. R. Damgaard & H. Huffel. 508p. 1987. 78.00 (ISBN 9971-50-254-2); pap. 32.00 (ISBN 9971-50-298-4). World Scientific Pub.
Stochastic Quantum Mechanics & Quantum Spacetime. Eduard Prugovecki. 1984. lib. bdg. 48.50 (ISBN 0-318-00434-8, Pub. by Reidel Holland). Kluwer Academic.
Stochastic Simulation. Brian D. Ripley. LC 86-15728. (Probabilbity & Mathematical Statistics Ser.). 237p. 1987. 32.95 (ISBN 0-471-81884-4). Wiley.
Stochastic Space-Time Models & Limit Theories. Ed. by L. Arnold & P. Kotelenz. (Mathematics & its Applications Ser.). 1985. lib. bdg. 44.00 (ISBN 90-277-2038-X, Pub. by Reidel Holland). Kluwer-Academic.
Stochastic Spatial Processes. Ed. by P. Tautu. (Lecture Notes in Mathematics Ser.: Vol. 1212). viii, 311p. 1986. pap. 27.50 (ISBN 0-387-16803-6). Springer-Verlag.
Stochastic Stability & Control. Harold J. Kushner. (Mathematics in Science & Engineering Ser.: Vol. 33). 1967. 47.00 (ISBN 0-12-430150-9). Acad Pr.
Stochastic Stability of Differential Equations. 2nd ed. R. Z. Has'Minskii. 360p. 50.00x (ISBN 90-286-0100-7, Pub. by Sijthoff & Noordhoff). Kluwer Academic.
Stochastic Storage Processes: Queues, Insurance Risk & Dams. N. U. Prabhu. (Applications of Mathematics Ser.: Vol. 15). 140p. 1980. 31.50 (ISBN 0-387-90522-7). Springer Verlag.

Stockroom Worker. Jack Rudman. (Career Examination Ser.: C-770). (Cloth bdg. avail. on request). pap. 12.00 (ISBN 0-8373-0770-8). Natl Learning.
Stocks & Bonds. Abiud Ramos-Ramos. LC 80-20002. (Illus.). 30p. 1980. pap. 3.50 (ISBN 0-8477-2637-1). U of PR Pr.
Stocks & Bonds, Profits & Losses: A Quick Look at Financial Markets. Elaine Scott. LC 84-25777. (Illus.). 96p. (gr. 7 up). 1984. lib. bdg. 11.90 (ISBN 0-531-04938-8). Watts.
Stocks, Bonds, Bills & Inflation. 1988 ed. Roger G. Ibbotson & Rex A. Sinquefield. 1988. 27.50 (ISBN 1-55623-140-7). Dow Jones-Irwin.
Stocks, Bonds, Options, Futures: Investments & Their Markets. NYIF Staff. (Illus.). 320p. 1987. 24.95 (ISBN 0-13-846718-8). NY Inst Finance.
Stocks on Target. Ken Schwab. (Illus.). 128p. 1986. 15.00 (ISBN 0-89962-537-1). Todd & Honeywell.
Stockton International Business Reports: Peoples Republic of China. InterMatrix Ltd. (Stockton International Business Reports Ser.). 100p. 1985. Looseleaf within ring binder cancelled 250.00x (ISBN 0-943818-28-1, Stockton Pr). Groves Dict Music.
Stockton International Business Reports: Egypt. InterMatrix Ltd. Staff. (Stockton International Business Reports Ser.). 100p. 1985. Looseleaf within ring binder, cancelled 250.00x (ISBN 0-943818-30-3, Stockton Pr). Groves Dict Music.
Stockton International Business Reports: Malaysia. InterMatrix Ltd. Staff. (Stockton International Business Reports Ser.). 100p. 1985. Looseleaf within ring binder, cancelled 250.00x (ISBN 0-943818-27-3, Stockton Pr). Groves Dict Music.
Stockton International Business Reports: Brazil. InterMatrix Ltd. Staff. (Stockton International Business Reports Ser.). 100p. 1985. cancelled 250.00x (ISBN 0-943818-24-9, Stockton Pr). Groves Dict Music.
Stockton International Business Reports: Indonesia. InterMatrix Ltd. Staff. (Stockton International Business Reports Ser.). 100p. 1985. Looseleaf within ring binder, cancelled 250.00x (ISBN 0-943818-22-2, Stockton Pr). Groves Dict Music.
Stockton International Business Reports: Thailand. InterMatrix Ltd. Staff. (Stockton International Business Reports Ser.). 100p. 1985. loose leaf, cancelled 250.00x (ISBN 0-943818-32-X, Stockton Pr). Groves Dict Music.
Stockton International Business Reports: India. InterMatrix Ltd. Staff. (Stockton International Business Reports Ser.). 100p. 1985. looseleaf, cancelled 250.00x (ISBN 0-943818-34-6, Stockton Pr). Groves Dict Music.
Stockton International Business Reports: Mexico. InterMatrix Ltd. Staff. (Stockton International Reports Ser.). 100p. 1985. looseleaf, cancelled 250.00x (ISBN 0-943818-35-4, Stockton Pr). Groves Dict Music.
Stockton International Business Reports: Saudi Arabia. InterMatrix Ltd. Staff. (Stockton International Business Reports Ser.). 100p. 1985. cancelled 250.00x (ISBN 0-943818-26-5, Stockton Pr). Groves Dict Music.
Stockton International Business Reports: South Korea. InterMatrix Ltd. Staff. (Stockton International Business Reports Ser.). 100p. 1985. Looseleaf within ring binder, cancelled 250.00x (ISBN 0-943818-23-0, Stockton Pr). Groves Dict Music.
Stockton Springs Vital Records 1859-1891. Ed. by Nancy S. Parsons. LC 79-55454. (Orig.). 1979. pap. 14.95x (ISBN 0-918768-02-0). Cay-Bel.
Stockton's Historic Public Schools. Robert Bonta & Horace A. Spencer. LC 81-52977. (Illus.). xii, 115p. 1981. 15.00 (ISBN 0-9607134-0-9). Stockton Unified Schl Dist.
Stockton's Stories, First Series. Frank R. Stockton. LC 74-98597. (Short Story Index Reprint Ser.). 1886. 17.00 (ISBN 0-8369-3271-4). Ayer Co Pubs.
Stockton's Stories, Second Series. Frank R. Stockton. LC 74-98597. (Short Story Index Reprint Ser.). 1886. 18.00 (ISBN 0-8369-3172-6). Ayer Co Pubs.
Stockwell Guide for Technical & Vocational Writing. 2nd ed. Richard E. Stockwell. LC 81-3675. (Engineering Technology Ser.). 354p. 1982. pap. text ed. write for info. (ISBN 0-201-07154-1); write for info. wkbk. (ISBN 0-201-07155-X). Addison-Wesley.
Stockyards. Rod Bellville & Cheryl W. Bellville. LC 83-18839. (Carolrhoda Photo Bks.). (Illus.). 32p. (gr. 1-5). 1984. PLB 9.95 (ISBN 0-87614-224-2). Carolrhoda Bks.
Stoddart Restaurant Guide to Toronto 1988. Dan Liebman. 1988. pap. 5.95 (ISBN 0-7736-7132-3). Longman Finan.
Stoddert's War: Naval Operations Against France, 1798-1801. Michael Palmer. Ed. by William Still, Jr. (Studies in Maritime History). 400p. 24.95 (ISBN 0-87249-499-3). U of SC Pr.
Stoff-und Motivgeschichte der Deutschen Literatur. 3rd ed. Franz A. Schmitt. 1976. 49.60x (ISBN 3-11-006506-1). De Gruyter.
Stogdill's Handbook of Leadership. 2nd rev. ed. Bernard M. Bass. (Illus.). 1057p. 1981. text ed. 45.00 (ISBN 0-02-901820-X). Free Pr.
Stoic. Theodore Dreiser. 1981. pap. 3.95 (ISBN 0-451-51549-8, CE1549, Sig Classics). NAL.
Stoic & Epicurean. Robert D. Hicks. LC 61-13090. 1962. Repr. of 1910 ed. 13.00x (ISBN 0-8462-0199-2). Russell.
Stoic, Christian & Humanist. Gilbert Murray. LC 75-99712. (Essay Index Reprint Ser.). 1940. 17.00 (ISBN 0-8369-1363-9). Ayer Co Pubs.
Stoic Comedians: Flaubert, Joyce & Beckett. Hugh Kenner. (Illus.). 1974. pap. 5.95x (ISBN 0-520-02584-9). U of Cal Pr.
Stoic Creed. William L. Davidson. Ed. by Gregory Vlastos. LC 78-19341. (Morals & Law in Ancient Greece Ser.). 1979. Repr. of 1907 ed. lib. bdg. 23.00x (ISBN 0-405-11535-0). Ayer Co Pubs.
Stoic Logic. Benson Mates. LC 53-9918. (California University Publications in Philosophy: Vol. 26). pap. 39.00 (ISBN 0-317-10250-8, 2021174). Bks Demand UMI.
Stoic Moral Philosphies: Their Counsel for Today. Ben F. Kimpel. LC 84-14894. 329p. 1985. 19.50 (ISBN 0-8022-2472-5). Philos Lib.
Stoic Philosophy. J. M. Rist. LC 79-85736. 1969. pap. 15.95 (ISBN 0-521-29201-8). Cambridge U Pr.
Stoic Philosophy of Life. Keith Campbell. LC 86-13351. 216p. (Orig.). 1986. lib. bdg. 22.50 (ISBN 0-8191-5529-2); pap. text ed. 13.00 (ISBN 0-8191-5530-6). U Pr of Amer.
Stoic Philosophy of Seneca. Moses Hadas. 15.25 (ISBN 0-8446-1214-6). Peter Smith.
Stoic Philosophy of Seneca: Essays & Letters. Lucius Annaeus Seneca. Ed. by Moses Hadas. 1968. pap. 6.95 (ISBN 0-393-00459-7, Norton Lib). Norton.
Stoichedon Style in Greek Inscriptions. Reginald P. Austin. LC 72-7884. (Greek History Ser). Repr. of 1938 ed. 19.00 (ISBN 0-405-04778-9). Ayer Co Pubs.
Stoichiometry & Its Influence on the Physical Properties of Crystalline Compounds. Ed. by Yu M. Popov. (Proceedings of the Lebedev Physics Institute of the Academy of Sciences of the U. S. S. R. Ser.: Vol. 177). 303p. 1988. text ed. 92.00 (ISBN 0-941743-21-5). Nova Sci Pubs.
Stoichiometry & Thermodynamics of Metallurgical Processes. Y. K. Rao. (Illus.). 800p. 1985. 57.50 (ISBN 0-521-25856-1). Cambridge U Pr.
Stoiciens: 1, Cleanthe; 2, Les Doctrines; 3, Les Directeurs de Conscience. 1512p. 45.00 (ISBN 0-686-56575-4). French & Eur.
Stoicism. William W. Capes. 1976. lib. bdg. 59.95 (ISBN 0-8490-2669-5). Gordon Pr.
Stoicism. S. George Stock. LC 75-38367. (Select Bibliographies Reprint Ser.). Repr. of 1908 ed. 13.00 (ISBN 0-8369-6784-4). Ayer Co Pubs.
Stoicism. St. George Stock. LC 71-101053. 1969. Repr. of 1908 ed. 16.50x (ISBN 0-8046-0718-4, Pub. by Kennikat). Assoc Faculty Pr.
Stoicism & the Epicurean Pursuit of Pleasure. William De Witt. (Illus.). 129p. 1988. 77.75 (ISBN 0-89920-181-4). Am Inst Psych.
Stoicorum Veterum Fragmenta, 4 vols. J. Von Arnim. (Classical Studies Ser.). 1054p. (Lat. & Gr.). 1986. Repr. of 1903 ed. Set. lib. bdg. 177.00 (ISBN 0-89197-950-6); Vol. 1 & 2. lib. bdg. 88.50 (ISBN 0-8290-1775-5); Vol. 3 & 4. lib. bdg. 88.50 (ISBN 0-8290-1776-3). Irvington.
Stoics. Ed. by John M. Rist. LC 75-27932. (Major Thinkers Ser.: No. 1). 1978. pap. 11.95x (ISBN 0-520-03675-1). U of Cal Pr.
Stoics & Sceptics. E. R. Bevan. 152p. 1980. Repr. of 1913 ed. 12.50 (ISBN 0-89005-364-2). Ares.
Stoics & Sceptics. Edwyn R. Bevan. Ed. by Gregory Vlastos. LC 78-15852. (Morals & Law in Ancient Greece Ser.). 1979. Repr. of 1913 ed. lib. bdg. 14.00x (ISBN 0-405-11530-X). Ayer Co Pubs.
Stoics, Epicureans & Skeptics. Edward Zeller. 75.00 (ISBN 0-8490-1125-6). Gordon Pr.
Stoke-by-Clare Cartulary I. Ed. by Christopher Harper-Bill & Richard Mortimer. (Suffolk Charters Ser.: No. IV). 150p. 1982. 36.00 (ISBN 0-85115-165-5, Pub. by Boydell & Brewer). Longwood Pub Group.
Stoke-by-Clare Cartulary II. Ed. by Christopher Harper-Bill & Richard Mortimer. (Suffolk Charters Ser.: No. V). 255p. 1983. 35.00 (ISBN 0-85115-179-5, Pub. by Boydell & Brewer). Longwood Pub Group.
Stoke-by-Clare Cartulary III. Christopher Harper-Bill & Richard Mortimer. 96p. 1984. 36.00 (ISBN 0-85115-198-1, Pub. by Boydell & Brewer). Longwood Pub Group.
Stokely Webster: Paintings Nineteen Twenty-Three to Nineteen Eighty-Four. Harry Rand. Ed. by Gary R. Libby. LC 85-60099. (Illus.). 104p. (Orig.). 1985. pap. 5.00 (ISBN 0-933053-00-2). Museum Art Sciences.
Stokers & Pokers. Francis B. Head. LC 69-10757. Repr. of 1849 ed. 25.00x (ISBN 0-678-05601-3). Kelley.
Stokers & Pokers: Or the London & North-Western Railway, the Electronic Telegraph & the Railway Clearing House. new ed. Francis B. Head. 278p. 1968. 26.00x (ISBN 0-7146-1440-8, F Cass Co). Biblio Dist.
Stokes Carson: Twentieth-Century Trading on the Navajo Reservation. Willow Roberts. LC 86-19207. 246p. 1987. 24.95x (ISBN 0-8263-0916-X); pap. 13.95 (ISBN 0-8263-0917-8). U of NM Pr.
Stokes County, N. C. Deeds, 1787-1797, Vols. 1-2. 200p. 1985. pap. 22.50 (ISBN 0-89308-556-1). Southern Hist Pr.
Stokes County, N. C., Wills, 1790-1864, Vols. 1-4. W. D. Abster. 181p. 1985. pap. 21.50 (ISBN 0-89308-557-X). Southern Hist Pr.
Stokey. Helen B. King. (Illus.). Date not set. pap. 4.95 (ISBN 0-9615366-1-6). King ME.
Stol Dolgoe Vozvrashchenie. Ester Markish. LC 84-60572. (Illus.). 320p. (Orig., Rus.). 1987. pap. 17.50 (ISBN 0-89830-084-3). Russica Pubs.
Stole Patterns. Jeff Wedge. 90p. 1985. pap. 8.95 (ISBN 0-8192-1373-X). Morehouse.
Stolen Air. Niall Quinn. 200p. 1988. 19.95 (ISBN 0-86327-157-X, Pub. by Wolfhound Pr Ireland); pap. 8.95 (ISBN 0-86327-158-8, Pub. by Wolfhound Pr Ireland). Irish Bks Media.
Stolen & Contaminated Poems. James Laughlin. 60p. 1985. text ed. 60.00 (ISBN 0-918824-47-8). Turkey Pr.
Stolen & Surreptitious Copies: A Comparative Study of Shakespeare's Bad Quartos. Alfred Hart. LC 77-3160. 1942. lib. bdg. 49.00 (ISBN 0-8414-4913-9). Folcroft.
Stolen Appaloosa & Other Indian Stories. Paul Levitt & Elissa Guralnick. (Illus.). 96p. (Orig.). (gr. 4 up). 1988. 12.95 (ISBN 0-917665-19-8). Bookmakers Guild.
Stolen Biography. 2nd ed. Szymon Szechter. Tr. by Frances Carroll & Nina Karsov. LC 84-70938. (Illus.). 1985. 12.95 (ISBN 0-907652-16-6). Dufour.
Stolen Ecstasy. Janelle Taylor. 1985. pap. 3.95 (ISBN 0-8217-1621-2). Zebra.
Stolen Faces. Michael Bishop. LC 76-26262. 176p. 1977. 15.00 (ISBN 0-06-010362-0). Ultramarine Pub.
Stolen Fire. Lyubomir Levchev. Tr. by Ewald Osers from Bulgarian. LC 85-82112. 105p. (Orig.). 1986. pap. 10.00 (ISBN 0-948259-04-3, Pub. by Forest Bks London). Three Continents.
Stolen Flower. Philip Carlo. 224p. 1986. 16.95 (ISBN 0-525-24484-0). Dutton.
Stolen Flower. Philip Carlo. 256p. 1988. pap. 3.50 (ISBN 0-671-64862-4). PB.
Stolen Goods. Susan Dworkin. LC 86-28615. 272p. 1987. 16.95 (ISBN 0-937858-90-0); pap. 3.95. Newmarket.
Stolen Goods. Susan Dworkin. LC 86-28615. 1988. pap. 4.50 (ISBN 1-55704-020-6). Newmarket.
Stolen Heritage: The Lost Becerra Grant in Texas. Abel Rubio. 256p. 1986. 14.95 (ISBN 0-89015-548-8). Eakin Pr.
Stolen Horse: Animal Rescue Farm, No. 1. Sharon M. Hart. 112p. (gr. 2-5). 1988. 2.50 (ISBN 0-590-41501-8). Scholastic Inc.
Stolen House. Jack Remick. LC 79-91912. (Fiction Ser.). 168p. (Orig.). 1980. pap. 4.95 (ISBN 0-917530-13-6). Pig Iron Pr.
Stolen Images. Ulli Beier. 64p. 1976. pap. 3.95x (ISBN 0-521-20901-3). Cambridge U Pr.
Stolen Kisses. Barbara Jacobs. (Heartlines Ser.: No. 3). (Orig.). (gr. 6 up). 1986. pap. 2.50 (ISBN 0-440-97734-7, LFL). Dell.
Stolen Kisses. Elizabeth Reynolds. (Sweet Dreams Ser.: No. 111). 144p. (Orig.). (YA) (gr. 7-12). 1986. pap. 2.50 (ISBN 0-553-25726-9). Bantam.
Stolen Lake. Joan Aiken. (gr. k-6). 1988. pap. 3.25 (ISBN 0-440-40037-6, YB). Dell.
Stolen Lake: A Novel. Joan Aiken. LC 81-5015. 256p. (YA) (gr. 7 up). 1981. 10.95 (ISBN 0-385-28982-0). Delacorte.
Stolen Law. Anne Mason. LC 85-45274. 224p. (YA) (gr. 7 up). 1986. 12.25i (ISBN 0-06-024118-7); PLB 11.89 (ISBN 0-06-024119-5). HarpJ.
Stolen Lightening: The Social Theory of Magic. Daniel L. O'Keefe. 600p. 1982. 27.50x (ISBN 0-8264-0059-0). Continuum.
Stolen Lightning: The Social Theory of Magic. Daniel L. O'Keefe. LC 83-3546. 608p. 1983. pap. 9.95 (ISBN 0-394-71634-5, Vin). Random.
Stolen Mind: The Slow Disappearance of Ray Doernberg. Myrna Doernberg. (Illus.). 224p. 1986. 14.95 (ISBN 0-912697-32-6). Algonquin Bks.
Stolen Mirror. Lidia Postma. LC 75-43888. (Illus.). 32p. (ps-3). 1976. McGraw.
Stolen Moments. Terri Herrington. (Candlelight Ecstasy Ser.: No. 489). (Orig.). 1987. pap. 2.25 (ISBN 0-440-18505-X). Dell.
Stolen Moments. Michael Jones. (Illus.). 143p. 1984. write for info. ltd. ed. (ISBN 0-89904-015-2). Crumb Elbow Pub.
Stolen Moments. Penelope Karageorge. 576p. 1988. pap. 4.50 (ISBN 1-55817-095-2). Windsor NY.
Stolen Moments. John Preston. (Mission of Alex Kane Ser.: Vol. 4). 120p. (Orig.). 1985. pap. 4.95 (ISBN 0-932870-71-6). Alyson Pubns.
Stolen Moments: Conversations with Contemporary Musicians. Tom Schabel. 220p. 1988. 19.95 (ISBN 0-918226-17-1); pap. 13.95 (ISBN 0-918226-22-8). Acrobat.
Stolen Paintings. Wolfgang Ecke. (Illus.). (gr. 5-9). 1981. 9.95 (ISBN 0-13-846865-6). P-H.
Stolen Paintings. Wolfgang Ecke. (Illus.). 144p. (gr. 5up). 1985. pap. 5.95 (ISBN 0-13-846916-4). P-H.
Stolen Past. John Knowles. 224p. 1984. pap. 3.50 (ISBN 0-345-31590-1). Ballantine.
Stolen Pay Train. Nicholas Carter. LC 74-15733. (Popular Culture in America Ser.). 128p. 1975. Repr. 13.00 (ISBN 0-405-06368-7). Ayer Co Pubs.
Stolen Pony. Glenn Rounds. 96p. (gr. 4-6). pap. 2.25 (ISBN 0-590-32297-4). Scholastic Inc.
Stolen Princess: A Northwest Indian Legend. Willard N. Morss & Janet M. Herren. LC 83-82920. (Illus.). 79p. (Orig.). (gr. 4-8). 1983. pap. 8.95 (ISBN 0-9613025-0-X). J M Herren.
Stolen Property Returned! John F. Avanzini. 116p. pap. 6.00 (ISBN 0-941117-03-0). HIM Publish.
Stolen Secrets. Marilyn Austin. (Orig.). 1981. pap. 1.95 (ISBN 0-8439-8045-1, Tiara Bks). Leisure NY.
Stolen Souls. Jeffrey Sackett. 320p. (Orig.). 1987. pap. 3.95 (ISBN 0-553-26937-2). Bantam.
Stolen Spring. Louisa Rawlings. 480p. (Orig.). 1988. pap. 3.95 (ISBN 0-445-20458-3, Pub. by Popular Lib). Warner Bks.
Stolen Spring. Hans Scherfig. Tr. by Frank Hugus from Danish. LC 82-82674. 196p. (Orig.). 1986. lib. bdg. 15.95 (ISBN 0-940242-20-6); pap. 7.95 (ISBN 0-940242-00-1). Fjord Pr.
Stolen Stallion. Max Brand. 1979. pap. 2.50 (ISBN 0-671-41581-6). PB.
Stolen Steers: A Tale of the Big Thicket. Bill Brett. LC 76-51651. (Illus.). 116p. 1977. 12.95 (ISBN 0-89096-026-7). Tex A&M Univ Pr.
Stolen Stories. Steve Katz. LC 83-27410. 149p. 1984. 12.95 (ISBN 0-914590-84-7); pap. 6.95 (ISBN 0-914590-85-5). Fiction Coll.
Stolen Story & Other Newspaper Stories. Jesse L. Williams. LC 76-98604. (Short Story Index Reprint Ser.). 1899. 18.00 (ISBN 0-8369-3178-5). Ayer Co Pubs.
Stolen Sun. K. Chukovsky. Tr. by Dorian Rottenberg. 18p. 1983. pap. 3.95 (ISBN 0-8285-2953-1, Pub. by Malysh Pubs USSR). Imported Pubns.
Stolen White Eagle. Pierce Mackenzie. (T. G. Horne Ser.: No. 1). 192p. 1987. pap. 2.50 (ISBN 0-451-14711-1, Sig). NAL.
Stolen White Elephant. Mark Twain. (Illus.). (gr. 4-8). 1988. 12.95 (ISBN 0-9587845-2-3). Publishers Group.
Stolen White Elephant, Etc. Samuel L. Clemens. LC 70-121530. (Short Story Index Reprint Ser). 1882. 17.00 (ISBN 0-8369-3486-5). Ayer Co Pubs.
Stolen Writings: Blake's "Milton", Joyce's "Ulysses", & the Nature of Influence. Murray McArthur. Ed. by Litz A. Walton. LC 87-28566. (Studies in Modern Literature: No. 87). 188p. 1988. 44.95 (ISBN 0-8357-1846-8). UMI Res Pr.
Stolen Years. Sara Zyskind. LC 81-1953. (Books for Adults & Young Adults). 288p. (gr. 6 up). 1981. 11.95 (ISBN 0-8225-0766-8, AACR2). Lerner Pubns.
Stolen Years. Sara Zyskind. 240p. 1983. pap. 3.50 (ISBN 0-451-14339-6, AE2011, Sig). NAL.
Stolia. Wilfredo Garrido, Jr. 169p. (Orig.). 1984. pap. 6.25x (ISBN 971-10-0109-8, Pub. by New Day Philippines). Cellar.
Stolypin: Russia's Last Great Reformer. Alexander V. Zenkovsky. Tr. by Margaret Patoski from Rus. 146p. 1986. 25.00 (ISBN 0-940670-25-9). Kingston Pr.
Stoma Therapy. Rainer Winkler. Tr. by Pola Nawrocki from Ger. (Illus.). 104p. 1985. text ed. 47.50 (ISBN 0-86577-215-0). Thieme Med Pubs.
Stomach. Ed. by L. Van der Reis. (Frontiers of Gastrointestinal Research Ser.: Vol. 6). (Illus.). xii, 188p. 1980. 61.50 (ISBN 3-8055-3071-4). S Karger.
Stomach Diseases: Current Status. Ed. by Van Maercke et al. (International Congress Ser.: Vol. 555). 434p. 1981. 127.00 (ISBN 0-444-90228-7, Excerpta Medica). Elsevier.
Stomach Ulcers & Acidity. Leonard Mervyn. 64p. (Orig.). 1986. pap. cancelled (ISBN 0-909911-52-5). Inner Tradit.
Stomach Ulcers & Acidity: Practical Measures to Help You Avoid & Treat These Painful Stomach Disorders. Leonard Mervyn. (Science of Life Ser.). 128p. (Orig.). 1988. pap. 2.99 (ISBN 0-909911-17-7, Pub. by Thorsons (England)). Sterling.
Stomata. E. Stephen Martin et al. 1985. 65.00x (ISBN 0-317-43662-7, Pub. by Arnold-Heineman). State Mutual Bk.
Stomata. C. Willmer. 166p. 1983. pap. 19.95 (ISBN 0-470-20396-X, Co-Pub. with Longman). Wiley.
Stomata. Colin M. Willmer. LC 82-6568. (Illus.). 166p. 1983. 14.95 (ISBN 0-582-44632-5). Wiley.
Stomatal Function. Ed. by Eduardo Zeiger et al. (Illus.). 520p. 1987. 65.00x (ISBN 0-8047-1347-2). Stanford U Pr.
Stomatal Physiology. Ed. by P. G. Jarvis & T. A. Mansfield. (Society for Experimental Biology Seminar Ser.: No. 8). 200p. 1981. text ed. 54.50 (ISBN 0-521-23683-5); pap. text ed. 22.95 (ISBN 0-521-28151-2). Cambridge U Pr.
Stomatognathic System. new ed. Mongini. (Illus.). 360p. 1984. text ed. 74.00 (ISBN 0-86715-146-3). Quint Pub Co.
Stomatopod Crustacea of the Western Atlantic. Raymond B. Manning. LC 68-30263. (Studies in Tropical Oceanography Ser: No. 8). 1969. 20.00x (ISBN 0-87024-089-7). U Miami Marine.
Stomping the Goyim. Michael Disend. LC 73-77370. 1969. 5.00 (ISBN 0-685-79019-3). Small Pr Dist.
Stonan! Chris Crutcher. (gr. k-12). 1988. pap. 3.25 (ISBN 0-440-20080-6, LFL). Dell.
Stone. Henry Gould. (Illus.). 46p. (Orig.). 1979. pap. 4.50 (ISBN 0-914278-23-1). Copper Beech.
Stone. James Tucker. (Orig.). 1981. pap. 2.95. Zebra.
Stone. John Unterecker. LC 76-26078. 64p. 1977. pap. 4.95 (ISBN 0-8248-0492-9). UH Pr.

Stonehenge & Its Environs. Royal Commission on Historical Monuments. (RCHM Inventory Vols.). (Illus.). 50p. 1979. pap. 15.00x (ISBN 0-85224-379-0, Pub. by Edinburgh U Pr Scotland). Columbia U Pr.
Stonehenge Complete. Christopher Chippindale. LC 83-70803. (Paperback Ser.). (Illus.). 300p. 1987. pap. 24.95 (ISBN 0-8014-9451-6). Cornell U Pr.
Stonehenge Decoded. Gerald S. Hawkins. 202p. 1978. pap. 4.50 (ISBN 0-385-28974-X, Delta). Dell.
Stonehenge Decoded. Gerald S. Hawkins. (Dorset Press Reprints Ser.). (Illus.). 240p. 1988. 18.95 (ISBN 0-88029-147-8). Hippocrene Bks.
Stonehenge People: An Exploration of Life in Neolithic Britain, 4700-2000 B.C. Rodney Castleden. (Illus.). 224p. 1987. text ed. 25.00 (ISBN 0-7102-0968-1, Pub. by Routledge UK). Routledge Chapman & Hall.
Stonehenge: The Indo-European Heritage. Leon E. Stover & Bruce Kraig. LC 77-25255. 224p. 1978. 29.95x (ISBN 0-88229-482-2); pap. 15.95x (ISBN 0-88229-612-4). Nelson-Hall.
Stonehenge...A Closer Look. Bonnie Gaunt. LC 79-51777. (Illus.). 236p. 1980. pap. 4.95 (ISBN 0-9602688-0-4). B Gaunt.
Stoneposts in the Sunset. Romeyn Berry. 1950. 5.00 (ISBN 0-87282-011-4). Am Life Foun.
Stoner. John E. Williams. LC 87-31948. (Reprint Ser.). 288p. 1988. pap. 11.95 (ISBN 1-55728-029-0). U of Ark Pr.
Stoner McTavish. Sarah Dreher. LC 85-60065. 200p. 1985. pap. 7.95 (ISBN 0-934678-06-5). New Victoria Pubs.
Stones. Janet Hickman. LC 76-11037. (Illus.). 116p. (gr. 3-6). 1976. 9.95 (ISBN 0-02-743760-4). Macmillan.
Stones. Erica Pedretti. Tr. by Judith Black from Ger. (Swiss Library). 220p. (Orig.). 1982. pap. 7.95 (ISBN 0-7145-3942-2). Riverrun NY.
Stones: A Litnay. James Chichetto. (Illus.). 20p. 1980. pap. 4.00 (ISBN 0-939622-06-8). Four Zoas Night.
Stones & Bones. Lisa Yount. 82p. (Orig.). 1986. pap. 4.95 (ISBN 0-9617366-0-7). Half Lump Pr.
Stones & Bones, Cemetery Records of Prince George's County Maryland. Ed. & illus. by Jean A. Sargent. LC 84-80257. (Illus.). 674p. 1984. 28.00. Prince Georges County Gen Soc.
Stones & Other Works. Alan Magee. (Illus.). 64p. 1987. pap. 16.95 (ISBN 0-8109-2341-6). Abrams.
Stones & Poets: An Anthology of Poetry. 2nd ed. Ed. by Patricia C. Groth & Kitty Druck. LC 80-66853. (Illus.). 90p. (Orig.). 1981. pap. 7.00 (ISBN 0-937158-01-1). Del Valley.
Stones & the Scriptures. Edwin Yamauchi. 1981. pap. 5.95 (ISBN 0-8010-9916-1). Baker Bk.
Stones by the River. Henry F. Flowers. 1988. 5.95 (ISBN 0-533-07455-X). Vantage.
Stones: Concepts About Print Test. Marie Clay. (Orig.). (ps-2). 1980. pap. text ed. 2.75x (00556). Heinemann Ed.
Stones Cry Out: A Cambodian Childhood, 1975-1980. Molyda Szymusiak. Tr. by Linda Coverdale from Fr. 1986. 17.95 (ISBN 0-8090-8844-4). Hill & Wang.
Stones Cry Out: A Cambodian Childhood, 1975-1980. Molyda Szymusiak. Tr. by Linda Coverdale from Fr. 256p. 1987. pap. 8.95 (ISBN 0-8090-1534-X). Hill & Wang.
Stones Cry Out: Sweden's Response to Persecution of Jews 1933-1945. Steven Koblik. 1988. 20.95 (ISBN 0-89604-118-2); pap. 13.95 (ISBN 0-89604-119-0). Holocaust Pubns.
Stones: Eighteenth Century Scottish Gravestones. Betty Willsher & Doreen Hunter. LC 78-62268. (Illus.). 128p. 1979. pap. 7.95 (ISBN 0-8008-7017-4). Taplinger.
Stones for Ibarra. Harriet Doerr. LC 83-47861. 215p. 1984. 16.95 (ISBN 0-670-19203-1). Viking.
Stones for Ibarra. Harriet Doerr. 214p. 1985. pap. 6.95 (ISBN 0-14-007562-3). Penguin.
Stones in a Glass House: CFCs & the Ozone Depletion Controversy. 100p. 1988. 35.00. IRRC Inc DC.
Stones in the Brook. Brian Morris. 53p. 1985. 25.00x (ISBN 0-85088-790-9, Pub. by Gomer Pr). State Mutual Bk.
Stones in the Lake. John M. Bennett. (Illus.). 20p. (Orig.). 1987. pap. 3.00 (ISBN 0-935350-14-4). Luna Bisonte.
Stones of Aran: Pilgrimage. Tim Robinson. (Illus.). 264p. 1986. 27.95 (ISBN 0-946640-10-6, Pub. by Wolfhound Pr Ireland); pap. 16.95 (ISBN 0-946640-12-2). Irish Bks Media.
Stones of Assyria. Cyril J. Gadd. LC 83-45767. Repr. of 1936 ed. 110.00 (ISBN 0-404-20104-0). AMS Pr.
Stones of Athens. R. E. Wycherley. LC 77-72142. (Illus.). 1977. 47.00 (ISBN 0-691-03553-9); pap. 16.50x (ISBN 0-691-10059-4). Princeton U Pr.
Stones of Bau. Nicholas Wollaston. 228p. 1988. 19.95 (ISBN 0-241-12041-1, Pub. by Hamish Hamilton). David & Charles.
Stones of Chile. Pablo Neruda. Tr. by Dennis Maloney from Span. 1987. 9.50 (ISBN 0-934834-01-6). White Pine.
Stones of Empire: The Buildings of the Raj. Jan Morris. (Illus.). 1984. 25.00x (ISBN 0-19-211449-2). Oxford U Pr.
Stones of Fire. Isobel Kuhn. 1951. pap. 3.95 (ISBN 9971-972-00-X). OMF Bks.
Stones of Florence. Mary McCarthy. LC 59-10257. (Illus.). 138p. 1976. 39.95 (ISBN 0-15-185079-8). HarBraceJ.
Stones of Florence. Mary McCarthy. LC 64-49015. 230p. 1963. pap. 5.95 (ISBN 0-15-685080-X, Harv). HarBraceJ.
Stones of Florence. Mary McCarthy. (Illus.). 1987. pap. 19.95 (ISBN 0-15-685081-8, Harv); text ed. 49.95 (ISBN 0-317-64159-X). HarBraceJ.
Stones of Silence: Journeys in the Himalaya. George B. Schaller. (Illus.). 1980. 15.95 (ISBN 0-670-67140-1). Viking.
Stones of Silence: Journeys in the Himalaya. George B. Schaller. (Illus.). xii, 292p. 1988. pap. 14.95 (ISBN 0-226-73646-6). U of Chicago Pr.
Stones of the Abbey. Fernand Pavillon. 1976. pap. 1.95 (ISBN 0-380-00737-1, 30106, Bard). Avon.
Stones of the Abbey. Fernand Pouillon. Tr. by Edward Gillot from Fr. LC 84-22440. 228p. 1985. pap. 7.95 (ISBN 0-15-685100-8, Harv). HarBraceJ.
Stones of the Sky. Pablo Neruda. Tr. by James Nolan from Span. LC 87-71140. 80p. (Orig.). 1987. 15.00 (ISBN 1-55659-006-7); pap. 9.00 (ISBN 1-55659-007-5). Copper Canyon.
Stones of the Wall. Dai Houying. Tr. by Frances Wood. 310p. 1986. 15.95 (ISBN 0-312-76215-1). St Martin.
Stones of Venice. John Ruskin. Ed. by J. G. Links. (Quality Paperbacks Ser.). 256p. 1985. pap. 9.95. Da Capo.
Stones: Poems by Daisy Aldan. Daisy Aldan. (Illus.). 1973. 4.95. Folder Edns.
Stones Refuse Their Peace. Mary Balazs. (Poetry Chapbooks: No. 2). 32p. 1979. pap. 2.50 (ISBN 0-913282-16-2). Seven Woods Pr.
Stones River: Bloody Winter in Tennessee. James L. McDonough. LC 80-11580. 286p. 1980. 18.95 (ISBN 0-87049-301-9); pap. 9.95 (ISBN 0-87049-373-6). U of Tenn Pr.
Stone's River: Turning Point of the Civil War. Wilson J. Vance. 1982. pap. text ed. 12.50 (ISBN 0-87556-584-0). Saifer.
Stones: Their Collection, Identification, & Uses. R. V. Dietrich. LC 79-24760. (Geology Ser.). (Illus.). 145p. 1980. pap. text ed. 11.95 (ISBN 0-7167-1139-7). W H Freeman.
Stone's Throw. Jennifer Stone. 200p. 1987. 20.00 (ISBN 1-55643-032-9); pap. 9.95 (ISBN 1-55643-031-0). North Atlantic.
Stone's Throw: Travels from Africa in Six Decades. Genesta Hamilton. (Illus.). 374p. 1987. 34.95 (ISBN 0-09-165910-8, Pub. by Century Hutchinson). David & Charles.
Stones Unturned. Napoleon St. Cyr. LC 67-8221. 1967. 4.00 (ISBN 0-910380-01-5). Cider Mill.
Stonewalkers. Vivien Alcock. LC 82-13956. 192p. (gr. 4-6). 1983. pap. 12.95 (ISBN 0-385-29233-3). Delacorte.
Stonewall. Jean Fritz. (Illus.). (gr. 3-7). 1979. 10.95 (ISBN 0-399-20698-1, Putnam). Putnam Pub Group.
Stonewall Brigade. James I. Robertson, Jr. LC 63-9648. (Illus.). xiii, 272p. 1963. pap. 9.95 (ISBN 0-8071-0396-9). La State U Pr.
Stonewall Brigade. Frank Slaughter. 749p. 1975. 18.95 (ISBN 0-317-52556-5). Thorndike Pr.
Stonewall Jackson & the American Civil War. abr. ed. G. F. Henderson. (Illus.). 15.50 (ISBN 0-8446-1232-4). Peter Smith.
Stonewall Jackson & the American Civil War. G. F. Henderson. (Quality Paperbacks Ser.). 740p. 1988. pap. 14.95 (ISBN 0-306-80318-6). Da Capo.
Stonewall Jackson's Way. John Wayland. 1984. 45.00 (ISBN 0-89029-083-0). Pr of Morningside.
Stonewall Ladies. Elizabeth O. Verner. 1963. 18.00 (ISBN 0-937684-07-4). Tradd St Pr.
Stoneware Monkey. R. Austin Freeman. (Dover Mystery Classics Ser.). 224p. 1987. pap. 5.95 (ISBN 0-486-25471-2). Dover.
Stonewares of Yi-Xing. K. S. Lo. 352p. 1984. 350.00x (ISBN 0-317-44211-2, Pub. by Han-Shan Tang Ltd). State Mutual Bk.
Stonewares of Yixing: From the Ming Period to the Present Day. K. S. Lo. LC 85-50363. (Illus.). 228p. 1986. 125.00 (ISBN 0-85667-181-9, Pub. by P Wilson Pubs). Sotheby Pubns.
Stonewycke Trilogy. Michael Phillips & Judith Pella. 1986. boxed set 17.85 (ISBN 0-87123-971-X, 252971). Bethany Hse.
Stoney Knows How: Life As a Tattoo Artist. Leonard L. St. Clair & Alan B. Govenar. LC 81-51018. (Illus.). 196p. 1981. 17.00 (ISBN 0-8131-1402-0). U Pr of Ky.
Stonington Cook Book. Young People's Society of Christian Endeavor. (Bicentennial Edition: 1776-1976). 98p. 1975. pap. 5.00 (ISBN 0-910258-04-X). Book & Tackle.
Stonor Eagles. William Horwood. 704p. 1982. 15.95 (ISBN 0-531-09873-7). Watts.
Stony Man Doctrine. (Executioner Ser.: No. 1). 384p. 1983. pap. 3.95 (ISBN 0-373-61401-2, Pub. by Worldwide). Harlequin Bks.
Stony Pass: The Tumbling & Impetuous Trail. Cathy E. Kindquist. (Illus.). 145p. (Orig.). 1988. pap. 8.95 (ISBN 0-9608000-5-0). San Juan County.
Stony the Road: Essays from the Hampton Institute Archives. Ed. by Keith L. Schall. LC 76-56224. (Illus.). 183p. 1977. 14.95x (ISBN 0-8139-0720-9). U Pr of Va.
Stoo Hample's Silly Joke Book. Stoo Hample. LC 78-50431. (Illus.). (gr. 1-6). 1978. pap. 5.47 (ISBN 0-440-08160-2); pap. 2.50 (ISBN 0-440-08154-8). Delacorte.
Stooge Chronicles. Jeffrey Forrester. (Illus.). 112p. 1982. pap. 8.95 (ISBN 0-8092-5666-5). Contemp Bks.
Stooge Fan's IQ Test: The Ultimate Challenge. Ronald L. Smith. (Illus.). 96p. (Orig.). 1988. pap. 6.95 (ISBN 0-8092-4613-9). Contemp Bks.
Stoogemania. Tom Hansen & Jeffrey Forrester. (Illus.). 160p. 1984. pap. 9.95 (ISBN 0-8092-5382-8). Contemp Bks.
Stoogephile Trivia Book. Jeffrey Forrester. (Illus., Orig.). 1982. pap. 7.95 (ISBN 0-8092-5613-4). Contemp Bks.
Stooges' Lost Episodes. Tom Forrester & Jeff Forrester. LC 87-35225. (Illus.). 128p. (Orig.). 1988. pap. 8.95 (ISBN 0-8092-4655-4). Contemp Bks.
Stoogism Anthology. Ed. by Paul F. Fericano. LC 77-76619. (Illus.). 1977. pap. 15.00 (ISBN 0-916296-01-6). Poor Souls Pr.
Stookie. Michael Elder. 1986. 34.75x (ISBN 1-85158-004-2, Pub. by Mainstream Scotland); pap. 19.75x (ISBN 1-85158-005-0). State Mutual Bk.
Stools & Bottles. 160p. 1955. 4.95 (ISBN 0-89486-027-5). Hazelden.
Stop. Richard S. Wheeler. 192p. 1988. 14.95 (ISBN 0-317-66670-3). M Evans.
Stop a Moment: A Group Leader's Handbook of Energizing Experiences. Jim Ballard. LC 77-81459. (Mandala Ser. in Education). (Illus.). 73p. 1982. pap. 5.95 (ISBN 0-8290-0981-7). Irvington.
Stop & Look! Illusions. Robyn Supraner. LC 80-23799. (Illus.). 48p. (gr. 1-5). 1981. PLB 9.49 (ISBN 0-89375-434-X); pap. 1.95 (ISBN 0-89375-435-8). Troll Assocs.
Stop Being Afraid. David Seabury. 96p. 1965. pap. 4.95 (ISBN 0-911336-19-2). Sci of Mind.
Stop Book. David Shevin. LC 78-11123. (Illus.). 1978. cloth 20.00 (ISBN 0-916906-20-5); signed ed. 50.00 (ISBN 0-916906-21-3); pap. 12.00 (ISBN 0-916906-19-1). Konglomerati.
Stop Burglary, Prevent Home Break-Ins. Robert Forte. (Illus.). 127p. (Orig.). 1987. 9.95 (ISBN 0-9609328-0-1). R Forte.
Stop Burning Your Money. John Rothchild. 258p. 1982. pap. 5.95 (ISBN 0-14-046551-0). Penguin.
Stop Calling Me Mr. Darling! Carol Burdick. 128p. 1988. 15.95 (ISBN 0-8397-7897-X). Eriksson.
Stop Crying at Your Own Movies: How to Solve Personal Problems & Open Your Life to Its Full Potential Using the Vector Method. George Burtt. LC 75-4770. 182p. 1975. 17.95x (ISBN 0-911012-83-4). Nelson-Hall.
Stop Dieting: Begin Losing with Gourmet Magic. rev. ed. Naomi Watson. LC 77-76948. 1978. 10.95 (ISBN 0-918766-05-2); spiral bdg. 7.95 (ISBN 0-918766-04-4). Butterfly Pr.
Stop Drinking & Live. 3.00 (SR10). Transitions.
Stop Drinking & Start Living. Stephen Schlesinger & John J. Gillick. (Illus.). 154p. 1985. 12.95 (ISBN 0-8306-1937-2, 1937H). TAB Bks.
Stop Drunk Driving: An Illustration of a Peace Game. (Analysis Ser.: No. 14). Date not set. 12.00 (ISBN 0-686-45486-3). Inst Analysis.
Stop DWI: Successful Community Responses to Drunk Driving. Ed. by Denis Foley. LC 85-45676. 208p. 1986. 29.00x (ISBN 0-669-12157-6). Lexington Bks.
Stop Forgetting. rev. ed. Bruno Furst. Rev. by Lotte Furst & Gerrit Storm. LC 75-164727. (Illus.). 1979. pap. 9.95 (ISBN 0-385-15401-1). Doubleday.
Stop-Go, Fast-Slow. Valjean McLenighan. LC 81-17080. (Rookie Readers Ser.). (Illus.). 32p. (ps-2). 1982. PLB 9.93 (ISBN 0-516-03617-3); pap. text ed. 2.50 (ISBN 0-516-43617-1). Childrens.
Stop! Go! Word Bird. Jane B. Moncure. LC 80-16273. (Word Birds for Early Birds Ser.: No. 33). (Illus.). 32p. (ps-1). 1981. PLB 11.93 (ISBN 0-516-06553-X). Childrens.
Stop! Go! Word Bird. Jane B. Moncure. LC 80-16273. (Early Bird Reader Ser.). (Illus.). 32p. (ps-2). 1980. PLB 7.45 (ISBN 0-89565-160-2). Childs World.
Stop Hair Loss. Paavo Airola. 32p. 1965. pap. 2.00 (ISBN 0-932090-06-0). Health Plus.
Stop Hair Loss. Paavo Airola. (Health Plus Bks). 1984. pap. 2.00 (ISBN 0-317-02879-0). Contemp Bks.
Stop in the Name of Love. Nancy Rue. Ed. by Roger Rosen. (Flipside Fiction Ser.). (YA) (gr. 7 up). 1988. lib. bdg. 12.95 (ISBN 0-8239-0794-5). Rosen Group.
Stop Insomnia: How to Sleep Well Through Bed Exercises. Richard R. Fuller. (Illus.). 1980. 5.00 (ISBN 0-682-49582-4). Exposition-Phoenix.
Stop It Now: How Targets & Managers Can End Sexual Harassment. Kenneth C. Cooper. LC 85-1280. (Illus.). 212p. (Orig.). 1985. pap. 9.95 (ISBN 0-932801-00-5). Total Comm.
Stop Justice Abuse. Eugene D. Wheeler & Robert E. Kallman. LC 85-72096. (Orig.). 1986. pap. 10.95 (ISBN 0-934793-02-6). Pathfinder CA.
Stop Killing Yourself: Make Stress Work for You. Susan Seliger. LC 83-24568. (Illus.). 256p. 1984. 16.95 (ISBN 0-399-12925-1, Putnam). Putnam Pub Group.
Stop Legal Stealing. John C. Lincoln. 1972. pap. 0.75 (ISBN 0-686-17296-5). Lincoln Inst Land.
Stop, Look, & Listen for Trains. Dorothy Chlad. LC 83-7213. (Safety Town Ser.). (Illus.). 32p. (ps-2). 1983. lib. bdg. 11.93 (ISBN 0-516-01988-0); pap. 2.95 (ISBN 0-516-41988-9). Childrens.
Stop, Look & Listen: Songs of Awareness for Young Children. Ginger Clarkson. (ps). 1986. pap. text ed. 4.95 (ISBN 0-8497-5924-2, WE8, Pub. by Kjos West). KJOS.
Stop, Look, Listen. Dorothy Johnston. (Illus.). 24p. (Orig.). (gr. k-2). 1977. pap. 1.29 (ISBN 0-87239-273-2, 2014). Standard Pub.
Stop Making Yourself Sick. Harold Adolph & David L. Bourne. 132p. 1986. pap. 5.50 (ISBN 0-89693-325-3). Victor Bks.
Stop Me Before I Plan Again. Richard Hedman. LC 77-73251. (Illus.). 112p. (Orig.). 1977. pap. 9.95 (ISBN 0-918286-10-7). Planners Pr.
Stop Me Before I Plan Again. Richard Hedman. 112p. 1977. pap. 9.95 (ISBN 0-318-13083-1). Am Plan Assn.
Stop Me Before I Write More. Scott Gardner. (Illus.). 104p. (Orig.). 1984. 14.95 (ISBN 0-9614112-1-X); pap. 6.95 (ISBN 0-9614112-0-1). Draydel Pr.
Stop Nuclear War! A Handbook. David P. Barash & Judith E. Lipton. LC 82-48162. 396p. 1982. pap. 7.95 (ISBN 0-394-62433-5, E835, Ever). Grove.
Stop Procrastinating - Do It! 2nd ed. James R. Shermman. 1988. pap. 2.95 (ISBN 0-935538-13-5). Pathway Bks.
Stop Procrastinating--Do It! James R. Sherman. LC 80-82893. (Orig.). 1981. pap. 2.25 (ISBN 0-935538-01-1). Pathway Bks.
Stop Procrastination & Do It Now. 3.00 (ISBN 0-686-40901-9, SR6). Transitions.
Stop Running Scared. H. Fensterheim & J. Baer. 1982. pap. 4.50 (ISBN 0-440-37734-X). Dell.
Stop School Failure. rev. ed. Louise B. Ames et al. LC 79-181603. 193p. 1987. tchrs.' ed. 14.95 (ISBN 0-317-59501-6, 105). Programs Educ.
Stop Smoking Activity Book. Edward Boggs. LC 84-28465. (Illus.). 96p. (Orig.). 1985. pap. 7.95 (ISBN 0-87879-464-6, Pub. by Arena Pr). Acad Therapy.
Stop Smoking & Start Living. M. Halayya. 188p. 1984. text ed. 13.95x (ISBN 0-86590-221-6, Pub. by Sterling Pubs India). Apt Bks.
Stop Smoking Book. Margaret K. McKean. LC 76-26302. 1987. pap. 6.95 (ISBN 0-915166-59-3). Impact Pubs Cal.
Stop Smoking Diet. Jane Ogle. LC 81-3181. 168p. 1983. pap. 5.95 (ISBN 0-87131-410-X). M Evans.
Stop Smoking, Lose Weight. Neil Solomon. 208p. 1986. pap. 2.95 (ISBN 0-8217-1776-6). Zebra.
Stop Smoking Program Guide. American Cancer Society. 184p. avail. (5003). Am Cancer NY.
Stop Smoking Soon. G-Jo Institute Staff. 1980. pap. 4.50 (ISBN 0-916878-09-0). Falkynor Bks.
Stop Smoking Through Self Hypnosis. rev. ed. Isabel Gilbert. Ed. by Suzanne Mikesell. 1987. pap. 6.95 (ISBN 0-914629-36-0, Dist. by St. Martin). Prima Pub Comm.
Stop Snoring Now. Dan Carlinsky. 1987. pap. 2.95 (ISBN 0-312-90612-9). St Martin.
Stop Snowing on My Secretary. Charles M. Schulz. LC 77-71355. (Peanuts Parade Bks.: No. 20). 1977. pap. 5.95 (ISBN 0-03-021391-6). H Holt & Co.
Stop, Start. Mary S. Shapiro. (Learn-to Read Ser.: Bk. 3). (Illus.). 14p. (ps-k). 1985. 3.50 (ISBN 0-934361-03-7); Set. write for info. (ISBN 0-934361-00-2). Kinder Read.
Stop-Start-Think! V. Stanford Hampson. LC 80-70231. 176p. (Orig.). 1981. pap. 5.50 (ISBN 0-87516-435-8). DeVorss.
Stop Stop. Edith T. Hurd. LC 61-12095. (Harper I Can Read Bks.). (Illus.). 64p. (gr. k-3). 1961. PLB 10.89 (ISBN 0-06-022746-X). HarpJ.
Stop Stress & Aging Now: The Methuselah Manual. David C. Gardner & Grace J. Beatty. LC 84-72980. (Illus.). 353p. (Orig.). 1985. pap. 12.95 (ISBN 0-9613999-9-6). ATRA.
Stop Struggling with Your Teen. Evonne Weinhaus & Karen Friedman. 96p. 1988. pap. 6.95 (ISBN 0-14-010604-9). Penguin.
Stop Struggling with Your Teen. Evonne Weinhaus et al. (Illus.). 64p. (Orig.). 1984. pap. text ed. 6.95 (ISBN 0-9613736-2-8). Speck Press.
Stop Studying, Start Learning: Or How to Jump-Start Your Brain. Richard Fenker, Jr. & Reverdy Mullins. LC 81-8797. 168p. 1981. pap. 11.95 (ISBN 0-940352-00-1, 4010). Res Press.
Stop Stuttering. Martin F. Schwartz & Grady L. Carter. LC 85-45230. 143p. 1986. 14.45i (ISBN 0-06-015525-6, HarpT). Har-Row.
Stop That Rabbit. Sharon Peters. (Illus.). 32p. (gr. k-2). 1980. PLB 5.41 (ISBN 0-89375-388-2); pap. 1.50 (ISBN 0-89375-288-6). Troll Assocs.
Stop That Witch! Mary Clark. LC 85-51048. (Crimson Crystal Adventures Ser.). (Illus.). 160p. (gr. 4-6). 1985. pap. 2.95 (ISBN 0-394-74241-9). Random.
Stop the Bed. Phyllis Adams et al. (BTR Ser.). (Illus.). 32p. (gr. k-3). 1982. PLB 4.95 (ISBN 0-02-188496-X, Dist. by Caroline Hse). Modern Curr.
Stop the Clock: The Tao of Time & Timelessness. John W. Flint. LC 84-51562. 85p. 1985. pap. 6.95 (ISBN 0-87516-546-X). DeVorss.

Storia Critico-Chronologica-Diplomatica del Patriarca S. Brunone e del Suo Ordine Cartusiano, 2 pts, Vol. 7. Benedetto Tromby. Ed. by James Hogg. (Analecta Cartusiana Ser.: No. 84/7). 637p. (Orig.). 1982. pap. 50.00 (ISBN 3-7052-0137-9, Pub. by Salzburg Studies). Longwood Pub Group.

Storia Critico-Chronologica-Diplomatica del Patriarca S. Brunone e del Suo Ordine Carusiano, 2 pts, Vol. 8. Benedetto Tromby. Ed. by James Hogg. (Analecta Cartusiana: No. 84-8). 574p. (Orig.). 1982. pap. 50.00 (ISBN 3-7052-0138-7, Pub. by Salzburg Studies). Longwood Pub Group.

Storia-Critico-Chronologica-Diplomatica del Patriarca S. Brunone e del Suo Cartusiano, 2 pts, Vol. 9. Benedetto Tromby. Ed. by James Hogg. (Analecta Cartusiana: No. 84-9). 638p. (Orig.). 1982. pap. 50.00 (ISBN 3-7052-0139-5, Pub. by Salzburg Studies). Longwood Pub Group.

Storia Critico-Chronologica-Diplomatica del Patriarca S. Brunone e del Suo Ordine Cartusiano, 3 pts, Vol. 10. Benedetto Tromby. Ed. by James Hogg. (Analecta Cartusiana Ser.: No. 84-10). 730p. (Orig.). 1982. pap. 85.00 (ISBN 3-7052-0140-9, Pub. by Salzburg Studies). Longwood Pub Group.

Storia Critico-Chronologica-Diplomatica del Patriarca S. Brunone e del Suo Ordine Cartusiano, Vol. 11. Benedetto Tromby. Ed. by James Hogg. (Analecta Cartusiana Ser.: No. 84-11). 31p. (Orig.). 1981. pap. 7.50 (ISBN 3-7052-0141-7, Pub. by Salzburg Studies). Longwood Pub Group.

Storia Del Metodo Sperimentale in Italia, 6 vols. Raffaello Caverni. xxii, 3478p. 1972. Repr. of 1891 ed. 300.00 (ISBN 0-384-07965-2). Johnson Repr.

Storia dell' eucaristia see Story of the Eucharist.

Storia dell'Arte Italiana: 1901-1940, 11. Vols. in 25 pts. Incl. Vol. 1. Dai primordi dell'arte cristiana al tempo di Giustiniano; Vol. 2. Dell'arte barbarica all romanica; Vol. 3. L'aret romanica; Vol. 4. La scultura del trecento e le sue origini; Vol. 5. La pittura del trecento e le sue origini; Vol. 6. La scultura del quattrocento; Vol. 7 (in 4 pts.) La pittura del quattrocento; Vol 8 (in 2 pts.) L'architetura del quattrocento; Vol. 9 (in 7 pts.) La pittura del cinquecento; Vol. 10 (in 3 pts.) La scultura del cinquecento; Vol. 11 (in 3 pts.) L'architettura del cinquecento. Set. 3475.00 (ISBN 0-8115-3505-3). Kraus Repr.

Storia dell'Economia Politica Nei Secoli Dix-Septieme e Dix-Huitieme Negli Stati della Repubblica Veneta, Corredata Da Documenti Inediti: Economica Politicanes Secoli 17e Negli Stati Del la Republica Veneta Corredate Da Documen; Inediti, 2 vols. Alberto Errera. 1965. 35.50 (ISBN 0-8337-1066-4). B Franklin.

Storia Di Panini see Breadtime Story.

Storia Di Sirio see Story of Sirio.

Storia Do Mogor, or Mogul India 1653-1708, 4 vols. Niccolao Manucci. Tr. by William Irvine. Repr. of 1907 ed. Set. text ed. 125.00x. Coronet Bks.

Stories. Richard L. Allington. Kathleen Krull. LC 82-10208. (E. G. Beginning to Learn about... Ser.). (Illus.). 32p. (gr. 1-2). 1985. pap. 9.27 (ISBN 0-8172-2490-4). Raintree Pubs.

Stories. Richard L. Allington & Kathleen Krull. LC 82-10208. (Beginning to Learn about Ser.). (Illus.). 32p. (gr. 1-2). 1982. PLB 15.33 (ISBN 0-8172-1386-4). Raintree Pubs.

Stories. Lorayne Ashton. 368p. (Orig.). 1987. pap. 3.95 (ISBN 0-8041-0134-5, Pub. by Ivy). Ballantine.

Stories. Brion Gysin. Ed. by Theo Green. 98p. (Orig.). 1984. pap. 7.00 (ISBN 0-934301-01-8). Inkblot Pubns.

Stories. Elizabeth Jolley. 308p. 1988. 17.95 (ISBN 0-670-82113-6). Viking.

Stories. Gottfried Keller. Ed. by Frank Ryder. LC 81-22067. (German Library: Vol. 44). 347p. 1982. 27.50x (ISBN 0-8264-0256-9); pap. 8.95 (ISBN 0-8264-0266-6). Continuum.

Stories. Ram Kumar. 1976. lib. bdg. 9.00 (ISBN 0-89253-085-5); flexible bdg. 6.00 (ISBN 0-89253-267-X). Ind-US Inc.

Stories. Doris Lessing. LC 77-20797. 1978. 17.00 (ISBN 0-394-50009-1). Knopf.

Stories. Doris Lessing. LC 79-22320. 1980. pap. 11.95 (ISBN 0-394-74249-4, Vin). Random.

Stories. Katherine Mansfield. Ed. by Elizabeth Bowen. 1956. pap. 4.95 (ISBN 0-394-70036-8, Vin). Random.

Stories. Tony Mendoza. Ed. by Gary Fisketjon. (Illus.). 96p. 1987. pap. 6.95 (ISBN 0-87113-146-3). Atlantic Monthly.

Stories. Leslie De Noronha. 8.00 (ISBN 0-89253-630-6); flexible cloth 4.80 (ISBN 0-89253-631-4). Ind-US Inc.

Stories. Cesare Pavese. Tr. & intro. by A. E. Murch. 415p. 1987. pap. 12.95 (ISBN 0-88001-124-6). Ecco Pr.

Stories. Dennis Turner. LC 87-90167. 194p. 1988. 11.95 (ISBN 0-533-07572-6). Vantage.

Stories About Children of the Bible. Hilda L. Rostron. (Ladybird Ser.). (Illus.). (gr. k-1). 1962. bds. 2.50 (ISBN 0-87508-860-0). Chr Lit.

Stories about How Things Fall Apart & What's Left When They Do. Ed. by Allen Woodman. 122p. (Orig.). 1985. pap. 7.95 (ISBN 0-912527-01-3). Word Beat.

Stories About Jesus the Friend. Hilda L. Rostron. (Ladybird Ser.). (Illus.). (gr. k-1). 1961. bds. 2.50 (ISBN 0-87508-862-7). Chr Lit.

Stories About Jesus the Helper. Hilda L. Rostron. (Ladybird Ser.). (Illus.). (gr. k-1). 1961. bds. 2.50 (ISBN 0-87508-864-3). Chr Lit.

Stories about Lenin & the Revolution. Z. Vosresentskaya et al. 175p. 1982. 5.95 (ISBN 0-8285-2348-7, Pub. by Progress Pubs USSR). Imported Pubns.

Stories about Magnitka. S. Alexeyev. Tr. by Natalia Belskaya. 102p. 1983. pap. 3.95 (ISBN 0-8285-2771-7, Pub. by Raduga Pubs USSR). Imported Pubns.

Stories about Rosie. Cynthia Voigt. LC 86-3640. (Illus.). 48p. (gr. 1-4). 1986. 12.95 (ISBN 0-689-31296-2, Atheneum Childrens Bk.). Macmillan.

Stories about Wooden Keyboards. Kendrick Smithyman. 1985. pap. 11.95x (ISBN 0-19-648049-3). Oxford U Pr.

Stories about Workers. Benjamin Piltch. (Illus.). 1983. pap. 3.75 (ISBN 0-88323-197-2, 208). Richards Pub.

Stories: Alchemy & Others. Andrew Lytle. 192p. 1984. pap. 9.95 (ISBN 0-918769-00-0). Univ South.

Stories & Essays. Richard Wagner. Selected by & Charles Osborne. 25.00 (ISBN 0-7206-9602-X, Pub. by P Owen Ltd). Dufour.

Stories & Fables of Ambrose Bierce. Ambrose Bierce. Ed. by Edward Wagenknecht. LC 77-20146. (Illus.). 368p. 1977. 14.95 (ISBN 0-916144-19-4). Stemmer Hse.

Stories & Games for Easy Lipreading Practice. rev. ed. Rose F. Broberg. LC 77-70167. 1963. softcover 7.95 (ISBN 0-88200-080-2, B0664). Alexander Graham.

Stories & Legends of the Bering Strait Eskimos. Clark M. Garber. LC 74-5835. 260p. 1975. Repr. of 1940 ed. 24.50 (ISBN 0-404-11640-X). AMS Pr.

Stories & Lore of the Zodiac. M. A. Jagendorf. LC 76-39724. 192p. (gr. 3-11). 1978. 10.95 (ISBN 0-8149-0752-0). Vanguard.

Stories & Parables. Satguru S. Keshavadas. (Illus.). 100p. 1979. 6.50 (ISBN 0-533-03818-9). Vishwa.

Stories & Parables for Preachers & Teachers. Paul J. Wharton. 1986. pap. 4.95 (ISBN 0-8091-2796-2). Paulist Pr.

Stories & Pictures. Isaac L. Peretz. 75.00 (ISBN 0-87968-376-7). Gordon Pr.

Stories & Pictures. facsimile ed. Isaac L. Perez. Tr. by Helena Frank from Yiddish. LC 75-152953. (Short Story Index Reprint Ser.). Repr. of 1906 ed. 23.50 (ISBN 0-8369-3868-2). Ayer Co Pubs.

Stories & Plays for Children. Sunanda. 91p. (gr. 3-8). 1984. pap. 1.50 (ISBN 0-89071-329-4, Pub. by Sri Aurobindo Ashram India). Aurobindo Assn.

Stories & Poems. Bret Harte. 1915. Repr. lib. bdg. 42.00 (ISBN 0-8414-5013-7). Folcroft.

Stories & Poems. Gailyn Saroyan. 1977. wrappers 2.25 (ISBN 0-939180-11-1). Tombouctou.

Stories & Poems about the Queenland Gemfields. Glen Gillard. 55p. 1985. pap. 7.50 (ISBN 0-908175-65-5, Pub. by Boolarong Pubn Australia). Intl Spec Bk.

Stories & Poems by the Co-Op Kids. Susan O. Higgins & The Co-Op Kids. (Co-Op Kids Series). (Illus.). 70p. (Orig.). (ps-3). 1987. pap. 4.00 (ISBN 0-939973-04-9). Pumpkin Pr Pub Hse.

Stories & Poems for Children. Ed. by I. Bronetsky. 143p. 1982. 7.95 (ISBN 0-8285-2361-4, Pub. by Raduga Pubs USSR). Imported Pubns.

Stories & Poems for Children. facsimile ed. Celia Thaxter. LC 73-167486. (Granger Index Reprint Ser.). Repr. of 1883 ed. 18.00 (ISBN 0-8369-6291-5). Ayer Co Pubs.

Stories & Poems from Close to Home. Ed. by Floyd Salas. LC 85-63696. (Illus.). 528p. (Orig.). 1986. pap. 9.95 (ISBN 0-9616101-3-1). Ortalda & Assocs.

Stories & Poems from the Old North State. facsimile ed. Ed. by Alga W. Leavitt. LC 71-163039. (Short Story Index Reprint Ser.). (Illus.). Repr. of 1923 ed. 20.00 (ISBN 0-8369-3953-0). Ayer Co Pubs.

Stories & Poems in Prose. Ivan S. Turgenev. 422p. 1982. 11.95 (ISBN 0-8285-2517-X, Pub. by Progress Pubs USSR). Imported Pubns.

Stories & Sketches. Saros Cowasjee. (Writers Workshop Greenbird Ser.). 85p. 1975. 11.00 (ISBN 0-88253-646-X); pap. text ed. 6.00 (ISBN 0-88253-645-1). Ind-US Inc.

Stories & Tales. Stephen Crane. Ed. by Robert W. Stallman. 1955. pap. 3.16 (ISBN 0-394-70010-4, Vin, V10). Random.

Stories & Tales, 7 Vols. Sarah O. Jewett. LC 83-45881. Repr. of 1910 ed. Set. 185.00 (ISBN 0-404-20136-9). AMS Pr.

Stories & Tales. N. S. Leskov. 368p. 1985. pap. 7.95 (ISBN 0-8285-3067-X, Pub. by Rus Lang Pubs USSR). Imported Pubns.

Stories & Texts for Nothing. Samuel Beckett. 1970. 10.00 (ISBN 0-394-47527-5, GP653). Grove.

Stories & Texts for Nothing. Samuel Beckett. 1967. pap. 6.95 (ISBN 0-394-17268-X, E466, Ever). Grove.

Stories & Verses. Hereward Wakefield. 1986. 8.95 (ISBN 0-533-06810-X). Vantage.

Stories Behind Everyday Things. Reader's Digest Editors. LC 79-88053. (Illus.). 416p. 1980. 21.50 (ISBN 0-89577-068-7, Pub. by RD Assn). Random.

Stories Behind Words. Peter Limburg. LC 85-26398. 288p. 1986. 30.00 (ISBN 0-8242-0718-1). Wilson.

Stories by American Authors, 10 vols in 5. Ed. by Scribner's, Charles, Sons Staff. 1972. Repr. of 1884 ed. lib. bdg. 150.00 set (ISBN 0-685-36668-5); Vols. 1-2. (ISBN 0-8422-8142-8); Vols. 3-4. (ISBN 0-8422-8143-6); Vols 5-6. (ISBN 0-8422-8144-4); Vols 7-8. (ISBN 0-8290-1658-9); Vols. 9-10. (ISBN 0-8422-8146-0); lib. bdg. 35.00 ea., 5 individual vols. Irvington.

Stories by English Authors, 10 vols in 5. Ed. by Scribner's, Charles, Sons Staff. 1972. Repr. of 1896 ed. Set. lib. bdg. 150.00 (ISBN 0-8290-1414-4); Vols. 1-2. 35.00 (ISBN 0-8422-8147-9); Vols 3-4. 35.00 (ISBN 0-8422-8148-7); Vols. 5-6. 35.00 (ISBN 0-8422-8149-5); Vols.-7-8. 35.00 (ISBN 0-8422-8150-9); Vols. 9-10. 35.00 (ISBN 0-8422-8151-7). Irvington.

Stories by Foreign Authors, 10 vols in 5. Ed. by Scribner's, Charles, Sons Staff. 1972. Repr. of 1896 ed. lib. bdg. 175.00 set (ISBN 0-685-36671-5); Vols 1-2. Fr. (ISBN 0-8422-8152-5); Vols 3-4. Fr. - Ger. (ISBN 0-8422-8153-3); Vols 5-6. Ger. - It. (ISBN 0-8422-8154-1); Vols. 7-8. Rus.-Scand. (ISBN 0-8422-8155-X); Vols. 9-10. Span. & Polish (ISBN 0-8422-8156-8); lib. bdg. 40.00 ea., 5 individual vols. Irvington.

Stories by Foreign Authors, Vols. 1 & 2. Ed. by Charles Scribners & Sons Staff. 1988. pap. text ed. 10.95 (ISBN 0-8290-2143-4). Irvington.

Stories by Foreign Authors, Vols. 5 & 6. Ed. by Scribners, Charles & Sons Staff. 1988. pap. text ed. 10.95 (ISBN 0-8290-2145-0). Irvington.

Stories by Foreign Authors, 2 vols, Vols. 7 & 8. Ed. by Scribners, Charles & Sons Staff. 1988. pap. text ed. 10.95 (ISBN 0-8290-2146-9). Irvington.

Stories by Foreign Authors, Vols. 9 & 10. Ed. by Charles Scribners & Sons Staff. 1988. pap. text ed. 10.95 (ISBN 0-8290-2147-7). Irvington.

Stories by Foreign Authors: German, 2 Vols. facsimile ed. LC 72-110211. (Short Story Index Reprint Ser.). 1898. 21.50 (ISBN 0-8369-3363-X). Ayer Co Pubs.

Stories by Foreign Authors: Italian. facsimile ed. LC 72-110211. (Short Story Index Reprint Ser.). 1898. 10.00 (ISBN 0-8369-3364-8). Ayer Co Pubs.

Stories by Foreign Authors: Polish Greek Belgian Hungarian. facsimile ed. LC 72-110211. (Short Story Index Reprint Ser.). 1898. 10.50 (ISBN 0-8369-3365-6). Ayer Co Pubs.

Stories by Foreign Authors: Russian. facsimile ed. LC 72-110211. (Short Story Index Ser.). 1898. 10.25 (ISBN 0-8369-3366-4). Ayer Co Pubs.

Stories by Foreign Authors: Scandinavian. facsimile ed. LC 72-110211. (Short Story Index Reprint Ser.). 1898. 10.25 (ISBN 0-8369-3367-2). Ayer Co Pubs.

Stories by Foreign Authors: Spanish. facsimile ed. LC 72-110211. (Short Story Index Reprint Ser.). 1898. 12.50 (ISBN 0-8369-3368-0). Ayer Co Pubs.

Stories by Meir Blinkin. Meir Blinkin. Tr. by Max Rosenfeld from Yiddish. LC 83-15564. (Modern Jewish Literature & Culture Ser.). 166p. 1984. 10.95 (ISBN 0-87395-818-7). State U NY Pr.

Stories California Indians Told. Anne B. Fisher. LC 57-8065. (Illus.). (gr. 3-7). 1957. 6.95 (ISBN 0-395-27723-X, Pub. by Parnassus). HM.

Stories, Dreams & Allegories. Olive Schreiner. Repr. of 1923 ed. 39.50. Darby Bks.

Stories, Et Cetera: A Country Lawyer Looks at Life & the Law. C. Lester Gaylord. LC 87-82962. 1988. 19.00. Lawyers Co-op.

Stories for a Prince. (Illus.). 48p. (ps-1). 1985. 12.95 (ISBN 0-241-11052-1, Pub. by Hamish Hamilton England). David & Charles.

Stories for Around the Campfire. Ray Harriot. (Illus.). 138p. (Orig.). (gr. 5-10). 1986. pap. 4.95 (ISBN 0-9617653-0-5). Campfire Pub.

Stories for Boys. facsimile ed. Richard H. Davis. LC 73-150472. (Short Story Index Reprint Ser.). Repr. of 1891 ed. 18.00 (ISBN 0-8369-3812-7). Ayer Co Pubs.

Stories for Children. Peter Bichsel. Tr. by Michael Hamberger from Ger. 60p. (gr. 3-6). 1984. pap. 5.95 (ISBN 0-7145-0689-3). M Boyars Pubs.

Stories for Children. Isaac Bashevis Singer. LC 84-13612. 338p. (gr. k up). 1984. 16.95 (ISBN 0-374-37266-7); signed, ltd. ed. 50.00 (ISBN 0-374-37267-5); pap. 7.95 (ISBN 0-374-46489-8). FS&G.

Stories for Children. Leo Tolstoy. Tr. by Jacob Guralsky. (Illus.). (ps-3). 1977. pap. 1.20 (ISBN 0-8285-8974-7, Pub. by Progress Pubs USSR). Imported Pubns.

Stories for Children. Konstantin Ushinsky. Tr. by Eve Manning. 34p. 1984. pap. 1.99 (ISBN 0-8285-2823-3, Pub. by Raduga Pubs USSR). Imported Pubns.

Stories for Communication. Kathy C. Patterson & Phyllis M. Niklaus. (Series I). (Illus.). 135p. 1985. instr. manual, score sheet 80.00 (ISBN 0-932361-00-5). Comm & Learning.

Stories for Communication. Kathy C. Patterson & Phyllis M. Niklaus. Ed. by Communication & Learning Innovators, Ltd. Staff et al. (Illus.). 13p. (ps-8). 1985. 6.00 (ISBN 0-932361-01-3). Comm & Learning.

Stories for Eight-Year-Olds & Other Young Readers. Ed. by Sara Corrin & Stephen Corrin. (Illus.). 192p. (gr. 2-4). 1984. 11.95 (ISBN 0-571-09332-9). Faber & Faber.

Stories for Every Holiday. Carolyn S. Bailey. LC 73-20149. 280p. 1974. Repr. of 1918 ed. 56.00x (ISBN 0-8103-3957-9). Gale.

Stories for Five Year-Olds & Other Young Readers. Sara Corrin et al. Ed. by Stephen Corrin. (Illus.). 168p. (ps-5). 1973. 12.95 (ISBN 0-571-10162-3). Faber & Faber.

Stories for Free Children. Letty C. Pogrebin. 144p. 1982. text ed. 14.95 (ISBN 0-07-050389-3). McGraw.

Stories for Free Children. Letty C. Pogrebin. 1983. pap. text ed. 9.95 (ISBN 0-07-050398-2). McGraw.

Stories for Killing Time. Darren O. Godfrey. 48p. 1985. 6.95 (ISBN 0-89962-484-7). Todd & Honeywell.

Stories for Lesley. Robert Frost. Ed. by Roger D. Sell. LC 83-19756. (Bibliographical Society of the University of Virginia). (Illus.). 77p. 1984. 16.95x (ISBN 0-8139-0979-1). U Pr of Va.

Stories for Nine-Year-Olds. Ed. by Sara Corrin & Stephen Corrin. LC 79-670371. (Illus.). 160p. (gr. 2-5). 1979. 11.95 (ISBN 0-571-11409-1). Faber & Faber.

Stories for Preachers. James A. Feehan. 148p. (Orig.). 1988. pap. 10.95 (ISBN 0-85342-840-9, Pub. by Mercier Pr Ireland). Irish Bks Media.

Stories for Ramu. Deepak Dubey. 10.00 (ISBN 0-89253-794-9); flexible cloth 5.00 (ISBN 0-89253-795-7). Ind-US Inc.

Stories for Seven-Year-Olds & Other Young Readers. Ed. by Sara Corrin & Stephen Corrin. (Illus.). 188p. (gr. 1-3). 1982. 12.95 (ISBN 0-571-05823-X). Faber & Faber.

Stories for Six-Year Olds & Other Young Readers. Ed. by Sara Corrin & Stephen Corrin. (Illus.). 198p. (gr. k-2). 1984. 12.95 (ISBN 0-571-08114-2). Faber & Faber.

Stories for Telling: A Treasury for Christian Storytellers. William R. White. LC 85-28980. 144p. (Orig.). 1986. pap. 7.95 (ISBN 0-8066-2192-3, 10-6023). Augsburg.

Stories for the Children of Light: Children's Sermons for the New Common Lectionary, Vol. 1. Thomas W. Goodhue. 56p. (Orig.). 1987. wkbk. 7.95 (ISBN 0-941850-25-0). Liturgical Pubns.

Stories for the Children's Hour. 2nd ed. Kenneth Taylor. (gr. 1-8). 1987. pap. 6.95 (ISBN 0-8024-2227-6). Moody.

Stories for the Children's Hour. rev. ed. Kenneth N. Taylor. LC 68-26408. (Illus.). (gr. k-6). 5.95 (ISBN 0-8024-8326-7). Moody.

Stories for the Journey: A Sourcebook for Christian Storytellers. William R. White. 128p. (Orig.). Date not set. pap. 7.95 (ISBN 0-8066-2364-0, 10-1026). Augsburg.

Stories for the Sophisticated. Lionel A. Canaan. 1981. 7.95 (ISBN 0-533-04871-0). Vantage.

Stories for the Third Ear: Using Hypnotic Fables in Psychology. Lee Wallas. (Professional Bks.). 1985. text ed. 17.95 (ISBN 0-393-70019-4). Norton.

Stories for Under-Fives. Ed. by Sara Corrin et al. (Illus.). 158p. (ps-5). 1974. 9.95 (ISBN 0-571-10371-5). Faber & Faber.

Stories from a Ming Collection. Tr. by Cyril Birch. 205p. 1968. pap. 9.95 (ISBN 0-394-17308-2, E473, Ever). Grove.

Stories from a Ming Collection: Translations of Chinese Short Stories Published in the 17th Century. Feng Meng-Lung. Tr. by Cyril Birch. LC 77-26340. (UNESCO Collection of Representative Works: Chinese Ser.). (Illus.). 1978. Repr. of 1959 ed. lib. bdg. 35.00x (ISBN 0-313-20067-X, FESM). Greenwood.

Stories from a Tearoom Window. Shigenori Chikamatsu. Ed. by Toshiko Mori. Tr. by Kozaburo Mori from Japanese. LC 82-80013. Orig. Title: Chaso Kanawa. (Illus.). 192p. 1982. 12.95 (ISBN 0-8048-1385-X). C E Tuttle.

Stories from Acts. G. L. LeFevre. (Bible Quiz 'n Tattletotals Ser.). 16p. (Orig.). (gr. 3-6). 1982. pap. 0.98 (ISBN 0-87239-581-2, 2808). Standard Pub.

Stories from Alaska. Edward W. Dolch & M. P. Dolch. (Dolch Folklore of the World Ser.). 176p. (gr. 2-8). 1961. PLB 7.29 (ISBN 0-8116-2554-0). Garrard.

Stories from American Business. Patricia Costello. (Illus.). 112p. 1987. pap. text ed. write for info. (ISBN 0-13-849811-3). P-H.

Stories from Ancient Canaan. Ed. by Michael D. Coogan. LC 77-20022. 120p. 1978. pap. 7.95 (ISBN 0-664-24184-0). Westminster John Knox.

Stories from Ancient China. Ed. by Mary Rouse & George A. Kennedy. 4.95 (ISBN 0-88710-113-5). Yale Far Eastern Pubns.

Stories from Ancient China see New Method Supplementary Readers.

Stories from Asia Today: A Collection for Young Readers, Bk. 1. Ed. by Asian Cultural Centre for UNESCO. LC 74-82605. (Illus.). 144p. (gr. 4-7). 1980. pap. 7.95 (ISBN 0-8348-1038-7). Weatherhill.

Stories from Asia Today: A Collection for Young Readers, Bk. 2. Ed. by Asian Cultural Center for UNESCO. LC 74-82605. (Illus.). 184p. (gr. 4-7). 1980. pap. 8.95 (ISBN 0-8348-1040-9). Weatherhill.

Stories from Bapu's Life. Uma Joshi. (Nehru Library for Children). (Illus.). (gr. 1-9). 1979. pap. 2.50 (ISBN 0-89744-180-X). Auromere.

Stories from Beyond the Double Rainbow. Elaine Hardt. (Orig.). (gr. 1-8). 1982. pap. 10.50 (ISBN 0-932960-03-0). Thinking Caps.

Stories from Black History: Nine Stories, 5 vols. Ed. by John McCluskey. Incl. Mr. Impossible. Edith Gaines (ISBN 0-913678-12-0, 205); Can You Count bnd. with Carpetbaggers in Action. Frank G. Ceasor, Sr (ISBN 0-913678-11-2, 204); Little Jess & the Circus bnd with Forty Acres. Mary Shepard (ISBN 0-913678-10-4, 203); Jubilee Day bnd. with Wildfire. Edith Gaines & Martha Smith (ISBN 0-913678-09-0); Henry Box Brown bnd. with Struggle for Freedom. Pamela Pruitt & Brenda Johnston (ISBN 0-913678-08-2, 201). (Series 2). (Illus., Orig.). (gr. 5 up). 1975. pap. 3.00 per set (ISBN 0-913678-07-4). New Day Pr.

Stories from Canada. Edward W. Dolch & M. P. Dolch. (Dolch Folklore of the World Ser.). 176p. (gr. 2-8). 1964. PLB 7.29 (ISBN 0-8116-2561-3). Garrard.

Stories from Central & Southern Africa. Paul A. Scanlon. (African Writers Ser.: No. 254). xii, 207p. (Orig.). 1983. pap. text ed. 7.50 (ISBN 0-435-90254-7). Heinemann Ed.

Stories from Chaucer. J. Walker McSpadden. 1912. 15.00 (ISBN 0-8274-3508-8). R West.

Stories from China's Past. Chinese Cultural Center Staff. 216p. 1987. 245.00x (ISBN 0-317-68593-7, Pub. by Han-Shan Tang Ltd). State Mutual Bk.

Stories from China's Past. Lucy Lim. (Illus.). 1987. 210p. 350.00x, (Pub. by Han-Shan Tang Ltd); pap. 220.00x, 216p. (Pub. by Han-Shan Tang Ltd). State Mutual Bk.

Stories from Dickens. J. Walker McSpadden. 20.00 (ISBN 0-8274-3509-6). R West.

Stories from France. Edward W. Dolch & M. P. Dolch. (Dolch Folklore of the World Ser.). (Illus.). 176p. (gr. 2-8). 1963. PLB 7.29 (ISBN 0-8116-2557-5). Garrard.

Stories from George Eliot. Amy Cruse. 1913. 20.00 (ISBN 0-8274-3510-X). R West.

Stories from Grandpa's Rocking Chair. Sarah Kaetler. (Kindred Press Sibling Ser.). 64p. (Orig.). (gr. 3-6). 1984. pap. 3.95 (ISBN 0-919797-11-3). Kindred Pr.

Stories from Greek Mythology. E. Constantopoulos. (Illus.). (gr. 3-4). 3.20 (ISBN 0-686-79632-2). Divry.

Stories from Hawaii. Edward W. Dolch & M. P. Dolch. (Dolch Folklore of the World Ser.). (Illus.). 176p. (gr. 2-8). 1960. PLB 7.29 (ISBN 0-8116-2550-8). Garrard.

Stories from Holy Writ. Helen Waddell. LC 74-25538. 280p. 1975. Repr. of 1949 ed. lib. bdg. 35.00x (ISBN 0-8371-7872-X, WAHW). Greenwood.

Stories from India. Edward W. Dolch & M. P. Dolch. (Dolch Folklore of the World Ser.). (Illus.). 176p. (gr. 2-8). 1961. PLB 7.29 (ISBN 0-8116-2553-2). Garrard.

Stories from Indian Wigwams & Northern Campfires. E. R. Young. 1977. lib. bdg. 59.95 (ISBN 0-8490-2671-7). Gordon Pr.

Stories from Italy. Edward W. Dolch & M. P. Dolch. (Dolch Folklore of the World Ser.). (Illus.). 176p. (gr. 2-8). 1962. PLB 7.29 (ISBN 0-8116-2556-7). Garrard.

Stories from Japan. Edward W. Dolch & M. P. Dolch. (Dolch Folklore of the World Ser.). (Illus.). 176p. (gr. 2-8). 1960. PLB 7.29 (ISBN 0-8116-2552-4). Garrard.

Stories from Latin America: An ESL-EFL Reader. Larry T. Myers. (Illus.). 96p. 1987. pap. text ed. write for info. P-H.

Stories from Mexico. Edward W. Dolch & M. P. Dolch. (Dolch Folklore of the World Ser.). (Illus.). 176p. (gr. 2-8). 1960. PLB 7.29 (ISBN 0-8116-2551-6). Garrard.

Stories from Miss A. Roz Abisch et al. Ed. by Ruth L. Perle. (Alpha Vowel Bks.). (Illus.). (gr. k-1). 1977. pap. text ed. 2.75 (ISBN 0-89796-850-6). Arista Corp NY.

Stories from Miss E. Roz Abisch et al. Ed. by Ruth L. Perle. (Alpha Vowel Bks.). (Illus.). (gr. k-1). 1977. pap. text ed. 2.75 (ISBN 0-89796-851-4). Arista Corp NY.

Stories from Miss I. Roz Abisch et al. Ed. by Ruth L. Perle. (Alpha Vowel Bks.). (Illus.). (gr. k-1). 1977. pap. text ed. 2.75 (ISBN 0-89796-852-2). Arista Corp NY.

Stories from Miss O. Roz Abisch et al. Ed. by Ruth L. Perle. (Alpha Vowel Bks.). (Illus.). (gr. k-1). 1977. pap. text ed. 2.75 (ISBN 0-89796-853-0). Arista Corp NY.

Stories from Miss U. Roz Abisch et al. Ed. by Ruth L. Perle. (Alpha Vowel Bks.). (Illus.). (gr. k-1). 1977. pap. text ed. 2.75 (ISBN 0-89796-854-9). Arista Corp NY.

Stories from Nicaragua. Sergio Ramirez. Tr. by Nick Caistor from Span. (Readers International Ser.). (Illus.). 130p. 1987. 14.95 (ISBN 0-930523-28-8, Dist. by Consortium); pap. 7.95 (ISBN 0-930523-29-6). Readers Intl.

Stories from Old China. Edward W. Dolch & M. P. Dolch. (Dolch Folklore of the World Ser.). (Illus.). 176p. (gr. 2-8). 1964. PLB 7.29 (ISBN 0-8116-2558-3). Garrard.

Stories from Old Egypt. Edward W. Dolch & M. P. Dolch. (Dolch Folklore of the World Ser.). (Illus.). 176p. (gr. 2-8). 1964. PLB 7.29 (ISBN 0-8116-2559-1). Garrard.

Stories from Old-Fashioned Children's Books. A. W. Tuer. 35.00 (ISBN 0-8490-1126-4). Gordon Pr.

Stories from Old Fashioned Children's Books. Andrew W. Tuer. LC 75-75059. (Illus.). 1969. Repr. of 1899 ed. 39.50x (ISBN 0-678-07507-7). Kelley.

Stories from Old-Fashioned Children's Books, Brought Together & Introduced to the Reader. Andrew W. Tuer. LC 68-31438. 456p. 1968. Repr. of 1899 ed. 34.00x (ISBN 0-8103-3489-5). Gale.

Stories from Old Russia. Edward W. Dolch & M. P. Dolch. (Dolch Folklore of the World Ser.). (Illus.). 176p. (gr. 2-8). 1964. PLB 7.29 (ISBN 0-8116-2560-5). Garrard.

Stories from Our House. Richard Tulloch. (Illus.). 32p. (ps-3). 1987. 9.95 (ISBN 0-521-33485-3). Cambridge U Pr.

Stories from Our Living Past. new ed. Francine Prose. Ed. by Jules Harlow. LC 74-8514. (Illus.). 128p. (gr. 3-4). 1974. 6.95x (ISBN 0-87441-081-9); wkbk. 1 2.75 (ISBN 0-87441-083-5); wkbk. 2 2.75 (ISBN 0-87441-084-3); tchr's guide 14.95 (ISBN 0-87441-082-7). Behrman.

Stories from Panchatantra. Bani R. Choudhary. (Illus.). (gr. 3-10). 1979. 7.50 (ISBN 0-89744-136-2). Auromere.

Stories from Panchatantra: Book I. Shivkumar. (Illus.). (gr. 1-9). 1979. 4.50 (ISBN 0-89744-162-1). Auromere.

Stories from Panchatantra: Book II. Shivkumar. (Illus.). (gr. 1-9). 1979. 4.50 (ISBN 0-89744-163-X). Auromere.

Stories from Panchatantra: Book III. Shivkumar. (Illus.). (gr. 1-9). 1979. 4.50 (ISBN 0-89744-164-8). Auromere.

Stories from Panchatantra: Book IV. Shivkumar. (Illus.). (gr. 1-9). 1979. 4.50 (ISBN 0-89744-165-6); pap. write for info. Auromere.

Stories from Pangirtung. Illus. by Germaine Arnaktauyok. (Illus.). 100p. 1976. 10.00 (ISBN 0-295-95972-X, Pub. by Hurtig Pubs). U of Wash Pr.

Stories from Pangnirtung. Illus. by Germaine Arnaktauyok. (Illus.). 100p. 1976. 10.00. U of Wash Pr.

Stories from Plutarch. F. J. Rowbotham. 1905. Repr. 20.00 (ISBN 0-8274-3512-6). R West.

Stories from Shakespeare. Marchette Chute. 320p. (YA) (gr. 7 up). 1971. pap. 3.95 (ISBN 0-451-62485-8, ME2183, Ment). NAL.

Stories from Shakespeare. Marchette Chute. Date not set. pap. 3.95 (ISBN 0-452-00895-6, Mer). NAL.

Stories from Shakespeare. (Classics Ser.). (gr. 4 up). 1988. pap. 3.95 (ISBN 0-582-52283-8). Longman.

Stories from Shakespeare see New Method Supplementary Readers.

Stories from Sikh History, 10 vols. Kartar Singh & Gurdial S. Dhillon. (Illus.). (gr. 1 up). 1971. Vol. I. pap. text ed. 2.25 (ISBN 0-89744-075-7); Vol. II. pap. text ed. 2.25 (ISBN 0-89744-076-5); Vol. III. pap. text ed. 2.25 (ISBN 0-89744-077-3); Vol. IV. pap. text ed. 2.50 (ISBN 0-89744-078-1); Vol. V. pap. text ed. 2.50 (ISBN 0-89744-079-X); Vol. VI. pap. text ed. 2.50 (ISBN 0-89744-080-3); Vol. VII. pap. text ed. 3.00 (ISBN 0-89744-081-1); Vol. VIII. pap. text ed. 4.00 (ISBN 0-89744-082-X); Vol. X. pap. text ed. 4.25 (ISBN 0-87944-083-8), Vol. IX, pap. text ed. 3.50 (ISBN 0-89744-084-6). Auromere.

Stories from Spain. Edward W. Dolch & M. P. Dolch. (Dolch Folklore of the World Ser.). (Illus.). 176p. (gr. 2-8). 1962. PLB 7.29 (ISBN 0-8116-2555-9). Garrard.

Stories from Sri Lanka. Ed. by Yasmine Gooneratne. (Writing in Asia Ser.). 1979. pap. text ed. 6.00x (ISBN 0-686-58249-7, 00218). Heinemann Ed.

Stories from Tagore. Rabindranath Tagore. 176p. Date not set. 4.00. Asia Bk Corp.

Stories from Tennessee. Linda Burton. LC 82-16016. 432p. 1983. text ed. 29.95x (ISBN 0-87049-376-0); pap. 14.95 (ISBN 0-87049-377-9). U of Tenn Pr.

Stories from the Arabian Nights. L. Housman. 144p. 1986. 70.00x (ISBN 1-85077-143-X, Pub. by Darf Pubs Ltd). State Mutual Bk.

Stories from the Arabian Nights. Retold by Naomi Lewis. LC 87-27134. (Illus.). 224p. (gr. 5 up). 1987. 19.95 (ISBN 0-8050-0404-1). H Holt & Co.

Stories from the Arabian Nights. Vernon Thomas. (Illus.). (YA) (gr. 8-12). 1979. 7.25 (ISBN 0-89744-142-7). Auromere.

Stories from the Bible. Walter De la Mare. (Illus.). 418p. (gr. 3). 1985. pap. 6.95 (ISBN 0-571-11086-X). Faber & Faber.

Stories from the Bible: From the Garden of Eden to the Promised Land. Walter De La Mare. (Illus.). 244p. (gr. 3 up). 1987. pap. 5.95 (ISBN 0-571-14946-4). Faber & Faber.

Stories from the Bible-Newly Retold. Sipke van der Land. LC 79-10049. pap. 51.30 (ISBN 0-317-39654-4, 2023224). Bks Demand UMI.

Stories from the Blue Road. Emily Crofford. LC 81-21229. (Illus.). 168p. (gr. 3-7). 1982. PLB 8.95 (ISBN 0-87614-189-0). Carolrhoda Bks.

Stories from the Country of Lost Borders. Ed. by Marjorie Pryse. (American Women Writers Ser.). 267p. 1987. text ed. 30.00 (ISBN 0-8135-1217-4); pap. text ed. 10.00 (ISBN 0-8135-1218-2). Rutgers U Pr.

Stories from The Delight of Hearts: The Memoirs of Haji Mirza Haydar-'Ali. A. Q. Faizi. LC 79-91219. (Illus.). 176p. 1980. 11.95 (ISBN 0-933770-11-1). Kalimat.

Stories from the Diary of a Doctor. L. T. Meade. LC 75-32767. (Literature of Mystery & Detection Ser.). (Illus.). 1976. Repr. of 1895 ed. 29.00x (ISBN 0-405-07886-2). Ayer Co Pubs.

Stories from the Four Corners. Ralph Cutlip. (gr. 7-12). 1975. pap. text ed. 8.33 (ISBN 0-87720-354-7). AMSCO Sch.

Stories from the Golden Goose Book. L. Leslie Brooke. (ps-3). 1987. 4.95 (ISBN 0-7232-3530-9). Warne.

Stories from the Greek Comedians Aristophanes, Philemon, Diphilus, Menander, Apollodorus. B. C. Burt. Repr. of 1893 ed. 17.50 (ISBN 0-686-20111-6). Quality Lib.

Stories from the Greek Comedians Aristophanes, Philemon, Piphilus, Menander, Apollodorus. Alfred J. Church. 1893. 17.50 (ISBN 0-8274-3940-7). R West.

Stories from the Land, Vol. 53, No. 2. 32p. 1981. pap. 3.00 (ISBN 0-686-94115-2). Mus Northern Ariz.

Stories from the Literary Review. Ed. by Charles Angoff. LC 68-21271. 312p. 1969. 20.00 (ISBN 0-8386-6899-2). Fairleigh Dickinson.

Stories from the Microwave. Willie Smith. 28p. 1983. pap. text ed. 2.50 (ISBN 0-686-38441-5). Skydog OR.

Stories from the Muslim World. Huda Khattab. (Stories from Religious World Ser.). (Illus.). 48p. (gr. 5 up). 1987. 7.96 (ISBN 0-382-09313-5). Silver.

Stories from the New Testament. G Polyzoides. (Illus.). 112p. 3.20 (ISBN 0-686-83966-8). Divry.

Stories from the Old Testament. David M. Harralson. (Literacy Volunteers of America Readers Ser.). 48p. (Orig.). 1983. pap. 1.95 (ISBN 0-8428-9607-4). Cambridge Bk.

Stories from the Old Testament. G. Polyzoides. (Illus.). 71p. (Gr.). (gr. 5 up). 3.20 (ISBN 0-686-80434-1). Divry.

Stories from the Rabbis. Abram S. Isaacs. LC 79-175868. Repr. of 1911 ed. 20.00 (ISBN 0-405-08661-X, Blom Pubns). Ayer Co Pubs.

Stories from the Rabbis. Abram S. Isaacs. Repr. of 1893 ed. 27.00. Darby Bks.

Stories from the Twilight Zone. Rod Serling. LC 86-47578. 432p. (Orig.). 1986. pap. 9.95 (ISBN 0-553-34329-7, Spectra). Bantam.

Stories from the Ukraine. Mykola Khvylovy. pap. 1.65 (ISBN 0-685-19413-2, 76, Pub. by Citadel Pr). Lyle Stuart.

Stories from the Ukraine. Mykola Knvylovy. (Philosophical Paperbook Ser.). 234p. 1983. pap. 6.95 (ISBN 0-8022-0850-9). Philos Lib.

Stories from the Warm Zone & Sydney Stories. Jessica Anderson. 1987. 15.95 (ISBN 0-670-81626-4). Viking.

Stories from Three Islands: Haiti, Jamaica, Puerto Rico. Ruth Montgomery & Edna Mc Guire. (gr. 1-7). 1977. 3.25 (ISBN 0-377-00064-7). Friendship Pr.

Stories from Ugidali: Cherokee Story Teller. Piper. 1981. pap. 1.95 (ISBN 0-89992-078-0). Coun India Ed.

Stories from Under the Sky. John Madson. (Iowa Heritage Collection Ser.). (Illus.). 205p. 1988. pap. 6.95 (ISBN 0-8138-0077-3). Iowa St U Pr.

Stories from Wagner. J. Walker McSpadden. 231p. 1981. Repr. of 1905 ed. lib. bdg. 30.00 (ISBN 0-89987-583-1). Darby Bks.

Stories in an Almost Classical Mode. Harold Brodkey. LC 88-45299. 624p. 1988. 24.95 (ISBN 0-394-50699-5). Knopf.

Stories in Another Language. Yannick Murphy. 1987. 15.95 (ISBN 0-394-55707-7). Knopf.

Stories in English Verse. George Loane. 1977. Repr. 20.00. Century Bookbindery.

Stories in English Verse. Ed. by George G. Loane. 256p. 1982. Repr. lib. bdg. 20.00. Century Bookbindery.

Stories in Light & Shadow. Bret Harte. LC 78-116952. (Short Story Index Reprint Ser). 1898. 17.00 (ISBN 0-8369-3455-5). Ayer Co Pubs.

Stories in Manx with English Translations. (Manx & Eng.). pap. 4.95 (ISBN 0-89979-030-5). British Am Bks.

Stories in Prose, Stories in Verse, Shorter Poems, Lectures & Essays. William Morris. Ed. by G. D. Cole. LC 75-41200. Repr. of 1934 ed. 31.50 (ISBN 0-404-14690-2). AMS Pr.

Stories in the Sky. Paul Thigpen. LC 85-29109. 160p. (gr. 4-6). 1986. pap. 7.95 (ISBN 0-89191-361-0). Cook.

Stories Jesus Told. Tim Dowley. (Moody Bible Storybooks Ser.). (Illus.). (gr. 1-4). 1988. pap. 3.95 (ISBN 0-8024-3237-9). Moody.

Stories Jesus Told. Gladys Hunt. (Fisherman Bible Studyguide Ser.). 96p. (Orig.). pap. 2.95 (ISBN 0-87788-791-8). Shaw Pubs.

Stories Jesus Told. Rawson Lloyd. (Children's Picture Bible Ser.). (gr. 4-6). 1982. 7.95 (ISBN 0-86020-516-9, Usborne-Hayes); PLB 12.96 (ISBN 0-88110-097-8); pap. 4.95 (ISBN 0-86020-521-5). EDC.

Stories Jesus Told. Patricia Mahany. (Standard's Coloring Bks.). (Illus.). 16p. (Orig.). (gr. k-3). 1982. pap. 0.89 (ISBN 0-87239-601-0, 2390). Standard Pub.

Stories Jesus Told see Historias Que Jesus Conto.

Stories Julian Tells. Ann Cameron. LC 80-18023. (Illus.). 96p. (gr. k-5). 1981. 8.95 (ISBN 0-394-84301-0); lib. bdg. 8.99 (ISBN 0-394-94301-5). Pantheon.

Stories Julian Tells. Ann Cameron. LC 80-18023. (Borzoi Sprinters Ser.). (Illus.). 96p. (gr. k-4). 1987. pap. 2.95 (ISBN 0-394-89262-3). Knopf.

Stories Made Easy for Spanish Speakers. Walker La Verne & Marta J. Planadeball. LC 86-6913. 75p. 1986. pap. 6.00 (ISBN 0-8477-3344-0). U of PR Pr.

Stories Made of Bible Stories. Abraham Cronbach. 1961. 17.95x (ISBN 0-8084-0386-9). New Coll U Pr.

Stories of a Salesman. Murli D. Melwani. 1976. lib. bdg. 8.00 (ISBN 0-89253-084-7); flexible bdg. 6.75 (ISBN 0-89253-268-8). Ind-US Inc.

Stories of a Western Town. Alice French. 1972. lib. bdg. 27.50 (ISBN 0-8422-8055-3); pap. text ed. 8.50x (ISBN 0-8290-0673-7). Irvington.

Stories of American Life, 3 vols. 1972. Repr. of 1830 ed. lib. bdg. 126.00 set (ISBN 0-8422-8097-9); lib. bdg. 42.00 ea. Irvington.

Stories of Authors, British & American. facs. ed. Edwin W. Chubb. LC 68-54338. (Essay Index Reprint Ser). 1926. 21.50 (ISBN 0-8369-0305-6). Ayer Co Pubs.

Stories of Baha'u'llah. Ali-Akbar Furutan. 128p. 1986. 14.75 (ISBN 0-317-55363-1); pap. 6.50 (ISBN 0-317-55364-X). G Ronald Pub.

Stories of Basel, Berne & Zurich. M. D. Hottinger. (Mediaeval Towns Ser.: Vol. 35). pap. 35.00 (ISBN 0-8115-0877-3). Kraus Repr.

Stories of Bernard Malamud. Bernard Malamud. LC 83-14100. 357p. 1983. 17.95 (ISBN 0-374-27037-6); signed, limited ed. 75.00 (ISBN 0-374-27038-4). FS&G.

Stories of Bernard Malamud. Bernard Malamud. 370p. 1984. pap. 8.95 (ISBN 0-452-25911-8, Plume). NAL.

Stories of Breece D'J Pancake. Breece D'J Pancake. 1983. 15.95 (ISBN 0-316-69012-0, Pub. by Atlantic Monthly Pr). Little.

Stories of Breece D'J Pancake. Breece D'J Pancake. 1984. pap. 6.95 (ISBN 0-03-070623-8, Owl Bks.). H Holt & Co.

Stories of Buddha's Births: A Jataka Reader. C. S. Jossan. LC 76-30762. (Foreign & Comparative Studies Program, South Asian Special Publications Ser.: No. 1). 130p. 1976. pap. text ed. 5.00x (ISBN 0-915984-77-6). Syracuse U Foreign Comp.

Stories of Central Queensland. Peter James. 105p. 1985. pap. 4.50 (ISBN 0-908175-40-X, Pub. by Boolarong Pubn Australia). Intl spec bk.

Stories of Charlemagne. Jennifer Westwood. LC 74-12435. (gr. 6 up). 1976. 14.95 (ISBN 0-87599-213-7). S G Phillips.

Stories of Christmas Carols. Ernest K. Emurian. (Paperback Program Ser). 1969. pap. 4.95 (ISBN 0-8010-3265-2). Baker Bk.

Stories of Composers for Young Musicians. Catherine W. Kendall. LC 83-103936. (Illus.). 192p. (Orig.). (gr. 1-10). 1982. pap. 12.95 (ISBN 0-9610878-0-3). Toadwood Pubs.

Stories of Crime & Detection. Ed. by Joan D. Berbrich. LC 73-8832. (Patterns in Literary Art Ser). (Illus.). 312p. (gr. 9-12). 1972. pap. 13.76 (ISBN 0-07-004826-6). McGraw.

Stories of Darkness & Dread. Joseph P. Brennan. 1973. 6.00 (ISBN 0-87054-064-5). Arkham.

Stories of Dixie. James W. Nicholson. 1965. 4.95 (ISBN 0-87511-153-X). Claitors.

Stories of Don Bosco. 2nd ed. Peter Lappin. LC 78-72525. (Illus.). 272p. (gr. 5-12). 1979. pap. 2.95 (ISBN 0-89944-036-3). Don Bosco Multimedia.

Stories of Elizabeth Spencer. Elizabeth Spencer. 542p. 1983. pap. 7.95 (ISBN 0-14-006436-2). Penguin.

Stories of Ernest Dowson. Ernest Dowson. Ed. by Mark Longaker. 1977. lib. bdg. 59.95 (ISBN 0-8490-2672-5). Gordon Pr.

Stories of Excellence: Ten Case Studies from a Study of Exemplary Mathematics Programs. Mark Driscoll. LC 86-33193. 106p. 1987. pap. 10.00 (ISBN 0-87353-236-8). NCTM.

Stories of F. Scott Fitzgerald. F. Scott Fitzgerald. 1951. pap. 12.95 (ISBN 0-684-71737-9, SL135, ScribT); lib. rep. ed. 35.00x (ISBN 0-684-15366-1). Scribner.

Stories of F. Scott Fitzgerald. F. Scott Fitzgerald. 480p. 1984. pap. 6.95 (ISBN 0-02-019940-6, Collier). Macmillan.

Stories of Faith. John Shea. 1980. pap. 9.95 (ISBN 0-88347-112-4). Thomas More.

Stories of Five Decades. Hermann Hesse. 20.95 (ISBN 0-89190-669-X, Pub. by Am Repr). Amereon Ltd.

Stories of Freedom: The 1988 Childcraft Annual. Ed. by World Book, Inc. Staff. LC 65-25105. (Illus.). 288p. (YA) (gr. 8-12). 1988. lib. bdg. write for info. (ISBN 0-7166-0688-7). World Bk.

Stories of Georgia. Joel C. Harris. LC 85-25490. (Illus.). 320p. 1971. Repr. of 1896 ed. bds. 9.50 (ISBN 0-87797-018-1). Cherokee.

Stories of Georgia. Joel C. Harris. LC 73-174943. 316p. 1975. Repr. of 1896 ed. 34.00x (ISBN 0-8103-4082-8). Gale.

Stories of God. rev. ed. Rainer M. Rilke. (Ger. & Eng.). 1963. pap. 6.95 (ISBN 0-393-00154-7, Norton Lib.). Norton.

Stories of God: An Unauthorized Biography. John Shea. 1978. pap. 9.95 (ISBN 0-88347-085-3). Thomas More.

Stories of Great Craftsmen. facs. ed. S. H. Glenister. LC 75-128247. (Essay Index Reprint Ser). 1939. 19.00 (ISBN 0-8369-1831-2). Ayer Co Pubs.

Stories of Great Muslims. K. H. Hayes. 4.75 (ISBN 0-686-18389-4). Kazi Pubns.

Stories of Great Muslims. 1985. 4.00 (ISBN 0-89259-020-3). Am Trust Pubns.

Stories of Great Writers. Henry Gilbert. 1973. Repr. of 1914 ed. 8.50 (ISBN 0-8274-0733-5). R West.

Stories of Hans Andersen. Hans Christian Andersen. Retold by Robert Mathias. LC 85-61399. (Illus.). 80p. (ps-4). 1985. 11.45 (ISBN 0-382-09153-1). Silver.

Stories of Happy People. Lars Gustafsson. Tr. by Yvonne L. Sandstroem & John Weinstock. LC 85-31052. 160p. 1986. 16.95 (ISBN 0-8112-0977-6); pap. 7.95 (ISBN 0-8112-0978-4, NDP616). New Directions.

Stories of Hawaii. Jack London. Ed. by A. Grove Day. LC 65-11682. 284p. 1985. pap. 3.95 (ISBN 0-935180-08-7). Mutual Pub HI.

Stories of Heinrich Boll. Heinrich Boll. Tr. by Leila Vennewitz from Ger. LC 85-40392. 576p. 1986. 24.50 (ISBN 0-394-51405-X). Knopf.

Stories of Heinrich Boll. Heinrich Boll. Tr. by Leila Vennewitz. 696p. 1987. pap. text ed. 9.95 (ISBN 0-07-006422-9). McGraw.

Stories of Here & Now. Dolores Seidman. (gr. 9 up). 1978. pap. text ed. 8.08 (ISBN 0-87720-309-1). AMSCO Sch.

Stories of Home Folks. Mabel Hale. 160p. pap. 1.50 (ISBN 0-686-29143-3). Faith Pub Hse.

Stories of Hospital & Camp. facsimile ed. Mrs. C. E. McKay. LC 70-37312. (Black Heritage Library Collection). Repr. of 1876 ed. 17.50 (ISBN 0-8369-8949-X). Ayer Co Pubs.

Stories of Jesus, Stories of Now. Alexander Campbell. 80p. (Orig.). (gr. 1-6). 1980. pap. 12.95 (ISBN 0-940754-04-5). Ed Ministries.

Stories of Jesus, Tell Them to Me. P. Gwyn Filby. 200p. 1986. 45.00x (ISBN 0-947939-01-6, Pub. by Elmcrest UK). State Mutual Bk.

Stories of Jesus, Tell Them to Me. P. Gwyn Filby. 200p. 1987. 60.00x (ISBN 0-317-62104-1, Michael Gardener Pubs). State Mutual Bk.

Stories of Jewish Home Life. facsimile ed. Salomon R. Von Mosenthal. LC 75-160945. (Short Story Index Reprint Ser.). Repr. of 1907 ed. 20.00 (ISBN 0-8369-3924-7). Ayer Co Pubs.

Stories of John Cheever. John Cheever. 1980. pap. 4.95 (ISBN 0-345-33567-8). Ballantine.

Stories of John Cheever. John Cheever. LC 78-106. 1978. 20.00 (ISBN 0-394-50087-3). Knopf.

Stories of King Arthur. Ed. by Blanche Winder. (Airmont Classics Ser.). (gr. 4 up). pap. 1.95 (ISBN 0-8049-0167-8, CL-167). Airmont.

Stories of King David. Lillian S. Freehof. (Illus.). (gr. 4-7). 1952. 5.95 (ISBN 0-8276-0162-X, 263). JPS Phila.

Stories of Kleist: A Critical Study. Denys Dyer. LC 76-58356. 210p. 1977. 32.50 (ISBN 0-8419-0303-4). Holmes & Meier.

Stories of Life & Death. Juan R. Jimenez. Tr. by Antonio T. De Nicholas. LC 85-28565. (Illus.). 185p. (Orig.). 1986. 18.95 (ISBN 0-913729-21-3); pap. 9.95 (ISBN 0-913729-07-8). Paragon Hse.

Stories of Lost Israel in Folklore. James A. Haggart. LC 80-65735. 144p. 1981. pap. 5.00 (ISBN 0-934666-08-3). Artisan Sales.

Stories of Love that Lasts. Don W. Hillis. 80p. (gr. 9-12). 1980. pap. 1.25 (ISBN 0-89323-015-4). Bible Memory.

Stories of Maasaw, a Hopi God. Ekkehart Malotki & Michael Lomatuway'ma. LC 87-164. (American Tribal Religions Ser.: Vol. 10). (Illus.). x, 347p. 1987. 24.95x (ISBN 0-8032-3117-2); pap. 14.95x (ISBN 0-8032-8147-1). U of Nebr Pr.

Stories of Men & Rats. Sam Spiller. 1982. 10.00 (ISBN 0-682-49882-3). Exposition-Phoenix.

Stories of Michael Robartes & His Friends. William B. Yeats. 58p. 1970. Repr. of 1931 ed. 15.00x (ISBN 0-7165-1373-0, BBA 02114, Pub. by Cuala Press Ireland). Biblio Dist.

Stories of Misbegotten Love. Herbert Gold. Bd. with Angel on My Shoulder & Other Stories. Don Asher. (Capra Back-to-Back Bks.). 128p. (Orig.). 1985. pap. 7.50 (ISBN 0-88496-234-2). Capra Pr.

Stories of Misbegotten Love; Angel on My Shoulder. Herbert Gold & Don Asher. (Capra Back-to-Back Ser.). 128p. 1988. Repr. lib. bdg. 19.95x (ISBN 0-8095-4103-3). Borgo Pr.

Stories of Mother Teresa: Her Smile & Her Words. Jose L. Balado. Tr. by Olimpia Diaz from Span. 96p. 1983. pap. 2.95 (ISBN 0-89243-181-4). Liguori Pubns.

Stories of Mukunda. Sri Kriyananda. LC 76-5748. (Illus.). 110p. 1976. pap. 4.95 (ISBN 0-916124-09-6). Crystal Clarity.

Stories of Muriel Spark. Muriel Spark. 320p. 1986. pap. 7.95 (ISBN 0-452-25880-4, Plume). NAL.

Stories of Mystery & Immagination see New Method Supplementary Readers.

Stories of New Jersey. Frank R. Stockton. (Illus.). 263p. 1984. pap. 9.95 (ISBN 0-8135-0369-8). Rutgers U Pr.

Stories of Old Daniel: Or Tales of Wonder & Delight. 2nd ed. Margaret J. Moore. (Early Children's Bks). 1969. Repr. of 1810 ed. 22.00 (ISBN 0-384-40000-0). Johnson Repr.

Stories of Old Ireland for Children. Edmund Lenihan. (Illus.). 90p. (Orig.). (ps-3). 1986. pap. 7.95 (ISBN 0-85342-777-1, Pub. by Mercier Pr Ireland). Irish Bks Media.

Stories of Old New Hampshire. Doris Piper. 1987. 7.95. Equity Pub NH.

Stories of Old New Spain. Thomas A. Janvier. 1972. Repr. of 1891 ed. lib. bdg. 26.50 (ISBN 0-8422-8081-2). Irvington.

Stories of Old New Spain. Thomas A. Janvier. 1986. pap. text ed. 6.95x (ISBN 0-8290-2031-4). Irvington.

Stories of Old Upland: Early Years Picture Album, Pt. 5. 3rd ed. Esther B. Black. Orig. Title: Stories of Old Upland for Young Listeners. (Illus.). 124p. 1979. pap. text ed. 7.00 (ISBN 0-9603586-0-9). Chaffey Commun Cult Ctr.

Stories of Old Upland for Young Listeners see Stories of Old Upland: Early Years Picture Album.

Stories of Our American Patriotic Songs. John H. Lyons. LC 42-24375. (Illus.). 72p. (gr. 5-12). 13.95 (ISBN 0-8149-0354-1). Vanguard.

Stories of Our Blackfeet Grandmothers. Mary C. Boss-Ribs & Jenny Running-Crane. (Indian Culture Ser.). (Orig.). (gr. 1-6). 1984. pap. 1.45 (ISBN 0-89992-096-9). Coun India Ed.

Stories of Our Favorite Hymns. Christopher Idle. (Illus.). 80p. 1980. 14.95 (ISBN 0-8028-3535-X). Eerdmans.

Stories of Peace & War. Frederic Remington. LC 75-125237. (Short Story Index Reprint Ser). 1899. 12.00 (ISBN 0-8369-3604-3). Ayer Co Pubs.

Stories of Persian Heroes. E. M. Wilmot-Buxton. 1976. lib. bdg. 59.95 (ISBN 0-8490-2673-3). Gordon Pr.

Stories of Prayer: Interviews with Leading Catholics on Their Experience of God. Betty Winter & Art Winter. LC 85-62159. (Orig.). 1985. pap. 8.95 (ISBN 0-934134-15-4). Sheed & Ward MO.

Stories of Ray Bradbury. Ray Bradbury. LC 80-7655. 928p. 1980. 24.50 (ISBN 0-394-51335-5). Knopf.

Stories of Red Hanrahan. William B. Yeats. 72p. 1971. Repr. of 1904 ed. 15.00x (ISBN 0-7165-1330-7, BBA 02115, Pub. by Cuala Press Ireland). Biblio Dist.

Stories of Rome. Tr. by Roger Nichols. Livy. LC 81-10227. (Translations from Greek & Roman Authors Ser.). (Illus.). 112p. pap. 5.95 (ISBN 0-521-22816-6). Cambridge U Pr.

Stories of Scientific Discovery. facs. ed. D. B. Hammond. LC 74-76901. (Essay Index Reprint Ser). 1923. 17.00 (ISBN 0-8369-0015-4). Ayer Co Pubs.

Stories of Sickness. Howard Brody. LC 87-10657. 1988. 27.50x (ISBN 0-300-03977-8). Yale U Pr.

Stories of Some of the Prophets, Vol. I. A. S. Hashim. (Islamic Books for Children: Bk. 8). pap. 4.95 (ISBN 0-686-18402-5); pap. 45.00 entire series (ISBN 0-686-18403-3). Kazi Pubns.

Stories of Some of the Prophets, Vol II. A. S. Hashim. (Islamic Books for Children: Bk. 9). pap. 4.95 (ISBN 0-686-18400-9); pap. 45.00 entire series (ISBN 0-686-18401-7). Kazi Pubns.

Stories of Survival. Remmelt Hummelen & Kathleen Hummelen. 1985. 5.95 (ISBN 0-377-00150-3). Friendship Pr.

Stories of the American Experience. Leonard Kriegel & Abraham Lass. 1973. pap. 4.95 (ISBN 0-451-62383-5, Ment). NAL.

Stories of the Ants. Robert L. Merriam. (Illus.). 19p. (Orig.). 1981. pap. 6.50x (ISBN 0-686-32495-1). R L Merriam.

Stories of the Arabian Nights. Tr. by Anthea Bell. LC 83-71485. (Illus.). 92p. (gr. 4-6). 1983. 12.95 (ISBN 0-911745-02-5). P Bedrick Bks.

Stories of the Army. facsimile ed. Brander Matthews et al. LC 76-113683. (Short Story Index Reprint Ser). Repr. of 1893 ed. 17.00 (ISBN 0-8369-3412-1). Ayer Co Pubs.

Stories of the Buddha. Intro. by C. Rhys Davids. LC 78-72444. Repr. of 1929 ed. 30.00 (ISBN 0-404-17316-0). AMS Pr.

Stories of the Cherokee Hills. Maurice Thompson. LC 77-113686. (Short Story Index Reprint Ser.). 1898. 19.00 (ISBN 0-8369-3415-6). Ayer Co Pubs.

Stories of the Falls of French Creek. W. Edmunds Claussen. (Illus.). 75p. (Orig.). pap. text ed. 2.50 (ISBN 0-9616068-3-5). Boyertown Hist.

Stories of the Fishfolk. Arthur Fripp. 1985. 18.95x (ISBN 0-901976-73-3, Pub. by United WRiters Pubns England). State Mutual Bk.

Stories of the Foot Hills. Margaret Graham. LC 76-94727. (Short Story Index Reprint Ser.). 1895. 17.00 (ISBN 0-8369-3106-8). Ayer Co Pubs.

Stories of the Gods & Heroes. Sally Benson. (Illus.). (gr. 4-6). 1940. 19.95 (ISBN 0-8037-8291-8, 01258-370). Dial Bks Young.

Stories of the Great Lakes see Early Stories of the Great Lakes.

Stories of the Great Operas & Their Composers, 3 vols. Ernest Newman. Repr. of 1930 ed. 195.00x (ISBN 0-403-01632-0). Scholarly.

Stories of the Great Operas & Their Composers, 3 vols. Ernest Newman. 1988. Repr. of 1930 ed. Set. lib. bdg. 249.00x. Am Biog Serv.

Stories of the Greeks. Rex Warner. 480p. 1978. 15.00 (ISBN 0-374-27056-2); pap. 9.95 (ISBN 0-374-50728-7). FS&G.

Stories of the Holy Fathers, 2 vols. Anan Isho. Tr. by E. A. Budge. 1980. Set. lib. bdg. 125.00 (ISBN 0-8490-3195-8). Gordon Pr.

Stories of the Hudson. Washington Irving. LC 84-12830. 320p. 1984. 16.95 (ISBN 0-916346-52-8). Harbor Hill Bks.

Stories of the Magicians. Alfred J. Church. Repr. of 1887 ed. 25.00. Darby Bks.

Stories of the Modern South. Ed. by Ben Forkner & Patrick Samway. 1984. 16.75 (ISBN 0-8446-6171-6). Peter Smith.

Stories of the Modern South. Expanded ed. Ed. by Benjamin Forkner & Patrick Samway. 512p. 1986. pap. 8.95 (ISBN 0-14-009695-7). Penguin.

Stories of the Nineteen Twenties. M. Zoshchenko. Ed. by A. B. Murphy. 96p. pap. 9.95x (ISBN 0-631-14398-X). Basil Blackwell.

Stories of the North Cornish Coast. Donald Bray. 1985. 15.00x (ISBN 0-907566-73-1, Pub. by Dyllansow & Truran). State Mutual Bk.

Stories of the Old Cherokees: A Collection. Ed. by F. Roy Johnson. (Illus.). 112p. (gr. 4-8). 1975. 7.50 (ISBN 0-930230-23-X). Johnson NC.

Stories of the Old Duck Hunters & Other Drivel. Gordon MacQuarrie. Ed. by Zack Taylor. 228p. 1985. Repr. of 1967 ed. 17.50 (ISBN 0-932558-25-9). Willow Creek Pr.

Stories of the Old Missions of California. Charles F. Carter. LC 71-116945. (Short Story Index Reprint Ser). 1917. 14.00 (ISBN 0-8369-3447-4). Ayer Co Pubs.

Stories of the Railway. George A. Hibbard et al. LC 70-113684. (Short Story Index Reprint Ser.). 1893. 17.00 (ISBN 0-8369-3413-X). Ayer Co Pubs.

Stories of the Sea. Ed. by Phyllis R. Fenner. (Illus.). (gr. 5-9). 1962. lib. bdg. 5.99 (ISBN 0-394-91678-6). Knopf.

Stories of the Sea. John R. Spears et al. LC 73-113685. (Short Story Index Reprint Ser). 1893. 18.00 (ISBN 0-8369-3414-8). Ayer Co Pubs.

Stories of the Seen & the Unseen. Margaret O. Oliphant. LC 72-113682. (Short Story Index Reprint Ser.). 1889. 33.00 (ISBN 0-8369-3411-3). Ayer Co Pubs.

Stories of the Sioux. Luther Standing Bear. LC 88-12221. (Illus.). x, 95p. 1988. 12.95x (ISBN 0-8032-4194-1); pap. 4.95 (ISBN 0-8032-9187-6, Bison). U of Nebr Pr.

Stories of the South. Thomas N. Page et al. LC 74-110217. (Short Story Index Reprint Ser.). 1893. 17.00 (ISBN 0-8369-3369-9). Ayer Co Pubs.

Stories of the South, Old & New. Ed. by Addison Hibbard. 1978. Repr. of 1931 ed. 35.00 (ISBN 0-8492-5311-X). R West.

Stories of the Steppe. Maxim Gorky. LC 72-121552. (Short Story Index Reprint Ser). 1918. 10.00 (ISBN 0-8369-3508-X). Ayer Co Pubs.

Stories of the Trees. S. L. Dyson. LC 78-175735. (Illus.). 274p. 1974. Repr. of 1890 ed. 40.00x (ISBN 0-8103-3033-4). Gale.

Stories of the Victorian Writers. facs. ed. Janie R. Walker. LC 68-26484. (Essay Index Reprint Ser). 1968. Repr. of 1922 ed. 15.00 (ISBN 0-8369-0964-X). Ayer Co Pubs.

Stories of the Wagner Operas. H. A. Guerber. 1977. lib. bdg. 59.95 (ISBN 0-8490-2674-1). Gordon Pr.

Stories of the Wagner Operas. H. A. Guerber. LC 77-90804. 1978. Repr. of 1895 ed. lib. bdg. 20.00 (ISBN 0-89341-421-2). Longwood Pub Group.

Stories of the World's Holidays. Grace Humphrey. LC 74-3023. 344p. 1974. Repr. of 1923 ed. 58.00x (ISBN 0-8103-3660-X). Gale.

Stories of Three Decades. Thomas Mann. 1936. 17.95 (ISBN 0-394-44734-4). Knopf.

Stories of Three Decades. Thomas Mann. Tr. by H. T. Lowe-Porter. LC 61-66696. 9.95 (ISBN 0-394-60483-0). Modern Lib.

Stories of Tommy's Toy Animal Collection. Pamela Peckham. 1988. 6.95 (ISBN 0-533-07906-3). Vantage.

Stories of Traditional Navajo Life & Culture. Ed. by Broderick H. Johnson. LC 77-22484. (Illus.). 335p. 1977. lib. bdg. 15.00x (ISBN 0-912586-23-0). Navajo Coll Pr.

Stories of Valour. Rajendra Awasthy. (Nehru Library for Children). (Illus.). (gr. 1-9). 1979. pap. 2.50 (ISBN 0-89744-182-6). Auromere.

Stories of Vanishing Peoples. John Mercer. (Illus.). 128p. 1982. 9.95 (ISBN 0-8052-8106-1, Pub. by Allison & Busby England). Schocken.

Stories of Vanishing Peoples. John Mercer. (Illus.). 128p. 1986. pap. 5.95 (ISBN 0-8052-8263-7, Pub. by Allison & Busby England). Schocken.

Stories of Wales: Told for Children. Elisabeth Sheppard-Jones. (Illus.). (gr. 3-6). 1978. pap. 5.95 (ISBN 0-902375-41-5). Academy Chi Pubs.

Stories of Willa Cather. Ed. by Sharon O'Brien. 1987. pap. 8.25 (ISBN 0-452-00874-3, Mer). NAL.

Stories of William Sansom. facsimile ed. William Sansom. LC 77-144171. (Short Story Index Reprint Ser.). Repr. of 1963 ed. 24.50 (ISBN 0-8369-3786-4). Ayer Co Pubs.

Stories of William Trevor. William Trevor. 799p. 1983. pap. 8.95 (ISBN 0-14-006092-8). Penguin.

Stories of Yesteryear: Horse & Buggy Days. Harry H. Brown. LC 82-90882. (Illus.). 74p. 1982. 6.95 (ISBN 0-9610806-0-4). Kemah Pr.

Stories on a String: The Brazilian Literatura De Cordel. Candace Slater. LC 80-29091. (Illus.). 360p. 1982. 35.00x (ISBN 0-520-04154-2). U of Cal Pr.

Stories on the Orift. Bill Roberts. LC 87-63108. (Illus.). 220p. 1988. pap. 8.00 (ISBN 0-944100-02-3). Pirogue Pub.

Stories Parents Seldom Hear: College Students Write about Their Lives & Families. Compiled by Harriet Harvey. 320p. 1923. pap. 14.95 (ISBN 0-385-29214-7, Sey Lawr). Delacorte.

Stories Revived. Henry James. (First Ser.). 428p. 1984. lib. bdg. 125.00 (ISBN 0-89984-718-8). Century Bookbindery.

Stories Revived. Henry James. (Second Ser.). 401p. 1984. lib. bdg. 125.00 (ISBN 0-89984-717-X). Century Bookbindery.

Stories Revived; First Series. Henry James. LC 72-12605. (Short Story Index Reprint Ser.). 1973. Repr. of 1885 ed. 27.00 (ISBN 0-8369-4237-X). Ayer Co Pubs.

Stories, Scripts, & Scenes: Aspects of Schema Theory. Jean M. Mandler. 144p. 1984. text ed. 19.95 (ISBN 0-89859-446-4). L Erlbaum Assocs.

Stories: Second Stories, Vol. 1. Henry C. Bunner. LC 72-5900. (Short Story Index Reprint Ser). Repr. of 1916 ed. 23.50 (ISBN 0-8369-4194-2). Ayer Co Pubs.

Stories, Songs, & Poetry for Teaching Reading & Writing: Literacy Through Language. Robert A. McCracken & Marlene J. McCracken. 176p. 1986. pap. text ed. 12.95x (ISBN 0-8077-2856-X). Tchrs Coll.

Stories, Songs & Poetry to Teach Reading & Writing: Langauge Through Literacy. Robert A. McCracken & Marlene J. McCracken. LC 86-1150. 160p. 1987. pap. text ed. 12.95x (ISBN 0-8389-0450-5). ALA.

Stories That Live. Ralph Cutlip. (gr. 7-12). 1973. 8.33 (ISBN 0-87720-352-0). AMSCO Sch.

Stories That Live, 6 vols. Peter Enns & Glen Forsberg. (Series I). (Illus.). 144p. (ps-5). 1985. books & cassettes 29.70 (ISBN 0-936215-00-3). STL Intl.

Stories That Never Grow Old. (Illus.). 48p. (gr. 1-7). 1978. 5.95 (ISBN 0-448-42004-X, G&D). Putnam Pub Group.

Stories the Feet Can Tell Thru Reflexology. rev. ed. Eunice D. Ingham. (Illus.). 109p. 1938. pap. 4.95 (ISBN 0-9611804-0-4). Ingham Pub.

Stories the Feet Can Tell Thru Reflexology. rev. ed. Eunice D. Ingham. Bd. with Stories the Feet Have Told Thru Reflexology. (Illus.). 226p. 1984. pap. 7.95 (ISBN 0-9611804-3-9). Ingham Pub.

Stories the Feet Have Told Thru Reflexology. rev. ed. Eunice D. Ingham. (Illus.). 110p. 1951. 4.95 (ISBN 0-9611804-1-2). Ingham Pub.

Stories the Feet Have Told Thru Reflexology see Stories the Feet Can Tell Thru Reflexology.

Stories to Dramatize. Winifred Ward. 1952. Anchorage.

Stories to Dramatize. Winifred Ward. 389p. pap. text ed. 15.00 (ISBN 0-87602-021-X). Anchorage.

Stories to Draw. Jerry J. Mallett & Marian R. Bartch. 52p. (Orig.). (ps-3). 1982. pap. 6.95x (ISBN 0-913853-00-3). Freline.

Stories to Grow On. Illus. by June Goldsborough. LC 73-7200. (Illus.). 64p. (ps-3). 6.95 (ISBN 0-528-82420-1). Macmillan.

Stories to Learn by. John Koenig. (Illus.). 5.00 (ISBN 0-8198-0333-2); pap. 4.00 (ISBN 0-8198-0334-0). Dghtrs St Paul.

Stories to Make You Feel Better. Bennett Cerf. 1972. 12.45 (ISBN 0-394-47553-4, BYR). Random.

Stories to Remember: David, God's Champion. Peter Enns. (Illus.). 32p. (ps-5). 1987. pap. 2.98 (ISBN 0-943593-04-2); cassette 5.98 (ISBN 0-943593-06-9); coloring bk. 0.98 (ISBN 0-943593-05-0). Kids Intl Inc.

Stories to Remember: Here Comes Jesus. Peter Enns. (Illus.). 32p. (ps-5). 1987. pap. 2.98 (ISBN 0-943593-12-3); coloring bk. 0.98 (ISBN 0-943593-13-1); cassette 5.98 (ISBN 0-943593-14-X). Kids Intl Inc.

Stories to Remember: Look What God Made. Peter Enns & Terry Ligon. (Illus.). 32p. (ps-5). 1987. pap. 2.98 (ISBN 0-943593-00-X); coloring bk. 0.98 (ISBN 0-943593-01-8); cassette 5.98 (ISBN 0-943593-02-6). Kids Intl Inc.

Stories to Remember: Walking with Jesus. Peter Enns. (Illus.). 32p. (ps-5). 1987. pap. 2.98 (ISBN 0-943593-08-5); coloring bk. 0.98 (ISBN 0-943593-09-3). Kids Intl Inc.

Stormy Patriot: The Life of Samuel Chase. James Haw et al. LC 80-83807. (Illus.). 305p. 1980. 14.95 (ISBN 0-938420-00-3). Md Hist.

Stormy Petrel & the Whale: Some Origins of Moby Dick. David Jaffe. 76p. 1976. pap. 2.50 (ISBN 0-9601782-1-X). Mardi Pr.

Stormy Petrel: N. G. Gonzales & His State. Lewis Pinckney Jones. LC 73-8792. xii, 340p. 1973. 19.95x (ISBN 0-87249-253-2). U of SC Pr.

Stormy Petrel: The Life & Times of General Benjamin F. Butler, 1818-1893. Howard P. Nash, Jr. LC 71-81498. 335p. 1969. 28.50 (ISBN 0-8386-7383-X). Fairleigh Dickinson.

Stormy Petrel: The Life & Work of Maxim Gorky. Dan Levin. LC 85-2485. 348p. 1986. pap. 11.95 (ISBN 0-8052-0788-0). Schocken.

Stormy Springtime. Betty Neels. (Romances Ser.: No. 2855). 192p. Date not set. pap. 1.95 (ISBN 0-317-63912-9). Harlequin Bks.

Stormy Surrender. Robin L. Hatcher. (Spring Haven Saga Ser.: Vol. 1). 432p. 1984. pap. 3.75 (ISBN 0-8439-2073-4, Leisure Bks). Leisure NY.

Stormy Surrender. Robin L. Hatcher. 432p. 1988. pap. 3.95 Mass Market (ISBN 0-8439-2585-X). Leisure NY.

Stormy the Dolphin. 2nd ed. Dorothy L. Hernandez. (Illus.). 83p. (gr. 3-8). 1988. pap. 4.95 (ISBN 0-9620342-0-7). D L Hernandez.

Stormy Vigil. Elizabeth Graham. (Harlequin Romances Ser.). 192p. 1982. pap. 1.75 (ISBN 0-373-10543-6). Harlequin Bks.

Stormy Weather. Sandra Clark. (Harlequin Romances Ser.). 192p. 1983. pap. 1.75 (ISBN 0-373-02569-6). Harlequin Bks.

Stormy Weather: The Music & Lives of a Century of Jazzwomen. Linda Dahl. LC 83-19456. (Illus.). 371p. 1984. pap. 12.95 (ISBN 0-394-72271-X). Pantheon.

Story. Catherine Booth. pap. 3.95 (ISBN 0-686-27773-2). Schmul Pub Co.

Story-a-Night. Linda Hayward. LC 85-71094. (Illus.). 744p. (ps-3). 1985. pap. 4.95 (ISBN 0-394-87330-0, BYR). Random.

Story, a Story. Gail E. Haley. LC 69-18961. (Illus.). 36p. (gr. k-3). 1970. PLB 14.95 Spartan ed. (ISBN 0-689-20511-2, Atheneum Childrens Bks). Macmillan.

Story,-A Story. Gail E. Haley. LC 87-17412. (Illus.). 36p. (ps-3). 1988. pap. 4.95 (ISBN 0-689-71201-4, Aladdin Bks). Macmillan.

Story about a Real Man. Boris N. Polevoi. 1970. Repr. of 1952 ed. lib. bdg. 41.50x (ISBN 0-8371-3993-7, PORM). Greenwood.

Story About Ping. Marjorie Flack. (Illus.). (gr. k-2). 1977. pap. 3.95 (ISBN 0-14-050241-6, Puffin). Penguin.

Story about Ping. Marjorie Flack. (Illus.). (ps-2). 1933. lib. bdg. 10.95 (ISBN 0-670-67223-8). Viking.

Story & Discourse: Narrative Structure in Fiction & Film. Seymour Chatman. (Paperback Ser.). 288p. 1978. 34.50x (ISBN 0-8014-1131-9); pap. 9.95x (ISBN 0-8014-9186-X). Cornell U Pr.

Story & Faith: A Guide to the Old Testament. James L. Crenshaw. 539p. 1986. text ed. write for info. (ISBN 0-02-325600-1). Macmillan.

Story & Its Writer: An Introduction to Short Fiction. Ed. by Ann Charters. LC 82-62584. 1986. text ed. write for info. (ISBN 0-312-76254-2). St Martin.

Story & Other Stories. Lydia Davis. 1983. pap. 5.00 (ISBN 0-317-28696-X). Figures.

Story & Situation: Narrative Seduction & the Power of Fiction. Ross Chambers. LC 83-14787. (Theory & History of Literature Ser.: No. 12). 279p. 1984. pap. 14.95 (ISBN 0-8166-1298-6). U of Minn Pr.

Story & Structure. 7th ed. Laurence Perrine & Thomas R. Arp. 563p. 1988. pap. text ed. 13.00 (ISBN 0-15-583790-7, HC); pap. text ed. 1.75 instr's. manual (ISBN 0-15-583791-5). HarBraceJ.

Story & the Fable: An Autobiography. Edwin Muir. LC 87-60854. 272p. 1987. pap. 13.95 (ISBN 0-937672-22-X). Rowan Tree.

Story & Verse for Children. 3rd ed. Miriam B. Huber. (gr. k-4). 1965. write for info. (ISBN 0-02-357500-X). Macmillan.

Story As Told. rev. ed. Jalil Mahmoudi. LC 79-65925. (Illus.). 80p. (Orig.). 1980. pap. 4.95 (ISBN 0-933770-10-3). Kalimat.

Story Bag: A Collection of Korean Folk Tales. Kim So-Un. Tr. by Setsu Higashi. LC 55-13738. (Illus.). (gr. 2-5). 1955. pap. 6.25 (ISBN 0-8048-0548-2). C E Tuttle.

Story Behind the Word. Morton S. Freeman. (Professional Writing Ser.). 275p. 1985. 19.95 (ISBN 0-89495-046-0); pap. 14.95 (ISBN 0-89495-047-9). ISI Pr.

Story Bible. Pearl S. Buck. 1984. lib. bdg. 18.95 (ISBN 0-8161-3661-0, Large Print Bks). G K Hall.

Story Bible: New Testament, Vol. 2. Pearl S. Buck. 1972. pap. 3.95 (ISBN 0-451-14639-5, AE2694, Sig). NAL.

Story Bible: Old Testament, Vol. 1. Pearl S. Buck. 1972. pap. 3.95 (ISBN 0-451-13458-3, Sig). NAL.

Story Book Prince. Joanne Oppenheim. LC 85-31745. (Illus.). 32p. (ps-3). 1987. 12.95 (ISBN 0-15-200590-0, Gulliver Bks). HarBraceJ.

Story Books for We Can Read. Illus. by Mary W. Walter. Incl. Eel, Ail, Ole (ISBN 0-917186-03-6); Happenings (ISBN 0-917186-04-4); We Learn at Play (ISBN 0-917186-05-2); Things for All Seasons (ISBN 0-917186-06-0); Tales & Tails (ISBN 0-917186-07-9); Just Like Me (ISBN 0-917186-08-7); All Around Me (ISBN 0-917186-09-5); Bridging the Summer (ISBN 0-917186-10-9). 5.40 ea. McQueen.

Story Builders Activity Book. Joan Lamport et al. (Tool Box Ser.). (Illus.). (gr. 2-3). 0.95 (ISBN 0-89796-844-1, XTW 03). Arista Corp NY.

Story Catcher. Mari Sandoz. LC 85-31810. (Illus.). 175p. (gr. 7-10). 1986. 5.95 (ISBN 0-8032-9163-9, Bison). U of Nebr Pr.

Story Experience. Jane B. Wilson. LC 79-13888. 177p. 1979. 16.00 (ISBN 0-8108-1224-X). Scarecrow.

Story: Fictions Past & Present. Boyd Litzinger & Joyce Carol Oates. LC 84-81089. 1077p. 1985. pap. text ed. 15.50 (ISBN 0-669-06687-7); instr's guide 2.00 (ISBN 0-669-06688-5). Heath.

Story First: The Writer As Insider. Kit Reed. Ed. by Joseph Reed. 150p. 1982. 19.95 (ISBN 0-13-850487-3). P-H.

Story for a Black Night. Clayton Bess. LC 81-13396. (gr. 7 up). 1982. 7.95 (ISBN 0-395-31857-2). HM.

Story from the Book. Ed. by Ted Miller. 400p. 1986. 4.95 (ISBN 0-8423-6677-6). Tyndale.

Story Hour. K. D. Wiggin & N. A. Smith. 185p. (gr. k up). 1980. Repr. PLB 20.00 (ISBN 0-8492-8803-7). R West.

Story Hour see Child Horizons.

Story I Love to Tell. Victor A. Myers. (Orig.). 1980. pap. 4.95 (ISBN 0-937172-02-2). JLJ Pubs.

Story in It see Daisy Miller.

Story Key to Geographic Names. Oscar D. Von Engeln & Jane M. Urquhart. LC 72-113299. 1970. Repr. of 1924 ed. 26.50x (ISBN 0-8046-1330-3, Pub. by Kennikat). Assoc Faculty Pr.

Story Key to Geographic Names. Oscar Dedrich Von Engeln & Jane M. Urquhart. LC 74-13855. 298p. 1976. Repr. of 1924 ed. 43.00x (ISBN 0-8103-4062-3). Gale.

Story Like the Wind. Laurens Van Der Post. LC 78-5688. 370p. 1978. pap. 8.95 (ISBN 0-15-685261-6, Harv). HarBraceJ.

Story-Lives of Master Musicians. facsimile ed. Harriette M. Brower. LC 74-167316. (Essay Index Reprint Ser). Repr. of 1922 ed. 24.00 (ISBN 0-8369-2338-3). Ayer Co Pubs.

Story-Lives of Master Writers. Charles H. Raymond. 1973. Repr. of 1927 ed. 30.00 (ISBN 0-8274-0971-0). R West.

Story, Myth & Celebration in Old French Narrative Poetry 1050-1200. Karl D. Uitti. LC 72-4048. 272p. 1973. 34.00x (ISBN 0-691-06242-0). Princeton U Pr.

Story of a Bad Boy. Thomas B. Aldrich. (Orig.). 1988. pap. 8.95 (ISBN 1-55709-119-6). Applewood.

Story of a Bohemian-American Village: A Study of Social Persistence & Change. Robert I. Kutak. LC 70-129406. (American Immigration Collection, Ser. 2). 1970. Repr. of 1933 ed. 13.00 (ISBN 0-405-00559-8). Ayer Co Pubs.

Story of a Bragging Duck. Juliet Kepes. LC 82-6180. (Illus.). 32p. (gr. k-3). 1983. PLB 8.95 (ISBN 0-395-32863-2). HM.

Story of a Cancer Cure: Book I. Thomas B. Caulfield. 224p. 1983. lib. bdg. 16.95 (ISBN 0-9611788-0-9). Ctr Adv Psychic Res.

Story of a Cannoneer Under Stonewall Jackson. facsimile ed. Edward A. Moore. LC 77-146866. (Select Bibliographies Reprint Ser). Repr. of 1907 ed. 22.00 (ISBN 0-8369-5633-8). Ayer Co Pubs.

Story of a Castle. John S. Goodall. LC 86-70130. (Illus.). 60p. (ps up). 1986. 14.95 (ISBN 0-689-50405-5, M K McElderry). Macmillan.

Story of a Civil Suit: Dominguez v. Scott's Food Stores. 2nd ed. David Crump & Jeffrey B. Berman. 129p. pap. text ed. 12.50 (ISBN 0-916081-03-6). J Marshall Pub Co.

Story of a Common Soldier. Stillwell. LC 83-17861. (Collector's Library of the Civil War). (gr. 7 up). 1984. 26.60 (ISBN 0-8094-4287-6, Pub. by Time-Life). Silver.

Story of a Confederate Boy in the Civil War. David E. Johnston. 1980. Repr. of 1914 ed. 17.95 (ISBN 0-89227-044-6). Commonwealth Pr.

Story of a Country Medical College: A History of the Clinical School of Medicine & the Vermont Medical College, Woodstock, Vermont, 1827-1856. Frederick C. Waite. (Illus.). 213p. 1945. 2.00x (ISBN 0-934720-12-6). VT Hist Soc.

Story of a Country Town. E. W. Howe. (Collected Works of E. W. Howe). 1988. Repr. of 1884 ed. lib. bdg. 59.00x. Am Biog Serv.

Story of a Country Town. Edgar W. Howe. Ed. by Sylvia E. Bowman. (Masterworks of Literature Ser.). 1962. 12.95x (ISBN 0-8084-0286-2); pap. 8.95x (ISBN 0-8084-0287-0). New Coll U Pr.

Story of a Country Town see Collected Works.

Story of a Cowhorse, Gotch. Luke D. Sweetman. LC 78-116053. (Illus.). pap. 80.50 (ISBN 0-317-28813-X, 2020334). Bks Demand UMI.

Story of a Criminal Case: The State v. Albert Delman Greene. David Crump & William J. Mertens. 154p. (Orig.). 1984. pap. text ed. 11.95x (ISBN 0-916081-00-1). J Marshall Pub Co.

Story of a Decedent's Estate: In Re Eaton, Text & Worksheet. David Crump. (Paralegal Studies Ser.). 86p. (Orig.). 1987. pap. text ed. 10.50 (ISBN 0-916081-11-7). J Marshall Pub Co.

Story of a Fair Greek of Yesteryear. Antoine-Francois Prevost. Tr. by James F. Jones, Jr. from Fr. 1984. 30.00. Scripta.

Story of a Fierce Bad Rabbit. Beatrix Potter. (ps-2). 1906. bds. 4.95 (ISBN 0-7232-0611-2). Warne.

Story of a Grain of Wheat. William C. Edgar. LC 72-4158. (Select Bibliographies Reprint Ser.). 1972. Repr. of 1903 ed. 26.50 (ISBN 0-8369-6877-8). Ayer Co Pubs.

Story of a Great Friendship: Charles Dickens & Clarkson Stanfield. Cumberland Clark. 1978. Repr. of 1918 ed. lib. bdg. 10.00 (ISBN 0-8495-0736-7). Arden Lib.

Story of a Great Friendship: Charles Dickens & Clarkson Stanfield. Cumberland Clark. LC 73-18187. Repr. of 1918 ed. lib. bdg. 20.00 (ISBN 0-8414-3522-7). Folcroft.

Story of a Happy Woman. Elizabeth Levin. 272p. 1988. 18.95 (ISBN 0-525-24696-7). Dutton.

Story of a Labor Agitator. facsimile ed. Joseph R. Buchanan. LC 75-148873. (Select Bibliographies Reprint Ser.). 1972. Repr. of 1903 ed. 26.50 (ISBN 0-8369-5644-3). Ayer Co Pubs.

Story of a Life. Guy Gaucher. LC 85-45715. 1986. 13.45 (ISBN 0-06-063095-7, HarpR). Har-Row.

Story of a Life. Claude Hartland. LC 85-12500. (Documents Ser.). 118p. 1985. 12.95 (ISBN 0-912516-93-3); pap. 7.95 (ISBN 0-912516-92-5). Grey Fox.

Story of a Main Street. John S. Goodall. LC 87-60644. (Illus.). 60p. (ps up). 1987. 14.95 (ISBN 0-689-50436-5, M K McElderry). Macmillan.

Story of a Main Street. John S. Goodall. (ps up). Date not set. 14.95 (ISBN 0-317-61919-5, M K McElderry Bks). Atheneum.

Story of a Musical Life. George F. Root. LC 71-174964. Repr. of 1891 ed. 20.00 (ISBN 0-404-07205-4). AMS Pr.

Story of a Musical Life: An Autobiography. George F. Root. LC 70-126072. (Music Ser.). 1970. Repr. of 1891 ed. lib. bdg. 35.00 (ISBN 0-306-70031-X). Da Capo.

Story of a Novel. Thomas Wolfe. (Hudson River Edition Ser.). 1936. 5.95 (ISBN 0-684-10683-3, ScribT); lib. rep. ed. 15.00 (ISBN 0-684-17937-7). Scribner.

Story of a Page: Thirty Years in the Public Service in the Editorial Columns of the New York World Under the Editorship of J. Pulitzer. John L. Heaton. LC 75-125698. (American Journalists Ser). 1970. Repr. of 1913 ed. 20.00 (ISBN 0-405-01677-8). Ayer Co Pubs.

Story of a Pathfinder. Philander Deming. LC 77-128731. (Short Story Index Reprint Ser). 1907. 17.00 (ISBN 0-8369-3622-1). Ayer Co Pubs.

Story of a Pioneer. Anna H. Shaw. Repr. of 1915 ed. 29.00 (ISBN 0-527-81900-X). Kraus Repr.

Story of a Poet: Madison Cawein. facsimile ed. Otto A. Rothert. LC 76-146871. (Select Bibliographies Reprint Ser). Repr. of 1921 ed. 38.50 (ISBN 0-8369-5640-0). Ayer Co Pubs.

Story of a Rising Race. facsimile ed. J. J. Pipkin. LC 70-173609. (Black Heritage Library Collection). Repr. of 1902 ed. 40.00 (ISBN 0-8369-8901-5). Ayer Co Pubs.

Story of a Shipwrecked Sailor. Gabriel Garcia Marquez. 1986. 13.95 (ISBN 0-394-54810-8). Knopf.

Story of a Shipwrecked Sailor. Gabriel Garcia Marquez. 1987. pap. write for info. (ISBN 0-345-33639-9). Ballantine.

Story of a Shipwrecked Sailor. Gabriel Garcia Marquez. 1987. pap. 4.95 (ISBN 0-394-75403-4, Vin). Random.

Story of a Soldier's Life, 2 Vols. in 1. G. J. Wolseley. Repr. of 1903 ed. 42.00 (ISBN 0-527-97800-0). Kraus Repr.

Story of a Soul: The Autobiography of St. Therese of Lisieux. Tr. by John Clarke from Fr. LC 76-43620. 1976. pap. 6.95x (ISBN 0-9600876-4-8). ICS Pubns.

Story of a Story & Other Stories. Brander Matthews. LC 70-98585. (Short Story Index Reprint Ser.). 1893. 18.00 (ISBN 0-8369-3159-9). Ayer Co Pubs.

Story of a Street. Frederick T. Hill. LC 73-78824. 1969. Repr. of 1908 ed. flexible cover 8.00 (ISBN 0-87034-038-7). Fraser Pub Co.

Story of a Throne: Catherine Second of Russia, 2 vols. facsimile ed. Kazimierz Waliszewski. LC 79-157358. (Select Bibliographies Reprint Ser.). Repr. of 1895 ed. Set. 40.00 (ISBN 0-8369-5819-5). Ayer Co Pubs.

Story of a Tlingit Community: Problem in the Relationship Between Archaeological, Ethnological & Historical Methods. Frederica De Laguna. Repr. of 1960 ed. 39.00x (ISBN 0-403-03698-4). Scholarly.

Story of a Varied Life. facs. ed. W. S. Rainsford. LC 70-126249. (Select Bibliographies Reprint Ser). (Illus.). 1922. 21.00 (ISBN 0-8369-5476-9). Ayer Co Pubs.

Story of a Whim. Grace L. Hill. 1976. Repr. of 1903 ed. lib. bdg. 16.95x (ISBN 0-89190-023-3, Pub. by River City Pr). Amereon Ltd.

Story of a Whim. Grace L. Hill. (Grace Livingston Hill Classic Ser.). 144p. 1982. 8.95 (ISBN 0-8007-1298-6). Revell.

Story of a Whim, No. 68. Grace L. Hill. 128p. 1985. pap. 2.75 (ISBN 0-553-26437-0). Bantam.

Story of a Wonder Man: Being the Autobiography of Ring Lardner. Ring W. Lardner. LC 75-26216. (Illus.). 151p. 1975. Repr. of 1927 ed. lib. bdg. 35.00x (ISBN 0-8371-8414-2, LAWOM). Greenwood.

Story of a Year: Eighty Forty-Eight. Raymond Postgate. LC 75-17508. (Illus.). 286p. 1975. Repr. of 1955 ed. lib. bdg. 35.00x (ISBN 0-8371-8249-2, POSY). Greenwood.

Story of Ab: A Tale of the Time of the Cave Man. Stanley Waterloo. LC 74-16524. (Science Fiction Ser). (Illus.). 366p. 1975. Repr. 26.50x (ISBN 0-405-06316-4). Ayer Co Pubs.

Story of Acadia National Park. George B. Dorr. (Illus.). 126p. 1985. pap. 7.95 (ISBN 0-934745-00-5). Acadia Pub Co.

Story of Adam & Eve. Gordon Lindsay. (Old Testament Ser.). 1.25 (ISBN 0-89985-124-X). Christ Nations.

Story of Adams County see Adams County.

Story of Adamsville. Agnes Riedmann. 115p. 1980. pap. text ed. write for info. (ISBN 0-534-00823-2). Wadsworth Pub.

Story of Adele H. Francois Truffaut. LC 75-42798. (Illus.). 1975. pap. 2.45 (ISBN 0-394-17908-0, B395, BC). Grove.

Story of Adirondac. Arthur H. Masten. (Illus.). 240p. 1968. Repr. of 1923 ed. 9.50 (ISBN 0-686-74842-5). Adirondack Mus.

Story of Adirondac. Arthur H. Masten. LC 68-20170. (Adirondack Museum Bks.). (Illus.). 1968. 9.50 (ISBN 0-8156-0062-3). Syracuse U Pr.

Story of Adoption: Why Do I Look Different? Darla Lowe. LC 87-46273. (Illus., Orig.). (gr. 3 up). 1987. pap. 5.95 (ISBN 0-9606090-2-4). East West Pr.

Story of Africa. A. J. Wills. LC 72-86247. 1973. 17.75 (ISBN 0-8419-0128-7, Africana). Holmes & Meier.

Story of Agricultural Economics in the United States, 1840-1932. Henry C. Taylor & Anne H. Taylor. LC 74-10646. (Illus.). 1121p. 1974. Repr. of 1952 ed. lib. bdg. 55.50x (ISBN 0-8371-7653-0, TAAE). Greenwood.

Story of Air Fighting. J. E. Johnson. (War Ser.). 368p. 1986. pap. 3.95 (ISBN 0-553-25732-3). Bantam.

Story of Aircraft & Travel by Air. Robert Hoare. (Junior Reference Ser.). (Illus.). (gr. 7 up). 1982. Repr. 13.95 (ISBN 0-7136-0115-9). Dufour.

Story of Ajax. Alva Noyes. LC 67-6837. (Studies in European Literature, No. 56). 1970. lib. bdg. 50.95x (ISBN 0-8383-1109-1). Haskell.

Story of Albert J. Iva Hamilton. (Illus., Orig.). 1985. pap. 6.95 (ISBN 0-87418-028-7, 162). Coleman Pub.

Story of Alchemy & the Beginnings of Chemistry. Matthew M. Muir. LC 79-8618. Repr. of 1903 ed. 27.50 (ISBN 0-404-18482-0). AMS Pr.

Story of Alfred the Great. Walter Hawkisn & Edward T. Smith. 142p. 1980. Repr. of 1900 ed. lib. bdg. 30.00 (ISBN 0-8495-2296-X). Arden Lib.

Story of Algiers Seventeen Eighteen to Eighteen Ninety-Six. William H. Seymour. (Illus.). 143p. 1981. pap. 6.95 (ISBN 0-911116-33-8). Pelican.

Story of Alice Paul & the National Woman's Part. Inez H. Irwin. LC 63-23006. (Illus.). 1977. pap. 6.95 (ISBN 0-87714-058-8). Denlingers.

Story of America. Reader's Digest Editors. LC 75-3837. (Illus.). 528p. 1975. 19.95 (ISBN 0-89577-024-5). RD Assn.

Story of America. LC 84-2018. (Illus.). (gr. 4-8). 1984. lib. bdg. 21.95 (ISBN 0-87044-535-9, 00535); 19.95 (ISBN 0-87044-508-1). Natl Geog.

Story of American Golf. 4th ed. Herbert W. Wind. 316p. 1986. Repr. of 1956 ed. 34.95 (ISBN 0-936557-02-8). Golf Shop Collect.

Story of American Painting: The Evolution of Painting in America from Colonial Times to the Present. Charles H. Caffin. LC 37-15304. (American Studies). 1970. Repr. of 1907 ed. 33.00. Johnson Repr.

Story of American Railroads. Stewart H. Holbrook. 1981. 6.98 (ISBN 0-517-00100-4). Crown.

Story of an African Famine: Gender & Famine in Twentieth Century Malawi. Megan Vaughan. (Illus.). 176p. 1987. 37.50 (ISBN 0-521-32917-5). Cambridge U Pr.

Story of an African Farm. Olive Schreiner. LC 77-21221. 258p. 1977. 9.95 (ISBN 0-915864-24-X); pap. 2.95 (ISBN 0-915864-23-1). Academy Chi Pubs.

Story of an African Farm. Olive Schreiner. Ed. by Robert L. Wolff. LC 75-1530. (Victorian Fiction Ser). 1975. Repr. of 1883 ed. lib. bdg. 73.00 (ISBN 0-8240-1602-5). Garland Pub.

Story of an African Farm. Olive Schreiner. 1983. pap. 4.95 (ISBN 0-14-043184-5). Penguin.

Story of an African Farm. Olive Schreiner. 12.00 (ISBN 0-8446-0247-7). Peter Smith.

Story of an African Farm. Olive Schreiner. (Illus.). 288p. 1988. 24.95 (ISBN 0-517-56803-9). Crown.

Story of an African Farm: A Novel. Olive Schreiner. 1978. Repr. of 1883 ed. lib. bdg. 37.50 (ISBN 0-8495-4832-2). Arden Lib.

Story of D-Day. R. Conrad Stein. LC 77-5089. (Cornerstones of Freedom Ser.). (Illus.). 32p. (gr. 3-5). 1977. PLB 11.67 (ISBN 0-516-04609-8). Childrens.

Story of D-Day: June 6, 1944. Bruce Bliven, Jr. (Landmark Ser.: No. 94). (Illus.). (gr. 6-8). 1963. (BYR); lib. bdg. 8.99 (ISBN 0-394-90362-5). Random.

Story of Dance Music. P. Nettl. (Ballroom Dance Ser.). 1985. lib. bdg. 79.95 (ISBN 0-87700-692-X). Revisionist Pr.

Story of Dance Music. P. Nettl. (Ballroom Dance Ser.). 1986. lib. bdg. 79.95 (ISBN 0-8490-3253-9). Gordon Pr.

Story of Dance Music. Paul Nettl. 1970. Repr. of 1947 ed. lib. bdg. 35.00 (ISBN 0-8371-2114-0, NEDM). Greenwood.

Story of Daniel. Lucy Diamond. (Ladybird Ser). (Illus.). 1958. bds. 2.50 (ISBN 0-87508-866-X). Chr Lit.

Story of Daniel & the Lions. Alice J. Davidson. (Alice in Bibleland Ser.). 32p. (ps-3). 1986. 4.95 (ISBN 0-8378-5079-7). Gibson.

Story of Daniel Boone. William Cunningham. 160p. (gr. 4-6). pap. 2.25 (ISBN 0-590-40536-5). Scholastic Inc.

Story of Daphnis & Chloe. Longus. Ed. by W. R. Connor. LC 78-18586. (Greek Texts & Commentaries Ser.). (Illus.). 1979. Repr. of 1908 ed. lib. bdg. 17.00x (ISBN 0-405-11428-1). Ayer Co Pubs.

Story of David & Goliath. Alice J. Davidson. (Alice in Bibleland Storybooks). (Illus.). 32p. (ps-3). 1985. 4.95 (ISBN 0-8378-5070-3). Gibson.

Story of David Grayson. Frank P. Rand. 160p. 1963. 9.95 (ISBN 0-686-31118-3). Jones Lib.

Story of Deborah. Constance Head. (Arch Bks.). (Illus.). (gr. k-3). 1978. 1.29 (ISBN 0-570-06116-4, 59-1234). Concordia.

Story of Dentistry. Kenneth Wilson. 88p. 1986. pap. 19.00X (ISBN 0-7223-1989-4, Pub. by A H Stockwell England). State Mutual Bk.

Story of Dinosaurs. David Eastman. LC 81-11363. (Now I Know Ser.). (Illus.). 32p. (gr. k-2). 1982. PLB 9.89 (ISBN 0-89375-648-2). Troll Assocs.

Story of Dion Fortune. Charles Fielding & Carr Collins. LC 85-72579. 320p. 1985. pap. 8.95 (ISBN 0-87728-658-2). Weiser.

Story of Dr. Dolittle. Hugh Lofting. (gr. k-6). 1969. pap. 2.95 (ISBN 0-440-48307-7, YB). Dell.

Story of Doctor Dolittle. Hugh Lofting. (gr. k-6). 1988. pap. 2.95 (YB). Dell.

Story of Doctor Dolittle. centenary ed. Hugh Lofting. (Illus.). 144p. (gr. 4-6). 1988. pap. 13.95 (ISBN 0-385-29662-2). Delacorte.

Story of Doctor Johnson. S. C. Roberts. LC 73-14816. 1973. lib. bdg. 27.00 (ISBN 0-8414-7205-X). Folcroft.

Story of Dona Gracia Mendes. Bea Stadtler. LC 70-83166. (Illus.). (gr. 6-9). 1969. 4.50 (ISBN 0-8381-0734-6). United Syn Bk.

Story of Dorothy Jordan. Clare A. Jerrold. LC 70-82555. (Illus.). 1914. 24.50 (ISBN 0-405-08672-5, Blom Pubns). Ayer Co Pubs.

Story of Droopy Doo. Maurice Selby. 1988. 5.95 (ISBN 0-533-07483-5). Vantage.

Story of Dublin. (Medieval Towns Ser.: Vol. 32). Repr. of 1932 ed. 44.00 (ISBN 0-8115-0874-9). Kraus Repr.

Story of Dwight W. Morrow. M. M. McBride. 59.95 (ISBN 0-8490-1131-0). Gordon Pr.

Story of Early Britain. Alfred J. Church. 375p. 1980. Repr. lib. bdg. 30.00 (ISBN 0-8495-0788-X). Arden Lib.

Story of Early Gaelic Literature. Douglas Hyde. LC 72-13812. 1972. Repr. lib. bdg. 35.50 (ISBN 0-8414-1296-0). Folcroft.

Story of Early Gaelic Literature. Douglas Hyde. LC 77-94587. 1978. Repr. of 1895 ed. lib. bdg. 20.00 (ISBN 0-89341-182-5). Longwood Pub Group.

Story of Easter. Alice J. Davidson. (Alice in Bibleland Ser.). (Illus.). 32p. (ps-3). 1988. 4.95 (ISBN 0-8378-1839-7). Gibson.

Story of Easter for Children. Date not set. pap. 3.95. Ideals.

Story of Easter for Children. Beverly Wiersum. Ed. by James A. Kuse. (Illus.). (ps-3). 1979. pap. 2.95 (ISBN 0-89542-452-5). Ideals.

Story of Eclipses. George F. Chambers. 1904. 15.00 (ISBN 0-686-17419-4). Ridgeway Bks.

Story of Edgar Cayce: There Is a River. Thomas Sugrue. 384p. 1984. pap. 4.50 (ISBN 0-87604-151-9). ARE Pr.

Story of Edinburgh. W. H. Smeaton. (Mediaeval Towns Ser.: Vol. 21). pap. 44.00 (ISBN 0-8115-0863-3). Kraus Repr.

Story of Effective Statesmanship see Strategy of St. Paul.

Story of "Eight Deer" in Codex Columbino. James C. Clark. Ed. by Karl Young. (Fourth Sun Ser.). (Illus.). lib. bdg. cancelled (ISBN 0-932282-34-2); pap. cancelled (ISBN 0-932282-33-4). Caledonia Pr.

Story of Electricity: With Twenty Easy-to-Perform Experiments. George D. Leon. (Illus.). 112p. 1988. pap. 4.95 (ISBN 0-486-25581-6). Dover.

Story of Elizabethan Drama. G. B. Harrison. LC 73-681. 134p. 1972. Repr. of 1924 ed. lib. bdg. 15.00x (ISBN 0-374-93688-9, Octagon). Hippocrene Bks.

Story of Elizabethan Drama. George B. Harrison. LC 73-11425. 1924. lib. bdg. 27.00 (ISBN 0-8414-4720-9). Folcroft.

Story of Ellis Island. R. Conrad Stein. LC 79-12225. (Cornerstones of Freedom Ser.). (Illus.). 32p. (gr. 3-6). 1979. PLB 11.67 (ISBN 0-516-04613-6). Childrens.

Story of England by Robert Manning of Brunne, from Manuscripts at Lambeth Palace & the Inner Temple, 2 vols. Ed. by Frederick Furnivall. (Rolls Ser.: No. 87). Repr. of 1887 ed. Set. 88.00 (ISBN 0-8115-1160-X). Kraus Repr.

Story of England's Architecture. Thomas E. Tallmadge. 363p. 1980. Repr. of 1934 ed. lib. bdg. 40.00 (ISBN 0-8495-5160-9). Arden Lib.

Story of English. Adult Learning Service Staff. 336p. 1986. pap. 18.95 (ISBN 0-8403-4035-4). Kendall-Hunt.

Story of English. Robert McCrum et al. LC 85-41070. (Illus.). 384p. 1986. 24.95 (ISBN 0-670-80467-3). Viking.

Story of English. Robert McCrum et al. (Illus.). 384p. 1987. pap. 12.95 (ISBN 0-14-009435-0). Penguin.

Story of English Literature. Edmund K. Broadus. 1933. Repr. 35.00 (ISBN 0-8274-3515-0). R West.

Story of English Literature. Gerald Bullett. LC 74-9776. 1935. 15.00 (ISBN 0-8414-3207-4). Folcroft.

Story of Ernie Pyle. Lee G. Miller. 1970. Repr. of 1950 ed. lib. bdg. 35.00x (ISBN 0-8371-3743-8, MIEP). Greenwood.

Story of Esther. Ruth F. Brin. LC 75-743. (Old Testament Bible Stories). 32p. (gr. k-5). 1976. PLB 6.95 (ISBN 0-8225-0364-6). Lerner Pubns.

Story of Euclid. F. W. Frankland. 59.95 (ISBN 0-8490-1132-9). Gordon Pr.

Story of Extinct Civilizations of the East. Robert E. Anderson. 1977. Repr. of 1904 ed. lib. bdg. 25.00 (ISBN 0-8492-0138-1). R West.

Story of Extinct Civilizations of the West. Robert Anderson. 59.95 (ISBN 0-8490-1133-7). Gordon Pr.

Story of Fabian Socialism. Margaret Cole. LC 61-16949. (Illus.). 1961. 37.50x (ISBN 0-8047-0091-5); pap. 12.95 (ISBN 0-8047-0092-3, SP105). Stanford U Pr.

Story of Faded Fobs. Ken Forsse. (Teddy Ruxpin Adventure Ser.). (Illus.). 26p. (ps). 1985. incl. audio-cassette 9.95 (ISBN 0-934323-02-X). Alchemy Comms.

Story of Fanny Burney. M. Masefield. LC 73-21629. (English Biography Ser., No. 31). 1974. lib. bdg. 51.95x (ISBN 0-8383-1786-3). Haskell.

Story of Fanny Burney. Muriel Masefield. LC 73-16151. 1927. Repr. lib. bdg. 25.75 (ISBN 0-8414-6089-2). Folcroft.

Story of Father Junipero Serra. Florence White. (gr. 3-6). pap. 2.95 (ISBN 0-317-62406-7, YB). Dell.

Story of Felicity. Anna Aragno. (Illus.). 64p. (gr. 2 up). 1980. 5.00 (ISBN 0-682-49633-2). Exposition-Phoenix.

Story of Ferdinand. Munro Leaf. (Illus.). 72p. (gr. k-3). 1977. pap. 3.95 (ISBN 0-14-050234-3, Puffin). Penguin.

Story of Ferdinand. Munro Leaf. (Illus.). (gr. k-3). 1936. lib. bdg. 11.95 (ISBN 0-670-67424-9). Viking.

Story of Ferdinand. Munro Leaf. (Illus.). (ps-3). 1988. pap. 9.95 bk. & t-shirt (ISBN 0-14-095075-3, Puffin Bks). Penguin.

Story of Ferrara. E. Noyes. (Mediaeval Towns Ser.: Vol. 2). pap. 44.00 (ISBN 0-8115-0844-7). Kraus Repr.

Story of Films. Ed. by Joseph P. Kennedy. LC 74-160236. (Moving Pictures Ser). xxi, 377p. 1971. Repr. of 1927 ed. lib. bdg. 23.95x (ISBN 0-89198-037-7). Ozer.

Story of Firearm Ignition. Edsall James. 3.50 (ISBN 0-913150-27-4). Pioneer Pr.

Story of Flight. Jim Robins. (Do You Know Ser.). (Illus.). 32p. (gr. k-6). 1987. lib. bdg. 11.90 (ISBN 0-531-19022-6, Warwick). Watts.

Story of Flight. Mary L. Settle. (Step-up Books Ser). (gr. 2-9). 1967. 3.95 (ISBN 0-394-80068-0, BYR). Random.

Story of Florence. E. Gardner. 1976. lib. bdg. 59.95 (ISBN 0-8490-2679-2). Gordon Pr.

Story of Folk Music. Melvin Berger. LC 76-18159. (Illus.). (gr. 6 up). 1976. PLB 14.95 (ISBN 0-87599-215-3). S G Phillips.

Story of Football. Dave Anderson. LC 85-7195. (Illus.). 192p. (gr. 5 up). 1985. 13.00 (ISBN 0-688-05634-2, Morrow Junior Books); pap. 8.95 (ISBN 0-688-05635-0). Morrow.

Story of Ford's Theatre & the Death of Lincoln. Zachary Kent. LC 87-17662. (Cornerstones of Freedom Ser.). (Illus.). 32p. (gr. 3-6). 1987. PLB 11.93 (ISBN 0-516-04729-9). Childrens.

Story of Fort Myers: The History of the Land of the Caloosahatchee & Southwest Florida. Karl H. Grismer. LC 82-80620. (Illus.). 360p. 1982. pap. 15.00 (ISBN 0-87208-226-1). Island Pr Pubs.

Story of Fowey. John Keast. 1985. 35.00x (ISBN 0-907566-72-3, Pub. by Dyllansow & Truran). State Mutual Bk.

Story of Free Enterprise. Joel R. Belknap. 1963. 9.95 (ISBN 0-8159-6825-6). Devin.

Story of Gandhi. R. Shankar. (Illus.). (gr. 3-10). 1979. 5.00 (ISBN 0-89744-166-4). Auromere.

Story of Gannon University: Education on the Square. Robert Barcio et al. LC 85-81770. 208p. (Orig.). 1985. 10.00 (ISBN 0-936063-00-9); pap. text ed. 5.00. Gannon U Pr.

Story of Genesis & Exodus an Early English Song. Ed. by R. Morris. (EETS OS Ser.: No. 7). Repr. of 1865 ed. 42.00 (ISBN 0-527-00006-X). Kraus Repr.

Story of George Washington Carver. Eva Moore. 96p. (gr. 2-5). pap. 2.25 (ISBN 0-590-09271-5). Scholastic Inc.

Story of Gilbert & Sullivan. Isaac Goldberg. LC 76-113194. Repr. of 1928 ed. 20.00 (ISBN 0-404-02858-6). AMS Pr.

Story of Gilbert & Sullivan. Isaac Goldberg. 59.95 (ISBN 0-8490-1134-5). Gordon Pr.

Story of Giuseppe Verdi. Gabriele Baldini. Tr. by Roger Parker from Ital. LC 79-41376. 330p. 1980. 47.50 (ISBN 0-521-22911-1); pap. 14.95 (ISBN 0-521-29712-5). Cambridge U Pr.

Story of Glendorgal. Nigel Tangye. 1985. 10.00x (ISBN 0-907566-87-1, Pub. by Dyllansow & Truran). State Mutual Bk.

Story of Godalming. John Janaway. 80p. 1987. pap. 30.00x (ISBN 0-86368-005-4, Countryside Bks). State Mutual Bk.

Story of God's Love. Elizabeth Friedrich. 144p. (gr. 6-9). 1985. 9.95 (ISBN 0-570-04122-8, 56-1533). Concordia.

Story of God's People. Clarence Y. Fretz. (Christian Day School Ser.). (gr. 7). pap. 5.90x (ISBN 0-87813-900-1); tchrs. guide 6.95x (ISBN 0-87813-901-X). Christian Light.

Story of Gold. Ruth Brindze. LC 55-11840. (Illus.). (gr. 4-8). 1954. 13.95 (ISBN 0-8149-0276-6). Vanguard.

Story of Gold Hill Colorado: Seventy-Odd Years in the Heart of the Rockies. rev. ed. Mabel G. Montgomery & Silvia Pettem. (Illus.). 37p. 1987. pap. 4.50 (ISBN 0-9617799-1-8). Book Lode.

Story of Greece. James A. Harrison. 1827. 35.00 (ISBN 0-8274-3954-7). R West.

Story of Gregg Shorthand. Louis A. Leslie. 1964. text ed. 16.65 (ISBN 0-07-037223-3). McGraw.

Story of Grettir the Strong. Tr. by Eirikr Magnusson & William Morris. 306p. 1980. Repr. of 1869 ed. 19.50x (ISBN 0-8154-0517-0). Cooper Sq.

Story of Griselda in Iceland. Griselda. Ed. by Halldor Hermannsson. (Islandica Ser.: Vol. 7). pap. 16.00 (ISBN 0-527-00337-9). Kraus Repr.

Story of Grump & Pout. Jamie McEwan. (Illus.). 40p. (ps up). 1988. PLB 12.95 (ISBN 0-517-56706-7). Crown.

Story of Guru Nanak. Mala Singh. (Illus.). (gr. 2-9). 1979. 6.50 (ISBN 0-89744-138-9). Auromere.

Story of Hamden: Land of the Sleeping Giant. rev. ed. Rachel Hartley. xiv, 98p. 1966. pap. 17.50 (ISBN 0-208-01648-1). Shoe String.

Story of Handball: The Game, the Players, the History. T. J. McElligott. (Illus.). 176p. 1984. 16.95 (ISBN 0-86327-018-2, Pub. by Wolfhound Pr Ireland). Irish Bks Media.

Story of Hanukkah. Charles Wengrov. (Shulsinger Holiday Ser.). (Illus.). (gr. k-7). 1965. pap. 1.50 (ISBN 0-914080-52-0). Shulsinger Sales.

Story of Hardwood Plywood. 11p. 1987. 1.00 (ISBN 0-318-23061-5). Hardwd Ply.

Story of Harold. Terry Andrews. (Illus.). 1985. pap. 2.95 (ISBN 0-380-49965-7, 49965-7, Bard). Avon.

Story of Hastings-Raydist. Carol H. Sanders. (Illus.). 116p. 1979. 20.00 (ISBN 0-9607696-3-3). Carol Mendel.

Story of Hay. Geoffrey Patterson. (Illus.). 32p. (gr. k-3). 1983. 9.95 (ISBN 0-233-97356-7). Andre Deutsch.

Story of Heart Disease. T. East. (Illus.). 148p. 1958. 14.95 (ISBN 0-8464-0886-4). Beekman Pubs.

Story of Henderson County. Sadie Patton. LC 76-4904. (Illus.). 310p. 1976. Repr. of 1947 ed. 25.00 (ISBN 0-87152-233-0). Reprint.

Story of Henri Tod. large print ed. William F. Buckley, Jr. LC 84-5973. 397p. 1984. Repr. of 1984 ed. 14.95 (ISBN 0-89621-537-7). Thorndike Pr.

Story of His Life from a Stonemason's Bench to the Treasury Bench, Told by Himself. Henry Broadhurst. LC 83-48475. (World of Labour: English Workers, 1850-1890 Ser.). 316p. 1984. lib. bdg. 40.00 (ISBN 0-8240-5703-1). Garland Pub.

Story of His Life, Told by Himself. Joseph Arch. LC 83-48472. (World of Labour-English Workers 1850-1890 Ser.). 412p. 1984. lib. bdg. 50.00 (ISBN 0-8240-5700-7). Garland Pub.

Story of HMS Fisgard. Philip Payton. 1985. 9.00x (ISBN 0-317-57990-8, Pub. by Dyllansow & Truran). State Mutual Bk.

Story of Holland. James E. Rogers. 1977. lib. bdg. 59.95 (ISBN 0-8490-2680-6). Gordon Pr.

Story of Holly & Ivy. Rumer Godden. LC 84-25799. (Illus.). 32p. (ps-5). 1985. 13.95 (ISBN 0-670-80622-6). Viking.

Story of Holly & Ivy. Rumer Godden. (Illus.). (gr. k-5). 1987. pap. 4.95 (ISBN 0-14-050723-X, Puffin Bks). Penguin.

Story of Hotel Polski. Abraham Shulman. 256p. 12.95 (ISBN 0-686-95088-7); pap. 5.95 (ISBN 0-686-99461-2). ADL.

Story of How the Easter Bunny Got His Wife. William E. Avant. 30p. (gr. k-4). 1987. 6.75 (ISBN 0-8062-2842-3). Carlton.

Story of Human Communication: Cave Painting to Microchip. Wilbur Schramm. 382p. 1987. pap. text ed. 20.95 (ISBN 0-06-045799-6, HarpC). Harrow.

Story of Human Error. facs. ed. Ed. by Joseph Jastrow. LC 67-30219. (Essay Index Reprint Ser). 1936. 18.50 (ISBN 0-8369-0568-7). Ayer Co Pubs.

Story of Human Evolution. Barborka. 7.95 (ISBN 0-8356-7550-5). Theos Pub Hse.

Story of Hungerford. Hugh Pihlens. 64p. 1987. 30.00x (ISBN 0-86368-000-3, Countryside Bks). State Mutual Bk.

Story of Hymns & Tunes. Hezekiah Butterworth. 1981. Repr. lib. bdg. 79.00x (ISBN 0-403-00107-2). Scholarly.

Story of Hymns & Tunes. Hezekiah Butterworth. 1988. Repr. of 1907 ed. lib. bdg. 99.00x. Am Biog Serv.

Story of Illinois. 3rd ed. Theodore C. Pease. Rev. by Marguerite J. Pease. LC 65-17299. pap. 95.80 (2026738). Bks Demand UMI.

Story of Illinois: Indian & Pioneer. rev. ed. Virginia S. Eifert. (Story of Illinois Ser.: No. 1). (Illus.). 24p. 1979. pap. 1.00x (ISBN 0-89792-039-2). Ill St Museum.

Story of Imelda, Who Was Small. Morris Lurie. (Illus.). 32p. (gr. k-3). 1988. 13.95. HM.

Story of Impacted Wisdom Teeth Kit. Joel M. Berns. 1980. pap. 28.00 (ISBN 0-931386-14-4). Quint Pub Co.

Story of Indian Music: Its Growth & Synthesis. O. Gosvami. LC 79-181165. 332p. 1961. Repr. 59.00x (ISBN 0-403-01567-7). Scholarly.

Story of Indian Music: Its Growth & Synthesis. O. Gosvami. 1988. Repr. of 1961 ed. lib. bdg. 79.00x. Am Biog Serv.

Story of Indira. Shakuntala Masani. (Illus.). 1975. 4.50x (ISBN 0-686-20309-7). Intl Bk Dist.

Story of Instructional Excellence: Say "Yes" For Learning! Don Stewart. (Chance for Instructional Excellence Ser.: Bk. 5). (Illus.). 250p. (Orig.). 1988. 11.95x (ISBN 0-913448-22-2); pap. 7.95x (ISBN 0-913448-23-0). Slate Servs.

Story of Integration: A New Interpretation of Princely States in India. Vanaja Rangaswami. 1982. 34.00x (ISBN 0-8364-0876-4, Pub. by Manohar India). South Asia Bks.

Story of Inyo. W. A. Chalfant. LC 33-19367. 1975. 18.95 (ISBN 0-912494-34-4); pap. 12.50 (ISBN 0-912494-35-2). Chalfant Pr.

Story of Ireland's National Theatre. Dawson Byrne. LC 70-119093. (Studies in Drama, No. 39). 1970. Repr. of 1929 ed. lib. bdg. 49.95x (ISBN 0-8383-1089-3). Haskell.

Story of Irving Berlin. Alexander Woollcott. LC 81-12535. (Music Ser.). (Illus.). 237p. 1982. Repr. of 1925 ed. lib. bdg. 32.50 (ISBN 0-306-76145-9). Da Capo.

Story of Islam. Anthony Kamm. (Religions Around the World Ser.). (Illus.). 32p. (gr. 4-8). 1987. pap. 3.95 (ISBN 0-317-59499-0). Cambridge U Pr.

Story of Islamic Culture. A. Rauf. 1981. 2.50 (ISBN 0-686-97868-4). Kazi Pubns.

Story of Israel. Mays. Date not set. 13.95 (Pub. by SCM Pr England). Fortress.

Story of Israel in Coins. Jean Gould & Maurice Gould. pap. 2.00 (ISBN 0-87980-150-6). Wilshire.

Story of Israel in Stamps. Maxim Shamir & Gabriel Shamir. pap. 1.00 (ISBN 0-87980-151-4). Wilshire.

Story of Jackie Robinson: Bravest Man in Baseball. Margaret Davidson. (Orig.). (gr. k-6). 1988. pap. 2.95 (ISBN 0-440-40019-8, YB). Dell.

Story of Jackie Robinson, the Bravest Man in Baseball: Yearling Biography Ser. Margaret Davidson. (gr. 3-6). 1988. 2.95 (ISBN 0-317-69319-0, YB). Dell.

Story of Jacob, Rachel & Leah. Yvonne H. McCall. (Arch Bks.). (Illus.). 24p. (gr. k-4). 1986. pap. 1.29 saddlestitched (ISBN 0-570-06205-5, 59-1428). Concordia.

Story of Jane Austen's Life. Oscar F. Adams. 277p. 1980. Repr. of 1891 ed. lib. bdg. 35.00 (ISBN 0-8495-0060-5). Arden Lib.

Story of Jane Austen's Life. Oscar F. Adams. LC 74-14568. 1974. Repr. of 1891 ed. lib. bdg. 29.00 (ISBN 0-8414-2861-1). Folcroft.

Story of Jazz. Rex Harris. Ed. by Thomas K. Scherman. LC 79-29696. (Little Music Library). 280p. 1980. Repr. of 1952 ed. lib. bdg. 35.00x (ISBN 0-313-22350-5, HASJ). Greenwood.

Story of Jazz. Marshall W. Stearns. 1956. 24.95x (ISBN 0-19-500115-X). Oxford U Pr.

Story of Jazz. Marshall W. Stearns. (Illus.). 1956. pap. 11.95 (ISBN 0-19-501269-0). Oxford U Pr.

Story of Jerusalem. C. M. Watson. (Mediaeval Towns Ser.: Vol. 26). Repr. of 1929 ed. 35.00 (ISBN 0-8115-0868-4). Kraus Repr.

Story of Jesus, 3 Pts. Frank C. Laubach. Incl. Jesus' Birth & Ministry: Pt. One; Jesus' Death & Resurrection: Pt. Two; Parables of Jesus: Pt. Three. 61p. Set. 6.95 (ISBN 0-88336-538-3); 2.50 ea. New Readers.

Story of Jesus. Mary P. Smith. (Illus.). 32p. (Orig.). (ps-2). 1980. pap. 1.95 (ISBN 0-87516-420-X). DeVorss.

Story of Jesus see Clothed with the Sun: The Mystery-Tale of Jesus the Avatara.

Story of Jesus Pop-Up Book. (Pop-Up Bks.). (Illus.). (ps-1). 1.98 (ISBN 0-517-43888-7). Outlet Bk Co.

Story of New York State. Schwarz & Goldberg. 1962. pap. 5.95 (ISBN 0-88323-098-4, 282). Richards Pub.
Story of Nigeria. 4th ed. Michael Crowder. 432p. 1978. pap. 9.95 (ISBN 0-571-04947-8). Faber & Faber.
Story of Nim: The Chimp Who Learned Language. Anna Michel. LC 79-17501. (Illus.). 72p. (gr. 3 up). 1980. 6.95 (ISBN 0-394-84444-0). Knopf.
Story of Noah. Alice J. Davidson. (Alice in Bibleland Storybooks). (Illus.). 32p. (gr. k-1). 1984. 4.95 (ISBN 0-8378-5067-3). Gibson.
Story of Notation. C. Abdy Williams. LC 69-16797. 280p. 1968. Repr. of 1903 ed. 40.00x (ISBN 0-8103-3557-3). Gale.
Story of Notation. C. Abdy Williams. LC 77-90803. 1978. Repr. of 1903 ed. lib. bdg. 25.00 (ISBN 0-89341-420-4). Longwood Pub Group.
Story of Notation. Charles F. Williams. LC 68-57648. (Illus.). 1970. Repr. of 1903 ed. lib. bdg. 35.00 (ISBN 0-8371-1622-8, WINO). Greenwood.
Story of Notation. Charles F. Williams. LC 68-25306. (Studies in Music, No. 42). (Illus.). 1969. Repr. of 1903 ed. lib. bdg. 47.95x (ISBN 0-8383-0317-X). Haskell.
Story of Nuclear Power. (Illus., Arabic.). (gr. 5-12). 3.50x (ISBN 0-86685-228-X). Intl Bk Ctr.
Story of Nuremberg. C. Headlam. 59.95 (ISBN 0-8490-2682-2). Gordon Pr.
Story of Nuremberg. C. Headlam. (Mediaeval Towns Ser.: Vol. 34). pap. 26.00 (ISBN 0-8115-0876-5). Kraus Repr.
Story of O. Pauline Reage. 1981. pap. 3.95 (ISBN 0-345-30111-0). Ballantine.
Story of O: Part Two, Return to the Chateau. Pauline Reage. Tr. by Sabine D'Estree from Fr. LC 77-155130. Orig. Title: Retour a Roissy. 158p. 1980. pap. 3.95 (ISBN 0-394-17658-8, B364, BC). Grove.
Story of Odette. (Red Stripe Ser.). 1988. pap. 4.50 (ISBN 0-8216-5050-5, Univ Bks). Lyle Stuart.
Story of Old Abe Wisconsin's Civil War Hero. Malcolm Rosholt & Margaret Rosholt. (Illus.). 110p. (gr. 4-12). 1987. 14.95 (ISBN 0-910417-09-1). Rosholt Hse.
Story of Old Chinese Ceramics. Koyama Fujio. 1949. 80.00x (ISBN 0-317-44215-5, Pub. by Han-Shan Tang Ltd). State Mutual Bk.
Story of Old Fort Loudon. facsimile ed. Mary N. Murfree. LC 73-104531. (Illus.). 409p. Repr. of 1899 ed. lib. bdg. 36.00 (ISBN 0-8398-1269-8). Irvington.
Story of Old Fort Loudon. Mary N. Murfree. 1986. pap. text ed. 10.95x (ISBN 0-8290-1941-3). Irvington.
Story of Old Glory. Albert I. Mayer. LC 79-110036. (Cornerstones of Freedom Bks). (Illus.). 32p. (gr. 4-8). 1970. PLB 11.67 (ISBN 0-516-04629-2); pap. 2.95 (ISBN 0-516-44629-0). Childrens.
Story of Old Ironsides. Norman Richards. LC 67-20099. (Cornerstones of Freedom Ser.). (Illus.). 32p. (gr. 2-5). 1967. PLB 11.67 (ISBN 0-516-04628-4). Childrens.
Story of Old Nantucket. Wm. F. Macy. (Illus.). 190p. 1983. Repr. of 1928 ed. 12.50 (ISBN 0-686-39887-4). Macys Mesa.
Story of Old New York. H. C. Brown. 1977. lib. bdg. 59.95 (ISBN 0-8490-2683-0). Gordon Pr.
Story of Old Ste. Genevieve. 4th ed. Gregory M. Franzwa. (Illus.). 169p. 1987. pap. 4.95 (ISBN 0-935284-54-0). Patrice Pr.
Story of Opera. Ernest M. Lee. LC 69-16803. (Music Story Ser). 292p. 1968. Repr. of 1909 ed. 30.00x (ISBN 0-8103-3359-7). Gale.
Story of Opera. Ernest M. Lee. 59.95 (ISBN 0-8490-1136-1). Gordon Pr.
Story of Optometry. James R. Gregg. LC 65-12749. (Illus.). pap. 78.80 (ISBN 0-317-07936-0, 2012411). Bks Demand UMI.
Story of Orange. Vernise E. Pelzel. Ed. by Lenore Monk. (Illus.). 48p. (gr. 3-12). 1987. pap. 6.95 (ISBN 0-944131-01-8). HPL Pub.
Story of Oregon, Illinois: Eighteen Eighty-Six to Nineteen Eighty-Six. Ed. by Charles Mongan, Sr. (Illus.). 300p. (YA) 1988. 20.00 (ISBN 0-9617730-0-6). Oregon Sesqui Celeb.
Story of Organ Music. C. Abdy Williams. LC 69-16789. 314p. 1968. Repr. of 1905 ed. 35.00x (ISBN 0-8103-3558-1). Gale.
Story of Organ Music. Charles F. Williams. LC 71-39643. (Select Bibliographies Reprint Ser). 1972. Repr. of 1905 ed. 20.25 (ISBN 0-8369-9948-7). Ayer Co Pubs.
Story of Oriental Philosophy. Adams L. Beck. 1931. 45.50 (ISBN 0-8495-6281-3). Arden Lib.
Story of Other Wise Man. Van Dyke. 5.95 (ISBN 0-88088-560-2). Peter Pauper.
Story of Our Army: From Colonial Days to the Present. Willis J. Abbott. 1977. lib. bdg. 59.95 (ISBN 0-8490-2684-9). Gordon Pr.
Story of Our Calendar. Ruth Brindze. (Illus.). (gr. 4-8). 1949. 13.95 (ISBN 0-8149-0278-2). Vanguard.
Story of Our Fruits & Vegetables. Dorothy Crispo. pap. 5.95 (ISBN 0-8159-6826-4). Devin.
Story of Our Inns of Court. D. Plunket Barton. LC 87-81958. 320p. 1987. Repr. of 1928 ed. lib. bdg. 38.50 (ISBN 0-89941-581-4). W S Hein.
Story of Our Lady of Guadalupe: Three People, Four Days, Many Miracles. J. Janda. 1988. pap. 2.95. Paulist Pr.
Story of Our Literature. John L. Haney. 1973. Repr. of 1923 ed. 15.00 (ISBN 0-8274-0217-1). R West.
Story of Our Lives. Mark Strand. LC 73-80756. 1973. pap. 4.95 (ISBN 0-689-10576-2). Atheneum.
Story of Our Money. Olive C. Dwinell. 1979. lib. bdg. 59.95 (ISBN 0-8490-3009-9). Gordon Pr.
Story of Our Names. Eldson C. Smith. (International Library of Names Ser.). 296p. 1984. Repr. of 1950 ed. text ed. cancelled (ISBN 0-8290-1244-3). Irvington.
Story of Our Post Office, 2 vols. Marshall Cushing. 1976. lib. bdg. 200.00 (ISBN 0-8490-1137-X). Gordon Pr.
Story of Our Rivers: Book II. Al. Valiappa. (Nehru Library for Children). (Illus.). (gr. 1-9). 1979. pap. 2.50 (ISBN 0-89744-184-2). Auromere.
Story of Oxford. C. Headlam. (Mediaeval Towns Ser.: Vol. 30). Repr. of 1931 ed. 44.00 (ISBN 0-8115-0872-2). Kraus Repr.
Story of Padua. C. Foligno. (Mediaeval Towns Ser.: Vol. 4). pap. 35.00 (ISBN 0-8115-0846-3). Kraus Repr.
Story of Painting. Peppin. (Story of Art Ser.). (gr. 6-9). 1980. 7.95 (ISBN 0-86020-442-1, Usborne-Hayes); PLB 12.96 (ISBN 0-88110-030-7); pap. 4.95 (ISBN 0-86020-441-3). EDC.
Story of Panama. Frank A. Gause & Charles C. Carr. LC 75-111714. (American Imperialism Ser.: Viewpoints of United States Foreign Policy, 1898-1941). 1970. Repr. of 1912 ed. 18.00 (ISBN 0-405-02022-8). Ayer Co Pubs.
Story of Paper. Odile Limousin. Tr. by Sarah Matthews from Fr. LC 87-31752. (Illus.). 38p. (gr. k-5). 1988. 4.95 (ISBN 0-944589-16-2, 162). Young Discovery Lib.
Story of Paris. T. Okey. (Mediaeval Towns Ser.: Vol. 15). Repr. of 1925 ed. 44.00 (ISBN 0-8115-0857-9). Kraus Repr.
Story of Passover. Charles Wengrov. (Shulsinger Holiday Ser.). (Illus.). (gr. k-7). 1965. pap. 1.50 (ISBN 0-914080-54-7). Shulsinger Sales.
Story of "Patria". Erich G. Steiner. LC 81-85302. 224p. 1982. 16.95 (ISBN 0-8052-5036-0); pap. 10.95 (ISBN 0-8052-5037-9). Holocaust Pubns.
Story of Paul J. Meyer. Gladys W. Hudson & Lois S. Strain. Ed. by Susan Snider. 1988. 14.95 (ISBN 0-8119-0720-1). Fell.
Story of Persia. S. G. Benjamin. 1977. lib. bdg. 59.95 (ISBN 0-8490-2685-7). Gordon Pr.
Story of Perugia. M. Symonds & C. L. Duff-Gordon. (Mediaeval Towns Ser.: Vol. 23). pap. 26.00 (ISBN 0-8115-0865-X). Kraus Repr.
Story of Perugia. Margaret Symonds & Lina D. Gordon. 1977. lib. bdg. 59.95 (ISBN 0-8490-2686-5). Gordon Pr.
Story of Peter Donders. Costanzo J. Antonellis. 115p. 3.50 (ISBN 0-8198-6834-5, BI0217); pap. 2.50 (ISBN 0-8198-6835-3). Dghtrs St Paul.
Story of Peter Rabbit. (Illus.). 24p. (ps-k). 1.29 (ISBN 0-317-68240-7, Checkerboard Pr). Macmillan.
Story of Peter the Fisherman. D. S. Hare. (Ladybird Ser.). (gr. 2-7). 1970. 2.50 (ISBN 0-87508-867-8). Chr Lit.
Story of Phallicism, with Other Essays on Related Subjects by Eminent Authorities. Lee A. Stone. LC 72-9682. Repr. of 1927 ed. 49.50 (ISBN 0-404-57500-5). AMS Pr.
Story of Philosophy. Will Durant. (gr. 11-12). 1961. pap. 11.95 (ISBN 0-671-20159-X, Touchstone Bks). S&S.
Story of Philospohy. Will Durant. 576p. 1969. pap. 5.95 (ISBN 0-671-49415-5). WSP.
Story of Photography. Michael Langford. (Illus.). 163p. 1980. pap. 19.95 (ISBN 0-240-51044-5). Focal Pr.
Story of Photography. Alfred T. Story. 1979. Repr. of 1904 ed. lib. bdg. 25.00 (ISBN 0-8495-4947-7). Arden Lib.
Story of Photography. Alfred T. Story. Ed. by Nathan Lyons. (Research & Reprint Ser.). (Illus.). 170p. 1974. 11.95 (ISBN 0-87992-003-3); pap. 6.75 (ISBN 0-87992-002-5). Visual Studies.
Story of Photography: An Illustrated History. Giovanni Chiaramonte. Tr. by W. S. Piero. LC 83-70829. (Illus.). 126p. 1983. 17.50 (ISBN 0-89381-122-X). Aperture.
Story of Pisa. J. A. Ross & N. Erichsen. LC 85-47864. (Mediaeval Towns Ser.: Vol. 3). pap. 44.00 (ISBN 0-8115-0845-5). Kraus Repr.
Story of Pollination. B. J. Meeuse. LC 61-15612. (Illus.). Repr. of 1961 ed. cancelled (ISBN 0-8357-9526-8, 2051299). Bks Demand UMI.
Story of Pop see Heinemann Guided Readers.
Story of Poppyseed. Bargi Sargent. (Illus.). 48p. (gr. k-2). 6.95 (ISBN 0-448-18966-6, G&D). Putnam Pub Group.
Story of Portland Glass. Thelma Ladd & Laurence Ladd. (Illus.). 1988. 60.00 (ISBN 0-89272-252-5). Down East.
Story of Portugal. Henry M. Stephens. LC 78-137293. 1971. Repr. of 1891 ed. 27.50 (ISBN 0-404-06255-5). AMS Pr.
Story of Portugal. Henry M. Stephens. 1976. lib. bdg. 59.95 (ISBN 0-8490-2687-3). Gordon Pr.
Story of Prague. C. Lutzow. 1976. lib. bdg. 59.95 (ISBN 0-8490-2688-1). Gordon Pr.
Story of Prague. F. H. Lutzow. (Mediaeval Towns Ser.: Vol. 12). pap. 26.00 (ISBN 0-8115-0854-4). Kraus Repr.
Story of "Primitive" Man. Edward Clodd. 1979. Repr. of 1910 ed. lib. bdg. 20.00 (ISBN 0-8492-4032-8). R West.
Story of Prince Rama. Brian Thompson. (Illus.). 64p. 1985. 12.95 (ISBN 0-670-80117-8). Viking.
Story of Private Security. John D. Peel. 168p. 1971. 19.75 (ISBN 0-398-01465-5). C C Thomas.
Story of Prophecy. Henry J. Forman. 388p. 1981. pap. 12.00 (ISBN 0-89540-089-8, SB-089). Sun Pub.
Story of Prophecy. Hannah G. Goodman. Ed. by Eugene B. Borowitz. LC 65-24925. (gr. 9 up). 1965. 5.95x (ISBN 0-87441-017-7). Behrman.
Story of Public Utilities. Edward Hungerford. LC 72-5053. (Technology & Society Ser.). (Illus.). 384p. 1972. Repr. of 1928 ed. 35.00 (ISBN 0-405-04705-3). Ayer Co Pubs.
Story of Punishment: A Record of Man's Inhumanity to Man. 2nd rev. ed. Harry E. Barnes. LC 74-108229. (Criminology, Law Enforcement, & Social Problems Ser.: No. 112). (Illus.). 1972. 20.00x (ISBN 0-87585-112-6); pap. 8.50x (ISBN 0-87585-913-5). Patterson Smith.
Story of Punxsutawney Phil, "The Fearless Forecaster". rev. ed. Julia S. Moutran. (Illus.). 64p. (gr. 4-10). 1988. 13.95; pap. 8.95. Lit Pubns.
Story of Purim. Charles Wengrov. (Shulsinger Holiday Ser.). (Illus.). (gr. k-7). 1965. pap. 1.50 (ISBN 0-914080-53-9). Shulsinger Sales.
Story of Pygmalion. Pamela Espeland. LC 80-15792. (Myths for Modern Children Ser.). (Illus.). 32p. (gr. 1-4). 1981. PLB 7.95 (ISBN 0-87614-127-0, AACR1). Carolrhoda Bks.
Story of Quailwood. Ethel H. Miller. (Illus.). 48p. 1952. 4.95 (ISBN 0-912142-07-3); pap. 2.00 (ISBN 0-912142-04-9). White S Bks.
Story of Quakerism. rev. ed. Elfrida Vipont. LC 77-71638. (Illus.). 1977. pap. 9.95 (ISBN 0-913408-31-X). Friends United.
Story of Rabbi Yisroel Salanter. Zalman F. Ury. 3.75 (ISBN 0-914131-60-5, D54). Torah Umesorah.
Story of Ramakrishna. Swami Smaranananda. (Illus., Orig.). (gr. k-5). 1976. pap. 2.25 (ISBN 0-87481-168-6). Vedanta Pr.
Story of Ramayan. Bani R. Choudhary. (Illus.). (gr. 3-10). 1979. 7.50 (ISBN 0-89744-133-8). Auromere.
Story of Ramses. Richard Sullivan. LC 86-12713. (Illus.). 212p. 1986. lib. bdg. 49.95x (ISBN 0-88946-046-9). E Mellen.
Story of Rauth & His Sons. Tr. by J. E. Turville-Petre. LC 77-90463. (Viking Society for Northern Research: Translation Ser.: Vol. 4). Repr. of 1947 ed. 16.00 (ISBN 0-404-60014-X). AMS Pr.
Story of Ravena. E. Hutton. (Mediaeval Towns Ser.: Vol. 19). Repr. of 1926 ed. 35.00 (ISBN 0-8115-0861-7). Kraus Repr.
Story of Reading. Daphne Phillips. 192p. 1987. pap. 30.00x (ISBN 0-905392-07-8, Countryside Bks). State Mutual Bk.
Story of Reb Baruch Ber: The Kamenitzer Rosh Yeshiba - Rabbi Baruch Ber Leibowitz & His Successor, Rabbi Reuven Grozovsky. Tzvi Z. Arem. (ArtScroll Youth Ser.). (Illus.). 128p. (YA) (gr. 6-12). 1987. 10.95 (ISBN 0-89906-804-9); pap. 7.95 (ISBN 0-89906-805-7). Mesorah Pubns.
Story of Reb Elchonon: The Life of Rabbi Elchonon Wasserman. Shimon Finkelman. (ArtScroll Youth Ser.). (Illus.). 160p. (YA) (gr. 6-12). 1984. 10.95 (ISBN 0-89906-770-0); pap. 7.95 (ISBN 0-89906-771-9). Mesorah Pubns.
Story of Reb Nachum'ke: The Nineteen Century Tzaddik - A Legend in His Time. Shimon Finkelman. (ArtScroll Youth Ser.). (Illus.). 144p. (YA) (gr. 6-12). 1985. 10.95 (ISBN 0-89906-781-6); pap. 7.95 (ISBN 0-89906-782-4). Mesorah Pubns.
Story of Reb Yisrael Salanter: The Legendary Founder of the Mussar Movement. Shimon Finkelman. (ArtScroll Youth Ser.). (Illus.). 96p. (YA) (gr. 6-12). 1986. 10.95 (ISBN 0-89906-797-2); pap. 7.95 (ISBN 0-89906-798-0). Mesorah Pubns.
Story of Reb Yosef Chaim: The Life & Times of Rabbi Yosef Chaim Sonnefield, the Guardian of Jerusalem. S. Finkelman. (ArtScroll Youth Ser.). (Illus.). 160p. (YA) (gr. 6-12). 1984. 10.95 (ISBN 0-89906-779-4); pap. 7.95 (ISBN 0-89906-780-8). Mesorah Pubns.
Story of Red Riding Hood. Kevin Scally. (Magic Road Bks.). (Illus.). 32p. (ps-3). 1984. 3.95 (ISBN 0-448-11126-8, G&D). Putnam Pub Group.
Story of Redemption. large print ed. 1980. pap. 7.95 (ISBN 0-8280-0058-1, 19654-3). Review & Herald.
Story of Renart the Fox. Pearcy. (Library of Medieval Texts). 1985. lib. bdg. 20.00 (ISBN 0-8240-9418-2). Garland Pub.
Story of Richard Storry & Japan, 1913-1982: A Biography by Dorothy Storry. Dorothy Storry. 1766p. 1987. 59.00x (ISBN 0-904404-58-7, Pub. by P Norbury Pubns Ltd). State Mutual Bk.
Story of Robert Emmet. Patita Nicholson. (Illus.). 79p. (gr. 4-8). 1974. 7.95 (ISBN 0-85342-402-0, Pub. by Mercier Pr Ireland). Irish Bks Media.
Story of Rock. 2nd ed. Carl Belz. (Illus.). 1972. 29.95x (ISBN 0-19-501554-1). Oxford U Pr.
Story of Rock. Carl Belz. 256p. Repr. of 1969 ed. lib. bdg. 39.00 (Pub. by Am Repr Serv). Am Biog Serv.
Story of Rock. 2nd ed. Carl Belz. pap. 7.95x (ISBN 0-06-132070-6, TB2070, Torch). Har-Row.
Story of Rock 'N ' Roll. Pete Fornatale. LC 86-28453. (Illus.). 224p. (gr. 5 up). 1987. 11.75 (ISBN 0-688-06276-8, Morrow Junior Books); pap. 7.95 (ISBN 0-688-06277-6, Morrow Junior Books). Morrow.
Story of Rome. N. Young. (Mediaeval Towns Ser.: Vol. 38). Repr. of 1953 ed. 26.00 (ISBN 0-8115-0880-3). Kraus Repr.
Story of Rome: From the Earliest Times to the End of the Republic. Arthur Gilman. 1827. 30.00 (ISBN 0-8274-3951-2). R West.
Story of Rouen. T. A. Cook. (Medieval Towns Ser.: Vol. 24). pap. 44.00 (ISBN 0-8115-0866-8). Kraus Repr.
Story of Royal Copenhagen Christmas Plates. Pat Owen. (Illus.). 1978. loose leaf 12.00 (ISBN 0-911576-01-0). Viking Import.
Story of Royal Worcester. (Illus.). 1973. pap. 3.00 (ISBN 0-685-57077-0). Ars Ceramica.
Story of Ruth. Morton Schatzman. 1981. pap. 2.95 (ISBN 0-89083-828-3). Zebra.
Story of Sahra. Hanan Al-Shaykh. 192p. 1987. 14.95 (ISBN 0-7043-2546-2, Pub. by Quartet Bks). Salem Hse Pubs.
Story of Sain Odile, the Pearl of Alsace. Francis X. McGowan. 1979. Repr. of 1899 ed. lib. bdg. 12.50 (ISBN 0-8495-3514-X). Arden Lib.
Story of Saint Francis de Sales: Patron of Catholic Writers. Katherine Bregy. 108p. 1982. Repr. of 1958 ed. lib. bdg. 35.00. Century Bookbindery.
Story of St. Paul. D. S. Hare. (Ladybird Ser.). (gr. 2-7). 1969. pap. 2.50 (ISBN 0-87508-869-4). Chr Lit.
Story of Samuel. Joan Kendall. (Very First Bible Stories Ser.). (gr. k-4). 1984. 1.59 (ISBN 0-87162-271-8, D8500). Warner Pr.
Story of San Michele. Axel Munthe. 351p. 1984. pap. 8.95 (ISBN 0-88184-109-9). Carroll & Graf.
Story of Sandy. rev. ed. Susan S. Wexler. 176p. (RL 10). pap. 1.50 (ISBN 0-451-08102-1, W8102, Sig). NAL.
Story of Santa Klaus: Told for Children of All Ages, from Six to Sixty. William S. Walsh. LC 68-58166. (Holiday Ser). (Illus.). 232p. 1970. Repr. of 1909 ed. 45.00x (ISBN 0-8103-3370-8). Gale.
Story of Sarada Devi. Smaranananda. (Illus.). 36p. (Orig.). (gr. k-4). 1987. pap. 2.50 (ISBN 0-87481-229-1, Pub. by Advaita Ashram India). Vedanta Pr.
Story of Saulte Ste. Marie & Chippewa County Michigan. Stanley Newton. LC 74-27236. (Illus.). 199p. 1975. 15.00 (ISBN 0-912382-17-1). Black Letter.
Story of Scary Squirrel. Meta G. Swanston. (ps up). 1986. cancelled (ISBN 0-8062-1996-3). Carlton.
Story of Science, Bk. 1. (Illus., Arabic.). (gr. 5-12). 3.50x (ISBN 0-86685-229-8). Intl Bk Ctr.
Story of Scotland in Stone. Ian C. Hannah. 350p. 1988. 100.00x (ISBN 1-871048-05-2, Pub. by S P A Bks Ltd). State Mutual Bk.
Story of Scottish Philosophy: A Compendium of Selections from the Writings of Nine Pre-Eminent Scottish Philosophers, with Biobibliographical Essays. Ed. by Daniel S. Robinson. LC 78-12114. (Illus.). 1979. Repr. of 1961 ed. lib. bdg. 35.00x (ISBN 0-313-21082-9, ROST). Greenwood.
Story of Seven Maidens: Classics of the Victorian Imagination. 192p. 1987. pap. 7.95 (ISBN 0-394-62299-5, Ever). Grove.
Story of Seven Princesses. Nizami. 174p. 1976. 35.00 (ISBN 0-317-39224-7, Pub. by Network Events Ltd). State Mutual Bk.
Story of Seville: With Three Chapters on the Artists of Seville. Walter M. Gallichan & C. G. Hartley. (Mediaeval Towns Ser.: Vol. 14). pap. 26.00 (ISBN 0-8115-0856-0). Kraus Repr.
Story of Seward's Folly. Susan Clinton. LC 86-30947. (Cornerstones of Freedom Ser.). (Illus.). 32p. (gr. 3-6). 1987. PLB 11.67 (ISBN 0-516-04727-2). Childrens.
Story of Shavuot. Charles Wengrov. (Shulsinger Holiday Ser.). (Illus.). (gr. k-7). 1965. pap. 1.50 (ISBN 0-914080-55-5). Shulsinger Sales.
Story of Shaw's Saint Joan. Brian Tyson. 180p. 1982. 27.95x (ISBN 0-7735-0378-1). McGill Queen's U Pr.
Story of Sherman's March to the Sea. Zachary Kent. LC 86-31054. (Cornerstones of Freedom Ser.). (Illus.). 32p. (gr. 3-6). 1987. PLB 11.67 (ISBN 0-516-04728-0); pap. 2.95 (ISBN 0-516-44728-9). Childrens.
Story of Siddhartha's Release. Richard Bartholomew. (Writers Workshop Redbird Ser.). 1975. 8.00 (ISBN 0-88253-648-6); pap. text ed. 4.00 (ISBN 0-88253-647-8). Ind-US Inc.
Story of Siegfried. James Baldwin. 1898. Repr. 30.00 (ISBN 0-8274-3520-7). R West.
Story of Siena & San Gimignano. E. G. Gardner. (Mediaeval Towns Ser.: Vol. 18). pap. 35.00 (ISBN 0-8115-0860-9). Kraus Repr.
Story of Sierra Leone. facsimile ed. Francis A. Utting. LC 77-37357. (Select Bibliographies Reprint Ser.). Repr. of 1931 ed. 17.00 (ISBN 0-8369-6704-6). Ayer Co Pubs.
Story of Sir Lancelot & His Companions. Howard Pyle. (Illus.). 360p. (YA) (gr. 7 up). 1985. 17.95 (ISBN 0-684-18313-7, Pub. by Scribner). Macmillan.
Story of Sir Walter Scott's First Love. Adam Scott. 1973. Repr. of 1896 ed. 20.00 (ISBN 0-8274-1086-7). R West.

Story of Sirio. Ferdinando Camon. Tr. by Cassandra Bertea from Ital. LC 84-63123. Orig. Title: Storia Di Sirio. 131p. (Orig.). 1985. pap. 8.00 (ISBN 0-910395-12-8). Marlboro Pr.

Story of Sitka. C. L. Andrews. 142p. (YA) (gr. 9 up). pap. 9.95 (ISBN 0-8466-0094-3, S94). Shorey.

Story of Slough. Judith Hunter. 96p. 1987. pap. 30.00x (ISBN 0-86368-006-2, Countryside Bks). State Mutual Bk.

Story of Social Philosophy. facs. ed. Charles A. Ellwood. LC 79-152169. (Essay Index Reprint Ser). 1938. 27.00 (ISBN 0-8369-2187-9). Ayer Co Pubs.

Story of Some Famous Books. Frederick Saunders. LC 72-5752. (Essay Index Reprint Ser.). 1972. Repr. of 1887 ed. 18.00 (ISBN 0-8369-7290-2). Ayer Co Pubs.

Story of Some Famous Books. Frederick Saunders. 1887. 15.00 (ISBN 0-8274-3521-5). R West.

Story of Southend Pier...and It's Associations. E. W. Shepherd. 120p. 1979. 27.50x (ISBN 0-905858-11-5, Pub. by Egon England). State Mutual Bk.

Story of Southern Hymnology. Arthur L. Stevenson. LC 72-1676. Repr. of 1931 ed. 17.50 (ISBN 0-404-08334-X). AMS Pr.

Story of Southwest Research Center. H. Vagtborg. 15.00 (ISBN 0-292-77508-3). Brown Bk.

Story of Space & Rockets. Roger Arno. (Illus.). (gr. 5). 1978. pap. 3.50 (ISBN 0-88388-063-6). Bellerophon Bks.

Story of Spain. Edward E. Hale & Susan Hale. 1978. Repr. of 1887 ed. lib. bdg. 30.00 (ISBN 0-8495-2227-7). Arden Lib.

Story of Spanish Painting. Charles H. Caffin. LC 72-100521. (BCL Ser. I). (Illus.). Repr. of 1910 ed. 17.50 (ISBN 0-404-01361-9). AMS Pr.

Story of Steel. Brenda Thompson & Rosemary Giesen. LC 76-22464. (Lerner First Fact Bks.). (Illus.). (gr. k-3). 1977. PLB 4.95 (ISBN 0-8225-1362-5). Lerner Pubns.

Story of Story Writing: Facts & Information about Literary Work of Practical Value to Both Amateur & Professional Writers. Nathaniel C. Fowler. 255p. 1982. Repr. of 1913 ed. lib. bdg. 40.00 (ISBN 0-89984-207-0). Century Bookbindery.

Story of Superstition. Philip F. Waterman. LC 78-107770. Repr. of 1929 ed. 15.00 (ISBN 0-404-06849-9). AMS Pr.

Story of Superstition Mountain & the Lost Dutchman Gold Mine. Robert J. Allen. Date not set. pap. 3.50 (ISBN 0-671-47674-2). PB.

Story of Superted. Mike Young. LC 84-61572. (Cuddle Shape Bks.). (Illus.). 14p. (ps-1). 1985. bds. 3.95 (ISBN 0-394-87152-9, BYR). Random.

Story of Surnames. William D. Bowman. LC 68-8906. 288p. 1968. Repr. of 1932 ed. 40.00x (ISBN 0-8103-3110-1). Gale.

Story of Susan B. Anthony. Susan Clinton. LC 86-9613. (Cornerstones of Freedom Ser.). (Illus.). 32p. (gr. 3-6). 1986. PLB 11.67 (ISBN 0-516-04705-1); pap. 2.95 (ISBN 0-516-44705-X). Childrens.

Story of Swarajya: Part I. Vishnu Prabhakar. (Nehru Library for Children). (Illus.). (gr. 1-10). 1979. pap. 2.50 (ISBN 0-89744-185-0). Auromere.

Story of Swarajya: Part II. Sumangal Prakash. (Nehru Library for Children). (Illus.). (gr. 1-10). 1979. pap. 2.50 (ISBN 0-89744-186-9). Auromere.

Story of Symphony. E. M. Lee. 59.95 (ISBN 0-8490-1138-8). Gordon Pr.

Story of Symphony. Ernest M. Lee. LC 69-16804. (Illus.). 260p. 1968. Repr. of 1916 ed. 38.00x (ISBN 0-8103-3568-9). Gale.

Story of Taize. J. L. Balado. (Illus.). 144p. (Orig.). 1981. pap. 4.95 (ISBN 0-8164-2321-0, HarpR). Har-Row.

Story of Tattersalls. Peter Willett. (Illus.). 192p. 1988. 34.95 (ISBN 0-09-171290-4, Pub. by Century Hutchinson). David & Charles.

Story of Television: The Life of Philo T. Farnsworth. George Everson. LC 74-4677. (Illus.). 270p. 1974. Repr. of 1949 ed. 18.00x (ISBN 0-405-06042-4). Ayer Co Pubs.

Story of Texas, 4 vols. John E. Weems. (Orig.). (gr. 2-6). 1986. Set. pap. 4.95 (ISBN 0-940672-35-9). Shearer Pub.

Story of Texas: A History Picture Book. Betsy Warren. (Illus.). 46p. (gr. 3 up). Date not set. pap. 3.50 (ISBN 0-9618660-1-2). Ranch Gate Bks.

Story of the Abbey Theatre. Peter Kavanagh. LC 84-60178. (Irish Art Ser.). (Illus.). 325p. 1984. 25.00x (ISBN 0-915032-29-5); pap. 12.95 (ISBN 0-915032-30-9). Natl Poet Foun.

Story of the Acadians. Amy Boudreau. (Illus.). 38p. 1971. pap. 2.75 (ISBN 0-911116-30-3). Pelican.

Story of the Alamo. Norman Richards. LC 70-100698. (Cornerstones of Freedom Ser.). (Illus.). 32p. (gr. 4-8). 1970. 11.67 (ISBN 0-516-04601-2); pap. 2.95 (ISBN 0-516-44601-0). Childrens.

Story of the Alphabet. Edward Clodd. 1979. Repr. of 1904 ed. lib. bdg. 25.00 (ISBN 0-8492-4034-4). R West.

Story of the American Board: An Account of the First Hundred Years of the American Board for Foreign Missions. William E. Strong. LC 79-83443. (Religion in America Ser). 1969. Repr. of 1910 ed. 26.50 (ISBN 0-405-00277-7). Ayer Co Pubs.

Story of the American Hymn. Edward S. Ninde. LC 72-1708. (Illus.). Repr. of 1921 ed. 29.75 (ISBN 0-404-09914-9). AMS Pr.

Story of the American Merchant Marine. John R. Spears. 1977. lib. bdg. 55.95 (ISBN 0-8490-2689-X). Gordon Pr.

Story of the American Revolution Coloring Book. Peter Copeland. (ps up). 1988. pap. 2.95 (ISBN 0-486-25648-0). Dover.

Story of the Amulet. E. Nesbit. (Orig.). (gr. k-6). 1987. pap. 4.95 (ISBN 0-440-47719-0, Pub. by Yearling Classics). Dell.

Story of the Arab Legion. John B. Glubb. LC 76-7060. (The Middle East in the 20th Century Ser.). 1976. Repr. of 1948 ed. lib. bdg. 42.50 (ISBN 0-306-70763-2). Da Capo.

Story of the Armory Show. Milton W. Brown. (Illus.). 400p. 1988. 29.95 (ISBN 0-89659-795-4). Abbeville Pr.

Story of the Art of Building: With an Account of Architecture in America. P. Leslie Waterhouse. (Illus.). 1979. Repr. of 1904 ed. lib. bdg. 25.00 (ISBN 0-8495-5701-1). Arden Lib.

Story of the Art of Music. Frederick J. Crowest. 1979. Repr. of 1904 ed. lib. bdg. 25.00 (ISBN 0-8495-0921-1). Arden Lib.

Story of the Assassination of John F. Kennedy. R. Conrad Stein. LC 85-10936. (Cornerstones of Freedom Ser.). (Illus.). 31p. (gr. 3-4). 1985. PLB 11.67 (ISBN 0-516-04693-4); pap. 2.95 (ISBN 0-516-44693-2). Childrens.

Story of the AT-6 Texan. Leo J. Kohn. 1975. pap. 6.95 (Pub. by AvPubns). Aviation.

Story of the Atlantic Telegraph. Henry M. Field. LC 72-5049. (Technology & Society Ser.). (Illus.). 415p. 1972. Repr. of 1893 ed. 24.00 (ISBN 0-405-04701-0). Ayer Co Pubs.

Story of the Bagpipe. William G. Flood. LC 76-22332. (Illus.). 1976. Repr. of 1911 ed. lib. bdg. 25.00 (ISBN 0-89341-009-8). Longwood Pub Group.

Story of the Baltimore & Ohio Railroad, 1827-1927, 2 vols. Edward Hungerford. LC 72-5054. (Technology & Society Ser.). (Illus.). 600p. 1972. Repr. of 1928 ed. Set. 66.00 (ISBN 0-405-04706-1); 33.00 ea. Vol. 1 (ISBN 0-405-04735-5). Vol. 2 (ISBN 0-405-04736-3). Ayer Co Pubs.

Story of the Barbary Corsairs. Stanley Lane-Poole. LC 73-97416. (Illus.). Repr. of 1901 ed. 35.00x (ISBN 0-8371-3231-2, LBC&, Pub. by Negro U Pr). Greenwood.

Story of the Barbary Pirates. R. Conrad Stein. LC 82-4436. (Cornerstones of Freedom Ser.). (Illus.). (gr. 3-6). 1982. PLB 11.67 (ISBN 0-516-04632-2); pap. 2.95 (ISBN 0-516-44632-0). Childrens.

Story of the Battle for Iwo Jima. R. Conrad Stein. LC 77-5088. (Cornerstones of Freedom Ser.). (Illus.). 32p. (gr. 3-5). 1977. PLB 11.67 (ISBN 0-516-04607-1). Childrens.

Story of the Battle Hymn of the Republic. facsimile ed. Florence H. Hall. LC 71-178474. (Black Heritage Library Collection). Repr. of 1916 ed. 15.25 (ISBN 0-8369-8923-6). Ayer Co Pubs.

Story of the Battle of Bull Run. Zachary Kent. LC 86-9642. (Cornerstones of Freedom Ser.). (Illus.). 32p. (gr. 3-6). 1986. PLB 11.67 (ISBN 0-516-04703-5); pap. 2.95 (ISBN 0-516-44703-3). Childrens.

Story of the Battle of the Bulge. R. Conrad Stein. LC 77-5431. (Cornerstones of Freedom Ser.). (Illus.). 32p. (gr. 3-5). 1977. PLB 11.67 (ISBN 0-516-04608-X). Childrens.

Story of the Bible. Edgar J. Goodspeed. LC 36-21666. Repr. of 1967 ed. 44.00 (ISBN 0-8357-9657-4, 2013612). Bks Demand UMI.

Story of the Bible. Ed. by Johnny Ramsey. pap. 3.95 (ISBN 0-89137-543-0). Quality Pubns.

Story of the Bible World see Fascinante Mundo de la Biblia.

Story of the Bicycle. John Woodforde. (Illus.). 1977. pap. 7.95 (ISBN 0-7100-8644-X). Routledge Chapman & Hall.

Story of the Black Hawk War. Jim Hargrove. LC 86-955. (Cornerstones of Freedom Ser.). (Illus.). 32p. (gr. 3-6). 1986. PLB 11.67 (ISBN 0-516-04696-9); pap. 2.95 (ISBN 0-516-44696-7). Childrens.

Story of the Bonhomme Richard. Norman Richards. LC 76-82961. (Cornerstones of Freedom Ser.). (Illus.). 32p. (gr. 3-5). 1969. 11.67 (ISBN 0-516-04602-0); pap. 2.95 (ISBN 0-516-44602-9). Childrens.

Story of the Boston Massacre. Mary K. Phelan. LC 75-25961. (Illus.). 160p. (gr. 5-9). 1976. 12.70i (ISBN 0-690-00716-7, Crowell Jr Bks). HarpJ.

Story of the Boston Tea Party. Illus. by Keith Neely. LC 83-27319. (Illus.). (gr. 3-5). Date not set. price not set (ISBN 0-516-04666-7). Childrens.

Story of the Boston Tea Party. Mary K. Phelan. LC 72-7554. (Illus.). (gr. 5-9). 1973. 12.70i (ISBN 0-690-77653-5, Crowell Jr Bks). HarpJ.

Story of the Boy Scouts. Wyatt Blassingame. LC 68-13593. (American Democracy Ser.). (Illus.). (gr. 3-6). 1968. PLB 7.12 (ISBN 0-8116-6500-3). Garrard.

Story of the Burning of Washington. R. Conrad Stein. LC 84-12124. (Cornerstones of Freedom Ser.). (Illus.). 32p. (gr. 3-6). 1985. lib. bdg. 11.67 (ISBN 0-516-04678-0). Childrens.

Story of the Calcutta Theatre, 1753-1980. Sushil K. Mukherjee. 1983. 32.00x (ISBN 0-8364-0994-9, Pub. by KP Bagchi India). South Asia Bks.

Story of the California Gold Rush Coloring Book. Peter Copeland. (Illus.). 32p. (gr. 2 up). 1988. pap. 2.95 (ISBN 0-486-25814-9). Dover.

Story of the Canadian Pacific Railway. Keith Morris. Ed. by Stuart Bruchey. LC 80-1332. (Railroads Ser.). (Illus.). 1981. Repr. of 1916 ed. lib. bdg. 18.00x (ISBN 0-405-13806-7). Ayer Co Pubs.

Story of the Capitol. Marilyn Prolman. LC 69-14681. (Cornerstones of Freedom Bks.). (Illus.). 32p. (gr. 3-5). 1969. PLB 11.67 (ISBN 0-516-04604-7); pap. 2.95 (ISBN 0-516-44604-5). Childrens.

Story of the Century. Michael A. Bass. (Divisional Ser.: No. 9). (Illus.). 1979. Repr. of 1946 ed. 25.00 (ISBN 0-89839-023-0). Battery Pr.

Story of the Challenger Disaster. Zachary Kent. LC 86-6822. (Cornerstones of Freedom Ser.). (Illus.). 32p. (gr. 3-6). 1986. PLB 11.67 (ISBN 0-516-04673-X); pap. 2.95 (ISBN 0-516-44673-8). Childrens.

Story of the Champions of the Round Table. Howard Pyle. (Illus.). xviii, 329p. (ps-4). 1968. pap. 6.95 (ISBN 0-486-21883-X). Dover.

Story of the Champions of the Round Table. Howard Pyle. (Illus.). (YA) (gr. 6-12). 15.50 (ISBN 0-8446-0229-9). Peter Smith.

Story of the Champions of the Round Table. Howard Pyle. LC 84-13881. (Illus.). 348p. (gr. k up). 1984. 17.95 (ISBN 0-684-18171-1, Pub. by Scribner). Macmillan.

Story of the Champions of the Round Table. Howard Pyle. 20.95 (ISBN 0-89190-661-4, Pub. by Am Repr). Amereon Ltd.

Story of the Chasam Sofer. Shubert Spero. (Illus.). 80p. 2.00 (ISBN 0-914131-61-3, D53). Torah Umesorah.

Story of the Cherokee People. Thomas B. Underwood. (Illus.). 48p. 1961. 3.50 (ISBN 0-935741-01-1). Cherokee Pubns.

Story of the Chevalier Boyard. M. De Berville. Ed. by Edith Walford. 1978. Repr. of 1880 ed. lib. bdg. 20.00 (ISBN 0-8492-3047-0). R West.

Story of the Chicago Fire. R. C. Stein. LC 81-15543. (Cornerstones of Freedom Ser.). (Illus.). 32p. (gr. 3-6). 1982. PLB 11.67 (ISBN 0-516-04633-0); pap. 2.95 (ISBN 0-516-44633-9). Childrens.

Story of the China Inland Mission. M. Geraldine Guinness. 512p. 1894. 245.00x (Pub. by Han-Shan Tang Ltd). State Mutual Bk.

Story of the Chofetz Chaim. Nosson Scherman & Eliezer Gevirtz. (ArtScroll Youth Ser.). (Illus.). 160p. (YA) (gr. 6-12). 1987. 10.95 (ISBN 0-89906-766-2); pap. 7.95 (ISBN 0-89906-767-0). Mesorah Pubns.

Story of the Chofetz Chaim. (Illus.). 160p. 9.85 (ISBN 0-89906-756-5); pap. 7.15 (ISBN 0-89906-757-3). Torah Umesorah.

Story of the Chokoloskee Bay Country, with the Reminiscences of T. S. "Ted" Smallwood. Charlton W. Tebeau. LC 75-43288. (Illus.). 1976. 3.00 (ISBN 0-916224-01-5). Banyan Bks.

Story of the Christian Church. rev. ed. Jesse L. Hurlbut. 192p. 1986. 12.95 (ISBN 0-310-26510-X, 6527). Zondervan.

Story of the Christian Year. Amy Boudreau. 1971. 4.50 (ISBN 0-685-27196-X). Claitors.

Story of the Christian Year. George M. Gibson. LC 71-142635. (Essay Index Reprint Ser.). (Illus.). Repr. of 1945 ed. 25.00 (ISBN 0-8369-2770-2). Ayer Co Pubs.

Story of the Christians. Jennifer Rye. (Religions Around the World). (Illus.). 32p. (gr. 4-8). 1987. 7.95 (ISBN 0-521-30118-1); pap. 3.95 (ISBN 0-521-31748-7). Cambridge U Pr.

Story of the Christians & Moors of Roman Spain. Charlotte M. Yonge. 1893. 30.00. Century Bookbindery.

Story of the Christmas Rose. I. M. Richardson. LC 87-13817. (Illus.). 32p. (gr. k-4). 1987. PLB 9.79 (ISBN 0-8167-1069-4); pap. text ed. 1.95 (ISBN 0-8167-1070-8). Troll Assocs.

Story of the Church. new ed. Inez S. Davis. 1981. pap. 18.00 (ISBN 0-8309-0188-4). Herald Hse.

Story of the Church. George Johnson et al. LC 80-51329. 521p. (gr. 9). 1980. pap. 13.50 (ISBN 0-89555-156-X). Tan Bks Pubs.

Story of the Church. 2nd. enl. ed. A. M. Renwick & A. M. Harman. 272p. (Orig.). 1985. pap. 9.95 (ISBN 0-8028-0092-0). Eerdmans.

Story of the Church of Egypt, 2 vols. Edith L. Butcher. LC 75-41459. Repr. of 1897 ed. Set. 87.50 (ISBN 0-404-56231-0). AMS Pr.

Story of the Church: Peak Moments from Pentecost to the Year 2000. Alfred McBride & O. Praem. (Illus.). 168p. (gr. 7-11). 1984. pap. text ed. 7.95 (ISBN 0-86716-029-2). St Anthony Mess Pr.

Story of the CIO. Benjamin Stolberg. LC 77-156426. (American Labor Ser., No. 2). 1971. Repr. of 1938 ed. 21.00 (ISBN 0-405-02944-6). Ayer Co Pubs.

Story of the City & of Its People During the 19th Century. Mary C. Drawford. 1979. Repr. of 1910 ed. lib. bdg. 30.00 (ISBN 0-8495-0943-2). Arden Lib.

Story of the Civil War, Vol. 4. John C. Ropes. 749p. 1980. Repr. of 1894 ed. lib. bdg. 475.00 (ISBN 0-8495-4634-6). Arden Lib.

Story of the Clipper Ships. R. Conrad Stein. LC 81-1299. (Cornerstones of Freedom Ser.). (Illus.). 32p. (gr. 3-6). 1981. PLB 11.67 (ISBN 0-516-04612-8); pap. 2.95 (ISBN 0-516-44612-6). Childrens.

Story of the Commonweal. Henry Vincent. LC 70-90194. (Mass Violence in America Ser). Repr. of 1894 ed. 11.00 (ISBN 0-405-01339-6). Ayer Co Pubs.

Story of the Confederate States; or, History of the War for Southern Independence Embracing the Early Settlement of the Country, Trouble with the Indians, the French, Revolutionary & Mexican Wars. Joseph T. Derry. 19.50 (ISBN 0-405-12295-0). Ayer Co Pubs.

Story of the Congo Free State. Henry W. Wack. (Illus.). 1970. Repr. of 1905 ed. 27.50 (ISBN 0-87266-042-7). Argosy.

Story of the Constitution. Sol Bloom. LC 86-12666. (Illus.). 192p. 1986. pap. text ed. 8.95 (ISBN 0-911333-45-2, 200046). Natl Archives & Records.

Story of the Constitution. Marilyn Prolman. LC 69-14680. (Cornerstones of Freedom Bks). (Illus.). 32p. (gr. 4-8). 1969. PLB 11.67 (ISBN 0-516-04605-5); pap. 3.25 (ISBN 0-516-44605-3). Childrens.

Story of the Dancing Frog. Quentin Blake. LC 84-12222. (Illus.). 32p. (ps-3). 1985. 10.95 (ISBN 0-394-87033-6); lib. bdg. 9.99 (ISBN 0-394-97033-0). Knopf.

Story of the Davis Cup. Alan Trengove. (Illus.). 577p. 1986. 24.95 (ISBN 0-09-159860-5, Pub. by Century Hutchinson). David & Charles.

Story of the Days to Come see Three Prophetic Novels.

Story of the Declaration of Independence. Norman Richards. LC 68-24379. (Cornerstones of Freedom Ser.). (Illus.). 32p. (gr. 2-5). 1968. PLB 11.67 (ISBN 0-516-04606-3); pap. 2.95 (ISBN 0-516-44606-1). Childrens.

Story of the Defenders of Bataan & Corregidor & Their Captivity. Mariano Villarin. (Illus.). 368p. 1986. 19.95 (ISBN 0-89962-536-3). Todd & Honeywell.

Story of the Dockers' Strike Told by Two East Londoners. H. Llewellyn Smith & Vaughn Nash. LC 83-48498. (World of Labour-English Workers 1850-1890 Ser.). 190p. 1984. lib. bdg. 20.00 (ISBN 0-8240-5725-2). Garland Pub.

Story of the Dutch East Indies. Bernard H. Vlekke. LC 71-161775. Repr. of 1945 ed. 22.00 (ISBN 0-404-09043-5). AMS Pr.

Story of the Earth. British Museum Geological Department Staff. (Illus.). 36p. (YA) (gr. 7 up). 1986. pap. 3.50 (ISBN 0-521-32413-0). Cambridge U pr.

Story of the Earth. Peter Cattermole & Patrick Moore. (Illus.). 224p. 1985. 29.95 (ISBN 0-521-26292-5). Cambridge U Pr.

Story of the Earth in Past Ages. H. G. Seeley. 1979. Repr. of 1904 ed. lib. bdg. 25.00 (ISBN 0-8495-4912-4). Arden Lib.

Story of the Earth's Atmosphere. Douglas Archibald. 1904. 15.00 (ISBN 0-686-17416-X). Ridgeway Bks.

Story of the Easter Bunny. Sheila Black. LC 87-81934. (Illus.). 32p. (ps-1). 1988. 3.95 (ISBN 0-307-10415-X, Pub. by Golden Bks). Western Pub.

Story of the Edinburgh Burns Relics with Fresh Facts About Burns & His Family. Robert Duncan. LC 75-42242. 1976. Repr. of 1910 ed. lib. bdg. 27.50 (ISBN 0-8414-3722-X). Folcroft.

Story of the Election of Abraham Lincoln. Zachary Kent. LC 85-23277. (Cornerstones of Freedom Ser.). (Illus.). 32p. (gr. 3-6). 1986. PLB 11.67 (ISBN 0-516-04669-1); pap. 2.95 (ISBN 0-516-44669-X). Childrens.

Story of the Empire State Building. Patrick Clinton. LC 87-25687. (Cornerstones of Freedom Ser.). (Illus.). 32p. (gr. 3-6). 1987. PLB 11.93 (ISBN 0-516-04730-2). Childrens.

Story of the Engineers, 1800-1845. James B. Jefferys. LC 75-136472. 1971. Repr. of 1945 ed. 27.00 (ISBN 0-384-27100-6). Johnson Repr.

Story of the Erie Canal. R. Conrad Stein. LC 84-28525. (Cornerstones of Freedom Ser.). (Illus.). 32p. (gr. 3-6). 1985. lib. bdg. 11.67 (ISBN 0-516-04682-9); pap. 2.95 (ISBN 0-516-44682-7). Childrens.

Story of the Eucharist. Inos Biffi. Tr. by John Drury from Ital. LC 85-82173. (Illustrated History of Christian Culture Ser.). Orig. Title: Storia dell' eucaristia. (Illus.). 125p. (gr. 5 up). 1986. 13.95 (ISBN 0-89870-089-2). Ignatius Pr.

Story of the Eye. Georges Bataille. Tr. by Joachim Neugroschal from Fr. 72p. (Orig.). pap. 5.95 (ISBN 0-87286-209-7). City Lights.

Story of the Falashas: "Black Jews" of Ethiopia. Simon D. Messing. (Illus.). 134p. 1982. pap. 7.50 (ISBN 0-9615946-9-1). Messing Pub.

Story of the Flight at Kitty Hawk. R. Conrad Stein. LC 81-1634. (Cornerstones of Freedom Ser.). (Illus.). 32p. (gr. 3-6). 1981. PLB 11.67 (ISBN 0-516-04614-4); pap. 2.95 (ISBN 0-516-44614-2). Childrens.

Story of the Four World Centres: For Girls & Leaders. rev. ed. World Association of Girl Guides & Girl Scouts. (Illus.). 51p. (gr. 4-8). 1982. pap. 2.25 (ISBN 0-900827-27-0, 23-123). Girl Scouts USA.

Story of the Freeman. Francis Neilson. 59.95 (ISBN 0-87700-011-5). Revisionist Pr.

Story of the Future. Ralph M. Riggs. LC 67-31330. 1968. 2.95 (ISBN 0-88243-742-9, 02-0742). Gospel Pub.

Story of the Gettysburg Address. Kenneth Richards. LC 70-82962. (Cornerstones of Freedom Ser.). (Illus.). 32p. (gr. 3-5). 1969. 11.67 (ISBN 0-516-04615-2); pap. 3.25 (ISBN 0-516-44615-0). Childrens.

Story of the Glittering Plain or the Land of Living Men: The 1894 Kelmscott Edition-with 23 Woodcuts by Walter Crane. William Morris. (Illus.). 192p. 1987. pap. 7.95 (ISBN 0-486-25467-4). Dover.

Story of the Glittering Plain, Which Has Been Also Called the Land of Living Men, or the Acre of the Undying. William Morris. Ed. by R. Reginald & Douglas Menville. LC 80-19460. (Newcastle Forgotten Fantasy Library Ser.: Vol. 1). 174p. 1980. Repr. of 1973 ed. lib. bdg. 22.95x (ISBN 0-89370-500-4). Borgo Pr.

Story of the Gold at Sutter's Mill. R. Conrad Stein. LC 81-6088. (Cornerstones of Freedom Ser.). (Illus.). 32p. (gr. 3-6). 1981. PLB 11.67 (ISBN 0-516-04617-9); pap. 2.95 (ISBN 0-516-44617-7). Childrens.

Story of the Golden Spike. R. Conrad Stein. LC 78-4042. (Cornerstones of Freedom Ser.). (Illus.). 32p. (gr. 3-6). 1978. PLB 11.67 (ISBN 0-516-04621-7); pap. 2.95 (ISBN 0-516-44621-5). Childrens.

Story of the Grail & the Passing of Arthur. Howard Pyle. LC 85-40302. (Illus.). 340p. (gr. 7 up). 1985. Repr. 17.95 (ISBN 0-684-18483-4, Pub. by Scribner). Macmillan.

Story of the Great American West. Reader's Digest Editors. LC 76-23542. (Illus.). 384p. 1977. 21.95 (ISBN 0-89577-039-3, Pub. by RD Assn). Random.

Story of the Great Armada. John R. Hale. lib. bdg. 59.95 (ISBN 0-8490-2690-3). Gordon Pr.

Story of the Great Depression. R. Conrad Stein. LC 85-11039. (Cornerstones of Freedom Ser.). (Illus.). 31p. (gr. 3-4). 1985. PLB 11.67 (ISBN 0-516-04694-2); pap. 2.95 (ISBN 0-516-44694-0). Childrens.

Story of the Great Geologists. facs. ed. Carroll L. Fenton & Mildred Fenton. LC 73-84306. (Essay Index Reprint Ser.). 1945. 22.00 (ISBN 0-8369-1130-X). Ayer Co Pubs.

Story of the Great March. George W. Nichols. 394p. 1972. Repr. of 1865 ed. 21.00 (ISBN 0-87928-031-X). Corner Hse.

Story of the Green Mountain Boys. Susan Clinton. LC 87-17380. (Cornerstones of Freedom Ser.). (Illus.). 32p. (gr. 3-6). 1987. PLB 11.93 (ISBN 0-516-04731-0). Childrens.

Story of the Gypsies. Konrad Bercovici. LC 78-164051. (Illus.). 310p. 1975. Repr. of 1928 ed. 37.00x (ISBN 0-8103-4042-9). Gale.

Story of the Harp. William Grattan Flood. LC 76-42036. 1977. Repr. of 1905 ed. lib. bdg. 25.00 (ISBN 0-89341-057-8). Longwood Pub Group.

Story of the Hays. Kenneth M. Hay. 131p. 1985. pap. 9.95 (ISBN 0-912951-25-7). ScotPr.

Story of the Hindus. Jacqueline S. Hirst. 32p. Date not set. price not set (ISBN 0-521-26261-5); pap. price not set (ISBN 0-521-26900-8). Cambridge U Pr.

Story of the Homestead Act. R. Conrad Stein. LC 78-4839. (Cornerstones of Freedom Ser.). (Illus.). 32p. (gr. 3-6). 1978. PLB 11.67 (ISBN 0-516-04616-0); pap. 2.95 (ISBN 0-516-44616-9). Childrens.

Story of the Hoover Dam. (Illus.). 144p. 1986. 17.50 (ISBN 0-913814-80-6); pap. 10.95 (ISBN 0-913814-79-2). Nevada Pubns.

Story of the House of Witmark: From Ragtime to Swingtime. Isidore Witmark & Isaac Goldberg. LC 76-20707. (Roots of Jazz Ser.). 1975. Repr. of 1939 ed. lib. bdg. 45.00 (ISBN 0-306-70686-5). Da Capo.

Story of the Huna Work. E. Otha Wingo. 1981. pap. 3.00x (ISBN 0-910764-06-9). Huna Res Inc.

Story of the Hutchinsons, 2 vols. John Wallace Hutchinson. Ed. by Charles E. Mann. LC 76-58562. (Music Reprint Ser.). 1977. Repr. of 1896 ed. Set. lib. bdg. 95.00 (ISBN 0-306-70864-7). Da Capo.

Story of the Hymns. H. Butterworth. 59.95 (ISBN 0-8490-1139-6). Gordon Pr.

Story of the Ice Age. Rose Wyler & Gerald Adams. (Illus.). 96p. (Orig.). (gr. 4-6). 1988. pap. 2.50 (ISBN 0-590-41446-1). Scholastic Inc.

Story of the Indian. George B. Grinnell. Repr. of 1909 ed. 35.00 (ISBN 0-8492-9965-9). R West.

Story of the Ingalls. William T. Anderson. (Laura Ingalls Wilder Family Ser.). (Illus.). 40p. (Orig.). 1971. pap. text ed. 3.95 (ISBN 0-9610088-0-6). Anderson MI.

Story of the Inns of Court. D. Plunket Barton et al. (Illus.). 320p. 1986. Repr. of 1924 ed. lib. bdg. 32.50x (ISBN 0-8377-1936-4). Rothman.

Story of the Integration of the Indian States. Vapal P. Menon. LC 72-4282. (World Affairs Ser.: National & International Viewpoints). (Illus.). 542p. 1972. Repr. of 1956 ed. 33.00 (ISBN 0-405-04575-1). Ayer Co Pubs.

Story of the Irish Citizen's Army. Sean O'Casey. 60p. (Orig.). 1985. pap. 4.50 (ISBN 0-904526-50-X, Pub. by Journeyman Pr Enlgand). Riverrun NY.

Story of the Irish Nation. Francis Hackett. 1930. Repr. 25.00 (ISBN 0-8274-3522-3). R West.

Story of the Irish Race: A Popular History of Ireland. Seumas MacManus. 1979. Repr. of 1922 ed. lib. bdg. 50.00 (ISBN 0-89987-550-5). Darby Bks.

Story of the Irish Race: A Popular History of Ireland. 40th rev. ed. Seumas MacManus. 740p. 12.95 (ISBN 0-8159-6827-2). Devin.

Story of the Jesus People: A Factual Survey. Ronald M. Enroth et al. (Illus.). 256p. 1972. pap. 3.95 (ISBN 0-85364-131-5). Attic Pr.

Story of the Jew. rev. ed. Harry Gersh et al. LC 64-22514. (Illus.). (gr. 8-11). 1965. 5.95x (ISBN 0-87441-019-3). Behrman.

Story of the Jewish People, 4 vols. Gilbert Klaperman & Libby Klaperman. Incl. Vol. 1. From Creation to the Second Temple. pap. text ed. 4.95x (ISBN 0-87441-207-2); Vol. 2. From the Building of the Second Temple Through the Age of the Rabbis. pap. text ed. 4.95x (ISBN 0-87441-208-0); Vol. 3. From the Golden Age in Spain Through the European Emancipation. pap. text ed. 5.95x (ISBN 0-87441-209-9); Vol. 4. From the Settlement of America Through Israel Today. pap. text ed. 5.95x (ISBN 0-87441-210-2). LC 56-12175. (Illus.). (gr. 5-9). 1974. pap. activity bks. 3.95. Behrman.

Story of the Jewish Way of Life. Meyer Levin & Toby Kurzband. LC 59-13487. (Jewish Heritage Ser.: Vol. 3). (gr. 4-6). 1959. 5.95x (ISBN 0-87441-003-7). Behrman.

Story of the Jews. Julia Neuberger. (Religions Around the World). (Illus.). 32p. (gr. 4-8). 1987. 7.95 (ISBN 0-521-30601-9); pap. 3.95 (ISBN 0-521-31580-8). Cambridge U Pr.

Story of the Johnstown Flood. R. Conrad Stein. LC 84-7824. (Cornerstones of Freedom Ser.). (Illus.). 32p. (gr. 3-6). 1985. lib. bdg. 11.67 (ISBN 0-516-04680-2). Childrens.

Story of the Jubilee Singers with Their Songs. rev. ed. J. B. Marsh. LC 72-165509. (Illus.). Repr. of 1880 ed. 14.00 (ISBN 0-404-04189-2). AMS Pr.

Story of the July Nineteen Thirty-One Cadet Class at Brooks, March & Randolph Fields: Forty-Four Years Later. Fred R. Freyer. (Illus.). 100p. 1977. pap. text ed. 10.00x (ISBN 0-89126-052-8). MA-AH Pub.

Story of the Kilmarnock Burns. John D. Ross. LC 76-153519. Repr. of 1933 ed. 12.50 (ISBN 0-404-08978-X). AMS Pr.

Story of the Kimmer Mennonite Brethren Church. C. F. Plett. pap. 12.00 (ISBN 0-919797-51-2). Herald Pr.

Story of the Kimono. Jill Liddell. Ed. by Cyril Nelson. (Illus.). 192p. 1988. 60.00 (ISBN 0-525-24574-X). Dutton.

Story of the Kind Wolf. Peter Nickl. (Illus.). 32p. (gr. k-3). 1988. 12.95 (ISBN 0-8050-0760-1, North South Bks); pap. 4.95 (ISBN 0-8050-0745-8, North South Bks). H Holt & Co.

Story of the Krimmer Mennonite Brethren Church. C. F. Plett. 338p. 1985. pap. 12.00 (ISBN 0-317-64807-1). Herald Pr.

Story of the Lafayette Escadrille. R. Conrad Stein. LC 82-23508. (Cornerstones of Freedom Ser.). (Illus.). 32p. (gr. 3-6). 1983. PLB 11.67 (ISBN 0-516-04660-8). Childrens.

Story of the Latter-day Saints. James B. Allen & Glen M. Leonard. LC 76-20376. (Illus.). 720p. 1976. 17.95 (ISBN 0-87747-594-6). Deseret Bk.

Story of the Lewis & Clark Expedition. R. Conrad Stein. LC 78-4648. (Cornerstones of Freedom Ser.). (Illus.). 32p. (gr. 3-6). 1978. PLB 11.67 (ISBN 0-516-04620-9); pap. 2.95 (ISBN 0-516-44620-7). Childrens.

Story of the Liberty Bell. Natalie Miller. LC 65-12215. (Cornerstones of Freedom Bks). (Illus.). 32p. (gr. 2-5). 1965. PLB 11.67 (ISBN 0-516-04622-5); pap. 2.95 (ISBN 0-516-44622-3). Childrens.

Story of the Life of John Anderson, the Fugitive Slave. facsimile ed. John Anderson. Ed. by Harper Twelvetrees. LC 72-164378. (Black Heritage Library Collection). Repr. of 1863 ed. 16.50 (ISBN 0-8369-8837-X). Ayer Co Pubs.

Story of the Life of the World's Favorite Author. Charles Dickens. 1927. 20.00 (ISBN 0-8274-3525-8). R West.

Story of the Lincoln Memorial. Natalie Miller. LC 66-10304. (Cornerstones of Freedom Bks). (Illus.). 32p. (gr. 2-5). 1966. PLB 11.67 (ISBN 0-516-04623-3). Childrens.

Story of the Little Big Horn: Custer's Last Fight. W. A. Graham. xi, 280p. 1988. 26.95x (ISBN 0-8032-2132-0); pap. 8.95 (Bison). U of Nebr Pr.

Story of the Little Red Engine. Diana Ross. (Illus.). (gr. k-2). 11.95 (ISBN 0-571-06421-3). Transatl Arts.

Story of the Little Round Barn. Velma Bright. LC 81-65540. (Illus.). 48p. (Orig.). (gr. 2-3). 1981. 9.95x (ISBN 0-9605968-2-8); pap. 3.95 (ISBN 0-9605968-3-6). Bright Bks.

Story of the Loaves & Fishes. Alice J. Davidson. (Alice in Bibleland Storybooks). (Illus.). 32p. (ps-3). 1985. 4.95 (ISBN 0-8378-5073-8). Gibson.

Story of the Lost Doll. Josephine Gates. LC 5-83020. (Illus.). 108p. (gr. 4 up). 1981. Repr. of 1905 ed. lib. bdg. 35.00 (ISBN 0-940070-06-5). Doll Works.

Story of the Lost Trail to Oregon. Ezra Meeker. 32p. 1984. pap. 4.95. Ye Galleon.

Story of the Louisiana Purchase. Mary K. Phelan. LC 78-22505. (Illus.). (gr. 4-6). 1979. 12.70 (ISBN 0-690-03955-7, Crowell Jr Bks); PLB 12.89 (ISBN 0-690-03956-5). HarpJ.

Story of the Lovat Scouts. Michael L. Melville. 118p. 1981. 35.00x (ISBN 0-7152-0474-2, Pub. by Engineering Ind). State Mutual Bk.

Story of the Lyric Theatre, Hammersmith. Nigel R. Playfair. LC 77-84524. (Illus.). 1925. 22.00 (ISBN 0-405-08858-2). Ayer Co Pubs.

Story of the Marches, Battles & Incidents of the Third United States Colored Cavalry. Edwin M. Main. LC 72-100268. Repr. of 1908 ed. cancelled (ISBN 0-8371-2865-X, MCO&, Pub. by Negro U Pr). Greenwood.

Story of the "Mary Celeste". Charles E. Fay. 320p. 1988. pap. 6.95 (ISBN 0-486-25730-4). Dover.

Story of the Mass. 1.00 (NCR 457). Paulist Pr.

Story of the Mass: From the Last Supper to the Present Day. Pierre Loret. LC 82-83984. 144p. 1983. pap. 3.50 (ISBN 0-89243-171-7). Liguori Pubns.

Story of the Mayflower Compact. Norman Richards. LC 67-22901. (Cornerstones of Freedom Ser.). (Illus.). 32p. (gr. 2-5). 1967. PLB 11.67 (ISBN 0-516-04625-X); pap. 2.95 (ISBN 0-516-44625-8). Childrens.

Story of the Meadowlark. Scott B. Smith. (Illus.). 47p. 1986. 15.00 (ISBN 0-937594-12-1). Bunkhouse.

Story of the Mennonites. C. Henry Smith. Ed. by Cornelius Krahn. LC 81-65130. (Illus.). 589p. 1981. pap. 17.95 (ISBN 0-87303-069-9). Faith & Life.

Story of the Mine. Charles Shinn. (Illus.). 277p. 6.50 (ISBN 0-317-64904-3). Nevada Pubns.

Story of the Monitor & the Merrimac. R. Conrad Stein. LC 82-23503. (Cornerstones of Freedom Ser.). (Illus.). 32p. (gr. 3-6). 1983. PLB 11.67 (ISBN 0-516-04662-4); pap. 2.95 (ISBN 0-516-44662-2). Childrens.

Story of the Montgomery Bus Boycott. R. Conrad Stein. LC 85-31349. (Cornerstones of Freedom Ser.). (Illus.). 32p. (gr. 3-6). 1986. PLB 11.67 (ISBN 0-516-04697-7); pap. 2.95 (ISBN 0-516-44697-5). Childrens.

Story of the Nations: the Story of Mediaeval France: From the Reign of Hughes Capet to the Beginning of the Eighteenth Century. Gustave Masson. 354p. 1980. Repr. of 1888 ed. lib. bdg. 40.00 (ISBN 0-8495-3793-2). Arden Lib.

Story of the New England Whalers. R. C. Stein. LC 81-18107. (Cornerstones of Freedom Ser.). (Illus.). (gr. 3-6). 1982. PLB 11.67 (ISBN 0-516-04634-9); pap. text ed. 2.95 (ISBN 0-516-44634-7). Childrens.

Story of the New York Times: The First Hundred Years, 1851-1951. Meyer Berger. LC 75-122933. (American Journalists Ser). 1970. Repr. of 1951 ed. 19.00 (ISBN 0-405-01652-2). Ayer Co Pubs.

Story of the Nineteenth Amendment. R. Conrad Stein. LC 82-4419. (Cornerstones of Freedom Ser.). (Illus.). (gr. 3-6). 1982. PLB 11.67 (ISBN 0-516-04639-X); pap. 2.95 (ISBN 0-516-44639-8). Childrens.

Story of the Nonpartisan League: A Chapter in American Evolution. facsimile ed. Charles E. Russell. Ed. by Dan C. McCurry & Richard E. Rubenstein. LC 74-30651. (American Farmers & the Rise of Agribusiness Ser.). (Illus.). 1975. Repr. of 1920 ed. 32.00x (ISBN 0-405-06823-9). Ayer Co Pubs.

Story of the Normans. S. Jewett. 59.95 (ISBN 0-8490-1140-X). Gordon Pr.

Story of the Novel. George Watson. LC 79-13093. 1979. pap. 9.95x (ISBN 0-06-497494-4). B&N Imports.

Story of the Nutcracker Ballet. Deborah Hautzig. (Illus.). 32p. (ps-1). 1986. pap. 4.95 (ISBN 0-394-88296-2, BYR). Random.

Story of the Nutcracker Ballet. Deborah Hautzig. LC 85-30149. (Picturebacks Ser.). (Illus.). 32p. (gr. 3-6). 1986. lib. bdg. 5.99 (ISBN 0-394-98178-2, BYR); pap. 1.95 (ISBN 0-394-88178-8, BYR). Random.

Story of the Old Testament Simply Told. Florence E. Waggener. (Illus.). 1979. 5.50 (ISBN 0-682-49375-9). Exposition-Phoenix.

Story of the Only Home Abraham Lincoln Ever Owned. Thomas J. Dyba. (Illus.). 16p. (Orig.). 1977. pap. 1.70 (ISBN 0-931090-00-8). I B C Pubns.

Story of the Oregon Trail. Illus. by David J. Catrow, III. LC 83-23997. (Illus.). 31p. (gr. 3-5). 1984. 6.75 (ISBN 0-516-04668-3). Childrens.

Story of the Organ. C. F. Williams. LC 78-90250. (Illus.). 342p. 1972. Repr. of 1903 ed. 40.00x (ISBN 0-8103-3067-9). Gale.

Story of the Original Dixieland Jazz Band. H. O. Brunn. LC 77-3791. (Roots of Jazz Ser.). (Illus.). 1977. Repr. of 1960 ed. lib. bdg. 32.50 (ISBN 0-306-70892-2). Da Capo.

Story of the Other Wise Man. Henry Van Dyke. 96p. 1986. pap. 2.95 (ISBN 0-345-31882-X, Pub. by Ballantine Epiphany). Ballantine.

Story of the Other Wise Man. Henry Van Dyke. 98p. 1985. pap. 3.95 (ISBN 0-89783-040-7). Larlin Corp.

Story of the Other Wise Man. Henry Van Dyke. 1987. pap. 2.95 (ISBN 0-345-00616-X, Pub. by Ballantine Epiphany). Ballantine.

Story of the Pall Mall Gazette. John W. Robertson-Scott. LC 73-141266. (Illus.). ix, 470p. 1971. Repr. of 1950 ed. lib. bdg. 35.00x (ISBN 0-8371-5826-5, ROPM). Greenwood.

Story of the Panama Canal. R. Conrad Stein. LC 82-4565. (Cornerstones of Freedom Ser.). (Illus.). (gr. 3-6). 1982. PLB 11.67 (ISBN 0-516-04640-3). Childrens.

Story of the Pennsylvania Germans: Embracing an Account of Their Origin, Their History, Their Dialect. William Beidelman. LC 70-81759. 262p. 1969. Repr. of 1898 ed. 43.00x (ISBN 0-8103-3571-9). Gale.

Story of the People of God. F. Burton Nelson. (Illus.). 436p. 1971. pap. 5.50 (ISBN 0-910452-17-2). Covenant.

Story of the Phillipines. Amos Fiske. 59.95 (ISBN 0-8490-1141-8). Gordon Pr.

Story of the Pilgrims & Their Indian Friends: A Thanksgiving Story for Children. 4th ed. Eunice Cauper. (Illus.). 16p. (gr. k). 1988. pap. 4.95 (ISBN 0-8283-1899-9). Branden Pub Co.

Story of the Plant Kingdom. rev. ed. Merle C. Coulter. Ed. by Howard J. Dittmer. LC 64-10093. 480p. 1973. pap. text ed. 4.95x (ISBN 0-226-11611-5, P494, Phoen). U of Chicago Pr.

Story of the Political Philosophers, 2 vols. George Catlin. Set. 250.00 (ISBN 0-87968-436-4). Gordon Pr.

Story of the Political Philosophers. George Catlin. (Illus.). 802p. 1985. Repr. of 1939 ed. lib. bdg. 85.00. Century Bookbindery.

Story of the Pony Express. R. Conrad Stein. LC 81-4558. (Cornerstones of Freedom Ser.). (Illus.). 32p. (gr. 3-6). 1981. PLB 11.67 (ISBN 0-516-04631-4). Childrens.

Story of the Powers of Congress. R. Conrad Stein. LC 85-10943. (Cornerstones of Freedom Ser.). (Illus.). 31p. (gr. 3-4). 1985. PLB 11.67 (ISBN 0-516-04695-0); pap. 2.95 (ISBN 0-516-44695-9). Childrens.

Story of the Powers of the President. R. Conrad Stein. LC 84-29257. (Cornerstones of Freedom Ser.). (Illus.). 32p. (gr. 3-6). 1985. lib. bdg. 11.67 (ISBN 0-516-04684-5). Childrens.

Story of the Prayer Book. Phillip Arian & Azriel Eisenberg. (gr. 7-9). 1971. pap. 5.95x. Prayer Bk.

Story of the Prayer Book. Azriel Eisenberg & Philip Arian. pap. 5.95x (ISBN 0-87677-017-0). Hartmore.

Story of the Psalters. Henry A. Glass. LC 72-1635. Repr. of 1888 ed. 18.50 (ISBN 0-404-08308-0). AMS Pr.

Story of the Pullman Car. Joseph Husband. LC 72-5055. (Technology & Society Ser.). (Illus.). 238p. 1972. Repr. of 1917 ed. 21.00 (ISBN 0-405-04707-X). Ayer Co Pubs.

Story of the Pullman Strike. R. C. Stein. LC 81-15512. (Cornerstones of Freedom Ser.). (Illus.). (gr. 3-6). 1982. PLB 11.67 (ISBN 0-516-04641-1); pap. text ed. 2.95 (ISBN 0-516-44641-X). Childrens.

Story of the Purr-Tenders. Cindy West. (Golden Story Book 'n' Tape Ser.). (Illus.). 24p. (Orig.). (ps-3). 1988. pap. 5.45 (ISBN 0-307-13961-1). Western Pub.

Story of the Purr-Tenders. Cindy West. LC 87-83196. (Golden Look-Look Bks.). (Illus.). 24p. (Orig.). (ps-3). 1988. pap. 1.60 (ISBN 0-307-11735-9). Western Pub.

Story of the Red Cross. Clara Barton. (Airmont Classics Ser.). (Illus.). (gr. 4 up). 1968. pap. 1.50 (ISBN 0-8049-0170-8, CL-170). Airmont.

Story of the Red Man. facs. ed. Flora W. Seymour. LC 79-124257. (Select Bibliographies Reprint Ser). 1929. 27.50 (ISBN 0-8369-5445-9). Ayer Co Pubs.

Story of the Renaissance. William H. Hudson. 1912. Repr. 30.00 (ISBN 0-8274-3524-X). R West.

Story of the Restoration. Bill J. Humble. 1969. pap. 2.75 (ISBN 0-88027-040-3). Firm Foun Pub.

Story of the Riot, Persecution of Negroes by Roughs & Policemen in the City of New York, August, 1900. Ed. by Frank Moss. LC 73-90186. (Mass Violence in America Ser). Repr. of 1900 ed. 9.00 (ISBN 0-405-01329-9). Ayer Co Pubs.

Story of the Salem Witch Trials. Zachary Kent. LC 86-9632. (Cornerstones of Freedom Ser.). (Illus.). 32p. (gr. 3-6). 1986. PLB 11.67 (ISBN 0-516-04704-3); pap. 3.25 (ISBN 0-516-44704-1). Childrens.

Story of the San Francisco Earthquake. R. C. Stein. LC 83-10135. (Cornerstones of Freedom Ser.). (Illus.). 32p. (gr. 3-6). 1983. PLB 11.67 (ISBN 0-516-04664-0); pap. 2.95 (ISBN 0-516-44664-9). Childrens.

Story of the Savannah: An Episode in Maritime Labor-Management Relations. David Kuechle. LC 78-131466. (Wertheim Publications in Industrial Relations Ser). (Illus.). 1971. 20.00x (ISBN 0-674-83961-7). Harvard U Pr.

Story of the Savoy Opera in Gilbert & Sullivan Days. S. J. Fitzgerald. (Music Reprint Ser.). 1979. Repr. of 1925 ed. lib. bdg. 35.00 (ISBN 0-306-79543-4). Da Capo.

Story of the Scottish Rite. Harold V. Voorhis. 72p. 1980. pap. 6.00 (ISBN 0-88053-063-4, M342). Macoy Pub.

Story, Sign, & Self: Phenomenology & Structuralism As Literary-Critical Methods. Robert Detweiler. Ed. by William A. Beardslee. LC 76-9713. (Semeia Studies). 240p. 1978. pap. 1.95 (ISBN 0-8006-1505-0, 1-1505). Fortress.
Story, Sign & Self: Phenomenology & Structuralism As Literary Critical Methods. Robert Detweiler. 1985. pap. 9.95 (06 06 06). Scholars Pr GA.
Story Snail. Anne Rockwell. LC 87-1097. (Ready-to-Read Ser.). (Illus.). 64p. (gr. 1-4). 1987. pap. 3.95 (ISBN 0-689-71164-6, Aladdin Bks). Macmillan.
Story Sunday: Christian Fairy Tales for Children, Parents & Educators. John R. Aurelio. LC 78-51587. 104p. 1978. pap. 3.95 (ISBN 0-8091-2115-8). Paulist Pr.
Story Teller. Compiled by Graham Barrett & Michael Morpurgo. 1985. 20.00x (ISBN 0-7062-3801-X, Pub. by Ward Lock Educ Co Ltd). State Mutual Bk.
Story Teller. Saki. LC 82-3149. 112p. 1986. pap. 9.95 (ISBN 0-87923-646-9). Godine.
Story-Teller. Saki. (Perfect Presents Story-Gifts Ser.). (Illus.). 32p. pap. 4.95 (ISBN 1-55628-018-1). Redpath Pr.
Story Teller. Peter Vansittart. 285p. 1968. 18.95 (ISBN 0-7206-7602-9). Dufour.
Story Teller & His Pack. Clifford H. Nowlin. 408p. 1981. Repr. of 1929 ed. lib. bdg. 35.00. Darby Bks.
Story Teller & His Pack. Clifford H. Nowlin. 408p. 1979. Repr. of 1931 ed. lib. bdg. 40.00 (ISBN 0-89987-601-3). Darby Bks.
Story-Teller Retrieves the Past: Historical Fiction & Fictitious History in the Art of Scott, Stevenson, Kipling, & Some Others. Mary Lascelles. 1980. 34.95x (ISBN 0-19-812802-9). Oxford U Pr.
Story-Teller's Holiday. George Moore. (Black & Gold Library). 1929. 7.95 (ISBN 0-87140-869-4). Liveright.
Story Teller's Tale. Sherwood Anderson. 24.95 (ISBN 0-88411-278-0, Pub. by Aeonian Pr). Amereon Ltd.
Story-Telling Poems. facs. ed. Compiled by Frances J. Olcott. LC 77-128155. (Granger Index Reprint Ser). 1913. 19.00 (ISBN 0-8369-6182-X). Ayer Co Pubs.
Story Telling: What to Tell & How to Tell It. 3rd ed. Edna Lyman, pseud. LC 74-167166. 234p. 1971. Repr. of 1911 ed. 50.00x (ISBN 0-8103-3403-8). Gale.
Story, Text, & Scripture: Literary Interests in Biblical Narrative. Wesley A. Kort. LC 87-42549. 180p. 1988. 20.00x (ISBN 0-271-00610-2). Pa St U Pr.
Story Theology. Terrence Tilley. LC 84-73564. (Theology & Life Ser.: Vol. 12). 1985. pap. 10.95 (ISBN 0-89453-464-5). M Glazier.
Story Time. Jean Warren. 80p. (gr. k-2). 1983. 7.95 (ISBN 0-912107-16-2). Monday Morning Bks.
Story Time with Grandma. Mary E. Yoder. 1979. 2.50 (ISBN 0-87813-514-6). Christian Light.
Story to Anti-Story. Mary Rohrberger. LC 78-69581. 1978. pap. text ed. 23.56 (ISBN 0-395-26387-5). HM.
Story to Tell. Dick Bruna. (Dick Bruna Bks.). 1984. 2.95 (ISBN 0-8431-1576-9). Price Stern.
Story Vine: A Source Book of Unusual & Easy-to-Tell Stories from Around the World. Anne Pellowski. LC 83-26756. (Illus.). 160p. 1984. 14.95 (ISBN 0-02-770590-0); pap. 7.95 (ISBN 0-02-044690-X, Collier). Macmillan.
Story Weaving. Peter Morgan. Ed. by Herbert Lambert. LC 86-6079. 128p. (Orig.). 1986. pap. 8.95 (ISBN 0-8272-3423-6). CBP.
Story-Weaving. Francis Vivian. 175p. 1981. Repr. of 1940 ed. lib. bdg. 25.00 (ISBN 0-8495-5522-1). Arden Lib.
Story Without an End. Mark Twain. LC 85-30885. (Creative's Classic Short Stories Ser.). 32p. (gr. 4 up). 1986. PLB 8.95 (ISBN 0-88682-064-2). Creative Ed.
Story Without Ending (Hekeyah bela Bidayah) Naguib Mahfouz. (Arabic.). 6.95x (ISBN 0-86685-155-0). Intl Bk Ctr.
Story Workshop. Wilbur L. Schramm. 458p. 1980. Repr. of 1938 ed. lib. bdg. 47.50 (ISBN 0-89984-423-5). Century Bookbindery.
Story Writing. Edith R. Mirrielees. LC 72-6277. pap. 8.95 (ISBN 0-87116-137-0). Writer.
Storyboard Prototyping for Systems Design: A New Approach to Requirements, Validation & System Sizing. Stephen J. Andriole. (Decision Support Systems Ser.). 160p. 1988. 29.95 (ISBN 0-89435-246-6, C882466). QED Info Sci.
Storybook & Heavenly Doll Costumes. Mary Hoyer. (Orig.). 1988. pap. 12.95 (ISBN 0-317-68998-3). Hobby Hse.
Storybook Classrooms: Using Children's Literature in the Learning Center-Primary Grades. Karla H. Wendelin & M. Jean Greenlaw. LC 83-81430. 220p. (Orig.). (ps-4). 1984. pap. 16.95 (ISBN 0-89334-043-X). Humanics Ltd.
Storybook Cookbook. Carol Mac Gregor. (Illus.). (gr. 3-7). pap. 1.95 (ISBN 0-13-850842-9, Pub. by Treehouse). P-H.
Storybook for Adults & Other Children: The Swan. Jerri Smock. (Illus.). 32p. (Orig.). (YA) (gr. 8 up). 1988. pap. 13.95 (ISBN 0-944586-00-7). WIN Pub.
Storybook Mazes. Dave Phillips. (Illus.). 62p. 1978. pap. 2.50 (ISBN 0-486-23628-5). Dover.
Storybook of Opera, Vol. II. Cyrus H. Biscardi. LC 86-81155. (Illus.). 224p. (YA) (gr. 7 up). 1987. lib. bdg. 23.95 (ISBN 0-918452-99-6); pap. 19.95 (ISBN 1-55691-006-1). Learning Pubns.
Storybook of Opera: Dramas, Vol. I. Cyrus H. Biscardi. LC 86-81155. (Illus.). 208p. 1987. lib. bdg. 23.95 (ISBN 0-918452-93-7); pap. 18.95 (ISBN 1-55691-007-X). Learning Pubns.
Storybook Quilting. Jennifer L. Baker & Laurie E. Mehalko. LC 84-45699. 224p. (Orig.). 1985. pap. 15.95 (ISBN 0-8019-7528-X). Chilton.
Storybooks. Francis H. Wise & Joyce M. Wise. (Learn to Read Ser. Books 16-20: Vol. 4). (Illus.). 105p. (gr. k-1). 1979. pap. 7.50. Wise Pub.
Storycrafting. Paul D. Boles. 243p. 1987. pap. 9.95 (ISBN 0-89879-298-3). Writers Digest.
Storylines: Conversation Skills Through Oral Histories. Priscilla Karant. 124p. 1988. pap. text ed. 11.95 (ISBN 0-06-632600-1). Newbury Hse.
Storyology: Essays in Folk-Lore, Sea-Lore, & Plant-Lore. Benjamin Taylor. 1979. Repr. of 1900 ed. lib. bdg. 35.00 (ISBN 0-8414-8416-3). Folcroft.
Storyology: Essays in Folklore, Sea-Lore, & Plant-Lore. Benjamin Taylor. 1976. lib. bdg. 59.95 (ISBN 0-8490-2693-8). Gordon Pr.
Storyteller. Harold Robbins. 1987. pap. 4.50 (ISBN 0-671-62740-6). PB.
Storyteller. Leslie M. Silko. LC 80-20251. (Illus.). 278p. 1981. 17.95 (ISBN 0-394-51589-7); pap. 9.95 (ISBN 0-394-17795-9). Seaver Bks.
Storyteller. Leslie M. Silko. 17.95 (ISBN 0-8050-0192-1); pap. 11.95 (ISBN 0-8050-0153-0). Seaver Bks.
Storyteller & a City: Sherwood Anderson's Chicago. Kenny J. Williams. (Illus.). 300p. 1988. text ed. 28.50 (ISBN 0-87580-135-8). N Ill U Pr.
Storyteller As Humanist: The Serees of Guillaume Bouchet. Hope H. Glidden. LC 80-70809. (French Forum Monographs: No. 25). 183p. (Orig.). 1981. pap. 12.95x (ISBN 0-917058-24-0). French Forum.
Storyteller-Korczak. Ed. by Robb DeWall. (Illus.). 60p. 1.90 (ISBN 0-318-17136-8). Crazy Horse.
Storyteller's Ghost Stories. Duane Hutchinson. 96p. (gr. 4 up). 1987. pap. 5.95 (ISBN 0-934988-07-2). Foun Bks.
Storytellers in Marguerite de Navarre's Heptameron. Betty J. Davis. LC 77-93406. (French Forum Monographs: No. 9). 203p. (Orig.). 1978. pap. 39.95 (ISBN 0-917058-08-9). French Forum.
Storyteller's Omnibus. John Harrell. LC 84-51770. 80p. (Orig.). 1985. 10.00x (ISBN 0-9615389-3-7). York Hse.
Storytellers One. Compiled by Roger Mansfield. 1982. 20.00x (ISBN 0-7217-0229-5, Pub. by Schofield & Sims). State Mutual Bk.
Storyteller's Sourcebook. Ed. by Margaret R. MacDonald. (Neal Schuman Bk.). 840p. 1982. 95.00x (ISBN 0-8103-0471-6). Gale.
Storytellers Two. Compiled by Roger Mansfield. 1982. 20.00x (ISBN 0-7217-0230-9, Pub. by Schofield & Sims). State Mutual Bk.
Storytelling. Gary Grim & Denny Dey. (gr. k-8). 1979. 8.95 (ISBN 0-916456-46-3, GA99). Good Apple.
Storytelling: A Selected Annotated Bibliography. Ellin Greene & George Shannon. LC 84-48877. (Garland Reference Library of Social Science). 125p. 1986. lib. bdg. 25.00 (ISBN 0-8240-8749-6). Garland Pub.
Storytelling: A Triad in the Arts. Gail N. Herman. 53p. 1986. pap. 8.95 (ISBN 0-936386-36-3). Creative Learning.
Storytelling Activities. Norma Livo & Sandra J. Rietz. 100p. 1987. lib. bdg. 15.50 (ISBN 0-87287-566-0). Libs Unl.
Storytelling & Mythmaking: Images from Film & Literature. Frank McConnell. (Illus.). 1979. pap. 8.95 (ISBN 0-19-503210-1). Oxford U Pr.
Storytelling: Art & Technique. 2nd ed. Augusta Baker & Ellin Greene. 182p. 1987. 29.95 (ISBN 0-8352-2336-1). Bowker.
Storytelling Folklore Sourcebook. Norma J. Livo & Sandra A. Rietz. 400p. 1989. lib. bdg. 28.50 (ISBN 0-87287-601-2). Libs Unl.
Storytelling, Imagination & Faith. William J. Bausch. LC 83-51515. 240p. (Orig.). 1984. pap. 7.95 (ISBN 0-89622-199-7). Twenty-Third.
Storytelling in Preaching. Bruce C. Salmon. LC 87-26810. 156p. (Orig.). 1988. pap. 6.95 (ISBN 0-8054-2118-1). Broadman.
Storytelling, It's Easy. Ethel Barrett. pap. 6.95 (ISBN 0-310-20561-1, 6832P). Zondervan.
Storytelling Mark Twain Style. Dale H. Janssen & Janice J. Beaty. LC 87-92177. (Illus.). 193p. (Orig.). 1988. pap. 13.95 (ISBN 0-9618217-1-X). Janssen Ed Enterp.
Storytelling: Process & Practice. Norma J. Livo & Sandra A. Reitz. 430p. 1986. lib. bdg. 25.00 (ISBN 0-87287-443-5). Libs Unl.
Storytelling Rights: The Use of Oral & Written Texts by Urban Adolescents. Amy Shuman. (Cambridge Studies in Oral & Literate Culture: No. 11). (Illus.). 256p. 1986. 32.50 (ISBN 0-521-32846-2). Cambridge U Pr.
Storytelling: Study Guide, The Enchantment of Theology Cassette Tapes. Belden C. Lane. LC 86-6079. 24p. (Orig.). 1982. pap. 2.50 (ISBN 0-8272-3419-8, 10S2113). CBP.
Storytelling Tips: How to Love, Learn & Relate a Story. Duane Hutchinson. 96p. 1985. pap. 5.95 (ISBN 0-934988-13-7). Foun Bks.
Storytelling with Puppets. Connie Champlin & Nancy Renfro. LC 84-18406. (Illus.). 308p. 1985. pap. text ed. 19.95x (ISBN 0-8389-0421-1). ALA.
Storytelling with the Computer. Connie Champlin & John DeVasure. (Illus.). 64p. (gr. k-6). 1986. pap. 24.95 (ISBN 0-938594-09-5); diskette incl. Spec Lit Pr.
Storytelling with the Flannel Board, 3 Bks. Paul S. Anderson. LC 21-650. (Illus.). 270p. (ps). 1963. Bk.1. 12.95 (ISBN 0-513-00105-0). Denison.
Storytelling with the Flannel Board, 3 Bks. Paul S. Anderson. LC 21-650. (Illus.). 260p. (ps). 1970. Bk. 2. 12.95 (ISBN 0-513-00137-9). Denison.
Storytelling with the Flannel Board, Bk. 3. Idalee Vonk. LC 21-650. 313p. (ps). 1983. 12.95 (ISBN 0-513-01762-3). Denison.
Storytime. Ed. by Reader's Digest Editors. LC 82-80898. (Illus.). 448p. (gr. 1-8). 1985. 17.00 (ISBN 0-89577-145-4, Pub. by RD Assn). Random.
Storytime Activity Book. Ed. by Jane Gerver. (Questron Electronic Bks.). (Illus.). 32p. (gr. 1-3). 1986. wkbk. 3.95 (ISBN 0-394-88168-0). Random.
Storytime Favorites: Six Big Little Golden Books. (Golden Boxed Ser.). (Illus.). (gr. 5-8). 1987. pap. write for info. (ISBN 0-307-15530-7, Pub. by Golden Bks). Western Pub.
Storytime Music. Judith Banja. 300p. 1988. pap. text ed. price not set (ISBN 1-55570-025-X). Neal-Schuman.
Storytime Science: Have You Clanged Your Hanger Banger Today? Virginia V. Baeckler. Ed. by Kenneth G. Van Wynen. LC 86-61013. (Illus.). 100p. 1986. pap. text ed. 10.00x (ISBN 0-9603232-2-8). Sources.
Storytimes for Two-Year-Olds. Judy Nichols. LC 86-32151. 152p. 1987. pap. text ed. 20.00x (ISBN 0-8389-0451-3). ALA.
Storyville, New Orleans: Being an Authentic Illustrated Account of the Notorious Redlight District. Al Rose. LC 74-491. (Illus.). 256p. 1974. pap. 12.95x (ISBN 0-8173-4404-7). U of Ala Pr.
Storyville to Harlem: Fifty Years in the Jazz Scene. Stephen Longstreet. 211p. 1986. 27.95 (ISBN 0-8135-1174-7); prepub. 24.95 Pre Dec. 31, 1986. Rutgers U Pr.
Stotan! Chris Crutcher. LC 85-12712. 192p. (gr. 7 up). 1986. reinforced trade ed. 10.25 (ISBN 0-688-05715-2). Greenwillow.
Stouffer Cookbook of Great American Food & Drink. Stouffer. 1974. 14.45 (ISBN 0-394-48810-5). Random.
Stoughton Musical Society's Centennial Collection of Sacred Music. Roger L. Hall. LC 80-11936. (Earlier American Music Ser.: No. 23). 304p. 1980. Repr. of 1878 ed. lib. bdg. 37.50 (ISBN 0-306-79618-X). Da Capo.
Stout Hearts: Traditional Oak Basket Makers of the South Carolina Upcountry. Gary Stanton & Tom Cowan. (Illus., Orig.). 1988. pap. 9.00. McKissick.
Stove. Jakov Lind. LC 82-10824. 110p. 1983. 13.95 (ISBN 0-935296-26-3); pap. 7.95 (ISBN 0-935296-27-1). Sheep Meadow.
Stove by a Whale: Owen Chase & the Essex. Thomas F. Heffernan. LC 80-21603. 274p. 1981. 25.00x (ISBN 0-8195-5052-3). Wesleyan U Pr.
Stove Haunting. Bel Mooney. LC 87-33901. 132p. (gr. 5-9). 1988. 12.95 (ISBN 0-395-46764-0). HM.
Stove Project Manual: Planning & Implementation. S. D. Joseph et al. (Illus.). 105p. (Orig.). 1985. pap. 22.50x (ISBN 0-946688-26-5, Pub. by Intermed Tech England). Intermediate Tech.
Stove-up Cowboy's Story. James E. McCauley. LC 65-4439. (Illus.). 100p. 1965. Repr. of 1943 ed. 9.95 (ISBN 0-87074-093-8). SMU Press.
Stover Manufacturing & Engine Company. Charles H. Wendel. LC 82-80676. (Power in the Past: Vol. 3). (Illus.). 96p. 1982. pap. 12.50 (ISBN 0-942804-00-7). Old Iron Bk Co.
Stoves & Trees: How Much Wood Would a Woodstove Save if a Woodstove Could Save Wood? Gerald Foley et al. (Illus.). 89p. 1986. pap. text ed. 8.50 (ISBN 0-905347-51-X, Pub. by Earthscan Pubns London). Longwood Pub Group.
Stow Affair: Anti-Semitism in the California Legislature. Budd Westreich. (Illus.). 84p. 1981. 10.00 (ISBN 0-936300-02-7). Pr Arden Park.
Stow Church Restored. Mark Spurrell. (Illus.). 256p. 1984. 36.00 (Pub. by Boydell & Brewer). Longwood Pub Group.
Stow Wengenroth, Artist-Lithographer: A Retrospective Exhibition. Norton (R. W.) Art Gallery. LC 76-26456. (Contemporary Realists Ser.). (Illus.). 1976. pap. 3.00x (ISBN 0-913060-10-0). Norton Art.
Stow Wengenroth's Lithographs: A Supplement. Ronald Stuckey & Joan Stuckey. LC 82-72164. (Illus.). 117p. 1982. 35.00 (ISBN 0-9608834-0-1). Black Oak NY.
Stowage: The Properties & Stowage of Cargoes. rev. ed. O. O. Thomas. (Illus.). 1983. 65.00 (ISBN 0-85174-450-8). Heinman.
Stowaway. Anne Weale. (Premiere Author Editions Ser.). 192p. 1983. pap. 1.95 (ISBN 0-373-80655-8). Harlequin Bks.
Stowaway to Texas. Ethel L. Evey. Ed. by Shelia S. Darst. 201p. (Orig.). (gr. 4-7). 1982. 8.95 (ISBN 0-89896-102-5, Post Oak Pr); pap. 5.95 (ISBN 0-89896-101-7). Larksdale.
Stowaway to the Mushroom Planet. Eleanor Cameron. (Illus.). (gr. 3-7). 1956. 14.95 (ISBN 0-316-12534-2, Joy St Bks). Little.
Stowaway to the Mushroom Planet. Eleanor Cameron. (gr. 3-7). 1988. pap. 4.95 (ISBN 0-316-12541-5, Joy St Bks). Little.
Stowboaters. Hervey Benham. 1981. 25.00x (ISBN 0-686-79166-5, Pub. by Essex County England). State Mutual Bk.
Stowboaters. Hervey Benham. (Illus.). 49p. 1977. 9.00 (ISBN 0-9505944-0-7, Pub. by Boydell & Brewer). Longwood Pub Group.
Stowe Psalter. Ed. by A. C. Kimmens. LC 78-23622. (Toronto Old English Ser.). 1979. 47.50x (ISBN 0-8020-2201-4). U of Toronto Pr.
Stowkowski: The Art of the Conductor. Paul Robinson. (Art of the Conductor Ser.). (Illus.). 1977. 11.95 (ISBN 0-685-77326-4). Vanguard.
Strabismus. J. Lang. LC 83-50673. 172p. 1984. 50.00 (ISBN 0-943432-18-9). Slack Inc.
Strabismus: A Programmed Text. 3rd ed. Robertk D. Reinecke & Marshall M. Parks. 1987. pap. 34.95 (ISBN 0-8385-8699-6). Appleton & Lange.
Strabismus & Amblyopia: Experimental Basis for Advances in Clinical Management. Ed. by G. Lennerstrand et al. (Wenner-Gren International Symposia Ser.: Vol. 49). (Illus.). 452p. 1988. 89.50x (ISBN 0-306-42943-8, Plenum Pr). Plenum Pub.
Strabismus & the Sensorimotor Reflex. Y. Mitsui. 228p. 1986. 68.00 (ISBN 4-900392-74-X). Elsevier.
Strabismus & Tumors of the Uvea. Ed. by H. Saraux. (Journal: Ophthalmologica: Vol. 182, No. 2). (Illus.). 84p. 1981. pap. 29.50 (ISBN 3-8055-3418-3). S Karger.
Strabismus II. Ed. by Robert D. Reinecke. 1040p. 1984. 95.00 (ISBN 0-8089-1424-3, 793527). Grune.
Strabismus Symposium, Amsterdam, September Third-Fourth, 1981. A. T. Van Balen & W. A. Houtman. 1982. lib. bdg. 59.50 (ISBN 90-6193-728-0, Pub. by Junk Pubs Netherlands). Kluwer Academic.
Strachey Boy. Richard Strachey. Ed. & frwd. by Simonette Strachey. 154p. 1980. 17.95 (ISBN 0-7206-0571-7, Pub. by P Owen Ltd). Dufour.
Strachey Line: An English Family in America, India & at Home, 1570 to 1902. Barbara Strachey. (Illus.). 192p. 1987. 30.95 (ISBN 0-575-03593-5, Pub. by Gollancz England). David & Charles.
Strad Facsimile: An Illustrated Guide to Violin Making. Edwin J. Ward. (Illus.). 1984. lib. bdg. 22.50x (ISBN 0-9613595-0-1). S E Ward.
Strad Model 'Cello, Plans. Harry S. Wake. 1975. 18.50 (ISBN 0-9607048-4-1). H S Wake.
Strada. Ed. by Peter Bondanella & Giere. (Rutgers Films in Print Ser). (Illus.). 200p. 1987. text ed. 25.00 (ISBN 0-8135-1236-0); pap. text ed. 12.00 (ISBN 0-8135-1237-9). Rutgers U Pr.
Strada. Louise Neaderland. (Illus.). 1986. 12.00 (ISBN 0-942561-06-6). Bone Hollow.
Stradivari-Cremona Mystery Disclosed. Pete Molenaar. LC 85-91055. (Illus.). 64p. 1986. pap. 25.00 (ISBN 0-682-40283-4). Exposition-Phoenix.
Stradivari Memorial. William D. Orcutt. LC 76-58561. (Music Reprint Ser.). 1977. Repr. of 1978 ed. lib. bdg. 21.50 (ISBN 0-306-70865-5). Da Capo.
Stradtrecht von Gortyn & Seine Beziehungen zum Gemeingriechischen Rechte. Josef Kohler. (Ger.). 12.00 (ISBN 0-405-11558-X). Ayer Co Pubs.
Strafford Reconsidered. Ashok Sengupta. Ed. by James Hogg. (Romantic Reassessment ser.). 117p. (Orig.). 1979. pap. 15.00 (ISBN 3-7052-0553-6, Pub. by Salzburg Studies). Longwood Pub Group.
Strafrecht Allgemeiner Teil: Die Grundiagen und die Zurechnungslehre lehrbuch. Gunther Jakobs. 787p. 1983. 75.20 (ISBN 3-11-009700-1). De Gruyter.
Strafrecht Allgemeiner Teil: Mit Einfuhrungen in Programmierter Form. 4th ed. Diethelm Kienapfel. 608p. (Ger.). 1984. 20.80 (ISBN 3-11-009804-0). De Gruyter.
Strafvollzug Im Europeaischen Verlgeich see Prison Systems & Correctional Laws: Europe, the United States & Japan, a Comparative Analysis.
Strafwuerdigkeit der Selbstverletzung der Drogenkonsum Im Deutschen und Brasilianischen Recht. Peter Hobbing. (European University Studies: No. 2, Vol. 295). xv, 400p. (Ger.). 1982. 40.55 (ISBN 3-8204-6278-3). P Lang Pubs.
Straight Ahead: The Story of Stan Kenton. Carol Easton. LC 81-7863. (Quality Paperbacks Ser.). (Illus.). 252p. 1981. pap. 7.95 (ISBN 0-306-80152-3). Da Capo.
Straight & Circular: A Study of Imagery in Greek Philosophy. Lynne Ballew. 158p. 1979. pap. text ed. 11.00 (ISBN 90-232-1676-8, Pub. by Van Gorcum Holland). Longwood Pub Group.
Straight Answers to Tough Questions About Sex. Rich Wilkerson. 224p. (Orig.). 1987. pap. text ed. 3.95 (ISBN 0-88368-191-9). Whitaker Hse.
Straight Arrow: The Art Schlichter Story. Ritter Collett. (Illus.). 160p. 1981. 10.95 (ISBN 0-913428-33-7). Landfall Pr.

Straight A's: How to Help Your Child Improve School Grades. Sal Di Francesca. Ed. by Ric Solano. LC 84-82154. (Illus.). 150p. 1985. 24.95 (ISBN 0-931657-00-8). Learning Proc Ctr.

Straight A's in Thirty Days: The Shocking Truth about Getting Good Grades. Howard Rosenthal. 64p. (Orig.). 1988. pap. 6.95 (ISBN 0-9618949-0-3). Genl Guid Grp.

Straight Back Home: To the Young Person Leaving Treatment. Jane Nakken. 16p. (Orig.). 1984. pap. 0.75 (ISBN 0-89486-250-2). Hazelden.

Straight Cut. Madison S. Bell. 240p. 1986. 15.95 (ISBN 0-89919-438-9). Ticknor & Fields.

Straight Cut. Madison S. Bell. 240p. 1987. pap. 3.95 (ISBN 0-14-010471-2). Penguin.

Straight Cut Ditch. Richard Andersen. Ed. by Debbie Hammond. LC 79-7034. 1979. 15.95 (ISBN 0-87949-139-6). Ashley Bks.

Straight Dope. Ceceil Adams. 1988. pap. 3.95 (ISBN 0-345-00757-3). Ballantine.

Straight Dope. Cecil Adams. Ed. by Ed Zotti. LC 84-17060. (Illus.). 320p. (Orig.). pap. 8.95 (ISBN 0-914091-54-9). Chicago Review.

Straight Down: Memoirs by the King of the Beach. Ron Bernstein. 218p. 1977. pap. 4.95 (ISBN 0-915520-08-7). Ross-Erikson.

Straight Forward BASIC. R. Barry Genzlinger et al. 163p. 1983. pap. 12.95 (ISBN 0-9612704-0-3). Champlain Coll Pr.

Straight Forward Managerial Accounting Applications Using Lotus 1-2-3. Nancy E. Wells. Ed. by Laurie E. Thompson. (Straight Forward Ser.). 1987. pap. 12.95 (ISBN 0-9612704-1-1). Champlain Coll Pr.

Straight from Boothill. William Hopson. 1978. pap. 1.25 (ISBN 0-8439-0555-7, Leisure Bks). Leisure NY.

Straight from the Heart. Karen Crawford. (Caprice Romance Ser.: No. 60). 144p. 1985. pap. 2.25 (ISBN 0-441-79021-6, Pub. by Tempo). Ace Bks.

Straight from the Heart. rev ed. Jesse L. Jackson. LC 86-19422. 320p. 1987. 18.95 (ISBN 0-8006-0862-3, 1-862). Fortress.

Straight from the Heart: A Call to the New Generation. John Bertolucci. 126p. 1986. pap. 5.95 (ISBN 0-89283-290-8). Servant.

Straight from the Heart: How to Talk to Your Teenagers about Love & Sex. Carol Cassell. 1987. 16.95 (ISBN 0-671-60521-6). S&S.

Straight from the Heart: How to Talk to Your Teenagers about Love & Sex. Carol Cassell. 1988. 6.95 (ISBN 0-671-66198-1, Fireside). S&S.

Straight from the Shoulder: Lawn Bowls. Vic Muir. (Illus.). 140p. 1986. pap. 11.50 (ISBN 0-86439-008-4, Pub. by Boolarong Pubns Australia). Intl Spec Bk.

Straight Hair, Curly Hair. Augusta Goldin. LC 66-12669. (Let's Read & Find out Science Bks.). (Illus.). (gr. k-3). 1966. PLB 12.89 (ISBN 0-690-77921-6, Crowell Jr Bks). HarpJ.

Straight Hearts' Delight: Love Poems & Selected Letters. Allen Ginsberg & Peter Orlovsky. Ed. by Winston Leyland. (Illus.). 240p. 1980. 20.00 (ISBN 0-917342-64-X, Gay Sunshine); pap. 8.95 (ISBN 0-917342-65-8). Gay Sunshine.

Straight Impressions. Lloyd J. Reynolds. Compiled by Rick Cusick. LC 78-60187. (Illus.). 1979. 12.50 (ISBN 0-931474-06-X). TBW Bks.

Straight Impressions. Lloyd J. Reynolds. Compiled by Rick Cusick. LC 78-60187. (Illus.). 1984. pap. 5.95 (ISBN 0-931474-07-8). TBW Bks.

Straight Life. Art Pepper & Laurie Pepper. 1983. pap. 9.95 (ISBN 0-02-872010-5). Schirmer Bks.

Straight Line & the Conic Section. P. H. Francis. (Oleander Mathematics Ser.: Vol. 2). (Illus.). 1975. pap. 13.50 (ISBN 0-902675-76-1). Oleander Pr.

Straight Lines & Curves. N. Vasilyev & V. Gutenmacher. 1980. 5.45 (ISBN 0-8285-1792-4, Pub. by Mir Pubs USSR). Imported Pubns.

Straight Look at the Third Reich. Austin J. App. 1984. lib. bdg. 79.95 (ISBN 0-87700-521-4). Revisionist Pr.

Straight Man. Kent Nelson. LC 77-88656. (Black Lizard Bks.). 144p. 1978. pap. 3.50 (ISBN 0-916870-11-1). Creative Arts Bk.

Straight Man. Roger L. Simon. LC 86-40105. 224p. 1986. 15.45 (ISBN 0-394-55837-5, Pub. by Villard Bks). Random.

Straight Man. Roger L. Simon. 240p. 1987. pap. 3.95 (ISBN 0-446-34389-7). Warner Bks.

Straight Mark. Hamilton. 3.95 (ISBN 0-318-18186-X). WCTU.

Straight Mark. Dorothy Hamilton. LC 76-26661. (Illus.). 128p. (gr. 4-8). 1976. pap. 3.95 (ISBN 0-8361-1342-X). Herald Pr.

Straight on Till Morning: A Biography of Beryl Markham. Mary S. Lovell. LC 87-16329. 256p. 1987. 16.95 (ISBN 0-312-01096-6). St Martin.

Straight on Till Morning: The Biography of Beryl Markham. Mary S. Lovell. (Illus.). 432p. 1988. pap. 10.95 (ISBN 0-312-01895-9). St Martin.

Straight Path: Studies in Medieval Philosophy & Culture. Ed. by Ruth Link-Salinger et al. (Essays in Honor of Arthur Hyman). 304p. 1988. 35.00x (ISBN 0-8132-0648-0). Cath U Pr.

Straight Poop. Peter A. Hemp. LC 85-18367. (Illus.). 176p. (Orig.). 1986. pap. 8.95 (ISBN 0-89815-146-5). Ten Speed Pr.

Straight Shootin' Lady, No. 220. Charlotte Sughes. 192p. 1987. pap. 2.50 (ISBN 0-553-21854-9, Loveswept). Bantam.

Straight Speaking from a Pacifist to a Militarist. Duke of Bedford. 1982. lib. bdg. 59.95 (ISBN 0-87700-337-8). Revisionist Pr.

Straight Talk: A Guide to Saying More with Less. Robert Maidment. LC 82-12211. 112p. (Orig.). 1983. pap. 4.95 (ISBN 0-88289-340-8). Pelican.

Straight Talk: A New Way to Get Close to Others by Saying What You Really Mean. Sherod Miller et al. 1982. pap. 4.50 (ISBN 0-451-12047-7, AE2047, Sig). NAL.

Straight Talk About American Education. Theodore M. Black. LC 81-48513. 288p. 1982. 14.95 (ISBN 0-15-185584-6). HarBraceJ.

Straight Talk about Attitude Research. Ed. by Joseph Chasin. LC 81-22916. (Proceedings Ser.). (Illus.). 225p. (Orig.). 1982. pap. text ed. 11.00 (ISBN 0-87757-156-2). Am Mktg.

Straight Talk about Drinking: Teenagers Speak Out about Alcohol. Wayne Coffey. LC 87-32446. 256p. (YA) (gr. 7 up). 1988. pap. 7.95 (ISBN 0-452-26061-2, Plume). NAL.

Straight Talk about Drugs & Alcohol. Elizabeth A. Ryan. (Straight Talk for Teens Ser.). 128p. (YA) 1988. 14.95x (ISBN 0-8160-1525-2). Facts on File.

Straight Talk about Mental Tests. Arthur R. Jensen. LC 80-83714. 1983. 8.95x (ISBN 0-02-916440-0). Free Pr.

Straight Talk about Parents. Elizabeth A. Ryan. (Straight Talk for Teens Ser.). 128p. (YA) 1989. 14.95x (ISBN 0-8160-1526-0). Facts on File.

Straight Talk about Small Business. Kenneth J. Albert. (Illus.). 256p. 1980. text ed. 23.50 (ISBN 0-07-000949-X). McGraw.

Straight Talk: Answers to Questions Young People Ask about Alcohol. Ralph E. Jones. Ed. by Lee M. Joiner. 64p. (Orig.). (YA) (gr. 10 up). 1988. pap. price not set (ISBN 0-943519-08-X, B1908). Human Servs Inst.

Straight Talk for Teens. Randy Simmons. 107p. (Orig.). 1987. pap. text ed. 4.95 (ISBN 0-89225-299-5). Gospel Advocate.

Straight Talk from Prison: A Convict Reflects on Youth, Crime & Society. Lou Torok. LC 74-1074. (Illus.). 142p. 1974. 24.95 (ISBN 0-87705-136-4). Human Sci Pr.

Straight Talk on Careers: Eighty Pros Take You into Their Professions. Mary Barbera-Hogan. 200p. (Orig.). 1987. pap. 15.00 (ISBN 0-912048-48-4). Garrett Pk.

Straight Talk on Raising Kids: Help for Concerned Parents of School Age Children. Curt Shreiner & Douglas Powelll. 76p. 1988. pap. text ed. 49.95 incl. 4 tapes (ISBN 1-55678-007-9). Learn Inc.

Straight Talk: Parent to Parent. Betty Pieper. 64p. 1.50 (ISBN 0-318-16610-0). Spina Bifida.

Straight Talk: Sexuality Education for Parents & Kids. Marilyn Ratner & Susan Chamlin. 48p. (gr. 4-7). 1987. 12.95 (ISBN 0-670-81317-6). Viking.

Straight Talk: Sexuality Education for Parents & Kids 4-7. Marilyn Ratner & Susan Chamlin. 48p. 1987. pap. 4.95 (ISBN 0-14-009413-X). Penguin.

Straight Talk to Men & Their Wives. James Dobson. (QP Proven-Word Ser.). 224p. 1984. pap. 7.99 (ISBN 0-8499-2981-4). Word Bks.

Straight Talk to Men & Their Wives. James C. Dobson. 1980. 12.95 (ISBN 0-8499-0260-6). Word Bks.

Straight Talk to Men & Wives see Esto Es Ser Hombre: Conversaciones Francas Con los Hombres y Sus Esposas.

Straight Talk to Parents: Cognitive Restructuring Training for Families. Rian E. McMullin et al. (Illus.). 63p. (Orig.). 1978. pap. 4.00 (ISBN 0-935205-03-9). Counseling Res.

Straight Teeth: Orthodontics for Everyone. Robert L. Holt. LC 80-10562. (Illus.). 283p. 1980. pap. 12.95 (ISBN 0-930926-07-2). Calif Health.

Straight Texas. Ed. by J. Frank Dobie et al. LC 77-8134. (Texas Folklore Society Publications: No. 13). 360p. 1984. Repr. of 1937 ed. 16.95 (ISBN 0-87074-164-0). SMU Press.

Straight Thinking in an Age of Exotic Beliefs. Dan Day. (Anchors Ser.). 124p. 1988. pap. 7.95 (ISBN 0-8163-0751-2). Pacific Pr Pub Assn.

Straight Through the Night. Edward Allen. 310p. 1989. 17.95 (ISBN 0-939149-19-2). Soho Press.

Straight Tongue: Minnesota Indian Art from the Bishop Whipple Collections. Louise B. Casagrande & Melissa M. Ringheim. LC 80-53670. (Illus.). 94p. (Orig.). 1980. pap. 9.95 (ISBN 0-295-96032-9). U of Wash Pr.

Straight with the Medicine: Narratives of Washoe Followers of the Tipi Way. Warren L. D'Azevedo. (Illus.). 64p. (Orig.). 1985. pap. 5.95 (ISBN 0-930588-19-3). Heyday Bks.

Straight Word to Kids & Parents. Anthony Campolo & Harold Hughes. (Illus.). 164p. 1987. pap. 3.50 (ISBN 0-87486-186-1). Plough.

Straight Word to Kids & Parents. Anthony Campolo et al. 150p. (Orig.). 1987. pap. 4.95 (ISBN 0-916035-21-2). Evangel Indiana.

Straightshooter's Guide to Marine Electronics. 2nd ed. Gordon West & Freeman Pittman. (Illus.). 160p. 1987. pap. 14.95 (ISBN 0-87742-241-9). Intl Marine.

Strain & Counterstrain. Lawrence H. Jones. LC 81-67256. (Illus.). 112p. (Orig.). 1981. text ed. 35.00 (ISBN 0-940668-00-9); pap. text ed. 25.00 (ISBN 0-940668-01-7). Am Acad Osteopathy.

Strain Facies. E. Hansen. LC 72-89551. (Minerals, Rocks & Inorganic Materials Ser.: Vol. 2). (Illus.). 1971. 34.00 (ISBN 0-387-05204-6). Springer-Verlag.

Strain Gauge Technology. A. L. Window & G. S. Holister. (Illus.). x, 356p. 1982. 73.00 (ISBN 0-85334-118-4, Pub. by Elsevier Applied Sci England). Elsevier.

Strain Measurement At High Temperatures: Proceedings, CEC Workshop, JRC Petten (N.H.), the Netherlands. Ed. by R. C. Hurst et al. 242p. 1986. 57.75 (ISBN 1-85166-056-9, Pub. by Elsevier Applied Sci England). Elsevier.

Strain of Violence: Historical Studies of American Violence & Vigilantism. Richard M. Brown. LC 75-7351. 1975. pap. 10.95x (ISBN 0-19-502247-5). Oxford U Pr.

Strain Your Brain. Becky Daniel & Charlie Daniel. (Gifted & Talented Ser.). 48p. (gr. 4-6). 1980. 4.95 (ISBN 0-88160-032-6, LW 217). Learning Wks.

Strained Alliance: Peking, P'yongyang, Moscow & the Politics of the Korean Civil War. Robert R. Simmons. LC 74-4891. 1975. 10.95 (ISBN 0-02-928880-0). Free Pr.

Strained Organic Molecules. Arthur Greenberg & Joel Liebman. (Organic Chemistry Ser.). 1978. 52.00 (ISBN 0-12-299550-3). Acad Pr.

Strained Relations: Ireland at Peace & the U. S. A. at War 1941-1945. T. Ryle Dwyer. 1988. 29.95 (ISBN 0-389-20774-8). B&N Imports.

Strains in International Finance & Trade. Fred H. Sanderson & Harold Van B. Cleveland. (Washington Papers: Vol. II, No. 14). 80p. (Orig.). 1974. pap. text ed. 7.95 (ISBN 0-8191-5973-5, Pub. by CSIS). U Pr of Amer.

Strains of Discord. facs. ed. Robert M. Adams. LC 75-142601. (Essay Index Reprint Ser). 1958. 16.00 (ISBN 0-8369-1917-3). Ayer Co Pubs.

Strains of Human Viruses. Ed. by M. Majer & S. A. Plotkin. 160p. 1972. 65.50 (ISBN 3-8055-1401-8). S Karger.

Strait: Book of Obenabi, His Songs. Fredy Perlman. 1988. 5.00x. Black & Red.

Strait Gate. John Bunyan. pap. 2.95 (ISBN 0-685-88394-9). Reiner.

Strait Is the Gate. Andre Gide. Tr. by Dorothy Bussy from Fr. LC 79-23999. Orig. Title: Porte Etroite. 1980. Repr. of 1924 ed. lib. bdg. 12.50x (ISBN 0-8376-0453-2). Bentley.

Strait Is the Gate. Andre Gide. Tr. by Dorothy Bussy. 1956. pap. 4.95 (ISBN 0-394-70027-9, V27, Vin). Random.

Strait of Dover. L. Cuyvers. 1986. lib. bdg. 45.50 (ISBN 90-247-3252-2, Pub. by Martinus Nijhoff Netherlands). Kluwer Academic.

Strait of Gibraltar & the Mediterranean. Scott G. Truver. (International Straits of the World Ser.: No. 4). 280p. 1980. 40.00x (ISBN 90-286-0709-9, Pub. by Sijthoff & Noordhoff). Kluwer Academic.

Straitjacket. Louise Neaderland. (Illus.). 1987. 5.00 (ISBN 0-942561-00-7). Bone Hollow.

Straits Chinese Porcelain: A Collector's Guide. Ho Wing Meng. 144p. 1983. 107.50x (ISBN 0-317-44213-9, Pub. by Han-Shan Tang Ltd). State Mutual Bk.

Straits Chinese Society: Studies in the Sociology of the Baba Communities of Malaysia & Singapore. John R. Clammer. 1981. 18.00x (ISBN 9971-69-009-8, Pub. by Singapore U Pr); pap. 8.95x (ISBN 9971-69-015-2, Pub. by Singapore U Pr). Ohio U Pr.

Straits in International Navigation: Contemporary Issues. Kheng-Lian Koh. LC 81-18977. 219p. 1982. lib. bdg. 35.00 (ISBN 0-379-20465-7). Oceana.

Straits of Mackinac & Mackinac Island. John S. Penrod. (YA) (gr. 7-12). 1988. pap. 2.95 (ISBN 0-942618-18-1). Penrod-Hiawatha.

Straits of Malacca, Indo-China, & China. John Thomson. 546p. 1987. 875.00x (ISBN 0-317-69737-4, Pub. by Han-Shan Tang Ltd). State Mutual Bk.

Straits of Messina. Samuel R. Delany. 200p. 1988. 19.95 (ISBN 0-934933-02-2). Serconia Pr.

Straits Settlements Law Reports, 1893-1923, 15 vols, Vols. 6-15. 1970. Repr. Set. 300.00 (ISBN 0-379-20610-2). Oceana.

Straits Settlements 1826-1867: Indian Presidency to Crown Colony. C. M. Turnbull. (Illus.). 428p. 1972. 48.50 (ISBN 0-485-13132-3, Pub. by Athlone Pr). Humanities.

Strana Slov: Opyt Sotsial'noi Istorii Sixty-x. Petr Vail & Alexandr Genis. (Rus.). 1988. pap. 17.50 (ISBN 0-87501-047-4). Ardis Pubs.

Strand. Violet V. Englund. LC 77-76176. (Illus.). 1977. pap. 6.95 (ISBN 0-9601258-0-9). Golden Owl Pub.

Strand see Trafalgar Square.

Stranded! Idella Bodie. LC 84-14098. (Illus.). 132p. (Orig.). (gr. 5-9). 1984. pap. 6.95 (ISBN 0-87844-060-7). Sandlapper Pub Co.

Stranded: Rock & Roll for a Desert Island. Ed. by Greil Marcus. LC 79-2225. 1979. 12.95 (ISBN 0-394-50828-9); pap. 5.95 (ISBN 0-394-73827-6). Knopf.

Strands. James Kisner. 368p. (Orig.). 1988. pap. 3.95 (ISBN 0-8439-2614-7, Pub. by Leisure Bks CT). Leisure NY.

Strands of Organic Chemistry: A Series of Lectures. Claude E. Wintner. LC 78-60358. 1978. pap. text ed. 13.95x (ISBN 0-8162-9661-8). Holden-Day.

Strands of War. Jean A. Kemeny. 325p. 1984. 16.95 (ISBN 0-395-36176-1). HM.

Strange Adventures of Andrew Battell of Leigh in Angola & the Adjoining Regions. Ed. by E. G. Ravenstein. Bd. with Concise History of Kongo & Angola. Andrew Battell. (Hakluyt Society Works Ser.: No. 2, Vol. 6). (Illus.). Repr. of 1900 ed. 35.00 (ISBN 0-8115-0329-1). Kraus Repr.

Strange Affair of Adelaide Harris. Leon Garfield. (gr. k-6). 1988. pap. 3.25 (ISBN 0-440-40057-0). Dell.

Strange Affinity. Paul Bennett. 1975. pap. 6.00 (ISBN 0-318-04215-0). Orchard.

Strange Ailments; Uncertain Cures. Bruce Goldsmith. LC 86-8361. 380p. 1986. 17.95 (ISBN 0-916515-11-7). Mercury Hse Inc.

Strange Allies: The United States & Poland, 1941-1945. Richard C. Lukas. LC 77-8585. Repr. of 1978 ed. 60.00 (2027566). Bks Demand UMI.

Strange & Amazing Facts about Star Trek. Daniel Cohen & Susan Cohen. (Illus.). (gr. 3-6). 1986. pap. 2.50 (ISBN 0-671-63014-8). Archway.

Strange & Amazing Wrestling Stories. Bill Gutman. (Illus.). (gr. 4 up). pap. 2.50 (ISBN 0-671-61125-9). Archway.

Strange & Dangerous Voyage of Captaine T. James. Thomas James. LC 68-54650. (English Experience Ser.: No. 58). 1968. Repr. of 1633 ed. 45.00 (ISBN 90-221-0058-8). Walter J Johnson.

Strange & Eerie Tales. new ed. Corinne Denan. LC 79-66336. (Illus.). 48p. (gr. 4-6). 1980. lib. bdg. 9.59 (ISBN 0-89375-338-6); pap. 1.95 (ISBN 0-89375-337-8). Troll Assocs.

Strange & Exciting Adventures of Jeramiah Hush. Uri Shulevitz. (Illus.). 96p. (gr. 2-5). 1986. 11.95 (ISBN 0-374-33656-3). FS&G.

Strange & Exciting Adventures of Jeremiah Hush. Uri Shulevitz. (Illus.). (gr. 3-7). 11.95 (ISBN 0-317-57825-1). FS&G.

Strange & Incredible Sports Happenings. Mac Davis. Ed. by Richard Powers. (Illus.). 128p. (gr. 3-7). 1982. pap. 4.95 (ISBN 0-448-12326-6, G&D). Putnam Pub Group.

Strange & Private War. Anthony LeJeune. LC 87-5306. (Crime Club Ser.). 192p. 1987. 12.95 (ISBN 0-385-24294-8). Doubleday.

Strange & the Impossible see And Hereby Hangs the Tale Series: Little Known Facts about Well-Known People, Places or Things.

Strange Appearance of Howard Cranebill Jr. Henrik Drescher. (Illus.). (ps-3). 1982. 11.75 (ISBN 0-688-00961-1); PLB 11.88 (ISBN 0-688-00962-X). Lothrop.

Strange Artifacts: A Sourcebook on Ancient Man, Vol. M1. William R. Corliss. LC 74-75256. (Illus.). 268p. 1974. 8.95x (ISBN 0-9600712-2-9). Sourcebook.

Strange Artifacts: A Sourcebook on Ancient Man, Vol. M2. William R. Corliss. LC 74-75256. (Illus.). 275p. 1976. 8.95x (ISBN 0-9600712-6-1). Sourcebook.

Strange Bedfellows. Evelyn Berckman. 15.95 (ISBN 0-88411-274-8, Pub. by Aeonian Pr). Amereon Ltd.

Strange Bedfellows. Herbert Burkholz. 256p. 1988. 18.95 (ISBN 0-689-11911-9). Atheneum.

Strange Breed of Cat: An Encounter in Human Sexuality. B. Mark Schoenberg. LC 74-5281. 336p. 1975. 12.95 (ISBN 0-88280-015-9). ETC Pubns.

Strange Brother. Blair Niles. LC 75-12341. (Homosexuality Ser.). 1975. Repr. of 1931 ed. 14.00x (ISBN 0-405-07390-9). Ayer Co Pubs.

Strange but True. Patrick M. Reynolds. 1978. pap. 3.25 (ISBN 0-932514-00-6). Red Rose Studio.

Strange but True Baseball Stories. Furman Bisher. (Major League Baseball Library). (Illus.). (gr. 5-9). 1966. (BYR). Random.

Strange But True Football Stories. Ed. by Zander Hollander. (NFL Punt, Pass & Kick Library: No. 8). (Illus.). (gr. 5-9). 1967. 2.95 (ISBN 0-394-80198-9, BYR). Random.

Strange but True: Twenty-Two Amazing Stories. David Duncan. (gr. 4-6). 1974. pap. 2.25 (ISBN 0-590-03528-2, Schol Pap). Scholastic Inc.

Strange but Wonderful Cosmic Awareness of Duffy Moon. Jean Robinson. LC 73-15526. (Illus.). 144p. (gr. 3-6). 1974. 6.95 (ISBN 0-395-28880-0, Clarion). HM.

Strange Career of Bishop Sterling. Walter A. Roberts. LC 73-18603. Repr. of 1932 ed. 21.50 (ISBN 0-404-11413-X). AMS Pr.

Strange Career of Jim Crow. 3rd rev. ed. C. Vann Woodward. 1974. pap. 7.95 (ISBN 0-19-501805-2). Oxford U Pr.

Strange Career of Marihuana: Politics & Ideology of Drug Control in America. Jerome L. Himmelstein. LC 82-12181. (Contributions in Political Science Ser.: No. 94). (Illus.). xii, 179p. 1983. lib. bdg. 35.00 (ISBN 0-313-23517-1, HSC/). Greenwood.

Strange Case of Dr. Jekyll & Mr. Hyde & Other Famous Tales. Robert Louis Stevenson. (Great Illustrated Classics Ser.). (Illus.). (YA) (gr. 9 up). 1979. 10.95 (ISBN 0-396-07758-7). Dodd.

Strange Case of Dr. Jekyll & Mr. Hyde & the Suicide Club. Robert Louis Stevenson. (Puffin Classics Ser.). 176p. (gr. 5 up). 1986. pap. 2.25 (ISBN 0-14-035047-0, Puffin). Penguin.

Strange Case of Dr. Jekyll & Mr. Hyde, the Merry Men, & Other Tales. Robert Louis Stevenson. 1977. (Evman); pap. 2.95x (ISBN 0-460-01767-5, Evman). Biblio Dist.

Strange Case of Dr. Jekyll & Mr. Hyde. Robert Louis Stevenson. Ed. by Raymond Harris. (Classics Ser.). (Illus.). 48p. (gr. 6-12). 1982. pap. text ed. 3.00x (ISBN 0-89061-253-6, 451); tchr's ed. 4.00x (ISBN 0-89061-254-4, 453); cassette 12.00 (452). Jamestown Pubs.

Strange Case of Richard Milhous Nixon. Jerry Voorhis. LC 72-83711. 352p. 1972. 8.95 (ISBN 0-8397-7917-8). Eriksson.

Strange Case of Rudi Schneider. Anita Gregory. LC 84-10591. 464p. 1985. 29.50 (ISBN 0-8108-1711-X). Scarecrow.

Strange Cases of Magistrate Pao. Leon Comber. (Writing in Asia Ser.). 1972. pap. text ed. 5.50x (ISBN 0-686-65343-2, 00200). Heinemann Ed.

Strange Child. E. T. Hoffmann. LC 84-8404. (Illus.). 28p. (gr. 3 up). 1984. 15.95 (ISBN 0-907234-60-7). Picture Bk Studio.

Strange Children. Caroline Gordon. LC 71-164525. 1972. Repr. of 1951 ed. 19.50x (ISBN 0-8154-0394-1). Cooper Sq.

Strange Coast. Graham Everett. (Illus., Orig.). 1979. pap. 5.00 (ISBN 0-918092-15-9). Tamarack Edns.

Strange Company. Leonard Blusse. 302p. 1986. pap. 119.00x (ISBN 0-317-69114-7, Pub. by Han-Shan Tang Ltd). State Mutual Bk.

Strange Contrarieties: Pascal in England During the Age of Reason. John C. Barker. (Illus.). 352p. 1976. 29.50x (ISBN 0-7735-0188-6). McGill-Queens U Pr.

Strange Country: A Study of Randolph Snow. Anthony J. Hassall. 256p. 1986. text ed. 32.50x (ISBN 0-7022-1866-9). U of Queensland Pr.

Strange Courage. Max Brand & Evan Evans. 256p. 1986. pap. 2.75 (ISBN 0-515-08582-0). Jove Pubns.

Strange Courage. Evan Evans, pseud. 213p. 1975. Repr. of 1952 ed. lib. bdg. 15.95 (ISBN 0-89190-211-2, Pub. by River City Pr). Amereon Ltd.

Strange Creatures. Simon Seymour. 48p. (gr. 3-7). 1981. 9.95 (ISBN 0-02-782860-3, Four Winds). Macmillan.

Strange Creatures of the Desert. Stanley Bank. LC 83-60112. (Strange but True Ser.). 1983. 10.96 (ISBN 0-382-06692-8). Silver.

Strange Creatures That Lived Long Age. Millicent Selsam. LC 86-29732. (Illus.). 32p. (gr. 4-6). 1987. 13.95 (ISBN 0-590-40707-4, Scholastic Hardcover). Scholastic Inc.

Strange Cults in America. abr. ed. Bob Larson. (Pocket Guides Ser.). 80p. 1986. pocket guide 1.95 (ISBN 0-8423-6675-X). Tyndale.

Strange Customs, Manners & Beliefs. facs. ed. Alpheus H. Verrill. LC 75-86791. (Essay Index Reprint Ser). 1946. 18.00 (ISBN 0-8369-1199-7). Ayer Co Pubs.

Strange Customs of Courtship & Marriage. William J. Fielding. 315p. 1980. Repr. of 1942 ed. lib. bdg. 39.50 (ISBN 0-89987-259-X). Darby Bks.

Strange Customs of Courtship & Marriage. William J. Fielding. 322p. 1985. Repr. of 1942 ed. lib. bdg. 75.00. Century Bookbindery.

Strange Days Ahead. Michael Brownstein. LC 75-26450. (Illus.). 98p. (Orig.). 1976. pap. 5.00 (ISBN 0-915990-01-6). Z Pr.

Strange Days: The Music of John, Paul, George & Ringo Twenty Years On. Walter Podrazik. (Rock & Roll Reference Ser.: No. 21). 1988. write for info. (ISBN 0-87650-206-0, 3390). Pierian.

Strange Death of Franklin Delano Roosevelt: A History of the Roosevelt-Delano Dynasty. new ed. Emanuel M. Josephson. 288p. 1976. 75.00 (ISBN 0-685-66413-9). Chedney.

Strange Death of Franklin Delano Roosevelt. Emanuel M. Josephson. 1979. write for info. (ISBN 0-685-96469-8). Revisionist Pr.

Strange Death of Franklin Roosevelt: A History of the Roosevelt-Delano Dynasty: America's Royal Family. Emanuel Josephson. (Blacked-Out History Ser.). 284p. 3.50 (ISBN 0-686-29296-0, Pub. by Chedney); pap. 3.00 (ISBN 0-686-29297-9). A-albionic Res.

Strange Death of Liberal England. George Dangerfield. 398p. 1989. pap. 8.95 (ISBN 0-89733-332-2). Academy Chi Pubs.

Strange Death of Liberal England, 1910-1914. George Dangerfield. (Illus.). 1961. pap. 4.95 (ISBN 0-399-50227-0, Perigee). Putnam Pub Group.

Strange Defeat: A Statement of Evidence Written in 1940. Marc Bloch. 1967. lib. bdg. 20.00x (ISBN 0-374-90665-3, Octagon). Hippocrene Bks.

Strange Defeat: A Statement of Evidence Written in 1940. Gerard Manley Hopkins. Tr. by Marc Bloch. 1968. pap. 6.95 (ISBN 0-393-00371-X, Norton Lib). Norton.

Strange Disappearance of Arthur Cluck. Nathaniel Benchley. LC 67-4151. (I Can Read Mystery Bks.). (Illus.). 64p. (gr. k-3). 1967. PLB 10.89 (ISBN 0-06-020478-8). HarpJ.

Strange Disappearances. Elliott O'Donnell. 1972. 7.95 (ISBN 0-8216-0155-5, Pub. by Univ Bks). Lyle Stuart.

Strange Eating Habits of Sea Creatures. Jean Sibbald. LC 85-11621. (Ocean World Library). (Illus.). 112p. (gr. 4 up). 1986. PLB 11.95 (ISBN 0-87518-349-2). Dillon.

Strange Encounters. 5th ed. Raymond Bernard. Tr. by AMORC Staff. 120p. (Orig.). Date not set. pap. price not set (ISBN 0-912057-52-1, G-665). AMORC.

Strange Encounters. Earl Murray. 1988. pap. 8.95. Contemp Bks.

Strange Encounters: A Graphic Novel. Fred Hull. Ed. by Joan Harryman. (Illus., Orig.). 1987. pap. 5.95 (ISBN 0-944099-05-X). CB Pubns.

Strange Eons. Robert Bloch. LC 78-66962. (Illus.). 1979. 12.00 (ISBN 0-918372-30-5); signed-slipcased ed 25.00x (ISBN 0-918372-29-1). Whispers.

Strange Experience: How to Become the World's Second Greatest Lover. Strange de Jim. LC 80-69868. (Illus.). 192p. (Orig.). 1980. perfect bdg. 6.95 (ISBN 0-9605308-1-9). Ash-Kar Pr.

Strange Facts & True About New Zealand. Patricia Chapman. 199p. 1984. pap. 9.95 (ISBN 0-86469-032-0, Pub. by Dunmore NZ). Intl Spec Bk.

Strange Fascination. Betty C. Mowery. 1985. 9.95 (ISBN 0-8034-8522-0, Avalon). Bouregy.

Strange Footprints on the Land. Constance Irwin. LC 78-19519. (Illus.). 192p. (YA) (gr. 7 up). 1980. PLB 13.89 (ISBN 0-06-022773-7). HarpJ.

Strange Fruit. Lillian Smith. LC 84-28073. (Brown Thrasher Bks.). 392p. 1985. pap. 9.95 (ISBN 0-8203-0779-3). U of Ga Pr.

Strange Fruit. Lillian E. Smith. LC 44-40028. 371p. 1948. 12.95 (ISBN 0-15-185769-5). HarBraceJ.

Strange Gifts: A Guide to Charismatic Renewal. Ed. by David Martin & Peter Mullen. 208p. 1984. pap. 9.95x (ISBN 0-631-13592-8). Basil Blackwell.

Strange Gifts: Eight Stories of Science Fiction. Ed. by Robert Silverberg. 15.95 (ISBN 0-89190-524-3, Pub. by Am Repr). Amereon Ltd.

Strange Gigs & Misadventures. Terry Hauptman. (Illus.). 80p. 1982. 25.00 (ISBN 0-939622-35-1); pap. 12.50 (ISBN 0-939622-34-3). Four Zoas Night.

Strange Glory. Ed. by G. Goldberg. (Illus.). 10.95 (ISBN 0-312-76387-5). Brown Bk.

Strange Gods Before Me. Mother Mary Francis. 199p. 1976. pap. 4.95 (ISBN 0-8199-0599-2). Franciscan Herald.

Strange Gods: Contemporary Religious Cults in America. William J. Whalen. LC 80-81451. 1981. pap. 4.95 (ISBN 0-87973-666-6, 666). Our Sunday Visitor.

Strange Gods: The Great American Cult Scare. David Bromley & Anson Shupe. LC 81-65763. 192p. 1982. pap. 9.95x (ISBN 0-8070-1109-6, BP641). Beacon Pr.

Strange Gravity: Songs Physical & Metaphysical. Paul Petrie. LC 84-50796. (Illus.). 77p. (Orig.). 1984. 17.50 (ISBN 0-930954-21-1); pap. 10.00 (ISBN 0-930954-22-X). Tidal Pr.

Strange Ground: American in Vietnam, 1945-1975. As told by Harry Maurer. 1988. 29.95 (ISBN 0-8050-0919-1). H Holt & Co.

Strange Happening at Vandenberg Surf. Norbert Schiller. (Illus.). 1984. ltd. ed. 50.00 (ISBN 0-943164-27-3). Geronima.

Strange Illusions: Strange Beliefs, Rituals & Cermonies of Primitive Peoples. Lloyd K. Ulery. 96p. 1986. 6.95 (ISBN 0-930984-05-6). Psychic Bks.

Strange Inheritance. Lorena A. Olmsted. (YA) (gr. 7 up). 1978. 9.95 (ISBN 0-685-86415-4, Avalon). Bouregy.

Strange Invasion of Catfish Bend. Ben L. Burman. 156p. (gr. 3-5). 1981. pap. 1.95 (ISBN 0-380-53520-3, 53520-3, Camelot). Avon.

Strange Invasion of Catfish Bend. Ben L. Burman. LC 79-67487. (Catfish Bend Stories Ser.). (Illus.). 160p. 1980. 12.95 (ISBN 0-8149-0828-4). Vanguard.

Strange Irish Tales for Children. Edmund Lenihan & Joseph Gervin. (Illus.). 128p. (gr. 4-8). 1987. pap. 9.95 (ISBN 0-85342-833-6, Pub. by Mercier Pr Ireland). Irish Bks Media.

Strange Lands. Michel Russell. 118p. 1986. 39.00x (ISBN 0-7212-0756-1, Pub. by Regency Pr). State Mutual Bk.

Strange Liberalism of Alexis de Tocqueville. Roger Boesche. LC 86-29141. 288p. 1987. 29.95x (ISBN 0-8014-1964-6). Cornell U Pr.

Strange Life: A Sourcebook on the Mysteries of Organic Nature. William R. Corliss. LC 75-6128. (Strange Life Ser.: Vol. B1). (Illus.). 275p. 1975. 8.95x (ISBN 0-9600712-8-8). Sourcebook.

Strange Life of Ivan Osokin. P. D. Ouspensky. 166p. 1986. pap. 6.95 (ISBN 0-7100-9419-1). Routledge Chapman & Hall.

Strange Life of Ivan Osokin. P. D. Ouspensky. (Arkana Fiction Ser.). 166p. 1987. pap. 9.95 (ISBN 1-85063-083-6, Pub. by Routledge UK). Routledge Chapman & Hall.

Strange Loop. Amanda Prantera. 176p. 1985. 14.95 (ISBN 0-525-24305-4). Dutton.

Strange Loops. David Evett. (Cleveland Poets Ser.: No. 38). 63p. (Orig.). 1985. pap. 5.00 (ISBN 0-914946-47-1). Cleveland St Univ Poetry Ctr.

Strange Loops. David Evett. 5.00. League Bks.

Strange Loyalty of Dr. Carlisle. Elizabeth Seifert. 1973. Repr. of 1952 ed. lib. bdg. 19.95x (ISBN 0-88411-026-5, Pub. by Aeonian Pr). Amereon Ltd.

Strange Maine. Ed. by Charles G. Waugh et al. (Illus.). 295p. (Orig.). 1986. pap. 9.95 (ISBN 0-912769-10-6). L Tapley.

Strange Malady: The Story of Allergy. Warren T. Vaughan. 1943. 25.00 (ISBN 0-8274-4268-8). R West.

Strange Man. Amu Djoleto. (African Writers Ser.). 1968. pap. text ed. 7.00 (ISBN 0-435-90041-2). Heinemann Ed.

Strange Manuscript Found in a Copper Cylinder. James De Mille. LC 74-15964. (Science Fiction Ser). (Illus.). 291p. 1975. Repr. 21.00x (ISBN 0-405-06285-0). Ayer Co Pubs.

Strange Masonic Stories. Alec Mellor. (Illus.). 208p. 1985. softcover 10.95 (ISBN 0-88053-082-0, M-313). Macoy Pub.

Strange Meat, Poems Nineteen Sixty-Eight to Nineteen Seventy-Four. Gloria Bosque. LC 74-23345. 2.00 (ISBN 0-914134-03-5). Sipapu-Konocti.

Strange Message in the Parchment. Carolyn Keene. (Nancy Drew Ser.: Vol. 54). (gr. 4-7). 1977. 4.50 (ISBN 0-448-09554-8, G&D). Putnam Pub Group.

Strange Monsters of the Sea. Richard Armour. LC 78-11263. (Illus.). 1979. text ed. 10.95 (ISBN 0-07-002294-1). McGraw.

Strange Mysteries. Thomas Gunning. (gr. 2-9). Date not set. pap. 2.95. Troll Assocs.

Strange Nation of Rafael Mendes. Moacyr Sciar. 1989. pap. 4.95. Ballantine.

Strange Nation of Rafael Mendes. Moacyr Scliar. Tr. by Eloah P. Giacomelli. 1988. 19.95 (ISBN 0-517-56776-8, Harmony). Crown.

Strange Necessity: Essays. Rebecca West. Repr. of 1928 ed. 19.00 (ISBN 0-403-08958-1). Somerset Pub.

Strange Necessity: Resolutions & Reminiscence to 1969. Margaret Anderson. LC 73-92708. (Illus.). 1969. pap. 8.95 (ISBN 0-8180-0212-3). Horizon.

Strange Negro Stories of the Old Deep South. Harry D. Howell, Sr. LC 78-122722. (Short Story Index Reprint Ser). 1937. 18.00 (ISBN 0-8369-3555-1). Ayer Co Pubs.

Strange Neutrality: Soviet - Japanese Relations During the Second World War, 1941-1945. George A. Lensen. LC 72-178091. (Illus.). 332p. 1972. 15.00 (ISBN 0-910512-14-0). Diplomatic IN.

Strange New Gospels. Edgar J. Goodspeed. 1979. Repr. of 1931 ed. lib. bdg. 22.50 (ISBN 0-8495-2000-2). Arden Lib.

Strange New Gospels. facsimile ed. Edgar J. Goodspeed. LC 70-156652. (Essay Index Reprint Ser). Repr. of 1931 ed. 12.00 (ISBN 0-8369-2364-2). Ayer Co Pubs.

Strange New Religions. Leon McBeth. LC 76-47780. 1977. pap. 4.95 (ISBN 0-8054-1806-7). Broadman.

Strange Night Writing of Jessamine Colter. Cynthia C. DeFelice. LC 88-4325. 56p. (gr. 5 up). 1988. 12.95 (ISBN 0-02-726451-3). Macmillan.

Strange Notions see Dark Ocean.

Strange Notions & the Dark Ocean. Jack Vance. Incl. Dark Ocean. 224p. 1986. Set. deluxe ed. 60.00x signed, slipcase ed. (ISBN 0-88733-015-0). Underwood-Miller.

Strange Occupation. Georgiana Melrose. 1987. 39.00x (ISBN 0-7223-2200-3, Pub. by A H Stockwell England). State Mutual Bk.

Strange Ordeal of Edwin Banquo & Other Stories. Ruth Jespersen. 85p. (Orig.). 1986. pap. 6.95 (ISBN 0-9617134-0-2). Biblia Candida.

Strange Papers of Dr. Blayre. Edward Heron-Allen. Ed. by R. Reginald & Douglas Menville. LC 76-14332. (Supernatural & Occult Fiction Ser.). 1976. Repr. of 1932 ed. lib. bdg. 21.00x (ISBN 0-405-08418-8). Ayer Co Pubs.

Strange Parallel: Zebulun a Tribe of Israel. Rev. ed. Helene Koppejan. LC 83-73689. (Illus.). 96p. 1984. pap. 4.00 (ISBN 0-934666-13-X). Artisan Sales.

Strange Partnership of George Alexander McGuire & Marcus Garvey. Bishop K. Pruter. LC 86-17628. 50p. 1986. lib. bdg. 19.95x (ISBN 0-89370-529-2). Borgo Pr.

Strange Peaches. Edwin Shrake. LC 86-30088. (Contemporary Fiction Ser.). 240p. 1987. pap. 9.95 (ISBN 0-87719-076-3). Texas Month Pr.

Strange People. Frank Edwards. 288p. 1986. Repr. of 1968 ed. write for info. (Pub. by Citadel Pr). Lyle Stuart.

Strange Phenomena: A Sourcebook of Unusual Natural Phenomena, Vol. G2. William R. Corliss. LC 73-9148. 1974. 8.95x (ISBN 0-9600712-5-3). Sourcebook.

Strange Planes: A Collection of Unusual Paper Airplanes. Mitchell D. Forcier. (Illus.). 60p. (Orig.). (gr. k up). 1987. pap. 6.95 (ISBN 0-9618419-4-X). Paper Press.

Strange Planet: A Sourcebook of Unusual Geological Facts. William R. Corliss. LC 74-26226. (Strange Planet Ser.: Vol. E2). 1978. 8.95x (ISBN 0-915554-04-6). Sourcebook.

Strange Planet: A Sourcebook of Unusual Geological Facts, Vol. E1. William R. Corliss. LC 74-26226. (Illus.). 283p. 1975. 8.95x (ISBN 0-9600712-3-7). Sourcebook.

Strange Reincarnations of Hendrik Verloom. Eth Clifford. (gr. 3-6). 1982. 8.95 (ISBN 0-395-32433-5); 8.70. HM.

Strange Ride of Rudyard Kipling. Angus Wilson. (Illus.). 1979. pap. 6.95 (ISBN 0-14-005122-8). Penguin.

Strange Routine. Tony Flynn. 56p. 1980. pap. 6.95 (ISBN 0-906427-20-7, Pub. by Bloodaxe Bks). Dufour.

"Strange Sapience": The Creative Imagination of D. H. Lawrence. Daniel Dervin. LC 84-2681. (Illus.). 256p. 1984. lib. bdg. 23.50x (ISBN 0-87023-455-2). U of Mass Pr.

Strange Schemes of Randolph Mason. Melville Post. LC 75-32776. (Literature of Mystery & Detection Ser.). 1976. Repr. of 1896 ed. 22.00x (ISBN 0-405-07895-1). Ayer Co Pubs.

Strange Schemes of Randolph Mason. Melville D. Post. LC 74-10490. (Milestones of Mystery Ser). 280p. 1975. Repr. of 1896 ed. 15.00 (ISBN 0-88355-204-3). Hyperion Conn.

Strange Schemes of Randolph Mason. Melville D. Post. 280p. 1980. Repr. of 1901 ed. lib. bdg. 14.25x (ISBN 0-89968-200-6). Lightyear.

Strange Scriptures That Perplex the Western Mind. Barbara M. Bowen. 1940. pap. 4.95 (ISBN 0-8028-1511-1). Eerdmans.

Strange Seas of Thought: Studies in William Wordsworth's Philosophy of Man & Nature. Newton P. Stallknecht. LC 77-22222. 1977. Repr. of 1958 ed. lib. bdg. 35.00x (ISBN 0-8371-9774-0, STSS). Greenwood.

Strange Seed. T. M. Wright. LC 79-93210. 240p. (Orig.). 1983. pap. 2.95. Playboy Pbks.

Strange Seed. T. M. Wright. 320p. 1987. pap. 3.95 (ISBN 0-8125-2762-3). Tor Bks.

Strange Sex Lives in the Animal Kingdom. Alice L. Hopf. 1981. text ed. 9.95 (ISBN 0-07-030319-3). McGraw.

Strange Shapes. Donald Keefe. Ed. by Marjorie Oelerich. (Baker Street Great Big Bks.). (Illus.). 16p. (gr. k-2). 1986. 14.95 (ISBN 0-914867-26-1). Baker St Prod.

Strange Silence of the Bible in the Church: A Study in Hermeneutics. James D. Smart. LC 72-118323. 184p. 1970. pap. 8.95 (ISBN 0-664-24894-2). Westminster John Knox.

Strange Sins. Jocelyn Christopher. (Orig.). 1988. pap. 3.95 (ISBN 0-440-20028-8). Dell.

Strange Sounds. Em McConnell. (Learn-a-Lot Ser.). (gr. k-3). Bk. & cassette 4.95 (ISBN 0-932715-09-5). Evans FL.

Strange Stories. Algernon Blackwood. Ed. by R. Reginald & Douglas Menville. LC 75-46255. (Supernatural & Occult Fiction Ser.). 1976. Repr. of 1929 ed. lib. bdg. 55.00x (ISBN 0-405-08114-6). Ayer Co Pubs.

Strange Stories, Amazing Facts. Reader's Digest Editors. LC 76-2966. (Illus.). 608p. 1976. 24.95 (ISBN 0-89577-028-8, Pub. by RD Assn). Random.

Strange Stories from a Chinese Studio. rev. ed. Linda Hsia & Roger Yue. 7.95 (ISBN 0-88710-114-3); tapes avail. (ISBN 0-88710-115-1). Yale Far Eastern Pubns.

Strange Stories of Life. Joann A. Lawless. LC 77-10866. (Great Unsolved Mysteries Ser.). (Illus.). 48p. (gr. 4-5). 1977. PLB 15.33 (ISBN 0-8172-1062-8). Raintree Pubs.

Strange Stories of Life. Joann A. Lawless. LC 77-10866. (Great Unsolved Mysteries Ser.). (Illus.). 48p. (gr. 4up). 1983. pap. 9.27 (ISBN 0-8172-2167-0). Raintree Pubs.

Strange Stories of the Animal World. John Timbs. Repr. of 1866 ed. lib. bdg. 45.00 (ISBN 0-8495-5328-8). Arden Lib.

Strange Stories of UFOs. Len Ortzen. LC 77-76726. 1977. 7.95 (ISBN 0-8008-7468-4). Taplinger.

Strange Story of False Teeth. John Woodforde. 152p. 1983. pap. 8.95 (ISBN 0-7100-9307-1). Routledge Chapman & Hall.

Strange Story of the Quantum. 2nd ed. Banesh Hoffman. 14.50 (ISBN 0-8446-0702-9). Peter Smith.

Strange Story of the Quantum. Banesh Hoffmann. 1959. pap. text ed. 5.95 (ISBN 0-486-20518-5). Dover.

Strange Studies from Life & Other Narratives: The Complete True Crime Writings of Sir Arthur Conan Doyle. Arthur Conan Doyle. (Conan Doyle Centennial Ser.). (Illus.). 104p. 1988. 15.95 (ISBN 0-934468-49-4). Gaslight.

Strange Survivals, Some Chapters in the History of Man. Sabine Baring-Gould. LC 67-23909. (Illus.). 296p. 1968. Repr. of 1892 ed. 35.00x (ISBN 0-8103-3422-4). Gale.

Strange Survivals: Some Chapters in the History of Man. Sabine Baring-Gould. 59.95 (ISBN 0-8490-1142-6). Gordon Pr.

Strange Swimming Coach. Jerry Jenkins. (Dallas O'Neil & the Baker Street Sports Club Ser.). (Orig.). (YA) (gr. 9-12). 1986. pap. text ed. 3.95 (ISBN 0-8024-8238-4). Moody.

Strange Tactics of Extremism. H. A. Overstreet & Bonaro Overstreet. 1964. 5.95 (ISBN 0-393-05268-0); pap. 4.95x (ISBN 0-393-09749-8). Norton.

Strange Tales. Mildred Sproxton. 1987. 29.00x (ISBN 0-7223-2131-7, Pub. by A H Stockwell England). State Mutual Bk.

Strange Tales. Mildred Sproxton. 56p. 1987. 35.00x (ISBN 0-317-62505-5, Pub. by A H Stockwell England). State Mutual Bk.

Strange Things Happen Here: Twenty-Six Short Stories & a Novel. Luisa Valenzuela. LC 78-22274. 264p. 1979. 9.95 (ISBN 0-15-185782-2). HarBraceJ.

Strange Things Happen in the Woods. Eve Bunting. Orig. Title: Cloverdale Switch. (gr. 7-9). 1984. pap. 1.95 (ISBN 0-671-41098-9). Archway.

Strangers in the Land. John Higham. LC 55-8601. (Illus.). 1963. pap. text ed. 6.95x (ISBN 0-689-70095-4, 32). Atheneum.
Strangers in the Land. Milt Machlin. 416p. 1985. pap. 3.95 (ISBN 0-345-31255-4). Ballantine.
Strangers in the Land: Patterns of American Nativism, 1860 to 1925. John Higham. LC 80-22204. (Illus.). xiv, 431p. 1981. Repr. of 1963 ed. lib. bdg. 52.50x (ISBN 0-313-22459-5, HISL). Greenwood.
Strangers in the Land: Patterns of American Nativism, 1860-1925. John Higham. 431p. 1988. text ed. 35.00 (ISBN 0-8135-1311-1); pap. text ed. 10.00 (ISBN 0-8135-1308-1). Rutgers U Pr.
Strangers in Their Midst: Small-Town Jews & Their Neighbors. Peter I. Rose. 1977. lib. bdg. 12.95 (ISBN 0-915172-32-1). Richwood Pub.
Strangers in Their Own Country: A Curriculum Guide on South Africa. William Bigelow. LC 85-71369. (Illus.). 104p. (Orig.). (YA) (gr. 8 up). 1987. pap. 12.95 (ISBN 0-86543-010-1). Africa World.
Strangers in Their Own Land. Peter Sichrovsky. Date not set. price not set. Bantam.
Strangers in Their Own Land: A Choctaw Portfolio. Carole Thompson. (State Historical Museum Catalog Ser.). (Illus.). 38p. 1983. pap. 3.00 (ISBN 0-938896-34-2). Mississippi Archives.
Strangers in Their Own Land: Young Jews in Germany & Austria Today. Peter Sichrovsky. Tr. by Jean Steinberg. LC 85-43108. 208p. 1986. 14.95 (ISBN 0-465-08211-4). Basic.
Strangers in Their Own Land: Young Jews in Germany & Austria Today. Peter Sichrovsky. 176p. 1987. pap. 5.95 (ISBN 0-14-009965-4). Penguin.
Strangers in this Land: Pluralism & the Response to Diversity in the United States. E. Allen Richardson. 240p. 1988. pap. 10.95 (ISBN 0-8298-0764-0). Pilgrim NY.
Stranger's Kiss. Jenny Loring. (Superromances Ser.). 384p. 1983. pap. 2.95 (ISBN 0-373-70074-1, Pub. by Worldwide). Harlequin Bks.
Strangers, Lovers, Friends. Urban G. Steinmetz. LC 80-69479. (Illus.). 176p. (Orig.). 1981. pap. 3.95 (ISBN 0-87793-242-5). Ave Maria.
Strangers May Marry see It's Rumoured in the Village.
Strangers No More. William Gellin. LC 85-63442. 192p. 1986. 11.95 (ISBN 0-88400-121-0). Shengold.
Strangers on a Train. Patricia Highsmith. (Crime Ser.). 1979. pap. 3.95 (ISBN 0-14-003796-9). Penguin.
Strangers on NMA-6. Harriette S. Abels. Ed. by Howard Schroeder. LC 79-4627. (Galaxy I Ser.). (Illus.). 48p. (gr. 3-5). 1979. PLB 7.95 (ISBN 0-89686-027-2). Crestwood Hse.
Strangers on the Mountain. Nina D. Santos. 128p. 1981. 19.00x (ISBN 0-85088-665-1, Pub. by Gomer Pr). State Mutual Bk.
Strangers or Friends: Principles for a New Alien Admission Policy. Mark Gibney. LC 86-7572. (Contributions in Political Science Ser.: No. 157). 184p. 1986. lib. bdg. 35.00 (ISBN 0-313-25344-7, GSG/). Greenwood.
Strangers Outside the Feast: A Choral Reading. Warren Mild. (gr. 9 up). 1966. pap. 0.75 (ISBN 0-377-80081-3). Friendship Pr.
Strangers' Sky see Celebration in Darkness.
Strangers: The Tragic World of Tristan l'Hermite. Claude K. Abraham. LC 66-64916. (University of Florida Humanities Monographs: No. 23). 1966. pap. 6.00x (ISBN 0-8130-0000-9). U Presses Fla.
Strangers to the City: Urban Man in Jos, Nigeria. Leonard Plotnicov. LC 67-13928. (Illus.). 1967. pap. 12.95x (ISBN 0-8229-5135-5). U of Pittsburgh Pr.
Strangers to These Shores: Race & Ethnic Relations in the United States. 2nd ed. Vincent N. Parrillo. LC 84-17435. 547p. 1985. text ed. write for info. (ISBN 0-02-391740-7); write for info. instr's manual avail. (ISBN 0-02-391770-9). Macmillan.
Strangers to This Ground: Cultural Diversity in Contemporary American Writing. Wilbur M. Frohock. LC 61-17183. 192p. 1961. 12.95x (ISBN 0-87074-055-5). SMU Press.
Strangers Within Our Gates. James S. Woodsworth. LC 76-163836. (Social History of Canada Ser.). 1972. pap. 9.95 (ISBN 0-8020-6149-4). U of Toronto Pr.
Strangers Within the Gate City: The Jews of Atlanta, 1845-1915. Steven Hertzberg. LC 78-1167. 352p. 1978. 12.00 (ISBN 0-8276-0102-6, 418). JPS Phila.
Strangest Friendship in History. George S. Viereck. LC 75-26222. 1976. Repr. of 1932 ed. lib. bdg. 35.00x (ISBN 0-8371-8413-4, VISF). Greenwood.
Strangest of All. Frank Edwards. 224p. 1987. pap. 5.95 (ISBN 0-8065-1023-4, Pub. by Citadel Pr). Lyle Stuart.
Strangled Cries. Julius Balbin. Ed. by Stanley H. Barkan. Tr. by Charlz Rizzuto. (Cross-Cultural Review Chapbook 8: Esperanto Poetry 1). 24p. (Esperanto & Eng.). 1980. pap. 2.50 (ISBN 0-89304-807-0). Cross Cult.
Strangled Prose. Joan Hess. 192p. 1985. 12.95 (ISBN 0-312-76428-6). St Martin.
Strangled Prose. Joan Hess. pap. 2.95 (ISBN 0-345-34059-0). Ballantine.
Stranglers. Loren D. Estleman. 176p. 1985. pap. 2.50 (ISBN 0-449-12848-2, GM). Fawcett.
Strangling Figs in Sanskrit Literature. Murray B. Emeneau. LC 49-2733. (University of California Publications in Classical Philology: Vol. 13, No. 10). pap. 20.00 (ISBN 0-317-09833-0, 2021166). Bks Demand UMI.
Strangling of Persia. W. Morgan Shuster. LC 86-31244. (Illus.). 496p. 1987. Repr. of 1912 ed. 20.00x (ISBN 0-934211-06-X). Mage Pubs Inc.
Strangpressen see Extrusion: Scientific & Technical Developments.
Strangulation. Bobby G. Price. (Illus.). 32p. (Orig.). 1983. pap. 3.00 (ISBN 0-932662-45-5). St Andrews NC.
Straniera. Vincenzo Bellini. Ed. by Philip Gosset & Charles Rosen. LC 76-49174. (Early Romantic Opera Ser.). 1982. 180.00 (ISBN 0-8240-2901-1). Garland Pub.
Stranitsky Diplomaticheskoi Istorii. V. M. Berezhkov. 502p. (Rus.). 1982. 59.00x (ISBN 0-317-40870-4, Pub. by Collets (UK)). State Mutual Bk.
Stranitsy Russkogo Realizma. Oleg Mikhailov. 288p. 39.00x (Pub. by Collets UK). State Mutual Bk.
Stranitzkys Drama Von Heiligen Nepomuck Mit Einem Neudruck Des Textes. Fritz Homeyer. 27.00 (ISBN 0-384-24110-7); pap. 22.00. Johnson Repr.
Strasberg's Method: As Taught by Lorrie Hull. S. Loraine Hull. 1985. 24.95 (ISBN 0-918024-38-2); pap. 15.95 (ISBN 0-918024-39-0). Ox Bow.
Strasbourg Agreement Concerning the International Patent Classification. 19p. 1971. pap. 7.50 (ISBN 0-686-53033-0, WIPO22, WIPO). UNIPUB.
Strasbourg Conference on the International Patent Classification. 1971. pap. 7.50 (ISBN 0-686-53034-9, WIPO23, WIPO). UNIPUB.
Strasburg Tapes. Henry Madden. Date not set. price not set. Daedalus Act.
Strastnaja Sedmitsa see Tserkovno-Pjevcheskiji Sbornik.
Strata Control in Meneral Engineering. Z. T. Bieniawski. 233p. 1987. text ed. 50.00 (ISBN 90-6191-608-9, Pub. by A A Balkema). Brookfield Pub Co.
Strata Control in Mineral Engineering. Bieniawski. 1986. 51.95 (ISBN 0-470-20329-3). Halsted Pr.
Strata Mechanics in Coal Mining. Ed. by M. L. Jeremic. 576p. 1985. text ed. 89.50 (ISBN 90-6191-508-2, Pub. by A A Balkema); pap. text ed. 48.50 (ISBN 0-317-65002-5, Pub. by A A Balkema). Brookfield Pub Co.
Strata Mechanics: Proceedings of the Symposium, Newcastle Upon Tyne, April 5-7, 1982. I. W. Farmer. (Developments in Geotechnical Engineering Ser.: Vol. 32). 290p. 1982. 118.50 (ISBN 0-444-42086-X). Elsevier.
Stratagem & Other Stories. facsimile ed. Aleister Crowley. LC 74-167446. (Short Story Index Reprint Ser.). Repr. of 1929 ed. 11.00 (ISBN 0-8369-3972-7). Ayer Co Pubs.
Stratagem & Other Stories. Aleister Crowley. 1973. lib. bdg. 79.95 (ISBN 0-87968-117-9). Krishna Pr.
Stratagem, Strategy. abr. ed. Luanna C. Blagrove. (Illus.). 275p. 1988. 24.95. Blagrove Pubns.
Stratagems. Julia Lorusso & Joel Glick. 108p. (Orig.). 1985. pap. 7.95 (ISBN 0-914732-15-3). Bro Life Inc.
Stratagems & Aqueducts. Sextus J. Frontinus. (Loeb Classical Library: No. 174). 13.95x (ISBN 0-674-99192-3). Harvard U Pr.
Stratagems & Spoils: A Social Anthropology of Politics. F. G. Bailey. (Pavilion Ser.). 254p. 1969. pap. 12.95x (ISBN 0-631-11760-1). Basil Blackwell.
Stratagems & Spoils: Stories of Love & Politics. William A. White. 1972. Repr. of 1901 ed. lib. bdg. 17.50 (ISBN 0-8422-8125-8). Irvington.
Stratagems & Spoils: Stories of Love & Politics. William A. White. (American Studies). Repr. of 1901 ed. 19.00 (ISBN 0-384-68100-X). Johnson Repr.
Stratagems & Spoils: Stories of Love & Politics. William A. White. 1986. pap. text ed. 8.95x (ISBN 0-8290-2033-0). Irvington.
Stratagems of War. Polyaenus. Tr. by R. Shepherd. 458p. 1974. 25.00 (ISBN 0-89005-020-1). Ares.
Stratas. Harry Rasky. (Illus.). 160p. 1988. 21.95 (ISBN 0-19-540598-6). Oxford U Pr.
Strategic Advertising Campaigns. 2nd ed. Don E. Schultz et al. LC 83-72177. 350p. 1984. 34.95 (ISBN 0-8442-3089-8, Crain Bks). Natl Textbk.
Strategic Air Attack in the United States Air Force: A Case Study. Thomas A. Fabyanic. 216p. 1977. pap. text ed. 22.00x (ISBN 0-89126-029-3). MA-AH Pub.
Strategic Air Command. Lindsay T. Peacock. (Illus.). 128p. 1988. 19.95 (ISBN 0-85368-864-8, Pub. by Arms & Armour). Sterling.
Strategic Air Command: People, Aircraft, & Missiles. Norman Polmar & John T. Bohn. 19.95 (ISBN 0-405-13275-1). Ayer Co Pubs.
Strategic Air War Against Germany & Japan: A Memoir. Haywood S. Hansell, Jr. LC 86-23749. (USAF Warrior Studies). (Illus.). 319p. (Orig.). 1986. pap. 14.00 (ISBN 0-318-22436-4, S/N 008-070-00583-2). USGPO.
Strategic Airline Management. Louis Gialloreto. 126p. 1988. 67.50x (ISBN 0-273-02857-X, Pub. by Pitman Pub Ltd London). Trans-Atl Phila.
Strategic Alliances in the Pacific Rim & India. LC 86-82940. 1987. 1500.00 (ISBN 0-914405-20-9). Electronic Trend.
Strategic Alternatives: Selection, Development & Implementation. William E. Rothschild. 1979. 16.95 (ISBN 0-8144-5514-X). AMACOM.
Strategic Analysis & Action: U. S. Edition. Joseph N. Fry & J. Peter Killing. 352p. 1986. pap. text ed. 23.00 (ISBN 0-13-850918-2). P-H.
Strategic Analysis for Hospital Management. Roger Kropf & James A. Greenberg. 330p. 1984. 49.95 (ISBN 0-89443-855-7). Aspen Pub.
Strategic Analysis for Venture Evaluation: The Safe Approach to Business Decisions. W. R. Park & J. B. Maillie. 224p. 1981. 26.95 (ISBN 0-442-24507-6). Van Nos Reinhold.
Strategic Analysis of AT&T. Gartner Group, Inc. Staff. 1987. pap. 995.00 (ISBN 0-9614408-1-3). Gartner Group.
Strategic Analysis of Science & Technology Policy. Harvey A. Averch. LC 84-47961. 232p. 1985. text ed. 22.50x (ISBN 0-8018-2467-2). Johns Hopkins.
Strategic Analysis, Selection, & Management of R & D Projects. D. Bruce Merrifield. LC 77-14599. 1977. 7.50 (ISBN 0-8144-2212-8). AMACOM.
Strategic Analysis, Selection, & Management of R & D Projects. D. Bruce Merrifield. LC 77-14599. (AMA Management Briefing Ser.). pap. 20.00 (ISBN 0-317-29944-1, 2051699). Bks Demand UMI.
Strategic Anatomy of the IBM PS-2: Product Opportunities(& Pitfalls) in Hardware Software & Systems. 130p. 495.00 (ISBN 0-317-65582-5). TBC Inc.
Strategic & Critical Materials. L. Harold Bullis & James E. Mielke. (Special Study Ser.). 245p. 1985. 60.50x (ISBN 0-86531-637-6). Westview.
Strategic & Long-Range Planning for Public Administrators: A Selective Bibliography. Lorna Peterson. (Public Administration Ser.: P 1805). 5p. 1985. 2.00 (ISBN 0-89028-635-3). Vance Biblios.
Strategic & Operational Deception in the Second World War. Michael I. Handel. 1987. 35.00 (ISBN 0-7146-3316-X, F Cass Co); pap. 18.50 (ISBN 0-7146-4056-5). Biblio Dist.
Strategic & Operational Planning for Information System. Chantico-QED Staff. LC 85-60179. (Chantico Technical Management Ser.). (Illus.). 200p. (Orig.). 1985. pap. 34.95 (ISBN 0-89435-151-6, CP 1516). QED Info Sci.
Strategic Antisubmarine Warfare & Naval Strategy. Tom A. Stefanick. LC 86-45596. 416p. 1987. 49.95x (ISBN 0-669-14015-5). Lexington Bks.
Strategic Approach to Business Marketing. Ed. by Robert E. Spekman & David T. Wilson. LC 84-18537. (Proceedings). (Illus.). 193p. (Orig.). 1985. pap. text ed. 8.00 (ISBN 0-87757-172-4). Am Mktg.
Strategic Arms Reductions. Michael M. May et al. 64p. 1988. pap. 8.95xt (ISBN 0-8157-5525-2). Brookings.
Strategic Atlas: A Comparative Geopolitics of the World's Powers. Gerald Chaliand & Jean-Pierre Rageau. Tr. by Tony Berrett. LC 84-48143. (Illus.). 224p. 1985. 26.45i (ISBN 0-06-015387-3, HarpT). Har-Row.
Strategic Atlas: A Comparative Geopolitics of the World's Power. Gerald Chaliand & Jean-Pierre Rageau. Tr. by Tony Berrett. LC 84-48143. 224p. 1985. pap. 16.95 (ISBN 0-06-091220-0, PL1220, PL). Har-Row.
Strategic Balance 1972. Edward Luttwak. (Washington Papers: Vol. I, No. 3). 146p. (Orig.). 1972. pap. text ed. 7.95 (ISBN 0-8191-5960-3, Pub. by CSIS). U Pr of Amer.
Strategic Behaviour & Industrial Competition. D. J. Morris et al. (Economic Papers Special Issues). 242p. 1987. pap. 22.00 (ISBN 0-19-828562-0). Oxford U Pr.
Strategic Bombers: How Many Are Enough? Jeffrey Record. LC 86-6. (National Security Papers: No. 3). 26p. 1986. 6.00 (ISBN 0-317-47180-5). Inst Foreign Policy Anal.
Strategic Bombers, 1945-1985. Michael J. Taylor. (Warbirds Illustrated Ser.: Vol. 30). (Illus.). 68p. (Orig.). 1985. pap. 9.95 (ISBN 0-85368-664-5, Pub. by Arms & Armour). Sterling.
Strategic Bombing in World War II: The Story of the United States Strategic Bombing Survey. David MacIsaac. LC 75-27037. 1976. 31.00 (ISBN 0-8240-2025-1). Garland Pub.
Strategic Bombing: The American Experience. Herman S. Wolk. 43p. 1981. pap. 10.00x (ISBN 0-89126-101-X). MA-AH Pub.
Strategic Budgeting: A Comparison Between U. S. & Japanese Companies. Akira Ishikawa. LC 84-18037. 240p. 1985. 33.95 (ISBN 0-275-90120-3, C0120). Praeger.
Strategic Budgeting: Japanese & American Methods & Cases. Akira Ishikawa. (Management & Management Accounting Ser.). 480p. text ed. cancelled (ISBN 0-910129-15-0); pap. text ed. cancelled (ISBN 0-910129-16-9). Wiener Pub Inc.
Strategic Business Messages: Applied Theory & Practice. Margaret F. Hauser. 240p. 1986. pap. text ed. 18.95 (ISBN 0-8403-4084-2). Kendall-Hunt.
Strategic Business Planning: The Pursuit of Competitive Advantage. George S. Day. (Strategic Marketing Ser.). (Illus.). 237p. 1984. pap. text ed. 20.00 (ISBN 0-314-77884-5). West Pub.
Strategic Career Planning & Development for Nurses. Russell C. Swansburg & Philip W. Swansburg. 370p. 1984. 46.25 (ISBN 0-89443-584-1). Aspen Pub.
Strategic Case Analysis. Garsombke. 144p. 1987. pap. text ed. 13.95 (ISBN 0-8403-4593-3). Kendall-Hunt.
Strategic Change & the Management Process. Gerry Johnson. 275p. Date not set. text ed. 39.95 (ISBN 0-631-14717-9). Basil Blackwell.
Strategic Command & Control: Redefining the Nuclear Threat. Bruce G. Blair. LC 84-73164. 341p. 1985. 32.95 (ISBN 0-8157-0982-X); pap. 12.95t (ISBN 0-8157-0981-1). Brookings.
Strategic Concepts in Fire Fighting. Edward McAniff. (Illus.). 1974. 26.95 (ISBN 0-912212-02-0). Fire Eng.
Strategic Consequences of Nuclear Proliferation in South Asia. Ed. by Neil Joeck. 120p. 1986. 25.00x (ISBN 0-7146-3300-3, F Cass Co). Biblio Dist.
Strategic Consequences of the Oil Price Collapse. Ed. by G. Henry & M. Schuler. (Significant Issues Ser.: Vol. 9, No. 2). 56p. (Orig.). 1987. pap. 7.95 (ISBN 0-89206-102-2). CSI Studies.
Strategic Control. Peter Lorange et al. 1986p. 1986. pap. text ed. 22.75 (ISBN 0-314-85258-1). West Pub.
Strategic Data Planning Methodologies. James Martin. (Illus.). 240p. 1982. text ed. 48.00 (ISBN 0-13-851113-6). P-H.
Strategic Data Processing: Considerations for Management. James W. Cortada. (Illus.). 224p. 1984. text ed. 43.00 (ISBN 0-13-851246-9). P-H.
Strategic Defense & Extended Deterrence. Jacquelyn K. Davis & Robert L. Pfaltzgraff. LC 86-69. (National Security Papers: No. 4). 56p. 1986. 8.00 (ISBN 0-317-47187-2). Inst Foreign Policy Anal.
Strategic Defense & the American Ethos: Can the Nuclear World Be Changed? Michael Vlahos. (SAIS Papers in International Affairs: No. 13). 122p. 1987. pap. 15.95 (ISBN 0-8133-0466-0). Westview.
Strategic Defense & the Future of the Arms Race: A Pugwash Symposium. Ed. by John Holdren & Joseph Rotblat. 256p. 1987. 37.50 (ISBN 0-312-00789-2); pap. 14.95 (ISBN 0-312-00790-6). St Martin.
Strategic Defense & the Western Alliance. Ed. by Sanford Lakoff & Randy Willoughby. 240p. 1987. 32.00x (ISBN 0-669-15839-9). Lexington Bks.
Strategic Defense & the Western Alliance. Dan Quayl1 et al. (Significant Issues Ser.: Vol. VIII, No. 6). 92p. (Orig.). 1986. pap. text ed. 8.95 (ISBN 0-89206-098-0). CSI Studies.
Strategic Defense Debate: Can "Star Wars" Make Us Safe? Ed. by Craig Snyder. (Illus.). 1987. pap. 16.95 (ISBN 0-8122-1233-9). U of Pa Pr.
Strategic Defense in the Twenty First Century. Ed. by Hans Binnendijk. LC 86-600547. (State Department Publication). 163p. (Orig.). 1986. pap. 5.50 (ISBN 0-318-21355-9, S/N 044-000-02135-8). USGPO.
Strategic Defense Initiative. Business Communications Staff. (Illus.). 300p. 1986. pap. 1750.00 (ISBN 0-89336-477-0, GB-088). BCC.
Strategic Defense Initiative - Update. Business Communications Staff. 1988. 2450.00 (ISBN 0-89336-669-2, GB-088N). BCC.
Strategic Defense Initiative: A Brief Bibliography. Alva W. Stewart. (Public Administration Ser.: P 2168). 11p. 1987. 3.75 (ISBN 1-55590-328-2). Vance Biblios.
Strategic Defense Initiative: An International Perspective. Ed. by C. James Haug. 1987. 18.00 (ISBN 0-88033-979-9). East Eur Quarterly.
Strategic Defense Initiative & American Security. Aspen Strategy Group. LC 87-1986. (Aspen Strategy Group Report). 82p. (Orig.). 1987. lib. bdg. 16.00 (ISBN 0-8191-6167-5, Pub. by Aspen Strategy Group); pap. text ed. 6.25 (ISBN 0-8191-6168-3, Pub. by Aspen Strategy Group). U Pr of Amer.
Strategic Defense Initiative: Folly or Future? Ed. by P. Edward Haley. Jack Merritt. 193p. 1986. 35.00 (ISBN 0-8133-0414-8); pap. 13.00 (ISBN 0-8133-0415-6). Westview.
Strategic Defense Initiative: Its Effect on the Economy & Arms Control. David Z. Robinson. (Joseph I. Lubin Memorial Lecture: No. 4). 88p. 1987. 12.50x (ISBN 0-8147-7404-0). NYU Pr.
Strategic Defense Initiative: Its Implications for Asia & the Pacific. Ed. by Jae K. Park & Byung-Joon Ahn. 274p. 1987. 35.00 (ISBN 0-8133-0591-8). Westview.
Strategic Defense Initiative: New Perspectives on Deterrence. Ed. by Dorinda G. Dallmeyer. (Dean Rusk Center Monograph Ser.). 112p. 1986. pap. 19.00 (ISBN 0-8133-7238-0). Westview.
Strategic Defense Initiative: Progress & Challenge. Douglas C. Waller et al. (Guides to Contemporary Issues: No. 7). (Illus.). xii, 174p. (Orig.). 1987. lib. bdg. 18.95x (ISBN 0-941690-24-5); pap. 10.95x (ISBN 0-941690-25-3). Regina Bks.
Strategic Defense Initiative: Shield or Snare? Ed. by Harold Brown. (Illus.). 304p. 1987. pap. 24.95 (ISBN 0-8133-0469-5). Westview.

Strategic Management: Public Planning at the Local Level. Leonard C. Moffitt. (Contemporary Studies in Economic & Financial Analysis: Vol. 45). 1984. 56.50 (ISBN 0-89232-428-7). Jai Pr.
Strategic Management Research: A European Perspective. Ed. by John McGee & Howard Thomas. LC 85-29592. 1986. 44.95 (ISBN 0-471-90992-0). Wiley.
Strategic Management Skills. Daniel J. Power et al. 300p. 1986. pap. write for info. (ISBN 0-201-13978-2). Addison-Wesley.
Strategic Management: Strategy Formulation & Implementation. 3rd ed. John A. Pearce & Richard B. Robinson. 1988. 38.95 (ISBN 0-256-06236-6). Irwin.
Strategic Management Techniques. Grant Robinson. (Illus.). 528p. 1986. text ed. 54.95 (ISBN 0-409-11088-4). Butterworth.
Strategic Management: Text & Cases. Glenn Boseman et al. LC 85-9553. (Management Ser.). 808p. 1986. write for info. (ISBN 0-471-88059-0). Wiley.
Strategic Management: Text & Cases. Robert McGlashan & Timothy M. Singleton. 800p. 1987. text ed. 37.95 (ISBN 0-675-20100-4). Merrill.
Strategic Management: Text & Cases on Business Policy. La Rue T. Hosmer. (Illus.). 736p. 1982. write for info (ISBN 0-13-851063-6). P-H.
Strategic Management: Text, Tools, & Cases for Business Policy. Ed. by Robert A. Comerford & Dennis W. Callaghan. LC 84-27827. 866p. 1985. text ed. 33.00 (ISBN 0-534-04518-9). PWS Kent Pub.
Strategic Managing of Human Resources. John Douglas et al. LC 84-17419. (Management Ser.: I-309). 619p. 1985. text ed. write for info. (ISBN 0-471-05315-5); study guide avail. (ISBN 0-471-89128-2); student manual avail. (ISBN 0-471-81815-1). Wiley.
Strategic Market Decisions: A Reader. Keith K. Cox & Vern J. McGinnis. (Illus.). 416p. 1982. pap. text ed. write for info. (ISBN 0-13-851022-9). P-H.
Strategic Market Management. 2nd ed. David A. Aaker. LC 87-31794. 364p. 1988. write for info. (ISBN 0-471-85262-7). Wiley.
Strategic Market Planning. Ed. by Fred S. Rosenau. LC 82-81837. 25.00 (ISBN 0-942774-05-1). Info Indus.
Strategic Market Planning: An Aid to the Evaluation of an Athletic Recreation Program. Earle F. Zeigler & John Cambell. (Stipes Monograph Series on Sport & Physical Education Management). 35p. (Orig.). 1984. pap. text ed. 3.00x. Stipes.
Strategic Market Planning: Problems & Analytical Approaches. Derek F. Abell & John Hammond. 1979. text ed. 42.00 (ISBN 0-13-851089-X). P-H.
Strategic Marketing. Associated Equipment Distributors Staff. 48p. 1984. 25.00 (ISBN 0-318-19175-X). Assn Equip Distrs.
Strategic Marketing. John Cady & Robert Buzzell. 1986. text ed. write for info. (ISBN 0-316-12328-5). Scott F.
Strategic Marketing. 2nd ed. David W. Cravens. 1987. 36.95x (ISBN 0-256-03370-6). Irwin.
Strategic Marketing: A Handbook for Entrepeneurs & Managers. B. M. Bradway & M. A. Frenzel. LC 81-3638. 1982. text ed. write for info. (ISBN 0-201-00079-2). Addison-Wesley.
Strategic Marketing & Management. Ed. by Howard Thomas & David Gardner. LC 83-25902. 509p. 1985. 73.95 (ISBN 0-471-90423-6). Wiley.
Strategic Marketing Cases & Applications. 2nd ed. David W. Cravens & Charles W. Lamb, Jr. 1985. 35.95x (ISBN 0-256-03371-4). Irwin.
Strategic Marketing for Educational Institutions. Philip Kotler & Karen F. Fox. (Illus.). 496p. 1985. text ed. 35.00 (ISBN 0-13-851403-8). P-H.
Strategic Marketing for Electric Utilities. Clark W. Gellings & Dilip Limaye. LC 86-46138. 250p. 1987. text ed. 74.95 (ISBN 0-88173-037-8). Fairmont Pr.
Strategic Marketing For Libraries: A Handbook. Elizabeth J. Wood. LC 87-15022. (Greenwood Library Management Collection). 240p. 1988. lib. bdg. 37.95 (ISBN 0-313-24405-7, WMK/). Greenwood.
Strategic Marketing for Nonprofit Organizations: Cases & Readings. 4th ed. Philip Kotler et al. (Illus.). 400p. 1987. pap. text ed. write for info. (ISBN 0-13-851312-0). P-H.
Strategic Marketing for Nonprofit Organizations. 3rd ed. Philip Kotler & Alan Andreasen. (Illus.). 560p. 1987. 42.00 (ISBN 0-13-851205-1). P-H.
Strategic Marketing for Not-for-Profit Organizations: Program & Resource Development. Armand Lauffer. LC 83-49509. 384p. 1984. 25.95x (ISBN 0-02-918260-3). Free pr.
Strategic Marketing Management. Lester A. Neidell. 648p. 1983. text ed. write for info. (ISBN 0-02-386240-8). Macmillan.
Strategic Marketing Management in a Dynamic Environment. Denis F. Healy. LC 77-70998. (Monograph Ser.). 1977. pap. text ed. 11.50x (ISBN 0-8046-9207-6, Pub. by Kennikat). Assoc Faculty Pr.
Strategic Marketing: Planning, Implementation & Control. Barton A. Weitz & Robin Wensley. LC 83-4324. 512p. 1984. text ed. 25.75 (ISBN 0-534-00971-9). PWS Kent Pub.
Strategic Marketing: Techniques, Technologies & Realities in the Electronic Information Marketplace. Ed. by Leslie R. Chase & Robert Landers. 1985. pap. 59.95 (ISBN 0-942774-20-5). Info Indus.
Strategic Materials: A World Survey. Rae Weston. LC 84-3358. 198p. 1984. 34.50x (ISBN 0-86598-165-5, Rowman & Allanheld). Rowman.
Strategic Metals Investment Handbook: How to Profit from the International Scramble for Resources. Mitchell J. Posner & Philip Goldberg. 384p. 1985. pap. text ed. 8.95 (ISBN 0-07-050577-2). McGraw.
Strategic Military Surprise: Incentives & Opportunities. Klaus Knorr & Patrick M. Morgan. LC 82-2784. 265p. (Orig.). 1982. pap. 18.95 (ISBN 0-87855-912-4). Transaction Bks.
Strategic Mineral Dependence: The Stockpile Dilemma. Amos A. Jordan & Robert A. Kilmarx. (Washington Papers: Vol. VII, No. 70). 84p. (Orig.). 1979. pap. text ed. 7.95 (ISBN 0-8191-6017-2, Pub. by CSIS). U Pr of Amer.
Strategic Minerals: A Resource Crisis. Economics & National Security Council. (Illus.). 105p. 1980. pap. text ed. 12.95x (ISBN 0-87855-913-2). Transaction Bks.
Strategic Minerals & International Security. Ed. by Uri Ra'anan & Charles M. Derry. (IFPA Foreign Policy Reports Ser.: No. 2). (Illus.). 104p. 1985. pap. 9.95 (ISBN 0-08-033157-2, Pub. by P-B). Pergamon.
Strategic Minerals: The Economic Impact of Supply Disruptions. James T. Bennett & Walter E. Williams. 59p. 1981. pap. 3.00 (ISBN 0-317-47060-4). Heritage Found.
Strategic Minerals: The Geopolitical Problems for the United States. Ewan W. Anderson. 1988. price not set (ISBN 0-275-93062-9, C3062). Praeger.
Strategic Minerals, Vol. I: Major Mineral Exporting Regions of the World. W. C. Van Rensburg. (Illus.). 720p. 1986. text ed. 110.00 (ISBN 0-13-851387-2). P-H.
Strategic Minerals, Vol. II: Major Mineral Consuming Regions of the World. W. C. Van Rensburg. (Illus.). 1986. text ed. 110.00 (ISBN 0-13-851411-9). P-H.
Strategic Missile Defense: Necessities, Prospects, & Dangers in the Near Term. (Special Report of the Center for International Security & Arms Control, Stanford University). 26p. (Orig.). 1985. pap. 5.00 (ISBN 0-935371-13-3). ISIS.
Strategic Model of Chinese Checkers: Power & Exchange in Beijing's Interactions with Washington & Moscow. Peter Kein-hong Yu. LC 84-47538. (American University Studies X (Political Science): Vol. 4). (Illus.). 233p. (Orig.). 1984. text ed. 27.25 (ISBN 0-8204-0123-4). P Lang Pubs.
Strategic Monitoring for Urban Planning in Developing Countries: Some Guidelines from British & Dutch Experience. Ian Masser. (UNCRD Working Paper: No. 85-7). 20p. (Orig.). 1986. pap. text ed. 5.00 (ISBN 0-318-21379-6, CRD186, CRD). UNIPUB.
Strategic Newspaper Management. Conrad Fink. 416p. 1988. text ed. 29.95x (ISBN 0-8093-1333-2). S Ill U Pr.
Strategic Newspaper Management. Conrad C. Fink. 464p. 1988. pap. text ed. 26.00 (ISBN 0-317-58322-0, RanC). Random.
Strategic Nuclear Arms Control Verification: An Annotated Bibliography. Ed. by Richard A. Scribner & Robert T. Scott. 90p. 1985. pap. 7.50 (ISBN 0-87168-276-1). AAAS.
Strategic Nuclear Arms Control Verification Terms & Concepts: A Glossary. Richard A. Scribner & Kenneth N. Luongo. 42p. 1985. pap. 2.50 (ISBN 0-87168-273-7). AAAS.
Strategic Nuclear Targeting. Ed. by Desmond Ball & Jeffrey Richelson. LC 85-48195. (Studies in Security Affairs). (Illus.). 367p. 1986. 29.95x (ISBN 0-8014-1898-4). Cornell U Pr.
Strategic Nuclear Targeting. Ed. by Desmond Ball & Jeffrey Richelson. LC 85-4195. (Paperback Ser.). 367p. 1988. pap. 9.95 (ISBN 0-8014-9507-5). Cornell U Pr.
Strategic Nuclear War: What the Superpowers Target & Why. William C. Martel & Paul L. Savage. LC 85-9869. (Contributions in Military Studies: No. 43). (Illus.). 280p. 1986. lib. bdg. 36.95 (ISBN 0-313-24192-9, SNU/). Greenwood.
Strategic Options for the Early 1980s. Ed. by William R. Van Cleave & Scott W. Thompson. 200p. 1979. pap. 14.95 (ISBN 0-87855-798-9). Transaction Bks.
Strategic Organization Design. David A. Nadler & Michael L. Tushman. (Filley Ser.). 1988. pap. text ed. write for info. (ISBN 0-673-15860-8). Scott F.
Strategic Organization Planning: Downsizing for Survival. David C. Dougherty. 1989. 39.85 (ISBN 0-89930-339-0, DYS/, Quorum Bks). Greenwood.
Strategic Organizational Communication. Charles R. Conrad. 340p. 1985. text ed. 24.95 (ISBN 0-03-061669-7). HR&W.
Strategic Outlook & Alliances. Incl. Support Every Outbreak of Protest & Rebellion. 28p. 1981. 1.00 (ISBN 0-89851-052-X); Charting the Uncharted Course: Proletarian Revolution in the U. S. 18p. 1982. 0.50 (ISBN 0-89851-054-6); Coming From Behind to Make Revolution & Crucial Questions in Coming From Behind. 80p. 1981. 1.25 (ISBN 0-89851-048-1); You Can't Beat the Enemy While Raising His Flag. 15p. 1981. 0.50 (ISBN 0-89851-050-3); Bob Avakian Replies to a Letter from Black Nationalist with Communistic Inclinations. Bob Avakian. 18p. 1981. 1.00 (ISBN 0-89851-046-5); Break the Chains! Unleash the Fury of Women as a Mighty Force for Revolution. 1979. 1.00 (ISBN 0-89851-031-7). 32p. 5.00. RCP Pubns.
Strategic Partnering in Advanced Materials: An Evaluation of Leading-Edge Companies. 275p. 1987. spiral-bound vinyl 1200.00 (ISBN 0-914993-43-7). Tech Insights.
Strategic Perspectives on Planning Practice. Barry Checkoway. (Politics of Planning Ser.). 288p. 1986. 32.00x (ISBN 0-669-10366-7); pap. text ed. 14.95x (ISBN 0-669-14227-1). Lexington Bks.
Strategic Petroleum Reserve: Planning, Implementation, & Analysis. David L. Weimer. LC 82-6184. (Contributions in Economics & Economic History Ser.: No. 48). (Illus.). xvii, 229p. 1982. lib. bdg. 35.00 (ISBN 0-313-23404-3, WPO/). Greenwood.
Strategic Planning. Cuns. 64p. 1987. saddle stitch 10.95 (ISBN 0-8403-4210-1). Kendall-Hunt.
Strategic Planning. Clark Holloway. LC 85-25837. 382p. 1986. 25.95x (ISBN 0-8304-1070-8). Nelson-Hall.
Strategic Planning: A Fitness Program for Wholesaler-Distributors. James W. Norris et al. 1988. 55.00. Natl Assn Wholesale Dists.
Strategic Planning & Forecasting: Political Risk & Economic Opportunity. William Ascher & William H. Overholt. LC 83-10166. 311p. 1983. 39.95 (ISBN 0-471-87342-X, Pub by Wiley-Interscience). Wiley.
Strategic Planning & Leadership In Continuing Education: Enhancing Organizational Vitality, Responsiveness & Identity. Robert G. Simerly. LC 86-27382. (Higher Education Ser.). 1987. text ed. 25.95x (ISBN 1-55542-034-6). Jossey-Bass.
Strategic Planning & Management: A Review of Recent Experiences. Nagy Hanna. (Working Paper: No. 751). 100p. 1985. 5.00 (ISBN 0-8213-0597-2, WP 0751). World Bank.
Strategic Planning & Management Control Systems for Survival & Success. John C. Camillus. LC 85-40001. 272p. 1986. 29.00X (ISBN 0-669-10315-2). Lexington Bks.
Strategic Planning & Management Handbook. Ed. by William R. King & David I. Cleland. LC 86-9058. (Professional Books Ser.). (Illus.). 644p. 1986. 44.95 (ISBN 0-442-24731-1). Van Nos Reinhold.
Strategic Planning & Modeling in Property-Liability Insurance. J. David Cummins. 1984. lib. bdg. 47.50 (ISBN 0-89838-159-2, Pub. by Kluwer-Academic (Netherlands)). Kluwer Academic.
Strategic Planning: Concepts & Implementation Text, Readings & Cases. John K. Ryans, Jr. & William L. Shanklin. (Illus.). 240p. 1984. pap. text ed. write for info (ISBN 0-394-33946-0, RanC). Random.
Strategic Planning Concepts: The Insurance Application. J. D. Hammond. Ed. by National Underwriter Company. 24p. (Orig.). 1984. pap. text ed. write for info. (ISBN 0-87218-350-5). Natl Underwriter.
Strategic Planning: Contemporary Viewpoints. Marie Ensign & Laurie N. Adler. LC 85-1342. (Dynamic Organization Ser.). 231p. 1985. lib. bdg. 39.00 (ISBN 0-87436-448-5). ABC-Clio.
Strategic Planning: Development & Implementation. Melcher & Kerzner. 1988. pap. 34.95 (ISBN 0-8306-9310-6, 3010). TAB Bks.
Strategic Planning for Churches & Ministries. R. Henry Migliore. 1988. pap. 5.95 (ISBN 0-317-68142-7). Harrison Hse.
Strategic Planning for Cogeneration & Energy Management. Association of Energy Engineers Staff. Ed. by F. William Payne. LC 85-80321. 600p. 1985. text ed. 62.95 (ISBN 0-88173-008-4); pap. text ed. 38.00 (ISBN 0-88173-009-2). Fairmont Pr.
Strategic Planning for Colleges & Universities: A Systems Approach to Planning & Resource Allocation. John C. Merson & Robert L. Qualls. LC 79-66068. 79p. 1979. 10.00 (ISBN 0-911536-82-5). Trinity U Pr.
Strategic Planning for Computer Integrated Manufacturing. Richard K. Miller. (Illus.). 459p. 1986. binder 495.00 (ISBN 0-89671-084-X). SEAI Tech Pubns.
Strategic Planning for Computer Integrated Manufacturing. 459p. 495.00 (ISBN 0-317-65604-X). TBC Inc.
Strategic Planning for Electronic Banking. Dimitris N. Chorasfas. write for info. Butterworth Legal Pubs.
Strategic Planning for Exploration Management. Allen N. Quick & Neal A. Buck. LC 83-12710. (Illus.). 161p. 1984. 32.00 (ISBN 0-934634-66-1). Intl Human Res.
Strategic Planning for Human Resources. Steven M. Director. (Studies in Productivity: No. 42). 46p. 1985. pap. 39.00 (ISBN 0-08-029516-9). Work in Amer.
Strategic Planning for Independent Schools. Susan C. Stone. 1987. pap. 10.00 (ISBN 0-934338-58-2). NAIS.
Strategic Planning for Information Resource Management: A Multinational Perspective. Gad J. Selig. LC 83-4997. (Management Information Systems Ser.: No. 4). 271p. pap. 70.50 (2070311). Bks Demand UMI.
Strategic Planning for Information Systems. rev. ed. Robert V. Head. LC 82-80713. (Illus.). 178p. 1982. pap. 29.95 (ISBN 0-89435-054-4). QED Info Sci.
Strategic Planning for Library Managers. Donald E. Riggs. LC 82-73735. 152p. 1984. lib. bdg. 33.00x (ISBN 0-89774-049-1). Oryx Pr.
Strategic Planning for Magazine Executives. 2nd ed. Richard Koff. 1987. 59.95 (ISBN 0-918110-16-5). Folio.
Strategic Planning for MIS. Ephraim R. McLean & John V. Soden. LC 77-58483. 489p. 1977. 47.95x (ISBN 0-471-58562-9, Pub. by Wiley-Interscience). Wiley.
Strategic Planning for Mortgage Bankers. 19p. 1988. 12.50. Mortgage Bankers.
Strategic Planning for Positive CAD-CAM Results. Stark. 128p. 1987. 495.00 (ISBN 0-8247-7757-3). Dekker.
Strategic Planning for Public & Nonprofit Organizations: A Guide to Strengthening & Sustaining Organizational Achievement. John M. Bryson. LC 87-46341. (Public Administration Ser.). 335p. 1988. text ed. 24.95x (ISBN 1-55542-087-7). Jossey-Bass.
Strategic Planning for Smaller Business: Improving Corporate Performance & Personal Reward. David A. Curtis. LC 82-48171. 224p. 1983. 29.00x (ISBN 0-669-06011-9); pap. text ed. 15.00x (ISBN 0-669-09815-9). Lexington Bks.
Strategic Planning for Sponsored Projects Administration: The Role of Information Management. Keith Harman & Charles M. McClure. LC 85-9881. (Emerging Patterns of Work & Communications in an Information Age Ser.: No. 1). (Illus.). xiii, 279p. 1985. lib. bdg. 46.95 (ISBN 0-313-24931-8, MST/). Greenwood.
Strategic Planning for the Industrial Engineering Function. Jack Byrd, Jr. & L. Ted Moore. 288p. 1986. 34.95 (ISBN 0-442-26185-3). Van Nos Reinhold.
Strategic Planning for the Real Estate Manager. Ken Reyhons. 101p. (Orig.). 1984. pap. text ed. 12.00 (ISBN 0-317-17696-X, BK. 133). Realtors Natl.
Strategic Planning for Workplace Drug Abuse Programs. Thomas E. Backer. LC 87-1538. (DHHS Publication ADM Ser.). 68p. 1987. pap. 3.25 (ISBN 0-318-23762-8, 017-024-01337-4). USGPO.
Strategic Planning in Action: The Impact of the Clyde Valley Regional Plan 1946-1982. Ed. by Roger Smith & Urlan Wannop. 288p. 1985. text ed. 34.50x (ISBN 0-566-00782-7). Gower pub Co.
Strategic Planning in Business & Government. Michael H. Moskow. LC 78-23401. (CED Supplementary Paper). 1978. pap. 3.50 (ISBN 0-87186-241-7). Comm Econ Dev.
Strategic Planning in Education: A Guide for Policymakers. 13p. 1985. 7.00 (ISBN 0-318-18983-6). NASBE.
Strategic Planning in Emerging Companies. Steven C. Brandt. (Illus.). 192p. 1981. text ed. 21.75 (ISBN 0-201-00942-0). Addison-Wesley.
Strategic Planning in Energy & Natural Resources: Proceedings of the 2nd Symposium in Analytic Techniques for Energy, Natural Resources, & Environmental Planning, Philadelphia PA, 3-4 April, 1986. Ed. by B. Lev et al. (Studies in Management Science & Systems: No. 15). 340p. 1987. 105.25 (ISBN 0-444-70230-X, North Holland). Elsevier.
Strategic Planning in Health Care Management. William Flexner et al. LC 81-2488. 408p. 1981. text ed. 55.50 (ISBN 0-89443-298-2). Aspen Pub.
Strategic Planning in International Banking. Ed. by Paola Savona & George Sutija. LC 85-30327. 256p. 1986. 32.50x (ISBN 0-312-76433-2). St Martin.
Strategic Planning in London: The Rise & Fall of the Primary Road Network. Douglas Hart. Ed. by Urban & Regional Planning Advisory Committee. 239p. 1976. 26.00 (ISBN 0-08-019780-9). Pergamon.
Strategic Planning in Small Business. Charles R. Stoner & Fred R. Fry. 1987. write for info. (ISBN 0-538-07060-9, G06). SW Pub.
Strategic Planning: Kit & Flyer 108. 136p. 1984. 20.00 (ISBN 0-318-18196-7); members 10.00 (ISBN 0-318-18197-5). OMS.
Strategic Planning Management. Thomas H. Naylor. 156p. 1980. pap. 13.00 (ISBN 0-912841-15-X, 03). Planning Forum.
Strategic Planning, Marketing & Public Relations, & Fund-raising in Higher Education: Perspectives, Reading, & Annotated Bibliography. Cynthia C. Ryans & William L. Shanklin. LC 86-3871. 280p. 1986. 20.00 (ISBN 0-8108-1891-4). Scarecrow.
Strategic Planning Process for Hospitals. Joseph P. Peters. 200p. 1985. pap. 34.95 (ISBN 0-939450-46-1, 127126). AHPI.

Strategies for Getting An Overseas Job. Kenneth O. Parsons. LC 83-12186. 32p. (Orig.). 1983. pap. 3.50 (ISBN 0-87576-105-4). Pilot Bks.
Strategies for Getting the Job You Want Now. Curtis Casewit. LC 76-2079. 48p. 1976. pap. 2.50 (ISBN 0-87576-053-8). Pilot Bks.
Strategies for Growing Your Church. C. Wayne Zunkel. 112p. 1986. pap. 12.95 (ISBN 0-89191-344-0). Cook.
Strategies for Growth in Religious Life. Gerald A. Arbuckle. LC 86-17359. 240p. (Orig.). 1986. pap. 11.95 (ISBN 0-8189-0505-0). Alba.
Strategies for Helping Parents of Exceptional Children: A Guide for Teachers. Milton Seligman. LC 78-24764. (Illus.). 1979. 18.95 (ISBN 0-02-928420-1). Free Pr.
Strategies for Helping Severely & Multiply Handicapped Citizens. John G. Greer & Robert M. Anderson. LC 81-11499. (Illus.). 448p. 1982. text ed. 24.00x (ISBN 0-8391-1692-6, 1221). Pro Ed.
Strategies for Helping Students. Calvin D. Catterall & George M. Gazda. (Illus.). 416p. 1978. 43.75x (ISBN 0-398-03686-1). C C Thomas.
Strategies for Helping Victims of Elder Mistreatment. Risa S. Breckman & Ronald D. Adelman. (Human Service Guides Ser.: Vol. 53). 160p. 1988. pap. text ed. 12.95 (ISBN 0-8039-3094-1). Sage.
Strategies for Human Settlements: Habitat & Environment. Ed. by Gwen Bell. LC 76-5416. (Illus.). 195p. (Orig.). 1976. (Eastwest Ctr); pap. 3.95x (ISBN 0-8248-0469-4). UH Pr.
Strategies for Identifying Words: A Workbook for Teachers & Those Preparing to Teach. 2nd ed. Dolores Durkin. 1980. pap. 22.00 (ISBN 0-205-07229-1, 2372290). Allyn.
Strategies for Improved Management of Latin American Drylands. Ed. by J. A. Mabbutt. H. J. Schneider et al. 29p. 1981. pap. 7.50 (ISBN 92-808-0227-5, TUNU127, UNU). UNIPUB.
Strategies for Improving Race Relations: The Anglo-American Experience. Ed. by John W. Shaw et al. 256p. 1987. 47.50 (ISBN 0-7190-1789-0, Pub. by Manchester Univ Pr). St Martin.
Strategies for Improving Reading in Social Studies. Fred Green et al. 1979. pap. text ed. 9.95 (ISBN 0-8403-2098-1). Kendall-Hunt.
Strategies for Individualizing Instruction in Content Areas. Walter J. Lamberg & Richard Ballard. Ed. by Donald E. Smith. (Michigan Learning Modules Ser.: No. 13). 67p. (Orig.). 1980. pap. 4.50x (ISBN 0-914004-16-6). Ulrich.
Strategies for Insurance Coverages: Continuing Manual. Bernard J. Daenzer & William R. Feldhaus. looseleaf 487.00x (ISBN 0-930868-57-9). Merritt Co.
Strategies for Integrated Communications. R. Scantlebury. (Computer State of the Art Report, Series 12: No. 5). (Illus.). 275p. 1984. 350.00x (ISBN 0-08-028590-2). Pergamon.
Strategies for International Industrial Marketing: The Management of Customer Relationships in European Industrial Markets. Ed. by Peter W. Turnbull & Jean-Paul Valla. LC 85-29047. 336p. 1986. 49.00 (ISBN 0-7099-2494-1, Pub. by Croom Helm Ltd). Routledge Chapman & Hall.
Strategies for Joint Ventures. Kathryn R. Harrigan. LC 85-40110. 448p. 1985. 40.00x (ISBN 0-669-10448-5). Lexington Bks.
Strategies for Joint Ventures in the People's Republic of China. Ike Mathur & Chen Jai-Sheng. LC 87-7033. 208p. 1987. lib. bdg. 35.00 (ISBN 0-275-92354-1, C2354). Praeger.
Strategies for Keeping Your State's Workforce Employed: Lessons from England, Sweden, & West Germany. (State Legislative Reports: Vol,12 No. 1). pap. 5.00 (ISBN 1-55516-174-X). Natl Conf State Legis.
Strategies for Library Administration: Concepts & Approaches. Charles R. McClure & Alan R. Samuels. LC 81-12408. 451p. 1982. lib. bdg. 28.50 (ISBN 0-87287-265-3); pap. 19.50 (ISBN 0-87287-390-0). Libs Unl.
Strategies for Lifelong Learning. Ed. by Per Himmelstrup et al. 1981. 7.95 (ISBN 0-87060-025-7, DAG 1). Syracuse U Cont Ed.
Strategies for Macro-Projects: Challenges & Opportunities. Ed. by Mel Horwitch. 280p. Date not set. cancelled (ISBN 0-88730-140-1). Ballinger Pub.
Strategies for Managing Behavior Problems in the Classroom. Mary M. Kerr & C. Michael Nelson. 448p. 1983. text ed. 31.95 (ISBN 0-675-20032-6). Merrill.
Strategies for Managing Nuclear Proliferation: Economic & Political Issues. Ed. by Dagobert Brito & Michael D. Intriligator. LC 82-49525. 336p. 1983. 39.00x (ISBN 0-669-06442-4). Lexington Bks.
Strategies for Mobilizing Black Voters: Four Case Studies. Ed. by Thomas E. Cavanagh. (Orig.). 1987. pap. 8.95 (ISBN 0-941410-48-X). Jt Ctr Pol Studies.
Strategies for Motivation. (Study Units Ser.). 1977. pap. 9.00 (ISBN 0-89401-116-2). Didactic Syst.
Strategies for Natural Language Processing. Ed. by Wendy G. Lehnert & Martin H. Ringle. (Illus.). 560p. 1982. 49.95x; pap. text ed. 29.95 (ISBN 0-89859-266-6). L Erlbaum Assocs.
Strategies for Needs Assessment in Prevention. Ed. by Alex Zautra et al. LC 83-10861. (Prevention in Human Services Ser.: Vol. 2, No. 4). 133p. 1983. text ed. 27.95 (ISBN 0-86656-187-0, B187). Haworth Pr.
Strategies for New Churches. Ezra E. Jones. LC 75-36731. 1979. pap. 7.95 (ISBN 0-06-064184-3, RD 276, HarpR). Har-Row.
Strategies for Office Automation: Planning for Success in the Office of 1990. Walter A. Kleinschrod. 122p. 1985. 21.95 (ISBN 0-916875-02-4); pap. 14.95 (ISBN 0-916875-03-2). Admin Mgmt.
Strategies for Passing the Georgia Regents' Exam. 3rd ed. Joan Elifson & Belita Gordon. 249p. 1985. pap. text ed. 17.95x (ISBN 0-89892-035-3). Contemp Pub Co of Raleigh.
Strategies for Personality Research: The Observation Versus Interpretation of Behavior. Donald W. Fiske. LC 78-1150. (Social & Behavioral Science Ser.). (Illus.). 1978. text ed. 42.95x (ISBN 0-87589-373-2). Jossey-Bass.
Strategies for Policy Making. Starling. 1988. text ed. 37.00 (ISBN 0-256-05531-9). Dorsey.
Strategies for Political Participation. 3rd ed. Frank Kendrick & Theodore Fleming. 208p. pap. text ed. 13.25 (ISBN 0-8191-3319-1). U Pr of Amer.
Strategies for Price & Quantity Measurement in External Trade. 1987. pap. 7.00 (ISBN 92-1-161174-1, E.82.XVII.3). UN.
Strategies for Primary Health Care: Technologies Appropriate for the Control of Disease in the Developing World. Ed. by Julia A. Walsh & Kenneth S. Warren. xii, 330p. 1986. 35.00x (ISBN 0-226-87207-6). U of Chicago Pr.
Strategies for Private Sector Participation in the Provision of Transportation Facilities. Edward Beimborn et al. (Publications in Architecture & Urban Planning: R85-4). v, 18p. 1985. 5.00 (ISBN 0-938744-40-2). U of Wis Ctr Arch-Urban.
Strategies for Productive Motor Carrier Sales Management. Paul Preston. 237p. 1987. pap. 18.00 (ISBN 0-88711-108-4). Am Trucking Assns.
Strategies for Readers: A Reading Communication Text for Students of ESL, Bk. 1. Christine P. Casanave. (Illus.). 192p. 1986. pap. text ed. write for info (ISBN 0-13-850728-7). P H.
Strategies for Readers: A Reading Communication Text for Students of ESL, Bk. 2. Christine P. Casanave. (Illus.). 144p. 1986. pap. text ed. write for info (ISBN 0-13-850744-9). P H.
Strategies for Reading Success. Earl H. Cheek, Jr. & Martha D. Collins. 256p. 1985. pap. text ed. 19.95 (ISBN 0-675-20227-2). Merrill.
Strategies for Real-Time System Specification. Derek J. Hatley & Imtiaz A. Pirhai. (Illus.). 400p. (Orig.). 1987. pap. 45.00 (ISBN 0-932633-04-8). Dorset Hse Pub Co.
Strategies for Recovery in the Eighties. Oil Daily Staff. Ed. by Marvin E. Murphy. 258p. 1983. 36.95 (ISBN 0-317-40488-1). Oil Daily.
Strategies for Reducing Gasoline Consumption Through Improved Motor Vehicle Efficiency. (Special Report). 51p. 1976. 2.40 (ISBN 0-309-02557-5). Transport Res Bd.
Strategies for Research & Development in Higher Education: Proceedings of Educational Research Symposium Organized by the Council of Europe & the Research & Development Unit of the Chancellor of Swedish Universities, Gotesburg, Sweden, Sept 7-12, 1975. Educational Research Symposium Staff. Ed. by Noel Entwistle. 282p. 1976. pap. text ed. 28.50 (ISBN 90-265-0242-7, Pub. by Swets & Zeitlinger Netherlands). Hogrefe Intl.
Strategies for Research on the Interactions of Drugs of Abuse. Monique C. Braude & Harold M. Ginzberg. (DHHS Publication (ADM) 86-1453 National Institute on Drug Abuse Research Monograph: Series 68). (Illus.). 237p. 1986. pap. 6.50 (ISBN 0-318-21356-7, S/N 017-024-01296-3). USGPO.
Strategies for River Basin Management: Environmental Integration of Land & Water in a River Basin. Ed. by Jan Lundqvist & Ulrik Lohm. LC 85-18293. 1985. lib. bdg. 56.00 (ISBN 90-277-2111-4, Pub. by Reidel Holland). Kluwer Academic.
Strategies for School Improvement: Cooperative Planning & Organization Development. Daniel C. Neale et al. 288p. 1980. text ed. 33.95x (ISBN 0-205-06950-9, 2369508, Pub. by Longwood Div). Allyn.
Strategies for Second Language Acquisition. Florence Stevens. 256p. (Orig.). 1984. pap. 18.95 (ISBN 0-920792-39-1). Eden Pr.
Strategies for Selling Ethical Pharmaceuticals. 340p. 1984. 1550.00 (ISBN 0-86621-607-3, E679). Frost & Sullivan.
Strategies for Selling to Automotive Aftermarket. Frost & Sullivan, Inc. Staff. 360p. 1987. 1900.00 (ISBN 0-86621-799-1, A1619). Frost & Sullivan.
Strategies for Short-Term Testing for Mutagens-Carcinogens. Byron E. Butterworth. 160p. 1979. 69.00 (ISBN 0-8493-5661-X). CRC Pr.
Strategies for Success: An Effective Guide for Teachers of Secondary Level Slow Learners. Gloria Wilkins & Susanne Miller. 364p. 1982. pap. text ed. 24.95x (ISBN 0-8077-2701-6). Tchrs Coll.
Strategies for Success in Real Estate. Sam Young. 1983. pap. 16.95 (ISBN 0-8359-7080-9, Reston). P-H.
Strategies for Success in Small Business. Donald R. Armstrong. (Illus.). 1977. text ed. 10.00 (ISBN 0-918464-15-3). D Armstrong.
Strategies for Successful Teaching in Urban Schools: Ideas & Techniques from Central City Teachers. Gordon L. Berry. Ed. by R. Reed. LC 81-84973. (Orig.). 1981. 14.95 (ISBN 0-88247-642-4); pap. 9.95 (ISBN 0-88247-632-7). R & E Pubs.
Strategies for Successful Writing. James A. Reinking & Andrew Hart. (Illus.). 550p. 1986. text ed. write for info (ISBN 0-13-851460-7). P H.
Strategies for Successful Writing: A Rhetoric Reader & Handbook. James A. Reinking & Andrew W. Hart. (Illus.). 640p. 1988. text ed. write for info (ISBN 0-13-851339-2). P-H.
Strategies for Sunday School Growth. George A. Edgerly & Harold E. Crosby. LC 83-80404. (Sunday School Staff Training Ser.). 128p. (Orig.). 1983. pap. 2.50 (ISBN 0-88243-591-4, 02-0591). Gospel Pub.
Strategies for Supporting Local Institutional Development. Gerard Finin et al. (Special Series on Local Institutional Development: No. 7). 99p. (Orig.). 1985. pap. text ed. 7.50 (ISBN 0-86731-114-2). Cornell CIS RDC.
Strategies for Survival: A Gay Men's Health Manual for the Age of AIDS. Martin Delaney & Peter Goldblum. 190p. 1987. pap. 10.95 (ISBN 0-312-00558-X). St Martin.
Strategies for Survival: American Indians in the Eastern United States. Ed. by Frank W. Porter, III. LC 85-30189. (Contributions in Ethnic Studies Ser.: No. 15). 248p. 1986. 36.95 (ISBN 0-313-25253-X, PST/). Greenwood.
Strategies for Survival: Cultural Behavior in an Ecological Context. Michael Jochim. LC 81-7887. 1981. 21.50 (ISBN 0-12-385460-1). Acad Pr.
Strategies for Taking Tests. James Divine & Judy Divine. 1982. pap. 8.95 (ISBN 0-8120-2565-2). Barron.
Strategies for Teachers: Information Processing Models in the Classroom. reference ed. Paul D. Eggen et al. (Curriculum & Teaching Ser.). (Illus.). 1979. write for info. (ISBN 0-13-851162-4). P-H.
Strategies for Teachers: Teaching Content & Thinking Skills. 2nd ed. Paul D. Eggen & Donald P. Kauchak. (Illus.). 320p. 1988. text ed. price not set (ISBN 0-13-851577-8). P-H.
Strategies for Teaching. Anthony S. Jones et al. LC 79-20596. 249p. 1979. 17.50 (ISBN 0-8108-1257-6). Scarecrow.
Strategies for Teaching. Phil Sciortino & William K. Esler. (Illus.). 211p. 1988. pap. text ed. 18.95 (ISBN 0-89892-070-1). Contemp Pub Co of Raleigh.
Strategies for Teaching Handicapped Adolescents. Patrick J. Schloss & Cynthia N. Schloss. LC 84-7449. 272p. 1985. pap. 26.00x (ISBN 0-936104-47-3, 1286). Pro Ed.
Strategies for Teaching Nursing. 2nd ed. Rheba De Tornyay & Martha A. Thompson. LC 82-2786. 274p. 1982. pap. 16.00 (ISBN 0-471-04523-3, Pub. by Wiley Medical). Wiley.
Strategies for Teaching Nursing. 3rd ed. Rheba De Tornyay & Martha A. Thompson. LC 86-19060. 353p. 1987. pap. 18.95 (ISBN 0-471-01197-5). Wiley.
Strategies for Teaching Retarded & Special Needs Learners. 4th ed. Edward A. Polloway. 1988. pap. 28.95 (ISBN 0-675-20994-3). Merrill.
Strategies for Teaching Retarded & Special Needs Learners. 3rd ed. Edward A. Polloway et al. 528p. 1985. 28.95 (ISBN 0-675-20291-4). Additional supplements may be obtained from publisher. Merrill.
Strategies for Teaching the Composition Process. Carl Koch & James Brazil. LC 77-26325. 1978. pap. 6.95 (ISBN 0-8141-4751-8). NCTE.
Strategies for Teaching with Learning & Behavior Disorders. Bos & Vaughan. 1988. pap. text ed. 24.00 (ISBN 0-205-11389-3). Allyn.
Strategies for Teaching Young Children. 2nd ed. Judith Schickedanz & Mary York. (Illus.). 416p. 1983. write for info. (ISBN 0-13-851139-X). P-H.
Strategies for Technical Writing: A Rhetoric with Readings. Mary M. Lay. LC 81-6802. 308p. 1982. pap. text ed. 18.95 (ISBN 0-03-053636-7). HR&W.
Strategies for Technology-Based Competition: Meeting the New Global Challenge. Albert N. Link & Gregory Tassey. LC 86-45885. 160p. 1987. 29.00x (ISBN 0-669-14574-2). Lexington Bks.
Strategies for Telecommunications Management. Thomas B. Cross. 320p. 1984. Binder 200.00 (ISBN 0-923426-01-9). Cross Info.
Strategies for the Nineteen Eighties: Lessons of Cuba, Vietnam & Afghanistan. Philip Van Slyck. LC 81-4627. (Studies in Freedom: No. 1). 104p. 1981. lib. bdg. 35.00 (ISBN 0-313-22975-9, VAS/); text ed. 19.95 (ISBN 0-317-43257-5). Greenwood.
Strategies for the Options Trader. Claud E. Cleeton. LC 78-11230. 172p. 1979. 42.95 (ISBN 0-471-04973-5, Pub. by Wiley-Interscience). Wiley.
Strategies for Theory Construction in Nursing. Lorraine O. Walker & Kay C. Avant. 208p. 1983. 19.95 (ISBN 0-8385-8686-4). Appleton & Lange.
Strategies for Vertical Integration. Kathryn R. Harrigan. LC 83-47513. 400p. 1983. 35.00x (ISBN 0-669-06694-X). Lexington Bks.
Strategies in Broadcast & Cable Promotion. Susan T. Eastman & Robert A. Klein. (Illus.). 355p. Date not set. pap. text ed. 17.95x (ISBN 0-88133-366-2). Waveland Pr.
Strategies in Business Communication. William J. Christen et al. (Illus.). 192p. 1981. pap. text ed. write for info (ISBN 0-13-851220-5). P-H.
Strategies in Clinical Hematology. Ed. by R. Gross. (Recent Results in Cancer Research Ser.: Vol. 69). (Illus.). 1979. 32.00 (ISBN 0-387-09578-0). Springer-Verlag.
Strategies in Genetic Counseling: The Challenge of the Future. Ed. by Susie Ball. 216p. 1988. 29.95x (ISBN 0-89885-388-5). Human Sci Pr.
Strategies in Global Competition. Ed. by Neil Hood & Jan-Erik Vahlne. 432p. 1988. lib. bdg. 65.00 (ISBN 0-7099-3796-2, Pub. by Croom Helm UK). Routledge Chapman & Hall.
Strategies in Gynecologic Surgery. Ed. by H. J. Buchsbaum & L. A. Walton. (Clinical Perspectives in Obstetrics & Gynecology Ser.). (Illus.). 256p. 1986. 65.00 (ISBN 0-387-96278-6). Springer-Verlag.
Strategies in Hospital Materiel Management: Case Analysis & Masterplanning. Charles E. Housley. LC 82-20620. 602p. 1982. 79.95 (ISBN 0-89443-668-6). Aspen Pub.
Strategies in Humanistic Education, 3 vols. Tim Timmermann & Jim Ballard. LC 75-25394. (Mandala Series in Education). 592p. 1976. Vol. 1. pap. 9.95 (ISBN 0-916250-03-2); Vol. 2. pap. 9.95 (ISBN 0-8290-0434-3); Vol. 3. pap. 9.95 (ISBN 0-916250-25-3). Irvington.
Strategies in Interlanguage Communication. Ed. by Claus Faerch & Gabriele Kasper. (Applied Linguistics & Language Study). 240p. (Orig.). 1983. pap. text ed. 14.95 (ISBN 0-582-55373-3). Longman.
Strategies in Occupational Safety & Health for Neighborhood Legal Services. Carol Oppenheimer & Deborah Greenfield. 144p. 1981. 12.75 (31,837). NCLS Inc.
Strategies in Prose. 5th ed. Ed. by Wilfred A. Ferrell & Nicholas A. Salerno. LC 82-15501. 385p. 1983. pap. text ed. 16.95 (ISBN 0-03-059324-7). HR&W.
Strategies in Rural Economic Development: A Case Study in Five Philippine Villages. Orlando J. Sacay et al. 109p. 1971. pap. text ed. 4.00 (ISBN 0-942717-15-5). Intl Inst Rural.
Strategies in Teaching Greek & Latin: Two Decades of Experimentation. Ed. by Floyd Moreland. LC 81-18428. (American Philological Association Pamphlet Ser.). 1981. pap. 10.50 (ISBN 0-89130-556-4, 40 06 07). Scholars Pr GA.
Strategies in Teaching Reading: Secondary. R. Baird Shuman. 128p. 1978. pap. 7.95 (ISBN 0-8106-1716-1). NEA.
Strategies Internationales, Croissance et Dimension des Nations. (Economies et Societes Series P: No. 5). 1961. pap. 19.00 (ISBN 0-8115-0773-4). Kraus Repr.
Strategies: Nurse Leaders' Role in Shaping Health Care. Ed. by Barbara B. Minckley & Lu Ann Young. 125p. (Orig.). 1984. pap. cancelled (ISBN 0-942146-08-5). Midwest Alliance Nursing.
Strategies of Action for Strengthening the Associated Schools Project in A & P. 129p. (Orig.). 1987. pap. text ed. 12.50 (ISBN 0-317-66952-4, UB361, UB). UNIPUB.
Strategies of British India: Britain, Iran, & Afghanistan, 1798-1850. M. E. Yapp. (Illus.). 1980. 98.00x (ISBN 0-19-822481-8). Oxford U Pr.
Strategies of Community Organization. 4th ed. Ed. by Fred M. Cox et al. LC 86-63526. 550p. 1987. pap. text ed. 23.95 (ISBN 0-87581-321-6). Peacock Pubs.
Strategies of Containment: A Critical Appraisal of Postwar American National Security Policy. John L. Gaddis. LC 81-772. 1982. 29.95x (ISBN 0-19-502944-5); pap. 10.95 (ISBN 0-19-503097-4). Oxford U Pr.
Strategies of Curriculum Development: The Works of Virgil E. Herrick. Virgil E. Herrick. Ed. by James Macdonald & Dan W. Andersen. LC 74-1781. 196p. 1975. Repr. of 1965 ed. lib. bdg. 35.00x (ISBN 0-8371-7400-7, HECD). Greenwood.
Strategies of Discourse Comprehension. Tuen A. Van Dijk & Walter Kintsch. LC 82-22671. (Monograph). 1983. 45.50 (ISBN 0-12-712050-5). Acad Pr.
Strategies of Educational Research: Qualitative Methods. Ed. by Robert G. Burgess. 336p. 1985. text ed. 38.00x (ISBN 1-85000-033-6, Falmer Pr); pap. text ed. 22.00x (ISBN 1-85000-034-4, Falmer Pr). Taylor & Francis.
Strategies of Industrialisation in the Developing Countries. Gyorgy Cukor. LC 73-89996. 288p. 1974. 26.00 (ISBN 0-312-76440-5). St Martin.
Strategies of International Mass Retailers. Charles Waldman. LC 78-19467. (Praeger Special Studies). 176p. 1978. 42.95 (ISBN 0-275-90319-2, C0319). Praeger.
Strategies of Intervention with Public Offenders. Ed. by Sol Chaneles. LC 82-15383. (Journal of Offender Counseling, Services & Rehabilitation Ser.: Vol. 6, Nos. 1-2). 137p. 1982. pap. text ed. 14.95 (ISBN 0-86656-171-4, B171). Haworth Pr.

Strategy of Computer Selection. Frederick T. Kelly & Peter J. Poggi. (Illus.). 1983. pap. text ed. 27.00 (ISBN 0-8359-7067-1, Reston). P-H.

Strategy of Conflict. Thomas C. Schelling. LC 60-11560. (Illus.). 1960. 22.95x (ISBN 0-674-84030-5); pap. text ed. 8.95x (ISBN 0-674-84031-3). Harvard U Pr.

Strategy of Decision: Policy Evaluation As a Social Process. David Braybrooke & Charles E. Lindblom. LC 63-13537. 1970. pap. text ed. 11.95 (ISBN 0-02-904610-6). Free Pr.

Strategy of Desire. Ernest Dichter. Ed. by Henry Assael & C. Samuel Craig. LC 84-46034. (History of Advertising Ser.). 314p. 1985. lib. bdg. 35.00 (ISBN 0-8240-6728-2). Garland Pub.

Strategy of Distribution Management. Martin Christopher. LC 84-18214. (Illus.). x, 192p. 1985. lib. bdg. 36.95 (ISBN 0-89930-114-2, CSD/, Quorum). Greenwood.

Strategy of Drug Design: A Guide to Biological Activity. William P. Purcell et al. LC 72-13240. pap. 38.00 (ISBN 0-8357-9983-2, 2055156). Bks Demand UMI.

Strategy of Economic Development. Albert O. Hirschman. (Encore Edition Ser.: No. 44). 218p. 1988. 40.00 (ISBN 0-8133-7419-7). Westview.

Strategy of Economy Development in the U. S. S. R. L. Abalkin. 228p. 1987. pap. 3.95 (ISBN 0-8285-3541-8, Pub. by Progress USSR). Imported Pubns.

Strategy of Electromagnetic Conflict. Ed. by Richard E. Fitts. 1979. Repr. of 1978 ed. 21.95 (ISBN 0-932146-02-3). Peninsula CA.

Strategy of Export-Led Growth. James K. Galbraith. (Working Paper Ser.: No. 43). 20p. 1988. 5.00. LBJ Sch Pub Aff.

Strategy of Ignorance: From Decision Logic to Evolutionary Epistemology. Soren Hallden. (Library Theoria: No. 17). 191p. (Orig.). 1986. pap. 57.50x (ISBN 91-87172-02-X). Coronet Bks.

Strategy of International Business. Maunuhal Singh. 240p. 1986. 19.00X (ISBN 81-7003-069-2, Pub. by South Asia Pubs). South Asia Bks.

Strategy of International Development: Essays in the Economics of Backwardness. Hans W. Singer. Ed. by Alec Cairncross & Mohinder Puri. LC 74-21810. Repr. of 1975 ed. 66.00 (2027624). Bks Demand UMI.

Strategy of Joy: An Essay on the Poetry of S. T. Coleridge. George H. Gilpin, Jr. Ed. by James Hogg. (Romantic Reassessment Ser.). 238p. (Orig.). 1972. pap. 15.00 (ISBN 0-317-40102-5, Pub. by Salzburg Studies). Longwood Pub Group.

Strategy of Life. Timothy Lenoir. 1982. 59.00 (ISBN 90-277-1363-4, Pub. by Reidel Holland). Kluwer Academic.

Strategy of Linguistics. Jan W. Mulder & Sandor G. Hervey. 256p. 1980. 17.50x (ISBN 0-7073-0248-X, Pub. by Scot Acad Pr). Longwood Pub Group.

Strategy of Marketing Research. Chester R. Wasson. LC 64-15387. (Illus.). 1964. 36.50x (ISBN 0-89197-426-1). Irvington.

Strategy of Meetings. George D. Kieffer. 1988. 17.95 (ISBN 0-317-66755-6). S&S.

Strategy of Peace in a Changing World. Arthur N. Holcombe. LC 67-27085. 1967. 24.50x (ISBN 0-674-84075-5). Harvard U Pr.

Strategy of Pitching Slow-Pitch Softball. 2nd ed. Michael Ivankovich. Ed. by Paul Johnson. (Illus.). 96p. 1987. pap. 8.95 (ISBN 0-9615843-4-3). Diamond Pr PA.

Strategy of St. Paul. Paul Campbell & Peter Howard. Orig. Title: Story of Effective Statesmanship. 85p. (Orig.). 1985. pap. 2.95 (ISBN 0-901269-69-7). Grosvenor USA.

Strategy of Satan. Warren W. Wiersbe. 1979. 4.95 (ISBN 0-8423-6665-2). Tyndale.

Strategy of Sea Power: Its Development & Application. Stephen W. Roskill. LC 80-27028. (Lees-Knowles Lecture Ser., Cambridge, 1961). 287p. 1981. Repr. of 1962 ed. lib. bdg. 35.00x (ISBN 0-313-22801-9, ROSSP). Greenwood.

Strategy of Service: Touching the Hurting & Needy of Your Community. June A. Williams. 112p. (Orig.). 1984. pap. 3.95 (ISBN 0-310-45761-0, 12046P). Zondervan.

Strategy of Social Choice. H. Moulin. (Advanced Textbooks in Economics Ser.: Vol. 18). 218p. 1983. 27.50 (ISBN 0-444-86371-0, North-Holland). Elsevier.

Strategy of Social Regulation: Decision Frameworks for Policy. Lester B. Lave. LC 81-7685. (Studies in the Regulation of Economic Activity). 166p. 1981. 26.95 (ISBN 0-8157-5162-1); pap. 9.95 (ISBN 0-8157-5161-3). Brookings.

Strategy of Soviet Imperialism: Expansion in Eurasia. Martin Sicker. LC 87-25882. 172p. 1988. lib. bdg. 37.95 (ISBN 0-275-92932-9, C2932). Praeger.

Strategy of the Dolphin. Dudley Lynch & Paul L. Kordis. (Illus.). 200p. (Orig.). 1988. pap. 29.95 (ISBN 0-945822-00-6). Brain Technologies.

Strategy of the Italian Communist Party. Donald Sassoon. 1981. 25.00x (ISBN 0-312-76478-2). St Martin.

Strategy of Trans-National Corporation. A. Z. Astapovich. 288p. 1983. 11.25x (ISBN 0-317-53793-8, Pub. by Collets (UK)). State Mutual Bk.

Strategy of Transnational Corporations. A. Z. Astapovich. 288p. 1983. pap. 3.95 (ISBN 0-8285-2601-X, Pub. by Progress Pubs USSR). Imported Pubns.

Strategy of Treaty Termination: Lawful Breaches & Retaliations. Arie E. David. LC 74-82748. 368p. 1975. 37.50x (ISBN 0-300-01718-9). Yale U Pr.

Strategy of Truth: A Study of Sir Thomas Browne. Leonard Nathanson. LC 67-18216. pap. 63.30 (ISBN 0-317-08080-6, 2020135). Bks Demand UMI.

Strategy of World Order, 4 vols. Ed. by Richard A. Falk & Saul H. Mendlovitz. Incl. Vol. 1. Toward a Theory of War Prevention. Frwd. by Harold D. Lasswell. pap. (ISBN 0-911646-01-9); Vol. 2. International Law. Frwd. by Wolfgang Friedmann. pap. 9.00 (ISBN 0-911646-02-7); Vol. 3. United Nations. Frwd. by Oscar Schacter. pap. 12.00 (ISBN 0-911646-03-5); Vol. 4. Disarmament & Economic Development. Frwd. by David Singer. pap. 10.00 (ISBN 0-911646-04-3). 1965. World Policy.

Strategy, Policy, & Central Management. 9th ed. William H. Newman et al. 1985. text ed. write for info. (ISBN 0-538-07500-7, G50). SW Pub.

Strategy, Politics & Defense Budgets. Warner R. Schilling et al. LC 62-17353. (Institute of War & Peace Studies). 1962. 40.00x (ISBN 0-231-02556-4). Columbia U Pr.

Strategy Process: Concepts, Contexts & Cases. James B. Quinn et al. (Illus.). 1040p. 1987. text ed. 43.00 (ISBN 0-13-850892-5). P-H.

Strategy, Risk, & Personality in Coalition Politics: The Case of India. Bruce Bueno de Mesquita. LC 75-3853. pap. 52.00 (ISBN 0-317-20837-3, 2024439). Bks Demand UMI.

Strategy, Structure & Economic Performance. Richard P. Rumelt. LC 86-278. (Harvard Business School Classics Ser.). 235p. 1986. pap. 12.95 (ISBN 0-87584-126-0, Dist. by Harper & Row Pubs., Inc.). Harvard Busn.

Strategy: The Logic of War & Peace. Edward N. Luttwak. LC 86-26975. 320p. 1987. 20.00 (ISBN 0-674-83995-1, Belknap Pr). Harvard U Pr.

Strategy to Revitalize the American Dream: Justice in Jeopardy. Albert B. Logan & Cheney William R. (Illus.). 260p. 1973. 8.95 (ISBN 0-398-02694-7); pap. 5.95 (ISBN 0-398-02764-1). NIJD Colorado.

Strategy Traps: And How to Avoid Them. Robert A. Stringer, Jr. & Joel Uchenick. LC 84-48444. 224p. 1986. 17.95 (ISBN 0-669-09362-9). Lexington Bks.

Strategy Without Slide Rule: British Air Strategy 1914-39. Barry D. Powers. 295p. 1976. 37.50 (ISBN 0-8419-5506-9). Holmes & Meier.

Stratemeyer Pseudonyms & Series Books: An Annotated Checklist of Stratemeyer & Stratemeyer Syndicate Publications. Ed. by Deidre Johnson. LC 81-23750. (Illus.). 343p. 1982. lib. bdg. 46.95 (ISBN 0-313-22632-6, JST/). Greenwood.

Stratford-On-Avon from the Earliest Times to the Death of Shakespeare. Sidney Lee. LC 71-109654. (Select Bibliographies Reprint Ser). 1890. 24.50 (ISBN 0-8369-5263-4). Ayer Co Pubs.

Stratford-on-Avon from the Earliest Times to the Death of Shakespeare. Sidney Lee. 1973. Repr. of 1890 ed. 20.00 (ISBN 0-8274-0318-6). R West.

Stratford to Dogberry: Studies in Shakespeare's Earlier Plays. John W. Draper. (Select Bibliographies Reprint Ser). 1961. 29.00 (ISBN 0-8369-5255-3). Ayer Co Pubs.

Stratford Upon Avon As It Was. Hendon Publishing Co., Ltd. Staff. 1986. 9.10x (ISBN 0-317-54181-1, Pub. by Hendon Pub UK). State Mutual Bk.

Strathcairn: A Novel, 2 vols. in 1. Charles A. Collins. LC 79-8257. Repr. of 1864 ed. 44.50 (ISBN 0-404-61832-4). AMS Pr.

Strathgallant. Laura Black. 1983. pap. 3.50 (ISBN 0-446-30318-6). Warner Bks.

Strathinver. Robin Bell. 1983. 30.00x (ISBN 0-86334-035-0, Pub. by Macdonald Pub UK); pap. 20.00x (ISBN 0-86334-036-9). State Mutual Bk.

Stratification & Organization: Selected Papers. Arthur L. Stinchcombe. (Studies in Rationality & Social Change). 350p. 1986. 42.50 (ISBN 0-521-32588-9). Cambridge U Pr.

Stratification, Class & Conflict. Irving Krauss. LC 75-12060. (Illus.). 1976. text ed. 15.95 (ISBN 0-02-917690-5). Free Pr.

Stratification: Leader Manual & Instructional Guide. Donald L. Dewar. (Advance Quality Circle Ser.). (Illus.). 42p. (Orig.). 1982. pap. 12.00 (ISBN 0-937670-18-9). Quality Circle.

Stratification: Member Manual. Donald L. Dewar. (Advance Quality Circle Ser.). (Illus.). 42p. (Orig.). 1982. pap. 8.00 (ISBN 0-937670-23-5). Quality Circle.

Stratification of a Tropical Forest As Seen in Dispersal Types. I Roth. (Tasks for Vegetation Science Ser.). 1986. lib. bdg. 130.00 (ISBN 90-6193-613-6, Pub. by Junk Pubs Netherlands). Kluwer Academic.

Stratification of Tropical Forests as seen in Leaf Structure. I. Roth. (Task for Vegetation Science). 1984. lib. bdg. 115.00 (ISBN 90-6193-946-1, Pub. by Junk Pubs Netherlands). Kluwer Academic.

Stratification: Socioeconomic & Sexual Inequality. Rae L. Blumberg. 128p. 1978. pap. text ed. write for info. (ISBN 0-697-07521-4). Wm C Brown.

Stratificational Grammar: A Definition & an Example. Geoffrey Sampson. LC 74-118282. (Janua Linguarum, Ser. Minor: No. 88). (Illus., Orig.). 1970. pap. text ed. 8.00x (ISBN 90-2790-712-9). Mouton.

Stratificational View of Linguistic Change. William M. Christie, Jr. LC 79-115787. (Edward Sapir Monograph Ser. in Language, Culture & Cognition: No. 4). viii, 71p. (Orig.). 1977. pap. 5.00x (ISBN 0-933104-04-9). Jupiter Pr.

Stratified Charge Engines. 190p. 1977. 35.00 (ISBN 0-85298-355-7, MEP-1). Soc Auto Engineers.

Stratified Charge Engines, Vol. 1. F. V. Bracco. 104p. 1973. pap. 58.00 (ISBN 0-677-05165-4). Gordon & Breach.

Stratified Charge Engines, Vol. 2. F. V. Bracco. 112p. 1976. pap. 68.00 (ISBN 0-677-05355-X). Gordon & Breach.

Stratified Flows. Chia-Shun Yih. LC 79-24817. 1980. 39.50 (ISBN 0-12-771050-7). Acad Pr.

Stratified Mappings: Structure & Triangulability. A. Verona. (Lecture Notes in Mathematics Ser.: Vol. 1102). ix, 160p. 1984. pap. 14.00 (ISBN 0-387-13898-6). Springer-Verlag.

Stratified Morse Theory. M. Goresky & R. Macpherson. (Ergebnisse, 3 Folge Ser.: Vol. 14). 290p. 1987. 75.00 (ISBN 0-387-17300-5). Springer-Verlag.

Stratified Polyhedra. D. A. Stone. LC 77-187427. (Lecture Notes in Mathematics: Vol. 252). 193p. 1972. pap. 15.00 (ISBN 0-387-05726-9). Springer-Verlag.

Stratigraphic Atlas: North & Central America. T. D. Cook. 1977. 73.50x (ISBN 0-691-08189-1); spiral bdg 26.50x (ISBN 0-691-08193-X). Princeton U Pr.

Stratigraphic Correlation Between Sedimentary Basins of the ESCAP Regions, Vol. IX: Proceedings of the Fourth Working Group Meeting, 1982. (Mineral Resources Development Ser.: No. 51). 82p. 11.50 (ISBN 92-1-119244-7, E.85.II.F.8). UN.

Stratigraphic Correlation Between Sedimentary Basins of the ESCAP Region: ESCAP Atlas of Stratigraphy Four. Peoples Republic of China, Vol. X. (Mineral Resources Development Ser.: No.52). 83p. 11.50 (E.85.II.F.13). UN.

Stratigraphic Correlation Between Sedimentary Basins of the ESCAP Region: ESCAP Atlas of Stratigraphy V - Republic of Korea, Vol. XI. (Mineral Resources Development Ser.: No. 53). 34p. 8.00 (ISBN 92-1-119406-7, E.86.II.F.5). UN.

Stratigraphic, Paleontologic, & Paleoenvironmental Analysis of the Upper Cretaceous Rocks of Cimarron County, Northwestern Oklahoma. Erle G. Kauffman et al. LC 76-47800. (Memoir Ser.: No. 149). (Illus.). 1977. 15.20 (ISBN 0-8137-1149-5). Geol Soc.

Stratigraphic Record of the Neogene Globorotalidradiation (Planktonic Foraminiferida) Richard Cifelli & George Scott. LC 84-600360. (Smithsonian Contributions to Paleobiology: No. 58). pap. 26.30 (2027135). Bks Demand UMI.

Stratigraphic, Tectonic, Thermal, & Diagenetic Histories of the Monterry Formation, Pismo & Huasna Basin, California. (Guidebook Ser.: No. 2). 96p. 1984. pap. 14.00 (ISBN 0-918985-44-7). SEPM.

Stratigraphic Type Oil Fields, 2 vols. Arville I. Levorsen. 1976. lib. bdg. 250.00 (ISBN 0-8490-2694-6). Gordon Pr.

Stratigraphical Index of British Ostracoda: Geological Journal Special Issue, Vol. 8. Ed. by Raymond H. Bate & Eric Robinson. (Liverpool Geological Society & the Manchester Geological Association Ser.). 552p. 1980. 195.00x (ISBN 0-471-27755-X, Pub. by Wiley-Interscience). Wiley.

Stratigraphical Index of Calcareous Nannofossils. Ed. by A. R. Lord. (British Micropalaeontological Society Series). 192p. 1982. 95.00x (ISBN 0-470-27338-0). Halsted Pr.

Stratigraphical Index of Conodonts. Ed. by A. C. Higgins & R. L. Austin. (Geology Ser.). 1985. 62.95 (ISBN 0-470-20232-7). Halsted Pr.

Stratigraphy. Roy R. Lemon. 640p. 1988. 37.95 (ISBN 0-675-20537-9). Merrill.

Stratigraphy & Archaeology of Ventana Cave. new ed. Emil W. Haury. LC 51-802. (Illus.). xxvii, 599p. 1975. 22.50x (ISBN 0-8165-0536-5). U of Ariz Pr.

Stratigraphy & Depositional History of the Star Peak Group (Triassic) Northwestern Nevada. K. M. Nichols & N. J. Silberling. LC 77-89753. (Special Paper: No. 178). (Illus.). 1977. pap. 6.20 (ISBN 0-8137-2178-4). Geol Soc.

Stratigraphy & Foraminifera of the Satsop River Area, Southern Olympic Peninsula, Washington. Weldon W. Rau. (Bulletin Ser.: No. 53). (Illus.). 66p. 1966. 1.50 (ISBN 0-686-34706-4). WA Div Geol.

Stratigraphy & Genera of Calcareous Foraminifera of the Fraileys Facies (Mississippian) of Central Kentucky see Bulletins of American Paleontology.

Stratigraphy & Glacial-Marine Sediments of the Amerasian Basin, Central Arctic Ocean. David L. Clark. LC 80-65270. (Geological Society of America Special Papers: No. 181). pap. 23.80 (ISBN 0-317-27883-5, 2025453). Bks Demand UMI.

Stratigraphy & Hydrocarbon Geology of the North Sea. C. Deegan & D. Pegrum. 1987. 84.59 (ISBN 0-86010-542-3). Graham & Trotman.

Stratigraphy & Life History. Marshall Kay & Edwin H. Colbert. LC 64-20072. pap. 160.00 (ISBN 0-317-28755-9, 2055486). Bks Demand UMI.

Stratigraphy & Paleobotany of the Golden Valley Formation (Early Tertiary) of Western North Dakota. Leo J. Hickey. LC 76-50970. (Memoir: No. 150). (Illus.). 1977. 21.00 (ISBN 0-8137-1150-9). Geol Soc.

Stratigraphy & Paleontology of the Brownsport Formation (Silurian) of Western Tennessee. Thomas W. Amsden. 1949. 85.00x (ISBN 0-686-50033-4). Elliots Bks.

Stratigraphy & Paleontology of the Maquoketa Group (Upper Ordovician) at Wequiock Creek, Eastern Wisconsin. Paul A. Sivon. (Contributions in Biology & Geology Ser.: No. 35). 45p. 1980. 3.50. Milwaukee Pub Mus.

Stratigraphy & Sedimentation. 2nd ed. William C. Krumbein & L. L. Sloss. LC 61-11422. (Illus.). 660p. 1963. 35.95 (ISBN 0-7167-0219-3). W H Freeman.

Stratigraphy & Uranium Deposits, Lisbon Valley District, San Juan County, Utah. G. C. Huber. Ed. by Jon W. Raese. LC 80-18873. (CSM Quarterly Ser.: Vol. 75, No. 2). (Illus.). 45p. (Orig.). 1980. pap. 8.00 (ISBN 0-686-63163-3). Colo Sch Mines.

Stratigraphy of Eocene Rocks in a Part of King County, Washington. James D. Vine. (Report of Investigations Ser.: No. 21). (Illus.). 20p. 1962. 0.50 (ISBN 0-686-34728-5). WA Div Geol.

Stratigraphy of the British Isles. 2nd ed. Dorothy H. Rayner. LC 79-8523. (Illus.). 400p. 1981. 77.00 (ISBN 0-521-23452-2). Cambridge U Pr.

Stratigraphy of the Pre-Simpson Paleozoic Subsurface Rocks of Texas & Southeast New Mexico, 2 Vols. V. E. Barnes et al. (Pub. Ser.: 5924). (Illus.). 836p. 1959. 7.75 (ISBN 0-318-03311-9). Bur Econ Geology.

Stratigraphy: Proceedings of the 27th International Geological Congress, Vol. 1. International Geological Congress Staff. 388p. 1984. lib. bdg. 88.50x (ISBN 90-6764-010-7). Coronet Bks.

Stratonikeia in Caria. M. Cetin Sahin. (Illus.). 53p. 1980. pap. 5.00 (ISBN 0-89005-266-2). Ares.

Stratospheric Aerosol Layer. Ed. by R. C. Whitten. (Topics in Current Physics Ser.: Vol. 28). (Illus.). 152p. 1982. 28.00 (ISBN 0-387-11229-4). Springer-Verlag.

Stratospheric & Mesopheric Circulation. A. L. Kats. 172p. 1970. text ed. 44.00x (ISBN 0-7065-0736-3, Pub. by Keter Pub Jerusalem). Coronet Bks.

Stratospheric Circulation. Ed. by Willis L. Webb. (Progress in Astronautics & Aeronautics: Vol. 22). 1969. 24.00 (ISBN 0-12-535122-4). Acad Pr.

Stratospheric Circulation, PAAS22. Ed. by W. L. Webb. LC 64-103. (Illus.). 600p. 1969. 49.50 (ISBN 0-317-36812-5). AIAA.

Stratospheric Ozone & Man, Vol. I: Stratospheric Ozone. Ed. by Frank A. Bower & Richard B. Ward. 232p. 1981. 89.00 (ISBN 0-8493-5753-5). CRC Pr.

Stratospheric Ozone & Man, Vol. II: Man's Interactions & Concerns. Ed. by Frank A. Bower & Richard B. Ward. 280p. 1981. 95.00 (ISBN 0-8493-5755-1). CRC Pr.

Stratospheric Ozone Reduction, Solar Ultraviolet Radiation & Plant Life. Ed. by R. C. Worrest & M. M. Caldwell. (NATO ASI Series, Series G: Ecological Sciences: No. 8). ix, 374p. 1986. 72.00 (ISBN 0-387-13875-7). Springer-Verlag.

Stratplan: A Participant's Guide. Roy W. Hinton & Daniel C. Smith. (Illus.). 144p. 1986. pap. write for info. (ISBN 0-13-851429-1). P-H.

Stratum Corneum. Ed. by R. Marks & G. Plewig. (Illus.). 300p. 1983. pap. 42.00 (ISBN 0-387-11704-0). Springer-Verlag.

Strauss' Air Pollution Control, Vol. 4. Jennifer Strauss. Ed. by Gordon Bragg. LC 79-28773. (Environmental Science & Technology: A Wiley-Interscience Series of Texts & Monographs). 356p. 1981. 79.00x (ISBN 0-471-07957-X, Pub. by Wiley-Interscience). Wiley.

Strauss' & Sayles' Behavioral Stategies for Managers. Leonard Sayles & George Strauss. 304p. 1980. text ed. write for info. (ISBN 0-13-791459-8). P-H.

Strauss-Rolland Correspondence. Ed. by Rollo Myers. 9.95 (ISBN 0-7145-0502-1); pap. 4.95 (ISBN 0-7145-0503-X). Riverrun NY.

Stravinsky. Ernest Ansermet. Tr. by Louise Guiney. (Performing Arts Ser.). (Illus.). 1982. 20.00 (ISBN 0-933806-08-6). Black Swan CT.

Stravinsky. Andre Boucourechliev. Tr. by Martin Cooper from Fr. LC 86-33488. 336p. 1987. 45.00 (ISBN 0-8419-1058-8); pap. 24.50 (ISBN 0-8419-1162-2). Holmes & Meier.

Stravinsky. Kenneth McLeish & Vallerie McLeish. (Composers & Their World Ser.). (Illus.). 90p. (YA) (gr. 9-12). 1983. 9.95 (Pub. by W Heinemann Ltd). David & Charles.

Stravinsky. Francis Routh. (Master Musicians Ser.: M-172). (Illus.). 1978. Littlefield.

Stravinsky. Francis Routh. (Master Musicians Ser.). (Illus.). 240p. 1975. text ed. 17.95x (ISBN 0-460-03138-4, BKA 01702, Pub. by J. M. Dent England). Biblio Dist.

Stravinsky. Robert Siohan. Tr. by Eric W. White. LC 76-94088. (Illus.). 192p. 1970. 15.00 (ISBN 0-670-67808-2); pap. 7.50x (ISBN 0-670-67809-0). Vienna Hse.

Streams in the Desert Sampler. Charles E. Cowman. 128p. 1983. pap. 4.95 (ISBN 0-310-37651-3, 6881P). Zondervan.

Streams of Civilization: The Modern World to the Nuclear Age, Vol. 2. Robert G. Clouse & Richard V. Pierard. LC 78-17811. (Illus.). (gr. 7-12). 1980. text ed. 14.95x (ISBN 0-915134-45-4); Tchrs Guide. pap. 3.95x (ISBN 0-915134-47-0). Mott Media.

Streams of Experience: Reflections on the History & Philosophy of American Culture. John J. McDermott. LC 85-16494. 296p. 1986. lib. bdg. 25.00x (ISBN 0-87023-496-X). U of Mass Pr.

Streams of Experience: Reflections on the History & Philosophy of American Culture. John J. McDermott. LC 85-16494. 296p. (Orig.). 1987. pap. 12.95 (ISBN 0-87023-597-4). U of Mass Pr.

Streams of Idealism & Health Care Innovation: An Assessment of Service Learning & Community Mobilization. Richard A. Couto. (Illus.). 1982. text ed. 18.95x (ISBN 0-8077-2724-5). Tchrs Coll.

Streams of Ocean. Aubrey De Selincourt. 1923. Repr. 15.00 (ISBN 0-8274-3527-4). R West.

Streams of Renewal. Peter Hocken. 288p. (Orig.). 1986. pap. 11.95 (ISBN 0-932085-03-2). Word Among Us.

Streams: Their Dynamics & Morphology. W. Morisawa. LC 68-12267. 1968. pap. text ed. 24.95 (ISBN 0-07-043123-X). McGraw.

Streams to the River, River to the Sea. Scott O'Dell. 176p. 1987. pap. 2.95 (ISBN 0-449-70244-8, Juniper). Fawcett.

Streams to the River, River to the Sea: A Novel of Sacagawea. Scott O'Dell. (YA) 1986. 14.95 (ISBN 0-395-40430-4). HM.

Strechting Turbo Pascal: Advanced Programming in the MS-DOS Environment. Kent Porter. 400p. 1987. pap. 21.95. Brady Comp Bks.

Street. Ann Petry. LC 85-47522. (Black Women Writers Ser.). 258p. 1985. pap. 8.95 (ISBN 0-8070-6357-6, BP699). Beacon Pr.

Street. Israel Rabon. Tr. by Leonard Wolf from Yiddish. 224p. 1985. Repr. of 1928 ed. 14.95 (ISBN 0-8052-3981-2). Schocken.

Street: An Autobiographical Novel. Aram Saroyan. 100p. 1974. pap. 5.00 (ISBN 0-912846-07-0). Bookstore Pr.

Street & Electric Railways. U.S. Census Office. LC 75-22867. (America in Two Centuries Ser). 1976. Repr. of 1903 ed. 18.00x (ISBN 0-405-07732-7). Ayer Co Pubs.

Street Art. Donald J. Davenport. (Illus.). 56p. 1982. pap. 15.00 trade manual saddle stitched (ISBN 0-9606640-0-9). D J Davenport.

Street Birth. Diana Bickston. (Prison Writing Ser.). 36p. 1982. pap. 2.00 (ISBN 0-912678-52-6). Greenfld Rev Pr.

Street Blues. T. A. Houlahan. 64p. 1986. 5.95 (ISBN 0-89962-472-3). Todd & Honeywell.

Street Cars of Boston: Closed Horse & Electric Cars to 1900, Vol. 1. O. R. Cummings. (Illus.). 92p. (Orig.). 1973. pap. 6.00 (ISBN 0-911940-18-9). Cox.

Street Children of Cali. Lewis Aptekar. LC 87-34234. (Illus.). 272p. 1988. lib. bdg. 38.50 (ISBN 0-8223-0834-7). Duke.

Street Cleaning Practice. 2nd ed. American Public Works Association, Street Sanitation Committee. (American Public Works Association Research Foundation Projects Ser.: No. 105). pap. 110.00 (ISBN 0-317-09892-6, 2015936). Bks Demand UMI.

Street Cleaning Practice. 3rd ed. APWA Research Foundation Staff. (Illus.). 1978. text ed. 28.00x (ISBN 0-917084-27-6). Am Public Works.

Street Club Worker. Jack Rudman. (Career Examination Ser.: C-1038). (Cloth bdg. avail. on request). pap. 12.00 (ISBN 0-8373-1038-5). Natl Learning.

Street Cop. 10/1986 ed. Michael C. Macdonald & John Bane, Jr. LC 86-60374. 200p. 16.95 (ISBN 0-933341-35-0). Quinlan Pr.

Street Corner Society: The Social Structure of an Italian Slum. 3rd ed. William F. Whyte. LC 81-10337. 1981. lib. bdg. 23.00x (ISBN 0-226-89542-4); pap. text ed. 9.00x (ISBN 0-226-89543-2). U of Chicago Pr.

Street Dance. Bill Kelly & Dolph Le Moult. 288p. (Orig.). 1987. pap. 3.95 (ISBN 0-441-79033-X, Charter Bks). Berkley Pub.

Street Directory of the Principal Cities of the United States: Embracing Letter-Carrier Offices Established to April 30, 1908. 5th ed. U. S. Post Office Department. LC 76-179692. 912p. Repr. of 1908 ed. 75.00x (ISBN 0-8103-3072-5). Gale.

Street Drugs: A Reference Guide to Controlled Substances. Carl L. Vidano. Ed. by Kenneth M. Goddard. (Illus.). 100p. (Orig.). 1986. pap. text ed. 10.95 (ISBN 0-9616606-0-0). C L Vidano Pub.

Street Economics. Rufus Shaw, Jr. 130p. (Orig.). 1984. pap. 10.50 (ISBN 0-936436-02-6). R S Publishing.

Street Family. Adrienne Jones. LC 85-45844. (Charlotte Zolotow Bks.). 288p. (YA) (gr. 7 up). 1987. 13.95i (ISBN 0-06-023049-5); PLB 13.89 (ISBN 0-06-023050-9). HarpJ.

Street Fighting Tactics From Karate-Do. Michael Rosenbaum. 96p. (Orig.). 1985. pap. 5.95 (ISBN 0-89826-015-9). Natl Paperback.

Street Fights. Joe Martori. Ed. by Toby Stein. 1987. 17.95 (ISBN 0-915643-24-3). Santa Barb Pr.

Street Fire. Daniel Halpern. LC 74-34025. Repr. of 1975 ed. 5.95. Small Pr Dist.

Street Food. Rose Grant. (Illus.). 192p. 1988. 20.95 (ISBN 0-89594-307-7). Crossing Pr.

Street French: How to Speak & Understand French Slang - a Self-Teaching Guide. David Burke. 304p. 1988. pap. 12.95 (ISBN 0-471-62876-X). Wiley.

Street Furniture Catalog. Ed. by Design Council. 192p. 1979. pap. 32.50x (ISBN 0-85072-082-6, Pub. by Design Council England). Intl Spec Bk.

Street Gangs. Sandra Gardner. (Single Titles Ser.). (Illus.). 128p. (YA) (gr. 7 up). PLB 12.90 (ISBN 0-531-04666-4). Watts.

Street Gangs: Yesterday & Today. James Haskins. (Illus.). (gr. 6 up). 1977. pap. 4.95 (ISBN 0-8038-6740-9). Hastings.

Street Gangs: Youth, Biker, & Prison Groups. James R. Davis. 160p. 1982. pap. text ed. 11.45 (ISBN 0-8403-2750-1). Kendall-Hunt.

Street Girl. Muriel Cerf. Tr. by Dominic Di Bernardi from Fr. 240p. 1988. 20.00 (ISBN 0-916583-33-3). Dalkey Arch.

Street Graphics. William Ewald & Daniel Mandelker. 175p. 1977. Repr. 15.00 (ISBN 0-318-14686-X); 10.50 (ISBN 0-318-14687-8). Landscape Architecture.

Street Graphics & the Law. 3rd ed. Daniel R. Mandelker & William R. Ewald, Jr. LC 87-71118. (Illus.). 225p. 1987. pap. 32.95 (ISBN 0-918286-50-6). Planners Pr.

Street Guide to Seattle Area Restaurants. Ed. by D. Craig Erken. 1985. 9.95 (ISBN 0-938047-00-0). Cedar River Pub.

Street-Hockey Lady. H. R. Sheffer. Ed. by Howard Schroeder. LC 80-29531. (Teamates Ser.). (Illus.). 48p. (gr. 3 up). 1981. PLB 7.95 (ISBN 0-89686-102-3). Crestwood Hse.

Street Hustler. Norman Rubington. 1975. pap. 1.50 (ISBN 0-685-57552-7, LB301DK, Leisure Bks). Leisure NY.

Street I Know. Harold Stearns. 1973. Repr. of 1935 ed. 25.00 (ISBN 0-8274-0875-7). R West.

Street in Marrakech. Elizabeth W. Fernea. LC 74-12686. 1976. pap. 7.95 (ISBN 0-385-12045-1, Anch). Doubleday.

Street in Moscow. Ilia G. Ehrenburg. Tr. by Sonia Volochova. LC 75-38496. (Soviet Literature in English Translation Ser.). (Illus.). 284p. 1977. Repr. of 1932 ed. 21.45 (ISBN 0-88355-400-3). Hyperion Conn.

Street in Petra. M. A. Murray & J. C. Ellis. (British School of Archaeology in Egypt Bks.). (Illus.). 38p. 1940. text ed. 17.50x (Pub. by Aris & Phillips UK). Humanities.

Street, Interurban & Rapid Transit Railways of the United States: A Selective Historical Bibliography. Thomas R. Bullard. (Illus.). 96p. (Orig.). 1984. pap. 10.00 (ISBN 0-911940-38-3). Cox.

Street Lavender. Chris Hunt. 288p. (Orig.). 1987. pap. 9.95 (ISBN 0-85449-035-3, Pub. by GMP England). Alyson Pubns.

Street Law. Jason Newman et al. (Course in Practical Law). (Illus.). 283p. (gr. 9-12). 1975. pap. text ed. 16.50 (ISBN 0-8299-1010-7); tchr's manual 16.50 (ISBN 0-8299-1011-5). West Pub.

Street Law: A Course in Practical Law. 2nd ed. Lee Arbetman et al. 365p. 1980. pap. text ed. 17.75 (ISBN 0-8299-1031-X). West Pub.

Street Law: A Course in Practical Law. 3rd ed. Edward T. McMahon et al. LC 85-26560. (Illus.). 446p. 1986. pap. text ed. 18.50 (ISBN 0-314-89283-4). West Pub.

Street Law: A Course in Practical Law: California Supplement. 2nd ed. Thomas A. Nazario. (Illus.). 80p. (gr. 9-12). 1984. pap. text ed. 19.75 (ISBN 0-314-84398-1). West Pub.

Street Law: A Course in Practical Law, with Florida Supplement. 2nd ed. Lee P. Arbetman et al. (Illus.). 480p. pap. text ed. write for info. (ISBN 0-314-63413-4). West Pub.

Street Law: A Course in the Law of Corrections. Jason Newman et al. 104p. 1976. pap. text ed. 7.50 (ISBN 0-8299-1013-1); tchr's ed 5.75 (ISBN 0-8299-1014-X). West Pub.

Street Law: New York Supplement. 2nd ed. Lee P. Arbetman & Edward T. McMahon. (Illus.). 441p. (gr. 9-12). 1982. 19.75 (ISBN 0-314-72084-7). West Pub.

Street-Level Bureaucracy: Dilemmas of the Individual in Public Services. Michael Lipsky. LC 79-7350. 275p. 1980. pap. 8.95x (ISBN 0-87154-526-8). Russell Sage.

Street Life in London. Adolphe Smith & John Thompson. LC 68-28169. (Illus.). 1968. Repr. of 1877 ed. 20.00 (ISBN 0-405-08982-1). Ayer Co Pubs.

Street Life in Medieval England. G. T. Salusbury-Jones. 1979. Repr. of 1938 ed. lib. bdg. 29.00 (ISBN 0-8495-4945-0). Arden Lib.

Street Light Inspections Foreman. Jack Rudman. (Career Examination Ser.: C-2961). 1988. pap. 14.00 (ISBN 0-8373-2961-2). Natl Learning.

Street Lighting: A Bibliography. Mary E. Huls. (Architecture Ser.: A 1655). 5p. 1986. 3.00 (ISBN 0-89028-985-9). Vance Biblios.

Street Lighting Installation Worker. Jack Rudman. (Career Examination Ser.: C-3108). 1988. pap. 14.00 (ISBN 0-8373-3108-0). Natl Learning.

Street Lighting Manual. 2nd ed. 186p. 1969. 7.50 (ISBN 0-317-34111-1, 046832). Edison Electric.

Street Literature in Great Britain & America: An Annotated Bibliography. Rainer Wehse. 250p. 1986. lib. bdg. 33.00 (ISBN 0-8240-8821-2). Garland Pub.

Street Map to Adobes, Bungalows, & Mansions of Riverside, California. Herbert L. Nickles & Michal J. Nickles. (Illus.). 1985. pap. 1.95x (ISBN 0-935661-13-1). Riverside Mus Pr.

Street Markets of London. L. Moholy-Nagy & Mary Benedetta. LC 72-84542. (Illus.). Repr. of 1936 ed. 33.00 (ISBN 0-405-08792-6, Pub. by Blom). Ayer Co Pubs.

Street Murals. Volker Barthelmeh. LC 82-80836. 1982. pap. 11.95 (ISBN 0-394-71196-3). Knopf.

Street of a Thousand Delights. facsimile ed. Jay Gelzer. LC 75-167449. (Short Story Index Reprint Ser.). Repr. of 1921 ed. 18.00 (ISBN 0-8369-3975-1). Ayer Co Pubs.

Street of Crocodiles. Bruno Schulz. (Writers from the Other Europe Ser). 1977. pap. 5.95 (ISBN 0-14-004227-X). Penguin.

Street of Ho's. Leo Guild. (Orig.). 1976. pap. 2.25 (ISBN 0-87067-025-5, BH025). Holloway.

Street of Mansions, No. 12. Dick Ferry. Ed. by Kerr Spooner. 23p. 1983. pap. 3.00 (ISBN 0-932884-11-3). Red Herring.

Street of No Return. rev. ed. David Goodis. LC 86-71911. 192p. 1988. pap. 3.95 (ISBN 0-88739-031-5, Pub. by Black Lizard). Creative Arts Bk.

Street of Queer Houses & Other Tales. David H. Keller. Ed. by R. Reginald & Douglas Menville. LC 75-46285. (Supernatural & Occult Fiction Ser.). 1976. Repr. of 1925 ed. lib. bdg. 18.00x (ISBN 0-405-08146-4). Ayer Co Pubs.

Street of the City. Grace L. Hill. 17.95 (ISBN 0-8488-0082-6, Pub. by Amereon Hse). Amereon Ltd.

Street of the Eye, & Nine Other Tales. facsimile ed. Gerald W. Bullett. LC 77-167444. (Short Story Index Reprint Ser). Repr. of 1923 ed. 18.00 (ISBN 0-8369-3970-0). Ayer Co Pubs.

Street of the Five Moons. Elizabeth Peters. 256p. 1987. pap. 3.50 (ISBN 0-8125-0766-5, Dist. by St Martin's Pr & Warner Pub Servs). Tor Bks.

Street of the Laughing Camel. Ben L. Burman. 4.95 (ISBN 0-685-20506-1). Taplinger.

Street of the Sun. Lance Horner. 1980. pap. 2.25 (ISBN 0-449-13972-7, GM). Fawcett.

Street or Pulpit? The Witness of Activist Monsignor Charles Owen Rice of Pittsburgh. Kenneth K. McNulty, Sr. (Answers Ser.). 288p. (Orig.). 1985. pap. 9.95 (ISBN 0-935025-00-6). Data & Res Tech.

Street Photographs of Roger Mayne. Intro. by Mark Haworth-Booth. (Illus.). 88p. (Orig.). 1986. pap. 10.95 (ISBN 1-85177-002-X). Faber & Faber.

Street Players. Donald Goines. 192p. (Orig.). 1973. pap. 2.25 (ISBN 0-87067-034-4, BH034). Holloway.

Street Poetry & Other Poems. Jesus P. Melendez. 80p. 1972. 12.95 (ISBN 0-87929-018-8). Barlenmir.

Street Power: Cultural & Politics in a Nicaraguan Neighbourhood. Stener Ekern. (Bergen Studies in Social Anthropology: No. 40). 240p. 1988. pap. text ed. 10.95x (ISBN 0-936508-70-1). Barber Pr.

Street Preachers, Faith Healers & Herb Doctors in Jamaica, 1890-1925. W. F. Elkins. (Caribbean Studies Ser). 1976. lib. bdg. 69.95 (ISBN 0-87700-241-X). Revisionist Pr.

Street Railway System of Philadelphia: Its History & Present Condition. Frederic W. Speirs. LC 78-63856. (Johns Hopkins University. Studies in the Social Sciences. Fifteenth Ser. 1897: 3-5). Repr. of 1897 ed. 11.50 (ISBN 0-404-61112-5). AMS Pr.

Street Railway System of Philadelphia: Its History & Present Condition. Frederic W. Speirs. Repr. of 1897 ed. 13.00 (ISBN 0-384-57013-5). Johnson Repr.

Street Railways of Birmingham. Alvin W. Hudson & Harold E. Cox. (Illus.). 216p. (Orig.). 1976. pap. 12.00 (ISBN 0-911940-25-1). Cox.

Street Railways of Harrisburg. Richard H. Steinmetz & Harold E. Cox. (Illus.). 96p. (Orig.). 1988. pap. 11.00 (ISBN 0-911940-44-8). Cox.

Street Railways of Louisiana. Louis G. Hennick & E. Harper Charlton. LC 76-30481. (Illus.). 143p. 1979. 19.95 (ISBN 0-88289-065-4). Pelican.

Street Railways of St. Petersburg, Florida. James Buckley. (Illus.). 48p. (Orig.). 1983. pap. 7.00 (ISBN 0-911940-37-5). Cox.

Street Railways of Trenton. Barker Gummere. (Illus.). 88p. (Orig.). 1986. pap. 10.00 (ISBN 0-911940-42-1). Cox.

Street Rod Buyer's Guide. Carl Hungness & Riley Tharp. 96p. 1985. pap. 4.95 (ISBN 0-915088-41-X). C Hungness.

Street Rodder's Handbook: How to Build a Street Rod. Frank Oddo. Ed. by Ron Sessions. LC 86-81201. (Illus.). 208p. 1986. pap. 14.95 (ISBN 0-89586-369-3, HP Bks). Price Stern.

Street Scenes: Afro-American Culture in Urban Trinidad. Michael Lieber. 120p. 1981. pap. 11.95. Schenkman Bks Inc.

Street Self-Defense. Don Sewalson. (Martial Arts Ser.: Vol. 1). (Illus.). 81p. (YA) (gr. 6-12). 1986. pap. 6.75 (ISBN 0-938419-01-3). DM Pub.

Street Self-Defense. Don Sewalson. (Martial Arts Ser.: Vol. 3). (Illus.). 63p. (YA) (gr. 6-12). 1986. pap. 6.75 (ISBN 0-938419-03-X). DM Pub.

Street Self-Defense. Don Sewalson. (Martial Arts Ser.: Vol. 2). (Illus.). 58p. (YA) (gr. 6-12). 1986. pap. 6.75 (ISBN 0-938419-02-1). DM Pub.

Street Self-Defense: Complete Edition. Don Sewalson. (Martial Arts Ser.). (Illus.). 193p. (YA) (gr. 6-12). 1986. 27.00 (ISBN 0-938419-04-8); pap. 16.95 (ISBN 0-938419-00-5). DM Pub.

Street Signs Chicago: Neighborhood & Other Illusions of Big City Life. Charles Bowden et al. (Illus.). 200p. 1981. 12.95 (ISBN 0-914091-05-0); pap. 7.95 (ISBN 0-914091-06-9). Chicago Review.

Street Smart Book. William Marsano. LC 84-27301. (Illus.). 64p. (gr. 4 up). 1986. 9.29 (ISBN 0-671-55035-7). Messner.

Street Smart Gun Book. John Farnum. 1986. pap. 11.95 (ISBN 0-936279-06-0). Police Bkshelf.

Street Smart Investing: A Price-Value Approach to Stock Market Profits. George B. Clairmont & Kiril Sokoloff. Date not set. pap. 8.95 (ISBN 0-394-72424-0, Vin). Random.

Street Smart Marketing. Levinson. 1988. pap. write for info. (ISBN 0-471-60874-2). Wiley.

Street Smart Real Estate Investing: Allen Cymrot's Strategies for Increasing Your Net Worth. Allen Cymrot. 220p. 1988. 19.95 (ISBN 1-55623-075-3). Dow Jones-Irwin.

Street Soldier's Handbook of Poetry. Rita C. Cordoze. 40p. 1987. 7.50 (ISBN 0-8062-3060-6). Carlton.

Street Song. Ann Charlton. (Harlequin Presents Ser.: No. 1008). 192p. Date not set. pap. 1.95 (ISBN 0-317-63755-X). Harlequin Bks.

Street Style: British Design in the 80's. Catherine McDermott. LC 86-43186. (Illus.). 172p. 1987. pap. 22.50 (ISBN 0-8478-0803-3). Rizzoli Intl.

Street Surface Railway Franchises of New York City. Harry J. Carman. LC 76-77998. (Columbia University Studies in the Social Sciences: No. 200). Repr. of 1919 ed. 20.00 (ISBN 0-404-51200-3). AMS Pr.

Street Survival: A Pratical Guide to Self Defense. Fumio Demura & Dan Ivan. LC 79-1946. (Illus.). 1979. pap. 11.50 (ISBN 0-87040-440-7). Japan Pubns USA.

Street Survival: Tactics for Armed Encounters. Ronald J. Adams et al. LC 79-57196. (Illus.). 416p. 1980. 25.95 (ISBN 0-935878-00-9). Calibre Pr.

Street Talk. Ann Turner. (gr. 3 up). 1985. 11.95. HM.

Street Talk in Real Estate. Bill W. West & Richard L. Dickinson. LC 86-50605. (Illus.). 217p. (Orig.). 1987. pap. 9.95 (ISBN 0-934189-01-3); pap. text ed. 9.95 (ISBN 0-934189-04-8). Unique Pub CA.

Street Talk: Notes from a Rescuer. Thom Dick. Ed. by Valla Howell. Ed. by Gary R. Williams. LC 88-80335. (Illus.). 192p. 1988. text ed. 15.95 (ISBN 0-936174-05-6). Jems Pub Co.

Street Theater. Doric Wilson. (JH Press Gay Play Script Ser.). (Illus.). 160p. (Orig.). 1983. pap. 6.95 (ISBN 0-935672-07-9). JH Pr.

Street Trees of Egypt. rev. ed. Loufty Boulos et al. (Illus.). 138p. 1988. 20.00 (ISBN 977-424-173-8, Pub. by Am Univ Cairo Pr). Columbia U Pr.

Street Vending in Washington, D.C. Reassessing the Regulation of a "Public Nuisance". Roberta M. Spalter-Roth & Eileen Zeitz. LC 85-240241. (Occasional Paper: No. 3). 50p. Date not set. 3.00. GWU CWAS.

Street Walkin' Ronal Charles. (Illus.). 120p. (Orig.). 1986. pap. 9.95 (ISBN 1-55630-020-4). Brentwood Comm.

Street Wars. Joseph Nazel. (Orig.). 1987. pap. 2.95 (ISBN 0-87067-284-3). Holloway.

Street Where I Live. Alan J. Lerner. (Illus.). 336p. 1980. pap. 5.95 (ISBN 0-393-00970-X). Norton.

Street Wisdom for Women: A Handbook for Urban Survival. Gerard Whittemore. LC 85-63395. 166p. 1986. pap. 10.95 (ISBN 0-933341-33-4). Quinlan Pr.

Street Without Joy. 4th ed. Bernard B. Fall. LC 64-23038. (Illus.). 408p. 1972. pap. 9.95 (ISBN 0-8052-0330-3). Schocken.

Street Woman. Eleanor M. Miller. LC 85-26133. (Women in the Political Economy Ser.). 1986. 24.95 (ISBN 0-87722-417-X). Temple U Pr.

Street Writers: A Guided Tour of Chicano Graffiti. Gusmano Cesaretti. (Illus.). 1975. pap. 9.95 (ISBN 0-918226-01-5). Acrobat.

Streetbird. Janwillem Van de Wetering. 288p. 1983. 13.95 (ISBN 0-399-12808-5, Putnam). Putnam Pub Group.

Streetbird. Janwillem Van de Wetering. pap. 3.50 (ISBN 0-671-47521-5). PB.

Streetcar Guide to Uptown New Orleans. Transitour, Inc. Ed. by Peter Raarup. (Illus.). 128p. 1982. pap. 7.95 (ISBN 0-88289-393-9). Pelican.

Streetcar Man: Tom Lowry & the Twin City Rapid Transit Company. Goodrich Lowry. LC 79-2584. (Books for Adults & Young Adults). (Illus.). (gr. 7 up). 1979. 7.95 (ISBN 0-8225-0764-1). Lerner Pubns.

Streetcar Named Desire. Tennessee Williams. 114p. 1984. pap. 3.50 (ISBN 0-451-14831-2, Sig). NAL.

Strengthening Informal Supports for the Aging: Theory, Practice, & Policy Implications. Marjorie H. Cantor & Sheila Kamerman. 59p. (Orig.). 1981. pap. 4.00 (ISBN 0-88156-007-3). Comm Serv Soc NY.
Strengthening Intergovernmental Management: An Agenda for Reform, a Special Report. 1980. 5.00 (ISBN 0-317-06623-4). Am Soc Pub Admin.
Strengthening Methods in Crystals. Ed. by A. Kelly & R. B. Nicholson. (Illus.). xii, 627p. 1971. 108.00 (ISBN 0-444-20105-X, Pub. by Elsevier Applied Sci England). Elsevier.
Strengthening of American Political Institutions. A. S. Monroney et al. LC 70-153232. (American Government & Politics Ser). 1971. Repr. of 1949 ed. 17.50x (ISBN 0-8046-1542-X, Pub. by Kennikat). Assoc Faculty Pr.
Strengthening of Ceramics. Kircher. (Manufacturing Engineering Ser.: Vol. 3). 1979. 65.00 (ISBN 0-8247-6851-5). Dekker.
Strengthening Regional Planning Capacities in Developing Countries. (Working Papers Ser.: No. 75-1). 26p. 1975. pap. 6.00 (ISBN 0-686-78502-9, CRD078, UNCRD). UNIPUB.
Strengthening State Departments of Education. Ed. by Roald F. Campbell. Gerald E. Sroufe & Donald H. Layton. LC 67-25738. 1967. pap. 4.00 (ISBN 0-931080-02-9). U Chicago Midwest Admin.
Strengthening Stepfamilies. Elizabeth Einstein & Linda Albert. 1986. complete program 89.50 (ISBN 0-88671-216-5). Am Guidance.
Strengthening Stepfamilies Leader's Guide. Elizabeth Einstein & Linda Albert. 1986. pap. 29.75 (ISBN 0-88671-218-1). Am Guidance.
Strengthening Teacher Education: The Challenges to College & University Leaders. C. Peter Magrath & Robert L. Egbert. LC 86-46336. (Higher Education Ser.). 1987. text ed. 22.95x (ISBN 1-55542-037-0). Jossey-Bass.
Strengthening the Adult Sunday School Class. Dick Murray. LC 81-3667. (Creative Leadership Ser.). 128p. (Orig.). 1981. pap. 7.95 (ISBN 0-687-39989-0). Abingdon.
Strengthening the Family. Wayne Rickerson. 128p. 1987. pap. 5.95 (ISBN 0-87403-206-7, 3186). Standard Pub.
Strengthening the Federal Budget: A Requirement for Effective Fiscal Control. (CED Statement on National Policy). 128p. (Orig.). 1983. 10.50 (ISBN 0-87186-777-X); pap. 8.50 (ISBN 0-87186-077-5). Comm Econ Dev.
Strengthening the International Monetary System: Exchange Rates, Surveillance & Objective Indicators. International Monetary Fund, Research Department. (Occasional Papers: No. 50). 84p. 1987. pap. 7.50 (ISBN 0-939934-76-0). Intl Monetary.
Strengthening the Legislative Process: An Agenda for Improvement. 32p. 1980. 5.00 (ISBN 1-55516-714-4). Natl Conf State Legis.
Strengthening the Teaching Assistant Faculty. Ed. by John D. Andrews. LC 84-82381. (Teaching & Learning Ser.: No. 22). (Orig.). 1985. pap. text ed. 12.95x (ISBN 0-87589-772-X). Jossey-Bass.
Strengthening the United Nations: A Bibliography on U. N. Reform & World Federalism. Compiled by Joseph P. Baratta. LC 87-134. (Bibliographies & Indexes in World History Ser.: No. 7). 361p. 1987. lib. bdg. 45.00 (ISBN 0-313-25840-6, BSU/). Greenwood.
Strengthening the World Bank. Escott Reid. LC 73-87437. (Illus.). xx, 290p. 1973. 20.00x (ISBN 0-226-70934-5). U of Chicago Pr.
Strengthening the World Monetary System. LC 73-84800. 87p. 1973. pap. 1.50 (ISBN 0-87186-051-1). Comm Econ Dev.
Strengthening Unemployment Insurance: Program Improvements. 55p. 1975. pap. 1.00 (ISBN 0-911558-23-3). W E Upjohn.
Strengthening Urban Management: International Perspectives. Ed. by Thomas L. Blair. (Urban Innovation Abroad Ser.). 368p. 1985. 45.00x (ISBN 0-306-42081-3, Plenum Pr). Plenum Pub.
Strengthening Vocational Education's Role in Decreasing the Dropout Rate. James Weber. 28p. 1987. 4.75 (ISBN 0-318-23417-3, RD 267). Natl Ctr Res Voc Ed.
Strengthening Young Families: The Parents Place Manual. Amy G. Rassen. 64p. 1986. 12.50 (ISBN 0-317-55088-8); write for info spiral bound paper (ISBN 0-936434-19-8). SF Study Ctr.
Strengthening Your Grip. Charles Swindoll. 1986. deluxe ed. 9.95 (ISBN 0-8499-3852-X). Word Bks.
Strengthening Your Grip. Charles R. Swindoll. 236p. 1982. 12.95 (ISBN 0-8499-0312-2). Word Bks.
Strengthening Your Grip. Charles R. Swindoll. 272p. 1986. pap. 3.50 (ISBN 0-553-25923-7). Bantam.
Strengthening Your Grip. Charles R. Swindoll. 1986. 3.50 (ISBN 0-8499-4176-8). Word Bks.
Strengthening Your Grip see Afirme Sus Valores.
Strengthening Your Marriage. Wayne Mack. (Christian Growth Ser.). 1977. pap. 5.95 (ISBN 0-87552-333-1). Presby & Reformed.
Strengthening Your Stepfamily. Elizabeth Einstein & Linda Albert. 1986. pap. 10.45 (ISBN 0-88671-217-3). Am Guidance.
Strengthening Your Stepfamily. Elizabeth Einstein & Linda Albert. 1987. pap. 10.95 (ISBN 0-394-75283-X). Random.
Strengths: African-American Children & Families. Asa G. Hilliard, III. 20p. (Orig.). 1982. pap. 3.00 (ISBN 0-317-45081-6). City Coll Wk.
Strengths of a Christian. Robert C. Roberts. LC 84-3498. (Spirituality & the Christian Life Ser.: Vol. 2). 118p. 1984. pap. 7.95 (ISBN 0-664-24613-3). Westminster John Knox.
Strenuous Age in American Literature. Grant C. Knight. LC 75-129461. 1970. Repr. of 1954 ed. 24.50x (ISBN 0-8154-0351-8). Cooper Sq.
Strenuous Life: Essays & Addresses. Theodore Roosevelt. 1902. 39.00x (ISBN 0-403-00311-3). Scholarly.
Streptococcal & Staphylococcal Infections: A Report. WHO Expert Committee, Geneva, 1967. (Technical Report Ser: No. 394). 56p. 1968. pap. 2.00 (ISBN 92-4-120394-3, 1490). World Health.
Streptococcal Diseases & the Immune Response. Ed. by Stanley E. Read & John B. Zabriskie. LC 79-26638. 1980. 68.50 (ISBN 0-12-583880-8). Acad Pr.
Streptococcal Genetics. Ed. by Joseph J. Ferretti & Roy Curtiss, III. (Illus.). 308p. 1987. text ed. 49.00 (ISBN 0-914826-93-X). Am Soc Microbio.
Streptococci. Ed. by F. A. Skinner & L. B. Quesnel. (Society for Applied Bacteriology Symposium Ser.). 1978. 86.00 (ISBN 0-12-648035-4). Acad Pr.
Streptokinase Treatment in Chronic Arterial Occlusions & Stenoses. Ed. by Michael Martin. 208p. 1982. 72.50 (ISBN 0-8493-5046-8). CRC Pr.
Streptozotocin: Fundamentals & Therapy. Ed. by M. K. Agarwal. viii, 310p. 1981. 140.75 (ISBN 0-444-80302-5). Elsevier.
Stresemann & the DNVP: Reconciliation or Revenge in German Foreign Policy, 1924-1928. Robert P. Grathwol. LC 79-28199. xiv, 302p. 1980. 29.95x (ISBN 0-7006-0199-6). U Pr of KS.
Stresemann & the Revision of Versailles. Henry L. Bretton. 1953. 18.50x (ISBN 0-8047-0444-9). Stanford U Pr.
Stresemann's Territorial Revisionism: Germany, Belgium & Europen-Malmedy Question, 1919-1929. Manfred J. Enssle. viii, 229p. 1980. text ed. 42.50x (ISBN 3-515-02959-1, Pub. by Franz Steiner). Coronet Bks.
Stress. Charles G. Edwards. (Outreach Ser.). 32p. 1982. pap. 1.25 (ISBN 0-8163-0468-8). Pacific Pr Pub Assn.
Stress. Walter McQuade & Ann Aikman. 256p. 1975. pap. 4.50 (ISBN 0-553-26086-3). Bantam.
Stress. Alan H. Rosenstein. Ed. by Margaret Chesney & Nancy Wiltsek. (Illus.). 23p. 1986. pap. 2.50 (ISBN 0-933161-06-9). Better H Prog.
Stress: A Nutritional Approach. Louise Tenney. (Todays Health Ser.: No. 5). Date not set. pap. 3.95 (ISBN 0-913923-32-X). Woodland UT.
Stress Analysis by Thermoelastic Techniques. Ed. by Gasper. 233p. 1987. 43.00 (ISBN 0-89252-766-8, 731). SPIE.
Stress Analysis for Creep. James T. Boyle & John Spence. 307p. 1983. 75.00 (ISBN 0-408-01172-6). Butterworth.
Stress Analysis of a Strapless Evening Gown. Ed. by Robert Baker. 192p. 1982. pap. 6.95 (ISBN 0-13-852608-7). P-H.
Stress Analysis of Notch Problems. Ed. by G. C. Sih. (Mechanics of Fracture Ser.: No. 5). 312p. 1978. 45.00x (ISBN 90-286-0166-X, Pub. by Sijthoff & Noordhoff). Kluwer Academic.
Stress & Addiction. Edward Gottheil et al. LC 87-7987. (Psychosocial Stress Ser.: No. 9). 352p. 1987. 40.00 (ISBN 0-87630-463-3). Brunner-Mazel.
Stress & Alcohol Use. Ed. by L. A. Pohorecky & J. Brick. 452p. 1983. 16.00 (ISBN 0-444-00730-X, Biomedical Pr). Elsevier.
Stress & Anxiety. Ed. by Charles D. Spielberger & Irwin G. Sarason. (Series in Clinical & Community Psychology: Vol. 4). 336p. 1977. 22.95x (ISBN 0-470-99016-3). Halsted Pr.
Stress & Anxiety, Vol. 7. Ed. by Irwin G. Sarason & Charles D. Spielberger. LC 74-28292. (Clinical & Community Psychology, Stress & Anxiety Ser.). (Illus.). 384p. 1980. text ed. 36.50 (ISBN 0-89116-183-X). Hemisphere Pub.
Stress & Anxiety, Vol. 8. Charles D. Spielberger et al. 1981. text ed. 34.95 (ISBN 0-07-060239-5). McGraw.
Stress & Anxiety, Vol. 8. Ed. by Charles D. Spielberger et al. LC 74-28292. (Clinical & Community Psychology, Stress & Anxiety Ser.). (Illus.). 456p. 1982. text ed. 39.95 (ISBN 0-89116-184-8). Hemisphere Pub.
Stress & Anxiety, Vol. 9. Ed. by Charles D. Spielberger et al. LC 74-28292. (Clinical & Community Psychology Ser.). (Illus.). 283p. 1985. text ed. 42.50 (ISBN 0-89116-310-7). Hemisphere Pub.
Stress & Anxiety, Vol. 11. Ed. by Chas. D. Spielberger et al. 258p. 1988. 49.95 (ISBN 0-89116-312-3). Hemisphere Pub.
Stress & Anxiety, Vol. 10: A Sourcebook of Theory & Research. Ed. by Charles D. Spielberger & Irwin G. Sarason. (Clinical & Community Psychology Ser.). (Illus.). 450p. 1985. text ed. 49.50 (ISBN 0-89116-311-5). Hemisphere Pub.
Stress & Burnout: A Primer for Special Education & Special Services Personnel. Stan F. Shaw & Jeffrey M. Bensky. LC 81-66270. 70p. 1981. pap. 5.50 (ISBN 0-86586-117-X). Coun Exc Child.
Stress & Burnout among Providers Caring for the Terminally Ill & Their Families. Ed. & intro. by Lenora F. Paridis. LC 87-25949. (Hospice Journal). 280p. 1988. text ed. 24.95 (ISBN 0-86656-674-0). Haworth Pr.
Stress & Burnout in the Human Service Professions. Ed. by Barry A. Farber. (Pergamon General Psychology Ser.). (Illus.). 272p. 1983. text ed. 37.00 (ISBN 0-08-028801-4). Pergamon.
Stress & Campus Response. Ed. by G. Kerry Smith. LC 68-57441. (Jossey-Bass Series in Higher Education). pap. 60.10 (ISBN 0-317-08577-8, 2013869). Bks Demand UMI.
Stress & Cancer. Ed. by Kurt Bammer & Benjamin H. Newberry. 264p. (Orig.). 1981. pap. text ed. 19.00 (ISBN 0-88937-003-6). Hogrefe Intl.
Stress & Cancer: An Annotated Bibliography. Gail A. Taff & Robert Friis. 32p. 1983. pap. 39.95 (ISBN 0-939552-07-8). Human Behavior.
Stress & Common Gastrointestinal Disorders: A Comprehensive Approach. Gerhard Dotevall. LC 85-6565. (Gastroenterology Ser.: Vol. 3). 192p. 1985. 36.95 (ISBN 0-275-91310-4, C1310). Praeger.
Stress & Coping, Vol. I. Ed. by Tiffany Field et al. 376p. 1985. text ed. 49.95 (ISBN 0-89859-564-9). L Erlbaum Assocs.
Stress & Coping Across Development. Tiffany M. Field et al. 280p. 1988. 34.95 (ISBN 0-89859-960-1). L Erlbaum Assocs.
Stress & Coping: An Anthology. 2nd ed. Alan Monat & Richard S. Lazarus. LC 77-3264. 560p. 1985. 39.50x (ISBN 0-231-05820-9); pap. 17.50x (ISBN 0-231-05821-7). Columbia U Pr.
Stress & Coping in Time of War: Generalizations from the Israeli Experience. Ed. by Norman Milgram. LC 86-9715. (Psychosocial Stress Ser.: No. 7). 416p. 1986. 45.00 (ISBN 0-87630-430-7). Brunner-Mazel.
Stress & Decision Making in the Dental Practice. James M. Dyce. (Illus.). 165p. 1973. 26.00 (ISBN 0-931386-72-1). Quint Pub Co.
Stress & Deflection Reduction in 2x4 Studs Spaced 24 Inches on Center Resulting from the Addition of Interior & Exterior Surfaces, Vol. 3. (Research Report Ser.). 46p. 1981. pap. 6.50 (ISBN 0-86718-117-6). Nat Assn H Build.
Stress & Disability in Childhood. N. Butler. (Illus.). 160p. 1984. 47.00 (ISBN 0-7236-0783-4). PSG Pub Co.
Stress & Fatigue in Human Performance. Robert Hockey. (Studies in Human Performance Ser.: I-507). 416p. 1983. 51.95x (ISBN 0-471-10265-2, Pub. by Wiley-Interscience). Wiley.
Stress & Fish. Ed. by A. D. Pickering. LC 81-67907. 1981. 67.50 (ISBN 0-12-554550-9). Acad Pr.
Stress & Health: Principles & Practice for Coping & Wellness. Phillip L. Rice. LC 86-26875. (Psychology Ser.). 416p. 1987. pap. text ed. 13.00 pub. net (ISBN 0-534-07608-4). Brooks-Cole.
Stress & Heart Disease. Ed. by R. E. Beamish et al. (Developments in Cardiovascular Medicine Ser.). 1985. lib. bdg. 55.00 (ISBN 0-89838-709-4, Pub. by Martinus Nijhoff Netherlands). Kluwer-Academic.
Stress & Hispanic Mental Health: Relating Research to Service Delivery. William A. Vega & Manuel R. Miranda. LC 85-600578. (Illus.). 203p. (Orig.). 1985. pap. 7.00 (ISBN 0-318-18845-7, S/N 017-024-01264-5). USGPO.
Stress & Hypertension. Ed. by J. Bahlmann & H. Liebau. (Contributions to Nephrology Ser.: Vol. 30). (Illus.). xiv, 206p. 1982. pap. 60.00 (ISBN 3-8055-3450-7). S Karger.
Stress & Hypertension. Aveline Kushi. Ed. by Helaine Honig. LC 86-62957. (Macrobiotic Food & Cooking Ser.). (Illus.). 144p. (Orig.). 1987. pap. 7.95 (ISBN 0-87040-679-5). Japan Pubns USA.
Stress & Hypertension. Michio Kushi. Ed. by Mark Mead. LC 86-62958. (Macrobiotic Health Education Ser.). (Illus.). 144p. (Orig.). 1987. pap. 7.95 (ISBN 0-87040-678-7). Japan Pubns USA.
Stress & Its Management by Yoga. K. N. Udupa. Ed. by R. C. Prasad. 395p. 1986. 25.00X (ISBN 81-208-0000-1, Pub. by Motilal Banarsidass). South Asia Bks.
Stress & Its Management by Yoga. K. N. Udupa. 1986. 34.95. Asia Bk Corp.
Stress & Mental Disorder. Ed. by James E. Barrett. LC 79-2202. (American Psychopathological Association Ser.). 310p. 1979. text ed. 52.00 (ISBN 0-89004-384-1). Raven.
Stress & Mental Health: A Bibliography, Vol. I. rev. ed. Robert Friis. 33p. 1981. pap. 39.95 (ISBN 0-939552-02-7, 003). Human Behavior.
Stress & Motor Performance: Understanding & Coping. David Pargman. (Illus.). 204p. 1986. pap. 15.95. Mouvement Pubns.
Stress & Nervous Disorders. Jan De Vries. 1987. 40.00x (Pub. by Mainstream Scotland); pap. 20.00x. State Mutual Bk.
Stress & Nervous Disorders. Jan De Vries. (By Appointment Only Ser.). 126p. 1988. pap. 8.95 (ISBN 0-906391-81-4, Pub. by Mnstream Scotland). David & Charles.
Stress & Non-Stress Accent. M. E. Beckmann. (Netherlands Phonetic Archives Ser.). xiv, 239p. 1986. write for info. (ISBN 90-6765-243-1); pap. write for info. (ISBN 90-6765-244-X). Foris Pubns.
Stress & Nutrition. Health Media of America Staff. (Health Media of America Nutrition Ser.). (Illus.). 80p. 1986. pap. 3.95 (ISBN 0-937325-03-1). Health Med Amer.
Stress & Old Age. Wilbur Watson. LC 79-65127. 144p. 1980. 24.95 (ISBN 0-87855-296-0). Transaction Bks.
Stress & Performance Effectiveness. Ed. by Earl A. Alluisi & Edwin A. Fleishman. (Human Performance & Productivity Ser.: Vol. 3). 256p. 1982. text ed. 29.95x (ISBN 0-89859-091-4). L Erlbaum Assocs.
Stress & Performance in Diving. Arthur J. Bachrach & Glen H. Egstrom. 183p. 1987. text ed. 26.50 (ISBN 0-941332-06-3). Best Pub Co.
Stress & Physical Health: A Bibliography, Vol. II. Robert Friis. (Orig.). 1981. pap. 39.95 (ISBN 0-939552-04-3). Human Behavior.
Stress & Physical Health: A Bibliography, Vol. I. rev. ed. Robert Friis. 37p. 1981. pap. 39.95 (ISBN 0-939552-01-9, 001). Human Behavior.
Stress & Physical Health: A Bibliography, Vol. III. Robert Friis. 34p. (Orig.). 1984. pap. 39.95 (ISBN 0-939552-08-6). Human Behavior.
Stress & Pregnancy. John J. Sullivan & Joyce C Foster. LC 86-82022. (Stress in Modern Society Ser.: No. 8). 1987. 32.50 (ISBN 0-404-63261-0). AMS Pr.
Stress & Productivity. Ed. by Leonard W. Krinsky et al. LC 83-22606. (Problems of Industrial Psychiatric Medicine Ser.: Vol. IX). 256p. 1984. 29.95x (ISBN 0-89885-137-8). Human Sci Pr.
Stress & Reading Difficulties: Research, Assessment, Intervention. Lance M. Gentile & Merna M. McMillan. 54p. 1987. pap. 5.00 (ISBN 0-87207-783-7). Intl Reading.
Stress & Recovery. Patricia Hoolihan. 24p. (Orig.). 1984. pap. 0.95 (ISBN 0-89486-236-7). Hazelden.
Stress & Response in Fieldwork. Frances Henry & Satish Saberwal. Ed. by George Spindler & Louise Spindler. (Studies in Anthropological Method). 96p. Date not set. pap. text ed. price not set (ISBN 0-8290-0316-9). Irvington.
Stress & Satisfaction on the Job: Work Meanings & Coping of Mid-Career Men. Patricia E. Benner. LC 84-3252. 176p. 1984. 35.00 (ISBN 0-275-91127-6, C1127). Praeger.
Stress & Service Needs of Those Who Care for the Aged. Joanna Mellor & George S. Getzel. 1980. pap. 2.00 (ISBN 0-88156-092-8). Comm Serv Soc NY.
Stress & Sexuality. Jerrold S. Greenberg. (Stress in Modern Society Ser.: No. 6). 1987. 32.50 (ISBN 0-404-63257-2). AMS Pr.
Stress & Stability in Late Eighteenth-Century Britain: Reflections on the British Avoidance of Revolution. Ian R. Christie. 1984. 37.00x (ISBN 0-19-820064-1). Oxford U Pr.
Stress & Stigma: Explanation & Evidence in the Sociology of Crime & Illness. Ed. by Uta E. Gerhardt & Michael E. Wadsworth. LC 84-17936. 206p. 1985. 29.95 (ISBN 0-312-76606-8). St Martin.
Stress & Strain: Basic Concepts of Continuum Mechanics for Geologists. W. D. Means. (Illus.). 336p. 1976. pap. text ed. 24.00 (ISBN 0-387-07556-9). Springer-Verlag.
Stress & Strain Data Handbook. Teng H. Hsu. LC 86-4663. (Illus.). 350p. 1986. 48.00x (ISBN 0-87201-159-3). Gulf Pub.
Stress & Stress Management: Research & Applications. Kevin Hamberger & Jeffrey Lohr. 288p. 1984. text ed. 25.95 (ISBN 0-8261-3950-7). Springer Pub.
Stress & Substance Abuse, Vol. I. rev. ed. Ed. by Robert Friis. 34p. 1981. pap. 39.95 (ISBN 0-939552-03-5, 004). Human Behavior.
Stress & Tension Control 1. Ed. by F. J. McGuigan et al. LC 80-16444. 332p. 1980. 55.00x (ISBN 0-306-40450-8, Plenum Pr). Plenum Pub.
Stress & Tension Control 2. Ed. by F. J. McGuigan et al. 420p. 1985. 65.00x (ISBN 0-306-41815-0, Plenum Pr). Plenum Pub.
Stress & the Bottom Line: A Guide to Personal Well-Being & Corporate Health. E. M. Gherman. 352p. 1981. 16.95 (ISBN 0-8144-5696-0). AMACOM.
Stress & the Classroom Teacher. (What Research Says to the Teacher Ser.). 2.50 (ISBN 0-8106-1063-9). NEA.
Stress & the Family: Vol. I Coping with Normative Transitions. Ed. by Hamilton I. McCubbin & Charles R. Figley. LC 83-6048. 300p. 1983. 27.50 (ISBN 0-87630-321-1). Brunner-Mazel.
Stress & the Family: Vol. II Coping with Catastrophe. Ed. by Charles R. Figley & Hamilton I. McCubbin. LC 83-6048. 272p. 1983. 27.50 (ISBN 0-87630-332-7). Brunner-Mazel.
Stress & the Healthy Family. Dolores Curran. 192p. 1985. 13.95 (ISBN 0-86683-863-5, HarpR). Harper Row.
Stress & the Heart. 2nd ed. Ed. by David Wheatley. 434p. 1981. pap. 45.50 (ISBN 0-89004-520-8). Raven.
Stress & the Heart: Storm in a Bottle. Sander Orent. 256p. 1988. text ed. 22.95 (ISBN 0-89876-139-5). Gardner Pr.
Stress & the Manager: Making It Work for You. Karl Albrecht. (Illus.). 1979. (Spec); pap. 8.95 (ISBN 0-13-852673-7). P-H.

Stress Relieving Heat Treatments of Welded Steel Constructions: Proceedings of the International Conference, Sofia, Bulgaria, 6-7 July 1987. Ed. by International Institute of Welding Staff. (Illus.). 420p. 1987. 110.00 (ISBN 0-08-035900-0, PBL). Pergamon.

Stress Research: Issues for the Eighties. Ed. by Cary L. Cooper. LC 82-11049. 149p. 1983. 47.00 (ISBN 0-471-10246-6). Wiley.

Stress Resource Syllubus. 2.00 (ISBN 0-317-15795-7); transparencies 5.00. Chr Marriage.

Stress Response Syndromes. 2nd ed. Mardi J. Horowitz. LC 85-71507. 358p. 1986. 35.00x (ISBN 0-87668-811-3). Aronson.

Stress-Rupture Parameters: Origin, Calculation, & Use. J. B. Conway. 318p. 1969. 108.00 (ISBN 0-677-01860-6). Gordon & Breach.

Stress, Sanity & Survival. Robert I. Woolfolk & Frank C. Richardson. 1979. pap. 3.95 (ISBN 0-451-14848-7, Sig). NAL.

Stress Skills Workbook. Donald A. Tubesing. 75p. 1979. wkbk. 10.00 (ISBN 0-938586-15-7). Whole Person.

Stress, Social Support & Women. Ed. by Stevan F. Hobfoll. (Clinical & Community Psychology Ser.). 225p. 1985. text ed. 42.00 (ISBN 0-89116-404-9). Hemisphere Pub.

Stress Solution: A Rational Approach to Increasing Corporate & Personal Effectiveness. Samuel H. Klarreich. 176p. 1988. 19.95 (ISBN 1-55013-074-9, Pub. by Key Porter Canada). U of Toronto Pr.

Stress-Strain Behaviour of Soils. Ed. by R. H. Parry. (Illus.). 1973. text ed. 95.00x (ISBN 0-85429-121-0). Trans-Atl Phila.

Stress-Strain Properties of Paper & Fibers. (Bibliographic Ser.: No. 217). 130p. 1965. 9.00 (ISBN 0-317-34448-X); Suppl. 1, 1971. 8.00 (ISBN 0-317-34449-8). Inst Paper Chem.

Stress Strategies. C. B. Scrignar. (Karger Biobehavioral Medicine Ser.: Vol. 1). (Illus.). 1983. 38.75 (ISBN 3-8055-3605-4). S Karger.

Stress Strategist. Dorothy M. Walters. (Illus.). 479p. 1986. 29.95 (ISBN 0-934344-19-1). Royal Pub.

Stress Test Biofeedback Card & Booklet. Alfred A. Barrios. 1985. 3.95 (ISBN 0-9601926-3-8). Self-Prog Control.

Stress Test for Children. Jerome Vogel & Richard Walsh. Ed. by Richard A. Passwater & Earl R. Mindell. (Good Health Guide Ser.). 32p. (Orig.). 1983. pap. 1.45 (ISBN 0-87983-299-1). Keats.

Stress Testing: Principles & Practice. 3rd ed. Myrvin H. Ellestad. LC 85-10413. (Illus.). 526p. 1985. text ed. 53.00 (ISBN 0-8036-3112-X). Davis Co.

Stress: The Hidden Adversary. C. B. Dobson. 1983. lib. bdg. 29.00 (ISBN 0-85200-381-1, Pub. by MTP Pr England). Kluwer Academic.

Stress: The Role of Catecholamines & Other Neurotransmitters. Earl Usdin et al. 1160p. 1984. text ed. 275.00 (ISBN 2-88124-102-6). Gordon & Breach.

Stress: Theory & Practice. King. Date not set. price not set (ISBN 0-8089-1874-5); pap. text ed. price not set. Grune.

Stress Transients in Solids. John S. Rinehart. 240p. 1975. pap. 8.95x (ISBN 0-913270-48-2). HyperDynamics.

Stress-Unstress. Keith W. Sehnert. LC 81-65647. 224p. (Orig.). 1981. pap. 4.50 (ISBN 0-8066-1883-3, 10-6065). Augsburg.

Stress, Vibration & Noise Analysis in Vehicles. Ed. by H. G. Gibbs & T. H. Richards. (Illus.). 485p. 1975. 106.25 (ISBN 0-85334-642-9, Pub. by Elsevier Applied Sci England). Elsevier.

Stress Walk: The Walking Cure. Richard L. Harding. (Illus.). 40p. (Orig.). 1988. pap. 4.95; audiocassette 9.95. Nutri-fit Intl.

Stress Wave Propagation in Solids. Richard J. Wasley. (Monographs & Textbooks in Material Science: Vol. 7). 328p. 1973. 75.00 (ISBN 0-8247-6039-5). Dekker.

Stress Waves in Non-Elastic Solids. Wojoiech Nowacki. 1978. 63.00 (ISBN 0-08-021294-8). Pergamon.

Stress Waves in Solids. 2nd ed. H. Kolsky. (Illus.). 1963. pap. text ed. 6.95 (ISBN 0-486-61098-5). Dover.

Stress Without Distress. Hans Selye. 1975. pap. 3.50 (ISBN 0-451-13635-7, AE2417, Sig). NAL.

Stress Without Distress: Rx for Burnout. George Manning & Kent Curtis. (Human Side of Work Ser.). 273p. 1988. pap. text ed. write for info. (ISBN 0-538-21250-0, U251). SW Pub.

Stress, Work Design & Productivity. Ed. by E. N. Corlett & J. Richardson. LC 81-13075. (Studies in Occupational Stress Ser.). 271p. 1981. 54.95x (ISBN 0-471-28044-5, Pub. by Wiley-Interscience). Wiley.

Stressed Ecosystems. John Cairns. 350p. 1989. 49.95. Lewis Pubs Inc.

Stressed Heart. Ed. by Marianne J. Legato. (Developments in Cardiovascular Medicine Ser.). 1987. lib. bdg. 82.50 (ISBN 0-89838-849-X, Pub. by Martinus Nijhoff Netherlands). Kluwer Academic.

Stressed Vowel Phonology of the Urkunden of St. Gallen in the First Half of the Fourteenth Century: German Language & Literature, Vol. 189. Terrence C. McCormick. (European University Studies: Ser. 1). xvi, 254p. 1977. pap. 28.70 (ISBN 3-261-02926-9). P Lang Pubs.

Stressed Vowels of Yiddish-American English see Selected List of Compounds from Present-Day Reading.

Stresses in Plates & Shells. Ansel C. Ugural. (Illus.). 352p. 1981. text ed. 52.95 (ISBN 0-07-065730-0). McGraw.

Stresses in Rock. G. Herget. 200p. 1987. text ed. 43.50 (ISBN 90-6191-685-2, Pub. by A A Balkema). Brookfield Pub Co.

Stresses in Shells. 2nd ed. W. Fluegge. LC 74-183604. (Illus.). 525p. 1973. 39.00 (ISBN 0-387-05322-0). Springer-Verlag.

Stresses in U. S.-Japanese Security Relations. Fred Greene. (Studies in Defense Policy). 110p. 1975. pap. 7.95 (ISBN 0-8157-3271-6). Brookings.

Stresses of Empire: Selected Articles on the British Empire in the Eighteenth Century. Ed. by Peter C. Hoffer. (Early American History Ser.). 310p. 1987. lib. bdg. 50.00 (ISBN 0-8240-6243-4). Garland Pub.

Stressfire. Massad F. Ayoob. (Gunfighting for Police: Advanced Tactics & Techniques Ser.: Vol. 1). (Illus.). 149p. 1986. pap. 9.95 (ISBN 0-936279-03-6). Police Bkshelf.

Stressful Life Events. Thomas W. Miller. (Stress & Health Ser.: No. 4). 640p. 1988. 60.00x (ISBN 0-8236-6165-2, BN#00165). Intl Univs Pr.

Stressful Life Events & Their Contexts. Ed. by Barbara S. Dohrenwend & Bruce P. Dohrenwend. (Monographs in Psychsocial Epidemiology). 287p. 1984. pap. text ed. 14.95 (ISBN 0-8135-1004-X). Rutgers U Pr.

Stressful Life Events, Social-Support Networks, & Gerontological Health. Thomas T. Wan. LC 81-48393. (Illus.). 176p. 1982. 24.00x (ISBN 0-669-05359-7). Lexington Bks.

Stressful Life Events: Their Nature & Effects. Barbara S. Dohrenwend & Bruce P. Dohrenwend. LC 74-6369. 340p. 1974. 52.50x (ISBN 0-471-21753-0). Wiley.

Stressing & Unstressing in a Tent: A Narrative Reminiscence. Stuart L. Burns. 200p. 1987. 14.95 (ISBN 0-8138-1726-9). Iowa St U Pr.

Stressless Home: A Step-by-Step Guide to Turning Your Home into the Haven You Deserve. Robert M. Bramson & Susan Bramson. 1987. pap. 3.95 (ISBN 0-345-33895-2). Ballantine.

Stressmap: Finding Your Pressure Points. 2nd ed. C. Michele Haney & Edmond Boenisch. LC 82-15391. 176p. 1987. pap. 7.95 (ISBN 0-915166-60-7). Impact Pubs Cal.

StressMap-Personal Diary Edition-The Ultimate Stress Measurement & Self-Assessment Guide Designed by Essi Systems. Esther M. Orioli et al. LC 87-12249. 80p. 1987. wiro-bound 14.95 (ISBN 0-937858-78-1). Newmarket.

Stresspoints: A Young Person's Guide to Peace of Heart. Joseph Moore & Douglas Fazzina. 1988. pap. 3.95. Paulist Pr.

Stretch. Edythe Draper. (gr. 5-9). 1983. kivar, girls' ed. 5.95 (ISBN 0-8423-6673-3). Tyndale.

Stretch & Relax. Maxine Tobias & Mary Stewart. LC 85-60489. (Illus.). 160p. 1985. pap. 12.95 (ISBN 0-89586-416-9). Price Stern.

Stretch & Strengthen. Judy Alter. 1986. pap. 9.95. HM.

Stretch & Strengthen for Rehabilitation & Development. Bob Anderson & Donald G. Bornell. (Illus.). 91p. (Orig.). 1984. pap. 5.95 wiro bdg. (ISBN 0-9601066-2-6); iso-band 5.50. Stretching Inc.

Stretch Exercise Program: A Program for Women Who Have Had Breast Cancer. Contrib. by Jane M. Colburn. (Illus.). 96p. 1988. pap. 20.00. U Ala Hospt Mktg.

Stretch on the River. Richard Bissell. LC 87-20390. (Borealis Books Reprint). 252p. 1987. pap. 8.95 (ISBN 0-87351-220-0). Minn Hist.

Stretch Out: Warmup & Beat Stress. Stephanie Sorine. 1984. pap. 2.95 (ISBN 0-517-55476-3). Crown.

Stretch! The Total Fitness Program. Ann Smith. LC 79-622. (Illus.). 176p. 1982. pap. 6.95 (ISBN 0-87491-239-3). Acropolis.

Stretch Think Program 1. Sydney B. Tyler. (Just Think Program Ser.). 144p. (gr. k-2). 1984. pap. 35.00 (ISBN 0-912781-12-2). Thomas Geale.

Stretch Think Program 2. Sydney B. Tyler. (Just Think Program Ser.). 140p. (gr. 2-4). 1984. pap. 35.00 (ISBN 0-912781-10-6). Thomas Geale.

Stretch Think Program 3. Mrs. Sydney B. Tyler. (Just Think Program Ser.). 138p. (gr. 5-8). 1984. pap. 35.00 (ISBN 0-912781-11-4). Thomas Geale.

Stretch Your Gas Dollars. P. Ross Aletto. LC 79-54982. (Illus.). 72p. (Orig.). 1979. pap. 2.95 (ISBN 0-935126-00-7). E & C Bks.

Stretched Out AASHO-PCI Beams Types III & IV for Longer Span Highway Bridges. (PCI Journal Reprints Ser.). 19p. pap. 5.00 (ISBN 0-318-19840-1, JR134). Prestressed Concrete.

Stretcher Bearers. Michael Slater. LC 85-8389. 168p. 1985. pap. 6.95 (ISBN 0-8307-1044-2, 5418505). Regal.

Stretcher Bearers. Michael Slater & Eric Nachtrieb. 64p. 1985. pap. 3.95 (ISBN 0-8307-1056-6, 6102137). Regal.

Stretchercize: Is Your Limber Lost? Mary Long. (Illus.). 75p. (Orig.). 1985. pap. 3.95 (ISBN 0-916005-03-8). Silver Sea.

Stretchers: The Story of a Hospital Unit on the Western Front. Frederick A. Pottle. 1929. 49.50x (ISBN 0-685-89785-0). Elliots Bks.

Stretching. Bob Anderson. LC 79-5567. (Illus.). 192p. (Orig.). 1980. pap. 9.95. Shelter Pubns.

Stretching Book. Nell Weaver. 1982. 11.95 (ISBN 0-89037-234-9); pap. 9.95 (ISBN 0-89037-242-X). Anderson World.

Stretching Dollars to Strengthen Infrastructure. Rick Watson. 1984. 15.00 (ISBN 0-87292-044-5). Coun State Govts.

Stretching for All Sports. John E. Beaulieu. LC 80-12695. (Illus.). 214p. pap. 8.95 (ISBN 0-87095-079-7, Athletic). Gldn West Bks.

Stretching for All Sports. pap. 8.95. Borden.

Stretching for Athletics. 2nd ed. Pat Croce. LC 83-80859. (Illus.). 128p. 1984. pap. 8.95 (ISBN 0-88011-119-4, PCRO0119). Leisure Pr.

Stretching: For Everyday Fitness & for Running, Tennis, Cycling, Swimming, Golf, Walking, Skiing & Other Sports. Bob Anderson. (Illus.). 1980. pap. 9.95 (ISBN 0-394-73874-8). Random.

Stretching Scientifically. Thomas Kurz. (Illus.). 96p. 1987. pap. 8.95 (ISBN 0-940149-25-7). Stadion Pub.

Stretching Scientifically. Thomas Kurz. (Illus.). 96p. (Orig.). 1985. pap. 8.95x (ISBN 0-940149-24-9). Stadion Pub.

Stretching Scientifically: A Guide to Flexibility Training. Thomas Kurz. 128p. 1988. lib. bdg. 19.95 (ISBN 0-940149-26-5); pap. 11.95 (ISBN 0-940149-28-1). Stadion Pub.

Stretching the Eyes' Distance Reflections on the Chesapeake Bay. Barclay Sheaks. Ed. by Nancy G. Harris. (Illus.). 72p. 1981. 25.00 (ISBN 0-941376-00-1). Bleecker St Pub.

Stretching the Truth. Created by Francine Pascal. (Sweet Valley Twins Ser.: No. 13). (gr. 3-7). 1987. pap. 2.75 (ISBN 0-553-15654-3, Skylark). Bantam.

Stretching Turbo Pascal: Advanced Programming in the MS-DOS Environment. Kent Porter. 1987. pap. 21.95 (ISBN 0-13-852757-1). P-H.

Stricken Deer or the Life of Cowper. David Cecil. 1929. 29.00 (ISBN 0-8274-3528-2). R West.

Stricken Field. Martha Gellhorn. (Virago Modern Classics Ser.). 1986. pap. 6.95 (ISBN 0-14-016140-6). Penguin.

Stricken Land, the Story of Puerto Rico. Rexford G. Tugwell. LC 68-23335. 1968. Repr. of 1946 ed. lib. bdg. 45.50x (ISBN 0-8371-0252-9, TUSL). Greenwood.

Stricken Lute. Roger B. Lloyd. LC 73-118535. 1971. Repr. of 1932 ed. 22.50x (ISBN 0-8046-1158-0, Pub. by Kennikat). Assoc Faculty Pr.

Stricker & Wernher: A View of Chivalry & Peasantry in Germany in the Late Middle Ages. Marion L. Huffines. 1978. lib. bdg. 69.95. Gordon Pr.

Strickers Daniel Von Dem Bluehenden Tal: Werkstruktur und Interpretation. Ingeborg Henderson. (German Language & Literature Monographs). viii, 206p. 1976. 30.00x (ISBN 90-272-0961-8). Benjamins North Am.

Strickly Fish Cookbook. Babe Winkelman & Charlie Winkelman. Ed. by Steve Grooms. LC 85-25247. 230p. (Orig.). 1985. pap. 11.95 (ISBN 0-915405-04-0). B Winkelman Prods.

Strickly for the Chickens. Frances Hamerstrom. LC 80-19387. pap. 46.00 (2026560). Bks Demand UMI.

Strict Convexity & Complex Strict Convexity. Istrautescu. (Lecture Notes in Pure & Applied Mathematics Ser.). 208p. 1984. 55.00 (ISBN 0-8247-1796-1). Dekker.

Strict Settlement: A Guide for Historians. B. English. Ed. by J. Saville. (Occasional Papers in Economic & Social History). 144p. 1983. pap. text ed. 12.50x (ISBN 0-85958-439-9, Pub. by U of Hull of UK). Humanities.

Strict Settlement: A Guide for Historians. Barbara English & John Saville. 1983. 30.00X (ISBN 0-317-52175-6, Pub. by Pinhorns UK). State Mutual Bk.

Strict Vegetarian Cookbook. Lorine Tadej. LC 84-61271. 160p. pap. 7.95 (ISBN 0-912145-02-1); comb. binding 7.95 (ISBN 0-912145-01-3). MMI Pr.

Strictly Academic: A Reading & Writing Text. Pat Currie & Ellen Cray. 288p. 1987. pap. text ed. 14.95 scp (ISBN 0-06-041411-1, HarpC); instr's manual avail. (ISBN 0-06-361406-5). Har-Row.

Strictly Dishonorable & Other Lost American Plays. Ed. by Richard Nelson. LC 86-5782. (Illus.). 260p. (Orig.). 1986. pap. 10.95 (ISBN 0-930452-55-0). Theatre Comm.

Strictly for Beginners CP-M Book or, How to Talk with Your New Personal Computer. Joseph T. Finnell, Jr. LC 83-51318. (Illus.). 304p. (Orig.). 1984. spiral bdg. 14.95 (ISBN 0-915767-00-7). Topaz Pr.

Strictly for Boys: A Cookbook for Boys from 8 to 80. 96p. 6.95 (ISBN 0-918544-47-5). Wimmer Bks.

Strictly for Laughs. Ellen Conford. LC 85-9450. 155p. (gr. 7-10). 1985. 12.95 (ISBN 0-448-47754-8, Putnam). Putnam Pub Group.

Strictly for Laughs. Ellen Conford. 100p. 1987. pap. 2.50 (ISBN 0-425-08883-9, Pub. by Berkley-Pacer). Berkley Pub.

Strictly for the Chickens. Frances Hamerstrom. 136p. 1980. 9.95 (ISBN 0-8138-0799-9). Iowa St U Pr.

Strictly Personal. W. Somerset Maugham. LC 75-25376. (Works of W. Somerset Maugham Ser.). 1977. Repr. of 1941 ed. 20.00x (ISBN 0-405-07829-3). Ayer Co Pubs.

Strictly Personal. Phyllis Schieber. 176p. 1987. pap. 2.75 (ISBN 0-449-70230-8, Juniper). Fawcett.

Strictly Personal: Black Vignettes. Mary Bohanon. LC 76-56031. 1977. 7.95 (ISBN 0-87881-058-7). Mojave Bks.

Strictly Seafood. Julie B. Perry. Ed. by Elizabeth Lacey. (Illus.). 80p. (Orig.). 1984. pap. text ed. 4.10 (ISBN 0-916427-00-5). Ravenel Bks.

Strictly South Coast: A Catalogue - A Guide to Southern California. 3rd, rev. ed. Uncle Jam Editors. (Illus.). 360p. 1984. pap. 9.95 (ISBN 0-916063-06-2). Fragments West.

Strictly Speaking. Edwin Newman. 1975. pap. 3.95 (ISBN 0-446-30900-1). Warner Bks.

Strictly Structured BASIC. Eli Berlinger. LC 85-21489. (Illus.). 372p. 1986. pap. text ed. 31.25 (ISBN 0-314-93152-X). West Pub.

Strictly Structured VAX BASIC. Eli Berlinger. 451p. 1988. pap. text ed. 31.25 (ISBN 0-314-64977-8). West Pub.

Strictures on a Life of William Wilberforce. facsimile ed. W. Wilberforce & S. Wilberforce. Ed. by Thomas Clarkson. LC 77-164398. (Black Heritage Library Collection). Repr. of 1838 ed. 15.25 (ISBN 0-8369-8857-4). Ayer Co Pubs.

Strictures on Mr. Colliers New Edition of Shakespeare, 1858. Alexander Dyce. LC 72-164816. Repr. of 1859 ed. 20.00 (ISBN 0-404-02231-6). AMS Pr.

Stride Across a Thousand Years. Ed. by S. Kovalenko. 245p. 1986. pap. 7.95 (ISBN 0-8285-3324-5, Pub. by Progress Pubs USSR). Imported Pubns.

Stride: The Music of Fats Waller. Paul S. Machlin. (Twayne Music Ser.). 192p. 1985. lib. bdg. 18.95 (ISBN 0-8057-9468-9, Twayne); pap. 9.95 (ISBN 0-8057-9470-0, Twayne). G K Hall.

Stride Toward Freedom: The Montgomery Story. Martin Luther King, Jr. LC 86-4813. 240p. 1987. 8.95 (ISBN 0-06-250490-8, HarpR). Har-Row.

Strider Incident: Regula 1 Space Laboratory Deck Plans, 2 bks. (Star Trek Ser.). 76p. (Orig.). 1987. Set. pap. 12.00 (ISBN 1-55560-003-4). FASA Corp.

Strides Across Images of Asia. Hiroshi Suga. 60p. 1988. 9.95 (ISBN 4-7683-0004-9). Bks Nippan.

Stridshasten see Battle Horse.

Strife. John Galsworthy. (Methuen Student Editions Ser.). 1984. pap. 3.95x (ISBN 0-413-54270-X, NO. 4097). Heinemann Ed.

Strife & Glory: A Translation of Berndt Krauthoff's "Ich Befehle". Berndt Krauthoff. LC 83-91451. 205p. 1985. pap. 4.95 (ISBN 0-533-06048-6). Vantage.

Strife of Brian. Andy Donato. 160p. Date not set. pap. 6.95 (ISBN 1-55013-058-7, Pub. by Key Porter Canada). U of Toronto Pr.

Strife of Interests: Politics & Policies in Australian Health Services. Sidney Sax. 350p. 1985. text ed. 34.95x (ISBN 0-86861-484-X). Unwin Hyman.

Strife of Systems: An Essay on the Grounds & Implications of Philosophical Diversity. Nicholas Rescher. LC 84-21958. (Illus.). 296p. 1985. 34.95x (ISBN 0-8229-3510-4). U of Pittsburgh Pr.

Strife of the Sea. Thornton J. Hains. LC 72-103515. (Short Story Index Reprint Ser.). 1903. 19.00 (ISBN 0-8369-3257-9). Ayer Co Pubs.

Strife of the Spirit. Adin Steinsaltz. LC 87-32173. 259p. 1988. 24.95 (ISBN 0-87668-986-1). Aronson.

Striga: Biology & Control. Ed. by H. Doggett et al. LC 84-12877. (Symposium Ser.: No. 2). 1984. 30.00 (ISBN 0-930357-01-9). ICSU Pr.

Strike! Jeremy Brecher. LC 77-82654. (Illus.). 327p. 1977. pap. 9.00 (ISBN 0-8467-0364-5). South End Pr.

Strike. Yvonne Burgess. LC 79-23680. 219p. 1980. 9.95 (ISBN 0-8008-7471-4). Taplinger.

Strike a Blow & Die: A Narrative of Race Relations in Colonial Africa. rev. ed. George S. Mwase. Ed. by Robert I. Rotberg. LC 66-21342. (Center for International Affairs Ser). (Illus.). xlviii, 135p. 1970. 13.50x (ISBN 0-674-84345-2). Harvard U Pr.

Strike a Giant Bell. John Davis. 1980. 3.00 (ISBN 0-8198-6815-9); pap. 2.00 (ISBN 0-8198-6816-7). Dghtrs St Paul.

Strike: A Handbook of Coastal & Offshore Angling in South Africa. S. Shoeman. 496p. 1982. pap. text ed. 33.00 (ISBN 0-86961-141-0, Pub. by A A Balkema). Brookfield Pub Co.

Strike: A Study in Collective Action. Ernest T. Hiller. LC 70-89738. (American Labor, from Conspiracy to Collective Bargaining, Ser. 1). 304p. 1969. Repr. of 1928 ed. 17.00 (ISBN 0-405-02127-5). Ayer Co Pubs.

Strike Aircraft: The Illustrated History of the Vietnam War. F. Clifton Berry, Jr. LC 87-47799. (Illus.). 160p. 1988. pap. 6.95 (ISBN 0-553-34508-7). Bantam.

Strike at Shane's: A Prize Story of Indiana. Limited ed. Gene Stratton-Porter. 91p. 1984. 17.50x (ISBN 0-9614522-0-X). J R Long Antiquarian.

Strike Contingency Plan. (Labor Relations Ser.). Date not set. 11.95 (ISBN 0-318-23211-1, LRN054700). Nat Grocers Assn.

Stringer & the Hanging Judge, No. 6. Lou Cameron. 1988. pap. 2.75 (ISBN 1-55773-028-8, Charter Bks). Berkley Pub.

Stringer & the Hangman's Rodeo, No. 4. Lou Cameron. 192p. 1988. pap. 2.75 (ISBN 0-441-79078-X, Charter Bks). Ace Bks.

Stringer on Assassin's Trail. Lou Cameron. 1987. pap. 2.75 (ISBN 0-441-79074-7, Charter Bks). Berkley Pub.

Stringer on Dead Man's Range, No. 2. Lou Cameron. 1987. pap. 2.75 (ISBN 0-441-79022-4, Charter Pub). Berkley Pub.

Strings: A Comparative View, Vol. I. Phyllis Skoldberg. LC 81-70184. 1982. pap. text ed. 19.95 (ISBN 0-89917-316-0). Alfred Pub.

Strings: A Comparative View, Vol. II. Phyllis Skoldberg. 1983. pap. text ed. 19.95 (ISBN 0-89917-367-5). Alfred Pub.

Strings: A Gathering of Family Poems. Ed. by Paul B. Janeczko. LC 83-21564. 176p. (YA) (gr. 7 up). 1984. 11.95 (ISBN 0-02-747790-8). Bradbury Pr.

Strings & Superstrings: Proceedings on the Third Jerusalem, Vol. 3. Ed. by S. Weinberg & T. Piran. 232p. 1987. 45.00 (ISBN 9971-50-374-3); pap. 28.00 (ISBN 9971-50-375-1). World Scientific Pub.

Strings & Superstrings: Proceedings of the XVIII Int'l Gift Seminar on Theoretical Physics. Ed. by Juan R. Mittebrunn et al. 550p. (Orig.). 1988. 87.00 (ISBN 9971-50-523-1); pap. 52.00 (ISBN 9971-50-524-X). World Scientific Pub.

Strings & Things: Poems & Other Messages for Children. Christy Kenneally. (Orig.). (gr. 2-3). 1984. pap. 3.50 (ISBN 0-8091-6555-4). Paulist Pr.

Strings, Lattice Gauge Theory & High Energy Phenomenology: Proceedings of the Winter School of Theoretical Particle Physics, Panchgani, India, January 25-February 5, 1986. Ed. by V. Singh & S. Wadia. 612p. 1987. 78.00 (ISBN 9971-50-157-0). World Scientific Pub.

Strings on a Kite: The Poetry of Max Hart. Max Hart. 78p. 1983. pap. 5.95 (ISBN 0-682-49994-3). Exposition-Phoenix.

Strings to Love. Anne Maguire. (YA) (gr. 7 up). 1981. 9.95 (ISBN 0-686-73959-0, Avalon). Bouregy.

Strip: An American Place. Richard P. Horwitz. LC 84-11897. (Illus.). xii, 188p. 1985. 25.95x (ISBN 0-8032-2332-3); pap. 14.95 (ISBN 0-8032-7228-6, BB 926, Bison). U of Nebr Pr.

Strip Death Naked. Norman Longmate. Ed. by J. Barzun & W. H. Taylor. LC 81-47351. (Crime Fiction 1950-1975 Ser.). 188p. 1983. lib. bdg. 18.00 (ISBN 0-8240-4972-1). Garland Pub.

Strip Method of Design. 2nd ed. Arno Hilleborg. (C & CA Viewpoint Publication Ser.). (Illus.). 1976. pap. text ed. 26.50x (ISBN 0-7210-1012-1, Pub. by C & CA London). Scholium Intl.

Strip-Mineable Coals Guidebook. LC 80-81269. 1980. 103.00 (ISBN 0-942218-08-6). Minobras.

Strip Mining. Susan Osterman. (Cambric Poetry Ser.). 72p. (Orig.). 1987. pap. 7.00 (ISBN 0-918342-26-0). Cambric.

Strip Mining: An Annotated Bibliography. Robert F. Munn. LC 72-96636. 110p. 1973. 4.00 (ISBN 0-937058-09-2). West Va U Pr.

Strip Quilting. Diane Wold. (Illus.). 160p. (Orig.). 1987. 21.95 (ISBN 0-8306-2522-4); pap. 12.95 (ISBN 0-8306-2822-3). TAB Bks.

Strip Quilting Projects: Quick Strip Quilting from the PBS-TV Series "Strip Quilting" by Kaye Wood. Kaye Wood. (Illus.). 1988. pap. 9.95 (ISBN 0-944588-11-5). K Wood Pub.

Strip Search. Rex Burns. (Crime Monthly Ser.). 272p. 1985. pap. 3.95 (ISBN 0-14-007747-2). Penguin.

Strip Searches. NCCL Staff. 1985. 20.00x (ISBN 0-946088-20-9, Pub. by NCCL UK). State Mutual Bk.

Strip Spring Making & Forming. Ed. by Spring Research Association, Sheffield. (Engineering Craftsmen: No. H7). (Illus.). 1977. spiral bdg. 39.95x. Trans-Atl Phila.

Strip Spring Making & Forming. 50.00x (Pub. by Engineering Ind). State Mutual Bk.

Strip-Squeezes. Hugh Kelsey. (Master Bridge Ser.). 128p. 1987. 20.95 (ISBN 0-575-03896-9, Pub. by Gollancz England). David & Charles.

Stripe & the Merbear. Dorothy Decker. LC 85-25433. (Stripe Adventures Ser.). (Illus.). 40p. (gr. k-3). 1986. lib. bdg. 10.95 (ISBN 0-87518-329-8, Gemstone Bks). Dillon.

Stripe Presents the ABC's. Dorothy Decker. LC 84-12180. (Stripe Adventures Ser.). (Illus.). 64p. (gr. k-3). 1984. PLB 10.95 (ISBN 0-87518-266-6, Gemstone Bks). Dillon.

Stripe Visits New York. Dorothy Decker. LC 85-6768. (Stripe Adventures Ser.). (Illus.). 48p. (gr. k-3). 1986. PLB 10.95 (ISBN 0-87518-267-4, Gemstone Bks). Dillon.

Striped Horses: The Story of a Zebra Family. Betty Dineen. LC 82-7786. (Illus.). 96p. (gr. 4-6). 1982. 9.95 (ISBN 0-02-732200-9). Macmillan.

Striped Ice Cream. Joan M. Lexau. (Illus.). (gr. 2-6). 1971. pap. 2.50 (ISBN 0-590-41307-4). Scholastic Inc.

Striped Skunk. Carl R. Green & William R. Sanford. Ed. by Howard Schroeder. LC 87-6652. (Wildlife Habits & Habitats Ser.). (Illus.). 48p. (gr. 5-6). 1987. PLB 10.95 (ISBN 0-89686-338-7). Crestwood Hse.

Stripers: The Economic Value of the Atlantic Coast Commerical & Recreational Striped Bass Fisheries. Ed. by Virgil Norton et al. pap. 4.00 (ISBN 0-943676-15-0). MD Sea Grant Col.

Stripes & Stars: The Evolution of the American Flag. Boleslaw Mastai & Marie-Louise D. Mastai. LC 73-87164. (Illus.). 72p. 1973. pap. 8.95 (ISBN 0-88360-001-3, Dist. by Univ. of Texas Pr). Amon Carter.

Stripline Circuit Design. Harlan Howe, Jr. LC 73-81242. 344p. 1975. 60.00 (ISBN 0-89006-020-7). Artech Hse.

Stripline-Line Transmission Lines for Microwave Integrated Circuits. Bherathi Bhat & Shiban K. Koul. 700p. 1988. 49.95 (ISBN 0-470-20700-0). Wiley.

Stripped Assets. Mike Hutton. 1986. 45.00x (ISBN 0-86332-141-0, Pub. by Book Guild Ltd). State Mutual Bk.

Stripper's Guide to Canoe-Building. David Hazen. LC 76-19972. 1982. 12.95 (ISBN 0-917436-00-8). Tamal Vista.

Stripping. Laura Boss. LC 82-4192. (Illus.). 52p. (Orig.). 1982. pap. 5.00 (ISBN 0-941608-01-8). Chantry Pr.

Stripping Analysis: Principles, Instrumentation & Applications. Ed. by Joseph Wang. 160p. 1985. 32.00 (ISBN 0-89573-143-6). VCH Pubs.

Stripping & Polishing Furniture. David Lawrence. 1985. 30.00x (Pub. by Bishopsgate Pr. Ltd.); pap. 21.00x. State Mutual Bk.

Stripping & Polishing Furniture: A Practical Guide. David Lawrence. (Illus.). 95p. 1987. 13.95 (ISBN 0-317-64163-8, Pub. by Bishopsgate Pr London); pap. 9.95 (ISBN 0-317-64165-4). Intl Spec Bk.

Stripping: The Assembly of Film Images. Harold L. Peck. LC 83-82330. 304p. 1984. 37.00 (ISBN 0-88362-049-9, 1507). Graphic Arts Tech Found.

Stripping the Trees. Harris Collingwood. (Chapbook Ser.: No. 2). (Illus.). 48p. (Orig.). 1980. pap. 4.95 (ISBN 0-937672-01-7). Rowan Tree.

Stripping Voltammetry in Chemical Analysis. K. Z. Brainina. 236p. 1974. text ed. 48.00x (ISBN 0-7065-1377-0, Pub. by Keter Pub Jerusalem). Coronet Bks.

Striptease. Elliot Fried. 36p. (Orig.). 1979. pap. 2.00 (ISBN 0-930090-09-8). Applezaba.

Striptease, Tango, Vatzlav: Three Plays. Slawomir Mrozek. Tr. by Lola Gruenthal et al from Pol. LC 81-47635. 224p. (Orig.). 1981. pap. 12.50 (ISBN 0-394-17933-1, E789, Ever). Grove.

Stripwell & Claw. Howard Barker. (Orig.). 1980. pap. 4.50 (ISBN 0-7145-3572-9). Riverrun NY.

Strive for the Truth: The World of Rav Dessler. E. E. Dessler. Tr. by Aryeh Carmell from Hebrew. 1978. 9.95 (ISBN 0-87306-139-X); pap. 7.95 (ISBN 0-87306-177-2). Feldheim.

Strive for Truth, Vol. 2. Eliyahu Dessler. 1985. 12.95 (ISBN 0-87306-395-3); pap. 9.95 (ISBN 0-87306-396-1). Feldheim.

Striving for Holiness. Bobbie C. Jobe. 2.70 (ISBN 0-89137-423-X). Quality Pubns.

Striving for Wholeness. Barbara Hannah. 316p. 1987. 24.95 (ISBN 0-938434-31-4); pap. 12.95 (ISBN 0-938434-32-2). Sigo Pr.

Striving; Keene State College, 1909-1984: The History of a Small Public Institution. James G. Smart. LC 84-5906. (Illus.). 400p. 1984. 25.00 (ISBN 0-914659-04-9). Phoenix Pub.

Stroboscopic Evaluation of the Larynx. Minora Hirano & Diane M. Bless. 250p. (Orig.). 1988. pap. text ed. 32.50 (ISBN 0-316-36463-0, 362630). College-Hill.

Strogaia Literatura. Boris Pankin. 400p. 1982. 39.00x (ISBN 0-317-40733-3, Pub. by Collets UK). State Mutual Bk.

Stroheim. Movie ed. Joel Finler. LC 68-17757. 1968. pap. 7.95 (ISBN 0-520-00413-2). U of Cal Pr.

Stroheim: A Pictorial Record of His Films. Herman G. Weinberg. 11.25 (ISBN 0-8446-5256-3). Peter Smith.

Stroka Prospekt. Richard Lupoff. Ed. by Thomas M. Disch. LC 82-19269. (Singularities Ser.). (Illus.). 48p. (Orig.). 1982. 40.00 (ISBN 0-915124-72-6, Pub. by Toothpaste); pap. 10.00 (ISBN 0-915124-73-4). Coffee Hse.

Stroke. Ed. by Moira A. Banks. (International Perspectives in Physical Therapy Ser.). (Illus.). 225p. 1986. pap. text ed. 27.00 (ISBN 0-443-02923-7). Churchill.

Stroke. Clark H. Milikan et al. LC 86-27379. (Illus.). 341p. 1987. text ed. 48.50 (ISBN 0-8121-1016-1). Lea & Febiger.

Stroke. Nexhat Thaqi. 144p. 1987. 8.95 (ISBN 0-8062-1846-0). Carlton.

Stroke. Ed. by Richard A. Thompson & John R. Green. LC 75-25129. (Advances in Neurology Ser.: Vol. 16). 250p. 1977. 44.50 (ISBN 0-89004-098-2). Raven.

Stroke. Derick Wade. (Practical Guides for General Practice: No. 4). (Illus.). 120p. 1988. pap. 12.95 (ISBN 0-19-261760-5). Oxford U Pr.

Stroke: A Clinical Approach. Louis R. Caplan & Robert W. Stein. (Illus.). 256p. 1986. text ed. 37.95 (ISBN 0-409-95157-9). Butterworth.

Stroke: A Guide for Patient & Family. Janice Frye-Pierson & James F. Toole. (Illus.). 224p. 1987. text ed. 26.50 (ISBN 0-88167-279-3); pap. text ed. 16.00 (ISBN 0-89004-637-9). Raven.

Stroke: A Guide for Patients & Their Families. rev ed. John E. Sarno & Martha T. Sarno. (Illus.). 1979. (ISBN 0-07-054732-7); pap. text ed. 5.95 (ISBN 0-07-054731-9). McGraw.

Stroke: A Guide to Recreational Rowing. Bruce Brown. (Illus.). 160p. 1986. pap. 14.95 (ISBN 0-87742-212-5). Intl Marine.

Stroke: A Practical Guide Towards Recovery. Richard L. Hewer & Derick T. Wade. (Illus.). 128p. 1986. pap. 9.95 (ISBN 0-668-06392-0). P-H.

Stroke: A Self-Help Manual for Stroke Sufferers & Their Relatives. R. M. Youngson. 144p. (Orig.). 1988. pap. 9.95 (ISBN 0-7153-8945-9, Pub. by David & Charles Pub England). Sterling.

Stroke a Slain Warrior. Frank M. Cortina. LC 70-133197. 231p. 1970. 30.00x (ISBN 0-231-03481-4); pap. 16.00x (ISBN 0-231-08658-X). Columbia U Pr.

Stroke & Heart Disease. Ed. by Dale C. Garell & Solomon H. Snyder. (Encyclopedia of Health Ser.). (Illus.). (YA) (gr. 7-12). 1989. 17.95 (ISBN 0-7910-0077-X). Chelsea Hse.

Stroke & Microcirculation. Ed. by J. Cervos-Navarro & R. Ferszt. (Illus.). 600p. 1988. text ed. 117.00 (ISBN 0-88167-313-7). Raven.

Stroke & the Extracranial Vessels. Ed. by Robert R. Smith et al. (Illus.). 390p. 1984. text ed. 115.50 (ISBN 0-89004-894-0). Raven.

Stroke: Animal Models: Proceedings of an International Symposium held at Wiesbaden, Germany, 16 November 1981. Ed. by Hoechst Stefanovich. (Illus.). 200p. 1982. 55.00 (ISBN 0-08-029799-4). Pergamon.

Stroke Diagnosis & Management: Current Procedures & Equipment. William S. Fields et al. LC 72-13847. (Illus.). 298p. 1973. 18.50 (ISBN 0-87527-101-4). Green.

Stroke: Epidemiological, Therapeutic & Socio-Economic Aspects. Ed. by F. Clifford Rose. (International Congress & Symposium Ser.: No. 99). 169p. 1986. pap. 28.00 (ISBN 0-317-58710-2, Pub. by Royal Society of Medicine Services Ltd). Longwood Pub Group.

Stroke Family Guide & Resource. Grady P. Bray & Gary S. Clark. (Illus.). 192p. 1984. 18.50x (ISBN 0-398-04856-8). C C Thomas.

Stroke: From Crisis to Victory - A Family Guide. John H. Lavin. 192p. 1985. 16.95 (ISBN 0-531-09787-0). Watts.

Stroke-Head Injury: A Guide to Functional Outcomes in Physical Therapy. Rehabilitation Institute of Chicago Procedure Manual. (Illus.). 325p. 1985. 49.50 (ISBN 0-87189-226-X). Aspen Pub.

Stroke in the Elderly: New Issues in Diagnosis, Treatment & Rehabilitation. Ed. by Ruth E. Dunkle & James Schmidley. 224p. 1987. text ed. 26.95 (ISBN 0-8261-5430-1). Springer Pub.

Stroke of Genius. Ted Mark. (Orig.). 1982. pap. 2.50 (ISBN 0-89083-976-X). Zebra.

Stroke of Genius: Graphic Programming in BASIC for the Apple Computer. Sid Caba & Norm Church. (Illus.). 128p. (gr. 4 up). 1985. pap. cancelled (ISBN 0-88056-311-7). Dilithium Pr.

Stroke of Lightning. Ted Mark. (Stroke Ser.). 1982. pap. cancelled (ISBN 0-8217-1078-8). Zebra.

Stroke of Luck & Dream of Destiny. Arnold Bennett. LC 74-17075. (Collected Works of Arnold Bennett: Vol. 76). 1976. Repr. of 1932 ed. 22.00 (ISBN 0-518-19157-5). Ayer Co Pubs.

Stroke: Pathophysiology, Diagnosis & Management, 2 vols. Ed. by Henry J. Barnett et al. (Illus.). 1985. text ed. 165.00 (ISBN 0-443-08260-X). Churchill.

Stroke Patient: A Team Approach. 3rd ed. Margaret Johnstone. LC 86-17584. (Illus.). 114p. (Orig.). 1987. pap. text ed. 11.00 (ISBN 0-443-03397-8). Churchill.

Stroke Patient's Own Story. Michael N. Prazich. 32p. 1985. pap. text ed. 1.50 (ISBN 0-8134-2499-2, 2499). Inter Print Pubs.

Stroke Prediction & Prevention. C. Raymond Van Dusen. (Royal Court Reports: No. 1). (Illus.). 14p. (Orig.). 1981. pap. 2.00 (ISBN 0-941354-00-8). Royal Court.

Stroke Rehabilitation. Murray E. Brandstater. (RML Ser.). (Illus.). 400p. 1987. 58.50 (ISBN 0-683-01013-1). Williams & Wilkins.

Stroke Rehabilitation. Paul E. Kaplan & Leonard J. Cerullo. (Illus.). 448p. 1986. text ed. 45.00 (ISBN 0-409-95122-6). Butterworth.

Stroke Rehabilitation: Basic Concepts & Research Trends. William S. Fields & William A. Spencer. LC 67-19383. (Illus.). 184p. 1967. 12.50 (ISBN 0-87527-034-4). Green.

Stroke Rehabilitation: The Recovery of Motor Control. Pamela Duncan. (Illus.). 226p. 1987. pap. text ed. 24.00 (ISBN 0-8151-2936-X). Year Bk Med.

Stroke: The Facts. Clifford Rose & Rudy Capildeo. (Facts Ser.). (Illus.). 1981. text ed. 14.95x (ISBN 0-19-261170-4); pap. 6.95 (ISBN 0-19-286029-1). Oxford U Pr.

Stroke! The Ordeal & the Rainbow. Sam Krupnick. Ed. by Gregory M. Franzwa. (Illus.). 116p. (Orig.). 1986. pap. 5.95 (ISBN 0-935284-43-5). Patrice Pr.

Strokes & Strokes: An Instructor's Manual for Developing Swim Programs for Stroke Victims. Jill Heckathorn. LC 83-190770. pap. 20.00 (ISBN 0-317-55560-X, 2029560). Bks Demand UMI.

Strokes: Essays & Reviews, 1966-1986. John Clute. 180p. 1988. 16.95 (ISBN 0-934933-03-0); pap. 8.95 (ISBN 0-934933-04-9). Serconia Pr.

Strokes of Genius. Thomas Boswell. LC 86-19697. (Illus.). 256p. 1987. pap. 19.95 (ISBN 0-385-19968-6). Doubleday.

Stroll down Millenium Alleys. Dokia Humenna. LC 87-60430. (Mini Short Stories Ser.). 170p. 1987. 7.50 (ISBN 0-914834-76-2). Smoloskyp.

Stroll in the Air. Eugene Ionesco. Tr. by Donald Watson from Fr. Bd. with Frenzy for Two or More. 1968. pap. 2.45 (ISBN 0-394-17311-2, E485, Ever). Grove.

Stroll Through Historic Salem. Samuel Chamberlain. LC 78-79738. (Illus.). 1969. student ed. 9.95 (ISBN 0-8038-6689-5). Hastings.

Stroll with William James. Jacques Barzun. LC 82-48108. 288p. 1983. 19.45i (ISBN 0-06-015090-4, HarpT). Har-Row.

Stroll with William James. Jacques Barzun. LC 84-2612. viii, 344p. 1984. pap. 12.95 (ISBN 0-226-03866-1); 25.00x (ISBN 0-226-03865-3). U of Chicago Pr.

Strolling Players & Drama in the Provinces, 1660-1765. Sybil Rosenfeld. LC 78-96167. 1970. Repr. lib. bdg. 23.00x (ISBN 0-374-96935-3, Octagon). Hippocrene Bks.

Strolling Through Istanbul. Hilary Sumner-Boyd & John Freely. (Illus.). 1972. 15.00x (ISBN 0-686-16866-6). Intl Learn Syst.

Strolling Through Istanbul: A Guide to the City. Hilary Sumner-Boyd & John Freely. 210p. 1987. pap. 16.95 (02142, Kegan Paul). Routledge Chapman & Hall.

Strom Toys: Classic Toys in Wood. rev. ed. Richard H. Strombeck & Janet A. Strombeck. (Illus.). 100p. (Orig.). 1984. pap. 9.95 (ISBN 0-912355-01-8). Sun Designs.

Stromatolites. M. R. Walter. (Developments in Sedimentology Ser.: Vol. 20). 790p. 1976. 176.50 (ISBN 0-444-41376-6). Elsevier.

Strong & Free. Amy Hagstrom. LC 87-3942. (Illus.). 24p. (gr. 1 up). 1987. 12.95 (ISBN 0-933849-08-7). Landmark Edns.

Strong & Tender Thread. Jackie Weger. (American Romance Ser.). 192p. 1983. pap. 2.25 (ISBN 0-373-16005-4). Harlequin Bks.

Strong & the Weak. Paul Tournier. LC 63-8898. 252p. 1976. pap. 6.95 (ISBN 0-664-24745-8). Westminster John Knox.

Strong & Ultrastrong Magnetic Fields. Ed. by F. Herlach. (Topics in Applied Physics Ser.: Vol. 57). (Illus.). 375p. 1985. 54.00 (ISBN 0-387-13504-9). Springer-Verlag.

Strong Asymptotics for Extremal Polynomials Associated with Weights on IR. D. S. Lubinsky & E. B. Saff. (Lecture Notes in Mathematics Ser.: Vol. 1305). vii, 153p. 1988. pap. 17.30 (ISBN 0-387-18958-0). Springer-Verlag.

Strong at the Broken Places. Max Cleland. LC 86-26814. (Illus.). 168p. 1986. Repr. of 1980 ed. 13.95 (ISBN 0-87797-126-9). Cherokee.

Strong Bones Diet: The High Calcium, Low Calorie Way to Prevent Osteoporosis. Lois Goulder & Leo Lutwak. 224p. 1988. 14.95 (ISBN 0-937404-20-9). Triad Pub FL.

Strong-Campbell Interest Inventory. David P. Campbell & Edward K. Strong, Jr. prices on request (ISBN 0-8047-1068-6). Stanford U. Pr.

Strong Choices, Weak Choices: The Challenge of Change in Recovery. Gayle Rosellini & Mark Worden. LC 87-46226. 144p. (Orig.). 1988. pap. 7.95 (ISBN 0-06-255484-0, PL-4285, HarpR). Har-Row.

Strong Cigars & Lovely Women. John Lardner. 16.95 (ISBN 0-8488-0124-5, Pub. by Amereon Hse). Amereon Ltd.

Strong City. Taylor Caldwell. 1974. Repr. of 1942 ed. lib. bdg. 29.95x (ISBN 0-88411-158-X, Pub. by Aeonian Pr). Amereon Ltd.

Strong Democracy: Participatory Politics for a New Age. Benjamin Barber. LC 83-4842. 320p. 1984. pap. 10.95x (ISBN 0-520-05616-7). U of Cal Pr.

Strong Fibers. Watt & Perov. (Handbook of Composites Ser.: Vol. 1). 1985. 122.00 (ISBN 0-444-87505-0). Elsevier.

Strong Ground Motion Seismology. Ed. by Mustafa O. Erdik & M. Nafi Toksoz. lib. bdg. 116.00 (ISBN 90-277-2532-2, Pub. by Reidel Holland). Kluwer Academic.

Strong Ground Motion Simulation & Earthquake Engineering Applications: A Technological Assessment. Ed. by R. Scholl & J. King. 400p. 1985. 10.00. Earthquake Eng.

Strong Hearts. facsimile ed. George W. Cable. LC 76-106254. (Short Story Index Reprint Ser.). 1899. 17.00 (ISBN 0-8369-3291-9). Ayer Co Pubs.

Strong Hearts. George W. Cable. 1972. Repr. of 1899 ed. lib. bdg. 16.00 (ISBN 0-8422-8020-0). Irvington.

Strong Hearts. George W. Cable. 1986. pap. text ed. 8.95x (ISBN 0-8290-1865-4). Irvington.

Strong Hearts see Collected Works.

Strong Interaction Physics. International Summer Institute in Theoretical Physics. (Springer Tracts in Modern Physics: Vol. 57). 1971. 56.70 (ISBN 0-387-05252-6). Springer-Verlag.

Strong Limit Theorems in Non-Commutative Probability. R. Jajte. (Lecture Notes in Mathematics Ser.: Vol. 1110). vi, 152p. 1985. pap. 14.00 (ISBN 0-387-13915-X). Springer-Verlag.

Strong, Loving & Wise: Presiding in Liturgy. Robert W. Hovda. (Illus.). 96p. 1983. pap. 5.95 (ISBN 0-8146-1253-9). Liturgical Pr.

Strong-Man from Piraeus: And Other Stories. George Johnston & Charmian Clift. Ed. by Garry Kinnane. 320p. 1986. pap. 6.95 (ISBN 0-14-008798-2). Penguin.

Strong Man of China. facs. ed. Robert Berkov. LC 70-124225. (Select Bibliographies Reprint Ser). (Illus.). 1938. 19.00 (ISBN 0-8369-5413-0). Ayer Co Pubs.

Strong Man's Prey. Ed. by A. J. Broomhall. 256p. 1953. 70.00x (Pub. by Han-Shan Tang Ltd). State Mutual Bk.

Strong Materials. J. W. Martin. (Wykeham Science Ser.: No. 21). 124p. 1972. pap. 18.00x (ISBN 0-85109-260-8). Taylor & Francis.

Strong Materials. J. W. Martin & R. A. Hull. LC 72-189452. (Wykeham Science Ser.: No. 21). 124p. 1972. 18.00x (ISBN 0-8448-1123-8, Pub. by Crane Russak & Co). Taylor & Francis.

Strong Measures. Ed. by Philip Dacey & David Jauss. LC 85-45186. 432p. 1986. 18.45i (ISBN 0-06-015484-5, HarpT). Har-Row.

Strong Measures: Contemporary American Poetry in Traditional Forms. Philip Dacey & David Jauss. 432p. 1985. pap. text ed. 16.50 (ISBN 0-06-041471-5, HarpC). Har-Row.

Strong Medicine. Arthur Hailey. 1986. pap. 4.95 (ISBN 0-440-18366-9). Dell.

Strong-Minded Women: And Other Lost Voices of Nineteenth-Century England. Janet H. Murray. (Illus.). 417p. 1982. 22.00 (ISBN 0-394-50459-3); pap. 11.95 (ISBN 0-394-71044-4). Pantheon.

Strong-Minded Women: The Emergence of the Woman-Suffrage Movement in Iowa. Louise R. Noun. (Iowa Heritage Collection Ser.). (Illus.). 322p. 1986. pap. 5.95 (ISBN 0-8138-1724-2). Iowa St U Pr.

Strong Mothers, Weak Wives. Miriam M. Johnson. 325p. 1988. 25.00 (ISBN 0-520-06161-6). U of Cal Pr.

Strong Name. James S. Stewart. (Scholar As Preacher Ser.). 268p. 1940. 16.95 (ISBN 0-567-04427-0, Pub. by T & T Clark Ltd UK). Fortress.

Strong Necessity of Time: The Philosophy of Time in Shakespeare & Elizabethan Literature. G. F. Waller. (Depropríetatibus Litterarum, Ser. Practica: No. 90). 1976. pap. text ed. 19.20x (ISBN 90-2793-254-9). Mouton.

Strong on Music: The New York Music Scene in the Days of George Templeton Strong, 1836-1875, Vol. 1: 1836-1849. Vera B. Lawrence. (Illus.). 750p. 1988. 85.00 (ISBN 0-19-504199-2). Oxford U Pr.

Strong Opinions. Vladimir Nabokov. LC 73-6604. 352p. 1973. text ed. 8.95 (ISBN 0-07-045737-9). McGraw.

Strong Place: Poems Seventy-Four to Eighty-Four. Paul Marion. LC 84-82241. 64p. (Orig.). 1984. pap. 4.95 (ISBN 0-931507-00-6). Loom Pr.

Strong Poison. Dorothy L. Sayers. LC 86-45144. 256p. 1987. 17.45i (ISBN 0-06-055025-2, HarpT). Har-Row.

Strong Poison: A Lord Peter Wimsey Mystery with Harriet Vane. Dorothy L. Sayers. LC 86-45144. 240p. 1987. pap. 4.50 (ISBN 0-06-080908-6, P-908, PL). Har-Row.

Strong Rigidity of Locally Symmetric Spaces. G. D. Mostow. (Annals of Mathematics Studies: No. 78). 220p. 1974. 27.00x (ISBN 0-691-08136-0). Princeton U Pr.

Strong Shall Live. Louis L'Amour. 1985. pap. 2.95 (ISBN 0-553-25200-3). Bantam.

Strong Societies & Weak States: State-Society Relations & State Capabilities in the Third World. Joel S. Migdal. (Illus.). 344p. 1988. 45.00 (ISBN 0-691-05669-2); pap. 13.95 (ISBN 0-691-01073-0). Princeton U Pr.

Strong Solids. 3rd ed. A. Kelly & N. H. MacMillan. (Monographs on the Physics & Chemistry of Materials). (Illus.). 420p. 1987. 89.00 (ISBN 0-19-851362-3). Oxford U Pr.

Strong Sunday Schools-Strong Churches: The Pastor's Role. Roy Ryan. LC 86-71810. 72p. (Orig.). 1986. pap. 4.95 (ISBN 0-88177-035-3, DR035B). Discipleship Res.

Strong Vocational Interest Blank. David P. Campbell & Edward K. Strong. prices on request (ISBN 0-8047-1069-4). Stanford U Pr.

Strong Voice. Ed. by Robert McGovern & Richard Snyder. 43p. 1972. pap. 1.95 (ISBN 0-912592-15-X). Ashland Poetry.

Strong Voice Three. Ed. by Robert McGovern & Richard Snyder. 63p. 1974. pap. 1.95 (ISBN 0-912592-19-2). Ashland Poetry.

Strong Voice Two. Ed. by Robert McGovern & Richard Snyder. 48p. 1973. pap. 1.95 (ISBN 0-912592-17-6). Ashland Poetry.

Strong-Willed Adult. Dennis L. Gibson. 160p. (Orig.). 1987. pap. 7.95 (ISBN 0-8010-3816-2). Baker Bk.

Strong-Willed Child. James C. Dobson. 1978. 10.95 (ISBN 0-8423-0664-1). Tyndale.

Strong-Willed Child. James C. Dobson. 240p. pap. 6.95 (ISBN 0-8423-6661-X). Tyndale.

Strongarm. Dan J. Marlowe. LC 87-72704. 160p. 1988. pap. 4.95 (ISBN 0-88739-041-2, Pub. by Black Lizard Bks). Creative Arts Bk.

Stronger see Three Plays.

Stronger by Far. Sandra James. (Superromance Ser.: No. 277). pap. 2.75 (ISBN 0-317-63895-5). Harlequin Bks.

Stronger Pump. Julia A. Purcell & Barbara Johnston. Ed. by Nancy R. Hull. LC 80-10191. (Illus., Orig.). (gr. 8-10). 1986. pap. text ed. 3.60 (ISBN 0-939838-05-2). Pritchett & Hull.

Stronger Than a Hundred Men: A History of the Vertical Water Wheel, No. 7. Terry S. Reynolds. LC 82-15346. (Studies in the History of Technology). (Illus.). 472p. 1983. 47.50x (ISBN 0-8018-2554-7). Johns Hopkins.

Stronger than Fear. Richard Tregaskis. 13.95 (ISBN 0-88411-878-9, Pub. by Aeonian Pr). Amereon Ltd.

Stronger Than Hatred: A Collection of Spiritual Writings. Maxmilian Kolbe. Tr. by Eduardo Flood from Ital. 136p. (Orig.). 1988. pap. 6.95 (ISBN 0-911782-64-8). New City.

Stronger Than Steel: The Wayne Alderson Story. R. C. Sproul. LC 80-7746. 208p. 1983. pap. 6.95 (ISBN 0-06-067503-9, RD445, HarpR). Har-Row.

Stronger Than Steel: The Wayne Alderson Story. Robert C. Sproul. LC 80-7746. 208p. 1980. 10.00 (ISBN 0-318-23249-9). W T Alderson.

Stronger than Yearning. Penny Jordan. pap. 3.50 (ISBN 0-373-83205-2). Harlequin Bks.

Strongest Ally. Stefan Troyanski. 1984. 25.00 (ISBN 0-900380-29-2, Pub. by FAP Co UK). State Mutual Bk.

Strongest Man in the World. Ed. by Dmitry Ivanov. LC 79-9425. (Illus.). 289p. 1979. 14.95 (ISBN 0-943071-09-7). Sphinx Pr.

Strongest Part of the Family: A Study of Lao Refugee Women in Columbus, Ohio. Karen L. Muir. (Immigrant Communities & Ethnic Minorities in the United States & Canada Ser: No. 17). 1988. 38.50. AMS Pr.

Stronghold. Phillips Kloss. LC 86-14557. 128p. 1987. 10.95 (ISBN 0-86534-093-5). Sunstone Pr.

Stronghold: A Story of Historic Northern Neck of Virginia & Its People. Miriam Haynie. 1959. 7.50 (ISBN 0-87517-042-0). Dietz.

Strongly Coupled Plasma Physics. Ed. by Forrest J. Rogers & Hugh E. Dewitt. (NATO ASI Series B, Physics: Vol. 154). (Illus.). 610p. 1987. 97.50x (ISBN 0-306-42581-5, Plenum Pr). Plenum Pub.

Strongly Interacting Particles. Riccardo Levi-Setti & Thomas Lasinski. (Chicago Lectures in Physics Ser). 1973. pap. 8.00x (ISBN 0-226-47445-3). U of Chicago Pr.

Strong's Book of Designs. 92p. 1982. Repr. of 1910 ed. 39.95 (ISBN 0-911380-61-2). Signs of Times.

Strong's Exhaustive Concordance. James Strong. 17.95 (ISBN 0-8010-8228-5); pap. 13.95 (ISBN 0-8010-8108-4). Baker Bk.

Strong's Exhaustive Concordance. James Strong. LC 78-73138. 1978. pap. 15.95 (ISBN 0-8054-1134-8). Broadman.

Strong's Exhaustive Concordance. James Strong. (Reference Set). 1547p. 1982. 17.95 (ISBN 0-88062-106-0). Mott Media.

Strong's Exhaustive Concordance of the Bible with the Exclusive Key-Word Comparison. rev. ed. James Strong. 1980. 23.95 (ISBN 0-687-40030-9); thumb-indexed 28.95 (ISBN 0-687-40031-7). Abingdon.

Strong's Exhaustive Concordance of the Bible. James Strong. 1552p. Date not set. 20.95 (ISBN 0-917006-01-1). Hendrickson MA.

Strong's Exhaustive Concordance of the Bible. James Strong. 19.95 (ISBN 0-87981-626-0). Holman Bible Pub.

Strong's Exhaustive Concordance of the Bible. Ed. by James Strong. 1552p. 1986. text ed. 12.95 (ISBN 0-529-06334-4); Thumb indexed ed. text ed. 15.95 (ISBN 0-529-06335-2). World Bible.

Strong's Exhaustive Concordance: Red-Letter, Easy to Read Edition. James Strong. 26.95; thumb-indexed ed. 29.95. Abingdon.

Strong's New Concordance of the Bible: Popular Edition. James Strong. 784p. 1985. text ed. 12.95 (ISBN 0-8407-4951-1). Nelson.

Strong's North Carolina Index, 13 Vols. LC 76-3380. write for info. Lawyers Co-Op.

Strontium Isotope Geology. G. Faure & J. L. Powell. LC 72-75720. (Minerals, Rocks & Inorganic Materials Ser.: Vol. 5). (Illus.). 200p. 1972. 24.80 (ISBN 0-387-05784-6). Springer-Verlag.

Stroop Report: The Jewish Quarter of Warsaw Is No More! Jurgen Stroop. LC 79-1900. 1980. 10.00 (ISBN 0-394-50443-7). Pantheon.

Stroop Report: The Jewish Quarter of Warsaw Is No More! Intro. by Andrzej Wirth. (Ger.). 1986. 9.95 (ISBN 0-394-73817-9). Pantheon.

Strophes; Etudes Historiques et Critiques Sur les Formes De la Poesie Lyrique En France Depuis la Renaissance. Philippe Martinon. 1969. Repr. of 1912 ed. 36.50 (ISBN 0-8337-2271-9). B Franklin.

Strosnider Family in America. Ruth C. Strosnider. 1982. 13.00 (ISBN 0-87012-442-0). McClain.

Stroud As It Was. Hendon Publishing Co., Ltd. Staff. 1986. 14.70x (ISBN 0-317-54183-8, Pub. by Hendon Pub UK). State Mutual BK.

Struck Copies of Early American Coins. E. Kenny. (Illus.). 1982. Repr. of 1952 ed. softcover 6.00 (ISBN 0-915262-91-6). S J Durst.

Structopathic Children, 2 pts. J. F. W. Kok. Incl. Pt. 1. Description of Disturbance Type & Strategies. 1126p (ISBN 90-237-4109-9); Pt. 2. Results of Experimental Research of Structuring Group Therapy. 122p (ISBN 90-237-4110-2). (Modern Approaches to the Diagnosis & Instruction of Multi-Handicapped Children Ser.: Vols. 9 & 10). 1972. text ed. 30.00 ea. (Pub. by Swets & Zeitlinger Netherlands). Hogrefe Intl.

Structual Equations with Latent Variables. Bollen. (Probability & Mathematical Statistics Ser.). 1988. write for info. (ISBN 0-471-01171-1). Wiley.

Structural. 25.00. Am Consul Eng.

Structural Adhesive Joints in Engineering. R. D. Adams & W. C. Wake. 320p. 1984. 77.50 (ISBN 0-85334-263-6, I-166-84, Pub. by Elsevier Applied Sci England). Elsevier.

Structural Adhesives & Bonding: Proceedings of a Special Conference, March 1979, El Segundo, California. (Illus.). 426p. 47.00 (ISBN 0-938648-07-1, 0111). T-C Pubns CA.

Structural Adhesives: Chemistry & Technology. Ed. by S. R. Hartshorn. (Topics in Applied Chemistry Ser.). 524p. 1986. 75.00x (ISBN 0-306-42121-6, Plenum Pr). Plenum Pub.

Structural Adhesives: Developments in Resins & Primers. Ed. by A. J. Kinloch. 322p. 1986. 74.25 (ISBN 1-85166-002-X, Pub. by Elsevier Appl Sci England). Elsevier.

Structural Adhesives with Emphasis on Aerospace Applications: A Report of the Ad Hoc Committee on Structural Adhesives for Aerospace Use, National Materials Advisory Board, National Research Council. National Research Council, Committee on Structural Adhesives for Aerospace Use. LC 75-17033. (Treatise on Adhesion & Adhesives Ser.: Vol. 4). pap. 66.00 (2027122). Bks Demand UMI.

Structural Adjustment & Economic Performance. OECD Staff. 372p. (Orig.). 1988. pap. 39.95x (ISBN 92-64-13006-3). OECD.

Structural Adjustment & Multinational Enterprises. OECD Staff. (Investment & Multinational Enterprises Ser.). 68p. (Orig.). 1985. pap. 11.00 (ISBN 0-318-18655-1). OECD.

Structural Adjustment in Developed Open Economies: Proceedings of a Conference of the International Economic Association Held at Yxtaholm, Sweden. Ed. by Karl Jungenfelt & Douglas C. Hague. LC 83-22966. 448p. 1985. 35.00 (ISBN 0-312-76662-9). St Martin.

Structural Adjustment in Europe. Pauline Creasey. 280p. 1988. 35.00 (ISBN 0-317-68231-8, Pub. by Pinter Pubs UK). Columbia U Pr.

Structural Adjustment in Lowinca: A Case Exercise in Economic Policy Analysis. Paul G. Clark et al. (EDI Development Policy Case Ser.). 256p. 1988. 12.95 (ISBN 0-8213-0974-9, BK0974). World Bank.

Structural Adjustment in the Federal Republic of Germany. Klaus W. Schatz et al. (Employment, Adjustment & Industrialisation Ser.: No. 4). vi, 141p. (Orig.). 1987. pap. 19.25 (ISBN 92-2-106114-0). Intl Labour Office.

Structural Adjustment Lending: An Evaluation of Program Design. Fahrettin Yagci et al. (Working Paper: No. 735). 150p. 1985. 8.00 (ISBN 0-8213-0545-X, WP 0735). World Bank.

Structural Adjustment Policies in Developing Economies. Bela Balassa. (Working Paper: No. 464). 36p. 1981. pap. 3.50 (ISBN 0-686-39748-7, WP-0464). World Bank.

Structural Allegory. Ed. by John Fekete. LC 83-19878. (Theory & History of Literature Ser.: Vol 11). xxiv, 269p. 1984. 29.50x (ISBN 0-8166-1271-4); pap. 14.95 (ISBN 0-8166-1270-6). U of Minn Pr.

Structural Ambiguity in Brahms: Analytical Approaches to Four Works. Jonathan Dunsby. LC 81-24. (Studies in British Musicology). pap. 33.30 (2070033). Bks Demand UMI.

Structural Analogy in Language. John M. Anderson. 201p. 1987. pap. 24.95 (ISBN 0-89720-083-7). Karoma.

Structural Analysis. Alexander Chajes. (Illus.). 384p. 1983. 48.00 (ISBN 0-13-853408-X). P-H.

Structural Analysis. 3rd ed. Coates. 1988. pap. 47.95 (ISBN 0-278-00035-5). Van Nos Reinhold.

Structural Analysis. Russell C. Hibbeler. 512p. 1985. text ed. write for info. (ISBN 0-02-354460-0). Macmillan.

Structural Analysis. Russell C. Hibbeler. 107p. 1985. pap. solutions manual avail. (ISBN 0-02-354470-8). Macmillan.

Structural Analysis. Jeffrey P. Laible. 902p. 1985. text ed. 44.95 (ISBN 0-03-063382-6, HoltC). HR&W.

Structural Analysis. 2nd ed. Harold I. Laursen. LC 77-21575. (Illus.). 1977. text ed. 48.95 (ISBN 0-07-036643-8). McGraw.

Structural Analysis. 3rd ed. Harold I. Laursen. 512p. 1988. text ed. 48.95 (ISBN 0-07-036645-4). McGraw.

Structural Analysis. 4th ed. Jack C. McCormac. 640p. 1984. text ed. 54.95 scp (ISBN 0-06-044342-1, HarpC). Har-Row.

Structural Analysis. S. M. Sack. 1984. text ed. 48.95 (ISBN 0-07-054392-5). McGraw.

Structural Analysis. J. C. Smith. 699p. 1988. text ed. 57.50 (ISBN 0-06-046317-1, HarpC). Har-Row.

Structural Analysis. Jan J. Tuma. (Schaum's Outline Ser). 1969. pap. text ed. 12.95 (ISBN 0-07-065422-0). McGraw.

Structural Analysis. Tung Au & Paul Christiano. (Illus.). 752p. 1987. text ed. write for info. (ISBN 0-13-853383-0). P-H.

Structural Analysis. G. B. Vine. LC 80-42209. (Constructions & Civil Engineering Sector: Technician Ser.). (Illus.). 288p. (Orig.). 1982. pap. text ed. 10.95 (ISBN 0-582-41618-3). Longman.

Structural Analysis: A Classical & Matrix Approach. 5th ed. Jack McCormac & Rudolph E. Elling. 608p. 1988. text ed. 56.50t (ISBN 0-06-044341-3, HarpC). Har-Row.

Structural Analysis: A Unified Classical & Matrix Approach. 2nd ed. A. Ghali & A. M. Neville. 1978. pap. 29.95x (ISBN 0-412-14990-7, 6122, Pub. by Chapman & Hall). Routledge Chapman & Hall.

Structural Analysis Activity Sheets. Wilma H. Miller. (Corrective Reading Skills Activity File Ser.). (Orig.). 1977. pap. 8.50x (ISBN 0-87628-223-0, C-2230-5). Ctr Appl Res.

Structural Analysis & Biblical Exegesis. R. Barthes et al. Tr. by Alfred M. Johnson, Jr. LC 74-31334. (Pittsburgh Theological Monographs: No. 3). 1974. pap. 9.95 (ISBN 0-915138-02-6). Pickwick.

Structural Analysis & Design. C. P. Heins, Jr. & K. Derucher. (Civil Engineering Ser.: Vol. 2). 1980. 59.75 (ISBN 0-8247-6922-8). Dekker.

Structural Analysis & Design, Vol. 1. Robert L. Ketter et al. (Illus.). 1979. text ed. 45.95 (ISBN 0-07-034291-1). McGraw.

Structural Analysis & Design of Multivariable Control Systems. Y. T. Tsay et al. (Lecture Notes in Control & Information Sciences Ser.: Vol. 107). vi, 208p. 1988. pap. 32.70 (ISBN 0-387-18916-5). Springer-Verlag.

Structural Analysis & Design of Nuclear Plant Facilities. LC 80-65828. (Manual & Report on Engineering Practice Ser.: No. 58). 571p. 1980. 140.00x (ISBN 0-87262-238-X). Am Soc Civil Eng.

Structural Analysis & Design of Process Equipment. Maan H. Jawad & James R. Farr. LC 83-12475. 704p. 1984. text ed. 73.50x (ISBN 0-471-09207-X, Pub. by Wiley-Interscience). Wiley.

Structural Analysis & Design of Process Equipment. 2nd ed. Maan H. Jawad & James R. Farr. LC 88-2796. 1988. 85.00 (ISBN 0-471-62471-3). Wiley.

Structural Analysis & Design of Tall Buildings. B. S. Taranath. 672p. 1988. text ed. 59.95 (ISBN 0-07-062878-5). McGraw.

Structural Analysis & Design: Some Minicomputer Applications, 2 pts. H. B. Harrison. (Illus.). 1980. Set. text ed. 120.00 (ISBN 0-08-023239-6); pap. text ed. 40.00 (ISBN 0-08-023240-X). Pergamon.

Structural Analysis & Synthesis: A Laboratory Course in Structural Geology. Stephen M. Rowland. LC 86-13631. (Illus.). 250p. 1986. pap. text ed. 29.95 (ISBN 0-86542-308-3). Blackwell Pubns.

Structural Analysis by Direct Moment Distribution. J. Rygol. 444p. 1968. 155.00 (ISBN 0-677-61190-0). Gordon & Breach.

Structural Analysis for Engineers. Nicholas Willems & William M. Lucas, Jr. (Illus.). 1977. text ed. 46.95 (ISBN 0-07-070295-0). McGraw.

Structural Analysis Learnt by Example: Simply Supported Beams Cantilevers, Vol. 1. J. Walter White. 1972. 25.00 (ISBN 0-8464-0888-0). Beekman Pubs.

Structural Analysis of Collision Amplitudes: Proceedings, les Houches June Institute of Physics, June 2-27, 1975. Ed. by R. Balian & D. Iagolnitzer. LC 76-17583. 1976. 118.50 (ISBN 0-7204-0506-8, North-Holland). Elsevier.

Structural Analysis of Complex Aerial Photographs. Ed. by Makoto Nagao & Takashi Matsuyama. (Advanced Applications in Pattern Recognition Ser.). 224p. 1980. 45.00x (ISBN 0-306-40571-7, Plenum Pr). Plenum Pub.

Structural Analysis of Discrete Data with Econometric Applications. Ed. by Charles F. Manski & Daniel McFadden. 588p. 1981. text ed. 42.50x (ISBN 0-262-13159-5). MIT Pr.

Structural Analysis of Granitic Rocks. J. Marre. 128p. 1986. 38.25 (ISBN 0-444-01078-5). Elsevier.

Structural Analysis of Kinship: Prolegomena to the Sociology of Kinship. Kingsley Davis. Ed. by Harriet Zuckerman & Robert K. Merton. LC 79-8990. (Dissertations on Sociology Ser.). 1980. lib. bdg. 38.00x (ISBN 0-405-12962-9). Ayer Co Pubs.

Structural Analysis of Laminated Anisotropic Plates. James M. Whitney. LC 87-50430. 200p. 1987. 55.00 (ISBN 0-87762-518-2); Book with LAMPCAL software. 135.00. Technomic.

Structural Analysis of Mozart's Piano Concertos. Hans Tischler. (Wissenschaftliche Abhandlungen-Musicological Studies Ser.: Vol. 10). 140p. (Eng., Ger. & Fr.). 1968. lib. bdg. 36.00 (ISBN 0-912024-80-1). Inst Mediaeval Mus.

Structural Analysis of Narrative. Tr. by Jean Calloud & Daniel Patte. 108p. 1976. pap. 8.95 (ISBN 0-89130-687-0, 06-06-04). Scholars Pr GA.

Structural Analysis of Narrative Texts, Conference Papers. Ed. by Andrej Kodjak et al. (New York University Slavic Papers: Vol. II). (Illus.). 203p. (Orig.). 1980. pap. 12.95 (ISBN 0-89357-071-0). Slavica.

Structural Analysis of Nucleic Acids. Ed. by J. C. Chirikjian & T. S. Papas. (Gene Amplification & Analysis Ser.: Vol. 2). 554p. 1981. 137.00 (ISBN 0-444-00636-2, Biomedical Pr). Elsevier.

Structural Analysis of Organic Compounds by Combined Application of Spectroscopic Methods. J. T. Clerc et al. (Studies in Analytical Chemistry: Vol. 1). 288p. 1982. 89.50 (ISBN 0-444-99748-2). Elsevier.

Structural Analysis of Pound's Usura Canto: Jakobson's Method Extended & Applied to Free Verse. Christine Brooke-Rose. (De Proprietatibus Litterarum Ser.: No. 26). 76p. 1976. pap. text ed. 12.00x (ISBN 90-2793-361-8). Mouton.

Structural Analysis of Shells. E. H. Baker et al. LC 79-27250. 364p. 1981. Repr. of 1972 ed. lib. bdg. 42.50 (ISBN 0-89874-118-1). Krieger.

Structural Analysis of the Sermon on the Mount. Andreij Kodjak. (Religion & Reasons Ser.: No. 34). (Illus.). x, 234p. 1986. lib. bdg. 59.50x (ISBN 0-89925-159-5). Mouton.

Structural Analysis Software for Micros. 2nd ed. Bernard J. Korites. Orig. Title: Sturctural Analysis for Micros. (Illus.). 222p. (Orig.). 1987. pap. 38.50 (ISBN 0-940254-07-7, 07-7). Kern Intl.

Structural Analysis System 4: CAD-CAM & Structural Analysis in Industry. Ed. by A. Niku-Lari. (Structural Analysis Systems). (Illus.). 284p. 1986. 72.00 (ISBN 0-08-034918-8). Pergamon.

Structural Analysis Systems: Finite, Boundary Element & Expert Systems in Structural Analysis. Ed. by A. Niku-Lari. (Structural Analysis Systems Ser.: No. 6). (Illus.). 210p. 1987. 63.00 (ISBN 0-08-034934-X). Pergamon.

Structural Analysis Systems I: Software, Hardware, Capability, Compatibility, Applications. Ed. by A. Niku-Lari. (Structural Analysis Systems Ser.: Vol. 1). (Illus.). 250p. 1986. 63.00 (ISBN 0-08-032577-7, Pub. by PPL). Pergamon.

Structural Analysis Systems II: Software, Hardware, Capability, Compatibility, Applications. Ed. by A. Niku-Lari. (Structural Analysis Systems Ser.: Vol. 2). (Illus.). 250p. 1986. 63.00 (ISBN 0-08-032578-5, Pub. by PPL). Pergamon.

Structural Analysis Systems III: Software, Hardward, Capability, Compatibility, Applications. Ed. by A. Niku-Lari. (Structural Analysis Systems Ser.: Vol. 3). (Illus.). 250p. 1986. 63.00 (ISBN 0-08-032582-3, Pub. by PPL). Pergamon.

Structural Analysis Systems, Vol. 5: Expert Systems in Structural Analysis. Ed. by A. Niku-Lari. (Illus.). 218p. 1986. 55.00 (ISBN 0-08-034919-6, PBL). Pergamon.

Structural Analysis Systems, Vol. 7: CAD-CAM & FEM in Metal Working. Ed. by A. Niku-Lari & S. K. Ghosh. LC 88-19669. (Technology Transfer Handbook Ser.). (Illus.). 300p. 1988. 87.00 (ISBN 0-08-035917-5). Pergamon.

Structural Analysis: The Solution of Statically Indeterminate Structures. 3rd ed. W. F. Cassie. LC 67-72611. pap. 73.80 (ISBN 0-317-11039-X, 2004914). Bks Demand UMI.

Structural Analysis Using Virtual Work. F. Thompson & G. G. Hayward. (Illus.). 320p. 1985. 59.95 (ISBN 0-412-22280-9, NO. 9128, Pub. by Chapman & Hall); 31.00 (ISBN 0-412-22290-6, NO. 9128, Pub. by Chapman & Hall). Routledge Chapman & Hall.

Structural & Chemical Aspects of High Temperature Superconductivity. C. N. Rao. 300p. (Orig.). 1988. 45.00 (ISBN 9971-50-607-6); pap. 27.00 (ISBN 9971-50-608-4). World Scientific Pub.

Structural & Cut-off Diaphragm Walls. R. G. Boyes. (Illus.). 181p. 1975. 43.00 (ISBN 0-85334-607-0, Pub. by Elsevier Applied Sci England). Elsevier.

Structural & Foundation Failures: A Casebook for Architects, Engineers & Lawyers. B. LePatner & Sidney M. Johnson. 1982. text ed. 51.00 (ISBN 0-07-032584-7). McGraw.

Structural & Functional Aspects of Enzyme Catalysis. Ed. by H. Eggerer & R. Hiber. (Colloquium Mosbach Ser.: Vol. 32). (Illus.). 280p. 1981. 33.00 (ISBN 0-387-11110-7). Springer-Verlag.

Structural & Functional Organization of the Placenta. Ed. by P. Kaufmann & B. F. King. (Bibliotheca Anatomica Ser.: No. 22). (Illus.). viii, 164p. 1982. 102.00 (ISBN 3-8055-3520-1). S Karger.

Structural & Lexical Comparison of the Tunica, Chitimacha & Atakapa Languages. John R. Swanton. Repr. of 1919 ed. 19.00x (ISBN 0-403-03699-2). Scholarly.

Structural & Resonance Techniques in Biological Research. Ed. by D. Rousseau. LC 54-11056. (Physical Techniques in Biology & Medicine Ser.). 1984. 82.00 (ISBN 0-12-599320-X). Acad Pr.

Structural & Semantic Analysis of the German Modal Moegen. Francis X. Allard. (Standford German Studies: Vol. 6). 117p. 1975. pap. 19.60. P Lang Pubs.

Structural & Specialty Adhesives. Business Communications Staff. 215p. 1988. 1750.00 (ISBN 0-89336-555-6, C-009U). BCC.

Structural & Statistical Problems for a Class of Stochastic Processes. Harald Cramer. LC 74-160260. (S. S. Wilks Memorial Lecture Ser.). 1971. pap. 14.50x (ISBN 0-691-08099-2). Princeton U Pr.

Structural & Thematic Analysis of George Meredith's Novel "Diana of the Crossways". Renate Bruckl. Ed. by James Hogg. (Romantic Reassessment Ser.). 191p. (Orig.). 1978. pap. 15.00 (ISBN 3-7052-0529-3, Pub. by Salzburg Studies). Longwood Pub Group.

Structural Anthropology, Vol. 1. Claude Levi-Strauss. LC 63-17344. 1963. pap. 13.95x (ISBN 0-465-09516-X, TB5017). Basic.

Structural Anthropology, Vol. 2. Claude Levi-Strauss. Tr. by Monique Layton. LC 82-16115. xvi, 384p. 1976. pap. 14.00x (ISBN 0-226-47491-7). U of Chicago Pr.

Structural Anthropology in the Netherlands. Ed. by P. E. De Josselin De Jong. (Translation Ser.: No. 17). (Illus.). 1977. pap. 31.00 (ISBN 90-247-1944-5, Pub. by Martinus Nijhoff Netherlands). Kluwer Academic.

Structural Approach in Psychological Testing. M. L. Kaplan et al. LC 70-93755. 1971. 34.00 (ISBN 0-08-006867-7). Pergamon.

Structural Approach to the Analysis of Drama. Paul M. Levitt. LC 79-159466. (De Proprietatibus Litterarum, Ser. Major: No. 15). 119p. 1971. text ed. 13.20x (ISBN 90-2791-841-4). Mouton.

Structural Approaches to South India Studies. Ed. by Harry M. Buck & Glenn A. Yocum. LC 74-77412. 1974. pap. 5.95 (ISBN 0-89012-000-5). Anima Pubns.

Structural Aspects of Homogeneous, Heterogeneous & Biological Catalysis. Ed. by L. J. Guggenberger et al. (Transactions of the American Crystallographic Association: Vol. 14). 141p. 1978. pap. 25.00x (ISBN 0-686-60384-2). Polycrystal Bk Serv.

Structural Aspects of Turkish Inflation: 1950-1979. M. Ataman Aksov. (Working Paper: No. 540). 118p. 1982. 5.00 (ISBN 0-8213-0098-9, WP 0540). World Bank.

Structural Assessment: The Use of Large & Full Scale Testing. F. K. Garas et al. (Illus.). 400p. 1988. text ed. 120.00 (ISBN 0-408-00356-1). Butterworth.

Structural Basis of Behavior. J. A. Deutsch. LC 60-12466. 1960. 16.00x (ISBN 0-226-14345-7). U of Chicago Pr.

Structural Basis of Muscular Contraction. John Squire. LC 81-2321. 716p. 1981. 95.00x (ISBN 0-306-40582-2, Plenum Pr). Plenum Pub.

Structural Basis of Neurobiology. Ed. by E. G. Jones. 224p. 1983. pap. text ed. 25.25 (ISBN 0-444-00795-4). Elsevier.

Structural Basis of Word Association Behaviour. Howard R. Pollio. (Janua Linguarum, Ser. Minor: No. 51). (Orig.). 1966. pap. text ed. 11.20x (ISBN 90-2790-583-5). Mouton.

Structural Biological Applications of X-Ray Absorption, Scattering & Diffraction. H. D. Bartunik & B. Chance. 1986. 65.50. Acad Pr.

Structural Budget Deficits in the Federal Government: Causes, Consequences, & Remedies. Khi V. Thai. LC 86-33961. (Illus.). 304p. (Orig.). 1987. lib. bdg. 27.50 (ISBN 0-8191-6138-1); pap. text ed. 15.25 (ISBN 0-8191-6139-X). U Pr of Amer.

Structural Carbohydrates in the Liver: Falk Symposium, No 34. Ed. by Hans Popper & Werner Reutter. 600p. 1983. text ed. write for info. (ISBN 0-85200-711-6, Pub. by MTP Pr England). Kluwer Academic.

Structural Ceramics & Design. Ed. by Samuel J. Acquaviva & Seymour A. Bortz. 240p. 1969. 95.00 (ISBN 0-677-13550-5). Gordon & Breach.

Structural Ceramics & Testing of Brittle Materials. Ed. by Samuel J. Acquaviva & Seymour A. Bortz. 232p. 1968. 115.00 (ISBN 0-677-12770-7). Gordon & Breach.

Structural Ceramics Joining. Ed. by R. Loehman & S. Johnson. (Advances in Ceramics Ser.: Vol. 26). Date not set. price not set (ISBN 0-916094-35-9). Am Ceramic.

Structural Change & Development Policy. Hollis B. Chenery. (World Bank Research Publications Ser.). (Illus.). 1979. 39.95x (ISBN 0-19-520094-2); pap. 14.95x (ISBN 0-19-520095-0). Oxford U Pr.

Structural Change & Economic Development: The Role of the Service Sector. Norman Gemmell. LC 85-24996. 214p. 1986. 32.50x (ISBN 0-312-76669-6). St Martin.

Structural Change & Economic Growth: A Theoretical Essay on the Dynamics of the Wealth of Nations. Luigi Pasinetti. LC 80-41496. 296p. 1983. pap. 17.95 (ISBN 0-521-27410-9). Cambridge U Pr.

Structural Change & Economic Policy in Israel. Howard Pack. LC 75-140536. (Economic Growth Center Ser.). 1971. 30.00x (ISBN 0-300-01415-5). Yale U Pr.

Structural Change & Prospects for Urbanization in Asian Countries. Gavin W. Jones. LC 83-16373. (Papers of East-West Population Institute: No. 88). vi, 46p. (Orig.). 1983. pap. 1.75 (ISBN 0-86638-047-7). EW Ctr HI.

Structural Change, Economic Interdependence & World Development: Economic Interdependence, Vol. 4. Ed. by John H. Dunning & Mikoto Usui. LC 86-31317. 390p. 1987. 42.50 (ISBN 0-312-00441-9). St Martin.

Structural Change, Economic Interdependence & World Development: Proceedings of the Seventh World Congress of the International Economic Association, Madrid, Spain, Vol. 1. Ed. by Victor L. Urquidi. LC 86-31371. 220p. 1987. Basic & Issues. 45.00 (ISBN 0-312-00415-X). St Martin.

Structural Change, Economic Interdependence & World Development: Structural Change & Adjustment in the World Economy, Vol. 3. Ed. by Luigi Pasinetti & Peter C. Lloyd. LC 86-29739. 350p. 1987. 45.00 (ISBN 0-312-00417-6). St Martin.

Structural Change, Economic Interdependence & World Development, Vol. 2: Natural & Financial Resources for Development. Ed. by Silvio Borner & Alwyn Taylor. LC 86-26311. 1987. 39.95 (ISBN 0-312-00416-8). St Martin.

Structural Change in a Developing Economy. Richard R. Nelson & T. P. Schultz. LC 79-148168. (Rand Corporation Research Study). 1971. 38.50x (ISBN 0-691-04163-6). Princeton U Pr.

Structural Change in an Urban Industrial Region: The Northeastern Ohio Case. Ed. by David L. McKee & Richard E. Bennett. LC 86-30652. 268p. 1987. lib. bdg. 39.95 (ISBN 0-275-92353-3, C2353). Praeger.

Structural Change in Macroeconomic Models. M. J. Vilares. 1986. lib. bdg. 70.50 (ISBN 90-247-3277-8, Pub. by Martinus Nijhoff Netherlands). Kluwer Academic.

Structural Change in the American Economy. Anne P. Carter. LC 73-95516. (Studies in Technology & Society). 1970. 24.50x (ISBN 0-674-84370-3). Harvard U Pr.

Structural Change in the U. S. Automobile Industry. Ed. by Jeffrey A. Hunker. LC 82-48529. 288p. 1983. 34.00x (ISBN 0-669-06267-7). Lexington Bks.

Structural Change in Trade in Manufactured Goods Between Industrial & Developing Countries. Bela Balassa. (Working Paper: No. 396). 46p. 1980. pap. 3.50 (ISBN 0-686-39774-6, WP-0396). World Bank.

Structural Change: The Challenge to Industrial Societies. Ed. by H. Hax et al. (Illus.). 210p. 1985. 24.50 (ISBN 0-387-15741-7). Springer-Verlag.

Structural Changes in Industry. 97p. 1981. pap. 5.00 (ISBN 0-686-79016-2, UN81/2B2, UNIDO). UNIPUB.

Structural Changes in International Steel Trade. 152p. 1988. pap. 23.00 (ISBN 92-1-116408-7, E.87.II.E.33). UN.

Structural Changes in Puerto Rico's Economy 1947-1976. Robert J. Tata. LC 80-19080. (Papers in International Studies: Latin America Ser.: No. 9). (Illus.). 104p. (Orig.). 1981. pap. 11.75x (ISBN 0-89680-107-1, Ohio U Ctr Intl). Ohio U Pr.

Structural Changes in the Economy & Future Job Prospects. Paul G. Craig. 16p. 1983. 2.50 (ISBN 0-318-22205-1, OC92). Natl Ctr Res Voc Ed.

Structural Changes in the World Economy. Bela Kadar. LC 83-10954. 250p. 1983. 25.00 (ISBN 0-312-76671-8). St Martin.

Structural Changes in World Industry: A Quantitative Analysis of Recent Developments. Chad Leechor et al. (World Bank Staff Technical Papers). 144p. 1985. 8.00 (ISBN 0-318-02965-0, BK0271). World Bank.

Structural Chemistry. L. D. Barron et al. (Topics in Current Chemistry. Fortschritte der Chemischen Forschung: Vol. 123). (Illus.). 200p. 1984. 44.00 (ISBN 0-387-13099-3). Springer Verlag.

Structural Chemistry of Boron & Silicon. (Topics in Current Chemistry Ser.: Vol. 131). (Illus.). 190p. 1986. 56.00 (ISBN 0-387-15811-1). Springer-Verlag.

Structural Chemistry of Phosphorus. S. Corbridge. LC 64-4605. 560p. 1974. 160.75 (ISBN 0-444-41073-2). Elsevier.

Structural Clay Products. W. E. Brownell. LC 76-40216. (Applied Mineralogy Ser: Vol. 9). 1976. 61.00 (ISBN 0-387-81382-9). Springer-Verlag.

Structural Communications & the Teacher of English. Charles L. Thompson et al. 139p. 1975. pap. text ed. 4.95x (ISBN 0-8422-0527-6). Irvington.

Structural Complexity I. J. L. Balcazar & J Diaz. (EATCS Monographs on Theoretical Computer Science: Vol. 11). (Illus.). ix, 191p. 1988. 29.50 (ISBN 0-387-18622-0). Springer-Verlag.

Structural Concepts & Systems for Architects & Engineers. rev. ed. T. Y. Lin & Sidney Stotesbury. (Illus.). 608p. 1988. text ed. 42.95 (ISBN 0-442-25903-4). Van Nos Reinhold.

Structural Concrete. C. B. Wilby. 264p. (Orig.). 1983. pap. text ed. 34.95 (ISBN 0-408-01170-X). Butterworth.

Structural Concrete Cost Estimating. John E. Clark. 256p. 1983. text ed. 38.50 (ISBN 0-07-011163-4). McGraw.

Structural Concrete Elements. E. W. Bennett. (Illus.). 1973. 21.95x (ISBN 0-412-09020-1, 6034, Pub. by Chapman & Hall). Routledge Chapman & Hall.

Structural Conflict: The Third World Against Global Liberalism. Stephen D. Krasner. (Studies in International Political Economy: No. 12). 1985. pap. 11.95x (ISBN 0-520-05478-4). U of Cal Pr.

Structural Considerations & Findings from Testing of Nuclear Components. Ed. by L. K. Severud et al. (PVP Ser.: Vol. 49). 99p. 1981. 24.00 (ISBN 0-686-34519-3, H00185). ASME.

Structural Control. Ed. by H. H. Leipholz. 1987. lib. bdg. 179.50 (ISBN 90-247-3429-0, Pub. by Martinus Nijhoff Netherlands). Kluwer Academic.

Structural Control: Proceedings of the Iutam Symposium, Waterloo, Ont. Canada, June, 1979. Ed. by H. H. Leipholz. 810p. 1980. 126.50 (ISBN 0-444-85485-1, North-Holland). Elsevier.

Structural Crashworthiness. Ed. by N. Jones & T. Wierzbicki. (Illus.). 320p. 1983. text ed. 95.00 (ISBN 0-408-01308-7). Butterworth.

Structural Cross Sections: Tertiary Formations, Texas Gulf Coast. 7.00 (ISBN 0-318-23687-7). U of Tex Econ Geology.

Structural Database Programming. H Wedekind. (Illus.). 1977. pap. cancelled (ISBN 3-446-12371-7). Adlers Foreign Bks.

Structural Depths of Indian Thought. P. T. Raju. (Philosophy Ser.). 599p. 1985. 59.50 (ISBN 0-88706-139-7); pap. 24.50x (ISBN 0-88706-140-0). State U NY Pr.

Structural Design & Analysis - Part 1 see Composite Materials.

Structural Design & Crashworthiness of Automobiles. Ed. by T. K. Murthy & C. A. Brebbia. 1987. 72.00 (ISBN 0-931215-21-8). Computational Mech MA.

Structural Design & Crashworthiness of Automobiles. Ed. by T. K. Murthy & C. A. Bregbia. 240p. 1987. 67.80 (ISBN 0-387-17504-0). Springer-Verlag.

Structural Design & Fire Extinguishing Systems. M. G. Stavitskiy et al. LC 83-1763. (Fire Fighting Aboard Ships Ser.: Vol. 2). 582p. (Orig.). 1983. pap. 79.00x (ISBN 0-87201-307-3). Gulf Pub.

Structural Design, Cementitious Products, & Case Histories: Proceedings of Three Sessions Sponsored by the Structural Division & the Michigan Section of ASCE. Ed. by Yogindra N. Anand. 129p. 1985. 16.00x (ISBN 0-87262-502-8). Am Soc Civil Eng.

Structural Design Guide for Hardwood Plywood, HP-SG - 86. 25p. 1986. 3.00 (ISBN 0-318-18928-3). Hardwd Ply.

Structural Design Guide to AISC Specifications for Buildings. Paul F. Rice & Edward S. Hoffman. LC 75-40491. (Illus.). pap. 92.00 (ISBN 0-317-11089-6, 2007877). Bks Demand UMI.

Structural Design Guide to the ACI Building Code. 3rd, rev. ed. Paul Rice et al. LC 85-3129. (Illus.). 512p. 1985. 51.95 (ISBN 0-442-27633-8). Van Nos Reinhold.

Structural Design in Architecture. 2nd ed. Mario Salvadori & M. Levy. 1981. 48.00 (ISBN 0-13-853473-X). P-H.

Structural Design in Metals. 2nd ed. Clifford D. Williams & Ernest C. Harris. LC 57-6824. pap. 160.00 (ISBN 0-317-08682-0, 2012442). Bks Demand UMI.

Structural Design in Wood. Ernest C. Harris & Judith J. Stalnaker. (Illus.). 500p. 1988. text ed. 47.95 (ISBN 0-442-23300-0). Van Nos Reinhold.

Structural Design of Asphalt Concrete Pavement Systems. (Special Report). 207p. 1971. 6.00 (ISBN 0-309-01972-9). Transport Res Bd.

Structural Design of Asphalt Concrete Pavements to Prevent Fatigue Cracking. (Special Report). 201p. 1973. 6.00 (ISBN 0-309-02160-X). Transport Res Bd.

Structural Design of Cable-Suspended Roofs. Janos Szabo & Lajos Kollar. (Ellis Horwood Series in Engineering Science: 1-467). 242p. 1984. 79.95x (ISBN 0-470-27188-4). Halsted Pr.

Structural Design of Nuclear Plant Facilities, 3 vols. 2118p. 1975. pap. 73.00x (ISBN 0-87262-172-3). Am Soc Civil Eng.

Structural Design of Nuclear Plant Facilities, 3 vols. 1263p. 1973. pap. 52.00x (ISBN 0-87262-155-3). Am Soc Civil Eng.

Structural Design of Nuclear Plant Facilities: Proceedings, American Nuclear Society Conference, New Orleans, December 8-10, 1975, 3 vols. 1668p. softcover 84.00 (ISBN 0-317-33012-8, 700014). Am Nuclear Soc.

Structural Design of Nuclear Plant Facilities: Proceedings, American Nuclear Society Conference, Chicago, December 17-18, 1973, 3 vols. 1240p. 60.00 (ISBN 0-317-33013-6, 700009). Am Nuclear Soc.

Structural Design of Steel Joist Roofs to Resist Ponding Loads. (Technical Digest Ser.: No. 3). 7.50 (ISBN 0-318-04227-4). Steel Joist Inst.

Structural Design of Steel Joist Roofs to Resist Uplift Loads. (Technical Digest Ser.: No. 6). 5.00 (ISBN 0-318-04230-4). Steel Joist Inst.

Structural Design with Plastics. 2nd ed. B. S. Benjamin. 416p. 1981. 41.95 (ISBN 0-442-20167-2). Van Nos Reinhold.

Structural Detailing for Technicians. Gerald L. Weaver. (Illus.). 256p. 1974. pap. 39.95 (ISBN 0-07-068712-9). McGraw.

Structural Determinants of Employment & Unemployment, Vol. II. (Document Ser.). 344p. 1979. 18.75x (ISBN 92-64-11940-X). OECD.

Structural Pattern Recognition. T. Pavlidis. LC 77-21105. (Springer Ser. in Electrophysics: Vol. 1). (Illus.). 1977. 30.00 (ISBN 0-387-08463-0). Springer-Verlag.
Structural Patterns of Pirandello's Work. Jorn Moestrup. (Etudes Romanes: No. 2). 294p. (Orig.). 1972. pap. 26.50x (ISBN 87-7492-056-1, Pub. by Odense Universitets Forlag (Odense Denmark)). Coronet Bks.
Structural Patterns of Tropical Barks. Ingrid Roth. (Encyclopedia of Plant Anatomy: Special Part Ser.: Vol. 9, Pt. 3). (Illus.). 609p. 1981. 150.00x (ISBN 3-443-14012-2). Lubrecht & Cramer.
Structural Phase in Transitions in Layered Transition Metal Compounds. Ed. by Kazuko Motizuki. 1986. lib. bdg. 94.50 (ISBN 90-277-2171-8, Pub. by Reidell Holland). Kluwer Academic.
Structural Phase Transitions. A. D. Bruce & R. A. Cowley. 325p. 1981. 35.00x (NO.6589, Pub by Pion England). Routledge Chapman & Hall.
Structural Phase Transitions, Vol. I. Ed. by K. A. Mueller & H. Thomas. (Topics in Current Physics Ser.: Vol. 23). (Illus.). 190p. 1981. 33.00 (ISBN 0-387-10329-5). Springer-Verlag.
Structural Plastics Design Manual: ASCE Manuals & Reports on Engineering Practice, No. 63. Task Committee on Design of the Structural Plastics Research Council. 1176p. 1984. 95.00x (ISBN 0-87262-391-2). Am Soc Civil Eng.
Structural Plastics: Properties & Possibilities. Structural Plastics Symposium (1st: 1969: Louisville. KY) LC 72-16688. (Illus.). pap. 61.50 (ISBN 0-317-08600-6, 2020824). Bks Demand UMI.
Structural Plastics Selection Manual: ASCE Manuals & Reports on Engineering Practice, No. 66. Task Committee on Properties of Selected Plastics Systems of the Structural Plastics Research Council. 584p. 1985. 64.00x (ISBN 0-87262-475-7). Am Soc Civil Eng.
Structural Polymers, 2 vols. Ed. by P. M. Ogibalov. 618p. 1973. Set. text ed. 125.00x (ISBN 0-7065-1338-X, Pub. by Keter Pub Jerusalem). Coronet Bks.
Structural Principles. Irving Engel. (Illus.). 384p. 1984. text ed. 40.00 (ISBN 0-13-854019-5). P-H.
Structural Principles in Inorganic Compounds. W. E. Addison. pap. 50.00 (ISBN 0-317-08948-X, 2006383). Bks Demand UMI.
Structural Principles of the Chinese Language, 3 vols. Sozef L. Mullie. 1976. lib. bdg. 300.00 (ISBN 0-8490-2698-9). Gordon Pr.
Structural Problem in Shakespeare's Henry the Fourth. Harold Jenkins. LC 73-4596. 1956. lib. bdg. 17.00 (ISBN 0-8414-2171-4). Folcroft.
Structural Problems. (Structure & Bonding Ser.: Vol. 37). (Illus.). 1979. 57.00 (ISBN 0-387-09455-5). Springer-Verlag.
Structural-Process Models of Complex Human Behavior, No. 26. M. N. Scandura. (NATO Advanced Study Applied Science Ser.). 620p. 1978. 49.00x (ISBN 9-0286-0578-9, Pub. by Sijthoff & Noordhoff). Kluwer Academic.
Structural Psychopathology: Structure & Evolution. Ed. by Zena Helman. LC 83-23935. (Illus.). 240p. 1984. 25.00 (ISBN 0-87630-355-6). Brunner-Mazel.
Structural Reform, Stabilization, & Growth in Turkey. George Kopits. (Occasional Papers: No. 52). 45p. 1987. pap. 7.50 (ISBN 0-939934-84-1). Intl Monetary.
Structural Reliability--Probabilistic Saftey Assessement. Ed. by Folker H. Wittmann. (Structural Mechanics in Reactor Technology Ser.: Vol. M). 498p. 1987. text ed. 63.00 (ISBN 90-6191-774-3, Pub. by A A Balkema). Brookfield Pub Co.
Structural Reliability: Analysis & Prediction. Melchers. (Engineering Science Ser.). 1987. 79.95 (ISBN 0-470-20873-2). Halsted Pr.
Structural Reliability Theory & Its Applications. P. Thoft-Christensen & M. J. Baker. (Illus.). 267p. 1982. 46.00 (ISBN 0-387-11731-8). Springer-Verlag.
Structural Research see Encyclopedia of Physics.
Structural Response to Explosion-Induced Ground Motions. 148p. 1975. pap. text ed. 8.00 (ISBN 0-87262-150-2). Am Soc Civil Eng.
Structural Revolution. Jean-Marie Benoist. LC 78-5298. 1978. 25.00x (ISBN 0-312-76698-X). St Martin.
Structural Safety Studies: Proceedings of a Symposium Sponored by the Structural Division. Ed. by James T. Yao. 205p. 1985. 24.00x (ISBN 0-87262-451-X). Am Soc Civil Eng.
Structural Semantics: An Attempt at a Method. A. J. Greimas. Tr. by Daniele McDowell et al from Fr. LC 83-5864. lvi, 325p. 1983. 31.50x (ISBN 0-8032-2112-6). U of Nebr Pr.
Structural Sensitivity in Econometric Models. Edwin Kuh et al. LC 84-23431. (Probability & Mathematical Statistics Ser.). 324p. 1985. 34.95 (ISBN 0-471-81930-1). Wiley.
Structural Shielding Design & Evaluation for Medical Use of X-Rays & Gamma-Rays of Energies up to Ten Mev. LC 76-22969. (NCRP Reports Ser.: No. 49). 1976. 14.00 (ISBN 0-913392-31-6); adjunct to NCRP Report No. 49 15.00 (ISBN 0-686-30845-X). NCRP Pubns.
Structural Sociology. Ed. by Ino Rossi. LC 81-12246. (Illus.). 416p. 1982. 45.00x (ISBN 0-231-04846-7); pap. 17.50 (ISBN 0-231-04847-5). Columbia U Pr.
Structural Solvability & Controllability. K. Murota. (Algorithms & Combinatorics Ser.: Vol. 3). (Illus.). 295p. 1987. pap. 48.00 (ISBN 0-387-17659-4). Springer-Verlag.
Structural Stability & Culture Change in a Mexican-American Community. Barbara J. Macklin. Ed. by Carlos E. Cortes. LC 76-1249. (Chicano Heritage Ser.). 1976. 23.50x (ISBN 0-405-09513-9). Ayer Co Pubs.
Structural Stability & Morphogenesis: An Outline of a General Theory of Models. R. Thom. Tr. by D. H. Fowler from Fr. pap. write for info. (ISBN 0-8053-9279-3). Addison-Wesley.
Structural Stability & Morphogenesis. Rene Thom. 1988. write for info. (ISBN 0-201-09419-3). Addison-Wesley.
Structural Stability in Physics: Proceedings of Two International Symposia. Ed. by W. Guettinger & H. Eikemeier. (Springer Ser. in Synergetics). (Illus.). 1979. 44.50 (ISBN 0-387-09463-6). Springer-Verlag.
Structural Stability: Theory & Implementation. W. F. Chen & E. N. Lui. LC 86-19931. 534p. 1987. 49.50 (ISBN 0-444-01119-6). Elsevier.
Structural Steel Design. Joseph E. Bowles. (Illus.). 1980. text ed. 50.95 (ISBN 0-07-006765-1). McGraw.
Structural Steel Design. 3rd ed. Jack C. McCormac. (Illus.). 661p. 1981. text ed. 53.50 scp (ISBN 0-06-044344-8, HarpC). Har-Row.
Structural Steel Design. 2nd ed. Lambert Tall. Ed. by Lambert Tall. LC 82-25853. 892p. 1983. Repr. of 1974 ed. text ed. 56.50 (ISBN 0-89874-602-7). Krieger.
Structural Steel Designer's Handbook. Ed. by Frederick S. Merritt. (Illus.). 1000p. 1972. text ed. 80.00 (ISBN 0-07-041507-2). McGraw.
Structural Steel in Architecture & Buildings Technology. Irvin Engel. (Illus.). 304p. 1988. text ed. 34.67 (ISBN 0-13-854894-3). P-H.
Structural Steel Shop Inspector Training Guide. 58p. 1985. 10.00 (ISBN 0-318-22855-6, F504). Am Inst Steel Construct.
Structural Steel (141 Standards) Concrete Reinforcing Steel, Pressure Vessel Plate & Forgings, Steel Rails, Wheels, & Tires, Fasteners see ASTM Annual Book of Standards, 1986.
Structural Steels. Earl Kent. 1977. pap. text ed. 10.00 (ISBN 0-918782-02-3). E Kent.
Structural Steelwork Design. L. J. Morris & D. R. Plum. 208p. 1988. pap. 29.95 (ISBN 0-89397-324-6). Nichols Pub.
Structural Steelwork: Design to Limit State Theory. T. J. MacGinley & T. C. Ang. (Illus.). 284p. 1987. 44.95 (ISBN 0-408-03020-8). Butterworth.
Structural Steelwork for Students. L. V. Leech. (Illus.). 96p. 1988. pap. text ed. 29.95 (ISBN 0-408-02970-6). Butterworth.
Structural Steelwork: Limit State Design to BS 5950. Antony B. Clarke & Sidney H. Coverman. 300p. 1987. text ed. 59.95 (ISBN 0-412-29660-8, Pub. by Chapman & Hall). Routledge Chapman & Hall.
Structural-Strategic Marriage & Family Therapy: A Training Handbook. John Friesen. 176p. 1985. pap. 22.50 (ISBN 0-89876-106-9). Gardner Pr.
Structural Studies of Macromolecules by Spectroscopic Methods. Ed. by K. J. Ivin. LC 75-19355. 1976. 94.95x (ISBN 0-471-43120-6, Pub. by Wiley-Interscience). Wiley.
Structural Studies of Macromolecules by Spectroscopic Methods. Ed. by Kenneth J. Ivin. LC 75-19355. 353p. pap. 91.80 (2030409). Bks Demand UMI.
Structural Studies of Surfaces. Ed. by G. Hoehler. (Springer Tracts in Modern Physics Ser.: Vol. 91). (Illus.). 190p. 1982. 33.00 (ISBN 0-387-10964-1). Springer-Verlag.
Structural Studies on Molecules of Biological Interest: A Volume in Honour of Professor Dorothy Hodgkin. Ed. by Guy Dodson et al. (Illus.). 1981. 42.50x (ISBN 0-19-855362-5). Oxford U Pr.
Structural Studies on Nucleic Acids & Other Biopolymers see Physico-Chemical Properties of Nucleic Acids.
Structural Study of Myth & Totemism. Ed. by Edmund Leach. (Orig.). 1968. pap. 12.95 (ISBN 0-422-72530-7, NO.2287, Pub by Tavistock England). Routledge Chapman & Hall.
Structural Styles in Petroleum Exploration. James D. Lowell. 460p. 1985. 45.00 (ISBN 0-930972-08-2). Oil & Gas.
Structural Stylistic Analysis of la Princesse De Cleves. Susan Tiefenbrun. (De Proprietatibus Litterarum Series Practica: No. 25). 185p. (Orig.). 1976. pap. text ed. 22.40x (ISBN 90-2793-263-8). Mouton.
Structural System. Henry J. Cowan. (Illus.). 356p. 1981. Van Nos Reinhold.
Structural Systems Design. Robert A. Coleman. (Illus.). 400p. 1983. 56.00 (ISBN 0-13-853978-2). P-H.
Structural Theory & Analysis. Joseph D. Todd. LC 75-327936. (Illus.). 1975. 32.50x (ISBN 0-333-18021-6, Pub. by Macmillan England). Scholium Intl.
Structural Theory of Distributed Systems. A. G. Butkovskiy. LC 83-10727. (Mathematics & Its Applications Ser.). 314p. 1983. 100.00x (ISBN 0-470-27469-7). Halsted Pr.
Structural Theory of the Emotions. Joseph De Rivera. LC 76-53916. (Psychological Issues Monograph: No. 40). 178p. 1977. text ed. 22.50x (ISBN 0-8236-6171-7); pap. text ed. 20.00x (ISBN 0-8236-6170-9). Intl Univs Pr.
Structural Thermodynamics of Alloys. J. Manenc. Tr. by N. Corcoran from Fr. LC 73-83564. Orig. Title: Thermodynamique Structurale Des Alliages. (Illus.). 1973. lib. bdg. 29.00 (ISBN 90-277-0346-9, Pub. by Reidel Holland). Kluwer Academic.
Structural Use of Wood in Adverse Environments. Ed. by Robert W. Meyer & Robert M. Kellogg. 1982. 52.95 (ISBN 0-442-28744-5). Van Nos Reinhold.
Structural Vibration Analysis: Modelling, Analysis & Damping of Vibrating Structures. C. F. Beards. LC 82-25482. 153p. 1983. 47.95x (ISBN 0-470-27422-0). Halsted Pr.
Structural Welder. Jack Rudman. (Career Examination Ser.: C-773). (Cloth bdg. avail. on request). pap. 14.00 (ISBN 0-8373-0773-2). Natl Learning.
Structural Welding Code-Aluminum: D1.2-83. 153p. 36.00 (ISBN 0-87171-238-5). Am Welding.
Structural Welding Code Steel: AWS D1-1. AWS Structural Welding Committee. (Illus.). 1979. 25.00 (ISBN 0-87171-125-7). Am Welding.
Structural Welding Code-Steel: AWS D1.1. 314p. 1982. 43.00 (ISBN 0-686-95786-5). Am Welding.
Structural Wood Composites: Meeting Today's Needs & Tomorrow's Challenges. 178p. (Orig.). 1986. pap. 20.00 (ISBN 0-935018-24-7). Forest Prod.
Structural Wood Research: State-of-the-Art & Research Needs: Proceedings of a Workshop Sponsored by the ASCE Committee on Wood, the National Science Foundation, & Washington State University. Ed. by Rafik Y. Itani & Keith F. Faherty. 214p. 1984. 24.00x (ISBN 0-87262-411-0). Am Soc Civil Eng.
Structuralism: An Interdisciplinary Study. Ed. by Susan Wittig. LC 76-899. (Pittsburgh Reprint Ser.: No. 3). 1976. pap. 4.75 (ISBN 0-915138-16-6). Pickwick.
Structuralism: An Introduction-Wolfson College Lectures 1972. Ed. by David Robey. 1973. pap. text ed. 12.95x (ISBN 0-19-874017-4). Oxford U Pr.
Structuralism & African Folklore. Ed. by S. O. Anozie. (Studies in African Semiotics Ser.). 1970. pap. 7.00 (ISBN 0-914970-05-4). Conch Mag.
Structuralism & Biblical Hermeneutics. Ed. & tr. by Alfred M. Johnson, Jr. LC 79-9411. (Pittsburgh Theological Monographs: No. 22). 1979. pap. 12.95 (ISBN 0-915138-18-2). Pickwick.
Structuralism & Education. Rex Gibson. (Studies in Teaching & Learning). 166p. (Orig.). 1984. pap. text ed. 14.95 (ISBN 0-340-33975-6). Princeton Bk Co.
Structuralism & Hermeneutics. T. K. Seung. 264p. 1982. 30.00x (ISBN 0-231-05278-2); pap. text ed. 14.00x (ISBN 0-231-05279-0). Columbia U Pr.
Structuralism & Marxism. A. Schaff. LC 77-30331. 256p. 1978. 46.00 (ISBN 0-08-020505-4). Pergamon.
Structuralism & Photography. Lew Thomas. LC 77-93057. (Illus.). 1978. pap. 25.00x (ISBN 0-917986-04-0). NFS Pr.
Structuralism & Semiotics. Terence Hawkes. LC 76-55560. 1977. pap. 9.95x (ISBN 0-520-03422-8). U of Cal Pr.
Structuralism & since. Ed. by John Sturrock. 1980. 24.95x (ISBN 0-19-215839-2). Oxford U Pr.
Structuralism & since: From Levi-Strauss to Derrida. Ed. by John Sturrock. 1979. pap. 7.95 (ISBN 0-19-289105-7). Oxford U Pr.
Structuralism & the Biblical Text. David C. Greenwood. (Religion & Reason Ser.: No. 32). xi, 155p. 1985. 41.50x (ISBN 0-89925-103-X). Mouton.
Structuralism in Literature: An Introduction. Robert Scholes. LC 73-90578. 250p. 1974. 25.00x (ISBN 0-300-01750-2); pap. 10.95x (ISBN 0-300-01850-9). Yale U Pr.
Structuralism in Sociology: An Approach to Knowledge. Fred Katz. LC 75-29015. 218p. 1976. 49.50x (ISBN 0-87395-318-5). State U NY Pr.
Structuralism, Moscow, Prague, Paris. J. M. Broekman. Tr. by J. F. Beekman & B. Helm. LC 74-79570. (Synthese Library: No. 67). Orig. Title: Strukturalismus. 175p. 1974. lib. bdg. 26.00 (ISBN 90-277-0478-3, Pub. by Reidel Holland). Kluwer Academic.
Structuralism or Criticism? Geoffrey Strickland. LC 80-40721. 209p. 1983. pap. 15.95 (ISBN 0-521-27657-8). Cambridge U Pr.
Structuralism or Criticism? Thought on How We Read. Geoffrey Strickland. 200p. 1981. 47.50 (ISBN 0-521-23184-1). Cambridge U Pr.
Structuralism: The Art of the Intelligible. Peter Caws. (Contemporary Studies in Philosophy & the Human Sciences). 1988. text ed. 39.95 (ISBN 0-391-02740-9). Humanities.
Structuralisme en Transformationeel Generative Grammatica. J. Kaldeway. (Geschuedenis van de Toalkunde Ser.), xii, 287p. 1986. pap. write for info. (ISBN 90-6765-154-0). Foris Pubns.
Structuralist Controversy: The Languages of Criticism & the Sciences of Man. Ed. by Richard Macksey & Eugenio Donato. LC 78-95789. 368p. 1972. pap. 9.95x (ISBN 0-8018-1381-6). Johns Hopkins.
Structuralist Interpretations of Biblical Myth. Edmund Leach & Alan Aycock. LC 82-25263. (Illus.). 176p. 1983. 34.50 (ISBN 0-521-25491-4); pap. 12.95 (ISBN 0-521-27492-3). Cambridge U Pr.
Structuralist Macroeconomics: Applicable Models for the Third World. Lance Taylor. 1983. text ed. 22.95x (ISBN 0-465-08239-4). Basic.
Structuralist Perspectives in Criticism of Fiction. Patrick Brady. (European University Studies: Series 18, Comparative Literature Vol. 16). 236p. 1978. pap. 26.85 (ISBN 3-261-03032-1). P Lang Pubs.
Structuralist Poetics: Structuralism, Linguistics & the Study of Literature. Jonathan Culler. LC 74-11608. (Paperback Ser.). 316p. 1976. pap. 9.95x (ISBN 0-8014-9155-X). Cornell U Pr.
Structuralist View of Theories: A Possible Analogue. W. Stegmueller. 1979. pap. 20.00 (ISBN 0-387-09460-1). Springer-Verlag.
Structure Activity Correlation as a Predictive Tool in Toxicology: Fundamentals, Methods, & Applications. Ed. by Leon Golberg. LC 82-3007. (Chemical Industry Institute of Toxicology Ser.). (Illus.). 330p. 1983. text ed. 69.50 (ISBN 0-89116-276-3). Hemisphere Pub.
Structure-Activity Relationships in Human Chemoreception. M. G. Beets. (Illus.). 408p. 1978. text ed. 90.00 (ISBN 0-85334-746-8, Pub. by Elsevier Applied Sci England). Elsevier.
Structure Analysis by Small-Angle X-Ray & Neutron Scattering. L. A. Feigin & D. I. Svergun. LC 87-25489. 350p. 1987. 79.50x (ISBN 0-306-42629-3, Plenum Pr). Plenum Pub.
Structure & Action of Proteins. Richard E. Dickerson & Irving Geis. LC 69-11112. 1969. pap. text ed. 21.95 (ISBN 0-8053-2391-0). Benjamin-Cummings.
Structure & Activity of Anti-Tumour Agents. D. N. Reinhoudt. 1983. 47.50 (ISBN 90-247-2783-9, Pub. by Martinus Nijhoff Netherlands). Kluwer Academic.
Structure & Activity of Natural Peptides: Selected Topics. Ed. by W. Voelter & G. Weitzel. 480p. 1980. 79.00x (ISBN 3-11-008264-0). De Gruyter.
Structure & Application of Galvanomagnetic Devices. H. Weiss. 1969. 93.00 (ISBN 0-08-012597-2). Pergamon.
Structure & Approximation in Physical Theories. Ed. by A. Hartkamper & H. J. Schmidt. LC 81-15846. 264p. 1981. text ed. 55.00x (ISBN 0-306-40882-1, Plenum Pr). Plenum Pub.
Structure & Bonding in Crystals, Vol. 2. Ed. by Michael O'Keeffe & Alexandra Navrotsky. LC 81-7924. 1981. 75.00 (ISBN 0-12-525102-5). Acad Pr.
Structure & Bonding in Crystals, Vol. 1. Ed. by Michael O'Keeffe & Alexandra Navrotsky. LC 81-7924. 1981. 75.00 (ISBN 0-12-525101-7). Acad Pr.
Structure & Bonding in Noncrystalline Solids. Ed. by George E. Walrafen & Akos G. Revesz. 442p. 1986. 75.00x (ISBN 0-306-42396-0, Pub by Plenum Pr.). Plenum Pub.
Structure & Bonding: Relationships Between Quantum Chemistry & Crystallography. Ed. by T. F. Koetzle. (Transactions of the ACA: Vol. 16). 95p. 1980. pap. 25.00x (ISBN 0-937140-25-2). Polycrystal Bk Serv.
Structure & Change in Economic History. Douglass C. North. 1981. 19.95 (ISBN 0-393-01478-9); pap. 8.95x (ISBN 0-393-95241-X). Norton.
Structure & Change in Indian Society. Ed. by Milton Singer & Bernard S. Cohn. LC 67-17609. (Viking Fund Publications in Anthropology: No. 47). pap. 130.80 (ISBN 0-317-26248-3, 2052137). Bks Demand UMI.
Structure & Chemistry of Solid Surfaces. G. A. Somorjai. LC 71-90401. 1576p. 1969. 66.00 (ISBN 0-471-81320-6, Pub. by Wiley). Krieger.
Structure & Classification of Paleocommunities. Ed. by Robert W. Scott & Ronald R. West. LC 76-4587. 352p. 1976. 70.50 (ISBN 0-12-787455-0). Acad Pr.
Structure & Cognition: Aspects of Hindu Caste & Ritual. 2nd ed. Veena Das. 1982. 29.95x (ISBN 0-19-561395-3). Oxford U Pr.
Structure & Cognition: Aspects of Hindu Caste & Ritual. 2nd ed. Veena Das. 177p. 1988. pap. 9.95 (ISBN 0-19-561979-X). Oxford U Pr.
Structure & Cognition in Art. Ed. by Dorothy K. Washburn. LC 82-14644. (New Directions in Archaeology Ser.). (Illus.). 180p. 1983. 47.50 (ISBN 0-521-23471-9). Cambridge U Pr.
Structure & Collisions of Ions & Atoms. Ed. by A. Sellin. (Topics in Current Physics: Vol 5). (Illus.). 1978. 48.00 (ISBN 0-387-08576-9). Springer-Verlag.
Structure & Confirmation of Evolutionary Theory. Elisabeth A. Lloyd. (Contributions in Philosophy Ser.: No. 37). 1988. lib. bdg. 35.85 (ISBN 0-313-25563-6, LVY/). Greenwood.
Structure & Conflict in Nigeria Nineteen Sixty to Nineteen Sixty-Five. Kenneth Post & Michael Vickers. 256p. 1974. 29.50x (ISBN 0-299-06470-0). U of Wis Pr.

Structure & Meaning of Second Baruch. Frederick J. Murphy. 1985. 16.50 (ISBN 0-89130-844-X, 06-01-78); pap. 10.95 (ISBN 0-89130-845-8). Scholars Pr GA.

Structure & Measurement of Intelligence. H. J. Eysenck & D. W. Fulker. (Illus.). 1979. 25.00 (ISBN 0-387-09028-2). Springer-Verlag.

Structure & Mechanism in Vinyl Polymerization. Ed. by Teiji Tsuruta & Kenneth F. O'Driscoll. LC 68-25345. pap. 138.00 (ISBN 0-317-08383-X, 2055022). Bks Demand UMI.

Structure & Mesomorphism of Cholesteric Liquid Crystals. A. I. Galatina et al. 80p. 1986. pap. text ed. 25.00 (ISBN 2-88124-178-6). Gordon & Breach.

Structure & Mobility in Molecular & Atomic Glasses, Vol. 371. Ed. by James M. O'Reilly. LC 81-14226. 354p. 1981. pap. 76.00x (ISBN 0-89766-132-X). NY Acad Sci.

Structure & Mobility: The Men & Women of Marseille, 1820-1870. William H. Sewell, Jr. (Illus.). 410p. 1985. 52.50 (ISBN 0-521-26237-2). Cambridge U Pr.

Structure & Molecular Organization of the Photosynthetic Apparatus, Vol. 3. Ed. by George Akoyunoglou. 1112p. cancelled 109.00 (Pub. by Balaban Intl Sci Serv). IPS.

Structure & Motion: Membranes, Nucleic Acids & Proteins. Ed. by E. Clementi et al. (Illus.). 582p. 1985. lib. bdg. 107.00 (ISBN 0-940030-12-8). Adenine Pr.

Structure & Organization of Multinational Enterprises. OECD. (International Investment & Multinational Enterprise Ser.). 59p. (Orig.). 1987. 13.00 (ISBN 92-64-13030-6). OECD.

Structure & Performance in Adult Education. Graham Mee & Harold Wiltshire. LC 77-7051. 1978. pap. text ed. 9.50x (ISBN 0-582-48944-X). Longman.

Structure & Performance of Cements. Ed. by P. Barnes. 576p. 1984. 133.25 (ISBN 0-85334-233-4, Pub. by Elsevier Applied Sci England). Elsevier.

Structure & Performance of Industries. T. Jones & T. Cockerill. (Industrial Studies). 224p. text ed. 28.50x (ISBN 0-86003-534-4, Pub. by Philip Allan UK); pap. text ed. 12.50x (ISBN 0-86003-636-7, Pub. by Philip Allan UK). Humanities.

Structure & Physical Properties of Paper. H. F. Rance. (Handbook of Paper Science: Vol. 2). 288p. 1982. 116.00 (ISBN 0-444-41974-8). Elsevier.

Structure & Physiology of the Slow Inward Calcium Channel. Ed. by J. Craig Venter & David Triggle. LC 87-2951. (Receptor Biochemistry & Methodology Ser.: Vol. 9). 292p. 1987. 70.00 (ISBN 0-8451-3708-5, 3708). A R Liss.

Structure & Process in Modern Societies. Talcott Parsons. 1960. 18.00 (ISBN 0-02-924340-8). Free Pr.

Structure & Process in Secondary Schools: The Academic Impact of Educational Climates. Edward L. McDill & Leo C. Rigsby. LC 73-8123. pap. 56.00 (ISBN 0-317-41751-7, 2025861). Bks Demand UMI.

Structure & Process in Southeastern Archaeology. Ed. by Roy S. Dickens, Jr. & H. Trawick Ward. LC 84-23. (Illus.). xiv, 347p. 1985. 35.00 (ISBN 0-8173-0216-6). U of Ala Pr.

Structure & Process in Speech Perception: Proceedings. Symposium on Dynamic Aspects of Speech Perception Held at I.P.O., Eindhoven, the Netherlands, Aug.4-6,1975. Ed. by A. Cohen & S. G. Nooteboom. (Communications & Cybernetics: Vol. II). (Illus.). 370p. 1975. 34.00 (ISBN 0-387-07520-8). Springer-Verlag.

Structure & Process of International Law. Ed. by Ronald S. Macdonald & Douglas M. Johnston. 1984. lib. bdg. 120.00 (ISBN 90-247-2882-7, Pub. by Martinus Nijhoff Netherlands). Kluwer Academic.

Structure & Process of International Law. Ed. by Ronald S. Macdonald & Douglas M. Johnston. 1986. pap. 75.00 (ISBN 90-247-3273-5, Pub. by Martinus Nijhoff Netherlands). Kluwer Academic.

Structure & Process: Readings in Introductory Sociology. Ed. by Richard J. Peterson & Charlotte A. Vaughan. 319p. 1986. pap. text ed. write for info. (ISBN 0-534-05172-3). Wadsworth Pub.

Structure & Processes of Organization. H. C. Ganguli. 1984. 14.00x (ISBN 0-8364-1163-3, Pub. by Allied India). South Asia Bks.

Structure & Profitability of the Antebellum Rice Industry: 1859. Dale E. Swan. LC 75-2598. (Dissertations in American Economic History). (Illus.). 1975. 31.00x (ISBN 0-405-07219-8). Ayer Co Pubs.

Structure & Properties of Amorphous Polymers: Proceedings of the 2nd Symposium Macromolecules Cleveland, October 31-November 2, 1978. Ed. by A. G. Walton. (Studies in Physical & Theoretical Chemistry: Vol. 10). 232p. 1980. 89.50 (ISBN 0-444-41905-5). Elsevier.

Structure & Properties of Cell Membranes, 3 vols. Ed. by Gheorghe Benga. 1985. Vol. I: A Survey on Molecular Aspects of Membrane Structures & Function, 240p. 99.00 (ISBN 0-8493-5764-0); Vol. II: Molecular Basis of Selected Transport Systems, 304p. 115.00 (ISBN 0-8493-5765-9); Vol. III: Methodology & Properties of Membranes, 304p. 130.00 (ISBN 0-8493-5766-7). CRC Pr.

Structure & Properties of Cellular Solids. L. J. Gibson & M. F. Ashby. (Illus.). 250p. 1988. text ed. 95.00 (ISBN 0-08-035910-8). Pergamon.

Structure & Properties of Crystal Defects. V. Paidar & L. Lejcek. (Materials Science Monographs: Vol. 20). 1984. 163.25 (ISBN 0-444-99627-3, I-037-84). Elsevier.

Structure & Properties of Engineering Materials. 4th ed. R. M. Brick et al. (McGraw-Hill Ser. in Materials Science & Engineering). (Illus.). 1977. text ed. 49.95 (ISBN 0-07-007721-5). McGraw.

Structure & Properties of Engineering Materials. Bryan Harris & A. R. Bunsell. LC 76-41771. (Introductory Engineering Ser.). (Illus.). pap. 90.80 (ISBN 0-317-08294-9, 2019608). Bks Demand UMI.

Structure & Properties of Engineering Alloys. W. F. Smith. 1980. text ed. 49.95 (ISBN 0-07-058560-1). McGraw.

Structure & Properties of Heat-Resistant Metals. Ed. by M. V. Pridantsev. 380p. 1970. text ed. 78.00x (ISBN 0-7065-0703-7, Pub. by Keter Pub Jerusalem). Coronet Bks.

Structure & Properties of Ionomers. Ed. by Michel Pineri & Adi Eisenberg. 1987. lib. bdg. 109.00 (ISBN 90-277-2458-X, Pub. by Reidel Holland). Kluwer Academic.

Structure & Properties of Magnetic Materials. D. J. Craik. 1971. (Pub. by Pion England); pap. 11.50x (ISBN 0-85086-018-0, 2903). Routledge Chapman & Hall.

Structure & Properties of Materials. A. T. DiBenedetto. LC 67-11602. pap. 138.50 (ISBN 0-317-11001-2, 2004413). Bks Demand UMI.

Structure & Properties of Materials, Vol. 2: Thermodynamics of Structure. Jere Brophy et al. pap. 57.00 (ISBN 0-317-28066-X, 2055769). Bks Demand UMI.

Structure & Properties of Matter. Ed. by T. Matsubara. (Springer Series in Solid-State Sciences: Vol. 28). (Illus.). 450p. 1982. 50.00 (ISBN 0-387-11098-4). Springer-Verlag.

Structure & Properties of MgO & Al2O3 Ceramics. Ed. by W. D. Kingery. (Advances in Ceramics Ser.: Vol. 10). 860p. 120.00 (ISBN 0-916094-62-6). Am Ceramic.

Structure & Properties of Nearby Galaxies: Proceedings. Symposium of the International Astronomical Union, No. 77. Ed. by Elly M. Berkhuijsen & Richard Wielebinski. 1978. lib. bdg. 39.50 (ISBN 90-277-0874-6, Pub. by Reidel Holland); pap. text ed. 26.00 (ISBN 90-277-0875-4). Kluwer Academic.

Structure & Properties of Oriented Polymers. I. M. Ward. (Illus.). 500p. 1975. 101.00 (ISBN 0-85334-600-3, Pub. by Elsevier Applied Sci England). Elsevier.

Structure & Properties of Silicate Melts. B. O. Mysen. (Developments in Geochemistry Ser.: Vol. 4). 368p. 1988. 84.25 (ISBN 0-444-42959-X). Elsevier.

Structure & Properties of Solids: An Introduction to Materials Science. Bruce Chalmers. 155p. 1982. 37.00x (ISBN 0-471-26214-5). Wiley.

Structure & Properties of Thin Films: Proceedings. International Conference on Structure & Properties of Thin Films (1959: Bolton Landing, NY) Ed. by C. A. Neugebauer & J. B. Newkirk. LC 59-15871. pap. 143.80 (ISBN 0-317-42403-3, 2056076). Bks Demand UMI.

Structure & Properties of Ultrahigh-Strength Steels. American Society for Testing & Materials Staff. LC 65-19686. (American Society for Testing & Materials Ser.: Special Technical Publication, No. 370). pap. 56.80 (ISBN 0-317-11239-2, 2000741). Bks Demand UMI.

Structure & Reactivity of Modified Zeolites: Proceedings of an International Conference, Prague, July 9-13, 1984. Ed. by P. A. Jacobs et al. (Studies in Surface Science & Catalysis: No. 18). 376p. 1984. 110.75 (ISBN 0-444-42351-6, I-234-84). Elsevier.

Structure & Realization Problems in the Theory of Dynamical Systems. M. Heymann. (International Centre for Mechanical Sciences: No. 204). 1976. soft cover 12.00 (ISBN 0-387-81348-9). Springer-Verlag.

Structure & Reform of the U. S. Tax System. Albert Ando et al. 184p. 1985. 17.95x (ISBN 0-262-01086-0). MIT Pr.

Structure & Relationship in Constitutional Law. Charles L. Black. LC 69-17621. (Edward Douglass White Lecture Ser.: 1968). pap. 26.80 (ISBN 0-317-28671-4, 2055300). Bks Demand UMI.

Structure & Relationship in Constitutional Law. Charles L. Black, Jr. LC 85-13904. 98p. 1986. 16.00 (ISBN 0-918024-42-0); pap. 7.95 (ISBN 0-918024-44-7). Ox Bow.

Structure & Representations of Jordan Algebras. Nathan Jacobson. LC 67-21813. (Colloquium Pbns. Ser.: Vol. 39). 455p. 1968. 42.00 (ISBN 0-8218-1039-1, COLL-39). Am Math.

Structure & Representations of Q-Groups. D. Kletzing. (Lecture Notes in Mathematics: Vol. 1084). vi, 290p. 1984. pap. 20.00 (ISBN 0-387-13865-X). Springer-Verlag.

Structure & Reproduction of Corn. T. A. Kiesselbach. LC 79-19648. viii, 96p. 1980. 9.50x (ISBN 0-8032-2703-5); pap. 2.95x (ISBN 0-8032-7751-2, BB 724, Bison). U of Nebr Pr.

Structure & Reproduction of the Algae. Felix E. Fritsch. LC 35-8014. Vol. 1: Introduction, Chlorophyceae, Xanthophyceae, Chrysophyseae, Bacillariophyceae, Crypotophyceae, Dinophyceae, Chloromonadineae Euglenineae, Colorless Flagellata. pap. 160.00 (ISBN 0-317-41818-1, 2025582). Bks Demand UMI.

Structure & Sacring: The Systematic Kingdom in Chretien's Erec. Donald Maddox. LC 77-93405. (French Forum Monographs: No. 8). 221p. (Orig.). 1978. pap. 9.95x (ISBN 0-917058-07-0). French Forum.

Structure & Sentiment: A Test Case in Social Anthropology. Ed. by Rodney Needham. LC 62-9738. xii, 136p. 1982. pap. 9.95x (ISBN 0-226-56989-6, Midway Reprint). U of Chicago Pr.

Structure & Society in Literary History: Studies in the History & Theory of Historical Criticism. Robert Weimann. LC 75-17719. 273p. 1976. 20.00x (ISBN 0-8139-0628-8). U Pr of Va.

Structure & Society in Literary History: Studies in the History & Theory of Historical Criticism. Robert Weimann. LC 84-9706. 1984. pap. text ed. 12.95x (ISBN 0-8018-3122-9). Johns Hopkins.

Structure & Spectra of Molecules. W. G. Richards & P. R. Scott. LC 84-15333. 1985. 24.95 (ISBN 0-471-90577-1). Wiley.

Structure & Spectroscopy see Pentacoordinated Phosphorus.

Structure & Stability of Salts of Halogen Oxyacids in the Solid Phase. F. Solymosi. LC 75-19287. 116.80 (ISBN 0-8357-9985-9, 2016157). Bks Demand UMI.

Structure & Statistics in Crystallography. Ed. by A. J. Wilson. 234p. 1985. lib. bdg. 72.00 (ISBN 0-940030-10-1). Adenine Pr.

Structure & Strategy in Sikh Society. Harry Izmirlian, Jr. 221p. 1979. 18.95. Asia Bk Corp.

Structure & Style. rev. enlarged ed. Leon Stein. LC 78-15541. (Illus.). xx, 297p. (Orig.). (gr. 9 up). 1979. pap. text ed. 16.95 (ISBN 0-87487-164-6). Birch Tree Gr.

Structure & Style in Javanese: A Semiotic View of Linguistic Etiquette. J. Joseph Errington. (Conduct & Communication Ser.). (Illus.). 288p. 1988. text ed. 29.95x (ISBN 0-8122-8103-9). U of Pa Pr.

Structure & Subject Interaction: Toward a Sociology of Knowledge in the Social Sciences. Stephen Bulick. (Books in Library & Information Science: Vol. 41). (Illus.). 256p. 1982. 45.00 (ISBN 0-8247-1847-X). Dekker.

Structure & Tectonics of Precambrian Rocks of India. S. Sinha-Roy. 252p. 1983. 59.95. Asia Bk Corp.

Structure & Texture of Beowulf. John A. Nist. LC 74-23587. 1974. Repr. of 1959 ed. lib. bdg. 30.00 (ISBN 0-8414-6253-4). Folcroft.

Structure & Texture: Selected Essays in Cheremis Verbal Art. Thomas A. Sebeok. LC 72-94505. (De Proprietatibus Litterarum, Ser. Practica: No. 44). (Illus.). 158p. (Orig.). 1974. pap. text ed. 19.20x (ISBN 90-2792-695-6). Mouton.

Structure & Theme: Don Quixote to James Joyce. Margaret Church. LC 83-2292. 219p. 1983. 20.00 (ISBN 0-8142-0348-5). Ohio St U Pr.

Structure & Transformation: Developmental & Historical Aspects. Ed. by Klaus F. Riegel & George C. Rosenwald. LC 75-15659. (The Origins of Behavior Ser.: Vol. 3). 1975. pap. 67.00 (ISBN 0-317-08075-X, 2016470). Bks Demand UMI.

Structure & Transformation: Developmental & Historical Aspects see Origins of Behavior.

Structure & Transformations of Organic Molecules. Ed. by F. Boschke et al. (Topics in Current Chemistry: Vol. 32). (Illus.). 110p. 1972. pap. 29.50 (ISBN 0-387-05936-9). Springer-Verlag.

Structure & Variability of Antarctic Circumpolar Current. E. I. Sarukhanyan. Tr. by M. N. Pillai from Rus. 110p. 1986. text ed. 36.00 (ISBN 90-6191-467-1, Pub. by A A Balkema). Brookfield Pub Co.

Structure & Weaving. Aan Sutton. LC 82-24941. (Illus.). 192p. 1982. 29.95 (ISBN 0-934026-38-6). Interweave.

Structure-Borne Sound. L. Cremer & M. Heckl. (Illus.). 550p. 1988. 75.00 (ISBN 0-387-18241-1). Springer-Verlag.

Structure Building Operations & Word Order. Michael Flynn. Ed. by Jorge Hankamer. (Outstanding Dissertations in Linguistics Ser.). 150p. 1985. 26.00 (ISBN 0-8240-5447-4). Garland Pub.

Structure, Consciousness, & History. Ed. by R. H. Brown & S. M. Lyman. LC 77-90212. (Illus.). 1978. 39.50 (ISBN 0-521-22047-5). Cambridge U Pr.

Structure, Constitution, & General Characteristics of Wrought Ferritic Stainless Steels-STP 619. J. J. Demo. 72p. 1976. 7.50 (ISBN 0-8031-0793-5, 04-619000-02). ASTM.

Structure, Context, Complexity & Organization: The Physics of Information & Value. Karl E. Eriksson. 256p. 1987. 39.00 (ISBN 9971-50-023-X). World Scientific Pub.

Structure-Contour Map on the Lower Permian Red Cave Formation, Panhandle Field & Adjacent Areas of the Texas Panhandle. R. T. Budnik (Illus.). 8p. 1987. 2.00 (ISBN 0-318-23679-6, MM 37). U of Tex Econ Geology.

Structure Data of Elements & Intermetallic Phases see Landolt-Boernstein Numerical Data & Functional Relationships in Science & Technology, New Series, Group 3: Crystal & Solid State Physics.

Structure Data of Organic Crystals see Landolt-Boernstein Numerical Data & Functional Relationships in Science & Technology, New Series, Group 3: Crystal & Solid State Physics.

Structure des Remunerations dans la Siderurgie Francaise see Cahiers de l'Institut de Science Economique Appliquee.

Structure Determination by X-Ray Crystallography. 2nd ed. M. F. Ladd & R. A. Palmer. 526p. 1985. 39.50x (ISBN 0-306-41878-9, Plenum Pr). Plenum Pub.

Structure Determination by X-Ray Crystallography. 2nd ed. M. F. Ladd & R. A. Palmer. 526p. 1986. pap. 19.95x (ISBN 0-306-42295-6, Plenum Pr). Plenum Pub.

Structure du Dialecte Basque de Maya. Genevieve N'Diaye. (Fr). 1970. pap. text ed. 26.40x (ISBN 0-686-22400-0). Mouton.

Structure d'un Mythe Vedique: Le Mythe Cosmogonique dans le Rgveda. B. L. Ogibenin. (Approaches to Semiotics: No. 30). 1973. 27.20x (ISBN 0-686-21821-3). Mouton.

Structure, Dynamics, & Biogenesis of Biomembranes. Ed. by Ryo Sato & Shun-Ichi Ohnishi. LC 83-51051. 188p. 1982. 49.50x (ISBN 0-306-41283-7, Plenum Pr). Plenum Pub.

Structure, Dynamics & Function of Biomolecules. Ed. by A. Ehrenberg et al. (Springer Series in Biophysics: Vol. 1). (Illus.). 315p. 1987. 71.50 (ISBN 0-387-17279-3). Springer-Verlag.

Structure, Dynamics, Interactions & Evolution of Biological Macromolecules. Helene. 1983. lib. bdg. 65.00 (ISBN 90-277-1531-9, Pub. by Reidel Holland). Kluwer Academic.

Structure Economique et Niveau de Revenu des Departements Francais see Complexe Agricole.

Structure et Croissance Regionale: Colloques 1961-1962 de L'Association de Science Regionale de Langue Francaise. (Economies et Societes Series L: No. 11). 1962. pap. 11.00 (ISBN 0-8115-0736-X). Kraus Repr.

Structure, Extractives, & Utilization of Bark. Jack Weiner & Vera Pollack. (Bibliographic Ser.: No. 191). 446p. 1960. 23.00 (ISBN 0-317-34450-1). Inst Paper Chem.

Structure, Extractives, & Utilization of Bark. Jack Weiner & Vera Pollock. LC 60-4278. (Bibliographic Ser.: No. 191, Supplement 2). 1973. pap. 10.00 (ISBN 0-87010-009-2). Inst Paper Chem.

Structure, Extractives, & Utilization of Bark. Jack Weiner & Vera Pollock. (Bibliographic Ser.: No. 191, Suppl. 1). 184p. 1968. 13.00 (ISBN 0-317-34451-X). Inst Paper Chem.

Structure for Population Education: Goals, Generalizations, & Behavioral Objectives. 2nd ed. Mary T. Lane & Ralph E. Wileman. LC 74-77985. 1978. pap. 4.00 (ISBN 0-89055-128-6). Carolina Pop Ctr.

Structure, Function & Genetics of Ribosomes. Ed. by B. Hardesty & G. Kramer. (Springer Series in Molecular Biology). (Illus.). 815p. 1986. 175.00 (ISBN 0-387-96233-6). Springer-Verlag.

Structure, Function & Metabolism of Plant Lipids: Proceedings of the International Symposium, 6th, Held in Neuchatel, Switzerland, July 16-20, 1984. Ed. by P. A. Siegenthaler & W. Eichenberger. (Developments in Plant Biology Ser.: Vol. 9). 634p. 1984. 197.00 (ISBN 0-444-80626-1). Elsevier.

Structure Function Correlation on Rat Kidney. W. Pfaller. (Advances in Anatomy, Embriology, & Cell Biology Ser.: Vol 70). (Illus.). 106p. 1982. pap. 30.00 (ISBN 0-387-11074-7). Springer-Verlag.

Structure in Architecture: The Building of Buildings. 3rd ed. Mario Salvadori. (Illus.). 448p. 1986. text ed. 40.00 (ISBN 0-13-854118-3). P-H.

Structure in Complexity Theory. Ed. by A. L. Selman. (Lecture Notes in Computer Science: Vol. 223). vi, 401p. 1986. pap. 25.00 (ISBN 0-387-16486-3). Springer-Verlag.

Structure in Complexity Theory Conference, 3rd, 1988: Proceedings. IEEE Staff. LC 87-83547. 303p. 1988. lib. bdg. 60.00 (ISBN 0-8186-8866-1, 866); pap. 60.00 (ISBN 0-8186-0866-8, 866); microfiche 60.00 (ISBN 0-8186-4866-X, 866). IEEE Comp Soc.

Structure in Fives: Designing Effective Organizations. Henry Mintzberg. (Illus.). 320p. 1983. text ed. 29.00 (ISBN 0-13-854349-6). P-H.

Structure in Medieval Narrative. William W. Ryding. LC 72-154531. (De Proprietatibus Litterarum, Ser. Major: No. 12). 177p. 1971. text ed. 18.00x (ISBN 90-2791-795-7). Mouton.

Structure in Milton's Poetry: From the Foundation to the Pinnacles. Ralph W. Condee. LC 73-12934. 240p. 1974. 23.50x (ISBN 0-271-01133-5). Pa St U Pr.

Structure in Process Control. Balchen & Mumme. 1987. 59.95 (ISBN 0-442-21155-4). Van Nos Reinhold.

Structure of Literary Understanding. Stein H. Olsen. 235p. 1985. pap. 14.95 (ISBN 0-521-31631-6). Cambridge U Pr.
Structure of Local Government in England & Wales. 4th ed. William Eric Jackson. LC 74-29792. 1976. Repr. of 1960 ed. lib. bdg. 35.00x (ISBN 0-8371-8001-5, JASL). Greenwood.
Structure of Locally Compact Abelian Groups. Armacost. 152p. 1981. 59.75 (ISBN 0-8247-1507-1). Dekker.
Structure of Love: Representational Patterns & Shakespeare's Love Tragedies. Michael Hall. 225p. Date not set. text ed. price not set (ISBN 0-8139-1207-5). U Pr of Va.
Structure of Lutheranism: The Theology & Philosophy of Life of Lutheranism, 16th & 17th Centuries, Vol. 1. Werner Elert. Tr. by Walter A. Hansen. LC 62-19955. 1974. pap. 16.95 (ISBN 0-570-03192-3, 12-2588). Concordia.
Structure of Magic, Vol. 1. Richard Bandler & John Grinder. LC 75-12452. 1975. 10.95 (ISBN 0-8314-0044-7). Sci & Behavior.
Structure of Magic, Vol. 2. John Grinder & Richard Bandler. LC 75-12452. 1976. 10.95 (ISBN 0-8314-0049-8). Sci & Behavior.
Structure of Marine Ecosystems. John H. Steele. LC 73-82350. 144p. 1974. pap. 4.95x (ISBN 0-674-84421-1). Harvard U Pr.
Structure of Marx's World-View. John McMurtry. LC 77-85552. 1978. 30.50x (ISBN 0-691-07229-9); pap. 9.95x (ISBN 0-691-01998-3). Princeton U Pr.
Structure of Material Systems: Ethnoarchaeology in the Maya Highlands. Brian Hayden & Aubrey Cannon. (SAA Papers: No. 3). 239p. 1984. 24.95 (ISBN 0-932839-06-1). Soc Am Arch.
Structure of Matter. Karl Schuster. (Siemens Programmed Instruction Ser.: No. 8). pap. 20.00 (ISBN 0-317-27769-3, 2052085). Bks Demand UMI.
Structure of Matter: A Survey of Modern Physics. Stephen Gasiorowicz. LC 78-18645. (Physics Ser.). (Illus.). 1979. text ed. write for info. (ISBN 0-201-02511-6). Addison-Wesley.
Structure of Matter: An Introduction to Atomic Nuclear & Particle Physics. R. M. Turnbull. (Illus.). 266p. 1979. pap. text ed. 22.50x (ISBN 0-216-90753-5). Trans-Atl Phila.
Structure of Medium-Heavy Nuclei 1979. (Institute of Physics Conference: No. 49). 1981. cancelled 68.00 (ISBN 0-85498-140-3, Pub. by Inst Physics England). IPS.
Structure of Membranes & Receptors. Ed. by Thomas C. Cheng. LC 83-23780. (Comparative Pathobiology Ser.: Vol. 5). 306p. 1984. 59.50x (ISBN 0-306-41503-8, Plenum Pr). Plenum Pub.
Structure of Metals: Crystallographic Methods, Principles & Data. 3rd rev. ed. C. S. Barrett & T. B. Massalski. LC 80-49878. (International Ser. on Materials Science & Technology: Vol. 14). (Illus.). 675p. 1980. pap. text ed. 29.50 (ISBN 0-08-026172-8). Pergamon.
Structure of Mind. Reinhardt S. Grossman. LC 65-13505. pap. 64.00 (ISBN 0-317-08118-7, 2002041). Bks Demand UMI.
Structure of Mind in History: Five Major Figures in Psychohistory. Philip Pomper. LC 84-22988. 192p. 1985. 21.50x (ISBN 0-231-06064-5). Columbia U Pr.
Structure of Modern Commerce. 7th ed. J. L. Hanson. 288p. (Orig.). 1986. pap. text ed. 17.95x (ISBN 0-273-02532-5). Trans-Atl Phila.
Structure of Modernist Poetry. Theo Hermans. 264p. 1982. 27.50 (ISBN 0-7099-0002-3, Pub. by Croom Helm Ltd). Routledge Chapman & Hall.
Structure of Modular Lattices of Width Four with Applications to Varieties of Lattices. R. S. Freese. LC 76-49468. (Memoirs: No. 181). 91p. 1977. pap. 15.00 (ISBN 0-8218-2181-4, MEMO-181). Am Math.
Structure of Monetarism. Thomas Mayer. 1978. 11.95x (ISBN 0-393-09045-0). Norton.
Structure of Moral Action: A Hermeneutic Study of Moral Conflict. M. J. Packer. (Contributions to Human Development Ser.: Vol. 13). (Illus.). xii, 164p. 1985. 64.75 (ISBN 3-8055-3999-1). S Karger.
Structure of Music. Percy Goetschius. LC 72-109736. 1971. Repr. of 1934 ed. lib. bdg. 35.00x (ISBN 0-8371-4226-1, GOSM). Greenwood.
Structure of Music: An Outline for Students. Reginald O. Morris. 1935. 8.25x (ISBN 0-19-317310-7). Oxford U Pr.
Structure of Nations & Empires: A Study of the Recurring Patterns & Problems of the Political Order in Relation to the Unique Problems of the Nuclear Age. Reinhold Niebuhr. LC 72-128064. 1977. Repr. of 1959 ed. 29.50x (ISBN 0-678-02755-2). Kelley.
Structure of Nematodes. Alan F. Bird. 1971. 45.00 (ISBN 0-12-099650-2). Acad Pr.
Structure of Nineteenth Century Cities. Ed. by J. H. Johnson & C. G. Pooley. LC 81-21280. 320p. 1982. 32.50x (ISBN 0-312-76781-1). St Martin.
Structure of Non-Crystalline Materials. Yoshio Waseda. (Illus.). 304p. 1980. text ed. 69.95 (ISBN 0-07-068426-X). McGraw.
Structure of Non-Crystalline Materials (1976) Ed. by P. H. Gaskell. 272p. 1977. 55.00x (ISBN 0-85066-120-X). Taylor & Francis.
Structure of Non-Crystalline Materials: 1982. Ed. by P. H. Gaskell et al. 610p. 1983. 75.00x (ISBN 0-85066-241-9). Taylor & Francis.
Structure of Non-Molecular Solids: A Coordinated Polyhedron Approach. G. M. Clark. (Illus.). 365p. 1972. 50.00 (ISBN 0-85334-544-9, Pub. by Elsevier Applied Sci England). Elsevier.
Structure of Nuclear Frechet Spaces. E. Dubinsky. (Lecture Notes in Mathematics: Vol. 720). 1979. pap. 14.00 (ISBN 0-387-09504-7). Springer-Verlag.
Structure of Nuclei: Trieste Lectures 1971. (Proceedings Ser.). (Illus.). 600p. (Orig.). 1973. pap. 45.00 (ISBN 92-0-130072-7, ISP305, IAEA). UNIPUB.
Structure of Obscurity: Gertrude Stein, Language, & Cubism. Randa Dubnick. LC 83-3603. (Illus.). 184p. 1984. 19.95 (ISBN 0-252-00909-6). U of Ill Pr.
Structure of Partially Ordered Sets with Transitive Automorphism Groups. Manfred Droste. LC 85-15625. (Memoirs of the AMS Ser.: No. 334). iv, 100p. 1985. pap. 13.00 (ISBN 0-8218-2335-3). Am Math.
Structure of Phonological Representation, Pt. One. Ed. by Harry V. Hulst & Norval Smith. 265p. 1982. 43.00 (ISBN 90-70176-53-X); pap. 24.90 (ISBN 90-70176-54-8). Foris Pubns.
Structure of Phonological Representation: Pt. Two. Ed. by Harry Van der Hulst & Norval Smith. 406p. 1983. pap. 28.90x (ISBN 90-70176-58-0). Foris Pubns.
Structure of Pindar's Epinician Odes. C. Greengard. viii, 135p. 1980. pap. text ed. 47.50x (ISBN 0-317-54496-9, Pub. by A. M. Hakkert). Coronet Bks.
Structure of Planets. G. H. Cole. (Wykeham Science Ser.: No. 45). 232p. 1977. 32.00 (ISBN 0-85109-610-7); pap. 18.00x (ISBN 0-85109-600-X). Taylor & Francis.
Structure of Plato's Philosophy. Jerry S. Clegg. LC 75-31467. 207p. 1978. 20.00 (ISBN 0-8387-1878-7). Bucknell U Pr.
Structure of Poetry. Elizabeth Sewell. LC 74-9584. 1951. lib. bdg. 35.00 (ISBN 0-8414-7760-4). Folcroft.
Structure of Police Organizations. Robert H. Langworthy. LC 86-21173. 176p. 1986. lib. bdg. 38.95 (ISBN 0-275-92328-2, C2328). Praeger.
Structure of Political Thought: A Study in the History of Political Ideas. Charles N. McCoy. LC 74-25996. 1978. Repr. of 1963 ed. lib. bdg. 41.50x (ISBN 0-8371-7880-0, MCPT). Greenwood.
Structure of Power in America: The Corporate Elite as a Ruling Class. Ed. by Michael Schwartz. 288p. 1987. 27.50 (ISBN 0-8419-0764-1); pap. 14.95 (ISBN 0-8419-0765-X). Holmes & Meier.
Structure of Power in North China During the Five Dynasties. Wang Gungwu. 1963. 25.00x (ISBN 0-8047-0786-3); pap. 6.95 (ISBN 0-8047-0603-4, SP61). Stanford U Pr.
Structure of Professionalism. John B. Cullen. (Illus.). 1979. text ed. 20.00 (ISBN 0-89433-084-5). Petrocelli.
Structure of Pronoun Incorporation in the Mayan Verbal Complex. John S. Robertson. Ed. by Jorge Hankamer. LC 79-55855. (Outstandinbg Dissertations in Linguistics Ser.). 415p. 1985. 56.00 (ISBN 0-8240-4558-0). Garland Pub.
Structure of Protection in Developing Countries. Balassa, Bela & Associates Staff. LC 77-147366. (World Bank Ser.). (Illus.). 384p. 1971. 34.50x (ISBN 0-8018-1257-7). Johns Hopkins.
Structure of Psychiatry in the U. S. S. R. Edward A. Babayan. LC 85-18100. 350p. 40.00x (ISBN 0-8236-6169-5). Intl Univs Pr.
Structure of Psychoanalytic Theory: A Systematizing Attempt. David Rapaport. (Psychological Issues Monograph: No. 6, Vol. 2, No. 2). 158p. (Orig.). 1967. text ed. 20.00x (ISBN 0-8236-6180-6). Intl Univs Pr.
Structure of Psychological Well-Being. Norman M. Bradburn. LC 67-27388. (NORC Monographs in Social Research Ser.: No. 15). (Illus.). 1969. 12.95x (ISBN 0-202-25029-6). NORC.
Structure of Psychopathological Experience. V. Siomopoulos. LC 83-7469. 136p. 1983. 20.00 (ISBN 0-87630-340-8). Brunner-Mazel.
Structure of Realism: The "Novelas Contemporaneas" de Benito Perez Galdos. Kay Engler. (Studies in the Romance Languages & Literatures Ser: No. 184). 193p. 1977. 15.00x (ISBN 0-8078-9184-3). U of NC Pr.
Structure of Recognizable Diatonic Tunings. Easley Blackwood. LC 85-42972. (Illus.). 360p. 1985. text ed. 50.00x (ISBN 0-691-09129-3). Princeton U Pr.
Structure of Regular Semigroups - I. K. S. S. Nambooripad. LC 79-21160. (Memoirs Ser.: No. 224). 119p. 1985. pap. 13.00 (ISBN 0-8218-2224-1, MEMO-224). Am Math.
Structure of Religious Experience. John MacMurray. LC 73-122406. xi, 77p. 1971. Repr. of 1936 ed. 15.00 (ISBN 0-208-00958-2, Archon). Shoe String.
Structure of Resurrection Belief. Peter Carnley. (Illus.). 408p. 1987. 69.00 (ISBN 0-19-826679-0). Oxford U Pr.
Structure of Retail Trade by Size of Store. new ed. Paul A. Vatter. Ed. by Stuart Bruchey & Vincent P. Carosso. LC 78-18151. (Small Business Enterprise in America Ser.). (Illus.). 1979. lib. bdg. 14.00x (ISBN 0-405-11509-1). Ayer Co Pubs.
Structure of Rings. rev. ed. Nathan Jacobson. LC 63-21795. (Colloquium Pbns. Ser.: Vol. 37). 299p. 1984. Repr. 31.00 (ISBN 0-8218-1037-5, COLL-37). Am Math.
Structure of School Improvement. Bruce Joyce et al. (Illus.). 304p. 1983. text ed. 20.95 (ISBN 0-582-28092-3). Longman.
Structure of Science. Ernest Nagel. LC 60-15504. 640p. 1979. lib. bdg. 35.00 (ISBN 0-915144-72-7); pap. text ed. 16.50 (ISBN 0-915144-71-9). Hackett Pub.
Structure of Scientific Revolutions. 2nd ed. Thomas S. Kuhn. LC 70-107472. (Foundations of the Unity of Science Ser: Vol. 2, No. 2). 1970. pap. 7.95 (ISBN 0-226-45804-0, P411, Phoen). U of Chicago Pr.
Structure of Scientific Revolutions. 2nd ed. Thomas S. Kuhn. LC 70-107472. (Foundations of the Unity of Science Ser: Vol. 2, No. 2). xii, 210p. 1970. 18.50x (ISBN 0-226-45803-2). U of Chicago Pr.
Structure of Scientific Theories. 2nd ed. Ed. by Frederick Suppe. LC 72-89604. (Illus.). 832p. 1977. 39.95 (ISBN 0-252-00655-0); pap. 19.95 (ISBN 0-252-00634-8). U of Ill Pr.
Structure of Shakespearean Scenes. James E. Hirsh. LC 81-2473. 224p. 1981. 26.50x (ISBN 0-300-02650-1). Yale U Pr.
Structure of Shock Waves in Magnetohydrodynamics. Mahmud Hesaaraki. LC 84-3085. (Memoirs: No. 302). 98p. 1984. pap. 12.00 (ISBN 0-8218-2303-5). Am Math.
Structure of Sidney's Arcadia. Nancy Lindheim. 232p. 1982. 30.00x (ISBN 0-8020-2374-6). U of Toronto Pr.
Structure of Singing: System & Art in Vocal Technique. Richard Miller. (Illus.). 384p. 1986. 27.95 (ISBN 0-02-872660-X). Schirmer Bks.
Structure of Social Action. Talcott Parsons. LC 49-49353. 1949. Vol. 1. pap. text ed. 10.95 (ISBN 0-02-924240-1); Vol. 2. pap. text ed. 16.95 (ISBN 0-02-924250-9). Free Pr.
Structure of Social Interaction: A Systematic Approach to the Semiotics of Service Encounters. Eija Ventola. 200p. 1986. 27.95 (ISBN 0-86187-626-1, Pub. by Frances Pinter). Longwood Pub Group.
Structure of Social Interaction: A Systemic Approach to the Semiotics of Service Encounters. Eija Ventola. (Open Linguistics Ser.). 289p. 1987. 47.50 (ISBN 0-317-61009-0, Pub. by Pinter Pubs UK). Columbia U Pr.
Structure of Social Science. Michael Lessnoff. (Studies in Sociology Ser.). 1978. pap. text ed. 14.95 (ISBN 0-04-300046-0). Unwin Hyman.
Structure of Social Systems. Frederick L. Bates & Clyde C. Harvey. LC 85-10009. 432p. 1986. Repr. of 1975 ed. lib. bdg. 30.50 (ISBN 0-89874-874-7). Krieger.
Structure of Social Theory: Strategies, Dilemmas & Projects. Terry Johnson et al. LC 84-13285. 262p. 1985. 29.95 (ISBN 0-312-76833-8); pap. 11.95 (ISBN 0-312-76834-6). St Martin.
Structure of Socialist Society. Andras Hegedus. LC 74-17724. 1977. 19.95x (ISBN 0-312-76825-7). St Martin.
Structure of Society. Julian Marias. Tr. by Harold C. Raley from Span. LC 84-185. 1987. 21.95 (ISBN 0-8173-0181-X). U of Ala Pr.
Structure of Sociological Theory. 4th ed. Jonathan H. Turner. 1986. 38.00x (ISBN 0-256-03408-7). Dorsey.
Structure of Soviet Wages: A Study in Socialist Economics. Abram Bergson. LC 44-1242. (Economic Studies: No. 76). 1944. 20.00x (ISBN 0-674-84480-7). Harvard U Pr.
Structure of State Legal Services. (Illus.). 62p. 1979. 4.50 (ISBN 0-318-15230-4). Natl Attys General.
Structure of Stichomythia in Attic Tragedy. J. L. Myers. 1949. pap. 5.50 (ISBN 0-85672-627-3, Pub. by British Acad). Longwood Pub Group.
Structure of Stratification in Thailand. Moshe Lissak. 1973. 4.95 (ISBN 0-87855-265-0). Transaction Bks.
Structure of Stuttering. M. E. Wingate. (Illus.). 335p. 1988. 67.00 (ISBN 0-387-96722-2). Springer-Verlag.
Structure of Surfaces. Ed. by M. A. Van Hove & S. Y. Tong. (Springer Series in Surface Sciences: Vol. 2). (Illus.). 470p. 1985. 55.00 (ISBN 0-387-15410-8). Springer-Verlag.
Structure of Surfaces II. Ed. by J. F. van der Veen & M. A. van Hove. (Surface Sciences Ser.: Vol. 11). (Illus.). 600p. 1988. 65.00 (ISBN 0-387-18784-7). Springer-Verlag.
Structure of Television. P. Gould et al. (Illus.). 178p. 1984. 29.95 (ISBN 0-85086-110-1, 9195, Pub. by Pion England). Routledge Chapman & Hall.
Structure of Texts & Semiotics of Culture. Ed. by Jan Van Der Eng & Mojmir Grygar. (Slavistic Printings & Reprintings: No. 294). 1973. 60.00x (ISBN 90-2792-514-3). Mouton.
Structure of the American Economy, 2 vols. in 1. United States National Resources Committee. LC 78-173418. (FDR & the Era of the New Deal Ser). 1972. Repr. of 1939 ed. lib. bdg. 55.00 (ISBN 0-306-70388-2). Da Capo.
Structure of the Artistic Text. Jurij Lotman. Tr. by Ronald Vroon from Rus. (Michigan Slavic Contributions: No. 7). 1977. pap. 10.00 (ISBN 0-930042-15-8). Mich Slavic Pubns.
Structure of the Autonomic Nervous System. G. Gabella. 1976. 75.00x (ISBN 0-412-13620-1, 6114, Pub. by Chapman & Hall). Routledge Chapman & Hall.
Structure of the Book of Job: A Form-Critical Analysis. Claus Westermann. LC 80-2379. pap. 40.00 (ISBN 0-317-55777-7, 2029297). Bks Demand UMI.
Structure of the British Isles. 2nd ed. J. G. Anderson & T. R. Owen. LC 80-41075. (Illus.). 242p. 1980. text ed. 44.00 (ISBN 0-08-023998-6); pap. text ed. 19.25 (ISBN 0-08-023997-8). Pergamon.
Structure of "The Brothers Karamazov". Robert L. Belknap. 122p. 1988. pap. 9.95 (ISBN 0-8101-0812-7). Northwestern U Pr.
Structure of the "Canterbury Tales". Helen Cooper. LC 83-13997. 256p. 1984. pap. 12.00x (ISBN 0-8203-0781-5). U of Ga Pr.
Structure of the Chemical Processing Industries: Function & Economics. James Wei et al. (Chemical Engineering Ser.). (Illus.). 1978. text ed. 52.95 (ISBN 0-07-068985-7). McGraw.
Structure of the Christian Science Textbook: Our Way of Life. Max Kappeler. LC 58-26857. 206p. 1954. 14.00 (ISBN 0-85241-071-9). Kappeler Inst Pub.
Structure of the Corporation. Melvin A. Eisenberg. 1976. pap. text ed. 11.95 (ISBN 0-316-22542-8). Little.
Structure of the Cotton Economy of the Antebellum South. Ed. by W. N. Parker. 1970. cancelled (ISBN 0-87461-046-X). McNally & Loftin.
Structure of the Defense Industry: An International Survey. Ed. by Milton Leitenberg & Nicole Ball. LC 82-42565. 1983. 29.95x (ISBN 0-312-76757-9). St Martin.
Structure of the Defense Market, 1955-1964. William L. Baldwin. LC 67-23730. Repr. of 1967 ed. 48.90 (2017880). Bks Demand UMI.
Structure of the Earth. Sydney P. Clark. (Foundations of Earth Science Ser). 1971. pap. text ed. write for info. (ISBN 0-13-854646-0). P-H.
Structure of the Eye. Ed. by J. G. Hollyfield. 382p. 1982. 146.00 (ISBN 0-444-00613-3, Biomedical Pr). Elsevier.
Structure of the Human Brain: A Photographic Atlas. 2nd ed. Stephen J. DeArmond et al. (Illus.). 1976. pap. text ed. 19.95x (ISBN 0-19-502073-1). Oxford U Pr.
Structure of the Indian Economy. Bharat Hazari. 1981. 12.50x (ISBN 0-8364-0675-3, Pub. by Macmillan India). South Asia Bks.
Structure of the International Environment see Future of the International Legal Order.
Structure of the Japanese Language. Susumu Kuno. 384p. 1973. 35.00x (ISBN 0-262-11049-0). MIT Pr.
Structure of the Level One Standard Modules for the Affine Lie Algebra. Mandia. LC 86-28797. (Memoirs of the American Mathematical Society Ser.: Vol. 362). 146p. 1987. pap. text ed. 19.00 (ISBN 0-8218-2423-6). Am Math.
Structure of the Literary Process: Studies Dedicated to the Memory of Felix Vodicka. Ed. by P. Steiner et al. (Linguistic & Literary Studies in Eastern Europe: No. 8). viii, 613p. 1982. 78.00x (ISBN 90-272-1512-X). Benjamins North Am.
Structure of the Metascientific Revolution: An Essay on the Growth of Modern Science. J. M. Zycinski. (Philosophy in Science Library: Vol. 3). 223p. (Orig.). 1988. pap. 14.95 (ISBN 0-88126-703-1). Pachart Pub Hse.
Structure of the Netherlands Indian Economy. Julius H. Boeke. LC 75-30047. (Institute of Pacific Relations). 1983. Repr. of 1942 ed. 29.50 (ISBN 0-404-59509-X). AMS Pr.
Structure of the Nigerian Economy. F. Akin Olaloku et al. LC 78-14765. 1980. 26.00x (ISBN 0-312-76777-3). St Martin.
Structure of the Noun Phrase in English & Hindi. M. K. Verma. (Eng. & Hindi.). 1971. 8.50 (ISBN 0-89684-322-X). Orient Bk Dist.
Structure of the Nucleus. M. A. Preston & R. K. Bharduri. 693p. 1975. text ed. 53.35 (ISBN 0-201-05976-2, Adv Bk Prog MSP). Addison-Wesley.
Structure of the Ottoman Dynasty. Anthony D. Alderson. LC 81-23751. xvi, 186p. 1982. Repr. of 1956 ed. lib. bdg. 52.50x (ISBN 0-313-22522-2, ALSO). Greenwood.
Structure of the Planets. Monograph ed. John W. Elder. (Academic Press Geology). 226p. 1987. 49.50 (ISBN 0-12-236452-X). Acad Pr.
Structure of the Proton: Deep Inelastic Scattering. R. G. Roberts. (Cambridge Monographs on Mathematical Physics). 200p. Date not set. price not set (ISBN 0-521-35159-6). Cambridge U Pr.
Structure of the Quiet Photosphere & the Low Chromosphere: Proceedings of the Biderberg Conference, Arnhem, Holland, April 17-21, 1967. Biderberg Conference Staff. Ed. by C. De Jager. 240p. 1968. lib. bdg. 47.50 (ISBN 90-277-0120-2, Pub. by Reidel Holland). Kluwer Academic.
Structure of the Retina. Santiago Ramon Y Cajal. Tr. by Sylvia A. Thorpe & Mitchell Glickstein. (Illus.). 224p. 1972. 26.00 (ISBN 0-398-02385-9). C C Thomas.
Structure of the Risk Management Process (for RM 54) 2nd, rev. ed. R. Robert Rackley. (ARM Ser.). 1984. 100.00 (ISBN 0-88171-093-8). Insurance Achiev.

Structured COBOL: Flowchart Edition. Gary B. Shelly & Thomas J. Cashman. (Anaheim Ser.). 540p. 1986. pap. text ed. 22.00 (ISBN 0-87835-197-3); tchr's. guide avail. (ISBN 0-87835-201-5). Boyd & Fraser.

Structured COBOL: Fundamentals. 2nd ed. Mike Murach & John J. Padgett. 384p. 1986. pap. text ed. write for info. (ISBN 0-574-21980-3, 13-4980); write for info. (ISBN 0-574-21981-1, 13-4981). Sci Res Assoc Coll.

Structured COBOL Programming. William M. Fuori & Stephen J. Gaughran. (Illus.). 544p. 1984. pap. text ed. write for info (ISBN 0-13-854430-1). P-H.

Structured COBOL Programming. Robert T. Grauer. (Illus.). 496p. 1985. pap. text ed. 32.33 (ISBN 0-13-854217-1). P-H.

Structured COBOL Programming. J. K. Pierson & Jeretta Horn. 1986. pap. text ed. write for info. (ISBN 0-673-15913-2). Scott F.

Structured COBOL Programming. 2nd ed. J. K. Pierson & Jeretta A. Horn. 1989. pap. text ed. price not set (ISBN 0-673-38469-1). Scott F.

Structured COBOL Programming. Morris Pollack & Harry Geist. 340p. (Orig.). 1982. pap. text ed. 24.15 scp (ISBN 0-672-97690-0). Bobbs.

Structured COBOL Programming. 5th ed. Nancy Stern & Robert A. Stern. LC 87-28003. 815p. 1988. write for info. (ISBN 0-471-63287-2). Wiley.

Structured COBOL Programming. J. M. Triance. 178p. 1984. pap. text ed. 21.55 (ISBN 0-471-81053-3, Pub by Wiley-Interscience). Wiley.

Structured COBOL Programming & Data Processing Methods. Richard McCalla. LC 84-21367. (Computer Science Ser.). 450p. 1985. pap. text ed. 22.00 pub net (ISBN 0-534-04488-3). Brooks-Cole.

Structured Cobol: Programming & Problem Solving. Fenton & Williams. 704p. 1988. pap. 31.95 (ISBN 0-8016-1662-X). Mosby.

Structured COBOL: Pseudocode Edition. Gary B. Shelly & Thomas J. Cashman. (Anaheim Ser.). 540p. 1986. pap. text ed. 22.00 (ISBN 0-87835-196-5); tchr's. guide avail. Boyd & Fraser.

Structured COBOL Reference Summary. National Computing Center. 100p. 1984. pap. text ed. 15.00 (ISBN 0-471-81056-8). Wiley.

Structured COBOL with Business Applications. Stanley E. Myers. (Illus.). 672p. 1987. pap. text ed. 30.67 (ISBN 0-13-854167-1). P-H.

Structured COBOLer's Guide. Thayne A. Shank. (Illus.). 144p. 1984. pap. 28.00 (ISBN 0-13-854448-4). P-H.

Structured Company Operational Review & Evaluation (SCORE) Andrew W. Poschmann. LC 84-45788. 432p. 1985. 59.95 (ISBN 0-8144-5814-9). AMACOM.

Structured Computer Organization. 2nd ed. Andrew S. Tanenbaum. (Illus.). 480p. 1984. text ed. 52.00 (ISBN 0-13-854489-1); tchr's manual avail. (ISBN 0-13-854423-9). P-H.

Structured Computer Vision: Machine Perception Through Hierarchical Computation Structures. Ed. by S. Tanimoto & A. Klinger. LC 80-14878. 1980. 35.00 (ISBN 0-12-683280-3). Acad Pr.

Structured Concurrent Programming with Operating Systems Applications. Richard C. Holt et al. 1978. pap. text ed. write for info. (ISBN 0-201-02937-5). Addison-Wesley.

Structured Crowd: Essays in English Social History. Harold Perkin. 250p. 1981. 28.50x (ISBN 0-389-20116-2). B&N Imports.

Structured Data Processing Design. Harry H. Ort. LC 84-14506. 224p. 1985. pap. write for info. (ISBN 0-201-05425-6); write for info. instr's manual (ISBN 0-201-05426-4). Addison-Wesley.

Structured DEC BASIC for Business Using Files. Allen M. Lewis. (Illus.). 208p. 1986. pap. text ed. write for info (ISBN 0-13-854746-7). P H.

Structured Design. 2nd ed. Edward Yourdon & Larry L. Constantine. LC 78-24465. 464p. 1978. pap. 27.95 (ISBN 0-917072-11-1, Yourdon). P-H.

Structured Design: Fundamentals of a Discipline of Computer Program & System Design. Edward Yourdon & Larry L. Constantine. 1979. text ed. 49.00 (ISBN 0-13-854471-9). P-H.

Structured Development & Evolution of Reptiles. Mark W. Ferguson. (Symposium Zoological Society: No. 52). 1984. 82.50 (ISBN 0-12-613352-2). Acad Pr.

Structured Development for Real-Time Systems. Comb Version, Vols. 1, 2 & 3. Paul Ward & Stephen J. Mellor. 468p. 1987. pap. text ed. 75.00 (ISBN 0-13-854654-1). P-H.

Structured Development for Real Time Systems: Essential Modeling Techniques, Vol. 2. Paul T. Ward & Stephen J. Mellor. 144p. (Orig.). 1985. pap. text ed. 28.95 (ISBN 0-917072-52-9, Yourdon). P-H.

Structured Development for Real-Time Systems: Implementation Modeling Techniques, Vol. 3. Paul T. Ward & Stephen J. Mellor. LC 85-50815. 168p. (Orig.). 1985. pap. text ed. 28.95 (ISBN 0-917072-53-7, Yourdon). P-H.

Structured Development for Real-Time Systems, Vol. 1: Introduction & Tools. Paul T. Ward & Stephen J. Mellor. LC 85-50815. (Illus.). 160p. (Orig.). 1985. pap. 28.95 (ISBN 0-917072-51-0, Yourdon). P-H.

Structured Digital Design Including MSI-LSI Components & Microprocessors. Raymond M. Kline. (Illus.). 544p. 1983. text ed. 39.95. P-H.

Structured EDP Auditing. Rothberg. 35.95 (ISBN 0-317-64293-6). Van Nos Reinhold.

Structured EDP Auditing. Gabriel B. Rothberg. (Data Processing Ser.). (Illus.). 302p. 1983. 31.50 (ISBN 0-534-97931-9, Lifetime Learn). Van Nos Reinhold.

Structured Enrichment Programs for Couples & Families. Luciano L'Abate & Steven Weinstein. LC 86-17128. 512p. 1987. 50.00 (ISBN 0-87630-407-2). Brunner-Mazel.

Structured Essay: A Formula for Writing. Mary Spangler & Rita Werner. 416p. 1986. pap. text ed. 29.95 (ISBN 0-8403-3813-9). Kendall-Hunt.

Structured Exercises in Stress Management, Vol. I. Ed. by Nancy L. Tubesing & Donald A. Tubesing. LC 83-61073. (Stress Management Handbook Ser.). 144p. 1983. spiral bound 24.95x (ISBN 0-938586-01-7). Whole Person.

Structured Exercises in Stress Management. Nancy Tubsing & Donald Tubsing. LC 83-61074. (Management Handbook Ser.). 144p. pap. 24.95. Whole Person.

Structured Exercises in Stress Management, Vol. 2. Ed. by Nancy L. Tubesing & Donald A. Tubesing. LC 83-61073. (Stress Management Handbook Ser.). 144p. 1984. spiral 24.95X (ISBN 0-938586-03-3). Whole Person.

Structured Exercises in Stress Management, Vol. 3. Nancy L. Tubesing & Donald A. Tubesing. LC 83-61073. (Stress Management Handbook Ser.). 144p. 1986. softcover, spiral bound 24.95x (ISBN 0-938586-06-8). Whole Person.

Structured Exercises in Stress Management, Vol. 4. Nancy L. Tubesing & Donald A. Tubesing. LC 83-61073. (Stress Management Handbook Ser.). 144p. 1988. spiral bdg. 24.95x (ISBN 0-938586-12-2). Whole Person.

Structured Exercises in Wellness Promotion, Vol. I. Ed. by Nancy L. Tubesing & Donald A. Tubesing. LC 83-61074. (Wellness Promotion Handbook Ser.). 144p. 1983. 24.95x (ISBN 0-938586-02-5). Whole Person.

Structured Exercises in Wellness Promotion, Vol. 2. Nancy L. Tubesing & Donald A. Tubesing. LC 83-61074. (Wellness Promotion Handbook Ser.). 144p. 1984. spiral 24.95X (ISBN 0-938586-04-1). Whole Person.

Structured Exercises in Wellness Promotion, Vol. 3. Nancy L. Tubesing & Donald A. Tubesing. LC 83-61074. (Wellness Promotion Handbook Ser.). 144p. 1986. softcover, spiral bound 24.95x (ISBN 0-938586-07-6). Whole Person.

Structured Exercises in Wellness Promotion, Vol. 4. Nancy L. Tubesing & Donald A. Tubesing. LC 83-61074. (Wellness Promotion Handbook Ser.). 144p. 1988. spiral bdg. 24.95x (ISBN 0-938586-13-0). Whole Person.

Structured Exercises in Wellness Promotion, Volume 4. Ed. by Nancy Tubesing & Donald Tubesing. LC 83-61074. (Promotion Handbook Ser.). 144p. pap. 24.95x. Whole Person.

Structured Family Facilitation Programs: Enrichment, Education, & Treatment. Margaret H. Hoopes et al. LC 83-22372. 480p. 1984. 38.00 (ISBN 0-89443-579-5). Aspen Pub.

Structured Formula Translation. Lester Klein. 250p. (Orig.). 1986. pap. text ed. write for info. (ISBN 0-89894-037-0). Advocate Pub Group.

Structured FORTRAN for Business. Charles E. Paddock. LC 84-18377. (Illus.). 272p. 1985. pap. text ed. 28.00 (ISBN 0-13-854233-3). P-H.

Structured FORTRAN IV Programming. V. Thomas Dock. (Data Processing & Information System Ser.). (Illus.). 344p. 1979. pap. text ed. 31.50 (ISBN 0-8299-0249-X). West Pub.

Structured FORTRAN WATFIV-S Programming. Jean-Paul Tremblay & Richard B. Bunt. 1979. pap. 26.95 (ISBN 0-07-065171-X). McGraw.

Structured FORTRAN with WATFIV-S. P. Cress et al. 1980. pap. write for info (ISBN 0-13-854752-1). P-H.

Structured FORTRAN 77 for Engineers & Scientists. 2nd ed. D. M. Etter. (Illus.). 500p. 1987. pap. 30.25 (ISBN 0-8053-2495-X); instr's guide avail. (ISBN 0-8053-2496-8); quiz bank 9.95 (ISBN 0-8053-2531-X); software pkg. avail. (ISBN 0-8053-2540-9). Benjamin-Cummings.

Structured FORTRAN 77 Programming. Seymour V. Pollack. LC 82-70214. 504p. (Orig.). 1982. pap. text ed. 25.00x (ISBN 0-87835-095-0); write for info. solutions manual. Boyd & Fraser.

Structured FORTRAN 77 Programming for Hewlett-Packard Computers. Seymour V. Pollack. 512p. (Orig.). 1983. pap. text ed. 25.00x (ISBN 0-87835-130-2). Boyd & Fraser.

Structured Groups for Facilitating Development: Acquiring Life Skills, Resolving Life Themes, & Making Life Transitions. David J. Drum & J. Eugene Knott. Ed. by Gary Walz & Benjamin B. Libby. LC 77-1947. (New Vistas in Counseling Ser.: Vol. I). 284p. 1977. 29.95 (ISBN 0-87705-308-1). Human Sci Pr.

Structured Hereditary Systems. Reneke. Ed. by Fennell & Minton. (Pure & Applied Mathematics Ser.). 232p. 1987. 79.75 (ISBN 0-8247-7772-7). Dekker.

Structured Induction in Expert Systems. Alen Shapiro. 256p. 1987. text ed. 28.95 (ISBN 0-201-17813-3). Addison-Wesley.

Structured Learning Therapy: Toward a Psychotherapy for the Poor. A. P. Goldstein. 1973. 27.50 (ISBN 0-12-288750-6). Acad Pr.

Structured Meanings: The Semantics of Propositional Attitudes. M. J. Cresswell. 1985. 25.00x (ISBN 0-262-03108-6). MIT Pr.

Structured Mediation in Divorce Settlements: A Handbook for Marital Mediators. O. J. Coogler. LC 77-15814. 1978. pap. 10.00x (ISBN 0-669-09747-0). Lexington Bks.

Structured Methods. Ed. by A. Bytheway. (Computer State of the Art Report, Series 12: No. 1). (Illus.). 250p. 1984. 350.00x (ISBN 0-08-028585-6). Pergamon.

Structured Methods Through COBOL. Robert T. Grauer. (Illus.). 384p. 1983. text ed. write for info (ISBN 0-13-854539-1). P-H.

Structured Microprocessor Programming. Morris Krieger et al. LC 79-67229. (Illus.). 240p. (Orig.). 1979. pap. 12.95 (ISBN 0-917072-18-9, Yourdon). P-H.

Structured Model of Bacterial Growth & Tests with Activated Sludge in a One-Stage & Two-Stage Chemostat. (Agricultural Research Reports: 886). 1979. pap. 18.00 (ISBN 90-220-0702-2, PDC116, PUDOC). UNIPUB.

Structured Mortgage & Receivable Financing. Practising Law Institute Staff & Rodney S. Dayan. LC 85-72525. (Real Estate Law & Practice Course Handbook Ser.: No. 264). 752p. 1985. 15.00 (N4-4443). PLI.

Structured Mortgage & Receivable Financing, 1987. (Real Estate Law & Practice Ser.). 581p. 1987. 45.00 (N4-4476). PLI.

Structured Pacing in Chemistry Education (SPICE) Hines et al. 272p. 1987. pap. text ed. 13.90 (ISBN 0-8403-4064-8). Kendall-Hunt.

Structured Pascal. Jean-Paul Tremblay & Richard B. Bunt. 448p. 1980. pap. 29.95 (ISBN 0-07-065159-0). McGraw.

Structured Personality Learning Theory: A Holistic Multivariate Research Approach. Raymond B. Cattell. LC 83-16103. (Centennial Psychology Ser.). 480p. 1983. 54.95 (ISBN 0-275-90958-1, C0958). Praeger.

Structured PL-Zero PL-One. Michael Kennedy & Martin B. Solomon. (Illus.). 1977. pap. write for info (ISBN 0-13-854901-X). P-H.

Structured PL-0 Plus PL-1. Michael Kennedy & Martin B. Solomon. (Illus.). 736p. 1987. pap. text ed. 28.00 (ISBN 0-13-854910-9). P-H.

Structured PL-1 (PL-C) Programming. Jean-Paul Tremblay & Richard B. Bunt. 1979. pap. 26.95x (ISBN 0-07-065173-6). McGraw.

Structured PL-1 Programming. 2nd ed. Clarence J. Rockey. 576p. 1985. pap. text ed. write for info. (ISBN 0-697-08180-X); solutions manual avail. (ISBN 0-697-00305-1). Wm C Brown.

Structured Polymer Properties. Robert J. Samuels. LC 73-21781. Repr. of 1974 ed. 50.40 (ISBN 0-8357-9986-7, 2015851). Bks Demand UMI.

Structured Preoperative Teaching. C. U. R. N. Project, Michigan Nurses Association. (Using Research to Improve Clinical Practice Ser.: Vol. I). (Illus.). 165p. 1980. pap. 13.50 (ISBN 0-8089-1311-5, 792065). Grune.

Structured Problem Analysis & Logic Design. Victor Broquard & John W. Westley. (Illus.). 304p. 1985. pap. text ed. 25.00 (ISBN 0-13-854712-2). P-H.

Structured Problem Solving with Pascal. Lawrence J. Mazlack. 1983. pap. text ed. 25.95 (ISBN 0-03-060153-3). HR&W.

Structured Program Design with the TRS-80 BASIC. Thomas A. Dwyer & Margot Critchfield. (Illus.). 352p. 1984. pap. text ed. 18.95 (ISBN 0-07-018493-3, BYTE Bks). McGraw.

Structured Programming. Infotech. (Infotech Computer State of the Art Reports). 495p. 1976. 61.00x (ISBN 0-08-028512-0). Pergamon.

Structured Programming Approach to Data. Derek Coleman. 222p. 1979. pap. 20.50 (ISBN 0-387-91138-3). Springer-Verlag.

Structured Programming Assembly Language for the IBM PC. William C. Runnion. 574p. 1988. text ed. 31.00 (ISBN 0-534-91480-2, PWS Computer Sci). PWS Kent Pub.

Structured Programming in BASIC-PLUS & BASIC PLUS-2: Including VAX-II BASIC Compatibility. C. Jinshing Hwang & Thomas I. Ho. LC 83-10259. 492p. 1984. pap. text ed. write for info. (ISBN 0-471-06338-X). Wiley.

Structured Programming in COBOL. Robert B. Boettcher. 620p. 1987. pap. text ed. write for info. (ISBN 0-03-070559-2). HR&W.

Structured Programming in FORTRAN. Louis A. Hill, Jr. LC 80-39567. (Illus.). 512p. 1981. text ed. write for info (ISBN 0-13-854612-6). P-H.

Structured Programming in Macro-11. Bob Southern. (DEC Books). 192p. 1984. pap. 22.00 (ISBN 0-932376-85-1, EY-00032-DP). Digital Pr.

Structured Programming in True BASIC. Wade Ellis, Jr. & Ed Lodi. 356p. 1988. pap. text ed. 19.00 net (ISBN 0-15-584076-2, HC). HarBraceJ.

Structured Programming Logic. Thomas Mason. 256p. 1988. pap. text ed. write for info. (ISBN 0-697-06776-9). Instr's manual (ISBN 0-697-06984-2). Wm C Brown.

Structured Programming Logic: A Flowcharting Approach. Jerry L. Jones. (Illus.). 144p. 1986. pap. text ed. 17.95 (ISBN 0-318-11865-3). P H.

Structured Programming: PL-1 with PL-C. Kathi H. Davis & Lyle Domina. LC 87-12473. 686p. Date not set. pap. text ed. 26.00 (ISBN 0-03-003723-9). HR&W.

Structured Programming: Practice & Experience, 5 vols. (Infotech Computer State of the Art Reports). 868p. 1978. Set. 1355.00 (ISBN 0-08-028555-4). Pergamon.

Structured Programming: Theory & Practice. R. C. Linger et al. LC 78-18641. 1979. text ed. write for info. (ISBN 0-201-14461-1). Addison-Wesley.

Structured Programming Using FORTRAN 77. Patrick G. McKeown. 482p. 1985. pap. text ed. 19.00 net (ISBN 0-15-584411-3, HC). HarBraceJ.

Structured Programming Using Pascal. J. Winston Crawley & William G. McArthur. (Illus.). 1008p. 1988. pap. text ed. 30.00 (ISBN 0-13-854035-7). P-H.

Structured Programming Using Pascal: A Brief Introduction. Margaret Anderson. 145p. 1988. pap. text ed. 6.00 net (ISBN 0-15-551150-5, HC). HarBraceJ.

Structured Programming Using PL-C. Joan K. Hughes & Barbara J. Lapearl. LC 81-4434. 414p. 1981. pap. write for info. (ISBN 0-471-04969-7); tchr's. manual avail. (ISBN 0-471-86939-2). Wiley.

Structured Programming Using PL-1 SP-K. 2nd ed. J. N. Hume & B. C. Holt. 1980. pap. text ed. write for info. (ISBN 0-8359-7131-7, Reston). P-H.

Structured Programming Using True Basic: An Introduction: Instructor's Manual. Wade Ellis, Jr. & Ed Lodi. 40p. 1988. pap. text ed. 1.75 net (ISBN 0-15-584077-0). HarBraceJ.

Structured Programming Using Turbo BASIC. Wade Ellis, Jr. & Ed Lodi. 307p. 1988. 42.50 (ISBN 0-12-237459-2); pap. 24.95 (ISBN 0-12-237460-6). Acad Pr.

Structured Programming Using WATFIV. Patrick G. McKeown. 405p. 1985. pap. text ed. 19.00 net (ISBN 0-15-584414-8, HC). HarBraceJ.

Structured Programming with COMAL. Roy Atherton. (Computers & Their Applications Ser.). 266p. 1982. 62.95x (ISBN 0-470-27318-6); pap. 31.95 (ISBN 0-470-27359-3). Halsted Pr.

Structured Programming with Lotus 1-2-3. Nancy Woodard Cain & Thomas Cain. (Illus.). 352p. 1989. pap. 23.95 (ISBN 0-13-853540-X). Brady Comp Bks.

Structured Programming with PL-1: An Introduction. Michael Marcotty. (Illus.). 1977. pap. text ed. write for info (ISBN 0-13-854885-4). P-H.

Structured Programming with True BASIC. Larry J. Goldstein et al. (Illus.). 512p. 1986. text ed. 29.00 (ISBN 0-13-855008-5). P-H.

Structured Programming with True BASIC. Harriet H. Morrill. 1986. pap. text ed. write for info. (ISBN 0-673-39061-6). Scott F.

Structured Reading. 2nd ed. Lynn Q. Troyka. (Illus.). 400p. 1984. write for info. (ISBN 0-13-854588-X). P-H.

Structured Receivables Financing: Managing Risks More Efficiently in Security Form. Edward F. Green & Walter G. McNeill. LC 85-241999. 270p. Date not set. price not set. HarBraceJ.

Structured Requirements Definition. Kenneth T. Orr. LC 81-80846. (Illus.). 237p. (Orig.). 1981. pap. 25.00 (ISBN 0-9605884-0-X). Orr & Assocs.

Structured Settlements. Paul J. Lesti & Brent B. Danninger. LC 86-80969. 1986. Updated annually. 72.50; Suppl. 1987. 24.00. Lawyers Co-Op.

Structured Settlements. Pennsylvania Bar Institute. 101p. 1983. 20.00 (ISBN 0-318-02167-6, 233). PA Bar Inst.

Structured Settlements. Arthur Simpson et al. 307p. 1984. looseleaf bdg. 35.00. NJ Inst CLE.

Structured Settlements: ALI-ABA Video Law Review Study Materials. ALI-ABA Committee on Continuing Professional Education. LC 84-210146. 95p. 1985. write for info. Am Law Inst.

Structured Settlements & Periodic Payment Judgements. Daniel W. Hindert et al. 522p. 1986. looseleaf 75.00 (ISBN 0-318-21441-5, 00598). NY Law Pub.

Structured Social Inequality: A Reader in Comparative Social Stratification. 2nd ed. Celia S. Heller. 989p. 1987. write for info. (ISBN 0-02-353430-3). Macmillan.

Structured System Analysis: A New Technique. Barbara F. Medina. 96p. 1981. 44.00 (ISBN 0-677-05570-6). Gordon & Breach.

Structured Systems Analysis: Tools & Techniques. C. Gane & Trish Sarson. 1979. 47.00 (ISBN 0-13-854547-2). P-H.

Structured Systems Analysis: Tools & Techniques. Chris Gane & Trish Sarson. 373p. (Orig.). 1977. 22.50 (ISBN 0-930196-00-7); pap. 15.00 (ISBN 0-686-37676-5). McDonnell Douglas.

Structured Systems Development. Kenneth T. Orr. LC 77-88593. (Illus.). 192p. (Orig.). 1977. 23.00 (ISBN 0-917072-08-1, Yourdon); pap. 19.95 (ISBN 0-917072-06-5). P-H.

Structured Systems Development Techniques: Strategic Planning to System Testing. Garfield L. Collins & Gillian L. Blay. 350p. 1983. 29.95x (ISBN 0-471-88773-0, Ronald Pr). Wiley.

Structured Systems Programming. J. Welsh & R. M. McKeag. (Ser. in Computer Science). (Illus.). 1980. text ed. 44.00 (ISBN 0-13-854562-6). P-H.

Structured Techniques: A Basis for CASE. rev. ed. James Martin & Carma L. McClure. (Illus.). 816p. 1988. text ed. 52.00 (ISBN 0-13-854936-2). P-H.
Structured Techniques for Computing. James Martin & Carma L. McClure. (Illus.). 736p. 1985. text ed. 59.00 (ISBN 0-13-855180-4). P-H.
Structured Techniques of System Analysis, Design, & Implementation. Sitansu S. Mittra. LC 87-28577. 392p. 1988. 42.95 (ISBN 0-471-83081-X). Wiley.
Structured Testing. Thomas J. McCabe. (Tutorial Texts Ser.). 132p. 1983. 30.00 (ISBN 0-8186-0452-2, Q452). IEEE Comp Soc.
Structured Tutoring. Grant V. Harrison & Ronald E. Guymon. Ed. by Danny G. Langdon. LC 79-23035. (Instructional Design Library). 108p. 1980. 23.95 (ISBN 0-87778-154-0). Educ Tech Pubns.
Structured Vacuum: Thinking about Nothing. J. Rafelski & B. Mueller. (Illus.). 182p. 1985. pap. 14.00 (ISBN 0-318-23064-X, Pub. by Verlag Harris Deusch). IPS.
Structured Vax BASIC. R. Hirschfelder & C. Hommel. 643p. 1987. pap. text ed. 29.95 (ISBN 0-8053-3690-7); instr's manual 15.95 (ISBN 0-8053-3691-5); magnetic tape avail. (ISBN 0-8053-3692-3). Benjamin-Cummings.
Structured VAX BASIC: A GOTO-less Approach. Wilson T. Price & Richard Spitzer. 581p. 1988. text ed. write for info. (ISBN 0-02-396620-3). Macmillan.
Structured VAX BASIC & BASIC PLUS. 2nd ed. Steve Teglovic & Kenneth D. Douglas. 1987. 26.95x (ISBN 0-256-03639-X). Irwin.
Structured Walkthroughs. 3rd ed. Edward Yourdon. LC 85-51717. (Illus.). 160p. 1985. pap. text ed. 19.95 (ISBN 0-917072-55-3, Yourdon). P-H.
Structured WATTIV: Problem Solving & Programming. D. M. Etter. 400p. 1985. pap. 29.95 (ISBN 0-8053-2502-6); instr's. guide 15.95 (ISBN 0-8053-2503-4); application software with tape 12.00 (ISBN 0-8053-2518-2). Benjamin Cummings.
Structured World of Jorge Guillen: A Study of Cantico & Clamor. Elizabeth Matthews. (Liverpool Monographs in Hispanic Studies: No. 4). 326p. 1986. text ed. 40.00 (ISBN 0-905205-23-5, Pub. by F Cairns). Longwood Pub Group.
Structures. Elementary Science Study Staff. 1970. tchr's guide 14.96 (ISBN 0-07-017696-5). McGraw.
Structures. 2nd ed. W. T. Marshall. (Illus.). 1977. pap. text ed. 19.95 (ISBN 0-8464-0889-9). Beekman Pubs.
Structures. D. Schodek. 1980. 42.00 (ISBN 0-13-855304-1). P-H.
Structures see Civil Engineering Practice.
Structures Agricoles & Developpement Economique. Bernard Rosier. (Publications de e'leuniversite des Sciences Sociales de Grenoble, Serie Economie du Developpement: No. 3). 1968. pap. 16.40 (ISBN 0-686-21785-3). Mouton.
Structures & Environment Handbook. rev. ed. Midwest Plan Service Engineers. LC 76-27983. (Illus.). 658p. 1983. pap. text ed. 25.00 (ISBN 0-89373-057-2, MWPS-1). Midwest Plan Serv.
Structures & Function of FC Receptors. Ed. by Arnold Froese & Frixos Paraskevas. (Receptors & Ligands in Intercellular Communication Ser.: Vol. 2). (Illus.). 312p. 1983. 59.75 (ISBN 0-8247-1814-3). Dekker.
Structures & Materials. Kathryn Whyman. (Science Today Ser.). (Illus.). 32p. 1987. lib. bdg. 11.90 (ISBN 0-531-17044-6, Gloucester Pr). Watts.
Structures & Materials: A Programmed Approach. P. C. Croxton et al. (Illus.). 300p. 1974. text ed. 22.95 (ISBN 0-8464-0890-2). Beekman Pubs.
Structures & Materials: Collection of Technical Papers, 10th Conference, New Orleans, Louisiana, April 14-16, 1969. AIAA-ASME Structures, Structural Dynamics & Material Conference Staff. (Illus.). pap. 120.30 (ISBN 0-317-08388-0, 2016452). Bks Demand UMI.
Structures & Patterns of Religion. G. Mensching. Tr. by V. S. Sharma & H. M. Klimkeit. 1976. 15.00 (ISBN 0-8426-0958-X). Orient Bk Dist.
Structures & Procedures Implicit Knowledge. Arthur C. Graesser & Leslie F. Clark. LC 85-7336. (Advances in Discourse Processes Ser.: Vol. 17). 336p. 1985. text ed. 49.50 (ISBN 0-89391-192-5); pap. 29.50 (ISBN 0-89391-362-6). Ablex Pub.
Structures & Properties of Fibres. R. Meredith. 85p. 1975. 70.00x (ISBN 0-686-63798-4). State Mutual Bk.
Structures & Reactions of the Aromatic Compounds. Geoffrey M. Badger. LC 54-3317. pap. 117.50 (ISBN 0-317-08966-8, 2051390). Bks Demand UMI.
Structures & Stochastic Methods. A. S. Cakmak. (Developments in Geotechnical Engineering Ser.: Vol. 45). 1987. 146.50 (ISBN 0-444-98955-2). Elsevier.
Structures & Stochastic Methods. Ed. by A. S. Cakmak. LC 87-70781. 500p. 1987. 134.00. Computational Mech MA.
Structures & Strategies of Human Memory. Leonard Stern. 392p. 1985. pap. 22.00x (ISBN 0-256-03250-5). Dorsey.
Structures & Their Functions in Usan: A Papuan Language of Papua New Guinea. Ger P. Reesink. LC 86-17518. (Studies in Language Companion Ser.: Vol. 13). xviii, 369p. 1987. 60.00x (ISBN 90-272-3015-3). Benjamins North Am.
Structures & Time: Narration, Poetry, Models. Cesare Segre. Tr. by John Meddemmen. LC 79-68. 1979. Repr. of 1974 ed. lib. bdg. 26.00x (ISBN 0-226-74476-0). U of Chicago Pr.
Structures & Transformations: The Romance Verb. Christopher J. Pountain. LC 83-12287. (Illus.). 272p. 1983. 28.50x (ISBN 0-389-20436-6, 07322). B&N Imports.
Structures: Business, Entrepreneurs, the Free Market. Robert E. Sonntag. (Illus.). 288p. (Orig.). 1986. pap. 14.95 (ISBN 0-938545-00-0). Philomod Corp.
Structures de Deux Testaments Fictionnels: Le Lais et le Testament de Francois Villon. A. J. Van Zoest. 320p. 1975. pap. text ed. 28.80x (ISBN 90-2793-133-X). Mouton.
Structures for Architects. 2nd ed. B. S. Benjamin. 1984. 41.95 (ISBN 0-442-21190-2). Van Nos Reinhold.
Structures for Business & Professional Speech: A Working Resource Manual. 2nd ed. Lawrence W. Hugenberg, Sr. & Alfred W. Owens, II. 144p. 1985. pap. text ed. 11.95 (ISBN 0-8403-3484-2). Kendall-Hunt.
Structures for Composition. 2nd ed. Bernard A. Drabeck et al. LC 77-77675. (Illus.). 1978. pap. text ed. 21.50 (ISBN 0-395-25567-8); instrs.' manual 0.50 (ISBN 0-395-25568-6). HM.
Structures: Fundamental Theory & Behavior. Richard M. Gutkowski. 592p. 1980. 41.95 (ISBN 0-442-22983-6). Van Nos Reinhold.
Structures in Beckett's Watt. John C. DiPierro. 116p. 1981. 11.95 (ISBN 0-917786-22-X). Summa Pubns.
Structures in Topology. Douglas Harris. LC 52-42839. (Memoirs Ser.: No. 115). 96p. 1971. pap. 11.00 (ISBN 0-8218-1815-5, MEMO-115). Am Math.
Structures Lexicales et Enseignement du Vocabulaire. Henri Holec. (Janua Linguarum Ser.: No. 5). pap. 10.80x (ISBN 90-2793-272-7). Mouton.
Structures, Mecanismes et Spectroscopie. J. Maire & B. Waegell. (Cours & Documents de Chimie Ser.). 312p. (Fr). 1969. 108.00 (ISBN 0-677-50160-9). Gordon & Breach.
Structures, Mechanisms & Spectroscopy: 120 Problems, 60 Solutions for the Organic Chemist. J. C. Maire & B. Waegell. LC 70-146808. (Documents in Chemistry Ser.). (Illus.). 312p. 1971. 108.00 (ISBN 0-677-30160-X). Gordon & Breach.
Structures of American Social History. Walter Nugent. LC 80-8634. (Midland Bks: No. 352). 224p. 1981. 25.00x (ISBN 0-253-10356-8); pap. 8.95X (ISBN 0-253-20352-X). Ind U Pr.
Structures of Consciousness: The Genius of Jean Gebser - an Introduction & Critique. Georg Feuerstein. LC 86-83184. (Illus.). 240p. (Orig.). 1987. pap. 14.95 (ISBN 0-941255-20-4). Integral Pub.
Structures of Crystalline Polymers. Ed. by I. H. Hall. 312p. 1984. 77.50 (ISBN 0-85334-236-9, I-523-83, Pub. by Elsevier Applied Sci England). Elsevier.
Structures of Discrete Event Simulation: An Introduction to the Engagement Strategy. J. B. Evans. (Artificial Intelligence Ser.). 272p. 1988. 39.95 (ISBN 0-470-21097-4). Wiley.
Structures of Domination & Peasant Movements in Latin America. Peter Singelmann. LC 79-48030. (Illus.). 224p. 1981. text ed. 28.00x (ISBN 0-8262-0307-8). U of Mo Pr.
Structures of Everyday Life. Fernand Braudel. LC 81-47653. (Illus.). 623p. 1982. 35.00i (ISBN 0-06-014845-4, HarpT). Har-Row.
Structures of Everyday Life, Vol. 1: Civilization & Capitalism 15th-18th Century. Fernand Braudel. LC 81-47653. (Illus.). 624p. 1985. pap. 17.95 (ISBN 0-06-091294-4, PL 1294, PL). Har-Row.
Structures of Experience: History, Society & Personal Life in the 18th Century British Novel. W. Austin Flanders. 308p. 1984. 24.95x (ISBN 0-87249-419-5). U of SC Pr.
Structures of Influence: A Comparative Approach to August Strindberg. Marilyn J. Blackwell. LC 80-29545. (Studies in the Germanic Languages & Literatures: No.98). xiv, 370p. 1982. 27.50x (ISBN 0-8078-8098-1). U of NC Pr.
Structures of Knowing. Richard C. Monk. 522p. (Orig.). 1986. lib. bdg. 38.75 (ISBN 0-8191-5580-2); pap. text ed. 23.00 (ISBN 0-8191-5581-0). U Pr of Amer.
Structures of Matter & Patterns of Science. Ed. by Marjorie Senechal. 200p. 1980. pap. text ed. 8.95x (ISBN 0-87073-909-3). Schenkman Bks Inc.
Structures of Modification in Contemporary American English. George A. Hough, III. (Janua Linguarum, Ser. Practica: No. 126). (Illus.). 124p. (Orig.). 1971. pap. text ed. 13.60x (ISBN 90-2791-909-7). Mouton.
Structures of Patriarchy: The State, the Community & the Household. Ed. by Bina Agarwal. 1988. text ed. 45.95 (ISBN 0-317-67829-9, Pub. by Zed Pr UK); pap. text ed. 12.95 (ISBN 0-317-67830-2, Pub. by Zed Pr). Humanities.
Structures of Power: An Introduction of Politics. John Schwarzmantel. LC 87-42775. 288p. 1987. 35.00 (ISBN 0-312-01208-X). St Martin.
Structures of Social Action: Studies in Conversation Analysis. Ed. by J. Maxwell Atkinson & John Heritage. 480p. 1985. 49.50 (ISBN 0-521-24815-9); pap. 20.95 (ISBN 0-521-31862-9). Cambridge U Pr.
Structures of Subjectivity: Explorations in Psychoanalytic Phenomenology, Vol. 4. George E. Atwood & Robert D. Stolorow. (Psychoanalytic Inquiry Book Ser.). 144p. 1984. 19.95 (ISBN 0-88163-012-8). Analytic Pr.
Structures of Technological Education & Contributing Social Factors. W. Fishwick. (Studies in Engineering Education: No. 11). 231p. 1988. pap. 16.50 (ISBN 92-3-102489-2, U1656, UNESCO). UNIPUB.
Structures of Television. Nicholas Garnham. (Television Monograph: No. 1). 58p. 1978. pap. 6.95 (ISBN 0-85170-035-7, Pub. by British Film Inst England). U of Ill Pr.
Structures of the Church. Hans Kung. LC 82-4706. 350p. 1982. pap. 12.95 (ISBN 0-8245-0508-5). Crossroad NY.
Structures of the Elements. Jerry Donohue. LC 80-15363. 448p. 1982. Repr. of 1974 ed. lib. bdg. 34.50 (ISBN 0-89874-230-7). Krieger.
Structures of the Life-World. Alfred Schutz & Thomas Luckmann. Tr. by Richard Zaner & Tristram Engelhardt, Jr. (Studies in Phenomenology & Existential Philosophy). 1973. text ed. 32.95x (ISBN 0-8101-0395-8); pap. 16.95 (ISBN 0-8101-0622-1). Northwestern U Pr.
Structures of Thinking. Karl Mannheim. Ed. by David Kettler et al. Tr. by Jeremy Shapiro & Shierry Weber. (International Library of Sociology). 240p. 1982. 32.00x (ISBN 0-7100-0936-4). Routledge Chapman & Hall.
Structures of Thinking. Karl Mannheim. Ed. by David Kettler et al. (International Library of Sociology). 240p. 1985. pap. 12.95 (ISBN 0-7102-0730-1). Routledge Chapman & Hall.
Structures of Working-Class Consciousness: The Chartist Experience. Thomas M. Kemnitz. 1979. lib. bdg. 25.00 (ISBN 0-89824-001-8); pap. 10.00 (ISBN 0-89824-002-6). Trillium Pr.
Structures on Manifolds. K. Yano & M. Kon. LC 85-675. (Pure Mathematics Ser.: Vol. 3). 450p. 1985. 59.00 (ISBN 9971-966-15-8); pap. 29.00 (ISBN 9971-966-16-6, Pub. by World Sci Singapore). World Scientific Pub.
Structures: Or Why Things Don't Fall Down. J. E. Gordon. LC 81-9755. (Quality Paperbacks Ser.). (Illus.). 395p. 1981. pap. 12.95 (ISBN 0-306-80151-5). Da Capo.
Structures: Or Why Things Don't Fall Down. Ed. by J. E. Gordon. LC 81-9755. 396p. 1978. 25.00x (ISBN 0-306-40025-1, Plenum Pr); pap. 11.95x. Plenum Pub.
Structures, Structural Dynamics & Materials Conference: Proceedings, 25th, 1984, 2 vols. (Illus.). 1188p. 1984. 125.00 (ISBN 0-317-36862-1, CP844 & 845). AIAA.
Structures, Structural Dynamics & Materials Conference, XXVIII: Proceedings, 1987, 2 vols. 1987. Set. pap. 200.00 (ISBN 0-317-58630-0). AIAA.
Structures Technology for Large Radio & Radar Telescope Systems. Ed. by James W. Mar. 1969. 50.00x (ISBN 0-262-13046-7). MIT Pr.
Structuring a General Practice Course. Stuart G. Gullickson. LC 76-7826. (Continuing Legal Education Library). (Illus.). 412p. 1976. 30.00 (B200). Am Law Inst.
Structuring Child Behavior Through Visual Art: A Therapeutic, Individualized Art Program to Develop Positive Behavior Attitudes in Children. photocopy ed. Florence Singer. (Illus.). 144p. 1980. 17.50 (ISBN 0-389-04114-9). C C Thomas.
Structuring Commercial Loan Agreements. Roger Tighe. (General Law Ser.). 450p. 1984. 84.00 (ISBN 0-88262-910-7). Warren Gorham & Lamont.
Structuring Committees for a Board of Directors. Ed. by Prentice-Hall Editorial Staff. 22p. 1984. 2.75x (ISBN 0-317-07503-9, 85526-2). P-H.
Structuring Complex Real Estate Transactions: Law, Procedure, Forms. James L. Lipscomb. LC 88-198. 1988. 95.00 (ISBN 0-471-84713-5). Wiley.
Structuring Cooperative Learning: Lesson Plans for Teachers, 1987. Ed. by Roger T. Johnson et al. 339p. (Orig.). 1987. pap. write for info. (ISBN 0-939603-00-4). Interaction Bk Co.
Structuring Exploration Deals, Vol. 1. Lewis G. Mosburg, Jr. 345p. 1983. text ed. 40.00x (ISBN 0-910649-02-2). Energy Textbks.
Structuring for Success in the English Classroom: Classroom Practices in Teaching English, 1981-1982. Candy Carter et al. LC 82-2309. 1982. pap. 11.00 (ISBN 0-8141-4760-7). NCTE.
Structuring Foreign Investment in U. S. Real Estate. W. Donald Knight, Jr. 400p. 1982. cancelled 75.00 (ISBN 90-654-4022-4, Pub. by Kluwer Law Netherlands). Kluwer Academic.
Structuring in Organizations: Ecosystem Theory Evaluated. Charles E. Bidwell et al. (Monographs in Organizational Behavior & Industrial Relations: Vol. 7). 1987. 56.50 (ISBN 0-89232-732-4). Jai Pr.
Structuring of a State: The History of Illinois, 1899-1928. Donald F. Tingley. LC 79-14964. (Sesquicentenniel History of Illinois Ser.: Vol. 5). (Illus.). 446p. 1980. 24.95 (ISBN 0-252-00736-0). U of Ill Pr.
Structuring of Experience. Ed. by I. C. Uzgiris & F. Weizman. LC 76-45357. (Illus.). 464p. 1977. 55.50x (ISBN 0-306-30961-0, Plenum Pr). Plenum Pub.
Structuring of Labor Markets: The Steel & Construction Industries in Italy. Paola Villa. (Library of Political Economy). (Illus.). 340p. 1986. text ed. 64.00x (ISBN 0-19-828508-6); pap. text ed. 32.00x (ISBN 0-19-828552-3). Oxford U Pr.
Structuring of Organizations. reference ed. Henry Mintzberg. (Theory of Management Policy Ser.). (Illus.). 1979. 39.00 (ISBN 0-13-855270-3). P-H.
Structuring Paragraphs: A Guide to Effective Writing. 2nd ed. A. Franklin Parks et al. LC 85-61251. 224p. 1985. pap. text ed. write for info. (ISBN 0-312-76861-3); instr's. manual avail. (ISBN 0-312-76862-1). St Martin.
Structuring Partnership Agreements: Forms, Analytical Text, State-by-State Requirements, 3 vols. Supplements avail. 210.00 (ISBN 0-317-29402-4, #H43910, Pub. by Law & Business). HarBraceJ.
Structuring Programs in Microsoft BASIC. Michael Cox & Kay Sullivan. 544p. (Orig.). 1986. pap. text ed. 22.00 (ISBN 0-87835-159-0); write for info. instr's manual (ISBN 0-87835-160-4). Boyd & Fraser.
Structuring Real Estate Investments in the Mid-Eighties. Ed. by Raymond J. Werner. LC 85-72126. 922p. 1985. 55.00 (ISBN 0-89707-188-3, PC: 5430070). Amer Bar Assn.
Structuring Speech: A How-to-Do-It-Book about Public Speaking. Gerald M. Phillips & J. Jerome Zolten. (Speech Communication Ser.). 1976. pap. 9.08 scp (ISBN 0-672-61366-2, SC-22). Bobbs.
Structuring State & Local Tax Reform Commissions. William R. Dodge. (Monograph: No. 86-2). 65p. 1986. pap. text ed. 12.00 (ISBN 0-318-20456-8). Lincoln Inst land.
Structuring the Therapeutic Process: Compromise with Chaos - a Therapist's Response to the Individual & the Group. Murray Cox. LC 77-4181. 1978. text ed. 55.00 (ISBN 0-08-020403-1); pap. text ed. 16.75 (ISBN 0-08-020402-3). Pergamon.
Structuring Unsecured Lending Transactions. 216p. 1984. 20.00 (V7-3932). PLI.
Structuring Your Classroom for Academic Success. Stan C. Paine et al. LC 83-61812. (Illus.). 176p. 1983. pap. 12.95 (ISBN 0-87822-228-6). Res Press.
Structuring Your Novel. Robert C. Meredith & John D. Fitzgerald. 1972. pap. 6.95 (ISBN 0-06-463325-X, EH 325, B&N Bks). Har-Row.
Structuro-Interaction Analysis in Time Domain. John P. Wolf. (Illus.). 416p. 1988. text ed. 52.00 (ISBN 0-13-822974-0). P-H.
Struder's Popular Ornithology: The Birds of North America. Jacob Struder. (Illus.). 1977. 39.95 (ISBN 0-517-22915-3); Special Imprint Society ed. 60.00 (ISBN 0-517-53204-2). Barre.
Struggle. Sara Zyskind. (YA) (gr. 6 up). Date not set. 14.95 (ISBN 0-8225-0772-2). Lerner Pubns.
Struggle see Age of the Democratic Revolution: A Political History of Europe & America, 1760-1800.
Struggle a Hard Battle: Essays on Working-Class Immigrants. Ed. by Dirk Hoerder. LC 85-25894. 384p. 1986. 25.00 (ISBN 0-87580-112-9); pap. 9.50 (ISBN 0-87580-533-7). N Ill U Pr.
Struggle Against Dependence: Nontraditional Export Growth in Central America & the Caribbean. Eva Paus. (Political Economics & Economic Development in Latin America). 225p. 1988. 35.00 (ISBN 0-8133-7559-2). Westview.
Struggle Against Fascism in Germany. Leon Trotsky. Ed. by George Breitman & Merry Maisel. LC 73-119532. 1970. 33.00 (ISBN 0-87348-135-6); pap. 10.95 (ISBN 0-87348-136-4). Path Pr NY.
Struggle Against Sleeping Sickness in Nyasaland & Northern Rhodesia. Norman H. Pollock. LC 82-91569. (Papers in International Studies: Africa Ser.: No. 5). 1969. pap. 3.00x (ISBN 0-89680-039-3, Ohio U Ctr Intl). Ohio U Pr.
Struggle Against the Historical Blackout. Harry E. Barnes. 59.95 (ISBN 0-87700-195-2). Revisionist Pr.
Struggle Against Tyranny & the Beginning of a New Era: Virginia, 1677-1699. Richard L. Morton. (Illus.). 80p. 1957. pap. 3.95 (ISBN 0-8139-0133-2). U Pr of Va.
Struggle & Submission: R. C. Zaehner on Mysticisms. William L. Newell. LC 80-6295. 402p. 1981. lib. bdg. 30.75 (ISBN 0-8191-1696-3); pap. text ed. 16.25 (ISBN 0-8191-1697-1). U Pr of Amer.
Struggle & Survival in Colonial America. Ed. by David G. Sweet & Gary B. Nash. 1981. pap. 10.95x (ISBN 0-520-04501-7). U of Cal Pr.
Struggle Between President Johnson & Congress over Reconstruction. Charles E. Chadsey. LC 79-181926. (Columbia University Studies in the Social Sciences: No. 19). Repr. of 1896 ed. 11.50 (ISBN 0-404-51019-1). AMS Pr.
Struggle Between the Civilization of Slavery & That of Freedom. facsimile ed. Edward C. Billings. LC 76-164379. (Black Heritage Library Collection). Repr. of 1873 ed. 10.75 (ISBN 0-8369-8838-8). Ayer Co Pubs.
Struggle Between the Two Princes: The Kingdom of Saudi Arabia in the Final Days of Ibn Saud. Ibrahim Al-Rashid. (Documents on the History of Arabia Ser.: Vol. VIII). 314p. 1985. text ed. 39.95x (ISBN 0-89712-112-0). Documentary Pubns.

Struggle for a Continent: The French & Indian Wars, 1690-1760. Albert Marrin. LC 86-26508. (Illus.). 232p. (gr. 5 up). 1987. 14.95 (ISBN 0-689-31313-6, Atheneum Childrens Bks). Macmillan.

Struggle for a Free Stage in London. Watson Nicholson. LC 65-27915. 1967. Repr. 22.00 (ISBN 0-405-08816-7, Pub. by Blom). Ayer Co Pubs.

Struggle for a Just World Order: An Agenda of Inquiry & Praxis for the 1980's. Saul H. Mendlovitz. (Working Papers: No. 20). 23p. 1982. pap. 2.00 (ISBN 0-911646-26-4). World Policy.

Struggle for a Proletarian Party. 2nd, rev. ed. James P. Cannon. Ed. by John G. Wright. LC 73-133396. 320p. 1972. pap. 7.95 (ISBN 0-87348-260-3). Path Pr NY.

Struggle for a State System of Public Schools in Tennessee, 1903-1936. A. D. Holt. LC 70-176876. (Columbia University. Teachers College. Contributions to Education: No. 753). Repr. of 1938 ed. 25.00 (ISBN 0-404-55753-8). AMS Pr.

Struggle for Afghanistan. Nancy P. Newell & Richard S. Newell. LC 80-69829. (Paperback Ser.). (Illus.). 236p. 1982. pap. 10.95 (ISBN 0-8014-9236-X). Cornell U Pr.

Struggle for Africa. Ed. by Mai Palmberg. Tr. by E. M. Andree et al from Swedish. (Illus.). 256p. 1983. 28.00x (ISBN 0-86232-100-X, Pub. by Zed Pr England); pap. 9.25 (ISBN 0-86232-101-8). Humanities.

Struggle for Africa: Politics of the Great Powers. Gerard Chaliand. LC 82-5967. 1982. 16.95 (ISBN 0-312-76868-0). St Martin.

Struggle for Airways in Latin America. William A. M. Burden. Ed. by Mira Wilkins. LC 76-29797. (European Business Ser.). (Illus.). 1977. Repr. of 1943 ed. lib. bdg. 32.00x (ISBN 0-405-09716-6). Ayer Co Pubs.

Struggle for American Independence, 2 vols. fascimile ed. Sydney G. Fisher. LC 78-37341. (Select Bibliographies Reprint Ser). Repr. of 1908 ed. Set. 64.00 (ISBN 0-8369-6688-0). Ayer Co Pubs.

Struggle for American Independence, Vol. II. facsimile ed. Sydney G. Fisher. LC 78-37341. (Illus.). 585p. Repr. of 1908 ed. lib. bdg. 30.00 (ISBN 0-8290-0499-8). Irvington.

Struggle for American Independence, Vol. 1. fascimile ed. Sydney G. Fisher. (Illus.). 1988. Repr. of 1908 ed. lib. bdg. 30.00 (ISBN 0-8290-2149-3). Irvington.

Struggle for Animal Rights. Tom Regan. 208p. (Orig.). 1987. pap. 5.95 (ISBN 0-9602632-1-7). ISAR Inc.

Struggle for Arab Independence. 2nd ed. Zeine N. Zeine. LC 77-5149. 280p. 1977. lib. bdg. 30.00x (ISBN 0-88206-002-3). Caravan Bks.

Struggle for Asia. Francis Low. LC 79-167379. (Essay Index Reprint Ser.). Repr. of 1955 ed. 18.00 (ISBN 0-8369-2699-4). Ayer Co Pubs.

Struggle for Asia, Eighteen Twenty Eight to Nineteen Fourteen. David Gillard. 1978. 31.50 (ISBN 0-8419-7000-9); pap. 13.95 (ISBN 0-8419-7003-3). Holmes & Meier.

Struggle for Baltic Markets: Power in Conflict, 1558-1618. Arthur Attman. (Acta Regiae Societas Scientarium et Litterarum Gothoburgensis, Humanoria Ser.: No. 14). 232p. (Orig.). 1979. pap. 29.50x (ISBN 0-317-68042-0, Pub. by Vetenskaps Gothenburg). Coronet Bks.

Struggle for Basic Needs in Nepal. OECD Staff et al. (Illus.). 100p. (Orig.). 1980. pap. 6.50x (ISBN 92-64-12101-3). OECD.

Struggle for Black Equality, 1954-1980. Harvard Sitkoff. (American Century Ser.). 259p. 1981. pap. 6.95 (ISBN 0-8090-0144-6). Hill & Wang.

Struggle for Black Political Empowerment in Three Georgia Counties. Lawrence J. Hanks. LC 86-24987. 248p. 1987. 24.95x (ISBN 0-87049-521-6). U of Tenn Pr.

Struggle for Change: International Economic Relations. K. B. Lal. 1984. 22.50x (ISBN 0-8364-1226-5, Pub. by Allied India). South Asia Bks.

Struggle for Change: (International Economic Relations) K. B. Lall. 327p. 1983. 34.95. Asia Bk Corp.

Struggle for Crete, 10 May-1 June 1941: A Story of Lost Opportunity. Ian M. Stewart. pap. 132.00 (ISBN 0-317-28731-1, 2051318). Bks Demand UMI.

Struggle for Cyprus. Charles Foley & W. I. Scobie. LC 74-10837. (Publications Ser.: No. 137). 187p. 1975. 9.95x (ISBN 0-8179-6371-5). Hoover Inst Pr.

Struggle for Economic Development: Readings in Problems & Policy. Michael Todaro. LC 82-7229. (Illus.). 320p. (Orig.). 1982. 16.95x (ISBN 0-582-28384-1). Longman.

Struggle for Education. Richard Bourne & Brian MacArthur. LC 79-136012. (Illus.). 128p. 1970. 20.00 (ISBN 0-8022-2041-X). Philos Lib.

Struggle for Empire: A Bibliography of the French & Indian Wars. James G. Lydon. LC 83-48203. (History Ser.). 275p. 1985. lib. bdg. 40.00 (ISBN 0-8240-9069-1). Garland Pub.

Struggle for Equality: Abolitionists & the Negro in the Civil War & Reconstruction. James M. McPherson. (Illus.). 1964. 47.00x (ISBN 0-691-04566-6); pap. 14.95x (ISBN 0-691-00555-9). Princeton U Pr.

Struggle for Equality: Blacks in Texas. James M. Smallwood. (Texas History Ser.). (Illus.). 46p. 1983. pap. text ed. 2.95x (ISBN 0-89641-120-6). American Pr.

Struggle for Equality: Urban Women Workers in Prestate Israeli Society. Deborah Bernstein. LC 86-8203. 219p. 1986. lib. bdg. 38.95 (ISBN 0-275-92139-5, C2139). Praeger.

Struggle for Europe. Chester Wilmont. 766p. 1986. pap. 14.95 (ISBN 0-88184-257-5). Carroll & Graf.

Struggle for Existence. G. F. Gause. (Illus.). 1969. Repr. of 1934 ed. 11.95x (ISBN 0-02-845200-3). Hafner.

Struggle for Federal Aid, First Phase: A History of the Attempts to Obtain Federal Aid for the Common Schools. Gordon C. Lee. LC 79-176979. (Columbia University. Teachers College. Contributions to Education: No. 957). Repr. of 1949 ed. 22.50 (ISBN 0-404-55957-3). AMS Pr.

Struggle for Freedom. Knofel Staton. LC 76-18381. 96p. 1977. pap. 2.25 (ISBN 0-87239-063-2, 40034). Standard Pub.

Struggle for Freedom & Henry Box Brown. Brenda A. Johnston & Pamela Pruitt. Ed. by John A. McCluskey. (Read-Along Bk.). (Illus.). 22p. (gr. 2-4). 1987. pap. 7.50 incl. audiocassette (ISBN 0-913678-16-3). New Day Pr.

Struggle for Freedom of the Press, 1819-1832. William H. Wickwar. Repr. of 1928 ed. 26.00 (ISBN 0-384-68281-2). Johnson Repr.

Struggle for Greece 1941-1949. C. M. Woodhouse. (Illus.). 1979. 29.95x (ISBN 0-8464-0042-1). Beekman Pubs.

Struggle for Greek Independence: Essays to Mark the 150th Anniversary of the Greek War of Independence. Ed. by Richard Clogg. vi, 259p. 1973. 27.50 (ISBN 0-208-01303-2, Archon). Shoe String.

Struggle for Grenada. 3rd, rev. ed. Richard Krooth. 1988. pap. 8.95 (ISBN 0-939074-12-5). Harvest Pubns.

Struggle for Humanity: Agents of Nonviolent Change in a Violent World. Marjorie Hope & James Young. LC 77-5573. 305p. (Orig.). 1977. pap. 6.95 (ISBN 0-88344-469-0). Orbis Bks.

Struggle for Indochina, 1940-1955. Ellen J. Hammer. 1955. 35.00x (ISBN 0-8047-0458-9). Stanford U Pr.

Struggle for Influence: The Impact of Minority Groups on Politics & Public Policy in the United States. Michael C. LeMay. LC 85-6105. (Illus.). 468p. (Orig.). 1985. lib. bdg. 40.25 (ISBN 0-8191-4653-6); pap. text ed. 22.00 (ISBN 0-8191-4654-4); pap. text ed. 22.50. U Pr of Amer.

Struggle for Inner Peace. rev. ed. Henry R. Brandt. 136p. 1984. pap. 5.50 (ISBN 0-88207-245-5). Victor Bks.

Struggle for Intimacy. Janet G. Woititz. 101p. 1985. pap. text ed. 6.95 (ISBN 0-932194-25-7, 22H103). Health Comm.

Struggle for Judicial Supremacy: A Study of a Crisis in American Power Politics. Robert H. Jackson. 1979. Repr. lib. bdg. 27.50x (ISBN 0-374-94130-0, Octagon). Hippocrene Bks.

Struggle for Justice. 1971. pap. 4.95 (ISBN 0-686-95388-6). Am Fr Serv Comm.

Struggle for Justice: A Report on Crime & Punishment in America. American Friends Service Committee. 186p. 1971. pap. 4.95 (ISBN 0-8090-1363-0). Hill & Wang.

Struggle for Land. J. Foweraker. (Illus.). 304p. 1981. 49.50 (ISBN 0-521-23555-3). Cambridge U Pr.

Struggle for Land in Ireland 1800-1923. John E. Pomfret. LC 68-27079. (Illus.). 1969. Repr. of 1930 ed. 11.00x (ISBN 0-8462-1292-7). Russell.

Struggle for Law. Rudolf von Jhering. 138p. 20.35. Hyperion-Conn.

Struggle for Law. Rudolf Von Jhering. Tr. by John Labor from Ger. LC 79-1610. 1980. Repr. of 1915 ed. 20.35 (ISBN 0-88355-913-7). Hyperion Conn.

Struggle for Liberation: From DuBois to Nyerere. Bert Thomas. LC 81-84242. 208p. 1982. 8.95 (ISBN 0-912444-23-1). Gaus.

Struggle for Mastery in Europe: 1848-1918. Alan J. Taylor. (Oxford History of Modern Europe Ser.). 1954. 42.00x (ISBN 0-19-822101-0); pap. 13.95x (ISBN 0-19-881270-1). Oxford U Pr.

Struggle for Men's Hearts & Minds. Charles Colson. 48p. 1986. 1.95 (ISBN 0-89693-166-8). Victor Bks.

Struggle for Mozambique. Eduardo Mondlane. 256p. 1983. pap. 9.25 (ISBN 0-86232-016-X, Pub. by Zed Pr England). Humanities.

Struggle for National Identity in the Third World. Kyu H. Rhee. LC 83-80008. 233p. 1983. 16.50x (ISBN 0-930878-31-0). Hollym Intl.

Struggle for Neutrality: Franco-American Diplomacy During the Federalist Era. Albert H. Bowman. LC 73-21917. 1974. 36.95x (ISBN 0-87049-152-0). U of Tenn Pr.

Struggle for North China. George E. Taylor. LC 75-30100. (Institute of Pacific Relations). Repr. of 1940 ed. 32.50 (ISBN 0-404-59566-9). AMS Pr.

Struggle for Pakistan. Lal Bahadur & J. C. Johari. 380p. 1988. text ed. 45.00x (ISBN 81-207-0802-4, Pub. by Sterling Pubs India). Apt Bks.

Struggle for Palestine. Jacob C. Hurewitz. LC 68-28594. (Illus.). 1968. Repr. of 1950 ed. lib. bdg. 35.00x (ISBN 0-8371-0111-5, HUSP). Greenwood.

Struggle for Religious Freedom in Germany. Arthur S. Duncan-Jones. LC 78-63664. (Studies in Fascism: Ideology & Practice). Repr. of 1938 ed. 34.00 (ISBN 0-404-16927-9). AMS Pr.

Struggle for Religious Freedom in Virginia. William T. Thom. LC 78-63877. (Johns Hopkins University. Studies in the Social Sciences. Eighteenth Ser. 1900: 10-12). Repr. of 1900 ed. 11.50 (ISBN 0-404-61133-8). AMS Pr.

Struggle for Religious Survival in the Soviet Union. Intro. by Ann Gillen. LC 86-72630. 76p. 1986. pap. 5.00 (ISBN 0-87495-085-6). Am Jewish Comm.

Struggle for Responsible Government in Marwar. Mathur Sobhag. 208p. 1982. 75.00x (ISBN 0-317-62317-6, Pub. by Scientific). State Mutual Bk.

Struggle for Responsible Government in the North-West Territories 1870-97. 2nd ed. Lewis H. Thomas. LC 56-3490. 1978. pap. 9.95c (ISBN 0-8020-6327-6). U of Toronto Pr.

Struggle for Rural Mexico. Gustavo Esteva. Orig. Title: Batalla En el Mexico Rural. (Illus.). 320p. 1983. text ed. 29.95 (ISBN 0-89789-025-6). Bergin & Garvey.

Struggle for Self-Government. Joseph L. Steffens. (American Studies). Repr. of 1906 ed. 26.00 (ISBN 0-384-57770-9). Johnson Repr.

Struggle for Sobriety: Protestants & Prohibition in Texas, 1919-1935. Jeanne McCarty. (Southwestern Studies: No. 62). 1980. pap. 5.00 (ISBN 0-87404-121-X). Tex Western.

Struggle for Social Security, 1900-1935. Roy Lubove. LC 85-40854. (Pitt Series in Policy & Institutional Studies). 296p. 1986. pap. 10.95x (ISBN 0-8229-5379-X). U of Pittsburgh Pr.

Struggle for Socialism in the "American Century" Writings & Speeches, 1945-1947. James P. Cannon. Ed. by Les Evans. LC 75-20719. (Writings & Speeches of James P. Cannon). 1977. 33.00 (ISBN 0-87348-550-5); pap. 10.95 (ISBN 0-87348-551-3). Path Pr NY.

Struggle for South Africa, Vol. 1. rev. ed. Rob Davies et al. LC 88-17180. 288p. 1987. text ed. 45.00 (ISBN 0-86232-760-1, Pub. by Zed Pr UK); pap. text ed. 15.00 (ISBN 0-86232-761-X, Pub. by Zed Pr UK). Humanities.

Struggle for South Africa, Vol. 2. rev. ed. Rob Davies et al. LC 88-17180. 240p. 1987. text ed. 45.00 (ISBN 0-86232-762-8, Pub. by Zed Pr UK); pap. text ed. 12.50 (ISBN 0-86232-763-6, Pub. by Zed Pr UK). Humanities.

Struggle for South Africa: A Reference Guide to Movements, Organizations & Institutions, 2 vols. Robert Davies et al. (Africa Ser.). 1984. Vol. 1, 278p. 29.50x (ISBN 0-86232-224-3, Pub. by Zed Pr England); pap. 10.75 (ISBN 0-86232-225-1, Pub. by Zed Pr England); Vol. 2, 206p. 29.50x (ISBN 0-86232-256-1); pap. 10.75 (ISBN 0-86232-257-X). Biblio Dist.

Struggle for South America: Economy & Ideology. J. F. Normano. 1977. lib. bdg. 59.95 (ISBN 0-8490-3067-6). Gordon Pr.

Struggle for South Yemen. Joseph Kostiner. LC 83-40529. 224p. 1984. 23.95 (ISBN 0-312-76872-9). St Martin.

Struggle for Stability in Early Modern Europe. Theodore K. Rabb. (Illus.). 1975. pap. 8.95x (ISBN 0-19-501956-3). Oxford U Pr.

Struggle for Status. Ed. by Prakash N. Pimpley & Satish K. Sharma. xv, 232p. 1986. text ed. 30.00x (ISBN 81-7018-265-4, Pub. by B R Pub Corp Delhi). Apt Bks.

Struggle for Succession, 1966-1970: Personal Account of the Nigerian Civil War. Ntieyong U. Akpan. 220p. 1972. (F Cass Co); pap. 9.95x (ISBN 0-7146-2949-9, BHA 02949, F Cass Co). Biblio Dist.

Struggle for Supremacy in the Baltic, 1600-1725. Jill Lisk. 1976. pap. 1.95 (ISBN 0-88254-419-5). Hippocrene Bks.

Struggle for Survival see No Break Here.

Struggle for Survival: Indian Cultures & the Protestant Ethic in British Columbia. Rev. ed. Forrest E. LaViolette. LC 73-84433. pap. 53.80 (ISBN 0-317-27022-2, 2023643). Bks Demand UMI.

Struggle for Survival: The Elephant Problem. John Hanks. (Illus.). 1979. 14.95 (ISBN 0-8317-2756-X, Mayflower Bks). Smith Pubs.

Struggle for Swazi Labour, 1890-1920. Jonathan Crush. 304p. 1987. 37.50x (ISBN 0-7735-0569-5). McGill-Queens U Pr.

Struggle for Synthesis: The Seventeenth Century Background of Leibniz's Synthesis of Order & Freedom. Leroy E. Loemker. LC 72-79308. 529p. 1972. 25.00x (ISBN 0-674-84545-5). Harvard U Pr.

Struggle for Syria: A Study in Post-War Arab Politics. Patrick Seale. LC 87-8265. 384p. 1987. text ed. 45.00 (ISBN 0-300-03944-1); pap. text ed. 15.95x (ISBN 0-300-03970-0). Yale U Pr.

Struggle for the American Curriculum 1893-1958. Herbert M. Kliebard. 293p. 1986. text ed. 24.95 (ISBN 0-7102-0055-2). Routledge Chapman & Hall.

Struggle for the American Curriculum: 1893-1958. Herbert M. Kliebard. pap. 13.95 (ISBN 0-317-65253-2, Pub. by Routledge UK). Routledge Chapman & Hall.

Struggle for the Arab World: Egypt's Nasser & the Arab League. Tawfig Y. Hasou. 300p. 1985. 49.95x (ISBN 0-7103-0080-8, Kegan Paul). Routledge Chapman & Hall.

Struggle for the Border. facsimile ed. Bruce Hutchinson. LC 70-140358. (Select Bibliographies Reprint Ser). Repr. of 1955 ed. 25.00 (ISBN 0-8369-5601-X). Ayer Co Pubs.

Struggle for the City: Migrant Labor, Capital & the State in Urban Africa. Ed. by Frederick Cooper. (Sage Series on African Modernization & Development: Vol. 8). 304p. 1983. 29.95 (ISBN 0-8039-2067-9). Sage.

Struggle for the Falkland Islands: A Study in Legal & Diplomatic History. Julius Goebel. 512p. 1982. text ed. 42.50x (ISBN 0-300-02943-8); pap. text ed. 13.95x (ISBN 0-300-02945-4, Y-445). Yale U Pr.

Struggle for the Film: Towards a Socially Responsible Cinema. Hans Richter. Ed. by Jurgen Romhild. Tr. by Ben Brewster. LC 85-10848. 176p. 1986. 25.00 (ISBN 0-312-76875-3). St Martin.

Struggle for the Freedom of the Press from Caxton to Cromwell. William M. Clyde. LC 70-122223. (Research & Source Works: No. 479). 1970. Repr. of 1934 ed. lib. bdg. 23.50 (ISBN 0-8337-0606-3). B Franklin.

Struggle for the Good, 2 pts. Ilija Poplasen. (Illus.). 1981. Repr. of 1978 ed. Pt. I, 61 Pgs. 15.00 (ISBN 0-935352-03-1); Pt. II, 128 Pgs. 25.00 (ISBN 0-935352-04-X). MIR PA.

Struggle for the Gulf Borderlands: The Creek War & the Battle of New Orleans, 1812-1815. Frank L. Owsley, Jr. LC 80-11109. (Illus.). vii, 255p. 1981. 25.00 (ISBN 0-8130-0662-7). U Presses Fla.

Struggle for the Himalayas: Study of Sino-Indian Relations. 2nd ed. S. P. Varma. 1979. 12.50 (ISBN 0-89684-557-5). Orient Bk Dist.

Struggle for the Jewish Mind: Debates & Disputes on Judaism Then & Now. Jacob Neusner. (Studies in Judaism). 200p. (Orig.). 1988. lib. bdg. 18.75 (ISBN 0-8191-6689-8). U Pr of Amer.

Struggle for the Mediterranean, 1939-1945. Raymond De Belot. Tr. by James A. Field, Jr. LC 51-12459. pap. 76.50 (ISBN 0-317-26671-3, 2055993). Bks Demand UMI.

Struggle for the Mind of German Youth, 1890-1914. Sterling Fishman. 1974. lib. bdg. 59.95 (ISBN 0-87700-229-0). Revisionist Pr.

Struggle for the Pacific. Gregory Bienstock. LC 76-115199. 1971. Repr. of 1937 ed. 23.00x (ISBN 0-8046-1092-4, Pub. by Kennikat). Assoc Faculty Pr.

Struggle for the Party Versus Chinese Revisionism. Marxist-Leninist Party, USA. Ed. by National Executive Committee of the MLP, USA. 73p. 1980. pap. 1.00 (ISBN 0-86714-005-4). Marxist-Leninist.

Struggle for the Third World. Brian Crozier. LC 66-18563. 1966. 10.95 (ISBN 0-8023-1035-4). Dufour.

Struggle for the Third World: Soviet Debates & American Options. Jerry F. Hough. LC 84-45856. 293p. 1986. 32.95 (ISBN 0-8157-3746-7); pap. 12.95 (ISBN 0-8157-3745-9). Brookings.

Struggle for the Victory of Good, Pt. II. Ilija Poplasen. (Illus.). 128p. 1984. 25.00 (ISBN 0-935352-19-8). MIR PA.

Struggle for the Victory of Good, Pt. I. Ilija Poplasen. (Illus.). 61p. 1984. 15.00 (ISBN 0-935352-18-X). MIR PA.

Struggle for Workers' Health. Ray H. Elling. 1987. text ed. 36.00 (ISBN 0-89503-047-0). Baywood Pub.

Struggle for World Power. George Knupffer. 240p. 1986. pap. 6.00 (ISBN 0-317-53307-X). Noontide.

Struggle for Zimbabwe. David Martin & Phyllis Johnson. LC 81-84556. 400p. (Orig.). 1982. pap. 8.95 (ISBN 0-85345-599-6). Monthly Rev.

Struggle for Zimbabwe: Battle in the Bush. Lewis H. Gann & Thomas H. Henriksen. LC 81-5190. 172p. 1981. 35.00 (ISBN 0-275-90630-2, C0630). Praeger.

Struggle from Sunday to Sabbath. Pearl Brians. 78p. 1988. pap. 8.00 (ISBN 1-55677-092-8). VHI Library.

Struggle in the Andes: Peasant Political Mobilization in Peru. Howard Handelman. (Latin American Monographs: No. 35). 321p. 1975. 18.50x (ISBN 0-292-77513-X). U of Tex Pr.

Struggle in the Coal Fields. Fred Mooney. Ed. by J. W. Hess. LC 67-30927. 194p. 1967. 5.00 (ISBN 0-937058-10-6). West Va U Pr.

Struggle in the Coal Fields: The Autobiography of Fred Mooney, Secretary-Treasurer, District 17, United Mine Workers of America. (Illus.). 1967. 6.00 (ISBN 0-685-30819-7). McClain.

Struggle Is My Life. rev. ed. Nelson Mandela. 280p. 1986. lib. bdg. 23.00 (ISBN 0-87348-662-5); pap. 6.95 (ISBN 0-87348-663-3). Path Pr NY.

Struggle of a Hong Kong Girl. Lily Chan. 1986. 12.95 (ISBN 0-533-06593-3). Vantage.

Struggle of Love. Cheryl Stoesz & Gilbert Brandt. 110p. (Orig.). 1983. pap. 4.95 (ISBN 0-919797-08-3). Kindred Pr.

Struggle of Muslim Women. Kaukab Siddique. LC 86-70641. 152p. (Orig.). 1986. pap. 9.95 (ISBN 0-942978-10-2). Am Soc Ed & Rel.

Struggle of Prayer. Donald G. Bloesch. LC 87-23764. 180p. 1988. pap. 7.95 (ISBN 0-939443-04-X). Helmers Howard Pub.

Struggle of Protestant Dissenters for Religious Toleration in Virginia. H. R. McIlwaine. pap. 9.00 (ISBN 0-384-34893-9). Johnson Repr.

Struggle of Protestant Dissenters for Religious Toleration in Virginia. Henry R. McIlwaine. LC 78-63830. (Johns Hopkins University. Studies in the Social Sciences. Twelfth Ser. 1894: 4). Repr. of 1894 ed. 11.50 (ISBN 0-404-61090-0). AMS Pr.

Struggle of the Cattleman, Sheepman & Settler for Control of Lands in Wyoming, 1867-1910. George W. Rollins. Ed. by Stuart Bruchey. LC 78-56671. (Management of Public Lands in the U. S. Ser.). (Illus.). 1979. lib. bdg. 32.50x (ISBN 0-405-11353-6). Ayer Co Pubs.

Struggle of the Dogs & the Black see Night Just Before the Forest.

Struggle of the U. S. S. R. for Peace & Security: History of U. S. S. R.: New Research. Collets Staff. 216p. 1984. 12.50x (ISBN 0-317-53823-3, Pub. by Collets (UK)). State Mutual Bk.

Struggle over Eritrea, 1962-1978: War & Revolution in the Horn of Africa. Haggai Erlich. (Publication Ser.: No. 260). 176p. 1982. pap. 10.95x (ISBN 0-8179-7602-7). Hoover Inst Pr.

Struggle over Lebanon. Tabitha Petran. LC 86-18284. 320p. 1987. 27.50 (ISBN 0-85345-651-8); pap. 12.00 (ISBN 0-85345-652-6). Monthly Rev.

Struggle over Reform in Rabbinic Literature. Alexander Guttman. LC 75-45046. 1977. 13.50 (ISBN 0-8074-0005-X, 382790). UAHC.

Struggle to Be Borne. Fran Adler. (Illus.). 68p. (Orig.). 1988. pap. 8.00 (ISBN 0-916304-84-1). SDSU Press.

Struggle to Be Free: My Story & Your Story. Wayne E. Oates. LC 83-5904. 164p. 1983. pap. 7.95 (ISBN 0-664-24500-5). Westminster John Knox.

Struggle to Preserve the First White House of the Confederacy. Cameron F. Napier. 1983. pap. 1.95 (ISBN 0-8173-0183-6). U of Ala Pr.

Struggle Within. Olgivanna L. Wright. 1971. pap. 5.95 (ISBN 0-8180-1313-3). Horizon.

Struggles & Accomplishments see Social Foundations of German Unification, 1858-1871.

Struggles & Sorrows: The Personal Testimony of a Chief Justice. Hardayal Hardy. 176p. 1984. text ed. 27.50x (ISBN 0-7069-2563-7, Pub. by Vikas India). Advent NY.

Struggles & Triumphs. P. T. Barnum. Ed. by Carl Bode. (Penguin American Library). 1981. pap. 6.95 (ISBN 0-14-039004-9). Penguin.

Struggles & Triumphs. Phineas T. Barnum. LC 77-125677. (American Journalists Ser). 1970. Repr. of 1869 ed. 48.50 (ISBN 0-405-01651-4). Ayer Co Pubs.

Struggles & Triumphs: Or the Life of P. T. Barnum, Written by Himself, 2 vols. P. T. Barnum. Ed. by George S. Bryan. (Illus.). 879p. 1986. Repr. of 1927 ed. Set. lib. bdg. 125.00 (ISBN 0-8495-0494-5). Arden Lib.

Struggles for Poland. Neal Ascherson. LC 88-42826. (Illus.). 256p. 1988. 19.95 (ISBN 0-394-55997-5). Random.

Struggles in an Alcoholic Family. Edward M. Scott. (Illus.). 280p. 1970. 19.75 (ISBN 0-398-01702-6). C C Thomas.

Struggles of Brown, Jones, & Robinson. Anthony Trollope. Ed. by N. John Hall. LC 80-1889. (Selected Works of Anthony Trollope Ser.). 1981. Repr. of 1870 ed. lib. bdg. 29.00 (ISBN 0-405-14156-4). Ayer Co Pubs.

Struggles of Gods. Ed. by Hans G. Kippenberg. LC 84-11501. (Religion & Reason Ser.: No. 31). vii, 296p. 1984. 50.50 (ISBN 90-279-3460-6). Mouton.

Struggles of the Italian Film Industry during Fascism, 1930-1935. Elaine Mancini. Ed. by Diane Kirkpatrick. LC 85-1069. (Studies in Cinema: No. 34). 310p. 1985. 44.95 (ISBN 0-8357-1655-4). UMI Res Pr.

Struggles of the Naga Tribe. Willibordus S. Rendra. Tr. by Max Lane from Indonesian. LC 79-16537. Orig. Title: Kisah Perjuangan Suku Naga. 1980. 20.00x (ISBN 0-312-76876-1). St Martin.

Struggling & Ruling: The Indian National Congress, Eighteen Eighty-Five to Nineteen Eighty-Five. Ed. by Jim Masselos. (South Asian Publications: No. 2). 224p. 1987. text ed. 37.50x (ISBN 81-207-0691-9, Pub. by Sterling Pubs India). Apt Bks.

Struggling for Wholeness. Ann K. Anderson & Jan K. Ream. LC 85-3185. 160p. 1986. 12.95 (ISBN 0-8407-9042-2). Oliver-Nelson.

Struggling Through Tight Times: Introductory Handbook for Women's & Other Non-Profit Organizations on Fiscal Management. Sara Gould. 125p. 1984. pap. 4.75 (ISBN 0-9605828-5-1). Women's Action.

Struggling to Survive in A Welfare Hotel. John H. Simpson et al. LC 85-105459. 47p. (Orig.). 1984. pap. 3.75 (ISBN 0-88156-037-5). Comm Serv Soc Ny.

Struggling to Swim on Concrete. Vassar Miller. Ed. by Maxine Cassin. (New Orleans Poetry Journal Press Bks.). (Illus.). 80p. (Orig.). 1984. pap. 5.00 (ISBN 0-938498-05-3). New Orleans Poetry.

Struggling Upward or Luke Larkin's Luck. Horatio Alger, Jr. 160p. 1984. pap. 4.50 (ISBN 0-486-24737-6). Dover.

Struggling with Sex: Serious Call to Marriage-Centered Sexual Life. Arthur A. Rouner, Jr. LC 86-32028. 112p. (Orig.). 1987. pap. 6.95 (ISBN 0-8066-2243-1, 10-6096). Augsburg.

Struktur Des Dramas Bei T. S. Eliot. Gerd Schmidt. Ed. by James Hogg. (Poetic Drama & Poetic Theory). 212p. (Orig.). 1978. pap. 15.00 (ISBN 3-7052-0872-1, Pub. by Salzburg Studies). Longwood Pub Group.

Struktur des Verhaltens. Maurice Merleau-Ponty. (Phaenomenologisch-Psychologische Forschungen: Vol. 13). xxvi, 278p. 1976. text ed. 31.20 (ISBN 3-11-004469-2). De Gruyter.

Struktur des Zylklus "Four Quartets" Von T. S. Eliot. Claudia Delank. (European University Studies: No. 14, Vol. 104). 327p. (Ger.). 1982. 37.35 (ISBN 3-8204-5810-7). P Lang Pubs.

Struktur und Bezeichnung des Scheltworts. Ludwig Markert. (Beiheft 40 zur fur die Alttesta-Mentliche Wissenschaft). 1977. text ed. 52.40x (ISBN 3-11-005813-8). De Gruyter.

Struktur und Dynamik von Waeldern: Rinteln, April 1981, Berichte der Internationalen Symposien der Intern'len Vereinigung fuer Vegetationskunde. Ed. by Hartmut Dierschke. (Illus.). 600p. (Orig., Ger.). 1983. lib. bdg. 92.00x (ISBN 3-7682-1334-X). Lubrecht & Cramer.

Struktur und Funktion Endothelialer Zellen. Ed. by K. Messmer & F. Hammersen. (Illus.). x, 150p. 1983. pap. 32.75 (ISBN 3-8055-3712-3). S Karger.

Struktur und Funktionen Mitochondrialer dna Bei Pilzen. H. U. Kueck. (No. 84, Bibliotheca Mycologica Ser.). (Illus.). 148p. (Ger.). pap. text ed. 24.00x (ISBN 3-7682-1323-4). Lubrecht & Cramer.

Struktur und Organisation des Pressevertriebs, Vol. 1: Der Deutsche Zeitungs-und ZeitschriftengroBhandel. Peter Brummund & Institut fur Zeitungsforschung Staff. (Dortmunder Beitrage: Vol. 40). 502p. 1985. pap. 17.50 (ISBN 3-598-21297-6). K G Saur.

Struktur und Organisation des Pressevertiiebs Vol. 2: Zeitungen und Zeitschriften im Einzelhandel. Peter Schwindt et al. (Dortmunder Beitrage: Vol. 41). 133p. 1985. pap. 18.00 (ISBN 3-598-21298-4). K G Saur.

Struktura Khudozhestvennogo Teksta. Iu. M. Lotman. LC 70-158681. (Brown University Slavic Reprint Ser.: No. 9). 391p. (Rus.). 1971. pap. 15.00x (ISBN 0-87057-129-X). U Pr of New Eng.

Strukturalismus see Structuralism, Moscow, Prague, Paris.

Strukturelemente der Deutschen Gegenwartshochsprache: Phone und Phonaden. B. F. Hildebrandt. (Janua Linguarum Ser: No. 231). 1976. 12.00x (ISBN 90-2793-405-3). Mouton.

Strukturelle und instrumentalphonetische Untersuchungen zur gesprochenen Sprache. Joachim Goeschel. LC 72-76054. (Studia Linguistica Germanica Vol. 9). (Illus.). 1973. 40.40x (ISBN 3-11-003624-X). De Gruyter.

Strukturen der Syntax. Noam Chomsky. (Janua Linguarum, Series Minor: No. 182). 1973. pap. 13.25x (ISBN 90-2792-490-2). Mouton.

Strukturen in Shakespeares King Henry the Sixth. Regina Dombrowa. (BAS Ser.: No. 18). x, 320p. (Orig.). 1985. pap. 77.00x (ISBN 90-6032-267-3, Pub by B R Gruner Netherlands). Benjamins North Am.

Strukturinterne und Umstrukturierende Neuerungen Dargestellt Am Beispiel der Forschung. Gerd Meyer. (VHS-V Ser.: Vol. 5). 339p. (Ger.). 1982. 28.95 (ISBN 3-261-04998-7). P Lang Pubs.

Strumard Face. Beverly A. Hightower. (Orig.). 6.95 (ISBN 0-8062-2457-6). Carlton.

Strumming, Finger-Picking, Playing the Melody: A Beginning Guitar Method for Group, Individual, or Self-Instruction. Michael Christiansen. 112p. 1980. pap. text ed. 12.95 (ISBN 0-8403-2247-X). Kendall-Hunt.

Strumpet City. James Plunkett. 578p. 1978. pap. 10.50 (ISBN 0-09-918750-7). Bks Britain.

Strumpet Muse: Art & Morals in Chaucer's Poetry. Alfred David. LC 76-11939. (Illus.). 288p. 1977. 22.50x (ISBN 0-253-35517-6). Ind U Pr.

Struthers Burt. Raymond C. Phillips, Jr. LC 82-74090. (Western Writers Ser.: No. 56). (Illus., Orig.). 1983. pap. 2.95x (ISBN 0-88430-030-7). Boise St Univ.

Strutts & the Arkwrights, 1758-1830. R. S. Fitton & A. P. Wadsworth. LC 72-375. 1968. Repr. of 1958 ed. 37.50x (ISBN 0-678-06758-9). Kelley.

Struttura Del Sistema Bancario Toscano Dal 1815 Al 1859, 2 vols. Anna Cecchi. Ed. by Stuart Bruchey. LC 80-2804. (Dissertations in European Economic History II). (Illus.). 1981. lib. bdg. 35.50x (ISBN 0-405-13988-8). Ayer Co Pubs.

Struve: Liberal on the Left, 1870-1905. Richard Pipes. (Russian Research Center Studies: No. 64). 1970. 29.50x (ISBN 0-674-84595-1). Harvard U Pr.

Struve: Liberal on the Right, 1905-1944. Richard Pipes. LC 79-16145. (Russian Research Center Studies: No. 80). 1980. 37.00x (ISBN 0-674-84600-1). Harvard U Pr.

Struwwelpeter. Heinrich Hoffmann. (Illus.). (gr. 1-5). 1909. 7.95 (ISBN 0-7100-1534-8). Routledge Chapman & Hall.

Stryker Family in America: A Genealogy of the Stryker & Striker Families. William N. Stryker. LC 78-75351. (Illus.). 500p. 1979. lib. bdg. 48.00 (ISBN 0-9602936-1-2). W N Stryker.

Stryker Family in America: A Genealogy of the Stryker & Striker Families, Vol. II. William N. Stryker. LC 78-75351. (Illus.). 210p. 1981. lib. bdg. 40.00 (ISBN 0-9602936-2-0). W N Stryker.

Stryker Family in America: A Genealogy of the Stryker & Striker Families, Vol. III. William N. Stryker. LC 78-75351. (Illus.). 226p. 1987. lib. bdg. 37.00 (ISBN 0-317-56281-9). W N Stryker.

Sts. Cyril & Methodius. 1966. pap. 0.50 (ISBN 0-317-30441-0). Holy Trinity.

STT 366: Deutungsbersuch 1982 & other articles. Karlheinz Deller & Kazuke Watanabe. (Assur Ser.: Vol. 3, Issue 4). 40p. (Ger.). 1983. pap. 6.00x. Undena Pubns.

Stu Apte's Fishing in the Florida Keys & Flamingo. 3rd ed. Stuart C. Apte. LC 76-360969. (Illus.). 96p. 1982. pap. 4.95 (ISBN 0-89317-006-2). Windward Pub.

Stuart Academica Drama: An Edition of Three University Plays. Ed. by Stephen Orgel. (Renaissance Imagination Ser.). 210p. 1987. lib. bdg. 30.00 (ISBN 0-8240-8414-4). Garland Pub.

Stuart Age. Barry Coward. LC 79-42887. (History of England Ser.). (Illus.). 512p. 1980. pap. text ed. 20.95x (ISBN 0-582-48833-8). Longman.

Stuart & Cromwellian Foreign Policy. G. M. Howat. LC 73-91111. 180p. 1974. 22.50 (ISBN 0-312-76895-8). St Martin.

Stuart Avenue Project. Ed. by Gary Cialdella & Lynwood Bartley. (Illus.). 16p. (Orig.). pap. 2.00 (ISBN 0-933742-02-9). Kalamazoo Inst Arts.

Stuart City Trend, Lower Cretaceous, South Texas--A Carbonate Shelf-Margin Model for Hydrocarbon Exploration. D. G. Bebout & R. G. Loucks. (Report of Investigations Ser.: RI 78). (Illus.). 80p. 1980. Repr. of 1974 ed. 3.00 (ISBN 0-318-03198-1). Bur Econ Geology.

Stuart Constitution: Documents & Commentary. 2nd ed. J. P. Kenyon. 550p. 1986. 65.00 (ISBN 0-521-30810-0); pap. 21.95 (ISBN 0-521-31327-9). Cambridge U Pr.

Stuart Davis. Karen Wilkin. (Illus.). 256p. 1987. 85.00 (ISBN 0-89659-755-5). Abbeville Pr.

Stuart Davis: Graphic Work & Related Paintings with a Catalogue Raisonne of the Prints. Jane Myers et al. (Illus.). 100p. 1986. 29.95 (ISBN 0-88360-054-4); pap. 14.95 (ISBN 0-88360-055-2). Amon Carter.

Stuart Davis' New York. Bruce Weber. LC 85-72521. (Illus.). 96p. 1985. pap. 12.95 (ISBN 0-943411-13-0). Norton Gal Art.

Stuart Davis: Sketchbooks. Stuart Davis. (Illus.). 140p. 1986. 65.00 (ISBN 0-8008-7483-8, Pub. by Grace Borgenicht Gallery). Taplinger.

Stuart England. J. P. Kenyon. 384p. 1986. pap. 5.95 (ISBN 0-14-022552-8, Pelican). Penguin.

Stuart England. Blair Worden. (Illus.). 272p. 1987. 34.95 (ISBN 0-7148-2391-0). Salem Hse Pubs.

Stuart Little. E. B. White. LC 45-9585. (Illus.). (ps-4). 1945. 10.70i (ISBN 0-06-026395-4); PLB 11.89 (ISBN 0-06-026396-2). HarpJ.

Stuart Little. E. B. White. LC 45-9585. (Trophy I Can Read Bks.). (Illus.). 132p. (ps-4). 1945. pap. 2.95 (ISBN 0-06-440056-5, Trophy). HarpJ.

Stuart Little see E. B. White Boxed Set.

Stuart Masques & the Renaissance Stage. Allardyce Nicoll. LC 63-23186. (Illus.). 1938. 37.15 (ISBN 0-405-08817-5, Pub. by Blom). Ayer Co Pubs.

Stuart of Dunleath: A Story of Modern Times, 3 vols. in 2. Caroline E. Norton. LC 79-8181. Repr. of 1851 ed. Set. 84.50 (ISBN 0-404-62073-6). AMS Pr.

Stuart Politics in Chapman's Tragedy of Chabot. Norma D. Solve. LC 74-1304. (English Literature Ser., No. 33). 1974. lib. bdg. 48.95x (ISBN 0-8383-2037-6). Haskell.

Stuart Politics in Chapman's Tragedy of Chabot. Norma D. Solve. 1928. 20.00 (ISBN 0-8274-3530-4). R West.

Stuart Royal Proclamations: Royal Proclamations of King James I 1603-1625, Vol. 1. Ed. by James F. Larkin & Paul L. Hughes. 1973. 115.00x (ISBN 0-19-822372-2). Oxford U Pr.

Stuart Royal Proclamations: Volume II: Royal Proclamations of King Charles I, 1625-46. Ed. by James F. Larkin. 1983. 145.00x (ISBN 0-19-822466-4). Oxford U Pr.

Stuart Tracts. C. H. Firth. LC 64-16747. (Arber's an English Garner Ser.). 1964. Repr. of 1890 ed. 23.50x (ISBN 0-8154-0071-3). Cooper Sq.

Stuart Tracts, Sixteen Hundred to Three to Sixteen Ninety-Three. Intro. by C. H. Firth. Ed. by Gerald M. Straka. LC 72-83161. (English Studies Ser.). 1972. Repr. of 1903 ed. lib. bdg. 43.00 (ISBN 0-8420-1419-5). Scholarly Res Inc.

Stuart: U. S. Light Tanks in Action. (Armor in Action Ser.). (Illus.). 1984. pap. 5.95 (ISBN 0-89747-084-2, 2018). Squad Sig Pubns.

Stuarts. Jennifer Ruby. (Costume in Context Ser.). (Illus.). 72p. (YA) (gr. 7-9). 1988. 19.95 (ISBN 0-7134-5604-3, Pub. by Batsford England). David & Charles.

Stub Entries to Indents Issued in Payment of Claims Against South Carolina Growing Out of the Revolution, 4 vols. Ed. by Alexander S. Salley, Jr. Incl. Books L-N. rev ed. 376p. 1959. Repr. of 1910 ed. 8.95x (ISBN 0-87249-925-1); Books O-Q. rev ed. 334p. 1960. Repr. of 1915 ed. 8.95x (ISBN 0-87249-926-X); Books R-T. rev ed. 320p. 1960. Repr. of 1917 ed. 8.95x (ISBN 0-87249-927-8); Books U-W. rev ed. 318p. 1960. Repr. of 1918 ed. 8.95x (ISBN 0-87249-928-6). LC 13-735. U of SC Pr.

Stub Entries to Indents Issued in Payment of Claims Against South Carolina Growing Out of the Revolution, Bk. K. Wylma A. Wates. LC 13-735. 1956. lib. bdg. 8.95x (ISBN 0-87249-924-3). U of SC Pr.

Stub Entries to Indents Issued in Payment of Claims Against South Carolina Growing Out of the Revolution, Bks. C-F. Ed. by Wylma A. Wates. LC 13-735. lib. bdg. 8.95x (ISBN 0-87249-921-9). U of SC Pr.

Stub Entries to Indents Issued in Payment of Claims Against South Carolina Growing Out of the Revolution, Bks. G-H. Ed. by Wylma A. Wates. LC 13-735. 1955. lib. bdg. 8.95x (ISBN 0-87249-922-7). U of SC Pr.

Stubborn, But Not Too Stubborn. Dave Jackson. (Storybooks for Caring Parents). 32p. 1986. 3.95 (ISBN 0-89191-271-1, 52712, Chariot Bks). Cook.

Stubborn Children. John Sutton. 1988. 37.50 (ISBN 0-520-06093-8). U of Cal Pr.

Stubborn Earth: American Agriculturalists on Chinese Soil, 1898-1937. Randy Stross. 468p. 1986. 25.00 (ISBN 0-520-05700-7). U of Cal Pr.

Stubborn Faith: Papers on Old Testament & Related Subjects Presented to Honor William Andrew Irwin. Ed. by Edward C. Hobbs. LC 56-12567. 184p. 1956. 13.95x (ISBN 0-87074-079-2). SMU Press.

Stubborn Fisherman. 2nd ed. Elda M. Roberts. LC 86-71820. (Illus.). 234p. 1987. 20.95 (ISBN 0-9617139-1-7); pap. 12.95 (ISBN 0-9617139-0-9). Creighton Pub.

Stubborn for Liberty: The Dutch in New York. Alice P. Kenney. LC 75-16403. (New York State Study Ser.). pap. 80.00 (ISBN 0-317-51999-9, 2027394). Bks Demand UMI.

Stubborn Forest. Paul Hyland. 1984. pap. 9.95 (ISBN 0-906427-59-2, Pub. by Bloodaxe Bks). Dufour.

Stubborn Old Woman. Clyde R. Bulla. LC 78-22506. (Illus.). 48p. (gr. 1-4). 1980. 11.70i (ISBN 0-690-03945-X, Crowell Jr Bks); PLB 11.89 (ISBN 0-690-03946-8). HarpJ.

Stubborn Weeds: Popular & Controversial Chinese Literature after the Cultural Revolution. Ed. by Perry Link. LC 82-48268. (Chinese Literature in Translation Ser.). (Illus.). 304p. 1984. 25.00x (ISBN 0-253-35512-5). Ind U Pr.

Stubborn Weeds: Popular & Controversial Chinese Literature after the Cultural Revolution. Ed. by Perry Link. LC 82-48268. (Chinese Literature in Translation: Midland Bks: No. 311). (Illus.). 304p. 1984. pap. 10.95X (ISBN 0-253-20311-2). Ind U Pr.

Stubbornness: A Field Guide. John Hildebidle. (Illus.). 194p. (Orig.). 1986. pap. 6.95 (ISBN 0-938621-00-9). MSS.

Stubbs & Wedgewood: Unique Alliance Between Artist & Potter. Bruce Tattersall & Basil Taylor. (Illus.). 120p. 10.95 (ISBN 0-900874-81-3). Salem Hse Pubs.

Stubbs' Dogs. Robert Fountain & Alfred Gates. 144p. 1984. 110.00x (ISBN 0-946186-04-9, Pub. by Arthur Ackermann Pub Ltd). State Mutual Bk.

Stubbs: Portraits in Detail. Intro. by Judy Egenton. (Illus.). 48p. 1985. pap. 8.95 (ISBN 0-946590-17-6). Salem Hse Pubs.

Stubby: Brave Soldier Dog. Richard Glendinning & Sally Glendinning. LC 78-4575. (Famous Animal Stories Ser.). (Illus.). (gr. 2-5). 1978. PLB 6.89 (ISBN 0-8116-4864-8). Garrard.

Stubs: London Edition of All the London (West End) & Select Regional Theatres, 1981 Edition. Ed. by Ronald S. Lee & Patricia Lee. (Illus.). 1981. pap. 6.95 (ISBN 0-911458-03-4). Stubs.

Stubs: The Seating Plan Guide for New York Theaters, Music Halls & Sports Stadia, 1986 Edition. Ed. by Ronald S. Lee & Patricia Lee. (Illus.). 1986. pap. 6.95 (ISBN 0-911458-06-9, MNYE9). Stubs.

Stucco & Decorative Plasterwork in Europe. Geoffrey Beard. LC 82-49006. (Icon Editions). (Illus.). 165p. 1983. 49.50i (ISBN 0-06-430383-7, HarpT). Har-Row.

Stucco Decoration & Architectural Assemblage of Structure 1-Sub Dzibilchaltun, Yucatan, Mexico. Chemency Coggins. (Publication: No. 49). 70p. 1983. pap. 15.00 (ISBN 0-939238-78-0). Tulane MARI.

Stucco Decoration & Architectural Assemblage of Structure 1-sub, Dzibilvhsltun, Yucatan, Mexico. Clemency Coggins. LC 83-61021. (Illus.). vii, 70p. 1983. 15.00. Tulane MARI.

Stucco from Chal Tarkhan-Eshqabad Near Rayy. Deborah Thompson. (Colt Archaeological Institute Ser.). 328p. 1976. text ed. 50.00x (ISBN 0-85668-062-1, Pub. by Aris & Phillips UK). Humanities.

Stuchka: Selected Writings on Soviet Law & Marxism. Piotr I. Stuchka. Intro. by Robert Sharlet et al. Tr. by Robert Sharlet et al from Rus. LC 87-36773. 280p. 1988. text ed. 60.00 (ISBN 0-87332-473-0). M E Sharpe.
Stuck Fast in Yesterday. Heather Kellerhals-Stewart. 136p. (Orig.). (gr. 7 up). 1986. pap. 5.95 (ISBN 0-88899-024-3, Pub. by Douglas & McIntyre-Grounwood). Salem Hse Pubs.
Stuck on Stickers. Linda W. Aber & Hal Aber. (Illus.). 48p. (Orig.). (ps). 1984. pap. 5.95 (ISBN 0-590-33272-4). Scholastic Inc.
Stuck on the Cubs. Rick Schwab. 192p. (Orig.). 1977. pap. 1.95 (ISBN 0-930528-01-8). Sassafras Pr.
Stuck on the Sox. Rick Lindberg. 192p. (Orig.). 1978. pap. 1.95 (ISBN 0-930528-02-6). Sassafras Pr.
Stuckenschmid. Tr. by H. H. Schoenberg from Ger. 400p. (Orig.). 1985. pap. 5.95 (ISBN 0-7145-0091-7). Riverrun NY.
Stucky Points for Weight Control see Calorie Points for Weight Control.
Stud. rev, abr. ed. Phil Andros, pseud. 216p. 1982. pap. 6.95 (ISBN 0-932870-02-3). Alyson Pubns.
Stud. Jackie Collins. 1982. pap. 3.95 (ISBN 0-451-13235-1, Sig). NAL.
Stud Farm Diary. Humphrey S. Finney. Repr. write for info. (ISBN 0-85131-194-6, NL51, Dist. by Miller). S R Smith Sporting Bks.
Stud Manager's Handbook: International Stockmen's School Handbooks, Vol. 19. Frank H. Baker. 500p. 1983. lib. bdg. 60.50X (ISBN 0-86531-675-9, Pub in cooperation with Winrock International). Westview.
Studded Tires & Highway Safety: An Accident Analysis. (National Cooperative Highway Research Program Report). 70p. 1978. 4.80. Transport Res Bd.
Studebaker Century. Asa E. Hall & Richard M. Langworth. LC 83-1912. (Illus.). 192p. 1983. 25.95 (ISBN 0-9606148-1-8). Dragonwyck Pub.
Studebaker: Less Than They Promised. Michael Beatty et al. LC 84-81548. (Illus.). 60p. 1984. 24.95 (ISBN 0-89708-150-1). And Bks.
Studebaker: Less Than They Promised. Michael Beatty et al. LC 84-81548. (Illus.). 94p. (Orig.). 1984. pap. 9.95 (ISBN 0-89708-129-3). And Bks.
Studebaker: The Complete Story. William A. Cannon & Fred K. Fox. (Illus.). 368p. 1982. 39.95 (ISBN 0-8306-2064-8, 2064). TAB Bks.
Student. W. P. Stanley. 1957. 4.95 (ISBN 0-87148-756-X). Pathway Pr.
Student Achievement Through Staff Developement. Bruce Joyce & Beverly Showers. 190p. 1987. pap. text ed. 13.95 (ISBN 0-582-28409-0). Longman.
Student Activism & Protest: Alternatives for Social Change. Edward E. Sampson & Harold A. Korn. LC 77-92898. (Jossey-Bass Higher Education Ser.). Repr. of 1970 ed. 54.00 (ISBN 0-8357-9349-4, 2013868). Bks Demand UMI.
Student Activities in Secondary Schools: A Bibliography. Compiled by Jackson et al. Battiste. 86p. 1980. pap. 7.00 (ISBN 0-88210-109-9). Natl Assn Principals.
Student Activities in the Secondary Schools: A Handbook & Guide. Ward Sybouts & Wayne J. Krepel. LC 83-18535. (Illus.). x, 428p. 1984. lib. bdg. 38.95 (ISBN 0-313-23379-9, SYS/). Greenwood.
Student Affairs: A Profession's Heritage. rev. ed. Gerald Saddlemire & Audrey Rentz. 1986. 20.00 (ISBN 1-55620-027-7, 72152C). Am Assn Coun Dev.
Student Affairs & the Law. Ed. by Margaret J. Barr. LC 82-84204. (Student Services Ser.: No. 22). 105p. 1983. 12.95x (ISBN 0-87589-970-6). Jossey-Bass.
Student Affairs Functions in Higher Education. Ed. by Audrey L. Rentz & Gerald L. Saddlemire. (Illus.). 386p. 1988. pap. 33.75x (ISBN 0-398-05480-0). C C Thomas.
Student Affairs 2001: A Paradigmatic Odyssey. George D. Kuh et al. 1987. 20.00 (ISBN 0-317-59913-5, 72153C). Am Assn Coun Dev.
Student Africanist's Handbook: A Guide to Resources. text ed. Gerald W. Hartwig & William M. O'Barr. 160p. 1974. 9.95x (ISBN 0-87073-218-8). Schenkman Bks Inc.
Student Aid & Public Higher Education: A Progress Report. Jacob O. Stampen & Roxanne W. Reeves. 1983. 5.00 (ISBN 0-317-40624-8). Am Assn Comm Jr Coll.
Student Aid & the Urban Poor. Ford Foundation Staff. Ed. by Washington Office of the College Board Staff. LC 80-29114. (Ford Foundation Series on Higher Education in the Cities). 48p. (Orig.). 1981. pap. text ed. 3.50 (ISBN 0-916584-16-X). Ford Found.
Student Aid: Bases of Selection of Students to Whom Loans, Scholarships & Fellowships Are Awarded in a Graduate School of Education. Margaret R. Smith. LC 75-177766. (Columbia University. Teachers College. Contributions to Education: No. 704). Repr. of 1937 ed. 22.50 (ISBN 0-404-55704-X). AMS Pr.
Student Aid in the Secondary Schools of the United States. V. A. Carley. LC 77-176626. (Columbia University. Teachers College. Contributions to Education: No. 594). Repr. of 1933 ed. 22.50 (ISBN 0-404-55594-2). AMS Pr.
Student Aide. Jack Rudman. (Career Examination Ser.: C-1496). (Cloth bdg. avail. on request). pap. 10.00 (ISBN 0-8373-1496-8). Natl Learning.
Student Alumni Associations & Foundations. Ed. by Patricia L. Alberger. 65p. 1980. 14.50 (ISBN 0-89964-163-6). Coun Adv & Supp Ed.
Student & His Studies. Esther Raushenbush. LC 64-22376. 1964. 12.50x (ISBN 0-8195-3045-X). Wesleyan U Pr.
Student & Singer. Charles Santley. LC 80-2756. Repr. of 1892 ed. 39.50 (ISBN 0-404-18866-4). AMS Pr.
Student Assistance Program: How it Works. rev. ed. Tom Griffin & Roger Svendsen. 68p. pap. 8.95 (ISBN 0-89486-350-9). Hazelden.
Student Assistance Program: How It Works. rev. ed. Roger Svendsen & Tom Griffin. 60p. 1980. pap. 8.95 (ISBN 0-89486-110-7). Hazelden.
Student Athlete: Eligibility & Academic Integrity. Clarence Underwood. 1984. 10.00x (ISBN 0-87013-236-9). Mich St U Pr.
Student-Athlete's Recruiting Handbook: Suiting up for Success. George A. Selleck. LC 83-26769. 80p. 1984. pap. 10.95 (ISBN 0-88011-240-9, PSEL0240). Leisure Pr.
Student Atlas of California. 3rd ed. Rice D. Oliver. (Illus.). 64p. (gr. 4 up). 1988. pap. text ed. 7.95 (ISBN 0-317-68211-3); tchr's ed. 8.95 (ISBN 0-936778-99-7). Calif Weekly.
Student Atlas of the Bible. American Map Corp. Staff. (Series 9500: No. 9559). (Illus.). 1978. 2.95 (ISBN 0-8416-9559-8); Span. lang. ed. write for info. Am Map.
Student, Behavior & Science Content Categories & Subcategories for a Science Program. Leopold E. Klopfer. 62p. 1970. 1.50 (ISBN 0-318-14740-8, ED 038 726). Learn Res Dev.
Student Body. J. S. Borthwick. 320p. 1986. 16.95 (ISBN 0-312-76934-2). St Martin.
Student Body. J. S. Borthwick. 1988. pap. 3.50 (ISBN 0-312-90738-9). St Martin.
Student Body Workbook. 32p. Date not set. 8.95 (ISBN 0-318-23894-2). Future Home.
Student-Centered Health Instruction: A Humanistic Approach. Jerrold S. Greenberg. (Illus.). 270p. 1978. text ed. 12.00 (ISBN 0-394-34874-5, RanC). Random.
Student-Centered Teaching for Increased Participation. James Kelly. 48p. 1985. 6.95 (ISBN 0-8106-1527-4). NEA.
Student Characteristics & Teaching. Jere Brophy et al. LC 80-32741. (Professional Ser.). 224p. 1981. text ed. 34.95x (ISBN 0-582-28152-0). Longman.
Student Chemist Explores Computations. Julian May. LC 74-8140. (Student Scientist Ser.). 140p. (YA) (gr. 7-12). 1975. PLB 10.97 (ISBN 0-8239-0301-X). Rosen Group.
Student Chemist Explores Organic Compounds. Ted Charney. LC 75-12904. (YA) (gr. 7-12). 1976. PLB 10.97 (ISBN 0-8239-0326-5). Rosen Group.
Student Competencies Guide: Survival Skills for a Changing World. 44p. 1977. 2.75 (ISBN 0-89354-602-X). Northwest Regional.
Student Concerto No. 2 in G Major for Violin & Piano, Op. 13. F. Seitz. (Carl Fischer Music Library: No. 591). 1904. pap. 4.00 (ISBN 0-8258-0078-1, L591). Fischer Inc NY.
Student Concerto No. 3 in G Minor, for Violin & Piano, Op. 12. Seitz. (Carl Fischer Music Library: No. 592). 1906. pap. 4.50 (ISBN 0-8258-0079-X, L592). Fischer Inc NY.
Student Contracts. Thorwald Esbensen. Ed. by Danny G. Langdon. LC 77-25411. (Instructional Design Library). (Illus.). 100p. 1978. 23.95 (ISBN 0-87778-121-4). Educ Tech Pubns.
Student Council Handbook. 104p. 1975. 9.00 (ISBN 0-318-15121-9, 6207523). Natl Assn Stud.
Student Council Projects. James Ferguson. Ed. by Patricia Lucas. 104p. 1982. pap. 9.00 (ISBN 0-88210-133-1). Natl Assn Principals.
Student Culture & Activism in Black South African Universities: The Roots of Resistance. Mokubung Nkomo. LC 84-3819. (Contributions in Afro-American & African Studies: No. 78). (Illus.). xxiii, 209p. 1984. lib. bdg. 35.00 (ISBN 0-313-24357-3, NSC/). Greenwood.
Student Culture: Social Structure & Continuity in a Liberal Arts College. Walter L. Wallace. LC 66-15212. (NORC Monographs in Social Research Ser.: No. 9). 1966. 9.50x (ISBN 0-202-09006-X). NORC.
Student Developement in Tomorrow's Higher Education. Robert Brown. 56p. 1972. pap. text ed. 4.00 (ISBN 0-911547-72-X, 72157W34). Am Assn Coun Dev.
Student Development & Education in College Residence Halls. David Decoster & Phylis Mable. (ACPA Student Personnel Monograph: No. 18). 278p. 1974. pap. 7.00; pap. 5.00 members (ISBN 0-911547-71-1, 72159W34). Am Assn Coun Dev.
Student Development in Higher Education. Don Creamer. 1980. 16.00 (ISBN 1-55620-029-3, 72608C). Am Assn Coun Dev.
Student Development Practices: Strategies for Making a Difference. F. B. Newton & K. L. Ender. (Illus.). 348p. 1980. 29.50 (ISBN 0-398-03997-6). C C Thomas.
Student Diagnosis, Placement, & Prescription: A Criterion-Referenced Approach. Roger B. Worner. LC 76-26432. (Illus.). Repr. of 1977 ed. 62.80 (ISBN 0-8357-9243-9, 2015839). Bks Demand UMI.
Student Dictionary. 1328p. (YA) (gr. 12 up). 1988. 15.95 (ISBN 0-673-12492-4). Scott F.
Student Dictionary with Merriam-Webster Phonetic Key. 1976. pap. 6.25 (ISBN 0-87738-021-X). Youth Ed.
Student Discipline & the Law. Eugene T. Connors. LC 79-83625. (Fastback Ser.: No. 121). 60p. 1979. pap. 0.90 (ISBN 0-87367-121-X). Phi Delta Kappa.
Student Discipline: Problems & Solutions. 9.95 (ISBN 0-686-36518-6, 021-00334). Am Assn Sch Admin.
Student Earth Scientist Explores Changing Earth. Constantine Constant. LC 75-8906. (Student Scientist Ser.). (YA) (gr. 7-12). 1976. PLB 10.97 (ISBN 0-8239-0330-3). Rosen Group.
Student Earth Scientist Explores Weather. Constantine Constant. LC 74-13746. (Student Scientist Ser.). (Illus.). 133p. (gr. 7-12). 1975. PLB 10.97 (ISBN 0-8239-0303-6). Rosen Group.
Student Employment Directory. 2nd ed. Ed. by Carolyn Schulze & Richard Schulze. 1977. 4.95 (ISBN 0-686-18796-2). Shaker Prairie.
Student Entrepreneur's Guide: How to Start & Run Your Own Business. 2nd, rev. ed. Brett Kingstone. 1988. pap. 9.95 (ISBN 0-317-67021-2). McGraw.
Student Evaluation Tests for the High School Equivalency (GED) Program. Trafalgar House Publishing, Inc. Staff. (McGraw-Hill Paperbacks Ser.). 256p. 1982. pap. text ed. write for info. (ISBN 0-07-065108-6). McGraw.
Student Evaluation Tests for the Pre-GED Basic Skills Program. Trafalgar House Publishing, Inc. Staff. 224p. 1982. pap. text ed. write for info. (ISBN 0-07-065109-4). McGraw.
Student Exercise Manual for Measurement & Evaluation in Teaching. 5th ed. Norman E. Gronlund. 224p. 1985. text ed. write for info. (ISBN 0-02-348010-6). Macmillan.
Student Experience of Higher Education. Ian Lewis. LC 84-45557. 180p. 1984. 27.50 (ISBN 0-7099-1666-3, Pub. by Croom Helm Ltd). Routledge Chapman & Hall.
Student-Faculty Relations in Medical School: A Study of Professional Socialization. David Caplovitz. Ed. by Harriet Zuckerman & Robert K. Merton. LC 79-8980. (Dissertations on Sociology Ser.). 1980. lib. bdg. 26.50x (ISBN 0-405-12956-4). Ayer Co Pubs.
Student Financial Aid & Women: Equity Dilemma. Mary Moran. Frwd. by Jonathan D. Fife. LC 86-72856. (ASHE-ERIC Higher Education Reports Series 1986: No. 5). 153p. (Orig.). 1987. pap. 10.00x (ISBN 0-913317-32-2). Assn Study Higher Ed.
Student Folkways & Spending at Indiana University, 1940-1941. Mary M. Crawford. LC 68-58563. (Columbia University. Studies in the Social Sciences: No. 499). Repr. of 1943 ed. 21.00 (ISBN 0-404-51499-5). AMS Pr.
Student Guide American Government I. 3rd ed. 304p. 1985. pap. 9.95 (ISBN 0-8403-3649-7). Kendall-Hunt.
Student Guide & Resource Manual to Accompany Human Development, 2nd ed. Lawrence B. Schiamberg & Gale S. Schiamberg. 179p. 1985. write for info. wkbk. (ISBN 0-02-406900-0). Macmillan.
Student Guide & Solutions Manual for Organic Chemistry. James D. Morrison. 176p. 1979. pap. 11.00 (ISBN 0-534-00720-1, WA). Krieger.
Student Guide for Canadian, Pt. 3. Ed. by Life Office Management Association Staff. (FLMI Insurance Education Program Ser.). 1976. pap. 8.00 workbook (ISBN 0-915322-20-X). LOMA.
Student Guide for Learning BASIC, for Classroom or Independent Study, Vol. II: TRS 80 Models III & IV. Fritz Erickson & John A. Vonk. LC 83-82120. 136p. (Orig.). 1983. pap. text ed. 9.95 (ISBN 0-918452-54-6). Learning Pubns.
Student Guide for Learning BASIC, for Classroom or Independent Study, Vol. I: Applesoft. John A. Vonk & Fritz J. Erickson. LC 83-82120. 125p. 1983. pap. text ed. 9.95 (ISBN 0-918452-53-8). Learning Pubns.
Student Guide Prentice Hall 1988 Federal Tax Course. Dale Bandy. (Illus.). 304p. 1988. write for info. (ISBN 0-13-313065-7). P-H.
Student Guide to Accompany Growing & Becoming: Development from Conception to Adolescence. Marilyn O. Karmel & Louis J. Karmel. Ed. by William J. Gnagey. 224p. 1984. write for info. study guide (ISBN 0-02-361960-0). Macmillan.
Student Guide to American Government II. 3rd ed. 320p. 1985. pap. 9.95 (ISBN 0-8403-3651-9). Kendall-Hunt.
Student Guide to American Government Survey. 3rd ed. 400p. 1985. pap. 14.95 (ISBN 0-8403-3658-6). Kendall-Hunt.
Student Guide to Campaign Politics. D. Herzberg & J. W. Peltason. 1970. pap. text ed. 2.45 (ISBN 0-07-028415-6). McGraw.
Student Guide to Catholic Colleges & Universities. John R. Crocker. LC 82-48923. 468p. (Orig.). 1983. pap. 9.95 (ISBN 0-06-061602-4, RD/459, HarpR). Har-Row.
Student Guide to Engineering Report Writing. 2nd ed. John F. Brown. 171p. 1985. 14.95 (ISBN 0-9612488-2-3). United Western Pr.
Student Guide to IFPS. Paul Gray. 384p. 1983. text ed. 23.95 (ISBN 0-07-024322-0). McGraw.
Student Guide to Language Skills. rev. ed. Keith D. Holmes. (Illus.). 95p. (Orig.). 1983. Repr. of 1960 ed. 7.75x (ISBN 0-9608250-2-9). Educ Serv Pub.
Student Guide to New York. Leslie Gourse. (Illus.). 1984. pap. 8.95 (ISBN 0-88254-895-6). Hippocrene Bks.
Student Guide to Richards Atlas of New York State. Jeanne Schwarz. 1976. pap. 6.95 ea. (ISBN 0-88323-108-5, 304). Richards Pub.
Student Guide to the Registered Nurse (R.N.) Examination. Maryanne C. Glynn. Ed. by David M. Tarlow. (Illus.). 1981. pap. 12.95 (ISBN 0-931572-03-7). Datar Pub.
Student Guide to the World's Medical Schools Where the Language of Instruction Is in English. David M. Tarlow. 1986. pap. 12.95 (ISBN 0-931572-02-9). Datar Pub.
Student Guide to Writing a Journal. 16p. 1977. 2.25 (ISBN 0-89354-601-1). Northwest Regional.
Student Handbook for the Profession of Dietetics. rev. ed. Burness G. Wenberg. 98p. 1977. pap. 6.25x (ISBN 0-87013-208-3). Mich St U Pr.
Student Handbook: How to Succeed in School & College. Charles A Heidenreich. 1973. 3.00 (ISBN 0-9600428-2-2). Heidenreich.
Student Hebrew & Chaldee Dictionary. Alexander Harkavy. 896p. 1914. 14.00 (ISBN 0-88482-686-4). Hebrew Pub.
Student Housing: Architectural & Social Aspects. William Mullins & Phyllis Allen. LC 76-159965. (Illus.). 1971. 94.50x (ISBN 0-89197-955-7). Irvington.
Student in Central America, 1914-1916. Dana G. Munro. (Publication: No. 51). 75p. 1983. pap. 10.00 (ISBN 0-939238-77-2). Tulane MARI.
Student Involvement-Implementing: A Computer Tutor Program. John T. Riley & Judie L. Hurtz. 21p. (Orig.). 1983. pap. 7.95 (ISBN 0-912007-01-X). Computer Direct.
Student Journalist & Broadcasting. John R. Rider. LC 68-12132. (Student Journalist Ser.). (Illus., Photos). (gr. 7-12). 1968. PLB 10.97 (ISBN 0-8239-0114-9). Rosen Group.
Student Journalist & Consumer Reporting. Rod Vahl. (Student Journalist Ser.). 142p. 1982. lib. bdg. 10.97 (ISBN 0-8239-0549-7). Rosen Group.
Student Journalist & Creative Photography. Bill Ward. LC 75-30781. (gr. 7-12). 1976. PLB 10.97 (ISBN 0-8239-0335-4). Rosen Group.
Student Journalist & Depth Reporting. Bill G. Ward. LC 70-163427. (Student Journalist Ser.). (gr. 7 up). 1972. PLB 10.97 (ISBN 0-8239-0251-X). Rosen Group.
Student Journalist & Designing the Opinion Pages. William G. Ward. LC 69-14235. (Student Journalist Ser.). (Illus.). (gr. 7 up). 1969. PLB 10.97 (ISBN 0-8239-0116-5). Rosen Group.
Student Journalist & Editing. Charles Garven. Ed. by Ruth C. Rosen. LC 68-11055. (Student Journalist Ser.). (Illus.). (gr. 7 up). 1968. PLB 10.97 (ISBN 0-8239-0117-3). Rosen Group.
Student Journalist & Editing the Yearbook. Edmund C. Arnold. LC 72-94929. (YA) (gr. 7-12). 1973. PLB 10.97 (ISBN 0-8239-0279-X). Rosen Group.
Student Journalist & Editorial Leadership. William G. Ward. LC 68-22157. (Student Journalist Ser.). (gr. 7 up). PLB 10.97 (ISBN 0-8239-0118-1). Rosen Group.
Student Journalist & Effective Writing Style. Bryan Reddick. LC 75-44487. (gr. 7 up). 1976. PLB 10.97 (ISBN 0-8239-0352-4). Rosen Group.
Student Journalist & Free-Lance Writing. Emalene Sherman. LC 67-14525. (Student Journalist Ser). (gr. 7 up). 1969. PLB 10.97 (ISBN 0-8239-0120-3). Rosen Group.
Student Journalist & Interviewing. rev. ed. Hazel Presson. LC 67-10292. (Student Journalist Ser.). (gr. 7 up). 1982. PLB 10.97 (ISBN 0-8239-0488-1). Rosen Group.
Student Journalist & Layout. Hazel Presson. LC 72-163949. (Illus.). 116p. (YA) (gr. 7 up). 1972. PLB 10.97 (ISBN 0-8239-0253-6). Rosen Group.
Student Journalist & Making Advertising Pay for the School Publication. Glen Wright. Ed. by Ruth C. Rosen. LC 68-10818. (Student Journalist Ser.). (Illus.). (gr. 7 up). 1968. PLB 10.97 (ISBN 0-8239-0123-8). Rosen Group.
Student Journalist & Mass Communication. Julian Adams. (Illus.). 190p. 1981. lib. bdg. 10.97 (ISBN 0-8239-0499-7); workbook 2.50 (ISBN 0-8239-0538-1). Rosen Group.
Student Journalist & Photographing Sports. Bill Ward. (gr. 7-12). 1981. PLB 12.50 (ISBN 0-8239-0520-9). Rosen Group.
Student Journalist & Photojournalism. Herb Germar. LC 67-15471. (Student Journalist Ser.). 188p. (gr. 7 up). 1967. PLB 10.97 (ISBN 0-8239-0125-4). Rosen Group.
Student Journalist & Reviewing the Performing Arts. Samuel L. Singer. LC 73-80359. (Student Journalist Ser.). (Illus.). 182p. (gr. 7 up). 1974. PLB 10.97 (ISBN 0-8239-0287-0). Rosen Group.
Student Journalist & Staff Management. John Reque. (gr. 7-12). 1979. PLB 10.97 (ISBN 0-8239-0442-3). Rosen Group.

Student Journalist & the Newsmagazine Format. Elaine Pritchett. LC 75-35664. (gr. 7 up). 1976. PLB 10.97 (ISBN 0-8239-0340-0). Rosen Group.

Student Journalist & Thinking Editorials. William G. Ward. Ed. by Ruth C. Rosen. LC 74-79745. (Student Journalist Ser.). (Illus.). (gr. 7 up). 1969. PLB 10.97 (ISBN 0-8239-0129-7). Rosen Group.

Student Journalist & Twenty-One Keys to News Reporting. Hazel Presson. (Student Journalist Ser.). 1982. lib. bdg. 10.97 (ISBN 0-8239-0519-5). Rosen Group.

Student Journalist: Producing Radio & Television Programs. Carl Levine. (Student Journalist Ser.). 157p. 1982. lib. bdg. 10.97 (ISBN 0-8239-0559-4). Rosen Group.

Student Journalist's Proofreader's Manual. Marion McCullo. LC 69-11852. (Student Journalist Ser.). (gr. 7 up). PLB 9.97 (ISBN 0-8239-0126-2). Rosen Group.

Student Laboratory Experiments in Operant Conditioning. Randall K. Flory & J. Gilmour Sherman. (Illus.). 100p. (Orig.). 1974. pap. text ed. 4.00 (ISBN 0-914044-02-8). Scholars Pr Ltd.

Student Lawyer: A Guide to Minnesota's Legal System. Minnesota State Bar Association Staff & Joseph L. Daly. 217p. 11.00 (ISBN 0-314-23039-4). West Pub.

Student Leadership Programs in Higher Education. Dennis Roberts. 1981. 17.00 (ISBN 1-55620-030-7, 72604C). Am Assn Coun Dev.

Student Learning: Research on Education & Cognitive Psychology. John T. Richardson & Michael W. Eysenck. 240p. 1987. 65.00x (ISBN 0-335-15601-0, Open Univ Pr.); pap. 29.00x (ISBN 0-335-15600-2). Taylor & Francis.

Student Learning Styles & Brain Behavior. Ed. by Thomas F. Koerner. 256p. (Orig.). 1982. pap. text ed. 9.00 (ISBN 0-88210-142-6). Natl Assn Principals.

Student-Level Observation of Beginning Reading Manual. Gaea Leinhardt & Andrea M. Seewald. 66p. 1980. 1.50 (ISBN 0-318-14741-6). Learn Res Dev.

Student Life & Customs. Henry D. Sheldon. LC 70-89233. (American Education: Its Men, Institutions & Ideas, Ser. 1). 1969. Repr. of 1901 ed. 28.00 (ISBN 0-405-01470-8). Ayer Co Pubs.

Student Life & Exams: Stresses & Coping Strategies. Daniel C. Albas & Cheryl M. Albas. 192p. 1984. pap. 11.95 (ISBN 0-8403-3362-5). Kendall-Hunt.

Student Life, & Other Essays. facs. ed. William Osler. LC 67-23256. (Essay Index Reprint Ser). 1931. 15.00 (ISBN 0-8369-0756-6). Ayer Co Pubs.

Student Life in Ave Maria College, Medieval Paris. Astrik L. Gabriel. (Mediaeval Studies Ser.: No. 14). (Illus.). 1955. 50.00 (ISBN 0-268-00265-7). U of Notre Dame Pr.

Student Litigation: A Compilation & Analysis of Civil Cases Involving Students, 1971-81. National Center for State Courts Staff. 208p. 1982. manuscript 12.48 (NCSC-016). Natl Ctr St Courts.

Student Loan Handbook: All About the Guaranteed Student Loan Program & Other Forms of Financial Aid. Lana J. Chandler & Michael D. Boggs. LC 87-15918. 160p. (Orig.). 1987. pap. 7.95 (ISBN 0-932620-82-5). Betterway Pubns.

Student Loans As a Means of Financing Higher Education: Lessons from International Experience. Maureen Woodhall. (Working Paper: No. 599). 119p. 1983. 5.00 (ISBN 0-8213-0206-X, WP 0599). World Bank.

Student Loans: Risks & Realities. Ed. by Joseph M. Cronin & Sylvia Q. Simmons. 1987. 24.95 (ISBN 0-86569-165-7). Auburn Hse.

Student Looks at His Teacher. John W. Riley, Jr. et al. LC 68-8234. 1969. Repr. of 1950 ed. 16.50x (ISBN 0-8046-0382-0, Pub. by Kennikat). Assoc Faculty Pr.

Student Lovers. Kristina Lindell. Ed. by John DeFrancis. LC 70-189615. (Pali Language Texts - Chinese). (Illus.). 40p. (Orig.). 1975. pap. text ed. 2.50x (ISBN 0-8248-0225-X). UH Pr.

Student Manual for Essential Mathematics. Rudolf A. Zimmer. 128p. 1985. pap. text ed. 5.00 (ISBN 0-8403-3880-5). Kendall-Hunt.

Student Manual for the Donut Franchise: A Microcomputer Simulation. P. C. Lewis & C. Lewis. 32[illegible] 1985. pap. text ed. 9.15 (ISBN 0-07-037604-2). McGraw.

Student Manual for Theory & Practice of Counseling & Psychotherapy see Theory & Practice of Group Counseling.

Student Manual to Accompany Computer-Based Information Systems: A Management Approach. Marianne M. Kroeber et al. 160p. 1984. pap. text ed. write for info. student manual (ISBN 0-02-365390-6). Macmillan.

Student Mission Power: Report of the First International Convention of the Student Volunteer Movement for Foreign Missions, 1891. John R. Mott et al. LC 79-92013. 235p. 1979. pap. 6.95 (ISBN 0-87808-736-2). William Carey Lib.

Student Moral Development in the Catholic School. Mary P. Traviss. 96p. 1986. 6.60 (ISBN 0-318-20565-3). Natl Cath Educ.

Student Nationalism in China, 1927-1937. John Israel. 1966. 25.00x (ISBN 0-8047-0280-2). Stanford U Pr.

Student Nurse. Patricia Rae. 1983. pap. 2.95 (ISBN 0-8217-1123-7). Zebra.

Student Paraprofessionals: A Working Model for Higher Education. Ursula Delworth et al. (ACPA Student Personnel Monograph: No. 17). 80p. 1974. pap. 4.00 a non member (ISBN 0-911547-73-8, 72158W34); pap. 3.00 members (ISBN 0-686-34306-9). Am Assn Coun Dev.

Student-Parent Socialization Study, 1965. M. Kent Jennings. 1971. codebk. write for info. (ISBN 0-89138-023-X). ICPSR.

Student Participation in Administration. R. C. Srivastava. LC 75-905820. 1975. 7.75x (ISBN 0-88386-657-9). South Asia Bks.

Student Personnel Work: A Program of Developmental Relationships. Edmund G. Williamson & Donald A. Biggs. LC 74-28492. pap. 100.00 (ISBN 0-317-09835-7, 2022501). Bks Demand UMI.

Student Physician As Psycho-therapist. Ed. by Ralph W. Heine. LC 62-19624. pap. 63.80 (ISBN 0-317-26509-1, 2024047). Bks Demand UMI.

Student-Physician: Introductory Studies in the Sociology of Medical Education. Ed. by Robert K. Merton et al. LC 57-12526. (Commonwealth Fund Publications Ser). (Illus.). Repr. of 1957 ed. 93.00 (ISBN 0-8357-9179-3, 2011023). Bks Demand UMI.

Student Pilot Guide. rev. ed. Federal Aviation Administration Staff. 36p. 1979. pap. text ed. 3.25. Flightshops.

Student Pilot Guide. rev. ed. (Advisory Circular Ser.: 61-12J). 36p. 1976. pap. 4.25 (ISBN 0-318-21917-4, S/N 050-007-00476-1). USGPO.

Student Pilot Guide (AC 61-12J) Federal Aviation Administration Staff. 1979. pap. text ed. 3.95 (Pub. by Natl Flightshops). Aviation.

Student Pilot's Flight Manual. 5th ed. William K. Kershner. (Illus.). 1979. pap. 17.95 (ISBN 0-8138-1610-6). Iowa St U Pr.

Student Pilot's Study Guide. William K. Kershner & Genie R. O'Kelley. (Illus.). 174p. (gr. 10-12). 1983. pap. 18.95 (ISBN 0-8138-0821-9). Iowa St U Pr.

Student Plan-It Calendar. Lee Sparks & Cindy Hansen. (Illus.). 120p. (YA) (gr. 9-12). Date not set. pap. 5.95 (ISBN 0-931529-50-6). Group Bks.

Student Planned Acquisition of Required Knowledge. Margaret Norton et al. Ed. by Danny G. Langdon. LC 79-23442. (Instructional Design Library). 104p. 1980. 23.95 (ISBN 0-87778-155-9). Educ Tech Pubns.

Student Political Involvement in the 1960's. Ed. by J. Peter Segall & Robert M. Pickett. 200p. 1978. 21.50x (9219). Assoc Faculty Pr.

Student Political Involvement in the 1970's. Ed. by J. Peter Segall & Robert M. Pickett. (National University Pubns. Ser. in American Studies). 1979. 21.50x (Pub. by Kennikat). Assoc Faculty Pr.

Student Politics in India. Subas C. Hazary. 1987. 34.00x (ISBN 81-7024-086-7, Pub. by Ashish India). South Asia Bks.

Student Politics: Perspectives for the Eighties. Ed. by Philip G. Altbach. LC 81-2725. 276p. 1981. 18.50 (ISBN 0-8108-1430-7). Scarecrow.

Student Projects: Ideas & Plans. Lois Roets. 272p. (gr. 3 up). 1987. pap. text ed. 30.00 (ISBN 0-911943-11-0). Leadership Pub.

Student Promise Pocketbook. 96p. 1982. pap. 2.50 (ISBN 0-87788-912-0). Shaw Pubs.

Student Protest, Nineteen-Sixty to Nineteen-Seventy: An Analysis of the Issues & Speeches-with a Comprehensive Bibliography. rev. ed. Donald E. Phillips. 536p. 1985. lib. bdg. 33.75 (ISBN 0-8191-4652-8). U Pr of Amer.

Student Reading Needs & Higher Education. Ed. by David Baker. 230p. 1986. 25.00x (ISBN 0-85365-926-5, L926-5, Pub. by Library Assn Pub London). ALA.

Student Record of Community Exploration. 24p. 1977. 2.25 (ISBN 0-89354-603-8). Northwest Regional.

Student Recruitment. Amy Gibson. (How To Ser.). 36p. 1986. 5.65. Natl Cath Educ.

Student Resource & Activity Manual: To Accompany Practical Introduction to Business. Goldman. 11.50 (ISBN 0-256-03031-6). Irwin.

Student Review Manual for Pathophysiology: Mechanisms & Expressions. Gary G. Ferguson. 112p. 1984. pap. 15.95 (ISBN 0-7216-3617-9). Saunders.

Student Review Manual for the Medical Office Assistant. 2nd ed. Mary E. Kinn. (Illus.). 298p. 1981. pap. 16.95 (ISBN 0-7216-5439-8). Saunders.

Student Revolution: A Global Confrontation. Joseph A. Califano, Jr. 1969. 3.95x (ISBN 0-393-05391-1, Norton Lib); pap. 1.50x (ISBN 0-393-00519-4). Norton.

Student Scientist Explores Energy & Fuels. rev. ed. William L. Kaplan & Melvyn Lebowitz. LC 74-34077. (gr. 7-12). 1981. PLB 10.97 (ISBN 0-8239-0338-9). Rosen Group.

Student Service: The New Carnegie Unit. Charles H. Harrison. LC 86-34304. 70p. 1987. pap. text ed. 6.50 (ISBN 0-931050-30-8). Carnegie Found.

Student Services: A Handbook for the Profession. Ursula Delworth et al. LC 80-8008. (Higher Education Ser.). 1980. text ed. 28.95x (ISBN 0-87589-476-3). Jossey-Bass.

Student Services & the Law: A Handbook for Practitioners. Margaret J. & Associates Barr. LC 87-46330. (Higher Education Ser.). 400p. 1988. text ed. 26.95x (ISBN 1-55542-079-6). Jossey-Bass.

Student Sociologist's Handbook. 4th ed. Pauline Bart & Linda Frankel. 228p. 1986. pap. text ed. write for info (ISBN 0-394-35109-6, RanC). Random.

Student Solutions Manual to Accompany Understanding Chemistry. Robert J. Ouellette. 137p. 1987. write for info. (ISBN 0-02-389640-X). Macmillan.

Student Stress: A Classroom Management System. Kevin J. Swick. 96p. 1987. 8.95 (ISBN 0-8106-1696-3). NEA.

Student Stress: Effects & Solutions. Neal A. Whitman et al. Ed. & frwd. by Jonathan D. Fife. LC 84-223037. (ASHE-ERIC Higher Education Report Ser.: No. 2, 1984). (Illus.). 125p. (Orig.). 1984. pap. 7.50x (ISBN 0-913317-11-X). Assn Study Higher Educ.

Student Study & Self Test Guide for Dental Anatomy. Teaching Research: Division of the Oregon State System of Higher Education. (Illus.). 93p. 1982. 9.00 (ISBN 0-8385-1568-1). Appleton & Lange.

Student Study Guide for Biological Science: An Ecological Approch. BSCS Staff. 112p. 1987. pap. text ed. 14.90 (ISBN 0-8403-4447-3). Kendall-Hunt.

Student Study Guide for Biological Science: An Ecological Approach. BSCS Staff. 112p. 1987. pap. text ed. 5.90 (ISBN 0-8403-4182-2). Kendall-Hunt.

Student Study Guide for Military History. Hugh G. Earnhart. (Illus.). 122p. (Orig.). 1985. pap. text ed. 10.95x (ISBN 0-8138-1161-9). Iowa St U Pr.

Student Study Guide to a Basic Course in American Sign Language. Frances De Capite. 1986. pap. 12.95 (ISBN 0-932666-33-7). T J Pubs.

Student Study Guide to Accompany Introductory Chemistry for Health Professionals. Ken Liska & Lucy T. Pryde. 272p. 1984. pap. text ed. write for info. study guide (ISBN 0-02-371010-1). Macmillan.

Student Success. 4th ed. Tim Walter & Al Siebert. 224p. 1987. pap. text ed. 10.95 (ISBN 0-03-009574-3). HR&W.

Student Success Secrets. Eric Jensen. (Illus.). 192p. (gr. 10-12). 1982. pap. 6.95 (ISBN 0-8120-2589-X). Barron.

Student Supplement to Accompany Calculus with Analytic Geometry. 3rd ed. Howard E. Campbell & Paul F. Dierker. 341p. 1982. pap. text ed. 10.00 (ISBN 0-87150-353-0, 2646, Prindle). PWS Kent Pub.

Student Survival Guide. Rev. ed. Gregory F. Kishel. Ed. by Patricia G. Kishel. LC 79-90414. (Illus.). 96p. (Orig.). 1982. pap. 8.95 (ISBN 0-935346-00-7). K & K Enter.

Student Survival Manual, Vol. I. Randy Rodden. (Illus.). (gr. 7-12). 1981. pap. 2.95 (ISBN 0-317-01576-1). Mott Media.

Student Teacher's Handbook. new ed. Virginia M. Sorenson & Mary L. Veele. LC 78-62768. 71p. 1978. pap. 2.95x (ISBN 0-918452-13-9); pap. 11.80 pkg. of 5. Learning Pubns.

Student Teacher's Handbook: A Step-by-Step Guide Through the Term. Andrew I. Schwebel et al. LC 79-2239. 1979. pap. 5.95 (ISBN 0-06-460186-2, CO 186, B&N Bks). Har-Row.

Student Teaching & Field Experience Handbook. Betty Roe et al. 1984. pap. text ed. 19.95 (ISBN 0-675-20169-1). Merrill.

Student Teaching, Classroom Management & Professionalism. W. Heitzman et al. 1974. text ed. 29.50x (ISBN 0-8422-5143-X); pap. text ed. 9.95x (ISBN 0-8422-0367-2). Irvington.

Student Teaching Guide for Blind & Visually Impaired University Students: Adapted Methods & Procedures. Lou Alonso. LC 86-7979. 55p. 1987. Large Print. pap. 5.00 (ISBN 0-89128-142-8, PES142); cassette incl. (PES916); Write for info. 0.00 (PES917). Am Foun Blind.

Student Teaching Survival Kit. Pat J. Wentz & James R. Yarling. (Illus.). 209p. (Orig.). 1982. pap. text ed. 8.50 incl. wkbk. (ISBN 0-686-37630-7). Gulf Coast Ed.

Student Team Learning: An Overview & Practical Guide. Robert E. Slavin. 56p. 1983. 8.95 (ISBN 0-8106-1827-3). NEA.

Student, the College, the Law. William T. O'Hara & John T. Hill, Jr. LC 72-87116. pap. 58.50 (ISBN 0-317-41886-6, 2026049). Bks Demand UMI.

Student-to-Student Counseling: An Approach to Motivating Academic Achievement. rev. ed. William F. Brown. (Hogg Foundation Research Ser). (Illus.). 370p. 1977. 14.95x (ISBN 0-292-77542-3). U of Tex Pr.

Student Trainee. Jack Rudman. (Career Examination Ser.: C-1039). (Cloth bdg. avail. on request). pap. 10.00 (ISBN 0-8373-1039-3). Natl Learning.

Student Transfers from White to Black Colleges. Narendra H. Patel. (National Association for Equal Opportunity in Higher Education Report Ser.: No. 3). 40p. (Orig.). 1988. pap. text ed. 7.50 (ISBN 0-8191-6952-8, Pub. by NAEOHE). U Pr of Amer.

Student Union Buildings, Nineteen Sixty to Nineteen Eighty-Five: A Bibliography. Mary E. Huls. (Architecture Ser.: A 1584). 7p. 1986. 3.00 (ISBN 0-89028-814-3). Vance Biblios.

Student Unrest in India: A Select Bibliography. S. M. Jafar. 1977. 12.50x (ISBN 0-8364-0095-X). South Asia Bks.

Student Voice & the Movement: Two Facsimile Editions. Ed. by Clayborne Carson. 1988. lib. bdg. 145.00 (ISBN 0-88736-323-7). Meckler Corp.

Student Workbook for Comprehensive Medical Assisting: Administration & Clinical Procedures. Anne L. Lilly & Mary A. Frew. 389p. (Orig.). 1988. pap. text ed. 14.95 (ISBN 0-8036-3865-5). Davis Co.

Student Workbook for Fundamental Skills & Concepts in Patient Care. 4th ed. Lewis et al. LC 64-5906. (Illus.). 280p. 1988. pap. 12.95 (ISBN 0-397-54691-2, Lippincott Nursing). Lippincott.

Student Workbook for Introduction to the Administration of Justice. Martin Carlsen et al. 1978. pap. text ed. 10.95 (ISBN 0-8403-1921-5). Kendall-Hunt.

Student Workbook for the Oklahoma Story by Arrell M. Gibson. Barbara Schindler. (Illus.). 49p. (gr. 6-12). 1982. pap. 2.25 (ISBN 0-8061-1766-4). U of Okla Pr.

Student Writer: Editor & Critic. B. Clouse. 416p. 1985. pap. 16.95 (ISBN 0-07-011410-2). McGraw.

Student Writer: Editor & Critic. 2nd ed. Barbara F. Clouse. 448p. 1988. pap. text ed. 18.95 (ISBN 0-07-011412-9). McGraw.

Student Writers at Work & in the Company of Other Writers: The Bedford Prizes. Nancy Sommers & Donald McQuade. (Second Ser.). Date not set. price not set (ISBN 0-312-76942-3). St Martin.

Student Writers at Work: The Bedford Prizes. Nancy Sommers & Donald McQuade. (Second Ser.). 1986. write for info. (ISBN 0-312-76940-7); instr's. manual avail. (ISBN 0-312-76941-5). St Martin.

Student Writers at Work: The Bedford Prizes. Ed. by Nancy Sommers & Donald McQuade. LC 83-61616. 350p. 1984. pap. text ed. 8.50 (ISBN 0-312-76938-5, Pub. by Bedford Bks); instr's. manual avail. St Martin.

Studentenfruendliche Lesebuch. Stevens et al. 288p. 1986. pap. text ed. 23.95 (ISBN 0-8403-4190-3). Kendall-Hunt.

Students' Accounting Vocabulary. Diane Houghton & Ralph G. Wallace. 278p. 1980. pap. text ed. 15.00x (ISBN 0-566-00330-9). Gower Pub Co.

Student's Aid to Gross Anatomy. Richard S. Snell. 544p. 1986. pap. 16.95 (ISBN 0-8385-8687-2). Appleton & Lange.

Students & Colleges: Higher Education in the GDR. Collets Staff. 64p. 1983. 8.75x (ISBN 0-317-53853-5, Pub. by Collets (UK)). State Mutual Bk.

Students & National Socialism in Germany. Geoffrey J. Giles. LC 85-42686. (Illus.). 384p. 1985. text ed. 52.50x (ISBN 0-691-05453-3). Princeton U Pr.

Students & Politics: A Case Study of Benares Hindu University, India. Anil Ray. 1978. 14.00x (ISBN 0-88386-789-3). South Asia Bks.

Students & Politics in India. A. B. Ray. 232p. 1977. 15.95. Asia Bk Corp.

Students & Society in Early Modern Spain. Richard L. Kagan. LC 74-6828. (Illus.). 303p. 1975. 32.50x (ISBN 0-8018-1583-5). Johns Hopkins.

Student's Answer Book to Abstract Algebra. Israel N. Herstein. 114p. 1986. pap. write for info. (ISBN 0-02-354720-0). Macmillan.

Students at a Disadvantage in Higher Education. Date not set. 3.10. Coun Soc Wk Ed.

Students at Risk. (Teaching Exceptional Children Ser.: Vol. 20, No. 4). 96p. 1988. 7.00 (B709). Coun Exc Child.

Students at Risk: Problems & Solutions. Ed. by Ben Brodinsky. (AASA Critical Issues Report). 80p. 1988. pap. text ed. 13.95 (ISBN 0-87652-123-5, 021-00213). Am Assn Sch Admin.

Student's Atlas. Date not set. write for info. Am Map.

Students Atlas of California. rev. ed. Rice D. Oliver & Barbara Paff. (Illus.). 72p. (gr. 4-8). 1988. pap. 7.95 (ISBN 0-936778-98-9); pap. 8.95. Calif Weekly.

Student's Bible Atlas. Ed. by H. H. Rowley. 40p. 1984. pap. 3.95 (ISBN 0-8170-1022-X). Judson.

Student's Book of College English. 4th ed. David Skwire. 560p. 1985. text ed. write for info. (ISBN 0-02-411530-4). Macmillan.

Student's Book of Lists. LC 87-81905. (Kid's Stuff People Ser.). 168p. 1988. pap. text ed. 4.95 (ISBN 0-86530-000-3, IP 47-1). Incentive Pubns.

Student's Career Guide to a Future in the Allied Health Professions. Craig R. Ilk. LC 81-10887. (Illus.). 208p. 1982. 9.95 (ISBN 0-668-04913-8). Appleton & Lange.

Student's Commentary - Genesis, 2 vols. C. C. Aalders. Set. 30.95 (ISBN 0-310-43968-X, 11755). Zondervan.

Student's Commentary on the Holy Scriptures. George Williams. LC 75-13929. 1971. 29.95 (ISBN 0-8254-4001-7). Kregel.

Student's Concerto for Violin & Piano, No. 5. (Carl Fischer Music Library: No. 594). 1904. pap. 5.00 (ISBN 0-8258-0081-1, L594). Fischer Inc NY.

Student's Concerto No. 1 in D Major for Violin & Piano, Op. 7. F. Seitz. (Carl Fischer Music Library: No. 590). 1904. pap. 3.95 (ISBN 0-8258-0077-3, L590). Fischer Inc NY.
Students Concerto No. 4 in D Major for Violin & Piano, Op..15. F. Seitz. (Carl Fischer Music Library: No. 593). 1904. pap. 4.50 (ISBN 0-8258-0080-3, L593). Fischer Inc NY.
Student's Cookbook. Jenny Baker. LC 85-1544. 144p. (Orig.). 1985. pap. 6.95 (ISBN 0-571-13522-6). Faber & Faber.
Student's Dictionary for Biblical & Theological Studies. F. B. Huey, Jr. & Bruce Corley. 1986. pap. 8.95 (ISBN 0-310-45951-6, 12726P). Zondervan.
Student's Dictionary of Anglo-Saxon. Henry Sweet. (Anglo-Saxon.). 1896. 27.50x (ISBN 0-19-863107-3). Oxford U Pr.
Student's Dictionary of Composers. Compiled by Harold Dexter. 168p. (Orig.). 1987. pap. 5.95 (ISBN 0-86359-120-5). H Leonard Pub Corp.
Student's Dictionary of Synonyms & Antonyms. 1983. pap. 2.95 (ISBN 0-89531-033-3). Sharon Pubns.
Student's Discourse: Paragraph to Essay. Valerie H. Weisberg. Ed. by George H. Herrick. (YA) (gr. 8 up). 1985. pap. 8.95 (ISBN 0-9610912-1-5). V H Pub.
Student's English-Sanskrit Dictionary. Vaman S. Apte. 501p. 1987. 12.50 (ISBN 81-208-0299-3, Pub. by Motilal Banarsidass India); pap. 9.50 (ISBN 81-208-0300-0, Pub. by Motilal Banarsidass India). Orient Bk Dist.
Student's First Aid to Writing. Theodore Grieder & Josephine Grieder. LC 72-81176. (Quality Paperback Ser.: No. 254). (Orig.). 1979. pap. 4.95 (ISBN 0-8226-0254-7). Littlefield.
Students for a Democratic Society Papers, 1958-1970: A Guide to the Microfilm Edition of the Original Records in the State Historical Society of Wisconsin. Ed. by Jack T. Ericson. 82p. 1986. pap. 30.00 (ISBN 0-667-00542-0); 2500 dollars 41 reels microfilm incl. guide 2500.00. Chadwyck-Healey.
Student's Grammar of English. Jan A. Van Ek & Nico J. Robat. 384p. 1985. 45.00x (ISBN 0-631-90050-0); pap. 15.95 (ISBN 0-631-90060-8). Basil Blackwell.
Student's Guide for Independent Study see Poetry Unfolding.
Students Guide for Writing College Papers. rev. 3rd expanded ed. Kate L. Turabian. LC 76-435. 1977. 16.00x (ISBN 0-226-81622-2); pap. 6.95 (ISBN 0-226-81623-0). U of Chicago Pr.
Student's Guide Through the Talmud. Chajes. 19.95 (ISBN 0-87306-089-X). Feldheim.
Students' Guide to Accounting, Vols. I & II. 4th ed. C. Edward Cavert et al. 467p. 1982. text ed. 18.95x (ISBN 0-931920-43-4). Dame Pubns.
Students Guide to Accounting, 2 vols. Edward C. Cavert et al. 512p. 1980. pap. text ed. 15.95 (ISBN 0-8403-2223-2). Kendall-Hunt.
Student's Guide to Accounting & Finance Abbreviations. Mark W. Greenia. (Orig.). 1988. pap. 6.95 (ISBN 0-944601-07-3). Lexikon Servs.
Student's Guide to Archaeological Illustrating. rev. ed. Ed. by Brian D. Dillon. (Archaeological Research Tools: 1). (Illus.). 185p. 1985. pap. 17.00x (ISBN 0-917956-38-9). UCLA Arch.
Student's Guide to Basic French. 2nd ed. Julius Arnold. 184p. (gr. 9-11). 1980. pap. text ed. 7.95x (ISBN 0-88334-021-6). Ind Sch Pr.
Student's Guide to Better Grades. J. A. Richard. pap. 3.00 (ISBN 0-87980-152-2). Wilshire.
Student's Guide to Better Grades with Less Work! How to Cope In College. Alphonse Thompson. Ed. by Ted Jones. LC 83-62069. (Illus.). 1983. pap. 7.95 (ISBN 0-916928-06-3). New Dimen Studio.
Student's Guide to Brown & Lemay--Chemistry--the Central Science. 4th ed. James C. Hill. (Illus.). 316p. 1988. pap. text ed. write for info. (ISBN 0-13-129859-3). P-H.
Student's Guide to Calculus, Vol. 3. F. Soon. (Illus.). 312p. 1986. pap. 14.95 (ISBN 0-387-96348-0). Springer-Verlag.
Student's Guide to "Calculus" by J. Marsden & A. Weinstein, Vol. 1. F. H. Soon. xiv, 312p. 1985. pap. 14.95 (ISBN 0-387-96207-7). Springer-Verlag.
Student's Guide to Calculus By J. Marsden & A. Weinstein, Vol. 2. F. H. Soon. (Illus.). xiv, 281p. 1986. pap. 14.95 (ISBN 0-387-96234-4). Springer-Verlag.
Students Guide to College Admissions: Everything Your Counselor Has No Time to Tell You. Harlow Unger. 160p. 1986. 19.95 (ISBN 0-8160-1418-3); pap. 8.95 (ISBN 0-8160-1542-2). Facts on File.
Student's Guide to Conducting Social Science Research. Barbara Bunker et al. LC 74-11814. 120p. 1975. pap. text ed. 12.95 (ISBN 0-87705-238-7). Human Sci Pr.
Student's Guide to Creative Writing. Naomi L. Madgett. LC 79-93055. 134p. 1980. pap. text ed. 11.00 (ISBN 0-916418-24-3, Penway Bks). Lotus.
Student's Guide to Finding a Superior Job. William A. Cohen. LC 87-4487. 160p. (Orig.). 1987. pap. 9.95 (ISBN 0-932238-41-6, Pub. Avant Bks). Slawson Comm.
Student's Guide to Freshman English. Philip J. Snyder. 96p. 1985. pap. text ed. 6.95 (ISBN 0-8403-3554-7). Kendall-Hunt.
Students Guide to Graduate Studies in the U. K. Ed. by Hobsons, Ltd. Staff. 512p. 1986. pap. 75.00x (ISBN 0-86021-815-5, Pub. by Hobsons Ltd UK). State Mutual Bk.
Student's Guide to History. 4th ed. Jules R. Benjamin. LC 86-60730. 167p. 1986. pap. text ed. write for info. (ISBN 0-312-77004-9). St Martin.
Student's Guide to Italian Film. Marga Cottino-Jones & Craig Kelly. 80p. 1983. pap. 11.95 (ISBN 0-8403-3041-3). Kendall-Hunt.
Students' Guide to Operations Research. Paul A. Jensen. LC 86-80839. 502p. 1986. 16.95 (ISBN 0-317-59480-X). Holden-Day.
Student's Guide to Philosophy. Peter Facione. 162p. 1988. pap. text ed. 9.95 (ISBN 0-87484-832-6). Mayfield Pub.
Student's Guide to Pulmonary Function Tests. Miller. LC 79-2923. 304p. 1987. 29.50 (ISBN 0-317-55901-X). Grune.
Student's Guide to Research Report Writing in Psychology. Paul R. Solomon. 1985. pap. text ed. write for info. (ISBN 0-673-15991-4). Scott F.
Student's Guide to Secured Transactions, Bulk Transfers, & Bankruptcy. Robert Laurence & Frederick M. Hart. LC 85-80583. (Student Guide Ser.). 1985. 19.00. Bender.
Student's Guide to Steinbeck's Literature: Primary & Secondary Sources. Tetsumaro Hayashi. 31p. 1986. 20.00 (ISBN 0-317-52444-5). Steinbeck Society.
Student's Guide to the Best Summer Jobs in Alaska. Josh Groves. LC 85-90485. (Illus.). 160p. (Orig.). 1986. pap. 7.95 (ISBN 0-914457-11-X). Mustang Pub.
Student's Guide to the Bible. Philip Yancey & Tim Stafford. 96p. 1988. pap. 3.95 (ISBN 0-310-58961-4, Pub. by Lamplighter). Zondervan.
Students Guide to the Doctrine & Covenants. F. Henry Edwards. 1980. pap. 9.00 (ISBN 0-8309-0267-8). Herald Hse.
Student's Guide to the Ferns of Singapore Island. Anne Johnson. 126p. 1977. pap. 9.00 (ISBN 0-8214-0468-7, Pub. by Singapore U Pr). Ohio U Pr.
Student's Guide to the Future: Value Dilemmas of the 21st Century. Carolyn Karr. LC 81-85981. 159p. (Orig.). 1985. pap. text ed. 9.95 (ISBN 0-88247-659-9). R & E Pubs.
Student's Guide to the Job Market of Tomorrow. Linda Hewitt. (Lenox Publishing Company Career Materials Ser.). (Illus.). 240p. (Orig.). 1985. pap. 11.95 (ISBN 0-917421-03-5). Lenox Pub.
Student's Guide to the Job Search. Emory L. Cooper. 95p. (Orig.). 1986. pap. 8.95 (ISBN 0-937355-00-3). Landon Pubns.
Student's Guide to the Plays of Samuel Beckett. John Fletcher et al. 288p. 1985. 23.95 (ISBN 0-571-13418-1); pap. 9.95 (ISBN 0-571-13419-X). Faber & Faber.
Student's Guide to the Selected Poems of Ezra Pound. Ed. by Peter Brooker. LC 79-670305. 368p. 1979. pap. 8.95 (ISBN 0-571-11012-6). Faber & Faber.
Student's Guide to Western Calligraphy: An Illustrated Survey. Joyce I. Whalley. LC 83-42805. (Illus.). 200p. 1984. pap. 14.95 (ISBN 0-394-72189-6). Shambhala Pubns.
Student's Guide to Word Processing with WordStar. Ira S. Luft. 90p. (YA) (gr. 10 up). 1988. pap. 7.95 (ISBN 0-318-23581-1). Automatic Manuals.
Student's Guide to Writing Across the Curriculum. Karen L. Pelz & Charles F. Meyer. 128p. 1985. pap. text ed. 14.95 (ISBN 0-8403-3604-7). Kendall-Hunt.
Student's Guide to Writing Better Compositions. Sharon Sorenson. 224p. 1986. pap. 7.95 (ISBN 0-668-06579-6). P-H.
Student's Handbook for the Fourth R: Relating. rev. ed. Richard D. Solomon & Elaine C. Solomon. (Illus.). 181p. 1987. pap. text ed. 14.95 (ISBN 0-9617198-2-6). NIRT Inc.
Student's Handbook of the Facts of English Literature. Karl Young. 1973. Repr. of 1915 ed. 15.00 (ISBN 0-8274-0722-X). R West.
Student's Hindi-Urdu Reference Manual. Franklin C. Southworth. LC 71-164367. pap. 62.30 (ISBN 0-317-09867-5, 2055354). Bks Demand UMI.
Student's History of Education. rev. ed. Frank P. Graves. LC 75-106716. (Illus.). xix, 567p. 1970. Repr. of 1936 ed. lib. bdg. 35.00x (ISBN 0-8371-3541-9, GRSH). Greenwood.
Students in Schools of Social Work. Date not set. 2.50. Coun Soc Wk Ed.
Students in Urban Settings: Achieving the Baccalaureate Degree. Richard C. Richardson & Louis W. Bender, Jr. Ed. by Jonathan D. Fife. LC 85-73509. (ASHE-ERIC Higher Education Report Ser., 1985: No. 6). 69p. (Orig.). 1985. pap. 10.00x (ISBN 0-913317-25-X). Assn Study Higher Ed.
Students Indexed World Atlas, No. 9551. American Map Corp. Staff. (Illus.). (gr. 7-12). 1983. pap. 1.50 (ISBN 0-8416-9551-2); Span. lang. ed. pap. write for info. Am Map.
Student's Introduction to Engineering Design. Harold A. Simon. LC 74-19010. 1975. 44.00 (ISBN 0-08-017103-6); pap. 28.00 (ISBN 0-08-018234-8). Pergamon.
Student's Introduction to History. Donald W. Whisenhunt. 31p. (Orig.). 1984. pap. text ed. 2.95x (ISBN 0-89641-146-X). American Pr.
Student's Manual for Balancing Body Chemistry with Nutrition. Robert J. Peshek. 1977. 20.00 (ISBN 0-9605902-1-8). Color Coded Charting.
Student's Manual of Auditing. 2nd ed. V. Cooper. 1983. pap. 34.95 (ISBN 0-85258-175-0). Van Nos Reinhold.
Students Manual of Auditing. 3rd ed. Coopers. 1985. pap. 44.95 (ISBN 0-85258-237-4). Van Nos Reinhold.
Student's Memory Book: Easy-to-Master Memory Techniques That Will Revolutionize Your Study Habits. Bill Adler, Jr. 1988. pap. 7.95 (ISBN 0-385-24559-9). Doubleday.
Students Must Write: A Guide to Better Writing in Course Work & Examinations. Robert Barrass. LC 82-8237. (Illus.). 120p. 1982. pap. 7.95 (ISBN 0-416-33620-5, NO. 3650). Routledge Chapman & Hall.
Students, My Friends: A Personal Journal of Experiences with Young People, Pt. 2. Don J. Black. 168p. (Orig.). (YA) (gr. 11 up). 1979. pap. 5.50 (ISBN 0-942241-20-7, 8709). Pubs Bk Sales.
Student's New Testament: The Greek Text & the American Translation. Edgar J. Goodspeed. pap. 160.00 (ISBN 0-317-20700-8, 2024115). Bks Demand UMI.
Student's New Testament: The Greek Text & the American Translation, 2 vols. Edgar J. Goodspeed. (Midway Reprint Ser.). Vol. 1. pap. 121.80 (2026775); Vol. 2. pap. 146.00. Bks Demand UMI.
Students Notes on the History of Africa in the 19th & 20th Centuries. Paul Thatcher. (Illus.). 138p. (Orig.). 1981. pap. text ed. 8.95 (ISBN 0-582-60362-5). Longman.
Students of Snow. Jane Flanders. LC 82-8461. 68p. 1982. lib. bdg. 8.50x (ISBN 0-87023-378-5); pap. 4.95 (ISBN 0-87023-379-3). U of Mass Pr.
Student's Partial Solutions Manual T-A Applied Regression Analysis. Hafner & Carr. 112p. 1988. pap. 9.00 (ISBN 0-534-91513-2, Duxbury Pr). PWS Kent Pub.
Students Partial Solutions Manual to Accompany Statistical Thinking for Managers. 2nd ed. Hildebrand. 272p. 1987. pap. text ed. 10.00 (ISBN 0-87150-053-1). PWS Kent Pub.
Student's Pocket Middle English Dictionary Speller: A Handy Reference Guide. Mike Gallatin. 63p. (Orig.). 1988. pap. 2.50 (ISBN 0-943851-08-4). QED Pr Ann Arbor.
Students Protest. Ed. by Philip G. Altbach & Robert Laufer. LC 72-160738. (Annals Ser: No. 395). 1971. pap. 7.95 (ISBN 0-87761-138-6). Am Acad Pol Soc Sci.
Student's Reading Test Book: Grades 2-6. Ruth E. Rogers et al. 31p. 1977. pap. 4.95x ea. (ISBN 0-918452-03-1); pap. 16.00 pkg. of 5. Learning Pubns.
Students Reports & Articles by "Outside" Authors As Published in "The White Light" (Vols. 1-10) Ed. by Nelson White & Anne White. LC 83-91007. (Illus.). 50p. (Orig.). 1983. pap. 18.00 (ISBN 0-939856-36-0). Tech Group.
Students' Right to Their Own Language. Melvin A. Butler et al. 32p. 1974. pap. 2.25 (ISBN 0-8141-4806-9). NCTE.
Student's Rorschach Manual: An Introduction to Administering, Scoring & Interpreting Researcher's Psychodiagnostic Inkblot Test. rev. ed. Robert M. Allen. LC 77-14710. 361p. 1978. text ed. 35.00x (ISBN 0-8236-6201-2). Intl Univs Pr.
Students' Sanskrit-English Dictionary. 2nd ed. Vaman S. Apte. 664p. 1986. 17.95 (ISBN 81-208-0044-3, Pub. by Motilal Banarsidass India); pap. 11.95 (ISBN 81-208-0045-1, Pub. by Motilal Banarsidass India). Orient Bk Dist.
Students Scholars & Saints. Louis Ginzberg. LC 85-9089. (Brown Classics in Judaica Ser.). 312p. 1985. pap. text ed. 13.50 (ISBN 0-8191-4490-8). U Pr of Amer.
Students Shop Reference Handbook. Compiled by Edward G. Hoffman. LC 85-8200. (Illus.). 530p. 1986. text ed. 15.00x (ISBN 0-8311-1161-5). Indus Pr.
Students, Society, & Politics in Imperial Germany: The Rise of Academic Illiberalism. Konrad H. Jarausch. LC 81-47926. 480p. 1982. 52.50x (ISBN 0-691-05345-6); pap. 19.95x LPE (ISBN 0-691-10131-0). Princeton U Pr.
Student's Solutions Manual to Accompany Probability & Statistics for Engineers & Scientists. 3rd ed. Ronald E. Walpole. 124p. 1985. write for info. (ISBN 0-02-424190-3). Macmillan.
Students Speak. Lucille Trucano. 151p. (Orig.). 1984. pap. 5.95 (ISBN 0-935529-02-0). Comprehen Health Educ.
Students' Technology of Breadmaking & Flour Confectionery. rev. ed. W. J. Fance. (Illus.). 464p. 1983. pap. 22.00 (ISBN 0-7100-9046-3). Routledge Chapman & Hall.
Students' Text-Book of Astrology. Vivian E. Robson. 243p. 1981. pap. 15.00 (ISBN 0-89540-117-7, SB-117). Sun Pub.
Students Themselves. Assembly on University Goals & Governance. 320p. 1974. text ed. 15.95x (ISBN 0-87073-432-6). Schenkman Bks Inc.
Student's Theory & Practice Workbook For Competency in Cosmetology - Spanish Version: A Professional Text. Anthony B. Colletti. (Illus., Span.). 1987. pap. text ed. 16.43 (ISBN 0-317-59336-6). Keystone Pubns.
Student's Theory & Practice Workbook for Competency in Cosmetology: A Professional Text. Anthony B. Colletti. (Illus.). 528p. (Orig.). 1987. pap. text ed. 24.21 tchr's. ed. (ISBN 0-912126-77-9); pap. text ed. 15.64 (ISBN 0-912126-76-0). Keystone Pubns.
Students under Stress: A Study in the Social Psychology of Adaptation. David Mechanic. LC 77-91058. 268p. 1978. 20.00x (ISBN 0-299-07470-6); pap. text ed. 10.95x (ISBN 0-299-07474-9). U of Wis Pr.
Students' Use in Leisure Time of Activities Learned in Physical Education in State Teachers College. Ethel J. Saxman. LC 78-177232. (Columbia University. Teachers College. Contributions to Education: No. 217). Repr. of 1926 ed. 22.50 (ISBN 0-404-55217-X). AMS Pr.
Students, Values & Politics: A Cross-Cultural Comparison. Otto Klineberg et al. LC 77-94082. 1979. 19.95 (ISBN 0-02-916770-1). Free Pr.
Student's Values in Drugs & Drug Abuse. Mary V. Sztorc. 1976. pap. 2.00 (ISBN 0-87507-000-0). Cath Lib Assn.
Students versus Parents: Problems & Conflicts. Samuel Perlman. LC 76-86341. 1969. 7.50x (ISBN 0-87299-006-0); pap. 4.95x (ISBN 0-87299-017-6). Howard Doyle.
Student's View of the College of St. James on the Eve of the Civil War: The Letters of W. Wilkins Davis (1842-1866) David Hein. (Studies in American Religion: Vol. 30). 175p. 1988. lib. bdg. 39.95 (ISBN 0-88946-674-2). E Mellen.
Student's Vocabulary for Biblical Hebrew & Aramaic. Larry A. Mitchel. 128p. 1984. pap. 10.95 (ISBN 0-310-45461-1, 11607P). Zondervan.
Student's Vocabulary of Biblical Hebrew. George M. Landes. 56p. (Orig.). 1961. pap. text ed. write for info. (ISBN 0-02-367410-5, Pub. by Scribner). Macmillan.
Student's Webster Dictionary. Ed. by Jess Stein. (Illus.). 48p. 1984. pap. 2.95 (ISBN 0-89531-075-9, 0114-72). Sharon Pubns.
Students with Learning Disabilities. Cecil D. Mercer. 544p. 1983. text ed. 27.95 (ISBN 0-675-20042-3). Merrill.
Students with Learning Disabilities. 3rd ed. Cecil D. Mercer. 672p. 1987. Additional supplements may be obtained from publisher. text ed. 32.95 (ISBN 0-675-20713-4). Merrill.
Students Without Teachers: The Crisis in the University. Harold Taylor. LC 70-79499. 348p. 1975. text ed. 5.95x (ISBN 0-8093-0750-2). S Ill U Pr.
Student's Workbook for the Art of Editing. 4th ed ed. Brian S. Brooks. viii, 247p. 1986. pap. write for info. (ISBN 0-02-315140-4). Macmillan.
Student's Workbook for the Buyer's Manual. 242p. pap. text ed. 13.00 (ISBN 0-87102-011-4, 45-9475). Natl Ret Merch.
Student's World Atlas. Vahe Movsessian. (Illus.). 48p. (Orig.). (gr. 2 up). 1981. pap. 3.95 (ISBN 0-89531-022-8, 0115-72). Sharon Pubns.
Students Write: A Collection of Essays. Leonora Woodman & C. Beth Burch. 1987. pap. text ed. write for info. (ISBN 0-673-18192-8). Scott F.
Student's Writing Guide for the Arts & Social Sciences. Gordon Taylor. (Illus.). 250p. Date not set. price not set (ISBN 0-521-36005-6); pap. price not set (ISBN 0-521-36905-3). Cambridge U Pr.
Studi Grammaticali. Gualtiero Calboli. (Studi Pubblicati Dall'Istituto di Filologia Classica (Universita di Bologna): No. XI). 258p. (Ital.). 1962. pap. text ed. 20.00 (ISBN 0-905205-45-6, Pub. by F Cairns). Longwood Pub Group.
Studi Salvianei, Vol. I. Giuseppe Vecchi. (Studi Pubblicati Dall'Istituto di Filologia Classica (Universita di Bologna): No. IV). 94p. (Ital.). 1951. pap. text ed. 4.95 (ISBN 0-905205-41-3, Pub. by F Cairns). Longwood Pub Group.
Studi su Polibio. Attilio Roveri. (Studi Pubblicati Dall'Istituto di Filologia Classica (Universita di Bologna): No. XVII). 270p. (Ital.). 1964. pap. text ed. 20.00 (ISBN 0-905205-51-0, Pub. by F Cairns). Longwood Pub Group.
Studia, Vols. 1-11. Anthropos Institute Staff. 375.00 (ISBN 0-384-01655-3). Johnson Repr.
Studia Arabica et Islamia: Festschrift for Ihsan Abbas. Ed. by Wadad Al-Qadi. 1981. 175.00x (ISBN 0-8156-6058-8, Am U Beirut). Syracuse U Pr.
Studia Belgica: Aufsaetze zur Literatur- und Kulturgeschichte Belgiens. Ed. by Hans-Joachim Lope. 231p. (Ger.). 1983. 23.15 (ISBN 3-8204-7321-1). P Lang Pubs.
Studia Hispanica I in Honor of Rodolfo Cardona. Ed. by Luis A. Ramos-Garcia & Nestor Lugones. 1982. 12.95 (ISBN 0-934840-01-6). Studia Hispanica.
Studia Iranica, Tome XV. (Illus.). 290p. 1986. 68.25x (ISBN 90-04-08275-1, Pub. by E J Brill). Heinman.
Studia Linguistica Alexandro Vasilii Filio Issatschenko: A Collegis Amicusque Oblata. Ed. by H. Birnbaum et al. xxvi, 517p. (Orig., Eng., Fr., Ger., & Rus.). 1978. pap. 77.00x (ISBN 0-686-32343-2). Benjamins North Am.

TITLE INDEX STUDIES IN ADAPTATION: THE

Studia Linguistica Diachronica et Synchronica. Ursula Pieper & Gerhard Stickel. 988p. 1985. text ed. 246.00. Mouton.

Studia nad Muzyka Polskiego Sredniowiecza. Hieronim Feicht. Ed. by Zofia Lissa. LC 75-543338. (Opera Musicologica Hieronymi Feicht Ser.: No. 1). (Illus.). 400p. (Eng., Ger. & Pol.). 1975. 10.00 (ISBN 0-934082-16-2, Pub. by PWM Edition Poland). Theodore Front.

Studia Otiosa. facsimile ed. Richard W. Bond. LC 71-99683. (Essay Index Reprint Ser.). 1938. 18.00 (ISBN 0-8369-1341-8). Ayer Co Pubs.

Studia Patristica XVII, 3 vols. Ed. by E. A. Livingstone. 1520p. 1982. Set. 240.00 (ISBN 0-08-025779-8). Pergamon.

Studia Patristica XVIII: Papers of the 1983 Oxford International Patristics Conference, Vol. 1. pap. 40.00 (ISBN 0-87907-350-0). Cistercian Pubns.

Studia Phycologica: Festschrift J. Gerloff. (Nova Hedwigia Ser.: No. 33). (Illus.). 1004p. 1980. pap. 110.00x (ISBN 0-686-33174-5). Lubrecht & Cramer.

Studia Pindarica. Elroy L. Bundy. LC 83-40482. 150p. 1987. text ed. 28.00x (ISBN 0-520-05098-3); pap. 14.95x (ISBN 0-520-05111-4). U of Cal Pr.

Studia Semitica, 2 vols. Erwin I. Rosenthal. Incl. Vol. 1. Jewish Themes. 59.50 (ISBN 0-521-07958-6); Vol. 2. Islamic Themes. 49.50 (ISBN 0-521-07959-4). (Oriental Publications Ser.: Nos. 16 & 17). 1971. Cambridge U Pr.

Studia Sino-Mongolica. Wolfgang Bauer. 470p. 1979. 70.00x (ISBN 0-317-68644-5, Pub. by Han-Shan Tang Ltd). State Mutual Bk.

Studia Sumiro-Hungarica, 3 vols. Ed. by Miklos Erdy. 1968-1974. Set. 44.00 (ISBN 0-914246-50-X). Gilgamesh Pub.

Studia Sumiro-Hungarica, 2 vols. Ed. by Matyas Feher & Miklos Erdy. Incl. Sumir Kerdes (the Sumerian Question) Janos Galgoczy. LC 79-7359. (Vol. 1). 270p (ISBN 0-914246-51-8); Szumirok Es Magyarok (Sumerians & Magyars) Ede Somogyi. LC 70-7362. (Vol. 2). 270p (ISBN 0-914246-52-6). (Illus.). 1968. Repr. 13.00 ea. Gilgamesh Pub.

Studied Madness. Heywood H. Broun. LC 79-84436. 1979. 15.95 (ISBN 0-933256-00-0); pap. 7.95 (ISBN 0-933256-03-5). Second Chance.

Studied Madness. Heywood H. Broun. LC 79-84436. 298p. 1983. pap. 5.95 (ISBN 0-933256-40-X). Second Chance.

Studien an eingebuergerten Arten der Gattung Solidago L. M. L. Voser-Huber. (Dissertationes Botanicae: No. 68). (Illus.). 158p. (Ger.). 1983. pap. text ed. 30.00x (ISBN 3-7682-1359-5). Lubrecht & Cramer.

Studien uber Salomon Ibn Gabirol. David Kaufmann. Ed. by Steven Katz. LC 79-7144. (Jewish Philosophy, Mysticism & the History of Ideas Ser.). (Ger. & Hebrew.). 1980. Repr. of 1899 ed. lib. bdg. 14.00x (ISBN 0-405-12272-1). Ayer Co Pubs.

Studien Uber Shakespeare's Wirkung auf Zeitgenossiche Dramatiker. E. Koeppel. (Material for the Study of the Old English Drama Ser.: No. 1, Vol. 9). pap. 16.00 (ISBN 0-8115-0258-9). Kraus Repr.

Studien ueber die saxicolen Arten der Flechtengattung Lecania II. Lecania s. Str. Michaela Mayrhofer. (Bibliotheca Lichenologica Ser.: Vol. 28). (Illus.). 134p. (Ger.). 1988. pap. text ed. 39.00x (ISBN 3-443-58007-6). Lubrecht & Cramer.

Studien und Berufsberatung Aus der Sicht Von Maturanden. Gerda Eberle. (European University Studies: No. 6, Vol. 95). 236p. (Ger.). 1982. 22.10 (ISBN 3-261-05022-5). P Lang Pubs.

Studien Zu Den Germanischen Volksrechten Gedaechtnisschrift Fuer Wilhelm Ebel. Gotz Landwehr. (Rechtshistorische Reihe: Vol. 1). 217p. (Ger.). 1982. 25.80 (ISBN 3-8204-6412-3). P Lang Pubs.

Studien Zu Den Klosterprivilegien der Paepste Im Fruehen Mittelalter Unter Besonderer Beruecksichtigung der Privilegierung Von St. Maurice D'agaune. Hans H. Anton. (Beitraege Zur Geschichte und Quellenkunde Des Mittelalters Ser.: Vol. 4). 1975. pap. 39.60x (ISBN 3-11-004686-5). De Gruyter.

Studien Zu Eichendorffs Prosastil. Gisela Jahn. 1937. 18.00 (ISBN 0-384-26701-7); pap. 13.00 (ISBN 0-384-26700-9). Johnson Repr.

Studien Zu Einer Ostturkischen Lautlehre. Gunnar Jarring. 53p. 1933. 64.00x (ISBN 0-317-68645-3, Pub. by Han-Shan Tang Ltd). State Mutual Bk.

Studien Zu Heines Reisebildern. Erich Loewenthal. pap. 13.00 (ISBN 0-384-33390-7). Johnson Repr.

Studien zu Much Ado About Nothing, Vol. 8. Norbert Greiner. (Trierer Studien zur Literatur). 188p. (Ger.). 1983. 22.10 (ISBN 3-8204-7794-2). P Lang Pubs.

Studien Zu Shelleys Lyrik. Herbert Huscher. 1919. 12.00 (ISBN 0-384-25030-0). Johnson Repr.

Studien zu Traditionellen Elementen des Geschichtsdenkens und der Bildlichkeit im Werk Johann Gottfried Herders. Peter Frenz. (Mikrokosmos: Vol. 12). 283p. (Ger.). 1983. 33.70 (ISBN 3-8204-7345-9). P Lang Pubs.

Studien Zum Altenglischen Computus. Heinrich Henel. 1934. pap. 8.00 (ISBN 0-384-22300-1). Johnson Repr.

Studien zum aristotelischen Materie-Begriff. Heinz H. Happ. 953p. 1971. 106.00x (ISBN 3-11-001796-2). De Gruyter.

Studien Zum Englischen Wortschatz der Gegenwart. Siegfried Bergerhoff. pap. 10.00 (ISBN 0-384-03985-5). Johnson Repr.

Studien zum juedischen Neuplatonismus: Die Religionsphilosophie des Abraham Ibn Ezra. Hermann Greive. (Studia Judaica Vol. 7). 225p. 1973. 35.60x (ISBN 3-11-004116-2). De Gruyter.

Studien Zum Problem des Metaphorischen Redens Am Beispiel Von Texten Aus Shakeskpeares "Richard II" und Marlowes "Edward II". Wilfried Malz. (European University Studies: No. 14, Vol. 105). 251p. (Ger.). 1982. 30.00 (ISBN 3-8204-5824-7). P Lang Pubs.

Studien zum Verstaendnis der Romischen Literatur. Wilhelm Kroll. Ed. by Steele Commager. LC 77-70839. (Latin Poetry Ser.: Vol. 23). 1978. lib. bdg. 50.00 (ISBN 0-8240-2972-0). Garland Pub.

Studien Zur Allegorischen Bildlichkeit In Den Parabolae Bernhards Von Clairvaux. Waltraud Timmermann. (Mikrokosmos: Vol. 10). 305p. (Ger.). 1982. 35.80 (ISBN 3-8204-6274-0). P Lang Pubs.

Studien Zur Alteren Athenischen Verfassungsgeschichte. Arthur Ledl. LC 72-7898. (Greek History Ser.). (Ger.). Repr. of 1914 ed. 29.00 (ISBN 0-405-04797-5). Ayer Co Pubs.

Studien zur antiken Literatur und Kunst. Paul Friedlaender. (Ger). 1969. 55.60x (ISBN 3-11-004049-2). De Gruyter.

Studien zur antiken Philosophie. Olof Gigon. Ed. by Andreas Graeser. 1972. 54.80x (ISBN 3-11-003928-1). De Gruyter.

Studien zur Arithmetik und Geometrie. E. Husserl. 1983. 91.50 (ISBN 90-247-2497-X, Pub. by Martinus Nijhoff Netherlands). Kluwer Academic.

Studien Zur Bestimmung Des Lebens In Meister Eckharts Deutschen Predigten. Till Beckmann. (European University Studies: No. 20, Vol. 85). 244p. (Ger.). 1982. 30.00 (ISBN 3-8204-5708-9). P Lang Pubs.

Studien zur Deutschen Kunstgeschichte: Nos. 1-50, Nos. 134 & 246, Strasbourg, etc, 1894-1904, 1911, 1927. 1986. 1416.00 (ISBN 0-8115-3167-8); pap. 1029.00 (ISBN 0-8115-3168-6). Kraus Repr.

Studien zur Deutschen Kunstgeschichte: Nos. 51-153 & No. 205, Strasbourg, etc., 1904-1910, 1918. 1986. 2330.00 (ISBN 0-8115-3169-4); pap. 1592.00 (ISBN 0-8115-3170-8). Kraus Repr.

Studien Zur Englischen Lautgeschichye, Von Karl Luick. Karl Luick. pap. 25.00 (ISBN 0-384-34200-0). Johnson Repr.

Studien Zur Englischen Literarkritik, 1910-30. Hans W. Haeusermann. 1938. 20.00 (ISBN 0-384-21810-5). Johnson Repr.

Studien Zur Geschichte der Alteren Arabischen Furstenspiegel. Gustav Richter. (Ger). 1932. pap. 12.00 (ISBN 0-384-50770-0). Johnson Repr.

Studien zur Geschichte des griechischen Alphabets. A. Kirchhoff. (Illus.). vi, 179p. (Ger.). 1970. pap. 35.00x (ISBN 90-70265-12-5, Pub. by Gieben Amsterdam). Benjamins North Am.

Studien Zur Geschichte Kapitalistischer Organisationsformen. Jakob Strieder. LC 77-161684. (Research & Source Works Ser.: No. 754). 1971. Repr. of 1925 ed. lib. bdg. 34.00 (ISBN 0-8337-3432-6). B Franklin.

Studien Zur Gliederung der Flechtengattung Lecanora. G. Eigler. (Illus.). 18.00x (ISBN 3-7682-0628-9). Lubrecht & Cramer.

Studien zur humanistischen Jurisprudenz. Guido Kisch. 1972. 48.40x (ISBN 3-11-003600-2). De Gruyter.

Studien Zur Hydronymie des Savesystems: Woerterbuch der Gewaessernamen, Auswertung. 2nd ed. (Ger.). 1966. pap. 32.50 (ISBN 3-533-00810-X, M-7629, Pub. by Carl Winter). French & Eur.

Studien Zur Klima- und Vegetations Kunde der Tropen. W. Lauer et al. 1952. 20.00 (ISBN 0-384-58675-9). Johnson Repr.

Studien Zur Konstituierung Einer Rezeptionsanalytisch Fundierten Literaturdidaktik. Reinhardt Pfleger. (European University Studies: No. 1, Vol. 545). 347p. (Ger.). 1982. 41.60 (ISBN 3-8204-6296-1). P Lang Pubs.

Studien Zur Kulturkunde, Vols. 1-8. 1933-43. 165.00 (ISBN 0-384-58680-5). Johnson Repr.

Studien zur Minne und Ehe in Wolframs Parzival und Hartmanns Artusepik. Herbert E. Wiegand. (Quellen und Forschungen Zur Sprach-und Kulturgeschichte der Germanischen Voelker, 49). 352p. (Ger.). 1972. 53.20x (ISBN 3-11-003672-X). De Gruyter.

Studien Zur Modernen Deutschen Lexikographie. Ruth Klappenbach. (Linguistik Aktuel: No. 1). xxiii, 313p. 1980. 36.00x (ISBN 90-272-2721-7). Benjamins North Am.

Studien Zur Osterreichischen Erzahlliteratur Der Gegenwart. H. Zeman. (Amsterdamer Beitrage Zur Neueren Germanistik Ser.: Band 14 - 1982). 344p. (Ger.). 1982. pap. text ed. 29.95x (ISBN 90-6203-674-0, Pub. by Rodopi Holland). Humanities.

Studien Zur Phanomenologie: 1930-1939. Fink. (Phaenomenologica Ser.: No. 21). 1966. lib. bdg. 24.00 (ISBN 90-247-0253-4, Pub. by Martinus Nijhoff Netherlands). Kluwer Academic.

Studien zur Rezeption des Franzoesischen Wortschatzes Im Mittelenglischen. Robert Feist. 1934. pap. 8.00 (ISBN 0-384-15420-4). Johnson Repr.

Studien Zur Short Story Als Fiktional-Narrative Textform und die Moeglichkeiten Einer Typenbildung, Vol. 20. Michael Thomas. (Sprache und Literatur). 390p. (Ger.). 1982. 40.00 (ISBN 3-8204-6267-8). P Lang Pubs.

Studien zur Theorie der Quadratischen Formen. H. Gross & B. Waerden. (Mathemische Reihe Ser.: No. 34). (Illus.). 254p. (Ger.). 1968. 41.95x (ISBN 0-8176-0401-4). Birkhauser.

Studies. Aeschylus. Ed. by R. P. Winnington-Ingram. LC 82-18155. 1983. 57.50 (ISBN 0-521-24938-4); pap. 20.95 (ISBN 0-521-27089-8). Cambridge U Pr.

Studies & Appreciations. Darrell Figgis. 258p. 1980. Repr. of 1912 ed. lib. bdg. 29.00 (ISBN 0-8495-1711-7). Arden Lib.

Studies & Appreciations. Darrell Figgis. LC 76-23186. 1976. Repr. of 1912 ed. lib. bdg. 37.00 (ISBN 0-8414-4200-2). Folcroft.

Studies & Appreciations. facs. ed. Lewis E. Gates. LC 76-134079. (Essay Index Reprint Ser). 1900. 18.00 (ISBN 0-8369-1927-0). Ayer Co Pubs.

Studies & Appreciations. facs. ed. William Sharp. Ed. by Mrs. W. Sharp. LC 67-26783. (Essay Index Reprint Ser). 1912. 19.00 (ISBN 0-8369-0871-6). Ayer Co Pubs.

Studies & Diversions in Greek Literature. Marshall MacGregor. LC 79-101047. 1969. Repr. of 1937 ed. 24.50x (ISBN 0-8046-0712-5, Pub. by Kennikat). Assoc Faculty Pr.

Studies & Documents Relating to the History of the Greek Church & People Under Turkish Domination. Theodore H. Papadopoullos. LC 78-38759. Repr. of 1952 ed. 27.50 (ISBN 0-404-56314-7). AMS Pr.

Studies & Essays in the History of Science & Learning. Ed. by Ashley Montagu. LC 74-26275. (History, Philosophy & Sociology of Science Ser). (Illus.). 1975. Repr. of 1944 ed. 47.50x (ISBN 0-405-06603-1). Ayer Co Pubs.

Studies & Essays on International Humanitarian Law & Red Cross Principles. Ed. by Christophe Swinarski. 1984. lib. bdg. 50.00 (ISBN 90-247-3078-3, Pub. by Martinus Nijhoff Netherlands). Kluwer Academic.

Studies & Executed Buildings by Frank Lloyd Wright. Vincent Scully. LC 85-43538. (Illus.). 124p. 1986. 65.00 (ISBN 0-8478-0687-1). Rizzoli Intl.

Studies & Further Studies in a Dying Culture. Christopher Caudwell. LC 77-142989. 544p. 1972. pap. 9.50 (ISBN 0-85345-218-0). Monthly Rev.

Studies & Issues in Smoking Behavior. National Research Conference on Smoking Behavior (2nd: 1966: University of Arizona) Staff. Ed. by Salvatore V. Zagona. LC 67-28650. pap. 72.10 (2031489). Bks Demand UMI.

Studies & Issues in Smoking Behavior. Ed. by Salvatore V. Zagona. 263p. 1967. 7.50x (ISBN 0-8165-0089-4). U of Ariz Pr.

Studies & Memories. Charles V. Stanford. LC 76-22352. (Illus.). 1976. Repr. of 1908 ed. lib. bdg. 25.00 (ISBN 0-89341-023-3). Longwood Pub Group.

Studies & Memories. Charles V. Stanford. 224p. 1984. pap. cancelled (ISBN 0-89341-526-X). Longwood Pub Group.

Studies & Sketches. Oxford & Herbert H. Asquith. LC 68-54366. (Essay Index Reprint Ser). 1924. 14.75 (ISBN 0-8369-0759-0). Ayer Co Pubs.

Studies & Texts in Folklore, Magic, Medieval Romance, Hebrew Apocrypha & Samaritan Archaeology, 3 Vols. rev. ed. Moses Gaster. 1970. Set. 45.00x (ISBN 0-87068-056-0). Ktav.

Studies & the Structure of National Elite of National Elite Groups. Ed. by Gwen Moore. (Research in Politics & Society Ser.: Vol. 1). 1985. 54.50 (ISBN 0-89232-335-3). Jai Pr.

Studies at Leisure. W. L. Courtney. 1973. Repr. of 1892 ed. 20.00 (ISBN 0-8274-1523-0). R West.

Studies by a Recluse in Cloister, Town & Country. 3rd ed. Augustus Jessopp. 1969. Repr. of 1883 ed. lib. bdg. 20.50 (ISBN 0-8337-1841-X). B Franklin.

Studies by Einar Haugen Presented on the Occasion of His 65th Birthday, April 19, 1971. Ed. by Evelyn S. Firchow et al. (Janua Linguarum Ser.: No. 49). 1972. 76.80x (ISBN 0-686-21225-8). Mouton.

Studies by Members of the English Department, University of Illinois, in Memory of John Jay Parry. facs. ed. University Of Illinois - English Dept. LC 68-58798. (Essay Index Reprint Ser). 1955. 18.00 (ISBN 0-8369-0120-7). Ayer Co Pubs.

Studies by Members of the French Department of Yale University. Yale University French Department. LC 72-1658. (Yale Romance Studies: No. 18). Repr. of 1941 ed. 34.00 (ISBN 0-404-53218-7). AMS Pr.

Studies by Samuel Horodezky: An Original Anthology. Ed. by Steven Katz. LC 79-51391. (Jewish Philosophy, Mysticism & History of Ideas Ser.). 1980. lib. bdg. 17.00x (ISBN 0-405-12233-0). Ayer Co Pubs.

Studies Concerning Organisms Occurring in Water Supplies. L. B. Walton. 1930. 2.00 (ISBN 0-86727-023-3). Ohio Bio Survey.

Studies Concerning the Origins of Milton's Paradise Lost. Heinrich Mutschmann. LC 79-163459. (Studies in Milton, No. 22). 1971. Repr. of 1924 ed. lib. bdg. 39.95x (ISBN 0-8383-1324-8). Haskell.

Studies Concerning the Origins of Milton's Paradise Lost. Heinrich Mutschmann. 1924. Repr. 15.00 (ISBN 0-8274-3532-0). R West.

Studies Critical & Comparative. Thomas B. Smith. LC 62-20563. 324p. 1962. 17.50 (ISBN 0-379-00118-7). Oceana.

Studies for a Byron Bibliography. Francis L. Randolph. LC 79-13752. 144p. 1979. 25.00 (ISBN 0-915010-26-7). Sutter House.

Studies for Einar Hauger Presented by Friends & Colleagues. Ed. by Evelyn S. Firchow. LC 72-889779. (Janua Linguarum, Ser. Major: No. 59). (Illus.). 573p. 1972. text ed. 59.20x (ISBN 90-2792-338-8). Mouton.

Studies for Violin, Op. 32, 2 pts. Hans Sitt. Ed. by G. Saenger. (Carl Fischer Music Library: Nos. 110 & 111). 1899. Pt. 1. pap. 6.00 (ISBN 0-8258-0017-X, L-110); Pt. 2, 19p. pap. 6.00 (ISBN 0-8258-0018-8, 111). Fischer Inc NY.

Studies for Violin, Op. 32. Hans Sitt. Ed. by Gustav Saenger. (Carl Fischer Music Library: No. 112). pap. 5.00 (ISBN 0-8258-0019-6, L112). Fischer Inc NY.

Studies for William A. Read: A Miscellany Presented by Some of His Colleagues & Friends. facs. ed. LC 68-22116. (Essay Index Reprint Ser). 1940. 14.50 (ISBN 0-8369-0912-7). Ayer Co Pubs.

Studies French & English. facs. ed. Frank L. Lucas. LC 69-17583. (Essay Index Reprint Ser). 1934. 19.00 (ISBN 0-8369-0084-7). Ayer Co Pubs.

Studies from Life. Hugh De Selincourt. 1978. Repr. of 1934 ed. lib. bdg. 20.00 (ISBN 0-8492-0671-5). R West.

Studies from Ten Literatures. Ernest Boyd. LC 68-16289. 1968. Repr. of 1925 ed. 25.75x (ISBN 0-8046-0038-4, Pub. by Kennikat). Assoc Faculty Pr.

Studies from Ten Literatures. facs. ed. Ernest A. Boyd. LC 68-20287. (Essay Index Reprint Ser). 1925. 20.00 (ISBN 0-8369-0236-X). Ayer Co Pubs.

Studies from Ten Literatures. Ernest A. Boyd. (English Literary Reference Ser.). Repr. of 1927 ed. 17.00 (ISBN 0-384-05330-0). Johnson Repr.

Studies from the Chemical Laboratory of the Sheffield Scientific School (Yale University, 2 vols. Horace L. Wells. 1901. 100.00x set (ISBN 0-685-89786-9). Elliots Bks.

Studies from the Psychological Laboratory of Oberlin College see Memory Defects in Organic Psychoses.

Studies, Green & Gray. facs. ed. Henry J. Newbolt. LC 68-8485. (Essay Index Reprint Ser). 1968. Repr. of 1926 ed. 17.50 (ISBN 0-8369-0740-X). Ayer Co Pubs.

Studies, Historical & Critical. facs. ed. Pasquale Villari. Tr. by L. Villari. LC 68-16983. (Essay Index Reprint Ser). 1968. Repr. of 1907 ed. 18.00 (ISBN 0-8369-0960-7). Ayer Co Pubs.

Studies Honoring Ignatius Charles Brady O. F. M. Ed. by Romano S. Almagno & Conrad L. Harkins. (Theology Ser). 1976. 25.00 (ISBN 0-686-17960-9). Franciscan Inst.

Studies in a Folk-Play-Li-Ching-Chi. Wu Shou-Li. (Asian Folklore & Social Life Monograph: No. 7). (Chinese.). 1970. 14.00x (ISBN 0-89986-010-9). Oriental Bk Store.

Studies in a Hawaiian Community: Na Makamaka o Nanakuli. Ed. by Ronald Gallimore & Alan Howard. LC 79-17014. (Bernice P. Bishop Museum, Pacific Anthropological Records: No. 1). pap. 38.50 (ISBN 0-317-28837-7, 2020786). Bks Demand UMI.

Studies in a Song Book - Pang Xie Duan Er. Taro Hatano. (Asian Folklore & Social Life Monograph: No. 9). (Japanese & Chinese.). 1970. 14.00x (ISBN 0-89986-012-5). Oriental Bk Store.

Studies in Abstract Families of Languages. Seymour Ginsberg et al. LC 52-42839. (Memoirs: No. 87). 51p. 1983. pap. 11.00 (ISBN 0-8218-1287-4, MEMO-87). Am Math.

Studies in Abstract Phonology. Edmund Gussmann. (Linguistic Inquiry Monographs). 176p. (Orig.). 1981. pap. text ed. 15.95x (ISBN 0-262-57057-2). MIT Pr.

Studies in Accounting Theory. 1985. 4.50 (ISBN 0-471-63952-4). Wiley.

Studies in Acts, Vol. II. Frances Easter. (Bible Study Ser.). 1986. pap. 3.50 (ISBN 0-8309-0442-5). Herald Hse.

Studies in Acts, Vol. II. Wallace Wartick. (Bible Student Study Guides Ser). 1978. pap. 3.95 (ISBN 0-89900-154-8). College Pr Pub.

Studies in Acts, Vol. I. Wallace Wartick. (Bible Student Study Guides Ser). 1977. pap. 3.95 (ISBN 0-89900-153-X). College Pr Pub.

Studies in Ada Style. 2nd ed. Peter Hibbard et al. (Illus.). 111p. 1983. pap. 17.50 (ISBN 0-387-90816-1). Springer-Verlag.

Studies in Adaptation: The Behavior of Higher Crustacea. Ed. by Steve Rebach & David W. Dunham. LC 82-13501. 282p. 1983. text ed. 53.00x (ISBN 0-471-89823-6, Pub. by Wiley Interscience). Wiley.

Studies in Administration & Finance, 1558-1825: With Special Reference to the History of Salt Taxation in England. Edward Hughes. LC 79-12656. 1980. Repr. of 1934 ed. lib. bdg. 45.00x (ISBN 0-87991-856-X). Porcupine Pr.

Studies in Administrative Theory. Robert L. Hefner. Ed. by Edward H. Seifert. 466p. 1980. pap. text ed. 19.95x (ISBN 0-89641-046-3). American Pr.

Studies in Adult Education 1969, Vol. 1, No's. 1-2. Ed. by T. Kelly. LC 73-110939. (Illus.). 1970. 19.95x (ISBN 0-678-05687-0). Kelley.

Studies in African Administration: Collected Essays. A. H. Kirk-Greene. 1986. 35.00x (ISBN 0-7146-3134-5, BHA-03134, F Cass Co). Biblio Dist.

Studies in African Music, 2 Vols. A. M. Jones. 1959. Set. 52.00x (ISBN 0-19-713512-9). Oxford U Pr.

Studies in Alchemy. St. Germain. LC 77-75411. (Alchemy Ser.). (Illus.). 116p. 1974. pap. 3.95 (ISBN 0-916766-00-4). Summit Univ.

Studies in Algebra & Number Theory. Ed. by Gian-Carlo Rota. LC 79-4638. (Advances in Mathematics Supplementary Studies: Vol. 6). 1979. 83.00 (ISBN 0-12-599153-3). Acad Pr.

Studies in Algebraic Geometry. Ed. by Abraham Seidenberg. LC 80-81041. (MAA Studies in Mathematics: No. 20). 1980. 18.50 (ISBN 0-88385-120-2). Math Assn.

Studies in Algebraic Logic. Ed. by Aubert Daigneauit. LC 74-84580. (Studies in Mathematics: No. 9). 1974. 20.50 (ISBN 0-88385-109-1). Math Assn.

Studies in Algebraic Topology. Ed. by Gian-Carlo Rota. (Advances in Mathematics Supplementary Studies: Vol. 5). 1979. 77.00 (ISBN 0-12-599152-5). Acad Pr.

Studies in American Church History, 25 vols. Catholic University of America Staff. Repr. of 1942 ed. 662.50 (ISBN 0-404-57750-4). AMS Pr.

Studies in American Historical Demography. Ed. by Maris A. Vinovskis. LC 78-25611. (Studies in Population Ser.). 1979. Repr. 29.50 (ISBN 0-12-722050-X). Acad Pr.

Studies in American Indian Languages. Jesse Sawyer. 1974. 36.50x (ISBN 0-520-02525-3). U of Cal Pr.

Studies in American Indian Literature: Critical Essays & Course Designs. Ed. by Paula G. Allen. LC 82-12516. (MLA Commission on the Literatures & Languages of America Ser.). 385p. 1983. 35.00x (ISBN 0-87352-354-7); pap. 18.00x (ISBN 0-87352-355-5). Modern Lang.

Studies in American Jewish History. Jacob R. Marcus. 1969. 15.00x (ISBN 0-87820-003-7, Pub. by Hebrew Union). Ktav.

Studies in American Jewish Literature: Isaac Bashevis Singer, 3 Vols. Ed. by Daniel Walden. Incl. Vol. 1. A Mosaic of Jewish Writers; Vol. 3. Jewish Women Writers & Women in Jewish Literature; Vol. 2. From Marginality to Mainstream: A Mosaic of Jewish Writers; Vol. 4. World of Chaim Potok. 1982. 12.95 ea. (ISBN 0-686-97287-2). State U NY Pr.

Studies in American Literature. Ed. by Waldo F. McNeir & Leo B. Levy. (Essay Index Reprint Ser.). Repr. of 1960 ed. 13.75 (ISBN 0-518-10152-5). Ayer Co Pubs.

Studies in American Literature. Charles Noble. 1973. Repr. of 1898 ed. 20.00 (ISBN 0-8274-1164-2). R West.

Studies in American Literature: Creative Scepticism in Emerson & Henry James. Margaret W. Marshall. LC 74-32433. 1960. Repr. lib. bdg. 15.50 (ISBN 0-8414-5988-6). Folcroft.

Studies in American Political Development, Vol. 2. Ed. by Karen Orren & Stephen Skowronek. (Illus.). 352p. 1988. pap. text ed. 40.00 (ISBN 0-300-04055-5); pap. text ed. 15.95x (ISBN 0-300-04056-3). Yale U Pr.

Studies in American Trade Unionism. Jacob H. Hollander & George E. Barnett. LC 73-89739. (American Labor, from Conspiracy to Collective Bargaining Ser., No. 1). 380p. 1969. Repr. of 1906 ed. 22.00 (ISBN 0-405-02128-3). Ayer Co Pubs.

Studies in American Trade Unionism. Ed. by Jacob H. Hollander & George E. Barnett. LC 77-120106. 1970. Repr. of 1912 ed. 39.50x (ISBN 0-678-00677-6). Kelley.

Studies in Analysis. Ed. by Gian-Carlo Rota. (Advances in Mathematics Supplementary Studies Ser.: Vol. 4). 1979. 83.00 (ISBN 0-12-599150-9). Acad Pr.

Studies in Analytical Geochemistry. Ed. by Denis M. Shaw. LC 64-6495. (Royal Society of Canada, Special Publications: No. 6). pap. 37.80 (ISBN 0-317-28231-X, 2014408). Bks Demand UMI.

Studies in Analytical Psychology. Gerhard Adler. LC 67-10652. (Illus.). 1967. 10.00x (ISBN 0-913430-14-5). C G Jung Foun.

Studies in Ancient American & European Art: The Collected Essays of George Kubler. George Kubler. Ed. by Thomas F. Reese. LC 84-13216. (Yale Publications in the History of Art Ser.: 30). (Illus.). 600p. 1985. text ed. 67.00t (ISBN 0-300-02662-5). Yale U Pr.

Studies in Ancient Greek Society: The Prehistoric Aegean. George Thomson. 1966. pap. 2.95 (ISBN 0-8065-0047-6, Pub. by Citadel Pr). Lyle Stuart.

Studies in Ancient Greek Topography, Pt. V. W. Kendrick Pritchett. (UC Publications in Classical Studies: Vol. 31). 1986. pap. 38.50x (ISBN 0-520-09698-3). U of Cal Pr.

Studies in Ancient Greek Topography: Battlefields, Part 2. William K. Pritchett. LC 65-65210. (University of California Publications: Classical Studies Ser.: Vol. 4). pap. 73.00 (ISBN 0-317-29555-1, 2021261). Bks Demand UMI.

Studies in Ancient Greek Topography: Part III (Roads) W. Kendrick Pritchett. (UC Publications in Classical Studies: Vol. 22). 436p. 1981. pap. 32.50x (ISBN 0-520-09635-5). U of Cal Pr.

Studies in Ancient Greek Topography: Pt IV (Passes) Kendrick W. Pritchett. LC 65-65210. (Publications in Classical Studies: Vol. 28). 374p. 1983. pap. text ed. 34.00x (ISBN 0-520-09660-6). U of Cal Pr.

Studies in Ancient Indian History: (D. C. Sircar Commemoration Volume) Ed. by K. K. Dasgupta et al. 1988. 110.00x (ISBN 81-85067-10-4, Pub. by Sundeep). South Asia Bks.

Studies in Ancient Israelite Wisdom. James L. Crenshaw. 1974. 59.50x (ISBN 0-87068-255-5). Ktav.

Studies in Anglo-French History During the Eighteenth, Nineteenth & Twentieth Centuries. facs. ed. Ed. by Alfred Coville et al. LC 67-23197. (Essay Index Reprint Ser). 1935. 17.00 (ISBN 0-8369-0343-9). Ayer Co Pubs.

Studies in Anglo-Scandinavian Literary Relations. H. G. Wright. LC 72-10784. 1973. Repr. of 1919 ed. lib. bdg. 35.55 (ISBN 0-8414-0716-9). Folcroft.

Studies in Animal & Human Behaviour, 2 vols. Konrad Lorenz. LC 75-11087. 390p. Vol. 2. 1971. 27.00x (ISBN 0-674-84631-1). Harvard U Pr.

Studies in Antarctic Meteorology. Ed. by M. J. Rubin. LC 66-6578. (Antarctic Research Ser.: Vol. 9). (Illus.). 231p. 1966. 18.00 (ISBN 0-87590-109-3). Am Geophysical.

Studies in Applied Mathematics. Ed. by A. H. Taub. LC 74-168565. (MAA Studies: No. 7). 217p. 1971. 21.00 (ISBN 0-88385-107-5). Math Assn.

Studies in Applied Mathematics: Volume Dedicated to Irving Segal. Ed. by Victor Guillemin. (Advances in Mathematics: Supplementary Studies: Vol. 8). 1983. 49.50 (ISBN 0-12-305480-X). Acad Pr.

Studies in Applied Probability & Management Science. Ed. by Kenneth J. Arrow et al. 1962. 27.50x (ISBN 0-8047-0099-0). Stanford U Pr.

Studies in Approximation & Analysis. vi, 195p. 1966. text ed. 18.00 (ISBN 0-89871-156-8). Soc Indus-Appl Math.

Studies in Arabic Linguistics. David Abdo. (Arabic.). 1973. 15.00x (ISBN 0-86685-053-8). Intl Bk Ctr.

Studies in Arabic Literary Papyri: Language & Literature, Vol. 3. Nabia Abbott. LC 56-5027. (Oriental Institute Pubns. Ser: No. 77). (Illus.). xvi, 216p. 1974. lib. bdg. 40.00x (ISBN 0-226-62178-2). U of Chicago Pr.

Studies in Arabic Philology. As-Sayyid Bakr. (Arabic.). 1969. 15.00x (ISBN 0-86685-055-4). Intl Bk Ctr.

Studies in Arabic Versions of Greek Texts & in Mediaeval Science. Shlomo Pines. (Collected Works of Shlomo Pines: Vol. 2). ix, 468p. 1986. 52.25 (ISBN 965-223-626-8, Pub. by E J Brill). Heinman.

Studies in Arcady & Other Essays for a Country Parsonage. Richard L. Gales. LC 70-107701. (Essay Index Reprint Ser.: No. 1). 1910. 24.50 (ISBN 0-8369-1502-X). Ayer Co Pubs.

Studies in Arcady & Other Essays from a Country Parsonage. Richard L. Gales. LC 70-107701. (Essay Index Reprint Ser.: No. 2). 1912. 25.50 (ISBN 0-8369-1589-5). Ayer Co Pubs.

Studies in Aristotle. Ed. by Dominic J. O'Meara. (Studies in Philosophy & the History of Philosophy: Vol. 9). 313p. 1981. 26.95x (ISBN 0-8132-0559-X). Cath U Pr.

Studies in Art, Architecture & Design: Victorian & After. Nikolaus Pevsner. LC 81-48077. (Illus.). 288p. (Orig.). 1982. 55.50x (ISBN 0-691-03998-4); pap. 19.50x (ISBN 0-691-00345-9). Princeton U Pr.

Studies in Art Education: Vols. 1-16, Washington, D. C., 1959-1974-75. 440.00 (ISBN 0-8115-3864-8); pap. 368.00 (ISBN 0-8115-3865-6). Kraus Repr.

Studies in Art History I: Studies in Italian Art & Architecture. Henry A. Millon. (Fifteenth-Eighteenth Centuries Ser.). 344p. 1980. 56.00x (ISBN 0-271-00457-6). Pa St U Pr.

Studies in Art History I. Studies in Italian Art & Architecture 15th Through 18th Centuries. (Memoirs: No. 35). (Illus.). 344p. 1980. 49.00 (ISBN 0-318-12335-5). Am Acad Rome.

Studies in Arthur Schnitzler. Ed. by Herbert W. Reichert & Herman Salinger. LC 63-62703. (North Carolina. University. Studies in the Germanic Languages & Literatures: No. 42). Repr. of 1963 ed. 27.00 (ISBN 0-404-50942-8). AMS Pr.

Studies in Asian Social Development, No. 2. S. N. Navalakha. 1974. 15.00 (ISBN 0-686-20310-0). Intl Bk Dist.

Studies in Athenian Architecture, Sculpture & Topography. American School of Classical Studies, at Athens Staff. LC 81-14994. (Hesperia Ser.: Suppl. 20). 1982. 15.00x (ISBN 0-87661-520-5). Am Sch Athens.

Studies in Athenian Politics & Genealogy. Peter J. Bicknell. 120p. (Orig.). 1972. pap. text ed. 24.00x (ISBN 3-515-00268-5, Pub by Franz Steiner). Coronet Bks.

Studies in Atmospheric Electricity. V. P. Kolokolov. 142p. 1974. text ed. 33.00x (ISBN 0-7065-1446-7, Pub. by Keter Pub Jerusalem). Coronet Bks.

Studies in Attic Epigraphy, History & Topography. American School of Classical Studies, at Athens Staff. LC 81-26460. (Hesperia Ser.: Suppl. 19). 1982. 15.00x (ISBN 0-87661-519-1). Am Sch Athens.

Studies in Attribution: Middleton & Shakespeare. MacDonald P. Jackson. Ed. by James Hogg. (Jacobean Drama Studies). 228p. (Orig.). 1979. pap. 15.00 (ISBN 3-7052-0370-3, Salzburg Studies). Longwood Pub Group.

Studies in Aulua Gellius. Barry Baldwin. 130p. 1975. 6.50x (ISBN 0-87291-071-7). Coronado Pr.

Studies in Australian Totemism. Adolphus P. Elkin. LC 76-44712. Repr. of 1933 ed. 31.50 (ISBN 0-404-15857-9). AMS Pr.

Studies in Austrian Capital Theory, Investment & Time. Ed. by M. Faber. (Lectures Notes in Economics & Mathematical Systems: Vol. 277). vi, 317p. 1986. pap. 30.30 (ISBN 0-387-16804-4). Springer-Verlag.

Studies in Austronesian Linguistics. Richard McGinn. (CIS Southeast Asia Ser.: No. 76). 650p. 1986. pap. text ed. 18.50x (ISBN 0-89680-137-3, Ohio U Ctr Intl). Ohio U Pr.

Studies in Autobiography. Ed. by James Olney. (Illus.). 256p. 1988. 24.95 (ISBN 0-19-505131-9). Oxford U Pr.

Studies in Automatic Programming Logic. Z. Manna et al. (Artificial Intelligence Ser.: Vol. 4). 192p. 1977. 40.75 (ISBN 0-444-00224-3, North Holland); pap. text ed. 23.25 (ISBN 0-444-00225-1). Elsevier.

Studies in Babi & Baha'i History, Vol. 1. Ed. by Moojan Momen. (Illus.). 1983. text ed. 19.95 (ISBN 0-933770-16-2). Kalimat.

Studies in Babi & Baha'i History: Covenant & Crisis, Vol. 7. Richard V. Hollinger. (Illus.). Date not set. 19.95 (ISBN 0-933770-43-X). Kalimat.

Studies in Babi & Baha'i History: Vol. 2: From Iran East & West. Ed. by Juan R. Cole & Moojan Momen. (Illus.). 205p. 1984. 19.95 (ISBN 0-933770-40-5). Kalimat.

Studies in Babi & Baha'i History Volume 3: In Iran. Ed. & intro. by Peter Smith. (Illus.). 1986. 19.95 (ISBN 0-933770-46-4). Kalimat.

Studies in Babi & Baha'i History, Vol. 4: Music, Devotions, & Mashriq'l-Adkhar. R. Jackson Armstrong-Ingram. (Illus.). 1988. 22.50 (ISBN 0-933770-62-6). Kalimat.

Studies in Babi & Baha'i History, Vol. 5: A Survey of Sources for Early Babi History & Doctrine. Denis MacEoin. 1988. 22.50 (ISBN 0-933770-63-4). Kalimat.

Studies in Babi & Baha'i History, Vol. 6: Baha'is in the West. Ed. by Peter Smith. 1988. 22.50 (ISBN 0-933770-64-2). Kalimat.

Studies in Banking Theory, Financial Theory & Vertical Control. Meyer Burstein. LC 87-30406. 1988. 45.00 (ISBN 0-312-01576-3). St Martin.

Studies in Bayesian Econometrics & Statistics. S. Fienberg. LC 73-86697. (Contributions to Economic Analysis: Vol. 86). 677p. 1975. 116.00 (ISBN 0-444-10579-4, North-Holland). Elsevier.

Studies in Beaumont, Fletcher & Massinger. Baldwin Maxwell. 1966. lib. bdg. 18.50x (ISBN 0-374-95396-1, Octagon). Hippocrene Bks.

Studies in Biblical & Jewish Folklore. Raphael Patai et al. LC 72-6871. (Studies in Comparitive Literature: No. 35). 1972. Repr. of 1960 ed. lib. bdg. 49.95x (ISBN 0-8383-1665-4). Haskell.

Studies in Biblical & Semitic Symbolism. Maurice H. Fairbridge. 1977. lib. bdg. 59.95 (ISBN 0-8490-2700-4). Gordon Pr.

Studies in Biblical Holiness. Donald Metz. 290p. 1971. 10.95 (ISBN 0-8341-0117-3). Beacon Hill.

Studies in Bibliography, Vol. XL. Ed. by Fredson Bowers. (Bibliographic Society of the University of Virginia Ser.). 265p. 1987. text ed. 30.00x (ISBN 0-8139-1133-8). U Pr of VA.

Studies in Bibliography, Vol. XLI. Ed. by Fredson Bowers. (Bibliographic Society of the University of Virginia Ser.). 325p. 1988. text ed. 30.00x (ISBN 0-8139-1175-3). U Pr of VA.

Studies in Bibliography, Vol. 32. Ed. by Fredson Bowers. LC 49-3353. (Illus.). 285p. 1979. 30.00x (ISBN 0-8139-0817-5). U Pr of Va.

Studies in Bibliography, Vol. 33. Ed. by Fredson Bowers. LC 49-3353. 282p. 1980. 30.00x (ISBN 0-8139-0860-4). U Pr of Va.

Studies in Bibliography, Vol. 34. Ed. by Fredson Bowers. LC 49-3353. 276p. 1981. 30.00x (ISBN 0-8139-0898-1). U Pr of Va.

Studies in Bibliography, Vol. 35. Ed. by Fredson Bowers. LC 49-3353. 338p. 1982. 30.00x (ISBN 0-8139-0948-1). U Pr of Va.

Studies in Bibliography, Vo.36. Fredson Bowers. LC 49-3353. 271p. 1983. text ed. 30.00x (ISBN 0-8139-0987-2). U Pr of Va.

Studies in Bibliography, Vol. 37. Ed. by Fredson Bowers. 312p. 1984. text ed. 30.00x (ISBN 0-8139-1029-3). U Pr of Va.

Studies in Bibliography, Vol. 38. Ed. by Fredson Bowers. 380p. 1985. text ed. 30.00x (ISBN 0-8139-1065-X). U Pr of Va.

Studies in Bibliography, Vol. 39. Ed. by Fredson Bowers. (Bibliographic Society of the University of Virginia Ser.). 375p. 1986. text ed. 30.00x (ISBN 0-8139-1095-1). U Pr of VA.

Studies in Bibliography: Papers of the Bibliographical Society of the University of Virginia, Vols. 1-31. Ed. by Fredson Bowers & L. A. Beaurline. Incl. Vol. 1. 1948-49. 204p (ISBN 0-8139-0032-8); Vol. 2. 1949-50. 211p (ISBN 0-8139-0033-6); Vol. 3. 1950-51. 306p (ISBN 0-8139-0034-4); Vol. 4. 1951-52. 237p (ISBN 0-8139-0035-2); Vol. 5. 1952-53. 230p (ISBN 0-8139-0036-0); Vol. 6. 1953-54. 288p (ISBN 0-8139-0037-9); Vol. 7. 1955. 240p (ISBN 0-8139-0038-7); Vol. 8. 1956. 272p (ISBN 0-8139-0039-5); Vol. 9. 1957. 268p (ISBN 0-8139-0040-9); Vol. 10. 1957. 192p; Vol. 11. 1958. 295p (ISBN 0-8139-0042-5); Vol. 12. 1959. 259p (ISBN 0-8139-0043-3); Vol. 13. 1960 (ISBN 0-8139-0044-1); Vol. 14. 1961. 290p (ISBN 0-8139-0045-X); Vol. 15. 1962. 311p (ISBN 0-8139-0046-8); Vol. 16. 1963. 276p (ISBN 0-8139-0047-6); Vol. 17. 1964. 258p (ISBN 0-8139-0048-4); Vol. 18. 1965. 312p (ISBN 0-8139-0049-2); Vol. 19. 1966. 282p (ISBN 0-8139-0050-6); Vol. 20. 1967. 298p (ISBN 0-8139-0051-4); Vol. 21. 1968. 290p (ISBN 0-8139-0052-2); Vol. 22. 1969. 341p (ISBN 0-8139-0053-0); Vol. 23. 1970. 280p (ISBN 0-8139-0309-2); Vol. 24. 1971. 240p (ISBN 0-8139-0331-9); Vol. 25. 1972. (ISBN 0-8139-0404-8); Vol. 26. 1973. (ISBN 0-8139-0468-4); Vol. 27. 1974. (ISBN 0-8139-0580-X); Vol. 28. 1975 (ISBN 0-8139-0636-9). Vol. 29 1976. (ISBN 0-8139-0687-3); Vol. 30 1977. (ISBN 0-8139-0717-9); Vol. 31. 1977. (ISBN 0-8139-0777-2). LC 49-3353. 30.00x ea. U Pr of Va.

Studies in Biography. Ed. by Daniel Aaron. (Harvard English Studies: No. 8). 200p. 1978. text ed. 16.00x (ISBN 0-674-84651-6); pap. text ed. 5.95x (ISBN 0-674-84652-4). Harvard U Pr.

Studies in Biography: Mr. Disraeli & Edward Gibbon. Spencer Walpole. 1979. Repr. of 1907 ed. lib. bdg. 30.00 (ISBN 0-8492-2988-X). R West.

Studies in Biological Control. Ed. by Vittorio L. Delucchi. LC 75-16867. (International Biological Programme Ser.: No. 9). pap. 80.00 (ISBN 0-317-29377-X, 2024479). Bks Demand UMI.

Studies in Black & White. Jerome Bruce. 18.75 (ISBN 0-8369-9160-5, 9035). Ayer Co Pubs.

Studies in British Imperial History: Essays in Honor of A. P. Thornton. Ed. by Gordon Martel. LC 85-8110. 256p. 1985. 25.00 (ISBN 0-312-77080-4). St Martin.

Studies in British Politics. 3rd. ed. Ed. by Richard Rose. LC 76-11279. 1977. 27.50x (ISBN 0-312-77070-7). St Martin.

Studies in Brown Humanity Being Scrawls & Smudges in Sepia, White & Yellow. Hugh C. Clifford. text ed. 16.00 (ISBN 0-8369-9240-7, 9094). Ayer Co Pubs.

Studies in Browning. Josiah Flew. LC 74-115859. (Studies in Browning, No. 4). 1970. Repr. of 1904 ed. lib. bdg. 44.95x (ISBN 0-8383-1071-0). Haskell.

Studies in Browning. Josiah Flew. 1979. Repr. lib. bdg. 22.50 (ISBN 0-8492-4608-3). R West.

Studies in Buddhism & Sikhism. Harcharan S. Sobti. 1986. 14.00 (ISBN 0-317-69974-1). Orient Bk Dist.

Studies in Buddhist Art of South Asia. A. K. Narain. (Illus.). 140p. 1986. 48.00X (ISBN 0-8364-1852-2, Pub. by Usha). South Asia Bks.

Studies in Buddhist Art of South Asia. Ed. by A. K. Narain. (Illus.). vi, 139p. 1985. 31.50 (ISBN 0-318-23246-4, Pub. by Kanak Pubns). Nataraj Bks.

Studies in Buddhist Iconography. Dipak C. Bhattacharya. 1978. 22.50x (ISBN 0-8364-0016-X). South Asia Bks.

Studies in Business-Cycle Theory. Robert E. Lucas, Jr. 312p. 1981. pap. 10.95x (ISBN 0-262-62044-8). MIT Pr.

Studies in Byzantine History & Modern Greek Folklore, Vol. I. Constantine N. Tsirpanlis. 180p. 1980. pap. 11.95 (ISBN 0-317-36319-0). EO Pr.

Studies in Byzantine Sigillography. Ed. by Nicolas Oikonomides. LC 87-22266. 128p. 1988. 18.00X (ISBN 0-88402-171-8). Dumbarton Oaks.

Studies in Capital Formation in the United Kingdom, 1750-1920. Ed. by Charles H. Feinstein & Sidney Pollard. 512p. 1988. 89.00 (ISBN 0-19-828408-X). Oxford U Pr.

Studies in Caribbean Spanish Dialectology. Intros. by Robert M. Hammond & Melvyn C. Resnick. 256p. 1988. pap. 12.95 (ISBN 0-87840-098-2). Georgetown U Pr.

Studies in Cassius Dio & Herodian. H. A. Andersen & E. Hohl. LC 75-7342. (Roman History Ser.). (Illus., Ger.). 1975. Repr. of 1975 ed. 17.00x (ISBN 0-405-07063-2). Ayer Co Pubs.

Studies in Castles & Castle-Building. A. J. Taylor. (Illus.). 350p. 1986. 45.00 (ISBN 0-907628-51-6). Hambledon Press.

Studies in Cephaloziellaceae. R. M. Schuster. (Illus.). 1977. 24.00x (ISBN 3-7682-0823-0). Lubrecht & Cramer.

Studies in Ch'an & Hua-Yen. Ed. by Robert M. Gimello & Peter N. Gregory. (Studies in East Asian Buddhism: No. 1). 406p. 1983. pap. text ed. 14.95x (ISBN 0-8248-0835-5). UH Pr.

Studies in Character Analysis. Manly P. Hall. pap. 3.95 (ISBN 0-89314-804-0). Philos Res.

Studies in Chaucer's House of Fame. Wilbur O. Sypherd. LC 65-26459. (Studies in Chaucer, No. 6). 1969. Repr. of 1907 ed. lib. bdg. 44.95x (ISBN 0-8383-0631-4). Haskell.

Studies in Child Development. Arnold L. Gesell. LC 76-138114. (Illus.). 224p. 1972. Repr. of 1948 ed. lib. bdg. 35.00x (ISBN 0-8371-5690-4, GECD). Greenwood.

Studies in Child Guidance. Jean W. Macfarlane. (SRCD M Ser.). 1938. 23.00 (ISBN 0-527-01506-7). Kraus Repr.

Studies in Child Language & Multilingualism. Ed. by Virginia Teller & Sheila J. White. LC 80-16810. (Annals of the New York Academy of Sciences: Vol. 345). 187p. 1980. 30.00x (ISBN 0-89766-078-1); pap. 30.00x (ISBN 0-89766-079-X). NY Acad Sci.

Studies in Child Psychoanalysis: Pure & Applied. Frwd. by Anna Freud. LC 74-20082. (Illus.). 250p. 1975. 27.50x (ISBN 0-300-01817-7). Yale U Pr.

Studies in Childhood. James Sully. LC 77-72191. (Contributions to the History of Psycholgy Ser.: Psychometrics & Educational Psychology). 486p. 1978. Repr. of 1978 ed. 30.00 (ISBN 0-89093-162-3). U Pubns Amer.

Studies in Chinese & Islamic Art, 2 vols. Basil Gray. 670p. 1986. 1330.00x (ISBN 0-317-69118-X, Pub. by Han-Shan Tang Ltd). State Mutual Bk.

Studies in Chinese Archaeology. Cheng Te-k'un. (Illus.). 160p. 1982. 35.00x (ISBN 0-295-95912-6, Pub. by Chinese Univ Hong Kong). U of Wash Pr.

Studies in Chinese Archaeology. Te-k'un Cheng. 160p. 1987. 189.00x (Pub. by Han-Shan Tang Ltd). State Mutual Bk.

Studies in Chinese Art. Te-k'un Cheng. LC 83-50019. (Illus.). 350p. 1983. 39.50x (ISBN 0-295-96053-1). U of Wash Pr.

Studies in Chinese Art. J. Hackin. lib. bdg. 79.95 (ISBN 0-87968-522-0). Krishna Pr.

Studies in Chinese Art. Cheng Te'k'un. (Illus.). 272p. 1983. 286.00x (ISBN 0-317-69215-1, Pub. by Han-Shan Tang Ltd). State Mutual Bk.

Studies in Chinese Art & Some Indian Influences. J. Hackin. 1976. lib. bdg. 59.95 (ISBN 0-8490-2701-2). Gordon Pr.

Studies in Chinese Art & Some Indian Influences. J. Hackin. 64p. 1938. 350.00x (ISBN 0-317-69116-3, Pub. by Han-Shan Tang Ltd). State Mutual Bk.

Studies in Chinese Diplomatic History. Ching-Lin Hsia. LC 75-32333. 226p. 1977. Repr. of 1925 ed. 17.00 (ISBN 0-89093-088-0). U Pubns Amer.

Studies in Chinese Institutional History. Yang Lieu-Shengyang. LC 61-8844. (Harvard-Yenching Institute Studies: No. 20). 1961. pap. 6.95x (ISBN 0-674-84660-5). Harvard U Pr.

Studies in Chinese Literary Genres. Ed. & intro. by Cyril Birch. LC 77-157825. 1975. 32.00x (ISBN 0-520-02037-5). U of Cal Pr.

Studies in Chinese Literature. John L. Bishop. 245p. 1965. pap. 175.00x (Pub. by Han-Shan Tang Ltd). State Mutual Bk.

Studies in Chinese Literature. Ed. by John L. Bishop. LC 65-13836. (Harvard-Yenching Institute Studies: No. 21). (Orig.). 1965. pap. 8.50x (ISBN 0-674-84705-9). Harvard U Pr.

Studies in Chinese Price History. Endymion P. Wilkinson. LC 78-24799. (Modern Chinese Economy Ser.). 285p. 1980. lib. bdg. 37.00 (ISBN 0-8240-4257-3). Garland Pub.

Studies in Chinese Proverbs. Chu Chien-Fan. (Asian Folklore & Social Life Monograph: No. 5). (Chinese.). 1972. 14.00x (ISBN 0-89986-008-7). Oriental Bk Store.

Studies in Chinese Society. Ed. by Arthur P. Wolf. LC 78-62272. 1978. 10.95x (ISBN 0-8047-1006-6). Stanford U Pr.

Studies in Chinese Thought. Arthur F. Wright. 317p. 1953. pap. 250.00x (Pub. by Han-Shan Tang Ltd). State Mutual Bk.

Studies in "Christ & Satan". Charles Sleeth. (McMaster Old English Studies & Texts). 160p. 1981. 27.50x (ISBN 0-8020-5484-6). U of Toronto Pr.

Studies in Christian Antiquity. Richard Hanson. 376p. 1986. 42.95 (ISBN 0-567-09363-8, Pub. by T & T Clark Ltd UK). Fortress.

Studies in Christian Doctrine, 4 Vols. G. P. Pardington. Rev. by H. M. Freligh & E. H. Schroeder. 312p. 1964. pap. 2.25 ea. Vol. 1 (ISBN 0-87509-135-0). Vol. 2 (ISBN 0-87509-136-9). Vol. 3 (ISBN 0-87509-137-7). Vol. 4 (ISBN 0-87509-138-5). Chr Pubns.

Studies in Christian Enthusiasm. Geoffrey F. Nuttall. 1948. pap. 2.50x (ISBN 0-87574-041-3, 041). Pendle Hill.

Studies in Christian Mysticism. W. H. Dyson. 1977. lib. bdg. 69.95 (ISBN 0-8490-2702-0). Gordon Pr.

Studies in Christianity. Borden P. Bowne. LC 75-3074. Repr. of 1909 ed. 28.50 (ISBN 0-404-59075-6). AMS Pr.

Studies in Church History. Henry C. Lea. LC 83-48780. 1988. Repr. of 1883 ed. 57.50 (ISBN 0-404-19154-1). AMS Pr.

Studies in Chuvash Etymology I. Ed. by A. Rona-Tas. (Studia Oralo-Altaica Ser.: No. 17). 240p. 1982. 30.00x (ISBN 0-686-36268-3). Benjamins North Am.

Studies in Cistercian Art & Architecture, I. Ed. by Meredith Lillich et al. (Cistercian Studies: No. 66). (Illus., Orig.). 1982. pap. 12.95 (ISBN 0-87907-866-9). Cistercian Pubns.

Studies in Cistercian Art & Architecture, II. Ed. by Meredith P. Lillich. (Cistercian Studies: No. 69). (Illus.). pap. 14.95 (ISBN 0-87907-869-3). Cistercian Pubns.

Studies in Cistercian Art & Architecture, III. Ed. by Meredith P. Lillich. (Cistercian Studies: No. 89). (Orig.). 1987. 49.95 (ISBN 0-87907-789-1); pap. 22.95. Cistercian Pubns.

Studies in Cistercian Medieval History: Presented to Jeremiah F. O'Sullivan. Ed. by J. F. O'Callahan. LC 77-152486. (Cistercian Studies: No. 13). 1971. 7.95 (ISBN 0-87907-813-8). Cistercian Pubns.

Studies in Civilization. Pennsylvania University Bicentennial Conference. Ed. by Alan Wace & Otto Neugebauer. LC 68-26197. Repr. of 1941 ed. 22.50x (ISBN 0-8046-0353-7, Pub. by Kennikat). Assoc Faculty Pr.

Studies in Classic American Literature. D. H. Lawrence. 1977. pap. 5.95 (ISBN 0-14-003300-9). Penguin.

Studies in Classical & Byzantine Manuscript Illumination. Kurt Weitzmann. Ed. by Herbert L. Kessler. LC 76-117623. (Illus.). 1971. 30.00x (ISBN 0-226-89246-8). U of Chicago Pr.

Studies in Classical Chinese Thought. Ed. by Henry Rosemont & Benjamin Schwartz. (AAR Thematic Studies). pap. 8.95 (ISBN 0-89130-677-3, 01-24-73). Scholars Pr GA.

Studies in Classics & Jewish Hellenism. Ed. by Richard Koebner. (Scripts Hierosolymitana Ser.: Vol. 1). pap. 39.00 (ISBN 0-317-28711-7, 2051594). Bks Demand UMI.

Studies in Clinical Psychology, Vol. 3. Ed. by Lee E. Travis. Bd. with Dynamic of Binocular Depth Perception. H. Werner. Repr. of 1937 ed; Plateaus & the Curve of Learning in Motor Skill. Dji-Lih Kao. Repr. of 1937 ed; Reminiscence & Rote Learning. L. B. Ward. Repr. of 1937 ed. (Psychology Monographs General & Applied: Vol. 49). pap. 36.00 (ISBN 0-8115-1448-X). Kraus Repr.

Studies in Cognitive Development: Essays in Honor of Jean Piaget. Ed. by David Elkind & John H. Flavell. 1969. pap. 12.95x (ISBN 0-19-500878-2). Oxford U Pr.

Studies in Colossiani. John Kackelman, Jr. 1986. pap. 5.50 (ISBN 0-89137-562-7). Quality Pubns.

Studies in Colossians & Philemon. H. C. Moule. LC 77-79185. (Kregel Popular Commentary Ser.). 196p. 1977. kivar 6.95 (ISBN 0-8254-3217-0). Kregel.

Studies in Colossians to Philemon. W. H. Thomas. LC 86-7178. 192p. 1986. pap. 6.95 (ISBN 0-8254-3834-9). Kregel.

Studies in Combinatorics. Ed. by Gian-Carlo Rota. LC 78-60730. (Studies in Mathematics: No. 17). 1978. 26.50 (ISBN 0-88385-117-2). Math Assn.

Studies in Communications: News & Knowledge, Vol. 3. Thelma McCormick. 1986. 52.50 (ISBN 0-89232-363-9). Jai Pr.

Studies in Comparative Aesthetics. Eliot Deutsch. LC 74-34028. (Society for Asian & Comparative Philosophy Monographs: No. 2). (Illus.). 112p. (Orig.). 1975. pap. text ed. 7.00x (ISBN 0-8248-0365-5). UH Pr.

Studies in Comparative Criminal Law. E. M. Wise & G. O. Mueller. (Illus.). 338p. 1975. 39.25 (ISBN 0-398-03168-1). C C Thomas.

Studies in Comparative Jurisprudence & the Conflict of Laws. George Merrill. xii, 247p. 1985. Repr. of 1886 ed. lib. bdg. 30.00x (ISBN 0-8377-0850-8). Rothman.

Studies in Comparative Jurisprudence & the Conflict of Laws. George Merrill. LC 33-33040. (Historical Reprints in Jurisprudence & Classical Legal Literature Ser.). xii, 247p. 1984. Repr. of 1886 ed. lib. bdg. 42.00 (ISBN 0-89941-340-4). W S Hein.

Studies in Comparative Semantics. Paul Canart. 1979. 19.95x (ISBN 0-312-77087-1). St Martin.

Studies in Compensatory Lengthening. Ed. by L. Wetzels & E. Sezer. (Publications in Language Sciences). viii, 353p. 1986. 49.00 (ISBN 90-6765-248-2); pap. 29.90 (ISBN 90-6765-247-4). Foris Pubns.

Studies in Complexity Theory. Ronald V. Book. Ed. by Ker-I Ko et al. 226p. 1986. pap. 22.95 (ISBN 0-470-20293-9). Halsted Pr.

Studies in Computer Science. Ed. by Seymour Pollack. LC 82-62390. (MAA Studies in Mathematics: No. 22). 408p. 1983. 30.00 (ISBN 0-88385-124-5). Math Assn.

Studies in Conservation of Natural Terrestrial Ecosystems in Japan, Part I: Vegetation & Its Conservation, Vol. 8. Ed. by M. Numata et al. (Japan International Biological Program Synthesis Ser.). 157p. 1975. pap. 22.50x (ISBN 0-86008-218-0, Pub. by U of Tokyo Japan). Columbia U Pr.

Studies in Conservation of Natural Terrestrial Ecosystems in Japan, Part II: Animal Communities, Vol. 9. Ed. by M. Numata et al. (Japan International Biological Program Synthesis Ser.). 91p. 1975. 15.00x (ISBN 0-86008-219-9, Pub. by U of Tokyo Japan). Columbia U Pr.

Studies in Constitutional Law: France-England-United States. 2nd ed. Emile Boutmy. Tr. by E. M. Dicey. xiv, 183p. 1982. Repr. of 1891 ed. lib. bdg. 22.50x (ISBN 0-8377-0332-8). Rothman.

Studies in Constructive Mathematics & Mathematical Logic. Ed. by A. O. Slisenko. LC 69-12507. (Seminars in Mathematics Ser.: Vol. 4, Pt. 1). pap. 24.00 (ISBN 0-317-08580-8, 2020696). Bks Demand UMI.

Studies in Contemporary Arabic Poetry & Criticism. Mounah Khouri. LC 86-82230. 150p. (Orig.). 1987. pap. 12.00 (ISBN 0-317-65709-7). Jahan Bk Co.

Studies in Contemporary Biography. facsimile ed. James B. Bryce. LC 77-156619. (Essay Index Reprint Ser). Repr. of 1903 ed. 25.50 (ISBN 0-8369-2271-9). Ayer Co Pubs.

Studies in Contemporary Jewry, Vol.I. Institute of Contemporary Jewry of The Hebrew University of Jerusalem. (Illus.). 608p. 1984. 22.50X (ISBN 0-253-39511-9). Ind U Pr.

Studies in Contemporary Jewry, Vol. II. Institute of Contemporary Jewry of the Hebrew University of Jerusalem. Ed. by Peter Y. Medding. 512p. 1986. 25.00x (ISBN 0-253-39512-7). Ind U Pr.

Studies in Contemporary Jewry, Vol. III: Jews & Other Ethnic Groups in a Multi-Ethnic World. Ed. by Ezra Mendelsohn. (Illus.). 360p. 1987. 29.95 (ISBN 0-19-504896-2). Oxford U Pr.

Studies in Contemporary Jewry: Vol.IV: The Jews & the European Crisis, 1914-1921. Ed. by Jonathan Frankel. 544p. 1987. 39.95 (ISBN 0-19-505113-0). Oxford U Pr.

Studies in Contemporary Music. Wilfrid H. Mellers. LC 74-24153. Repr. of 1947 ed. 17.50 (ISBN 0-404-13046-1). AMS Pr.

Studies in Contemporary Superstition. W. H. Mallock. 1973. Repr. of 1895 ed. 25.00 (ISBN 0-8274-1566-4). R West.

Studies in Contract Law. 3rd ed. Edward J. Murphy & Richard E. Speidel. LC 84-6083. (University Casebook Ser.). 1376p. 1984. 31.00 (ISBN 0-88277-177-9). Foundation Pr.

Studies in Convection: Theory Measurement & Applications, Vol. 2. Ed. by B. E. Launder. 1978. 61.00 (ISBN 0-12-438002-6). Acad Pr.

Studies in Country Malay. C. C. Brown. 259p. 1956. 35.00x (ISBN 0-317-39156-9, Pub. by Luzac & Co Ltd). State Mutual Bk.

Studies in Creation: A General Introduction to the Creation-Evolution Debate. John Klotz. 224p. (Orig.). 1985. pap. 9.95 (ISBN 0-570-03969-X, 12-3004). Concordia.

Studies in Creative Partnership: Federal Aid to Public Libraries During the New Deal. Ed. by Daniel F. Ring. LC 80-15762. 154p. 1980. 16.50 (ISBN 0-8108-1319-X). Scarecrow.

Studies in Crisis Behavior. Ed. by Michael Brecher. 384p. 1979. text ed. 39.95 (ISBN 0-87855-292-8). Transaction Bks.

Studies in Cromwell's Family Circle. Robert W. Ramsey. LC 76-118497. 1971. Repr. of 1930 ed. 22.50x (ISBN 0-8046-1245-5, Pub. by Kennikat). Assoc Faculty Pr.

Studies in Cross-Cultural Psychology, Vol. 2. Ed. by Neil Warren. LC 76-48386. (Serial Publication). 1981. 82.50 (ISBN 0-12-609202-8). Acad Pr.

Studies in Cryobiology. L. K. Lozina-Lozinski. 270p. 1974. text ed. 56.00x (ISBN 0-7065-1403-3, Pub. by Keter Pub Jerusalem). Coronet Bks.

Studies in Cultural Anthropology. Ed. by Frederick C. Gamst. (Rice University Studies: Vol. 61, No. 2). (Illus.). 161p. 1975. pap. 10.00x (ISBN 0-89263-224-0). Rice Univ.

Studies in Culture, Linguistics, & Speechology. Ed. by A. W. Entwistle. 1985. 22.50x (ISBN 0-8364-1257-5, Pub. by Swati Pub). South Asia Bks.

Studies in Currency Eighteen Ninety-Eight. Thomas H. Farrer. LC 67-19961. 1968. Repr. of 1898 ed. 45.00x (ISBN 0-678-00397-1). Kelley.

Studies in Cypriote Archaeology. Ed. by Jane C. Biers & David Soren. (Monograph xviii). 189p. 1981. pap. 15.00x (ISBN 0-917956-23-0). UCLA Arch.

Studies in Dante, First Series. E. Moore. LC 68-24955. (Studies in Dante, No. 9). 1969. Repr. of 1896 ed. lib. bdg. 39.95x (ISBN 0-8383-0217-3). Haskell.

Studies in Dante, Fourth Series: A Textual Criticism of the Convivo & Miscellaneous Essays. E. Moore. LC 68-29737. (Studies in Dante, No. 9). 1968. Repr. lib. bdg. 39.95x (ISBN 0-8383-0220-3). Haskell.

Studies in Dante, Second Series. E. Moore. LC 68-24956. (Studies in Dante, No. 9). 1969. Repr. of 1899 ed. lib. bdg. 49.95x (ISBN 0-8383-0218-1). Haskell.

Studies in Dante, Second Series: Miscellaneous Essays. Edward Moore. LC 68-57628. (Illus.). 1969. Repr. of 1899 ed. lib. bdg. 35.00 (ISBN 0-8371-0908-6, MOSD). Greenwood.

Studies in Dante, Third Series. E. Moore. LC 68-24957. (Studies in Dante, No. 9). (Illus.). 1969. Repr. of 1903 ed. lib. bdg. 39.95x (ISBN 0-8383-0219-X). Haskell.

Studies in Decision Making. Ed. by Martin Irle & Lawrence B. Katz. 917p. 1982. 92.50x (ISBN 3-11-008087-7). De Gruyter.

Studies in Demetrius on Style. D. M. Schenkeveld. 186p. 1964. lib. bdg. 48.50x (Pub. by A M Hakkert). Coronet Bks.

Studies in Dependency Syntax. Igor A. Melcuk. Ed. by Paul T. Roberge. Tr. by Lev Stern from Rus. (Linguistica Extranea: Studia 2). 172p. 1979. pap. 7.25 (ISBN 0-89720-001-2). Karoma.

Studies in Developmental Neurobiology: Essays in Honor of Viktor Hamburger. Ed. by W. Maxwell Cowan. (Illus.). 1981. text ed. 49.50x (ISBN 0-19-502927-5). Oxford U Pr.

Studies in Developmental Planning. Hollis B. Chenery. LC 70-143227. (Economic Studies: No. 136). 1971. 30.00x (ISBN 0-674-84725-3). Harvard U Pr.

Studies in Devorim (Deuteronomy) 1982. 12.95 (ISBN 0-686-76264-9). Feldheim.

Studies in Dharmasastra. Ed. by Richard W. Lariviere. 1984. 14.50x (ISBN 0-8364-1124-2, Pub. by Mukhopadhyay India). South Asia Bks.

Studies in Diachronic, Synchronic & Typological Linguistics: Festschrift for Oswald Szemerenyi on the Occasion of His 65th Birthday, 2 vols. Ed. by Bela Brogyanyi. (Current Issues in Linguistic Theory: No. 11). 1979. Set. 110.00 (ISBN 90-272-3504-X). Benjamins North Am.

Studies in Dickens. Mabel S. Smith. LC 72-3291. (Studies in Dickens, No. 52). 1972. Repr. of 1910 ed. lib. bdg. 49.95x (ISBN 0-8383-1499-6). Haskell.

Studies in Dickens. Mabel S. Smith. 1973. Repr. of 1910 ed. 25.00 (ISBN 0-8274-1263-0). R West.

Studies in Differential Equations. Harold T. Davis. Ed. by Walter Scott. LC 56-14277. (Northwestern University Series in Mathematical & Physical Sciences: No. 3). pap. 30.00 (ISBN 0-317-08636-7, 2006876). Bks Demand UMI.

Studies in Diplomatic History: Essays in Memory of David Bayne Horn. Ed. by R. Hatton & M. S. Anderson. LC 73-18965. xiv, 384p. 1970. 35.00 (ISBN 0-208-01039-4, Archon). Shoe String.

Studies in Discipleship. Charles P. Conn & Donald S. Aultman. LC 75-14887. 1975. pap. 1.99 (ISBN 0-87148-772-1). Pathway Pr.

Studies in Discourse Analysis. Ed. by Martin Montgomery & Malcolm Coulthard. 1981. pap. 15.95x (ISBN 0-7100-0510-5). Routledge Chapman & Hall.

Studies in Discourse Representation Theory & the Theory of Generalized Quantifiers. Ed. by J. Groenendyk & M. Stokhof. (Groningen-Amsterdam Studies in Semantics). 200p. 1986. write for info.; pap. write for info. Foris Pubns.

Studies in Disease Ecology see Studies in Medical Geography.

Studies in Divergent Series & Summability & the Asymptotic Development of Functions. Walter B. Ford. LC 60-16836. 371p. 1985. text ed. 19.50 (ISBN 0-8284-0143-8). Chelsea Pub.

Studies in Dogmatics: Theology. Gerrit C. Berkouwer. Incl. Vol. 1. Faith & Sanctification; Vol. 2. Providence of God. 11.95 (ISBN 0-8028-3029-3); Vol. 3. Faith & Justification; Vol. 4. Person of Christ; Vol. 5. General Revelation. 11.95 (ISBN 0-8028-3032-3); Vol. 6. Faith & Perseverance. 9.95 (ISBN 0-8028-3033-1); Vol. 7. Divine Election; Vol. 8. Man-The Image of God. 13.95 (ISBN 0-8028-3035-8); Vol. 9. Work of Christ. 10.95 (ISBN 0-8028-3036-6); Vol. 10. Sacraments; Vol. 11. Sin. 17.95 (ISBN 0-8028-3027-7); Vol. 12. Return of Christ; The Church; Holy Scripture. 12.95 (ISBN 0-8028-3394-2). 1952. Eerdmans.

Studies in Dryden's Dramatic Technique: The Use of Scenes Depicting Persuasion & Accusation. Richard L. Larson. Ed. by James Hogg. (Poetic Drama & Poetic Theory). 317p. (Orig.). 1975. pap. 15.00 (ISBN 3-7052-0833-0, Pub. by Salzburg Studies). Longwood Pub Group.

Studies in Dyadic Communication: Proceedings of a Research Conference on the Interview. Aron Wolfe Siegman & Benjamin Pope. 356p. 1972. text ed. 34.00 (ISBN 0-08-015867-6). Pergamon.

Studies in Earlier Old English Prose: Sixteen Original Contributions. Ed. by Paul E. Szarmach. LC 84-8849. 420p. 1985. 49.50x (ISBN 0-87395-947-7); pap. 19.50x (ISBN 0-87395-948-5). State U NY Pr.

Studies in Early Buddhist Architecture of India. H. Sarkar. (Illus.). 1966. 20.00x. Coronet Bks.

Studies in Early Chinese Culture. Herrlee G. Creel. LC 78-14504. (Perspectives in Asian History Ser: No. 3). xxii, 266p. 1979. Repr. of 1937 ed. lib. bdg. 29.50x (ISBN 0-87991-601-X). Porcupine Pr.

Studies in Early Christianity. Shirley J. Case. 1928. 35.00 (ISBN 0-932062-35-0). Sharon Hill.

Studies in Early French Poetry. Walter Besant. LC 72-13206. (Essay Index Reprint Ser.). Repr. of 1868 ed. 20.00 (ISBN 0-8369-8147-2). Ayer Co Pubs.

Studies in Early French Poetry. Walter Besant. LC 72-13206. (Essay Index Reprint Ser.). 319p. Repr. of 1868 ed. lib. bdg. 19.00 (ISBN 0-8290-0522-6). Irvington.

Studies in Early German Comedy: 1500-1650. Richard E. Schade. LC 86-71135. (Studies in German Literature, Linguistics, & Culture: Vol. 24). (Illus.). 280p. 1986. 32.50x (ISBN 0-938100-41-6). Camden Hse.

Studies in Early Graduate Education. W. Carson Ryan. LC 73-165729. (American Education Ser, No. 2). 1971. Repr. of 1939 ed. 10.00 (ISBN 0-405-03718-X). Ayer Co Pubs.

Studies in Early Impressionism. Kermit S. Champa. LC 70-151569. (Publications in the History of Art Ser.: No. 22). (Illus.). Repr. of 1973 ed. 58.00 (ISBN 0-8357-1111-0, 2011110). Bks Demand UMI.

Studies in Early Impressionism. Kermit S. Champa. LC 84-81040. (Illus.). 106p. 1985. Repr. of 1973 ed. lib. bdg. 75.00 (ISBN 0-87817-299-8). Hacker.

Studies in Early Petroleum History. R. J. Forbes. LC 75-6471. (History & Politics of Oil Ser.). (Illus.). ix, 199p. 1976. Repr. of 1957 ed. 21.50 (ISBN 0-88355-290-6). Hyperion Conn.

Studies in Early Victorian Literature. Frederic Harrison. LC 72-194439. 1895. lib. bdg. 32.00 (ISBN 0-8414-5007-2). Folcroft.

Studies in Earth & Space Sciences: A Memoir in Honor of Harry Hammond Hess. Ed. by R. Shagam et al. LC 76-190172. (Geological Society of America Memoir Ser.: No. 132). pap. 160.00 (ISBN 0-317-29124-6, 2025026). Bks Demand UMI.

Studies in Earth Sciences. T. V. Murty. 614p. 1971. 25.00 (ISBN 0-88065-164-4, Pub. by Messers Today & Tomorrows Printers & Publishers India). Scholarly Pubns.

Studies in East African Geography & Development. Ed. by S. H. Ominde. (Illus.). 1971. 44.00x (ISBN 0-520-02073-1). U of Cal Pr.

Studies in East African History. Norman R. Bennett. LC 63-11193. (Pub. by Boston U Pr). 1963. 12.50 (ISBN 0-8419-8701-7, Africana). Holmes & Meier.

Studies in East Christian & Roman Art. Walter Dennison. (Humanistic Ser.: Vol. 12). Repr. of 1918 ed. 37.00 (ISBN 0-384-38812-4). Johnson Repr.

Studies in East European Folk Narrative. Ed. by Linda Degh. (AFS Bibliographic & Special Ser.: No. 30). 696p. 1978. 25.00x (ISBN 0-292-77544-X). U of Tex Pr.

Studies in East European Jewish Mysticism. Joseph Weiss. Ed. by David Goldstein. (Littman Libray of Jewish Civilazation). 1985. 29.95x (ISBN 0-19-710034-1). Oxford U Pr.

Studies in Eastern Chant, Vol. IV. Ed. by Milos Velimirovic. 248p. 1979. pap. text ed. 10.95 (ISBN 0-913836-57-5). St Vladimirs.

Studies in Econometrics, Time Series & Multivariate Statistics: Monograph. Ed. by Samuel Karlin et al. 1983. 48.50 (ISBN 0-12-398750-4). Acad Pr.

Studies in Economic Appraisal in Health Care, 2 vols. M. F. Drummond. 1981. Vol. 1. text ed. 35.00x (ISBN 0-19-261274-3); Vol. 2. text ed. 49.00x (ISBN 0-19-261398-7). Oxford U Pr.

Studies in Economic Planning Over Space & Time. G. G. Judge & T. Takayama. (Contributions to Economic Analysis Ser.: Vol. 82). 450p. 1973. 97.75 (ISBN 0-444-10515-8, North-Holland). Elsevier.

Studies in Economic Planning Over Space & Time. Ed. by George G. Judge & Takashi Takayama. 1976. Vol. 1. pap. 25.75 (ISBN 0-7204-0536-X, North-Holland); Vol. 2. pap. 21.00 (ISBN 0-7204-0535-1). Elsevier.

Studies in Economic Policy of Frederick the Great. W. O. Henderson. 205p. 1963. 29.50x (ISBN 0-7146-1321-5, F Cass Co). Biblio Dist.

Studies in Economic Theory & Practice: Essays in Honor of Edward Lipinski. Ed. by N. Assorodobraj-Kula et al. 252p. 1981. 87.00 (ISBN 0-444-86010-X). Elsevier.

Studies in Economics & Industrial Relations. Pennsylvania University Bicentennial Conference. Ed. by Wesley Mitchell & Herbert Hoover. LC 68-26198. Repr. of 1941 ed. 21.95x (ISBN 0-8046-0354-5, Pub. by Kennikat). Assoc Faculty Pr.

Studies in Ecstatic Kabbalah. Moshe Idel. LC 87-6522. (Judaica: Hermeneutics, Mysticism, & Religion Ser.). 160p. 1988. 39.50x (ISBN 0-88706-604-6); pap. 12.95x (ISBN 0-88706-605-4). State U NY Pr.

Studies in Educational Costs. C. E. Cummings. 1972. 15.00x (ISBN 0-7073-0197-1, Pub. by Scot Acad Pr). Longwood Pub Group.

Studies in Eighteenth Century British Art & Aesthetics. Ed. by Ralph Cohen. LC 84-2693. (Clark Library Professorship, UCLA: No. 9). 1985. 34.00x (ISBN 0-520-05258-7). U of Cal Pr.

Studies in Eighteenth-Century Culture, Vol. 17. Ed. by John Yolton & Leslie E. Brown. 384p. 1987. 25.00 (ISBN 0-937191-04-3). Colleagues Pr Inc.

Studies in Eighteenth-Century Diplomacy, 1740-1748. Richard Lodge. 1970. Repr. of 1930 ed. lib. bdg. 35.00 (ISBN 0-8371-4261-X, LODI). Greenwood.

Studies in Eighteenth-Century Islamic History. Ed. by Thomas Naff & Roger Owen. LC 77-22012. 462p. 1977. 26.50x (ISBN 0-8093-0819-3). S Ill U Pr.

Studies in Eighteenth Century Music: A Tribute to Karl Geiringer on His 70th Birthday. Robbins H. Landon & Roger Chapman. (Music Reprint Ser.). 1979. Repr. of 1970 ed. lib. bdg. 49.50 (ISBN 0-306-79519-1). Da Capo.

Studies in Elizabethan Drama. Percy Simpson. LC 72-194468. 1955. lib. bdg. 35.00 (ISBN 0-8414-8058-3). Folcroft.

Studies in Elizabethan Foreign Trade. Thomas S. Willan. LC 74-878. 1959. 39.50x (ISBN 0-678-06772-4). Kelley.

Studies in Elizabethan Literature. P. S. Shastry. 1972. text ed. 25.00x. Coronet Bks.

Studies in Empowerment: Steps Toward Understanding & Action. Ed. by Julian Rappaport & Robert Hess. LC 84-4461. (Prevention in Human Services Ser.: Vol. 3, Nos. 2-3). 230p. 1984. text ed. 24.95 (ISBN 0-86656-283-4). Haworth Pr.

Studies in English. Max Apple et al. (Rice University Studies: Vol. 61, No. 1). 150p. (Orig.). 1975. pap. 10.00x (ISBN 0-89263-223-2). Rice Univ.

Studies in English Adverbial Usage. Sidney Greenbaum. LC 70-90047. (Miami Linguistics Ser: No. 5). 1969. 13.95x (ISBN 0-87024-137-0). U of Miami Pr.

Studies in English & Comparative Literature by Former & Present Students at Radcliffe College. Agnes Irwin. LC 72-194993. 1910. lib. bdg. 35.00 (ISBN 0-8414-5065-X). Folcroft.

Studies in English & Hungarian Contrastive Linguistics. L. Dezso & W. Nemser. 590p. 1980. 118.00x (ISBN 0-569-08680-9, Pub. by Collets (UK)). State Mutual Bk.

Studies in English by Members of University College, Toronto. Ed. by M. W. Wallace. LC 68-26286. 1969. Repr. of 1931 ed. 21.00x (ISBN 0-8046-0484-3, Pub. by Kennikat). Assoc Faculty Pr.

Studies in English Commerce & Exploration in the Reign of Elizabeth, 2 vols. in 1. Albert L. Rowland & G. B. Manhart. (Research & Source Works Ser.: No. 213). 1968. Repr. of 1924 ed. 22.50 (ISBN 0-8337-3081-9). B Franklin.

Studies in English in Honor of Raphael Dorman O'Leary & Seldon Lincoln Whitcomb. Kansas Univ. Humanistic Studies, Vol. 6, No. 4. facs. ed. University Of Kansas - Department Of English. LC 68-20340. (Essay Index Reprint Ser). 1940. 15.00 (ISBN 0-8369-0913-5). Ayer Co Pubs.

Studies in English Legal History. T. F. Plucknett. 350p. 1983. 40.00 (ISBN 0-907628-11-7). Hambledon Press.

Studies in English Literature: Pope, Defoe, Matthew Prior, Steele, the Wartons, Southey, the English Sonnet. John Dennis. 1973. Repr. of 1883 ed. 35.00 (ISBN 0-8274-1642-3). R West.

Studies in English Official Historical Documents. Hubert Hall. LC 73-106063. (Bibliography & Reference Ser: No. 267). 1970. Repr. of 1908 ed. lib. bdg. 25.50 (ISBN 0-8337-1549-6). B Franklin.

Studies in English Poetry. Joseph Payne. 1863. Repr. 30.00 (ISBN 0-8274-3533-9). R West.

Studies in English Prose. Joseph Payne. 1881. 45.00 (ISBN 0-8274-3534-7). R West.

Studies in English Prose. Joseph Payne. 435p. 1983. Repr. of 1872 ed. lib. bdg. 50.00 (ISBN 0-89984-835-4). Century Bookbindery.

Studies in English Puritanism from the Restoration to the Revolution, 1660-1688. Charles E. Whiting. LC 68-56060. 1968. Repr. of 1931 ed. 45.00x (ISBN 0-678-05203-4). Kelley.

Studies in English Renaissance Literature. Waldo F. McNeir. (Essay Index Reprint Ser.). Repr. of 1962 ed. 20.75 (ISBN 0-518-10153-3). Ayer Co Pubs.

Studies in English Usage: The Resources of a Present-Day English Corpus for Linguistic Analysis. Ed. by Wolf-Dietrich Bald & Robert Ilson. (Forum Linguisticum: Vol. 6). 230p. 1977. pap. 22.30 (ISBN 3-261-01701-5). P Lang Pubs.

Studies in English-World Literature. Ottis B. Sperlin. 1978. Repr. of 1923 ed. lib. bdg. 30.00 (ISBN 0-8495-4866-7). Arden Lib.

Studies in Entertainment: Critical Approaches to Mass Culture. Ed. by Tania Modleski. LC 85-45980. (Theories of Contemporary Culture Series: Midland Bks.: No. 395). (Illus.). 224p. 1986. 27.50x (ISBN 0-253-35566-4); pap. 8.95x (ISBN 0-253-20395-3). Ind U Pr.

Studies in Ephesians. R. C. Bell. 1971. pap. 2.75 (ISBN 0-88027-041-1). Firm Foun Pub.

Studies in Ephesians. H. C. Moule. LC 77-79179. (Kregel Popular Commentary Ser.). 176p. 1977. kivar 7.95 (ISBN 0-8254-3218-9). Kregel.

Studies in Ephesians. W. Leon Tucker. LC 83-6115. 136p. 1983. pap. 4.95 (ISBN 0-8254-3828-4). Kregel.

Studies in Epistemology. Ed. by Peter A. French et al. (Midwest Studies in Philosophy: Vol. 5). 1980. 35.00x (ISBN 0-8166-0944-6); pap. 16.95 (ISBN 0-8166-0947-0). U of Minn Pr.

Studies in Ergativity. R. M. Dixon. 1987. 73.25 (ISBN 0-444-70275-X). Elsevier.

Studies in Essentialism. Ed. by Peter A. French et al. LC 86-11240. (Midwest Studies in Philosophy: Vol. XI). 528p. 1987. 49.50 (ISBN 0-8166-1551-9); pap. 19.95 (ISBN 0-8166-1552-7). U of Minn Pr.

Studies in Ethical Theory. Ed. by Peter A. French et al. (Midwest Studies in Philosophy: Vol. 3). 1980. 25.00x (ISBN 0-8166-0968-3); pap. 12.95 (ISBN 0-8166-0971-3). U of Minn Pr.

Studies in Ethnomethodology. Harold Garfinkel. 1967. text ed. write for info. (ISBN 0-13-858381-1). P-H.

Studies in Ethnomethodology. Harold Garfinkel. (Polity Press Bk.). 304p. 1985. pap. 12.95x (ISBN 0-7456-0005-0). Basil Blackwell.

Studies in Euripides: Phoenissae & Andromache. M. V. Valk. viii, 104p. 1985. lib. bdg. 27.50x (ISBN 0-317-54498-5, Pub. by A. M. Hakkert). Coronet Bks.

Studies in European Literature. Janko Lavrin. LC 74-103230. 1970. Repr. of 1929 ed. 24.00x (ISBN 0-8046-0867-9, Pub. by Kennikat). Assoc Faculty Pr.

Studies in European Literature: A Series of Studies (Montaigne, Hugo, Balzac, Goethe, Ibsen) Chautauqua Literary & Scientific Circle. 302p. 1985. Repr. of 1908 ed. lib. bdg. 40.00 (ISBN 0-8414-4100-6). Folcroft.

Studies in European Literature, Being the Taylorian Lectures 1920-1930. Oxford University. Taylor Institution. LC 76-90673. (Essay Index Reprint Ser). 1930. 24.50 (ISBN 0-8369-1232-2). Ayer Co Pubs.

Studies in European Politics. Mountstuart E. Grant-Duff. LC 72-110901. 1970. Repr. of 1866 ed. 36.50x (ISBN 0-8046-0884-9, Pub. by Kennikat). Assoc Faculty Pr.

Studies in Evolution. Charles E. Beecher. Ed. by Stephen J. Gould. LC 79-8324. (History of Paleontology Ser.). (Illus.). 1980. Repr. of 1901 ed. lib. bdg. 55.50x (ISBN 0-405-12704-9). Ayer Co Pubs.

Studies in Exodus, Vol. 2. Clifford A. Cole. (Bible Study Ser.). 1986. pap. 3.50 (ISBN 0-8309-0462-X). Herald Hse.

Studies in Fascism: Ideology & Practice, 101 titles in 113 vols. (AMS Press Reprint Ser.). Repr. Set. write for info. (ISBN 0-404-56100-4). AMS Pr.

Studies in Faulkner. Carnegie Institute of Technology, Department of English Staff & Ann L. Hayes. LC 72-1325. (Essay Index Reprint Ser.). Repr. of 1961 ed. 14.00 (ISBN 0-8369-2839-3). Ayer Co Pubs.

Studies in Fiction. enl. 3rd ed. Blaze O. Bonazza et al. 880p. 1982. pap. text ed. 16.50 scp (ISBN 0-06-040832-4, HarpC). Har-Row.

Studies in Fifth-Century Attic Epigraphy. Donald W. Bradeen & Malcolm F. McGregor. LC 72-9258. (Illus.). 150p. 1974. 16.95x (ISBN 0-8061-1064-3); pap. 8.95x (ISBN 0-8061-1364-2). U of Okla Pr.

Studies in Financial Organization. Thomas Balogh. LC 82-48174. (Gold, Money, Inflation & Deflation Ser.). 332p. 1983. lib. bdg. 44.00 (ISBN 0-8240-5225-0). Garland Pub.

Studies in Finger Action & Position Playing. Gaylord Yost. 3.50 (ISBN 0-913650-54-4). Columbia Pictures.

Studies in Finnic Folklore. Felix J. Oinas. LC 84-80930. (Uralic & Altaic Ser.: Vol. 147). 219p. (Orig.). 1985. pap. 12.00 (ISBN 0-933070-15-2). Ind U Res Inst.

Studies in Finno-Ugric Linguistics: In Honor of Alo Raun. Ed. by Denis Sinor. LC 81-622858. (Indiana University Uralic & Altaic Ser.: Vol. 131). 440p. 1977. 70.00 (ISBN 0-933070-00-4). Ind U Res Inst.

Studies in First & Second Samuel. Willard W. Winter. LC 70-1508. (Bible Study Textbook Ser.). 1967. 16.95 (ISBN 0-89900-011-8). College Pr Pub.

Studies in First & Second Thessalonians. Robert R. Taylor, Jr. 1977. pap. 2.50 (ISBN 0-89315-285-4). Lambert Bk.

Studies in First & Second Timothy. Robert Taylor, Jr. 2.50 (ISBN 0-89315-286-2). Lambert Bk.

Studies in First Corinthians. Paul T. Butler. (Bible Study Textbook Ser.). 416p. text ed. 14.95 (ISBN 0-89900-063-0). College Pr Pub.

Studies in First Corinthians. Don Compier. (Bible Study Ser.). 1987. pap. 3.50 (ISBN 0-8309-0448-4). Herald Hse.

Studies in First, Second Peter. Robert R. Taylor, Jr. pap. 2.50 (ISBN 0-89315-294-3). Lambert Bk.

Studies in First, Second, Third John. Robert R. Taylor, Jr. pap. 2.50 (ISBN 0-89315-295-1). Lambert Bk.

Studies in Folk Life: Essays in Honor of Iorwerth C. Peate, John G. Jenkins. Ed. by Richard M. Dorson. LC 77-70603. (International Folklore Ser.). 1977. lib. bdg. 30.00x (ISBN 0-405-10102-3). Ayer Co Pubs.

Studies in Folklore: In Honor of Distinguished Service Professor Stith Thompson. Ed. by Winthrop E. Richmond. LC 72-163547. (Illus.). 270p. 1972. Repr. of 1957 ed. lib. bdg. 15.00x (ISBN 0-8371-6208-4, RISF). Greenwood.

Studies in Foraminifera. A. B. Loeblich et al. 1970. 42.00x (ISBN 0-934454-75-2). Lubrecht & Cramer.

Studies in Foreign Literature. Virginia M. Crawford. LC 70-103221. 1970. Repr. of 1899 ed. 25.50x (ISBN 0-8046-0858-X, Pub. by Kennikat). Assoc Faculty Pr.

Studies in Foreign Literature: (Daudet, Huysmans, Verhaeren, Maeterlinck, & D'annunzio) Virginia M. Crawford. 1908. Repr. 20.00 (ISBN 0-8274-3535-5). R West.

Studies in Forensic Psychiatry. Bernard Glueck. LC 16-20410. (Criminal Science Monograph: No. 2). 1968. Repr. of 1915 ed. 21.00 (ISBN 0-527-34112-6). Kraus Repr.

Studies in Forensic Psychiatry. Bernard Glueck. 269p. 1983. Repr. of 1916 ed. lib. bdg. 85.00 (ISBN 0-8495-2141-6). Arden Lib.

Studies in Formal Historical Linguistics. H. M. Hoenigswald. LC 72-95891. (Formal Linguistics Ser: No. 3). 63p. 1973. lib. bdg. 16.00 (ISBN 90-277-0270-5, Pub. by Reidel Holland). Kluwer Academic.

Studies in Formal Semantics: Intentionality, Temporality, Negation. Ed. by F. Guenthner & C. Rohrer. (North Holland Linguistics Ser.: Vol. 35). 266p. 1978. 66.00 (ISBN 0-7204-0508-4, LIS, 35, North-Holland). Elsevier.

Studies in Foundational Philosophy. Klaus Hartmann. (Elementa (Band ILVII-1988) Ser.: Vol. 47). 448p. 1988. pap. text ed. 99.00 (ISBN 90-6203-989-8, Pub. by Rodopi Holland). Humanities.

Studies in Foundations & Combinatorics: Advances in Mathematics Supplementary Studies, Vol. 1. Ed. by Gian-Carlo Rota. 1978. 83.00 (ISBN 0-12-599101-0). Acad Pr.

Studies in Frankness. Charles Whibley. LC 79-122969. 1970. Repr. of 1898 ed. 24.50x (ISBN 0-8046-1350-8, Pub. by Kennikat). Assoc Faculty Pr.

Studies in Free Russia. Franco Venturi. Tr. by Fausta S. Walsby from Ital. LC 81-23149. 1982. lib. bdg. 30.00x (ISBN 0-226-85272-5). U of Chicago Pr.

Studies in French. Madeleine Alcover et al. (Rice University Studies: Vol. 63, No. 1). 133p. 1977. pap. 10.00x (ISBN 0-89263-231-3). Rice Univ.

Studies in French & Comparative Phonetics. Pierre Delattre. (Janua Linguistica, Ser. Major: No. 18). (Fr. & Eng.). 1966. text ed. 35.20x (ISBN 90-2790-610-6). Mouton.

Studies in French-Classical Tragedy. Lacy Lockert. LC 59-298. 1958. 19.95x (ISBN 0-8265-1049-3). Vanderbilt U Pr.

Studies in French Education from Rabelais to Rosseau. Geraldine E. Hodgson. LC 72-80233. 1969. Repr. of 1908 ed. lib. bdg. 20.50 (ISBN 0-8337-1713-8). B Franklin.

Studies in French in Honor of Andre Bourgeois. Catharine S. Brosman et al. (Rice University Studies: Vol. 59, No. 3). 100p. 1973. pap. 10.00x (ISBN 0-89263-217-8). Rice Univ.

Studies in French Language & Mediaeval Literature. facs. ed. LC 70-84340. (Essay Index Reprint Ser). 1939. 24.25 (ISBN 0-8369-1109-1). Ayer Co Pubs.

Studies in French Language, Literature & History. facs. ed. LC 76-80400. (Essay Index Reprint Ser). 1949. 15.00 (ISBN 0-8369-1067-2). Ayer Co Pubs.

Studies in French Literature. Andre Bourgeois et al. (Rice University Studies: Vol. 57, No. 2). 127p. 1971. pap. 10.00x (ISBN 0-89263-208-9). Rice Univ.

Studies in Functional Analysis. R. G. Bartle. LC 80-81042. (MAA Studies in Mathematics: No. 21). 229p. 1981. 24.50 (ISBN 0-88385-121-0). Math Assn.

Studies in Functional Grammar. Simon Dik. 1981. 66.00 (ISBN 0-12-216350-8). Acad Pr.

Studies in Functional Logical Semiotics of Natural Languages. Jerzy Pelc. (Janua Linguarum, Ser. Minor: No. 90). 1971. text ed. 18.40x (ISBN 90-2791-599-7). Mouton.

Studies in Galatians. R. C. Bell. 1954. pap. 2.75 (ISBN 0-88027-042-X). Firm Foun Pub.

Studies in GDR Culture & Society Eight: Selected Papers from the Thirteenth New Hampshire Symposium on the German Democratic Republic. Ed. by Margy Gerber. (Illus.). 214p. (Orig.). 1988. lib. bdg. 28.25 (ISBN 0-8191-7046-1, Pub. by Intl Symposium on the German Democratic Republic); pap. text ed. 14.25 (ISBN 0-8191-7047-X, Pub. by Intl Symposium on the German Democratic Republic). U Pr of Amer.

Studies in GDR Culture & Society Four: Selected Papers from the Ninth New Hampshire Symposium on the German Democratic Republic. Ed. by Margy Gerber et al. Tr. by Volker Gransow et al. (Illus.). 316p. (Orig.). 1984. lib. bdg. 29.00 (ISBN 0-8191-4015-5); pap. text ed. 15.50 (ISBN 0-8191-4016-3). U Pr of Amer.

Studies in GDR Culture & Society: Proceedings. International Symposium on the German Democratic Republic, 6th. Ed. by Margy Gerber et al. LC 80-6255. 324p. (Orig.). 1981. lib. bdg. 33.75 (ISBN 0-8191-1735-8); pap. text ed. 16.25 (ISBN 0-8191-1736-6). U Pr of Amer.

Studies in GDR Culture & Society: Selected Papers from the Twelfth New Hampshire Symposium on the German Democratic Republic, No. 7. Ed. by Margy Gerber. (Illus.). 246p. (Orig.). 1987. lib. bdg. 24.50 (ISBN 0-8191-6485-2, Pub. by Intl Symposium on the German Democratic Republic); pap. text ed. 13.50 (ISBN 0-8191-6486-0, Pub. by Intl Symposium on the German Democratic Republic). U Pr of Amer.

Studies in GDR Culture & Society Three: Selected Papers from the Eighth International Symposium on the German Democratic Republic. Ed. by Margy Gerber & Christine Cosentino. Tr. by Nancy A. Lauckner & Duncan Smith. LC 83-6763. (Illus.). 270p. (Orig.). 1983. lib. bdg. 30.25 (ISBN 0-8191-3278-0); pap. text ed. 14.25 (ISBN 0-8191-3279-9). U Pr of Amer.

Studies in GDR Culture & Society 2: Proceedings of the Seventh International Symposium on the German Democratic Republic. Ed. by Margy Gerber & Christine Cosentino. LC 81-43512. (Illus.). 298p. (Orig.). 1982. lib. bdg. 32.00 (ISBN 0-8191-2524-5); pap. text ed. 14.00 (ISBN 0-8191-2525-3). U Pr of Amer.

Studies in GDR Culture & Society 6: Selected Papers from the Eleventh New Hampshire Symposium on the German Democratic Republic. Ed. by Margy Gerber et al. 214p. (Orig.). 1986. lib. bdg. 23.75 (ISBN 0-8191-5468-7, Pub. by Intl Symposium on the General Democratic Republic); pap. text ed. 12.75 (ISBN 0-8191-5469-5, Pub. by Intl Symposium on the General Democratic Republic). U Pr of Amer.

TITLE INDEX

STUDIES IN ITALIAN RENAISSANCE

Studies in General Psychology see Studies in the Psychology of Art.
Studies in Genesis. John B. Burke. 1979. pap. 4.95 (ISBN 0-88469-048-2). BMH Bks.
Studies in Genesis, 2 vols. in one. Robert S. Candlish. LC 79-14084. (Kregel Bible Study Classics Ser.). 854p. 1979. 22.95 (ISBN 0-8254-2315-5). Kregel.
Studies in Genesis, Vol. 1. Wayne Ham. 1987. pap. 3.50 (ISBN 0-8309-0482-4). Herald Hse.
Studies in Genesis, Vol. 2. Wayne Ham. (Bible Study Ser.). 1987. pap. 3.50 (ISBN 0-8309-0483-2). Herald Hse.
Studies in Genesis One. Edward J. Young. LC 64-17028. pap. 4.95 (ISBN 0-87552-550-4). Presby & Reformed.
Studies in Genevan Government, 1536-1605. W. Monter. 132p. (Orig.). 1964. pap. text ed. 26.50x (ISBN 0-317-56048-4, Pub. by Droz Switzerland). Coronet Bks.
Studies in Genius. Walter Bowerman. 5.95 (ISBN 0-8022-0163-6). Philos Lib.
Studies in Georgia Local Government Law. 3rd ed. R. Perry Sentell, Jr. 969p. 1977. 40.00x (ISBN 0-87215-189-1). Michie Co.
Studies in Geriatric Psychiatry. Ed. by Anthony D. Isaacs & F. Post. LC 77-9990. pap. 70.00 (ISBN 0-317-07821-6, 2022402). Bks Demand UMI.
Studies in German Colonial History. W. O. Henderson. 150p. 1962. 28.00x (ISBN 0-7146-1674-5, F Cass Co). Biblio Dist.
Studies in German in Memory of Andrew Louis. Ed. by Robert L. Kahn. (Rice University Studies: Vol. 55, No. 3). 250p. 1969. pap. 10.00x (ISBN 0-89263-201-1). Rice Univ.
Studies in German in Memory of Robert L. Kahn. Ernst Behler et al. Ed. by Hans Eichner & Lisa Kahn. (Rice University Studies: Vol. 57, No. 4). 134p. 1971. pap. 10.00x (ISBN 0-89263-210-0). Rice Univ.
Studies in German Literature. Ed. by Carl Hammer. LC 82-15862. (Louisiana State University Studies: Humanities Ser.: No. 13). xviii, 172p. 1982. Repr. of 1963 ed. lib. bdg. 45.50x (ISBN 0-313-23735-2, HASGL). Greenwood.
Studies in German Literature. Bayard Taylor. 1979. Repr. of 1893 ed. lib. bdg. 30.00 (ISBN 0-8495-5139-0). Arden Lib.
Studies in German Literature. Baynard Taylor. LC 72-1145. (Essay Index Reprint Ser.). Repr. of 1877 ed. 23.00 (ISBN 0-8369-2865-2). Ayer Co Pubs.
Studies in Goethe's Lyric Cycles. Meredith Lee. (Studies in the Germanic Languages & Literatures: No. 93). xii, 191p. 1978. 17.50x (ISBN 0-8078-8093-0). U of NC Pr.
Studies in Golden-Age Drama. (Bulletin of Hispanic Studies: LXIV-1, January 1987). 104p. (Eng. & Span.). 1987. pap. text ed. 19.95 (ISBN 0-85323-006-4, Pub. by Liverpool U Pr). Humanities.
Studies in Graph Theory: Part I. Ed. by D. R. Fulkerson. LC 75-24987. (MAA Studies in Mathematics: No. 11). 19.00 (ISBN 0-88385-111-3). Pt. 2, 1976, 212p. Math Assn.
Studies in Graph Theory: Part II. Ed. by D. R. Fulkerson. LC 75-24987. (MAA Studies: No. 12). 212p. 1976. 19.00 (ISBN 0-88385-112-1). Math Assn.
Studies in Greek & Roman History. E. Badian. 290p. 1964. 24.95x (ISBN 0-631-08140-2). Basil Blackwell.
Studies in Greek Elegy & Iambus. Martin West. LC 73-93168. (Untersuchungen zur antiken Literatur & Geschichte, Vol. 14). ix, 198p. 1974. 51.00x (ISBN 3-11-004585-0). De Gruyter.
Studies in Guidance see This Is the Way.
Studies in Hadith Methodology & Literature. Mustafa Azami. Ed. by Anwer Beg. LC 77-90335. 1978. pap. 5.50 (ISBN 0-89259-011-4); pap. text ed. 5.50. Am Trust Pubns.
Studies in Harmonic Analysis. Ed. by Marshall J. Ash. LC 76-16431. (MAA Studies Ser.: No. 13). 319p. 1976. 26.50 (ISBN 0-88385-113-X). Math Assn.
Studies in Hausa Language & Linguistics. Graham Furniss & Philip J. Jagger. 320p. 1988. lib. bdg. 65.00 (ISBN 0-7103-0282-7). Routledge Chapman & Hall.
Studies in Health. Date not set. lib. bdg. price not set (ISBN 0-86663-650-1); pap. text ed. price not set (ISBN 0-86663-651-X). Ide Hse.
Studies in Heat Transfer. Hartnett. 516p. 1979. 68.95 (ISBN 0-89116-516-9). Hemisphere Pub.
Studies in Hebrew Proper Names. George B. Gray. (International Library of Names). 338p. 1984. Repr. of 1896 ed. text ed. cancelled (ISBN 0-8290-1232-X). Irvington.
Studies in Hebrews. James D. Bales. pap. 3.95 (ISBN 0-89315-260-9). Lambert Bk.
Studies in Hebrews. H. C. Moule. LC 77-79181. (Kregel Popular Commentary Ser.). 120p. 1977. kivar 5.95 (ISBN 0-8254-3223-5). Kregel.
Studies in Hegelian Cosmology. John McTaggart & Ellis McTaggart. LC 83-48513. (Philosophy of Hegel Ser.). 312p. 1984. lib. bdg. 38.00 (ISBN 0-8240-5636-1). Garland Pub.
Studies in Hegelian Cosmology. 2nd ed. John M. McTaggart. 1986. lib. bdg. 25.00x (ISBN 0-935005-59-5); pap. text ed. 13.00x (ISBN 0-935005-60-9). Ibis Pub VA.
Studies in Henry James. R. P. Blackmur. Ed. by Veronica A. Makowsky. LC 82-18911. 256p. 1983. 19.50 (ISBN 0-8112-0863-X); pap. 9.25 (ISBN 0-8112-0864-8, NDP552). New Directions.
Studies in Herodotus. facs. ed. Joseph Wells. LC 77-137388. (Select Bibliographies Reprint Ser). 1923. 18.00 (ISBN 0-8369-5589-7). Ayer Co Pubs.
Studies in Herodotus & Plato. I. M. Linforth. Ed. by Leonardo Taran. (Ancient Greek Literature Ser.). 350p. 1987. lib. bdg. 40.00 (ISBN 0-8240-7772-5). Garland Pub.
Studies in Hindu Political Thought & Its Metaphysical Foundations. rev. ed. V. P. Varma. 1974. 18.25. Orient Bk Dist.
Studies in Hinduism. Rene Guenon. 1986. 18.50x (ISBN 0-8364-1548-5, Pub. by Navrang). South Asia Bks.
Studies in Historical & Political Science, 1882-1965. Johns Hopkins University. Repr. of 1965 ed. Set. write for info. (ISBN 0-404-61000-5). AMS Pr.
Studies in Historical German Phonology: A Phonological Comparison of MHG & NHG with Reference to Modern Dialects. Charles V. Russ. (German Language & Literature-European University Studies: No. 1, Vol. 616). 214p. 1982. pap. 24.80 (ISBN 3-261-05070-5). P Lang Pubs.
Studies in Historiography. A. D. Momigliano. Ed. by Robin W. Wicks. LC 83-49156. (History & Historigraphy Ser.). 256p. 1985. lib. bdg. 30.00 (ISBN 0-8240-6372-4). Garland Pub.
Studies in History. Katherine F. Drew et al. (Rice University Studies: Vol. 58, No. 4). 155p. 1972. pap. 10.00x (ISBN 0-89263-214-3). Rice Univ.
Studies in History. Henry C. Lodge. LC 70-39132. (Essay Index Reprint Ser.). Repr. of 1884 ed. 25.50 (ISBN 0-8369-2698-6). Ayer Co Pubs.
Studies in History & Jurisprudence, 2 Vols. facs. ed. James B. Bryce. LC 68-8444. (Essay Index Reprint Ser). 1968. Repr. of 1901 ed. Set. 44.00 (ISBN 0-8369-0261-0). Ayer Co Pubs.
Studies in History & Letters. Thomas W. Higginson. 1973. Repr. of 1900 ed. 25.00 (ISBN 0-8274-0249-X). R West.
Studies in History & Politics. facs. ed. Herbert A. Fisher. LC 67-26740. (Essay Index Reprint Ser). 1920. 18.00 (ISBN 0-8369-0441-9). Ayer Co Pubs.
Studies in History, Economics & Public Law see Columbia University Studies in the Social Sciences.
Studies in History, Legend & Literature. H. Schutz Wilson. 1977. Repr. of 1884 ed. lib. bdg. 37.00 (ISBN 0-8492-2884-0). R West.
Studies in History of Biology, Vol. 5. Ed. by William Coleman & Camille Limoges. LC 78-647138. 224p. 1981. text ed. 24.50x (ISBN 0-8018-2566-0). Johns Hopkins.
Studies in History of Biology, Vol. 6. Ed. by William Coleman & Camille Limoges. LC 76-47139. 240p. 1983. text ed. 25.00x (ISBN 0-8018-2856-2). Johns Hopkins.
Studies in History of Biology, Vol. 7. Ed. by William Coleman & Camille Limoges. LC 78-647138. 160p. 1984. text ed. 20.00x (ISBN 0-8018-2995-X). Johns Hopkins.
Studies in History of Biology, Vol. 1. Ed. by William Coleman & Camille Limoges. LC 76-47139. (Historical Studies in the Life Sciences). 232p. 1977. 25.00x (ISBN 0-8018-1862-1). Johns Hopkins.
Studies in Honor of A. H. R. Fairchild. Arthur H. Fairchild. Ed. by Charles T. Prouty. 1946. Repr. 30.00 (ISBN 0-8274-3536-3). R West.
Studies in Honor of Albert H. Markwardt. Ed. by James E. Alatis. 166p. 1972. 4.00 (ISBN 0-939791-27-7). Tchrs Eng Spkrs.
Studies in Honor of Dewitt T. Starnes. Ed. by Thomas P. Harrison et al. LC 66-64359. (Illus.). 1967. 7.50 (ISBN 0-87959-058-0). U of Tex H Ransom Ctr.
Studies in Honor of Everett W. Hesse. William C. McCrary & Jose A. Madrigal. LC 80-53824. pap. 52.00 (2027062). Bks Demand UMI.
Studies in Honor of Frederick W. Shipley, by His Colleagues. Washington Univ. Studies NS No. 14. facs. ed. Washington University, St. Louis. LC 68-20341. (Essay Index Reprint Ser). 1942. 20.00 (ISBN 0-8369-0914-3). Ayer Co Pubs.
Studies in Honor of George R. Hughes. Ed. by Janet H. Johnson. Edward F. Wente. LC 76-47851. (Studies in Ancient Oriental Civilization Ser.: No. 39). (Illus.). 1977. pap. 10.00x (ISBN 0-918986-01-X). Oriental Inst.
Studies in Honor of Gertrude Rosenthal: Annual IV, Pt. II. (Illus.). 1972. pap. 7.50 (ISBN 0-912298-31-6). Baltimore Mus.
Studies in Honor of Gertrude Rosenthal: Annual III, Pt. I. 1970. pap. 7.50 (ISBN 0-912298-27-8). Baltimore Mus.
Studies in Honor of Hermann Collitz. facs. ed. LC 76-84339. (Essay Index Reprint Ser). 1930. 14.50 (ISBN 0-8369-1196-2). Ayer Co Pubs.
Studies in Honor of John A. Wilson. Oriental Institute. LC 76-81081. 1969. pap. 9.00x (ISBN 0-226-62408-0, SAOC35). U of Chicago Pr.
Studies in Honor of John Albrecht Walz. facs. ed. LC 68-29249. (Essay Index Reprint Ser). 1968. Repr. of 1941 ed. 20.00 (ISBN 0-8369-0915-1). Ayer Co Pubs.
Studies in Honor of Jose Rubia Barcia. Ed. by Roberta Johnson & Paul Smith. LC 81-86349. (Illus.). 180p. (Orig.). 1982. pap. 30.00 (ISBN 0-89295-020-X). Society Sp & Sp-Am.
Studies in Honor of Samuel Montifiore Waxman. Herbert Golden. LC 68-59217. 263p. 1969. 19.50 (ISBN 0-8419-8715-7). Holmes & Meier.
Studies in Honor of Sumner M. Greenfield. Ed. by H. L. Boudreau & Luis T. Gonzalez-del-Valle. LC 83-51006. 220p. 1985. pap. 25.00 (ISBN 0-89295-030-7). Society Sp & Sp-Am.
Studies in Honor of Tatiana Fotitch. Ed. by Jose M. Sola-Sole et al. LC 78-339493. pap. 92.80 (ISBN 0-317-55472-7, 2029526). Bks Demand UMI.
Studies in Honor of William C. McCrary. Ed. by Robert Fiore et al. LC 83-51007. 220p. 1986. pap. 25.00 (ISBN 0-89295-029-3). Society Sp & Sp-Am.
Studies in Honor of Xenia Gasiorowska. Ed. by Lauren Leighton. (Illus.). 191p. (Orig.). 1983. pap. 12.95 (ISBN 0-89357-102-4). Slavica.
Studies in Honour of T. B. L. Webster. Ed. by J. H. Betts et al. 264p. 1986. 39.50x (ISBN 0-8453-4515-X, Pub. by Bristol Classical Pr). Assoc Univ Prs.
Studies in Human Development: Selections from the Publications & Addresses of Harold Ellis Jones. Ed. by Herbert S. Conrad. (Century Psychology Ser.). (Illus.). 1966. 64.50x (ISBN 0-89197-581-0). Irvington.
Studies in Human Sexual Behavior: The American Scene. Ed. by Ailon Shiloh. (Illus.). 488p. 1970. 25.50 (ISBN 0-398-01746-8). C C Thomas.
Studies in Human Sexuality: A Guide to the Most Informative & Influential Sex Books of Our Times. Suzanne G. Frayser & Thomas J. Whitby. 550p. 1987. lib. bdg. 47.50 (ISBN 0-87287-422-2). Libs Unl.
Studies in Human Time. Georges Poulet. Tr. by Elliot Coleman. LC 78-13572. 1979. Repr. of 1956 ed. lib. bdg. 37.50x (ISBN 0-8371-9348-6, POSH). Greenwood.
Studies in Humanism. facs. ed. John W. Mackail. LC 73-84322. (Essay Index Reprint Ser). 1938. 17.75 (ISBN 0-8369-1092-3). Ayer Co Pubs.
Studies in Humanism. F. C. Schiller. 1907. 35.00. Century Bookbindery.
Studies in Humanism. facsimile ed. Ferdinand C. Schiller. LC 76-102255. (Select Bibliographies Reprint Ser). 1907. 33.00 (ISBN 0-8369-5140-9). Ayer Co Pubs.
Studies in Humanism, 2 vols. facsimile ed. Ferdinand C. Schiller. (Select Bibliographies Reprint Ser.). 492p. Repr. of 1907 ed. Set. lib. bdg. 32.00 (ISBN 0-8290-0518-8). Irvington.
Studies in I Nephi. Steven L. Shields. (Book of Mormon Study Ser.). 40p. 1987. pap. 3.50 (ISBN 0-8309-0489-1). Herald Hse.
Studies in Ice Physics & Ice Engineering. G. N. Yakovlev. 200p. 1972. text ed. 44.00x (ISBN 0-7065-1275-8, Pub. by Keter Pub Jerusalem). Coronet Bks.
Studies in Iconology: Humanistic Themes in the Art of the Renaissance. Erwin Panofsky. (Icon Editions). (Illus.). 306p. 1972. pap. 10.95 (ISBN 0-06-430025-0, IN-25, HarpT). Har-Row.
Studies in Idealism. Hugh L. Fausset. LC 65-18603. Repr. of 1923 ed. 23.00x (ISBN 0-8046-0140-2, Pub. by Kennikat). Assoc Faculty Pr.
Studies in III Nephi. Steven L. Shields. (Book of Mormon Study). 1987. pap. 3.50 (ISBN 0-8309-0485-9). Herald Hse.
Studies in Impressionism. John Rewald. Ed. by Irene Gordon & Frances Weitzenhoffer. (Illus.). 232p. 1986. 37.50 (ISBN 0-8109-1617-7). Abrams.
Studies in Income & Wealth. Conference on Research in National Income & Wealth. LC 75-19704. (National Bureau of Economic Research Ser.). (Illus.). 1975. Repr. 26.50x (ISBN 0-405-07589-8). Ayer Co Pubs.
Studies in Indian Agricultural Economics. Ed. by J. P. Bhattacharjee. LC 75-26296. (World Food Supply Ser). (Illus.). 1976. Repr. of 1958 ed. 27.50x (ISBN 0-405-07769-6). Ayer Co Pubs.
Studies in Indian Archaeology. Ed. by S. B. Deo & M. K. Dhavaliker. 1985. 28.50x (ISBN 0-8364-1404-7, Pub. by Popular Prakashan). South Asia Bks.
Studies in Indian Coins. D. C. Sircar. (Illus.). 1968. 24.00 (ISBN 0-89684-323-8). Orient Bk Dist.
Studies in Indian Economic Problems. C. Ganguli. 1978. 11.00x (ISBN 0-8364-0242-1). South Asia Bks.
Studies in Indian English Literature. 1st ed. M. K. Naik. 179p. 1987. text ed. 25.00x (ISBN 81-207-0657-9, Pub. by Sterling Pubs India). Apt Bks.
Studies in Indian Folk Traditions. Ved P. Vatuk. 221p. 1979. 17.95. Asia Bk Corp.
Studies in Indian Metal Sculptures. Bandyopadhyay. 250p. 1987. 44.00x (ISBN 0-8364-2180-9, Pub. by Sundeep). South Asia Bks.
Studies in Indian Thought: The Collected Papers of Professor TRV Murti. T. R. Murty. Ed. by Harold Coward. 1983. 25.00x (ISBN 0-8364-0866-7); text ed. 17.00x (ISBN 0-8364-0984-1). South Asia Bks.
Studies in Indian Urban Development. Edwin S. Mills & Charles M. Becker. (World Bank Publication). 224p. 1986. 29.95x (ISBN 0-19-520507-3). Oxford U Pr.
Studies in India's Economic Problems. N. C. Saha. 1985. 79.00x (ISBN 0-317-38796-0, Pub. by Current Dist). State Mutual Bk.
Studies in Indo-Soviet Relations. Ed. by V. D. Chopra. 288p. 1987. text ed. 32.50 (ISBN 81-7050-028-1, Pub. by Patriot Pubs). Advent NY.
Studies in Inductive Logic & Probability, Vol. II: (Rudolf Carnap) Ed. by Richard C. Jeffrey. 312p. 1980. 38.00x (ISBN 0-520-03826-6). U of Cal Pr.
Studies in Inductive Probability & Rational Expectation. Theo A. Kuipers. (Synthese Library: No. 123). 1978. lib. bdg. 26.00 (ISBN 90-277-0882-7, Pub. by Reidel Holland). Kluwer Academic.
Studies in Inflationary Dynamics: Financial Repression & Financial Liberalization in Less-Developed Countries. Basant K. Kapur. 146p. 1987. pap. 15.95x (ISBN 9971-69-099-3, Pub. by Singapore U Pr). Ohio U Pr.
Studies in Innovation in the Steel & Chemical Industries. James A. Allen. LC 68-583. 246p. 1967. lib. bdg. 29.50x (ISBN 0-678-06790-2). Kelley.
Studies in Integer Programming: Proceedings of a Workshop Held in Bonn. Institute of Operations Research, Sponsored by IBM, University of Bonn, Germany, Sept. 8-12, 1975. Ed. by P. L. Hammer. (Annals of Discrete Mathematics: Vol. 1). 562p. 1977. 137.00 (ISBN 0-7204-0765-6, North-Holland). Elsevier.
Studies in Intellectual Breakthrough: Freud, Simmel, & Buber. Charles D. Axelrod. LC 78-53177. 112p. 1979. lib. bdg. 12.00x (ISBN 0-87023-256-8). U of Mass Pr.
Studies in International History. Ed. by K. Bourne & D. C. Watt. 460p. 1967. 37.50 (ISBN 0-208-00406-8, Archon). Shoe String.
Studies in International Law. Nathan Feinberg. 640p. 1979. text ed. 49.50x (ISBN 0-86598-051-9, Pub. by Allanheld). Rowman.
Studies in International Law. R. C. Hingorani. 115p. 1981. 30.00 (ISBN 0-379-20719-2). Oceana.
Studies in International Law. Thomas E. Holland. LC 4-14210. (Historical Reprints in Jurisprudence & Classical Legal Literature Ser.). viii, 314p. 1984. Repr. of 1898 ed. lib. bdg. 38.00 (ISBN 0-89941-342-0). W S Hein.
Studies in International Law. 2nd ed. Stuart S. Malawer. LC 77-71708. 1977. lib. bdg. 35.00 (ISBN 0-9601384-1-2). W S Hein.
Studies in International Macroeconomics. Jagdeep S. Bhandari. LC 86-8095. 279p. 1986. lib. bdg. 50.95 (ISBN 0-275-92087-9, C2087). Praeger.
Studies in Interpersonal Relationships. Date not set. lib. bdg. price not set; pap. text ed. price not set. Ide Hse.
Studies in Interpretation. William H. Hudson. LC 76-23270. 1896. lib. bdg. 32.00 (ISBN 0-8414-4837-X). Folcroft.
Studies in Invalid Occupation: A Manual for Nurses & Attendants. Susan R. Tracy. Ed. by William R. Phillips & Janet Rosenberg. LC 79-6926. (Physically Handicapped in Society Ser.). (Illus.). 1980. Repr. of 1912 ed. lib. bdg. 17.00x (ISBN 0-405-13133-X). Ayer Co Pubs.
Studies in Irish & Scandinavian Folktales. Reider T. Christiansen. Ed. by Richard M. Dorson. LC 80-741. (Folklore of the World Ser.). 1980. Repr. of 1959 ed. lib. bdg. 26.50x (ISBN 0-405-13307-3). Ayer Co Pubs.
Studies in Ishcali Documents. S. Greengus. (Bibliotheca Mesopotamica Ser.: Vol. 19). 1986. 44.00x (ISBN 0-89003-166-5); pap. 34.00x (ISBN 0-89003-167-3). Undena Pubns.
Studies in Islamic & Judaic Traditions. Ed. by William M. Brinner & Stephen D. Ricks. LC 86-15552. (Brown Judaic Studies). 287p. 1986. 29.95 (ISBN 1-55540-047-7, 14-01-10); pap. 24.95 (ISBN 1-55540-048-5). Scholars Pr GA.
Studies in Islamic Economics. Ed. by Khurshid Ahmad. 390p. (Orig.). 1980. 31.50x (ISBN 0-86037-066-6, Pub. by Islamic Found UK); pap. 15.95 (ISBN 0-86037-067-4). New Era Pubns MI.
Studies in Islamic History & Civilization. Ed. by Uriel Heyd. (Scripta Hierosolymitana Ser.: Vol. 9). pap. 60.00 (ISBN 0-317-08597-2, 2051596). Bks Demand UMI.
Studies in Islamic History & Civilization. M. Sharon. (Illus.). 611p. 1987. 66.00 (ISBN 90-04-08473-8, Pub. by E J Brill). Heinman.
Studies in Islamic Mysticism. Reynold A. Nicholson. LC 78-73958. 1979. pap. 16.95 (ISBN 0-521-29546-7). Cambridge U Pr.
Studies in Israel Law. G. Tedeschi. (Hebrew University Legal Studies: No. 7). vi, 302p. 1960. 10.00x (ISBN 0-8377-1200-9). Rothman.
Studies in Israeli Ethnicity after the Ingathering. Ed. by Alex Weingrod. 345p. 1985. text ed. 49.00 (ISBN 2-88124-007-0). Gordon & Breach.
Studies in Israelite Poetry & Wisdom. Patrick W. Skehan. LC 77-153511. (Catholic Biblical Quarterly Monographs: II). xii, 265p. 1971. pap. 9.00 (ISBN 0-915170-00-0). Catholic Biblical.
Studies in Italian Art & Architecture: 15th Through 18th Centuries. Ed. by Henry Millon. (American Academy in Rome Studies in Art History). (Illus.). 1980. 70.00x (ISBN 0-262-13156-0). MIT Pr.
Studies in Italian Renaissance Architecture. Wolfgang Lotz. LC 76-44833. (Illus.). 256p. 1976. pap. 10.95 (ISBN 0-262-62036-7). MIT Pr.

Studies in Item Analysis & Prediction. Ed. by Herbert Solomon. 1961. 30.00x (ISBN 0-8047-0590-9). Stanford U Pr.
Studies in Jacobean Drama, Nineteen Seventy-Three to Nineteen Eighty-Four: An Annotated Bibliogrpahy. Mark J. Lidman. LC 85-45141. (Literature Ser.). 275p. 1985. lib. bdg. 37.00 (ISBN 0-8240-8725-9). Garland Pub.
Studies in Jainism. Ed. by M. P. Marathe et al. 267p. 1986. pap. 9.50X (ISBN 0-8364-1665-1, Pub. by Abhinav India). South Asia Bks.
Studies in James & Jude. Robert Taylor. 2.50 (ISBN 0-89315-293-5). Lambert Bk.
Studies in Japanese Buddhism. A. K. Reischauer. LC 73-107769. Repr. of 1917 ed. 24.50 (ISBN 0-404-05237-1). AMS Pr.
Studies in Japanese Buddhism. August Reischauer. 75.00 (ISBN 0-8490-1147-7). Gordon Pr.
Studies in Japanese Folklore. Ed. by Richard M. Dorson. LC 80-744. (Folklore of the World Ser.). (Illus.). 1980. Repr. of 1963 ed. lib. bdg. 34.50x (ISBN 0-405-13310-3). Ayer Co Pubs.
Studies in Jazz Discography, I. Studies in Jazz Discography. LC 78-5037. pap. 30.50 (ISBN 0-317-27281-0, 2024161). Bks Demand UMI.
Studies in Jewish & Christian History, Pt. 3. Elias Bickerman. (Arbeiten zur Geschichte des antiken Judentums und des Urchritentums Ser.: Band 9). xvi, 392p. 1986. 100.00 (ISBN 90-04-07480-5, Pub. by E J Brill). Heinman.
Studies in Jewish & World Folklore. Haim Schwarzbaum. (Fabula Supplement Ser., No. B 3). 1968. 97.50x (ISBN 3-11-000393-7). De Gruyter.
Studies in Jewish Bibliography & Related Subjects in Memory of Abraham Solomon Freidus (1867-1923) Georg Schweinfurth. 814p. 1929. Repr. text ed. 124.20x (ISBN 0-576-80130-5, Pub. by Gregg Intl Pubs England). Gregg Intl.
Studies in Jewish Bibliography, History & Literature: In Honor of I. Edward Kiev. Charles Berlin. 1971. 50.00x (ISBN 0-87068-143-5). Ktav.
Studies in Jewish Demography. U. O. Schmelz. 1983. 25.00x (ISBN 0-88125-013-9). Ktav.
Studies in Jewish Education & Judaica in Honor of Louis Newman. Alexander M. Shapiro & Burton I. Cohen. 1984. 20.00 (ISBN 0-317-13172-9). Ktav.
Studies in Jewish Ethnopoetry. Heda Jason. (Asian Folklore & Social Life Monograph: No. 72). 1975. 19.00x (ISBN 0-89986-068-0). Oriental Bk Store.
Studies in Jewish Folklore. Dov Noy. 1981. 25.00x (ISBN 0-87068-802-2). Ktav.
Studies in Jewish Folklore: Proceedings of a Regional Conference Held at the Spertus College of Judaica in May, 1977. Ed. by Frank Talmage. 408p. 1980. 25.00 (Dist. by KTAV). Assn for Jewish Studies.
Studies in Jewish History & Booklore. A. Marx. 472p. 1944. text ed. 49.68x (ISBN 0-576-80136-4, Pub. by Gregg Intl Pubs England). Gregg Intl.
Studies in Jewish Jurisprudence: Criminal Law. Ed. by Abraham Fuss. (Studies in Jewish Jurisprudence Ser.: Vol. 4). 320p. 1975. 16.95 (ISBN 0-87203-058-X). Hermon.
Studies in Jewish Law & Philosophy. I. Twersky. 39.50x (ISBN 0-87068-335-7). Ktav.
Studies in Jewish Law I: The Touro Conference Volume. Bernard S. Jackson & Jewish Law Association, International Congress Staff. LC 84-1329. (SP Occasional Papers & Proceedings: No. 3). 1985. 26.75 (ISBN 0-89130-732-X, 15-00-01); pap. 17.75 (ISBN 0-89130-868-7). Scholars Pr GA.
Studies in Jewish Literature Issued in Honor of Professor Kaufmann Kohler, Ph.D. David Philipson et al. Ed. by Steven Katz. LC 79-7167. (Jewish Philosophy, Mysticism & History of Ideas Ser.). 1980. Repr. of 1913 ed. lib. bdg. 26.50x (ISBN 0-405-12283-7). Ayer Co Pubs.
Studies in Jewish Music: The Collected Writings of the Noted Musicologist. Abraham W. Binder. Ed. by Irene Heskes. LC 72-136423. 1971. 15.00x (ISBN 0-8197-0272-2). Bloch.
Studies in Jewish Mysticism. Ed. by Joseph Dan. 220p. 1981. 25.00 (Dist by Ktav). Assn for Jewish Studies.
Studies in Jewish Mysticism. Ed. by Joseph Dan & Frank Talmage. 25.00x (ISBN 0-87068-803-0). Ktav.
Studies in Jewish Nationalism. Leon Simon. LC 75-6458. (Rise of Jewish Nationalism & the Middle East Ser.). xi, 174p. 1975. Repr. of 1920 ed. 19.80 (ISBN 0-88355-343-0). Hyperion Conn.
Studies in Jewish Philosophy: Collected Essays of the Academy for Jewish Philosophy, 1980-1985. Ed. by Norbert M. Samuelson. LC 87-14691. (Studies in Judaism). (Illus.). 600p. (Orig.). 1987. lib. bdg. 42.00 (ISBN 0-8191-6508-5, Pub. by Studies in Judaism); pap. text ed. 27.50 (ISBN 0-8191-6509-3). U Pr of Amer.
Studies in Jewish Preaching: Middle Ages. D. D. Israel-Bettan. LC 87-6125. (Brown Classics in Judaica Ser.). 424p. 1987. pap. text ed. 18.75 (ISBN 0-8191-6268-X). U Pr of Amer.
Studies in Jewish Theology. A. Marmorstein. 376p. Repr. of 1950 ed. text ed. 49.68x (ISBN 0-576-80153-4, Pub. by Gregg Intl Pubs England). Gregg Intl.
Studies in Jewish Theology: The Arthur Marmorstein Memorial Volume. Arthur Marmorstein. Ed. by Joseph Rabbinowitz & Meyer S. Lew. LC 76-39174. (Essay Index Reprint Ser.). Repr. of 1950 ed. 21.00 (ISBN 0-8369-2702-8). Ayer Co Pubs.
Studies in Jewish Thought: An Anthology of German Jewish Scholarship. Alfred Jospe. LC 80-29338. pap. 112.90 (2032035). Bks Demand UMI.
Studies in Jocular Literature. William C. Hazlitt. LC 67-24352. 240p. 1969. Repr. of 1890 ed. 35.00x (ISBN 0-8103-3529-8). Gale.
Studies in Jocular Literature. William C. Hazlitt. 59.95 (ISBN 0-8490-1148-5). Gordon Pr.
Studies in John's Epistles: Fellowship in Life Eternal. George G. Findlay. 448p. (YA) (gr. 7 up). 1989. pap. 14.95 (ISBN 0-8254-2629-4). Kregel.
Studies in Jonah. John L. Kachelman. pap. 5.50 (ISBN 0-89137-319-5). Quality Pubns.
Studies in Jonson's Comedies. Elizabeth M. Woodbridge. LC 66-29470. 101p. 1966. Repr. of 1898 ed. 15.00x (ISBN 0-87752-123-9). Gordian.
Studies in Joshua-Job. William R. Newell. LC 83-19899. (Old Testament Studies). 224p. 1983. kivar 7.95 (ISBN 0-8254-3314-2). Kregel.
Studies in Joshua, Judges, Ruth. Willard W. Winter. (Bible Study Textbook Ser.). (Illus.). 1969. 15.95 (ISBN 0-89900-010-X). College Pr Pub.
Studies in Joyce. Nathan Halper. LC 83-1360. (Studies in Modern Literature Ser.: No. 5). 177p. pap. 46.10 (2070316). Bks Demand UMI.
Studies in Judaism. facsimile ed. Solomon Schechter. LC 78-38775. (Essay Index Reprint Ser). Repr. of 1896 ed. 19.50 (ISBN 0-8369-2670-6). Ayer Co Pubs.
Studies in Judges. John Kackelman, Jr. 1986. pap. 5.95 (ISBN 0-89137-564-3). Quality Pubns.
Studies in Kabuki: Its Acting, Music, & Historical Context. James R. Brandon et al. LC 77-5336. 198p. 1978. pap. 9.00x (ISBN 0-8248-0452-X, Eastwest Ctr). UH Pr.
Studies in Kant's Aesthetics. Eva Schaper. 139p. 1979. 16.50x (ISBN 0-85224-359-6, Pub. by Edinburgh U Pr Scotland). Columbia U Pr.
Studies in Karnataka History. B. Vasantha Shetty. 144p. 1984. text ed. 15.00x (ISBN 0-86590-206-2, Pub. By Sterling Pubs India). APT Bks.
Studies in Keats. John M. Murry. LC 78-185023. (Studies in Keats, No. 19). 1969. Repr. of 1930 ed. lib. bdg. 49.95x (ISBN 0-8383-0671-3). Haskell.
Studies in Keats, New & Old. John M. Murry. LC 74-9966. 1939. 32.50 (ISBN 0-8414-6150-3). Folcroft.
Studies in Labor Market Behavior: Sweden & the United States. Ed. by G. Eliasson et al. 442p. (Orig.). 1981. pap. text ed. 32.00 (ISBN 9-172041-39-0, Pub. by Almqvist & Wiksell). Coronet Bks.
Studies in Labor Market Dynamics. Ed. by G. R. Neumann & N. C. Westergard-Nielsen. (Studies in Contemporary Economics: Vol. 11). x, 285p. 1984. pap. 26.00 (ISBN 0-387-13942-7). Springer-Verlag.
Studies in Labor Markets. Ed. by Sherwin Rosen. LC 81-7488. (National Bureau of Economic Research Ser.: Universities-Nat'l Conference Series No. 31). (Illus.). 400p. 1981. lib. bdg. 47.00x (ISBN 0-226-72628-2). U of Chicago Pr.
Studies in Labor Theory & Practice. Ed. by William L. Rowe. LC 81-82455. (Studies in Marxism: Vol. 12). 100p. 1982. 16.25x (ISBN 0-930656-23-7); pap. 6.50 (ISBN 0-930656-24-5). MEP Pubns.
Studies in Land & Credit in Ancient Athens, 500-200 B. C. The Horos Inscriptions. Moses I. Finley. LC 72-7890. (Greek History Ser.). Repr. of 1952 ed. 29.00 (ISBN 0-405-04786-X). Ayer Co Pubs.
Studies in Land & Credit in Ancient Athens, 500-200 B.C. The Horos Inscriptions. Moses I. Finley. 340p. 1986. text ed. 39.95x (ISBN 0-88738-066-2). Transaction Bks.
Studies in Language see Syntax & Semantics.
Studies in Language & Reason. Ilham Dilman. LC 79-55527. 228p. 1981. text ed. 29.50x (ISBN 0-389-20229-0). B&N Imports.
Studies in Late Greek Epic Poetry. Heather White. (London Studies in Classical Philology). 160p. 1987. text ed. 70.00 (ISBN 90-70265-39-7, Pub. by Gieben Holland). Humanities.
Studies in Late Greek Epic Poetry. Heather White. (London Studies in Classical Philology: Vol. 18). (Illus.). 153p. 1987. 41.00x (ISBN 90-70265-39-7, Pub. by Gieben Amsterdam). Benjamins North Am.
Studies in Late Medieval & Renaissance Painting in Honor of Millard Meiss. Ed. by Irving Lavin & John Plummer. LC 75-27118. 550p. 1978. 200.00x set (ISBN 0-8147-4963-1); Vol. I (ISBN 0-8147-5001-X); Vol. II (ISBN 0-8147-4978-X). NYU Pr.
Studies in Later Greek Comedy. Thomas B. Webster. LC 81-5016. (Illus.). xiv, 282p. 1981. Repr. of 1970 ed. lib. bdg. 35.00x (ISBN 0-313-23050-1, WESL). Greenwood.
Studies in Latin American Popular Culture, Vol. I. Ed. by Harold E. Hinds, Jr. & Charles M. Tatum. 1982. pap. 30.00 (ISBN 0-9608664-0-X). Studies Lat Am.
Studies in Latin American Popular Culture, Vol. 2. Ed. by Harold E. Hinds, Jr. & Charles M. Tatum. 1983. pap. 30.00 (ISBN 0-9608664-1-8). Studies Lat Am.
Studies in Latin American Popular Culture, Vol. 4. Ed. by Harold E. Hinds, Jr. & Charles M. Tatum. 1985. pap. 30.00 (ISBN 0-9608664-3-4). Studies Lat Am.
Studies in Latin American Popular Culture, Vol. 5. Ed. by Harold E. Hinds, Jr. & Charles M. Tatum. 1986. pap. 30.00 (ISBN 0-9608664-4-2). Studies Lat Am.
Studies in Latin American Popular Culture, Vol. 6. Ed. by Harold E. Hinds, Jr. & Charles M. Tatum. 1987. pap. text ed. 30.00 (ISBN 0-9608664-5-0). Studies Lat Am.
Studies in Latin American Popular Culture, Vol. 7. Ed. by Harold E. Hinds, Jr. & Charles M. Tatum. 1988. pap. text ed. 40.00. Studies Lat Am.
Studies in Latin Moods & Tenses. Herbert C. Elmer. 1898. 24.00 (ISBN 0-384-14275-3). Johnson Repr.
Studies in Latin Syntax, 2 Vols. Herbert C. Nutting. pap. 42.00 ea. Vol. 1 (ISBN 0-384-42411-2). Vol. 2 (ISBN 0-384-42413-9). Johnson Repr.
Studies in Law & Politics. facs. ed. Harold J. Laski. LC 68-22106. (Essay Index Reprint Ser). 1932. 18.00 (ISBN 0-8369-0608-X). Ayer Co Pubs.
Studies in Law & Politics. Harold J. Laski. LC 69-12933. 299p. 1969. Repr. of 1932 ed. 28.00 (ISBN 0-208-00731-8, Archon). Shoe String.
Studies in Leadership. A. W. Gouldner. Ed. by Arthur P. Brief. (Continuity in Administrative Science & Ancestral Books in the Management of Organizations). 736p. 1987. lib. bdg. 95.00 (ISBN 0-8240-8230-3). Garland Pub.
Studies in Learning & Memory: Selected Papers. Benton J. Underwood. Ed. by Charles D. Spielberger. LC 81-22694. (Centennial Psychology Ser.). 346p. 1982. 35.00 (ISBN 0-275-90917-4, C0917). Praeger.
Studies in Legal Terminology. Erwin Hexner. vi, 150p. 1981. Repr. of 1941 ed. lib. bdg. 20.00x (ISBN 0-8377-0635-1). Rothman.
Studies in Legato for Trombone. Reginald H. Fink. 1967. pap. 3.00 (ISBN 0-8258-0245-8, 04767). Fischer Inc NY.
Studies in Levitical Terminology: Vol. 1, The Encroacher & the Levite. The Term Aboda. Jacob Milgrom. LC 76-626141. (Univeraity of California Publications. Near Eastern Studies: Vol. 14). pap. 30.00 (ISBN 0-317-10194-3, 2021380). Bks Demand UMI.
Studies in Leviticus. Samuel H. Kellogg. LC 88-12062. 574p. 1988. lib. bdg. 22.95 (ISBN 0-8254-3043-7); pap. 16.95 (ISBN 0-8254-3041-0). Kregel.
Studies in Lexicography. Ed. by Robert W. Burchfield. (Illus.). 240p. 1987. 55.00 (ISBN 0-19-811945-3). Oxford U Pr.
Studies in Library Management, Vol. 1. Ed. by Brian Redfern. 168p. 1972. 17.50 (ISBN 0-208-01071-8, Linnet). Shoe String.
Studies in Library Management, Vol. 2. Ed. by Gileon Holroyd. (Illus.). 167p. 1975. 19.50 (ISBN 0-208-01357-1, Linnet). Shoe String.
Studies in Library Management, Vol. 3. Ed. by Gileon Holroyd. 192p. (Orig.). 1976. 21.50 (ISBN 0-208-01526-4, Linnet). Shoe String.
Studies in Library Management, Vol. 4. Ed. by Gileon Holroyd. 178p. 1977. 19.50 (ISBN 0-208-01547-7, Linnet). Shoe String.
Studies in Library Management, Vol. 5. Ed. by Anthony Vaughan. 168p. 1979. 14.00 (ISBN 0-85157-265-0, Pub. by Bingley England). ALA.
Studies in Library Management, Vol. 7. Ed. by Anthony Vaughan. 237p. 1982. 23.50 (ISBN 0-85157-322-3, Pub. by Bingley England). ALA.
Studies in Library Management: The Coming of Age of Library Management, 1960-1980, Vol. 6. Ed. by Anthony Vaughan. 214p. 1980. 22.00 (ISBN 0-85157-301-0, Pub. by Bingley England). ALA.
Studies in Linear & Non-Linear Programming. Kenneth J. Arrow et al. (Illus.). 1958. pap. 20.00x (ISBN 0-8047-0562-3). Stanford U Pr.
Studies in Linear Programming. Ed. by H. M. Salkin & J. Saha. LC 74-28998. (Studies in Management Science & Systems: Vol. 2). 322p. 1975. 66.00 (ISBN 0-444-10884-X, North-Holland). Elsevier.
Studies in Linguistic Geography: The Dialects of English in Britain & Ireland. Ed. by John M. Kirk et al. LC 84-23118. (Illus.). 208p. 1985. 60.00 (ISBN 0-7099-1502-0, Pub. by Croom Helm Ltd). Routledge Chapman & Hall.
Studies in Linguistic Semantics. Ed. by Charles J. Fillmore & D. Terence Langendoen. LC 74-140383. 307p. Date not set. Repr. of 1971 ed. price not set (ISBN 0-8290-0982-5). Irvington.
Studies in Linguistics, Vol. 1-17. Set. 395.00 (ISBN 0-384-58682-1); Set. pap. 290.00 (ISBN 0-685-02166-1). Johnson Repr.
Studies in Linguistics in Honor of George L. Trager. Ed. by M. E. Smith. (Janua Linguarum, Series Maior: No. 52). 1972. 64.80 (ISBN 90-2792-309-4). Mouton.
Studies in Linguistics in Honor of Raven I. McDavid Jr. Lawrence M. Davis et al. LC 77-156749. 461p. 1972. 26.75 (ISBN 0-8173-0010-4); limited edition 39.50 (ISBN 0-8173-0005-8). U of Ala Pr.
Studies in Linnaean Method & Nomenclature, Vol. 7. John L. Heller. (Marburger Schriften zur Medicingeschichte). 328p. 1983. 31.05 (ISBN 3-8204-7344-0). P Lang Pubs.
Studies in Literary Modes. Arthur M. Clark. LC 76-58436. 1946. lib. bdg. 25.00 (ISBN 0-8414-3428-X). Folcroft.
Studies in Literature. Henry Bett. LC 68-8220. 1929. Repr. of 1929 ed. 21.50x (ISBN 0-8046-0028-7, Pub. by Kennikat). Assoc Faculty Pr.
Studies in Literature. G. W. Griffin. 1973. Repr. of 1870 ed. 20.00 (ISBN 0-8274-0204-X). R West.
Studies in Literature. Alfred C. Lyall. 1978. Repr. of 1915 ed. lib. bdg. 30.00 (ISBN 0-8495-3230-2). Arden Lib.
Studies in Literature. Arthur T. Quiller-Couch. (Third Ser.). 1919. 29.00 (ISBN 0-8274-3538-X). R West.
Studies in Literature. Arthur T. Quiller-Couch. (Second Series). 1973. 30.00 (ISBN 0-8274-0979-6). R West.
Studies in Literature & Belief. facsimile ed. Martin Jarrett-Kerr. LC 74-134101. (Essay Index Reprint Ser). Repr. of 1954 ed. 18.00 (ISBN 0-8369-1978-5). Ayer Co Pubs.
Studies in Literature & History. facs. ed. Alfred C. Lyall. LC 68-29227. (Essay Index Reprint Ser). 1968. Repr. of 1915 ed. 21.50 (ISBN 0-8369-0637-3). Ayer Co Pubs.
Studies in Literature & History (Thackeray, Heroic Poetry, Byron. Alfred C. Lyall. 1973. lib. bdg. 15.00 (ISBN 0-8414-5631-3). Folcroft.
Studies in Literature from the Ancient Near East: Dedicated to Samuel Noah Kramer. Ed. by Jack M. Sasson. (American Oriental Ser.: Vol. 65). 1984. 25.00x (ISBN 0-940490-65-X). Am Orient Soc.
Studies in Literature (Shakespeare, Hawthorne, Shelley, Thackeray, Dante, Hugo) G. W. Griffin. 1978. Repr. of 1870 ed. lib. bdg. 29.00 (ISBN 0-8414-2007-6). Folcroft.
Studies in Literature (Wordsworth, Browning, Etc.) John Morley. 1973. lib. bdg. 25.50 (ISBN 0-685-38012-2). Folcroft.
Studies in Literature, 1789-1877. Edward Dowen. 523p. 1981. Repr. of 1902 ed. lib. bdg. 65.00 (ISBN 0-8495-1135-6). Arden Lib.
Studies in Logic: By Members of the Johns Hopkins University (1883) Ed. by Charles S. Peirce. (Foundations of Semiotics Ser.: 1). xl, 203p. 1983. Repr. 40.00x (ISBN 90-272-3271-7). Benjamins North Am.
Studies in Logical Theory. John Dewey. LC 75-3128. Repr. of 1903 ed. 34.50 (ISBN 0-404-59129-9). AMS Pr.
Studies in Long Term Memory. Ed. by Alan Kennedy & Alan Wilkes. LC 74-13149. pap. 94.50 (ISBN 0-317-30318-X, 2024801). Bks Demand UMI.
Studies in Love & in Terror. facsimile ed. Marie A. Lowndes. LC 74-167462. (Short Story Index Reprint Ser.). Repr. of 1913 ed. 19.00 (ISBN 0-8369-3988-3). Ayer Co Pubs.
Studies in Lucian's De Syria Dea. Robert A. Oden, Jr. LC 76-54988. (Harvard Semitic Monograph). (Illus.). 1976. 10.50 (ISBN 0-89130-123-2, 040015). Scholars Pr GA.
Studies in Lutheran Doctrine. Paul F. Keller. LC 60-15574. (YA) (gr. 7-8). 1959. pap. 6.00 (ISBN 0-570-03517-1, 14-1265); correction & profile chart 0.40 (ISBN 0-570-03526-0, 14-1267); tests 0.60 (ISBN 0-570-03525-2, 14-1266). Concordia.
Studies in Machiavellianism. Richard Christie et al. (Social Psychology Ser). 1970. 39.95 (ISBN 0-12-174450-7). Acad Pr.
Studies in Macroeconomic Theory Taxation, Vol. 2: Redistribution & Growth. Ed. by Edmund S. Phelps. (Economic Theory, Econometrics & Mathematics Ser.). 1980. 34.50 (ISBN 0-12-554002-7). Acad Pr.
Studies in Macroeconomics Theory: Employment & Inflation, Vol. 1. Ed. by Edmund S. Phelps. (Economic Theory Econometrics, & Mathematical Economics Ser.). 1979. 39.50 (ISBN 0-12-554001-9). Acad Pr.
Studies in Macromolecular Biosynthesis. Ed. by Richard B. Roberts. (Illus.). 702p. 1964. 29.00 (ISBN 0-87279-635-3, 624). Carnegie Inst.
Studies in Magic from Latin Literature. Eugene Tavenner. LC 16-25151. Repr. of 1916 ed. 16.50 (ISBN 0-404-06350-0). AMS Pr.
Studies in Maimonidean Medicine. Ed. by J. I. Dienstag. (Texts, Studies & Translations in Maimonidean Thought & Scholarship: Vol.2). 35.00x (ISBN 0-87068-449-3). Ktav.
Studies in Maimonides & Spinoza. Ed. by J. I. Dienstag. (Texts, Studies & Translations in Maimonidean Thought & Scholarship: Vol. 3). 35.00x (ISBN 0-87068-330-6). Ktav.
Studies in Malory. Ed. by James W. Spisak. LC 84-16542. (Illus.). vii, 319p. 1985. 22.95x (ISBN 0-918720-54-0); pap. 13.95x (ISBN 0-918720-55-9). Medieval Inst.
Studies in Manorial History. A. E. Levett. 375p. 1962. 17.00 (ISBN 0-85036-063-3, Pub. by Merlin Pr UK). Longwood Pub Group.
Studies in Maritime Economics. R. O. Goss. LC 68-29328. (Illus.). 1968. 42.50 (ISBN 0-521-07329-4). Cambridge U Pr.
Studies in Marriage & Funerals of Taiwan Aborigines. Ch'en Kou-Chun. (Asian Folklore & Social Life Monograph: No. 4). (Chinese.). 1970. 14.00x (ISBN 0-89986-007-9). Oriental Bk Store.
Studies in Mass Communication & Technology. Ed. by Sari Thomas. LC 83-25746. (Studies in Communication: Vol. 1). 272p. 1984. text ed. 39.50 (ISBN 0-89391-133-X). Ablex Pub.

TITLE INDEX STUDIES IN MUSICAL INTERPRETATION.

Studies in Mathematical Analysis & Related Topics: Essays in Honor of George Polya. Ed. by Gabor Szego et al. 1962. 40.00x (ISBN 0-8047-0140-7). Stanford U Pr.

Studies in Mathematical Biology. Ed. by Simon Levin. Incl. Part 1, Cellular Behavior & Development of Pattern. (Vol. 15). 329p. 1978. 24.00 (ISBN 0-88385-115-6); Part 2, Populations & Communities. (Vol. 16). 328p. 1978. 24.00 (ISBN 0-88385-116-4). (Studies in Mathematics). Math Assn.

Studies in Mathematical Economics. Ed. by Stanley Reiter. LC 85-63770. (Studies in Mathematics: Vol. 25). 420p. 1986. 46.50 (ISBN 0-88385-127-X). Math Assn.

Studies in Mathematical Economics & Econometrics in Memory of Henry Schultz. facs. ed. Ed. by O. Lange et al. LC 68-8498. (Essay Index Reprint Ser). 1942. 21.50 (ISBN 0-8369-0916-X). Ayer Co Pubs.

Studies in Mathematical Geology. Andrei Vistelius. LC 65-25266. pap. 77.50 (ISBN 0-317-28726-5, 2020676). Bks Demand UMI.

Studies in Mathematical Learning Theory. Ed. by Robert R. Bush & William K. Estes. 1959. 40.00x (ISBN 0-8047-0563-1). Stanford U Pr.

Studies in Mathematical Physics: Essays in Honor of Valentine Bargmann. Ed. by E. H. Lieb et al. LC 76-4057. (Princeton Series in Physics). (Illus.). 472p. 1976. 58.50x (ISBN 0-691-08180-8); pap. 17.50x (ISBN 0-691-08185-9). Princeton U Pr.

Studies in Mathematical Physics: Lectures in Mathematical Physics at the NATO Advanced Study Institute, Istanbul, Turkey, August, 1970, Vol. 1. NATO Advanced Study Institute Staff. Ed. by A. O. Barut. LC 73-88587. (NATO Advanced Study Institutes Ser.: No. C-1). 1973. lib. bdg. 39.50 (ISBN 90-277-0405-8, Pub. by Reidel Holland). Kluwer Academic.

Studies in Mathematical Psychology. Ed. by Richard C. Atkinson. 1964. 40.00x (ISBN 0-8047-0181-4). Stanford U Pr.

Studies in Mathematical Statistics: Proceedings. Steklov Institute of Mathematics, Academy of Sciences, USSR. Ed. by J. V. Linnick. (Proceedings of the Steklov Institute of Mathematics: No. 104). 1971. 46.00 (ISBN 0-8218-3004-X, STEKLO-104). Am Math.

Studies in Mathematics Education. R. Morris. (Illus.). 135p. (Orig.). 1987. pap. 12.00 (ISBN 92-3-102526-0, U1635, UNESCO). UNIPUB.

Studies in Mathematics Education, 2 Vols. Robert Morris. Incl. Vol. 1. 129p. 1980. pap. 7.00 (ISBN 92-3-101779-9, U1013). UNIPUB; Vol. 2. 179p. 1981. pap. 9.25 (ISBN 92-3-101905-8, U1101). UNIPUB; Vol. 3. Mathematical Education of Primary-School Teachers. 258p. 1985. pap. 18.75 (ISBN 92-3-102141-9, U1370). UNIPUB. (Teaching of Basic Sciences Ser.). (Illus.). 179p. Vol. 1, 1980, 129p. pap. 7.00 (ISBN 92-3-101779-9, U1013, UNESCO); Vol. 2, 1981, 179p. pap. 9.25 (ISBN 92-3-101905-8, U1101). UNIPUB.

Studies in Mathematics Education: Geometry in Schools, Vol. 5. Ed. by Robert Morris. (Illus.). 197p. (Orig.). 1986. text ed. 10.00 (ISBN 92-3-102373-X, U1518, UNESCO). UNIPUB.

Studies in Mathematics Education: The Education of Secondary School Teachers of Mathematics, Vol. 4. Ed. by Robert Morris. (Teaching of Basic Sciences Mathematics Ser.). 175p. 1986. pap. text ed. 12.00 (ISBN 92-3-102142-7, U1494, Pub. by Unesco). UNIPUB.

Studies in Mathematics Education: The Mathematical Education of Primary-School Teachers. Ed. by Robert Morris. (Teaching of Basic Sciences: Vol. 3). 258p. 1985. pap. 10.50 (ISBN 92-3-102141-9, U1370, UNESCO). UNIPUB.

Studies in Medical Geography, 14 vols. Ed. by Jacques M. May & Donna L. McLellan. Incl. Vol. 2. Studies in Disease Ecology. (Illus.). 1961. 27.95x (ISBN 0-02-848980-2); Vol. 3. Ecology of Malnutrition in the Far & Near East. (Illus.). 1961. 24.95x (ISBN 0-02-849010-X); Vol. 4. Ecology of Malnutrition in Five Countries of Eastern & Central Europe: East Germany,Poland, Yugoslavia, Albania, Greece. (Illus.). 1964. 18.95x (ISBN 0-02-848970-5); Vol. 5. Ecology of Malnutrition in Middle Africa: Ghana, Nigeria, Republic of the Congo, Rwanda & Burundi & the Former French Equatorial Africa. (Illus.). 1965. 16.95x (ISBN 0-02-848990-X); Vol. 6. Ecology of Malnutrition in Central & Southern Europe: Austria, Hungary, Romania, Bulgaria & Czechoslovakia. (Illus.). 1966. 18.95x (ISBN 0-02-849000-2); Vol. 7. Ecology of Malnutrition in Northern Africa: Libya, Tunisia, Algeria, Morocco, Spanish Sahara & Ifni, Mauretania. (Illus.). 1967. 18.95x (ISBN 0-02-848950-0); Vol. 8. Ecology of Malnutrition in the French-Speaking Countries of West Africa & Madagascar: Senegal, Guinea, Ivory Coast, Togo, Dahomey, Cameroon, Niger, Mali, Upper Volta, & Madagascar. (Illus.). 1968. 21.95x (ISBN 0-02-848960-8); Vol. 9. Ecology of Malnutrition in Eastern Africa: Equatorial Guinea, the Gambia, Liberia, Sierra Leone, Malawi, Rhodesia, Zambia, Kenya, Tanzania, Uganda, Ethiopia, the French Territory of the Atars & Issas, the Somali Republic & Sudan. 1970. 32.95x (ISBN 0-02-849020-7); Vol. 10. Ecology of Malnutrition in Seven Countries of Southern Africa and in Portuguese Guinea: The/Republic of South Africa, South West Africa (Namibia), Botswana, Lesotho, Swaziland, Mozambique, Angola, Portuguese Guinea. 1971. 27.95x (ISBN 0-02-848940-3); Vol. 11. Ecology of Malnutrition in Mexico & Central America. 1972. 24.95x (ISBN 0-02-848930-6); Vol. 12. Ecology of Malnutrition in the Caribbean. 1973. 21.95x (ISBN 0-02-848920-9); Vol. 13. Ecology of Malnutrition in Eastern South America. 1975. 41.95x (ISBN 0-02-849060-6); Vol. 14. Ecology of Malnutrition in Western South America. 1975. 32.95x (ISBN 0-02-849070-3). Hafner.

Studies in Medieval & Modern German History. Walther Hubatsch. LC 83-4508. (Illus.). 190p. 1985. 25.00 (ISBN 0-312-77096-0). St Martin.

Studies in Medieval & Renaissance Culture: Medieval Poetics see Medievalia et Humanistica.

Studies in Medieval & Renaissance Culture Transformation & Continuity see Medievalia et Humanistica.

Studies in Medieval & Renaissance Culture. Ed. by Paul M. Clogan. LC 75-32451. (Medievalie et Humanistica; New Series: No. 9). pap. 67.30 (2027282). Bks Demand UMI.

Studies in Medieval & Renaissance History, Vol. IX. Ed. by J. A. Evans & R. W. Unger. LC 63-22098. 45.00 (ISBN 0-404-62859-1). AMS Pr.

Studies in Medieval & Renaissance History. Studies in Medieval & Renaissance History. LC 63-22098. Vol. 1, 1964. pap. 75.00 (ISBN 0-317-27624-7, 2023489); Vol. 4, 1967. pap. 63.00 (ISBN 0-317-27625-5); Vol. 5, 1968. pap. 71.30 (ISBN 0-317-27626-3); Vol. 6, 1969. pap. 88.00 (ISBN 0-317-27627-1); Vol. 7, 1970. pap. 63.80 (ISBN 0-317-27628-X); Vol. 8, 1971. pap. 54.30 (ISBN 0-317-27629-8). Bks Demand UMI.

Studies in Medieval & Renaissance History, 4 vols. Studies in Medieval & Renaissance History. LC 63-22098. Vol. 2. pap. 79.50 (2056180); Vol. 3. pap. 80.30; Vol. 9. pap. 55.80; Vol. 10. pap. 51.00. Bks Demand UMI.

Studies in Medieval & Renaissance History, Vol. 9. J. A. Evans & R. W. Unger. LC 63-22098. 1978. 45.00 (ISBN 0-404-62850-8). Ams Pr.

Studies in Medieval & Renaissance Literature. Clive S. Lewis. 1980. 34.50 (ISBN 0-521-05545-8); pap. 11.95 (ISBN 0-521-29701-X). Cambridge U Pr.

Studies in Medieval Cistercian History, Vol. 2. Ed. by J. R. Sommerfeldt. (Studies Ser.: No. 24). 1977. pap. 10.95 (ISBN 0-87907-824-3). Cistercian Pubns.

Studies in Medieval Culture, Vol. III. 1970. pap. 5.00x (ISBN 0-686-14884-3). Medieval Inst.

Studies in Medieval Culture, Vol. IV-1. 1974. pap. 5.00x (ISBN 0-686-14886-X). Medieval Inst.

Studies in Medieval Culture, Vols. 6 & 7. combined ed. Ed. by John R. Sommerfeldt & E. Rozanne Elder. 1976. pap. 5.00x (ISBN 0-686-86322-4). Medieval Inst.

Studies in Medieval Culture, Vols. 8 & 9. combined ed. Ed. by John R. Sommerfeldt & Rozanne E. Elder. 1976. pap. 5.00x (ISBN 0-686-86323-2). Medieval Inst.

Studies in Medieval Culture, Vol. 11. Ed. by John R. Sommerfeldt & Thomas H. Seiler. 1977. pap. 5.00x (ISBN 0-686-86325-9). Medieval Inst.

Studies in Medieval Culture, Vol. 12. Ed. by John R. Sommerfeldt & Thomas H. Seiler. 1978. pap. 5.00x (ISBN 0-686-86326-7). Medieval Inst.

Studies in Medieval Culture, Kalamazoo, Vol. V. 1975. pap. 5.00x (ISBN 0-686-14892-4). Medieval Inst.

Studies in Medieval Culture, Kalamazoo, Vol. IV-3. 1974. pap. 5.00x (ISBN 0-686-14890-8). Medieval Inst.

Studies in Medieval History. Ed. by Henry Mayr-Harting & R. I. Moore. (Illus.). 330p. 1985. 40.00 (ISBN 0-907628-68-0). Hambledon Press.

Studies in Medieval History Presented to Frederick Maurice Powicke. Ed. by Richard W. Hunt et al. LC 79-14227. 1979. Repr. of 1948 ed. lib. bdg. 45.50x (ISBN 0-313-21484-0, SMFM). Greenwood.

Studies in Medieval Jewish History & Literature. Ed. by Isadore Twersky. LC 79-11588. (Judaic Monographs: No. 2). 1979. text ed. 25.00x (ISBN 0-674-85192-7). Harvard U Pr.

Studies in Medieval Jewish History & Literature, Vol. 2. Ed. by Isadore Twersky. (Harvard Judaic Monographs: No. V). 460p. 1985. text ed. 25.00x (ISBN 0-674-85193-5). Harvard U Ctr Jewish.

Studies in Medieval Jewish Philosophy. Israel I. Efros. LC 73-12512. 279p. pap. 72.60 (2029826). Bks Demand UMI.

Studies in Medieval Life & Literature. Edward T. McLaughlin. LC 74-39101. (Essay Index Reprint Ser.). Repr. of 1894 ed. 15.00 (ISBN 0-8369-2701-X). Ayer Co Pubs.

Studies in Medieval Linguistic Thought. Ed. by Konrad Koerner et al. (Studies in the History of Linguistics: No. 26). vi, 321p. 1980. 52.00x (ISBN 90-272-4508-8). Benjamins North Am.

Studies in Medieval Literature: A Memorial Collection of Essays. Ed. by Roger S. Loomis. LC 73-135508. (Research & Source Works Ser.: No. 599). (Bibl. of loomis's writings by ruth roberts). 1970. Repr. 23.50 (ISBN 0-8337-4733-9). B Franklin.

Studies in Medieval Painting. Bernard Berenson. LC 73-153884. (Graphic Art Ser.). (Illus.). 148p. 1971. Repr. of 1930 ed. lib. bdg. 39.50 (ISBN 0-306-70292-4). Da Capo.

Studies in Medieval Painting. Bernard Berenson. LC 74-22036. (Graphic Art Ser.). (Illus.). xxii, 148p. 1975. pap. 5.95 (ISBN 0-306-80010-1). Da Capo.

Studies in Medieval Philosophy. Ed. by John F. Wippel. (Studies in Philosophy & the History of Philosophy: Vol. 17). 1987. 36.95 (ISBN 0-8132-0640-5). Cath U Pr.

Studies in Medieval Science: Alchemy, Astrology, Mathematics & Medicine. Pearl Kibre. 355p. 1983. 40.00 (ISBN 0-907628-21-4). Hambledon Press.

Studies in Medieval Thought & Learning from Abelard to Wyclif. Beryl Smally. (Illus.). 455p. 1982. 45.00 (ISBN 0-9506882-6-6). Hambledon Press.

Studies in Medieval Trade & Finance. E. B. Fryde. 430p. 1983. 40.00 (ISBN 0-907628-10-9). Hambledon Press.

Studies in Melody: Studies in Melody see Study of Sensory Control in the Rat.

Studies in Memory of Frank Martindale Webster. Frank M. Webster. 1951. Repr. 30.00 (ISBN 0-8274-3539-8). R West.

Studies in Memory of Ramon Menendez Pidal: Hispanic Review Special Issue, November 1970. Hispanic Review Editors. (Illus.). 114p. 1970. pap. 4.00 (ISBN 0-87535-117-4). Hispanic Soc.

Studies in Memory of Warren Cowgill (1929-1985) Ed. by Calvert Watkins. (Studies in Indo-European Language & Culture Band 3: Vol. 3). 327p. 1987. lib. bdg. 115.00x (ISBN 0-89925-422-5). De Gruyter.

Studies in Metaphysical Poetry. Theodore Spencer & Mark Van Doren. LC 64-15543. Repr. of 1939 ed. 15.50x (ISBN 0-8046-0436-3, Pub. by Kennikat). Assoc Faculty Pr.

Studies in Metaphysics. Ed. by Peter French et al. (Midwest Studies in Philosophy: Vol. 4). 1979. 29.50x (ISBN 0-8166-0887-3); pap. 14.95 (ISBN 0-8166-0888-1). U of Minn Pr.

Studies in Mexican Compositae One see Memoirs of the New York Botanical Garden.

Studies in Micropublishing: A Reader. Allen B. Veaner. (Meckler Publishing's Series in Library Micrographics Management: No. 2). 440p. 1977. 24.50x (ISBN 0-913672-07-6). Meckler Corp.

Studies in Middle America. Incl. A Maya Skull from Uloa Valley, Honduras. Frans Blom. (Illus.). 3.00; Dermatoglyphics & Functional Lateral Dominance in Mexican Indians (Mayas & Tarahumaras) Stella M. Leche. 2.50; Manuscripts in the Department of Middle American Research. Arthur e. Gropp. 81p. 5.00; Relation of the Synodical Month & Eclipses to the Maya Correlation Problem. Hermann Beyer. 2.50; Mexican Bone Rattles. Hermann Beyer. (Illus.). 3.00. (Illus.). 401p. 1934. Set. 30.00 (ISBN 0-939238-06-3). Tulane MARI.

Studies in Middle American Anthropology. Incl. The Extent of Dominance of Tenochtitlan During the Reign of Mocteuczoma Ilhuicamina. H. Barry Holt. (Illus.). 1975. 2.00; A Critical Analysis of Yuri Knoeozov's Decipherment of the Maya Hieroglyphics. Arthur A. Demarest. (Illus.). 1976. 1.00; A Re-Evaluation of the Archaeological Sequences of Preclassic Chaipas. Arthur A. Demarest. (Illus.). 1976. 3.50. 107p. 1976. 10.00 (ISBN 0-939238-24-1). Tulane MARI.

Studies in Midrash & Related Literature. Judah Goldin. Ed. by Jeffery Tigay & Barry Eichler. (Scholars of Distinction Ser.). 456p. 1988. 39.95 (ISBN 0-8276-0277-4). JPS Phila.

Studies in Migration: Internal & International Migration in India. M. S. Rao. 410p. 1986. 34.00 (ISBN 81-85054-08-8, Pub. by Manohar India). South Asia Bks.

Studies in Milton. Sten Liljegren. LC 67-30816. (Studies in Milton, No. 22). 1969. Repr. of 1918 ed. lib. bdg. 75.00x (ISBN 0-8383-0718-3). Haskell.

Studies in Milton. Sten B. Liljegren. 1918. lib. bdg. 30.50 (ISBN 0-8414-5707-7). Folcroft.

Studies in Milton & an Essay on Poetry. Alden Sampson. LC 71-126686. 1970. Repr. of 1913 ed. 24.00 (ISBN 0-404-05555-9). AMS Pr.

Studies in Mineralogy & Precambrian Geology: A Volume in Honor of John W. Gruner. Ed. by B. R. Doe & D. K. Smith. LC 70-190173. (Geological Society of America Memoir Ser.: No. 135). pap. 93.00 (ISBN 0-317-30052-0, 2025029). Bks Demand UMI.

Studies in Model Theory. Ed. by Michael D. Morley. LC 73-86564. (MAA Studies: No. 8). 197p. 1974. 21.00 (ISBN 0-88385-108-3). Math Assn.

Studies in Modeltheoretic Semantics. Ed. by Ter A. Meulen. (GRABS (Groninger-Amsterdam Studies in Semantics)). x, 206p. 1983. write for info. (ISBN 90-70176-81-5); pap. write for info. (ISBN 90-70176-80-7). Foris Pubns.

Studies in Modern Analysis. Ed. by R. C. Buck. LC 62-11884. (MAA Studies: No. 1). 182p. 1962. 19.00 (ISBN 0-88385-101-6). Math Assn.

Studies in Modern Arabic Poetry: Thought & Criticism. Mounah A. Khouri. (Middle Eastern Ser.: No. 16). 120p. (Orig.). 1986. pap. 9.00x (ISBN 0-936665-02-5). Jahan Bk Co.

Studies in Modern Choice-of-Law: Torts, Insurance, Land Titles. Moffatt Hancock. LC 84-80150. xviii, 446p. 1984. lib. bdg. 48.00 (ISBN 0-89941-320-X). W S Hein.

Studies in Modern European Literature, 10 vols. Ed. by Richard A. Koenigsberg. 1979. Set. 100.00 (ISBN 0-915042-13-4). Lib Soc Sci.

Studies in Modern Fiction. Shiva M. Pandeya. 1983. text ed. 30.00x (ISBN 0-7069-2272-7, Pub. by Vikas India). Advent NY.

Studies in Modern German Literature. facs. ed. Otto Heller. LC 67-26748. (Essay Index Reprint Ser). 1905. 18.00 (ISBN 0-8369-0531-8). Ayer Co Pubs.

Studies in Modern German Literature. Otto Heller. 1973. lib. bdg. 17.00 (ISBN 0-8414-5037-4). Folcroft.

Studies in Modern Guitar. Gary R. Smith & Martin Stuart. LC 77-75479. 1977. pap. 9.95 (ISBN 0-8497-5500-X, WE4, Pub by Kjos West). Kjos.

Studies in Modern Hebrew Syntax & Semantics: Transformational Generative Approach. new ed. Ed. by Peter Cole. (North Holland Linguistics Ser.: Vol. 32). 286p. 1976. pap. 47.50 (ISBN 0-7204-0543-2, North-Holland). Elsevier.

Studies in Modern History. facs. ed. George P. Gooch. LC 68-16934. (Essay Index Reprint Ser). 1931. 20.00x (ISBN 0-8369-0482-6). Ayer Co Pubs.

Studies in Modern Indian Art. R. Paramoo. (Illus.). 246p. 1975. pap. 10.95. Asia Bk Corp.

Studies in Modern Indian Fiction in English, 2 vols. Haydn M. Williams. (Greybird Book). 182p. 1975. Set. text ed. 24.00 (ISBN 0-88253-652-4); Set. pap. text ed. 15.00 (ISBN 0-88253-651-6). Ind-US Inc.

Studies in Modern Indian History. Ed. by B. R. Nanda & V. C. Joshi. 1972. 19.50x (ISBN 0-8046-8819-2, Pub. by Kennikat). Assoc Faculty Pr.

Studies in Modern Italian History: From the 'Risorgimento' to the Republic. Ed. by Frank J. Coppa. 392p. 1986. text ed. 34.50 (ISBN 0-8204-0180-3). P Lang Pubs.

Studies in Modern Italian Literature. Ernesto Grillo. 1973. Repr. of 1930 ed. 25.00 (ISBN 0-8274-0203-1). R West.

Studies in Modern Kentish History. Date not set. 95.00x (ISBN 0-906746-05-1, Pub. by Kent Cty Coun UK). State Mutual Bk.

Studies in Modern Portuguese Literature, Vol. 4. 104p. 1971. pap. 7.00 (ISBN 0-912788-03-8). Tulane Romance Lang.

Studies in Modern Topology. Ed. by P. J. Hilton. LC 68-11402. (MAA Studies: No. 5). 212p. 1968. 21.00 (ISBN 0-88385-105-9). Math Assn.

Studies in Monastic Theology. Odo Brooke. (Cistercian Studies Ser.: No. 37). 1980. 8.95 (ISBN 0-87907-837-5). Cistercian Pubns.

Studies in Montaigne. Grace Norton. 1973. Repr. of 1904 ed. 25.00 (ISBN 0-8274-0303-8). R West.

Studies in Mother Infant Interaction. Ed. by H. R. Schaffer. 1977. 69.00 (ISBN 0-12-622560-5). Acad Pr.

Studies in Mulk Raj Anand. P. K. Rajan. viii, 122p. 1986. 11.00 (ISBN 81-7017-207-1, Pub. by Abhinav India). South Asia Bks.

Studies in Murder. Edmund L. Pearson. 295p. 1982. Repr. of 1924 ed. lib. bdg. 30.00 (ISBN 0-8495-4406-8). Arden Lib.

Studies in Music. Robin Grey. LC 74-24092. Repr. of 1901 ed. 27.50 (ISBN 0-404-12937-4). AMS Pr.

Studies in Music History: Essays for Oliver Strunk. Ed. by Harold Powers. LC 80-14086. (Illus.). x, 527p. 1980. Repr. of 1968 ed. lib. bdg. 45.50x (ISBN 0-313-22501-X, POSM). Greenwood.

Studies in Musical Interpretation. Alfred Cortot. (Music Reprint Ser.). 1989. 37.50 (ISBN 0-306-79715-1). Da Capo.

Studies in Musicology: Essays in History, Style & Bibliography of Music in Memory of Glenn Haydon. Compiled by James W. Pruett. LC 76-7574. (Illus.). 1976. Repr. of 1969 ed. lib. bdg. 35.00x (ISBN 0-8371-8883-0, PRSM). Greenwood.
Studies in Musicology, 1935-1975. Charles Seeger. LC 76-19668. 1977. 45.00x (ISBN 0-520-02000-6). U of Cal Pr.
Studies in Muslim Philosophy. M. Saeed. 14.50 (ISBN 0-686-18601-X). Kazi Pubns.
Studies in Muslim Political Thought & Administration. H. K. Sherwani. 14.95 (ISBN 0-686-18544-7). Kazi Pubns.
Studies in Mystical Religion. Jones M. Rufus. 1978. Repr. of 1919 ed. lib. bdg. 45.00 (ISBN 0-8492-1257-X). R West.
Studies in Napoleonic Statesmanship: Germany. Herbert Fisher. LC 68-25230. (World History Ser., No. 48). 1969. Repr. of 1903 ed. lib. bdg. 54.95x (ISBN 0-8383-0939-9). Haskell.
Studies in Natyasastra. G. H. Tarlekar. 1975. 14.00 (ISBN 0-8426-0843-5). Orient Bk Dist.
Studies in Network Thermodynamics. L. Peusner. (Studies in Modern Thermodynamics: No. 5). 370p. 1986. 129.00 (ISBN 0-444-42580-2). Elsevier.
Studies in Neurolinguistics, 2 vols. Ed. by Haiganoosh Whitaker & Harry A. Whitaker. LC 75-13100. (Perspectives in Neurolinguistics & Psycholinguistics). Vol. 1, 1976. 39.95 (ISBN 0-12-746301-1); Vol. 2, 1976. 39.95 (ISBN 0-12-746302-X); Vol. 3, 1977. 39.95 (ISBN 0-12-746303-8); Vol. 4, 1979. 39.95 (ISBN 0-12-746304-6). Acad Pr.
Studies in Neurophysiology: Presented to A. K. McIntyre. Ed. by Robert Porter. LC 78-1695. (Illus.). 470p. pap. 122.20 (2030614). Bks Demand UMI.
Studies in Neuropsychology: Selected Papers of Arthur Benton. Arthur Benton. Ed. by Otfried Spreen & Louis Costa. (Illus.). 1985. 41.95x (ISBN 0-19-503636-0). Oxford U Pr.
Studies in New Age Prediction. John Soric. 70p. 1985. 7.95 (ISBN 0-86690-323-2, 2471-01). Am Fed Astrologers.
Studies in New England Geology: A Memoir in Honor of C. Wroe Wolfe. Ed. by Paul C. Lyons & Arthur Brownlow. LC 75-30494. (Memoir: No. 146). (Illus.). 1976. 20.50 (ISBN 0-8137-1146-0). Geol Soc.
Studies in New England Puritanism. Ed. by Winfried Herget. 240p. 1983. 28.95. P Lang Pubs.
Studies in New England Transcendentalism. H. C. Goddard. 1978. Repr. of 1960 ed. lib. bdg. 30.00 (ISBN 0-8492-4906-6). R West.
Studies in New Testament & Gnosticism. George W. MacRae. 1988. pap. 12.95 (ISBN 0-89453-648-6). M Glazier.
Studies in Nietzsche & the Classical Tradition. Ed. by James C. O'Flaherty et al. (Germanic Languages & Literatures Ser: No. 85). xiii, 278p. 1976. 20.00x (ISBN 0-8078-8085-X). U of NC Pr.
Studies in Nietzsche & the Judeo-Christian Tradition. Ed. by James C. O'Flaherty et al. LC 84-11963. (Studies in the Germanic Language & Literature: No. 103). 424p. 1985. 32.00x (ISBN 0-8078-8104-X). U of NC Pr.
Studies in Nigerian Administration. 2nd ed. D. J. Murray. 342p. 1980. pap. 13.75 (ISBN 0-8419-6602-8, Africana). Holmes & Meier.
Studies in Nineteenth Century Literature. James Hogg. (Romantic Reassessment Ser.). (Orig.). 1987. pap. 15.00 (ISBN 3-7052-0551-X, Pub. by Salzburg Studies). Longwood Pub Group.
Studies in Niuean Syntax. William J. Seiter. Ed. by Jorge Hankamer. LC 79-55857. (Outstanding Dissertations in Linguistics Ser.). 367p. 1985. lib. bdg. 53.00 (ISBN 0-8240-4560-2). Garland Pub.
Studies in Non-Deterministic Psychology. Ed. by Gerald Epstein. LC 80-13820. (New Directions in Psychotheraphy Ser.: Vol. V). 294p. (Series editor Paul T. Olsen). 1980. 36.95 (ISBN 0-87705-654-4). Human Sci Pr.
Studies in Non-Linear Stability Theory. Viktor Eckhaus. (Springer Tracts in Natural Philosophy: Vol. 6). (Illus.). 1965. 19.00 (ISBN 0-387-03407-2). Springer-Verlag.
Studies in Numerical Analysis. Ed. by Gene H. Golub. 422p. 1985. 46.50 (ISBN 0-88385-126-1, MAS-24). Math Assn.
Studies in Numerical Analysis 1. Ed. by W. J. Jameson, Jr. v, 133p. 1968. text ed. 15.50 (ISBN 0-89871-042-1). Soc Indus-Appl Math.
Studies in Numismatic Method. Ed. by C. N. Brooke et al. LC 81-15524. (Illus.). 368p. 1983. 110.00 (ISBN 0-521-22503-5). Cambridge U Pr.
Studies in Occult Philosophy. G. De Purucker. LC 73-81739. 1973. 15.00 (ISBN 0-911500-52-9); pap. 9.00 (ISBN 0-911500-53-7). Theos U Pr.
Studies in Occultism. Helena P. Blavatsky. LC 67-18822. 1973. 7.50 (ISBN 0-911500-08-1); pap. 4.00 (ISBN 0-911500-09-X). Theos U Pr.
Studies in Ohio Archaeology. rev. ed. Ed. by Olaf H. Prufer & Douglas H. McKenzie. LC 75-45380. pap. 100.00 (ISBN 0-317-28372-3, 2025452). Bks Demand UMI.
Studies in Old English. H. M. Chadwick. 1978. Repr. of 1899 ed. lib. bdg. 42.50 (ISBN 0-8495-0844-4). Arden Lib.
Studies in Old English. H. M. Chadwick. LC 73-20322. Repr. of 1899 ed. lib. bdg. 37.00 (ISBN 0-8414-3538-3). Folcroft.
Studies in Old English Fractured "EA". H. Hallovist. (Lund Studies in English: Vol. 14). pap. 18.00 (ISBN 0-8115-0557-X). Kraus Repr.
Studies in Old English Phonology. R. Lass & J. M. Anderson. LC 74-80360. (Studies in Linguistics: No. 14). 352p. 1975. 49.50 (ISBN 0-521-20531-X). Cambridge U Pr.
Studies in Old Prussian. William R. Schmalstieg. LC 76-19017. 1977. text ed. 26.50x (ISBN 0-271-01231-5). Pa St U Pr.
Studies in Open Education. Ed. by Bernard Spodek & Herbert Walberg. LC 73-19109. 256p. 1975. 15.00x (ISBN 0-87586-045-1). Agathon.
Studies in Operating Systems. R. M. McKeag & R. Wilson. (APIC Ser.). 1976. 69.00 (ISBN 0-12-484350-6). Acad Pr.
Studies in Opposition. Ed. by Rodney Barker. LC 70-167757. 300p. 1972. 25.00 (ISBN 0-312-77105-3). St Martin.
Studies in Optics. Albert A. Michelson. 1962. pap. 2.45x (ISBN 0-226-52388-8, P514, Phoen). U of Chicago Pr.
Studies in Optimization. Ed. by G. B. Dantzig & B. C. Eaves. LC 74-21481. (MAA Studies: No. 10). 174p. 1975. 21.00 (ISBN 0-88385-110-5). Math Assn.
Studies in Optimization. Ed. by T. E. Hull. (Proceedings Ser.: 1). v, 137p. 1970. text ed. 15.00 (ISBN 0-89871-152-5). Soc Indus-Appl Math.
Studies in Ordinary Differential Equations. Jack Hale. LC 77-8289. (MAA Studies: No. 14). 278p. 1977. 26.50 (ISBN 0-88385-114-8). Math Assn.
Studies in Oriental Musical Instruments, 2 vols. in 1. Henry G. Farmer. LC 77-75185. 1977. Repr. of 1939 ed. lib. bdg. 30.00 (ISBN 0-89341-056-X). Longwood Pub Group.
Studies in Otomanguean Phonology. Ed. by William Merrifield. (SIL Publications in Linguistics: No. 54). 180p. 1977. 8.00x (ISBN 0-88312-067-4); microfiche (2) 4.00 (ISBN 0-88312-467-X). Summer Inst Ling.
Studies in Outdoor Recreation. Robert E. Manning. LC 85-15447. (Illus.). 184p. 1986. pap. text ed. 13.95x (ISBN 0-87071-345-0). Oreg St U Pr.
Studies in Overseas Settlement & Population. Anthony Lemon & Norman Pollock. LC 79-42738. pap. 33.30 (ISBN 0-317-30106-3, 2025274). Bks Demand UMI.
Studies in Paleontology & Stratigraphy. Ed. by J. Pojeta, Jr. & J. K. Pope. (Illus.). 456p. 1975. 25.00 (ISBN 0-87710-296-1). Paleo Res.
Studies in Parapsychology. Sigmund Freud. 224p. 1985. pap. 4.95 (ISBN 0-02-076550-9, Collier). MacMillan.
Studies in Parasitology in Memory of Clark P. Read. C. Arme et al. Ed. by J. E. Byram & George Stewart. (Rice University Studies: Vol. 62, No. 4). 236p. 1977. pap. 10.00x (ISBN 0-89263-230-5). Rice Univ.
Studies in Partial Differential Equations. Ed. by Walter Littman. LC 82-62782. (MAA Studies in Mathematics Ser.: No. 23). 280p. 1983. 30.00 (ISBN 0-88385-125-3). Math Assn.
Studies in Paul's Epistles. Frederic L. Godet. LC 84-7138. 352p. 1984. 14.95 (ISBN 0-8254-2723-1). Kregel.
Studies in Peerage & Family History. Horace Round. (Genealogy Ser.: No. 2). 496p. 1971. Repr. of 1907 ed. 45.00x (Pub. by Woburn Pr England). Biblio Dist.
Studies in Peerage & Family History. John H. Round. LC 72-124475. 496p. 1970. Repr. of 1901 ed. 22.50 (ISBN 0-8063-0426-X). Genealog Pub.
Studies in Peirce's Semiotic: A Symposium. Institute for Studies in Pragmaticism. LC 79-90875. (Peirce Studies Ser.). 108p. 1979. 22.50x (ISBN 0-936842-01-6); pap. 10.95x (ISBN 0-936842-00-8). Ind U Pr.
Studies in Perception. Ross H. Day & Gordon V. Stanley. 1977. 14.50x (ISBN 0-85564-121-5, Pub. by U of W Austral Pr). Intl Spec Bk.
Studies in Perception: Interrelations in the History of Philosophy & Science. Ed. by Peter K. Machamer & Robert G. Turnbull. LC 77-10857. (Illus.). 577p. 1978. 37.50x (ISBN 0-8142-0244-6). Ohio St U Pr.
Studies in Perfectionism. B. B. Warfield. 15.95 (ISBN 0-8010-9587-5). Baker Bk.
Studies in Perfectionism. Benjamin B. Warfield. LC 58-11208. 1958. 15.95 (ISBN 0-87552-528-8). Presby & Reformed.
Studies in Personalism. Edgar S. Brightman. Ed. by Warren Steinkraus & Robert Beck. (Signature Series of Philosophy & Religion). 1988. 25.00 (ISBN 0-86610-067-9). Meridian Pub.
Studies in Peruvian Indian Languages I. Mildred Larson et al. (Publications in Linguistics & Related Fields Ser.: No. 9). 220p. 1963. microfiche (3) 6.00 (ISBN 0-88312-409-2). Summer Inst Ling.
Studies in Pessimism. Arthur Schopenhauer. 1903. Repr. 29.00x (ISBN 0-403-00044-0). Scholarly.
Studies in Pessimism. Arthur Schopenhauer. 1988. Repr. of 1903 ed. lib. bdg. 49.00x. Am Biog Serv.
Studies in Phenomenology. Sinha. (Phaenomenologica Ser: No. 30). 1969. lib. bdg. 21.00 (ISBN 90-247-0267-4, Pub. by Martinus Nijhoff Netherlands); pap. 13.00 (ISBN 90-247-0266-6). Kluwer Academic.
Studies in Phenomenology & Psychology. Aron Gurwitsch. (Studies in Phenomenology & Existential Philosophy Ser). 1966. 36.95 (ISBN 0-8101-0110-6); pap. 16.95 (ISBN 0-8101-0592-6). Northwestern U Pr.
Studies in Philemon. W. Graham Scroggie. LC 77-79186. (W. Graham Scroggie Library). 136p. 1982. pap. 4.50 (ISBN 0-8254-3739-3). Kregel.
Studies in Philippians. R. C. Bell. 1956. pap. 7.50 (ISBN 0-88027-043-8). Firm Foun Pub.
Studies in Philippians. H. C. Moule. LC 77-79184. (Kregel Popular Commentary Ser.). 136p. 1977. kivar 6.95 (ISBN 0-8254-3216-2). Kregel.
Studies in Philosophy. Reinhold F. Hoernle. Ed. by Daniel S. Robinson. LC 72-5614. (Essay Index Reprint Ser.). 1972. Repr. of 1952 ed. 22.00 (ISBN 0-8369-2992-6). Ayer Co Pubs.
Studies in Philosophy. George H. Howison. (Publications in Philosophy Ser: Vol. 1). 1904. 24.00 (ISBN 0-384-24480-7). Johnson Repr.
Studies in Philosophy: A Symposium on Gilbert Ryle. Ed. by Konstantin Kolenda. (Rice University Studies: No. 58, No. 3). 134p. 1972. pap. 10.00x (ISBN 0-89263-213-5). Rice Univ.
Studies in Philosophy & in the History of Science. Ed. by Richard Tursman. 220p. 1970. 7.50x (ISBN 0-87291-007-5). Coronado Pr.
Studies in Philosophy & Psychology. Ed. by James H. Tufts et al. LC 75-3153. 1976. Repr. of 1906 ed. 29.50 (ISBN 0-404-59159-0). AMS Pr.
Studies in Philosophy & the History of Philosophy, Vol. 2. Ed. by John K. Ryan. LC 61-66336. pap. 66.50 (2029505). Bks Demand UMI.
Studies in Philosophy & the History of Philosophy, Vol. 4. Ed. by John K. Ryan. LC 61-66336. Repr. of 1969 ed. 59.50 (ISBN 0-8357-9057-6, 2017279). Bks Demand UMI.
Studies in Philosophy & the History of Philosophy: Ancients & Moderns, Vol.5. Ed. by John K. Ryan. LC 61-66336. pap. 93.50 (ISBN 0-317-12990-2, 2017280). Bks Demand UMI.
Studies in Philosophy & Theology. Ed. by Emil C. Wilm. LC 75-3078. Repr. of 1922 ed. 17.00 (ISBN 0-404-59079-9). AMS Pr.
Studies in Philosophy, British Academy Lectures. Ed. by John N. Findlay. (Oxford Paperbacks Ser). (Orig.). 1966. pap. 6.95x (ISBN 0-19-283004-X). Oxford U Pr.
Studies in Phonetics. Milan Romportle. (Janua Linguarum, Ser. Major: No. 61). 217p. 1973. text ed. 24.00x (ISBN 90-2792-667-0). Mouton.
Studies in Physical Oceanography, 2 vols. A. Gordon. 456p. 1972. Set. 152.00 (ISBN 0-677-12910-6); Vol. 1. 80.00 (ISBN 0-677-15160-8); Vol. 2. 92.00 (ISBN 0-677-15170-5). Gordon & Breach.
Studies in Plant Ecology. Ed. by Erik Sjogren. (Illus.). 192p. (Orig.). 1980. pap. text ed. 23.50x (ISBN 0-317-46474-4, Pub. by Almqvist & Wiksell). Coronet Bks.
Studies in Platonic Political Philosophy. Leo Strauss et al. Ed. by Thomas L. Pangle. LC 83-5064. 264p. 1985. lib. bdg. 27.50x (ISBN 0-226-77703-0); 8.95x (ISBN 0-226-77700-6). U of Chicago Pr.
Studies in Play & Games, 21 vols. Ed. by Brian Sutton-Smith. 1976. Set. 536.00x (ISBN 0-405-07912-5). Ayer Co Pubs.
Studies in Poetry & Criticism. John C. Collins. LC 72-12568. 1973. lib. bdg. 27.00 (ISBN 0-8414-0928-5). Folcroft.
Studies in Poetry & Philosophy. J. C. Shairp. LC 70-113345. 1970. Repr. of 1868 ed. 24.50x (ISBN 0-8046-1052-5, Pub. by Kennikat). Assoc Faculty Pr.
Studies in Poetry & Philosophy. J. C. Shairp. 1973. 35.00 (ISBN 0-8274-1370-X). R West.
Studies in Polish Civilization: Selected Papers. Polish Institute of Arts & Sciences in America, N.Y., 1966. Ed. by Damian Wandycz. 1971. 9.00 (ISBN 0-940962-43-8). Polish Inst Art & Sci.
Studies in Polish Life & History. A. E. Tennant. 1977. lib. bdg. 59.95 (ISBN 0-8490-2703-9). Gordon Pr.
Studies in Political Economy. Anthony Musgrave. LC 67-18581. 1968. Repr. of 1875 ed. 27.50x (ISBN 0-678-00337-8). Kelley.
Studies in Political Science & Sociology. Pennsylvania University Bicentennial Conference. Ed. by Hu Shih & Newton Edwards. LC 68-26201. Repr. of 1941 ed. 22.50x (ISBN 0-8046-0357-X, Pub. by Kennikat). Assoc Faculty Pr.
Studies in Politics: National & International. M. S. Rajan. 1971. 15.00 (ISBN 0-89684-502-8). Orient Bk Dist.
Studies in Population & Economic Development, 2 vols. B. N. Ghosh. 1987. Set. 80.00x (ISBN 81-7100-025-8, Pub. by Deep) (ISBN 81-7100-024-X). South Asia Bks.
Studies in Portuguese Literature. A. F. Bell. 69.95 (ISBN 0-87968-243-4). Gordon Pr.
Studies in Post-Impressionism. John Rewald. (Illus.). 296p. 1986. 37.50 (ISBN 0-8109-1632-0). Abrams.
Studies in Post Samkara Dialectics. 2nd ed. Ashutash Bhattacharya. 339p. 1987. 28.00 (ISBN 81-7030-035-5, Pub. by SRI SATGURU Pubns India). Orient Bk Dist.
Studies in Power & Class in Africa. Ed. by Irving L. Markovitz. (Illus.). 415p. 1987. 36.00 (ISBN 0-19-504129-1); pap. text ed. 14.95 (ISBN 0-19-504130-5). Oxford U Pr.
Studies in Pre-School Education. Ed. by M. M. Clark & W. M. Cheyne. (SCRE Ser.: No. 70). 292p. 1979. text ed. 22.50x (ISBN 0-901116-68-8, Pub. by Scot Council Research). Humanities.
Studies in Primitive Looms. H. Ling Roth. 1977. pap. 7.95 (ISBN 0-686-19834-4). Robin & Russ.
Studies in Probability & Ergodic Theory: Advances in Mathematics Supplementary Studies, Vol. 2. Ed. by Gian-Carlo Rota. 1978. 89.00 (ISBN 0-12-599102-9). Acad Pr.
Studies in Probability & Statistics. Ed. by E. J. Williams. 172p. 1976. 68.50 (ISBN 0-7204-0434-7, North-Holland). Elsevier.
Studies in Probability Theory. Ed. by Murray Rosenblatt. LC 78-71935. (MAA Studies in Mathematics: Vol. 18). 268p. 1978. 26.50 (ISBN 0-88385-118-0). Math Assn.
Studies in Prose & Poetry. Algernon C. Swinburne. 14.00 (ISBN 0-8369-7331-3, 8124). Ayer Co Pubs.
Studies in Prose & Verse. Arthur Symons. LC 78-148315. Repr. of 1922 ed. 14.50 (ISBN 0-404-07827-3). AMS Pr.
Studies in Proverbs. William Arnot. LC 78-6014. (Reprint Library). Orig. Title: Laws From Heaven for Life on Earth. 584p. 1986. pap. 14.95 (ISBN 0-8254-2123-3). Kregel.
Studies in Proverbs. Maurice Meredith. pap. 2.50 (ISBN 0-89315-261-7). Lambert Bk.
Studies in Proverbs: Wise Words in a Wicked World. Charles W. Turner. (Contemporary Discussion Ser.). 1977. pap. 3.50 (ISBN 0-8010-8815-1). Baker Bk.
Studies in Psalms, Vol. I. Joseph B. Rotherham. Ed. by Don DeWelt. (Bible Study Textbook Ser.). (Illus.). 1970. Repr. 14.95 (ISBN 0-89900-016-9). College Pr Pub.
Studies in Psalms, Vol. II. rev. ed. Joseph B. Rotherham. Ed. by Don DeWelt. (Bible Study Textbook Ser.). (Illus.). 1971. Repr. of 1901 ed. 14.95 (ISBN 0-89900-017-7). College Pr Pub.
Studies in Psalms. Robert R. Taylor, Jr. pap. 5.95 (ISBN 0-89137-560-0). Quality Pubns.
Studies in Psychiatric Art: Its Psychodynamics, Therapeutic Value & Relationship to Modern Art. photocopy ed. R. W. Pickford. (Illus.). 360p. 1967. 40.75 (ISBN 0-398-01487-6). C C Thomas.
Studies in Psychiatry. New York Psychiatrical Society. (Nervous & Mental Disease Monographs: No. 9). 1912. 19.00 (ISBN 0-384-41249-1). Johnson Repr.
Studies in Psychical Research. Frank Podmore. LC 75-7393. (Perspectives in Psychical Research Ser.). 1975. Repr. of 1897 ed. 35.50x (ISBN 0-405-07042-X). Ayer Co Pubs.
Studies in Psychoanalysis: An Account of Twenty-Seven Concrete Cases Preceded by a Theoretical Exposition. Comprising Lectures Delivered in Geneva at the Jean Jacques Rousseau Institute and at the Faculty of Letters in the University. Charles Baudouin et al. Tr. by Eden Paul & Cedar Paul. 1979. Repr. of 1922 ed. lib. bdg. 30.00 (ISBN 0-8495-0532-1). Arden Lib.
Studies in Psychology from Smith College see Serial Reactions Considered As Conditioned Reactions.
Studies in Psychology from the University of Illinois see On the Melodic Relativity of Tones.
Studies in Psychology of Reading. William C. Morse et al. LC 68-54427. (Michigan University Monographs in Education: No. 4). 1968. Repr. of 1951 ed. lib. bdg. 35.00 (ISBN 0-8371-0176-X, MOPR). Greenwood.
Studies in Psychology of Reading see Studies in the Psychology of Art.
Studies in Psychology: The Collective & the Individual. A. V. Petrovsky. 254p. 1985. 7.95 (ISBN 0-8285-3062-9, Pub. by Progress Pub USSR). Imported Pubns.
Studies in Public Enterprise. V. V. Ramanadham. 275p. 1986. 32.50x (ISBN 0-7146-3267-8, F Cass Co). Biblio Dist.
Studies in Public Finance. Edwin R. Seligman. LC 68-58013. 1969. Repr. of 1925 ed. 39.50x (ISBN 0-678-00490-0). Kelley.
Studies in Public Regulation. Ed. by Gary Fromm. (Regulation of Economic Activity Ser.). (Illus.). 400p. 1981. 60.00x (ISBN 0-262-06074-4). MIT Pr.
Studies in Public Regulation. Ed. by Gary Fromm & Schmalensee. (Regulation of Economic Activity Ser. (REA)). (Illus.). 368p. 1981. pap. text ed. 17.50x (ISBN 0-262-56028-3). MIT Pr.
Studies in Punjab Economy. R. S. Johar & J. S. Khanna. 1983. 14.50x (ISBN 0-8364-1602-3, Pub. by Nanak Dev Univ India). South Asia Bks.
Studies in Pure Mathematics: To the Memory of Paul Turan. Ed. by Paul Erdoes. 400p. 1983. 78.00 (ISBN 0-8176-1288-2). Birkhauser.
Studies in Qualitative Methodology, Vol. 1. Ed. by Robert Burgess. 1988. 58.50 (ISBN 0-89232-762-6). Jai Pr.
Studies in Qur'an & Hadith: The Formation of the Islamic Law of Inheritance. David S. Powers. 1986. text ed. 30.00x (ISBN 0-520-05558-6). U of Cal Pr.

Studies in Qur'an & Tafsir. Ed. by Alford Welch. (Thematic Studies). 1980. pap. 8.95 (ISBN 0-89130-678-1, 01-24-74). Scholars Pr GA.

Studies in Radiation Effects in Solids, 3 vols. G. J. Dienes. LC 66-24006. 992p. Set. 73.00 (ISBN 0-685-58276-0, 450001). Am Nuclear Soc.

Studies in Radiotherapeutics. Joseph S. Mitchell. LC 60-3368. (Illus.). 1960. 18.50x (ISBN 0-674-84930-2). Harvard U Pr.

Studies in Railway Expansion & the Capital Market in England: 1825-73. Seymour Broadbridge. 216p. 1970. 35.00x (ISBN 0-7146-1287-1, F Cass Co). Biblio Dist.

Studies in Real & Complex Analysis. Ed. by I. I. Hirschmann, Jr. LC 65-22403. (MAA Studies: No. 3). 213p. 1965. 21.00 (ISBN 0-88385-103-2). Math Assn.

Studies in Recent Australian Novel. Ed. by K. G. Hamilton. 257p. 1979. 34.50x (ISBN 0-7022-1247-4). U of Queensland Pr.

Studies in Regional Consciousness & Environment: Essays Presented to H. J. Fleure. facs. ed. Ed. by I. C. Peate. LC 68-26478. (Essay Index Reprint Ser). (Illus.). 1968. Repr. of 1930 ed. 20.00 (ISBN 0-8369-0917-8). Ayer Co Pubs.

Studies in Relational Grammar. David M. Perlmutter et al. LC 82-6945. (No. 2). 1984. lib. bdg. 35.00x (ISBN 0-226-66051-6). U of Chicago Pr.

Studies in Relational Grammar 1. Ed. by David M. Perlmutter. LC 82-6945. xvi, 412p. 1986. lib. bdg. 34.00x (ISBN 0-226-66050-8); pap. 15.95x (ISBN 0-226-66052-4). U of Chicago Pr.

Studies in Relevance: Romantic & Victorian Writers in 1972. Thomas M. Harwell. Ed. by James Hogg. (Romantic Reassessment Ser.). 171p. (Orig.). 1973. pap. 15.00 (Pub. by Salzburg Studies). Longwood Pub Group.

Studies in Religion & Education. J. Hull. 292p. 1984. 36.00x (ISBN 0-905273-52-4, Falmer Pr); pap. 20.00x (ISBN 0-905273-51-6). Taylor & Francis.

Studies in Religious Fundamentalism. Ed. by Lionel Caplan. LC 86-30026. 240p. 1988. 49.50 (ISBN 0-88706-518-X); pap. 14.95x (ISBN 0-88706-519-8). State U NY Pr.

Studies in Religious Philosophy & Mysticism. Alexander Altmann. (New Reprints in Essay & General Literature Index Ser.). 1975. Repr. of 1969 ed. 24.25 (ISBN 0-518-10194-0). Ayer Co Pubs.

Studies in Religious Poetry of the Seventeenth Century: Essays on Henry Vaughn, Francis Quarles, Richard Crawshaw, John Davies, Henry More & Thomas Traherne. W. L. Doughty. LC 68-26278. Repr. of 1946 ed. 23.00x (ISBN 0-8046-0113-5, Pub. by Kennikat). Assoc Faculty Pr.

Studies in Remembering: The Reproduction of Connected & Extended Verbal Material. I. H. Paul. (Psychological Issues Monograph: No. 2, Vol. 1, No. 2). 152p. (Orig.). 1959. text ed. 20.00x (ISBN 0-8236-6240-3). Intl Univs Pr.

Studies in Renaissance & Baroque Music in Honor of Arthur Mendel. Ed. by Robert L. Marshall. 1974. 37.00 (ISBN 0-913574-26-0, EAMARS). Eur-Am Music.

Studies in Renewable Resource Policy, 2 vols. Michael Barker. 1981. pap. write for info. (ISBN 0-934842-74-4). CSPA.

Studies in Resource Allocation Process. Ed. by K. J. Arrow & L. Hurwicz. LC 76-9171. (Illus.). 1977. 62.50 (ISBN 0-521-21522-6). Cambridge U Pr.

Studies in Revelation. W. M. Davis. 1976. pap. 2.75 (ISBN 0-88027-044-6). Firm Foun Pub.

Studies in Revelation. Herman A. Hoyt. pap. 5.95 (ISBN 0-88469-118-7). BMH Bks.

Studies in Revelation. W. Leon Tucker. LC 80-16206. (Kregel Bible Study Classics Ser.). 400p. 1980. 14.95 (ISBN 0-8254-3826-8). Kregel.

Studies in Roman Economic & Social History in Honor of Allan Chester Johnson. facs. ed. Ed. by Paul R. Coleman-Norton. LC 70-80384. (Essay Index Reprint Ser). 1951. 23.75 (ISBN 0-8369-1027-3). Ayer Co Pubs.

Studies in Roman Literature, Culture & Religion. Hendrik Wagenvoort. Ed. by Steele Commager. LC 77-70817. (Latin Poetry Ser.: Vol. 31). 1978. lib. bdg. 40.00 (ISBN 0-8240-2981-X). Garland Pub.

Studies in Roman Property. Ed. by M. I. Finley. (Classical Studies). (Illus.). 192p. 1976. 17.95 (ISBN 0-521-21115-8). Cambridge U Pr.

Studies in Romance Languages: Selected Proceedings of the 15th Linguistic Symposium on Romance Languages. Ed. by C. Neidle & R. A. Nunez-Cedeno. (Publications in Language Sciences). xiv, 318p. 1987. 49.00 (ISBN 90-6765-293-8); pap. 29.00 (ISBN 90-6765-294-6). Foris Pubns.

Studies in Romance Linguistics: Selected Papers of the Fourteenth Linguistics Symposium on romance Languages. Ed. by O. Jaeggli & C. Silva-Corvalan. (Publications in Language Sciences). viii, 452p. 1986. pap. 26.90 (ISBN 90-6765-253-9). Foris Pubns.

Studies in Romans. R. C. Bell. 1957. pap. 2.75 (ISBN 0-88027-025-X). Firm Foun Pub.

Studies in Romans. W. Leon Tucker. LC 83-6114. 112p. 1983. pap. 4.95 (ISBN 0-8254-3827-6). Kregel.

Studies in Romans, Vol. 2. Richard A. Brown. (Bible Study Ser.). 1986. pap. 3.50 (ISBN 0-8309-0454-9). Herald Hse.

Studies in Romans: A Suggestive Commentary on Paul's Epistle to the Romans, 2 vols. in 1. Thomas Robinson. LC 82-7795. (Kregel Bible Study Classics Ser.). 912p. 1982. 24.95 (ISBN 0-8254-3625-7). Kregel.

Studies in Romanticism. Kenneth Hunt. 1980. Set. 60.00 (ISBN 0-915042-18-5). Lib Soc Sci.

Studies in Ruskin: Some Aspects of the Work & Teaching of John Ruskin. Edward T. Cook. 1978. Repr. of 1890 ed. lib. bdg. 25.00 (ISBN 0-8495-0728-6). Arden Lib.

Studies in Russian Historical Geography. James H. Bater & R. Anthony French. 1983. Vol. 1. 52.00 (ISBN 0-12-081201-0); Vol. 2. 44.50 (ISBN 0-12-081202-9). Acad Pr.

Studies in Russian Literature. C. E. Turner. Repr. of 1882 ed. 23.00 (ISBN 0-527-91150-X). Kraus Repr.

Studies in Russian Literature in Honor of Vsevolod Setchkarev. Ed. by Julian W. Connolly & Sonia I. Ketchian. (Illus.). 288p. (Orig.). 1987. pap. 15.95 (ISBN 0-89357-174-1). Slavica.

Studies in Russian Music. Gerald Abraham. 1988. Repr. of 1935 ed. lib. bdg. 49.00x. Am Biog Serv.

Studies in Russian Music. facs. ed. Gerald E. Abraham. LC 68-20285. (Essay Index Reprint Ser). 1936. 18.00 (ISBN 0-8369-0133-9). Ayer Co Pubs.

Studies in Russian Music. Gerald E. Abraham. 1976. Repr. of 1935 ed. lib. bdg. 16.00x (ISBN 0-403-03700-X). Scholarly.

Studies in Ruth. Brenda Robertson. (Bible Studies). (Illus.). 32p. 1988. pap. 3.50 (ISBN 0-8309-0523-5). Herald Hse.

Studies in Sanskrit Dramatic Criticism. T. G. Mainkar. 1971. 10.50 (ISBN 0-89684-324-6). Orient Bk Dist.

Studies in Sardinian Archaeology. Ed. by Miriam S. Balmuth & Robert J. Rowland. 1986. 25.00x (ISBN 0-472-10047-5). U of Mich Pr.

Studies in Sardinian Archaeology, Vol. II: Sardinia in the Mediterranean. Ed. by Miriam S. Balmuth. (Illus.). 320p. 1986. text ed. 30.00 (ISBN 0-472-10081-5). U of Mich Pr.

Studies in Scarlet: Essays on Mystery & Detective Fiction. Frank D. McSherry, Jr. LC 84-12353. (I. O. Evans Studies in the Philosophy & Criticism of Literature: No. 16). 144p. (Orig.). Date not set. lib. bdg. 19.95x (ISBN 0-89370-310-9); pap. 9.95x (ISBN 0-89370-410-5). Borgo Pr.

Studies in School Self-Evaluation. P. S. Clift et al. 180p. 1987. 37.00x (ISBN 1-85000-242-8, Falmer Pr); pap. 18.00x (ISBN 1-85000-241-X, Falmer Pr). Taylor & Francis.

Studies in Science. Ed. by William C. Coker. LC 77-39098. (Essay Index Reprint Ser.). (University of North Carolina sesquicentennial publications). Repr. of 1946 ed. 40.00 (ISBN 0-8369-2683-8). Ayer Co Pubs.

Studies in Scottish Antiquity. D. J. Breeze & N. Reynolds. (Illus.). 1984. text ed. 60.00 (ISBN 0-85976-075-8, Pub. by John Donald Pub UK). Humanities.

Studies in Scottish Business History. Ed. by P. L. Payne. 435p. 1967. 37.50x (ISBN 0-7146-1349-5, F Cass Co). Biblio Dist.

Studies in Scottish Business History. Ed. by Peter L. Payne. LC 67-20815. (Illus.). 1967. 39.50x (ISBN 0-678-05076-7). Kelley.

Studies in Scripture: Acts to Revelation, Vol. 6. Ed. by Robert L. Millet. LC 87-70686. 304p. 1987. 14.95 (ISBN 0-87579-084-4). Deseret Bk.

Studies in Scripture: The Gospels, Vol. 5. Compiled by Kent P. Jackson & Robert Millet. LC 86-23981. 490p. 1986. text ed. 15.95 (ISBN 0-87579-064-X). Deseret Bk.

Studies in Scripture: The Old Testament, Vol. III. Robert Millett & Kent Jackson. 345p. 1985. 13.95 (ISBN 0-934126-81-X). Randall Bk Co.

Studies in Scripture: The Pearl of Great Price, Vol. II. Robert Millett & Kent Jackson. 446p. Date not set. price not set (ISBN 0-934126-74-7). Randall Bk Co.

Studies in Scripture: 1 Nephi - Alma 29, Vol. 7. Ed. by Kent P. Jackson. LC 87-27030. 372p. 1987. 15.95 (ISBN 0-87579-117-4). Deseret Bk.

Studies in Scriptures: The Doctrine & Covenants, Vol. I. Kent Jackson & Robert Millett. 615p. Date not set. 15.95 (ISBN 0-934126-60-7). Randall Bk Co.

Studies in Second Corinthians. Don Compier. (Bible Study Ser.). 1987. pap. 3.50 (ISBN 0-8309-0479-4). Herald Hse.

Studies in Second Corinthians. Wallace Wartick. (Bible Student Study Guides Ser.). 1977. pap. 3.95 (ISBN 0-89900-155-6). College Pr Pub.

Studies in Second Timothy. H. C. Moule. LC 77-79182. (Kregel Popular Commentary Ser.). 180p. 1977. kivar 6.95 (ISBN 0-8254-3219-7). Kregel.

Studies in Seicento Art & Theory. Denis Mahon. LC 73-114544. (Illus.). 1971. Repr. of 1947 ed. lib. bdg. 27.50x (ISBN 0-8371-4743-3, MAST). Greenwood.

Studies in Semitic Syntax, Vol. 38. Geoffrey Khan. (London Oriental Ser.). (Illus.). 288p. 1988. 69.00 (ISBN 0-19-713607-9). Oxford U Pr.

Studies in Sephardic Culture: The David N. Barocas Memorial Volume. Ed. by Marc D. Angel. LC 79-92737. (Illus.). 190p. 1980. 15.00 (ISBN 0-87203-090-3). Hermon.

Studies in Seven Arts. Arthur Symons. 1978. Repr. of 1910 ed. lib. bdg. 25.00 (ISBN 0-8492-8078-8). R West.

Studies in Seven Arts. Arthur Symons. LC 82-4901. (Degeneration & Regeneration Ser.). 403p. 1984. lib. bdg. 52.00 (ISBN 0-8240-5562-4). Garland Pub.

Studies in Seventeenth Century English Literature, History & Bibliography. G. Janssens & F. Aarts. (Costerus New Ser.: No. 46). 268p. 1984. pap. text ed. 28.50x (ISBN 90-6203-736-4, Pub. by Rodopi Holland). Humanities.

Studies in Seventeenth Century Imagery, 2 vols. in 1. Manrio Praz. LC 40-3654. Repr. 79.00x (ISBN 0-403-07208-5). Somerset Pub.

Studies in Seventeenth-Century Poetic. Ruth C. Wallerstein. (Illus.). 432p. 1950. pap. 7.50x (ISBN 0-299-00654-9). U of Wis Pr.

Studies in Several Literatures. facs. ed. Harry T. Peck. LC 68-16967. (Essay Index Reprint Ser). 1909. 18.00 (ISBN 0-8369-0781-7). Ayer Co Pubs.

Studies in Several Literatures. Harry T. Peck. 1973. Repr. of 1909 ed. 33.00 (ISBN 0-8274-1228-2). R West.

Studies in Sexual Inversion. John A. Symonds. LC 72-9683. Repr. of 1928 ed. 32.50 (ISBN 0-404-57503-X). AMS Pr.

Studies in Shakespeare. John C. Collins. LC 72-944. Repr. of 1904 ed. 12.50 (ISBN 0-404-01637-5). AMS Pr.

Studies in Shakespeare. Ed. by Arthur D. Matthews & Clark M. Emery. LC 79-144658. Repr. of 1953 ed. 17.25 (ISBN 0-404-04267-8). AMS Pr.

Studies in Shakespeare. Allardyce Nicoll. LC 73-470. lib. bdg. 35.50 (ISBN 0-8414-1558-7). Folcroft.

Studies in Shakespeare. 3rd ed. Richard G. White. LC 74-177834. Repr. of 1887 ed. 17.50 (ISBN 0-404-06935-5). AMS Pr.

Studies in Shakespeare, Milton & Donne. Oscar J. Campbell et al. Ed. by Eugene S. McCartney. LC 78-93244. (University of Michigan Publications: Vol. 1). 235p. 1970. Repr. of 1925 ed. 27.50x (ISBN 0-87753-020-3). Phaeton.

Studies in Shakespeare, Milton & Donne. Michigan University Department of English. LC 65-15881. (Studies in English Literature, No. 33). 1972. Repr. of 1925 ed. lib. bdg. 75.00x (ISBN 0-8383-0638-1). Haskell.

Studies in Shelley. M. M. Bhalla. 1973. 10.50 (ISBN 0-686-20311-9). Intl Bk Dist.

Studies in Shelley. Amiyakuman Sen. LC 72-194999. 1936. lib. bdg. 29.00 (ISBN 0-8414-8131-8). Folcroft.

Studies in Shinto Thought, 10 vols. Tsunetsugu Muraoka. Tr. by Delmer M. Brown & James T. Araki. (Documentary Reference Collection). 1988. Set. 395.00 (CMJ/); 49.85 (ISBN 0-313-26555-0, MTO/). Greenwood.

Studies in Siberian Ethnogenesis. LC 67-53579. (Arctic Institute of North America Ser. Anthropology of the North; Translations from Russian Sources: No. 2). pap. 80.30 (ISBN 0-317-10879-4, 2019172). Bks Demand UMI.

Studies in Sir Thomas Browne. Robert Cawley & George Yost. LC 65-29995. 1965. 5.00 (ISBN 0-87114-011-X). U of Oreg Bks.

Studies in Social & General Psychology from the University of Illinois see Mental Measurements of the Blind.

Studies in Social & Legal Theories: An Historical Account of the Social, Ethical, Political & Legal Doctrines of the Foremost Ancient & Medieval Philosophers. Meyer B. Barr. 148p. 1982. Repr. of 1932 ed. lib. bdg. 20.00x (ISBN 0-8377-0327-1). Rothman.

Studies in Social & Private Accounting. Solomon Fabricant. LC 82-82488. (Accountancy in Transition Ser.). 300p. 1982. lib. bdg. 44.00 (ISBN 0-8240-5337-0). Garland Pub.

Studies in Social Change Since 1948, Vol. 1: Methodological. James A. Davis. (Report Ser: No. 127-A). 1976. 4.50x (ISBN 0-932132-19-7). NORC.

Studies in Social Change Since 1948, Vol. 2: Substantive. James A. Davis. (Report Ser: No. 127-B). 1976. 7.00x (ISBN 0-932132-20-0). NORC.

Studies in Social History. facs. ed. Ed. by John H. Plumb. LC 71-80395. (Essay Index Reprint Ser). 1955. 22.00 (ISBN 0-8369-1063-X). Ayer Co Pubs.

Studies in Social Identity. Theodore R. Sarbin & Karl Scheibe. LC 82-16580. 410p. 1983. 42.95 (ISBN 0-275-91073-3, C1073). Praeger.

Studies in Social Interaction. D. Sudnow. LC 79-168542. 1972. 23.95 (ISBN 0-02-932360-6). Free Pr.

Studies in Social Movements. Ed. by Barry McLaughlin. LC 69-17783. 1969. 19.95 (ISBN 0-02-920560-3). Free Pr.

Studies in Social Power. Ed. by Dorwin P. Cartwright. LC 59-63036. 225p. 1959. 12.00x (ISBN 0-87944-230-1). Inst Soc Res.

Studies in Social Psychology in World War 2, 3 vols. Ed. by Robert K. Merton. Incl. Vol. 1. American Soldiers: Adjustment During Army Life; Vol. 2. American Soldiers: Combat & Its Aftermath; Vol. 3. Experiments on Mass Communication. LC 73-14180. (Perspectives in Social Inquiry Ser.). 1662p. 1974. Repr. 88.00 (ISBN 0-405-05523-4). Ayer Co Pubs.

Studies in Social Psychology in World War II, Prepared & Edited under the Auspices of a Special Committee of the Social Science Research Council: Volume 3 - Experiences on Mass Communication. C. I. Hovland et al. pap. 88.80 (ISBN 0-317-10520-5, 2000439). Bks Demand UMI.

Studies in Socialism. Authorized English Edition ed. J. L. Jaures. Repr. of 1906 ed. 23.00 (ISBN 0-8115-0017-9). Kraus Repr.

Studies in Socialist Pedagogy. Ed. by Theodore M. Norton & Bertell Ollman. LC 77-91734. 405p. 1979. 16.50 (ISBN 0-85345-440-X); pap. 6.50 (ISBN 0-85345-500-7). Monthly Rev.

Studies in Socialist Pedogogy. Ed. by Bertell Ollman. 405p. 1978. 16.50 (ISBN 0-317-61681-1); pap. 6.50 (ISBN 0-317-61682-X). Monthly Rev.

Studies in Southeastern Indian Languages. Ed. by James D. Crawford. (Illus.). 453p. 1975. 25.00 (ISBN 0-8203-0334-8). Brown Bk.

Studies in Southeastern Indian Languages. James M. Crawford. LC 73-90840. (Illus.). 464p. 1975. 25.00 (ISBN 0-87797-112-9). Cherokee.

Studies in Southern History & Politics. Compiled by William A. Dujning. 1964. Repr. of 1914 ed. 24.50x (ISBN 0-8046-0451-7, Pub. by Kennikat). Assoc Faculty Pr.

Studies in Southern Nigerian History. Ed. by Boniface I. Obichere. 278p. 1982. 32.50x (ISBN 0-7146-3106-X, F Cass Co). Biblio Dist.

Studies in Southern Presbyterian Theology. Morton H. Smith. LC 87-7368. 367p. 1987. Repr. 11.95 (ISBN 0-87552-449-4). Presby & Reformed.

Studies in Soviet Economic Planning. Aron Katsenelinboigen. Tr. by Arlo Schultz. LC 77-90277. pap. 61.30 (ISBN 0-317-41954-4, 2026133). Bks Demand UMI.

Studies in Soviet Thought. Ed. by J. M. Bochenski & T. J. Blakeley. (Sovietica Ser.: No. 7). 141p. 1961. lib. bdg. 24.00 (ISBN 90-277-0051-6, Pub. by Reidel Holland). Kluwer Academic.

Studies in Spanish-American Literature. Isaac Goldberg. 59.95 (ISBN 0-8490-1149-3). Gordon Pr.

Studies in Spanish-American Literature. Issac Goldberg. LC 67-27600. 1968. Repr. of 1920 ed. 25.50 (ISBN 0-8046-0171-2, Pub. by Kennikat). Assoc Faculty Pr.

Studies in Spanish Literature of the Golden Age. Ed. by R. O. Jones. (Serie A: Monagrafias, XXX). 372p. (Orig.). 1973. pap. 20.00 (ISBN 0-900411-68-6, Pub. by Tamesis Bks Ltd). Longwood Pub Group.

Studies in Spanish Phonology. Tomas Navarro. Tr. by Richard D. Abraham. LC 68-31043. (Miami Linguistics Ser: No. 4). 1968. 9.95x (ISBN 0-87024-096-X). U of Miami Pr.

Studies in Spanish Renaissance Thought. Norena. (International Archives of the History of Ideas Ser: No. 82). 1975. lib. bdg. 50.00 (ISBN 90-247-1727-2, Pub. by Martinus Nijhoff Netherlands). Kluwer Academic.

Studies in Speculative Philosophy. James E. Creighton. Ed. by H. R. Stuart. 1925. 31.00 (ISBN 0-527-20500-1). Kraus Repr.

Studies in Speculative Philosopy. James E. Creighton. 290p. 1982. Repr. of 1925 ed. lib. bdg. 35.00. Darby Bks.

Studies in Spenser. M. M. Bhattacherje. LC 74-13422. 1929. lib. bdg. 20.00 (ISBN 0-8414-3253-8). Folcroft.

Studies in Spenser's Complaints. Harold Stein. LC 72-191961. 1934. lib. bdg. 35.00 (ISBN 0-8414-7818-X). Folcroft.

Studies in Spenser's Historical Allegory. Edwin Greenlaw. 1978. Repr. of 1932 ed. lib. bdg. 35.00 (ISBN 0-8414-4463-3). Folcroft.

Studies in Spinoza: Critical & Interpretative Essays. Ed. by S. Paul Kashap. LC 71-174459. 360p. 1973. pap. 10.95x (ISBN 0-520-02590-3). U of Cal Pr.

Studies in Stagecraft. Clayton Hamilton. 1975. Repr. of 1914 ed. 20.00 (ISBN 0-8274-4123-1). R West.

Studies in Stagecraft. Clayton Hamilton. 298p. 1983. Repr. of 1914 ed. lib. bdg. 40.00 (ISBN 0-89987-424-X). Darby Bks.

Studies in Standard Samples of Silicate Rocks & Minerals: Edition of Usable Values, Pt. 4. 1974. pap. 5.00 (SSC77, SSC). UNIPUB.

Studies in Starlight: Understanding Our Universe. Charles J. Caes. LC 87-33515. (Illus.). 256p. 1987. 18.95 (ISBN 0-8306-0946-6, 2946); pap. 12.95 (ISBN 0-8306-2946-7). TAB Bks.

Studies in State & Local Public Finance. Ed. by Harvey S. Rosen. (NBER Project Report Ser.). x, 236p. 1986. 33.00x (ISBN 0-226-72621-5). U of Chicago Pr.

Studies in State Development Policy, 12 vols, Vol. 1. Ed. by Michael Barker. 1979. pap. 100.00x (ISBN 0-934842-24-8). CSPA.

Studies in State Taxation with Particular Reference to the Southern States. J. H. Hollander. 1973. Repr. of 1900 ed. 26.00 (ISBN 0-384-23971-4). Johnson Repr.

Studies in State Taxation with Particular Reference to the Southern States. Ed. by Jacob H. Hollander. LC 78-63873. (Johns Hopkins University. Studies in the Social Sciences. Eighteenth Ser. 1900: 1-4). Repr. of 1900 ed. 19.50 (ISBN 0-404-61129-X). AMS Pr.

Studies in Statecraft. Geoffrey Butler. LC 79-110899. 1970. Repr. of 1920 ed. 17.00x (ISBN 0-8046-0882-2, Pub. by Kennikat). Assoc Faculty Pr.

Studies in Statesmanship. David C. Somervell. LC 75-110934. 1970. Repr. of 1923 ed. 31.50x (ISBN 0-8046-0916-0, Pub. by Kennikat). Assoc Faculty Pr.

Studies in Statistics. Ed. by Robert V. Hogg. LC 78-71936. (MAA Studies in Mathematics: Vol. 19). 213p. 1978. 23.50 (ISBN 0-88385-119-9). Math Assn.

Studies in Stock Speculation, 2 vols. H. J. Wolf. LC 65-29150. 1966. Repr. of 1924 ed. Vol. 1. flexible cover 8.00 (ISBN 0-87034-017-4); Vol. 2. flexible cover 8.00 (ISBN 0-87034-018-2). Fraser Pub Co.

Studies in Strange Souls. Arthur Symons. LC 72-195777. 1929. lib. bdg. 35.00 (ISBN 0-8414-8029-X). Folcroft.

Studies in Structure of American Economy: Theoretical & Empirical Explorations in Input-Output Analysis. Wassily W. Leontief. LC 76-16433. 562p. 1976. Repr. of 1953 ed. 50.00 (ISBN 0-87332-086-7). M E Sharpe.

Studies in Structure: The Stages of the Spiritual Life in Four Modern Authors. Robert J. Andreach. LC 64-24755. xii, 177p. 1965. 25.00 (ISBN 0-8232-0630-0). Fordham.

Studies in Subjective Probability. 2nd ed. Henry E. Kyburg & Howard E. Smokler. LC 79-16294. 272p. 1980. pap. 14.00 (ISBN 0-88275-296-0). Krieger.

Studies in Sublime Failure. Shane Leslie. LC 70-117817. (Essay Index Reprint Ser). 1932. 20.00 (ISBN 0-8369-1670-0). Ayer Co Pubs.

Studies in Substantive Tax Reform. American Bar Foundation Staff. 198p. 1969. 10.00 (ISBN 0-317-63749-5, 765-0036-01); pap. 5.00 (ISBN 0-317-63750-9, 765-0036-01). Amer Bar Assn.

Studies in Symbolic Interaction, Vol. 2. Ed. by Norman K. Denzin. (Orig.). 1979. lib. bdg. 42.50 (ISBN 0-89232-105-9). Jai Pr.

Studies in Symbolic Interaction, Vol. 3. Ed. by Norman K. Denzin. 304p. 1980. 56.50 (ISBN 0-89232-153-9). Jai Pr.

Studies in Symbolic Interaction, Vol. 4. Ed. by Norman K. Denzin. 350p. 1981. 56.50 (ISBN 0-89232-232-2). Jai Pr.

Studies in Symbolic Interaction, Vol. 5. Norman K. Denzin. 47.50 (ISBN 0-89232-362-0). Jai Pr.

Studies in Symbolic Interaction, Vol. 6. Norman Denzin. 1986. 52.50 (ISBN 0-89232-625-5). Jai Pr.

Studies in Symbolic Interaction, Vol. 8. Ed. by Norman K. Denzin. 1988. 58.50 (ISBN 0-89232-719-7). Jai Pr.

Studies in Symbolic Interaction, Vol. 9. Norman K. Denzin. 1988. 58.50 (ISBN 0-89232-924-6). Jai Pr.

Studies in Symbolic Interaction: An Annual Compilation of Research, Vol. 1. Norman K. Denzin. 1978. lib. bdg. 56.50 (ISBN 0-89232-065-6). Jai Pr.

Studies in Syntactic Typology. Ed. by Michael T. Hammond et al. (Typological Studies in Language: Vol. 17). 350p. 1988. 56.00x (ISBN 1-55619-020-4); pap. 29.95 (ISBN 1-55619-021-2). Benjamins North Am.

Studies in Syntax & Semantics. Ed. by F. Kiefer. (Foundations of Language Supplementary Ser: No. 10). 242p. 1969. lib. bdg. 34.00 (ISBN 90-277-0027-3, Pub. by Reidel Holland); pap. 21.00 (ISBN 90-277-0597-6). Kluwer Academic.

Studies in Syntax of Mixtecan Languages. Ed. by C. Henry Bradley & Barbara E. Hollenbach. (Publications in Linguistics: No. 83). 525p. 1988. Vol. I. price not set (ISBN 0-88312-107-7); Three-Volume Set. price not set (ISBN 0-88312-110-7). Summer Inst Ling.

Studies in Tape Reading. Rolo Tape. LC 82-71246. 1982. Repr. of 1910 ed. flexible cover 10.00 (ISBN 0-87034-064-6). Fraser Pub Co.

Studies in Tape Reading. Richard D. Wyckoff. (New Stock Market Library). (Illus.). 1978. Repr. of 1921 ed. 175.50 (ISBN 0-89266-134-8). Am Classical Coll Pr.

Studies in Targum Jonathan to the Prophets. Pinchas Churgin & Leivy Smolar. 59.50x (ISBN 0-87068-109-5). Ktav.

Studies in Tennyson. Ed. by Hallam Tennyson. LC 79-55520. 244p. 1981. text ed. 28.50x (ISBN 0-389-20236-3). B&N Imports.

Studies in Tennyson. Henry Van Dyke. LC 66-25949. Repr. of 1920 ed. 21.00x (ISBN 0-8046-0476-2, Pub. by Kennikat). Assoc Faculty Pr.

Studies in Tennyson. Henry Van Dyke. 1973. Repr. of 1920 ed. 11.00 (ISBN 0-8274-0585-5). R West.

Studies in Territorial History. Ed. by T. C. Hinckley. (Illus.). 68p. (Orig.). 1981. pap. text ed. 9.95x (ISBN 0-89745-014-0). Sunflower U Pr.

Studies in Tertullian & Augustine. Benjamin B. Warfield. 1970. Repr. of 1930 ed. lib. bdg. 35.00x (ISBN 0-8371-4490-6, WATT). Greenwood.

Studies in Text Grammar. Ed. by J. S. Petofi & H. Rieser. LC 73-75766. (Foundations of Language Supplementary Ser.: No. 19). 370p. 1973. lib. bdg. 53.00 (ISBN 90-277-0368-X, Pub. by Reidel Holland). Kluwer Academic.

Studies in the Acoustic Characteristics of Hungarian Speech Sounds. Klara Magdics. LC 68-65314. (Uralic & Altaic Ser: Vol. 97). (Illus.). 141p. 1969. pap. text ed. 7.00x (ISBN 0-87750-041-X). Res Ctr Lang Semiotic.

Studies in the Acquisition of Anaphora. Ed. by Barbara Lust. 1986. lib. bdg. 64.95 (ISBN 90-277-2121-1, Pub. by Reidel Holland); pap. 24.00 (ISBN 90-277-2122-X, Pub. by Reidel Holland). Kluwer Academic.

Studies in the Acquisition of Anaphora. Ed. by Barbara Lust. 1987. lib. bdg. 79.00 (ISBN 1-55608-022-0, Pub. by Reidel Holland); pap. text ed. 24.00 (ISBN 0-317-67682-2). Kluwer Academic.

Studies in the Acquisition of Deictic Terms. Christine Tanz. LC 79-12272. (Cambridge Studies in Linguistics: No. 26). (Illus.). 1980. 39.50 (ISBN 0-521-22740-2). Cambridge U Pr.

Studies in the Administration of International Law & Organization, Vols. 1-9. 1944-48. 212.00 (ISBN 0-527-00878-8). Kraus Repr.

Studies in the African Diaspora: A Memorial to James R. Hooker (1929-1976) Ed. by John P. Henderson & Harry A. Reed. (Illus.). 250p. 1988. text ed. 34.95 (ISBN 0-912469-25-0). Majority Pr.

Studies in the Age of Chaucer, Vol. VII. T. J. Heffernan. 1986. 40.00 (ISBN 0-933784-06-6). New Chaucer Soc.

Studies in the Age of Chaucer, Vol. IV. Roy J. Pearcy. 1982. 40.00 (ISBN 0-933784-03-1). New Chaucer Soc.

Studies in the Age of Chaucer, Vol. 1. Roy D. Pearcy. 1979. 40.00 (ISBN 0-933784-00-7). New Chaucer Soc.

Studies in the Age of Chaucer, Vol. 2. Roy J. Pearcy. 1980. 40.00 (ISBN 0-933784-01-5). New Chaucer Soc.

Studies in the Age of Chaucer, Vol. 3. Roy J. Pearcy. 1981. 40.00 (ISBN 0-933784-02-3). New Chaucer Soc.

Studies in the Age of Chaucer, Vol. 5. T. J. Heffernan. 1983. 40.00 (ISBN 0-937664-64-2). New Chaucer Soc.

Studies in the Age of Chaucer, Vol. 6. T. J. Heffernan. 1984. 40.00 (ISBN 0-933784-05-8). New Chaucer Soc.

Studies in the Age of Chaucer, Vol. 8. T. J. Heffernan. 353p. 1986. 30.00. New Chaucer Soc.

Studies in the Age of Chaucer, Vol. 9. T. J. Heffernan. 1987. 30.00 (ISBN 0-933784-10-4). New Chaucer Soc.

Studies in the Age of Chaucer, Proceedings II: Philadelphia Proceedings. 1987. 30.00. New Chaucer Soc.

Studies in the Age of Chaucer, Proceedings I: York Proceedings. 1985. 30.00 (ISBN 0-933784-07-4). New Chaucer Soc.

Studies in the Age of Goethe. Marshall Montgomery. LC 77-9357. 1977. lib. bdg. 35.00 (ISBN 0-8414-6208-9). Folcroft.

Studies in the Ajanta Paintings. D. Schlingloff. 500p. 1987. 70.00x (ISBN 81-202-0173-6, Pub. by Ajanta). South Asia Bks.

Studies in the American Jewish Experience II: Contributions from the Fellowship Programs of the American Jewish Archives. Ed. by Jacob R. Marcus & Abraham J. Peck. 228p. (Orig.). 1984. lib. bdg. 26.75 (ISBN 0-8191-3714-6); pap. text ed. 13.00 (ISBN 0-8191-3715-4). U Pr of Amer.

Studies in the American Renaissance, 1983. Ed. by Joel Myerson. (Illus.). x, 417p. 1983. 35.00x (ISBN 0-8139-0997-X). U Pr of VA.

Studies in the American Renaissance, 1984. Ed. by Joel Myerson. (Illus.). vii, 458p. 1984. 35.00x (ISBN 0-8139-1021-8). U Pr of VA.

Studies in the American Renaissance, 1985. Ed. by Joel Myerson. (Illus.). x, 410p. 1985. 35.00x (ISBN 0-8139-1060-9). U Pr of Va.

Studies in the American Renaissance 1986. Ed. by Joel Myerson. (Illus.). x, 450p. 1986. 35.00x (ISBN 0-8139-1106-0). U Pr of VA.

Studies in the Anthropology of Bougainville, Solomon Islands. D. L. Oliver. (HU PMP Ser.). Repr. of 1949 ed. 26.00 (ISBN 0-527-01274-2). Kraus Repr.

Studies in the Antiquities of Stobi, 3 Vol. Set, Vol. III. Ed. by James Wiseman & Blaga Aleksova. LC 75-641175. (Illus.). 323p. 1981. 73.00x (ISBN 0-691-03563-6); Set Price o.p. 72.50. Princeton U Pr.

Studies in the Antiquities of Stobi, 3 vol. set, Vol. II. Ed. by James Wiseman & Djordje Mano-Zissi. LC 75-641175. (Illus.). 190p. 1975. 23.00x (ISBN 0-691-03558-X). Princeton U Pr.

Studies in the Antiquities of Stobi, 3 vol. set, Vol. I. Ed. by James Wiseman & Djordje Mano-Zissi. LC 75-641175. (Illus.). 268p. 1973. 22.00x (ISBN 0-691-03557-1). Princeton U Pr.

Studies in the Application of Free Text Package Systems for Information Storage & Retrieval in Libraries & Related Information Centres. John Ashford & Derek Matkin. 64p. 1982. pap. 12.95x (ISBN 0-85365-535-9, Pub. by Library Assn Pub London). ALA.

Studies in the Archaeological History of the Deh Luran Plain: The Excavation of Chagha Sefid. Frank Hole. (Memoirs Ser.: No. 9). (Illus.). 1976. pap. 10.00x (ISBN 0-932206-71-9). U Mich Mus Anthro.

Studies in the Archaeology & Palaeoanthropology of South Asia. Ed. by K. Kennedy & G. Possehl. 144p. 1984. text ed. 22.50x (ISBN 0-391-03049-3). Humanities.

Studies in the Archaeology of Coastal Yucatan & Campeche, Mexico. (Illus.). x, 146p. 1978. 20.00 (ISBN 0-939238-51-9). Tulane MARI.

Studies in the Archaeology of India & Pakistan. Ed. by Jerome Jacobson. 335p. 1986. 45.00X (ISBN 81-204-0085-2, Pub. by Oxford IBH). South Asia Bks.

Studies in the Archaeology of India & Pakistan. Ed. by Jerome Jacobson. (Illus.). 352p. 1987. text ed. 45.00 (ISBN 0-85668-385-X, Pub. by Aris & Phillips). Humanities.

Studies in the Art of China & South-East Asia. Michael Sullivan. 405p. 1987. 1330.00x (ISBN 0-317-68571-6, Pub. by Han-Shan Tang Ltd). State Mutual Bk.

Studies in the Arts at Sinai. Kurt Weitzmann. LC 81-47959. (Illus.). 450p. 1982. 67.50x (ISBN 0-691-03993-3); pap. 22.50x (ISBN 0-691-00342-4). Princeton U Pr.

Studies in the Autograph of George Chapman. L. A. Cummings. Ed. by James Hogg. (Elizabethan & Renaissance Studies). (Orig.). 1985. pap. 15.00 (ISBN 3-7052-0773-3, Pub. by Salzburg Studies). Longwood Pub Group.

Studies in the Baroque From Montaigne to Rotrov. Imbrie Buffum. 1957. 75.00x (ISBN 0-686-83793-2). Elliots Bks.

Studies in the Book of Esther. Carey A. Moore. 1982. 79.50x (ISBN 0-87068-718-2). Ktav.

Studies in the Book of Job. Ed. by Walter Aufrecht. (SR Supplements Ser.: No. 16). 104p. 1985. pap. text ed. 8.50x (ISBN 0-88920-179-X, Pub. by Wilfrid Laurier Canada). Humanities.

Studies in the Book of Jonah. Karin Almbladh. (Studia Semitica Upsaliensia: No. 7). 54p. (Orig.). 1986. pap. text ed. 14.95x (ISBN 91-554-1535-0, Pub. by Uppsala Univ Acta Univ Uppsaliensis (Uppsala Sweden)). Coronet Bks.

Studies in the Buddhistic Culture of India. 2nd rev. ed. Lalman Joshi. 1977. 28.00 (ISBN 0-89684-325-4, Pub. by Motilal Banarsidass India). Orient Bk Dist.

Studies in the Buddhistic Culture of India. Lalmani Joshi. 500p. 1987. Repr. of 1977 ed. 28.00x (ISBN 81-208-0281-0, Pub. by Motilal Banarsidass). South Asia Bks.

Studies in the Byzantine Monetary Economy: 300-1450. Michael Hendy. (Illus.). 596p. 1985. 130.00 (ISBN 0-521-24715-2). Cambridge U Pr.

Studies in the Cartesian Philosophy. N. Kemp Smith. LC 62-8404. 1962. Repr. of 1902 ed. 15.00x (ISBN 0-8462-0276-X). Russell.

Studies in the Cartesian Philosophy. Norman K. Smith. Ed. by Willis Doney. (Philosophy of Descartes Ser.). 290p. 1987. lib. bdg. 45.00 (ISBN 0-8240-4673-0). Garland Pub.

Studies in the Chinese Drama. K. Buss. 1977. lib. bdg. 59.95 (ISBN 0-8490-2704-7). Gordon Pr.

Studies in the Chinese Drama. Kate Buss. 77p. 1922. 385.00x (ISBN 0-317-69220-8, Pub. by Han-Shan Tang Ltd). State Mutual Bk.

Studies in the Chronology & Regional Style of Old Babylonian Cylinder Seals. Lamia W. Al-Gailani. (Bibliotheca Mesopotamica: Vol. 23). 166p. 1988. 25.00x; pap. 18.00. Undena Pubns.

Studies in the Civil Law & Its Relations to the Law of England & America. William W. Howe. xv, 340p. 1980. Repr. of 1896 ed. lib. bdg. 27.50x (ISBN 0-8377-0631-9). Rothman.

Studies in the Classical Theories of Money. Karl H. Niebyl. LC 70-173795. Repr. of 1946 ed. 18.75 (ISBN 0-404-04709-2). AMS Pr.

Studies in the Cognitive Basis of Language Development. Harry Beilen. (Child Psychology Ser.). 1975. 65.50 (ISBN 0-12-085650-6). Acad Pr.

Studies in the Colonial History of Spanish America. Mario Gongora. LC 74-19524. (Cambridge Latin America Studies: vol. 20). pap. 76.30 (ISBN 0-317-28400-2, 2022450). Bks Demand UMI.

Studies in the Comic. B. H. Bronson et al. LC 76-29415. Repr. of 1941 ed. 23.50 (ISBN 0-404-15324-0). AMS Pr.

Studies in the Comic. Bertrand H. Bronson et al. LC 74-3333. lib. bdg. 25.50 (ISBN 0-8414-3128-0). Folcroft.

Studies in the Contemporary Spanish-American Short Story. David W. Foster. LC 79-1558. 144p. 1979. text ed. 16.00x (ISBN 0-8262-0279-9). U of Mo Pr.

Studies in the Contemporary Theatre. John L. Palmer. LC 70-97716. (Essay Index Reprint Ser.). 1927. 18.00 (ISBN 0-8369-1369-8). Ayer Co Pubs.

Studies in the Continental Background of Renaissance English Literature: Essays Presented to John L. Lievsay. Ed. by Dale B. Randall & George W. Williams. LC 77-78523. xiii, 235p. 1977. 25.00 (ISBN 0-8223-0388-4). Duke.

Studies in the Control of Radio, Nos. 1-6. Radio Broadcasting Research Project. LC 79-161174. (History of Broadcasting: Radio to Television Ser). 1971. Repr. of 1948 ed. 29.00 (ISBN 0-405-03581-0). Ayer Co Pubs.

Studies in the Covenant of Grace. David L. Neilands. 1981. pap. 5.75 (ISBN 0-87552-365-X). Presby & Reformed.

Studies in the Development of Capitalism. rev. ed. Maurice Dobb. LC 74-13744. 415p. (Orig.). 1964. pap. 4.95 (ISBN 0-7178-0197-7). Intl Pubs Co.

Studies in the Development of the Fool in the Elizabethan Drama. Olive M. Busby. LC 72-39567. Repr. of 1923 ed. 5.00 (ISBN 0-404-07849-4). AMS Pr.

Studies in the Development of the Fool in the Elizabethan Drama. Olive M. Busby. LC 75-17871. 1923. lib. bdg. 22.50 (ISBN 0-8414-3223-6). Folcroft.

Studies in the Early British Church. Nora K. Chadwick et al. LC 73-673. vii, 374p. 1973. Repr. of 1958 ed. 32.50 (ISBN 0-208-01315-6, Archon). Shoe String.

Studies in the Early History of Judaism, 2 vols. Solomon Zeitlin. 1973. Vol. 1. 59.50x (ISBN 0-87068-208-3); Vol. 2. 59.50x (ISBN 0-87068-209-1). Ktav.

Studies in the Early History of Judaism. Solomon Zeitlin. Vol. 3. 59.50x (ISBN 0-87068-278-4); Vol. 4. 59.50x (ISBN 0-87068-454-X). Ktav.

Studies in the East-West Philosophy. G. Srinivasan. (Orig.). 1979. pap. 3.95 (ISBN 0-89684-084-0). Orient Bk Dist.

Studies in the Economic & Social History of Palestine in the 19th & 20th Centuries. Ed. by Roger Owen. LC 82-80662. 271p. 1982. 29.95x (ISBN 0-8093-1089-9). S Ill U Pr.

Studies in the Economic History of Orissa from Ancient Times to 1833. Binod S. Das. 1978. 11.50x (ISBN 0-8364-0200-6). South Asia Bks.

Studies in the Economic History of the Ohio Valley. Louis C. Hunter. LC 72-98689. (American Scene Ser.). 1973. Repr. of 1933 ed. lib. bdg. 24.50 (ISBN 0-306-71837-5). Da Capo.

Studies in the Economic History of the Ohio Valley. Louis C. Hunter. LC 36-6753. (History of American Economy Ser). Repr. of 1934 ed. 13.00 (ISBN 0-384-24945-0). Johnson Repr.

Studies in the Economics of Income Maintenance. Ed. by Otto Eckstein. LC 77-592. (Brookings Institution Studies of Government Finance). 1977. Repr. of 1967 ed. lib. bdg. 35.00x (ISBN 0-8371-9488-1, ECTE). Greenwood.

Studies in the Economics of Overhead Costs. John M. Clark. (Midway Reprint). 1981. pap. 27.00x (ISBN 0-226-10851-1). U of Chicago Pr.

Studies in the Economics of Transportation. Martin Beckmann et al. 1956. 65.00x (ISBN 0-685-89787-7). Elliots Bks.

Studies in the Eighteenth Century Background of Hume's Empiricism. Mary S. Kuypers. LC 82-48337. (Philosophy of David Hume Ser.). 148p. 1983. lib. bdg. 28.00 (ISBN 0-8240-5413-X). Garland Pub.

Studies in the Eighteenth Century English Novel. Arthur Sherbo. 180p. 1969. 6.00 (ISBN 0-87013-140-0). Mich St U Pr.

Studies in the Elizabethan Drama. Arthur Symons. LC 75-155222. Repr. of 1919 ed. 14.00 (ISBN 0-404-06331-4). AMS Pr.

Studies in the English Mystery Plays. Charles Davidson. LC 68-752. (Studies in Drama, No. 39). 1969. Repr. of 1892 ed. lib. bdg. 49.95x (ISBN 0-8383-0536-9). Haskell.

Studies in the English Mystics: Book to a Mother, No. 1. Adrian J. McCarthy. Ed. by James Hogg. (Elizabethan & Renaissance Studies). 275p. (Orig.). 1981. pap. 15.00 (ISBN 3-7052-0742-3, Pub. by Salzburg Studies). Longwood Pub Group.

Studies in the English Outlook in the Period Between the World Wars. Conrad G. Weber. 1945. Repr. 25.00 (ISBN 0-8274-3543-6). R West.

Studies in the English Social & Political Thinkers of the Nineteenth Century. Robert H. Murray. 940p. Repr. of 1929 ed. text ed. 99.36x (ISBN 0-576-29354-7, Pub. by Gregg Intl Pubs England). Gregg Intl.

Studies in the Evolution of English Criticism: A Thesis Presented to the Philosophical Faculty of Yale University in Candidacy for the Degree of Doctor of Philosophy. Laura J. Wylie. 1979. Repr. of 1903 ed. lib. bdg. 25.50 (ISBN 0-8495-5720-8). Arden Lib.

Studies in the Evolution of the English Criticism. Laura J. Wylie. LC 76-43988. 1903. lib. bdg. 35.50 (ISBN 0-8414-9478-9). Folcroft.

Studies in the Exact Islamic Sciences. E. S. Kennedy. 790p. 1983. text ed. 80.00x (ISBN 0-8156-6067-7, Am U Beirut). Syracuse U Pr.

Studies in the Fairy Mythology of Arthurian Romance. L. A. Paton. 69.95 (ISBN 0-8490-1150-7). Gordon Pr.

Studies in the Fairy Mythology of Arthurian Romance. 2nd enl. ed. Lucy A. Paton. Ed. by Roger S. Loomis. 1963. 22.50 (ISBN 0-8337-2683-8). B Franklin.

Studies in the Period of David & Solomon & Other Essays: Papers Read at the International Symposium for Biblical Studies, 6-7 December 1979. Ed. by T. Ishida. LC 82-11183. 409p. 1982. text ed. 35.00x (ISBN 0-931464-16-1). Eisenbrauns.

Studies in the Personal Imagery of Cosimo I De'Medici, Duke of Florence. Paul W. Richelson. LC 77-94714. (Outstanding Dissertations in the Fine Arts Ser.). 208p. 1978. lib. bdg. 25.00 (ISBN 0-8240-3247-0). Garland Pub.

Studies in the Philosophy of Aristotle's Rhetoric. M. A. William & S. J. Grimaldi. 159p. (Orig.). 1972. pap. 27.50x (ISBN 3-515-00246-4, Pub. by Franz Steiner). Coronet Bks.

Studies in the Philosophy of Biology: Reduction & Related Problems. Ed. by Francisco J. Ayala & Theodosius Dobzhansky. LC 73-90656. 1974. 45.00x (ISBN 0-520-02649-7). U of Cal Pr.

Studies in the Philosophy of David Hume. Charles W. Hendel. LC 82-48334. (Philosophy of David Hume Ser.). 567p. 1983. lib. bdg. 55.00 (ISBN 0-8240-5406-7). Garland Pub.

Studies in the Philosophy of History. Ed. by George H. Nadel. 1965. lib. bdg. 20.00x (ISBN 0-88307-212-2). Gannon.

Studies in the Philosophy of J. N. Findlay. Ed. by Robert S. Cohen et al. LC 83-18219. (Philosophy Ser.). 478p. 1985. 59.50 (ISBN 0-87395-795-4); pap. 24.50x (ISBN 0-87395-794-6). State U NY Pr.

Studies in the Philosophy of Kant. Lewis W. Beck. LC 81-7247. (Essay & Monograph Series of the Liberal Arts Press). viii, 242p. 1981. Repr. of 1965 ed. lib. bdg. 35.00x (ISBN 0-313-23183-4, BESK). Greenwood.

Studies in the Philosophy of Kierkegaard. Klemke. 1976. pap. 16.00 (ISBN 90-247-1852-X, Pub. by Martinus Nijhoff Netherlands). Kluwer Academic.

Studies in the Philosophy of Paul Ricoeur. Ed. by Charles Reagan. LC 79-10343. xxvi, 194p. 1979. 22.95x (ISBN 0-8214-0223-4). Ohio U Pr.

Studies in the Philosophy of Religion. A. Seth Pringle-Pattison. LC 77-27204. (Gifford Lectures: 1923). Repr. of 1930 ed. 30.00 (ISBN 0-404-60474-9). AMS Pr.

Studies in the Phonology of Asian Languages, IX: Word Accent in Japanese. Raymond S. Weitzman. LC 73-141215. 128p. 1970. 19.00 (ISBN 0-403-04545-2). Scholarly.

Studies in the Phonology of Colloquial English. Ken Lodge. 160p. 1984. 27.50 (ISBN 0-7099-1631-0, Pub. by Croom Helm Ltd). Routledge Chapman & Hall.

Studies in the Pollen Morphology of Indian Heteromerae. P. K. Nair & Sushma Kothari. (Advances in Pollen Spore Research Ser.: Vol. 13). xii, 90p. 1985. 15.00 (ISBN 1-55528-055-2, Pub. by Messers Today & Tomorrow Printers & Publishers). Scholarly Pubns.

Studies in the Pollen Morphology of Rosales. Kamlesh Katiyar. Ed. by P. K. Nair. (Advances in Pollen Spore Research Ser.: Vol. 8). (Illus.). 150p. 1982. 15.00 (ISBN 0-88065-226-8, Pub. by Messers Today & Tomorrow Printers & Publishers). Scholarly Pubns.

Studies in the Pollen Morphology of South Indian Rubiaceae. P. M. Mathew & Omana Philip. (Advances in Pollen Spore Research Ser.: Vol. 10). viii, 80p. 1983. 20.00 (ISBN 1-55528-056-0, Pub. by Messers Today & Tomorrow Printers & Publishers). Scholarly Pubns.

Studies in the Posthumous Works of Spinoza: On Style, Earliest Translation & Reception, Earliest & Modern Edition of Some Texts. Fokke Akkerman. vi, 285p. (Orig.). 1980. pap. 22.00x (ISBN 0-317-19838-6, Pub. by Boumas Boekhuis Netherlands). Benjamins North AM.

Studies in the Pragmatics of Discourse. Teun A. van Dijk. (Janua Linguarum Series Maior: No. 101). 332p. 1981. 44.75x (ISBN 90-279-3249-2). Mouton.

Studies in the Prehistory of Psychoanalysis: The Etiology of Psychoneuroses & Some Related Themes in Sigmund Freud's Scientific Writings & Letters, 1886-1896. Ola Andersson. 245p. 1962. pap. text ed. 20.00x (ISBN 0-686-27249-8). Gach Bks.

Studies in the Problem of Sovereignty. Harold J. Laski. 1968. Repr. 35.00x (ISBN 0-86527-191-7). Fertig.

Studies in the Problems of Norms: Lectures. University Of California Philosophical Union - 1924-1925. (Publications in Philosophy Ser: Vol. 7). 1925. 20.00 (ISBN 0-384-07180-5). Johnson Repr.

Studies in the Problems of Relations: Lectures. University Of California Philosophical Union - 1930. (Publications in Philosophy Ser: Vol. 13). 1930. 20.00 (ISBN 0-384-07190-2). Johnson Repr.

Studies in the Processing, Marketing & Distribution of Commodities: The Processing & Marketing of Coffee: Areas For International Co-Operation. LC 84-46787. 51p. 7.00 (ISBN 92-1-112179-5, 84.II.O.11). UN.

Studies in the Processing, Marketing & Distribution of Commodities: The Processing Before Export of Cocoa: Areas for International Cooperation. (Illus.). 81p. 1985. pap. 9.50 (E.84.II.D.16). UN.

Studies in the Processing, Marketing & Distribution of Commodities: The Processing & Marketing of Copper: Areas for International Co-operation. 73p. 1985. pap. 9.50 (ISBN 92-1-112183-3, E.84.II.D.24). UN.

Studies in the Processing, Marketing & Distribution of Commodities: The Processing & Marketing of Manganese: Areas for International Cooperation. UNCTAD Secretariat. 57p. 1985. pap. 8.00 (E.84.II.D.18). UN.

Studies in the Processing, Marketing & Distribution of Commodities: The Processing & Marketing of Bauxite, Alumina, Aluminum: Areas for International Cooperation. UNCTAD Secretariat. 89p. 1985. pap. 11.00 (E.84.II.D.15). UN.

Studies in the Processing, Marketing & Distribution of Commodities: The Marketing of Hard Fibres (Sisal & Henequen): Areas for International Cooperation. United Nations Conference on Trade & Development. 77p. 1985. pap. 9.50 (ISBN 92-1-112167-1, E.84.II.D.21). UN.

Studies in the Processing, Marketing & Distribution of Commodities: The Processing & Marketing for Phosphates: Areas of International Cooperation. United Nations Conference on Trade & Development. 72p. 1985. pap. 9.50 (E.84.II.D.13). UN.

Studies in the Prophecy of Jeremiah. G. Campbell & Morgan. 288p. 13.95 (ISBN 0-8007-0298-0). Revell.

Studies in the Prose Style of Joseph Addison. J. Lannering. (Essays & Studies on English Language & Literature: Vol. 9). pap. 19.00 (ISBN 0-8115-0207-4). Kraus Repr.

Studies in the Prose Style of Joseph Addison. Jan Lannering. LC 72-194448. 1951. lib. bdg. 20.00 (ISBN 0-8414-5669-0). Folcroft.

Studies in the Psychology of Art. Ed. by Christian A. Ruckwick. Bd. with Experimental Study of Factors Influencing Consonance Judgements. E. G. Bugg. Repr. of 1933 ed; Binocular & Monocular Relation in Foveal Dark Adaptations. T. W. Cook. Repr. of 1934 ed; Brain Fields & Learning Process. J. A. Gengerelli. Repr. of 1934 ed; Practice & Variability: A Study in Psychological Method. A. Anastasi. Repr. of 1934 ed. (Psychology Monographs General & Applied: Vol. 45). pap. 44.00 (ISBN 0-8115-1444-7). Kraus Repr.

Studies in the Psychology of Art, Vol. 2. Ed. by Norman C. Meier. Bd. with Vol. 2. Studies in General Psychology. Ed. by C. A. Ruckwick; Vol. 1. Studies in Psychology of Reading. Ed. by J. Tiffin. Repr. of 1937 ed; Etiology of Mental Deficiency. A. J. Rosanoff. Repr. of 1937 ed. (Psychology Monographs: General & Applied: Vol. 48). Repr. of 1936 ed. 44.00 (ISBN 0-8115-1447-1). Kraus Repr.

Studies in the Psychology of Art, Vol 3. Ed. by Norman C. Meier. LC 73-2977. (Classics in Psychology Ser.). Repr. of 1939 ed. 14.00 (ISBN 0-405-05149-2). Ayer Co Pubs.

Studies in the Psychology of Art see Differential Forecasts of Achievement & Their Use in Educational Counseling.

Studies in the Psychology of Intemperance. G. E. Partridge. Ed. by Gerald N. Grob. LC 80-1244. (Addiction in America Ser.). 1981. Repr. of 1912 ed. lib. bdg. 25.00x (ISBN 0-405-13614-5). Ayer Co Pubs.

Studies in the Puranic Records on Hindu Rites & Customs. 2nd ed. R. C. Hazra. 1975. 28.00 (ISBN 0-8426-0965-2). Orient Bk Dist.

Studies in the Quantity Theory of Money. Ed. by Milton Friedman. LC 56-10999. 1973. pap. 4.75x (ISBN 0-226-26406-8, P561, Phoen). U of Chicago Pr.

Studies in the Reformation: Luther to Hooker. W. D. Cargill Thompson. Ed. by C. W. Dugmore. 259p. 1980. 58.50 (ISBN 0-485-11187-X, Pub. by Athlone Pr UK). Humanities.

Studies in the Reign of Constantius II. Mary M. Mudd. 144p. 1988. 9.95 (ISBN 0-8062-3234-X). Carlton.

Studies in the Reign of Tiberius. Robert S. Rogers. LC 77-152601. 181p. 1972. Repr. of 1943 ed. lib. bdg. 35.00x (ISBN 0-8371-6036-7, RORT). Greenwood.

Studies in the Religious Life of Ancient & Medieval India. D. C. Sircar. 1971. 9.95 (ISBN 0-89684-326-2). Orient Bk Dist.

Studies in the Religious Tradition of the Old Testament. Ackroyd. Date not set. 22.95 (Pub. by SCM Pr England). Fortress.

Studies in the Revolution of English Criticism. Laura J. Wylie. 212p. 1980. Repr. of 1903 ed. text ed. 25.00 (ISBN 0-8492-2997-9). R West.

Studies in the Romance Verb. Nigel Vincent & Martin Harris. 200p. 1982. 32.00 (ISBN 0-7099-2602-2, Pub. by Croom Helm). Routledge Chapman & Hall.

Studies in the Romano-British Villa. Malcolm Todd. LC 79-315069. (Illus.). 61.00 (ISBN 0-317-10627-9, 2017340). Bks Demand UMI.

Studies in the Romantics, Vol. IV. James Hogg. (Romantic Reassessment Ser.). (Orig.). 1985. pap. 15.00 (ISBN 3-7052-0542-0, Pub. by Salzburg Studies). Longwood Pub Group.

Studies in the Romantics, Vol. I. Betty T. Mann. Ed. by James Hogg. (Romantic Reassessment Ser.). 129p. (Orig.). 1978. pap. 15.00 (ISBN 3-7052-0539-0, Pub. by Salzburg Studies). Longwood Pub Group.

Studies in the Romantics, Vol. II. Leonard Orr. Ed. by James Hogg. (Romantic Reassessment Ser.). 103p. (Orig.). 1981. pap. 15.00 (ISBN 3-7052-0540-4, Pub. by Salzburg Studies). Longwood Pub Group.

Studies in the Romantics, Vol. III. Erwin A. Sturzl. Ed. by James Hogg. (Romantic Reassessment Ser.). 83p. (Orig.). 1982. pap. 15.00 (ISBN 3-7052-0541-2, Pub. by Salzburg Studies). Longwood Pub Group.

Studies in the Russian Historical Song. Carl Stief. LC 79-3073. (Illus.). 274p. 1981. Repr. of 1953 ed. 25.50 (ISBN 0-8305-0092-8). Hyperion Conn.

Studies in the Science of Society Presented to Albert Galloway Keller. facs. ed. LC 68-55860. (Essay Index Reprint Ser). 1937. 28.25 (ISBN 0-8369-1157-1). Ayer Co Pubs.

Studies in the Scientific & Mathematical Philosophy of Charles S. Pierce: Essays by Carolyn Eisele. Ed. by Carolyn Eisele & Richard M. Martin. (Studies in Philosophy). 1979. text ed. 50.50x (ISBN 90-279-7808-5). Mouton.

Studies in the Scottish Lateglacial Environment. Ed. by J. M. Gray & J. J. Lowe. 1977. 46.00 (ISBN 0-08-020498-8). Pergamon.

Studies in the Scriptures, 1946. A. W. Pink. pap. 11.95 (ISBN 0-85151-346-8). Banner of Truth.

Studies in the Scriptures, 1947. A. W. Pink. 298p. pap. 11.95 (ISBN 0-85151-347-6). Banner of Truth.

Studies in the Semantic Structure of Hindi, Two. Kali C. Bahl. 1979. 17.50x (ISBN 0-8364-0513-7). South Asia Bks.

Studies in the Sermon on the Mount. Oswald Chambers. 1973. pap. 5.95. Chr Lit.

Studies in the Sermon on the Mount. D. Martyn Lloyd-Jones. 1984. 12.95 (ISBN 0-8028-0036-X). Eerdmans.

Studies in the Short Story. 6th ed. Ed. by David Madden & Virgil Scott. LC 83-8590. 536p. 1984. pap. text ed. 16.95 (ISBN 0-03-063644-2). HR&W.

Studies in the Social & Economic Development of the Netherlands East Indies, 3 vols. in 1. John S. Furnivall. LC 77-87488. Repr. of 1934 ed. 21.50. AMS Pr.

Studies in the Social & Economic History of the Witwatersrand 116-1914: New Babylon, Vol. 1. Charles Van Onselen. (Illus.). 1982. 29.95x (ISBN 0-582-64382-1). Longman.

Studies in the Social Aspects of the Depression: Social Science Research Council, 13 Vols. Ed. by Alex Baskin. 1972. Repr. Set. 219.00 (ISBN 0-405-00840-6). Ayer Co Pubs.

Studies in the Social History of Modern Egypt. Gabriel Baer. Ed. by William R. Polk. LC 69-17537. (Publications of the Center for Middle Eastern Studies Ser.: No. 4). 1969. 20.00x (ISBN 0-226-03405-4). U of Chicago Pr.

Studies in the Social Services. S. M. Ferguson & H. Fitzgerald. 1978. 53.00. Kraus Intl.

Studies in the Social War: Kiene, Marcks, Haug, Voirol: An Original Anthology. Adolf Kiene. LC 75-7343. (Roman History Ser.). (Illus., Ger.). 1975. 34.00 (ISBN 0-405-07064-0). Ayer Co Pubs.

Studies in the Sociology of Music. Louis Wildman. (Orig.). 1981. pap. text ed. 8.00 (ISBN 0-939630-08-7). Inst Qual Hum Life.

Studies in the Sociology of Social Problems. Joseph Schneider & John I. Kitsuse. Ed. by Gerald Platt. LC 84-14549. (Modern Sociology Ser.). 240p. 1984. text ed. 34.50 (ISBN 0-89391-053-8); pap. 19.95 (ISBN 0-89391-450-9). Ablex Pub.

Studies in the Sociology of Sport. Ed. by Aidan O. Dunleavy & Andrew W. Miracle. LC 82-16807. 402p. 1982. pap. 15.00x (ISBN 0-912646-78-0). Tex Christian.

Studies in the Sources on the History of Pre-Islamic Central Asia. Ed. by J. Harmatta. 162p. 1979. 44.00x (ISBN 0-569-08582-9, Pub. by Collets (UK)). State Mutual Bk.

Studies in the Structure & Innervation of the Sensory Epithelium of the Cristae Ampullares in the Guinea Pig. Jan Wersall. Repr. of 1956 ed. 12.00 (ISBN 0-384-66900-X). Johnson Repr.

Studies in the Structure of the Urban Economy. Edwin S. Mills. LC 71-179873. (Resources for the Future, Inc. Ser). (Illus.). 162p. 1972. 15.95x (ISBN 0-8018-1367-0); pap. 9.95x (ISBN 0-8018-1595-9). Johns Hopkins.

Studies in the Structure, Physiology & Ecology of Molluscs. Zoological Society Of London - 22nd Symposium. Ed. by Fretter. 1968. 72.00 (ISBN 0-12-613322-0). Acad Pr.

Studies in the Syntax of Relative & Comparative Clauses. Andrews D. Avery, III. Ed. by Jorge Hankamer. (Outstanding Dissertations in Linguistics Ser.). 200p. 1985. 26.00 (ISBN 0-8240-5419-9). Garland Pub.

Studies in the Syntax of the Gathas of Zarathushtra. Maria W. Smith. (LD). 1929. 13.00 (ISBN 0-527-00750-1). Kraus Repr.

Studies in the Syntax of the Old English Passive. Louise G. Frary. (LD). 1929. pap. 16.00 (ISBN 0-527-00751-X). Kraus Repr.

Studies in the Technological Development of the American Economy During the First Half of the Nineteenth Century. Paul J. Uselding. LC 75-2600. (Dissertations in American Economic History). (Illus.). 1975. 21.00x (ISBN 0-405-07221-X). Ayer Co Pubs.

Studies in the Terminology of Early Stoic Ethics. Damianos Tsekourakis. 154p. (Orig.). 1974. pap. 33.50x (ISBN 3-515-01914-6, Pub. by Franz Steiner). Coronet Bks.

Studies in the Text History of the Life & Fables of Aesop. Ben E. Perry. LC 81-13575. (American Philological Association Monograph Ser.). 1981. pap. 22.50 (ISBN 0-89130-534-3, 40 00 07). Scholars Pr GA.

Studies in the Text of Jeremiah. John G. Janzen. LC 73-81265. (Harvard Semitic Monographs: Vol. 6). pap. 64.00 (ISBN 0-317-09145-X, 2021591). Bks Demand UMI.

Studies in the Text of Matthew Arnold's Prose Works. Edward K. Brown. 59.95 (ISBN 0-8490-1151-5). Gordon Pr.

Studies in the Theory of Business Cycles, 1933-39. Michal Kalecki. LC 66-31550. 1969. 15.00x (ISBN 0-678-06269-2). Kelley.

Studies in the Theory of Descent, 2 vols. in 1. August Weismann. LC 72-1661. Repr. of 1882 ed. 72.00 (ISBN 0-404-08192-4). AMS Pr.

Studies in the Theory of Functions of Several Real Variables & the Approximation of Functions. Ed. by Sobolev. (Proceedings of the Steklov Institute of Mathematics Ser.: Vol. 172). 392p. 1988. pap. text ed. price not set. Am Math.

Studies in the Theory of Ideology. John B. Thompson. LC 84-16129. (Illus.). 360p. 1985. 37.50x (ISBN 0-520-05411-3); pap. 12.95x (ISBN 0-520-05412-1). U of Cal Pr.

Studies in the Theory of Money, 1690-1776. Douglas Vickers. LC 59-9191. 1959. 35.00x (ISBN 0-678-08048-8). Kelley.

Studies in the Theory of Numbers. Leonard E. Dickson. LC 61-13494. 13.95 (ISBN 0-8284-0151-9). Chelsea Pub.

Studies in the Theory of Welfare Economics. Melvin W. Reder. LC 68-54288. (Columbia University. Studies in the Social Sciences: No. 534). Repr. of 1947 ed. 14.00 (ISBN 0-404-51534-7). AMS Pr.

Studies in the Transformation of U. S. Agriculture. Ed. by A. Eugene Havens et al. (Rural Studies). 330p. 1985. pap. text ed. 34.00x (ISBN 0-8133-7058-2). Westview.

Studies in the Use of Fire in the Ancient Greek Religion. rev. ed. William D. Furley. Ed. by W. R. Connor. LC 80-2650. (Monographs in Clasical Studies). (Illus.). 1981. lib. bdg. 29.00 (ISBN 0-405-14037-1). Ayer Co Pubs.

Studies in the Vedanta Sutras of Badarayana. Srisa C. Vasu. LC 73-3815. (The Sacred Books of the Hindus Ser.: Vol. 22, Part 2). Repr. of 1919 ed. 18.00 (ISBN 0-404-57843-8). AMS Pr.

Studies in the Vegetation History of the British Isles. Ed. by D. Walker & R. G. West. 89.50 (ISBN 0-521-07565-3). Cambridge U Pr.

Studies in the Wagnerian Drama. Henry Krehbiel. LC 76-56860. (Studies in Music: No. 42). 1977. lib. bdg. 42.95x (ISBN 0-8383-2137-2). Haskell.

Studies in the Wagnerian Drama: 1935, I. Henry E. Krehbiel. LC 74-24133. (M). Repr. of 1891 ed. 12.50 (ISBN 0-404-12993-5). AMS Pr.

Studies in the Work of Colley Cibber. DeWitt C. Croissant. (English Literature Ser., No. 33). 1970. pap. 27.95x (ISBN 0-8383-0088-X). Haskell.

Studies in the Yorkshire Coal Industry. Ed. by John Benson & Robert G. Neville. LC 76-11778. 1976. lib. bdg. 27.50x (ISBN 0-678-06793-7). Kelley.

Studies in Theatre & Drama. Ed. & frwd. by Oscar G. Brockett. (De Proprietatibus Litterarum, Ser. Major: No. 23). 217p. 1972. text ed. 29.60 (ISBN 90-2792-112-1). Mouton.

Studies in Theism. Borden P. Bowne. LC 7-25071. 1968. Repr. of 1907 ed. 28.00 (ISBN 0-527-10450-7). Kraus Repr.

Studies in Theocritus & Other Hellenistic Poets. Heather White. (London Studies in Classical Philology: Vol. 3). (Illus.). 89p. 1979. 21.00 (ISBN 90-70265-81-8, Pub. by Gieben Amsterdam). Benjamins North Am.

Studies in Theology. Loraine Boettner. 1947. 7.95 (ISBN 0-87552-131-2). Presby & Reformed.

Studies in Theology & Education. John L. Elias. LC 85-9887. 240p. 1986. lib. bdg. 16.50 (ISBN 0-89874-841-0). Krieger.

Studies in Thirteenth Century Justice & Administration. C. A. Meekings. 342p. 1982. 40.00 (ISBN 0-9506882-3-1). Hambledon Press.

Studies in Thought & Language. Ed. by Joseph L. Cowan. LC 75-89620. 1970. pap. 58.00 (ISBN 0-317-08180-2, 2022755). Bks Demand UMI.

Studies in Three Literatures: English, Latin & Greek: Contrasts & Comparisons. M. R. Ridley. 1979. Repr. of 1962 ed. lib. bdg. 30.00 (ISBN 0-8495-4602-8). Arden Lib.

Studies in Three Literatures: English, Latin & Greek Contrasts & Comparisons. Maurice R. Ridley. LC 78-42. 1978. Repr. of 1962 ed. lib. bdg. 35.00x (ISBN 0-313-20189-7, RISTL). Greenwood.

Studies in Titus & Philemon. Robert Taylor, Jr. 2.50 (ISBN 0-89315-287-0). Lambert Bk.

Studies in Tourism, Wildlife Parks & Conservation. Tej Vir Singh et al. (Illus.). 300p. 1982. 30.00 (ISBN 0-935638-07-5). Travel & Tourism.

Studies in Trade Liberalization: Problems & Prospects for the Industrial Countries. Bela A. Balassa & M. E. Kreinin. LC 67-22889. pap. 90.50 (ISBN 0-317-19827-0, 2023080). Bks Demand UMI.

Studies in Training & Development, No. 1. Ed. by Richard D. Peterson. (ASTD Research Ser.). 196p. soft cover 9.50 (ISBN 0-318-13283-4, &ESTP); members 7.50 (ISBN 0-318-13284-2). Am Soc Train & Devel.

Studies in Transnational Economic Law. Ed. by Norbert Horn & Clive M. Schmitthoff. 1983. write for info. (Pub. by Kluwer Law Netherlands). Kluwer Academic.

Studies in Tropical American Mollusks. Ed. by Frederick M. Bayer & Gilbert L. Voss. LC 70-170142. 1971. 10.00x (ISBN 0-87024-230-X). U of Miami Pr.

Studies in Tudor History. W. P. Kennedy. LC 73-118480. 1971. Repr. of 1916 ed. 23.50x (ISBN 0-8046-1229-3, Pub. by Kennikat). Assoc Faculty Pr.

Studies in Turkish Linguistics. Ed. by Dan I. Slobin & Karl Zimmer. LC 86-11777. (Typological Studies in Language: Vol. 8). vi, 294p. 1986. 56.00x (ISBN 0-915027-35-6); pap. 29.95x (ISBN 0-915027-36-4). Benjamins North Am.

Studies in Two Literatures. Arthur Symons. 1978. Repr. of 1924 ed. lib. bdg. 29.00 (ISBN 0-8495-4847-0). Arden Lib.

Studies in Two Literatures. Arthur Symons. LC 72-193757. 1924. lib. bdg. 35.50 (ISBN 0-8414-8003-6). Folcroft.

Studies in Two Literatures. Arthur Symons. LC 76-20002. (Decadent Consciousness Ser.: Vol. 25). 1977. Repr. of 1897 ed. lib. bdg. 46.00 (ISBN 0-8240-2774-4). Garland Pub.

Studies in U. S.- Asia Economic Relations. Ed. by Manoranjan Dutta. LC 83-70889. (Acorn Economic Communication Ser.: No. 2). xvi, 578p. 1985. 58.50x (ISBN 0-89386-010-7). Acorn NC.

Studies in Upplandic Runography. Claiborne W. Thompson. LC 74-22284. (Illus.). 218p. 1975. 22.50x (ISBN 0-292-77511-3). U of Tex Pr.

Studies in Urban Public Sector, India. N. Nageswara Rao. 1985. 30.00x (ISBN 0-8364-1386-5, Pub. by Ashish India). South Asia Bks.

Studies in Utilitarianism. Thomas K. Hearn, Jr. LC 79-151031. (Century Philosophy Ser). (Orig.). 1971. 29.50 (ISBN 0-89197-431-8); pap. text ed. 10.95x (ISBN 0-89197-432-6). Irvington.

Studies in Uto-Aztecan Grammar: Modern Aztec Grammatical Sketches, Vol. 2. Ed. by Ronald W. Langacker. LC 78-56488. (Publications in Linguistics: No. 56). 380p. 1979. pap. 13.50x (ISBN 0-88312-072-0); microfiche (4) 8.00 (ISBN 0-88312-405-X). Summer Inst Ling.

Studies in Uto-Aztecan Grammar: Overview of Uto-Aztecan Grammar, Vol. 1. Ed. by Ronald W. Langacker. (Publications in Linguistics & Related Fields Ser.: No. 56). 199p. 1977. o. p. 13.00x (ISBN 0-88312-070-4); microfiche (3) 6.00 (ISBN 0-88312-469-6). Summer Inst Ling.

Studies in Uto-Aztecan Grammar: Southern Uto-Aztecan Grammatical Sketches, Vol. 4. Ed. by Ronald W. Langacker. LC 84-51054. (Publications in Linguistics Ser.: No. 56). 459p. (Orig.). 1984. microfiche (5) 10.00 (ISBN 0-88312-402-5); pap. 18.00x. Summer Inst Ling.

Studies in Uto-Aztecan Grammar: Uto-Aztecan Grammatical Sketches, Vol. 3. Ed. by Ronald W. Langacker. LC 82-+025. (Publications in Linguistics: No. 56). 393p. 1982. pap. text ed. 14.00; microfiche (5) 10.00 (ISBN 0-88312-403-3). Summer Inst Ling.

Studies in Verbal Behavior: An Empirical Approach. Kurt Salzinger & Richard S. Feldman. LC 76-179073. 474p. 1973. 42.00 (ISBN 0-08-016926-0). Pergamon.

Studies in Victorian Drama: An Appraisal of the Poetic Plays of Browning, Tennyson & Other Victorians. Virendra Sharma. Ed. by James Hogg. (Poetic Drama & Poetic Theory Ser.). 203p. (Orig.). 1979. pap. 15.00 (ISBN 3-7052-0839-X, Pub. by Salzburg Studies). Longwood Pub Group.

Studies in Vocabulary see Word Studies in the Greek New Testament, for the English Reader.

Studies in Walt Whitman's Leaves of Grass. Ed. by Harry R. Warfel. LC 54-8472. 1978. Repr. of 1954 ed. 35.00x (ISBN 0-8201-1226-7). Schol Facsimiles.

Studies in War & Peace. Ed. by Oyvind Osterud. (Norwegian University Press Publication Series). 230p. 45.00x (ISBN 82-00-07749-7). Oxford U Pr.

Studies in Weather & Climate. 2nd ed. Philip Suckling & Roy Doyon. 1987. pap. text ed. 18.95x (ISBN 0-317-56975-9). Contemp Pub Co of Raleigh.

Studies in Welsh History. 2nd ed. Frederick Rees. 212p. 1965. text ed. 12.50x (ISBN 0-7083-0079-0, Pub. by U of Wales). Humanities.

Studies in West African Islamic History: The Cultivators of Islam, Vol. I. Ed. by John R. Willis. (Illus.). 325p. 1979. 39.50x (ISBN 0-7146-1737-7, F Cass Co). Biblio Dist.

Studies in Western Australian History II: March 1978. 1978. pap. 5.50x (ISBN 0-89955-408-3, Pub. by U of W Austral Pr). Intl Spec Bk.

Studies in Western Australian History, No. 1. 1978. pap. 5.50x (ISBN 0-89955-407-5, Pub. by U of W Austral Pr). Intl Spec Bk.

Studies in Words. 2nd ed. Clive S. Lewis. 1960. 37.50 (ISBN 0-521-05547-4); pap. 14.95 (ISBN 0-521-09371-6). Cambridge U Pr.

Studies in Wordsworth. Henry N. Hudson. LC 76-42991. 1884. lib. bdg. 30.00 (ISBN 0-8414-4938-4). Folcroft.

Studies in World Economics. facs. ed. George D. Cole. LC 67-23195. (Essay Index Reprint Ser). 1934. 18.00 (ISBN 0-8369-0324-2). Ayer Co Pubs.

Studies in World Public Order. Myres S. McDougal & Associates et al. 1986. lib. bdg. 149.50 (ISBN 0-89838-900-3, Pub. by Martinus Nijhoff Netherlands). Kluwer Academic.

Studies Literary & Historical in the Odes of Horace. A. W. Verrall. LC 68-26258. 1969. Repr. of 1884 ed. 21.50x (ISBN 0-8046-0480-0, Pub. by Kennikat). Assoc Faculty Pr.

Studies, Military & Diplomatic, 1775-1865. facs. ed. Charles F. Adams. LC 73-150168. (Select Bibliographies Reprint Ser). 1911. 23.50 (ISBN 0-8369-5681-8). Ayer Co Pubs.

Studies, Military & Diplomatic, 1775-1865. facsimile ed. Charles F. Adams. LC 73-150168. (Select Biographics Reprint Ser.). 424p. 1982. Repr. of 1911 ed. 22.50 (ISBN 0-8290-0474-2). Irvington.

Studies of a Biographer, 4 vols. Leslie Stephen. LC 78-128115. 1973. Repr. of 1898 ed. lib. bdg. 79.50 (ISBN 0-8337-3394-X). B Franklin.

Studies of a Biographer, Vol. 3. Leslie Stephen. 13.25 (ISBN 0-8369-7236-8, 8035). Ayer Co Pubs.

Studies of a Biographer, Vol. 4. Leslie Stephen. text ed. 13.25 (ISBN 0-8369-7346-1, 8139). Ayer Co Pubs.

Studies of a Booklover. facs. ed. Thomas M. Parrott. LC 67-28763. (Essay Index Reprint Ser). 1904. 18.00 (ISBN 0-8369-0771-X). Ayer Co Pubs.

Studies of A. J. Wensinck: An Original Arno Press Anthology. Ed. by Kees W. Bolle. LC 77-82275. (Mythology Ser.). 1978. lib. bdg. 17.00x (ISBN 0-405-10567-3). Ayer Co Pubs.

Studies of a Litterateur. facs. ed. George E. Woodberry. LC 68-26486. (Essay Index Reprint Ser). 1968. Repr. of 1921 ed. 17.75 (ISBN 0-8369-1009-5). Ayer Co Pubs.

Studies of American Fungi: Mushrooms, Edible, Poisonous, Etc. G. F. Atkinson. (Illus.). 1961. Repr. of 1903 ed. 24.95x (ISBN 0-02-840600-1). Hafner.

Studies of Arianism: Chiefly Referring to the Character & Chronology of the Reaction Which Followed the Council of Nicaea. 2nd ed. Henry M. Gwatkin. LC 77-84703. Repr. of 1900 ed. 38.00 (ISBN 0-404-16110-3). AMS Pr.

Studies of Azorin: In Memoriam of L. D. Joiner. Lawrence D. Joiner. Ed. by Joseph W. Zdenek. LC 82-60058. 88p. 1982. pap. 7.00x (ISBN 0-938972-03-0). Spanish Lit Pubns.

Studies of Biosynthesis in Escherichia Coli. Richard B. Roberts et al. (Illus.). 521p. 1958. pap. 21.50 (ISBN 0-87279-618-3, 607). Carnegie Inst.

Studies of Birds Killed in Nocturnal Migration. Harrison B. Tordoff & Robert M. Mengel. (Museum Ser.: Vol. 10, No. 1). 44p. 1956. pap. 2.50 (ISBN 0-317-04637-3). U of KS Mus Nat Hist.

Studies of British Newspapers & Periodicals from Their Beginning to 1800. Katherine K. Weed & Richmond P. Bond. Repr. of 1946 ed. 12.00 (ISBN 0-384-66370-2). Johnson Repr.

Studies of Carboniferous Crinoids: Oklahoma & Nebraska see Palaeontographica Americana.

Studies of Cellular Function Using Radiotracers. Ed. by Mervyn W. Billinghurst. 272p. 1981. 89.00 (ISBN 0-8493-6025-0). CRC Pr.

Studies of Certain Nineteenth Century Poets. Martha H. Shackford. LC 76-16833. 1976. lib. bdg. 17.00 (ISBN 0-8414-7815-5). Folcroft.

Studies of College Teaching: Experimental Results, Theoretical Interpretations & New Perspectives. Carolyn L. Ellner & Carol P. Barnes. LC 82-47853. 240p. 1983. 29.00x (ISBN 0-669-05656-1). Lexington Bks.

Studies of Company Records: Eighteen Thirty to Nineteen Seventy-Four. J. R. Edwards. LC 83-49439. (Accounting History & the Development of a Profession Ser.). 344p. 1984. lib. bdg. 35.00 (ISBN 0-8240-6306-6). Garland Pub.

Studies of Congress. Glenn Parker & C Q Press Staff. LC 84-16993. 570p. 1985. pap. 17.95 (ISBN 0-87187-333-8). Congr Quarterly.

Studies of Contemporary Poets. Mary C. Sturgeon. LC 78-105839. 1970. Repr. of 1920 ed. 26.50x (ISBN 0-8046-1055-X, Pub. by Kennikat). Assoc Faculty Pr.

Studies of Contemporary Superstition. William H. Mallock. LC 72-333. (Essay Index Reprint Ser.). Repr. of 1895 ed. 20.00 (ISBN 0-8369-2804-0). Ayer Co Pubs.

Studies of Coprophilous Sphaeriales in Ontario. Roy L. Cain. (Illus.). 1968. Repr. of 1934 ed. 24.00x (ISBN 3-7682-0531-2). Lubrecht & Cramer.

Studies of Development & Change in the Modern World. Ed. by Michael T. Martin & Terry R. Kandal. (Illus.). 368p. 1989. 39.95 (ISBN 0-19-505646-9); pap. text ed. 14.95 (ISBN 0-19-505647-7). Oxford U Pr.

Studies of Early Fossil Primates in North America. William K. Gregory et al. LC 78-72713. 1980. Repr. 34.50 (ISBN 0-404-18283-6). AMS Pr.

Studies of Engine Bearings & Lubrication. 80p. 1983. 20.00 (ISBN 0-89883-310-8, SP539). Soc Auto Engineers.

Studies of English Mystics. facs. ed. William R. Inge. LC 69-17578. (Essay Index Reprint Ser). 1906. 15.00 (ISBN 0-8369-0081-2). Ayer Co Pubs.

Studies of English Poets. facs. ed. John W. Mackail. LC 68-25604. (Essay Index Reprint Ser). 1968. Repr. of 1926 ed. 17.50 (ISBN 0-8369-0651-9). Ayer Co Pubs.

Studies of English Poets (Pope, Shakespeare, Young, Collins, Keats, Morris, Swinburne, Tennyson) J. W. Mackail. 1973. lib. bdg. 27.00 (ISBN 0-8414-6432-4). Folcroft.

Studies of Field Systems in the British Isles. Ed. by Alan R. Baker & R. A. Butlin. (Illus.). 728p. 1980. pap. 34.50 (ISBN 0-521-29790-7). Cambridge U Pr.

Studies of Food Microstructure. Ed. by O. Johari et al. LC 81-84080. (Illus.). x, 342p. 1981. 49.00 (ISBN 0-931288-22-3). Scanning Microscopy.

Studies of Food Preference, Appetite & Dietary Habit. P. T. Young & J. P. Chaplin. Incl. Pt. III. Palatability & Appetite in Relation to Bodily Need. pap. 10.00; Pt. V. Techniques for Testing Food Preference, & the Significance of Results Obtained with Different Methods; Pt. IX. Palatability Versus Appetite As Determinants of the Critical Concentrations of Sucrose & Sodium Chloride. write for info. (ISBN 0-527-24933-5); Pt. X. Preferences Adrenalectomized Rats for Salt Solutions of Different Concentrations. pap. write for info.. (Comp. Psych. Monographs). 1945. Kraus Repr.

Studies of Foreign Competition Policy & Practice, 2 vols. 1976. (SSC); pap. 12.50 ea. (ISBN 0-686-67774-9, SSC101). UNIPUB.

Studies of French Criminals of the Nineteenth Century. Henry B. Irving. LC 74-10428. (Classics of Crime & Criminology Ser). 356p. 1975. Repr. of 1901 ed. 17.60 (ISBN 0-88355-195-0). Hyperion Conn.

Studies of Governmental Institutions in Chinese History. Ed. by John L. Bishop. LC 68-17622. (Harvard-Yenching Institute Studies: No. 23). 1968. pap. 8.50x (ISBN 0-674-85110-2). Harvard U Pr.

Studies of Illnesses of Children Followed from Birth to Eighteen Years. Isabelle Valadian et al. (SRCD M). 1961. 16.00 (ISBN 0-527-01590-3). Kraus Repr.

Studies of Irving. Charles D. Warner et al. LC 73-9634. 1974. Repr. of 1880 ed. lib. bdg. 30.00 (ISBN 0-8414-2848-4). Folcroft.

Studies of Israeli Society: Politics & Society in Israel, Vol. III. Ed. by Ernest Krausz. 400p. 1984. deluxe ed. 34.95x; pap. 14.95x. Transaction Bks.

Studies of Language, Thought & Verbal Communication. Ed. by R. Rommetveit & R. M. Blaker. 1979. 98.00 (ISBN 0-12-594660-0). Acad Pr.

Studies of Law in Social Change & Development: Law & Social Enquiry-Case Studies of Research. Ed. by R. Luckham. 20.00 (ISBN 0-686-35903-8); pap. 12.00 (ISBN 0-686-37206-9). Intl Ctr Law.

Studies of Law in Social Change & Development: Lawyers in the Third World-Comparative & Developmental Perspectives. Ed. by C. J. Dias & R. Luckham. 25.00 (ISBN 0-686-35898-8); pap. 12.00 (ISBN 0-686-37202-6). Intl Ctr Law.

Studies of Law in Social Change & Development: Law in the Political Economy of Public Enterprise - African Perspectives. Ed. by Y. Ghai. 15.00 (ISBN 0-686-35892-9); pap. 10.00 (ISBN 0-686-37198-4). Intl Ctr Law.

Studies of Law in Social Change & Development: Legal Roles in Columbia, No. 4. Ed. by D. O. Lynch. 14.00 (ISBN 0-686-35900-3); pap. 7.00 (ISBN 0-686-37204-2). Intl Ctr Law.

Studies of Law in Social Change & Development: Urban Legal Problems in Eastern Africa. Ed. by G. W. Kanyeihamba & J. P. McAuslan. 15.00 (ISBN 0-686-35896-1); pap. 10.00 (ISBN 0-686-37200-X). Intl Ctr Law.

Studies of Managerial Work: Results & Methods. Morgan W. McCall, Jr. et al. (Technical Report Ser.: No. 9). 49p. 1978. pap. 10.00 (ISBN 0-912879-08-4). Ctr Creat Leader.

Studies of Mascarene Island Birds. A. W. Diamond. 450p. 1987. 125.00 (ISBN 0-521-25808-1). Cambridge U Pr.

Studies of Men. George W. Smalley. 1973. Repr. of 1895 ed. 25.00 (ISBN 0-8274-0895-1). R West.

Studies of Mind & Brain. Stephen Grossberg. 1982. 59.50 (ISBN 90-277-1359-6, Pub. by Reidel Holland); pap. 23.95 (ISBN 90-277-1360-X). Kluwer Academic.

Studies of Mineral Deposits. Ed. by V. Smirnov. 288p. 1983. 11.95 (ISBN 0-8285-2763-6, Pub. by Mir Pubs USSR). Imported Pubns.

Studies of Organic Molecules. Ed. by J. F. Liebman & A. Greenberg. (Molecular Structure & Energetics Ser.: Vol. 3). (Illus.). 400p. 1986. lib. bdg. 84.00 (ISBN 0-89573-141-X). VCH Pubs.

Studies of Paris. Edmondo De Amicis. LC 72-3348. (Essay Index Reprint Ser.). Repr. of 1879 ed. 19.00 (ISBN 0-8369-2888-1). Ayer Co Pubs.

Studies of Paris: (Victor Hugo, Emile Zola) Edmondo Deamicis. 276p. 1981. Repr. of 1882 ed. lib. bdg. 35.00 (ISBN 0-8495-1062-7). Arden Lib.

Studies of Parydrinae (Diptera: Ephydridae) A Review of the Genus Brachydeutere Loew from the Oriental, Australian & Oceanian Regions, Pt. 1. Wayne N. Mathis & Kumar D. Ghorpade. LC 84-600345. (Smithsonian Contributions to Zoology Ser.: No. 406). pap. 20.00 (ISBN 0-317-30040-7, 2025043). Bks Demand UMI.

Studies of Parydrinae (Diptera: Ephydridae) Revision of the Shore Fly Genus Pelinoides Cresson, Pt. 2. Wayne N. Mathis. LC 84-600299. (Smithsonian Contributions to Zoology Ser.: No. 410). pap. 20.00 (ISBN 0-317-30174-8, 2025356). Bks Demand UMI.

Studies of Passive Clauses. Paul M. Postal. LC 84-26850. (Linguistics Ser.). 271p. 1985. 59.50 (ISBN 0-88706-083-8); pap. 24.50x (ISBN 0-88706-084-6). State U NY Pr.

Studies of Play: An Original Anthology. Judith K. Gardner & Howard Gardner. LC 74-21429. (Classics in Child Development Ser). 198p. 1975. Repr. 19.00x (ISBN 0-405-06478-0). Ayer Co Pubs.

Studies of Political Thought from Gerson to Grotius, 1414-1625. John N. Figgis. LC 75-41092. 1976. Repr. of 1907 ed. 21.00 (ISBN 0-404-14540-X). AMS Pr.

Studies of Psychosocial Risk: The Power of Longitudinal Data. Ed. by Michael Rutter. (Illus.). 440p. Date not set. price not set (ISBN 0-521-35330-0). Cambridge U Pr.

Studies of Reading & Arithmetic in Mentally Retarded Boys. L. Dunn & R. J. Capobianco. (SRCD M Ser.). 1954. pap. 13.00 (ISBN 0-527-01560-1). Kraus Repr.

Studies of Relief & Rehabilitation in China. Owen L. Dawson. LC 78-74350. (Modern Chinese Economy Ser.). 126p. 1980. lib. bdg. 20.00 (ISBN 0-8240-4285-9). Garland Pub.

Studies of Research in Social Work Practice: Harriett M. Bartlett Practice Effectiveness Project Bibliography. Ed. by Lynn Videcka-Sherman. 64p. 1986. 8.95 (ISBN 0-87101-146-8). Natl Assn Soc Wkrs.

Studies of Sargassum & the Sargassum Community. James N. Butler et al. (Bermuda Biological Station Special Publications: No. 22). (Illus.). 307p. 1983. pap. 12.50 (ISBN 0-917642-22-8). Bermuda Bio.

Studies of Savages & Sex. Alfred E. Crawley. Ed. by Theodore Besterman. (Landmarks in Anthropology Ser). 1969. Repr. of 1929 ed. 16.00 (ISBN 0-384-10140-2). Johnson Repr.

Studies of Savages & Sex. facs. ed. Ernest Crawley. Ed. by Theodore Besterman. LC 77-102231. (Select Bibliographies Reprint Ser). 1929. 26.50 (ISBN 0-8369-5116-6). Ayer Co Pubs.

Studies of Schizophrenia: Papers Read at the World Psychiatric Association Symposium, "Current Concepts of Schizophrenia", London, November, 1972. Ed. by Malcolm H. Lader. LC 76-382728. (British Journal of Psychiatry. Special Publication: No. 10). pap. 44.20 (2031465). Bks Demand UMI.

Studies of Shakespeare. Charles Knight. LC 72-171547. Repr. of 1849 ed. 25.00 (ISBN 0-404-03733-X). AMS Pr.

Studies of Shang Archaeology: Selected Papers from the International Conference on Shang Civilization. K. C. Chang. LC 85-10044. 336p. 1986. 32.50x (ISBN 0-300-03578-0). Yale U Pr.

Studies of Shiftwork. Ed. by W. P. Colquhoun & J. Rutenfanz. (Illus.). 468p. 1980. 44.00x (ISBN 0-85066-210-9). Taylor & Francis.

Studies of Small Mammal Populations at Three Sites on the Northern Great Plains. Jaime E. Pefaur & Robert S. Hoffmann. (Occasional Papers: No. 37). 27p. 1975. pap. 1.50 (ISBN 0-317-04897-X). U of KS Mus Nat Hist.

Studies of Some of Longfellow's Poems. Frank Walters. LC 77-22319. 1892. lib. bdg. 17.00 (ISBN 0-8414-9465-7). Folcroft.

Studies of Some of Robert Browning's Poems. F. Walters. LC 79-184648. (Studies in Browning, No. 4). 180p. 1972. Repr. of 1893 ed. lib. bdg. 49.95x (ISBN 0-8383-1380-9). Haskell.

Studies of Some Shakespeare's Plays. Frank Walters. 1977. Repr. of 1902 ed. lib. bdg. 20.00 (ISBN 0-8495-5610-4). Arden Lib.

Studies of South India: An Anthology of Recent Research & Scholarship. Ed. by Robert E. Frykenbert & Pauline Kolenda. 464p. 1986. 32.00X (ISBN 0-8364-1675-9, Pub. by Manohar India). South Asia Bks.

Studies of Suburbanization in Connecticut. Ed. by Richard C. Wade. Incl. No. 1. Windsor; No. 2. Norwich; No. 3. Wilton. LC 73-11933. (Metropolitan America Ser.). (Illus.). 402p. 1974. Repr. 30.00x (ISBN 0-405-05427-0). Ayer Co Pubs.

Studies of Terelliinae (Diptera: Tephritidae) A Revision of the Genus Neaspilota Osten Sacken. Amnon Freidberg & Wayne N. Mathis. LC 85-600299. (Smithsonian Contribution to Zoology Ser: No. 439). pap. 20.00 (ISBN 0-317-55745-9, 2029360). Bks Demand UMI.

Studies of Tertiary & Quaternary Mammals of North America. Carnegie Institution of Washington Staff. Repr. of 1936 ed. 19.00 (ISBN 0-685-02165-3). Johnson Repr.

Studies of the Book of Mormon. B. H. Roberts. Ed. by Brigham D. Madsen. LC 84-236. (Illus.). 412p. 1985. 21.95 (ISBN 0-252-01043-4). U of Ill Pr.

Studies of the Bronze Chueh-Cup. Li Chi & Wang Chia-Pao. (Archaeologia Sinica, New Ser.: No. 2). 140p. 1966. 400.00x (Pub. by Han-Shan Tang Ltd). State Mutual Bk.

Studies of the Bronze Ku-Beaker. Li Chi & Wang Chia-Pao. (Archaeologica Sinica, New Ser.: No. 1). 130p. 1964. 400.00x (Pub. by Han-Shan Tang Ltd). State Mutual Bk.

Studies of the Church in History: Essays Honoring Robert S. Paul on His Sixty-Fifth Birthday. Ed. by Horton Davies. LC 83-9715. (Pittsburgh Theological Monographs. New Series: No. 5). 276p. (Orig.). 1983. pap. 16.95 (ISBN 0-915138-55-7). Pickwick.

Studies of the Design of Steel Castings & Steel Weldments As Related to Methods of Their Manufacture: Castings vs. Weldments. 1959. 6.00 (ISBN 0-686-44993-2). Steel Founders.

Studies of the Economics of Search. Ed. by S. A. Lippman & J. J. McCall. (Contributions to Economic Analysis Ser.: Vol. 123). 1979. 40.50 (ISBN 0-444-85222-0, North Holland). Elsevier.

Studies of the Eighteenth Century in Italy. Vernon Lee. LC 77-17466. (Music Reprint Ser.: 1978). 1978. Repr. of 1887 ed. lib. bdg. 37.50 (ISBN 0-306-77517-4). Da Capo.

Studies of the Greek Poets, 2 Vols. John Addington Symonds. 932p. 1983. Repr. of 1893 ed. lib. bdg. 97.00 set (ISBN 0-89987-978-0). Darby Bks.

Studies of the Human Aura. Kuthumi. LC 74-24022. (Illus.). 166p. 1975. pap. 5.95 (ISBN 0-916766-09-8). Summit Univ.

Studies of the Location, Planning, Zoning & Development of Civil Airports in the U. S. A Selected Bibliography of Sources for the Period 1920-1974, No. 830. Ed. by Eugene C. Kirchherr. 1975. 5.00 (ISBN 0-686-20360-7). CPL Biblios.

Studies of the Middle Atmosphere. Intro. by J. A. Pyle et al. (Series A: Vol. 323). (Illus.). 185p. 1988. text ed. 95.00x (ISBN 0-85403-334-3, Pub. by Royal Soc London). Scholium Intl.

Studies of the Modern World System. Ed. by Albert Bergesen. LC 80-10871. (Studies in Social Discontinuity). 1980. 38.50 (ISBN 0-12-090550-7). Acad Pr.

Studies of the Normal & Abnormal Development of the Nervous System. Ed. by W. Lierse & F. Beck. (Bibliotheca Anatomica Ser.: No. 19). (Illus.). 1981. soft cover 124.75 (ISBN 3-8055-1039-X). S Karger.

Studies of the Pleistocene Palaeobotany of California. Carnegie Institution of Washington Staff. Repr. of 1934 ed. 19.00 (ISBN 0-685-02051-7). Johnson Repr.

Studies of the Pliocene Palaeobotany of California. Carnegie Institution of Washington Staff. Repr. of 1933 ed. 19.00 (ISBN 0-685-02164-5). Johnson Repr.

Studies of the Pollution of the Tennessee River System. G. R. Scott. LC 77-125764. (American Environmental Studies). 1970. Repr. of 1941 ed. 20.00 (ISBN 0-405-02690-0). Ayer Co Pubs.

Studies of the Spanish & Portuguese Ballad. Ed. by N. D. Shergold. (Serie A: Monagrafias, XXVI). 176p. (Orig., Span., Eng. & Port.). 1972. pap. 18.00 (ISBN 0-900411-39-2, Pub. by Tamesis Bks Ltd). Longwood Pub Group.

Studies of the Spanish Mystics, 3 vols. E. A. Peers. 1977. lib. bdg. 300.00 (ISBN 0-8490-2706-3). Gordon Pr.

Studies of the Stage. Brander Matthews. 213p. 1982. Repr. of 1894 ed. lib. bdg. 30.00 (ISBN 0-8495-3930-7). Arden Lib.

Studies of the Stage. Brander Matthews. LC 72-294. (Essay Index Reprint Ser.). Repr. of 1894 ed. 18.00 (ISBN 0-8369-2806-7). Ayer Co Pubs.

Studies of the Surfaces of Solids by Electron Microscopy...Recent Trends. Intro. by Ronald Mason et al. (Philosophical Trans. of the Royal Society, Series A, 1986: Vol. 318). (Illus.). 284p. 1986. lib. bdg. 110.00x (ISBN 0-85403-269-X, Pub. by Royal Soc London). Scholium Intl.

Studies of the Virginia Eastern Shore in the Seventeenth Century. Susie M. Ames. LC 73-76918. (Illus.). x, 274p. 1973. Repr. of 1940 ed. 17.00x (ISBN 0-8462-1730-9). Russell.

Studies of the Wild Turkey in Florida. Lovett Williams, Jr. & David H. Austin. 1988. 27.50x (ISBN 0-8130-0874-3). U Presses Fla.

Studies of the Yaqui Indians of Sonora, Mexico. William C. Holden et al. LC 76-43747. (Texas Tech. College, Bulletin: 12). Repr. of 1936 ed. 19.00 (ISBN 0-404-15586-3). AMS Pr.

Studies of Tropical American Birds. Alexander F. Skutch. (Publications: No. 10). (Illus.). 228p. 1972. 12.00 (ISBN 0-686-35798-1). Nuttall Ornith.

Studies of Vortex Dominated Flows. Ed. by M. Y. Hussaini & M. Salas. (Illus.). xii, 364p. 1986. pap. 28.00 (ISBN 0-387-96430-4). Springer-Verlag.

Studies of Woman. Eric Gill. (Illus.). 1982. 20.00 (ISBN 0-933806-12-4). Black Swan CT.

Studies on Agrarian Reform & Rural Poverty. R. P. Sinha & K. H. Parsons. (Economic & Social Development Ser.: No. 27). (Illus.). 104p. 1985. pap. 19.50 (ISBN 92-5-101371-3, F2677, FAO). UNIPUB.

Studies on Aquatic Vascular Plants: Proceedings of the International Colloquium on Aquatic Vascular Plants, Brussels. J. J. Symoens & S. S. Hooper. (Illus.). 424p. 1982. pap. text ed. 66.00x (ISBN 3-87429-202-9). Lubrecht & Cramer.

Studies on Archaeology of Michoacan Mexico. Leon & Holmes. 33p. pap. 3.95 (ISBN 0-8466-4012-0, I12). Shorey.

Studies on Art & Archeology in Honor of Ernst Kitzinger. Ed. by William Tronzo et al. LC 42-6499. (Dumbarton Oaks Papers: No. 41). (Illus.). 528p. 1987. 65.00X (ISBN 0-88402-169-6). Dumbarton Oaks.

Studies on Asia. Studies on Asia. LC 60-15432. (No. 1). Vol. 1, 1960. pap. 26.80 (ISBN 0-317-27609-3, 2023481); Vol. 2, 1961. pap. 23.80 (ISBN 0-317-27610-7); Vol. 3, 1962. pap. 24.30 (ISBN 0-317-27611-5); Vol. 4, 1963. pap. 51.50 (ISBN 0-317-27612-3); Vol. 5, 1964. pap. 49.50 (ISBN 0-317-27613-1); Vol. 6, 1965. pap. 54.80 (ISBN 0-317-27614-X); Vol. 7, 1966. pap. 48.80 (ISBN 0-317-27615-8); Vol. 8, 1967. pap. 50.50 (ISBN 0-317-27616-6). Bks Demand UMI.

Studies on Botel Tobago & Yap. Inez De Beauclair. (Asian Folklore & Social Life Monograph: No. 19). (Eng. & Ger.). 1971. 19.00 (ISBN 0-89986-021-4). Oriental Bk Store.

Studies on Byzantine Literature of the Eleventh & Twelfth Centuries. Alexander Kazhdan. LC 83-7442. (Past & Present Publications Ser.). 320p. 1984. 54.50 (ISBN 0-521-24656-3). Cambridge U Pr.

Studies on Byzantium, Seljuks & Ottomans: Reprinted Studies. Speros Vryonis, Jr. LC 81-51168. (Byzantina kai Metabyzantina Ser.: Vol. 2). x, 343p. 1981. 29.50x (ISBN 0-89003-072-3); pap. 19.50x (ISBN 0-89003-071-5). Undena Pubns.

Studies on Camille Pissaro. Ed. by Christopher Lloyd. (Illus.). 192p. 1986. pap. 28.00 (ISBN 0-7102-0928-2, 09882, Pub. by Routledge UK). Routledge Chapman & Hall.

Studies on Carbohydrate Metabolism in Fish. Sadao Shimeno. 136p. 1982. text ed. 23.00 (ISBN 90-6191-215-6, Pub. by A A Balkema). Brookfield Pub Co.

Studies on Cenozoic Vertebrates of Western America. Carnegie Institution of Washington Staff. Repr. of 1938 ed. 28.00 (ISBN 0-685-02176-9). Johnson Repr.

Studies on Chaucer & His Audience. Mary E. Giffin. LC 74-18083. 1974. Repr. of 1956 ed. lib. bdg. 37.00 (ISBN 0-8414-4570-2). Folcroft.

Studies on Child Language & Aphasia. Roman Jakobson. (Janua Linguarum, Ser. Minor: No. 114). (Orig.). 1971. pap. text ed. 14.25x (ISBN 90-2791-640-3). Mouton.

Studies on Christiean Huygens: Invited Papers. Symposium on the Life & Work of Christiaan Huygens, Amsterdam, 22-25 August 1979. Ed. by H. J. Bos et al. 1980. text ed. 42.00 (ISBN 90-265-0333-4, Pub. by Swets Pub Serv Holland). Swets North Am.

Studies on Chronic Mental Illness: New Horizons for Social Work Researchers. Ed. by Joan P. Bowker & Allen Rubin. Date not set. 6.50 (ISBN 0-87293-015-7). Coun Soc Wk Ed.

Studies on Clarin: An Annotated Bibliographies. David Torres. LC 87-4362. (Scarecrow Author Bibliographies Ser.: No. 79). 224p. 1987. 20.00 (ISBN 0-8108-1993-7). Scarecrow.

Studies on Co-ordinate Expressions in Middle English. U. Ohlander. (Lund Studies in English: Vol. 5). pap. 22.00 (ISBN 0-8115-0548-0). Kraus Repr.

Studies on Crisis Management. C. F. Smart & W. T. Stanbury. 195p. 1978. pap. text ed. 9.95x (ISBN 0-920380-03-4, Pub. by Inst Res Pub Canada). Brookfield Pub Co.

Studies on Don Quijote & Other Cervantine Works. Donald W. Bleznick. LC 83-51090. 79p. 1984. 12.00x (ISBN 0-938972-07-3). Spanish Lit Pubns.

Studies on Ethnicity: The East European Experience in America. Ed. by Charles A. Ward et al. (East European Monographs: No. 73). 254p. 1980. 25.00x (ISBN 0-914710-67-2). East Eur Quarterly.

Studies on Excitation & Inhibition in the Retina. Ed. by Floyd Ratliff. LC 73-89539. (Illus.). 688p. 1974. 17.50x (ISBN 0-87470-044-2). Rockefeller.

Studies on Gandhi. Ed. by V. T. Patil. viii, 296p. 1984. text ed. 30.00x (ISBN 0-86590-520-7, Pub. by Sterling Pubs India). Apt Bks.

Studies on German Grammar. Ed. by Jindrich Toman. (Studies in Generative Grammar: No. 21). x, 452p. (Orig.). 1985. pap. 33.90 (ISBN 9-067-65113-3); 49.00. Foris Pubns.

Studies on Gottlob Frege & Traditional Philosophy. I. Angelelli. 291p. 1967. lib. bdg. 34.00 (ISBN 90-277-0067-2, Pub. by Reidel Holland). Kluwer Academic.

Studies on Graphs & Discreet Programming. P. Hansen. (Mathematics Studies: Vol. 59). 396p. 1982. 131.75 (ISBN 0-444-86216-1, North Holland). Elsevier.

Studies on Greek & Roman History & Literature. B. Baldwin. (London Studies in Classical Philology: Vol. 15). 604p. 1985. 75.00x (ISBN 90-70265-09-5, Pub. by Gieben Holland). Humanities.

Studies on Greek & Roman History & Literature. Barry Baldwin. (London Studies in Classical Philology: Vol. 15). xiv, 588p. 1985. 92.00x (ISBN 90-70265-09-5, Pub. by Gieben Amsterdam). Benjamins North Am.

Studies on Gregarines. Minnie E. Kamm. 1916. 22.00 (ISBN 0-384-28550-3). Johnson Repr.

Studies on Gregarines 2: Synopsis of the Polycystid Gregarines of the World, Excluding Those from the Myriapoda, Orthoptera & Coleoptera. Minnie E. Kamm. (Illinois Biological Monographs: Vol. 7, No. 1). 1922. 8.00 (ISBN 0-384-28560-0). Johnson Repr.

Studies on Homer & the Homeric Age, 3 vols. W. E. Gladstone. LC 77-94580. 1978. Repr. of 1858 ed. lib. bdg. 75.00 (ISBN 0-89341-176-0). Longwood Pub Group.

Studies on Human Voice Production. E. Vilkman. 74p. (Orig.). 1987. pap. 28.00x (ISBN 951-44-2159-0). Coronet Bks.

Studies on Hysteria. Josef Breuer & Sigmund Freud. LC 57-12310. 1982. 17.00x (ISBN 0-465-08274-2); pap. 12.95x (ISBN 0-465-08276-9, TB-5123). Basic.

Studies on India & Vietnam. Helen B. Lamb. Ed. by Corliss Lamont. LC 76-1668. 288p. 1976. 16.50 (ISBN 0-85345-384-5). Monthly Rev.

Studies on Indian Agromyzidae (Diptera) M. Ipe et al. 1971. 30.00. Oriental Insects.

Studies on Indian Chelonethi. V. A. Murthy & T. N. Ananthakrishnan. (Oriental Insects Monograph: No. 4). 1977. 45.00x (ISBN 0-318-01587-0). Oriental Insects.

Studies on Indian Medical History: Papers Presented at the International Workshop on the Study of Indian Medicine Held at the Wellcome Institute for the History of Medicine, Sept. 2-4, 1985. Ed. by G. Jan Meulenbeld & Dominik Wujastyk. (Groningen Oriental Studies: Vol. II). 247p. (Orig.). 1987. pap. 39.00 (ISBN 90-6980-015-2, Pub. by Egbert Forsten Holland). Benjamins North Am.

Studies on Industrial Relations (I. L. O.) Studies & Reports, Vol. II. (Series A: No. 35, vol. 6). Repr. of 1932 ed. 40.00 (ISBN 0-8115-3238-0). Kraus Repr.

Studies on International Political Economy: A Select Bibliography. Mohammed B. Alam. (Public Administration Ser.: P 2305). 10p. 1987. 3.00 (ISBN 1-55590-605-2). Vance Biblios.

Studies on Iroquoian Culture. Nancy Bonvillain. (Occasional Publications in Northeastern Anthropology: No. 6). 1980. 6.00 (ISBN 0-318-19885-1). Fund Anthrop.

Studies on Iroquoian Culture. Ed. by Nancy Sonvillain. (Occasional Publications in Northeastern Anthropology: No. 6). (Illus.). 148p. 6.00 (ISBN 0-318-22326-0). F Pierce College.

Studies on Islam. Merlin L. Swartz et al. 1981. 22.50x (ISBN 0-19-502716-7); pap. 10.95x (ISBN 0-19-502717-5). Oxford U Pr.

Studies on Japanese Ostracoda. Tetsuro Hanai. (Illus.). 300p. 1982. 77.50 (ISBN 0-86008-314-4, Pub. by U of Tokyo Japan). Columbia U Pr.

Studies on Jorge de Sena. Ed. by Harvey L. Sharrer & Frederick G. Williams. LC 81-85956. 280p. (Orig.). 1981. pap. 18.00x (ISBN 0-942208-20-X). Bandanna Bks.

Studies on Korea: A Scholar's Guide. Ed. by Han-Kyo Kim. LC 79-26491. 458p. 1980. text ed. 27.50x (ISBN 0-8248-0673-5). UH Pr.

Studies on Korea in Transition. Ed. by David R. McCann et al. LC 78-67859. (Occasional Papers: No. 9). 245p. 1979. pap. 8.00x (ISBN 0-917536-13-4). UH Manoa CKS.

Studies on Kosova. Ed. by Arshi Pippa & Sami Repishti. 279p. 1984. 30.00x (ISBN 0-88033-047-3). East Eur Quarterly.

Studies on Lake Vechten & Tjeukemeer: The Netherlands. R. D. Gulati & S. Parma. 1982. 87.00 (ISBN 90-6193-762-0, Pub. by Junk Pubs Netherlands). Kluwer Academic.

Studies on Late Roman & Byzantine History, Literature & Language. B. Baldwin. (London Studies in Classical Philology: Vol. 12). 502p. 1984. text ed. 70.00x (ISBN 90-70265-56-7, Pub. by Gieben Holland). Humanities.

Studies on Late Roman & Byzantine History, Literature & Language. Barry Baldwin. (London Studies in Classical Philology: Vol. 12). xii, 502p. 1984. 85.00x (ISBN 90-70265-56-7, Pub. by Gieben Amsterdam). Benjamins North Am.

Studies on Mathematical Programming. Prekopa. (Mathematical Method Operations Research Ser.: Vol. 1). 1979. cancelled 21.00 (ISBN 963-05-1854-6, Pub. by Akademiai Kaido Hungary). IPS.

Studies on Mathematical Programming. A. Prekopa. 200p. 1980. 74.00x (ISBN 0-569-08626-4, Pub. by Collets (UK)). State Mutual Bk.

Studies on Mesozoic & Caenozoic Dinoflagellate Cysts. R. J. Davey et al. (Illus.). 272p. 1983. pap. text ed. 101.50x (ISBN 0-565-00879-X, Pub. by Brit Mus Nat Hist England). Sabbot-Natural Hist Bks.

Studies on Methods of Estimating Population Density, Biomass & Productivity in Terrestrial Animals, Vol. 17. Ed. by T. Morisita. (Japan International Biological Program Synthesis Ser.). 237p. 1977. 32.50 (ISBN 0-86008-227-X, Pub. by U of Tokyo Japan). Columbia U Pr.

Studies on Middle English Local Surnames. M. T. Lofvenberg. (Lund Studies in English: Vol. 11). pap. 30.00 (ISBN 0-8115-0554-5). Kraus Repr.

Studies on Modern Painters. facs. ed. Arthur Symons. LC 67-30233. (Essay Index Reprint Ser). 1925. 17.00 (ISBN 0-8369-0920-8). Ayer Co Pubs.

Studies on Money in Early America. Ed. by Eric P. Newman & Richard G. Doty. (Illus.). 216p. 1976. 10.50 (ISBN 0-89722-065-X). Am Numismatic.

Studies on Myxosporidia. Roksabro Kudo. (Illus.). 1920. Repr. of 1920 ed. 22.00 (ISBN 0-384-30620-9). Johnson Repr.

Studies on Nehru. Ed. by V. T. Patil. 421p. 1987. text ed. 45.00x (ISBN 81-207-0624-2, Pub. by Sterling Pubs India). Apt Bks.

Studies on Neotropical Water Mites. David Cook. (Memoir Ser.: No. 31). (Illus.). 644p. 1980. 50.00x (ISBN 0-686-27979-4). Am Entom Inst.

Studies on Neuromuscular Diseases: Proceedings. Quantitative Methods of Investigations in the Clinics of Neuromuscular Diseases International Symposium, Giessen, April 1974. Ed. by K. Kunze & J. E. Desmedt. 250p. 1975. 101.50 (ISBN 3-8055-1749-1). S Karger.

Studies on Non-Alignment. M. S. Rajan. 1986. 25.00x (ISBN 0-8364-1917-0, Pub. by ABC Pub India). South Asia Bks.

Studies on North American Polystomidae Aspidogastridae & Paramphistomidae. Horace W. Stunkard. (Illus.). Repr. of 1917 ed. 12.00 (ISBN 0-384-58730-5). Johnson Repr.

Studies on Ohio Diatoms: Diatoms of the Scioto River Basin & Referenced Checklist from Ohio Exclusive of Lake Erie & the Ohio River. Gary B. Collins & Robert G. Kalinsky. 1977. 7.00 (ISBN 0-86727-080-2). Ohio Bio Survey.

Studies on Oriental Pipunculidae (Diptera) D. Elmo Hardy. 1972. 30.00. Oriental Insects.

Studies on Plant Demography: A Festschrift for John L. Harper. Ed. by James White. 1986. 66.00 (ISBN 0-12-746630-4); pap. 32.50 (ISBN 0-12-746631-2). Acad Pr.

Studies on Public Employment & Compensation in Canada. Meyer W. Bucovetsky. 177p. 1979. pap. text ed. 14.95x (ISBN 0-409-88601-7, Pub. by Inst Res Pub Canada). Brookfield Pub Co.

Studies on Regulation in Canada. W. T. Stanbury. 249p. 1978. pap. text ed. 9.95x (ISBN 0-920380-04-2, Pub. by Inst Res Pub Canada). Brookfield Pub Co.

Studies on Religion & Politics. Ed. by Jerome J. Hanus & James V. Schall. LC 86-9166. 120p. (Orig.). 1986. lib. bdg. 30.00 (ISBN 0-8191-5391-5); pap. text ed. 13.50 (ISBN 0-8191-5392-3). U Pr of Amer.

Studies on Rural Development: Experiences & Issues. Ajit K. Danda. xii, 96p. 1984. text ed. 18.95x (ISBN 0-86590-389-1, Pub. by Inter Pubns N Delhi). Apt Bks.

Studies on Scarab Seals. W. A. Ward. (Pre-12th Dynasty Scarab Amulets Ser.: Vol. I). (Illus.). 116p. 1978. text ed. 55.00x (ISBN 0-85668-124-5, Pub. by Aris & Phillips UK). Humanities.

Studies on Scarab Seals: Vol. 2: Scarab Seals & Their Contribution to History in the Early Second Millennium, 2 pts. Olga Tufnell. LC 82-102187. (Illus.). 220p. 1984. pap. text ed. 75.00x (Pub. by Aris & Phillips UK). Pt. 1 (ISBN 0-85668-130-X). Pt. 2 (ISBN 0-85668-279-9). Humanities.

Studies on Scipio Africanus. Richard M. Haywood. LC 78-64148. (Johns Hopkins University. Studies in the Social Sciences. Fifty-First Ser. 1933: 1). Repr. of 1933 ed. 11.50 (ISBN 0-404-61259-8). AMS Pr.

Studies on Semantics in Generative Grammar. Noam Chomsky. LC 74-189711. (Janua Linguarum, Ser. Minor: No. 107). 207p. (Orig.). 1972. pap. text ed. 16.75x (ISBN 90-2797-964-2). Mouton.

Studies on Slavery, in Easy Lessons. facs. ed. John Fletcher. LC 70-83962. (Black Heritage Library Collection Ser). 1851. 27.50 (ISBN 0-8369-8572-9). Ayer Co Pubs.

Studies on Slavic Derivation. Kristine Heltberg. 160p. (Orig.). 1970. pap. 23.50x (ISBN 87-7492-001-4, Pub. by Odense Universitets Forlag (Odense Denmark)). Coronet Bks.

Studies on Some of Shakespeare's Plays. Frank Walters. 172p. 1984. Repr. of 1889 ed. lib. bdg. 35.00 (ISBN 0-918377-25-0). Russell Pr.

Studies on Sulphur Isotope Variations in Nature. (Panel Proceedings Ser.). 124p. (Orig.). 1987. pap. text ed. 21.00 (ISBN 0-317-68050-1, ISP747A, IAEA). UNIPUB.

Studies on Syntactic Topology & Contrastive Grammar. Laslo Dezsoe. (Janua Linguarum, Series Maior 89). 307p. 1982. pap. text ed. 44.25x (ISBN 90-279-3108-9). Mouton.

Studies on Thackeray. James Hannay. LC 73-103191. 1970. Repr. of 1868 ed. 19.50x (ISBN 0-8046-0828-8, Pub. by Kennikat). Assoc FAculty Pr.

Studies on the Animal Ecology of the Hocking River Basin: The Bottom Invertebrates of the Hocking River & the Plankton of the Hocking River. William B. Ludwig & Lee S. Roach. 1932. 2.00 (ISBN 0-86727-025-X). Ohio Bio Survey.

Studies on the Avian Species of the Cestode Family Hymenolepididae. Roy L. Mayhew. (Illinois Biological Monographs: Vol. 10, No. 1). Repr. of 1925 ed. 12.00 (ISBN 0-384-36080-7). Johnson Repr.

Study & Management of Large Mammals. Thane Riney. LC 81-11519. 552p. 1982. 106.00 (ISBN 0-471-10062-5, Pub. by Wiley-Interscience). Wiley.

Study & Notebook for Organic Chemistry. George Newkome & N. H. Fischer. 1982. spiral bdg. 7.95 (ISBN 0-88252-027-X). Paladin Hse.

Study & Practice of Astral Projection. Robert Crookall. 1977. pap. 5.95 (ISBN 0-8065-0547-8, Pub. by Citadel Pr). Lyle Stuart.

Study & Practice of Astral Projection. Robert Crookall. 1966. 7.50 (ISBN 0-8216-0154-7, Pub. by Univ Bks). Lyle Stuart.

Study & Prevention of Corrosion. 1983. 40.00 (ISBN 0-89883-309-4, SP538). Soc Auto Engineers.

Study & Reading Skills. (Basic Academics Ser.: Module 1). (Illus.). 80p. 1982. spiral binding 18.50x (ISBN 0-87683-225-7). GP Pub.

Study & Research Opportunities in the Middle East & North Africa. Ed. by Leslie C. Schmida & Andrea Lorenz. 170p. 1985. pap. 7.95 (ISBN 0-913957-02-X). AMIDEAST.

Study & Teaching of Law in Africa, with a Survey of Institutions of Legal Education in Africa. John S. Bainbridge & Terry Wood. x, 342p. 1972. text ed. 12.50x (ISBN 0-8377-0304-2). Rothman.

Study & Thinking Skills in College. Kathleen T. McWhorter. (Orig.). 1988. pap. text ed. write for info. (ISBN 0-673-39739-4). Scott F.

Study & Writing of Poetry: American Women Poets Discuss Their Craft. Ed. by Wauneta Hackleman. LC 82-50773. 420p. 1983. 27.50X (ISBN 0-87875-259-5); pap. 12.50X. Whitston Pub.

Study Atlas of Electron Micrographs. rev. ed. Judy M. Strum. LC 86-80327. (Illus.). 208p. 1986. text ed. 25.00 (ISBN 0-9608786-1-0). Univ Maryland.

Study Break. Alison Blair. (Roommates Ser.: No. 15). (YA) (gr. 10 up). 1988. pap. 2.95 (ISBN 0-8041-0327-5, Pub. by Ivy). Ballantine.

Study Circles: Coming Together for Personal Growth and Social Change. Leonard P. Oliver. (Illus.). 152p. (Orig.). 1987. pap. 9.95 (ISBN 0-932020-47-X). Seven Locks Pr.

Study Course in Homeopathy. Phyllis Speight. 145p. 1979. text ed. 27.95x (ISBN 0-8464-1052-4). Beekman Pubs.

Study Course in Homeopathy. Phyllis Speight. 1980. 17.50x (ISBN 0-85032-164-6, Pub. by Daniel Co England). State Mutual Bk.

Study Design, Procedures & Available Data for 1968-1972 Interviewing Years see Panel Study of Income Dynamics: Complete Documentation for Interviewing Years 1968-1981.

Study Edition (Lectors' Guide) of the Lectionary for Mass, Cycle A Sundays & Solemnities. Catholic Church, Sacred Congregation of Divine Worship Staff. Tr. by International Committee on English in the Liturgy, Confraternity of Christian Doctrine for the New American Bible. (The Study Edition (Lector's Guide) of the Lectionary for Mass Ser.: Texts from the New American Bible). 1977. pap. 6.95 (ISBN 0-916134-04-0). Pueblo Pub Co.

Study Edition (Lectors' Guide) of the Lectionary for Mass, Cycle B Sundays & Solemnities. Catholic Church, Sacred Congregation of Divine Worship Staff. 1978. pap. 6.95 (ISBN 0-916134-05-9). Pueblo Pub Co.

Study Edition (Lectors' Guide) of the Lectionary for Mass, Cycle C, Sunday & Solemnities. Tr. by International Committee on English in the Liturgy. (Study Edition (Lectors' Guide) of the Lectionary for Mass Ser.: Texts from the New American Bible). 1976. pap. 6.95 (ISBN 0-916134-06-7). Pueblo Pub Co.

Study English for Science. A. R. Bolitho & P. L. Sandler. (English As a Second Language Bk.). 104p. 1980. pap. text ed. 6.95 (ISBN 0-582-55248-6); tchr's ed. 4.50 (ISBN 0-582-74821-6). Longman.

Study English-Korean - Korean-English Dictionary. (Illus., Eng. & Korean.). 1987. 14.95 (ISBN 0-89346-300-0). Heian Intl.

Study for Applying Computer-Generated Images to Visual Stimulation. Robert A. Schumaker et al. LC 74-131394. 142p. 1969. 19.00 (ISBN 0-403-04536-3). Scholarly.

Study for Success. Meredith D. Gall & Joyce P. Gall. LC 84-14993. (Illus.). 165p. (Orig.). 1985. pap. 7.95 (ISBN 0-930539-01-X); pap. instr's. manual avail. (ISBN 0-930539-03-6); pap. avail. (ISBN 0-930539-04-4). M Damien Pubs.

Study for the Birmingham (AL) Municipal Court. National Center for State Courts Staff. 228p. 1980. manuscript 13.68 (SRO-003). Natl Ctr St Courts.

Study Group Leader's Manual. Vicki Soltz. 1967. pap. 5.00x (ISBN 0-918560-09-8). A Adler Inst.

Study Group on the Russian Revolution: Publications, Vols. 2-7. Ed. by Maureen Perrie et al. (Orig.). 1982. lib. bdg. 362.00. Kraus Intl.

Study Group on the Russian Revolution: Protokoly vtorogo (ekstrennago) s"ezda Partii Sotsialistov - Revolution, Vol. 10. Intro. by Christopher J. Rice. 218p. (Rus.). 1986. lib. bdg. 72.00 (ISBN 0-527-87322-5). Kraus Intl.

Study Group on the Russian Revolution: Spisok Provremennykh Izdanii Za, 1917, No. 1. Ed. by David R. Jones. LC 82-49046. 280p. (Rus.). 1986. lib. bdg. 83.00 (ISBN 0-527-87313-6). Kraus Intl.

Study Group on the Russian Revolution: Vtoroi Vserosskii s"ezd Konstitutsionnov-Demokraticheskoi Partii, No. 8. Ed. by Raymond Pearson. 392p. (Rus.). 1986. lib. bdg. 106.00 (ISBN 0-527-87320-9). Kraus Intl.

Study Group Readings. Compiled by Associations for Research & Enlightenment, Readings Research Department Staff. (Library: Vol. 7). 545p. 1977. 10.95 (ISBN 0-87604-094-6). ARE Pr.

Study Group Report: Classification & Nomenclature Systems for Petroleum Reserves. 10p. 1984. pap. 19.95 (ISBN 0-471-90427-9). Wiley.

Study Guide & Manual for the National Certification Examinations for Nurse Practitioners & Other Primary Health Care Providers. Patricia Martinell & Patricia Seaman. 125p. 1988. pap. text ed. 19.95x (ISBN 0-8290-1279-6). Irvington.

Study Guide & Review Manual of Human Embryology. 2nd ed. Keith L. Moore. 304p. 1982. pap. 22.95 (ISBN 0-7216-6476-8). Saunders.

Study Guide & Review Manual of Human Embryology. 3rd ed. Keith L. Moore. (Illus.). 210p. 1988. write for info. (ISBN 0-7216-2412-X). Saunders.

Study Guide & Review of the Nervous System. 2nd ed. Keith L. Moore et al. (Illus.). 285p. 1986. 22.95 (ISBN 0-7216-1524-4). Saunders.

Study Guide & Self-Assessment for the American Psychiatric Press Textbook of Psychiatry. Michael Franzen & Mark Lovell. 1988. pap. 20.00. Am Psychiatric.

Study Guide & Self-Assessment for the American Psychiatric Press Textbook of Neuropsychiatry. Michael D. Franzen & Mark R. Lovell. LC 87-1057. 144p. 1987. study guide 20.00 (ISBN 0-88048-293-1). Am Psychiatric.

Study Guide & Workbook for Nursing Fundamentals. Catherine W. Bevil. 400p. 1986. pap. 14.95 (ISBN 0-8385-7035-6). Appleton & Lange.

Study Guide Book. ACCESS Staff. (Mathematics for Modern Living Ser.). 1980. pap. text ed. 25.00 (ISBN 1-55740-000-8). Magna Systems.

Study Guide Exercise Book to Accompany Business Communication, by Richard C. Huseman, James M. Lahiff, John M. Penrose jr. Westley King & Edward Miles. (Illus.). 576p. 1988. pap. price not set. Dryden Pr.

Study Guide for ACSW Certification. 2nd ed. Ed. by Ruth R. Middleman. 64p. 1987. 6.95 (ISBN 0-87101-150-6). Natl Assn Soc Wkrs.

Study Guide for Advanced Life Support: Problem Solving in Cardiac Arrest. Ken Grauer. 222p. 1984. 18.95. Soc Tchrs Fam Med.

Study Guide for Agricultural Pest Control Advisors: Insects, Mites & Other Invertebrates & Their Control in California. rev. ed. Vernon Burton et al. LC 81-68756. 128p. 1981. pap. 4.00x (ISBN 0-931876-49-4, 4044). ANR Pubns CA.

Study Guide for Archbishop Hunthausen's Pastoral on Matrimony. rev. ed. Thomas L. Vandenberg. LC 82-62716. 59p. 1984. pap. text ed. 2.95 (ISBN 0-911905-02-2). Past & Mat Rene Ctr.

Study Guide for Competency Tests in the Basic Skills. Pauline Hodges et al. 176p. 1983. 15.95 (ISBN 0-8403-2962-8). Kendall-Hunt.

Study Guide for Efficient Reading: Alternate Edition. James I. Brown & Karyn S. Prois. Ed. by W. W. Kemmerer. 52p. pap. text ed. 4.95 (ISBN 0-943000-05-X). Telstar Inc.

Study Guide for Efficient Reading: Form B. James I. Brown & Karyn Prois. 52p. 1982. pap. text ed. 4.95 (ISBN 0-943000-06-8). Telstar Inc.

Study Guide for Ezra, Nehemiah, Esther. John F. Brug. (Study Guide for People's Bible Ser.). 60p. (Orig.). 1985. pap. 2.25 (ISBN 0-938272-53-5). Wels Board.

Study Guide for Federal Tax Course, 1984. Foth. 428p. pap. 9.50 (ISBN 0-317-04203-3). Commerce.

Study Guide for Genesis. Hagen Staack. 1984. pap. 3.95 (ISBN 0-9613270-0-6). G McBride.

Study Guide for Hebrews. Richard E. Lauersdorf. Ed. by William E. Fischer. (Study Guide for People's Bible Ser.). 48p. (Orig.). 1986. pap. 1.95 (ISBN 0-938272-56-X). WELS Board.

Study Guide for Introduction to Computers & Information Processing. 2nd ed. Nancy Long & Larry Long. (Illus.). 256p. 1988. write for info. (ISBN 0-13-480708-1). P-H.

Study Guide for Invitation to Economics. James Pinto. 196p. 1984. pap. 7.95 (ISBN 0-86576-075-6). W Kaufmann.

Study Guide for Ministry & Counsel. Revised ed. 30p. (Orig.). 1985. pap. 1.50x (ISBN 0-942727-11-8). NC Yrly Pubns Bd.

Study Guide for Nineteen Eighty-Eight CCH Federal Taxation: Advanced Topics. Foth. 296p. 1987. pap. 15.00 (5316). Commerce.

Study Guide for Nineteen Eighty-Eight CCH Federal Taxation: Basic Principles. Foth. 392p. 1987. pap. 15.00 (5318). Commerce.

Study Guide for Nineteen Eighty-Eight Federal Tax Course. Foth. 416p. (Orig.). 1987. pap. 15.00 (5324). Commerce.

Study Guide for Nineteen Eighty-Six Federal Tax Course. Foth. 428p. 1985. 12.50 (ISBN 0-317-44565-0, 4718). Commerce.

Study Guide for (Patrick) Medical-Surgical Nursing. Felver. LC 64-5054. 1986. 12.95 (ISBN 0-397-54576-2). Lippincott.

Study Guide for Paul's Letters to the Thessalonians. David P. Kuske. 41p. (Orig.). 1984. pap. 1.75 (ISBN 0-938272-51-9). WELS Board.

Study Guide for Philippians-Colossians & Philemon. Harlyn J. Kuschel. Ed. by William E. Fischer. (Study Guide for People's Bible Ser.). 48p. (Orig.). 1987. pap. text ed. 2.50 (ISBN 0-938272-57-8). Wels Board.

Study Guide for Porth's Pathophysiology: Concepts of Altered Health States. 2nd ed. E. Ronald Wright. (Illus.). 417p. 1986. pap. text ed. 13.75 (ISBN 0-397-54483-9, Lippincott Nursing). Lippincott.

Study Guide for Radiologic Technologists. Judith P. Baron. (Illus.). 560p. 1978. 54.75x (ISBN 0-398-03726-4). C C Thomas.

Study Guide For Real Estate License Examinations. R. Ripley. (Orig.). pap. 3.95 (ISBN 0-13-858753-1, Reward). P-H.

Study Guide for the Associate CET Test. 3rd ed. Ed. by Sam Wilson. 28p. pap. 5.00. Intl Soc Cert Elect.

Study Guide for the CET Test: Computer Option. 2nd ed. Ed. by Elmer Poe. 12p. pap. 5.00. Intl Soc Cert Elect.

Study Guide for the New Birth. Neil Stegall & David Bernard. LC 87-10491. 116p. (Orig.). 1987. pap. 5.95 spiral bd. (ISBN 0-932581-15-3). Word Aflame.

Study Guide for the R. D. A. Practical Exam. Catherine M. Germano. (Course Syllabus Ser.). (Illus.). 83p. (Orig.). 1987. pap. text ed. 16.95 (ISBN 0-942801-03-2). Apogee Pr.

Study Guide for the Registration Examination for Dietetic Technicians. Commission on Dietetic Registration Staff & The American Dietetic Association Staff. 28p. (Orig.). 1987. pap. text ed. 7.15 (ISBN 0-88091-030-5). Am Dietetic Assn.

Study Guide for What Is Economics? James Pinto. 108p. 1987. pap. 5.95 (ISBN 0-86576-105-1). W Kaufmann.

Study Guide in Alternating Current Circuits: A Personalized System of Instruction. Irving L. Kosow. LC 77-22152. (Electronic Technology Ser.). pap. 128.80 (ISBN 0-317-10110-2, 2015180). Bks Demand UMI.

Study Guide in Direct Current Circuits: A Personalized System of Instruction. Irving L. Kosow. LC 77-1739. (Ser. in Electronic Technology). Repr. of 1977 ed. 99.80 (ISBN 0-8357-9873-9, 2015181). Bks Demand UMI.

Study Guide to Bible Prayers see Prayers That Make a Difference.

Study Guide to Core Curriculum for Critical Care Nursing. Maureen A. Harvey. (Illus.). 243p. 1986. pap. 15.95 (ISBN 0-7216-1856-1). Saunders.

Study Guide to Greater Bible Knowledge. Wayne Jackson. 156p. (Orig.). 1986. pap. 5.00 (ISBN 0-932859-12-7). Apologetic Pr.

Study Guide to Introduction to Literature: Reading, Analyzing & Writing. Northern Virginia Community College Staff & Sara M. Miller. 160p. 1983. pap. 18.95 (ISBN 0-8403-3231-9). Kendall-Hunt.

Study Guide to Steinbeck, Pt. II. Tetsumaro Hayashi. LC 74-735. 252p. 1979. 17.50 (ISBN 0-8108-1220-7). Scarecrow.

Study Guide to Steinbeck: A Handbook to His Major Works. Tetsumaro Hayashi. LC 74-735. 332p. 1974. 19.00 (ISBN 0-8108-0706-8). Scarecrow.

Study Guide to Steinbeck's The Long Valley. Ed. by Tetsumaro Hayashi. LC 76-42125. 1976. 19.50 (ISBN 0-87650-074-2). Pierian.

Study Guide to Textbook of Medical-Surgical Nursing. 6th ed. Boyer & Lillian S. Brunner. LC 64-5997. 1987. text ed. 12.95 (ISBN 0-397-54701-3, Lippincott Nursing). Lippincott.

Study Guide to the ARI-GAMA Competency in HVACR, 1987-1988. ARI Staff & PES Staff. 80p. 1988. pap. text ed. 6.00 study guide (ISBN 0-13-855636-9). P-H.

Study Guide to the Multiple-Choice Examination for Chief Mate & Master. 3rd, rev. ed. Richard James & Richard M. Plant. LC 82-2441. 686p. 1987. pap. text ed. 32.00x (ISBN 0-87033-371-2). Cornell Maritime.

Study Guide to the Multiple Choice Examinations for Lifeboatmen & Able Seamen. William B. Hayler & Paul M. Seiler. LC 85-48289. (Cornell Study Guides). (Illus.). 112p. 1986. pap. text ed. 12.50 (ISBN 0-87033-346-1). Cornell Maritime.

Study Guide to the Multiple-Choice Examinations for Third & Second Assistant Engineers. William D. Eglinton. LC 85-47836. 264p. (Orig.). 1985. pap. 27.50x (ISBN 0-87033-339-9). Cornell Maritime.

Study Guide to the Multiple Choice Examinations for Third & Second Mates. 4th ed. ed. Richard James & Richard M. Plant. LC 82-2438. 1982. pap. 24.50x (ISBN 0-87033-289-9). Cornell Maritime.

Study Guide to the Professional Engineer's Examination for Industrial Engineers. 2nd ed. Robert P. Davis & Richard A. Wysk. 1987. 49.95. Inst Indus Eng.

Study Guide to Understanding Human Behavior Telecourse. 2nd ed. Coast Community College Staff. 512p. 1986. pap. 12.95 (ISBN 0-03-063588-8, HoltC). HR&W.

Study Guide: Workbook for Biology 102. Arnold J. Karpoff. 176p. 1982. pap. text ed. 15.95 (ISBN 0-8403-4207-1, 4042074). Kendall-Hunt.

Study Guide-Workbook to Accompany Speech & Hearing Science Anatomy & Physiology. Eileen Zemlin & W. R. Zemlin. (Illus.). 300p. 1988. 14.80x (ISBN 0-87563-314-5). Stipes.

Study-Habits Inventory. rev. ed. C. Gilbert Wrenn. 1941. pap. 0.12x (ISBN 0-8047-1070-8). Stanford U Pr.

Study in Aesthetics. Louis A. Reid. 415p. 1980. Repr. of 1931 ed. lib. bdg. 45.00 (ISBN 0-8495-4635-4). Arden Lib.

Study in Aesthetics. Louis A. Reid. LC 70-114546. 415p. 1973. Repr. of 1954 ed. lib. bdg. 35.00x (ISBN 0-8371-4794-8, RESA). Greenwood.

Study in Anti-Gnostic Polemics: Irenaeus, Hippolytus & Epiphanius. Gerard Vallee. 128p. 1981. pap. text ed. 8.95x (ISBN 0-919812-14-7, Pub. by Wilfrid Laurier Canada). Humanities.

Study in Association Reaction & Reaction Time see Mental & Physical Measurements of Working Children.

Study in Austrian Intellectual History from Late Baroque to Romanticism. Robert A. Kann. LC 73-16356. 367p. 1973. Repr. lib. bdg. 27.50x (ISBN 0-374-94504-7, Octagon). Hippocrene Bks.

Study in Austrian Romanticism: Hungarian Influences in Lenau's Poetry. Agnes H. Vardy. LC 73-620154. 1974. 9.00 (ISBN 0-914648-05-5). Hungarian Cultural.

Study in Boss Politics: William Lorimer of Chicago. Joel A. Tarr. LC 72-133945. (Illus.). 392p. 1971. 34.95 (ISBN 0-252-00139-7). U of Ill Pr.

Study in Consciousness. 6th ed. Annie Besant. 1972. 8.25 (ISBN 0-8356-7287-5). Theos Pub Hse.

Study in Corneille. Lee D. Lodge. LC 70-132812. (Literary Criticism Ser). 1970. Repr. of 1891 ed. lib. bdg. 21.50 (ISBN 0-8337-2133-X). B Franklin.

Study in Corneille. Lee D. Lodge. 1976. lib. bdg. 59.95 (ISBN 0-8490-2707-1). Gordon Pr.

Study in Creative History. O. E. Burton. LC 71-105821. (Classics Ser). 1971. Repr. of 1932 ed. 26.00x (ISBN 0-8046-1197-1, Pub. by Kennikat). Assoc Faculty Pr.

Study in Creative History: The Interaction of the Eastern & Western Peoples to 500 B. C. O. E. Burton. 1977. lib. bdg. 59.95 (ISBN 0-8490-2708-X). Gordon Pr.

Study in Culture Contact & Culture Change: The Whiterock Utes in Transition. Gottfried O. Lang. (Utah Anthropological Papers: No. 15). Repr. of 1953 ed. 10.50 (ISBN 0-404-60615-6). AMS Pr.

Study in Daniel. Howard B. Rand. 1948. 12.00 (ISBN 0-685-08814-6). Destiny.

Study in Depth. Doris W. Gilbert. (Orig.). 1966. pap. text ed. write for info. (ISBN 0-13-858902-X). P-H.

Study in Disguised Intelligence Tests: Interview Form. Donald S. Snedden. LC 71-177765. (Columbia University. Teachers College. Contributions to Education: No. 291). Repr. of 1927 ed. 22.50 (ISBN 0-404-55291-9). AMS Pr.

Study in Educational Prognosis. Elbert K. Fretwell. LC 72-177603. (Columbia University. Teachers College. Contributions to Education: No. 99). Repr. of 1919 ed. 22.50 (ISBN 0-404-55099-1). AMS Pr.

Study in English Metrics. Adelaide Crapsey. LC 77-6978. 1977. Repr. of 1918 ed. lib. bdg. 10.00 (ISBN 0-89341-169-8). Longwood Pub Group.

Study in English Metrics. Adelaide Crapsey. 1918. Repr. 10.00 (ISBN 0-8274-3547-9). R West.

Study in Hosea. Howard B. Rand. 1955. 5.00 (ISBN 0-685-08815-4). Destiny.

Study in Jeremiah. Howard B. Rand. 1947. 12.00 (ISBN 0-685-08816-2). Destiny.

Study in Karma. Besant. 3.95 (ISBN 0-8356-7292-1). Theos Pub Hse.

Study in Latin Prognosis. William S. Allen. LC 70-176513. (Columbia University. Teachers College. Contributions to Education: No. 135). Repr. of 1923 ed. 22.50 (ISBN 0-404-55135-1). AMS Pr.

Study in Law of Evidence. M. S. Prasad. 292p. 1982. 45.00x (ISBN 0-317-54676-7, Pub. by Eastern Bk India). State Mutual Bk.

Study in Lilac. Maria-Antonia Oliver. Tr. by Kathleen McNerney from Catalan. (International Women's Crime Ser.). 161p. (Orig.). 1987. pap. 8.95 (ISBN 0-931188-52-0). Seal Pr Feminist.

Study in Memorizing Various Materials by the Reconstruction Method see Johns Hopkins University Psychology Laboratories: Studies.

Study in Metaphysics. Henri Bergson. LC 61-10604. 1961. pap. 5.00 (ISBN 0-8022-0107-5). Philos Lib.

Study in Methodist Discipline. C. R. Nichol. Date not set. pap. 1.95 (ISBN 0-915547-50-3). Abilene Christ U.

Study in Milton's Christian Doctrine. Arthur Sewell. LC 72-193159. 1939. lib. bdg. 32.50 (ISBN 0-8414-8118-0). Folcroft.

Study in Milton's Christian Doctrine. Arthur Sewell. LC 67-26661. xiii, 214p. 1967. Repr. of 1939 ed. 22.50 (ISBN 0-208-00416-5, Archon). Shoe String.

Study in Nationality. J. Vyrnwy Morgan. LC 74-118491. 1971. Repr. of 1911 ed. 38.50x (ISBN 0-8046-1239-0, Pub. by Kennikat). Assoc Faculty Pr.

Study in Public Finance. 3rd rev. ed. Arthur C. Pigou. 1975. Repr. of 1947 ed. lib. bdg. 35.50x (ISBN 0-678-07009-1). Kelley.

Study in Pyramidology. E. Raymond Capt. LC 86-70103. (Illus.). 264p. (Orig.). 1986. 15.00 (ISBN 0-934666-20-2); pap. 10.00 (ISBN 0-934666-21-0). Artisan Sales.

Study in Reaction Time & Movement. T. V. Moore. Bd. with Individual & His Relation to Society. J. H. Tufts. Repr. of 1904 ed; Time & Reality. J. E. Boddin. Repr. of 1904 ed; Differentiation of the Religious Consciousness. Irving King. Repr. of 1905 ed; No. 4. Iowa University Studies in Psychology. Ed. by C. E. Seashore. Repr. of 1905 ed. (Psychology Monographs General & Applied: Vol. 6). pap. 29.00 (ISBN 0-8115-1405-6). Kraus Repr.

Study in Realism. facsimile ed. John Laird. LC 77-152991. (Select Bibliographies Reprint Ser). Repr. of 1920 ed. 18.00 (ISBN 0-8369-5743-1). Ayer Co Pubs.

Study in Revelation. Howard B. Rand. 1941. 12.00 (ISBN 0-685-08817-0). Destiny.

Study in Robert Browning. K. C. Chakravarti. 1973. lib. bdg. 12.50 (ISBN 0-8414-3011-X). Folcroft.

Study in Scarlet. Arthur Conan Doyle. lib. bdg. 15.95x (ISBN 0-89966-231-5). Buccaneer Bks.

Study in Scarlet. Arthur Conan Doyle. 1982. pap. 2.95 (ISBN 0-14-005707-2). Penguin.

Study in Scarlet & the Sign of the Four. Arthur Conan Doyle. 256p. (gr. 10 up). 1985. pap. 2.50 (ISBN 0-425-09577-0). Berkley Pub.

Study in Shelley Criticism. Francis C. Mason. LC 77-5507. 1937. lib. bdg. 35.50 (ISBN 0-8414-6165-1). Folcroft.

Study in Smollett Chiefly "Peregrine Pickle". Howard S. Buck. 228p. Repr. of 1925 ed. 10.00x (ISBN 0-911858-09-1). Appel.

Study in Southsea: The Unrevealed Life of Dr. Arthur Conan Doyle, the Creator of Sherlock Holmes. Geoffrey Stavert. 192p. 1988. 19.95 (ISBN 0-903852-92-6, Pub. by Milestone Pubns UK). Seven Hills Bks.

Study in String Processing Languages. P. Klint. (Lecture Notes in Computer Science Ser.: Vol. 205). vii, 165p. 1986. pap. 14.50 (ISBN 0-387-16041-8). Springer-Verlag.

Study in Student Development: Rebellion & Delinquency As Alternative Responses to Schooling. Richard P. Rettig. LC 79-65273. 130p. 1979. perfect bdg. 15.00 (ISBN 0-88247-589-4). R & E Pubs.

Study in Surmise: The Making of Sherlock Holmes. Michael Harrison. LC 81-82193. (Illus.). 274p. 1985. 29.95 (ISBN 0-934468-10-9). Gaslight.

Study in Surmise: The Making of Sherlock Holmes. Michael Harrison. (Illus.). 254p. 1985. 29.95 (ISBN 0-317-30095-4). Vanguard.

Study in Symbolism: An Empirical Foundation of Graphology. Ralph V. Gologie. LC 73-86368. 256p. 1973. pap. 5.95x (ISBN 0-915286-00-9). Landrum & Assocs.

Study in the Etymology of the Indian Place Name. G. McAleer. 1977. 59.95 (ISBN 0-8490-2709-8). Gordon Pr.

Study in the Language of Scottish Prose Before 1600. William P. Reeves. LC 74-13972. 1974. Repr. of 1893 ed. lib. bdg. 25.00 (ISBN 0-8414-7337-4). Folcroft.

Study in the Narrative Structure of Three Epic Poems: Gilgamesh, Odyssey, & Beowulf. Hope N. Wolff. Ed. by James J. Wilhelm & Richard Saez. (Harvard Dissertations in Comparative Literature Ser.). 176p. 1987. lib. bdg. 25.00 (ISBN 0-8240-8438-1). Garland Pub.

Study in the Philosophy of Malebranche. Ralph W. Church. LC 74-102564. 1970. Repr. of 1931 ed. 31.50x (ISBN 0-8046-0724-9, Pub. by Kennikat). Assoc Faculty Pr.

Study in the Psychology of Learning in Geometry. Winona M. Perry. LC 72-177149. (Columbia University. Teachers College. Contributions to Education: No. 179). Repr. of 1925 ed. 22.50 (ISBN 0-404-55179-3). AMS Pr.

Study in the Theory & Practice of German Liberalism: Eduard Lasker, 1829-1884. James F. Harris. (Illus.). 194p. (Orig.). 1984. lib. bdg. 26.25 (ISBN 0-8191-4174-7); pap. text ed. 12.50 (ISBN 0-8191-4175-5). U Pr of Amer.

Study in the Theory of Economic Expansion. Erik Lundberg. 1964. Repr. of 1937 ed. 29.50x (ISBN 0-678-00046-8). Kelley.

Study in the Theory of Inflation & Unemployment. C. H. Siven. LC 78-24271. (Studies in Monetary Economics: Vol. 4). 372p. 1979. 94.75 (ISBN 0-444-85252-2, North Holland). Elsevier.

Study in the Theory of Investment. Trygve Haavelmo. LC 60-13057. (Economic Research Ser). 1960. pap. text ed. 17.00x (ISBN 0-226-31141-4). U of Chicago Pr.

Study in the United Kingdom & Ireland, Nineteen Eighty-Eight to Nineteen Eighty-Nine. Ed. by Edrice Howard. (Orig.). 1988. pap. text ed. 14.95 (ISBN 0-87206-157-4). Inst Intl Educ.

Study in the Warwickshire Dialect. 3rd ed. Ed. by James A. Morgan. LC 76-169927. (Shakespeare Society of New York. Publications: No. 10). Repr. of 1899 ed. 26.00 (ISBN 0-404-54210-7). AMS Pr.

Study in Tolerance As Practiced by Muhammed & His Immediate Successors. Adolph L. Wismar. LC 27-24455. (Columbia University. Contributions to Oriental History & Philology: No. 13). Repr. of 1927 ed. 14.00 (ISBN 0-404-50543-0). AMS Pr.

Study in Zodiacal Symbology. J. Henry Van Stone. 1973. pap. 2.95 (ISBN 0-912504-19-6). Sym & Sign.

Study Lists Chronological Tables & Maps. Henry S. Pancoast. 1973. Repr. of 1908 ed. 12.50 (ISBN 0-8274-1245-2). R West.

Study Manual for E.I.T. Examination. 2nd, rev. ed. Young C. Kim. LC 82-82593. (Illus.). 480p. 1987. 35.00 (ISBN 0-944999-01-8). EPDS.

Study Materials for Clarinet, Vols. 1 & 2. Phillip Rehfeldt. (Clarinet Ser.). 1985. 9.50x ea. (ISBN 0-933251-05-X). Mill Creek Pubns.

Study Materials for Project Universe: Astronomy. John L. Safko. 174p. 1986. pap. text ed. 12.95 shrink wrapped (ISBN 0-8403-3888-0). Kendall-Hunt.

Study Notes in System Dynamics. Michael R. Goodman. LC 74-84407. (Illus.). 300p. 1974. pap. 19.95x (ISBN 0-262-57051-3). MIT Pr.

Study of a Child. Louise E. Hogan. LC 74-21416. (Classics in Child Development Ser.). (Illus.). 1975. Repr. of 1898 ed. 29.00x (ISBN 0-405-06466-7). Ayer Co Pubs.

Study of a Community & Its Groups & Institutions Conceived of As Behaviors of Individuals see Iowa University Studies in Psychology.

Study of a Group of Children of Exceptionally High Intelligence Quotient in Situations Partaking of the Nature of Suggestion. Rachel Simmons. LC 71-177781. (Columbia University. Teachers College. Contributions to Education: No. 788). Repr. of 1940 ed. 22.50 (ISBN 0-404-55788-0). AMS Pr.

Study of a Recordkeeping System for Inprocessing of Transient Workers at Nuclear Power Plants: AIF-NESP-025. (National Environmental Studies Project: NESP Reports). 1982. 50.00 (ISBN 0-318-02233-8). US Coun Energy Awareness.

Study of a Sixteenth-Century Tagalog Manuscript on the Ten Commandments: Its Significance & Implications. Antonio Rosales. (Illus.). 166p. 1985. text ed. 16.00x (ISBN 0-8248-0971-8). UH Pr.

Study of a Static Screen, Jig, Spiral, & a Compound Water Cyclone in a Placer Gold Recovery Plant. Daniel E. Walsh & Donald J. Cook. LC 87-62002. (Mirl Report Ser.: No. 73). (Illus.). 57p. Date not set. pap. text ed. 10.00 (ISBN 0-911043-01-2). UAKF Min Ind Res Lab.

Study of Ability Grouping in the Elementary School in Terms of Variability of Achievement. Parl West. LC 72-177646. (Columbia University. Teachers College. Contributions to Education: No. 588). Repr. of 1933 ed. 22.50 (ISBN 0-404-55588-8). AMS Pr.

Study of Abortion in Primitive Societies. rev. ed. George Devereux. LC 75-10572. 390p. 1976. text ed. 42.50x (ISBN 0-8236-6245-4); pap. text ed. 17.95 (ISBN 0-8236-8311-7, 26245). Intl Univs Pr.

Study of Administration Revisited: A Report on the Centennial Agendas Project of the American Society for Public Administration. Ed. by James D. Carroll & Alfred M. Zuck. 34p. (Orig.). 1983. pap. text ed. 5.00 (ISBN 0-936678-07-0). Am Soc Pub Admin.

Study of Adverbs. Shuan-Fan Huang. (Janua Linguarum, Ser. Minor: No. 213). 96p. (Orig.). 1975. pap. text ed. 13.50x (ISBN 90-2793-363-4). Mouton.

Study of Aggregate Consumption Functions. Robert Ferber. 7.00 (ISBN 0-405-18755-6, 16467). Ayer Co Pubs.

Study of Agricultural Systems. Ed. by G. E. Dalton. (Illus.). xiv, 441p. 1975. 99.00 (ISBN 0-85334-640-2, Pub. by Elsevier Applied Sci England). Elsevier.

Study of Alastor. William H. Hildebrand. LC 75-23022. 1974. Repr. of 1954 ed. lib. bdg. 27.00 (ISBN 0-8414-4701-2). Folcroft.

Study of Alcohol Prevention Grants in the State of Nebraska, 1973-1979. CAUR Staff. 40p. (Orig.). 1980. pap. 3.00 (ISBN 1-55719-090-9). U NE Ctr Applied Urban Rsch.

Study of Amber Spiders. Alexander Petrunkevich. (CT Academy of Arts & Science Transactions Ser.: Vol. 34). 1942. pap. 75.00x (ISBN 0-686-51318-5). Elliots Bks.

Study of Ambrosiaster. A. Souter. (Text & Studies Series 1: Vol. 7, Pt. 4). pap. 19.00 (ISBN 0-8115-1706-3). Kraus Repr.

Study of American & Korean Attitudes & Values Through Associative Group Analysis. Lorand B. Szalay et al. LC 71-135080. 107p. 1970. 19.00 (ISBN 0-403-04541-X). Scholarly.

Study of American English. William A. Craigie. LC 77-965. 1926. lib. bdg. 17.00 (ISBN 0-8414-3405-0). Folcroft.

Study of American English see Society's Work.

Study of American Folklore. 3rd ed. Jan H. Brunvand. 1986. text ed. 22.95x (ISBN 0-393-95495-1); instr's. manual avail. (ISBN 0-393-95580-X). Norton.

Study of American Indian Religions. Ake Hulkrantz. 176p. 1983. 12.95 (ISBN 0-8245-0558-1). Crossroad NY.

Study of American Indian Religions. Ake Hultkrantz. Ed. by Christopher Vecsey. LC 82-10533. (American Academy of Religion - Studies in Religion). 142p. 1983. 12.95 (01 00 29). Scholars Pr GA.

Study of American Intelligence. C. C. Brigham. LC 23-6849. Repr. of 1923 ed. 26.00 (ISBN 0-527-10891-X). Kraus Repr.

Study of Americanization in Carneta. new ed. Clement L. Valletta. LC 74-17958. (Italian American Experience Ser). (Illus.). 522p. 1975. 34.50x (ISBN 0-405-06427-6). Ayer Co Pubs.

Study of Americans' Awareness & Attitudes Toward Vacation Timesharing. 1985. 65.00 (ISBN 0-318-03349-6). ARRDA.

Study of an Interest Test & Affectivity Test in Forecasting Freshman Success in College. Charles A. Drake. LC 76-176729. (Columbia University. Teachers College. Contributions to Education: No. 504). Repr. of 1931 ed. 22.50 (ISBN 0-404-55504-7). AMS Pr.

Study of an Italian Village. A. L. Maraspini. 1968. pap. text ed. 21.60x (ISBN 90-2796-039-9). Mouton.

Study of Ancient Judaism, 2 vols. Jacob Neusner. 1982. Vol. I. 37.50x ea. (ISBN 0-87068-892-8). Ktav.

Study of Anglicanism. Ed. by Stephen Sykes & John Booty. LC 87-45906. 1988. pap. 29.95 (ISBN 0-8006-2087-9). Fortress.

Study of Animal Behavior. F. A. Huntingford. (Illus.). 411p. 1984. 49.95x (ISBN 0-412-22320-1, NO. 6884); pap. 22.00x (ISBN 0-412-22330-9, NO. 6885). Routledge Chapman & Hall.

Study of Anthroposophy As an Aspect of the Free Spiritual Life. Alan Howard. 1985. pap. 2.00 (ISBN 0-916786-80-3). St George Bk Serv.

Study of Archeology. Walter W. Taylor. LC 83-71270. (Center for Archaeological Investigations). xvi, 263p. pap. 8.00 (ISBN 0-88104-009-6). Center Archaeo.

Study of Argumentation. F. H. Van Eemeren & R. Grootendorst. 333p. 1986. text ed. 37.50x (ISBN 0-8290-0978-7). Irvington.

Study of Assimilation Among the Roumanians in the United States. Christine A. Galitzi. LC 72-76634. (Columbia University. Studies in the Social Sciences: No. 315). 1969. Repr. of 1929 ed. 21.00 (ISBN 0-404-51315-8). AMS Pr.

Study of Astrology, Vol. II. Henry Weingarten. 1987. pap. 9.95 (ISBN 0-88231-030-5). ASI Pubs Inc.

Study of Astrology: Vol. I. Henry Weingarten. LC 77-314. 1977. 7.95 (ISBN 0-88231-029-1). ASI Pubs Inc.

Study of Ballad Rhythm with Special Reference to Ballad Music. Joseph W. Hendren. LC 66-29463. (Princeton Studies in English: No. 14). 1966. Repr. of 1936 ed. 20.00x (ISBN 0-87752-052-6). Gordian.

Study of Basketmaker II Settlement on Northern Black Mesa: Excavations 1973-1979. Susan E. Bearden. LC 84-72847. (Center for Archaeological Investigations Research Paper: No. 44). (Illus.). xii, 198p. 1984. softcover 12.00 (ISBN 0-88104-021-5). Center Archaeo.

Study of Ben Jonson. Algernon C. Swinburne. LC 68-24922. (Studies in Drama, No. 39). 1969. Repr. of 1889 ed. lib. bdg. 75.00x (ISBN 0-8383-0245-9). Haskell.

Study of Ben Jonson. Algernon Charles Swinburne. Ed. by Howard B. Norland. LC 69-12400. xxxii, 212p. 1969. pap. 3.65x (ISBN 0-8032-5709-0, BB 326, Bison). U of Nebr Pr.

Study of Benthic Communities. R. Parker. LC 73-20941. (Oceanography Ser.: Vol. 9). 279p. 1975. 97.50 (ISBN 0-444-41203-4). Elsevier.

Study of Bible Leaders. J. J. Turner. pap. 2.50 (ISBN 0-89315-290-0). Lambert Bk.

Study of Biology. 4th ed. Jeffrey J. Baker & Garland A. Allen. LC 81-17550. (Illus.). 1040p. 1982. text ed. write for info. (ISBN 0-201-10180-7); instr's. manual o.p. 3.50 (ISBN 0-201-10181-5); write for info. study guide (ISBN 0-201-10182-3). Addison-Wesley.

Study of Biology Notebook Work in New York State. Don O. Baird. LC 71-176532. (Columbia University. Teachers College. Contributions to Education: No. 400). Repr. of 1929 ed. 22.50 (ISBN 0-404-55400-8). AMS Pr.

Study of Black Self Help. William L. Pollard. LC 78-62225. 1978. soft cover 12.95 (ISBN 0-88247-532-0). R & E Pubs.

Study of BMD Mobilization Base Requirements & Constraints. Martin Zlotnick. 12p. 1984. pap. text ed. 12.00 (HI-3660). Hudson Inst.

Study of Boat Ownership in the Omaha-Council Bluffs Metropolitan Area. Paul S. Lee & Yeshen Chen. 26p. (Orig.). 1978. pap. 2.50 (ISBN 1-55719-079-8). U NE Ctr Applied Urban Rsch.

Study of Books Privately Owned in England, 1300-1450. Susan H. Cavanaugh. (Manuscript Studies: No. IV). 1988. 29.50 (ISBN 0-85991-239-6, Pub. by Boydell & Brewer). Longwood Pub Group.

Study of Boy Life in Our Cities. Ed. by E. J. Urwick. LC 79-56942. (English Working Class Ser.). 1980. lib. bdg. 37.00 (ISBN 0-8240-0125-7). Garland Pub.

Study of Brief Psychotherapy. D. H. Malan. LC 75-30916. 326p. 1976. pap. 15.95x (ISBN 0-306-20019-8, Plenum Pr). Plenum Pub.

Study of British Genius. Havelock Ellis. 1978. Repr. of 1926 ed. lib. bdg. 30.00 (ISBN 0-8495-1319-7). Arden Lib.

Study of Browning's Ring & the Book. James A. Cassidy. LC 74-117581. (Studies in Browning, No. 4). 1970. Repr. of 1924 ed. lib. bdg. 39.95x (ISBN 0-8383-1014-1). Haskell.

Study of Cafeteria Plans & Flexible Spending Accounts. 112p. 1985. 6.00 (ISBN 0-317-44604-5, 5487). Commerce.

Study of Capital Mobilization: The Life Insurance Industry of the 19th Century. Bruce M. Pritchett. Ed. by Stuart Bruchey. LC 76-45109. (Nineteen Seventy-Seven Dissertations Ser.). (Illus.). 1977. lib. bdg. 37.50x (ISBN 0-405-09921-5). Ayer Co Pubs.

Study of Cardboard Voids for Prestressed Concrete Box Slabs. 56p. 10.00 (ISBN 0-318-17394-8, JR284). Prestressed Concrete.

Study of Caseflow Management. National Center for State Courts. (Paul Reardon Ser.). 71p. 1981. manuscript 4.26 (PRS-004). Natl Ctr St Courts.

Study of Cases: A Course of Instruction in Reading & Stating Reported Cases, Composing Head-notes & Briefs, Criticising & Comparing Authorities, & Compiling Digests. Eugene Wambaugh. xi, 306p. 1981. Repr. of 1892 ed. lib. bdg. 28.50x (ISBN 0-8377-1310-2). Rothman.

Study of Cataloguing Computer Software: Applying AACR2 to Microcomputer Programs. Ray Templeton & Anita Witten. (LIR Report 28). 85p. (Orig.). 1984. pap. 16.50 (ISBN 0-7123-3041-0, Pub. by British Lib). Longwood Pub Group.

Study of Cathodic Protection of Buried Steel Pipeline Within a Steel Casing. 222p. 25.00 (ISBN 0-318-12704-0, L51382). Am Gas Assn.

Study of Changing Pre-Columbian Commercial Systems: Cozumel, Mexico. Ed. by Jeremy A. Sabloff & William L. Rathje. LC 75-20624. (Peabody Museum Monographs: No. 3). 1975. pap. 12.00x (ISBN 0-87365-902-3). Peabody Harvard.

Study of Characterization of Women in the Plays of Bertolt Brecht. Bernhard Fenn. (European University Studies, German Language & Literature: Ser. 1, Vol. 383). 290p. 1981. pap. 27.35 (ISBN 3-8204-6865-X). P Lang Pubs.

Study of Child Nature from the Kindergarten Standpoint. Elizabeth Harrison. Ed. by Sheila M. Rothman & David J. Rothman. (Women & Children First Ser.). 207p. 1986. lib. bdg. 30.00 (ISBN 0-8240-7658-3). Garland Pub.

Study of Child Variance, 2 vols. Ed. by William C. Rhodes & Michael L. Tracy. Incl. Vol. 1. Conceptual Models. 628p (ISBN 0-472-08758-4); Vol. 2. Interventions. 700p (ISBN 0-472-08759-2). (Conceptual Project in Emotional Disturbance Ser). (Illus.). 1974. pap. text ed. 7.95x ea. U of Mich Pr.

Study of Child Welfare in a Rural New York County. Abd-El-Hamid Zaki. LC 72-177611. (Columbia University. Teachers College. Contributions to Education: No. 927). Repr. of 1947 ed. 22.50 (ISBN 0-404-55927-1). AMS Pr.

Study of Chinese Alchemy. Obed S. Johnson. LC 74-352. (Gold Ser.: Vol. 12). 156p. 1974. Repr. of 1928 ed. 18.00x (ISBN 0-405-05914-0). Ayer Co Pubs.

Study of Chinese Boycotts, with Special References to Their Economic Effectiveness. Charles F. Remer. 25.50 (ISBN 0-405-10620-3). Ayer Co Pubs.

Study of Chinese Paintings in the Collection of Ada Small Moore. Louise W. Hackney & Yau Chang-foo. 279p. 1940. 1750.00x (ISBN 0-317-69121-X, Pub. by Han-Shan Tang Ltd). State Mutual Bk.

Study of Chinese Society: Essays by Maurice Freedman. Maurice Freedman. Ed. by G. William Skinner. LC 78-65395. 1979. 42.50x (ISBN 0-8047-0964-5). Stanford U Pr.

Study of Chord Frequencies Based on the Music of the Eighteenth & Nineteenth Centuries. Helen Budge. LC 75-176604. (Columbia University. Teachers College. Contributions to Education: No. 882). Repr. of 1943 ed. 22.50 (ISBN 0-404-55882-8). AMS Pr.

Study of Circulation Control Systems: Public Libraries, College & University Libraries, Special Libraries. George Fry. LC 61-16167. (American Library Association - Library Technology Project Ser.: No. 1). pap. 36.50 (ISBN 0-317-26364-1, 2024222). Bks Demand UMI.

Study of Classic Maya Sculpture. Tatiana A. Proskouriakoff. LC 77-11515. (Carnegie Institution of Washington. Publication: No. 593). Repr. of 1950 ed. 62.50 (ISBN 0-404-16275-4). AMS Pr.

Study of Combined School-Public Libraries. Shirley L. Aaron. LC 80-19785. (School Media Centers: Focus on Trends & Issues Ser.: No. 6). 120p. 1980. pap. 7.00x (ISBN 0-8389-3247-9). ALA.

Study of Comparative Politics. David Roth & Paul Warwick. 432p. 1988. text ed. 27.95t (ISBN 0-06-045626-4, HarpC). Har-Row.

Study of Contemporary Law School Curricula. ABA, Legal Education & Admissions to the Bar Section. 174p. 1987. pap. 4.00. Amer Bar Assn.

Study of Conversion among the Angas of Plateau State of Nigeria with Emphasis on Christianity. Daniel N. Wambutda. (European University Studies: Series 23, Theology: Vol. 289). 230p. 1986. 25.00 (ISBN 3-8204-9780-3). P Lang Pubs.

Study of Counterpoint. Johann J. Fux. Ed. & tr. by Alfred Mann. Orig. Title: Gradus Ad Parnassum. 1965. pap. 6.95 (ISBN 0-393-00277-2, Norton Lib). Norton.

Study of Court Filing Fees. National Center for State Courts Staff. 138p. 1975. manuscript 8.28 (MAB-114). Natl Ctr St Courts.

Study of Coverage Overlap Among Major Science & Technology Abstracting & Indexing Services. Toni C. Bearman & William Kunberger. 1977. 20.00 (ISBN 0-942308-12-3). NFAIS.

Study of Cranial & Skeletal Material Excavated at Nippur. D. R. Swindler. (University Museum Monographs: No. 12). (Illus.). v, 40p. 1956. pap. 10.00 (ISBN 0-934718-04-0). Univ Mus of U PA.

Study of Credentialing in Nursing: A New Approach, Staff Working Papers, Vol. II. (No. G-138). 500p. 1979. 24.00 (ISBN 0-686-40435-1, G-138). ANA.

Study of Credentialing in Nursing: A New Approach, the Report of the Committee, Vol. 1. (No. G-136). 125p. 1979. 18.25 (ISBN 0-686-40434-3, G-136). ANA.

Study of Credentialing in Nursing Recommendations, 1979: Where Are We Now? Elizabeth W. Carter. (Credentialing in Nursing: Contemporary Developments & Trends Ser.). 14p. (Orig.). 1987. pap. 100.00 set of 10 monographs (ISBN 0-317-60352-3, G-172). ANA.

Study of Critical Reading Comprehension in the Intermediate Grades. Roma Gans. (Columbia University. Teachers College. Contributions to Education: No. 811). Repr. of 1940 ed. 22.50 (ISBN 0-404-55811-9). AMS Pr.

Study of Cuba's Material Product System, Its Conversion to the System of National Accounts, & Estimation of Gross Domestic Product per Capita & Growth Rates. Carmelo Mesa-Lago & Jorge Perez-Lopez. (Working Paper: No. 770). 120p. 1985. 5.00 (ISBN 0-8213-0638-3, WP 0770). World Bank.

Study of Culture. L. L. Langness. LC 74-88. (Publications in Anthropology Ser.). 200p. 1974. pap. 9.95 (ISBN 0-88316-507-4). Chandler & Sharp.

Study of Culture. rev. ed. L. L. Langness. LC 86-32716. (Publications in Anthropology & Related Fields). (Illus.). 288p. 1987. pap. 10.95x (ISBN 0-88316-556-2). Chandler & Sharp.

Study of Culture Change in Modern Puerto Rico. Irwin B. Blatt. LC 78-68459. 1979. perfect bdg. 13.95 (ISBN 0-88247-558-4). R & E Pubs.

Study of Damage to a Residential Structure from Blast Vibrations. 71p. 1974. pap. 5.00x (ISBN 0-87262-074-3). Am Soc Civil Eng.

Study of Daniel. John A. Copeland. 1973. pap. 4.50 (ISBN 0-89137-703-4). Quality Pubns.

Study of "Daphnis & Chloe". Richard L. Hunter. LC 83-3929. (Cambridge Classical Studies). 144p. 1984. 34.50 (ISBN 0-521-25452-3). Cambridge U Pr.

Study of Data Base Access Alternatives: Final Report. M. Lynne Neufeld & Martha Cornog. 1981. 25.00 (ISBN 0-942308-14-X). NFAIS.

Study of Data Base Processor Technology. Laura A. Gregory. LC 79-66678. (Data Base Monograph: No. 8). (Illus.). 77p. (Orig.). pap. 15.00x (ISBN 0-89435-035-8). QED Info Sci.

Study of Data Base Processor Technology. Laura A. Gregory. LC 79-119010. (QED Monograph Series. Data Base Management: No. 8). pap. 21.40 (2031752). Bks Demand UMI.

Study of Day Calendars. Herman Oliphant & Theodore S. Hope. 12.00 (ISBN 0-405-10618-1). Ayer Co Pubs.

Study of Death: Works of Henry Mills Alden. Henry M. Alden. (Works of Henry Mills Alden). vii, 335p. 1985. Repr. of 1895 ed. 49.00 (Pub. by Am Repr Serv). Am Biog Serv.

Study of Delaware Indian Medicine Practice & Folk Beliefs. Gladys Tantaquidgeon. LC 76-43864. (Pennsylvania Historical Commission). Repr. of 1942 ed. 18.00 (ISBN 0-404-15724-6). AMS Pr.

Study of Deviates in Versatility & Sociability of Play Interest. Paul A. Witty. LC 73-177630. (Columbia University. Teachers College. Contributions to Education: No. 470). Repr. of 1931 ed. 28.50 (ISBN 0-404-55470-9). AMS Pr.

Study of Dialect: An Introduction to Dialectology. Student ed. K. M. Petyt. (Language Library). 236p. 1984. pap. 16.95 (ISBN 0-631-13845-5). Basil Blackwell.

Study of Donne's Imagery: A Revelation of His Outlook on the World & His Vision of a Christian Monarchy. Kaichi Matsuura. LC 72-7223. Repr. of 1953 ed. lib. bdg. 32.00 (ISBN 0-8414-0270-1). Folcroft.

Study of Drama. H. Granville-Barker. 1934. lib. bdg. 22.00 (ISBN 0-8414-4624-5). Folcroft.

Study of Drama. Harley Granville-Barker. 92p. 1983. Repr. of 1934 ed. lib. bdg. 16.50 (ISBN 0-8492-5025-0). R West.

Study of Economic History: Collected Inaugural Lectures, 1893-1970. Ed. by N. B. Harte. 385p. 1971. 32.50x (ISBN 0-7146-2905-7, F Cass Co). Biblio Dist.

Study of Economic History: Collected Inaugural Lectures, 1893-1970. Ed. by N. B. Harte. 390p. 1975. pap. 12.50x (ISBN 0-7146-4013-1, F Cass Co). Biblio Dist.

Study of Economics: Principles, Concepts & Applications. 3rd ed. LC 83-16993. (Illus.). 544p. 1987. pap. 21.95 (ISBN 0-87967-638-8). Dushkin Pub.

Study of Education: A Collection of Inaugural Lectures: The Changing Scene, Vol. III. Ed. by Peter Gordon. 1988. 29.50 (Pub. by Wolburn Pr England). Biblio Dist.

Study of Education: A Collection of Inaugural Lectures, Vol. I--Early & Modern, Vol. II--The Last Decade. Ed. by Peter Gordon. (Woburn Education Ser.). 662p. 1980. Vol. I. 32.50x (ISBN 0-7130-0171-2, Pub. by Woburn Pr England); pap. 15.00x (ISBN 0-7130-4005-X); Vol.II. 32.50x (ISBN 0-7130-0170-4); pap. 15.00x (ISBN 0-7130-4006-8). Biblio Dist.

Study of Educational Achievement of Problem Children. facsimile ed. Richard H. Paynter & Phyllis Blanchard. LC 74-160985. (Select Bibliographies Reprint Ser). Repr. of 1929 ed. 13.00 (ISBN 0-8369-5853-5). Ayer Co Pubs.

Study of Eighty-One Principal American Markets. Leslie M. Barton. LC 75-22800. (America in Two Centuries Ser). (Illus.). 1976. Repr. of 1925 ed. 34.50x (ISBN 0-405-07672-X). Ayer Co Pubs.

Study of Elizabeth Barrett Browning. Lilian Whiting. LC 71-148332. Repr. of 1899 ed. 9.50 (ISBN 0-404-08924-0). AMS Pr.

Study of English. D. G. Crawford. 1928. 15.00 (ISBN 0-8274-3549-5). R West.

Study of English & American Writers: A Laboratory Method. John S. Clark & John P. Odell. LC 72-1070. Repr. of 1916 ed. 34.50 (ISBN 0-404-01559-X). AMS Pr.

Study of English Literature. John C. Collins. 1891. lib. bdg. 27.00 (ISBN 0-8414-2365-2). Folcroft.

Study of English Literature. Walter Raleigh. 1900. 10.00 (ISBN 0-8274-3550-9). R West.

Study of English Poetry. Henry Newbolt. 1979. Repr. of 1917 ed. lib. bdg. 30.00 (ISBN 0-8492-1977-9). R West.

Study of English Romanticism. Northrop Frye. LC 82-11018. viii, 180p. 1983. pap. 5.95x (ISBN 0-226-26651-6). U of Chicago Pr.

Study of Enzyme Mechanisms. Eugene Zeffren & Philip L. Hall. LC 72-13751. 298p. 1973. 42.95x (ISBN 0-471-98150-8, JW). Krieger.

Study of Ethics: A Syllabus. John Dewey. 1976. lib. bdg. 59.95 (ISBN 0-8490-2710-1). Gordon Pr.

Study of Ethnomusicology: Twenty-Nine Issues & Concepts. Bruno Nettl. LC 82-7065. 424p. 1983. 29.95 (ISBN 0-252-00986-X); pap. 13.95 (ISBN 0-252-01039-6). U of Ill Pr.

Study of Exhaust Emmissions from Natural Gas Pipeline Compressor Engines. Charles M. Urban & Karl J. Springer. 100p. 1975. pap. 5.00 softcover (ISBN 0-318-12705-9, L22276). Am Gas Assn.

Study of Expenditures & Service in Physical Education: An Analysis of Variations in Expenditure, Extent of Service, Personnel, Facilities, & Program of Physical Education in Selected Schools of New York State. Ruth Abernathy. LC 77-176685. (Columbia University. Teachers College, Contributions to Education: No. 904). Repr. of 1944 ed. 22.50 (ISBN 0-404-55904-2). AMS Pr.

Study of Factors Suspected of Influencing the Settling Velocity of Fine Gold Particles. Daniel E. Walsh & P. D. Rao. (MIRL Report: No. 76). (Illus.). 51p. (Orig.). 1988. pap. 10.00 (ISBN 0-911043-05-5). UAKF Min Ind Res Lab.

Study of Fast Processes & Transient Species by Electron Pulse Radiolysis. J. Baxendale & F. Busi. 1982. 74.50 (ISBN 90-277-1431-2, Pub. by Reidel Holland). Kluwer Academic.

Study of Feasibility of Basing Natural Gas Pipeline Operating Pressure on Hydrostatic Test Pressure. Batelle Columbus Labs. Staff & A. R. Duffy. 100p. 1968. softcover 10.00 (ISBN 0-318-12706-7, L30050). Am Gas Assn.

Study of Federal Tax Law 1985-1986 Edition: Business Enterprises Income Tax (STDB) 800p. 1985. 44.50 (ISBN 0-317-44571-5, 4716). Commerce.

Study of Federal Tax Law 1985-1986 Edition: Estate & Gift Tax. 944p. 1985. 44.50 (ISBN 0-317-44573-1, 4717). Commerce.

Study of Federal Tax Law 1985-1986 Edition: Individuals' Income Tax (STDI) 1040p. 1985. 44.50 (ISBN 0-317-44572-3, 4715). Commerce.

Study of Federal Tax Law 1985-1986 Edition: Transnatinal Transactions (STDT) 1168p. 1983. 48.50 (ISBN 0-317-44574-X, 4891). Commerce.

Study of Federal Tax Law, 1987-1988: Business Enterprises Income Tax (STDB) 848p. 1987. 49.50 (5322). Commerce.

Study of Federal Tax Law, 1987-1988: Individuals' Income Tax (STDI) 1044p. 1987. 49.50 (5323). Commerce.

Study of Federal Tax Law, 1987-1988: Taxation of Estates, Gifts & Trusts (STDE) 976p. 1987. 49.50 (5321). Commerce.

Study of Federal Tax Law, 1987-1988: Transnational Transactions (STDT) 642p. 1987. 49.50 (5320). Commerce.

Study of Film As an Art Form in American Secondary Schools. S. A. Selby. LC 77-22913. 1978. lib. bdg. 22.00x (ISBN 0-405-10755-2). Ayer Co Pubs.

Study of Financial Management Issues & Reporting Requirements of South Bronx Community Organizations: Problems & Recommendations. Herzog & Kirshner, Inc. Staff. 1981. pap. 2.50 (ISBN 0-88156-046-4). Comm Serv Soc NY.

Study of Fish Populations by Capture Data & the Value of Tagging Experiments. (General Fisheries Council of the Mediterranean (GFCM): Studies & Reviews: No. 54). 75p. (Eng. & Fr.). 1974. pap. 7.50 (ISBN 92-5-001973-4, F924, FAO). UNIPUB.

Study of Fluid Milk Prices. John M. Cassels. LC 75-39237. (Getting & Spending: the Consumer's Dilemma). (Illus.). 1976. Repr. of 1937 ed. 26.50x (ISBN 0-405-08014-X). Ayer Co Pubs.

Study of Folk Music in the Modern World. Philip V. Bohlman. LC 87-45401. 192p. 1988. 35.00 (ISBN 0-253-35555-9); pap. 10.95 (ISBN 0-253-20464-X). Ind U Pr.

Study of Folklore. Alan Dundes. (Illus.). 1965. text ed. write for info. (ISBN 0-13-858944-5). P-H.

Study of Form & the Renewal of Poetry. F. T. Prince. (Warton Lectures on English Poetry Ser.). 1964. pap. 5.50 (ISBN 0-85672-347-9, Pub. by British Acad). Longwood Pub Group.

Study of Freshwater Fishery Regulation Based on North American Experience. W. J. Christie. (Fisheries Technical Papers: No. 180). 53p. 1978. pap. 7.50 (ISBN 92-5-100579-6, F1464, FAO). UNIPUB.

Study of Fugue. Alfred Mann. LC 81-4183. (Illus.). x, 341p. 1981. Repr. of 1958 ed. lib. bdg. 35.00x (ISBN 0-313-22623-7, MASF). Greenwood.

Study of Fugue. Alfred Mann. 352p. 1987. pap. 8.95 (ISBN 0-486-25439-9). Dover.

Study of Future Worlds. Richard A. Falk. LC 74-10139. (Preferred Worlds for the 1990's Ser.). (Illus.). 1975. pap. text ed. 16.95 (ISBN 0-02-910080-1). Free Pr.

Study of Games. Elliott M. Avedon & Brian Sutton-Smith. LC 79-21194. 544p. 1979. Repr. of 1971 ed. lib. bdg. 38.50 (ISBN 0-89874-045-2). Krieger.

Study of German Hymns in Current English Hymnals. J. S. Andrews. (German Language & Literature-European University Studies: No. 1, Vol. 614). 398p. 1982. pap. 36.30 (ISBN 3-261-05068-3). P Lang Pubs.

Study of Gersonides in His Proper Perspective. Nima H. Adlerblum. LC 73-158229. Repr. of 1926 ed. 14.50 (ISBN 0-404-00296-X). AMS Pr.

Study of Global Interdependence: Essays on the Transnationalization of World Affairs. James N. Rosenau. (Essays on the Analysis of World Politics). 350p. 1980. 39.50 (ISBN 0-89397-078-6); pap. 23.50x (ISBN 0-89397-079-4). Nichols Pub.

Study of Goethe. Barker Fairley. LC 76-56253. 1977. Repr. of 1947 ed. lib. bdg. 27.50x (ISBN 0-8371-9330-3, FASG). Greenwood.

Study of Good, 10 vols. Kitaro Nishida. Tr. by V. H. Viglielmo. (Documentary Reference Collection). 1988. Set. 395.00 (CMJ/); price not set (ISBN 0-313-26560-7, NSG/). Greenwood.

Study of Greatness in Men. facsimile ed. Josephus N. Larned. LC 73-156677. (Essay Index Reprint Ser). Repr. of 1911 ed. 20.00 (ISBN 0-8369-2557-2). Ayer Co Pubs.

Study of Gregory Palamas. John Meyendorff. LC 65-56528. 245p. 1964. 12.95 (ISBN 0-913836-14-1). St Vladimirs.

Study of Hake (Merluccius Merluccius L.) Biology & Population Dynamics in the Adriatic. (General Fisheries Council of the mediterranean (GFCM): Studies & Reviews: No. 32). 24p. (Summary in Fr., 2nd Printing 1969). 1968. pap. 7.50 (ISBN 92-5-101951-7, F1793, FAO). UNIPUB.

Study of Hamlet. Cumberland Clark. LC 77-6817. 1926. lib. bdg. 25.00 (ISBN 0-8414-1801-2). Folcroft.

Study of Hamlet. John Connolly. LC 73-517. 1973. Repr. of 1863 ed. lib. bdg. 27.00 (ISBN 0-8414-1490-4). Folcroft.

Study of Hamlet. John Conolly. LC 72-942. Repr. of 1863 ed. 17.00 (ISBN 0-404-01695-2). AMS Pr.

Study of Hamlet. Francis A. Marshall. LC 78-135729. Repr. of 1875 ed. 19.50 (ISBN 0-404-04191-4). AMS Pr.

Study of Handedness. Wallace F. Jones. LC 78-72804. (Brainedness, Handedness & Mental Abilities Ser.). Repr. of 1918 ed. 21.50 (ISBN 0-404-60867-1). AMS Pr.

Study of Handwriting Movement: Peripheral Models & Signal Processing Techniques. F. J. Maarse. 160p. 1987. pap. 14.80 (Pub. by Swets Pub Serv Holland). Taylor & Francis.

Study of Handwriting Movement: Peripheral Models & Signal Processing Techniques. Frans J. Maarse. 168p. (Orig.). 1987. pap. 14.80 (ISBN 90-265-0812-3, Pub. by Zeitlinger Netherlands). Hogrefe Intl.

Study of Hawthorne. George P. Lathrop. LC 70-86168. Repr. of 1876 ed. 17.50 (ISBN 0-404-03884-0). AMS Pr.

Study of Hawthorne. George P. Lathrop. LC 78-107178. 1970. Repr. of 1876 ed. 16.00x (ISBN 0-403-00237-0). Scholarly.

Study of Heart-Rate Variability. R. I. Kitney & O. Rompelman. (Illus.). 1980. text ed. 80.00x (ISBN 0-19-857533-5). Oxford U Pr.

Study of Hegel's Logic. Geoffrey R. Mure. LC 83-26391. viii, 375p. 1984. Repr. of 1950 ed. lib. bdg. 52.50x (ISBN 0-313-24397-2, MUSH). Greenwood.

Study of Heliocentric Science. Swami Abhedananda. 5.95 (ISBN 0-87481-619-X). Vedanta Pr.

Study of Henry D. Thoreau. Helena Dickinson. 59.95 (ISBN 0-8490-1152-3). Gordon Pr.

Study of Hindu Criminology. V. Upadhyaya. 504p. 1978. 28.95. Asia Bk Corp.

Study of History. Arnold J. Toynbee. (Royal Institute of International Affairs Ser.). 1961. Vol. 12, Reconsiderations. maroon cloth 25.00x (ISBN 0-19-500197-4); Vol. 11; 1959, Historical Atlas & Gazetteer. green cloth 36.50x (ISBN 0-19-215223-8); Vol. 12; 1961. green cloth o.p 37.50x (ISBN 0-19-215225-4). Oxford U Pr.

Study of History, 2 vols. Arnold J. Toynbee. Abridged by D. C. Somervell. Vol. 1, 638p: Abridgement of Volumes I-VI. pap. 12.95 (ISBN 0-317-66467-0); Vol. 2, 428p: Abridgement of Volumes VII-X. pap. 12.95 (ISBN 0-317-66468-9). Oxford U Pr.

Study of History, Vols. 1-10. abr. ed. Arnold J. Toynbee. Ed. by D. C. Somervell. Incl. Vols. 1-6. 1946. 25.00x (ISBN 0-19-500198-2); Vols. 7-10. 1957. 25.00x (ISBN 0-19-500199-0). (Royal Institute of International Affairs Ser.). Oxford U Pr.

Study of History, Vols. 7-10. Arnold J. Toynbee. Incl. Vol. 7. Universal States; Universal Churches. Greencloth. 37.50x (ISBN 0-19-215215-7); Vol. 8. Heroic Ages; Contacts Between Civilization in Space; Vol. 9. Contacts Between Civilizations in Time; Law & Freedom in History; the Prospects of the Western Civilization; Vol. 10. The Inspirations of Historians. 29.00x (ISBN 0-19-215218-1). 1954. Oxford U Pr.

Study of History: A Bibliographical Guide. R. C. Richardson. 112p. 1988. 55.00 (ISBN 0-7190-1881-1, Pub. by Manchester Univ Pr). St Martin.

Study of History: A Collection of Inaugural Lectures in Two Volumes. Ed. by Arthur J. Taylor. Incl. Vol. 1. Beginnings to Nineteen Forty-Five; Vol. 2. Nineteen Forty-Five to Present. 1980. 30.00x set (ISBN 0-7146-3125-6, F Cass Co). Vol. 1, beginnings to 1945. Vol. 2, 1945 to Present. Biblio Dist.

Study of History: Abridgement of Volumes I-VI, Part I of II. Arnold Toynbee. 640p. 1987. pap. 12.95 (ISBN 0-19-505080-0). Oxford U Pr.

Study of History: Abridgement of Volumes VII-X, Part II of II. Arnold Toynbee. 432p. 1987. pap. 12.95 (ISBN 0-19-505081-9). Oxford U Pr.

Study of History in England & Scotland. Paul Fredericq. LC 78-63776. (Johns Hopkins University. Studies in the Social Sciences. Fifth Ser. 1887: 10). Repr. of 1887 ed. 11.50 (ISBN 0-404-61042-0). AMS Pr.

Study of History in Germany & France. Paul Fredericq. LC 78-63795. (Johns Hopkins University. Studies in the Social Sciences. Eighth Ser. 1890: 5-6). Repr. of 1890 ed. 11.50 (ISBN 0-404-61060-9). AMS Pr.

Study of History in Germany & France see Early Presbyterianism in Maryland.

Study of History in Holland & Belgium. Paul Fredericq. LC 78-63797. (Johns Hopkins University. Studies in the Social Sciences. Eighth Ser. 1890: 10). Repr. of 1890 ed. 11.50 (ISBN 0-404-61062-5). AMS Pr.

Study of History in Holland & Belgium see Educational Aspects of the United States National Museum.

Study of Homogeneous Grouping in Terms of Individual Variations & the Teaching Problem. M. Y. Burr. LC 70-176616. (Columbia University. Teachers College. Contributions to Education Ser.: No. 457). Repr. of 1931 ed. 22.50 (ISBN 0-404-55457-1). AMS Pr.

Study of Human Abilities. Shao Liu. (American Oriental Ser.). 1937. 20.00 (ISBN 0-527-02685-9). Kraus Repr.

Study of Human Communication. Nan Lin. LC 72-77128. 1973. pap. 9.63 scp (ISBN 0-672-61206-2). Bobbs.

Study of Human Evolution. Robert B. Eckhardt. (Illus.). 1979. text ed. 42.95 (ISBN 0-07-018902-1). McGraw.

Study of Human Nature. Ed. by Leslie Stevenson. 1981. pap. text ed. 9.95x (ISBN 0-19-502827-9). Oxford U Pr.

Study of Humor in Greek Tragedy. A. Reardon. 59.95 (ISBN 0-8490-1153-1). Gordon Pr.

Study of Husband-Wife Interaction in Three Cultures. Fred L. Strodtback. Ed. by Harriet Zuckerman & Robert K. Merton. LC 79-9032. (Dissertation on Sociology Ser.). 1980. lib. bdg. 53.50x (ISBN 0-405-12998-X). Ayer Co Pubs.

Study of Husserl's Formal & Transcendental Logic. Suzanne Bachelard. Tr. by Lester E. Embree. LC 68-15330. (Studies in Phenomenology & Existential Philosophy Ser). 1968. 23.95x (ISBN 0-8101-0028-2). Northwestern U Pr.

Study of Illumination (Henry Vaughan, William Wordsworth, Robert Browning, Thompson) Geraldine E. Hodgson. LC 76-10164. 1973. lib. bdg. 27.00 (ISBN 0-8414-4849-3). Folcroft.

Study of Imagination in Early Childhood & Its Function in Mental Development: Imaginary Playmates & Other Mental Phenomena of Children. Ruth Griffiths & Nathan A. Harvey. LC 74-21411. (Classics in Child Development Ser). 390p. 1975. Repr. 34.00x (ISBN 0-405-06463-2). Ayer Co Pubs.

Study of Incunibula. K. Haebler. Tr. by Lucy E. Osborne. Repr. of 1933 ed. 48.00 (ISBN 0-527-37100-9). Kraus Repr.

Study of Indonesia's Economically Active Population. Soeharsono Soemantri. LC 82-95024. (Illus.). xiv, 118p. 1980. pap. 7.00x (ISBN 0-8214-0776-7). Ohio U Pr.

Study of Industrial Fluctuation. Dennis H. Robertson. Repr. of 1915 ed. cancelled (ISBN 0-678-01244-X). Kelley.

Study of Information: Interdisciplinary Messages. Fritz Machlup & Una Mansfield. LC 83-12147. 743p. 1984. 47.50x (ISBN 0-471-88717-X, Wiley-Interscience). Wiley.

Study of Infra-Red Energy Generated by Radiant Gas Burners. D. W. DeWerth. 61p. 1962. 2.00 (ISBN 0-318-12707-5, U71141). Am Gas Assn.

Study of Institutional Children with Particular Reference to the Caloric Value As Well As Other Factors of the Dietary. Pauline B. Mack & C. Urbach. (SRCD M Ser.). 1948. pap. 16.00 (ISBN 0-527-01543-1). Kraus Repr.

Study of Intelligence Test Elements. Elizabeth L. Vincent. (Columbia University. Teachers College. Contributions to Education Ser.: No. 152). Repr. of 1924 ed. 22.50 (ISBN 0-404-55152-1). AMS Pr.

Study of International Attitudes of High School Students with Special Reference to Those Nearing Completion of Their High School Courses. George B. Neumann. LC 77-177118. (Columbia University. Teachers College. Contributions to Education Ser.: No. 239). Repr. of 1926 ed. 22.50 (ISBN 0-404-55239-0). AMS Pr.

Study of International Relations: A Guide to Information Sources. Ed. by Robert Pfaltzgraff, Jr. LC 73-17511. (International Relations Information Guide Ser.: Vol. 5). 168p. 1977. 68.00x (ISBN 0-8103-1331-6). Gale.

Study of Introvert-Extrovert Responses to Certain Test Situations. Raymond A. Schwegler. LC 76-177805. (Columbia University. Teachers College. Contributions to Education Ser.: No. 361). Repr. of 1929 ed. 22.50 (ISBN 0-404-55361-3). AMS Pr.

Study of Israeli Nuclear Armament, No. 6. 1982. pap. 4.00 (ISBN 92-1-142011-3, E.82.IX.2). UN.

Study of Japan in the Behavioral Sciences. Ed. by Edward Norbeck & Susan Parman. (Rice University Studies: Vol. 56, No. 4). 309p. 1970. pap. 10.00x (ISBN 0-89263-206-2). Rice Univ.

Study of Japanese Syntax. Kazuko Inoue. LC 68-17883. (Janua Linguarum, Ser. Practica: No. 41). (Orig.). 1969. pap. text ed. 21.60x (ISBN 90-2790-692-0). Mouton.

Study of Jazz. 5th ed. Paul Tanner & Maurice Gerow. 256p. 1983. pap. text ed. write for info. (ISBN 0-697-03567-0); instr's. manual avail. (ISBN 0-697-03568-9). Wm C Brown.

Study of Jean-Jacques Bernard's Theatre De L'inexprime. Kester A. Branford. LC 76-58424. (Romance Monographs: No. 24). 1977. 25.00x (ISBN 84-399-6422-6). Romance.

Study of John Keats's "Isabella". Eve Leoff. Ed. by James Hogg. (Romantic Reassessment Ser.). 217p. (Orig.). 1972. pap. 15.00 (ISBN 0-317-40104-1, Pub. by Salzburg Studies). Longwood Pub Group.

Study of John Webster's Use of Renaissance Natural & Moral Philosophy. William G. Dwyer. Ed. by James Hogg. (Jacobean Drama Studies). 206p. (Orig.). 1973. pap. 15.00 (ISBN 3-7052-0317-7, Pub. by Salzburg Studies). Longwood Pub Group.

Study of Judaism: Bibliographical Essays, Vol. 1. 229p. 12.50 (ISBN 0-686-95147-6). ADL.

Study of Judaism: Vol. 2. Ed. by Lawrence V. Berman et al. 25.00x (ISBN 0-87068-486-8). Ktav.

Study of Judicial Administration in the State of Maryland. George K. Reiblich. LC 78-64131. (Johns Hopkins University. Studies in the Social Sciences. Forty-Seventh Ser. 1929: 2). Repr. of 1929 ed. 18.00 (ISBN 0-404-61244-X). AMS Pr.

Study of Judicial Review in Virginia, 1789-1928. Margaret V. Nelson. LC 47-31482. (Columbia University. Studies in the Social Sciences: No. 532). Repr. of 1947 ed. 20.00 (ISBN 0-404-51532-0). AMS Pr.

Study of Jury Management in Selected Pennsylvania Counties: Berks, Blair, Chester, McKean, Northumberland & Westmoreland. National Center for State Courts Staff. 160p. 1984. manuscript 10.00 (NERO-147). Natl Ctr St Courts.

Study of Kansu & Honan Aeneolithic Skulls & Specimens from Later Kansu Prehistoric Sites in Comparison with North China & Other Recent Crania. Davidson Black. LC 77-86444. (China. Geological Survey. Palaeontologia Sinica. Ser. D.: Vol. 6., Fasc. 1). Repr. of 1928 ed. 21.00 (ISBN 0-404-16687-3). AMS Pr.

Study of Kant. James Ward. Ed. by Lewis W. Beck. Bd. with Immanual Kant (Seventeen Twenty-Four to Eighteen Hundred Four) The British Academy Annual Philosophical Lecture. LC 75-32045. (Philosophy of Immanuel Kant Ser.: Vol. 9). 1976. Repr. of 1922 ed. lib. bdg. 29.00 (ISBN 0-8240-2333-1). Garland Pub.

Study of Kant's Psychology see On Sensations from Pressure & Impact.

Study of Kindergarten Activities for Language Development. Eileen G. Cowe. LC 74-83368. 10.95 (ISBN 0-88247-301-8). R & E Pubs.

Study of Land Reforms in Uttar Pradesh. Baljit Singh & Shridhar Misra. (Illus.). 1965. 14.00x (ISBN 0-8248-0020-6, Eastwest Ctr). UH Pr.

Study of Landforms. 2nd ed. R. J. Small. LC 77-71427. 1978. pap. 27.95x (ISBN 0-521-29238-7). Cambridge U Pr.

Study of Language: An Introduction. George Yule. 250p. 1985. 32.50 (ISBN 0-521-30531-4); pap. 10.95 (ISBN 0-521-31877-7). Cambridge U Pr.

Study of Language in England: Seventeen Eighty to Eighteen Sixty. Hans Aarsleff. LC 78-13573. 1979. Repr. of 1967 ed. lib. bdg. 35.00x (ISBN 0-313-21046-2, AASL). Greenwood.

Study of Language in England: Seventeen Eighty to Eighteen Sixty. Hans Aarsleff. 288p. 1984. pap. 14.95 (ISBN 0-8166-1253-6). U of Minn Pr.

Study of Language in 17th-Century England. Vivian Salmon. (Studies in the History of Linguistics Ser.: No. 17). x, 218p. 1979. 36.00x (ISBN 90-272-0958-8). Benjamins North Am.

Study of Lapses see On Inhibition.

Study of Latent Fingerprints: A Science. Wendell W. Clements. (Illus.). 144p. 1987. 27.50x (ISBN 0-398-05290-5). C C Thomas.

Study of Learning & Retention in Young Children. Lois Hayden Stolz. LC 71-177067. (Columbia University. Teachers College. Contributions to Education: No. 164). Repr. of 1925 ed. 22.50 (ISBN 0-404-55164-5). AMS Pr.

Study of Learning Environments. Ed. by Barry J. Fraser. 85p. 1986. pap. text ed. 15.00 (ISBN 0-937987-00-X). Assessment Res.

Study of Leon Bopp. C. Duckworth. 290p. (Orig.). 1955. pap. text ed. 20.00x (ISBN 0-317-56049-2, Pub. by Droz Switzerland). Coronet Bks.

Study of Liberty. Horace M. Kallen. LC 72-7964. 151p. 1973. Repr. of 1959 ed. lib. bdg. 35.00x (ISBN 0-8371-6554-7, KASL). Greenwood.

Study of Library Cooperatives, Networks & Demonstration Projects, 2 vols. in 1. Ruth J. Patrick et al. 280p. 1980. Set. 42.50 (ISBN 0-208-01942-1, Linnet). Vol. 1: Findings & Recomendations. Vol. 2: Case Study Reports. Shoe String.

Study of Library Reading in the Primary Grades. C. D. Boney. LC 76-176579. (Columbia University. Teachers College. Contributions to Education: No. 578). Repr. of 1933 ed. 22.50 (ISBN 0-404-55578-0). AMS Pr.

Study of Life: A Naturalist's View. R. D. Lawrence. (Illus.). 43p. 1980. pap. 1.50 (ISBN 0-913098-37-X). Myrin Institute.

Study of Literature for Readers & Critics. David Daiches. LC 71-152593. 240p. 1972. Repr. of 1948 ed. lib. bdg. 35.00x (ISBN 0-8371-6026-X, DARC). Greenwood.

Study of Liturgy. Ed. by Cheslyn Jones et al. 1978. 27.00x (ISBN 0-19-520075-6); pap. 13.95x (ISBN 0-19-520076-4). Oxford U Pr.

Study of Lorenzo De'Medici's Villa at Poggio a Caiano, 2 vols. Philip E. Foster. LC 77-94695. (Outstanding Dissertations in the Fine Arts Ser.). 776p. 1978. lib. bdg. 88.00 Set (ISBN 0-8240-3227-6). Garland Pub.

Study of Love's Labour's Lost. Frances A. Yates. 1979. Repr. of 1936 ed. lib. bdg. 35.00 (ISBN 0-8495-6123-X). Arden Lib.

Study of Macbeth. Cumberland Clark. LC 77-10885. 1977. Repr. lib. bdg. 35.00 (ISBN 0-8414-1839-X). Folcroft.

Study of Macbeth for the Stage. Francis Neilson. 1981. lib. bdg. 59.95 (ISBN 0-686-72851-3). Revisionist Pr.

Study of Macroeconomics. M. Mussa. LC 75-38905. (Studies in Monetary Economics: Vol. 3). 316p. 1976. 68.50 (ISBN 0-444-10908-0, North-Holland). Elsevier.

Study of Mammalia & Geology Across the Cretaceous-Tertiary Boundary in Garfield County, Montana. J. David Archibald. (U C Publications in Geological Sciences: Vol. 122). 1982. pap. 36.00x (ISBN 0-520-09639-8). U of Cal Pr.

Study of Man. Alfred C. Haddon. LC 76-44729. Repr. of 1898 ed. 47.00 (ISBN 0-404-15930-3). AMS Pr.

Study of Man. Alfred C. Haddon. (Classics of Anthropology Ser.). 74.00 (ISBN 0-8240-9647-9). Garland Pub.

Study of Man. Michael Polanyi. LC 59-4021. 1963. pap. 9.00 (ISBN 0-226-67292-1, P128, Phoen). U of Chicago Pr.

Study of Man: General Education Course. 2nd ed. Rudolf Steiner. Tr. by Daphne Harwood & Helen Fox. 191p. 1981. 20.00 (ISBN 0-85440-104-0, Pub by Steinerbooks); pap. 10.95 (ISBN 0-85440-292-6). Anthroposophic.

Study of Maria Edgeworth. Grace A. Oliver. 1973. Repr. of 1882 ed. 45.00 (ISBN 0-8274-1009-3). R West.

Study of Mary Wollstonecraft & the Rights of Woman. E. R. Clough. 1972. 59.95 (ISBN 0-8490-1154-X). Gordon Pr.

Study of Mary Wollstonecraft & the Rights of Woman. Emma R. Clough. LC 74-9555. 1898. lib. bdg. 37.00 (ISBN 0-8414-3364-X). Folcroft.

Study of Massachusetts Court Facilities: Summary & Evaluation Volume With Recommendations. National Center for State Courts Staff. 183p. 1975. manuscript 10.98 (NERO-021). Natl Ctr St Courts.

Study of Maya Art. H. J. Spinden. 1976. lib. bdg. 39.95 (ISBN 0-8490-2711-X). Gordon Pr.

Study of Maya Art: Its Subject Matter & Historical Development. Herbert J. Spinden. LC 74-20300. (Illus.). 352p. 1975. pap. text ed. 11.95 (ISBN 0-486-21235-1). Dover.

Study of Maya Art: Its Subject Matter & Historical Development. Herbert J. Spinden. (HUPMM Ser.: Vol. 6). Repr. of 1913 ed. 88.00 (ISBN 0-527-01168-1). Kraus Repr.

Study of Maya Art: Its Subject Matter & Historical Development. Herbert J. Spinden. (Illus.). 16.50 (ISBN 0-8446-5246-6). Peter Smith.

Study of Mechanism in Education. W. L. Patty. LC 71-177146. (Columbia University. Teachers College. Contributions to Education Ser.: No. 739). Repr. of 1938 ed. 22.50 (ISBN 0-404-55739-2). AMS Pr.

Study of Medical Sciences (Theodor Billroth & Abraham Flexner) An Analysis from Past to Present. K. B. Absolon. (Illus.). 170p. 1986. pap. 39.50 (ISBN 0-930329-10-4). Kabel Pubs.

Study of Memory see Sociality & Sympathy.

Study of Methodologies for Forecasting Aquaculture Development. Rev. ed. (Fisheries Technical Papers: No. 248). 47p. pap. 7.50 (ISBN 92-5-102132-5, F2684, FAO). UNIPUB.

Study of Methods & Cost Factors in the Stock & Shipping Department of Men's & Boys' Clothing Factory. 10p. 1955. 5.00 (ISBN 0-318-19661-1). Clothing Mfrs.

Study of Methods of Preparation & Properties of Synthetic Inorganic Coatings on Copper: The Corrosion of Copper in Acidic Chlorate Solution. University of Utah. 178p. 1971. 26.70 (ISBN 0-317-34550-8, 94). Intl Copper.

Study of Metre. T. S. Omond. LC 72-195002. 1920. lib. bdg. 25.50 (ISBN 0-8414-6669-6). Folcroft.

Study of Milton's Paradise Lost. John A. Himes. LC 76-17888. 1976. lib. bdg. 50.00 (ISBN 0-8414-4841-8). Folcroft.

Study of Minor Prophets. Brodie Crouch. pap. 2.50 (ISBN 0-89315-291-9). Lambert Bk.

Study of Modern Parody. David Kiremidjian. LC 84-48374. 225p. 1985. lib. bdg. 33.00 (ISBN 0-8240-6701-0). Garland Pub.

Study of Modern Society: Perspectives from Classic Sociology. Philip Olson. 9.25 (ISBN 0-8446-0831-9). Peter Smith.

Study of Moneyflows in the United States. Morris A. Copeland. 30.00 (ISBN 0-405-07586-3, 16432). Ayer Co Pubs.

Study of Mothers' Practices & Children's Activities in a Co-Operative Nursery School. Clara Tucker. LC 79-177696. (Columbia University Teachers College. Contributions to EDucation: No. 810). Repr. of 1940 ed. 22.50 (ISBN 0-404-55810-0). AMS Pr.

Study of Mozart's Last Three Symphonies. Alan E. Dickinson. LC 73-181142. 1927. Repr. 29.00x (ISBN 0-403-01543-X). Scholarly.

Study of Mozart's Last Three Symphonies. Alan E. Dickinson. 1988. Repr. of 1927 ed. lib. bdg. 49.00x. Am Biog Serv.

Study of Music in the Elementary School: A Conceptual Approach. Music Educators National Conference. Ed. by Flavis Evenson & Charles L. Gary. LC 67-31352. 182p. (Orig.). 1967. pap. 7.00 (ISBN 0-940796-19-8, 1048). Music Ed Natl.

Study of Mutual Funds: Report of the Committee on Interstate & Foreign Commerce (87th Congress, 2nd Session, House Report No. 2274) Wharton School of Finance & Commerce, University of Pennsylvania. LC 62-62400. xxxiii, 595p. 1982. Repr. of 1962 ed. lib. bdg. 45.00 (ISBN 0-89941-181-9). W. S. Hein.

Study of Navajo Symbolism, 3 pts. in 1. Franc J. Newcomb. Incl. Pt. 1. Navajo Symbols in Sandpaintings & Ritual Objects; Pt. 2. Navajo Picture Writing. S. A. Fishler; Pt. 3. Notes on Corresponding Symbols in Various Parts of the World. Mary C. Wheelwright. 1956. Set. 23.00 (ISBN 0-527-01284-X, HU.PMP). Kraus Repr.

Study of Nehru. 2nd rev. ed. Ed. by Rafiq Zakaria. (Illus.). 478p. 1964. Repr. of 1959 ed. 25.00x (ISBN 0-7146-1574-9, F Cass Co). Biblio Dist.

Study of Neurosis: Library of Congress Catalog Card Number. John S. Duryee. LC 84-18699. 300p. 1984. text ed. 29.95 (ISBN 0-940524-02-3); pap. text ed. 19.95 (ISBN 0-940524-03-1). G Handwerk.

Study of New Jersey's Public Defender's Appellate Office. 48p. 1986. manuscript 3.00 (ISBN 0-317-59214-9, NERO-189). Natl Ctr St Courts.

Study of Nietzsche. J. P. Stern. LC 78-54328. (Major European Authors Ser.). 1979. 39.50 (ISBN 0-521-22126-9). Cambridge U Pr.

Study of Nietzsche. J. P. Stern. LC 78-54328. (Major European Authors Ser.). 1982. pap. 16.95 (ISBN 0-521-28380-9). Cambridge U Pr.

Study of Nine & Eighty-Five Widows Known to Certain Charity Organization Societies in 1910. Mary E. Richmond & Fred S. Hall. LC 74-3971. (Women in America Ser). (Illus.). 84p. 1974. Repr. of 1913 ed. 13.00x (ISBN 0-405-06119-6). Ayer Co Pubs.

Study of Nineteenth Century Society. Ed. by E. A. Wrigley. LC 71-174258. (Illus.). 512p. 1972. 57.50 (ISBN 0-521-08412-1). Cambridge U Pr.

Study of Nonstandard English. rev. ed. William Labov. LC 70-114999. 1970. pap. 4.95 (ISBN 0-8141-4849-2). NCTE.

Study of Numbers. R. A. Schwaller de Lubicz. 1986. pap. 6.95 (ISBN 0-89281-112-9). Inner Tradit.

Study of Numbers. J. Adrian Verkouteren. 355p. (gr. 5-8). 1981. pap. text ed. 9.95x (ISBN 0-88334-153-0). Ind Sch Pr.

Study of Obituaries As a Source for Polish Genealogical Research. Thomas E. Golembiewski. (Illus.). 63p. 1985. pap. 10.95 (ISBN 0-318-17020-5). Polish Genealog.

Study of Olmec Iconography see Olmec Paintings of Oxtotitlan Cave, Guerrero, Mexico.

Study of Olmec Sculptural Chronology. Susan Milbrath. LC 79-89248. (Studies in Pre-Columbian Art & Archaeology: No. 23). (Illus.). 75p. 1979. pap. 8.00x (ISBN 0-88402-093-2). Dumbarton Oaks.

Study of Omaha Indian Music with a Report of the Structural Peculiarities of the Music by J. C. Fillmore. Alice C. Fletcher & Francis LaFlesche. (HU PMP). 1893. 20.00 (ISBN 0-527-01187-8). Kraus Repr.

Study of Opinions of Some International Problems As Related to Certain Experience & Background Factors. Arthur Kolstad. LC 70-176947. (Columbia University. Teachers College. Contributions to Education Ser.: No. 555). Repr. of 1933 ed. 22.50 (ISBN 0-404-55555-1). AMS Pr.

Study of Orchestration. Samuel Adler. 400p. 1982. text ed. 22.95x (ISBN 0-393-95188-X); wkbkx 7.95x (ISBN 0-393-95213-4); tapes 395.00 (ISBN 0-393-95217-7). Norton.

Study of Organization & Method of the Course of Study in Agriculture in Secondary Schools. Theodore H. Eaton. LC 78-176740. (Columbia University. Teachers College. Contributions to Education Ser.: No. 86). Repr. of 1917 ed. 22.50 (ISBN 0-404-55086-X). AMS Pr.

Study of Organizational Leadership. Ed. by Office of Military Leadership, United States Military Academy Staff. LC 76-25242. 600p. 1976. pap. 14.95 (ISBN 0-8117-2059-4). Stackpole.

Study of Organizations: Findings from Field & Laboratory. Ed. by Daniel Katz et al. LC 80-15488. (Social & Behavioral Science Ser.). 1980. text ed. 49.95x (ISBN 0-87589-464-X). Jossey-Bass.

Study of Oscar Wilde. Walter W. Kenilworth. LC 72-3091. (English Literature Ser.: No. 33). 1972. Repr. of 1912 ed. lib. bdg. 39.95x (ISBN 0-8383-1524-0). Haskell.

Study of Passive Resistance in Foundation Structures, Pt. 2. M. Reimbert & A. Reimbert. LC 74-77789. (Rock & Soil Mechanics Ser.). (Illus.). 200p. 1976. text ed. 30.00x (ISBN 0-87849-013-2). Trans Tech.

Study of Patriotism in the Elizabethan Drama. Richard V. Lindabury. LC 68-54170. (Studies in Drama, No. 39). 1969. Repr. of 1931 ed. lib. bdg. 75.00x (ISBN 0-8383-0584-9). Haskell.

Study of Personality. Georgia Babladelis. 400p. 1984. text ed. 29.95 (ISBN 0-03-063662-0). HR&W.

Study of Philosophy: An Introduction. rev. ed. S. Morris Engel. 360p. 1988. pap. text ed. 21.80 (ISBN 0-939693-02-X). Collegiate Pr.

Study of Play Selection in Women's Colleges. Sr. Mary P. Doyle. LC 72-176728. (Columbia University. Teachers College. Contributions to Education Ser.: No. 648). Repr. of 1935 ed. 12.50 (ISBN 0-404-55648-5). AMS Pr.

Study of Plea Bargaining in Municipal Courts of the State of New Jersey. National Center for State Courts Staff. 106p. 1974. manuscript 6.36 (NERO-050). Natl Ctr St Courts.

Study of Poetry. Heathcote W. Garrod. LC 72-196082. 1974. Repr. of 1936 ed. lib. bdg. 15.00 (ISBN 0-8414-4562-1). Folcroft.

Study of Poetry. Bliss Perry. 1977. Repr. of 1920 ed. lib. bdg. 32.00 (ISBN 0-8414-9221-2). Folcroft.

Study of Poetry. Bliss Perry. LC 72-86052. 1969. Repr. of 1920 ed. 27.50x (ISBN 0-8046-0632-3, Pub. by Kennikat). Assoc Faculty Pr.

Study of Poetry. Bliss Perry. 1973. Repr. of 1920 ed. 14.50 (ISBN 0-8274-1319-X). R West.

Study of Poetry. Bliss Perry. 396p. 1986. 47.50 (ISBN 0-8495-4447-5). Arden Lib.

Study of Policy Formation. R. A. Bauer & K. J. Gergen. 1971. pap. text ed. 12.95 (ISBN 0-02-901930-3). Free Pr.

Study of Political Adaptation. James N. Rosenau. (Essays on the Analysis of World Politics Ser.). 300p. 1981. 39.50 (ISBN 0-89397-076-X); pap. 23.50x (ISBN 0-89397-077-8). Nichols Pub.

Study of Politics. Duverger. pap. 21.95 (ISBN 0-442-30698-9). Van Nos Reinhold.

Study of Politics. 2nd ed. Andrew Hacker. LC 72-4851. (Foundations of American Government & Political Science Ser.). (Illus.). 144p. 1972. pap. text ed. 19.95 (ISBN 0-07-025394-3). McGraw.

Study of Politics: Inaugural Lectures. Ed. by Preston King. 341p. 1977. 32.50x (ISBN 0-7146-3084-5, F Cass Co). Biblio Dist.

Study of Politics: The/Present State of American Political Science. Charles S. Hyneman. LC 59-10554. 243p. 1959. 17.95 (ISBN 0-252-72671-5). U of Ill Pr.

Study of Population. Ed. by Philip M. Hauser & Otis D. Duncan. (Illus.). 1959. 30.00x (ISBN 0-226-31951-2). U of Chicago Pr.

Study of Population: A Geographic Approach. George A. Schnell & Mark S. Monmonier. 362p. 1983. text ed. 33.95 (ISBN 0-675-20046-6). Merrill.

Study of Populations. Ed. by H. Messel. (Illus.). 266p. 1986. pap. text ed. 16.50 (ISBN 0-08-029877-X, Pub. by PPA). Pergamon.

Study of Porous Plate Flameholders. S. A. Weil. (Research Bulletin Ser.: No. 35). iv, 30p. 1964. 3.50 (ISBN 0-317-56887-6). Inst Gas Tech.

Study of Possible Societies. Walter Firey. LC 76-55578. (Illus.). 1977. 10.00 (ISBN 0-9603066-0-9). Firey.

Study of Precis Writing As Composition Technique. G. E. Jencke. LC 70-176907. (Columbia University. Teachers College. Contributions to Education Ser.: No. 644). Repr. of 1935 ed. 22.50 (ISBN 0-404-55644-2). AMS Pr.

Study of Prehistoric Social Change: The Development of Complex Societies in the Hawaiian Islands. Ross Cordy. LC 81-10825. (Studies in Archaeology). 1981. 33.00 (ISBN 0-12-188450-3). Acad Pr.

Study of Primary Education: A Source Book: Classroom & Teaching Studies, Roles & Relationships, Vol. 3. Ed. by Colin Richards & Brenda Lofthouse. 126p. 1985. text ed. 29.00x (ISBN 1-85000-061-1, Falmer Pr); pap. text ed. 14.00x (ISBN 1-85000-060-3, Falmer Pr). Taylor & Francis.

Study of Primary Education: A Source Book, Vol. 1. Colin Richards. 330p. 1984. 39.00x (ISBN 0-905273-64-8, Falmer Pr); pap. 21.00x (ISBN 0-905273-63-X). Taylor & Francis.

Study of Primary Education: A Source Book: The Curriculum, Vol. 2. Ed. by Colin Richards & Brenda Lofthouse. 260p. 1985. 36.00x (ISBN 1-85000-044-1, Falmer Pr); pap. 20.00x (ISBN 1-85000-043-3, Falmer Pr). Taylor & Francis.

Study of Problem Material in High School Algebra. Jesse J. Powell. LC 71-177162. (Columbia University. Teachers College. Contributions to Education Ser.: No. 405). Repr. of 1929 ed. 22.50 (ISBN 0-404-55405-9). AMS Pr.

Study of Problem Pupils. Louise E. Tucker. LC 70-177691. (Columbia University. Teachers College. Contributions to Education Ser.: No. 720). Repr. of 1937 ed. 22.50 (ISBN 0-404-55720-1). AMS Pr.

Study of Professional Training & Development Roles & Competencies. Patrick R. Pinto. 124p. softcover 9.00 (ISBN 0-318-13285-0, PWBCP); members 6.95 (ISBN 0-318-13286-9). Am Soc Train & Devel.

Study of Prose Fiction. Bliss Perry. 1902. Repr. lib. bdg. 32.00 (ISBN 0-8414-9222-0). Folcroft.

Study of Psychology & Mind As a Function of the Organism see Problems of Life & Mind.

Study of Public Administration. Keith M. Henderson. LC 83-16648. 122p. 1984. lib. bdg. 23.25 (ISBN 0-8191-3541-0); pap. text ed. 9.25 (ISBN 0-8191-3542-9). U Pr of Amer.

Study of Raptor Populations. 2nd ed. Donald R. Johnson. LC 81-50768. (Gem Books Natural History Ser.). (Illus.). 64p. 1981. 5.95 (ISBN 0-89301-079-0). U of Idaho Pr.

Study of Regulations, Codes & Standards Related to Energy Use in Buildings. (ECE Committee on Housing, Building & Planning Ser.: No. 41). (Illus.). 54p. 1985. pap. 8.50 (ISBN 92-1-116189-4, E.84.II.E.7). UN.

Study of Relationships Between Diet & Dental Health, United States, 1971-1974. Brian A. Burt et al. Ed. by Klaudia Cox. 100p. 1981. pap. text ed. 5.00 (ISBN 0-8406-0235-9). Natl Ctr Health Stats.

Study of Relationships Between Level of College Education & Police Patrolmen's Performance. Gerald R. Griffin. LC 79-65262. 120p. 1980. 11.95 (ISBN 0-86548-012-5). R & E Pubs.

Study of Religion. Morris Jastrow, Jr. Ed. by William A. Clebsch. LC 81-9184. (Classics & Reprints Series of the American Academy of Religion & Scholars Press). 1981. text ed. 10.95 (ISBN 0-89130-519-X, 01-05-01). Scholars Pr GA.

Study of Religion & Its Meaning. J. Barnhart. 1977. 25.50x (ISBN 90-279-7762-3). Mouton.

Study of Religion in Colleges & Universities. Paul Ramsey. Ed. by John F. Wilson. LC 70-90957. 336p. 1970. 41.00x (ISBN 0-691-07161-6). Princeton U Pr.

Study of Religion in Two-Year Colleges. C. Freeman Sleeper & Robert A. Spivey. LC 75-28158. (American Academy of Religion, Individual Volumes). 1975. pap. 8.95 (ISBN 0-89130-031-7, 010801). Scholars Pr GA.

Study of Religious Thought at Oxford & Cambridge: 1590-1640. Stewart A. Dippel. LC 87-8306. 136p. (Orig.). 1987. lib. bdg. 19.25 (ISBN 0-8191-6387-2); pap. text ed. 9.75 (ISBN 0-8191-6388-0). U Pr of Amer.

Study of Representative Indo-English Novelists. Uma Parameswaran. 1976. 13.50 (ISBN 0-7069-0410-9). Intl Bk Dist.

Study of Retroactive Inhibition see On the Function of the Cerebrum.

Study of Rhetorical Patterns in John Donne's Epicedes & Obsequies. Issac I. Elimimian. 120p. 1987. 10.00 (ISBN 0-533-07391-X). Vantage.

Study of Rhythmic Structure in the Verse of William Butler Yeats. Adelyn Dougherty. (De Proprietatibus Litterarum, Ser. Practica: No. 38). (Illus.). 135p. 1973. pap. text ed. 17.60x (ISBN 90-2792-506-2). Mouton.

Study of Richard Symonds: His Italian Notebooks & Their Relevance to Seventeenth Century Painting Techniques. Mary Beal. LC 83-48688. (Theses from the Courtauld Institute of Art Ser.). 420p. 1984. lib. bdg. 50.00 (ISBN 0-8240-5976-X). Garland Pub.

Study of Roles in the Arashiyama West Troop of Japanese Monkeys (Macaca Fuscata) L. M. Fedigan. Ed. by F. S. Szalay. (Contributions to Primatology Ser.: Vol. 9). (Illus.). 116p. 1976. 32.75 (ISBN 3-8055-2334-3). S Karger.

Study of Rural Society. John H. Kolb. LC 70-136074. (Illus.). 1971. Repr. of 1952 ed. lib. bdg. 35.00x (ISBN 0-8371-5224-0, KORS). Greenwood.

Study of Russian Folklore. Felix J. Oinas & Stephen Soudakoff. (Indian Univ. Folklore Ser.: No. 25). 341p. 1975. text ed. 38.40x (ISBN 90-2793-147-X). Mouton.

Study of Russian History from British Archival Sources. Ed. by Janet Hartley. 184p. 1986. 55.00x (ISBN 0-7201-1784-4). Mansell.

Study of Sacred Scripture. Paul Y. Taguchi. 1988. 3.00 (ISBN 0-8198-6821-3, SC0446); pap. write for info. (ISBN 0-8198-6822-1). Dghtrs St Paul.

Study of St. Paul: His Character & Opinions. S. Baring-Gould. 1977. lib. bdg. 59.95 (ISBN 0-8490-2712-8). Gordon Pr.

Study of Samurai Income & Entrepreneurship. Kozo Yamamura. LC 73-87378. (East Asian Ser.: No. 76). 256p. 1974. text ed. 19.50x (ISBN 0-674-85322-9). Harvard U Pr.

Study of Saving in the United States, 3 Vols. Raymond W. Goldsmith. LC 69-13910. 1969. Repr. of 1956 ed. Vol. 1. lib. bdg. 41.80 (GOST); Vol. 2. lib. bdg. 41.80 (ISBN 0-8371-0999-X, GOSU); Vol. 3. lib. bdg. 41.80 (ISBN 0-8371-1000-9, GOSV). Greenwood.

Study of Schooling: Field-Based Methodologies in Educational Research & Evaluation. Thomas S Popkewitz & B. Robert Tabachnick. LC 81-1416. 316p. 1981. 38.95 (ISBN 0-275-90705-8, C0705). Praeger.

Study of Selected Concepts for Government Financial Accounting & Reporting. William W. Holder. LC 85-50315. 69p. 1980. pap. 5.00 (ISBN 0-686-84264-2). Municipal.

Study of Selected English Critical Terms from 1650 to 1800. Edward A. Watson. (American University Studies IV: English Language & Literature: Vol. 55). 686p. 1987. text ed. 78.95 (ISBN 0-8204-0518-3). P Lang Pubs.

Study of Sensory Control in the Rat. Florence Richardson. Bd. with On the Influence of Complexity & Dissimilarity on Memory. H. A. Peterson. Repr. of 1909 ed; Studies in Melody: Studies in Melody. W. Van Dyke Bingham. Repr. of 1910 ed; Report Presented 1909. American Psychology Association Committee on Teaching of Psychology. Repr. of 1910 ed; Some Mental Processes of the Rhesus Monkey. W. T. Shepherd. Repr. of 1910 ed. (Psychology Monographs General & Applied: Vol. 12). pap. 36.00 (ISBN 0-8115-1411-0). Kraus Repr.

Study of Several Linguistic Functions of Mexican-American Children in a Two Language Environment. George B. Linn. LC 70-163940. pap. 9.95 (ISBN 0-88247-152-X). R & E Pubs.

Study of Shakespeare. Una Ellis-Fermor. LC 76-46453. 1947. lib. bdg. 15.00 (ISBN 0-8414-3949-4). Folcroft.

Study of Shakespeare. Russell Potter. LC 73-15569. 1926. Repr. lib. bdg. 17.00 (ISBN 0-8414-6734-X). Folcroft.

Study of Shakespeare. Algernon C. Swinburne. LC 9-30432. Repr. of 1880 ed. 27.50 (ISBN 0-404-06315-2). AMS Pr.

Study of Shakespeare's Henry VIII. Cumberland Clark. LC 78-7503. 1978. Repr. of 1931 ed. lib. bdg. 35.00 (ISBN 0-8414-0059-8). Folcroft.

Study of Shakespeare's Versification. M. A. Bayfield. LC 74-4224. 1920. lib. bdg. 40.00 (ISBN 0-8414-9920-9). Folcroft.

Study of Shakespeare's Versification, with an Inquiry into the Trustworthiness of the Early Texts. Matthew A. Bayfield. LC 77-130616. Repr. of 1920 ed. 34.50 (ISBN 0-404-00695-7). AMS Pr.

Study of Shelley. P. Edgar. LC 70-116792. (Studies in Shelley, No. 25). 1970. Repr. of 1899 ed. lib. bdg. 39.95x (ISBN 0-8383-1034-6). Haskell.

Study of Shelley. Pelham Edgar. LC 76-26146. 1899. lib. bdg. 30.00 (ISBN 0-8414-3933-8). Folcroft.

Study of Shelley with Special References to His Nature Poetry. Edgar Pelham. 1978. Repr. of 1899 ed. lib. bdg. 25.00 (ISBN 0-8492-0762-2). R West.

Study of Shelley's "A Defence of Poetry" A Textual & Critical Evaluation, 2 vols. Fanny Delisle. Ed. by James Hogg. (Romantic Reassessment Ser.). 633p. (Orig.). 1974. pap. 30.00 (ISBN 0-317-40105-X, Pub. by Salzburg Studies). Longwood Pub Group.

Study of Shelley's Defence of Poetry. Lucas Verkoren. 1937. lib. bdg. 27.50 (ISBN 0-8414-9195-X). Folcroft.

Study of Shelley's Defense of Poetry. L. Verkoren. LC 72-95451. (Studies in Shelley, No. 25). 1970. Repr. lib. bdg. 39.95x (ISBN 0-8383-1208-X). Haskell.

Study of Shelley's Drama-The Cenci. Ernest S. Bates. LC 73-16185. 1908. lib. bdg. 20.00 (ISBN 0-8414-3343-7). Folcroft.

Study of Shelley's Poetry. Seymour Reiter. LC 67-22735. 1967. 17.50 (ISBN 0-8263-0085-5). Lib Soc Sci.

Study of Shelly. John Todhunter. LC 75-40238. 1880. lib. bdg. 45.00 (ISBN 0-8414-8521-6). Folcroft.

Study of Shorthand Reporter Transcript Production Costs. LC 82-216768. 1982. pap. 10.00 (ISBN 0-318-01733-4). Natl Shorthand Rptr.

Study of Shorthand Teaching: Comparison & Outcomes in the Learning of Effected by Differences in Teaching Methodology. Benjamin F. Davis. LC 78-176716. (Columbia University. Teachers College. Contributions to Education Ser.: No. 693). Repr. of 1936 ed. 22.50 (ISBN 0-404-55693-0). AMS Pr.

Study of Simon Willard's Clocks. R. W. Husher & W. W. Welch. LC 80-65021. (Illus.). 292p. 1980. 49.50 (ISBN 0-9603944-0-0). Husher & Welch.

Study of Siouan Cults. James O. Dorsey. (Illus.). 208p. pap. 11.95 (ISBN 0-8466-4055-4, I55). Shorey.

Study of Slavery in New Jersey. Henry S. Cooley. LC 78-63853. (Johns Hopkins University. Studies in the Social Sciences. Fourteenth Ser. 1896: 9-10). Repr. of 1896 ed. 11.50 (ISBN 0-404-61109-5). AMS Pr.

Study of Slavery in New Jersey. Henry S. Cooley. 1973. pap. 9.00 (ISBN 0-384-09779-0). Johnson Repr.

Study of Slavery in New Jersey see Early Studies of Slavery by States.

Study of Social & Constitutional Tendencies in the Early Years of Edward Three. Dorothy Hughes. LC 78-14508. (Perspectives in European History Ser.: No. 16). viii, 245p. 1979. Repr. of 1915 ed. lib. bdg. 29.50x (ISBN 0-87991-623-0). Porcupine Pr.

Study of Social Effects. Jacques Vallee et al. (Group Communication Through Computers: Vol. 2). 160p. 1974. 10.50 (ISBN 0-318-14424-7, R33). Inst Future.

Study of Social Problems. 4th ed. Earl Rubington & Martin Weinberg. (Illus.). 304p. 1989. pap. text ed. 10.95 (ISBN 0-19-505723-6). Oxford U Pr.

Study of Social Problems: Five Perspectives. 3rd ed. Ed. by Earl Rubington & Martin S. Weinberg. 1981. pap. text ed. 10.95x (ISBN 0-19-502825-2). Oxford U Pr.

Study of Social Status, Personality Characteristics, & Motor Ability of Mentally Handicapped Girls. Betty S. Baker. LC 74-28604. 1975. soft bdg. 10.95 (ISBN 0-88247-311-5). R & E Pubs.

Study of Society: An Integrated Anthology. 4th ed. Ed. by Peter I. Rose. 1977. pap. text ed. write for info (ISBN 0-394-31229-5, RanC). Random.

Study of Sociology. Herbert Spencer. 446p. 1985. Repr. of 1903 ed. lib. bdg. 45.00 (ISBN 0-89984-641-6). Century Bookbindery.

Study of Some Aspects of Satisfaction in the Vocation of Stenography. Margaret S. Quayle. LC 76-177174. (Columbia University. Teachers College. Contributions to Education Ser.: No. 659). Repr. of 1935 ed. 22.50 (ISBN 0-404-55659-0). AMS Pr.

Study of Some Negro-White Families in the U. S. Caroline Day. LC 76-106857. (Illus.). 1971. Repr. of 1932 ed. 35.00x (ISBN 0-8371-3479-X, DNF&, Pub. by Negro U Pr). Greenwood.

Study of Some of the Influences of Regents Requirements & Examinations in French. Arnold L. Frizzle. LC 70-176789. (Columbia University. Teachers College. Contributions to Education Ser.: No. 964). Repr. of 1950 ed. 22.50 (ISBN 0-404-55964-6). AMS Pr.

Study of Some Personality Aspects of Deaf Children. L. Brunschwig. LC 70-176608. (Columbia University. Teachers College. Contributions to Education Ser.: No. 687). Repr. of 1936 ed. 22.50 (ISBN 0-404-55687-6). AMS Pr.

Study of Some Problems Arising in the Admission of Students As Candidates for Professional Degrees in Education. Clarence Linton. LC 73-176999. (Columbia University. Teachers College. Contributions to Education Ser.: No. 285). Repr. of 1927 ed. 22.50 (ISBN 0-404-55285-4). AMS Pr.

Study of Spinoza. 3rd facsimile ed. James Martineau. LC 78-152994. (Select Bibliographies Reprint Ser). Repr. of 1895 ed. 23.50 (ISBN 0-8369-5746-6). Ayer Co Pubs.

Study of Spinoza's Ethics. Jonathan Bennett. LC 83-18568. 416p. 1984. lib. bdg. 32.00 (ISBN 0-915145-82-0); pap. text ed. 16.50 (ISBN 0-915145-83-9). Hackett Pub.

Study of Spirituality. Cheslyn Jones et al. (Illus.). 664p. 1986. 32.00 (ISBN 0-19-504169-0); pap. text ed. 14.95 (ISBN 0-19-504170-4). Oxford U Pr.

Study of Structural Characteristics, Policies, & Operational Procedures in Metropolitan Juvenile Courts: Executive Summary. National Center for State Courts Staff. 177p. 1982. manuscript 10.62 (NCSC-017). Natl Ctr St Courts.

Study of Structural Characteristics, Policies & Operational Procedures in Metropolitan Juvenile Center, 2 vols. National Center for State Courts Staff. 1982. Vol. I, 302 pgs. manuscript 18.12 (NCSC-018); Vol. II, 131 pgs. manuscript 7.86 (NCSC-019). Natl Ctr St Courts.

Study of Subject Bibliography with Special Reference to the Social Sciences. Ed. by Christopher D. Needham & Esther Herman. LC 75-630095. (Student Contribution Ser.: No. 3). 1970. pap. 5.00 (ISBN 0-911808-05-1). U of Md Lib Serv.

Study of Sung Underglaze Blue & Red Porcelain. Lee Yu-Kuan. 242p. 1982. 315.00x (ISBN 0-317-68499-X, Pub. by Han-Shan Tang Ltd). State Mutual Bk.

Study of Svatantrika. Donald S Lopez, Jr. 490p. (Orig.). 1987. lib. bdg. 35.00 (ISBN 0-937938-20-3); pap. 19.95 (ISBN 0-937938-19-X). Snow Lion.

Study of Swinburne. T. Earle Welby. 1973. lib. bdg. 27.00 (ISBN 0-8414-9689-7). Folcroft.

Study of Teacher Training in Vermont. Robert M. Steele. LC 70-177743. (Columbia University. Teachers College. Contributions to Education Ser.: No. 243). Repr. of 1926 ed. 22.50 (ISBN 0-404-55243-9). AMS Pr.

Study of Teaching. M. Dunkin & J. Biddle. 1982. Repr. of 1974 ed. text ed. cancelled (ISBN 0-8290-0603-6). Irvington.

Study of Teaching. Michael J. Dunkin & Bruce J. Biddle. LC 81-40903. (Illus.). 508p. 1982. pap. text ed. 19.75 (ISBN 0-8191-2259-9). U Pr of Amer.

Study of Temperament: Changes, Continuities & Challenges. Ed. by Robert Plomin & Judy Dunn. 192p. 1986. text ed. 24.95 (ISBN 0-89859-670-X). L Erlbaum Assocs.

Study of Textile Mill Closings in Selected New England Communities. W. Stanley Devino et al. 1966. pap. 6.95x (ISBN 0-89101-014-9). U Maine Orono.

Study of Thailand: Analyses of Knowledge. Ed. by Eliezer B. Ayal. LC 79-4544. (Papers in International Studies: Southeast Asia Ser.: No. 54). 1979. pap. 13.50x (ISBN 0-89680-079-2, 82-90553, Ohio U Ctr Intl). Ohio U Pr.

Study of the Absorption Spectra of Solutions of Certain Salts of Potassium, Cobalt, Nickel, Copper, Chromium, Erbium, Praseodymium, Neodymium & Uranium. Harry C. Jones. LC 11-670. (Carnegie Institute of Washington Publication Ser.: No. 130). pap. 90.80 (ISBN 0-317-29734-1, 2015701). Bks Demand UMI.

Study of the Achievement of College Students in Beginning Courses in Food Preparation & Serving & Related Factors. Mary K. Wilson. LC 75-177628. (Columbia University. Teachers College. Contributions to Education Ser.: No. 958). Repr. of 1949 ed. 22.50 (ISBN 0-404-55958-1). AMS Pr.

Study of the Appellate System in Minnesota. National Center for State Courts Staff. 58p. 1974. manuscript 3.48 (MAB-116). Natl Ctr St Courts.

Study of the Application of an Educational Theory to Science Instruction. Eugene A. Waters. LC 76-177663. (Columbia University. Teachers College. Contributions to Education Ser.: No. 864). Repr. of 1942 ed. 22.50 (ISBN 0-404-55864-X). AMS Pr.

Study of the Bible. rev. ed. Ernest C. Colwell. LC 64-23411. (Midway Reprint Ser.). pap. 54.50 (2026769). Bks Demand UMI.

Study of the Bible in the Middle Ages. Beryl Smalley. 1964. pap. 11.95 (ISBN 0-268-00267-3). U of Notre Dame Pr.

Study of the Book of Genesis. Gordon Talbot. LC 81-65578. 288p. (Orig.). 1981. pap. 5.95 (ISBN 0-87509-253-5); leader's guide 2.95 (ISBN 0-87509-311-6). Chr Pubns.

Study of the Book of Jonah. Jonathan Magonet. 1985. 10.00x (ISBN 0-317-62185-8, Guild of Pastoral Psych). State Mutual Bk.

Study of the Boston Housing Court. National Center for State Courts Staff. 91p. 1974. manuscript 5.46 (MAB-117). Natl Ctr St Courts.

Study of the Boston Mechanic Arts High School. Charles A. Prosser. LC 77-177169. (Columbia University. Teachers College. Contributions to Education Ser.: No. 74). Repr. of 1915 ed. 22.50 (ISBN 0-404-55074-6). AMS Pr.

Study of the Bronze Age Pottery of Great Britain & Ireland: Its Associated Grave Goods, 2 vols. John Abercromby. LC 77-86419. (Illus.). Repr. of 1912 ed. 70.00 set (ISBN 0-404-15850-1). AMS Pr.

Study of the Bronze Drums of South China. Princeton S. Hsu. (Asian Folklore & Social Life Monographs: Vol. 95). (Chinese.). 1977. 14.00x (ISBN 0-89986-327-2). Oriental Bk Store.

Study of the Results of Planning for Home Economics Education in the Southern States As Organized Under the National Acts for Vocational Education. Druzilla C. Kent. LC 77-176965. (Columbia University. Teachers College. Contributions to Education: No. 689). Repr. of 1936 ed. 22.50 (ISBN 0-404-55689-2). AMS Pr.

Study of the Revelation. John A. Copeland. 1971. pap. 4.50 (ISBN 0-89137-702-6). Quality Pubns.

Study of the Sea: The Development of Marine Research Under the Auspices of the International Council for the Exploration of the Sea. Ed. by Fishing News Books Ltd. 272p. 1981. 90.00x (Pub. by Fishing News England). State Mutual Bk.

Study of the Sea: The Development of Marine Research under the Auspices of the International Council for the Exploration of the Sea. Compiled by E. M. Thomasson. (Illus.). 272p. 1981. 52.95 (ISBN 0-85238-112-3, FN92, FNB). UNIPUB.

Study of the Securities Industry, 3 Bks, Pts. 1-9. U. S. Congress House. 1982. Repr. of 1972 ed. Set. lib. bdg. 140.00 (ISBN 0-89941-228-9). W S Hein.

Study of the Short Story. Henry S. Canby. Ed. by Alfred Dashiell. LC 83-45726. Repr. of 1935 ed. 33.00 (ISBN 0-404-20050-8). AMS Pr.

Study of the Small-Mouth Bass, Micropterus Dolomieu (Lacepede) in Rearing Ponds in Ohio. T. H. Langlois. 1936. 2.00 (ISBN 0-86727-032-2). Ohio Bio Survey.

Study of the Sociability of Elementary School Children. Jui-Ching Hsia. LC 70-176884. (Columbia University. Teachers College. Contributions to Education: No. 322). Repr. of 1928 ed. 22.50 (ISBN 0-404-55322-2). AMS Pr.

Study of the Social & Economic Needs Created by the Proposed Craig Power Plant Installation. 119p. 1974. 15.00 (ISBN 0-686-64166-3). U CO Busn Res Div.

Study of the Social Attitudes & Information on Public Problems of Women Teachers in Secondary Schools. John C. Sullivan. LC 72-177733. (Columbia University. Teachers College. Contributions to Education Ser.: No. 791). Repr. of 1940 ed. 22.50 (ISBN 0-404-55791-0). AMS Pr.

Study of the Source of the Tales & Romances Written by Nathaniel Hawthorne. Elizabeth L. Chandler. LC 75-9569. Repr. of 1926 ed. lib. bdg. 25.00 (ISBN 0-8414-3645-2). Folcroft.

Study of the Sources of Bunyan's Allegories. James B. Wharey. 59.95 (ISBN 0-8490-1158-2). Gordon Pr.

Study of the Sources of Bunyan's Allegories(with Special Reference to Deguileville's Pilgrimage of Man. James B. Wharey. LC 68-59038. 136p. 1968. Repr. of 1904 ed. 20.00x (ISBN 0-87752-120-4). Gordian.

Study of the Sources of Han D'Islande & Their Significance in the Literary Development of Victor Hugo. Mary I. O'Connor. LC 76-115357. (Catholic University Romance Languages Ser: No. 24). Repr. of 1942 ed. 20.00 (ISBN 0-404-50324-1). AMS Pr.

Study of the Sources of the Tales & Romances Written by Nathaniel Hawthorne Before 1853. Elizabeth L. Chandler. 1978. Repr. of 1926 ed. lib. bdg. 27.50 (ISBN 0-8495-0832-0). Arden Lib.

Study of the Standard of Living of Working Families in Shanghai. Simon Yang & L. K. Tao. Ed. by Ramon H. Myers. LC 80-8826. (China During the Interregnum 1911-1949, The Economy & Society Ser.). 142p. 1982. lib. bdg. 22.00 (ISBN 0-8240-4681-1). Garland Pub.

Study of the State. Ed. by Henri J. Claessen & Peter Skalnik. (New Babylon Studies in the Social Sciences Ser.: No.35). 535p. 1981. 55.50 (ISBN 90-279-3348-0). Mouton.

Study of the Stated Aims & Purposes of the Departments of Military Science & Tactics & Physical Education in the Land-Grant Colleges of the United States. Willard L. Nash. LC 79-177105. (Columbia University. Teachers College. Contributions to Education: No. 614). Repr. of 1934 ed. 22.50 (ISBN 0-404-55614-0). AMS Pr.

Study of the Stipitate Hydunums from the Southern Appalachian Mountains - Genera: Bankera, Hydnellum, Phellodon, Sarcodon. Richard E. Baird. (Bibliotheca Mycologica Ser.: Vol. 104). (Illus.). 158p. 1986. pap. 45.00x (ISBN 3-443-59005-5). Lubrecht & Cramer.

Study of the Summer High School. Willis H. Reals. LC 79-177180. (Columbia University. Teachers College. Contributions to Education: No. 337). Repr. of 1928 ed. 22.50 (ISBN 0-404-55337-0). AMS Pr.

Study of the Supernatural in Three Plays of Shakespeare. Edwin Wiley. LC 74-32191. 1913. lib. bdg. 20.00 (ISBN 0-8414-9382-0). Folcroft.

Study of the Teaching of English Composition in Teachers Colleges of the United States, with a Suggested Course of Procedure. Leon R. Meadows. LC 78-177066. (Columbia University. Teachers College. Contributions to Anthropology: No. 311). Repr. of 1928 ed. 22.50 (ISBN 0-404-55311-7). AMS Pr.

Study of the Test-Performance of American, Mexican & Negro Children see On the Melodic Relativity of Tones.

Study of the Topography & Municipal History of Praeneste. Ralph V. Magoffin. LC 78-63928. (Johns Hopkins University. Studies in the Social Sciences. Twenty-Sixth Ser. 1908: 9-10). Repr. of 1908 ed. 15.00 (ISBN 0-404-61178-8). AMS Pr.

Study of the Toyota Production System from Industrial Engineering Viewpoint. Shigeo Shingo. Ed. by Constance E. Dyer. (Japanese Management Ser.). (Illus.). 300p. 1987. 35.00 (ISBN 0-915299-19-4). Prod Press.

Study of the Tragoediae Sacrae of Father Caussin, 1583-1651. G. D. Hocking. 1973. Repr. of 1943 ed. 14.00 (ISBN 0-384-23783-5). Johnson Repr.

Study of the Traite des Indivisibles of Gilles Persone de Roberval. Evelyn Walker. LC 78-177669. (Columbia University. Teachers College. Contributions to Education: No. 446). Repr. of 1932 ed. 22.50 (ISBN 0-404-55446-6). AMS Pr.

Study of the Treatment of the Philippines in Selected Social Studies Textbooks Published in the U. S. for Use in Elementary & Secondary Schools. Socorro C. Espiritu. LC 74-76469. 1974. Repr. of 1954 ed. soft bdg. 12.95 (ISBN 0-88247-234-8). R & E Pubs.

Study of the Types. Ada R. Habershon. LC 67-24340. 240p. 1975. pap. 7.95 (ISBN 0-8254-2850-5). Kregel.

Study of the United States Steel Corporation in Its Industrial & Legal Aspects. Horace L. Wilgus. LC 73-2541. (Big Business; Economic Power in a Free Society Ser.). Repr. of 1901 ed. 19.00 (ISBN 0-405-05120-4). Ayer Co Pubs.

Study of the Upper Limits of the Development of Intelligence. Florence M. Teagarden. LC 75-177723. (Columbia University. Teachers College. Contributions to Education: No. 156). Repr. of 1924 ed. 22.50 (ISBN 0-404-55156-4). AMS Pr.

Study of the "Villancico" up to Lope De Vega. Sr. M. Paulina St. Amour. LC 78-94170. (Catholic University of America Studies in Romance Languages & Literatures Ser: No. 21). Repr. of 1940 ed. 22.00 (ISBN 0-404-50321-7). AMS Pr.

Study of the Whole of Man: The Significance of the Seven Principles of Man & the Significance of the Monad. Elsie Benjamin. (Study Ser.: No. 6). 41p. 1981. pap. 3.00 (ISBN 0-913004-41-3). Point Loma Pub.

Study of the Works of Alfred Lord Tennyson. Edward C. Tainsh. LC 76-15984. 1974. Repr. of 1893 ed. lib. bdg. 35.00 (ISBN 0-8414-8614-X). Folcroft.

Study of the Works of Alfred Lord Tennyson. Edward C. Tainsh. 1983. Repr. of 1893 ed. lib. bdg. 35.00 (ISBN 0-8492-8412-0). R West.

Study of Theater Organ Style. 1968. pap. 25.00 (ISBN 0-686-09506-5, Pub. by Peer-Southern). Columbia Pictures.

Study of Theology. Gerhard Ebeling. Tr. by Duane A. Priebe. LC 78-5393. pap. 76.50 (2026983). Bks Demand UMI.

Study of Thinking. Jerome Bruner et al. (Social Science Classics Ser.). 352p. 1986. pap. 19.95 (ISBN 0-88738-656-3). Transaction Bks.

Study of Thomas Hardy. Arthur Symons. LC 77-160427. (Studies in Thomas Hardy, No. 14). 1971. Repr. of 1927 ed. lib. bdg. 27.95x (ISBN 0-8383-1297-7). Haskell.

Study of Thomas Hardy & Other Essays. D. H. Lawrence. Ed. by Bruce Steele. (Cambridge Edition of the Works of D. H. Lawrence). 400p. 1985. 44.50 (ISBN 0-521-25252-0); pap. 15.95 (ISBN 0-521-27248-3). Cambridge U Pr.

Study of Thomas Middleton's Tragicomedies. Carolyn Asp. Ed. by James Hogg. (Jacobean Drama Studies). 282p. (Orig.). 1974. pap. 15.00 (ISBN 0-317-40106-8, Pub. by Salzburg Studies). Longwood Pub Group.

Study of Those Who Influence & of Those Who Are Influenced in a Discussion. Ray H. Simpson. LC 70-177778. (Columbia University. Teachers College. Contributions to Education: No. 748). Repr. of 1938 ed. 22.50 (ISBN 0-404-55748-1). AMS Pr.

Study of Time. Incl. Vol. 1. Ed. by J. T. Fraser et al. (Illus.). 550p. 1972. 27.90 (ISBN 0-387-05824-9, Pub. by Springer Vlg); Vol. 2. Ed. by J. T. Fraser & N. Lawrence. (Illus.). 486p. 1975. 28.20 (Pub. by Springer Vlg); Vol. 3. Ed. by J. T. Fraser et al. (Illus.). 727p. 1978. 24.80 (Pub. by Springer Vlg); Vol. 4. Ed. by J. T. Fraser et al. (Illus.). 286p. 1981. avail. (Pub. by Springer Vlg); Vol. 5. Ed. by J. T. Fraser et al. 1985. write for info.. U of Mass Pr.

Study of Time II: 2nd Conference of the International Society for the Study of Time, Summer, 1973. Ed. by J. T. Fraser et al. (Illus.). ix, 487p. 1975. 47.90 (ISBN 0-387-07321-3). Springer-Verlag.

Study of Time III: 3rd Conference of the International Society for the Study of Time. Ed. by J. T. Fraser et al. 1978. 45.00 (ISBN 0-387-90311-9). Springer-Verlag.

Study of Time IV: Proceedings. Ed. by J. T. Fraser et al. (Illus.). 286p. 1981. 56.00 (ISBN 0-387-90594-4). Springer-Verlag.

Study of Tindale's Genesis: Compared with the Genesis of Coverdale & of the Authorized Version. Elizabeth W. Cleaveland. LC 72-341. (Yale Studies in English Ser.: No. 43). xiiii, 258p. 1972. Repr. of 1911 ed. 27.50 (ISBN 0-208-01126-9, Archon). Shoe String.

Study of Tooth Shapes: A Systematic Procedure. Horst Grundler. (Illus.). 104p. 1976. 32.00 (ISBN 3-87652-561-6). Quint Pub Co.

Study of Trade among Developing Countries, 1950-1980: An Appraisal of the Emerging Pattern. H. C. Thomas. 242p. 1988. 65.75 (ISBN 0-444-70385-3, North Holland). Elsevier.

Study of Transfer of Training from High School Subjects to Intelligence. Alexander G. Wesman. LC 78-177650. (Columbia University. Teachers College. Contributions to Education: No. 909). Repr. of 1945 ed. 22.50 (ISBN 0-404-55909-3). AMS Pr.

Study of Travelling Interplanetary Phenomena. Ed. by M. A. Shea et al. (Astrophysics & Space Science Library: No. 71). 1977. lib. bdg. 50.00 (ISBN 90-277-0860-6, Pub. by Reidel Holland). Kluwer Academic.

Study of Trends in World Supply & Demand of Major Agricultural Commodities: Report by the Secretary-General. (Illus.). 1976. 13.50x (ISBN 92-64-11549-8). OECD.

Study of Turnover. James L. Price. 1977. text ed. 10.95x (ISBN 0-8138-1645-9). Iowa St U Pr.

Study of Twentieth-Century Harmony: Harmony in France to 1914 & Contemporary Harmony, 2 vols. in 1. Rene Lenormand & Mosco Carner. LC 76-40058. (Music Reprint Ser). 1975. Repr. of 1940 ed. lib. bdg. 32.50 (ISBN 0-306-70717-9). Da Capo.

Study of Two Levels of Bread Enrichment in Children's Diets. Pauline B. Mack et al. (SRCD M Ser.: Vol. 18, No. 2). 1953. pap. 15.00 (ISBN 0-527-01558-X). Kraus Repr.

Study of Two Methods for Repairing Defects in Line Pipe. J. F. Kiefner & A. R. Duffy. 175p. 1974. 12.00 (ISBN 0-318-12709-1, L22275). Am Gas Assn.

Study of Two, Three & Four Year Interior Design Programs in the United States & Canada, Phase II: Research Report. 61p. 15.00 (ISBN 0-931007-02-X). Foun Int Design.

Study of Two, Three & Four Year Interior Design Programs in the United States & Canada, Phase III: Research Report. 28p. 10.00 (ISBN 0-931007-03-8). Foun Int Design.

Study of Urban Geography. 2nd ed. Harold Carter. LC 76-22730. 398p. 1976. 28.95x (ISBN 0-470-98911-4). Wiley.

Study of Urban History. H. J. Dyos. LC 68-29379. (Illus.). 1969. 27.50 (ISBN 0-312-77280-7). St Martin.

Study of Urbanization. Philip M. Hauser & L. F. Schnore. LC 65-24223. Repr. of 1965 ed. 141.00 (ISBN 0-8357-9987-5, 2013058). Bks Demand UMI.

Study of Values. 3rd ed. Gordon W. Allport et al. test booklets 14.64 (ISBN 0-395-08460-1); instrs' manual 2.40 (ISBN 0-395-08466-0). HM.

Study of Variable Stars Using Small Telescopes. Ed. by John R. Percy. (Illus.). 272p. 1987. 34.50 (ISBN 0-521-33300-8). Cambridge U Pr.

Study of Vasyl' Stefanyk: The Pain at the Heart of Existence. D. S. Struk. LC 72-89110. (Ukrainian Research Foundation Ser.). 200p. 1973. lib. bdg. 13.50 (ISBN 0-87287-056-1). Ukrainian Acad.

Study of Vegetation. Ed. by M. J. Werger. (Illus.). 1979. lib. bdg. 60.50 (ISBN 90-6193-594-6, Pub. by Junk Pubs Netherlands). Kluwer Academic.

Study of Verbal Accompaniments to Educational Motion Pictures. Leon H. Westfall. LC 76-177647. (Columbia University. Teachers College. Contributions to Education: No. 617). Repr. of 1934 ed. 22.50 (ISBN 0-404-55617-5). AMS Pr.

Study of Vermeer. Edward A. Snow. LC 75-32675. pap. 49.00 (ISBN 0-317-55479-4, 2029592). Bks Demand UMI.

Study of Victor Hugo. Algernon Swinburne. LC 76-25888. 1976. Repr. of 1866 ed. lib. bdg. 25.00 (ISBN 0-8414-7781-7). Folcroft.

Study of Victor Hugo. Algernon C. Swinburne. LC 78-113323. 1970. Repr. of 1886 ed. 18.50x (ISBN 0-8046-1000-2, Pub. by Kennikat). Assoc Faculty Pr.

Study of Walter Pater. Arthur Symons. LC 72-195644. 1932. lib. bdg. 32.00 (ISBN 0-8414-8004-4). Folcroft.

Study of War. Reginald Custance. LC 76-110929. 1970. Repr. of 1924 ed. 25.50x (ISBN 0-8046-0912-8, Pub. by Kennikat). Assoc Faculty Pr.

Study of War. Quincy Wright. LC 83-50443. 1983. pap. 22.00x (ISBN 0-226-91001-6, Midway). U of Chicago Pr.

Study of War As a Contribution to Peace. Wolf Mendl. (Orig.). 1983. pap. 2.50x (ISBN 0-87574-247-5, 247). Pendle Hill.

Study of War for Statesmen & Citizens. Ed. by George Aston. LC 72-89260. 216p. 1973. Repr. of 1927 ed. 23.50x (ISBN 0-8046-1762-7, Pub. by Kennikat). Assoc Faculty Pr.

Study of William Shenstone & His Critics. Alice I. Hazeltine. LC 74-1053. 1918. Repr. lib. bdg. 17.00 (ISBN 0-8414-4807-8). Folcroft.

Study of Winchester: Archaeology & History in a British Town, 1961-1983. Martin Biddle. (Albert Reckitt Archaeological Lectures). (Illus.). 43p. 1985. pap. 4.25 (ISBN 0-85672-488-2, Pub. by British Acad). Longwood Pub Group.

Study of Women Delinquents in New York State. Mabel R. Fernald et al. LC 68-55770. (Criminology, Law Enforcement, & Social Problems Ser.: No. 23). 1968. Repr. of 1920 ed. 20.00x (ISBN 0-87585-023-5). Patterson Smith.

Study of Wordsworth. J. C. Smith. LC 68-26218. 1969. Repr. of 1944 ed. 17.00x (ISBN 0-8046-0427-4, Pub. by Kennikat). Assoc Faculty Pr.

Study of Workload Policies & Faculty Resources in Graduate Schools of Social Work. Robert T. Constable & Samuel Weingarten. Date not set. 1.00 (77-550-12). Coun Soc WK Ed.

Study of Workmen's Compensation In Relation To Sheltered Workshops. Henry Viscardi, Jr. & Irving M. Friedman. 68p. 1971. 1.50 (ISBN 0-686-38807-0). Human Res Ctr.

Study of Writing. rev. ed. Ignace J. Gelb. LC 52-10599. (Illus.). 1963. pap. 12.00x (ISBN 0-226-28606-1, P109, Phoen). U of Chicago Pr.

Study of Yoga. J. Ghosh. 276p. 1977. 16.95. Asia Bk Corp.

Study of Yoga. 2nd rev. ed. Jajneshwar Ghosh. 1977. 16.95 (ISBN 0-89684-014-X, Pub. by Motilal Banarsidass India); pap. 12.50 (ISBN 0-89684-015-8). Orient Bk Dist.

Study of Young Gifted Children in Senior High School. Edna E. Lamson. LC 73-176972. (Columbia University. Teachers College. Contributions to Education: No. 424). Repr. of 1930 ed. 22.50 (ISBN 0-404-55424-5). AMS Pr.

Study of Young High School Graduates. Margaret Moore. LC 74-177081. (Columbia University. Teachers College. Contributions to Education: No. 583). Repr. of 1933 ed. 22.50 (ISBN 0-404-55583-7). AMS Pr.

Study of Your Bible. Harold Mackay. 1988. pap. 2.95 (ISBN 0-937396-68-0). Walterick Pubs.

Study on Conventional Disarmament. (Disarmament Study Ser.: No. 12). 67p. 9.50 (ISBN 92-1-142077-6, E.85.IX.1). UN.

Study on Deterrence: Its Implications for Disarmament & the Arms Race, Negotiated Arms Reductions & International Security & Other Related Matters. (Study Ser.: No.17). 142p. 1987. 15.00 (ISBN 92-1-142127-6, E.87.IX.2). UN.

Study on Evaluation of Driver Education. William A. Lybrand et al. LC 75-121262. 225p. 1968. 19.00 (ISBN 0-403-04515-0). Scholarly.

Study on Generation-Skipping Transfers Under the Federal State Tax: Discussion Draft No. 1, Parts 1-3. 206p. 1984. write for info. Am Law Inst.

Study on Inflation & Unemployment. Hak-Un Kim. LC 80-8618. (Outstanding Dissertations in Economics Ser.). 1984. lib. bdg. 24.00 (ISBN 0-8240-4175-5). Garland Pub.

Study on Institutional Advertising. 289p. 1980. pap. 7.50 (ISBN 0-686-47808-8). Amer Bar Assn.

Study on Israeli Nuclear Armament. (Disarmament Study Ser.: No. 6). pap. 4.00 (E.82.1X.2). UN.

Study on Jerusalem. Hassan bin Talal Crown Prince of Jordan. LC 80-506808. 64p. pap. 20.00 (2030349). Bks Demand UMI.

Study on Papuan Music. Jaap Kunst. LC 75-35130. (Illus.). Repr. of 1931 ed. 20.00 (ISBN 0-404-14146-3). AMS Pr.

Study on State-of-the-Art of Dioxin from Combustion Sources. Ed. by Research Committee on Industrial & Municipal Wastes, ASME & A. D. Little, Inc. 1981. 20.00 (ISBN 0-686-34520-7, H00180). ASME.

Study on the Dynamics, Evolution & Consequences of Migrations, II: Three Centuries of Spatial Mobility in France, No. 51. 64p. 1983. pap. text ed. 5.00 (ISBN 92-3-102086-2, U1294, UNESCO). UNIPUB.

Study on the Historiography of the British West Indies to the End of the Nineteenth Century. Elsa V. Goveia. LC 75-20036. 192p. 1980. pap. 8.95 (ISBN 0-88258-048-5). Howard U Pr.

Study on the Library Resources at the Military Institutions in Japan, the United States, England, France, Belgium, the Netherlands, Germany, & Switzerland. Joseph D. Lowe. iii, 13p. 1973. pap. 5.00 (ISBN 0-9605506-1-5). Lowe Pub.

Study on the Origins of Mental Retardation. Matti Iavanainen. (Clinics in Developmental Medicine Ser.: Vol. 51). 182p. 1974. text ed. 23.00 (ISBN 0-433-16300-3, Pub. by Spastics Intl England). Lippincott.

Study on the Potentialities of the Use of a Nuclear Reactor for the Industrialization of Southern Tunisia. (Technical Reports Ser.: No. 35). (Illus.). 30p. 1964. pap. 9.00 (ISBN 92-0-155164-9, IDC35, IAEA). UNIPUB.

Study on the Pure Theory of Production. Sune Carlson. LC 65-18333. 1965. Repr. of 1939 ed. 19.50x (ISBN 0-678-00009-3). Kelley.

Study on the Synoptic Gospels. Eduardo Martinez Dalmau. 1964. 5.95 (ISBN 0-8315-0013-1). Speller.

Study on the Transmission of the Most Noted Masterpieces of "Karae". Takagi Bun. 9p. 1926. 600.00x (Pub. by Han-Shan Tang Ltd). State Mutual Bk.

Study out the Land. facs. ed. Thomas K. Whipple. LC 76-134158. (Essay Index Reprint Ser). 1943. 18.00 (ISBN 0-8369-2088-0). Ayer Co Pubs.

TITLE INDEX

STUFFED OWL: AN ANTHOLOGY

Study Outline & Workbook in the Elements of Music. 8th ed. Frank W. Hill & Roland Searight. 224p. 1984. write for info. wire coilbinding (ISBN 0-697-03608-1); instr's. manual avail. (ISBN 0-697-03622-7). Wm C Brown.
Study Outline & Workbook in the Fundamentals of Music. 9th ed. Frank W. Hill et al. 256p. 1988. write for info. plastic comb. bdg. (ISBN 0-697-03665-0); Instr's Manual. avail. (ISBN 0-697-03666-9). Wm C Brown.
Study Outlines in Physics; Construction & Experimental Evaluation. Jessie Clemensen. LC 71-176654. (Columbia University. Teachers College. Contributions to Education: No. 553). Repr. of 1933 ed. 22.50 (ISBN 0-404-55553-5). AMS Pr.
Study Paper on Parliamentary Procedure. Ira Grinnell. 1971. 5.00 (ISBN 1-55614-008-8). U of SD Gov Res Bur.
Study Power Leader's Guide. The American College Testing Program Staff. (Study Power Ser.). 99p. (Orig.). (YA) (gr. 7 up). 1987. tchr's. ed. 4.00 (ISBN 0-937734-63-2). Am Coll Testing.
Study Power, Managing Time & Environment. The American College Testing Program Staff. (Study Power Ser.). 30p. (Orig.). (YA) (gr. 7 up). 1987. wkbk. 1.00 (ISBN 0-937734-65-9). Am Coll Testing.
Study Power, Preparing for Tests. The American College Testing Program Staff. (Study Power Ser.). 14p. (Orig.). (YA) (gr. 7 up). 1987. wkbk. 1.00 (ISBN 0-937734-69-1). Am Coll Testing.
Study Power, Reading Textbooks. The American College Testing Program Staff. (Study Power Ser.). 21p. (Orig.). (YA) (gr. 7 up). 1987. wkbk. 1.00 (ISBN 0-937734-66-7). Am Coll Testing.
Study Power, Student Workbook Set. The American College Testing Program Staff. (Study Power Ser.). (Orig.). (YA) (gr. 7 up). 1987. wkbk. 5.00 (ISBN 0-937734-64-0). Am Coll Testing.
Study Power, Taking Class Notes. The American College Testing Program Staff. (Study Power Ser.). 22p. (Orig.). (YA) (gr. 7 up). 1987. wkbk. 1.00 (ISBN 0-937734-67-5). Am Coll Testing.
Study Power, Taking Tests. The American College Testing Program Staff. (Study Power Ser.). 13p. (Orig.). (YA) (gr. 7 up). 1987. wkbk. 1.00 (ISBN 0-937734-70-5). Am Coll Testing.
Study Power, Using Resources. The American College Testing Program Staff. (Study Power Ser.). 14p. (Orig.). (YA) (gr. 7 up). 1987. wkbk. 1.00 (ISBN 0-937734-68-3). Am Coll Testing.
Study-Reading & Test-Taking Skills. (Fossil Power Plant Startup Training Ser.: Module 1). (Illus.). 69p. spiral bdg. 18.50 (ISBN 0-87683-358-X). GP Pub.
Study References Useful for the Architect Registration Examination. David K. Ballast. (Architecture Ser.: A 1909). 11p. 1987. 3.75 (ISBN 1-55590-499-8). Vance Biblios.
Study Scores of Historical Styles, Vol. II. Harry B. Lincoln & Stephen Bonta. (Illus.). 400p. 1986. pap. text ed. write for info. (ISBN 0-13-858853-8). P H.
Study Scores of Historical Styles, Vol. 1. Harry Lincoln & Stephen Bonta. 400p. 1986. text ed. write for info. (ISBN 0-13-698267-0). P H.
Study Scrapbook of Virginia. (Illus.). 5.00 (ISBN 0-318-01325-8). VA Chamber Com.
Study Skills: A Student's Guide for Survival. 2nd ed. Robert A. Carman & Royce W. Adams, Jr. LC 83-5925. (Self-Teaching Guides Ser.: No. 1-581). 272p. 1984. pap. 8.95 (ISBN 0-471-88911-3, 1-591). Wiley.
Study Skills: A Student's Guide for Survival. Robert A. Carman & W. Royce Adams, Jr. LC 72-4506. (Wiley-Self Teaching Guides). 256p. 1972. 6.95x (ISBN 0-471-13491-0, Pub. by Wiley Pr). Wiley.
Study Skills Advantage. 1987. Teacher Guide. 1.50 (ISBN 0-88047-080-1); Student Book. 3.95 (ISBN 0-88047-081-X). DOK Pubs.
Study Skills & Writing Process Workbook. 2nd ed. Phyllis Duda & Patrick Sebranek. (Illus.). 160p. (gr. 9-10). 1984. pap. text ed. 5.00x (ISBN 0-9605312-2-X); tchr's ed. 5.00 (ISBN 0-9605312-3-8). Write Source.
Study Skills: Establishing a Comprehensive Program at the College Level. Joseph E. Talley & Lawrence H. Henning. (Illus.). 86p. 1981. spiral bdg. 12.00 (ISBN 0-398-04561-5). C C Thomas.
Study Skills for Adults Returning to School. 2nd ed. Jerold W. Apps. 240p. 1982. pap. text ed. 16.95x (ISBN 0-07-002165-1). McGraw.
Study Skills for College. Eleanor C. Haburton. (Orig.). 1981. pap. text ed. write for info. (ISBN 0-673-39267-8). Scott F.
Study Skills for College Athletes. Walter Pauk. LC 86-60912. (Illus.). 105p. 1987. pap. 8.95 (ISBN 0-9614487-0-9). Reston-Stuart Pub.
Study Skills for Community & Junior Colleges. Walter Pauk. LC 87-60317. (Illus.). 126p. 1987. pap. text ed. 8.95 (ISBN 0-9614487-1-7). Reston-Stuart Pub.
Study Skills for Students of English as a Second Language. 2nd ed. Richard C. Yorkey. (Illus.). 256p. (gr. 11-12). 1982. pap. 7.52x (ISBN 0-07-072316-8). McGraw.
Study Skills for Success: How to Learn Effectively. William M. Saleebey. LC 81-83180. (Illus.). xii, 112p. pap. text ed. 7.95x (ISBN 0-935920-25-0). Natl Pub Black Hills.
Study Skills GED Student Textbook. E. C. Keroack et al. Ed. by P. Klein. 132p. (Orig.). 1986. pap. text ed. 5.25 (ISBN 0-88210-177-3). Natl Assn Principals.
Study Skills GED Teachers Manual. E. C. Keroack et al. Ed. by P. Klein. 52p. (Orig.). 1986. pap. 4.50 (ISBN 0-88210-178-1). Natl Assn Principals.
Study Skills Handbook. Harry S. Dahlstrom. (Illus.). 50p. (Orig., Prog. Bk.). 1987. pap. text ed. 3.79 (ISBN 0-940712-10-5, Study Buddy). Dahlstrom & Co.
Study Skills Handbook: A Guide for All Teachers. Kenneth G. Graham & H. Alan Robinson. (IRA Bk.: No. 858). 136p. 1984. 8.00 (ISBN 0-87207-858-2). Intl Reading.
Study Skills in the Content Areas. Eunice N. Askov & Karlyn Kamm. 1985. 25.00 (ISBN 0-205-07743-9, 237743). Allyn.
Study Skills Shortcake. Linda Schwartz. (Study Skills Ser.). 32p. (gr. 4-6). 1979. 3.95 (ISBN 0-88160-071-7, LW 804). Learning Wks.
Study Skills Sorcery. Leslie S. Zakalik. (Study Skills Ser.). 48p. (gr. 4-6). 1978. 4.95 (ISBN 0-88160-028-8, LW 213). Learning Wks.
Study Skills Strategies. Uelaine Lengefeld. LC 85-72810. (Fifty-Minute Guide Ser.). (Illus.). 72p. (Orig.). 1987. pap. 6.95 (ISBN 0-931961-05-X). Crisp Pubns.
Study Skills Strategies. rev. ed. Uelaine Lengefeld. (CRISP Publications 50-Minute Ser.). Date not set. 6.95. Human Res Dev Pr.
Study Skills: The Parent Connection. Patricia S. Olson. Ed. by Karen M. Hess. (Illus.). 50p. 1988. pap. text ed. 7.50 (ISBN 0-929168-00-3). Milestone Pub.
Study Skills Workout, Gr 5-8. Susan C. Bartoletti & Elaine S. Lisandrelli. 1987. pap. 8.95 (ISBN 0-673-18995-3). Scott F.
Study Skills Workshop Kit. Incl. Level 1. (gr. 5-9). 1980 (ISBN 0-88210-112-9); Level II. (gr. 8-10). 1979 (ISBN -088210-113-7). 13.75 (ISBN 0-317-31958-2). Natl Assn Principals.
Study Smarter-Save Time-Learn More: A Home Study Course. Michael A. Lisausky. (Home Study Ser.). 40p. wkbk. 28.00 (ISBN 0-939926-36-9); audio tape incl. (ISBN 0-939926-35-0). Fruition Pubns.
Study Smarts: How to Learn More in Less Time. Judi Kesselman-Turkel & Franklynn Peterson. 64p. 1981. pap. 4.95 (ISBN 0-8092-5852-8). Contemp Bks.
Study Tactics. William H. Armstrong. 272p. (gr. 10-12). 1983. pap. text ed. 6.95 (ISBN 0-8120-2590-3). Barron.
Study Techniques. Linda F. Annis. 136p. 1983. pap. text ed. write for info. (ISBN 0-697-06069-1). Wm C Brown.
Study Text II: Pastoral Care of Sick & Dying. 56p. 1984. pap. 3.95 (ISBN 1-55586-918-1). US Catholic.
Study Text III: Ministries in the Church. 68p. 1973. pap. 3.95 (ISBN 1-55586-304-3). US Catholic.
Study Text IX: Liturgical Year Celebrating Mystery of Christ & His Saints. 112p. 1985. pap. 6.95 (ISBN 1-55586-930-0). US Catholic.
Study Text 11: Eucharistic Worship & Devotion Outside Mass. Anthony S. Dann. (Study Texts Ser.). 56p. (Orig.). 1987. pap. 5.95 (ISBN 1-55586-178-4). US Catholic.
Study Tips: How to Study Effectively & Get Better Grades. 2nd ed. William H. Armstrong. LC 75-16482. (gr. 7-12). 1983. pap. text ed. 4.95 (ISBN 0-8120-2366-8). Barron.
Study to Evaluate the Stability of Underground Gas Storage Reservoirs. American Gas Association, Pipeline Research Committee & H. Reginald Hardy. 404p. 1972. 10.00 (ISBN 0-318-12710-5, L19724). Am Gas Assn.
Study War No More. Ed. by David S. Young. (Orig.). 1981. pap. 3.95 (ISBN 0-87178-822-5). Brethren.
Study: With Critical & Explanatory Notes of Alfred Tennyson's Poem "the Princess". Samuel E. Dawson. LC 72-13042. 1973. lib. bdg. 17.00 (ISBN 0-8414-1040-2). Folcroft.
Study Writing. L. Hamp-Lyons & B. Heasley. 176p. 1987. pap. 8.95 (ISBN 0-521-31558-1). Cambridge U Pr.
Studying a Study & Testing a Test: How to Read the Medical Literature. Richard K. Riegelman. 1981. pap. text ed. 18.50 (ISBN 0-316-74518-9). Little.
Studying Africa in Elementary & Secondary Schools. 3rd ed. Leonard S. Kenworthy. LC 70-105869. (World Affairs Guides). pap. 20.00 (ISBN 0-317-41867-X, 2026030). Bks Demand UMI.
Studying American Music. Richard Crawford. (I. S. A. M. Special Publications Ser.: No. 3). 24p. (Orig.). 1985. pap. 3.00 (ISBN 0-914678-25-6). Inst Am Music.
Studying Art History. Charles R. Jansen. (Illus.). 96p. 1986. pap. text ed. write for info (ISBN 0-13-858705-1). P-H.
Studying Behavior in Natural Settings. Richard M. Brandt. LC 81-40189. (Illus.). 416p. 1981. lib. bdg. 35.75 (ISBN 0-8191-1829-X); pap. text ed. 18.50 (ISBN 0-8191-1830-3). U Pr of Amer.
Studying Birds in the Garden. T. Jennings. (YA) 1975. 9.45 (ISBN 0-08-017802-2). Pergamon.
Studying Children: An Introduction to Research Methods. Ross Vasta. LC 78-25941. (Psychology Ser.). (Illus.). 212p. 1979. pap. text ed. 11.95 (ISBN 0-7167-1068-4). W H Freeman.
Studying Children: Observing & Participating. Draper. 1977. pap. text ed. 15.00 (ISBN 0-02-665770-8). Bennett IL.
Studying China in Elementary & Secondary Schools. Leonard S. Kenworthy. LC 74-23808. (World Affairs Guides). pap. 20.00 (ISBN 0-317-41908-0, 2026033). Bks Demand UMI.
Studying Cultures. C. Cherryholmes & G. Manson. (Illus.). (gr. 4). 1979. text ed. 22.40 (ISBN 0-07-011984-8). McGraw.
Studying Drug Abuse. Ed. by Lee N. Robins. (Psychosocial Epidemiology Ser.: Vol. 6). (Illus.). 256p. 1985. text ed. 35.00 (ISBN 0-8135-1085-6); pap. text ed. 16.00 (ISBN 0-8135-1086-4). Rutgers U Pr.
Studying Effectively. C. Gilbert Wrenn & Robert P. Larsen. 1955. pap. 0.95x (ISBN 0-8047-1071-6). Stanford U Pr.
Studying for a Drivers License. rev. ed. Donald Joyce. Ed. by Mary Ann Lapinski. (Wheels Ser.). (Illus.). 64p. (gr. 10-12). 1985. pap. text ed. 3.88 (ISBN 0-88336-441-7). New Readers.
Studying Health & Disease. Open University Health & Disease Course Team. (Health & Disease Ser.). 112p. 1985. pap. 21.00x (ISBN 0-335-15050-0, Open U Pr). Taylor & Francis.
Studying History: An Introduction to Methods & Structure. Paul L. Ward. LC 84-73235. (Discussions on Teaching Ser.: No. 1). 35p. 1985. pap. 3.50 (ISBN 0-87229-026-3). Am Hist Assn.
Studying History: How & Why. 3rd ed. Robert V. Daniels. LC 80-18406. 128p. 1981. pap. text ed. write for info. (ISBN 0-13-858738-8). P-H.
Studying Implementation: Methodological & Administrative Issues. Walter Williams et al. LC 81-21734. (Chatham House Series on Change in American Politics). 192p. (Orig.). 1982. pap. text ed. 12.95x (ISBN 0-934540-12-8). Chatham Hse Pubs.
Studying India in Elementary & Secondary Schools. Leonard S. Kenworthy. LC 74-23809. (World Affairs Guides). pap. 20.00 (ISBN 0-317-41905-6, 2026034). Bks Demand UMI.
Studying Japan in Elementary & Secondary Schools. Leonard S. Kenworthy. LC 74-23896. (His World Affairs Guides Ser.). (Illus.). 68p. pap. 20.00 (2056464). Bks Demand UMI.
Studying Latin America: Essays in Honor of Preston E. James. Ed. by David J. Robinson. LC 80-12413. (Dellplain Latin American Studies Ser.: No. 4). pap. 72.30 (ISBN 0-317-28159-3, 2022591). Bks Demand UMI.
Studying Law: An Introduction. Charles D. Kelso & Randall R. Kelso. LC 84-7345. (American Casebook Ser.). 587p. 1984. text ed. 25.95 (ISBN 0-314-81472-8). West Pub.
Studying Mathematics. Kay Hudspeth & Lewis Hirsh. 64p. 1982. saddle stitch 6.25 (ISBN 0-8403-2768-4). Kendall-Hunt.
Studying Music History: Learning, Reasoning & Writing about Music History & Literature. David Poultney. 256p. 1983. pap. text ed. write for info (ISBN 0-13-858860-0). P-H.
Studying Organizational Communication. Nancy Wyatt & Gerald M. Phillips. Ed. by Lee Thayer. LC 87-33443. (People, Communication, Organization Ser.). 288p. 1988. text ed. 45.00 (ISBN 0-89391-473-8). Ablex Pub.
Studying People: A Primer in the Ethnics of Social Research. Robert D. Reece & Harvey A. Siegel. LC 86-18059. 272p. (Orig.). 1986. 29.95 (ISBN 0-86554-220-1, H198); pap. 18.75 (ISBN 0-86554-221-X, P28). Mercer Univ Pr.
Studying Personality: Student Booklet. American Psychological Association Staff. (Human Behavior Curriculum Project Ser.). 75p. (Orig.). (gr. 9-12). 1981. pap. text ed. 3.95x (ISBN 0-8077-2627-3). Tchrs Coll.
Studying Personality: Teachers Manual & Duplication Masters. American Psychological Association Staff. (Human Behavior Curriculum Project Ser.). (Orig.). (gr. 9-12). 1981. pap. 9.95x (ISBN 0-8077-2628-1). Tchrs Coll.
Studying Russian & Soviet History. Ed. by Abraham S. Ascher. 122p. (Orig.). 1987. pap. 9.95 (ISBN 0-89994-317-9). Soc Sci Ed.
Studying School Children in Uganda: Four Reports of Exploratory Research. Millie Almy et al. LC 74-122748. Repr. of 1970 ed. 21.30 (ISBN 0-8357-9607-8, 2017763). Bks Demand UMI.
Studying School Effectiveness. Ed. by David Reynolds. 216p. 1985. text ed. 33.00x (ISBN 1-85000-023-9, Falmer Pr); pap. text ed. 18.00x (ISBN 1-85000-024-7, Falmer Pr). Taylor & Francis.
Studying Shakespeare: An Introduction. Andrew Gurr. 96p. 1988. pap. text ed. 9.95 (ISBN 0-7131-6539-1, Pub. by E Arnold UK). Routledge Chapman & Hall.
Studying Smart: Time Management for College Students. Diana Schard & Pam Hait. LC 84-43238. 96p. (Orig.). 1985. pap. 4.95 (ISBN 0-06-464111-2, BN 4111, B&N Bks). Har-Row.
Studying Society: An Introduction to Social Science. G. B. Atkinson et al. 192p. 1987. 39.95x (ISBN 0-19-878013-3); pap. 12.95 (ISBN 0-19-878012-5). Oxford U Pr.
Studying South America in Elementary & Secondary Schools. 2nd ed. Leonard S. Kenworthy. LC 65-19211. (World Affairs Guides). pap. 20.00 (ISBN 0-317-41865-3, 2026031). Bks Demand UMI.
Studying Student Attrition. Ed. by Ernest T. Pascarella. LC 81-48576. (Institutional Research Ser.: No. 36). 1982. pap. text ed. 12.95x (ISBN 0-87589-906-4). Jossey-Bass.
Studying Suzuki Piano: More Than Music: A Handbook for Teachers, Parents & Students. Carole L. Bigler & Valery Lloyd-Watts. LC 78-73088. (Illus., Orig.). 1979. pap. 24.95 (ISBN 0-918194-06-7, Pub. by Ability Devel). Accura.
Studying Teaching. 2nd ed. James Raths et al. LC 70-123086. 1971. P-H.
Studying, Teaching & Learning: Trends in Soviet & American Research. Ed. by Robert Tabachnick et al. LC 80-27528. (Comparative Education Ser.). 270p. 1981. 38.95 (ISBN 0-275-90729-5, C0729). Praeger.
Studying the Content Areas: Mathematics & Business, Bk. 2. Carole Bogue. Ed. by Karen H. Davis. (Illus.). 467p. 1988. pap. 28.00 (ISBN 0-943202-28-0). H & H Pub.
Studying the Content Areas: Social Sciences & the Sciences. Carole Bogue. Ed. by Karen H. Davis. (Illus.). 455p. 1988. pap. 28.00 (ISBN 0-943202-26-4). H & H Pub.
Studying the Ground for Holes. Michael Andre. LC 78-5184. (Illus.). 1978. pap. 3.00 (ISBN 0-913722-14-6, Pub by Release). Small Pr Dist.
Studying the Middle East in Elementary & Secondary Schools. Leonard S. Kenworthy. LC 65-19213. pap. 15.00 (ISBN 0-8357-9608-6, 2016935). Bks Demand UMI.
Studying the New Testament. Morna D. Hooker. LC 82-70959. 224p. (Orig.). 1982. pap. 12.95 (ISBN 0-8066-1934-1, 10-6140). Augsburg.
Studying the Novice Programmer. E. Soloway & J. C. Spohrer. (Interacting with Computers: IWC Ser.). 224p. Date not set. price not set (ISBN 0-8058-0002-6); pap. price not set (ISBN 0-8058-0003-4). L Erlbaum Assocs.
Studying the Old Testament. Henry McKeating. LC 82-70960. 224p. (Orig.). 1982. pap. 10.95 (ISBN 0-8066-1935-X, 10-6141). Augsburg.
Studying the Old Testament. Annemarie Ohler. 400p. 42.95 (ISBN 0-567-09335-2, Pub. by T & T Clard Ltd UK). Fortress.
Studying the Presidency. Ed. by George C. Edwards, III & Stephen J. Wayne. LC 82-17472. 320p. 1983. text ed. 19.95x (ISBN 0-87049-378-7); pap. text ed. 12.95x (ISBN 0-87049-379-5). U of Tenn Pr.
Studying the Short-Story. J. Berg Esenwein. 440p. 1983. Repr. of 1928 ed. lib. bdg. 40.00 (ISBN 0-89987-222-0). Darby Bks.
Studying the U. S. S. R. in Elementary & Secondary Schools. Leonard S. Kenworthy. LC 77-94510. (World Affairs Guides Ser.). pap. 20.00 (ISBN 0-317-41914-5, 2026032). Bks Demand UMI.
Studying Visual Communication. Sol Worth. Ed. by Larry Gross. (Conduct & Communication Ser.). 1981. 30.95x (ISBN 0-8122-7791-0); pap. 15.95x (ISBN 0-8122-1116-2). U of Pa Pr.
Studying with the Masters. Dean Larson. (Illus.). 144p. 1986. 24.95 (ISBN 0-8230-4994-9). Watson-Guptill.
Studying Your Community. Roland L. Warren. LC 55-7727. 1965. pap. 9.95 (ISBN 0-02-933990-1). Free Pr.
Stufen des Organischen und der Mensch: Einleitung in die philosophische Anthropologie. 3rd ed. Helmuth Plessner. (Sammlung Goeschen: No. 2200). 373p. 1975. 9.95x (ISBN 3-11-005985-1). De Gruyter.
Stuff! Good Players Should Know. Dick DeVenzio. (Illus.). 320p. 1983. 13.95 (ISBN 0-910305-00-5). Fool Court.
Stuff of Dreams. Beryl Walthew. 1985. 24.95x (ISBN 0-7090-2209-3, Pub. by R Hale Ltd UK). State Mutual Bk.
Stuff of Dreams: Native America Dolls. Mary J. Lenz. LC 86-61168. (Illus.). 96p. 1986. pap. 15.95 (ISBN 0-934490-43-0). Mus Am Ind.
Stuff of Fiction. Gerald W. Brace. LC 71-77391. 1969 o.p. 4.50 (ISBN 0-393-04312-6, Norton Lib); pap. 1.95x 1972 (ISBN 0-393-00648-4). Norton.
Stuff of Sleep & Dreams: Experiments in Literary Psychology. Leon Edel. LC 81-47787. 224p. 1982. 19.50i (ISBN 0-06-014929-9, HarpT). Har-Row.
Stuff of Sleep & Dreams: Experiments in Literary Psychology. Leon Edel. 368p. 1983. pap. 4.95 (ISBN 0-380-63719-7, 63719, Discus). Avon.
Stuff the Lady's Hatbox. Carlton E. Morse. (I Love a Mystery Novel Ser.). 342p. (Orig.). 1988. 16.95 (ISBN 0-940249-03-0); pap. 9.95 (ISBN 0-940249-04-9). Seven Stones Pr.
Stuff We're Made Of: The Positive Approach to Health Through Nutrition. Jorian Jenks. 1959. 5.00 (ISBN 0-8159-6829-9). Devin.
Stuffed Feet. Mike Thaler. (Illus.). 107p. (Orig.). (gr. k up). 1983. pap. 2.50 (ISBN 0-380-84673-X, 84673, Camelot). Avon.
Stuffed Owl: An Anthology of Bad Verse. Ed. by D. Wyndham Lewis & Charles Lee. 296p. 1978. 9.95x (ISBN 0-460-00186-8, Evman). Biblio Dist.

Stuffed Owl: An Anthology of Bad Verse. Selected by D. Wyndham Lewis & Charles Lee. 296p. 1984. pap. 5.95x (ISBN 0-460-01186-3, DEL-05219, Pub. by Evman England). Biblio Dist.
Stuffed Owl: An Anthology of Bad Verse. Ed. by Dominic B. Lewis & Charles Lee. LC 76-42707. (Illus.). Repr. of 1948 ed. 16.50 (ISBN 0-404-15371-2). AMS Pr.
Stuffed Peacocks. facsimile ed. Emily Clark. LC 75-110181. (Short Story Index Reprint Ser.). 1927. 18.00 (ISBN 0-8369-3332-X). Ayer Co Pubs.
Stuffed Shirts. facsimile ed. Clare Booth Luce. LC 77-163043. (Short Story Index Reprint Ser.). Repr. of 1931 ed. 22.00 (ISBN 0-8369-3957-3). Ayer Co Pubs.
Stuffed Spuds: One Hundred Meals in a Potato. Jeanne Jones. LC 82-11361. 132p. (Orig.). 1982. o. p. 11.95 (ISBN 0-87131-392-8); pap. 5.95 (ISBN 0-87131-385-5). M Evans.
Stuffin' Muffin: Muffin Pan Cooking for Kids. Strom Scherie. (Illus.). 100p. (Orig.). (gr. 4-7). 1982. pap. 9.95 (ISBN 0-9606964-9-0). Yng Peoples Pr.
Stuffy: The Life of Newspaper Pioneer Basil "Stuffy" Walters. Raymond Moscowitz. 196p. 1982. 12.95 (ISBN 0-8138-1896-6). Iowa St U Pr.
Stuka-JU-87. A. J. Barker. (Illus.). 64p. 1983. pap. write for info (ISBN 0-13-858837-6). P-H.
Stuka Pilot. Hans-Ulrich Rudel. 240p. 1987. 12.95. Noontide.
Stumbling Block: A Sociological Study of the Relationship Between Selected Religious Norms & Drinking Behavior. Jerome H. Skolnick. Ed. by Harriet Zuckerman & Robert K. Merton. LC 79-9028. (Dissertations on Sociology). 1980. lib. bdg. 40.00x (ISBN 0-405-12995-5). Ayer Co Pubs.
Stumbling Blocks or Stepping Stones: Spiritual Answers to Psychological Questions. J. Groeschel. 180p. 1987. pap. 8.95 (ISBN 0-8091-2896-9). Paulist Pr.
Stumbling on Melons. T. R. Garnett. 253p. 1986. 24.95 (ISBN 0-85091-187-7, Pub. by Lothian). Intl Spec Bk.
Stumbling Toward Maturity. Arnold T. Olson. LC 81-66943. (Heritage Ser.: Vol. 3). 208p. 1981. 8.95 (ISBN 0-911802-50-9). Free Church Pubns.
Stumped: The Forest Industry in Transition. Ken Drushka. (Illus.). 304p. pap. 16.95 (ISBN 0-295-96299-2). U of Wash Pr.
Stumpwork: Historical & Contemporary Raised Embroidery. Muriel Best. (Illus.). 136p. 1987. 29.95 (ISBN 0-7134-5572-1, Pub. by Batsford England). David & Charles.
Stung by Salt & War: Creative Texts of the Italian Avant-Gardist F.T. Marinetti. Richard Pioli. (Reading Plus Ser.: Vol. 2). 187p. 1987. text ed. 31.50 (ISBN 0-8204-0381-4). P Lang Pubs.
Stunning the Punters. Robert Sproat. 200p. (Orig.). 1986. pap. 11.95 (ISBN 0-571-13823-3). Faber & Faber.
Stunt Dogs. Jane M. Leder. Ed. by Howard Schroeder. LC 85-19469. (Working Dogs Ser.). (Illus.). 48p. (gr. 5-6). 1985. 9.95 (ISBN 0-89686-289-5). Crestwood Hse.
Stunt People. R. Hepworth. (Dangerous Jobs Ser.). (Illus.). 32p. (gr. 4 up). Date not set. PLB 13.27 (ISBN 0-86592-415-5). Rourke Corp.
Stunt Planes. Rosemary Grimm. Ed. by Carnival Enterprises Staff. LC 87-29020. (Super-Charged! Ser.). (Illus.). 48p. (gr. 5-6). 1988. PLB 10.95 (ISBN 0-89686-363-8). Crestwood Hse.
Stunt Riding. Norman Barrett. (Picture Library). (Illus.). 32p. (gr. k-3). 1987. PLB 9.90 (ISBN 0-531-10276-9). Watts.
Stuntmen & Special Effects. (Ripley's Believe It or Not Ser.). (Illus.). (gr. 8-12). 1982. 7.95 (ISBN 0-698-20564-2, Coward). Putnam Pub Group.
Stunts & Tumbling Skills & Activities. Ellen Curtis-Pierce & Janet Wessel. (ps). 1998. pap. 7.95 (ISBN 0-8224-5358-4). D S Lake Pubs.
Stupid American. Frank Taberski, Jr. 1986. 8.95 (ISBN 0-533-06773-1). Vantage.
Stupid Bar Tricks. Adam Steinfeld & Bret McCormick. (Illus.). 96p. (Orig.). 1986. pap. 5.95 (ISBN 0-939639-00-9). Variety Artists Bks.
Stupid Bar Tricks. Adam Steinfeld & Bret McCormick. LC 87-43260. (Illus.). 96p. 1988. lib. bdg. 12.90 (ISBN 0-89471-620-4); pap. 4.95 (ISBN 0-89471-619-0). Running Pr.
Stupids Die. Harry Allard & James Marshall. (Illus.). (gr. k-3). 1981. 12.95 (ISBN 0-395-30347-8). HM.
Stupids Die. James Marshall. (gr. k-3). 1985. 3.95 (ISBN 0-317-18512-8). HM.
Stupids Have a Ball. Harry Allard. LC 77-27660. (Illus.). (gr. k-3). 1978. PLB 12.95 (ISBN 0-395-26497-9). HM.
Stupids Have a Ball. Harry Allard. (Illus.). 32p. (gr. k-3). pap. 3.95 (ISBN 0-395-36169-9, 4-90940). HM.
Stupids Step Out. Harry Allard. LC 73-21698. (Illus.). 32p. (gr. k-3). 1974. PLB 12.95 (ISBN 0-395-18513-0). HM.
Stupids Step Out. Harry Allard & James Marshall. (Illus.). (gr. k-3). 1977. pap. 3.95 (ISBN 0-395-25377-2). HM.
Sturctural Analysis for Micros see Structural Analysis Software for Micros.
Sturge Moore & the Life of Art. Frederick L. Gwynn. 159p. 1980. Repr. of 1952 ed. lib. bdg. 30.00 (ISBN 0-89984-249-6). Century Bookbindery.
Sturgeon Fishing. Larry Leonard. (Illus.). 1987. pap. 7.95 (ISBN 0-936608-57-9). F Amato Pubns.
Sturla the Historian. William P. Ker. pap. 20.00 (ISBN 0-317-08057-1, 2051176). Bks Demand UMI.
Sturlanga Saga: Including the Islendinga Saga of Lawman Sturla Thordsson & Other Works, 2 vols. Ed. by Gudbrand Vigfusson. (Illus.). Vol. 1. pap. 157.30 (ISBN 0-317-10727-5, 2051168); Vol. 2. pap. 138.50 (ISBN 0-317-10728-3). Bks Demand UMI.
Sturlunga Saga. Julia H. McGrew. Incl. Vol.1. (Vol. 9). 1970. 10.50 (ISBN 0-89067-020-X); Vol. 2. (Vol. 10). 550p. 1974. 12.50 (ISBN 0-89067-025-0). LC 71-120536. (Library of Scandinavian Literature Ser.). Am Scandinavian.
Sturlunga Saga, Vol. 1: The Saga of Hvamm-Sturla & the Sage of the Icelanders. Ed. by Julia H. McGrew. LC 71-120536. (Library of Scandinavian Literature). (Illus.). 1970. lib. bdg. 49.00 (ISBN 0-8057-3364-7); pap. text ed. 9.75x (ISBN 0-8290-2036-5). Irvington.
Sturlunga Saga, Vol. 2: Shorter Sagas of the Icelanders. Ed. by Julia H. McGrew & George Thomas. LC 71-120536. (Library of Scandinavian Literature). (Illus.). 1974. lib. bdg. 49.00 (ISBN 0-8057-3365-5); pap. text ed. 11.75x (ISBN 0-8290-2035-7). Irvington.
Sturm: A Focus of Expressionism. M. S. Jones. LC 83-72542. (Studies in German Literature, Linguistics & Culture: Vol. 16). (Illus.). 275p. 1984. 26.50x (ISBN 0-938100-26-2). Camden Hse.
Sturm-Liouville Operators & Applications. Vladimir A. Marchenko. (Operator Theory Ser.: Vol. 22). 392p. 1986. 71.50 (ISBN 0-8176-1794-9). Birkhauser.
Sturm, Ruger 10-22 Rifle & .44 Magnum Carbine. Duncan Long. (Illus.). 108p. 1988. pap. text ed. 10.00 (ISBN 0-87364-449-2). Paladin Pr.
Sturman Collection: Twentieth Century Works on Paper. Tucson Museum of Art Staff et al. LC 86-51143. (Illus.). 43p. 1986. pap. 12.00 (ISBN 0-911611-12-6). Tucson Mus Art.
Sturmgeschutz III in Action. (Armor in Action Ser.). (Illus.). 1984. pap. 5.95 (ISBN 0-89747-047-8, 2014). Squad Sig Pubns.
Sturmian Theory for Ordinary Differential Equations. William T. Reid. (Applied Mathematical Sciences: Vol. 31). 559p. 1980. pap. 41.00 (ISBN 0-387-90542-1). Springer-Verlag.
Sturtevant's Edible Plants of the World. Hedrick. 686p. 1972. pap. 10.95 (ISBN 0-486-20459-6). Dover.
Sturz Des Antichrist see Fall of Antichrist.
Stutterer's Story. Frederick P. Murray & Susan G. Edwards. 164p. 1980. pap. 8.95x. Inter Print Pubs.
Stutterin' Boy: The Autobiography of Mel Tillis, America's Beloved Star of Country Music. Mel Tillis & Walter Wager. LC 83-43114. (Illus.). 288p. 1984. 15.95 (ISBN 0-89256-263-3). Rawson Assocs.
Stuttering. Edward G. Conture. (Illus.). 208p. 1982. write for info. (ISBN 0-13-858977-1). P-H.
Stuttering: A New Look at an Old Problem Based on Neurophysiological Aspects. Charles P. Overstake. (Illus.). 160p. 1979. 17.25 (ISBN 0-398-03896-1). C C Thomas.
Stuttering: A Psychoanalytic Understanding. I. Peter Glauber. Ed. by Helen M. Glauber. LC 82-8125. 208p. 1982. 29.95 (ISBN 0-89885-154-8). Human Sci Pr.
Stuttering: An Integration of Contemporary Therapies, No. 16. Theodore Peters & Barry Guitar. LC 80-51679. 1980. pap. 1.50 (ISBN 0-933388-15-2). Speech Found Am.
Stuttering & Personality Dynamics: Play Therapy, Projective Therapy, & Counseling. Albert T. Murphy & Ruth M. Fitzsimons. LC 60-14180. pap. 131.80 (ISBN 0-317-07907-7, 2012382). Bks Demand UMI.
Stuttering Behavior Therapy: Current Status & Experimental Foundations. Roger J. Ingham. LC 83-7593. 486p. 1984. text ed. 46.50 (ISBN 0-316-41810-2, 418102). College-Hill.
Stuttering: Differential Evaluation & Therapy. Hugo H. Gregory. Ed. by Harvey Halpern. LC 86-490. (The Pro-Ed Studies in Communicative Disorders). (Illus.). 64p. (Orig.). 1986. pap. text ed. 7.00x (ISBN 0-89079-093-0, 1383). Pro Ed.
Stuttering Disorders, Vol. 8: Current Therapy of Communication Disorders. William H. Perkins. 255p. 1985. text ed. 17.50 (ISBN 0-86577-102-2). Thieme Med Pubs.
Stuttering-In Perspective: Practical Advice for Those Who Must Deal with Stuttering-For Adult Stutterers & Parents of Young Stutterers. Lloyd M. Hulit. 152p. 1985. 21.75x (ISBN 0-398-05125-9). C C Thomas.
Stuttering: Significant Theories & Therapies. rev. ed. Eugene F. Hahn. Ed. by Elise S. Hahn. 1956. 15.00x (ISBN 0-8047-0376-0). Stanford U Pr.
Stuttering: Successes & Failures in Therapy, No. 6. Ed. by Harold L. Luper. LC 82-170724. 148p. 1968. pap. 1.50 (ISBN 0-933388-04-7). Speech Found Am.
Stuttering: The Disorder of Many Theories. Gerald Jonas. 68p. 1977. pap. 2.95 (ISBN 0-374-51429-1). FS&G.
Stuttering: Then & Now. George Shames & Herbert Rubin. 496p. 1986. text ed. 33.95 (ISBN 0-675-20125-X). Merrill.
Stuttering Therapies: Practical Approaches. Ed. by Celia Levy. 224p. 1987. pap. text ed. 25.95x (ISBN 0-7099-4145-5, Pub. by Croom Helm UK). Routledge Chapman & Hall.
Stuttering Therapy: A Guide to the Charles Van Riper Approach. Lloyd M. Hulit. 92p. 1985. 16.25x (ISBN 0-398-05124-0). C C Thomas.
Stuttering Therapy: Prevention & Intervention with Children, No. 20. Ed. by Gregory H. Hugo. LC 85-189819. 152p. pap. 1.50 (ISBN 0-933388-22-5). Speech Found Am.
Stuttering Therapy, Transfer & Maintenance, No. 19. Ed. by Jane Fraser Gruss. LC 83-240657. 112p. 1985. pap. 1.50 (ISBN 0-933388-19-5). Speech Found Am.
Stuttering: Training the Therapist, No. 5. Ed. by Charles Van Riper. LC 66-7072. 96p. 1966. pap. 0.50 (ISBN 0-933388-03-9). Speech Found Am.
Stuttering Treatment: A Comprehensive Clinical Guide. G. Beverly Wells. (Illus.). 208p. 1987. pap. text ed. write for info. (ISBN 0-13-859000-1). P-H.
Stuttering: What It Is & What to Do About It. Stanley Ainsworth. LC 74-76252. (Speech & Hearing Ser.). 101p. (Orig.). 1975. pap. text ed. 4.95 (ISBN 0-8220-1805-5). Cliffs.
Stuttering Words. LC 86-82260. (Publications on Stuttering: No. 2). 64p. pap. 0.50 (ISBN 0-933388-25-X). Speech Found Am.
Stuttgart's Profile Catalog: Experimental Results from the Laminar Wind Tunnel of the Institute for Aero- & Gas-Dynamics. D. Althaus & F. X. Wortmann. 1981. 125.00 (ISBN 3-528-08464-2, Pub. by Vieweg & Sohn Germany). IPS.
Stuyvesant Square. Margaret Lewerth. 576p. 1987. 18.95 (ISBN 0-525-24538-3). Dutton.
Stygofauna Mundi: A Faunistic, Distributional & Ecological Synthesis of the World Fauna Inhabiting Subterranean Waters, including the Marine Interstitial. Lazare Botosaneanu. vi, 740p. 1986. 218.25 (ISBN 90-04-07571-2, Pub. by E J Brill). Heinman.
Stylasteridae (Hydrozoa: Hydroida) of the Galapagos Islands. Stephen D. Cairns. LC 85-600176. (Smithsonian Contributions to Zoology: No. 426). pap. 20.00 (2027139). Bks Demand UMI.
Style. Walter Raleigh. LC 73-16467. 1973. lib. bdg. 30.50 (ISBN 0-8414-7272-6). Folcroft.
Style. Walter Raleigh. Ed. by Fredeman & Nadel. (Victorian Muse: Selected Criticism & Parody of the Period Ser.). 137p. 1986. lib. bdg. 25.00 (ISBN 0-8240-8615-5). Garland Pub.
Style: An Anti-Textbook. Richard A. Lanham. LC 73-86906. 144p. 1974. 17.50x (ISBN 0-300-01720-0); pap. 7.95x (ISBN 0-300-02243-3). Yale U Pr.
Style & Authenticity in Postmodern Poetry. Jonathan Holden. LC 85-20966. 184p. 1986. text ed. 21.00 (ISBN 0-8262-0600-X). U of Mo Pr.
Style & Class. Sietze Buning. LC 82-14541. 1982. pap. 7.95 (ISBN 0-931940-06-0). Middleburg Pr.
Style & Conscious in Middle English Narrative. John M. Ganim. LC 83-42559. 212p. 1983. 27.50x (ISBN 0-691-06580-2). Princeton U Pr.
Style & Content in Christian Art. Jane Dillenberger. 320p. 1986. pap. 17.95 (ISBN 0-8245-0782-7). Crossroad NY.
Style & Content in Christian Art: From the Catacombs to the Chapel Designed by Matisse at Vence, France. Jane Dillenberger. LC 65-22293. pap. 80.50 (ISBN 0-317-10399-7, 2001274). Bks Demand UMI.
Style & Epoch. Moisei Ginzburg. Tr. by Anatole Senkevitch, Jr. from Rus. (Oppositions Bks.). (Illus.). 200p. 1982. 37.50 (ISBN 0-262-07088-X). MIT Pr.
Style & Evolution of the Earliest Modets. Hans Tischler. (Wissenschaftliche Adhandlungen-Musicological Studies). 224p. 1981. Pt. I. lib. bdg. 55.00 (ISBN 0-931902-30-4); Pt. II, Tabular Analysis, 208p. lib. bdg. 55.00 (ISBN 0-931902-31-2); Pt. IIIa, Catalogue Raisonne. lib. bdg. 45.00 (ISBN 0-931902-32-0); Pt. IIIb, Catalogue Raisonne. lib. bdg. 45.00. Inst Mediaeval Mus.
Style & Evolution of the Earliest Motets, Pts. 1, 2, 3A & 3B. Hans Tischler. Incl. Pt. 1. Text. 344p. lib. bdg. 55.00; Pt. 2. Tabular Analyses. 308p. lib. bdg. 55.00; Catalogue Raisonne (A & B, 2 pts. 568p. Pt. 3A. lib. bdg. 45.00 ea. Pt. 3B. (Wissenschaftliche Abhandlungen - Musicological Studies: Vol. 40). 1985. Inst Mediaeval Mus.
Style & Form in American Prose. Gorham B. Munson. LC 68-26291. 1969. Repr. of 1929 ed. 25.50x (ISBN 0-8046-0328-6, Pub. by Kennikat). Assoc Faculty Pr.
Style & Idea: Selected Writings of Arnold Schoenberg. Arnold Schoenberg. Ed. by Leonard Stein. Tr. by Leo Black from Ger. LC 84-2604. 560p. 1985. 55.00x (ISBN 0-520-05286-2); pap. 12.95 (ISBN 0-520-05294-3). U of Cal Pr.
Style & Literary Method of Luke, 2 Vols. in 1. H. J. Cadbury, (Harvard Theo. Studies: No. 6). 1919-1920. 24.00 (ISBN 0-527-01006-5). Kraus Repr.
Style & Orchestration. Gardner Read. LC 77-15884. 1979. 29.95 (ISBN 0-02-872110-1). Schirmer Bks.
Style & Readability in Business Writing. Gary Olson et al. 200p. 1984. pap. text ed. write for info (ISBN 0-394-33151-6, RanC). Random.
Style & Rhetoric in Bertrand Russell's Work. Mary L. Jackson. (European University Studies: No. 14, Vol. 116). 234p. (Ger.). 1983. 27.90 (ISBN 3-8204-7855-8). P Lang Pubs.
Style & Sense: Court Reporting, Transcribing, Legal. Audrey A. Fatooh et al. LC 84-28744. 192p. 1986. spiral wire 15.95 (ISBN 0-88280-109-0). ETC Pubns.
Style & Society in German Literary Expressionism. Egbert Krispyn. LC 64-63741. (University of Florida Humanities Monographs: No. 15). 1964. pap. 6.00x (ISBN 0-8130-0136-6). U Presses Fla.
Style & Strategy of the Business Letter. Jacqueline Trace. (Illus.). 208p. 1985. text ed. 18.00 (ISBN 0-13-858895-3); pap. 8.95 (ISBN 0-13-858887-2). P-H.
Style & Strategy of the Business Letter. Jacqueline Trace. Date not set. write for info. S&S.
Style & Structure in Shakespeare. Henry Wells & H. H. Gowda. 1979. text ed. 14.95x (ISBN 0-7069-0711-6). Humanities.
Style & Structure in the Praeludia of Dietrich Buxtehude. Lawrence Archbold. Ed. by George Buelow. LC 85-1064. (Studies in Musicology: No. 82). 358p. 1985. 49.95 (ISBN 0-8357-1646-5). UMI Res Pr.
Style & Structure in the Prose of Isaak Babel. Efraim Sicher. 169p. (Orig.). 1986. pap. 14.95 (ISBN 0-89357-163-6). Slavica.
Style & Substance. Judith Martin. LC 86-47672. 320p. 1986. 15.95 (ISBN 0-689-11514-8). Atheneum.
Style & Substance in Writing. Adrienne Wade. 176p. 1985. pap. 15.95 (ISBN 0-8403-3623-3). Kendall Hunt.
Style & Substance: Leadership & the College Presidency. Louis Benezet. 1981. 18.50 (ISBN 0-02-902540-0). ACE.
Style & Symbolism in Piers Plowman: A Modern Critical Anthology. Ed. by Robert J. Blanch. LC 69-20115. (Illus., Orig.). 1969. pap. text ed. 12.95x (ISBN 0-87049-101-6). U of Tenn Pr.
Style & Symbolism in Piers Plowman: A Modern Critical Anthology. Ed. by Robert J. Blanch. LC 69-20115. pap. 72.50 (ISBN 0-317-55785-8, 2029372). Bks Demand UMI.
Style & Vernacular: A Guide to the Architecture of Lane County, Oregon. Southern Oregon Chapter-AIA. (Illus.). 160p. (Orig.). 1983. pap. 9.95 (ISBN 0-87595-085-X, Western Imprints). Oregon Hist.
Style & Vocabulary: Numerical Studies. C. B. Williams. 162p. 1972. pap. text ed. 21.75x (ISBN 0-85264-164-8). Lubrecht & Cramer.
Style as Argument: Comtemporary American Nonfiction. Chris Anderson. 224p. 1987. text ed. 19.95x (ISBN 0-8093-1314-6); pap. 11.95x (ISBN 0-8093-1373-1). S Ill U Pr.
Style As Structure & Meaning: William Bradford's "Of Plymouth Plantation". Floyd Ogburn, Jr. LC 80-5879. 169p. 1981. pap. text ed. 11.50 (ISBN 0-8191-1591-6). U Pr of Amer.
Style de la Lyrique Courtoise en France aux Douzieme et Triezieme Siecles. Hyacinthe Binet. 1968. Repr. of 1891 ed. 21.00 (ISBN 0-8337-0278-5). B Franklin.
Style in Art History: An Introduction to Theories of Style & Sequence. Margaret Finch. LC 73-14705. 178p. 1974. lib. bdg. 15.00 (ISBN 0-8108-0679-7). Scarecrow.
Style in Fiction. G. N. Leech & M. H. Short. (English Language Ser.). 384p. 1981. text ed. 28.00x (ISBN 0-582-29102-X); pap. text ed. 16.95 (ISBN 0-582-29103-8). Longman.
Style in History. Peter Gay. 1988. pap. 7.95 (ISBN 0-393-30558-9). Norton.
Style in Modern British Fiction: Studies in Joyce, Lawrence, Forster, Lewis & Green. John Russell. LC 77-22477. (Illus.). 208p. 1978. text ed. 21.50x (ISBN 0-8018-2029-4). Johns Hopkins.
Style in Musical Art. Charles Parry. lib. bdg. 25.00 (ISBN 0-403-01752-1). Scholarly.
Style in Musical Art. Charles Parry. 1988. Repr. lib. bdg. 49.00x. Am Biog Serv.
Style in Musical Art. Charles H. Parry. LC 78-13864. (Encore Music Editions Ser.). 1979. Repr. of 1924 ed. 32.45 (ISBN 0-88355-807-6). Hyperion Conn.
Style in Old English Poetry: The Test of the Auxiliary. Daniel Donoghue. LC 87-13264. 256p. 1988. text ed. 30.00 (ISBN 0-300-03956-5). Yale U Pr.
Style in Piano Playing. Peter Cooper. 1986. 11.95 (ISBN 0-7145-3512-5). Riverrun NY.
Style in Prose Fiction. Ed. by Harold C. Martin. LC 59-11178. (Essays of the English Institute). 1959. 25.00 (ISBN 0-231-02353-7). Columbia U Pr.
Style in Prose Fiction see English Institute Essays.
Style in Technical Writing. Gary Olson & James DeGeorge. 1983. pap. text ed. write for info (ISBN 0-394-33152-4, RanC). Random.
Style in Technical Writing: A Text Workbook. Ronald K. Messer. 1982. pap. text ed. write for info. (ISBN 0-673-15529-3). Scott F.
Style in the Arts of China. William Watson. (Illus.). 256p. (Orig.). 1974. pap. 7.95 (ISBN 0-14-021863-7, Pelican). Penguin.
Style Louis XV see Histoire de l'Architecture Classique en France.
Style Louis XVI see Histoire de l'Architecture Classique en France.

Style Manual. American Physical Therapy Association Staff. 1985. Vinyl bdg. 40.00. Am Phys Therapy Assn.

Style Manual: A Guide for the Preparation of Reports & Dissertations. Martha L. Manheimer. (Bks. in Library & Information Science: Vol. 5). 176p. 1973. 19.75 (ISBN 0-8247-6046-8). Dekker.

Style Manual for Citing Microform & Nonprint Media. Eugene B. Fleischer. LC 78-9375. 76p. 1978. pap. 6.00x (ISBN 0-8389-0268-5). ALA.

Style Manual for College Students: A Guide to Written Assignments & Papers. rev ed. Margaret L. Ranald et al. 1982. pap. 1.00 (ISBN 0-930146-07-7). Queens Coll Pr.

Style Manual for the Law Office. 32p. 1978. pap. 15.00 (ISBN 0-89707-059-3). Amer Bar Assn.

Style Manual for Writers. 2nd ed. Mary E. Pitts & Pat Collins. 128p. 1985. pap. text ed. 9.95 (ISBN 0-8403-3609-8). Kendall-Hunt.

Style Manual for Written Communication. 2nd ed. Arno F. Knapper & Loda I. Newcomb. LC 82-6053. 222p. 1984. pap. text ed. 14.95 (ISBN 0-471-84213-3, Pub. by Grid). Wiley.

Style Manuals of the English-Speaking World: A Guide. John B. Howell. LC 82-42916. 152p. 1983. lib. bdg. 36.00x (ISBN 0-89774-089-0). Oryx Pr.

Style Name Directory for Carpets & Rugs. 96p. pap. 30.00 (ISBN 0-89275-016-2). Carpet Rug Inst.

Style Nineteen Thirty. Klaus-Jurgen Sembach. LC 76-162926. (Illus.). 175p. 1986. pap. 14.95 (ISBN 0-87663-865-5). Universe.

Style of Aeschylus. Frank R. Earp. LC 79-102489. 1970. Repr. of 1948 ed. 9.00x (ISBN 0-8462-1494-6). Russell.

Style of Bana: An Introduction to Sanskrit Prose Poetry. Robert A. Hueckstedt. 228p. (Orig.). 1986. lib. bdg. 29.00 (ISBN 0-8191-4998-5); pap. text ed. 13.50 (ISBN 0-8191-4999-3). U Pr of Amer.

Style of Connectedness: "Gravity's Rainbow" & Thomas Pynchon. Thomas Moore. LC 86-16093. 352p. 1987. text ed. 30.00 (ISBN 0-8262-0625-5, 83-36331). U of Mo Pr.

Style of J. S. Bach's Chorale Preludes. 2nd ed. Robert L. Tusler. LC 68-13275. (Music Ser). 1968. Repr. of 1956 ed. lib. bdg. 19.50 (ISBN 0-306-70942-2). Da Capo.

Style of John Wyclif's English Sermons. P. Knapp. 1977. 16.00x (ISBN 90-279-3156-9). Mouton.

Style of Lord Byron's Plays. Paulino M. Lim, Jr. Ed. by James Hogg. (Poetic Drama & Poetic Theory ser.). 177p. (Orig.). 1973. pap. 15.00 (ISBN 3-7052-0827-6, Pub. by Salzburg Studies). Longwood Pub Group.

Style of Nerval's Aurelia. William Beauchamp. (De Proprietatibus Litterarum Series Practica: No. 109). 108p. 1976. pap. text ed. 15.20x (ISBN 90-2793-284-0). Mouton.

Style of Pope St. Leo the Great, No. 59. William J. Halliwell. (Patristic Studies). 114p. 1984. 26.00x (ISBN 0-939738-25-2). Zubal Inc.

Style of Robert Louis Stevenson. James Leatham. LC 72-192989. lib. bdg. 15.00 (ISBN 0-8414-5696-8). Folcroft.

Style Profile for Communication at Work. 2nd ed. Susan K. Gilmore & Patrick W. Fraleigh. (Illus.). 1988. pap. 5.00 (ISBN 0-938070-08-8). Friendly Oregon.

Style Sheets for Business Documents. Martha Lubow & Jesse Berst. LC 88-61188. (Illus.). 320p. 1988. pap. 19.95 (ISBN 0-934035-32-6); Business Documents Disk Set 21.95 (ISBN 0-934035-37-7). New Riders Pub.

Style Sheets for Newsletters. Martha Lubow. (Illus.). 320p. 1988. pap. 19.95 (ISBN 0-934035-30-X); Newsletters Disk Set 21.95 (ISBN 0-934035-39-3). New Riders Pub.

Style Sheets for Newsletters: A Guide to Advanced Designs for Xerox Ventura Publisher. (Desktop Power Ser.). (Illus.). 320p. 1988. Book & disk set. pap. 39.95 (ISBN 0-934035-31-8). New Riders Pub.

Style Sheets for Technical Documentation: A Guide to Advanced Designs for Xerox Ventura Publisher. Byron Canfield & Chad Canty. (Desktop Power Ser.). (Illus.). 320p. 1988. Book & disk set. pap. 39.95 (ISBN 0-934035-29-6). New Riders Pub.

Style Sheets for Technical Documents. Byron Canfield & chad Canty. LC 88-61189. (Illus.). 320p. 1988. pap. 19.95 (ISBN 0-934035-28-8); Technical Documentation Disk Set 21.95 (ISBN 0-934035-38-5). New Riders Pub.

Style Strategy: Winning the Appearance Game. Jane Segerstrom. LC 88-15877. (Illus.). 160p. (Orig.). 1988. pap. 14.95 (ISBN 0-936740-12-4). Triad Pr TX.

Style: Ten Lessons in Clarity & Grace. 2nd ed. Joseph M. Williams. 1985. pap. text ed. write for info. (ISBN 0-673-18058-1). Scott F.

Style: Ten Lessons in Clarity & Grace. 3rd ed. Joseph M. Williams. 1988. pap. text ed. write for info. (ISBN 0-673-38186-2). Scott F.

Style: The Problem & Its Solution. Bennison Gray. (De Proprietatibus Litterarum Ser. Major: No. 3). 1969. text ed. 13.20x (ISBN 90-2790-441-3). Mouton.

Style Theories As Found in Stylistic Studies of Romance Scholars - 1900-1950. Sr. Clare E. Craddock. LC 70-94184. (Catholic University of America Studies in Romance Languages & Literatures Ser: No. 43). Repr. of 1952 ed. 26.00 (ISBN 0-404-50343-8). AMS Pr.

Style Versus Substance: Boston, Kevin White & the Politics of Illusion. George V. Higgins. 256p. 1984. 15.95 (ISBN 0-02-551450-4). Macmillan.

Style Wheel of Furniture & Decoration. A. Allen Dizik. (Illus.). 12.95 (ISBN 0-686-86777-7). Stratford Hse.

Style: Writing & Reading As the Discovery of Outlook. 3rd ed. Richard M. Eastman. 1984. pap. 13.95x (ISBN 0-19-503395-7). Oxford U Pr.

Styled for Living. Ed. by Sherman R. Emery. LC 83-50429. (Illus.). 240p. 1983. 40.00 (ISBN 0-943370-00-0). Inter Design.

Styles. Paul V. Carter. Ed. by Kathy R. Aszkenas. 224p. 1987. 15.95 (ISBN 0-682-40354-7). Exposition-Phoenix.

Styles & Structures: Alternative Approaches to College Writing. Charles K. Smith. 340p. 1974. pap. text ed. 12.95x (ISBN 0-393-09273-9). Norton.

Styles, Eighteen Fifty to Nineteen Hundred. Kathryn B. Hiesinger. LC 83-6229. (Guides to European Decorative Arts: No. 2). (Illus.). 48p. (Orig.). 1984. pap. 3.50 (ISBN 0-87633-051-0). Phila Mus Art.

Styles in Painting: A Comparative Study. Paul Zucker. (Illus.). 1950. pap. 6.95 (ISBN 0-486-20760-9). Dover.

Styles of Acting: A Scenebook for the Advanced Acting Student. Elaine Novak. LC 85-6407. 240p. 1985. pap. 8.95 (ISBN 0-13-858796-5). P H.

Styles of Discourse. Ed. by Nikolaus Coupland. 240p. 1988. lib. bdg. 72.50x (ISBN 0-7099-4852-2, Pub. by Croom Helm UK). Routledge Chapman & Hall.

Styles of English Architecture. Hubert Pragnell. (Illus.). 176p. 1985. 24.95 (ISBN 0-7134-3768-5, Pub. by Batsford England). David & Charles.

Styles of Folding: Mechanics & Mechanisms of Folding of Natural Elastic Materials. A. M. Johnson. (Developments in Geotectonics: Vol. 11). 406p. 1977. 76.75 (ISBN 0-444-41496-7). Elsevier.

Styles of Loving: Why You Love the Way You Do. Marcia Lasswell & Norman M. Lobsenz. 192p. 1981. pap. 2.50 (ISBN 0-345-29228-6). Ballantine.

Styles of Ornament. Alexander Speltz. Tr. by David O'Connor. pap. 9.95 (ISBN 0-486-20557-6). Dover.

Styles of Political Action in America. Ed. by Robert P. Wolff. LC 81-40796. 256p. 1981. pap. text ed. 10.00 (ISBN 0-8191-1802-8). U Pr of Amer.

Styles of Radical Will. Susan Sontag. 1978. pap. 5.75 (ISBN 0-385-28909-X, Delta). Dell.

Styles of Radical Will. Susan Sontag. 280p. 1987. pap. 7.95 (ISBN 0-374-51364-3). FS&G.

Styles of the Emerging Nation. Ed. by Lisa C. Mullins. (Architectural Treasures of Early America Ser.). (Illus.). 224p. 1988. 19.95 (ISBN 0-918678-35-8). Historical Times.

Styles of Urban Policing: Organization, Environment & Police Styles in Selected American Cities. Jeffrey S. Slovak. LC 86-5440. 236p. 1986. 35.00x (ISBN 0-8147-7855-0). NYU Pr.

Styles of Urban Policing: Organization, Environment, & Police Styles in Selected American Cities. Jeffrey S. Slovak. 236p. 1988. pap. 15.00x (ISBN 0-8147-7875-5). NYU Pr.

Stylewise: A Man's Guide to Looking Good for Less. Leonard McGill. LC 82-21513. (Illus.). 208p. 1983. 15.95 (ISBN 0-399-12792-5, Putnam). Putnam Pub Group.

Styling vs. Safety: The American Automobile Industry & the Development of Automobile Safety, 1900-1966. Joel W. Eastman. 296p. (Orig.). 1984. lib. bdg. 29.25 (ISBN 0-8191-3685-9); pap. text ed. 14.50 (ISBN 0-8191-3686-7). U Pr of Amer.

Stylish Knitting: From Handspun or Commercial Yarns. Nina Shuttlewood. (Illus.). 152p. 1988. 34.95 (ISBN 0-7134-5167-X, Pub. by Batsford England). David & Charles.

Stylistic Analysis of Arshile Gorky's Art from 1943-1948. Robert F. Reiff. LC 76-23679. (Outstanding Dissertations in the Fine Arts-American). (Illus.). 345p. 1977. Repr. of 1961 ed. lib. bdg. 63.00 (ISBN 0-8240-2719-1). Garland Pub.

Stylistic Arrangements: A Study of William Butler Yeat's "A Vision". Barbara L. Croft. LC 84-45453. (Illus.). 200p. 1987. 28.50x (ISBN 0-8387-5087-7). Bucknell U Pr.

Stylistic Criticism & the African Novel. Emmanuel Ngara. (Studies in African Literature). 151p. 1982. pap. 14.00x (ISBN 0-435-91720-X). Heinemann Ed.

Stylistic Development of Edgar Allen Poe. Richard M. Fletcher. LC 72-94467. (Janua Linguarum, Ser. Practica: No. 55). 192p. 1974. pap. text ed. 20.80x (ISBN 90-2792-508-9). Mouton.

Stylistic Development of Keats. Walter J. Bate. LC 83-48836. Repr. of 1958 ed. 23.00 (ISBN 0-404-20019-2). AMS Pr.

Stylistic Evaluation of Aeschines in Antiquity. Jan F. Kindstrand. (Studia Graeca Upsaliensia: No. 18). 104p. (Orig.). 1982. pap. 15.00x (ISBN 91-554-1320-X, Pub. by Uppsala Univ Acta Univ Uppsaliensis (Uppsala Sweden)). Coronet Bks.

Stylistic Life of Samuel Johnson. William Vesterman. 1977. 23.00 (ISBN 0-8135-0839-8). Rutgers U Pr.

Stylistic Options: The Sentence & the Paragraph. Walter H. Beale et al. 1982. pap. text ed. write for info. (ISBN 0-673-15444-0). Scott F.

Stylistic Relationship Between Poetry & Prose in the Cantico Espiritual of San Juan De la Cruz. Sr. Rosa M. Icaza. LC 76-94191. (Catholic University of America Studies in Romance Languages & Literatures Ser: No. 54). 1969. Repr. of 1957 ed. 21.00 (ISBN 0-404-50354-3). AMS Pr.

Stylistic Variation in Prehistoric Ceramics. Stephen Plog. (New Studies in Archaeology). (Illus.). 40p. 1980. 34.50 (ISBN 0-521-22581-7). Cambridge U Pr.

Stylistics & Psychology: Investigations of Foregrounding. Willie Van Peer. 224p. 1986. 43.00 (ISBN 0-7099-2604-9, Pub. by Croom Helm Ltd). Routledge Chapman & Hall.

Stylometric Study of the New Testament. Anthony Kenny. 160p. 1986. text ed. 42.00x (ISBN 0-19-826178-0). Oxford U Pr.

Styrbiorn the Strong. Eric R. Eddison. Ed. by R. Reginald & Douglas Melville. LC 77-84222. (Lost Race & Adult Fantasy Ser.). 1978. Repr. of 1926 ed. lib. bdg. 24.50x (ISBN 0-405-10975-X). Ayer Co Pubs.

Styrene Polymers: Technology & Environmental Aspects. C. A. Brighton et al. (Illus.). 284p. 1979. 66.75 (ISBN 0-85334-810-3, Pub. by Elsevier Applied Sci England). Elsevier.

Styrenics. Business Communications Staff. 202p. 1984. 1750.00 (ISBN 0-89336-385-5, P-076). BCC.

Styria. (Panorama Bks.). (Illus., Eng. & Fr.). 3.95 (ISBN 0-685-11576-3). French & Eur.

Styrian Estates, 1740-1848: A Century of Transition. Christine L. Mueller. Ed. by William H. McNeill & Enno E. Kraehe. (Modern European History Ser.). 428p. 1987. lib. bdg. 65.00 (ISBN 0-8240-8049-1). Garland Pub.

Systematic Design of Training Courses. Ed. by Bob Wilson. (Training Technology Programme Ser.). (Illus.). 310p. 1987. 45.00 (ISBN 0-940813-30-0). Parthenon NJ.

Su Historia: Los Pentecostales del Siglo Veinte. Fred Foster. Ed. by Mary H. Wallace. Tr. by Jerry Burns & Beth Burns. (Illus.). 192p. (Span.). 1988. pap. 5.95 (ISBN 0-932581-35-8). Word Aflame.

Su Man-Shu. Liu Wu-Chi. (Twayne's World Authors Ser.). 1971. lib. bdg. 17.95 (ISBN 0-8057-2870-8). Irvington.

Su Poder Espiritual Y Emocional. Richard D. Dobbins. Tr. by Eliezer Oyola from Eng. Orig. Title: Your Spiritual & Emotional Power. 171p. (Span.). 1985. pap. 2.95 (ISBN 0-8297-0705-0). Life Pubs Intl.

SU Site Excavations at a Mongollon Village, Western New Mexico, 1st, 2nd, & 3rd Seasons. Paul S. Martin. (Field Museum of Natural History Ser.). (Illus.). 1940-1947. 34.00 (ISBN 0-527-01892-9). Kraus Repr.

Su-Su, the Fremont School Panda. Henry Eisemann. (Illus.). 22p. (Orig.). (gr. k-6). 1987. pap. 4.95 (ISBN 0-938129-03-1). Emprise Pubns.

Suakin & Massawa under Egyptian Rule, 1865-1885. Ghada H. Talhami. LC 79-66418. 1979. pap. text ed. 15.25 (ISBN 0-8191-0828-6). U Pr of Amer.

Suarez: Disputation Six, on Formal & Universal Unity. Tr. by James F. Ross. (Medieval Philosophical Texts in Translation: No. 15). 1965. pap. 7.95 (ISBN 0-87462-215-8). Marquette.

Suarez on Individuation. Jorge J. Gracia. Ed. by James Robb. 304p. 1981. pap. 24.95 (ISBN 0-87462-223-9). Marquette.

Sub & Supersonic Experimental Rocket Computer Programs: Fourth Order Range-Kutta, Altitude Prediction, Drag, Center of Pressure. Charles E. Rogers. 1983. 49.00 (ISBN 0-912468-13-0). CA Rocketry.

Sub Arbor Vitae (Under the Tree of Life) Americus L. McQueen. 25p. 1988. 5.95 (ISBN 0-533-07734-6). Vantage.

Sub-Clinical Lead Poisoning. D. Stofen & H. A. Walsren. 1974. 64.00 (ISBN 0-12-671650-1). Acad Pr.

Sub Commander: Tactics & Strategy for WWII Submarine Simulations. Richard G. Scheffield. 1987. 12.95 (ISBN 0-87455-127-7). Compute Pubns.

Sub-Orbital Project Documentation & Computer Runs. Jerry Irvine et al. 50p. 1985. 19.95 (ISBN 0-912468-27-0). CA Rocketry.

Sub Rosa: The O.S.S. & American Espionage. Stewart Alsop & Thomas Branden. LC 64-57431. 272p. 1964. pap. 1.65 (ISBN 0-15-686300-6, Harv). HarBraceJ.

Sub-Saharan Africa. Ed. by Chris Allen & Gavin Williams. LC 81-16902. (Sociology of "Developing Societies" Ser.). 240p. 1982. 18.00 (ISBN 0-85345-597-X); pap. 8.00 (ISBN 0-85345-598-8). Monthly Rev.

Sub-Saharan Africa: A Guide to Information Sources. Ed. by W. A. Skurnik. LC 73-17513. (International Relations Information Guide Ser.: Vol. 3). 144p. 1977. 68.00x (ISBN 0-8103-1391-X). Gale.

Sub-Saharan Africa: An Introduction. Edmund C. Gannon. (JSPES Monograph: No. 6). 1978. pap. 20.00 (ISBN 0-930690-09-5). Coun Soc Econ.

Sub-Saharan Africa & the United States. rev. ed. Philip R. Cook. (State Department Publication: No. 9112). (Illus.). 48p. (Orig.). 1985. pap. 2.50 (ISBN 0-318-20151-8, S/N 044-000-02114-5). USGPO.

Sub-Saharan African Films & Filmakers: An Annotated Bibliography. Ed. by Nancy J. Schmidt. 400p. 1988. lib. bdg. 86.00 (ISBN 3-598-10659-9). K G Saur.

Sub-Saharan Agriculture: Synthesis & Trade Prospects. Shamsher Singh. (Working Paper: No. 608). 172p. 1983. 8.00 (ISBN 0-8213-0221-3, WP 0608). World Bank.

Sub-Sea Explorers. T. Hayward. (Dangerous Jobs Ser.). (Illus.). 32p. (gr. 4 up). Date not set. PLB 13.27 (ISBN 0-86592-413-9). Rourke Corp.

Sub Specie Historiae: Essays in the Manifestations of Historical & Moral Consciousness. John T. Marcus. LC 76-50285. 328p. 1979. 29.50 (ISBN 0-8386-2057-4). Fairleigh Dickinson.

Sub Survival: A Handbook for the Substitute Elementary Teacher. Rev. ed. Danna Downing. 150p. 1981. pap. text ed. 19.95 (ISBN 0-918452-85-6, 80-83081). Learning Pubns.

Sub-Tropical Rambles in the Land of the Aphanapteryx: Personal Experiences, Adventures & Wanderings in & Around the Island of Mauritus. Nicholas Pike. LC 72-4081. (Black Heritage Library Collection Ser.). Repr. of 1873 ed. 40.25 (ISBN 0-8369-9103-6). Ayer Co Pubs.

Sub vs. Sub: The Tactics & Technology of Underwater Warfare. Richard Compton-Hall. (Illus.). 192p. 1988. 24.95 (ISBN 0-517-56617-6, Orion Bks). Crown.

Sub Wars, No. 1: Target Delta V. James Good. (Orig.). 1982. pap. 2.50 (ISBN 0-8217-1046-X). Zebra.

Sub Wars, No. 2: Target Sosus. James Good. 1982. pap. 2.50 (ISBN 0-8217-1092-3). Zebra.

Sub-Zero! Robert W. Walker. 1979. pap. 1.75 (ISBN 0-505-51395-1, Pub. by Tower Bks). Leisure NY.

Subacute Sclerosing Panencephalitis: A Reappraisal. Ed. by F. Bertamini et al. 440p. 1986. 121.75 (ISBN 0-444-80790-X, Excerpta Medica). Elsevier.

Subaltern Studies, Vol. III. Ed. by Ranajit Guha. 1985. 27.95x (ISBN 0-19-561653-7). Oxford U Pr.

Subaltern Studies, Vol. V. Ed. by Ranajit Guha. 320p. 1988. 24.95 (ISBN 0-19-562004-6). Oxford U Pr.

Subaltern Studies, Vol. IV. Ed. by Ranajit Guha. 396p. 1988. 24.95 (ISBN 0-19-561840-8). Oxford U Pr.

Subaltern Studies I: Writings on South Asian History & Society. Ed. by Ranajit Guha. (Illus.). 1982. 24.95x (ISBN 0-19-561355-4). Oxford U Pr.

Subaltern Studies II: Writings on South Asian History & Society. Ed. by Ranajit Guha. (Illus.). 1984. 27.50x (ISBN 0-19-561502-6). Oxford U Pr.

Subaltern's War. Charles Edmonds. 224p. 1984. pap. 7.50 (ISBN 0-907746-38-1, Pub. by A Mott Ltd). Longwood Pub Group.

Subaltern's War: Being a Memoir of the Great War from the Point of View of a Romantic Young Man. Charles E. Carrington. LC 72-4273. (World Affairs Ser.: National & International Viewpoints). (Illus.). 236p. 1972. Repr. of 1930 ed. 20.00 (ISBN 0-405-04562-X). Ayer Co Pubs.

Subantarctic Campbell Island. Alfred M. Bailey & J. H. Sorenson. (Proceedings: No. 10). 1962. pap. 2.00 (ISBN 0-916278-63-8). Denver Mus Natl Hist.

Subaqueous Slope Failures: Experiments & Modern Occurences. H. Schwarz. (Contributions to Sedimentology: No. 11). (Illus.). 116p. 1982. pap. text ed. 48.00x (ISBN 3-510-57011-1). Lubrecht & Cramer.

Subarachnoid Haemorrhage. R. P. Sengupta & V. L. McAllister. (Illus.). 390p. 1986. 135.00 (ISBN 0-387-15534-1). Springer-Verlag.

Subarctic. Ed. by June Helm. LC 77-17162. (Handbook of North American Indians: Vol. 6). (Illus.). 836p. 1981. 25.00x (ISBN 0-87474-186-6, HEV6). Smithsonian.

Subarctic Athabascans: A Selected, Annotated Bibliography. Arthur E. Hippler & John R. Wood. LC 74-620010. (ISER Report: No. 39). 380p. 1974. pap. 15.00 (ISBN 0-88353-012-0). U Alaska Inst Res.

Subarea Projections Model (SAM) Allocating Employment & Population, Projecting Household Income, & Land Use Accounting. 55p. 1986. 55.00 (ISBN 0-318-22685-5). Assn Bay Area.

Subarrachnoid Hemorrhage. Maurice-Williams. 624p. 1987. 124.00 (ISBN 0-7236-0742-7). PSG Pub Co.

Subaru Service Repair Handbook: All Models, 1300-1800, Brat, MPV, 1972-1984. Ray Hoy. (Illus.). pap. 14.95 (ISBN 0-89287-146-6, A186). Clymer Pub.

Subatomic Monster. Isaac Asimov. 272p. 1986. pap. 3.95 (ISBN 0-451-62530-7, Ment). NAL.

Subatomic Physics. Hans Frauenfelder & Ernest M. Henley. (Illus.). 544p. 1974. write for info (ISBN 0-13-859082-6). P-H.

Subatomic Physics: Nuclei & Particles, 2 vols. L. Valentin. 600p. 1981. Set. 131.75 (ISBN 0-444-86117-3, North-Holland). Elsevier.

Subcelluar Taxonomy: An Ultrastructural Classification System with Diagnostic Applications. Ed. by A. L. McLay & Peter G. Toner. LC 83-10856. (Ultrastructural Pathology Publication Ser.). 86p. 1985. 49.50 (ISBN 0-89116-293-3). Hemisphere Pub.
Subcellular Biochemistry, Vol. 9. Ed. by Donald B. Roodyn. LC 73-643479. 442p. 1983. 69.50x (ISBN 0-306-41091-5, Plenum Pr). Plenum Pub.
Subcellular Biochemistry, Vol. 10. Ed. by Donald B. Roodyn. LC 73-643479. 568p. 1984. 85.00x (ISBN 0-306-41528-3, Plenum Pr). Plenum Pub.
Subcellular Biochemistry, Vol. 11. Ed. by Donald B. Roodyn. LC 73-643479. 308p. 1985. 59.50x (ISBN 0-306-41959-9, Plenum Pr). Plenum Pub.
Subcellular Biochemistry, Vol. 12: Immunological Aspects. Ed. by J. R. Harris. LC 73-643479. (Illus.). 400p. 1988. 69.50x (ISBN 0-306-42737-0, Plenum Pr). Plenum Pub.
Subcellular Biochemistry, Vol. 13: Fluorescence Studies on Biological Membranes. Ed. by H. Hilderson. (Illus.). 460p. 1988. 85.00x (ISBN 0-306-42940-3, Plenum Pr). Plenum Pub.
Subcellular Biochemistry, Vol. 14: Artificial & Reconstituted Membrane Systems. Ed. by J. R. Harris & A. E. Etemadi. (Illus.). 455p. Date not set. price not set (ISBN 0-306-43055-X, Plenum Pr). Plenum Pub.
Subcellular Factors Immunity. Ed. by Herman Friedman. LC 79-24875. (Annals of the New York Academy of Sciences: Vol. 332). 625p. 1979. 112.00x (ISBN 0-89766-035-8). NY Acad Sci.
Subcellular Pathology of Systemic Disease. Ed. by T. J. Peters. 456p. 1987. text ed. 135.00 (ISBN 0-412-26550-8, Pub. by Chapman & Hall). Routledge Chapman & Hall.
Subchapter S Revision Act of 1982 - Law & Explanations. 136p. pap. 6.50 (ISBN 0-317-04221-1, 4958). Commerce.
Subchapter S Revisions of 1982. Pennsylvania Bar Institute. 21p. 1983. incl. audiocassettes 30.00 (ISBN 0-318-02162-5, 219). PA Bar Inst.
Subchapter S Taxation. 2nd ed. Irving M. Grant. LC 80-10826. (Tax & Estate Planning Ser.). 762p. 1980. text ed. 120.00 (ISBN 0-07-024072-8). Shepards-McGraw.
Subchaser to Sicily. Edward P. Stafford. (Illus.). 320p. 1988. 17.95 (ISBN 0-87021-692-9). Naval Inst Pr.
Subclinical Hepatocellular Carcinoma. Ed. by Z. Y. Tang. (Illus.). 400p. 1985. 110.00 (ISBN 0-387-12664-3). Springer-Verlag.
Subconscious. Joseph Jastrow. 1979. Repr. of 1905 ed. lib. bdg. 50.00 (ISBN 0-8495-2745-7). Arden Lib.
Subconscious Orthodoxy of the Spanish Race. Archimandrite P. DeBallester. Ed. by Orthodox Christian Educational Society. 8p. (Orig.). 1978. pap. 0.30x (ISBN 0-938366-46-7). Orthodox Chr.
Subcontinent in World Politics: India, Its Neighbors & the Great Powers. 2nd, rev. ed. Ed. by Lawrence Ziring. LC 82-7634. 268p. 1982. 36.95 (ISBN 0-275-90930-1, C0930). Praeger.
Subcontract Management Handbook. George Sammet & Clifton G. Kelley. LC 80-69698. pap. 64.00 (ISBN 0-317-26704-3, 2023510). Bks Demand UMI.
Subcontracting in the Public Sector: The New York State Experience. Ronald Donovan & Marsha J. Orr. LC 82-6379. (IPE Monograph: No. 10). 44p. 1982. pap. 4.95 (ISBN 0-87546-095-X). ILR Pr.
Subcortical Visual Systems. Ed. by D. Ingle & G. E. Schneider. (Journal: Brain, Behavior & Evolution Ser.: Vol. 3, No. 1-4). 1970. pap. 61.50 (ISBN 3-8055-1149-3). S Karger.
Subcritical Crack Growth & Fracture of Bridge Steels. (National Cooperative Highway Research Program Report). 82p. 1977. 5.60 (ISBN 0-309-02755-1). Transport Res Bd.
Subcritical Crack Growth Due to Fatigue, Stress Corrosion & Creep: Selected Proceedings of the Third Advanced Seminar on Fracture Mechanics (ASFM 3), Joint Research Centre, Ispra, Italy, 19-23 October 1981. Ed. by L. H. Larsson. (Illus.). 640p. 1985. 165.75 (ISBN 0-85334-289-X, Pub. by Elsevier Applied Sci England). Elsevier.
Subculture of Pregnancy in a College Community. Jean H. Thrasher. 78p. 1963. pap. text ed. 1.50 (ISBN 0-89143-051-2). U NC Inst Res Soc Sci.
Subculture of Violence: Towards an Integrated Theory in Criminology. Marvin E. Wolfgang & Franco Ferracuti. (Illus.). 416p. 1982. 29.95 (ISBN 0-8039-1808-9); pap. 14.95 (ISBN 0-8039-1809-7). Sage.
Subculture: The Meaning of Style. Dick Hebdige. 1979. pap. 9.50x (ISBN 0-416-70860-9, NO. 2378). Routledge Chapman & Hall.
Subcutaneously, My Dear Watson: Sherlock Holmes & the Cocaine Habit. Jack Tracy & Jim Barkey. (Illus.). 91p. Date not set. pap. 8.95 (ISBN 0-317-30096-2). Vanguard.
Subcutaneously, My Dear Watson: Sherlock Holmes & the Cocaine Habit. Jack Tracy & Jim Berkey. (Illus.). 91p. (Orig.). 1978. pap. 8.95 (ISBN 0-317-11849-8). Gaslight.
Subdivision Analysis. Robert W. Dombal. 20p. 1978. pap. 2.00. Am Inst Real Estate Appraisers.
Subdivision & Site Plain Handbook. David Listokin & Carole W. Baker. 432p. 1987. 45.00 (ISBN 0-88285-123-3). Transaction Bks.
Subdivision Map Act Manual. 4th, rev. ed. Daniel J. Curtin, Jr. 136p. 1988. pap. 20.00x (ISBN 0-9614657-6-X). Solano Pr.
Subdivision Regulation Handbook. National Association of Home Builders. (Cost Effective Residential Development Standards Ser.). (Illus.). 40p. 1978. pap. 6.00 (ISBN 0-86718-048-X). Nat Assn H Build.
Subdivision Regulations in North Carolina: An Introduction. Richard D. Ducker. 1980. pap. 2.50. U of NC Inst Gov.
Subdivisions & Development Design: An Annotated Bibliography of Recent Publications. T. William Patterson. (Public Administration Ser.: P 2296). 15p. 1987. 3.75 (ISBN 1-55590-576-5). Vance Biblios.
Subdrainage & Soil Moisture. (Transportation Research Record Ser.). 76p. 1979. 4.00 (ISBN 0-309-02951-1). Transport Res Bd.
Subduction of Aseismic Oceanic Ridges: Effects on Shape, Seismicity, & Other Characteristics of Consuming Plate Boundaries. Peter R. Yogt et al. LC 75-40900. (Geological Society of America, Special Paper: No. 172). pap. 20.00 (2027367). Bks Demand UMI.
Subduction Zone Metamorphism. Ed. by W. G. Ernst. LC 74-25224. (Benchmark Papers in Geology Ser: No. 19). 1975. 85.50 (ISBN 0-12-786448-2). Acad Pr.
Subdue Sins. large print ed. Ellen White. 41p. 1985. pap. 5.50 (ISBN 0-914009-44-3). VHI Library.
Subdued Southern Nobility: A Southern Ideal, by One of the Nobility. LC 72-2035. (Black Heritage Library Collection Ser.). Repr. of 1882 ed. 20.50 (ISBN 0-8369-9070-6). Ayer Co Pubs.
Sube Tu Apuesta. new ed. Glen Chase. Tr. by Jacinto De Torres from Eng. (Pimienta Collection, Cereza Delicias: No. 4). 160p. (Span.). 1974. pap. 1.00 (ISBN 0-88473-220-7). Fiesta Pub.
Subgroup Structure of the Finite Classical Groups. P. B. Kleidman & M. W. Liebeck. (London Mathematical Society Lecture Note: No. 129). 250p. Date not set. pap. price not set (ISBN 0-521-35949-X). Cambridge U Pr.
Subharmonic Functions, Vol 1. W. K. Hayman & P. B. Kennedy. (London Mathematical Society Ser.). 1977. 76.00 (ISBN 0-12-334801-3). Acad Pr.
Subhas Chandra Bose & Indian Freedom Struggle. Edmund Muller & Arun Bhattacharjee. 1985. 17.50x (ISBN 0-8364-1452-7, Pub. by Ashish India). South Asia Bks.
Subhas Chandra Bose & the Indian National Movement. Hari H. Das. text ed. 37.50x (ISBN 0-86590-104-X, Pub. by Sterling Pubs India). Apt Bks.
Subhas Chandra Bose: From Kabul to Battle of Imphal. H. N. Pandit. 360p. 1988. text ed. 40.00x (Pub. by Sterling Pubs India). Apt Bks.
Subhash Chandra Bose: The Springing Tiger. Hugh Toye. 1970. pap. 2.80 (ISBN 0-88253-190-5). Ind-US Inc.
Subhasita Samgraha, Vol. III & IV. Vol. III - 142 p. pap. 2.00 (ISBN 0-686-95449-1); Vol. IV - 128 p. pap. 2.00 (ISBN 0-686-99508-2). Ananda Marga.
Subhasitaratnakosa. Vidyakara. Ed. by D. D. Kosambi & V. V. Gokhale. LC 57-9076. (Oriental Ser: No. 42). 1958. 27.50x (ISBN 0-674-85380-6). Harvard U Pr.
Subject. Bernard Lonergan. LC 68-22238. (Aquinas Lectures Ser). 1968. 7.95 (ISBN 0-87462-133-X). Marquette.
Subject Access Systems. Milstead. 1984. 31.00 (ISBN 0-12-498120-8). Acad Pr.
Subject Access to Visual Resources Collections: A Model for the Computer Construction of Thematic Catalogs. Karen Markey. LC 86-7658. (New Directions in Information Management Ser.; No. 11). 209p. 1986. 36.95 (ISBN 0-313-24031-0, MSI/). Greenwood.
Subject Analysis in Online Catalogs. Rao Aluri & D. A. Kemp. 300p. 1989. lib. bdg. 29.50 (ISBN 0-87287-670-5). Libs Unl.
Subject & Author Index to Chinese Literature Monthly. Donald A. Gibbs. (Sinology Ser.). 173p. 1978. pap. text ed. 5.95 (ISBN 0-88710-135-6). Yale Far Eastern Pubns.
Subject & Object: As Connected with Our Double Brain & a New Theory of Causation. Robert Verity. LC 78-72828. (Brainedness, Handedness, & Mental Ability Ser.). Repr. of 1870 ed. 21.50 (ISBN 0-404-60896-5). AMS Pr.
Subject & Object in Modern English. Barbara H. Partee. Ed. by Jorge Hankamer. LC 78-66576. (Outstanding Dissertations in Linguistics Ser.). 1985. 20.00 (ISBN 0-8240-9679-7). Garland Pub.
Subject & Place for Watercolour Landscapes. John Fletcher-Watson. (Illus.). 144p. 1985. 25.95 (ISBN 0-7134-3748-0, Pub. by Batsford England). David & Charles.
Subject & Predicate in Logic & Grammar. P. F. Strawson. (University Paperbacks Ser.). 144p. 1974. pap. 13.95x (ISBN 0-416-82200-2, NO.2539). Routledge Chapman & Hall.
Subject & Strategy: A Rhetoric Reader. 4th ed. Ed. by Paul A. Eschholz & Alfred Rosa. LC 87-60568. 600p. 1988. pap. text ed. write for info. (ISBN 0-312-00277-7); write for info. instr.'s manual. St Martin.
Subject & Structure: An Anthology for Writers. 8th ed. John M. Wasson. 1984. pap. text ed. write for info. (ISBN 0-673-39241-4). Scott F.
Subject & Topic: Proceedings. Symposium, University of California, Santa Barbara, Mar. 1975. Ed. by Charles N. Li. 1976. 68.00 (ISBN 0-12-447350-4). Acad Pr.
Subject Approach to Information. 4th ed. A. C. Foskett. 480p. 1982. 27.50 (ISBN 0-85157-313-4, Pub. by Bingley England); pap. 18.50 (ISBN 0-85157-339-8, Pub. by Bingley England). ALA.
Subject Area Reading in the Middle School. David Bishop. 45p. 1982. 4.25 (ISBN 0-318-18691-8). Natl Middle Schl.
Subject Bibliography of Aphid Parasitoids: Hymenoptera: Aphidiidae of the World (1758-1982) Peter Stary. (Monographs in Applied Entomology: Vol. 25). 150p. (Orig.). 1986. pap. text ed. 33.00x (ISBN 3-490-11018-8). Parey Sci Pubs.
Subject Bibliography of the History of American Higher Education. Compiled by Mark Beach. LC 83-22565. vii, 165p. 1984. lib. bdg. 36.95 (ISBN 0-313-23276-8, BEH/). Greenwood.
Subject Bibliography of the Second World War: Books in English, 1975-1983. A. G. Enser. LC 84-13619. 225p. 1985. text ed. 35.50 (ISBN 0-566-03514-6). Gower Pub Co.
Subject Catalog Africa - Fachkatalog Afrika, Vol. 11: Indian Ocean. Compiled by Irmtraud D. Wolke-Renk. 260p. (Eng. & Ger.). 1988. lib. bdg. 119.00 (ISBN 3-598-20931-2). K G Saur.
Subject Catalog: Africa, Vol. 1: Geschichte (Volume 1: History, 2 vols. 2nd, rev., enl. ed. Ed. by Stadt-und Universitat Bibliothek Frankfurt. 781p. (Ger.). 1987. Complete set. lib. bdg. 240.00 (ISBN 3-598-20920-7). K G Saur.
Subject Catalog of the Institute of Governmental Studies Library, 26 Vols. University of California, Berkeley Institute of Governmental Studies Library. 1970. Set. 2570.00 (ISBN 0-8161-0907-9, Hall Library). G K Hall.
Subject Catalog of the Institute of Governmental Studies Library First Supplement. (Reference Supplements Ser.). 1978. lib. bdg. 680.00 (ISBN 0-8161-0963-X, Hall Library). G K Hall.
Subject Cataloging: Critiques & Innovations. Ed. by Sanford Berman. LC 84-10554. (Technical Services Quarterly Ser.: Vol. 2, No. 1/2). 252p. 1985. text ed. 29.95 (ISBN 0-86656-265-6, B265). Haworth Pr.
Subject Catalogue Africa: Vol 10-1: East Africa, Kenya, Vol 10-2: Tanzania, Uganda, 2 Vols. Ed. by Irmtraud D. Wolcke-Renk. xvi, 1403p. 1985. Set. lib. bdg. 165.00 (ISBN 3-598-20929-0). K G Saur.
Subject Catalogue Africa, Vol. 2: Politics, Holdings as of September 1977. Ed. by Stadt und Universitatsbibliothek & Frankfurt am Main. 279p. 1979. lib. bdg. 50.00 (ISBN 3-598-02852-0). K G Saur.
Subject Catalogue Africa, Vol. 3: Literature Holdings as of December 1977. Ed. by Stadt und Universitatsbibliothek & Frankfurt am Main. 368p. 1979. lib. bdg. 50.00 (ISBN 3-598-02853-9). K G Saur.
Subject Catalogue Africa, Vol. 4: Social & Cultural Anthropology Holdings as of December 1978. Ed. by Stadt und Universitatsbibliothek Staff & Frankfurt am Main Staff. 598p. 1980. lib. bdg. 100.00 (ISBN 3-598-20924-X). K G Saur.
Subject Catalogue Africa, Vol. 5: Geography & Social Science Holding As of March 1980. Ed. by Stadt und Universitatsbibliothek & Frankfurt am Main. 589p. 1981. lib. bdg. 100.00 (ISBN 3-598-20925-8). K G Saur.
Subject Catalogue Africa, Vol. 6: Languages-Liguistics. Ed. by Stadt und Universitatsbibiliothek & Frankfurt am Main. 470p. 1982. lib. bdg. 75.00 (ISBN 3-598-20926-6). K G Saur.
Subject Catalogue Africa, Vol. 7: Library Science Education Sciences. Ed. by Stadt und Universitatsbibliothek Frankfurt am Main. Frankfurt A. Main. 414p. 1983. lib. bdg. 100.00 (ISBN 3-598-20927-4). K G Saur.
Subject Catalogue Film, Vol. 1: Individual Holding as of July 1981. Ed. by Stadt und Universitatsbucherei & Frankfurt am Main. 397p. 1982. lib. bdg. 40.00 (ISBN 3-598-10414-6). K G Saur.
Subject Catalogue of the History of Medicine & Related Sciences, 18 vols. Ed. by Wellcome Institute for the History of Medicine, London. 1980. lib. bdg. 2400.00 (ISBN 3-601-00000-8). Kraus Intl.
Subject Catalogue of the House of Commons Parliamentary Papers, 1801-1900, 5 vols. Compiled by Peter Cockton. 4000p. 1987. lib. bdg. 1500.00 (ISBN 0-85964-133-3). Chadwyck-Healey.
Subject Catalogue of the Library of the Royal Empire Society, 1930-1937, 4 vols. Evans Lewin. Incl. Vol. 1. British Empire. 850p. Repr. of 1930 ed; Vol. 2. Australia, New Zealand, South Pacific, Antarctic. 770p. Repr. of 1931 ed; Vol. 3. Canada, Newfoundland, West Indies, Colonial America. 830p. Repr. of 1932 ed; Vol. 4. Mediterranean Colonies, Middle East, Indian Empire, Far East. 820p. Repr. of 1937 ed. 1967. 40.00 ea.; 160.00x set (ISBN 0-8464-0894-5). Beekman Pubs.
Subject Catalogue of the Royal Commonwealth Society, 7 vols. Royal Commonwealth Society, London. 1971. Set. 725.00 (ISBN 0-8161-0885-4, Hall Library). G K Hall.
Subject Classification for the Arrangement of Libraries & the Organization of Information with Tables, Indexes, Etc. For the Subdivision of Subjects. James D. Brown. 1976. lib. bdg. 59.95 (ISBN 0-8490-2715-2). Gordon Pr.
Subject Collections, 2 vols. 6th ed. Lee Ash. 2144p. 1985. 175.00 (ISBN 0-8352-1917-8). Bowker.
Subject Compilations of State Laws, Nineteen Seventy-Nine to Nineteen Eighty-Three: Research Guide & Annotated Bibliography. Cheryl Nyberg & Carol Boast. LC 84-12813. x, 556p. 1984. lib. bdg. 56.95 (ISBN 0-313-23335-7, BSL/). Greenwood.
Subject Compilations of State Laws: Research Guide & Annotated Bibliography. Lynn Foster & Carol Boast. LC 80-1788. 473p. 1981. lib. bdg. 56.95 (ISBN 0-313-21255-4, FOS/). Greenwood.
Subject Compilations of State Laws 1983-1985: An Annotated Bibliography. Cheryl R. Nyberg. LC 85-73774. 595p. 1986. text ed. 78.00 (ISBN 0-9616293-0-4). C Boast & C Nyberg.
Subject Directory of Special Libraries & Information Centers 1988, 5 vols. 11th ed. Ed. by Brigitte T. Darnay. 1987. Set. 685.00x (ISBN 0-8103-4342-8). Gale.
Subject Directory of Special Libraries & Information Centers 1988: Business & Law Libraries, Vol. 1. 11th ed. Ed. by Brigitee T. Darnay. 381p. 1987. 160.00x (ISBN 0-8103-4343-6). Gale.
Subject Directory of Special Libraries & Information Centers 1988: Education & Information Science Libraries, Vol. 2. 11th ed. Ed. by Brigitte T. Darnay. 279p. 1987. 160.00x (ISBN 0-8103-4344-4). Gale.
Subject Directory of Special Libraries & Information Centers 1988: Health Sciences Libraries, Vol. 3. 11th ed. Ed. by Brigitte T. Darnay. 348p. 1987. 160.00x (ISBN 0-8103-4345-2). Gale.
Subject Directory of Special Libraries & Information Centers 1988: Social Sciences & Humanities Libraries, Vol. 4. 11th ed. Ed. by Brigitte T. Darnay. 794p. 1987. 160.00x (ISBN 0-8103-4346-0). Gale.
Subject Directory of Special Libraries & Information Centers 1988: Science & Engineering Libraries, Vol. 5. 11th ed. Ed. by Brigitte T. Darnay. 609p. 1987. 160.00x (ISBN 0-8103-4347-9). Gale.
Subject Directory of Special Libraries, Vol. 1: Business & Law Libraries. Ed. by Brigitte I. Darnay. 1988. 160.00 (ISBN 0-8103-2788-0). Gale.
Subject Directory of Special Libraries, Vol. 2: Social Science, Humanities, Education Libraries. Ed. by Brigitte I. Darnay. 1988. 160.00 (ISBN 0-8103-2789-9). Gale.
Subject Directory of Special Libraries, Vol. 3: Health Sciences Libraries. Ed. by Brigitte I. Darnay. 1988. 160.00 (ISBN 0-8103-2790-2). Gale.
Subject Directory of Special Libraries, Vol. 4: Science & Engineering Libraries. Ed. by Brigitte I. Darnay. 1988. 160.00 (ISBN 0-8103-2791-0). Gale.
Subject Guide to Abstracts: III International Conference on Aids. Ed. by Hovey Smith. 92p. (Orig.). 1987. pap. 10.00 (ISBN 0-317-65394-6). Whitehall Pr.
Subject Guide to AORN Journal Columns, 1982-1984. 1985. 3.00 (ISBN 0-939583-20-8). Assn Oper Rm Nurses.
Subject Guide to Books in Print, 1988-89, 4 vols. Ed. by Bowker, R. R., Staff. 1988. 199.95 (ISBN 0-8352-2493-7); Full year. microfiche 399.00 (ISBN 0-8352-2524-0); Quarterly. microfiche 210.00. Bowker.
Subject Guide to Children's Books in Print, 1988-89. Ed. by Bowker, R. R., Staff. 1988. 89.95 (ISBN 0-8352-2512-7). Bowker.
Subject Guide to Humor: Anecdotes, Facetiae & Satire from 365 Periodicals, 1968-74. Jean S. Kujoth. LC 76-4865. 206p. 1976. 17.50 (ISBN 0-8108-0924-9). Scarecrow.
Subject Guide to Major United States Government Publications. Ellen P. Jackson. LC 68-25844. pap. 46.80 (ISBN 0-317-41822-X, 2025613). Bks Demand UMI.
Subject Guide to Major United States Government Publications. 2nd ed. Rev. by Wiley J. Williams. LC 87-1152. 208p. 1987. 21.95x (ISBN 0-8389-0475-0). ALA.
Subject Guide to Microforms in Print, 1987. Ed. by Microforms in Print Staff. 1987. lib. bdg. 149.50x (ISBN 0-88736-182-X). Meckler Corp.
Subject Guide to Microforms in Print, 1988. Ed. by Microforms in Print Staff. 1988. lib. bdg. 189.50x (ISBN 0-88736-279-6). Meckler Corp.
Subject Guide to Publications of the International Labour Office, with Geographical Index, 1919-1964. 1968. Set. 5.60 (ISBN 92-2-100930-0). Intl Labour Office.
Subject Guide to Publications of the International Labour Office 1980-85. (International Labour Bibliography: No. 1). viii, 614p. (Orig.). 1987. pap. 21.00 (ISBN 92-2-106076-4). Intl Labour Office.
Subject Guide to Reference Books, 1970-1975. M. Balachandran & S. Balachandran. LC 79-83698. 1980. 60.00 (ISBN 0-87650-102-1). Pierian.

Submersible Pumps & Their Applications. H. H. Anderson. 370p. 1985. text ed. 116.00 (ISBN 0-85461-098-7, Pub. by Trade & Tech England). Brookfield Pub Co.

Submersible Sewage Pumping Systems Handbook. Ed. by Durward Humes. (Illus.). 120p. 1986. 27.95 (ISBN 0-87371-085-1). Lewis Pubs Inc.

Submersible Technology & Adapting to Change. Ed. by Society for Underwater Technology. 1988. lib. bdg. 120.00 (ISBN 0-86010-896-1, Pub. by Graham & Trotman UK). Kluwer Academic.

Submersibles & Their Use in Oceanography & Ocean Engineering. R. A. Geyer. (Elsevier Oceanography Ser.: Vol. 17). 384p. 1977. 108.00 (ISBN 0-444-41545-9). Elsevier.

Submicroscopic Cytochemistry, 2vols. Ed. by Isidore Gersh. Incl. Vol. 1. Protein & Nucleic Acids. 1974; Vol.2. Membranes,Mitochondria, & Connective Tissue. 1974. 54.00 (ISBN 0-12-281402-9). Acad Pr.

Submicroscopic Studies of Soils. Ed. by E. B. Bisdom & J. Duclox. (Developments in Soil Science Ser.: Vol. 12). 352p. 1983. Repr. 113.25 (ISBN 0-444-42195-5, I-308-83). Elsevier.

Submillimeter Waves see Microwave Research Institute Symposia.

Submillimetre Wave Astronomy. J. E. Beckman & J. P. Phillips. LC 82-4487. (Illus.). 370p. 1982. 54.50 (ISBN 0-521-24733-0). Cambridge U Pr.

Submillimetre Waves & Their Applications: Proceedings. International Conference on Submillimetre Waves & Their Applications, 3rd, 1978. LC 79-40065. (Illus.). 1979. 71.00 (ISBN 0-08-023817-3). Pergamon.

Subminiature Camera. William White, Jr. (Illus.). 288p. Date not set. 24.95 (ISBN 0-240-51710-5). Focal Pr.

Submission Is for Husbands, Too. Mark R. Littleton. LC 87-71221. 160p. 1988. pap. 6.95 (ISBN 0-89636-239-6). Accent Bks.

Submissions to the Royal Commission on Criminal Procedure. NCCL Staff. 1979. 20.00x (ISBN 0-317-54922-7, Pub. by NCCL UK). State Mutual Bk.

Submissive Wife & other Legends. Marsha Drake. 176p. (Orig.). 1987. pap. 5.95 (ISBN 0-87123-926-4). Bethany Hse.

Submitting. Churches Alive, Inc. Staff. LC 79-52131. (Love One Another Bible Study Ser.). (Illus.). 1979. wkbk. 3.00 (ISBN 0-934396-04-3). Churches Alive.

Submitting an Idea. 7p. 1974. pap. 1.00 (ISBN 0-317-30712-6). Amer Bar Assn.

Submitting To A Sinning Husband. Wanda Burkhart. 64p. 1984. pap. 2.95 (ISBN 0-88144-042-6). Christian Pub.

Submolecular Biology & Cancer. Ciba Foundation Staff. LC 79-10949. (Ciba Foundation Ser.: No. 67). 360p. 1979. 60.00 (ISBN 0-444-90078-0, Excerpta Medica). Elsevier.

Submolecular Biology & Cancer. Ciba Foundation Staff. LC 79-14324. (Ciba Foundation Symposium, New Ser.: 67). pap. 90.00 (ISBN 0-317-29763-5, 2022187). Bks Demand UMI.

Subnational Politics in the 1980's: Organization, Reorganization & Economic Development. Ed. by Louis A. Picard & Raphael Zariski. LC 86-20479. 276p. 1986. lib. bdg. 40.95 (ISBN 0-275-92314-2, C2314). Praeger.

Subnational Politics: Readings in State & Local Government. David C. Saffell & Terry Gilbreth. (Political Science Ser.). (Illus.). 320p. 1981. pap. write for info (ISBN 0-394-34939-3, RanC). Random.

Subnormal Operators & Representations of Algebras of Bounded Analytic Functions & Other Uniform Algebras. Olin et al. LC 86-17381. (Memoirs of the American Mathematical Society Ser.: Vol. 354). 125p. 1986. pap. text ed. 20.00 (ISBN 0-8218-2415-5). Am Math.

Subnormal Subgroups of Groups. John C. Lennox & Stewart Stonehewer. (Oxford Mathematical Monographs). (Illus.). 268p. 1987. 69.00 (ISBN 0-19-853552-X). Oxford U Pr.

Subordinate Sex: A History of Attitudes Towards Women. Vern L. Bullough & Bonnie Bullough. LC 72-91079. pap. 72.80 (ISBN 0-317-09711-3, 2014930). Bks Demand UMI.

Subordinated Sex: A History of Attitudes Toward Women. rev. ed. Vern L. Bullough et al. LC 87-23292. 488p. 1988. 40.00x (ISBN 0-8203-1002-6); pap. 17.95 (ISBN 0-8203-1003-4). U of Ga Pr.

Subordination: Feminism & Social Theory. Clare Burton. 146p. 1985. text ed. 34.95x (ISBN 0-86861-718-0); pap. text ed. 10.50x (ISBN 0-86861-710-5). Unwin Hyman.

Subordination or Liberation? The Development & Conflicting Theories of Black Education in Nineteenth Century Alabama. Robert G. Sherer. LC 75-44050. 224p. 1977. 18.75 (ISBN 0-8173-9111-8). U of Ala Pr.

Subpoemas. Lennart Bruce. 68p. 1974. pap. 6.00 (ISBN 0-915572-06-0). Panjandrum.

Subpulmonic Ventricular Septal Defect: Proceedings of the Third Asian Congress on Pediatric Neurosurgery Held in November 1983. Ed. by A. Takao & H. C. Lue. 70p. 1986. pap. 45.00 (ISBN 0-387-70014-5). Springer-Verlag.

Subramanyam: Scientific & Technical Information. 1981. 39.75 (ISBN 0-8247-1356-7). Dekker.

Subrecursion: Functions & Hierarchies. H. E. Rose. (Oxford Logic Guides). 1984. 35.00x (ISBN 0-19-853189-3). Oxford U Pr.

Subscribe Now: Building Arts Audiences Through Dynamic Subscription Promotion. 3rd ed. Danny Newman. LC 77-81452. (Illus.). 288p. 1977. pap. 11.95 (ISBN 0-930452-01-1). Theatre Comm.

Subscribe Now! Building Arts Audiences Through Dynamic Subscription Promotion. Danny Newman. 276p. pap. 10.95. Am Council Arts.

Subscription Television - A Study for the Home Office. 180p. (Orig.). 1987. pap. text ed. 17.50 (ISBN 0-11-340855-2, HM1, HMSO). UNIPUB.

Subscription Television: History, Current Status & Economic Projections. 200p. 20.00 (ISBN 0-317-34984-8). Natl Assn Broadcasters.

Subsea Blowout Preventers & Marine Riser Systems. (Rotary Drilling Ser.: Unit III, Lesson 4). (Illus.). 57p. (Orig.). 1976. pap. text ed. 6.95 (ISBN 0-88698-052-6, 2.30410). PETEX.

Subsea Technology. (Advances in Underwater Technology & Offshore Engineering: Vol. 5). (Illus.). 500p. 1986. 106.50 (ISBN 0-86010-771-X). Graham & Trotman.

Subseciva Groningana I. Ed. by J. H. Lokin et al. 142p. (Orig., Ger. & Eng.). 1984. pap. 23.00x (ISBN 90-6088-086-2, Pub. by Boumas Boekhuis Netherlands). Benjamins North Am.

Subseciva Groningana II. Ed. by C. J. Lokin et al. iv, 146p. (Fr., Ger., & Ital.). 1985. pap. 24.00x (ISBN 90-6980-006-3, Pub. by Egbert Forsten Holland). Benjamins North Am.

Subsequent Performances. Jonathan Miller. LC 85-41088. 288p. 1986. 25.00 (ISBN 0-670-81234-X). Viking.

Subset FORTRAN-77. Max W. Durgin. (Illus.). 320p. (Orig.). 1983. pap. text ed. 24.95x (ISBN 0-935920-11-0). Natl Pub Black Hills.

Subsidence Over Mines & Caverns, Moisture & Frost Actions & Classification. (Transportation Research Record Ser.). 83p. 1976. 3.60 (ISBN 0-309-02588-5). Transport Res Bd.

Subsidies for the Theatre: A Study of the Central European System of Financing Drama, Opera & Ballet. Wallace Dace. LC 72-84841. 188p. 1973. pap. 7.95 (ISBN 0-686-05610-8). AG Pr.

Subsidies in International Trade. Gary C. Hufbauer & Joanna S. Erb. LC 84-12825. 299p. (Orig.). 1984. 35.00 (ISBN 0-88132-004-8). Inst Intl Eco.

Subsidies to Higher Education: The Issues. Ed. by Howard P. Tuckman & Edward L. Whalen. LC 80-18241. 320p. 1980. 42.95 (ISBN 0-275-90562-4, C0562). Praeger.

Subsidised Public Transport & the Demand for Travel. Bailey Goodwin et al. 234p. 1983. text ed. 33.95x (ISBN 0-566-00654-5). Gower Pub Co.

Subsidized Housing Handbook: How to Provide, Preserve & Manage Housing for Lower-Income People. National Housing Law Project. 500p. (Orig.). 1982. pap. 35.00 (ISBN 0-9606098-3-0). Natl Housing Law.

Subsidized Housing in Chicago: A Spatial Survey & Analysis, No. 6. Elizabeth Warren. LC 80-120114. (Illus.). 70p. 1980. pap. 3.00 (ISBN 0-911531-05-X). Loyola U Ctr Urban.

Subsidized Housing in the Chicago Suburbs. Elizabeth Warren. LC 83-110654. (Urban Insights Ser.: No. 8). (Illus.). 80p. 1981. pap. 4.50 (ISBN 0-911531-06-8). Loyola U Ctr Urban.

Subsidized Programs for Low Income People. Ed. by Lloyd Hogan. LC 80-53746. 192p. 1981. pap. text ed. 12.95 (ISBN 0-87855-864-0). Transaction Bk.

Subsidizing Industrial Location: A Conceptual Framework with Application to Korea. Michael P. Murray. LC 88-45375. (World Bank Occasional Papers, New Ser.: No. 3). 160p. (Orig.). 1988. pap. text ed. 14.95x (ISBN 0-8018-3752-9). Johns Hopkins.

Subsidizing Inefficiency: A Study of State Aid & Local Government Productivity. Richard H. Silkman. 124p. 1985. 35.00 (ISBN 0-275-90164-5, C0164). Praeger.

Subsidizing Shelter: The Relationship Between Welfare & Housing Assistance. Sandra J. Newman & Ann B. Schnare. LC 87-34026. (Report Ser.: No. 1). (Illus.). 206p. (Orig.). 1988. pap. text ed. 14.95 (ISBN 0-87766-414-5). Urban Inst.

Subsidizing Success: The Export-Import Bank in the United States Economy. Richard E. Feinberg. LC 81-4702. (Illus.). 192p. 1982. 42.50 (ISBN 0-521-23427-1). Cambridge U Pr.

Subsistence Agriculture in Melanesia, 2 vols. Jacques Barrau. (BMB). 1958-1961. Repr. of 1958 ed. Vol. 1. 15.00 (ISBN 0-527-02327-2); Vol. 2. 16.00 (ISBN 0-527-02331-0). Kraus Repr.

Subsistence & Change: Lessons of Agropastoralism in Somalia. Garth Massey. (Westview Special Studies in Social, Political & Economic Development). 238p. 1987. pap. 34.50 (ISBN 0-8133-7294-1). Westview.

Subsistence & Conflict in Kona, Hawai'i: An Archaeological Study of the Kuakini Highway Realignment Corridor. Rose Schlit. (Departmental Report Ser.: No. 84-1). (Illus.). 427p. 1984. 15.00 (ISBN 0-910240-96-5). Bishop Mus.

Subsistence & Survival: Rural Ecology in the Pacific. Ed. by Timothy Bayliss-Smith & Richard Feachem. 1978. 94.00 (ISBN 0-12-083250-X). Acad Pr.

Subsistence & the North Slope Inupiat: The Effects of Energy Development. John A. Kruse. (ISER Report Ser.: No. 56). 45p. 1982. pap. 6.50 (ISBN 0-88353-034-1). U Alaska Inst Res.

Subsistence Farming in Roman Italy. J. Frayn. 1981. 40.00x (ISBN 0-900000-92-9, Pub. by Centaur Bks). State Mutual Bk.

Subspace Explorers. E. E. Smith. 256p. 1984. pap. 2.75 (ISBN 0-425-07480-3). Berkley Pub.

Subspace Explorers. Edward E. Smith. LC 64-25828. 1965. 15.00x (ISBN 0-940724-15-4). A E Ryter Bks.

Subspace Methods of Pattern Recognition. E. Oja. (Pattern Recognition & Image Processing Research Studies Ser.). 186p. 1984. Repr. 77.95x (ISBN 0-471-90311-6, 1-516, Pub. by Wiley-Interscience). Wiley.

Substance Abuse. Mario Orlandi & Donald Prue. (Encyclopedia of Health Ser.). (gr. 5 up). 1988. 16.95x (ISBN 0-8160-1669-0). Facts On File.

Substance Abuse Accounts Auditor. (Career Examination Ser.: C-3478). Date not set. pap. 16.00 (ISBN 0-8373-3478-0). Natl Learning.

Substance Abuse & Family Therapy. Edward Kaufman. 256p. 1985. 27.50 (ISBN 0-8089-1679-3, 792254). Grune.

Substance Abuse & Psychopathology. Ed. by Arthur I. Alterman. (Applied Clinical Psychology Ser.). 412p. 1985. 45.00x (ISBN 0-306-41849-5, Plenum Pr). Plenum Pub.

Substance Abuse & Psychopathology. Steven M. Mirin. LC 84-6291. (Clinical Insights Monograph). 176p. 1984. pap. text ed. 12.00x (ISBN 0-88048-059-9, 48-059-9). Am Psychiatric.

Substance Abuse: Bibliography. 7.50 (ISBN 0-317-59914-3, 72509C). Am Assn Coun Dev.

Substance Abuse: Genetic, Perinatal, & Developmental Aspects. Ed. by Monique C. Braude. Date not set. price not set (ISBN 0-89004-413-9). Raven.

Substance Abuse, Habitual Behavior & Self-Control. Ed. by Peter K. Levison. (American Association for the Advancement of Science Selected Symposium Ser.: No. 59). 185p. 1984. lib. bdg. 39.00x (ISBN 0-86531-034-3). Westview.

Substance Abuse Materials for School Libraries: An Annotated Bibliography. Theodora Andrews. 225p. 1985. lib. bdg. 22.50 (ISBN 0-87287-476-1). Libs Unl.

Substance Abuse: Pharmacologic & Developmental Perspectives. Purcell Taylor. (Illus.). 120p. 1988. text ed. 24.75x (ISBN 0-398-05484-3). C C Thomas.

Substance Abuse: Pharmacologic, Developmental & Clinical Perspectives. 2nd ed. Bennett. 1988. price not set (ISBN 0-471-63499-9). Wiley.

Substance Abuse: Pharmacologic, Developmental & Clinical Perspectives. Gerald Bennett et al. LC 82-13583. 453p. 1983. 35.00 (ISBN 0-471-08537-5). Wiley.

Substance Abuse Prevention Activities for Elementary Children. Timothy Gerne, Jr. & Patricia Gerne. LC 86-3176. 244p. 1986. pap. 18.95x (ISBN 0-13-859075-3, Busn Pro Bks). P-H.

Substance Abuse: Prevention & Cures. Edwin Dobb. (Encyclopedia of Psychoactive Drugs Ser.: No. 2). (Illus.). 104p. (gr. 5 up). 1988. lib. bdg. 17.95x (ISBN 1-55546-219-7). Chelsea Hse.

Substance Abuse Problems. Sidney Cohen. LC 80-21280. 392p. 1981. text ed. 39.95 (ISBN 0-917724-18-6, B18); pap. text ed. 22.95 (ISBN 0-917724-22-4, B22). Haworth Pr.

Substance Abuse Problems, Vol. 2: New Issues for the 1980's. Sidney Cohen. LC 80-21280. 323p. 1985. text ed. 39.95 (ISBN 0-86656-368-7); pap. text ed. 19.95 (ISBN 0-86656-369-5). Haworth Pr.

Substance Abuse Program Specialist. (Career Examination Ser.: C-3336). Date not set. pap. 14.00 (ISBN 0-8373-3336-9). Natl Learning.

Substance Abuse Treatment Program Assistant. (Career Examination Ser.: C-3479). Date not set. pap. 14.00 (ISBN 0-8373-3479-9). Natl Learning.

Substance Abusers, Criminality & Aftercare. Robert M. Owings. LC 85-82110. 80p. (Orig.). 1985. pap. 4.95 (ISBN 0-930823-01-X). Lifeline Pubs.

Substance & Form in History. Ed. by Leon Pompa & Williams Dray. 198p. 1981. 22.50 (ISBN 0-85224-413-4, Pub. by Edinburgh U Pr Scotland). Columbia U Pr.

Substance & Function & Einstein's Theory of Relativity. Ernst Cassirer. pap. 7.95 (ISBN 0-486-20050-7). Dover.

Substance & Manner: Studies in Music & the Other Arts. Audrey Davidson. (Illus.). 1977. pap. 4.95 (ISBN 0-930276-00-0). Hiawatha Pr.

Substance & Modern Science. Richard J. Connell. LC 87-73319. 1988. text ed. 29.95x (ISBN 0-268-01731-X); pap. text ed. 16.95x (ISBN 0-268-01732-8). U of Notre Dame Pr.

Substance & Shadow: Or, Morality & Religion in Their Relation to Life, an Essay upon the Physics of Creation. Henry James, Sr. LC 72-915. (Selected Works of Henry James, Sr.: Vol. 8). 552p. 1983. Repr. of 1863 ed. 49.50 (ISBN 0-404-10088-0). AMS Pr.

Substance & the Dream. Lorice F. Mulhern. 288p. 1988. 14.95 (ISBN 0-89962-620-3). Todd & Honeywell.

Substance, Body & Soul: Aristotelian Investigations. Edwin Hartman. LC 77-71984. 1977. text ed. 36.50x (ISBN 0-691-07223-X). Princeton U Pr.

Substance, Form, & Psyche: An Aristolelean Methaphysics. Montgomery Furth. 304p. Date not set. price not set (ISBN 0-521-34143-4). Cambridge U Pr.

Substance of a Journal During a Residence at the Red River Colony. John West. 19.00 (ISBN 0-384-66930-1). Johnson Repr.

Substance of Cervantes. John G. Weiger. 320p. 1985. 44.50 (ISBN 0-521-30516-0). Cambridge U Pr.

Substance of Greek & Shakespearan Tragedy under Special Consideration of Shakespeare's King Lear, Macbeth, Othello & Romeo & Juliet. Gerhard W. Kaiser. Ed. by James Hogg. (Elizabethan & Renaissance Studies). 291p. (Orig.). 1977. pap. 15.00 (ISBN 3-7052-0710-5, Pub. by Salzburg Studies). Longwood Pub Group.

Substance of Muhammahan Law. A. R. Chaudhri. 1970. 4.25x (ISBN 0-87902-157-8). Orientalia.

Substance of the Descent of Man. Charles Darwin. 1978. Repr. of 1926 ed. lib. bdg. 32.50 (ISBN 0-8492-0685-5). R West.

Substance of Things Hoped for: Fiction & Faith - Outstanding Modern Short Stories. John B. Breslin, Jr. 1988. pap. 8.95 (ISBN 0-385-24692-7). Doubleday.

Substance of Things Hoped for Short Fiction by Modern Catholic Authors. Intro. by John B. Breslin. LC 86-16656. 336p. 1987. pap. 17.95 (ISBN 0-385-23428-7). Doubleday.

Substance P & Neurokinins. Ed. by J. Henry. (Illus.). 390p. 1987. 79.00 (ISBN 0-387-96421-5). Springer-Verlag.

Substance P in the Nervous System: Symposium, No. 91. CIBA Foundations Symposium Staff. 360p. 1986. Repr. 54.95 (ISBN 0-471-91060-0). Wiley.

Substance P: Metabolism & Biological Actions. Ed. by C. C. Jordan & P. Oehme. 260p. 1985. 66.00x (ISBN 0-85066-324-5). Taylor & Francis.

Substance under Pressure: Artistic Coherence & Evolving Form in the Novels of Doris Lessing. Betsy Draine. LC 82-70556. 240p. 1983. 21.50x (ISBN 0-299-09230-5). U of Wis Pr.

Substance X. David Houston. (Tales of Tomorrow Ser.: No. 3). 208p. (Orig.). 1982. pap. 2.25 (ISBN 0-8439-0961-7, Leisure Bks). Leisure NY.

Substantial Holdings. M. Truman Cooper. (Orig.). 1987. pap. 4.50 (ISBN 0-317-66653-3). Pudding Hse Pubns.

Substantial Proofs of Being: Osip Mandelstam's Literary Prose. Charles Isenberg. 179p. (Orig.). 1987. pap. 14.95 (ISBN 0-89357-169-5). Slavica.

Substantive Criminal Law. M. Cherif Bassiouni. 676p. 1978. 61.50x (ISBN 0-398-03628-4). C C Thomas.

Substantive Criminal Law. 2nd ed. Wayne R. LaFave & Austin W. Scott, Jr. LC 86-7795. (Criminal Practice Ser.). 1300p. 1986. text ed. write for info. (ISBN 0-314-98403-8). West Pub.

Substantive Due Process of Law: A Dichotomy of Sense & Nonsense. Frank R. Strong. LC 86-71003. 316p. 1987. lib. bdg. 24.95 (ISBN 0-89089-313-6). Carolina Acad Pr.

Substantive Evidence in Phonology: The Evidence from Finnish & French. Royal Skousen. LC 74-84242. (Janua Linguarum Ser. Minor). (Illus.). 135p. (Orig.). 1975. pap. text ed. 16.00x (ISBN 0-686-22595-3). Mouton.

Substantive Grammar of Shakespeare's Non-Dramatic Texts. Ashley C. Partridge. LC 75-44106. 232p. 1976. 22.50x (ISBN 0-8139-0619-9, Bibliographical Soc., U of VA). U Pr of Va.

Substantivized Adjectives in Old Norse. C. D. Buchanan. (LD). pap. 16.00 (ISBN 0-527-00761-7). Kraus Repr.

Substanz und Qualitaet: Ein Beitrag zur Interpretation der plotinischen Traktate Vi 1, 2, und 3. Klaus Wurm. LC 72-81572. (Quellen und Studien zur Philosophie, Vol. 5). 276p. 1973. 33.60x (ISBN 3-11-001899-3). De Gruyter.

Substate Regional Planning in Virginia: A Bibliographical Essay, No. 1086. Walter J. Raymond. 1976. 5.00 (ISBN 0-686-20402-6). CPL Biblios.

Substituent Effects in Radical Chemistry. Ed. by Heinz G. Viehe et al. 1986. lib. bdg. 79.50 (ISBN 90-277-2340-0, Pub. by Reidel Holland). Kluwer Academic.

Substitute Bride. Margaret Pargeter. (Harlequin Presents Ser.). 192p. 1983. pap. 1.95 (ISBN 0-373-10580-0). Harlequin Bks.

Substitute Bridegroom. Jeanne Abbott. 256p. 1985. pap. 2.50 (ISBN 0-449-20804-4, Crest). Fawcett.

Substitute Care Programs for Young Mothers & Their Infants: An Overview. 70p. 1984. 9.50 (ISBN 0-87868-230-9, 2309). Child Welfare.

Substitute Doctor. Elizabeth Seifert. 1974. Repr. of 1957 ed. lib. bdg. 19.95x (ISBN 0-88411-036-2, Pub. by Aeonian Pr). Amereon Ltd.

Substitute Foods Industry. Business Communications Staff. 185p. 1986. 1250.00 (ISBN 0-89336-481-9, GA-052). BCC.

Substitute for Holiness, Or Antinomianism Revived. Daniel Steele. (Higher Christian Life Ser.). 370p. 1985. lib. bdg. 45.00 (ISBN 0-8240-6445-3). Garland Pub.

Substitute Guest. Grace L. Hill. 17.95 (ISBN 0-89190-065-9, Pub. by Am Repr). Amereon Ltd.

Subway Slams. Ed. by Barbara Fisher & Richard Spiegel. (Illus.). 48p. (Orig.). (gr. k-8). 1981. pap. 2.00 (ISBN 0-934830-22-3). Ten Penny.

Subway Survival: The Art of Self-Defense on American Public Transit Facilities. B. J. Steiner. 1986. lib. bdg. 79.95 (ISBN 0-8490-3554-6). Gordon Pr.

Subway Survival: The Art of Self Defense on American Public Transit Facility. Bradley J. Steiner. 1980. pap. 7.95 (ISBN 0-686-29512-9). Loompanics.

Succasunna New Jersey. Sander Zulauf. 64p. (Orig.). 1987. pap. 6.00 (ISBN 0-917020-03-0). Breaking Point.

Succeed. Rob Narke. LC 83-71420. (Illus.). 336p. (Orig.). 1983. pap. 7.95 (ISBN 0-9611336-0-0). Dreaming.

Succeeding at Business & Technical Presentations. Meuse. 1988. 29.95 (ISBN 0-471-62486-1). Wiley.

Succeeding in High Tech: A Guide to Building Your Career. Marlene Shigekawa. LC 86-33953. 368p. 1987. 29.95 (ISBN 0-471-85636-3). Wiley.

Succeeding in the World of Work. rev. ed. Grady Kimbrell & Ben S. Vineyard. (gr. 10-12). 1981. text ed. 25.32 (ISBN 0-02-669650-9); filmstrip set 612.00 (ISBN 0-02-669690-8); instr's guide 7.80 (ISBN 0-02-669670-3); activities 8.60. Glencoe Bennett & McKnight.

Succeeding John Bull: America in Britain's Place, 1900-1975. D. C. Watt. LC 83-7813. (Wiles Lectures Ser.). 288p. 1984. 42.50 (ISBN 0-521-25022-6). Cambridge U Pr.

Succeeding on the Job: A Self-Study Guide for Students. Patricia M Rath. 1970. pap. text ed. 8.00x (ISBN 0-8134-1167-X, 1167). Inter Print Pubs.

Succesful Machine Applique. Ed. by S. Gail Reeder. LC 78-72878. (Illus.). 48p. 1978. pap. 6.00 (ISBN 0-932946-01-1). Burdett CA.

Success. Martin Amis. LC 87-7564. 224p. 1987. 15.95 (ISBN 0-517-56649-4, Harmony). Crown.

Success. Lion Feuchtwanger. 652p. 1984. pap. 10.95 (ISBN 0-88184-078-5). Carroll & Graf.

Success. Lion Feuchtwanger. 781p. 1986. Repr. of 1930 ed. lib. bdg. 47.50 (ISBN 0-8495-1742-7). Arden Lib.

Success. Robert B. Graham. LC 71-103512. (Short Story Index Reprint Ser.). 1902. 17.00 (ISBN 0-8369-3254-4). Ayer Co Pubs.

Success! Michael Korda. (Illus.). 1977. 8.95 (ISBN 0-394-40866-7). Random.

Success. Janet McDonnell. LC 88-4348. (What Is It?--A Values Ser.). (Illus.). 32p. (gr. k-3). 1988. PLB 7.95 (ISBN 0-89565-376-1). Childs World.

Success. Sue Riley. LC 77-20992. (What Does It Mean? Ser.). (Illus.). (ps-2). 1978. PLB 6.75 (ISBN 0-89565-016-9). Childs World.

Success. Sue Riley. LC 77-20992. (What Does It Mean? Ser.). (Illus.). 32p. (ps-2). 1978. 10.33 (ISBN 0-516-06146-1). Childrens.

Success & Betrayal: The Crisis of Women in Corporate America. Sarah Hardesty & Nehama Jacobs. 464p. 1986. 18.95 (ISBN 0-531-15027-5). Watts.

Success & Betrayal: The Crisis of Women in Corporate America. Sarah Hardesty & Nehama Jacobs. 480p. 1987. 8.95 (ISBN 0-671-64563-3, Touchstone Bks). S&S.

Success & Failure in Europe's Intellectual Development, 2 vols. John W. Draper. (Illus.). 187p. 1986. Repr. of 1876 ed. two vols. 187.50 (ISBN 0-89901-251-5). Found Class Reprints.

Success & Failure in Israeli Elementary Education: An Evaluation Study with Special Emphasis on Disadvantaged Students. Avram Minkowich. LC 80-19873. 539p. 1981. 49.95 (ISBN 0-87855-370-3). Transaction Bks.

Success & Failure in Psychoanalysis & Psychotherapy. Ed. by Benjamin Wolman. 1972. 7.95 (ISBN 0-02-896120-X). Macmillan.

Success & Failure in Small Business. John Lewis & John Stanworth. LC 83-16447. 304p. 1984. text ed. 36.00x (ISBN 0-566-00645-6). Gower Pub Co.

Success & Failure of Picasso. John Berger. (Illus.). 1980. pap. 7.95 (ISBN 0-394-73900-0). Pantheon.

Success & Failure of Primal Therapy: An Empirical Study of Patients at the Primal Institute in Los Angeles. T. Videgard. 302p. 1984. text ed. 28.50x (ISBN 91-22-00698-2, Pub. by Almqvist & Wiksell). Humanities.

Success & Failure of the Anglo-American Committee of Inquiry, 1945-1946: Last Chance in Palestine. Allen H. Podet. LC 87-1635. (Jewish Studies: Vol. 3). 384p. 1987. lib. bdg. 59.95x (ISBN 0-88946-255-0). E Mellen.

Success & Failure on Parole in California. Date not set. price not set. Natl Coun Crime.

Success & Harmony in Life. Elfrida Muller-Kainz. 112p. 1987. 15.00 (ISBN 0-8062-2814-8). Carlton.

Success & Health Conscious Thoughts & Actions for Business People. Herbert L. Beierle. 1982. 10.00 (ISBN 0-940480-17-4). U of Healing.

Success & Survival in the Family Owned Business. Pat B. Alcorn. 272p. 1986. pap. 9.95 (ISBN 0-446-38326-0). Warner Bks.

Success & Survival in the Family-Owned Business. Pat B. Alcorn. LC 80-28976. pap. 68.90 (ISBN 0-317-58110-4, AU00346). Bks Demand UMI.

Success & Survival in the Family Owned Business. 253p. 17.50 (ISBN 0-318-15925-2). Natl Water Well.

Success & the Fear of Success in Women. David W. Krueger. LC 83-48706. 224p. 1984. 29.95x (ISBN 0-02-918040-6). Free Pr.

Success & the Single Woman. Gwendolyn L. Baines. Ed. by Jane Whitehead. 80p. (Orig.). 1985. pap. 7.95 (ISBN 0-9614505-0-9). Baines.

Success & Understanding. Jean Piaget. LC 78-16435. (Illus.). 1978. 17.50x (ISBN 0-674-85387-3). Harvard U Pr.

Success at O Level Physics. K. N. Gravelle. 108p. 1985. 13.50x (ISBN 0-85088-654-6, Pub. by Gomer Pr). State Mutual Bk.

Success at the Harness Races. Barry Meadow. 1970. 4.95 (ISBN 0-685-08136-2, Pub. by Citadel Pr). Lyle Stuart.

Success at the Harness Races. Barry Meadow. 1976. pap. 5.00 (ISBN 0-87980-320-7). Wilshire.

Success Book for Landlords: A Money-Making Guide for Property Owners, Managers & Investors. David N. Siegel. (Illus.). 272p. 1983. 13.00 (ISBN 0-682-49992-7). Exposition-Phoenix.

Success Control: Positive Thinking. Enoch A. Gyamfi. 1985. 6.50 (ISBN 0-8062-2464-9). Carlton.

Success Cybernetics. Uell S. Andersen. pap. 7.00 (ISBN 0-87980-155-7). Wilshire.

Success Easier Than Failure. E. W. Howe. (Collected Works of E. W. Howe). 1988. Repr. of 1917 ed. lib. bdg. 59.00x. Am Biog Serv.

Success Easier Than Failure see Collected Works.

Success Ethic & the Shattered American Dream. Blaine Taylor. (Illus.). 270p. 1976. 8.95 (ISBN 0-87491-387-X); pap. 4.95 (ISBN 0-87491-039-0). Acropolis.

Success Factor. Fred Good. LC 85-50414. 84p. 1985. pap. 3.95 (ISBN 0-931117-02-X). Univ Pub.

Success Factor. Sydney Lecker. 112p. 1986. 10.95 (ISBN 0-8160-1271-7). Facts on File.

Success Fantasy. Anthony Campolo. LC 79-67852. 144p. 1980. pap. 5.95 (ISBN 0-88207-796-1). Victor Bks.

Success Guide to Exciting Fashion Shows. Thelma H. Shirley. LC 78-75210. (Illus., Orig.). 1978. pap. 10.00x (ISBN 0-686-52691-0). Fashion Imprints.

Success Guide to Managerial Achievement. Robin Stuart-Kotze & Rick Roskin. 1983. text ed. 26.00 (ISBN 0-8359-7141-4, Reston); pap. text ed. 18.95 (ISBN 0-8359-7142-2). P-H.

Success How-To's of Money-Making Direct Mail. Galen Stilson. (Mail Order Success Ser.: No.4). 32p. 1985. pap. 11.00 (ISBN 0-915665-10-7). Premier Publishers.

Success Image: A Guide for the Better-Dressed Businesswoman. Vicki Keltner & Mike Holsey. LC 82-3127. 96p. (Orig.). 1982. pap. 8.00x (ISBN 0-87201-034-1). Gulf Pub.

Success in a Small Business is a Laughing Matter. 2nd rev. ed. J. Phillips Johnston. LC 82-14277. (Illus.). 224p. 1982. 14.95 (ISBN 0-939710-11-0). Meridional Pubns.

Success in America: The Yeoman Dream & the Industrial Revolution. Rex Burns. LC 75-32482. (Illus.). 224p. 1976. 17.50x (ISBN 0-87023-207-X). U of Mass Pr.

Success in Answering Reference Questions: Two Studies. Frances Benham & Ronald R. Powell. LC 86-14629. (Illus.). 313p. 1987. 29.50 (ISBN 0-8108-1940-6). Scarecrow.

Success in Athletics. Carl Johnson. (Success Sportbooks Ser.). (Illus.). 1977. 12.00 (ISBN 0-7195-3375-9). Transatl Arts.

Success in Beginning Reading & Writing: Grade 1. Anne H. Adams. (gr. 1-3). 1978. 14.95 (ISBN 0-673-16551-5). Scott F.

Success in British History Seventeen Sixty to Nineteen Fourteen. Peter Lane. (Success Ser). (Illus.). 1978. pap. 12.00 (ISBN 0-7195-3483-6). Transatl Arts.

Success in Chemistry. John Bandtock & Paul Hanson. (Success Studybooks Ser.). (Illus.). 380p. 1975. pap. 12.00 (ISBN 0-7195-2914-X). Transatl Arts.

Success in College: The Role of Personal Qualities & Academic Ability. Warren W. Willingham. 240p. (Orig.). 1985. 26.95 (ISBN 0-87447-229-6); pap. 16.95 (ISBN 0-87447-228-8). College Bd.

Success in Court. Francis L. Wellman. xviii, 404p. 1982. Repr. of 1941 ed. lib. bdg. 35.00x (ISBN 0-8377-1326-9). Rothman.

Success in Economics. Derek Lobley. (Illus.). 363p. 1975. pap. 12.00. Transatl Arts.

Success in Football (Soccer) 3rd ed. Mike Smith. (Illus.). 96p. 1984. 12.00 (ISBN 0-7195-2822-4). Transatl Arts.

Success in God's Word: Bible Scriptures for a Fulfilling Life. Ed. by Charles R. Adams & William J. Seno. 112p. 1986. pap. 2.95 (ISBN 0-933437-01-3). Round River Pub.

Success in Golf. Ken Redford & Nick Tremayne. (Success Sportbooks Ser.). (Illus.). 1977. 12.00 (ISBN 0-7195-2862-3). Transatl Arts.

Success in Kindergarten Reading & Writing. Anne Adams et al. (gr. k). 1980. 13.95 (ISBN 0-673-16437-3). Scott F.

Success in Literature. W. Morris Colles & Henry Cresswell. LC 70-105771. 1970. Repr. of 1911 ed. 27.50x (ISBN 0-8046-0944-6, Pub. by Kennikat). Assoc Faculty Pr.

Success in Literature. W. Morris Colles & Henry Cresswell. 1911. 20.00 (ISBN 0-8274-3902-4). R West.

Success in Marriage. David R. Mace. (Festival Ser.). 160p. 1980. pap. 3.95 (ISBN 0-687-40555-6). Abingdon.

Success in Mathematics. (Success Studybooks Ser.). (Illus.). 609p. 1975. 12.00 (ISBN 0-7195-2901-8). Transatl Arts.

Success in Newsletter Publishing: A Practical Guide. 256p. 1985. 37.50 (ISBN 0-318-03791-2). Newsletter Assn.

Success in Practical Nursing: Personal & Vocational Issues. Signe S. Hill & Helen A. Howlett. 288p. 1988. 14.95 (ISBN 0-7216-2133-3). Saunders.

Success in Reading & Writing. Anne H. Adams et al. (gr. 5). 1982. 15.95 (ISBN 0-673-16546-9). Scott F.

Success in Reading & Writing: Grade 2. Anne Adams et al. 1980. 14.95 (ISBN 0-673-16435-7). Scott F.

Success in Reading & Writing: Grade 3. Anne H. Adams. 1980. 14.95 (ISBN 0-673-16436-5). Scott F.

Success in Reading & Writing: Grade 4. Anne H. Adams et al. 1982. 15.95 (ISBN 0-673-16545-0). Scott F.

Success in Reading & Writing: Grade 6. Anne H. Adams & Elisabeth L. Bebensee. 1983. 16.95 (ISBN 0-673-16586-8). Scott F.

Success in Reading & Writing: Phonics Sheets, Grade 1. Anne H. Adams. 1978. pap. 6.95 (ISBN 0-673-16433-0). Scott F.

Success in School. Karen Levy. 64p. 1988. 7.95 (ISBN 0-8062-3288-9). Carlton.

Success in Swimming. John Hogg. (Success Sportbooks Ser.). (Illus.). 1977. 12.00 (ISBN 0-7195-3376-7). Transatl Arts.

Success in Twentieth Century World Affairs. (Success Studybooks Ser.). (Illus.). 387p. 1975. pap. 12.00 (ISBN 0-7195-2919-0). Transatl Arts.

Success Is a Choice. Richard C. Nelson. (Orig.). 1979. pap. write for info. (ISBN 0-932570-01-1). Guidelines Pr.

Success Is a Good Word. Janice Ching Yee. (gr. 9 up). 1979. pap. 5.00 (ISBN 0-931420-22-9). Pi Pr.

Success Is a Way of Life. Christopher Hills. LC 83-19417. 96p. (Orig.). 1983. 3.95 (ISBN 0-916438-49-X). Univ of Trees.

Success Is Never Ending - Failure Is Never Final. Robert H. Schuller. 1988. 14.95 (ISBN 0-8407-5529-5). Nelson.

Success Is the Quality of Your Journey. expanded ed. Jennifer James. LC 85-73148. 144p. (Orig.). 1986. pap. 8.95 (ISBN 0-937858-66-8). Newmarket.

Success Is the Quality of Your Journey. Jennifer James. 1988. pap. 8.95. Newmarket.

Success Made Fun. Jim Brancaleone. LC 81-90660. (Orig.). 1981. pap. 9.95 (ISBN 0-9601186-2-4). Brancaleone Educ.

Success, Motivation, & the Scriptures. new ed. William H. Cook. LC 74-82582. 192p. 1975. kivar 6.95 (ISBN 0-8054-5226-5). Broadman.

Success Motivation Through the Word. Charles Capps. 272p. 1982. pap. 3.95 (ISBN 0-89274-183-X, HH-183). Harrison Hse.

Success Now, Why Wait! Learning Annex Staff. 1987. pap. 2.95 (ISBN 0-425-07377-7). Berkley Pub.

Success of a Business-Failure of Its Partners. Barry Oshry. (Notes on Power Ser.). (Orig.). 1980. pap. text ed. 4.00 (ISBN 0-910411-07-7). Power & Sys.

Success of Failure. Joel Fisher. (Illus.). 45p. 1987. 9.00 (ISBN 0-916365-20-4). Ind Curators.

Success of Modern Private Enterprise. Roland W. Bartlett. LC 70-106133. 1970. 7.95 (ISBN 0-8134-1148-3, 1148); text ed. 5.95x. Inter Print Pubs.

Success or Failure. Henry Trueba. 421p. 1987. pap. text ed. 21.95 (ISBN 0-06-632547-1). Newbury Hse.

Success or Failure? Family Planning Programs in the Third World. Donald J. Hernandez. LC 84-6653. (Studies in Population & Urban Demography Ser.: No. 4). (Illus.). xviii, 161p. 1984. lib. bdg. 35.00 (ISBN 0-313-24401-4, HSU/). Greenwood.

Success Oriented Supervision. rev. ed. Ed. by Albert St. Denis. 1980. 44.15 (ISBN 0-87771-019-8). Grad School.

Success over Sixty. Albert Myers & Christopher Andersen. 1984. 15.95 (ISBN 0-671-49460-0). Summit Bks.

Success over Sixty. Albert Myers & Christopher P. Andersen. 1986. pap. 8.95 (ISBN 0-671-62013-4). Summit Bks.

Success over Sixty. Albert Myers & Christopher Anderson. (General Ser.). 1985. lib. bdg. 16.95 (ISBN 0-8161-3801-X, Large Print Bks). G K Hall.

Success Process. Brown Landone. 232p. 1981. pap. 8.00 (ISBN 0-89540-075-8, SB-075). Sun Pub.

Success Profile: A Leading Headhunter Tells You How to Get to the Top. Lester Korn. 1989. 17.95 (ISBN 0-671-55263-5). S&S.

Success-Pure & Simple: How to Make It in Business, Sports & the Arts. Dominic N. Certo. LC 83-90470. (Self-Help Bks.). (Illus.). 200p. (Orig.). 1983. pap. 9.95x (ISBN 0-915755-00-9). Hillside Pubns.

Success Shortcuts. Jimmy Calano & Jeff Salzman. 1988. 8.95 (ISBN 1-55525-234-6). Nightingale-Conant.

Success Signs. Marlene M. Rathgeb. (Illus.). 224p. 1981. pap. 5.95 (ISBN 0-312-77486-9). St Martin.

Success Stories. Russell Banks. LC 85-45617. 192p. 1986. 15.45 (ISBN 0-06-015567-1, HARPT). Har-Row.

Success Stories. Russell Banks. 208p. 1987. pap. 3.95 (ISBN 0-345-34235-6). Ballantine.

Success Stories in Productivity Improvement. Ed. by Jerry Hamlin. 1985. 29.95 (ISBN 0-89806-071-0). Inst Indus Eng.

"Success Story" of Peasant Tobacco Production in Tanzania. Jannik Boesen & A. T. Mohele. (Centre for Development Research Studies: No. 2). (Illus.). 169p. 1983. pap. 14.50 (ISBN 0-8419-9757-8, Africana). Holmes & Meier.

Success Strategies for Design Professionals: Super Positioning for Architecture & Engineering Firms. Cox Group & W. Coxe. 1987. text ed. 29.50 (ISBN 0-07-013311-5). McGraw.

Success Strategies for Investment Real Estate: The Professionals Guide to Better Service & Increased Commissions. 2nd ed. Jerry Anderson. (Illus.). 334p. 1987. pap. 25.95 (ISBN 0-13-859257-8). P-H.

Success Strategies for Investment Real Estate: The Professionals Guide to Better Service & Increased Commissions. 2nd ed. Jerry D. Anderson. Ed. by Helene Berlin. LC 82-61402. (Illus.). 322p. (Orig.). 1985. pap. text ed. 17.95 (ISBN 0-913652-33-4, BK 153); pap. text ed. 14.36 members. Realtors Natl.

Success Strategies for the New Sales Manager. Mack Hanan et al. 1982. pap. 8.95 (ISBN 0-8144-7566-3). AMACOM.

Success Syndrome: Hitting Bottom When You Reach the Top. Steven Berglas. 300p. 1986. 18.95 (ISBN 0-306-42349-9, Plenum Pr). Plenum Pub.

Success System That Never Fails. W. Clement Stone. 1983. pap. 4.50 (ISBN 0-671-52462-3). PB.

Success: The Glenn Bland Method. Glenn Bland. 1983. pap. 3.50 (ISBN 0-8423-6689-X). Tyndale.

Success Through a Positive Mental Attitude. Napoleon Hill & W. Clement Stone. 1983. pap. 4.50 (ISBN 0-671-50447-9). PB.

Success Through a Positive Mental Attitude. Napoleon Hill & W. Clement Stone. 1985. pap. 6.95 (ISBN 0-13-859422-8). P-H.

Success Through a Positive Mental Attitude. Napoleon Hill & W. Clement Stone. 320p. 1987. pap. 4.50 (ISBN 0-671-62224-2). PB.

Success Through Color Charisma. Ruth Miller & Sandy Parks. LC 83-73079. 133p. (Orig.). 1983. pap. 12.00 (ISBN 0-916359-38-7). Color Pr.

Success Through Communication. L. Ron Hubbard. 72p. 1980. pap. 9.00 (ISBN 0-88404-076-3). Bridge Pubns Inc.

Success Through Handwriting Analysis. Malcolm W. Ater, Jr. (Illus.). 1985. pap. 4.95 (ISBN 0-8283-1900-6). Branden Pub Co.

Success Through Mind Power. 2nd ed. Roy Hunter. Ed. by Gil Boyne. 136p. (Orig.). 1986. pap. 7.95 (ISBN 0-930298-27-6). Westwood Pub Co.

Success Through Partnership. Reinhard Mohn. 1988. 16.95 (ISBN 0-385-24789-3). Doubleday.

Success Through Transactional Analysis. Jut Meininger. 224p. 1974. pap. 3.50 (ISBN 0-451-12637-8, Sig). NAL.

Success to the Brave. Alexander Kent. LC 83-11238. 284p. 1983. 13.95 (ISBN 0-399-12878-6, Putnam). Putnam Pub Group.

Success with Algebra. Lucreda A. Hutton et al. (Illus.). 512p. 1985. pap. text ed. 32.00 (ISBN 0-13-859372-8). P-H.

Success with Educational Software. Frederick Williams & Victoria Williams. LC 85-5679. 192p. 1985. 36.95 (ISBN 0-275-90186-6, C0186). Praeger.

Success with House Plants. Reader's Digest Editors. LC 78-59802. (Illus.). 480p. 1979. 23.95 (ISBN 0-89577-052-0, Pub. by RD Assn). Random.

Success with Parts. Robert A. Pearson. (Illus.). 42p. (Orig.). 1976. pap. 4.20 (ISBN 0-9608378-0-9). B Pearson.

Success with Scientology. Church of Scientology Information Service Staff & L. Ron Hubbard. 112p. pap. cancelled (ISBN 0-915598-01-9). Church of Scient Info.

Success with the Pole. Dickie Carr. 1985. 29.00x (ISBN 0-317-39178-X, Pub. by BeeKay Pubs Ltd). State Mutual Bk.

Success with Words. Reader's Digest Editors. LC 82-62542. 704p. 1983. 24.95 (ISBN 0-89577-168-3, Pub. by RD Assn). Random.

Success Without Compromise: There's Only One Way to Succeed & Be Happy. 2nd ed. Richard H. LeTourneau. LC 77-80947. (LeTourneau One-Way Ser.: Vol. 4). 176p. 1985. pap. 5.95 (ISBN 0-88207-757-0). LeTourneau Pr.

Successes & Failures in Meeting the Management Challenge: Strategies & Their Implementation. Milan Kubr & John Wallace. (Working Paper: No. 585). 120p. 1983. 5.00 (ISBN 0-8213-0254-X, WP 0585). World Bank.

Successes in Small & Medium-Scale Enterprises: The Evidence from Colombia. Mariluz Cortes et al. (World Bank Publication). 304p. 1987. 27.50 (ISBN 0-19-520593-6). Oxford U Pr.

Successful Acquisition of Unquoted Companies. 2nd ed. Barrie Pearson. 120p. 1985. text ed. 42.50x (ISBN 0-566-02609-0, Pub. by Gower Pub England). Gower Pub Co.

Successful Market Penetration: How to Shorten the Sales Cycle by Making the First Sale the First Time. Mack Hanan. 224p. 1987. 16.95 (ISBN 0-8144-5934-X). AMACOM.

Successful Marketing for Small Business. William A. Cohen & Marshall E. Reddick. 288p. 1981. 17.95 (ISBN 0-8144-5611-1). AMACOM.

Successful Marketing for Small Business. William A. Cohen & Marshall E. Reddick. LC 80-69699. pap. 72.00 (ISBN 0-317-19830-0, 2023077). Bks Demand UMI.

Successful Marketing for Small Business. Brian R. Smith. LC 83-22219. 256p. 1984. pap. text ed. 10.95 (ISBN 0-86616-033-7). Greene.

Successful Marketing Strategies in American Industry. Jon G. Udell. Ed. by Gay Leslie. (Illus.). 1972. 9.50x (ISBN 0-912084-07-3). Mimir.

Successful Marriage: A Family Systems Approach to Couples Therapy. W. Robert Beavers. 1985. 19.95 (ISBN 0-393-70006-2). Norton.

Successful Mass Catering & Volume Feeding. rev. ed. Matteo A. Casola. Ed. by Mary Darveau. LC 80-66708. 329p. 1980. Repr. of 1969 ed. text ed. 24.95x (ISBN 0-916096-25-4). Books Bakers.

Successful Media Relations: A Practitioner's Guide. Judith Ridgway. LC 84-6128. 214p. 1984. text ed. 32.95x (ISBN 0-566-02469-1). Gower Pub Co.

Successful Meetings. Public Management Institute Staff. LC 80-80198. 1980. 3 ring binder 39.00x (ISBN 0-916664-23-6). Public Management.

Successful Men of To-Day: And What They Say of Success. Wilbur F. Crafts. LC 73-2500. (Big Business; Economic Power in a Free Society Ser.). Repr. of 1883 ed. 18.00 (ISBN 0-405-05081-X). Ayer Co Pubs.

Successful Methods in Cost Engineering. Hira N. Ahuja & Michael A. Walsh. LC 82-17316. 398p. (Orig.). 1983. 51.95 (ISBN 0-471-86435-8, JW). Krieger.

Successful Midlife Career Change. Paula I. Robbins. 1980. pap. 7.95 (ISBN 0-8144-7536-1). AMACOM.

Successful Model Business Contracts & Agreements. Ed. by Alan M. Shaver. (Illus.). 550p. 1988. loose leaf 99.95 (ISBN 0-929321-01-4, 10600). Weka-Pub.

Successful Model Letters for Executives. Ed. by Nina H. Frost. (Illus.). 550p. 1988. loose leaf 99.95 (ISBN 0-929321-00-6, 10200). Weka-Pub.

Successful Movement Challenges: Movement Activities for the Developing Child. Jack Capon. Ed. by Frank Alexander & Diane Alexander. (Illus.). 129p. (Orig.). 1981. pap. 9.95 (ISBN 0-915256-07-X). Front Row.

Successful Negotiating in Local Government. Ed. by Nancy A. Huelsberg & William F. Lincoln. LC 85-8275. (Practical Management Ser.). (Illus.). 211p. 1985. pap. text ed. 21.00 (ISBN 0-87326-045-7). Intl City Mgt.

Successful Negotiating Skills for Women. John Ilich & Barbara S. Jones. 116p. pap. 6.95 (ISBN 0-935650-06-7). Bengal Pr.

Successful Negotiation. rev ed. Robert B. Maddux. LC 85-73178. (Fifty-Minute Guide Ser.). (Illus.). 80p. (Orig.). 1987. pap. 6.95 (ISBN 0-931961-09-2). Crisp Pubns.

Successful Negotiation. Robert B. Maddux. (CRISP Publications 50-Minute Ser.). Date not set. 6.95. Human Res Dev Pr.

Successful Negotiation of Commercial Contracts a Businessman's Guide. Patrick Hearn. 142p. 1979. text ed. 32.00x (ISBN 0-566-02365-2). Gower Pub Co.

Successful Negotiation, Trieste 1954: An Appraisal by the Five Participants. Ed. by John C. Campbell. LC 75-2981. 225p. 1975. 29.00x (ISBN 0-691-05658-7). Princeton U Pr.

Successful Newsletter Publishing for the Consultant. Herman Holtz. (Consultant's Library). 135p. 1983. 25.00 (ISBN 0-930686-20-9, Pub. by Consultants Library). Bermont Bks.

Successful Newspaper Advertising for Restaurants. John J. Prizzia, Jr. 68p. (Orig.). 1986. pap. 3.95 (ISBN 0-940373-00-9). Unltd Pub.

Successful Nonverbal Communication: Principles & Applications. Dale G. Leathers. 415p. 1986. pap. write for info. (ISBN 0-02-369010-0). Macmillan.

Successful Ocean Game Fishing. Frank T. Moss. LC 72-132081. pap. 63.80 (ISBN 0-317-27674-3, 2019512). Bks Demand UMI.

Successful On-Site Manager. Carol S. King et al. Ed. by Mark E. Ingebretsen. LC 83-82536. (Illus.). 353p. 1984. 27.95 (ISBN 0-912104-62-7, 811). Inst Real Estate.

Successful Outdoor Writing. Jack Samson. LC 79-11854. 244p. 1979. 11.95 (ISBN 0-911654-66-6). Writers Digest.

Successful Parenting. Ann Murphy & John Murphy. 260p. 1983. 4.95 (ISBN 0-8198-6841-8); pap. 3.95 (ISBN 0-8198-6842-6). Dghtrs St Paul.

Successful Parenting for Stressful Times. Dennis Lees. LC 85-61381. 100p. (Orig.). 1986. pap. 7.95 (ISBN 0-88247-744-7). R & E Pubs.

Successful Parishes: How They Meet the Challenge of Change. Thomas P. Sweetser. 204p. 1983. pap. 9.95 (ISBN 0-86683-694-2, HarpR). Har-Row.

Successful Participative Management in Smaller Companies. Robert E. Cope. 125p. (Orig.). 1982. pap. text ed. 18.00 (ISBN 0-9610044-0-1). QDP Inc.

Successful Parties: Simple & Elegant. Martin Johner & Gary Goldberg. Ed. by Jean Atcheson. LC 83-71040. (Great American Cooking School Ser.). (Illus.). 84p. 1983. pap. 5.95 (ISBN 0-941034-19-4). I Chalmers.

Successful Pension Design for Small to Medium Sized Businesses. Robert F. Slimmon. 1984. text ed. 39.33 (ISBN 0-8359-7146-5, Reston). P-H.

Successful Pension Design for Small to Medium-Sized Businesses. 2nd ed. Robert F. Slimmon. (Illus.). 480p. 1987. 44.00 (ISBN 0-13-860255-7). P-H.

Successful People: What Makes Them That Way? Alice Dunkle. 1987. pap. text ed. 14.00 (ISBN 0-910609-14-4). Gifted Educ Pr.

Successful Perennial Gardening: A Practical Guide. Lewis Hill & Nancy Hill. Ed. by Sarah M. Clarkson. LC 87-45582. (Illus.). 254p. (Orig.). 1988. 29.95 (ISBN 0-88266-473-5, Garden Way Pub); pap. 16.95 (ISBN 0-88266-472-7, Garden Way Pub). Storey Comm Inc.

Successful Policy Implementation. Ed. by Daniel Mazmanian & Paul Sabatier. (Orig.). 1980. pap. 8.00 (ISBN 0-918592-37-2). Policy Studies.

Successful Practice of Law. John E. Tracy. LC 72-6212. (Illus.). 470p. 1973. Repr. of 1947 ed. lib. bdg. 22.50x (ISBN 0-8371-6455-9, TRPL). Greenwood.

Successful Private Eyes & Private Spies: Private Spies. Barbara L. Thomas & Ralph D. Thomas. (Private Investigation Ser.). 100p. 1986. pap. text ed. 19.95 (ISBN 0-317-45231-2). Thomas Pubns TX.

Successful Private Practice: A Guide to Effective Medical Practice Management. Maxine Buchele & Susan Wynn-Williams. LC 86-9547. (Illus.). 238p. 1987. text ed. 48.00 (ISBN 0-443-03456-7). Churchill.

Successful Problem Management. Michael Sanderson. LC 78-21050. 227p. 1979. 33.95 (ISBN 0-471-04871-2, Pub. by Wiley-Interscience). Wiley.

Successful Problem Solving. David A. Thomas & Maridell Fryar. 64p. 1983. pap. 6.60 (ISBN 0-8442-5239-5, Passport Bks.). Natl Textbk.

Successful Product & Business Development. N. Giragosian. 1978. 59.75 (ISBN 0-8247-6770-5). Dekker.

Successful Professional Practice. Robert P. Levoy. LC 74-97581. (Illus.). 192p. 1970. 39.95x (ISBN 0-13-868307-7, Busn). P-H.

Successful Programs for the Gifted & Talented. Ed. by Joyce E. Juntune. 250p. 1986. pap. 12.00 (ISBN 0-912723-01-7). Nat Assn Gift Child.

Successful Project Management. Rosenau. 36.95 (ISBN 0-317-64294-4). Van Nos Reinhold.

Successful Project Management: A Step-by-Step Approach with Practical Examples. Milton D. Rosenau, Jr. LC 80-24720. 266p. 1981. text ed. 38.95 (ISBN 0-534-97977-7, Lifetime Learn). Van Nos Reinhold.

Successful Projects--With a Moral for Management. O. P. Kharbanda & E. A. Stallworthy. 300p. 1986. text ed. 47.50x (ISBN 0-566-02651-1, Pub. by Gower Pub England). Gower Pub Co.

Successful Public Relations Techniques. Public Management Institute Staff. LC 79-93010. 400p. 1979. 3 ring binder 59.00x (ISBN 0-916664-15-5). Public Management.

Successful Public Speaking: A Practical Guide. Williams Haskins & Joseph M. Staudacher. 1987. pap. text ed. write for info. (ISBN 0-673-18204-5). Scott F.

Successful Quality Management. Frank H. Squires. Ed. by Robert T. Linke. 342p. (Orig.). 1980. pap. 22.50 (ISBN 0-933931-03-4). Hitchcock Pub.

Successful Real Estate Investing: A Practical Guide to Profits after Tax Reform for the Small Investor. Peter G. Miller. LC 87-46157. 320p. 1988. 18.95 (ISBN 0-06-015943-X). Har-Row.

Successful Real Estate Sales Agreements. 4th ed. Erik Jorgensen. 370p. 1986. pap. 17.95 (ISBN 0-933800-03-7). Axiom Pr Pubs.

Successful Recareering: How to Shift Gears Before You're over the Hill. Roger W. Axford. (Illus.). 154p. 1983. 15.95 (ISBN 0-939644-11-8); pap. 12.95 (ISBN 0-939644-10-X). Media Prods & Mktg.

Successful Restaurant Design. Regina S. Baraban & Joseph F. Durocher. (Illus.). 256p. 1988. 37.95 (ISBN 0-442-21839-7). Van Nos Reinhold.

Successful Restaurant Operation. T. F. Chiffriller, Jr. 290p. 1983. 31.95 (ISBN 0-8436-2221-0). Van Nos Reinhold.

Successful Retail Sales. Kenneth H. Mills & J. Paul. 1979. pap. write for info (ISBN 0-13-869602-0). P-H.

Successful Sales Assistant's Handbook. New York Institute of Finance. (Illus.). 288p. wkbk. 25.00 (ISBN 0-13-860305-7). NY Inst Finance.

Successful Sales Management: A New Strategy for Modern Sales Managers. Hal Fahner. LC 82-24085. 264p. 1983. 29.95 (ISBN 0-13-870402-3). P-H.

Successful Sales Managing. pap. 1.95x (ISBN 0-686-02549-0). Dun.

Successful Sales Training: How to Build a Program That Works. Ian E. McLaughlin. 168p. 1983. 22.95 (ISBN 0-8436-0863-3). Van Nos Reinhold.

Successful Salon Management for Cosmetology Students. E. J. Tezak. 1985. 11.35 (ISBN 0-87350-404-6); wkbk. 6.10 (ISBN 0-87350-411-9). Milady Pub.

Successful School Commmunications: A Manual & Guide for Administrators. William Goldstein & Joseph DeVita. (Illus.). 1977. 22.95x (ISBN 0-13-872036-3, Parker). P-H.

Successful Schools for Young Adolescents. Joan Lipsitz. 240p. 1983. 27.95 (ISBN 0-87855-487-4); pap. text ed. 14.95x (ISBN 0-87855-947-7). Transaction Bks.

Successful Scriptwriting. Jurgen Wolff & Kerry Cox. 288p. 1988. 18.95 (ISBN 0-89879-325-4). Writers Digest.

Successful Secretary: You, Your Boss, & the Job. Loren B. Belker. LC 81-66239. pap. 56.00 (ISBN 0-317-26943-7, 2023590). Bks Demand UMI.

Successful Secretary's Handbook. Esther R. Becker & Evelyn Anders. 480p. 1984. pap. 6.95 (ISBN 0-06-463593-7, EH 593, B&N Bks). Har-Row.

Successful Seed Programs: A Planning & Management Guide. Johnson E. Douglas. (Winrock Development Oriented Literature Ser.). 330p. 1980. pap. 40.00x (ISBN 0-89158-793-4). Westview.

Successful Self-Management. Paul R. Trim. Ed. by Michael G. Crisp. LC 86-72080. (Fifty-Minute Guide Ser.). (Illus.). 80p. (Orig.). 1987. pap. 6.95 (ISBN 0-931961-26-2). Crisp Pubns.

Successful Self-Management. Paul R. Trimm. (CRISP Publications 50-Minute Ser.). Date not set. 6.95. Human Res Dev Pr.

Successful Self-Publishing. Jack Erbe & Anitra Earle. 1983. pap. 20.00 (ISBN 0-910795-02-9). Ondine Pr.

Successful Self Publishing on a Shoestring. Bruce David & Gary Tartaglia. (Illus.). 75p. (Orig.). wkbk. 8.95x (ISBN 0-9609734-5-1). Worthprinting.

Successful Selling Strategies. David El Fattal. 56p. (Orig.). 1988. pap. 6.00. El Fattal Enterprises.

Successful Seminars, Conferences & Workshops. Public Management Institute Staff. LC 80-65013. 400p. 1980. 3 ring binder 59.00x (ISBN 0-916664-19-8). Public Management.

Successful Sewing. Mary Westfall. LC 86-29606. 368p. 1987. text ed. 10.80 (ISBN 0-87006-631-5); instr's guide 5.20 (ISBN 0-87006-632-3). Goodheart.

Successful Sewing: A Modern Guide. Nesta Hollis. LC 76-84974. (Illus.). (gr. 8 up). 8.75 (ISBN 0-8008-7490-0). Taplinger.

Successful Single Adult Ministry. Linda Cahill et al. 144p. 1987. pap. 6.95 (ISBN 0-87403-229-6, 3219). Standard Pub.

Successful Single Parenting: A Practical Guide. Anne Wayman. 180p. 1987. pap. 4.95 (ISBN 0-317-61927-6). Meadowbrook.

Successful Sitcom Writing. Jurgen Wolff. 224p. 1988. 16.95x (ISBN 0-312-01514-3). St Martin.

Successful Small Business Management. Forest H. Frantz. LC 77-14385. 1978. text ed. write for info (ISBN 0-13-872119-X). P-H.

Successful Small Business Management. 5th ed. Leon C. Megginson et al. 1988. 36.95 (ISBN 0-256-05813-X). Business Pubns.

Successful Small Business Management. 4th ed. Curtis E. Tate, Jr. et al. 1985. 36.95 (ISBN 0-256-03278-5). Business Pubns.

Successful Small Business Management. Leon Wortman. LC 76-18160. (AMACOM Executive Books). 272p. 1978. pap. 8.95 (ISBN 0-8144-7503-5). AMACOM.

Successful Small Business Management. Leon A. Wortman. (Illus.). 1976. 12.95 (ISBN 0-8144-5394-5). AMACOM.

Successful Small Business Management: It's Your Business.... Mind It! David Seigel & Harold L. Goldman. LC 81-71604. pap. 93.60 (2030991). Bks Demand UMI.

Successful Software Evaluation & Rating: A Quantitative Approach. Michael L. Dean. (Illus.). 250p. (Orig.). 1986. 39.95 (ISBN 0-87007-996-4); pap. 19.95 (ISBN 0-87007-997-2). SourceView.

Successful Software Project Management. Rosenau. 39.95 (ISBN 0-317-64295-2). Van Nos Reinhold.

Successful Software Project Management. Milton D. Rosenau & Marsha D. Lewin. (Computers Ser.). 300p. 1984. 30.00 (Lifetime Learn). Van Nos Reinhold.

Successful Songwriting. 2nd ed. Lou Herscher. Ed. by Paul Mills. LC 66-6554. (Orig.). 1966. pap. 4.95 (ISBN 0-913754-01-3). P Mills.

Successful Soul Winning. Paul Sherrod. (Illus.). 1978. 6.95 (ISBN 0-686-14476-7, 1730394523). P Sherrod.

Successful Sound System Operation. F. Alton Everest. (Illus.). 336p. (Orig.). 1985. 24.95 (ISBN 0-8306-0306-9, 2606). Tab Bks.

Successful Sport Management. Guy Lewis & Herb Appenzeller. 377p. 1985. 60.00x (ISBN 0-87215-925-6). Michie Co.

Successful Stock Investing. 2nd ed. 1984. pap. 10.00 (ISBN 0-318-19199-7). Truth Seeker.

Successful Stock Selecting Methods in Wall Street. William D. Gann. (Illus.). 159p. 1985. 177.45. Inst Econ Finan.

Successful Storytelling. Leila Ashton. Ed. by Penny E. Wheeler. 128p. 1988. pap. write for info. (ISBN 0-8280-0412-9). Review & Herald.

Successful Strategies for Real Estate Agents: A Step-by-Step System on How to Succeed in Today's Real Estate World. Floyd Wickman. 260p. 1987. 14.95 (ISBN 0-939975-01-7). Exec Pr NC.

Successful Strategies for Real Estate Agents. Floyd Wickman. 256p. 1987. 14.95 (ISBN 0-8403-4185-7). Kendall-Hunt.

Successful Strategies for Recruiting Family Day Care Providers. Tom Copeland & Megan Roach. Ed. by Jill Hix. (Illus.). 110p. (Orig.). 1986. pap. text ed. 17.95 (ISBN 0-934140-32-4). Toys 'n Things.

Successful Strategies for Sales Managers: A Guide to Get the Best from Salespeople. Floyd Wickman. 249p. 1987. 14.95 (ISBN 0-939975-00-9). Exec Pr NC.

Successful Stress Control: The Natural Way. David Hoffman. 192p. (Orig.). 1987. pap. 6.95. Inner Tradit.

Successful Student Teaching: A Handbook for Elementary & Secondary Student Teachers. Fillmer Hevener, Jr. LC 80-69332. 125p. 1981. perfect bdg. 9.95 (ISBN 0-86548-040-0). R & E Pubs.

Successful Study Skills. Wayne R. Herlin & Craig Mayfield. 120p. 1981. pap. 10.95 (ISBN 0-8403-2524-X). Kendall-Hunt.

Successful Style: A Man's Guide to a Complete Professional Image. Doris Pooser. (Illus.). 208p. 1988. 16.95 (ISBN 0-937359-37-8). HDL Pubs.

Successful Sunday School & Teachers Guidebook. revised ed. Elmer Towns. LC 75-23009. (Illus.). 430p. 1986. pap. 10.95 (ISBN 0-88419-118-4, Creation Hse). Strang Comms Co.

Successful Sunday School & Teacher's Guidebook. 3rd, rev. ed. Elmer Towns. 399p. 1987. pap. 10.95 (Creation Hse). Strang Comms Co.

Successful Sunday School Teaching. Myer Pearlman. (Sunday School Staff Training Ser.). 112p. 1935. pap. 1.35 (ISBN 0-88243-606-6, 02-0606). Gospel Pub.

Successful Sunfish Racing. Derrick R. Fries. LC 83-72325. 1984. 12.95 (ISBN 0-8286-0095-3). J De Graff.

Successful Supervision. John H. Jackson & Timothy J. Keaveny. (Illus.). 1980. text ed. write for info. (ISBN 0-13-872796-1). P-H.

Successful Supervision. 2nd ed. James R. White. 272p. 1987. pap. 12.95 (ISBN 0-07-084925-0). McGraw.

Successful Supervisor: In Government & Business. rev. ed. William R. Van Dersal. LC 73-4134. 220p. 1985. 17.45i (ISBN 0-06-015476-4, HarpT). Har-Row.

Successful Teacher: Essays in Secondary School Instruction. Ed. by James L. Kelly. 146p. 1982. pap. text ed. 7.95x (ISBN 0-8138-0196-6). Iowa St U Pr.

Successful Teacher Evaluation. Thomas L. McGreal. LC 83-71704. 176p. 1983. 8.75 (ISBN 0-87120-120-8, 611-83300). Assn Supervision.

Successful Teaching in Secondary Schools: A Guide for Student & In-Service Teachers. 2nd ed. Sterling G. Callahan. 1971. text ed. write for info. (ISBN 0-673-07720-9). Scott F.

Successful Team Building Through TA. Dudley Bennett. 1980. 14.95 (ISBN 0-8144-5607-3). AMACOM.

Successful Techniques for Civil Trials. Ronald L. Carlson. LC 83-81617. 1983. 72.50 (ISBN 0-318-00076-8); Suppl. 1987. 26.00. Lawyers Co-Op.

Successful Techniques for Higher Profits. Robert Rachlin. LC 80-85150. 260p. 1981. 16.95 (ISBN 0-938712-02-0). Marr Pubns.

Successful Techniques for Improving Productivity in On-Site Construction. Clarkson H. Oglesby et al. (Illus.). 512p. 1988. 46.95 (ISBN 0-07-047802-3). McGraw.

Successful Techniques for Solving Employees Compensation Problems. Don R. Marshall. LC 77-17964. (Illus.). pap. 53.00 (ISBN 0-317-09588-9, 2020189). Bks Demand UMI.

Successful Telemarketing. Bob Stone & John Wyman. LC 85-63834. (Illus.). 236p. (Orig.). 1986. 29.95 (ISBN 0-8442-3134-7, Crain Bks); pap. 15.95 (ISBN 0-8442-3133-9). Natl Textbk.

Successful Telemarketing. Bob Stone & John Wyman. (Illus.). 236p. 1987. 29.95 (ISBN 0-8442-3136-3, NTC Busn Bks). Natl Textbk.

Successful Telemarketing: Opportunities & Techniques for Increasing Sales & Profits. Bob Stone & John Wyman. Date not set. write for info. S&S.

Successful Telephone Selling in the Eighties. Robert L. Shook & Martin D. Shafiroff. 176p. 1983. pap. 6.95 (ISBN 0-06-463569-4, EH 569, B&N Bks). Har-Row.

Successful Textbook Publishing: The Author's Guide. Thomas D. Brock. LC 84-27541. 1985. 28.50 (ISBN 0-910239-01-0). Sci Tech Pubs.

Successful Time Management. Jack D. Ferner. LC 79-13680. (Self-Teaching Guide Ser.). 296p. 1980. pap. text ed. 12.95x (ISBN 0-471-03911-X). Wiley.

Successful Time Management for Hospital Administrators. Merrill E. Douglass & Phillip H. Goodwin. LC 79-55063. pap. 37.50 (ISBN 0-317-26716-7, 2023519). Bks Demand UMI.

Successful Tourism Management. Pran N. Seth. 1986. text ed. 45.00x (ISBN 0-317-43219-2, Pub. by Sterling Pubs India). Apt Bks.

Successful Trading Techniques in the Commodity Futures Market. Curtis Dahl. (Illus.). 147p. 1987. Repr. of 1960 ed. 189.55 (ISBN 0-86654-215-9). Inst Econ Finan.

Successful Training Strategies: Twenty-Six Innovative Corporate Models - A Work in America Institute Publication. LC 88-42781. Date not set. 32.95x (ISBN 1-55542-101-6). Jossey-Bass.

Successful Transitions: A Guide Through the Employment Process. 3rd ed. 1982. pap. 7.95 (ISBN 1-55549-015-8). Ed Assocs Ky.

Successful Turkey Hunting. J. Wayne Fears. Ed. by Glenn Helgeland. LC 82-74192. (On Target Ser.). (Illus.). 92p. (Orig.). 1984. pap. 5.95 (ISBN 0-913305-01-4). Target Comm.

Successful Tutoring: A Practical Guide to Adult Learning Processes. David P. Moore & Mary A. Poppino. (Illus.). 178p. 1983. 19.75 (ISBN 0-398-04763-4). C C Thomas.

Successful Volunteer Organization. Joan Flanagan. 320p. 1981. pap. 13.95 (ISBN 0-8092-5837-4). Contemp Bks.

Successful Volunteer Organization: Getting Started & Getting Results in Nonprofit, Charities, Grass Roots, & Community Groups. Joan Flanagan. 376p. 1981. pap. 9.50 (ISBN 0-318-17155-4, C78). VTNC Arlington.

Successful Waitresses' Guide to More & Bigger Tips. Justin St. James & Nita Lynn. 18p. (Orig.). 1987. pap. 4.00 (ISBN 0-9617479-8-6). Palamora Pub.

Successful Winemaking at Home. rev. ed. H. E. Bravery. LC 62-12119. (Illus.). 1967. pap. 4.50 (ISBN 0-668-00861-X, 843). Arco.

Successful Women, Angry Men: Backlash in the Two-Career Marriage. Bebe M. Campbell. LC 86-10240. 256p. Date not set. 15.95 (ISBN 0-394-55149-4). Random.

Successful Women: With Portraits. Sarah K. Bolton. LC 74-936. (Essay Index Reprint Ser.). (Illus.). Repr. of 1888 ed. 15.75 (ISBN 0-518-10143-6). Ayer Co Pubs.

Successful Writing. 2nd ed. Maxine Hairston. 1986. text ed. 14.95x (ISBN 0-393-95416-1); tchr's. ed. avail. (ISBN 0-393-95419-6). Norton.

Successful Writing at Work. 2nd ed. Philip C. Kolin. LC 85-81812. 546p. 1986. pap. text ed. 19.50 (ISBN 0-669-07695-3); instr's guide 2.00 (ISBN 0-669-07694-5). Heath.

Successfully Developing Your Accounting Practice: A Practical Guide with Forms, Letters & Checklists. Dana M. Ronald. LC 86-32388. 314p. 1987. 39.95 (ISBN 0-471-84736-4). Wiley.

Successfully Managing Stress. Lynn Brallier. 297p. 1982. pap. 9.95 (ISBN 0-917010-10-8). Natl Nursing.

Successfully Managing Your Accounting Career. Labus. (National Association of Accountants Ser.). 1988. 24.95 (ISBN 0-471-63388-7). Wiley.

Successfully Single. Yvonne G. Baker. LC 85-7089. 196p. 1985. pap. 6.95 (ISBN 0-89636-163-2). Accent Bks.

Succession. Joyce Carlow. 1986. pap. 3.95 (ISBN 0-451-14205-5, Sig). NAL.

Succession. Mary Swander. LC 79-12392. (Contemporary Poetry Ser.). 60p. 1979. 9.95x (ISBN 0-8203-0479-4); pap. 5.95 (ISBN 0-8203-0486-7). U of Ga Pr.

Succession in Fen Woodland Ecosystems in the Dutch Haf District with Special Reference to Betula Pubescens Ehrh. J. Wiegers. (Dissertationes Botanicae Ser.: No. 86). (Illus.). 152p. 1985. pap. text ed. 30.00x (ISBN 3-7682-1441-9). Lubrecht & Cramer.

Succession in the Muslim Family. N. J. Coulson. 1971. 54.50 (ISBN 0-521-07852-0). Cambridge U Pr.

Succession Laws of Christian Countries with Special Reference to the Law of Primogeniture As It Exists in England. Eyre Lloyd. xi, 108p. 1985. Repr. of 1877 ed. lib. bdg. 20.00x (ISBN 0-8377-0816-8). Rothman.

Succession of New States to International Treaties. Okon Udokang. LC 79-38029. 552p. 1972. lib. bdg. 30.00 (ISBN 0-379-00168-3). Oceana.

Succession of Shakespere's Works. Ed. by Frederick J. Furnivall. LC 76-137318. Repr. of 1874 ed. 11.50 (ISBN 0-404-02663-X). AMS Pr.

Succession Planning Handbook for the Chief Executive. Walter R. Mahler & Stephen J. Drotter. 300p. 1986. 45.00 (ISBN 0-914431-01-3). Mahler Pub Co.

Succession Planning: Key to Corporate Excellence. Arthur X. Deegan. LC 85-22776. 253p. 1986. pap. 39.95 (ISBN 0-471-82527-1, Pub. by Wiley-Interscience). Wiley.

Succession-Replacement Planning: Programs & Practices. Joseph Carnazza. 1982. pap. 12.00 (ISBN 0-317-11511-1). CU Ctr Career Res.

Succession to the Rule in Islam. A. Chejne. 1960. 5.30x (ISBN 0-87902-158-6). Orientalia.

Successions of Meniscomyine & Allomyine Rodents (Aplodontidae) in the Oligo-Miocene John Day Formation, Oregon. John M. Rensberger. LC 83-1403. (UC Publications in Geological Sciences: Vol. 124). 176p. 1983. pap. text ed. 23.50x (ISBN 0-520-09668-1). U of Cal Pr.

Successor Generation: Its Challenges & Responsibilities. Robert E. Osgood. 45p. 1983. pap. 7.95 (ISBN 0-87855-874-8). Transaction Bks.

Successor: My Life. Kosho K. Otani. LC 84-23016. (Illus.). 114p. 1985. 18.95x (ISBN 0-914910-50-7). Buddhist Bks.

Successors of Alexander the Great. C. A. Kinkaid. 192p. 1980. pap. 12.50 (ISBN 0-89005-352-9). Ares.

Successors of Drake. Julian S. Corbett. (Research & Source Works Ser.: No. 176). 1968. Repr. of 1900 ed. 25.50 (ISBN 0-8337-0662-4). B Franklin.

Successors of Genghis Khan. Rashid A. Tabib. LC 70-135987. (Persian Heritage Ser.: No. 10). pap. 99.90 (ISBN 0-317-58197-X, 2029718). Bks Demand UMI.

Successors of Homer. W. C. Lawton. LC 69-17001. Repr. of 1898 ed. 21.50x (ISBN 0-8154-0276-7). Cooper Sq.

Succinct View of the Origin of Our Colonies. William Bollan. LC 75-31084. 1976. Repr. of 1766 ed. 21.00 (ISBN 0-404-13503-X). AMS Pr.

Succos: Its Significance, Law, & Prayers. Hersh Goldwurm & Meir Zlotowitz. (ArtScroll Mesorah Ser.). (Illus.). 128p. 1982. 11.95 (ISBN 0-89906-166-4); pap. 8.95 (ISBN 0-89906-167-2). Mesorah Pubns.

Succubus. Kenneth R. Johnson. (Orig.). 1980. pap. 2.25 (ISBN 0-440-17716-2). Dell.

Succulent Flora of Southern Africa: A Comprehensive & Authoritative Guide to the Indigenous Succulents of S Africa, Botswana, S-W Africa, Namibia, Angola, Zambia, Zimbabwe, Rhodesia & Mozambique Incorporating the Latest Research & Changes in Nomenclature. Doreen Court. 240p. 1981. text ed. 60.00 (ISBN 90-6191-091-9, Pub. by A A Balkema). Brookfield Pub Co.

Succulent Plants. 3.95 (ISBN 0-686-21138-3). Bklyn Botanic.

Sucess in Marriage-Guaranteed !!! The Secret of Making Friends & Keeping them. John Bryant. (Orig.). 1987. pap. 7.95 (ISBN 0-9617444-4-8). Socratic Pr.

Sucessful Techniques for Criminal Trials. 2nd ed. F. Lee Bailey & Henry B. Rothblatt. LC 84-82304. 1985. 69.50 (ISBN 0-318-04533-8). Lawyers Co-Op.

Sucessful Telemarketing Manual. Peg Fisher. 300p. 1985. 61.95 (ISBN 0-85013-152-9). Dartnell Corp.

Such a Candle. Douglas C. Wood. 1980. pap. 9.95 (ISBN 0-87552-946-1, Evangel Pr UK). Presby & Reformed.

Such a Good Baby. Ruby J. Jensen. 320p. 1988. pap. 3.95 (ISBN 0-8125-1977-9). Tor Bks.

Such a Life. Edith La Zebnik. 1979. pap. 2.50 (ISBN 0-671-82282-9). PB.

Such a Pretty Face: Being Fat in America. Marcia Millman. (Illus.). 1980. 12.95 (ISBN 0-393-01317-0). Norton.

Such a Vision of the Street: Mother Teresa-The Spirit & the Work. Eileen Egan. LC 81-43570. (Illus.). 528p. 1986. pap. 9.95 (ISBN 0-385-17491-8, Im). Doubleday.

Such Agreeable Friends. Gay L. Balliet. 266p. (Orig.). 1987. pap. write for info. (ISBN 0-910119-33-3). Soco Pubns.

Such Are the Valiant. John C. Andrews. (Inflation Fighter Ser.). 160p. 1982. pap. write for info. (ISBN 0-8439-1122-0, Leisure Bks). Leisure NY.

Such Are the Valiant. John C. Andrews. 1978. pap. 1.50 (ISBN 0-505-51314-5, Pub. by Tower Bks). Leisure NY.

Such As Us: Southern Voices of the Thirties. Ed. by Tom E. Terrill & Jerrold Hirsch. LC 77-14248. (Illus.). xxvi, 302p. 1978. 22.50x (ISBN 0-8078-1318-4). U of NC Pr.

Such As Us: Southern Voices of the Thirties. Ed. by Tom E. Terrill & Jerrold Hirsch. LC 77-14248. xxvi, 302p. 1987. 22.50x; pap. 9.95x (ISBN 0-8078-4191-9). U of NC Pr.

Such Bright Hopes. Walter R. Scragg. Ed. by Raymond Woolsey. 384p. 1987. 8.50 (ISBN 0-8280-0389-0). Review & Herald.

Such Devoted Sisters. Cathy Linton. 1978. 15.00 (ISBN 0-86025-068-7, Pub. by Ian Henry Pubns England). State Mutual Bk.

Such Friends Are Dangerous. Walter Tyrer. Ed. by J. Barzun & W. H. Taylor. LC 81-47390. (Crime Fiction 1950-1975 Ser.). 224p. 1983. lib. bdg. 18.00 (ISBN 0-8240-4974-8). Garland Pub.

Such Friends As These. Alexander G. Rose, III & Jeffrey A. Savoye. 1986. pap. 5.00 (ISBN 0-910556-24-5). Enoch Pratt.

Such Good Friends. Lois Gould. 1971. pap. 2.25 (ISBN 0-440-18376-6). Dell.

Such Good Friends. Lois Gould. 288p. 1988. pap. 6.95 (ISBN 0-374-52086-0). FS&G.

Such Is Death. Leo Bruce, pseud. 1985. 14.95 (ISBN 0-89733-159-1); pap. 4.95 (ISBN 0-89733-160-5). Academy Chi Pubs.

Such Is My Love: A Study of Shakespeare's Sonnets. Joseph Pequigney. LC 85-984. x, 264p. 1985. lib. bdg. 22.50x (ISBN 0-226-65563-6). U of Chicago Pr.

Such Is My Love: A Study of Shakespeare's Sonnets. Joseph Pequigney. LC 85-984. x, 250p. 1987. pap. 9.95 (ISBN 0-226-65564-4). U of Chicago Pr.

Such Is the Real Nature of Horses. Robert Vavra. LC 79-52901. (Illus.). 1979. 39.95 (ISBN 0-688-03504-3). Morrow.

Such Men Are Dangerous. Lawrence Block. 192p. 1985. pap. 2.95 (ISBN 0-515-08170-1). Jove Pubns.

Such Nice People. Sandra Scoppettone. 288p. 1981. pap. 2.75 (ISBN 0-449-24420-2, Crest). Fawcett.

Such Nonsense! An Anthology. Carolyn Wells. 1978. Repr. of 1918 ed. lib. bdg. 25.00 (ISBN 0-8492-2950-2). R West.

Such Pretty Toys. S. F. Dean. 224p. 1986. pap. 2.95 (ISBN 0-8125-0184-5, Dist. by Warner Pub Services & St. Martin's Press). Tor Bks.

Such Prompt Eloquence: Language As Agency & Character in Milton's Epics. Leonard Mustazza. LC 86-48007. 176p. 1988. 28.50x (ISBN 0-8387-5121-0). Bucknell U Pr.

Such Sweet Compulsion: The Autobiography of Geraldine Farrar. Geraldine Farrar. LC 72-107802. (Select Bibliographies Reprint Ser). 1938. 25.50 (ISBN 0-8369-5205-7). Ayer Co Pubs.

Such Sweet Compulsion, the Autobiography of Geraldine Farrar. Geraldine Farrar. LC 70-100656. (Music Ser.). 1970. Repr. of 1938 ed. lib. bdg. 37.50 (ISBN 0-306-71863-4). Da Capo.

Such Sweet Magic. Rosalind Carson. (Superromances Ser.). 384p. 1983. pap. 2.95 (ISBN 0-373-70091-1, Pub. by Worldwide). Harlequin Bks.

Such Waltzing Was Not Easy: Stories. Gordon Weaver. LC 75-2288. (Illinois Short Fiction Ser.). 144p. 1974. pap. 8.95 (ISBN 0-252-00533-3). U of Ill Pr.

Such Was Saratoga. facsimile ed. Hugh Bradley. LC 75-1832. (Leisure Class in America Ser.). 1975. Repr. of 1940 ed. 25.50x (ISBN 0-405-06901-4). Ayer Co Pubs.

Such Was the Season. Clarence Major. LC 87-7760. 213p. 1987. 16.95 (ISBN 0-916515-20-6). Mercury Hse Inc.

Such Were the Joys. Griselda Scott. 160p. 1985. 34.00x (ISBN 0-901976-89-X, Pub. by United Writers Pubns England). State Mutual Bk.

Sucinta Historia de la Cartuja de Valldemossa. Luis Ripoll. Ed. by james Hogg. (Analecta Cartusiana Ser.: No. 41-4). (Illus.). 179p. (Orig., Span.). 1978. pap. 25.00 (ISBN 3-7052-0052-6, Pub by Salzburg Studies). Longwood Pub Group.

Suck Cumin. Eilah Scaccia & Michael Scaccia. LC 81-67394. (Illus.). 128p. (Orig.). 1981. pap. 10.00 (ISBN 0-940204-00-2). Fredonia.

Sucker. Carson McCullers. LC 85-29114. (Creative's Classic Short Stories Ser.). 40p. (gr. 4 up). 1986. PLB 8.95 (ISBN 0-88682-053-7). Creative Ed.

Sucker Bet. Zeke Masters. (Faro Blake Ser.: No. 17). 176p. (Orig.). 1982. pap. 1.95 (ISBN 0-671-43816-6). PB.

Suckers Progress: An Informal History of Gambling in America from the Colonies to Canfield. Herbert Asbury. LC 69-14909. (Criminology, Law Enforcement, & Social Problems Ser.: No. 51). (Illus.). 1969. Repr. of 1938 ed. 17.50x (ISBN 0-87585-051-0). Patterson Smith.

Sucking Lice of North America: An Illustrated Manual for Identification. Ke C. Kim et al. LC 84-43060. (Illus.). 256p. 1987. 39.50x (ISBN 0-271-00395-2). Pa St U Pr.

Sucrochemistry. Ed. by John L. Hickson. LC 77-1296. (ACS Symposium Ser.: No. 41). 1977. 34.95 (ISBN 0-8412-0290-7). Am Chemical.

Sucrose. Ed. by G. Vettorazzi & I. Macdonald. (ILSI Human Nutrition Reviews Ser.). (Illus.). 210p. 1988. 39.50 (ISBN 0-387-19526-2). Springer-Verlag.

Sucrose Crystal & Its Solutions. F. H. Kelly & F. Mark. 272p. 1975. pap. 17.50x (ISBN 0-8214-0497-0, Pub. by Singapore U Pr). Ohio U Pr.

Suction Lipectomy & Body Sculpturing. Teimourian. (Illus.). 608p. 1986. 209.00 (ISBN 0-8016-4923-4). Mosby.

Sudan. M. W. Daly. (World Bibliographical Ser.: No. 40). 175p. 1983. lib. bdg. 26.75 (ISBN 0-903450-70-4). ABC-Clio.

Sudan. (Let's Visit Places & Peoples - - Nations, Dependencies, & Sovereignties of the World Ser.). (Illus.). (gr. 5 up). 1988. 12.95 (ISBN 0-222-00964-0). Chelsea Hse.

Sudan. Nick Worrall. 30.00 (ISBN 0-7043-2242-0, Pub. by Quartet England). Charles River Bks.

Sudan: A Country Study. 3rd ed. Harold D. Nelson. LC 83-2718. (Area Handbook Ser.: DA Pam 550-27). (Illus.). 393p. 1983. 10.00 (ISBN 0-318-21918-2, S/N 008-020-00955-5). USGPO.

Sudan: A Second Challenge to Nationhood. Bona Malwal. LC 85-4761. (Illus.). 48p. (Orig.). 1985. pap. text ed. 3.95x (ISBN 0-936508-13-2). Barber Pr.

Sudan in Evolution: A Study of the Economic, Financial & Administrative Conditions of the Anglo-Egyptian Sudan. Percy F. Martin. LC 75-90122. Repr. of 1921 ed. 28.00x (ISBN 0-8371-2896-X, MSE&, Pub. by Negro U Pr). Greenwood.

Sudan in Original Photographs. Lesley Forbes & Martin Daly. (Illus.). 128p. 1988. text ed. 65.00 (ISBN 0-7103-0273-8, Kegan Paul). Routledge Chapman & Hall.

Sudan in Pictures. Department of Geography, Lerner Publications. (Visual Geography Ser.). (Illus.). 64p. (gr. 5 up). 1988. PLB 9.95 (ISBN 0-8225-1839-2). Lerner Pubns.

Sudan Law Reports: Civil Cases, 1900-1940, 2 vols. LC 69-15390. 1969. Repr. Set. 90.00 (ISBN 0-379-12750-4); Vol. 1, 1900-1931. 40.00 ea. Vol. 2, 1932-1940. Oceana.

Sudan Memoirs of Carl Christian Giegler Pasha, 1873-83. Richard Hill. (Illus.). 1984. 45.00x (ISBN 0-19-726028-4). Oxford U Pr.

Sudan: Pricing Policies & Structural Balance. 254p. 1985. 10.00 (ISBN 0-8213-0621-9, BK 0621). World Bank.

Sudan Since Independence: Studies of the Political Development Since 1956. Ed. by Peter Woodward. 180p. 1987. text ed. 43.95 (ISBN 0-566-00991-9). Gower Pub Co.

Sudan since Nimeiri. Ed. by Peter Woodward. 176p. 1988. lib. bdg. 39.95x (ISBN 0-7099-5223-6, Pub. by Croom Helm UK). Routledge Chapman & Hall.

Sudan since Nimeiri. Ed. by Peter Woodward. 176p. 1988. lib. bdg. 52.50 (ISBN 0-415-00480-2). Routledge Chapman & Hall.

Sudan: State, Capital & Transformation. Ed. by Tony Barnett & Abbas A. Karim. 288p. 1988. lib. bdg. 75.00x (ISBN 0-7099-5902-8, Pub. by Croom Helm UK). Routledge Chapman & Hall.

Sudan Tales: Reminiscences of Sudan Political Service Wives, 1926-56. Ed. by Rosemary Kenrick. 174p. 1986. 26.50 (ISBN 0-906672-31-7); pap. 16.50 (ISBN 0-906672-32-5). Oleander Pr.

Sudan under Wingate: Administration in the Anglo-Egyptian Sudan, 1899 to 1916. Gabriel Warburg. (Illus.). 245p. 1971. 29.50x (ISBN 0-7146-2612-0, F Cass Co). Biblio Dist.

Sudan: Unity & Diversity in a Multicultural State. John O. Voll & Sarah P. Voll. (Profiles-Nations of Contemporary Middle East Ser.). 178p. 1985. 39.50x (ISBN 0-86531-302-4). Westview.

Sudanese Bourgeoisie-Vanguard of Development? Fatima B. Mahmoud. (Middle East Ser.). (Illus.). 180p. 1984. 26.25x (ISBN 0-86232-183-2, Pub. by Zed Pr England); pap. 10.25 (ISBN 0-86232-184-0, Pub. by Zed Pr England). Humanities.

Sudanna, Sudanna. Brian Herbert. 208p. 1986. pap. 2.95 (ISBN 0-425-08786-7). Berkley Pub.

Sudbury Region: An Illustrated History. Graeme S. Mount. LC 86-5653. (Illus.). 144p. 1986. 24.95 (ISBN 0-89781-177-1). Windsor Pubns Inc.

Sudden & Gradual: Approaches to Enlightenment in Chinese Thought. Ed. by Peter N. Gregory. LC 87-26688. (Studies in East Asian Buddhism: No. 5). 474p. 1987. text ed. 37.50X (ISBN 0-8248-1118-6). UH Pr.

Sudden Apprehension: Aspects of Knowledge in Paradise Lost. Lee A. Jacobus. (Studies in English Literature: No. 94). 225p. 1976. text ed. 27.20x (ISBN 90-2793-253-0). Mouton.

Sudden Around the Bend. Gary Sange. LC 81-68477. 4.75 (ISBN 0-933532-30-X). BKMK.

Sudden Cardiac Death. Ed. by Mark E. Josephson. LC 70-6558. (Cardiovascular Clinics Ser.: Vol. 15 No. 3). (Illus.). 328p. 1985. 50.00 (ISBN 0-8036-5098-1). Davis Co.

Sudden Cardiac Death. Ed. by Joel Morganroth & Leonard Horowitz. LC 79-2965. 352p. 1986. 49.50 (ISBN 0-8089-1725-0, 792965). Grune.

Sudden Cardiac Death. Ed. by R. J. Myerburg. (Journal: Cardiology: Vol. 74, Suppl. 2, 1987). (Illus.). iv, 72p. 1987. pap. 18.00 (ISBN 3-8055-4629-7). S Karger.

Sudden Cardiac Death. Ed. by Edmund Sonnenblick & Michael Lesch. 352p. 1981. 49.50 (ISBN 0-8089-1460-X, 794181). Grune.

Sudden Cardiac Death. (Technical Report Ser.: No. 726). 25p. 1985. pap. 2.40 (ISBN 92-4-120726-4). World Health.

Sudden Cardiac Death & Congestive Heart Failure. Joel Morganroth & E. Neil Moore. 1983. lib. bdg. 45.00 (ISBN 0-89838-580-6, Pub. by Martinus Nijhoff Netherlands). Kluwer Academic.

Sudden Cardiac Death in the Community. Ed. by Mickey Eisenberg et al. LC 83-21156. 163p. 1984. 35.00 (ISBN 0-275-91428-3, C1428). Praeger.

Sudden Clash of Thunder. Bhagwan Shree Rajneesh. Ed. by Ma Yoga Anurag. LC 78-901998. (Zen Ser.). (Illus.). 284p. (Orig.). 1977. 9.95 (ISBN 0-88050-135-9). Chidvilas Inc.

Sudden Coronary Death, Vol. 382. Ed. by Henry M. Greenberg. 484p. 1982. 102.00x (ISBN 0-89766-153-2); pap. 102.00x (ISBN 0-89766-154-0). NY Acad Sci.

Sudden Coronary Death: Proceedings. Paavo Nurmi Symposium, 4th, Helsinki, September 15-17, 1977. Ed. by V. Manninen. (Advances in Cardiology Ser.: Vol. 25). (Illus.). 1978. 78.75 (ISBN 3-8055-2881-7). S Karger.

Sudden Dancing. Gene Zeiger. (Amherst Writers & Artists Chapbook Ser.). 30p. (Orig.). 1988. pap. 4.95 (ISBN 0-941895-03-3). Amherst Wri Art.

Sudden Death. Rita Mae Brown. 256p. 1984. pap. text ed. 4.50 (ISBN 0-553-24030-7). Bantam.

Sudden Death. William X. Kienzie. 1986. pap. 3.95 (ISBN 0-345-32851-5). Ballantine.

Sudden Death. William X. Kienzle. (Large Print Bks.). 445p. 1986. lib. bdg. 16.95 (ISBN 0-8161-3965-2). G K Hall.

Sudden Death. Ed. by H. E. Kulbertus & H. J. Wellens. (Developments in Cardiovascular Medicine: Vol. 4). (Illus.). xiv, 406p. 1980. lib. bdg. 68.50 (ISBN 90-247-2290-X, Martinus Nijhoff Pubs). Kluwer Academic.

Sudden Death. (Mack Bolan Ser.: No. 7). 384p. 1987. pap. 3.95 (ISBN 0-373-61407-1, Pub. by Gold Eagle). Harlequin Bks.

Sudden Death Finish. Tucker Halleran. 1986. pap. 3.50 (ISBN 0-312-90483-5). St Martin.

Sudden Death in Infancy. Preben Geertinger. (Illus.). 128p. 1968. photocopy ed. 16.00x (ISBN 0-398-00663-6). C C Thomas.
Sudden Death in Infancy. Bernard Knight. LC 82-25501. 176p. (Orig.). 1983. pap. 7.95 (ISBN 0-571-13066-6). Faber & Faber.
Sudden Death: Medical Subject Analysis & Research Directory with Bibliography. Samuel Shapiro. LC 81-71810. 134p. 1983. 34.95 (ISBN 0-941864-34-0); pap. 26.50 (ISBN 0-941864-35-9). ABBE Pubs Assn.
Sudden Death of Athletes. Ernst Jokl. 142p. 1985. 21.75x (ISBN 0-398-05088-0). C C Thomas.
Sudden Departures. Jonathan Ross. 192p. 1988. 14.95 (ISBN 0-312-02292-1). St Martin.
Sudden Door. Madeline Benedict. 1960. 2.75 (ISBN 0-8233-0005-6). Golden Quill.
Sudden Dozen. D. W. Meyer. 224p. 1981. 12.50 (ISBN 0-89962-224-0). Todd & Honeywell.
Sudden Engagement. Penny Jordon. (Harlequin Presents Ser.). 192p. 1983. pap. 1.95 (ISBN 0-373-10618-1). Harlequin Bks.
Sudden Family. Steven Standiford & Deborah Standiford. 160p. 1986. 9.95 (ISBN 0-8499-0567-2). Word Bks.
Sudden Fear: The Horror & Dark Suspense Novels of Dean R. Koontz. Ed. by Bill Munster. (Studies in Literary Criticism: No. 24). 1988. 19.95; pap. 10.95. Starmont Hse.
Sudden Fear: The Horror & Dark Suspense Novels of Dean R. Koontz. Ed. by Bill Munster. (Starmont Studies in Literary Criticism: No. 24). 182p. 1988. Repr. lib. bdg. 19.95x (ISBN 0-8095-5104-7). Borgo Pr.
Sudden Fiction: American Short-Short Stories. Ed. by Robert Shapard & James Thomas. 280p. 1986. pap. 10.95 (ISBN 0-87905-265-1). Gibbs Smith Pub.
Sudden Glory. Vernon F. Anderson. (Caribbean Writers Ser.). 274p. (Orig.). 1987. pap. 8.50 (ISBN 0-435-98808-5). Heinemann Ed.
Sudden Hunger. Debra Bruce. LC 86-16091. 80p. 1987. 10.50 (ISBN 0-938626-81-7); pap. 6.95 (ISBN 0-938626-82-5). U of Ark Pr.
Sudden Ice. Jim Leeke. LC 87-26771. (Illus.). 188p. (Orig.). 1988. pap. 8.95 (ISBN 0-89407-073-8). Strawberry Hill.
Sudden Impact. Joe Stinson. 224p. (Orig.). 1984. pap. 2.95 (ISBN 0-446-32203-2). Warner Bks.
Sudden Impulse. Georgia M. Shewmake. (YA) (gr. 7 up). 1984. 9.95 (ISBN 0-8034-8448-8, Avalon). Bouregy.
Sudden Infant Death- S.I.D.S. Probable Causes & Simple Prevention. James W. Tyler. LC 85-32325. 96p. (Orig.). 1986. pap. 5.95 (ISBN 0-8069-6346-8). Sterling.
Sudden Infant Death: Patterns, Puzzles, & Problems. Jean Golding et al. LC 85-15008. 272p. 1985. 25.00x (ISBN 0-295-96302-6). U of Wash Pr.
Sudden Infant Death Syndrome. Tyson Tildon & Lois Roedes. Ed. by Alfred Steinschneider. (Symposium). 1983. 59.00 (ISBN 0-12-691050-2). Acad Pr.
Sudden Infant Death Syndrome: Journal: Pediatrician, Vol. 15, No. 4, 1988. Ed. by D. W. Kaplan. (Illus.). 76p. 1988. pap. 30.00 (ISBN 3-8055-4892-3). S Karger.
Sudden Infant Death Syndrome: Medical Aspects & Psychological Management. Ed. by Jan L. Culbertson et al. LC 88-45399. (Contemporary Medicine & Public Health Ser.). 288p. 1988. text ed. 39.50x (ISBN 0-8018-3679-4). Johns Hopkins.
Sudden Infant Death Syndrome: Risk Factors & Basic Mechanisms. Ed. by Ronald Harper & Howard Hoffman. LC 87-2365. 1988. 150.00 (ISBN 0-89335-248-9). PMA Pub Corp.
Sudden Infant Death Syndrome: The Possible Role of "The Fear of Paralysis Reflex". Ed. by Birger Kaada & Stavanger. (Illus.). 64p. 1986. pap. 18.95 (ISBN 82-00-18204-5). Oxford U Pr.
Sudden Land. Dale Oldham. 192p. 1985. pap. 2.25 (ISBN 0-8439-2233-8, Leisure Bks). Leisure NY.
Sudden Loss of Chochlear & Vestibular Function. Ed. by M. Hoke. (Advances in Oto-Rhino-Laryngology Ser.: Vol. 27). (Illus.). x, 198p. 1981. 98.75 (ISBN 3-8055-2630-X). S Karger.
Sudden Loss of Cochlear & Vestibular Function. Ed. by M. Hoke. (Advances in Oto-Rhino-Laryngology Ser.: Vol. 27). (Illus.). x, 198p. 1981. 98.75 (ISBN 3-8055-2630-X). S Karger.
Sudden Madness. Ralph Hayes. (Orig.). 1981. pap. 2.25 (ISBN 0-505-51693-4, Pub. by Tower Bks). Leisure NY.
Sudden Music. Roger White. 200p. 14.50 (ISBN 0-85398-162-0); pap. 8.50 (ISBN 0-85398-163-9). G Ronald Pub.
Sudden Ripples. Virginia McKinney. Ed. by Barbara Fischer. 1974. 2.95x (ISBN 0-912658-28-2). J Mark Pr.
Sudden Shelter. Jesse D. Jennings et al. (University of Utah Anthropological Papers: No. 103). (Illus., Orig.). 1980. pap. 25.00x (ISBN 0-87480-166-4). U of Utah Pr.
Sudden Silence. Eve Bunting. 112p. (YA) (gr. 12 up). 1988. 13.95 (ISBN 0-15-282058-2). HarBraceJ.
Sudden Spring Wind. Bill Kunz. 1985. 5.00 (ISBN 0-931611-01-6). D R Benbow.
Sudden Star. Pamela Sargent. 1979. pap. 1.95 (ISBN 0-449-14114-4, GM). Fawcett.
Sudden Twists. Burton Goodman. 120p. (gr. 6-8). 1988. pap. text ed. 7.20x (ISBN 0-89061-501-2). Jamestown Pubs.
Suddenly. Hila Colman. LC 86-28460. 160p. (YA) (gr. 7 up). 1987. 11.75 (ISBN 0-688-05865-5, Morrow Junior Books). Morrow.
Suddenly Alone: A Progression of Emotions Embraced by a Widow on the Path of Healing. Dolores Dahl. (Illus.). 144p. 1987. pap. 9.95 (ISBN 0-9608960-5-8). Single Vision.
Suddenly & Gently: Visions of Elvis Through the Art of Betty Harper. Betty Harper. 96p. 1987. pap. 9.95 (ISBN 0-312-00707-8). St Martin.
Suddenly at His Residence. Christianna Brand. 176p. (Orig.). 1988. pap. 3.50 (ISBN 0-553-25465-0). Bantam.
Suddenly in Her Sorbet. Joyce Christmas. 1988. pap. 3.50 (ISBN 0-449-13311-7, GM). Fawcett.
Suddenly in Rome. Max Davidson. 224p. 1988. 19.95 (ISBN 0-340-41514-2, Pub. by Hodder & Stoughton UK). David & Charles.
Suddenly It's Christmas. Vernon Thomas. (Writers Workshop Greenbird Ser.). 70p. 1976. 10.00 (ISBN 0-86578-112-5); flexible cloth 6.00 (ISBN 0-86578-113-3). Ind-US Inc.
Suddenly It's Evening. Ryah T. Goodman. LC 77-9026. 1977. 5.95 (ISBN 0-87233-042-7). Bauhan.
Suddenly It's Springtime. Vessa Harper. 1967. pap. 3.50 (ISBN 0-88027-050-0). Firm Foun Pub.
Suddenly Last Summer see Theatre of Tennessee Williams.
Suddenly Love. Rebecca Flanders. (Harlequin American Romance Ser.). 256p. 1984. pap. 2.25 (ISBN 0-373-16041-0). Harlequin Bks.
Suddenly Single. Jim Smoke. 120p. 1984. pap. 5.95 (ISBN 0-8007-5152-3, Power Bks). Revell.
Suddenly Single: Learning to Start Over, a Personal Guide. John Robertson & Betty Utterback. 200p. 1986. 15.95 (ISBN 0-671-54442-X). S&S.
Suddenly Successful Student: A Parents' & Teachers' Guide to Learning & Behavior Problems: How Behavioral Optometry Helps. Ellis S. Edelman et al. LC 85-30343. 48p. 1986. pap. 7.95 (ISBN 0-915010-34-8). Sutter House.
Suddenly Thunder. Ruth L. Schechter. LC 76-176098. 96p. 1972. 12.95 (ISBN 0-87929-004-8). Barlenmir.
Sudek. Sonja Bullaty. (Illus.). 192p. 1986. 35.00 (ISBN 0-517-56419-X, C N Potter Bks). Crown.
Sudeten-German Tragedy. Austin J. App. (Illus.). 84p. (Orig.). 1979. pap. 3.00x (ISBN 0-911038-66-3, Inst Hist Rev). Noontide.
Sudeten German Tragedy. Austin J. App. 1984. lib. bdg. 79.95 (ISBN 0-87700-523-0). Revisionist Pr.
Sudhin N. Ghose. S. A. Narayan. (Indian Writers Ser.). 8.50 (ISBN 0-89253-557-1). Ind-US Inc.
Sudie. Sara Flanigan. 288p. 1985. 15.95 (ISBN 0-312-77519-9). St Martin.
Sudman's Bubble-ology Guide. Louis Pearl. (Illus.). 32p. (Orig.). 1985. pap. 7.95 (ISBN 0-932165-07-9). Tangent Pr.
Suds. Judie Angell. LC 82-22732. 167p. (gr. 6-9). 1983. 10.95 (ISBN 0-02-705570-1). Bradbury Pr.
Sue Bradley's Cotton Collection. Sue Bradley. 1988. 18.95 (ISBN 0-8050-0674-5). H Holt & Co.
Sue Coe: Police State. Sue Coe et al. Ed. by Marilyn A. Zeitlin. (Illus., Orig.). 1987. pap. text ed. 30.00x (ISBN 0-935519-07-6). Anderson Gal.
Sue Kreitzman's Sunday Best. Sue Kreitzman. Ed. by Becky Hoollingsworth. (Illus.). 304p. (Orig.). 1981. pap. 9.95 (ISBN 0-939114-33-X). Wimmer Bks.
Sue Likes Blue. Barbara Gregorich. Ed. by Joan Hoffman. (Start To Read! Ser.). (Illus.). 16p. (Orig.). (gr. k-2). 1984. pap. 1.95 (ISBN 0-88743-011-2, 06011). Sch Zone Pub Co.
Sue Me. Warren Murphy & Richard Sapir. (Destroyer Ser.: No. 66). 1986. pap. 2.95 (ISBN 0-451-14556-9, Sig). NAL.
Sue Your Boss. E. Richard Larson. 316p. 1981. pap. 9.95 (ISBN 0-374-51608-1). FS&G.
Suede Holloway. William Baldwin. 1978. pap. 3.95 (ISBN 0-9602170-0-2). Ars Eterna.
Suedhuegel Kerameikos, Vol. 9. Ursula Knigge. 1976. 144.00x (ISBN 3-11-004879-5). De Gruyter.
Sueno. Sov J. De la Cruz. Tr. by John Campion. LC 83-4719. pap. 5.00 (ISBN 0-914476-93-9). Thorp Springs.
Sueno de Colibri: Hummingbird Dream. Naomi Quinonez. (Illus.). 80p. (Orig., Eng. & Span.). 1985. pap. 4.95 (ISBN 0-931122-38-4). West End.
Sueno de Rosita. Mary-Ann S. Bruni. Tr. by Rogelio De Castro from Eng. (Texas Ser.: Vol. 1). (Illus.). 48p. (Span.). (gr. k-8). 1985. 13.95 (ISBN 0-935857-02-8); pap. write for info. (ISBN 0-935857-04-4) (ISBN 0-935857-11-7) (ISBN 0-935857-12-5). Texart.
Sueno de Rosita. Mary-Ann S. Bruni. Tr. by Rocelio de Casho. (Illus.). 48p. (gr. k-8). 1987. price not set. Texart.
Sueno de Sor Juana Ines de La Cruz: Tradiciones Literarias Y Originalidad. Georgina S. De Rivers. (Serie A: Monagrafias, LXIII). 180p. (Span.). 1976. 25.50 (ISBN 0-7293-0030-7, Pub. by Tamesis Bks Ltd). Longwood Pub Group.
Sueno (Rimas al Recuerdo) Myriam Y. Aguiar. LC 84-80617. 64p. (Orig., Span.). 1984. pap. 6.00 (ISBN 0-89729-348-7). Ediciones.
Sue's. Agatha M. Thrash & Phylis A. Austin. 1984. pap. write for info. (ISBN 0-942658-07-8). Yuchi Pines.
Suesswasser-Diatomeen des indo-Malayischen Archipels und der Hawaii-Inseln. Friedrich Hustedt. (Ger.). 1979. Repr. of 1942 ed. lib. bdg. 105.00x (ISBN 3-87429-162-6). Lubrecht & Cramer.
Suesswasserfauna Deutchlands. A. Brauer. (Illus.). 1961. Repr. of 1909 ed. 210.00x (ISBN 3-7682-0045-0). Lubrecht & Cramer.
Suesswasserflora von Mitteleuropa: Chlorophyta I: Phytomonadma, Vol. 9. H. Ettl. Ed. by A. Pascher & J. Gerloff. (Illus.). 807p. (Ger.). 1983. lib. bdg. 99.00x (ISBN 3-437-30408-9). Lubrecht & Cramer.
Suesswasserflora von Mitteleuropa: Conjugatophyceae I. Chlorophyta VIII Zygnemales, Vol. 16. J. Z. Kadlubowska. Ed. by A. Pascher & H. Ettl. (Illus.). 532p. (Ger.). 1984. lib. bdg. 82.80x (ISBN 3-437-30415-1). Lubrecht & Cramer.
Suesswasserflora von Mitteleuropa: Pteridophyta und Antophyta, Part 1 - Lycopodiaceae bis Orchidaceae, Vol. 23. S. J. Casper & H. D. Krausch. Ed. by A. Pascher et al. (Illus.). 403p. (Ger.). 1980. lib. bdg. 50.00x (ISBN 3-437-30309-0). Lubrecht & Cramer.
Suesswasserflora von Mitteleuropa: Starmach K. Chrysophyceae und Haptophyceae, Vol. 1. Ed. by A. Pascher. (Illus.). 515p. 1985. lib. bdg. 82.80x (ISBN 3-437-30402-X). Lubrecht & Cramer.
Suesswasserflora von Mitteleuropa, Vol. 14: Mrozinska, T. Chlorophyta VI. Oedogoniophyceae: Oedogoniales. T. Mrozinska. Ed. by A. Pascher. (Illus., Ger.). 1985. lib. bdg. 94.80x (ISBN 3-437-30413-5). Lubrecht & Cramer.
Suesswasserflora von Mitteleuropa. Vol. 4: Xanthophyceae, Part 2. A. Rieth. Ed. by A. Pascher et al. (Illus.). 147p. (Ger.). 1978. lib. bdg. 40.00x (ISBN 3-437-30304-X). Lubrecht & Cramer.
Suesswasserflora von Mitteleuropa: Xanthophyceae, Part 1, Vol. 3. Ed. by A Pascher et al. (Illus.). 530p. (Ger.). 1978. lib. bdg. 58.80x (ISBN 3-437-30250-7). Lubrecht & Cramer.
Suesswasserflora von Mittelieuropa, Vol. 20: Schyzomyceten-Bakterien, von J. Haeisler. A. Pascher. Ed. by H. Ettl & J. Gerloff. (Illus.). 588p. (Ger.). 1982. lib. bdg. 80.95x (ISBN 3-437-30344-9). Lubrecht & Cramer.
Suesswasserflora von Mitteluropa Vol. 2: Bacillariophyceae Pt. 1: Naviculaceae. K. Krammer & H. Lange-Bertalot. Ed. by A. Pascher. (Illus.). 876p. (Ger.). 1986. lib. bdg. 130.00x (ISBN 3-437-30403-8). Lubrecht & Cramer.
Suesswasserflora von Suedeuropa, Vol. 24: Pteridophyta und Antophyta, Part 2-Saururaceae bis Asteraceae. A. Pascher. Ed. by H. Ettl et al. (Illus.). 540p. 1981. lib. bdg. 82.80x (ISBN 3-437-30341-4). Lubrecht & Cramer.
Suetonio De Poetis E Biografi Minori. Suetonius. Ed. by W. R. Connor. LC 78-67147. (Latin Texts & Commentaries Ser.). (Lat. & Eng.). 1979. Repr. of 1944 ed. lib. bdg. 17.00x (ISBN 0-405-11615-2). Ayer Co Pubs.
Suetonius: Claudius. J. Mottershead. 190p. 1986. 15.25 (ISBN 0-86292-080-9, Pub. by Bristol Classical UK). Focus Info Gr.
Suetonius: Divus Augustus. J. M. Carter. 236p. 16.00 (ISBN 0-906515-55-6, Pub. by Bristol Classical Pr). Focus Info Gr.
Suetonius: Divus Julius. H. Butler & M. Cary. 186p. 1983. Repr. of 1927 ed. 16.00 (ISBN 0-86292-026-4, Pub. by Bristol Classical UK). Focus Info Gr.
Suetonius: Nero. B. Warmington. 120p. 1977. 12.25 (ISBN 0-906515-06-8, Pub. by Bristol Classical UK). Focus Info Gr.
Suetonius: The Biographer of the Caesars. B. Baldwin. 579p. 1983. lib. bdg. 87.50x (ISBN 0-317-46477-9, Pub. by A M Hakkert). Coronet Bks.
Suetonius: The Scholar & His Caesars. Andrew Wallace-Hadrill. LC 83-50728. 288p. 1984. 25.00x (ISBN 0-300-03000-2). Yale U Pr.
Suez & Sinai. Harry Browne. LC 72-101536. (Flashpoints Ser.). pap. 34.00 (ISBN 0-317-09516-1, 2004920). Bks Demand UMI.
Suez Canal. Sean Garrett. Ed. by Malcolm Yapp et al. (World History Ser.). (Illus.). 32p. (gr. 6-11). 1980. lib. bdg. 6.95 (ISBN 0-89908-230-0); pap. text ed. 2.45 (ISBN 0-89908-205-X). Greenhaven.
Suez Canal: A Selection of Documents Relating to the International Status of the Suez Canal & the Position of the Suez Canal Company, November 30,1854-July 26, 1958. (International & Comparative Law Quarterly Special Supplement Ser.: No. 1). pap. 15.00 (ISBN 0-317-17905-5). UNIPUB-Kraus Intl.
Suez Canal Company. Jean B. D'Humieres et al. Ed. by Leonard H. Hartmann. LC 85-90306. (Private Ship Letter Stamps of the World Ser.: Pt. 3). (Illus.). 288p. 1985. 45.00 (ISBN 0-917528-07-7). L H Hartmann.
Suez Canal: Its Past, Present, & Future. Arnold T. Wilson. Ed. by Mira Wilkins. LC 76-29990. (European Business Ser.). (Illus.). 1977. Repr. of 1933 ed. lib. bdg. 19.00x (ISBN 0-405-09722-0). Ayer Co Pubs.
Suez Canal: Letters & Documents Descriptive of Its Rise & Progress in 1854-56. Ferdinand M. De Lesseps. LC 74-83185. (Islam & Mideast Ser.). 1976. Repr. of 1876 ed. 31.00 (ISBN 0-8420-1748-8). Scholarly Res Inc.
Suez Crisis. (Flashpoints Ser.). (Illus.). (YA) (gr. 7 up). Date not set. write for info. Rourke Corp.
Suez Crisis, Nineteen Fifty-Six. Gerald Kurland. Ed. by D. Steve Rahmas. LC 73-78400. (Events of Our Times Ser.: No. 9). 32p. (Orig.). (YA) (gr. 7-12). 1973. lib. bdg. 3.75 incl. catalog cards (ISBN 0-87157-711-9); pap. 2.50 vinyl laminated covers (ISBN 0-87157-211-7). SamHar Pr.
Suez Nineteen Fifty-Six. Robert R. Bowie. (International Crisis & the Role of Law Ser). 1974. pap. 5.95x (ISBN 0-19-519805-0). Oxford U Pr.
Suffer a Sea Change. Celeste De Blasis. 1979. pap. 1.95 (ISBN 0-449-23954-3, Crest). Fawcett.
Suffer a Sea Change. Celeste De Blasis. 256p. 1986. pap. 3.50 (ISBN 0-553-26023-5). Bantam.
Suffer a Witch. Nigel Fitzgerald. Ed. by J. Barzun & W. H. Taylor. LC 81-47411. (Crime Fiction 1950-1975 Ser.). 256p. 1983. lib. bdg. 18.00 (ISBN 0-8240-5001-0). Garland Pub.
Suffer & Be Still: Women in the Victorian Age. Ed. by Martha Vicinus. LC 71-184524. (Midland Bks.: No. 168). (Illus.). 256p. 1972. 18.50x (ISBN 0-253-35572-9); pap. 9.95x (ISBN 0-253-20168-3). Ind U Pr.
Suffer the Children. John Saul. 384p. 1986. pap. 4.50 (ISBN 0-440-18293-X). Dell.
Suffer the Future: Policy Choices in Southern Africa. Robert I. Rotberg. LC 79-25845. 1980. text ed. 21.00x (ISBN 0-674-85401-2). Harvard U Pr.
Suffer the Little Children: The Battle Against Childhood Cancer. Jocelyn Demers. Tr. by James Parry from Fr. 192p. 1986. pap. 10.95 (ISBN 0-920792-62-6). Eden Pr.
Suffer the Little Children: Two Children's Bureau Bulletins, Original Anthology. Ed. by Leon Stein. LC 77-70552. (Work Ser.). (Illus.). 1977. lib. bdg. 24.50x (ISBN 0-405-10206-2). Ayer Co Pubs.
Sufferers & Healers: The Experience of Illness in Seventeenth-Century England. Lucinda M. Beier. (Social & Economic History Ser.). (Illus.). 288p. 1988. text ed. 67.50 (ISBN 0-7102-1053-1, Pub. by Routledge UK). Routledge Chapman & Hall.
Suffering. Dorothee Soelle. Tr. by Everett R. Kalin from Ger. LC 75-13036. 192p. 1975. pap. 6.95 (ISBN 0-8006-1813-0, 1-1813). Fortress.
Suffering: A Test of Theological Method. Arthur C. McGill. LC 82-6934. 130p. 1982. pap. 7.95 (ISBN 0-664-24448-3). Westminster John Knox.
Suffering & Evil. John Heagle. (Guidelines for Contemporary Catholics Ser.). (Orig.). 1987. pap. 7.95 (ISBN 0-88347-212-0). Thomas More.
Suffering & Hope: The Biblical Vision & the Human Predicament. J. Christiaan Beker. LC 86-46418. 96p. 1987. pap. 4.95 (ISBN 0-8006-1999-4). Fortress.
Suffering & Martyrdom in the New Testament. Ed. by W. Horbury & B. McNeil. LC 80-40706. 240p. 1981. 49.50 (ISBN 0-521-23482-4). Cambridge U Pr.
Suffering & the Saints. John D. Clark. Ed. by James Goodman. 272p. (Orig.). 1988. pap. text ed. cancelled (ISBN 0-89896-129-7, Linolean). Larksdale.
Suffering & the Spirit. Scott J. Hafemann. 258p. 1986. text ed. 55.00x (ISBN 3-16-144973-8, Pub. by J C B Mohr BRD). Coronet Bks.
Suffering: Eighteen Eighty-Seven to Eighteen Ninety-Five. Alphonse Daudet. 1934. 39.50x (ISBN 0-686-51319-3). Elliots Bks.
Suffering from Illusion: The Secret Victory of Self-Defeat. Sayers R. Brenner. 310p. 1988. text ed. 43.40 (ISBN 0-8204-0540-X). P Lang Pubs.
Suffering God: Selected Letters to Galatea & to Papastephanou. Nikos Kazantzakis. Tr. by Philip Ramp & Katerina Rooke. LC 78-75133. 1979. 20.00 (ISBN 0-89241-088-4). Caratzas.
Suffering: Indian Perpsective. Kapil N. Tiwari. 302p. 1986. 22.00x (ISBN 0-317-60582-8, Pub. by Motilal Banarsidass India). Orient Bk Dist.
Suffering: Indian Perspectives. K. N. Tiwari. 1986. 22.50 (ISBN 81-208-0092-3, Pub. by Motilal Banarsidass). South Asia Bks.
Suffering Is Optional! The Myth of the Innocent Bystander. Morris L. Haimowitz & Natalie R. Haimowitz. LC 77-72839. (Illus.). 1977. pap. 6.00 (ISBN 0-917790-01-4). Haimowoods.
Suffering: Issues of Emotional Living in an Age of Stress for Clergy & Religious. John A. Struzzo et al. Ed. by Richard J. Gilmartin. LC 84-9334. 144p. 1984. pap. 8.00 (ISBN 0-89571-020-X). Affirmation.
Suffering: Its Meaning & Ministry. James G. Emerson. 176p. (Orig.). 1986. pap. 8.95 (ISBN 0-687-40573-4). Abingdon.
Suffering of God: An Old Testament Perspective. Terence E. Fretheim. Ed. by Walter Brueggemann. LC 84-47921. (Overtures to Biblical Theology Ser.). 224p. 1984. pap. 10.95 (ISBN 0-8006-1538-7). Fortress.
Suffering, of Tests, Trials & Other Troubles. Myrna L. Etheridge. (Illus.). 75p. (Orig.). 1988. pap. 5.00x (ISBN 0-937417-03-3). Etheridge Minist.
Suffering Presence: Theological Reflections on Medicine, the Mentally Handicapped & the Church. Stanley Hauerwas. LC 85-40603. 224p. (Orig.). 1986. text ed. 19.95x (ISBN 0-268-01721-2); pap. text ed. 9.95 (ISBN 0-268-01722-0). U of Notre Dame Pr.

Sugar Creek Gang on the Mexican Border. Paul Hutchens. (gr. 3-7). 1968. pap. 3.50 (ISBN 0-8024-4818-6). Moody.

Sugar Creek: Life on the Illinois Praire. John M. Faragher. LC 86-5622. 320p. 1987. text ed. 30.00x (ISBN 0-300-03545-4). Yale U Pr.

Sugar Creek: Life on the Illinois Prairie. John M. Faragher. 1988. pap. 12.95x (ISBN 0-300-04263-9). Yale U Pr.

Sugar Economy of Puerto Rico. Arthur D. Gayer et al. 1976. lib. bdg. 59.95 (ISBN 0-8490-2717-9). Gordon Pr.

Sugar Factory. Robert Carter. LC 87-12625. 144p. 1987. 14.95 (ISBN 0-689-11926-7). Atheneum.

Sugar Free Cakes & Biscuits: Recipes for Diabetics & Dieters. Elsie Lebrecht. LC 85-10365. (Illus.). 96p. (Orig.). 1985. pap. 6.95 (ISBN 0-571-13668-0). Faber & Faber.

Sugar Free: Goodies. Judith S. Majors. LC 87-70318. pap. 6.95 (ISBN 0-941905-00-4). Apple Pr.

Sugar Free: Hawaiian Cookery. Judith S. Majors. LC 87-70229. pap. 6.95 (ISBN 0-9602238-9-4). Apple Pr.

Sugar Free: Kids Cookery. Judith S. Majors. LC 79-66220. 1979. pap. 4.95 (ISBN 0-9602238-1-9). Apple Pr.

Sugar Free... Microwavery. Judith S. Majors. LC 80-67167. pap. 6.95 (ISBN 0-9602238-3-5). Apple Pr.

Sugar Free: Sweets & Treats. Judith S. Majors. 1985. pap. 6.95 (ISBN 0-345-32345-9). Ballantine.

Sugar Free-That's Me. Judith S. Majors. LC 78-74029. (Illus.). 1978. pap. 6.95 (ISBN 0-9602238-0-0). Apple Pr.

Sugar Free...Family Favorites. Judith S. Majors. LC 84-72670. 1985. pap. 5.95 (ISBN 0-9602238-7-8). Apple Pr.

Sugar Free...Good & Easy. Judith S. Majors. LC 85-72597. 1985. pap. 5.95 (ISBN 0-9602238-8-6). Apple Pr.

Sugar Free...Sweets & Treats. Judith S. Majors. LC 82-73049. 1982. pap. 6.95 (ISBN 0-9602238-6-X). Apple Pr.

Sugar Free...That's Me! Judith S. Majors. 1980. pap. 6.95 (ISBN 0-345-28708-8). Ballantine.

Sugar Gets the Skunk. Martha M. Moran. (Illus.). (gr. k-4). 1977. 4.50 (ISBN 0-682-48778-3). Exposition-Phoenix.

Sugar Hill. Amanda H. Douglass. 1979. pap. 2.25 (ISBN 0-505-51412-5, Pub. by Tower Bks). Leisure NY.

Sugar Industry in Pernambuco, 1840-1910: Modernization Without Change. Peter L. Eisenberg. LC 75-117340. 1973. 42.00x (ISBN 0-520-01731-5). U of Cal Pr.

Sugar Is Made with Blood: The Conspiracy of La Escalera & the Conflict Between Empires over Slavery in Cuba. Robert L. Paquette. (Illus.). 352p. 1988. 29.95 (ISBN 0-8195-5192-9). Wesleyan U Pr.

Sugar Isn't Everything: A Support Book, in Fiction Form, for the Young Diabetic. Willo D. Roberts. LC 86-17275. 208p. (gr. 4 up). 1987. 12.95 (ISBN 0-689-31316-0, Atheneum Childrens Bks). Macmillan.

Sugar Isn't Everything: A Support Book, in Fiction Form, for the Young Diabetic. Willo D. Roberts. LC 88-3358. 192p. (gr. 3-7). Date not set. pap. 3.95 (ISBN 0-689-71225-1, Aladdin Bks). Macmillan.

Sugar Loaf Springs: Heber's Elegant Watering Place. Evalena Beary. (Illus.). 120p. 1985. write for info. River Road Pr.

Sugar: Major Trade & Stabilization Issues in the Eighties. (Economic & Social Development Papers: No. 50). 37p. 1985. pap. 7.50 (ISBN 92-5-102205-4, F2755, FAO). UNIPUB.

Sugar Maple. Rosamond S. Metcalf. LC 82-595. (Illus.). 40p. (gr. 3-5). 1982. pap. 3.50x (ISBN 0-914016-87-3). Phoenix Pub.

Sugar Mother. Elizabeth Jolley. LC 87-46274. 192p. 1988. 16.95 (ISBN 0-06-015940-5, HarpT). Har-Row.

Sugar Petite. Mildred L. McVea. 8.95 (ISBN 0-87511-083-5). Claitors.

Sugar Plantations in the Formation of Brazilian Society, Bahia, Fifteen Fifty to Eighteen Thirty-Five. Stuart B. Schwartz. (Cambridge Latin American Studies 52). 608p. 1986. 70.00 (ISBN 0-521-30934-4); pap. 24.95 (ISBN 0-521-31399-6). Cambridge U Pr.

Sugar-Plum Christmas Book. Jean Chapman. (Teacher Resource Collections Ser.). (Illus.). 190p. (ps-6). 1982. lib. bdg. 21.27 (ISBN 0-516-08952-8). Childrens.

Sugar Prince. Fiona Moodie. (Illus.). (ps-3). 1987. 12.95 (ISBN 1-55774-005-4, Dist. by Watts). Adama Pubs Inc.

Sugar-Processing: The Development of a Third-World Technology. Raphael Kaplinsky. (Illus.). 148p. (Orig.). 1983. pap. 13.50x (ISBN 0-903031-98-1, Pub. by Intermediate Tech England). Intermediate Tech.

Sugar Production in Northeastern Brazil & Cuba. David Denslow. Ed. by Stuart Bruchey. (South American & Latin American Economic History Ser.). 182p. 1987. lib. bdg. 30.00 (ISBN 0-8240-1357-3). Garland Pub.

Sugar Program: Large Costs & Small Benefits. D. Gale Johnson. 1974. pap. 7.00 (ISBN 0-8447-3126-9). Am Enterprise.

Sugar Ray Leonard. James Haskins. LC 82-15227. (Illus.). 160p. (gr. 4 up). 1982. 12.95 (ISBN 0-688-01436-4). Lothrop.

Sugar Ray Leonard: And Other Noble Warriors. Sam Toperoff. 208p. 1986. text ed. 15.95 (ISBN 0-07-065003-9). McGraw.

Sugar Ray Leonard: The Baby-faced Boxer. Bert Rosenthal. LC 82-4472. (Sports Stars Ser.). (Illus.). (gr. 2-8). 1982. PLB 11.27 (ISBN 0-516-04326-9); pap. 2.95 (ISBN 0-516-44326-7). Childrens.

Sugar Rose. Susan Carroll. 208p. (Orig.). 1987. pap. 2.50 (ISBN 0-449-21238-6, Crest). Fawcett.

Sugar: Science & Technology. Ed. by G. G. Birch & K. J. Parker. (Illus.). 475p. 1979. 122.50 (ISBN 0-85334-805-7, Pub. by Elsevier Applied Sci England). Elsevier.

Sugar Snow Spring. Lillian Hoban. LC 72-9866. (Illus.). 48p. (ps-3). 1973. PLB 11.89 (ISBN 0-06-022334-0). HarpJ.

Sugar, Sweeteners & Substitutes. Business Communications Staff. 141p. 1983. 1250.00 (ISBN 0-89336-091-0, C-005R). BCC.

Sugar Teat. Robin K. Willoughby. 1981. 2.50 (ISBN 0-934834-25-3). White Pine.

Sugar: Threat or Challenge, An Assessment of the Impact of Technological Developments in the High Fructose Corn Syrup & Sucrochemicals Industries. Clive Y. Thomas. (Illus.). 140p. (Orig.). 1986. pap. text ed. 12.00 (ISBN 0-88936-451-6, IDRC244, Pub. by IDRC). UNIPUB.

Sugar Transport & Metabolism in Gram-Positive Bacteria. Jonathan Reizer & Alan Peterkofsky. (Topics in Enzyme & Fermentation Biotechnology Ser.). 560p. 1987. 158.00 (ISBN 0-470-20818-X). Halsted Pr.

Sugar Work. P. Boyle. 1987. 29.95 (ISBN 0-442-20994-0). Van Nos Reinhold.

Sugarbeet Pest Management: Aphid-Borne Viruses. F. J. Hills et al. (Illus.). 12p. (Orig.). 1982. pap. 2.00 (ISBN 0-931876-60-5, 3277). ANR Pubns CA.

Sugarbeet Pest Management: Leaf Diseases. F. J. Hills et al. (Illus.). 12p. (Orig.). 1982. pap. 2.00 (ISBN 0-931876-59-1, 3278). ANR Pubns CA.

Sugarbeet Pest Management: Nematodes. Philip S. Roberts & Ivan J. Thomason. (Illus.). 36p. 1981. pap. text ed. 3.00 (ISBN 0-931876-52-4, 3272). ANR Pubns CA.

Sugarbush: Making Maple Syrup. Nancy H. Gokay. LC 80-17582. (Illus.). 32p. (Orig.). (gr. 3-4). 1980. pap. 2.00 (ISBN 0-910726-95-7). Hillsdale Educ.

Sugarcane & Sugar in Gorakpur: An Inquiry into Peasant Production for Capitalist Enterprises in Colonial India. Shahid Amin. (Illus.). 1984. 29.95x (ISBN 0-19-561545-X). Oxford U Pr.

Sugarcane Crop Logging & Crop Control: Principles & Practices. Harry F. Clements. LC 79-9894. (Illus.). 540p. 1980. text ed. 40.00x (ISBN 0-8248-0508-9). UH Pr.

Sugarcane Improvement Through Breeding. Ed. by D. J. Heinz. (Developments in Crop Science Ser.: No. 11). (Illus.). 604p. 1987. text ed. 131.75 (ISBN 0-444-42769-4). Elsevier.

Sugarcane Island. Edward Packard. (Which Way Bks.: No. 6). (Illus.). (gr. 3-6). 1978. pap. 1.95 (ISBN 0-671-44189-2). Archway.

Sugarcane Island. Edward Packard. (Choose Your Own Adventure Ser.: No. 62). 128p. (gr. 4). 1986. pap. 2.25 (ISBN 0-553-26040-5). Bantam.

Sugarcane Island. Incl. Space Raiders & the Planet of Doom; Trapped in the Black Box; Starship Warrior. (Which Way Ser.). 1984. boxed set 7.80 (ISBN 0-671-90085-4). PB.

Sugarcane Physiology. A. G. Alexander. 1973. 208.00 (ISBN 0-444-41016-3). Elsevier.

Sugarcane Production in Asia. 339p. 1980. pap. 14.75 (ISBN 0-686-97527-8, APO120, APO). UNIPUB.

Sugaring Time. Kathryn Lasky. LC 82-23928. (Illus.). 64p. (gr. 4-7). 1983. 10.95 (ISBN 0-02-751680-6). Macmillan.

Sugaring Time. Kathryn Lasky. LC 86-3468. (Illus.). 64p. (gr. 3-7). 1986. pap. 3.95 (ISBN 0-689-71081-X, Aladdin Bks). Macmillan.

Sugarless Baking Book: The Natural Way to Prepare America's Favorite Breads, Pies, Cakes, Puddings & Desserts. Patricia T. Mayo. LC 82-42757. (Illus.). 116p. (Orig.). 1983. pap. 5.95 (ISBN 0-87773-227-2). Shambhala Pubns.

Sugarless Cookery. Florence Murphy. 1978. pap. 3.95 (ISBN 0-8323-0306-2). Binford-Metropolitan.

Sugarless Desserts, Jams & Salads Cookbook. Addie Gonshorowski. 150p. 1988. pap. 7.99 (ISBN 0-318-23890-X). Ad-dee Pubs Inc.

Sugarmill. Manuel M. Fraginals. Tr. by Cedric Belfrage from Span. LC 73-90074. (Illus.). 1978. pap. 10.95 (ISBN 0-85345-432-9). Monthly Rev.

Sugarpink Rose. Adela Turin & Nella Bosnia. 32p. 4.95 (ISBN 0-904613-20-8). Writers & Readers.

Sugarplum Visions: Old Christmases Made New. Susan A. McCreary. LC 83-18300. (Illus.). 160p. 1983. pap. 6.00 (ISBN 0-9608428-3-7). Straw Patchwork.

Sugars in Nutrition. Ed. by Horace Sipple & Kristen W. McNutt. 1974. 98.00 (ISBN 0-12-646750-1). Acad Pr.

Sugartown. Loren D. Estleman. LC 84-12910. 220p. 1984. 13.95 (ISBN 0-395-36449-3). HM.

Sugartown. Loren D. Estleman. pap. 3.50 (ISBN 0-317-43030-0). Fawcett.

Sugartown. Loren D. Estleman. LC 84-12910. 220p. 1984. 15.00 (ISBN 0-317-57641-0). Ultramarine Pub.

Sugawara & the Secrets of Calligraphy. Stanleigh H. Jones, Jr. (Translations from the Oriental Classics Ser.). 272p. 1984. 29.00x (ISBN 0-231-05974-4); pap. 15.00x (ISBN 0-231-05975-2). Columbia U Pr.

Sugawara no Michizane & the Early Heian Court. Robert Borgen. (Harvard East-Asian Monographs: No. 120). (Illus.). 426p. 1986. text ed. 22.00x (ISBN 0-674-85415-2). Harvard U Pr.

Suger et la Monarchie Francaise Au XIIe Siecle (1108-1152) Alexandre Huguenin. 383p. (Fr.). Repr. of 1857 ed. lib. bdg. 67.50x. Coronet Bks.

Suggested Chart of Accounts for the Hot Mix Industry. Felix Rollaritsch. (Management Ser.: No. 1). 14p. 1971. 20.00 (ISBN 0-317-58424-3). Natl Asphalt Pavement.

Suggested Course Outline for Training NDT Personnel. Ed. by Vernon L. Stokes. 16p. 1977. member 2.00 (ISBN 0-318-21495-4, 107); non-member 3.00. Am Soc Nondestructive.

Suggested Curriculum for the Day School. N. W. Dessler. 7.00 (ISBN 0-914131-63-X, C01). Torah Umesorah.

Suggested Fertilizer-Related Policies for Government & International Agencies. C. R. Amstrup et al. (Technical Bulletin T-10). 67p. (Orig.). 1977. pap. 4.00 (ISBN 0-88090-009-1). Intl Fertilizer.

Suggested Guidelines for Nutrition Management of the Critically Ill Patient. The American Dietetic Association Staff. 104p. 1984. pap. text ed. 22.75 (ISBN 0-88091-011-9). Am Dietetic Assn.

Suggested Guidelines for Reducing Adverse Effects of Case Continuances & Delays on Crime Victims & Witnesses. 47p. 1986. pap. 6.00 (ISBN 0-317-63273-6, 509-0024-01). Amer Bar Assn.

Suggested Nicaraguan Pottery Sequence Based on the Museum Collection. Lydia L. Wyckoff. LC 75-139868. (Illus.). 1971. pap. 2.50 (ISBN 0-934490-35-X). Mus Am Ind.

Suggested Pattern Jury Instructions: Vol. I: Civil Cases. 2nd ed. Council of Superior Court Judges of Georgia Committee. 379p. 1984. looseleaf 50.00 (ISBN 0-318-03835-8). U of GA Inst Govt.

Suggested Pattern Jury Instructions, Vol. II: Criminal Cases. Council of Superior Court Judges of Georgia Committee. Ed. by Institute of Government Staff. 201p. 1985. looseleaf 50.00 (ISBN 0-89854-132-8). U of GA Inst Govt.

Suggested Program of Teacher Training for Mission Schools Among the Batetela. John G. Barden. LC 75-176517. (Columbia University. Teachers College. Contributions to Education: No. 853). Repr. of 1941 ed. 22.50 (ISBN 0-404-55853-4). AMS Pr.

Suggested Safe Practices for Gas Distribution Workers. 53p. 1975. pap. 1.00 (ISBN 0-318-12712-1, J00400); pap. 0.80 ea. 11 to 100 copies; pap. 0.75 ea. 101 or more copies. Am Gas Assn.

Suggested Services & Policies Related to Adolescent Parenthood. 104p. 1981. 9.50 (ISBN 0-318-15055-7). NASBE.

Suggested State Legislation, 1941-1980, 39 vols. in 19. Ed. by Council of State Governments Staff. LC 72-86156. 1972. Repr. Ser. lib. bdg. 995.00x (ISBN 0-912004-05-3). W W Gaunt.

Suggested State Legislation 1982. 254p. 1982. 15.00 (ISBN 0-87292-022-4); back issues avail. Coun State Govts.

Suggested State Legislation, 1983, Vol. 42. 395p. (Orig.). 1982. pap. 15.00 (ISBN 0-87292-032-1). Coun State Govts.

Suggested State Legislation 1984, Vol. 43. Ed. by L. Edward Purcell. (Orig.). 1983. pap. 15.00 (ISBN 0-87292-042-9). Coun State Govts.

Suggested State Legislation 1985, Vol. 44. Ed. by L. E. Purcell. 178p. (Orig.). 1984. pap. 15.00 (ISBN 0-87292-053-4). Coun State Govts.

Suggested State Legislation 1986, Vol. 45. Ed. by L. E. Purcell. 220p. (Orig.). 1986. pap. 15.00 (ISBN 0-87292-060-7). Coun State Govts.

Suggested Statistical Tables & Figures for Ohio Courts: A Trial Court Technical Assistance Project Report. 59p. 1987. manuscript 4.00 (ISBN 0-317-59217-3, NERO, T/A-537). Natl Ctr St Courts.

Suggestion & Psycho Therapy. George W. Jacoby. Repr. of 1912 ed. 30.00. Darby Bks.

Suggestion & Statement in Poetry. Krishna Rayan. 182p. 1972. 36.50 (ISBN 0-485-11134-9, Pub. by Athlone Pr UK). Humanities.

Suggestion of His Climate. Tony Nolan. 1977. pap. 5.00 (ISBN 0-931350-00-X). Moonlight Pubns.

Suggestion of the Devil. Judith S. Neaman. 1976. Repr. of 1975 ed. lib. bdg. 17.00 (ISBN 0-374-96038-0, Octagon). Hippocrene Bks.

Suggestions. Ernest E. Kellett. LC 79-99705. (Essay Index Reprint Ser). 1923. 18.00 (ISBN 0-8369-1357-4). Ayer Co Pubs.

Suggestions for Becoming Self Sufficient. Center for Self-Sufficiency, Research Division Staff. LC 83-90723. 90p. 1983. pap. text ed. 3.00 (ISBN 0-910811-29-6, Pub. by Center Self Suff). Prosperity & Profits.

Suggestions for Hunting Aluminum Cans & Other Aluminum. Center for Self Sufficiency, Research Division Staff. 26p. 1983. pap. text ed. 1.95 (ISBN 0-910811-26-1, Pub. by Center Self Suff). Prosperity & Profits.

Suggestions for Improved Case Processing & Case Assignment in the Portage County (OH) Municipal Court: Technical Assistance Report. National Center for State Courts Staff. 92p. 1981. manuscript 5.52 (NERO, T/A-510). Natl Ctr St Courts.

Suggestions for Improvement of Jury Management in Rhode Island. National Center for State Courts Staff. 25p. 1982. manuscript 1.50 (NERO-102). Natl Ctr St Courts.

Suggestions for Improving Juror Utilization in the United States District Court for the Southern District of New York. 99p. 1971. 10.00 (ISBN 0-318-14446-8). IJA NYU.

Suggestions for Making Money Addressing & Stuffing Envelopes Or How to Run a Small Letter Shop Service. Center for Self-Sufficiency, Research Division Staff. 26p. 1983. pap. text ed. 3.25 (ISBN 0-910811-20-2, Pub. by Center Self Suff). Prosperity & Profits.

Suggestions for Self-Evaluation of Geography Programs with Self-Study Data Forms. AAG Consulting Services Panel Staff. 1974. pap. 2.50 (ISBN 0-89291-141-7). Assn Am Geographers.

Suggestions for Starting a Business from Businesses that are Going Out of Business, Bankrupt Business, Etc. Center for Self-Sufficiency, Research Division Staff. LC 83-90720. 26p. 1983. pap. text ed. 4.00 (ISBN 0-910811-25-3, Pub. by Center Self Suff). Prosperity & Profits.

Suggestions for Telemarketing Operations. Center for Self-Sufficiency, Research Division Staff. 26p. 1983. pap. text ed. 2.95 (ISBN 0-910811-27-X, Pub. by Center Self Suff). Prosperity & Profits.

Suggestions for the Beginning Teacher of English. 3rd ed. Mercedes A. Saez. 1.50 (ISBN 0-8477-2719-X). U of PR Pr.

Suggestions for the Future Provision of Criminal Lunatics see On the Different Forms of Insanity in Relation to Jurisprudence.

Suggestions for the Repression of Crime: With Introduction & Essay Added. Matthew D. Hill. LC 70-172581. (Criminology, Law Enforcement, & Social Problems Ser.: No. 169). 1975. 30.00x (ISBN 0-87585-169-X). Patterson Smith.

Suggestions in the Planning of a New Hotel. rev. ed. Ad Wittemann. 175p. (Orig.). 1986. pap. 50.00 (ISBN 0-938481-36-3). Camelot Consult.

Suggestions, Literary Essays. E. E. Kellett. 1979. Repr. of 1923 ed. lib. bdg. 20.00 (ISBN 0-8492-1482-3). R West.

Suggestions on Academical Organisation with Especial Reference to Oxford. Mark Pattison. Ed. by Walter P. Metzger. (Academic Profession Ser.). 1977. lib. bdg. 26.50x (ISBN 0-405-10027-2). Ayer Co Pubs.

Suggestive-Accelerative Learning & Teaching. Owen L. Caskey. Ed. by Danny G. Langdon. LC 79-26386. (Instructional Design Library). 136p. 1980. 23.95 (ISBN 0-87778-156-7). Educ Tech Pubns.

Suggestive Accelerative Learning Techniques: Theory & Applications. Donald H. Schuster & Charles E. Gritton. 236p. 1986. text ed. 50.00 (ISBN 2-88124-055-0); pap. text ed. 25.00 (ISBN 2-88124-054-2). Gordon & Breach.

Suggestive Inquiry into the Hermetic Mystery. Mary A. Atwood. LC 75-36825. (Occult Ser.). 1976. Repr. of 1920 ed. 51.00x (ISBN 0-405-07938-9). Ayer Co Pubs.

Suggestive Inquiry into the Hermetic Mystery. Mary Anne Atwood. 597p. 1976. Repr. of 1918 ed. 15.50 (ISBN 0-911662-64-2). Yoga.

Suggestology & Outlines of Suggestopedy. G. Lozanov. (Psychic Studies). 380p. 1978. 28.00 (ISBN 0-677-30940-6). Gordon & Breach.

Suggin Cookbook. Josephine Graham. 164p. 1974. pap. 6.98 (ISBN 0-686-09048-9). J Graham.

Suggin Painting. Josephine Graham. 1976. pap. 3.00 (ISBN 0-686-17966-8). J Graham.

SUGI Supplemental Library User's Guide, Version 5 Edition. SAS Institute Inc. Staff. 662p. 1986. pap. 17.95 (ISBN 1-55544-000-2). SAS Inst.

Sugums' Boat. Paula J. Bussard. Ed. by Shirley Wigginton. (Critter County Ser.). (Illus.). 32p. (gr. k-4). 1987. 1.39 (ISBN 0-87403-251-2, 3451). Standard Pub.

Suharto & His Generals: Indonesian Military Politics, 1975-83. David Jenkins. (Monograph: No. 64). 300p. 1984. 12.50 (ISBN 0-87763-030-5). Cornell Mod Indo.

Suharto's Indonesia. Hamish McDonald. 277p. 1981. pap. text ed. 5.95x (ISBN 0-8248-0781-2). UH Pr.

Suho & the White Horse. Yuzo Otsuka. Tr. by Ann Herring from Japanese. LC 80-26789. (Illus.). 48p. (gr. k-3). 1981. 11.95 (ISBN 0-670-68149-0, Viking Kestrel). Viking.

Suhrab & Rustam: A Poem from the Shah Namah of Firdausi. Firdawsi. Tr. by James Atkinson from Persian. LC 72-3772. Orig. Title: Soohrab, a Poem. (Eng. & Persian, Modern.). 1972. Repr. of 1814 ed. 30.00x (ISBN 0-8201-1103-1). Schol Facsimiles.

Sui Dynasty. Arthur Wright. 237p. 1978. pap. 80.00x (ISBN 0-317-69124-4, Pub. by Han-Shan Tang Ltd). State Mutual Bk.

Suivez la Piste. Emile De Harven. LC 77-10091. 1972. pap. 5.95 (ISBN 0-912022-30-2, 40257). EMC.

Sukarno. 2nd ed. J. D. Legge. (Illus.). 330p. 1985. pap. text ed. 15.95x (ISBN 0-86861-463-7). Unwin Hyman.

Sukarno. Sidharth Varadarajan. (World Leaders--Past & Present Ser.). (Illus.). 112p. (gr. 5 up). Date not set. 16.95x (ISBN 1-55546-853-5). Chelsea Hse.

Sukey's Songbook of Multiple Sclerosis. Sheila Siegelman. (Illus., Orig.). 1988. pap. 6.95 (ISBN 0-944066-00-3). Scheherazade Bks.

Sukhoveis & Drought Control. B. L. Dzerdzeevskii. 376p. 1963. text ed. 73.50x (ISBN 0-7065-0260-4, Pub. by Keter Pub Jerusalem). Coronet Bks.

Suki. Matthew Lipman. (Philosophy for Children Ser). 153p. (Orig.). (gr. 9-10). 1978. pap. 8.00 (ISBN 0-916834-08-5, TX86-788). Inst Advncmnt Philos Child.

Suki: A Novel for Young People. 153p. (gr. 7-9). 6.50 (ISBN 0-686-74923-5). ADL.

Sukkah, 1 vol. (Hebrew & Eng.). 15.00 (ISBN 0-910218-58-7). Bennet Pub.

Sukkah & the Big Wind. Lily Edelman. (Holiday Series of Picture Storybooks). (Illus.). (gr. k-2). 1956. 5.95 (ISBN 0-8381-0716-8). United Syn Bk.

Sukkot. Ed. by Hayyim H. Donin. 128p. pap. 4.50 (ISBN 0-686-95148-4). ADL.

Sukkot: A Time to Rejoice. Malka Drucker. LC 82-80814. (Jewish Holidays Bks.). (Illus.). 96p. (gr. 5 up). 1982. Reinforced bdg. 10.95 (ISBN 0-8234-0466-8). Holiday.

Sukkot-Simhat Torah Anthology. Philip Goodman. 475p. 1988. 12.95 (ISBN 0-8276-0302-9). JPS Phila.

Sukraniti. Sukra. Ed. & tr. by Benoy K. Sarkar. LC 73-3801. (Sacred Books of the Hindus: No. 13). Repr. of 1914 ed. 32.50 (ISBN 0-404-57813-6). AMS Pr.

Sul Ross: Soldier, Statesman, Educator. Judith A. Benner. LC 82-45891. (Centennial Series of the Association of Former Students: No. 13). (Illus.). 286p. 1983. 19.50 (ISBN 0-89096-142-5). Tex A&M Univ Pr.

Sul Ross State University: The Cultural Center of Trans-Pecos Texas 1917-1975. Clifford B. Casey. (Illus.). 416p. 1976. 9.50 (ISBN 0-933512-25-2). Pioneer Bk Tx.

Sula. Toni Morrison. 1974. 14.95 (ISBN 0-394-48044-9). Knopf.

Sula. Toni Morrison. LC 87-15237. 176p. 1982. pap. 6.95 (ISBN 0-452-26010-8, Z5476, Plume). NAL.

Sulcorebutia & Weingartia: A Collector's Guide. John Pilbeam. (Illus.). 144p. 1985. 32.95 (ISBN 0-88192-053-3). Timber.

Suleiman the Elephant. Margret Rettich. Tr. by Elizabeth D. Crawford. LC 86-2737. (Illus.). 32p. (ps-3). 1986. 11.75 (ISBN 0-688-05741-1); PLB 11.88 (ISBN 0-688-05742-X). Lothrop.

Suleyman & the Ottoman Empire. John Addison et al. Ed. by Malcolm Yapp & Margaret Killingray. (Illus.). (gr. 6-10). 1980. lib. bdg. 6.95 (ISBN 0-89908-038-3); pap. text ed. 2.45 (ISBN 0-89908-013-8). Greenhaven.

Suleymanname: The Illustrated History of Suleyman the Magnificent. Esin Atil. (Illus.). 256p. 1986. 75.00 (ISBN 0-8109-1505-7). Abrams.

Sulfatases of Microbial Origin, Vols. 1 & 2. Ed. by K. S. Dodgeson et al. 1982. Vol. 1, 216p. 67.00 (ISBN 0-8493-6035-8); Vol. 2, 208p. 67.00 (ISBN 0-8493-6036-6). CRC Pr.

Sulfate Metabolism & Sulfate Conjugation. Ed. by G. J. Mulder & J. Caldwell. 312p. 1982. 64.00x (ISBN 0-8002-3665-3). Taylor & Francis.

Sulfate-Reducing Bacteria. 2nd ed. J. R. Postgate. LC 83-15307. 250p. 1984. 44.50 (ISBN 0-521-25791-3). Cambridge U Pr.

Sulfation of Drugs & Related Compounds. Gerald J. Mulder. 248p. 1981. 87.00 (ISBN 0-8493-5920-1). CRC Pr.

Sulfide Inclusions in Steel: An International Symposium, 7-8 November, 1974, Port Chester, New York Proceedings. Ed. by John J. DeBarbadillo & Edwin Snape. LC 75-19315. (Materials-Metalworking Technology Ser.: No. 6). (Illus.). pap. 127.00 (ISBN 0-317-09688-5, 2051903). Bks Demand UMI.

Sulfide Mineralogy. Ed. by P. H. Ribbe. (Reviews in Mineralogy: Vol. 1). 284p. 1974. 13.00 (ISBN 0-939950-01-4). Mineralogical Soc.

Sulfilimines & Related Derivatives. Ed. by Shigeru Oae & Naomichi Furukawa. LC 83-12220. (ACS Monographs: No. 179). 340p. 1983. lib. bdg. 84.95 (ISBN 0-8412-0705-4). Am Chemical.

Sulfite Pulping Process, 2 Vols, Vols. 1 & 2. (Bibliographic Ser.). 269p. 1966. Series No. 225, 269p. 15.00, (ISBN 0-317-34452-8); Supplement 1, 1972. 12.00 (ISBN 0-317-34453-6); Series No. 226, 138p. 9.00, (ISBN 0-317-34454-4); Supplement 1, 1972. 8.00 (ISBN 0-317-34455-2). Inst Paper Chem.

Sulfites, Selenites & Tellurites. Ed. by M. R. Masson et al. (IUPAC Solubility Data Ser.). (Illus.). 451p. 1986. 110.00 (ISBN 0-08-032517-3, E125, E120, PBL). Pergamon.

Sulfonyl Isocyanates & Sulfonyl Isothiocyanates. J. W. McFarland. (Sulfur Reports Ser.). 54p. 1981. flexicover 25.00 (ISBN 3-718-60255-5). Harwood Academic.

Sulfur Amino Acids: Biochemical & Clinical Aspects. Kinya Kuriyama et al. LC 83-7982. (Progress in Clinical & Biological Research Ser.: Vol. 125). 510p. 1983. 95.00 (ISBN 0-8451-0125-0). A R Liss.

Sulfur Bacteria - STP 650. Ed. by E. Fjerdingstad. 129p. 1979. pap. 15.00x (ISBN 0-8031-0582-7, 04-650000-16). ASTM.

Sulfur Containing Radio-Protective Agents. Z. M. Bacq. 344p. 1975. 145.00 (ISBN 0-08-016298-3). Pergamon.

Sulfur Dioxide & Vegetation: Physiology, Ecology, & Policy Issues. Ed. by William E. Winner et al. LC 83-51323. (Illus.). 624p. 1986. 65.00x (ISBN 0-8047-1234-4). Stanford U Pr.

Sulfur Dioxide, Chlorine, Fluorine & Chlorine Oxides. A. S. Young. 1983. 110.00x (ISBN 0-08-026218-X). Pergamon.

Sulfur Dioxide Processing. LC 74-331468. 117p. 1975. pap. 12.00 (ISBN 0-8169-0055-8, R-7). Am Inst Chem Eng.

Sulfur Electrode: Fused Salts & Solid Electrolytes. Ed. by R. P. Tischer. LC 82-22753. 1983. 81.00 (ISBN 0-12-691680-2). Acad Pr.

Sulfur Emissions Policies, Oil Prices, & the Appalachian Coal Industry. Robin C. Landis. LC 80-8625. (Outstanding Dissertations in Economics Ser.). 270p. 1984. lib. bdg. 36.00 (ISBN 0-8240-4182-8). Garland Pub.

Sulfur, Energy, & Environment. B. Meyer. 448p. 1977. 113.25 (ISBN 0-444-41595-5). Elsevier.

Sulfur in Organic & Inorganic Chemistry, Vol. 1. Ed. by Alexander Senning. 1971. 99.75 (ISBN 0-8247-1615-9). Dekker.

Sulfur in Organic & Inorganic Chemistry, Vol. 4. Alexander Senning. 416p. 1982. 110.00 (ISBN 0-8247-1350-8). Dekker.

Sulfur in Pesticide Action & Metabolism. Ed. by Joseph D. Rosen et al. LC 81-7916. (ACS Symposium Ser.: No. 158). 1981. 34.95 (ISBN 0-8412-0635-X). Am Chemical.

Sulfur in Proteins. Yu. M. Torchinsky. (Illus.). 304p. 1981. 130.00 (ISBN 0-08-023778-9). Pergamon.

Sulfur in Texas. S. P. Ellison, Jr. (Handbook Ser.: No. 2). (Illus.). 48p. 1971. 2.00 (ISBN 0-686-29324-X). Bur Econ Geology.

Sulfur in the Environment: Ecological Impacts, Pt. 2. Jerome O. Nriagu. LC 78-6807. (Environmental Science & Technology Ser.). 482p. 1978. 115.00x (ISBN 0-471-04255-2). Wiley.

Sulfur in the Tropics. Graeme Blair. (Technical Bulletin Ser.: T-12). (Illus.). 71p. (Orig.). 1979. pap. 4.00 (ISBN 0-88090-011-3). Intl Fertilizer.

Sulfur: Its Significance for Chemistry, for the Geo-, Bio- & Cosmosphere & Technology. Ed. by A. Muller & B. Krebs. (Studies in Organic Chemistry: Vol. 5). 512p. 1984. 160.75 (ISBN 0-444-42355-9). Elsevier.

Sulfur: New Sources & Uses. Ed. by Michael E. Raymont. LC 82-1645. (ACS Symposium Ser.: No. 183). 1982. 33.95 (ISBN 0-8412-0713-5). Am Chemical.

Sulfur Poisoning of Nickel Catalysts. C. H. Riesz et al. (Research Bulletin Ser.: No. 10). iv, 23p. 1951. 2.50 (ISBN 0-317-56798-5). Inst Gas Tech.

Sulfur Removal & Recovery from Industrial Processes. Ed. by John B. Pfeiffer. LC 75-11557. (Advances in Chemistry Ser.: No. 139). 1975. 24.95 (ISBN 0-8412-0217-6). Am Chemical.

Sulfuric Acid-Based Partially Acidulated Phosphate Rock: Its Production, Cost & Use. James J. Schultz et al. Ed. by E. N. Roth & E. D. Frederick. LC 86-93. (Technical Bulletin Ser.: T-31). (Illus.). 30p. (Orig.). 1986. pap. text ed. 4.50 (ISBN 0-88090-056-3). Intl Fertilizer.

Sulfuric-Phosphoric Acid Plant Operations. LC 82-6873. (AIChE CEP Technical Manual Ser.). pap. 34.00 (ISBN 0-8169-0221-6, T-75). Am Inst Chem Eng.

Sulieman the Magnificent. Anthony Bridge. (Dorset Press Reprints Ser.). (Illus.). 220p. 1988. 21.95 (ISBN 0-88029-169-9). Hippocrene Bks.

Sulindac: A Five-Year Perspective. Ed. by J. J. Calabro & A. Calin. 1982. text ed. 5.50. Raven.

Sulla Lirica Romanza Delle Origini. Guido Errante. 441p. (Ital.). 1943. pap. 8.50x (ISBN 0-913298-44-1). S F Vanni.

Sulla: The Last Republican. Arthur Keaveney. 256p. 1983. 33.00 (ISBN 0-7099-1507-1, Pub. by Croom Helm Ltd). Routledge Chapman & Hall.

Sulla: The Last Republican. Arthur Keaveney. (Classical Lives Ser.). 256p. 1987. pap. 13.50 (ISBN 0-7099-3104-2, Pub. by Croom Helm Ltd). Routledge Chapman & Hall.

Sullen Weedy Lakes. William Logan. 1988. 9.95 (ISBN 0-87923-730-9); 15.95 (ISBN 0-87923-729-5). Godine.

Sullied Poem. Ferreira Gullar. Tr. & intro. by Leland Guyer. LC 86-32212. (Modern & Contemporary Literature Ser.). 216p. (Eng. & Port.). 1987. Repr. of 1981 ed. text ed. 24.95x (ISBN 0-8046-9407-9, 9407). Assoc Faculty Pr.

Sullivan & the Scott Russells. John Wolfson. 1979. 30.00x (ISBN 0-900000-93-7, Pub. by Centaur Bks). State Mutual Bk.

Sullivan & the Scott Russells: A Victorian Love Affair Told Through the Letters of Rachel & Louise Scott Russell to Arthur Sullivan, 1864-1870. John Wolfson. 1985. 35.00x (ISBN 0-906527-14-7, Pub. by Packard Pub Ltd.). State Mutual bk.

Sullivan Basal Mathematics Program, 37 bks. Sullivan Associates Staff. pap. text ed. 3.50 ea. (ISBN 0-8449-0304-3); Set. 129.50. Learning Line.

Sullivan Fun Readers, 12 vols. Sullivan Associates Staff. 1972. pap. 3.50 ea. (ISBN 0-8449-4080-1); 35.00 set. Learning Line.

Sullivan Reading Plays, 1 bk. Sullivan Associates Staff. pap. text ed. 2.50 (ISBN 0-8449-4050-X). Learning Line.

Sullivan Reading Program, 25 texts. Sullivan Associates Staff. 1980. pap. text ed. 3.25 ea. (ISBN 0-8449-1902-0); 6 tchr's. manual, 6 tests avail.; Set of 25 Texts. 181.25. Learning Line.

Sullivan Topic Readers, 20 vols. Sullivan Associates Staff. 1972. pap. 2.00 ea. (40.00 if purchased as set with guide & dictionary) (ISBN 0-8449-4202-2). Learning Line.

Sullivan's Comic Operas: A Critical Appreciation. Thomas F. Dunhill. (Music Ser.). 256p. 1981. Repr. of 1928 ed. lib. bdg. 32.50 (ISBN 0-306-76080-0). Da Capo.

Sullivan's Guide to Learning Centers in Higher Education. LeRoy L. Sullivan. 1978. pap. text ed. 49.50 (ISBN 0-87567-074-1). Entelek.

Sully, Colbert & Turgot. Eleanor C. Lodge. LC 70-110911. 1970. Repr. of 1931 ed. 23.00x (ISBN 0-8046-0893-8, Pub. by Kennikat). Assoc Faculty Pr.

Sully, Colbert & Turgot: A Chapter in French Economic History. Eleanor Lodge. LC 71-178939. (Selected Essays in History, Economics & Social Science Ser.). 279p. 1972. Repr. of 1931 ed. lib. bdg. 14.00 (ISBN 0-8337-4237-X). B Franklin.

Sulod Society. F. Landa Jocano. 318p. 1968. 10.00x (ISBN 0-8248-0438-4). UH Pr.

Sulphide Deposits in Mafic & Ultramafic Rocks: Proceedings of Nickel Sulphide Field Conference III, Western Australia, 1982. Ed. by D. L. Buchanan & M. J. Jones. (Orig.). 1984. pap. text ed. 78.00x (ISBN 0-900488-71-9). Imm North Am.

Sulphide Minerals. Crystal Chemistry, Parageneses and Systematics. I. Kostov & J. M. Stefanova. (Illus.). 212p. 1982. text ed. 44.00x (ISBN 3-510-65110-3). Lubrecht & Cramer.

Sulphides: The Art of Cameo Incrustation. Paul Jokelson. LC 68-25513. (Illus.). 159p. 1968. 15.00 (ISBN 0-933756-08-9). Paperweight Pr.

Sulphides-the Art of Cameo Incrustation. Paul Jokelson. LC 68-25513. (Illus.). 159p. 1968. incl. slipcase 15.00 (ISBN 0-317-61126-7, Dist. by Charles Tuttle Publishing Co.). Paperweight Pr.

Sulphur & Lime Sulphur. (Specifications for Plant Protection Products: No. 24). pap. 7.50 (F2009, FAO). UNIPUB.

Sulphur in Biology. Ciba Foundation Staff. (Ciba Symposium Ser.: Vol. 72). 1980. 69.00 (ISBN 0-444-90108-6). Elsevier.

Sulphur in Biology. Ciba Foundation Staff. LC 79-24939. (Ciba Foundation Symposium, New Ser.: 72). pap. 81.00 (ISBN 0-317-29756-2, 2022191). Bks Demand UMI.

Sulphur in the Atmosphere: Proceedings. International Symposium, Dubrovnik, Yugoslavia, 7-14 Sept. 1977. Ed. by R. B. Husar et al. 1978. 100.00 (ISBN 0-08-022932-8). Pergamon.

Sulphur, Sulphur Dioxide, Sulphuric Acid. Ed. by U. Sander et al. Tr. by A. I. More. 428p. 1984. Repr. of 1982 ed. text ed. 45.00x (ISBN 0-902777-64-5). VCH Pubs.

Sulphuric Acid Recovery. 15.00 (ISBN 0-318-03195-7, 7520). Wire Assn Intl.

Sulpiride & Other Benzamides. Ed. by Pier F. Spano et al. 326p. 1979. text ed. 50.50 (ISBN 0-89004-502-X). Raven.

Sultan of Batan. (Sharazad Stories Ser.). (Illus., Arabic.). (gr. 5-12). pap. 3.50x (ISBN 0-86685-230-1). Intl Bk Ctr.

Sultan to Sultan: Adventures Among the Masai & Other Tribes of East Africa. Mary Sheldon. LC 72-5615. (Black Heritage Library Collection Ser). 1972. Repr. of 1892 ed. 65.00 (ISBN 0-8369-9149-4). Ayer Co Pubs.

Sultana & Miriam: Two Hundred Fifty Creative Writing Ideas. Diana Doore & Debra Johnson. LC 83-62301. 75p. (Orig.). 1985. pap. text ed. 4.95 (ISBN 0-88247-718-8). R & E Pubs.

Sultana's Dream & Selections from the Secluded Ones. Rokeya S. Hossain. Ed. & tr. by Roushan Jahan. 100p. 1988. 16.95 (ISBN 0-935312-98-6); pap. 6.95 (ISBN 0-935312-83-8). Feminist Pr.

Sultanate of Bornu. P. A. Benton. Tr. by A. Shultze. 401p. 1968. Repr. of 1913 ed. 35.00x (ISBN 0-7146-1717-2, F Cass Co). Biblio Dist.

"Sultangalievisme" Au Tatarstan see Mouvements Nationaux Chez les Musulmans De Russie.

Sultan's Gift. Marguerite Henry. (King of the Wind Ser.). (Illus.). 24p. (ps-3). 1988. pap. 1.95 (ISBN 0-02-688803-3, Checkerboard Pr). Macmillan.

Sultan's Secret. Peter Lerangis. (G. I. Joe Ser.). (YA) (gr. 8 up). 1988. pap. 2.95. Ballantine.

Sultan's Servants: The Transformation of Ottoman Provincial Government, 1550-1650. I. M. Kunt. LC 82-19800. 200p. 1983. 37.50x (ISBN 0-231-05578-1). Columbia U Pr.

Sum. Alan Stephens. LC 58-13024. (New Poetry Ser.: No. 19). 47p. 1958. 4.95 (ISBN 0-8040-0285-1, Pub. by Swallow). Ohio U Pr.

Sum. Alan A. Stephens. LC 70-179819. (New Poetry Ser). Repr. of 1958 ed. 16.00 (ISBN 0-404-56019-9). AMS Pr.

Sum of Good Government. Philip M. Crane. LC 76-43560. 210p. 1976. pap. 1.95 (ISBN 0-916054-07-1). Green Hill.

Sum Phun with Phobias. Bessie D. Price. 1977. 3.00 (ISBN 0-87012-282-7). McClain.

Sum Plus Exercise in Radiology & Pathology Transcription. 56p. 1988. pap. 50.00 (ISBN 0-934385-07-6); 1 one hr. cass. incl. Prima Vera Pubns.

S.U.M. Poems Nineteen Seventy-Eight. Ed. by Selwyn Kittredge et al. 40p. (Orig.). 1978. pap. 1.00 (ISBN 0-89120-011-8). From Here.

Sum Program Pathology Transcription Unit. 64p. 1987. pap. 200.00 (ISBN 0-934385-06-8); 4 one hr. cass. incl. Prima Vera Pubns.

Sum Program Radiology Transcription Unit. 65p. 1987. pap. 150.00 (ISBN 0-934385-05-X); 3 one hr. cass. incl. Prima Vera Pubns.

Suma Cervantina. Ed. by J. B. Avalle-Arce & E. C. Riley. (Serie A: Monagrafias, XIV). 452p. (Orig., Span.). 1973. pap. 18.00 (ISBN 0-900411-66-X, Pub. by Tamesis Bks Ltd). Longwood Pub Group.

Suma Oriental of Tome Pires, an Account of the East Fifteen Twelve to Fifteeen Fifteen & the Book of Francisco Rodriguez, Rutter of a Voyage in the Red Sea: Vol. 89 & Vol. 90, 2 vols. in one. Ed. by Armando Cortesad. (Hakluyt Society Works Series: No. 2, Vol. 89 & 90). (Illus.). Repr. of 1944 ed. 95.00 (ISBN 0-8115-0387-9). Kraus Repr.

Sumangala-Vilasini, 3 vols. Buddhaghosa. LC 78-72390. Repr. of 1886 ed. Set. 110.00 (ISBN 0-404-17580-5). Vol. 1 (ISBN 0-404-17581-3). Vol. 2 (ISBN 0-404-17582-1). Vol. 3 (ISBN 0-404-17583-X). AMS Pr.

Sumario de Derecho Procesal Penal Puertorriqueno. 2nd ed. Dora Nevares-Muniz. 296p. (Span.). 1986. pap. text ed. 20.00 (ISBN 0-317-38881-9); supplement 10.00. Instituto Desarrollo.

Sumario de Doctrina Cristiana. 5th ed. Louis Berkhof. Tr. by David Vila from Eng. 240p. (Span.). 1986. pap. 3.25 (ISBN 0-939125-05-6). Evangelical Lit.

Sumatran Contributions to the Development of Indonesian Literature, 1920-1942. Alberta J. Freidus. (Asian Studies at Hawaii Ser.: No. 19). 76p. 1977. pap. text ed. 7.50x (ISBN 0-8248-0462-7). UH Pr.

Sumatran Rhinoceros-Dicerorhinus Sumatr ensis Fischer, 1814 - In the Gunung Leuser National Park, Sumatra, Indonesia: Its Distribution, Ecology & Conservation. Nico J. Van Strien. (Mammalia Depicta Ser.: Vol. 12). (Illus.). 200p. (Orig.). 1986. pap. text ed. 49.00 (ISBN 3-490-11118-4). Parey Sci Pubs.

Sumer Is Icumen in. Jamieson B. Hurry. LC 77-75217. 1977. Repr. of 1914 ed. lib. bdg. 15.00 (ISBN 0-89341-117-5). Longwood Pub Group.

Sumerian Administrative Documents Dated in the Reigns of the Kings of the Second Dynasty of the Ur from the Temple Archives of Nippur Preserved in Philadelphia. David V. Myhrman. LC 11-1230. (University of Pennsylvania, Babylonian Expedition, Series A: Cuneiform Texts: Vol. 3, Pt. 1). pap. 60.50 (ISBN 0-317-29805-4, 2052013). Bks Demand UMI.

Sumerian Administrative Documents from the Reigns of ISBI-ERRA. Marc Van de Mieroop. 144p. 1987. text ed. 37.50 (ISBN 0-300-03805-4). Yale U Pr.

Sumerian & Akkadian Administrative Texts: From Pre-Dynastic Times to the End of the Akkad Dynasty. George G. Hackman. LC 78-63527. (Babylonian Inscriptions in the Collection of James B. Nies: No. 8). Repr. of 1958 ed. 45.00 (ISBN 0-404-60138-3). AMS Pr.

Sumerian & Akkadian Royal Inscriptions: Presargonic Inscriptions. Jerrold S. Cooper. (American Oriental Society Translation Ser.: Vol. 1). 1986. 17.50x (ISBN 0-940490-82-X). Am Orient Soc.

Sumerian Dictionary of the University Museum of the University of Pennsylvania, Vol. B. PSD 2. xxviii, 220p. 1984. 40.00x (ISBN 0-934718-64-4). Univ Mus of U PA.

Sumerian Economic Texts from the Drehem Archive, Vol.1. Shin T. Kang. LC 78-162290. (Illus.). 312p. 1971. 35.00 (ISBN 0-252-00204-0). U of Ill Pr.

Sumerian Economic Texts from the First Dynasty of Isin. Vaughn E. Crawford. LC 78-63528. (Babylonian Inscriptions in the Collection of James B. Nies: No. 9). Repr. of 1954 ed. 38.00 (ISBN 0-404-60139-1). AMS Pr.

Sumerian Economic Texts from the Umma Archive, Vol.2. Shin T. Kang. LC 73-84697. (Illus.). 463p. 1973. 35.00 (ISBN 0-252-00425-6). U of Ill Pr.

Sumerian Grammatical Texts. Stephen H. Langdon. LC 17-16093. (University of Pennsylvania, The University Museum, Publications of the Babylonian Section: Vol. 12, No. 1). pap. 25.80 (ISBN 0-317-28543-2, 2052028). Bks Demand UMI.

Sumerian Hymnology: The Ersemma. Mark E. Cohen. 1981. 18.75x (ISBN 0-87820-601-9). Ktav.

TITLE INDEX SUMMARY REPORT & SELECTED

Sumerian Hymns from Cuneiform Texts in the British Museum. Ed. by Frederick A. Vanderburgh. LC 68-23118. (Columbia University. Contributions to Oriental History & Philology: No. 1). Repr. of 1908 ed. 14.00 (ISBN 0-404-50531-7). AMS Pr.
Sumerian King List. Thorkild Jacobsen. LC 39-19328. 1939. pap. 12.00x (ISBN 0-226-62273-8, AS11). U of Chicago Pr.
Sumerian Literary Fragments from Nippur. J. Heimerdinger. (Occasional Publications of the Babylonian Fund: Vol. 4 OPBF 4). 1979. 20.00x (ISBN 0-934718-31-8). Univ Mus of U PA.
Sumerian Literary Texts in the Ashmolean Museum. Ed. by Oliver R. Gurney & Samuel N. Kramer. (Oxford Editions of Cuneiform Texts). (Illus.). 1976. pap. 45.00x (ISBN 0-19-815450-X). Oxford U Pr.
Sumerian Liturgical Texts. Stephen H. Langdon. LC 17-16092. (University of Pennsylvania, University Museum, Publications of the Babylonian Section: Vol. 10, No. 2). pap. 40.80 (ISBN 0-317-28546-7, 2052026). Bks Demand UMI.
Sumerian Mythology: A Study of Spiritual & Literary Achievement in the Third Millennium B. C. Samuel N. Kramer. LC 88-163. (Illus.). 148p. 1988. Repr. of 1972 ed. lib. bdg. 39.75x (ISBN 0-313-26363-9, KRSM). Greenwood.
Sumerian Records from Drehem. William M. Nesbit. LC 15-2779. (Columbia University. Oriental Studies: No. 8). (Illus.). Repr. of 1914 ed. 12.50 (ISBN 0-404-50498-1). AMS Pr.
Sumerian Tablets in the Harvard Semitic Museum, 2 Vols. Ed. by Mary I. Hussey. 1912-1915. Vol. 3. 25.00 ea. (ISBN 0-384-25090-4); Vol. 4. (ISBN 0-384-25091-2). Johnson Repr.
Sumerian, Ural-Altaic, Magyar Relationship: A History of Research, Pt. 1, the 19th Century. Miklos Erdy. LC 72-112303. (Studia Sumiro-Hungarica: Vol. 3). (Illus.). 530p. (Bilingual text). 1974. 18.00 (ISBN 0-914246-53-4). Gilgamesh Pub.
Sumerian Vistas: Poems. A. R. Ammons. 1987. 15.95 (ISBN 0-393-02468-7); pap. 7.95 (ISBN 0-393-30425-6). Norton.
Sumeriana. Duncan McNaughton. (Illus.). 1976. pap. 3.00 (ISBN 0-939180-04-9). Tombouctou.
Sumerians. C. Leonard Woolley. LC 79-120570. Repr. of 1929 ed. 29.50 (ISBN 0-404-07029-9). AMS Pr.
Sumerians. C. Leonard Woolley. (Illus.). 1965. pap. 7.95 (ISBN 0-393-00292-6, Norton Lib). Norton.
Sumerians: Their History, Culture & Character. Samuel N. Kramer. LC 63-11398. (Illus.). 1971. pap. 12.95 (ISBN 0-226-45238-7, P422, Phoen). U of Chicago Pr.
Sumero-Babylonian Sign List. Samuel A. Mercer. LC 18-16548. (Columbia University. Oriental Studies: No. 14). Repr. of 1918 ed. 21.50 (ISBN 0-404-50504-X). AMS Pr.
Sumero-Babylonian Sign List to Which Is Added an Assyrian Sign List & a Catalogue of the Numerals, Weights & Measures used at Various Periods. Compiled by Samuel A. Mercer. 244p. 1983. Repr. of 1918 ed. lib. bdg. 200.00 (ISBN 0-89987-632-3). Darby Bks.
Sumero-Babylonian Year-Formulae. S. A. Mercer. 121p. 1946. 30.00x (ISBN 0-317-39162-3, Pub. by Luzac & Co Ltd). State Mutual Bk.
Sumerological Studies in Honor of Thorkild Jacobsen: On His Seventieth Birthday, June 7, 1974. Stephen J. Lieberman. LC 75-42584. (Assyriological Studies: No. 20). 1977. 20.00x (ISBN 0-226-62282-7). U of Chicago Pr.
Sumi-E: An Introduction to Ink Painting. Nanae Momiyama. LC 67-15320. (Illus.). (gr. 7-9). 1967. pap. 3.50 (ISBN 0-8048-0554-7). C E Tuttle.
Sumi-E Just for You. Hakuho Hirayama. LC 79-84653. (Illus.). 96p. 1980. pap. 14.95 (ISBN 0-87011-369-0). Kodansha.
Sumi-e Painting Lessons for Beginners: Painting for Beginners. Judith Armbruster. (Illus.). 30p. 1987. pap. 8.95 (ISBN 0-9619502-0-X). Maple Tree Studio.
Sumi Painting: Study of Japanese Brush Painting. Tahahiko Mikami. (Illus.). 48p. 1965. pap. 6.50 (ISBN 4-07-971229-4, Pub. by Shufunotomo Co. Ltd Japan). C E Tuttle.
Sumida, Edition I. A. Wallen Burgh. 222p. 1959. write for info. Rural Life.
Sumida-Curious. A. Wollenburg. 256p. 1974. pap. 3.95 (ISBN 0-686-02473-7). Rural Life.
Sumir Kerdes (the Sumerian Question) see Studia Sumiro-Hungarica.
Sumitra's Story. Rukshana Smith. LC 82-19794. 168p. (gr. 6). 1983. 9.95 (ISBN 0-698-20579-0, Coward). Putnam Pub Group.
Summa Contra Gentiles, 4 bks. St. Thomas Aquinas. Incl. Bk. 1. God. Tr. by Anton C. Pegis. 317p. pap. 8.95x (ISBN 0-268-01678-X); Bk. 2. Creation. Tr. by James F. Anderson. 351p. text ed. 16.95 (ISBN 0-268-01679-8); pap. 8.95 (ISBN 0-268-01680-1); Bk. 3. Providence, 2 bks. in 1. Tr. by Vernon J. Bourke. 560p. text ed. 27.95x (ISBN 0-268-01681-X); pap. 15.00x (ISBN 0-268-01682-8); Bk. 4. Salvation. Tr. by Charles J. O'Neil. 360p. text ed. 16.95 (ISBN 0-268-01683-6); pap. 8.95x (ISBN 0-268-01684-4). LC 75-19883. 1975. Set. pap. 40.00. U of Notre Dame Pr.
Summa De Literis Missilibus. Petrus De Hallis. Repr. of 1853 ed. 23.00 (ISBN 0-384-46030-5). Johnson Repr.
Summa Insolubilium Johannis Wyclif. Ed. by Paul V. Spade & Gordon A. Wilson. (Medieval & Renaissance Texts & Studies: Vol. 41). 176p. 19.00 (ISBN 0-86698-074-1). Medieval & Renaissance NY.
Summa Modorum Significandi: Sophismata. Sigerius De Cortraco. (Studies in the History of Linguistics Ser.: No. 14). xii, 108p. 1977. 26.00x (ISBN 90-272-0955-3). Benjamins North Am.
Summa of the Christian Life, 3 vols. Louis Of Granada. Tr. by Jordan Aumann from Span. LC 79-65716. 1979. Set. pap. 27.00 (ISBN 0-89555-121-7). Vol. 1 (ISBN 0-89555-118-7). Vol. 2 (ISBN 0-89555-119-5). Vol. 3 (ISBN 0-89555-120-9). TAN Bks Pubs.
Summa Theologiae, 61 vols. 1981. Set. 2000.00x (ISBN 0-686-75401-8, Pub. by Eyre & Spottiswoode England). State Mutual Bk.
Summa virtutum de remediis Anime. Ed. by Siegfried Wenzel. LC 82-13430. (Chaucer Library). 352p. 1984. 35.00x (ISBN 0-8203-0638-X). U of Ga Pr.
Summability Through Functional Analysis. A. Wilansky. (Mathematics Studies: Vol. 85). 1984. 68.50 (ISBN 0-444-86840-2, I-550-83, North-Holland). Elsevier.
Summaries of Graduate Programs for Physical Therapists. pap. 6.00 (ISBN 0-912452-62-5). Am Phys Therapy Assn.
Summaries of Leading Cases on the Constitution. 12th ed. Paul C. Bartholomew. (Quality Paperback Ser.: No. 50). 460p. (Orig.). 1983. pap. text ed. 8.95 (ISBN 0-8226-0364-0, Helix Bks). Rowman.
Summaries of Safety Defect Recall Campaigns for American Motors Corporation Vehicles (1966-1986) Donald J. Schallau. 33p. 1986. 100.00. DJS Ent.
Summaries of Safety Defect Recall Campaigns for Chrysler Corporation Vehicles (1966-1986) Donald J. Schallau. 75p. 1986. 100.00 (ISBN 0-933634-04-8). DJS Ent.
Summaries of Safety Defect Recall Campaigns for Ford Motor Company Vehicles (1966-1986) Donald J. Schallau. 124p. 1986. 100.00 (ISBN 0-933634-05-6). DJS Ent.
Summaries of Safety Defect Recall Campaigns for General Motors Corporation Vehicles (1966-1987) Donald J. Schallau. 134p. 1986. 100.00 (ISBN 0-933634-06-4). DJS Ent.
Summaries of Safety Defect Recall Campaigns for Harley-Davidson Motor Company Vehicles (1966-1986) Donald J. Schallau. 14p. 1986. 100.00 (ISBN 0-933634-11-0). DJS Ent.
Summaries of Safety Defect Recall Campaigns for International Harvester Vehicles (1966-1986) Donald J. Schallau. 37p. 1986. 100.00 (ISBN 0-933634-07-2). DJS Ent.
Summaries of Safety Defect Recall Campaigns for Mack Trucks Inc. Vehicles (1966-1986) Donald J. Schallau. 40p. 1986. 100.00 (ISBN 0-933634-08-0). DJS Ent.
Summaries of Safety Defect Recall Campaigns for Vehicle Tires (All Manufacturers & Distributors), 1966-1986. Donald J. Schallau. 112p. 1986. 100.00 (ISBN 0-933634-12-9). DJS Ent.
Summaries of Safety Defect Recall Campaigns for Volkswagen Vehicles: VW-Porsche-Audi (1966-1986) 36p. 1986. 100.00 (ISBN 0-933634-09-9). DJS Ent.
Summaries of Safety Defect Recall Campaigns for White Motor Corporation Vehicles (1966-1986) Donald J. Schallau. 32p. 1986. 100.00 (ISBN 0-933634-10-2). DJS Ent.
Summaries of State Laws Relating to the Insane. John Koren. Ed. by Gerald N. Grob. LC 78-22570. (Historical Issues in Mental Health Ser.). 1979. Repr. of 1917 ed. lib. bdg. 18.00x (ISBN 0-405-11923-2). Ayer Co Pubs.
Summaries of Three Bilateral Conferences: Held in Beijing & Shanghai, the People's Republic of China, October 15-30, 1986. Pacific Forum Staff et al. 88p. 1988. pap. text ed. 9.95x (ISBN 0-8248-1175-5, Pub. by Pacific Forum). UH Pr.
Summarium Heinrici, Vol. 1: Textkritische Ausgabe der ersten Fassung, Buch I-X. Ed. by Reiner Hildebrandt. LC 73-75487. (Quellen und Forschungen Zur Sprach-und Kulturgeschichte der Germanischen Voelker N. F. 61). 1974. text ed. 96.00 (ISBN 3-11-003750-5). De Gruyter.
Summary & Analysis of Statutory Provisions Relating to the Records of the Circuit Courts, District Courts, & Magistrates of Virginia. National Center for State Courts Staff. 91p. 1976. manuscript 5.46 (MAB-119). Natl Ctr St Courts.
Summary Description of Design Criteria, Codes, Standards, & Regulatory Provisions Typically Used for the Civil & Structural Design of Nuclear Fuel Cycle Facilities, A. 128p. 1988. 16.00 (ISBN 0-87262-651-2). Am Soc Civil Eng.
Summary Groundwater Resources of Lebanon County, Pennsylvania. Denise W. Royer. (Water Resource Report Ser.: No. 55). (Illus.). 84p. (Orig.). 1983. pap. 14.55 (ISBN 0-8182-0026-X). Commonweal PA.
Summary, Historical & Political, of the First Planting, Progressive Improvements, & Present State of the British Settlements in North-America. William Douglass. LC 74-141084. (Research Library of Colonial Americana). 1971. Repr. of 1749 ed. 79.50 (ISBN 0-405-03279-X). Ayer Co Pubs.
Summary Information on Master of Social Work Programs, 1987. 8.00. Coun Soc Wk Ed.
Summary Information on Master of Social Work Programs: 1985. Date not set. 6.95 (85-320-41). Coun Soc WK Ed.
Summary of American Law. 2nd ed. Martin Weinstein. LC 87-82759. 1988. 32.50. Lawyers Co-Op.
Summary of Arizona Community Property Law. Charles M. Smith. 144p. 1981. 12.65 (ISBN 0-910039-07-0). Az Law Inst.
Summary of CETA Employment & Training Activities on the Criminal Justice Field During FY 79. 80p. 1981. pap. 3.50 (ISBN 0-686-47920-3). Amer Bar Assn.
Summary of Christian Doctrine. Louis Berkhof. 1939. pap. 7.95 (ISBN 0-8028-1513-8). Eerdmans.
Summary of Christian History. Robert A. Baker. (Illus.). 1959. 16.95 (ISBN 0-8054-6502-2). Broadman.
Summary of Christian History see Compendio de la Historia Cristiana.
Summary of Conference Agreement on H. R. 3838 (Tax Reform Act of 1986) Joint Committee on Taxation Staff. 73p. 1986. pap. text ed. write for info. (ISBN 0-314-34290-7). West Pub.
Summary of Consumer Protection Seminar. 75p. 1976. avail. Natl Attys General.
Summary of Coopers & Lybrand Study of Computer-Assisted Legal Research for the Department of Justice. Fred M. Greguras. (Computer Law Monograph Ser). 19p. (Orig.). 1980. 5.00 (ISBN 0-935200-02-9). Ctr Comp Law.
Summary of Data on Handicapped Children & Youth. 231p. 1985. pap. 6.00 (ISBN 0-318-21357-5, S/N 065-000-00247-7). USGPO.
Summary of Earth Processes & Environments. John Tomikel. LC 74-28957. 1975. 8.00 (ISBN 0-910042-19-5). Allegheny.
Summary of Employment in Fifty Top-Paying Fields. Work for Hire Staff. 1984. 2.50x (ISBN 0-917421-01-9, Career Materials Inc.). Lenox Pub.
Summary of Financial & Cost Data Survey. 58p. Date not set. 750.00 (FCD). Prestressed Concrete.
Summary of Groundwater Resources of Perry County, Pennsylvania. Denise W. Royer. (Water Resource Report: No. 59). (Illus.). 70p. 1984. pap. 15.35 (ISBN 0-8182-0059-6). Commonweal PA.
Summary of Investigations Relating to Reading: July 1, 1982 to June 30, 1983. Samuel Weintraub et al. pap. 91.60 (ISBN 0-317-58125-2, 2029732). Bks Demand UMI.
Summary of Mississippi Law, 3 Vols. Leslie B. Grant. LC 78-76760. write for info. Lawyers Co-Op.
Summary of Oil & Gas Developments in Pennsylvania: 1955 to 1959. William S. Lytle et al. (Mineral Resource Report Ser.: No. 45). (Illus.). 133p. pap. 14.40 (ISBN 0-8182-0036-7). Commonweal PA.
Summary of Precision Bidding. C. C. Wei. 10p. 1978. folder 1.00. Barclay Bridge.
Summary of Preliminary Crop Germplasm Evaluation for Resistance to Root-Knot Nematodes. J. N. Sasser et al. 87p. (Orig.). 1987. pap. text ed. write for info. (ISBN 0-931901-07-3). NCSU Plant Pathol.
Summary of Proceedings. American Bar Association, Patent, Trademark & Copyright Law Staff. 1986. pap. 5.00. Amer Bar Assn.
Summary of Proceedings & Selected Papers: Symposium on the Planning & Implementation of Fisheries Management & Development, Lusaka, Zamvia, 7-11 October, 1985. Ed. by J. L. Gaudet & O. Parker. (Fisheries Report Ser.: No. 360). 155p. (Orig.). 1986. pap. text ed. 12.50 (ISBN 92-5-102438-3, F2947, FAO). UNIPUB.
Summary of Proceedings: The 80's: Decade for Decisions. 319p. 1981. 19.50 (ISBN 0-686-40431-9, G-150). ANA.
Summary of Publications & Hearings, Vol. 4. Chadbourne et al. (Municipal Securities Regulation Ser.). 1977. pap. text ed. 70.00 (ISBN 0-916450-11-2). Nat Civic League.
Summary of Reports (Articles 19, 22 & 35 of Constitution) ILO Conference: 72nd Session, 1986. (International Labour Conference Reports Ser.). 41p. 1987. pap. text ed. 8.75 (ISBN 92-2-105170-6, ILO619, ILO). UNIPUB.
Summary of Reports Presented at April 28, 1984 CMA Production Management Seminar on: New Developments in Trouser Technology, Tailored Clothing Technology Corporation, Manufacturer's Experience with New Technology. 36p. 1984. 50.00 (ISBN 0-318-19699-9). Clothing Mfrs.
Summary of Reports Presented at April 20, 1985 CMA Production-Management Seminar of Survey of Retail Alterations Problems & Impact of Wider Lining Widths on Clothing Manufacturers Operations. 30p. 1985. 50.00 (ISBN 0-318-19703-0). Clothing Mfrs.
Summary of Research in Science Education 1983. william G. Holiday et al. 176p. 1985. pap. 19.95 (ISBN 0-471-83747-4). Wiley.
Summary of Research in Science Education 1984. Anton E. Lawson et al. 35p. 1986. pap. 23.95 (ISBN 0-471-85460-3). Wiley.
Summary of Research in Science Education, 1984. Roger G. Olstad & David L. Haury. (Science Education Ser.: Vol. 68, No. 3). 363p. 1984. pap. text ed. 25.95x (ISBN 0-471-81740-6). Wiley.
Summary of Research in Science Education 1980. Ed. by H. Craig Sipe & Walter A. Farmer. 503p. 1983. 29.95x (ISBN 0-471-87028-5, Pub. by Wiley Interscience). Wiley.
Summary of Research in Science Education 1981. Burton E. Voss. 424p. 1983. pap. 21.95 (ISBN 0-471-88199-6). Wiley.
Summary of Research Studies of Interviewing Methodology, 1959-1970. Charles F. Cannell & Kent H. Marquis. (Ser. 2: No. 69). 70p. 1976. pap. text ed. 2.00 (ISBN 0-8406-0062-3). Natl Ctr Health Stats.
Summary of Scholastic Principles. Bernard Wuellner. LC 56-10903. 1956. 1.50 (ISBN 0-8294-0084-2). Loyola.
Summary of Size & Weight Limits. American Trucking Associations, Inc., Department of State Laws. 1988. pap. 3.00 (ISBN 0-88711-101-7). Am Trucking Assns.
Summary of Speeches: Seminar for Attorneys General. 49p. 1979. 4.00 (ISBN 0-318-15235-5). Natl Attys General.
Summary of State Activities: Fall, 1979 Consumer Protection Seminar. 60p. 1979. write for info. Natl Attys General.
Summary of State Ground Water Quality Monitoring Well Regulations. Date not set. 8.75 (ISBN 0-318-23013-5). Natl Water Well.
Summary of State Legislation-Savings Banks, Credit unions, Savings & Loan Associations. American Bankers Association, Office of the General Counsel Staff. LC 84-189061. write for info. Am Bankers.
Summary of Systemic Opthamology & Indices see System of Ophthalmology Series.
Summary of the Basics in Solar Energy: Supplement-Tutorials to the 1978 Annual Meeting of the American Section of the International Solar Energy Society. International Solar Energy Society, American Section. Ed. by Karl W. Boer. 1978. pap. text ed. 18.00x (ISBN 0-89553-013-9). Am Solar Energy.
Summary of the Colloquium on Public Law 94-210. Ed. by John H. Davis. (Lincoln Institute Monograph: No. 77-3). 1977. pap. text ed. 1.00 (ISBN 0-686-20039-X). Lincoln Inst Land.
Summary of the Law of Contracts. C. C. Langdell. xiv, 278p. 1980. Repr. of 1880 ed. lib. bdg. 26.00x (ISBN 0-8377-0809-5). Rothman.
Summary of the Literatures of Modern Europe from the Origins to 1400. Marian Edwardes. LC 7-20970. 1968. Repr. of 1907 ed. 48.00 (ISBN 0-527-26400-8). Kraus Repr.
Summary of the Principal Legal Decisions Affecting Auditors. Hugh Cocke. Ed. by Richard P. Brief. LC 80-1480. (Dimensions of Accounting Theory & Practice Ser.). 1981. Repr. of 1946 ed. lib. bdg. 14.00x (ISBN 0-405-13510-6). Ayer Co Pubs.
Summary of the Public Hearings: The National Commission on Nursing. 77p. 1981. 9.00 (ISBN 0-87914-056-9, C-654635). Am Hospital.
Summary of the Recommendations of Recent Commission Reports on Improving Undergraduate Education: Five Reports. 48p. 1985. 7.00 (ISBN 0-318-22554-9, PS-85-3). Ed Comm States.
Summary of the Roman Civil Law, Illustrated by Commentaries on & Parallels from the Mosaic, Canon, Mohammedan, English, & Foreign Law, with an Appendix, Map, & General Index, 4 vols. Patrick M. De Colquhoun. 1988. Repr. of 1849 ed. Set. lib. bdg. 150.00 (ISBN 0-8377-2036-2). Rothman.
Summary of the Seven Sacraments. Daughters of St. Paul. 2.75 (ISBN 0-8198-6858-2). Dghtrs St Paul.
Summary of the Work of Rudyard Kipling Including Items Ascribed to Him. Lloyd H. Chandler. 465p. 1986. Repr. of 1930 ed. lib. bdg. 200.00 (ISBN 0-8492-9724-9). R West.
Summary of Unidentified Flying Objects & Related Events in Malaysia (1950-1980) Ahmad Jamaludin. (Illus.). xvii, 88p. 1981. pap. 11.00. J A Hynek Ctr UFO.
Summary Plan Descriptions. Barbara Boettcher. (Requirements for Qualification of Plans Ser.). 42p. 1979. pap. 2.00 (ISBN 0-317-31167-0, B359). Am Law Inst.
Summary Record of the Eighth Session of FAO Advisory Committee on Forestry Education. 47p. 1980. pap. 7.50 (ISBN 92-5-100480-3, F1968, FAO). UNIPUB.
Summary Report & Recommendations of the First Session of the Joint FAO-IOC Panel of Experts on the Aquatic Sciences & Fisheries Information Systems (ASFIS), 1978. (Fisheries Reports Ser.: No. 168). 1976. pap. 7.50 (ISBN 0-685-68959-X, F815, FAO). UNIPUB.
Summary Report & Selected Papers Presented at the IPFC Workshop on Inland Fisheries for Planners: Indo-Pacific Fisheries Commission (IPFC), Manila, the Philippines, August 1982. (Fisheries Reports: No. 288). 197p. 1984. pap. 7.50 (ISBN 92-5-101380-2, F2494, FAO). UNIPUB.

Summary Report, Conference on Research & Development of Vegetables in the Tropics. Ed. by Mason E. Miller & E. Denise Felton. 88p. 1986. 11.00 (ISBN 0-933595-04-2). Winrock Intl.

Summary Report of the FAO Regional Population Workshop for Latin America, Santiago, Chile, 1974. FAO Regional Population Workshop for Latin America Staff. (Illus.). 40p. 1976. pap. 7.50 (ISBN 0-685-66343-4, F1214, FAO). UNIPUB.

Summary Report of the Modoc Rock Shelter, 1952-1956. facsimile ed. Melvin L. Fowler. (Reports of Investigations Ser.: No. 8). (Illus.). 72p. 1971. pap. 3.00x (ISBN 0-89792-019-8). Ill St Museum.

Summary Report on Adult College Students. Alan B. Knox. 1959. 2.50 (ISBN 0-87060-086-9, PUC 8). Syracuse U Cont Ed.

Summary Reporting of Financial Information, 2 vols, Vols. 1 & 2. Deloitte, Haskins & Sells Staff. 20.00 (ISBN 0-910586-52-7). Finan Exec.

Summary View of the Courses of Crops in the Husbandry of England & Maryland. John B. Bordley. LC 72-89075. (Rural America Ser.). 1973. Repr. of 1784 ed. 8.00 (ISBN 0-8420-1477-2). Scholarly Res Inc.

Summary View of the Millennial Church, or United Society of Believers, Commonly Called Shakers. Shakers. LC 72-2993. Repr. of 1848 ed. 38.50 (ISBN 0-404-10755-9). AMS Pr.

Summary View of the Rights of British America. Thomas Jefferson. (Research & Source Works Ser.: No. 833). 1971. Repr. of 1892 ed. wrappers 13.00 (ISBN 0-8337-1834-7). B Franklin.

Summary View of the Rights of British America. Thomas Jefferson. 1976. 5.00 (ISBN 0-940550-07-5). Caxton Club.

Summary View of the Rights of British America. Thomas Jefferson. LC 76-2728. 1977. Repr. of 1774 ed. 30.00x (ISBN 0-8201-1170-8). Schol Facsimiles.

Summary View of the Rights of British America see Writings.

Summation. Lawrence J. Smith. (Art of Advocacy Ser.). 1978. looseleaf 90.00 (030); Updates avail. 1985 37.50; 1986 39.50. Bender.

Summation of Infinitesimal Quantities. I. Natanson. (Russian Tracts on the Physical Sciences Ser.). 74p. 1962. 30.00 (ISBN 0-677-20450-7). Gordon & Breach.

Summation of Series. Harold T. Davis. 140p. 1962. 6.00 (ISBN 0-911536-19-1). Trinity U Pr.

Summations. Moe Levine. (Best of Moe Ser.). 256p. 1983. Repr. of 1968 ed. 30.00 (ISBN 0-379-01065-8). Oceana.

Summe & Substance of the Conference at Hampton Court, January 14, 1603. William Barlow. LC 74-28829. (English Experience Ser.: No. 711). 1975. Repr. of 1604 ed. 30.00 (ISBN 90-221-0711-6). Walter J Johnson.

Summe & Substance of the Conference. William Barlow. LC 65-10395. 1965. Repr. of 1604 ed. 30.00x (ISBN 0-8201-1004-3). Schol Facsimiles.

Summer. Richard L. Allington. Kathleen Krull. LC 80-25097. (Beginning to Learn about Ser.). (Illus.). 32p. (ps-2). 1985. pap. 9.27 (ISBN 0-8172-2491-2). Raintree Pubs.

Summer. Richard L. Allington & Kathleen Krull. LC 80-25097. (Beginning to Learn about Ser.). (Illus.). 32p. (gr. k-2). 1981. PLB 15.33 (ISBN 0-8172-1341-4). Raintree Pubs.

Summer. Jane Factor. LC 87-50990. (Illus.). 32p. (ps-3). 1988. 10.95 (ISBN 0-670-81157-2). Viking.

Summer. Lisa Grunwald. LC 85-40115. 224p. 1985. 15.45 (ISBN 0-394-54535-4). Knopf.

Summer. Lisa Grunwald. 320p. 1987. pap. 3.95 (ISBN 0-446-34377-3). Warner Bks.

Summer. Robert Highsmith. (Illus.). 26p. (ps). 1986. 2.95 (ISBN 0-02-747920-X). Macmillan.

Summer. Bela Liscsinszky. (Foods for All Seasons Ser.). (Illus.). 104p. 1986. 9.95 (ISBN 963-13-2032-4, Pub. by Corvina Kiado Hungary). Intl Spec Bk.

Summer. Colin McNaughton. LC 83-45234. (Very First Bks.). (Illus.). 10p. (ps-k). 1983. 4.95 (ISBN 0-8037-0042-3). Dial Bks Young.

Summer. Sean O'Leary. (Busy Fingers Ser.). (Illus.). 16p. (gr. 1-4). 1987. pap. 3.95 (ISBN 0-86278-125-6, Pub. by O'Brien Pr Ireland). Irish Bks Media.

Summer. Louis Santrey. LC 82-19384. (Discovering the Seasons Ser.). (Illus.). 32p. (gr. 4-7). 1982. lib. bdg. 10.79 (ISBN 0-89375-911-2); pap. text ed. 2.50 (ISBN 0-89375-912-0). Troll Assocs.

Summer. C. S. Vendrell & J. M. Parramon. (Exploring the Seasons Ser.). (Illus.). 32p. (ps-3). 1981. 11.93 (ISBN 0-516-02382-9). Childrens.

Summer. Edith Wharton. LC 79-5266. 1980. pap. 4.95 (ISBN 0-06-080507-2, P 507, PL). Har-Row.

Summer. Edith Wharton. LC 73-115288. 1970. Repr. of 1917 ed. 39.00x (ISBN 0-403-00259-1). Scholarly.

Summer. Edith Wharton. (Twentieth Century Classics Ser.). 320p. 1987. pap. 4.95 (ISBN 0-02-055440-0, Collier). Macmillan.

Summer. Ralph Whitlock. (Seasons Ser.). (Illus.). 48p. 1987. lib. bdg. 12.90 (ISBN 0-531-18106-5, Pub. by Bookwright Pr). Watts.

Summer after Summer. Richard Sullivan. 25.50 (ISBN 0-405-10860-5, 11858). Ayer Co Pubs.

Summer Ago. George Scarbrough. LC 86-6758. 214p. 1986. 13.95 (ISBN 0-918518-46-6, St Luke TN). Peachtree Pubs.

Summer Aide. Jack Rudman. (Career Examination Ser.: C-1498). (Cloth bdg. avail. on request). pap. 12.00 (ISBN 0-8373-1498-4). Natl Learning.

Summer Air Conditioning. Seichi Konzo et al. pap. 138.50 (ISBN 0-317-10814-X, 2003090). Bks Demand UMI.

Summer & Fables. Edward Bond. (Modern Plays Ser.). 100p. 1983. pap. 6.95 (ISBN 0-413-50970-2, NO. 3789). Heinemann Ed.

Summer & Fall Wildflowers of New England. Dwelley. (Illus.). 1975. 10.95 (ISBN 0-89272-020-4). Down East.

Summer and Smoke see Theatre of Tennessee Williams.

Summer & Winter. Illus. by Peter Firmin. (What's the Difference Ser.). (Illus.). 16p. (ps-1). 1986. 2.95 (ISBN 0-86020-964-1). EDC.

Summer & Winter. Harriet Tidball. LC 76-24010. (Shuttle Craft Guild Monograph: No. 19). (Illus.). 58p. 1966. pap. 8.45 (ISBN 0-916658-19-8). Shuttle Craft.

Summer & Winter Knitting. Ed. by Stephen Sheard. LC 87-14783. (Illus.). 160p. 1987. 24.95 (ISBN 0-938953-02-8). Westminster Trading.

Summer Anniversaries. Donald Justice. LC 60-7256. (Wesleyan Poetry Program: Vol. 6). (Orig.). 1960. 17.00x (ISBN 0-8195-2105-1); pap. 8.95 (ISBN 0-8195-1105-6). Wesleyan U Pr.

Summer at Awakopu. Robyn Donald. (Harlequin Presents Ser). (Orig.). 1979. pap. 1.25 (ISBN 0-373-70785-1). Harlequin Bks.

Summer at Fairacre. Miss Read. (Illus.). 256p. 1985. 14.95 (ISBN 0-395-38016-2). HM.

Summer Awakening. Anita Eires. (Heartlines Ser.: No. 1). (gr. 6 up). 1986. pap. 2.50 (ISBN 0-440-98369-X, LFL). Dell.

Summer Before. Patricia Windsor. 176p. (gr. 7 up). 1974. pap. 1.95 (ISBN 0-440-98382-7, LFL). Dell.

Summer before Dark. Doris Lessing. LC 82-40421. 256p. 1983. pap. 4.95 (ISBN 0-394-71095-9, Vin). Random.

Summer Bird-Cage. Margaret Drabble. 1985. pap. 6.95 (ISBN 0-452-25761-1, Plume). NAL.

Summer Birds. Penelope Farmer. (Orig.). (gr. k-6). 1987. pap. 2.50 (ISBN 0-440-47737-9, YB). Dell.

Summer Blues. Emily Chase. (Girls of Canby Hall Ser.: No. 5). 192p. (Orig.). (gr. 7 up). 1984. pap. 2.25 (ISBN 0-590-40082-7). Scholastic Inc.

Summer Blues. Joyce Lezan. (Orig.). 1984. pap. 1.95 (ISBN 0-87067-230-4, BH230). Holloway.

Summer Book. Tove Jansson. Tr. by Thomas Teal from Swedish. LC 87-42995. 176p. 1988. pap. 6.95 (ISBN 0-8052-0850-X). Pantheon.

Summer Brave. William Inge. Orig. Title: Picnic. pap. 3.50x (ISBN 0-686-62807-1). Dramatists Play.

Summer Break. Victoria Althoff. 112p. (gr. 6-8). 1987. 2.25 (ISBN 0-87406-196-2). Willowisp Pr.

Summer Business. Charles E. Martin. LC 83-25422. (Illus.). 32p. (gr. k-3). 1984. 10.25 (ISBN 0-688-03863-8); PLB 10.88 (ISBN 0-688-03864-6). Greenwillow.

Summer by the Sea. Marian F. Bray. (gr. 7-9). 1988. pap. 3.95 (ISBN 1-55513-408-4, Chariot Bks). Cook.

Summer Cabin Cartoons. 2nd ed. Wm. Armstrong. (Armstrong Cartoon Ser.). (Illus.). 48p. (gr. 1-6). 1972. pap. 1.00 (ISBN 0-913452-11-4). Jesuit Bks.

Summer Camp. Judy Gitenstein. (Skylark Choose Your Own Adventure Ser.: No. 18). 64p. (Orig.). (gr. 2-4). 1984. pap. 2.25 (ISBN 0-553-15562-8, Skylark). Bantam.

Summer Camp: A Guidebook for Parents. Alice Van Krevelen. LC 80-26726. (Illus.). 168p. 1981. 17.95 (ISBN 0-88229-296-X). Nelson-Hall.

Summer Camp Adventure. (ALF Storybooks). (Illus.). 24p. (ps-3). 1987. pap. 1.95 (ISBN 0-02-688553-0, Checkerboard Pr). Macmillan.

Summer Camp Creeps. Tim Schoch. 160p. (Orig.). (gr. 3-7). 1987. pap. 2.50 (ISBN 0-380-75343-X, Camelot). Avon.

Summer-Camp Nurse. Mary Lupton. 1985. 9.95 (ISBN 0-8034-8521-2, Avalon). Bouregy.

Summer Camps & Teen Tours: Everything Parents & Kids Should Know. Adrienne Popper. 68p. 1988. pap. 6.95 (ISBN 0-671-64726-1). PB.

Summer Captive. Penny Pollock. LC 86-63075. 184p. (YA) (gr. 7 up). 1987. 14.95 (ISBN 0-936915-06-4). McDonald Shoe Tree Pr.

Summer Cat. Howard Knotts. LC 79-9610. (Illus.). 48p. (gr. k-4). 1981. PLB 11.89 (ISBN 0-06-023179-3). HarpJ.

Summer Celestial. Stanley Plumly. (American Poetry Ser.: No. 27). 75p. 1983. 13.50 (ISBN 0-88001-029-0). Ecco Pr.

Summer Celestial, No. 27. Stanley Plumly. (American Poetry Ser.). 75p. 1985. pap. 7.50 (ISBN 0-88001-084-3). Ecco Pr.

Summer Charade. Karen T. Whittenburg. (American Romance Ser.: No. 197). 245p. Date not set. pap. 2.50 (ISBN 0-317-63682-0). Harlequin Bks.

Summer Children: Ready of Not for School. James K. Uphoff et al. (Illus.). 114p. 1986. pap. 12.95 (ISBN 0-9618561-0-6). J&J Pub Co.

Summer Chills. J. H. Rodes. (YA) (gr. 7 up). 1985. 9.95 (ISBN 0-8034-8507-7, Avalon). Bouregy.

Summer Companions. Olivia Manning. (Inflation Fighter Ser.). 192p. 1982. pap. write for info. (ISBN 0-8439-1120-4, Leisure Bks). Leisure NY.

Summer Computer Simulation Conference Proceedings, Boston, 2 vols. 1984. Set. 90.00 (ISBN 0-317-17120-8). Soc Computer Sim.

Summer Computer Simulation Conference Proceedings: Chicago. 1985. 75.00 (ISBN 0-317-60945-9). Soc Computer Sim.

Summer Computer Simulation Conference Proceedings: Reno. 1986. 90.00 (ISBN 0-317-60949-1). Soc Computer Sim.

Summer Computer Simulation Conference Proceedings: Vancouver, Vol. 2. 1983. 30.00 (ISBN 0-317-17119-4). Soc Computer Sim.

Summer Computer Simulation Conference Proceedings, 1987: Montreal. 1987. 90.00 (ISBN 0-911801-20-0). Soc Computer Sim.

Summer Computer Simulation Conference Proceedings: 1981 (Washington, D. C.) 750p. pap. 50.00 ea. Soc Computer Sim.

Summer Computer Simulation Conference, 1982: Proceedings (Denver) 678p. 1982. softbound 50.00 (ISBN 0-686-38788-0). Soc Computer Sim.

Summer Cooking. Elizabeth David. (Illus.). 1980. pap. 5.95 (ISBN 0-14-046100-0). Penguin.

Summer Cooking. Elizabeth David. 240p. 1988. pap. 8.95 (ISBN 0-14-046794-7). Penguin.

Summer Cottages & Castles. Patricia Corbin. (Illus.). 160p. 1987. pap. 15.95 (ISBN 0-525-48357-8). Dutton.

Summer Cottages & Castles: Scenes from the Good Life. Patricia Corbin. (Illus.). 144p. 1983. 29.95 (ISBN 0-525-93279-8, 02908-870). Dutton.

Summer Cottages of Edwin Hale Lincoln. Ed. by Sno Publications. (Illus.). 72p. (Orig.). 1981. pap. 15.00. Sno Pubns.

Summer Cottages of Edwin Hale Lincoln see Pride of Palaces: Lenox Summer Cottages 1883-1933.

Summer Crossing. Steve Tesich. LC 82-40125. 373p. 1982. 14.45 (ISBN 0-394-52759-3). Random.

Summer Day. Douglas Florian. LC 87-8484. (Illus.). 24p. (ps-1). 1988. 11.95 (ISBN 0-688-07564-9); lib. bdg. 11.88 (ISBN 0-688-07565-7). Greenwillow.

Summer Days Gone: Thoughts & Reflections. J. P. Ballard. 37p. (Orig.). 1987. pap. text ed. 5.00 (ISBN 0-318-23405-X). Common Mans Symposium.

Summer Days with the Treelo Triplets. Mary M. Landis. 192p. (YA) 1971. 6.15 (ISBN 0-686-05591-8). Rod & Staff.

Summer Delights: Cooking with Fresh Herbs. Noel Richardson. (Illus.). 128p. 1986. spiral bd. 9.95 (ISBN 0-317-60787-1). Aris Bks Harris.

Summer Dreams. Patricia Bird. 1986. 9.95 (ISBN 0-8034-8611-1, Avalon). Bouregy.

Summer Dreams. Bill Gutman. (Going for it Ser.: No. 3). 144p. 1985. pap. 2.50 (ISBN 0-380-89901-9, Flare). Avon.

Summer Dreams. Dorothy Oxley. LC 84-71420. Orig. Title: Wheelchair Summer. 144p. (gr. 6-10). 1984. pap. 3.95 (ISBN 0-89107-319-1, Crossway Bks). Good News.

Summer Dresses. Stephanie Hallgren. Ed. by Desert First Works, Inc. 1977. pap. text ed. 2.50 (ISBN 0-916556-08-5). Desert First.

Summer Employment Directory of U. S., 1989. Ed. by Pat Beusterien. 312p. 1988. pap. 10.95 (ISBN 0-89879-340-8). Writers Digest.

Summer Employment Examination. Jack Rudman. (Career Examination Ser.: C-1663). (Cloth bdg. avail. on request). 1988. pap. 12.00 (ISBN 0-8373-1663-4). Natl Learning.

Summer Ends Now. John Emery. 164p. 1980. 15.95x (ISBN 0-7022-1467-1); pap. 7.95 (ISBN 0-7022-1468-X). U of Queensland Pr.

Summer Exhibition: Umezawg Gallery. Umezawa Gallery Staff. 1968. 60.00x (ISBN 0-317-45274-6, Pub. by Han-Shan Tang Ltd). State Mutual Bk.

Summer Feasts. Molly Finn. 1985. pap. 6.95 (ISBN 0-671-55453-0, Fireside). S&S.

Summer Fire. Douglas H. Thayer. 258p. (Orig.). 1983. pap. 7.95 (ISBN 0-941214-18-4, Orion). Signature Bks.

Summer Fires: New Poetry of Africa. Ed. by Angus Calder et al. (African Writers Ser.: No. 257). xii, 116p. 1984. pap. text ed. 7.00 (ISBN 0-435-90257-1). Heinemann Ed.

Summer Food. Judith Olney. LC 77-15870. 272p. 1983. pap. 7.95 (ISBN 0-689-70643-X, 292). Atheneum.

Summer Food Service Program for Children in New York City: Part 2, Report on Monitoring the Summer Food Service Program for Children in New York City. 1978. 1.00 (ISBN 0-686-05507-1). Comm Coun Great NY.

Summer for Joey. Lyle Glazier. LC 86-63092. 256p. 1987. pap. 9.95 (ISBN 0-912395-08-7). Millers River Pub Co.

Summer Friends. Peter McCurtin. 400p. (Orig.). 1983. pap. 3.50 (ISBN 0-8439-1167-0, Leisure Bks). Leisure NY.

Summer Fun. Carolyn Haywood. LC 85-25864. (Illus.). 128p. (gr. 1-4). 1986. 10.25 (ISBN 0-688-04958-3, Morrow Junior Books); lib. bdg. 10.88 (ISBN 0-688-04959-1). Morrow.

Summer Fun. Carolyn Haywood. (gr. 2-4). 1987. pap. 2.95 (ISBN 0-8167-1037-6). Troll Assocs.

Summer Game. Roger Angell. pap. 3.95 (ISBN 0-345-34192-9). Ballantine.

Summer Games Access, 1988: A Viewer's Guide to the Sports, Athletes, Records & Sites. Created by Richard S. Wurman. (Illus.). 108p. 1988. pap. 6.95 (ISBN 0-13-875840-9). P-H.

Summer Games for Adults & Children. Hereward Zigo. (Oleander Games & Pastimes Ser.: Vol. 6). (Illus.). 64p. 1982. 9.95 (ISBN 0-906672-05-8); pap. 4.95 (ISBN 0-906672-06-6). Oleander Pr.

Summer Ghost. Ruth Tomalin. (gr. 5-9). 1986. 15.95 (ISBN 0-571-13826-8). Faber & Faber.

Summer Ghost. Ruth Tomalin. (Lythway Ser.). (gr. 4-8). 1987. lib. bdg. 12.95x (ISBN 0-7451-0630-7, Pub. by Chivers Pr UK). G K Hall.

Summer Girls, Love Boys & Other Short Stories. Norma F. Mazer. LC 82-70320. 192p. (gr. 7 up). 1982. pap. 11.95 (ISBN 0-385-28930-8). Delacorte.

Summer Girls, Love Boys: And Other Short Stories. Norma F. Mazer. 256p. (gr. 7 up). 1986. pap. 2.95 (ISBN 0-440-98375-4, LFL). Dell.

Summer Harvest. Madge Swindells. 1986. pap. 3.95 (ISBN 0-451-13555-5, Sig). NAL.

Summer Heat! M. E. Cooper. (Couples (Special Edition) Ser.). 288p. (Orig.). (YA) (gr. 7 up). 1986. pap. 2.95 (ISBN 0-590-40236-6). Scholastic Inc.

Summer Heat. Maura Seger. (Now & Forever Ser.: No. 3). 1988. pap. 2.95 (Pageant). Crown.

Summer Helmets of the U. S. Army, 1875-1910. 2nd ed. Gordon Chappell. (Illus.). 34p. 1976. pap. 2.00 (ISBN 0-943398-05-3). Wyoming State Press.

Summer Holds Too Long & Rooting. Leslie C. Tompkins & Lynn H. Burgess. (Juniper Books: No. 52). 50p. 1988. 16.00 (ISBN 1-55780-105-3); pap. 9.00 (ISBN 1-55780-099-5). Juniper Pr WI.

Summer House Cookbook. Chris C. Madden. LC 78-71062. 192p. 1979. pap. 5.95 (ISBN 0-15-686302-2, Harv). HarBraceJ.

Summer Hum. Cornelia P. Draves. Ed. by Cornelia D. Baker. LC 84-60279. (Illus.). 160p. 1984. lib. bdg. 11.95 (ISBN 0-916335-00-3). Mimosa Pubns.

Summer in a Jar: Making Pickles, Jams & More. Andrea Chesman. Ed. by Susan Williamson. (Illus.). 160p. 1985. pap. 7.95 (ISBN 0-913589-14-4). Williamson Pub Co.

Summer in El Salvador. Larry K. Jones. Ed. by Tom McKernan & Lana H. Davis. 310p. 1988. 19.95 (ISBN 0-940513-00-5). World Promos.

Summer in Italy. Sean O'Faolain. 9.95 (ISBN 0-8159-6831-0). Devin.

Summer in the City: A Novel. Mark Stevens. 1984. 16.45 (ISBN 0-394-53187-6). Random.

Summer in the Enchanted Forest. (Enchanted Forest Ser.). (Illus.). (ps-1). 1985. 2.98 (ISBN 0-517-46981-2). Outlet Bk Co.

Summer in the South. James Marshall. (Illus.). (gr. 1 up). 1977. 6.95 (ISBN 0-395-25840-5). HM.

Summer in the Spring: Ojibwe Lyric Poems & Tribal Stories. Gerald Vizenor. (Illus.). 157p. 1981. pap. 1.00 (ISBN 0-931714-15-X). Nodin Pr.

Summer in the Street of the Prophets & A Voyage to Ur of the Chaldees: The First Two Novels of the Palace of Shattered Vessels. David Shahar. Tr. by Dalya Bilu. 1988. 22.50 (ISBN 1-55584-068-X). Weidenfeld.

Summer in the Sun. Jan Gelman. 1983. pap. text ed. 1.95 (ISBN 0-671-46393-4). Archway.

Summer in the Twenties. Peter Dickinson. LC 80-8652. 256p. 1987. pap. 4.95 (ISBN 0-394-75186-8). Pantheon.

Summer in Williamsburg. Daniel Fuchs. 380p. 1983. pap. 8.95 (ISBN 0-88184-006-8). Carroll & Graf.

Summer Institute of Linguistics: Its Works & Contributions. Ed. by Ruth M. Brend & Kenneth L. Pike. 1977. pap. 26.25x (ISBN 90-279-3355-3). Mouton.

Summer Intern. Jack Rudman. (Career Examination Ser.: C-1499). (Cloth bdg. avail. on request). pap. 12.00 (ISBN 0-8373-1499-2). Natl Learning.

Summer Is... Charlotte Zolotow. LC 82-45185. (Illus.). 32p. (gr. k-4). 1983. 13.70i (ISBN 0-690-04303-1, Crowell Jr Bks); PLB 13.89 (ISBN 0-690-04304-X). HarpJ.

Summer Is from Winter Until Winter. Sigrid Olesen. (Illus.). 80p. 1980. 4.95 (ISBN 0-936748-02-8); pap. 3.50. Fade In.

Summer Is Here! Jane B. Moncure. LC 75-12945. (Illus.). (ps-2). 1975. 7.95 (ISBN 0-913778-12-5). Childs World.

Summer Is Here! Jane B. Moncure. LC 75-12945. (Seasons Awareness Bks.). (Illus.). 24p. (ps-2). 1975. PLB 11.93 (ISBN 0-516-05858-4). Childrens.

Summer Is the Cote d'Azur. Michael Gifkins. 144p. 1987. pap. 6.95 (ISBN 0-14-009732-5). Penguin.

Summer Isn't Forever. Patricia S. Rivas. 176p. 1984. pap. 2.25 (ISBN 0-441-79093-3, Pub by Tempo). Ace Bks.

Summer Jobs: Finding Them, Getting Them, Enjoying Them. Sandra Schocket. LC 84-22645. 170p. (Orig.). 1985. pap. 5.95 (ISBN 0-87866-325-8). Petersons Guides.

Summer Jobs in Britain, 1989. Ed. by Susan Griffith. 174p. (Orig.). 1988. pap. 9.95 (ISBN 0-907638-93-7, Pub. by Vacation-Work England). Writers Digest.

Summer Journey in the West. facsimile ed. Eliza R. Steele. LC 75-123. (Mid-American Frontier Ser.). 1975. Repr. of 1841 ed. 24.50x (ISBN 0-405-06888-3). Ayer Co Pubs.

Summerhaven. Linda Masterson. (Illus.). 1979. pap. 1.95 (ISBN 0-89083-471-7). Zebra.
Summerhays' Encyclopedia for Horsemen. R. S. Summerhays. 1988. 90.00x (ISBN 0-901366-44-7, Pub. by Harrap Ltd England). State Mutual Bk.
Summerhaze. Kate O'Hara. (Harlequin Romances Ser.). 192p. 1983. pap. 1.75 (ISBN 0-373-02560-2). Harlequin Bks.
Summerhill: A Radical Approach to Child Rearing. A. S. Neill. 1984. pap. 4.95 (ISBN 0-671-81302-1, Wallaby). PB.
Summerhills. D. E. Stevenson. 311p. 1976. lib. bdg. 18.95x (ISBN 0-89966-162-9). Buccaneer Bks.
Summering on Nantucket. Ed. by Bruce Courson. (Illus.). 49p. 1986. 9.95 (ISBN 0-9607340-6-6). Nantucket Hist Assn.
Summerisch-Akkadische Parallelen Zum Aufbau Alttestamentlicher Psalmen. Friedrich Stummer. Repr. of 1922 ed. 15.00 (ISBN 0-384-58710-0). Johnson Repr.
Summerland. Ed. by Alec Shoate & Barbara Y. Main. 242p. 1980. 21.95x (ISBN 0-85564-166-5, Pub. by U of West Australia Pr Australia). Intl Spec Bk.
Summers & Sabbaticals: Selected Papers on Psychology & Education. Fred S. Keller. 169p. 1986. 19.95 (ISBN 0-8290-1968-5). Irvington.
Summer's Chance. Patricia H. Easton. LC 87-17728. 160p. (YA) (gr. 12 up). 1988. 13.95 (ISBN 0-15-200591-9, Gulliver Bks). HarBraceJ.
Summer's Day. Joel Meyerowitz. LC 84-40642. (Illus.). 156p. 1985. 39.45 (ISBN 0-8129-1182-2); special ltd. ed. A 750.00 (ISBN 0-8129-1194-6); special ltd. ed. B 750.00 (ISBN 0-8129-1195-4); special ltd. ed. C 750.00 (ISBN 0-8129-1196-2). Times Bks.
Summer's Day. Photos by Joel Meyerowitz. (Illus.). 1987. pap. 17.95 (ISBN 0-8129-1643-3). Times Bks.
Summer's End. Danielle Steel. 384p. 1980. pap. 4.95 (ISBN 0-440-18405-3). Dell.
Summers Fly, Winters Walk. Charles M. Schulz. LC 77-73859. (Peanuts Parade Books: No. 21). (Illus.). 192p. (gr. 4-6). 1977. pap. 4.95 (ISBN 0-8050-0216-2). H Holt & Co.
Summer's King. Cherry Wilder. LC 85-20057. 264p. (gr. 7-12). 1986. 15.95 (ISBN 0-689-31118-4, Atheneum Children Bks). Macmillan.
Summer's King. Cherry Wilder. 1987. pap. 2.95 (ISBN 0-671-65617-1). Baen Bks.
Summer's Lease. John Mortimer. 1988. 19.95 (ISBN 0-670-81984-0). Viking.
Summer's Lease. Marilyn Sachs. LC 78-12486. (gr. 5 up). 1979. 9.25 (0898-270). Dutton.
Summers of the Wild Rose. Rosemary Harris. 188p. 1988. 11.95 (ISBN 0-571-14702-X). Faber & Faber.
Summers on Oil & Gas. write for info. West Pub.
Summers on the Saranacs. Maitland C. De Sormo. LC 80-81853. (Illus.). 1980. 30.00 (ISBN 0-9601158-6-2). North Country.
Summer's Quest. Suzanne Elliott. (Lindsey Ser.). (Illus.). 144p. (YA) (gr. 7-9). 1987. pap. 3.95 (ISBN 0-87403-269-5, 2946). Standard Pub.
Summer's Tale. Marcia S. Andrews. LC 86-51051. 240p. (Orig.). 1987. pap. 10.95 (ISBN 0-931328-10-1). Timely Bks.
Summer's Witness. Saranne Dawson. (American Romance Ser.). pap. 2.75 (ISBN 0-373-16222-7). Harlequin Bks.
Summertime. David L. Fleming. LC 85-20827. (Illus.). 410p. (Orig.). 1986. 22.50 (ISBN 0-87565-060-0); pap. 12.95 (ISBN 0-87565-061-9). Tex Christian.
Summertime. Maureen McCoy. 288p. 1987. 15.95 (ISBN 0-671-62187-4, Poseidon). PB.
Summertime. Maureen McCoy. 304p. 1988. pap. 6.95 (ISBN 0-671-62188-2). WSP.
Summertime, Bibletime. William DeAngelis. LC 86-51543. (Illus.). 144p. (Orig.). 1987. pap. 19.95 (ISBN 0-89622-322-1). Twenty-Third.
Summertime Eating for a Healthy Heart: Cook Out-Camp Out-Eat Out the Low Cholesterol Way. Eleanor P. Betz et al. (Illus.). 60p. 1981. pap. 3.95 (ISBN 0-686-31628-2). Rush-Presby-St Lukes.
Summertime Soldiers. Susan Kelley. 192p. 1986. 14.95 (ISBN 0-8027-5646-8). Walker & Co.
Summing & Nuclear Norms in Banach Space Theory. (London Mathematical Society Students Text Ser.: No. 8). 192p. 1987. 39.50 (ISBN 0-521-34134-5); pap. 13.95 (ISBN 0-521-34937-0). Cambridge U Pr.
Summing up. W. Somerset Maugham. LC 75-25377. (Works of W. Somerset Maugham Ser.). 1977. Repr. of 1938 ed. 20.00x (ISBN 0-405-07830-7). Ayer Co Pubs.
Summing Up. W. Somerset Maugham. 1978. pap. 4.95 (ISBN 0-14-001852-2). Penguin.
Summing Up the Black Panther Party see Leadership.
Summing up: The Science of Reviewing Research. Richard J. Light & David B. Pillemer. LC 84-4506. (Illus.). 224p. 1984. text ed. 18.50x (ISBN 0-674-85430-6); pap. text ed. 7.95x (ISBN 0-674-85431-4). Harvard U Pr.
Summit. Richard Bowker. (Spectra Ser.). 288p. 1989. pap. 3.95 (ISBN 0-553-27710-3, Spectra). Bantam.
Summit. D. M. Thomas. 1988. 15.95 (ISBN 0-670-81921-2). Viking.
Summit: A Gold Rush History of Summit County, Colorado. Mary E. Gilliland. LC 80-65781. (Illus.). 336p. (Orig.). 1980. pap. text ed. 13.50 (ISBN 0-9603624-0-1). Alpenrose Pr.
Summit Conference. Robert D. MacDonald. (Illus.). 64p. 1983. pap. 4.00 (ISBN 0-88145-009-X). Broadway Play.
Summit Conferences, 1919-1960. Keith Eubank. (Illus.). 1966. 16.50x (ISBN 0-8061-0716-2). U of Okla Pr.
Summit County Cemetary Inscriptions, 2 vols. 100p. 1980. Vol. 1. 7.00 (ISBN 0-686-28156-X); Vol. 2. 7.00 (ISBN 0-686-28157-8). Summit Cnty OH.
Summit Diplomacy. Elmer Plischke. LC 73-16629. 125p. 1974. Repr. of 1958 ed. lib. bdg. 35.00x (ISBN 0-8371-7199-7, PLSD). Greenwood.
Summit Diplomacy: A Learning Package. Gary K. Bertsch & James M. Rosenbluth. (CISE Learning Packages in International Studies). 49p. (Orig.). 1980. pap. text ed. 4.00x (ISBN 0-936876-37-9). LRIS.
Summit Hiker. Mary E. Gilliland. LC 83-71361. (Illus.). 97p. (Orig.). 1983. pap. text ed. 9.95 (ISBN 0-9603624-2-8). Alpenrose Pr.
Summit Living. Norman P. Grubb. 368p. 1985. 9.95 (ISBN 0-317-43397-0); pap. 7.95 (ISBN 0-87508-267-X). Chr Lit.
Summit Meetings & Collective Leadership in the 1980's. William C. Turner & Harold B. Malmgren. 69p. 1980. 5.00 (ISBN 0-317-33698-3). Atlantic Council US.
Summit of Sun. Joe D. Johnson. 35p. 1977. pap. 3.00 (ISBN 0-915564-03-3). Joe D Johnson.
Summit Season. Nancy E. Lay. (Illus.). 1988. price not set (ISBN 0-88011-339-1). Leisure Pr.
Summit: Treaty of Peace. Edward S. Lax. 90p. Date not set. lib. bdg. 30.00 (ISBN 0-9620530-0-7). Hist Bks Ltd.
Summits, Level 1, Bk. B. Jo M. Stanchfield et al. LC 77-83336. (Vistas Ser.). (Illus., Gr. 7). (gr. 7). 1978. pap. text ed. 8.92 (ISBN 0-395-25226-1); tchr's guide 7.28 (ISBN 0-395-25232-6); skillbk 5.08 (ISBN 0-395-25238-5); tchr's annot ed. skillbk 5.44 (ISBN 0-395-25244-X). HM.
Summits Move with the Tide. 2nd ed. Mei Mei Berssenbrugge. 70p. (Orig.). pap. 4.00 (ISBN 0-912678-56-9). Greenfld Rev Pr.
Summits of God Life: Samadhi & Siddhi. Sri Chinmoy. LC 80-65397. 145p. 1984. pap. 4.95 (ISBN 0-88497-145-7). Aum Pubns.
Summits of Samivel. Samivel. (Illus.). 108p. 1986. 29.95 (ISBN 0-9616970-0-8). Alta House.
Summits to Reach: Report on the Topography of the San Juan Country. Franklin Rhoda. Ed. by Mike Foster. LC 84-15135. (Illus.). 168p. 1984. pap. 7.95 (ISBN 0-87108-667-0). Pruett.
Summitt. William P. McGivern. 496p. 1986. pap. 4.50 (ISBN 0-441-79089-5, Pub. by Charter Bks). Ace Bks.
Summon Up Remembrance. Marzieh Gail. (Illus.). 320p. 1987. 28.50 (ISBN 0-85398-258-9); pap. 15.75 (ISBN 0-85398-259-7). G Ronald Pub.
Summoned by Knox: Poems in Scots. Alan Bold. 84p. 1985. pap. 12.95 (ISBN 0-905075-20-X, Pub. by Wilfion Bks Scotland). Dufour.
Summoned by Love. Carlo Carretto. Tr. by Alan Neame from Ital. LC 78-962. Orig. Title: Padre Mio me abbandono a Te. 1978. pap. 5.95 (ISBN 0-88344-472-0). Orbis Bks.
Summoned: Poems. Diana O'Hehir. LC 76-16011. (Breakthrough Books). 64p. 1976. 6.95 (ISBN 0-8262-0204-7). U of Mo Pr.
Summoning. Dana Reed. 368p. (Orig.). 1988. pap. 3.95 (ISBN 0-8439-2656-2, Pub. by Leisure Bks CT). Leisure NY.
Summoning of Every Man. LC 71-133741. (Tudor Facsimile Texts. Old English Plays: No. 5). Repr. of 1912 ed. 49.50 (ISBN 0-404-53305-1). AMS Pr.
Summoning Tablets of Guilds in Hungary. P. Bagybakay. 1981. 18.00x (ISBN 0-317-57365-9, Pub. by Collets UK). State Mutual Bk.
Summoning the Familiar: Powers & Rites of Common Life. Eileen Gregory. 90p. 1984. pap. 8.00 (ISBN 0-911005-04-8). Dallas Inst Pubns.
Summoning the Gods: Sandpainting of the Native American Southwest. Ronald McCoy. (Plateau Ser.). (Illus.). 32p. 1988. pap. 4.95 (ISBN 0-89734-059-0). Mus Northern Ariz.
Summons & Sign. Dagmar Nick. Tr. by Jim Barnes from Ger. LC 80-18367. Orig. Title: Zeugnis & Zeichen. (Illus.). 124p. (Orig.). 1980. pap. 3.00 (ISBN 0-933428-02-2). Chariton Review.
Summons of Death on the Medieval & Renaissance English Stage. Phoebe S. Spinrad. LC 87-5487. 304p. 1987. 30.00x (ISBN 0-8142-0443-0). Ohio St U pr.
Summons of the Trumpet. Dave R. Palmer. 384p. 1984. pap. 3.95 (ISBN 0-345-31583-9). Ballantine.
Summons of the Trumpet: U. S.-Vietnam in Perspective. Dave R. Palmer. LC 77-28339. (Illus.). 294p. 1978. 17.95 (ISBN 0-89141-041-4). Presidio Pr.
Summons to Memphis. Peter Taylor. LC 86-45417. 224p. 1986. 15.95 (ISBN 0-394-41062-9). Knopf.
Summons to Memphis. Peter Taylor. 224p. 1987. pap. 4.95 (ISBN 0-345-34660-2). Ballantine.
Summons to Memphis. Peter Taylor. 319p. 1987. 18.95 (ISBN 0-8161-4305-6). G K Hall.
SUMMUM: Sealed, Except to the Open Mind. Summum Bonum Amen Ra. LC 87-91265. 126p. 1988. pap. 7.00 (ISBN 0-943217-00-8); wkbk. 11.00 (ISBN 0-943217-01-6). Summum.
Summur Bird Feeding: Audubon Workshop Guide to Feeding Wild Birds in Summer. John V. Dennis. (Illus.). 130p. 1989. pap. 8.95 (ISBN 0-9620001-0-8). Audubon Workshop.
Summy Piano Solo Package: Advanced, No. 501. (Summy Piano Solo Package Ser.). (Illus.). 32p. (gr. 10-12). 1976. pap. text ed. 5.95 (ISBN 0-87487-656-7). Birch Tree Gr.
Summy Piano Solo Package: Elementary, No. 101. (Summy Piano Solo Package Ser.). (Illus.). 32p. (Orig.). (gr. k-2). 1976. pap. text ed. 5.95 (ISBN 0-87487-652-4). Birch Tree Gr.
Summy Piano Solo Package: Intermediate, No.301. (Summy Piano Solo Package Ser.). (Illus.). 32p. (Orig.). (gr. 5-8). 1976. pap. text ed. 5.95 (ISBN 0-87487-654-0). Birch Tree Gr.
Summy Piano Solo Package: Late Elementary, No.201. (Summy Piano Solo Package Ser.). (Illus.). 32p. (Orig.). (gr. 2-6). 1976. pap. text ed. 5.95 (ISBN 0-87487-653-2). Birch Tree Gr.
Sumner County, Tennessee: Abstracts of Will Books 1 & 2 (1788-1842) Edythe R. Whitley. LC 78-60960. 84p. 1980. pap. 6.00 (ISBN 0-8063-0825-7). Genealog Pub.
Sumo: From Rite to Sport. P. L. Cuyler. (Illus.). 232p. pap. 12.50 (ISBN 0-8348-0203-1). Weatherhill.
Sumo: History, Rites, Traditions. Patricia L. Cuyler. LC 79-18859. (Illus.). 1979. 16.50 (ISBN 0-8348-0145-0). Weatherhill.
Sumo: Le Sport et le Sacre. Laurent R. Martres. (Illus.). 144p. (Fr.). 1985. pap. text ed. 12.95 (ISBN 0-916189-01-5). Graphie Intl.
Sumo: The Sport & the Tradition. J. A. Sargeant. LC 59-5993. (Illus.). 1959. pap. 4.95 (ISBN 0-8048-1084-2). C E Tuttle.
Sumptuary Law in Nuernberg: A Study in Paternal Government. Kent R. Greenfield. LC 78-63964. (Johns Hopkins University. Studies in the Social Sciences. Thirty-Sixth Ser. 1918: 2). Repr. of 1918 ed. 16.50 (ISBN 0-404-61211-3). AMS Pr.
Sumptuary Legislation & Personal Regulation in England. Frances E. Baldwin. LC 78-64119. (Johns Hopkins University. Studies in the Social Sciences. Forty-Fourth Ser. 1926: 1). Repr. of 1926 ed. 24.50 (ISBN 0-404-61233-4). AMS Pr.
Sums of Independent Random Variables. V. V. Petrov. Tr. by A. A. Brown. LC 75-5766. (Ergebuisse der Mathematik Ser.: Vol. 82). 360p. 1975. text ed. 56.00 (ISBN 0-387-06635-7). Springer-Verlag.
Sun. Isaac Asimov. LC 87-42595. (Isaac Asimov's Library of the Universe). (Illus.). 32p. (gr. 3-4). 1988. PLB 10.95 (ISBN 1-55532-350-2). Stevens Inc.
Sun. George Blattman. 240p. (Orig.). 1985. pap. text ed. 16.95 (ISBN 0-88010-148-2). Anthroposophic.
Sun. Keith Brandt. LC 84-2715. (Illus.). 32p. (gr. 3-6). 1985. PLB 8.45 (ISBN 0-8167-0190-3); pap. text ed. 1.95 (ISBN 0-8167-0191-1). Troll Assocs.
Sun. Heather Couper & Nigel Henhest. LC 85-51135. (Space Scientist Ser.). (Illus.). 32p. (gr. 4-9). 1987. PLB 11.90 (ISBN 0-531-10055-3). Watts.
Sun. Karl O. Kiepenheuer. Tr. by A. J. Pomerans. LC 59-7294. (Ann Arbor Science Library). pap. 40.00 (ISBN 0-317-09534-X, 2051047). Bks Demand UMI.
Sun. Christopher Lampton. (First Bks). (Illus.). 72p. (gr. 4 up). 1982. PLB 10.40 (ISBN 0-531-04390-8). Watts.
Sun. Patrick Moore. (Illus.). 1968. 4.95 (ISBN 0-393-06276-7). Norton.
Sun. Kate Petty. (First Library). (Illus.). 32p. (gr. 1-6). 1985. PLB 10.90 (ISBN 0-531-10027-8). Watts.
Sun. Seymour Simon. LC 85-32018. (Illus.). 32p. (ps-3). 1986. 13.95 (ISBN 0-688-05857-4, Morrow Junior Books); lib. bdg. 12.88 (ISBN 0-688-05858-2, Morrow Junior Books). Morrow.
Sun Also Rises. Ernest Hemingway. (Arabic.). pap. 8.95x (ISBN 0-686-63550-7). Intl Bk Ctr.
Sun Also Rises. Ernest Hemingway. (Library Reprint Editions). 1984. 27.50x (ISBN 0-684-15327-0, ScribT); pap. 8.95 (ISBN 0-684-71808-1, ScribT). Scribner.
Sun Also Rises. Ernest Hemingway. 256p. 1982. pap. 4.95 rack size (ISBN 0-684-17472-3, ScribT). Scribner.
Sun Also Rises. Ernest Hemingway. 256p. 1983. 18.95 (ISBN 0-684-10250-1, ScribT). Scribner.
Sun Also Rises. Ernest Hemingway. 48p. (Orig.). 1987. pap. 9.95 (ISBN 1-55651-825-0); cassette (ISBN 1-55651-826-9). Cram Cassettes.
Sun Also Rises. Ernest Hemingway. 256p. 1987. pap. 4.95 (ISBN 0-02-051870-6, Collier). Macmillan.
Sun Also Rises see Three Novels.
Sun Also Rises: A Novel of the Twenties. Michael S. Reynolds. (Masterwork Studies). 118p. 1988. 17.95 (ISBN 0-8057-7962-0, Twayne); pap. 6.95 (ISBN 0-8057-8015-7, Twayne). G K Hall.
Sun Also Rises: Hemingway. Dunn. (Book Notes Ser.). 1984. pap. 2.50 (ISBN 0-8120-3443-0). Barron.
Sun Also Rises Notes. Gary K. Carey. (Orig.). 1968. pap. 3.50 (ISBN 0-8220-1237-5). Cliffs.
Sun Always Shines for the Cool; Midnight Moon at the Greasy Spoon; Eulogy for a Small Time Thief. Miguel Pinero. LC 83-72582. 128p. (Orig.). 1983. pap. 10.00 (ISBN 0-934770-25-5). Arte Publico.
Sun & Catriona. Rosemary Pollock. (Harlequin Romance Ser.). 192p. 1982. pap. 1.50 (ISBN 0-373-02486-X). Harlequin Bks.
Sun & Earth: A Scientific American Book. H. Friedman. 251p. 1987. 32.95 (ISBN 0-317-63619-7). W H Freeman.
Sun & Its Family. rev. ed. Irving Adler. LC 68-57377. (Illus.). (gr. 5-9). 1969. PLB 12.89 (ISBN 0-381-99983-1, A76000, Crowell Jr Books). HarpJ.
Sun & Light. Neil Ardley. (Action Science Ser.). 32p. (gr. k-3). 1983. PLB 11.90 (ISBN 0-531-04616-8). Watts.
Sun & Moon: Fairy Tales from Korea. Adapted by Kathleen Seros. LC 82-82510. (Illus.). 61p. (gr. 3-9). 1982. PLB 14.50x (ISBN 0-930878-25-6). Hollym Intl.
Sun & Moon Polarity in Your Horoscope. Robert Hughes. LC 77-92771. 6.00 (ISBN 0-86690-116-7). Am Fed Astrologers.
Sun & Planetary System. Ed. by W. Fricke & G. Teleki. 1982. 65.00 (ISBN 90-277-1429-0, Pub. by Reidel Holland). Kluwer Academic.
Sun & Saddle Leather. Reissue ed. Badger Clark. 190p. 9.95 (ISBN 0-318-02288-5). Westerners Intl.
Sun & Solar System Debris. William R. Corliss. LC 86-60231. (Catalog of Astronomical Anomalies Ser.). (Illus.). 300p. 1986. 17.95 (ISBN 0-915554-20-8). Sourcebook.
Sun & Stars. Norman Barrett. LC 85-50161. (Picture Library Ser.). (Illus.). 32p. (gr. k-6). 1986. lib. bdg. 10.90 (ISBN 0-531-10007-3). Watts.
Sun & Steel. Yukio Mishima. Tr. by John Bester from Japanese. 176p. 1972. pap. 4.95 (ISBN 0-394-17765-7, E583, Ever). Grove.
Sun & the Clouds. Menahem Stern. (gr. 3-6). 1972. 6.95x (ISBN 0-87068-389-6). Ktav.
Sun & the Heliosphere in Three Dimensions. Ed. by R. G. Marsden. (Astrophysics & Space Science Library). 1986. lib. bdg. 79.00 (ISBN 90-277-2198-X, Pub. by Reidel Holland). Kluwer-Academic.
Sun & the Ionosphere: Short-Wave Solar Radiation and Its Effects on the Ionosphere. G. S. Ivanov-Kholodnyi et al. 376p. 1971. text ed. 72.50x (ISBN 0-7065-1180-8, Pub. by Keter Pub Jerusalem). Coronet Bks.
Sun & the Moon. Adapted by & tr. by Mark C. Setton. (Korean Folk Tales Ser.: No. 10). (Illus.). 32p. (Eng. & Korean.). (gr. 1-8). 1986. PLB write for info. (ISBN 0-87296-009-9, Pub. by Si-sa-yong-o-sa Korea); bilingual cassette incl. Si-sa-yong-o-sa.
Sun & the Moon. Niccolo Tucci. 1977. 13.95 (ISBN 0-394-46640-3). Knopf.
Sun & the Shade: Florida Photography, 1885-1983. Bruce Weber. LC 83-50606. (Illus.). 95p. 1983. pap. 10.00 (ISBN 0-943411-14-9). Norton Gal Art.
Sun & the Shadow: My Experiment with Lucid Dreaming. Kenneth Kelzer. 332p. (Orig.). 1987. pap. 9.95 (ISBN 0-87604-195-0). ARE Pr.
Sun & the Wind. Cornelia Lehn. (Illus.). 32p. (gr. k-5). 1983. 7.95 (ISBN 0-87303-072-9). Faith & Life.
Sun & the Wind. Cornelia Lehn. LC 32-+010. 32p. 1987. 7.95 (ISBN 0-8361-3466-4). Herald Pr.
Sun & Time Dial Book. John Mellor. (Illus.). 32p. (gr. 3 up). 1985. pap. cancelled (ISBN 0-317-30503-4). Parkwest Pubns.
Sun Angles for Design. Robert Bennett. LC 78-103157. 1978. pap. 10.00 (ISBN 0-9601718-1-9). Bennett Arch & Eng.
Sun Artists (Original Series, Nos. 1-8. Ed. by W. Arthur Boord. LC 72-9184. (Literature of Photography Ser.). Repr. of 1891 ed. 44.00 (ISBN 0-405-04895-5). Ayer Co Pubs.
Sun As Architect's Helper: Solar Houses - The Popular View, 1980-1985. Dale E. Casper. (Architecture Ser.: A 1583). 9p. 1986. 3.00 (ISBN 0-89028-813-5). Vance Biblios.
Sun at Noon: An Anatomy of Modern Japan. Dick Wilson. 266p. 1988. 32.95 (ISBN 0-241-11839-5, Pub. by Hamish Hamilton). David & Charles.
Sun Bear: The Path of Power. Sun Bear et al. LC 83-72949. (Illus.). 272p. 1984. pap. 9.95 (ISBN 0-943404-03-7). Bear Tribe.
Sun Bear the Path of Power: Sun Bear, Wabun & Barry Weinstock. (Illus.). 272p. (Orig.). 1987. pap. 9.95 (ISBN 0-13-653403-1). P-H.
Sun Bear's Book of the Vision Quest: Personal Transformation in the Wilderness. Steven Foster & Meredith Little. (Illus.). 172p. (Orig.). 1987. pap. 9.95 (ISBN 0-13-080110-0). P-H.
Sun Betrayed: A Report on the Corporate Seizure of U. S. Solar Energy Development. Ray Reece. LC 79-66992. 234p. 1979. 20.00 (ISBN 0-89608-072-2); pap. 7.50 (ISBN 0-89608-071-4). South End Pr.
Sun-Blazoned. Judy Hogan. 90p. 1983. pap. 5.00 (ISBN 0-916324-11-7, Sunbury Pressbooks). Carolina Wren.
Sun Calendar. Una Jacobs & Una Jacobs. LC 85-30317. (Illus.). 40p. (gr. 3 up). 1986. 8.96 (ISBN 0-382-09217-1); pap. 5.75 (ISBN 0-382-09220-1). Silver.
Sun Came Down: The History of the World as My Blackfeet Elders Told It. Percy Bullchild. LC 85-42771. (Illus.). 384p. 1985. 22.45 (ISBN 0-06-250107-0, HarpR). Har-Row.

Sunan Abu Dawud, Vol. I-III. A. Hasan. 85.00 (ISBN 0-317-14639-4). Kazi Pubns.
Sunbathing with the Professors: Poems of the Eastern Shore. Gilbert Byron. (Illus., Orig.). 1982. 17.95 (ISBN 0-9615275-1-X); pap. 5.95 (ISBN 0-9615275-0-1). Unicorn Bkshop.
Sunbeam Alpine & Tiger, 1959-1967. R. M. Clarke. (Brooklands Bks.). (Illus., Orig.). 1980. pap. 13.95 (ISBN 0-906589-57-6, Pub. by Brooklands Bks England). Motorbooks Intl.
Sunbeam Owners Handbook of Maintenance & Repair: Rapier, Alpine, & Tiger. Clymer Publications Staff. (Illus.). pap. 8.95 (ISBN 0-89287-253-5, A189). Clymer Pub.
Sunbeam Portable Electric Cookery. Bonnie Brown. LC 74-121732. 6.95 (ISBN 0-87502-008-9); pap. 1.95 (ISBN 0-685-30861-8). Benjamin Co.
Sunbeam S7 & S8. (Super Profile MC Ser.). 8.95 (ISBN 0-85429-363-9, F363, Pub. by G T Foulis Ltd). Haynes Pubns.
Sunbeams & Golden Nuggets. James Weekley. (Orig.). 1988. pap. 2.25 (ISBN 0-937172-80-4). JLJ Pubs.
Sunbelly. Kenneth Fields. Ed. by Jan Schreiber. LC 73-81066. (Chapbook Series One). 1974. 5.00 (ISBN 0-87923-078-9). Godine.
Sunbelt Cities: Politics & Growth since World War II. Ed. by Richard M. Bernard & Bradley R. Rice. LC 83-10222. 358p. 1983. pap. 12.95 (ISBN 0-292-77580-6). U of Tex Pr.
Sunbelt City? A Study of Economic Change in Britain's M4 Growth Corridor. Martin Boddy et al. (Inner City in Context Ser.). (Illus.). 240p. 1986. pap. 16.95x (ISBN 0-19-823265-9). Oxford U Pr.
Sunbelt Designs, No. A72: Outdoor Living...Indoors. Ed. by National Plan Service Staff. (Illus., Orig.). 1988. pap. 3.95 (ISBN 0-934039-27-5). Natl Plan Serv.
Sunbelt Retirement. updated & exp. ed. Peter A. Dickinson. 367p. 1986. pap. 11.95 (ISBN 0-673-24832-1). Am Assn Retire.
Sunbelt-Snowbelt Controversy: The War over Federal Funds. Robert J. Dilger. 240p. 1984. 35.00x; pap. 12.50x. NYU Pr.
Sunbelt-Snowbelt: Urban Development & Regional Restructuring. Ed. by Larry Sawers & William K. Tabb. 1984. pap. 11.95x (ISBN 0-19-503265-9). Oxford U Pr.
Sunbird. Arthur Dobrin. (Illus.). 64p. signed ed. 15.00 (ISBN 0-89304-046-0); pap. 3.95 (ISBN 0-89304-012-6). Cross Cult.
Sunbonnet Babies Book. (gr. k-2). 5.35 (ISBN 0-87497-104-7, 2373B). Merrimack.
Sunbonnet Babies Primer. (gr. k-2). 5.00 (ISBN 0-87497-105-5, 23735). Merrimack.
Sunbonnet Family of Quilt Patterns. Dolores A. Hinson. LC 83-7113. 280p. 1984. 19.95 (ISBN 0-668-05864-1, 5864); pap. 13.95 (ISBN 0-668-05987-7). Arco.
Sunbrite Laundry Company: A Computerized Practice Set for a Service Establishment - Apple & IBM Edition. Rocco M. Santoro et al. (Career Accounting Ser.). 25p. 1984. pap. 8.95 (ISBN 0-471-80857-1). Wiley.
Sunburn, Vol 1, No. 1. Ed. by H. Dieter Rickford. Bd. with Vol. 1, No. 1. Fogbound. 84p. (Orig.). 1986. pap. 10.00 (ISBN 0-942098-07-2). Class Media Prod.
Sunburn Lake. Tom De Haven. LC 87-40456. 320p. 1988. 18.95 (ISBN 0-670-80930-6). Viking.
Sunburst. Phyllis Gotlieb. LC 78-21557. 160p. 1978. 15.00 (ISBN 0-8398-2500-5). Ultramarine Pub.
Sunburst. Mauricio Magdaleno. Tr. by Anita Brenner from Span. LC 74-25390. Repr. of 1944 ed. 17.50 (ISBN 0-404-58449-7). AMS Pr.
Sunburst Farm Family Cookbook. rev. ed. Susan Duquette. LC 78-70916. (Illus.). 256p. (Orig.). 1978. pap. 7.95 (ISBN 0-912800-60-7). Woodbridge Pr.
Sunburst Production Manual. International Export Trading & Supply, Inc. 86p. 1984. text ed. 20.00 (ISBN 0-89904-021-7); composition 10.00 (ISBN 0-89904-022-5). Crumb Elbow Pub.
Sunburst Tropical Fruit Company Cookbook. Nita Grochowski & Mel Meo. (Illus.). 1987. 20.00. Sunburst Tropical Fruit.
Sunburstay. Jeanne Grant. (To Have & to Hold Ser.: No. 14). Date not set. pap. 1.95 (ISBN 0-317-04566-0). Jove Pubns.
Sunbursts for the Spirit. C. W. Vandenbergh. LC 79-90313. (Sunbursts for the Spirit Ser.: Vol. 1). (Illus.). 56p. (Orig.). 1979. pap. 3.25 (ISBN 0-935238-02-6). Pine Row.
Suncatchers Stained Glass Pattern Book: One Hundred Nineteen Designs. Connie Eaton. (Illus.). 64p. (Orig.). 1987. pap. 3.95 (ISBN 0-486-25470-4). Dover.
Suncell: Energy, Economy & Photovoltaics. Christopher C. Swan. LC 85-18394. (Illus.). 240p. 1986. 17.95 (ISBN 0-87156-751-2, Dist. by Random). Sierra.
Suncoast Seasons. Dunedin Youth Guild Staff. (Illus.). 430p. 1984. 13.95 (ISBN 0-9613858-0-4). Dunedin Youth.
SUNCODE Documentation & User's Manual. Larry Palmiter & Terry Wheeling. 235p. 1981. ringbinder 35.00 (ISBN 0-934478-29-5). Ecotope.
Sunda & Sahul: Prehistoric Studies in Southeast Asia, Melenasia & Australia. Ed. by J. Allen et al. 1977. 106.00 (ISBN 0-12-051250-5). Acad Pr.
Sundance: Apache War. Peter McCurtin. (Sundance Ser.: No. 34). 192p. 1985. pap. 2.25 (ISBN 0-8439-2285-0, Leisure Bks). Leisure NY.
Sundance: Scorpion. Peter McCurtin. (Sundance Ser.). 208p. 1985. pap. 2.25 (ISBN 0-8439-2223-0, Leisure Bks). Leisure NY.
Sundance: Trail Drive. Peter McCurtin. 192p. 1986. pap. 2.50 (ISBN 0-8439-2384-9, Leisure Bks). Leisure NY.
Sundancer. Edward Hays. LC 82-83135. (Illus.). 64p. (Orig.). 1982. pap. 5.95 (ISBN 0-939516-04-7). Forest Peace.
Sundara Kandam of Srimad Valmiki Ramayana. Valmiki. Tr. by Swami Tapasyananda. 286p. 1984. 11.50 (ISBN 0-87481-527-4, Pub. by Ramakrishna Math Madras India). Vedanta Pr.
Sunday. Denys Cazet. LC 87-15313. (Illus.). 64p. (gr. 1-4). 1988. PLB 11.95 (ISBN 0-02-717970-2). Bradbury Pr.
Sunday. Phoebe MacAdams. 100p. (Orig.). 1983. pap. 6.00 (ISBN 0-939180-20-0). Tombouctou.
Sunday after Sunday: Preaching the Homily as a Story. Robert Waznak. LC 82-62922. 128p. (Orig.). 1983. pap. 4.95 (ISBN 0-8091-2540-4). Paulist Pr.
Sunday Afternoon: Grande Ronde. George Venn. (Illus.). 1975. 5.00 (ISBN 0-915986-03-5); pap. 2.50 (ISBN 0-915986-04-3). Prescott St Pr.
Sunday Best. Bernice Rubens. 224p. 1984. pap. 3.95 (ISBN 0-671-50279-4). WSP.
Sunday Best. John K. Sherman. 4.95 (ISBN 0-87018-057-6). Ross.
Sunday Bloody Sunday. Penelope Gilliatt. 126p. 1986. 16.95 (ISBN 0-396-08492-3); pap. 8.95 (ISBN 0-396-08539-3). Dodd.
Sunday Came Early This Week. Luleen S. Anderson. 140p. 1982. pap. 9.95 (ISBN 0-87073-575-6). Schenkman Bks Inc.
Sunday Church School Teacher. Richard S. Hanson. 1986. 5.95 (ISBN 0-89536-796-3, 6814); leader's guide 1.75 (ISBN 0-89536-806-4, 6824). CSS of Ohio.
Sunday: Day of Light. H. Boone Porter. 104p. 1988. pap. 6.95 (ISBN 0-912405-40-6). Pastoral Pr.
Sunday Dinner. William H. Willimon. LC 81-52215. 1981. pap. 4.50x (ISBN 0-8358-0429-1). Upper Room.
Sunday Doorposts. Timothy R. Botts. LC 87-6177. (Illus.). 128p. (Orig.). 1987. pap. 9.95 (ISBN 1-55612-078-8). Sheed & Ward MO.
Sunday Driver. Brock Yates. (Illus.). 258p. 1972. 7.95 (ISBN 0-374-27183-6). FS&G.
Sunday Express Book of European Holidays. Lewis De Fries. (Illus.). 202p. 1985. pap. 7.95 (ISBN 0-86072-076-4, Pub. by Quartet Bks). Salem Hse Pubs.
Sunday Father. John Neufeld. (Signet Young Adult Mystery Ser.). 160p. (YA) (RL 6). 1977. pap. 1.50 (ISBN 0-451-07292-8, W7292, Sig Vista). NAL.
Sunday Habit. Jim Mele. 1978. pap. 3.00 (ISBN 0-916696-07-3). Cross Country.
Sunday in the Park with George: A Musical. Stephen Sondheim & James Lapine. LC 85-27473. 204p. 1986. 16.95 (ISBN 0-396-08600-4). Dodd.
Sunday Laws of the United States & Leading Judicial Decisions Having Special Reference to the Jews. Albert M. Friedenberg. LC 12-23685. 42p. 1986. pap. 18.00 (ISBN 0-89941-475-3). W S Hein.
Sunday Mass: What Part Do You Play? Robert Rietcheck & Daniel Korn. 32p. 1985. pap. 1.50 (ISBN 0-89243-235-7). Liguori Pubns.
Sunday Mayhem: A Celebration of Pro Football in America. Dick Whittingham. (Illus.). 368p. 1987. pap. 13.95 (ISBN 0-87833-548-X). Taylor Pub.
Sunday Morning. David Rogers. LC 86-90807. 95p. (Orig.). 1986. pap. 6.95 (ISBN 0-9618064-0-0). D Rogers NY.
Sunday Morning. Judith Viorst. LC 68-24333. (Illus.). 32p. (ps-2). 1968. pap. 3.95 (ISBN 0-689-70447-X, Aladdin). Macmillan.
Sunday Morning: A Time for Worship. Ed. by Mark Searle. LC 82-15306. 200p. (Orig.). 1982. pap. 5.95 (ISBN 0-8146-1259-8). Liturgical Pr.
Sunday Morning Alive, Bk. I. Shirley Pollock. (Orig.). 1987. pap. 6.50 (ISBN 0-89536-887-0, 7873). CSS of Ohio.
Sunday Morning: Aspects of Urban Ritual. Michael H. Ducey. LC 76-25342. 1977. 17.00 (ISBN 0-02-907640-4). Free Pr.
Sunday Morning Insights. Eugene F. Lauer. 252p. 1984. pap. 8.95 (ISBN 0-8146-1361-6). Liturgical Pr.
Sunday Morning We Went to the Zoo. Deborah Ray. LC 80-7915. (Illus.). 32p. (ps-2). 1981. PLB 10.89 (ISBN 0-06-024842-4). HarpJ.
Sunday Night Sermons. Edward Fudge. pap. 2.00 (ISBN 0-686-12685-8). E Fudge.
Sunday No Sabbath: A Sermon. John Pocklington. LC 74-28881. (English Experience Ser.: No. 759). 1975. Repr. of 1636 ed. 20.00 (ISBN 90-221-0759-0). Walter J Johnson.
Sunday of Life. Raymond Queneau. Tr. by Barbara Wright from Fr. LC 76-49628. 1977. 12.00 (ISBN 0-8112-0645-9); pap. 3.95 (ISBN 0-8112-0646-7, NDP433). New Directions.
Sunday Readings. Albert J. Nevins. LC 84-60748. 172p. 1984. pap. 2.95 (ISBN 0-87973-734-4, 734). Our Sunday Visitor.
Sunday Readings. Kevin O'Sullivan. Incl. Cycle A. 428p. 1971. (ISBN 0-8199-0481-3); Cycle B. 487p. 1972. (ISBN 0-8199-0482-1); Cycle C. 444p. 1970. (ISBN 0-8199-0483-X). LC 74-141766. 9.00 ea. Franciscan Herald.
Sunday School Basics. Ed. by Floyd D. Carey. 1976. 5.25 (ISBN 0-87148-778-0); pap. 4.25 (ISBN 0-87148-777-2). Pathway Pr.
Sunday School Evangelical Commentary. Ed. by James Humbertson. write for info. (ISBN 0-87148-315-7). Pathway Pr.
Sunday School Evangelism. Earl P. Paulk. 1958. 4.95 (ISBN 0-87148-759-4). Pathway Pr.
Sunday School Growth. J. Martin Baldree. 1971. 5.25 (ISBN 0-87148-761-6); pap. 4.25 (ISBN 0-87148-762-4). Pathway Pr.
Sunday School Growth & Renewal: How to Reach, Teach, Care, Share. Millie S. Goodson. LC 84-71642. 76p. (Orig.). 1984. DR014B. pap. 3.75 (ISBN 0-88177-014-0). Discipleship Res.
Sunday-School Movement, 1780-1917, & the American Sunday-School Union, 1817-1917. Edwin W. Rice. LC 70-165728. (American Education Ser, No. 2). (Illus.). 1971. Repr. of 1917 ed. 36.00 (ISBN 0-405-03717-1). Ayer Co Pubs.
Sunday School Outreach. W. W. Thomas. 112p. 1979. 5.25 (ISBN 0-87148-787-X); pap. 4.25 (ISBN 0-87148-788-8). Pathway Pr.
Sunday School Outreach Instructor's Guide. 1979. pap. 4.95 (ISBN 0-87148-789-6). Pathway Pr.
Sunday School Spirit. Stephen V. Rexroat. LC 79-51833. (Sunday School Staff Training Ser.). 128p. (Orig.). 1979. pap. 1.50 (ISBN 0-88243-594-9, 02-0594). Gospel Pub.
Sunday School Teacher. O. W. Polen. 1956. pap. 5.25 (ISBN 0-87148-765-9). Pathway Pr.
Sunday School Teacher's Guide, 1984. William S. Deal. 1984. pap. 3.95 (ISBN 0-318-18717-5). Crusade Pubs.
Sunday School: The Formation of an American Institution. Anne M. Boylan. LC 87-34588. 1988. text ed. 26.50 (ISBN 0-300-04019-9). Yale U Pr.
Sunday Scriptures. Daniel Sullivan & Judy Andrews. 4.95 (ISBN 0-8091-9336-1). Paulist Pr.
Sunday Seducer. Linda DuBreuil. 1975. pap. 1.50 (ISBN 0-685-52173-7, LB246DK, Leisure Bks). Leisure NY.
Sunday Services of the Methodists in North America. John Wesley. 144p. (Orig.). 1984. pap. 4.95 (ISBN 0-687-40632-3). Abingdon.
Sunday Sister. large print ed. Charline Brians. 24p. 1985. pap. 4.00 (ISBN 0-914009-53-2). VHI Library.
Sunday Song. Shaerie Cosgrove. (Sing! Ser.). 32p. (ps-3). 1988. pap. 7.95 (ISBN 0-8249-7272-4). Ideals.
Sunday Suppers: Informal American Home Cooking. Melanie Barnard & Brooke Dojny. (Illus.). 256p. 1989. pap. 19.45 (ISBN 0-13-875832-8). Prentice Hall Pr.
Sunday Telegraph Business Finance Directory 1987. Ed. by J Carr. 1987. lib. bdg. 158.00 (ISBN 0-86010-828-7, Pub. by Graham & Trotman UK); pap. 123.00 (ISBN 0-86010-827-9). Kluwer Academic.
Sunday the Rabbi Stayed Home. Harry Kemelman. (Rabbi Ser.). 224p. 1985. pap. 3.50 (ISBN 0-449-21000-6, Crest). Fawcett.
Sunday Throughout the Week. Gaynell Cronin. LC 81-68992. (Illus.). 176p. (Orig.). 1981. pap. 6.95 (ISBN 0-87793-241-7). Ave Maria.
Sunday Times Book of Brain Teasers. Bryant & Ronald Posthill. 1988. pap. 3.95 (ISBN 0-312-90338-3). St Martin.
Sunday Times Book of Brain Teasers. Victor Bryant & Ronald Postill. LC 81-21429. (Illus.). 160p. 1982. pap. 5.95x (ISBN 0-312-77565-2). St Martin.
Sunday Times Book of Woodland & Wildflower Gardening. Graham Rose. (Illus.). 128p. 1988. 24.95 (ISBN 0-7153-9112-7). David & Charles.
Sunday Times Guide to Enlightened Eating: How to Buy, Cook & Store Food for Pleasure, Nourishment & Health. Lis Leigh. (Illus.). 128p. 1987. pap. 18.95 (ISBN 0-7126-1400-1, Pub. by Century Hutchinson). David & Charles.
Sunday Times Self Help Directory. Gillel Price. 300p. 1980. 15.95x (ISBN 0-8464-1241-1). Beekman Pubs.
Sunday Word: A Commentary on the Sunday Readings. Dom H. Wansbrough. 400p. 1984. pap. 14.95 (ISBN 0-225-66254-X, HarpR). Har-Row.
Sunday Words for a Monday World. Gaylord L. Lehman. 75p. (Orig.). 1986. pap. 6.95 (ISBN 0-938828-03-7). Falls Tar.
Sunday Work, 1794-1856. LC 72-2547. (British Labour Struggles Before 1850 Ser). (7 pamphlets). 1972. 12.00 (ISBN 0-405-04438-0). Ayer Co Pubs.
Sunday Worship. Kevin W. Irwin. 1983. pap. 14.95 (ISBN 0-916134-52-0). Pueblo Pub Co.
Sunday Zebras. Art Holst. 1981. 12.00 (ISBN 0-9605118-0-6). Forest Pub.
Sunday 2.0 Documentation & User's Manual. Davis Straub. Ed. by Larry Palmiter et al. (Illus.). 57p. 1984. looseleaf binder 35.00 (ISBN 0-934478-36-8). Ecotope.
Sunday's Child. Joyce Bright. 256p. 1988. pap. 8.95 (ISBN 0-941483-12-6). Naiad Pr.
Sunday's Child. Gudrun Mebs. LC 85-20629. 144p. (gr. 3-6). 1986. 10.95 (ISBN 0-8037-0192-6, 01063-320); PLB 10.89 (ISBN 0-8037-0197-7). Dial Bks Young.
Sunday's Child. Edward Phillips. 240p. 1987. 15.95 (ISBN 0-312-01097-4). St Martin.
Sunday's Child. Edward Phillips. (Stonewall Inn Editions Ser.). 240p. 1988. pap. 7.95 (ISBN 0-312-02294-8). St Martin.
Sunday's Children: Prayers in the Language of Children. James L. Bitney & Suzanne Schaffhausen. LC 86-60172. (Illus.). 65p. (Orig.). 1986. 9.95 (ISBN 0-89390-076-1); pap. 5.95 (ISBN 0-89390-110-5). Resource Pubns.
Sunday's Foyer. Calvin Grondahl. (Illus.). 96p. 1983. pap. 4.95 (ISBN 0-9606760-3-1). Sunstone Found.
Sunday's Mail. Gene S. Jones. Ed. by John Sollami. 96p. (Orig.). 1987. pap. 7.95 (ISBN 0-9618601-0-3). Gladiola Pr.
Sunday's Women: Lesbian Life Today. Sasha G. Lewis. LC 78-53655. 232p. 1981. pap. 9.95 (ISBN 0-8070-3795-8, BP622). Beacon Pr.
Sundial. Gillian Clarke. 55p. 1984. 21.00x (ISBN 0-85088-540-X, Pub. by Gomer Pr). State Mutual Bk.
Sundial. Shirley Jackson. (Penguin Fiction Ser.). 256p. 1986. pap. 5.95 (ISBN 0-14-008317-0). Penguin.
Sundial. L. C. Morse. LC 86-60034. 192p. 1986. 15.00 (ISBN 0-937167-00-2). Stonehill Pr.
Sundial Years. Alida Harvie. (Illus.). 152p. 1984. 30.00 (ISBN 0-7212-0663-8, Pub. by Regency Pr). State Mutual Bk.
Sundials: How to Know, Use, & Make Them. 2nd ed. R. Newton Mayall & Margaret W. Mayall. LC 73-76242. (Illus.). 1973. 12.95 (ISBN 0-933346-11-5). Sky Pub.
Sundials, Their Theory & Construction. Albert E. Waugh. (Illus.). 14.75 (ISBN 0-8446-4835-3). Peter Smith.
Sundials: Theory & Construction. Albert E. Waugh. (Orig.). 1973. pap. 4.50 (ISBN 0-486-22947-5). Dover.
Sundiver. David Brin. 1980. pap. 3.95 (ISBN 0-553-25594-0). Bantam.
Sundown. John J. Mathews. LC 88-40214. 328p. 1988. pap. 11.95 (ISBN 0-8061-2160-2). U of Okla Pr.
Sundown Breed. Dan Parkinson. 240p. 1986. pap. 2.50 (ISBN 0-8217-1860-6). Zebra.
Sundown Man-Sunday in Choctaw Country. Shad Denver & Brett McKinley. 1980. pap. 1.75 (ISBN 0-8439-0732-0, Leisure Bks). Leisure NY.
Sundown Searchers. Jon Sharpe. (Trailsman Ser.: No. 4). (Orig.). 1980. pap. 2.50 (ISBN 0-451-12200-3, AE2200, Sig). NAL.
Sundowners. Jon Cleary. 22.95 (ISBN 0-88411-467-8, Pub. by Aeonian Pr). Amereon Ltd.
Sundrinker. Zach Hughes. 272p. 1987. pap. 3.50 (ISBN 0-88677-213-3). DAW Bks.
Sundry Great Gentlemen. Marjorie Bowen. 359p. 1980. Repr. lib. bdg. 30.00. Century Bookbindery.
Sundry Great Gentlemen: Some Essays in Historical Biography. facs. ed. Marjorie Bowen. LC 68-29192. (Essay Index Reprint Ser). 1968. Repr. of 1928 ed. 20.00 (ISBN 0-8369-0230-0). Ayer Co Pubs.
SUNE Ceramic Designs. Jan Wirgen. (Illus.). 43p. 1979. 65.00 (ISBN 0-87556-746-0). Saifer.
Sunfall. C. J. Cherryh. 1983. pap. 2.50 (ISBN 0-87997-881-3, UE1881). DAW Bks.
Sunfire Boxed Set, 3 vols. Incl. Laura. Vivian Schurfranz; Susannah. Candice F. Ransom; Joanna. Jane C. Miner. (gr. 7 up). 1985. Set. pap. 8.85 (ISBN 0-590-37817-1, Sunfire). Scholastic Inc.
Sunflower. Leo Aylen. 1983. pap. text ed. cancelled (ISBN 0-8290-1300-8). Irvington.
Sunflower. Walt Curtis. 1975. pap. 2.00 (ISBN 0-685-65549-0). Out of the Ashes.
Sunflower. Charles B. Heiser, Jr. LC 74-15906. (Illus.). 198p. 1981. pap. 7.95 (ISBN 0-8061-1743-5). U of Okla Pr.
Sunflower. Jill M. Landis. 1988. pap. 3.95 (ISBN 0-425-11171-7). Jove Pubns.
Sunflower. P. S. Vasudev. 15.00 (ISBN 0-89253-776-0); flexible cloth 6.75 (ISBN 0-89253-777-9). Ind-US Inc.
Sunflower. Rebecca West. 320p. 1987. 18.95 (ISBN 0-670-81386-9). Viking.
Sunflower. Rebecca West. 288p. 1988. pap. 7.95 (ISBN 0-14-009497-0). Penguin.
Sunflower Forest. Torey L. Hayden. 1984. 15.95 (ISBN 0-399-12946-4, Putnam). Putnam Pub Group.
Sunflower Forest. Torey L. Hayden. 416p. 1985. pap. 3.95 (ISBN 0-380-69922-2). Avon.
Sunflower Sampler. Ed. by Junior League of Wichita, Inc. LC 73-88177. 236p. 1985. pap. 9.95 (ISBN 0-9609676-0-5). Jr League Wichita.
Sunflower School. Doris Stupka & Joe Jenkins. (Orig.). 1987. pap. 5.00 (ISBN 0-916801-01-2). Inst Univ.
Sunflower Science & Technology. Ed. by Jack Carter. 1978. 17.50 (ISBN 0-89118-054-0). Am Soc Agron.
Sunflower Splendor. Liu Wu-Chi & Lo. 630p. 1975. pap. 42.00x (ISBN 0-317-69415-4, Pub. by Han-Shan Tang Ltd). State Mutual Bk.
Sunflower: With a Symposium. Simon Wiesenthal. LC 75-35446. 1977. pap. 7.95 (ISBN 0-8052-0578-0). Schocken.
Sunflowering. Bob Stanish. (gr. 4-12). 1977. 7.95 (ISBN 0-916456-12-9, GA69). Good Apple.
Sunflowers. Cynthia Overbeck. LC 80-27797. (Lerner Natural Science Bks.). (Illus.). (gr. 4-10). 1981. PLB 12.95 (ISBN 0-8225-1457-5). Lerner Pubns.

TITLE INDEX SUNSHINE BOYS: LOBBYISTS, INTEREST

Sunflowers. Kathleen Pohl. (Nature Close-Ups Ser.). (Illus.). 32p. (gr. 3-4). 1986. PLB 15.33 (ISBN 0-8172-2710-5); pap. text ed. 9.27 (ISBN 0-8172-2728-8). Raintree Pubs.
Sunflowers. facs. ed. Compiled by Willard Wattles. LC 78-133077. (Granger Index Reprint Ser). 1916. 16.00 (ISBN 0-8369-6207-9). Ayer Co Pubs.
Sung Biographies, 3 Vols. Herbert Franke. xxxii, 1272p. (Orig.). 1976. Parts 1-3. 125.00 set (ISBN 3-515-02412-3, Pub. by Franz Steiner). Coronet Bks.
Sung Biographies: Painters, Pt. 4. Herbert Franke. viii, 158p. (Orig.). 1976. pap. text ed. 20.00x (ISBN 3-515-02547-2, Pub. by Franz Steiner). Coronet Bks.
Sung Ceramic Designs. Jan Wirgin. 274p. 1979. 130.00 (ISBN 0-317-43709-7, Pub. by Han-Shan Tang Ltd). State Mutual Bk.
Sung-Ming. Jan Wirgin. 76p. 1965. pap. 170.00x (Pub. by Han-Shan Tang Ltd). State Mutual Bk.
Sung-Ming: Treasures from the Holgar Lauritzer Collection. Jan Wirgin. 76p. 1965. 75.00x (ISBN 0-317-45276-2, Pub. by Han-Shan Tang Ltd). State Mutual Bk.
Sung Porcelain & Stoneware. Basil Gray. LC 83-20668. (Illus.). 205p. 1984. 65.00 (ISBN 0-571-13048-8). Faber & Faber.
Sung Porcelain & Stoneware. Basil Gray. 205p. 1984. 300.00x (ISBN 0-317-44217-1, Pub. by Han-Shan Tang Ltd). State Mutual Bk.
Sung Sherds. N. Palmgren & W. Steger. 505p. 1963. lacquered leather bdg. 1300.00x (Pub. by Han-Shan Tang Ltd). State Mutual Bk.
Sung Sherds. N. Palmgren et al. 505p. 1963. 550.00x (ISBN 0-317-45280-0, Pub. by Han-Shan Tang Ltd). State Mutual Bk.
Sung to Sharyar. E. P. Mathers. 128p. 1987. 70.00x (ISBN 1-85077-146-4, Pub. by Darf Pubs Ltd). State Mutual Bk.
Sungates: A Testimony Carved in Wood. Victor Hajdu. Tr. by Rose Stein. (Illus., Hungarian.). 1980. 15.00 (ISBN 0-933652-16-X). Domjan Studio.
Sunk-in Action. R. H. Freeman. 380p. 1986. 19.95 (ISBN 0-931099-05-6). Shellback Pr.
Sunken Pirate or, Frank Reade Jr. in Search of Treasure at the Bottom of the Sea, Vol. 5. Luis Senarens. (Frank Reade Library). 1985. lib. bdg. 57.00 (ISBN 0-8240-3544-5). Garland Pub.
Sunken Red. Jeroen Brouwers. 144p. 1988. 15.95 (ISBN 0-941533-19-0). New Amsterdam Bks.
Sunken Ships & Treasure. John C. Fine. LC 86-3652. (Illus.). 128p. (gr. 3 up). 1986. 16.95 (ISBN 0-689-31280-6, Atheneum Childrens Bk). Macmillan.
Sunken Treasure. Gail Gibbons. LC 87-30114. (Illus.). 32p. (gr. 1-5). 1988. 12.95i (ISBN 0-690-04734-7, Crowell Jr Bks); PLB 12.89 (ISBN 0-690-04736-3, Crowell Jr Bks). HarpJ.
Sunken Treasure. Edward Packard. 1982. 6.95 (ISBN 0-553-05018-4); 2.25 (ISBN 0-553-15464-8). Bantam.
Sunken Treasure Mystery. Jack Long. (O'Reilly Mysteries Ser.). (Illus.). 24p. (ps-3). 1987. 3.95 (ISBN 0-02-688776-2, Checkerboard Pr). Macmillan.
Sunken Treasure: Six Who Found Fortunes. Robert F. Burgess. (Illus.). 224p. 1988. 19.95 (ISBN 0-396-08848-1). Dodd.
Sunkist Case: A Study in Legal-Economic Analysis. Willard F. Mueller et al. LC 86-46242. 288p. 1987. 34.95x (ISBN 0-669-15189-0). Lexington Bks.
Sunlight & Health. Michael J. Lillyquist. LC 84-21084. 272p. 1985. 15.95 (ISBN 0-396-08482-6). Dodd.
Sunlight & Health: The Positive & Negative Effects of the Sun on You. Michael J. Lillyquist. 1987. pap. 7.95 (ISBN 0-396-08957-7). Dodd.
Sunlight & Shadow. Ed. by Adams W. Lincoln. LC 76-24669. (Sources of Modern Photography Ser.). (Illus.). 1979. Repr. of 1897 ed. lib. bdg. 17.00x (ISBN 0-405-09646-1). Ayer Co Pubs.
Sunlight & Shadow: The Art of Alfred R. Mitchell, 1888-1972. Thomas R. Anderson & Bruce A. Kamerling. LC 88-11429. (Illus.). 84p. pap. 24.95 (ISBN 0-918740-08-8). San Diego Hist.
Sunlight & Shadow: The Life & Art of Willard Leroy Metcalf. Elizabeth De Veer & Richard J. Boyle. (Illus.). 288p. 1988. 85.00 (ISBN 0-89659-753-9). Abbeville Pr.
Sunlight & Shadows: Portraits of Priorities for Living & Dying. Louis R. Batzler. (Illus.). 60p. (Orig.). 1986. pap. 4.95 (ISBN 0-936241-39-X). Hid Valley MD.
Sunlight & Song: A Singer's Life. Maria Jeritza. Ed. by Andrew Farkas. Tr. by Frederick H. Martens. LC 76-29942. (Opera Biographies). (Illus.). 1977. Repr. of 1929 ed. lib. bdg. 27.50x (ISBN 0-405-09684-4). Ayer Co Pubs.
Sunlight Could Save Your Life. Zane R. Kime. LC 80-51038. 312p. 1980. 15.95 (ISBN 0-9604268-0-9); pap. 11.95 (ISBN 0-9604268-1-7). World Health.
Sunlight Dialogues. John Gardner. LC 86-40156. 758p. 1987. pap. 6.95 (ISBN 0-394-74394-6, Vin). Random.
Sunlight Dialogues. John C. Gardner. 1982. pap. 6.95. Ballantine.
Sunlight Dialogues. John C. Gardner. 1973. pap. 1.95. Ballantine.
Sunlight: Friend or Foe. David J. Gerrick. 1978. 20.00 (ISBN 0-916750-56-6). Dayton Labs.
Sunlight in the Morning: Songs from the Farm. Rochester Folk Art Guild. (Illus.). 40p. (gr. k-6). 1983. 15.00 (ISBN 0-686-40298-7); cassette tape 5.00. Rochester Folk Art.
Sunlight on a Broken Column. Attia Hosain. 319p. 1981. pap. 5.25 (ISBN 0-86578-066-8). Ind-US Inc.
Sunlight on the Wall: Selected Poems. Bert Meyers. 1977. pap. 50.00 (ISBN 0-685-67045-7). Story Line.
Sunlight on Your Doorstep. Bradley L. Morison. 3.95 (ISBN 0-87018-044-4); pap. 1.95 (ISBN 0-87018-073-8). Ross.
Sunlight to Electricity: Prospects for Solar Energy Conversion by Photovoltaics. Joseph A. Merrigan. LC 75-6933. 192p. (Orig.). 1975. pap. 6.95 (ISBN 0-262-63072-9). MIT Pr.
Sunlighting As Formgiver for Architecture. William Lam. (Illus.). 576p. 1986. 78.95x (ISBN 0-442-25941-7). Van Nos Reinhold.
Sunlit Path. Mother. 194p. 1984. pap. 4.95 (ISBN 0-89071-318-9, Pub. by Sri Aurobindo Ashram India). Aurobindo Assn.
Sunlit Road: Readings in Verse & Prose for Every Day. Horder W. Garrett. 1978. Repr. of 1908 ed. lib. bdg. 20.00 (ISBN 0-8492-5242-3). R West.
Sunlit Slopes. Priscilla Klepser. 68p. 1984. 7.95 (ISBN 0-533-05870-8). Vantage.
Sunnah. S. M. Yousaf. pap. 1.50 (ISBN 0-686-18419-X). Kazi Pubns.
Sunnier Side: Twelve Arcadian Tales. facsimile ed. Charles R. Jackson. LC 70-157779. (Short Story Index Reprint Ser.). Repr. of 1950 ed. 19.00 (ISBN 0-8369-3891-7). Ayer Co Pubs.
Sunny Day Bunny. Linda Hayward. (Happy Day Shape Bks.). (Illus.). 12p. (ps-1). 1986. 5.95 (ISBN 0-448-10452-0, G&D). Putnam Pub Group.
Sunny Days, Lonely Nights: Sunshine Hawks. Ed. by Thomas L. Hakes. (Illus.). 20p. pap. 3.00x (ISBN 0-317-38232-2). Bardic.
Sunny, Funny Stories. Betty Donatelli. (Happy Learning Ser.). (Illus.). 11p. (Orig.). (gr. 1-2). 1984. pap. 1.00 (ISBN 0-912981-08-3). Hse Bon Giovanni.
Sunny Hours. Alice Usher. LC 83-82780. (Illus.). 40p. (Orig.). (ps-2). 1983. pap. 8.95 (ISBN 0-88138-018-0). Green Tiger Pr.
Sunny Morning: Teddy Horsley Celebrates the New Life of Easter. Leslie J. Francis & Nicola M. Slee. (Teddy Horsley Books for Young Christians). (Illus.). 24p. (ps-2). 1986. pap. 1.25 (ISBN 0-00-599781-X, Collins Liturgical). HarpR.
Sunny Sentences: Sight Word Activities to Cut & Paste. Ellen Sussman. (Illus.). (gr. 1-2). 1978. pap. 4.95 (ISBN 0-933606-02-8, MS-600). Monkey Sisters.
Sunny Side of Castro Street. Dan Vojir. LC 81-14344. (Illus., Orig.). 1982. pap. 6.95 (ISBN 0-89407-034-7). Strawberry Hill.
Sunny Side of Genealogy. Fonda D. Baselt. 102p. 1988. 8.95 (385). Genealog Pub.
Sunny-Side Up. Alma Barkman. (Quiet Time Bks.). 1984. pap. 3.50 (ISBN 0-8024-8431-X). Moody.
Sunny Side Up. Patricia R. Giff. (Kids of the Polk Street School Ser.: No. 11). (Orig.). (gr. k-3). 1986. pap. 2.50 (ISBN 0-440-48406-5, YB). Dell.
Sunny Side Up. Patricia R. Giff. (Kids of the Polk Street School Ser.). (Illus.). (ps-2). 1986. pap. 8.95 (ISBN 0-385-29476-X). Delacorte.
Sunny Side Up. Valiska Gregory. LC 85-27418. (Mr. Poggle & Scamp Bks.). (Illus.). 24p. (ps-k). 1986. 8.95 (ISBN 0-02-738050-5, Four Winds); bds. 3.95 (ISBN 0-02-738060-2). Macmillan.
Sunny Side Up. Compiled By Junior League of Ft. Lauderdale. (Illus.). 1980. stacon binder 11.95 (ISBN 0-9604158-0-7). Jr League Ft Lauderdale.
Sunny Side Up: Diet Cooking the Hospital Way. Alan McLaren & Indianapolis Community Hospital Staff. LC 76-11308. 1977. 15.95 (ISBN 0-87949-062-4). Ashley Bks.
Sunny Slopes of Long Ago. Ed. by Wilson M. Hudson & Allen Maxwell. LC 65-24930. (Texas Folklore Society Publications: No. 33). (Illus.). 214p. 1966. 12.95 (ISBN 0-87074-082-2). SMU Press.
Sunny Start: Getting Ready for Kindergarten. Ellen Sussman & Helen Johnson. (Illus.). 44p. (Orig.). (ps). 1983. pap. 5.95 (ISBN 0-933606-20-6, MS-611). Monkey Sisters.
Sunny Sunflower. Illus. by Pat Paris & Wendy All. (Rose-Petal Place Ser.). (Illus.). 14p. (ps-3). 1984. cancelled 4.00 (ISBN 0-910313-55-5). Parker Bros.
Sunny: The Death of a Pet. Judith E. Greenberg & Helen H. Carey. LC 85-29549. (My World Ser.). (Illus.). 32p. (gr. k-6). 1986. lib. bdg. 9.90 (ISBN 0-531-10102-9). Watts.
Sunny: The Life & Times of Sunny Von Bulow. James Southwood. Date not set. price not set. S&S.
Sunnyside Up. Martin Charlot. LC 73-173473. (Illus.). (gr. 1-7). 1972. 5.95. Island Heritage.
Sunpiper. Thompson. 1988. pap. 3.50 (ISBN 0-312-90706-0). St Martin.
Sunrise. Dominic Cooper. 224p. (Orig.). pap. 6.95 (ISBN 0-571-13956-6). Faber & Faber.
Sunrise. Grace L. Hill. 17.95 (ISBN 0-8488-0088-5, Pub. by Amereon Hse). Amereon Ltd.
Sunrise. Frederick Seidel. 1980. pap. 6.95 (ISBN 0-14-042280-3). Penguin.
Sunrise. 2nd ed. Yu Tsao. Tr. by A. C. Barnes from Chinese. (Illus.). 168p. 1978. 6.95 (ISBN 0-917056-73-6, Pub. by Foreign Lang Pr China). Cheng & Tsui.
Sunrise. White Eagle. 1958. 4.50 (ISBN 0-85487-016-4). DeVorss.
Sunrise All Day Long: Anthology. (Illus.). 24p. (Orig.). 1986. 5.00 (ISBN 0-914473-04-2). Stone Man Pr.
Sunrise & Shadow. Arthur O. Roberts. LC 84-62861. 112p. (Orig.). 1985. pap. 7.95 (ISBN 0-913342-48-3). Barclay Pr.
Sunrise & Sunset Tables for Key Cities & Weather Stations in the United States. United States. Nautical Almanac Office & Gale Research Company. LC 76-24796. 376p. 1977. 82.00x (ISBN 0-8103-0464-3). Gale.
Sunrise at Abadan: The British & Soviet Invasion of Iran, 1941. Richard A. Stewart. 1988. price not set (ISBN 0-275-92793-8, C2793). Praeger.
Sunrise Europe: The Dynamics of Information Technology. Ian Mackintosh. 304p. 1986. text ed. 24.95 (ISBN 0-631-14406-4). Basil Blackwell.
Sunrise in the Ricefield: Filipina's Life in the Philippines & in the United States. Date not set. price not set. Trudco Pub.
Sunrise Over Jordan: A Twenty-First Century College. Niels T. Andersen. LC 82-84240. 283p. 1982. 11.95 (ISBN 0-910213-01-1); pap. 6.95 (ISBN 0-910213-00-3). Jordan Pub.
Sunrise Route: A History of the Railroads of Washington County, Maine. Michael W. Zimmermann. (Illus.). 240p. (Orig.). 1985. 20.00 (ISBN 0-941216-27-6); pap. 12.50 (ISBN 0-941216-26-8). Cay-Bel.
Sunrise Song. Minnie Gilbert. (Illus.). 96p. 1984. 8.95 (ISBN 0-89015-468-6). Eakin Pr.
Sunrise-Sunset: Challenging the Myth of Industrial Obsolescence. Harvard Business Review Staff. Ed. by Alan M. Kantrow. LC 84-19580. (Harvard Business Review Executive Book Ser.: 1-583). (Illus.). 552p. 1985. 24.95 (ISBN 0-471-80573-4). Wiley.
Sunrise to Eternity: A Study in Jacob Boehme's Life & Thought. John J. Stoudt. LC 79-8626. Repr. of 1957 ed. 34.50 (ISBN 0-404-18492-8). AMS Pr.
Sunrise to Windward. Miles Smeeton. 272p. 1987. pap. 12.95 (ISBN 0-246-13171-3, Pub. by Collins England). Sheridan.
Sunrise Tomorrow: Coping with a Child's Death. Elizabeth B. Brown. 160p. 1988. 8.95 (ISBN 0-8007-1576-4). Revell.
Sunrise with Seamonsters. Paul Theroux. 1986. pap. 7.95 (ISBN 0-395-41501-2). HM.
Sunrise with Seamonsters: Travels & Discoveries 84. Paul Theroux. 365p. 1985. 18.95 (ISBN 0-395-38221-1). HM.
Sunrising. David Cook. LC 85-31045. 248p. 1986. 16.95 (ISBN 0-87951-253-9). Overlook Pr.
Sun's Asleep Behind the Hill. Mirra Ginsburg. LC 81-6615. (Illus.). 32p. (ps-1). 1982. 12.95 (ISBN 0-688-00824-0); PLB 12.88 (ISBN 0-688-00825-9). Greenwillow.
Sun's End. Richard A. Lupoff. 288p. 1984. pap. 2.95 (ISBN 0-425-08381-0). Berkley Pub.
Suns, Myths & Men. rev. ed. Patrick Moore. LC 68-27145. (Illus.). 1969. 7.95 (ISBN 0-393-06364-X). Norton.
Sun's Not Broken, A Cloud's Just in the Way. Sydney G. Clemens. (Illus.). 138p. 1987. pap. 8.95 (ISBN 0-87659-109-8). Acropolis.
Sun's Not Broken, A Cloud's Just in the Way: On Child-Centered Teaching. Sydney G. Clemens. 137p. (Orig.). 1984. pap. 8.95. Gryphon Hse.
Suns of Independence. Ahmadou Kourouma. Tr. by Adrian Adams from Fr. LC 80-8891. 160p. 1982. 17.50 (ISBN 0-8419-0626-2, Africana); pap. 11.50 (ISBN 0-8419-0747-1, Africana). Holmes & Meier.
Sun's Up. Illus. by Teryl Euvremer. (Illus.). (ps-2). 1987. PLB 9.95 (ISBN 0-517-56432-7). Crown.
Sunscream. (Executioner Ser.: No. 85). Date not set. pap. 2.25 (ISBN 0-317-63953-6, Pub. by Worldwide). Harlequin Bks.
Sunset. Hanoch Teller. 288p. 1987. 9.95 (ISBN 0-9614772-2-9). NYC Pub Co.
Sunset. 2nd ed. Hanoch Teller. (Illus.). 288p. (YA) (gr. 12). 1988. Repr. of 1987 ed. 9.95 (ISBN 0-317-68545-7). NYC Pub Co.
Sunset: A Schedule of State Sunset Reviews. 36p. 1983. 15.00 (ISBN 0-317-45882-5, RM 715). Coun State Govts.
Sunset at Izilwane. Yvonne Whittal. (Harlequin Presents Ser.: No. 1022). 192p. Date not set. pap. 1.95 (ISBN 0-317-63779-7). Harlequin Bks.
Sunset Bomber. D. Kincaid. 1986. 16.95 (ISBN 0-671-60444-9, Pub. by Linden Pr). S&S.
Sunset Bomber. D. Kincaid. 336p. 1987. pap. 4.50 (ISBN 0-451-15126-7, Sig). NAL.
Sunset Boulevard: America's Dream Street. Joe Kennelley & Roy Hankey. (Illus.). 256p. 1982. 34.95 (ISBN 0-933506-06-6). Darwin Pubns.
Sunset California Freeway: Exit Guide. Bill Cima & Saundra Cima. (Illus.). 352p. (Orig.). 1985. pap. 9.95 (ISBN 0-936929-01-4). Am Travel Pubns.
Sunset Evaluation Report: Report to the Governor & the Legislature of the State of Hawaii. Hawaii, Office of the Legislative Auditor Staff. LC 84-621439. 38p. write for info. HI Auditor.
Sunset Handbook II. (State Legislation Department Publications). 1982. write for info. Am Inst CPA.
Sunset High, No. 5. 160p. (Orig.). 1986. pap. 2.50 (ISBN 0-449-12884-9, Pub. by Girls Only). Ballantine.
Sunset High, No. 6. Linda A. Cooney. (Orig.). 1986. pap. 2.50 (ISBN 0-449-13002-9, Pub. by Girls Only). Ballantine.
Sunset in Biafra. Elechi Amadi. (African Writers Ser.). 1973. pap. text ed. 6.50 (ISBN 0-435-90140-0). Heinemann Ed.
Sunset Lines: The Story of the Chicago Aurora & Elgin Railroad, 3 vols. Larry Plachno. Incl. Vol. 1. Trackage. 1986; Vol. 2. Operations & Equipment. Date not set; Vol. 3. History. Date not set. (Illus.). 1986. write for info. Transport Trails.
Sunset Lines: The Story of the Chicago Aurora & Elgin Railroad, Number 1, Trackage. Larry Plachno. Ed. by Eric Bronsky. (Illus.). 160p. 1987. 32.00 (ISBN 0-933449-02-X). Transport Trails.
Sunset Maker. Donald Justice. LC 86-47917. 192p. 1987. 16.00 (ISBN 0-689-11903-8); pap. 8.95 (ISBN 0-689-11904-6). Atheneum.
Sunset of the Sikh Empire. Sita Ram Kohli. Ed. by Khushwant Singh. 1967. 21.00x (ISBN 0-8046-8814-1, Pub. by Kennikat). Assoc Faculty Pr.
Sunset on the Window Panes. Walter Macken. 255p. 1978. pap. 6.95 (ISBN 0-330-25313-1). Bks Britain.
Sunset Possibilities & Other Poems. Gabriel Preil. Tr. by Robert Friend from Hebrew. (Jewish Poetry Ser.). 150p. 1985. 12.95 (ISBN 0-8276-0240-5); pap. 8.95 (ISBN 0-8276-0241-3). JPS Phila.
Sunset Review of Accounting Principles. write for info. Am Inst CPA.
Sunset Song. Lewis G. Gibbon. 288p. 1988. pap. 8.95 (ISBN 0-86241-179-3, Pub. by Canongate Class). David & Charles.
Sunset to Sunrise. Lee Minchey. 1976. 4.95x (ISBN 0-913078-26-3). Sheriar Pr.
Sunset Warrior. Eric Van Lustbader. 1983. pap. 3.50 (ISBN 0-425-09786-2). Berkley Pub.
Sunset Wings. William P. Fowler. 96p. 1981. 8.50 (ISBN 0-914339-03-6). P E Randall Pub.
Sunsets. Benjamin Darling. (Illus.). 72p. (Orig.). Date not set. pap. 8.95. Green Tiger Pr.
Sunsets into Sunrises. Bischof Martin. Tr. by Violet Ozols. 560p. 1985. cancelled (ISBN 0-934616-14-0). Valkyrie Pub Hse.
Sunsets, Twilights, & Evening Skies. Aden Meinel & Marjorie Meinel. LC 83-1794. (Illus.). 200p. 1983. 39.50 (ISBN 0-521-25220-2). Cambridge U Pr.
Sunshine. Norma Klein. 224p. 1982. pap. 2.75 (ISBN 0-380-00049-0, 89506-4, Flare). Avon.
Sunshine. Jan Ormerod. LC 80-84971. (Illus.). 32p. (ps-1). 1981. 10.25 (ISBN 0-688-00552-7); PLB 10.88 (ISBN 0-688-00553-5). Lothrop.
Sunshine. Jan Ormerod. (Picture Puffin Ser.). (Illus.). 32p. (ps-k). 1984. pap. 2.95 (ISBN 0-14-050362-5, Puffin). Penguin.
Sunshine. Bob Reese. Ed. by Dan Wasserman. (Ten Word Bks.). (Illus.). (gr. k-1). 1979. PLB 5.95 (ISBN 0-89868-073-5); pap. 1.95 (ISBN 0-89868-084-0). ARO Pub.
Sunshine & Dark Clouds. James A. Logue. 141p. 1988. 10.95 (ISBN 0-533-07641-2). Vantage.
Sunshine & Promises. Geraldine M. Leach. 500p. write for info. (ISBN 0-9605274-1-9); pap. write for info. (ISBN 0-9605274-2-7). Albion Am Bks.
Sunshine & Shadow. Tom Curtis & Sharon Curtis. 368p. (Orig.). 1986. pap. 3.95 (ISBN 0-553-25047-7). Bantam.
Sunshine & Shadow of Slave Life. Isaac D. Williams. LC 73-168152. Repr. of 1885 ed. 12.50 (ISBN 0-404-00262-5). AMS Pr.
Sunshine & Shadow: Recent Painting in Southern California. Susan C. Larsen. LC 84-73006. (Illus.). 78p. (Orig.). 1985. pap. write for info. (ISBN 0-911291-10-5). Fellows Cont Art.
Sunshine & Shadow: The Amish & Their Quilts. rev. ed. Phyllis Haders. LC 84-909. (Illus.). 88p. 1984. pap. 8.95 (ISBN 0-915590-43-3). Main Street.
Sunshine & Shadows. Ed. by Travis D. Anthony. LC 81-70847. (Illus.). 223p. 1981. 12.95x (ISBN 0-9604686-1-7). T D Anthony.
Sunshine & Shadows: Poetry. Ida R. Bellegarde. LC 83-72335. 62p. 1984. 4.45x (ISBN 0-918340-12-8). Bell Ent.
Sunshine & Storm in Rhodesia. 2nd ed. Frederick C. Selous. LC 69-18660. (Illus.). 1969. Repr. of 1896 ed. 35.00x (ISBN 0-8371-4947-9, SES&, Pub. by Negro U Pr). Greenwood.
Sunshine & the Moon's Delight: A Centenary Tribute to J. M. Synge. Ed. by Suhbil B. Bushrui. 1979. 32.50 (ISBN 0-900675-55-1, Pub. by Colin Smythe Ltd Britain); pap. 10.95. Dufour.
Sunshine & Wealth: Los Angeles in the Twenties & Thirties. Bruce Henstell. LC 84-17595. 132p. (Orig.). 1984. pap. 12.95 (ISBN 0-87701-275-X). Chronicle Bks.
Sunshine at Home & Other Stories. facs. ed. Timothy S. Arthur. LC 77-137722. (American Fiction Reprint Ser). Repr. of 1864 ed. 18.00 (ISBN 0-8369-7021-7). Ayer Co Pubs.
Sunshine Basket. Lula Guthrie. (Illus.). 1986. pap. 1.95 (ISBN 0-89265-112-1). Randall Hse.
Sunshine Boys. Neil Simon. 1973. 9.95 (ISBN 0-394-48808-3, 48808). Random.
Sunshine Boys: Lobbyists, Interest Groups & Disclosure Laws. Neil Upmeyer. 7.50 (ISBN 0-943136-18-0). Ctr Analysis Public Issues.

Sunshine Country. Cristina Roy. 160p. (YA) 6.50 (ISBN 0-686-05594-2); pap. 4.35 (ISBN 0-686-05595-0). Rod & Staff.
Sunshine Crime. Ed. by Frank McSherry, Jr. et al. LC 87-24330. 240p. 1987. pap. 8.95 (ISBN 0-934395-64-0). Rutledge Hill Pr.
Sunshine Days & Foggy Nights. James Kavanaugh. (Illus.). 1975. 9.95 (ISBN 0-87690-167-4). Dutton.
Sunshine, Fruit & Flowers. Pref. by Charles M. Shortridge. (Illus.). 325p. 1986. Repr. of 1895 ed. 25.00 (ISBN 0-914139-03-7). San Jose His Mus Assn.
Sunshine Grows the Day. S. Bradford Williams, Jr. LC 83-7314. 80p. (Orig.). 1983. pap. 4.00 (ISBN 0-9608522-1-2). Copper Orchid.
Sunshine in the Shadows. Peter Lappin. LC 79-57184. 218p. 1980. pap. 6.95 (ISBN 0-89944-042-8). Don Bosco Multimedia.
Sunshine Lost. Patricia Bird. (YA) (gr. 7 up). 1979. 9.95 (ISBN 0-685-65276-9, Avalon). Bouregy.
Sunshine Makes the Seasons. rev. ed. Franklyn M. Branley. LC 85-47540. (Let's-Read-&-Find-Out Science Bks.). (Illus.). 32p. (ps-3). 1985. 12.70 (ISBN 0-690-04481-X, Crowell Jr Bks); PLB 12.89 (ISBN 0-690-04482-8). HarpJ.
Sunshine Makes the Seasons. rev. ed. Franklyn M. Branley. LC 85-42750. (Trophy Let's-Read-&-Find-Out Bks.). (Illus.). 32p. (gr. k-3). 1986. pap. 4.95 (ISBN 0-06-445019-8, Trophy). HarpJ.
Sunshine Makes the Seasons. rev. ed. Franklyn M. Branley. LC 85-42750. (Trophy Let's-Read-&-Find-Out Book & Cassette Set). (Illus.). 32p. (ps-3). 1988. pap. 7.95 incl. cassette (ISBN 0-694-00203-8, Trophy). HarpJ.
Sunshine of Joy. Helen S. Rice. 1988. 8.95 (ISBN 0-317-68175-3). Revell.
Sunshine on the Soapsuds. Beneth P. Jones. 86p. (Orig.). 1977. pap. 3.95 (ISBN 0-89084-054-7). Bob Jones Univ Pr.
Sunshine: Our Gift of Love. B. R. Schmalzried. 1988. 5.00 (ISBN 0-317-67495-1, BI0220); pap. 4.00 (ISBN 0-317-67496-X). Dghtrs St Paul.
Sunshine Patriots: Punishment & the Vietnam Offender. David Curry. LC 81-40450. 192p. 1985. 14.95 (ISBN 0-268-01706-9). U of Notre Dame Pr.
Sunshine Preferred: The Philosophy of an Ordinary Woman. Anne Ellis. LC 84-5141. vi, 249p. 1984. 21.95x (ISBN 0-8032-1810-9); pap. 6.95 (ISBN 0-8032-6709-6, BB 880, Bison). U of Nebr Pr.
Sunshine, Rainbows & Friends. Judith Beyl. LC 80-50828. (Illus.). 83p. (Orig.). (ps-k). 1980. pap. 5.95 (ISBN 0-933308-01-9, HarpR). Har-Row.
Sunshine Road. David Chagall & Juneau Chagall. 1988. pap. 7.95 (ISBN 0-8407-7623-3). Nelson.
Sunshine Sketches of a Little Town. Stephen B. Leacock. LC 71-125228. (Short Story Index Reprint Ser). 1912. 21.95 (ISBN 0-8369-3595-0). Ayer Co Pubs.
Sunshine Thoughts Poster Book: Self-esteem Builders for Children. David Thornburg. (Illus.). 48p. (gr. 3-8). 1988. pap. 5.95 (ISBN 0-942207-06-8, Pub. by Starsong Pubns). Innovision.
Sunshine Through the Shadows. Hulen Jackson. 4.95 (ISBN 0-89315-283-8). Lambert Bk.
Sunshine Tree: And Other Tales From Around the World. Wendy Heller. (Illus.). 96p. 11.50 (ISBN 0-85398-153-1). G Ronald Pub.
Sunship Earth. Steve Van Matre. 265p. 1979. pap. 13.50 (ISBN 0-87603-046-0). Am Camping.
Sunship Earth: An Acclimatization Program for Outdoor Learning. Steve Van Matre. 13.50 (ISBN 0-87603-007-X). Inst Earth.
Sunspace Primer Guide for Solar Heating. R. Jones. 1984. 40.95 (ISBN 0-442-24575-0). Van Nos Reinhold.
Sunspacer. George Zebrowski. LC 79-2670. 320p. (YA) (gr. 6-9). 1984. pap. 7.95 (ISBN 0-06-026849-2). HarpJ.
Sunspaces: New Vistas for Living & Growing. Peter Clegg & Derry Watkins. Ed. by Sarah Clarkson. Tr. by Peter Clegg. LC 86-45974. (Illus.). 304p. 1987. 29.95 (ISBN 0-88266-453-0, Garden Way Pub); pap. 16.95 (ISBN 0-88266-452-2, Garden Way Pub). Storey Comm Inc.
Sunspot Cycles. Ed. by D. Justin Schove. LC 82-15657. (Benchmark Papers In Geology: Vol. 68). 416p. 1983. 44.50 (ISBN 0-87933-424-X). Van Nos Reinhold.
Sunspots. Steve Baer. LC 75-20779. 1977. pap. 6.95 (ISBN 0-686-21779-9). Zomeworks Corp.
Sunspots. R. J. Bray & R. E. Loughhead. (Illus.). 1979. pap. 9.50 (ISBN 0-486-63731-X). Dover.
Sunspots, Dust & Rainfall. George N. Newhall. (Illus.). 208p. (Orig.). 1988. text ed. 20.00 (ISBN 0-9619881-0-X); pap. 16.00 (ISBN 0-9619881-1-8). S & G Pub.
Sunstar: Sun of Superlove. Superlove. LC 80-53694. (Illus.). 200p. (Orig.). (gr. 7 up). 1980. pap. 7.00 (ISBN 0-9602334-1-5); 20.00. Superlove.
Sunstroke. Arthur Hansl. 1987. pap. 3.95 (ISBN 0-312-90757-5). St Martin.
Sunswept Summer. Kathleen O'Brien. (Harlequin Presents Ser.: No. 1011). 192p. Date not set. pap. 1.95 (ISBN 0-317-63758-4). Harlequin Bks.
Suntanned Days. (Follow Your Heart Ser.: No. 9). (YA) (gr. 7 up). pap. 2.25 (ISBN 0-671-55824-2). Archway.
Suomi-Poula Suomi Dictionary: Finnish-Polish-Finnish. A. Krawczykiewicz. 687p. (Finnish & Pol.). 1979. pap. 49.95 (ISBN 951-0-08000-4, M-9638). French & Eur.
Suomiria: A Fantasy. James Carnegie. Ed. by R. Reginald & Douglas Menville. LC 75-46307. (Supernatural & Occult Fiction Ser.). 1976. Repr. of 1899 ed. lib. bdg. 24.50x (ISBN 0-405-08170-7). Ayer Co Pubs.
Sup with the Devil. Sara Craven. (Harlequin Presents Ser.). 192p. 1983. pap. 1.95 (ISBN 0-373-10599-1). Harlequin Bks.
Supai Group of the Grand Canyon. Edwin D. McKee. (Illus.). 515p. 1982. 33.00 (ISBN 0-318-11751-7, S/N 024-001-03501-4). USGPO.
SUPCE & SUREA: Publications & Resources for Educators of Adults. Harold Shufflefield. 1983. 5.00 (ISBN 0-87060-026-5, MSS 31). Syracuse U Cont Ed.
Super. John Cornwell. 1972. pap. 2.25 (ISBN 0-8439-0682-0, Leisure Bks). Leisure NY.
Super & Parallel Computers & Their Impact on Civil Engineering. Ed. by Manohar P. Kamat. (Sessions Proceedings Ser.). 54p. 1986. 10.00x (ISBN 0-87262-551-6). Am Soc Civil Eng.
Super & Superman. Philip Guedalla. 1924. Repr. 20.00 (ISBN 0-8274-3554-1). R West.
Super Babies: A Handbook of Enriched & Accelerated Childhood Development. Robert L. Johnson & Pamela G. Johnson. (Illus.). 1982. pap. 7.95 (ISBN 0-682-49680-4, Banner). Exposition-Phoenix.
Super Banking: Innovative Management Strategies That Work. Richard B. Miller. 1988. 42.50 (ISBN 1-55623-114-8). Dow Jones-Irwin.
Super Bible Heroes. Dick Wright. 96p. 1987. pap. 5.95 (ISBN 0-345-34391-3). Pharos Bks NY.
Super Bodies in Twelve Weeks. Frank Zane & Christine Zane. 256p. 1986. pap. 8.95 (ISBN 0-671-60269-1, Fireside). S&S.
Super Bowl. Leonard Kessler. LC 80-10171. (Greenwillow Read-Alone Bks.). (Illus.). 56p. (gr. 1-4). 1980. PLB 8.88 (ISBN 0-688-84270-4). Greenwillow.
Super Bowl. updated ed. George Vecsey. (Illus.). 176p. (gr. 5 up). 1986. pap. 2.25 (ISBN 0-590-40451-2). Scholastic Inc.
Super Bowl by the Bay. Ed. by Karen E. Sweetland. (Illus.). 288p. 1984. 18.95 (ISBN 0-930965-00-0); softcover 14.95 (ISBN 0-930965-01-9); pap. 7.95 128pp. (ISBN 0-930965-02-7). Bohn Bland Pub.
Super Bowl II: Green Bay Packers vs. Oakland Raiders. Ward. (Super Bowl Champions Ser.). (Illus.). 32p. (gr. 3-8). PLB 8.95. Creative Ed.
Super Bowl Sunday. Mitch Gelman. (A Play it Your Way Sports Ser.: Bk. 4). (Orig.). (gr. 9 up). 1984. pap. 2.25 (ISBN 0-671-47578-9). Archway.
Super Bowl Superstars: The Most Valuable Players in the NFL's Championship Game. Pete Alfano. LC 82-368. (Random House Sports Library). (Illus.). 144p. (gr. 5-9). 1982. pap. 4.95 (ISBN 0-394-85017-3). Random.
Super Boxers. John Byrne & Ron Wilson. (Marvel Graphic Novel Ser.: No. 8). 5.95 (ISBN 0-939766-77-9). Marvel Comics.
Super Brain Breathing. 18th ed. Paul C. Bragg & Patricia Bragg. pap. 1.75 (ISBN 0-87790-014-0). Health Sci.
Super Bull & Other True Escapades. Max Evans. LC 85-16369. (Illus.). 198p. 1985. 16.95 (ISBN 0-8263-0838-4). U of NM Pr.
Super Car. Mike Trier. Ed. by FS-Aladdin Staff. (Engineers at Work Ser.). (Illus.). 32p. (gr. 4-9). 1988. 10.90 (ISBN 0-531-17098-5, Gloucester Pr). Watts.
Super Carrier: An Inside Account of Life on the World's Most Powerful Ship, the U.S.S. Kennedy. George C. Wilson. (Illus.). 320p. 1986. 19.95 (ISBN 0-02-630120-2). Macmillan.
Super Champ. David R. Collins. 1982. 6.95 (ISBN 0-89015-349-3). Eakin Pr.
Super-Champions of Auto Racing. Ross R. Olney. LC 83-14407. (Illus.). 128p. (Orig.). (gr. 6up). 1984. PLB 11.95 (ISBN 0-89919-259-9, Clarion); pap. 4.95 (ISBN 0-89919-289-0). HM.
Super Chest. Robert Kennedy. LC 86-30114. (Musclebuilder's Body Parts Ser.). (Illus.). 128p. (Orig.). 1987. pap. 7.95 (ISBN 0-8069-6412-X). Sterling.
Super Chief: Earl Warren & His Supreme Court, A Judicial Biography. Bernard Schwartz. (Illus.). 864p. 1983. 50.00x (ISBN 0-8147-7825-9); pap. 20.00x (ISBN 0-8147-7826-7). NYU Pr.
Super-Chords Made Super-Simple. Duane Shinn. 1976. pap. 10.00 (ISBN 0-912732-20-2); incl. cassette 19.95. Duane Shinn.
Super-Colossal Book of Puzzles, Tricks & Games. Sheila A. Barry. LC 77-93325. (Illus.). 640p. (gr. 3 up). 1985. Repr. 6.98 (ISBN 0-8069-4720-9). Sterling.
Super Course for the SAT. Thomas Martinson. 784p. (Orig.). (YA) (gr. 7-8). 1988. pap. 12.95 (ISBN 0-13-788506-7). S&S.
Super Depth Force: Project Discovery. Irving A. Greenfield. 400p. 1988. pap. 3.95 (ISBN 0-8217-2352-9). Zebra.
Super Dooper Jezebel. Tony Ross. (Illus.). 32p. (ps up). 1988. 11.95 (ISBN 0-374-33660-1). FS&G.
Super Dot to Dot, No. 1. (Super Activity Bks.). (Illus.). 48p. (gr. 1-4). 1988. pap. 2.95 (ISBN 0-8431-2267-6). Price Stern.
Super Dot to Dot, No. 2. (Super Activity Bks.). (Illus.). 48p. (gr. 1-4). 1988. pap. 2.95 (ISBN 0-8431-2268-4). Price Stern.
Super Duper Story Problems. Ginger Wentrcek. (gr. 1-4). 1986. pap. 4.50 (ISBN 0-8224-6570-1). D S Lake Pubs.
Super Dynamic Kicks. Chong Lee. LC 80-84496. (Korean Arts Ser.). (Illus.). 1980. pap. 8.95 (ISBN 0-89750-072-5, 409). Ohara Pubns.
Super-Easy Step-by-Step Cheesemaking. Yvonne Y. Tarr. (Orig.). 1975. pap. 3.95 (ISBN 0-394-72009-1, Vin). Random.
Super-Easy-Step-by-Step Sausagemaking. Yvonne Y. Tarr. (Orig.). 1975. pap. 5.95 (ISBN 0-394-72011-3, Vin). Random.
Super Easy-Step-by-Step Winemaking. Yvonne Y. Tarr. (Orig.). 1975. pap. 7.95 (ISBN 0-394-72012-1, Vin). Random.
Super Eight Book. Lenny Lipton. 1975. 9.95 (ISBN 0-671-22082-9, Fireside). S&S.
Super Eight Filmaking from Scratch. reference ed. Bebe F. McClain. (Illus.). 1978. 23.33 (ISBN 0-13-876128-0); pap. 19.95 (ISBN 0-13-876110-8). P-H.
Super Eight in the Video Age. 3rd ed. Bob Brodsky & Toni Treadway. 1988. pap. text ed. 16.95 (ISBN 0-9610914-4-4). B&T.
Super Eight: The Modest Medium. (Monographs on Communication Technology & Utilization: No. 1). (Illus.). 92p. 1976. pap. 5.00 (ISBN 92-3-101368-8, U644, UNESCO). UNIPUB.
Super Etendard. (Super Profile AC Ser.). 8.95 (ISBN 0-85429-378-7, F378, Pub. by G T Foulis Ltd). Haynes Pubns.
Super Executive's Guide to Getting Things Done. Charles H. Ford. 272p. 1983. 14.95 (ISBN 0-8144-5724-X). AMACOM.
Super Faculties & Their Culture. Manly P. Hall. pap. 2.95 (ISBN 0-89314-358-8). Philos Res.
Super Feds: A Facsimile Selection of Dynamic G-Man Stories from the 1930s. Compiled by Don Hutchison. (Popular Culture Studies: No. 8). 1988. 19.95; pap. 9.95. Starmont Hse.
Super Feds: A Facsimile Selection of Dynamic G-Man Stories from the 1930s. Ed. by Don Hutchison. (Starmont Popular Culture Studies). 160p. 1988. Repr. lib. bdg. 19.95x (ISBN 0-8095-5304-X). Borgo Pr.
Super Field Theories. Ed. by H. C. Lee et al. LC 87-14159. (NATO ASI Series B, Physics: Vol. 160). (Illus.). 608p. 1987. 110.00x (ISBN 0-306-42660-9, Plenum Pr). Plenum Pub.
Super-Fit for Business. Graham Price & Gerry Rickards. 1987. 15.50 (ISBN 0-906619-14-9, Pub. by Milestone Pubns UK). Seven Hills Bks.
Super Flyers. Neil Francis. (Illus.). 80p. (gr. 1-12). 1988. pap. 6.95 (ISBN 0-201-14519-7). Addison-Wesley.
Super Foods Diet. Mary A. Crenshaw. 256p. 1983. 12.95 (ISBN 0-02-528820-2). Macmillan.
Super Foods Diet Guide. Prevention Magazine Editors. Ed. by Sharon Faelten. 96p. 1987. pap. 4.95 (ISBN 0-87857-708-4). Rodale Pr Inc.
Super Friend. Dandi D. Knorr. (Jenny & Josh Bks.). (Illus.). 32p. (gr. 1-3). 1987. 4.95 (ISBN 0-87403-316-0, 3546). Standard Pub.
Super Fullback for the Super Bowl. Clare Gault & Frank Gault. (gr. k-3). 1978. pap. 1.50 (ISBN 0-590-11904-4). Scholastic Inc.
Super Good Cents: Construction Manual. Anne W. Smith. (Illus.). 261p. 1986. looseleaf, binder 26.00 (ISBN 0-318-22444-5, S/N 061-000-00684-2). USGPO.
Super Good Cents: Technical Reference Manual. Ed. by Anne W. Smith. (Illus.). 274p. 1986. looseleaf binder 34.00 (ISBN 0-318-22443-7, S/N 061-000-00683-4). USGPO.
Super Gran. Forrest Wilson. (Illus.). (gr. 3-7). Date not set. pap. 3.95 (ISBN 0-317-62162-9, Puffin Bks). Penguin.
Super Gran Rules OK! Forrest Wilson. (Illus.). (gr. 3-7). Date not set. pap. 3.95 (ISBN 0-317-62168-8, Puffin Bks). Penguin.
Super-Heavy Elements: Theoretical Predictions & Experimental Generation-(Proceedings of the 27th Nobel Symposium) Ed. by Sven Nilsson & Nils Nilsson. 184p. (Orig.). 1974. pap. text ed. 27.50x (Pub. by Almqvist & Wiksell). Coronet Bks.
Super Hedging. Thomas C. Noddings. 232p. 1985. 29.50 (ISBN 0-917253-21-3). Probus Pub Co.
Super High-Intensity Bodybuilding. Ellington Darden. (Illus.). 1986. pap. 11.95 (ISBN 0-399-51220-9, Perigee). Putnam Pub Group.
Super Horoscopes 1985: Gemini. 256p. 1984. pap. 3.50 (ISBN 0-441-79302-9). Ace Bks.
Super Horoscopes 1985: Leo. 256p. 1984. pap. 3.50 (ISBN 0-441-79304-5). Ace Bks.
Super Horoscopes 1985: Libra. 256p. 1984. pap. 3.50 (ISBN 0-441-79306-1). Ace Bks.
Super Horoscopes 1985: Pisces. 256p. 1984. pap. 3.50 (ISBN 0-441-79311-8). Ace Bks.
Super Horoscopes 1985: Sagittarius. 256p. 1984. pap. 3.50 (ISBN 0-441-79308-8). Ace Bks.
Super Horoscopes 1985: Scorpio. 256p. 1984. pap. 3.50 (ISBN 0-441-79307-X). Ace Bks.
Super Horoscopes 1985: Taurus. 256p. 1984. pap. 3.50 (ISBN 0-441-79301-0). Ace Bks.
Super Horoscopes 1985: Virgo. 256p. 1984. pap. 3.50 (ISBN 0-441-79305-3). Ace Bks.
Super Horoscopoes. 256p. 1987. pap. 3.95 (ISBN 0-317-59757-4, Charter Bks). Berkley Pub.
Super Ideas for Youth Groups. Wayne Rice & Mike Yaconelli. (Orig.). 1979. pap. 8.95 (ISBN 0-310-34981-8, 10773P). Zondervan.
Super Insulation. James M. Shepherd. (Illus.). 36p. 1983. pap. 3.95 (ISBN 0-9607308-1-8). Shepherd Pubs VA.
Super Job Search: The Complete Manual for Job-Seekers & Career-Changers. Peter K. Studner. LC 86-50476. 330p. 1987. softcover 22.95 (ISBN 0-938667-00-9). Jamenair Ltd.
Super Joke Book. Gyles Brandreth. (Illus.). 128p. (gr. 3 up). 1985. 10.95 (ISBN 0-8069-6200-3); pap. 3.95 (ISBN 0-8069-4672-5). Sterling.
Super Joy: In Love with Living. Paul Pearsall. 1988. 18.95 (ISBN 0-385-24459-2). Doubleday.
Super Kid? Or Kids Who Are Super? Elaine McEwan. 196p. 1988. 11.95 (ISBN 1-55513-633-8, LifeJourney). Cook.
Super Kids & Their Parents. Robert L. Johnson. LC 86-914000. (Illus.). 1987. 12.50 (ISBN 0-682-40322-9). Exposition-Phoenix.
Super Machine Knits. Judy Dodson. LC 87-46095. (Illus.). 144p. (Orig.). 1987. pap. 15.95 (ISBN 0-937274-42-9, Dist. by Sterling). Lark Bks.
Super Machines. John Freeman. LC 85-40204. (Let's Look Up Ser.). (Illus.). 32p. (gr. 3-6). PLB 7.96 (ISBN 0-382-09076-4). Silver.
Super Machines. Ralph Hancock. LC 78-2202. (Illus.). (gr. 4-9). 1978. 11.50 (ISBN 0-670-68446-5). Viking.
Super Mafia. Jonathan Harris. LC 84-10867. (Illus.). 192p. (gr. 7 up). 1985. 9.97 (ISBN 0-671-49368-X). Messner.
Super Managing: How to Harness Change for Personal & Organizational Success. A. Brown & E. Weiner. 1985. pap. 4.95 (ISBN 0-451-62382-7, Sig). NAL.
Super Marital Sex. Paul Pearsall. 1988. pap. 4.95. Ivy Books.
Super Marital Sex: Loving for Life. Paul Pearsall. LC 87-6705. 408p. 1987. 18.95 (ISBN 0-385-24018-X). Doubleday.
Super Market Crafts. Betty A. Vaughan. (Illus.). 12p. (Orig.). 1983. pap. 1.95 (ISBN 0-9605172-2-7). Betom Pubns.
Super Menus for Football Fans. Candy Coleman. (Illus.). 48p. (Orig.). 1981. pap. text ed. 3.00 (ISBN 0-943768-04-7). C Coleman.
Super Mom's Country Cookin' Cookbook. Ophelia Warner. 400p. 1988. 21.95 (ISBN 0-89896-089-4). Larksdale.
Super Motion. Philip Watson. LC 82-80990. (Science Club Ser.). (Illus.). 48p. (gr. 3-6). 1983. PLB 10.88 (ISBN 0-688-00971-9); pap. 6.95 (ISBN 0-688-00976-X). Lothrop.
Super Natural Cookery. Jim Corlett. pap. 6.95 (ISBN 0-87491-058-7). Acropolis.
Super Natural Dessert Cookbook. Lois Fishkin & Susan DiMarco. LC 84-45095. (Illus.). 132p. (Orig.). 1984. pap. 6.95 (ISBN 0-916870-61-8). Creative Arts Bk.
Super Natural Living. Betty Malz. 1983. pap. 2.50 (ISBN 0-451-12517-7, Sig). NAL.
Super Natural Selling for Everyday People. Danielle Kennedy. 176p. text ed. 8.95 (ISBN 0-9613396-0-8, Dist. by Publishers Group West). Craig Pubns.
Super-Nutrition. Richard A. Passwater. 1983. pap. 3.50 (ISBN 0-671-45640-7). PB.
Super Official NFL Trivia Book. Ted Brock & Jim Campbell. 1985. pap. 3.95 (ISBN 0-451-13822-8, Sig). NAL.
Super Official TV Trivia Quiz Book. Bart Andrews. 1985. pap. 3.95 (ISBN 0-451-13507-5, Sig). NAL.
Super Plastic Model Manual: Macross, Vol. 1. (Illus.). 1984. 8.95 (ISBN 0-318-02677-5). Bks Nippan.
Super Plastic Model Manual: Macross & Orguss, Vol. 2. (Illus.). 1984. 8.95 (ISBN 0-318-02678-3). Bks Nippan.
Super-Power Golf. Gary Wiren & Dawson Taylor. (Illus.). 160p. (Orig.). 1984. pap. 9.95 (ISBN 0-8092-5465-4). Contemp Bks.
Super Power Rivalry in the Indian Ocean. V. K. Bhasin. 229p. 1981. 24.95x (ISBN 0-940500-16-7, Pub. by S Chand India). Asia Bk Corp.
Super Power Rivalry in the Indian Ocean. V. K. Bhasin. 236p. 1981. text ed. 20.00x. Coronet Bks.
Super Power Rivalry in the Indian Ocean. V. K. Bhasin. 238p. 17.50X (ISBN 0-317-52157-8, Pub. by S Chand India). State Mutual Bk.
Super Powers & Their Spheres of Influence. Edy Kaufman. LC 76-24651. 1977. 25.00x (ISBN 0-312-77630-6). St Martin.
Super Powers Anti-Coloring Book. Susan Striker. (Illus.). (ps up). 1984. pap. 3.95 (ISBN 0-448-07932-1, G&D). Putnam Pub Group.
Super Powers in the Horn of Africa. Madan M. Sauldie. LC 82-71853. 300p. 1987. text ed. 30.00x (ISBN 0-86590-092-2). Apt Bks.
Super Procrastinators. Joe Barnes. (Illus.). 224p. 1988. 14.95 (ISBN 0-917732-36-7); pap. text ed. 10.95 (ISBN 0-917732-37-5). Barnes-Bks.
Super Profile: Austin-Healey 'Frogeye' Sprite. Lindsay Porter. (Illus.). 56p. 1983. 8.95 (ISBN 0-85429-343-4, F343, Pub. by G T Foulis Ltd). Haynes Pubns.

Supercomputers & Fluid Dynamics. Ed. by K. Kuwahara et al. (Lecture Notes in Engineering: Vol. 24). viii, 200p. 1986. pap. 21.70 (ISBN 0-387-17051-0). Springer-Verlag.

Supercomputers & Parallel Computations. Ed. by D. J. Paddon. (Institute of Mathematics & Its Applications Conference Ser.). (Illus.). 1984. 55.95x (ISBN 0-19-853601-1). Oxford U Pr.

Supercomputers & Their Use. Christopher Lazou. LC 86-8643. 227p. 1987. 49.95 (ISBN 0-19-853720-4). Oxford U Pr.

Supercomputers & Their Use. rev. ed. Christopher Lazou. (Illus.). 250p. 1988. 59.95 (ISBN 0-19-853815-4); pap. 29.95 (ISBN 0-19-853759-X). Oxford U Pr.

Supercomputers: Class VI Systems, Hardware & Software. Ed. by S. Fernbach. 260p. 1986. 47.75 (ISBN 0-444-87981-1, North-Holland). Elsevier.

Supercomputers in Chemistry. Ed. by Peter Lykos & Isaiah Shavitt. LC 81-17630. (ACS Symposium Ser.: No. 173). 1981. 34.95 (ISBN 0-8412-0666-X). Am Chemical.

Supercomputers in Theoretical & Experimental Science. Ed. by Jozef T. Devreese & P. E. Van Camp. 238p. 1985. 59.50x (ISBN 0-306-42107-0, Plenum Pr). Plenum Pub.

Supercomputers: Materials, Components, Software. Business Communications Staff. (Illus.). 236p. 1986. pap. 1750.00 (ISBN 0-89336-494-0, G-102). BCC.

Supercomputers Structured Software Development, 2 vols. Jesshope Staff. (Infotech Computer State of the Art Reports). 580p. 1979. 61.00x (ISBN 0-08-028505-8). Pergamon.

Supercomputing. Ed. by E. N. Houstis et al. (Lecture Notes in Computer Science Ser.: Vol. 297). x, 1093p. 1988. pap. 75.00 (ISBN 0-387-18991-2). Springer-Verlag.

Supercomputing: State of the Art. A. Lichnewsky & Z. C. Sague. 1987. 88.00 (ISBN 0-444-70320-9). Elsevier.

Superconcious Meditation. Pandit U. Arya. 150p. 1978. pap. 6.95 (ISBN 0-89389-035-9). Himalayan Pubs.

Superconducting D. C. Machines. A. D. Appleton. 1984. write for info. Elsevier.

Superconducting Magnet Systems. H. Brechna. LC 72-96051. (Technische Physik in Einveldarstellungen: Vol. 18). (Illus.). 480p. 1973. 110.00 (ISBN 0-387-06103-7). Springer-Verlag.

Superconducting Magnets. Martin Wilson. (Monographs on Cryogenics: No. 2). (Illus.). 352p. 1987. pap. 23.95 (ISBN 0-19-854810-9). Oxford U Pr.

Superconducting Magnets. Martin N. Wilson. (Monographs on Cryogenics). (Illus.). 1983. 45.00x (ISBN 0-19-854805-2). Oxford U Pr.

Superconducting Rotating Electrical Machines. J. R. Bumby. (Monographs in Electrical & Electronic Engineering). (Illus.). 1983. 49.95x (ISBN 0-19-859327-9). Oxford U Pr.

Superconductive Particle Detectors. Antonio Barone. (Advances in the Physics of Condensed Matter - ISI - 87 Ser.). 350p. 1988. 42.00 (ISBN 9971-50-611-4). World Scientific Pub.

Superconductivity in Magnetic & Exotic Materials: Proceedings of the Sixth Taniguchi International Symposium, Kashikojima, Japan, Nov. 14-18, 1983. Ed. by T. Matsubara & A. Kotani. (Springer Series in Solid-State Sciences Ser.: Vol. 52). (Illus.). 225p. 1984. 32.50 (ISBN 0-387-13324-0). Springer-Verlag.

Superconductivity. 2nd ed. David Shoenberg. (Cambridge Monographs on Physics). pap. 67.50 (ISBN 0-317-09142-5, 2051478). Bks Demand UMI.

Superconductivity. A. W. Taylor. 110p. 1970. pap. 18.00x (ISBN 0-85109-120-2). Taylor & Francis.

Superconductivity. A. W. Taylor & G. R. Noakes. (Wykeham Science Ser.: No. 11). 110p. 1970. 18.00x (ISBN 0-8448-1113-0, Pub. by Crane Russak & Co). Taylor & Francis.

Superconductivity. M. Tinkham. (Documents on Modern Physics Ser.). 142p. 1964. pap. 27.00 (ISBN 0-677-00065-0). Gordon & Breach.

Superconductivity, Vol 1. Ed. by R. D. Parks. LC 68-23775. pap. 160.00 (ISBN 0-317-08358-9, 2055056). Bks Demand UMI.

Superconductivity, Vol. 2. Ed. by R. D. Parks. LC 68-23775. (Illus.). pap. 160.00 (ISBN 0-317-07985-9, 2055076). Bks Demand UMI.

Superconductivity - The Threshold of a New Technology. Jonathan L. Mayo. 1988. 18.95 (ISBN 0-8306-9122-7, 3022); pap. 12.95 (ISBN 0-8306-9322-X). TAB Bks.

Superconductivity & Its Applications. J. E. Williams. 1970. 22.00x (ISBN 0-85086-010-5, 2921, Pub. by Pion England). Routledge Chapman & Hall.

Superconductivity & Quantum Fluids. Z. M. Galasiewicz. 1970. 50.00 (ISBN 0-08-013089-5). Pergamon.

Superconductivity & Superconducting Materials. A. V. Narlikar & S. N. Ekbote. LC 83-188223. (Solid Physics Ser.: No. 1). (Illus.). 306p. 1983. 39.00 (ISBN 0-9605004-9-9, Pub. by South Asian Pubs India). Eng Pubns.

Superconductivity Directory, 1988. Ed. by Sally Anderson & Jane Glass. 376p. 1988. pap. 195.00 (ISBN 0-935453-21-0). Pasha Pubns.

Superconductivity: Experiments in a New Technology. Dave Prochnow. (Advanced Technology Ser.). (Illus.). 208p. 1988. 22.95 (ISBN 0-8306-1432-X, 3132); pap. 14.95 (ISBN 0-8306-3132-1, 3132). TAB Bks.

Superconductivity: Guide to the Corporate Players. 100p. 1987. spiral-bound 295.00 (ISBN 0-914993-42-9). Tech Insights.

Superconductivity in D- & F- Band Metals: Proceedings of the AIP Conference, Univ. of Rochester, 1971, No. 4. American Institute of Physics. Ed. by D. H. Douglass. LC 74-188879. 375p. 1972. 14.00 (ISBN 0-88318-103-7). Am Inst Physics.

Superconductivity in D & F-Band Metals. Ed. by Harry Suhl & M. Brian Maple. LC 80-12907. 1980. 65.50 (ISBN 0-12-676150-7). Acad Pr.

Superconductivity in Science & Technology. Ed. by Morrel H. Cohen. LC 67-25534. pap. 42.80 (ISBN 0-317-08095-4, 2020047). Bks Demand UMI.

Superconductivity in Ternary Compounds II: Superconductivity & Magnetism. Ed. by M. B. Maple & O. Fischer. (Topics in Current Physics: Vol. 34). (Illus.). 335p. 1982. 43.50 (ISBN 0-387-11814-4). Springer-Verlag.

Superconductivity in Ternary Compounds I: Structural, Electronics & Lattices Properties. Ed. by O. Fischer & M. B. Maple. (Topics in Current Physics Ser.: Vol. 32). (Illus.). 320p. 1982. 43.50 (ISBN 0-387-11670-2). Springer-Verlag.

Superconductivity: McGill Summer School Proceedings, 2 vols. Ed. by P. R. Wallace. 1969. Vol. 1, 544p. 160.00 (ISBN 0-677-13810-5); Vol. 2, 420p. 127.00 (ISBN 0-677-13820-2); Set. 250.00 (ISBN 0-677-13210-7). Gordon & Breach.

Superconductivity of Transition Metals: Their Alloys & Compounds. S. V. Vonsovsky et al. (Springer Series in Solid-State Sciences: Vol. 27). (Illus.). 512p. 1982. 47.50 (ISBN 0-387-11382-7). Springer-Verlag.

Superconductivity: Research, Applications & Potential Markets. T. A. Heppenheimer. 220p. 1988. pap. 194.00 (ISBN 0-935453-19-9). Pasha Pubns.

Superconductivity: The Threshold of a New Technology. Jonathan L. Mayo. (Illus.). 160p. 1988. 18.95 (ISBN 0-317-67252-5); pap. 12.95 (ISBN 0-317-67253-3). TAB Bks.

Superconductor Component Industry. Business Communications Staff. 177p. 1988. pap. 1950.00 (ISBN 0-89336-616-1, GB-106). BCC.

Superconductor Materials Science: Metallurgy, Fabrication, & Applications. Ed. by Simon Foner & Brian B. Schwartz. LC 81-8669. (NATO ASI Series B, Physics: Vol. 68). 1000p. 1981. 150.00x (ISBN 0-306-40750-7, Plenum Pr). Plenum Pub.

Superconductors: Conquering Technology's New Frontier. Randy Simon & Andrew Smith. (Illus.). 325p. 1988. 23.95 (ISBN 0-306-42959-4, Plenum Pr). Plenum Pub.

Superconductors: Proceedings. Ed. by M. Tanenbaum & W. V. Wright. LC 62-18707. pap. 40.30 (ISBN 0-317-08032-6, 2000686). Bks Demand UMI.

Superconscious World. Peter Reveen. 160p. 1987. 19.95 (ISBN 0-920792-86-3). Eden Pr.

Supercook: The Complete Encyclopedia of Cooking. (Illus.). 3186p. 1978. lib. bdg. 199.50x (ISBN 0-85685-534-0). Marshall Cavendish.

Supercookery! (Illus.). 384p. 12.98 (ISBN 0-8317-7980-2). Smith Pubs.

Supercounties, U. S. A. G. Etzel Pearcy. LC 75-36700. (Monograph: No.3). (Illus.). 1976. 11.95 (ISBN 0-916434-15-X). Plycon Pr.

Supercourse for the ACT. Thomas Martinson & Juliana Fazzane. (Arco Academic Test Preparation Ser.). 784p. 1988. pap. 14.95 (ISBN 0-13-003170-4). Prentice Hall Pr.

Supercourse for the GMAT. Thomas Martinson. (Arco Academic Test Preparation Ser.). 1988. pap. 12.95 (ISBN 0-13-357427-X). Prentice Hall Pr.

Supercourse for the GRE. Thomas Martinson. (Arco Academic Test Preparation Ser.). 1988. pap. 12.95 (ISBN 0-13-363516-3). Prentice Hall Pr.

Supercourse for the LSAT. Thomas Martinson. (Arco Academic Test Preparation Ser.). 784p. 1988. pap. 12.95 (ISBN 0-13-541145-9). Prentice Hall Pr.

Supercritical Fluid Chromatology. Intro. by Roger M. Smith. (Chromatology Monographs). (Illus.). 200p. 1988. text ed. 59.00x (ISBN 0-85186-577-1, Pub. by Royal Soc Chem). Scholium Intl.

Supercritical Fluid Extraction. Mark McHugh & Val Krukonis. (Illus.). 200p. 1986. text ed. 44.95 (ISBN 0-409-90015-X). Butterworth.

Supercritical Fluid Extraction & Chromatography: Techniques & Applications. Ed. by Bonnie A. Carpentier & Michael R. Sevenants. LC 88-3466. (Symposium Ser.: No. 366). (Illus.). ix, 253p. 1988. 59.95 (ISBN 0-8412-1469-7). Am Chemical.

Supercritical Fluid Technology: Process Technology Proceedings, No. 3. Ed. by J. M. Penninger et al. 468p. 1985. 152.75 (ISBN 0-444-42552-7). Elsevier.

Supercritical Fluids. Ed. by Thomas G. Squires & Michael E. Paulaitis. LC 86-26480. (ACS Symposium Ser.: No. 329). (Illus.). x, 294p. 1986. 59.95 (ISBN 0-8412-1010-1). Am Chemical.

Superculture: American Popular Culture & Europe. C. W. Bigsby. LC 74-84638. 1975. 13.95 (ISBN 0-87972-070-0). Bowling Green Univ.

Supercut: Nutrition for the Ultimate Physique. Bill Reynolds & Joyce L. Vedral. (Illus.). 320p. (Orig.). 1985. pap. 12.95 (ISBN 0-8092-5387-9). Contemp Bks.

Superdeep Well of the Kola Peninsula. Ed. by Y. A. Kozlovsky. (Exploration of the Deep Continental Crust Ser.). (Illus.). 590p. 1987. 118.00 (ISBN 0-387-16416-2). Springer-Verlag.

Superdrivers: Three Auto Racing Champions. Bill Libby. LC 76-47475. (Garrard Sports Library). (Illus.). 96p. (gr. 3-6). 1977. PLB 7.12 (ISBN 0-8116-6681-6). Garrard.

Superduper Collector. Susan C. Poskanzer. LC 85-14051. (Illus.). 48p. (Orig.). (gr. 1-3). 1986. PLB 9.49 (ISBN 0-8167-0606-9); pap. text ed. 1.95 (ISBN 0-8167-0607-7). Troll Assocs.

Supererogation: Its Status in Ethical Theory. David Heyd. LC 81-15476. (Cambridge Studies in Philosophy). 180p. 1982. 37.50 (ISBN 0-521-23935-4). Cambridge U Pr.

Superfairness: Applications & Theory. William J. Baumol. (Illus.). 280p. 1986. text ed. 22.00x (ISBN 0-262-02234-6). MIT Pr.

Superfairness: Applications & Theory. William J. Baumol. 280p. 1988. pap. text ed. 12.50x (ISBN 0-262-52131-8). MIT Pr.

Superficial Bladder Tumors: EORTC Genitourinary Group Monograph Two, Part B. Fritz H. Schroeder & Brian Richards. LC 85-10206. (Progress in Clinical & Bioligical Research Ser.: Vol. 185B). 198p. 1985. 34.00 (ISBN 0-8451-0189-7). A R Liss.

Superficial Estimation. John Wieners. (Illus., Orig.). 1987. pap. 4.00 (ISBN 0-937815-00-4). Hanuman Bks.

Superficial Fungal Infections. Ed. by J. L. Verbox. (New Clinical Applications Dermatology Ser.). 1986. lib. bdg. 41.95 (ISBN 0-85200-943-7, Pub. by MTP Pr England). Kluwer Academic.

Superficial Journey Through Tokyo & Peking. P. A. Quennell. 250p. 1986. pap. 35.00x (ISBN 0-317-69418-9, Pub. by Han-Shan Tang Ltd). State Mutual Bk.

Superficial Journey Through Tokyo & Peking. Peter Quennell. (Oxford in Asia Paperbacks Ser.). (Illus.). 296p. 1987. pap. 9.95 (ISBN 0-19-584099-2). Oxford U Pr.

Superficial Keratitis. Ed. by P. C. Maudgal & L. Missotten. 1981. lib. bdg. 45.00 (ISBN 90-6193-801-5, Pub. by Junk Pubs Netherlands). Kluwer Academic.

Superficial Veins of the Human Brain: Veins of the Brain Stem & of the Base of the Brain. H. M. Duvernoy. (Illus.). viii, 110p. 1975. pap. 52.00 (ISBN 0-387-06876-7). Springer-Verlag.

Superfiction, or the American Story Transformed: An Anthology. Ed. by Joe D. Bellamy. (Orig.). 1975. pap. 6.95 (ISBN 0-394-71523-3, Vin). Random.

Superfilms: An International Guide to Award Winning Educational Films. Salvatore J. Parlato, Jr. LC 76-10801. 365p. 1976. 22.50 (ISBN 0-8108-0953-2). Scarecrow.

Superfitness Handbook. Ellington Darden. (Illus.). 296p. 1980. 14.95 (ISBN 0-89313-016-8). G F Stickley Co.

Superflex: Ms. Olympia's Guide to Building a Strong & Sexy Body. Corinna Everson & Jeff Everson. (Illus.). 224p. (Orig.). 1987. pap. 11.95 (ISBN 0-8092-4865-4). Contemp Bks.

Superflirt. Helen Cavanagh. 176p. (Orig.). (gr. 7 up). 1980. pap. 1.95 (ISBN 0-590-30951-X, Wildfire). Scholastic Inc.

Superfluid Hydrodynamics. S. J. Putterman. LC 74-75578. (Low Temperature Physics Ser.: Vol. 3). 443p. 1975. 66.00 (ISBN 0-444-10681-2, North-Holland); pap. 34.25 (ISBN 0-444-10713-4). Elsevier.

Superfluid Phases of Helium-3. Ed. by P. Wolfe & D. Vollhardt. 300p. 1988. 66.00x (ISBN 0-85066-412-8). Taylor & Francis.

Superfluidity & Superconductivity. 2nd ed. D. R. Tilley & J. Tilley. (Graduate Student Series in Physics). (Illus.). 440p. 1986. 95.00x (ISBN 0-85274-807-8, Pub. by A Hilger UK); pap. 49.00x (ISBN 0-85274-791-8, Pub. by A Hilger UK). Taylor & Francis.

Superfluous Anarchist: Albert Jay Nock. Michael Wreszin. LC 75-154339. Repr. of 1972 ed. 52.00 (2027526). Bks Demand UMI.

Superfluous Men & the Post-Stalin Thaw: The Alienated Hero in Soviet Prose During the Decade 1953-1963. Thomas F. Rogers. 1972. text ed. 45.60x (ISBN 90-2792-118-0). Mouton.

Superfluous Men: Conservative Critics of American Culture, 1900-1945. Ed. by Robert M. Crunden. 309p. 1977. 17.50 (ISBN 0-292-77527-X). U of Tex Pr.

Superflyer: Captain John Champion Flyer. Jonathon Thompson. 40p. (gr. 3-6). 3.95 (ISBN 0-933479-08-5). Thompson.

Superforce: The Search for a Grand Unified Theory of Nature. Paul Davies. LC 84-5473. 288p. 1984. 8.95 (ISBN 0-671-47685-8). S&S.

Superforce: The Search for a Grand Unified Theory of Nature. Paul Davies. Date not set. pap. 8.95 (ISBN 0-671-60573-9, Touchstone Bks.). S&S.

Superfortress. (Super Profile AC Ser.). 8.95 (ISBN 0-85429-339-6, F339, Pub. by G T Foulis Ltd). Haynes Pubns.

Superfortress-The Boeing B-29. Steve Birdsall. (Illus.). 1984. pap. 7.95 (ISBN 0-89747-104-0, 6028). Squad Sig Pubns.

Superfortress: The Story of the B-29 & American Air Power in World War II. Curtis E. LeMay & Bill Yenne. 264p. 1988. text ed. 18.95 (ISBN 0-07-037164-4). McGraw.

Superfudge. Judy Blume. 176p. (gr. 2-6). 1981. pap. 3.25 (ISBN 0-440-48433-2, YB). Dell.

Superfudge. Judy Blume. LC 80-10439. 176p. (gr. 3-6). 1980. 10.95 (ISBN 0-525-40522-4). Dutton.

Superfudge. Judy Blume. 239p. (gr. 2-6). 1987. Repr. of 1980 ed. lib. bdg. 13.95 (ISBN 1-55736-014-6). ABC-Clio.

Superfudge see Judy Blume.

Superfudge see Judy Blume Collection.

Superfund: A Legislative History, 3 Vols. Ed. by Helen C. Needham & Mark Menefee. LC 84-10208. 1982. Set. looseleaf bindings 215.00 (ISBN 0-911937-08-0). Environ Law Inst.

Superfund & RCRA: Litigation with Forms. Christopher Schraff & Robert Steinberg. 750p. 1988. 95.00 (ISBN 0-8240-7328-2). Garland Pub.

Superfund Deskbook. Environmental Law Reporter Staff. 380p. 1986. pap. 75.00 (ISBN 0-911937-21-8). Environ Law Inst.

Superfund II: A New Mandate. 165p. 1987. 50.00 (ISBN 0-87179-923-5). BNA.

Superfund Manual: Legal & Management Strategies. Ridgway M. Hall, Jr. et al. 224p. 1985. pap. text ed. 46.00 (ISBN 0-86587-047-0). Gov Insts.

Superfund Manual: Legal & Management Strategies. 2nd ed. Ridgway M. Hall, Jr. et al. (Superfund Manual Ser.). 506p. 1987. pap. text ed. 87.00 (ISBN 0-86587-704-1). Gov Insts.

Superfund Report: What Do Responsible Parties Do Now. LC 86-32208. 89.50 (ISBN 0-317-55240-6). Aspen Pub.

Superfund: The 1986 Amendments. Michael A. Brown & Practising Law Institute Staff. LC 86-63317. (Litigation & Administration Practice Ser.: No. 315). 531p. 1986. 45.00 (ISBN 0-317-59124-X, H45009). PLI.

Supergirl. Norma F. Mazer. (Illus.). 256p. (Orig.). 1984. pap. 2.95 (ISBN 0-446-32367-5). Warner Bks.

Supergirl Activity Book of Fun, 36 bks. (Illus.). 48p. (gr. 4 up). Set of 12. pap. 23.40 (ISBN 0-448-81758-6); Set of 24. pap. 46.80 (ISBN 0-448-81716-0). Putnam Pub Group.

Supergirl: The Girl of Steel. Andrew Helfer. (Super Powers Which Way Bks.: No. 2). (Illus.). 128p. (Orig.). (gr. 3-6). 1984. pap. 1.95 (ISBN 0-671-47566-5). Archway.

Supergranny & the Mystery of the Shrunken Heads. Beverly H. Van Hook. Ed. by Andrea Nelken. (Holderby Mystery Ser.: No. 1). (Illus.). 96p. (Orig.). (gr. 3-6). 1985. pap. 2.50 (ISBN 0-916761-01-0). Holderby & Bierce.

Supergranny: The Case of the Riverboat Riverbelle. Beverly H. Van Hook. Ed. by Andrea Nelken. (Holderby Mystery Ser.: No. 2). (Illus.). 112p. (Orig.). (gr. 3-6). 1986. pap. 2.50 (ISBN 0-916761-02-9). Holderby & Bierce.

Supergranny: The Ghost of Heidelberg Castle, No. 3. Beverly H. Van Hook. Ed. by Andrea Nelken. (Illus.). 112p. (Orig.). (gr. 3-6). 1987. pap. 2.50 (ISBN 0-916761-03-7). Holderby & Bierce.

Supergrasses: The Use of Accomplice Evidence in Northern Ireland. Tony Gifford. 1984. 20.00x (ISBN 0-900137-21-5, Pub. by NCCL UK). State Mutual Bk.

Supergravity. Ed. by P. Van Nieuwenhuizen & D. Z. Freedman. 342p. 1980. 97.50 (ISBN 0-444-85438-X, North-Holland). Elsevier.

Supergravity Nineteen Eighty One. Ed. by S. Ferrara & J. G. Taylor. LC 82-1204. 512p. 1982. 47.50 (ISBN 0-521-24738-1). Cambridge U Pr.

Supergravity Theories, Anomalies & Compactification: Commentary & Reprints, 2 vols. Ed. by A. Salam & E. Sezgin. 1400p. 1988. Set. 97.00 (ISBN 9971-50-119-8); Set. pap. 48.00 (ISBN 9971-50-122-8, Pub. by World Sci Singapore). World Scientific Pub.

Supergravity Theory: A Geomatric Perspective, 2 vols. L. Castellani et al. 1200p. 1988. 99.00 (ISBN 9971-50-037-X); pap. 55.00 (ISBN 9971-50-038-8). World Scientific Pub.

Superhard Materials, Convection, & Optical Devices. Ed. by R. B. Heimann et al. (Crystals - Growth, Properties, & Applications Ser.). (Illus.). 200p. 1988. 101.80 (ISBN 0-387-18602-6). Springer-Verlag.

Superheavy Elements: Proceedings. International Symposium on Superheavy Elements, March 9-11, 1978, Lubbock, Texas. Ed. by M. A. Lodhi. 604p. 1979. 110.00 (ISBN 0-08-022946-8). Pergamon.

Superheroes. Nancy L. Dehnbostel & Mary E. Hartman. (P.E.P.P.E.R. Ser.). (Illus.). 48p. (gr. 1-6). 1983. pap. 5.95 Tchr Enrichment Bk (ISBN 0-88047-026-7, 8306). DOK Pubs.

Superhistorians: Makers of Our Past. John Barker. 365p. 1983. pap. text ed. write for info. (ISBN 0-02-306070-0, Pub. by Scribner). Macmillan.

Superhuman Life of Gesar of Ling. Alexandra David-Neel & Lama Yongden. Ed. by Kees W. Bolle. LC 77-79120. (Mythology Ser.). 1978. Repr. of 1934 ed. lib. bdg. 34.50x (ISBN 0-405-10532-0). Ayer Co Pubs.

Supernatural Fiction Writers: Fantasy & Horror, 2 vols. Ed. by Everette F. Bleiler. 1985. lib. bdg. 130.00 (ISBN 0-684-17808-7, ScribR). Scribner.
Supernatural Hawaii. Margaret Stone. LC 87-125359. (Hawaiiana Ser.). (Illus.). 38p. (Orig.). 1979. pap. 3.95 (ISBN 0-941351-03-3). Aloha Pub.
Supernatural Horizons: From Glory to Glory. Charles Hunter & Frances Hunter. 1983. pap. 5.95 (ISBN 0-917726-52-9). Hunter Bks.
Supernatural Horror in Literature. Howard P. Lovecraft. Ed. by E. F. Bleiler. 1973. pap. 3.50 (ISBN 0-486-20105-8). Dover.
Supernatural in Early Spanish Literature. Frank Callcott. 158p. 1.00 (ISBN 0-318-14309-7). Hispanic Inst.
Supernatural in English Romantic Poetry. Sukumar Dutt. LC 72-197457. 1938. lib. bdg. 35.00 (ISBN 0-8414-3883-8). Folcroft.
Supernatural in Fiction. Ed. by Leo P. Kelley. (Patterns in Literary Art Ser.). 324p. (gr. 10-12). 1973. pap. 13.80 (ISBN 0-07-033497-8). McGraw.
Supernatural in Modern Fiction. Dorothy Scarborough. 1967. lib. bdg. 20.50 (ISBN 0-374-97049-1, Octagon). Hippocrene Bks.
Supernatural in Relation to the Natural. James McCosh. LC 75-3267. Repr. of 1862 ed. 38.00 (ISBN 0-404-59255-4). AMS Pr.
Supernatural in Romantic Fiction. Edward Yardley. LC 78-3504. 1979. Repr. of 1880 ed. lib. bdg. 29.50 (ISBN 0-8495-6124-8). Arden Lib.
Supernatural in Romantic Fiction. Edward Yardley. LC 76-40241. 1880. lib. bdg. 30.50 (ISBN 0-8414-9761-3). Folcroft.
Supernatural in Romantic Fiction. Edward Yardley. 1979. 42.50 (ISBN 0-685-94350-X). Bern Porter.
Supernatural in Shakespeare. Helen H. Stewart. LC 72-13282. 1972. Repr. of 1908 ed. lib. bdg. 35.50 (ISBN 0-8414-1168-9). Folcroft.
Supernatural in the Modern German Drama. G. Baerg. 59.95 (ISBN 0-8490-1160-4). Gordon Pr.
Supernatural in the Tragedies of Euripides. Ernest H. Klotsche. 107p. 1980. 10.00 (ISBN 0-89005-343-X). Ares.
Supernatural Intervention in the Tempest & Sakuntala. Mandakranta Bose. Ed. by James Hogg. (Jacobean Drama Studies). 71p. (Orig.). 1980. pap. 15.00 (ISBN 3-7052-0401-7, Salzburg Studies). Longwood Pub Group.
Supernatural Marine Ring. Mary J. Nesbit. (Illus.). 128p. 1987. 8.95 (ISBN 0-8059-3081-7). Dorrance.
Supernatural Omnibus. Montague Summers. Repr. lib. bdg. 34.95x (ISBN 0-88411-989-0, Pub. by Aeonian Pr). Amereon Ltd.
Supernatural Power & the Occult. Lynn Walker. 1977. pap. 4.00 (ISBN 0-88027-093-4). Firm Foun Pub.
Supernatural Power of Jesus. John MacArthur, Jr. (John MacArthur's Bible Studies). 1985. pap. 4.95 (ISBN 0-8024-5113-6). Moody.
Supernatural Short Stories of Charles Dickens. Ed. by Michael Hayes. 1979. 11.95 (ISBN 0-7145-3678-4). Riverrun NY.
Supernatural Short Stories of Robert Louis Stevenson. 188p. (Orig.). 1986. pap. 11.95 (ISBN 0-7145-3550-8). Riverrun NY.
Supernatural Short Stories of Sir Walter Scott. Ed. by Michael Hayes. 224p. (Orig.). 1986. pap. 9.95 (ISBN 0-7145-4086-2). Riverrun NY.
Supernatural Solution: Chilling Stories of Spooks & Sleuths. Ed. by Michel Parry. LC 75-27979. 224p. 1976. 8.95 (ISBN 0-8008-7497-8). Taplinger.
Supernatural Stories: Thirteen Tales of the Unexpected. Jean Russell. LC 87-7881. 160p. (gr. 4-7). 1987. 11.95 (ISBN 0-531-05723-2); PLB 11.99 (ISBN 0-531-08323-3). Orchard Bks Watts.
Supernatural Tales: Excursions into Fantasy. Vernon Lee. LC 87-60976. 222p. 1987. 18.95 (ISBN 0-7206-0680-2, Pub. by P Owen Ltd). Dufour.
Supernatural Tales of Sir Arthur Conan Doyle. Ed. by Peter Haining. (Illus.). 272p. 1988. 27.50x (ISBN 0-572-01453-8, Pub. by W Foulsham UK). Trans-Atl Phila.
Supernaturals Among Carolina Folk & Their Neighbors. F. Roy Johnson. (Illus.). 256p. (gr. 8-12). 1974. 9.50 (ISBN 0-930230-25-6). Johnson NC.
Supernova! Christopher Lampton. Ed. by Maury Solomon. (Impact Ser.). (Illus.). 128p. (YA) (gr. 7 up). 1988. 12.90 (ISBN 0-531-10602-0). Watts.
Supernova One: S. F. Introduction. 1977. 8.95 (ISBN 0-571-10984-5). Transatl Arts.
Supernova Search Charts & Handbook. Gregg D. Thompson & James T. Bryan, Jr. (Illus.). 96p. Date not set. price not set hbk. (ISBN 0-521-26721-8); charts avail. Cambridge U Pr.
Supernova Story. Laurence A. Marschall. (Illus.). 305p. 1988. 22.95 (ISBN 0-306-42955-1, Plenum Pr). Plenum Pub.
Supernova 1987A: Astronomy's Explosive Enigma. Russell M. Genet. Ed. by Donald S. Hayes & Douglas S. Hall. (Illus.). 210p. 1987. 23.95 (ISBN 0-944389-01-5). Fairborn AZ.
Supernova 1987A in the Large Magellanic Cloud. Ed. by Minas Kafatos. 420p. 1988. 64.50 (ISBN 0-521-35575-3). Cambridge U Pr.
Supernovae. Paul Murdin & Lesley Murdin. 260p. 1985. 24.95 (ISBN 0-521-30038-X). Cambridge U Pr.
Supernovae. Ed. by David Schramm. (Astrophysics & Space Science Library: No. 66). 1977. lib. bdg. 29.00 (ISBN 90-277-0806-1, Pub. by Reidel Holland). Kluwer Academic.
Supernovae: A Survey of Current Research. M. Rees & R. Stoneham. 1982. 69.00 (ISBN 90-277-1442-8, Pub. by Reidel Holland). Kluwer Academic.
Supernovae & Supernova Remnants: Proceedings. The International Conference on Supernovae; May 7-11, 1973, Lecce, Italy. Ed. by Cosmovici. LC 73-91428. (Astrophysics & Space Science Library: No. 45). 400p. 1974. lib. bdg. 55.00 (ISBN 90-277-0427-9, Pub. by Reidel Holland). Kluwer Academic.
Supernovae & Their Remnants: Proceedings of a Conference Held at Goddard Space Center, 1967. Ed. by Peter J. Brancazio & A. G. Cameron. (Illus.). 248p. 1969. 96.00 (ISBN 0-677-13290-5). Gordon & Breach.
Supernovae As Distance Indicators. Ed. by N. Bartel. (Lecture Notes in Physics: Vol. 224). vi, 226p. 1985. pap. 15.00 (ISBN 0-387-15206-7). Springer-Verlag.
Supernovae Spectra: La Jolla Institute, 1980. Ed. by Roland Meyerhoff & George H. Gillespie. (AIP Conference Proceedings: No. 63). 173p. 1980. lib. bdg. 18.25 (ISBN 0-88318-162-2). Am Inst Physics.
Supernutrition: Megavitamin Revolution. Richard Passwater. Date not set. pap. 3.95 (ISBN 0-671-62012-6). PB.
Superoxide & Superoxide Dismutase in Chemistry, Biology & Medicine. Ed. by G. Rotillo. 688p. 1986. 193.75 (ISBN 0-444-80797-7). Elsevier.
Superoxide Dismutase, Vols. I & II. Ed. by Larry W. Oberley. 1982. Vol. I, 168p. 75.00 (ISBN 0-8493-6240-7); Vol. II, 192p. 75.00 (ISBN 0-8493-6241-5). CRC Pr.
Superoxide Dismutase: Pathological States, Vol. III. Ed. by Larry W. Oberley. 280p. 1985. 125.00 (ISBN 0-8493-6242-3). CRC Pr.
SuperPaint Secrets. Gia L. Rozells. 1988. pap. 19.95 (ISBN 0-673-38190-0). Scott F.
Superplastic Forming of Structural Alloys: Proceedings of a Symposium. The Metallurgical Society of Aime. Ed. by N. E. Paton & C. H. Hamilton. LC 82-81860. pap. 106.50 (ISBN 0-317-42099-2, 2026228). Bks Demand UMI.
Superplasticizers in Concrete. CANMET-ACI International Symposium on Superplasticizers in Concrete (1st: 1978: Ottawa, Ont) Staff. LC 79-89813. (American Concrete Institute, ACI Publication Ser.: No. SP-62). (Illus.). 433p. pap. 112.60 (2030037). Bks Demand UMI.
Superposition & Interaction: Coherence in Physics. Richard Schlegel. LC 80-11119. (Illus.). 1980. lib. bdg. 22.50x (ISBN 0-226-73841-8). U of Chicago Pr.
Superpower: A Portrait of America in the 70's. Robert Hargreaves. LC 72-88430. 600p. 1973. 10.95 (ISBN 0-312-77665-9). St Martin.
Superpower Arms Control: Setting the Record Straight. Ed. by Albert Carnesale & Richard Haass. LC 87-1372. 392p. 1987. 34.95x (ISBN 0-88730-228-9); pap. text ed. 14.95x (ISBN 0-88730-229-7). Ballinger Pub.
Superpower at Sea: U. S. Ocean Policy. Finn Laursen. LC 83-21222. 224p. 1983. 35.00 (ISBN 0-275-91033-4, C1033). Praeger.
Superpower: Comparing American & Soviet Foreign Policy. Christer Jonsson. LC 83-40585. 248p. 1984. 29.95 (ISBN 0-312-77622-5). St Martin.
Superpower Competition & Security in the Third World. Ed. by Robert S. Litwak & Samuel F. Wells. LC 87-24187. (Wilson Center Series on International Security Studies). 296p. 1987. 29.95x (ISBN 0-88730-253-X). Ballinger Pub.
Superpower Detente: A Reappraisal. Mike Bowker & Phil Williams. (Royal Institute of International Affairs). 288p. 1988. text ed. 49.95 (ISBN 0-8039-8041-8); pap. text ed. 20.95 (ISBN 0-8039-8042-6). Sage.
Superpower Diplomacy in the Horn of Africa. Samuel M. Makinda. LC 86-31379. 272p. 1987. 45.00 (ISBN 0-312-00548-2). St Martin.
Superpower Games: Applying Game Theory to Superpower Conflict. Steven J. Brams. LC 84-21876. (Illus.). 192p. 1985. text ed. 25.00x (ISBN 0-300-03323-0, Y-529); pap. 9.95x (ISBN 0-300-03364-8). Yale U Pr.
Superpower Involvement in the Middle East: The Dynamics of Foreign Policy. Ed. by Paul Marantz. (Westview Special Studies in International Relations). 300p. 1985. pap. 28.00x (ISBN 0-8133-7100-7). Westview.
Superpower Rivalry & Third World Radicalism: The Idea of National Liberation. S. Neil MacFarlane. LC 84-43081. 236p. 1985. text ed. 24.50x (ISBN 0-8018-2671-3). Johns Hopkins.
Superpower Rivalry in the Indian Ocean: Indian & American Perspectives. Ed. by Selig S. Harrison & K. Subrahmanyam. 288p. 1988. 36.00 (ISBN 0-19-505497-0). Oxford U Pr.
Superpower: The Making of a Steam Locomotive. David Weitzman. 1987. 24.95 (ISBN 0-87923-671-X). Godine.
Superpowers & International Conflict. Carsten Holbraad. LC 79-9942. 1979. 26.00x (ISBN 0-312-77674-8). St Martin.
Superpowers & Regional Crises in Central America & the Middle East. Ed. by P. Shearman & P. Williams. 240p. 1988. 36.00 (ISBN 0-08-035814-4, Pub. by Pergamon-Brasseys). Pergamon.
Superpowers & Revolution. Ed. by Jonathan R. Adelman. LC 86-21273. 316p. 1986. lib. bdg. 40.95 (ISBN 0-275-92166-2, C2166). Praeger.
Superpowers & the Balance of Power in the Arab World. Enver M. Koury. LC 79-131974. 208p. 1970. pap. 8.00 (ISBN 0-934484-01-5). Inst Mid East & North Africa.
Superpowers & the Third World: Turkish-American Relations & Cyprus. Suha Bolukbasi. LC 88-10343. (Exxon Education Foundation Series on Rhetoric & Political Discourse: Vol. 15). 288p. (Orig.). 1988. lib. bdg. 27.50 (ISBN 0-8191-6977-3, Co-pub. by White Miller Center); pap. text ed. 14.75 (ISBN 0-8191-6978-1, Co-pub. by White Miller Center). U Pr of Amer.
Superpowers in Crisis: Implications of Domestic Discord. R. J. Krickus. 248p. 1987. text ed. 30.00 (ISBN 0-08-034705-3, PDP); pap. text ed. 14.95 (ISBN 0-08-035158-1, PDP). Pergamon.
Superpremium Ice Cream Market. 270p. 1986. 1250.00 (ISBN 0-931634-62-8). FIND SVP.
SuperPro-crastinators. Joseph E. Barnes. LC 84-71554. 200p. 1985. 14.95 (ISBN 0-917732-34-0, 765); pap. 10.95 (ISBN 0-917732-35-9). Barnes-Bks.
Superprofits & Crises: Modern U. S. Capitalism. Victor Perlo. (Illus.). 504p. 1988. 21.00 (ISBN 0-7178-0665-0); pap. 9.95 (ISBN 0-7178-0662-6). Intl Pubs Co.
Superpump! Hardcore Women's Bodybuilding. Ben Weider & Robert Kennedy. LC 86-6034. (Illus.). 192p. (Orig.). 1986. pap. 9.95 (ISBN 0-8069-4800-0). Sterling.
Superpuppy: How to Choose, Raise, & Train the Best Possible Dog for You. Daniel M. Pinkwater & Jill Pinkwater. (Illus.). 208p. 1982. pap. 4.95 (ISBN 0-89919-084-7, Clarion). HM.
Superpuppy: How to Choose, Raise & Train the Best Possible Dog for You. Jill Pinkwater & Daniel M. Pinkwater. LC 76-8825. (Illus.). 208p. (gr. 6 up). 1976. 13.95 (ISBN 0-395-28878-9, Clarion). HM.
Superquake: Why Earthquakes Occur & When the Big One Will Hit Southern California. David Ritchie. (Illus.). 224p. 1988. 18.95 (ISBN 0-517-56699-0). Crown.
Supersaurus. Francine Jacobs. (Illus.). 48p. 1982. PLB 6.99 (ISBN 0-399-61150-9). Putnam Pub Group.
Superschool & the Superstate: American Education in the Twentieth Century, 1918-1970. Edgar B. Gumbert & Joel H. Spring. LC 73-22226. (Studies in the History of American Education Ser.). pap. 55.50 (ISBN 0-317-09296-0, 2013572). Bks Demand UMI.
Superscripted Revelation. Lois Griffith. 1988. price not set. Dovetree Pr.
Supersearch Software: Documentation Plus Three Media Disks. Peter K. Studner. 52p. (For IBM-PC & 100 percent Compatibles). 1987. pap. 59.95 (ISBN 0-938667-01-7). Jamenair Ltd.
Supersellers. Gerhard Gschwandtner & Laura B. Gschwandtner. LC 86-47586. 192p. 1986. 15.95 (ISBN 0-8144-5883-1). AMACOM.
Supersensible Knowledge. Rudolf Steiner. Tr. by Rita Stebbing from Ger. Orig. Title: Die Erkenntnis des Uebersinnlichen in unserer Zeit und deren Bedeutung fuer. 230p. (Eng.). 1988. 20.00 (ISBN 0-88010-190-3); pap. 9.95 (ISBN 0-88010-191-1). Anthroposophic.
Supersensitivity Following Lesions of the Nervous System: An Aspect of the Relativity of Nervous Intergration. George W. Stavraky. (Illus.). pap. 55.00 (ISBN 0-317-07847-X, 2014419). Bks Demand UMI.
Supersensonics: The Science of Radiational Paraphysics. Christopher Hills. LC 75-46093. (Illus.). 609p. (Orig.). 1978. pap. 24.95 (ISBN 0-916438-18-X, Dist. by New Era Pr). Univ of Trees.
Supershow! Pref. by Elke Solomon. LC 79-90496. (Illus.). 32p. 1979. 6.00 (ISBN 0-916365-08-5). Ind Curators.
Supershow! Educational Supplement. Susan Sollins et al. LC 79-90496. (Illus.). 54p. 1979. 6.00 (ISBN 0-916365-09-3). Ind Curators.
Supersoaps. Chris Stacey & Darcy Sullivan. 160p. 1988. 39.00x (ISBN 1-85283-206-1, Pub. by Boxtree Ltd UK). State Mutual Bk.
Supersonic. Basil Jackson. 234p. 1975. 6.95 (ISBN 0-393-08701-8). Norton.
Supersonic Cruise Technology. F. Edward McLean. LC 83-26912. (NASA SP Ser.: No. 472). (Illus.). 199p. (Orig.). 1985. pap. 6.50 (S/N 033-000-00944-5). USGPO.
Supersonic Fighter Developments. Roy Braybrock. (Illus.). 225p. 1987. 24.95 (ISBN 0-85429-582-8, Pub. by GT Foulis Ltd). Haynes Pubns.
Supersonic Flow & Shock Waves. R. Courant & K. O. Friedrichs. (Applied Mathematical Sciences: Vol. 21.). 1948. 53.00 (ISBN 0-387-90232-5). Springer-Verlag.
Supersonic Sounds: A Business Record-Keeping Practice Set. 3rd ed. N. Fritz & Richard H. Wirth. 1981. text ed. 11.76 (ISBN 0-07-022562-1). McGraw.
Superspace & Supergravity: Proceedings of the Nuffield Workshop, Cambridge, June 16-July 12, 1980. Ed. by S. W. Hawking & M. Roicek. LC 80-42091. pap. 134.50 (ISBN 0-317-39713-3, 2055939). Bks Demand UMI.
Superspace or One Thousand & One Lessons in Super Symmetry. S. J. Gates et al. LC 83-5986. 1985. 59.25 (Adv Bk Prog MSP, Adv Bk Prog MSP). Addison-Wesley.
SuperSpan: The Golden Gate Bridge. Tom Horton. LC 82-17746. (Illus.). 96p. (Orig.). 1983. pap. 10.95 (ISBN 0-87701-277-6). Chronicle Bks.
Superspies: The Secret Side of Government. Jules Archer. LC 77-72640. (gr. 7up). 1977. pap. 7.95 (ISBN 0-440-08136-X). Delacorte.
Superstar. Barry Mazer. 1977. pap. 1.50 (ISBN 0-505-51200-9, Pub. by Tower Bks). Leisure NY.
Superstar Called Sweetpea. Mary S. Davidson. LC 80-11985. 144p. 1980. 11.50 (ISBN 0-670-68478-3). Viking.
Superstar Word Search. Sonia Black & Chip Lovitt. 64p. (YA) (gr. 7 up). pap. 1.95 (ISBN 0-590-33969-9). Scholastic Inc.
Superstars: How Stellar Explosions Shape the Destiny of Our Universes. David H. Clark. (Illus.). 224p. 1984. text ed. 17.95 (ISBN 0-07-011152-9). McGraw.
Superstars of Rock: Their Lives & Their Music. Gene Busnar. LC 80-18912. (Illus.). 224p. (gr. 7 up). 1980. PLB 10.79 (ISBN 0-671-32967-7); pap. 4.95 (ISBN 0-671-32968-5). Messner.
Superstars of Rock Two. Gene Busnar. LC 84-10831. (Illus.). 192p. (gr. 7 up). 1984. 9.79 (ISBN 0-671-45626-1). Messner.
Superstars Stopped Short. Nathan Aaseng. LC 81-12431. (Sports Heroes Library). (Illus.). 80p. (gr. 4 up). 1982. PLB 7.95 (ISBN 0-8225-1326-9). Lerner Pubns.
Supersticiones y Buenos Consejos. Lydia Cabrera. LC 86-83335. (Coleccion del Chichereku). 62p. (Orig., Span.). 1988. pap. 7.95 (ISBN 0-89729-433-5). Ediciones.
Superstition. F. E. Planer. 400p. 1988. pap. 15.95 (ISBN 0-87975-494-X). Prometheus Bks.
Superstition & Force. Henry C. Lea. LC 79-148823. (World History Ser., No. 48). 1971. Repr. of 1870 ed. lib. bdg. 75.00x (ISBN 0-8383-1228-4). Haskell.
Superstition & the Press. Curtis D. MacDougall. LC 83-61115. (Science & the Paranormal Ser.). 616p. 1983. 29.95 (ISBN 0-87975-211-4); pap. 18.95 (ISBN 0-87975-212-2). Prometheus Bks.
Superstition, Are You Superstitious? Maple. pap. 2.00 (ISBN 0-87980-245-6). Wilshire.
Superstition in All Ages. Paul H. D'Holbach & Jean Meslier. 69.95 (ISBN 0-87968-108-X). Gordon Pr.
Superstition in All Ages. Jean Meslier. Tr. by Anna Knoop from Fr. LC 77-161337. (Atheist Viewpoint Ser). (Illus.). 346p. 1972. Repr. of 1890 ed. 23.50 (ISBN 0-405-03795-3). Ayer Co Pubs.
Superstition in All Ages. Jean Meslier. Tr. by Anna Knopp. 346p. 1974. pap. 13.95 (ISBN 0-88697-008-3). Life Science.
Superstitions from North Carolina, 2 vols, Vols. 6-7. Wayland D. Hand. LC 58-10967. (Frank C. Brown Collection of North Carolina Folklore Ser.). Vol. 6. 29.95 (ISBN 0-8223-0258-6); Vol. 7. 29.95 (ISBN 0-8223-0259-4). Duke.
Superstitions from Seven Towns of the United States. Catherine H. Ainsworth. LC 43-7320. (Clyde Press Folklore Bks.). vi, 58p. 1973. 4.00 (ISBN 0-933190-00-X). Clyde Pr.
Superstitions of Sailors. Angelo S. Rappoport. LC 71-158207. 290p. 1971. Repr. of 1928 ed. 43.00x (ISBN 0-8103-3739-8). Gale.
Superstitions of the Highlands & Islands of Scotland. John G. Campbell. LC 71-173104. (Illus.). Repr. of 1900 ed. 18.00 (ISBN 0-405-08337-8, Blom Pubns). Ayer Co Pubs.
Superstitions of the Highlands & Islands of Scotland. John G. Campbell. 344p. 1970. 43.00x (ISBN 0-8103-3589-1). Gale.
Superstitions of the Irish Country People. rev. ed. Padraic O'Farrell. 92p. 1982. pap. 7.95 (ISBN 0-85342-530-2, Pub. by Mercier Pr Ireland). Irish Bks Media.
Superstitions of the Irreligious. George P. Hedley. LC 78-10274. 1979. Repr. of 1951 ed. lib. bdg. 35.00x (ISBN 0-313-20755-0, HESU). Greenwood.
Superstitions, Talismans, Amulets, Crystal Gazing see Mystical Lore of Precious Stones.
Superstitious Mind: French Peasants & the Supernatural in the Nineteenth Century. Judith Devlin. LC 86-23341. 336p. 1987. text ed. 30.00 (ISBN 0-300-03710-4). Yale U Pr.
Superstocks. Hugh Ferguson. 1979. 25.00 (ISBN 0-685-49183-8). Windsor.
Superstring Theory, 2 vols. Michael B. Green & John H. Schwarz. (Cambridge Monographs on Mathematical Physics). 1988. Vol. 1, Introduction, 467p. pap. 19.95 (ISBN 0-521-35752-7); Vol. 2, Phenomenology & Field Theory. pap. 24.95 (ISBN 0-521-35753-5). Cambridge U Pr.
Superstring Theory. Michael B. Green et al. (Cambridge Monographs on Mathematical Physics). 1987. Vol. 1: Introduction, 350p. 39.50 (ISBN 0-521-32384-3); Vol. 2: Phenomenology & Field Theory, 400p. 49.50 (ISBN 0-521-32999-X). Cambridge U Pr.

Superstring Theory: DST Workshop on Superstring. Ed. by R. Ramachandran & H. S. Mari. 600p. 1988. 84.00 (ISBN 9971-50-592-4). World Scientific Pub.

Superstrings. Ed. by P. G. Freund & K. T. Mahanthappa. LC 88-6032. (NATO ASI Series B, Physics: Vol. 175). (Illus.). 360p. 1988. 75.00x (ISBN 0-306-42908-X, Plenum Pr). Plenum Pub.

Superstrings, 2 Vols. John H. Schwartz. 950p. 1986. 99.00 (ISBN 9971-978-66-0); pap. 46.00 (ISBN 9971-978-67-9). World Scientific Pub.

Superstrings: A Theory of Everything? Ed. by P. C. W. Davies & J. Brown. 180p. 1988. 34.50 (ISBN 0-521-35462-5); pap. 10.95 (ISBN 0-521-35741-1). Cambridge U Pr.

Superstrings & Grand Unification: Proceedings of the Winter School on High Energy Physics. Ed. by T. Pradhan. 400p. (Orig.). 1988. 69.00 (ISBN 9971-50-527-4); pap. 41.00 (ISBN 9971-50-528-2). World Scientific Pub.

Superstrings & the Search for the Theory of Everything. F. David Peat. 256p. 1988. 19.95 (ISBN 0-8092-4637-6). Contemp Bks.

Superstrings, Anomalies & Unification: Proceedings of the Adriatic Meeting on Particle Physics, 5th, Dubrovnik, Yugoslavia, June 16-28, 1986. Ed. by M. Martinis. 584p. 1987. 60.00 (ISBN 9971-50-232-1); pap. 32.00 (ISBN 9971-50-233-X). World Scientific Pub.

Superstrings, Composite Structures & Cosmology. Ed. by S. Gates, Jr. & R. N. Mohapatra. 604p. 1987. 94.00 (ISBN 9971-50-373-5); pap. 44.00 (ISBN 9971-50-384-0). World Scientific Pub.

Superstrings Nineteen Eighty-Seven: Proceedings of the Trieste Spring School on Superstrings, 1987. Ed. by L. Alvarez-Gaume et al. 432p. (Orig.). 1988. 64.00; pap. 44.00 (ISBN 9971-50-518-5). World Scientific Pub.

Superstrings, Supergravity, & Unified Theories. Ed. by G. Furlan et al. LC 85-31450. (ICTP Series in Theoretical Physics: Vol. 2). 560p. 1986. 82.00 (ISBN 9971-50-035-3); pap. 41.00 (ISBN 9971-50-036-1). World Scientific Pub.

Superstrings, Unified Theories & Cosmology: Proceedings of the Summer Workshop on High Energy Physics & Cosmology, Trieste, Italy, June 30-August 15, 1986. Ed. by G. Furlan et al. (ICTP Theoretical Physics Ser.: Vol. 3). 464p. 1987. 78.00x (ISBN 9971-50-271-2); pap. 32.00 (ISBN 9971-50-280-1). World Scientific Pub.

Superstructuralism: The Philosophy of Structuralism & Post-Structuralism. Richard Harland. LC 86-23627. 213p. 1987. 37.50 (ISBN 0-416-03232-X); pap. 10.95 (ISBN 0-416-03242-7). Routledge Chapman & Hall.

Supersubs of Pro Sports. Nathan Aaseng. LC 83-738. (Sports Heroes Library). (Illus.). 80p. (gr. 4up). 1983. PLB 7.95 (ISBN 0-8225-1328-5). Lerner Pubns.

Supersymetry: A Decade of Development. Ed. by Peter C. West & R. F. Streater. 496p. 1986. 72.00x (ISBN 0-85274-572-9, Pub. by A Hilger UK). Taylor & Francis.

Supersymmetry. Ed. by K. Dietz et al. (NATO ASI Series B, Physics: Vol. 125). 716p. 1985. 95.00x (ISBN 0-306-42012-0, Plenum Pr). Plenum Pub.

Supersymmetry. S. Ferrara. 1376p. 1987. 97.00 (ISBN 9971-966-21-2); pap. 48.00 (ISBN 9971-966-22-0, Pub. by Sci Singapore). World Scientific Pub.

Supersymmetry. S. Ferrara. 1987. 42.00 (ISBN 0-444-87085-7). Elsevier.

Supersymmetry. S. Ferrara. 1987. 84.00 (ISBN 0-444-87079-2). Elsevier.

Supersymmetry: An Introduction with Conceptual & Calculational Details. Ed. by H. Muller-Kirsten & A. Wiedemann. (Lecture Notes in Physics Ser.: Vol. 7). 608p. 1987. 78.00; pap. 38.00 (ISBN 9971-50-355-7). World Scientific Pub.

Supersymmetry & Its Applications: Proceedings of the Nuffield Workshop, Cambridge, 24 June to 12 July, 1985. G. Gibbons et al. 500p. 1986. 54.50 (ISBN 0-521-30721-X). Cambridge U Pr.

Supersymmetry & Supergravity. Julius Wess & Jonathan Bagger. (Princeton Series in Physics). 192p. 1983. 50.00x (ISBN 0-691-08327-4); pap. 14.95 (ISBN 0-691-08326-6). Princeton U Pr.

Supersymmetry & Supergravity: A Reprint Volume of Physics Reports. Ed. by M. Jacob. 968p. 1986. 76.50 (ISBN 0-444-87022-9, North Holland). Elsevier.

Supersymmetry & Supergravity: Collected Articles from Physics Report. Ed. by M. Jacob. 600p. 1986. 67.00 (ISBN 9971-978-74-1); pap. 41.00 (ISBN 9971-978-75-X). World Scientific Pub.

Supersymmetry & Supergravity-Nonperturbative QCD. Ed. by P. Roy & V. Singh. (Lecture Notes in Physics Ser.: Vol. 208). vi, 389p. 1984. pap. 26.00 (ISBN 0-387-13390-9). Springer-Verlag.

Supersymmetry & Supergravity, 1983: Proceedings of the XIX Winter School & Workshop Theoretical Physics, Karpacz, Poland, February 14-26, 1983. B. Milewski. 588p. 1983. 67.00 (ISBN 9971-950-23-5); pap. 36.00 (ISBN 9971-950-97-9, Pub. by World Sci Singapore). World Scientific Pub.

Supersymmetry & Supergravity '82: Proceedings of the Trieste Workshop Sept. 1982 School. Ed. by S. Ferrara & J. G. Taylor. vi, 334p. 1983. 54.00 (ISBN 9971-950-67-7); pap. 23.00 (ISBN 9971-950-68-5, Pub. by World Sci Singapore). World Scientific Pub.

Supersymmetry in Physics: Proceedings of the Conference on Supersymmetry in Physics Held at the Center for Nonlinear Studies, Los Alamos, NM. Ed. by V. A. Kostelecky & D. K. Campbell. 294p. 1985. Repr. 68.50 (ISBN 0-444-86935-2, North-Holland). Elsevier.

Supersymmetry, Superfields & Supergravity: An Introduction. Prem P. Srivastava. (Graduate Student Series in Physics). (Illus.). 172p. 1986. 68.00x (ISBN 0-85274-571-0, Pub. by A Hilger UK); pap. 34.00x (ISBN 0-85274-575-3, Pub. by A Hilger UK). Taylor & Francis.

Supersymmetry, Supergravity & Related Topics: Proceedings of the XVth GIFT International Seminar on Theoretical Physics, Sant Feliu de Guixols, Girona, Spain, June 4-9, 1984. Ed. by F. Del Aguila et al. 550p. 1985. 67.00 (ISBN 9971-966-79-4); pap. 31.00 (ISBN 9971-966-92-1, Pub. by World Sci Singapore). World Scientific Pub.

Supersymmetry, Supergravity & Superstrings '86: Proceedings of the Trieste Spring School ICTP, Trieste, Italy 7-15 April 1986. Ed. by B. De Wit et al. 576p. 1987. 78.00 (ISBN 9971-50-144-9); pap. 34.00. World Scientific Pub.

Supersymmetry Supergravity 1984: Proceedings of Trieste Spring School, Italy 1984. Ed. by B. De Wit et al. 500p. 1984. 67.00 (ISBN 9971-966-75-1); pap. 31.00 (ISBN 9971-966-76-X, Pub. by World Sci Singapore). World Scientific Pub.

Supertanks. Ed. by Joe Haldeman et al. 272p. 1987. pap. 3.50 (ISBN 0-441-79106-9, Pub. by Ace Science Fiction). Ace Bks.

Superteam Solution: Successful Teamworking in Organizations. Colin Hasting et al. 208p. 1986. text ed. 35.50x (ISBN 0-566-02621-X, Pub. by Gower Pub England). Gower Pub Co.

Superteam Solution: Successful Teamworking in Organizations. 2nd ed. Colin Heastings et al. (Illus.). 192p. 1987. pap. text ed. 15.95 (ISBN 0-88390-206-0). Univ Assocs.

SuperTed & the Birthday Search. Mike Young. LC 85-42717. (Sniffy Bks.). (Illus.). 24p. (ps-1). 1985. 4.95 (ISBN 0-394-87462-5, BYR). Random.

SuperTed & the Stolen Rocket Ship. Mike Young. LC 84-61460. (SuperTed Mini-Storybooks). (Illus.). 24p. (gr. 1-5). 1984. pap. 1.25 (ISBN 0-394-87154-5, BYR). Random.

SuperTed & the Train Robbers. Mike Young. LC 85-42710. (Picturebacks). (Illus.). 32p. (gr. 1-5). 1985. pap. 1.95 (ISBN 0-394-87463-3, BYR). Random.

SuperTed at the Funfair. Mike Young. LC 85-42718. (Illus.). 24p. (gr. 1-5). 1985. pap. 1.25 (ISBN 0-394-87464-1, BYR). Random.

SuperTed in the Artic. Mike Young. LC 85-42719. (SuperTed Minibooks). (Illus.). 24p. (gr. 1-5). 1985. pap. 1.25 (ISBN 0-394-87465-X, BYR). Random.

SuperTed on the Planet Spot. Mike Young. LC 84-61459. (SuperTed Mini-Storybooks). (Illus.). 24p. (gr. 1-5). 1984. pap. 1.25 (ISBN 0-394-87153-7, BYR). Random.

Supertongue & Other Turn Ons. William Rotsler. 1975. pap. 1.50 (ISBN 0-87067-478-1, BH478, Melrose Sq). Holloway.

Supertot: Creative Learning Activities for Children One to Three & Sympathetic Advice for Their Parents. Jean Marzollo. LC 76-47265. (Illus.). 1979. pap. 7.95 (ISBN 0-06-090657-X, CN 657, PL). Har-Row.

Supertrains. rev. ed. Rutland. (Young Engineer Bks.). (gr. 4-6). 1984. (Usborne-Hayes); PLB 12.96 (ISBN 0-88110-125-7); pap. 4.95 (ISBN 0-86020-180-5). EDC.

Supertramp: Paris. 1980. 9.95 (ISBN 0-89898-021-6). Almo Pubns.

Supertrucks. Sloan Walker & Andrew Vasey. LC 85-5379. (Crazy Car Ser.). (Illus.). 48p. (gr. 1-4). 1985. 12.95 (ISBN 0-8027-6586-6); PLB 12.85 (ISBN 0-8027-6606-4). Walker & Co.

Supertuning Your Firebird Trans-Am. Joe Oldham. (Illus.). 288p. 1982. pap. 12.95 (ISBN 0-8306-2088-5, 2088P). TAB Bks.

Superturbulent Combustion Noise. A. A. Putnam et al. 136p. 1976. softcover 5.25 (ISBN 0-318-12713-X, M40077). Am Gas Assn.

Superunification & Extra Dimensions: Proceedings of the First Torino Meeting on Superunification & Extra Dimensions, Torino, Italy, September 1985. Ed. by P. Fre. 750p. 1986. 78.00 (ISBN 9971-50-101-5). World Scientific Pub.

Supervised Occupational Experience Manual. 2nd ed. Merle A. Carwin. 242p. 1982. pap. text ed. 5.50x (ISBN 0-8134-2228-0, 2228). Inter Print Pubs.

Supervising. Christina Christenson & Thomas W. Johnson. 336p. 1982. write for info. (ISBN 0-201-03431-X); write for info. instrs' manual (ISBN 0-201-03432-8). Addison-Wesley.

Supervising: A Guide for All Levels. Paul O. Radde. LC 81-1827. 235p. 1981. text ed. 27.95 (ISBN 0-89384-053-X). Univ Assocs.

Supervising Account Clerk. Jack Rudman. (Career Examination Ser.: C-1884). (Cloth bdg. avail. on request). pap. 14.00 (ISBN 0-8373-1884-X). Natl Learning.

Supervising Accountant. Jack Rudman. (Career Examination Ser.: C-1040). (Cloth bdg. avail. on request). pap. 16.00 (ISBN 0-8373-1040-7). Natl Learning.

Supervising Addiction Specialist. Jack Rudman. (Career Examination Ser.: C-1501). (Cloth bdg. avail. on request). pap. 14.00 (ISBN 0-8373-1501-8). Natl Learning.

Supervising Admitting Clerk. Jack Rudman. (Career Examination Ser.: C-1041). (Cloth bdg. avail. on request). pap. 14.00 (ISBN 0-8373-1041-5). Natl Learning.

Supervising Air Pollution Inspector. Jack Rudman. (Career Examination Ser.: C-1502). (Cloth bdg. avail. on request). pap. 16.00 (ISBN 0-8373-1502-6). Natl Learning.

Supervising Appraiser. Jack Rudman. (Career Examination Ser.: C-1699). (Cloth bdg. avail. on request). pap. 14.00 (ISBN 0-8373-1699-5). Natl Learning.

Supervising Appraiser (Real Estate) Jack Rudman. (Career Examination Ser.: C-1680). (Cloth bdg. avail. on request). pap. 14.00 (ISBN 0-8373-1680-4). Natl Learning.

Supervising Assessor. Jack Rudman. (Career Examination Ser.: C-1042). (Cloth bdg. avail. on request). pap. 14.00 (ISBN 0-8373-1042-3). Natl Learning.

Supervising Audiologist. Jack Rudman. (Career Examination Ser.: C-2237). (Cloth bdg. avail. on request). pap. 16.00. Natl Learning.

Supervising Audit Clerk. Jack Rudman. (Career Examination Ser.: C-887). (Cloth bdg. avail. on request). pap. 14.00 (ISBN 0-8373-0887-9). Natl Learning.

Supervising Auditor. Jack Rudman. (Career Examination Ser.: C-2681). (Cloth bdg. avail. on request). pap. 16.00 (ISBN 0-8373-2681-8). Natl Learning.

Supervising Automotive Facilities Inspector. Jack Rudman. (Career Examination Ser.: C-2215). (Cloth bdg. avail. on request). pap. 16.00 (ISBN 0-8373-2215-4). Natl Learning.

Supervising Automotive Mechanic. Jack Rudman. (Career Examination Ser.: C-2575). (Cloth bdg. avail. on request). pap. 16.00 (ISBN 0-8373-2575-7). Natl Learning.

Supervising Beverage Control Investigator. Jack Rudman. (Career Examination Ser.: C-2824). (Cloth bdg. avail. on request). 1988. pap. 16.00 (ISBN 0-8373-2824-1). Natl Learning.

Supervising Bookkeeper. Jack Rudman. (Career Examination Ser.: C-2682). (Cloth bdg. avail. on request). pap. 14.00 (ISBN 0-8373-2682-6). Natl Learning.

Supervising Building Inspector. Jack Rudman. (Career Examination Ser.: C-2840). (Cloth bdg. avail. on request). 1988. pap. 16.00 (ISBN 0-8373-2840-3). Natl Learning.

Supervising Building Plan Examiner. Jack Rudman. (Career Examination Ser.: C-862). (Cloth bdg. avail. on request). pap. 16.00 (ISBN 0-8373-0862-3). Natl Learning.

Supervising Campus Security Officer. Jack Rudman. (Career Examination Ser.: C-1703). (Cloth bdg. avail. on request). pap. 16.00 (ISBN 0-8373-1703-7). Natl Learning.

Supervising Cashier. Jack Rudman. (Career Examination Ser.: C-774). (Cloth bdg. avail. on request). pap. 14.00 (ISBN 0-8373-0774-0). Natl Learning.

Supervising Children's Counselor. Jack Rudman. (Career Examination Ser.: C-2010). (Cloth bdg. avail. on request). pap. 16.00 (ISBN 0-8373-2010-0). Natl Learning.

Supervising Claim Examiner. Jack Rudman. (Career Examination Ser.: C-2322). (Cloth bdg. avail. on request). pap. 14.00 (ISBN 0-8373-2322-3). Natl Learning.

Supervising Clerk. Jack Rudman. (Career Examination Ser.: C-775). (Cloth bdg. avail. on request). pap. 14.00 (ISBN 0-8373-0775-9). Natl Learning.

Supervising Clerk (Income Maintenance) Jack Rudman. (Career Examination Ser.: C-1706). (Cloth bdg. avail. on request). pap. 14.00 (ISBN 0-8373-1706-1). Natl Learning.

Supervising Clerk-Stenographer. 4th ed. Arco Editorial Board. LC 67-25272. 1977. pap. 8.00 (ISBN 0-668-04309-1). Arco.

Supervising Community Service Worker. Jack Rudman. (Career Examination Ser.: C-2677). (Cloth bdg. avail. on request). pap. 14.00 (ISBN 0-8373-2677-X). Natl Learning.

Supervising Computer Operator. Jack Rudman. (Career Examination Ser.: C-776). (Cloth bdg. avail. on request). pap. 14.00 (ISBN 0-8373-0776-7). Natl Learning.

Supervising Construction Inspector. Jack Rudman. (Career Examination Ser.: C-1043). (Cloth bdg. avail. on request). pap. 16.00 (ISBN 0-8373-1043-1). Natl Learning.

Supervising Consumer Affairs Inspector. Jack Rudman. (Career Examination Ser.: C-1657). (Cloth bdg. avail. on request). pap. 14.00 (ISBN 0-8373-1657-X). Natl Learning.

Supervising Counselors & Therapists: A Developmental Approach. Cal D. Stoltenberg & Ursula Delworth. LC 87-45415. (Social & Behavioral Science Ser.). 1987. text ed. 22.95x (ISBN 1-55542-066-4). Jossey-Bass.

Supervising Court Officer. Jack Rudman. (Career Examination Ser.: C-1503). (Cloth bdg. avail. on request). pap. 16.00 (ISBN 0-8373-1503-4). Natl Learning.

Supervising Custodial Foreman. Jack Rudman. (Career Examination Ser.: C-1044). (Cloth bdg. avail. on request). pap. 16.00 (ISBN 0-8373-1044-X). Natl Learning.

Supervising Demolition Inspector. Jack Rudman. (Career Examination Ser.: C-777). (Cloth bdg. avail. on request). pap. 16.00 (ISBN 0-8373-0777-5). Natl Learning.

Supervising Departmental Specialist. Jack Rudman. (Career Examination Ser.: C-935). (Cloth bdg. avail. on request). pap. 14.00 (ISBN 0-8373-0924-7). Natl Learning.

Supervising Deputy Sheriff. Jack Rudman. (Career Examination Ser.: C-1666). (Cloth bdg. avail. on request). pap. 16.00 (ISBN 0-8373-1666-9). Natl Learning.

Supervising Developmental Specialist. Jack Rudman. (Career Examination Ser.: C-924). 1988. pap. 16.00 (ISBN 0-317-44909-5). Natl Learning.

Supervising Dietician. Jack Rudman. (Career Examination Ser.: C-1968). (Cloth bdg. avail. on request). pap. 14.00 (ISBN 0-8373-1968-4). Natl Learning.

Supervising Drug & Alcohol Community Coordinator. Jack Rudman. (Career Examination Ser.: C-2777). (Cloth bdg. avail. on request). 1980. pap. 16.00 (ISBN 0-8373-2777-6). Natl Learning.

Supervising Economist. Jack Rudman. (Career Examination Ser.: C-2202). (Cloth bdg. avail. on request). pap. 16.00 (ISBN 0-8373-2202-2). Natl Learning.

Supervising Electrical Inspector. Jack Rudman. (Career Examination Ser.: C-778). (Cloth bdg. avail. on request). pap. 16.00 (ISBN 0-8373-0778-3). Natl Learning.

Supervising Electronic Computer Operator. Jack Rudman. (Career Examination Ser.: C-1549). (Cloth bdg. avail. on request). pap. 14.00 (ISBN 0-8373-1549-2). Natl Learning.

Supervising Elevator Inspector. Jack Rudman. (Career Examination Ser.: C-1955). (Cloth bdg. avail. on request). pap. 16.00 (ISBN 0-8373-1955-2). Natl Learning.

Supervising Emergency Medical Service Specialist. (Career Examination Ser.: C-3480). Date not set. pap. 16.00 (ISBN 0-8373-3480-2). Natl Learning.

Supervising Employment Consultant (Testing) Jack Rudman. (Career Examination Ser.: C-2464). (Cloth bdg. avail. on request). pap. 16.00 (ISBN 0-8373-2464-5). Natl Learning.

Supervising Environmentalist. Jack Rudman. (Career Examination Ser.: C-1586). (Cloth bdg. avail. on request). pap. 16.00 (ISBN 0-8373-1586-7). Natl Learning.

Supervising Examiner - Social Services. Jack Rudman. (Career Examination Ser.: C-2140). (Cloth bdg. avail. on request). 1988. pap. 16.00 (ISBN 0-8373-2140-9). Natl Learning.

Supervising Fire Alarm Dispatcher. Jack Rudman. (Career Examination Ser.: C-1695). (Cloth bdg. avail. on request). pap. 16.00 (ISBN 0-8373-1695-2). Natl Learning.

Supervising Fire Marshal (Uniformed) Jack Rudman. (Career Examination Ser.: C-1817). (Cloth bdg. avail. on request). pap. 16.00 (ISBN 0-8373-1817-3). Natl Learning.

Supervising Food Inspector. Jack Rudman. (Career Examination Ser.: C-2055). (Cloth bdg. avail. on request). pap. 16.00 (ISBN 0-8373-2055-0). Natl Learning.

Supervising Grants Analyst. Jack Rudman. (Career Examination Ser.: C-2834). (Cloth bdg. avail. on request). 1988. pap. 16.00 (ISBN 0-8373-2834-9). Natl Learning.

Supervising Hearing Examiner. Jack Rudman. (Career Examination Ser.: C-2327). (Cloth bdg. avail. on request). pap. 18.00 (ISBN 0-8373-2327-4). Natl Learning.

Supervising Hearing Officer. Jack Rudman. (Career Examination Ser.: C-2328). (Cloth bdg. avail. on request). pap. 18.00 (ISBN 0-8373-2328-2). Natl Learning.

Supervising Highway Engineer. Jack Rudman. (Career Examination Ser.: C-2523). (Cloth bdg. avail. on request). pap. 16.00 (ISBN 0-8373-2523-4). Natl Learning.

Supervising Highway Maintenance Supervisor. Jack Rudman. (Career Examination Ser.: C-2632). (Cloth bdg. avail. on request). pap. 16.00 (ISBN 0-8373-2632-X). Natl Learning.

Supervising Hospital Care Investigator. Jack Rudman. (Career Examination Ser.: C-779). (Cloth bdg. avail. on request). pap. 16.00 (ISBN 0-8373-0779-1). Natl Learning.

Supervising Housing Groundsman. Jack Rudman. (Career Examination Ser.: C-780). (Cloth bdg. avail. on request). pap. 14.00 (ISBN 0-8373-0780-5). Natl Learning.

Supervising Housing Inspector. Jack Rudman. (Career Examination Ser.: C-1045). (Cloth bdg. avail. on request). pap. 16.00 (ISBN 0-8373-1045-8). Natl Learning.

Supervising Housing Sergeant. Jack Rudman. (Career Examination Ser.: C-1667). (Cloth bdg. avail. on request). pap. 16.00 (ISBN 0-8373-1667-7). Natl Learning.

Supervising Housing Teller. Jack Rudman. (Career Examination Ser.: C-781). (Cloth bdg. avail. on request). pap. 14.00 (ISBN 0-8373-0781-3). Natl Learning.

Supervising Housing Teller. Jack Rudman. (Career Examination Ser.: C-781). 1985. pap. 14.00 (ISBN 0-317-44910-9). Natl Learning.

Supervising Human Resources Specialist. (Career Examination Ser.: C-1046). Date not set. pap. 14.00 (ISBN 0-8373-1046-6). Natl Learning.

Supervising Human Rights Specialist. Jack Rudman. (Career Examination Ser.: C-1613). 1988. pap. 14.00 (ISBN 0-8373-1613-8). Natl Learning.

Supervising Identification Specialist. Jack Rudman. (Career Examination Ser.: C-2513). (Cloth bdg. avail. on request). pap. 16.00 (ISBN 0-8373-2513-7). Natl Learning.

Supervising in the Human Services: The Politics of Practice. Stephen M. Holloway & George Brager. 320p. 1988. 27.50 (ISBN 0-02-914810-3). Free Pr.

Supervising Incinerator Stationary Engineer. Jack Rudman. (Career Examination Ser.: C-2638). pap. 18.00 (ISBN 0-8373-2638-9). Natl Learning.

Supervising Inspector of Markets, Weights & Measures. Jack Rudman. (Career Examination Ser.: C-1047). (Cloth bdg. avail. on request). pap. 16.00 (ISBN 0-8373-1047-4). Natl Learning.

Supervising Investigator. Jack Rudman. (Career Examination Ser.: C-2106). (Cloth bdg. avail. on request). 1988. pap. 16.00 (ISBN 0-8373-2106-9). Natl Learning.

Supervising Janitor. Jack Rudman. (Career Examination Ser.: C-2065). (Cloth bdg. avail. on request). 1988. pap. 14.00 (ISBN 0-8373-2065-8). Natl Learning.

Supervising Labor Specialist. Jack Rudman. (Career Examination Ser.: C-2382). (Cloth bdg. avail. on request). pap. 16.00 (ISBN 0-8373-2382-7). Natl Learning.

Supervising Laundry Worker. Jack Rudman. (Career Examination Ser.: C-2200). (Cloth bdg. avail. on request). pap. 14.00 (ISBN 0-8373-2200-6). Natl Learning.

Supervising Legal Stenographer. Jack Rudman. (Career Examination Ser.: C-2635). (Cloth bdg. avail. on request). pap. 14.00 (ISBN 0-8373-2635-4). Natl Learning.

Supervising Manpower Counselor. Jack Rudman. (Career Examination Ser.: C-2437). (Cloth bdg. avail. on request). pap. 16.00 (ISBN 0-8373-2437-8). Natl Learning.

Supervising Meat Inspector. Jack Rudman. (Career Examination Ser.: C-2056). (Cloth bdg. avail. on request). pap. 14.00 (ISBN 0-8373-2056-9). Natl Learning.

Supervising Medicaid Claims Examiner. Jack Rudman. (Career Examination Ser.: C-2693). (Cloth bdg. avail. on request). pap. 16.00 (ISBN 0-8373-2693-1). Natl Learning.

Supervising Medical Care Representative. Jack Rudman. (Career Examination Ser.: C-3148). 1988. pap. 16.00 (ISBN 0-8373-3148-X). Natl Learning.

Supervising Medical Social Worker. Jack Rudman. (Career Examination Ser.: C-2630). (Cloth bdg. avail. on request). pap. 16.00 (ISBN 0-8373-2630-3). Natl Learning.

Supervising Mortgage Administrator. Jack Rudman. (Career Examination Ser.: C-2312). (Cloth bdg. avail. on request). 1988. pap. 16.00 (ISBN 0-8373-2312-6). Natl Learning.

Supervising Motor Vehicle License Examiner. Jack Rudman. (Career Examination Ser.: C-2390). (Cloth bdg. avail. on request). pap. 14.00 (ISBN 0-8373-2390-8). Natl Learning.

Supervising Motor Vehicle Representative. (Career Examination Ser.: C-3300). Date not set. pap. 14.00 (ISBN 0-8373-3300-8). Natl Learning.

Supervising Museum Instructor. Jack Rudman. (Career Examination Ser.: C-1048). (Cloth bdg. avail. on request). pap. 16.00 (ISBN 0-8373-1048-2). Natl Learning.

Supervising Nurse. Jack Rudman. (Career Examination Ser.: C-1883). (Cloth bdg. avail. on request). pap. 16.00 (ISBN 0-8373-1883-1). Natl Learning.

Supervising Office Systems Personnel: Strategies for Professional Management of the Automated Office. Gerald L. Hershey. (Illus.). 512p. 1985. text ed. write for info (ISBN 0-13-876749-1). P-H.

Supervising on the Job: A Self-Study Guide for Students. Patricia M Rath et al. 1971. pap. text ed. 8.00x (ISBN 0-8134-1238-2, 1238). Inter Print Pubs.

Supervising on the Line. Gene Gagnon. (Illus.). 131p. (Orig.). 1988. pap. 12.95 (ISBN 0-944671-00-4). Margo.

Supervising Painter. Jack Rudman. (Career Examination Ser.: C-3254). 1988. pap. 14.00 (ISBN 0-8373-3254-0). Natl Learning.

Supervising Parking Enforcement Agent. Jack Rudman. (Career Examination Ser.: C-2143). (Cloth bdg. avail. on request). 1988. pap. 14.00 (ISBN 0-8373-2143-3). Natl Learning.

Supervising Parking Meter Collector. Jack Rudman. (Career Examination Ser.: C-782). (Cloth bdg. avail. on request). pap. 14.00 (ISBN 0-8373-0782-1). Natl Learning.

Supervising Photographer. Jack Rudman. (Career Examination Ser.: C-2504). (Cloth bdg. avail. on request). pap. 14.00 (ISBN 0-8373-2504-8). Natl Learning.

Supervising Physical Therapist. Jack Rudman. (Career Examination Ser.: C-2904). (Cloth bdg. avail. on request). pap. 16.00 (ISBN 0-8373-2904-3). Natl Learning.

Supervising Physician & Surgeon. Jack Rudman. (Career Examination Ser.: C-2195). (Cloth bdg. avail. on request). pap. 29.95 (ISBN 0-8373-2195-6). Natl Learning.

Supervising Plumbing Inspector. Jack Rudman. (Career Examination Ser.: C-1049). (Cloth bdg. avail. on request). pap. 16.00 (ISBN 0-8373-1049-0). Natl Learning.

Supervising Police Personnel: Back to the Basics. Paul Whisenand & George Rush. (Illus.). 432p. 1987. text ed. 36.00 (ISBN 0-13-876178-7). P-H.

Supervising Probation Officer. Jack Rudman. (Career Examination Ser.: C-2591). (Cloth bdg. avail. on request). pap. 14.00 (ISBN 0-8373-2591-9). Natl Learning.

Supervising Professional Conduct Investigator. Jack Rudman. (Career Examination Ser.: C-2299). (Cloth bdg. avail. on request). 1988. pap. 14.00 (ISBN 0-8373-2299-5). Natl Learning.

Supervising Program Research Specialist. Jack Rudman. (Career Examination Ser.: C-3201). 1988. pap. 18.00 (ISBN 0-8373-3201-X). Natl Learning.

Supervising Public Health Adviser. Jack Rudman. (Career Examination Ser.: C-3176). 1988. pap. 14.00 (ISBN 0-8373-3176-5). Natl Learning.

Supervising Public Health Nurse. Jack Rudman. (Career Examination Ser.: C-1748). (Cloth bdg. avail. on request). 1988. pap. 16.00 (ISBN 0-8373-1748-7). Natl Learning.

Supervising Public Health Sanitarian. Jack Rudman. (Career Examination Ser.: C-2275). (Cloth bdg. avail. on request). 1988. pap. 14.00 (ISBN 0-8373-2275-8). Natl Learning.

Supervising Real Estate Manager. Jack Rudman. (Career Examination Ser.: C-1860). (Cloth bdg. avail. on request). pap. 16.00 (ISBN 0-8373-1860-2). Natl Learning.

Supervising Rent Examiner. Jack Rudman. (Career Examination Ser.: C-1818). (Cloth bdg. avail. on request). pap. 16.00 (ISBN 0-8373-1818-1). Natl Learning.

Supervising Sanitary Engineer. Jack Rudman. (Career Examination Ser.: C-2447). (Cloth bdg. avail. on request). pap. 16.00 (ISBN 0-8373-2447-5). Natl Learning.

Supervising Sanitation Inspector. Jack Rudman. (Career Examination Ser.: C-2455). (Cloth bdg. avail. on request). pap. 16.00 (ISBN 0-8373-2455-6). Natl Learning.

Supervising Security Officer. Jack Rudman. (Career Examination Ser.: C-2205). (Cloth bdg. avail. on request). pap. 14.00 (ISBN 0-8373-2205-7). Natl Learning.

Supervising Senior Citizens Club Leader. Jack Rudman. (Career Examination Ser.: C-2829). (Cloth bdg. avail. on request). pap. 16.00. Natl Learning.

Supervising Social Welfare Examiner. Jack Rudman. (Career Examination Ser.: C-2379). (Cloth bdg. avail. on request). pap. 16.00 (ISBN 0-8373-2379-7). Natl Learning.

Supervising Special Officer. Jack Rudman. (Career Examination Ser.: C-1766). (Cloth bdg. avail. on request). pap. 14.00 (ISBN 0-8373-1766-5). Natl Learning.

Supervising Stenographer. Jack Rudman. (Career Examination Ser.: C-783). (Cloth bdg. avail. on request). pap. 14.00 (ISBN 0-8373-0783-X). Natl Learning.

Supervising Storekeeper. Jack Rudman. (Career Examination Ser.: C-861). (Cloth bdg. avail. on request). pap. 14.00 (ISBN 0-8373-0861-5). Natl Learning.

Supervising Street Club Worker. Jack Rudman. (Career Examination Ser.: C-1050). (Cloth bdg. avail. on request). pap. 14.00 (ISBN 0-8373-1050-4). Natl Learning.

Supervising Student Internships in Human Services. Ed. by Carlton E. Munson. LC 83-26393. (The Clinical Supervisor: Vol. 2, No. 1). 84p. 1984. text ed. 22.95 (ISBN 0-86656-301-6). Haworth Pr.

Supervising Student Teachers the Professional Way: A Guide for Cooperating Teachers. 3rd rev. ed. Marvin A. Henry & W. Wayne Beasley. LC 81-50782. 244p. 1982. pap. text ed. 12.95 (ISBN 0-916768-05-8). Sycamore Pr.

Supervising Support Investigator. Jack Rudman. (Career Examination Ser.: C-2766). (Cloth bdg. avail. on request). 1988. pap. 14.00 (ISBN 0-8373-2766-0). Natl Learning.

Supervising Systems Analyst. Jack Rudman. (Career Examination Ser.: C-2387). (Cloth bdg. avail. on request). pap. 16.00 (ISBN 0-8373-2387-8). Natl Learning.

Supervising Tabulator Operator. Jack Rudman. (Career Examination Ser.: C-1681). (Cloth bdg. avail. on request). pap. 14.00 (ISBN 0-8373-1681-2). Natl Learning.

Supervising Target Teaching. 3rd ed. Richard H. Ehrgott & F. William Luehe. 98p. 1983. pap. text ed. 7.95 (ISBN 0-943141-02-8). Key Pubns CA.

Supervising Taxi & Limosine Inspector. Jack Rudman. (Career Examination Ser.: C-2554). (Cloth bdg. avail. on request). pap. 14.00 (ISBN 0-8373-2554-4). Natl Learning.

Supervising Technical & Professional People. 2nd ed. Martin Broadwell & Ruth S. House. LC 85-26628. 300p. 1986. 24.95 (ISBN 0-471-81785-6). Wiley.

Supervising the Electronic Office. Caroline Blaazer & Eric Molyneux. 202p. 1984. text ed. 27.95x (ISBN 0-566-02448-9). Gower Pub Co.

Supervising the Union-Free Workforce: A Pro-Employee Approach. Doug Kalish. 112p. (Orig.). 1986. pap. text ed. write for info. (ISBN 0-938883-00-3). SERA Presents.

Supervising Therapist. Jack Rudman. (Career Examination Ser.: C-2253). (Cloth bdg. avail. on request). 1988. pap. 16.00 (ISBN 0-8373-2253-7). Natl Learning.

Supervising Thermostat Repairer. (Career Examination Ser.: C-3409). Date not set. pap. 16.00 (ISBN 0-8373-3409-8). Natl Learning.

Supervising Today: A Guide for Positive Leadership. 2nd ed. Martin Broadwell. LC 85-29576. (Training & Development Ser.). 267p. 1986. pap. 14.95 (ISBN 0-471-83674-5). Wiley.

Supervising Typist. Jack Rudman. (Career Examination Ser.: C-1928). (Cloth bdg. avail. on request). pap. 14.00 (ISBN 0-8373-1928-5). Natl Learning.

Supervising Vocational Counselor. Jack Rudman. (Career Examination Ser.: C-2439). (Cloth bdg. avail. on request). pap. 16.00 (ISBN 0-8373-2439-4). Natl Learning.

Supervising Water Use Inspector. Jack Rudman. (Career Examination Ser.: C-1051). (Cloth bdg. avail. on request). pap. 14.00 (ISBN 0-8373-1051-2). Natl Learning.

Supervising Youth Division Counselor. Jack Rudman. (Career Examination Ser.: C-2501). (Cloth bdg. avail. on request). pap. 16.00 (ISBN 0-8373-2501-3). Natl Learning.

Supervision. 2nd ed. Keys. 1988. pap. write for info. (ISBN 0-471-63545-6). Wiley.

Supervision. Bernard Keys & Joy Henshall. LC 83-14713. (Management Ser.: 1-309). 399p. 1984. write for info. (ISBN 0-471-07820-4); tchrs manual avail. (ISBN 0-471-80374-X). Wiley.

Supervision. Lussier. 1989. 29.95 (ISBN 0-256-06502-0). Irwin.

Supervision. R. Wayne Mondy & Jerry M. DeHay. 345p. 1983. text ed. write for info (ISBN 0-394-33102-8, RanC). Random.

Supervision. Charles M. Ray & Charles L. Eison. 396p. 1983. text ed. 30.95x (ISBN 0-03-054556-0); instr's manual 19.95 (ISBN 0-03-054561-7). Dryden Pr.

Supervision. Coursebook ed. 1988. write for info. (ISBN 0-471-61349-5). Wiley.

Supervision. rev. ed. George R. Terry & Leslie W. Rue. (Plaid Ser.). 141p. 1981. pap. 10.95 (ISBN 0-256-02718-8). Dow Jones-Irwin.

Supervision. Paul R. Timm. (Illus.). 503p. 1984. text ed. 36.50 (ISBN 0-314-77836-5); instrs.' manual avail. (ISBN 0-314-77837-3). West Pub.

Supervision: A Decision-Making Approach. Eileen Gambrill & Theodore J. Stein. (Vol. 35). 192p. 1983. pap. 12.95 (ISBN 0-8039-2149-7). Sage.

Supervision: A Guide to Practice. 2nd ed. Jon Wiles & Joseph Bondi. 384p. 1986. text ed. 34.95 (ISBN 0-675-20485-2). Merrill.

Supervision: A Situational Approach. Thomas Kirkpatrick. 624p. 1987. text ed. 28.00 (ISBN 0-534-07314-X). PWS Kent Pub.

Supervision: An Introduction to Business Management. Steven L. Shapiro. 1978. 13.50 (ISBN 0-87005-213-6); instructor's guide o.p. 2.50 (ISBN 0-87005-306-X). Fairchild.

Supervision & Management of Quantity Preparation: Principles & Procedures. 2nd, rev ed. William J. Morgan, Jr. LC 80-83876. (Illus.). 1981. 28.50 (ISBN 0-8211-1254-6); text ed. 26.00x 10 or more copies. McCutchan.

Supervision & Performance: Managing Professional Work in Human Service Organizations. Douglas R. Bunker & Marion H. Wijnberg. LC 88-42779. 1988. 29.95x (ISBN 1-55542-099-0). Jossey-Bass.

Supervision & Teaching of Reading. Julia A. Harris. 1927. 20.00 (ISBN 0-932062-75-X). Sharon Hill.

Supervision & Training: Models, Dilemmas, & Challenges. Ed. by Florence W. Kaslow. LC 85-27037. (Clinical Supervisor Ser.: Vol.4 (1-2)). 259p. 1986. text ed. 32.95 (ISBN 0-86656-528-0); pap. text ed. 19.95 (ISBN 0-86656-529-9). Haworth Pr.

Supervision Can Be Easy. David K. Lindo. (Illus.). 1979. 14.95 (ISBN 0-8144-5548-4). AMACOM.

Supervision Can Be Easy! David K. Lindo. LC 79-17682. pap. 70.50 (ISBN 0-317-26952-6, 2023582). Bks Demand UMI.

Supervision Card Course. pap. 7.95. Looseleaf Law.

Supervision: Concepts & Practices of Management. 4th ed. Theo Haimann & Raymond L. Hilgert. 1987. pap. text ed. write for info. (ISBN 0-538-07940-1, G94). SW Pub.

Supervision, Consultation, & Staff Training in the Helping Professions. Florence W. Kaslow et al. LC 77-82819. (Social & Behavioral Science Ser). 1977. text ed. 29.95x (ISBN 0-87589-353-8). Jossey-Bass.

Supervision Course. 9th ed. Hy Hammer. LC 83-8843. 240p. (Orig.). 1984. pap. 10.00 (ISBN 0-668-05618-5). Arco.

Supervision CSS. write for info. Looseleaf Law.

Supervision Evaluation of Teaching: A Due Process Model. Robert Furman. 1988. 13.95 (ISBN 0-533-07333-2). Vantage.

Supervision: Focus on Instruction. Don M. Beach & Judy Reinhartz. 1988. text ed. 31.05t (ISBN 0-06-040558-9, HarpC). Har-Row.

Supervision for Better Instruction: Practical Techniques for Improving Staff Performance. Marcia Knoll. 256p. 1987. 27.50 (ISBN 0-13-876426-3). P-H.

Supervision for Better Schools. 5th ed. John T. Lovell & Kimball Wiles. (Illus.). 352p. 1983. 33.67 (ISBN 0-13-876169-8). P-H.

Supervision for Staff Development: Ideas & Application. Ronald C. Doll. 450p. 1983. 38.00 (ISBN 0-205-07854-0, 237854); write for info. Allyn.

Supervision for Today's Schools. 2nd ed. Peter F. Oliva. LC 83-5417. 480p. pap. text ed. 29.95 (ISBN 0-582-28420-1). Longman.

Supervision: Human Perspectives. 3rd ed. Thomas J. Sergiovanni & Robert J. Starratt. (Illus.). 384p. 1983. text ed. 34.95 (ISBN 0-07-056312-8). McGraw.

Supervision in Action. 4th ed. Claude S. George. 1985. text ed. write for info. (ISBN 0-8359-7160-0, Reston); instr's. manual avail. (ISBN 0-8359-7161-9). P-H.

Supervision in Communication Disorders. Stephen S. Farmer & Judith Farmer. 416p. 1988. 29.95 (ISBN 0-675-20963-3). Merrill.

Supervision in Early Childhood Education. Joseph J. Caruso & M. Temple Fawcett. (Early Childhood Education Ser.). 256p. 1986. pap. text ed. 16.95x (ISBN 0-8077-2802-0). Tchrs Coll.

Supervision in Education: Problems & Practices. Daniel Tanner & Laurel Tanner. x, 1093p. 1987. text ed. write for info. (ISBN 0-02-418950-2). Macmillan.

Supervision in European Community Law: Observance by the Member States of Their Treaty Obligations - A Treatise on International & Supranational Supervision. H. Audretsch. 304p. 1978. 61.75 (ISBN 0-444-85037-6, North-Holland). Elsevier.

Supervision in European Community Law: Observance by the Member States of their Treaty Obligations-A Treatise on International & Supra-National Supervision. 2nd ed. H. A. H. Audretsch. 782p. 1986. 144.75 (ISBN 0-444-70027-7, North-Holland). Elsevier.

Supervision in German Elementary Education, 1918-1933. Clara G. Stratemeyer. LC 73-177815. (Columbia University. Teachers College. Contributions to Education: No. 734). Repr. of 1938 ed. 22.50 (ISBN 0-404-55734-1). AMS Pr.

Supervision in Human Communication Disorders: Perspectives on a Process. Ed. by Martha B. Crago & Marisue Pickering. LC 87-3757. (Illus.). 250p. (Orig.). 1987. pap. text ed. 22.00 (ISBN 0-316-15907-7, 159077). College-Hill.

Supervision in International Economic Organizations: The NIEO-Perspective. Ed. by P. Van Dijk. 450p. 1983. 53.00 (ISBN 90-65-44076-3). Kluwer Academic.

Supervision in Social Work. 2nd ed. Alfred Kadushin. LC 84-21397. 608p. 1985. 25.00 (ISBN 0-231-06008-4). Columbia U Pr.

Supervision in the Administration of Justice: Police, Corrections, Courts. 2nd ed. Paul B. Weston. (Illus.). 224p. 1978. 28.25 (ISBN 0-398-03762-0). C C Thomas.

Supervision in the Health Care Organizations. Richard I. Lyles & Carl Joiner. LC 85-17799. 245p. 1986. 18.95 (ISBN 0-471-80459-2, Wiley Medical). Wiley.

Supervision in the Hospitality Industry. 2nd ed. John P. Daschler & Jack D. Ninemeier. (Illus.). 350p. 1989. text ed. 36.95 (ISBN 0-86612-052-1). Educ Inst Am Hotel.

Supervision in the Hospitality Industry. John P. Daschler & Jack D. Nineneier. Ed. by Marj Harless. LC 83-20722. (Illus.). 332p. 1984. 36.95 (ISBN 0-86612-016-5). Educ Inst Am Hotel.

Supervision in the Hospitality Industry. Jack E. Miller & Mary Porter. LC 84-11861. (Service Management Ser.). 347p. 1985. write for info. (ISBN 0-471-88706-4). Wiley.

Supervision in Thought & Action. 3rd ed. William H. Lucio & John D. McNeil. (Illus.). 1979. text ed. 36.95 (ISBN 0-07-038952-7). McGraw.

Supervision: Key Link to Productivity. 2nd ed. Leslie W. Rue & Lloyd L. Byars. 1986. pap. 25.95 (ISBN 0-256-03366-8); pap. 9.95x study guide (ISBN 0-256-03367-6). Irwin.

Supervision Made Simple. William Goldstein. LC 82-60800. (Fastback Ser.: No. 180). 50p. 1982. pap. 0.90 (ISBN 0-87367-180-5). Phi Delta Kappa.

Supervision of Applied Training: A Comparative Review. Ed. by DeWayne J. Kurpius et al. LC 76-28640. 1977. lib. bdg. 67.95 (ISBN 0-8371-9288-9, KSA/). Greenwood.

Supervision of Bilingual Programs. Juan C. Munguia. Ed. by Francesco Cordasco. LC 77-90555. (Bilingual-Bicultural Education in the U. S. Ser.). 1978. lib. bdg. 24.50x (ISBN 0-405-11093-6). Ayer Co Pubs.

Supervisory Management: Guidelines for Application. Robert C. Lowery. (Illus.). 640p. 1985. text ed. write for info. (ISBN 0-13-877176-6). P-H.

Supervisory Management: The Art of Working with & Through People. 2nd ed. Donald C. Mosley et al. 588p. 1989. text ed. write for info. (ISBN 0-538-80026-7, GZ66BA). SW Pub.

Supervisory Management: The Art of Work with & Through People. Donald C. Mosley et al. 1985. write for info. (ISBN 0-538-07660-7, G66). SW Pub.

Supervisory Mechanisms in International Economic Organizations. Ed. by Pieter Van Dijk. 1984. lib. bdg. 140.00 (ISBN 90-6544-076-3, Pub. by Kluwer Law Netherlands). Kluwer Academic.

Supervisory Personnel Management: Building Work Relationships. Institute of Financial Education Staff. 1988. pap. 19.95 (ISBN 0-912857-45-5). Inst Finan Educ.

Supervisory Process in Speech-Language Pathology & Audiology. Jean L. Anderson. 1988. text ed. 29.50 (ISBN 0-316-03959-4, 039594). College-Hill.

Supervisory Skills. Harold M. Emanuel et al. LC 85-81542. 251p. 1985. pap. text ed. 25.00 (ISBN 0-89462-024-X). IIA.

Supervisory Skills. Howard Wilson. 1973. pap. 1.50 (ISBN 0-910022-17-8). ARA.

Supervisory Skills in Marketing. Lucy Crawford. Ed. by Eugene L. Dorr. (Occupational Manuals & Projects in Marketing Ser.). (Illus.). (gr. 9-10). 1977. pap. 12.04 (ISBN 0-07-013471-5). McGraw.

Supervisory Studies. 4th ed. P. W. Betts. (Illus.). 498p. 1983. pap. text ed. 26.50x (ISBN 0-7121-1992-2). Trans-Atl Phila.

Supervisory Techniques for the Security Professional. Guy Wanat et al. 160p. 1981. text ed. 22.95 (ISBN 0-409-95035-1). Butterworth.

Supervisory Training. Walter S. Wikstrom. (Report Ser: No. 612). 57p. (Orig.). 1973. pap. 15.00 (ISBN 0-8237-0052-6). Conference Bd.

Supervisory Training Approaches & Methods. Compiled by Bradford B. Boyd. 162p. 8.25 (ISBN 0-318-13287-7, BOSTP); members 6.50 (ISBN 0-318-13288-5). Am Soc Train & Devel.

SuperVocabulary Builder: A Strategies Approach. Rose Wassman & Gail Benchener. 1986. IBM version. pap. write for info. (ISBN 0-673-18634-2); Apple version. write for info. (ISBN 0-673-18633-4). Scott F.

Superweapon: The Making of MX. John Edwards. 288p. 1982. 16.95 (ISBN 0-393-01523-8). Norton.

Superwest. Massimo Mattioli. Ed. by Bernd Metz. Tr. by Tom Leighton from Fr. (Illus.). 48p. 1987. 12.95 (ISBN 0-87416-035-9). Catalan Communs.

Superwoman Sydrome. Marjorie H. Shaevitz. LC 84-40091. 17.50 (ISBN 0-446-51310-5). Warner Bks.

Superwoman Syndrome. Marjorie H. Shaevitz. 1985. pap. 3.95 (ISBN 0-446-32979-7). Warner Bks.

Superwoman Turns Forty: The Story of One Woman's Intentions to Grow Up. Donna Schaper. Ed. by Marcia Broucek. (Women's Ser.). (Illus.). 80p. (Orig.). 1988. pap. 7.95 (ISBN 0-931055-57-1). LuraMedia.

Superworld. Steven Otfinoski. (Magic Micro Ser.: No. 2). 80p. (Orig.). (gr. 2-5). 1985. pap. 1.95 (ISBN 0-590-33477-8). Scholastic Inc.

Superwreck: Amoco Cadiz--The Shipwreck That Had to Happen. Rudolph Chelminski. LC 86-23831. (Illus.). 288p. 87. 17.95 (ISBN 0-688-06954-1). Morrow.

Superzap: IBM-PC Version 1.0. Dale Buscaino & Scott Daniel. Ed. by David Moore & Charles Trapp. (Illus.). 104p. 1985. softcover & disk 49.95 (ISBN 0-932679-00-5). Blue Cat.

Suplementum Epigraphicum Graecum, Vol. 33. Ed. by H. W. Pleket & R. S. Stroud. (Lat. & Gr.). 1986. 65.00 (ISBN 0-89005-449-5). Ares.

Supper Club Chez Martha Rose: A Cookbook of Parties & Tables from Paris. Martha R. Shulman. (Illus.). 320p. 1988. 24.95 (ISBN 0-689-11990-9). Atheneum.

Supper in the Evening: Pioneer Tales of Michigan. rev. 2nd ed. Al Barnes. LC 67-26278. (Illus.). 254p. 1985. pap. 10.95 (ISBN 0-915937-01-8). Hor Bks MI.

Supper of the Lamb: A Culinary Reflection. Robert F. Capon. LC 78-14937. 271p. 1979. pap. 3.95 (ISBN 0-15-686893-8, Harv). HarBracej.

Supper of the Lord. Deborah J. Baker et al. (Orig.). 1988. pap. 1.75 (ISBN 1-55673-023-3, 8807). CSS of Ohio.

Supper of the Lord: The New Testament, Ecumenical Dialogues & Faith & Order on "Eucharist". John Reumann. LC 84-47932. 224p. 1984. pap. 13.95 (ISBN 0-8006-1816-5). Fortress.

Supper Table. Maurice L. Monette. LC 85-62299. 74p. (Orig.). 1987. pap. 8.95 (ISBN 0-934134-48-0). Sheed & Ward MO.

Suppers & Snacks. Carol Bowen. LC 85-60085. (Creative Cuisine Ser.). 80p. 1985. pap. 4.95 (ISBN 0-89586-345-6). Price Stern.

Suppertime for Baby Ben. Harriet Ziefert. LC 84-61324. (Baby Ben Bks.). (Illus.). 16p. (ps). 1985. 3.95 (ISBN 0-394-87024-7, BYR). Random.

Suppertime for Frieda Fuzzypaws. Cyndy Szekeres. (Cyndy Szekeres Board Bks.). (Illus.). 16p. (ps-k). 1985. 4.95 (ISBN 0-307-12234-4, Pub. by Golden Bks). Western Pub.

Supplement a la Revue de la Musique Dramatique en France see Revue de la Musique Dramatique en France.

Supplement: A Narrative of the Vice-Regal Embassy to Vilcabamba, 1571, & of the Execution of the Inca Tupac Amaru, December, 1571 see History of the Incas.

Supplement: An Annotated Bibliography of Oceanic Music & Dance. Mervyn McLean. 74p. 1981. pap. text ed. 8.00x (ISBN 0-8248-0862-2). UH Pr.

Supplement au Dictionnaire de la Bible, 7 vols. H. Cazelles et al. 128p. (Fr.). 1967. Set. 1995.00 (ISBN 0-686-56943-1, M-6065). French & Eur.

Supplement Au Voyage de Bougainville: Avec: Pensees Philosophiques, Lettre sur les Aveugles. Denis Diderot & Antoine Adam. 192p. 1972. 9.95 (ISBN 0-686-56030-2). French & Eur.

Supplement au Voyage de Cook. Jean Giraudoux. pap. 9.95 (ISBN 0-685-33929-7). French & Eur.

Supplement au Voyage de Cook see Theatre.

Supplement Aux Dictionnaire Arabe (Arabic-French, 2 vols. R. Dozy. (Arabic & Fr.). 1969. 80.00x (ISBN 0-86685-106-2). Intl Bk Ctr.

Supplement aux supercheries litteraires. Brunet. 99.95 (ISBN 0-685-35982-4). French & Eur.

Supplement C: The Chemistry of Triple Bonded Groups. Saul Patai & Zvi Rappoport. (Chemistry of Functional Groups Ser.). 1983. Repr. Pt. 1, 736p. 310.00 (ISBN 0-471-28030-5); Pt. 2, 785p. 310.00 (ISBN 0-471-28031-3). Wiley.

Supplement Drawings for Embryology. Graham P. DuShane. LC 55-5121. pap. 20.00 (ISBN 0-317-28105-4, 2024091). Bks Demand UMI.

Supplement E: Chemistry of Ethers, Crown Ethers, Hydroxyl Group & Their Sulphur Analogs. Ed. by Saul Patai. LC 80-41256. (Chemistry of Functional Group Ser.). 1142p. 1981. Set. 550.00 (ISBN 0-471-27618-9, Pub. by Wiley-Interscience); Pt. 1 - 608 Pgs. 285.00 (ISBN 0-471-27771-1); Pt. 2 - 534 Pgs. pap. 285.00 (ISBN 0-471-27772-X). Wiley.

Supplement for the Days of Remembrance & Thanksgiving. Norman Lamm. 1973. 0.85x (ISBN 0-87306-079-2). Feldheim.

Supplement Four, Nineteen Seventy-Eight to Nineteen Eighty-Five: Water Law Bibliography. John E. Christensen & Deann E. Hupe. Ed. by Carolyn S. Dickerson. 424p. 1987. text ed. write for info. (ISBN 0-87084-922-0). Anderson Pub Co.

Supplement Guide to Manuscripts Relating to the American Indian in the Library of the American Philosophical Society, Vol. 65S. Daythal Kendall. LC 81-65976. (Memoirs Ser.: 65S). 1983. 15.00 (ISBN 0-87169-650-9). Am Philos.

Supplement No. 1 1987: Resolutions & Decisions of the Economic & Social Council. Organizational Session for 1987 New York, 3-6 February 1987 First Regular Session of 1987 New York, 4-29 May 1987. 66p. 1988. pap. 9.00 (E.1987/87). UN.

Supplement Number 1 to the 1977 Edition of the Code for the Construction & Equipment of Ships Carrying Dangerous Chemicals in Bulk. 24p. 1978. 7.00 (ISBN 0-686-70789-3, IMCO049, Pub. by Intl Maritime Orgn). UNIPUB.

Supplement of "Helium". Evgenii M. Lifshits & E. L. Andronikashvili. LC 59-8465. pap. 44.00 (ISBN 0-317-08930-7, 2003365). Bks Demand UMI.

Supplement of the Dictionary of the English Language of the XII, XIII, XIV, & XV Centuries. 3rd ed. Franz H. Stratmann. 93p. 1980. Repr. of 1881 ed. lib. bdg. 32.00 (ISBN 0-8492-8111-3). R West.

Supplement on Aging (SOA) to the 1984 National Health Interview Survey. Joseph E. Fitti & Mary G. Kovar. Ed. by Klaudia Cox. LC 87-1323. (Series 1: No. 21). 263p. Date not set. pap. 6.00 (ISBN 0-8406-0369-X). Natl Ctr Health Stats.

Supplement Relating to the Annex to the Convention on Facilitation...International Maritime Traffic. 64p. (Orig.). 1987. pap. text ed. 7.50 (ISBN 92-801-1219-8, IMCO362 87 03E, Pub. by Intl Maritime Orgn). UNIPUB.

Supplement Six. Committee for Development Planning, 1986: Report on the Twenty-Second Session. (Official Records). 1986. pap. 7.00 (ISBN 0-317-52476-3). UN.

Supplement to a Bibliography of George Moore. Edwin Gilcher. 200p. 1988. lib. bdg. 29.95x (ISBN 0-88736-199-4). Meckler Corp.

Supplement to a Bibliography of United States-Latin American Relations Since 1810. Ed. by Michael C. Meyer. LC 79-1243. xxvi, 193p. 1979. 21.50x (ISBN 0-8032-3051-6). U of Nebr Pr.

Supplement to a Bio-Bibliography for the History of the Biochemical Sciences Since 1800. Joseph S. Fruton. LC 82-72158. (Special Publications Ser.: No. 395). 262p. 1986. 15.00 (ISBN 0-87169-980-X). Am Philos.

Supplement to a California Flora. Philip A. Munz. 1968. pap. 22.50x (ISBN 0-520-00904-5). U of Cal Pr.

Supplement to a Guide to Jim Beam Bottles. 12th ed. Al Cembura & Constance Avery. (Illus.). 24p. 1987. pap. 5.60 (ISBN 0-317-64505-6). Cembura.

Supplement to "A Monograph of Clavaria & Allied Genera". E. Corner. (Illus.). 1970. pap. 74.00x (ISBN 3-7682-5433-X). Lubrecht & Cramer.

Supplement to ABA Standards for Criminal Justice. American Bar Association Staff. 1986. pap. 48.00 (ISBN 0-316-03724-9). Little.

Supplement to Allibone's Critical Dictionary of English Literature & British & American Authors, 2 vols. J. F. Kirk. 200.00 (ISBN 0-8490-1161-2). Gordon Pr.

Supplement to American Criminal Procedure, Cases & Commentary, 1988. 2nd ed. Stephen A. Saltzburg. (American Casebook Ser.). 1988. pap. text ed. write for info. (ISBN 0-314-44486-6). West Pub.

Supplement to Analytical Toxicology Methods Manual with Cumulative Index. Ed. by H. M. Stahr. 312p. 1981. 18.00x (ISBN 0-8138-1626-2). Iowa St U Pr.

Supplement to Antitrust Civil Jury Instructions. LC 80-67740. 88p. 1986. looseleaf 30.00 (ISBN 0-89707-215-4, 503-0060-01). Amer Bar Assn.

Supplement to Bell's British Theatre, Farces-1784, 4 vols. Ed. by John Bell. LC 76-44552. (Illus.). 1977. 42.50 ea.; 170.00 set (ISBN 0-404-00830-5). AMS Pr.

Supplement to Bibliography on Deafness: 1977 to 1979. Ed. by George W. Fellendorf. 1980. pap. text ed. 3.95 (ISBN 0-88200-139-6, L9435). Alexander Graham.

Supplement to Birds of the World in Philately. Beverly S. Ridgely & Gustavs E. Eglaus. (Illus.). 62p. 1986. pap. text ed. 6.00 (ISBN 0-935991-00-X). Am Topical Assn.

Supplement to Black African Literature in English: 1777-1981. Ed. by Bernth Linfors. 290p. 1986. 24.50 (ISBN 0-8419-0962-8, Africana). Holmes & Meier.

Supplement to Charles Evans' American Bibliography. Roger P. Bristol. LC 73-94761. (Bibliographical Society Ser). 640p. 1970. 50.00x (ISBN 0-8139-0287-8). U Pr of Va.

Supplement to Children's Books on Africa & Their Authors. Nancy J. Schmidt. LC 78-24102. (African Bibliographic Ser.: Vol. 5). 1979. 35.00 (ISBN 0-8419-0433-2, Africana). Holmes & Meier.

Supplement to Constitutional Law, the American Constitution, Constitutional Rights & Liberties. 6th ed. William B. Lockhart et al. (American Casebook Ser.). 1988. pap. text ed. write for info. (ISBN 0-314-44485-8). West Pub.

Supplement to Corporations 1986: Law & Policy, Materials & Problems, 1982. Lewis D. Solomon et al. (American Casebook Ser.). 345p. 1986. pap. 10.95 (ISBN 0-314-26047-1). West Pub.

Supplement to Criminal Law: Theory & Process. Loftus E. Becker & Joseph Goldstein. 1982. pap. 9.95x (ISBN 0-02-912320-8). Free Pr.

Supplement to Dodsley's Old Plays, Vol. 1: The Chester Plays, a Collection of Mysteries. Ed. by T. Amyot et al. (Shakespeare Society of London Publications: Vol. 1). pap. 52.00 (ISBN 0-8115-0160-4). Kraus Repr.

Supplement to Dodsley's Old Plays, Vol. 2: Ludus Coventriae, a Collection of Mysteries; The Marriage of Wit & Wisdom; The Moral Play of Wit & Science. Ed. by T. Amyot et al. (Shakespeare Society of London Publications: Vol. 2). pap. 52.00 (ISBN 0-8115-0161-2). Kraus Repr.

Supplement to Dodsley's Old Plays, Vol. 3: Patient Grissil, a Play; Sir Thomas More, a Play; Ralph Roister Doister, a Comedy; The Tragedie of Gorboduc. Ed. by T Amyot et al. (Shakespeare Society of London Publications: Vol. 3). pap. 52.00 (ISBN 0-8115-0162-0). Kraus Repr.

Supplement to Dodsley's Old Plays, Vol. 4: The First Sketch of Shakespeare's Merry Wives of Windsor; the First Sketches of the Second & Third Parts of Henry VI; the True Tragedy of Richard III; the Old Taming of the Shrew. Ed. by T. Amyot et al. (Shakespeare Societyof London Publications: Vol. 4). pap. 52.00 (ISBN 0-8115-0163-9). Kraus Repr.

Supplement to Dodson-Dotson Family of Southwest Virginia. (Illus.). 125p. 1965. 15.00 (ISBN 0-89308-025-X, FH 8). Southern Hist Pr.

Supplement to Doing Business in Saudi Arabia & the Arab Gulf States, 1977. LC 77-86478. 1977. 40.00 (ISBN 0-916400-02-6). Inter-Crescent.

Supplement to Duthie's Flora of the Upper Gangetic Plain & of the Adjacent Siwalik & Sub-Himalayan Tracts. M. B. Raizada. 1978. 18.75x (ISBN 0-89955-305-2, Pub. by Intl Bk Dist). Intl Spec Bk.

Supplement to E. J. Labarre's Dictionary & Encyclopaedia of Paper & Paper-Making. Ed. by E. G. Loeber. 114p. text ed. 28.25 (ISBN 90-265-0038-6, Pub. by Swets Pub Serv). Swets North Am.

Supplement to Edward S. Corwin's Constitution & What It Means Todays. Edward S. Corwin. Ed. by Harold W. Chase & Craig R. Ducat. 1981. pap. 3.50x (ISBN 0-691-02761-7). Princeton U Pr.

Supplement to Edwin S. Corwin's "The Constitution & What It Means Today," 1979. Harold W. Chase & Craig R. Ducat. LC 79-2504. 1981. pap. 3.50 (ISBN 0-691-02762-5). Princeton U Pr.

Supplement to Federal Income Taxation, 1985. Boris Brittker et al. 1985. pap. text ed. write for info. Little.

Supplement to Federal Wage & Hour Law, 1980: No. B244. Louis Weiner. 50p. 1980. pap. 4.00 (ISBN 0-317-30800-9). Am Law Inst.

Supplement to Finding Birds in Mexico, 1985. Ernest P. Edwards et al. LC 84-81944. (Illus.). 176p. 1985. pap. 12.00 (ISBN 0-911882-08-1). E P Edwards.

Supplement to Guide to Publishers & Distributors Serving Minority Languages. Harpreet K. Sandhu. 26p. 1982. 3.90 (ISBN 0-317-15085-5). Natl Clearinghse Bilingual Ed.

Supplement to Gwinnett County, Georgia, Families, 1818-1968. Alice S. McCabe. 32p. (Orig.). 1988. pap. write for info. (ISBN 0-914923-08-0). Gwinnett Hist.

Supplement to Illinois Handbook of Criminal Law Decisions. Robert E. Davison. 1985. pap. text ed. 17.00 (ISBN 0-318-18986-0). Illinois Bar.

Supplement to Index of Artists. D. T. Mallett. 19.00 (ISBN 0-8446-1298-7). Peter Smith.

Supplement to Judicial Remedies in the European Communities. L. J. Brinkhorst & H. G. Schermers. xii, 183p. 1972. pap. text ed. 10.00x (ISBN 90-268-0641-8). Rothman.

Supplement to Let's Make It Happen. 32p. 1983. pap. 2.25 (ISBN 0-88441-333-0, 20-817). Girl Scouts USA.

Supplement to Livelys of America, 1972. John Vallentine. 1973. 8.00 (ISBN 0-87012-159-6). McClain.

Supplement to Making It on Your Own. Nancy Chandler & Jo Wintker. 21p. (Orig.). 1984. pap. text ed. 3.50 (ISBN 0-89695-013-1). U Tenn CSW.

Supplement to Maritime History. pap. 5.00 (ISBN 0-916617-01-7). J C Brown.

Supplement to Max Farrand's Records of the Federal Convention of 1787. James Hutson. LC 86-51340. 512p. 1987. text ed. 45.00 (ISBN 0-300-03903-4); pap. 14.95x (ISBN 0-300-03904-2, Y-652). Yale U Pr.

Supplement to Mister Warburton's Edition of Shakespeare. Thomas Edwards. LC 76-164762. Repr. of 1748 ed. 11.50 (ISBN 0-404-02262-6). AMS Pr.

Supplement to Modern Criminal Procedure & Basic Criminal Procedure, 1988. 6th ed. Yale Kamisar et al. (American Casebook Ser.). 1988. pap. text ed. write for info. (ISBN 0-314-44483-1). West Pub.

Supplement to National Legislation & Regulations Relating to Transnational Corporations. pap. 9.00 (ISBN 92-1-104025-6, E.80.II.A.5). UN.

Supplement to Railway Stamps. Howard J. Burkhalter & Allen Pollock. 52p. 1988. pap. 5.00. Am Topical Assn.

Supplement to Reference Guide to Minnesota History: A Subject Bibliography 1970-80. Michael Brook & Sarah P. Rubinstein. LC 83-5438. 69p. 1983. pap. 6.95 (ISBN 0-87351-160-3). Minn Hist.

Supplement to Register of Northfield, Pt. 1. 1987. 35.00x (Pub. by Birmingham Midland Soc UK). State Mutual Bk.

Supplement to Russian-English Dictionary of Electrotechnology & Applied Sciences. Paul Macura. LC 85-8652. 240p. 1986. lib. bdg. 19.50 (ISBN 0-89874-873-9). Krieger.

Supplement to South Carolina Marriages, 1688-1820. Brent H. Holcomb. LC 84-80460. 57p. 1984. pap. 6.00 (ISBN 0-8063-1075-8). Genealog Pub.

Supplement to Standardized Quantity Recipe File - for Quality & Cost Control. Institution Management Department, Iowa State University. 1984. 16.95x (ISBN 0-8138-1566-5). Iowa St U Pr.

Supplement to Table of Sines & Cosines to Ten Decimal Places at Thousandths of a Degree. Herbert E. Salzer & Norman Levine. LC 85-73900. 66p. 1987. pap. 3.50 (ISBN 0-915061-02-3). Applied Sci Pubns.

Supplement to the Bibliography of the Works of Rudyard Kipling, 1927. Flora V. Livingston. 333p. Repr. of 1938 ed. lib. bdg. 75.00 (ISBN 0-89987-487-8). Darby Bks.

Supplement to the Bibliography of Walter Gropius see American Association of Architectural Bibliographers' Papers.

Supplement to the Book of Hymns. Ed. by Carlton R. Young. 160p. (Orig.). 1981. pap. 4.75 (ISBN 0-687-03757-3); pap. 6.75 accompanist ed. (ISBN 0-687-03758-1). Abingdon.

Supplement to the Bright Star Catalogue. Dorrit Hoffleit et al. vi, 135p. (Orig.). 1984. pap. 12.00 (ISBN 0-914753-01-0). Yale U Observ.

Supplement to the Check List of Plant & Soil Nematodes, 1961-1965: A Nomenclatorial Compilation. Armen C. Tarjan. LC 60-10226. 129p. pap. 33.60 (2030012). Bks Demand UMI.

Supplement to the Code of Safe Practice for Ships Carrying Timber Deck Cargoes. 18p. 1979. 7.00 (ISBN 0-686-70784-2, INCO54, Pub. by Intl Maritime Orgn). UNIPUB.

Supplement to the Dictionary of American Library Biography. Ed. by Wayne A. Wiegand. 250p. 1989. lib. bdg. 35.00 (ISBN 0-87287-586-5). Libs Unl.

Supplement to the Dictionary of the English Language of the 12th, 13th, 14th, & 15th Centuries. 3rd ed. Franz H. Stratmann. LC 76-30620. 1977. Repr. of 1881 ed. lib. bdg. 35.00 (ISBN 0-8414-7554-7). Folcroft.

Supplement to the Fact Book-1986: Statistics & Market Data. rev. ed. (Illus.). 100p. 1986. pap. 39.95 (ISBN 0-933641-06-5). Direct Mkt.

Supplement to the Fire Litigation Handbook. National Fire Protection Association Staff. 25.00 (ISBN 0-317-46512-0, B7-SPP-79S). Natl Fire Prot.

Supplies & Office Maintenance, Vol. 8. A. Ziegler. (Illus.). 1982. pap. 21.95 (ISBN 0-87489-157-4). Med Economics.
Supplies for the Confederate Army. 1976. pap. 5.00 (ISBN 0-89029-036-9). Pr of Morningside.
Supplies Management for Health Service. Stanley Hyman. 244p. 1979. 30.00x (ISBN 0-85664-707-1, Pub. by Croom Helm Ltd). Routledge Chapman & Hall.
Supply & Costs in the U. S. Petroleum Industry: Two Econometric Studies. Franklin M. Fisher. LC 77-86394. (Resources for the Future, Inc. Publications). 192p. Repr. of 1964 ed. 42.50 (ISBN 0-404-60332-7). AMS Pr.
Supply & Demand for College Graduates in the South, 1985. Marilu H. McCarty & Eva C. Galambos. 1978. pap. text ed. 2.50 (ISBN 0-686-23907-5). S Regional Ed.
Supply & Demand for Foster Family Care in the Southeast. George Thomas et al. 115p. 1977. 3.50 (ISBN 0-318-16358-6, B26). Regional Inst Social Welfare.
Supply & Demand for Money. Keith Cuthbertson. 352p. 1985. 39.95x (ISBN 0-631-14339-4). Basil Blackwell.
Supply & Price Outlook for Crops. S. L. Bapna & K. R. Rao. 262p. 1987. 18.50x (ISBN 81-204-0218-9, Pub. by Oxford IBH). South Asia Bks.
Supply & Quality of Rural Transport Services in Developing Countries: A Comparative Review. S. Carapetis et al. (Working Paper: No. 654). 64p. 1984. 5.00 (ISBN 0-8213-0390-2, WP 0654). World Bank.
Supply & Welfare Effects of Rice-Pricing Policy in Thailand. Gerald O'Mara & Vinh Le-Si. (Staff Working Paper: No. 0714). 138p. 1985. 8.00 (ISBN 0-318-11909-9, WP 0714). World Bank.
Supply Clerk. (Career Examination Ser.: C-3340). Date not set. pap. 12.00 (ISBN 0-8373-3340-7). Natl Learning.
Supply Management: Material for Management Training in Agricultural Cooperatives (MATCOM, Viena. 4th ed. 1986. 24.50. Intl Labour Office.
Supply of & Demand for Qualified Librarians. 72p. 1977. pap. text ed. 10.50x (ISBN 0-85365-870-6, Pub. by Library Assn Pub London). ALA.
Supply of Heroes. James Carroll. 432p. 1987. pap. 4.95 (ISBN 0-451-14875-4, Sig). NAL.
Supply of Heroes. James Carroll. 1986. 17.95 (ISBN 0-525-24450-6). Dutton.
Supply of Heroes. James Carroll. 614p. 1987. lib. bdg. 19.95x (ISBN 0-8161-4264-5, Large Print Bks). G K Hall.
Supply of Natural Resources: The Case of Oil & Natural Gas. Robert M. Spann. Ed. by Stuart Bruchey. LC 78-22748. (Energy in the American Economy Ser.). (Illus.). 1979. lib. bdg. 12.00x (ISBN 0-405-12013-3). Ayer Co Pubs.
Supply of Petroleum Reserves in South-East Asia. Corazon M. Siddayao. 260p. 1980. 32.00. Graham & Trotman.
Supply Response for Rubber in Sri Lanka: A Preliminary Analysis. Michael J. Hartley et al. (Working Paper: No. 657). 96p. 1984. 5.00 (ISBN 0-8213-0403-8, WP 0657). World Bank.
Supply Side: Debating Current Economic Policies. Thomas R. Swartz et al. LC 83-70925. (Contemporary Focus Paperback Ser.). (Illus.). 252p. 1983. pap. text ed. 9.95 (ISBN 0-87967-476-8). Dushkin Pub.
Supply-Side Economics: A Critical Appraisal. Intro. by Richard H. Fink. LC 82-51294. (Illus.). 488p. 1982. lib. bdg. 27.50 (ISBN 0-89093-460-6, Aletheia Bks); pap. 12.00. U Pubns Amer.
Supply-Side Economics in the Nineteen Eighties: Conference Proceedings. Federal Reserve Bank of Atlanta Staff & Emory University Law & Economics Center Staff. LC 82-15025. (Illus.). 572p. 1982. lib. bdg. 36.95 (ISBN 0-89930-045-6, FSU/, Quorum). Greenwood.
Supply-Side Portfolio Strategies. Ed. by Victor A. Canto & Arthur B. Laffer. LC 87-13091. 200p. 1988. lib. bdg. 35.00 (ISBN 0-89930-286-6, LFP/, Quorum Bks). Greenwood.
Supply-Side Revolution: An Insider's Account of Policymaking in Washington. Paul C. Roberts. (Illus.). 328p. 1984. 25.00x (ISBN 0-674-85620-1). Harvard U Pr.
Supply-Side Revolution: An Insider's Account of Policymaking in Washington. Paul C. Roberts. 328p. 1985. pap. 9.95 (ISBN 0-674-85621-X). Harvard U Pr.
Supply-Side Solution. Ed. by Bruce Bartlett & Timothy P. Roth. LC 83-7619. 1983. pap. text ed. 18.95x (ISBN 0-934540-18-7). Chatham Hse Pubs.
Supply-Side Tax Policy: Its Relevance to Developing Countries. Ved P. Gandhi et al. LC 87-29890. 400p. 1987. pap. 20.00 (ISBN 0-939934-91-4). Intl Monetary.
Supplycacyon of Soulys: Agaynst the Supplycacyon of Beggars. Thomas More. LC 72-220. (English Experience Ser.: No. 353). 88p. 1971. Repr. of 1529 ed. 25.00 (ISBN 90-221-0353-6). Walter J Johnson.
Supplying Energy Through Greater Efficiency: The Potential for Conservation in California's Residential Sector. Alan K. Meier et al. LC 83-47661. (Illus.). 200p. 1983. 28.00x (ISBN 0-520-04848-2). U of Cal Pr.
Supplying Household Heating Services by High Temperature Circulating Liquids & Vapors. E. F. Davis et al. (Research Bulletin Ser.: No. 3). iv, 23p. 1948. 2.50. Inst Gas Tech.
Supplying Repression: U. S. Support for Authoritarian Regimes Abroad. rev. ed. Michael T. Klare & Cynthia Arnson. 165p. 1981. 9.95 (ISBN 0-89758-033-8); pap. 4.95 (ISBN 0-89758-024-9). Inst Policy Stud.
Supplying War. Martin L. Van Creveld. LC 77-5550. 1979. pap. 14.95 (ISBN 0-521-29793-1). Cambridge U Pr.
Support & Struggle. Ed. by Joseph L. Tropea et al. 1984. 12.95 (ISBN 0-317-54016-5). Am Italian.
Support Collector. Jack Rudman. (Career Examination Ser.: C-2800). (Cloth bdg. avail. on request). 1988. pap. 14.00 (ISBN 0-8373-2800-4). Natl Learning.
Support Costs in the Defense Budget: The Submerged One-Third: A Staff Paper. Martin Binkin. LC 72-646. (Studies in Defense Policy Ser.). pap. 20.00 (2027739). Bks Demand UMI.
Support Every Outbreak of Protest & Rebellion see Strategic Outlook & Alliances.
Support for Independent Scholarship & Research. Elbridge Sibley. LC 51-5070. (Social Science Research Council Bulletin). 1951. pap. 10.00 (ISBN 0-527-03310-3). Kraus Repr.
Support for Parents & Infants: A Manual for Parent Organization & Professionals. Ed. by C. F. Boukydis. 256p. 1986. 29.95 (ISBN 0-7102-0038-2, 0038W, Pub. by Routledge UK). Routledge Chapman & Hall.
Support for School Management. A. J. Bailey. 192p. 1987. 31.00 (ISBN 0-7099-5033-0, Pub. by Croom Helm UK). Routledge Chapman & Hall.
Support for Secession: Lancashire & the American Civil War. Mary Ellison. LC 72-80158. 276p. 1973. 17.00x (ISBN 0-226-20593-2). U of Chicago Pr.
Support for Social Work Education. Date not set. 1.10. Coun Soc Wk Ed.
Support for the Poor in the Mishnaic Law of Agriculture: Tractate Peah. Roger Brooks. LC 83-8719. (Brown Judaic Studies: No. 43). 220p. 1983. pap. 21.00 (ISBN 0-89130-632-3, 14 00 43). Scholars Pr GA.
Support Groups for Caregivers of the Aged: A Training Manual for Facilitators. Harriet Rzetelny & Jonna Mellor. LC 84-167188. 72p. (Orig.). 1981. pap. 7.50 (ISBN 0-88156-008-1). Comm Serv Soc NY.
Support Investigator. Jack Rudman. (Career Examination Ser.: C-2765). (Cloth bdg. avail. on request). 1988. pap. 14.00 (ISBN 0-8373-2765-2). Natl Learning.
Support Library Reference Manual for DOS 8087 Systems. Intel Staff. 406p. 1985. pap. 20.00 (ISBN 0-917017-64-1, 122406). Intel Corp.
Support Library Reference 80287: DOS. Intel Staff. 180p. 1985. pap. 18.00 (ISBN 0-917017-78-1, 122461). Intel Corp.
Support Network in a Caring Community. Ed. by J. A. Yoder et al. 1985. text ed. 24.50 (ISBN 90-247-3200-X, Pub. by Martinus Nijhoff Netherlands). Kluwer Academic.
Support of Life. Gene Liberty. (Orig.). (YA) (gr. 7-10). 1975. pap. text ed. 10.33 (ISBN 0-87720-011-4). AMSCO Sch.
Support of Schools in Colonial New York by the Society for the Propagation of the Gospel in Foreign Parts. William W. Kemp. LC 78-176933. (Columbia University. Teachers College. Contributions to Education: No. 56). Repr. of 1913 ed. 22.50 (ISBN 0-404-55056-8). AMS Pr.
Support of Schools in Colonial New York by the Society for the Propagation of the Gospel in Foreign Parts. William W. Kemp. LC 72-89192. (American Education: Its Men, Institutions, & Ideas, Ser. 1). 1969. Repr. of 1913 ed. 12.00 (ISBN 0-405-01430-9). Ayer Co Pubs.
Support of State Educational Programs by Dedication of Specific Revenues & by General Revenue Appropriations: A Study of Certain Factors Which Relate to the Adoption & Use of These General Policies by State Governments. William I. Pearman. LC 75-177147. (Columbia University. Teachers College. Contributions to Education: No. 591). Repr. of 1933 ed. 22.50 (ISBN 0-404-55591-8). AMS Pr.
Support of the Shaken Sangat: Meetings with Three Masters. A. S. Oberoi. Ed. by Russell Perkins. LC 84-50911. (Illus.). 256p. (Orig.). 1984. pap. 15.00 (ISBN 0-89142-043-6). Sant bani Ash.
Support Organizations for the Engineering Community. National Research Council. (Engineering Education & Practice in the United States Ser.). 80p. 1985. pap. text ed. 10.50x (ISBN 0-309-03629-1). Natl Acad Pr.
Support Practice Handbook: Preparation, Negotiation, Trial. Neil Hurowitz. LC 85-24069. (Kluwer Family Law Library). 628p. 1985. text ed. 80.00 (ISBN 0-930273-14-1). Kluwer Law Bk.
Support-Raising Handbook: A Guide for Christian Workers. Brian Rust & Barry McLeish. LC 84-22448. 156p. (Orig.). 1984. pap. 9.95 (ISBN 0-87784-326-0). Inter-Varsity.
Support Services Review: Problem Identification & Analysis of Patient Care. (QRB Special Edition Ser.). 64p. 1981. pap. 20.00 (ISBN 0-86688-048-8). Joint Comm Hlthcare.
Support Staff Desk Manual. Carol Mosely & Billy Bitely. 160p. 1983. 11.50 (37,530). NCLS Inc.
Support Staff Development. Rex P. Gatto. (Illus.). 161p. 1987. teacher's ed. 67.95 (ISBN 0-945997-13-2); wrkbk. 52.50. GATTO Training Assocs.
Support Systems & Mutual Help. Ed. by Gerald Caplan & Marie Killilea. LC 76-7473. (Illus.). 336p. 1976. 64.50 (ISBN 0-8089-0927-4, 790785). Grune.
Support Systems for Buildings. Jack R. Lewis. (Illus.). 608p. 1986. text ed. 50.00 (ISBN 0-13-877184-7). P-H.
Supported Employment: A Community Implementation Guide. G. Thomas Bellamy et al. LC 87-14367. 304p. (Orig.). 1988. pap. text ed. 21.00 (ISBN 0-933716-83-4). P H Brookes.
Supported Metal Complexes: A New Generation of Catalysts. F. R. Hartley. LC 85-19362. 1985. lib. bdg. 59.00 (ISBN 90-277-1855-5, Pub. by Reidel Holland). Kluwer Academic.
Supported Self-Study in Secondary Education. Philip Waterhouse. (Orig.). 1983. pap. text ed. 21.00x (ISBN 0-86184-112-3). Trans Atl Phila.
Supporting an Adoption. Pat Holmes. 28p. 1986. pap. 3.50 (ISBN 0-9611872-1-2). Our Child Pr.
Supporting Art & Culture. DeGrazia. 12.95x (ISBN 0-317-07058-4); pap. 6.95 (ISBN 0-88311-913-7). Lieber-Atherton.
Supporting Classroom Instruction Through the School Media Center: A Collection of Case Studies. Ed. by George K. Sheppard. 53p. (Orig.). 1984. pap. 5.95 (ISBN 0-914677-02-0). Contemp Issues.
Supporting Documents: Transborder Data Flows: Concerns in Privacy Protection & Free Flow of Information, Vol. II. Ed. by Rein Turn & Alexander D. Roth. 300p. 1979. pap. 28.75 (ISBN 0-88283-024-4). AFIPS Pr.
Supporting Families Who Care for Severely Disabled Children at Home: A Public Policy Perspective. Susan Cina & Francis G. Caro. 74p. (Orig.). 1984. pap. 6.00 (ISBN 0-88156-038-3). Comm Serv Soc Ny.
Supporting K-5 Reading Instruction in the School Library Media Center. Lea-Ruth C. Wilkens. LC 84-460. 144p. 1984. pap. text ed. 12.50x (ISBN 0-8389-0397-5). ALA.
Supporting Literacy: Developing Effective Learning Environments for the Classroom. Catherine E. Loughlin & Mavis D. Martin. 208p. 1987. pap. 15.95x (ISBN 0-8077-2859-4). Tchrs Coll.
Supporting the Changing Family: A Guide to the Parent-to-Parent Model. B. Reschly. 90p. 1979. pap. 10.00. High-Scope.
Supporting the Eighteen Percent: The Experience of the Six LEA's. Harriet Gross & Caroline Gipps. 200p. 1987. 36.00x (ISBN 1-85000-141-3, Falmer Pr); pap. 19.00x (ISBN 1-85000-142-1, Falmer Pr). Taylor & Francis.
Supporting Young Adolescents: A Guide to Leading Parent Meetings. rev. ed. Linda Barr. Ed. by Hank Resnik. (Skills for Adolescence Ser.). (Illus.). 128p. 1988. 10.50 (ISBN 0-933419-27-9). Quest Intl.
Supporting Yourself As An Artist: A Practical Guide. Deborah A. Hoover. LC 85-8787. 1985. 17.95 (ISBN 0-19-503669-7). Oxford U Pr.
Supporting Yourself As an Artist: A Practical Guide. Deborah A. Hoover. 246p. 1986. pap. 7.95 (ISBN 0-19-504215-8). Oxford U Pr.
Supportive Care for the Patient with Cancer. Christine Miaskowski et al. 48p. (Orig.). 1988. write for info. (ISBN 0-936445-01-7). MMI Press.
Supportive Care in Cancer Patients. Ed. by H. J. Senn & L. Schmid. (Recent Results in Cancer Research Ser.: Vol. 108). (Illus.). 350p. 1988. 110.00 (ISBN 0-387-17150-9). Springer-Verlag.
Supportive Care in Cancer Therapy. Ed. by Donald J. Higby. (Cancer Treatment & Research Ser.). 1983. lib. bdg. 80.00 (ISBN 0-89838-569-5, Pub. by Martinus Nijhoff Netherlands). Kluwer Academic.
Supportive Care of the Child with Cancer. A. Oakhill et al. (Illus.). 328p. 1988. pap. 45.00 (ISBN 0-7236-0745-1). PSG Pub Co.
Supportive Fellow Speakers & Cooperative Conversations: Discourse Topics & Topical Actions, Participant Roles & 'Recipient Action' in a Particular Type of Everyday Conversation. Wolfram Bublitz. LC 88-10119. xii, 308p. 1988. 48.00x (ISBN 1-55619-047-6); pap. 19.95x (ISBN 1-55619-048-4). Benjamins North Am.
Supportive Ministries. Michael Landsman. 1981. pap. 1.95 (ISBN 0-89274-181-3). Harrison Hse.
Supportive Network. Claire G. Wenger. 1984. 38.75x (ISBN 0-317-40641-8, Pub. by Natl Inst Social Work). State Mutual Bk.
Supportive Network: Coping with Old Age. G. Clare Wenger. (National Institute Social Services Library: No. 46). 224p. 1984. 34.95x (ISBN 0-04-362056-6); pap. text ed. 14.95x (ISBN 0-04-362057-4). Unwin Hyman.
Supportive Personnel Training Manuals, 2 vols. (Illus.). 1978. pap. 24.00 set (ISBN 0-917330-22-6); Pharmacist's Manual. pap. 15.00 (ISBN 0-686-96654-6); Trainee's Manual. pap. 15.00 (ISBN 0-686-96655-4). Am Pharm Assn.
Supportive Services for Disadvantaged Workers & Trainees. Deborah Heskes. (Key Issues Ser.: No. 12). 48p. 1973. pap. 2.00 (ISBN 0-87546-225-1). ILR Pr.
Supportive Therapy in Haematology. Ed. by P. C. Das et al. LC 85-4977. 1985. lib. bdg. 79.95 (ISBN 0-89838-700-0, Pub. by Martinus Nijhoff Netherlands). Kluwer Academic.
Supports for Family Caregivers of the Elderly: Highlights of a National Symposium. Lorraine Lidoff. 60p. 1985. 9.00 (ISBN 0-910883-08-4, 2009). Natl Coun Aging.
Supports for Family Caregivers: Opportunities for National Organizations. Lorraine N. Ross & George T. Beall. (Patterns of Progress in Aging Among National Voluntary Organizations Ser.: Vol. II). 1985. 2.00 (ISBN 0-910883-23-8, 2004). Natl Coun Aging.
Suppose a Man. John Levy. 1977. in wraps 4.00 (ISBN 0-685-88979-3). Elizabeth Pr.
Suppose the Wolf Were An Octopus: A Guide to Creative Questioning for Primary Grade Literature, Grades K-2. Michael T. Bagley & Joyce P. Foley. 9.95 (ISBN 0-89824-087-5). Trillium Pr.
Suppose You Were a Kitten. Phyllis J. Neuberger. LC 82-91105. (Illus.). (gr. 1-3). 1982. pap. 2.95 (ISBN 0-9610050-0-9). P J Neuberger.
Suppressed Book About Slavery. Ed. by George W. Carleton. LC 68-28987. (American Negro: His History & Literature Ser., No. 1). (Illus.). 1968. Repr. of 1864 ed. 19.00 (ISBN 0-405-01806-1). Ayer Co Pubs.
Suppressed Commentaries on the Wiseian Forgeries: Addendum to an Enquiry. William B. Todd. LC 77-89555. (Bibliographical Monograph: No. 1). (Illus.). 1974. Repr. of 1969 ed. 50.00 (ISBN 0-87959-052-1). U of Tex H Ransom Ctr.
Suppressed Inventions & How They Work. 1986. lib. bdg. 79.95 (ISBN 0-8490-3605-4). Gordon Pr.
Suppressed Madness of Sane Men: Forty-Four Years of Exploring Psycho-Analysis. Marion Milner. (Illus.). 250p. 1987. lib. bdg. 47.50x (ISBN 0-422-61020-8, Pub. by Tavistock England); pap. 19.95x (ISBN 0-422-61690-7, Pub. by Tavistock England). Routledge Chapman & Hall.
Suppressed Truth about the Assassination of Abraham Lincoln. Burke McCarthy. 255p. 1976. 50.00 (ISBN 0-685-66405-8). Chedney.
Suppressed Truth About the Assassination of Abraham Lincoln. Burke McCarty. 255p. 1960. Repr. of 1870 ed. 5.00 (ISBN 0-686-29301-0, Pub. by Chedney). A-albionic Res.
Suppressed Truth About the Assassination of Lincoln. Burke McCarty. 69.95 (ISBN 0-87968-169-1). Gordon Pr.
Suppressing the Ku Klux Klan: The Enforcement of the Reconstruction Amendments, 1870-1877. Everette Swinney. Ed. by Harold Hyman & Stuart Bruchey. (American Legal & Constitutional History Ser.). 360p. 1987. lib. bdg. 40.00 (ISBN 0-8240-8297-4). Garland Pub.
Suppression. Francisco H. Mosti. 64p. 1981. 9.00 (ISBN 0-682-49691-X). Exposition-Phoenix.
Suppression of Drama in 19th Century India. Pramila Pandhe. 1978. 7.50x (ISBN 0-8364-0237-5). South Asia Bks.
Suppression of Experimental Allergic Encephalomyelitis & Multiple Sclerosis. Ed. by A. N. Davison & M. L. Cuzner. LC 79-41796. 1980. 76.00 (ISBN 0-12-206660-X). Acad Pr.
Suppression of John F. Deitz: An Episode of the Progressive Era in Wisconsin. (Wisconsin Stories Ser.). 55p. 1979. pap. 1.75 (ISBN 0-87020-184-0). State Hist Soc Wis.
Suppression of the African Slave Trade, 1638-1870. W. E. B. Dubois. LC 65-18803. xx, 336p. 1970. pap. text ed. 9.95 (ISBN 0-8071-0149-4). La State U Pr.
Suppression of the African Slave-Trade see Writings.
Suppression of the African Slave Trade to the United States of America, 1638-1870. W. E. B. Dubois. 325p. 1970. Repr. of 1896 ed. 20.00 (ISBN 0-87928-011-5). Corner Hse.
Suppression of the African Slave Trade to the United States of America, 1638-1870. W. E. B. Dubois. 335p. 1973. Repr. of 1896 ed. 20.00 (ISBN 0-527-25335-9). Kraus Intl.
Suppression of the Automobile: Skulduggery at the Crossroads. David Beasley. LC 87-31788. (Contributions in Economics & Economic History: No. 81). 192p. 1988. 35.95 (ISBN 0-313-26144-X, BSY/). Greenwood.
Suppressive Soils & Plant Diseases. Ed. by Raymond W. Schneider. LC 82-72591. 88p. 1982. pap. 12.00 (ISBN 0-89054-048-9). Am Phytopathol Soc.
Suppressor Cells. Ed. by B. Serrou & C. Rosenfeld. (Human Cancer Immunology Ser.: Vol. 2). 261p. 1981. 118.50 (ISBN 0-444-80306-8, Biomedical Pr). Elsevier.
Suppressor Cells & Their Factors. Ed. by Randall S. Krakauer & John D. Clough. 184p. 1981. 75.00 (ISBN 0-8493-6185-0). CRC Pr.
Suppressor Cells in Human Disease. James S. Goodwin. (Immunology Ser: Vol. 14). (Illus.). 376p. 1981. 65.00 (ISBN 0-8247-1290-0). Dekker.
Suppressors, 6 Vols. 1986. lib. bdg. 500.00 (ISBN 0-8490-3590-2). Gordon Pr.
Suprafamilial Authority & Economic Process in Micronesian Atolls see Commerce des Hommes.

Supreme Court Review, 1966. Ed. by Philip B. Kurland. LC 60-14353. 1966. 25.00x (ISBN 0-226-46417-2). U of Chicago Pr.
Supreme Court Review, 1967. Ed. by Philip B. Kurland. LC 60-14353. 1967. 25.00x (ISBN 0-226-46418-0). U of Chicago Pr.
Supreme Court Review, 1968. 1968 ed. Ed. by Philip B. Kurland. LC 60-14357. 25.00x (ISBN 0-226-46419-9). U of Chicago Pr.
Supreme Court Review, 1969. Ed. by Philip B. Kurland. LC 60-14353. 1969. 25.00x (ISBN 0-226-46420-2). U of Chicago Pr.
Supreme Court Review, 1970. Ed. by Philip B. Kurland. LC 60-14353. 1970. 25.00x (ISBN 0-226-46421-0). U of Chicago Pr.
Supreme Court Review, 1971. Ed. by Philip B. Kurland. LC 60-14353. 1971. 25.00x (ISBN 0-226-46422-9). U of Chicago Pr.
Supreme Court Review, 1972. Ed. by Philip B. Kurland. LC 60-14353. 1973. 25.00x (ISBN 0-226-46423-7). U of Chicago Pr.
Supreme Court Review, 1973. Ed. by Philip B. Kurland. LC 60-14353. viii, 252p. 1974. 25.00x (ISBN 0-226-46424-5). U of Chicago Pr.
Supreme Court Review, 1974. Ed. by Philip B. Kurland. LC 60-14353. 1975. 25.00x (ISBN 0-226-46425-3). U of Chicago Pr.
Supreme Court Review, 1975. Ed. by Philip B. Kurland. LC 60-14353. 1976. 25.00x (ISBN 0-226-46426-1). U of Chicago Pr.
Supreme Court Review, 1976. Ed. by Philip B. Kurland. LC 76-14353. 1977. lib. bdg. 25.00x (ISBN 0-226-46428-8). U of Chicago Pr.
Supreme Court Review, 1977. Ed. by Philip B. Kurland. LC 60-14353. (Supreme Court Review). 1978. lib. bdg. 25.00x (ISBN 0-226-46429-6). U of Chicago Pr.
Supreme Court Review, 1978. Ed. by Philip B. Kurland & Gerhard Casper. LC 60-14353. 1979. 30.00x (ISBN 0-226-46431-8). U of Chicago Pr.
Supreme Court Review, 1979. Ed. by Philip B. Kurland & Gerhard Casper. LC 60-14353. 1980. lib. bdg. 35.00x (ISBN 0-226-46432-6). U of Chicago Pr.
Supreme Court Review, 1980. Ed. by Philip B. Kurland & Gerhard Casper. LC 60-14353. 416p. 1980. 30.00x (ISBN 0-226-46433-4). U of Chicago Pr.
Supreme Court Review, 1981. Philip B. Kurland et al. LC 60-14353. 376p. 1982. lib. bdg. 30.00x (ISBN 0-226-46434-2). U of Chicago Pr.
Supreme Court Review, 1982. 2nd ed. Ed. by Philip B. Kurland & Gerhard Casper. LC 60-14353. (Supreme Court Review Ser.). 432p. 1983. lib. bdg. 30.00x (ISBN 0-226-46435-0). U of Chicago Pr.
Supreme Court Review, 1983. Ed. by Philip B. Kurland et al. LC 60-14353. 570p. 1984. 39.00x (ISBN 0-226-46436-9). U of Chicago Pr.
Supreme Court Review, 1984. Ed. by Philip G. Kurland et al. LC 60-14353. vii, 410p. 1985. 35.00x (ISBN 0-226-46437-7). U of Chicago Pr.
Supreme Court Review, 1986. Ed. by Philip B. Kurland et al. LC 60-14353. 402p. 1987. 37.50x (ISBN 0-226-46439-3). U of Chicago Pr.
Supreme Court Rules Nineteen Sixty-Six. K. K. Malik. 119p. 1984. 60.00x (ISBN 0-317-54869-7, Pub. by Eastern Bk India). State Mutual Bk.
Supreme Court Says Minority Enterprises Must Be Given a Piece of the Action. Michael Langley. 1980. 1.00 (ISBN 0-686-38005-3). Voter Ed Proj.
Supreme Court Speaks. facsimile ed. United States Supreme Court & Jerre S. Williams. LC 71-121509. (Essay Index Reprint Ser). Repr. of 1956 ed. 29.00 (ISBN 0-8369-1855-X). Ayer Co Pubs.
Supreme Court Statecraft: The Rule of Law & Men. Wallace Mendelson. 352p. 1985. text ed. 24.95x (ISBN 0-8138-1047-7). Iowa St U Pr.
Supreme Court: The Way It Was--the Way It Is. William H. Rehnquist. LC 87-12271. 388p. 1987. 18.95 (ISBN 0-688-05714-4). Morrow.
Supreme Court: Trends & Developments, Vols. 1-5. Jesse Choper et al. Set. 150.00 (ISBN 0-318-24003-3, 811B). Natl Prac Inst.
Supreme Court: Trends & Developments, Vol. 1: 1978-79. Jesse Choper et al. Ed. by Laurence Tribe & Yale Kamisar. LC 79-93039. 370p. 1979. 30.00 (ISBN 0-686-31601-0, 760B). Natl Prac Inst.
Supreme Court: Trends & Developments, Vol. 2: 1979-80. Ed. by Jesse Choper et al. 322p. 1981. 30.00 (ISBN 0-686-31602-9, 770B). Natl Prac Inst.
Supreme Court: Trends & Developments, Vol. 3: 1980-81. Jesse Choper et al. 40.00 (ISBN 0-318-24000-9, 780B). Natl Prac Inst.
Supreme Court: Trends & Developments, Vol. 4: 1981-82. Jesse Choper et al. 40.00 (ISBN 0-318-24001-7, 800B). Natl Prac Inst.
Supreme Court: Trends & Developments, Vol. 5: 1982-83. Jesse Choper et al. 40.00 (ISBN 0-318-24002-5, 810B). Natl Prac Inst.
Supreme Court Under Marshall & Taney. R. Kent Newmyer. LC 68-29540. (American History Ser.). (Orig.). 1969. pap. 8.95x (ISBN 0-88295-746-5). Harlan Davidson.
Supreme Court Under Warren. Gerald Kurland. Ed. by D. Steve Rahmas. LC 72-89222. (Topics of Our Times Ser.: No. 5). 32p. 1973. lib. bdg. 3.75 incl. catalog cards (ISBN 0-87157-805-0); pap. 2.50 vinyl laminated covers (ISBN 0-87157-305-9). SamHar Pr.
Supreme Court: Views from the Inside. Alan F. Westin. LC 83-6722. 192p. 1983. Repr. of 1961 ed. lib. bdg. 35.00 (ISBN 0-313-24062-0, WSUP). Greenwood.
Supreme Court Yearly Digest Series. Surendra Malik. write for info. (Pub. by Eastern Bk Mutual). State Mutual Bk.
Supreme Courts & Judicial Law-Making: Constitutional Tribunals & Constitutional Review. E. J. McWhinney. 1986. lib. bdg. 67.00 (ISBN 90-247-3203-4, Pub. by Martinus Nijhoff Netherlands). Kluwer Academic.
Supreme Court's Constitution. Bernard Siegan. 305p. 1987. 29.95 (ISBN 0-88738-127-8); pap. 14.95 (ISBN 0-88738-671-7). Transaction Bks.
Supreme Court's Impact on Public Education. Edmund E. Reutter, Jr. LC 81-60805. 200p. 1982. 9.00 (ISBN 0-87367-783-8); pap. 7.00 (ISBN 0-87367-784-6). Phi Delta Kappa.
Supreme Doctrine: Discourses on the Kenopanishad. Bhagwan S. Rajneesh. 356p. (Orig.). 1980. pap. 12.95 (ISBN 0-7100-0572-5). Routledge Chapman & Hall.
Supreme Doctrine: Psychological Studies in Zen Thought. Hubert Benoit. 272p. 1984. pap. 8.95 (ISBN 0-89281-058-0). Inner Tradit.
Supreme Fictions: Studies in the Work of William Blake, Thomas Carlyle, W. B. Yeats & D. H. Lawrence. Brian John. 336p. 1974. 29.95x (ISBN 0-7735-0213-0). McGill-Queens U Pr.
Supreme Godhead. Kenneth V. Reeves. Ed. by Mary H. Wallace. (Illus.). 100p. (Orig.). 1984. pap. 5.50 (ISBN 0-912315-74-1). Word Aflame.
Supreme, I Sing Only for You. Sri Chinmoy. 105p. (Orig.). 1974. pap. 2.00 (ISBN 0-88497-079-5). Aum Pubns.
Supreme Identity. Alan W. Watts. 1972. pap. 4.95 (ISBN 0-394-71835-6, Vin). Random.
Supreme Initiation. Shoko Asahara. Tr. by Fumihiro Joyu & Jaya P. Nepal. LC 88-70339. (Illus.). 300p. (Orig.). 1988. pap. 5.95 (ISBN 0-945638-00-0). AUM USA.
Supreme Instants: The Photography of Edward Weston. Beaumont Newhall. 191p. 1986. 50.00 (ISBN 0-317-53697-4). Little.
Supreme Instants: The Photography of Edward Weston. Beaumont Newhall. (Illus.). 1986. 50.00 (ISBN 0-8212-1621-X). NYGS.
Supreme Koan: An Artist's Spiritual Journey. Frederick Franck. LC 81-22037. (Illus.). 1982. pap. 12.95 (ISBN 0-8245-0430-5). Crossroad NY.
Supreme Labor Court in Nazi Germany. Marc Linder. 290p. 1987. write for info. (Pub. by Vittorio Klostermann W. Germany). Transnatl Pubs.
Supreme Law. Maurice Maeterlinck. LC 75-86042. (Essay & General Literature Index Reprint Ser). 1969. Repr. of 1935 ed. 18.50x (ISBN 0-8046-0571-8, Pub. by Kennikat). Assoc Faculty Pr.
Supreme Life: The History of a Negro Life Insurance Company. Robert C. Puth. LC 75-41780. (Companies & Men: Business Enterprises in America). 1976. 25.00x (ISBN 0-405-08095-6). Ayer Co Pubs.
Supreme Mastery of Fear. Joseph Murphy. pap. 1.50 (ISBN 0-87516-340-8). DeVorss.
Supreme Philosophy of Man: The Laws of Life. Alfred A. Montapert. 1977. pap. 2.95 (ISBN 0-686-85728-3). Borden.
Supreme Philosphy of Man. 7th ed. Alfred A. Montapert. LC 70-119515. 1977. 2.95 (ISBN 0-9603174-2-2). Bks of Value.
Supreme Publications Master Index. 49p. pap. 8.00 (ISBN 0-938630-21-0, I-1). Ars Enterprises.
Supreme Publications Specialty Manuals Index. 25p. pap. 7.00 (ISBN 0-938630-22-9, SI-1). ARS Enterprises.
Supreme Self: A Modern Upanishad. Swami Abhayananda. (Illus.). 180p. (Orig.). 1984. pap. 9.95 (ISBN 0-914557-01-7). Atma Bks.
Supreme Souvenir Factory. James Stevenson. LC 87-33390. (Illus.). 56p. (gr. 1-4). 1988. 11.95 (ISBN 0-688-07782-X). Greenwillow.
Supreme Soviet: Politics & the Legislative Process in the Soviet Political System. Peter Vanneman. LC 75-25107. (Comparative Legislative Studies). xii, 256p. 1977. 27.95 (ISBN 0-8223-0357-4). Duke.
Supreme, Teach Me How to Cry. Sri Chinmoy. 100p. (Orig.). 1974. pap. 2.00 (ISBN 0-88497-120-1). Aum Pubns.
Supreme, Teach Me How to Surrender. Sri Chinmoy. 100p. (Orig.). 1975. pap. 2.00 (ISBN 0-88497-237-2). Aum Pubns.
Supremes: Triumph & Tragedy. Marianne Ruuth. 1987. pap. 2.95 (ISBN 0-87067-725-X, BH725). Holloway.
Supression of Immoral Traffic in Women & Girls Act, 1956. Mazhar Husain. 236p. 1979. 75.00x (ISBN 0-317-54675-9, Pub. by Eastern Bk India). State Mutual Bk.
Suprise Dinosaur! (Suprise Board Bks.). (ps-1). 1988. bds. 3.95 (ISBN 0-671-66712-2, Little Simon). S&S.
Suprofen. Ed. by M. E. Rosenthale. (Journal-Pharmacology: Vol. 27, Suppl. 1). (Illus.). viii, 96p. 1983. pap. 25.50 (ISBN 3-8055-3789-1). S Karger.
Sur: A Study of the Argentine Literary Journal & Its Role in the Development of a Culture, 1931-1970. John King. (Cambridge Iberian & Latin American Studies). 300p. 1987. 44.50 (ISBN 0-521-26849-4). Cambridge U Pr.
Sur ce Rivage: Le Periple, Vol. 1. Vercors. 160p. 1958. 4.95 (ISBN 0-686-55139-7). French & Eur.
Sur ce Rivage: Monsieur Prousthe, Vol. 2. Vercors. 192p. 1958. 4.95 (ISBN 0-686-55140-0). French & Eur.
Sur Das: Poet, Singer, Saint. John S. Hawley. LC 84-40327. (Publications on Asia of the Henry M. Jackson School of International Studies: No. 40). (Illus.). 256p. 1984. text ed. 25.00x (ISBN 0-295-96102-3). U of Wash Pr.
Sur la Definition du Progres par Francois Perroux see Cahiers de L'Institut de Science Economique Appliquee.
Sur la Liberte de la Presse. Denis Diderot & Jacques Proust. 1975. 9.95 (ISBN 0-686-56031-0). French & Eur.
Sur la Poesie. Rene Char. 35p. 1974. 8.95 (ISBN 0-686-54171-5). French & Eur.
Sur la Politique Rationnelle. facsimile ed. Alphonse de Lamartine. 164p. 1978. Repr. of 1831 ed. 28.00 (ISBN 0-686-54279-7). French & Eur.
Sur la Route de la Contrebande. Joseph F. Conroy. LC 81-7817. (L'aventure! Ser.: 3). (Illus.). 40p. (Orig., Fr.). (YA) (gr. 7-12). pap. 1.95 (ISBN 0-88436-856-4, 40261). EMC.
Sur la Voie Glorieuse. Anatole France. 102p. 1916. 25.00 (ISBN 0-686-55878-2). French & Eur.
Sur L'amour. Pierre Teilhard De Chardin. pap. 6.25 (ISBN 0-685-36602-2). French & Eur.
Sur l'Art et les Artistes. Denis Diderot. 220p. 1967. 9.95 (ISBN 0-686-56032-9). French & Eur.
Sur le Bonheur. Pierre Teilhard De Chardin. pap. 6.25 (ISBN 0-685-36603-0). French & Eur.
Sur le Fil ou la Ballade du Train Fantome. Fernando Arrabal. 118p. 1974. 9.95 (ISBN 0-686-54463-3). French & Eur.
Sur le Materialisme: De l'Atomisme a la Dialectique Revolutionnaire. Philippe Sollers. 192p. 1974. 11.95 (ISBN 0-686-55017-X). French & Eur.
Sur le Vif. Madeleine Le Cunff. LC 77-10091. (Illus., Fr.). 1977. pap. text ed. 8.95 (ISBN 0-88436-454-2, 40254). EMC.
Sur l'Eau. Guy De Maupassant. 1972. 9.95 (ISBN 0-686-54800-0). French & Eur.
Sur les Femmes. Henry De Montherlant. 14.95 (ISBN 0-685-36988-9). French & Eur.
Sur les sections analytiques de la courbe universelle de Teichmuller. John H. Hubbard. LC 75-41604. (Memoirs: No. 166). 137p. 1976. pap. 16.00 (ISBN 0-8218-1866-X, MEMO-166). Am Math.
Sur L'internationalisme. Libres Entretiens. (Library of War & Peace; Int'l. Organization, Arbitration & Law). 1972. lib. bdg. 46.00 (ISBN 0-8240-0354-3). Garland Pub.
Sur Quelques Myrionemacees. C. Sauvageau. 1897. Repr. 24.00x (ISBN 3-7682-0705-6). Lubrecht & Cramer.
Sur Racine. Roland Barthes. 1963. 29.95 (ISBN 0-686-53942-7). French & Eur.
Surcharge Litigation & How to Avoid It. 235p. 1981. pap. 15.00 (ISBN 0-686-48274-3). Amer Bar Assn.
Sure Could Use a Friend. Dan Day. (Lifestyle Ser.). 31p. 1986. pap. 0.75 (ISBN 0-8163-0656-7). Pacific Pr Pub Assn.
Sure-Fire Kid & Wildcats of Tonto Basin. Nelson Nye. (Double Barrel Western Ser.: No. 2). 448p. 1987. pap. 3.95 (ISBN 0-8439-2474-8, Leisure Bks). Leisure NY.
Sure Foundation. T. David Sustar. LC 80-84008. 124p. (Orig.). 1980. pap. text ed. 3.00 (ISBN 0-87148-795-0); 2.00 (ISBN 0-87148-436-6). Pathway Pr.
Sure Hands, Strong Heart: The Life of Daniel Hale Williams. Lillie Patterson. LC 81-2660. (Illus.). 142p. (gr. 3-7). 1981. 8.95 (ISBN 0-687-40700-1). Abingdon.
Sure Recompense. Richard T. Bickers. 24.95x (ISBN 0-7090-1069-9, Pub. by R Hale Ltd UK). State Mutual Bk.
Sure Salvation. John Hearne. LC 85-6852. 224p. 1985. pap. 8.95 (ISBN 0-571-13452-1). Faber & Faber.
Sure Shot: One Hundred Golf Errors & How to Correct Them. Gary Wirne & Dawson Taylor. (Illus.). 192p. (Orig.). 1987. pap. 10.95 (ISBN 0-8092-5104-3). Contemp Bks.
Sure Signs: New & Selected Poems. Ted Kooser. LC 79-21725. (Pitt Poetry Ser.). 1980. 16.95x (ISBN 0-8229-3410-8); pap. 8.95 (ISBN 0-8229-5313-7). U of Pittsburgh Pr.
Sure Steps to Reading & Spelling: The Weiss Method of Teaching English. rev. ed. M. Herbert Weiss. 1976. text ed. write for info (ISBN 0-916720-07-1); pap. text ed. 6.75 (ISBN 0-916720-02-0); The Science of Reading & Spelling. tchr's manual for use with Sure Steps to Reading & Spelling 2.00 (ISBN 0-916720-01-2). Weiss Pub.
Sure Thing. Warren Murphy. 448p. 1988. pap. 4.50 (ISBN 1-55817-129-0). Windsor NY.
Sure Thing. Cornelius Plantinga, Jr. LC 86-8280. (Illus.). 300p. (gr. 8-10). 1986. lib. bdg. 12.95 (ISBN 0-930265-27-0); incl. tchr's. manual 9.30 (ISBN 0-930265-28-9). CRC Pubns.
Sure Thing Commodity Trading. Larry Williams & Michelle Noseworthy. 1977. 50.00 (ISBN 0-930233-04-2). Windsor.
Sure-Thing Options Trading. George Angell. 1984. pap. 7.95 (ISBN 0-452-25614-3, Plume). NAL.
Sure-Thing Options Trading: A Money-Making Guide to the New Listed Stock & Commodity Options Markets. George Angell. LC 84-6812. 288p. 1988. pap. 9.95 (ISBN 0-452-26110-4, Plume). NAL.
Sure to Endure. Danny Lynchard. 43p. 1983. pap. 1.95 (ISBN 0-88144-043-4). Christian Pub.
Sure Way to Get Job Interviews. 1980. pap. 9.00 (ISBN 0-936510-00-5); 5.95 (ISBN 0-936510-01-3); 5.95 (ISBN 0-936510-02-1). Diamond Pubs.
Sure You Can! Extra-Musical Guidance for the Young Choral Conductor. Theron Kirk. LC 77-76867. 1978. pap. text ed. 11.95 (ISBN 0-916656-02-0). Mark Foster Mus.
Sure You Can Sing. Fral Berkman. 1983. 12.95 (ISBN 0-317-03727-7). Melrose Bk Co.
Surefire Programming in C. Warren A. Stewart. LC 84-26898. (Illus.). 288p. (Orig.). 1985. pap. 17.95 (ISBN 0-8306-1873-2). TAB Bks.
Surefire Ways to Beat Stress. Don Osgood. (Pocket Guides Ser.). 96p. 1988. pap. 2.25 (ISBN 0-8423-6693-8). Tyndale.
Surely You Bluff...& Other Works on End-User Computing. Naomi Karten. 164p. (Orig.). 1988. pap. 19.00 (ISBN 0-929154-00-2). TLI Pubns.
Surely You're Joking, Mr. Feynman! Richard P. Feynman. 352p. 1986. pap. 4.50 (ISBN 0-553-25649-1). Bantam.
Surely You're Joking, Mr. Feynman! Adventures of a Curious Character. Richard P. Feynman. Ed. by Edward Hutchings. 1984. 16.95 (ISBN 0-393-01921-7). Norton.
Surena, General Des Parthes. Pierre Corneille. 248p. 1970. 12.95 (ISBN 0-686-54623-7). French & Eur.
Surest Path: The Political Treatise of a Nineteenth-Century Muslim Statesman. Khayr Al Tunisi. Tr. by Leon C. Brown. LC 67-25399. (Middle Eastern Monographs Ser: No. 16). pap. 5.00x (ISBN 0-674-85695-3). Harvard U Pr.
Sureste de Asia. Rosenfeld & Geller. Tr. by Sonia Casasnovas from Eng. LC 76-14401. (Illus., Span., Span. ed. of Unit 7-Afro-Asian Culture Studies). (gr. 7-12). 1976. pap. text ed. 4.95 (ISBN 0-8120-0615-1). Barron.
Surety Law Topical Index. American Bar Association, Tort & Insurance Practice Staff. 1987. write for info. Amer Bar Assn.
Surety Underwriting Manual. Edward J. McKenna. 15.00 (ISBN 0-942326-19-9, 26620). Rough Notes.
Surf City-Drag City. Rob Burt. (Illus.). 128p. 1986. (Pub. by Blandford Pr England); pap. 12.95 (ISBN 0-7137-1891-9). Sterling.
Surf Club. Ed Harsen. 32p. (Orig.). 1982. pap. 3.00 (ISBN 0-935252-35-5). Street Pr.
Surface! Alexander Fullerton. 176p. pap. 4.95 (ISBN 0-583-12295-7, Pub. by Granada England). Academy Chi Pubs.
Surface Acoustic Wave Designs & Their Signal Processing Applications. Colin Campbell. 700p. 1989. price not set (ISBN 0-12-157345-1). Acad Pr.
Surface Acoustic Wave Devices. Supriyo Datta. (Illus.). 208p. 1986. text ed. 54.00 (ISBN 0-13-877911-2). P-H.
Surface Acoustic Wave Devices. 1982. 3 ring bdg. 130.00 (ISBN 0-87739-052-5). Optosonic Pr.
Surface Active Agents: Their Chemistry & Technology, Vol. 1. Anthony M. Schwartz et al. LC 74-11051. 592p. 1978. Repr. of 1949 ed. lib. bdg. 32.50 (ISBN 0-88275-684-2). Krieger.
Surface Alloying by Ion, Electron & Laser Beams, No. 6725. 432p. 1986. 120.00 (ISBN 0-87170-274-6). ASM.
Surface Analysis & Pretreatment of Plastics & Metals. Ed. by D. M. Brewis. (Illus.). xii, 266p. 1982. 55.00 (ISBN 0-85334-992-4, Pub. by Elsevier Applied Sci England). Elsevier.
Surface Analysis of High Temperature Materials. Ed. by G. Kemeny. (Illus.). 184p. 1984. 48.75 (ISBN 0-85334-264-4, Pub. by Elsevier Applied Sci England). Elsevier.
Surface Analysis Techniques for Metallurgical Applications - STP 596. 146p. 1976. pap. 15.00 (ISBN 0-8031-0584-3, 04-596000-28). ASTM.
Surface Anatomy. Joseph Royce. (Illus.). 270p. 1973. pap. text ed. 15.00x (ISBN 0-8036-7641-7). Davis Co.
Surface Anatomy: Abdomen. David J. Gerrick. (Illus.). 1978. 20.00 (ISBN 0-916750-57-4). Dayton Labs.
Surface Anatomy for Coaches & Athletic Trainers. photocopy ed. Hubert F. Riegler & Alan P. Peppard. (Illus.). 80p. 1979. spiral bdg. 15.25 (ISBN 0-398-03856-2). C C Thomas.
Surface Anatomy for Radiographers. D. W. McKears & R. Owen. 124p. 1980. pap. 15.00 (ISBN 0-7236-0511-4). PSG Pub Co.
Surface Anatomy: The Arm. David J. Gerrick. (Illus.). 1978. 20.00 (ISBN 0-916750-58-2). Dayton Labs.
Surface Anatomy: The Back. David J. Gerrick. (Illus.). 1978. 20.00 (ISBN 0-916750-59-0). Dayton Labs.
Surface Anatomy: The Head. David J. Gerrick. (Illus.). 1978. 20.00 (ISBN 0-916750-60-4). Dayton Labs.
Surface Anatomy: The Leg. David J. Gerrick. 1979. 20.00 (ISBN 0-916750-61-2). Dayton Labs.

Surface Transportation Regulation & Railroad Planning. (Transportation Research Record Ser.). 58p. 1978. 3.40 (ISBN 0-309-02832-9). Transport Res Bd.

Surface Treatment. (Publications for Developing Countries: Compendium 12). 285p. 1980. 12.00 (ISBN 0-309-03057-9). Transport Res Bd.

Surface Treatment & Finishing of Aluminium. R. G. King. (Materials Engineering Practice Ser.). 150p. 1988. text ed. 40.00 (ISBN 0-08-031137-7); pap. text ed. 19.95 (ISBN 0-08-031138-5). Pergamon.

Surface Treatment of Aluminium: Dictionary of Technical Terms. W. F. Kehler. (Eng., Fr., & Ger.). 1975. cancelled 12.00 (ISBN 3-87017-121-9, Pub. by Aluminium W Germany). IPS.

Surface Treatment of Aluminiun & Its Alloys. Ed. by Portcullis Press Ltd. Staff. 1985. 410.00x (Pub. by Portcullis Pr UK). State Mutual Bk.

Surface Treatments for Improved Performance & Properties. Ed. by John J. Burke & Volker Weiss. (Sagamore Army Materials Research Conference Proceedings Ser.: Vol. 26). 226p. 1982. 49.50x (ISBN 0-306-40897-X, Plenum Pr). Plenum Pub.

Surface Treatments for Protection. 343p. 1978. pap. text ed. 30.40x (ISBN 0-318-20352-9, Pub. by Inst Metals). Brookfield Pub Co.

Surface Vehicle Sound Measurement Procedures. 82p. 1979. 20.00 (ISBN 0-89883-367-1, HS-184). Soc Auto Engineers.

Surface Warships: An Introduction to Design Principles. P. J. Gates. (SEAP Ser.). (Illus.). 170p. 1987. 28.00 (ISBN 0-08-034753-3, BDP); pap. 15.95 (ISBN 0-08-034754-1, BDP). Pergamon.

Surface Water. R. N. Bowen. (Illus.). vii, 278p. 1982. 43.00 (ISBN 0-85334-128-1, Pub. by Elsevier Applied Sci England). Elsevier.

Surface Water & Groundwater Interaction: A Contribution to the International Hydrological Programme Report Prepared for the International Commission on Groundwater. C. E. Wright. (Studies & Reports in Hydrology: No. 29). (Illus.). 123p. 1980. pap. 9.50 (ISBN 92-3-101862-0, U1078, UNESCO). UNIPUB.

Surface Water Impoundments, 2 vols. Ed. by H. Stefan. LC 81-67445. 1724p. 1981. Set. pap. 115.00x (ISBN 0-87262-271-1). Am Soc Civil Eng.

Surface Water Sewerage. 2nd ed. Ronald E. Bartlett. (Illus.). vii, 148p. 1981. 37.00 (ISBN 0-85334-925-8, Pub. by Elsevier Applied Sci England). Elsevier.

Surface-Wave Devices for Signal Processing. D. P. Morgan. LC 85-10330. (Studies in Electrical & Electronic Engineering Ser.: No. 19). 432p. 1985. 129.00 (ISBN 0-444-42511-X). Elsevier.

Surface Wave Filters: Design, Construction & Use. Ed. by Herbert Matthews. LC 77-3913. pap. 101.70 (ISBN 0-317-09163-8, 2019522). Bks Demand UMI.

Surface Waves & Discontinuities. P. Malischewsky. (Development in Solid Earth Geophysics Ser.: Vol. 16). 1987. 85.50 (ISBN 0-444-98959-5). Elsevier.

Surface Waves in Plasmas & Solids: Proceedings of the Second International Conference on Surface Waves in Plasmas & Solids, Ohrid, Yugoslavia 5-11 September 1985. Ed. by S. Vukovic. 712p. 1986. 71.00 (ISBN 9971-50-139-2, Z0298P-P). World Scientific Pub.

Surfaces. 2nd ed. H. B. Griffiths. 131p. 1981. 39.50 (ISBN 0-521-23570-7); pap. 15.95 (ISBN 0-521-29977-2). Cambridge U Pr.

Surfaces. Avrum Stroll. LC 87-35541. (Illus.). 240p. 1988. 39.50x (ISBN 0-8166-1693-0); pap. 15.95 (ISBN 0-8166-1694-9). U of Minn Pr.

Surfaces Aleatoires. M. Wschebor. (Lecture Notes in Mathematics Ser.: Vol. 1147). vii, 111p. 1985. pap. 11.00 (ISBN 0-387-15688-7). Springer-Verlag.

Surfaces & Coatings Related to Paper & Wood. Ed. by R. H. Marchessault & Christen Skaar. LC 66-27617. 1967. 24.95x (ISBN 0-8156-5017-5). Syracuse U Pr.

Surfaces & Disorder. Ed. by J. W. Halley. (Material Science Forum SEr.: Vol. 4). 224p. 1985. text ed. 55.00x (ISBN 0-87849-532-0). Trans Tech.

Surfaces & Interfaces: Physics & Electronics. Ed. by R. S. Bauer. 650p. 1984. 113.25 (ISBN 0-444-86784-8, I-200-84, North Holland). Elsevier.

Surfaces & Masks. Clarence Major. 1988. pap. 8.95 (ISBN 0-918273-43-9). Coffee Hse.

Surfaces Fibrees en Courbes de Genre Deux. G. Xiao. (Lecture Notes in Mathematics: Vol. 1137). ix, 103p. 1985. pap. 11.00 (ISBN 0-387-15662-3). Springer-Verlag.

Surfaces in CAGD '84. Ed. by R. E. Barnhill & W. Boehm. 236p. 1985. 79.00 (ISBN 0-444-87798-3, North-Holland). Elsevier.

Surfaces in Computer Aided Geometric Design: Proceedings of a Conference, Mathematisches Forschungsinstitut, Oberwolfach, F.R.G., April 25-30, 1982. Ed. by Robert E. Barnhill & Wolfgang Boehm. xvi, 216p. 1983. 66.00 (ISBN 0-444-86550-0, I-32-83, North-Holland). Elsevier.

Surfaces of a Diamond, Novel. Louis D. Rubin, Jr. LC 81-6034. 232p. 1981. 16.95 (ISBN 0-8071-0897-9). La State U Pr.

Surfaces of Nonpositive Curvature. Patrick Eberlein. LC 79-15112. (Memoirs: No. 218). 90p. 1979. pap. 12.00 (ISBN 0-8218-2218-7, MEMO-218). Am Math.

Surfaces of Normal & Malignant Cells. Richard O. Hynes. LC 78-16184. (Illus.). 479p. pap. 124.60 (2030418). Bks Demand UMI.

Surfacing. Margaret Atwood. 224p. 1983. pap. 3.50 (ISBN 0-446-31107-3). Warner Bks.

Surfacing. Margaret Atwood. 240p. 1987. pap. 4.50 (ISBN 0-449-21375-7, Crest). Fawcett.

Surfactant Based Separation Processes. Scamehorn & Harwell. (Surfactant Science Ser.). 269p. 1988. 99.75 (ISBN 0-8247-7929-0). Dekker.

Surfactant Biodegradation. Robert D. Swisher. LC 79-107757. (Surfactant Science Ser.: Vol. 3). Repr. of 1970 ed. cancelled (ISBN 0-8357-9094-0, 2055031). Bks Demand UMI.

Surfactant in Emerging Technologies. Rosen. (Surfactant Science Ser.). 232p. 1987. 65.00 (ISBN 0-8247-7801-4). Dekker.

Surfactant Science & Technology. D. Y. Myers, Jr. 351p. 1988. lib. bdg. 35.00 (ISBN 0-89573-339-0). VCH Pubs.

Surfactant Solutions: New Methods & Investigations. Zana. (Surfactant Science Ser.). 538p. 1986. 99.75 (ISBN 0-8247-7623-2). Dekker.

Surfactant Systems: Their Chemistry, Pharmacy & Biology. D. Attwood & A. T. Florence. 1982. 105.00x (ISBN 0-412-14840-4, 6714, Pub. by Chapman & Hall). Routledge Chapman & Hall.

Surfactants. Tharwat F. Tadros. 1984. 38.50 (ISBN 0-12-682180-1). Acad Pr.

Surfactants & Interfacial Phenomena. 2nd ed. Milton Rosen. LC 88-5404. 1988. 50.00 (ISBN 0-471-83651-6). Wiley.

Surfactants & Interfacial Phenomena. Milton J. Rosen. LC 77-19092. 304p. 1978. 46.50 (ISBN 0-471-73600-7, Pub. by Wiley-Interscience). Wiley.

Surfactants & the Lining of the Lung. Emile M. Scarpelli. LC 87-29861. (Contemporary Medicine & Public Health Ser.). (Illus.). 160p. 1988. text ed. 42.50x (ISBN 0-8018-3633-6). Johns Hopkins.

Surfactants, Detergents & Sequestrants: Developments since 1979. Ed. by J. I. DiStasio. LC 81-38360. (Chem. Tech. Rev. 192). 353p. 1981. 48.00 (ISBN 0-8155-0856-5). Noyes.

Surfactants in Chemical & Process Engineering. Wasan. Ed. by Shah Ginn. (Surfactant Science Ser.). 560p. 1988. 99.75 (ISBN 0-8247-7830-8). Dekker.

Surfactants in Consumer Products. Ed. by J. Falbe. (Illus.). 600p. 1987. 126.50 (ISBN 0-387-17019-7). Springer-Verlag.

Surfactants in Cosmetics. Rieger. (Surfactant Science Ser.). 576p. 1985. 99.75 (ISBN 0-8247-7262-8). Dekker.

Surfactants in Solution, 3 Vols. Ed. by K. L. Mittal. LC 83-19170. 712p. 1984. Set. 285.00x (Plenum Pr); 115.00x ea. Vol. 1, 712p (ISBN 0-306-41483-X). Vol. 2, 718p (ISBN 0-306-41484-8). Vol. 3, 740p (ISBN 0-306-41485-6). Plenum Pub.

Surfactants in Solution, Vol. 4: Theoretical & Applied Aspects. Ed. by K. L. Mittal. 550p. 1987. 97.50x (ISBN 0-306-42468-1, Plenum Pr); Set with Vol. 5 & 6. 250.00. Plenum Pub.

Surfactants in Solution, Vol. 5. Ed. by K. L. Mittal. 575p. 1987. 97.50x (ISBN 0-306-42469-X, Plenum Pr); Set with Vol. 4 & 6. 250.00. Plenum Pub.

Surfactants in Solution, Vol. 6: Theoretical & Applied Aspects. Ed. by K. L. Mittal. 600p. 1987. 97.50x (ISBN 0-306-42470-3, Plenum Pr); Set with Vol.4 & 5. 250.00. Plenum Pub.

Surfactants in Textile Processing. Arved Datyner. (Surfactant Science Ser.: No. 14). (Illus.). 232p. 1983. 65.50 (ISBN 0-8247-1812-7). Dekker.

Surfboard to Peril: A Miss Mallard Mystery. Robert Quackenbush. (Illus.). 48p. (gr. 1-5). 1986. PLB 10.95 (ISBN 0-13-877986-4). P-H.

Surfeit of Suitors. Barbara Hazard. 224p. 1987. pap. 2.50 (ISBN 0-451-13887-2, Sig). NAL.

Surfer & the City Girl. Betty Cavanna. LC 80-25901. (Hiway Bk.: A High Interest-Low Reading Level Book). 96p. (gr. 7-9). 1981. 8.95 (ISBN 0-664-32679-X). Westminster John Knox.

Surfer Girl. Frances L. Lantz. (Caprice Romance Ser.). 148p. 1983. pap. 1.95 (ISBN 0-441-79101-8). Ace Bks.

Surfer Sex: True Gay Encounters from Australia. Rusty Winter. 96p. (Orig.). 1985. pap. 7.95 (ISBN 0-917342-10-0, Dist. by Bookpeople, Berkeley, Ca). Gay Sunshine.

Surfers of the Zuvuya: Tales of Interdimensional Travel. Jose Arguelles. LC 88-18091. 176p. (Orig.). 1988. pap. 9.95 (ISBN 0-939680-55-6). Bear & Co.

Surficial Deposits of the United States. Charles B. Hunt. LC 85-15692. (Illus.). 208p. 1986. 41.95 (ISBN 0-442-23231-4). Van Nos Reinhold.

Surficial Geology of the New Brighton Quadrangle, Minnesota. J. E. Stone. LC 68-22771. (Geologic Map Series: No. 2). 1966. 1.75x (ISBN 0-8166-0376-6). Minn Geol Survey.

Surfiction: Fiction Now & Tomorrow. Ed. by Raymond Federman. LC 73-13215. 294p. 1973. 18.00x (ISBN 0-8040-0651-2, Pub. by Swallow). Ohio U Pr.

Surfiction: Fiction Now & Tomorrow. 2nd ed. Ed. by Raymond Federman. LC 80-54657. viii, 316p. 1981. pap. 8.95x (ISBN 0-8040-0652-0, Pub by Swallow). Ohio U Pr.

Surfing. Jerolyn Nentl. Ed. by Howard Schroeder. LC 78-8723. (Funseekers Ser.). (Illus.). 32p. (gr. 3-4). 1978. PLB 8.95 (ISBN 0-913940-93-3). Crestwood Hse.

Surfing California. Allan B. Wright. LC 73-78956. 176p. (Orig.). 1973. pap. 5.95 (ISBN 0-911449-02-7). Mountain Sea.

Surfing Fundamentals: How to Ride a Modern Short Board, the Art of Riding a Malibu, Kneeboard, Wave-Ski & Bogie Board. Nat Young. LC 87-23065. (Illus.). 128p. (Orig.). 1988. pap. 10.95 (ISBN 0-89586-688-9, HP Bks). Price Stern.

Surfing Guide to Southern California. David Stern & Bill Cleary. LC 63-17835. 256p. 1977. 8.95 (ISBN 0-911449-06-X). Mountain Sea.

Surfing Hawaii. Bank Wright. LC 72-81871. (Illus.). 96p. (Orig.). 1971. pap. 4.95 (ISBN 0-911449-07-8). Mountain Sea.

Surfing off the Ark, Poems: 1965-1969. Bill Pearlman. 1970. pap. 1.50 (ISBN 0-685-27722-4, Pub. by Grasshopper Pr). Small Pr Dist.

Surfing Samurai Robots. Mel Gilden. 256p. (Orig.). 1988. pap. 3.95 (ISBN 1-55802-001-2, Omeiga). Lynx Bks.

Surfing Subcultures of Australia & New Zealand. Kent Pearson. (Illus.). 1980. 34.50x (ISBN 0-7022-1398-5). U of Queensland Pr.

Surfing, the Big Wave. new ed. Don Smith. LC 75-21847. (Illus.). 32p. (gr. 5-10). 1976. PLB 9.79 (ISBN 0-89375-011-5); pap. 2.50 (ISBN 0-89375-027-1). Troll Assocs.

Surfing: The Ultimate Pleasure. Leonard Lueras. LC 83-40541. (Illus.). 244p. pap. 16.95 (ISBN 0-89480-708-0, 708). Workman Pub.

Surfmen & Lifesavers. Paul Giambarba. (Illus.). 1985. pap. 6.95 (ISBN 0-87155-117-9). Scrimshaw.

Surf's Up! Janet Quin-Harkin. (Sugar & Spice Ser.). 192p. 1987. pap. 2.50 (ISBN 0-8041-0063-2, Pub. by Ivy). Ballantine.

Surf's Up for Laney. Claire Caldwell. 187p. (YA) (gr. 7 up). 1984. pap. 1.95 (ISBN 0-671-53390-8). PB.

Surf's Up! The Beach Boys on Record, 1961-1981. Brad Elliott. LC 81-80190. (Rock & Roll Reference Ser.: No. 6). (Illus.). 512p. 1984. 29.50 (ISBN 0-87650-118-8). Pierian.

Surge & Thunder: Trends of Civilization & Culture. Charles G. Shaw. LC 75-3377. Repr. of 1932 ed. 47.50 (ISBN 0-404-59371-2). AMS Pr.

Surgeon. Jack Rudman. (Career Examination Ser.: C-790). (Cloth bdg. avail. on request). pap. 23.95 (ISBN 0-8373-0790-2). Natl Learning.

Surgeon. Lynn Strongin. LC 79-12821. 70p. 1979. 6.95 (ISBN 0-934332-17-7). L'Epervier Pr.

Surgeon! A Year in the Life of an Innercity Surgeon. Richard Caleel & John Littell. 1988. pap. 3.95 (ISBN 0-317-62245-5). St Martin.

Surgeon from Another World. George Chapman & Roy Stemman. LC 88-2640. 192p. 1988. Repr. lib. bdg. 22.95x (ISBN 0-8095-7049-1). Borgo Pr.

Surgeon in Charge. Elizabeth Seifert. 1973. Repr. of 1942 ed. lib. bdg. 17.95x (ISBN 0-88411-007-9, Pub. by Aeonian Pr). Amereon Ltd.

Surgeon on Iwo: Up Front with the 27th Marines. James S. Vedder. (Illus.). 232p. 1984. 15.95 (ISBN 0-89141-199-2). Presidio Pr.

Surgeon on Safari. Paul J. Jorden & James R. Adair. (Living Bks.). 192p. (Orig.). 1985. pap. 3.95 (ISBN 0-8423-6686-5). Tyndale.

Surgeon Probationers. R. S. Allison. (Illus.). 142p. 1979. 1.00 (ISBN 0-85640-145-5, Pub. by Blackstaff Pr). Longwood Pub Group.

Surgeon: The Making of an Inner-City Doctor. Richard Caleel & John Littell. LC 85-43091. 256p. 1986. 15.95 (ISBN 0-89256-307-9). Rawson Assocs.

Surgeon: The View from Behind the Mask. Richard S. Weeder. 208p. 1988. 17.95 (ISBN 0-8092-4606-6). Contemp Bks.

Surgeon to Washington: Dr. John Cochran (1730-1807) Morris H. Saffron. LC 77-2675. 1977. 35.00x (ISBN 0-231-04186-1). Columbia U Pr.

Surgeons at the Bailey: English Forensic Medicine to 1878. Thomas R. Forbes. LC 85-8191. 352p. 1986. text ed. 28.00x (ISBN 0-300-03338-9). Yale U Pr.

Surgeon's Book of Hope. William A. Nolen. 1982. pap. 2.95 (ISBN 0-425-05334-2). Berkley Pub.

Surgeon's Boy. Eve Sutton. 138p. 1985. 16.00x (ISBN 0-907349-60-9, Pub by Spindlewood). State Mutual Bk.

Surgeon's Guide to Intraocular Lens Implantation. Henry Clayman. LC 84-50461. 169p. 1985. text ed. 60.00 (ISBN 0-943432-26-X). Slack Inc.

Surgeon's Handbook. Frank T. Kurzweg. (Other Medical Bks.: Vol. 10). 1982. pap. text ed. 31.25 (ISBN 0-87488-732-1). Med Exam.

Surgeon's Log. Andrew V. Mason. 410p. 1980. 9.75 (ISBN 0-8158-0394-X); pap. 6.95. Chris Mass.

Surgeon's Surgeon: Theodor Billroth (1829-1894, Vol. II. Karel B. Absolon. (Illus.). 232p. 1981. 28.50x (ISBN 0-87291-146-2). Coronado Pr.

Surgeon's Surgeon: Theodor Billroth, 1829-1894, Vol. 1. Karel B. Absolon. (Illus.). 1979. 15.00 (ISBN 0-87291-129-2). Coronado Pr.

Surgery. Maynard Kirk & Henry Kirk. (Illus.). 1974. text ed. 20.00x (ISBN 0-272-00099-X); pap. text ed. 12.00x (ISBN 0-272-00112-0). State Mutual Bk.

Surgery. (National Medical Series for Independent Study). 517p. 1986. pap. 23.00 (ISBN 0-471-82342-2, Wiley Medical). Wiley.

Surgery! A Layman's Guide to Common Operations. Edward L. Stern. Ed. by Ron Stern. LC 88-81920. (Illus.). 132p. (Orig.). 1989. pap. 9.95 (ISBN 0-944711-01-4). Lawman Pr.

Surgery: A Textbook for Students. R. M. Kirk et al. (Illus.). 1974. text ed. 24.00x (ISBN 0-8464-0901-1); pap. text ed. 29.95 (ISBN 0-8464-0902-X). Beekman Pubs.

Surgery & Arthroscopy of the Knee. Ed. by W. Muller & W. Hackenbruch. (Illus.). 800p. 1988. 180.60 (ISBN 0-387-17982-8). Springer-Verlag.

Surgery & Arthroscopy of the Knee. Ed. by E. L. Trickey & P. Hertel. (Illus.). 420p. 1986. 81.40 (ISBN 0-387-16274-7). Springer-Verlag.

Surgery & Pathology of the Middle Ear. Ed. by Jean F. Marquet. 1985. lib. bdg. 84.00 (ISBN 0-89838-707-8, Pub. by Martinus Nijhoff Netherlands). Kluwer-Academic.

Surgery & Support of the Premature Infant. Ed. by P. Puri. (Modern Problems in Paediatrics Ser.: Vol. 23). (Illus.). x, 210p. 1985. 108.75 (ISBN 3-8055-4073-6). S Karger.

Surgery Annual, 1982, Vol. 14. Ed. by Lloyd M. Nyhus. 1982. 52.00 (ISBN 0-8385-8719-4). Appleton & Lange.

Surgery Annual, 1983, Vol. 15. Lloyd M. Nyhus. 416p. 1983. 52.00 (ISBN 0-8385-8721-6). Appleton & Lange.

Surgery Annual, 1984, Vol. 16. L. M. Nyhus. LC 69-18093. 432p. 1984. 52.00 (ISBN 0-8385-8722-4). Appleton & Lange.

Surgery Annual, 1985, Vol. 17. Ed. by Lloyd M. Nyhus. 400p. 1984. 59.95 (ISBN 0-8385-8723-2). Appleton & Lange.

Surgery Annual, 1986, Vol. 18. Lloyd Nyhus. 416p. 1985. 59.95 (ISBN 0-8385-8725-9). Appleton & Lange.

Surgery Annual, 1987, Vol. 19. Ed. by Lloyd M. Nyhus. 368p. 1986. 65.00 (ISBN 0-8385-8794-1). Appleton & Lange.

Surgery Annual, 1988, Vol. 20. 1988. text ed. 69.95 (ISBN 0-8385-8728-3). Appleton & Lange.

Surgery: Current Aspects with Medical Subject Analysis & Reference Bibliography. Peter B. Zeiderhof. LC 85-48082. 150p. 1987. 34.50 (ISBN 0-88164-436-6); pap. 26.50 (ISBN 0-88164-437-4). ABBE Pubs Assn.

Surgery Examination Review. Simon Wapnick & Nino Carnevale. LC 81-20503. (Medical Review Ser.). (Illus.). 112p. (Orig.). 1982. pap. 17.95 (ISBN 0-668-05107-8). Appleton & Lange.

Surgery for Cancer of the Larynx. C. E. Silver. 1981. text ed. 69.00 (ISBN 0-443-08064-X). Churchill.

Surgery for Congenital Heart Defects in Infants. Ed. by J. Stark & M. De Leval. 1983. 225.00 (ISBN 0-8089-1161-9, 794309). Grune.

Surgery for Morbid Obesity. J. H. Linner. (Illus.). 275p. 1984. 85.00 (ISBN 0-387-90888-9). Springer Verlag.

Surgery for Phonatory Disorders. Tucker. (Illus.). 1981. text ed. 35.00 (ISBN 0-443-08058-5). Churchill.

Surgery for the Morbidly Obese Patient. Ed. by Mervyn Deitel. (Illus.). 300p. 1989. price not set (ISBN 0-8121-1136-2). Lea & Febiger.

Surgery in America: From the Colonial Era to the Twentieth Century. 2nd ed. A. S. Earle. LC 83-17808. (Illus.). 350p. 1983. 60.95 (ISBN 0-275-91389-9, C1389). Praeger.

Surgery in & Around the Brain Stem & Third Ventricle. Ed. by M. Samii. (Illus.). 625p. 1986. 147.50 (ISBN 0-387-16581-9). Springer-Verlag.

Surgery in Chronic Renal Failure. Friedrich W. Eigler & Hans D. Jakubowski. (Illus.). 256p. 1984. pap. text ed. 47.50 (ISBN 0-317-13126-5). Thieme Med Pubs.

Surgery in Gynecological Oncology. Ed. by A. P. Heintz & C. T. Griffiths. (Developments in Oncology Ser.). 1983. lib. bdg. 52.00 (ISBN 0-89838-604-7, Pub. by Martinus Nijhoff Netherlands). Kluwer Academic.

Surgery in Maryland Hospitals Nineteen Seventy-Nine & Nineteen Eighty Charges & Deaths. Eve Bargmann & Cynthia Grove. 158p. (Orig.). 1982. pap. 5.00 (ISBN 0-937188-13-1). Pub Citizen Inc.

Surgery in Rheumatoid Arthritis. Ed. by I. Goldie. (Reconstruction Surgery & Traumatology Ser.: Vol. 18). (Illus.). vi, 214p. 1981. 73.50 (ISBN 3-8055-1445-X). S Karger.

Surgery in the Aged. Lazar J. Greenfield. LC 75-8177. (Major Problems in Clinical Surgery Ser.: Vol. 17). pap. 40.80 (ISBN 0-317-26435-4, 2024990). Bks Demand UMI.

Surgery of Basal Cell Carcinoma. D. Marchac. (Illus.). 130p. 1987. 89.50 (ISBN 0-387-18034-6). Springer-Verlag.

Surgery of Facial Bone Fractures. Ed. by Craig A. Foster & John E. Sherman. (Illus.). 273p. 1986. text ed. 75.00 (ISBN 0-443-08436-X). Churchill.

Surgery of Facial Fractures. Reed O. Dingman & Paul Natvig. LC 63-14507. (Illus.). 1964. 68.00 (ISBN 0-7216-3085-5). Saunders.

Surgery of Female Incontinence. 2nd, rev. ed. Ed. by S. L. Stanton & E. A. Tanagho. (Illus.). 304p. 1986. 73.00 (ISBN 0-387-15821-9). Springer-Verlag.

Surgery of Hand Unit in Adults & Children, 2 vols. 5th ed. H. A. Motamed. LC 77-78228. (Illus.). 1614p. 1988. Repr. of 1979 ed. Set. 250.00 (ISBN 0-910161-02-X). Vol. I (ISBN 0-910161-03-8). Vol. II (ISBN 0-910161-04-6). Motamed Med Pub.

Surgery of Inflammatory Bowel Disorders: Vol. 14, CSI. Lee & Nolan. 1987. 65.00 (ISBN 0-443-03439-7). Churchill.

Surgical Infections. Alan Pollock. 233p. 1987. 39.95 (ISBN 0-683-06916-0). Williams & Wilkins.

Surgical Infections. M. Robson. 1988. 33.00 (ISBN 0-8151-7309-1). Year Bk Med.

Surgical Infectious Disease. 2nd ed. Richard J. Howard & Richard L. Simmons. 1987. 159.00 (ISBN 0-8385-8733-X). Appleton & Lange.

Surgical Instruments in Greek & Roman Times. J. G. Milne. (Illus.). 25.00 (ISBN 0-89005-127-5). Ares.

Surgical Instruments in Greek & Roman Times. John S. Milne. LC 70-95630. (Illus.). 1970. Repr. of 1907 ed. 29.50x (ISBN 0-678-03755-8). Kelley.

Surgical Instruments of the Hindus, 2 vols. Girindranath Mukhopadhyaya. LC 75-23714. Repr. of 1914 ed. 47.50 set (ISBN 0-404-13340-1). AMS Pr.

Surgical Intensive Care: Practical Guide. Kortz & Lumb. 1984. 20.00 (ISBN 0-8151-5650-2). Year Bk Med.

Surgical Intervention in Corneal & External Diseases. Ed. by Richard L. Abbott. 1987. 86.50 (ISBN 0-8089-1850-8, 790004). Grune.

Surgical Judgement Using Decision Sciences. John R. Clarke. LC 83-24594. (Surgical Science Ser.: Vol. III). 124p. 1984. 35.00 (ISBN 0-275-91425-9, C1425). Praeger.

Surgical MCQ's. 2nd ed. J. L. Craven & J. S. Lumley. LC 84-12147. 243p. 1985. pap. text ed. 18.00 (ISBN 0-443-03052-9). Churchill.

Surgical Malpractice. M. Levine. 554p. 1970. 25.00 (ISBN 0-913338-11-7). Condyne-Oceana.

Surgical Management of Acquired Heart Disease. Fred A. Crawford, Jr. & Harvey I. Pass. 306p. 1988. 52.50 (ISBN 0-87527-338-6). Green.

Surgical Management of Cerebrovascular Diseases. 2nd ed. Robert Ojemann. 496p. 1987. 110.95 (ISBN 0-683-06640-4). Williams & Wilkins.

Surgical Management of Degenerative Arthritis of the Lower Limb. Ed. by Richard L. Cruess & Nelson S. Mitchell. LC 75-20440. (Illus.). Repr. of 1975 ed. 62.00 (ISBN 0-8357-9421-0, 2014539). Bks Demand UMI.

Surgical Management of Juvenile Chronic Polyarthritis. Ed. by G. P. Arden & B. M. Ansell. 300p. 1979. 55.00 (ISBN 0-8089-1104-X, 790150). Grune.

Surgical Management of Morbid Obesity. Griffen & Printen. (Science & Practice of Surgery Ser.). 296p. 1987. 79.75 (ISBN 0-8247-7381-0). Dekker.

Surgical Management of Soft Tissue Sarcomas. Myron Arlen & Ralph C. Marcove. (Illus.). 344p. 1987. 79.00 (ISBN 0-7216-1399-3). Saunders.

Surgical Management of Soft Tissue Sarcoma. Ed. by Man H. Shiu & Murray F. Brennan. (Illus.). 400p. 1989. price not set (ISBN 0-8121-1152-4). Lea & Febiger.

Surgical Management of the Burn Wound. David M. Heimbach & Loren H. Engrav. (Illus.). 176p. 1984. text ed. 100.00 (ISBN 0-89004-914-9). Raven.

Surgical Management of Urologic Disease. Droller. (Illus.). 900p. 1990. 95.00 (ISBN 0-8016-0398-6). Mosby.

Surgical Neonate. 2nd ed. Howard C. Filston & Robert Izant, Jr. 320p. 1985. 39.95 (ISBN 0-8385-8717-8). Appleton & Lange.

Surgical Neuroangiography, Vol. 1. P. Lasjaunias & A. Berenstein. (Functional Anatomy of Craniofacial Arteries Ser.). (Illus.). 450p. 1986. 165.50 (ISBN 0-387-16534-7). Springer-Verlag.

Surgical Neuroangiography, Vol. 2. P. Lasjaunias & A. Berenstein. (Endovascular Treatment of Craniofacial Lesions Ser.). (Illus.). 450p. 1987. 180.50 (ISBN 0-387-16535-5). Springer-Verlag.

Surgical Nutrition. Josef E. Fischer. 1983. 77.50 (ISBN 0-316-28371-1). Little.

Surgical Oncology. Ed. by Edward M. Copeland. LC 82-8608. 723p. 1983. 70.00x (ISBN 0-471-07997-9, Pub. by Wiley Med). Wiley.

Surgical Oncology. Ed. by Y. H. Pilch. (Illus.). 1200p. 1984. text ed. 125.00 (ISBN 0-07-049997-7). McGraw.

Surgical Operations in Short-Stay Hospitals, U. S. 1971. Gary E. Blanken. LC 74-6259. (Data from the Hospital Discharge Survey Ser. 13: No. 18). 62p. 1974. pap. text ed. 1.50 (ISBN 0-8406-0017-8). Natl Ctr Health Stats.

Surgical Operations in Short-Stay Hospitals: United States, 1978. Robert Pokras et al. Ed. by Mary Olmstead. (Series 13: No. 61). 64p. 1981. pap. text ed. 4.25 (ISBN 0-8406-0238-3). Natl Ctr Health Stats.

Surgical Operations in Short-Stay Hospitals United States-1975. Abraham L. Ranofsky. Ed. by Margot Kemper. (Ser. 13-34). 1978. pap. text ed. 2.00 (ISBN 0-8406-0122-0). Natl Ctr Health Stats.

Surgical Operations in Short-Stay Hospitals, U. S. 1973. Abraham L. Ranofsky. Ed. by Audrey M. Shipp. (Ser. 13: No. 24). 61p. 1976. pap. text ed. 1.25 (ISBN 0-8406-0069-0). Natl Ctr Health Stats.

Surgical-Orthodontic Treatment: A Contemporary Synthesis. Proffit & White. (Illus.). 750p. 1990. 125.00 (ISBN 0-8016-5291-X). Mosby.

Surgical Pathology, 2 vols. 2nd ed. Walter F. Coulson. LC 65-7743. (Illus.). 1824p. 1988. 195.00 (ISBN 0-397-50609-0, Lippincott Medical). Lippincott.

Surgical Pathology in Urologic Disease. Nasser Javadpour. (Illus.). 312p. 1986. 85.95 (ISBN 0-683-04359-5). Williams & Wilkins.

Surgical Pathology of Bone Marrow: Core Biopsy Diagnosis. Benjamin Wittels. (Major Problems in Pathology Ser.). (Illus.). 162p. 1985. 58.00 (ISBN 0-7216-1434-5). Saunders.

Surgical Pathology of Diffuse Infiltrative Lung Disease. Flint & Colby. LC 79-1284. 256p. 1987. 49.50 (ISBN 0-317-55906-0). Grune.

Surgical Pathology of Lymph Nodes & Related Organs. Elaine S. Jaffe. (Major Problems in Pathology Ser.). (Illus.). 455p. 1985. 73.00 (ISBN 0-7216-1027-7). Saunders.

Surgical Pathology of Non-Neoplastic Lung Disease. Anna-Louise Katzenstein & Frederic Askin. (Major Problems in Pathology Ser.: Vol. 13). (Illus.). 488p. 1982. 83.00 (ISBN 0-7216-5301-4). Saunders.

Surgical Pathology of the Head & Neck, 2 vols. Barnes. 1032p. 1985. Vol. 1. 125.00 (ISBN 0-8247-7216-4); Vol. 2. 125.00 (ISBN 0-8247-7269-5); Set. 250.00. Dekker.

Surgical Pathology of the Mediastinum. Alberto M. Marchevsky & Mamoru Kaneko. (Illus.). 304p. 1984. text ed. 73.00 (ISBN 0-88167-005-7). Raven.

Surgical Pathology of the Nervous System & Its Coverings. 2nd ed. Peter C. Burger & F. Stephen Vogel. LC 81-16250. 739p. 1982. pap. 65.00 (ISBN 0-471-12347-1). Wiley.

Surgical Pediatric Urology. H. B. Eckstein et al. (Illus.). 533p. 1978. 89.00 (ISBN 0-7216-3325-0). Saunders.

Surgical Pediatrics: Nonoperative Care. 2nd ed. Stephen Gans. 352p. 1980. 53.50 (ISBN 0-8089-1197-X, 791516). Grune.

Surgical Pharmacology of the Eye. Ed. by Marvin L. Sears & Ahti Tarkkanen. 608p. 1985. text ed. 73.00 (ISBN 0-88167-047-2). Raven.

Surgical Physiology. John F. Burke. (Illus.). 592p. 1983. write for info. (ISBN 0-7216-2183-X). Saunders.

Surgical Problems in Immuno-Depressed Patients. Richard E. Wilson. (Major Problems in Clinical Surgery Ser.: Vol. 30). (Illus.). 304p. 1984. 49.95 (ISBN 0-7216-9454-3). Saunders.

Surgical Product Comparison System, 1988, 2 vols. Ed. by Walter Hook. 1000p. 1988. Set. 245.00 (ISBN 0-941417-04-2); renewal 225.00 (ISBN 0-317-65022-X). ECRI.

Surgical Radiology: A Complement in Radiology & Imaging to the Sabiston-Davis-Christopher Textbook of Surgery, 3 vols. J. George Teplick & Marvin E. Haskin. (Illus.). 1152p. 1981. text ed. write for info. (ISBN 0-7216-8783-0); Vol. 1. 100.00 (ISBN 0-7216-8781-4); Vol. 2. text ed. 105.00 (ISBN 0-7216-8782-2); Vol. 3. text ed. 105.00 (ISBN 0-7216-8791-1). Saunders.

Surgical Research: Recent Concepts & Results. A. Baethmann & K. Messmer. 260p. 1987. 83.70 (ISBN 0-387-18492-9). Springer-Verlag.

Surgical Research: Recent Developments: Proceedings of the First Annual Scientific Session of the Academy of Surgical Research, San Antonio, TX, U. S. A., 18-19 October, 1985. Ed. by C. W. Hall. (Illus.). 200p. 1985. pap. 40.00 (ISBN 0-08-033138-6, Pub. by PPI). Pergamon.

Surgical Secrets. Abernathy & Abernathy. 1986. 21.00 (ISBN 0-8016-0070-7). Mosby.

Surgical Secrets: Questions you will be asked on Rounds, in the OR, on Oral Exams. Ed. by Charles M. Abernathy & Brett B. Abernathy. (Illus.). 300p. 1985. pap. 20.00 (ISBN 0-932883-00-1). Hanley & Belfus.

Surgical Strike. Jerry Ahern. 1988. pap. 3.95 (ISBN 1-55773-036-9, Charter Pub). Berkley Pub.

Surgical Technology Examination Review. 3rd ed. Norma C. Allen & Diane Gulczynski. (Allied Health Bks.: Vol. 25). 1984. pap. text ed. 26.75 (ISBN 0-87488-651-1). Med Exam.

Surgical Technology: Principles & Practice. 2nd ed. Joanna R. Fuller. (Illus.). 610p. 1986. 37.95 (ISBN 0-7216-1960-6). Saunders.

Surgical Tips. Ed. by Thomas L. Dent & John Kukora. (Illus.). 300p. 1988. pap. 30.00 (ISBN 0-07-016374-X). McGraw.

Surgical Treatment Objective: A Systematic Approach to the Prediction Tracing. Wolford et al. 1984. 250.00 (ISBN 0-8016-5609-5). Mosby.

Surgical Treatment of Aortic Aneurysms. Ed. by Charles D. Campbell. LC 81-69572. (Illus.). 208p. 1981. monograph 25.00 (ISBN 0-87993-162-0). Futura Pub.

Surgical Treatment of Aortic Aneurysms. Denton A. Cooley. (Illus.). 215p. 1986. 68.00 (ISBN 0-7216-1398-5). Saunders.

Surgical Treatment of Bronchial Carcinoma. J. Hasse. (Illus.). 160p. 1986. 53.50 (ISBN 0-387-16230-5). Springer-Verlag.

Surgical Treatment of Congenital Heart Disease. 3rd ed. Grady L. Hallman et al. LC 86-21062. (Illus.). 234p. 1987. text ed. 45.00 (ISBN 0-8121-1069-2). Lea & Febiger.

Surgical Treatment of Metastatic Cancer. Steven A. Rosenberg. LC 65-9459. (Illus.). 286p. 1987. text ed. 62.50 (ISBN 0-397-50781-X, Lippincott Medical). Lippincott.

Surgical Treatment of Middle Ear Cholesteatoma. M. Wayoff et al. (Advances in Oto-Rhino-Laryngology Ser.: Vol.36). (Illus.). x, 238p. 1987. 130.00 (ISBN 3-8055-4441-3). S Karger.

Surgical Treatment of Mitral Stenosis. Ed. by A. N. Bakulev. 304p. 1961. text ed. 67.50x (ISBN 0-7065-0099-7, Pub. by Keter Pub Jerusalem). Coronet Bks.

Surgical Treatment of Ocular Inflammatory Disease. Joseph B. Michelson & Robert Nozik. LC 65-9277. (Illus.). 304p. 1988. 49.50 (ISBN 0-397-50763-1, Lippincott Medical). Lippincott.

Surgical Treatment of the Epilepsies. Ed. by Jerome Engel, Jr. (Illus.). 727p. 1987. text ed. 135.00 (ISBN 0-88167-226-2). Raven.

Surgical Treatment of the Infertile Female. Veasy C. Buttram, Jr. & Robert C. Reiter. 350p. 1985. 59.50 (ISBN 0-683-01251-7). Williams & Wilkins.

Surgical Urology. 5th ed. Culp. 1985. 89.00 (ISBN 0-8151-2070-2). Year Bk Med.

Surgical Uses of Fluorescein. David G. Silverman & Bert Meyers. 128p. 1987. cancelled (ISBN 0-03-063398-2). Praeger.

Surgical Voice Restoration: Evaluation & Management. Alison Perry. (Illus.). 1989. text ed. 29.50 (ISBN 0-316-69999-3, 699993). College-Hill.

Surgical Word Book. Claudia J. Tessier. LC 81-40485. 507p. 1981. pap. text ed. 24.95 (ISBN 0-7216-8805-5). Saunders.

Surimi. Sunee C. Sonu. (NOAA Technical Memorandum NMFS-SWR 013). (Illus.). 130p. 1986. pap. 6.00 (ISBN 0-318-21358-3, S/N 003-018-00112-8). USGPO.

Surimono from the Chester Beatty Collection. Ed. by Roger S. Keyes. (Illus.). 160p. 1987. pap. 105.00x (Pub. by Han-Shan Tang Ltd). State Mutual Bk.

Surimono: Privately Published Japanese Prints in the Spencer Museum of Art. Roger Keyes. LC 83-48879. (Illus.). 199p. 1984. 50.00 (ISBN 0-87011-650-9). Kodansha.

Surinaamse Slangeninkleur: Surinam Snakes in Color. Joep Moonen et al. (Illus.). 119p. 1979. pap. 29.95x (ISBN 0-88359-016-6). R Curtis Bks.

Surinam: Politics, Economics & Society. H. E. Chin. (Marxist Regimes Ser.). 220p. 1987. 35.00 (ISBN 0-86187-516-8, Pub. by Pinter Pubs UK); pap. 12.50 (ISBN 0-86187-517-6). Columbia U Pr.

Suriname. Noelle B. Beatty. (Places & Peoples of the World Ser.). (Illus.). 96p. (gr. 5 up). 1988. lib. bdg. 12.95x (ISBN 1-55546-196-4). Chelsea Hse.

Suriname. (Let's Visit Places & Peoples - - Nations, Dependencies, & Sovereignties of the World Ser.). (Illus.). (gr. 5 up). 1988. 12.95. Chelsea Hse.

Suriname see Statements of the Laws of the OAS Member States in Matters Affecting Business.

Suriname Folk-Lore. Melville J. Herskovits & Frances S. Herskovits. LC 71-82365. (Columbia Univ. Contributions to Anthropology Ser.: No. 27). (Illus.). Repr. of 1936 ed. 67.50 (ISBN 0-404-50577-5). AMS Pr.

Suriname: Recent Developments Relating to Human Rights: Report of a Mission to Suriname in February 1981. John Griffiths. pap. 20.00 (2027736). Bks Demand UMI.

Surly Bonds of Earth. Edward D. McKenzie. (Illus.). 160p. 1987. 20.00 (ISBN 0-9617909-0-3). E D McKenzie.

Surly Tim & Other Stories. facsimile ed. Frances Burnett. LC 77-103500. (Short Story Index Reprint Ser). 1877. 19.00 (ISBN 0-8369-3242-0). Ayer Co Pubs.

Surmale. Alfred Jarry. 154p. 1970. 5.95 (ISBN 0-686-54212-6). French & Eur.

Surname Index File. Ed. by Elise H. Jennings. 110p. Date not set. pap. 4.50. Prince Georges County Gen Soc.

Surname Index to Forty-Three Westmoreland County, PA. Cemeteries, Vol. 2. Bob Closson & Mary Closson. 127p. 1986. PLB 9.50 (ISBN 0-933227-52-3). Closson Pr.

Surname Index to Sixty-Five Volumes of Colonial & Revolutionary Pedigrees. Rodney G. Crowther. 143p. lib. bdg. 17.25 (ISBN 0-915156-27-X). Natl Genealogical.

Surnames & Genetic Structure. G. W. Lasker. (Cambridge Studies in Biological Anthropology). 150p. 1985. 24.95 (ISBN 0-521-30285-4). Cambridge U Pr.

Surnames of Ireland. 6th ed. Edward MacLysaght. 334p. 1985. 22.50x (ISBN 0-7165-2367-1, BBA 05252, Pub by Irish Academic Pr Ireland); pap. 10.00x (ISBN 0-7165-2366-3, BBA 05251, Pub by Irish Academic Pr Ireland). Biblio Dist.

Surnames of Ireland. 5th ed. Edward Maclysaght. 340p. 1980. pap. 9.50x (ISBN 0-7165-2300-0, BBA 02174, Pub. by Irish Academic Pr). Biblio Dist.

Surnames of Scotland: Their Origin, Meaning & History. George F. Black. LC 47-1716. 838p. 1986. Repr. of 1946 ed. 25.00 (ISBN 0-87104-172-3). NY Pub Lib.

Surpassing the Love of Men: Love Between Women from the Renaissance to the Present. Lillian Faderman. Ed. by Maria D. Guarnaschelli. LC 80-24482. (Illus.). 488p. 1981. 18.95 (ISBN 0-688-03733-X); pap. 12.95 (ISBN 0-688-00396-6, Quill). Morrow.

Surpassing Wit: Oliver St. John Gogarty, His Poetry & His Prose. James F. Carens. LC 78-12644. 304p. 1979. 32.00x (ISBN 0-231-04642-1). Columbia U Pr.

Surplus. Sylvia Stevenson. 336p. 1986. pap. 7.95 (ISBN 0-930044-78-9). Naiad Pr.

Surplus Dollars. 3rd ed. Ed Bennington, Jr. LC 75-23177. (Illus.). 80p. 1982. pap. 4.95 (ISBN 0-686-34360-3). E Bennington.

Surplus Love. Rose G. Ignatow. LC 85-11012. 132p. (Orig.). 1985. pap. 7.95 (ISBN 0-914278-44-4). Copper Beech.

Surplus People: Forced Removals in South Africa. Laurine Platzky & Cherryl Walker. LC 82-95958. 250p. 1985. pap. text ed. 16.95x (ISBN 0-86975-255-3, Pub. by Ravan Pr). Ohio U Pr.

Surplus Powerlessness. Michael Lerner. LC 85-62314. 320p. 1986. 14.95 (ISBN 0-935933-01-8); pap. 9.95 (ISBN 0-935933-02-6). Inst Labor & Mental.

Surplus School Space: Options & Opportunities. LC 76-21173. 72p. 1976. pap. 4.00 (ISBN 0-88481-220-0). Ed Facilities.

Surplus Space in Schools: An Opportunity. OECD Staff. 132p. (Orig.). 1985. pap. 19.00x (ISBN 92-64-12732-1). OECD.

Surplus Species: Need Man Prevail? Walter H. Slack. LC 81-40833. 172p. (Orig.). 1982. lib. bdg. 27.75 (ISBN 0-8191-2231-9); pap. text ed. 12.25 (ISBN 0-8191-2232-7). U Pr of Amer.

Surplussed Barrelware. Vasily Aksyonov. Ed. by Joel Wilkinson & Slava Yastremski. LC 84-6348. 228p. 1985. 23.50 (ISBN 0-88233-904-4); pap. 5.95 (ISBN 0-88233-905-2). Ardis Pubs.

Surprise! Winsom Amos. 63p. (Orig.). 1982. pap. 2.00 (ISBN 0-932510-01-9). Soma Pr.

Surprise. Winsom Amos. 63p. 1987. pap. 2.50 (ISBN 0-932510-02-7). Soma Pr.

Surprise. George Shannon. LC 83-1434. (Illus.). 32p. (gr. k-3). 1983. 11.75 (ISBN 0-688-02313-4); PLB 11.88 (ISBN 0-688-02314-2). Greenwillow.

Surprise. Z. Voskrenskaya. 32p. 1974. pap. 0.99 (ISBN 0-8285-1236-1, Pub. by Progress Pubs USSR). Imported Pubns.

Surprise! Harriet Ziefert. (Illus., Orig.). (ps-3). 1988. pap. 2.95 (ISBN 0-14-050814-7, Puffin Bks). Penguin.

Surprise! Harriet Ziefert. LC 87-26217. (Hello Reading Ser.). (Illus.). 32p. (ps-3). 1988. 8.95 (ISBN 0-670-82036-9, Viking Kestrel). Viking.

Surprise, No. 30. Emily Chase. (Girls of Canby Hall Ser.). (gr. 7-10). 1988. 2.50 (ISBN 0-590-41672-3). Scholastic Inc.

Surprise at Muddy Creek. Leone C. Anderson. LC 84-7072. (Illus.). 32p. (gr. 1-2). 1984. lib. bdg. 4.95 (ISBN 0-89693-222-2). Dandelion Hse.

Surprise Attack in Mathematical Problems. Lloyd A. Graham. (Illus., Orig.). 1968. pap. 4.50 (ISBN 0-486-21846-5). Dover.

Surprise Attack: Lessons for Defense Planning. Richard K. Betts. LC 82-70887. 318p. 1982. 32.95 (ISBN 0-8157-0930-7); pap. 12.95 (ISBN 0-8157-0929-3). Brookings.

Surprise Attack: The Victim's Perspective. Ephraim Kam. (Illus.). 304p. 1988. text ed. 25.00 (ISBN 0-674-85745-3). Harvard U Pr.

Surprise Bear! (Surprise Board Bks.). (Illus.). (ps-1). 1987. bds. 3.95 (ISBN 0-317-66510-3, Little Simon). S&S.

Surprise Cat! (Surprise Board Bks.). (Illus.). (ps-1). 1987. bds. 3.95 (ISBN 0-317-66511-1, Little Simon). S&S.

Surprise Fire Engine! (Surprise Board Bks.). (Illus.). (ps-1). 1987. bds. 3.95 (ISBN 0-317-66512-X, Little Simon). S&S.

Surprise for Baby Blueberry Muffin. Susan C. Poskanzer. (Baby Strawberry Shortcake Ser.). (Illus.). 40p. (ps-3). 1984. cancelled 5.95 (ISBN 0-910313-23-7). Parker Bros.

Surprise for Lunchbox. Paula J. Bussard. (Critter County Ser.). (Illus.). 32p. (gr. k-6). 1986. 1.29 (ISBN 0-87403-104-4, 3434). Standard Pub.

Surprise for Mrs. Pinkerton-Trunks. Shirley Isherwood. (Illus.). 96p. (gr. k-2). 1986. 12.95 (ISBN 0-09-160380-3, Pub. by Century Hutchinson). David & Charles.

Surprise for Mrs. Rabbit see Peter Rabbit's First Library.

Surprise for Perky Pup. May Justus. LC 74-155569. (Garrard Venture Ser.). (Illus.). 40p. (gr. k-3). 1971. PLB 6.69 (ISBN 0-8116-6704-9); pap. 1.19 (9025). Garrard.

Surprise in the Mountains. Natalie S. Carlson. LC 82-47716. (Illus.). 32p. (gr. 1-3). 1983. 12.70 (ISBN 0-06-021008-7); PLB 12.89 (ISBN 0-06-021009-5). HarpJ.

Surprise Island. Gertrude C. Warner. LC 49-49618. (Boxcar Children Mysteries Ser.). (Illus.). (gr. 3-7). PLB 8.95 (ISBN 0-8075-7673-5). A Whitman.

Surprise of Being. Fernando Pessoa. Tr. by James Greene & Clara de Azevedo Mafra. LC 86-82063. 64p. 1987. 16.95 (ISBN 0-946162-23-9, Pub. by Angel Bks); pap. 9.95 (ISBN 0-946162-24-7, Pub. by Angel Bks). Dufour.

Surprise of Burning. Michael Doane. LC 87-45259. 288p. 1988. 17.95 (ISBN 0-394-55879-0). Knopf.

Surprise of Excellence: Modern Essays on Max Beerbohm. Ed. by J. G. Riewald. LC 74-5181. (Illus.). xiii, 265p. 1974. 27.50 (ISBN 0-208-01443-8, Archon). Shoe String.

Surprise Paper Tearing Talks, No. 9. Arnold C. Westphal. 1976. pap. 3.95 (ISBN 0-915398-08-7). Visual Evangels.

Surprise Party. Sharon Gordon. LC 81-4869. (Illus.). 32p. (gr. k-2). 1981. PLB 9.89 (ISBN 0-89375-521-4); pap. 2.95 (ISBN 0-89375-522-2). Troll Assocs.

TITLE INDEX SURVEILLANCE RADAR PERFORMANCE PREDICTION.

Surprise Party. Pat Hutchins. (Illus.). 32p. (ps-3). 1986. 10.95 (ISBN 0-02-745930-6). Macmillan.
Surprise Party. William Katz. 304p. 1987. pap. 3.50 (ISBN 0-446-32778-6). Warner Bks.
Surprise Party. Annabelle Prager. LC 87-20649. (Step into Reading Bks.). (Illus.). 48p. (Orig.). (gr. 1-3). 1988. PLB 6.99 (BYR); pap. 2.95 (ISBN 0-394-89596-7). Random.
Surprise Picnic. Illus. by John S. Goodall. LC 76-28455. (Illus.). 64p. (ps up). 1977. 6.95 (ISBN 0-689-50074-2, M K McElderry). Macmillan.
Surprise Robot! (Surprise Board Bks.). (Illus.). (ps-1). 1987. bds. 3.95 (ISBN 0-317-66513-8, Little Simon). S&S.
Surprise Surprise. Agatha Christie. 1971. pap. 2.50 (ISBN 0-440-18389-8). Dell.
Surprise! Surprise! Gyo Fujikawa. (Fujikawa Board Books). (Illus.). (gr. k-3). 1978. 3.50 (ISBN 0-448-14557-X, G&D). Putnam Pub Group.
Surprise! Surprise! A Reproduction of An Antique Book of Magical Moving Pictures. Lothar Meggendorfer. LC 81-52199. (Illus.). 12p. 1982. 9.95 (ISBN 0-670-68483-X). Viking.
Surprised by Joy: The Shape of My Early Life. C. S. Lewis. LC 56-5329. 248p. 1956. 12.95 (ISBN 0-15-187011-X). HarBraceJ.
Surprised by Joy: The Shape of My Early Life. C. S. Lewis. LC 56-5329. 1966. pap. 5.95 (ISBN 0-15-687011-8, Harv). HarBraceJ.
Surprised by Sin: The Reader in Paradise Lost. Stanley E. Fish. 1971. pap. 10.95x (ISBN 0-520-01897-4). U of Cal Pr.
Surprised by the Spirit. Edward Farrell. 4.95 (ISBN 0-87193-030-7). Dimension Bks.
Surpriser: The Life of Rowland, Lord Hill. Gordon L. Teffeteller. LC 81-72058. (Illus.). 272p. 1983. 32.50 (ISBN 0-87413-212-6). U Delaware Pr.
Surprises! Dick Hilliard & Beverly Valenti-Hilliard. (Center Celebration Ser.). (Illus.). 48p. (Orig.). (gr. 1 up). 1981. pap. text ed. 4.95 (ISBN 0-89390-031-1). Resource Pubns.
Surprises. Lee B. Hopkins. LC 83-47712. (Charlotte Zolotow Bk.: Trophy I Can Read Bk.). (Illus.). 64p. (gr. k-3). 1986. pap. 3.50 (ISBN 0-06-444105-9, Trophy). HarpJ.
Surprises. Ed. by Lee B. Hopkins. LC 83-47712. (Trophy I Can Read Bks.). (Illus.). 64p. (gr. k-3). 1984. 9.70i (ISBN 0-06-022584-X); PLB 10.89g (ISBN 0-06-022585-8). HarpJ.
Surprises. Kenneth G. Mills. (Illus.). 135p. 1980. 24.95 (ISBN 0-919842-06-2). Sun-Scape Pubns.
Surprises in Theoretical Physics. Rudolf Peierls. LC 79-84009. (Princeton Ser. in Physics). 1979. 27.00x (ISBN 0-691-08241-3); pap. 10.00x (ISBN 0-691-08242-1). Princeton U Pr.
Surprises of Life. facs. ed. Georges E. Clemenceau. Tr. by Grace Hall. LC 77-132113. (Short Story Index Reprint Ser). 1920. 18.00 (ISBN 0-8369-3670-1). Ayer Co Pubs.
Surprising Account of the Captivity & Escape of Philip M'Donald & Alexander M'Leod, from the Chikkamaugga Indians. M'Donald & M'Leod. 23p. 1973. 7.50. Ye Galleon.
Surprising Adventures of the Magical Monarch of Mo & His People. L. Frank Baum. (Illus.). (ps-4). 1968. pap. 5.95 (ISBN 0-486-21892-9). Dover.
Surprising Adventures of the Magical Monarch of Mo & His People. L. Frank Baum. (gr. 5-6). 17.95 (ISBN 0-88411-771-5, Pub. by Aeonian Pr). Amereon Ltd.
Surprising Citrus: A Cookbook. Audra Hendrickson & Audra Hendrickson. (Illus.). 1988. 15.95 (ISBN 0-88266-514-6, Garden Way Pub); pap. 7.95 (ISBN 0-88266-515-4). Storey Comm Inc.
Surprising Effects of Sympathy: Marivaux, Diderot, Rousseau, & Mary Shelley. David Marshall. (Illus.). x, 286p. 1988. 27.50x (ISBN 0-226-50710-6). U of Chicago Pr.
Surprising Gift: The Story of Holden Village, Church Renewal Center. Charles P. Lutz. (Illus.). 144p. (Orig.). 1987. pap. 6.00 (ISBN 0-9618617-0-3). Holden Village.
Surprising Gospel: Intriguing Psychological Insights from the New Testament. Wilhelm H. Wuellner & Robert C. Leslie. 176p. (Orig.). 1983. pap. 11.95 (ISBN 0-687-40724-9). Abingdon.
Surprising Myself. Christopher Bram. (Owl Bks.). 1988. pap. 8.95 (ISBN 0-8050-0669-9). H Holt & Co.
Surprising Myself. LC 86-82182. 400p. 1987. 17.95 (ISBN 1-55611-007-3). D I Fine.
Surprising People. Christopher Carrie. (Crayola Laugh & Play Bks.). (Illus.). 48p. (Orig.). (gr. k-4). 1981. pap. cancelled (ISBN 0-86696-031-7). Binney & Smith.
Surprising Pictures for Little Folk. Ernest Nister. (Illus.). (ps up). 1987. 10.95 (ISBN 0-399-21423-2, Philomel Bks). Putnam Pub Group.
Surprising Rise of Luke Vanner. Robert M. Moore. LC 86-23395. 192p. (Orig.). 1986. pap. 7.95 (ISBN 0-915175-16-9). Knights Pr.
Surprising Years: Understanding Your Changing Adolescent. Cliff Schimmels & Hank Resnik. (Illus.). 140p. (Orig.). 1985. pap. 7.50 (ISBN 0-933419-08-2). Quest Intl.
Surprising Years: Understanding Your Changing Adolescent. rev. ed. Cliff Schimmels & Hank Resnik. Ed. by Linda Barr & Marba Wojcicki. (Skills for Adolescence Ser.). (Illus.). 144p. 1988. pap. text ed. 6.00 (ISBN 0-933419-25-2). Quest Intl.
Surprizing Narrative: Olaudah Equiano & the Beginnings of Black Autobiography. Angelo Costanzo. LC 86-25748. (Contributions in Afro-American & African Studies: No. 104). 156p. 1987. lib. bdg. 29.95 (ISBN 0-313-25633-0, CZO/). Greenwood.
Surreal Numbers. Donald E. Knuth. LC 74-5998. 1974. pap. text ed. write for info. (ISBN 0-201-03812-9). Addison-Wesley.
Surreal Songs. John Judson. (Juniper Bk.: No. 1). 1968. 5.00 (ISBN 1-55780-000-6). Juniper Pr WI.
Surrealism. Yves Duplessis. Tr. by Paul Capon. LC 77-17880. 1978. Repr. of 1963 ed. lib. bdg. 35.00x (ISBN 0-313-20110-2, DUSU). Greenwood.
Surrealism. Julien Levy. LC 68-9469. Repr. of 1936 ed. 16.00 (ISBN 0-405-00299-8, Pub. by Ind. Pubns.). Ayer Co Pubs.
Surrealism. Ed. by Herbert E. Read. LC 37-1497. 251p. 1936. Repr. 49.00x (ISBN 0-403-07248-4). Somerset Pub.
Surrealism. (Yale French Studies). pap. 16.00 (ISBN 0-527-01735-3). Kraus Repr.
Surrealism. Patrick Waldberg. (World of Art Ser.). (Illus.). 128p. 1985. pap. 11.95 (ISBN 0-500-20040-8). Thames Hudson.
Surrealism & Film. J. H. Matthews. LC 75-163624. pap. 56.50 (2056146). Bks Demand UMI.
Surrealism & Its Affinities: The Mary Reynolds Collection. 2nd ed. Hugh Edwards. LC 73-132025. (Illus.). 147p. pap. 1.50 (ISBN 0-86559-003-6). Art Inst Chi.
Surrealism & Its Popular Accomplices. Ed. by Franklin Rosemont. (Illus.). 112p. 1980. pap. 4.95 (ISBN 0-87286-121-X). City Lights.
Surrealism & Language: Seven Essays. Ed. by Ian Higgins. 104p. 1987. 12.00 (ISBN 0-7073-0454-7, Pub. by Scot Acad Pr). Longwood Pub Group.
Surrealism & Quebec Literature: History of a Cultural Revolution. Andre G. Bourassa. Tr. by Mark Czarnecki. (University of Toronto Romance Ser.: 50). 416p. 1984. 20.00 (ISBN 0-8020-6528-7). U of Toronto Pr.
Surrealism & Spain Nineteen Twenty to Nineteen Thirty-Six. C. B. Morris. LC 74-190414. (Illus.). 1979. o.p 52.50 (ISBN 0-521-08529-2); pap. 12.95x (ISBN 0-521-29457-6). Cambridge U Pr.
Surrealism in Literature. Paul W. Memrey. 236p. 1983. 10.95 (ISBN 0-935539-08-5). Heroica Bks.
Surrealism, Insanity, & Poetry. J. H. Matthews. LC 82-3165. (Illus.). 168p. 1982. 22.00x (ISBN 0-8156-2273-2). Syracuse U Pr.
Surrealism of the Movies. William Earle. 1986. 23.95 (ISBN 0-913750-42-5, Dist. by Transaction Bks). Precedent Pub.
Surrealism Pro & Con. Kenneth Burke et al. 1973. pap. 2.50 (ISBN 0-910664-27-7). Gotham.
Surrealism, Quantum Philosophy, & World War I. Virginia P. Williams. Ed. by William H. McNeill. (Modern European History Ser.). 328p. 1987. lib. bdg. 50.00 (ISBN 0-8240-8068-8). Garland Pub.
Surrealism: The Road to the Absolute. Anna Balakian. LC 76-87200. (Illus.). 266p. 1986. pap. 12.50 (ISBN 0-226-03560-3). U of Chicago Pr.
Surrealisme au Service de la Revolution. Andre Breton. 59.95 (ISBN 0-686-51938-8). French & Eur.
Surrealisme au Service de la Revolution, Nos. 1-6. Ed. by Andre Breton. LC 68-28661. (Contemporary Art Ser). (Illus., Fr.). 1968. Repr. of 1930 ed. 66.00 (ISBN 0-405-00707-8). Ayer Co Pubs.
Surrealist Art. Sarane Alexandrian. (World of Art Ser.). (Illus.). 1985. pap. 11.95 (ISBN 0-500-20097-1). Thames Hudson.
Surrealist Image: A Stylistic Study. Gerald Mead. (Utah Studies in Literature & Linguistics: Vol. 9). 161p. 1977. pap. 19.25 (ISBN 3-261-02995-1). P Lang Pubs.
Surrealist Movement in England. Paul C. Ray. LC 70-145626. 352p. 1971. 35.00x (ISBN 0-8014-0621-8). Cornell U Pr.
Surrealist Movement in England. Paul C. Ray. LC 70-145626. 331p. 1971. 20.00x. Lib Soc Sci.
Surrealist Painting. Simon Wilson. (Phaidon Color Library). (Illus.). 84p. 1983. pap. 18.95 (ISBN 0-7148-2244-2). Salem Hse Pubs.
Surrealist Philosophy. 2nd ed. Tom Hibbard & Joseph Uphoff. LC 87-17519. 46p. 1987. pap. text ed. 3.00 (ISBN 0-943123-00-3). Arjuna Lib Pr.
Surrealist Poetry in France. J. H. Matthews. LC 71-96815. 1969. 24.95x (ISBN 0-8156-2144-2). Syracuse U Pr.
Surrealist Revolution in France. Herbert S. Gershman. (Illus.). 268p. 1973. pap. 5.95 (ISBN 0-472-06188-7, AA). U of Mich Pr.
Surrealist Voice of Robert Desnos. Mary Ann Caws. LC 76-25145. (Illus.). 208p. 1977. 17.50x (ISBN 0-87023-223-1). U of Mass Pr.
Surrealists & Surrealism. Gaeton Picon & Skira-Rizzoli. (Illus.). 220p. 1983. pap. 25.00 (ISBN 0-8478-0486-0). Rizzoli Intl.
Surrealist's Bible. Dierdre Luzwick. LC 75-44001. (Illus.). 128p. 1976. 15.00 (ISBN 0-8246-0206-4). Jonathan David.
Surrealists Look at Art. Andre Breton et al. Ed. by Pontus Hulten. LC 85-81092. (Illus.). 96p. (Orig.). 1988. price not set (ISBN 0-932499-08-2); pap. price not set (ISBN 0-932499-09-0). Lapis Pr.
Surrender. Emily Carmichael. 432p. 1988. pap. 3.95 (ISBN 0-446-35200-4). Warner Bks.
Surrender. (Pocket Power Ser.). 16p. (Orig.). 1986. pap. 0.50 (ISBN 0-89486-325-8). Hazelden.
Surrender. Irma Walker. (Love & Life Romance Ser.). 176p. (Orig.). 1983. pap. 1.75 (ISBN 0-345-30450-0). Ballantine.
Surrender: A Guide to Prayer. Nancy Schreck & Maureen Leach. (Take & Receive Ser.). 153p. (Orig.). 1986. pap. 6.95 (ISBN 0-88489-171-2). St Mary's.
Surrender & Catch: Experience & Inquiry Today. new ed. Kurt H. Wolff. (Synthese Library: No. 105). 1976. lib. bdg. 47.40 (ISBN 90-277-0758-8, Pub. by Reidel Holland); pap. 18.50 (ISBN 90-277-0765-0). Kluwer Academic.
Surrender & Other Poems. Cosmo E. Damiani. 96p. 1987. 8.95 (ISBN 0-8062-3074-6). Carlton.
Surrender & the Singing: Happiness Through Letting Go. Ray Ashford. 168p. (Orig.). 1985. pap. 7.95 (ISBN 0-86683-964-X, AY8546, HarpR). Har-Row.
Surrender by Moonlight. Bonnie Drake. (Canlelight Ecstasy Ser.: No. 9). (Orig.). 1986. pap. 1.50 (ISBN 0-440-18426-6). Dell.
Surrender in Moonlight. Jennifer Blake. 416p. 1984. pap. 6.95 (ISBN 0-449-90082-7, Columbine). Fawcett.
Surrender in Moonlight. Jennifer Blake. 1988. pap. 4.95 (GM). Fawcett.
Surrender in Panama: The Case Against the Treaty. Philip M. Crane. LC 77-93941. 180p. 1978. 7.95 (ISBN 0-916054-57-8, Dist. by Kampmann). Green Hill.
Surrender Mountain. Joan Gimbel. 192p. 1985. 13.95 (ISBN 0-8027-0854-4). Walker & Co.
Surrender of An Empire. Nesta Webster. 75.00 (ISBN 0-8490-1162-0). Gordon Pr.
Surrender of An Empire. Nesta H. Webster. 392p. 1972. pap. 5.00 (ISBN 0-913022-07-1). Angriff Pr.
Surrender or Starve: The Wars Behind the Famine. Robert D. Kaplan. 192p. 1988. 26.95 (ISBN 0-8133-0754-6). Westview.
Surrender Proceedings, April Ninth, 1865, Appomattox Court House. Frank P. Cauble. (Illus.). 141p. 1987. 16.00 (ISBN 0-930919-40-8). H E Howard.
Surrender Sweet Stranger. De Wanna Pace. 1988. price not set. Outlet Bk Co.
Surrender the Dawn. Jan Mathews. Ed. by Joan Marlowe. (Second Chance at Love Ser.: No. 434). 192p. (Orig.). 1988. pap. 2.50 (ISBN 0-425-10682-9). Berkley Pub.
Surrender the Night. Christine Monson. 400p. 1987. pap. 3.95 (ISBN 0-380-89969-8). Avon.
Surrender the Stars. Cynthia Wright. 416p. (Orig.). 1987. pap. 3.95 (ISBN 0-345-33484-1). Ballantine.
Surrender to a Stranger. Sibylle Garrett. (Intimate Moments Ser.). pap. 2.75 (ISBN 0-373-07211-2). Harlequin Bks.
Surrender to Ecstasy. Rochelle Wayne. 1984. pap. 3.95 (ISBN 0-8217-1307-8). Zebra.
Surrender to Love. Rosemary Rogers. 624p. 1982. pap. 4.50 (ISBN 0-380-80630-4, 60166-4). Avon.
Surrendering to the Real Things: The Archetypal Experience of C. Wordsworth Crockett. Jeff Gundy. (Pikestaff Poetry Chap Bks.: No. 2). 16p. (Orig.). 1986. pap. 2.50 (ISBN 0-936044-04-7). Pikestaff Pr.
Surreptitious Printing in England, 1550 to 1640. Denis B. Woodfield. 203p. 1973. 17.50 (ISBN 0-914930-04-4). Biblio Soc Am.
Surreptitious Printing in England, 1550-1640. Denis B. Woodfield. LC 75-185916. (Illus.). 203p. 1973. 17.50x (ISBN 0-8139-0940-6, Bibliographical Society of America). U Pr of Va.
Surrey: A Photographic Record 1850-1920. John Janaway. 96p. 1987. 30.00x (ISBN 0-905392-38-8, Countryside Bks). State Mutual Bk.
Surrey Rambles. Derek Palmer. 64p. 1987. 30.00x (ISBN 0-905392-77-9, Countryside Bks). State Mutual Bk.
Surrey Village Book. Graham Collyer. 168p. 1987. 30.00x (ISBN 0-905392-32-9, Countryside Bks). State Mutual Bk.
Surrogate. Elizabeth Hanley. 1977. pap. 1.50 (ISBN 0-8439-0443-7, Leisure Bks). Leisure NY.
Surrogate. Willa Ramsaran. 234p. 1986. 11.95 (ISBN 0-533-06097-4). Vantage.
Surrogate Motherhood. Martha A. Field. 224p. 1988. 22.50 (ISBN 0-674-85748-8). Harvard U Pr.
Surrogate Motherhood: The Ethics of Using Human Beings. Thomas A. Shannon. 212p. 1988. 17.95 (ISBN 0-8245-0899-8). Crossroad NY.
Surrogate Mothers. Elaine Landau. Ed. by Iris Rosoff. (Illus.). 144p. (YA) (gr. 7 up). 1988. 11.90 (ISBN 0-531-10603-9). Watts.
Surrogate Mother's Story. Patricia Adair. LC 86-20817. 140p. 1987. 14.95 (ISBN 0-933703-19-8). Loiry Pubs Hse.
Surrogate Parenting. Amy Z. Overvold. LC 87-50915. 224p. 1988. 16.95 (ISBN 0-345-35225-4). Pharos Bks NY.
Surrogate Parenting: An Annotated Review of the Literature. Sara Robbins. LC 84-1824. (CompuBibs Ser.: No. 3). 40p. 1984. pap. 10.00x (ISBN 0-914791-04-4). Vantage Info.
Surrogate Parenting & the Law of Adoption. Irving J. Sloan. (Legal Almanac Ser.: No. 3). 1988. lib. bdg. 10.00 (ISBN 0-379-11169-1). Oceana.
Surrogate Proletariat: Moslem Women & Revolutionary Strategies in Soviet Central Asia, 1919-1929. Gregory L. Massell. (Center of International Studies, Princeton Univ.). 452p. 1974. 54.00x (ISBN 0-691-07562-X). Princeton U Pr.
Surrogate Sister. Eve Bunting. LC 83-49483. 192p. (YA) (gr. 7 up). 1984. 13.70i (ISBN 0-397-32098-1, Lipp Jr Bks); PLB 12.89g (ISBN 0-397-32099-X). HarpJ.
Surrogate's Court Clerk. Jack Rudman. (Career Examination Ser.: C-2135). (Cloth bdg. avail. on request). 1988. pap. 14.00 (ISBN 0-8373-2135-2). Natl Learning.
Surrogate's Court Procedure Act (N. Y.) Gould Editorial Staff. (Supplemented annually). looseleaf 7.50 (ISBN 0-87526-129-9). Gould.
Surrogates Court Procedure Act, N.Y.S. write for info. Looseleaf Law.
Surrogates in New Jersey: Final Report. National Center for State Courts Staff. 230p. 1981. manuscript 13.80 (NERO-080). Natl Ctr St Courts.
Surrounded. D'Arcy McNickle. LC 77-91886. (Zia Bks Ser.). 311p. 1978. pap. 8.95x (ISBN 0-8263-0469-9). U of NM Pr.
Surrounded by His Love. Dixie Duncan. 1988. 7.95 (ISBN 0-533-07524-6). Vantage.
Surrounded by Mystery: Living with the Contradictions of Faith. Ruth Senter. 144p. 1988. pap. 6.95 (ISBN 0-310-38871-6, 11229P). Zondervan.
Surry County Marriages, 1768-1825. Catherine L. Knorr. 124p. 1982. Repr. of 1960 ed. 20.00 (ISBN 0-89308-256-2, VA 14). Southern Hist Pr.
Surry County, N. C., Court Minutes, 1768-1789, Vols. 1 & 2. W. O. Absher. 168p. pap. 18.50 (ISBN 0-89308-554-5). Southern Hist Pr.
Surry County, N. C., Deeds, 1779-1797, Bks. D, E, & F. 128p. 1985. pap. 15.00 (ISBN 0-89308-555-3). Southern Hist Pr.
Surry County Records, Surry County, Virginia, 1652-1684. Eliza T. Davis. LC 80-52582. 156p. 1980. Repr. of 1950 ed. 12.50 (ISBN 0-8063-0904-0). Genealog Pub.
Surry County Wills, Estate Accounts & Inventories, 1730-1800. Lyndon H. Hart, III. 182p. 1983. pap. 25.00 (ISBN 0-89308-325-9). Southern Hist Pr.
Surry Light Artillery of Virginia. Jones, Jr. Ed. by Lee A. Wallace. (Illus.). 1975. Repr. 20.00 (ISBN 0-89029-020-2). Pr of Morningside.
Surry of Eagle's Nest: Or, the Memoirs of a Staff Officer Serving in Virginia. John E. Cooke. LC 68-23718. (Americans in Fiction Ser.). 484p. Repr. of 1866 ed. lib. bdg. 34.00 (ISBN 0-8398-0273-0). Irvington.
Surry of Eagle's Nest: Or, the Memoirs of a Staff Officer Serving in Virginia. John E. Cooke. (Americans in Fiction Ser.). 484p. 1986. pap. text ed. 8.95x (ISBN 0-8290-2037-3). Irvington.
Sursis. Jean-Paul Sartre. (Folio Ser.: No. 866). 250p. 1945. 11.95 (ISBN 0-686-55002-1); pap. 8.95 (ISBN 0-686-55003-X). Schoenhof.
Surti Touch: Adventures in Indian Cooking. Malvi Doshi. LC 80-21487. (Illus., Orig.). 1980. pap. 7.95 (ISBN 0-89407-042-8). Strawberry Hill.
Surveillance. Ed. by Deborah Irmas & Branda Miller. (Illus.). 55p. (Orig.). 1987. pap. 7.00 exhib. catalogue (ISBN 0-937335-02-9). LA Contemp Exhib.
Surveillance & Target Acquisition. (Brassey's Battlefield Weapons Systems & Technology Ser.: Vol. 7). 160p. 1983. text ed. 33.00 (ISBN 0-08-028334-9); pap. text ed. 15.75 (ISBN 0-08-028335-7). Pergamon.
Surveillance & Undercover Investigation. Art Buckwalter. LC 83-15425. (Library of Investigation Ser.). 208p. 1984. 22.95 (ISBN 0-409-95098-X). Butterworth.
Surveillance in Health & Disease. Ed. by W. J. Eylenbosch & N. D. Noah. (Illus.). 320p. 1988. 65.00 (ISBN 0-19-261611-0). Oxford U Pr.
Surveillance Methods & Ways & Means of Communicating with Drivers. (National Cooperative Highway Research Program Report). 66p. 1966. 2.60 (ISBN 0-317-36106-6, 1473). Transport Res Bd.
Surveillance of Items Important to Safety in Nuclear Power Plants: A Safety Ser. (Safety Ser.: No. 50-SG-08). 48p. 1983. pap. 9.25 (ISBN 92-0-123282-9, ISP640, IAEA). UNIPUB.
Surveillance of Reproductive Health in the U. S. Survey of Activity Within & Outside Industry. Maureen Hatch et al. LC 85-71881. (Orig.). 1985. pap. text ed. 12.00 (ISBN 0-89364-053-0, 847-8800). Am Petroleum.
Surveillance Radar Performance Prediction. P. Rohan. Ed. by J. R. Wait et al. (Electromagnetic Waves Ser.). 336p. 1983. casebound 82.00 (ISBN 0-906048-98-2, EW017). Inst Elect Eng.

Surveiors Dialogue... for All Men to Peruse, That Have to Do with the Revenues of Land, or the Manurance, Use or Occupation. Third Time Imprinted & Enlarged. John Norden. LC 79-84126. (English Experience Ser.: No. 945). 280p. 1979. Repr. of 1618 ed. lib. bdg. 26.00 (ISBN 90-221-0945-3). Walter J Johnson.

Survey & Analysis of Flue Gas Treatment Methods. 80p. softcover 15.00 (ISBN 0-318-12714-8, L51386). Am Gas Assn.

Survey & Critique of World Bank Supported Research in International Comparisons of Real Product. Robin Marris. (Working Paper: No. 365). ii, 56p. 1979. 5.00 (ISBN 0-686-36093-1, WP-0365). World Bank.

Survey & Evaluation of Factors Affecting Heat Transfer Performance & Cost of Steam Condensers. North Carolina State University. 93p. 1967. 13.95 (ISBN 0-317-34551-6, 104). Intl Copper.

Survey & Evaluation of Handling & Disposing of Solid Low-Level Nuclear Fuel Cycle Wastes (AIF-NESP-008) NUS Corporation. (National Environmental Studies Project: NESP Reports). 125p. 1976. 24.00 (ISBN 0-318-13596-5); to NESP sponsors 12.00 (ISBN 0-318-13597-3). US Coun Energy Awareness.

Survey & Evaluation of the Education of School Music Teachers in the United States. Edna McEachern. LC 78-177023. (Columbia University. Teachers College. Contributions to Education: No. 701). Repr. of 1937 ed. 22.50 (ISBN 0-404-55701-5). AMS Pr.

Survey & Excavations North & East of Navajo Mountain, Utah, 1959-1962. Alexander J. Lindsay, Jr. et al. (Glen Canyon Ser.: No. 8). 400p. 1968. pap. 12.50 (BS-45). Mus Northern Ariz.

Survey & Public Opinion Research. 2nd ed. Lois F. Roets. 120p. (gr. 3 up). 1988. 14.00 (ISBN 0-911943-14-5). Leadership Pub.

Survey & Questionnaire Design: A Bibliography. Anthony G. White. (Public Administration Ser.: P 2021). 8p. 1986. 3.00 (ISBN 1-55590-041-0). Vance Biblios.

Survey Course in Christian Doctrine, Vols. III & IV. C. C. Crawford. LC 71-1388. (Bible Study Textbook Ser.). 1964. 13.95 (ISBN 0-89900-054-1). College Pr Pub.

Survey Design & Analysis. F. R. Jolliffe. LC 85-24866. (Mathematics & its Applications Ser.). 184p. 1986. 64.95 (ISBN 0-470-20272-6). Halsted Pr.

Survey Drafting: Drafting Practices in Surveying & Engineering Offices. 2nd ed. Gurdon H. Wattles. LC 81-52885. 382p. 1981. problems with answers 28.00 (ISBN 0-9606962-0-2). Wattles Pubns.

Survey Errors & Survey Cost. Groves. 1988. price not set (ISBN 0-471-61171-9). Wiley.

Survey Graphic. Ed. by Alain L. Locke. (Illus.). 92p. 1980. pap. 10.00 (ISBN 0-933121-05-9). Black Classic.

Survey Graphic "New Negro" A Facsimile of the 1925 Magazine Issue. Ed. by Alain Locke. (Critical Studies on Black Life & Culture). 1981. lib. bdg. 33.00 (ISBN 0-8240-9458-1). Garland Pub.

Survey in Basic Christianity. Jean Gibson. (Believer's Bible Lessons Ser.). 1979. pap. 6.00 (ISBN 0-937396-41-9). Walterick Pubs.

Survey in Seating. Earnest A. Hooton. 1970. Repr. of 1945 ed. lib. bdg. 35.00x (ISBN 0-8371-3952-X, HOSS). Greenwood.

Survey in Zeelandia of Formosa. Lin Yung. (Asian Folklore & Social Life Monographs: Vol. 96). (Chinese.). 1977. 14.00x (ISBN 0-89986-328-0). Oriental Bk Store.

Survey Interviewing: Theory & Techniques. Ed. by Terence W. Beed & Robert J. Stimson. 224p. 1985. text ed. 34.95x (ISBN 0-86861-436-X). Unwin Hyman.

Survey Method in the Social & Political Sciences: Achievements, Failures, Prospects. William L. Miller. LC 83-40095. 250p. 1983. 27.50 (ISBN 0-312-77721-3). St Martin.

Survey Method: The Contribution of Surveys to Sociological Explanation. Catherine Marsh. (Contemporary Social Research Ser.: No. 6). 272p. 1982. pap. text ed. 15.95x (ISBN 0-04-310015-5). Unwin Hyman.

Survey Methods for Ecosystem Management. Wayne L. Myers & Ronald L. Shelton. LC 79-25404. 384p. 1980. 45.95x (ISBN 0-471-62735-6, Pub. by Wiley Interscience). Wiley.

Survey Methods in Community Medicine: An Introduction to Epidemiological & Evaluative Studies. 3rd ed. J. H. Abramson. 1984. pap. text ed. 22.00 (ISBN 0-443-03068-5). Churchill.

Survey Methods in Social Investigation. 2nd ed. Ed. by C. A. Moser & G. Kalton. LC 76-182200. 1972. text ed. 19.95x (ISBN 0-465-08340-4). Basic.

Survey of a Public School System. Henry L. Smith. LC 75-177774. (Columbia University. Teachers College. Contributions to Education: No. 82). Repr. of 1917 ed. 22.50 (ISBN 0-404-55082-7). AMS Pr.

Survey of Accountants' Views on the Desirability & Method of Inflation Accounting. Rosalie C. Hallbauer & Surendra P. Agrawal. LC 83-6900. (Illus.). 350p. (Orig.). 1983. lib. bdg. 34.25 (ISBN 0-8191-3212-8); pap. text ed. 17.75 (ISBN 0-8191-3213-6). U Pr of Amer.

Survey of Accounting. 6th ed. Gary Schugart et al. 1988. 33.95 (ISBN 0-256-06534-9); study guide 12.95; 12.95. Irwin.

Survey of Adult Aphasia. G. Albyn Davis. (Illus.). 384p. 1983. write for info. (ISBN 0-13-878207-5). P-H.

Survey of Advanced Sales. 140p. pap. text ed. 23.95 (ISBN 0-317-57623-2). Longman Finan.

Survey of African Marriage & Family Life. Arthur Phillips. LC 74-15079. Repr. of 1953 ed. 67.50 (ISBN 0-404-12128-4). AMS Pr.

Survey of Afro-American Experience in the U. S. Economy. Martin O. Ijere. 1978. 8.50 (ISBN 0-682-49029-6, University). Exposition-Phoenix.

Survey of Agricultural Economics Literature: Quantitative Methods in Agricultural Economics, 1940's to 1970's, Vol. II. Ed. by Lee R. Martin et al. LC 76-27968. (Illus.). 1977. 29.50x (ISBN 0-8166-0818-0). U of Minn Pr.

Survey of Agricultural Economics Literature: Traditional Fields of Agricultural Economics, 1940s to 1970s, Vol. I. Ed. by Lee R. Martin. LC 76-27968. 1977. 29.50x (ISBN 0-8166-0801-6). U of Minn Pr.

Survey of Algebraic Coding Theory. CISM (International Center for Mechanical Sciences) Staff. Ed. by E. R. Berlekamp. (CISM Pubns. Ser.: No. 28). (Illus.). 75p. 1973. pap. 12.40 (ISBN 0-387-81088-9). Springer-Verlag.

Survey of American City Energy Programs. 53p. 1982. 8.00 (ISBN 0-317-36376-X, 4002); 4.00, member (ISBN 0-317-36377-8). Natl League Cities.

Survey of American Foreign Relations: 1928, 1929, 1930, 1931, 4 vols. Charles P. Howland. Ea. 75.00x (ISBN 0-686-50174-8). Elliots Bks.

Survey of American Gambling Attitudes & Behavior. Maureen Kallick et al. 560p. (Orig.). 1979. pap. 25.00x (ISBN 0-87944-245-X). Inst Soc Res.

Survey of American Genealogical Periodicals & Periodical Indexes. Ed. by Kip Sperry. LC 78-55033. (Genealogy & Local History Ser.: Vol. 3). 216p. 1978. 68.00x (ISBN 0-8103-1401-0). Gale.

Survey of American Philosophy. Ed. by Ralph B. Winn. (Quality Paperback: No. 162). 1965. pap. 2.95 (ISBN 0-8226-0162-1). Littlefield.

Survey of American Poetry: Civil War & Aftermath (1861-1889), Vol. V. Granger Book Company, Editorial Board Staff. LC 81-83526. 400p. 1985. lib. bdg. 39.95x (ISBN 0-89609-217-8). Roth Pub Inc.

Survey of American Poetry: Early Nineteenth Century (1800-1829, Vol. III. Ed. by Granger Book Company, Editorial Board Staff. LC 81-83526. (Series II). 286p. 1984. 39.95x (ISBN 0-89609-215-1). Roth Pub Inc.

Survey of American Poetry: First Great Period (1830-1860, Vol. IV. Granger Book Company, Editorial Board Staff. LC 81-83526. (No. II). 1984. 39.95x (ISBN 0-89609-216-X). Roth Pub Inc.

Survey of American Poetry: Revolutionary Era, 1766-1799, Vol. II. Granger Book Company, Editorial Board Staff. LC 81-83526. 200p. 1983. 39.95x (ISBN 0-89609-214-3). Roth Pub Inc.

Survey of American Poetry: Twilight Interval (1890-1912, Vol. VI. Granger Book Company, Editorial Board Staff. LC 81-83526. 400p. 1986. 39.95x (ISBN 0-89609-218-6). Roth Pub Inc.

Survey of American Poetry, Vol. I: Colonial Period, 1607-1765. Granger Book Company, Editorial Board Staff. LC 81-83526. 220p. 1982. 39.95x (ISBN 0-89609-213-5). Roth Pub Inc.

Survey of American Poetry, Vol. IX: World War II & Aftermath (1940-1950) Roth Publishing Editorial Board. LC 81-83526. 1986. 39.95 (ISBN 0-89609-221-6). Roth Pub Inc.

Survey of American Poetry, Vol. VII: Poetic Renaissance (1913-1919) Roth Publishing Editorial Board. LC 81-83526. 380p. 1986. 39.95x (ISBN 0-89609-219-4). Roth Pub Inc.

Survey of American Poetry, Vol. VIII: Interval Between World Wars (1920-1939) Roth Publishing Editorial Board. LC 81-83526. 380p. 1986. 39.95x (ISBN 0-89609-220-8). Roth Pub Inc.

Survey of American Poetry, Vol. X: Midcentury to 1984. Roth Publishing Editorial Board. LC 81-83526. 370p. 1986. 39.95x (ISBN 0-89609-222-4). Roth Pub Inc.

Survey of Applied Linguistics. Ed. by Ronald Wardhaugh & H. Douglas Brown. LC 75-31053. 1976. pap. 12.95x (ISBN 0-472-08959-5). U of Mich Pr.

Survey of Arab History. rev. ed. Bernard G. Weiss & Arnold H. Green. 320p. 1988. 20.00x (ISBN 977-424-180-0, Pub. by Am Univ Cairo Pr). Columbia U Pr.

Survey of Architectural History in Cambridge. Cambridge Historical Commission Staff. Incl. Report One: East Cambridge; Report Two: Mid Cambridge. 1967; Report Three: Cambridgeport. 1971. pap. 10.95 (ISBN 0-262-53013-9); Report Four: Old Cambridge. 1973; Report Five: Northwest Cambridge. 1977. pap. 10.95 (ISBN 0-262-53032-5). pap. write for info. MIT Pr.

Survey of Arts Administration Training: 1987-88. 6th ed. Ed. by E. Arthur Prieve. 87p. (Orig.). 1987. pap. 8.95 (ISBN 0-915400-55-3). Am Council Arts.

Survey of Attitudes in Oklahoma Toward DUI. F. Ted Hebert. 32p. 1983. 3.50 (ISBN 0-318-01370-3). Univ OK Gov Res.

Survey of Attorneys in the District of Columbia Regarding Their Experiences with Court Reporting Services in the Superior Court. Barbara Kajdan & Jill B. Wilson. LC 83-244782. (Illus.). Date not set. 0.50. Natl Shorthand Rptr.

Survey of Bar Foundations. National Conference of Bar Foundations. 16p. 1981. pap. 4.00 (ISBN 0-317-63155-1, 572-0001-01). Amer Bar Assn.

Survey of Basic Accounting. 5th ed. Edwards et al. 1988. 34.95 (ISBN 0-256-06976-X). Irwin.

Survey of Basic Accounting. 4th ed. R. F. Salmonson et al. 1985. 33.95 (ISBN 0-256-03203-3); workbook 12.95 (ISBN 0-256-03204-1). Irwin.

Survey of Basic Mathematics. 4th ed. Fred W. Sparks & Charles S. Rees. (Illus.). 1979. pap. text ed. 34.95 (ISBN 0-07-059902-5). McGraw.

Survey of Bible Doctrine. Charles C. Ryrie. LC 72-77958. 192p. 1972. pap. 6.95 (ISBN 0-8024-8435-2). Moody.

Survey of Bible Prophecy. Raymond Ludwigson. (Contemporary Evangelical Perspective Ser.). Orig. Title: Outlines to Bible Eschatology. 192p. 1973. Repr. 8.95 (ISBN 0-310-28421-X, 10100P). Zondervan.

Survey of Biomedical & Clinical Engineering Department In U. S. Hospitals, 1981. Allan F. Pacela. 27p. (Orig.). 1985. pap. text ed. 40.00x (ISBN 0-930844-18-1). Quest Pub.

Survey of Black Newspapers in America. Henry G. La Brie, III. LC 80-80551. (Mass Communication & Journalism Ser.). 72p. (Orig.). 1980. 6.00 (ISBN 0-89080-034-0). Mercer Hse.

Survey of Black School Board Members in the South. Richard A. Hudlin & Shelby Lewis. 1981. 3.00 (ISBN 0-686-36623-9). Voter Ed Proj.

Survey of British Commonwealth Affairs: Problems of Wartime Cooperation & Post-War Change 1939-1952. Nicholas Mansergh. 470p. 1968. Repr. of 1958 ed. 35.00x (ISBN 0-7146-1496-3, F Cass Co). Biblio Dist.

Survey of British Commonwealth Affairs, 2 vols. William K. Hancock. LC 74-15049. Repr. of 1942 ed. Set. 62.50 (ISBN 0-404-12084-9). AMS Pr.

Survey of British Poetry, Vol. 1. Ed. by Roth Publishing, Inc. Editorial Board. 400p. 1988. 59.95x (ISBN 0-89609-274-7). Roth Pub Inc.

Survey of Cable Subscribers: Viewing Preferences for Channels 4, 13, & 19. CAUR Staff. 25p. (Orig.). 1985. pap. 2.50 (ISBN 1-55719-037-2). U NE Ctr Applied Urban Rsch.

Survey of Cenozoic Volcanism on Mainland Asia. Ed. by J. L. Whitford-Stark. (Special Paper Ser.: No. 213). (Illus.). 1987. 15.00 (ISBN 0-8137-2213-6). Geol Soc.

Survey of Chester County Pennsylvania Architecture. Margaret B. Schiffer. 396p. 1976. 35.00 (ISBN 0-916838-02-1). Schiffer.

Survey of Chinese Art. John C. Ferguson. 153p. 1940. 525.00x (ISBN 0-317-69127-9, Pub. by Han-Shan Tang Ltd). State Mutual Bk.

Survey of Choral Music. Homer Ulrich. (Harbrace History of Musical Forms Ser.). 245p. 1973. pap. text ed. 11.00 net (ISBN 0-15-584863-1, HC). HarBraceJ.

Survey of Christian Epistemology. Cornelius Van Til. 1967. pap. 6.95 (ISBN 0-87552-495-8). Presby & Reformed.

Survey of Christian Ethics. Edward L. Long, Jr. 1967. pap. 12.95x (ISBN 0-19-503242-X). Oxford U Pr.

Survey of Christian Hymnody. rev. ed. William J. Reynolds & Milburn Price. LC 87-81996. (Illus.). 300p. 1987. pap. text ed. 19.95 (ISBN 0-916642-32-1, 904). Hope Pub.

Survey of Church History. J. D. O'Donnell. 1973. pap. 4.95 (ISBN 0-89265-009-5). Randall Hse.

Survey of Citizen Attitudes & Opinions Regarding the Austin, Texas, Police Department & its Relations with the Community. James W. Stevens et al. 68p. (Orig.). 1986. pap. text ed. write for info (ISBN 0-936440-72-4). Inst Urban Studies.

Survey of Classical Roman Literature, 2 Vols. Dean P. Lockwood. LC 34-40316. 1962. Vol. 1. pap. 14.00x (ISBN 0-226-48962-0, Midway Reprint); Vol. 2. pap. 16.00x (ISBN 0-226-48963-9, Midway Reprint). U of Chicago Pr.

Survey of Climatology. John F. Griffiths & Dennis M. Driscoll. 368p. 1982. text ed. 35.95 (ISBN 0-675-09994-3). Merrill.

Survey of CMEA Activities in 1981. 84p. 1982. 7.50x (Pub. by Collets (UK)). State Mutual BK.

Survey of Combinatorial Theory. J. N. Srivastava et al. LC 72-88578. 470p. 1973. 63.25 (ISBN 0-444-10425-9, North-Holland). Elsevier.

Survey of Commercial Turnkey CAD-CAM Systems. 2nd ed. 96.00 (ISBN 0-686-31441-7). C I M Systems.

Survey of Community Workers in the United Kingdom. David Francis et al. 1984. 15.00x (ISBN 0-317-40619-1, Pub. by Natl Soc Work). State Mutual Bk.

Survey of Concrete Research in Australia: A Report on Information Subjects Allied to Concrete. 86p. (Orig.). 1979. pap. text ed. 18.00x (ISBN 0-85825-108-6, Pub. by Inst Engineering Australia). Brookfield Pub Co.

Survey of Constitutional Development in China. Hawkling L. Yen. LC 72-76693. (Columbia University, Studies in the Social Sciences Ser.: No. 104). Repr. of 1911 ed. 12.50 (ISBN 0-404-51104-X). AMS Pr.

Survey of Construction Materials & Corrosion in Sour Water Strippers, 1978. American Petroleum Institute, Division of Refining Staff. (API Publication Ser.: No. 950, April, 1983). (Illus.). 95p. pap. 24.70 (2029896). Bks Demand UMI.

Survey of Consumer Attitudes to Food, 2 vols. (Orig.). 1987. Vol. 1, 51 pgs. pap. 23.00 (ISBN 0-11-242801-0, HM1423, Pub. by Her Maj Station Ofc); Vol. 2, 122 pgs. pap. 34.00 (ISBN 0-11-242802-9, HM1424, Pub. by Her Maj Station Ofc). UNIPUB.

Survey of Contemporary Literature, 12 vols. new ed. Ed. by Frank N. Magill. LC 77-79874. 8531p. 1977. Set. 350.00x (ISBN 0-89356-050-2). Salem Pr.

Survey of Contemporary Music. Cecil Gray. LC 75-93341. (Essay Index Reprint Ser). 1924. 19.00 (ISBN 0-8369-1294-2). Ayer Co Pubs.

Survey of Contemporary Music. 2nd ed. Cecil Gray. LC 78-163551. 266p. 1972. Repr. of 1927 ed. lib. bdg. 35.00x (ISBN 0-8371-6211-4, GRCM). Greenwood.

Survey of Contemporary Toxicology, Vol. 1. Ed. by Anthony T. Tu. LC 79-25224. pap. 95.50 (2032003). Bks Demand UMI.

Survey of Corporate Contributions, 1988. Linda C. Platzer. (Report Ser.: No. 906). (Illus.). ix, 58p. (Orig.). 1988. pap. text ed. 75.00 (ISBN 0-8237-0350-9). Conference Bd.

Survey of Corporate Government Affairs Departments. Rebecca S. Fahrlander. 48p. (Orig.). 1984. pap. 3.50 (ISBN 1-55719-004-6). U NE Ctr Applied Urban Rsch.

Survey of Corrosion Inhibitors & Related Additives to Improve the Corrosion Resistance & Heat Transfer of Copper & Its Alloys. Battelle Memorial Institute Staff. 59p. 1969. 8.85 (ISBN 0-317-34552-4, 148). Intl Copper.

Survey of Counseling Methods. 2nd ed. Samuel H. Osipow et al. 1984. pap. 22.00x (ISBN 0-256-03048-0). Dorsey.

Survey of Criminal Justice in Israel. Gad J. Bensinger. LC 83-188743. 120p. 1983. 5.00 (ISBN 0-911531-11-4). Loyola U Ctr Urban.

Survey of Cripples in New York City: Under the Auspices of a Special Committee on Survey of Cripples. Henry C. Wright. Ed. by William R. Phillips & Janet Rosenberg. LC 79-6014. (Physically Handicapped in Society Ser.). 1980. Repr. of 1920 ed. lib. bdg. 12.00x (ISBN 0-405-13137-2). Ayer Co Pubs.

Survey of Current Structural Research. (Manual & Report on Engineering Practice Ser.: No. 51). 335p. 1970. pap. 30.00x (ISBN 0-87262-225-8). Am Soc Civil Eng.

Survey of Cybernetics. Ed. by J. Rose. 394p. 1970. 97.00 (ISBN 0-677-60560-9). Gordon & Breach.

Survey of Documentary Sources for Property Holding in London Before the Great Fire. Compiled by Derek Keene & Vanessa Harding. (Illus.). 248p. 1986. lib. bdg. 35.00 (ISBN 0-900952-22-9). Chadwyck-Healey.

Survey of Early American Design. Ed. by Lisa C. Mullins. (Architectural Treasures of Early America Ser.). (Illus.). 248p. 1987. 19.95 (ISBN 0-918678-20-X). Historical Times.

Survey of Early American Design. Ed. by Lisa C. Mullins. LC 87-7442. (Architectural Treasures of Early America Ser.: Vol. I). (Illus.). 248p. 1987. 19.95 (ISBN 1-55562-038-8). Main Street.

Survey of Early Childhood Software, 1988. rev. ed. Warren Buckleither. (Annual Software Survey Ser.). (Illus.). 160p. 1988. pap. text ed. 20.00 (ISBN 0-931114-78-0). High-Scope.

Survey of Early Childhood Software, 1988. Warren Buckleitner. 128p. (Orig.). 1988. pap. 20.00. High Scope.

Survey of Economic & Social Conditions in Africa. 1987. pap. 13.00 (ISBN 92-1-125044-7, E.87.II.K.3). UN.

Survey of Economic & Social Conditions in Africa, 1983-1984. 82p. 1987. 15.00 (ISBN 92-1-125043-9, E.87.II.K.2). UN.

Survey of Economic Theory on Technological Change & Employment. Alexander Gourvitch. LC 66-23421. 1966. Repr. of 1940 ed. 35.00x (ISBN 0-678-00113-8). Kelley.

Survey of Economics. James S. Lassiter & Jim Gilbertie. (Illus.). 412p. 1988. pap. text ed. 24.00 (ISBN 0-943437-51-2). CAT Pub.

Survey of Electronics. 3 ed. Leland P. Schwartz. 224p. 1985. text ed. 25.95 (ISBN 0-675-20162-4). Merrill.

Survey of Energy Demand Elasticity Estimates in Developing Countries. Corazon M. Siddavao. (Technical Memorandum: No. 80-7). pap. 20.00 (ISBN 0-317-42012-7, 2025970). Bks Demand UMI.

Survey of English Literature: Eighteen Thirty to Eighteen Eighty, 2 vols. Oliver Elton. (Vol. I 434 pp., Vol. II 432 pp.). 1980. Repr. of 1932 ed. Set. lib. bdg. 150.00 (ISBN 0-8492-0786-X). R West.

Survey of English Literature: Seventeen Eighty to Eighteen Thirty, 2 vols. Oliver Elton. (Vol. I 456 pp., Vol. II 475 pp.). 1980. Repr. of 1912 ed. Set. lib. bdg. 150.00 (ISBN 0-8492-0785-1). R West.

TITLE INDEX SURVEY OF RESEARCH IN

Survey of English Literature: Seventeen Thirty to Seventeen Eighty, 2 vols. Oliver Elton. 1980. Set. lib. bdg. 150.00 (ISBN 0-8492-0784-3). R West.
Survey of English Literature, 1730-1780, 2 vols. Oliver Elton. LC 77-3043. 1977. 125.00 (ISBN 0-8414-3961-3). Folcroft.
Survey of English Literature, 1780-1830, 2 vols. Oliver Elton. LC 77-5511. 1977. Repr. of 1912 ed. Set. 125.00 (ISBN 0-8414-3963-X). Folcroft.
Survey of English Literature, 1830-1880, 2 vols. Oliver Elton. LC 75-41086. (BCL Ser. II). Repr. of 1932 ed. Set. 75.00 (ISBN 0-404-14900-6). AMS Pr.
Survey of English Literature: 1830-1880, 2 vols. Oliver Elton. LC 77-7594. 1977. Repr. of 1932 ed. lib. bdg. 125.00 (ISBN 0-8414-3967-2). Folcroft.
Survey of European Civilization. 4th ed. Wallace K. Ferguson & Geoffrey Bruun. Incl. Pt. 1. To 1660; Complete. 1969. 44.36 (ISBN 0-395-04425-1). HM.
Survey of Existing & Promising New Methods of Surface Preparation. John D. Keane et al. (Illus.). 165p. 1982. pap. text ed. 40.00 (ISBN 0-938477-12-9). SSPC.
Survey of Export Markets for Sorghum. (Commodity Bulletins: No. 49). 40p. (Orig.). 1971. pap. 6.00 (ISBN 92-5-101644-5, F453, FAO). UNIPUB.
Survey of Factors Affecting the Use of Copper in Steel. Southern Research Institute. 58p. 1966. 8.70 (ISBN 0-317-34553-2, 84). Intl Copper.
Survey of Folklife along the Big South Fork of the Cumberland River. Benita J. Howell. (University of Tennessee, Department of Anthropology, Report of Investigations Ser.: No. 30). (Illus.). 454p. pap. 118.10 (2029848). Bks Demand UMI.
Survey of Fortune 100 Companies' Personnel Activities, Projects, & Staffs. 1987. 125.00. BNA.
Survey of French Literature, 2 vols. rev. ed. Morris Bishop. Incl. Vol. 1. The Middle Ages to 1800. 462p (ISBN 0-15-584963-8, HC); Vol. 2. The Nineteenth & Twentieth Centuries. 462p (ISBN 0-15-584964-6, HC). 1965. text ed. 22.00 net ea. (HC). HarBraceJ.
Survey of Functional Neuroanatomy. Bill Garoutte. LC 80-84809. (Illus.). 217p. 1982. pap. text ed. 9.75x (ISBN 0-930010-04-3). Jones Med.
Survey of Gas Utility & Pipeline Research & Development. J. Glenn Seay & Institute of Gas Technology. 246p. 1972. pap. 10.00 softcover (ISBN 0-318-12715-6, M21173). Am Gas Assn.
Survey of German Literature: Old High German to Storm & Stress, Vol. I. Ed. by Kim Vivian et al. 616p. (Orig.). 1987. lib. bdg. 38.50 (ISBN 0-8191-6541-7); pap. text ed. 26.75 (ISBN 0-8191-6542-5). U Pr of Amer.
Survey of German Literature, Volume II: Classicism to Naturalism. Ed. by Kim Vivian et al. LC 86-24620. 628p. (Orig.). 1987. lib. bdg. 40.50 (ISBN 0-8191-5719-8); pap. text ed. 28.25 (ISBN 0-8191-5720-1). U Pr of Amer.
Survey of Grant-Making Foundations 1983-1984. Ed. by Public Service Materials Center. 1982. pap. 15.95 (ISBN 0-686-37910-1). Public Serv Materials.
Survey of Graves in the Cemeteries of Northwest Pasco County, Florida. West Pasco Genealogical Society Staff. Ed. by Bea Boisselle. (Illus.). 151p. 1984. 15.00 (ISBN 0-9614369-0-5). West Pasco Genealogical.
Survey of Greek Alchemy. Frank S. Taylor. LC 79-8627. Repr. of 1930 ed. 21.50 (ISBN 0-404-18493-6). AMS Pr.
Survey of Greek Civilization. J. P. Mahaffy. 1896. 39.50 (ISBN 0-8274-3965-2). R West.
Survey of Health Careers. Ann Hackleman. 88p. 1981. pap. text ed. 8.95 (ISBN 0-8403-2460-X). Kendall-Hunt.
Survey of Hinduism. Klaus K. Klostermaier. 608p. 1988. 56.60x (ISBN 0-88706-807-3); pap. 18.95x (ISBN 0-88706-809-X). State U NY Pr.
Survey of Historic Costume. Phyllis Tortora & Keith Eubank. (Illus.). 400p. 1988. text ed. 30.00 (ISBN 0-87005-632-8). Fairchild.
Survey of Historical Source Materials in Java & Manila. Robert Van Niel. LC 72-132554. (Asian Studies at Hawaii Ser.: No. 5). 255p. (Orig.). 1971. pap. text ed. 10.00x (ISBN 0-87022-841-2). UH Pr.
Survey of Idea Law for the Texas General Practitioner. Texas Young Lawyers Association. Ed. by Lester L. Hewitt. LC 78-58705. 285p. 1978. 30.00 (ISBN 0-938160-19-2, 6314). State Bar TX.
Survey of Income & Expenditure of Urban Households in China, 1985. People's Republic of China, State Statistical Bureau Staff. LC 87-36588. 200p. 1988. pap. text ed. 29.95x (ISBN 0-86638-105-8, Eastwest Ctr Pr). UH Pr.
Survey of Indian Metal Sculpture. B. Bandopadhyay. 217p. 1987. 99.95. Asia Bk Corp.
Survey of Indian Metal Sculpture. B. Bandyopahyay. 217p. 1987. 65.00x (ISBN 0-8364-2035-7, Pub. by Usha). South Asia Bks.
Survey of Indian River Archeology, Florida. Irving Rouse. LC 76-43813. (Yale Univ. Publications in Anthropology: No. 45). 376p. Repr. of 1951 ed. 32.50 (ISBN 0-404-15668-1). AMS Pr.
Survey of Indian Sculpture. S. K. Saraswati. (Illus.). 1975. 28.50x. Coronet Bks.
Survey of Industrial Chemistry. Philip J. Chenier. LC 86-7813. 432p. 1987. 45.00 (ISBN 0-471-01077-4). Wiley.
Survey of Industrial Robots. 2nd ed. 143.00 (ISBN 0-686-31442-5). C I M Systems.
Survey of Information Systems Interests Report July 1987. American Trucking Associations. 29p. 1987. pap. 125.00 (ISBN 0-88711-109-2). Am Trucking Assns.
Survey of Inmates of State Correctional Facilities, 1979. 2ND ed. U. S. Dept of Justice, Bureau of Justice Statistics. LC 81-85743. 1981. write for info., codebk (ISBN 0-89138-941-5). ICPSR.
Survey of Institutions in the Federal Republic of Germany Co-operating with Developing Countries in Science & Technology. Ed. by Research Unit Gottstein & Max Planck Society. 340p. 1987. lib. bdg. 20.00 (ISBN 3-598-10626-2). K G Saur.
Survey of Instructional Development Models. Kent L. Gustafson. 60p. 1981. 6.00 (ISBN 0-937597-00-7, IR-54). ERIC Clear.
Survey of Interim Committee & Long-Term Research Studies. Melissa Davis & Tami Yellico. (State Legislative Reports: Vol. 13, No. 7). 1988. text ed. 5.00 (ISBN 1-55516-192-8). Natl Conf State Legis.
Survey of International Affairs, Indexes, 1920-1930. Repr. of 1932 ed. 50.00, incl. suppl. vols (ISBN 0-384-58817-4). Johnson Repr.
Survey of International Affairs, 1962. D. C. Watt. (Royal Institute of International Affairs Ser). 1970. 26.00x (ISBN 0-19-214732-3). Oxford U Pr.
Survey of International Arbitration Sites. American Arbitration Association Staff. LC 84-81526. 107p. 1984. pap. 15.00 (ISBN 0-943001-09-9); pap. 10.00 members. Am Arbitration.
Survey of International Arbitrations, 1794-1970. Alexander M. Stuyt. LC 72-79626. 587p. 1972. lib. bdg. 32.50 (ISBN 0-379-00008-3). Oceana.
Survey of Israel's History. rev. ed. Leon Wood & David O'Brien. 416p. 1986. 20.95 (ISBN 0-310-34770-X, 6505). Zondervan.
Survey of Jewish Affairs 1982. Ed. by William Frankel. LC 83-48732. 289p. 1984. 25.00 (ISBN 0-8386-3206-8). Fairleigh Dickinson.
Survey of Jewish Affairs 1983. Ed. by William Frankel. 320p. 1985. 25.00 (ISBN 0-8386-3244-0). Fairleigh Dickinson.
Survey of Jewish Affairs, 1985. Ed. by William Frankel. 280p. 1985. 25.00x (ISBN 0-8386-3269-6). Fairleigh Dickinson.
Survey of Jewish Affairs 1987. William Frankel. LC 84-645587. (Illus.). 304p. 1988. 25.00x (ISBN 0-8386-3322-6). Fairleigh Dickinson.
Survey of Judicial Salaries in State Court System: Volumes I-III. National Center for State Courts Staff. 107p. 1974. manuscript 6.42 (MAB-120). Natl Ctr St Courts.
Survey of Jurors in Selected Pennsylvania Counties. National Center for State Courts Staff. 25p. 1983. manuscript 1.50 (NERO-136). Natl Ctr St Courts.
Survey of Known Mineral Deposits in Canada That Are Not Being Mined. (Mineral Bulletins: No. 181). 159p. 1980. pap. 7.50 (SSC138, SSC). UNIPUB.
Survey of Labor Relations. 2nd ed. Lee Balliet. 200p. 1987. pap. text ed. 17.00 (ISBN 0-87179-544-2, 0544). BNA.
Survey of Lawyer Disciplinary Procedures in the United States. American Bar Association Center for Professional Responsibility Staff. LC 84-250556. 355p. write for info. Amer Bar Assn.
Survey of Legal Literature on Woman Offenders. S. Livesay. i, 16p. 1975. pap. 2.00 (ISBN 0-938876-01-5). Entropy Ltd.
Survey of Library networks & Cooperative Library Organizations: 1985-86. Donald W. King. (Education Department Publications CS: No. 87-349c). 162p. 1987. pap. 8.00 (ISBN 0-317-62899-2, S-N 065-000-00289-2). USGPO.
Survey of London, 36 Vols. London County Council. Ed. by F. W. Sheppard et al. Repr. write for info (ISBN 0-404-51650-5). AMS Pr.
Survey of London. John Stow. 1987. (Evman); pap. 12.95 (ISBN 0-460-11589-8). Biblio Dist.
Survey of Lubbock's Growth As a Medical Center, 1909-1954. William R. Dunnagan. 65p. 1980. 5.00 (ISBN 0-911618-05-8). West Tex Mus.
Survey of Macro Processors: A Machine-Independent Assembly Language for Systems Programs see Annual Review in Automatic Programming.
Survey of Maintenance & Management Needs in Omaha Housing Authority's Apartments for Senior Citizens. Rebecca S. Fahrlander & Joan V. Holley. 46p. (Orig.). 1982. pap. 3.50 (ISBN 1-55719-017-8). U NE Ctr Applied Urban Rsch.
Survey of Manuscripts used in Editions of the Greek New Testament. J. K. Elliott. (Novum Testamentum Ser.: Supplement 57). 150p. 1987. 38.25x (ISBN 90-04-08109-7, Pub. by E J Brill); Novum Testamentum subscription. 32.75 (ISBN 0-317-60880-0, Pub. by E J Brill). Heinman.
Survey of Marketing Research, 1983. Dik W. Twedt. LC 84-259. 82p. 1984. text ed. 40.00 (ISBN 0-87757-166-X). Am Mktg.
Survey of Mass Communication. Ronald G. Hicks. LC 77-8438. 372p. 1977. pap. text ed. 7.95x (ISBN 0-88289-164-2). Pelican.
Survey of Mathematical Logic see Logic, Computers & Sets.
Survey of Mathematical Programming: Proceedings of the 9th Math Programming Symposium, Budapest, 1976, 3 vols. Ed. by A. Prekopa. 1554p. 1980. Set. 268.50 (ISBN 0-444-85033-3, North Holland). Elsevier.
Survey of Medieval Winchester, 2 vols. Derek J. Keene. (Illus.). 1490p. 1985. Set. 225.00x (ISBN 0-19-813181-X). Oxford U Pr.
Survey of Mental Health Nursing Practices see Critical Behaviors in Psychiatric-Mental Health Nursing: Monograph.
Survey of Metaphysics & Esoterism. Frithjof Schuon. Tr. by Gustavo Polit from Fr. LC 86-13261. (Library of Traditional Wisdom). Orig. Title: Resume de Metaphysique Integral Sur les Traces de la Religion Perenne. 224p. (Orig.). 1986. pap. 12.00 (ISBN 0-941532-06-2). Wrld Wisdom Bks.
Survey of Minimal Surfaces. Robert Osserman. 192p. 1986. pap. 8.00 (ISBN 0-486-64998-9). Dover.
Survey of Minority-Owned Business Enterprises, 1982: Minority-Owned Businesses: Black. LC 83-600199. (MB82-1 Ser.). 110p. 1985. pap. 4.00 (ISBN 0-318-19596-8, S/N 003-024-06351-4). USGPO.
Survey of Minority-Owned Business Enterprises, 1982, Minority Owned Businesses: Hispanic. LC 83-600139. (MB82-2 Ser.). (Illus.). 230p. 1986. pap. 11.00 (S/N 003-024-06214-3). USGPO.
Survey of Minority-Owned Business Enterprises, 1982, Minority-Owned Businesses: Asian Americans, American Indians, & Other Minorities. LC 83-600199. (MB82-3 Ser.). (Illus.). 256p. 1986. pap. 12.00 (ISBN 0-318-21816-X, S/N 003-024-06223-2). USGPO.
Survey of Modern Fantasy Literature, 5 vols. Ed. by Frank N. Magill. LC 83-15189. 2589p. 1983. Set. 275.00x (ISBN 0-89356-450-8). Salem Pr.
Survey of Modernist Poetry. Laura R. Jackson & Robert Graves. LC 73-155122. 1927. Repr. lib. bdg. 49.50 (ISBN 0-8414-5356-X). Folcroft.
Survey of Modernist Poetry. Laura Riding & R. Graves. LC 76-95444. (Studies in Poetry, No. 38). 1969. Repr. of 1927 ed. lib. bdg. 75.00x (ISBN 0-8383-1200-4). Haskell.
Survey of Modernist Poetry. Laura Riding & Robert Graves. LC 76-145263. 1971. Repr. of 1928 ed. 19.00x (ISBN 0-403-01178-7). Scholarly.
Survey of Musical Instrument Collections in the United States & Canada. Ed. by MLA Committee. 135p. 1974. 8.50 (ISBN 0-318-14925-7); pap. 6.50 (ISBN 0-318-14927-3). Music Library Assn.
Survey of Mutualistic Communities in America. Ralph Albertson. LC 72-2934. (Communal Societies in America Ser.). Repr. of 1936 ed. 19.50 (ISBN 0-404-10700-1). AMS Pr.
Survey of National & State Regulatory Agency Effluent Toxicity Testing & Procedures. Ecological Analysts Inc. & Environmental Affairs Dept., American Petroleum Institute. LC 83-127589. (Illus.). ix, 52p. 1983. 7.25 (841-43530). Am Petroleum.
Survey of National Sources of Income Distribution Statistics. (Statistical Papers Ser.: No. 72). pap. 24.00 (ISBN 92-1-161187-3, E.81.XVII.7). UN.
Survey of Nebraska Women's Employment Participation, Attitudes, & Needs. Murray Frost. 105p. (Orig.). 1979. pap. 6.50 (ISBN 1-55719-063-1). U NE Ctr Applied Urban Rsch.
Survey of Non-Degree Legal Assistant Training in U. S. 77p. 1976. pap. 2.00 (ISBN 0-686-48060-0). Amer Bar Assn.
Survey of Nucleonic Heat Transfer Research & Development. American Society of Mechanical Engineers, Committee on Nucleonics Heat Transfer. LC 72-185848. (American Society of Mechanical Engineers, Heat Transfer Division Ser.: Vol. 1). pap. 20.00 (ISBN 0-317-09936-1, 2016900). Bks Demand UMI.
Survey of Numerical Mathematics, 2 vols. David M. Young & Robert T. Gregory. 1248p. 1988. Vol. I. pap. text ed. 13.95t (ISBN 0-486-65691-8); Vol. II. pap. text ed. 13.95t (ISBN 0-486-65692-6). Dover.
Survey of Numerical Methods for Partial Differential Equations. Ed. by I. Gladwell & R. Wait. (Illus.). 1979. 52.00x (ISBN 0-19-853351-9). Oxford U Pr.
Survey of Numerical Methods for the Solution of Fredholm Integer Equations of the Second Kind. Kendall E. Atkinson. LC 75-28900. vii, 230p. (Orig.). 1976. pap. text ed. 31.00 (ISBN 0-89871-034-0). Soc Indus-Appl Math.
Survey of Numismatic Research, 1966-71, 3 vols. American Numismatic Society Staff. 1133p. 1973. 40.00 set (ISBN 0-89722-069-2). Am Numismatic.
Survey of Objective Studies of Psychoanalytic Concepts. Robert R. Sears. LC 79-4476. 1979. Repr. of 1943 ed. lib. bdg. 35.00x (ISBN 0-313-21249-X, SESO). Greenwood.
Survey of Objective Studies of Psychoanalytic Concepts. Robert R. Sears. LC 77-27635. (Social Science Research Council Bulletin 51). 1979. pap. 16.00 (ISBN 0-527-03293-X). Kraus Repr.
Survey of Old Testament Introduction. Gleason L. Archer. LC 64-20988. 582p. 1973. 16.95 (ISBN 0-8024-8447-6). Moody.
Survey of Organ Literature & Editions. Marilou Kratzenstein. 1980. text ed. 18.95x (ISBN 0-8138-1050-7). Iowa St U Pr.
Survey of Organic Syntheses, 2 vols. Calvin A. Buehler & Donald E. Pearson. LC 73-112590. 1985. Vol. 1, 1970, 1166p. 95.00 (ISBN 0-471-11670-X); Vol. 2, 1977, 1105p. 85.00 (ISBN 0-471-11671-8); Set. 155.00 (ISBN 0-471-01178-9). Wiley.
Survey of Organizational & Instructional Practices in Michigan Middle Schools, 1988. Katherine Gilliland. Ed. by Louis G. Romano. 1988. pap. 3.50 (ISBN 0-918449-12-X). MI Middle Educ.
Survey of Organizations. James C. Taylor & David G. Bowers. LC 72-619571. 172p. 1972. 16.00x (ISBN 0-87944-124-0). Inst Soc Res.
Survey of Pathology: With Color Microfiche, Illustrations, & Instructional Objectives. Donald W. King et al. (Illus.). 1976. pap. text ed. 29.95x (ISBN 0-19-502104-5). Oxford U Pr.
Survey of Pending State Legislation Pertaining to Utility Regulation. 53p. 1984. 6.50 (ISBN 0-318-17660-2). NARUC.
Survey of Persian Art, 16 Vols. rev. ed. Ed. by Arthur U. Pope & Phyllis Ackerman. Incl. Vols. I & II. PreIslamic Persian Art. Incl. Plate Vol. VII. 200.00 (ISBN 4-89360-012-5); Vol. III. Architecture. Incl. Plate Vol. VIII. 200.00 (ISBN 4-89360-013-3); Vol. IV. Ceramics (Pottery & Falence) Incl. Plate Vol. IX. 200.00 (ISBN 4-89360-014-1); Vol. Va. Art of the Book (Miniatures & Calligraphy) Incl. Plate Vol. X. 200.00 (ISBN 4-89360-015-X); Vol. Vb. Textiles. Incl. Plate Vol. XI. 200.00 (ISBN 4-89360-016-8); Vol. VIa. Carpets. Incl. Plate Vol. XII. 225.00 (ISBN 4-89360-017-6); Vol. VIb. Metalwork & Minor Arts. Incl. Plate Vol.XIII. 200.00 (ISBN 4-89360-018-4); Vol. XIII. Fascicle, Addendum A. - The Andarz Nama. 20.00 (ISBN 4-89360-022-2); Vol. XIV. New Studies 1939-1960-First Addendum. 50.00 (ISBN 4-89360-019-2); Vol. XV. Bibliography-PreIslamic Persian Art to 1939. 75.00 (ISBN 4-89360-020-6); Vol. XVI. Bibliography-Islamic Persian Art to 1939. 75.00 (ISBN 4-89360-021-4). (Illus.). 3816p. 1981. Set. 1200.00 (ISBN 4-89360-011-7, Pub. by Personally Oriented Japan). C E Tuttle.
Survey of Persian Handicraft. J. Gluck & S. Gluck. 416p. 1977. 210.00x (ISBN 0-317-39200-X, Pub. by Luzac & Co Ltd). State Mutual Bk.
Survey of Persian Handicraft. Jay Gluck & Sami Gluck. (Survey of Persian Art Ser.). (Illus.). 416p. 1977. 125.00 (ISBN 4-89360-024-9, Pub. by Personally Oriented Ltd.SoPA (Ashiya, Japan)). C E Tuttle.
Survey of Persian Handicraft. Jay Gluck & Sumi Gluck. (Illus.). 416p. 125.00 (ISBN 0-317-55043-8). Apollo.
Survey of Petroleum Industry. Muhammed Aruna. (Illus.). 170p. 1987. notebook 200.00 (ISBN 0-934355-05-3). Huddleston-Brown Pubs.
Survey of Phenomena in Ionized Gases: Invited Papers. (Proceedings Ser.). (Illus., Eng., Fr., Rus. & Ger.). 1968. pap. 48.50 (ISBN 92-0-030068-5, ISP178, IAEA). UNIPUB.
Survey of Precast Prestressed Concrete Parking Structures. 73p. Date not set. 24.00 (R&D7). Prestressed Concrete.
Survey of Prehistoric Sites in the Region of Flagstaff, Arizona. Harold S. Colton. Repr. of 1932 ed. 29.00x (ISBN 0-403-03702-6). Scholarly.
Survey of Press Freedom in Latin America 1985-1986. Ed. by Cecilio J. Morales, Jr. et al. 64p. (Orig.). 1986. pap. 8.95 (ISBN 0-937551-00-7). Coun Hemispheric Aff.
Survey of Primitive Money: The Beginnings of Currency. Alison H. Quiggin. LC 76-44779. Repr. of 1949 ed. 36.50 (ISBN 0-404-15964-8). AMS Pr.
Survey of Private Sector Work & Family Policy. 41p. 1986. 12.50 (ISBN 0-940173-19-0). New Ways Work.
Survey of Progress in Chemistry, Vols. 1-9. Ed. by Arthur F. Scott. Incl. Vol. 1. 1963; Vol. 2. 1965; Vol. 3. 1966; Vol. 4. 1968; Vol. 5. 1969; Vol. 6. 1973; Vol. 7. 1976; Vol. 8. 1978; Vol. 9. 1980; Vol. 10. 1983. 65.00. Acad Pr.
Survey of Progress in Chemistry, Vol. 10. Ed. by Arthur F. Scott. (Serial Publication). 1983. 59.00 (ISBN 0-12-610510-3). Acad Pr.
Survey of Public Attitudes Toward Refugees & Immigrants: Report of Findings. 1984. write for info. US Comm Refugees.
Survey of Recent Christian Ethics. Edward L. Long, Jr. 1982. pap. 8.95x (ISBN 0-19-503160-1). Oxford U Pr.
Survey of Research & Investigations in Agricultural Engineering, 1978. Intro. by J. A. O'Shea. 129p. (Orig.). 1978. pap. text ed. 20.25x (ISBN 0-85825-098-5, Pub. by Inst Engineering Australia). Brookfield Pub Co.
Survey of Research & Investigations in Agricultural Engineering, 1980. Intro. by J. A. O'Shea. 134p. (Orig.). 1980. pap. text ed. 22.50x (ISBN 0-686-42704-1, Pub. by Inst Engineering Australia). Brookfield Pub Co.
Survey of Research & Investigations in Agricultural Engineering, 1982. Intro. by J. A. O'Shea. 110p. (Orig.). 1982. pap. text ed. 18.00x (ISBN 0-85825-180-9, Pub. by Inst Engineering Australia). Brookfield Pub Co.
Survey of Research in Economic & Social History of India. R. S. Sharma. 1986. 30.00 (ISBN 81-202-0142-6, Pub. by Ajanta). South Asia Bks.

Survey of Research in Economics: Vol. 1, Methods & Techniques. Ed. by D. T. Lakdawal. 1978. 14.00x (ISBN 0-8364-0224-3). South Asia Bks.
Survey of Research in Economics: Vol. 2, Macroeconomics. D. T. Lakdawala. LC 76-904977. 1976. 14.50x (ISBN 0-88386-878-4). South Asia Bks.
Survey of Research in Geography, Nineteen Sixty-Nine to Nineteen Seventy-Two (India) 1979. 12.50x (ISBN 0-8364-0524-2). South Asia Bks.
Survey of Research in Management, Vol. 1. Indian Council of Social Science Research. 1973. 15.00 (ISBN 0-686-20313-5). Intl Bk Dist.
Survey of Research in Management, Vol. 2. Indian Council of Social Science Research. 1977. 27.00 (ISBN 0-686-21733-0). Intl Bk Dist.
Survey of Research in Management, Vol. 2. 1978. 22.50x (ISBN 0-8364-0165-4). South Asia Bks.
Survey of Research in Management, India, Vol. 1. 1973. 14.00x (ISBN 0-8364-0471-8). South Asia Bks.
Survey of Research in Political Science, Vol. 4: Political Dynamics. 1983. 14.00x (ISBN 0-8364-1020-3, Pub. by Allied India). South Asia Bks.
Survey of Research: Public Administration, Vol. 2. 1975. 15.00 (ISBN 0-89684-522-2). Orient Bk Dist.
Survey of Residents' Perceptions of Neighborhood Services in the South Bronx. Louis Harris & Associates, Inc. 1979. pap. 2.50 (ISBN 0-88156-096-0). Comm Serv Soc NY.
Survey of Resistivities of Water from Subsurface Formations in West Texas & Southeastern New Mexico. 248p. 1982. 17.00 (ISBN 0-89520-316-2, 31632). Soc Petrol Engineers.
Survey of Retail Furniture Distribution in France. 1981. 95.00x (ISBN 0-317-43722-4, Pub. by F I R A). State Mutual Bk.
Survey of Rock-Cut Chamber-Tombs in Caria: Part I, South-Eastern Caria & the Lyco-Carian Borderland. Paavo Roos. (Studies in Mediterranean Archaeology: Vol. LXXII, No. 1). (Illus.). 132p. 1985. pap. text ed. 80.00 (ISBN 91-86098-25-X, Pub. by P Astrom Pubs Sweden). Humanities.
Survey of Rock-Cut Chamber-Tombs in Caria, Pt. I: Southeastern Caria & the Lyco-Carian Borderland. Paavo Roos. (Studies in Mediterranean Archaeology). (Illus.). 132p. (Orig.). 1985. pap. text ed. 110.00x (Pub. by Almqvist & Wiksell). Coronet Bks.
Survey of Sardis & the Major Monuments Outside the City Walls. George M. Hanfmann & Jane C. Waldbaum. LC 75-1746. (Archaeological Explorations of Sardis Ser.: Report No. 1). (Illus.). 416p. 1976. text ed. 37.00x (ISBN 0-674-85751-8). Harvard U Pr.
Survey of Science & Technology Needs in Barbados: Studies on Scientific & Technological Development. (Science). 132p. 1977. 3.00 (ISBN 0-8270-6450-0). OAS.
Survey of Science Fiction Literature, 5 vols. Ed. by Frank N. Magill. LC 79-64639. 2549p. 1979. Set. 250.00x (ISBN 0-89356-194-0). Salem Pr.
Survey of Selected Local Government Energy Emergency Planning Programs. 84p. 1982. 15.00 (ISBN 0-318-17337-9, DG/82-321). Pub Tech Inc.
Survey of Semiconductor Radiation Techniques. Ed. by L. S. Smirnov. 288p. 1983. 10.95 (ISBN 0-8285-2568-4, Pub. by Mir Pubs USSR). Imported Pubns.
Survey of Significant Court Decisions of the Rights of Federal Employees Since the Civil Reform Act of 1978. Arthur L. Burnett. 123p. 10.00 (ISBN 0-318-14098-5). Federal Bar.
Survey of SLA Software Users. SLA. (SLA Research Ser.). 1988. pap. 15.00 (ISBN 0-87111-336-8). SLA.
Survey of Small Business Experience with & Perceptions of the Legal Professions. 18p. 1980. pap. 5.00 (ISBN 0-317-31051-8). Amer Bar Assn.
Survey of Small Business Experience with & Perceptions of the Legal Profession. 18p. 1980. pap. 5.00 (ISBN 0-317-63649-9, 351-0003-01). Amer Bar Assn.
Survey of Social Psychology. 3rd ed. Leonard Berkowitz. 592p. 1986. text ed. 34.95 (ISBN 0-03-070438-3, HoltC). HR&W.
Survey of Some Japanese Tax Laws. Eric V. De Becker. LC 78-78358. (Studies in Japanese Law & Government). 182p. 1979. Repr. of 1931 ed. 18.50 (ISBN 0-89093-218-2). U Pubns Amer.
Survey of Spousal Violence Against Women in Kentucky. Louis Harris. (Louis Harris Publications Ser.). 1981. lib. bdg. 24.00 (ISBN 0-8240-9373-9). Garland Pub.
Survey of State Actions Promoting AIDS Education. 42p. 1987. 4.50. NASBE.
Survey of State Blue Sky Laws Applicable to Tax Exempt Bonds. National Association of Bond Lawyers Committee on State Blue Sky & Legal Investment Laws Staff & Peter M. Wright. LC 85-227123. vi, 222p. 1987. 28.00. Nat Assn Bond.
Survey of State Supreme Courts With Intermediate Appellate Courts: Technical Assistance Report. National Center for State Courts Staff. 114p. 1980. manuscript 6.84 (NERO, T/A-508). Natl Ctr St Courts.
Survey of States' Teacher Policies. 117p. 1983. 7.00 (ISBN 0-318-17969-5, EG-83-2). Ed Comm States.
Survey of Structural Linguistics. 2nd ed. G. C. Lepschy. (Language Library). 206p. 1984. pap. 12.95x (ISBN 0-233-97415-6). Basil Blackwell.
Survey of Taiwanese Family-Life. Toshio Ikeda. (Asian Folklore & Social Life Monograph: No. 11). (Japanese.). 1972. 18.00x (ISBN 0-89986-014-1). Oriental Bk Store.
Survey of the Administration of Criminal Justice in Oregon: Final Report on 1771 Felony Cases in Multnomah County Report Number One. facsimile ed. Wayne L. Morse & Ronald H. Beattie. LC 74-3838. (Criminal Justice in America Ser.). 1974. Repr. of 1932 ed. 22.00x (ISBN 0-405-06155-2). Ayer Co Pubs.
Survey of the Almagest. Olaf Pedersen. (Acta Historica Scientarium Ser.: No. 30). 454p. (Orig.). 1974. pap. 48.50x (Pub. by Odense Universitets Forlag (Odense Denmark)). Coronet Bks.
Survey of the Application of Simulation to Health Care. Ed. by Stephen D. Roberts & William L. England. (SCS Simulation Ser.: Vol. 10, No. 1). 1981. 36.00 (ISBN 0-686-36678-6). Soc Computer Sim.
Survey of the Atlantic Beaches. Don Hendrie, Jr. 1988. 13.95 (ISBN 0-517-56691-5). Crown.
Survey of the Benthis Algal Vegetation of the Dyrafjordur, Northwest Iceland. I. M. Munda. (Offprint from Nova Hedwigia Ser.: No. 29). (Illus.). 1978. pap. text ed. 24.00x (ISBN 3-7682-1201-7). Lubrecht & Cramer.
Survey of the Bible. William Hendriksen. 1977. pap. 18.95 (ISBN 0-87552-967-4, Evangel Pr UK). Presby & Reformed.
Survey of the Birdlife of Northwestern Florida. Francis M. Weston. (Tall Timbers Resaerch Station Bulletin Ser.: No. 5). pap. 37.80 (2026818). Bks Demand UMI.
Survey of the Books of History. J. D. O'Donnell & Ralph Hampton, Jr. 1976. pap. 3.25 (ISBN 0-89265-032-X). Randall Hse.
Survey of the Books of Poetry. J. D. O'Donnell & Ralph Hampton, Jr. 1976. pap. 2.25 (ISBN 0-89265-033-8). Randall Hse.
Survey of the Development of the Intellectuals. T. Huszar. 560p. text ed. 65.00 (ISBN 0-317-65685-6, Pub. by Akademiai Kiado). Humanities.
Survey of the Dragonflies (Order Odonata) of Eastern Africa. E. C. Pinhey. (Illus.). vii, 214p. 1961. 18.00x (ISBN 0-565-00216-3, Pub. by Brit Mus Nat Hist England). Sabbot-Natural Hist Bks.
Survey of the Duchy of Lancaster Lordships in Wales 1609-1613. Williams Rees. (History & Law Ser.: No. 12). 303p. 1953. text ed. 28.50x (ISBN 0-7083-0117-7, Pub. by U of Wales). Humanities.
Survey of the Electronic Funds Transfer Transaction System, 1986. 66p. 1986. 90.00 (685). Bank Admin Inst.
Survey of the Epistles. Charles W. Conn. 112p. 1969. 5.25 (ISBN 0-87148-007-7); pap. 4.25 (ISBN 0-87148-008-5). Pathway Pr.
Survey of the Fertilizer Sector in India. Balu Bumb. (Working Paper: No. 331). iv, 216p. 1979. 10.00 (ISBN 0-686-36189-X, WP-0331). World Bank.
Survey of the Fossil Cephalopoda of the Chalk of Great Britain. C. W. Wright & E. V. Wright. pap. 6.00 (ISBN 0-384-69440-3). Johnson Repr.
Survey of the General Epistles & Revelation. Stanley Outlaw et al. 1976. pap. 2.95 (ISBN 0-89265-036-2). Randall Hse.
Survey of the Gospels. Stanley Outlaw & Charles Thigpen. 1976. pap. 1.95 (ISBN 0-89265-031-1). Randall Hse.
Survey of the Great Dukes State of Tuscany, in 1596. Robert Dallington. LC 74-80171. (English Experience Ser.: No. 650). 74p. 1974. Repr. of 1605 ed. 17.50 (ISBN 90-221-0650-0). Walter J Johnson.
Survey of the History, Biology, & Preservation of Some Retreating Synanthropic Plants. Roger Svensson & Marita Wigren. (Illus.). 74p. (Orig.). 1986. pap. text ed. 19.00x (ISBN 91-554-1880-5, Pub. by Uppsala Univ Acta Univ Uppsaliensis (Uppsala Sweden)). Coronet Bks.
Survey of the Honour of Denbigh 1334. Ed. by P. Vinogradoff & F. Morgan. (British Academy, London, Record of the Social & Economic History of Wngland & Wales. Ser.: Vol. 1). pap. 45.00 (ISBN 0-8115-1241-X). Kraus Repr.
Survey of the Impact of Manufactured Exports from Industrializing Countries in Asia & Latin America: Must Export-Oriented Growth Be Disruptive? Lawrence G. Franko. LC 79-91759. (Committee on Changing International Realities Ser.). 56p. 1979. 4.50 (ISBN 0-89068-051-5). Natl Planning.
Survey of the Influence of Sir Walter Scott in Spain. P. H. Churchman & E. A. Peers. LC 73-9842. 1922. lib. bdg. 15.00 (ISBN 0-8414-1848-9). Folcroft.
Survey of the International Sale of Goods. Ed. by Louis Lafili & Franklin Gervutz. 375p. 44.00 (ISBN 90-6544-241-3). Kluwer Academic.
Survey of the Jury Systems in Virginia. (On Loan Through NCSC Library). 67p. 1983. write for info. (CJS-003). Natl Ctr St Courts.
Survey of the Law of Property. 3rd ed. Ralph E. Boyer. 766p. 1981. text ed. 23.95 (ISBN 0-8299-2128-1). West Pub.
Survey of the Life of Christ, 2 vols. Melvin J. Wise. 2.50 ea.; Vol. 1. (ISBN 0-89315-288-9); Vol. 2. (ISBN 0-89315-289-7). Lambert Bk.
Survey of the Major Prophets. Robert Picirilli & Ralph Hampton, Jr. 1976. pap. 1.50 (ISBN 0-89265-034-6). Randall Hse.
Survey of the Management & Utilization of Electronics Data Processing Systems in Admission, Records, & Registration, 1969-70. American Association of Collegiate Registrars & Admissions Officers Staff. pap. 34.80 (ISBN 0-317-26616-0, 2024076). Bks Demand UMI.
Survey of the Manor of Wye. Ed. by Helen E. Muhlfeld. LC 74-5047. 256p. 1974. Repr. of 1933 ed. lib. bdg. 18.00x (ISBN 0-374-95991-9, Octagon). Hippocrene Bks.
Survey of the Moon. Patrick Moore. (Illus.). 1963. 6.95 (ISBN 0-393-06330-5). Norton.
Survey of the Movements Culminating in Industrial Arts Education in Secondary Schools. Ray M. Stombaugh. LC 76-177821. (Columbia University. Teachers College. Contributions to Education: No. 670). Repr. of 1936 ed. 22.50 (ISBN 0-404-55670-1). AMS Pr.
Survey of the Negro Convention Movement. Howard H. Bell. LC 74-94129. (American Negro: His History & Literature, Ser. No. 3). 1970. Repr. of 1953 ed. 19.00 (ISBN 0-405-01915-7). Ayer Co Pubs.
Survey of the New Testament. Robert H. Gundry. (Illus.). 432p. 1982. 20.95 (ISBN 0-310-25410-8, 18280). Zondervan.
Survey of the New Testament. Outlaw et al. Ed. by Harrold D. Harrison. (Orig.). 1984. pap. 5.95 (ISBN 0-89265-090-7). Randall Hse.
Survey of the Non-Pronominal Non-Formative Affixes of the Blackfoot Verb. C. C. Uhlenbeck. Repr. of 1920 ed. 40.00x (ISBN 3-253-02068-1). Adlers Foreign Bks.
Survey of the Old Testament. Paul Benware. (Everyman's Bible Commentary). 1988. pap. text ed. 8.95 (ISBN 0-8024-2091-5). Moody.
Survey of the Old Testament. Outlaw et al. Ed. by Harrold D. Harrison. (Orig.). 1984. pap. 6.95 (ISBN 0-89265-089-3). Randall Hse.
Survey of the Old Testament. Stanley Outlaw. 1977. pap. 2.75 (ISBN 0-89265-048-6). Randall Hse.
Survey of the Pauline Epistles. Leroy Forlines & Robert Picirilli. 1976. pap. 3.75 (ISBN 0-89265-035-4). Randall Hse.
Survey of the Pentateuch. Stanley Outlaw & J. D. O'Donnell. 93p. 1975. pap. 2.95 (ISBN 0-89265-027-3). Randall Hse.
Survey of the Pretended Holy Dicipline. Richard Bancroft. LC 78-38148. (English Experience Ser.: No. 428). 472p. 1972. Repr. of 1593 ed. 75.00 (ISBN 90-221-0428-1). Walter J Johnson.
Survey of the Profession: Photogrammetry, Surveying, Mapping, Remote Sensing. 1985. pap. 70.00 (ISBN 0-937294-79-9). ASP & RS.
Survey of the Scientific Manuscripts in the Egyptian National Library. David A. King. LC 85-29369. (American Research Center in Egypt, Catalogs: Vol. 5). (Illus.). xiv, 331p. 1986. text ed. 59.50x (ISBN 0-936770-15-5, Pub. by Am Res Ctr Egypt); pap. text ed. 49.50x (ISBN 0-936770-12-0, Pub. by Am Res Ctr Egypt). Eisenbrauns.
Survey of the Social & Business Usage of Arithmetic. Guy M. Wilson. LC 74-177633. (Columbia University. Teachers College. Contributions to Education: No. 100). Repr. of 1919 ed. 22.50 (ISBN 0-404-55100-9). AMS Pr.
Survey of the Social Structure of England & Wales. A. M. Carr-Saunders & D. Caradog-Jones. 246p. 1985. lib. bdg. 33.00 (ISBN 0-8240-7606-0). Garland Pub.
Survey of the Spherical Space Form Problem. James F. Davis. (Mathematical Reports Ser.: vol.2, pt. 2). 72p. 1985. pap. text ed. 19.00 (ISBN 3-7186-0250-4). Harwood Academic.
Survey of the State of Maine in Reference to Its Geographical Features, Statistics & Political Economy. Moses Greenleaf. LC 71-128108. 1970. 14.00 (ISBN 0-913764-00-0). Maine St Mus.
Survey of the State of the Art in Footwear Manufacturing, 2 vols. 633p. 1983. Set. 105.00 (ISBN 0-318-17524-X); members 35.00 (ISBN 0-318-17525-8). Footwear Indus.
Survey of the Status of Judicial Planning in State Courts: Paper Number Five. National Center for State Courts Staff. 147p. 1978. manuscript 8.82 (DC-007). Natl Ctr St Courts.
Survey of the Summe of Church-Discipline Wherein the Way of the Congregational Churches of Christ in New England Is Warranted & Cleared, by Scripture & Argument. Thomas Hooker. LC 78-141113. (Research Library of Colonial Americana). 1971. Repr. of 1648 ed. 40.00 (ISBN 0-405-03326-5). Ayer Co Pubs.
Survey of the Teaching of English to Non-English Speakers in the United States. Harold B. Allen. Ed. by Francesco Cordasco. LC 77-90403. (Bilingual-Bicultural Education in the U. S. Ser.). 1978. Repr. of 1966 ed. lib. bdg. 20.00x (ISBN 0-405-11072-3). Ayer Co Pubs.
Survey of the Turkish Empire. William Eton. LC 73-6278. (Middle East Ser.). Repr. of 1798 ed. 37.50 (ISBN 0-405-05334-7). Ayer Co Pubs.
Survey of the United States Government's Investment in Africa. David L. Duffy. 1978. pap. 10.00 (ISBN 0-918456-22-3, Crossroads). African Studies Assn.
Survey of the Woman Problem. Rosa Mayreder. Tr. by Scheffauer Herman from Ger. LC 79-2944. 275p. 1983. Repr. of 1913 ed. 25.75 (ISBN 0-8305-0108-8). Hyperion Conn.
Survey of Tidal River Systems in the Northern Territory & Their Crocodile Populations: Monographs, Nos. 2-8. H. Messel et al. Incl. No. 2. Victoria & Fitzmaurice River Systems. 52p. 1979. pap. 24.00 (ISBN 0-08-023098-9); No. 3. Adelaide, Daly & Moyle Rivers. 58p. 1979. pap. 24.00 (ISBN 0-08-023099-7); No. 4. Alligator Region River System: Murgenella & Cooper's Creeks; East, South & West Alligator Rivers & Wildman River. 70p. 1979. pap. 24.00 (ISBN 0-08-024789-X); No. 5. Goodmadeer & King River Systems: Majarie, Wurugoij & All Night Creeks. 62p. 1979. pap. 24.00 (ISBN 0-08-024790-3); No. 6. Some River & Creek Systems on Melville & Grant Islands: North & South Creeks on Grant Island. 64p. 1979. pap. 24.00 (ISBN 0-08-024784-9); No. 7. Liverpool-Tomkinson River Systems & Nungbulgarri Creek. 84p. 1979. pap. 24.00 (ISBN 0-08-024785-7); No. 8. Some Rivers & Creeks on the Western Shore of the Gulf of Carpentaria: Rose River, Muntak Creek; Hart, Walker & Koolatong Rivers. 40p. 1979. pap. 24.00 (ISBN 0-08-024786-5). (Illus.). 1979. pap. write for info. Pergamon.
Survey of Trace Forms of Algebraic Number Fields. P. E. Connor & R. Perlis. (Lecture Notes on Pure Mathematics: Vol. 2). 325p. 1984. 38.00 (ISBN 9971-966-04-2); pap. 21.00x (ISBN 9971-966-05-0, Pub. by World Sci Singapore). World Scientific Pub.
Survey of Traditional Chinese Medicine. Claude Larre et al. Tr. by Sarah E. Stang. (Illus.). 231p. (Orig., Fr.). 1986. pap. 15.00 (ISBN 0-912381-00-0). Trad Acupuncture.
Survey of Turkish & Japanese Folklore. Lou Tsu-K'uang. (Asian Folklore & Social Life Monograph: No. 53). 162p. (Chinese.). 1973. 14.00x (ISBN 0-89986-050-8). Oriental Bk Store.
Survey of Ufologists & Their Use of the Library. George M. Eberhart. 24p. 1978. pap. 2.00. J A Hynek Ctr UFO.
Survey of Underground Gas Storage Facilities in the United States & Canada 1978. 64p. 1978. pap. 4.00 (ISBN 0-318-12716-4, XU0678). Am Gas Assn.
Survey of United States & Total World Production, Proved Reserves, & Remaining Recoverable Resources of Fossil Fuels & Uranium, as of December 31, 1982. Joseph D. Parent. xviii, 250p. 1984. 30.00 (ISBN 0-910091-52-8). Inst Gas Tech.
Survey of United States International Finance, 1949-1953 5 Vols. Ed. by Gardner Patterson et al. LC 70-159075. 1971. Repr. of 1954 ed. Set. 137.50x (ISBN 0-8046-1670-1, Pub. by Kennikat). Assoc Faculty Pr.
Survey of U. S. Naval Affairs, 1865-1917. Paolo E. Coletta. LC 87-10394. (Illus.). 272p. (Orig.). 1987. lib. bdg. 28.50 (ISBN 0-8191-6397-X); pap. text ed. 15.75 (ISBN 0-8191-6398-8). U Pr of Amer.
Survey of Urban Arterial Design Standards. (Illus.). 91p. 1969. 10.00x (ISBN 0-917084-21-7). Am Public Works.
Survey of Vegetation in Glen Canyon Reservoir Basin. Angus M. Woodbury & Stephen D. Durrant. (Glen Canyon Series: No. 5). Repr. of 1959 ed. 20.00 (ISBN 0-404-60636-9). AMS Pr.
Survey of Vegetation in the Curecanti Reservoir Basins. Angus M. Woodbury et al. (Upper Colorado Ser.: No. 6). Repr. of 1962 ed. 17.50 (ISBN 0-404-60656-3). AMS Pr.
Survey of Vegetation in the Flaming Gorge Basin. Angus M. Woodbury & Stephen D. Durrant. (Upper Colorado Series: No. 2). Repr. of 1960 ed. 30.00 (ISBN 0-404-60645-8). AMS Pr.
Survey of Vegetation in the Navajo Reservoir Basin. Angus M. Woodbury et al. (Upper Colorado Ser.: No. 4). Repr. of 1961 ed. 25.00 (ISBN 0-404-60651-2). AMS Pr.
Survey of Vehicle Fire Causes. Lee S. Cole. (Illus.). 123p. (Orig.). 1988. pap. 32.00 (ISBN 0-939818-16-7). Lee Bks.
Survey of Verification Techniques for Parallel Programs. H. Barringer. (Lecture Notes in Computer Science: Vol. 191). vi, 115p. 1985. pap. 12.50 (ISBN 0-387-15239-3). Springer-Verlag.
Survey of Vertebrate Pretectal Areas & the Accessory Optic System. Ed. by J. Wallman & K. V. Fite. (Journal: Brain, Behavior Evolution: Vol. 26, No. 2, 1985). (Illus.). 76p. 1985. pap. 36.75 (ISBN 3-8055-4247-X). S Karger.
Survey of Virulence Genes in Wheat Stem Rust, Puccinia Graminis. Norbert H. Luig. (Advances in Plant Breeding Ser.: No. 11). (Illus.). 199p. 1983. pap. text ed. 25.20x (ISBN 3-489-74110-2). Parey Sci Pubs.
Survey of Water Utility Salaries, Wages & Employee Benefits, 1981. 248p. 21.00 (20216); members 15.75 (ISBN 0-317-33299-6). Am Water Wks Assn.
Survey of Weed Problems & Management Technologies in Organic Agriculture. 8.50 (ISBN 0-317-57592-9); 1.50 (ISBN 0-317-57593-7). Organic Agri.

Surveys of the Confederate Postmasters' Provisionals. Francis J. Crown, Jr. lib. bdg. 100.00x (ISBN 0-88000-124-0). Quarterman.

Surveys of Tidal River Systems in the Northern Territory & Their Crocodile Populations. Ed. by H. Messel. Incl. Tidal Waterways of Castlereagh Bay & Hutchinson & Cadell Straits: Bennett, Darbitla, Djigaglia Djabura, Ngandadauda Creeks & the Glyde & Woolen Rivers. (Monograph: No. 9). 1980. pap. 31.00 (ISBN 0-08-024801-2); Tidal Waterways of Buckingham & Ulundurwi Bays: Buckingham, Kalarwoi, Warawuruwoi & Kurala Rivers & Slippery Creek. (Monograph: No. 10). 1980. pap. 23.00 (ISBN 0-08-024802-0); Tidal Waterways of Arnhem Bay: Darwarunga, Habgood, Baralminer, Gobalpa, Coromuro, Cato, Peter John & Burungbirinung Rivers. (Monograph: No. 11). 1980. pap. 28.00 (ISBN 0-08-024803-9); Tidal Waterways on the South-Western Coast of the Gulf of Carpentaria: Limmen Bight Towns, Roper, Phelp & Wilson Rivers; Nayarnpi, Wungguliyanga, Painnyilatya, Mangkurdurrungku & Yiwapa Creeks. (Monograph: No. 12). 1980. pap. 22.00 (ISBN 0-08-024804-7); Tidal Waterways on the Southern Coast of the Gulf of Carpentaria: Calvert, Robinson, Wearyan & McArthur Rivers & Some Intervening Creeks. (Monograph: No. 13). 1980. pap. 24.00 (ISBN 0-08-024805-5); Tidal Waterways of the Van Diemen Gulf: Ilamary; River, Iwalg, Saltwater & Minimini: Creeks & Coastal Arms on Cobourg Peninsula. Resurveys of the Alligator Region Rivers. (Monograph: No. 14). 1980. pap. 26.00 (ISBN 0-08-024806-3); Some River & Creek Systems on the West Coast of Cape York Peninsula in the Gulf of Carpentaria: Nassau, Staaten & Gilbert Rivers & Duck Creek. (Monograph: No. 16). 1981. pap. 28.00 write for info. (ISBN 0-08-024807-1). (Monographs: Nos. 9-14 & 16). (Illus.). 1980. write for info. Pergamon.

Surveys of Tidal River Systems in the Northern Territory & Their Crocodile Populations. H. Messel et al. (Monograph: No. 17). (Illus.). 92p. 1981. pap. 24.00 (ISBN 0-08-024818-7). Pergamon.

Surveys of Tidal River Systems in the Northern Territory & Their Crocodile Population. H. Messel et al. (Monograph: No. 1). (Illus.). 464p. 1982. 140.00 (ISBN 0-08-024819-5, G135). Pergamon.

Surveys of Tidal River Systems in the Northern Territory & Their Crocodile Populations. M. Messel. (Monograph: No. 15). (Illus.). 368p. 1982. 125.00 (ISBN 0-08-024831-4). Pergamon.

Surveys of Tidal River Systems in the Northern Territory & Their Crocodile Population: Monograph, No. 18. Ed. by H. Messel et al. (Illus.). 308p. 1985. 105.00 (ISBN 0-08-029858-3). Pergamon.

Surveys of Tidal River Systems in the Northern Territory of Australia: Resurveys of the Tidal Waterways of Van Diemen Gulf & the Southern Gulf of Carpentaria 1984 & 1985. H. Messel et al. (Surveys of Tidal Rivers Monographs: No. 19). (Illus.). 118p. 1986. 65.00 (ISBN 0-08-029882-6, Pub. by PPA). Pergamon.

Surveys of Tidal Waterways in the Kimberley Region, Western Australia & Their Crocodile Populations: Monograph 20 - Tidal Waterways of the Kimberley Surveyed During 1977, 1978 & 1986. H. Messel et al. (Surveys of Tidal Rivers Ser.: No. 20). 256p. 1988. 74.50 (ISBN 0-08-034429-1, PPA). Pergamon.

Surveys, Polls, Censuses, & Forecasts Directory. 284p. 1983. 240.00x (ISBN 0-8103-1692-7). Gale.

Surveys 1: Eight State-of-the Art Articles on Key Areas in Language Teaching. Ed. by Valerie Kinsella. LC 82-4332. (Cambridge Language Teaching Surveys). 159p. 1983. 24.95 (ISBN 0-521-24886-8); pap. 10.95 (ISBN 0-521-27046-4). Cambridge U Pr.

Surveys 2: Eight State-of-the Art Articles on Key Areas in Language Teaching. Ed. by Valerie Kinsella. LC 82-45961. (Cambridge Language Teaching Surveys). 156p. 1983. 24.95 (ISBN 0-521-24887-6); pap. 10.95 (ISBN 0-521-27047-2). Cambridge U Pr.

Survival! Gordon R. Dickson. (Orig.). 1984. pap. 2.75 (ISBN 0-671-55927-3). PB.

Survival. Vernon L. Doss. (Orig.). 1981. pap. 2.50 (ISBN 0-505-51727-2, Pub. by Tower Bks). Leisure NY.

Survival. Vernon L. Doss. 288p. 1986. pap. 2.95 (ISBN 0-8439-2429-2, Leisure Bks). Leisure NY.

Survival. Hester S. McKenzie. 32p. 1988. 6.95 (ISBN 0-89962-681-5). Todd & Honeywell.

Survival. 2nd ed. (Department of the Army Field Manual: No. 21-76). (Illus.). 407p. 1986. pap. 11.00 (ISBN 0-318-22953-6, S/N 008-020-01106-1). USGPO.

Survival: A Guide to Living on Your Own. Joan Kelly & Valerie M. Chamberlain. (Illus.). 1979. text ed. 24.88 (ISBN 0-07-033870-1). McGraw.

Survival-A Sequential Program for College Writing. 3rd, rev. ed. Robert Frew et al. 350p. 1985. pap. 16.95x (ISBN 0-917962-50-8). T H Peek.

Survival: A Thematic Guide to Canadian Literature. Margaret Atwood. LC 72-91501. 287p. (Orig.). 1972. pap. 8.95 (ISBN 0-88784-613-0, Pub. by Hse Anansi Pr Canada). U of Toronto Pr.

Survival Acre. 1984. 7.95 (ISBN 0-317-43191-9). North Country.

Survival Acre-Fifty Nationwide Wild Foods & Medicines. Linda Runyon. (Illus.). 43p. (Orig.). 1985. pap. 7.95 (ISBN 0-918517-03-6). Runyon Pub.

Survival Against All Odds: The First 100 Years of Anatolia College. Everett Stephens & Mary Stephens. (Illus.). 224p. 1986. lib. bdg. 37.50x (ISBN 0-89241-421-9). Caratzas.

Survival! Air Force Manual 64-5. Department of the Air Force. (Illus.). 144p. 1979. pap. 8.00 (ISBN 0-87364-167-1). Paladin Pr.

Survival Analysis. Ed. by John Crowley et al. LC 82-84316. (IMS Lecture Notes-Monograph Ser.: Vol. 2). x, 302p. (Orig.). 1982. pap. 25.00 (ISBN 0-940600-02-1). Inst Math.

Survival Analysis. Gross et al. (Probability & Mathematical Statistics Ser.). 1988. write for info. (ISBN 0-471-83936-1). Wiley.

Survival Analysis. Rupert G. Miller, Jr. LC 81-4437. (Wiley Series in Probability & Mathematical Statistics: Applied Probability & Statistics Section). 238p. 1981. pap. 29.95x (ISBN 0-471-09434-X, Pub. by Wiley-Interscience). Wiley.

Survival & Challenge: Proceedings. Pacific Northwest Conference on Higher Education, 1972. Ed. by R. J. Leskiw. LC 48-10303. 1973. pap. 5.00x (ISBN 0-87071-272-1). Oreg St U Pr.

Survival & Change in the Third World. B. Crow et al. 400p. 1988. text ed. 36.00 (ISBN 0-19-520716-5); pap. 15.95 (ISBN 0-19-520717-3). Oxford U Pr.

Survival & Dormancy of Microorganisms. Ed. by Yigal Henis. LC 87-3472. 355p. 1988. 49.95 (ISBN 0-471-80054-6). Wiley.

Survival & Growth for Small Business. Theodore Cohn & Roy A. Lindberg. 200p. 1980. pap. 6.95 (ISBN 0-8144-7541-8). AMACOM.

Survival & Growth: Management Strategies for the Small Firm. Theodore Cohn & Roy A. Lindberg. LC 73-92163. pap. 60.00 (ISBN 0-317-29948-4, 2051700). Bks Demand UMI.

Survival & Progress: The Afro-American Experience. L. Alex Swan. LC 80-1197. (Contributions in Afro-American & African Studies: No. 58). (Illus.). xxiii, 251p. 1981. lib. bdg. 35.00x (ISBN 0-313-22480-3, SSU/). Greenwood.

Survival & Success in a Shrinking Economy. Rodney Cron. (Illus.). 16.95 (ISBN 0-442-21756-0). Brown Bk.

Survival & the Bomb: Methods of Civil Defense. Ed. by Eugene Paul Wigner. LC 69-16003. pap. 79.30 (ISBN 0-317-12974-0, 2015520). Bks Demand UMI.

Survival Arts. Ian Wedde. 176p. 1988. pap. 6.95 (ISBN 0-14-010503-4). Penguin.

Survival Arts of the Primitive Paiutes. Margaret M. Wheat. LC 67-30392. (Illus.). xiii, 119p. 1967. pap. 12.95 (ISBN 0-87417-048-6). U of Nev Pr.

Survival at Sea. Mary Erickson. (Jesus the Wonder Worker Ser.). 48p. (gr. 3-6). 1985. pap. 2.95 (ISBN 0-89191-695-4, 56952, Chariot Bks). Cook.

Survival at Sea. Montgomery. (Choose Your Adventure Ser.: No. 16). (ps-7). 1987. pap. 2.25 (ISBN 0-553-26560-1). Bantam.

Survival at Sea: The Lifeboat & Liferaft. 4th ed. C. H. Wright. (Illus.). 353p. 1988. pap. text ed. 35.00 (ISBN 0-85174-540-7, Pub. by Brown Son Ferg). Sheridan.

Survival Bartering. Duncan Long. LC 86-80537. 56p. 1986. pap. text ed. 6.95 (ISBN 0-915179-37-7). Loompanics.

Survival Basics for Kids. Cindy Coble & Maureen Stoffel. (Illus.). 32p. pap. 2.50 (ISBN 0-913724-26-2). Emerg Response Inst.

Survival: Black & White. Florence Halpern. 225p. 1973. pap. 13.25 (ISBN 0-08-017193-1). Pergamon.

Survival: Body, Mind & Death in the Light of Psychic Experience. David Lorimer. 288p. (Orig.). 1984. pap. 12.95 (ISBN 0-7102-0003-X). Routledge Chapman & Hall.

Survival Books, Nineteen Eighty-One. Bruce Clayton. LC 81-80117. (Illus.). 180p. (Orig.). 1981. pap. 14.95 (ISBN 0-939216-00-0). Media West.

Survival Chemist. David A. Howard. (Illus.). 64p. (Orig.). 1987. pap. 7.00 (ISBN 0-918751-08-X). J O Flores.

Survival Communication: Writing & Speaking for Law Enforcement Officers. Steve Gladis. 96p. 1987. pap. 7.95 (ISBN 0-8403-4151-2). Kendall-Hunt.

Survival: Cycle of a Black Woman. Ed. by Mordecia D. Strickland. LC 85-70302. 64p. (Orig.). 1985. pap. 5.00 (ISBN 0-940248-23-9). Guild Pr.

Survival Distributions: Reliability Applications in the Biomedical Sciences. Alan J. Gross & Virginia A. Clark. LC 75-6808. (Wiley Series in Probability & Mathematical Statistics). pap. 86.50 (ISBN 0-317-28063-5, 2055770). Bks Demand UMI.

Survival Economy: Micro-Enterprises in Latin America. Paul F. Nevin. 94p. (Orig.). 1985. pap. 4.95x (ISBN 0-89192-385-3). Interbk Inc.

Survival English. Lee Mosteller & Bobbi Paul. (Illus.). 200p. 1984. pap. text ed. write for info (ISBN 0-13-879172-4). P-H.

Survival English: English Through Conversations, BK. 1B. Lee Mosteller & Bobbi Paul. (Illus.). 144p. 1988. pap. text ed. price not set (ISBN 0-13-879222-4). P-H.

Survival English: English Through Conversations, Bk. 2A. Lee Mosteller & Michele A. Haight. (Illus.). 128p. 1988. pap. text ed. price not set (ISBN 0-13-879230-5). P-H.

Survival English: English Through Conversations, Bk. 2B. Lee Mosteller & Michele A. Haight. (Illus.). 128p. 1988. pap. text ed. price not set (ISBN 0-13-879263-1). P-H.

Survival-Fighting Knives. Leroy Thompson. (Illus.). 104p. (Orig.). 1986. pap. text ed. 14.00 (ISBN 0-87364-347-X). Paladin Pr.

Survival for All: The Alternative to Nuclear War with a Practical Plan for Total Denuclearization. A. J. Aizenstat. LC 84-28231. 224p. 1985. 14.95 (ISBN 0-932755-14-3). Billner & Rouse.

Survival for Busy Women. Emilie Barnes. LC 85-82153. 224p. (Orig.). 1986. pap. 5.95 (ISBN 0-89081-492-9). Harvest Hse.

Survival for What. Zvi Kolitz. LC 70-75761. 234p. 1969. 10.00 (ISBN 0-8022-2272-2). Philos Lib.

Survival Game. Philip Kerrigan. 1987. 17.95 (ISBN 0-517-56582-X). Crown.

Survival Game: Strategies & Tactics. Bill Barnes. LC 88-60658. (Illus.). 128p. (Orig.). 1989. pap. 7.95 (ISBN 0-914457-25-X). Mustang Pub.

Survival Gardening Cookbook: Low Cost Nutritious. John A. Freeman. Ed. by Grace B. Freeman. (Illus.). 104p. (Orig.). 1985. pap. 10.95 (ISBN 0-9607730-8-8). Johns Pr.

Survival Gardening: Enough Nutrition to Live on... Just in Case. 2nd ed. John A. Freeman. (Illus.). 104p. 1983. pap. 8.95 (ISBN 0-9607730-5-3). Johns Pr.

Survival Guide for a Weekend Father. P. Platt. LC 87-60315. (Illus.). 256p. (Orig.). 1987. pap. 10.95 (ISBN 0-9618546-0-X). Orcas Pr.

Survival Guide for the Jr. High - Middle School Math Teacher. G. Baur & D. Pigford. 1983. 22.95x (ISBN 0-13-879156-2, Busn). P-H.

Survival Guide for the Secondary School Counselor. Kenneth Hitchner. 256p. 1987. pap. 24.95 (ISBN 0-87628-781-X). Ctr Appl Res.

Survival Guide for Tough Times. Mike Phillips. LC 79-4261. 176p. 1979. pap. 3.95 (ISBN 0-87123-498-X, 210498). Bethany Hse.

Survival Guide for Widows. Betty J. Wylie. 160p. 1986. pap. 2.95 (ISBN 0-345-33008-0). Ballantine.

Survival Guide to Rats & Stats. Jerry Kroth. (Illus.). 192p. 1988. pap. text ed. 15.95 (ISBN 0-936618-02-7). Genotype.

Survival Guide to the Last Times. James A. Aderman. Ed. by William E. Fischer. (Bible Class Course for Young Adults Ser.). (Illus.). 36p. (Orig.). 1987. pap. text ed. 2.95 (ISBN 0-938272-30-6); tchr's ed. 2.95 (ISBN 0-938272-31-4). Wels Board.

Survival Guns. Mel Tappan. LC 75-17327. 1987. 14.95. Janus Pr.

Survival Guns & Ammo. John J. Williams. (Illus.). 52p. 1979. pap. 15.00 (ISBN 0-934274-00-2). Consumertronics.

Survival Handbook for Preschool Mothers. Helen W. Smith. 163p. pap. 7.40 (ISBN 0-8428-2278-X). Cambridge Bk.

Survival Handbook for Small Business. Frieda Carrol. LC 80-70496. 73p. 1981. pap. 5.00 (ISBN 0-9605246-4-9, Pub. by Biblio Pr GA). Prosperity & Profits.

Survival Handbook for the Newly Recovering. Scott Sheperd. 70p. (Orig.). 1988. pap. 3.95 (ISBN 0-89638-149-8). CompCare.

Survival Handbook for the School Library Media Specialist. Betty Martin. LC 83-14851. xi, 146p. 1984. 24.50 (ISBN 0-208-02047-0, Library Prof Pubs); pap. 17.50x. Shoe String.

Survival Handbook for Widows (& for Relatives & Friends Who Want to Understand) Ruth J. Loewinsohn. 141p. 1984. pap. 5.95 (ISBN 0-673-24820-8). Am Assn Retire.

Survival Improvised Weapons. (Weaponry Ser.). 1986. lib. bdg. 79.95 (ISBN 0-8490-3846-4). Gordon Pr.

Survival in Auschwitz. Primo Levi. 160p. 1988. pap. 4.95 (ISBN 0-02-034310-8, Collier). Macmillan.

Survival in Auschwitz & the Reawakening. Primo Levi. Bd. with Reawakening. 384p. 1986. 19.95 (ISBN 0-671-60541-0). Summit Bks.

Survival in Business. Michael Allsopp. 139p. 1977. text ed. 24.50x (ISBN 0-220-66320-3, Pub. by Busn Bks England). Brookfield Pub Co.

Survival in Space. Richard Harding. 256p. 1988. 22.00 (ISBN 0-415-00253-2). Routledge Chapman & Hall.

Survival in the Air Age. U. S. President's Air Policy Commission. Ed. by Richard H. Kohn. LC 78-22406. (American Military Experience Ser.). 1979. Repr. of 1948 ed. lib. bdg. 14.00x (ISBN 0-405-11880-5). Ayer Co Pubs.

Survival in the Cold: Hibernation & Other Adaptations. Ed. by X. J. Musacchia & L. Jansky. 226p. 1981. 87.00 (ISBN 0-444-00635-4, Biomedical Pr). Elsevier.

Survival in the Corporate Fishbowl: Making It into Middle & Upper Management. John P. Fernandez. 336p. 1987. 24.95 (ISBN 0-669-10336-5). Lexington Bks.

Survival in the Doldrums: The American Women's Rights Movement, 1945 to the 1960s. Leila J. Rupp & Verta Taylor. 256p. 1987. 19.95 (ISBN 0-19-504938-1). Oxford U Pr.

Survival in Your Own Backyard. Shirley G. Baber. LC 82-99943. (First Edition). (Illus.). 60p. (Orig.). 1982. pap. 10.00 (ISBN 0-686-42957-5). Shirleys Pub.

Survival into the Twenty-First Century. Viktoras Kulvinskas. Ed. by Hermine Hurlbut & Joan Newman. (Illus.). 1975. pap. 12.95 (ISBN 0-933278-04-7). Twen Fir Cent.

Survival Is Not Enough. Richard Pipes. 288p. 1984. 16.45 (ISBN 0-671-49535-6). S&S.

Survival Is not Enough: Soviet Realities & America's Future. rev. ed. Richard Pipes. 304p. 1986. pap. 9.95 (ISBN 0-671-60614-X, Touchstone Bks.). S&S.

Survival Kit: A Complete Guidance Manual for Gay Men Everywhere. Ed. by Perry Brass & Lou Thomas. (Illus.). 240p. 1988. pap. 9.95 (ISBN 0-943383-00-5). FirstHand Ltd.

Survival Kit for Directors. Early Childhood Directors Association. Ed. by Sue Baldwin. (Illus.). 100p. (Orig.). pap. 5.95 (ISBN 0-934140-24-3). Toys 'n Things.

Survival Kit for Marriage. Carolyn S. Self & William L. Self. LC 81-66091. 1981. pap. 5.95 (ISBN 0-8054-5643-0). Broadman.

Survival Kit for New Bar Presidents. 150p. 1985. looseleaf 5.00 (ISBN 0-317-63158-6, 171-0033-01). Amer Bar Assn.

Survival Kit for Overseas Living. L. Robert Kohls. LC 79-65061. 100p. 1984. pap. text ed. 6.95 (ISBN 0-933662-04-1). Intercult Pr.

Survival Kit for Teachers (& Parents) Myrtle T. Collins & Dwane R. Collins. LC 74-10230. 1975. pap. 11.95 (ISBN 0-673-16443-8). Scott F.

Survival Kit for Teachers of Composition: Skill-by-Skill Writing Improvement Program. Robert J. Leonard & Peter H. De Beer. 1982. comb-bound 22.95x (ISBN 0-87628-777-1); 2.95x. Ctr Appl Res.

Survival Kit for Wives. Donald Martin & Renee Martin. 1986. pap. 12.95 (ISBN 0-394-74361-X, Pub. by Villard Bks). Random.

Survival Kit: Triumph over Suffering Break Through to Serenity with These Life-Saving Tools. rev. ed. Susan B. Anthony. LC 81-9771. 279p. 1981. pap. 7.95 (ISBN 0-89638-050-5). CompCare.

Survival Knife Reference Guide. Douglas C. Berner. (Illus.). 207p. 1986. pap. 12.95 (ISBN 0-937083-09-7). Bee Tree.

Survival: Life & Art of the Alaskan Eskimo. Barbara Lipton. LC 76-53613. 1977. 7.95 (ISBN 0-932828-04-3). Newark Mus.

Survival: Live off the Land in the City & Country. Pagnar Benson & Devon Christensen. 262p. 1983. pap. 9.95 (ISBN 0-8065-0867-1, Pub. by Citadel Pr). Lyle Stuart.

Survival Manual for Consumers: Get Mad then Get Even. James McTigue. (Self-Confidence-Self-Competence Ser.). 200p. (Orig.). 1987. pap. 11.95 (ISBN 0-932123-03-1). Stone Trail Pr.

Survival Manual for Small Business. Selma H. Lamkin. (Orig.). 15.00 (ISBN 0-686-32947-3). Nikmal Pub.

Survival Manual for the Independent Woman Traveler. Roberta Mendel. LC 82-80695. 128p. (Orig.). 1982. 12.95 (ISBN 0-936424-06-0). Pin Prick.

Survival Manual for Widows & Widowers. Florence P. Kulick. 200p. 1988. 16.95 (ISBN 0-939713-01-2). Carriage House.

Survival Math. Edward Williams & Jacob Cohen. (gr. 9-12). 1982. pap. 9.95 (ISBN 0-8120-2012-X). Barron.

Survival Models & Data Analysis. Regina C. Elandt-Johnson & Norman L. Johnson. LC 79-22836. (Wiley Series in Probability & Mathematical Statistics: Applied Probability & Statistics). 457p. 1980. 51.95x (ISBN 0-471-03174-7, Pub. by Wiley-Interscience). Wiley.

Survival Munitions: How to Reuse Spent Primers, How to Make Your Own Small Arms Rifle Powder, Flash Powder for Hand Grenades, Land Mines & Napalm from Everyday Supermarket Items. (Weaponry Ser.). 1986. lib. bdg. 79.95 (ISBN 0-8490-3844-8). Gordon Pr.

Survival Notes. John Herndon. 1987. pap. 9.00 (ISBN 0-941179-00-1). Latitudes Pr.

Survival of a Counterculture: Ideological Work & Everyday Life Among Rural Communards. Bennett M. Berger. LC 72-93531. 251p. 1981. 23.00x (ISBN 0-520-02388-9); pap. 9.95x (ISBN 0-520-04950-0). U of Cal Pr.

Survival of American Innocence: Catholicism in An Era of Disillusionment, 1920-1940. William M. Halsey. LC 79-63360. (Studies in American Catholicism: No. 2). 1980. 22.95x (ISBN 0-268-01699-2). U of Notre Dame Pr.

Survival of Antiquity. Ed. by Nelly Hoyt. LC 80-53219. (Studies in History Ser.: No. 48). (Illus.). 1980. pap. 14.40 (ISBN 0-87391-019-2). Smith Coll.

Survival of Capitalism: The Re-Production of the Relations of Production. Henri Lefebver. LC 75-32932. 208p. 1976. 20.00 (ISBN 0-312-77910-0). St Martin.

Survival of Charles Darwin: A Biography of a Man & an Idea. Ronald W. Clark. LC 84-42507. (Illus.). 544p. 1985. 19.45 (ISBN 0-394-52134-X). Random.

Surviving Difficult Church Members. Robert D. Dale. 128p. (Orig.). 1984. pap. 8.95 (ISBN 0-687-40763-X). Abingdon.

Surviving Divorce: A British Handbook for Men. Gay Search. (Illus.). 128p. 1983. 17.95 (ISBN 0-241-10954-X, Pub. by Hamish Hamilton England). David & Charles.

Surviving Divorce: Men Beyond Marriage. Peter Ambrose & John Harper. LC 82-22717. 206p. 1983. text ed. 25.95x (ISBN 0-86598-122-1, Rowman & Allanheld). Rowman.

Surviving English Carthusian Remains, Vol. 1. Ed. by James Hogg. (Analecta Cartusiana Ser.: No. 36). (Orig.). 1986. pap. 25.00 (ISBN 3-7052-0042-9, Pub by Salzburg Studies). Longwood Pub Group.

Surviving English Carthusian Remains: Beauvale, Coventry, Mountgrace Album. James Hogg. (Analecta Cartusaina Ser.: No. 36-2). (Illus., Orig.). 1976. pap. 25.00 (ISBN 3-7052-0043-7, Pub by Salzburg Studies). Longwood Pub Group.

Surviving Excercise. Judy Alter. 1989. pap. 7.95 (ISBN 0-395-50073-7). HM.

Surviving Exercise: Judy Alter's Safe & Sane Exercise Program. Judy Alter. 1983. 11.95 (ISBN 0-395-33112-9); pap. 5.95 (ISBN 0-395-33113-7). HM.

Surviving Family Life: The Seven Crises of Living Together. Sonya Rhodes & Josleen Wilson. 299p. 1986. pap. 16.95x (ISBN 0-935005-06-4). Ibis Pub VA.

Surviving Family Life: The Seven Crises of Living Together. Sonya Thodes & Josleen Wilson. 300p. 1981. 13.95 (ISBN 0-399-12507-8). Putnam Pub Group.

Surviving Freshman Composition: Straight Talk about How to Get the Best Possible Start in Your College Career. Scott Edelstein. 192p. (Orig.). 1988. pap. 7.95 (ISBN 0-8184-0463-9). Lyle Stuart.

Surviving Hard Times: The Working People of Lowell. Ed. by Mary H. Blewett. LC 81-86362. (Illus.). xii, 178p. (Orig.). 1982. pap. 6.95 (ISBN 0-942472-05-5). Lowell Museum.

Surviving High School. Ed. by Verne Becker. (Campus Life Ser.). 144p. 1986. pap. 5.95 (ISBN 0-8423-0295-6). Tyndale.

Surviving in College. David J. Yarington. 1977. pap. text ed. 10.83 scp (ISBN 0-672-61372-7); scp tchr's manual 3.67 (ISBN 0-672-61373-5). Bobbs.

Surviving in Corrections: A Guide for Corrections Professionals. David B. Kalinich & Terry Pitcher. (Illus.). 206p. 1984. 27.00x (ISBN 0-398-04999-8). C C Thomas.

Surviving in General Music I. Michael D. Bennett. 97p. (Orig.). 1979. pap. 8.95 (ISBN 0-934019-00-2). Pop Hits Pub.

Surviving in General Music II. Michael D. Bennett. 95p. (Orig.). 1978. pap. 18.95 (ISBN 0-934019-01-0); 3 game boards, pictures, 7" LP incl. Pop Hits Pub.

Surviving in the Newspaper Business: Newspaper Management in Turbulent Times. Jim Willis. LC 87-37685. 223p. 1988. lib. bdg. 39.95 (ISBN 0-275-92862-4, C2862); pap. 15.95 (ISBN 0-275-92863-2, B2863). Praeger.

Surviving in the Restaurant Jungle: Tips for Everyone. Claudia Carr. (Illus.). 100p. 1985. spiral bdg. 5.95 (ISBN 0-318-18460-5). C Carr.

Surviving ina Ex Steel Town. Herman A. Talley. 128p. 1988. 8.95 (ISBN 0-8062-3293-5). Carlton.

Surviving Junior High. Martha E. Chamberlain. LC 88-2937. 296p. (Orig.). (YA) (gr. 7-9). 1988. pap. 9.95 (ISBN 0-8361-3462-1). Herald Pr.

Surviving Major Chemical Accidents & Chemical-Biological Warfare. Duncan Long. LC 86-80536. 152p. (Orig.). 1986. pap. text ed. 14.95 (ISBN 0-915179-38-5). Loompanics.

Surviving Merger & Acquisition. Michael L. McManus & Michael L. Hergert. 1988. 18.95 (ISBN 0-673-18854-X). Scott F.

Surviving Middle Age. Mike Hepworth & Mike Featherstone. (Understanding Everyday Experience Ser.). 216p. 1982. 34.95x (ISBN 0-631-12751-8); pap. 6.95 (ISBN 0-631-12955-3). Basil Blackwell.

Surviving Motherhood. Donna L. Montgomery. (Illus.). 200p. (Orig.). 1986. pap. 6.95 (ISBN 0-938577-00-X). St Johns Pub.

Surviving Nuclear Disaster. Cresson Kearny & Conrad Chester. (Illus.). 240p. 1987. pap. cancelled (ISBN 0-915463-44-X, Pub. by Jameson Bks). Green Hill.

Surviving Nursing: A Coping Manual. Emily E. Smythe. 300p. 1984. pap. write for info. (ISBN 0-201-16418-3, Hlth-Sci). Addison-Wesley.

Surviving on the Job. Jay Como. 1983. 10.00 (ISBN 0-02-670180-4); instr's. guide 6.64 (ISBN 0-02-670190-1). Glencoe Bennett & McKnight.

Surviving Passages. Andrew Grieg. 1982. 12.95 (ISBN 0-86241-025-8); pap. 4.95 (ISBN 0-86241-026-6). Dufour.

Surviving Popular Psychology: Debriefing the Me Degeneration. Clint Weyand. 148p. (Orig.). 1980. pap. 4.95 (ISBN 0-686-28854-8). Being Bks.

Surviving Pregnancy Loss. Rochelle Friedman & Bonnie Gradstein. 1982. 16.45 (ISBN 0-316-29349-0); pap. 10.95 (ISBN 0-316-29348-2). Little.

Surviving Proposition Thirteen: Fiscal Crisis in California Counties. Valerie Raymond. LC 88-2766. 84p. (Orig.). 1988. pap. 6.95 (ISBN 0-87772-315-X). UCB IGS.

Surviving Retirement. John H. Graves. 64p. 1987. 7.95 (ISBN 0-8062-3082-7). Carlton.

Surviving Schizophrenia. E. Fuller Torrey. LC 82-48138. 288p. 1983. 20.00i (ISBN 0-06-015112-9, HarpT). Har-Row.

Surviving Schizophrenia: A Family Manual. rev. ed. E. F. Torrey. LC 87-45673. (Illus.). 400p. 1988. 22.95 (ISBN 0-06-055119-4). Har-Row.

Surviving Schizophrenia: A Family Manual. rev. ed. E. F. Torrey. LC 87-45673. (Illus.). 400p. 1988. pap. 9.95 (ISBN 0-06-096249-6, PL6249, PL). Har-Row.

Surviving Separation & Divorce. Sharon Marshall. 96p. (Orig.). 1988. pap. 5.95 (ISBN 0-8010-6228-4). Baker Bk.

Surviving Sexual Assault. Los Angeles Commission on Assaults Against Women. (Illus.). 64p. 1983. pap. 4.95 (ISBN 0-312-92796-7); 49.50, set of 10 (ISBN 0-312-92798-3). Congdon & Weed.

Surviving Sexual Assault. Los Angeles Commission on Assaults Against Women. 96p. Date not set. 4.95 (ISBN 0-86553-093-9). Congdon & Weed.

Surviving Sobriety: The Woman. Marwood Wegner. 24p. 1983. pap. 1.15 (ISBN 0-89486-191-3). Hazelden.

Surviving Steam Railways. Jeoffry Spence. 1979. pap. 9.95 (ISBN 0-7134-0641-0, Pub. by Batsford England). David & Charles.

Surviving: The Best Game on Earth. Ed. by Norrie Huddle. LC 83-42722. 320p. 1984. 16.95 (ISBN 0-8052-3871-9). Schocken.

Surviving the Breakup: How Children & Parents Cope with Divorce. Judith S. Wallerstein & Joan B. Kelly. 1982. pap. 11.95x (ISBN 0-465-08339-0, TB-5094). Basic.

Surviving the Eighties: Strategies & Procedures for Solving Fiscal & Enrollment Problems. Lewis B. Mayhew. LC 79-88773. (Higher Education Ser.). 1979. text ed. 27.95x (ISBN 0-87589-428-3). Jossey-Bass.

Surviving the Flood. Stephen Minot. LC 85-63551. (Illus.). 306p. 1986. Repr. of 1981 ed. 18.95 (ISBN 0-933256-62-0). Second Chance.

Surviving the Flood. Stephen Minot. LC 85-63551. 306p. 1987. 12.95 (ISBN 0-933256-63-9). Second Chance.

Surviving the Great Depression of 1990. Ravi Batra. 288p. 1988. 18.95 (ISBN 0-671-66324-0). S&S.

Surviving the Law. CWL. LC 86-61881. (Breaking the Law Ser.: Vol. 2). (Illus.). 55p. (Orig.). 1986. pap. 13.00 (ISBN 0-939856-62-X). Tech Group.

Surviving the Raw & the Cooked. David Nolf. LC 80-82717. (Lightning Tree Contemporary Poets Ser.: No. 6). (Illus.). 63p. 1980. 12.95 (ISBN 0-89016-060-0); pap. 4.95 (ISBN 0-89016-059-7). Lightning Tree.

Surviving the Seasons. Fern Kupfer. 360p. 1987. 17.95 (ISBN 0-385-29534-0). Delacorte.

Surviving the Secret. Pamela Vredevelt & Kathryn Rodriguez. 192p. (YA) (gr. 9-12). 1987. 9.95 (ISBN 0-8007-1543-8). Revell.

Surviving the Siege of Beirut: A Personal Account. Lina Mikdadi. 152p. 1983. casebound 22.00 (ISBN 0-906383-21-8, Pub. by Onyx Pr UK). Three Continents.

Surviving the Teenage Years: A Guide to Early Adolescence. Gary Hunt & Angela Hunt. 128p. (Orig.). 1988. pap. 5.95 (ISBN 0-89840-205-0). Heres Life.

Surviving the Ten Ordeals of the Takeover. Robert Bell. 192p. 1988. 17.95 (ISBN 0-8144-5902-1). AMACOM.

Surviving the Unexpected: A Curriculum Guide for Wilderness Survival & Survival from Natural & Man Made Disasters. rev., 3rd ed. Ed. by Daniel E. Fear. (Illus.). 91p. 1974. spiral bdg. 5.00 (ISBN 0-913724-00-9). Emerg Response Inst.

Surviving the Unexpected Wilderness Emergency: A Text for Body Management Under Stress. rev., 6th ed. Eugene H. Fear. LC 73-78035. (Illus.). 1979. pap. 6.00 (ISBN 0-913724-02-5). Emerg Response Inst.

Surviving Transition: Rational Management in a World of Mergers, Layoffs, Start-Ups, Takeovers, Divestitures, Deregulation & New Technologies. William Bridges. LC 87-19978. 216p. 1988. pap. 18.95 (ISBN 0-385-23761-8). Doubleday.

Surviving with Kids: A Lifeline for Overwhelmed Parents. Wayne Bartz & Richard Rasor. LC 78-13328. (Illus.). 184p. 1978. pap. 6.95 (ISBN 0-915166-55-0). Impact Pubs Cal.

Surviving Without Governing: The Italian Parties in Parliament. Guiseppe DiPalma. LC 75-46035. (Institute of International Studies, UC Berkeley). 1977. 42.00x (ISBN 0-520-03195-4). U of Cal Pr.

Surviving World War Two Aircraft. Chaz Bowyer. (Illus.). 64p. 1981. pap. 9.95 (ISBN 0-7134-3431-7, Pub. by Batsford England). David & Charles.

Surviving Your Role As a Lawyer. rev. 2nd ed. David H. Barber. (Illus.). 166p. 1987. pap. text ed. 17.95 (ISBN 0-915667-07-X). Spectra Pub Co.

Survivor. Christina Crawford. (Illus.). 1988. 17.95 (ISBN 1-55611-118-5). D I Fine.

Survivor. Terrence DesPres. 1983. pap. 3.95 (ISBN 0-671-46687-9). WSP.

Survivor. James Forman. LC 76-2478. 288p. (gr. 7 up). 1976. 8.95 (ISBN 0-374-37312-4). FS&G.

Survivor. James Herbert. 208p. (Orig.). 1988. pap. 3.95 (ISBN 0-451-15655-2, Sig). NAL.

Survivor. Herbert James. 1979. pap. 2.50 (ISBN 0-451-11395-0, Sig). NAL.

Survivor. Arun Joshi. 136p. 1975. pap. 2.50 (ISBN 0-88253-777-6). Ind-US Inc.

Survivor. Thomas Keneally. (Fiction Ser.). 288p. 1985. pap. 5.95 (ISBN 0-14-003217-7). Penguin.

Survivor. Knute Lee. LC 84-81767. 224p. 1984. pap. 9.95 (ISBN 0-8187-0057-2). Harlo Pr.

Survivor. Fritz Raddatz. Tr. by Ralph Manheim. 1989. 15.95 (ISBN 0-316-73213-3). Little.

Survivor: An Anatomy of Life in the Death Camps. Terrence Des Pres. 1976. 21.95x (ISBN 0-19-501952-0). Oxford U Pr.

Survivor: An Anatomy of Life in the Death Camps. Terrence Des Pres. (Illus.). 1976. pap. 8.95 (ISBN 0-19-502703-5). Oxford U Pr.

Survivor & Other Poems. Tadeusz Rozewicz. Tr. by Magnus J. Krynski et al. (Lockert Library of Poetry in Translation). 1976. 25.00x (ISBN 0-691-06315-X). Princeton U Pr.

Survivor: Cadwallader Colden II in Revolutionary America. Eugene R. Fingerhut. LC 82-20092. (Illus.). 200p. (Orig.). 1983. lib. bdg. 29.00 (ISBN 0-8191-2868-6); pap. text ed. 13.00 (ISBN 0-8191-2869-4). U Pr of Amer.

Survivor in Us All: Four Young Sisters in the Holocaust. Erna F. Rubinstein. 185p. 1986. 19.50 (ISBN 0-208-02025-X, Archon); pap. 12.50 (ISBN 0-208-02128-0, Archon). Shoe String.

Survivor of a Tarnished Ministry. Betty E. De Blase. 176p. (Orig.). 1983. pap. text ed. 6.95 (ISBN 0-913621-00-5). Truth CA.

Survivor of Mars. John R. Fearn. 39p. 1983. Repr. of 1982 ed. lib. bdg. 19.95x (ISBN 0-89370-796-1). Borgo Pr.

Survivor of Nam. Donald E. Zlotnik. (P.O.W. Ser.: No. 2). 192p. (Orig.). 1988. pap. 2.95 (ISBN 0-445-20602-0, Pub. by Popular Lib). Warner Bks.

Survivor of Nam: Court-Martial, No. 4. Donald E. Zlotnik. 192p. (Orig.). Date not set. pap. 2.95 (ISBN 0-445-20606-3, Pub. by Popular Lib). Warner Bks.

Survivor of Nam, No. 1: Baptism. Donald E. Zlotnik. 1988. pap. 2.95 (ISBN 0-317-67191-X, Pub. by Popular Lib). Warner Bks.

Survivor of Nam, No. 3: Black Market. Donald E. Zlotnik. Date not set. pap. 2.95 (ISBN 0-445-20604-7, Pub. by Popular Lib). Warner Bks.

Survivors. Clint Berrywell. 196p. 1983. pap. 5.00 (ISBN 0-942698-13-4). Trends & Events.

Survivors. Marion Zimmer Bradley & Paul E. Zimmer. (Science Fiction Ser.). (Orig.). 1983. pap. 2.95 (ISBN 0-87997-861-9). DAW Bks.

Survivors. Mary Canon. (O'Hara Dynasty Ser.). 1982. pap. 2.95 (ISBN 0-373-89002-8). Harlequin Bks.

Survivors. Anne Edwards. 1969. pap. 1.50 (ISBN 0-440-18397-9). Dell.

Survivors. Zalin Grant. 345p. 1975. 12.95 (ISBN 0-393-08727-1). Norton.

Survivors. John Nahmlos. (Orig.). 1982. pap. 3.25 (ISBN 0-8217-1071-0). Zebra.

Survivors. Georges Simenon. Tr. by Stuart Gilbert from Fr. LC 84-22385. (Helen & Kurt Wolff Bk.). 180p. 1985. 14.95 (ISBN 0-15-187047-0). HarBraceJ.

Survivors. (Firebrats Ser.). (gr. 7 up). 1987. pap. 2.50 (ISBN 0-671-55733-5). Archway.

Survivors. R. T. Wilkinson. 1971. pap. 1.00 (ISBN 0-685-27776-3). Stone-Marrow Pr.

Survivors: A Personal Story of the Holocaust. Jacob Biber. LC 85-22415. (Studies in Judaica & the Holocaust: No. 2). 200p. 1986. lib. bdg. 19.95x (ISBN 0-89370-370-2); pap. text ed. 9.95x (ISBN 0-89370-470-9). Borgo Pr.

Survivors: After a Suicide What Can We Do. Bill Steele. 1985. pap. text ed. 10.00 (ISBN 0-317-59339-0). Ann Arbor FL.

Survivors: American POW's in Vietnam. Grant Zalin. 336p. 1987. pap. 3.95 (ISBN 0-425-09689-0). Berkley Pub.

Survivors: And Other New York Poems. Ilsa Gilbert. 24p. (Orig.). 1985. pap. 3.50 (ISBN 0-934776-05-9). Bard Pr.

Survivors & Others. Robert Drake. LC 87-5644. 208p. 1987. 24.95 (ISBN 0-86554-253-8, MUP H-218); pap. 14.95 (ISBN 0-86554-254-6, MUP P-41). Mercer Univ Pr.

Survivors: Children of the Holocaust. Judith Hemmendinger. 200p. (Orig.). 1986. Repr. of 1984 ed. 15.95 (ISBN 0-915765-24-1). Natl Pr Inc.

Survivors: Documentary Account of the Victims of Northern Ireland. Alf McCreary. 1977. 24.95 (ISBN 0-8464-0904-6). Beekman Pubs.

Survivors of Successful Sales: A Guide to Organizing Fundraising Sales. Lois B. Hart et al. LC 86-80036. (Illus.). 120p. 1986. pap. 19.95spiral bind (ISBN 0-911777-08-3). Leadership Dyn.

Survivors of Suicide. Ed. by Albert C. Cain. (Illus.). 324p. 1972. 30.75x. C C Thomas.

Survivors of the Chicano Titanic. Reyes Cardenas. LC 81-81742. (Illus.). 80p. 1982. lib. bdg. 25.00 (ISBN 0-916908-20-8); pap. 5.95 (ISBN 0-916908-15-1). Place Herons.

Survivors of the Stone Age: Nine Tribes Today. Rebecca Marcus. (Illus.). 160p. (gr. 7 up). 1975. PLB 9.95 (ISBN 0-8038-6726-3). Hastings.

Survivors: Poems. Frederick Feirstein. LC 74-12385. 1976. 12.50 (ISBN 0-89366-125-2); pap. 7.50 (ISBN 0-89366-126-0). Ultramarine Pub.

Survivor's Primer & Up-Dated Retreater's Bibliography. Don Stephens & Barbie Stephens. (Illus.). 1976. pap. 12.00 (ISBN 0-686-21855-8). Stephens Pr.

Survivors, Victims & Perpetrators: Essays on the Nazi Holocaust. Ed. by Joel E. Dimsdale. LC 79-24834. (Illus.). 474p. 1980. text ed. 42.50 (ISBN 0-89116-145-7); pap. text ed. 36.00 (ISBN 0-89116-351-4). Hemisphere Pub.

Surya Siddhanta. Tr. by Ebeneezer Burgess from Sanskrit. LC 74-78001. (Secret Doctrine Reference Ser.). 368p. 1977. Repr. of 1860 ed. 20.00 (ISBN 0-913510-13-0). Wizards.

Sus. Barrie Keefe. 1981. pap. 4.95 (ISBN 0-413-46870-4, 2073). Heinemann Ed.

Susan & Gordon Adopt a Baby. Judy Freudberg & Tony Geiss. LC 86-2951. (Sesame Street Bks.). (Illus.). 24p. (ps-2). 1986. 3.95 (ISBN 0-394-88341-1, BYR); lib. bdg. 4.99 (ISBN 0-394-98341-6). Random.

Susan Anthony: Champion of Women's Rights. Helen A. Monsell. LC 83-19737. (Childhood of Famous Americans Ser.). 192p. 1984. pap. 3.95 (ISBN 0-672-52799-5). Bobbs.

Susan B. Anthony. Ilene Cooper. (Impact Biography Ser.). 128p. (gr. 7 up). 1984. lib. bdg. 12.90 (ISBN 0-531-04750-4). Watts.

Susan B. Anthony. (Childhood of Famous Americans Ser.). 1984. pap. 3.95. Bobbs.

Susan B. Anthony. Barbara Weisberg. (American Women of Achievement Ser.). (Illus.). 112p. (gr. 5 up). 1988. lib. bdg. 16.95x (ISBN 1-55546-639-7). Chelsea Hse.

Susan B. Anthony - A Biography: A Singular Feminist. Kathleen L. Barry. (Illus.). 416p. 1988. 27.95 (ISBN 0-8147-1105-7). NYU Pr.

Susan B. Anthony: A Crusader for Women's Rights. Barbara Salsini. Ed. by D. Steve Rahmas. LC 72-89211. (Outstanding Personalities Ser.: No. 49). 32p. 1972. lib. bdg. 3.75 incl. catalog cards (ISBN 0-87157-544-2); pap. 2.50 vinyl laminated covers (ISBN 0-87157-044-0). SamHar Pr.

Susan B. Anthony: Champion of Women's Rights. Helen A. Monsell. LC 86-10716. (Macmillan Childhood of Famous Americans Ser.). (Illus.). 192p. (gr. 2-6). 1986. pap. 3.95 (ISBN 0-02-041800-0, Aladdin Bks). Macmillan.

Susan B. Anthony: Mini-Play. (Women Studies Ser.). (gr. 7 up). 1974. 6.50 (ISBN 0-89550-365-4). Stevens & Shea.

Susan B. Anthony: Pioneer in Woman's Rights. Helen S. Peterson. LC 76-151991. (Americans All Ser.). (Illus.). 96p. (gr. 3-6). 1971. PLB 7.12 (ISBN 0-8116-4570-3). Garrard.

Susan B. Anthony: Rebel, Crusader, Humanitarian. Alma Lutz. LC 75-37764. 1976. Repr. of 1959 ed. 19.95 (ISBN 0-89201-017-7). Zenger Pub.

Susan B. Anthony, The Woman Who Changed the Mind of a Nation. Rheta C. Dorr. LC 74-100519. Repr. of 1928 ed. 47.50 (ISBN 0-404-00626-4). AMS Pr.

Susan Clegg & Her Friend Mrs. Lathrop. Anne French. LC 71-94723. (Short Story Index Reprint Ser.). 1904. 17.00 (ISBN 0-8369-3102-5). Ayer Co Pubs.

Susan Clegg & Her Neighbors' Affairs. facsimile ed. Anne French. LC 70-150474. (Short Story Index Reprint Ser.). Repr. of 1906 ed. 17.00 (ISBN 0-8369-3814-3). Ayer Co Pubs.

Susan Comes Through the Fire. Lois Eddy McDonnell. LC 68-56619. (Orig.). (gr. 1-3). 1969. pap. 1.75 (ISBN 0-377-09701-2). Friendship Pr.

Susan Constant, 1607. Brian Lavery. (Anatomy of the Ship Ser.). (Illus.). 120p. 1988. 21.95 (ISBN 0-87021-583-3). Naval Inst Pr.

Susan Duckworth's Knitting. Susan Duckworth. LC 87-48000. (Illus.). 144p. 1988. 25.00 (ISBN 0-345-35276-9, Del Rey Bks). Ballantine.

Susan Ferrier. Mary Cullinan. (English Authors Ser.: No. 392). 1984. lib. bdg. 20.95 (ISBN 0-8057-6878-5, Twayne). G K Hall.

Susan Glaspell. Arthur E. Waterman. (Twayne's United States Authors Ser). 1966. pap. 8.95x (ISBN 0-8084-0288-9, T101, Twayne). New Coll U Pr.

Susan Glaspell. Arthur E. Waterman. LC 66-17062. (Twayne's United States Authors Ser.). 1966. lib. bdg. 17.95 (ISBN 0-89197-958-1); pap. text ed. 7.75x (ISBN 0-8290-0016-X). Irvington.

Susan Haywood: Portrait of a Survivor. Beverly Linet. 352p. 1984. pap. 3.95 (ISBN 0-425-10383-8). Berkley Pub.

Susan Hiller 1973-1984: The Muse My Sister. 48p. 1984. 24.00x (ISBN 0-907797-15-6, Pub. by Third Eye Centre). State Mutual Bk.

Susan Hopley: Or, the Adventures of a Maidservant, 3 vols. in 2. Catherine S. Crowe. LC 79-8258. Repr. of 1841 ed. Set. 84.50 (ISBN 0-404-61836-7). Vol. 1 (ISBN 0-404-61837-5). Vol. 2. AMS Pr.

Susan Kahn. Lincoln Rothschild. LC 79-5388. (Illus.). 164p. 1980. 35.00 (ISBN 0-87982-031-4). Art Alliance.

Susan L. Mitchell. Richard M. Kain. LC 78-126275. (Irish Writers Ser.). 1972. 4.50 (ISBN 0-8387-7768-6); pap. 1.95 (ISBN 0-8387-7627-2). Bucknell U Pr.

Susan Lee's ABZs of Economics. Susan Lee. 224p. (Orig.). Date not set. pap. 6.95 (ISBN 0-671-64911-6). PB.

TITLE INDEX SUTTER BUTTES: A NATURALIST'S

Susan Lee's ABZ's of Economics: From Arbitrage to Zero Sum. Susan Lee. (Illus.). 224p. 1987. 16.95 (ISBN 0-671-55711-4, Poseidon). S&S.
Susan Lee's ABZ's of Money & Finance: From Annuities to Zero Coupon Bonds. Susan Lee. 1988. 16.95 (ISBN 0-671-55712-2, Poseidon Pr). PB.
Susan Lenox: Her Fall & Rise, 2 vols. David C. Phillips. (Collected Works of David G. Phillips). 1988. Repr. of 1917 ed. Set. lib. bdg. 99.00x. Am Biog Serv.
Susan Lenox, Her Fall & Rise, 2 vols. in 1. David G. Phillips. LC 70-121842. (Illus.). Repr. of 1937 ed. 18.00 (ISBN 0-404-05029-8). AMS Pr.
Susan Lenox: Her Fall & Rise, 2 vols. in 1. David G. Phillips. 489p. 1980. Repr. of 1937 ed. lib. bdg. 35.00 (ISBN 0-8495-4384-3). Arden Lib.
Susan Lenox: Her Fall & Rise, 2 vols. David G. Phillips. LC 68-57548. (Muckrakers Ser.). 1076p. Repr. of 1917 ed. Set. lib. bdg. 16.00 (ISBN 0-8398-1568-9). Irvington.
Susan Lenox: Her Fall & Rise, 2 vols. David G. Phillips. (Muckrakers Ser.). 1076p. 1986. Set. pap. text ed. 12.50x (ISBN 0-8290-2038-1). Irvington.
Susan Lenox: Her Fall & Rise see Collected Works.
Susan Lenox, Her Fall & Rise. A Novel. David G. Phillips. LC 76-21767. (Lost American Fiction Ser.). 986p. 1977. Repr. of 1917 ed. 12.95 (ISBN 0-8093-0773-1). S Ill U Pr.
Susan Lucci. Siegel & Siegel. 1988. pap. 3.50 (ISBN 0-312-90639-0). St Martin.
Susan Lucci: The Woman Behind Erica Kane. Barbara Siegel & Scott Siegel. (Illus.). 160p. 1986. 13.95 (ISBN 0-312-77963-1). St Martin.
Susan Rios. Matthew Fabris. (Illus.). 144p. 1987. 50.00 (ISBN 0-88363-587-9). H L Levin.
Susan Rothenberg. Eliza Rathbone. Ed. by Sara Hutchinson. LC 85-21538. (Illus.). 1985. pap. text ed. 9.50 (ISBN 0-943044-06-5). Phillips Coll.
Susan Rothenberg - The Prints: A Catalogue Raisonne. Rachel R. Maxwell et al. (Illus.). 104p. (Orig.). 1987. pap. 20.00 (ISBN 0-944751-00-8). Maxwells Busn.
Susan Scott. (Cost Containment Learning Modules Ser.: No. 9). (Orig.). 1985. pap. text ed. 47.50 (ISBN 0-931369-11-8). Southern IL Univ Sch.
Susan Sontag Reader. Susan Sontag. 446p. 1982. 17.95 (ISBN 0-374-27215-8); slip-cased ltd. ed. 60.00 (ISBN 0-374-27216-6). FS&G.
Susan Sontag Reader. Susan Sontag. LC 83-5767. 464p. 1983. pap. 9.95 (ISBN 0-394-71569-1, Vin). Random.
Susan Witt's Classics for Needlepoint. Susan Witt. LC 80-84410. (Illus.). 128p. 1981. 19.95 (ISBN 0-8487-0525-4). Oxmoor Hse.
Susana y Javier en Espana. Marvin Wasserman & Carol Wasserman. (Orig.). (gr. 7-12). 1975. pap. text ed. 8.50 (ISBN 0-87720-502-7). AMSCO Sch.
Susann Folk Cross-Stitch Charts see Charted Folk Designs for Cross-Stitch Embroidery.
Susanna. Glen Williamsen & Isabel Anders. 240p. (Orig.). 1985. pap. 3.95 (ISBN 0-8423-6691-1). Tyndale.
Susanna, "Jeanie," & "The Old Folks at Home" The Songs of Stephen C. Foster from His Time to Ours. 2nd ed. William W. Austin. LC 87-13931. (Music in American Life Ser.). 456p. 1988. 29.95 (ISBN 0-252-01476-6). U of Ill Pr.
Susanna Moodie: Letters of a Lifetime. Carl Ballstadt et al. 400p. 1985. 29.95 (ISBN 0-8020-2580-3). U of Toronto Pr.
Susanna: Mother of the Wesleys. rev. ed. Rebecca L. Harmon. 1968. 7.50 (ISBN 0-687-40766-4). Abingdon.
Susanna of the Alamo: A True Story. John Jakes. LC 85-27143. (Illus.). 32p. (gr. 1-5). 1986. 13.95 (ISBN 0-15-200592-7, Gulliver Bks). HarBraceJ.
Susanna Rowson. Patricia L. Parker. (Twayne United States Authors Ser.: No. 498). 160p. 1986. lib. bdg. 19.95x (ISBN 0-8057-7458-0, Twayne). G K Hall.
Susanna Wesley. Charles Ludwig. LC 84-60314. (Sower Ser.). 195p. (gr. 3-6). 1984. 8.95 (ISBN 0-88062-111-7); pap. 4.95 (ISBN 0-88062-110-9). Mott Media.
Susanna Wesley, a Study Guide. Joe Ponzani & Mrs. Joe Ponzan. 1983. 1.75 (ISBN 0-89536-607-X, 1930). CSS of Ohio.
Susanna Wesley: Servant of God. Sandy Dengler. (Preteen Biographies Ser.). (YA) (gr. 9-12). 1987. pap. text ed. 3.95 (ISBN 0-8024-8414-X). Moody.
Susannah, No. 2. Candice F. Ransom. 368p. (gr. 7 up). 1984. pap. 2.95 (ISBN 0-590-33064-0, Sunfire). Scholastic Inc.
Susannah see Sunfire Boxed Set.
Susannah & the Blue House Mystery. Patricia Elmore. LC 79-20491. (Illus.). 176p. (gr. 4-7). 1980. 10.25 (ISBN 0-525-40525-9). Dutton.
Susannah & the Blue House Mystery. Patricia Elmore. (Orig.). (gr. 4-6). 1984. pap. 1.95 (ISBN 0-671-43493-4). Archway.
Susannah & the Poison Green Halloween. Patricia Elmore. LC 82-2493. (Illus.). 128p. (gr. 4-7). 1982. 9.95 (ISBN 0-525-44019-4). Dutton.
Susan's Story: My Struggle with Dyslexia. Susan Hampshire. 168p. 1983. pap. 5.95 (ISBN 0-312-77967-4). St Martin.
Sushi: A Light & Right Diet. Asako Kishi. LC 85-80535. (Illus.). 136p. (Orig.). 1986. pap. 12.95 (ISBN 0-87040-576-4). Japan Pubns USA.
Sushi: An Indispensable Handbook for Sushi Lovers. Mia Detrick. LC 81-12224. (Illus.). 96p. (Orig.). 1981. pap. 9.95 (ISBN 0-87701-238-5). Chronicle Bks.
Sushi at Home. Kay Shimizu. 142p. 1988. pap. 14.95 (ISBN 0-87040-767-8). Japan Pubns USA.
Sushi at Home. Kay Shimizu et al. (Illus.). 140p. 1983. 12.95 (ISBN 0-87040-572-1). Japan Pubns USA.
Sushi Handbook. Kenji Kumagai. (Illus.). 94p. (Orig.). 1983. pap. 8.95 (ISBN 0-89346-211-X). Heian Intl.
Sushi Made Easy. Nobuko Tsuda. LC 82-7097. (Illus.). 152p. (Japanese.). 1982. pap. 9.95 (ISBN 0-8348-0173-6). Weatherhill.
Susie. Jennie Tremaine, pseud. (Orig.). 1981. pap. 2.95 (ISBN 0-440-18391-X). Dell.
Susie Goes Shopping. Rose Greydanus. (Illus.). 32p. (gr. k-2). 1980. PLB 5.41 (ISBN 0-89375-389-0); pap. 1.50 (ISBN 0-89375-289-4). Troll Assocs.
Susie's Girls. Susanna Sheldon. 1975. pap. 1.50 (ISBN 0-685-61050-0, LB314DK, Leisure Bks). Leisure NY.
Susie's Girls. Susanna Sheldon. 1979. pap. 1.75 (ISBN 0-505-51362-5, Pub. by Tower Bks). Leisure NY.
Suslov: Selected Speeches & Writings. Mikhail A. Suslov. LC 79-41075. 368p. 1980. 59.00 (ISBN 0-08-023602-2). Pergamon.
Suspect. B. M. Gill. 192p. 1985. pap. 2.95 (ISBN 0-345-32514-1). Ballantine.
Suspect. Martin Meyers. 224p. 1987. pap. 3.95 (ISBN 0-553-27076-1). Bantam.
Suspect. L. R. Wright. (Fiction Ser.). 224p. 1985. 15.95 (ISBN 0-670-80596-3). Viking.
Suspect. L. R. Wright. 224p. 1987. pap. 3.95 (ISBN 0-14-010477-1). Penguin.
Suspect Documents: Their Scientific Examination. Wilson R. Harrison. LC 80-22803. (Illus.). 594p. 1981. text ed. 41.95x (ISBN 0-88229-759-7). Nelson-Hall.
Suspects. William J. Caunitz. 384p. 1986. 17.95 (ISBN 0-517-55864-5). Crown.
Suspects. William J. Caunitz. 384p. 1987. pap. 4.95 (ISBN 0-553-26705-1). Bantam.
Suspects. William J. Caunitz. 589p. 1988. lib. bdg. 19.95 (ISBN 0-8161-4337-4, Large Print Bks). G K Hall.
Suspects. David Thomson. LC 84-48665. 288p. 1985. 16.45 (ISBN 0-394-54226-6). Knopf.
Suspects. David Thomson. LC 86-40145. 288p. 1986. pap. 6.95 (ISBN 0-394-74468-3, Vin). Random.
Suspended Fictions: Reading Novels by Manuel Puig. Lucille Kerr. 280p. 1987. 21.95 (ISBN 0-252-01329-8). U of Ill Pr.
Suspended Judgments, Essays on Books & Sensations. John C. Powys. LC 76-29700. 1916. lib. bdg. 57.50 (ISBN 0-8414-6786-2). Folcroft.
Suspense Thriller: Films in the Shadow of Alfred Hitchcock. Charles Derry. LC 87-46381. 375p. 1988. lib. bdg. 35.00x (ISBN 0-89950-332-2). McFarland & Co.
Suspension & Steering. James G. Hughes. 256p. 1987. pap. text ed. write for info. (ISBN 0-15-584985-9, SUSPEN, HC). HarBraceJ.
Suspension Bridge. Rod McKuen. LC 84-47589. 216p. 1984. 10.95i (ISBN 0-06-015348-2). Har-Row.
Suspension of Mercy. Patricia Highsmith. 1982. pap. 3.95 (ISBN 0-14-003470-6). Penguin.
Suspension of the Power of Alienation, & Postponement of Vesting, Under the Laws of New York, Michigan, Minnesota & Wisconsin. Stewart Chaplin. xxxix, 370p. 1981. Repr. of 1891 ed. lib. bdg. 30.00x (ISBN 0-8377-0428-6). Rothman.
Suspicion. Jo Sullivan. (Harlequin Romances Ser.). 192p. 1983. pap. 1.75 (ISBN 0-373-02544-0). Harlequin Bks.
Suspicion: Park Avenue. Lorayne Ashton. 368p. (Orig.). 1987. pap. 3.95 (ISBN 0-8041-0159-0, Pub. by Ivy). Ballantine.
Suspicious Characters. Bill Pronzini & Martin H. Grunberg. 240p. 1987. pap. 2.95 (ISBN 0-8041-0126-4, Pub. by Ivy). Ballantine.
Suspicious Death. Dorothy Simpson. 272p. 1988. 15.95 (ISBN 0-684-19026-5). Scribner.
Suspicious Origins. Perry Glasser. 1983. 6.00 (ISBN 0-89823-049-7). New Rivers Pr.
Susquehanna. Harriet Segal. 1988. pap. 4.50 (ISBN 0-451-15304-9, Sig). NAL.
Susquehanna: From New York to the Chesapeake. Elizabeth Carmer & Carl Carmer. LC 64-10245. (Rivers of the World Ser.). (Illus.). 96p. (gr. 4-7). 1964. PLB 3.98 (ISBN 0-8116-6360-4). Garrard.
Susquehanna: Images of the Settled Landscape. Roger B. Stein. Ed. by Lawrence B. Bothwell. LC 81-50681. (Illus.). 144p. 1981. pap. 10.00 (ISBN 0-937318-08-6, Pub. by Roberson Ctr). Pub Ctr Cult Res.
Susquehanna: NYS&W. Krause & Crist. (Carstens Hobby Bks.: No. C38). (Illus.). 1980. pap. 12.00 (ISBN 0-911868-38-0). Carstens Pubns.
Susquehanna's Indians. Barry C. Kent. (Pennsylvania Historical & Museum Commission Anthropological Ser.: No. 6). (Illus.). 438p. 1984. 15.95 (ISBN 0-89271-024-1). Pa Hist & Mus.
Susquehannock: An Anthology of Bioregional Literature. Ed. by Walt Franklin & Michael Czarnecki. 52p. 1986. pap. 5.95 (ISBN 0-9613465-4-X). Great Elm.
Sussex. Wilfrid Ball. 1906. 20.00 (ISBN 0-686-17218-3). Scholars Ref Lib.
Sussex. Jim Cleland. (Vistor's Guide Ser.). (Illus.). 160p. 1986. pap. 8.95 (ISBN 0-935161-32-5). Hunter Pub NY.
Sussex County, a Tale of Three Centuries. Writers Program, Virginia. LC 73-3659. (American Guide Ser.). 1942. Repr. 16.00 (ISBN 0-404-57959-0). AMS Pr.
Sussex County Marriages, 1754-1810. Catherin L. Knorr. 118p. 1980. Repr. of 1952 ed. 16.00 (ISBN 0-89308-257-0, VA 20). Southern Hist Pr.
Sussex Garland. Tony Wales. 128p. 1987. 30.00x (ISBN 0-905392-64-7, Countryside Bks). State Mutual Bk.
Sussex Ghosts. Judy Middleton. 96p. 1987. 30.00x (ISBN 0-905392-90-6, Countryside Bks). State Mutual Bk.
Sussex Scandals. Rupert Taylor. 96p. 1987. 30.00x (ISBN 0-905392-81-7, Countryside Bks). State Mutual Bk.
Sussex Songs. H. F. Reynardson. 1978. lib. bdg. 30.00 (ISBN 0-8492-2292-3). R West.
Sustainability Issuses in Agricultural Development. Ed. by Ted J. Davis & Isabelle A. Schirmer. (Proceedings of the Seventh Agricultural Sector Symposium). 392p. 1987. 23.00 (ISBN 0-8213-0909-9). World Bank.
Sustainable Clean Water. R. P. Lim et al. (Advances in Limnology Ser.: Heft 28). (Illus.). 571p. 1987. pap. text ed. 156.10x (ISBN 3-510-47026-5). Lubrecht & Cramer.
Sustainable Communities: A New Design Synthesis for Cities, Suburbs, & Towns. Sim Van der Ryn & Peter Calthorpe. LC 83-4676. (Illus.). 256p. 1986. 25.00 (ISBN 0-87156-800-4). Sierra.
Sustainable Corporate Growth: A Model & Management Planning Tool. John J. Clark et al. 1989. 39.85 (ISBN 0-89930-238-6, CKS/, Quorum Bks). Greenwood.
Sustainable Development: Constraints & Opportunities. Mostafa K. Tolba. 232p. 1987. pap. 75.00 (ISBN 0-408-00877-6). Butterworth.
Sustainable Development: Exploring the Contradictions. Michael Redclift. 200p. 1987. lib. bdg. 45.00x (ISBN 0-416-90240-5); pap. 13.95x (ISBN 0-416-90250-2). Routledge Chapman & Hall.
Sustainable Development of Agriculture. Ed. by Jyoti K. Parikh. 1988. lib. bdg. 105.00 (ISBN 90-247-3642-0, Pub. by Martinus Nijhoff). Kluwer Academic.
Sustainable Development of the Biosphere. Ed. by W. C. Clark & R. E. Munn. (Illus.). 450p. 1987. 29.50 (ISBN 0-521-32369-X); pap. 17.95 (ISBN 0-521-31185-3). Cambridge U Pr.
Sustainable Environmental Management: Principles & Practice. R. Kerry Turner. 292p. 1988. 37.50 (ISBN 0-8133-0744-9). Westview.
Sustainable Industrial Development. Intro. by Marilyn Carr. 208p. 1988. pap. 17.50x (ISBN 0-942850-12-2). Intermediate Tech.
Sustainable Resource Development in the Third World. Ed. by Douglas D. Southgate & John F. Disinger. (Special Studies in Natural Resources & Energy Management). 192p. 1987. pap. 22.00 (ISBN 0-8133-7522-3). Westview.
Sustained & Controlled Release Drug Delivery System. 2nd ed. Robinson & Lee. (Drug & Pharmaceutical Science Ser.). 808p. 1987. 125.00 (ISBN 0-8247-7588-0). Dekker.
Sustained Attention in Human Performance. Ed. by Joel S. Warm. LC 83-10946. (Studies in Human Performance Ser.: 1-507). 368p. 1984. text ed. 59.95 (ISBN 0-471-10322-5). Wiley.
Sustained Release Medications. Ed. by J. C. Johnson. LC 80-23455. (Chemical Technology Review: No. 177). (Illus.). 412p. 1981. 54.00 (ISBN 0-8155-0826-3). Noyes.
Sustained Release Theophylline: A Biopharmaceutical Challenge to a Clinical Need. Ed. by F. W. Merkus & L. Hendeles. (Current Clinical Practice Ser.: Vol. 3). 175p. 1983. 60.00 (ISBN 0-444-90318-6, Excerpta Medica). Elsevier.
Sustained Release Theophylline & Nocturnal Asthma: Current Clinical Practice, Vol. 18. Ed. by A. F. Isles & P. Von Wichert. 182p. 1985. 78.00 (ISBN 0-444-90404-2). Elsevier.
Sustained Timed Writings. 4th ed. Robert L. Grubbs & James L. White. 96p. 1982. pap. 10.36 (ISBN 0-07-025063-4). McGraw.
Sustaining. Connie Rector. 79p. 1985. 7.95 (ISBN 0-934126-59-3). Randall Bk Co.
Sustaining Agriculture near Cities. Ed. by William Lockeretz. (Orig.). 1988. pap. text ed. 12.00 (ISBN 0-935734-17-1). Soil & Water Conserv.
Sustaining Hand: Community Leadership & Corporate Power. Bryan D. Jones et al. (Studies in Government & Public Policy). xii, 260p. 1986. 27.50x (ISBN 0-7006-0278-X); pap. 9.95x (ISBN 0-7006-0279-8). U Pr of KS.
Sustaining Love: Healing & Growth in the Passages of Marriage. David Augsburger. Ed. by Earl Roe. 196p. 1988. 14.95 (ISBN 0-8307-1318-2, 5111782). Regal.
Sustaining Power of Hope. Leslie B. Flynn. 132p. 1985. pap. 5.50 (ISBN 0-89693-600-7). Victor Bks.
Sustaining Systems: A Preventive Maintenance Program. Michael P. Seidler. (Illus.). 34p. 1986. 3-ring binder 39.95 (ISBN 0-939335-01-8). Sustaining Syst.
Sustaining Tomorrow: A Strategy for World Conservation & Development. Ed. by Francis R. Thibodeau & Hermann H. Field. LC 84-40297. (Illus.). 198p. 1984. 30.00x (ISBN 0-87451-305-7); pap. 15.00x (ISBN 0-87451-306-5). U Pr of New Eng.
Sustaining World Economic Recovery: The Challenges Ahead. Jean Baneth & Enzo Grilli. (Working Paper: No. 737). 82p. 1985. 5.00 (ISBN 0-8213-0546-8, WP 0737). World Bank.
Sustancia Mas Extraordinaria en el Mundo. I. V. Petrianov. 109p. 1980. pap. 2.75 (ISBN 0-8285-1864-5, Pub. by Mir Pubs USSR). Imported Pubns.
Susto: A Folk Illness. Arthur J. Rubel et al. Ed. by Charles Leslie. LC 84-214. (Comparative Studies of Health Systems & Medical Care: Vol. 12). (Illus.). 170p. 1985. text ed. 27.50x (ISBN 0-520-05196-3). U of Cal Pr.
Susu & the Mother Earth Family: A Foster Mothers Story. G. Elaine Anderson. Ed. by Gayle Landow & Grace M. Sandness. (Illus.). 250p. (Orig.). 1986. pap. write for info. Mini-World Pubns.
Susurros del Ser. Validivar. Tr. by AMORC Staff. 85p. (Orig., Span.). 1981. pap. 6.50 (ISBN 0-912057-80-7, GS-510). AMORC.
Susurrus. Jane B. Gillespie. LC 87-16829. (Orig.). 1987. pap. 7.95 (ISBN 0-87233-091-5). Bauhan.
Susy & Grand Unification from Strings to Collider Phenomenology: Proceedings of the 3rd CSIC Workshop; Madrid, Spain Jan-Feb 1985. Ed. by J. Leon et al. 530p. 1986. 64.00 (ISBN 9971-978-62-8). World Scientific Pub.
Susy's Scoundrel. Harold Keith. LC 74-1052. (Illus.). 160p. (gr. 5 up). 1974. 12.70 (ISBN 0-690-00496-6, Crowell Jr Bks). HarpJ.
Sut Lovingood: Yarns Spun by a Nat'ral Born Durn'd Fool. George W. Harris. Ed. by M. Thomas Inge. LC 87-20635. 324p. 1987. pap. 9.95 (ISBN 0-918518-59-8, St Luke TN). Peachtree Pubs.
Sut Lovingood's Yarns. George W. Harris. Ed. by M. Thomas Inge. (Masterworks of Literature Ser). 1966. pap. 8.95x (ISBN 0-8084-0290-0). New Coll U Pr.
Sutherland & Bonynge: An Intimate Biography. Quaintance Eaton. (Illus.). 1987. 21.95 (ISBN 0-396-08945-3). Dodd.
Sutherland, Lucy Stuart, Nineteen Three to Nineteen Eighty. Anne Whiteman. (Memoirs of the Fellows of the British Academy Ser.). (Illus.). 20p. 1985. pap. 5.50 (ISBN 0-85672-506-4, Pub. by British Acad). Longwood Pub Group.
Sutherland Statutory Construction, 6 vols. 4th ed. C. Sands. LC 84-22974. 1981. 280.00. Callaghan.
Sutherland: The Wartime Drawings. Roberto Tassi. Ed. & tr. by Julian Andrews. (Illus.). 172p. 1980. 29.95 (ISBN 0-85667-095-2). Sotheby Pubns.
Sutherland's War. Douglas Sutherland. (Illus.). 186p. 1985. 22.95 (ISBN 0-436-50601-7, Pub. by Secker & Warburg UK). David & Charles.
Sutivan: A Dalmatian Village in Social & Economic Transition. Brian C. Bennett. LC 73-80724. (Illus.). 1974. 10.00 (ISBN 0-88247-226-7). Ragusan Pr.
Sutra in Forty-Two Sections. Commentary by Tripitaka Master Hua. Tr. by Buddhist Text Translation Society. (Illus.). 114p. (Orig.). 1977. pap. 5.00 (ISBN 0-917512-15-4). Buddhist Text.
Sutra of the Past Vows of Earth Store Bodhisattva. Tr. by Buddhist Text Translation Society Staff. (Illus.). 120p. (Orig.). 1982. pap. text ed. 6.00 (ISBN 0-88139-502-1). Buddhist Text.
Sutra of the Past Vows of Earth Store Bodhisattva. Commentary by Tripitaka Master Hua. Tr. by Buddhist Text Translation Society Staff. LC 74-18135. (Illus.). 235p. (Orig.). 1976. 16.00. Buddhist Text.
Sutra of the Past Vows of Earthstore Bodhisattva: The Collected Lectures of Tripitaka Master Hsuan Hua. Husan Hua. Tr. by Heng Ching from Chinese. (IASWR Ser.). 235p. 1974. 12.75 (ISBN 0-686-47598-4, S-10); pap. 6.75 (ISBN 0-915078-00-7, S-11). Inst Adv Stud Wld.
Sutra of Wei Lang. Hui-neng. Tr. by Wong Mou-lam from Chinese. LC 73-879. (China Studies: from Confucius to Mao Ser.). 128p. 1973. Repr. of 1944 ed. 15.75 (ISBN 0-88355-073-3). Hyperion Conn.
Sutra on the Eight Realizations of the Great Beings. Thich Nhat-Hahn. Tr. by Diem T. Truong & Carole Melkonian. 22p. 1987. pap. 3.00 (ISBN 0-938077-07-4). Parallax Pr.
Sutra on the Full Awareness of Breathing. Thich Nhat-Hanh. Tr. by Annabel Laity from Vietnamese. 72p. (Orig.). 1988. pap. 6.00 (ISBN 0-938077-04-X). Parallax Pr.
Sutra Spoken by Vimilakirti. Ed. by Kevin O'Neil. pap. 6.00 (ISBN 0-86627-009-4). Crises Res Pr.
Sutta-Nipata. Ed. by Dines Andersen & Helmer Smith. LC 78-70124. Repr. of 1913 ed. 27.00 (ISBN 0-404-17383-7). AMS Pr.
Sutta-Nipata. Ed. & tr. by H. Saddhatissa. 160p. 1988. pap. 40.00x (ISBN 0-7007-0181-8, Pub. by Curzon Pr Ltd UK). State Mutual Bk.
Sutta Nipata: Or Dialogues & Discourses of Gotama Buddha. Intro. by Swamy M. Coomara. LC 78-70125. 1980. Repr. of 1874 ed. 23.00 (ISBN 0-404-17384-5). AMS Pr.
Sutter Buttes: A Naturalist's View. Walt Anderson. LC 82-90753. (Illus.). 346p. 1983. 18.95 (ISBN 0-9610722-0-2). Nat Select.

Sutter Buttes of California: A Study of Plio-Pleistocene Volcanism. Howell Williams & G. H. Curtis. (UC Publications in Social Sciences: Vol. 116). 1979. Repr. of 1977 ed. 22.50x (ISBN 0-520-03808-8). U of Cal Pr.

Sutter of California. James Dana. lib. bdg. 29.00 (ISBN 0-403-08971-9). Scholarly.

Sutton Hoo: The Excavation of a Royal Ship-Burial. Charles Green. 1988. 24.95 (ISBN 0-389-20775-6). B&N Imports.

Suttons Synagogue: Or the English Centurion (A Sermon) Percival Burrell. LC 74-28822. (English Experience Ser.: No. 647). 1974. Repr. of 1629 ed. 3.50 (ISBN 90-221-0647-0). Walter J Johnson.

Sutton's Warbler: A Critical Review & Summation of Current Data. Carl W. Carlson et al. (Atlantic Naturalist Ser.: Vol. 34). 24p. 1981. 3.50 (ISBN 0-318-20252-2). Audubon Naturalist.

Suttree. Cormac McCarthy. LC 86-40171. 480p. 1986. pap. 6.95 (ISBN 0-394-74145-5, Vin). Random.

Sutured Words: Contemporary Poetry about Medicine. Jon Mukand. LC 87-71549. (Illus.). 424p. (Orig.). 1987. pap. 18.00x (ISBN 0-9619150-0-5). Aviva Pr.

Su'udi Relations with Eastern Arabia & Uman, 1800-1871. Z. M. Al-Rashid. 192p. 1981. 60.00x (ISBN 0-317-39159-3, Pub. by Luzac & Co Ltd). State Mutual Bk.

Suum Cuique. facs. ed. Oscar G. Sonneck. LC 70-76916. (Essay Index Reprint Ser). 1916. 18.00 (ISBN 0-8369-0031-6). Ayer Co Pubs.

Suwanee River Tales. facsimile ed. Sherwood Bonner. LC 73-38641. (Black Heritage Library Collection). (Illus.). Repr. of 1884 ed. 20.25 (ISBN 0-8369-8999-6). Ayer Co Pubs.

Suwannee River: Strange Green Land. Cecile H. Matschat. LC 79-5190. (Brown Thrasher Bks.). (Illus.). 308p. 1980. 20.00x (ISBN 0-8203-0508-1); pap. 7.95 (ISBN 0-8203-0496-4). U of Ga Pr.

Suye Mura: A Japanese Village. John F. Embree. LC 40-1477. (Illus.). 1939. 15.00x (ISBN 0-226-20631-9). U of Chicago Pr.

Suye Mura: A Japanese Village. John F. Embree. LC 40-1477. (Illus.). 1964. pap. 3.25 (ISBN 0-226-20632-7, P173, Phoen). U of Chicago Pr.

Suzannah, Teach Me to Love - Grace, Sing to Me. Judy Hogan. 82p. 1986. 14.95 (ISBN 0-89002-259-3); pap. 6.95 (ISBN 0-317-65407-1). Carolina Wren.

Suzanne & the Pacific. Jean Giraudoux. Tr. by Ben R. Redman from Fr. 286p. 1975. Repr. of 1923 ed. 25.00x (ISBN 0-86527-311-1). Fertig.

Suzanne et le Pacifique. Jean Giraudoux. pap. 9.95 (ISBN 0-685-33930-0). French & Eur.

Suzanne et les Jeunes Hommes see Chronique des Pasquier.

Suzanne et les Juenes Hommes see Chronique des Pasquier.

Suzanne Helmuth & Jack Reynolds: Photographas & Documents, 1975-1985. Philip Brookman. (Illus.). 46p. 1986. write for info. (ISBN 0-939982-06-4). Sesnon Art Gall.

Suzanne Stephens: Writings on Architecture. Lamia Doumato. (Architecture Ser.: A 1946). 14p. 1987. 3.75 (ISBN 1-55590-556-0). Vance Biblios.

Suzanne Valadon. Jeanine Warnod. (Illus.). 1981. 14.95 (ISBN 0-517-54499-7). Crown.

Suzanne White's Book of Chinese Chance. Suzanne White. 384p. 1980. pap. 2.50 (ISBN 0-449-24194-7, Crest). Fawcett.

Suzanne's Cooking Secrets. Suzanne W. Pierot. (Illus.). 1981. pap. 5.95 (ISBN 0-393-00055-9). Norton.

Suzette & Nicholas & the Seasons Clock. Marie-France Mangin. (Illus.). 32p. (ps-k). 1982. 8.95 (ISBN 0-399-20832-1, Philomel). Putnam Pub Group.

Suzette & Nicholas in the Garden. Satomi Ichikawa. LC 86-10194. (Illus.). 32p. (ps-2). 1986. 7.95 (ISBN 0-312-77982-8). St Martin.

Suzhou. Compiled by An Chunyang. (Illus.). 142p. 1984. 70.00x (ISBN 0-317-69223-2, Pub. by Han-Shan Tang Ltd). State Mutual Bk.

Suzi Sinzinnati. Joe D. Bellamy. 1989. 18.95 (ISBN 0-916366-56-1). Pushcart Pr.

Suzuki. Geoff Aspel. LC 83-73616. (Illus.). 64p. (Orig.). 1984. pap. 3.95 (ISBN 0-668-06171-5). Arco.

Suzuki ALT & LT185 & 125: 1983-85. 207p. (Orig.). 1985. pap. 13.95 (ISBN 0-89287-393-0, M381). Clymer Pub.

Suzuki Cello School, Cello Part, Vol. 2. Shinichi Suzuki. (Suzuki Cello School Ser.). 24p. (Japanese.). (gr. k-12). 1980. pap. text ed. 6.50 (ISBN 0-87487-258-8, Suzuki Method). Birch Tree Gr.

Suzuki Cello School, Cello Part, Vol. 3. Shinichi Suzuki. (Suzuki Cello School Ser.). 32p. (Japanese.). (gr. k-12). 1980. pap. text ed. 6.50 (ISBN 0-87487-259-6, Suzuki Method). Birch Tree Gr.

Suzuki Cello School, Cello Part, Vol. 7. Shinichi Suzuki. (Suzuki Cello School Ser.). 24p. (gr. k-12). 1987. pap. text ed. 6.50 (ISBN 0-87487-360-6, Suzuki Method). Birch Tree Gr.

Suzuki Cello School: Piano Accompaniment, Vol. 5. Shinichi Suzuki. (Suzuki Cello School (Suzuki Method) Ser.). 24p. (gr. k-12). 1983. pap. text ed. 6.50 (ISBN 0-87487-270-7, Suzuki Method). Birch Tree Gr.

Suzuki Cello School, Piano Accompaniments, Vol. 7. Shinichi Suzuki. (Suzuki Cello School Ser.). 32p. (gr. k-12). 1987. pap. text ed. 6.50 (ISBN 0-87487-361-4, Suzuki Method). Birch Tree Gr.

Suzuki Cello School, Vol. 1: Piano Accompaniment. Shinichi Suzuki. (Suzuki Cello School Ser.). 24p. (gr. k-12). 1982. pap. text ed. 6.50 (ISBN 0-87487-263-4, Suzuki Method). Birch Tree Gr.

Suzuki Cello School, Vol. 2: Piano Accompaniment. Shinichi Suzuki. (Suzuki Cello School Ser.). 24p. (gr. k-12). 1982. pap. text ed. 6.50 (ISBN 0-87487-264-2, Suzuki Method). Birch Tree Gr.

Suzuki Cello School, Vol. 3: Piano Accompaniment. Shinichi Suzuki. 32p. (gr. k-12). 1983. pap. text ed. 6.50 (ISBN 0-87487-265-0, Suzuki Method). Birch Tree Gr.

Suzuki Cello School, Vol. 4: Cello Part. Shinichi Suzuki. (Suzuki Cello School (Suzuki Method) Ser.). 16p. (gr. k-12). 1983. pap. text ed. 6.50 (ISBN 0-87487-266-9, Suzuki Method). Birch Tree Gr.

Suzuki Cello School, Vol. 4: Piano Accompaniment. Shinichi Suzuki. (Suzuki Cello School (Suzuki Method) Ser.). 24p. (gr. k-12). 1983. pap. text ed. 6.50 (ISBN 0-87487-269-3, Suzuki Method). Birch Tree Gr.

Suzuki Cello School, Vol. 5: Cello Part. Shinichi Suzuki. (Suzuki Cello School (Suzuki Method) Ser.). 24p. (gr. k-12). pap. text ed. 6.50 (ISBN 0-87487-267-7, Suzuki Method). Birch Tree Gr.

Suzuki Cello School, Vol 6: Cello Part. Shinichi Suzuki. 16p. (gr. k-12). pap. text ed. 6.50 (ISBN 0-87487-268-5, Suzuki Method). Birch Tree Gr.

Suzuki Cello School, Vol. 6: Piano Accompaniments. Shinichi Suzuki. (Suzuki Cello School (Suzuki Method) Ser.). 24p. (Orig.). (gr. 6-12). 1984. pap. text ed. 6.50 (ISBN 0-87487-271-5, Suzuki Method). Birch Tree Gr.

Suzuki Changed My Life. Maasaki Honda. (Illus.). 320p. 1976. pap. text ed. 12.95 (ISBN 0-87487-084-4, Suzuki Method). Birch Tree Gr.

Suzuki Concept: An Introduction to a Successful Method for Early Music Education. Ed. by Elizabeth Mills & Sr. Therese Murphy. (Illus.). 220p. 1973. pap. 7.95 (ISBN 0-87297-003-5). Diablo.

Suzuki Education in Action: A Story of Talent Training from Japan. Clifford A. Cook. LC 74-136977. 1970. 7.50 (ISBN 0-682-47192-5, University). Exposition-Phoenix.

Suzuki Flute School, Piano Accompaniments, Vol. 1. Shinichi Suzuki. 24p. (Orig.). 1971. pap. text ed. 6.50 (ISBN 0-87487-166-2, Suzuki Method). Birch Tree Gr.

Suzuki Flute School, Piano Accompaniments, Vol. 4. Shinichi Suzuki. 24p. (Orig.). 1971. pap. text ed. 6.50 (ISBN 0-87487-172-7, Suzuki Method). Birch Tree Gr.

Suzuki Flute School: Piano Accompaniments, Vol. 2. Shinichi Suzuki. 16p. (Orig.). (gr. k-6). 1971. pap. text ed. 6.50 (ISBN 0-87487-168-9, Suzuki Method). Birch Tree Gr.

Suzuki Flute School: Vol. 1-Flute Part. Shinichi Suzuki. 24p. (gr. k-6). 1971. pap. text ed. 6.50 (ISBN 0-87487-165-4). Birch Tree Gr.

Suzuki Flute School: Vol. 3-Flute Part. Shinichi Suzuki. 16p. (Orig.). (gr. k-8). 1971. pap. text ed. 6.50 (ISBN 0-87487-169-7, Suzuki Method). Birch Tree Gr.

Suzuki Flute School, Vol. 3: Piano Accompaniments. Shinichi Suzuki. 32p. (Orig.). 1971. pap. text ed. 6.50 (ISBN 0-87487-170-0, Suzuki Method). Birch Tree Gr.

Suzuki Flute School: Vol. 4-Flute Part. Shinichi Suzuki. 16p. (Orig.). (gr. k-8). 1971. pap. text ed. 6.50 (ISBN 0-87487-171-9, Suzuki Method). Birch Tree Gr.

Suzuki Flute School: Vol. 5-Flute Part. Shinichi Suzuki. 24p. (gr. 6-12). 1971. pap. text ed. 6.50 (ISBN 0-87487-173-5, Suzuki Method). Birch Tree Gr.

Suzuki Flute School, Vol. 5: Piano Accompaniments. Shinichi Suzuki. 32p. (Orig.). 1971. pap. text ed. 6.50 (ISBN 0-87487-174-3, Suzuki Method). Birch Tree Gr.

Suzuki GS & GSX1100 Chain Drive Fours: 1980-1981 (Service, Repair, Performance) David Sales. (Illus., Orig.). 1981. pap. 17.95 (ISBN 0-89287-353-1, M378). Clymer Pub.

Suzuki: GS400-450 Twins 1977-1983 Service, Repair, Performance. (Illus.). pap. 13.95 (ISBN 0-89287-237-3, M372). Clymer Pub.

Suzuki: GS550 Fours, 1977-1986 - Service, Repair, Performance. (Illus.). pap. 17.95 (ISBN 0-89287-273-X, M373). Clymer Pub.

Suzuki GS650 Fours, 1981 to 1983: Service Repair Performance. (Illus.). 326p. 1983. 17.95 (ISBN 0-89287-367-1, M364). Clymer Pub.

Suzuki GS750 Fours, 1977-1982: Service, Repair, Performance. (Illus.). pap. 17.95 (ISBN 0-89287-189-X, M370). Clymer Pub.

Suzuki GS850 & GS1100 Shaft Drive Fours 1979-1984: Service, Repair, Maintenance. (Illus., Orig.). pap. text ed. 17.95 (ISBN 0-89287-305-1, M376). Clymer Pub.

Suzuki Harp School, Vol. 1. Mary K. Waddington. Ed. by Shinichi Suzuki. (Suzuki Harp Method Ser.). 32p. (Orig.). 1985. pap. text ed. 6.50 (ISBN 0-87487-290-1, Suzuki Method). Birch Tree Gr.

Suzuki in the String Class: An Adaptation of the Teachings of Shinichi Suzuki. Paul Zahtilla. LC 70-178376. pap. 48.30 incl. tchr.'s manual (score) & pts. for bass, cello, viola & violin (ISBN 0-317-26425-7, 2024981). Bks Demand UMI.

Suzuki LT230, 1985-1986: Service, Repair, Maintenance. (Illus.). 247p. (Orig.). pap. 14.95 (ISBN 0-89287-423-6, M475). Clymer Pub.

Suzuki Outboard Shop Manual: 2-140 HP 1977-1984. (Illus.). 368p. (Orig.). 1985. pap. 24.95 (B780). Clymer Pub.

Suzuki Parent's Diary: Or How I Survived My First 10,000 Twinkles. Carroll Morris. (Illus.). 1984. pap. 6.95 (ISBN 0-918194-14-8, Pub. by Ability Devel). Accura.

Suzuki PE175-400 Singles 1977-1981 Service, Repair, Performance. (Illus., Orig.). pap. text ed. 13.95 (ISBN 0-89287-328-0, M377). Clymer Pub.

Suzuki Pianist's List of Supplementary Materials: An Annotated Bibliography. Beverly T. Graham. LC 81-65666. 1981. pap. 4.95 (ISBN 0-918194-11-3, Pub. by Ability Devel). Accura.

Suzuki Piano School, Vol. 1. Ed. by Shinichi Suzuki. 32p. (Orig.). (gr. k-3). 1978. pap. text ed. 6.50 (ISBN 0-87487-160-3, Suzuki Method). Birch Tree Gr.

Suzuki Piano School, Vol. 2. Shinichi Suzuki. (Suzuki Piano School Ser.). 24p. (Ger., Fr., Span. & Japanese.). (gr. k-12). 1978. pap. text ed. 6.50 (ISBN 0-87487-161-1, Suzuki Method). Birch Tree Gr.

Suzuki Piano School, Vol. 3. Shinichi Suzuki. (Suzuki Piano School Ser.). 32p. (Ger., Fr., Span. & Japanese.). (gr. k-12). 1970. pap. text ed. 6.50 (ISBN 0-87487-162-X, Suzuki Method). Birch Tree Gr.

Suzuki Piano School, Vol. 4. Shinichi Suzuki. (Suzuki Piano School Ser.). 32p. (Ger., Fr., Span. & Japanese.). (gr. 3-12). 1978. pap. text ed. 6.50 (ISBN 0-87487-163-8, Suzuki Method). Birch Tree Gr.

Suzuki Piano School, Vol. 5. Shinichi Suzuki. (Suzuki Piano School Ser.). 48p. (Japanese.). (gr. 4-12). 1973. pap. text ed. 8.50 (ISBN 0-87487-099-2, Suzuki Method). Birch Tree Gr.

Suzuki Piano School, Vol. 6. Shinichi Suzuki. (Suzuki Piano School Ser.). 48p. (Japanese.). (gr. 4-12). 1973. pap. text ed. 8.50 (ISBN 0-87487-101-8, Suzuki Method). Birch Tree Gr.

Suzuki RM 125-500 Single Shock: 1981-1984 Service Repair Performance. (Illus.). 242p. 1985. pap. 13.95 (ISBN 0-89287-385-X, M379). Clymer Pub.

Suzuki RM 50-400cc Twin Shock, 1975-81: Service, Repair, Performance. (Illus.). pap. 13.95 (ISBN 0-89287-196-2, M371). Clymer Pub.

Suzuki Service-Repair Handbook 125-500cc Twins: 1964-1976. 3rd rev. ed. Ray Hoy. (Illus.). pap. 13.95 (ISBN 0-89287-132-6, M 366). Clymer Pub.

Suzuki Viola School. Ed. by Doris Preucil & Shinichi Suzuki. (Piano Accompaniment Ser.). 64p. (gr. k-12). 1982. pap. text ed. 10.95 (ISBN 0-87487-245-6, Suzuki Method). Birch Tree Gr.

Suzuki Viola School: Piano Accompaniment, Vol. 3. Doris Preucil. Ed. by Shinichi Suzuki. 32p. (gr. k-12). 1983. pap. text ed. 6.50 (ISBN 0-87487-246-4, Suzuki Method). Birch Tree Gr.

Suzuki Viola School: Piano Accompaniment, Vol. 4. Shinichi Suzuki. Ed. by Doris Preucil. 64p. (gr. k-12). 1983. pap. text ed. 10.95 (ISBN 0-87487-275-8, Suzuki Method). Birch Tree Gr.

Suzuki Viola School, Piano Accompaniments, Vol. 5. Shinichi Suzuki. (Suzuki Viola School Ser.). 52p. (gr. k-12). 1986. pap. text ed. 6.50 (ISBN 0-87487-250-2, Suzuki Method). Birch Tree Gr.

Suzuki Viola School, Viola Part, Vol. 1. Doris Preucil. Ed. by Shinichi Suzuki. (Suzuki Viola School Ser.). 32p. (gr. k-12). 1981. pap. text ed. 6.50 (ISBN 0-87487-241-3). Birch Tree Gr.

Suzuki Viola School, Viola Part, Vol. 2. Doris Preucil. Ed. by Shinichi Suzuki. (Suzuki Viola School Ser.). 32p. (gr. k-12). 1982. pap. text ed. 6.50 (ISBN 0-87487-242-1). Birch Tree Gr.

Suzuki Viola School: Viola Part, Vol. 3. Shinichi Suzuki. Ed. by Doris Preucil. (Suzuki Viola School Ser.). 24p. (gr. k-12). 1983. pap. text ed. 6.50 (ISBN 0-87487-243-X, Suzuki Method). Birch Tree Gr.

Suzuki Viola School: Viola Part, Vol. 4. Shinichi Suzuki. Ed. by Doris Preucil. (Suzuki Viola School Ser.). 32p. (gr. k-12). 1983. pap. text ed. 6.50 (ISBN 0-87487-244-8, Suzuki Method). Birch Tree Gr.

Suzuki Viola School, Viola Part, Vol. 5. Shinichi Suzuki. Ed. by Doris Preucil. (Suzuki Cello School Ser.). 32p. 1986. pap. text ed. 6.50 (ISBN 0-87487-249-9). Birch Tree Gr.

Suzuki Violin Method in American Music Education. rev. ed. John Kendall. 40p. 1985. pap. text ed. 6.50 (ISBN 0-87487-280-4, Suzuki Method). Birch Tree Gr.

Suzuki Violin School, Piano Accompaniments, Vol. B. Shinichi Suzuki. (Suzuki Violin School Ser.). 192p. (Japanese.). 1980. pap. text ed. 24.95 (ISBN 0-87487-228-6). Birch Tree Gr.

Suzuki Violin School, Piano Accompaniments, Vol. 1. Shinichi Suzuki. 24p. 1978. pap. text ed. 6.50 (ISBN 0-87487-145-X, Suzuki Method). Birch Tree Gr.

Suzuki Violin School, Piano Accompaniments, Vol. 2. Shinichi Suzuki. 32p. (Ger., Fr., Span. & Japanese.). 1970. pap. text ed. 6.50 (ISBN 0-87487-147-6, Suzuki Method). Birch Tree Gr.

Suzuki Violin School, Piano Accompaniments, Vol. 3. S inichi Suzuki. 32p. (Ger., Fr., Span. & Japanese.). 1970. pap. text ed. 6.50 (ISBN 0-87487-149-2, Suzuki Method). Birch Tree Gr.

Suzuki Violin School, Piano Accompaniments, Vol. 4. Shinichi Suzuki. 32p. (Ger., Fr., Span. & Japanese.). 1970. pap. text ed. 6.50 (ISBN 0-87487-151-4, Suzuki Method). Birch Tree Gr.

Suzuki Violin School: Piano Accompaniments, Vol. 5. 39p. (Ger., Fr., Span. & Japanese.). 1971. pap. text ed. 7.50 (ISBN 0-87487-153-0). Birch Tree Gr.

Suzuki Violin School, Violin Part, Vol. 6. Shinichi Suzuki. (Suzuki Violin School Ser.). 24p. (Ger., Fr., Span. & Japanese.). (gr. 5-12). 1978. pap. text ed. 6.50 (ISBN 0-87487-154-9). Birch Tree Gr.

Suzuki Violin School, Violin Part, Vol. 7. Shinichi Suzuki. (Suzuki Violin School Ser.). 24p. (Ger., Fr., Span. & Japanese.). (gr. 6-12). 1978. pap. text ed. 6.50 (ISBN 0-87487-156-5). Birch Tree Gr.

Suzuki Violin School, Violin Part, Vol. 8. Shinichi Suzuki. (Suzuki Violin School Ser.). 24p. (Ger., Fr., Span. & Japanese.). (gr. 6-12). 1978. pap. text ed. 6.50 (ISBN 0-87487-158-1). Birch Tree Gr.

Suzuki Violin School, Violin Part, Vol. 9. Shinichi Suzuki. (Suzuki Violin School Ser.). 48p. (Japanese.). (gr. 6-12). 1975. pap. text ed. 8.50 (ISBN 0-87487-225-1). Birch Tree Gr.

Suzuki Violin School, Violin Part, Vol. 10. Shinichi Suzuki. (Suzuki Violin School Ser.). 48p. (Japanese.). (gr. 6-12). 1976. pap. text ed. 8.50 (ISBN 0-87487-226-X). Birch Tree Gr.

Suzuki Violinist. William Starr. (Illus.). 142p. 1976. pap. 9.95 (ISBN 0-317-06502-5). Kingston Ellis.

Suzuki: 125-400cc Singles, 1964-1981 Service, Repair, Performance. 3rd ed. (Illus.). pap. 13.95 (ISBN 0-89287-280-2, M369). Clymer Pub.

Suzuki: 2-140 Hp Outboards, 1977-1988. (Illus.). 300p. 1988. pap. 24.95 (ISBN 0-89287-406-6). Western Marine Ent.

Suzuki: 380-750cc Triples, 1972-1977 Service, Repair, Maintenance. Clymer Publications Staff. (Illus.). 1977. pap. 13.95 (ISBN 0-89287-285-3, M368). Clymer Pub.

Suzy McKee Charnas, Octavia Butler, & Joan D. Vinge. Marleen S. Barr et al. LC 86-34308. (Starmont Reader's Guides Ser.: No. 23). 96p. 1986. Repr. lib. bdg. 17.95x (ISBN 0-89370-950-6). Borgo Pr.

Suzy Prudden's Exercise Program for Young Children. Suzy Prudden. LC 82-40506. (Illus.). 192p. 1983. pap. 6.95 (ISBN 0-89480-371-9, 371). Workman Pub.

Suzy Prudden's I Can Exercise Anywhere Book. Suzy Prudden & Jeffrey Sussman. LC 81-40507. (Illus.). 160p. 1981. pap. 4.95 (ISBN 0-89480-186-4, 468). Workman Pub.

Suzy Prudden's Pregnancy & Back-to-Shape Exercise Program. Suzy Prudden & Jeffrey Sussman. LC 80-51614. (Illus.). 224p. 1980. pap. 7.95 (ISBN 0-89480-129-5, 430). Workman Pub.

Suzy Prudden's Spot Reducing Program. Suzy Prudden & Jeffrey Sussman. LC 79-64784. (Illus.). 224p. 1979. pap. 7.95 (ISBN 0-89480-114-7, 288). Workman Pub.

Suzy Swoof. Michael P. Waite. LC 87-5269. (Christian Character Builders Ser.). (ps-3). 1987. 5.95 (ISBN 1-55513-219-7, Chariot Bks). Cook.

Suzy Who? Winifred Madison. 172p. (Orig.). (gr. 7 up). 1981. pap. 1.95 (ISBN 0-590-31822-5, Wildfire). Scholastic Inc.

SU3 X SU2 X U1 & Beyond: Proceedings of the XIIIth GIFT International Seminar on Theoretical Physics & Xth Winter Meeting on Fundamentals Physics Masella, Girona, Spain, Jan. 28-Feb. 6, 1982. Ed. by A. Ferrando et al. 516p. 1983. 67.00 (ISBN 9971-950-79-0). World Scientific Pub.

Svan-English Dictionary. Chato Gudjedjiani & Letas Palmaitis. LC 85-4089. 1985. 55.00x (ISBN 0-88206-062-7). Caravan Bks.

Svayamvara & Other Poems. Jayanta Mahapatra. (Redbird Bk.). 1976. 6.75 (ISBN 0-89253-558-X); flexible bdg. 4.00 (ISBN 0-89253-091-X). Ind-US Inc.

Svea: The Dancing Moose. LaVere Anderson. LC 77-13922. (Famous Animal Stories Ser.). (Illus.). 48p. (gr. 2-5). 1978. PLB 6.89 (ISBN 0-8116-4862-1). Garrard.

Svengali's Secrets & Memoirs of the Golden Age. J. H. Duval. 5.95 (ISBN 0-8315-0014-X). Speller.

Sven's Bridge. Anita Lobel. LC 65-14491. (Illus.). (gr. k-3). 1965. PLB 11.89 (ISBN 0-06-023926-3). HarpJ.

Svensk-Dansk Ordbog. V. Palmgen & E. Hartmann. 251p. (Slovene & Danish.). 1978. 39.95 (ISBN 87-01-52371-6, M-1287). French & Eur.

Svenska-Engelsk Ordbok, Vol. I. Karre. 1986. 95.00x (ISBN 91-241-4308-1, S132). Vanous.

Svenska Fur Er, Part 1. S. Higelin et al. (Illus.). Set. pap. text ed. 27.50x exercise, wordlist (S174); tchr's manual o.p. 8.50 (S174T); 4 cassettes 70.00x (S174C). Vanous.

Svenska Fur Er, Part 2. S. Higelin et al. (Illus.). 1971. Set. pap. text ed. 27.50x exercise wordlist (ISBN 0-89918-188-0, S188). 3 cassettes 60.00 (S188). Vanous.

Svenska Fur Nyborjaae, Vol. 1. E. Heider et al. 1978. 22.00x ea. (ISBN 0-89918-212-7, S212); Vanous.

Svetasvatara Upanisad, 2 pts. in 1. Tr. by Siddhesvar Varma Shastri. LC 73-3810. (Sacred Books of the Hindus: Vol. 18, Pt. 2). Repr. of 1916 ed. 18.00 (ISBN 0-404-57840-3). AMS Pr.

Svetasvataropanisad. Tr. by Swami Tyagisananda. (Sanskrit & Eng.). pap. 2.50 (ISBN 0-87481-418-9). Vedanta Pr.

Svetlana Beriosova: A Biography. A. H. Franks. (Series in Dance). 1978. Repr. of 1958 ed. 25.00 (ISBN 0-306-79537-X). Da Capo.

Sviatoslav the Conqueror: Emperor of Rus'-Ukraine. Jurij A. Luciw. 1985. 30.00 (ISBN 0-317-12226-6). Slavia Lib.

Svidetelstvo Obvineniya. Vladimir Stepanov. (Illus.). 350p. Date not set. 20.00 (ISBN 0-9616413-2-0). Multilingual.

Svjatejshij Tikhon, Patrijarkh Moskovskij i Vseja Rossij. 80p. 1965. pap. 3.00 (ISBN 0-317-29216-1). Holy Trinity.

Svjatitel' Tikhon, Episkop Voronjezhskij i Zadonskij. N. Sergijevsky. 213p. pap. 8.00 (ISBN 0-317-29184-X). Holy Trinity.

Svjatoj Ioann (Pommer) Arkiepiskop Rihskij i Latvijskij. Lugmilla Koehler. (Illus.). 72p. 1985. pap. 3.00 (ISBN 0-317-29224-2). Holy Trinity.

Svjatoj Mark Efesskij i Florentijskaja Unia. Archimandrite Amvrossy Pogodin. 436p. (Orig.). 1963. pap. 15.00x (ISBN 0-88465-026-X). Holy Trinity.

Svjelij Otrok; Sbornik Statej o Tsarevichje Mutchenikje Alekseje i drugikh Tsarstvennikh Mutchenikakh. (Illus.). 105p. pap. 5.00 (ISBN 0-317-29229-3). Holy Trinity.

Svoboda: Wagner: Joseph Svoboda's Scenography for Richard Wagner's Opera. Jarka Burian. 1983. 35.00 (ISBN 0-8195-5088-4). Wesleyan U Pr.

Svyata Ukrayina. Oles Berdnyk. LC 80-51598. 208p. (Ukrainian.). 1980. pap. 8.75 (ISBN 0-914834-29-0). Smoloskyp.

Swabian Kreis: Institutional Growth in the Holy Roman Empire, 1648-1715. James Allen Vann. 1982. pap. 30.55. P Lang Pubs.

Swadeshi Bank from South India: A History of the Indian Bank 1907-1982. R. K. Seshadri. (Illus.). 249p. 1982. text ed. 27.50x (ISBN 0-86131-341-0, Pub. by Orient Longman Ltd India). Apt Bks.

Swag. Elmore Leonard. 240p. 1976. pap. 7.95 (ISBN 0-440-08449-0). Delacorte.

Swag. Elmore Leonard. 1984. pap. 3.95 (ISBN 0-440-18424-X). Dell.

Swahili: A Foundation for Speaking, Reading & Writing. Thomas J Hinnebusch & Sarah M Mirza. LC 78-65430. (Illus., English & Swahili). 1978. pap. 12.25 (ISBN 0-8191-0659-3). U Pr of Amer.

Swahili: Active Introduction-General Conversation. Foreign Service Institute Staff. 159p. 1966. with 2 cassettes 39.00x (ISBN 0-88432-110-X, W300). J Norton Pubs.

Swahili Basic Course. Foreign Service Institute Staff. 560p. (Swahili.). 1980. 215.00x (ISBN 0-88432-041-3, W426); 20 audio-cassettes incl. J Norton Pubs.

Swahili Chronicle of Ngazija. Said B. Ahmed. Ed. by Lyndon Harries. (African Humanities Ser.). (Illus.). 136p. (Orig.). 1977. pap. text ed. 5.00 (ISBN 0-941934-20-9). Indiana Africa.

Swahili Coast: Politics, Diplomacy & Trade on the East African Littoral, 1798-1856. C. S. Nicholls. LC 78-180670. 419p. 1971. 55.00 (ISBN 0-8419-0099-X, Africana). Holmes & Meier.

Swahili: Conversation & Grammar. 2nd ed. John Indakwa. LC 72-84022. pap. 130.00 (ISBN 0-317-26821-X, 2024309). Bks Demand UMI.

Swahili-English Dictionary. F. Johnson. 35.00 (ISBN 0-87557-079-8). Saphrograph.

Swahili Exercises. rev. ed. Edward Steere. Ed. by A. B. Heller. 1977. pap. 7.95x (ISBN 0-19-572433-X). Oxford U Pr.

Swahili for Travellers. Berlitz Editors. 1974. pap. 4.95 (ISBN 0-02-964220-5, Berlitz). Macmillan.

Swahili Grammar. 2nd ed. E. O. Ashton. 1976. pap. text ed. 6.50x (ISBN 0-582-62701-X). Longman.

Swahili Language: A Descriptive Language. E. N. Myachina. (Languages of Asia & Africa Ser.). 96p. (Orig.). 1981. pap. 15.95x (ISBN 0-7100-0849-X). Routledge Chapman & Hall.

Swahili Phrase Book. Theopolis L. Gilmore & Shadrack O. Kwasa. 384p. 1987. pap. 6.95 (ISBN 0-8044-6176-7, 0073). Hippocrene Bks.

Swahili Phrasebook. Robert Leonard. (Illus.). 104p. (Orig.). 1988. pap. 2.95 (ISBN 0-86442-025-0). Lonely Planet.

Swahili: Reconstructing the History & Language of An African Society, 800-1500. Derek Nurse & Thomas Spear. LC 84-3659. (Ethnohistory Ser.). (Illus.). 152p. 1985. pap. 13.95 (ISBN 0-8122-1207-X). U of Pa Pr.

Swahili Syntax. Anthony J. Vitale. 260p. 1981. 33.00x (ISBN 90-70176-38-6); pap. 22.90x (ISBN 90-70176-25-4). Foris Pubns.

Swahili Tales. Edward Steere. LC 78-63225. (Folktale). Repr. of 1870 ed. 38.00 (ISBN 0-404-16164-2). AMS Pr.

Swahili Tales, as Told by the Natives of Zanzibar. Edward Steere. 1870. 42.00 (ISBN 0-8115-3003-5). Kraus Repr.

S.W.A.K. Sealed with a Kiss. (Caprice Ser.: No. 14). 144p. 1985. pap. 2.25. Ace Bks.

Swallow. D. M. Thomas. LC 83-40666. 320p. 1984. 16.95 (ISBN 0-670-68609-3). Viking.

Swallow. D. M. Thomas. 1985. pap. 4.50 (ISBN 0-671-60607-7). WSP.

Swallow Barn; or, a Sojourn in the Old Dominion, Novel: Library of Southern Civilization Ser. John P. Kennedy. LC 85-23215. 535p. 1986. pap. text ed. 11.95 (ISBN 0-8071-1322-0). LA State U Pr.

Swallow-Book. Ernst Toller. LC 74-7005. (Studies in German Literature, No. 13). 1974. lib. bdg. 49.95x (ISBN 0-8383-1902-5). Haskell.

Swallow Island. Julia Ferrarie. (Illus.). 28p. 1981. 25.00 (ISBN 0-939622-14-9); pap. 7.00 (ISBN 0-939622-13-0). Four Zoas Night.

Swallow Right-or Else! Daniel Garliner. LC 78-75294. 110p. 1979. 9.00 (ISBN 0-87527-195-2). Green.

Swallow Shelter & Associated Sites. Gardiner F. Dalley. (University of Utah Anthropological Papers: No. 96). (Illus.). 1978. pap. 15.00x (ISBN 0-87480-143-5). U of Utah Pr.

Swallow the Lake. Clarence Major. LC 79-120258. (Wesleyan Poetry Program: Vol. 54). (Orig.). 1970. 17.00x (ISBN 0-8195-2054-3); pap. 8.95 (ISBN 0-8195-1054-8). Wesleyan U Pr.

Swallow the Sun, the Poetry of Lorinc Szabo. Anton N. Nyerges. 274p. 1986. pap. 21.00 (ISBN 0-9600954-4-6). Nyerges.

Swallowdale. Arthur Ransome. LC 84-48802. 448p. 1985. pap. 8.95 (ISBN 0-87923-572-1). Godine.

Swallowing Dust. Robert J. Stout. 1976. pap. 1.50 (ISBN 0-88031-033-2). Invisible-Red Hill.

Swallowing the Anchor. William McFee. LC 70-128275. (Essay Index Reprint Ser). 1925. 19.00 (ISBN 0-8369-1986-6). Ayer Co Pubs.

Swallows. Roland Duhlliard. Tr. by Barbara Wright from Fr. 128p. (Orig.). 1986. pap. 4.95 (ISBN 0-7145-0648-6). Riverrun NY.

Swallows. Peter Tate. (Illus.). 96p. 1988. 13.95 (ISBN 0-85493-140-6, Pub. by Gollancz England). David & Charles.

Swallows & Amazons. Arthur Ransome. (Illus.). 343p. 1980. Repr. of 1931 ed. lib. bdg. 25.00. Darby Bks.

Swallows & Amazons. Arthur Ransome. LC 84-48803. 352p. 1985. pap. 7.95 (ISBN 0-87923-573-X). Godine.

Swallowtail Butterflies. Jane Dallinger & Cynthia Overbeck. LC 82-15294. (Lerner Natural Science Bks.). (Illus.). 48p. (gr. 4-10). 1982. PLB 12.95 (ISBN 0-8225-1465-6). Lerner Pubns.

Swallowtail Butterflies of East Africa. R. H. Carcasson. 1984. 30.00x (ISBN 0-317-07177-7, Pub. by FW Classey UK). State Mutual Bk.

Swallowtail Butterflies of North America. Hamilton A. Tyler. LC 75-30569. (Illus.). 192p. (Orig.). 1975. 14.95 (ISBN 0-87961-039-5); pap. 8.95 (ISBN 0-87961-038-7). Naturegraph.

Swallowtail Butterfly. Hidetomo Oda. Ed. by Kathy Pohl. LC 85-28229. (Nature Close-Ups Ser.). (Illus.). 32p. (gr. 4). 1986. PLB 15.33 (ISBN 0-8172-2542-0); pap. text ed. 9.27 (ISBN 0-8172-2567-6). Raintree Pubs.

Swami Adbhutananda: Teachings & Reminiscences. Swami Chetanananda. LC 80-50962. (Illus.). 175p. 1980. pap. 6.95 (ISBN 0-916356-59-0). Vedanta Soc St Louis.

Swami & Friends. R. K. Narayan. LC 80-16119. 192p. 1980. lib. bdg. 13.00x (ISBN 0-226-56829-6); pap. 6.95 (ISBN 0-226-56831-8). U of Chicago Pr.

Swami & Sam: A Yoga Book. Brandt Dayton. (Illus.). 95p. (Orig.). pap. 0.95 (ISBN 0-89389-014-6). Himalayan Pubs.

Swami & the Comrade. K. K. Roy. 1975. 40.00 (ISBN 0-8283-1633-3). Branden Pub Co.

Swami Dayanand Saraswati. Krishna Singh Arya. 355p. 1987. 23.00x (ISBN 81-85054-22-3, Pub. by Manohar India). South Asia Bks.

Swami Dayananda Sarasvati. Krishan S. Arya. 355p. 1987. 23.00x (ISBN 0-8364-2096-9, Pub. by Manohar India). South Asia Bks.

Swami Krishnananda: In Conversation. 1983. 30.00x (ISBN 0-7069-2346-4, Pub. by Vikas India). Advent NY.

Swami Rama of the Himalayas. Ed. by L. K. Misra. (Illus.). 90p. (Orig.). 1976. pap. 4.95 (ISBN 0-89389-013-8). Himalayan Pubs.

Swami Ramakrishnananda: The Apostle of Sri Ramakrishna to the South. Swami Tapasyananda. 276p. 1973. 3.95 (ISBN 0-87481-453-7). Vedanta Pr.

Swami Shraddhanands: His Life & Causes. J. T. Jordens. 1981. 27.50x (ISBN 0-19-561252-3). Oxford U Pr.

Swami Turiyananda. Swami Ritajananda. (Illus.). pap. 1.95 (ISBN 0-87481-473-1). Vedanta Pr.

Swami Vijanananda: A Short Life. Compiled by Apurvananda. 173p. 1987. pap. 3.50 (ISBN 0-87481-547-9, Pub. by Ramakrishna Math Madras India). Vedanta Pr.

Swami Vijnanananda: His Life & Sayings. Swami Vishwashrayananda. Tr. by Devavrata Basu Ray from Bengali. 72p. 1981. pap. 1.95 (ISBN 0-87481-502-9). Vedanta Pr.

Swami Vivekananda & the Indian Quest for Socialism. Arun K. Biswas. 300p. 35.00 (ISBN 0-8364-1949-9, Pub. by KL Mukhopadhyay). South Asia Bks.

Swami Vivekananda in the West. Marie L. Burke. (Pt. III). (Illus.). 639p. 1987. 12.95x (ISBN 0-87481-220-8, Pub. by Advaita Ashram India). Vedanta Pr.

Swami Vivekananda in the West: New Discoveries: His Prophetic Mission, 2 Vols, Vol. 1. new ed. Marie L. Burke. (Illus.). 515p. text ed. 12.50x (ISBN 0-317-03702-1, Pub. by Advaita Ashrama India). Vedanta Pr.

Swami Vivekananda in the West: New Discoveries, Vol. II. Marie L. Burke. (Illus.). 457p. 1985. 12.50x (ISBN 0-87481-219-4, Pub. by Advaita Ashrama India). Vedanta Pr.

Swami Vivekananda: The Educator. V. Sukumaran Nair. 1987. text ed. 11.95x (ISBN 81-207-0610-2, Pub. by Sterling Pubs India). Apt Bks.

Swami Vivekananda's Contribution to the Present Age. Swami Satprakashananda. (Illus.). 249p. 1978. 9.50 (ISBN 0-916356-58-2, 77-91628). Vedanta Soc St Louis.

Swamp. Bill Thomas. (Illus.). 1976. 29.95 (ISBN 0-393-08747-6). Norton.

Swamp Angel. Dorothy Langley. 237p. 1982. o. p. 14.95 (ISBN 0-89733-060-9); pap. 6.95 (ISBN 0-89733-061-7). Academy Chi Pubs.

Swamp Fox. Robert Bass. LC 59-5368. (Illus.). 1982. pap. 7.50 (ISBN 0-87844-007-0). Sandlapper Pub Co.

Swamp Fox, Francis Marion. Noel B. Gerson. 19.95 (ISBN 0-88411-642-5, Pub. by Aeonian Pr). Amereon Ltd.

Swamp Man. Donald Goines. (Orig.). 1974. pap. 2.25 (ISBN 0-87067-026-3, BH026). Holloway.

Swamp Monsters. Mary B. Christian. LC 82-1574. (Easy-to-Read Bks.). (Illus.). 56p. (ps-3). 1983. PLB 8.89 (ISBN 0-8037-7616-0); pap. 3.95 (ISBN 0-8037-7614-4, 0383-120). Dial Bks Young.

Swamp Rice Farming: The Indigenous Pahang Malay Agricultural System. Donald H. Lambert. (Westview Replica Ser.). 230p. 1985. pap. 28.00x (ISBN 0-86531-892-1). Westview.

Swamp-Sago Industry in West Malaysia: A Study of the Sungei Batu Pahat Floodplain. Tan Koonlin. 174p. 1984. pap. text ed. 24.50x (ISBN 9971-902-66-4, Pub. by Inst Southeast Asian Stud). Gower Pub Co.

Swamp Sailors: Riverine Warfare in the Everglades, 1835-1842. George E. Buker. LC 74-186326. 152p. 1975. 10.00x (ISBN 0-8130-0352-0). U Presses Fla.

Swamp Sister. Robert E. Alter. LC 85-72783. 192p. 1986. pap. 3.95 (ISBN 0-88739-007-2, Pub. by Black Lizard Bks). Creative Arts Bk.

Swamp Water. Vereen Bell. LC 80-24570. (Brown Thrasher Bks.). 282p. 1981. 16.00x (ISBN 0-8203-0553-7); pap. 7.95 (ISBN 0-8203-0546-4). U of Ga Pr.

Swamp Water & Wiregrass: Historical Sketches of Coastal Georgia. George A. Rogers & R. Frank Saunders. LC 84-701. x, 254p. 1984. 19.95 (ISBN 0-86554-099-3, MUP/H91). Mercer Univ Pr.

Swamp Witch, No. 6. Laurie Bridges & Paul Alexander. (Dark Forces Ser.). 160p. (Orig.). (YA) (gr. 7-12). 1987. pap. 2.50 (ISBN 0-553-26792-2). Bantam.

Swampland Flowers: The Letters & Lectures of Zen Master Ta Hui. Ta Hui. Tr. by Christopher Cleary. LC 77-77853. 1977. pap. 3.95 (ISBN 0-394-17011-3, E696, Ever). Grove.

Swamps & Marshes. Francene Sabin. LC 84-2717. (Illus.). 32p. (gr. 3-6). 1985. PLB 8.45 (ISBN 0-8167-0280-2); pap. text ed. 1.95 (ISBN 0-8167-0281-0). Troll Assocs.

Swan. Naomi Lewis. LC 85-15961. (Illus.). 32p. (gr. k-3). 1986. 11.75 (ISBN 0-688-05534-6); PLB 11.88 (ISBN 0-688-05535-4). Lothrop.

Swan Among the Indians: Life of James Swan, 1818-1900. Lucile McDonald. LC 72-85230. (Illus.). 272p. 1972. 11.95 (ISBN 0-8323-0066-7). Binford-Metropolitan.

Swan & the Eagle: Essays on Indian English Literature. C. D Narasimhaiah. 220p. 1987. Repr. of 1968 ed. 16.50x (ISBN 81-208-0327-2, Pub. by Motilal Banarsidass). South Asia Bks.

Swan at the Well: Shakespeare Reading Chaucer. E. Talbot Donaldson. LC 84-21913. 192p. 1985. text ed. 20.00 (ISBN 0-300-03349-4). Yale U Pr.

Swan Cove. Jane W. Canfield. LC 77-11832. (Early I Can Read Bks.). (Illus.). 32p. (ps-3). 1978. PLB 11.89 (ISBN 0-06-020949-6). HarpJ.

Swan Dive: A Novel of Suspense. Jerimiah Healy. LC 87-46272. 224p. 1988. 16.95 (ISBN 0-06-015921-9, HarpT). Har-Row.

Swan Family. G. T. Ridlon. LC 70-142770. (Saco Valley Settlements Ser). 1970. pap. 1.50 (ISBN 0-8048-0840-6). C E Tuttle.

Swan Knight. W. Ray Rine. 1986. 7.50 (ISBN 0-8062-3003-7). Carlton.

Swan Lake. Anthea Bell. LC 86-9509. (Illus.). 28p. (gr. 1 up). 1986. 14.95 (ISBN 0-88708-028-6). Picture Bk Studio.

Swan Lake. Illus. & adapted by Donna Diamond. LC 79-11179. (Illus.). 32p. (gr. 2-6). 1980. reinforced bdg. 10.95 (ISBN 0-8234-0356-4). Holiday.

Swan Lake. As told by Mark Helprin. 1989. price not set. HM.

Swan Lake. Pam Kennedy. (Illus.). 48p. (gr. k-5). 1986. 5.95 (ISBN 0-8249-8151-0). Ideals.

Swan Lake. Anne Nugent. (Stories of the Ballets Ser.). (Illus.). 48p. 1985. 8.95 (ISBN 0-8120-5674-4). Barron.

Swan Lake. Catherine Storr. (Easy Piano Picture Bk.). 32p. 1987. 15.00 (ISBN 0-571-10077-5); pap. 7.95 (ISBN 0-571-10078-3). Faber & Faber.

Swan on the Lake. Jennifer Coldrey. LC 86-5719. (Animal Habitats Ser.). (Illus.). 32p. (gr. 4-6). 1987. 9.95 (ISBN 1-55532-066-X). Stevens Inc.

Swan Prince. Mikhail Baryshnikow & Peter Anastos. LC 87-47574. 80p. 1987. 16.95 (ISBN 0-553-05218-7). Bantam.

Swan Research. Grace Cavalieri. LC 78-64529. (Illus.). 1979. perfect bdg. 7.00 (ISBN 0-915380-08-0). Word Works.

Swan Sky. Keizaburo Tejima. (Illus.). 48p. (ps-2). 1988. 13.95 (ISBN 0-399-21547-6, Philomel Bks). Putnam Pub Group.

Swan Song. T. J. Binyon. 288p. 1986. pap. 3.50 (ISBN 0-8125-8095-8, Dist. by Warner Pub Services & Saint Martin's Press). Tor Bks.

Swan Song. Edmund Crispin. 192p. Repr. of 1947 ed. lib. bdg. 15.95 (ISBN 0-89190-692-4, Pub. by River City Pr). Amereon Ltd.

Swan Song. Robert McCammon. 1987. pap. 4.95 (ISBN 0-671-62413-X). PB.

Swan Song. Helen Robertson. Ed. by J. Barzun & W. H. Taylor. LC 81-47394. (Crime Fiction 1950-1975 Ser.). 192p. 1983. lib. bdg. 18.00 (ISBN 0-8240-4957-8). Garland Pub.

Swan Song: The Undiscovered Portrait of a Dying Swan. Henry Van McNeal. 90p. (Orig.). 1987. pap. 9.95 (ISBN 0-916641-26-0). Amer Songwriters Assn.

Swan: The History of a Brewery. Suzanne Welborn. (Illus.). 308p. 1987. 39.00 (ISBN 0-85564-271-8, Pub. by U of W Austral Pr); pap. 27.50 (ISBN 0-85564-272-6, Pub. by U of W Austral Pr). Intl Spec Bk.

Swan Villa. Martin Walser. Tr. by Leila Vennewitz. 1982. 14.95 (ISBN 0-03-059372-7). H Holt & Co.

Swan Villa. Martin Walser. 1987. pap. 7.95 (ISBN 0-317-58525-8). H Holt & Co.

Swann. Dan Sherman. 1979. pap. 1.95 (ISBN 0-449-24132-7, Crest). Fawcett.

Swann, Gibbons, Burrows, Slotznik, Galler. (Poetry Ser.: Vol. XX). 304p. 1980. 20.00 (ISBN 0-686-37991-8); pap. 10.00. Quarterly Rev.

Swann in Love. Marcel Proust. Tr. by C. K. Moncrieff & Terence Kilmartin. LC 84-7318. 320p. 1984. pap. 3.95 (ISBN 0-394-72769-X, Vin). Random.

Swann Song. Gibbs Davis. 176p. (YA) (gr. 7 up). 1989. pap. 2.50 (ISBN 0-380-75609-9, Flare). Avon.

Swann's Way. Marcel Proust. Tr. by C. K. Scott-Moncrieff. (YA) 1964. pap. write for info (ISBN 0-394-30967-7, T67, RanC). Random.

Swann's Way: The School Busing Case & the Supreme Court. Bernard Schwartz. 256p. 1986. 24.95x (ISBN 0-19-503888-6). Oxford U Pr.

Swans. Althea Braithwaite. (Life Cycle Bks.). (ps-6). 1988. PLB 7.95 (ISBN 0-88462-194-4); pap. 2.95 (ISBN 0-88462-195-2). Longman Crown.

Swans. Jack D. Scott. 64p. (gr. 5 up). 1987. 13.95 (ISBN 0-399-21406-2). Putnam Pub Group.

Swans: An Opera Libretto in Three Acts. Janet Lewis. 96p. (Orig.). 1986. pap. 10.00 (ISBN 0-936784-07-5). J Daniel.

Swans & Amber: Some Early Greek Lyrics. Dorothy B. Thompson. LC 49-6415. pap. 50.30 (ISBN 0-317-28162-3, 2014434). Bks Demand UMI.

Swan's Chance. Celeste De Blasis. LC 85-5999. 688p. (Orig.). 1986. pap. 4.50 (ISBN 0-553-25692-0). Bantam.

Swan's Chance. Celeste De Blasis & Celeste De Blasis. 560p. 1985. 16.95 (ISBN 0-553-05092-3). Bantam.

Swan's Island. Elizabeth Spires. 1985. pap. 8.95 (ISBN 0-03-004423-5, Owl Bks). H Holt & Co.

Swans of Brhyadr. Vivienne Couldrey. 224p. 1981. pap. 1.75 (ISBN 0-449-50166-3, Coventry). Fawcett.

Swans of the World. Sylvia B. Wilmore. LC 74-3669. (Illus.). 224p. 1974. 14.95 (ISBN 0-8008-7524-9). Taplinger.

Swans of the World. Sylvia B. Wilmore. LC 74-3669. (Illus.). 1979. pap. 8.50 (ISBN 0-8008-7523-0). Taplinger.

Swan's Wide Waters: Ramakrishna & Western Culture. new ed. Harold W. French. LC 74-77657. (National University Publications Ser.). 214p. 1974. 23.50x (ISBN 0-8046-9055-3, Pub by Kennikat). Assoc Faculty Pr.

Swan's Wing. Ursula Synge. 160p. 1985. pap. 2.75 (ISBN 0-441-79094-1, Pub. by Ace Science Fiction). Ace Bks.

Swanscombe Skull. A. T. Marston. Bd. with Report on the Swanscombe Skull. Swanscombe Committee of the Royal Anthropological Society. LC 78-72701. Repr. of 1938 ed. 27.50 (ISBN 0-404-18271-2). AMS Pr.

Swansdowne. Daniel Farson. 416p. 1987. 18.95 (ISBN 0-312-00690-X). St Martin.

Swansdowne. Daniel Farson. 402p. 1988. pap. 3.95 (ISBN 1-55547-245-1). Critics Choice Paper.

Swansong. Richard Francis. LC 86-47661. 304p. 1986. 15.95 (ISBN 0-689-11843-0). Atheneum.

Swansongs: Poems. Susan J. Lenier. (Oleander Modern Poets Ser.: Vol. 12). (Illus., Orig.). 1982. 15.00 (ISBN 0-906672-04-X); pap. 8.95 (ISBN 0-906672-03-1). Oleander Pr.

Swap. Norma Klein. LC 83-3383. 1983. 13.95 (ISBN 0-312-77988-7, Pub. by Marek). St Martin.

Swap. Norma Klein. 320p. 1984. pap. 3.75 (ISBN 0-380-68528-0). Avon.

Swap. Walter Wager. 320p. 1988. pap. 3.95 (ISBN 0-8125-1031-3). Tor Bks.

Swap & Go: Home Exchanging Made Easy. Albert C. Beerbower & Verna E. Beerbower. Date not set. write for info. S&S.

Swap & Go-Home Exchanging Made Easy. Albert C. Beerbower & Verna E. Beerbower. 248p. 1985. pap. 10.95 (ISBN 0-671-60228-4). Prentice Hall Pr.

Swap Finance Service. 394p. 1986. pap. 240.00 (ISBN 0-8002-4073-1). Intl Pubns Serv.

Swap Financing Techniques. Ed. by Boris Antl. (Euromoney Ser.). 168p. (Orig.). 1983. pap. 150.00 (ISBN 0-903121-49-2, Pub. by Woodhead-Faulkner). Longwood Pub Group.

Swapping. Shirley Lowe & Angela Ince. 240p. 1988. 17.95 (ISBN 0-316-53381-5). Little.

Swaraj: Cultural & Political. Pramatha N. Bose. 1986. Repr. 32.50 (ISBN 0-8364-1950-2, Pub. by Usha). South Asia Bks.

Swaraj in One Year. 2nd ed. Mohandas K. Gandhi. 1921. 14.50 (ISBN 0-404-02676-1). AMS Pr.

Swaraj Party & the Indian National Congress. S. R. Bakshi. 1986. text ed. 25.00x (ISBN 0-7069-2837-7, Pub. by Vikas India). Advent NY.

Swaraj: The Problem of India. J. E. Ellam. xiii, 288p. 1984. Repr. of 1930 ed. text ed. 40.00x (ISBN 0-86590-328-X, Pub by B R Publishing Corp). Apt Bks.

Sward & Johnston, Biographical Sketches of Augustana Leaders. Oscar N. Olson. LC 56-5870. (Augustana Historical Society Ser.: No. 15). 80p. 1955. pap. 3.00 (ISBN 0-910184-15-1). Augustana.

Swarm Studies & Inelastic Electron-Molecule Collisions. Ed. by L. C. Pitchford et al. (Illus.). xi, 403p. 1986. 49.00 (ISBN 0-387-96402-9). Springer-Verlag.

Swarms of Ions & Electrons in Gases. Ed. by W. Lindinger et al. (Illus.). 320p. 1984. 41.00 (ISBN 0-387-81823-5). Springer-Verlag.

Swartkrans Ape-Man: Paranthropus Crassidens. Robert Broom & J. T. Robinson. LC 76-44697. Repr. of 1952 ed. 32.50 (ISBN 0-404-15911-7). AMS Pr.

Swarts Ruin: A Typical Mimbres Site in Southwestern New Mexico. Harriet S. Cosgrove & C. B. Cosgrove. (HU PMP Ser.). 1932. 60.00 (ISBN 0-527-01234-3). Kraus Repr.

Swashbuckler. Lee Lynch. 256p. (Orig.). 1985. pap. 8.95 (ISBN 0-930044-66-5). Naiad Pr.

Swastika Night. Katharine Burdekin. 208p. (Orig.). 1985. pap. 8.95 (ISBN 0-935312-56-0). Feminist Pr.

Swastika on the Synagogue Door. J. Leonard Romm. LC 83-27263. (Lazarus Family Mystery Ser.). 180p. (Orig.). (gr. 3-10). 1984. pap. 6.95 (ISBN 0-940646-53-6). Rossel Bks.

Swastika Outside Germany. Donald M. McKale. LC 77-22304. 288p. 1977. 19.00x (ISBN 0-87338-209-9). Kent St U Pr.

Swastika Poems. William Heyen. LC 76-39729. 1977. 8.95 (ISBN 0-8149-0780-6). Vanguard.

SWAT (Special Weapons & Tactics) Phillip L. Davidson. (Illus.). 148p. 1979. photocopy ed. 18.50x (ISBN 0-398-03890-2). C C Thomas.

S.W.A.T. Tactics. Jeffrie Jacobs. (Illus.). 98p. 1983. pap. 10.00 (ISBN 0-87364-265-1). Paladin Pr.

S.W.A.T. Tactics: The Tactical Handling of Barricaded Suspects, Snipers and Hostage-Takers. J. Jacobs. 1986. lib. bdg. 79.95 (ISBN 0-8490-3704-2). Gordon Pr.

S.W.A.T Team Manual. R. Cappel. 1986. lib. bdg. 79.95 (ISBN 0-8490-3669-0). Gordon Pr.

SWAT Training & Employment. Steven Mattoon. (Illus.). 152p. (Orig.). 1987. pap. text ed. 14.00 (ISBN 0-87364-439-5). Paladin Pr.

Swath. John Perlman. 1978. 20.00 (ISBN 0-686-59675-7); pap. 8.00 (ISBN 0-686-59676-5). Elizabeth Pr.

Swatow in Het Princessehof. Barbara Harrison. 140p. 1979. 112.50x (ISBN 0-317-44218-X, Pub. by Han-Shan Tang Ltd). State Mutual Bk.

Swatow in Het Princesshof. Barbara Harrisson. 131p. 1979. 116.00x (ISBN 0-317-69129-5, Pub. by Han-Shan Tang Ltd). State Mutual Bk.

Swayam's Authentic Cookbook of India: Healthy No Preservatives Recipes. rev. ed. Swayam P. Singh. Ed. by Mike Danovich. 100p. 1987. pap. 12.95 (ISBN 0-935380-01-9). S Singh.

Swayam's India Cook Book. Swayam Singh. Ed. by Mike Donavich. Date not set. price not set. S Singh.

Swayed Pines Song Book. Henry B. Hays. x, 88p. 1981. wirebound 7.95 (ISBN 0-8146-1238-5). Liturgical Pr.

Swaying Pillars. E. X. Ferrars. 1985. 20.00x (ISBN 0-86025-232-9, Pub. by Ian Henry Pubns England). State Mutual Bk.

Swazi. 2nd ed. Hilda Kuper. 208p. 1986. pap. text ed. 10.95 (ISBN 0-03-070239-9, HoltC). HR&W.

Swaziland. Balem Nyeko. (World Bibliographical Ser.: No. 24). 135p. 1982. lib. bdg. 25.50 (ISBN 0-903450-35-6). ABC-Clio.

Swaziland. (Let's Visit Places & Peoples - - Nations, Dependencies, & Sovereignties of the World Ser.). (Illus.). (gr. 5 up). 1989. 12.95 (ISBN 0-7910-0131-8). Chelsea Hse.

Swaziland: Tradition & Change in a Southern African Kingdom. Alan R. Booth. LC 83-6511. (Profiles-Nations of Contemporary Africa). 144p. 1984. lib. bdg. 31.50x (ISBN 0-86531-233-8). Westview.

Sweat. Mikkel Aaland. Ed. by Noel Young. LC 77-28114. (Illus.). 256p. 1978. pap. 7.95 (ISBN 0-88496-124-9). Capra Pr.

Sweat. Mikkel Aaland. (Illus.). 256p. 1988. Repr. lib. bdg. 19.95x (ISBN 0-8095-4023-1). Borgo Pr.

Sweat & the Gold. Harriet M. Savitz. (Illus.). 154p. (Orig.). 1984. pap. 7.95. Veep.

Sweat Equity: What it Really Takes to Build America's Best Small Companies - By the Guys Who Did It. Geoffrey Smith & Paul B. Brown. 246p. 1986. 17.95 (ISBN 0-671-55210-4). S&S.

Sweat of the Sun & Tears of the Moon: Gold & Silver in Pre-Columbian Art. Andre Emmerich. LC 77-72685. (Illus.). 1977. Repr. of 1965 ed. 35.00 (ISBN 0-87817-208-4). Hacker.

Sweated Industries & Sweated Labor: The London Clothing Trades, 1860-1914. James A. Schmiechen. LC 82-17357. (Working Class in European History Ser.). 236p. 1984. 23.95 (ISBN 0-252-01024-8). U of Ill Pr.

Sweated Trade: Outwork in Nineteenth Century Britain. Duncan Bythell. LC 78-451. 1979. 27.50 (ISBN 0-312-77999-2). St Martin.

Sweater. Diane Tippell. LC 86-42828. (Where Does It Come From Ser.). (Illus.). 20p. (gr. k-4). 1986. 6.95 (ISBN 0-382-09363-1). Silver Burdett Pr.

Sweater Book. Ed. by Amy Carroll. 144p. 1983. pap. 11.95 (ISBN 0-345-34341-7). Ballantine.

Sweater Connection: Over 25 Designs for Preteens & Teens. Michele Maks. 1988. pap. 9.95 (ISBN 0-345-33278-4). Ballantine.

Sweater Workshop. Jacqueline Fee. LC 83-80246. (Illus.). 160p. 1983. spiral bdg. 15.00 (ISBN 0-934026-12-2). Interweave.

Sweater Workshop. Jacqueline Fee. (Interweave Press Bk). 1986. spiral bdg. 15.00. Contemp Bks.

Sweaters by Hand: Designs for Spinners & Knitters. Helene Rush & Rachael Emmons. (Illus.). 160p. 1988. pap. 17.95 (ISBN 0-934026-37-8). Interweave.

Sweathouses. L. Satterthwaite, Jr. (Piedras Negras Archaeology: Architecture: Pt. 5). (Illus.). 93p. 1952. 10.00 (ISBN 0-318-01004-6). Univ Mus of U PA.

Sweats & Swigs Workout for Men. Carla Dijs. 1988. 4.95 (ISBN 0-8362-1800-0). Andrews & McMeel.

Sweats & Swigs Workout for Women. Carla Dijs. 1988. 4.95 (ISBN 0-8362-1801-9). Andrews & McMeel.

Sweaty Palms: The Neglected Art of Being Interviewed. H. Anthony Medley. (Illus.). 191p. 1978. 7.95 (ISBN 0-534-97999-8, Lifetime Learn). Van Nos Reinhold.

Sweaty Palms: The Neglected Art of Being Interviewed. H. Anthony Medley. LC 78-1258. (Illus.). 208p. 1984. pap. 8.95 (ISBN 0-89815-139-2). Ten Speed Pr.

Sweden. Walter Imber & Wolf Tieze. LC 78-66110. (Illus.). 1979. 50.00 (ISBN 0-89674-004-8). J J Binns.

Sweden. Intro. by C. Johnson. (Panorama Bks.). (Illus., Fr.). 3.95 (ISBN 0-685-11577-1). French & Eur.

Sweden. Hannes Lange. (Visitor's Guide Ser.). (Illus.). 210p. (Orig.). 1987. pap. 9.95 (ISBN 0-935161-14-7). Hunter Pub NY.

Sweden. Brian McIlroy. (World Cinema Ser.: No. 2). 1988. 24.95 (ISBN 0-948911-48-4). U of Ill Pr.

Sweden. Leland B. Sather & Alan Swanson. 370p. 1987. 55.00 (ISBN 1-85109-035-5). ABC-Clio.

Sweden. Ralph Zickgraf. (Places & Peoples of the World Ser.). (Illus.). 96p. (gr. 5 up). 1988. lib. bdg. 12.95x (ISBN 1-55546-797-0). Chelsea Hse.

Sweden: A Good Life for All. Kari Olsson. LC 82-17683. (Discovering Our Heritage Ser.). (Illus.). 112p. (gr. 5 up). 1983. PLB 12.95 (ISBN 0-87518-231-3). Dillon.

Sweden: A Short Survey of the Kingdom of Sweden. LC 79-84139. (English Experience Ser.: No. 956). 116p. 1979. Repr. of 1632 ed. lib. bdg. 11.50 (ISBN 90-221-0956-9). Walter J Johnson.

Sweden & the American Revolution. Adolph B. Benson. 1926. 20.00x (ISBN 0-686-17387-2). R S Barnes.

Sweden: Coat of Arms Ore Values 1858-1872. Per Sjoman et al. Ed. by Lauson Stone et al. Tr. by Sven Ahman from Swedish. (Illus.). 113p. (Orig.). 1984. pap. text ed. 17.50 (ISBN 0-936493-04-6). Scand Philatelic.

Sweden in the Nineteen Eighty's. Michael Stevenson. (Public Administration Ser.: P 1664). 13p. 1985. 2.00 (ISBN 0-89028-374-5). Vance Biblios.

Sweden in World Society: Thoughts About the Future. Secretariat for Futures Studies, Stockholm, Sweden. LC 80-40321. (Illus.). 228p. 1980. 48.00 (ISBN 0-08-025456-X); pap. 23.00 (ISBN 0-08-025455-1). Pergamon.

Sweden: Its People & Industry, 2 vols. Ed. by Raoul Gordon. 1976. lib. bdg. 250.00 (ISBN 0-8490-2719-5). Gordon Pr.

Sweden: Lion Type Stamps 1862-1872 & Ring Type Stamps 1872-1892. Georg Menzinsky & Erik Blomberg. Ed. by Lauson Stone & Alan Warren. Tr. by Sven Ahman from Swedish. (Illus.). 123p. (Orig.). 1985. pap. text ed. 17.50 (ISBN 0-936493-05-4). Scand Philatelic.

Sweden: Penal Code of Sweden. (American Series of Foreign Penal Codes: Vol. 17). x, 114p. 1972. 15.00x (ISBN 0-8377-0037-X). Rothman.

Sweden: Skilling Banco Stamps 1855-1858. Georg Menzinsky et al. Ed. by Lauson Stone et al. Tr. by Sven Ahman from Swedish. Bd. with Black Local Stamp & 1862 Provisional of Local Stamp Type. 41p. (Illus.). 91p. (Orig.). 1985. pap. text ed. 17.50 (ISBN 0-936493-06-2). Scand Philatelic.

Sweden: the Middle Way on Trial. Marquis W. Childs. LC 79-24714. 188p. 1984. pap. 9.95x (ISBN 0-300-03181-5, Y 483). Yale U Pr.

Sweden: The Nation's History. Franklin D. Scott. LC 76-51154. 1977. 30.00 (ISBN 0-8166-0804-0). Am Scandinavian.

Sweden: The Nation's History. Franklin D. Scott. LC 88-6931. 688p. 1988. text ed. 45.00x (ISBN 0-8093-1513-0); pap. text ed. 24.95x (ISBN 0-8093-1489-4). S Ill U Pr.

Sweden, the Welfare State. Wilfrid Fleisher. LC 72-10696. (Illus.). 255p. 1973. Repr. of 1956 ed. lib. bdg. 35.00x (ISBN 0-8371-6611-X, FLSW). Greenwood.

Swedenborg: A Hermetic Philosopher. Ethan A. Hitchcock. 59.95 (ISBN 0-8490-1164-7). Gordon Pr.

Swedenborg & the New Age. Edmund A. Beaman. LC 77-134422. (Communal Societies in America Ser.). Repr. of 1881 ed. 29.00 (ISBN 0-404-08458-3). AMS Pr.

Swedenborg Epic. Cyriel O. Sigstedt. LC 78-137269. (Illus.). Repr. of 1952 ed. 34.50 (ISBN 0-404-05999-6). AMS Pr.

Swedenborg, Fourier & the America of the 1840's. Robert W. Gladish. 123p. 1983. pap. 8.00 (ISBN 0-915221-61-6). Swedenborg Sci Assn.

Swedenborg's Journal of Dreams. Ed. by Wilson Van Dusen. LC 86-70341. pap. 8.95 (ISBN 0-317-66525-1). Swedenborg.

Swedenborg's System of Degrees. Hugo LJ. Odhner. 25p. 1970. pap. 1.00 (ISBN 0-915221-16-0). Swedenborg Sci Assn.

Sweden's Age of Greatness: Sixteen Thirty-Two to Seventeen Eighteen. Ed. by Michael Roberts. LC 73-77736. (Problems in Focus Ser.). 288p. 1973. 25.00 (ISBN 0-312-78015-X). St Martin.

Sweden's Best Stories: An Introduction to Swedish Fiction. facsimile ed. Ed. by Hanna A. Larsen. Tr. by Charles W. Stork from Swedish. LC 70-37276. (Short Story Index Reprint Ser.). Repr. of 1928 ed. 20.00 (ISBN 0-8369-4087-3). Ayer Co Pubs.

Sweden's Capital Imports & Exports. Jucker Fleetwood & Erin Elver. Ed. by Mira Wilkins. LC 76-29743. (European Business Ser.). (Illus.). 1977. Repr. of 1947 ed. lib. bdg. 37.50x (ISBN 0-405-09760-3). Ayer Co Pubs.

Sweden's Day Nurseries: Focus on Programs for Infants & Toddlers. Joan L. Bergstrom & Jane R. Gold. (Illus.). 144p. pap. 5.25 (ISBN 0-936746-08-4, L56). Day Care Coun.

Sweden's Trade with the Dutch Republic 1738-1795: A Quantitative Analysis of the Relationship Between Economic Growth & International Trade in the Eighteenth Century. J. Thomas Lindblad. (Aspects of Economic History Ser.: The Low Countries: No. 4). 216p. 1982. pap. text ed. 14.50 (ISBN 90-232-1953-8, Pub. by Van Gorcum Holland). Longwood Pub Group.

Swedes & Dutch at New Castle. C. A. Weslager. (Illus., Orig.). 1987. pap. 9.95 (ISBN 0-912608-50-1). Mid Atlantic.

Swedes & Finns in New Jersey. Federal Writers' Project, New Jersey. LC 73-3640. (American Guide Ser.). (Illus.). Repr. of 1938 ed. 20.00 (ISBN 0-404-57940-X). AMS Pr.

Swedes & the Swedish Settlements in North America, 2 vols. in one. Helge Nelson. Ed. by Franklyn D. Scott. LC 78-15197. (Scandinavians in America Ser.). (Illus.). 1979. Repr. of 1943 ed. lib. bdg. 46.00x (ISBN 0-405-11654-3). Ayer Co Pubs.

Swedes in America. Percie V. Hillbrand. LC 66-10152. (In America Bks.). (Illus.). (gr. 5-11). 1966. PLB 8.95 (ISBN 0-8225-0201-1); pap. 3.95 (ISBN 0-8225-1023-5). Lerner Pubns.

Swedes in America, 1638-1938. A. Benson & A. Hedin. LC 73-98681. (American History & Americana Ser., No. 47). 1969. Repr. of 1938 ed. lib. bdg. 59.95x (ISBN 0-8383-0326-9). Haskell.

Swedes: In Their Homeland, in America, in Connecticut. David E. O'Connor & Arthur E. Soderlind. (Peoples of Connecticut Ser.). 238p. 1983. 8.00. I N Thut World Educ Ctr.

Swedish. 2nd ed. Gladys Hird. LC 78-74534. 1980. 22.95 (ISBN 0-521-22644-9). Cambridge U Pr.

Swedish see Sparkerpolice Guidebook: How to Play Sparkerpolice.

Swedish, A Practical Grammar. rev. ed. Allan L. Rice. LC 58-13379. pap. 27.50 (2026950). Bks Demand UMI.

Swedish America, 1914-1932. Sture Lindmark. 360p. 1971. 7.50 (ISBN 0-318-16622-4). Swedish-Am.

Swedish-American Colonization in the San Joaquin Valley in California. Phebe Fjellstrom. 158p. (Orig.). 1970. pap. text ed. 22.50x (Pub. by Almqvist & Wiksell). Coronet Bks.

Swedish-American Newspapers: A Guide to the Microfilms Held by Swenson Swedish Immigration Research Center. Compiled by Lilly Setterdahl. LC 81-68299. (Augustana College Library Ser.: No. 35). 36p. 1981. pap. 3.00x (ISBN 0-910182-41-8). Augustana Coll.

Swedish-American Periodicals. E. Walfred Erickson. Ed. by Franklyn D. Scott. LC 78-15206. (Scandinavians in America Ser.). 1979. lib. bdg. 16.00x (ISBN 0-405-11635-7). Ayer Co Pubs.

Swedish Americans. Allyson McGill. (Peoples of North America Ser.). (Illus.). 112p. (gr. 5 up). 1988. lib. bdg. 16.95 (ISBN 1-55546-135-2). Chelsea Hse.

Swedish & Hungarian Historical Studies. Collets Holdings Ltd. Staff. 122p. 1975. 14.00x (ISBN 0-569-08238-2, Pub. by Collets (UK)). State Mutual Bk.

Swedish & Soviet Energy Problems. Ed. by Kurt Wickman. 373p. (Orig.). 1987. pap. 34.00x. Coronet Bks.

Swedish Arbetshafte. A. Svenssons. 116p. 1978. pap. 22.00x (ISBN 91-738-2449-6, S-211). Vanous.

Swedish Aspirations & the Russian Market During the 17th Century. Artur Attman. Tr. by Eva Green & Allen Green. (Acta: Regiae Societatis Scientiarum et Litterarum Gothoburgensis Ser.: No. 44). (Illus.). 44p. 1985. pap. text ed. 9.95 (ISBN 91-85252-35-2, Pub. by Acta Universitat Sweden). Humanities.

Swedish Attendant Care Programs for the Disabled & Elderly: Description, Analysis, & Research Issues from a Consumer Perspective. Adolf D. Ratzka. (Monograph: No. 34). 96p. 1986. pap. text ed. 3.00 (ISBN 0-939986-48-5). World Rehab Fund.

Swedish Basic Course. Foreign Service Institute Staff. 384p. 1980. plus 8 audio-cassettes 149.00x (ISBN 0-88432-045-6, K501). J Norton Pubs.

Swedish Basic Grammar. 3rd ed. Beite Hildeman. 1982. text ed. 23.00x (ISBN 9-1210-1551-1, S145). Vanous.

Swedish Beauty Secrets. Paavo Airola. 32p. 1972. pap. 2.00 (ISBN 0-932090-07-9). Health Plus.

Swedish Beauty Secrets: How to feel & Look Healthier, Younger & More Beautiful with Internal & External Natural Cosmetics. Paavo Airola. (Health Plus Bks). 1984. pap. 2.00 (ISBN 0-317-02878-2). Contemp Bks.

Swedish Bullionist Controversy: P. N. Christiernin's Lectures on the High Price of Foreign Exchange in Sweden, 1761. P. N. Christiernin. Ed. by Robert V. Eagly. LC 74-161990. (American Philosophical Society Memoirs Ser.: Vol. 87). pap. 32.30 (ISBN 0-317-27884-3, 2025137). Bks Demand UMI.

Swedish Church. Herbert M. Waddams. LC 81-7021. (Illus.). viii, 70p. 1981. Repr. of 1946 ed. lib. bdg. 35.00x (ISBN 0-313-22184-7, WASW). Greenwood.

Swedish Code of Judicial Procedure. rev ed. Ed. by Anders Bruzelius & Krister Thelin. (American Ser. of Foreign Penal Codes: No. 24). xvii, 253p. 1979. 28.50x (ISBN 0-8377-0044-2). Rothman.

Swedish Code of Judicial Procedure. National Council for Crime Prevention Staff. 230p. (Orig.). 1985. pap. text ed. 24.50x (Pub. by Almqvist & Wiksell). Coronet Bks.

Swedish Commentators on America: Sixteen Thirty-Eight to Eighteen Sixty-Five. Esther E. Larson. Ed. by Franklyn D. Scott. LC 78-15194. (Scandinavians in America Ser.). 1979. Repr. of 1963 ed. lib. bdg. 14.00x (ISBN 0-405-11647-0). Ayer Co Pubs.

Swedish Connections. Connie K. Heckert. LC 86-90361. (Illus.). 110p. 1986. 13.95 (ISBN 0-930942-10-8); pap. 6.95 (ISBN 0-930942-09-4). Sutherland FL.

Swedish Contributions to Modern Theology: With Special Reference to Lundensian Thought. Nels F. Ferre. 1967. lib. bdg. 20.00x (ISBN 0-88307-092-8). Gannon.

Swedish Contributions to the Polish Resistance Movement During World War II. J. Lewandowski. 114p. (Orig.). 1979. pap. text ed. 16.50x (ISBN 0-317-46423-X, Pub. by Almqvist & Wiksell). Coronet Bks.

Swedish Development Aid in Perspective: Policies, Problems & Results Since 1952. Pierre Fruhling. 327p. 1986. text ed. 47.50x (ISBN 91-22-00835-7, Pub. by Almqvist & Wiksell). Coronet Bks.

Swedish Economic Policy. Assar Lindbeck. 1973. 35.95x (ISBN 0-520-02422-2). U of Cal Pr.

Swedish Economy. Ed. by Barry P. Bosworth & Alice M. Rivlin. LC 86-29920. 338p. 1987. 32.95 (ISBN 0-8157-1042-9); pap. 12.95 (ISBN 0-8157-1041-0). Brookings.

Swedish-English Dictionary. Ruben & M. Angstrom. (Swedish & Eng.). 29.50 (ISBN 0-87557-082-8, 082-8). Saphrograph.

Swedish-English, English-Swedish Dictionary, 2 vols. R. Santesson. (Swedish & Eng.). Set. 185.00; Swedish-English. 85.00; English-Swedish. 100.00. Heinman.

Swedish-English, English-Swedish Pocket Dictionary. (Swedish & Eng.). 10.00 (ISBN 91-46-18459-7). Heinman.

TITLE INDEX SWEET FRIDAY ISLAND.

Swedish-English, English-Swedish Technical Dictionary, 2 vols. rev. enl ed. E. Engstroem. (Swedish & Eng.). Set. 150.00; Swedish-English. 75.00; English-Swedish. 75.00. Heinman.
Swedish-English Fact Ordbok (Technical Terms) 2nd ed. Ingvar E. Gullberg. (Swedish & Eng.). 1977. 225.00x (ISBN 91-177-5052-0, S-207). Vanous.
Swedish-English, Swedish Ordbok: Prisma Modern Pocket Dictionary. 2nd ed. 1985. 14.00x (ISBN 91-518-1148-0, SW-208). Vanous.
Swedish-English-Swedish Pocket Dictionary. A. Hills. 1978. 14.00x (ISBN 91-461-8459-7, S134). Vanous.
Swedish-English Technical Dictionary. Gullberg. 1722p. 225.00 (ISBN 91-177-5052-0, SW207). Vanous.
Swedish Exodus. Lars Ljungmark. Tr. by Kermit B. Westerberg from Swedish. LC 79-10498. 192p. 1979. 19.95x (ISBN 0-8093-0905-X). S Ill U Pr.
Swedish Exodus. Lars Ljungmark. 165p. 1979. 19.95 (ISBN 0-318-16623-2). Swedish-Am.
Swedish Film Classics: A Pictorial Study or Twenty-Five Films from 1913-1957. Alexsander Kwiatkowski. (Illus.). 144p. 1983. pap. 7.95 (ISBN 0-486-24304-4). Dover.
Swedish-Finnish Dictionary. L. Lampen. 548p. (Swedish & Finnish.). 1980. Leatherette 59.95 (ISBN 951-0-08621-5, M-9656). French & Eur.
Swedish for Travel Cassettepack. Berlitz Editors. 1983. 14.95 (ISBN 0-02-962860-1, Berlitz); cassette incl. Macmillan.
Swedish Foreign Policy During the Second World War. M. W. Carlgren. LC 77-78681. (Illus.). 1977. 25.00x (ISBN 0-312-78058-3). St Martin.
Swedish Immigrants in Lincoln's Time. Nels Hokanson. Ed. by Franklyb D. Scott. LC 78-15187. (Scandinavians in America Ser.). 1979. Repr. of 1942 ed. lib. bdg. 25.50x (ISBN 0-405-11640-3). Ayer Co Pubs.
Swedish Imperial Experience, 1560-1718. Michael Roberts. LC 78-58799. 166p. 1984. pap. 13.95 (ISBN 0-521-27889-9). Cambridge U Pr.
Swedish in Three Months. (Hugo's Language Courses Ser.: No. 531). 160p. 1960. pap. 4.95 (ISBN 0-8226-0531-7). Littlefield.
Swedish in Three Months. (Hugo's Language Bks.). 192p. (Orig.). 1987. pap. 6.95 (ISBN 0-935161-89-9); pap. 39.95 (ISBN 0-935161-06-6); 4 tapes incl. Hunter Pub NY.
Swedish Industry & Industrial Policy 1985. Ministry of Industry Staff. (Illus.). 122p. (Orig.). 1985. pap. text ed. 82.00x (Pub. by Almqvist & Wiksell). Coronet Bks.
Swedish Karre Dictionary, Vol. 1: Svensk-Engelsk. K. Karre. (Swedish & Eng.). 1986. 95.00x (ISBN 91-24-14308-1, S132). Vanous.
Swedish Karre Dictionary, Vol. 2: Engelsk-Svensk. 3rd ed. K. Karre. (Swedish & Eng.). 1981. text ed. 95.00x (ISBN 91-24-29824-7, SW133). Vanous.
Swedish, Learn: Reader for Beginners. 4th ed. N. Hildeman et al. (Swedish Language Ser.). 1977. text ed. 23.00x (ISBN 9-1210-3042-1, S143); 5 45 rpm records o.p. 90.00x (ISBN 91-21-90171-6, SW143R); 5 tapeso.p. 90.00x (ISBN 91-21-90332-8, SW143T); 2 cassettes 90.00x (ISBN 91-219-1742-6, S146). Vanous.
Swedish Legends & Folktales. John Lindow. LC 77-7830. 1978. 25.00x (ISBN 0-520-03520-8). U of Cal Pr.
Swedish Literature in America. A. H. Edgren. 59.95 (ISBN 0-8490-1165-5). Gordon Pr.
Swedish Lotto Systems: Guaranteed & Tested Strategies. Thomas Ollson. (LOMAP Ser.: Vol. 4). (Illus.). 80p. 1986. pap. 9.95 (ISBN 0-317-47680-7). Intergalactic NJ.
Swedish Medieval Ballads: Ballads of the Supernatural, Vol. 1. Svenskt Visarkiv et al. Ed. by Bengt R. Jonsson. 496p. 1983. text ed. 47.50x (ISBN 0-317-56997-X, Pub. by Nordiska Afrikainstitutet (Uppsala Sweden)). Coronet Bks.
Swedish Medieval Ballads, Vol. 2: Legendary & Historical Ballads. Svenskt Visarkiv et al. Ed. by Bengt Jonsson. 292p. 1986. text ed. 54.00x (ISBN 0-317-56998-8). Coronet Bks.
Swedish Modern Pocket Dictionary: Svensk-Engelsk, Engelsk-Svensk Grammatik Parlor. E. Gomer. 1985. text ed. 14.00x (ISBN 91-518-1148-0, SW-208). Vanous.
Swedish Notebooks for the Returning Student, 3 Vols. T. A. T. Larke. (Returning Student Ser.: No. 1). (Illus.). 1981. Set. looseleaf 12.95 (ISBN 0-9608460-0-X, SV1); Vol. 1. looseleaf 4.95 (ISBN 0-9608460-1-8, SV1); Vol. 2. looseleaf 4.95 (ISBN 0-9608460-2-6, SV1); Vol. 3. looseleaf 4.95 (ISBN 0-9608460-3-4, SV1). Answer-Bk.
Swedish Passenger Arrivals in New York 1820-1850. Nils W. Olsson. LC 67-21056. 1967. 15.00 (ISBN 0-318-03677-0). Swedish Am.
Swedish Passenger Arrivals in New York, 1820-1850. Nils W. Olsson. 392p. 1967. 15.00 (ISBN 0-318-16625-9). Swedish-Am.
Swedish Passenger Arrivals in U. S. Ports 1820-1850, Except New York. Nils W. Olsson. 1979. 15.00 (ISBN 0-318-03678-9). Swedish Am.
Swedish Philosopher Axel Haegerstroem & His Relationship to Finland's Struggle to Preserve Her Legal Order, 1899-1917. Jacob W. Sundberg. ix, 77p. (Orig.). 1983. pap. text ed. 10.00x (ISBN 0-8377-1129-0). Rothman.
Swedish Place-Names in North America. Otto R. Landelius. Ed. by Raymond Jarvi. Tr. by Karin Franzen. 376p. 1985. text ed. 24.95x (ISBN 0-8093-1204-2). S Ill U Pr.
Swedish Public & Nuclear Energy: The Referendum 1980. 54p. 1981. pap. 5.00 (ISBN 92-808-0155-4, TUNU137, UNU). UNIPUB.
Swedish Reader. Ed. by P. Brandenberg & R. J. McLean. 174p. 1953. 19.50 (ISBN 0-485-11013-X, Pub. by Athlone Pr UK). Humanities.
Swedish-Russian Dictionary. D. Milanova. 760p. (Swedish & Rus.). 1973. 59.95 (ISBN 0-686-92499-1, M-9077). French & Eur.
Swedish Settlements on the Delaware: Their History & Relation to the Indians, Dutch & English, 1638-1664, 2 vols. Amandus Johnson. LC 69-17934. (Research & Source Works: No. 427). (Illus.). 1970. Repr. of 1911 ed. Set. text ed. 43.00 (ISBN 0-8337-1858-4). B Franklin.
Swedish Settlements on the Delaware 1638-1664, 2 Vols. Amandus Johnson. LC 76-80644. (Illus.). 879p. 1969. Repr. of 1911 ed. Set. 50.00 (ISBN 0-8063-0194-5). Genealog Pub.
Swedish Symposium on Classical Fatigue. Ed. by N. G. Ohlson & I. Wester. (Illus.). 418p. 1985. text ed. 87.00x (ISBN 91-22007-70-9, Pub. by Almqvist & Wiksell). Coronet Bks.
Swedish Theatre of Chicago: 1868-1950. Henriette C. Naeseth. LC 51-14886. (Augustana College Library Ser.: No. 22). 390p. 1951. 4.95x (ISBN 0-910182-17-5). Augustana Coll.
Swedish Theatre of Chicago, 1869-1950. Henriette C. Naeseth. LC 51-14886. (Augustana Historical Society Ser.: Vol. 12). 390p. 1951. 4.95 (ISBN 0-910184-12-7). Augustana.
Swedish Tvistsom Embroidery: Technique & 42 Charted Designs. Pamela M. Ness. (Illus.). 48p. (Orig.). 1981. pap. 2.25 (ISBN 0-486-24149-1). Dover.
Sweelinck. Frits Noske. (Studies of Composers: No. 22). (Illus.). 128p. 1988. 32.50 (ISBN 0-19-315259-2); pap. 14.95 (ISBN 0-19-315258-4). Oxford U Pr.
Sweelinck's Keyboard Music. Curtis. (Publications of Sir Thomas Browne Institute: No. 4). 1972. lib. bdg. 23.00 (ISBN 90-6021-062-X, Pub. by Leiden Univ. Holland). Kluwer Academic.
Sweeney Astray. Seamus Heaney. LC 84-1512. 96p. 1984. 13.95 (ISBN 0-374-27221-2); limited ed. 60.00 (ISBN 0-374-27222-0); pap. 7.95 (ISBN 0-374-51894-7). FS&G.
Sweeney Todd: Demon Barber of the Barbary Coast. Tim Kelly. 52p. 1978. pap. 2.75 (ISBN 0-88680-189-3); royalty 35.25 (ISBN 0-317-03595-9). I E Clark.
Sweeney Todd, the Demon Barber of Fleet Street. Stephen Sondheim & Wheeler Hugh. LC 79-18468. (Illus.). 1979. 12.95 (ISBN 0-396-07776-5). Dodd.
Sweeney Todd: The Demon Barber of Fleet Street-A Musical Thriller. Stephen Sondheim et al. (Illus.). 224p. 1985. pap. 6.95 (ISBN 0-396-08598-9). Dodd.
Sweeneys from 9D. Ethel Kessler & Leonard Kessler. LC 84-20156. (Illus.). 56p. (gr. 1-4). 1985. 9.95 (ISBN 0-02-750230-9). Macmillan.
Sweeney's Honor. Brian Garfield. 192p. 1980. pap. 1.95 (ISBN 0-449-24330-3, Crest). Fawcett.
Sweeny's Honor. Brian Garfield. 1987. pap. 2.75 (ISBN 0-553-26711-6). Bantam.
Sweep of American History, 2 vols. 3rd ed. Robert R. Jones & Gustav L. Seligmann. 1981. Vol. 1, 352pgs. pap. text ed. 11.00 (ISBN 0-394-34191-0, RanC); Vol. 2, 405pgs. pap. text ed. 11.00 (ISBN 0-394-34192-9). Random.
Sweeper to Saint: Stories of Holy India. Baba Hari Dass. Ed. by Ma Renu. LC 80-52021. (Illus.). 208p. (Orig.). 1980. pap. 6.95 (ISBN 0-918100-03-8). Sri Rama.
Sweepers of Slaughterhouse: Conflict & Survival in a Karachi Neighborhood. Pieter Streefland. (Studies of Developing Countries: No. 23). 150p. 1979. pap. text ed. 12.50 (ISBN 90-232-1665-2, Pub. by Van Gorcum Holland). Longwood Pub Group.
Sweeping Beauty; Or, Notes on Cinderella. Laurie Fox. (Pictograms Ser.). 32p. (Orig.). 1984. pap. 2.95 (ISBN 0-89807-114-3). Illuminati.
Sweeping It Under the Drug: A Complete Book about Recreational Drugs & How to Create a Satisfying Life Without Them. Dennis Marcellino. LC 88-2083. 192p. 1988. cancelled (ISBN 0-945272-05-7); pap. 9.95 (ISBN 0-945272-04-9). Lighthouse Reseda.
Sweeping Statements: Writings from the Women's Liberation Movement 1981-1983. Hannah Kanter et al. 336p. (Orig.). 1984. pap. 9.95 (ISBN 0-7043-3930-7, Pub. by Quartet Bks). Salem Hse Pubs.
Sweeping the Cobwebs. Lillien J. Martin & Clare De Grucy. Ed. by Robert Kastenbaum. LC 78-22209. (Aging & Old Age Ser.). 1979. Repr. of 1933 ed. lib. bdg. 14.00x (ISBN 0-405-11823-6). Ayer Co Pubs.
Sweeps. Bill Granger. 1980. pap. 2.50 (ISBN 0-449-14351-1, GM). Fawcett.
Sweepstakes. Judith A. Magarian & Patricia M. Horton. (Illus.). 13p. (gr. 4-6). 1980. pap. 5.95 (ISBN 0-933358-74-1, 72204). Enrich.
Sweepstakes, Prize Promotions, Games & Contests. Jeffrey P. Feinman & Robert D. Blashek. 200p. 1986. 25.00 (ISBN 0-87094-643-9). Dow Jones-Irwin.
Sweet Adelaide. Julian Symons. 384p. 1981. pap. 3.95 (ISBN 0-14-005792-7). Penguin.
Sweet Adventure, No. 17. Barbara Cartland. Date not set. pap. 2.25 (ISBN 0-515-06390-8). Jove Pubns.
Sweet Adversity. Donald Newlove. 1978. pap. 2.95 (ISBN 0-380-38364-0, 38364-0, Bard). Avon.
Sweet Agony Two: A Writing Book of Sorts. Gene Olson. 194p. 1983. pap. 7.97 (ISBN 0-913366-07-2). Windyridge.
Sweet & Hard Cider: Making It, Using It, & Enjoying It. rev. ed. Annie Proulx & Lew Nichols. LC 80-19701. (Illus.). 188p. 1984. pap. 9.95 (ISBN 0-88266-352-6, Garden Way Pub). Storey Comm Inc.
Sweet & Low. Emma Lathen. 1983. pap. 2.95 (ISBN 0-671-45527-3). PB.
Sweet & Lowdown: America's Popular Song Writers. Warren Craig. LC 77-20223. 1978. 40.00 (ISBN 0-8108-1089-1). Scarecrow.
Sweet & Natural Desserts: East West's Best & Most Wholesome, Sugar- & Dairy-Free Treats. Ed. by East West Journal Editors. (Illus.). 120p. (Orig.). 1986. pap. 7.95 (ISBN 0-936184-05-1). East West Health.
Sweet & Natural: Desserts without Sugar, Honey, Molasses, or Artifical Sweeteners. Janet Warrington. LC 82-4962. 143p. 1982. 22.95 (ISBN 0-89594-073-6); pap. 8.95 (ISBN 0-89594-072-8). Crossing Pr.
Sweet & Sassy: Counted Cross Stitch Designs for Children & Beginners. Annette Bradshaw & Gwyn Franson. 32p. (Orig.). 1983. pap. 5.00 (ISBN 0-88290-216-4). Horizon Utah.
Sweet & Sour Capitalism: An Analysis of Socialism with Chinese Characteristics. Don J. Senese. (Journal of Social Political & Economic Studies Monograph Ser.: No. 15). 180p. 1986. pap. 20.00x (ISBN 0-930690-18-4). Coun Soc Econ.
Sweet & Sour: Couples, No. 27. M. E. Cooper. (Illus.). 192p. (Orig.). (YA) (gr. 7 up). 1987. pap. 2.50 (ISBN 0-590-40797-X). Scholastic Inc.
Sweet & Sour Hippo. Paul White. (Jungle Doctor Picture Fable Ser.). 21p. (gr. 1-7). 1986. Set of 8. pap. 26.50 (ISBN 0-85364-376-8, Pub. by Paternoster UK). Attic Pr.
Sweet & Sour Romance. Giovanni Vitacolonna. 156p. (Orig.). 1982. pap. 6.50 (ISBN 0-907040-15-2, Pub. by GMP England). Alyson Pubns.
Sweet & Sour: Tales from China. Carol Kendall & Li Yao-wen. LC 78-24349. (Illus.). 112p. (gr. 3-6). 1979. 7.95 (ISBN 0-395-28958-0, Clarion). HM.
Sweet & Sugar Free: Nutritional Sweets Cookbook. Karen E. Barkie. 5.95 ea. Hypoglycemia Foun.
Sweet Anticipation. Kathy Clark. (American Romance Ser.). pap. 2.75 (ISBN 0-373-16224-3). Harlequin Bks.
Sweet Bells Jangled Out of Tune. Robin Brancato. LC 81-14283. 224p. 1982. 10.95 (ISBN 0-394-84809-8); lib. bdg. 10.99 (ISBN 0-394-94809-2). Knopf.
Sweet Bells Jangled out of Tune. Robin Brancato. 182p. (gr. 7 up). 1983. pap. 2.50 (ISBN 0-590-40459-8, Point). Scholastic Inc.
Sweet Bird of Youth. Tennessee Williams. LC 59-9492. 128p. 1975. pap. 5.95 (ISBN 0-8112-0596-7, NDP409). New Directions.
Sweet Bird of Youth see Theatre of Tennessee Williams.
Sweet Cane. Bruce McGinnis. LC 79-16126. 256p. 1982. 11.95 (ISBN 0-8149-0857-8). Vanguard.
Sweet Charity - Broadway Vocal Selections. 1986. pap. 10.95 (ISBN 0-89898-471-8). Columbia Pictures.
Sweet Comfort for Feeble Saints. C. H. Spurgeon. 1978. pap. 0.95 (ISBN 0-686-28282-5). Pilgrim Pubns.
Sweet Country. Caroline Richards. 1986. pap. 7.95 (ISBN 0-671-62285-4, Fireside). S&S.
Sweet Creek Holler. Ruth White. 168p. (YA) 1988. 11.95 (ISBN 0-374-37360-4). FS&G.
Sweet Danger. Margery Allingham. 256p. 1988. pap. 5.95 (ISBN 0-14-008779-6). Penguin.
Sweet Deals. Brian Lysaght. 256p. pap. 2.95 (ISBN 0-8125-0644-8, Dist. by Warner Pub Services & St. Martin's Press). Tor Bks.
Sweet Death. Claude Tardat. Tr. by Linda Coverdale from Fr. 154p. 1988. 15.95 (ISBN 0-87951-291-1). Overlook Pr.
Sweet Death, Kind Death. Amanda Cross. 192p. 1987. pap. 3.50 (ISBN 0-345-35254-8). Ballantine.
Sweet Desire. Sara Orwig. 1988. pap. 3.95 (ISBN 0-451-40071-2, Onyx). NAL.
Sweet Disorder. Claudette Williams. 224p. 1981. pap. 1.50 (ISBN 0-449-50206-6, Coventry). Fawcett.
Sweet Dove Died. Barbara Pym. LC 86-45682. 208p. 1987. pap. 6.95 (ISBN 0-06-097072-3, PL 7072, PL). Har-Row.
Sweet Dove Died. Barbara Pym. 208p. 1988. pap. 7.95 (ISBN 0-525-48380-2, Obelisk). Dutton.
Sweet Drams: The Perfect Catch, No. 153. Laurie Lykken. (YA) (gr. 6 up). 1988. pap. 2.50 (ISBN 0-553-27475-9). Bantam.
Sweet Dreams. William W. Johnstone. 368p. 1985. pap. 3.50 (ISBN 0-8217-1553-4). Zebra.
Sweet Dreams. B. Neasi. LC 87-15083. (Rookie Readers Ser.). (Illus.). 32p. (ps-2). 1987. PLB 9.93 (ISBN 0-516-02084-6); pap. 2.50 (ISBN 0-516-42084-4). Childrens.
Sweet Dreams. John Preston. (Mission of Alex Kane Ser.: vol. 1). 130p. (Orig.). 1984. pap. 4.95 (ISBN 0-932870-57-0). Alyson Pubns.
Sweet Dreams. 1988. pap. 3.95 (ISBN 0-8216-5012-2). Blue Moon Bks.
Sweet Dreams. Vecsey. 1988. pap. 3.95 (ISBN 0-312-90340-5). St Martin.
Sweet Dreams, No. 153. Cloverdale Press Staff. 176p. (Orig.). 1988. pap. 2.50 (ISBN 0-553-27414-7). Bantam.
Sweet Dreams, No. 159. Cloverdale Press Staff. 176p. 1988. pap. 2.50 (ISBN 0-317-69925-3). Bantam.
Sweet Dreams, No. 160. Cloverdale Press Staff. 176p. 1989. pap. 2.50 (ISBN 0-553-27648-4). Bantam.
Sweet Dreams, No. 161. Cloverdale Press Staff. 176p. 1989. pap. 2.50 (ISBN 0-553-27649-2). Bantam.
Sweet Dreams, No. 162. Cloverdale Press Staff. 176p. (Orig.). 1989. pap. 2.50 (ISBN 0-553-27719-7). Bantam.
Sweet Dreams: A Guide to Productive Sleep. Frank B. Minirth et al. (Life Enrichment Ser.). pap. 3.95 (ISBN 0-8010-6206-3). Baker Bk.
Sweet Dreams & Monsters: A Beginner's Guide to Dreams & Nightmares & Things That Go Bump under the Bed. Peter Mayle. (Illus.). (gr. k up). 1986. 9.95 (ISBN 0-517-55972-2, Harmony). Crown.
Sweet Dreams Book. Alida Allison. 32p. 1984. pap. 3.95 (ISBN 0-8431-1037-6). Price Stern.
Sweet Dreams, Clown-Arounds. Joanna Cole. LC 85-6348. (Illus.). 48p. (ps-3). 1985. 5.95 (ISBN 0-8193-1138-3). Parents.
Sweet Dreams, Clown Arounds! Joanna Cole. (Illus.). (ps-2). 1987. pap. 2.95 (ISBN 0-517-56747-4). Crown.
Sweet Dreams: Cross-Country Match, No. 152. Ann Richards. (Orig.). 1988. pap. 2.50 (ISBN 0-553-27413-9). Bantam.
Sweet Dreams: Crossed Signals, No. 158. Janice Boies. 176p. 1988. pap. 2.50 (ISBN 0-553-27593-3). Bantam.
Sweet Dreams for Little Ones. Michael G. Pappas. (Illus.). 64p. (Orig.). 1982. pap. 6.95 (ISBN 0-86683-641-1, AY8156, HarpR). Har-Row.
Sweet Dreams for Sally. Amelia Hubert. (Care Bears Ser.). (Illus.). 40p. (ps-3). 1983. 5.95 (ISBN 0-910313-01-6, 7002). Parker Bros.
Sweet Dreams, Lady Moon. Marsena Shane. (Critic's Choice Paperbacks Ser.). 1988. pap. 2.95 (ISBN 1-55547-223-0, Univ Bks). Lyle Stuart.
Sweet Dreams: Long Shot, No. 159. Joanne Simbal. (YA) (gr. 6 up). 1988. pap. 2.50. Bantam.
Sweet Dreams: Love Lines, No. 154. Frances H. Grimes. (YA) (gr. 6 up). 1988. pap. 2.50. Bantam.
Sweet Dreams: Mr. Perfect, No. 157. Stefanie Curtis. 176p. (Orig.). 1988. pap. 2.50 (ISBN 0-553-27553-4). Bantam.
Sweet Dreams: My Greatest Desserts. Renny Darling. (Illus.). 1980. pap. 9.95 (ISBN 0-930440-13-7). Royal Hse.
Sweet Dreams Nantucket. Tom Simms. LC 84-62252. (Illus.). 128p. (Orig.). 1985. pap. 12.95 (ISBN 0-932493-00-9). Rejected Works.
Sweet Dreams: No. 150. Cloverdale Press Staff. 176p. (Orig.). 1988. pap. 2.50 (ISBN 0-553-27357-4). Bantam.
Sweet Dreams: No. 151. Cloverdale Press Staff. 176p. (Orig.). 1988. pap. 2.50 (ISBN 0-553-27358-2). Bantam.
Sweet Dreams of Gingerbread. Jann Johnson. (Illus.). 168p. 1986. 19.95 (ISBN 0-02-496780-7). Macmillan.
Sweet Dreams on Sesame Street. Sesame Street. Ed. by Janet Schulman. LC 82-80572. (Little Pops Ser.). (Illus.). 12p. (ps-3). 1983. pap. 2.50 (ISBN 0-394-85448-9). Random.
Sweet Dreams, Spot! Eric Hill. (Soft Spots Ser.). (Illus.). 8p. (gr. k-1). 1984. 2.95 (ISBN 0-399-21069-5, Putnam). Putnam Pub Group.
Sweet Dreams, Sweet Princes. Mack Reynolds & Michael Banks. 1986. 2.95 (ISBN 0-671-65595-7). Baen Bks.
Sweet Dreams: The Art of Bessie Pease Gutman. Pamela Prince & Bessie Pease. 10.95 (ISBN 0-517-55672-3). Crown.
Sweet Dreams: The Game of Love, No. 155. Susan Gorman. (YA) (gr. 6 up). 1988. pap. 2.50 (ISBN 0-553-27476-7). Bantam.
Sweet Dreams: Two Boys Too Many, No. 156. Janet A. Bloss. 176p. (Orig.). 1988. pap. 2.50 (ISBN 0-553-27552-6). Bantam.
Sweet Ember. Bonnie Drake. (Candlelight Ecstacy Ser.: No. 18). (Orig.). 1981. pap. 1.50 (ISBN 0-440-18459-2). Dell.
Sweet Fierce Fires. Joyce Myrus. 576p. 1984. pap. 3.95 (ISBN 0-8217-1401-5). Zebra.
Sweet Fire. Kate Fairfax. 272p. pap. 2.95 (ISBN 0-441-79119-0); pap. text ed. 3.25 (ISBN 0-441-79120-4). Ace Bks.
Sweet Flypaper of Life. rev. ed. Langston Hughes. 112p. 1985. Repr. of 1955 ed. 24.95 (ISBN 0-88258-152-X). Howard U Pr.
Sweet Freedom: The Struggle for Women's Liberation. 2nd ed. Anna Coote & Beatrix Campbell. 300p. (Orig.). Date not set. text ed. 34.95 (ISBN 0-631-14957-0); pap. text ed. 16.95 (ISBN 0-631-14958-9). Basil Blackwell.
Sweet Friday Island. Theodore Taylor. 150p. (gr. 7 up). 1984. pap. 2.25 (ISBN 0-590-33174-4, Point). Scholastic Inc.

Sweet Gogarty. Matthew Hochberg. LC 75-19570. (Illus.). 111p. 1975. pap. 7.50x (ISBN 0-913204-04-8). December Pr.

Sweet Grass Lives On: Fifty Contemporary North American Indian Artists. Jamake Highwater. LC 80-7776. (Illus.). 192p. 1980. 35.00 (ISBN 0-690-01925-4). Har-Row.

Sweet Gwendolyn & the Countess. Edward Field. (Illus.). 1974. pap. 12.00 (ISBN 0-916906-03-5); pap. 20.00 signed (ISBN 0-686-86246-5). Konglomerati.

Sweet Hearts for Dolly. Ruth Brook. LC 86-30732. (Illus.). 32p. (gr. k-3). 1987. PLB 10.89 (ISBN 0-8167-0906-8); pap. text ed. 2.95 (ISBN 0-8167-0907-6). Troll Assocs.

Sweet Herbs & Sundry Flowers: Medieval Gardens & the Gardens of the Cloisters. Tania Bayard. LC 85-7133. 104p. 1986. 12.95 (ISBN 0-87923-593-4). Godine.

Sweet Here & Now. Geoffrey E. Garne. (Anchor Ser.). 1984. 6.95 (ISBN 0-8163-0543-9). Pacific Pr Pub Assn.

Sweet Hollow: Stories. Lou Crabtree. LC 83-14934. (Illus.). 106p. 1984. pap. 9.95 (ISBN 0-8071-1133-3). La State U Pr.

Sweet Home Chicago. Joel Lipmann. 1980. pap. 2.00 (ISBN 0-686-70612-9). Quixote.

Sweet Home Chicago: The Real City Guide. Sherry Kent & Mary Szpur. 240p. (Orig.). 1987. pap. 8.95 (ISBN 1-55652-006-9). Chicago Review.

Sweet Home in the Oregon Cascades. Margaret S. Carey & Patricia H. Hainline. (Illus.). 140p. 1979. pap. 7.95 (ISBN 0-934784-04-3). Calapooia Pubns.

Sweet Hoyden. Rachelle Edwards. 1988. pap. 2.95 (ISBN 0-449-21605-5, Crest). Fawcett.

Sweet Illusions. Walter D. Myers. 146p. (Orig.). (YA) 1987. 9.95 (ISBN 0-915924-14-5); pap. 3.95. Tchrs & Writers Coll.

Sweet Illusions. Walter D. Myers. 146p. Date not set. 9.95; pap. 3.95. Morning Glory.

Sweet Instruction: Franklin's Journalism a Literary Apprenticeship. James A. Sappenfield. LC 73-7808. (New Horizons in Journalism Ser.). 247p. 1973. 8.95x (ISBN 0-8093-0610-7). S Ill U Pr.

Sweet Justice. Jerry Oster. LC 84-48186. 224p. 1985. 13.45i (ISBN 0-06-015401-2, HarpT). Har-Row.

Sweet Justice. Jerry Oster. 288p. 1986. pap. 3.95 (ISBN 0-441-79126-3, Pub. by Charter Bks). Ace Bks.

Sweet Kate, A Time Remembered: Dangerous Stranger. Lucy Gillen. (Harlequin Romances Ser.). 576p. 1982. pap. 3.50 (ISBN 0-373-20060-9). Harlequin Bks.

Sweet Land of Liberty. O. Z. Tyler, Jr. LC 86-91399. (Illus.). 288p. 1987. text ed. 17.50 (ISBN 0-682-40315-6). Exposition-Phoenix.

Sweet Land of Liberty? The Supreme Court & Individual Rights. Henry M. Holzer. 198p. 1983. 14.95 (ISBN 0-917572-03-3). Common Sense.

Sweet Lass of Richmond Hill. Jean Plaidy. 384p. 1988. 17.95 (ISBN 0-399-13362-3). Putnam Pub Group.

Sweet Laughter. Carolyn J. Coleman. 32p. 1987. 6.50 (ISBN 0-8062-3158-0). Carlton.

Sweet Liberty. Cynthia Blair. (Orig.). 1987. pap. 2.50 (ISBN 0-449-70263-4, Juniper). Fawcett.

Sweet Life: Adventures on the Way to Paradise. Barry Manilow. (Illus.). 288p. 1987. text ed. 17.95 (ISBN 0-07-039904-2). McGraw.

Sweet Life! Macrobiotic Desserts. Marcea Weber. (Illus.). 1981. pap. 12.50 (ISBN 0-87040-493-8). Japan Pubns USA.

Sweet Life of Jimmy Riley. James Reardon. 1981. 14.95 (ISBN 0-671-61014-7, Wyndham Bks). S&S.

Sweet Little Alice. Mabel Johnson. (Illus.). (gr. 5 up). 1978. pap. 3.50 (ISBN 0-9600838-4-7). M Johnson.

Sweet Little Jesus Boy: A Soliloquy. Robert H. McGimsey. 32p. 1973. pap. 2.95 (ISBN 0-911336-53-2). Sci of Mind.

Sweet Lou. Lou Piniella & Maury Allen. 304p. 1987. pap. 3.95 (ISBN 0-553-26459-1). Bantam.

Sweet Love Survive. Susan Johnson. 1987. pap. 3.50 (ISBN 0-441-79121-2, Pub. by Charter Bks). Ace Bks.

Sweet Madness: A Study of Humor. William F. Fry, Jr. LC 63-17821. (Pacific Books Paperbounds, PB-3). 1968. pap. 6.95 (ISBN 0-87015-163-0). Pacific Bks.

Sweet Medicine: The Continuing Role of the Sacred Arrows, The Sun Dance, & The Sacred Buffalo Hat in Northern Cheyenne History, 2 vols. Peter J. Powell. (Civilization of the American Ser.: Vol. 100). (Illus.). 986p. 1979. 57.50 (ISBN 0-8061-0885-1). U of Okla Pr.

Sweet Medicine's Propehcy: Sun Dancer's Passion. Karen A. Bale. 1981. pap. 2.95 (ISBN 0-89083-776-7). Zebra.

Sweet Medicine's Prophecy, No. 3: Winter's Love Song. Karen A. Bale. 1983. pap. 3.50 (ISBN 0-8217-1154-7). Zebra.

Sweet Medicine's Prophecy, No. 5: Sun Dancer's Legacy. Karen A. Bale. 496p. 1986. pap. 3.95 (ISBN 0-8217-1878-9). Zebra.

Sweet Memories. Lavyrle Spencer. 384p. 1984. pap. 3.95 (ISBN 0-373-97008-0). Harlequin Bks.

Sweet Nelly. Maurice Callard. 1982. 15.00x (ISBN 0-903653-00-1, Pub. by New Playwrights Network). State Mutual Bk.

Sweet Nutcracker. David Kossoff. LC 86-60935. (Illus.). 50p. (gr. 5-9). 1986. 8.95 (ISBN 0-88186-378-5, Pub. by Tarquin). Parkwest Pubns.

Sweet on Construction Industry Contracts: Major AIA Documents. Justin Sweet. LC 87-2192. (Construction Law Library). 656p. 1987. 85.00 (ISBN 0-471-85232-5). Wiley.

Sweet on Construction Industry Contracts: 1988 Supplement. Justin Sweet. (Construction Law Library). 1988. pap. price not set (ISBN 0-471-60631-6). Wiley.

Sweet Ones. Len Roberts. LC 87-63529. (Lakes & Prairies Award Bk.). (Illus.). 80p. (Orig.). 1988. pap. 6.95 (ISBN 0-915943-24-7). Milkweed Ed.

Sweet Pain. Richard Posner. 224p. (gr. 12 up). 1987. 11.95 (ISBN 0-87131-501-7). M Evans.

Sweet Paradise. Jolene Prewit-Parker. 448p. (Orig.). 1988. pap. 3.95 (ISBN 0-8439-2639-2, Pub. by Leisure Bks CT). Leisure NY.

Sweet Paradise. Diana H. Young. 144p. 1986. 24.95 (ISBN 0-317-56892-2). Mutual Pub HI.

Sweet Passion's Pain. Karen Harper. pap. 3.75 (ISBN 0-8217-1367-1). Zebra.

Sweet Peter Deeder. Rev. ed. Odie Hawkins. (Orig.). 1983. pap. 2.25 (ISBN 0-87067-223-1, BH223). Holloway.

Sweet Potato & Oceania: An Essay in Ethnobotany. Douglas E. Yen. LC 74-75842. (Bulletin Ser: No. 236). (Illus.). 389p. 1974. 25.00 (ISBN 0-910240-17-5). Bishop Mus.

Sweet Potato Products: A Natural Resource for the Tropics. Ed. by John C. Bouwkamp. 280p. 1985. 110.00 (ISBN 0-8493-5428-5). CRC Pr.

Sweet Prairie Passion. Rosanne F. Bittner. (Savage Destiny Ser.: No. 1). 1983. pap. 3.50 (ISBN 0-8217-1251-9). Zebra.

Sweet Pretender. Violet Hamilton. 352p. 1986. pap. 3.50 (ISBN 0-8217-1883-5). Zebra.

Sweet Promised Land. Robert Laxalt. (Illus.). 180p. 1986. Repr. 16.95 (ISBN 0-87417-114-8); deluxe ed. 125.00 (ISBN 0-87417-118-0). U of Nev Pr.

Sweet Promised Land. Robert Laxalt. (Basque Ser.). 183p. 1988. pap. 9.95 (ISBN 0-87417-137-7). U of Nev Pr.

Sweet Reason. Robert Littell. 224p. (Orig.). 1986. pap. 3.50 (ISBN 0-553-25547-9). Bantam.

Sweet Reckoning. Eugenia Riley. (Orig.). 1987. pap. 3.95 (ISBN 0-446-34266-1). Warner Bks.

Sweet Revenge. Dick Beaird. (Orig.). 1982. pap. 2.95 (ISBN 0-89083-911-5). Zebra.

Sweet Revenge. Dick Beaird. 416p. 1986. pap. 3.50 (ISBN 0-8217-1904-1). Zebra.

Sweet Revenge. Patricia Pellicane. pap. 3.50 (ISBN 0-317-61761-3). PB.

Sweet Revenge. Dorothy Wakeley. 176p. 1984. pap. 2.95 (ISBN 0-441-79122-0). Ace Bks.

Sweet Ride. Richard S. Prather. 256p. 1988. pap. 3.95 (ISBN 0-8125-0785-1). Tor Bks.

Sweet Salt. Felix Goodson. LC 75-40585. 1976. 8.95 (ISBN 0-8048-1173-3). C E Tuttle.

Sweet Salt. Robert Mayer. 144p. (Orig.). 14.95 (ISBN 0-933553-02-1); pap. 9.95 (ISBN 0-933553-03-X). Mariposa Print Pub.

Sweet, Savage Death. Orania Papazoglou. (Crime Monthly Ser.). 192p. 1985. pap. 3.50 (ISBN 0-14-007745-6). Penguin.

Sweet Savage Eden. Heather Graham. (American Woman Ser.). (Orig.). (YA) 1989. pap. price not set (ISBN 0-440-20235-3). Dell.

Sweet Savage Heart. Janelle Taylor. (Zebra Romance Ser.). 560p. 1986. pap. 3.95 (ISBN 0-8217-1900-9). Zebra.

Sweet Savage Heathcliff. George Gately. 128p. 1982. pap. 4.95 (ISBN 0-441-32198-4). Ace Bks.

Sweet Savage Love. Rosemary Rogers. (Steve & Ginny Ser.: Bk. 1). 640p. 1979. pap. 4.50 (ISBN 0-380-00815-7, 60011-0). Avon.

Sweet Savage Sophmore Year, No. 1. 160p. (Orig.). (YA) 1989. pap. 2.95 mass mrkt. (ISBN 1-55802-077-2). Lynx Bks.

Sweet-Scented Name & Other Fairy Tales & Stories. Fiodor K. Sologub. Ed. by S. Graham. LC 76-23900. (Classics of Russian Literature). 1977. 15.00 (ISBN 0-88355-519-0). Hyperion Conn.

Sweet-Scented Name, & Other Fairy Tales, Fables, & Stories. facsimile ed. Fedor K. Teternikov. Ed. by Stephen Graham. LC 73-37565. (Short Story Index Reprint Ser.). Repr. of 1915 ed. 18.00 (ISBN 0-8369-4124-1). Ayer Co Pubs.

Sweet Science. A. J. Liebling. (Autographed Sports Classics Ser.). 1981. Repr. of 1951 ed. 19.95 (ISBN 0-941372-06-5). Holtzman Pr.

Sweet Science. A. J. Liebling. Ed. by Dick Schaap. (Penguin Sports Library). 306p. 1982. pap. 6.95 (ISBN 0-14-006191-6). Penguin.

Sweet Sea: The Princess of Coral Kingdom. Patricia Relf. (Illus.). 48p. (ps-3). 1985. 6.95 (ISBN 0-448-18974-7, G&D). Putnam Pub Group.

Sweet Seasons: Baseball's Greatest Teams Since 1920. Howard Siner. LC 87-50914. (Illus.). 240p. (Orig.). 1988. pap. 8.95 (ISBN 0-345-35229-7). Pharos Bks NY.

Sweet Secrets. Elisabeth Kidd. 384p. (Orig.). 1988. pap. 3.95 (ISBN 0-446-34652-7). Warner Bks.

Sweet Shallin. Rheunick Greene. 1988. 10.95 (ISBN 0-533-07764-8). Vantage.

Sweet-Shop Owner. Graham Swift. 222p. 1985. pap. 7.95 (ISBN 0-671-54611-2). WSP.

Sweet Silver Blues. Glen Cook. 256p. 1987. pap. 3.50 (ISBN 0-451-15061-9, Sig). NAL.

Sweet Singer. Marla Martin. (gr. 2-4). 1976. 2.50 (ISBN 0-686-15487-8). Rod & Staff.

Sweet Singer of Israel: Unfinished Poems & Devotional Thoughts. Max I. Reich. LC 70-38312. (Biography Index Reprint Ser). Repr. of 1948 ed. 15.50 (ISBN 0-8369-8127-8). Ayer Co Pubs.

Sweet Sinner. Lorinda Hagen. 1979. pap. 1.95 (ISBN 0-505-51330-7, Pub. by Tower Bks). Leisure NY.

Sweet Sixteen. Leonore Fleischer. Ed. by Jim Connor. 160p. (Orig.). 1988. pap. 3.50 (ISBN 0-7701-0931-4). PaperJacks US.

Sweet Sixteen & Never... Jeanne Betancourt. 144p. (Orig.). (YA) (gr. 7-12). 1987. pap. 2.75 (ISBN 0-553-25534-7, Starfire). Bantam.

Sweet Slow Death. Lawrence Bloch. 144p. 1986. pap. 2.95 (ISBN 0-515-08645-2). Jove Pubns.

Sweet Smell of Christmas. Patricia M. Scarry. (Golden Scratch & Sniff Bks.). (Illus.). 32p. (ps-2). 1970. 5.95 (ISBN 0-307-13527-6, Golden Bks). Western Pub.

Sweet Smell of Success. Ernest Lehman. 14.95 (ISBN 0-88411-447-3, Pub. by Aeonian Pr). Amereon Ltd.

Sweet, Soft, & Country. Pat McClure. (Illus.). 32p. 1984. pap. 6.50 (ISBN 0-941284-25-5). Deco Design Studio.

Sweet Songbird. Teresa Crane. 608p. 1988. 22.95 (ISBN 0-312-01831-2). St Martin.

Sweet Songs for Gentle Americans. Nicholas Tawa. LC 78-71394. 1980. 21.95 (ISBN 0-87972-130-8); pap. 10.95 (ISBN 0-87972-157-X). Bowling Green Univ.

Sweet Soul Music: Rhythm & Blues & the Southern Dream of Freedom. Peter Guralnick. (Illus.). 480p. 1986. 24.45i (ISBN 0-06-015514-0, HarpT). Har-row.

Sweet Soul Music: Rhythm & Blues & the Southern Dream of Freedom. Peter Guralnick. (Illus.). 480p. 1986. pap. 14.95 (ISBN 0-06-096049-3, PL6049, PL). Har-Row.

Sweet Sounds of Life. Janelle C. Lapaglia. 1979. 5.00 (ISBN 0-682-49332-5). Exposition-Phoenix.

Sweet Starfire. Jayne A. Krentz. 1986. pap. 3.95 (ISBN 0-445-20034-0, Pub. by Popular Lib). Warner Bks.

Sweet Street Blues. rev. ed. Laurence Blaine. (Orig.). 1985. pap. 2.50 (ISBN 0-87067-260-6, BH260). Holloway.

Sweet Subsidy: The Economic & Diplomatic Effects of the U. S. Sugar Acts, 1934-1974. Thomas J. Heston. Ed. by Stuart Bruchey. (Foreign Economic Policy of the United States Ser.). 537p. 1987. lib. bdg. 80.00 (ISBN 0-8240-8084-X). Garland Pub.

Sweet Success: How to Understand the Men in Your Business Life - & Win with Your Own Rules. Kathryn B. Stechert. 256p. 1986. 17.95 (ISBN 0-02-614380-1). Macmillan.

Sweet Suffering: Woman As Victim. Natalie Shainess. LC 83-18762. 256p. 1984. 15.95 (ISBN 0-672-52766-9). Bobbs.

Sweet Suffering: Woman As Victim. Natalie Shainess. 1985. pap. 3.50 (ISBN 0-671-61894-6). PB.

Sweet Surrender. Catherine Coulter. LC 99-943913. 1984. pap. 3.95 (ISBN 0-451-14200-4, Sig). NAL.

Sweet Talk. Eileen Goudge. (Senior Ser.: No. 7). (Orig.). (gr. k-12). 1986. pap. 2.25 (ISBN 0-440-98411-4, LFL). Dell.

Sweet Talk. Eileen Goudge. (Seniors Ser.: No. 15). 160p. 1986. pap. 2.95 (ISBN 0-553-17220-4). Bantam.

Sweet Talk: Media Coverage of Artificial Sweeteners. Philip F. Lawler. Ed. by The Media Institute. LC 85-63769. (Media in Society Ser.). 100p. (Orig.). 1986. pap. 12.95 (ISBN 0-937790-33-8). Media Inst.

Sweet Temptation. Shannon Clare. (Superromances). 384p. 1982. pap. 2.50 (ISBN 0-373-70043-1, Pub. by Worldwide). Harlequin Bks.

Sweet Temptation. Caroline Standish. 320p. 1982. pap. 3.25 (ISBN 0-441-79124-7). Ace Bks.

Sweet Temptations Natural Dessert Book: Delicious Desserts That Need No Cooking. Francis Kendall. 160p. 1988. pap. 8.95 (ISBN 0-89529-355-2). Avery Pub.

Sweet Things. A. Wilkes. (Usborne First Cookbooks Ser.). (Illus.). 24p. (gr. k-3). 1983. 5.95 (ISBN 0-86020-763-3). EDC.

Sweet Thunder. Lynn Scott-Drennan. LC 86-24222. (Starlight Romance Ser.). 192p. 1987. 12.95 (ISBN 0-385-23531-3). Doubleday.

Sweet Thursday. John Steinbeck. 1979. pap. 3.95 (ISBN 0-14-004889-8). Penguin.

Sweet Tomorrow. Ross Laursen. LC 75-16009. 80p. 1975. pap. 1.95x (ISBN 0-914024-21-3). SF Arts & Letters.

Sweet Tooth. Yves Navarre. Tr. by Donald Watson from Fr. 1980. 8.95 (ISBN 0-7145-3522-2). Riverrun NY.

Sweet Torment. Elaine Barbieri. 496p. 1984. pap. 3.75 (ISBN 0-8217-1385-X). Zebra.

Sweet Touch. Lorna Balian. 48p. (Orig.). (gr. 1-2). pap. 5.95 (ISBN 0-687-40774-5). Abingdon.

Sweet Track to Glastonbury. Bryony Coles & John Coles. LC 85-51949. (New Aspects of Antiquity Ser.). (Illus.). 200p. 1986. 29.95 (ISBN 0-500-39022-3). Thames Hudson.

Sweet Valley High, No. 47. Francine Pascal. 160p. (Orig.). 1988. pap. 2.95 (ISBN 0-553-27359-0). Bantam.

Sweet Valley High, No. 48. Francine Pascal. 160p. (Orig.). 1988. pap. 2.95 (ISBN 0-553-27416-3). Bantam.

Sweet Valley High, No. 50. Created by Francine Pascal. 160p. 1988. pap. 2.95 (ISBN 0-553-27596-8). Bantam.

Sweet Valley High, No. 51. Created by Francine Pascal. 160p. 1989. pap. 2.95 (ISBN 0-553-27650-6). Bantam.

Sweet Valley High, No. 52. Created by Francine Pascal. 160p. (Orig.). 1989. pap. 2.95 (ISBN 0-553-27720-0). Bantam.

Sweet Valley High No. Forty-Four: Pretenses. Created by Francine Pascal. 1988. pap. 2.95 (ISBN 0-553-27064-8). Bantam.

Sweet Valley High Slam. Date not set. pap. 3.95 (ISBN 0-553-05496-1). Bantam.

Sweet Valley High Super Edition: Spring Break. Francine Pascal. (Sweet Valley High Ser.: No. 3). 240p. (Orig.). 1986. pap. 2.95 (ISBN 0-553-25537-1). Bantam.

Sweet Valley High Super Edition: Winter Carnival. Francine Pascal. (Orig.). (YA) (gr. 7-12). 1986. pap. 2.95 (ISBN 0-553-26159-2). Bantam.

Sweet Valley High Super Thriller, No. 3. Created by Francine Pascal. 240p. (Orig.). Date not set. pap. 2.95 (ISBN 0-553-27554-2). Bantam.

Sweet Valley Twins. Francine Pascal. (Sweet Valley High Ser.: No. 5). 96p. (Orig.). (YA) (gr. 7-12). 1987. pap. 2.50 (ISBN 0-553-15474-5). Bantam.

Sweet Valley Twins. Francine Pascal. (Skylark Old Ser.: No. 7). 112p. (Orig.). 1987. pap. 2.50 (ISBN 0-553-15500-8). Bantam.

Sweet Valley Twins. Francine Pascal. (ps-7). 1987. pap. 2.50 (ISBN 0-553-15510-5). Bantam.

Sweet Valley Twins, No. 24. Created by Francine Pascal. 112p. (Orig.). 1988. pap. 2.75 (ISBN 0-553-15635-7). Bantam.

Sweet Valley Twins, No. 25. Created by Francine Pascal. 112p. 1989. pap. 2.75 (ISBN 0-553-15653-5). Bantam.

Sweet Valley Twins, No. 26. Created by Francine Pascal. 112p. (Orig.). 1989. pap. 2.75 (ISBN 0-553-15669-1). Bantam.

Sweet Valley Twins No. Eighteen: Center of Attention. Francine Pascal. 1988. pap. 2.50 (ISBN 0-553-15581-4, Skylark). Bantam.

Sweet Valley Twins: No. 14. Francine Pascal. (Skylark Ser.). 112p. (Orig.). 1988. pap. 2.75 (ISBN 0-553-15609-8, Skylark). Bantam.

Sweet Valley Twins No. 17: Boys Against Girls. Created by Francine Pascal. Date not set. pap. 2.50 (ISBN 0-553-15571-7). Bantam.

Sweet Valley Twins Super Book, No. 2. Francine Pascal. 144p. 1988. pap. 2.95 (ISBN 0-553-15641-1, Skylark). Bantam.

Sweet Vietnam. Richard Parque. 288p. 1984. pap. 3.50 (ISBN 0-8217-1423-6). Zebra.

Sweet Water Sea: A Guide to Lake Huron's Georgian Bay. Marjorie C. Brazer. (Illus.). 200p. 1987. Repr. of 1984 ed. 18.95 (ISBN 0-942603-01-X). Heron Bks MI.

Sweet Waters, a Chilean Farm. Charles J. Lambert. LC 75-14091. (Illus.). 212p. 1975. Repr. of 1952 ed. lib. bdg. 35.00x (ISBN 0-8371-8201-8, LASWA). Greenwood.

Sweet Whispers. Samantha Harte. 336p. (Orig.). 1986. pap. 3.50 (ISBN 0-7701-0496-7). Paperjacks US.

Sweet Whispers, Brother Rush. Virginia Hamilton. 224p. (gr. 7 up). 1982. 12.95 (ISBN 0-399-20894-1, Philomel). Putnam Pub Group.

Sweet Whispers, Brother Rush. Virginia Hamilton. 220p. (gr. 5 up). 1983. pap. 2.95 (ISBN 0-380-64824-5, Camelot). Avon.

Sweet Wild World: Selections from Thoreau's Journals. Illus. by Georgia Dearborn. (Illus.). 142p. (Orig.). 1982. 12.95 (ISBN 0-89182-059-0); pap. 6.95 (ISBN 0-89182-060-4). Charles River Bks.

Sweet Wild World: Thoreau on Birds & Small Creatures. William M. White. (Illus.). 146p. (Orig.). 1981. 14.95 (ISBN 0-85699-112-0); pap. 9.95 (ISBN 0-85699-115-5). Chatham Pr.

Sweet Will. Philip Levine. LC 84-45781. 96p. 1985. 10.95 (ISBN 0-689-11585-7); pap. 5.95 (ISBN 0-689-11586-5). Atheneum.

Sweet William. Beryl Bainbridge. LC 75-43672. 192p. 1976. 7.95 (ISBN 0-8076-0816-5). Braziller.

Sweet Words: Storytelling Events in Benin. Dan Ben-Amos. LC 75-26677. (Illus.). 96p. 1975. text ed. 7.95 (ISBN 0-915980-00-2). ISHI PA.

Sweetbriar. Jude Deveraux. (Gregg Hardcovers Ser.). 1985. lib. bdg. 12.95 (ISBN 0-8398-2874-8, Gregg). G K Hall.

Sweetbriar. Jude Deveraux. 1985. pap. 3.95 (ISBN 0-671-60074-5). PB.

Sweetbriar. Jude Devereaux. (Tapestry Romance Ser.). (Orig.). 1983. pap. 2.50 (ISBN 0-671-45035-2). PB.

Sweetbriar. Brenda Wilbee. LC 83-80122. 208p. (Orig.). 1983. pap. 5.95 (ISBN 0-89081-336-1). Harvest Hse.

Sweetbriar Bride. Brenda Wilbee. (Pioneer Romance Ser.). 240p. (Orig.). 1986. pap. 5.95 (ISBN 0-89081-482-1). Harvest Hse.

Sweetco: Business Model & Activity File. 2nd ed. Lester R. Bittel & Ronald S. Burke. 320p. 1984. pap. text ed. 13.35 (ISBN 0-07-005516-5). McGraw.

Swimming for Children with Physical & Sensory Impairments. photocopy ed. Judy Newman. (Illus.). 208p. 1976. 25.25 (ISBN 0-398-03442-7). C C Thomas.
Swimming for Seniors. Edward J. Shea. LC 85-23787. 142p. (Orig.). 1986. pap. 10.95 (ISBN 0-88011-271-9, PSHE0271). Leisure Pr.
Swimming for Total Fitness: A Progressive Aerobic Program. Jane Katz & Nancy P. Bruning. LC 80-708. (Illus.). 380p. 1981. pap. 14.95 (ISBN 0-385-15932-3, Dolp). Doubleday.
Swimming: Gift for Life, Vol. I. Elise T. Lawton. (Illus.). 64p. 1986. pap. text ed. 3.00 (ISBN 0-9617193-0-3). Lawton E T.
Swimming: Going for Strength & Stamina. Marianne Brems. (Sportsperformance Ser.). (Illus.). 176p. (Orig.). 1988. pap. 7.95 (ISBN 0-8092-4573-6). Contemp Bks.
Swimming Hole Disaster. Gerald D. O'Nan & Lawrence W. O'Nan. (Adventures of Andy Ant Ser.: Vol. 2). (Illus.). 32p. (gr. 3-5). 1988. 6.95 (ISBN 0-8423-0316-2). Tyndale.
Swimming: Index of Modern Information with Bibliography. Irwin E. Herold. LC 88-47799. 150p. (Orig.). 1988. 34.50 (ISBN 0-88164-878-7); pap. 26.50 (ISBN 0-88164-879-5). ABBE Pubs Assn.
Swimming Is for Me. Lowell A. Dickmeyer. LC 80-15366. (Sports for Me Bks.). (Illus.). (gr. 2-5). 1980. PLB 7.95 (ISBN 0-8225-1084-7). Lerner Pubns.
Swimming Lessons. Rohinton Mistry. 1989. 16.95 (ISBN 0-395-49862-7). HM.
Swimming-Pool Library. Alan Hollinghurst. LC 88-42653. 1988. 16.95 (ISBN 0-394-57025-1). Random.
Swimming Pool Management. Roger Warren & Phillip Rea. LC 84-25220. (Parks and Recreation Ser.). (Illus.). 79p. (Orig.). 1985. pap. text ed. 15.00 (ISBN 0-88244-282-1); pap. 16.95. Pub Horizons.
Swimming Pool Season. Rose Tremain. LC 85-2781. 1985. 16.95 (ISBN 0-671-50464-9). Summit Bks.
Swimming Pool Season. Rose Tremain. 288p. 1986. pap. 7.95 (ISBN 0-8050-0127-1). H Holt & Co.
Swimming Pools. Kent Keegan & Pamela J. Keegan. Ed. by Shirley Horowitz & Gail Kummings. LC 81-69642. (Illus.). 160p. 1982. pap. 7.95 (ISBN 0-932944-50-7). Creative Homeowner.
Swimming Pools. 2nd ed. P. H. Perkins. (Illus.). 395p. 1978. 56.00 (ISBN 0-85334-769-7, Pub. by Elsevier Applied Sci England). Elsevier.
Swimming Pools. 5th ed. Sunset Editors. LC 80-53488. (Illus.). 128p. 1981. pap. 6.95 (ISBN 0-376-01608-6, Sunset Bks.). Sunset-Lane.
Swimming Pools: A Bibliography. Sara S. Richardson. (Architectural Ser.: A 1722). 34p. 1986. 8.75 (ISBN 1-55590-112-3). Vance Biblios.
Swimming Pools: A Guide to Their Operation & Maintenance. Gerald C. Parker. (Illus.). 53p. (Orig.). 1981. pap. 4.95x (ISBN 0-9609588-0-0). Pool Pubns.
Swimming Pools: A Guide to Their Planning, Design, & Operation. 4th ed. M. Alexander Gabrielsen. LC 86-15255. (Illus.). 328p. 1987. 32.00x (ISBN 0-87322-075-7, BGAB0075). Human Kinetics.
Swimming Pools at War. Yves Navarre. Tr. by Donald Watson from Fr. (Ubu Repertory Theater Publications Ser.: No. 1). 168p. (Orig.). 1983. pap. 6.25 (ISBN 0-913745-00-6). Ubu Repertory.
Swimming Science V. Ed. by Bodo E. Ungerechts et al. LC 87-4002. (International Sport Sciences Ser.: Vol. 18). (Illus.). 416p. 1988. text ed. 38.00x (ISBN 0-87322-108-7, BUNG0108). Human Kinetics.
Swimming Skill Book. (Illus.). 32p. (gr. 3-4). 1977. pap. 1.08x (ISBN 0-8395-6591-7); tchr's. guide 0.50x (ISBN 0-8395-8231-5); Troop leader's can-do-kit 0.50x (ISBN 0-8395-8211-0). BSA.
Swimming: Steps to Success. David G. Thomas. (Steps to Success Activity Ser.). (Illus.). 1988. pap. text ed. 9.95x (ISBN 0-88011-309-X, PHTO0309). Leisure Pr.
Swimming the Channel. Richard Meade. LC 80-26545. 80p. 1981. 7.95 (ISBN 0-931704-07-3); pap. 3.95 (ISBN 0-931704-06-5). Story Pr.
Swimming the English Channel. Susan Bright. (Fastbook 1985 Ser.). 20p. 1985. 6.00. Plain View.
Swimming to Cambodia. Spalding Gray. LC 85-20875. 160p. 1985. pap. 7.95 (ISBN 0-930452-50-X). Theatre Comm.
Swimmy. Leo Lionni. (Illus., Eng.). (ps-2). 1963. lib. bdg. 11.99 (ISBN 0-394-91713-8). Pantheon.
Swimmy. Leo Lionni. LC 63-8504. (Knopf Children's Paperbacks Ser.). (Illus.). 32p. (ps-6). 1987. pap. 2.95 (ISBN 0-317-53621-4). Knopf.
Swimwear in Vogue since 1910. Christina Probert. LC 81-67879. (Accessories in Vogue Ser.). (Illus.). 96p. 1981. pap. 12.95 (ISBN 0-89659-242-1). Abbeville Pr.
Swinburne. Samuel C. Chew. Repr. of 1931 ed. 30.00 (ISBN 0-8274-4332-3). R West.
Swinburne. Samuel C. Chew. LC 66-15385. (Illus.). viii, 335p. 1966. Repr. of 1929 ed. 29.00 (ISBN 0-208-00557-9, Archon). Shoe String.
Swinburne. J. W. Mackail. 1909. 20.50. Folcroft.
Swinburne. Harold G. Nicolson. 1973. 12.00 (ISBN 0-8274-0305-4). R West.
Swinburne. Harold G. Nicolson. LC 70-145208. 1971. Repr. of 1928 ed. 39.00 (ISBN 0-403-00807-7). Scholarly.
Swinburne: A Critical Evaluation. George E. Woodberry. 1973. lib. bdg. 20.50 (ISBN 0-8414-9793-1). Folcroft.
Swinburne: A Critical Evaluation. George E. Woodberry. LC 65-18614. Repr. of 1905 ed. 16.50x (ISBN 0-8046-0512-2, Pub by Kennikat). Assoc Faculty Pr.
Swinburne: A Lecture Delivered Before the University on April 30, 1909. John W. Mackail. LC 74-20655. 1974. Repr. of 1909 ed. lib. bdg. 15.50 (ISBN 0-8414-5946-0). Folcroft.
Swinburne: A Literary Biography. Georges Lafourcade. LC 73-12878. 1979. Repr. of 1932 ed. lib. bdg. 37.00 (ISBN 0-8414-5843-X). Folcroft.
Swinburne: A Nineteenth Century Hellene. William R. Rutland. LC 72-187516. 1931. lib. bdg. 42.50 (ISBN 0-8414-7497-4). Folcroft.
Swinburne: A Nineteenth Century Hellene. William R. Rutland. 1980. Repr. of 1931 ed. lib. bdg. 30.00 (ISBN 0-8492-7704-3). R West.
Swinburne: A Study of Romantic Mythmaking. David G. Riede. LC 78-4940. 227p. 1978. 17.95x (ISBN 0-8139-0745-4). U Pr of Va.
Swinburne: An Essay Written in 1875 & Now First Printed. Edmund Gosse. LC 73-7959. 1925. lib. bdg. 17.00 (ISBN 0-8414-2036-X). Folcroft.
Swinburne: An Experiment in Criticism. Jerome J. McGann. LC 72-77598. 352p. 1972. 22.00x (ISBN 0-226-55846-0). U of Chicago Pr.
Swinburne & Baudelaire. Harold Nicolson. LC 73-787. 1930. lib. bdg. 20.50 (ISBN 0-8414-1618-4). Folcroft.
Swinburne & Landor: A Study of Their Spiritual Relationships & Its Effect on Swinburne's Moral & Poetic Development. W. Brooks Henderson. LC 72-7221. Repr. of 1918 ed. lib. bdg. 32.00 (ISBN 0-8414-0266-3). Folcroft.
Swinburne As I Knew Him. Coulson Kernahan. LC 76-17889. 1976. Repr. of 1919 ed. lib. bdg. 25.00 (ISBN 0-8414-5517-1). Folcroft.
Swinburne, Hardy, Lawrence, & the Burden of Belief. Ross C. Murfin. LC 78-3564. 1978. 18.00x (ISBN 0-226-55150-4). U of Chicago Pr.
Swinburne Letters. Algernon C. Swinburne. Ed. by Cecil Y. Lang. LC 59-12698. Vol. 3: 1875-1877. pap. 85.80 (ISBN 0-317-29712-0, 2022043); Vol. 5: 1883-1890. pap. 74.50 (ISBN 0-317-29713-9). Bks Demand UMI.
Swinburne Letters, 6 vols, Vols. 1-5. Algernon C. Swinburne. Ed. by Cecil Y. Lang. Incl. Vol. 1. 1854-1869. (Illus.). i, 315p. 1959 (ISBN 0-300-00665-9); Vol. 2. 1869-1875. vi, 378p. 1959 (ISBN 0-300-00666-7); Vol. 3. 1875-1877. (Illus.). vii, 335p. 1960; Vol. 4. 1877-1882. vi, 325p. 1960; Vol. 5. 1883-1890. (Illus.). vii, 290p. 1962. 42.00x ea. Yale U Pr.
Swinburne Replies. Algernon Swinburne. Ed. by Clyde K. Hyder. Bd. with Notes on Poems & Reviews; Under the Microscope; Dedicatory Epistle. LC 66-19436. 136p. 1966. 14.00x (ISBN 0-8156-2098-5). Syracuse U Pr.
Swinburne: The Critical Heritage. Ed. by Clyde K. Hyder. 1970. 29.95x (ISBN 0-7100-6656-2). Routledge Chapman & Hall.
Swinburne: The Critical Heritage. Ed. by Clyde K. Hyder. (Critical Heritage Ser.). 1984. pap. 15.00 (ISBN 0-7102-0398-5). Routledge Chapman & Hall.
Swinburne: The Poet of His World. Donald Thomas. 1979. 22.95x (ISBN 0-19-520136-1). Oxford U Pr.
Swinburne's Flowers of Evil: Baudelaire's Influence. Anne Walder. 157p. 1976. pap. text ed. 16.00x (ISBN 0-317-46475-2, Pub. by Almqvist & Wiksell). Coronet Bks.
Swinburne's Hyperion & Other Poems. LaFourcade. 175p. 1980. Repr. of 1927 ed. lib. bdg. 29.00 (ISBN 0-8492-1628-1). R West.
Swinburne's Hyperion & Other Poems. Algernon C. Swinburne. LC 77-21921. 1977. Repr. of 1927 ed. lib. bdg. 35.00 (ISBN 0-8414-5829-4). Folcroft.
Swinburne's Literary Career & Fame. Clyde K. Hyder. LC 75-30031. 1984. Repr. of 1933 ed. 34.50 (ISBN 0-404-14034-3). AMS Pr.
Swinburne's Medievalism: A Study in Victorian Love Poetry. Antony H. Harrison. LC 87-3345. 208p. 1988. text ed. 27.50 (ISBN 0-8071-1327-1). La State U Pr.
Swinburne's Poems & Ballads. William M. Rossetti. LC 72-193680. 1886. lib. bdg. 42.50 (ISBN 0-8414-7482-6). Folcroft.
Swinburne's Poems & Ballads: A Criticism. William M. Rossetti. LC 73-130623. Repr. of 1866 ed. 5.00 (ISBN 0-404-05416-1). AMS Pr.
Swinburne's Theory of Poetry. Thomas E. Connolly. LC 64-17576. 1964. 39.50x (ISBN 0-87395-013-5). State U NY Pr.
Swindler & Other Stories. facs. ed. Ethel M. Dell. LC 72-140329. (Short Story Index Reprint Ser.). 1914. 21.00 (ISBN 0-8369-3721-X). Ayer Co Pubs.
Swindlers & Rogues in French Drama. Hilda Norman. LC 68-26280. 1968. Repr. of 1928 ed. 22.50x (ISBN 0-8046-0337-5, Pub by Kennikat). Assoc Faculty Pr.
Swindler's Trail, No. 68. J. D. Hardin. 192p. 1987. pap. 2.50 (ISBN 0-425-09480-4). Berkley Pub.
Swindon Fifty Years Ago (More or Less) Reminiscences, Notes & Relics of Ye Olde Wiltshire Town. William Morris. 527p. 1971. Repr. of 1885 ed. 22.50x (ISBN 0-7130-0023-6, Pub. by Woburn Pr England). Biblio Dist.
Swine Feeding & Nutrition. Ed. by Cunha. (Animal Feeding & Nutrition Ser). 1977. 39.95 (ISBN 0-12-196550-3). Acad Pr.
Swine Housing & Equipment Handbook. 4th ed. Midwest Plan Service Engineers. Ed. by Midwest Plan Service Staff. LC 82-2292. (Illus.). 112p. 1983. pap. 6.00 (ISBN 0-89373-054-8, MWPS-8). Midwest Plan Serv.
Swine in Biomedical Research, Vols 1-3. Ed. by M. E. Tumbleson. 1986. Set. 245.00 (Plenum Pr); Vol. 1, 684 p. 95.00x.; Vol. 2, 690 p. 95.00x; Vol. 3, 750 p. 95.00x. Plenum Pub.
Swine Lake. Charles Lake. (Illus.). 48p. (gr. 3-7). 1985. 9.95 (ISBN 0-13-879743-9). P-H.
Swine Production. Clarence E. Bundy et al. (gr. 10-12). 1976. text ed. 31.52 (ISBN 0-13-879783-8). P-H.
Swine Production. 5th ed. J. L. Krider et al. (Agricultural Science Ser.). 688p. 1982. text ed. 49.95 (ISBN 0-07-035503-7). McGraw.
Swine Production in Temperate & Tropical Environments. Wilson G. Pond & Jerome H. Maner. LC 73-16068. (Illus.). 646p. 1974. text ed. 38.95 (ISBN 0-7167-0840-X). W H Freeman.
Swine Raising. Ricardo El Dayrit. 1976. write for info. (ISBN 0-942717-22-8). Intl Inst Rural.
Swine Science. 5th ed. Eugene M. Ensminger & Richard Parker. LC 82-84359. (Illus.). (gr. 9-12). 1984. 53.25 (ISBN 0-8134-2289-2); text ed. 39.95x. Inter Print Pubs.
Swineherd. Hans Christian Andersen. LC 84-9460. (Illus.). 28p. (ps up). 1986. pap. 5.95 (ISBN 0-88708-011-1). Picture Bk Studio.
Swineherd. Hans Christian Andersen. Tr. by Naomi Lewis. LC 86-62521. (Illus.). 32p. (gr. k-3). 1987. 13.95 (ISBN 0-8050-0232-4, North South Bks). H Holt & Co.
Swing. Earl Atkinson. (Ballroom Dancing Ser.). 1983. lib. bdg. 79.95 (ISBN 0-87700-470-6). Revisionist Pr.
Swing. R. Ezera. 318p. 1985. pap. 4.00 (ISBN 0-8285-2965-5, Pub. by Raduga Pubs USSR). Imported Pubns.
Swing. Joyce L. Wilson. Ed. by Adrian Wilson. (Illus.). (ps-5). 1981. pap. 35.00x (ISBN 0-915918-04-8). Pr Tuscany.
Swing & a Miss. Anne B. Jones. 25p. 1988. 4.95 (ISBN 0-533-07193-3). Vantage.
Swing-Bed Planning Guide for Rural Hospitals. Ed. by John T. Supplitt. LC 83-25752. (Illus.). 220p. 1984. 3-ring binder 37.50 (ISBN 0-939450-07-0, 130500). AHPI.
Swing Dancer, Version 1.0: A Swing Dancer's Manual. Craig R. Hutchinson. LC 88-90818. (Illus.). 212p. (Orig.). 1988. pap. 20.00. Potomac Swing Dance Club.
Swing Era: The Development of Jazz 1933-1945. Gunther Schuller. (History of Jazz Ser.: No. 2: Vol. 2). (Illus.). 640p. 1988. 32.50 (ISBN 0-19-504312-X). Oxford U Pr.
Swing Low, Sweet Harriet. George Baxt. (Library of Crime Classics). 250p. 1987. pap. 4.95 (ISBN 0-930330-56-0). Intl Polygonics.
Swing Made Easy. (Ballroom Dance Ser.). 1985. lib. bdg. 79.95 (ISBN 0-87700-675-X). Revisionist Pr.
Swing Shift: Building the Liberty Ships. Joseph Fabry. LC 81-14449. (Illus.). 224p. (Orig.). 1982. pap. 7.95 (ISBN 0-89407-049-5). Strawberry Hil.
Swing, Swing Together. Peter Lovesey. (Crime Ser.). 1978. pap. 3.95 (ISBN 0-14-004618-6). Penguin.
Swing, Swing Together. Peter Lovesey. 16.95 (ISBN 0-89190-093-4, Pub. by Am Repr). Amereon Ltd.
Swing the Clubhead. Ernest Jones. LC 85-30241. (Illus.). 126p. 1986. Repr. of 1952 ed. 9.95 (ISBN 0-914178-91-1). Golf Digest.
Swing to Bop: An Oral History of the Transition in Jazz in the 1940s. Ira Gitler. (Illus.). 331p. 1985. 24.95 (ISBN 0-19-503664-6). Oxford U Pr.
Swing to Bop: An Oral History of the Transition in Jazz in the 1940's. Ira Gitler. 352p. 1987. pap. 9.95 (ISBN 0-19-505070-3). Oxford U Pr.
Swing Your Partner: Old Time Dances of New Brunswick & Nova Scotia. Lois S. Fahs. 1939. pap. 12.95 (ISBN 0-931814-01-4). Comn Studies.
Swingbeds: Assessing Flexible Health Care in Rural Communities. Ed. by Joshua M. Wiener. LC 86-73150. (Dialogue on Public Policy Ser.). 140p. pap. 11.95 (ISBN 0-8157-9283-2). Brookings.
Swinger of Birches: Poems of Robert Frost for Young People. Robert Frost. LC 82-5517. (Illus.). 80p. (gr. 4 up). 1982. 17.95 (ISBN 0-916144-92-5); pap. 9.95 (ISBN 0-916144-93-3); cassette & Bk. 21.90 (102-5); cassette only 8.95 (ISBN 0-88045-099-1). Stemmer Hse.
Swingers. Carter Brown. (Orig.). 1980. pap. 1.75 (ISBN 0-505-51583-0, Pub. by Tower Bks). Leisure NY.
Swingers Guide for the Single Girl. Marie Roget & Hector Roget. (Orig.). 1966. pap. 0.95 (ISBN 0-87067-156-1, BH156). Holloway.
Swingers Three. Cherri Grant. (Orig.). 1974. pap. 2.25 (ISBN 0-87067-047-6, BH047). Holloway.
Swingin' Round the Cirkle. David R. Locke. LC 72-91085. (American Humorists Ser.). (Illus.). 307p. Repr. of 1867 ed. lib. bdg. 26.50 (ISBN 0-8398-1167-5). Irvington.
Swinging Approach to Raquetball. Charles Smith. 64p. 1981. pap. text ed. 7.95 (ISBN 0-8403-4130-X, 40316302). Kendall-Hunt.
Swinging Caravan. Achmed Abdullah. LC 75-103485. (Short Story Index Reprint Ser.). 1925. 18.00 (ISBN 0-8369-3077-0). Ayer Co Pubs.
Swinging High: Dr. Wise Reader. Francis H. Wise. Ed. by Joyce M. Wise. (A Learn to Read Ser.: No. 8). (Illus.). 21p. 1983. pap. 1.50 (ISBN 0-915766-61-2). Wise Pub.
Swinging Mad. (Mad Ser.: No.46). (Illus.). 192p. (Orig.). 1977. pap. 1.95 (ISBN 0-446-30418-2). Warner Bks.
Swinging with Gar. Gar Witherspoon. (Illus.). 114p. (Orig.). 1987. pap. 9.95 (ISBN 0-9618178-0-1). G Witherspoon.
Swinglische Bekenntuis see Acconmpt Rekenynge & Confession of the Faith of Huldrik Zwinglius.
Swing's the Thing. Ben Hines & Bob McBee. LC 85-6349. 112p. (Orig.). 1986. pap. 9.95 (ISBN 0-9609500-1-X). McBee Sports.
Swirl Flows, Vol. 3. A. K. Gupta & D. G. Lilley. 475p. 1984. 56.00 (ISBN 0-85626-175-0). Abacus Pr.
Swirling Flow Problems at Intakes: Hydraulic Structures Design Manual, No. 1. Ed. by J. Knauss. 168p. 1987. text ed. 43.50 (ISBN 90-6191-643-7, Pub. by A A Balkema). Brookfield Pub Co.
Swiss Abduction. Mark Denning. 1981. pap. 1.95 (ISBN 0-8439-0858-0, Leisure Bks). Leisure NY.
Swiss Architecture: A General Sourcelist. Anthony G. White. (Architecture Ser.: A 1384). 9p. 1985. 2.00 (ISBN 0-89028-394-X). Vance Biblios.
Swiss Army Knife Companion: The Improbable History of the World's Handiest Knife. Rick Wall. LC 86-62852. (Illus.). 64p. 1986. pap. 5.95 (ISBN 0-9618035-0-9). Swiss Army Knife Soc.
Swiss Army Knife Handbook: The Official History & Owner's Guide. Kathryn Kane. (Illus.). 104p. (Orig.). 1988. pap. 7.50 (ISBN 0-929180-00-3). Birdworks Pubns.
Swiss Capital Market. Henri M. Neier. 130p. 1983. 120.00 (ISBN 0-8002-3403-0). Intl Pubns Serv.
Swiss Civil Code. Eugen Huber. LC 79-1609. 1985. Repr. of 1925 ed. 27.00 (ISBN 0-88355-912-9). Hyperion Conn.
Swiss Civil Code: English Version, with Vocabularies & Notes, 4 vols. Ivy Williams. 1976. Repr. of 1923 ed. Set. lib. bdg. 100.00x (ISBN 0-686-81316-2); Vol. 1. (ISBN 3-85856-000-6); Vol. 2. (ISBN 3-85856-002-2); Vol. 3. (ISBN 3-85856-003-0); Vol. 4. (ISBN 3-85856-004-9). Rothman.
Swiss Cookbook. Nika Hazelton. LC 67-23573. 1973. pap. 8.95 (ISBN 0-689-70363-5, 200). Atheneum.
Swiss Cooking. Anne Mason. 160p. 1984. pap. 9.95 (ISBN 0-233-97494-6, Pub. by A Deutsch England). David & Charles.
Swiss Country Inns & Chalets. Karen Brown. 1988. pap. 12.95 (ISBN 0-446-38816-5). Warner Bks.
Swiss Country Inns & Chalets. rev., 2nd ed. Karen Brown & Clare Brown. LC 84-52123. (Karen Brown's: European Country Inn Ser.). (Illus.). 256p. (Orig.). 1985. pap. 9.95 (ISBN 0-930328-11-6). Travel Pr.
Swiss Equity Market. Henri B. Meier. LC 85-12195. (Illus.). xiv, 210p. 1985. lib. bdg. 38.95 (ISBN 0-89930-147-9, MEQ/, Quorum Bks.). Greenwood.
Swiss Family Perelman. S. J. Perelman. 216p. 1987. pap. 6.95 (ISBN 0-14-008040-6). Penguin.
Swiss Family Robinson. Ed. by S. E. Paces. 1985. 20.00x (ISBN 0-7062-4169-X, Pub. by Ward Lock Educ Co Ltd). State Mutual Bk.
Swiss Family Robinson. (Illustrated Junior Library). (Illus.). 384p. (gr. 3-9). 1981. pap. 7.95 (ISBN 0-448-11022-9, G&D). Putnam Pub Group.
Swiss Family Robinson. (Classics Ser.). (ps-6). 1988. pap. 3.95 (ISBN 0-582-54157-3). Longman.
Swiss Family Robinson. J. D. Wyss. (Puffin Classics Ser.). (gr. 4-6). 1986. pap. 2.25 (ISBN 0-14-035044-6, Puffin). Penguin.
Swiss Family Robinson. J. R. Wyss. (Dent's Illustrated Children's Classics Ser.). (Illus.). 350p. (gr. 6 up). 1977. Repr. of 1957 ed. 13.95x (ISBN 0-460-05008-7, BKA 01637, Pub. by J. M. Dent England). Biblio Dist.
Swiss Family Robinson. Johann Wyss. (Airmont Classics Ser.). (gr. 5 up). 1964. pap. 1.95 (ISBN 0-8049-0013-2, CL-13). Airmont.
Swiss Family Robinson. Johann Wyss. 288p. (gr. 5-9). 1979. pap. 2.95 (ISBN 0-440-98440-8, LFL). Dell.
Swiss Family Robinson. Johann Wyss. (Illus.). (gr. 4-6). PLB 3.79 (ISBN 0-448-13454-3, G&D); deluxe ed. 12.95 (ISBN 0-448-06022-1). Putnam Pub Group.
Swiss Family Robinson. Johann Wyss. Ed. by Naunerle Farr. (Now Age Illustrated IV Ser.). (Illus.). (gr. 4-12). 1978. text ed. 7.50 (ISBN 0-88301-335-5); pap. text ed. 2.95 (ISBN 0-88301-323-1); activity bk. 1.25 (ISBN 0-88301-347-9). Pendulum Pr.
Swiss Family Robinson. Johann Wyss. (Bambi Classics Ser.). (Illus.). 432p. (Orig.). (YA) (gr. 9-12). 1981. pap. 3.95 (ISBN 0-89531-064-3, 0221-48). Sharon Pubns.
Swiss Family Robinson. Johann Wyss. 1981. Repr. lib. bdg. 18.95x (ISBN 0-89966-421-0). Buccaneer Bks.
Swiss Family Robinson. Johann Wyss. (Classics Ser.). (gr. 6-7). Date not set. pap. 3.95. Longman Trade.
Swiss Family Robinson. Johann D. Wyss. 21.95 (ISBN 0-8488-0108-3, Pub. by Amereon Hse). Amereon Ltd.
Swiss Family Robinson see Good Literature for Slow Readers.

Sword of Caesar. Stevenson. (Time Machine Ser.: No. 18). (ps-7). 1987. pap. 2.50 (ISBN 0-553-26531-8). Bantam.
Sword of Calandra. Susan Dexter. 352p. 1986. pap. 2.95 (ISBN 0-345-29717-2, Del Rey). Ballantine.
Sword of Chaos. Marion Zimmer Bradley. 1987. pap. 3.50 (ISBN 0-88677-172-2). DAW Bks.
Sword of Fire. Ward Hawkins. 304p. (Orig.). 1987. pap. 2.95 (ISBN 0-345-32348-3, Del Rey). Ballantine.
Sword of Forbearance. Paul O. Williams. (Pelbar Cycle Ser.: Bk. 7). 256p. (Orig.). 1985. pap. 2.95 (ISBN 0-345-32504-4, Del Rey). Ballantine.
Sword of Glory, No. 8. Peter Danielson. (Children of the Lion Ser.). 432p. (Orig.). 1987. pap. 4.50 (ISBN 0-553-26800-7). Bantam.
Sword of Gnosis: Metaphysics, Cosmology, Tradition, Symbolism. Ed. by John Needleman. 448p. 1986. pap. 10.95 (ISBN 0-317-40557-8). Routledge Chapman & Hall.
Sword of Hachiman. Guest. 1981. text ed. 12.95 (ISBN 0-07-025108-8). McGraw.
Sword of Hachiman. Lynn Guest. 416p. 1982. pap. 3.50 (ISBN 0-8217-1104-0). Zebra.
Sword of His Mouth. Robert Tannehill. 224p. 1975. pap. 9.95 (ISBN 0-89130-684-6, 06-06-01). Scholars Pr GA.
Sword of Islam. Raphael Sabatini. 1976. Repr. of 1939 ed. lib. bdg. 22.95 (ISBN 0-89190-745-9, Pub. by River City Pr). Amereon Ltd.
Sword of Light: From the Four Masters to Douglas Hyde, 1636-1938. Desmond Ryan. LC 78-5092. 1979. Repr. of 1939 ed. lib. bdg. 37.50 (ISBN 0-8495-4607-9). Arden Lib.
Sword of Light, from the Four Masters to Douglas Hyde, 1636-1938. Desmond Ryan. LC 74-9698. 1939. 35.00 (ISBN 0-8414-7307-2). Folcroft.
Sword of Nemesis. Robert A. Tracy. LC 73-18609. Repr. of 1919 ed. 24.50 (ISBN 0-404-11419-9). AMS Pr.
Sword of No-Sword: Life of the Master Warrior Tesshu. John Stevens. LC 84-5468. (Illus.). 171p. 1984. pap. 9.95 (ISBN 0-87773-284-1, 72770-3). Shambhala Pubns.
Sword of Shannara. Terry Brooks. 1983. pap. 9.95 (ISBN 0-345-33686-0, Del Rey). Ballantine.
Sword of the Dawn. Michael Moorcock. (Science Fiction Ser.: No. III). 224p. 1985. pap. 2.95 (ISBN 0-88677-173-0). DAW Bks.
Sword of the Heart. Maureen Kurr. 480p. (Orig.). 1987. pap. 3.95 (ISBN 0-8439-2467-5, Leisure Bks). Leisure NY.
Sword of the Lictor. Gene Wolfe. pap. 3.50 (ISBN 0-671-49945-9). PB.
Sword of the Lord. Wim Malgo. pap. 2.95 (ISBN 0-937422-24-X). Midnight Call.
Sword of the Lord & Gideon. James C. Kelly & William C. Baker. LC 80-15899. 1980. pap. 2.95 (ISBN 0-686-37452-5). Appalach Consortium.
Sword of the North. Richard White. LC 83-147510. 400p. 1983. 13.95 (ISBN 0-89803-122-2, Dist. by Kampmann). Green Hill.
Sword of the Prophet. Robert Goldston. 224p. 1982. pap. 2.50 (ISBN 0-449-24393-1, Crest). Fawcett.
Sword of the Prophet: A History of the Arab World from the Time of Mohammed to the Present Day. Robert Goldston. (Illus.). 1979. 11.95 (ISBN 0-8037-8372-8). Dial Bks Young.
Sword of the Republic: The United States Army on the Frontier, 1783-1846. Francis P. Prucha. LC 86-6951. (Illus.). xviii, 458p. 1986. 31.00x (ISBN 0-8032-3676-X); pap. 12.95 (ISBN 0-8032-8713-5, Bison). U of Nebr Pr.
Sword of the Samurai. Steve Jackson & Ian Livingstone. (Fighting Fantasy Gamebooks: No. 20). (Orig.). (gr. k-12). 1987. pap. 2.50 (ISBN 0-440-97795-9, LFL). Dell.
Sword of the Samurai. Michael Reaves. (Time Machine Ser.: No. 3). (Illus.). 144p. (gr. 4 up). 1984. pap. 2.50 (ISBN 0-553-26427-3). Bantam.
Sword of the Samurai: The Classical Art of Japanese Swordsmanship. George R. Parulski, Jr. (Illus.). 144p. 1985. 21.95 (ISBN 0-87364-332-1). Paladin Pr.
Sword of the Spirit. John Christopher. (gr. 6-12). 1984. 13.50 (ISBN 0-8446-6158-9). Peter Smith.
Sword of the Spirit. John E. Steinmueller. 108p. 1977. pap. 3.50 (ISBN 0-912103-00-0). Stella Maris Bks.
Sword of the Spirit: Puritan Responses to the Bible. John R. Knott, Jr. LC 79-23424. 1980. lib. bdg. 20.00x (ISBN 0-226-44848-7). U of Chicago Pr.
Sword of the Spirits see Sword of the Spirits Trilogy.
Sword of the Spirits Trilogy, 1 bk. John Christopher. Incl. Beyond the Burning Lands; Prince in Waiting; Sword of the Spirits. 192p. (gr. 5-9). pap. 3.95 (ISBN 0-02-042640-2, Collier). (gr. 6 up). 1980. (Collier). Macmillan.
Sword of Tipu Sultan. B. S. Gidwani. 372p. 1983. 7.50. Asia Bk Corp.
Sword of Truth: The Life & Times of the Shehu Usuman Dan Fodio. Mervyn Hiskett. (Illus.). 1973. pap. 3.00x (ISBN 0-19-501647-5). Oxford U Pr.
Sword of Vengeance. Alexander Karol. 1977. pap. 1.50 (ISBN 0-505-51150-9, Pub. by Tower Bks). Leisure NY.
Sword of Welleran & Other Wonder Tales. Lord Dunsany. 16.50 (ISBN 0-8159-6833-7). Devin.
Sword of Winter. Randall. Date not set. pap. 3.50 (ISBN 0-671-55456-5). PB.
Sword of Winter. Marta Randall. LC 83-4830. 271p. 1983. 15.00. Ultramarine Pub.
Sword of Wood. G. K. Chesterton. 1928. lib. bdg. 22.00 (ISBN 0-8414-0902-1). Folcroft.
Sword Over America. Richard Ruhling. (Illus.). 55p. (Orig.). pap. 2.00x (ISBN 0-317-55134-5). Total Health.
Sword over Richmond: An Eyewitness History of McClellan's Peninsula Campaign. Richard Wheeler. LC 85-45240. (Illus.). 400p. 1986. 21.45i (ISBN 0-06-015529-9, HarpT). Har-Row.
Sword Point. Harold Coyle. 388p. 1988. 18.95 (ISBN 0-671-66553-7). S&S.
Sword-Singer. Jennifer Roberson. 384p. 1988. pap. 3.95 (ISBN 0-88677-295-8). DAW Bks.
Sword, the Jewel, & the Mirror. John M. Roberts. 288p. 1988. pap. 3.50 (ISBN 0-8125-5204-0, Dist. by St Martin's Pr & Warner Pub Servs). Tor Bks.
Sword Woman. Robert E. Howard. 1987. pap. 2.95 (ISBN 0-317-63419-4, Pub by Ace Science Fiction). Ace Bks.
Swordbearer. Glen Cook. (Orig.). 1982. pap. 2.75 (ISBN 0-671-83687-0, Timescape). PB.
Swordbearers: Supreme Command in the First World War. Correlli Barnett. LC 74-19057. (Midland Bks.: No. 175). (Illus.). 416p. 1975. 30.00x (ISBN 0-253-35584-2); pap. 12.50x (ISBN 0-253-20175-6). Ind U Pr.
Swordfish Tooth: Poems. Cynthia Zarin. LC 88-45264. 64p. 1989. 16.95 (ISBN 0-394-57320-X); pap. 8.95 (ISBN 0-679-72140-1). Knopf.
Swords Against Carthage. Friedrich Donauer. Tr. by F. T. Cooper. LC 61-12878. (Illus.). (gr. 7-11). 1932. 15.00 (ISBN 0-8196-0112-8). Biblo.
Swords Against Darkness, No. 4. Ed. by Andrew J. Offutt. 1981. pap. 2.50 (ISBN 0-89083-784-8). Zebra.
Swords Against Darkness Five. Ed. by Andrew J. Offutt. 1981. pap. 2.50 (ISBN 0-89083-839-9). Zebra.
Swords Against Death. Fritz Leiber. (Fafhrd & the Grey Mouser Ser.). 1982. pap. 2.95 (ISBN 0-441-79193-X). Ace Bks.
Swords & Camellias. Teresa Moore. 400p. (Orig.). 1987. pap. 3.95 (ISBN 0-8439-2479-9, Leisure Bks). Leisure NY.
Swords & Deviltry. Fritz Leiber. 256p. 1985. pap. 2.95 (ISBN 0-441-79197-2) (ISBN 0-317-31890-X). Ace Bks.
Swords & Ice Magic. Fritz Leiber. 1986. pap. 2.95 (ISBN 0-441-79196-4). Ace Bks.
Swords & Ploughshares; Or, the Supplanting of the System of War by the System of Law. Lucia A. Mead. LC 71-143431. (Peace Movement in America Ser.). xiv, 249p. 1972. Repr. of 1912 ed. lib. bdg. 18.95x (ISBN 0-89198-079-2). Ozer.
Swords & Plowshares: The United States & Disarmament 1898-1979. Patrick J. Gallo. 101p. (Orig.). 1980. pap. 13.00x (ISBN 0-89126-090-0). MA-AH Pub.
Swords & Roses. facsimile ed. Joseph Hergesheimer. LC 70-167355. (Essay Index Reprint Ser). Repr. of 1929 ed. 19.00 (ISBN 0-8369-2650-1). Ayer Co Pubs.
Swords & Scales: The Development of the Uniform Code of Military Justice. William T. Generous, Jr. LC 72-91173. 1973. 26.50x (ISBN 0-8046-9039-1, Pub by Kennikat). Assoc Faculty Pr.
Swords & Shields: New Choices for Offense & Defense. Fred S. Hoffman et al. 384p. 35.00x (ISBN 0-669-14249-2). Lexington Bks.
Swords Around a Throne: Napoleon's Grande Armee. John R. Elting. (Illus.). 550p. 1988. 35.00 (ISBN 0-02-909501-8). Free Pr.
Swords from Plowshares: The Military Potential of Civilian Nuclear Energy. Albert Wohlstetter et al. LC 78-56373. 1979. 16.50x (ISBN 0-226-90476-8); pap. 5.95x (ISBN 0-226-90477-6). U of Chicago Pr.
Swords in the North. Paul L. Anderson. LC 57-9448. 270p. (gr. 7-11). 1935. 15.00 (ISBN 0-8196-0103-9). Biblo.
Swords into Ploughshares. Mary H. Jones. LC 70-109757. (Illus.). 1971. Repr. of 1937 ed. lib. bdg. 25.00x (ISBN 0-8371-4247-4, JOSP). Greenwood.
Swords into Plowshares. Ernest M. Eller. (Orig., Eng. & Japanese.). 1986. pap. 1.50 (ISBN 0-934841-12-8). Adm Nimitz Foun.
Swords into Plowshares. Ed. by Arthur Laffin & Anne Montgomery. 192p. 1987. pap. 8.95 (ISBN 0-06-064911-9, HarpR). Har-Row.
Swords into Plowshares: A Collection of Plays About Peace & Social Justice. Ingrid Rogers. 288p. (Orig.). 1983. pap. 8.95 (ISBN 0-87178-827-6). Brethren.
Swords into Plowshares: The Problems & Progress of International Organization. 4th ed. Inis L. Claude, Jr. 1971. text ed. write for info (ISBN 0-394-34053-1, RanC). Random.
Swords of Anjou. Mario Pei. 310p. 1953. 8.95x (ISBN 0-913298-66-2). S F Vanni.
Swords of God. Alan Caillou. (Ian Quayle Ser.: No. 2). 256p. (Orig.). 1987. pap. 3.50 (ISBN 1-55547-180-3). Critics Choice Paper.
Swords of Mars. Edgar Rice Burroughs. 1985. pap. 2.50 (ISBN 0-345-32956-2). Ballantine.
Swords of Shahrazar. Robert E. Howard. LC 76-16707. 1976. 12.95x (ISBN 0-913960-08-X). Fax Collect.
Swords of the Britons. A. J. Young. 200p. 1984. 40.00x (ISBN 0-7212-0624-7, Pub. by Regency Pr). State Mutual Bk.
Swords of the Horseclans. Robert Adams. (Horseclans Ser.: No. 2). 1983. pap. 2.95 (ISBN 0-451-14025-7, E9988, Sig). NAL.
Swords of the Legion. Harry Turtledove. (Videssos Cycle Ser.: Bk. 4). 408p. 1987. pap. 3.95 (ISBN 0-345-33070-6, Del Rey). Ballantine.
Swords of the Swashbucklers. Bill Mantlo & Jackson Guice. (Marvel Graphic Novel Ser.: No. 14). 5.95 (ISBN 0-87135-002-5). Marvel Comics.
Swords of WWII Germany. Thomas M. Johnson & John R. Omsby. (Illus.). 66p. pap. 5.00 (ISBN 0-317-55220-1). Johnson Ref Bks.
Swords or Plowshares: South Africa & Political Change; An Introduction. Vincent V. Razis. 162p. 1980. pap. text ed. 10.95x (ISBN 0-86975-123-9, Pub. by Ravan Pr). Ohio U Pr.
Swords Trilogy. Michael Moorcock. 1984. pap. 3.95 (ISBN 0-425-10333-1). Berkley Pub.
Swordsman. Terry L. Craig. 304p. (Orig.). 1987. pap. 7.95 (ISBN 0-9618852-0-3). Berachah Pub.
Swordsmen of the Screen: From Douglas Fairbanks to Michael York. Jeffrey Richards. (Cinema & Society Ser.). (Illus.). 312p. 1980. pap. 10.95 (ISBN 0-7100-0681-0). Routledge Chapman & Hall.
Swordsplay & the Elizabethan & Jacobean Stage. Robert E. Morsberger. Ed. by James Hogg. (Jacobean Drama Studies). 129p. (Orig.). 1974. pap. 15.00 (ISBN 0-317-40107-6, Pub. by Salzburg Studies). Longwood Pub Group.
Swordspoint. Ellen Kushner. 272p. 1987. 15.95 (ISBN 0-87795-923-4, Arbor Hse). Morrow.
Swordspoint. Ellen Kushner. 336p. 1989. pap. price not set. Tor Bks.
Swordswoman. Jessica A. Salmons. 320p. 1988. pap. 3.50 (ISBN 0-8125-5350-0). Tor Bks.
Swordwield. Aedric. 240p. 1987. 10.95 (ISBN 0-8062-3046-0). Carlton.
Sworn Book of Honourius the Magician. Tr. by Daniel J. Driscoll. LC 76-57011. 1983. 20.00 (ISBN 0-935214-00-3). Heptangle.
Sworn Enemies, No. 7. Linda A. Cooney. (Couples Ser.). (YA) (gr. 7-12). 1988. pap. 2.50 (ISBN 0-590-33970-2). Scholastic Inc.
SX-Seventy Art. LC 79-2426. (Illus.). 140p. 1979. 20.00 (ISBN 0-912810-23-8). Lustrum Pr.
Sybaris & Other Homes. Edward E. Hale. LC 70-155158. (Utopian Literature Ser). 1971. Repr. of 1869 ed. 18.00 (ISBN 0-405-03551-9). Ayer Co Pubs.
Sybelle. Roberta Gellis. (Roselynde Chronicles Ser.). 1984. lib. bdg. 13.95 (ISBN 0-8398-2865-9, Gregg). G K Hall.
SYBEX Computer Blue Book. National Association of Computer Dealers (NACD) Staff. 421p. (Orig.). 1987. pap. 9.95 (ISBN 0-89588-460-7). Sybex.
SYBEX Computer Blue Books. National Association of Computer Dealers (NACD) Staff. 380p. (Orig.). 1988. pap. 9.95 (ISBN 0-89588-526-3). Sybex.
SYBEX WordPerfect Study Guide. Milano et al. 175p. (Orig.). 1987. pap. 10.95 (ISBN 0-89588-434-8). Sybex.
Sybil. Louis Auchincloss. LC 75-108840. 284p. 1972. Repr. of 1952 ed. lib. bdg. 35.00x (ISBN 0-8371-3728-4, AUSY). Greenwood.
Sybil. Benjamin Disraeli. Ed. by Sheila Smith. (World's Classics Paperback Ser.). 1981. pap. 7.95 (ISBN 0-19-281551-2). Oxford U Pr.
Sybil. Benjamin Disraeli. Ed. by Thom Braun. (English Library). 1980. pap. 6.95 (ISBN 0-14-043134-9). Penguin.
Sybil. Flora R. Schreiber. (Illus.). 464p. 1974. pap. 4.50 (ISBN 0-446-32154-0). Warner Bks.
Sybil; Or, the Two Nations. Benjamin Disraeli. LC 83-45412. Repr. of 1925 ed. 42.50 (ISBN 0-404-20022-2). AMS Pr.
Sybil Rides for Independence. Drollene Brown. Ed. by Abby Levine. (Illus.). 48p. (gr. 2-5). 1985. 9.75 (ISBN 0-8075-7684-0). A Whitman.
Sybil Sadie. Illus. by Lucinda McQueen & Jeremy Guitar. (Cabbage Patch Kids Ser.). (Illus.). 12p. (gr. 1-5). 1984. 4.00 (ISBN 0-910313-32-6). Parker Bros.
Sybil; Tancred see Works of Benjamin Disraeli, Earl of Beaconsfield.
Sybilla. Joan Hessayon. 251p. 1987. 18.95 (ISBN 0-7126-1276-9, Pub. by Century Hutchinson). David & Charles.
Sycamore Hill. Francine Rivers. 320p. 1985. pap. 3.50 (ISBN 0-515-08181-7). Jove Pubns.
Sycamore Steeple. Suzanne P. Ellison. 224p. 1987. pap. 5.95 (ISBN 0-310-47721-2, 15625P). Zondervan.
Sycamore Stories. Jerome Koch. pap. 3.50 (ISBN 0-8006-1945-5). Fortress.
Sycamore Year. Mildred Lee. LC 74-6409. 160p. (gr. 6 up). 1974. PLB 11.88 (ISBN 0-688-51643-2). Lothrop.
Sycophancy in Athens. J. O. Lofberg. xii, 104p. 1976. 15.00 (ISBN 0-89005-115-1). Ares.
Sycophancy in Athens & Capital Punishment in Ancient Athens. John O. Lofbarg & Irving Barkan. Ed. by Gregory Vlastos. LC 78-14609. (Morals & Law in Ancient Greece Ser.). 1979. Repr. of 1936 ed. lib. bdg. 14.00x (ISBN 0-405-11585-7). Ayer Co Pubs.
Syd Hoff Shows You How to Draw Cartoons. Syd Hoff. (Illus.). (gr. k-3). 1979. pap. 1.50 (ISBN 0-590-05777-4). Scholastic Inc.
Syd Hoff's Animal Jokes. Syd Hoff. LC 84-48353. (Illus.). 48p. (gr. k-3). 1985. (Lipp Jr Bks); PLB 12.89 (ISBN 0-397-32117-1). HarpJ.
Sydney. (Frommer's City Guides Ser.). (Illus.). 224p. 1988. pap. 5.95 (ISBN 0-13-332073-1). Prentice Hall Pr.
Sydney & Frances Lewis Contemporary Art Fund Collection. Rebecca Massie. LC 80-14914. (Illus.). 112p. (Orig.). 1980. pap. 7.95 (ISBN 0-917046-09-9). VA Mus Arts.
Sydney by Ferry & Foot. John Gunter. 160p. (Orig.). 1985. pap. 10.95 (ISBN 0-949924-51-2, Pub. by Kangaroo Pr). Intl Spec Bk.
Sydney Circle. Alice Ekert-Rotholz. Tr. by Catherine Hutter from Ger. LC 83-1448. 392p. 1983. 15.95 (ISBN 0-88064-009-X). Fromm Intl Pub.
Sydney Circle. Alice Ekert-Rotholz. 400p. 1986. pap. 3.95 (ISBN 0-445-20069-3, Pub. by Popular Lib). Warner Bks.
Sydney Cove Medallion see Emile Lessore, 1805-1876: His Life & Work.
Sydney Learns to Share. Paula Bussard. (Critter County Ser.). (Illus.). 28p. (gr. k-3). 1985. 1.29 (ISBN 0-87239-961-3, 3381). Standard Pub.
Sydney Omarr's Astrological Guide for You in 1988. Sydney Omarr. 256p. 1987. pap. 3.95 (ISBN 0-451-14940-8, Sig). NAL.
Sydney Omarr's Astrological Guide for You in 1989. Sydney Omarr. 256p. (Orig.). 1988. pap. 3.95 (ISBN 0-451-15479-7, Sig). NAL.
Sydney Omarrs Day-by-Day Astrological Guide for Aquarius: 1986. 1985. pap. 3.50 (ISBN 0-451-14908-4, Sig). NAL.
Sydney Omarrs Day-by-Day Astrological Guide for Aries: 1986. 1985. pap. 3.50 (ISBN 0-451-14897-5, Sig). NAL.
Sydney Omarrs Day-by-Day Astrological Guide for Capricorn: 1986. 1985. pap. 3.50 (ISBN 0-451-14907-6, Sig). NAL.
Sydney Omarrs Day-by-Day Astrological Guide for Cancer: 1986. 1985. pap. 3.50 (ISBN 0-451-14900-9, Sig). NAL.
Sydney Omarrs Day-by-Day Astrological Guide for Gemini: 1986. 1985. pap. 3.50 (ISBN 0-451-14899-1, Sig). NAL.
Sydney Omarrs Day-by-Day Astrological Guide for Libra: 1986. 1985. pap. 3.50 (ISBN 0-451-14903-3, Sig). NAL.
Sydney Omarrs Day-by-Day Astrological Guide for Leo: 1986. 1985. pap. 3.50 (ISBN 0-451-14901-7, Sig). NAL.
Sydney Omarrs Day-by-Day Astrological Guide for Pisces: 1986. 1985. pap. 3.50 (ISBN 0-451-14909-2, Sig). NAL.
Sydney Omarrs Day-by-Day Astrological Guide for Sagittarius: 1986. 1985. pap. 3.50 (ISBN 0-451-14906-8, Sig). NAL.
Sydney Omarrs Day-by-Day Astrological Guide for Scorpio: 1986. 1985. pap. 3.50 (ISBN 0-451-14904-1, Sig). NAL.
Sydney Omarrs Day-by-Day Astrological Guide for Taurus: 1986. 1985. pap. 3.50 (ISBN 0-451-14898-3, Sig). NAL.
Sydney Omarrs Day-by-Day Astrological Guide for Virgo: 1986. 1985. pap. 3.50 (ISBN 0-451-14902-5, Sig). NAL.
Sydney Parkinson: Artist of Cook's Endeavor Voyage. Ed. by D. J. Carr. (Illus.). 315p. 1983. text ed. 45.00X (ISBN 0-8248-0889-4). UH Pr.
Sydney Smith. Alan Bell. (Illus.). 1980. 38.00x (ISBN 0-19-812050-8). Oxford U Pr.
Sydney Smith. George W. E. Russell. 1973. lib. bdg. 25.00 (ISBN 0-8414-7488-5). Folcroft.
Sydney Smith. George W. E. Russell. LC 79-156929. 254p. 1971. Repr. of 1905 ed. 35.00x (ISBN 0-8103-3720-7). Gale.
Sydney Smith: A Biography & a Selection. Gerald W. Bullett. LC 77-138578. (Illus.). 1971. Repr. of 1951 ed. lib. bdg. 35.00x (ISBN 0-8371-5777-3, BUSS). Greenwood.
Sydney the Koala. (Zoo Babies Ser.). 16p. (gr. k-6). 1982. pap. 1.25 (ISBN 0-8249-8033-6). Ideals.
Sydney to the Rescue. Paula Bussard. (Critter County Ser.). (Illus.). 28p. (gr. k-3). 1985. 1.29 (ISBN 0-87239-964-8, 3384). Standard Pub.
Sydney Traders: Simeon Lord & His Comtemporaries 1788-1821. D. R. Hains. 264p. 1982. pap. 21.00x (ISBN 0-522-84217-8, Pub. by Melbourne U Pr). Intl Spec Bk.
Sydney Walkabout, No. 1. Janice Dewhurst & Margaret White. (Heritage Field Guides Ser.). (Illus.). 160p. 1987. pap. 10.95 (ISBN 0-86417-069-6, Pub. by Kangaroo Pr). Intl Spec Bk.
Sydney's Soup-Can Message. Paula J. Bussard. (Critter County Ser.). (Illus.). 32p. (gr. k-6). 1986. 1.29 (ISBN 0-87403-101-X, 3431). Standard Pub.
Syed Amanuddin: His Mind & Art. A. N. Dwivedi. vii, 143p. 1988. text ed. 25.00x (ISBN 81-207-0824-5, Pub. by Sterling Pubs India). Apt Bks.
Sykaos Papers. E. P. Thompson. LC 88-42596. 1988. 19.95 (ISBN 0-394-56828-1). Pantheon.
Syllabic Inscriptions from Byblos. George E. Mendenhall. 194p. 1986. text ed. 40.00x (ISBN 0-8156-6077-4, Am U Beirut). Syracuse U Pr.
Syllabic Reading. Bernice C. Kramkowski. LC 83-90226. (Illus.). 118p. (Orig.). (gr. 1-5). 1983. comb bdg. 9.95 (ISBN 0-912145-00-5). MMI Pr.

Symbiosis In Parent-Offspring Interactions. Ed. by Leonard A. Rosenblum. Howard Moltz. 300p. 1983. 39.50x (ISBN 0-306-41410-4, Plenum Pr). Plenum Pub.

Symbiosis: Popular Culture & Other Fields. Ed. by Ray B. Browne & Marshall Fishwick. LC 88-71361. 224p. 1988. lib. bdg. 31.95 (ISBN 0-87972-440-4); pap. text ed. 15.95 (ISBN 0-87972-439-0). Bowling Green Univ.

Symbiotic Imperative: A Blueprint for Living Together Campatibly. W. D. Taylor. 165p. 1981. 9.50 (ISBN 0-682-49675-8). Exposition-Phoenix.

Symbiotic Nitrogen Fixation in Plants. Ed. by P. S. Nutman. LC 75-2732. (International Biological Programme Ser.: No. 7). (Illus.). 652p. 1976. 130.00 (ISBN 0-521-20645-6). Cambridge U Pr.

Symbiotic Nitrogen Fixation Technology. Elkan. 456p. 1987. 125.00 (ISBN 0-8247-7751-4). Dekker.

Symbiotic Phenomenon. Ed. by Joanna Mikolajewska et al. 1988. lib. bdg. 99.00 (ISBN 90-277-2723-6). Kluwer Academic.

Symbiotic Stars. S. J. Kenyon. (Illus.). 200p. 1987. 54.50 (ISBN 0-521-26807-9). Cambridge U Pr.

Symbiotic Universe: An Unorthodox Look at the Origin of the Cosmos & the Development of Life. George Greenstein. LC 87-17391. (Illus.). 1988. 18.95 (ISBN 0-688-07604-1). Morrow.

Symbol & Art in Worship. Ed. by Luis Maldonado & David Power. (Concilium Ser.: Vol. 132). 128p. (Orig.). 1980. pap. 5.95 (ISBN 0-8164-2274-5, HarpR). Har-Row.

Symbol & Empowerment: Paul Tillich's Post-Theistic System. Richard Grigg. LC 85-7214. xvi, 148p. 1985. text ed. 14.50 (ISBN 0-86554-163-9, MUP H153). Mercer Univ Pr.

Symbol & Idea in Henry Adams. Melvin Lyon. LC 67-20597. xii, 326p. 1970. 27.50x (ISBN 0-8032-0729-8). U of Nebr Pr.

Symbol & Meaning Beyond the Closed Community: Essays in Mesoamerican Ideas. Gary H. Gossen. LC 86-82620. (Studies on Culture & Society: No. 1). (Illus.). 278p. (Orig.). 1987. pap. text ed. 25.00 (ISBN 0-942041-10-0). SUNYA Inst Mesoam.

Symbol & Myth: Humbert De Superville's Essay on Absolute Signs in Art. Barbara Stafford. LC 76-19842. 206p. 1979. 50.00 (ISBN 0-87413-120-0). U Delaware Pr.

Symbol & Myth in Ancient Poetry. Herbert A. Musurillo. LC 77-2395. 1977. Repr. of 1961 ed. lib. bdg. 35.00x (ISBN 0-8371-9554-3, MUSM). Greenwood.

Symbol & Neurosis: Selected Papers of Lawrence S. Kubie. Ed. by Herbert J. Schlesinger. LC 77-92177. (Psychological Issues Monograph: No. 44, Vol. 11, No. 4). 280p. 1978. text ed. 30.00x (ISBN 0-8236-6291-8); pap. text ed. 22.50 (ISBN 0-8236-6290-X). Intl Univs Pr.

Symbol & Politics in Communal Ideology: Cases & Questions. Ed. by Sally F. Moore & Barbara G. Myerhoff. LC 75-16810. (Symbol, Myth & Ritual Ser.). (Illus.). 240p. 1975. pap. 9.95x (ISBN 0-8014-9157-6). Cornell U Pr.

Symbol & Privilege: The Ritual Context of British Royalty. Ilse Hayden. LC 86-25093. 214p. 1987. 27.95 (ISBN 0-8165-0906-9). U of Ariz Pr.

Symbol & Sacrament: A Contemporary Sacramental Theology. Michael G. Lawler. 304p. 1988. pap. 11.95 (ISBN 0-8091-2924-8). Paulist Pr.

Symbol & Satire in the French Revolution: With 171 Illustrations. Ernest F. Henderson. 1977. lib. bdg. 69.95 (ISBN 0-8490-2724-1). Gordon Pr.

Symbol & Substance in American Indian Art. Zena Pearlstone Mathews. Ed. by Amy Horbar. LC 83-26407. 24p. (Orig.). 1984. pap. 2.95 (ISBN 0-87099-363-1). Metro Mus Art.

Symbol & Symbolism. (YFS Ser.: No. 9). 1952. pap. 16.00 (ISBN 0-527-01717-5). Kraus Repr.

Symbol & the Symbolic: Ancient Egypt, Science, & the Evolution of Consciousness. R. A. Schwaller De Lubicz. Tr. by Robert Lawlor & Deborah Lawlor. LC 81-13375. (Illus.). 100p. 1981. pap. 5.95 (ISBN 0-89281-022-X). Inner Tradit.

Symbol & Theory. John Skorupski. LC 76-3037. 1976. 39.50 (ISBN 0-521-21200-6). Cambridge U Pr.

Symbol & Theory: A Philosophical Study of Theories of Religion in Social Anthropology. John Skorupski. LC 76-3037. 280p. 1983. pap. 14.95 (ISBN 0-521-27252-1). Cambridge U Pr.

Symbol & Truth in Blake's Myth. Leopold Damrosch, Jr. LC 80-7515. (Illus.). 504p. 1980. 44.50x (ISBN 0-691-06433-4); pap. 14.50x o.p (ISBN 0-691-10095-0). Princeton U Pr.

Symbol Art: Thirteen Squares, Circles & Triangles from Around the World. Leonard E. Fisher. LC 85-42805. (Illus.). 64p. (gr. 4-6). 1986. 12.95 (ISBN 0-02-735270-6, Four Winds). Macmillan.

Symbol Communication Technique (SCT) A Self-Motivating Method of Learning to Write. rev. ed. Alfred W. Munzert. Ed. by Karen K. Elskamp. LC 70-134719. 88p. 1987. pap. 8.95 (ISBN 0-917292-04-9). H-U Public.

Symbol Discrimination & Sequencing. Reusable ed. W. Edwards & S. Edwards. (Ann Arbor Tracking Program Ser.). (gr. 2). 1976. wkbk. 6.50 (ISBN 0-89039-154-8). Ann Arbor FL.

Symbol Discrimination Series: Books 1, 2, 3, 4, 5, & 6. Reusable ed. Ann Arbor Publishers Editorial Staff. (Symbol Discrimination Series). (Illus.). 16p. (gr. k-1). 1974. 3.00 ea.; Book 1. 3.00 (ISBN 0-89039-078-9); Book 2. 3.00 (ISBN 0-89039-079-7); Book 3. 3.00 (ISBN 0-89039-080-0); Book 4. 3.00 (ISBN 0-89039-081-9); Book 5. 3.00 (ISBN 0-89039-082-7); Book 6. 3.00 (ISBN 0-89039-083-5). Ann Arbor FL.

Symbol, Dream & Psychosis. Robert Fliess. LC 72-184212. (Psychoanalytic Ser.: Vol. 3). 435p. 1973. text ed. 42.50x (ISBN 0-8236-6287-X). Intl Univs Pr.

Symbol Formation: An Organismic-Developmental Approach to the Psychology of Language. Ed. by Heinz Werner & Bernard Kaplan. 544p. 1984. pap. text ed. 19.95 (ISBN 0-89859-370-0). L Erlbaum Assocs.

Symbol Manipulation Techniques for Physics. T. A. Brody. (Documents on Modern Physics Ser.). 104p. 1968. 59.00 (ISBN 0-677-01820-7). Gordon & Breach.

Symbol, Myth & Culture: Essays & Lectures of Ernst Cassirer 1935-45. Ernst Cassirer. Ed. by Donald P. Verne. LC 78-9887. 1979. 40.00x (ISBN 0-300-02306-5); pap. 12.95x (ISBN 0-300-02666-8). Yale U Pr.

Symbol, Myth, & Rhetoric: The Politics of Culture in an Armenian-American Population. Jenny K. Phillips. LC 87-45788. (Immigrant Communities & Ethnic Minorities in the United States & Canada Ser.: No. 23). 1988. 47.50 (ISBN 0-404-19433-8). AMS Pr.

Symbol of Liberty. Linda B. Vasilaki & Theodore C. Merritt. (Illus.). 26p. (gr. 1-6). 1987. 7.95 (ISBN 0-8059-3066-3); cassette incl. Dorrance.

Symbol of Man. G. Wilson Knight. LC 81-40003. (Illus.). 194p. 1981. lib. bdg. 25.50 (ISBN 0-8191-1588-6); pap. text ed. 11.50 (ISBN 0-8191-1589-4). U Pr of Amer.

Symbol of Man. G. Wilson Knight. 192p. 1984. 25.00 (ISBN 0-317-43712-7, Pub. by Regency Pr). State Mutual Bk.

Symbol of the Soul from Holderlin to Yeats: A Study in Metonymy. Suzanne Nalbantian. LC 76-25550. 151p. 1976. 25.00x (ISBN 0-231-04148-9). Columbia U Pr.

Symbol Patterns: Ideas for Banners, Posters, Bulletin Boards. 40p. (Orig.). 1981. pap. 5.95 (ISBN 0-8066-1897-3, 10-6173). Augsburg.

Symbol-Psychology. Adolph Roeder. 204p. 1981. Repr. of 1903 ed. lib. bdg. 50.00 (ISBN 0-89987-724-9). Darby Bks.

Symbol Sourcebook: An Authoritative Guide to International Graphic Symbols. Henry Dreyfuss. LC 83-12514. (Illus.). 292p. 1984. pap. 24.95 (ISBN 0-442-21806-0). Van Nos Reinhold.

Symbol, Status, & Personality. Samuel I. Hayakawa. LC 63-1772. 188p. 1966. pap. 5.95 (ISBN 0-15-687611-6, Harv). HarBraceJ.

Symbol to Vortex: Poetry, Painting & Ideas, 1885-1914. Alan Robinson. LC 83-24449. 280p. 1985. 25.00 (ISBN 0-312-78188-1). St Martin.

Symbolae Ad Mycologiam Fennicam. P. A. Karsten. 1966. Repr. of 1895 ed. 96.00x (ISBN 3-7682-0352-2). Lubrecht & Cramer.

Symbolae Ad Mycologiam Fennicam. Peter A. Karsten. 1870-1895. 85.00 (ISBN 0-384-28690-9). Johnson Repr.

Symbolae Mycologicae. K. Leopold Fuckel. (Illus.). Repr. of 1877 ed. 90.00 (ISBN 0-384-17190-7). Johnson Repr.

Symbolae Mycologicae & Supplements. L. Fuckel. (Illus.). 1966. Repr. of 1877 ed. 120.00x (ISBN 3-7682-0358-1). Lubrecht & Cramer.

Symbolae Osloenses, Vol. LXIII. Egil Kraggerud. (Norwegian University Press Publication Ser.). (Illus.). 130p. 1988. 36.00 (ISBN 82-00-18123-5). Oxford U Pr.

Symbolae Osloenses, Vol. LIX. Ed. by Egil Kraggerud & L. Amundsen. 144p. (Orig.). 1984. pap. 25.00x (ISBN 82-00-06883-8). Oxford U Pr.

Symbolae Osloenses LXI. Ed. by Egil Kraggerud. (Norwegian University Press Publication). 112p. 1986. pap. 27.00x (ISBN 82-00-07381-5). Oxford U Pr.

Symbolae Osloenses LXI. Ed. by Egil Kraggerud. (Norwegian University Press Publication). 160p. 1986. 36.00 (ISBN 82-00-07709-8). Oxford U Pr.

Symbolae Osloenses LXII. Ed. by L. Amundsen et al. (Norwegian University Press Publication). (Illus.). 130p. 1987. 39.95 (ISBN 82-00-07068-9). Oxford U Pr.

Symbolaeographia Which Termed the Art, Description of Instruments, Covenants, Contracts, Etc. William West. LC 74-28892. (English Experience Ser.: No. 768). 1975. Repr. of 1590 ed. 60.00 (ISBN 90-221-0768-X). Walter J Johnson.

Symbole litteraire: Essai sur la signification du symbole chez Wagner, Baudelaire, Mallarme, Bergson, et Marcel Proust. Emeric Fiser. LC 77-10260. Repr. of 1941 ed. 27.50 (ISBN 0-404-16315-7). AMS Pr.

Symbolic Action in the Plays of the Wakefield Master. Jeffrey Helterman. LC 80-18273. (South Atlantic Modern Language Association Award Study). 208p. 1981. 20.00x (ISBN 0-8203-0534-0). U of Ga Pr.

Symbolic Analysis Cross Culturally: The Rorschach Test. George De Vos & L. Bryce Boyer. 1988. 40.00x (ISBN 0-520-06086-5). U of Cal Pr.

Symbolic & Algebraic Computation by Computers: Proceedings of the International Symposium, 2nd, Institute of Physical & Chemical Research (RIKEN), Saitama, Japan, August 21-22, 1984. Ed. by N. Inada & T. Soma. LC 85-20323. (World Scientific Series in Computer Science: Vol. 2). 256p. 1985. 33.00 (ISBN 9971-50-021-3). World Scientific Pub.

Symbolic & Pragmatic Semantics: A Kannada System of Address. Susan S. Bean. LC 77-18198. (Illus.). 1978. lib. bdg. 17.00x (ISBN 0-226-03989-7). U of Chicago Pr.

Symbolic & Structural Archaeology. Ed. by Ian Hodder. LC 81-17992. (New Directions in Archaeology Ser.). (Illus.). 250p. 1982. o. p. 44.50 (ISBN 0-521-24406-4). Cambridge U Pr.

Symbolic & the Real. Ira Progoff. LC 63-18865. (Holistic Depth Psyhcology Trilogy). 256p. 1973. pap. text ed. 7.95 (ISBN 0-07-050892-5). McGraw.

Symbolic Anthropology: A Reader in the Study of Symbols & Meanings. Ed. by Janet L. Dolgin et al. LC 77-3176. 523p. 1977. 47.50x (ISBN 0-231-04032-6); pap. 22.50x (ISBN 0-231-04033-4). Columbia U Pr.

Symbolic Art of Gogol: Essays on His Short Fiction. James B. Woodward. 131p. 1982. 12.95 (ISBN 0-89357-093-1). Slavica.

Symbolic Communication: Signifying Calls & Police Response. Peter K. Manning. (Organization Studies: No. 9). 290p. 1988. text ed. 35.00x (ISBN 0-262-13234-6). MIT Pr.

Symbolic Communities: The Persistence & Change of Chicago's Local Communities. Albert Hunter. LC 74-75612. (Studies of Urban Society Ser.). xviii, 254p. 1982. pap. 7.95x (ISBN 0-226-36081-4, Phoen). U of Chicago Pr.

Symbolic Computing with Lisp & Prolog. Page. 1988. price not set (ISBN 0-471-60771-1). Wiley.

Symbolic Consumer Behavior. Ed. by Elizabeth C. Hirschman & Morris B. Holbrook. 109p. 1981. pap. 15.00 (ISBN 0-915552-16-7). Assn Consumer Res.

Symbolic Crusade: Status Politics & the American Temperance Movement. Joseph R. Gusfield. LC 80-13342. viii, 198p. 1980. Repr. of 1963 ed. lib. bdg. 35.00x (ISBN 0-313-22423-4, GUSC). Greenwood.

Symbolic Crusade: Status Politics & the American Temperance Movement. 2nd ed. Joseph R. Gusfield. LC 85-28858. 240p. 1986. 24.95 (ISBN 0-252-01321-2); pap. 8.95 (ISBN 0-252-01312-3). U of Ill Pr.

Symbolic Directions: Modern Astrology. Carter. 8.75 (ISBN 0-7229-5145-0). Theos Pub Hse.

Symbolic Domination: Cultural Symbols & Historical Change in Morocco. Paul Rabinow. LC 74-7565. (Midway Reprint). 1978. pap. text ed. 10.00x (ISBN 0-226-70149-2). U of Chicago Pr.

Symbolic Dynamics of Trapezoidal Maps. J. D. Louck & N. Metropolis. (Mathematics & Its Applications (Main Ser.)). 1986. lib. bdg. 59.00 (ISBN 90-277-2197-1, Pub. by Reidel Holland). Kluwer-Academic.

Symbolic Essays. Manly P. Hall. pap. 3.50 (ISBN 0-89314-822-9). Philos Res.

Symbolic Experience: A Study of Poems by Pedro Salinas. Rupert C. Allen. LC 81-10307. 180p. 1982. text ed. 20.00 (ISBN 0-8173-0081-3). U of Ala Pr.

Symbolic Experiential Journeys: A Tribute to Carl Whitaker, a Special Issue of Journal of Contemporary Family Therapy. Ed. by Robert Garfield et al. 159p. 1987. pap. 14.95 (ISBN 0-89885-340-0). Human Sci Pr.

Symbolic Functioning in Childhood. Ed. by Nancy R. Smith & Margery B. Franklin. 256p. 1979. 29.95x (ISBN 0-89859-491-X). L Erlbaum Assocs.

Symbolic Images: Studies in the Art of the Renaissance, No. II. E. H. Gombrich. LC 84-28111. (Illus.). xii, 356p. 1985. pap. 14.95 (ISBN 0-226-30217-2). U of Chicago Pr.

Symbolic Imagination: Coleridge & the Romantic Tradition. J. R. Barth. LC 76-44333. (Princeton Essays in Literature). 1977. 26.50x (ISBN 0-691-06320-6). Princeton U Pr.

Symbolic Inducement & Knowing: A Study in the Foundations of Rhetoric. Richard B. Gregg. LC 83-26113. 160p. 1984. 21.95x (ISBN 0-87249-434-9). U of SC Pr.

Symbolic Interactionism: An Introduction, An Interpretation, An Integration. 2nd ed. Joel M. Charon. (Illus.). 208p. 1985. pap. text ed. write for info (ISBN 0-13-879966-0). P-H.

Symbolic Interactionism: Genesis, Varieties & Criticsms. B. N. Meltzer et al. (Monographs in Social Theory). 1977. pap. 8.95x (ISBN 0-7100-8056-5). Routledge Chapman & Hall.

Symbolic Interactionism: Perspective & Method. Herbert Blumer. 1986. pap. 9.95x (ISBN 0-520-05676-0). U of Cal Pr.

Symbolic Language of Geometrical Figures. Omraam M. Aivanhov. (Izvor Collection: Vol. 218). (Orig.). 1985. pap. 5.95 (ISBN 2-85566-366-0, Pub. by Prosveta France). Prosveta USA.

Symbolic Leaders: Public Dramas & Public Men. Orrin E. Klapp. LC 64-23369. 1964. 37.50x (ISBN 0-202-30024-2); pap. 4.95x (ISBN 0-8290-0688-5). Irvington.

Symbolic Life. C. G. Jung. 1985. 10.00x (ISBN 0-317-62191-2, Guild of Pastoral Psych). State Mutual Bk.

Symbolic Logic. 5th ed. Irving M. Copi. 1979. text ed. write for info. (ISBN 0-02-324980-3). Macmillan.

Symbolic Logic. John Venn. LC 70-165345. (Research & Source Works Ser.: No. 778). 1971. Repr. of 1894 ed. lib. bdg. 32.00 (ISBN 0-8337-3626-4). B Franklin.

Symbolic Logic. 2nd ed. John Venn. LC 79-119161. 1971. text ed. 19.50 (ISBN 0-8284-0251-5). Chelsea Pub.

Symbolic Logic & Mechanical Theorem Proving. Chin-Liang Chang & Richard C. Lee. (Computer Science & Applied Mathematics Ser). 1973. 71.50 (ISBN 0-12-170350-9). Acad Pr.

Symbolic Logic & the Game of Logic. Lewis Carroll. pap. 5.95 (ISBN 0-486-20492-8). Dover.

Symbolic Meaning. D. H. Lawrence. Ed. by Arnold. 1985. 60.00x (ISBN 0-317-39029-5, Pub. by Centaur Bks). State Mutual Bk.

Symbolic Meaning, Uncollected Versions of 'Studies in Classic American Literature' D. H. Lawrence. Ed. by Armin Arnold. 264p. 1962. 25.00 (ISBN 0-87556-147-0). Saifer.

Symbolic Method of Coleridge, Baudelaire, & Yeats. Anca Vlasopolos. LC 82-20079. 232p. 1983. 24.95x (ISBN 0-8143-1730-8). Wayne St U Pr.

Symbolic Persons in the Masques of Ben Jonson. Allan H. Gilbert. LC 79-85910. (BCL Ser.: I). Repr. of 1948 ed. 23.00 (ISBN 0-404-02759-8). AMS Pr.

Symbolic Play: The Developmental Psychology of Social Cognition. Ed. by Inge Bretherton. LC 83-11958. 1984. 39.95 (ISBN 0-12-132680-2). Acad Pr.

Symbolic Process & It's Integration in Children: A Study in Social Psychology. John F. Markey. LC 78-56924. (Midway Reprint Ser.). 1978. pap. text ed. 9.00x (ISBN 0-226-50585-5). U of Chicago Pr.

Symbolic Profile. Ruth T. Fry & Joyce Hall. LC 76-5085. 94p. 1976. 16.00x (ISBN 0-87201-815-6). Gulf Pub.

Symbolic Prophecy of the Great Pyramid. Lewis H. Spencer. LC 37-3808. (Illus.). 192p. 1988. pap. write for info. (ISBN 0-912057-55-6, G-680). AMORC.

Symbolic Quest: Basic Concepts of Analytical Psychology. Edward C. Whitmont. 1978. 41.00x (ISBN 0-691-08609-5); pap. 9.95x (ISBN 0-691-02454-5). Princeton U Pr.

Symbolic Realization: A New Method of Psychotherapy Applied to a Case of Schizophrenia. M. A. Sechehaye. (Monograph Ser. on Schizophrenia: No. 2). 184p. 1960. text ed. 25.00x (ISBN 0-8236-6300-0). Intl Univs Pr.

Symbolic Regression Psychology. Paul D. Fairweather & Donovan Johnson. 231p. 1982. text ed. 19.50x (ISBN 0-8290-0420-3). Irvington.

Symbolic Self Completion. R. A. Wicklund & P. M. Gollwitzer. 256p. 1982. text ed. 29.95x (ISBN 0-89859-213-5). L Erlbaum Assocs.

Symbolic Sit-Ins: Protest Occupations at the California Capitol. John Lofland & Michael Fink. LC 81-40725. 128p. (Orig.). 1982. PLB 26.25 (ISBN 0-8191-2503-2); pap. text ed. 9.75 (ISBN 0-8191-2504-0). U Pr of Amer.

Symbolic State Politics: Education Funding in Ohio, 1970-1980. Linda L. Bennett. LC 83-48760. (American University Studies X, Political Science: Vol. 1). 160p. 1983. pap. text ed. 17.35 (ISBN 0-8204-0052-1). P Lang Pubs.

Symbolic Stories. Derek Brewer. 190p. 1981. 36.00 (ISBN 0-85991-063-6, Pub. by Boydell & Brewer). Longwood Pub Group.

Symbolic Stories: Traditional Narratives of the Family Drama in English Literature. Derek Brewer. 200p. (Orig.). 1988. pap. text ed. 14.95 (ISBN 0-582-01879-X). Longman.

Symbolic Structures: An Exploration of the Culture of the Dowayos. Nigel Barley. LC 82-23651. (Illus.). 160p. 1983. 29.95 (ISBN 0-521-24745-4). Cambridge U Pr.

Symbolic Tendency in Irish Renaissance. K. C. Bhatnagar. 1973. Repr. of 1962 ed. 15.00 (ISBN 0-8274-1798-5). R West.

Symbolic Tendency in the Irish Renaissance. K. C. Bhatnager. LC 74-7226. lib. bdg. 18.50 (ISBN 0-8414-3182-5). Folcroft.

Symbolic Uses of Politics. With a New Afterword. Murray Edelman. LC 84-16195. 232p. 1985. pap. 6.95 (ISBN 0-252-01202-X). U of Ill Pr.

Symbolic Vision in Biblical Tradition. Susan Niditch. LC 83-8643. (Harvard Semitic Monographs). 270p. 1983. 15.00 (ISBN 0-89130-627-7, 04 00 30). Scholars Pr GA.

Symbolic World of Federico Garcia Lorca. Rupert C. Allen. LC 72-80890. 1972. 17.50 (ISBN 0-8263-0245-9). Lib Soc Sci.

Symbolical Consciousness: A Commentary on Love's Body. William C. Shepherd. LC 76-26582. (American Academy of Religion. Aids for the Study of Religion Ser.). 1976. pap. 9.95 (ISBN 0-89130-083-X, 010304). Scholars Pr GA.

Symbols of Power: Studies on the Political Status of Women in India. Vina Mazumdar. 1979. 17.50x (ISBN 0-8364-0528-5). South Asia Bks.
Symbols of Power: The Esthetics of Political Legitimation in the Soviet Union & Eastern Europe. Claes Arvidsson & Lars E. Blomqvist. (Illus.). 185p. 1987. 38.50x (ISBN 91-22-00843-8, Pub. by Almqvist & Wiksell). Coronet Bks.
Symbols of Sovereignty. Brian Barker. (Illus.). 254p. 1979. 21.50x (ISBN 0-8476-6192-X). Rowman.
Symbols of Sovereignty: Feather Girdles of Tahiti & Hawai'i. Roger S. Rose. LC 78-65065. (Pacific Anthropological Records: No. 28). 69p. 1978. pap. 6.00 (ISBN 0-686-47665-4). Bishop Mus.
Symbols of the Church. Ed. by Carroll E. Whittemore. 64p. 1983. pap. 2.25 (ISBN 0-687-40786-9). Abingdon.
Symbols of the Nations. A. Guy Hope. 1973. 15.00. Pub Aff Pr.
Symbols of Trade. Stanley Sacharow. (Illus.). 163p. 1983. 14.50 (ISBN 0-88108-003-9); pap. 9.95 (ISBN 0-910158-98-3). Art Dir.
Symbols of Transformation in Dreams. Jean Clift & Wallace Clift. 144p. 1986. pap. 9.95 (ISBN 0-8245-0727-4). Crossroad NY.
Symbols of Transformation in Poetry. Alan Hobson. 1985. 10.00x (ISBN 0-317-62198-X, Guild of Pastoral Psych). State Mutual Bk.
Symbols of War: Pershing II & Cruise Missiles in Europe. Andrew White. 75p. 1983. pap. 3.50 (ISBN 0-85036-320-9, Pub. by Merlin Pr UK). Longwood Pub Group.
Symbols: Our Universal Language. LC 62-20744. 1962. pap. 5.95 (ISBN 0-912504-44-7). Sym & Sign.
Symbols: Public & Private. Raymond Firth. LC 72-11806. (Symbol, Myth & Ritual Ser). 469p. 1975. pap. 12.95x (ISBN 0-8014-9150-9); 34.50x (ISBN 0-8014-0760-5). Cornell U Pr.
Symbols, Sex, & the Stars. Ernest Busenbark. (Illus.). 396p. 6.00 (ISBN 0-318-16751-4). Truth Seeker.
Symbols, Signs & Signets. Ernst Lehner. (Illus.). 1950. pap. 6.95 (ISBN 0-486-22241-1). Dover.
Symbols, Signs & Signets. Ernst Lehner. (Illus.). 16.50 (ISBN 0-8446-0771-1). Peter Smith.
Symbols That Stand for Themselves. Roy Wagner. LC 85-16448. (Illus.). 1986. lib. bdg. 27.00x (ISBN 0-226-86928-8); pap. text ed. 9.95x (ISBN 0-226-86929-6). U of Chicago Pr.
Symeon Neos Theologos, Hymnen Einleitung und kritischer Text. Ed. by Athanasios Kambylis. (Supplementa Byzantina, Vol. 3). 1976. 234.00x (ISBN 3-11-004888-4). De Gruyter.
Symeon, the New Theologian: The Discourses. C. J. De Catanzaro. LC 80-82414. (Classics of Western Spirituality Ser.). 416p. 1980. 13.95 (ISBN 0-8091-0292-7); pap. 9.95 (ISBN 0-8091-2230-8). Paulist Pr.
Symeonis Monachi Opera Omnia, 2 vols. Ed. by Thomas Arnold. Incl. Vol. 1. Historia Ecclesiae Dunelmensis (ISBN 0-8115-1143-X); Vol. 2. Historia Regum (ISBN 0-8115-1144-8). (Rolls Ser.: No. 75). Repr. of 1885 ed. Set. 88.00. Kraus Repr.
Symlog: A Manual for the Case Study of Groups. Robert F. Bales et al. LC 79-7480. (Illus.). 1979. 33.95 (ISBN 0-02-901300-3). Free Pr.
Symlog Case Study Kit: With Instructions for a Group Self-Study. Robert F. Bales. LC 79-7480. 1980. pap. text ed. 15.95 (ISBN 0-02-901310-0). Free Pr.
Symlog Practitioner: Applications of Small Group Research. Ed. by Richard B. Polley et al. LC 87-37684. (Illus.). 427p. 1988. lib. bdg. 49.95 (ISBN 0-275-92364-9, C2364). Praeger.
Symmes Hole. Ian Wedde. 328p. 1987. pap. 7.95 (ISBN 0-14-008840-7). Penguin.
Symmetric Banach Manifolds & Jordan C-Algebras. H. Upmeier. (Mathematics Studies: Vol. 104). 444p. 1985. 84.25 (ISBN 0-444-87651-0, North-Holland). Elsevier.
Symmetric Bilinear Forms. J. Milnor & D. Husemoller. LC 72-90190. (Ergebnisse der Mathematik und Ihrer Greuzgebiete: Vol. 73). (Illus.). 147p. 1973. 34.00 (ISBN 0-387-06009-X). Springer-Verlag.
Symmetric Designs: An Algebraic Approach. Eric Lander. LC 82-9705. (London Mathematical Society Lecture Note Ser.: Note 74). 175p. 1983. pap. 34.50 (ISBN 0-521-28693-X). Cambridge U Pr.
Symmetric Function & Allied Tables. F. N. David et al. 278p. 1966. lib. bdg. 32.50x. Lubrecht & Cramer.
Symmetric Functions & Hall Polynomials. I. G. MacDonald. (Oxford Mathematical Monographs). 1979. 45.00x (ISBN 0-19-853530-9). Oxford U Pr.
Symmetric Generalized Topological Structures. C. J. Mozzochi et al. LC 76-15121. 1976. text ed. 7.50 (ISBN 0-682-48584-5, University). Exposition-Phoenix.
Symmetric Hilbert Spaces & Related Topics. A. Guichardet. LC 72-76390. (Lecture Notes in Mathematics: Vol. 261). 102p. 1972. pap. 15.00 (ISBN 0-387-05803-6). Springer-Verlag.
Symmetric Markov Processes. M. L. Silverstein. LC 74-22376. (Lecture Notes in Mathematics Ser.: Vol. 426). 1974. pap. 18.00 (ISBN 0-387-07012-5). Springer-Verlag.
Symmetric Spaces: Short Courses Presented at Washington University. Ed. by William M. Boothby et al. LC 74-182213. (Pure & Applied Mathematics: No. 8). (Illus.). pap. 125.50 (ISBN 0-317-08008-3, 2021506). Bks Demand UMI.
Symmetric Structures in Banach Spaces. W. B. Johnson et al. LC 79-10225. (Memoirs Ser.: No. 217). 298p. 1981. pap. 16.00 (ISBN 0-8218-2217-9). Am Math.
Symmetrical Components. L. J. Myatt. 1968. pap. text ed. 13.00 (ISBN 0-08-012978-1). Pergamon.
Symmetrical Components. C. F. Wagner & R. D. Evans. LC 82-14051. 454p. 1982. Repr. of 1933 ed. lib. bdg. 33.50 (ISBN 0-89874-556-X). Krieger.
Symmetrical English. John Watson. 1988. pap. 14.95 (ISBN 0-02-026241-8, Collier). Macmillan.
Symmetrie. 2nd ed. Hermann Weyl. (Science & Society Ser.: No. 11). 158p. (Ger.). 1981. text ed. 15.95x (ISBN 0-8176-1280-7). Birkhauser.
Symmetries. Tom Johnson. 1981. 6.95 (ISBN 0-938690-02-7). Two Eighteen.
Symmetries. Richard Kostelanetz. 1983. pap. 12.00 (ISBN 0-918406-24-2); signed 100.00 (ISBN 0-686-84605-2). Future Pr.
Symmetries & Elementary Particles. F. Low. (Documents on Modern Physics Ser.). 112p. (Orig.). 1967. 43.00 (ISBN 0-677-01750-2). Gordon & Breach.
Symmetries & Nonlinear Phenomena, Paipa, Colombia, Feb 22-26, 1988. Ed. by D. Levi & P. Winternitz. 400p. 1988. 56.00 (ISBN 9971-50-663-7, ZB0656PP). World Scientific Pub.
Symmetries & Nuclear Structure. Richard A. Meyer & Vladimir Paar. (Nuclear Science Research Conference Ser.: Vol. 13). 620p. Date not set. flexicover 86.00 (ISBN 3-7186-0400-0). Harwood Academic.
Symmetries & Properties of Non-Rigid Molecules: A Comprehensive Survey. Ed. by J. Maruani & J. Serre. (Studies in Physical & Theoretical Chemisty Ser.: Vol. 23). 520p. 1983. 163.25 (ISBN 0-444-42174-2). Elsevier.
Symmetries & Quark Models. Ed. by Ramesh Chand. 420p. 1970. 108.00 (ISBN 0-677-13880-6). Gordon & Breach.
Symmetries & Reflections. Eugene P. Wigner. LC 79-89843. 1979. pap. 12.00 (ISBN 0-918024-16-1). Ox Bow.
Symmetries & Semiclassical Features of Nuclear Dynamics. Ed. by A. Raduta. (Lecture Notes in Physics Ser.: Vol. 279). 1987. 35.70 (ISBN 0-387-17926-7). Springer-Verlag.
Symmetries Asymmetries, & the World of Particles. T. D. Lee. (Illus.). 80p. 1987. 9.95 (ISBN 0-295-96519-3). U of Wash Pr.
Symmetries in Nuclear Structure. Ed. by K. Abrahams et al. LC 83-2455. (NATO ASI Series B, Physics: Vol. 93). (Illus.). 312p. 1983. 57.50x (ISBN 0-306-41341-8, Plenum Pr). Plenum Pub.
Symmetries in Particle Physics. Ed. by Itzhak Bars et al. 320p. 1984. 57.50x (ISBN 0-306-41801-0, Plenum Pr). Plenum Pub.
Symmetries in Physics. W. Ludwig & C. Falter. (Solid-State Sciences Ser.: Vol. 64). (Illus.). 470p. 1988. 59.50 (ISBN 0-387-18021-4). Springer-Verlag.
Symmetries In Science I. Ed. by Bruno Gruber & Richard S. Millman. LC 80-18665. 506p. 1980. 75.00x (ISBN 0-306-40541-5, Plenum Pr). Plenum Pub.
Symmetries in Science II. Ed. by Bruno Gruber & Romuald Lenczewski. 590p. 1986. 85.00x (ISBN 0-306-42461-4, Plenum Pr). Plenum Pub.
Symmetries of Culture: Theory & Practice of Plane Pattern Analysis. Dorothy K. Washburn & Donald W. Crowe. (Illus.). 304p. 1988. 35.00 (ISBN 0-295-96586-X). U of Wash Pr.
Symmetries of Maxwell's Equations. W. I. Fushchich & A. G. Nikitin. 1987. lib. bdg. 74.00 (ISBN 90-277-2320-6, Pub. by Reidel Holland). Kluwer Academic.
Symmetry. Ed. by I. Hargittai. (International Series on Modern Applied Mathematics & Computer Science). 1000p. 1986. 140.00. Pergamon.
Symmetry. Hermann Weyl. 1952. pap. 7.95 (ISBN 0-691-02374-3). Princeton U Pr.
Symmetry: An Analytical Treatment. J. Lee Kavanau. LC 80-52565. 656p. 1980. 34.95x (ISBN 0-937292-00-1). Science Software.
Symmetry Analysis of Upper Gila Area Ceramic Design. Dorothy K. Washburn. LC 76-53125. (Peabody Museum Papers: Vol. 68). (Illus.). 1977. pap. 20.00x (ISBN 0-87365-193-6). Peabody Harvard.
Symmetry & Function of Biological Systems at the Macromolecular Level: Proceedings of the Eleventh Nobel Symposium. Ed. by Arne Engstrom & Bror Strandberg. (Illus.). 436p. 1969. text ed. 37.50x (Pub. by Almqvist & Wiksell). Coronet Bks.
Symmetry & Spectroscopy: An Introduction to Vibrational & Electronic Spectroscopy. Daniel C. Harris & Michael D. Bertolucci. (Illus.). 1978. 18.95x (ISBN 0-19-855152-5). Oxford U Pr.
Symmetry & Structure. S. A. Kettle. LC 84-17365. 340p. 1985. Repr. 44.95 (ISBN 0-471-90501-1). Wiley.
Symmetry Discovered. J. Rosen. LC 75-6006. (Illus.). 150p. 1975. 24.95 (ISBN 0-521-20695-2). Cambridge U Pr.
Symmetry Groups & Their Applications. Willard Miller, Jr. (Pure & Applied Mathematics Ser.: Vol. 50). 1972. 89.50 (ISBN 0-12-497460-0). Acad Pr.
Symmetry Groups: Theory & Chemical Applications. Robert L. Flurry, Jr. (Illus.). 1980. text ed. write for info. (ISBN 0-13-880013-8). P-H.
Symmetry in Chemical Theory: Application of Group Theoretical Techniques to the Solution of Chemical Problems. Ed. by J. P. Fackler, Jr. LC 73-12620. (Benchmark Papers in Inorganic Chemistry: Vol. 4). 508p. 1974. 59.95 (ISBN 0-87933-018-X). Van Nos Reinhold.
Symmetry in Chemistry. H. H. Jaffe & Milton M. Orchin. LC 76-7534. 206p. 1977. pap. text ed. 8.50 (ISBN 0-88275-414-9). Krieger.
Symmetry in Physics, Vols. 1 & 2. J. P. Elliott & P. G. Dawber. 1985. Vol. 1. pap. 17.95x (ISBN 0-19-520455-7); Vol. 2. pap. 17.95x (ISBN 0-19-520456-5). Oxford U Pr.
Symmetry in World of Molecules. I. S. Dmitriev. 148p. 1979. pap. 4.45 (ISBN 0-8285-1519-0, Pub. by Mir Pubs USSR). Imported Pubns.
Symmetry of Crystals. E. S. Fedorov. LC 75-146982. (American Crystallographic Association Monograph: Vol. 7). 315p. 1971. 25.00 (ISBN 0-686-60371-0). Polycrystal Bk Serv.
Symmetry of Polycentric Systems: The Polycentric Tensor Algebra for Molecules. G. Fieck. (Lecture Notes in Physics: Vol. 167). 137p. 1982. pap. 10.00 (ISBN 0-387-11589-7). Springer-Verlag.
Symmetry of Sailing: The Physics of Sailing for Yachtsmen. Ross Garrett. (Illus.). 278p. 1987. 45.00 (ISBN 0-229-11759-7, Pub. by Adlar Coles). Sheridan.
Symmetry Primer for Scientists. Joe Rosen. LC 82-10876. 192p. 1983. 35.95 (ISBN 0-471-87672-0, Pub. by Wiley-Interscience). Wiley.
Symmetry Principles in Elementary Particle Physics. W. M. Gibson & B. R. Pollard. LC 74-31796. (Cambridge Monographs on Physics). (Illus.). 395p. 1980. o. p. 85.00 (ISBN 0-521-20787-8); pap. 32.50 (ISBN 0-521-29964-0). Cambridge U Pr.
Symmetry Principles in Quantum Physics. L. Fonda & G. C. Ghirardi. (Theoretical Physics Ser: Vol. 1). 1970. 55.00 (ISBN 0-8247-1213-7). Dekker.
Symmetry Properties of Molecules. G. S. Ezra. (Lecture Notes in Chemistry Ser.: Vol. 28). 202p. 1982. pap. 19.90 (ISBN 0-387-11184-0). Springer-Verlag.
Symmetry Properties of Nuclei. Solvay Conference on Physics. 372p. 1974. 140.00 (ISBN 0-677-14450-4). Gordon & Breach.
Symmetry Rules for Chemical Reactions: Orbital Topology & Elementary Processes. Ralph G. Pearson. LC 76-10314. pap. 139.30 (ISBN 0-317-28061-9, 2055771). Bks Demand UMI.
Symmetry, Structure & Spectroscopy of Atoms & Molecules. Harter et al. 1988. write for info. (ISBN 0-471-05020-2). Wiley.
Symmetry Through the Eyes of a Chemist. Ed. by I. Hargittai & M. Hargittai. 460p. 1986. lib. bdg. 103.00 (ISBN 0-89573-520-2). VCH pubs.
Symmetry through the Eyes of a Chemist. Istvan Hargittai & Magdolna Hargittai. (Illus.). 458p. 1987. pap. text ed. 24.95 (ISBN 0-89573-681-0). VCH Pubs.
Symmetry: Unifying Human Understanding. Ed. by I. Hargittai. (International Series on Modern Applied Mathematics & Computer Science: Vol. 10). 1058p. 1986. 140.00 (ISBN 0-08-033986-7, C110, D110, H100, E110, K105, PBI). Pergamon.
Symonds Family. G. T. Ridlon. LC 74-142771. (Saco Valley Settlements Ser). 1970. pap. 1.50 (ISBN 0-8048-0841-4). C E Tuttle.
Symozia: Voyage of Discovery. J. C. Symmes. LC 74-16520. (Science Fiction Ser). (Illus.). 248p. 1975. Repr. 23.50x (ISBN 0-405-06312-1). Ayer Co Pubs.
Sympathetic History of Jonestown: The Moore Family Involvement in Peoples Temple. Rebecca Moore. LC 85-11632. (Studies in Religion & Society: Vol. 14). (Illus.). 448p. 1985. lib. bdg. 69.95x (ISBN 0-88946-860-5). E Mellen.
Sympathetic Journalism. C. L. Morrison. 16p. 1986. pap. 1.00 (ISBN 0-318-23500-5). Samisdat.
Sympathetic Magic. Michael Blumenthal. LC 80-50812. (Illus.). 96p. (Orig.). 1980. 30.00 (ISBN 0-931956-04-8); pap. 9.00 (ISBN 0-931956-03-X); handbound o.p. 60.00 (ISBN 0-686-70197-6). Water Mark.
Sympathetic Manifesto: Poems. Doren Robbins. LC 87-42791. 91p. (Orig.). 1987. pap. 7.95 (ISBN 0-912288-26-4). Perivale Pr.
Sympathetic Response: George Eliot's Fictional Rhetoric. Mary E. Doyle. LC 80-65908. (Illus.). 192p. 1981. 19.50 (ISBN 0-8386-3065-0). Fairleigh Dickinson.
Sympathetic Strikes & Sympathetic Lockouts. Frederick S. Hall. LC 78-76665. (Columbia University. Studies in the Social Sciences: No. 26). Repr. of 1898 ed. 16.50 (ISBN 0-404-51026-4). AMS Pr.
Sympathetic Understanding of the Child: Birth to Sixteen. 2nd ed. David Elkind. 1978. text ed. 24.00 (ISBN 0-205-06015-3, 246015). Allyn.
Sympathetic Vibrations: Reflections on Physics As a Way of Life. K. C. Cole. LC 85-7555. (Illus.). 352p. 1985. pap. 9.95 (ISBN 0-553-34234-7). Bantam.
Sympathoadrenal System: Physiology & Pathophysiology. Ed. by Niels J. Christensen et al. (Alfred Benzon Symposium Ser.: Vol. 23). 512p. 1986. text ed. 73.50 (ISBN 0-88167-149-5). Raven.
Sympathy & Science: Women Physicians in American Medicine. Regina M. Morantz-Sanchez. 464p. 1985. 24.95 (ISBN 0-19-503627-1). Oxford U Pr.
Sympathy & Science: Women Physicians in American Medicine. Regina M. Morantz-Sanchez. 480p. 1987. pap. 10.95 (ISBN 0-19-504985-3). Oxford U Pr.
Sympathy for the Devil. Kent Anderson. LC 87-630. 316p. 1987. 17.95 (ISBN 0-385-23943-2). Doubleday.
Sympathy fot the Devil. Kent Anderson. 1988. pap. 4.95. Warner Bks.
Symphonia: A Critical Edition of the Symphonia Armonie Celestium Revelationum (Symphony of the Harmony of Celestial Revelations) St. Hildegard of Bingen. Ed. & tr. by Barbara Newman. LC 88-47739. 288p. 1989. 32.50x (ISBN 0-8014-2009-1); pap. 9.95x (ISBN 0-8014-9514-8). Cornell U Pr.
Symphonic Masterpieces. Olin Downes. LC 72-5560. (Essay Index Reprint Ser). 1972. Repr. of 1935 ed. 22.00 (ISBN 0-8369-2987-X). Ayer Co Pubs.
Symphonic Music: Its Evolution Since the Renaissance. Homer Ulrich. LC 52-12033. 352p. 1952. 36.00x (ISBN 0-231-01908-4). Columbia U Pr.
Symphonic Portraits: A Classical Portfolio. Ramon Scavelli & Theodore Libby. (Illus.). 150p. 1988. 50.00 (ISBN 0-89526-557-5). Regnery Gateway.
Symphonic Theology: The Validity of Multiple Perspectives in Theology. Vernon S. Poythress. 128p. (Orig.). 1987. pap. 9.95 (ISBN 0-310-45221-X, 12358P). Zondervan.
Symphonie Concertante. Jean-Baptiste Davauz et al. Ed. by Barry S. Brook et al. (Symphony Ser.). 568p. 1983. lib. bdg. 90.00 (ISBN 0-8240-3835-5). Garland Pub.
Symphonie Pastorale. Andre Gide. (Folio Ser.: No. 18). 1972. 5.95 (ISBN 0-686-56058-2). Schoenhof.
Symphonie Pastorale. Andre Gide. Ed. by Justin O'Brien & M. Shackleton. 1954. pap. text ed. 7.00 (ISBN 0-669-27383-X). Heath.
Symphonie Pastorale. Andre Gide. 1972. write for info. French & Eur.
Symphonies Concertantes I. Ed. by Ernest Warburton. (Johann Christian Bach, 1735-1782 The Collected Works Ser.). 75.00 (ISBN 0-8240-6079-2). Garland Pub.
Symphonies Concertantes II. Ed. by Ernest Warburton. (Johnathan Christian Bach, 1735-1782 The Collected Works Ser.). 75.00 (ISBN 0-8240-6080-6). Garland Pub.
Symphonies De Beethoven. 13th ed. J. G. Prod'Homme. LC 76-52485. (Music Reprint Ser.). (Illus., Fr.). 1977. Repr. of 1906 ed. lib. bdg. 55.00 (ISBN 0-306-70859-0). Da Capo.
Symphonies I. Johann C. Bach. LC 83-48727. (Johann Christian Bach: The Collected Works Ser.). 300p. 1984. lib. bdg. 45.00 (ISBN 0-8240-6075-X). Garland Pub.
Symphonies II. Johann C. Bach. Ed. by Ernest Warburton. (Johann Christian Bach: The Collected Works Ser.). 330p. 1984. lib. bdg. 75.00 (ISBN 0-8240-6076-8). Garland Pub.
Symphonies III. Ed. by Ernest Warburton. (Johann Christian Bach Ser., 1735-1782). 75.00 (ISBN 0-8240-6077-6). Garland Pub.
Symphonies IV. Ed. by Ernest Warburton. (Johann Christian Bach Ser., 1735-1782). 75.00 (ISBN 0-8240-6078-4). Garland Pub.
Symphonies Nos. 1 & 2 in Full Score. Gustav Mahler. 1987. pap. 14.95 (ISBN 0-486-25473-9). Dover.
Symphonies of Gustav Mahler: A Critical Discography. Lewis M. Smoley. LC 86-14222. (Discographies Ser.: No. 23). 206p. 1986. 36.95 (ISBN 0-313-25189-4, SSY/). Greenwood.
Symphonies of Havergal Brian. Malcolm MacDonald. LC 78-110357. (Illus.). 1978. Vol. 1. symphonies 1 to 12 11.95 (ISBN 0-8008-7527-3, Crescendo); Vol. 2. symphonies 13 to 29 13.95 (ISBN 0-8008-7528-1). Taplinger.
Symphonies of Havergal Brian, Vol.3. Malcolm MacDonald. LC 78-110357. 256p. 1984. 13.95 (ISBN 0-8008-7530-3, Crescendo). Taplinger.
Symphonies of Mozart. Georges P. Saint-Foix. 1980. lib. bdg. 55.00 (ISBN 0-8490-3191-5). Gordon Pr.
Symphonies of Ralph Vaughan Williams. Elliott S. Schwartz. LC 81-12513. (Music Reprint Ser.). (Illus.). 242p. 1982. Repr. of 1964 ed. lib. bdg. 32.50 (ISBN 0-306-76137-8). Da Capo.
Symphonies, Vol. 6: Symphony No. 1 in E-flat, op. 20; Symphony No. 2 in D Minor, op. 49; Symphony No. 5 in C Minor, op. 102. Ed. by Clive Brown. (Selected Works of Louis Spohr (1784-1859)). 440p. 1987. lib. bdg. 115.00 (ISBN 0-8240-1505-3). Garland Pub.
Symphony. Ed. by Ralph Hill. LC 72-181174. 416p. 1961. Repr. 59.00 (ISBN 0-403-01578-2). Scholarly.
Symphony. Ed. by Ralph Hill. 1988. Repr. of 1961 ed. lib. bdg. 79.00x. Am Biog Serv.
Symphony. reference ed. Preston Stedman. (Illus.). 1979. write for info. (ISBN 0-13-880062-6). P-H.
Symphony: An Advanced Course. ComputerKnowledge, Inc. Staff. 111p. 1986. pap. 180.00 (ISBN 0-471-84418-7). Wiley.

TITLE INDEX SYMPOSIUM ON EDWARDS LIMESTONE

Symphony: An Introduction. ComputerKnowledge, Inc. Staff. 81p. 1986. pap. 180.00 (ISBN 0-471-84422-5). Wiley.
Symphony & Overture in Great Britain. William Croft. Ed. by Brook Barrys & Richard Platt. LC 83-20758. (Symphony Ser.). 1984. lib. bdg. 90.00 (ISBN 0-8240-3840-1). Garland Pub.
Symphony & Song: The Saint Louis Symphony Orchestra. Katherine G. Wells. LC 80-14322. 142p. 1980. 18.95 (ISBN 0-914378-62-7). Countryman.
Symphony & the Symphonic Poem. 6th rev. ed. Earl V. Moore & Theodore E. Heger. LC 57-63375. 1974. text ed. 15.95x (ISBN 0-914004-01-8). Ulrich.
Symphony Applications: A Manager's Toolkit. Estoppel. 1985. pap. 19.95. Wiley.
Symphony Book. Edward M. Baras. 300p. (Orig.). 1984. pap. text ed. 19.95 (ISBN 0-07-881160-0). Osborne-McGraw.
Symphony Command Language Programmer's Guide. Weber Systems Inc. Staff et al. (Application Software Ser.). 250p. (Orig.). 1985. pap. 17.95 (ISBN 0-938862-39-1). Weber Systems.
Symphony, Eighteen Hundred to Nineteen Hundred. Ed. by Paul H. Lang. LC 75-77392. (Music Anthology Ser). 1969. pap. text ed. 16.95x (ISBN 0-393-09865-6, NortonC). Norton.
Symphony Fantastique & Harold in Italy in Full Score. Hector Berlioz. (Music Scores & Music to Play Ser.). 320p. 1984. pap. 11.95 (ISBN 0-486-24657-4). Dover.
Symphony: First Introduction to Business Software. Donald Beil. 1984. cancelled (ISBN 0-8359-7440-5, Reston). P-H.
Symphony for Business. (Symphony Ser.). pap. cancelled (ISBN 0-88022-140-2). Que Corp.
Symphony for the Devil: The Rolling Stones Story. Philip Norman. (Illus.). 448p. 1984. 17.95 (ISBN 0-671-44975-3, Linden Pr). S&S.
Symphony Hall, Boston. H. Earle Johnson. LC 78-31124. (Music Reprint Ser.). 1979. Repr. of 1950 ed. lib. bdg. 42.50. Da Capo.
Symphony in B Minor: The Passion of Peter Ilitch Tchaikovsky. Larry Holdridge. LC 78-2284. (Illus.). 64p. 1978. 10.95 (ISBN 0-916144-26-7); pap. 3.95 (ISBN 0-916144-27-5). Stemmer Hse.
Symphony in C Minor Resurrection Facsimile, No. 2. Gustav Mahler. (Illus.). 1986. 150.00x (ISBN 0-571-10064-3, Pub. by Kaplan Foundation). Faber & Faber.
Symphony in Denmark. Simoni dall Croubelis et al. Ed. by Barry S. Brook et al. LC 83-21125. (Symphony Ser.). 424p. 1983. lib. bdg. 90.00 (ISBN 0-8240-3822-3). Garland Pub.
Symphony in Naples. Domenico Tritto et al. Ed. by Barry S. Brook & Rey M. Longyear. LC 83-14011. (Symphony Ser.). 320p. 1983. lib. bdg. 90.00 (ISBN 0-8240-3831-2). Garland Pub.
Symphony in Poland. Ed. by B. Muchenberg & J. Prosnak. (Symphony 1720-1840 Series F: Vol. 7). 1982. lib. bdg. 90.00 (ISBN 0-8240-3820-7). Garland Pub.
Symphony in Portugal & Spain. Antonio L. Moreira et al. Ed. by Barry S. Brooks et al. LC 83-14188. (Symphony Ser.). 424p. 1983. lib. bdg. 90.00 (ISBN 0-8240-3837-1). Garland Pub.
Symphony in Steam. Jan Gleysteen. LC 66-17851. (Illus.). 1972. 7.50 (ISBN 0-9600578-1-1). Trogon Pubns.
Symphony in Sweden, Pt. II. Ferinand Zellbell, Sr. et al. LC 82-772149. (Symphony Ser.). 406p. 1983. lib. bdg. 90.00 (ISBN 0-8240-3827-4). Garland Pub.
Symphony in Sweden, Pt. 1. Ed. by Ingmar Bengtsson & Bertil H. Van Boer, Jr. (Symphony 1720-1840 Series F: Vol. II). 1982. lib. bdg. 90.00 (ISBN 0-8240-3811-8). Garland Pub.
Symphony Master: The Expert's Guide. Edward M. Baras. 352p. (Orig.). 1985. pap. text ed. 19.95 (ISBN 0-07-881170-8). Osborne McGraw.
Symphony Mastery. Daniel H. Harris. 432p. 1985. text ed. 38.95 (ISBN 0-13-880022-7). P-H.
Symphony No. Forty Five. Lazlo SomFai. 1959. cancelled 32.50 (Pub. by Akademiai Kaido Hungary). IPS.
Symphony No. Four for Orchestra. Elie Siegmeister. 159p. 1981. pap. 50.00 (ISBN 0-8258-0188-5, 05049). Fischer Inc NY.
Symphony No. One: Opus 23. John K. Paine. LC 73-171077. (Earlier American Music Ser.: No. 1). 180p. 1972. Repr. of 1908 ed. lib. bdg. 32.50 (ISBN 0-306-77301-5). Da Capo.
Symphony No. Two: In B Flat, Opus 21. facsimile ed. George W. Chadwick. LC 71-170930. (Earlier American Music Ser.: No. 3). 216p. 1972. Repr. of 1888 ed. 35.00 (ISBN 0-306-77304-X). Da Capo.
Symphony Number Thirty Five in D. K. 385: The Haffner Symphony. facsimile ed. Wolfgang Amadeus Mozart. 1968. Set. boxed o.p. 32.50 (ISBN 0-19-393180-X); pap. 8.00x (ISBN 0-19-385289-6). Oxford U Pr.
Symphony of Life: Letters by Ludwig van Beethoven. Ludwig Van Beethoven. Tr. by Ulrich L. Steindorff. LC 74-24037. pap. 17.50 (ISBN 0-404-12860-2). AMS Pr.
Symphony of Light. Jack McKinney. (Robotech Ser.: No. 12). 224p. 1987. pap. 2.95 (ISBN 0-345-34145-7, Del Rey). Ballantine.
Symphony of Songs. Georgiana L. Lahr. 1985. 8.95 (ISBN 0-533-06179-2). Vantage.
Symphony of the Planets. Sylvia Sherman & Jori F. Manske. 1986. 19.95 (ISBN 0-9618457-0-8). Am Sch Astrol.
Symphony of the Zodiac. Torkom Saraydarian. LC 79-53516. 1980. pap. 12.00 (ISBN 0-911794-05-0). Aqua Educ.
Symphony Orchestras of the United States: Selected Profiles. Ed. by Robert R. Craven. LC 85-7637. 544p. 1986. lib. bdg. 56.95 (ISBN 0-313-24072-8, CRU/). Greenwood.
Symphony Orchestras of the World. Robert R. Craven. LC 86-29452. 464p. 1987. lib. bdg. 75.00 (ISBN 0-313-24073-6, CRW/). Greenwood.
Symphony Revealed. Dan Shaffer. Date not set. price not set. P-H.
Symphony since Beethoven. Felix Weingartner. 59.95 (ISBN 0-8490-1169-8). Gordon Pr.
Symphony since Beethoven. Felix Weingartner. 1980. lib. bdg. 49.95 (ISBN 0-8490-3143-5). Gordon Pr.
Symphony: Structure & Style. Roland Nadeau. 1974. pap. 7.50 (ISBN 0-8008-7526-5, Crescendo). Taplinger.
Symphony: The Decision Maker's Guide to Business Applications. Brian L. King et al. 258p. Date not set. pap. cancelled (ISBN 0-394-73819-5, RanC). Random.
Symphony Themes. Raymond M. Burrows. 295p. Repr. of 1942 ed. lib. bdg. 39.00 (Pub. by Am Repr Serv). Am Biog Serv.
Symphony Writers since Beethoven. Felix Weingartner. Tr. by Arthur Bles from Ger. LC 77-109878. (Illus.). vii, 168p. (Second impression, with notice of the author's own no. 5 Symphony by D.C. Parker added to this issue). Repr. of 1925 ed. lib. bdg. 25.00x (ISBN 0-8371-4369-1, WESW). Greenwood.
Symphony Writers since Beethoven. Felix Weingartner. 1976. lib. bdg. 29.00 (ISBN 0-403-03756-5). Scholarly.
Symphorien Champier & the Reception of the Occultist Tradition in Renaissance France. Brian Copenhaver. 1978. text ed. 38.80x (ISBN 90-279-7647-3). Mouton.
Symplectic Corbordism Ring I. Stanley O. Kochman. LC 79-27872. 206p. 1980. pap. 15.00 (ISBN 0-8218-2228-4, MEMO-228). Am Math.
Symplectic Corbordism Ring II. Stanley O. Kochman. LC 79-27872. (Memoirs of the American Mathematical Society Ser.: No. 271). 172p. 1982. pap. 14.00 (ISBN 0-8218-2271-3, MEMO/271). Am Math.
Symplectic Framework for Field Theories. J. Kijowski & W. M. Tulczyjew. (Lecture Notes in Physics: Vol. 107). 1979. pap. 19.00 (ISBN 0-387-09538-1). Springer-Verlag.
Symplectic Geometry. A. Crumeyrolle. 264p. 1983. pap. 24.95 (ISBN 0-470-20461-3, Co-Pub. with Longman). Wiley.
Symplectic Geometry & Analytical Mechanics. Paulette Libermann & Charles-Michel Marle. 1987. lib. bdg. 89.00 (ISBN 90-277-2438-5, Pub. by Reidel Holland). Kluwer Academic.
Symplectic Geometry & Secondary Characteristic Classes. Izu Vaisman. (Progress in Mathematics Ser.: No. 72). 232p. 1987. 39.00 (ISBN 0-8176-3356-1). Birkhauser.
Symplectic Groups, Vol. 16. Timothy O'Meara. LC 78-19101. (Mathematical Surveys Ser.). 122p. 1982. pap. 39.00 (ISBN 0-8218-1516-4, SURV 16). Am Math.
Symplectic Techniques in Physics. Victor Guillemin & Shlomo Sternberg. LC 83-7762. 464p. 1984. 54.50 (ISBN 0-521-24866-3). Cambridge U Pr.
Symposia & Symposium Publications: A Guide for Organisers, Lecturers, & Editors of Scientific Meetings. A. A. Manten. LC 76-837. (Illus.). pap. 44.00 (ISBN 0-317-09783-0, 2051677). Bks Demand UMI.
Symposia Mathematica, Vol. 24. 1981. 47.50 (ISBN 0-12-612224-5). Acad Pr.
Symposia Mathematica, Vol. 26. (Serial Publication). 243p. 1982. 37.50 (ISBN 0-12-612226-1). Acad Pr.
Symposia Mathematica, Vol. 27. Instituto Nazaionale di Alta Mathematica Francesco Severi Staff. 285p. 1986. 65.00 (ISBN 0-12-612227-X). Acad Pr.
Symposia Mathematica, Vol. 28. 255p. 1987. 65.00 (ISBN 0-12-612228-8). Acad Pr.
Symposia Mathematica: Proceedings. Italian National Institute of Higher Mathematics Conventions. Incl. Vol. 1. Group Theory. 1970. 68.50 (ISBN 0-12-612201-6); Vol. 2. Functional Analysis & Geometry. 1970. 65.00 (ISBN 0-12-612202-4); Vol. 3. Problems in the Evolution of the Solar System. 1970. 79.00 (ISBN 0-12-612203-2); Vol. 4. 1971. 76.50 (ISBN 0-12-612204-0); Vol. 5. 1971. 73.50 (ISBN 0-12-612205-9); Vol. 6. 1971. 62.50 (ISBN 0-12-612206-7); Vol. 7. 1972. 85.00 (ISBN 0-12-612207-5); Vol. 8. 1972. 44.50 (ISBN 0-12-612208-3); Vol. 9. 1973. 82.50 (ISBN 0-12-612209-1); Vol. 10. 1973. 69.50 (ISBN 0-12-612210-5); Vol. 18. 1977. 85.00 (ISBN 0-12-612218-0); Vol. 19. 1977. 66.00 (ISBN 0-12-612219-9). Acad Pr.
Symposia of the Royal Entomological Society of London: Insect Reproduction. K. C. Highnam. 120p. 1984. 35.00x (ISBN 0-317-07179-3, Pub. by FW Classey Uk). State Mutual Bk.
Symposia of the Royal Entomological Society of London: Insect Polymorphism. Ed. by J. S. Kennedy. 115p. 1984. 35.00x (ISBN 0-317-07178-5, Pub. by FW Classey UK). State Mutual Bk.
Symposia of the Royal Entomological Society of London: Insect Ultrastructure. A. C. Neville. 190p. 1984. 35.00x (ISBN 0-317-07180-7, Pub. by FW Classey UK). State Mutual Bk.
Symposia of the Zoological Society of London, Vol. 51. (Serial Publication). 1984. 58.50 (ISBN 0-12-613351-4). Acad Pr.
Symposia on Theoretical Physics & Mathematics: Lectures Presented at the Anniversary Symposium of the Institute of Mathematical Sciences, Madras, India, 8 Vols. Institute of Mathematical Sciences (India) Ed. by Alladi Ramakrishnan. LC 65-31184. Vol. 1, 1963. pap. 45.30 (ISBN 0-317-11136-1, 2019402); Vol. 2, 1964. pap. 62.00 (ISBN 0-317-11137-X); Vol. 3, 1964. pap. 48.50 (ISBN 0-317-11138-8); Vol. 5, 1965. pap. 57.50 (ISBN 0-317-11139-6); Vol. 7, 1966. pap. 51.30 (ISBN 0-317-11140-X); Vol. 8, 1967. pap. 53.00 (ISBN 0-317-11141-8); Vol. 9, 1968. pap. 72.30 (ISBN 0-317-11142-6); Vol. 10, 1969. pap. 42.80 (ISBN 0-317-11143-4). Bks Demand UMI.
Symposium. Plato. Tr. by Benjamin Jowett. 1956. pap. 3.03 scp (ISBN 0-672-60169-9, LLA7). Bobbs.
Symposium. Plato. Ed. by K. J. Dover. LC 78-67430. (Cambridge Greek & Latin Classics Ser.). 1980. 39.50 (ISBN 0-521-20081-4); pap. 16.95x (ISBN 0-521-29523-8). Cambridge U Pr.
Symposium. Plato. Tr. by W. Hamilton. (Classics Ser.). (Orig.). 1952. pap. 3.50 (ISBN 0-14-044024-0). Penguin.
Symposium: An Entertainment. Geoffrey R. Simm. LC 84-14347. 226p. (Orig.). 1984. pap. 6.95 (ISBN 0-915175-02-9). Knights Pr.
Symposium & Other Dialogues. Plato. Tr. by Michael Joyce et al. 1964. Repr. of 1979 ed. 14.95x (ISBN 0-460-00418-2, Evman). Biblio Dist.
Symposium & the Phaedo: Plato. Ed. & tr. by Raymond Larson. LC 79-55931. (Crofts Classics Ser.). (Orig.). 1980. text ed. 14.95x (ISBN 0-88295-119-X); pap. text ed. 3.95x (ISBN 0-88295-122-X). Harlan Davidson.
Symposium by God & the Devil. John R. Stahl. (Illus.). 32p. 1971. 10.00 (ISBN 0-945303-00-9). Evanescent Pr.
Symposium: Factors that Regulate the Wax & Wane of Algal Populations. Ed. by R. G. Wetzel. (International Associatiation of Theoretical & Applied Limnology, Communications Ser.). (Illus.). 318p. 1971. pap. text ed. 84.50x (ISBN 3-510-52019-X). Lubrecht & Cramer.
Symposium in Honor of C. C. Lin: Proceedings. Ed. by D. Benney et al. 434p. 1987. 64.00 (ISBN 9971-50-245-3). World Scientific Pub.
Symposium in Memoriam Dr. Ernst Berliner on the Occasion of the 75th Anniversary of the Primary Description of Bacillus Thuringiensis. Ed. by A. Krieg & A. M. Huger. (Mitteilungen der Biologischen Bundesanstalt Fuer Land-Und Forstwirtschaft Berlin: Vol. 233). (Illus.). 111p. (Orig.). 1986. pap. text ed. 10.00x (ISBN 3-489-23300-X). Parey Sci Pubs.
Symposium in Music Education: A Festschrift for Charles Leonhard. Ed. by Richard Colwell. LC 81-71592. 329p. 15.00 (ISBN 0-686-38473-3). U IL Sch Music.
Symposium: Looking at the Principles Behind Affirmative Action. William B. Reynolds & Richard Wasserstrom. (Working Papers on Civil Rights). Date not set. 2.50 (CR1). IPPP.
Symposium of North Eastern Accelerator Personnel: Proceedings of the Twentieth Symposium SNEAPXX. Ed. by C. Browne et al. 500p. 1987. 71.00 (ISBN 9971-50-325-5). World Scientific Pub.
Symposium of Plato. 2nd ed. Ed. by R. G. Bury. (Classical Texts-Greek Texts Ser.). 258p. 1986. Repr. of 1973 ed. text ed. 37.50 (ISBN 0-85270-039-3, Pub. by Aris & Phillips). Humanities.
Symposium of Plato. Plato. Tr. by Benjamin Jowett. pap. 3.00 (ISBN 0-8283-1456-X, 17, IPL). Branden Pub Co.
"Symposium" of Plato. Plato. Ed. by John A. Brentlinger. Tr. by Suzy Q Groden. LC 79-103478. (Illus.). 144p. 1970. 12.00x (ISBN 0-87023-039-5); pap. 6.95x (ISBN 0-87023-076-X). U of Mass Pr.
Symposium of the International Society for Research in Stereoencephalotomy, 7th, Sao Paulo, June 24, 1977. Ed. by P. L. Gildenberg. (Advances in Stereoencephalotomy Ser.: Vol. 8). (Illus.). 1978. pap. 65.50 (ISBN 3-8055-2946-5). S Karger.
Symposium of the Whole: A Range of Discourse Toward an Ethnopoetics. Jerome Rothenberg & Diane Rothenberg. 526p. 1983. 27.50x (ISBN 0-520-04530-0); pap. 14.95x (ISBN 0-520-04531-9). U of Cal Pr.
Symposium on Air Pollution. H. W. Kennedy et al. LC 75-152831. (Symposia on Law & Society Ser). 1971. Repr. of 1968 ed. lib. bdg. 22.50 (ISBN 0-306-70143-X). Da Capo.
Symposium on Air-Pollution Measurement Methods. LC 63-21664. (American Society for Testing & Materials. Special Technical Publications Ser.: No. 352). pap. 21.00 (ISBN 0-317-10904-9, 2000117). Bks Demand UMI.
Symposium on Algebraic Topology, in Honor of Jose Adem: Proceedings. Ed. by Samuel Gitler. LC 82-13812. (Contemporary Mathematics Ser.: Vol. 12). 372p. 1982. pap. 27.00 (ISBN 0-8218-5010-5, CONM-12). Am Math.
Symposium on Analgesics. E. Vizi. 207p. 1976. 66.00x (ISBN 0-569-08376-1, Pub. by Collets (UK)). State Mutual Bk.
Symposium on Analgesics, Vol. 1: 1974. Vizi. 1979. cancelled 20.00 (Pub. by Akademiai Kaido Hungary). IPS.
Symposium on Applications of Micro-Electronics, 27th March, 1968, University of Birmingham. LC 73-435862. (Institution of Electrical Engineers Conference Publications: No. 49). pap. 22.00 (ISBN 0-317-10137-4, 2007387). Bks Demand UMI.
Symposium on Aquaculture in Latin America: Proceedings, 1972. (Fisheries Reports: No. 159, Annex F, Revision 1). 44p. 1977. pap. 7.50 (ISBN 92-5-100214-2, F802, FAO). UNIPUB.
Symposium on Aspirin & Related Drugs: Their Actions & Uses. Ed. by K. D. Rainsford & K. Brune. Tr. by M. W. Whitehouse. (Agents & Actions Suppl. Ser.: No. 1). 118p. 1977. pap. 25.95x (ISBN 0-8176-0902-4). Birkhauser.
Symposium on Aspirin & Related Drugs: Their Action & Uses. Ed. by K. D. Rainsford et al. (Illus.). 1977. pap. 49.00 (ISBN 3-7643-0902-4). Adlers Foreign Bks.
Symposium on Atomic Energy & Its Implications. facs. ed. LC 74-84341. (Essay Index Reprint Ser). 1946. 15.75 (ISBN 0-8369-1110-5). Ayer Co Pubs.
Symposium on Automatic Control in Electricity Supply, 29-31 March, 1966 in Manchester, England. Automatic Control in Electricity Supply Staff. (IEE Conference Publication Ser.: No. 16, Pt. 1). (Illus.). pap. 98.00 (ISBN 0-317-09932-9, 2051588). Bks Demand UMI.
Symposium on Byzantine Medicine. Ed. by John Scarborough. LC 85-25967. (Dumbarton Oaks Papers: No. 38). (Illus.). 298p. 1985. 40.00x (ISBN 0-88402-139-4). Dumbarton Oaks.
Symposium on Cinema in Developing Countries. 171p. 1979. 6.95. Asia Bk Corp.
Symposium on Cleaning & Materials Processing for Electronics & Space Apparatus. American Society for Testing & Materials Staff. LC 63-15794. (American Society for Testing & Materials: Special Technical Publication: No. 342). pap. 68.30 (ISBN 0-317-08016-4, 2000138). Bks Demand UMI.
Symposium on Community Studies in Anthropology: American Ethnological Society Proceedings, 1963. American Ethnological Society Staff. LC 84-45550. 1988. pap. 18.50 (ISBN 0-404-62657-2). AMS Pr.
Symposium on Computer Applications in Medical Care, 9th 1985: Proceedings. 913p. 1985. 88.00 (ISBN 0-8186-0647-9, Q647); microfiche 88.00 (ISBN 0-8186-4647-0). IEEE Comp Soc.
Symposium on Concrete 1983: The Material for Tomorrow's Demands. 136p. (Orig.). 1984. pap. text ed. 28.00x (ISBN 0-85825-201-5, Pub. by Inst. Engineering Australia). Brookfield Pub Co.
Symposium on Conodont Biostratigraphy. Symposium on Conodont Biostratigraphy 1969:(Ohio State University) Ed. by Walter C. Sweet & Stig M. Bergstrom. (Geological Society of America Memoir Ser.: No. 127). pap. 128.80 (ISBN 0-317-28379-0, 2025461). Bks Demand UMI.
Symposium on Corrosion Fundamentals: A Series of Lectures Presented at the University of Tennessee Corrosion Conference at Knoxville on March 1-3, 1955. Ed. by Anton De Brasunas & E. E. Stansbury. LC 56-13073. pap. 65.30 (ISBN 0-317-10658-9, 2022212). Bks Demand UMI.
Symposium on Cotton Dust: Sampling, Monitoring & Control. 65p. 1980. 12.00 (ISBN 0-317-33625-8, 100136); members 6.00 (ISBN 0-317-33626-6). ASME.
Symposium on Creation, No. 4. Ed. by Donald W. Patten. pap. 3.95 (ISBN 0-8010-6925-4). Baker Bk.
Symposium on Creation VI. Donald W. Patten. 1977. pap. 3.95 (ISBN 0-685-52492-2). Pacific Mer.
Symposium on Design for Elevated Temperature Environment. Ed. by S. Y. Zamrik. LC 79-173043. pap. 20.00 (ISBN 0-317-10994-4, 2013307). Bks Demand UMI.
Symposium on Diseases of Fishes & Shellfishes. Ed. by S. F. Snieszko. (AFS Special Publications: No. 5). 528p. 1970. text ed. 16.00. Am Fisheries Soc.
Symposium on Dravidian Civilization. Ed. by Andree F. Sjoberg. LC 72-169898. 1971. 7.50 (ISBN 0-8363-0091-2). Jenkins.
Symposium on Drought in Botswana. Ed. by Madalon T. Hinchey. 15.00 (ISBN 0-87451-171-2). Clark U Pr.
Symposium on Dynamic Behavior of Materials. American Society for Testing & Materials Staff. LC 63-20729. (American Society for Testing & Materials. Special Technical Publication Ser.: No. 336). pap. 80.80 (ISBN 0-317-10854-9, 2000144). Bks Demand UMI.
Symposium on Edwards Limestone in Central Texas. F. E. Lozo et al. (Pub Ser.: 5905). (Illus.). 235p. 1959. 5.00 (ISBN 0-318-03309-7). Bur Econ Geology.

Symposium on Electronic Phenomena in Chemisorption & Catalysis on Semiconductors. Ed. by T. Wolkenstein & K. Hauffe. 1969. 37.60x (ISBN 3-11-000846-7). De Gruyter.
Symposium on Ethics: The Role of Moral Values in Contemporary Thought. Bernard D. Ouden. 104p. (Orig.). 1983. lib. bdg. 25.25 (ISBN 0-8191-2763-9); pap. text ed. 9.75 (ISBN 0-8191-2764-7). U Pr of Amer.
Symposium on Fatigue & Symposium on Human Factors in Equipment Design, 2 vols. in one. Ed. by W. F. Floyd & A. T. Welford. LC 77-70494. (Work Ser.). (Illus.). 1977. Repr. of 1954 ed. lib. bdg. 32.00x (ISBN 0-405-10165-1). Ayer Co Pubs.
Symposium on Fatigue Tests of Aircraft Structures: Low-Cycle, Full-Scale, & Helicopters. American Society for Testing & Materials Staff. LC 63-15793. (American Society for Testing & Materials. Special Technical Publication Ser.: No. 338). pap. 69.80 (ISBN 0-317-09223-5, 2000142). Bks Demand UMI.
Symposium on Flameproofing, Intrinsic Safety & Other Safeguards in Electrical Instrument Practice, 27th April, 1962. (Institution of Electrical Engineers Conference Report Ser.: No. 3). pap. 24.00 (ISBN 0-317-10109-9, 2007382). Bks Demand UMI.
Symposium on Graphite Fiber Composites: An Integrated Approach to Their Development & Use Presented at ASME Winter Meeting, Pittsburgh, PA., Nov. 1967. American Society of Mechanical Engineers, Rubber & Plastic Division Staff. LC 67-31228. pap. 20.00 (ISBN 0-317-08656-1, 2012303). Bks Demand UMI.
Symposium on Hong Kong: 1997. Ed. by Hungdah Chiu. (Occasional Papers-Reprints Series in Contemporary Asian Studies: No. 3-1985 (68)). 100p. (Orig.). 1986. pap. 4.00 (ISBN 0-942182-70-7). Occasional Papers.
Symposium on Idiopathic Low Back Pain. American Academy of Orthopedic Surgeons Staff. Ed. by Agustus A. White & Stephen L. Gordon. (Illus.). 448p. 1982. text ed. 65.00 (ISBN 0-8016-0059-6). Mosby.
Symposium on Infinite Dimensional Topology. Ed. by R. D. Anderson. LC 69-17445. (Annals of Mathematic Studies, 69). 230p. 1972. text ed. 34.00x (ISBN 0-691-08087-9). Princeton U Pr.
Symposium on Investigations & Resources of the Caribbean Sea & Adjacent Regions (CICAR) Proceedings. (Fisheries Reports: No. 71.2). 353p. 1971. pap. 18.00 (ISBN 0-686-92975-6, F1678, FAO). UNIPUB.
Symposium on Investigations & Resources of the Caribbean Sea & Adjacent Regions: Preparatory to the Co-operative Investigations of the Caribbean & Adjacent Regions (CICAR) Organized Jointly by UNESCO & FAO, Willemstad, Curacao, Netherlands Antilles, 18-26 Nov. 1968. 545p. (Eng. & Span.). 1971. 14.75 (U649, UNESCO). UNIPUB.
Symposium on Language & Culture: American Ethnological Society Proceedings, 1962. Ed. by Viola E. Garfield & Wallace L. Chafe. LC 84-45549. 1988. pap. 21.50 (ISBN 0-404-62656-4). AMS Pr.
Symposium on Local Diversity in Iroquois Culture. Ed. by William N. Fenton. Repr. of 1951 ed. 39.00 (ISBN 0-403-03704-2). Scholarly.
Symposium on Logic in Computer Science, 3rd, 1988: Proceedings. IEEE Staff. LC 88-45439. 1988. lib. bdg. 75.00 (ISBN 0-8186-8853-X, 853); pap. 75.00 (ISBN 0-8186-0853-6, 853); microfiche 75.00 (ISBN 0-8186-4853-8, 853). IEEE Comp Soc.
Symposium on Love. Ed. by Mary E. Curtin. LC 73-10475. 244p. 1973. text ed. 29.95 (ISBN 0-87705-116-X). Human Sci Pr.
Symposium on Lubricants for Automotive Equipment. American Society for Testing & Materials Staff. LC 63-15729. (American Society for Testing & Materials. Special Technical Publication Ser.: No. 334). pap. 64.80 (ISBN 0-317-09152-2, 2000122). Bks Demand UMI.
Symposium on Materials & Processes - Continuing Innovations: Meeting Held April 12-14, 1983, Anaheim , California. (Science of Advanced Materials & Process Engineering Ser.: Vol. 28). 1549p. 1983. 60.00 (ISBN 0-938994-22-0). Soc Adv Material.
Symposium on Materials for Aircraft, Missiles, & Space Vehicles. American Society for Testing & Materials Staff. LC 63-20730. (American Society for Testing & Materials. Special Technical Publication Ser.: 345). pap. 37.30 (ISBN 0-317-09214-6, 2000136). Bks Demand UMI.
Symposium on Materials Overview for 1982 - Including Electronics: Meeting Held May 4-6, 1982, San Diego, California. (Science of Advanced Materials & Processes Engineering Ser.: Vol. 27). 1062p. 1983. 60.00 (ISBN 0-938994-20-4). Soc Adv Material.
Symposium on Measurement in Unsteady Flow: Presented at the ASME Hydraulic Division Conference, Worcester, Mass., May 21-23, 1962. Symposium on Measurement in Unstaedy Flow, Worcester, Mass., 1962. LC 63-2546. pap. 29.50 (ISBN 0-317-11163-9, 2050440). Bks Demand UMI.
Symposium on Medical Therapy in Gloucoma. Ed. by E. L. Greve. (Documenta Ophthalmologica Proceedings: Vol. 12). 1976. lib. bdg. 26.00 (ISBN 90-6193-152-5, Pub. by Junk Pubs Netherlands). Kluwer Academic.
Symposium on Mineral Resources of the Southeastern United States: 1949 Proceedings. Tennessee University, Department of Geology & Geography. Ed. by F. G. Snyder. pap. 68.00 (ISBN 0-317-29304-4, 2022223). Bks Demand UMI.
Symposium on Mining, Hydrology, Sedimentology & Reclamation: Proceedings, 1986. R. William DeVore & Donald H. Graves. LC 83-60966. (Illus.). 283p. (Orig.). 1986. pap. 45.00 (ISBN 0-89779-067-7, UKY BU142). OES Pubns.
Symposium on New Approaches to the Study of Religion: American Ethnological Society Proceedings, 1964. Ed. by June Helm. LC 84-45551. 1988. pap. 27.50 (ISBN 0-404-62658-0). AMS Pr.
Symposium on Newer Structural Materials for Aerospace Vehicles. LC 65-16809. (American Society for Testing & Materials: No. 379). pap. 31.30 (ISBN 0-317-09248-0, 2000735). Bks Demand UMI.
Symposium on Nuclear Energy & Latin American Development: Proceedings. AEC Technical Information Center Staff. 166p. 1968. pap. 18.95 (ISBN 0-87079-358-6, PRNC-112). DOE.
Symposium on Nucleic Acid Metabolism of Placenta & Fetus. Ed. by T. Hayashi. (Journal: Gynecologic Investigation Ser.: Vol. 8, No. 3). (Illus.). 1977. 20.00 (ISBN 3-8055-2771-3). S Karger.
Symposium on Oneness Pentecostalism 1986. Compiled by United Pentecostal Church Int. & J. L. Hall. LC 86-19024. (Orig.). pap. 7.95 (ISBN 0-932581-03-X). Word Aflame.
Symposium on Paleolimnology. Ed. by David Frey. (Communications of the International Association of Theoretical & Applied Limnology: No. 17). (Illus.). 448p. (Orig.). 1969. pap. text ed. 115.00x (ISBN 3-510-52017-3, Pub. by E Schweizerbartsche). Coronet Bks.
Symposium on Pharmachaminergic & Serotonergic Mechanisms, Vol. 3. Magyar. 1979. cancelled 20.00 (ISBN 963-05-0923-7, Pub. by Akademiai Kaido Hungary). IPS.
Symposium on Pharmacological Agents & Biogenic Amines in the Central Nervous System. K. Magyar. 274p. 1973. 53.00x (ISBN 0-569-08072-X, Pub. by Collets (UK)). State Mutual Bk.
Symposium on Pharmacology of Catecholaminergic Serotonergic Mechanisms. K. Magyar. 203p. 1976. 66.00x (ISBN 0-569-08374-5, Pub. by Collets (UK)). State Mutual Bk.
Symposium on Pharmacology of the Heart, Vol. 6. Szekeres. 1979. pap. 36.00 cancelled (ISBN 963-05-0976-8, Pub. by Akademiai Kaido Hungary). IPS.
Symposium on Pharmacology of Vinca Alkaloids. G. Fekete. 106p. 1976. 30.00x (ISBN 0-569-08373-7, Pub. by Collets (UK)). State Mutual Bk.
Symposium on Pharmacology of Vinca Alkaloids, Vol. 5. Fekete. 1979. cancelled 14.00 (ISBN 963-05-0925-3, Pub. by Akademiai Kaido Hungary). IPS.
Symposium on Photofinishing Technology: 2nd International: Programs & Paper Summaries. Society of Photographic Scientists & Engineers. Ed. by Kenneth T. Lassiter. pap. 20.00 (ISBN 0-317-28479-7, 2019236). Bks Demand UMI.
Symposium on Prostaglandins: 1974, Vol. 2. Kelemen. cancelled 23.00 (ISBN 963-05-0922-9, Pub. by Akademiai Kaido Hungary). IPS.
Symposium on Prostoglandins. K. Kelemen. 235p. 1976. 70.00x (ISBN 0-569-08375-3, Pub. by Collets (UK)). State Mutual Bk.
Symposium on Radiation Effects on Metals & Neutron Dosimetry. American Society for Testing & Materials Staff. LC 63-12698. (American Society for Testing & Materials Ser.: Special Technical Publication, No. 341). pap. 103.80 (ISBN 0-317-10870-0, 2000139). Bks Demand UMI.
Symposium on Recent & Fossil Diatoms Proceedings Budapest Sept. 1980, Taxonomy, Morphology, Ecology, Biology, 6th. Ed. by R. Ross. (Illus.). 500p. 1982. text ed. 145.00x (ISBN 3-87429-192-8). Lubrecht & Cramer.
Symposium on Recent & Fossil Marine Diatoms, 3rd, Oslo, 1976: Proceedings. Ed. by R. Simonsen. (Illus.). 1977. text ed. 120.00x (ISBN 3-7682-5453-4). Lubrecht & Cramer.
Symposium on Recent Developments in Nondestructive Testing of Missiles & Rockets. American Society for Testing & Materials Staff. (American Society for Testing & Materials. Special Technical Publication Ser.: No. 350). pap. 30.30 (ISBN 0-317-09141-7, 2000116). Bks Demand UMI.
Symposium on Recent Trends in Development of Drug Metabolism, Vol. 4. Javor. 1979. cancelled 12.00 (ISBN 963-05-0924-5, Pub. by Akademiai Kaido Hungary). IPS.
Symposium on River & Floodplain Fisheries in Africa: Review & Experience Papers, Bujumbura, Burundi, 21-23 November 1977. R. L. Welcomme. (Commission for Inland Fisheries of Africa (CIFA): Technical Papers: No. 5). 390p. (Eng. & Fr.). 1978. pap. 26.25 (ISBN 92-5-000674-8, F1561, FAO). UNIPUB.
Symposium on Rolling Fatigue Performance: Testing of Lubricants. Ed. by R. Tourret & E. P. Wright. 324p. 1979. 88.95 (ISBN 0-471-25823-7). Wiley.
Symposium on Salt, Vol. 1: Introduction, Geology, Tectonics, Mineralology, Dry Mining, Rock Mechanics. Alan H. Coogan & Lukas Hauber. 495p. 1980. text ed. 110.00x (ISBN 0-317-63440-2, Pub. by E Schweizerbartsche). Coronet Bks.
Symposium on Salt, Vol. 2: Solution Mining, Salt Production, Salt Markets, Nutrition, Environmental Problems. Ed. by Alan H. Coogan & Lukas Hauber. 555p. 1980. text ed. 117.50x (ISBN 0-317-63444-5, Pub. by E Schweizerbartsche). Coronet Bks.
Symposium on Saprobiology. Ed. by Vladimir Sladecek. (Limnology Report: No. 9). (Illus.). 249p. (Orig.). 1978. pap. text ed. 73.50x (ISBN 3-510-47007-9, Pub. by E Schweizerbartsche). Coronet Bks.
Symposium on Small Hydropower & Fisheries. Ed. by F. W. Olson et al. 497p. 1985. text ed. 25.00 (ISBN 0-913235-37-7, 85-72260). Am Fisheries Soc.
Symposium on Spectrochemical Analysis for Trace Elements. American Society for Testing & Materials Staff. LC 58-3176. (American Society for Testing & Materials Special Technical Publications Ser: No. 221). pap. 21.30 (ISBN 0-317-09810-1, 2000112). Bks Demand UMI.
Symposium on Spectroscopy. American Society for Testing & Materials Staff. LC 60-9523. (American Society for Testing & Materials, Special Technical Publication: No. 269). pap. 62.80 (ISBN 0-317-09560-9, 2000106). Bks Demand UMI.
Symposium on Sports Medicine: The Knee. American Academy of Orthopaedic Surgeons Staff. 1984. text ed. 61.00 (ISBN 0-8016-0025-1). Mosby.
Symposium on Standards for Filament-Wound Reinforced Plastics. American Society for Testing & Materials Staff. LC 62-22246. (American Society for Testing & Materials Ser.: Special Technical Publication, No. 327). pap. 84.00 (ISBN 0-317-10780-1, 2000120). Bks Demand UMI.
Symposium on Stress-Strain-Time-Temperature Relationships in Materials. American Society for Testing & Materials Staff. LC 62-22248. (American Society for Testing & Materials: Special Publication, No. 325). pap. 33.80 (ISBN 0-317-10835-2, 2000133). Bks Demand UMI.
Symposium on Support & Testing of Large Astronomical Mirrors: Proceedings Held in Tuscon, Arizona, December 4-6, 1966. Ed. by David L. Crawford et al. (Arizona University, Optical Sciences Center, Technical Report: Vol. 30). pap. 63.00 (ISBN 0-317-28566-1, 2055253). Bks Demand UMI.
Symposium on the Biological Significance of Estuaries. Ed. by Philip A. Douglas & Richard H. Stroud. 1971. 4.00 (ISBN 0-686-21854-X). Sport Fishing.
Symposium on the Biology of the California Islands: Proceedings. Ed. by Ralph N. Philbrick. (Illus.). 1967. 12.50 (ISBN 0-916436-01-2). Santa Barb Botanic.
Symposium on the Chemical & Physical Effects of High-Energy Radiation on Inorganic Substances. American Society for Testing & Materials Staff. LC 64-14646. (American Society for Testing & Materials Special Technical Publication Ser.: No. 359). pap. 29.80 (ISBN 0-317-09795-4, 2000748). Bks Demand UMI.
Symposium on the Development & Exploitation of Artificial Lakes: Proceedings, Dominican Republic, Nov.-Dec. 1981. (Fisheries Reports: No. 273). 22p. (Eng. & Span.). 1982. pap. 7.50 (ISBN 92-5-001246-2, F2347, FAO). UNIPUB.
Symposium on the Engineering of Computer-Based Medical Systems, 1st, 1988: Proceedings. IEEE Staff. LC 88-81027. 174p. 1988. lib. bdg. 50.00 (ISBN 0-8186-8863-7, 863); pap. 50.00 (ISBN 0-8186-0863-3, 863); microfiche 50.00 (ISBN 0-8186-4863-5, 863). IEEE Comp Soc.
Symposium on the Foot & Ankle. American Academy of Orthopaedic Surgeons Staff. Ed. by Richard H. Kiene & Kenneth A. Johnson. LC 82-21716. (Illus.). 250p. 1983. text ed. 57.00 (ISBN 0-8016-0133-9). Mosby.
Symposium on the Foot & Leg in Running Sports. American Academy of Orthopaedic Surgeons Staff. LC 82-8188. (Illus.). 208p. 1982. text ed. 50.00 (ISBN 0-8016-0054-5). Mosby.
Symposium on the House Sparrow (Passer domesticus) & European Tree Sparrow (P. montanus) in North America. Ed. by S. Charles Kendeigh. 121p. 1973. 6.00 (ISBN 0-943610-14-1). Am Ornithologists.
Symposium on the Laser in Opthalmology & Glaucoma Update: Transcripts of the New Orleans Academy of Opthalmology. New Orleans Academy & Caldwell. 1984. 75.00 (ISBN 0-8016-3669-8). Mosby.
Symposium on the Magisterium: A Positive Statement. Ed. by John J. O'Rourke & S. Thomas Greenburg. 1978. 5.95 (ISBN 0-8198-0559-9); pap. 4.50 (ISBN 0-8198-0560-2). Dghtrs St Paul.
Symposium on the Muscle. Biro. 1976. cancelled 11.50 (Pub. by Akademiai Kaido Hungary). IPS.
Symposium on the Numerical Treatment of O.D.E. Integral & Integro-Differential Equations. Rome 1960. 680p. 1961. 36.95x (ISBN 0-8176-0378-6). Birkhauser.
Symposium on the Orion: Nebula to Honor Henry Draper, December 4-5, 1981. Ed. by A. E. Glassgold & P. J. Huggins. 338p. 1982. 65.00x (ISBN 0-89766-180-X, VOL. 395C); pap. write for info. (ISBN 0-89766-181-8). NY Acad Sci.
Symposium on the Phycology of Large Lakes of the World. Ed. by M. Munawar. (Limnology Report: No. 22). (Illus., Orig.). 1985. pap. text ed. 87.50x (ISBN 0-317-63452-6, Pub. by E Schweizerbartsche). Coronet Bks.
Symposium on the Siting of Nuclear Facilities: Proceedings. (Illus.). 1975. pap. 68.00 (ISBN 92-0-020175-X, ISP384, IAEA). UNIPUB.
Symposium on the Use of Isotopes in Biology & Medicine. Symposium on the Use of Isotopes in Biology & Medicine (1947: University of Wisconsin) et al. LC 48-2939. pap. 117.00 (ISBN 0-317-41734-7, 2021131). Bks Demand UMI.
Symposium on Trazodone. Ed. by C. L. Cazzullo et al. (Journal: Neuropsychobiology Ser.: Vol. 15, Suppl. 1, 1986). (Illus.). iv, 52p. 1986. pap. 18.75 (ISBN 3-8055-4338-7). S Karger.
Symposium on Upper Extremity Injuries in Athletes. American Academy of Orthopaedic Surgeons Staff. 1986. text ed. 50.00 (ISBN 0-8016-0026-X). Mosby.
Symposium: Our Living History: Reminiscences of Black Participants in NAWDAC. National Association for Women Deans, Administrators & Counselors. 1980. pap. 3.00 (ISBN 0-686-28001-6). Natl Assn Women.
Symposium Papers & Related Information on Nondestructive Testing for Pipe Systems: Sponsored by Institute of Gas Technology, June 7-10, 1976, Chicago, Illinois. Institute of Gas Technology. LC 76-382339. pap. 83.80 (ISBN 0-317-30071-7, 2019243). Bks Demand UMI.
Symposium: Patterns of Land Utilization & Other Papers: American Ethnological Society Proceedings, 1961. Ed. by Viola E. Garfield. LC 84-45548. 1988. pap. 27.50 (ISBN 0-404-62655-6). AMS Pr.
Symposium Plato. Benjamin Jowett. 1956. pap. text ed. write for info. (ISBN 0-02-360760-2). MacMillan.
Symposium sur les tumeurs cutanees des enfants. Gent. November 1978. Ed. by J. De Bersaques. (Journal: Dermatologica: Vol. 161, Suppl. 1, 1980). (Illus.). iv, 160p. 1981. pap. 12.00 (ISBN 3-8055-2238-X). S Karger.
Symposium Transsonicum 2. Ed. by K. Oswatitsch & D. Rues. (International Union of Theoretical & Applied Mechanics). 1976. 63.80 (ISBN 0-387-07526-7). Springer-Verlag.
Symposium Zoological Society London, No. 50. Ed. by Marcia Edwardss & Unity McDonnell. (Serial Publication). 336p. 1982. 68.00 (ISBN 0-12-613350-6). Acad Pr.
Symposiums see Republic & Other Works.
Symptom Analysis & Physical Diagnosis. 2nd ed. Ed. by A. Davis et al. 328p. 1985. text ed. 29.00 (ISBN 0-08-029870-2, Pub. by PPA); pap. text ed. 19.95 (ISBN 0-08-029869-9). Pergamon.
Symptom Control. Ed. by T. Declan Walsh. (Illus.). 450p. 1988. 25.00 (ISBN 0-86542-050-5). Blackwell Sci.
Symptom des Schreibens: Roman und Absolutes Buch in der Fruehromantik. Jens Schreiber. (European University Studies: No. 1, Vol. 649). 286p. (Ger.). 1983. 34.20 (ISBN 3-8204-7378-5). P Lang Pubs.
Symptom Management in Multiple Sclerosis. Randall T. Schapiro. LC 86-72100. (Illus.). 128p. 1987. text ed. 15.95 (ISBN 0-939957-02-7, 00S7); pap. 10.95 (ISBN 0-939957-03-5). Demos Pubns Inc.
Symptom-Oriented Guide to Adverse Drug Reactions. Mark L. Braunstein & John D. James. 560p. Date not set. pap. price not set (ISBN 0-07-032252-X). McGraw.
Symptom Reduction Through Clinical Biofeedback. Ivan Wentworth-Rohr. 273p. 1988. text ed. 34.95 (ISBN 0-89885-135-1); pap. 16.95 (ISBN 0-89885-366-4). Human Sci Pr.
Symptomatic Affective Disorders. F. A. Whitlock. (Personality & Psychopathology Ser.). 1983. 35.00 (ISBN 0-12-747580-X). Acad Pr.
Symptomatology & Differential Diagnosis: A Conspectus of Clinical Semeiographies. R. C. Schafer. LC 85-71673. (Illus.). 1088p. 1986. text ed. 90.00 (ISBN 0-9606618-1-6, K-18). Am Chiro Assn.
Symptoms after Forty. Kenneth Anderson. 384p. 1987. 19.95 (ISBN 0-87795-879-3). Morrow.
Symptoms after Forty. Kenneth Anderson. 384p. 1988. pap. 8.95 (ISBN 0-688-08245-9, Quill). Morrow.
Symptoms & Illness. David Locker. 1981. 29.95x (ISBN 0-422-77460-X, NO.6498, Pub. by Tavistock). Routledge Chapman & Hall.
Symptoms & Signs of Vitamin A Deficiency & Their Relationship to Applied Nutrition. Elmer J. Ballintine et al. (Illus., Orig.). 1981. pap. text ed. 3.50 (ISBN 0-935368-26-4). Nutrition Found.
Symptoms in Eye Examination. Geoffrey V. Ball. 154p. 1982. 59.95 (ISBN 0-407-00205-7). Butterworth.

Synodicon Vetus. Ed. by John Duffy. John Parker. LC 79-52935. (Dumbarton Oaks Texts: Vol. 5). 209p. 1979. 35.00x (ISBN 0-88402-088-6). Dumbarton Oaks.

Synonomy, Repetition & Restatement in the Vocabulary of Herman Melville's Moby Dick. James W. Nechas. 286p. 1980. Repr. of 1978 ed. lib. bdg. 35.00 (ISBN 0-8414-6311-5). Folcroft.

Synonym Dictionary. Norman Crozer. 240p. 1985. pap. text ed. 14.95 (ISBN 0-8403-3705-1). Kendall-Hunt.

Synonym Finder. rev. ed. J. I. Rodale. 1978. 21.95 (ISBN 0-87857-236-8). Rodale Pr Inc.

Synonym Finder. J. I. Rodale & Lawrence Urdang. 1376p. 1986. pap. 12.95 (ISBN 0-446-37029-0). Warner Bks.

Synonym-Word Finder Box Set. J. I. Rodale. 1987. 43.90 (ISBN 0-87857-711-4). Rodale Pr Inc.

Synonymic Catalogue of Homoptera, Pt. 1, Cicadidae. William L. Distant. 1906. 19.00. Johnson Repr.

Synonymized Checklist of the Vascular Flora of the United States, Canada, & Greenland. John T. Kartesz & Rosemarie Kartesz. xlviii, 494p. 1980. 40.00x (ISBN 0-8078-1422-9). U of NC Pr.

Synonyms, Antonyms, Homonyms. Sheldon Tilkin. (Horizons II Ser.). (Illus.). 24p. (gr. 3-4). 1980. wkbk. 2.50 (ISBN 0-89403-603-3). EDC.

Synonyms for "Child", "Boys", "Girl" in Old English: An Etymological-Semiasiological Investigation. H. Back. (Lund Studies in English: Vol. 2). pap. 30.00 (ISBN 0-8115-0545-6). Kraus Repr.

Synonyms of the Old Testament. Robert B. Girdlestone. 1948. pap. 6.95 (ISBN 0-8028-1548-0). Eerdmans.

Synonyms of the Old Testament: Numerically Coded to Strong's Exhaustive Concordance. Robert B. Girdlestone. Ed. by Donald R. White. 400p. 1983. pap. 17.95 kivar bdg. (ISBN 0-8010-3789-1). Baker Bk.

Synonymy & Linguistic Analysis. Roy Harris. LC 73-160625. (Language & Style Ser.: No. 12). pap. 43.00 (2026524). Bks Demand UMI.

Synonymy & Semantic Classification. Karen S. Jones. 256p. 22.50 (ISBN 0-85224-517-3, Pub. by Edinburgh U Pr Scotland). Columbia U Pr.

Synopses of English Fiction. Nora I. Sholto-Douglas. LC 72-5373. 1972. Repr. lib. bdg. 55.00 (ISBN 0-8414-0029-6). Folcroft.

Synopsis & Classification of Living Organism, 2 vols. McGraw-Hill Editors. Ed. by Sybil P. Parker. 2424p. 1982. Set. text ed. 265.00 (ISBN 0-07-079031-0). McGraw.

Synopsis der Fische Des Rothen Meeres, 2 parts in 1 vol. C. B. Klunzinger. (Illus.). 1964. Repr. of 1871 ed. 60.00x (ISBN 3-7682-7115-3). Lubrecht & Cramer.

Synopsis Fungorum Carolinea Superioris. L. D. Von Schweinitz. 1976. Repr. of 1822 ed. 24.00x (ISBN 3-7682-1065-0). Lubrecht & Cramer.

Synopsis Fungorum in America Boreali Media Degentium. L. D. Schweinitz. 1962. Repr. of 1834 ed. 60.00x (ISBN 3-7682-0117-1). Lubrecht & Cramer.

Synopsis Hepaticarum. K. M. Gottsche et al. 1967. Repr. of 1844 ed. 96.00x (ISBN 3-7682-0516-9). Lubrecht & Cramer.

Synopsis Medica Lichenum. E. Acharius. (Illus.). 424p. (Lat.). 1977. Repr. of 1814 ed. 116.95x (ISBN 0-916422-29-1, Pub. by Richmond Pub Co). Mad River.

Synopsis Methodica Animalium Quadrupedum et Serpentini Generis. John Ray. Ed. by Keir B. Sterling. LC 77-81111. (Biologists & Their World Ser.). (Lat.). 1978. Repr. of 1693 ed. lib. bdg. 29.00x (ISBN 0-405-10694-7). Ayer Co Pubs.

Synopsis Methodica Avium & Piscium. John Ray. Ed. by William Derham & Keir B. Sterling. LC 77-81111. (Biologists & Their World Ser.). (Illus., Lat.). 1978. Repr. of 1713 ed. lib. bdg. 35.50x (ISBN 0-405-10695-5). Ayer Co Pubs.

Synopsis of American History, 2 vols. 6th ed. Charles Sellers et al. Incl. Vol. I. Through Reconstruction. pap. text ed. 21.16 (ISBN 0-395-36194-X); Since the Civil War. pap. text ed. 21.16 (ISBN 0-395-36195-8). (Illus.). 448p. 1985. instr's manual 2.36 (ISBN 0-395-36196-6). HM.

Synopsis of American History. 6th ed. Charles Sellers et al. 1985. pap. text ed. 26.76 (ISBN 0-395-36193-1); write for info. instr's. manual. HM.

Synopsis of Anaesthesia. 9th ed. R. S. Atkinson et al. (Illus.). 976p. 1982. pap. text ed. 42.00 (ISBN 0-7236-0621-8). PSG Pub Co.

Synopsis of Anaesthesia. 10th ed. R. S. Atkinson et al. 912p. 1987. 55.00 (ISBN 0-7236-0807-5). PSG Pub Co.

Synopsis of Biological Data on Catla: Catla Catla (Hamilton, 1822) Y. G. Jhingram. (Fisheries Synopses: No. 32). 78p. 1966. pap. 7.50 (ISBN 0-686-92723-0, F1759, FAO). UNIPUB.

Synopsis of Biological Data on European Grayling: Thymallus Thymallus (Linnaeus, 1758) D. Jankovic. (Fisheries Synopses: No. 24, Rev. 1). 50p. 1964. pap. 7.50 (ISBN 0-686-92726-5, F1754, FAO). UNIPUB.

Synopsis of Biological Data on Haddock, Melanogrammus Aeglefinus (Linnaeus, 1758) R. W. Blacker. (Fisheries Synopses: No. 84). 41p. 1971. pap. 7.50 (ISBN 0-686-92727-3, F1179, FAO). UNIPUB.

Synopsis of Biological Data on Indian Mackerel, Rastrelliger Kanagurta (Cuvier, 1817) & Short-Bodied Mackerel, Rastrelliger Brachymosa (Bleeker, 1851) (Fisheries Synopses: No. 29). 34p. 1965. pap. 7.50 (ISBN 92-5-101890-1, F1758, FAO). UNIPUB.

Synopsis of Biological Data on North Atlantic Sand Eels of the Genus Ammodytes, CA. Tobianus, A. Dubius, A. Americanus & A. Marinus. (Fisheries Synopses: No. 82). 42p. 1970. pap. 7.50 (ISBN 0-686-92730-3, F1765, FAO). UNIPUB.

Synopsis of Biological Data on Scallops: Chlamys (Aequipecten) Opercularis (Linaeus) Argopecten Irradians (Lamarck) Argopecten Gibbus (Linnaeus) M. J. Broon. (Fisheries Synopses: No. 114). (Illus.). 44p. 1976. pap. 7.50 (ISBN 92-5-100213-4, F846, FAO). UNIPUB.

Synopsis of Biological Data on Sprat, Sprattus Sprattus (Linnaeus, 1758) (Mediterranean & Adjacent Seas) M. Demir. (Fisheries Synopses: No. 27, Rev. 1). 39p. 1966. pap. 7.50 (ISBN 0-686-93016-9, F1756, FAO). UNIPUB.

Synopsis of Biological Data on the Anchoveta, Cetengraulis Mysticetus (Gunther, 1866) W. H. Bayliff. (Fisheries Synopses: No. 43). 46p. 1969. pap. 7.50 (ISBN 92-5-101896-0, F1764, FAO). UNIPUB.

Synopsis of Biological Data on the Eel: Anguilla anguilla (Linnaeus, 1758) C. L. Deelder. (Fisheries Synopsis Ser.: No. 80, Rev. 1). 73p. 1985. pap. 7.50 (ISBN 92-5-102166-X, F2724, FAO). UNIPUB.

Synopsis of Biological Data on the Green Turtle: Chylonia Mydas (Linnaeus, 1758) H. F. Hirth. (Fisheries Synopses: No. 85). 71p. 1971. pap. 7.50 (ISBN 92-5-101901-0, F1180, FAO). UNIPUB.

Synopsis of Biological Data on the Hawksbill Turtle: Bretmochelys Imbricata (Linnaeus, 1766) W. N. Witzel. (Fisheries Synopses: No. 137). 82p. 1983. pap. text ed. 7.50 (ISBN 92-5-101356-X, F2455, FAO). UNIPUB.

Synopsis of Biological Data on the Lumpsucker: Cyclopterus Lumpus (Linnaeus, 1758) J. Davenport. (FAO Fisheries Synopsis: No. 147). (Illus.). 30p. (Orig.). 1986. pap. text ed. 7.50 (ISBN 92-5-102330-1, F2874, FAO). UNIPUB.

Synopsis of Biological Data on the Western Rock Lobster: Panulirus cygnus (George, 1962) B. F. Philipps & G. R. Morgan. (Fisheries Synopses: No.128). 69p. 1980. pap. 7.50 (ISBN 92-5-101025-0, F2166, FAO). UNIPUB.

Synopsis of Biological Data on West African Croakers: Pseudotolithus Typus, P. Elongatus. A. R. Longhurst. (Fisheries Synopses: No. 35). 44p. 1966. pap. 7.50 (ISBN 0-686-93037-1, F1762, FAO). UNIPUB.

Synopsis of California Stalk - Eyed Crustacea. Samuel J. Holmes. (California Academy of Sciences, Occasional Papers: No. 7). (Illus.). 262p. 1900. 37.00 (ISBN 0-384-24040-2). Johnson Repr.

Synopsis of Cancer Chemotherapy. 2nd ed. Richard T. Silver et al. LC 86-50564. (Illus.). 150p. 1987. 39.95 (ISBN 0-914316-39-7, Yorke Medical Bks). Butterworth.

Synopsis of Cardiology. S. C. Jordan. (Illus.). 352p. 1979. pap. 22.00 (ISBN 0-7236-0533-5). PSG Pub Co.

Synopsis of Chest Diseases. J. Collins. (Illus.). 224p. 1979. pap. 22.00 (ISBN 0-7236-0526-2). PSG Pub Co.

Synopsis of Children's Diseases. 6th ed. Rendle-Short et al. (Illus.). 568p. 1985. 42.00 (ISBN 0-7236-0743-5). PSG Pub Co.

Synopsis of Clinical Pulmonary Disease. 4th ed. Mitchell et al. (Illus.). 352p. 1988. pap. text ed. 24.95 (ISBN 0-8016-3908-5). Mosby.

Synopsis of Complete Dentures. Charles W. Ellinger. LC 74-23703. pap. 91.30 (ISBN 0-317-28606-4, 2055422). Bks Demand UMI.

Synopsis of Contents & Index to Sir George Scott Robertson, the Kafirs of the Hindu-Kush. Lennart Edelberg. (Illus.). 59p. 1896-1900. Repr. 13.00 (ISBN 0-384-13850-0). Johnson Repr.

Synopsis of Critical Care. 3rd ed. William Sibbald. 350p. 1988. 29.95 (ISBN 0-317-67384-X). Williams & Wilkins.

Synopsis of Dicken's Novels. J. Walker McSpadden. LC 72-195399. 1904. lib. bdg. 45.00 (ISBN 0-8414-5961-4). Folcroft.

Synopsis of Diseases of the Chest. J. A. Pare & Robert Fraser. (Illus.). 896p. 1983. 58.00 (ISBN 0-7216-7068-7). Saunders.

Synopsis of Endocrinology & Metabolism. 3rd ed. Ramsay. 1986. 33.00 (ISBN 0-7236-0852-0). PSG Pub Co.

Synopsis of English Syntax. Eugene A. Nida. (Janua Linguarum, Ser. Practica: No. 19). (Orig.). 1966. pap. text ed. 19.20x (ISBN 90-2792-430-9). Mouton.

Synopsis of Eugen Bleuler's Dementia Praecox or the Group of Schizophrenias. Ed. by Nathan S. Kline. (Monograph Ser. on Schizophrenia). 57p. 1966. text ed. 17.50x (ISBN 0-8236-6320-5). Intl Univs Pr.

Synopsis of Gastroenterology. R. H. Salter. 176p. 1980. pap. 35.00 (ISBN 0-7236-0536-X). PSG Pub Co.

Synopsis of Gross Anatomy: With Clinical Correlations. 5th ed. John B. Christensen & Ira R. Telford. LC 65-10150. (Illus.). 468p. 1988. 23.50 (ISBN 0-397-50850-6, Lippincott Medical). Lippincott.

Synopsis of Haematology. J. Richards et al. (Illus.). 320p. 1983. pap. 24.00 (ISBN 0-7236-0650-1). PSG Pub Co.

Synopsis of Infectious & Tropical Diseases. 3rd ed. Woodruff & Wright. 352p. 1987. 32.00 (ISBN 0-7236-0826-1). PSG Pub Co.

Synopsis of Invertebrate Pathology: Exclusive of Insects. Ed. by A. K. Sparks. 424p. 1985. 120.50 (ISBN 0-444-80678-4). Elsevier.

Synopsis of Neuroanatomy. 4th ed. Howard A. Matzke & Floyd M. Foltz. (Illus.). 1983. pap. 9.95x (ISBN 0-19-503244-6). Oxford U Pr.

Synopsis of North American Desmids, Pt. II: Desmidiaceae; Placodermae, Section 4. G. W. Prescott & Carlos E. Bicudo. LC 70-183418. x, 700p. 1982. 66.50x (ISBN 0-8032-3650-6). U of Nebr Pr.

Synopsis of North American Desmids Part II: Desmidiaceae: Placodermae Section 5. The Filamentous Genera. Hannah Croasdale & Carlos E. Bicudo. LC 70-183418. (Illus.). vi, 117p. 1983. 26.50x (ISBN 0-8032-3661-1). U of Nebr Pr.

Synopsis of North American Desmids, Part II: Desmidiaceae, Placodermae, Section 2. G. W. Prescott & Hannah T. Croasdale. LC 70-183418. (Illus.). x, 413p. 1977. 36.50x (ISBN 0-8032-0899-5). U of Nebr Pr.

Synopsis of North American Desmids, Part II: Desmidiaceae, Placodermae, Section 1. G. W. Prescott et al. LC 70-183418. (Illus.). x, 275p. 1975. 31.50x (ISBN 0-8032-0854-5). U of Nebr Pr.

Synopsis of North American Desmids Part II: Desmidiaceae, Placodermae, Section 3. G. W. Prescott et al. LC 70-183418. (Illus.). x, 720p. 1981. 61.50x (ISBN 0-8032-3660-3). U of Nebr Pr.

Synopsis of Occupational Medicine. 2nd ed. F. H. Tyrer & K. Lee. (Illus.). 240p. 1985. pap. 28.00 (ISBN 0-7236-0798-2). PSG Pub Co.

Synopsis of Ophthalmology. 5th ed. J. Martin-Doyle. (Illus.). 300p. 1975. 24.00. PSG Pub Co.

Synopsis of Oral Pathology. 7th ed. Bhaskar. 1986. 37.95 (ISBN 0-8016-1243-8). Mosby.

Synopsis of Otolaryngology. 4th ed. J. Groves & R. Gray. (Illus.). 570p. 1985. 40.00 (ISBN 0-7236-0772-9). PSG Pub Co.

Synopsis of Pathology. 10th ed. W. A. Anderson & W. A. Scotti. LC 80-13985. (Illus.). 798p. 1980. pap. text ed. 35.95 (ISBN 0-8016-0231-9). Mosby.

Synopsis of Pediatrics. 6th ed. James G. Hughes. (Illus.). 1086p. 1984. pap. text ed. 44.95 (ISBN 0-8016-2310-3). Mosby.

Synopsis of Pharmacology for Students in Dentistry. Thomas J. Pallasch & Richard M. Oksas. LC 74-8951. Repr. of 1974 ed. 28.90 (ISBN 0-8357-9422-9, 2014571). Bks Demand UMI.

Synopsis of Psychiatry. J. Harding Price. (Illus.). 512p. 1982. pap. text ed. 42.00 (ISBN 0-7236-0611-0). PSG Pub Co.

Synopsis of Psychiatry. 5th ed. Harold I. Kaplan & Benjamin Sadock. (Illus.). 576p. 1987. 24.95 (ISBN 0-317-67388-2). Williams & Wilkins.

Synopsis of Publications. AFA Staff. 108p. 1983. 3.00 (ISBN 0-318-01887-X). Am Fed Astrologers.

Synopsis of Radiologic Anatomy with Computed Tomography. rev. ed. Isadore Meschan. LC 80-5042. (Illus.). 762p. 1980. Repr. of 1978 ed. text ed. 67.95 (ISBN 0-7216-6296-X). Saunders.

Synopsis of Rheumatic Disease. 4th ed. D. Golding. 314p. 1982. 30.00 (ISBN 0-7236-0627-7). PSG Pub Co.

Synopsis of Rheumatic Diseases. D. N. Golding. (Illus.). 344p. 1988. price not set (ISBN 0-7236-0850-4). PSG Pub Co.

Synopsis of Surgery. 5th ed. Richard D. Liechty & Robert T. Soper. LC 80-12884. (Illus.). 716p. 1985. pap. text ed. 41.95 (ISBN 0-8016-3099-1). Mosby.

Synopsis of the Avifauna of China. Cheng Tso-hsin. (Illus.). 1224p. 1987. lib. bdg. 163.00x. Parey Sci Pubs.

Synopsis of the Biology of the Middle American Highland Frog Rana Maculata Brocchi. Jaime Villa. (Contributions in Biology & Geology Ser.: No. 21). 1979. 1.00 (ISBN 0-89326-037-1). Milwaukee Pub Mus.

Synopsis of the Birds of India & Pakistan: Together with Those of Nepal, Bhutan, Bangladesh, & Sri Lanka. Sidney D. Ripley, II. (Illus.). 652p. 1988. 45.00 (ISBN 0-19-562164-6). Oxford U Pr.

Synopsis of the Books of the Bible, 5 vols. J. N. Darby. Set. 27.50 (ISBN 0-88172-070-4). Believers Bkshelf.

Synopsis of the Chrysididae in America North of Mexico. R. M. Bohart & Lynn S. Kimsey. (Memoir Ser: No.33). (Illus.). 266p. 1982. 26.00x (ISBN 0-686-40423-8). Am Entom Inst.

Synopsis of the First Three Gospels With the Addition of the Johannine Parallels. Albert Huck. 1982. 22.50x (ISBN 0-8028-3568-6). Eerdmans.

Synopsis of the Four Gospels (English Only) Ed. by K. Aland. 361p. 1983. 5.95x (ISBN 0-8267-0500-6, 08564). Am Bible.

Synopsis of the Four Gospels in a New Translation: Arranged According to the Two Gospel Hypothesis. John B. Orchard. LC 81-18753. 319p. 1982. English 19.95 (ISBN 0-86554-024-1, MUP-H22); Greek 31.95 (ISBN 0-86554-061-6, MUP-H70). Mercer Univ Pr.

Synopsis of the Herpetofauna of Mexico. Hobart M. Smith & Rozella B. Smith. Incl. Vol. 1. Analysis of the Literature on the Mexican Axolotl. 1971. 10.00x (ISBN 0-910914-06-0); Vol. 2. Analysis of the Literature Exclusive of the Mexican Axolotl. 1973. 12.50x (ISBN 0-910914-07-9); Vol. 3. Source Analysis & Index for Mexican Reptiles. 1976. 25.00x (ISBN 0-910914-08-7); Vol. 4. Source Analysis & Index for Mexican Amphibians. 1976. 12.50x (ISBN 0-910914-09-5); Vol. 5. Guide to Mexican Amphisbaenians & Crocodilians. 1977. 12.50x (ISBN 0-910914-10-9); Vol. 6. Guide to Mexican Turtles. (Illus.). 1980. 40.00x (ISBN 0-910914-11-7). J Johnson.

Synopsis of the Heteroptera or True Bugs of the Galapagos Islands. Richard C. Froeschner. LC 84-600217. (Smithsonian Contributions to Zoology Ser.: No. 407). pap. 22.00 (ISBN 0-317-30173-X, 2025355). Bks Demand UMI.

Synopsis of the Indian Tribes Within the U. S. East of the Rocky Mountains & in British & Russian Possessions in North America. Albert Gallatin. LC 78-168093. Repr. of 1836 ed. 27.50 (ISBN 0-404-07127-9). AMS Pr.

Synopsis of the Law of Libel & the Right of Privacy. Bruce W. Sanford. 1986. pap. 2.95 (ISBN 0-915106-19-1). Newspaper Ent.

Synopsis of the Law of Partnership. Lewis Mayers. LC 78-78635. (Quality Paperback: No. 235). 184p. (Orig.). 1973. pap. 4.95 (ISBN 0-8226-0235-0). Littlefield.

Synopsis of the Marine Prosobranch Gastropod & Bivalve Mollusks in Alaskan Waters. Nora R. Foster. (IMS Report Ser.: No. R81-3). 499p. 37.50 (ISBN 0-914500-14-7). U of Ak Inst Marine.

Synopsis of the Military Career of General Joseph Wheeler: Commander of the Cavalry Corps, Army of the West. Ed. & intro. by George R. Stewart. (Eyewitness Accounts of the Civil War Ser.). (Illus.). 38p. 1988. pap. 7.50 (ISBN 0-942301-05-6). Birm Pub Lib.

Synopsis of the Nomenclature of the Fixed Stars. A. Werner & T. Schmeidler. (Illus.). 510p. 1986. 155.00 (ISBN 3-8047-0739-4, Pub by Wissenschaftliche Verlagsgesselshaft). IPS.

Synopsis of the North American Microtine Rodents. E. Raymond Hall & E. Lendell Cockrum. (Museum Ser.: Vol. 5, No. 27). 126p. 1953. pap. 6.50 (ISBN 0-686-80288-8). U of KS Mus Nat Hist.

Synopsis of the Siphonophora. A. K. Totton. (Illus.). viii, 231p. 1965. 54.00x (ISBN 0-565-00642-8, Pub. by Brit Mus Nat Hist). Sabbot-Natural Hist Bks.

Synopsis of the Stratigraphy in the Western Grand Canyon, Arizona. George H. Billingsley. (Research Ser.). 36p. 1978. pap. 3.50 (RS-16). Mus Northern Ariz.

Synopsis of World Civilization. Charles Cox. 192p. 1987. pap. text ed. 16.95 (ISBN 0-8403-4214-4). Kendall Hunt.

Synopsis: Painting, Architecture, Sculpture. 2nd ed. Alvar Aalto. (Geschichte und Theorie der Architektur: No. 12). (Illus.). 240p. (Eng., Ger. & Fr.). 1980. 81.95x (ISBN 0-8176-1109-6). Birkhauser.

Synoptic Abstract. Joseph B. Tyson & Thomas R. W. Longstaff. Ed. by J. Arthur Baird & David Noel Freedman. (The Computer Bible Ser.: Vol. XV). 1978. pap. 15.00 (ISBN 0-935106-05-7). Biblical Res Assocs.

Synoptic Approach to the Riddle of Existence: Toward an Adequate World View for a World Civilization. Arthur W. Munk. LC 77-818. 264p. 1977. 15.00. Green.

Synoptic Approach to the Riddle of Existence. Arthur W. Munk. LC 77-818. 264p. 1977. 15.00 (ISBN 0-87527-165-0). Fireside Bks.

Synoptic Classification of Living Organisms. R. S. Barnes. LC 84-1237. (Illus.). 276p. (Orig.). 1984. pap. text ed. 16.95x (ISBN 0-87893-048-5). Sinauer Assocs.

Synoptic Climatology: Methods & Applications. R. G. Barry & A. H. Perry. 500p. 1973. 66.00x (ISBN 0-416-08500-8, 2078). Routledge Chapman & Hall.

Synoptic Concordance of Aramaic Inscriptions. Walter E. Aufrecht & John Hurd. (International Concordance Library: Vol. I). 1975. pap. 20.00 (ISBN 0-935106-24-3). Biblical Res Assocs.

Synoptic Eddies in the Ocean. A. S. Monin et al. 1985. lib. bdg. 79.00 (ISBN 90-277-1925-X, Pub. by Reidel Holland). Kluwer Academic.

Synoptic Flora of Mysore District. R. R. Rao & B. A. Razi. (International Bio-Science Ser.: No. 7). 694p. 1981. 65.00 (ISBN 0-88065-180-6, Pub. by Messers Today & Tomorrows Printers & Publishers India). Scholarly Pubns.

Synoptic Gospels: An Introduction. Keith F. Nickle. LC 79-92069. (Orig.). 1980. pap. 9.95 (ISBN 0-8042-0422-5, John Knox). Westminster John Knox.

Synoptic Harmony of Samuel, Kings, & Chronicles. James D. Newsome, Jr. 272p. 1986. text ed. 16.95 (ISBN 0-8010-6744-8). Baker Bk.

Synoptic History of Classical Rhetoric. Ed. by James J. Murphy. 199p. (Orig.). 1983. pap. text ed. 8.50 (ISBN 0-9611800-0-5). Hermagoras Pr.

Synoptic Meteorology in China. C. Bao. (Illus.). vi, 269p. 1988. 77.60 (ISBN 0-387-16715-3). Springer-Verlag.

Synoptic Problem. Robert H. Stein. 280p. 1987. 17.95 (ISBN 0-8010-8272-2). Baker Bk.

Synoptic Problem: A Critical Analysis. William R. Farmer. LC 76-13764. xi, 308p. 1981. 18.95 (ISBN 0-915948-02-8, MUP-H005). Mercer Univ Pr.

Synoptic Supplement to T. Wright's Monograph on the Lias Ammonites of the British Islands. D. T. Donovan. 1954. pap. 12.00 (ISBN 0-384-12325-2). Johnson Repr.

Synoptic Vision: Essays on the Philosophy of Wilfrid Sellars. C. F. Delaney et al. LC 76-22406. 1977. text ed. 17.95x (ISBN 0-268-01596-1). U of Notre Dame Pr.

Synopticon: The Verbal Agreement Between the Greek Texts of Matthew, Mark & Luke Contextually Exhibited. Ed. by William R. Farmer. LC 78-77287. pap. 62.20 (2031647). Bks Demand UMI.

Synovial Lining in Health & Disease. J. C. Edwards & B. Henderson. 368p. 1987. text ed. 79.50x (ISBN 0-412-26200-2, Pub. by Chapman & Hall UK). Sheridan Med Bks.

Synphore Dans "la Jeune Parque" De Paul Valery. Grace Campbell. LC 74-28038. (Romance Monographs: No. 12). 1975. 10.00x (ISBN 84-399-3510-2). Romance.

Syntactic Analysis of Selected Middle High German Prose As a Basis for Stylistic Differentiations: German Language & Literature, Vol. 127. Heidi M. Rockwood. (European University Studies: Ser. 1). 152p. 1976. pap. 18.25 (ISBN 3-261-01657-4). P Lang Pubs.

Syntactic & Structural Pattern Recognition: Theory & Applications. Ed. by H. Bunke & A. Sanfeliu. 500p. (Orig.). 1988. 87.00 (ISBN 9971-50-552-5); pap. 51.00 (ISBN 9971-50-566-5). World Scientific Pub.

Syntactic Argumentation. Donna J. Napoli & Emily Rando. 422p. 1979. pap. text ed. 9.95 (ISBN 0-87840-180-6); with teacher's guide course order 2.50 (ISBN 0-87840-181-4). Georgetown U Pr.

Syntactic Argumentation & the Structure of English. Scott Soames & David M. Pelmutter. LC 78-65471. 1979. 40.00x (ISBN 0-520-03828-2); pap. 12.95x (ISBN 0-520-03833-9). U of Cal Pr.

Syntactic Blends in English Parole. Gerald L. Cohen. (Forum Anglicum Ser.: Vol. 15). viii, 178p. 1987. pap. 26.25 (ISBN 3-8204-9836-2). P Lang Pubs.

Syntactic Case & Morphological Case in the History of English. A. Van Kemeuade. xi, 249p. 1987. pap. write for info. (ISBN 90-6765-342-X). Foris Pubns.

Syntactic Chains. Kenneth J. Safir. (Cambridge Studies in Linguistics: 40). (Illus.). 400p. 1985. 39.50 (ISBN 0-521-25980-0). Cambridge U Pr.

Syntactic Change & Syntactic Reconstruction: A Tagmemic Approach. John R. Costello. LC 83-60279. (Publications in Linguistics Ser.: No. 68). 78p. (Orig.). 1983. pap. 9.00x (ISBN 0-88312-092-5); microfiche (2) 4.00 (ISBN 0-88312-404-1). Summer Inst Ling.

Syntactic Derivation of Tagalog Verbs. Videa P. DeGuzman. LC 78-11029. (Oceanic Linguistic Special Publication: No. 16). 1978. pap. text ed. 15.00x (ISBN 0-8248-0627-1). UH Pr.

Syntactic Development of the Gerund in Middle English. Matsuji Tajima. xii, 154p. 1985. 38.00x (ISBN 0-317-38862-2, Pub. by Nan Un-do). Benjamins North Am.

Syntactic Development of the Infinitive in Indo-European. Dorothy Disterheft. 220p. (Orig.). 1980. pap. 16.95 (ISBN 0-89357-058-3). Slavica.

Syntactic Factors in Memory? Samuel Fillenbaum. (Janua Linguarum Ser. Minor: No. 168). 1973. pap. text ed. 10.80x (ISBN 0-686-22590-2). Mouton.

Syntactic Methods in Pattern Recognition. K. S. Fu. (Mathematics & Science Engineering Ser.). 1974. 79.50 (ISBN 0-12-269560-7). Acad Pr.

Syntactic Modularity. Gabriella Hermon. (Studies Generative Grammar: No. 20). 265p. 1985. pap. 26.90 (ISBN 9-067-65111-7); pap. 49.00 (ISBN 90-6765-110-9). Foris Pubns.

Syntactic Pattern Recognition & Applications. King Sun Fu. (Advances in Computing Science & Technology Ser.). (Illus.). 640p. 1982. text ed. 64.00 (ISBN 0-13-880120-7). P-H.

Syntactic Pattern Recognition, Applications. Ed. by King Sun Fu. (Communication & Cybernetics: Vol. 14). (Illus.). 1977. 56.00 (ISBN 0-387-07841-X). Springer-Verlag.

Syntactic Phenomena of English, Vol. 1. James D. McCawley. (Illus.). 416p. 1988. 60.00x (ISBN 0-226-55623-9); pap. 19.95x (ISBN 0-226-55624-7). U of Chicago Pr.

Syntactic Phenomena of English, Vol. 2. James D. McCawley. (Illus.). 464p. 1988. 60.00x (ISBN 0-226-55625-5); pap. 19.95x (ISBN 0-226-55626-3). U of Chicago Pr.

Syntactic Revolution. Abraham L. Gillespie. Ed. by Richard Milazzo. LC 75-22994. (Illus.). 190p. 1981. pap. 12.95 (ISBN 0-915570-05-X). Oolp Pr.

Syntactic Structures. Noam Chomsky. (Janua Linguarum Ser. Minor: No. 4). 1978. 6.95 (ISBN 90-279-3385-5). Mouton.

Syntactic Study of Egyptian Colloquial Arabic. Saad M. Gamal-Eldin. (Janua Linguarum, Ser. Practica: No. 34). 1967. pap. text ed. 22.00x (ISBN 90-2790-648-3). Mouton.

Syntactic Theory. Emmon Bach. LC 81-40918. 310p. 1982. pap. text ed. 15.25 (ISBN 0-8191-2258-0). U Pr of Amer.

Syntactic Theory in the High Middle Ages: Modistic Models of Sentence Structure. Michael A. Covington. (Studies in Linguistics: No. 39). (Illus.). 200p. 1985. 39.50 (ISBN 0-521-25679-8). Cambridge U Pr.

Syntactic Typology: Studies in the Phenomenology of Language. Ed. by Winfred P. Lehmann. LC 78-56377. 477p. 1978. 22.50x (ISBN 0-292-77545-8). U of Tex Pr.

Syntactical & Critical Concordance to the Greek Text of Baruch & the Epistle of Jeremiah. R. A. Martin. (Computer Bible Ser.: Vol. XII). (Gr.). 1977. pap. 15.00 (ISBN 0-935106-09-X). Biblical Res Assocs.

Syntactical Causes of Case Reduction in Old French. G. G. Laubscher. (Elliott Monographs: Vol. 7). 1921. 15.00 (ISBN 0-527-02611-5). Kraus Repr.

Syntagma Musicum of Michael Praetorius, Vol. 2: De Organographica. Michael Praetorius. Tr. by Harold Blumenfeld. LC 79-20847. (Music Reprint Ser.). (Illus.). 1980. Repr. of 1962 ed. 29.50 (ISBN 0-306-70563-X). Da Capo.

Syntagma Musicum: Tomus Secundus se Organographie. Michael Praetorius. Ed. by Robert Eitner. (Publikation aelterer praktischer und theoretischer Musikwerke Ser.: Vol. XIII). (Illus., Ger.). 1967. Repr. of 1618 ed. 30.00x. Broude.

Syntagme Verbal en Envietnamien: Materiaux Pour l'Etude de l'Extreme-Orient Moderne et Contemporain. Phu P. Nguyen. (Etudes Linguistiques: No. 5). 1976. pap. 9.60x (ISBN 90-2797-553-1). Mouton.

Syntaktische Bedeutung des Mittelhochdeutschen Enjambements. Friedrich Wahnschaffe. 27.00 (ISBN 0-384-65491-6); pap. 22.00 (ISBN 0-384-65490-8). Johnson Repr.

Syntaktische Verandering in Kontrolezinnen: Een Sociolinguistische Studie van het Brugs van de 13 tot de 17 eeuw. M. Gerritsen. xv, 274p. 1987. pap. write for info. (ISBN 90-6765-367-5). Foris Pubns.

Syntax. 2nd ed. Peter W. Culicover. 356p. 1982. 29.50 (ISBN 0-12-199256-X). Acad Pr.

Syntax. Ralph Gibson. LC 82-83708. (Illus.). 80p. 1983. 24.95 (ISBN 0-912810-39-4). Lustrum Pr.

Syntax. P. H. Matthews. LC 80-41664. (Cambridge Textbooks in Linguistics Ser.). (Illus.). 325p. 1981. 49.50 (ISBN 0-521-22894-8); pap. 15.95 (ISBN 0-521-29709-5). Cambridge U Pr.

Syntax: A Functional-Typological Introduction, Vol. 1. T. Givon. LC 84-6195. xx, 440p. 1984. 42.00x (ISBN 0-915027-07-0); pap. text ed. 21.95 (ISBN 0-915027-08-9). Benjamins North Am.

Syntax Analysis & Software Tools. K. John Gough. (Illus.). 352p. 1988. pap. 32.25x (ISBN 0-201-18048-0). Addison-Wesley.

Syntax & Interpretation of the Relative Clause Constructure in Swahili. Ed. by Camillia N. Barrett-Keach. (Outstanding Dissertations in Linguistics Ser.). 255p. 1985. lib. bdg. 32.00 (ISBN 0-8240-5432-6). Garland Pub.

Syntax & Pragmatics in Functional Grammar. Ed. by M. Bolkestein et al. (Functional Grammar Ser.). xiv, 223p. 1985. pap. write for info. (ISBN 90-6765-097-8). Foris Pubns.

Syntax & Semantics, 13 vols. John P. Kimball et al. Incl. Vol. 1. Studies in Language. 260p. 1973. 71.50 (ISBN 0-12-785421-5); Vol. 2. 1973. 71.50 (ISBN 0-12-785422-3); Vol. 3. 1975. 39.50 (ISBN 0-12-785423-1); Vol. 4. 1975. 71.50 (ISBN 0-12-785424-X); Vol. 5. Japanese Generative Grammar. 1976. 71.50 (ISBN 0-12-785425-8); Vol. 6. 1976. 71.50 (ISBN 0-12-785426-6); Vol. 7. 1976. 39.50 (ISBN 0-12-613507-X); Vol. 8. 1977. 71.50 (ISBN 0-12-613508-8); Vol. 9. Pragmatics. 1978. 39.50 (ISBN 0-12-613509-6); Vol. 10. Selections from the Third Groningen Round Table. Ed. by Frank W. Heny & Helmut Schnelle. 1979. 71.50 (ISBN 0-12-613510-X); Vol. 11. Presupposition. 1979. 71.50 (ISBN 0-12-613511-8); Vol. 12. Discourse & Syntax. 1979. 39.50 (ISBN 0-12-613512-6); Vol. 13. Current Approaches to Syntax. 1980. 39.50 (ISBN 0-12-613513-4). Acad Pr.

Syntax & Semantics, Vol. 20. Ed. by Geoffrey J. Huck & Almerindo E. Ojeda. 306p. 1987. 72.00 (ISBN 0-12-613520-7); pap. 24.95 (ISBN 0-12-606101-7). Acad Pr.

Syntax & Semantics of Complex Nominals. Judith N. Levi. 1978. 29.50 (ISBN 0-12-445150-0). Acad Pr.

Syntax & Semantics of Infinitary Languages. Ed. by J. Barwise. LC 68-57175. (Lecture Notes in Mathematics: Vol. 72). 1968. pap. 14.70 (ISBN 0-387-04242-3). Springer-Verlag.

Syntax & Semantics of Questions in Navajo. Ellen Schauber. Ed. by Jorge Hankamer. LC 78-66568. (Outstanding Dissertations in Linguistics Ser.). 1979. lib. bdg. 43.00 (ISBN 0-8240-9676-2). Garland Pub.

Syntax & Semantics of the English Verb Phrase. Michael Grady. LC 75-118277. (Janua Linguarum, Ser. Practica: No. 112). (Illus., Orig.). 1970. pap. text ed. 9.60x (ISBN 90-2790-745-5). Mouton.

Syntax & Semantics of the Verb in Classical Greek: An Introduction. Albert Rijksbaron. xi, 176p. 1984. 24.00x (ISBN 90-70265-36-2, Pub. by Gieben Amsterdam). Benjamins North Am.

Syntax & Semantics of WH-Constructions. Paul Hirsschbuhler. (Outstanding Dissertations in Linguistics Ser.). 190p. 1986. 25.00 (ISBN 0-8240-5449-0). Garland Pub.

Syntax & Semantics, Vol. 14: Tense & Aspect. Ed. by John P. Kimball & Philip Tedesch. 1981. 65.00 (ISBN 0-12-613514-2). Acad Pr.

Syntax & Semantics: Vol. 15, Studies in Transivity. Ed. by Paul Hopper. Sandra Thompson. (Syntax & Semantics Ser.). 1982. 65.00 (ISBN 0-12-613515-0). Acad Pr.

Syntax & Semantics: Vol. 16: The Syntax of Native American Languages. Eung-Do Cook & Donna B. Gerdts. LC 83-17265. (Serial Publication). 1984. 65.00 (ISBN 0-12-613516-9). Acad Pr.

Syntax & Semantics: Vol. 17, Composite Predicates in English. Ed. by R. Cattell. 310p. 1984. 65.00 (ISBN 0-12-613517-7). Acad Pr.

Syntax & Semantics, Vol. 21. Ed. by Wendy Wolkins. (Thematic Relations). 308p. 1988. 65.00; pap. 24.95 (ISBN 0-12-606102-5). Acad Pr.

Syntax & Speech. William E. Cooper & Jeanne Paccia-Cooper. LC 80-16614. (Cognitive Science Ser.: No. 3). 284p. 1980. text ed. 25.00x (ISBN 0-674-86075-6). Harvard U Pr.

Syntax & Style. Clarence E. Schneider. LC 72-97330. 342p. 1974. pap. 9.95x (ISBN 0-88316-019-6). Chandler & Sharp.

Syntax & Style in Chaucer's Poetry. Gregory Roscow. (Chaucer Studies: VI). 158p. 1981. 42.50x (ISBN 0-8476-7053-8). Rowman.

Syntax & Style in Old English. Samuel O. Andrew. LC 66-13220. 1966. Repr. of 1940 ed. 14.00x (ISBN 0-8462-0762-1). Russell.

Syntax & Style in Old English: A Comparison of the Two Versions of Waerferth's Translation of Gregory's Dialogues. David Yerkes. LC 81-14200. (Medieval & Renaissance Texts & Studies: Vol. 5). 112p. 1982. 15.00 (ISBN 0-86698-011-3). Medieval & Renaissance NY.

Syntax Criticism of the Synoptic Gospels. Raymond A. Martin. LC 87-5646. (Studies in Bible & Early Christianity: Vol. 10). 220p. 1987. lib. bdg. 49.95 (ISBN 0-88946-610-6). E Mellen.

Syntax Des Superlativs Im Gotischen, Altniederdeutschen, Althochdeutschen, Fruemittelhochdeutsc Im Beowulf und in der Aelteren Edda. Reinhard Wagner. 18.00 (ISBN 0-384-65440-1); pap. 13.00 (ISBN 0-685-13614-0). Johnson Repr.

Syntax: Internatonal Edition. Peter W. Culicover. 1977. 13.50 (ISBN 0-12-199230-6). Acad Pr.

Syntax of Apollonius Dyscolus. Fred W. Householder. Tr. by Fred W. Householder from Lat. (Studies in the History of Linguistics Ser.: Vol. 23). vi, 281p. 1981. 40.00x (ISBN 90-272-4504-5). Benjamins North Am.

Syntax of Causative Constructions. Judith Aissen. Ed. by Jorge Hankamer. LC 78-66533. (Outstanding Dissertations in Linguistics Ser.). 1979. lib. bdg. 35.00 (ISBN 0-8240-9690-8). Garland Pub.

Syntax of Classical Greek from Homer to Demosthenes: First Part-The Syntax of the Simple Sentence Embracing the Doctrine of the Moods & TENSES, Second Part-The Syntax of Simple Sentence Continued Embracing the Doctrine of the Article. Basil L. Gildersleeve. 1980. Repr. 49.00x (ISBN 90-6088-071-4, Pub. by Boumas Boekhuis Netherlands). Benjamins North AM.

Syntax of Coordination. Robert R. Van Dirsouw. 250p. 1988. lib. bdg. 75.00x (ISBN 0-7099-2639-1, Pub. by Croom Helm UK). Routledge Chapman & Hall.

Syntax of Crossing Conference Sentences. Pauline I. Jacobson. LC 79-6625. (Outstanding Dissertations in Linguistics Ser.). 270p. 1980. 38.00 (ISBN 0-8240-4553-X). Garland Pub.

Syntax of Early Latin, 2 Vols. Charles E. Bennett. Repr. of 1910 ed. Set. cancelled (ISBN 3-487-01345-2). Adlers Foreign Bks.

Syntax of English Phrasal Verbs. Kazimierz A. Sroka. LC 74-151657. (Janua Linguarum, Ser. Practica: No. 129). 216p. (Orig.). 1972. pap. text ed. 26.00x (ISBN 90-2792-218-7). Mouton.

Syntax of Il Fiore & of Dante's Inferno As Evidence in the Question of the Authorship of Il Fiore. Sr. Mary D. Ramacciotti. LC 72-115356. (Catholic University of America. Studies in Romance Languages & Literatures: No. 12). Repr. of 1936 ed. 23.00 (ISBN 0-685-05985-5). AMS Pr.

Syntax of Japanese Honorifics. Gary D. Prideaux. (Janua Linguarum, Ser. Practica: No. 102). 1970. pap. text ed. 15.20x (ISBN 90-2790-741-2). Mouton.

Syntax of Mandarin Interrogatives. Earl Rand. LC 78-626766. (University of California Publications in Linguistics: Vol. 55). (Illus.). pap. 30.80 (ISBN 0-317-10083-1, 2011788). Bks Demand UMI.

Syntax of Modern Arabic Prose. Vicente Cantarino. Incl. Vol. I. The Simple Sentence. 184p. 1974; Vol. 2. The Expanded Sentence. 544p. 1976; Vol. III. The Compound Sentence. (Oriental Ser.). 424p. 1976. 22.50x (ISBN 0-253-39506-2). LC 69-16996. Ind U Pr.

Syntax of Modern Arabic Prose, Vol. 1: The Simple Sentence. Vicente Cantarino. LC 69-16996. 184p. pap. 47.90 (2056415). Bks Demand UMI.

Syntax of Modern Colloquial Japanese. E. H. Jorden. (LD). 1955. 16.00 (ISBN 0-527-00798-6). Kraus Repr.

Syntax of Modern Literary Ukranian. George Y. Shevelov. 1963. text ed. 35.20x (ISBN 90-2790-186-4). Mouton.

Syntax of Moods & Tenses of New Testament Greek. Ernest D. Burton. 240p. 1898. 16.95 (ISBN 0-567-01002-3, Pub. by T & T Clark Ltd UK). Fortress.

Syntax of New Testament Greek. James A. Brooks & Carlton L. Winbery. LC 78-51150. 1978. pap. text ed. 8.50 (ISBN 0-8191-0473-6). U Pr of Amer.

Syntax of Pronominal Cities, Vol 19. Hagit Borer. (Syntax & Semantics Ser.). 365p. 1986. 57.50 (ISBN 0-12-613519-3). Acad Pr.

Syntax of Serial Verbs: An Investigation into Serialization in Sranan & Other Languages. Mark Sebba. LC 86-31017. (Creole Language Library: Vol. 2). xv, 218p. 1987. 32.00x (ISBN 0-915027-95-X). Benjamins North Am.

Syntax of Social Life: The Theory & Method of Comparative Narratives. Peter Abell. 192p. 1987. 36.00 (ISBN 0-19-827271-5). Oxford U Pr.

Syntax of Spanish Reflexive Verbs: The Parameters of the Middle Verb. Sandra S. Babcock. LC 74-106468. (Janua Linguarum, Ser. Practica: No. 105). (Orig.). 1970. pap. text ed. 12.80 (ISBN 90-2790-742-0). Mouton.

Syntax of Spoken Brazilian Portuguese. Earl W. Thomas. LC 69-11280. (Eng. & Port.). 1969. 12.95x (ISBN 0-8265-1130-9). Vanderbilt U Pr.

Syntax of Spoken Brazilian Portuguese. Earl W. Thomas. (Vanderbilt University Press Bks.). 363p. 1969. 12.95. U of Ill Pr.

Syntax of Spoken Brazilian Portuguese. 2nd ed. Earl W. Thomas. LC 69-11280. 383p. pap. 14.95 (ISBN 0-8265-1221-6). Vanderbilt U Pr.

Syntax of the Albanian Verb Complex. Philip L. Hubbard. (Outstanding Dissertations in Linguistics Ser.). 200p. 1985. 25.00 (ISBN 0-8240-5431-8). Garland Pub.

Syntax of the Declinable Words in the Roman de la Rose. Sr. M. Calixta Garvey. LC 74-94208. (Catholic University in Romance Languages & Literatures Ser: No. 13). Repr. of 1936 ed. 26.00 (ISBN 0-404-50313-6). AMS Pr.

Syntax of the English Language of St. Thomas More: The Verb, Pt. 1. F. T. Visser. (Materials for the Study of the Old English Drama Series 2: Vol. 19). pap. 36.00 (ISBN 0-8115-0312-7). Kraus Repr.

Syntax of the English Language of St. Thomas More: The Verb, Pt. 2. F. T. Visser. (Materials for the Study of the Old English Drama Series 2: Vol. 24). pap. 30.00 (ISBN 0-8115-0317-8). Kraus Repr.

Syntax of the English Language of St. Thomas More: The Verb, Pt. 3. F. R. Visser. (Materials for the Study of the Old English Drama 2: Vol. 26). pap. 21.00 (ISBN 0-8115-0319-4). Kraus Repr.

Syntax of the Gesta Francorum. John J. Gavigan. (L. D. Mono. Ser.: No.37). 1943. pap. 16.00 (ISBN 0-527-00783-8). Kraus Repr.

Syntax of the Moods & Tenses of New Testament Greek. Ernest D. Burton. LC 76-25360. 238p. 1976. 12.95 (ISBN 0-8254-2256-6). Kregel.

Syntax of the Moods & Tenses of the Greek Verb. William W. Goodwin. (Illus.). 264p. 1981. Repr. of 1878 ed. lib. bdg. 49.50 (ISBN 0-8495-1972-1). Arden Lib.

Syntax of the Old French Subjunctive. Frede Jensen. LC 73-79890. (Janua Linguarum, Ser. Practica: No. 220). 134p. (Orig.). 1974. pap. text ed. 22.40x (ISBN 90-2792-691-3). Mouton.

Syntax of the Old Spanish Subjunctive. Frede Jensen & Thomas A. Lathrop. (Janua Linguarum Ser. Practica: No. 182). 1973. pap. text ed. 13.20x (ISBN 90-2792-450-3). Mouton.

Syntax of the Simple Sentence in Proto - Germanic. Paul J. Hopper. LC 72-94524. (Janua Linguarum, Series Practice, No. 143). 104p. (Orig.). 1975. pap. text ed. 17.60x (ISBN 90-2793-282-4). Mouton.

Syntax of Urban Hijazi Arabic. Mahmoud Sieny. (Arabic.). 12.00x (ISBN 0-86685-051-1). Intl Bk Ctr.

Syntax of Verbs: From Verb Movement Rules in the Kru Language to Univiersal Grammar. H. Koopman. Ed. by J. Kaster & H. Van Riemsdyk. (Studies in Generative Grammar: No. 15). viii, 242p. (Orig.). 1984. pap. write for info. (ISBN 90-6765-027-7). Foris Pubns.

Syntax of Welsh. Gwen Awbery. LC 76-11489. (Cambridge Studies in Linguistics: No. 18). 1977. 42.50 (ISBN 0-521-21341-X). Cambridge U Pr.

Syntax of Western Middle Iranian. Christopher J. Brunner. LC 75-17528. (Persian Studies Ser.). 311p. 1977. text ed. 35.00x (ISBN 0-88206-005-8). Caravan Bks.

Syntax of Words. Elisabeth O. Selkirk. (Linguistic Inquiry Monographs: No. 7). 160p. 1982. pap. 13.95x (ISBN 0-262-69079-9). MIT Pr.

Syntax Oriented Translator. Peter Z. Ingerman. 1966. 24.50 (ISBN 0-12-370850-8). Acad Pr.

Syntax, Speech & Hearing: Applied Linguistics for Teachers of Children with Language & Hearing Disabilities. Alice Streng. LC 72-1072. 288p. 1972. 47.50 (ISBN 0-8089-0756-5, 794414). Grune.

Syntaxe de l'Haitien. Claire Lefebvre. Ed. by Helene Magloire-Holly & Nanie Piou. xiv, 251p. (Fr.). 1982. pap. 15.00 (ISBN 0-89720-055-1). Karoma.

Syntaxe des Verbes de mouvement en Coreen Contemporain. Chai-Song Hong. (Lingvisticae Investigationes Supplementas: No. 12). xv, 309p. (Fr.). 1985. 40.00x (ISBN 90-272-3122-2). Benjamins North Am.

Syntaxe du Francais Moderne, 2 tomes. Le Bidois. Set. 35.90 (ISBN 0-685-36655-3). French & Eur.

Syntaxe du verbe Italien, Vol. 1: Les Constructions a Completives des Verbes a un Complement. Annibale Elia. (Lingvisticae Investigationes Supplementa Ser.: No. 7). 250p. (Fr.). 1988. Repr. of 1983 ed. 28.00. Benjamins North Am.

Syntaxis en Lexicon. Ed. by C. Hoppenbrouwers et al. viii, 192p. pap. write for info. (ISBN 90-6765-280-6). Foris Pubns.

Syntaxis van het Nederlands: Een Inleiding in de Regeer - en Bindtheorie. 4th ed. H. Bennis & T. Hoekstra. viii, 158p. 1987. pap. write for info. (ISBN 90-70176-64-5). Foris Pubns.

Synthese des ARN & son Role dans le Developpement Primitif & la Differenciation de l 'Embryon. Ed. by E. Wolff. (Cours et Documents De Biologie Ser.). 166p. (Fr.). 1971. 55.00 (ISBN 0-677-50260-5). Gordon & Breach.

Syntheses & Reactions in Organic Chemistry. William E. Parham. LC 74-1410. 558p. 1974. pap. text ed. 14.50 (ISBN 0-88275-171-9). Krieger.

Syntheses & Separations Using Functional Polymers. Sherrington. 400p. 1988. write for info. (ISBN 0-471-91848-2). Wiley.

Syntheses of Fluoroorganic Compounds. Ed. by I. L. Knunyants & G. G. Yakobson. 260p. 1985. 109.00 (ISBN 0-387-15077-3). Springer-Verlag.

Syntheses with Stable Isotopes of Carbon, Nitrogen, & Oxygen. Donald G. Ott. LC 80-19076. 224p. 1981. 39.50 (ISBN 0-471-04922-0, Pub. by Wiley-Interscience). Wiley.

Syntheses with Stable Isotopes of Carbon, Nitrogen & Oxygen. Donald G. Ott. LC 80-19076. pap. 57.80 (ISBN 0-317-55607-X, 2056348). Bks Demand UMI.

Synthesis. Theodore Enslin. 400p. 1975. pap. 6.00 (ISBN 0-913028-36-3). North Atlantic.

Synthesis. Torkom Saraydarian. 1983. pap. 2.50 (ISBN 0-911794-18-2). Aqua Educ.

Synthesis: An Introduction to the History, Theory & Practice of Electronic Music. rev. ed. Herbert A. Deutsch. LC 85-30824. (Illus.). 120p. (Orig.). 1985. pap. 14.95 (ISBN 0-88284-348-6, 1439). Alfred Pub.

Synthesis & Analysis Methods for Safety & Reliability Studies. Ed. by G. Apostolakis et al. LC 79-21315. 474p. 1980. 79.50x (ISBN 0-306-40316-1, Plenum Pr). Plenum Pub.

Synthesis & Applications of DNA & RNA. Ed. by Saran A. Narang. 1987. 45.00 (ISBN 0-12-514030-4). Acad Pr.

Synthesis & Applications of Isotopically Labelled Compounds. W. P. Duncan & A. B. Susan. 1983. 144.75 (ISBN 0-444-42152-1, I-472-82). Elsevier.

Synthesis & Applications of Isotopically Labeled Compounds, 1985. Ed. by R. R. Muccino. 558p. 1986. 184.25 (ISBN 0-444-42612-4). Elsevier.

Synthesis & Characterization of Inorganic Compounds. W. Jolly. 1970. 44.00 (ISBN 0-13-879932-6). P-H.

Synthesis & Chemistry of Agrochemicals. Ed. by Don R. Baker et al. LC 87-22304. (Symposium Ser.: No. 355). (Illus.). ix, 465p. 1987. 99.95 (ISBN 0-8412-1434-4). Am Chemical.

Synthesis & Decline see Vorticism & Abstract Art in the First Machine Age.

Synthesis & Degradation-Rheology & Extrusion. Ed. by H. J. Cantow et al. (Advances in Polymer Science: Vol. 47). (Illus.). 170p. 1982. 43.00 (ISBN 0-387-11774-1). Springer-Verlag.

Synthesis & Fertility of Brassicoraphanus & Ways of Transferring Raphanus Characters to Brassica. O. Dolstra. (Agricultural Research Reports: No. 917). 98p. 1982. pap. 14.50 (ISBN 90-220-0805-3, PDC256, PUDOC). UNIPUB.

Synthesis & Modeling of Inermittent Estuaries. Ed. by W. R. Cuff & M. Tomczak, Jr. (Lecture Notes on Coastal and Estuarine Studies Ser.: Vol. 3). 302p. 1983. pap. 29.00 (ISBN 0-387-12681-3). Springer Verlag.

Synthesis & Properties of Anticancer & Inerferon Inducing Agents (TBC) Ottenberite & Butler. 360p. 1984. 75.00 (ISBN 0-8247-7189-3). Dekker.

Synthesis & Properties of Low-Dimensional Materials, Vol. 313. Ed. by Joel S. Miller & Arthur J. Epstein. (Annals of the New York Academy of Sciences). 828p. 1978. pap. 82.00x (ISBN 0-89072-069-X). NY Acad Sci.

Synthesis & Release of Adenohypophyseal Hormones. Ed. by Marian Jutisz & Kenneth W. McKerns. LC 80-96. (Biochemical Endocrinology Ser.). (Illus.). 822p. 1980. 115.00 (ISBN 0-306-40247-5, Plenum Pr). Plenum Pub.

Synthesis & Technique in Inorganic Chemistry. 2nd ed. Robert J. Angelici. (Illus.). 235p. 1987. pap. text ed. 28.00x (ISBN 0-935702-53-9). Univ Sci Bks.

Synthesis, Assembly & Turnover of Cell Surface Components. Poste & Nicholson. (Cell Surface Reviews: Vol. 4). 884p. 1978. 84.75 (ISBN 0-444-00232-4, Biomedical Pr). Elsevier.

Synthesis bei Kant: Das Problem der Verbindung von Vorstellungen. Hansgeorg Hoppe. 252p. 1983. 41.60 (ISBN 3-11-008981-5). De Gruyter.

Synthesis, Crystal Growth & Characterization: Proceedings of the International School on Synthesis Crystal Growth, October, '81. Ed. by K. Lal. 400p. 1984. 100.00 (ISBN 0-444-86435-0, I-497-83, North Holland). Elsevier.

Synthesis for Economic Performance in Latin America During 1979. OAS General Secretariat Planning & Statistics. (Statistics Ser.). 40p. 1979. pap. 3.00 (ISBN 0-8270-1160-1). OAS.

Synthesis in Language Teaching: An Introduction to Languistics. Hector Hammerly. (Languistics ser.: Vol.1). (Illus.). 693p. 1986. pap. 22.95 (ISBN 0-919950-04-3). Second Lang.

Synthesis of Acetylenes, Allenes & Cumulenes: A Laboratory Manual. L. Bradsma & H. D. Verkruijsse. (Studies in Organic Chemistry: Vol. 8). 276p. 1981. 97.50 (ISBN 0-444-42009-6). Elsevier.

Synthesis of Carbon-Phosphorus Bonds. Ed. by Robert Engel. 160p. 1988. 95.50 (ISBN 0-8493-4930-3, 4930). CRC Pr.

Synthesis of Deep Sea Drilling Results in the Indian Ocean. Ed. by C. C. Von Der Borch. (Oceanography Ser.: Vol. 21). 176p. 1978. 89.50 (ISBN 0-444-41675-7). Elsevier.

Synthesis of Digital Design from Recursive Equations. Steven D. Johnson. (ACM Distinguished Dissertation Ser.). (Illus.). 200p. 1984. text ed. 32.50x (ISBN 0-262-10029-0). MIT Pr.

Synthesis of Electrical Networks. H. Baher. 285p. 1985. Repr. 61.95 (ISBN 0-471-90399-X, Pub. by Wiley-Interscience). Wiley.

Synthesis of Fused Heterocycles. Gwyn P. Ellis. LC 86-28944. (Chemistry of Heterocyclic Compounds Ser.). 800p. 1987. Repr. 288.00 (ISBN 0-471-91431-2, Wiley-Interscience). Wiley.

Synthesis of High-Silica Aluminosilicate Zeolites. P. A. Jacobs & J. A. Martens. 390p. 1987. 147.50 (ISBN 0-444-42814-3). Elsevier.

Synthesis of Macrocycles: The Design of Selective Complexing Agent. Reed M. Izatt & James J. Christensen. (Progress in Macrocyclic Chemistry Ser.). 480p. 1986. write for info. (ISBN 0-471-82589-1). Wiley.

Synthesis of Natural Products see Eleventh IUPAC International Symposium on Chemistry: Bulgarian Academy of Sciences.

Synthesis of Natural Products Problems of Stereoselectivity, Vols. I & II. Pavel Kocovsky et al. 1986. Vol. I, 248 pgs. 2 vol. set 198.00 (ISBN 0-8493-6418-3). Vol. II 304 pgs. CRC Pr.

Synthesis of Passive Networks: Theory & Methods Appropriate to the Realization & Approximation Problems. Ernest A. Guillemin. LC 76-50044. 760p. 1977. Repr. of 1957 ed. 46.00 (ISBN 0-88275-481-5). Krieger.

Synthesis of Penicillin, Cephaloaporin C, & Analogs. Maghar S. Manhas & Ajay K. Bose. LC 69-13151. (New Directions in Organic Chemistry Ser.). pap. 33.00 (2027101). Bks Demand UMI.

Synthesis of Planar Antenna Sources. Donald R. Rhodes. (Oxford Engineering Science Ser.). (Illus.). 1974. 65.00x (ISBN 0-19-856123-7). Oxford U Pr.

Synthesis of Polymers by Polycondensation. L. B. Sokolov. 272p. 1968. text ed. 54.00x (ISBN 0-7065-0603-0, Pub. by Keter Pub Jerusalem). Coronet Bks.

Synthesis of Prostaglandins. Szantay. 1978. cancelled 18.50 (ISBN 963-05-1303-X, Pub. by Akademiai Kaido Hungary). IPS.

Synthesis of Self, 4 vols. Roy M. Mendelsohn. LC 87-25798. (Illus.). 1987. Set. 115.00x (ISBN 0-317-66308-9, Plenum Med Bk); Vol. 1, 370p: The I of Consciousness: Development from Birth to Maturity. 37.50x (ISBN 0-306-42711-7); Vol. 2, 272p: It All Depends on How You Look at It: The Development of Pathology in the Cohesive Disorders. 29.50x (ISBN 0-306-42712-5); Vol. 3, 392p: Believing Is Seeing: The Pathology of Development in the Noncohesive Disorders. 29.50x (ISBN 0-306-42713-3); Vol. 4, 266p: The Principles that Guide the Ideal Therapist. 39.50x (ISBN 0-306-42714-1). Plenum Pub.

Synthesis of Subsonic Airplain Design. E. Torenbeek. 1986. Repr. of 1982 ed. lib. bdg. 34.50 (ISBN 90-247-2724-3, Pub. by Martinus Nijhoff Netherlands). Kluwer Academic.

Synthesis of Switching Circuits. J. Klir & L. Seidl. 326p. 1966. 107.00 (ISBN 0-677-61830-1). Gordon & Breach.

Synthesis of the Benzo(C) Phenanthridine Alkaloids. The Chemistry the Vancomycin Group of Antibiotics. I. Ninomiya. 210p. 1984. 96.00x (ISBN 0-569-08788-0, Pub. by Collets (UK)). State Mutual Bk.

Synthesis of the Caledonian Rocks of Britain. Ed. by D. J. Fettes & A. L. Harris. 1986. lib. bdg. 64.95 (ISBN 90-277-2235-8, Pub. by Reidel Holland). Kluwer Academic.

Synthesis of Yoga. 6th ed. Sri Aurobindo. 1979p. 36.00 (ISBN 0-89744-931-2). Auromere.

Synthesis of Yoga. Sri Aurobindo. 1979p. 30.00 (ISBN 0-89744-932-0). Auromere.

Synthesis of Yoga. Sri Aurobindo. (Life Companion Bible Bks.). 1984p. 24.95 (ISBN 0-89744-017-X). Auromere.

Synthesis of Yoga. Sri Aurobindo. 899p. 1984. 16.75 (ISBN 0-89071-313-8, Pub. by Sri Aurobindo Ashram India); pap. 12.50 (ISBN 0-89071-312-X, Pub. by Sri Aurobindo Ashram India). Aurobindo Assn.

Synthesis, Storage & Secretion of Adrenal Catecholamines: Proceedings of a Satellite Symposium to the 8th International Congress of Pharmacology, 19-24 July 1981, Tokyo, Japan. Ed. by F. Izumi & M. Oka. (Illus.). 302p. 1982. 79.00 (ISBN 0-08-028012-9). Pergamon.

Synthesizer & Electronic Keyboard Handbook. David Crombie. LC 84-47863. (Illus.). 1984. 24.50 (ISBN 0-394-54084-0); pap. 13.95 (ISBN 0-394-72711-8). Knopf.

Synthesizer Basics. Rev. ed. Ed. by Keyboard Magazine Editors. (Keyboard Synthesizer Library). (Illus.). 1987. pap. 12.95 (ISBN 0-88188-714-5, HL00183705). H Leonard Pub Corp.

Synthesizer Programming. Ed. by Dominic Milano. (Keyboard Magazine Synthesizer Library). (Illus.). 120p. (Orig.). 1987. pap. 14.95 (ISBN 0-88188-550-9, HL00183703). H Leonard Pub Corp.

Synthesizer Technique. Rev. ed. Ed. by Keyboard Magazine Editors. (Keyboard Synthesizer Library). 120p. 1987. pap. 12.95 (ISBN 0-88188-290-9, HL00183706). H Leonard Pub Corp.

Synthesizer Technique. Rev. ed. Ed. by Keyboard Magazine Staff. (Illus.). 136p. 1988. pap. 14.95 (ISBN 0-88188-715-3, Pub. by GPI Pubns). H Leonard Pub Corp.

Synthesizers & Computers. Rev. ed. Ed. by Keyboard Magazine Editors. 136p. 1987. pap. 12.95 (ISBN 0-88188-716-1). H Leonard Pub Corp.

Synthetic Adjuvants: Modern Concepts in Immunology Ser. Arlette Adam. LC 85-6331. 239p. 1985. 62.95 (ISBN 0-471-86450-1, Interscience). Wiley.

Synthetic & Structural Problems. Ed. by M. J. Dewar et al. (Topics in Current Chemistry Ser.: Vol. 106). (Illus.). 170p. 1982. 43.00 (ISBN 0-387-11766-0). Springer-Verlag.

Synthetic Antidiarrheal Drugs. William Van Bever & Harbans Lal. (Modern Pharmacology-Toxicology Ser.: Vol.7). 296p. 1976. 65.00 (ISBN 0-8247-6370-X). Dekker.

Synthetic Aperture Radar. J. P. Fitch. (Illus.). 170p. 36.00 (ISBN 0-387-96665-X). Springer-Verlag.

Synthetic Aperture Radar. John J. Kovaly. LC 76-42314. (Artech Radar Library). (Illus.). 357p. pap. 92.90 (2030128). Bks Demand UMI.

Synthetic Aperture Radar. Ed. by John J. Kovaly. LC 76-42314. (Artech Radar Library). 329p. 1976. 40.00 (ISBN 0-89006-056-8). Artech Hse.

Synthetic Aperture Radar: Systems & Signal Processing. Mcdonough. (Remote Sensing & Image Processing Ser.). 1988. price not set (ISBN 0-471-85770-X). Wiley.

Synthetic Aperture Radar with Remote Sensing Applications. Mccandless. 300p. 1987. write for info. (ISBN 0-471-89606-3). Wiley.

Synthetic Approach to Lip Reading. George S. Haspiel. 1973. text ed. 4.00 (ISBN 0-686-09401-8). Expression.

Synthetic Aspects of Aminodeoxy Sugars of Antibiotics. I. F. Pelyvas et al. (Illus.). 490p. 1988. 102.00 (ISBN 0-387-18877-0). Springer-Verlag.

Synthetic Automotive Engine Oils. 1981. 58.00 (ISBN 0-89883-110-5, PT22). Soc Auto Engineers.

Synthetic Binders in Paper Coatings: A Project of the Coating Binders Committee. Technical Association of the Pulp & Paper Industry. Ed. by Alvin R. Sinclair. LC 75-7557. (TAPPI Monograph Ser.: No. 37). pap. 37.80 (ISBN 0-317-28872-5, 2020305). Bks Demand UMI.

Synthetic Biomedical Polymers: Concepts & Applications. Ed. by Michael Szycher & William J. Robinson. LC 80-52137. (Illus.). 235p. 1980. 29.00 (ISBN 0-87762-290-6). Technomic.

Synthetic Crude from Oil Sands. VDI. (Progress Report of the VDI-Z, Series 3: No. 80). 108p. (Orig.). 1983. pap. 38.00 (ISBN 3-18-148003-7, Pub. by VDI W Germany). IPS.

Synthetic Detergents. 6th ed. A. Davidsohn & B. M. Milwidski. LC 77-13133. 265p. 1978. 41.95 (ISBN 0-470-99312-X). Halsted Pr.

Synthetic Detergents. 7th ed. Alfred S. Davidsohn. LC 86-20035. 288p. 1987. 59.95 (ISBN 0-470-20722-1, Co-Pub. with Longman). Wiley.

Synthetic Differential Geometry. Anders Kock. LC 81-6099. (London Mathematical Society Lecture Note Ser.: No. 51). 328p. 1981. pap. 37.50 (ISBN 0-521-24138-3). Cambridge U Pr.

Synthetic Dyeing: For Spinners, Weavers, Knitters & Embroiderers. Frances Tompson & Tony Tompson. (Illus.). 136p. 1988. 19.95 (ISBN 0-7153-8874-6, Pub. by David & Charles Pub England). Sterling.

Synthetic Dyes for Natural Fibers. rev. ed. Linda Knutson. LC 86-80912. (Illus.). 168p. 1986. pap. 12.00 (ISBN 0-934026-23-8). Interweave.

Synthetic Economics. Henry L. Moore. LC 67-18571. 1967. Repr. of 1929 ed. 25.00x (ISBN 0-678-00233-9). Kelley.

Synthetic Elements. 1983. 2.00 (ISBN 0-471-63857-9). Wiley.

Synthetic Estimation of State Health Characteristics Based on the Health Interview Survey. Ed. by Taloria Stevenson. (Ser. 2, No. 75). 1977. pap. text ed. 1.75 (ISBN 0-8406-0107-7). Natl Ctr Health Stats.

Synthetic Feelings & Popular Culture. Ala Glasser. LC 78-24017. 1979. 14.95 (ISBN 0-87949-132-9). Ashley Bks.

Synthetic Fibers for Papermaking. (Bibliographic Ser.: No. 223). 172p. 1965. 12.00 (ISBN 0-317-34456-0); Supplement 1, 1972. 8.00 (ISBN 0-317-34457-9). Inst Paper Chem.

Synthetic Fibers for the Wet System & Thermal Bonding Applications Seminar, 1986: Boston Park Plaza, Boston, MA, October 9-10. Technical Association of the Pulp & Paper Industry Staff. (TAPPI Notes Ser.). (Illus.). pap. 20.10 (ISBN 0-317-58155-4, 2029693). Bks Demand UMI.

Synthetic Fibers in Papermaking. Ed. by O. A. Battista. LC 64-13211. 340p. 1964. text ed. 23.50 (ISBN 0-470-05894-3, Pub. by Wiley). Krieger.

Synthetic Foam & Combined Agent Systems. (Ten Ser.). 1974. pap. 2.00 (ISBN 0-685-58132-2, 11B). Natl Fire Prot.

Synthetic Fuels. R. F. Probstein & R. E. Hicks. (Chemical Engineering Ser.). 576p. 1982. text ed. 43.50x (ISBN 0-07-050908-5). McGraw.

Synthetic Fuels from Coal. VDI. (Progress Report of the VDI-Z, Series 3: No. 79). 226p. (Orig.). 1983. pap. 68.00 (ISBN 3-18-147903-9, Pub. by VDI W Germany). IPS.

Synthetic Fuels from Coal: Overview & Assessment. Larry L. Anderson & David A. Tillman. LC 79-17786. 158p. 1979. 40.00 (ISBN 0-471-01784-1, Pub. by Wiley-Interscience). Wiley.

Synthetic Fuels from Coal: Overview & Assessment. Larry L. Anderson & David A. Tillman. LC 79-17786. (Wiley-Interscience Publication). pap. 43.00 (ISBN 0-317-26175-4, 2025184). Bks Demand UMI.

Synthetic Fuels from Coal: Status of the Technology. Ed. by P. F. Paul et al. 1988. lib. bdg. 112.00 (ISBN 1-85333-103-1, Pub. by Graham & Trotman UK). Kluwer Academic.

Synthetic Fuels from Oil Shale & Tar Sands (Symposium III) 707p. 1983. 75.00 (ISBN 0-910091-48-X). Inst Gas Tech.

Synthetic Fuels from Oil Shale Symposium I, December 1979. (Synthetic Fuels). 684p. 60.00 (ISBN 0-910091-44-7). Inst Gas Tech.

Synthetic Fuels from Oil Shale Symposium II. 624p. 1981. 60.00 (ISBN 0-910091-45-5). Inst Gas Tech.

Synthetic Fuels Processing. Arnold H. Pelofsky. (Energy Library Ser: Vol. 1). 1977. 95.00 (ISBN 0-8247-6544-3). Dekker.

Synthetic Fuels Research: A Bibliography. 4th ed. Ruby L. Mathison. 218p. 1980. softcover 15.00 (ISBN 0-318-12717-2, H01980). Am Gas Assn.

Synthetic Hetero-Chain Polyimides. V. V. Korshak & T. M. Frunze. 574p. text ed. 115.00x (ISBN 0-7065-0527-1, Pub. by Keter Pub Jerusalem). Coronet Bks.

Synthetic Latex Polymer Market. Frost & Sullivan, Inc. Staff. 288p. 1986. 1950.00 (ISBN 0-86621-790-8, A1610). Frost & Sullivan.

Synthetic Ligaments: Scaffolds, Stents & Prostheses. Frederick C. Balduini. LC 86-42514. 96p. 1986. pap. 29.95 (ISBN 0-943432-70-7). Slack Inc.

Synthetic Liquid Fuels: An IEA Seminar. OECD. 152p. (Orig.). 1985. pap. 22.00x (ISBN 0-318-18427-3). OECD.

Synthetic Lubricants Market. 259p. 1984. 1750.00 (ISBN 0-86621-298-1, A1375). Frost & Sullivan.

Synthetic Materials for Electronics: Proceedings of the 2nd International Summer School, Jachranka, October, '79. Ed. by B. Jakowlew et al. (Materials Science Monograph: Vol. 8). 350p. 1982. 97.50 (ISBN 0-444-99741-5). Elsevier.

Synthetic Membrane Process: Fundamentals & Water Applications. Georges Belfort. LC 83-2654. (Water Pollution Ser.). 1984. 60.00 (ISBN 0-12-085480-5). Acad Pr.

Synthetic Membranes, 2 vols. Ed. by Albin Turbak. Incl. Vol. I, Desalination. 49.95 (ISBN 0-8412-0622-8); Vol. II, Hyper & Ultrafiltration Uses. 49.95 (ISBN 0-8412-0623-6). LC 81-1259. (ACS Symposium Ser.: Nos. 153 & 154). 1981. Set. 94.95 (ISBN 0-8412-0625-2). Am Chemical.

Synthetic Membranes: MMI Press Symposium Ser. Ed. by Maynard B. Chenoweth. (Vol. 5). 298p. 1986. text ed. 80.00 (ISBN 3-7186-0327-6). Harwood Academic.

Synthetic Membranes: Science, Engineering & Applications. Ed. by P. M. Bungay & H. K. Lonsdale. 1986. lib. bdg. 124.00 (ISBN 90-277-2293-5, Pub. by Reidel Holland). Kluwer Academic.

Synthetic Methods for Carbohydrates. Ed. by Hassan S. El Khadem. LC 76-58888. (ACS Symposium Ser: No. 39). 1977. 29.95 (ISBN 0-8412-0365-2). Am Chemical.

TITLE INDEX

SYSTEM & PROCESS IN

Synthetic Methods of Organic Chemistry: Synthetische Methoden der Organischen Chemie, 32 vols. Ed. by W. Theilheimer. Incl. Vol. 1. A Thesaurus. 2nd ed. Tr. by H. Wynberg from Ger. 1975. 50.75 (ISBN 3-8055-2226-6); Vol. 2. A Thesaurus. 2nd ed. Tr. by A. Ingberman from Ger. 1975. 64.75 (ISBN 3-8055-2227-4); Repertorium. (With Eng. index key). Vol. 3. 1975. 94.75 (ISBN 3-8055-2228-2); Vol. 4. 1966. 84.00 (ISBN 3-8055-0640-6); Vol. 5. Annual Survey, 1951. 2nd ed. 1966. 139.50 (ISBN 3-8055-0641-4); Annual Survey, 1952. 2nd ed. 1975. Vol. 6 1952. 80.00 (ISBN 3-8055-2229-0); Vol. 7 1953. 90.00 (ISBN 3-8055-2230-4); Vol. 8. Annual Survey, 1954. 2nd ed. (With cumulative index to vols. 6-8). 1975. 101.50 (ISBN 3-8055-2231-2); Vol. 9. Annual Survey, 1955. 1955. 62.75 (ISBN 3-8055-0643-0); Vol. 10. Yearbook, 1956. 2nd ed. (With Reaction titles & cumulative index to vols. 6-10). 1975. 148.75 (ISBN 3-8055-2232-0); Yearbooks, 1957. 2nd ed. 1975. Vol. 11. 1957. 98.75 (ISBN 3-8055-2233-9); Vol. 12. 1958. 108.75 (ISBN 3-8055-2234-7); Vol. 13. 1959. 120.00 (ISBN 3-8055-2235-5); Vol. 14. 1960. 109.50 (ISBN 3-8055-2236-3); Vol. 15. Yearbook, 1961. (With Reaction titles & cumulative index to vols. 11-15; Ger. word key). 1961. 144.00 (ISBN 3-8055-0646-5); Yearbook, 1962. (With ger. word key). Vol. 16. 1962. 120.00 (ISBN 3-8055-0647-3); Vol. 17. 1963. 120.00 (ISBN 3-8055-0648-1); Vol. 18. 1964. 136.00 (ISBN 3-8055-0650-3); Vol. 19. 1965. 136.00 (ISBN 3-8055-0651-1); Vol. 20. Yearbook, 1966. (With Reaction titles & cumulative index to vols. 16-20; Ger. word key). 1966. 196.75 (ISBN 3-8055-0653-8); Yearbooks, 1967. (With Ger. word key). Vol. 21. 1967. 156.00 (ISBN 3-8055-0654-6); Vol. 22. 1968. 181.50 (ISBN 3-8055-0655-4); Vol. 23. 1969. 211.50 (ISBN 3-8055-0656-2); Vol. 24. 1970. 200.00 (ISBN 3-8055-0657-0); Vol. 25. Yearbook, 1971. (With Reaction titles & cumulative index to vols. 21-25; Ger. word key). 1971. 197.50 (ISBN 3-8055-1198-1); Yearbooks, 1972. (With Ger. word key). Vol. 26. 1972. 190.00 (ISBN 3-8055-1390-9); Vol. 27. 1973. 212.75 (ISBN 3-8055-1565-0); Vol. 28. 1974. 326.75 (ISBN 3-8055-1680-0); Vol. 29. 1975. 306.75 (ISBN 3-8055-2095-6); Vol. 30. Yearbook, 1976. (With Reaction titles & cumulative index to vols. 26-30; Ger. word key). 350.00 (ISBN 3-8055-2256-8); Yearbooks, 1977. (With Ger. word key). Vol. 31, 1977. 332.00 (ISBN 3-8055-2432-3); Vol. 32. 1978. 326.75 (ISBN 3-8055-2818-3). S Karger.

Synthetic Modulated Structures. Ed. by Leroy L. Chang & B. C. Giessen. (Materials Science & Technology Ser.). 1985. 98.00 (ISBN 0-12-170470-X). Acad Pr.

Synthetic Multidentate Macrocyclic Compounds. Ed. by Reed M. Izatt & James J. Christensen. 1978. 65.50 (ISBN 0-12-377650-3). Acad Pr.

Synthetic Organic Chemistry. (Topics in Current Chemistry Ser.: Vol. 130). (Illus.). 250p. 1985. 53.00 (ISBN 0-387-15810-3). Springer-Verlag.

Synthetic Organic Photochemistry. Ed. by William M. Horspool. LC 84-10480. 552p. 1984. 79.50x (ISBN 0-306-41449-X, Plenum Pr). Plenum Pub.

Synthetic Peptides, Vol. 3. George R. Pettit. 1975. 96.50 (ISBN 0-12-552403-X). Acad Pr.

Synthetic Peptides, Vol. 4. G. R. Pettit. 478p. 1977. 152.75 (ISBN 0-444-41521-1). Elsevier.

Synthetic Peptides, Vol. 5. G. R. Pettit. 404p. 1980. 152.75 (ISBN 0-444-41895-4). Elsevier.

Synthetic Peptides, Vol. 6. G. R. Pettit. 512p. 1982. 200.00 (ISBN 0-444-42080-0). Elsevier.

Synthetic Peptides As Antigens: Symposium, No. 119. CIBA Foundation Symposium Ser. 1986. 47.50 (ISBN 0-471-99838-9). Wiley.

Synthetic Peptides in Biology & Medicine. Ed. by K. Alitalo et al. 256p. 1986. 92.00 (ISBN 0-444-80753-5). Elsevier.

Synthetic Polymeric Membranes: A Structural Perspective. 2nd ed. Robert E. Kesting. LC 85-6162. 348p. 1985. 57.50 (ISBN 0-471-80717-6). Wiley.

Synthetic Polymeric Membranes: Proceedings of the 29th Microsymposium on Macromolecules, Prague, Czechoslovakia, July 7-10, 1986. Ed. by J. Kahovec & B. Sedlacek. xiv, 717p. (Orig.). 1987. lib. bdg. 212.00 (ISBN 0-89925-151-X). De Gruyter.

Synthetic Polymers-Building the Giant Molecule, 1st ed. Fred W. Billmeyer. LC 77-171279. (Science Study Ser.). pap. 51.00 (2026508). Bks Demand UMI.

Synthetic Procedures in Nucleic Acid Chemistry: Vol. 2. Ed. by W. Werner Zorbach & R. Stuart Tipson. 686p. (Orig.). 1973. 54.25 (ISBN 0-471-98418-3, JW). Krieger.

Synthetic Pyrethroids. Ed. by Michael Elliott. LC 77-1810. (ACS Symposium Ser.: No. 42). 1977. 27.95 (ISBN 0-8412-0368-7). Am Chemical.

Synthetic Reagents: Chloramine-T; Hydrogen Peroxide; Polyphosphoric Acid, Vol. 6. J. S. Pizey. (Synthetic Reagents Ser.). 160p. 1985. 89.95 (ISBN 0-470-20152-5). Halsted Pr.

Synthetic Reagents: Dimethylformamide: Lithium Aluminum Hybride: Mercuric Oxide: Thionyl Chloride, Vols. 1-2. J. S. Pizey. LC 73-14417. (Ellis Horwood Synthetic Reagents Ser.). 353p. 1974. Repr. Vol. 1, 411p. 111.00 (ISBN 0-470-69104-2); Vol. 2, 353p. 111.00 (ISBN 0-470-69107-7). Halsted Pr.

Synthetic Reagents: Synthetic Reagents. Diborane; 2, 3-Dichloro-5, 6-Dicyanobenzoquinone (DDQ): Iodine: Lead Tetra-Acetate. Vol. 3, Vol. 3. Ed. by J. S. Pizey. LC 73-14417. (Synthetic Reagents Ser.). 447p. 1977. Repr. 94.95 (ISBN 0-470-99118-6). Halsted Pr.

Synthetic Reagents: Thallium (III) Acetate & Trifluoroacetate; Ammonia; Iodine Monochloride, Vol. 5. Ed. by J. S. Pizey. LC 73-14417. (Ellis Horwood Synthetic Reagents Ser.). 261p. 1983. Repr. 94.95 (ISBN 0-470-27455-7). Halsted Pr.

Synthetic Reagents Vol. 4: Mercuric Acetate Periodic Acid & Periodates Sulfuryl Chloride. Ed. by J. S. Pizey. LC 80-41742. 426p. 1981. Repr. 146.00 (ISBN 0-470-27133-7). Halsted Pr.

Synthetic Repertory, 3 vols. 3rd ed. Incl. Vol. 1. Mental Symptoms. H. Barthel. 734p. 125.00 (ISBN 3-7760-0559-9); Vol. 2. General Symptoms. H. Barthel. 491p. 110.00 (ISBN 3-7760-0560-2); Vol. 3. Sleeping & Sexual Symptoms. W. Klunker. 434p. 105.00 (ISBN 3-7760-0561-0). (Eng., Fr. & Ger.). 1987. Set. 300.00 (Pub. by K F Haug Pubs). Medicina Bio.

Synthetic Rubber: A Project That Had to Succeed. Vernon Herbert & Attilio Bisio. LC 85-948. (Contributions in Economics & Economic History Ser.: No. 63). (Illus.). xi, 243p. 1985. lib. bdg. 46.95 (ISBN 0-313-24634-3, BSR/). Greenwood.

Synthetic Rubbers: Their Chemistry & Technology. D. C. Blackley. (Illus.). 372p. 1983. 88.25 (ISBN 0-85334-152-4, I-462-82, Pub. by Elsevier Applied Sci England). Elsevier.

Synthetic Streamflows. Ed. by Myron B. Fiering & Barbara B. Jackson. LC 77-172418. (Water Resources Monograph: Vol. 1). (Illus.). 1971. pap. 10.00 (ISBN 0-87590-300-2). Am Geophysical.

Synthetic Substrates & Synthetic Inhibitors: The Use of Chromogenic Substrates in Studies of the Haemostatic Mechanism. Ed. by M. Blomback & P. Brakman. (Haemostasis: Vol. 7, Nos. 2-3). (Illus.). 1978. pap. 25.50 (ISBN 3-8055-2907-4). S Karger.

Synthetic Substrates in Clinical Blood Coagulation Assays. Ed. by H. R. Lijnen et al. (Developments in Hematology Ser.: No. 1). 142p. 1981. PLB 23.50 (ISBN 90-247-2409-0, Pub. Bymartinus Nijhoff). Kluwer Academic.

Synthetic Zeolites: Crystallization, Structural-Chemical Modification & Absorption Properties. S. P. Zhdanov et al. 600p. 1988. write for info. (ISBN 2-88124-675-3). Gordon & Breach.

Syntony & Spark: The Origins of Radio. Hugh G. Aitken. LC 84-26408. (Illus.). 368p. 1985. 43.00x (ISBN 0-691-08377-0); pap. 13.95x (ISBN 0-691-02392-1). Princeton U Pr.

Syphilis & Other Venereal Diseases. William J. Brown et al. LC 77-88803. pap. 65.80 (ISBN 0-317-55361-5, 2029170). Bks Demand UMI.

Syphilis; Or a Poetical History of the French Disease. Fracastorius. 69.95 (ISBN 0-8490-1170-1). Gordon Pr.

Syphilis Serology: Principles & Practice. G. D. Wasley & Helen H. Wong. (Illus.). 130p. 1989. 35.00 (ISBN 0-19-261530-0). Oxford U Pr.

Syphilis Today & among the Ancients, 3 vols. in 2. Frederic Buret. LC 72-9627. Repr. of 1895 ed. Set. 81.50 (ISBN 0-404-57422-X). AMS Pr.

Syr Gawayne. Frederic Madden. 59.95 (ISBN 0-8490-1171-X). Gordon Pr.

Syr Gawayne: A Collection of Ancient Romance Poems. Ed. by Frederick Madden. Repr. of 1839 ed. 45.00 (ISBN 0-384-17820-0). Johnson Repr.

Syr Gawayne: A Collection of Ancient Romance Poems by Scottish & English Authors. Ed. by Frederic Madden. LC 71-144420. (Bannatyne Club. Edinburgh. Publications: No. 61). Repr. of 1839 ed. 35.00 (ISBN 0-404-52772-8). AMS Pr.

Syracuse & South Bay Railway to Oneida Lake. William R. Gordon & Joseph G. Platukis. Ed. by Harold E. Cox. (Illus.). 48p. (Orig.). 1985. pap. 7.00 (ISBN 0-911940-40-5, Dist. by Rochester Chapter, N. R. H. S.). W R Gordon.

Syracuse Black Community, 1970: A Comparative Study. new ed. Seymour Sacks & Ralph Andrew. LC 73-21186. (Occasional Papers Ser.: No. 41). 77p. 1974. pap. 3.00 (ISBN 0-87060-065-6, OCP 41). Syracuse U Cont Ed.

Syracuse Football Story. Ken Rappoport. LC 75-6096. (College Sports Ser.). 1975. 10.95 (ISBN 0-87397-061-6). Strode.

Syracuse Journal of International Law & Commerce: 1972-1985, 12 vols. Bound set. 360.00x (ISBN 0-686-90050-2). Rothman.

Syracuse University History. William F. Galpin. Incl. Vol. 1. Pioneer Days. (Illus.). 270p. 1952 (ISBN 0-8156-2010-1). LC 52-2118. 20.00x. Syracuse U Pr.

Syracuse University History: The Critical Years, Vol.3. Richard Wilson et al. LC 52-2118. (Illus.). 464p. 1984. text ed. 20.00x (ISBN 0-8156-8108-9). Syracuse U Pr.

Syria. (Let's Visit Places & Peoples - - Nations, Dependencies, & Sovereignties of the World Ser.). (Illus.). (gr. 5 up). 1988. 12.95 (ISBN 0-7910-0095-8). Chelsea Hse.

Syria & Egypt: From the Tell El Amarna Letters. Flinders Petrie. 196p. 1978. 12.50 (ISBN 0-89005-234-4). Ares.

Syria & Egypt, from the Tell El Amarna Letters. W. M. Flinders Petrie. 187p. 1983. Repr. of 1898 ed. lib. bdg. 65.00 (ISBN 0-89984-831-1). Century Bookbindery.

Syria & Egypt under the Last Five Sultans of Turkey, 2 vols. in 1. Ed. by Edward B. Barker. LC 73-6269. (Middle East Ser.). Repr. of 1876 ed. 51.00 (ISBN 0-405-05324-X). Ayer Co Pubs.

Syria & Iran: Three Studies in Medieval Ceramics. Ed. by J. W. Allan & Caroline Roberts. (Studies in Islamic Art: No. IV). (Illus.). 248p. 1988. 69.00 (ISBN 0-19-728007-2); pap. 48.00 (ISBN 0-19-728008-0). Oxford U Pr.

Syria & Lebanon. A. H. Hourani. 20.00x (ISBN 0-86685-015-5). Intl Bk Ctr.

Syria & Lebanon. Nicola Ziadeh. (Arab Background Ser.). 1968. 18.00x (ISBN 0-86685-034-1). Intl Bk Ctr.

Syria & Lebanon: A Political Essay. A. H. Hourani. 1977. lib. bdg. 59.95 (ISBN 0-8490-2714-4). Gordon Pr.

Syria & Lebanon under French Mandate. Stephen H. Longrigg. 1972. lib. bdg. 29.00x (ISBN 0-374-95088-1, Octagon). Hippocrene Bks.

Syria & Lebanon under French Mandate, 1968. Stephen Longrigg. (Arab Background Ser.). 16.00x (ISBN 0-86685-021-X). Intl Bk Ctr.

Syria & the CGIAR Centers: A Study of Their Collaboration in Agricultural Research. Hisham El-Akhrass. (CGIAR Study Paper: No. 13). 61p. 1986. 5.00 (ISBN 0-317-59165-7, BK 0822). World Bank.

Syria & the French Mandate: The Politics of Arab Nationalism, 1920-1945. Philip S. Khoury. (Studies in the Near East). 650p. 1986. text ed. 55.00 (ISBN 0-691-05486-X). Princeton U Pr.

Syria & the Lebanese Crisis. Adeed I. Dawisha. LC 80-85. 200p. 1980. 27.50 (ISBN 0-312-78203-9). St Martin.

Syria: Development & Monetary Policy. Edmund Y. Asfour. LC 59-13357. (Middle Eastern Monographs Ser: No. 1). (Illus.). 1959. pap. 5.95x (ISBN 0-674-86190-6). Harvard U Pr.

Syria: Fragile Mosaic of Power. Martha N. Kessler. (Illus.). 159p. (Orig.). 1987. pap. 3.75 (S/N 008-020-0117-7). USGPO.

Syria: Land of Contrast. Peter Lewis. (Illus.). 160p. (Orig.). 1984. pap. 14.95 (ISBN 0-7043-3442-9, Pub. by Quartet Bks). Salem Hse Pubs.

Syria: Modern State in an Ancient Land. John F. Devlin. LC 82-15909. 135p. 1982. lib. bdg. 29.50x (ISBN 0-86531-185-4); pap. text ed. 14.95x (ISBN 0-8133-0021-5). Westview.

Syria the Desert & the Sown. G. L. Bell. 352p. 1984. 250.00x (ISBN 1-85077-062-X, Pub. by Darf Pubs Ltd). State Mutual Bk.

Syria: The Desert & the Sown. Gertrude L. Bell. LC 73-6270. (Middle East Ser.). Repr. of 1908 ed. 32.00 (ISBN 0-405-05325-8). Ayer Co Pubs.

Syria: Torture by the Security Forces. Amnesty International Staff. 44p. (Orig.). 1987. pap. 5.00 (ISBN 0-939994-33-X, Pub by Amnesty Intl Pubns UK). Amnesty Intl USA.

Syria under Assad: Domestic Constraints & Regional Risks. Ed. by Moshe Maoz & Avner Yaniv. LC 85-18274. 320p. 1986. 35.00 (ISBN 0-312-78206-3). St Martin.

Syria under Islam: Empire on Trial, 634-1097. Kamal S. Salibi. LC 77-24197. 1977. 30.00x (ISBN 0-88206-013-9). Caravan Bks.

Syria under the Ba'th, 1963-1966: Army-Party Symbiosis. Itamar Rabinovitch. 276p. 1972. casebound 15.95x (ISBN 0-87855-163-8). Transaction Bks.

Syria, 1945-1986: Politics & Society. Derek Hopwood. 176p. 1988. 45.00 (ISBN 0-04-445039-7); pap. 14.95 (ISBN 0-04-445046-X). Unwin Hyman.

Syriac Chronicle Known As That of Zachariah of Mitylene. Zacharias. LC 76-24991. (Byzantine Texts: No. 5). Repr. of 1899 ed. 37.00 (ISBN 0-404-60005-0). AMS Pr.

Syriac Chronicle of Pseudo-Dionysius of Tel-Mahre: A Study in the History of Historiography. Witold Witakowski. (Studia Semitica Upsaliensia: Vol. 9). 182p. (Orig.). 1987. pap. text ed. 27.50x (ISBN 91-554-1967-4, Pub. by Uppsala Univ Acta Univ Uppsaliensis (Uppsala Sweden)). Coronet Bks.

Syriac Manuscripts in the Harvard College Library: A Catalogue. Moshe H. Goshen-Gottstein. LC 77-13132. (Harvard Semitic Studies: No. 23). 1979. 15.00 (ISBN 0-89130-189-5, 040423). Scholars Pr GA.

Syriac Version of the Ps. Nonnos Mythological Scholia. Sebastian Brock. LC 79-139712. (Oriental Publications: No. 20). 1971. 62.50 (ISBN 0-521-07990-X). Cambridge U Pr.

Syriac Version of the Psalms of Solomon. Joseph L. Trafton. (SBL Septuagint & Cognate Studies). 1985. 22.95 (ISBN 0-89130-910-1, 06-04-11); pap. 15.95 (ISBN 0-89130-911-X). Scholars Pr GA.

Syrian-African Rift & Other Poems. Avoth Yeshurun. Ed. by Yehuda Amichai & Allen Mandelbaum. Tr. by Harold Schimmel. LC 80-13630. (Jewish Poetry Ser.). 160p. 1980. 11.95 (ISBN 0-8276-0181-6, 464); pap. 7.95 (ISBN 0-8276-0182-4, 463). JPS Phila.

Syrian Arab Republic. Ed. by Anne Sinai & Allen Pollack. 1976. pap. text ed. 2.95 (ISBN 0-917158-00-8). AAAPME.

Syrian Christians in Muslim Society: An Interpretation. Robert M Haddad. LC 81-6202. (Princeton Studies on the Near East). viii, 118p. 1981. Repr. of 1970 ed. lib. bdg. 35.00x (ISBN 0-313-23054-4, HASYC). Greenwood.

Syrian Desert. Christian P. Grant. LC 78-63341. (Crusades & Military Orders: Second Ser.). (Illus.). Repr. of 1937 ed. 41.00 (ISBN 0-404-17017-X). AMS Pr.

Syrian Hamster in Toxicology & Carcinogenesis: Proceedings. Symposium on the Syrian Hamster in Toxicology & Carcinogenesis Research, Boston, November 30-December 2, 1977. Ed. by F. Homburger. (Progress in Experimental Tumor Research Ser.: Vol. 24). (Illus.). 1979. 108.75 (ISBN 3-8055-2890-6). S Karger.

Syrian Intervention in Lebanon. Naomi Weinberger. (Illus.). 352p. 1986. text ed. 32.00x (ISBN 0-19-504010-4). Oxford U Pr.

Syrian Pageant: The History of Syria & Palestine, 1000 B.C. to A.D. 1945. Wilfrid T. Castle. 1977. lib. bdg. 59.95 (ISBN 0-8490-2716-0). Gordon Pr.

Syrian Social Nationalist Party: An Ideological Analysis. Labib Zuwiyya-Yamak. LC 66-24812. (Middle Eastern Monographs Ser: No. 14). (Illus.). 1966. pap. 4.50x (ISBN 0-674-86236-8). Harvard U Pr.

Syrian Tetradrachmas of Caracalla & Macrinus. 1980. Repr. of 1940 ed. lib. bdg. 30.00 (ISBN 0-915262-57-6). S J Durst.

Syrians in Egypt 1725-1975. Thomas Philipp. (Illus.). 203p. (Orig.). 1985. pap. 48.50x (ISBN 3-515-04031-5, Pub. by Franz Steiner). Coronet Bks.

Syringobulbia: A Contribution to the Pathophysiology of the Brainstem. N. Jonesco-Sisesti. Ed. & tr. by R. T. Ross. LC 86-9489. 328p. 1986. lib. bdg. 50.95 (ISBN 0-275-92123-9, C2123). Praeger.

Syrinx Or a Sevenfold History. W. Warner. Ed. by Wallace A. Bacon. LC 72-128939. (Northwestern University. Humanities Series: No. 26). Repr. of 1950 ed. 25.00 (ISBN 0-404-50726-3). AMS Pr.

Syrische Kirchenbau. Hermann W. Beyer. (Studien Zur Spaetantiken Kunstgeschichte Ser.: Vol. 1). (Illus.). viii, 183p. 1978. Repr. of 1925 ed. 60.00x (ISBN 3-11-005705-0). De Gruyter.

Syrische Verskunst. Gustav Hoelscher. (Ger). 1932. 19.00 (ISBN 0-384-23860-2). Johnson Repr.

Syrphidae of the Ethiopian Region. Mario Bezzi. Repr. of 1915 ed. 16.00 (ISBN 0-384-04095-0). Johnson Repr.

Syst-O-Color, Vier-Kleurensysteem, 2 vols. Paul Schuitema. (Illus.). 1966. loose-leaf bdg. 106.00x (ISBN 0-686-21790-X). Mouton.

System Analysis & Design Projects. Harpool et al. 1986. pap. 24.95 (ISBN 0-8016-2068-6). Mosby.

System Analysis & Design: Traditional, Structured & Advanced Concepts & Techniques (International Ed) 2nd ed. James C. Wetherbe. LC 80-27802. (Illus.). 401p. 1984. 22.50 (ISBN 0-314-77859-4). West Pub.

System Analysis & Mathematical Modeling in the U. S. S. R. Avgustin Tuzhilin. Ed. by Cynthia Corell. (Illus., Orig.). Date not set. pap. text ed. 35.00 (ISBN 1-55831-054-1). Delphic Associates.

System Analysis & Simulation in Ecology, Vol. 4. Ed. by Bernard C. Patten. 1976. 92.50 (ISBN 0-12-547204-8). Acad Pr.

System Analysis & Simulation 1985. Ed. by Collet's Staff. 1986. 160.00x (ISBN 0-317-52964-1, Pub. by Collets (UK)). State Mutual Bk.

System Analysis of Ambulatory Care in Selected Countries. Ed. by P. L. Reichertz et al. (Lecture Notes in Medical Informatics Ser.: Vol. 29). vi, 197p. 1987. pap. 23.90 (ISBN 0-387-17159-2). Springer-Verlag.

System Analysis of Biological Processes. Ed. by D. Moeller. (Advances in Systems Analysis Ser.: Vol. 2). 224p. 1987. pap. 42.50 (ISBN 3-528-08983-0, Pub. by Vieweg & Sohn). IPS.

System Analyzer. George F. Forbes. 1961. pap. text ed. 2.25 (ISBN 0-685-10948-8). G F Forbes.

System & Function: Toward a Theory of Society. Piotr Sztompka. 1974. 19.95 (ISBN 0-12-681850-9). Acad Pr.

System & History in Philosophy: On the Unity of Thought & Time, Text & Explanation, Solitude & Dialogue, Rhetoric & Truth in the Practice of Philosophy & Its History. Adriaan T. Peperzak. LC 85-27679. (Contemporary Continental Philosophy Ser.). 172p. (Orig.). 1986. 52.50 (ISBN 0-88706-273-3); pap. 17.95 (ISBN 0-88706-275-X). State U NY Pr.

System & Process in Southeast Asia: The Evolution of a Region. Donald G. McCloud. 300p. 1985. 36.00x (ISBN 0-86531-587-6); pap. text ed. 16.95x (ISBN 0-86531-588-4). Westview.

System & Profits: Early Management Accounting at Dupont & General Motors. original anthology ed. Thomas H. Johnson. Ed. by Richard P. Brief. LC 80-1458. (Dimensions of Accounting Theory & Practice Ser.). 1981. lib. bdg. 28.50x (ISBN 0-405-13481-9). Ayer Co Pubs.
System & Structure: Essays in Communication & Exchange. 2nd ed. Anthony Wilden. (Illus.). 1980. 42.00x (ISBN 0-422-76700-X, 2585, Pub. by Tavistock England); pap. 21.00x (ISBN 0-422-76710-7, 2879). Routledge Chapman & Hall.
System & Succession: The Social Bases of Political Elite Recruitment. John D. Nagle. LC 77-3936. 284p. 1977. text ed. 19.50x (ISBN 0-292-77537-7). U of Tex Pr.
System Approach for Development: Proceedings of the IFAC-IFIP-IFORS Conference, 3rd, Rabat, Morocco, Nov., 1980. IFAC-IFIP-IFORS Conference Staff. Ed. by M. Najim & Y. M. Abdel-Fettah. LC 80-41530. 592p. 1981. 170.00 (ISBN 0-08-025670-8). Pergamon.
System Architecture. John Zarrella. LC 80-82932. (Microprocessor Software Engineering Concepts Ser.). (Illus.). 240p. (Orig.). 1980. pap. 18.95 (ISBN 0-935230-02-5). Microcomputer Appns.
System Architecture: Software & Hardware Concepts. William E. Leigh & Dia L. Ali. 1988. pap. text ed. write for info. (ISBN 0-538-10880-0, J88). SW Pub.
System: As Uncovered by the San Francisco Graft Prosecution. Franklin Hichborn. LC 69-14933. (Criminology, Law Enforcement, & Social Problems Ser.: No. 38). 1969. Repr. of 1915 ed. 15.00x (ISBN 0-87585-038-3). Patterson Smith.
System Builders: The Story of SDC. Claude Baum. (Illus.). ix, 302p. 1981. 20.00x (ISBN 0-916368-02-5). System Dev CA.
System der Wissenschaften nach Gegenstanden und Methoden see System of the Sciences According to Objects & Methods.
System Derparadigmatischen Suffixmorpheme Des Wogulischen Dialektes an der Tawda.Aus Dem Ungarischen Ubersetzt Von Regina Hessky. Laszlo Honti. (Janua Linguarum Ser.: No. 246). pap. 24.25x (ISBN 90-2793-406-1). Mouton.
System Description Methodologies: Proceedings of the IFIP TC2 Conference, Kecskemet, Hungary, 23-27 May, 1984. Ed. by D. Teichroew & G. David. 616p. 1985. 65.00 (ISBN 0-444-87731-2, North-Holland). Elsevier.
System Design. Henderson. (Infotech Computer State of the Art Reports). 1981. 61.00x (ISBN 0-08-028559-7). Pergamon.
System Design Approaches to Public Services. John H. Burgess. LC 76-737. (Illus.). 300p. 1978. 25.00 (ISBN 0-8386-1892-8). Fairleigh Dickinson.
System Design: Behavioral Perspectives on Designers, Tools, & Organization. (Norht Holland Series Systems Science & Engineering: Vol. 13). 1987. 47.25 (ISBN 0-444-01230-3). Elsevier.
System Design for Computer Applications. Hyman N. Laden & T. R. Gildersleeve. LC 63-17363. pap. 84.00 (ISBN 0-317-09782-2, 2007075). Bks Demand UMI.
System Design for Human Development & Productivity: Participation & Beyond. Ed. by P. Docherty et al. 462p. 1987. 100.00 (ISBN 0-444-70251-2, North Holland). Elsevier.
System Design for Human Interaction. Andrew P. Sage. LC 87-4225. 496p. 1987. 69.95 (ISBN 0-87942-218-1, PCO2113). Inst Electrical.
System Design with Microprocessors. 2nd ed. Zissos. 1984. pap. 21.50 (ISBN 0-12-781740-9). Acad Pr.
System Development & Ada. Ed. by A. N. Habermann & U. Montanari. (Lecture Notes in Computer Science: Vol. 275). v, 305p. 1987. pap. 25.70 (ISBN 0-387-18341-8). Springer-Verlag.
System Development Audit Review Guide. Coopers & Lybrand. 76p. 1986. pap. text ed. 15.00 (ISBN 0-89413-161-3). Inst Inter Aud.
System Development Methodology. 2nd, rev. ed. G. F. Hice et al. 450p. 1978. 73.75 (ISBN 0-444-85143-7, North-Holland). Elsevier.
System Developments Standards. C. Candullo. 544p. 1985. text ed. 54.95 (ISBN 0-07-009724-0). McGraw.
System Disorders & Atrophies see Handbook of Clinical Neurology.
System Dynamics. Ed. by A. A. Legasto, Jr. et al. (TIMS Studies in the Management Sciences: Vol. 14). 282p. 1981. pap. 36.50 (ISBN 0-444-85491-6, North-Holland). Elsevier.
System Dynamics. Katsuhiko Ogata. LC 77-20180. (Illus.). 1978. 54.00 (ISBN 0-13-880385-4). P-H.
System Dynamics: A Unified Approach. Dean C. Karnopp & Ronald C. Rosenberg. LC 74-22466. 402p. 1975. 53.50 (ISBN 0-471-45940-2). Wiley.
System Dynamics & the Analysis of Change: Proceedings of the 6th International Conference, University of Paris, Dauphine, November, '80. Ed. by B. E. Paulre. 382p. 1981. 94.75 (ISBN 0-444-86251-X, North-Holland). Elsevier.
System Effectiveness. A. R. Habayeb. 450p. 1987. 120.00 (ISBN 0-08-034814-9, PBL). Pergamon.
System Fault Diagnostics, Reliability & Related Knowledge-Based Approaches, Vols. 1 & 2. Ed. by Tzafestas. 1987. Set. lib. bdg. 136.00 (ISBN 9-0277-2550-0, Pub. by Reidel Holland); Vol. I: Fault Diagnostics & Reliability. lib. bdg. 78.00 (ISBN 90-277-2551-9); Vol. II: Knowledge-Based & Fault Tolerant Techniques. lib. bdg. 78.00 (ISBN 90-277-2550-0). Kluwer Academic.
System for Assessing Affectivity. Robert E. Bills. LC 73-22712. 240p. 1975. 21.75 (ISBN 0-8173-9107-X). U of Ala Pr.
System for Caring: Supportive Counseling Techniques for Professionals & Families. Timothy J. Shannon. Ed. by Bradley L. Winch. LC 88-80771. (Creative Parenting & Teaching Ser.). (Illus.). 128p. (Orig.). 1988. pap. 9.95 (ISBN 0-915190-55-9, JP9055-9). Jalmar Pr.
System for Development Planning & Budgeting. Arie Beenhakker. 200p. 1980. text ed. 37.95x (ISBN 0-566-00326-0). Gower Pub Co.
System for Evaluating the Performance of Government-Invested Enterprises in the Republic of Korea. Young C. Park. (Discussion Paper: No. 3). 60p. 1986. 5.00 (ISBN 0-8213-0859-9, DP 0003). World Bank.
System for Keeping Genealogical Research Records. 101p. 1982. pap. 5.40 (ISBN 0-942574-00-1). Ciga Pr.
System for Ophthalmic Dispensing. Clifford F. Brooks & Irving Borish. LC 76-5734. (Illus.). 472p. 1979. 60.00 (ISBN 0-87873-025-7). Prof Pr Bks NYC.
System for Settlement of Disputes under the United Nations Convention on the Law of the Sea. A. O. Adede. LC 86-5373. (Publications on Ocean Development Ser.: Vol. 10). 1987. write for info. (ISBN 9-02-473324-3, Pub. by Kluwer-Nijhoff (Netherlands)). Kluwer Academic.
System for Teaching Business Education. A. Schrag & R. P. Poland. 576p. 1986. pap. text ed. 30.20 (ISBN 0-07-055602-4). McGraw.
System FORE, 5 Vols. Ed. by Eric Bagai & Judith Bagai. (Illus.). 1328p. 1979. wkbk. 90.00x (ISBN 0-943292-00-X). Foreworks.
System FORE Handbook. Eric Bagai & Judith Bagai. (System FORE Ser.: Vol. 1). 96p. (Orig.). 1979. pap. text ed. 7.00x (ISBN 0-943292-01-8). Foreworks.
System Identification. Andrew P. Sage & James L. Melsa. (Mathematics in Science & Engineering Ser: Vol. 80). 1971. 69.50 (ISBN 0-12-614450-8). Acad Pr.
System Identification for Self-Adaptive Control. W. D. Davies. LC 70-128756. pap. 98.50 (ISBN 0-317-08013-X, 2022540). Bks Demand UMI.
System Identification of Vibrating Structures: Mathematical Models from Test Data Presented at 1972 Winter Annual Meeting of the American Society of Mechanical Engineers. Ed. by W. D. Pilkey & R. Cohen. LC 72-92594. (Illus.). pap. 51.50 (ISBN 0-317-08340-6, 2019473). Bks Demand UMI.
System Identification Parameter & State Estimation. P. Eykhoff. LC 73-2781. 555p. 1974. 152.95x (ISBN 0-471-24980-7, Pub. by Wiley-Interscience). Wiley.
System Identification: Theory for the User. Lennant Ljung. (Illus.). 384p. 1987. text ed. 50.00 (ISBN 0-13-881640-9). P-H.
System Integration, Vol. 8. Ed. by James E. Rush. LC 83-9584. (Library Systems Evaluation Guides). (Illus.). 240p. 1987. velo bd. 59.50 (ISBN 0-912803-08-8). Rush Assoc.
System-M CAD: Computer-Aided Drafting Software from Macmillan. T&W Systems, Inc. Staff. 287p. Date not set. write for info. (ISBN 0-02-421840-5). Macmillan.
System-M CAM. Scott M. Stevens. 300p. Date not set. write for info. (ISBN 0-02-417190-5). Macmillan.
System Management: Planning & Control. H. W. Lanford. (National University Publications Ser.). 200p. 1981. 23.50x (ISBN 0-8046-9223-8, Pub by Kennikat). Assoc Faculty Pr.
System Modeling & Control. J. Schwarzenbach & K. F. Gill. LC 78-40537. 229p. 1978. pap. 27.95x (ISBN 0-470-26457-8). Halsted Pr.
System Modeling & Optimization, New York 1981: Proceedings. Ed. by R. F. Drenick & F. Kozin. (Lecture Notes in Control & Information Sciences: Vol. 38). 894p. 1982. pap. 59.00 (ISBN 0-387-11691-5). Springer-Verlag.
System Modeling & Optimization: Proceedings. IFIP Conference, 11th, Copenhagen, DK, July 25-29, 1983. Ed. by P. Thoft-Christian. (Lectures Notes in Control & Information Sciences: Vol. 59). x, 892p. 1984. pap. 66.00 (ISBN 0-387-13185-X). Springer-Verlag.
System Modelling & Optimization. M. Iri & K. Yajma. (Lecture Notes in Control & Information Sciences Ser.: Vol. 113). (Illus.). 787p. 1988. pap. 120.00 (ISBN 0-387-19238-7). Springer-Verlag.
System Modelling & Optimization. Ed. by A. Prekopa et al. (Lecture Notes in Control & Information Sciences: Vol. 84). (Illus.). 1060p. 1986. pap. 120.00 (ISBN 0-387-16854-0). Springer-Verlag.
System of Accentuation for Sumero-Akkadian Signs. Clarence E. Keiser. LC 78-63553. (Yale Oriental Ser. Researches: No. 9). Repr. of 1919 ed. 20.00 (ISBN 0-404-60279-7). AMS Pr.
System of Adult Education in Yugoslavia. Dusan Savicevic. LC 69-17692. (Notes & Essays Series, No. 59). 1968. pap. text ed. 2.50 (ISBN 0-87060-023-0, NES 59). Syracuse U Cont Ed.
System of Aeronautics. John Wise. (Illus.). 319p. 1980. 14.95 (ISBN 0-87770-227-6). Ye Galleon.
System of Ayurveda. Shiv Sharma. 356p. 1983. Repr. of 1929 ed. text ed. 40.00x (ISBN 0-86590-188-0). Apt Bks.
System of Complete Medical Police: Selections from Johann Peter Frank. Johann P. Frank. Ed. by Erna Lesky. LC 75-39820. pap. 123.30 (ISBN 0-317-07932-8, 2020757). Bks Demand UMI.
System of Courtly Love. Lewis F. Mott. LC 65-26458. (Studies in Comparative Literature, No. 35). 1969. Repr. of 1924 ed. lib. bdg. 49.95x (ISBN 0-8383-0599-7). Haskell.
System of Criminal Justice. 2nd ed. M. Gary Holten & Melvin E. Jones. 1982. text ed. write for info. (ISBN 0-673-39445-X). Scott F.
System of Economic Contradictions; Or, the Philosophy of Misery. Pierre J. Proudhon. Tr. by Benjamin R. Tucker. LC 75-38261. (Evolution of Capitalism Ser.). 482p. 1972. Repr. of 1888 ed. 28.00 (ISBN 0-405-04134-9). Ayer Co Pubs.
System of Elocution with Special Referance to Gesture, to the Treatment of Stammering & Defective Articulation. Andrew Comstock. 1841. 25.00 (ISBN 0-8274-3561-4). R West.
System of English Grammar. Ralph B. Long & Dorothy R. Long. LC 75-159449. 531p. 1980. text ed. 15.00 (ISBN 0-8477-3325-4); pap. text ed. 12.00 (ISBN 0-8477-3326-2). U of PR Pr.
System of Ethics. Leonard Nelson. 1956. 65.00x (ISBN 0-685-69846-7). Elliots Bks.
System of Experimental Design: Engineering Methods to Optimize Quality & Minimize Cost, 2 vols. Taguchi. 1176p. 1987. Set. 150.00 (ISBN 0-317-59599-7, 3876-UPB137). UNIPUB-Kraus Intl.
System of Financial Administration in British India. P. K. Wattal. xv, 412p. 1985. Repr. of 1923 ed. text ed. 45.00x (ISBN 0-317-18507-1, Pub. by Daya Pub Hse India). Apt Bks.
System of Hypnotherapy. B. J. Hartman. LC 79-16980. 332p. 1980. 24.95x (ISBN 0-88229-449-0). Nelson-Hall.
System of Incomes & Incentives in Hungary. Katalin Falus-Szikra. Tr. by Istvan Kollar from Hungarian. (Illus.). 332p. 1985. 29.95x (ISBN 963-05-4208-0, Pub. by Akademiai Kiado Hungary). Humanities.
System of International Comparisons of Gross Product & Purchasing Power, Phase 1. Irving B. Kravis et al. LC 73-19352. (World Bank Ser). (Illus.). 308p. 1975. 30.50x (ISBN 0-8018-1606-8). Johns Hopkins.
System of Justice. Mike Fitzgerald & John Muncie. 200p. 1984. pap. 14.95x (ISBN 0-631-13249-X). Basil Blackwell.
System of Logic. 8th ed. John S. Mill. 1986. lib. bdg. 40.00X (ISBN 0-935005-29-3); pap. text ed. 25.00X (ISBN 0-935005-34-X). Ibis Pub VA.
System of Logic: Ratiocinative & Inductive, 2 vols. John S. Mill. Ed. by J. M. Robson. LC 73-78926. (Collected Works of John Stuart Mill). 1974. Set. 85.00x (ISBN 0-8020-1875-0). U of Toronto Pr.
System of Marker Variables for the Field of Learning Disabilities. Barbara Keogh et al. LC 81-18202. 104p. 1982. 14.95x (ISBN 0-8156-2257-0). Syracuse U Pr.
System of Metaphysics. George S. Fullerton. 1968. Repr. of 1904 ed. 39.00x (ISBN 0-403-00125-0). Scholarly.
System of Mineralogy: Halides, Nitrates, Borates, Carbonates, Sulfates, Phosphates, Arsenates, Tungstates, Molybdate, etc. see Systems of Minerology.
System of Mineralogy: Silica Minerals see Systems of Minerology.
System of Monitoring & Evaluating Agricultural Extension Projects. Michael M. Cernea & Benjamin J. Tepping. (Working Paper: No. 272). vi, 115p. 1977. 5.00 (ISBN 0-686-36079-6, WP-0272). World Bank.
System of Nature, 3 Vols. Paul H. Holbach. Ed. by Burton Feldman & Robert D. Richardson. LC 78-60890. (Myth & Romanticism Ser.). 1984. lib. bdg. 240.00 (ISBN 0-8240-3562-3). Garland Pub.
System of Nature Or, Laws of the Moral & Physical World, 2 vols. in 1. Ed. by Paul T. D'Holbach & Diderot. Tr. by H. D. Robinson. LC 79-143669. (Research & Source Works Ser.: No. 618). 1971. Repr. of 1836 ed. lib. bdg. 29.50 (ISBN 0-8337-0753-1). B Franklin.
System of Nomenclature for Terpene Hydrocarbons: Acyclics, Monocyclics, Bicyclics. American Chemical Society, Division of Organic Chemistry Staff & Industrial & Engineering Chemistry. LC 55-4170. (American Chemical Society Advances in Chemistry Series: No. 14). pap. 37.50 (ISBN 0-317-08703-7, 2050183). Bks Demand UMI.
System of Open Star Clusters & the Galaxy Atlas of Open Star Clusters. G. Alter & J. Ruprecht. 1963. 86.00 (ISBN 0-12-054250-1). Acad Pr.
System of Ophthalmology Series. Ed. by Stewart Duke-Elder. Incl. Vol. 1. Eye in Evolution. (Illus.). 859p. 1958. 65.00 (ISBN 0-8016-8282-7); Vol. 2. Anatomy of the Visual System. (Illus.). 923p. 1961. 67.50 (ISBN 0-8016-8283-5); Vol. 3, Pt. 1. Normal & Abnormal Development: Embryology. (Illus.). 372p. 1963. 51.50 (ISBN 0-8016-8285-1); Vol. 3, Pt. 2. Normal & Abnormal Development: Congenital Deformities. (Illus.). 1190p. 1964. 72.50 (ISBN 0-8016-8286-X); Vol. 4. Physiology of the Eye & of Vision. (Illus.). 754p. 1968. 79.50 (ISBN 0-8016-8296-7); Vol. 5. Ophthalmic Optics & Refraction. (Illus.). 899p. 1970. 69.50 (ISBN 0-8016-8298-3); Vol. 7. Foundations of Ophthalmology: Heredity, Pathology, Diagnosis & Therapeutics. (Illus.). 851p. 1962. 69.50 (ISBN 0-8016-8284-3); Vol. 8. Diseases of the Outer Eye: Conjunctiva, Cornea & Sclera, 2 parts. (Illus.). 1273p. 1965. Pt. 1. 75.00 (ISBN 0-8016-8288-6); Pt. 2. 75.00 (ISBN 0-8016-8289-4); Vol. 9. Diseases of Uveal Tract. (Illus.). 994p. 1966. 85.00 (ISBN 0-8016-8290-8); Vol. 10. Diseases of the Retina. (Illus.). 894p. 1967. 85.00 (ISBN 0-8016-8295-9); Vol. 11. Diseases of the Lens & Vitreous. (Illus.). 799p. 1969. 85.00 (ISBN 0-8016-8297-5); Vol. 12. Neuro-Ophthalmology. (Illus.). 1278p. 1971. 89.50 (ISBN 0-8016-8299-1); Vol. 14. Injuries, 2 vols. 1378p. 1972. Set. 125.00 (ISBN 0-8016-8300-9); Vol. 15. Summary of Systemic Opthamology & Indices. 499p. 1976. cloth 61.50 (ISBN 0-8016-8301-7). 657.75 (ISBN 0-8016-8310-6). Mosby.
System of Opthalmology Series: The Ocular Adnexa, Vol. 13. Elder Duke & MacFaul. 1974. 120.00 (ISBN 0-8016-8303-3). Mosby.
System of Oyster Culture on Floating Shellfish Parks. M. Nikolic & I. Stojmic. (GFCM Studies & Reviews: No. 18). 15p. (Eng., Fr. & Span., 2nd Printing 1965). 1962. pap. 7.50 (ISBN 92-5-101953-3, F1781, FAO). UNIPUB.
System of Physical Education in the U. S. S. R. G. I. Kukushkin. 231p. 1983. 7.95 (ISBN 0-8285-2608-7, Pub. by Raduga Pubs USSR). Imported Pubns.
System of Plotinus. H. T. S. 1985. pap. 7.95 (ISBN 0-916411-75-3, Pub by Alexandrian Pr). Holmes Pub.
System of Practical Anatomy for Dental Students: A Guide & Atlas. Lord Zuckerman et al. (Illus.). 280p. 1986. 32.50 (ISBN 0-19-267005-0). Oxford U Pr.
System of Professions: An Essay on the Division of Expert Labor. Andrew Abbott. xvi, 436p. 1988. 49.95x (ISBN 0-226-00068-0); pap. 19.95x (ISBN 0-226-00069-9). U of Chicago Pr.
System of Quality Control for a CPA Firm. (Statement on Quality Control Standards Ser.: No. 1). 6p. 1979. pap. 3.25 (ISBN 0-686-70248-4). Am Inst CPA.
System of Scientific Medicine. Howard Berliner. 180p. 1985. 29.95 (ISBN 0-422-79520-8, 9619, Pub. by Tavistock England); pap. 12.95 (ISBN 0-422-79530-5, 9620, Pub. by Tavistock England). Routledge Chapman & Hall.
System of Social Science: Papers Relating to Adam Smith. Andrew S. Skinner. 1979. text ed. 34.95x (ISBN 0-19-828422-5). Oxford U Pr.
System of Stages for Correlation of Magallanes Basin Sediments. Manley L. Natland et al. LC 74-75964. (Geological Society of America Memoir Ser.: No. 139). pap. 50.50 (ISBN 0-317-28976-4, 2023735). Bks Demand UMI.
System of Target Selection Applied by the German Air Force in WW II. Paul Deichmann. 425p. pap. 50.00. MA-AH Pub.
System of Taxation in China in the Tsing Dynasty, 1644-1911. Shao-Kwan Chen. LC 79-120215. (Columbia University Studies in the Social Sciences: No. 143). 1970. Repr. of 1914 ed. 12.50 (ISBN 0-404-51143-0). AMS Pr.
System of the Earth, 1785. James Hutton. Ed. & frwd. by George W. White. Bd. with Theory of the Earth, 1788; Observations on Granite, 1795; Biography of Hutton. John Playfair. (Contributions to the History of Geology Ser.: Vol. 5). 1970. Repr. 20.95x (ISBN 0-02-846220-3). Hafner.
System of the Hungarian Sentence Patterns. Janos Zsilka. LC 66-63663. (Uralic & Altaic Ser: Vol. 67). 1967. pap. text ed. 7.00x (ISBN 0-87750-023-1). Res Ctr Lang Semiotic.
System of the Law of Nations: State Responsibility, Pt. 1. Ian Brownlie. 1983. 55.00x (ISBN 0-19-825452-0). Oxford U Pr.
System of the Laws of the State of Connecticut, 2 vols. Zephaniah Swift. LC 73-37991. (American Law Ser.: The Formative Law). 962p. 1972. Repr. of 1795 ed. Set. 55.00 (ISBN 0-405-04036-9); 27.50 ea. Vol. 1 (ISBN 0-405-04037-7). Vol. 2 (ISBN 0-405-04038-5). Ayer Co Pubs.
System of the Modern Roman Law, Vol. I. Frederich Von Savigny. Tr. by William Holloway from Ger. LC 79-14142. 1980. Repr. of 1867 ed. 30.00 (ISBN 0-88355-923-4). Hyperion Conn.
System of the Quadriliteral Verb in Akkadian. Alexander Heidel. LC 78-72739. (Ancient Mesopotamian Texts & Studies). Repr. of 1940 ed. 24.50 (ISBN 0-404-18177-5). AMS Pr.

Systematic Monograph of the Dermaptera of the World, Part 1: Pygidicranidae, Subfamily Diplatyinae. W. D. Hincks. (Illus.). 132p. 1955. pap. 15.50x (ISBN 0-565-00568-5, Pub. by Brit Mus Nat Hist England). Sabbot-Natural Hist Bks.
Systematic Monograph of the Dermaptera of the World, Part 2: Pygidicranidae, Excluding Diplatyinae. W. D. Hincks. (Illus.). 218p. 1959. pap. 23.50x (ISBN 0-565-00459-X, Pub. by Brit Mus Nat Hist England). Sabbot-Natural Hist Bks.
Systematic Monograph of the Tongue Soles of the Genus Cynoglossus Hamilton-Buchanan (Pisces, Cynoglossidae) A. G. Menon. LC 76-608109. (Smithsonian Contributions to Zoology Ser.: No. 238). pap. 33.30 (ISBN 0-317-28685-4, 2055286). Bks Demand UMI.
Systematic New Product Development. A. G. Douglas et al. LC 78-2398. 173p. 1978. 42.95x (ISBN 0-470-26328-8). Halsted Pr.
Systematic New Product Development. 2nd ed. G. Douglas et al. 196p. 1983. text ed. 37.00x (ISBN 0-566-02412-8). Gower Pub Co.
Systematic Nursing Care. Rosemary Long. (Illus.). 96p. 1981. pap. 7.95. Faber & Faber.
Systematic Philosophy: An Overview of Metaphysics Showing the Development from the Greeks to the Contemporaries with Specified Directions & Projections. John E. Van Hook. (Illus.). 1979. 8.50 (ISBN 0-682-49398-8, University). Exposition-Phoenix.
Systematic Planning for Educational Change. William Cunningham. LC 81-84692. 323p. 1982. text ed. 24.95 (ISBN 0-87484-551-3). Mayfield Pub.
Systematic Planning of Industrial Facilities, 2 vols. Richard Muther & Lee Hales. LC 79-84256. Set. 80.00 (ISBN 0-933684-00-2). Vol I, 1979. Vol. II, 1980. Mgmt & Indus Res Pubns.
Systematic Planning of Industrial Facilities, Vol. I. Richard Muther & Lee Hales. LC 79-84256. 1979. 18.00 (ISBN 0-933684-01-0). Mgmt & Indus Res Pubns.
Systematic Planning of Industrial Facilities, Vol. II. Richard Muther & Lee Hales. LC 79-84256. 1980. 68.00 (ISBN 0-933684-02-9). Mgmt & Indus Res Pubns.
Systematic Political Geography. 3rd ed. Martin I. Glassner & Harm J. DeBlij. LC 79-26750. 537p. 1980. text ed. write for info. (ISBN 0-471-05228-0). Wiley.
Systematic Political Geography. 4th. ed. Martin I. Glassner & Harm J. DeBlij. LC 88-2655. 576p. 1988. write for info. (ISBN 0-471-63583-9). Wiley.
Systematic Politics. Charles E. Merriam. 1966. pap. 2.45x (ISBN 0-226-52060-9, P228, Phoen). U of Chicago Pr.
Systematic Process for Planning Media Programs. James W. Liesener. LC 76-3507. 166p. 1976. pap. text ed. 9.00x (ISBN 0-8389-0176-X). ALA.
Systematic Programming: An Introduction. Niklaus Wirth. (Illus.). 208p. 1973. 46.00 (ISBN 0-13-880369-2). P-H.
Systematic Relationships of Neotropical Horned Frogs, Genus Hemiphractus (Anura: Hylidae) Linda Trueb. (Occasional Papers: No. 29). 60p. 1974. pap. 3.25 (ISBN 0-686-80386-8). U of KS Mus Nat Hist.
Systematic Review of the Marsupial Frogs (Hylidae Gastrotheca) of the Andes of Ecuador. William E. Duellman. (Occasional Papers: No. 22). 27p. 1974. pap. 1.50 (ISBN 0-686-80347-7). U of KS Mus Nat Hist.
Systematic Revision of Diplocentrid Scorpions (Diplocentridae) from Circum - Caribbean Lands. Oscar F. Francke. (Special Publications: No. 14). (Illus.). 92p. (Orig.). 1978. pap. 7.00 (ISBN 0-89672-062-4). Tex Tech Univ Pr.
Systematic Revision of the Genus Cybianthus Subgenus Grammadenia (Myrsinaceae) J. J. Pipoly. (Memoirs of the New York Botanical Garden Ser.: Vol. 43). 1987. pap. 17.50 (ISBN 0-89327-314-7). NY Botanical.
Systematic Selling: How to Influence the Buying Decision Process. Terry A. Mort. LC 77-5937. pap. 49.50 (ISBN 0-317-26910-0, 2023552). Bks Demand UMI.
Systematic Settlements. 2nd ed. Sanford W. Hornwood & I. Lucretia Hollingsworth. LC 85-82120. 1986. 74.50 (ISBN 0-318-19872-X); Suppl. 1987. 22.50; Suppl. 1988. 24.50. Lawyers Co-Op.
Systematic Significance of Leaf Structure in the Cyperaceae-Mapanieae see Memoirs of the New York Botanical Garden.
Systematic Significance of Leaf Structure in the Tribe Sclerieae (Cyperaceae) see Memoirs of the New York Botanical Garden.
Systematic Sociology: An Introduction to the Study of Society. Karl Mannheim. Ed. by J. S. Eros & W. A. Stewart. LC 83-22743. (International Library of Sociology & Social Reconstruction). xxx, 169p. 1984. Repr. of 1957 ed. lib. bdg. 35.00x (ISBN 0-313-24378-6, MASY). Greenwood.
Systematic Sociology of Australian Education. R. J. King & R. E. Young. 204p. 1986. text ed. 29.95x (ISBN 0-86861-897-7). Unwin Hyman.
Systematic Sociology: On the Basis of the Beziehungslebre & Gebildelebre. Leopold Von Wiese. LC 73-14186. 798p. 1974. Repr. 40.00x (ISBN 0-405-05532-3). Ayer Co Pubs.
Systematic Software Development Using VDM. Cliff B. Jones. (Illus.). 336p. 1986. text ed. 44.00 (ISBN 0-13-880725-6). P-H.
Systematic Status & Relationships of the Hylid Frog Nyctimantis Rugiceps Boulenger. William E. Duellman & Linda Trueb. (Occasional Papers: No. 58). 14p. 1976. pap. 1.25 (ISBN 0-686-80350-7). U of KS Mus Nat Hist.
Systematic Studies in Polygonaceae of Kashmir Himalaya. A. H. Munshi & G. N. Javeid. 215p. 1986. 75.00x (ISBN 81-85046-32-8, Pub. by Scientific). State Mutual Bk.
Systematic Studies of Darters of the Subgenus Catonotus (Percidae), with the Description of a New Species from Caney Fork, Tennessee. Marvin E. Braasch & Lawrence M. Page. (Occasional Papers: No. 78). 10p. 1979. 1.25 (ISBN 0-317-04822-8). U of KS Mus Nat Hist.
Systematic Studies of Darters of the Subgenus Catonotus (Percidae), with the Description of a New Species from the Lower Cumberland & Tennessee River Systems. Lawrence M. Page & Marvin E. Braach. (Occasional Papers: No. 60). 18p. 1976. pap. 1.25 (ISBN 0-686-79828-7). U of KS Mus Nat Hist.
Systematic Studies of Darters of the Subgenus Catonotus with the Description of a New Species from the Duck River System. Lawrence M. Page & Marvin E. Braasch. (Occasional Papers: No. 63). 18p. 1977. pap. 1.25 (ISBN 0-686-79827-9). U of KS Mus Nat Hist.
Systematic Studies of the Genus Pyrrhopappus (Compositae, Cichorieae) David K. Northington. (Special Publications: No. 6). 38p. 1974. pap. 2.00 (ISBN 0-89672-031-4). Tex Tech Univ Pr.
Systematic Study in the Elementary Schools. Lida B. Earhart. LC 73-176739. (Columbia University. Teachers College. Contributions to Education: No. 18). Repr. of 1908 ed. 22.50 (ISBN 0-404-55018-5). AMS Pr.
Systematic Survey of the Mesozoic Bivalvia from Japan. Ed. by Itaru Hayami. 249p. 1976. 42.50 (ISBN 0-86008-152-4, Pub. by U of Tokyo Japan). Columbia U Pr.
Systematic Survey of the Paleozoic & Mesozoic Gastropoda & Paleozoic Bivalvia from Japan. Ed. by Itaru Hayami & Tomoki Kase. 153p. 1978. 35.00 (ISBN 0-86008-198-2, Pub. by U of Tokyo Japan). Columbia U Pr.
Systematic Systems Approach: An Integrated Method for Solving Systems Problems. Thomas H. Athey. (Illus.). 416p. 1982. text ed. 41.00 (ISBN 0-13-880914-3). P-H.
Systematic Tabulation of Indo-European Animal Names. E. Gottlieb. (LD). 1931. pap. 16.00 (ISBN 0-527-00754-4). Kraus Repr.
Systematic Theology. Louis Berkhof. 1978. 24.95 (ISBN 0-8028-3020-X). Eerdmans.
Systematic Theology. R. L. Dabney. 903p. 1985. 23.95 (ISBN 0-85151-453-7). Banner of Truth.
Systematic Theology, 3 Vols. Charles Hodge. 1960. Set. 59.95 (ISBN 0-8028-8135-1). Eerdmans.
Systematic Theology. abr. ed. Charles Hodge. Ed. by Edward N. Gross. 544p. 1988. 24.95 (ISBN 0-8010-4321-2). Baker Bk.
Systematic Theology, 3 Vols in 1. Augustus H. Strong. 21.95 (ISBN 0-8170-0177-8). Judson.
Systematic Theology. Augustus H. Strong. Incl. Doctrine of God; Doctrine of Man; Doctrine of Salvation. 1168p. 24.95 (ISBN 0-8007-0302-2). Revell.
Systematic Theology, 3 vols. in 1. Paul Tillich. LC 51-2235. 950p. 1967. 49.95x (ISBN 0-226-80336-8). U of Chicago Pr.
Systematic Theology, 3 vols. Ernest S. Williams. Incl. Vol. 1. 294p. (02-0643); Vol. 2. 294p. (02-0644); Vol. 3. 280p. pap. (ISBN 0-88243-645-7, 02-0645). 1953. pap. 18.00 Set 3 vol (ISBN 0-88243-650-3, 02-0650); pap. 6.95 ea. Gospel Pub.
Systematic Theology, Vol. 1. Paul Tillich. LC 51-2235. 1973. pap. 11.00x (ISBN 0-226-80337-6, P556, Phoen). U of Chicago Pr.
Systematic Theology, Vol. 2. Paul Tillich. LC 51-2235. xii, 188p. 1975. pap. 7.50X (ISBN 0-226-80338-4, P633, Phoen). U of Chicago Pr.
Systematic Theology: A Modern Protestant Approach. Kenneth Cauthen. LC 86-23807. (Toronto Studies in Theology: Vol. 25). 480p. 1986. lib. bdg. 69.95x (ISBN 0-88946-769-2). E Mellen.
Systematic Theology: Life & the Spirit History & the Kingdom of God, Vol. 3. Paul Tillich. LC 51-2235. 1976. pap. 11.00x (ISBN 0-226-80339-2, P706, Phoen). U of Chicago Pr.
Systematic Theology of the Christian Religion. James O. Buswell, Jr. 25.95 (ISBN 0-310-22190-0, 9364). Zondervan.
Systematic Thinking for Social Action. Alice M. Rivlin. LC 74-161600. 150p. 1971. 22.95 (ISBN 0-8157-7478-8); pap. 8.95 (ISBN 0-8157-7477-X). Brookings.
Systematic Training for Effective Parenting of Teens - Step-Teen: The Parents Guide. Don Dinkmeyer et al. LC 82-74394. (Illus.). 160p. 1983. pap. text ed. 9.95 (ISBN 0-913476-82-X). Am Guidance.
Systematic Training for Effective Parenting of Teens - Step-Teen: Leader's Guide. Don Dinkmeyer et al. 135p. 1983. pap. text ed. 29.75 (ISBN 0-913476-83-8). Am Guidance.
Systematic Training for Effective Teaching (STET) Leader's Manual. Don Dinkmeyer & Gary McKay. 149p. 1980. vinyl cover 31.00 (ISBN 0-913476-74-9). Am Guidance.
Systematic Training for Effective Teaching (STET) Teacher's Resource Book: Activities for Teachers & Students. Don Dinkmeyer et al. (Illus.). 161p. (Orig.). 1980. pap. 9.75 (ISBN 0-913476-76-5). Am Guidance.
Systematic Training for Effective Teaching: Teacher's Handbook. Don Dinkmeyer et al. (Illus.). 291p. (Orig.). 1980. pap. text ed. 15.50 (ISBN 0-913476-75-7). Am Guidance.
Systematic Translation of Hindi-Urdu into English. Anoop Chandola. LC 79-127886. 365p. 1970. pap. 12.50x (ISBN 0-8165-0289-7). U of Ariz Pr.
Systematic Treatise, Historical, Etiological & Practical on the Principal Diseases of the Interior Valley of North America, 8 Pts. in 2 Vols. Daniel Drake. 1971. Repr. of 1850 ed. lib. bdg. 89.00 (ISBN 0-8337-0907-0). B Franklin.
Systematic View of the Science of Jurisprudence. Sheldon Amos. xxii, 545p. 1982. Repr. of 1872 ed. lib. bdg. 39.50x (ISBN 0-8377-0210-0). Rothman.
Systematics. Don Hegberg. 748p. (Orig.). 1977. pap. 10.00 (ISBN 0-686-32735-7). Systematic Dev.
Systematics: A New Approach to Systems Analysis. Kit Grindley. (Illus.). 1977. text ed. 13.95 (ISBN 0-89433-020-9). Petrocelli.
Systematics & Biogeography: Cladistics & Vicariance. Gareth Nelson & Norman I. Platnick. LC 80-20828. (Illus.). 592p. 1981. 65.00x (ISBN 0-231-04574-3). Columbia U Pr.
Systematics & Bionomics of Anthophora: The Bomboides Group & Species Groups of the New World (Hymenoptera: Apoidea, Anthophoridae) Robert W. Brooks. LC 82-40445. (UC Publications in Entomology: Vol. 98). 96p. 1983. pap. text ed. 14.00x (ISBN 0-520-09658-4). U of Cal Pr.
Systematics & Ecology of the Sea-Urchin Genus Centrostephanus Echinodermata: Echinodea) from the Altantic & Eastern Pacific Oceans. David L. Pawson & John E. Miller. LC 83-600054. (Smithsonian Contributions to the Marine Sciences: No. 20). pap. 20.00 (ISBN 0-317-29916-6, 2021766). Bks Demand UMI.
Systematics & Economic Botany of the Oenocarpus - Jessenia (Palmae) Complex. Michael J. Balick. (Advances in Economic Botany Ser.: Vol. 3). 1986. pap. text ed. 29.25x (ISBN 0-89327-311-2). NY Botanical.
Systematics & Evolution of Cordylanthus(Scrophulariaceae-Pedicularieae) Tsan I. Chuang & Lawrence R. Heckard. Ed. by Christiane Anderson. LC 86-3546. (Systematic Botany Monographs: Vol. 10). (Illus.). 105p. 1986. 13.00 (ISBN 0-912861-10-X). Am Soc Plant.
Systematics & Evolution of Dicerandra (Labiatae) R. B. Huck. (Phanerogamarum Monographiae Ser.: Vol. 19). (Illus.). 344p. 1987. text ed. 96.00x (ISBN 3-443-78001-6). Lubrecht & Cramer.
Systematics & Evolution of the Greater Antillean Hylid Frogs. Linda Trueb & Michael J. Tyler. (Occasional Papers: No. 24). 60p. 1974. pap. 3.25 (ISBN 0-686-80385-X). U of KS Mus Nat Hist.
Systematics & Evolutionary Relationships of Spiny Pocket Mice, Genus Liomys. Hugh H. Genoways. (Special Publications: No. 5). (Illus.). 368p. (Orig.). 1973. pap. 10.00 (ISBN 0-89672-030-6). Tex Tech Univ Pr.
Systematics & Life History of the Great Barracuda, Sphyraena barracuda (Walbaum) Donald P. De Sylva. (Studies in Tropical Oceanography Ser: No. 1). 1970. 7.95x (ISBN 0-87024-082-X). U Miami Marine.
Systematics & Nesting Behavior of Australian Bembix Sand Wasps -(Hymenoptera, Sphecidae) Evans & Matthews. (Memoirs Ser: No. 20). (Illus.). 1973. 35.00x (ISBN 0-686-17148-9). Am Entom Inst.
Systematics & Pollination of the "Closed Flowered" Species of Calathea (Marantacae) Helen Kennedy. (Publications in Botany: No. 71). 1978. pap. 15.50x (ISBN 0-520-09572-3). U of Cal Pr.
Systematics & the Origin of Species. Ernst Mayr. Ed. by Niles Eldrige & Stephen J. Gould. LC 82-4215. (Classics in Evolution Ser.). 384p. 1982. pap. 18.00x (ISBN 0-231-05449-1). Columbia U Pr.
Systematics & the Properties of the Lanthanides. Ed. by Shyama Sinha. 1983. lib. bdg. 85.00 (ISBN 90-2771-613-7, Pub. by Reidel Holland). Kluwer Academic.
Systematics & Zoogeography of Middle American Shrews of the Genus Cryptotis. Jerry R. Choate. (Museum Ser.: Vol. 19, No. 3). 123p. 1970. 6.25 (ISBN 0-317-04961-5). U of KS Mus Nat Hist.
Systematics, Breeding & Seed Production of Potatoes. Tr. by A. K. Dhote from Rus. 219p. 1986. text ed. 41.00 (ISBN 90-6191-452-3, Pub. by A A Balkema). Brookfield Pub Co.
Systematics Community. Stephen R. Edwards et al. 275p. 1985. spiral bound 20.00 (ISBN 0-942924-12-6). Assn Syst Coll.
Systematics of a Species Complex in the Deep-Sea Genus Eurycope, with a Revision of Six Previously Described Species (Crustacea, Isopoda, Eurycopidae) George D. Wilson. LC 83-5917. (Bulletin of the Scripps Institution of Oceanography: Vol. 25). 70p. 1983. pap. text ed. 12.95x (ISBN 0-520-09678-9). U of Cal Pr.
Systematics of Acmella (Asteraceae-Heliantheae) Robert K. Jansen. Ed. by Christiane Anderson. LC 85-15844. (Systematic Botany Monographs: Vol. 8). (Illus.). 115p. (Orig.). 1985. pap. 13.50 (ISBN 0-912861-08-8). Am Soc Plant.
Systematics of Antirrhinum (Scrophulariaceae) in the New World. David M. Thompson. Ed. by Christiane Anderson. (Systematics Botany Monographs: Vol. 22). (Illus.). 142p. (Orig.). 1988. lib. bdg. 17.00 (ISBN 0-912861-22-3). Am Soc Plant.
Systematics of Bees of the Genus Eufriesea (Hymenoptera, Apidae) Lynn S. Kimsey. LC 81-7400. (University of California Publications in Entomology: Vol. 95). 136p. 1982. pap. 20.00x (ISBN 0-520-09643-6). U of Cal Pr.
Systematics of Coursetia - Leguminosae-Papilionoideae. Matt Lavin. Ed. by Christiane Anderson. (Systematic Botany Monographs: Vol. 21). (Illus.). 167p. 1988. lib. bdg. 20.00 (ISBN 0-912861-21-5). Am Soc Plant.
Systematics of Frankenia (Frankeniaceae) in North & South America. M. A. Whalen. Ed. by Christiane Anderson. (Systematic Botany Monographs: Vol. 17). (Illus., Orig.). 1987. lib. bdg. 11.00 (ISBN 0-912861-17-7). Am Soc Plant.
Systematics of Montanoa (Asteraceae-Heliantheae) Vicki Ann Funk. (Memoirs of the New York Botanical Garden Ser.: Vol. 36). (Illus.). 1982. pap. 21.00x (ISBN 0-89327-243-4). NY Botanical.
Systematics of Nearctic Telenomus: Classification & Revisions of the Podisi & Phymatae Species Groups (Hymenopetra Scelionidae) Norman F. Johnson. Ed. by Veda M. Cafazzo & Karen J. Reese. (Bulletin New Ser.: Vol. 6, No. 3). 113p. 1984. 10.00 (ISBN 0-86727-094-2). Ohio Bio Survey.
Systematics of Oenothera Section Oenothera Subsection Raimannia & Subsection Nutantigemma (Onagraceae) Werner Dietrich & Warren L. Wagner. Ed. by Christiane Anderson. (Systematic Botany Monographs: Vol. 24). (Illus.). 91p. (Orig.). 1988. lib. bdg. 10.50 (ISBN 0-912861-24-X). Am Soc Plant.
Systematics of Rhynchospora Section Dichromena. W. W. Thomas. (Memoirs of the New York Botanical Garden Ser.: Vol. 37). 1984. 21.00x (ISBN 0-89327-251-5). NY Botanical.
Systematics of Simple Sulfide Structures. rev. ed. Tibor Zoltai. 93p. 1974. pap. 4.50x (ISBN 0-686-47229-2). Polycrystal Bk Serv.
Systematics of Smaller Asian Night Birds Based on Voice. Joe T. Marshall. 58p. 1978. 7.00 (ISBN 0-943610-25-7). Am Ornithologists.
Systematics of Sympatric Species in West Indian Spatangoids: A Revision of the Genera Brissopsis, Plethotaenia, Paleopneustes, & Saviniaster. Richard H. Chesher. LC 68-30264. (Studies in Tropical Oceanography Ser: No. 7). 1968. 12.00x (ISBN 0-87024-088-9). U Miami Marine.
Systematics of Tetramerium (Acanthaceae) Thomas F. Daniel. Ed. by Christiane Anderson. LC 86-10852. (Systematic Botany Monographs: Vol. 12). (Illus.). 134p. 1986. 16.50 (ISBN 0-912861-12-6). Am Soc Plant.
Systematics of the Acutae Group of Carex (Cyperaceae) in the Pacific Northwest. Lisa A. Standley. Ed. by Christiane Anderson. LC 85-9024. (Systematic Botany Monographs: Vol. 7). (Illus.). 106p. (Orig.). 1985. pap. 13.00 (ISBN 0-912861-07-X). Am Soc Plant.
Systematics of the Calamarina Group of the Colubrid Snake Genus Tantilla. Larry D. Wilson & John R. Meyer. (Contributions in Biology & Geology Ser.: No. 42). 1981. 3.25 (ISBN 0-89326-069-X). Milwaukee Pub Mus.
Systematics of the Colletidae Based on Mature Larvae with Phenetic Analysis of Apoid Larvae (Hymenoptera, Apoidea) Ronald J. McGinley. (UC Publications in Entomology: Vol. 91). 332p. 1981. pap. 20.50x (ISBN 0-520-09623-1). U of Cal Pr.
Systematics of the Genus Didelphis (Marsupialia: Didelphidae) in North & Middle America. Alfred L. Gardner. (Special Publications: No. 4). (Illus.). 81p. (Orig.). 1973. pap. 4.00 (ISBN 0-89672-029-2). Tex Tech Univ Pr.
Systematics of the Green Algae. Ed. by David E. Irvine & David M. John. (Systematics Association Ser.: Vol. 27). 1985. 88.00 (ISBN 0-12-374040-1). Acad Pr.
Systematics of the Legume Genus Harpalyce: Leguminosae. Lotoideae. Mary T. Arroyo. Incl. Monographs of the Genus Hamelia: Rubiaceae. Thomas S. Elias. LC 66-6394. (Memoirs of the New York Botanical Garden: Vol. 26, No. 4). 1976. pap. 16.00x (ISBN 0-89327-001-6). NY Botanical.
Systematics of the Neotropical Characiform Genus Potamorhina. Richard P. Vari. LC 84-1398. (Smithsonian Contributions to Zoology Ser.: No. 400). pap. 20.00 (ISBN 0-317-26576-8, 2023958). Bks Demand UMI.
Systematics of the New World Species of Marsilea (Marsileaceae) David M. Johnson. Ed. by Christiane Anderson. LC 86-7949. (Systematic Botany Monographs: Vol. 11). (Illus.). 87p. 1986. 10.00 (ISBN 0-912861-11-8). Am Soc Plant.

Systems Analysis of Ecosystems. Ed. by G. S. Innis & R. V. O'Neill. (Statistical Ecology Ser.: Vol. 9). 1979. 45.00 (ISBN 0-89974-006-5). Intl Co-Op.
Systems Analysis of International Crises. Richard S. Beal. LC 79-66860. 1979. text ed. 28.25 (ISBN 0-8191-0858-8). U Pr of Amer.
Systems Analysis of Political Life. David Easton. LC 78-71148. 1979. pap. 8.95x (ISBN 0-226-18016-6, P833, Phoen). U of Chicago Pr.
Systems Analysis of Storage, Hauling & Discharge of Hot Asphalt Paving Mixtures. Texas A & M University Staff. (Quality Improvement Program Ser.: No. 94). 170p. 1972. 12.00 (ISBN 0-317-58427-8). Natl Asphalt Pavement.
Systems Analysis of the New York City Home Attendant Program: With Recommendations for a Home Care Service Delivery System. 1977. 4.00 (ISBN 0-86671-040-X). Comm Coun Great NY.
Systems Analyst. Jack Rudman. (Career Examination Ser.: C-2168). (Cloth bdg. avail. on request). 1988. pap. 16.00 (ISBN 0-8373-2168-9). Natl Learning.
Systems & Computer Science. Conference on Systems & Computer Science, 1965: University of Western Ontario. Ed. by John F. Hart & Satoru Takasu. LC 68-114245. pap. 65.30 (ISBN 0-317-10999-5, 2014240). Bks Demand UMI.
Systems & Control Encyclopedia: Theory, Technology, Applications. Ed. by M. G. Singh. LC 86-15085. (Illus.). 5500p. 1987. 2300.00 (ISBN 0-08-028709-3). Pergamon.
Systems & Data Processing in Insurance Companies: Student Guide. rev. ed. Charles H. Cissley. LC 82-80670. (FLMI Insurance Education Program Ser.). 287p. 1982. text ed. 12.00 (ISBN 0-915322-55-2); wkbk. 7.00 (ISBN 0-915322-56-0). LOMA.
Systems & Medical Care. Ed. by Alan Sheldon et al. 1970. 27.50x (ISBN 0-262-19077-X). MIT Pr.
Systems & Models for Developing Programs for the Gifted & Talented. Ed. by Joseph S. Renzulli. 1986. pap. text ed. 34.95 (ISBN 0-936386-44-4). Creative Learning.
Systems & Models for Energy & Environmental Analysis. Ed. by T. R. Lakshmanan & Peter Nijkamp. 240p. 1983. text ed. 35.50x (ISBN 0-566-00558-1). Gower Pub Co.
Systems & Optimization. Ed. by A. Bagchi & H. T. Jongen. (Lecture Notes in Control & Information Sciences Ser.: Vol. 66). x, 206p. 1985. pap. 18.50 (ISBN 0-387-15004-8). Springer-Verlag.
Systems & Procedures: A Handbook for Business & Industry. 2nd ed. Victor Lazzaro. 1968. text ed. 41.00 (ISBN 0-13-881425-2). P-H.
Systems & Procedures Including Office Management Information Sources. Ed. by Chester Morrill, Jr. LC 67-31261. (Management Information Ser.: No. 12). 380p. 1967. 68.00x (ISBN 0-8103-0812-6). Gale.
Systems & Process in International Politics. Morton A. Kaplan. LC 74-13081. 324p. 1975. pap. 11.50 (ISBN 0-88275-212-X). Krieger.
Systems & Processes: Collected Works in Sociology. Ed. by Mario Reda et al. 1968. pap. 14.95x (ISBN 0-8084-0292-7). New Coll U Pr.
Systems & Programming Exercises in Data Processing. W. Skok. 128p. 1982. 30.00x (ISBN 0-905435-30-3, Pub. by DP Pubns). State Mutual Bk.
Systems & Signals. N. Levan. (University Series in Modern Engineering). 173p. 1983. pap. 22.00 (ISBN 0-387-90900-1). Springer Verlag.
Systems & Signals. 2nd, rev. ed. N. Levan. (University Series in Modern Engineering). 176p. 1987. text ed. 29.50 (ISBN 0-911575-40-5). Optimization Soft.
Systems & Simulation in the Service of Society. Ed. by D. D. Sworder. (SCS Simulation Ser.: Vol. 1, No. 2). 1971. 36.00 (ISBN 0-686-36655-7). Soc Computer Sim.
Systems & Specifications see Steel Structures Painting Manual.
Systems & Specifications, Supplement to the 3rd Edition. 1985. 15.00 (ISBN 0-938477-03-X). SSPC.
Systems & Theories in Psychology. 4th ed. Melvin H. Marx & W. A. Cronan-Hillix. (McGraw-Hill Series in Psychology). 576p. 1987. text ed. 36.95 (ISBN 0-07-040680-4). McGraw.
Systems & Theories in Psychology. 3rd ed. Melvin H. Marx & William A. Hillix. (Illus.). 1979. text ed. 44.95 (ISBN 0-07-040679-0). McGraw.
Systems & Theories in Psychology: A Reader. 2nd ed. William A. Hillix & Melvin H. Marx. 1987. pap. 28.00 (ISBN 0-914525-07-7). Waterfront Bks.
Systems & Transforms with Applications in Optics. Athanasios Papoulis. LC 81-5995. 484p. 1981. Repr. of 1968 ed. lib. bdg. 35.00 (ISBN 0-89874-358-3). Krieger.
Systems Approach. C. West Churchman. 1969. pap. 3.95 (ISBN 0-385-28998-7, Delta). Dell.
Systems Approach. rev. & updated ed. C. West Churchman. (YA) (gr. 7-12). 1983. pap. 3.95 (ISBN 0-440-38407-9, LE). Dell.
Systems Approach for Development: Proceedings of the IFAC Conference, Cairo Egypt, Nov., 1977. IFAC Conference Staff. Ed. by M. A. Ghonaimy. (IFAC Proceedings). 658p. 1979. 180.00 (ISBN 0-08-022017-7). Pergamon.
Systems Approach in Vision: Proceedings of a Workshop Held in Amsterdam, the Netherlands, 27-29 August 1984. Ed. by D. Regan et al. (Illus.). 226p. 1986. 55.00 (ISBN 0-08-032033-3, Pub. by PPL). Pergamon.
Systems Approach to Air Pollution Control. Robert J. Bibbero & Irving G. Young. LC 74-8905. pap. 135.50 (ISBN 0-317-11255-4, 2055157). Bks Demand UMI.
Systems Approach to Appropriate Technology Transfer: Proceedings of the IFAC Symposium, Laxenburg, Austria, March, 1983. IFAC Symposium Staff & Alonso-Conchiero. (IFAC Proceedings Ser.). 206p. 1983. 67.00 (ISBN 0-08-029979-2). Pergamon.
Systems Approach to Architecture. A. Benjamin Handler. LC 79-100397. (Elsevier Architectural Science Ser.). pap. 48.00 (ISBN 0-317-10850-6, 2007768). Bks Demand UMI.
Systems Approach to Civil Engineering. Thomas K. Jewell. 576p. 1986. text ed. 48.95 scp (ISBN 0-06-043317-5, HarpC). Har-Row.
Systems Approach to Handicapped Children: Helping Children Grow. Lauren C. Bradway. (Illus.). 242p. 1984. 27.25x (ISBN 0-398-05025-2). C C Thomas.
Systems Approach to Hospital Medical Device Safety. Marvin D. Shepherd. (Illus.). 48p. 1983. pap. text ed. 30.00 (ISBN 0-910275-31-9). Assn Adv Med Instrs.
Systems Approach to Hydrology: Proceedings of the Bilateral U. S.-Japan Seminar in Hydrology, 1st, Honolulu, Jan. 11-17, 1971. U. S.-Japan Seminar Staff. Ed. by Vujica Yevjevich. LC 71-168496. 1971. 21.00 (ISBN 0-918334-02-0). WRP.
Systems Approach to Instructional Design. Ed. by Thomas T. Liao & David C. Miller. LC 77-86497. (Technology of Learning Systems Ser.: Vol. 1). (Illus.). 1978. pap. 10.00x (ISBN 0-89503-004-7). Baywood Pub.
Systems Approach to Library Program Development. Robert L. Goldberg. LC 76-18157. 189p. 1976. 16.50 (ISBN 0-8108-0944-3). Scarecrow.
Systems Approach to Recreation Programming. Frederick C. Patterson. LC 87-12682. (Recreation Ser.). (Illus.). 181p. (Orig.). 1987. pap. text ed. 17.00 (ISBN 0-942280-26-1); pap. 19.00. Pub Horizons.
Systems Approach to Small Group Interaction. 2nd ed. Stewart L. Tubbs. 400p. 1984. text ed. write for info (ISBN 0-394-34993-8, RanC). Random.
Systems Approach to Small Group Interaction. Stewart L. Tubbs. 400p. 1988. text ed. 21.00 (ISBN 0-394-36539-9, RanCC). Random.
Systems Approach to Social Impact Assessment: Two Alaskan Case Studies. Ed. by Lawrence A. Palinkas et al. (Special Study Ser.). 280p. 1985. softcover 35.50x (ISBN 0-8133-7031-0). Westview.
Systems Approach to Teaching & Learning Procedures: A Guide for Educators. 2nd, Rev. & Expanded ed. (Illus.). 203p. 1981. pap. 8.50 (ISBN 92-3-101826-4, U1168, UNESCO). UNIPUB.
Systems: Approaches, Theories, Applications. Ed. by William E. Hartnett. (Epistome Ser.: No. 3). 1977. lib. bdg. 42.00 (ISBN 90-277-0822-3, Pub. by Reidel Holland). Kluwer Academic.
Systems Architecture & Systems Design. Dimitris N. Chorafas. (Illus.). 400p. 1988. 44.95 (ISBN 0-07-010890-0). McGraw.
Systems Aspects of Chronic Mental Illness: A Special Issue of Community Mental Health Journal. Ed. by Michael R. Berren & Jose M. Dantiago. 96p. (Orig.). 1986. pap. 12.95 (ISBN 0-89885-353-2). Human Sci Pr.
Systems Auditability & Control Study, 3 Vols. Ed. by Tom S. Eason et al. Susan H. Russell & Brian Ruder. Incl. Data Processing Audit Practices Report. pap. text ed. 15.00 (ISBN 0-89413-052-8); Data Processing Control Practices Report. pap. text ed. 15.00 (ISBN 0-89413-051-X); Executive Report. pap. text ed. 15.00 (ISBN 0-89413-050-1). (Illus.). 1977. Set. pap. text ed. 37.50 (ISBN 0-686-86121-3). Inst Inter Aud.
Systems Building for Bridges. (Special Report). 76p. 1972. 2.40 (ISBN 0-309-02063-8). Transport Res Bd.
Systems Change Strategies in Educational Settings. Richard I. Arends & Jane H. Arends. Ed. by Garry R. Walz & Libby Benjamin. LC 77-22315. (New Vistas in Counseling Ser.: Vol. III). 120p. 1977. 26.95 (ISBN 0-87705-310-3). Human Sci Pr.
Systems: Concepts, Methodologies & Applications. Brian Wilson. LC 84-3703. 400p. 1984. 44.95 (ISBN 0-471-90443-0). Wiley.
Systems Consultation: A New Perspective for Family Therapy. Ed. by Lyman C. Wynne et al. LC 86-4778. (Guilford Family Therapy Ser.). 487p. 1986. text ed. 40.00 (ISBN 0-89862-068-6); pap. 24.95 (ISBN 0-89862-908-X). Guilford Pr.
Systems Contracting. Ralph Bolton. 1979. pap. 7.50 (ISBN 0-8144-2236-5). AMACOM.
Systems: Decomposition, Optimisation & Control. M. G. Singh & A. Titli. 1978. pap. text ed. 37.00 (ISBN 0-08-023238-8). Pergamon.
Systems Design for Data Protection. Michael Wood & Tony Elbra. 170p. 1984. pap. text ed. 21.55 (ISBN 0-471-81051-7). Wiley.
Systems Design for, with, & by the Users. Ed. by U. Briefs et al. 424p. 1983. 68.50 (ISBN 0-444-86613-2, I-174-83, North Holland). Elsevier.
Systems Design from Provably Correct Constructs. James Martin. (Illus.). 480p. 1985. text ed. 53.33 (ISBN 0-13-881483-X). P-H.
Systems Design under CICS Command & VSAM. Alex Varsegi. (Illus.). 272p. 1987. 28.95 (ISBN 0-8306-2843-6, 2843, TAB-TPR). TAB Bks.
Systems Design: VLSI for Digital Signal Processing, Vol. II. B. A. Bowen & William R. Brown. (Illus.). 432p. 1985. text ed. 40.00 (ISBN 0-317-20146-8). P-H.
Systems Design with Ada. Raymond Buhr. (Illus.). 288p. 1984. text ed. 44.00 (ISBN 0-13-881623-9). P-H.
Systems Design with Advanced Microprocessors. John Freer. 288p. 1987. pap. 26.95 (ISBN 0-672-22595-6). Sams.
Systems Development: A Practical Approach. William Amadio. 500p. 1989. text ed. price not set (ISBN 0-394-39232-9). Mitchell Pub.
Systems Development: Analysis, Design, & Implications. Alan L. Eliason. 1987. pap. text ed. 25.25 (ISBN 0-316-23256-4); tchr's. ed. avail.; wkbk. 8.75 (ISBN 0-316-23258-0). Scott F.
Systems Development Documentation: Forms Method. Steve J. Ayer & Frank S. Patrinostro. (Illus.). 430p. (Orig.). pap. cancelled (ISBN 0-9611694-0-0). Tech Comm Assoc.
Systems Development Methodology. 3rd ed. W. S. Turner et al. 600p. 1987. 122.00 (ISBN 0-444-70268-7). Elsevier.
Systems Development Without Pain: A User's Guide to Modeling Organizational Patterns. Paul T. Ward. LC 83-27368. (Illus.). 288p. 1984. pap. 27.95 (ISBN 0-917072-40-5, Yourdon). P-H.
Systems Documentation: Techniques of Persuasion in Large Organizations. Frank Whitehouse. 1973. 27.00 (ISBN 0-8464-0906-2). Beekman Pubs.
Systems Drafting. Fred A. Stitt. (Illus.). 1980. text ed. 44.50 (ISBN 0-07-061550-0). McGraw.
Systems Echantillonnes Nonlineaires-Exercises et Problemes: Exercises et Problemes. P. Vidal. (Theorie des Systemes Ser.). 124p. (Fr.). 1970. 55.00 (ISBN 0-677-50500-0). Gordon & Breach.
Systems Ecology: An Introduction. Howard T. Odum. LC 82-8650. (Environmental Science & Technology Ser.). 644p. 1983. 62.95 (ISBN 0-471-65277-6, Wiley-Interscience). Wiley.
Systems Ecology: An Introduction to Ecological Modelling. R. L. Kitching. LC 82-20032. (Illus.). 280p. 1984. text ed. 29.95 (ISBN 0-7022-1813-8). U of Queensland Pr.
Systems Economics: Concepts, Models & Multidisciplinary Perspectives. Ed. by Karl A. Fox & Don G. Miles. 252p. 1987. 24.50x (ISBN 0-8138-1738-2). Iowa St U Pr.
Systems Education: Perspectives, Programs, & Methods. Ed. by Bela H. Banathy. (Systems Inquiry Ser.). 177p. 1983. pap. 16.95x (ISBN 0-914105-02-7). Intersystems Pubns.
Systems Engineering. Richard R. Sylvester. Date not set. 49.95 (ISBN 0-932010-25-3). PhD Pub.
Systems Engineering & Analysis. B. Blanchard & Walter J. Fabrycky. 1981. 46.00 (ISBN 0-13-881631-X). P-H.
Systems Engineering Management Guide. (Illus.). 309p. (Orig.). 1986. pap. 17.00 (ISBN 0-318-22438-0, S/N 008-020-01099-5). USGPO.
Systems Engineering: Methodology & Applications. Ed. by Andrew P. Sage. LC 77-82294. 408p. 1977. 36.95 (ISBN 0-87942-097-9, PP00950). Inst Electrical.
Systems Engineering Methods. Harold Chestnut. LC 67-17336. (Wiley Ser. on Systems Engineering & Analysis). pap. 101.00 (ISBN 0-317-08335-X, 2051601). Bks Demand UMI.
Systems Engineering Models of Human Machine Interactions. W. B. Rouse. (Systems Science & Engineering Ser.: Vol. 6). 152p. 1980. 52.50 (ISBN 0-444-00366-5, North-Holland). Elsevier.
Systems Engineering of Education: Anasynthesis of the Education & Training Supersystem, No. 9. Leonard C. Silvern. 1970. pap. 2.00 (ISBN 0-87657-126-7). Ed & Training.
Systems Engineering of Education: Application of Systems Thinking to the Administration of Instruction, 2 vols, No. 2. Leonard C. Silvern. LC 75-27690. (Illus.). 178p. 1976. 25.00 (ISBN 0-87657-114-3). Ed & Training.
Systems Engineering of Education: General Systems Model for Effective Curriculums, No. 7. Leonard C. Silvern. (Illus.). 1971. incl. cassettes & charts 25.00 (ISBN 0-87657-120-8). Ed & Training.
Systems Engineering of Education: Logos Language for Flowchart Modeling, No. 10. Leonard C. Silvern. 1970. Set. 60.00 (ISBN 0-685-03525-5); wkbk., slides cassette (ISBN 0-87657-108-9). Ed & Training.
Systems Engineering of Education: Model for Producing a System, No. 11. Leonard C. Silvern. 1970. Set. 20.00 (ISBN 0-87657-109-7); slides & cassette incl. Ed & Training.
Systems Engineering of Education: Model for Producing Models, No. 13. Leonard C. Silvern. 1971. incl. slides & cassette 25.00 (ISBN 0-87657-111-9). Ed & Training.
Systems Engineering of Education: Preparing Occupational Instruction, No. 19. Leonard C. Silvern. LC 77-74289. 1977. text ed. 18.00 (ISBN 0-87657-115-1, ETC 3.1.3.219). Ed & Training.
Systems Engineering of Education: Principles of Computer-Assisted Instruction Systems, No. 6. Leonard C. Silvern. LC 70-76367. (Illus.). 1970. 15.00 (ISBN 0-87657-104-6). Ed & Training.
Systems Engineering of Education: Quantitative Concepts for Education Systems, No. 5. Leonard C. Silvern. LC 69-19555. (Illus.). iv, 144p. 1972. 16.00 (ISBN 0-87657-105-4). Ed & Training.
Systems Engineering of Education: Quantitative Models for Occupational Teacher Utilization of Government Published Information, No. 8. Leonard C. Silvern & Carl N. Brooks. LC 79-91932. (Illus.). 1969. 10.00 (ISBN 0-87657-101-1). Ed & Training.
Systems Engineering of Education: Roles of Feedback & Feedforward During Simulation, No. 18. Leonard C. Silvern. LC 74-79181. 1974. text ed. 6.00 (ISBN 0-87657-113-5). Ed & Training.
Systems Engineering of Education: Simulating a Real-Life Problem on the General System Model for Effective Curriculums, No. 15. Leonard C. Silvern. (Illus.). 1972. incl. wrkbk. 2 cassettes & 1 chart 30.00 (ISBN 0-87657-121-6). Ed & Training.
Systems Engineering of Education: Synthesis As a Process, No. 16. Leonard C. Silvern. LC 73-76218. 1973. incl. slides & cassette 40.00 (ISBN 0-87657-122-4). Ed & Training.
Systems Engineering of Education: Systems Analysis & Synthesis Applied to Occupational Instruction in Secondary Schools, No. 3. Leonard C. Silvern. LC 67-31679. (Illus.). 99p. 1967. text ed. 10.00 (ISBN 0-87657-123-2). Ed & Training.
Systems Engineering of Education: Systems Analysis & Synthesis Applied Quantitatively to Create an Instructional System, No. 4. Leonard C. Silvern. LC 65-27696. (Illus.). 120p. 1969. text ed. 18.00 (ISBN 0-87657-124-0). Ed & Training.
Systems Engineering of Education: System Conceptualizations, No. 17. Leonard C. Silvern. 1973. 80.00, incl. cassette & slides (ISBN 0-87657-125-9). Ed & Training.
Systems Engineering of Education: Systems Engineering Applied to Training, No. 20. Leonard C. Silvern. (Illus.). Date not set. 25.00 (ISBN 0-87657-127-5). Ed & Training.
Systems Engineering of Education: Systems Techniques for Pretesting Mediated Instructional Materials, No. 14. Jay M. Sedlik. LC 79-162916. (Illus.). 1971. text ed. 18.00 (ISBN 0-87657-112-7). Ed & Training.
Systems Engineering of Education: Systems Using Feedback, No. 12. Leonard C. Silvern. 1971. incl. slides workbk & cassette 45.00 (ISBN 0-87657-110-0). Ed & Training.
Systems Engineering of Education: The Evolution of Systems Thinking in Education, No. 1. 3rd ed. Leonard C. Silvern. LC 73-150823. (Illus.). vi, 128p. 1975. 20.00 (ISBN 0-87657-107-0). Ed & Training.
Systems Engineering Tools. Harold Chestnut. LC 65-19484. (Wiley Series on Systems Engineering & Analysis). (Illus.). pap. 160.00 (ISBN 0-317-08334-1, 2055158). Bks Demand UMI.
Systems Far from Equilibrium: Sitges Conference. Ed. by L. Garrido. (Lecture Notes in Physics Ser.: Vol. 132). 403p. 1980. pap. 32.00 (ISBN 0-387-10251-5). Springer Verlag.
Systems for Cytogenetic Analysis in Vicia faba L. Ed. by G. P. Chapman & S. A. Tarawall. (Advances in Agricultural Biotechnology). 1984. lib. bdg. 38.00 (ISBN 90-247-3089-9, Pub. by Martinus Nijhoff Netherlands). Kluwer Academic.
Systems Horti-Culturae: The Art of Gardening. John Worlidge. Ed. by John D. Hunt. LC 79-57001. (English Landscape Garden Ser.). 325p. 1982. lib. bdg. 53.00 (ISBN 0-8240-0153-2). Garland Pub.
Systems Implementation. Dennis Guster. 168p. 1986. pap. text ed. 13.95 (ISBN 0-8403-4054-0). Kendall-Hunt.
Systems in Action. R. J. Allen & Bennett P. Lientz. 1978. pap. text ed. write for info. (ISBN 0-673-16150-1). Scott F.
Systems in Organizations: Bugs & Features. M. Lynne Markus. LC 83-22121. 256p. 1984. text ed. 28.00x (ISBN 0-88730-202-5). Ballinger Pub.
Systems in Stochastic Equilibrium. Peter Whittle. LC 85-17923. (Probability & Mathematical Statistics Ser.). 460p. 1986. 84.95 (ISBN 0-471-90887-8). Wiley.
Systems Inquiring - Applications, Theory, Philosophy & Methodology: Proceedings of the Society for General Systems Research, 1985, Vols. 1 & 2. Ed. by Bela H. Banathy. 1200p. 1985. Set. pap. text ed. 86.00x (ISBN 0-914105-36-1). Intersystems Pubns.
Systems Laboratory for Information Management. James F. Courtney, Jr. & Ronald Jensen. 1981. pap. 12.95x (ISBN 0-256-02574-6). Business Pubns.
Systems Life Cycle Guide: A Systems Development Methodology. Raymond T. Clarke et al. (Illus.). 240p. 1987. text ed. 80.00 (ISBN 0-13-881574-7). P-H.
Systems Management. John S. Baumgartner. LC 79-11634. pap. 130.30 (2026799). Bks Demand UMI.
Systems Management & Change. Martin Carter & Munday Mayblin. 1984. pap. text ed. 7.00 (ISBN 0-06-318272-6). Har-Row.

Systems Management under UNIX. Nigel Backhurst & Paul Davies. 232p. 1987. text ed. 25.95 (ISBN 1-85058-049-9, Pub. by Sigma Pr UK). Bk Clearing Hse.

Systems Methodologies, Isomorphies & Applications: Proceedings of the Society for General Systems Research, 1984, Vols. 1 & 2. Ed. by August W. Smith. 660p. 1984. Set. pap. text ed. 66.00x (ISBN 0-914105-29-9). Intersystems Pubns.

Systems Methodology in Social Science Research: Recent Developments. Roger Cavallo. (Frontiers in Systems Research Ser.). 1982. lib. bdg. 35.50 (ISBN 0-89838-044-8, Pub. by Kluwer-Nijhoff (Netherlands)). Kluwer Academic.

Systems Modeling & Computer Simulation. Kheir. (Electrical Engineering Ser.). 736p. 1988. 99.75 (ISBN 0-8247-7812-X). Dekker.

Systems, Modeling, & Decision Making. John P. Novosad. 280p. 1981. pap. text ed. 23.95 (ISBN 0-8403-2676-9). Kendall-Hunt.

Systems Modeling & Response: Theoretical & Experimental Approaches. Ernest O. Doebelin. LC 79-27609. 587p. 1980. text ed. write for info. (ISBN 0-471-03211-5). Wiley.

Systems Modelling & Optimisation. P. Nash. (IEE Control Engineering Ser.: No. 16). 224p. 1981. casebound 54.00 (ISBN 0-906048-63-X, CE016). Inst Elect Eng.

Systems Models for Counselor Supervision. T. Antoinette Ryan. (ACES Monograph). 52p. 1977. pap. 5.75 (ISBN 0-911547-75-4, 72175W34). Am Assn Coun Dev.

Systems Network Architecture: A Tutorial. Anton Meijer. 223p. 1988. 34.95 (ISBN 0-470-21015-X). Wiley.

Systems, Networks & Computation: Basic Concepts. Michael Dertouzos et al. LC 79-4556. 528p. 1979. Repr. of 1972 ed. lib. bdg. 35.50 (ISBN 0-88275-916-7). Krieger.

Systems of Cities & Facility Location. Pierre Hansen et al. (Fundamentals of Pure & Applied Economics Ser.: Vol. 22). 132p. 1987. pap. text ed. 32.00 (ISBN 3-7186-0403-5). Harwood Academic.

Systems of Cities: Readings on Structure Growth & Policy. Ed. by Larry S. Bourne & James W. Simmons. (Illus.). 1978. pap. text ed. 16.95x (ISBN 0-19-502264-5). Oxford U Pr.

Systems of Discourse: Structures & Semiotics in the Social Sciences. George V. Zito. LC 83-26668. (Contributions in Sociology Ser.: No. 51). (Illus.). xiv, 158p. 1984. lib. bdg. 35.00 (ISBN 0-313-24446-4, ZSD/). Greenwood.

Systems of Family Therapy: An Adlerian Integration. Robert Sherman & Don Dinkmeyer. LC 86-29897. 300p. 1987. 35.00 (ISBN 0-87630-457-9). Brunner-Mazel.

Systems of Formal Logic. I. H. Hackstaff. 354p. 1966. lib. bdg. 42.00 (ISBN 90-277-0077-X, Pub. by Reidel Holland). Kluwer Academic.

Systems of Formal Logic. L. H. Hackstaff. 366p. 1967. 82.00 (ISBN 0-677-01280-2). Gordon & Breach.

Systems of Frequency Curves. William Elderton & Norman L. Johnson. LC 69-10571. pap. 56.00 (ISBN 0-317-26324-2, 2024451). Bks Demand UMI.

Systems of Higher Education: Australia. Bruce Williams. (Publication of the International Council for Educational Development). 103p. 1978. pap. 4.00 (ISBN 0-89192-199-0). Interbk Inc.

Systems of Higher Education: Canada. rev. ed. Edward Sheffield et al. 219p. 1982. pap. 8.00 (ISBN 0-89192-204-0, Pub. by ICED). Interbk Inc.

Systems of Higher Education: France. Alain Bienayme. 144p. 1978. pap. 7.00 (ISBN 0-89192-205-9, Pub. by ICED). Interbk Inc.

Systems of Higher Education: Iran. M. Reza Vaghefi et al. 43p. 1978. pap. 3.50 (ISBN 0-89192-207-5, Pub. by ICED). Interbk Inc.

Systems of Higher Education: Japan. Katsuya Narita. (Systems of Higher Education Ser.). 154p. (Orig.). 1978. pap. text ed. 5.50 (ISBN 0-89192-202-4, Pub. by ICED). Interbk Inc.

Systems of Higher Education: Mexico. Alfonso R. Guerra. (Systems of Higher Education). 98p. 1978. pap. 5.00 (ISBN 0-89192-203-2, Pub. by ICED). Interbk Inc.

Systems of Higher Education: United Kingdom. Tony Becher et al. 1978. pap. 6.00 (ISBN 0-89192-200-8, Pub. by ICED). Interbk Inc.

Systems of Individualized Education. Ed. by Harriet Talmage. LC 74-24478. 200p. 1975. 23.00x (ISBN 0-8211-1904-4); text ed. 20.75x 10 or more copies. McCutchan.

Systems of Land Tenure in Various Countries. facs. new ed. Ed. by John W. Probyn. LC 75-153000. (Select Bibliographies Reprint Ser.). Repr. of 1881 ed. 27.50 (ISBN 0-8369-5752-0). Ayer Co Pubs.

Systems of Linear Inequalities. A. S. Solodovnikov. 123p. 1979. pap. 3.95 (ISBN 0-8285-1515-8, Pub. by Mir Pubs USSR). Imported Pubns.

Systems of Linear Inequalities. A. S. Solodovnikov. Tr. by Lawrence M. Glasser & Thomas P. Branson. LC 79-16106. (Popular Lectures in Mathematics Ser.). 1980. pap. text ed. 6.00x (ISBN 0-226-76786-8). U of Chicago Pr.

Systems of M. R. Shurnas. David Nemec. 152p. (Orig.). 1984. pap. 6.95 (ISBN 0-86676-011-3). Riverrun NY.

Systems of Microdifferential Equations. Masaki Kashiwara. Tr. by Teresa M. Fernandes. (Progress in Mathematics Ser.). 200p. 1983. text ed. 22.50 (ISBN 0-8176-3138-0). Birkhauser.

Systems of Minerology, 3 vols. 7th ed. James D. Dana et al. Incl. Vol. 1. Elements of Mineralogy: Elements, Sulfides, Sulfosalts, Oxides. 7th ed. James D. Dana et al. 834p. 1944. 95.00 (ISBN 0-471-19239-2); Vol. 2. System of Mineralogy: Halides, Nitrates, Borates, Carbonates, Sulfates, Phosphates, Arsenates, Tungstates, Molybdate, etc. James D. Dana et al. 1951. 94.95 (ISBN 0-471-19272-4); Vol. 3. System of Mineralogy: Silica Minerals. 7th ed. James D. Dana et al. 334p. 1962. 60.00 (ISBN 0-471-19287-2). Pub. by Wiley-Interscience). Wiley.

Systems of Modern Psychology: A Critical Approach. Daniel N. Robinson. LC 79-15778. 333p. 1979. pap. 16.00x (ISBN 0-231-04309-0). Columbia U Pr.

Systems of Nonlinear Partial Differential Equations. Ed. by J. M. Ball. 1983. lib. bdg. 65.00 (ISBN 90-277-1629-3, Pub. by Reidel Holland). Kluwer Academic.

Systems of Order & Inquiry in Later Eighteenth-Century Fiction. Eric Rothstein. LC 74-16716. 284p. 1975. 33.00x (ISBN 0-520-02862-7). U of Cal Pr.

Systems of Organization: Management of the Human Resource. David Bowers. LC 75-31052. 1977. pap. text ed. 10.95x (ISBN 0-472-08173-X). U of Mich Pr.

Systems of Partial Differential Equations & Lie Pseudogroups. J. Pommaret. (Mathematics & Its Applications Ser.). 426p. 1978. 90.00 (ISBN 0-677-00270-X). Gordon & Breach.

Systems of Political Control & Bureaucracy in Human Societies: American Ethnological Society Proceedings, 1958. Ed. by Verne F. Ray. LC 84-45545. 1988. pap. 18.50 (ISBN 0-404-62652-1). AMS Pr.

Systems of Positive Polity, 4 vols. August Comte. LC 66-20689. 1973. Repr. of 1875 ed. Set. 115.00 (ISBN 0-8337-0636-5). B Franklin.

Systems of Profit Measure. Bailie. pap. 21.95 (ISBN 0-85258-234-X). Van Nos Reinhold.

Systems of Prosodic & Paralinguistic Features in English. David Crystal & Randolph Quirk. (Janua Linguarum, Ser. Minor: No. 39). (Orig.). 1964. pap. text ed. 14.00x (ISBN 90-2790-574-6). Mouton.

Systems of Psychotherapy: A Transtheoretical Analysis. 2nd ed. James O. Prochaska. 1984. 37.00x (ISBN 0-256-03049-9). Dorsey.

Systems of Psychotherapy: An Empirical Analysis of Theoretical Models. Kenneth U. Gutsch et al. (Illus.). 340p. 1984. 32.50x (ISBN 0-398-04922-X). C C Thomas.

Systems of Quasilinear Equations & Their Applications to Gas Dynamics. B. L. Rozdestvenskii & N. N. Janenko. LC 82-24488. (Translations of Mathematical Monographs: Vol. 55). 163.00 (ISBN 0-8218-4509-8). Am Math.

Systems of Singular Integral Equations. N. P. Vekua. 216p. 1967. 75.00 (ISBN 0-677-61340-7). Gordon & Breach.

Systems of Society: An Introduction to Social Science. 4th ed. Manual G. Mendoza & Vince Napoli. LC 85-81121. 752p. 1986. text ed. 23.00 (ISBN 0-669-07580-9); instr's guide 2.00 (ISBN 0-669-07582-5); study guide 8.00 (ISBN 0-669-07581-7); test item file 2.00 (ISBN 0-669-15084-3); Archive test prog. Apple 150.00 (ISBN 0-669-14596-3). Heath.

Systems of the Hellenistic Age: A History of Ancient Philosophy, Vol. III. Giovanni Reale. Tr. by John R. Catan. LC 79-13867. 499p. 1985. 44.50x (ISBN 0-88706-027-7); pap. 14.95x (ISBN 0-88706-008-0). State U NY Pr.

Systems of the Horse. Jeremy H. Brown & Vincent Powell-Smith. LC 87-7963. (Illus.). 144p. 1987. 14.95 (ISBN 0-87605-866-7). Howell Bk.

Systems of the Human Body. Carla Overbeck. (Science Ser.). 24p. (gr. 5 up). 1979. wkbk. 5.00 (ISBN 0-8209-0150-4, S-12). ESP.

Systems of Therapy in Cerebral Palsy. Harriet E. Gillette. (Illus.). 96p. 1974. 15.25x (ISBN 0-398-00680-6). C C Thomas.

Systems of Units, National & International Aspects: A Symposium Organized by Section M on Engineering. American Association for the Advancement of Science, Section on Engineering Staff. Ed. by Carl F. Kayan. LC 59-15335. (American Association for the Advancement of Science Publication Ser.: No. 57). pap. 76.80 (ISBN 0-317-27548-8, 2015170). Bks Demand UMI.

Systems on Silicon. Ed. by P. B. Denyer et al. (Digital Electronics, Computing & Software Engineering Ser.). 96p. 1984. pap. 23.00 for info. (ISBN 0-86341-020-0, CM003). Inst Elect Eng.

Systems One Thousand & Thirty-Two Reference Booklet. Karen Molloy. 90p. 1987. spiral bdg. 12.00 (ISBN 0-317-61662-5). CompuServe Data Tech.

Systems One Thousand & Thirty Two Reference Booklet. rev. ed. Karen Molloy. 91p. 1987. 12.00 (ISBN 0-317-62431-8). CompuServe Data Tech.

Systems One Thousand & Twenty-Two Primer. Ken Jackson. 142p. 1982. spiral 25.00 (ISBN 0-317-61663-3). CompuServe Data Tech.

Systems Programmer. Jack Rudman. (Career Examination Ser.: C-2187). 1988. pap. 16.00 (ISBN 0-8373-2187-5). Natl Learning.

Systems Programming. John J. Donovan. LC 79-172263. (Computer Science Ser). (Illus.). 480p. 1972. text ed. 52.95 (ISBN 0-07-017603-5). McGraw.

Systems Programming for Small Computers. Daniel H. Marcellus. 1983. text ed. 36.00 (ISBN 0-13-881664-6); pap. text ed. 21.95 (ISBN 0-13-881656-5). P-H.

Systems Programming in Turbo C. Michael J. Young. 503p. (Orig.). 1988. pap. 24.95. Sybex.

Systems Psychology in the Schools. Jeanne M. Plas. (General Psychology Ser.: No. 141). 19209p. 1986. 24.50 (ISBN 0-08-033144-0, J115, PBI); pap. 12.95 (ISBN 0-08-033143-2, PBI). Pergamon.

Systems Quality--Reliability Handbook Nineteen Eighty-Seven. Intel Staff. 160p. 1987. pap. 20.00 (ISBN 1-55512-053-9, 231762). Intel Corp.

Systems Quality-Reliability Handbook, 1988. Intel Staff. 160p. (Orig.). 1988. pap. 20.00 (ISBN 1-55512-027-X, 231762). Intel Corp.

Systems Reliability & Risk Analysis. 2nd, rev. ed. E. G. Frankel. 1988. lib. bdg. 99.00 (ISBN 90-247-3665-X, Pub. by Graham & Trotman UK). Kluwer Academic.

Systems Reliability & Risk Analysis. Ernst G. Frankel. 1984. lib. bdg. 40.00 (ISBN 90-247-2895-9, Pub. by Martinus Nijhoff Netherlands). Kluwer Academic.

Systems Reliability, Maintainability & Management. Balhir Dhillon. (Illus.). 376p. 1983. text ed. 32.50 (ISBN 0-89433-195-7). Petrocelli.

Systems Research II: Methodological Problems. Ed. by J. M. Gvishiani. (Advances in Systems Research Ser.). (Illus.). 280p. 1985. 52.00 (ISBN 0-08-030556-3, Pub. by PPL). Pergamon.

Systems Research: Methodological Problems. Ed. by J. M. Gvishiani. 380p. 1983. 89.00 (ISBN 0-08-030000-6). Pergamon.

Systems Safety: Technology & Application. Sol Malasky. 300p. 1982. lib. bdg. 41.00 (ISBN 0-8240-7280-4). Garland Pub.

Systems Science. Ed. by Collet's Holdings, Ltd. Staff. 140p. 1983. 40.00x (ISBN 0-317-46746-8, Pub. by Collets (UK)). State Mutual Bk.

Systems Science & Engineering. Ching Weimin. (IAPS Ser.). 1000p. 1988. 200.00 (ISBN 0-08-036387-3); 150.00 (ISBN 0-08-036388-1). Pergamon.

Systems Science & Modeling in Insect Pest Management. Shoemaker. (Environmental Science & Technology Ser.). 1988. write for info. (ISBN 0-471-05329-5). Wiley.

Systems Science & World Order: Selected Studies. E. Laszlo. (Systems Science & World Order Library). 278p. 1983. text ed. 53.00 (ISBN 0-08-028924-X). Pergamon.

Systems Science in Health Care. Ed. by A. M. Coblentz & J. R. Walter. LC 77-21046. 1978. text ed. 35.00 (ISBN 0-89433-067-5). Petrocelli.

Systems Science in Health Care. Ed. by A. M. Coblentz & J. R. Walter. 452p. 1977. cancelled (ISBN 0-85066-118-8). Taylor & Francis.

Systems Science in Health Care: Proceedings of the International Conference on Systems in Health Care, July 1980, Montreal, Quebec, Canada. C. Tilquin. LC 81-94784. 1888p. 1981. 370.00 (ISBN 0-08-025370-9, PBL). Pergamon.

Systems Sciences & Modelling. Ed. by A. Ruberti. (Trends in Scientific Research Ser.: No. 1). 159p. 1985. pap. 25.50 (ISBN 92-3-102138-9, U1408 5071, UNESCO). UNIPUB.

Systems Selling: A Marketing Guide for Wholesaler-Distributors. William Hannaford. 1988. 39.00. Natl Assn Wholesale Dists.

Systems Selling Strategies. Mack Hanan & James Cribbin. LC 77-25034. pap. 51.30 (ISBN 0-317-10206-0, 2022620). Bks Demand UMI.

Systems Selling Strategies: How to Justify Premium Prices for Commodity Products. Mack Hanan et al. 1978. 14.95 (ISBN 0-8144-5460-7). AMACOM.

Systems Selling to Industrial Markets. William J. Hannaford. 112p. 30.00 (ISBN 0-318-15155-3); NAW commodity line association members 25.00 (ISBN 0-318-15156-1); NAW members 22.00 (ISBN 0-318-15157-X). Natl Assn Wholesale Dists.

Systems Simulation in Agriculture. J. B. Dent & M. J. Blackie. (Illus.). x, 180p. 1979. 45.00 (ISBN 0-85334-827-8, Pub. by Elsevier Applied Sci England). Elsevier.

Systems Simulation: The Art & Science. Robert E. Shannon. (Illus.). 368p. 1975. ref. ed. 46.00 (ISBN 0-13-881839-8). P-H.

Systems Software Tools. Ted J. Biggerstaff. (Illus.). 320p. 1986. text ed. 32.00 (ISBN 0-13-821869-2). P-H.

Systems Software Tools, Software Builder's Kit Version 1.0. rev. ed. Ted J. Biggerstaff. 48p. 1987. write for info. P-H.

Systems Specifications for a Micro-or-Mini-Computer Based Accountant's Client Write-Up Systems. Gordon E. Louvau & Arnold J. Carvajal. (Accounting Ser.). (Illus.). 135p. 1982. 32.50 (Lifetime Learn). Van Nos Reinhold.

Systems, States, Diplomacy & Rules. John W. Burton. 256p. 1968. 34.50 (ISBN 0-521-07316-2). Cambridge U Pr.

Systems That Learn: Introduction to Learning Theory for Cognitive & Computer Scientist. Daniel N. Osherson et al. (MIT Press Series in Learning Development & Conceptual Change). 232p. 1986. text ed. 27.50x (ISBN 0-262-15030-1, Pub by Bradford). MIT Pr.

Systems That Work: Government Financial Manuals, Analyses & Operating Procedures. Municipal Finance Officers Association Staff & Girard Miller. LC 83-62575. (Illus.). ix, 273p. Date not set. price not set. Municipal.

Systems Theory & Family Therapy: A Primer. Raphael J. Becvar & Dorothy S. Becvar. LC 81-43721. 104p. (Orig.). 1982. PLB 26.00 (ISBN 0-8191-2443-5); pap. text ed. 9.25 (ISBN 0-8191-2444-3). U Pr of Amer.

Systems Theory & Scientific Philosophy. John Bryant. Date not set. price not set (ISBN 0-9617444-3-X). Socratic Pr.

Systems Theory for Organization Development. Ed. by Thomas G. Cummings. LC 79-42906. (Wiley Series on Individuals, Groups, & Organizations). pap. 95.00 (2026691). Bks Demand UMI.

Systems Theory in Immunology. Ed. by C. Bruni. (Lecture Notes in Biomathematics: Vol. 32). 273p. 1979. pap. 19.00 (ISBN 0-387-09728-7). Springer-Verlag.

Systems Theory Research. Systems Theory Research Staff. Vol. 18. pap. 81.50 (ISBN 0-317-28435-5, 2020694); Vol. 19. pap. 81.80 (ISBN 0-317-28436-3); Vol. 20. pap. 69.50 (ISBN 0-317-28437-1); Vol. 21. pap. 66.30 (ISBN 0-317-28438-X); Vol. 22. pap. 75.30 (ISBN 0-317-28439-8); Vol. 23. pap. 80.30 (ISBN 0-317-28440-1). Bks Demand UMI.

Systems Thinking. Nicolas Kramer & Jacob De Smit. 1977. 15.50 (ISBN 90-207-0587-3, Martinus Nijhoff Pubs). Kluwer Academic.

Systems Thinking in Library & Information Management. David Smith. 144p. 1980. 15.95 (ISBN 0-85157-333-9, B333-9, Pub. by C Bingley Ltd London). ALA.

Systems Thinking, Systems Practice. P. B. Checkland. LC 80-41381. 330p. 1981. 53.95 (ISBN 0-471-27911-0, Pub. by Wiley-Interscience). Wiley.

Systems Tools for Project Planning. Peter Delp. LC 77-7588. 1976. pap. text ed. 15.00 (ISBN 0-89249-021-7). Intl Development.

Systems Transfer Characteristics of Firms in Spain: A Comparative Management Study of American & Spanish Business Organizations. Bernard D. Estafen. (International Business Research Institute Ser: No. 5). 160p. 1973. 5.00 (ISBN 0-87925-005-4). Ind U Busn Res.

Systems Under Indirect Observation: Casualty Structure Prediction, 2 vols. K. G. Joreskog & H. Wold. (Contributions to Economic Analysis Ser.: Vol. 139). 636p. 1982. Set. 155.25 (ISBN 0-444-86301-X, I-114-82, North-Holland). Elsevier.

Systems Understanding Aid for Auditing. Rev. ed. Alvin A. Arens & D. Dewey Ward. 128p. 1983. pap. text ed. 12.95x (ISBN 0-912503-00-9). Systems Pubns.

Systems Understanding Aid for Financial Accounting. Donald E. Kieso et al. 128p. (Orig.). 1983. pap. text ed. 12.95x (ISBN 0-912503-01-7). Systems Pubns.

Systems Understanding Aid: Microcomputer Version. Alvin A. Arens & D. Dewey Ward. 160p. (Orig.). 1985. pap. text ed. 14.95x (ISBN 0-912503-05-X); diskette incl. Systems Pubns.

Systems View of Education: A Model for Change. John A. Scileppi. 246p. (Orig.). 1984. lib. bdg. 26.25 (ISBN 0-8191-3853-3); pap. text ed. 13.00 (ISBN 0-8191-3854-1). U Pr of Amer.

Systems View of Education: A Model for Change. rev. ed. John A. Scileppi. 236p. 1988. lib. bdg. 23.25 (ISBN 0-8191-6763-0); pap. text ed. 12.75 (ISBN 0-8191-6764-9). U Pr of Amer.

Systems View of Man: Collected Essays. Ludwig Von Bertalanffy. Ed. by Paul LaViolette. 190p. 1981. lib. bdg. 34.00x (ISBN 0-86531-084-X); pap. 17.95x (ISBN 0-86531-094-7). Westview.

Systems View of Planning: Towards a Theory of the Urban & Regional Planning Process. 2nd ed. George Chadwick. (Urban & Regional Planning Ser.: Vol. 2). (Illus.). 1978. pap. text ed. 24.00 (ISBN 0-08-020625-5). Pergamon.

Systems View of the World. Ervin Laszlo. LC 71-188357. 1972. 7.95 (ISBN 0-8076-0637-5); pap. 5.95 (ISBN 0-8076-0636-7). Braziller.

Systems with Small Dissipation. V. B. Braginsky et al. Tr. by Erast Gliner. LC 85-20876. (Illus.). xii, 148p. 1986. lib. bdg. 28.00x (ISBN 0-226-07072-7); pap. 12.00x (ISBN 0-226-07073-5). U of Chicago Pr.

Systemtik fur Bibliotheken (SfB) Sonderlieferung Musikalien. Ed. by Bibliotekare an Offentlichen Bibliotheken Staff. 29p. (Ger.). 1985. lib. bdg. 16.00 (ISBN 3-598-20574-0). K G Saur.

Systolic Arrays: Proceedings of the International Workshop University of Oxford, July 1986. Ed. by W. R. Moore et al. 336p. 1987. 61.00x (ISBN 0-85274-826-4, Pub. by A Hilger). Taylor & Francis.

Systolic Signal Processing Systems. Swartzlander. (Electrical Engineering, & Electronics Ser.). 416p. 1987. 75.00 (ISBN 0-8247-7717-4). Dekker.

Systolic Time Intervals. Ed. by W. List et al. (International Boehringer Mannheim Symposia). (Illus.). 300p. 1980. pap. 36.00 (ISBN 0-387-09871-2). Springer-Verlag.

Syzgies. E. G. Evans & P. Griffith. (London Mathematical Society Lecture Note Ser.: No. 106). 160p. 1985. pap. 15.95 (ISBN 0-521-31411-9). Cambridge U Pr.

Szabo Dezso Es a Magyar Miniszterelnokok. Ed. by Gyula Gombos. (Hungarian.). 1975. 6.00 (ISBN 0-911050-43-4). Occidental.

Szajrol Szajra. Ferenc Somogyi. (Reference Books of Hungarian Self Knowledge). (Illus.). 1978. 12.00 (ISBN 0-918570-02-6). Karpat.

Szamuzott a Szabadsag Igajaban. Istvan Eszterhas. 1978. perfect bdg. 10.00 (ISBN 0-912404-10-8). Alpha Pubns.

Szechwan & Northern Cooking: From Hot to Cold. Rhoda Yee. LC 82-50788. (Illus.). 102p. 1983. pap. 5.95 (ISBN 0-394-71433-4, Dist. by Random). Taylor & Ng.

Szechwan & the Chinese Republic: Provincial Militarism & Central Power, 1911-1938. Robert A. Kapp. LC 73-77155. (Yale Historical Publications Miscellany Ser.: No. 96). (Illus.). pap. 52.00 (ISBN 0-317-11081-0, 2022008). Bks Demand UMI.

Szechwan Pottery. Cheng Te-K'un. 16p. 1948. 30.00x (ISBN 0-317-43850-6, Pub. by Han-Shan Tang Ltd). State Mutual Bk.

Szeletian: And the Transition from Middle to Upper Paleolithic in Central Europe. P. Allsworth-Jones. 448p. 105.00 (ISBN 0-19-813401-0). Oxford U Pr.

Szerelmes Foldrajz. 2nd ed. Zoltan Szabo. LC 63-14466. 198p. (Hungarian). 1964. 6.00 (ISBN 0-911050-20-5). Occidental.

Szigeti on the Violin. Joseph Szigeti. LC 78-6800. 1979. pap. 5.00 (ISBN 0-486-23763-X). Dover.

Szilagyi. Bibo Tanulmanyok. 104p. 1985. Framo Pub.

Szivarvany, No. 22. 160p. 1987. pap. 10.00 (ISBN 0-936398-44-2). Framo Pub.

Szivarvany, No. 23. 160p. 1987. pap. 10.00 (ISBN 0-936398-45-0). Framo Pub.

Szivarvany Konyvek. (No. 9). cancelled. Framo Pub.

Szivarvany Konyvek: Ferdinandy Avadak Utjan, No. 11. 128p. 1986. Framo Pub.

Szombathelyi Ferenc Visszaemlekezesei. Ed. by Peter Gosztonyi. 64p. 1980. 6.00 (ISBN 0-911050-50-7). Occidental.

Szuletesnap korul: Vazlat egy letunt korszakrol (1950-1953)-Krudy Gyula Szellemenek. Rozsa Ignacz. x, 111p. 1983. 15.00x (ISBN 0-933104-15-4). Jupiter Pr.

Szumirok Es Magyarok (Sumerians & Magyars) see Studia Sumiro-Hungarica.

Szymanowski. Teresa Chylinska. Tr. by A. T. Jordan. (Library of Polish Studies: Vol. 1). (Illus.). 1973. text ed. 5.00 (ISBN 0-917004-04-3). Kosciuszko.

Szymborska, Hirshfield, Bursk, Bouvard, Gustafsson. (Poetry Ser.: Vol. XXIII). 344p. 1983. pap. 20.00. Quarterly Rev.

T

T. A. T., C. A. T., & S. A. T. in Clinical Use. 4th ed. Leopold Bellak. 408p. 1986. 36.50 (ISBN 0-8089-1815-X, 790516). Grune.

T A Today: A New Introduction to Transactional Analysis. Ian Stewart & Vann Joines. 342p. 1987. pap. text ed. 12.95 (Pub. by Lifespace UK). V Joines.

T. A. Willard: Wizard of the Storage Battery. Edna R. Webster. 1976. 8.95 (ISBN 0-686-21901-5); pap. 5.00 (ISBN 0-686-21902-3). Wilmar Pubs.

T & B Lymphocytes: Proceedings of the ICN-UCLA Symposia on Molecular & Cellular Biology, 1979, Vol. XVI. ICN-UCLA Symposia Staff. Ed. by Fritz H. Bach et al. LC 79-26438. (Recognition & Function Ser.). 1979. 83.00 (ISBN 0-12-069850-1). Acad Pr.

T & V Approach to Agricultural Extension Services. 171p. 1986. pap. text ed. 14.75 (ISBN 92-833-2031-X, APO182, APO). UNIPUB.

T-Ball Is Our Game. Leila B. Gemme. LC 77-17173. (Sport Primer Ser.). (Illus.). 32p. (gr. k-3). 1978. PLB 12.60 (ISBN 0-516-03630-0). Childrens.

T-Boat Handbook. Richard A. Block. (Illus.). 172p. (Orig.). 1986. pap. text ed. 18.00 (ISBN 0-934114-76-5, BK-115). Marine Educ.

T-Boy & the Trial for Life: Tim Edler's Tales from the Atchafalaya Ser. Timothy J. Edler. (Illus.). 36p. (gr. k-8). 1978. pap. 6.00 (ISBN 0-931108-02-0). Little Cajun Bks.

T-Boy in Mossland. Timothy J. Edler. (Tim Edler's Tales from the Atchafalaya Ser.). (Illus.). 48p. (gr. k-8). 1978. pap. 6.00 (ISBN 0-931108-03-9). Little Cajun Bks.

T-Boy the Little Cajun. Timothy J. Edler. (Tim Edler's Tales from the Atchafalaya Ser.). (Illus.). 36p. (gr. k-8). 1978. pap. 6.00 (ISBN 0-931108-01-2). Little Cajun Bks.

T-Cell. Feldman. (Cell Biology Ser.). 1986. write for info. (ISBN 0-471-89169-X). Wiley.

T Cell Clones: Research Monographs in Immunology, Vol. 8. Ed. by H. Von Boehmer et al. 340p. 1985. 144.25 (ISBN 0-444-80600-8). Elsevier.

T Cell Hybridomas. M. J. Taussig. 296p. 1984. 110.00 (ISBN 0-8493-5202-9). CRC Pr.

T Cell Hybridomas: A Workshop at the Basle Institute for Immunology. Ed. by H. V. Boehmer et al. (Current Topics in Microbiology & Immunology Ser.: Vol. 100). 262p. 1982. 38.00 (ISBN 0-387-11535-8). Springer-Verlag.

T-Cell Receptor. Ed. by Mark M. Davis & John Kappler. LC 87-29301. (UCLA Symposia on Molecular & Cellular Biology, New Ser.: Vol. 73). 432p. 1987. 76.00 (ISBN 0-8451-2672-5, 2672). A R Liss.

T-Cell Receptor. Ed. by Mark M. Davis & John Kappler. 1988. write for info. (ISBN 0-471-60999-4). Wiley.

T-Cell Receptors. Ed. by T. W. Mak. LC 87-38495. (Illus.). 254p. 1988. 42.50x (ISBN 0-306-42708-7, Plenum Pr). Plenum Pub.

T Directorate. Tuck. 1988. pap. 3.95 (ISBN 0-312-90835-0). St Martin.

T E A T: The Saga of Isaiah Dorman, American Frontiersman, Interpreter for General Custer & Friend to Chief Sitting Bull. Theodore A. Gould. LC 86-62332. 491p. 1987. 16.95 (ISBN 0-317-56105-7). World Promos.

T. E. Hulme. Michael Roberts. LC 72-169106. (English Biography Ser., No. 31). 1971. Repr. of 1938 ed. lib. bdg. 49.95x (ISBN 0-8383-1342-6). Haskell.

T. E. Hulme. Michael Roberts. Intro. by Anthony Quinton. 310p. 1982. 21.00 (ISBN 0-85635-411-2). Carcanet.

T. E. Lawrence. Charles Edmonds. LC 76-52954. (English Biography Ser, No. 31). 1977. lib. bdg. 49.95x (ISBN 0-8383-2177-1). Haskell.

T. E. Lawrence--"Lawrence of Arabia". J. M. Wilson. (Illus.). 30p. (Orig.). 1976. Set of slides incl. pap. 7.50 (ISBN 0-317-58702-1, Pub. by Ashmolean Mus). Longwood Pub Group.

T. E. Lawrence: A Bibliography. Elizabeth W. Duval. LC 74-185877. (Reference Ser., No. 44). 1972. Repr. of 1938 ed. lib. bdg. 75.00x (ISBN 0-8383-1385-X). Haskell.

T. E. Lawrence: A Bibliography. Jeffrey Meyers. LC 74-11361. (Reference Library of the Humanities: No. 5). 50p. 1975. lib. bdg. 19.00 (ISBN 0-8240-1052-3). Garland Pub.

T. E. Lawrence: A Bibliography. Philip O'Brien. (G. K. Hall Reference Bks.). 416p. 1988. 35.00 (ISBN 0-8161-8945-5); lib. bdg. 60.00x. G K Hall.

T. E. Lawrence: A Critical Study. Robert Warde. Ed. by Stephen Orgel. (Harvard Dissertations in American & English Literature Ser.). 550p. 1987. lib. bdg. 85.00 (ISBN 0-8240-0082-X). Garland Pub.

T. E. Lawrence: A Portrait in Paradox Controversy & Caricature in the Biographies of T. E. Lawrence. Jill M. Phillips. 600p. 1975. 75.00 (ISBN 0-8490-1172-8). Gordon Pr.

T. E. Lawrence: A Reader's Guide. Frank Clements. LC 72-8438. 208p. 1973. 25.00 (ISBN 0-208-01313-X, Archon). Shoe String.

T. E. Lawrence by His Friends. A. W. Lawrence. 1937. Repr. 35.00 (ISBN 0-8274-3575-4). R West.

T. E. Lawrence by His Friends. Ed. by A. W. Lawrence. 576p. 1980. Repr. of 1937 ed. 50.00x (ISBN 0-87752-196-4). Gordian.

T. E. Lawrence: Lawrence of Arabia. J. M. Wilson. (Illus.). 30p. (Orig.). 1976. pap. 20.00x (ISBN 0-900090-35-9, Pub. by Ashmolean Museum). State Mutual Bk.

T. E. Lawrence (of Arabia) Charles Edmonds. 1936. Repr. 20.00 (ISBN 0-8274-3576-2). R West.

T. E. Lawrence Puzzle. Ed. by Stephen E. Tabachnick. LC 83-1119. (Illus.). 288p. 1984. 22.50 (ISBN 0-8203-0669-X). U of Ga Pr.

T. E. Rhine, M.D. Recollections of an Arkansas Country Doctor. Pat R. Brown. LC 85-13559. (Illus.). 400p. 1985. 14.95 (ISBN 0-935304-94-0). August Hse.

T. E. T. (Teacher Effectiveness Training) Thomas Gordon. 14.95 (ISBN 0-317-63114-4). McKay.

T. F. H. Book of Snakes. Thomas Leetz. (T.F.H. Book Ser.). (Illus.). 80p. 1983. 6.95 (ISBN 0-87666-561-X, HP-017). TFH Pubns.

T. F. Powys. H. Coombes. Repr. of 1960 ed. 20.00 (ISBN 0-8274-4333-1). R West.

T. F. Powys: A Modern Allegorist. Marius Buning. (Costerus, New Ser.: Vol.56). (Illus.). 272p. 1986. pap. text ed. 35.00 (ISBN 90-6203-718-6, Pub. by Rudophi Holland). Humanities.

T. F. Wade in China. James C. Cooley, Jr. 160p. 1981. 126.00x (ISBN 0-317-68598-8, Pub. by Han-Shan Tang Ltd). State Mutual Bk.

T for Texas: A State Full of Folklore. Ed. by Francis E. Abernethy. LC 82-70089. (Texas Folklore Society Publications Ser.: No. 44). (Illus.). 250p. (Orig.). 1982. 15.95 (ISBN 0-935014-03-9). E-Heart Pr.

T for Tommy. Joan M. Lexau. LC 74-161032. (Garrard Venture Ser.). (Illus.). 40p. (gr. k-3). 1971. PLB 6.69 (ISBN 0-8116-6719-7); pap. 1.19 (9026). Garrard.

T. G. I. M. Strategies to Increase Work Satisfaction. Charles Cameron & Suzanne Elusorr. 1986. 8.95 (ISBN 0-317-42720-2). J P Tarcher.

T. G. I. M. (Thank God It's Monday) Making Your Work Fulfilling & Finding Fulfilling Work. Charles Cameron & Suzanne Elusorr. LC 85-27736. 224p. 1986. pap. 8.95 (ISBN 0-87477-357-1). J P Tarcher.

T. G. Masaryk Revisited. Hanus J. Hajek. (East European Monographs: No. 139). 194p. 1983. 24.00x (ISBN 0-88033-030-9). East Eur Quarterly.

T-Groups & Therapy Groups in a Changing Society. Dee G. Appley & Alvin E. Winder. LC 73-10934. (Jossey-Bass Behavioral Science Ser.). Repr. of 1973 ed. 58.00 (ISBN 0-8357-9350-8, 2013913). Bks Demand UMI.

T. H. Green: Lectures on the Principles of Political Obligation & Other Writings. Ed. by Paul Harris & John Morrow. 350p. 1986. 47.50 (ISBN 0-521-26035-3); pap. 15.95 (ISBN 0-521-27810-4). Cambridge U Pr.

T. H. Huxley: Man's Place in Nature. James G. Paradis. LC 78-5492. xiv, 226p. 1978. 21.00x (ISBN 0-8032-0917-7). U of Nebr Pr.

T. H. Huxley on Education: A Selection of His Writings. Thomas H. Huxley. LC 72-154507. (Cambridge Texts & Studies in the History of Education). pap. 60.00 (ISBN 0-317-26091-X, 2024417). Bks Demand UMI.

T. H. Huxley's Place in Natural Science. Mario A. Di Gregorio. LC 84-2375. 280p. 1984. 27.50x (ISBN 0-300-03062-2). Yale U Pr.

T. H. White: An Annotated Bibliography. Francois Gallix. LC 86-18444. (Reference Library of the Humanities Ser.). 160p. 1986. lib. bdg. 27.00 (ISBN 0-8240-8589-2). Garland Pub.

T. H. White & the Matter of Britain: A Literary Overview. Martin Kellman. LC 87-24677. (Studies in the Historical Novel: Vol. 2). 256p. 1988. lib. bdg. 49.95x (ISBN 0-88946-231-3). E Mellen.

T-Hold Kubotan. Takayuki Kubota. 28p. (Orig.). 1983. pap. 3.95 (ISBN 0-86568-111-2). Unique Pubns.

T I N A. Bart Mills. Date not set. pap. 2.95 (ISBN 0-446-34044-8). Warner Bks.

T in CETA: Local & National Perspectives. Ed. by Sar A. Levitan & Garth L. Mangum. LC 81-19791. 433p. 1981. text ed. 20.95 (ISBN 0-911558-94-2); pap. text ed. 13.95 (ISBN 0-911558-93-4). W E Upjohn.

T Is for Touching. Carol Grimm & Becky Montgomery. (gr. k up). 1985. manual & 3-filmstrip series 79.00 (ISBN 0-317-40553-5); manual & videotape one half inch 79.00 (ISBN 0-914633-09-0); manual & videotape three quarter inch 95.00 (ISBN 0-914633-08-2). Rape Abuse Crisis.

T. J. Folger. Thief. Steven Kroll. LC 77-24575. (Illus.). 40p. (gr. 1-3). 1978. reinforced bdg. 5.95 (ISBN 0-8234-0313-0). Holiday.

T. L. Yuan Bibliography of Western Writings. Harrie A. Vanderstappen. 654p. 1975. 385.00x (Pub. by Han-Shan Tang Ltd). State Mutual Bk.

T. Lucreti Cari de Rerum Natura Libri Sex. Ed. by Karl Lachmann. (Latin Poetry Ser.). 439p. 58.00 (ISBN 0-8240-2956-9). Garland Pub.

T Lymphocytes Today. Ed. by J. R. Inglis. 200p. 1983. 22.00 (ISBN 0-444-80524-9, I-331-83, Biomedical Pr). Elsevier.

T. Macci Plauti Aulularia: With Critical & Exegetical Notes & an Introduction. Plautus. Ed. by W. R. Connor. LC 78-67156. (Latin Texts & Commentaries Ser.). (Lat. & Eng.). 1979. Repr. of 1876 ed. lib. bdg. 12.00x (ISBN 0-405-11623-3). Ayer Co Pubs.

T. Macci Plauti Epidicus. Plautus. Ed. by W. R. Connor. (Latin Texts & Commentaries Ser.). (Lat. & Eng.). 1979. Repr. of 1940 ed. lib. bdg. 34.50x (ISBN 0-405-11600-4). Ayer Co Pubs.

T. Macci Plauti Pseudolus. Plautus. Ed. by W. R. Connor. LC 78-11622. (Latin Texts & Commentaries Ser.). (Lat. & Eng.). 1979. Repr. of 1932 ed. lib. bdg. 12.00x (ISBN 0-405-11622-5). Ayer Co Pubs.

T. Macci Plauti Rudens. Plautus. Ed. by W. R. Connor & Edward A. Sonnenschein. LC 78-67153. (Latin Texts & Commentaries Ser.). (Lat. & Eng.). 1979. Repr. of 1891 ed. lib. bdg. 23.50x (ISBN 0-405-11620-9). Ayer Co Pubs.

T. N. Hasselquist. Oscar F. Ander. Ed. by Franklyn D. Scott. LC 78-15208. (Scandinavians in America Ser.). 1979. Repr. of 1931 ed. lib. bdg. 21.00x (ISBN 0-405-11630-6). Ayer Co Pubs.

T-O-R-A-H see Kadima Kesher Series.

T. P. O'Connor & the Liverpool Irish. L. W. Brady. (Royal Historical Society Ser.: No. 39). 304p. 1983. 38.00 (ISBN 0-901050-92-X, Pub. by Boydell & Brewer). Longwood Pub Group.

T Programming Language: A Dialect of LISP. Stephen Slade. (Illus.). 448p. 1987. pap. text ed. 22.00 (ISBN 0-13-881905-X). P-H.

T-R-A-I-N up the Children. Linda J. Burba & Keith V. Burba. 111p. 1985. pap. 4.50 (ISBN 0-8341-1062-8). Beacon Hill.

T. R. Goes to School. Terrance Hellard. (T. R. Bear Ser.). (Illus.). 56p. (gr. 2-4). 1988. pap. 2.95 (ISBN 0-8120-4106-2). Barron.

T-Rings & Wreath Product Representations. P. Hoffman. (Lecture Notes in Mathematics: Vol. 746). 1979. pap. 14.00 (ISBN 0-387-09551-9). Springer-Verlag.

T. R's Day Out. Terrance Dicks. (T. R. Bear Ser.). (Illus.). 56p. (gr. 2-4). 1988. pap. 2.95 (ISBN 0-8120-4107-0). Barron.

T. R's Halloween. Terrance Dicks. (T. R. Bear Ser.). (Illus.). 56p. (gr. 2-4). 1988. pap. 2.95 (ISBN 0-8120-4108-9). Barron.

T. S. Bayer, 1649-1738: Pioneer Sinologist. Knud Lundbaek. (Scandinavian Institute of Asian Studies Monograph: Vol. 54). (Illus.). 256p. 1986. pap. text ed. 25.00 (ISBN 0-7007-0189-3, Pub. by Curzon Pr UK). Humanities.

T. S. Eliot. Intro. by Harold Bloom. (Modern Critical Views Ser.). 126p. 1985. 19.95 (ISBN 0-87754-601-0). Chelsea Hse.

T. S. Eliot. Angus Calder. LC 86-21488. (Harvester New Reading Ser.). 192p. 1987. text ed. 29.95 (ISBN 0-391-03472-3); pap. text ed. 9.95 (ISBN 0-391-03532-0). Humanities.

T. S. Eliot. Ed. by William Cookson & Peter Dale. (Agenda Critical Editions). (Illus.). 200p. (Orig.). 1988. pap. 17.50 (ISBN 0-933806-50-7). Black Swan CT.

T. S. Eliot. Ed. by Laura Cowan. (Man & Poet Ser.). 1989. price not set (ISBN 0-943373-09-3); pap. price not set (ISBN 0-943373-10-7). Natl Poet Foun.

T. S. Eliot. Sandra Gilbert. (Feminist Readings Ser.). 160p. 1989. text ed. 29.95 (ISBN 0-391-03516-9); pap. text ed. 12.50 (ISBN 0-391-03517-7). Humanities.

T. S. Eliot. Philip Headings. (Twayne's United States Authors Ser). 1964. pap. 8.95x (ISBN 0-8084-0293-5, T57, Twayne). New Coll U Pr.

T. S. Eliot. Rev. ed. Philip R. Headings. (United States Authors Ser.). 1982. lib. bdg. 15.95 (ISBN 0-8057-7357-6, Twayne). G K Hall.

T. S. Eliot. rev ed. Philip R. Headings. (United States Authors Ser.). 1985. pap. 7.95 (ISBN 0-8057-7443-2, Twayne). G K Hall.

T. S. Eliot. Thomas McGreevy. 84p. 42.50 (ISBN 0-686-74430-6). Bern Porter.

T. S. Eliot. facs. ed. Compiled by Richard March. LC 68-55850. (Essay Index Reprint Ser.). 1949. 18.50 (ISBN 0-8369-0676-4). Ayer Co Pubs.

T. S. Eliot. Compiled by Richard March & Tambimuttu. 259p. 1979. Repr. of 1948 ed. lib. bdg. 30.00 (ISBN 0-89984-300-X). Century Bookbindery.

T. S. Eliot. Burton Raffel. LC 81-70119. (Literature and Life Ser.). 253p. 1982. 16.95x (ISBN 0-8044-2708-9). Ungar.

T. S. Eliot. Leonard Unger. (Pamphlets on American Writers Ser: No. 8). (Orig.). 1961. pap. 1.25x (ISBN 0-8166-0235-2, MPAW8). U of Minn Pr.

T. S. Eliot. Linda Wagner. 160p. 1974. pap. text ed. 2.25 (ISBN 0-07-067675-5). McGraw.

T. S. Eliot - The Critic: A Study in Critical Ideology & Method. Sourindra Mitra. xx, 279p. 1985. 16.00 (ISBN 0-318-23238-3, Pub. by Mittal Pubs Dist India). Nataraj Bks.

T. S. Eliot: A Bibliography of Secondary Works. Compiled By Beatrice Ricks. LC 79-21305. (Author Ser.: No. 45). 392p. 1980. 29.00 (ISBN 0-8108-1262-2). Scarecrow.

T. S. Eliot: A Chronology of His Life & Work. Caroline Behr. LC 82-16716. 250p. 1983. 25.00x (ISBN 0-312-82185-9). St Martin.

T. S. Eliot: A Collection of Critical Essays. Ed. by H. Kenner. 1962. pap. 4.95 (ISBN 0-13-274324-8, Spec). P-H.

T. S. Eliot: A Life. Peter Ackroyd. (Illus.). 338p. 1984. 24.95 (ISBN 0-671-53043-7). S&S.

T. S. Eliot: A Life. Peter Ackroyd. pap. 12.95 (ISBN 0-671-60572-0, Touchstone Bks.). S&S.

T. S. Eliot: A Memoir. Joseph Chiari. (Illus.). 1982. 12.00 (ISBN 0-905289-33-1). Small Pr Dist.

T. S. Eliot: A Study in Character & Style. Ronald Bush. LC 83-4259. (Illus.). 1984. 29.95x (ISBN 0-19-503376-0). Oxford U Pr.

T. S. Eliot: A Study in Character & Style. Ronald Bush. (798). (Illus.). 320p. 1985. pap. 7.95 (ISBN 0-19-503726-X). Oxford U Pr.

T. S. Eliot: A Study of His Writings by Several Hands. B. Rajan. LC 65-15865. (Studies in T. S. Eliot, No. 11). 1969. Repr. of 1947 ed. lib. bdg. 75.00x (ISBN 0-8383-0545-8). Haskell.

T. S. Eliot: A Symposium for His Seventieth Birthday. facsimile ed. Ed. by Neville Braybrooke. LC 68-58773. (Essay Index Reprint Ser). Repr. of 1958 ed. 20.00 (ISBN 0-8369-0100-2). Ayer Co Pubs.

T. S. Eliot Als Kritiker: Eine Untersuchung Anhand Der Ungesammelten Kritischen Schriften. Elisabeth Baun. Ed. by James Hogg. (Poetic Drama & Poetic Theory Ser.). 215p. (Orig.). 1980. pap. 15.00 (ISBN 3-7052-0891-8, Pub. by Salzburg Studies). Longwood Pub Group.

T. S. Eliot: An Introduction. Northrop Frye. LC 80-29344. 110p. 1981. pap. 6.50x (ISBN 0-226-26649-4). U of Chicago Pr.

T. S. Eliot & Hermeneutics: Absence & Interpretation in "The Waste Land". Harriet Davidson. LC 84-21757. 143p. 1985. text ed. 20.00 (ISBN 0-8071-1208-9). La State U Pr.

Table of Offerings: Seventeen Years of Acquisitions of Egyptian & Ancient Near Easter Art by William Kelly Simpson for the Museum of Fine Arts, Boston. William K. Simpson & The Egyptian Dept. of the MFA, Boston. Ed. by Cynthia Purvis. LC 87-50312. (Illus.). 112p. 1987. pap. write for info. (ISBN 0-87846-280-5). Mus Fine Arts Boston.

Table of Radioactive Isotopes. Edgardo Browne & Richard B. Firestone. LC 86-9069. 1056p. 1986. 62.95 (ISBN 0-471-84909-X, Wiley-Interscience). Wiley.

Table of the Lord. Gaynell B. Cronin. LC 86-70131. (Illus., Orig.). (gr. 1-3). 1986. Child's Bk, 104 pgs. pap. text ed. 4.50 (ISBN 0-87793-299-9); Director's Manual, 168 pgs. 9.75 (ISBN 0-87793-325-1); Parent's Bk, 96 pgs. 3.50 (ISBN 0-87793-326-X). Ave Maria.

Table of the Sin Function & Sin Squared Function for Values from 2 Degrees to 87 Degrees. H. Anne Plettinger. 46p. 1965. 39.00 (ISBN 0-677-01100-8). Gordon & Breach.

Table Prayers. A. Dellinger & S. Fletcher. (ps-3). pap. 0.59 (ISBN 0-570-08316-8, 56HH1448). Concordia.

Table Prayers: New Prayers, Old Favorites, Songs, & Responses. Compiled by Mildred Tengbom. LC 77-72451. 1977. pap. 4.95 (ISBN 0-8066-1594-X, 10-6185). Augsburg.

Table Rock Basin in Barry County, Missouri. Lee M. Adams. Ed. by Carl H. Chapman. (Memoir Ser.: No. 1). (Illus.). 63p. (Orig.). 1950. pap. 1.00 (ISBN 0-943414-17-2). MO Arch Soc.

Table Saw Book. R. J. De Cristpforo. (Illus.). 352p. 1987. 23.95 (ISBN 0-8306-7789-5, 2789); pap. 15.95 (ISBN 0-8306-2789-8). TAB Bks.

Table Saw Techniques. Roger W. Cliffe. LC 84-8676. (Illus.). 352p. 1985. cancelled (ISBN 0-8069-5540-6); pap. 14.95 (ISBN 0-8069-7912-7). Sterling.

Table Setting Guide. Sharon Dlugosch. LC 82-74344. 64p. (Orig.). 1982. pap. 6.95 (ISBN 0-918420-07-5); tchr's manual 8.00 (ISBN 0-918420-05-9). Brighton Pubns.

Table Settings. James Lapine. LC 82-80614. 106p. 1982. pap. 4.95 (ISBN 0-933826-32-X). PAJ Pubns.

Table Swift Construction Manual. Richard Schneider & Myrna Schneider. (Spinster-Helper Ser.). (Illus., Orig.). 1984. pap. 1.95 (ISBN 0-936984-04-X). Schneider Pubs.

Table Talk. A. Bronson Alcott. 208p. 1969. 12.50x (ISBN 0-87556-010-5). Saifer.

Table-Talk, 2 vols. John Selden. 1973. Repr. of 1868 ed. Set. 50.00 (ISBN 0-8274-1299-1). R West.

Table-Talk. large type ed. John Selden. Ed. by Edward Arber. 1972. Repr. of 1869 ed. 10.00x (ISBN 0-87556-314-7). Saifer.

Table-Talk & Bon-Mots of Samuel Foote. Ed. by William Cooke. Repr. of 1902 ed. 20.00 (ISBN 0-8274-4153-3). R West.

Table Talk: From Bridge to Brunches. Becky Bowdre et al. (Illus.). 202p. (Orig.). 1986. pap. 8.00x spiral bound (ISBN 0-9616705-0-9). Table Talk Bridge.

Table-Talk of G. B. S. Archibald Henderson. LC 74-16315. (George Bernard Shaw Ser., No. 92). 1974. lib. bdg. 75.00x (ISBN 0-8383-1890-8). Haskell.

Table-Talk of John Selden: With a Biographical Preface & Notes by S.W. Singer; to Which Is Added Spare Minutes; Or, Resolved Meditations & Premeditated Resolutions by Arthur Warwick. rev. ed. John Selden. LC 74-39207. (Select Bibliographies Reprint Ser.). Repr. of 1855 ed. 21.00 (ISBN 0-8369-6809-3). Ayer Co Pubs.

Table Talk of Samuel Taylor Coleridge. Samuel Taylor Coleridge. 1884. 37.50 (ISBN 0-8274-3563-0). R West.

Table Tennis. Martin Sklorz. (EP Sports Ser.). (Illus.). 1971. 6.95 (ISBN 0-7158-0582-7). Charles River Bks.

Table, the Donkey & the Stick. Jacob Grimm & Wilhelm K. Grimm. (Illus.). (ps-3). 1976. PLB 7.95 (ISBN 0-07-022701-2). McGraw.

Table Treasures Cookbook. 15.95 (ISBN 0-88466-000-1). NPGA.

Table Wines: The Technology of Their Production. 2nd ed. Maynard A. Amerine & M. A. Joslyn. LC 69-12471. (Illus.). 1970. 40.00x (ISBN 0-520-01657-2). U of Cal Pr.

Table with People. Marc Kaminsky. LC 81-8913. 117p. (Orig.). 1982. pap. 7.00 (ISBN 0-915342-36-7). SUN.

Tableau see Theatre.

Tableau Chronologique des Oeuvres de Ronsard. 2nd rev. enl. ed. Paul Laumonier. 1969. Repr. of 1911 ed. 22.50 (ISBN 0-8337-2023-6). B Franklin.

Tableau Economique de F. Quesnay see Deux Etudes de V. S. Nemtchinov.

Tableau Politique de la France de L'ouest Sous la Troisieme Republique: The Political Map of Western France Under the Third Republic. Andre Siegfried. LC 74-25784. (European Sociology Ser.). 566p. 1975. Repr. 42.00x (ISBN 0-405-06537-X). Ayer Co Pubs.

Tableau Systems for First Order Number Theory & Certain Higher Order Theories. S. A. Toledo. LC 75-6738. (Lecture Notes in Mathematics Ser.: Vol. 447). iii, 339p. 1975. pap. 20.00 (ISBN 0-387-07149-0). Springer-Verlag.

Tableaux, Charades, & Pantomimes: Adapted Alike to Parlor Entertainments, School & Church Exhibitions, & for Use on the Amateur Stage. facsimile ed. LC 70-167485. (Granger Index Reprint Ser.). Repr. of 1889 ed. 10.50 (ISBN 0-8369-6290-7). Ayer Co Pubs.

Tableaux Du Temple Des Muses, Repr. Of 1655 Ed. Michel de Marolles. Bd. with Iconologia or Moral Problems. Cesare Ripa. Repr. of 1709 ed. LC 75-27876. (Renaissance & the Gods Ser.: Vol. 31). (Illus.). 1976. lib. bdg. 80.00 (ISBN 0-8240-2080-4). Garland Pub.

Tableaux: Nine Contemporary Sculptors. Michael R. Klein & Robert Stearns. (Illus.). 1983. 10.00 (ISBN 0-917562-23-2). Contemp Arts.

Tableaux Pour le Trianon De Marbre, 1688-1714. Antoine Schnapper. (Illus.). 1967. 24.00 (ISBN 90-2796-407-6). Mouton.

Tables. Ed. by Tony Curtis. (Illus.). 1978. 2.00 (ISBN 0-902921-86-X). Apollo.

Tables Alphabetiques des Noms Cites, 4 vols. Stendhal. Set. 195.00 (ISBN 0-686-55082-X). French & Eur.

Tables & Chairs: Easy to Make. Sunset Editors. LC 75-26492. (Illus.). 80p. 1976. pap. 4.95 (ISBN 0-376-01654-X, Sunset Bks.). Sunset-Lane.

Tables & Figures for Use with Thermodynamics. Kenneth Wark. 128p. 1988. pap. text ed. 5.95 (ISBN 0-07-068288-7). McGraw.

Tables & Formulas see World Book Desk Reference Set.

Tables & Nomograms of Hydrochemical Analysis. Igor' I Sokolov. LC 60-13952. pap. 22.30 (ISBN 0-317-09355-X, 2020662). Bks Demand UMI.

Tables Are Turning: German & Japanese Multinational Companies in the United States. Anant R. Negandhi & R. R. Baliga. LC 81-1445. 188p. 1981. text ed. 35.00 (ISBN 0-89946-088-7). Oelgeschlager.

Tables for Active Filter Design: Cauer & MCPER Functions. Mario Biey & Amedeo Premoli. 580p. 1985. pap. text ed. 72.00 (ISBN 0-89006-159-9). Artech Hse.

Tables for Aspect Research. Mark Pottenger & Scott G. Vail. 128p. 1986. pap. 9.95 (ISBN 0-917086-90-2). A C S Pubns Inc.

Tables for Converting Polynomials & Power Series into Chebyshev Series. Herbert E. Salzer & Norman Levine. LC 83-73685. 1984. pap. 12.00 (ISBN 0-915061-01-5). Applied Sci Pubns.

Tables for Estimating Median Fatigue Limits - STP 731. Ed. by R. Little. 176p. 1981. 15.00 (ISBN 0-8031-0718-8, 04-731000-30). ASTM.

Tables for Investment Decision Making. Ramon E. Johnson & Richard T. Pratt. 272p. 1980. pap. text ed. 16.95 (ISBN 0-8403-3587-3). Kendall-Hunt.

Tables for Lagrangian Interpolation Using Chebyshev Points. Herbert E. Salzer et al. LC 83-73684. 1984. pap. 28.00 (ISBN 0-915061-00-7). Applied Sci Pubns.

Tables for Microscopic Identification of Ore Minerals. E. W. Uytenbogaardt & E. A. Burke. (Earth Science Ser.). 430p. 1985. pap. 11.95 (ISBN 0-486-64839-7). Dover.

Tables for Multi-Server Queues. L. P. Seelen et al. 450p. 1985. 105.25 (ISBN 0-444-87722-3, North Holland). Elsevier.

Tables for Normal Sampling with Unknown Variances: The Student Distribution & Economically Optimal Sampling Plans. Jerome Bracken & Arthur Schliefer. LC 64-13716. pap. 52.00 (ISBN 0-317-08675-8, 2002196). Bks Demand UMI.

Tables for Normal Tolerance Limits, Sampling Plans, & Screening. Ed. by E. Oden & D. Owen. (Statistics Textbooks & Monographs: Vol. 32). 328p. 1980. 69.75 (ISBN 0-8247-6944-9). Dekker.

Tables for Numerical Integration. H. V. Smith. (Charles Griffin Bk.). (Illus.). 1982. pap. 7.50 (ISBN 0-19-520586-3). Oxford U Pr.

Tables for Numerical Integration of Functions with Logarithmic & Power Singularities. V. I. Krylov & A. A. Pal'tsev. 176p. 1971. text ed. 37.00x (ISBN 0-7065-1107-7, Pub. by Keter Pub Jerusalem). Coronet Bks.

Tables for Old English Sound-Changes. Alan S. Ross. LC 77-22642. 1951. lib. bdg. 20.00 (ISBN 0-8414-7290-4). Folcroft.

Tables for Old English Sound-Changes. Alan S. Ross. 1980. Repr. of 1951 ed. lib. bdg. 17.50 (ISBN 0-8492-7727-2). R West.

Tables for Rapid Sub-Frame Analysis. S. Rajendran. 367p. 1979. pap. 20.00x (ISBN 0-8214-0517-9, Pub. by Singapore U Pr). Ohio U Pr.

Tables for Statisticians. 2nd ed. Herbert Arkin & Raymond R. Colton. (Illus.). 168p. 1971. pap. 5.95 (ISBN 0-06-460075-0, CO 75, B&N Bks). Harper-Row.

Tables for Statisticians. John White et al. 61p. 1984. pap. text ed. 5.00x (ISBN 0-7022-1146-X). U of Queensland Pr.

Tables for Tests Confidence Limits & Plans Based on Proportions. Owen & Oden. (Statistics, Textbooks & Monographs). 400p. 1983. 78.00 (ISBN 0-8247-7136-2). Dekker.

Tables for Texture Analysis of Cubic Crystals. J. Hansen et al. 1978. pap. 99.20 (ISBN 0-387-08689-7). Springer-Verlag.

Tables for the Automotive Trade. 1986. 4.50 (ISBN 0-471-63941-9). Wiley.

Tables for the Design & Analysis of Stiffened Steel Plates. N. W. Murray & G. Thierauf. 1981. 46.00 (ISBN 3-528-08673-4, Pub. by Vieweg & Sohn Germany). IPS.

Tables for the Hydraulic Design of Pipes & Sewers. 4th ed. Hydraulics Research Station Limited Staff. 158p. 1983. 21.00 (ISBN 0-317-59742-6, Pub. by T Telford UK). Am Soc Civil Eng.

Tables for Traffic Management & Design. Theodore Frankel. 1977. 12.95 (ISBN 0-686-98071-9). Telecom Lib.

Tables for Use in High Resolution Mass Spectrometry. Robert Binks et al. Incl. Chemical Formulae from Mass Determinations. D. Henneberg & K. Casper. LC 75-130645. pap. 52.00 (ISBN 0-317-29340-0, 2024031). Bks Demand UMI.

Tables of Antenna Characteristics. Ronald W. King. LC 74-157425. 400p. 1971. 95.00x (ISBN 0-306-65154-8, IFI Plenum). Plenum Pub.

Tables of Ascendants & Midheavens. Ernest R. Grant. 136p. 1954. 7.00 (ISBN 0-86690-108-6, 1151-01). Am Fed Astrologers.

Tables of Bessel Transforms. F. Oberhettinger. LC 72-88727. 289p. 1972. pap. 20.00 (ISBN 0-387-05997-0). Springer-Verlag.

Tables of Bullet Performance. Philip Mannes. Ed. by Dave Wolfe. 407p. (Orig.). 1980. text ed. write for info. (ISBN 0-935632-06-9); pap. text ed. 17.50 (ISBN 0-935632-05-0). Wolfe Pub Co.

Tables of Clebsch-Gordan, Racah, & Subduction Coefficients of SU(n) Groups. Jin-Quan Chen & Pei-Ning Wang. 240p. 1987. 78.00 (ISBN 9971-50-072-8); pap. 44.00 (ISBN 9971-50-073-6, Pub. by World Sci Singapore). World Scientific Pub.

Tables of Compound Interest Functions & Logarithms of Compound Interest Functions. James W. Glover & Henry C. Carver. 1921. 7.50x (ISBN 0-685-21808-2). Wahr.

Tables of Definite & Infinite Integrals. A. Apelblat. (Physical Sciences Data Ser.: Vol. 13). 458p. 1983. 144.75 (ISBN 0-444-42151-3, I-470-82). Elsevier.

Tables of Dimensions, Indices, & Branching Rules for Representations of Simple Lie Algebras. W. G. McKay & J. Patera. (Lecture Notes in Pure & Applied Mathematics Ser.: Vol. 69). (Illus.). 336p. 1981. 75.00 (ISBN 0-8247-1227-7). Dekker.

Tables of Diurnal Planetary Motion. 176p. 8.00 (ISBN 0-86690-055-1, 1005-01). Am Fed Astrologers.

Tables of Dominant Weight Multiplicites of Simple Life Algebras of Rank Less Than or Equal to 8. Bremmer. (Pure & Applied Mathematics: Monographs & Textbooks). 232p. 1985. 75.00 (ISBN 0-8247-7270-9). Dekker.

Tables of Events. Reinhold Ebertin. 48p. 1975. 4.50 (ISBN 0-86690-185-X, 1100-01). Am Fed Astrologers.

Tables of Functions with Formulae & Curves. 4th ed. Eugene Jahnke & Fritz Emde. (Ger & Eng). 1945. pap. text ed. 7.50 (ISBN 0-486-60133-1). Dover.

Tables of Houses Campanus. Astro Numeric Service Staff. LC 77-77345. 208p. 1977. 12.00 (ISBN 0-86690-054-3, 2005-05). Am Fed Astrologers.

Tables of Houses Koch. Astro Numeric Service Staff. LC 77-77346. 208p. 1977. 12.00 (ISBN 0-86690-251-1, 2006-05). Am Fed Astrologers.

Tables of Houses Placidus. Astro Numeric Service Staff. LC 77-77344. 208p. 1977. 12.00 (ISBN 0-86690-252-X, 2007-05). Am Fed Astrologers.

Tables of Huckel Molecular Orbitals see HMO Model & Its Application.

Tables of Indefinite Integrals. G. Petit Bois. 1906. pap. text ed. 6.95 (ISBN 0-486-60225-7). Dover.

Tables of Integrals & Other Mathematical Data. 4th ed. Herbert B. Dwight. 1961. write for info. (ISBN 0-02-331170-3, 33117). Macmillan.

Tables of Integrals, Series & Products. I. S. Gradshteyn et al. 1980. 39.95 (ISBN 0-12-294760-6). Acad Pr.

Tables of Ion Implantation Spatial Distribution. A. F. Burenkov et al. 465p. 1986. text ed. 125.00 (ISBN 2-88124-071-2). Gordon & Breach.

Tables of Laplace Transforms. F. Oberhettinger & L. Badii. LC 73-81328. vii, 428p. 1973. pap. 38.00 (ISBN 0-387-06350-1). Springer-Verlag.

Tables of Light-Scattering Functions: Relative Indices of Less Than Unity & Infinity. Richard Henry Boll. LC 57-7175. pap. 93.00 (ISBN 0-317-08493-3, 2011234). Bks Demand UMI.

Tables of Mathematical Functions, Vol. 3. Harold T. Davis & Vera Fisher. 1962. 8.75 (ISBN 0-911536-17-5). Trinity U Pr.

Tables of Mellin Transforms. F. Oberhettinger. vii, 275p. 1974. pap. 24.00 (ISBN 0-387-06942-9). Springer-Verlag.

Tables of Nuclear Quadrupole Resonance Frequencies. I. P. Biryukov et al. 144p. 1971. text ed. 31.00 (ISBN 0-7065-0621-9, Pub. by Keter Pub Jerusalem). Coronet Bks.

Tables of Physical & Chemical Constants: And Some Mathematical Functions. 15th ed. G. W. Kaye & T. H. Laby. 432p. 1986. 39.95 (ISBN 0-470-20662-4, Co-Pub. with Longman). Wiley.

Tables of Physical & Chemical Constants. 15th rev. ed. G. W. Kaye & T. H. Laby. Ed. by A. E. Bailey et al. LC 73-85205. (Illus.). 320p. 1973. text ed. 39.95x (ISBN 0-582-46354-8). Wiley.

Tables of Progressive Gravity Waves. John M. Williams. 640p. 1986. 135.00 (ISBN 0-470-20685-3, Co-Pub. with Longman). Wiley.

Tables of Random Permutations. Lincoln E. Moses & Robert V. Oakford. LC 63-12041. 1963. 22.50x (ISBN 0-8047-0148-2). Stanford U Pr.

Tables of Screening Design. Donald J. Wheeler. 239p. 1987. pap. text ed. 35.00 (ISBN 0-945320-02-7). Stat Process Controls.

Tables of Spectral Lines. 3rd. ed. A. N. Zaidel' et al. LC 70-120028. 782p. 1970. 125.00x (ISBN 0-306-65151-3, IFI Plenum). Plenum Pub.

Tables of Standard Electrode Potentials. Guilio Milazzo & Sergio Caroli. LC 77-8111. 437p. pap. 113.70 (2030411). Bks Demand UMI.

Tables of the Anger & Lommel-Weber Functions. Gary D. Bernard & Akira Ishimaru. LC 62-17144. (Illus.). 74p. 1962. pap. 15.00x (ISBN 0-295-73956-8). U of Wash Pr.

Tables of the F-E Related Distribution Algorithms. K. Mardia & Zemroch. 1979. 66.00 (ISBN 0-12-471140-5). Acad Pr.

Tables of the Hypergeometric Probability Distribution. Gerald J. Lieberman & Donald B. Owen. 1961. 60.00x (ISBN 0-8047-0057-5). Stanford U Pr.

Tables of the Incomplete Beta-Function. K. Pearson. 505p. 1968. 95.00x (ISBN 0-85264-704-2, Pub. by England Griffin). State Mutual Bk.

Tables of the Incomplete Beta Function. Karl Pearson. 205p. 1968. lib. bdg. 37.95x (ISBN 0-521-05922-4). Lubrecht & Cramer.

Tables of the Incomplete Gamma Function. Karl Pearson. 164p. 1965. lib. bdg. 27.00x (ISBN 0-521-05924-0). Lubrecht & Cramer.

Tables of the Motion of the Moon, 3 vols. Ernest Brown & Henry B. Hedrick. 1920. pap. 350.00x set (ISBN 0-685-89789-3). Elliots Bks.

Tables of the Non-Central T-Distribution: Density Function, Cumulative Distribution Function, & Percentage Points. George J. Resnikoff & Gerald J. Lieberman. LC 57-7832. 1957. 38.50x (ISBN 0-8047-0492-9). Stanford U Pr.

Tables of Thermodynamic Data. (Technical Reports Ser.: No. 38). 96p. 1964. pap. 10.50 (ISBN 92-0-145264-0, IDC38, IAEA). UNIPUB.

Tables of Transformation Brackets for Nuclear Shell-Model Calculations. 2nd ed. T. A. Brody & M. Moshinsky. 250p. 1967. 94.00 (ISBN 0-677-01320-5). Gordon & Breach.

Tables of Trigonometric Functions for the Numerical Computation of Electron Density in Crystals. I. M. Kuntsevich et al. 220p. 1971. text ed. 44.00x (ISBN 0-7065-1108-5, Pub. by Keter Pub Jerusalem). Coronet Bks.

Tables of Wavenumbers for the Calibration of Infrared Spectrometers, Vol. 9. 2nd ed. Ed. by Howard Cole. 1977. text ed. 53.00 (ISBN 0-08-021247-6). Pergamon.

Tables of Working Life: The Increment-Decrement Model. (Labor Statistics Bureau Bulletin Ser.: No. 2135). (Illus.). 72p. 1982. pap. 5.00 (ISBN 0-318-20383-9, S/N 029-001-02728-1). USGPO.

Tables Turned. James Bonar. LC 70-107918. 1970. Repr. of 1931 ed. 25.00x (ISBN 0-678-00633-4). Kelley.

Tablet Machine Instrumentation in Pharmaceutics. Watt. (Pharmaceutical Technology Ser.). 416p. 1988. 69.95 (ISBN 0-470-21088-5). Wiley.

Tablet of Cebes. Cebes. Ed. by Stephen Orgel. LC 78-68186. (Philosophy of Images Ser.). 1980. lib. bdg. 80.00 (ISBN 0-8240-3693-X). Garland Pub.

Tablet of the Heart: God & Me. Abdu'l-Baha. Ed. by Betty J. Fisher & Leslie Lundberg. (Illus.). (ps-2). 1987. PLB 12.95 (ISBN 0-87743-207-4). Baha'i.

Tableting Specification Manual. rev. ed. American Pharmaceutical Association, Committee on Tableting Specifications. (Illus.). 39p. 1981. pap. text ed. 42.00 (ISBN 0-917330-36-6). Am Pharm Assn.

Tabletop & Giftwares. Fairchild Market Research Division Staff. (Fairchild Fact Files Ser.). (Illus.). 50p. 1986. pap. 17.50 (ISBN 0-87005-557-7). Fairchild.

Tabletop Learning Series, 16 bks. Imogene Forte. 480p. 1987. Set. 60.50 (ISBN 0-86530-095-X, IP95-3). Incentive Pubns.

Tabletop Presentations: A Guide for the Foodservice Professional. Irving Mills. (Illus.). 256p. 1988. 34.95 (ISBN 0-442-26472-0). Van Nos Reinhold.

Tablets. A. Bronson Alcott. 208p. 1969. Repr. of 1868 ed. 12.50x (ISBN 0-87556-011-3). Saifer.

Tablets. A. Bronson Alcott. 1868. 30.00 (ISBN 0-932062-02-4). Sharon Hill.

Tablets of Baha'u'llah Revealed Before the Kitab-i-Aqdas. Baha'u'llah. Compiled by Universal House of Justice Staff. Tr. by Habib Taherzadeh from Persian. LC 88-6250. 299p. 1988. pap. 5.95 (ISBN 0-87743-216-3). Baha'i.

Tablets of Ebla: Concordance & Bibliography. Scott G. Beld et al. 70p. (Orig.). 1984. text ed. 6.50x (ISBN 0-931464-21-8). Eisenbrauns.

Tablets of the Divine Plan. rev. ed. Abdu'l-Baha. LC 76-10624. 1977. o.s.i 10.95 (ISBN 0-87743-107-8, 106-010); pap. 9.95 (ISBN 0-87743-116-7, 106-011). Baha'i.

Tablets XVI-XVIII. Armand Schwerner. 1976. pap. 20.00 (ISBN 0-686-67895-8). Heron Pr.

Taekwon-Do. Y. K. Kim. Ed. by Christine Miller. LC 83-70220. (Illus.). 184p. (Orig.). 1983. 26.95 (ISBN 0-89305-052-0); pap. 16.95 (ISBN 0-89305-049-0). Anna Pub.

Taekwon-Do: A Guide to the Theories of Defensive Movement. Mark McCarthy et al. (Illus.). 160p. 1984. pap. 8.95 (ISBN 0-8092-5404-2). Contemp Bks.

Taekwon Do Handbook, 1977-1980. cancelled (ISBN 0-686-43038-7). AAU Pubns.

Taekwon-Do Hyungs for Blue & Red Belt Levels. James S. Benko. LC 81-82100. (Illus.). 121p. (Orig.). 1981. cancelled (ISBN 0-937314-05-6, Intl Taekwon-Do); pap. 12.00 (ISBN 0-937314-04-8, 048S). ITA Pubns MI.

Taekwon-Do Hyungs for White, Yellow & Green Belt Levels. James S. Benko. LC 81-81353. (Illus.). 121p. (Orig.). 1981. cancelled (ISBN 0-937314-01-3, Intl Taekwon-Do); pap. 12.00 (ISBN 0-937314-02-1, 021S). ITA Pubns MI.

Taekwon-Do, Self-Defense Against Weapons. James S. Benko. LC 80-82015. (Illus.). 111p. 1981. cancelled (ISBN 0-937314-03-X, Intl Taekwon-Do); pap. 12.00 (ISBN 0-937314-00-5, 005S). ITA Pubns MI.

Taekwon Do: The Korean Martial Art & National Sport. Richard Chun. LC 74-1799. (Illus.). 544p. 1976. 45.00i (ISBN 0-06-010779-0, HarpT). Har-Row.

Taezhnyi Brodiaga. Mikhail Dyomin. LC 84-62843. 336p. (Orig.). 1986. pap. 19.00 (ISBN 0-89830-094-0). Russica Pubs.

Taffy Finds a Halloween Witch. Donna L. Pape. LC 75-11590. (Easy Venture Ser.). (Illus.). 32p. (gr. k-2). 1975. PLB 6.69 (ISBN 0-8116-6067-2). Garrard.

Taffy Sinclair & the Melanie Makeover. Betsy Haynes. (Taffy Sinclair Bks.). (gr. 2-6). 1988. pap. 2.50 (ISBN 0-317-68881-2, Skylark). Bantam.

Taffy Sinclair & the Romance Machine Disaster. Betsy Hanes. 128p. (Orig.). 1987. pap. 2.50 (ISBN 0-553-15494-X, Skylark). Bantam.

Taffy Sinclair & the Secret Admirer Epidemic. Betsy Haynes. (Taffy Sinclair Bks.). (gr. 2-6). 1988. pap. 2.50 (ISBN 0-553-15582-2, Skylark). Bantam.

Taffy Sinclair, Baby Ashley, & Me. Betsy Haynes. 128p. (gr. 4-7). 1988. pap. 2.50 (ISBN 0-553-15557-1, Skylark). Bantam.

Taffy Sinclair, Queen of the Soaps. Betsy Haynes. (ps-7). 1987. pap. 2.50 (ISBN 0-553-15330-7, Skylark). Bantam.

Taffy Sinclair Strikes Again. Betsy Haynes. (Skylark Choose Your Own Adventure Bks.). 128p. (gr. 4-6). 1984. pap. 2.50 (ISBN 0-553-15417-6, Skylark). Bantam.

Tafhimul - Quran: Urdu Translation & Commentary. A. A. Maudadi. 95.00 (ISBN 0-686-18523-4). Kazi Pubns.

Taflak Lysandra. L. Neil Smith. (Thomas Paine Maru Ser.). 240p. (Orig.). 1988. pap. 3.50 (ISBN 0-380-75323-5). Avon.

Tafsir-ul-Quran, Vol. I-IV. A. Majid Daryabadi. 75.00 (ISBN 0-317-14641-6). Kazi Pubns.

Taft & Roosevelt, 2 Vols. Archibald W. Butt. LC 71-137968. (American History & Culture in the Twentieth Century Ser). 1971. Repr. of 1930 ed. Set. 70.00x (ISBN 0-8046-1425-3, Pub by Kennikat). Assoc Faculty Pr.

Taft Architects: A Bibliography. Mary E. Huls. (Architecture Ser.: A 1891). 5p. 1987. 3.00 (ISBN 1-55590-461-0). Vance Biblios.

Taft Corporate Directory see Taft Corporate Giving Directory: Comprehensive Profiles & Analyses of Major American Corporate Philanthropic Programs, 1986.

Taft Corporate Giving Directory: Comprehensive Profiles & Analyses of Major American Corporate Philanthropic Programs. Rev., 1985 ed. Ed. by Taft Corporation. 733p. 267.00 (ISBN 0-914756-75-3). Taft Group.

Taft Corporate Giving Directory: Comprehensive Profiles & Analyses of Major American Corporate Philanthropic Programs, 1986. rev. ed. The Taft Group, Inc. Orig. Title: Taft Corporate Directory. 800p. 1985. 267.00 (ISBN 0-914756-76-1). Taft Group.

Taft Foundation Reporter: Comprehensive Profiles & Analyses of Major American Private Foundations. rev. ed. Ed. by Taft Corporation. 827p. 1985. 267.00 (ISBN 0-914756-21-4). Taft Group.

Taft Museum: A Cincinnati Legacy. Ed. by Dottie L. Lewis. (Illus.). 64p. (Orig.). 1988. pap. text ed. 7.50 (ISBN 0-911497-09-9). Cinc Hist Soc.

Taft Papers on the League of Nations. William H. Taft. Ed. by T. Marburg & H. Flack. Repr. of 1920 ed. 24.00 (ISBN 0-527-88618-1). Kraus Repr.

Tag. Lee Dalton. LC 81-82053. 140p. 1982. 8.95 (ISBN 0-88290-193-1, 2020). Horizon Utah.

Tag-A-Long: Timless Relax Time Story for Children. Wilma Andrews. (Illus.). 29p. (Orig.). (ps-3). 1984. pap. 5.95 (ISBN 0-943049-00-8). Tag A Long.

Tag Alongs. Joyce M. Burkes. (Funny Flippin's Ser.: Bk. 4). (Illus.). 8p. (ps-6). 1987. book & cassette 4.95 (ISBN 0-931218-53-5, 4604). Joybug.

TAGA Proceedings: Graphic Arts. annual 750p. 55.00 (ISBN 0-318-16654-2); 2.00 (ISBN 0-318-16655-0). Tech Assn Graphic.

Tagalog Beginning Course. Neonetta C. Cabrera & Augustina S. Cunanan. Tr. by J. Donald Bowen. (Illus.). 399p. 1968. 295.00x (ISBN 0-88432-103-7, TG10); cassettes incl. J Norton Pubs.

Tagalog Dictionary. Teresita V. Ramos. LC 71-152471. (PALI Language Texts: Philippines). 373p. (Orig., Tagalog.). 1971. pap. text ed. 8.50x (ISBN 0-87022-676-2). UH Pr.

Tagalog for Beginners. Teresita V. Ramos & Videa De Guzman. LC 77-148651. (Pacific & Asian Linguistics Institute PALI Language Texts: Philippines Ser.). pap. 160.00 (ISBN 0-317-55727-0, 2029584). Bks Demand UMI.

Tagalog Poetry, Fifteen Seventy to Eighteen Ninety-Eight: Tradition & Influence in Its Development. Bienvenido L. Lumbera. xii, 267p. 1986. 18.75x (ISBN 971-113-052-1, Pub by Ateneo de Manila U Pr Philippines); pap. 11.75x (ISBN 971-113-051-3). Cellar.

Tagalog Reference Grammar. Paul Schachter & Fe T. Otanes. 600p. 1983. text ed. 45.00x (ISBN 0-520-04943-8). U of Cal Pr.

Tagalog-Russian Dictionary. M. Cruz & S. P. Ignashev. 388p. (Tagalog & Rus.). 1959. leatherette 14.95 (ISBN 0-686-92479-7, M-9052). French & Eur.

Tagalog Structures. Teresita V. Ramos. LC 75-152472. (PALI Language Texts: Philippines). 186p. (Orig.). 1971. pap. text ed. 8.50x (ISBN 0-87022-677-0). UH Pr.

Tagasode: Whose Sleeves.... Nishimura Hyobu et al. 125p. 1976. 245.00x (ISBN 0-317-68504-X, Pub. by Han-Shan Tang Ltd). State Mutual Bk.

Tage Frid Teaches Woodworking: Furnituremaking, Bk. 3. Tage Frid. LC 78-65178. (Illus.). 240p. 1985. text ed. 18.95 (ISBN 0-918804-40-X, Dist. by W W Norton). Taunton.

Tage Frid Teaches Woodworking: Joinery, Bk. 1. Tage Frid. LC 78-65178. (Illus.). 224p. 1979. 18.95 (ISBN 0-918804-03-5, Dist. by W W Norton). Taunton.

Tage Frid Teaches Woodworking: Shaping, Veneering, Finishing, Bk. 2. Tage Frid. LC 78-65178. (Illus.). 224p. 1981. 18.95 (ISBN 0-918804-11-6, Dist. by W W Norton). Taunton.

Tagebuch ueber die Informationstheorie. A. Renyi. (Wissenschalt & Kultur Ser.: No. 34). 174p. 1983. 19.95 (ISBN 0-8176-1006-5). Birkhauser.

Tagebucher von Joseph Goebbels: Samtliche Fragmente. Teil I: Die Handschriftlichen Tagebucher. Juli 1924 bis Juli 1941, 4 vols. & index. Ed. by Elke Frohlich. 2831p. (Ger.). 1987. lib. bdg. 200.00 (ISBN 3-598-21915-6). K G Saur.

Taggart. Louis L'Amour. 160p. 1982. pap. 2.95 (ISBN 0-553-25477-4). Bantam.

Taggart: Murder in Season. Peter Cave. 1986. 34.75x (ISBN 0-906391-94-6, Pub. by Mainstream Scotland); pap. 9.75x (ISBN 0-906391-95-4). State Mutual Bk.

Tagging Procedures. Center for Occupational Research & Development Staff. (EUTEC Power Plant Operator Curriculum Ser.). (Illus.). 18p. 1985. pap. text ed. write for info. (ISBN 1-55502-223-5). Ctr Res & Dev.

Tagmeme Sequences in the English Noun Phrase. Peter H. Fries. (Publications in Linguistics & Related Fields Ser.: No. 36). 247p. 1970. microfiche (3) 6.00 (ISBN 0-88312-438-6). Summer Inst Ling.

Tagmemic Analysis of Mexican Spanish Clauses. Ruth M. Brend. (Janua Linguarum, Ser. Practica: No. 52). 1968. text ed. 18.40x (ISBN 90-2790-662-9). Mouton.

Tagmemic & Matrix Linguistics Applied to Selected African Languages. Kenneth L. Pike. (Publications in Linguistics & Related Fields Ser.: No. 23). 122p. 1970. microfiche (2) 4.00 (ISBN 0-88312-425-4). Summer Inst Ling.

Tagmemic Comparison of the Structure of English & Vietnamese Sentences. Duong T. Binh. LC 74-123126. (Janua Linguarum, Ser. Practica: No. 110). (Orig.). 1971. pap. text ed. 35.20x (ISBN 90-2791-598-9). Mouton.

Tagmemics, Discourse & Verbal Art. Kenneth L. Pike. LC 81-9541. (Michigan Studies in the Humanities: No. 3). 1981. pap. 6.00 (ISBN 0-936534-02-8). Mich Slavic Pubns.

Tagore-Gandhi Controversy. M. K. Gandhi & Rabindranath Tagore. Ed. by R. K. Prabhu. 155p. (Orig.). 1983. pap. 3.00 (ISBN 0-934676-52-6). Greenlf Bks.

Tagore, India & Soviet Union. A. P. Gnatyuk Danil'chuk. 400p. 1986. 48.50x (ISBN 0-8364-1831-X, Pub. by Firma KLM). South Asia Bks.

Tagore Reader. Rabindranath Tagore. Ed. by Amiya Chakravarty. 1966. pap. 14.95x (ISBN 0-8070-5971-4, BP234). Beacon Pr.

Tagore Testament. Rabindranath Tagore. Tr. by Indu Dutt from Bengali. 115p. 1979. pap. 3.95 (ISBN 0-88253-188-3). Ind-US Inc.

Tagore: The Novelist. G. V. Raj. 1983. 11.50x (ISBN 0-8364-0981-7, Pub. by Sterling India). South Asia Bks.

Tagore's Last Poems. Rev. ed. Shyamasree Devi & P. Lal. 29p. (Bengali.). 1980. 8.00 (ISBN 0-86578-120-6); pap. 4.00 (ISBN 0-86578-121-4). Ind-US Inc.

Tagore's Vision of a Global Family. Vivek R. Bhattacharya. 226p. 1987. text ed. 27.50x (ISBN 81-85148-10-4, Pub. by Enkay Pubs Ltd). Advent NY.

Taguchi Techniques for Quality Engineering: Loss Function, Orthgonal Experiments, Parameter & Tolerance Design. Phillip J. Ross. 1988. text ed. 39.95 (ISBN 0-07-053866-2). McGraw.

Tagungsbericht der 14. Tonmeistertagung Munchen, 1986: Internationaler Kongress mit Fachausstellung im Kongressbau des Deutschen Museums 19.-22.November 1986. Hrsg. Bildungswerk des Verbands Deutscher Tonmeister. Compiled by Michael Dickreiter. (Ger.). 1988. lib. bdg. 30.00 (ISBN 3-598-20355-1). K G Saur.

Tah-Koo Wah-Kan; Or, the Gospel Among the Dakotas. Stephen R. Riggs. LC 78-38460. (Religion in America, Ser. 2). 534p. 1972. Repr. of 1869 ed. 33.00 (ISBN 0-405-04081-4). Ayer Co Pubs.

Tahafatul Falasifa. S. A. Kamali. 19.95 (ISBN 0-686-18600-1). Kazi Pubns.

Tahafut Al-Falasifah. Al-Ghazzali. 8.25x (ISBN 0-87902-054-7). Orientalia.

Taharath Hamishpacha: Jewish Family Laws. Zev Schostak. 1982. 4.95 (ISBN 0-87306-100-4). Feldheim.

Tahin Salakhov. 50p. 1980. 69.00x (ISBN 0-317-14302-6, Pub. by Collets (UK)). State Mutual Bk.

Tahir Salakhov: Introduction in English & Russian. 1980. 66.00X (ISBN 0-317-57455-8, Pub. by Collets UK). State Mutual Bk.

Tahirih: The Poetry of Qurratu'l-'Ayn. Ed. by Amin Banani. 1988. 19.95 (ISBN 0-933770-55-3). Kalimat.

Tahirih the Pure. Rev. ed ed. Martha L. Root. LC 80-39945. (Illus.). 1981. Repr. of 1938 ed. casebound 10.95 (ISBN 0-933770-14-6). Kalimat.

Tahiti. Henry Adams. Ed. by Robert E. Spiller. LC 47-3845. (Illus.). 216p. 1976. Repr. 45.00x (ISBN 0-8201-1213-5). Schol Facsimiles.

Tahiti. P. I. Nordmann. 69.95 (ISBN 0-8490-1175-2). Gordon Pr.

Tahiti. (Times Travel Library). (Illus.). 128p. (Orig.). 1988. pap. text ed. 12.95 (ISBN 1-55650-102-1). Hunter Pub NY.

Tahiti: A Paradise Lost. David Howarth. 224p. 1985. pap. 7.95 (ISBN 0-14-008095-3). Penguin.

Tahiti & French Polynesia: A Travel Survival Kit. Rob Kay. (Illus.). 136p. (Orig.). 1985. pap. 7.95 (ISBN 0-908086-80-6). Lonely Planet.

Tahiti & French Polynesia: A Travel Survival Kit. 2nd ed. Rob Kay. (Illus.). 160p. 1988. pap. 9.95 (ISBN 0-86442-049-8). Lonely Planet.

Tahiti: Complete Travel Guide to All of the Islands. Vicki Poggioli. (Illus.). 216p. (Orig.). 1987. pap. 9.95 (ISBN 0-87052-363-5). Hippocrene Bks.

Tahiti Nui. Eric Debischop. Tr. by Edward Young. (Illus.). 1959. 15.95 (ISBN 0-8392-1109-0). Astor-Honor.

Tahiti Nui: Change & Survival in French Polynesia, 1767-1945. Colin Newbury. LC 79-23609. (Illus.). 396p. 1980. text ed. 25.00x (ISBN 0-8248-0630-1). UH Pr.

Tahiti: Romance & Reality. James Siers. (Illus.). 204p. 1983. 30.00 (ISBN 0-312-78281-0). St Martin.

Tahiti: The Marriage of Loti. Pierre Loti. Tr. by Clara Bell. 217p. 1987. pap. 12.95 (ISBN 0-7103-0231-2, 02312, Kegan Paul). Routledge Chapman & Hall.

Tahiti Traveler's Guide. 4th & rev. ed. Rose Corser. 150p. pap. 6.95 (ISBN 0-9608636-1-3). F & R Corser.

Tahitian & English Dictionary. John Davies. LC 75-35188. (Eng. & Tahitian.). Repr. of 1851 ed. 34.50 (ISBN 0-404-14217-6). AMS Pr.

Tahitian-English, English-Tahitian Dictionary. Leonard Clairmont. 22.50 (ISBN 0-87559-053-5). Shalom.

Tahitian Society: Before the Arrival of the Europeans. 2nd ed. Edmond De Bovis. (Monograph Ser.: No. 1). pap. 6.95 (ISBN 0-939154-04-8). Inst Polynesian.

Tahitians: Mind & Experience in the Society Islands. Robert I. Levy. LC 73-77136. (Illus.). 1973. 14.00x (ISBN 0-226-47605-7). U of Chicago Pr.

Tahitians: Mind & Experience in the Society Islands. Robert I. Levy. (Illus.). 576p. 1988. pap. 19.95x (ISBN 0-226-47611-1, Midway Reprint). U of Chicago Pr.

Tahoe: An Environmental History. Douglas H. Strong. LC 83-6523. (Illus.). xviii, 252p. 1984. 17.95 (ISBN 0-8032-4141-0). U of Nebr Pr.

Tahoe Lake in the Sky. Anne Seagraves & Wes Seagraves. LC 86-91667. (Illus.). 81p. 1987. 12.95 (ISBN 0-9619088-0-7). Wesanne Ent.

Tahoe Place Names. Barbara Lekisch. Ed. by Peter Browning. LC 88-80574. (Illus.). 125p. (Orig.). 1988. pap. 9.95 (ISBN 0-944220-01-0). Great West Bks.

Tahoe Rock Climbs. Christine Jenkewitz-Meytras. (Illus.). 192p. 1987. pap. text ed. 13.95 (ISBN 0-934641-04-8). Chockstone Pr.

Tahoe Sierra. 3rd ed. Jeffrey Schaffer. LC 87-6198. (Illus.). 320p. 1987. pap. 15.95 (ISBN 0-89997-082-6). Wilderness Pr.

Tahoe-Yosemite Trail. 5th ed. Thomas Winnett. LC 87-6216. (Illus.). 136p. (Orig.). 1987. pap. 7.95 (ISBN 0-89997-039-7). Wilderness Pr.

Tahquamenon in Michigan's Upper Peninsula. John S. Penrod. (YA) (gr. 7-12). 1988. pap. 2.95 (ISBN 0-942618-12-2). Penrod-Hiawatha.

Tai Ahom System of Government. A. C. Sharma. xii, 372p. 1986. text ed. 37.50x (ISBN 81-7018-103-8, Pub by B R Pub Corp Delhi). Apt Bks.

T'ai Chan. Edouard Chavannes. 596p. (Fr.). Repr. of 1910 ed. text ed. 99.36x (ISBN 0-576-03443-6, Pub. by Gregg Intl Pubs England). Gregg Intl.

Tai Chen's Inquiry into Goodness. Chung-Ying Cheng. LC 70-113573. 187p. 1971. 12.00x (ISBN 0-8248-0093-1, Eastwest Ctr). UH Pr.

Tai Chi. Cheng & Smith. 22.50x (ISBN 0-685-22124-5). Wehman.

T'ai Chi Chih! Joy Thru Movement. rev. ed. Justin F. Stone. (Illus.). 136p. 1986. pap. 9.95 (ISBN 0-937277-02-9). Satori Resources.

T'ai Chi Ch'uan. Y. Ming-Shih. 6.95x (ISBN 0-685-63782-4). Wehman.

T'ai Chi Ch'uan. Yang Ming-shih. (Quick & Easy Ser.). (Illus.). 60p. (Orig.). 1974. pap. 4.95 (ISBN 4-07-973783-1, Pub. by Shufunmato Co Ltd Japan). C E Tuttle.

T'ai Chi Ch'uan: A Simplified Method of Calisthenics for Health. Cheng Man-Ching. Tr. by Beauson Tseng from Chinese. (Illus.). 160p. (Orig.). 1981. pap. 8.95 (ISBN 0-913028-85-1). North Atlantic.

T'ai Chi Ch'uan & I Ching: A Choreography of Body & Mind. Liu Da. LC 79-183640. 1987. pap. 6.95 (ISBN 0-06-091309-6, PL-1309, PL). Har-Row.

T'ai Chi Ch'uan & Meditation. Da Liu. LC 85-25071. 192p. 1986. 15.95 (ISBN 0-8052-4011-X). Schocken.

T'ai Chi Ch'uan: Body & Mind in Harmony (Integration of Meaning & Method) Sophia Delza. Ed. by Robert C. Neville. LC 84-23916. 244p. 1985. 49.50 (ISBN 0-88706-029-3); pap. 16.95x (ISBN 0-88706-030-7). State U NY Pr.

Tai-Chi-Ch'uan: Effects & Practical Applications. Y. K. Chen. 9.95 (ISBN 0-685-70710-5). Wehman.

T'ai Chi Ch'uan for Health & Self-Defense: Philosophy & Practice. T. T. Liang. 1977. pap. 5.95 (ISBN 0-394-72461-5, Vin). Random.

T'ai Chi Ch'uan: Its Effects & Practical Applications. Y. K. Chen. 1979. pap. 6.95 (ISBN 0-87877-043-7). Newcastle Pub.

Tai-Chi Ch'uan: Its Effects & Practical Applications. Yen-Lin Chen. LC 80-19810. 184p. 1980. Repr. of 1979 ed. lib. bdg. 19.95x (ISBN 0-89370-643-4). Borgo Pr.

Tai-Chi Ch'uan: The Chinese Way. Foen Tjoeng Lie. LC 87-35928. (Illus.). 128p. (Orig.). 1988. pap. 8.95 (ISBN 0-8069-6826-5). Sterling.

T'ai Chi Ch'uan the Philosophy of Yin & Yang & Its Applications. Douglas Lee. Ed. by Charles Lucas. LC 76-6249. (Chinese Arts Ser.). (Illus.). 1976. pap. text ed. 6.95x (ISBN 0-89750-044-X, 317, Dist. by Wehman). Ohara Pubns.

T'ai Chi Ch'uan: The Technique of Power. Ed. by Susan Kimmelman & Tem Horwitz. LC 76-41613. (Illus.). 1980. pap. 9.95 (ISBN 0-914090-24-0). Chicago Review.

Tai Chi Chuan: The Twenty-Seven Forms. Marshall Ho'o. Ed. by Mike Lee. LC 86-51059. (Chinese Arts Ser.). 112p. 1986. pap. 6.95 (ISBN 0-89750-109-8, 449). Ohara Pubns.

T'ai Chi Ch'uan: Yang Style. Yang Jwing-Ming. LC 81-50513. (Illus.). 250p. (Orig.). 1981. pap. 11.50 (ISBN 0-86568-023-X, 210). Unique Pubns.

T'ai Chi Handbook: Exercise, Meditation, Self-Defense. Herman Kauz. LC 73-10552. (Illus.). 192p. 1974. pap. 10.95 (ISBN 0-385-09370-5, Dolp). Doubleday.

T'ai Chi Sword, Sabre & Staff: Complete Secret Works of Yang-Style T'ai Chi Weapons. Stuart A. Olson. Tr. by Stuart A. Olson from Chinese. (Illus.). 178p. 1986. pap. 10.95 (ISBN 0-938045-03-2). Bubbling-Well.

T'ai Chi: Ten Minutes to Health. Chia S. Pang & Goh E. Hock. LC 85-22388. (Illus.). 131p. (Orig.). 1986. pap. 14.95 (ISBN 0-916360-30-X). CRCS Pubns CA.

T'ai Chi: The Supreme Ultimate. Lawrence Galante. LC 84-50665. (Illus.). 208p. 1981. pap. 10.95 (ISBN 0-87728-497-0). Weiser.

T'ai-Chi the Supreme Ultimate Exercise for Health, Sport, & Self-Defense. Man-Ch'ing Cheng & Robert W. Smith. LC 67-23009. (Illus.). 1967. 22.50 (ISBN 0-8048-0560-1). C E Tuttle.

T'ai Chi Touchstones: Yang Family Secret Transmissions. 3rd ed. Ed. by Douglas Wile. (Illus.). 159p. (Orig.). 1983. 17.95 (ISBN 0-912059-02-8); pap. 11.95 (ISBN 0-912059-01-X). Sweet Ch'i Pr.

T'ai Chi Workbook. Paul Crompton. LC 87-9736. (Illus.). 157p. 1987. pap. 14.95 (ISBN 0-87773-424-0). Shambhala Pubns.

T'ai-Chung, T'ai-Wan: Structure & Function. Clifton W. Pannell. LC 72-91223. (Research Papers Ser.: No. 144). (Illus., Orig.). 1973. pap. 12.00 (ISBN 0-89065-051-9, 144). U Chicago Comm Geo.

T'ai-Lin-Chi: Waiting for the Unicorn: Poems & Lyrics of China's Last Dynasty 1644-1911. LC 85-42816. (Chinese Literature in Translation; & Midland Bks: No. 403). (Illus.). 416p. 1986. pap. 15.95x (ISBN 0-253-20403-8). Ind U Pr.

Tai-Pan. James Clavell. 1986. pap. 4.95 (ISBN 0-440-18462-2). Dell.

Tai-Pan. James Clavell. 1983. 19.95 (ISBN 0-385-29218-X). Delacorte.

TITLE INDEX

TAKE A GOOD LOOK.

Tai-Pan see **James Clavell Library.**

Tai Race, Elder Brother of the Chinese. William C. Dodd. 1976. lib. bdg. 59.95 (ISBN 0-8490-2726-8). Gordon Pr.

T'ai Shan: An Account of the Sacred Eastern Peak of China. Dwight C. Baker. lib. bdg. 79.95 (ISBN 0-87968-474-7). Krishna Pr.

T'ai Shan: An Account of the Sacred Eastern Peak of China. Dwight C. Baker. 225p. 1925. 180.00x (ISBN 0-317-68659-3, Pub. by Han-Shan Tang Ltd). State Mutual Bk.

Tai Yu Shan: Traditional Ecological Adaptation in a South Chinese Island. Armando Da Silva. (Asian Folklore & Social Life Monograph: No. 32). 1972. 14.00x (ISBN 0-89986-032-X). Oriental Bk Store.

TAICH Directory 1983: U. S. Nonprofit Organizations in Development Assistance Abroad. 8th. ed. Ed. by Wynta Boynes & Florence M. Lowenstein. 584p. 1983. pap. 24.50 (ISBN 0-932140-02-5, TAICH100, TAICH). UNIPUB.

Taif: The Summer Capital of Saudi Arabia. A. Pesce. 120p. 1984. 95.00x (ISBN 0-907151-27-2, Pub. by IMMEL UK). State Mutual Bk.

Taigu Genci Male-Sterile Wheat. Ed. by D. Jingyang. (Developments in Crop Science Ser.: No. 9). 176p. 1988. 100.00 (ISBN 0-444-42644-2). Elsevier.

Taiheiki: A Chronicle of Medieval Japan. Tr. by Helen C. McCullough from Japanese. LC 79-64824. (Illus.). 1979. pap. 12.95 (ISBN 0-8048-1322-1). C E Tuttle.

Taijutsu: Ninja Art of Unarmed Combat. Charles Daniel. LC 86-51212. 200p. (Orig.). 1986. pap. 8.95 (ISBN 0-86568-085-X, 125). Unique Pubns.

Taijutsu Tactics: Ninja Close-Quarter Grappling. Omoto Saiji. (Illus.). 112p. (Orig.). 1987. pap. text ed. 10.00 (ISBN 0-87364-401-8). Paladin Pr.

Tail Arse Charlie. John Millet. 24p. 1984. pap. 2.00 (ISBN 0-317-07609-4). Samisdat.

Tail Feathers from Mother Goose: The Opie Rhyme Book. Ed. by Peter Opie & Iona Opie. (Illus.). (ps up). 1988. 19.95 (ISBN 0-316-65081-1). Little.

Tail-Holt College: How It Was Then Ozarks 1910-1918. L. Virgil Hogg. (Illus.). 128p. 1984. 6.95 (ISBN 0-89962-360-3). Todd & Honeywell.

Tail of the Arabian Knight. Geoffrey Marsh. 288p. 1988. pap. 3.95 (ISBN 0-8125-0652-9). Tor Bks.

Tail of the Comet. Mary Cable Dennis. 1937. 30.00 (ISBN 0-8274-3564-9). R West.

Tail of the Dragon & Other Works. Gloria Merchant. write for info. (ISBN 0-932298-41-9). Copple Hse.

Tail of Three Tails. (gr. 1-6). 1975. pap. 1.95 (ISBN 0-8431-0563-1). Price Stern.

Tail Tigerswallow & the Great Tobacco War. Arthur L. Hoffman. LC 87-72579. (Orig.). 1988. pap. 8.00 (ISBN 0-938513-04-4). Amador Pubs.

Tail Toes Eyes Ears Nose. Marilee R. Burton. LC 87-33276. (Illus.). 32p. (ps-1). 1988. 11.95i (ISBN 0-06-020873-2); PLB 11.89 (ISBN 0-06-020874-0). HarpJ.

Tail Waggings of Maggie. Margaret W. Baender. (Illus.). 64p. (gr. 8-10). 1982. pap. 6.00x (ISBN 0-88100-012-4). Philmar Pub.

Tailchaser's Song. Tad Williams. 400p. 1986. 15.95 (ISBN 0-8099-0002-5); pap. 4.50 (ISBN 0-88677-278-8). DAW Bks.

Taildraggers High. Larry Sutton. LC 85-47592. 161p. (gr. 5 up). 1985. 11.95 (ISBN 0-374-37372-8). FS&G.

Tailed Amphibians of Europe. J. W. Steward. LC 79-97191. (Illus.). 1970. 8.50 (ISBN 0-8008-7540-0). Taplinger.

Tailed Head-Hunters of Nigeria: An Account of an Official's Seven Years of Experience in the Northern Nigerian Pagan Belt, & a Description of the Manners, Habits & Customs of Some of Its Native Tribes. A. J. Tremearne. 1912. 32.00 (ISBN 0-8115-3058-2). Kraus Repr.

Tailgate Parties. Susan Wyler. (Particular Palate Cookbooks Ser.). 1984. pap. 6.95 (ISBN 0-517-55441-0, Harmony). Crown.

Tailgate Picnics for the Southwest Conference. Candy Coleman. (Illus.). 48p. (Orig.). 1981. pap. text ed. 4.00 (ISBN 0-943768-05-5). C Coleman.

Tailgater's Cookbook. Vick L. McLaughlin & Roger F. McLaughlin. (Illus.). 248p. (Orig.). 1984. 9.95 (ISBN 0-9613456-0-8). V R McLaughlin.

Tailgaters Cookbook; Second Down. Vicki McLaughlin & Roger F. McLaughlin. 201p. 1987. 9.95 (ISBN 0-9613456-1-6). V R McLaughlin.

Tailgating: The Lincoln-Douglas Debates: A Tour of the Seven Original Debate Sites on the Eve of Their 125th Anniversary. B. C. Corrigan. LC 82-73684. (Illus.). 60p. 1984. pap. 2.95 (ISBN 0-9612956-0-0). ADS Pr.

Tailholt Tales. Frank F. Latta. (Illus.). 1979. 18.75 (ISBN 0-686-26703-6). Bear State.

Tailless Batrachians of Europe, 2 parts in one. George A. Boulenger. Ed. by Keir B. Sterling. LC 77-81096. (Biologists & Their World Ser.). (Illus.). 1978. Repr. of 1898 ed. lib. bdg. 38.50x (ISBN 0-405-10679-3). Ayer Co Pubs.

Tailleur de Gloucester. Beatrix Potter. Tr. by Deborah Chattaway. LC 68-10151. (Illus., Fr.). (gr. 3-7). 1967. 5.00 (ISBN 0-7232-0658-9). Warne.

Tailor. Jack Rudman. (Career Examination Ser.: C-1512). (Cloth bdg. avail. on request). pap. 16.00 (ISBN 0-8373-1512-3). Natl Learning.

Tailor & Ansty. 2nd ed. Eric Cross. 168p. 1985. pap. 9.95 (ISBN 0-85342-050-5, Pub. by Mercier Pr Ireland). Irish Bks Media.

Tailor-Made Friendship. Ane Weber & Ron Krueger. (Tell Me a Story Ser.). (Illus.). 26p. (ps up). 1988. incl. cassette 7.95 (ISBN 1-55578-913-7). Worlds Wonder.

Tailor-Made Friendship. Ane Weber et al. (Land of Pleasant Dreams Ser.). (Illus.). 26p. (ps up). 1986. Book & Cassette. 7.95 (ISBN 1-55578-107-1). Worlds Wonder.

Tailor of Gloucester. Beatrix Potter. (Illus.). 57p. (gr. k-3). 1973. pap. 1.75 (ISBN 0-486-20176-7). Dover.

Tailor of Gloucester. facsimile ed. Beatrix Potter. (Illus.). 30.00 (ISBN 0-911132-11-2). Phila Free Lib.

Tailor of Gloucester. Beatrix Potter. (Illus.). 1984. pap. 2.25 (ISBN 0-553-15220-3). Bantam.

Tailor of Gloucester. Beatrix Potter. LC 88-11510. (Illus.). 44p. (ps up). 1988. 14.95 (ISBN 0-88708-080-4); bk. & cass. pkg. 19.95 (ISBN 0-88708-085-5). Picture Bk Studio.

Tailor of Gloucester Model Book. Beatrix Potter. (Illus.). (ps-3). 1987. pap. 3.95 (ISBN 0-7232-3455-8). Warne.

Tailored Metal Catalysts. Yasuhiro Iwasawa. 1986. lib. bdg. 59.50 (ISBN 90-277-1866-0, Pub. by Reidel Holland). Kluwer Academic.

Tailoring. Cy DeCosse Inc. Staff. (Singer Sewing Reference Library). (Illus.). 128p. 1988. 14.95 (ISBN 0-86573-241-8); pap. 11.95 (ISBN 0-86573-242-6). Cy De Cosse.

Tailoring & Repair. rev. ed. (Illus.). 170p. 1985. 10.00 (ISBN 0-318-18629-2). Master Design.

Tailoring Environmental Standards to Control Contract Requirements: Proceedings of the 1st National Conference & Workshop, June 1984. LC 62-38584. 200p. (Orig.). 1984. pap. text ed. 30.00 (ISBN 0-915414-79-1). Inst Environ Sci.

Tailoring Genes for Crop Improvements: An Agricultural Perspective. Ed. by George Bruening et al. (Basic Life Sciences Ser.: Vol. 41). (Illus.). 223p. 1987. 49.50x (ISBN 0-306-42579-3, Plenum Pr). Plenum Pub.

Tailoring Multiphase & Composite Ceramics. Ed. by Richard E. Tressler et al. (Material Science Research Ser.: Vol. 20). 796p. 1986. 115.00x (ISBN 0-306-42381-2, Plenum Pr). Plenum Pub.

Tailoring of Melville's White Jacket. Howard P. Vincent. 240p. 1970. 21.95x (ISBN 0-8101-0310-9). Northwestern U Pr.

Tailoring RT-11: System Management & Programming Facilities. Simon Clinch & Stephen Peters. (DEC Books). (Illus.). 220p. 1984. pap. 38.00 (ISBN 0-932376-34-7, EY-00024-DP). Digital Pr.

Tailoring Software for Multiple Processor Systems. Karsten Schwan. Ed. by Harold Stone. LC 84-28081. (Computer Science: Distributed Database Systems Ser.: No. 16). 202p. 1985. 44.95 (ISBN 0-8357-1645-7). UMI Res Pr.

Tailoring: Traditional & Contemporary Techniques. Linda Thiel & Marie Ledbetter. (Illus.). 384p. 1980. text ed. 30.00 (ISBN 0-8359-7534-7, Reston); instructor's manual (ISBN 0-8359-7535-5). P-H.

Tailoring Vocational Education to Adult Needs. Norma B. Brewer. 30p. 1981. 2.80 (ISBN 0-318-22206-X, IN226). Natl Ctr Res Voc Ed.

Tailor's Dummy. Irving Weinman. LC 85-47775. 192p. 1986. 13.95 (ISBN 0-689-11654-3). Atheneum.

Tailor's Dummy. Irving Weinman. 1987. pap. 3.95 (ISBN 0-449-21201-7, Crest). Fawcett.

Tailor's Pattern Book: From Spain in the Year 1589. Juan De Alcega. 279p. limited ed 50.00x (ISBN 0-318-01133-6). Robin & Russ.

Tails Are Not for Painting. Bernard Wiseman. LC 79-18373. (Bernard Wiseman Bks.). (Illus.). 32p. (gr. k-4). 1980. PLB 6.69 (ISBN 0-8116-6078-8). Garrard.

Tails, Claws, Fangs & Paws: An AlphaBet Caper. Terry Small. (Illus.). 32p. (ps-3). Date not set. price not set. Bantam.

Tails' of a Dog Psychoanalyst. C. W. Meisterfeld. LC 78-58492. (Illus.). 1978. 15.95 (ISBN 0-9601292-2-7). M R K.

Tails of a Dog Shrink. C. W. Meisterfeld. (Illus.). 48p. (Orig.). (gr. 3 up). 1980. pap. 5.95 (ISBN 0-9601292-4-3). M R K.

Tails of the Famous. Margaret J. Brown & Elizabeth Edwards. 1986. 38.00x (ISBN 0-946041-42-3, Pub. by Kensal Pr UK). State Mutual Bk.

Tails Up! Ray R. Kepley. LC 80-81060. (Illus.). 466p. 1980. 14.95x (ISBN 0-9604248-0-6). Kepley.

Tailypo. Joanna Galdone. LC 77-23289. (ps-4). 1977. 8.95 (ISBN 0-395-28809-6, Clarion); pap. 4.95 (ISBN 0-395-30084-3). HM.

Taimanov & Knights Tour Benoni. John L. Watson. 86p. (Orig.). 1985. pap. 5.00 (ISBN 0-931462-39-8). Chess Ent Inc.

Tain. Gregory Frost. 368p. 1986. pap. 3.50 (ISBN 0-441-79534-X, Pub. by Ace Science Fiction). Ace Bks.

Tain. Thomas Kinsella. (Illus.). 1970. pap. 9.95x (ISBN 0-19-281090-1). Oxford U Pr.

Tain. Tr. by Thomas Kinsella from Gaelic. LC 81-16175. (Illus.). 304p. 1985. Repr. of 1969 ed. text ed. 34.95 (ISBN 0-8122-7837-2). U of Pa Pr.

Tain of the Mirror. Rodolphe Gasche. LC 86-4673. 384p. 1986. text ed. 25.00x (ISBN 0-674-86700-9). Harvard U Pr.

Tain of the Mirror: Derrida & the Philosophy of Reflection. Rodolphe Gasche. 360p. 1988. pap. text ed. 12.95 (ISBN 0-674-86701-7). Harvard U Pr.

Taine & Brunetiere on Criticism. Giovanni Gullace. 158p. 1982. 10.00x (ISBN 0-87291-160-8). Coronado Pr.

Taine's Notes on England. facs. ed. Hippolyte A. Taine. LC 74-142704. (Essay Index Reprint Ser). 1957. 21.00 (ISBN 0-8369-2139-9). Ayer Co Pubs.

Taint. Patricia Wallace. 1983. pap. 2.95 (ISBN 0-8217-1174-1). Zebra.

Tainted Booze: The Consumer's Guide to Urethane in Alcoholic Beverages. Charles Mitchell & Michael Jacobson. 65p. (Orig.). 1987. pap. 3.95 (ISBN 0-89329-017-3). Ctr Sci Public.

Tainted War: Culture & Identity in Vietnam War Narratives. Lloyd B. Lewis. LC 84-27929. (Contributions in Military History Ser.: No. 44). xvi, 193p. 1985. lib. bdg. 35.00 (ISBN 0-313-23723-9, LVW/). Greenwood.

Tainyi Sovetnik. Loseff Lev. LC 87-35388. 128p. (Orig., Rus.). 1988. pap. 8.00 (ISBN 0-938920-97-9). Hermitage.

Taipei. (Times Travel Library). (Illus.). 104p. (Orig.). 1988. pap. text ed. 12.95 (ISBN 1-55650-104-8). Hunter Pub NY.

Taiping Ideology. Vincent Y. Shih. 553p. 1968. 40.00x (ISBN 0-317-68662-3, Pub. by Han-Shan Tang Ltd). State Mutual Bk.

Taiping Ideology: Its Sources, Interpretations & Influences. Vincent Y. Shih. LC 66-19571. (Publications on Asia of the School of International Studies: No. 15). 576p. 1967. 20.00x (ISBN 0-295-73957-6, PAI15); pap. 7.95x (ISBN 0-295-95243-1). U of Wash Pr.

Taiping Rebel: The Deposition of Li Hsiu-Ch'eng. Charles A. Curwen. LC 76-8292. (Cambridge Studies in Chinese History, Literature & Institutions). 365p. pap. 94.90 (2030588). Bks Demand UMI.

Taiping Rebellion: Documents & Comments. Franz Michael & Chung-Li Chang. Incl. Vol. 2. 756p (ISBN 0-295-73959-2); Vol. 3. 1107p (ISBN 0-295-73958-4). LC 66-13538. (Publications on Asia of the Institute for Foreign & Area Studies: No. 14, Pt. 2). 1971. 35.00x ea. U of Wash Pr.

Taiping Rebellion: History, Vol. 1. Franz Michael & Chung-Li Chang. (Publications on Asia of the Institute for Foreign & Area Studies: No. 14, Pt. 1). 256p. 1966. pap. 8.95x (ISBN 0-295-95244-X). U of Wash Pr.

Taiping Rebellion: History & Documents. Franz Michael & Chang Chung-li. 244p. 1966. Vol. 1: History. 56.00x (ISBN 0-317-68664-X, Pub. by Han-Shan Tang Ltd). State Mutual Bk.

Tairora Culture: Contingency & Pragmatism. James B. Watson. LC 82-23776. (Anthropological Studies in the Eastern Highlands of New Guinea: Vol. 5). (Illus.). 346p. 1983. 35.00x (ISBN 0-295-95799-9). U of Wash Pr.

Tait & LaPlante's Handbook of Connecticut Evidence. 2nd ed. Colin Tait. 608p. 1988. 75.00 (ISBN 0-316-83178-6). Little.

Taitiriya Samhita of the Black Yajurveda, 10 vols. Ed. by A. Mahadeva & K. Rangacharya. 1986. Repr. of 1984 ed. 185.00x (ISBN 81-208-0228-4, Pub. by Motilal Banarsidass). South Asia Bks.

Taitiriya Upanisat. Tr. by Srisa Chandra Vidyarnava & Mohan L. Sandal. LC 73-3824. (Sacred Books of the Hindus: No. 30, Pt 3). Repr. of 1925 ed. 17.00 (ISBN 0-404-57833-0). AMS Pr.

Taitiriya Upanishad. Tr. by Alladi M. Sastry. 93p. 1980. 36.00 (ISBN 0-89744-145-1, Pub. by Samata Bks India). Auromere.

Taiwan. Ed. by Harrap Limited Staff. 1986. 49.75X (ISBN 0-245-54128-4, Pub. by Harrap Ltd England). State Mutual Bk.

Taiwan. (Insight Guides Ser.). 384p. 1984. pap. 16.95 (ISBN 0-13-882192-5). P-H.

Taiwan. rev. ed. (Hildebrand Travel Guides). (Illus.). 190p. (Orig.). 1988. pap. text ed. 10.95 (ISBN 3-88989-078-4). Hunter Pub NY.

Taiwan. (Let's Visit Places & Peoples - - Nations, Dependencies, & Sovereignties of the World Ser.). (Illus.). (gr. 5 up). 1988. 12.95 (ISBN 1-55546-180-8). Chelsea Hse.

Taiwan: A Comprehensive Bibliography of English-Language Publications. Bruce Jacobs et al. (Occasional Papers of the East Asian Institute). 214p. 1984. pap. 12.50 (ISBN 0-913418-09-9). Columbia U E Asian Inst.

Taiwan: A Travel Survival Kit. Robert Storey. (Illus.). 256p. (Orig.). 1987. pap. 8.95 (ISBN 0-86442-014-5). Lonely Planet.

Taiwan Buyer's Guide, 1986-87. 1986. 180.00x (ISBN 0-8002-3993-8). Intl Pubns Serv.

Taiwan Economy in Transition. Shirley W. Y. Kuo. LC 82-63192. 362p. 1983. lib. bdg. 35.50x (ISBN 0-86531-611-2). Westview.

Taiwan: Facing Mounting Threats. Ed. by Martin Lasater. 82p. 1987. pap. 7.00 (ISBN 0-89195-220-9). Heritage Found.

Taiwan: Guide to Taipei & All Taiwan. 8th rev & enl ed. J. J. Nerbonne. (Illus.). 1985. pap. 25.00. Heinman.

Taiwan-Ilha Formosa. Hsieh Chiao-min. 372p. 1964. 60.00x (ISBN 0-317-69131-7, Pub. by Han-Shan Tang Ltd). State Mutual Bk.

Taiwan in China's Foreign Relations, 1836-1874. Sophia S. Yen. LC 65-7577. pap. 104.00 (ISBN 0-317-11218-X, 2010227). Bks Demand UMI.

Taiwan Issue in Sino-American Strategic Relations. Martin L. Lasater. (Replica Edition). 200p. 1984. pap. 32.50x (ISBN 0-86531-842-5). Westview.

Taiwan Journal: Ten Historic Days. John Tomikel. LC 79-53164. (Illus.). 1979. lib. bdg. 10.00 (ISBN 0-910042-37-3); pap. 4.00 (ISBN 0-910042-36-5). Allegheny.

Taiwan Relations Act & the Defense of the Republic of China. Edwin K. Snyder et al. LC 80-81294. (Policy Papers in International Affairs Ser.: No. 12). 132p. 1980. pap. 7.50x (ISBN 0-87725-512-1). U of Cal Intl St.

Taiwan Shokai Saishin Shashinshu. Katsuyama Yoshiasaku. 308p. 1931. 630.00x (ISBN 0-317-68506-6, Pub. by Han-Shan Tang Ltd). State Mutual Bk.

Taiwan: Studies in Chinese Local History. Ed. by Leonard H. Gordon. LC 78-108096. (East Asian Institute Ser). 124p. 1970. 18.00x (ISBN 0-231-03376-1). Columbia U Pr.

Taiwan, Technology Transfer & Transnationalism: The Political Management of Dependency. Denis F. Simon. LC 81-12980. (Special Studies on East Asia). 325p. Date not set. lib. bdg. 26.00x (ISBN 0-86531-246-X). Westview.

Taiwan Trade Directory. 1987. lib. bdg. 75.50 (ISBN 0-8490-3909-6). Gordon Pr.

Taiwanese Ballads: A Catalogue. Wolfram Eberhard. (Asian Folklore & Social Life Monograph: No. 22). 1972. 14.00x (ISBN 0-89986-024-9). Oriental Bk Store.

Taiwanese Folkliterature, 2 vols. Teito Hirasawa. (Asian Folklore & Social Life Monographs: Vols. 78-79). (Japanese.). 1917. 22.00x (ISBN 0-89986-290-X). Oriental Bk Store.

Taiwan's Changing Rural Society, 2 vols. Wu Tsong-Shien. (Asian Folklore & Social Life Monograph: Nos. 44-45). (Chinese & Eng.). 1972. 25.00x (ISBN 0-89986-043-5). Oriental Bk Store.

Taiwan's Security & United States Policy: Executive & Congressional Strategies. Michael S. Frost. (Occasional Papers-Reprints Contemporary Asian Studies in 1978-1979: No. 4). 39p. (Orig.). 1982. pap. text ed. 2.50 (ISBN 0-942182-48-0). Occasional Papers.

Taiwan's Social Construction, Nineteen Forty-Five to Nineteen Seventy-Five. Yang Chai-Ling. (Asia Folklore & Social Life Monograph: No. 77). (Chinese.). 1976. 14.00x (ISBN 0-89986-255-1). Oriental Bk Store.

Taize Picture Bible. Ed. by Eric De Suassure. LC 69-11860. (Illus.). 298p. 1968. 9.95 (ISBN 0-8006-0005-3, 1-5). Fortress.

Taj Mahal. Photos by Raghu Rai. (Illus.). 160p. 1987. 65.00 (ISBN 0-317-66279-1). Vendome.

Taj Mahal in Starlight. R. H. Linn. 64p. 1987. 7.95 (ISBN 0-8062-3112-2). Carlton.

Tajaliat. Mir-Ghotbeddin M. Angha. 104p. (Persian.). 1982. 16.00 (ISBN 0-910735-15-8); pap. 11.00 (ISBN 0-910735-16-6). MTO Printing & Pubn Ctr.

Tajan. Nader Majd. 100p. (Orig., Persian.). 1987. pap. 5.00x. Iran Bks.

Tajin Totonac. Isabel T. Kelly & Angel Palerm. LC 76-44746. Repr. of 1952 ed. 38.75 (ISBN 0-404-15865-X). AMS Pr.

Tajinstvennij Starets Theodor Kuzmitch v Siberia i Imperator Aleksandr 1. 112p. pap. 5.00 (ISBN 0-317-29253-6). Holy Trinity.

Taji's Syndrome. Chelsea Q. Yarbro. 448p. (Orig.). Date not set. pap. 3.95 (ISBN 0-445-20474-5, Pub. by Popular Lib). Warner Bks.

Tajmahal & Its Incarnation. R. Nath. 232p. 1985. 79.95. Asia Bk Corp.

Takamiyama: The World of Sumo. Jesse Kuhaulua & John Wheeler. LC 72-96129. (Illus.). 176p. 1973. 15.95 (ISBN 0-87011-195-7). Kodansha.

Take. Eugene Izzi. 256p. 1987. 16.95 (ISBN 0-312-01038-9). St Martin.

Take. Eugene Izzi. 1988. pap. 3.50. St Martin.

Take a Bible Break. William McCumber. 115p. 1986. pap. 3.95 (ISBN 0-8341-1080-6). Beacon Hill.

Take a Bow, Victoria. Shelly Nielsen. (Victoria Ser.). 130p. (gr. 5-6). 1986. pap. 3.95 (ISBN 0-89191-470-6). Cook.

Take a Break. 272p. Date not set. incl. 3 cassettes 49.50 (ISBN 0-88432-197-5, S32516). J Norton Pubs.

Take a Break, Vol. 1. 2nd ed. Albert DiNicola. LC 86-91043. (Orig.). 1986. pap. write for info. Lumen Series.

Take a Chance on Love. Jan Gelman. (Follow Your Heart Romance Ser.: No. 6). 128p. (Orig.). (gr. 5 up). 1984. pap. 1.95 (ISBN 0-671-52408-9). Archway.

Take a Chance on Me. Clint Berryhill. 268p. 1983. pap. 5.00. Trends & Events.

Take a Chance to Be First: Hands-on Advice from America's Number One Entrepreneur. Warren Avis. (Paperbacks Ser.). 240p. 1987. pap. text ed. 6.95 (ISBN 0-07-002547-9). McGraw.

Take a Deep Breath. James E. Loehr & Jeffrey Migdow. 1986. pap. 9.95 (ISBN 0-394-74360-1, Pub. by Villard Bks). Random.

Take a Good Look. Ken Forsse. (Teddy Ruxpin Adventure Ser.). (Illus.). 26p. (ps). 1985. incl. audio-cassette 9.95 (ISBN 0-934323-08-9). Alchemy Comms.

Take a Letter: Powerful, Professional Letterstyles. David O. Lynch. LC 85-80700. (Illus.). 208p. (Orig.). 1985. pap. 12.95 (ISBN 0-9615490-0-9). Jantrex & Co.
Take a Look at Kansas. Pat Stinson & Robert Richmond. LC 78-67273. (Illus.). (gr. 2-5). 1979. text ed. 5.95x (ISBN 0-88273-003-7). Forum Pr IL.
Take a Look at Yourself: Self-in-System Sensitizers. Barry Oshry. (Notes on Power Ser.). (Orig.). 1978. pap. text ed. 6.00 (ISBN 0-910411-05-0). Power & Sys.
Take a Murder, Darling. Richard S. Prather. 256p. 1988. pap. 3.50 (ISBN 0-8125-0781-9, Dist. by St Martin's Pr & Warner Pub Servs). Tor Bks.
Take a Stand: Discussion Topics for Intermediate Adult Students. L. G. Alexander et al. (English As a Second Language Bk.). (Illus.). 1978. pap. text ed. 5.95 (ISBN 0-582-79721-7); cassettes 12.95x (ISBN 0-582-79722-5). Longman.
Take a Trip to Antartica. Keith Lye. LC 83-50997. (Take A Trip to Ser.). (Illus.). 32p. (gr. 2-4). 1984. PLB 10.90 (ISBN 0-531-04514-5). Watts.
Take a Trip to Argentina. Keith Lye. LC 86-50018. (Take a Trip Ser.). (Illus.). 32p. (gr. 1-6). 1986. PLB 10.90 (ISBN 0-531-10194-0). Watts.
Take a Trip to Australia. David Truby. LC 80-52721. (Take a Trip Ser.). (gr. 1-3). 1981. PLB 10.90 (ISBN 0-531-00988-2). Watts.
Take a Trip to Austria. Keith Lye. (Take a Trip to... Ser.). (Illus.). 32p. (gr. k-3). 1987. PLB 10.90 (ISBN 0-531-10365-X). Watts.
Take a Trip to Belgium. Keith Lye. (Take a Trip to Ser.). 32p. (gr. k-7). 1984. lib. bdg. 10.90 (ISBN 0-531-04871-3). Watts.
Take a Trip to Brazil. Keith Lye. (Easy-Read Fact Bks.). (Illus.). 32p. (ps-4). 1984. lib. bdg. 10.90 (ISBN 0-531-04736-9). Watts.
Take a Trip to Canada. Keith Lye. (Take a Trip to Ser.). (Illus.). 32p. (gr. k-3). 1983. PLB 10.90 (ISBN 0-531-03757-6). Watts.
Take a Trip to Central America. Keith Lye. LC 85-50162. (Take a Trip to Ser.). (Illus.). 32p. (gr. 1-6). 1985. PLB 10.90 (ISBN 0-531-10010-3). Watts.
Take a Trip to China. Sally Mason. (Take a Trip to Ser.). (Illus.). 32p. (gr. 1-3). 1981. lib. bdg. 10.90 (ISBN 0-531-04317-7). Watts.
Take a Trip to Cuba. Keith Lye. LC 86-50896. (Take a Trip Ser.). (Illus.). 32p. (ps-4). 1987. lib. bdg. 10.90 (ISBN 0-531-10286-6). Watts.
Take a Trip to Czechoslovakia. Keith Lye. LC 86-50018. (Take a Trip Ser.). (Illus.). 32p. (gr. 1-6). 1986. PLB 10.90 (ISBN 0-531-10195-9). Watts.
Take a Trip to Denmark. Keith Lye. (Take a Trip to Ser.). (Illus.). 32p. (gr. k-5). 1985. PLB 10.90 (ISBN 0-531-04884-5). Watts.
Take a Trip to East Germany. Keith Lye. (Take a Trip Ser.). (Illus.). 32p. (ps-4). 1987. lib. bdg. 10.90 (ISBN 0-531-10287-4). Watts.
Take a Trip to Egypt. Keith Lye. (Take a Trip to Ser.). (Illus.). 32p. (gr. k-3). 1983. PLB 10.90 (ISBN 0-531-03758-4). Watts.
Take a Trip to England. Chris Fairclough. (Take a Trip Ser.). (Illus.). 32p. (gr. 1-3). 1982. PLB 10.90 (ISBN 0-531-04416-5). Watts.
Take a Trip to Ethiopia. Keith Lye. (Take a Trip To... Ser.). (Illus.). 32p. (gr. k-6). 1986. lib. bdg. 10.90 (ISBN 0-531-10103-7). Watts.
Take a Trip to Finland. Keith Lye. (Take a Trip To... Ser.). (Illus.). 32p. (gr. k-6). 1986. lib. bdg. 10.90 (ISBN 0-531-10104-5). Watts.
Take a Trip to Greece. Keith Lye. (Take a Trip to Ser.). (Illus.). 32p. (gr. k-3). 1983. PLB 10.90 (ISBN 0-531-03759-2). Watts.
Take a Trip to Hawaii. Keith Lye. Ed. by Franklin Watts Ltd. (Take a Trip Ser.). (Illus.). 32p. (ps-9). 1988. 10.90 (ISBN 0-531-10466-4). Watts.
Take a Trip to Hungary. Keith Lye. (Take a Trip To...Ser.). (Illus.). 32p. (gr. k-6). 1986. lib. bdg. 10.90 (ISBN 0-531-10105-3). Watts.
Take a Trip to India. Keith Lye. (Take a Trip to Ser.). 32p. (gr. 1-3). 1982. PLB 10.90 (ISBN 0-531-04347-9). Watts.
Take a Trip to Indonesia. Keith Lye. LC 84-51806. (Take a Trip to Ser.). (Illus.). 32p. (gr. k-3). 1985. PLB 10.90 (ISBN 0-531-04940-X). Watts.
Take a Trip to Ireland. Keith Lye. (Take a Trip to Ser.). (Illus.). 32p. (gr. 1-3). 1984. lib. bdg. 10.90 (ISBN 0-531-04741-5). Watts.
Take a Trip to Israel. Jonathan Rutland. (Take a Trip to Ser.). (Illus.). 32p. (gr. 1-3). 1981. lib. bdg. 10.90 (ISBN 0-531-04318-5). Watts.
Take a Trip to Italy. Chris Fairclough. (Take a Trip to Ser.). (Illus.). 32p. (gr. 1-3). 1981. lib. bdg. 10.90 (ISBN 0-531-04319-3). Watts.
Take a Trip to Jamaica. Keith Lye. Ed. by FS Staff. (Take a Trip Ser.). (Illus.). 32p. (gr. 1-6). 1988. 10.90 (ISBN 0-531-10558-X). Watts.
Take a Trip to Japan. Gwynneth Ashby. LC 80-52719. (Take a Trip Ser.). (gr. 1-3). 1981. PLB 10.90 (ISBN 0-531-00990-4). Watts.
Take a Trip to Kenya. Keith Lye. LC 85-50163. (Take a Trip to Ser.). (Illus.). 32p. (gr. 1-6). 1985. PLB 10.90 (ISBN 0-531-10011-1). Watts.
Take a Trip to Malaysia. Bruce Elder. LC 84-51807. (Take a Trip to Ser.). (Illus.). 32p. (gr. k-3). 1985. PLB 10.90 (ISBN 0-531-04941-8). Watts.
Take a Trip to Mexico. Keith Lye. LC 82-50061. (Take a Trip to Ser.). 32p. (gr. 1-3). 1982. PLB 10.90 (ISBN 0-531-04471-8). Watts.
Take a Trip to Morocco. Keith Lye. Ed. by Franklin Watts Ltd. (Take a Trip Ser.). (Illus.). 32p. (ps-9). 1988. pap. 10.90 (ISBN 0-531-10467-2). Watts.
Take a Trip to Nepal. Keith Lye. Ed. by FS Staff. (Take a Trip Ser.). (Illus.). 32p. (gr. 1-6). 1988. 9.90 (ISBN 0-531-10557-1). Watts.
Take a Trip to Nicaragua. Keith Lye. Ed. by FS Staff. (Take a Trip Ser.). (Illus.). 32p. (gr. 2-5). 1988. 10.90 (ISBN 0-531-10559-8). Watts.
Take a Trip to Nigeria. Keith Lye. (Take a Trip to Ser.). (Illus.). 32p. (gr. 1-3). 1984. lib. bdg. 10.90 (ISBN 0-531-04742-3). Watts.
Take a Trip to Norway. Keith Lye. (Take a Trip to Ser.). (Illus.). (gr. k-3). 1985. PLB 10.90 (ISBN 0-531-04885-3). Watts.
Take a Trip to Pakistan. Keith Lye. (Take a Trip to Ser.). (Illus.). 32p. (gr. k-3). 1985. PLB 10.90 (ISBN 0-531-04886-1). Watts.
Take a Trip to Peru. Keith Lye. (Take a Trip to... Ser.). (Illus.). 32p. (gr. k-3). 1987. PLB 10.90 (ISBN 0-531-10363-3). Watts.
Take a Trip to Poland. Keith Lye. (Take a Trip to Ser.). (Illus.). (gr. k-3). 1985. PLB 10.90 (ISBN 0-531-04887-X). Watts.
Take a Trip to Portugal. Keith Lye. LC 86-50019. (Take a Trip Ser.). (Illus.). 32p. (gr. 1-6). 1986. PLB 10.90 (ISBN 0-531-10196-7). Watts.
Take a Trip to Romania. Keith Lye. Ed. by Franklin Watts Ltd. (Take a Trip Ser.). (Illus.). 32p. (ps-9). 1988. 10.90 (ISBN 0-531-10468-0). Watts.
Take a Trip to Russia. Keith Lye. LC 82-50062. (Take a Trip to Ser.). (gr. 1-3). 1982. PLB 10.90 (ISBN 0-531-04472-6). Watts.
Take a Trip to Saudi Arabia. Keith Lye. (Take a Trip to Ser.). 32p. (gr. k-7). 1984. lib. bdg. 10.90 (ISBN 0-531-04872-1). Watts.
Take a Trip to Singapore. Bruce Elder. LC 84-51808. (Take a Trip to Ser.). (Illus.). 32p. (gr. k-3). 1985. PLB 10.90 (ISBN 0-531-04942-6). Watts.
Take a Trip to South Korea. Keith Lye. (Take a Trip to Ser.). (Illus.). 32p. (gr. 1-6). 1985. PLB 10.90 (ISBN 0-531-10012-X). Watts.
Take a Trip to Spain. Jonathan Rutland. LC 80-52718. (Take a Trip Ser.). (gr. 1-3). 1981. PLB 10.90 (ISBN 0-531-00991-2). Watts.
Take a Trip to Sri Lanka. Ohanapala Samarasekara. (Take a Trip Ser.). (Illus.). 32p. (ps-4). 1987. lib. bdg. 10.90 (ISBN 0-531-10288-2). Watts.
Take a Trip to Sweden. Keith Lye. (Take a Trip to Ser.). (Illus.). 32p. (gr. k-3). 1983. PLB 10.90 (ISBN 0-531-03760-6). Watts.
Take a Trip to Switzerland. Keith Lye. (Take a Trip to Ser.). 32p. (gr. k-7). 1984. lib. bdg. 10.90 (ISBN 0-531-04874-8). Watts.
Take a Trip to Syria. Keith Lye. Ed. by FS Staff. (Take a Trip Ser.). (Illus.). 32p. (gr. 1-6). 1988. 10.90 (ISBN 0-531-10560-1). Watts.
Take a Trip to Thailand. Keith Lye. (Take a Trip To... Ser.). (Illus.). 32p. (gr. k-6). 1986. lib. bdg. 10.90 (ISBN 0-531-10106-1). Watts.
Take a Trip to the Philippines. Keith Lye. LC 85-50164. (Take a Trip to Ser.). (Illus.). 32p. (gr. 1-6). 1985. PLB 10.90 (ISBN 0-531-10013-8). Watts.
Take a Trip to the West Indies. Keith Lye. (Take a Trip to Ser.). 32p. (gr. 1-4). 1984. lib. bdg. 10.90 (ISBN 0-531-03762-2). Watts.
Take a Trip to Turkey. Keith Lye. (Take a Trip to... Ser.). (Illus.). 32p. (gr. k-3). PLB 10.90 (ISBN 0-531-10366-8). Watts.
Take a Trip to Venezuela. Keith Lye. Ed. by Franklin Watts Ltd. (Take a Trip Ser.). (Illus.). 32p. (ps-9). 1988. 10.90 (ISBN 0-531-10469-9). Watts.
Take a Trip to Wales. Keith Lye. LC 86-50020. (Take a Trip Ser.). 32p. (gr. 1-6). 1986. PLB 10.90 (ISBN 0-531-10197-5). Watts.
Take a Trip to West Germany. Chris Fairclough. (Take a Trip to Ser.). (Illus.). 32p. (gr. 1-3). 1981. lib. bdg. 10.90 (ISBN 0-531-04320-7). Watts.
Take a Trip to Yugoslavia. Keith Lye. (Take a Trip Ser.). (Illus.). 32p. (ps-4). 1987. lib. bdg. 10.90 (ISBN 0-531-10289-0). Watts.
Take a Trip to Zimbabwe. Keith Lye. (Take a Trip to... Ser.). (Illus.). 32p. (gr. k-3). 1987. PLB 10.90 (ISBN 0-531-10364-1). Watts.
Take a Walk, Beetle Bailey, No. 12. Mort Walker. 128p. 1986. pap. 1.95 (ISBN 0-441-05267-3, Pub. by Charter Bks). Ace Bks.
Take a Walk, Johnny. Margaret Hillert. (Illus.). 32p. (ps-2). 1981. lib. bdg. 4.39 (ISBN 0-8136-5111-5, Dist. by Caroline Hse); pap. 1.95 (ISBN 0-8136-5611-7). Modern Curr.
Take a Walk with Jesus. Genevieve Parkhurst. pap. 0.40 ea. 3 for 1.00 (ISBN 0-910924-31-7). Macalester.
Take Advantage of the Ever Increasing Value of Your Money. Malcolm Haley. LC 76-58116. (A Browser Spellbinder Special). 1977. 4.95 (ISBN 0-918582-01-6). Tenameca.
Take Aim, Vol. I. James H. Clark. (Illus.). 400p. 1981. pap. 19.95 (ISBN 0-916460-29-0, Matrix Pubs Inc). Weber Systems.
Take All to Nebraska. Sophus K. Winther. LC 75-11672. vi, 306p. 1976. 24.95x (ISBN 0-8032-0861-8); pap. 7.50 (ISBN 0-8032-5831-3, BB 611, Bison). U of Nebr Pr.
Take-Along Crafts. Susan P. Curtis. (Illus.). 72p. (Orig.). 1982. pap. 2.50 (ISBN 0-918178-28-2). Simplicity.
Take & Read: Gems from the Bible. Alvin Manni. 298p. (Orig.). 1981. pap. 7.50 (ISBN 0-89944-054-1). Don Bosco Multimedia.
Take Another Look. E. Carini. (ps-3). 1969. pap. 1.50. P-H.
Take Another Look. Tana Hoban. LC 80-21342. (Illus.). 32p. (ps-3). 1981. 13.95 (ISBN 0-688-80298-2); PLB 13.88 (ISBN 0-688-84298-4). Greenwillow.
Take Another Look at Linear Bass Patterns. William L. Fowler. LC 82-90965. (Illus.). 82p. 1983. pap. text ed. 10.00 (ISBN 0-943894-01-8). Fowler Music.
Take Another Look at the Keyboard. William L. Fowler. LC 82-90364. (Illus.). 100p. 1982. pap. text ed. 12.00 (ISBN 0-943894-00-X). Fowler Music.
Take Another Look at the Keyboard. rev. ed. William L. Fowler. LC 82-90364. (Illus.). 76p. 1986. pap. text ed. 10.00 (ISBN 0-943894-11-5). Fowler Music.
Take Away Monsters. Colin Hawkins. (Pull-the-Tab Bk.). (Illus.). 12p. (ps-2). 1984. 10.95 (ISBN 0-399-20962-X, Putnam). Putnam Pub Group.
Take Away One. Thomas Froncek. 1988. pap. 4.50 (ISBN 0-312-90509-2). St Martin.
Take Away the Darkness. Witter Bynner. LC 83-45725. Repr. of 1947 ed. 22.50 (ISBN 0-404-20049-4). AMS Pr.
Take Back the Moment. Janice Stevens. 144p. (YA) (gr. 7 up). 1983. pap. 1.95 (ISBN 0-451-12025-6, Sig Vista). NAL.
Take Back the Night: Women on Pornography. Ed. by Laura Lederer. LC 80-17084. 352p. 1980. 14.95 (ISBN 0-688-03728-3). Morrow.
Take Back the Night: Women on Pornography. Ed. by Laura Lederer. LC 80-23701. 352p. (Orig.). 1980. pap. 9.95 (ISBN 0-688-08728-0, Quill NY). Morrow.
Take Better Pictures. LC 82-62973. (Kodak Library of Creative Photography). (gr. 7 up). 1983. lib. bdg. 15.94 (ISBN 0-86706-201-0, Pub. by Time-Life). Silver.
Take Better Travel Photos. LC 82-62979. (Kodak Library of Creative Photography). (gr. 7 up). 1983. lib. bdg. 15.94 (ISBN 0-86706-219-3, Pub. by Time-Life). Silver.
Take Care. C. W. Brister. LC 76-51022. 1979. pap. 3.95 (ISBN 0-8054-5578-7). Broadman.
Take Care: A Guide for Responsible Living. L. David Brown. LC 78-52200. 1978. pap. 7.95 (ISBN 0-8066-1665-2, 10-6190). Augsburg.
Take Care of Dexter. Clyde R. Bulla. (ps-3). pap. 1.50 (ISBN 0-590-05400-7). Scholastic Inc.
Take Care of Millie. Jessie R. Hull. (Sundown Fiction Ser.). 64p. 1980. 2.95 (ISBN 0-88336-704-1). New Readers.
Take Care of Your Heart. Ezra A. Amsterdam & Ann M. Holmes. (Illus.). 356p. 1984. 21.95x (ISBN 0-87196-731-6). Facts on File.
Take Care of Yourself. Donald M. Vickery & James F. Fries. Date not set. pap. write for info. Addison-Wesley.
Take Care with Yourself: A Young Person's Guide to Understanding, Preventing & Healing from the Hurts of Child Abuse. Laurie A. White & Steven L. Spencer. (Illus.). 36p. (Orig.). (gr. k-7). 1983. pap. 5.95 (ISBN 0-9612024-0-8). White & Spencer.
Take Charge! A Guide to Feeling Good. W. W. Johnston. (Illus.). 159p. (Orig.). 1986. pap. 6.95 (ISBN 0-9619220-1-X); pap. 7.95 wire bdg. (ISBN 0-9619220-0-1). Acorn Endeavors.
Take Charge of Your Body. Susan P. Schutz & Katherine F. Carson. 500p. 1983. text ed. 15.95 (ISBN 0-88396-199-7). Blue Mtn Pr Co.
Take Charge of Your Health: Healing with Yogatherapy & Nutrition. Christopher S. Kilham. (Illus.). 176p. (Orig.). 1985. pap. 12.95 (ISBN 0-317-19308-2). Japan Pubns USA.
Take Charge of Your Health: The Complete Nutrition Book. Gladys Lindberg & Judy L. McFarland. LC 81-47836. 272p. 1982. 15.95 (ISBN 0-06-250519-X). Lippincott.
Take Charge of Your Health: The Guide to Personal Health Competence. Peter Ways. (Illus.). 288p. 1985. pap. 12.95 (ISBN 0-8289-0548-7). Greene.
Take Charge of Your Life. 4th ed. Patricia D. Cota-Robles. Ed. by Elvira Dunlap & Kay Meyer. 179p. Date not set. pap. 8.95 (ISBN 0-9615287-0-2). New Age Study Human.
Take Charge of Your Own Career. 2nd ed. Donna J. Moore. LC 79-88808. (Illus.). 184p. (Orig.). 1981. 10.00 (ISBN 0-9605466-0-X). Moore D.
Take Charge: Success Tactics for Business & Life. John K. Cannie. (Illus.). 1980. 12.95 (ISBN 0-13-882621-8, Spec); (Spec). P-H.
Take Control of Your Life: A Complete Guide to Stress Relief. Sharon Faelten & David Diamond. 448p. 1988. 24.95 (ISBN 0-87857-757-2). Rodale Pr Inc.
Take Control of Your Money: A Life Guide to Financial Freedom. Barbara Lee & Paula M. Siegel. LC 86-40097. 208p. 1986. 16.45 (ISBN 0-394-54392-0, Pub. by Villard Bks). Random.
Take Control: Weight Reduction. Judd Biasiotto. (Illus.). 134p. (Orig.). 1986. pap. 8.00 (ISBN 0-933079-05-2). World Class Enterprises.
Take Dominion. Bob Weiner. 224p. 1988. 11.95 (ISBN 0-8007-9119-3). Revell.
Take Effective Control of Your Life. William Glasser. LC 84-47574. 256p. 1984. 14.95i (ISBN 0-06-015342-3, HarpT). Har-Row.
Take 'Em Along: Sharing the Wilderness with Your Children. Barbara J. Euser. (Illus.). 126p. (Orig.). 1987. pap. 11.95 (ISBN 0-917895-12-6). Cordillera CO.
Take Five. Steven Mosley. (Anchors Ser.). 92p. 1987. pap. 6.95 (ISBN 0-8163-0752-0). Pacific Pr Pub Assn.
Take Five: Collected Poems. Kenneth A. McClane. LC 87-23699. (Contributions in Afro-American & African Studies: No. 109). 296p. 1988. lib. bdg. 35.00 (ISBN 0-313-25761-2, MTA/). Greenwood.
Take Five: Integrated Assignments for Pre-Vocational Education. John Davis et al. 200p. 1987. 170.00x (ISBN 1-85008-060-7, Pub. by Framework UK). State Mutual Bk.
Take Heart. Oglesby Paul. LC 86-3170. (Francis A. Countway Library of Medicine). (Illus.). 336p. 1986. text ed. 19.95x (ISBN 0-674-86745-9). Harvard U Pr.
Take Heart, Father: A Hope-Filled Vision for Today's Priest. William J. Bausch. LC 86-50893. 216p. (Orig.). 1986. pap. 9.95 (ISBN 0-89622-309-4). Twenty-Third.
Take Her Deep! A Submarine Against Japan in World War II. I. J. Galatin. (Illus.). 312p. 1987. 17.95 (ISBN 0-912697-64-4). Algonquin Bks.
Take Hold of Your Future: A Career Planning Guide. JoAnn Harris-Bowlsbey et al. (Illus.). 137p. 1986. pap. text ed. 8.95x (ISBN 0-937734-11-X); pap. text ed. 6.95x leader's manual (ISBN 0-937734-10-1). Am Coll Testing.
Take Hold of Your Future: Leader's Manual. JoAnn Harris-Bowlsbey et al. 152p. (Orig.). 1982. pap. text ed. 6.95 (ISBN 0-937734-03-9). Am Coll Testing.
Take Home Games: Motivational Activities for Articulation Carryover (S R L) Debbie H. Wieser. 72p. (Orig.). 1986. pap. text ed. 19.95 tchrs. manual & games (ISBN 0-88450-940-0). Communication Skill.
Take It Easy. Steven Kroll. 144p. (gr. 7 up). 1984. pap. 2.25 (ISBN 0-590-32306-7, Point). Scholastic Inc.
Take It Easy, 2 vols. Bhagwan Shree Rajneesh. Ed. by Ma Yoga Anurag & Ma Ananda Vandana. LC 83-177521. (Zen Ser.). (Illus., Orig.). 1979. Vol. I, 584 pgs. 10.95 ea. (ISBN 0-88050-141-3). Vol. II, 584 pgs (ISBN 0-88050-142-1). Chidvilas Inc.
Take It Easy: American Idioms & Two Word Verbs for Students of English As a Foreign Language. Pamela McPartland. (ESL Ser.). 176p. 1981. 38.00 (ISBN 0-13-882910-1). P-H.
Take It Easy: The Art of Conquering Your Nerves. Arthur G. Mathews. (Illus.). 1945. 11.50x (ISBN 0-911378-25-1). Sheridan.
Take It Home & Try It Out. Bill VanderWerf. 278p. 1985. pap. text ed. 10.00 net (ISBN 0-15-585530-1, HC); net cassettes tapes 12.00 (ISBN 0-15-585532-8); instr's. manual avail. (ISBN 0-15-585531-X). HarBraceJ.
Take It, It's Yours. Lester Sumrall. 140p. (Orig.). 1986. pap. text ed. 3.95 (ISBN 0-88368-174-9). Whitaker Hse.
Take It or Leave It. Raymond Federman. LC 75-21556. 426p. 1976. pap. 8.95 (ISBN 0-914590-23-5). Fiction Coll.
Take It to the Hoop. Ed. by Daniel Rudman. (Illus.). 300p. (Orig.). 1980. 25.00 (ISBN 0-686-77638-0); pap. 8.95 (ISBN 0-913028-76-2). North Atlantic.
Take It to the Limit: Put Yourself on a Path to Life Without Limits. Julie Ridge & Judith Zimmer. LC 84-42934. 1985. 16.95 (ISBN 0-89256-281-1). Rawson Assocs.
Take Jesus for Example. Thomas Babaja. (Illus.). 66p. (Orig.). 1985. pap. text ed. 3.50 (ISBN 0-318-18797-3). Dovehaven Pr Ltd.
Take Joy: The Tasha Tudor Christmas Book. Tasha Tudor. LC 66-10645. (Illus.). (gr. k up). 1980. 16.95 (ISBN 0-399-20766-X, Philomel); PLB 12.99 (ISBN 0-399-61169-X). Putnam Pub Group.
Take Judaism, for Example: Studies Toward the Comparison of Religion. Ed. by Jacob Neusner. LC 82-16039. 1983. 22.50x (ISBN 0-226-57618-3). U of Chicago Pr.
Take Me Along. Lynn Videon et al. 1987. pap. 6.95 (ISBN 0-8224-6719-4). D S Lake Pubs.
Take Me As I Am & Other Poems. Linda I. Henry. 40p. 1988. 7.50 (ISBN 0-8062-3374-5). Carlton.
Take Me Back. M. E. Cooper. (Couples Ser.: No. 29). 192p. (Orig.). (gr. 7 up). 1988. pap. 2.50 (ISBN 0-590-41264-7). Scholastic Inc.
Take Me Back to Dear Old Blighty: The First World War Through the Eyes of the Heraldic China Manufacturers. Robert Southall. (Illus.). 168p. 1985. 17.95 (ISBN 0-903852-14-4, Pub. by Milestone Pubns UK). Seven Hills Bks.
Take Me for a Ride. Michel Gay. LC 84-19088. (Illus.). 32p. (ps). 1985. 10.25 (ISBN 0-688-04135-3, Morrow Junior Books); PLB 10.88 (ISBN 0-688-04136-1, Morrow Junior Books). Morrow.
Take Me for a Ride. Michel Gay. (ps-1). 1987. pap. 3.95 (ISBN 0-14-050655-1, Puffin Bks). Penguin.
Take Me Home. Bonnie Jamison. (Living Books). 176p. 1986. pap. 3.50 (ISBN 0-8423-6901-5). Tyndale.
Take Me Home Again. Celia Dimmette. 1979. 8.00. M Jones.

Take Me Like a Photograph. 2nd ed. Chocolate Waters. 1980. 4.75 (ISBN 0-935060-02-2). Eggplant Pr.

Take Me Out to the Ball Game. Dennis Fertig. Ed. by Ann Fay. (Illus.). 40p. (ps-3). 1987. PLB 9.95 (ISBN 0-8075-7735-9). A Whitman.

Take Me out to the Ball Park. rev. ed. 288p. 1987. pap. 17.95 (ISBN 0-89204-262-1). Sporting News.

Take Me to Your Leader: A Game about Presidential Elections. Edward Dye. (Illus.). 12p. (gr. 4-12). 1982. inc. game 9.95 (ISBN 0-910141-02-9, KP116). Kino Pubns.

Take My Advice. rev. ed. Ed. by John E. Rotelle. 64p. 1987. pap. 1.00 (ISBN 0-941491-02-1). Augustinian Pr.

Take My Hands. D. Schrader. (gr. k-8). Date not set. 4.95 (ISBN 0-570-04035-3, 61HH1019). Concordia.

Take My Jokes, Please! Henny Youngman. 160p. 1986. pap. 2.95 (ISBN 0-931773-78-4). Critics Choice Paper.

Take My Jokes-Please. Henry Youngman. (Critic's Choice PaperBacks Ser.). 1988. pap. 3.50 (ISBN 1-55547-279-6, Univ Bks). Lyle Stuart.

Take My Word for It. William Safire. LC 85-40808. (Illus.). 320p. 1986. 22.00 (ISBN 0-8129-1323-X, Dist. by Random House). Times Bks.

Take My Word for It. William Safire. 1987. pap. 9.95 (ISBN 0-8050-0606-0). H Holt & Co.

Take New York Home. Cari J. Aratoon. (Illus.). (YA) (gr. 9-12). 1988. write for info. (ISBN 0-929644-01-8). Panavision Intl Inc.

Take Nine Spys. Fitzroy Maclean. LC 77-15315. (Illus.). 1978. 11.95 (ISBN 0-689-10854-0). Atheneum.

Take No Prisoners. John Crosby. 320p. (Orig.). 1985. pap. 3.95 (ISBN 0-446-32777-8). Warner Bks.

Take Note of College Study Skills. Anne Bradley. 1983. pap. text ed. write for info. (ISBN 0-673-15578-1). Scott F.

Take Nothing for the Journey: Solitude as the Foundation for Non-Possessive Life. Mary Fritz. 88p. (Orig.). 1985. pap. 3.95 (ISBN 0-8091-2722-9). Paulist Pr.

Take Off... Jenny Armour. 180p. 1980. pap. text ed. 15.00x (ISBN 0-85365-673-8, Pub by Lib Assn England). ALA.

Take Off. Paul Kropp. (Encounters Ser.). 96p. 1986. pap. text ed. 3.95 (ISBN 0-8219-0231-8, 35359); 1.20 (ISBN 0-8219-0232-6, 35718). EMC.

Take-Off Companies. Ed. by Raymond W. Smilor & Robert L. Kuhn. LC 85-16745. 204p. 1985. 35.00 (ISBN 0-275-90226-9, C0226). Praeger.

Take off the Masks. Malcolm Boyd. 178p. 1984. lib. bdg. 24.95 (ISBN 0-86571-048-1); pap. 7.95 (ISBN 0-86571-047-3). New Soc Pubs.

Take off with the Electron & BBC Micro. Audrey Bishop & Owen Bishop. (Illus.). 144p. (Orig.). 1984. pap. 11.95 (ISBN 0-246-12356-7, Pub. by Granada England). Sheridan.

Take off Your Mask. Ludwig Eidelberg. LC 48-4537. pap. 57.80 (ISBN 0-317-10378-4, 2010699). Bks Demand UMI.

Take off Your Shoes. Stefan C. Nadzo. 120p. 1981. pap. 4.57. Coleman Pub.

Take off Your Shoes: A Guide to the Nature of Reality. Stefan C. Nadzo. LC 81-66185. 140p. (Orig.). 1981. pap. 5.95. Eden's Work.

Take-offs & Landings. Leighton Collins. 1982. 19.95 (ISBN 0-02-527240-3). Macmillan.

Take One for Murder. Eileen Fulton. (Take One for Murder Ser.: Bk. 1). 1988. pap. 3.50 (ISBN 0-8041-0194-9). Ivy Books.

Take Out Hunger: Two Case Studies of Rural Development in Basutoland. Sandra Wallman. (London School of Economics Monographs on Social Anthropology: No. 39). 1969. 52.50 (ISBN 0-485-19539-9, Pub. by Athlone Pr UK). Humanities.

Take Out Market. National Restaurant Association Staff. 140p. 1986. pap. 50.00 (ISBN 0-317-57893-6, CS935). Natl Restaurant Assn.

Take-Over. Louis Rossetto, Jr. 1974. 6.95 (ISBN 0-8184-0205-9). Lyle Stuart.

Take Over. Jeffrey C. Wright. (Orig.). 1983. pap. 6.00 (ISBN 0-915124-85-8, Pub. by Toothpaste). Coffee Hse.

Take Pride in Your Work & Build Team Effectiveness. Darby V. Checketts. LC 87-70380. (Illus.). 132p. (Orig.). 1987. pap. 7.95 (ISBN 0-9618170-0-3). Corner Prof Devel.

Take Sky. David McCord. (Illus.). (gr. 4 up). 1962. 12.95 (ISBN 0-316-55509-6). Little.

Take Something to Work with You: A Primer to Enhance Success & Effectiveness on the Job. Catherine I. Williams. 160p. 1984. pap. text ed. 18.95 (ISBN 0-8403-3374-9). Kendall-Hunt.

Take Ten...Steps to Successful Research. Liz Rothlein & Anita M. Meinbach. 1988. pap. 8.95 (ISBN 0-673-38087-4). Scott F.

Take That Hill! Royal Marines in the Falklands War. N. F. Vaux. (Illus.). 256p. 1987. 21.95 (ISBN 0-08-035548-X, Pub. by PDP). Pergamon.

Take the Crazy Out of Christmas Hints & Holiday Planner, 1987. 1987. 5.50 (ISBN 0-943786-05-3). Hollyday.

Take the High Road: Mist on the Moorland. Michael Elder. 1986. pap. 9.75x (ISBN 0-906391-89-X, Pub. by Mainstream Scotland). State Mutual Bk.

Take the High Road: Summer's Gloaming. Don Houghton. 1986. pap. 9.75x (ISBN 0-906391-34-2, Pub. by Mainstream Scotland). State Mutual Bk.

Take the High Road: The Last of the Lairds. Michael Elder. 184p. (Orig.). 1987. 40.00x (ISBN 1-85158-082-4, Pub. by Mainstream Scotland); pap. 10.00x (ISBN 1-85158-081-6, Pub. by Mainstream Scotland). State Mutual Bk.

Take the High Road: The Man from France. Michael Elder. 184p. 1986. 34.75x (ISBN 1-85158-034-4, Pub. by Mainstream Scotland); pap. 9.75x (ISBN 1-85158-035-2). State Mutual Bk.

Take the IQ Challenge, No. 2. Philip J. Carter & Ken Russell. 112p. (Orig.). 1988. pap. 4.95 (ISBN 0-7137-2000-X, Pub. by Javelin Pr England). Sterling.

Take the IQ Challenge: A Mensa Book of Puzzles. Philip J. Carter. 124p. (Orig.). 1986. pap. 4.95 (ISBN 0-7137-1736-X, Pub. by Javelin England). Sterling.

Take the Money & Strut! A Private Investigator's Guide To Collecting a Bad Debt. Fay Faron. 128p. (Orig.). 1988. pap. 9.95 (ISBN 0-9620096-0-1). Zero Sixty Pub.

Take the Road to Creativity & Get off Your Dead End. David P. Campbell. 136p. 1985. pap. 4.50 (ISBN 0-912879-91-2). Ctr Creat Leader.

Take the Wrists Out: A Life in Golf. Howard Capps. LC 85-60492. 158p. (Orig.). 1985. pap. 7.00 (ISBN 0-937088-12-9). Illum Pr.

Take Them up Tenderly: A Collection of Profiles. Margaret C. Harriman. LC 72-5763. (Essay Index Reprint Ser.). 1972. Repr. of 1944 ed. 23.50 (ISBN 0-8369-2991-8). Ayer Co Pubs.

Take These Men. Cyril Joly. (Echoes of War Ser.). 1987. pap. text ed. 11.95 (ISBN 0-907675-40-9, Pub. by Buchan & Enright England). Seven Hills Bks.

Take Thirty Dictionary. Ernest Beaucamp & Dorothea Hansen. (gr. 12). 1971. pap. 5.25 (ISBN 0-89420-099-2, 219905). Natl Book.

Take Thirty Shorthand: Student Syllabus, 2 vols. Ernest Beaucamp & Dorthea Hansen. (gr. 11-12). 1976. Vol. 1. pap. text ed. 5.95 (ISBN 0-89420-097-6, 218999); cassette recordings 244.75 (ISBN 0-89420-211-1, 219105); Vol. 2. pap. text ed. 5.80 (ISBN 0-89420-098-4, 219105). Natl Book.

Take This Book to the Hospital with You: A Consumer's Guide to Surviving Your Hospital Stay. Charles B. Inlander & Ed Weiner. 304p. 1987. pap. 4.50 (ISBN 0-446-34610-1). Warner Bks.

Take This Book to the Hospital with You. Charles B. Inlander & Ed Weiner. (Illus.). 240p. 1985. pap. 9.95 (ISBN 0-87857-537-5). Rodale Pr Inc.

Take This House, Please! The Complete Guide to Buying Real Estate Owned by Lenders, 2 vols. John Beck & Ronald Starr. Ed. by Jonathan Albert. 535p. (Orig.). 1985. Set. pap. 95.00 comb bdg. (ISBN 0-934521-02-6); Vol. 1. pap. 65.00 (ISBN 0-934521-00-X); Vol. 2. pap. 65.00 (ISBN 0-934521-01-8). Unlimited Golden Pr.

Take This Job & Love It. Stanley Baldwin. 144p. (Orig.). (YA) (gr. 7-12). 1988. pap. 6.95 (ISBN 0-8308-1250-4). Inter-Varsity.

Take This Man. Frederick Busch. 264p. 1981. 11.95 (ISBN 0-374-27246-8). FS&G.

Take Three Doctors. Elizabeth Seifert. 1973. Repr. of 1947 ed. lib. bdg. 16.95x (ISBN 0-88411-018-4, Pub. by Aeonian Pr). Amereon Ltd.

Take Time to Focus. Juanita Boggs & Carole Starr. (Illus.). 60p. 1983. pap. text ed. 5.50 (ISBN 0-910817-01-4). Collaborative Learn.

Take Twenty-Two: Moviemakers on Moviemaking. Judith Crist. LC 83-47934. 496p. 1984. 25.00 (ISBN 0-670-49185-3). Viking.

Take Two: A Guide to Ithaca's Movie Making Past. Colleen Kaplin. 1988. pap. 7.95 (ISBN 0-9615964-5-7). I Stephanus Pub.

Take Two & Rolling. Susan B. Pfeffer. (Make Me a Star Ser.). 192p. (Orig.). (gr. 5 up). 1985. pap. 2.50 (ISBN 0-448-47737-8). Putnam Pub Group.

Take Two &...Rolling, No. 2. Susan B. Pfeffer. 1988. pap. 2.50 (ISBN 0-425-08401-9, Pub. by Berkley Pacer). Berkley Pub.

Take Two, They're Small. Elizabeth Levy. (Orig.). (gr. k-6). 1986. pap. 2.95 (ISBN 0-440-48517-7, YB). Dell.

Take Up the Bodies: Theater at the Vanishing Point. Herbert Blau. LC 81-19774. (Illus.). 328p. 1982. 24.95 (ISBN 0-252-00945-2); pap. 10.95 1985 (ISBN 0-252-01245-3). U of Ill Pr.

Take up the Song! Edna St. Vincent Millay & Ivan Hassar. LC 86-45129. (Illus.). 160p. 1986. 19.50i (ISBN 0-06-015461-6, HarpT); pap. cancelled (ISBN 0-317-44437-9, HarpT). Har-Row.

Take up Thy Bed & Walk. David Hinshaw. Ed. by William R. Phillips & Janet Rosenberg. LC 79-6905. (Physically Handicapped in Society Ser.). (Illus.). 1980. Repr. of 1948 ed. lib. bdg. 25.50x (ISBN 0-405-13114-3). Ayer Co Pubs.

Take up Your Cross: Invitation to Abundant Life. Wallace D. Drotts. LC 84-61032. 80p. (Orig.). 1985. pap. 3.95 (ISBN 0-8091-2655-9). Paulist Pr.

Take Your Choice-Separation or Mongrelization. Theodore G. Bilbo. 330p. 1986. pap. 9.00 (ISBN 0-317-53018-6). Noontide.

Take Your Hands off My Attitude: Your Right to a Bad Attitude; Alyce P. Cornyn-Selby. 48p. (Orig.). 1987. pap. 6.95 (ISBN 0-941383-02-4). Beynch Pr.

Take Your Hat Off When the Flag Goes By. Janeen Brady. (Illus., Orig.). (gr. k-6). 1987. activity bk. 2.25 (ISBN 0-944803-31-8); cassette & bk. 9.95 (ISBN 0-944803-32-6); dialogue bk. 1.25 (ISBN 0-944803-33-4). Brite Music Inc.

Take Your Hat Off When the Flag Goes By. Janeen Brady. (Orig.). (gr. k-6). Date not set. pap. text ed. price not set songbook (ISBN 0-944803-29-6). Brite Music Inc.

Take Your Life Off Hold. Ted Dreier. 1988. pap. 13.95 (ISBN 1-55591-038-6). Fulcrum Inc.

Take 22-Crist. J. Crist. pap. write for info. (ISBN 0-14-009462-8). Penguin.

Taken by Surprise. J. Grevin. Ed. by L. Lieblein & R. McGillivray. Tr. by L. Lieblein & R. McGillivray. (Carleton Renaissance Plays in Translation). 84p. 1985. pap. text ed. 9.95x (ISBN 0-919473-51-2, Pub. by Dovehouse Editions Canada). Humanities.

Taken for Granted: How Grout Thornton's Business Climate Index Leads States Astray. Corporation for Enterprise Development Staff et al. 101p. (Orig.). 1986. pap. 10.00 (ISBN 0-9605804-3-3). Corp Ent Dev.

Takenaka Komuten: Japan's "Total Design" Construction Firm. James P. Noffsinger. (Architecture Ser.: A 1922). 26p. 1987. 7.50 (ISBN 1-55590-512-9). Vance Biblios.

Takeoff. Randall Garrett. Ed. by Polly Freas & Kelly Freas. LC 79-9140. (Illus.). 250p. 1980. pap. 7.95 (ISBN 0-915442-84-1, Starblaze). Donning Co.

Takeoff!! The Story of America's First Woman Pilot for a Major Airline. Bonnie Tiburzi. LC 83-18909. 328p. 1984. 15.95 (ISBN 0-517-55263-9, E Friede). Crown.

Takeoff, Too. Randall Garrett. Ed. by Kay Reynolds. LC 86-4256. (Illus.). 311p. (Orig.). 1986. pap. 7.95 (ISBN 0-89865-455-6, Starblaze). Donning Co.

Takeoffs & Touchdowns: My Sixty Years of Flying. Fred E. Jacob. LC 80-28865. (Illus.). 304p. 1981. 14.95 (ISBN 0-498-02540-3). A S Barnes.

Takeoffs from Tension. Mary J. Irion et al. (Orig.). 1969. pap. 0.85 (ISBN 0-377-80571-8). Friendship Pr.

Takeover. G. C. Edmondson & C. M. Kotlan. 288p. 1984. pap. 2.75 (ISBN 0-441-79540-4). Ace Bks.

Takeover. Jonathan Evans. pap. 3.50 (ISBN 0-523-48044-X, Dist. by Warner Pub. Services & St. Martin's Press). Tor Bks.

Takeover. Arthur Herzog. 1987. pap. 3.95 (ISBN 0-425-10503-2). Berkley Pub.

Takeover Defenses - Profiles of the Fortune 500: 1987 Update. Virginia K. Rosenbaum. 33p. (Orig.). 1988. pap. 40.00 (ISBN 0-931035-23-6). IRRC Inc DC.

Takeover Defenses: Profiles of the Fortune 500. Virginia K. Rosenbaum. Ed. by Peg O'Hara. 240p. (Orig.). 1987. pap. 175.00 (ISBN 0-931035-13-9). IRRC Inc DC.

Takeover Dialogues: A Discussion of Hostile Takeovers. Edmund J. Kelly. 160p. 1988. pap. 14.95 (ISBN 0-9620193-0-5). Washington Network.

Takeover Game. John Brooks. 416p. 1988. pap. 9.95 (ISBN 0-525-48440-X, 0966-290, Pub. by Truman Talley Bk). Dutton.

Takeover: Promises vs. Realities. rev. ed. Dennis Meehan. (Illus.). 25p. 1986. pap. 1.00 (ISBN 0-317-59996-8). Reddy Comm.

Takeover: The New Wall Street Warriors - the Men, the Money, Impact. Moira Johnston. 1986. 19.95 (ISBN 0-87795-784-3). Morrow.

Takeover: The New Wall Street Warriors. Moira Johnston. 416p. 1987. pap. 7.95 (ISBN 0-14-010505-0). Penguin.

Takeover Time. Arthur R. Solmssen. 1986. 17.95 (ISBN 0-316-80370-7). Little.

Takeovers & Freezeouts, 3 vols. Martin Lipton & Erica H. Steinberger. 2000p. 1978. Set. 195.00 (00551). NY Law Pub.

Takeovers & the Theory of the Firm: An Empirical Analysis for the United Kingdom. Douglas Kuehn. 189p. 1975. 35.00 (ISBN 0-8419-5000-8). Holmes & Meier.

Takeovers: Attack & Survival, A Strategist's Manual. Ralph Ferrara et al. 1987. 95.00 (ISBN 0-88063-099-X). Butterworth Legal Pubs.

Takeovers of Banks. 35.00 (ISBN 0-317-29540-3, #CO2151, Law & Business). HarBraceJ.

Takeovers of Broadcast Licensees. LC 86-201327. Date not set. price not set. Amer Bar Assn.

Takers. Jerry Ahern. 1984. pap. 3.50 (ISBN 0-373-62401-8, Pub. by Worldwide). Harlequin Bks.

Takers River of Gold. Jerry Ahern & S. A. Ahern. 1987. pap. 3.50 (ISBN 0-373-62402-6, Pub. by Gold Eagle). Harlequin Bks.

Takes from the Talmud, 1906. E. R. Montague. 1977. 22.50 (ISBN 0-686-19672-4). Mill Bks.

Takigi Noh. K. Tanaka. 96p. 1986. 28.95 (ISBN 4-766-10426-9, Pub. by Graphic Sha Japan). Bks Nippan.

Taking. Rev. ed. Joseph M. Gughemetti & Eugene D. Wheeler. (Illus.). 197p. lib. bdg. cancelled (ISBN 0-9608474-1-3); pap. 9.95 (ISBN 0-9608474-0-5). Terra View.

Taking a Chance on God: A Liberating Theology for Gays, Lesbians & Their Lovers, Families & Friends. John J. McNeill. LC 87-47875. 224p. 1988. 17.95 (ISBN 0-8070-7902-2). Beacon Pr.

Taking a Chance on Love. Emily Marlin. LC 84-1352. 128p. 1984. 11.95 (ISBN 0-8052-3913-8). Schocken.

Taking a Line for a Walk. Martin Wiener. LC 84-27735. (Illus.). 166p. 1985. 24.50 (ISBN 0-8108-1781-0). Scarecrow.

Taking a Look at Your Leadership Styles see How to be a More Effective Church Leader: A Special Edition for Pastors & Other Church Leaders.

Taking a Sex History: Interviewing & Recording. Wardell B. Pomeroy et al. 353p. 1981. text ed. 35.00 (ISBN 0-02-925370-5). Free Pr.

Taking Action: Writing, Reading, Speaking & Listening Through Simulation Games. Lynn Q. Troyka & Jerrold Nudelman. (Illus.). 176p. 1975. pap. text ed. write for info. (ISBN 0-13-882571-8). P-H.

Taking Active Charge of Your Life: Facilitator's Manual. Ed Harmon & Marge Jarmin. (Illus.). 149p. (gr. 5-12). 1987. Repr. of 1984 ed. bk. & video or Filmstrip 175.00 (ISBN 0-918588-09-X). Barksdale Foun.

Taking Advantage of Media: A Manual for Parents & Teachers. Laurene K. Brown. 208p. 1986. 18.95 (ISBN 0-7102-0402-7). Routledge Chapman & Hall.

Taking Advantage of the Natural Gas Surplus. 35p. pap. 5.00 (ISBN 0-913359-29-7). Assn Phys Plant Admin.

Taking Agricultural Censuses: Guidelines Supplementing the Program for the 1980 World Census of Agriculture. (Economic & Social Development Papers: No. 1). 135p. (Eng., Fr. & Span.). 1978. pap. 9.50 (ISBN 92-5-100569-9, F1483, FAO). UNIPUB.

Taking America: How We Got from the First Hostile Takeover to Mega-Mergers, Corporate Raiding & Scandal. Jeff Madrick. 356p. 1987. 19.95 (ISBN 0-553-05229-2). Bantam.

Taking & Defending Depositions: ALI-ABA Video Law Review - Satellite Videolaw Seminar: Materials. ALI-ABA Committee on Continuing Professional Education & American Bar Association, Discovery Committee. LC 84-192327. (Illus.). vii, 525p. 1984. 40.00. Am Law Inst.

Taking Another Look. Charles Saltzman. (Illus.). 260p. (Orig.). 1988. lib. bdg. 15.95 laminated; pap. 5.95 (ISBN 0-935343-77-6). Peartree.

Taking Better Travel Photos. (Kodak Library of Creative Photography). 1988. 11.95 (ISBN 0-86706-220-7). Time-Life.

Taking Big Bucks: Solving the Whitetail Riddle. Ed Wolff. (Illus.). 176p. 1987. 14.95 (ISBN 0-912299-25-8); pap. 9.95. Stoneydale Pr Pub.

Taking Books to Heart: How to Develop a Love of Reading in Your Child-For Parents of Children 2 to 9. Paul Copperman. LC 86-7923. 288p. 1986. pap. 9.95 (ISBN 0-201-05717-4). Addison-Wesley.

Taking C Book. Richard J. Leider & James S. Harding. Ed. by Roger Hangen. (Illus.). 133p. (Orig.). 1985. 14.95 (ISBN 0-9607504-1-X). Leider-Harding.

Taking Care: A Self-Help Guide to Coping with an Elderly, Chronically Ill or Disabled Relative. Jill Watt & Ann Calder. 128p. 1986. pap. 7.95 (ISBN 0-88908-628-1, 9547P). ISC Pr.

Taking Care of Business. David Viscott. pap. 6.95 (ISBN 0-671-62529-2). PB.

Taking Care of Business: A Decision Maker's Guide to Worksite Health Promotion. Donald M. Vickery et al. Ed. by Catherine Reef. 200p. (Orig.). 1988. price not set (ISBN 0-9616506-2-1). Ctr Corporate Hlth.

Taking Care of Business: The Economics of Crime by Heroin Abusers. Bruce D. Johnson et al. LC 84-48480. 304p. 1985. 32.00x (ISBN 0-669-09535-4). Lexington Bks.

Taking Care of Carruthers. James Marshall. (Illus.). (gr. 4-6). 1981. 9.95 (ISBN 0-395-28593-3). HM.

Taking Care of Clothes. Jones. 1988. pap. 4.95 (ISBN 0-312-90355-3). St Martin.

Taking Care of Eyeglasses. Dennis Tucker & Madeline Caruthers. (Project MORE Daily Living Skills Ser.). (Illus.). 32p. 1979. pap. text ed. 5.95 (ISBN 0-8331-1238-4). Hubbard Sci.

Taking Care of Mommy. Paula Linden & Susan Gross. (Family Bk.). 239p. 1983. pap. 7.95 (ISBN 0-318-19491-0). M E Pinkham.

Taking Care of Mommy. Paula Linden & Susan Gross. 240p. 1987. pap. 7.95 (ISBN 0-531-15066-6). Watts.

Taking Care of Mrs. Carroll. Paul Monette. (Gay Bks.). 288p. 1988. pap. 7.95x (ISBN 0-312-01515-1). St Martin.

Taking Care of Strangers: The Rule of Law in Doctor-Patient Relations. Robert A. Burt. LC 79-7364. 1979. 15.95 (ISBN 0-02-905090-1). Free Pr.

Taking Care of Terrific. Lois Lowry. LC 82-23331. 160p. (gr. 5 up). 1983. 8.95 (ISBN 0-395-34070-5). HM.

Taking Care of Terrific. Lois Lowry. 176p. (gr. 4-7). 1984. pap. 2.95 (ISBN 0-440-48494-4, YB). Dell.

Taking Care of the Law. Griffin B. Bell & Ronald J. Ostrow. LC 86-23884. 256p. 1986. 29.95 (ISBN 0-86554-265-1, MUP H-226). Mercer Univ Pr.

Taking Care of Yoki. Barbara Campbell. LC 85-46040. (Trophy I Can Read Bks.). 160p. (gr. 3-7). 1986. pap. 2.95 (ISBN 0-06-440173-1, Trophy). HarpJ.

Taking Care of Your Aging Family Members: A Practical Guide. Nancy R. Hooyman & Wendy Lustbader. 336p. 1988. pap. 9.95 (ISBN 0-02-914901-0). Free Pr.

Taking Care of Your Back: A Guide for Healthcare Professionals. Gary Martel. 90p. 1988. Home Study Course. pap. 26.97 (ISBN 0-942028-31-7). R D Anderson.

Taking Care of Your Cat. Sheldon L. Gerstenfeld. LC 79-2338. (Illus.). 1979. o. p. 11.95 (ISBN 0-201-03058-6); pap. 9.95 (ISBN 0-201-03059-4). Addison-Wesley.

Taking Care of Your Cat. Joyce Pope. LC 85-51605. (Taking Care of Your Pet Ser.). (Illus.). 32p. (gr. 4-8). 1987. lib. bdg. 10.90 (ISBN 0-531-10159-2). Watts.

Taking Care of Your Child. rev. ed. R. H. Pantell et al. 1984. pap. 14.95 (ISBN 0-201-08278-0). Addison-Wesley.

Taking Care of Your Complexion. Ingo Keilitz & Don R. Horner. (Project MORE Daily Living Skills Ser.). (Illus.). 48p. 1979. pap. text ed. 7.95 (ISBN 0-8331-1239-2). Hubbard Sci.

Taking Care of Your Dog. Sheldon L. Gerstenfeld. LC 79-2339. (Illus.). 1979. o. p. 11.95 (ISBN 0-201-03060-8); pap. 9.95 (ISBN 0-201-03061-6). Addison-Wesley.

Taking Care of Your Dog. Joyce Pope. LC 85-51604. (Taking Care of Your Pet Ser.). (Illus.). 32p. (gr. 4-8). 1987. lib. bdg. 10.90 (ISBN 0-531-10160-6). Watts.

Taking Care of Your Fish. Joyce Pope. Ed. by Franklin Watts Ltd. (Taking Care of Your Pets Ser.). (Illus.). 32p. (YA) (gr. 7-9). 1988. 10.90 (ISBN 0-531-10192-4). Watts.

Taking Care of Your Gerbils. Joyce Pope. (Taking Care of Your Pet Ser.). (Illus.). 32p. (gr. 4-8). 1987. PLB 10.90 (ISBN 0-531-10190-8). Watts.

Taking Care of Your Guinea Pig. Joyce Pope. (Taking Care of Your Pet Ser.). (Illus.). 32p. (gr. 4-9). 1986. PLB 10.90. Watts.

Taking Care of Your Hamster. Joyce Pope. (Taking Care of Your Pet Ser.). (Illus.). 32p. (gr. 4-9). 1986. PLB 10.90 (ISBN 0-531-10162-2). Watts.

Taking Care of Your New Baby: A Guide to Infant Care for the First Six Months of Life. Marsha Walker & Jeanne Driscoll. 124p. (Orig.). 1988. pap. 6.95 (ISBN 0-89529-397-8). Avery Pub.

Taking Care of Your Parents. Donald M. Vickery et al. (Illus.). 250p. (Orig.). 1987. write for info. (ISBN 0-9616506-1-3). Ctr Corporate Hlth.

Taking Care of Your Rabbit. Joyce Pope. (Taking Care of Your Pet Ser.). (Illus.). 32p. (gr. 4-6). 1987. PLB 10.90 (ISBN 0-531-10189-4). Watts.

Taking Care of Your Rats & Mice. Joyce Pope. Ed. by Franklin Watts Ltd. (Taking Care of Your Pets Ser.). (Illus.). 32p. (YA) (gr. 7-9). 1988. 10.90 (ISBN 0-531-10191-6). Watts.

Taking Care: Supporting Older People & Their Families. Nancy R. Hooyman & Wendy Lustbader. 320p. 24.95x (ISBN 0-02-914900-2). Free Pr.

Taking Care: Understanding & Encouraging Self-Protective Behavior. Ed. by Neil Weinstein. (Illus.). 320p. 1987. 39.50 (ISBN 0-521-32435-1). Cambridge U Pr.

Taking Cash Out of the Closely Held Corporation. 4th ed. Lawrence C. Silton. 460p. 69.95 (ISBN 0-13-882713-3, Busn). P-H.

Taking Cash Out of the Closely-Held Corporation: Taking Opportunities, Strategies & Techniques. 3rd ed. Lawerence C. Silton. LC 84-25249. 380p. 1985. 59.95 (ISBN 0-87624-536-X, Inst Busn Plan). P-H.

Taking Chances. M. J. Farrell. 288p. 1987. pap. 6.95 (ISBN 0-14-016173-2). Penguin.

Taking Chances: Abortion & the Decision Not to Contracept. Kristin Luker. LC 74-22965. 200p. 1975. pap. 8.95x (ISBN 0-520-03594-1). U of Cal Pr.

Taking Chances: Derrida, Psychoanalysis, & Literature. Ed. by Joseph H. Smith & William Kerrigan. LC 83-49198. 216p. 1984. 24.50x (ISBN 0-8018-3232-2). Johns Hopkins.

Taking Chances: Derrida, Psychoanalysis, & Literature. Ed. by Joseph H. Smith & William Kerrigan. LC 83-49198. (Psychiatry & the Humanities Ser.: No. 7). 216p. 1988. pap. 9.95x (ISBN 0-8018-3749-9). Johns Hopkins.

Taking Charge. Compiled by Dale Dieleman. (Good Things for Youth Leaders Ser.). pap. 3.45 (ISBN 0-8010-2911-2). Baker Bk.

Taking Charge. Richard J. Leider & James S. Harding. (3 components) 49.95 (ISBN 0-9607504-4-4). Leider-Harding.

Taking Charge. National Center for Research in Vocational Education Staff. 1982. instr's. guide 12.00 (ISBN 0-318-22207-8, RD217A); filmstrip/tape incl. (RD217B). Natl Ctr Res Voc Ed.

Taking Charge: A Manager's Guide to Leadership. Perry M. Smith. 240p. (Orig.). 1988. pap. 9.95 (ISBN 0-89529-383-8). Avery Pub.

Taking Charge: A Practical Guide for Leaders. Perry M. Smith. LC 86-18014. 258p. (Orig.). 1986. pap. 7.00 (ISBN 0-318-21815-1, S/N 008-020-01098-7). USGPO.

Taking Charge: How Families Can Climb Out of the Chaos of Addiction...& Flourish. Stephen E. Schlesinger & Lawrence K. Horberg. (Illus.). 272p. 1988. pap. 9.95 (ISBN 0-671-64261-8, Fireside). S&S.

Taking Charge: Management & Marketing for the Media Arts. Ed. by Evelyn Goldstein et al. 165p. 1986. pap. 27.50 (ISBN 0-915339-01-3). Media All.

Taking Charge: Management Guide to Troubled Companies & Turnarounds. John O. Whitney. 275p. 1986. 25.00 (ISBN 0-87094-940-3). Dow Jones-Irwin.

Taking Charge: Managing Conflict. Joseph B. Stulberg. 192p. 1987. 22.95 (ISBN 0-669-14014-7). Lexington Bks.

Taking Charge of Change. Shirley M. Hord & William L. Rutherford. LC 87-70644. 98p. 1987. pap. text ed. 8.00 (ISBN 0-87120-144-5, 611-87022). Assn Supervision.

Taking Charge of Manufacturing: How Companies Are Combining Technological & Organizational Innovations to Compete Successfully. John E. Ettlie. LC 87-46333. (Management Ser.). 1988. text ed. 22.95x (ISBN 1-55542-086-9). Jossey-Bass.

Taking Charge of My Life: Choices, Changes & Me. Ed Harmon & Marge Jarmin. LC 88-988. (Illus.). 184p. (Orig.). (gr. 5 up). 1988. pap. write for info. (ISBN 0-918588-10-3). Barksdale Foun.

Taking Charge of Our Lives: Living Responsibly in the World. American Friends Service Committee of San Francisco. Ed. by Joan Bodner. LC 83-48981. (Illus.). 256p. 1984. pap. 9.95 (ISBN 0-06-250019-8, CN 4085, HarpR). Har-Row.

Taking Charge of Your Life. rev. ed. Ernest Wood. LC 84-40512. 136p. 1985. pap. 4.75 (ISBN 0-8356-0594-9). Theos Pub Hse.

Taking Charge of Your Medical Fate. Lawrence C. Horowitz. LC 88-2001. (Illus.). 288p. 1988. 18.95 (ISBN 0-394-56336-0). Random.

Taking Charge of Your Smoking. Joyce Nash. 250p. (Orig.). 1981. leader manual 3.95 (ISBN 0-915950-52-9); student manual 12.95 (ISBN 0-915950-50-2). Bull Pub.

Taking Charge of Your Social Life. rev. ed. Eileen Gambrill & Cheryl Richey. (Illus.). 346p. 1988. Repr. of 1985 ed. 15.95 (ISBN 0-9619781-0-4). Behavioral Options.

Taking Charge of Your Weight & Well-Being. Joyce D. Nash & Linda Ormiston. 492p. 1978. leader manual 3.95 (ISBN 0-915950-28-6); student manual 14.95 (ISBN 0-915950-21-9). Bull Pub.

Taking Charge on the Job. Lyn Taetzsch & Eileen Benson. pap. 2.95 (ISBN 0-345-33204-0). Ballantine.

Taking Charge on the Job: Techniques for Assertive Management. Lyn Taetzsch. Ed. by Eileen Benson. 1978. 15.95 (ISBN 0-917386-22-1). Exec Ent Pubns.

Taking Charge Personal Management System. Richard J. Leider & James S. Harding. Ed. by Roger Hangen. 216p. (Orig.). 1985. 29.95 (ISBN 0-9607504-2-8). Leider-Harding.

Taking Control. Mary H. Ponce. LC 87-70272. 128p. (Orig.). 1987. 8.50 (ISBN 0-934770-70-0). Arte Publico.

Taking Control Counter Display. Garfield. 1988. pap. 49.75 (ISBN 0-471-61363-0). Wiley.

Taking Control: New Hope for Substance Abusers & Their Families. Frank Minirth et al. 176p. (Orig.). 1988. pap. 7.95 (ISBN 0-8010-6234-9). Baker Bk.

Taking Control of Your Office Records: A Manager's Guide. Ed. by Katherine Aschner. (Illus.). 264p. 1984. pap. text ed. 22.95x (ISBN 0-471-81860-7). Wiley.

Taking Creative Chances in Your Paintings. Alfred C. Chadbourn. (Illus.). 144p. 1986. cancelled (ISBN 0-89134-131-5). North Light Bks.

Taking Darwin Seriously: A Naturalistic Approach to Philosophy. Michael Ruse. 250p. 1986. 24.95 (ISBN 0-631-14145-6). Basil Blackwell.

Taking Darwin Seriously: A Naturalistic Approach to Philosophy. Michael Ruse. 250p. 1987. pap. 15.95 (ISBN 0-631-15478-7). Basil Blackwell.

Taking Deadlock Out of Wedlock. Robert Wieland. (Outreach Ser.). 32p. 1985. pap. 1.25 (ISBN 0-8163-0605-2). Pacific Pr Pub Assn.

Taking Discipleship Seriously. Tom Sine. 80p. 1985. pap. 5.95 (ISBN 0-8170-1085-8). Judson.

Taking Dreams Off Hold. Clark B. McCall. (Out Ser.). 1984. pap. 1.25 (ISBN 0-8163-0551-X). Pacific Pr Pub Assn.

Taking Flight: A Book of Story-Meditations. Anthony De Mello. 1988. 14.95 (ISBN 0-385-23586-0). Doubleday.

Taking Freshwater Game Fish: A Treasury of Expert Advice. rev. ed. Todd Swainbank et al. (Illus.). 288p. 1988. pap. 14.95 (ISBN 0-88150-113-1). Countryman.

Taking Glasnost Seriously: Toward an Open Soviet Union. Micheal Novak. LC 87-34895. 180p. 1988. 22.50 (ISBN 0-8447-3641-4); pap. 9.75 (ISBN 0-8447-3642-2). Am Enterprise.

Taking God Seriously. Stuart Briscoe. 192p. 1986. 10.95 (ISBN 0-8499-0523-0, 0523-0). Word Bks.

Taking High Tech Companies Public. Justin P. Klein & Ross J. Reese. 35p. (Orig.). 1983. pap. text ed. 12.50 (ISBN 0-936093-36-6). Packard Pr Fin.

Taking It All In. Pauline Kael. LC 83-8445. 508p. 1984. 25.00 (ISBN 0-03-069362-4, William Abrahams Bk); pap. 14.95 (ISBN 0-03-069361-6). H Holt & Co.

Taking Japan Seriously: A Confucian Perspective on Leading Economic Issues. Ronald Dore. LC 86-61030. 240p. 1987. text ed. 35.00x (ISBN 0-8047-1350-2); pap. text ed. 11.95x (ISBN 0-8047-1401-0). Stanford U Pr.

Taking Juvenile Justice Seriously. Ruth M. Adler. 172p. 1985. 26.50 (ISBN 0-7073-0466-0, Pub. by Scot Acad Pr). Longwood Pub Group.

Taking Laughter Seriously. John Morreall. LC 82-5858. 144p. 1983. 52.50 (ISBN 0-87395-642-7); pap. 14.95x (ISBN 0-87395-643-5). State U NY Pr.

Taking Leave. Janet Shaw. 320p. 1987. 17.95 (ISBN 0-670-80054-6). Viking.

Taking Liberties: A Compendium of Hard Cases, Legal Dilemmas & Bum Raps. Alan M. Dershowitz. LC 88-2716. 336p. 1988. 19.95 (ISBN 0-8092-4616-3). Contemp Bks.

Taking Liberty with the Lady. Dani Aguila. (Illus.). 240p. (Orig.). 1986. pap. 12.95 (ISBN 0-9616392-0-2). Eaglenest Pub.

Taking Lives: Genocide & State Power. 3rd, augmented ed. Irving L. Horowitz. LC 79-66341. 230p. 1981. pap. 12.95 (ISBN 0-87855-882-9). Transaction Bk.

Taking My Cat to the Vet. Susan Kuklin. LC 88-5052. (Illus.). 32p. (ps-k). 1988. 12.95 (ISBN 0-02-751233-9). Bradbury Pr.

Taking My Dog to the Vet. Susan Kuklin. LC 88-5047. (Illus.). 32p. (ps-k). 1988. 12.95 (ISBN 0-02-751234-7). Bradbury Pr.

Taking Note of Music: Beginning Theory & Songwriting. Robert Engle. 224p. 1988. pap. text ed. price not set (ISBN 0-13-882705-2). P-H.

Taking Notice. Marilyn Hacker. LC 79-28166. 128p. 1980. pap. 5.95 (ISBN 0-394-73917-5). Knopf.

Taking of Agnes. Jennifer Potter. LC 87-7839. 208p. 1987. Repr. of 1985 ed. 15.95 (ISBN 0-916515-26-5). Mercury Hse Inc.

Taking of Getty Oil: From the Oil Patch to Wall Street - The Full Story of the Most Spectacular & Catastrophic Takeover of All Time. Steve Coll. LC 87-11467. 484p. 1987. 19.95 (ISBN 0-689-11860-0). Atheneum.

Taking of Mariasburg. Julian F. Thompson. 288p. (YA) (gr. 7 up). 1988. 12.95 (ISBN 0-590-41247-7, Scholastic Hardcover). Scholastic Inc.

Taking of Pelham One, Two, Three. John Godey. 19.95 (ISBN 0-88411-649-2, Pub. by Aeonian Pr). Amereon Ltd.

Taking of the USS Tunny. William G. Davis. 288p. 1989. pap. price not set. Tor Bks.

Taking off the Patriarchal Glasses. Cora E. Cypser. 237p. 1987. 14.95 (ISBN 0-533-07214-X). Vantage.

Taking Off: Travel Tips for a Carefree Trip. Joanne E. Bernstein. LC 85-45440. (Trophy Nonfiction Bks.). (Illus.). 224p. (YA) (gr. 7 up). 1986. pap. 3.95 (ISBN 0-06-446047-9, Trophy). HarpJ.

Taking Off: Travel Tips for a Carefree Trip. Joanne E. Bernstein. LC 85-45171. (Illus.). 224p. (YA) (gr. 7 up). 1986. PLB 12.89 (ISBN 0-397-32107-4, Lipp Jr Bks). HarpJ.

Taking off with BASIC on the Commodore 64. Nancy R. Watson. (Illus.). 208p. (gr. 5 up). 1984. pap. 12.95 (ISBN 0-89303-868-7). Brady Comp Bks.

Taking on General Motors: A Case Study of the UAW Campaign to Keep GM Van Nuys Open. Eric Mann. (Illus.). 408p. (Orig.). 1988. pap. 20.00 (ISBN 0-89215-141-2). U Cal La Indus Rel.

Taking on the Heart of Christ. John H. Newman. Date not set. Repr. 4.95 (ISBN 0-87193-114-1). Dimension Bks.

Taking on the Local Color. Cynthia Genser. LC 76-41486. (Wesleyan Poetry Program: Vol. 85). 1977. 17.00x (ISBN 0-8195-2085-3); pap. 8.95 (ISBN 0-8195-1085-8). Wesleyan U Pr.

Taking on the Press: Constitutional Rights in Conflict. Melvyn B. Zerman. LC 85-47896. (Illus.). 192p. (YA) (gr. 7 up). 1986. 11.70i (ISBN 0-690-04301-5, Crowell Jr Bks); PLB 11.89 (ISBN 0-690-04302-3). HarpJ.

Taking on Tomorrow. Ned White. 26p. 1980. 2.35 (ISBN 0-318-22208-6, SN25). Natl Ctr Res Voc Ed.

Taking Our Time: Feminist Perspectives on Temporality. Frieda J. Forman & Caoran Sowton. (Athene Ser.). (Illus.). 256p. 1988. 36.01 (ISBN 0-08-036478-0); pap. text ed. 14.51 (ISBN 0-08-036477-2). Pergamon.

Taking Over. Jennifer Sarasin. (Cheerleaders Ser.: No. 26). 176p. (Orig.). (gr. 6-10). 1987. pap. 2.50 (ISBN 0-590-40447-4). Scholastic Inc.

Taking Pictures. Nina Leen. (Illus.). 48p. (ps-5). 1980. pap. 1.75 (ISBN 0-380-49205-9, 49205-9, Camelot). Avon.

Taking Possession. Bert Almon. 1976. 5.25 (ISBN 0-941490-17-3). Solo Pr.

Taking Profits From the OEX: How to Start & Sustain a Winning Pattern of Trading Stock Index Options. Arthur Darack. (Illus., Orig.). 1988. 19.95 (ISBN 0-933893-58-2). Bonus Books.

Taking Reform Seriously: Perspectives on Public Interest Liberalism. Michael W. McCann. LC 86-47647. 348p. 1986. 29.95 (ISBN 0-8014-1952-2). Cornell U Pr.

Taking Reform Seriously: Perspectives on Public Interest Liberalism. Michael W. McCann. LC 86-47647. (Paperback Ser.). 348p. 1987. pap. 12.95x (ISBN 0-8014-9415-X). Cornell U Pr.

Taking Refuge in L. A. Life in a Vietnamese Buddhist Temple. Photos by Don Farber. (Illus.). 108p. 1987. pap. 14.95 (ISBN 0-89381-261-7). Aperture.

Taking Rights Seriously. Ronald Dworkin. 1977. 21.00x (ISBN 0-674-86710-6); pap. 10.95x (ISBN 0-674-86711-4). Harvard U Pr.

Taking Risks. Anne Reynolds. (Cheerleaders Ser.: No. 17). 160p. (Orig.). (gr. 7 up). 1986. pap. 2.25 (ISBN 0-590-40187-4). Scholastic Inc.

Taking Risks: The Management of Uncertainty. Kenneth R. Maccrimmon & Donald A. Wehrung. (Illus.). 384p. 1988. pap. 12.95 (ISBN 0-02-919563-2). Free Pr.

Taking Risks: The Mangement of Uncertainty. Kenneth R. MacCrimmon & Donald A. Wehrung. 384p. 1986. 26.95 (ISBN 0-02-919560-8). Free Pr.

Taking Root: The Workshop Center at City College. Beth Alberty et al. 45p. (Orig.). 1983. pap. 3.00 (ISBN 0-317-45084-0). City Coll Wk.

Taking Root to Fly. Irene Dowd. (Illus.). 48p. (Orig.). pap. 5.00x (ISBN 0-937645-00-1). Contact Edit.

Taking Sides. Stephen Green. 370p. 1987. pap. 9.95 (ISBN 0-915597-54-3). Amana Bks.

Taking Sides. Stephen Green. 368p. 10.00 (ISBN 0-88728-189-3). Inst Palestine.

Taking Sides. Norma Klein. 144p. 1982. pap. 2.25 (ISBN 0-380-00528-X, 60054-4, Flare). Avon.

Taking Sides. Albert Nolan. 16p. 1984. 3.00x (ISBN 0-946848-40-8, Pub. by CIIR). State Mutual Bk.

Taking Sides. Created by Francine Pascal. (Sweet Valley High Ser.: No. 31). 160p. (Orig.). (YA) (gr. 7-12). 1986. pap. 2.75 (ISBN 0-553-25886-9). Bantam.

Taking Sides: America's Secret Relations with a Militant Israel. Stephen Green. LC 83-61736. 320p. 1984. 14.95 (ISBN 0-688-02643-5). Morrow.

Taking Sides: Clashing Views on Controversial Bioethical Issues. 2nd ed. Carol Levine. LC 86-71775. (Illus.). 372p. 1987. pap. text ed. 9.95. Dushkin Pub.

Taking Sides: Clashing Views on Controversial Economic Issues. 4th ed. Frank J. Bonello & Thomas R. Swartz. LC 87-72958. (Illus.). 396p. 1988. pap. text ed. 9.95 (ISBN 0-87967-740-6). Dushkin Pub.

Taking Sides: Clashing Views on Controversial Environmental Issues. 2nd ed. Theodore Goldfarb. LC 86-71776. (Illus.). 336p. 1987. pap. text ed. 9.95 (ISBN 0-87967-656-6). Dushkin Pub.

Taking Sides: Clashing Views on Controversial Educational Issues. 4th ed. James W. Noll. LC 86-48003. (Illus.). 384p. 1987. pap. text ed. 9.95 (ISBN 0-87967-660-4). Dushkin Pub.

Taking Sides: Clashing Views on Controversial Issues in American History, Vol. I. 2nd ed. Larry Madaras. LC 86-48001. (Illus.). 396p. 1987. pap. text ed. 9.95 (ISBN 0-87967-658-2). Dushkin Pub.

Taking Sides: Clashing Views on Controversial Issues in American History, Vol. II. 2nd ed. Larry Madaras. LC 86-48004. (Illus.). 396p. 1987. pap. text ed. 9.95 (ISBN 0-87967-659-0). Dushkin Pub.

Taking Sides: Clashing Views on Controversial Issues in Human Sexuality. Robert T. Francoeur. LC 86-48002. (Illus.). 360p. (Orig.). 1987. pap. text ed. 9.95 (ISBN 0-87967-661-2). Dushkin Pub.

Taking Sides: Clashing Views on Controversial Issues in World Politics. John T. Rourke. LC 87-72264. (Illus.). 336p. (Orig.). 1988. pap. text ed. 9.95 (ISBN 0-87967-737-6). Dushkin Pub.

Taking Sides: Clashing Views on Controversial Moral Issues. LC 87-72957. (Illus.). 336p. (Orig.). 1988. pap. text ed. 9.95 (ISBN 0-87967-739-2). Dushkin Pub.

Taking Sides: Clashing Views on Controversial Political Issues. 5th ed. George McKenna. LC 86-71774. (Illus.). 372p. 1987. pap. text ed. 9.95 (ISBN 0-87967-655-8). Dushkin Pub.

Taking Sides: Clashing Views on Controversial Psychological Issues. 5th ed. Joseph Rubinstein & Brent Slife. LC 87-72959. (Illus.). 396p. 1988. pap. text ed. 9.95 (ISBN 0-87967-741-4). Dushkin Pub.

Taking Sides: Clashing Views on Controversial Social Issues. 5th ed. Kurt Finsterbusch & George McKenna. LC 87-72960. (Illus.). 396p. 1988. pap. text ed. 9.95 (ISBN 0-87967-742-2). Dushkin Pub.

Taking Sides in the Financial Revolution. Michael Kieschnick. 1987. 4.95 (ISBN 0-317-62722-8). NCPA Washington.

Taking Sides: The Fiction of John LeCarre. Tony Barley. LC 85-28434. 192p. 1986. 65.00x (ISBN 0-335-15251-1, Open Univ Pr); pap. 21.00x (ISBN 0-335-15252-X). Taylor & Francis.

Taking Sides: The War at Home. Jerold M. Starr & Charles Di Benedetti. (Lessons of the Vietnam War Ser.). (Illus.). 32p. 1988. pap. text ed. 3.00 (ISBN 0-945919-07-7). Ctr Social Studies.

Taking Soaps Seriously: The World of Guiding Light. Michael J. Intintoli. LC 83-27232. 208p. 1984. 27.95 (ISBN 0-275-91738-X, C1738). Praeger.

Taking Stock: A Daily Journal. James Harding & Richard Leider. (Skill Builder Ser.). 154p. (Orig.). 1987. pap. 9.95 (ISBN 0-943920-76-0). Metamorphous Pr.

Taking Stock: A Personal Inventory. Terence Williams & Harold Swift. 52p. 1980. 1.75 (ISBN 0-89486-117-4). Hazelden.

Tale of Lanherne. Charles Lee. 1985. 15.00x (ISBN 0-907566-45-6, Pub. by Dyllansow & Truran). State Mutual Bk.

Tale of Little Pig Robinson. Beatrix Potter. (ps-2). 1930. bds. 4.95 (ISBN 0-7232-0610-4). Warne.

Tale of Love. Lori Copeland. (Orig.). 1988. pap. 3.95 (ISBN 0-440-20173-X). Dell.

Tale of Lumbdoom, The Long-Tailed Langoor. Uma Anand. (Illus.). 1968. 1.00 (ISBN 0-88253-325-8). Ind-US Inc.

Tale of Marvel & Wonder. Ngoc M. Thai et al. Ed. by Lawrence Stolurow. Tr. by Enrique Cubillos from Span. (Eng.). (gr. 4 up). 1985. pap. text ed. 5.25 (ISBN 0-88670-280-1, 8144); tchr's guide 7.50, (ISBN 0-88670-284-4, 8149). U IA Ctr Ed Experiment.

Tale of Mr. Jeremy Fisher. Beatrix Potter. LC 74-75269. (Illus.). 59p. (gr. 2-4). 1974. pap. 1.75 (ISBN 0-486-23066-X). Dover.

Tale of Mr. Jeremy Fisher. Beatrix Potter. (Illus.). (ps-2). 1906. bds. 4.95 (ISBN 0-7232-0598-1); pap. 4.95 (ISBN 0-7232-6231-4). Warne.

Tale of Mr. Jeremy Fisher. Beatrix Potter. (Beatrix Potter's Timeless Tales Ser.). (Illus.). 1983. pap. 2.25 (ISBN 0-553-15221-1). Bantam.

Tale of Mister Tod. Beatrix Potter. (Illus.). (ps-2). 1912. bds. 4.95 (ISBN 0-7232-0605-8). Warne.

Tale of Mrs. Tiggy-winkle. Beatrix Potter. (Illus.). 57p. (gr. k-6). 1973. pap. 1.75 (ISBN 0-486-20546-0). Dover.

Tale of Mrs. Tiggy-Winkle. Beatrix Potter. (Illus.). (ps-2). 1905. bds. 4.95 (ISBN 0-7232-0597-3); pap. 2.25 (ISBN 0-7232-6230-6). Warne.

Tale of Mrs. Tiggy-Winkle. Beatrix Potter. (Illus.). 1984. pap. 2.25 (ISBN 0-553-15204-1). Bantam.

Tale of Mrs. Tiggy-Winkle. Beatrix Potter. (Illus.). 64p. (ps-3). 1987. bds. 3.95 (ISBN 0-671-63235-3, Little Simon). S&S.

Tale of Mrs. Tittlemouse. Beatrix Potter. (Illus.). (ps-2). 1910. bds. 4.95 (ISBN 0-7232-0602-3); pap. 2.25 (ISBN 0-7232-6235-7). Warne.

Tale of Mrs. Tittlemouse. Beatrix Potter. 64p. 1986. pap. 1.75 (ISBN 0-486-25230-2). Dover.

Tale of Mrs. Tittlemouse & Other Mouse Stories. Beatrix Potter. LC 85-40386. (Illus.). 80p. (ps-3). 1985. 10.95 (ISBN 0-7232-3324-1). Warne.

Tale of Mrs. Tittlemouse & Other Mouse Stories. Beatrix Potter. (ps-3). 1988. pap. 5.95 (ISBN 0-317-69624-6, Puffin Bks). Penguin.

Tale of Nezame: Part Three of Yowa no Nezame Monogatari. Tr. by Carol Hochstedler. LC 79-130060. (East Asia Papers: No. 22). 273p. 1979. 5.00 (ISBN 0-939657-22-8). Cornell East Asia Pgm.

Tale of "O"-- On Being Different in An Organization. Rosabeth M. Kanter & Barry Stein. LC 79-2625. (Illus., Orig.). 1980. pap. 6.95x (ISBN 0-06-132064-1, TB 2064, Torch). Har-Row.

Tale of One January. Albert Maltz. (Orig.). pap. 2.95 (ISBN 0-7145-0544-7). Riverrun NY.

Tale of Pausanian Love. Edward P. Warren. LC 78-22236. (Gay Experience). Repr. of 1927 ed. 16.50 (ISBN 0-404-61518-X). AMS Pr.

Tale of Peter Rabbit. Beatrix Potter. (Illus.). 60p. (gr. 1-5). 1972. pap. 1.75 (ISBN 0-486-22827-4). Dover.

Tale of Peter Rabbit. new ed. Beatrix Potter. LC 78-18071. (Illus.). 32p. (gr. k-3). 1979. PLB 9.79 (ISBN 0-89375-124-3); pap. 1.95 (ISBN 0-89375-102-2). Troll Assocs.

Tale of Peter Rabbit. Beatrix Potter. (Illus.). (ps-2). 1902. bds. 4.95 (ISBN 0-7232-0592-2); pap. 2.25 (ISBN 0-7232-6225-X). Warne.

Tale of Peter Rabbit. Beatrix Potter. (Golden Storytime Bks.). (Illus.). 24p. (ps-1). 1982. pap. 2.95 (ISBN 0-307-11950-5, Golden Bks). Western Pub.

Tale of Peter Rabbit. Beatrix Potter. (Illus.). 64p. (Orig.). 1984. pap. 2.50 (ISBN 0-553-15470-2). Bantam.

Tale of Peter Rabbit. Beatrix Potter. LC 85-70809. (Pudgy Pal Board Bks.). (Illus.). 13p. (ps). 1986. 3.95 (ISBN 0-448-10224-2, G&D). Putnam Pub Group.

Tale of Peter Rabbit. Beatrix Potter. (Easy to Read Folktales Ser.). (Illus.). 32p. (Orig.). (gr. k-3). 1988. pap. 2.50 (ISBN 0-590-33848-X); incl. cassette 5.95 (ISBN 0-590-63091-1). Scholastic Inc.

Tale of Peter Rabbit. Beatrix Potter. 1985. pap. 2.95 (ISBN 0-7232-2938-4). Warne.

Tale of Peter Rabbit. Beatrix Potter. (Illus.). 64p. (ps-3). 1986. pap. 3.95 (ISBN 0-671-62924-7, Little Simon). S&S.

Tale of Peter Rabbit. Beatrix Potter. LC 87-40282. (Illus.). (ps up). 1988. incl. audio cassettes 5.95 (ISBN 1-55782-015-5). Warner Bks.

Tale of Peter Rabbit. Beatrix Potter. LC 88-11509. (Illus.). 36p. (ps up). 1988. 14.95; bk. & cass. pkg. 19.95 (ISBN 0-88708-084-7). Picture Bk Studio.

Tale of Peter Rabbit. Beatrix Potter. (Illus.). (ps-3). Date not set. 4.95 (ISBN 0-7232-3460-4). Warne.

Tale of Peter Rabbit. (Read Along with Me Ser.). (ps). 1988. pap. 1.29 (ISBN 0-317-69606-8, Checkerboard Pr). Macmillan.

Tale of Peter Rabbit. Illus. by Tony Tallarico. (Tote Bks). (Illus.). 12p. (ps). 1988. price not set (ISBN 0-89828-322-1). Tuffy Bks.

Tale of Peter Rabbit: A Coloring Book in Signed English. Beatrix Potter. (Signed English Ser.). (Illus.). 64p. 1986. pap. 4.95 (ISBN 0-930323-29-7, Clerc Bks). Gallaudet Univ Pr.

Tale of Peter Rabbit & Chicken Little, 2 bks. (Illus.). 40p. (ps-k). 1989. Set. pap. 4.95 incl. audio cassette (ISBN 0-448-10232-3, G&D). Putnam Pub Group.

Tale of Peter Rabbit & Other Favorite Stories, 7 vols. Beatrix Potter. 447p. (gr. 2 up). Boxed Set. pap. 12.25 (ISBN 0-486-23903-9). Dover.

Tale of Peter Rabbit & Other Stories. Beatrix Potter. LC 82-47808. (Illus.). 1982. 17.95 (ISBN 0-394-52845-X). Knopf.

Tale of Peter Rabbit & Other Stories. Beatrix Potter. (Illus.). 1985. 6.95. Wanderer Bks.

Tale of Peter Rabbit & Other Stories. Beatrix Potter. 6.95 (ISBN 0-317-43245-1, Little Simon). S&S.

Tale of Peter Rabbit & Other Stories. Beatrix Potter. (Picture Storybooks Ser.). (Illus.). 1987. 6.95 (ISBN 0-671-52403-8, Little Simon). S&S.

"Tale of Peter Rabbit" in French: L'Histoire de Pierre Lapin. Beatrix Potter. Tr. by Judith L. Greenberg from Eng. 64p. (Orig.). 1987. pap. 2.50 (ISBN 0-486-25313-9). Dover.

"Tale of Peter Rabbit" in Spanish: El Cuento de Pedro, el Conejo. Beatrix Potter. Tr. by Esperanza G. Saludes from Eng. 64p. (Orig.). 1987. pap. 2.50 (ISBN 0-486-25314-7). Dover.

Tale of Peter Rabbit Paint with Water Book. Beatrix Potter. (Illus.). (gr. 1 up). 1988. 1.49 (ISBN 0-671-62983-2). Wanderer Bks.

Tale of Peter Rabbit Sticker Book. Beatrix Potter. (Illus.). (gr. 1 up). 1988. 1.49 (ISBN 0-671-62579-9). Wanderer Bks.

Tale of Pierrot: & Other Stories. George Dennison. LC 86-46056. 352p. 1987. 17.45i (ISBN 0-06-055079-1, HarpT). Har-Row.

Tale of Pierrot: And Other Stories. George Dennison. 352p. 1987. pap. 8.95 (ISBN 0-06-096169-4, PL6169, PL). Har-Row.

Tale of Pigling Bland. Beatrix Potter. (Illus.). (ps-2). 1913. bds. 4.95 (ISBN 0-7232-0606-6). Warne.

Tale of Poor Lovers. Vasco Pratolini. (Voices of Resistance Ser.). 368p. 1988. pap. 7.50. Monthly Rev.

Tale of Ringy. Meyer Azaad. Tr. by Mohammad R. Ghanoonparvar & Diane L. Wilcox. (Illus.). 24p. (Orig.). (gr. 3 up). 1983. pap. 4.95 (ISBN 0-686-43078-6). Mazda Pubs.

Tale of Sir Gawain. As told by Neil Philip. (Illus.). 112p. (gr. 5 up). 1987. 11.95 (ISBN 0-399-21488-7, Philomel). Putnam Pub Group.

Tale of Squirrel Nutkin. Beatrix Potter. (Illus.). 60p. (gr. 1-5). 1972. pap. 1.75 (ISBN 0-486-22828-2). Dover.

Tale of Squirrel Nutkin. Beatrix Potter. (Illus.). (ps-2). 1903. bds. 4.95 (ISBN 0-7232-0593-0); bds. 5.00 French Ed. (ISBN 0-7232-0654-6); pap. 2.25 (ISBN 0-7232-6226-8). Warne.

Tale of Squirrel Nutkin. Beatrix Potter. (Illus.). 64p. 1984. pap. 2.25 (ISBN 0-553-15205-X). Bantam.

Tale of Squirrel Nutkin. Beatrix Potter. (Illus.). 64p. (ps-3). 1986. pap. 3.95 (ISBN 0-671-62926-3, Little Simon). S&S.

Tale of Sunlight. Gary Soto. LC 77-18743. (Pitt Poetry Ser.). 1978. 16.95x (ISBN 0-8229-3375-6); pap. 8.95 (ISBN 0-8229-5293-9). U of Pittsburgh Pr.

Tale of Tall Toothbrush. Elayne Reiss & Rita Friedman. (gr. k-1). 1978. 7.50 (ISBN 0-89796-869-7). Arista Corp NY.

Tale of the Armament of Igor, A.D. 1185, A Russian Historical Epic. Ed. by Leonard A. Magnus. 1977. lib. bdg. 59.95 (ISBN 0-8490-2727-6). Gordon Pr.

Tale of the Bad Macocha & the Fable of the Underground Punkva River. Karel B. Absolon. Ed. & illus. by K. B. Absolon. (Moravian Tales, Legends, Myths Ser.). (Illus.). 40p. (Orig.). (gr. 4). 1984. pap. text ed. 12.00 (ISBN 0-930329-02-3). KABEL Pubs.

Tale of the Battle on the Kulikovo Field: From the Illuminated Codex of the 16th Century. D. S. Likhachev. 194p. 1980. 112.00x (ISBN 0-317-57458-2, Pub. by Collets UK). State Mutual Bk.

Tale of the Battle on the Kulikovo Field. Ed. by D. S. Likhachev. 392p. 1984. 131.00 (ISBN 0-569-08657-4, Pub. by Collets (UK)). State Mutual Bk.

Tale of the Bunny Picnic: A Jim Henson Picture Book. Louise Gikow. (Illus.). (gr. k-3). 1987. 12.95 (ISBN 0-590-40443-1, Scholastic Hardcover). Scholastic Inc.

Tale of the Bunny Picnic: A Jim Henson Picture Book. Louise Gikow. (Illus.). 40p. (ps-4). 1988. pap. 3.95 (ISBN 0-590-40837-2). Scholastic Inc.

Tale of the Butterscotch Bears. Janice Davis. (Scratch-Sniff-Color Ser.). (Illus.). (gr. 4-9). 1980. pap. 2.95 (ISBN 0-931318-05-X). Walnut AZ.

Tale of the Campaign of Igor. Tr. by Robert C. Howes. 1974. pap. text ed. 2.95x (ISBN 0-393-09310-7). Norton.

Tale of the Dead Princess & the Seven Knights. Aleksandr Pushkin. 36p. 1984. pap. 1.99 (ISBN 0-8285-2962-0, Pub. by Raduga Pubs USSR). Imported Pubns.

Tale of the Faithful Dove. Beatrix Potter. LC 75-109403. (Illus.). (gr. k-3). 1970. 5.95 (ISBN 0-7232-1336-4). Warne.

Tale of the Flopsy Bunnies. Beatrix Potter. (Illus.). (gr. k-2). 1909. bds. 4.95 (ISBN 0-7232-0601-5); pap. 2.25 (ISBN 0-7232-6234-9). Warne.

Tale of the Flopsy Bunnies. Beatrix Potter. (Juveniles Ser.). 64p. (gr. 1 up). 1985. pap. 1.75 (ISBN 0-486-24806-2). Dover.

Tale of the Flopsy Bunnies. Beatrix Potter. (Illus.). 64p. (ps-3). 1987. bds. 3.95 (ISBN 0-671-63237-X, Little Simon). S&S.

Tale of the Future: From the Beginning to the Present Day. 3rd ed. Ed. by I. F. Clarke. 374p. 1978. pap. 15.00x (ISBN 0-8389-3225-8). ALA.

Tale of the Great Mutiny. W. H. Fitchett. Repr. of 1909 ed. 25.00 (ISBN 0-686-19880-8). Ridgeway Bks.

Tale of the Heike, 2 Vols. Tr. by Hiroshi Kitagawa & Bruce T. Tsuchida. Vol. 1, 1975, 391 p. pap. 17.50 (ISBN 0-86008-188-5, Pub. by U of Tokyo Japan); Vol. 2, 1977, 416 p. pap. 17.50 (ISBN 0-86008-189-3). Columbia U Pr.

Tale of the Heike. Helen C. McCullough. 608p. 1987. 294.00x (Pub. by Han-Shan Tang Ltd). State Mutual Bk.

Tale of the Heike. Tr. by Helen C. McCullough from Japanese. LC 87-18001. (Illus.). 504p. 1987. text ed. 60.00x (ISBN 0-8047-1418-5). Stanford U Pr.

Tale of the Host of Igor. V. Rzhiga. 100p. 1985. 315.00x (ISBN 0-317-61403-7, Pub. by Collets (UK)). State Mutual Bk.

Tale of the House of the Wolfings & All the Kindreds of the Mark. William Morris. Ed. by R. Reginald & Douglas Menville. LC 80-19670. (Newcastle Forgotten Fantasy Library Ser.: Vol. 16). 199p. 1980. Repr. of 1978 ed. lib. bdg. 19.95x (ISBN 0-89370-515-2). Borgo Pr.

Tale of the Mackinaw Fur Trade: Sandy MacDonald's Man. R. Clyde Ford. LC 85-70345. (Illus.). 1985. pap. 7.49 (ISBN 0-932212-41-7). Avery Color.

Tale of the Mermaid. LeeEllen Griffith. (Illus.). 56p. 1986. pap. 9.00 (ISBN 0-913346-12-8). Phila Maritime Mus.

Tale of the Mouse: The Family Book on Dying. Patricia Shelton. (Illus.). 60p. 1985. write for info. Sarasvati.

Tale of the Nisan Shamaness: A Manchu Folk Epic. Margaret Nowak & Stephen Durrant. LC 76-49171. (Publications on Asia of the School of International Studies: No. 31). 192p. 1977. 15.00x (ISBN 0-295-95548-1). U of Wash Pr.

Tale of the Porcelain God. Lafcadio Hearn. 1973. 30.00 (ISBN 0-686-23324-7). Rochester Folk Art.

Tale of the Ring: A Kaddish. Frank Stiffel. LC 83-63000. 320p. 1984. 22.50 (ISBN 0-916366-21-9). Pushcart Pr.

Tale of the Rout of Mamai: Illuminated Manuscript of the 17th Century from the History Museum Collection. L. A. Dmitriev. 270p. 1980. 280.00x (ISBN 0-317-57460-4, Pub. by Collets UK). State Mutual Bk.

Tale of the Soga Brothers. Tr. by Thomas Cogan. 310p. (Japanese.). 1987. 34.50 (ISBN 0-86008-411-6, Pub. by U of Tokyo Japan). Columbia U Pr.

Tale of the Solovetsky Insurrection: Povest' O Solovetskom Vosstanii. O. B. Fedorova. 96p. 1982. 154.00x (ISBN 0-317-57462-0, Pub. By Collets UK). State Mutual Bk.

Tale of the Tailor of Gloucester. Beatrix Potter. (Illus.). 64p. (ps-3). 1987. bds. 3.95 (ISBN 0-671-63234-5, Little Simon). S&S.

Tale of the Tell: Archaeological Studies by Paul W. Lapp. Ed. by Nancy L. Lapp. LC 75-5861. (Pittsburgh Theological Monographs: No. 5). 1975. pap. text ed. 9.25 (ISBN 0-915138-05-0). Pickwick.

Tale of the Tribe: Ezra Pound & the Modern Verse Epic. Michael A. Bernstein. LC 80-129. 1980. 41.00x (ISBN 0-691-06434-2); pap. 15.95x LPE (ISBN 0-691-10105-1). Princeton U Pr.

Tale of the Tsar Saltan. Aleksandr Pushkin & I. Bilibin. (Illus.). 18p. 1978. pap. 3.45 (ISBN 0-8285-1240-X, Pub. by Progress Pubs USSR). Imported Pubns.

Tale of the Wise Little Sea Turtle. David E. Beverly. 27p. (gr. 1-3). 1986. 4.95 (ISBN 0-533-05506-7). Vantage.

Tale of the Yellow Triangle. Gustaf Sobin. (Illus.). 64p. (gr. 1-6). 1973. 4.95 (ISBN 0-8076-0686-3). Braziller.

Tale of Thebes. R. L. Green. LC 76-22979. (Illus.). 1977. Cambridge U Pr.

Tale of Theodore Bear. Cecile Green. LC 68-56812. (Illus.). 32p. (gr. 1-2). 1968. PLB 9.95 (ISBN 0-87783-038-X). Oddo.

Tale of Theodore Bear. Cecile Green. (Illus.). (gr. 1-2). 1978. pap. 1.25 (ISBN 0-89508-060-5). Rainbow Bks.

Tale of Thomas Mead. Pat Hutchins. LC 79-6398. (Greenwillow Read-Alone Bks.). (Illus.). 32p. (gr. 1-4). 1980. 10.95 (ISBN 0-688-80282-6); PLB 10.88 (ISBN 0-688-84282-8). Greenwillow.

Tale of Thomas Mead. Pat Hutchins. Date not set. pap. 2.95 (ISBN 0-688-08422-2). Morrow.

Tale of Three Cities: Boston, Birmingham, Hartford. Ford Foundation Staff & Ernest Lynton. LC 81-9790. (Ford Foundation Series on Higher Education in the Cities). 80p. (Orig.). 1981. pap. text ed. 4.00 (ISBN 0-916584-18-6). Ford Found.

Tale of Three Cities: Elsinore-Montreal-Tokyo. James R. Kidd. LC 74-9351. (Landmark Ser.). 1974. pap. 2.00 (ISBN 0-87060-066-4, LNH 3). Syracuse U Cont Ed.

Tale of Three Heads. Irina Ratushinskaia. Tr. & intro. by Diane N. Ignashev. LC 86-25623. 128p. (Eng. & Rus.). 1986. pap. 7.50 (ISBN 0-938920-83-9). Hermitage.

Tale of Three Kings. Gene Edward. 120p. 1980. pap. 6.95 (ISBN 0-940232-03-0). Christian Bks.

Tale of Three Wishes. Isaac Bashevis Singer. LC 75-43632. (Illus.). 32p. (ps-3). 1976. 11.95 (ISBN 0-374-37370-1). FS&G.

Tale of Time City. Diana W. Jones. LC 86-33304. (Illus.). 288p. (YA) (gr. 7 up). 1987. 11.75 (ISBN 0-688-07315-8). Greenwillow.

Tale of Timmy Tiptoes. Beatrix Potter. (Illus.). (ps-2). 1911. bds. 4.95 (ISBN 0-7232-0603-1); pap. 2.25 (ISBN 0-7232-6236-5). Warne.

Tale of Timmy Tiptoes. Beatrix Potter. (Illus.). 64p. (gr. 3 up). 1987. pap. 1.75 (ISBN 0-486-25541-7). Dover.

Tale of Timmy Tiptoes see Tonton-le-Vonltigeur.

Tale of Tom Kitten. Beatrix Potter. (Illus.). (ps-2). 1907. bds. 4.95 (ISBN 0-7232-0599-X); pap. 2.25 (ISBN 0-7232-6232-2). Warne.

Tale of Tom Kitten. Beatrix Potter. (Illus.). 58p. (gr. k up). 1983. pap. 1.75 (ISBN 0-486-24502-0). Dover.

Tale of Tom Kitten. Beatrix Potter. (Illus., X). 1983. pap. 2.25 (ISBN 0-553-15224-6). Bantam.

Tale of Tom Kitten. Beatrix Potter. (Illus.). 64p. (ps-3). 1986. pap. 3.95 (ISBN 0-671-62927-1, Little Simon). S&S.

Tale of Tom Kitten. Beatrix Potter. LC 87-40285. (Illus.). (ps up). 1988. incl. audio cassettes 5.95 (ISBN 1-55782-018-X). Warner Bks.

Tale of Tom Kitten. Beatrix Potter. (Illus.). (ps-3). Date not set. 4.95 (ISBN 0-7232-3467-1). Warne.

Tale of Troy. Roger L. Green. (Illus., Orig.). (gr. 5-7). 1974. pap. 3.95 (ISBN 0-14-030120-8, Puffin). Penguin.

Tale of Tsarevich Ivan, the Firebird & the Grey Wolf. Illus. by I. Bilibin. (Illus.). 16p. 1979. pap. 2.45 (ISBN 0-8285-1241-8, Pub. by Goznak Pubs USSR). Imported Pubns.

Tale of Tuppenny. Beatrix Potter. LC 72-89477. (Illus.). 40p. (gr. k-3). 1973. PLB 5.95 (ISBN 0-7232-6097-4). Warne.

Tale of Two Agencies: A Comparative Analysis of the General Accounting Office & the Office of Management & Budget. Frederick C. Mosher. LC 83-10634. (Miller Center Series on the American Presidency). xxvi, 219p. 1986. pap. text ed. 9.95 (ISBN 0-8071-1305-0). LA State U Pr.

Tale of Two Bad Mice. Beatrix Potter. LC 74-75268. (Illus.). 59p. (gr. 2-4). 1974. pap. 1.75 (ISBN 0-486-23065-1). Dover.

Tale of Two Bad Mice. Beatrix Potter. (Illus.). (ps-2). 1904. bds. 4.95 (ISBN 0-7232-0596-5); pap. 2.25 (ISBN 0-7232-6229-2). Warne.

Tale of Two Bad Mice. Beatrix Potter. 64p. (Orig.). (ps). 1984. pap. 2.25 (ISBN 0-553-15219-X). Bantam.

Tale of Two Bad Mice. Beatrix Potter. (Illus.). (ps-3). Date not set. 4.95 (ISBN 0-7232-3464-7). Warne.

Tale of Two Bridges & the Battle for the Skies over North Vietnam. Delbert Corum et al. (USAF Southeast Asia Monograph Ser.: Vol., Monogrphs 1 & 2). (Illus.). 193p. 1986. pap. write for info. (ISBN 0-912799-26-9). Off Air Force.

Tale of Two Brothers. Charles E. Moldenke. 60p. 1988. pap. 6.95 (ISBN 0-933121-16-4). Black Classic.

Tale of Two Cabins. Helen H. Danforth. (Illus.). 36p. (Orig.). (gr. 7 up). 1985. pap. 4.95 (ISBN 0-9614899-0-1). Pioneer Farm.

Tale of Two Churches: Can Protestants & Catholics Get Together? George Carey. LC 84-28858. 180p. (Orig.). 1985. pap. 5.95 (ISBN 0-87784-972-2). Inter-Varsity.

Tale of Two Cities. Charles Dickens. (Airmont Classics Ser.). (gr. 9 up). 1964. pap. 2.50 (ISBN 0-8049-0021-3, CL-21). Airmont.

Tale of Two Cities. Charles Dickens. (Literature Ser). (gr. 7-12). 1969. pap. text ed. 8.33 (ISBN 0-87720-716-X). AMSCO Sch.

Tale of Two Cities. Charles Dickens. 368p. (gr. 9-12). 1984. pap. 2.25 (ISBN 0-553-21176-5, Bantam Classics); tchr's. guide avail. Bantam.

Tale of Two Cities. Charles Dickens. 1983. 12.95x (ISBN 0-460-10102-1, DEL-04393, Evman); pap. 2.95x (ISBN 0-460-01102-2, Evman). Biblio Dist.

Tale of Two Cities. Charles Dickens. (Illus.). (gr. 4-6). 1948. pap. 5.95 (ISBN 0-448-11023-7, G&D); deluxe ed. 11.95 (ISBN 0-448-06023-X). Putnam Pub Group.

Tale of Two Cities. Charles Dickens. Ed. by A. G. Eyre. (Longman Simplified English Ser.). 143p. 1947. pap. 3.95 (ISBN 0-582-52821-6). Longman.

Tale of Two Cities. Charles Dickens. 384p. (RL 7). 1960. pap. 2.25 (ISBN 0-451-51959-0, Sig Classics). NAL.

Tale of Two Cities. new ed. Charles Dickens. Ed. by Naunerle Farr. (Now Age Illustrated Ser., No. 2). (Illus.). 64p. (gr. 5-10). 1974. 7.50 (ISBN 0-88301-217-0); pap. text ed. 2.95 (ISBN 0-88301-134-4). Pendulum Pr.

Tale of Two Cities. Charles Dickens. Ed. by George Woodcock. (English Library Ser). 1970. pap. 2.25 (ISBN 0-14-043054-7). Penguin.

Tales from Gray's: Selections from Gray's Sporting Journal, 1975-1985. Ed. by Ed Gray. LC 86-83015. (Illus.). 272p. 1987. text ed. 25.00 (ISBN 0-9609842-3-2). GSJ Press.
Tales from Greenery Street. facs. ed. Denis G. Mackail. LC 75-140335. (Short Story Index Reprint Ser). 1928. 20.00 (ISBN 0-8369-3727-9). Ayer Co Pubs.
Tales from Grimm. Wanda Gag. 1981. pap. 5.95 (ISBN 0-698-20533-2, Coward). Putnam Pub Group.
Tales from Hans Andersen see New Method Supplementary Readers.
Tales from Hans Christian Andersen. Mary J. Evans & Deborah Anderson. (gr. k up). 1983. pap. 3.50 (ISBN 0-87602-257-3). Anchorage.
Tales from Hans Christian Andersen One to Four, 4 bks. Val Biro. (Illus., Orig.). (gr. 2-3). 1986. Set. pap. text ed. 16.80 (ISBN 1-55624-007-4). Wright Group.
Tales from Hollywood. Christopher Hampton. 1986. pap. 7.95 (ISBN 0-317-46858-8). Faber & Faber.
Tales from Indian Classics. Rupa Gupta. (Illus.). 136p. (gr. 1-9). 1981. 7.50 (ISBN 0-89744-233-4, Pub. by Hemkunt India). Auromere.
Tales from Indian Classics, Bk. I. Savitri. (Illus.). (gr. 3-9). 1979. 4.50 (ISBN 0-89744-167-2). Auromere.
Tales from Indian Classics, Bk. II. Savitri. (Illus.). (gr. 3-9). 1979. 4.50 (ISBN 0-89744-168-0). Auromere.
Tales from Indian Classics, Bk. III. Savitri. (Illus.). (gr. 3-9). 1979. 4.50 (ISBN 0-89744-169-9); pap. write for info. Auromere.
Tales from Indian Mythology. Rupa Gupta. (Illus.). 96p. (gr. 2-8). 1982. text ed. 7.50 (ISBN 0-89744-058-7, Pub. by Hemkunt Indig). Auromere.
Tales from Indian Mythology. Rupa Gupta. (Illus.). 96p. (gr. 2-8). 1982. text ed. 7.50 (ISBN 0-89744-058-7, Pub. by Hemkunt Indig). Auromere.
Tales from Indochina. Ed. by Marilyn Gregerson et al. LC 82-81681. 106p. 1987. pap. 11.00 (ISBN 0-88312-169-7); microfiche (2) 4.00 (ISBN 0-88312-258-8). Summer Inst Ling.
Tales from Isaac Asimov's Science Fiction Magazine: Short Stories for Young Adults. Sheila Williams & Cynthia Manson. LC 86-7591. 352p. (gr. 7 up). 1986. 15.95 (ISBN 0-15-239050-2, HJ). HarBraceJ.
Tales from Isaac Asimov's Science Fiction Magazine: Short Stories for Young Adults. Selected by Sheila Williams & Cynthia Manson. (gr. 7 up). 1986. 15.95 (ISBN 0-15-284209-8). HarBraceJ.
Tales from Jalisco, Mexico. Howard T. Wheeler. LC 44-5764. (American Folklore Society Memoirs). Repr. of 1943 ed. 48.00 (ISBN 0-527-01087-1). Kraus Repr.
Tales from Jokai. facsimile 3rd ed. Mor Jokai. Tr. by R. Nisbet Bain from Hungarian. LC 76-163032. (Short Story Index Reprint Ser.). Repr. of 1904 ed. 5.37 (ISBN 0-8369-3946-8). Ayer Co Pubs.
Tales from Long Ago, 8 bks. Ben Butterworth. (Illus., Orig.). (gr. 2-3). 1986. Set. pap. text ed. 22.40 (ISBN 1-55624-004-X). Wright Group.
Tales from Luristan. Ed. by Sekandar Amanolahi & Wheeler M. Thackston. (Harvard Iranian Ser.). (Illus.). 276p. 1986. pap. text ed. 19.95x (ISBN 0-674-86780-7). Harvard U Pr.
Tales from Old Carolina. F. Roy Johnson. LC 65-8878. (Illus.). 1980. Repr. of 1965 ed. 9.50 (ISBN 0-930230-38-8). Johnson NC.
Tales from Old Fiji. Lorimer Fison. LC 75-32816. Repr. of 1904 ed. 20.00 (ISBN 0-404-14120-X). AMS Pr.
Tales from Our Cornish Island. E. Atkins. 1986. 44.75X (ISBN 0-245-54265-5, Pub. by Harrap Ltd England). State Mutual Bk.
Tales from Paradise. June Knox-Mawer. 136p. 1987. pap. 5.95 (ISBN 0-563-20460-5, Pub. by BBC). Parkwest Pubns.
Tales from Peking Opera. (Illus.). 232p. (Orig.). 1985. pap. 6.95 (ISBN 0-8351-1399-X). China Bks.
Tales from Ramakrishna. Swami Ramakrishna. (Illus.). 54p. (Orig.). (gr. 1-5). 1975. pap. 1.95 (ISBN 0-87481-152-X). Vedanta Pr.
Tales from Reb Nachman: Parables Told by Rabbi Nachman of Breslov. David Sears. (Artscroll Youth Ser.). (Illus.). 32p. (gr. k-6). 1987. 8.95 (ISBN 0-89906-808-1); pap. 5.95 (ISBN 0-89906-809-X). Mesorah Pubns.
Tales from Sacchetti. Franco Sacchetti. Tr. by Mary G. Steegmann from Ital. LC 76-48457. (Library of World Literature Ser.). 1977. Repr. of 1918 ed. lib. bdg. 24.75 (ISBN 0-88355-608-1). Hyperion Conn.
Tales from Shakespeare. Charles Lamb. (Illus.). 337p. 1988. 147.75 (ISBN 0-89901-367-8). Found Class Reprints.
Tales from Shakespeare. Charles Lamb & Mary Lamb. 1981. 13.95x (ISBN 0-460-00008-X, Evman); pap. 2.95x (ISBN 0-460-01008-5, Evman). Biblio Dist.
Tales from Shakespeare. Charles Lamb & Mary Lamb. 336p. 1986. pap. 2.95 (ISBN 0-451-52065-3, Sig Classics). NAL.
Tales from Shakespeare. Charles Lamb & Mary Lamb. (gr. k-6). 1986. 8.98 (621568). Outlet Bk Co.
Tales from Shakespeare. Charles Lamb & Mary Lamb. LC 79-89991. (Illus.). Date not set. 29.50 (ISBN 0-918016-04-5). Folger Bks.
Tales from Shakespeare. Charles Lamb & Mary Lamb. (gr. 5 up). 1988. pap. 2.25 (ISBN 0-14-035088-8, Puffin Bks). Penguin.
Tales from Shakespeare. 1987. 50.00x (ISBN 0-948397-45-4, Pub. by M O'Mara UK). State Mutual Bk.
Tales from Shakespeare: Children's Illustrated Classics. Charles Lamb. (Illus.). 316p. (gr. 6 up). 1982. Repr. of 1957 ed. 11.95x (ISBN 0-460-05039-7, Pub. by J M Dent England). Biblio Dist.
Tales from Silver Lands. Charles J. Finger. (Illus.). 225p. (gr. 7 up). 1965. pap. 15.95 (ISBN 0-385-07513-8). Doubleday.
Tales from Southern Africa. Retold by A. C. Jordan. (Perspectives on Southern Africa: No. 4). (Illus.). 1973. pap. 5.95x (ISBN 0-520-03638-7). U of Cal Pr.
Tales from Spanish Picaresque Novels: A Motif-Index. James W. Childers. LC 77-8780. 262p. 1977. 44.50 (ISBN 0-87395-188-3). State U NY Pr.
Tales from Ten Poets (Swinburne, George Eliot, Etc.) Harrison Morris. 1973. Repr. of 1892 ed. 25.00 (ISBN 0-8274-1565-6). R West.
Tales from Thailand: Folklore, Culture, & History. Marian D. Toth. LC 77-125563. (Illus.). 184p. (YA) (gr. 7 up). 1983. 14.50 (ISBN 0-8048-0563-6). C E Tuttle.
Tales from the Adirondack Foothills: Two-Page Yarns about the Foothills. Howard Thomas. 1973. Repr. of 1956 ed. 7.95 (ISBN 0-913710-03-2). North Country.
Tales from the Amazon. Martin Elbl. (Illus.). 32p. (gr. k-3). 1986. PLB 11.66 (ISBN 0-87617-032-7, Pub. by C Hayes Pr). Penworthy Pub.
Tales from the American Attic. Shepherd Welsh. 256p. (Orig.). 1988. pap. 9.95 (ISBN 0-9620361-0-2). Pemaquid Pr.
Tales from the Arab Tribes. Charles G. Campbell. Ed. by Richard M. Dorson. LC 80-790. (Folklore of the World Ser.). (Illus.). 1980. Repr. of 1950 ed. lib. bdg. 23.00x (ISBN 0-405-13329-4). Ayer Co Pubs.
Tales from the Arabian Nights. Michael B. Dixon. (Stage Magic Plays for Children's Theatre Ser.). (Illus.). 52p. (Orig.). 1985. pap. 3.00 (ISBN 0-88680-239-3); piano & vocal score 5.00 (ISBN 0-88680-240-7). I E Clark.
Tales from the Arabian Nights. James Riordan. LC 84-62456. (Illus.). 128p. (gr. 4 up). 1985. 11.95 (ISBN 0-528-82672-7, Checkerboard Pr). Macmillan.
Tales from the Arabian Nights see New Method Supplementary Readers.
Tales from the Argentine. Ed. by Waldo Frank. Tr. by Anita Brenner. 1977. lib. bdg. 59.95 (ISBN 0-8490-2728-4). Gordon Pr.
Tales from the Argentine. Ed. by Waldo D. Frank. Tr. by Anita Brenner from Sp. LC 78-122706. (Short Story Index Reprint Ser). (Illus.). 1930. 17.00 (ISBN 0-8369-3539-X). Ayer Co Pubs.
Tales from the Beechy Woods: Fluff's Birthday. Gerda Neubacher. (Illus.). 32p. (ps-k). 1983. PLB 10.39 (ISBN 0-88625-044-7). C Hayes Pr.
Tales from the Big Thicket. Ed. by Francis E. Abernethy. (Illus.). 256p. 1966. pap. 8.95 (ISBN 0-292-78083-4). U of Tex Pr.
Tales from the Cherokee Hills. Jean Starr. (Orig.). 1988. pap. 8.95 (ISBN 0-89587-062-2). Blair.
Tales from the Clubroom. Bernard Bragg & Eugene Bergman. LC 81-81925. (Illus.). xxii, 118p. (Orig.). 1981. 8.95 (ISBN 0-913580-73-2). Gallaudet Univ Pr.
Tales from the Darkside, Vol. 1. Ed. by Mitchell Galin & Tom Allen. 1988. pap. 3.50 (ISBN 0-425-11095-8). Berkley Pub.
Tales from the Derrick Floor: A People's History of the Oil Industry. Mody C. Boatright & William A. Owens. LC 81-19725. (Illus.). xx, 284p. 1982. 25.95x (ISBN 0-8032-1177-5); pap. 7.95 (ISBN 0-8032-6067-9, BB 804, Bison). U of Nebr Pr.
Tales from the Dramatists 1580 to 1780, 2 vols. in 1. Charles Morris. 1975. Repr. of 1898 ed. 40.00 (ISBN 0-8274-4009-X). R West.
Tales from the East see New Method Supplementary Readers.
Tales from the Enchanted World. Anabel Williams-Ellis. (Illus.). (gr. 3-7). 1988. 17.95 (ISBN 0-316-94133-6). Little.
Tales from the Fjeld. Peter C. Asbjornsen. Tr. by George W. Dasent. LC 69-13232. (Illus.). 1969. Repr. of 1896 ed. 20.00 (ISBN 0-405-08217-7). Ayer Co Pubs.
Tales from the French Folk-Lore of Missouri. Joseph M. Carriere. LC 79-128989. (Northwestern University. Humanities Ser.: No. 1). Repr. of 1937 ed. 24.00 (ISBN 0-404-50701-8). AMS Pr.
Tales from the Front. Laura Kavesh & Cheryl Lavin. 1989. 7.95 (ISBN 0-671-67541-9, Fireside). S&S.
Tales from the Front: Real People Report from the Singles Scene. Cheryl Lavin & Laura Kavesh. LC 87-19854. 216p. 1988. pap. 16.95 (ISBN 0-385-24159-3, Dolp). Doubleday.
Tales from the Greek Drama. H. R. Jolliffe. xi, 320p. 10.00 (ISBN 0-86516-013-9). Bolchazy-Carducci.
Tales from the Japanese Storytellers As Collected in the Ho-Dan Zo. Post Wheeler. Ed. by Harold G. Henderson. LC 73-90236. 1974. pap. 3.95 (ISBN 0-8048-1132-6). C E Tuttle.
Tales from the Jungle Book. Rudyard Kipling. Adapted by Robin McKinley. LC 84-11724. (Looking Glass Library). (Illus.). 64p. (gr. k-3). 1985. 7.95 (ISBN 0-394-86940-0, BYR); lib. bdg. 8.99 (ISBN 0-394-96940-5). Random.
Tales from the Land under My Table. Hans Wilhelm. LC 83-4471. (Illus.). 64p. (gr. k-3). 1983. Random.
Tales from the Levee: The Folklore of St. John the Baptist Parish. Marcia G. Gaudet. (Louisiana Folklife Ser.). 116p. 1984. 10.95 (ISBN 0-940984-21-0). U of SW LA Ctr LA Studies.
Tales from the Mabinogion. Owen Bowen. LC 78-155665. (Illus.). (gr. 3-11). 1974. 12.95 (ISBN 0-8149-0706-7). Vanguard.
Tales from the Mabinogion. Tr. by Gwyn Thomas & Kevin Crossley-Holland. LC 84-14777. (Illus.). 88p. (gr. 7 up). 1985. 16.95 (ISBN 0-87951-987-8). Overlook Pr.
Tales from the Mines. Geoffrey Carr. 44p. 1987. 25.00x (ISBN 0-907496-45-8, Pub. by JNM Pubns UK). State Mutual Bk.
Tales from the Mohaves. Herman Grey. LC 69-16731. (Civilization of the American Indian Ser.: Vol. 107). 96p. 1980. pap. 4.95 (ISBN 0-8061-1655-2). U of Okla Pr.
Tales from the New Life with Meher Baba. Eruch et al. 191p. 1976. 9.95 (ISBN 0-940700-10-7); pap. 6.95 (ISBN 0-940700-09-3). Meher Baba Info.
Tales from the Next Village: Fictions of Mary Caponegro (No. 28) Mary Caponegro. LC 85-14888. (Lost Roads Ser.: No. 28). 112p. (Orig.). 1985. pap. 6.95 (ISBN 0-918786-32-0). Lost Roads.
Tales from the Nightside. Charles L. Grant. (Illus.). 240p. 1981. 11.95 (ISBN 0-87054-091-2). Arkham.
Tales from the Opera. Anthony J. Rudel. 379p. 1985. 17.95 (Fireside); pap. 9.95. S&S.
Tales from the Panchatantra. Tr. by Alfred Williams from Sanskrit. 207p. 1985. Repr. of 1930 ed. text ed. 35.00x (ISBN 0-86590-713-7, Pub. by Eastern Bk Hse India). Apt Bks.
Tales from the Planet Earth. Ed. by Frederik Pohl & Elizabeth A. Hull. 1987. pap. 3.95 (ISBN 0-312-90779-6). St Martin.
Tales from the Planet Earth: A Novel with Nineteen Authors. Ed. by Frederik Pohl & Elizabeth A. Hull. 290p. 1986. 15.95 (ISBN 0-312-78420-1). St Martin.
Tales from the Prairie, 3 vols, Vols. 1-4. Dorothy W. Creigh. Incl. Vol. 1. 1970; Vol. 2. 1973; Vol. 3. 1976. pap. 7.95 (ISBN 0-934858-05-5); Vol. 4. 1979. pap. 9.95 (ISBN 0-934858-06-3). LC 74-157038. (Illus.). Set. pap. 6.95 (ISBN 0-934858-09-8); pap. 5.95; pap. 9.95; write for info. (ISBN 0-934858-10-1). Adams County.
Tales From the Pump Room: Nine Hundred Years of Bath: The Place, Its People, & Its Gossip. Thomas Hinde. (Illus.). 252p. (Orig.). 1988. pap. 13.95 (ISBN 0-575-04193-5, Pub. by Gollancz England). David & Charles.
Tales From the Rebbe's Table. Nosson Scherman. (ArtScroll Youth Ser.). (Illus.). 32p. 1986. 8.95 (ISBN 0-89906-789-1); pap. 5.95 (ISBN 0-89906-790-5). Mesorah Pubns.
Tales from the Roof of The World: Folktales of Tibet. Gioi Timpanelli. LC 83-19826. (Illus.). 64p. (gr. 3-7). 1984. 11.95 (ISBN 0-670-71249-3, Viking Kestrel). Viking.
Tales from the Sidewalk Benches. Jimmy C. Acton. (Illus.). 103p. (Orig.). 1988. pap. 7.50 (ISBN 0-943487-06-4). Sevgo Pr.
Tales from the South Pacific Islands. Anne Gittins. LC 76-5411. (Illus.). 96p. (gr. 3 up). 1977. 7.95 (ISBN 0-916144-02-X). Stemmer Hse.
Tales from the Spaceport Bar. Ed. by George H. Scithers & Darrell Schweitzer. 256p. 1987. pap. 3.50 (ISBN 0-380-89943-4). Avon.
Tales from the Uncertain Country. Jacques Ferron. Tr. by Betty Bednarski from Fr. LC 71-190704. (Anansi Fiction Ser.: No. 19). 24p. 1977. (Pub. by Hse Anansi Pr Canada); study guide by Mary Ziroff 1.00x (ISBN 0-88784-053-1). U of Toronto Pr.
Tales from the Weird Zone, Bk. II. Jim Razzi. (Illus.). 64p. (gr. 4-7). 1988. pap. 2.50 (ISBN 0-671-62704-X, Minstrel Bks). S&S.
Tales from the Weird Zone. (gr. 2-5). 1988. pap. 2.50 (ISBN 0-317-69585-1). PB.
Tales from the Weird Zone, Bk. 1. Jim Razzi. (gr. 7-10). 1987. pap. 2.50 (ISBN 0-671-63240-X, Minstrel Bks). S&S.
Tales from the White Hart. Arthur C. Clarke. 1981. pap. 2.95 (ISBN 0-345-34322-0). Ballantine.
Tales from the White Hart. Arthur C. Clarke. 12.95 (ISBN 0-89190-249-X, Pub. by Am Repr). Amereon Ltd.
Tales from the Wind in the Willows. Kenneth Grahame. (Young Puffins Ser.). (Illus.). 64p. (gr. 1-4). 1986. pap. 2.95 (ISBN 0-14-031877-1, Puffin). Penguin.
Tales from the Yeshiva World. Nosson Scherman. (ArtScroll Youth Ser.). (Illus.). 32p. 1986. 8.95 (ISBN 0-89906-791-3); pap. 5.95 (ISBN 0-89906-792-1). Mesorah Pubns.
Tales from Third Street. Carol Jordan. (Illus.). 100p. 1980. pap. 3.50 (ISBN 0-9605360-0-0). C Jordan.
Tales from Tibetan Opera. Wang Yao. (Illus.). 214p. 1986. pap. 6.95 (ISBN 0-8351-1657-3). China Bks.
Tales from Tiburon: An Anthology of Adventures in Seriland. Ed. by Neil B. Carmony & David E. Brown. LC 82-51171. (Illus.). 146p. (Orig.). 1983. 15.95 (ISBN 0-9610126-1-7); pap. 9.95 (ISBN 0-9610126-0-9). SW Nat Hist Assn.
Tales from Two Hemispheres. facsimile ed. Hjalmar H. Boyesen. LC 78-98563. (Short Story Index Reprint Ser.). 1877. 18.00 (ISBN 0-8369-3137-8). Ayer Co Pubs.
Tales from Ye Olde Bard Barbershop. Thomas L. Hakes. (Illus.). 15p. Date not set. pap. 3.75x (ISBN 0-915020-46-7). Bardic.
Tales I Told My Mother. Robert Nye. 171p. 1982. pap. text ed. 7.95 (ISBN 0-7145-2741-6, Dist by Scribner). M Boyars Pubs.
Tales in Scarlet - Hematouria. Catherine Kirsch. (Illus.). 1978. 20.00 (ISBN 0-916750-64-7). Dayton Labs.
Tales Mummies Tell. Patricia Lauber. LC 83-46172. (Illus.). 128p. (gr. 5-9). 1985. 12.70 (ISBN 0-690-04388-0, Crowell Jr Bks); PLB 12.89 (ISBN 0-690-04389-9). HarpJ.
Tales, Now First Collected. facsimile ed. Leigh Hunt. LC 79-178441. (Short Story Index Reprint Ser.). Repr. of 1891 ed. 21.00 (ISBN 0-8369-4042-3). Ayer Co Pubs.
Tales of a Chinese Grandmother. Frances Carpenter. LC 72-77514. (Illus.). 302p. (gr. 3-8). 1972. pap. 6.95 (ISBN 0-8048-1042-7). C E Tuttle.
Tales of a Chinese Grandmother. Francis Carpenter. 293p. (gr. 5-6). Repr. of 1937 ed. lib. bdg. 19.95x (ISBN 0-89190-481-6, Pub. by River City Pr). Amereon Ltd.
Tales of a Country Judge. Robert H. Gollmar. LC 79-65286. (Illus.). 192p. 1981. 9.95x (ISBN 0-87319-018-1). Hallberg Pub Corp.
Tales of a Cruel Country. facsimile ed. Charles F. Kenyon. LC 74-150546. (Short Story Index Reprint Ser.). Repr. of 1919 ed. 19.00 (ISBN 0-8369-3843-7). Ayer Co Pubs.
Tales of a Dalai Lama. Pierre Delattre. LC 74-153958. (Fiction Ser.). 160p. 1978. pap. 5.95 (ISBN 0-916870-10-3). Creative Arts Bk.
Tales of a Fledging Homestead. Joe E. Armstrong. LC 84-25389. (Illus.). 110p. (Orig.). 1985. pap. 7.95 (ISBN 0-930079-00-0). Misty Hill Pr.
Tales of a Fourth Grade Nothing. Judy Blume. (gr. k-6). 1986. pap. 2.95 (ISBN 0-440-48474-X, YB). Dell.
Tales of a Fourth Grade Nothing. Judy Blume. LC 70-179050. (Illus.). 128p. (gr. 2-5). 1972. 9.95 (ISBN 0-525-40720-0). Dutton.
Tales of a Fourth Grade Nothing. Judy Blume. (Illus.). 174p. (gr. 2-6). 1987. Repr. of 1972 ed. lib. bdg. 13.95 (ISBN 1-55736-015-4). ABC-Clio.
Tales of a Fourth Grade Nothing see Judy Blume.
Tales of a Fourth Grade Nothing see Judy Blume Collection.
Tales of a Gambling Grandma. Dayal K. Khalsa. (Illus.). 32p. (gr. 1 up). 1986. 11.95 (ISBN 0-517-56137-9, C N Potter Bks). Crown.
Tales of a Greek Island. Julia D. Dragoumis. LC 76-110184. (Short Story Index Reprint Ser.). 1912. 21.00 (ISBN 0-8369-3335-4). Ayer Co Pubs.
Tales of a Japanese Grandmother, 5 Vols. Yasuko Hashimoto & Jean Edades. (Illus., Orig.). (gr. k-3). 1982. Set. pap. 12.00 (ISBN 0-686-37564-5, Pub. by New Day Philippines). Cellar.
Tales of a Korean Grandmother. Frances Carpenter. LC 72-77515. (Illus.). (gr. 3-8). 1972. pap. 8.95 (ISBN 0-8048-1043-5). C E Tuttle.
Tales of a Long Night. Alfred Doblin. Tr. by Robert Kimber & Rita Kimber. LC 84-18798. 496p. 1984. 18.95 (ISBN 0-88064-016-2); pap. 12.95 (ISBN 0-88064-017-0). Fromm Intl Pub.
Tales of a Louisiana Duck Hunter. Fielding Lewis. 1988. 14.95 (ISBN 0-533-07843-1). Vantage.
Tales of a Low-Rent Birder. Peter Dunne. 175p. 1986. 15.95 (ISBN 0-8135-1139-9). Rutgers U Pr.
Tales of a Low-Rent Birder: 19 Flights of Fancy by North America's Second-Best-Known Bird-Watcher. Pete Dunne. 1988. 6.95 (ISBN 0-671-66099-3, Fireside). S&S.
Tales of a Magic Monastery. Theophane The Monk. LC 81-9765. (Illus.). 96p. 1981. pap. 8.95 (ISBN 0-8245-0085-7). Crossroad NY.
Tales of a New America. Robert B. Reich. 1987. 19.95 (ISBN 0-8129-1624-7). Times Bks.
Tales of a New America: The Anxious Liberal's Guide to the Future. Robert B. Reich. Ed. by Peter Dimock. LC 87-45915. 304p. Date not set. pap. 8.95 (ISBN 0-394-75706-8, Vin). Random.
Tales of a Nomad; Or, Sport & Strife. Charles Montague. LC 72-5559. (Black Heritage Library Collection Ser). 1972. Repr. of 1894 ed. 15.00 (ISBN 0-8369-9144-3). Ayer Co Pubs.
Tales of a Pueblo Boy. Lawrence Vallo. LC 86-5876. (Illus.). 48p. (Orig.). 1987. pap. 5.95 (ISBN 0-86534-089-7). Sunstone Pr.
Tales of a Rambler. John Ellberg. LC 70-110185. (Short Story Index Reprint Ser.: Vol. 1). (Illus.). 1938. 19.00 (ISBN 0-8369-3336-2). Ayer Co Pubs.
Tales of a Rat-Hunting Man. D. Brian Plummer. (Illus.). 1978. 18.00 (ISBN 0-85115-097-7, Pub. by Boydell & Brewer). Longwood Pub Group.
Tales of a Teller: An Informal Guide to a Fine Art. Morton G. Zimmerman. Ed. by Dave Johnson. (Illus.). 156p. (Orig.). 1975. 18.95 (ISBN 0-9608944-0-3, 7039104). AppleSeeds.

TITLE INDEX

TALES OF NEW ENGLAND.

Tales of a Time & Place. Grace E. King. LC 76-122593. Repr. of 1892 ed. 16.00 (ISBN 0-404-03690-2). AMS Pr.
Tales of a Time & Place. facsimile ed. Grace E. King. 1972. lib. bdg. 14.00 (ISBN 0-8422-8086-3); pap. text ed. 6.95x (ISBN 0-8290-0675-3). Irvington.
Tales of a Tour Guide. (Illus.). 50p. 1983. 4.00 (ISBN 0-931440-04-1). Stoneback Pub.
Tales of a Traveler. Washington Irving. Ed. by Judith G. Haig. (Twayne's Critical Editions Program - The Works of Washington Irving). 500p. 1987. lib. bdg. 60.00x (ISBN 0-8057-8515-9, Twayne). G K Hall.
Tales of a Traveller. facsimile ed. Washington Irving. LC 71-37551. (Short Story Index Reprint Ser.). Repr. of 1825 ed. 17.00 (ISBN 0-8369-4110-1). Ayer Co Pubs.
Tales of a Wandering Warthog. Tom Sinclair. Ed. by Abby Levine. LC 84-19621. (Illus.). 134p. (gr. 4 up). 1985. PLB 8.95 (ISBN 0-8075-7754-5). A Whitman.
Tales of a Western Mountaineer. C. E. Rusk. LC 78-54427. (Illus.). 400p. 1978. pap. 7.95 (ISBN 0-916890-62-7). Mountaineers.
Tales of a Wilderness Trapper. Neil M. Lindsey. 66p. 1973. pap. 1.50 (ISBN 0-936622-21-0). A R Harding Pub.
Tales of Afghanistan. Amina Shah. 1982. 17.95 (ISBN 0-900860-94-4, Pub. by Octagon Pr England). Ins Study Human.
Tales of All Countries. Anthony Trollope. Ed. by N. John Hall. LC 80-1879. (Selected Works of Anthony Trollope Ser.). 1981. Repr. of 1861 ed. Vol. 1 First Ser. lib. bdg. 35.00x (ISBN 0-405-14138-6); Vol. 2 Second Ser. lib. bdg. 39.00x (ISBN 0-405-14139-4). Ayer Co Pubs.
Tales of All Times. Mother. Orig. Title: Youth's Noble Path. (Illus.). 138p. (gr. 3-8). 1983. pap. 2.50 (ISBN 0-89071-321-9, Pub. by Sri Aurobindo Ashram India). Aurobindo Assn.
Tales of Amadou Koumba. Birago Diop. 1988. pap. 8.95 (ISBN 0-582-78587-1). Longman.
Tales of Amanda Pig. Jean Van Leeuwen. LC 82-23545. (Easy-to-Read Bks.). (Illus.). 56p. (ps-3). 1983. PLB 9.89 (ISBN 0-8037-8450-3); pap. 4.95 (ISBN 0-8037-8443-0, 0481-140). Dial Bks Young.
Tales of Amherst: A Look Back. Daniel Lombardo. LC 85-23791. 140p. 1986. 13.95x (ISBN 0-9616559-1-7); pap. 7.95x (ISBN 0-9616559-0-9). Jones Lib.
Tales of an American Hobo. Charles E. Fox. 1988. 15.95 (ISBN 0-913211-57-5, Am Liberty Pub). Jackson Assocs.
Tales of an Ashanti Father. Peggy Appiah. LC 88-19059. (Night Lights Ser.). (Illus.). 160p. (YA) (gr. 7-11). 1989. lib. bdg. 12.95 (ISBN 0-8070-8312-7); pap. 5.95 (ISBN 0-8070-8313-5). Beacon Pr.
Tales of an Old Horsetrader: The First Hundred Years. Leroy J. Daniels. As told to Helen S. Herrick. LC 87-10932. 235p. 1987. price not set; pap. 9.95 (ISBN 0-87745-187-7). U of Iowa Pr.
Tales of Ancient Egypt. Roger L. Green. (gr. k-3). 1972. pap. 2.95 (ISBN 0-14-030438-X, Puffin). Penguin.
Tales of Ancient Greece. George W. Cox. LC 77-94559. 1979. Repr. of 1880 ed. lib. bdg. 40.00 (ISBN 0-89341-308-9). Longwood Pub Group.
Tales of Ancient India. Tr. by J. A. Van Buitenen. LC 59-10430. 1969. pap. 5.95 (ISBN 0-226-84647-4, P341, Phoen). U of Chicago Pr.
Tales of Ardent & Whimsical Love. Boccaccio. (Illus.). 151p. 1984. 147.45 (ISBN 0-89901-189-6). Found Class Reprints.
Tales of Art & Life. Henry James. LC 83-51481. (Signature Ser.). 316p. (Orig.). 1984. pap. 14.75 (ISBN 0-912756-14-4); pap. text ed. 5.75 (ISBN 0-912756-12-8). Union Coll.
Tales of Atlantis & the Enchanted Islands. Thomas W. Higginson. LC 80-21017. (Newcastle Mythology Library Ser.: Vol. 3). 259p. 1980. Repr. of 1977 ed. lib. bdg. 22.95x (ISBN 0-89370-642-6). Borgo Pr.
Tales of Ayelsfarn: An Aetheral Menagerie. Robert B. Reinhardt. 48p. 1985. 5.95 (ISBN 0-8059-2988-6). Dorrance.
Tales of Ayrshire. Anna Blair. 192p. 1983. 11.95 (ISBN 0-85683-068-2, Pub. by Shepheard-Walwyn UK); pap. 5.95 (ISBN 0-85683-069-0). Dufour.
Tales of Baldy Mt. (Illus.). 120p. 1987. 5.00 (ISBN 0-931440-12-2). Stoneback Pub.
Tales of Beaufort. Nell S. Graydon. 13.95 (ISBN 0-685-06835-8). Beaufort SC.
Tales of Belkin. Aleksandr Pushkin. Tr. by Gillon Aitken & David Budgen. 1983. 19.95 (ISBN 0-946162-04-2). Dufour.
Tales of Belkin by A. S. Pushkin. J. Van Der Eng et al. 1968. pap. text ed. 16.80x (ISBN 90-2790-437-5). Mouton.
Tales of Bequia. Thomas C. Thomsen. Ed. by Eleanor Mann. (Illus.). 160p. 1988. 12.95 (ISBN 0-945288-00-X). Crss River Pr.
Tales of Canterbury: Complete. Geoffrey Chaucer. Ed. by Robert A. Benson. LC 72-9380. (Illus.). 587p. 1974. text ed. 26.50 (ISBN 0-395-14052-8). HM.
Tales of Cedar Lawn Farm. Dale Fields. (Illus.). 360p. pap. 9.95 (ISBN 0-87770-278-0). Ye Galleon.
Tales of Chekhov, 13 vols. Chekhov. Tr. by Constance Garnett from Rus. 1987. Set. pap. 95.00 (ISBN 0-88001-175-0); Vol.1, The Darling & Other Stories. pap. 9.50 (ISBN 0-88001-038-X); Vol. 2, The Duel & Other Stories. pap. 9.50 (ISBN 0-88001-039-8). Ecco Pr.
Tales of Chinatown. facsimile ed. Sax Rohmer, pseud. LC 75-178459. (Short Story Index Reprint Ser.). Repr. of 1922 ed. 19.50 (ISBN 0-8369-4060-1). Ayer Co Pubs.
Tales of Christian Unity: The Adventures of An Ecumenical Pilgrim. Thomas P. Ryan. LC 82-60748. 224p. 1983. pap. 9.95 (ISBN 0-8091-2502-1). Paulist Pr.
Tales of Civilians see In the Midst of Life.
Tales of Country Folks Down Carolina Way. F. Roy Johnson. (Illus.). 1978. 9.50 (ISBN 0-930230-36-1). Johnson NC.
Tales of Courtship by Jeremias Gotthelf. Tr. by Robert Godwin-Jones from Ger. LC 84-48102. (American University Studies I (Germanic Languages & Literature): Vol. 35). 241p. 1984. text ed. 28.00 (ISBN 0-8204-0177-3). P Lang Pubs.
Tales of D. H. Lawrence, 2 vols. David H. Lawrence. LC 73-145135. (Literature Ser). 1138p. 1972. Repr. of 1934 ed. 70.00 (ISBN 0-403-01068-3). Scholarly.
Tales of Darkest America. facsimile ed. Fenton Johnson. LC 72-178477. (Black Heritage Library Collection). Repr. of 1920 ed. 10.00 (ISBN 0-8369-8926-0). Ayer Co Pubs.
Tales of Database Pitfalls. Frank Sweet. (Illus.). 80p. (Orig.). 1988. pap. 6.50 (ISBN 0-939479-05-2). Boxes & Arrows.
Tales of Destiny. Elizabeth G. Jordan. LC 79-103522. (Short Story Index Reprint Ser.). 1902. 19.00 (ISBN 0-8369-3264-1). Ayer Co Pubs.
Tales of Dunstable Weir. Gwendoline Keats. LC 70-94736. (Short Story Index Reprint Ser.). 1901. 17.00 (ISBN 0-8369-3116-5). Ayer Co Pubs.
Tales of E. T. A. Hoffmann. E. T. Hoffmann. Ed. by Leonard J. Kent & Elizabeth C. Knight. Landau Jacob. (Illus.). xl, 280p. 1972. pap. 10.95x (ISBN 0-226-34789-3, P452, Phoen). U of Chicago Pr.
Tales of Early Poland. Sigmund H. Uminski. (Illus.). 1968. 3.00 (ISBN 0-685-09288-7). Endurance.
Tales of East & West. Sax Rohmer. 1976. 8.50 (ISBN 0-685-79490-3). Bookfinger.
Tales of Edgar Allan Poe. Edgar Allan Poe. LC 80-14064. (Short Classics Ser.). (Illus.). 48p. (gr. 4 up). 1980. PLB 15.99 (ISBN 0-8172-1662-6); pap. 9.27 (ISBN 0-8172-2023-2). Raintree Pubs.
Tales of Edisto. Nell S. Graydon. (Illus.). 166p. 1983. Repr. of 1955 ed. 12.95 (ISBN 0-87844-053-4). Sandlapper Pub Co.
Tales of Edisto. rev. ed. Nell S. Graydon. (Illus.). 180p. 1986. 12.95 (ISBN 0-87844-071-2). Sandlapper Pub Co.
Tales of El Huitlacoche. Gary D. Keller. Ed. by Alurista & Xelina. LC 83-62552. 78p. (Orig.). 1984. pap. 6.95 (ISBN 0-939558-05-X). Maize Pr.
Tales of Enchantment from Spain. Elsie Eells. LC 78-67706. (Folktale). (Illus.). Repr. of 1920 ed. 21.50 (ISBN 0-404-16079-4). AMS Pr.
Tales of Erotic Fantasy. Richard K. Floyd. LC 85-90497. 328p. (Orig.). 1986. pap. 6.95 (ISBN 0-9616060-1-0). Poopsies.
Tales of Espionage & Intrigue: The Secret Agent in Literature. Arthur Liebman. (Masterworks of Mystery). 180p. (gr. 7-12). 1977. PLB 10.97 (ISBN 0-8239-0311-7); tchr's. manual 3.95 (ISBN 0-685-66609-3). Rosen Group.
Tales of Fantasy & Fact. Brander Matthews. LC 73-98586. (Short Story Index Reprint Ser.). 1896. 17.00 (ISBN 0-8369-3160-2). Ayer Co Pubs.
Tales of Fear & Frightening Phenomena. Ed. by Helen Hoke. 144p. (gr. 7 up). 1982. 10.50 (ISBN 0-525-66789-X, 01019-310). Lodestar Bks.
Tales of Firenzuola. rev. ed. Intro. by Eileen Gardiner. LC 86-82698. (Illus.). 130p. 1987. pap. 7.95 (ISBN 0-934977-04-6). Italica Pr.
Tales of Four Lakes. Duane R. Lund. 1977. 7.95 (ISBN 0-934860-04-1). Adventure Pubns.
Tales of Freshwater Fishing. Zane Grey. Ed. by George Erikson. (Illus.). 320p. 1986. pap. 14.50 (ISBN 0-915643-11-1). Santa Barb Pr.
Tales of Frontier Texas: 1830-1860. Ed. by John Q. Anderson. LC 66-19620. 328p. 1984. Repr. of 1966 ed. 16.95 (ISBN 0-87074-202-7). SMU Press.
Tales of Fuzzy Mouse. Jan Wahl. LC 87-81785. (Illus.). 48p. (ps-2). 1988. 6.95 (ISBN 0-307-15846-2). Western Pub.
Tales of Fuzzy Mouse: Six Cozy Stories for Bedtime. Jan Wahl. (Illus.). (ps-6). Date not set. price not set (Golden Pr). Western Pub.
Tales of Galloway. Alan Temperley. 320p. 1986. 20.00x (ISBN 1-85158-026-3, Pub. by Mainstream Scotland). State Mutual Bk.
Tales of Glauber-Spa, 2 vols. Ed. by William C. Bryant. 1972. Repr. of 1832 ed. Vol. 1. lib. bdg. 26.00 (ISBN 0-8422-8012-X); Vol. 2. lib. bdg. 26.00 (ISBN 0-8422-8013-8). Irvington.
Tales of Gold: The Oral History of the Olympic Games Told by America's Gold Medal Winners. Lewis H. Carlson & John J. Fogarty. (Illus.). 400p. 1987. 25.00 (ISBN 0-8092-5067-5). Contemp Bks.
Tales of Great Dragons. John K. Anderson. (Illus.). 64p. 1980. pap. 3.50 (ISBN 0-88388-075-X). Bellerophon Bks.
Tales of Greek Heroes. Roger L. Green. (Orig.). (gr. 5-7). 1974. pap. 2.95 (ISBN 0-14-030119-4, Puffin). Penguin.
Tales of Henry James. Henry James. Ed. by Christof Weglin. (Critical Editions Ser.). (Orig.). 1984. pap. text ed. 11.95x (ISBN 0-393-95359-9); 29.95x (ISBN 0-393-01824-5). Norton.
Tales of Henry James: Vol. 1, 1864-1869. Henry James. Ed. by Maqbool Aziz. (Illus.). 1973. 55.00x (ISBN 0-19-812457-0). Oxford U Pr.
Tales of Henry James, Vol. 2: 1870-1874. Henry James. Ed. by Madbool Aziz. 1979. 55.00x (ISBN 0-19-812572-0). Oxford U Pr.
Tales of Henry James: 1875-1879, Vol. 3. Henry James. Ed. by Maqbool Aziz. (Illus.). 1984. 65.00x (ISBN 0-19-812573-9). Oxford U Pr.
Tales of Hoffmann. E. T. Hoffmann. 1982. pap. 4.95 (ISBN 0-14-044392-4). Penguin.
Tales of Hoffmann. E. T. Hoffmann. Tr. by Michael Bullock. LC 63-21988. 1963. pap. 7.95x (ISBN 0-8044-6275-5). Ungar.
Tales of Horror & Fantasy. Ambrose Bierce. 228p. Repr. of 1907 ed. lib. bdg. 16.95x (ISBN 0-89190-187-6, Pub. by River City Pr). Amereon Ltd.
Tales of Horror & the Supernatural: The Occult in Literature. Arthur Liebman. (Masterworks of Mystery). 274p. (gr. 7-12). 1975. PLB 10.97 (ISBN 0-8239-0299-4); tchr's. manual 3.95 (ISBN 0-686-67049-3). Rosen Group.
Tales of Horsemen. Cunningham Graham. Ed. & illus. by Alexander Maitland. (Illus.). 137p. 1981. pap. 8.95 (ISBN 0-86241-122-X). Dufour.
Tales of Hulan River see Field of Life & Death & Tales of Hulan River.
Tales of Imagination & Suspense. LC 80-54130. (Silver Burdett Classics for Kids Ser.). 288p. (gr. 6 up). 1985. pap. 3.67 (ISBN 0-382-09995-8). Silver.
Tales of India, Vol. 1. Daulat Panday. 114p. (gr. 3-8). 1985. pap. 2.25 (ISBN 0-89071-330-8, Pub. by Sri Aurobindo Ashram India). Aurobindo Assn.
Tales of India, Vol. 2. Daulat Panday. 110p. (gr. 3-8). 1985. pap. 2.25 (ISBN 0-89071-331-6, Pub. by Sri Aurobindo Ashram India). Aurobindo Assn.
Tales of India, Vol. 3. Daulat Panday. 126p. (gr. 3-8). 1985. pap. 2.25 (ISBN 0-89071-332-4, Pub. by Sri Aurobindo Ashram India). Aurobindo Assn.
Tales of Intrigue & Revenge. Stephen McKenna. LC 72-128738. (Short Story Index Reprint Ser). 1925. 17.00 (ISBN 0-8369-3629-9). Ayer Co Pubs.
Tales of Irish Enchantment. Patricia Lynch. (Illus.). 128p. (gr. 5 up). 1980. pap. 7.95 (ISBN 0-85342-608-2, Pub. by Mercier Pr Ireland). Irish Bks Media.
Tales of Irish Life & Character. facs. ed. Anna M. Hall. LC 74-134964. (Short Story Index Reprint Ser). 1910. 21.00 (ISBN 0-8369-3694-9). Ayer Co Pubs.
Tales of Irish Life & Character. Anna M. Hall. LC 78-174395. Repr. of 1913 ed. 26.50 (ISBN 0-405-08592-3, Blom Pubns). Ayer Co Pubs.
Tales of Ise. H. Jay Harris. 247p. 1984. 74.00x (ISBN 0-317-69144-9, Pub. by Han-Shan Tang Ltd). State Mutual Bk.
Tales of Ise. Tr. by H. Jay Harris. LC 70-167934. (Illus.). 1972. 10.50 (ISBN 0-8048-0745-0). C E Tuttle.
Tales of Ise: Lyrical Episodes from Tenth-Century Japan. Tr. by Helen C. McCullough. 1968. 25.00x (ISBN 0-8047-0653-0). Stanford U Pr.
Tales of Ivan Belkin. Aleksandr Pushkin. 12.95 (ISBN 0-8488-0111-3, Pub. by Amereon Hse). Amereon Ltd.
Tales of Japan: Scrolls & Prints from the New York Public Library. Miyeko Murase. (Illus.). 256p. 1986. 34.50x (ISBN 0-19-504020-1); pap. 16.95 (ISBN 0-19-504021-X). Oxford U Pr.
Tales of Kankakee Land. Charles H. Bartlett. (Illus.). 1977. Repr. of 1907 ed. 7.50 (ISBN 0-915056-07-0). Hardscrabble Bks.
Tales of King Arthur. James Riordan. LC 81-86152. (Illus.). 128p. (gr. 4-7). 1982. 11.95 (ISBN 0-528-82383-3, Checkerboard Pr). Macmillan.
Tales of King Saul. Charles Wengrov. (Shulsinger Biblical Ser.). (Illus.). (gr. 5-10). 1969. 4.00 (ISBN 0-914080-21-0). Shulsinger Sales.
Tales of Known Space: The Universe of Larry Niven. Larry Niven. 256p. (Orig.). 1975. pap. 3.50 (ISBN 0-345-33469-8). Ballantine.
Tales of Life among the Indians. James W. Schultz. Ed. by Warren L. Hanna. 165p. 1988. pap. 9.95 (ISBN 0-87842-221-8). Mountain Pr.
Tales of Lonely Trails. 3rd ed. Zane Grey. LC 86-60518. (Illus.). 350p. 1986. pap. 14.95 (ISBN 0-87358-410-4). Northland.
Tales of Lonely Trails II. Zane Grey. 1988. pap. 2.95 (ISBN 1-55773-027-X, Charter Bks). Berkley Pub.
Tales of Louisiana Treasure. Paul F. Serpas. 1967. 3.95 (ISBN 0-87511-102-5). Claitors.
Tales of Love. Julia Kristeva. Tr. by Leon S. Roudiez from Fr. LC 86-28311. 448p. 1987. text ed. 27.50 (ISBN 0-231-06024-6). Columbia U Pr.
Tales of Love & Mystery. James Hogg. Intro. by David Groves. LC 85-73028. (Orig.). 1985. 18.95 (ISBN 0-86241-085-1, Pub. by Canongate Pub Ltd); pap. 10.95 (ISBN 0-86241-103-3, Pub. by Canongate Pub Ltd). Dufour.
Tales of Love & Terror: Booktalking the Classics, Old & New. Hazel Rochman. LC 86-32285. 128p. 1987. pap. text ed. 15.95x (ISBN 0-8389-0463-7). ALA.
Tales of Love, Sex, & Danger. Sudhir Kakar & John M. Ross. 250p. 1987. 16.95 (ISBN 1-55786-000-9). Basil Blackwell.
Tales of Madness. Luigi Pirandello. Tr. by Giovanni R. Bussino from Ital. 1984. 14.50 (ISBN 0-937832-26-X, Dist. by Branden). Dante U Am.
Tales of Magic & Spells. Corinne Denan. (Illus.). 48p. (gr. 3-6). 1980. PLB 9.59 (ISBN 0-89375-318-1); pap. text ed. 1.95 (ISBN 0-89375-317-3); cassette avail. Troll Assocs.
Tales of Maritime Maine. Bruce Clark. write for info. B Clark ME.
Tales of Maritime Maine: The Vanished Years of the Maine Coast Brought to Life in Three Absorbing Tales. Bruce Clark. Ed. by Jill Mason. LC 86-51015. 168p. 1987. 12.95 (ISBN 0-89909-122-9). Yankee Bks.
Tales of Marvel & Wonder. 2nd ed. Nocg M. Thai et al. Ed. by Lawrence Stolurow. Tr. by Hong-Cuc Nguyen from Eng. & Vietnamese. (gr. 4 up). 1985. pap. 7.50 tchr's guide (ISBN 0-88670-285-2, 8150). U IA Ctr Ed Experiment.
Tales of Marvel & Wonder: English. 2nd ed. Ngoc M. Thai et al. Ed. by Lawrence Stolurow. (Illus.). (gr. 4 up). 1981. pap. text ed. 5.25 (ISBN 0-88670-277-1, 8141). U IA Ctr Ed Experiment.
Tales of Marvel & Wonder: Lao. 2nd ed. Ngoc M. Thai et al. Ed. by Lawrence Stolurow. Tr. by Bounling Phommasouvangh from Eng. (Illus.). (gr. 4 up). 1985. pap. text ed. 5.25 (ISBN 0-88670-279-8, 8143); tchr's guide 7.50 (ISBN 0-88670-283-6, 8148). U IA Ctr Ed Experiment.
Tales of Marvel & Wonder Student Text: Hmong. Ngoc M. Thai et al. Ed. by Lawrence Stolurow. Tr. by Pha Thao from Eng. (Illus.). (gr. 4 up). 1985. pap. text ed. 5.25 (ISBN 0-88670-278-X, 8142); tchr's guide 7.50 (ISBN 0-88670-282-8, 8147). U IA Ctr Ed Experiment.
Tales of Marvel & Wonder Student Text: Cambodian. 2nd ed. Ngoc M. Thai et al. Ed. by Lawrence Stolurow. Tr. by Khuy T. Omg from Eng. (Illus.). (gr. 4 up). 1981. pap. text ed. 5.25 (ISBN 0-88670-276-3, 8140); 7.50 (ISBN 0-317-66040-3, 8146). U IA Ctr Ed Experiment.
Tales of Marvel & Wonder Teacher's Guide: ESL Grammer Workbook. 2nd ed. Ncog M. Thai et al. Ed. by Lawrence Stolurow. (Illus.). (gr. 4 up). 1985. pap. text ed. 7.50 (ISBN 0-88670-286-0, 8151). U IA Ctr Ed Experiment.
Tales of Marvel & Wonder Teacher's Guide: English-Lao. 2nd ed. Ngoc M. Thai et al. Ed. by Lawrence Stolurow. Tr. by Bounlieng Phommasouvanh. (gr. 4 up). 1985. pap. text ed. 7.50 (ISBN 0-317-66053-5, 8148). U IA Ctr Ed Experiment.
Tales of Mean Streets. Arthur Morrison. LC 78-128742. (Short Story Index Reprint Ser). 1921. 17.00 (ISBN 0-8369-3633-7). Ayer Co Pubs.
Tales of Mean Streets. Arthur Morrison. 175p. pap. 6.95 (ISBN 0-85115-221-X, Pub. by Boydell & Brewer). Academy Chi Pubs.
Tales of My Native Town. Gabriele D'Annunzio. Tr. by Rafael Mantellini. LC 69-10065. Repr. of 1920 ed. lib. bdg. 35.00x (ISBN 0-8371-0056-9, DANT). Greenwood.
Tales of My People. facs. ed. Sholem Asch. Tr. by Meyer Levin. LC 75-128752. (Short Story Index Reprint Ser). 1948. 20.00 (ISBN 0-8369-3609-4). Ayer Co Pubs.
Tales of Mysterious & Macabre, Vol. 1. Algernon Blackwood. 15.95 (ISBN 0-8488-0193-8). Amereon Ltd.
Tales of Mystery & Imagination. Edgar Allan Poe. 1975. 12.95x (ISBN 0-460-00336-4, Evman); pap. 4.95x (ISBN 0-460-01336-X, Evman). Biblio Dist.
Tales of Mystery & Imagination. Edgar Allan Poe. 438p. 1981. Repr. lib. bdg. 19.95. Lightyear.
Tales of Mystery & Imagination. Edgar Allan Poe. 1981. Repr. lib. bdg. 19.95x (ISBN 0-89966-434-2). Buccaneer Bks.
Tales of Mystery & Imagination. Edgar Allan Poe. (Illus.). 320p. 1987. 59.00x (ISBN 0-948397-46-2, Pub. by M O'Mara UK). State Mutual Bk.
Tales of Mystery & Imagination. Edgar Allan Poe. LC 88-40069. 304p. 1988. 25.00 (ISBN 0-89296-350-6). Mysterious Pr.
Tales of Mystery & Imagination. Edgar Allan Poe. (Classics Ser.). (YA) (gr. 7 up). Date not set. pap. 3.95. Longman Trade.
Tales of Mystery & Imagination. Poe Rackham. 1986. 19.75X (ISBN 0-245-52953-5, Pub. by Harrap Ltd England). State Mutual Bk.
Tales of Mystery & Imagination. (Classics Ser.). (ps-6). 1988. pap. 3.95 (ISBN 0-582-54159-X). Longman.
Tales of Mystery & Imagination, Retold by Henniker-Major. Edgar Allan Poe. (Oxford Progressive English Readers Ser.). (Illus.). (gr. 3 up). 1975. pap. text ed. 3.75x (ISBN 0-19-580511-9). Oxford U Pr.
Tales of Nasr-ed-Din Khoja. Nasr Al-Din. Tr. by Henry D. Barnham from Turkish. LC 77-87632. 1977. Repr. of 1923 ed. 23.00 (ISBN 0-404-16457-9). AMS Pr.
Tales of Natural & Unnatural Catastrophes. Patricia Highsmith. 1989. 16.95 (ISBN 0-87113-251-6). Atlantic Monthly.
Tales of New England. Sarah O. Jewett. LC 77-110223. (Short Story Index Reprint Ser.). 1894. 16.00 (ISBN 0-8369-3362-1). Ayer Co Pubs.

Tales of Old Cairo: Qahira Al Jadida. Nagib Mahfouz. pap. 6.95x (ISBN 0-86685-150-X). Intl Bk Ctr.
Tales of Old Dorset. Sean Street. 96p. 1987. 30.00x (ISBN 0-905392-44-2, Countryside Bks). State Mutual Bk.
Tales of Old Hertfordshire. Doris Jones-Baker. 96p. 1987. pap. 30.00x (ISBN 0-905392-82-5, Countryside Bks). State Mutual Bk.
Tales of Old Japan. A. B. Mitford. 383p. 1983. Repr. of 1874 ed. lib. bdg. 150.00 (ISBN 0-8495-3902-1). Arden Lib.
Tales of Old Japan. A. B. Mitford. LC 66-25436. (Illus.). 430p. 1966. pap. 8.95 (ISBN 0-8048-1160-1). C E Tuttle.
Tales of Old Japan. 2nd ed. A. B. Mitford. 383p. 1893. Repr. 250.00x (Pub. by Han-Shan Tang Ltd). State Mutual Bk.
Tales of Old Kent. Alan Bignell. 96p. 1987. pap. 30.00x (ISBN 0-905392-75-2, Countryside Bks). State Mutual Bk.
Tales of Old Malawi. Ed. by Ellis Singano & Adrian Roscoe. (Malawian Writers Ser.: No. 1). 106p. (Orig.). (gr. 9-12). 1974. pap. 7.00x (ISBN 0-89410-274-5). Three Continents.
Tales of Old Oxfordshire. Cecillia Millson. 96p. 1987. pap. 30.00x (ISBN 0-905392-20-5, Countryside Bks). State Mutual Bk.
Tales of Old Surrey. Matthew Alexander. 96p. 1987. 30.00x (ISBN 0-905392-41-8, Countryside Bks). State Mutual Bk.
Tales of Old Sussex. Lillian Candlin. 96p. 1987. 30.00x (ISBN 0-905392-45-0, Countryside Bks). State Mutual Bk.
Tales of Old-Time Texas. J. Frank Dobie. 1955. 16.45 (ISBN 0-316-18801-8); pap. 8.95 (ISBN 0-316-18802-6). Little.
Tales of Old-Time Texas. J. Frank Dobie. (Illus.). 350p. 1984. pap. 9.95 (ISBN 0-292-78069-9). U of Tex Pr.
Tales of Old Wiltshire. Cecilia Millson. 96p. 1987. 30.00x (ISBN 0-905392-12-4, Countryside Bks). State Mutual Bk.
Tales of Olga da Polga. Michael Bond. (gr. 7 up). 1974. pap. 3.50 (ISBN 0-14-030500-9, Puffin). Penguin.
Tales of Oliver Pig. Jean Van Leeuwen. LC 79-4276. (Easy-to-Read Bks.). (Illus.). 64p. (ps-3). 1979. PLB 9.89 (ISBN 0-8037-8736-7); pap. 4.95 (ISBN 0-8037-8737-5, 0481-140). Dial Bks Young.
Tales of One-Who-Seeks. Colin Berg. (Illus.). 128p. (Orig.). 1983. pap. 9.50 (ISBN 0-9608720-1-9). Schofield Pub.
Tales of Ordinary Madness. Charles Bukowski. 1983. pap. 6.95 (ISBN 0-87286-155-4). City Lights.
Tales of Our Coast. S. R. Crockett et al. LC 70-116966. (Short Story Index Reprint Ser). (Illus.). 1896. 17.00 (ISBN 0-8369-3470-9). Ayer Co Pubs.
Tales of Pan. Mordicai Gerstein. LC 83-49484. (Illus.). 64p. (gr. 2-5). 1986. 12.70i (ISBN 0-06-021996-3); PLB 12.89 (ISBN 0-06-021997-1). HarpJ.
Tales of Parker Parrot. Calvert Estill. (Illus.). 36p. (gr. 3 up). Date not set. pap. price not set (ISBN 0-934750-65-3). Jalamap.
Tales of Patrick Merla. Patrick Merla. (Orig.). Date not set. pap. 3.95 (ISBN 0-345-32252-5, Pub. by Available Pr). Ballantine.
Tales of Persia: A Book for Children. William M. Miller. (Illus.). 145p. (gr. 1-6). 1988. pap. 5.95 (ISBN 0-87552-292-0). Presby & Reformed.
Tales of Physicists & Mathematicians. S. G. Gindikin. 200p. 1987. 29.50 (ISBN 0-8176-3317-0). Birkhauser.
Tales of Pirx the Pilot. Stanislaw Lem. 224p. 1981. pap. 2.95 (ISBN 0-380-55665-0, 55665-0, Bard). Avon.
Tales of Potosi. Bartolome Arzans De Orsua Y Vela. Ed. by R. C. Padden. LC 74-6574. 245p. 1975. 20.00x (ISBN 0-87057-144-3). U Pr of New Eng.
Tales of Power. Carlos Castaneda. 1982. pap. 4.95 (ISBN 0-671-55329-1). WSP.
Tales of Power. Carlos Castaneda. 287p. 1975. pap. 4.95 (ISBN 0-671-22144-2, Touchstone Bks). S&S.
Tales of Quails n' Such. Havilah Babcock. (Illus.). 237p. 1985. Repr. of 1951 ed. 19.95 (ISBN 0-87249-441-1). U of SC Pr.
Tales of Rabbi Nachman. Martin Buber. LC 56-12330. 214p. 1972. 5.95 (ISBN 0-8180-1325-7). Horizon.
Tales of Rabbi Nachman. Martin Buber. LC 87-22906. 1988. pap. text ed. 15.00 (ISBN 0-391-03548-7). Humanities.
Tales of Racing & Chasing. Terry Biddlecombe. (Illus.). 96p. 1986. 20.95 (ISBN 0-09-162690-0, Pub. by Century Hutchinson). David & Charles.
Tales of Richland, White Bluffs & Hanford 1805-1943. Martha B. Parker. (Illus.). 407p. 1987. 22.50 (ISBN 0-87770-223-3); 16.95. Ye Galleon.
Tales of Robin Hood. Clayton Emory. (Orig.). 1988. pap. 3.50 (ISBN 0-671-65397-0). Baen Bks.
Tales of St. Francis: Ancient Stories for Contemporary Living. Murray Bodo. 1988. pap. 14.95 (ISBN 0-385-23824-X). Doubleday.
Tales of Samurai Honor. Ihara Saikaku. 156p. 1983. pap. 39.00x (ISBN 0-317-69421-9, Pub. by Han-Shan Tang Ltd). State Mutual Bk.
Tales of San Francisco. Samuel Dickson. 1955. 19.95 (ISBN 0-8047-0488-0). Stanford U Pr.
Tales of Sea & Shore. Juliet Heslewood. (Illus.). 152p. (ps-6). 1987. 12.95 (ISBN 0-19-278105-7). Oxford U Pr.
Tales of Secret Egypt. Sax Rohmer. 1976. Repr. of 1918 ed. lib. bdg. 19.95x (ISBN 0-89190-809-9, Pub. by River City Pr). Amereon Ltd.
Tales of Sevastopol: The Cossacks. Leo Tolstoy. 367p. 1982. 10.95 (ISBN 0-8285-2346-0, Pub. by Progress Pubs USSR). Imported Pubns.
Tales of Sex & Viloence: Folklore, Sacrifice, & Danger in the Jaiminiya Brahmana. Wendy D. O'Flaherty. 145p. 1987. 11.50x (ISBN 81-208-0267-5, Pub. by Motilal Banarsidass India). Orient Bk Dist.
Tales of Sex & Violence: Folklore, Sacrifice & Danger in the Jaiminya Brahmana. Wendy D. O'Flaherty. LC 84-16393. (Illus.). 128p. 1985. lib. bdg. 16.95x (ISBN 0-226-61852-8). U of Chicago Pr.
Tales of Socialist Yugoslavia. Milos Acin-Kosta. Ed. by Sandra K. Lindsa. LC 84-52846. 287p. (Eng.). pap. 15.00 (ISBN 0-931931-15-0). Ravnogorski.
Tales of Soldiers see In the Midst of Life.
Tales of Soldiers & Civilians. facs. ed. Ambrose Bierce. LC 70-121522. (Short Story Index Reprint Ser). 1891. 21.00 (ISBN 0-8369-3478-4). Ayer Co Pubs.
Tales of South Asia, 4 bks. Beulah Candappa. (Illus.). 64p. (Orig.). (gr. 4-7). 1986. Set. pap. text ed. 19.80 incl. teacher's notes (ISBN 1-55624-012-0). Wright Group.
Tales of Space & Time. H. G. Wells. LC 72-3285. (Short Story Index Reprint Ser). Repr. of 1899 ed. 24.50 (ISBN 0-8369-4166-7). Ayer Co Pubs.
Tales of Suicide. Luigi Pirandello. Tr. by Giovanni R. Bussino. 1988. 11.95 (ISBN 0-937832-31-6). Dante U Am.
Tales of Teevee. Jeanne G. Smith. (Illus.). 1985. 16.00x (ISBN 0-317-46996-7); plastic bd. 12.00 (ISBN 0-317-46998-3). Jeannes Dreams.
Tales of Ten Worlds. Arthur C. Clarke. (YA) (gr. 7 up). 1987. pap. 3.50 (ISBN 0-451-14978-5, Sig). NAL.
Tales of Terror. (Enchanted World Ser.). 143p. 1987. 16.95 (ISBN 0-8094-5277-4); lib. bdg. write for info. (ISBN 0-8094-5278-2). Time Life.
Tales of Terror & Mystery. Arthur Conan Doyle. 1982. Repr. lib. bdg. 16.95x (ISBN 0-89966-429-6). Buccaneer Bks.
Tales of Terror & the Supernatural. Wilkie Collins. Ed. & intro. by Herbert Van Thal. LC 75-189974. 305p. (Orig.). 1972. pap. 6.50 (ISBN 0-486-20307-7). Dover.
Tales of Terror & Wonder. M. G. Lewis. 283p. 1980. Repr. of 1887 ed. lib. bdg. 37.00 (ISBN 0-8492-6304-2). R West.
Tales of Terror & Wonder. Henry Morley. 1887. Repr. 30.00 (ISBN 0-8274-3566-5). R West.
Tales of Terror: Ten Short Stories. Edgar Allan Poe. LC 84-22290. (Illus.). 208p. (gr. 5 up). 1985. 11.95 (ISBN 0-13-884214-0). P-H.
Tales of Texas & Beyond. Charles A. Watson. LC 86-71449. 130p. 1986. 11.95 (ISBN 0-9617161-0-X). Cedar Elm Pub.
Tales of the Alimentary Canal. Richard Kent. 17.95 (ISBN 0-317-27923-8, Pub. by Amereon Hse). Amereon Ltd.
Tales of the Amazon. Martin Elbl. (Illus.). 32p. (gr. k-3). 1985. 9.95 (ISBN 0-88625-127-3). C Hayes Pr.
Tales of the Anna Karrue. Leon B. Ward, III. (Orig.). 1988. pap. 15.00 (ISBN 0-937684-25-2). Tradd St Pr.
Tales of the Argonauts & Other Sketches. facsimile ed. Bret Harte. LC 78-152943. (Short Story Index Reprint Ser.). Repr. of 1875 ed. 16.00 (ISBN 0-8369-3802-X). Ayer Co Pubs.
Tales of the Banshee. Patrick F. Byrne. 104p. (Orig.). 1987. pap. 7.95 (ISBN 0-85342-821-2, Pub. by Mercier Pr Ireland). Irish Bks Media.
Tales of the Big Bend. Elton Miles. LC 76-17977. (Illus.). 200p. (Orig.). 1976. pap. 10.95 (ISBN 0-89096-360-6). Tex A&M Univ Pr.
Tales of the Black Cat: Khamarat Quet Aswad. Nagib Mahfouz. (Arabic.). pap. 6.95x (ISBN 0-86685-157-7). Intl Bk Ctr.
Tales of the Black Hills. Helen Rezatto. LC 83-61869. (Illus.). 288p. 1983. pap. 9.95 (ISBN 0-87970-161-7). North Plains.
Tales of the Black Widowers. Isaac Asimov. 224p. 1980. pap. 1.95 (ISBN 0-449-23788-5, Crest). Fawcett.
Tales of the Black Widowers. Isaac Asimov. 16.95 (ISBN 0-89190-278-3, Pub. by Am Repr). Amereon Ltd.
Tales of the British Isles, 4 bks. Kenneth McLeish. (Illus.). 64p. (Orig.). (gr. 4-7). 1986. Set. pap. text ed. 19.80 incl. teacher's notes (ISBN 1-55624-015-5). Wright Group.
Tales of the Cakchiquels. Ed. by Larry L. Richman. 102p. 9.95 (ISBN 0-941846-01-6). Richman Pub.
Tales of the Caribbean, 4 bks. Evan Jones. (Illus.). 48p. (Orig.). (gr. 4-7). 1986. Set. pap. text ed. 19.80 incl. teacher's notes (ISBN 1-55624-014-7). Wright Group.
Tales of the Chesapeake. facs. ed. George A. Townsend. LC 74-83904. (Black Heritage Library Collection Ser). 1880. 14.50 (ISBN 0-8369-8668-7). Ayer Co Pubs.
Tales of the City. Armistead Maupin. LC 77-11781. 1978. pap. 10.95 (ISBN 0-06-090654-5, CN-654, PL). Har-Row.
Tales of the City Room. Elizabeth G. Jordan. LC 70-116958. (Short Story Index Reprint Ser). 1898. 17.00 (ISBN 0-8369-3462-8). Ayer Co Pubs.
Tales of the Cloister. Elizabeth G. Jordan. LC 76-110204. (Short Story Index Reprint Ser.). 1901. 18.00 (ISBN 0-8369-3355-9). Ayer Co Pubs.
Tales of the Club Expert. Jimmy Tait. 144p. (Orig.). 1987. pap. 6.95 (ISBN 0-571-14870-0). Faber & Faber.
Tales of the Cochiti Indians. Ruth Benedict. 1976. lib. bdg. 59.95 (ISBN 0-8490-2729-2). Gordon Pr.
Tales of the Cochiti Indians. Ruth Benedict. Repr. of 1931 ed. 29.00 (ISBN 0-403-03705-0). Scholarly.
Tales of the Cochiti Indians. Ruth Benedict. LC 81-16426. pap. 70.20 (2030998). Bks Demand UMI.
Tales of the Comet. Douglas Campbell & John Higgins. LC 86-15992. 224p. 1986. Repr. lib. bdg. 24.95x (ISBN 0-89370-536-5). Borgo Pr.
Tales of the Comet: Digressions & Fantasies Concerning the Good Dr. Halley & the Wondrous Reappearances of His Celestial Namesake. Douglas Campbell & John Higgins. LC 85-24960. (Illus.). 288p. (Orig.). 1986. pap. 9.95 (ISBN 0-89793-038-X). Hunter Hse.
Tales of the Congaree. Edward C. L. Adams. Intro. by Robert G. O'Meally. LC 86-30912. xx, 367p. 1987. 29.95x (ISBN 0-8078-1709-0); pap. 12.50 (ISBN 0-8078-4188-9). U of NC Pr.
Tales of the Dark. Ed. by Lincoln Child. 1988. pap. 3.50 (ISBN 0-312-90339-1). St Martin.
Tales of the Dark II. Ed. by Child. 1988. pap. 3.50 (ISBN 0-312-90769-9). St Martin.
Tales of the Dervishes. Idries Shah. 1967. 18.95 (ISBN 0-900860-47-2, Pub. by Octagon Pr England). Ins Study Human.
Tales of the Dervishes. Idries Shah. pap. 8.95 (ISBN 0-525-48368-3). Dutton.
Tales of the Enlightened. S. Z. Kahana. Ed. by Philip S. Berg. 160p. 1987. 14.95 (ISBN 0-943688-39-6); pap. 9.95 (ISBN 0-943688-40-X). Res Ctr Kabbalah.
Tales of the Fairies & the Ghost-World. Jeremiah Curtin. LC 75-152760. Repr. of 1895 ed. 20.00 (ISBN 0-405-08416-1, Blom Pubns). Ayer Co Pubs.
Tales of the Far North. Eva Martin. LC 85-46068. (Illus.). 124p. (ps up). 1987. 12.95 (ISBN 0-8037-0319-8, 01258-440). Dial Bks Young.
Tales of the Field: On Writing Ethnography. John Van Maanen. (Chicago Guides to Writing, Editing, & Publishing). xvi, 174p. 1988. 25.00x (ISBN 0-226-84961-9); pap. 7.95 (ISBN 0-226-84962-7). U of Chicago Pr.
Tales of the Fish Patrol. Jack London. LC 72-4454. (Short Story Index Reprint Ser). Repr. of 1905 ed. 22.00 (ISBN 0-8369-4181-0). Ayer Co Pubs.
Tales of the Fish Patrol. Jack London. (Illus.). 244p. 1982. pap. 6.95 (ISBN 0-932458-07-6). Star Rover.
Tales of the Five Towns. Arnold Bennett. LC 74-17131. (Collected Works of Arnold Bennett: Vol. 77). 1976. Repr. of 1910 ed. 21.75 (ISBN 0-518-19158-3). Ayer Co Pubs.
Tales Of The Flying Mountains. Poul Anderson. 288p. (Orig.). 1984. pap. 2.95 (ISBN 0-8125-3073-X, Dist. by Warner Pub. Services & Saint Martin's Press). Tor Bks.
Tales of the Foreign Settlements in Japan. Harold S. Williams. LC 72-77513. (Illus.). 351p. (Orig.). 1972. pap. 7.95 (ISBN 0-8048-1051-6). C E Tuttle.
Tales of the Four Dervishes of Amir Khusru. Amina Shah. 1976. 17.95 (ISBN 0-318-22031-8, Pub. by Octagon Pr England); pap. 5.95 (ISBN 0-318-22032-6). Ins Study Human.
Tales of the Frontier: From Lewis & Clark to the Last Roundup. Everett Dick. LC 62-14664. (Illus.). x, 390p. 1963. 32.50x (ISBN 0-8032-0038-2); pap. 7.50 (ISBN 0-8032-5744-9, BB 539, Bison). U of Nebr Pr.
Tales of the Gods & Heroes. George W. Cox. LC 77-94564. 1979. Repr. of 1895 ed. lib. bdg. 25.00 (ISBN 0-89341-309-7). Longwood Pub Group.
Tales of the Great Game Fish. Zane Grey. 304p. Repr. of 1928 ed. lib. bdg. 18.95x (ISBN 0-89190-767-X, Pub. by River City Pr). Amereon Ltd.
Tales of the Great Western. O. S. Nock. (Illus.). 176p. 1984. 22.95 (ISBN 0-7153-8347-7). David & Charles.
Tales of the Grotesque & Arabesque. Edgar Allan Poe. 12.00 (ISBN 0-8446-1352-5). Peter Smith.
Tales of the Hasidim, 2 vols. Martin Buber. Incl. The Early Masters. pap. 8.95 (ISBN 0-8052-0001-0); The Later Masters. pap. 9.95 (ISBN 0-8052-0002-9). LC 47-2952. 1961. pap. Schocken.
Tales of the Home Folks in Peace & War. Joel C. Harris. LC 75-98573. (Short Story Index Reprint Ser.). 1898. 24.50 (ISBN 0-8369-3147-5). Ayer Co Pubs.
Tales of the Horseclans. Robert Adams. 1985. pap. 8.95 (ISBN 0-452-25726-3, Plume). NAL.
Tales of the Kingdom. Karen B. Mains & David Mains. (Illus.). 96p. (gr. 1 up). 1983. 12.95 (ISBN 0-89191-560-5). Cook.
Tales of the Late Ivan Petrovich Belkin. Aleksandr Pushkin. Ed. by Norman Henly. (Library of Russian Classics). 136p. pap. text ed. 9.95x (ISBN 0-631-14503-6). Basil Blackwell.
Tales of the Little Quarter. Jan Neruda. Tr. by Edith Pargeter from Czech. 1977. Repr. of 1957 ed. lib. bdg. 35.00x (ISBN 0-8371-9344-3, NELQ). Greenwood.
Tales of the Maine Coast. Noah Brooks. 1980. 8.50 (ISBN 0-686-64301-1). Bookfinger.
Tales of the Malayan Coast. facs. ed. Rounsevelle Wildman. LC 72-90593. (Short Story Index Reprint Ser.). (Illus.). 1899. 19.00 (ISBN 0-8369-3076-2). Ayer Co Pubs.
Tales of the Maori Bush. James Cowan. LC 75-35248. Repr. of 1934 ed. 24.50 (ISBN 0-404-14422-5). AMS Pr.
Tales of the Mediterranean, 4 bks. Kenneth McLeish. Ed. by Maria Roussou. (Illus.). 56p. (Orig.). (gr. 4-7). 1986. Set. pap. text ed. 19.80 incl. teachers notes (ISBN 1-55624-013-9). Wright Group.
Tales of the Mississippi. rev ed. Ray Samuel et al. LC 81-5937. (Illus.). 240p. 1981. Repr. of 1955 ed. 19.95 (ISBN 0-88289-291-6). Pelican.
Tales of the Nashramh: Rinim Poodor, Pt. 2. Diane J. Bothell. (Illus.). 104p. (Orig.). 1987. pap. text ed. 7.95 (ISBN 0-933673-10-8). Three-Stones Pubns.
Tales of the Nashramh: Scoffing Marah, Pt. 1. Sarah Cohen. (Illus.). 82p. (Orig.). 1987. pap. 7.95 (ISBN 0-933673-09-4). Three-Stones Pubns.
Tales of the Nez Perce. Donald M. Hines. 232p. 1984. 19.95 (ISBN 0-87770-311-6). Ye Galleon.
Tales of the Night. Sarah Wood. LC 82-61086. 126p. 1982. Repr. of 1827 ed. 15.00 (ISBN 0-89725-025-7). NH Pub Co.
Tales of the North American Indians. Ed. by Stith Thompson. LC 66-22898. (Midland Bks.: No. 91). (Illus.). 416p. 1966. pap. 9.95x (ISBN 0-253-20091-1). Ind U Pr.
Tales of the Northwest. William J. Snelling. Ed. by David Stinebeck. (Masterworks of Literature Ser.). 1975. pap. 6.95x (ISBN 0-8084-0418-0). New Coll U Pr.
Tales of the Northwest. William J. Snelling. Repr. 10.00 (ISBN 0-87018-058-4). Ross.
Tales of the Ohio Land. Jack Matthews. (Illus.). 186p. 1978. 11.95 (ISBN 0-87758-011-1). Ohio Hist Soc.
Tales of the Old Stock Exchange Before the Big Bang. Donald Cobbett. (Illus.). 128p. 1987. pap. 6.95 (ISBN 0-903852-99-3, Pub. by Milestone Pubns UK). Seven Hills Bks.
Tales of the Old U. P. A Second Northwoods Reader. 4th ed. Cully Gage. (Illus.). 1981. 7.49 (ISBN 0-932212-23-9). Avery Color.
Tales of the Orishas. M. G. Wippler. pap. 7.95 (ISBN 0-317-58910-5). Original Pubns.
Tales of the Pampas. W. H. Hudson. (Illus.). 264p. 1979. pap. 5.95 (ISBN 0-916870-23-5). Creative Arts.
Tales of the Plainsman. George Stucker. (Illus.). 32p. 1982. 5.95 (ISBN 0-89962-264-X). Todd & Honeywell.
Tales of the Prophet Samuel. Charles Wengrov. (Shulsinger Biblical Ser.). (Illus.). (gr. 5-10). 1969. 4.00 (ISBN 0-914080-22-9). Shulsinger Sales.
Tales of the Prophets. A. H. Nadvi. pap. 2.50 (ISBN 0-686-18388-6). Kazi Pubns.
Tales of the Punjab. Flora A. Steel. LC 78-63222. (Folktale). pap. 33.00 (ISBN 0-404-16159-6). AMS Pr.
Tales of the Quintana Roo. James Tiptree, Jr. (Illus.). 112p. 1986. 11.95 (ISBN 0-87054-152-8). Arkham.
Tales of the Real Gypsy. Paul Kesler. LC 77-142004. 330p. 1971. Repr. of 1897 ed. 40.00x (ISBN 0-8103-3633-2). Gale.
Tales of the Resistance. Karen Mains & David Mains. (Illus.). (gr. 4-7). 1986. 12.95 (ISBN 0-89191-938-4). Cook.
Tales of the Sacred & the Supernatural. Mircea Eliade. LC 81-12924. 108p. 1981. pap. 7.95 (ISBN 0-664-24391-6). Westminster John Knox.
Tales of the Samurai. James S. De Benneville. 480p. 1987. pap. 16.95 (ISBN 0-7103-0233-9, 02339, Kegan Paul). Routledge Chapman & Hall.
Tales of the Scottish Highlands. Gerald Warner. (Illus.). 192p. 1982. 11.95 (ISBN 0-85683-060-7); pap. 11.95 (ISBN 0-85683-061-5). Dufour.
Tales of the Sea. Tim Diet. Ed. by Susan Jack. 160p. 1983. pap. 7.95 (ISBN 0-930096-51-7). G Gannett.
Tales of the Sexy Snake: The Art of Healing Through Touch & Language. Jan Kennedy. LC 83-73352. (Illus.). 320p. (Orig.). 1983. pap. 9.95 (ISBN 0-938954-03-2). Cosmoenergetics Pubns.
Tales of the Sonotia. 2nd ed. Frank M. Siebold. LC 73-21889. (Illus.). 100p. Date not set. pap. 12.95 (ISBN 0-9612152-1-6). A & W Limited.
Tales of the South Carolina Low Country. Nancy Rhyne. LC 82-9710. 112p. 1982. pap. 5.95 (ISBN 0-89587-027-4). Blair.
Tales of the South Pacific. James A. Michener. 1984. pap. 3.95 (ISBN 0-449-20652-1, Crest). Fawcett.
Tales of the Spring Rain. Ed. by Akinari Uyeda. Tr. by Barry Jackman. 249p. 1979. pap. 15.00x (ISBN 0-86008-251-2, Pub. by U of Tokyo Japan). Columbia U Pr.
Tales of the Sun: Folklore of Southern India. Ed. by Richard M. Dorson. LC 77-70604. (International Folklore Ser.). 1977. Repr. of 1890 ed. lib. bdg. 24.50x (ISBN 0-405-10103-1). Ayer Co Pubs.
Tales of the Sun: Folklore of Southern India. Georgiana Kingscote & Pandit Natesa Sastri. LC 78-67728. (Folktale). Repr. of 1890 ed. 28.00 (ISBN 0-404-16137-5). AMS Pr.
Tales of the Sunshine Coast. Alf Woods. 118p. 1985. pap. 6.95 (ISBN 0-317-39572-6, Pub. by Boolarong Pubn Australia). Intl spec bk.

Talk Less & Say More: Vermont Proverbs. Wolfgang Mieder. LC 86-50974. (Illus.). 64p. (Orig.). 1986. pap. 5.95 (ISBN 0-933050-42-9). New Eng Pr VT.
Talk Like an Eagle. Dan Zadra. (Adventures in Human Potential Ser.). (Illus.). 32p. (gr. 6 up). PLB 8.95 (ISBN 0-88682-021-9). Creative Ed.
Talk Never Dies: The Language of Huli Disputes. Laurence Goldman. LC 83-18294. 352p. 1984. 49.95x (ISBN 0-422-78210-6, NO. 4009). Routledge Chapman & Hall.
Talk-Power: How to Speak Without Fear. Natalie H. Rogers. LC 82-5174. 1982. 13.95 (ISBN 0-396-08080-4). Dodd.
Talk Radio. Eric Bogosian. (Orig.). 1988. 6.95 (ISBN 0-394-75946-X, Vin). Random.
Talk Radio. Adult ed. Edgar Sather & Catherine Sadow. (Illus.). 1987. pap. text ed. 12.95 (ISBN 0-201-16836-7). Addison-Wesley.
Talk Radio & the American Dream. Murray B. Levin. 192p. 1986. 25.00x (ISBN 0-669-13216-0); pap. 10.95 (ISBN 0-669-13217-9). Lexington Bks.
Talk Sense to Yourself: A Guide to Cognitive Restructuring Therapy. Rian E. McMullin & Bill Caesy. (Illus.). 57p. (Orig.). 1975. pap. 4.00 (ISBN 0-935205-02-0). Counseling Res.
Talk Sense to Yourself: A Guide to Cognitive Restructuring Therapy see Hablese con Sentido A Si Mismo: Una Guia de Terapia de Restructuracion Cognitiva.
Talk Sense to Yourself: Language & Personal Power. Chick Moorman. 200p. 1985. 9.95 (ISBN 0-9616046-0-3). Prsnl Power Pr.
Talk Show Guest Directory of Experts, Authorities & Spokespersons, 1987-1988. 4th ed. Ed. by Mitchell P. Davis. 1987. pap. 25.00 (ISBN 0-934333-02-5). Broadcast Inter.
Talk Show: Selects. Ed. by Mitchell P. Davis. 254p. 1987. pap. text ed. 185.00 (ISBN 0-934333-25-4); Mailing list 175.00 (ISBN 0-934333-27-0); Rolodex 242.25 (ISBN 0-934333-26-2). Broadcast Inter.
Talk Story. Mallie Moore et al. (Illus.). 115p. (Orig.). 1987. 7.95 (ISBN 0-9618620-0-9). Bright Design.
Talk Story: An Anthology of Hawaii's Local Writers. Ed. by Eric Chock. 1978. pap. 3.95 (ISBN 0-932136-03-6). Petronium Pr.
Talk Thru the Bible: A Survey of a Setting & Content of Scripture. Bruce Wilkinson & Kenneth Boa. LC 83-13343. (Illus.). 469p. 1983. Repr. of 1981 ed. 16.95 (ISBN 0-8407-5286-5). Nelson.
Talk to God about The Sabbath. large type ed. Calkins & White. 70p. 1984. pap. 8.50x (ISBN 0-914009-22-2). VHI Library.
Talk to God... I'll Get the Message: Black Version. Norman Geller. (Illus.). 23p. (gr. 1-4). 1985. pap. 4.95 (ISBN 0-915753-08-1). N Geller Pub.
Talk to God... I'll Get the Message: Spanish Version. Norman Geller. Tr. by Bonnie Galway from Eng. (Illus.). 23p. (gr. 1-4). 1985. pap. 4.95 (ISBN 0-915753-07-3). N Geller Pub.
Talk to God...I'll Get the Message: Catholic Version. Norman Geller. (Illus.). 23p. (gr. 1-4). 1983. pap. 4.95 (ISBN 0-915753-03-0). N Geller Pub.
Talk to God...I'll Get the Message: Jewish Version. Norman Geller. (Illus.). 23p. (gr. 1-4). 1983. pap. 4.95 (ISBN 0-915753-02-2). N Geller Pub.
Talk to God...I'll Get the Message: Protestant Version. Norman Geller. (Illus.). 23p. (gr. 1-4). 1983. pap. 4.95 (ISBN 0-915753-04-9). N Geller Pub.
Talk to Me, My Love. Deborah Kent. (Orig.). (gr. k-12). 1987. pap. 2.75 (ISBN 0-440-97810-6, LFL). Dell.
Talk to the Deaf: A Manual of Approximately 1,000 Signs Used by the Deaf of North America. Lottie Riekehof. LC 63-17975. (Illus.). 154p. 1963. 7.95 (ISBN 0-88243-612-0, 02-0612). Gospel Pub.
Talk to Win: Six Steps to a Successful Vocal Image. Lillian Glass. (Illus.). 224p. 1988. pap. 9.95 (ISBN 0-399-51386-8, Perigee Bks). Putnam Pub Group.
Talk to Your Child: How to Develop Reading & Language Skills Through Conversation at Home. Harvey S. Wiener. 1989. 7.95 (ISBN 0-14-009652-3). Penguin.
Talk, Tour, & Taste: A Practical Introduction to Spanish Conversation, Culture, & Vocabulary. Del Bye & Kendra Ettenhofer. LC 88-61794. (Illus.). 134p. (Orig.). (YA) (gr. 9 up). 1989. pap. text ed. 10.95 (ISBN 0-944208-03-7); tchr's. ed. 3.95 (ISBN 0-944208-04-5). Seventh-Wing Pubns.
Talk Two: Children Using English as a Second Language. Joan Tough. vii, 216p. pap. text ed. 16.50x (ISBN 0-906383-27-7, 00588, Pub. by Onyx Pr UK). Heinemann Ed.
Talk with Angels. Desmond Meiring. 352p. Date not set. pap. 3.95 (ISBN 0-373-62106-X, Pub. by Worldwide). Harlequin Bks.
Talk with Me: Communication with the Multi-Handicapped Deaf. California State Department of Health Staff. LC 75-70066. 24.95 (ISBN 0-917002-05-9). Joyce Media.
Talk with the Angels. Desmond Meiring. 304p. 1985. 15.95 (ISBN 0-312-78476-7). St Martin.
Talk with Us, Work with Us. 1986. 8.50 (ISBN 0-318-22547-6, TR-86-4). Ed Comm States.
Talk with Your Child. Harvey S. Weiner. 280p. 1988. 16.95 (ISBN 0-670-81411-3). Viking.
Talk Your Fat Off. Maye Keao. 150p. 1988. price not set. Keaos Enterprises.
Talk Your Way to Success. Lilyan Wilder. (Illus.). 320p. 1987. pap. 8.95 (ISBN 0-671-63956-0, Fireside). S&S.
Talk Your Way to the Top. James C. Humes. (McGraw-Hill Paperbacks Ser.). 192p. (Orig.). 1980. pap. text ed. 4.95 (ISBN 0-07-031160-9). McGraw.
Talkabout Animals. (Illus., Arabic.). (gr. 1-3). 3.50x (ISBN 0-86685-231-X). Intl Bk Ctr.
Talkabout the Beach. (Illus., Arabic.). (gr. 1-3). 3.50x (ISBN 0-86685-232-8). Intl Bk Ctr.
Talkabout the Home. (Illus., Arabic.). (gr. 1-3). 3.50x (ISBN 0-86685-233-6). Intl Bk Ctr.
Talkative Man. R. K. Narayan. 1988. pap. 5.95 (ISBN 0-14-010134-9). Penguin.
Talkative Man: A Novel of Malgudi. R. K. Narayan. 128p. 1987. 15.95 (ISBN 0-670-81341-9). Viking.
Talked to Death: The Life & Murder of Alan Berg. Stephen Singular. LC 86-22250. (Illus.). 352p. 1987. 17.95 (ISBN 0-688-06154-0, Pub. by Beech Tree Bks). Morrow.
Talkin' about My G-G-Generation. G. B. Trudeau. (Owl Bks.). 1988. pap. 5.95 (ISBN 0-8050-0791-1). H Holt & Co.
Talkin & Testifyin: The Language of Black America. Geneva Smitherman. LC 85-22615. 246p. 1986. pap. 9.95x (ISBN 0-8143-1805-3). Wayne St U Pr.
Talkin' B.A. Blues: The Life & a Couple of Deaths of Ed Teashack...etc. George Starbuck. 45p. 1980. 5.00 (ISBN 0-913219-22-3); pap. 2.50 (ISBN 0-913219-23-1); signed 10.00 (ISBN 0-913219-24-X). Pym-Rand Pr.
Talkin' Dan Gable. Ed. by Stephen T. Holland. 100p. 1983. pap. 7.95 (ISBN 0-9612582-0-9). Limerick Pubns.
Talkin' Socialism: J.A. Wayland & the Role of the Press in American Radicalism, 1890-1912. Elliott Shore. LC 87-37255. (Illus.). x, 278p. 1988. 25.00x (ISBN 0-7006-0352-2). U Pr of KS.
Talking. Richard L. Allington. Kathleen Krull. LC 80-17021. (E. G. Beginning to Learn about... Ser.). (Illus.). 32p. (ps-2). 1985. pap. 9.27 (ISBN 0-8172-2492-0); PLB 15.33. Raintree Pubs.
Talking. David Antin. pap. 3.50 (ISBN 0-686-09756-4). Kulchur Foun.
Talking about Death: A Dialogue Between Parent & Child; With Parent's Guide & Recommended Resources. new ed. Earl A. Grollman. LC 75-36042. (Illus.). 112p. (YA) (gr. k-4). 1976. pap. 6.95 (ISBN 0-8070-2373-6, BP531). Beacon Pr.
Talking about Divorce & Separation: A Dialogue Between Parent & Child. Earl A. Grollman. LC 75-5289. (Illus.). (YA) (gr. k-4). pap. 6.95 (ISBN 0-8070-2375-2, BP524). Beacon Pr.
Talking about Dreams: Dream Reports As Personal Narratives. Roger Elbourne. 320p. Date not set. text ed. price not set (ISBN 0-8290-1582-5). Irvington.
Talking about Films: A Discussion Guide. Robert Selinske. (Illus.). 432p. (Orig.). 1983. Filmquest Bks.
Talking about Films: A Discussion Guide. 2nd ed. Robert Selinske. (Illus.). 464p. 1988. pap. 20.00x (ISBN 0-9610670-2-0). Filmquest Bks.
Talking about God Is Dangerous: The Diary of a Russian Dissident. Tatiana Goricheva. 144p. 1987. 11.95 (ISBN 0-8245-0798-3). Crossroad NY.
Talking about Pianos. Corby Kummer. Ed. by William Zinsser et al. LC 81-84064. (Illus.). 80p. (Orig.). 1982. pap. write for info. (ISBN 0-9607196-0-1). Steinway.
Talking about Prayer. Richard Bewes. LC 80-7781. 128p. (Orig.). 1980. pap. 2.95 (ISBN 0-87784-465-8). Inter-Varsity.
Talking about Something Important. Stan Stewart & Pauline Hubner. 128p. (Orig.). 1981. pap. 8.95 (ISBN 0-85819-328-0, Pub. by JBCE). ANZ Religious Pubns.
Talking about Writing: A Guide for Tutor & Teacher Conferences. Beverly L. Clark. (Illus.). 192p. 1985. pap. text ed. 9.95x (ISBN 0-472-08062-8). U of Mich Pr.
Talking Across the World: The Love Letters of Olaf Stapledon & Agnes Miller, 1913-1919. Ed. by Robert Crossley. LC 87-8119. (Illus.). 424p. 1987. 30.00x (ISBN 0-87451-423-1). U pr of New Eng.
Talking All Morning. Robert Bly. (Poets on Poetry Ser.). 316p. 1980. pap. 8.95 (ISBN 0-472-15760-4). U of Mich Pr.
Talking American: Cultural Discourses on Donahue. Donal Carbaugh. Ed. by Brenda Dervin. (Communication & Information Science Ser.). 272p. 1988. text ed. 39.50 (ISBN 0-89391-477-0); pap. text ed. 22.50 (ISBN 0-89391-492-4). Ablex Pub.
Talking & Learning: A Guide to Fostering Communication in Nursery & Infant Schools. Joan Tough. 328p. (Orig.). 1983. pap. text ed. 17.50 (ISBN 0-7062-3603-3, 00574). Heinemann Ed.
Talking & Learning: A Guide to Fostering Communication Skills. Ed. by Ward Lock Educational Staff. 309p. 1985. 25.00x (ISBN 0-317-42645-1, Pub. by Ward Lock Educ Co Ltd). State Mutual Bk.
Talking & Listening: Guide to Helping Interview. Laura Epstein. 1985. pap. text ed. 19.95 (ISBN 0-675-20595-6). Merrill.
Talking Animals. Charles Waterman. (Juniper Bks: No. 24). (Orig.). 1978. pap. 5.00 (ISBN 1-55780-023-5). Juniper Pr WI.
Talking Animals & Other People: The Autobiography of One of Animation's Legendary Figures. Shamus Culhane. (Illus.). 416p. 1986. 24.95 (ISBN 0-312-78473-2). St Martin.
Talking at the Boundaries. David Antin. LC 76-15374. 1976. 11.95 (ISBN 0-8112-0559-2); pap. 3.95 (ISBN 0-8112-0560-6, NDP388). New Directions.
Talking Back. Lisa Norby. (Cheerleaders Ser.: No. 38). 176p. (Orig.). (gr. 7 up). 1988. pap. 2.50 (ISBN 0-590-41370-8). Scholastic Inc.
Talking Back: Citizen Feedback & Cable Technology. Ed. by Ithiel De Sola Pool. 320p. 1973. 32.50x (ISBN 0-262-16056-0). MIT Pr.
Talking Back to the Media. Peter Hannaford. 192p. 1986. 21.95 (ISBN 0-87196-815-0). Facts on File.
Talking Behind Masks: Socio-Drama for ESL Students. Bill Grout. Ed. by Helen Munch. (Orig.). 1982. pap. text ed. 5.95 (ISBN 0-88084-051-X); tchr's ed. 4.95 (ISBN 0-88084-050-1); class set 52.95 (ISBN 0-88084-052-8). Alemany Pr.
Talking Between Lines. Julius Fast & Barbara Fast. 1980. pap. 2.50 (ISBN 0-671-83244-1). PB.
Talking Bird & the Story Pouch. Amy Lawson. LC 86-45493. (Illus.). 96p. (gr. 5up). 1987. 11.50i (ISBN 0-06-023833-X); PLB 11.89 (ISBN 0-06-023834-8). HarpJ.
Talking Business In. Incl. French. Beppie LeGal (ISBN 0-8120-3745-6); German. Henry Strutz (ISBN 0-8120-3747-2); Italian. Frank Rakus (ISBN 0-8120-3754-5); Spanish. T. Bruce Fryer & Hugo Faria (ISBN 0-8120-3769-3). 1987. pap. 6.95 ea. Barron.
Talking Business in Japanese. Carol Akiyama & Nubuo Akiyama. 256p. 1987. soft cloth cover 6.95 (ISBN 0-8120-3848-7). Barron.
Talking Cat & Other Stories of French Canada. Natalie S. Carlson. LC 52-5429. (Illus.). (gr. 3-6). 1952. PLB 12.89 (ISBN 0-06-021081-8). HarpJ.
Talking Computers & Telecommunications. John A. Kuecken. 256p. 1982. 35.95 (ISBN 0-442-24721-4). Van Nos Reinhold.
Talking Culture: Ethnography & Conversational Analysis. Michael Moerman. (Conduct & Communication Ser.). 256p. 1987. text ed. 25.95x (ISBN 0-8122-8072-5); pap. text ed. 14.95x. U of Pa Pr.
Talking Cure. Lisa Zeidner. LC 81-52502. 81p. 1982. 10.95 (ISBN 0-89672-095-0); pap. 5.95 (ISBN 0-89672-094-2). Tex Tech Univ Pr.
Talking Cure: A Descriptive Guide to Psychoanalysis. J. D. Lichtenberg. (Psychoanalytic Inquiry Bk. Ser.). 168p. 1984. text ed. 19.95 (ISBN 0-88163-008-X). Analytic Pr.
Talking Cure: Essays in Psychoanalysis & Language. Ed. by Colin MacCabe. LC 79-28551. 243p. 1986. pap. 11.95 (ISBN 0-312-78475-9). St Martin.
Talking Cure: Essays in Psychoanalysis. Colin MacCabe. 1981. 27.50 (ISBN 0-312-78474-0). St Martin.
Talking Cure: Literary Representations of Psychoanalysis. Jeffrey Berman. 368p. (Orig.). 1986. pap. text ed. 15.00x (ISBN 0-8147-1091-3). NYU Pr.
Talking Dictionary. Richard Ballard. (Michigan Learning Modules Ser.: No. 21). 1978. pap. 2.45x (ISBN 0-914004-24-7). Ulrich.
Talking Dog Stories. Walker Gould. LC 83-5733. (Walker's Learn to Read Ser.). (Illus.). 1984. PLB 12.85 (ISBN 0-8027-9195-6); pap. 6.95 (ISBN 0-8027-9196-4). Walker & Co.
Talking Drums of Africa. John F. Carrington. LC 70-77195. (Illus.). 1969. Repr. of 1949 ed. 35.00x (ISBN 0-8371-1292-3, CDA&, Pub. by Negro U Pr). Greenwood.
Talking Drums of Africa. John F. Carrington. (Illus.). 96p. 1949. 15.00. G Vanderstoel.
Talking Earth. Jean C. George. LC 82-48850. 160p. (gr. 6 up). 1983. 12.70i (ISBN 0-06-021975-0); PLB 12.89 (ISBN 0-06-021976-9). HarpJ.
Talking Earth. Jean C. George. LC 82-48850. (Trophy Bks.). 160p. (gr. 5 up). 1987. pap. 2.95 (ISBN 0-06-440212-6, Trophy). HarpJ.
Talking Girl & Other Poems. John Thompson. 33p. 1968. pap. 2.00 (ISBN 0-913219-02-9). Pym-Rand Pr.
Talking Heads. Jerome Davis. LC 85-40146. (Illus.). 224p. 1987. pap. 6.95 (ISBN 0-394-74131-5, Vin). Random.
Talking Heads. David Gans. 1985. pap. 9.95 (ISBN 0-380-89954-X). Avon.
Talking Horse. facsimile ed. Thomas A. Guthrie. LC 79-103514. (Short Story Index Reprint Ser.). 1891. 18.00 (ISBN 0-8369-3256-0). Ayer Co Pubs.
Talking in Flowers: Japanese Botanical Art. Compiled by J. V. Brindle & J. J. White. (Illus.). 96p. 1982. pap. 15.00x (ISBN 0-913196-40-1). Hunt Inst Botanical.
Talking in Whispers. James Watson. LC 83-17595. 144p. (YA) (gr. 7-12). 1984. lib. bdg. 10.99 (ISBN 0-394-96538-8); pap. 10.95 (ISBN 0-394-86538-3). Knopf.
Talking into Writing: Exercises for Basic Writers. Donald L. Rubin & William M. Dodd. (Orig.). 1987. pap. 6.00 (ISBN 0-8141-5005-5). NCTE.
Talking It Out: A Guide to Effective Communication & Problem Solving. Joseph M. Strayhorn, Jr. LC 77-81298. 186p. 1977. pap. text ed. 9.95 (ISBN 0-87822-140-9, 1409). Res Press.
Talking It Out: A Guide to Groups for Abused Women. Ginny NiCarthy et al. LC 84-23404. (New Leaf Ser.). 192p. (Orig.). 1984. pap. 9.95 (ISBN 0-931188-24-5). Seal Pr Feminist.
Talking Jars: An Exhibition of Oriental Ceramic Folwares Found in Southeast Asia. Centennial Museum Staff. 1976. 30.00x (ISBN 0-317-43815-8, Pub. by Han-Shan Tang Ltd). State Mutual Bk.
Talking Jazz. Mark Jones. (Illus.). 1988. 19.95 (ISBN 0-393-02494-6). Norton.
Talking Leaves: Panjandrum No. 4. Ed. by Dennis Koran & David Guss. 1975. pap. 6.95 (ISBN 0-915572-33-8). Panjandrum.
Talking, Listening, Communicating. Jeffrey S. Bormaster & Carol L. Treat. LC 82-3702. 120p. (Orig.). 1982. pap. text ed. 18.00x (ISBN 0-936104-26-0, 072). Pro Ed.
Talking Machine Madness: The Story of America's Early Phonograph Shows. Randy McNutt & Cheryl Bauer. (Illus.). 30p. 1985. pap. 4.00 (ISBN 0-940152-02-9). McNutt Pubns.
Talking Man. Terry Bisson. 192p. 1986. 14.95 (ISBN 0-87795-813-0). Morrow.
Talking Man. Terry Bisson. 192p. 1987. pap. 2.95 (ISBN 0-380-75141-0). Avon.
Talking Minds: The Study of Language in Cognitive Sciences. Ed. by Thomas Bever et al. 296p. 1986. pap. text ed. 9.95 (ISBN 0-262-52114-8). MIT Pr.
Talking Minds: The Study of Language in the Cognitive Sciences. Ed. by Thomas Bever & John M. Carroll. 296p. 1984. 21.95x (ISBN 0-262-02181-1); pap. 9.95. MIT Pr.
Talking of Books: Conrad, Shakespeare, Bennett. Oliver Edwards. 306p. 1981. Repr. of 1957 ed. lib. bdg. 25.00 (ISBN 0-8495-1357-X). Arden Lib.
Talking of Moths. P. B. Allan. 340p. 1943. 30.00x (ISBN 0-317-07181-5, Pub. by FW Classey UK). State Mutual Bk.
Talking of Shakespeare. facsimile ed. Ed. by John Garrett. LC 70-157334. (Select Bibliographies Reprint Ser). Repr. of 1954 ed. 20.00 (ISBN 0-8369-5794-6). Ayer Co Pubs.
Talking of Wales: A Companion to Wales & the Welsh. Trevor Fishlock. 191p. 1978. pap. 4.95 (ISBN 0-586-04555-4, Pub. by Granada England). Academy Chi Pubs.
Talking Parcel. Gerald Durrell. LC 74-23367. (Illus.). (gr. 4-7). 1975. 12.70i (ISBN 0-397-31608-9, Lipp Jr Bks). HarpJ.
Talking Pictures. B. Brown. 1976. lib. bdg. 69.95 (ISBN 0-8490-2730-6). Gordon Pr.
Talking Pictures: Screenwriters in the American Cinema. Richard Corliss. 1985. 27.95; pap. 10.95 (ISBN 0-87951-159-1). Overlook Pr.
Talking Pictures: The Story of Hollywood. Barry Norman. LC 87-31268. 320p. 1988. 19.95 (ISBN 0-453-00589-6). NAL.
Talking Pine. George Moore. LC 76-44812. 1976. Repr. of 1931 ed. lib. bdg. 25.50 (ISBN 0-8414-6059-0). Folcroft.
Talking Poetics from Naropa Institute: Annals of the Jack Kerouac School of Disembodied Poetics, 2 vols. Ed. by Anne Waldman & Marilyn Webb. LC 77-90884. (Illus.). 1978. pap. 6.95 ea.; Vol. 1, 220p. 6.95 (ISBN 0-87773-117-9); Vol. 2, 208p. (ISBN 0-394-73691-5). Shambhala Pubns.
Talking Poetics from Naropa Institute: Annals of the Jack Kerouac School of Disembodied Poetics, Vol. I. Ed. by Anne Waldman & Marilyn Webb. pap. 6.95 (ISBN 0-394-73569-2). Shambhala Pubns.
Talking Poetry: Conversations in the Workshop with Contemporary Poets. Lee Bartlett. LC 86-16163. (Illus.). 320p. 1987. 29.95x (ISBN 0-8263-0911-9); pap. 15.95 (ISBN 0-8263-0912-7). U of NM Pr.
Talking Points. Pamela J. Maraldo & Sally B. Solomon. (Illus.). 48p. (Orig.). 1986. pap. 12.95 (ISBN 0-88737-211-2, 41-1993). Natl League Nurse.
Talking Points in Dermatology - I. Ed. by J. L. Verbov. (New Clinical Applications Dermatology Ser.). 1987. lib. bdg. 38.75 (ISBN 0-85200-939-9, Pub. by MTP Pr England). Kluwer Academic.
Talking Points in Dermatology II. Ed. by J. L. Verbov. (New Clinical Applications Dermatology). 112p. 1988. lib. bdg. 40.00 (ISBN 0-85200-689-6, Pub. by MTP Pr England). Kluwer Academic.
Talking Room. Marianne Hauser. LC 75-21557. 158p. 1976. 11.95 (ISBN 0-914590-20-0); pap. 6.95 (ISBN 0-914590-21-9). Fiction Coll.
Talking Scots Quiz Book. William Graham. 90p. 1985. 20.00x (ISBN 0-907526-07-1, Pub. by Alloway Pub). State Mutual Bk.
Talking Sex with Your Kids. Lois B. Morris. (Orig.). 1984. pap. 6.95 (ISBN 0-671-50022-8, Fireside). S&S.
Talking Sociology. Fine. 1985. 18.00 (ISBN 0-205-08358-7, 818358). Allyn.
Talking Soft Dutch. Linda McCarriston. LC 83-51718. 71p. (Orig.). 1984. 10.95 (ISBN 0-89672-116-7); pap. 6.95 (ISBN 0-89672-115-9). Tex Tech Univ Pr.
Talking Sparrow Murders. Darwin L. Teilhet. 301p. 1985. pap. 4.95 (ISBN 0-930330-29-3). Intl Polygonics.
Talking Story with Nona Beamer: Stories of a Hawaiian Family. Winona D. Beamer. LC 83-70357. (Illus.). 80p. (gr. 2-6). 1984. 8.95 (ISBN 0-935848-20-7). Bess Pr.

Tall Phil & Small Bill. Patricia McKissack & Fredrick McKissack. (Reading Well Ser.). (Illus.). 30p. (Orig.). (gr. 1-3). 1987. text ed. 9.95 (ISBN 0-88335-727-5); pap. text ed. 4.95 (ISBN 0-88335-747-X). Milliken Pub Co.
Tall Ship to America: Log of the Christian Radich. Kjell Thorsen. Tr. by Lizann Disch from Norwegian. LC 79-91578. (Illus.). 128p. 1980. 18.50 (ISBN 0-89096-096-8). Tex A&M Univ Pr.
Tall Ships of the World. C. Keith Wilbur. LC 86-11994. (Illus.). 96p. (Orig.). 1986. pap. 9.95 (ISBN 0-87106-898-2). Globe Pequot.
Tall Ships on the High Seas. Beken of Cowes. 1986. 35.00 (ISBN 0-525-24394-1). Dutton.
Tall Ships Pass: The Story of the Last Years of Deepwater Square-Rigged Sail. William L. Derby. LC 72-121378. pap. 125.30 (ISBN 0-317-08228-0, 2001853). Bks Demand UMI.
Tall Ships, 1986: Collector's Edition. Cy Liberman & Pat Liberman. (Illus.). 64p. (Orig.). 1986. pap. 5.95 (ISBN 0-912608-29-3). Mid Atlantic.
Tall Soldier: My Forty Year Search for the Man Who Saved My Life. Manuel Alvarez. 236p. 1980. lib. bdg. 16.95 (ISBN 0-920528-13-9); pap. 7.95 (ISBN 0-919573-19-3). Left Bank.
Tall Stacks: A Decade of Illegal Use, a Decade of Damage Downwind. R. Ayres. 50p. 1985. 5.00 (ISBN 0-318-20487-8). Natl Resources Defense Coun.
Tall Stance. Elois S. Sampson. 1979. 5.50 (ISBN 0-682-49434-8). Exposition-Phoenix.
Tall Stranger. Louis L'Amour. 128p. (Orig.). 1986. pap. 2.95 (ISBN 0-553-25876-1). Bantam.
Tall Tale America: A Legendary History of Our Humorous Heroes. Walter Blair. (Illus.). 288p. 1987. pap. 9.95 (ISBN 0-226-05596-5). U of Chicago Pr.
Tall Tale in American Folklore & Literature. Carolyn S. Brown. LC 86-25125. (Illus.). 192p. 1987. lib. bdg. 18.95x (ISBN 0-87049-529-1). U of Tenn Pr.
Tall Tales. Henry F. Young. 1982. write for info. (ISBN 0-9609074-0-8). McClain.
Tall Tales: American Myths. Tom Lisker. LC 77-11104. (Myth, Magic & Superstition Ser.). (Illus.). (gr. 4-5). 1977. PLB 14.65 (ISBN 0-8172-1039-3). Raintree Pubs.
Tall Tales from an Island. P. A. Macnab. 245p. 1986. 24.00x (ISBN 0-946487-07-3, Pub. by Luath Pr UK). State Mutual Bk.
Tall Tales from Texas Cow Camps. Mody C. Boatright. LC 82-3186. (Illus.). 144p. 1982. Repr. of 1946 ed. 8.95 (ISBN 0-87074-181-0). SMU Press.
Tall Tales of Davy Crockett: The Second Nashville Series of Crockett Almanacs, 1839-1841. Michael A. Lofaro. (Tennesseana Editions Ser.). (Illus.). 164p. 1987. 24.95x (ISBN 0-87049-525-9); pap. 12.95 (ISBN 0-87049-526-7). U of Tenn Pr.
Tall Tales of the Devil's Apron. Herbert M. Sutherland. 314p. 1988. Repr. of 1970 ed. 14.95 (ISBN 0-932807-27-5). Overmountain Pr.
Tall Tales of the Southwest. Franklin J. Meine. LC 78-166809. (Illus.). 1971. Repr. of 1946 ed. 49.00x (ISBN 0-403-01424-7). Scholarly.
Tall Tales of the Southwest. Franklin J. Meine. 1988. Repr. of 1946 ed. lib. bdg. 49.00x. Am Biog Serv.
Tall Tales Teacher's Guide. Joseph Anderson & Alisse Seelig. Ed. by Ethelyn Simon & Beth Nelson. (Illus.). 80p. (Orig.). 1983. pap. text ed. 4.95 (ISBN 0-939144-08-5). EKS Pub Co.
Tall Tales Told & Retold in Biblical Hebrew. Joseph Anderson & Devora Lipshitz. (Illus.). 96p. (Orig., Hebrew.). 1983. pap. text ed. 9.95 (ISBN 0-939144-07-7). EKS Pub Co.
Tall Timber. Fred Thompson & Tom Bacig. (Illus.). 160p. 1982. 19.95 (ISBN 0-89658-025-3). Voyageur Pr Inc.
Tall Timber Tales: More Paul Bunyan Stories. Dell J. McCormick. LC 39-20778. (Illus.). (gr. 4-6). 1939. 7.95 (ISBN 0-87004-094-4). Caxton.
Tall Timbers Conference on Ecological Animal Control by Habitat Management: Proceedings, No. 1. Tall Timbers Research Station Staff. pap. 62.50 (2026824). Bks Demand UMI.
Tall Timbers Conference on Ecological Animal Control by Habitat Management: Proceedings, No. 3. Tall Timbers Research Station Staff. pap. 73.50 (2026823). Bks Demand UMI.
Tall Timbers Fire Ecology Conference Proceedings No. 11: Five in Africa April 22-23, 1971, Meeting at Auditorium, Sheraton Motor Inn, Tallahassee, FL. Tall Timbers Fire Ecology Conference Staff. pap. 132.00 (2026822). Bks Demand UMI.
Tall Trees & Far Horizons: Adventures & Discoveries of Early Botanists in America. Virginia L. Eifert. LC 70-39100. (Essay Index Reprint Ser.). (Illus.). Repr. of 1965 ed. 27.50 (ISBN 0-8369-2686-2). Ayer Co Pubs.
Tall Trees, Tough Men. Robert E. Pike. (Illus.). 320p. 1984. pap. 8.95 (ISBN 0-393-30185-0). Norton.
Tall Truths from Short Stories. Crate H. Jones. (Orig.). 1987. pap. 6.95 (ISBN 0-8054-5729-1). Broadman.
Tall Woman. Wilma Dykeman. LC 62-11580. 315p. 1982. pap. 8.95 (ISBN 0-9613859-1-X). Wakestone Bks.
Tallahassee Higgins. Mary D. Hahn. LC 86-17513. 192p. (gr. 5-7). 1987. 12.95 (ISBN 0-89919-495-8, Pub. by Clarion). Ticknor & Fields.
Tallahassee Higgins. Mary D. Hahn. 1988. pap. 2.50 (ISBN 0-380-70500-1, Camelot). Avon.
Talley & Son. Lanford Wilson. 13.95 (ISBN 0-317-40302-8); pap. 7.95 (Hill & Wang). Hill & Wang.
Talleyman. John James. 247p. 1988. 18.95 (ISBN 0-575-03791-1, Pub. by Gollancz England). David & Charles.
Talleyrand. Duff Cooper. 1932. 32.50x (ISBN 0-8047-0616-6). Stanford U Pr.
Talleyrand: A Biography. Duff Cooper. LC 86-12093. 408p. 1986. pap. 9.95 (ISBN 0-88064-065-0). Fromm Intl Pub.
Talleyrand in America As a Financial Promoter, 1794-96. Ed. by H. Huth & W. Pugh. LC 76-75323. (American Scene Ser). 1971. Repr. of 1942 ed. lib. bdg. 27.50 (ISBN 0-306-71286-5). Da Capo.
Talley's Folly. Lanford Wilson. (Mermaid Dramabook Ser.). 60p. 1980. pap. 5.95 (ISBN 0-8090-1242-1). Hill & Wang.
Talley's Truth. Philip Ross. 288p. 1987. 15.95 (ISBN 0-312-93015-1, Dist. by St. Martin's Pr & Warner Pub Servs). Tor Bks.
Talley's Truth. Philip Ross. 256p. 1988. pap. 3.50 (ISBN 0-8125-8784-7, Dist. by St Martin's Pr & Warner Pub Servs). Tor Bks.
Tallgrass Prairie: The Inland Sea. Patricia D. Duncan. LC 78-60177. (Illus.). 1979. 20.00 (ISBN 0-913504-44-0). Lowell Pr.
Tallien: A Brief Romance. Frederic Tuten. 230p. 1988. 16.95 (ISBN 0-374-27249-2). FS&G.
Tallinn in 19th Century Engravings. Collets Staff. 1983. 165.00x (ISBN 0-317-57465-5, Pub. by Collets UK). State Mutual Bk.
Tallis. 2nd ed. Paul Doe. (Oxford Studies of Composers). (Illus.). 1976. pap. 9.95x (ISBN 0-19-314122-1). Oxford U Pr.
Tallit see Mitzvah of the Month.
Tallulah Bankhead Murder Case. George Baxt. 240p. 1987. 15.95 (ISBN 0-312-01098-2). St Martin.
Tally-ho! Amrjit S. Kullar. 88p. 1982. pap. text ed. 2.95x (ISBN 0-86131-394-1). Apt Bks.
Tally of Types, with Additions by Several Hands. rev. ed. Stanley Morison. Ed. by Brooke Crutchley. LC 72-90486. (Illus.). 138p. 1973. 55.00 (ISBN 0-521-20043-1). Oak Knoll.
Tallyho, Pinkerton! Steven Kellogg. LC 82-70198. (Illus.). 32p. (ps-3). 1982. 14.95 (ISBN 0-8037-8731-6); PLB 14.89 (ISBN 0-8037-8743-X). Dial Bks Young.
Tallyho, Pinkerton! Steven Kellogg. LC 82-2341. (Pied Piper Bk.). (Illus.). 32p. (ps-3). 1985. 4.95 (ISBN 0-8037-0166-7, 0481-140). Dial Bks Young.
Tally's Corners. Elliot Liebow. 1967. pap. 7.95 (ISBN 0-316-52514-6). Little.
Talmadge: A Political Legacy, A Politician's Life. Herman E. Talmadge & Mark R. Winchell. LC 87-80973. (Illus.). 371p. 1987. 17.95 (ISBN 0-934601-23-2). Peachtree Pubs.
Talmage on Palestine: Series of Sermons. Thomas Talmage. Ed. by Moshe Davis. LC 77-70747. (America & the Holy Land Ser.). 1977. Repr. of 1890 ed. lib. bdg. 17.00x (ISBN 0-405-10293-3). Ayer Co Pubs.
Talmud, 64 vols. (Hebrew & Eng.). Complete Set. 995.00 (ISBN 0-910218-50-1). Bennet Pub.
Talmud: An Analytical Guide. Isaac Unterman. LC 73-148291. 351p. 1985. text ed. 17.95x (ISBN 0-8197-0189-0); pap. text ed. 10.95x (ISBN 0-8197-0005-3). Bloch.
Talmud & Apocrypha. Herford. Date not set. 11.95. Ktav.
Talmud As Law Or Literature: An Analysis of David W. Halivni's Mekorot Umasorot. Irwin H. Haut. x, 83p. pap. 6.95 (ISBN 0-87203-107-1). Hermon.
Talmud: Law & Commentary. Harry Gersh. 64p. (YA) (gr. 9 up). 1986. pap. text ed. 2.95x (ISBN 0-87441-434-2); By Derek J. Penslar. tchr's. ed. 6.95 (ISBN 0-87441-435-0). Behrman.
Talmud of Babylonia: An American Translation VII Tractate Besah. Tr. by Alan J. Avery-Peck from Hebrew-Aramaic. LC 86-20237. (Brown Judaic Studies). 358p. 1986. pap. 39.95 (ISBN 1-55540-054-X, 14-01-17). Scholars Pr GA.
Talmud of Babylonia: An American Translation XXXV Meilah & Tamid. Tr. by Peter J. Haas from Hebrew-Aramaic. LC 86-26036. (Brown Judaic Studies). 180p. 1986. 29.95 (ISBN 1-55540-086-8, 14-01-09). Scholars Pr GA.
Talmud of Babylonia, an American Translation xxvi: Tractate Horayot. Martin S. Jaffee. LC 87-4783. (Brown Judaic Studies). 233p. 1987. 27.95 (ISBN 1-55540-119-8, 14-00-90). Scholars Pr Ga.
Talmud of Babylonia: An American Translation XXIII: Tractate Sanhedrin-Chap. 9-11. Tr. by Jacob Neusner. (Brown Judiac Studies). 1985. 29.95 (ISBN 0-89130-803-2, 14-0087); pap. 23.00 (ISBN 0-89130-804-0). Scholars Pr GA.
Talmud of the Land of Israel: A Preliminary Translation & Explanation- Vol. 25, Gittin. Ed. by Jacob Neusner. (Chicago Studies in the History of Judaism). 270p. 1985. 33.00x (ISBN 0-226-57684-1). U of Chicago Pr.
Talmud of the Land of Israel: A Preliminary Translation & Explanation- Vol. 24, Nazir. Ed. by Jacob Neusner. (Chicago Studies in the History of Judaism). 268p. 1985. 33.00x (ISBN 0-226-57683-3). U of Chicago Pr.
Talmud of the Land of Israel: A Preliminary Translation & Explanation- Vol. 23, Nedarim. Ed. & tr. by Jacob Neusner. (Chicago Studies in the History of Judaism). 248p. 1985. 31.00x (ISBN 0-226-57682-5). U of Chicago Pr.
Talmud of the Land of Israel: A Preliminary Translation & Explanation - Maaserot, Vol. 7. Ed. by Jacob Neusner & Martin S. Jaffee. LC 87-5852. (Chicago Studies in the History of Judaism). xii, 284p. 1987. 25.00x (ISBN 0-226-57664-7). U of Chicago Pr.
Talmud of the Land of Israel: A Preliminary Translation & Explanation: Hagigah & Moed Qatan, Vol. 20. Ed. & tr. by Jacob Neusner. LC 85-29037. (Chicago Studies in the History of Judaism). 242p. 1986. 35.00x (ISBN 0-226-57679-5). U of Chicago Pr.
Talmud of the Land of Israel: A Preliminary Translation & Explanation, Rosh Hashanah, Vol. 16. Jacob Neusner. Tr. by Edward A. Goldman. (Chicago Studies in the History of Judaism Ser.). 136p. 1988. 26.00x (ISBN 0-226-57675-2). U of Chicago Pr.
Talmud of the Land of Israel: A Preliminary Translation & Explanation, Sukkah, Vol. 17. Jacob Neusner. (Chicago Studies in the History of Judaism Ser.). 160p. 1988. 26.00x (ISBN 0-226-57676-0). U of Chicago Pr.
Talmud of the Land of Israel: A Preliminary Translation & Explanation, Vol. 22: Ketubot. Ed. by Jacob Neusner. (Chicago Studies in the History of Judaism). 384p. 1985. lib. bdg. 49.00x (ISBN 0-226-57681-7). U of Chicago Pr.
Talmud of the Land of Israel: A Preliminary Translation & Explanation-Vol. 26, Qiddushin. Ed. & tr. by Jacob Neusner. 1984. 25.00x (ISBN 0-226-57686-8). U of Chicago Pr.
Talmud of the Land of Israel: A Preliminary Translation & Explanation-Vol. 27, Sotah. Ed. & tr. by Jacob Neusner. 1984. 25.00x (ISBN 0-226-57687-6). U of Chicago Pr.
Talmud of the Land of Israel: A Preliminary Translation & Explanation-Vol. 28, Baba Qamma. Ed. & tr. by Jacob Neusner. 1984. 25.00x (ISBN 0-226-57688-4). U of Chicago Pr.
Talmud of the Land of Israel: A Preliminary Translation & Explanation-Vol. 29, Baba Mesia. Ed. & tr. by Jacob Neusner. 1984. 25.00x (ISBN 0-226-57689-2). U of Chicago Pr.
Talmud of the Land of Israel: A Preliminary Translation & Explanation-Vol. 30, Baba Batra. Ed. & tr. by Jacob Neusner. 1984. 25.00x (ISBN 0-226-57690-6). U of Chicago Pr.
Talmud of the Land of Israel: A Preliminary Translation & Explanation-Vol. 31, Sanhedrin & Makkot. Ed. & tr. by Jacob Neusner. 1984. 45.00x (ISBN 0-226-57691-4). U of Chicago Pr.
Talmud of the Land of Israel: A Preliminary Translation & Explanation-Vol. 32, Shebuot. Ed. & tr. by Jacob Neusner. 1983. 31.00x (ISBN 0-226-57692-2). U of Chicago Pr.
Talmud of the Land of Israel: A Preliminary Translation & Explanation-Vol. 33, Abodah Zarah. Ed. & tr. by Jacob Neusner. 1982. 27.00x (ISBN 0-226-57693-0). U of Chicago Pr.
Talmud of the Land of Israel: A Preliminary Translation & Explanation-Vol. 34, Horayot & Niddah. Ed. & tr. by Jacob Neusner. 1982. 29.00x (ISBN 0-226-57694-9). U of Chicago Pr.
Talmud of the Land of Israel: A Preliminary Translation & Explanation-Vol. 35, Introduction & Taxonomy. Ed. & tr. by Jacob Neusner. 1984. 19.00x (ISBN 0-226-57695-7). U of Chicago Pr.
Talmud of the Land of Israel: A Preliminary Translation & Explanation: Vol. 19, Megillah. Ed. by Jacob Neusner. LC 86-25284. (Chicago Studies in the History of Judaism). x, 188p. 1987. text ed. 29.00x (ISBN 0-226-57678-7). U of Chicago Pr.
Talmud of the Land of Israel: A Preliminary Translation & Explanation: Vol. 18, Besah & Taanit. Ed. by Jacob Neusner. (Chicago Studies in the History of Judaism). x, 314p. 1987. text ed. 37.50x (ISBN 0-226-57677-9). U of Chicago Pr.
Talmud of the Land of Israel: A Preliminary Translation & Explanation-Yebamot, Vol. 21. Ed. & tr. by Jacob Neusner. LC 86-11406. (Chicago Studies in the History of Judaism). x, 514p. 1987. text ed. 58.00x (ISBN 0-226-57680-9). U of Chicago Pr.
Talmud of the Land of Isreal: A Preliminary Translation & Explanation, 2 Vols. Ed. by Jacob Neusner. Tr. by Alan J. Avery-Peck & Martin S. Jaffee. (Chicago Studies in the History Judaism). xii, 570p. 1987. Vol. 6: Terumot, 504p. 75.00x (ISBN 0-226-57663-9); Vol. 7: Maaserot, 272p. 21.00 (ISBN 0-317-60146-6). U of Chicago Pr.
Talmud Today. Ed. by Alexander Feinsilver. 320p. 1980. 14.95 (ISBN 0-312-78479-1). St Martin.
Talmud Torah see Mitzvah of the Month.
Talmud Unmasked. Prainatis. 1979. lib. bdg. 59.95 (ISBN 0-8490-3010-2). Gordon Pr.
Talmudic & Rabbinical Chronology. Edgar Frank. 1978. 6.95 (ISBN 0-87306-050-4). Feldheim.
Talmudic Anthology. Ed. by Louis I. Newman. LC 45-9682. 1978. pap. text ed. 14.95x (ISBN 0-87441-303-6). Behrman.
Talmudic Argument: A Study in Talmudic Reasoning & Methodology. Louis Jacobs. LC 84-4351. 240p. 1984. 47.50 (ISBN 0-521-26370-0). Cambridge U Pr.
Talmudic Law & the Modern State. Moshe Silberg. 1973. 9.00x (ISBN 0-8381-3112-3). United Syn Bk.
Talmudische Archaeologie, 3 vols. Samuel Krauss. Ed. by Moses Finley. LC 79-4988. (Ancient Economic History). (Illus., Ger.). 1980. Repr. of 1912 ed. Set. lib. bdg. 172.00x (ISBN 0-405-12373-6); lib. bdg. 57.50x ea. Vol. 1 (ISBN 0-405-12374-4). Vol. 2 (ISBN 0-405-12375-2). Vol. 3 (ISBN 0-405-12376-0). Ayer Co Pubs.
Talons: North American Birds of Prey. Millie Miller & Cyndi Nelson. (Pocket Nature Guide Ser.). 1988. pap. 4.95. Johnson Bks.
Talons of Time. Paul Twitchell. LC 74-21136. 1974. pap. 6.95 (ISBN 0-914766-23-6). Illum Way Pub.
Taltos. Steven Burst. 1988. pap. 2.95 (ISBN 0-317-67113-8). Ace Bks.
Taluqdari Settlement in Oudh. Raj K. Sarvadhikari. 1986. Repr. of 1882 ed. 18.00x (ISBN 0-8364-1582-5, Pub. by Usha). South Asia Bks.
Tam, Gde Vyros Kiev. D. J. Telegin. 94p. (Rus.). 1982. 25.00x (ISBN 0-317-40783-X, Pub. by Collets (UK)). State Mutual Bk.
Tamagno, Il Piu Grande Fenomeno Canoro Dell'ottocento: Tamagno, the Greatest Singing Phenomenon of the Nineteenth Century. Mario Corsi. Ed. by Andrew Farkas. LC 76-29931. (Opera Biographies). (Illus., Ital.). 1977. Repr. of 1937 ed. lib. bdg. 24.50x (ISBN 0-405-09673-9). Ayer Co Pubs.
Taman Budiman: Memoirs of an Unorthodox Civil Servant. Mubin Sheppard. 278p. (Orig.). 1979. pap. text ed. 17.50x. Heinemann Ed.
Tamar & the Desert Adventure. Joann Knox. (Junior Adventure Ser.). 64p. (gr. 4-8). 1973. pap. 1.00 (ISBN 0-88243-770-4, 02-0770). Gospel Pub.
Tamar & the Tiger. Susan Jeschke. LC 79-22591. (Illus.). 40p. (gr. k-2). 1980. 8.95 (ISBN 0-03-052176-9). H Holt & Co.
Tamara. Eva Kilpi. Tr. by Philip Binham. 1978. pap. 8.95 (ISBN 0-440-08494-6, Sey Lawr). Delacorte.
Tamara de Lempicka. E. Ishioka. (Illus.). 230p. 1980. pap. 75.00 (ISBN 4-8-9194049-2, Parco Pub Japan). Bks Nippan.
Tamarack Review: Nos. 1-41 & General Index, Toronto, 1956-1966. 550.00 (ISBN 0-8115-3866-4). Kraus Repr.
Tamarack Tree. Patricia Clapp. LC 86-108. 224p. (YA) (gr. 7 up). 1986. 10.25 (ISBN 0-688-02852-7). Lothrop.
Tamarack Tree. Patricia Clapp. 256p. (Orig.). (gr. 5-9). Date not set. pap. 3.95 (ISBN 0-14-032406-2, Puffin Bks). Penguin.
Tamara's Ecstasy. Sylvie F. Sommerfield. 1982. pap. 3.50 (ISBN 0-89083-998-0). Zebra.
Tamarind Book of Lithography: Art & Techniques. Garo Z. Antreasian & Clinton Adams. LC 76-121328. 29.95 (ISBN 0-8109-9017-2). Abrams.
Tamarind Tree. Romen Basu. 227p. 1976. 7.95 (Pub. by Writers Wksp India). R Basu.
Tamarindo Puppy & Other Poems. Charlotte Pomerantz. LC 79-16584. (Illus.). 32p. (gr. k-3). 1980. PLB 11.88 (ISBN 0-688-84251-8). Greenwillow.
Tamar's Revenge, Eng. & Span. Tirso De Molina. Ed. by John Lyon. (Hispanic Classics--The Golden Age Ser.). 1988. text ed. 49.95 (ISBN 0-85668-323-X, Pub. by Aris & Phillips UK); pap. text ed. 16.50 (ISBN 0-85668-324-8, Pub. by Aris & Phillips UK). Humanities.
Tamar's Son & Other Christmas Sonnets. Esther M. Leiper. 28p. 1987. pap. 3.95 (ISBN 0-9617284-2-6). Sand & Silk.
Tamar's Sukkah. Ellie Gellman. (Illus.). 32p. (ps-2). 1988. pap. 4.95 (ISBN 0-930494-79-2). Kar Ben.
Tamasi Monografiaja. Laszlo L. Konnyu. LC 78-74527. (Monograph of the Hungarian Town of Tamasi). (Illus.). 1979. pap. 5.00 (ISBN 0-685-67251-4). Hungarian Rev.
Tamate-A King: James Chalmers in New Guinea, 1877-1901. Diane Langmore. (Illus.). xvi, 169p. 1974. 19.00x (ISBN 0-522-84079-5, Pub. by Melbourne U Pr). Intl Spec Bk.
Tamayo. Jose Corredor-Matheos. LC 87-45384. (Illus.). 128p. 1987. 19.95 (ISBN 0-8478-0855-6). Rizzoli Intl.
Tamazight of the Ayt Ndhir. Thomas G. Penchoen. LC 73-91702. (Afroasiatic Dialects Ser.: Vol. 1). (Illus.). 122p. 1973. pap. 16.00x (ISBN 0-89003-000-6). Undena Pubns.
Tamazight Verb Stucture: A Generative Approach. Ernest T. Abdel-Massih. LC 72-633892. (African Ser: Vol. 2). (Orig.). 1968. pap. text ed. 15.00 (ISBN 0-87750-160-2). Res Ctr Lang Semiotic.
Tamazine. Edwin Harrington. LC 82-80349. (Illus.). 160p. 1982. pap. 10.95 (ISBN 0-941066-02-9). Hillside Pr.
Tamba Pottery. Daniel Rhodes. 178p. 1970. 140.00x (Pub. by Han-Shan Tang Ltd). State Mutual Bk.
Tamba Pottery: The Timeless Art of a Japanese Village. Daniel Rhodes. LC 74-113180. (Illus.). 180p. 1982. pap. 14.95 (ISBN 0-87011-520-0). Kodansha.
Tambia Bourri. Evelyn F. Updite. 224p. 1987. text ed. 16.00 (ISBN 0-682-40306-7). Exposition-Phoenix.
Tambourines! Tambourines to Glory! Prayers & Poems. Nancy Larrick. LC 81-23158. (Illus.). 122p. (gr. 3-7). 1982. 8.95 (ISBN 0-664-32689-7). Westminster John Knox.

Tamburlaine. Christopher Marlowe. Ed. by J. W. Harper. (New Mermaid Ser.). 1976. pap. 4.95x (ISBN 0-393-90021-5). Norton.

Tamburlaine & Edward II. George L. Geckle. (Text & Performance Ser.). 1988. pap. text ed. 8.50 (ISBN 0-391-03573-8). Humanities.

Tamburlaine, Part One: And Its Audience. Frank B. Fieler. LC 62-62580. (University of Florida Humanities Monographs: No. 8). 1961. pap. 6.00x (ISBN 0-8130-0077-7). U Presses Fla.

Tamburlaine the Great, 2 pts. Christopher Marlowe. Ed. by V. M. Ellis-Fermor. LC 66-23027. (Works & Life of Christopher Marlowe Ser.: Vol. 2). 321p. 1966. Repr. of 1930 ed. 25.00x (ISBN 0-87752-192-1). Gordian.

Tamburlaine the Great. Christopher Marlowe. Ed. by J. S. Cunningham. LC 81-47596. (Revels Plays Ser.). 354p. 1981. text ed. 25.00x (ISBN 0-8018-2669-1). Johns Hopkins.

Tamburlaine the Great, Parts I & II. Christopher Marlowe. Ed. by John D. Jump. LC 67-10666. (Regents Renaissance Drama Ser). xxvi, 205p. 1967. pap. 6.50x (ISBN 0-8032-5271-4, BB 222, Bison). U of Nebr Pr.

Tame a Proud Heart. Jeneth Murrey. (Harlequin Romances Ser.). 192p. 1983. pap. 1.75 (ISBN 0-373-02559-9). Harlequin Bks.

Tame Algebras & Integral Quadratic Forms. C. M. Ringel. (Lecture Notes in Mathematics Ser.: Vol. 1099). xiii, 376p. 1984. pap. 26.00 (ISBN 0-387-13905-2). Springer-Verlag.

Tame My Wild Heart. Sylvie F. Sommerfield. 1984. pap. 3.95 (ISBN 0-317-02887-1). Zebra.

Tame Representations of Local Weil Groups & of Chain Groups of Local Principle Orders. A. Frohlich. (Sitzungsberichte der Heidelberger Akademie der Wissenschaften, Jahrgang 1986: 3. Adhandlung). 100p. 1987. pap. 33.30 (ISBN 0-387-17340-4). Springer-Verlag.

Tame the Restless Heart. Patricia Matthews. LC 85-47765. 352p. (Orig.). 1986. pap. 6.95 (ISBN 0-553-34220-7). Bantam.

Tame the Wild Heart. Ellen T. Marsh. 448p. 1988. pap. 3.95 (ISBN 0-380-75219-0). Avon.

Tame the Wild Heart. Serita Stevens. (Tapestry Romance Ser.: No. 25). 320p. 1983. pap. 2.95 (ISBN 0-671-49398-1). PB.

Tame the Wild Stallion. Jeanne Williams. LC 84-16257. (Chaparral Bks.). (Illus.). 181p. (gr. 4 up). 1985. 14.95 (ISBN 0-87565-002-3); pap. 8.95 (ISBN 0-87565-009-0). Tex Christian.

Tame the Wild Wind. Katherine Vickery. 1988. pap. 3.95 (ISBN 0-451-40068-2, Onyx). NAL.

Tame Wilderness. Dennis Fritzinger. 1979. wrappers 5.00 (ISBN 0-913537-11-X). Arif.

Tamer. Nicolas Fokker. LC 78-2056. 1979. 10.00i (ISBN 0-06-011299-9, HarpT). Har-Row.

Tamerlane. Edward D. Sokol. 1977. 12.50x (ISBN 0-87291-093-8). Coronado Pr.

Tamerlane. Dennis Wepman. (World Leaders--Past & Present Ser.). (Illus.). 112p. 1987. lib. bdg. 16.95 (ISBN 0-87754-442-5). Chelsea Hse.

Tamerlane: The Earth Shaker. Harold Lamb. 340p. 1985. Repr. of 1928 ed. lib. bdg. 40.00 (ISBN 0-8414-6920-2). Folcroft.

Tamerlano. George F. Handel & Howard M. Brown. LC 76-21083. (Italian Opera 1640-1770 Ser.). 1978. lib. bdg. 77.00 (ISBN 0-8240-2626-8). Garland Pub.

Tami. Cyclone Millsap. (Illus.). 160p. 1987. 9.95 (ISBN 0-8059-3078-7). Dorrance.

Tamil. R. E. Asher. (Descriptive Grammars Ser.). 280p. 1982. 50.00 (ISBN 0-7099-0563-7, Pub. by Croom Helm Ltd). Routledge Chapman & Hall.

Tamil-English Dictionary. Miron Winslow. Ed. by Kalus L. Janert. xvi, 976p. 1978. Repr. of 1862 ed. text ed. 115.00x (ISBN 3-515-02703-3, Pub. by Franz Steiner). Coronet Bks.

Tamil-English, English-Tamil Comprehensive Dictionary. 3rd, rev. ed. M. Winslow. (Eng. & Tamil.). Set. 70.00; Tamil-English. 35.00; English-Tamil, 3rd, rev. ed. 35.00. Heinman.

Tamil Prose Reader. G. U. Pope. 132p. 1986. Repr. of 1906 ed. 12.50X (ISBN 0-8364-1679-1, Pub. by Abhinav India). South Asia Bks.

Tamil Revivalism in the 1930's. Eugene Irschick. 372p. 1986. 32.00 (ISBN 0-8364-1918-9, Pub. by Manohar India). South Asia Bks.

Tamil Short Stories. Ed. by Ka Naa Subramanyam. 1981. text ed. 15.00x (ISBN 0-7069-1241-1, Pub by Vikas India). Advent NY.

Tamil Short Stories. Ed. by Kanaa Subramanyam. 202p. 1980. 9.50. Asia Bk Corp.

Tamil Studies. Srinivasa Aiyangar. (Illus.). 428p. 1986. Repr. of 1914 ed. 22.00X (ISBN 0-8364-1714-3, Pub. by Abhinav India). South Asia Bks.

Tamil Temple Myths: Sacrifice & Divine Marriage in the South Indian Saiva Tradition. David D. Shulman. LC 79-17051. 1980. 50.00x (ISBN 0-691-06415-6). Princeton U Pr.

Tamil Veda of Tiruvalluvar see Sacred Kural.

Tamilee Webb's Original Rubber Band Workout. Tamilee Webb. LC 85-40987. (Illus.). 144p. 1986. pap. 8.95 (ISBN 0-89480-056-6). Workman Pub.

Taming. Aleen Malcolm. 480p. 1979. pap. 3.50 (ISBN 0-440-18510-6). Dell.

Taming a Sea-Horse. Robert B. Parker. 250p. 1987. pap. 4.50 (ISBN 0-440-18841-5, Sey Lawr). Dell.

Taming a Sea-Horse. Robert B. Parker. (Large Print Bks). 362p. 1987. lib. bdg. 18.95x (ISBN 0-8161-4166-5, Large Print Bks). G K Hall.

Taming a Tartar see Modern Mephistopheles.

Taming Ancient Rivers of Greece. Jack Moore. 337p. 1981. 60.00x (ISBN 0-9507476-0-2, Pub. by Faraway Bks). State Mutual Bk.

Taming & Training African Grey Parrots. Risa Teitler. (Illus.). 1979. 9.95 (ISBN 0-87666-994-1, KW-025). TFH Pubns.

Taming & Training Conures. Risa Teitler. (Illus.). 96p. 1981. 9.95 (ISBN 0-87666-842-2, KW-139). TFH Pubns.

Taming & Training Parrots. Edward J. Mulawka. (Illus.). 1981. 19.95 (ISBN 0-87666-989-5, H-1019). TFH Pubns.

Taming Butterflies. Dawn Aiken. Ed. by Dianne Draze & Dixie Ryder. (Illus.). 96p. (gr. 4-7). tchrs. ed. 8.50 (ISBN 0-931724-25-2). Dandy Lion.

Taming Monsters, Slaying Dragons: The Revolutionary Family Approach to Overcoming Childhood Fears & Anxieties. Joel Feiner & Graham Yost. 256p. 1988. 17.95 (ISBN 0-87795-939-0, Arbor Hse). Morrow.

Taming MS-DOS. Thom Hogan. 1986. pap. 19.95 (ISBN 0-934375-24-0); bk. & disk 34.95 (ISBN 0-934375-59-3). M & T Pub Inc.

Taming MS-DOS. 2nd ed. Thom Hogan. 288p. 1988. pap. 19.95 (ISBN 0-934375-87-9); Book & disk. 34.95 (ISBN 0-934375-92-5). M & T Pub Inc.

Taming New Guinea. Charles A. Monckton. LC 75-35143. (Illus.). Repr. of 1921 ed. 28.50 (ISBN 0-404-14159-5). AMS Pr.

Taming of a Dream. Agustin Lopez. LC 86-913600. 256p. 1987. text ed. 17.50 (ISBN 0-682-40320-2). Exposition-Phoenix.

Taming of a Shrew. LC 79-133743. (Tudor Facsimile Texts. Old English Plays: No. 69). Repr. of 1912 ed. 49.50 (ISBN 0-404-53369-8). AMS Pr.

Taming of Annabelle. Marion Chesney. 176p. 1987. pap. 2.50 (ISBN 0-449-21457-5, Crest). Fawcett.

Taming of Evolution: The Persistence of Non-Evolutionary Views in the Study of Humans. Davydd J. Greenwood. LC 84-45147. (Illus.). 232p. 1984. 26.50x (ISBN 0-8014-1743-0). Cornell U Pr.

Taming of Fidel Castro. Maurice Halperin. LC 80-18581. 1981. 30.00x (ISBN 0-520-04184-4). U of Cal Pr.

Taming of Government: Micro-Macro Disciplines on Whithall & Town Hall. Lord Robbins et al. (Institute of Economic Affairs Readings Ser.: No. 21). (Orig.). 1979. technical 10.95 (ISBN 0-255-36125-4). Transatl Arts.

Taming of Romanticism: European Literature & the Age of the Biedermeier. Virgil Nemoianu. (Harvard Studies in Comparative Literature: No. 37). 336p. 1984. text ed. 27.00x (ISBN 0-674-86802-1). Harvard U Pr.

Taming of the C. A. N. D. Y. Monster. rev. ed. Vicki Lansky. 156p. 1988. lib. bdg. 7.95 (ISBN 0-916773-08-6); pap. 7.95 (ISBN 0-916773-07-8). Book Peddlers.

Taming of the C.A.N.D.Y. Monster. Vicki Lansky. 160p. 1985. pap. 2.95 (ISBN 0-553-24977-0). Bantam.

Taming of the Frontier. facs. ed. Ed. by Duncan Aikman. LC 67-26711. (Essay Index Reprint Ser). 1925. 20.00 (ISBN 0-8369-0141-X). Ayer Co Pubs.

Taming of the Nations: A Study of the Cultural Bases of International Policy. F. S. Northrop. LC 86-28587. xvi, 362p. 1987. 30.00 (ISBN 0-918024-45-5); pap. 16.00 (ISBN 0-918024-46-3). Ox Bow.

Taming of the Screw: Several Million Homeowner's Problems. Dave Barry. (Illus.). 96p. (Orig.). 1983. pap. 5.95 (ISBN 0-87857-484-0). Rodale Pr Inc.

Taming of the Shrew. Bay Area Community College Staff. 32p. 1982. 4.50 (ISBN 0-8403-2707-2). Kendall-Hunt.

Taming of the Shrew. Berger. 1986. lib. bdg. 54.00 (ISBN 0-8240-8892-1). Garland Pub.

Taming of the Shrew. Adapted by Charlotte Brown. (Illus.). 32p. (gr. 5 up). 1987. pap. 1.50 (ISBN 0-88680-276-8). I E Clark.

Taming of the Shrew. H. B. Charlton. 1932. lib. bdg. 15.00 (ISBN 0-8414-3564-2). Folcroft.

Taming of the Shrew. Ed. by A. L. Rowse. LC 85-681. (Contemporary Shakespeare Ser.: Vol. III). 130p. (Orig.). 1985. pap. text ed. 3.45 (ISBN 0-8191-3921-1). U Pr of Amer.

Taming of the Shrew. William Shakespeare. (Airmont Shakespeare Ser.). (gr. 10 up). pap. 1.75 (ISBN 0-8049-1010-3, S10). Airmont.

Taming of the Shrew. William Shakespeare. Ed. by Robert Heilman. pap. 2.50 (ISBN 0-451-52126-9, Sig Classics). NAL.

Taming of the Shrew. William Shakespeare. Ed. by G. R. Hibbard. 1981. pap. 3.75 (ISBN 0-14-070710-7). Penguin.

Taming of the Shrew. William Shakespeare. Ed. by Richard Hosley. (Shakespeare Ser.). 1964. pap. 2.95 (ISBN 0-14-071425-1, Pelican). Penguin.

Taming of the Shrew. William Shakespeare. Ed. by Louis B. Wright & Virginia A. LaMar. (Folger Library). (Illus.). 272p. (gr. 11 up). 1963. pap. text ed. 3.75. WSP.

Taming of the Shrew. William Shakespeare. Ed. by Brian Morris. LC 81-16785. 1982. 37.00x (ISBN 0-416-47580-9, NO. 3590); pap. 7.95 (ISBN 0-416-17800-6, NO. 3589). Routledge Chapman & Hall.

Taming of the Shrew. William Shakespeare. (Classics Ser.). 160p. 1988. pap. 2.50 (ISBN 0-553-21306-7, Bantam Classics). Bantam.

Taming of the Shrew. William Shakespeare. Ed. by Ann Thompson. (New Cambridge Shakespeare Ser.). (Illus.). 204p. 1984. 29.95 (ISBN 0-521-22195-1); pap. 6.95 (ISBN 0-521-29388-X). Cambridge U Pr.

Taming of the Shrew. William Shakespeare & H. J. Oliver. (Oxford Shakespeare Ser.). 254p. 1982. 26.00x (ISBN 0-19-812907-6); pap. 6.95x (ISBN 0-19-281440-0). Oxford U Pr.

Taming of the Shrew. (Book Notes Ser.). 1985. pap. 2.50 (ISBN 0-8120-3544-5). Barron.

Taming of the Shrew for Young People. William Shakespeare. Ed. by Diane Davidson. LC 86-5934. (Shakespeare for Young People Ser.: Vol. 3). 64p. (YA) (gr. 5-8). 1986. pap. 2.95 (ISBN 0-934048-20-7). Swan Books.

Taming of the Shrew Notes. L. L. Hillegass. (Orig.). 1971. pap. 3.25 (ISBN 0-8220-0081-4). Cliffs.

Taming of the Text: Explorations in Language, Literature & Culture. Ed. by Willie Van Peer. 328p. 1988. lib. bdg. 59.50 (ISBN 0-415-01309-7). Routledge Chapman & Hall.

Taming of the Troops: Social Control in the United States Army. Lawrence B. Radine. LC 76-5262. (Contributions in Sociology Ser.: No. 22). (Orig.). 1976. lib. bdg. 35.00 (ISBN 0-8371-8911-X, RTT/). Greenwood.

Taming of the West: Laramie. (Orig.). 1987. pap. 3.50 (ISBN 0-553-26463-X). Bantam.

Taming Philippine Headhunters: A Study of Government & of Cultural Change in Northern Luzon. Felix M. Keesing & Marie Keesing. LC 77-86953. (Ethnology-South East Asia Ser.). (Illus.). 288p. 1984. Repr. of 1934 ed. 31.50 (ISBN 0-404-16747-0). AMS Pr.

Taming Tension. Phillip W. Keller. 224p. pap. 5.95 (ISBN 0-8010-5407-9). Baker Bk.

Taming Tension Through Total Health. Leo R. Van Dolson. Ed. by Richard W. Coffen. LC 83-23028. (Illus.). 96p. (Orig.). 1984. pap. 6.50 (ISBN 0-8280-0224-X). Review & Herald.

Taming the Anthill (Middle School Music: An Uncommon Handbook for Common Problems) Jean Spanko. Ed. by Michael D. Bennett. (Illus.). 76p. (Orig.). 1985. pap. text ed. 9.50 (ISBN 0-934017-07-7). Memphis Musicraft.

Taming the Atom: Facing the Future with Nuclear Power. I. Blair. 1983. 53.00x (ISBN 0-85274-414-5, Pub. by A Hilger UK); pap. 21.00x (ISBN 0-85274-483-8, Pub. by A Hilger UK). Taylor & Francis.

Taming the Buck. William Pettus Buck. 1979. 1.98 (ISBN 0-934530-02-5). Buck Pub.

Taming the Criminal: Adventures in Penology. John L. Gillin. LC 69-14927. (Criminology, Law Enforcement, & Social Problems Ser.: No. 71). (Illus.). 1969. Repr. of 1931 ed. 15.00x (ISBN 0-87585-071-5). Patterson Smith.

Taming the Federal Budget: Fiscal Year 1986. Ed. by Stuart M. Butler. 51p. 1985. pap. 5.00 (ISBN 0-317-47103-1). Heritage Found.

Taming the Flood: Rivers & Wetlands in Britain. Jeremy Purseglove. (Illus.). 288p. 1988. 35.00 (ISBN 0-19-215891-0). Oxford U Pr.

Taming the Forest King. Claudia J. Edwards. 224p. 1986. pap. 3.50 (ISBN 0-445-20308-0, Pub. by Popular Lib). Warner Bks.

Taming the Gentle Giant: A Guide to Hot Air Ballooning. Amogene B. Norwood. LC 86-80816. (Illus.). 120p. (Orig.). 1986. pap. 15.95 (ISBN 0-9616608-0-5). Land O' Sky Aero.

Taming the Megalopolis: A Design for Urban Growth. Lauchlin Currie. 1976. pap. 15.25 (ISBN 0-08-021397-9). Pergamon.

Taming the Nueces Strip: The Story of McNelly's Rangers. George Durham. (Illus.). 198p. 1962. pap. 7.95 (ISBN 0-292-78048-6). U of Tex Pr.

Taming the Paper Tiger: Organizing the Paper in Your Life. Barbara Hemphill. (Illus.). 192p. 1988. pap. 9.95 (ISBN 0-396-09198-9, Gamut Bk). Dodd.

Taming the Prince: The Necessary Contradictions of Modern Executive Power. Harvey Mansfield, Jr. 310p. 1989. 24.95 (ISBN 0-02-919980-8). Free Pr.

Taming the Sasquatch & Other Big Foot Tales. Lee Nelson. 90p. 1983. pap. 5.95 (ISBN 0-936860-13-8). Liberty Pr.

Taming the Savage River. Margaret M. Streaker. 1968. 5.25 (ISBN 0-87012-032-8). McClain.

Taming the Star Runner. S. E. Hinton. Date not set. price not set. Delacorte.

Taming the Tiger. Richard Jackman & Kurt Klappholz. (Hobart Papers Special Ser.: No. 63). 1976. pap. 4.25 technical (ISBN 0-255-36073-8). Transatl Arts.

Taming the Tiger: Software Engineering & Software Economics. L. S. Levy. (Books on Professional Computing). (Illus.). viii, 248p. 1986. pap. 25.00 (ISBN 0-387-96468-1). Springer-Verlag.

Taming the Tiger: The Struggle to Control Technology. Witold Rybczynski. (Nonfiction Ser.). 256p. 1985. pap. 6.95 (ISBN 0-14-007564-X). Penguin.

Taming the Tongue: Why Christians Should Care about What They Say. Mark Kinzer. (Living as a Christian Ser.). 1982. pap. 3.95 (ISBN 0-89283-165-0). Servant.

Taming Your Gremlin: A Guide to Enjoying Yourself. Richard D. Carson. LC 86-45310. (Illus.). 128p. 1986. pap. 7.95 (ISBN 0-06-096102-3, PL/6102, PL). Har-Row.

Taming Your Junk Jungle: Trash to Cash! Sell Your Stash! Make Your Garage Sale a Successful Bash! Lois B. Hart et al. LC 86-80039. 104p. (Orig.). 1986. pap. 7.95 (ISBN 0-911777-09-1). Leadership Dyn.

Taming Your Mind. Ken Keyes, Jr. LC 75-4297. 246p. 1975. 7.95 (ISBN 0-9600688-7-2). Love Line Bks.

Taming Your Turbulent Past. Gayle Rosellini. 1987. pap. 8.95 (ISBN 0-932194-50-8). Health Comm.

Tamirie-Seven Geese. (Sharazad Stories Ser.). (Illus., Arabic.). (gr. 4-6). pap. 3.50x (ISBN 0-86685-234-4). Intl Bk Ctr.

Tammany Hall. Morris R. Werner. Repr. of 1932 ed. lib. bdg. 35.00x (ISBN 0-8371-0746-6, WETH). Greenwood.

Tammany Hall & the New Immigrants: The Progressive Years. Thomas M. Henderson. LC 76-6347. (Irish Americans Ser). (Illus.). 1976. 24.00 (ISBN 0-405-09341-1). Ayer Co Pubs.

Tammuz & Ishtar. Stephen H. Langdon. LC 78-72750. (Ancient Mesopotamian Texts & Studies). Repr. of 1914 ed. 34.50 (ISBN 0-404-18193-7). AMS Pr.

Tammy & Dolls You Love to Dress. John Axe. (Illus.). 81p. pap. 5.95 (ISBN 0-87588-155-6, 2186). Hobby Hse.

Tammy & the Gigantic Fish. Catherine D. Gray & James Gray. LC 82-47732. (Illus.). 32p. (ps-2). 1983. PLB 11.89g (ISBN 0-06-022139-9). HarpJ.

Tammy's Smile. Sharon Otis & Lois Walker. (Illus., Orig.). (ps-7). 1985. wkbk. 6.00 (ISBN 0-9617737-0-7). Total Lrn.

Tamotzu in Haiku. Harriet Kimbro. LC 77-10844. (Illus.). 1977. pap. 4.95 (ISBN 0-913270-78-4). Sunstone Pr.

Tampa: A Pictorial History. Hampton Dunn. Ed. by Nancy Morgan. LC 85-4450. (Portrait of American Cities Ser.). (Illus.). 224p. 1985. 20.95 (ISBN 0-89865-408-4); pap. 14.95 (ISBN 0-89865-409-2). Donning Co.

Tampa Bay Buccanneers. James R. Rothaus. (NFL Today Ser.). 48p. (gr. 4 up). 1986. PLB 10.45 (ISBN 0-88682-050-2). Creative Ed.

Tampa Bay Career Guide. George Fencl. Ed. by Janie Pritchett. 112p. (Orig.). 1987. 16.95 (ISBN 0-942827-01-5). Edge Pub.

Tampa: The Treasure City. new ed. Gary R. Mormino & Anthony P. Pizzo. Ed. by Sharon Mason. LC 83-70417. (American Portrait Ser.). (Illus.). 272p. 1983. 29.95 (ISBN 0-932986-38-2). Continent Herit.

Tampa: Yesterday, Today & Tomorrow. Michael Bane & Ellen Moore. (Illus.). 180p. (Orig.). 1982. 19.95 (ISBN 0-9609530-0-0); pap. 12.95 (ISBN 0-9609530-2-7). King Co.

Tamper Resistant Packaging: What's Ahead? Business Communications Staff. 194p. 1984. pap. 1500.00 (ISBN 0-89336-394-4, GB-067). BCC.

Tampons & Other Catamenial Receptors. M. H. Gutcho. LC 79-84431. (Chemical Technology Review Ser.: No. 129). (Illus.). 294p. 1979. 39.00 (ISBN 0-8155-0753-4). Noyes.

Tamsen. David Galloway. 448p. 14.95 (ISBN 0-15-187992-3). HarBraceJ.

Tamsen Donner: A Woman's Journey. Ruth Whitman. LC 77-90508. 75p. 1977. pap. 7.95 (ISBN 0-914086-20-0). Alicejamesbooks.

Tamworth Pig Stories. Gene Kemp. (Illus.). 224p. (ps-4). 1987. laminated boards 9.95 (ISBN 0-571-14931-6). Faber & Faber.

Tan-Gun & To-San of Tae Kwon Do Hyung. Jhoon Rhee. LC 71-150320. (Korean Arts Ser.). (Illus.). 1971. pap. text ed. 9.95x (ISBN 0-89750-001-6, 106, Dist. by Wehman). Ohara Pubns.

Tan Kah-Kee: The Making of an Overseas Chinese Legend. C. F. Yong. (Illus.). 288p. 1987. 48.00 (ISBN 0-19-582678-7). Oxford U Pr.

T'an Ssu-t'ung: An Annotated Bibliography. Chan Sin-wai. viii, 117p. 1980. text ed. 27.50x (ISBN 962-201-210-8, Pub. by Chinese U HK). Coronet Bks.

Tan Your Hide: Home Tanning Leathers & Furs. Phyllis Hobson. LC 77-2593. (Illus.). 144p. 1977. pap. 6.95 (ISBN 0-88266-101-9, Garden Way Pub). Storey Comm Inc.

Tana Maguire. Diana Saunders. LC 85-70273. 304p. 1985. 16.95 (ISBN 0-917657-21-7). D I Fine.

Tanagers: Natural History, Distribution, & Identification. Morton L. Isler & Phyllis R. Isler. LC 85-11747. (Illus.). 464p. 1987. 70.00x (ISBN 0-87474-552-7, ISTA); pap. 49.95x (ISBN 0-87474-553-5, ISTAP). Smithsonian.

Tanagra & the Figurines. Reynold Higgins. (Illus.). 248p. 1987. text ed. 50.00 (ISBN 0-691-04044-3). Princeton U Pr.

Tanagrafiguren: Untersuchengen zur hellenistischen Kunst und Geschichte. Gerhard Kleiner. (Illus.). 368p. 1983. 79.20 (ISBN 3-11-008982-3). De Gruyter.

Tanah Air Kita: A Book of the Country & People of Indonesia. 2nd ed. Niels A. Douwes Dekker. LC 77-86970. Repr. of 1951 ed. 46.00 (ISBN 0-404-16705-5). AMS Pr.

Tanaina Tales from Alaska. Bill Vaudrin. LC 69-16717. (Civilization of the American Indians Ser.: Vol. 96). 133p. 1981. pap. 5.95 (ISBN 0-8061-1414-2). U of Okla Pr.

Tanaka Giichi & Japan's China Policy. William F. Morton. LC 79-27570. 330p. 1980. 30.00 (ISBN 0-312-78500-3). St Martin.

TANAKH: A New Translation of the Holy Scriptures According to the Traditional Hebrew Text. 1656p. 1985. 21.95 (ISBN 0-8276-0252-9); leatherette 29.95. JPS Phila.

Tanala, a Hill Tribe of Madagascar. R. Linton. (Chicago Field Museum of Natural History Fieldiana Anthropology Ser). 1933. 36.00 (ISBN 0-527-01882-1). Kraus Repr.

Tanamono Shusei. Sadajiro Yamanaka. 43p. 1933. 340.00x (ISBN 0-317-69149-X, Pub. by Han-Shan Tang Ltd). State Mutual Bk.

Tanaquil: The Hardest Thing of All. Donald Windham. 1972. wrappers, ltd. ed. 100.00x (ISBN 0-917366-02-6). S Campbell.

Tanar of Pellucidar. Edgar Rice Burroughs. (Pellucidar Ser.: No. 3). 256p. 1985. pap. 1.95 (ISBN 0-441-79796-2). Ace Bks.

Tanar of Pellucidar see Pellucidar Novels.

Tanat Valley. Wilfrid J. Wren. LC 68-141249. (Illus.). 1968. 22.95x (ISBN 0-678-05748-6). Kelley.

Tancook Whalers: Origins, Rediscovery & Revival. Robert C. Post. LC 85-63457. (Illus.). 113p. (Orig.). 1986. pap. 15.00 (ISBN 0-937410-05-5). Me Maritime Mus.

Tancred: A Study of His Career & Work. Robert L. Nicholson. LC 79-29847. Repr. of 1940 ed. 29.50 (ISBN 0-404-15425-5). AMS Pr.

Tancred & Gismund. Robert Wilmot et al. LC 70-133765. (Tudor Facsimile Texts. Old English Plays: No. 60). Repr. of 1912 ed. 49.50 (ISBN 0-404-53360-4). AMS Pr.

Tancredi, 2 vols. Gioachino Rossini. Ed. by Philip Gossett. Tr. by Bruno Cagli et al from Ital. (Works of Gioachino Rossini Ser.). xix, 818p. 1986. One vol. pap., 200 p. text ed. 260.00x (ISBN 0-317-46892-8, 718382, Pub. by Fondazione Rossini). U of Chicago Pr.

Tancreds Andre Campra see Chefs-D'oeuvres Classiques De L'opera Francais Ser.

Tancy. Belinda Hurmence. LC 83-19035. 224p. (gr. 6 up). 1984. PLB 11.95 (ISBN 0-89919-228-9, Clarion). HM.

Tandem Mass Spectrometry. F. W. McLafferty. LC 83-10528. 506p. 1983. 60.00 (ISBN 0-471-86597-4, Pub. by Wiley-Interscience). Wiley.

Tandy. B. J. Benson. 179p. (YA) Date not set. pap. 6.95 (ISBN 1-55523-169-1). Winston-Derek.

Tandy. James Traill-Hill. (Private Library Collection). 1986. mini-bound 6.95 (ISBN 0-938422-29-4). SOS Pubns CA.

Tanelorn Archives: A Primary & Secondary Bibliography of the Works of Michael Moorcock,1949-1979. Richard Bilyeu. 108p. 1981. lib. bdg. 19.95x (ISBN 0-919695-04-3). Borgo Pr.

Tang. Eskenazi Ltd. Staff. (Illus.). 85p. 1987. 280.00x (ISBN 0-317-69227-5, Pub. by Han-Shan Tang Ltd). State Mutual Bk.

Tang & Liao Ceramics. William Watson. 283p. 1984. 550.00x (Pub. by Han-Shan Tang Ltd). State Mutual Bk.

Tang Ceramics with the Liao Dynasty. William Watson. 300p. 1984. 200.00x (ISBN 0-317-45292-4, Pub. by Han-Shan Tang Ltd). State Mutual Bk.

Tang Changan Daming Gong. Academia Sinica. 62p. 1959. pap. 315.00x (Pub. by Han-Shan Tang Ltd). State Mutual Bk.

Tang Changean Cheng Jiao Sui Tang Mu. 89p. 1980. 168.00x (ISBN 0-317-69423-5, Pub. by Han-Shan Tang Ltd). State Mutual Bk.

T'ang Code: General Principles, Vol. I. Tr. by Wallace Johnson from Chinese. LC 78-51172. (Studies in East Asia Law Ser.). 1979. 41.00x (ISBN 0-691-09239-7). Princeton U Pr.

T'Ang Dynasty Poems. John Knoefle & Wang Shouyi. 73p. (Orig., Chinese & Eng.). 1986. 11.95 (ISBN 0-933180-84-5, Dist. by Bookslinger); pap. 4.95 (ISBN 0-933180-76-4). Spoon Riv Poetry.

Tang Dynasty Stories. Tr. by Xianyi Yang & Gladys Yang. 149p. (Orig.). 1986. pap. 4.95 (ISBN 0-8351-1602-6). China Bks.

T'Ang Gold & Silver. Bo Gyllensvard. 370p. 1957. 420.00x (Pub. by Han-Shan Tang Ltd). State Mutual Bk.

Tang-Plastik-Chinesische Grabkeramik: Des VLL Bis X Jahrhunderts. Edward Fuchs. 62p. 1924. 300.00x (ISBN 0-317-43761-5, Pub. by Han-Shan Tang Ltd). State Mutual Bk.

T'ang Poet-Monk Chiao-Jan. Thomas P. Nielson. 64p. 1972. 3.00 (ISBN 0-939252-01-5). ASU Ctr Asian.

T'ang Poetic Vocabulary. Hugh M. Stimson. 9.95 (ISBN 0-88710-121-6). Yale Far Eastern Pubns.

Tang Three Colored Pottery, Nos. 1 & 2. 354p. 1984. 315.00x (ISBN 0-317-69152-X, Pub. by Han-Shan Tang Ltd). State Mutual Bk.

Tang Yan Liben Bunian Tu. Yan Liben. 1959. 250.00x (Pub. by Han-Shan Tang Ltd). State Mutual Bk.

T'ang-Yin-Pi-Shih: Parallel Cases from Under the Pear Tree. Tr. by Robert H. Van Gulik. LC 79-1605. 1985. Repr. of 1956 ed. 22.00 (ISBN 0-88355-908-0). Hyperion Conn.

T'ang-Yin-Pi-shih: Parallel Cases from Under the Pear Tree. Tr. by Robert H. Van Gulik. LC 79-1605. 1988. Repr. of 1956 ed. 23.00. Hyperion Conn.

Tanganyika: Preplanning. Fred G. Burke. LC 65-25989. (National Planning Ser.: No. 3). pap. 34.50 (ISBN 0-317-28737-0, 2020396). Bks Demand UMI.

Tangent & Cotangent Bundles: Differential Geometry. Kentaro Yano & Shigeru Ishihara. LC 72-91438. (Pure & Applied Mathematics Ser.: 16). pap. 108.00 (ISBN 0-317-07841-0, 2055025). Bks Demand UMI.

Tangent Factor. Lawrence Sanders. 352p. 1985. pap. 3.95 (ISBN 0-425-10062-6). Berkley Pub.

Tangent Objective. Lawrence Sanders. 352p. 1987. pap. 3.95 (ISBN 0-425-10331-5). Berkley Pub.

Tangents. Lynn Leone. (Illus.). 44p. (Orig.). 1983. pap. 4.00 (ISBN 0-9611742-0-X, 10 LL). Tangents.

Tangerine. Linda C. Gray. 352p. 1988. pap. 3.95 (ISBN 0-8125-1876-4). Tor Bks.

Tangi. Witi Ihimaera. 207p. (Orig.). 1983. pap. 4.95x (ISBN 0-89955-372-9, Pub. by Heinemann Pub New Zealand). Intl Spec Bk.

Tangible Evidence: How to Use Exhibits at Trial. Deanne C. Siemer. 380p. 1984. 55.00 (ISBN 0-15-004366-X, Law & Business). HarBraceJ.

Tangible Personal Property: Assessment & Taxation. Robert M. Clatanoff. (Bibliographic Ser.). 20p. 1982. 9.00 (ISBN 0-88329-112-6). IAAO.

Tangier: A Different Way. Lawdom Vaidon. LC 77-8601. (Illus.). 444p. 1977. 30.00 (ISBN 0-8108-1072-7). Scarecrow.

Tangle. Meg E. Atkins. (Iris Ser.). 224p. 1988. 18.95 (ISBN 0-7145-2877-3, Dist. by Kampmann & Co). M Boyars Pubs.

Tangle & the Firesticks. Benedict Blathwayt. LC 87-2591. (Illus.). (gr. k-3). 1987. 9.95 (ISBN 0-394-88827-8); lib. bdg. 11.99 (ISBN 0-394-98827-2). Knopf.

Tangle of Robots. Barbara Girion. 100p. 1987. pap. 2.50 (ISBN 0-317-56945-7, Pub. by Berkley-Pacer). Berkley Pub.

Tangle of Roots. Barbara Girion. 160p. (Orig.). (gr. 5 up). 1985. pap. 2.25 (ISBN 0-448-47747-5). Putnam Pub Group.

Tangle of Roots. Barbara Girion. (gr. 8 up). 1987. 2.50 (ISBN 0-425-09781-1, Pub. by Berkley-Pacer). Berkley Pub.

Tangled Butterfly. Marion D. Bauer. LC 79-23405. 162p. (gr. 6 up). 1980. 12.95 (ISBN 0-395-29110-0, Clarion). HM.

Tangled Chain: The Structure of Disorder in the Anatomy of Melancholy. Ruth Fox. LC 75-17296. 1976. 27.50x (ISBN 0-520-03085-0). U of Cal Pr.

Tangled Dreams. Lynn Erickson. (Superromance Ser.: No. 255). 308p. Date not set. pap. 2.75 (ISBN 0-317-63873-4). Harlequin Bks.

Tangled Emotions. Billie J. Longstreth et al. LC 82-80742. 357p. 1986. 10.95 (ISBN 0-9608142-0-5); pap. 2.95 (ISBN 0-9608142-1-3). Shamrock Pubns.

Tangled Fire of William Faulkner. William Van O'Connor. LC 68-22386. 191p. 1968. Repr. of 1953 ed. 20.00x (ISBN 0-87752-078-X). Gordian.

Tangled Hair: Love Poems of Yosano Akiko. Yosano Akiko. Tr. by Dennis Maloney & Hide Oshiro. (Illus.). 1986. 7.50 (ISBN 0-934834-05-9). White Pine.

Tangled Hair: Selected Tanka from Midaregami. Akiko Yosano. Ed. by Florence Sakade & Lora Sharnoff. Tr. by Sanford Goldstein & Seishi Shinoda. LC 87-50164. Orig. Title: Midaregami. 166p. (Orig.). 1987. pap. 6.95 (ISBN 0-8048-1522-4). C E Tuttle.

Tangled Harvest. L. G. Layberry. Ed. by Kathleen Morley-Clarke. 192p. 1986. 35.00x (ISBN 0-317-57995-9, Pub. by Spellmount Ltd Pubs). State Mutual Bk.

Tangled Justice: Some Reasons for a Change of Policy in Africa. Charles C. Roberts. LC 72-89011. 157p. Repr. of 1937 ed. cancelled (ISBN 0-8371-1724-0, ROT&, Pub. by Negro U Pr). Greenwood.

Tangled Sheets. Gerard Curry. 128p. (Orig.). 1986. pap. 7.95 (ISBN 0-934411-02-6, Banned Bks). Edward-William Austin.

Tangled Tale. Lewis Carroll. LC 87-50437. (Illus.). 208p. (gr. 5-12). 1987. pap. 7.95 (ISBN 0-940561-06-9). White Rose Pr.

Tangled Tongue: Living with a Stutter. Jock A. Carlisle. 272p. 1985. 25.00x (ISBN 0-8020-2558-7); pap. 9.95 (ISBN 0-8020-6577-5). U of Toronto Pr.

Tangled Tongue: Living with a Stutter. Jock A. Carlisle. LC 86-8029. 272p. 1986. pap. write for info. (ISBN 0-201-11243-4). Addison-Wesley.

Tangled Vines. Mary J. Roberts. LC 86-21683. 252p. 1987. 16.95 (ISBN 0-916515-16-8). Mercury Hse Inc.

Tangled Vines: A Collection of Mother & Daughter Poems. Ed. by Lyn Lifshin. LC 77-88340. 1978. pap. 7.95 (ISBN 0-8070-6367-3, BP574). Beacon Pr.

Tangled Vows. Anne Moore. (Tapestry Ser.: No. 56). (Orig.). 1985. pap. 2.95 (ISBN 0-671-52626-X). PB.

Tangled Web. Nicholas Blake. 224p. 1987. 3.50 (ISBN 0-88184-292-3). Carroll & Graf.

Tangled Web. Barbara Hazard. 224p. 1981. pap. 1.95 (ISBN 0-449-50177-9, Coventry). Fawcett.

Tangled Web. B. J. Hoff. LC 87-70365. (Daybreak Mystery Ser.). 194p. 1988. pap. 6.95 (ISBN 0-89636-242-6). Accent Bks.

Tangled Web. Hannelore Valencak. Tr. by Patricia Crampton from Ger. (gr. 7-9). 1978. 11.75 (ISBN 0-688-22169-6); PLB 11.88 (ISBN 0-688-32169-0). Morrow.

Tangled Web of Price Variation Accounting: The Development of Ideas Underlying Professional Prescriptions in Six Counties. F. L. Clarke. LC 82-82485. (Accountancy in Transition Ser.). 466p. 1982. lib. bdg. 61.00 (ISBN 0-8240-5300-1). Garland Pub.

Tangled Webb. E. B. Wight. 1981. 18.00x (ISBN 0-686-87220-7, Pub. by A H Stockwell England). State Mutual Bk.

Tangled Webs: The U. S. in Greece 1947-1967. Yiannis P. Roubatis. LC 87-60390. 228p. (Orig.). 1987. 25.00 (ISBN 0-317-64511-0); pap. 12.00 (ISBN 0-918618-34-7). Pella Pub.

Tangled Wing: Biological Constraints on the Human Spirit. Melvin Konner. 564p. 1983. pap. 10.95x (ISBN 0-06-132066-8, TB2066, Torch). Har-Row.

Tangled Worlds: The Story of Maria Hertogh. Tom E. Hughes. 64p. (Orig.). 1980. pap. text ed. 12.00x (ISBN 9971-902-12-5, Pub. by Inst Southeast Asian Stud). Gower Pub Co.

Tangles. Marie L. Wallin. 122p. (YA) (gr. 6-9). 1980. pap. 1.50 (ISBN 0-440-99055-6, LFL). Dell.

Tanglewood Murder. Lucille Kallen. 1981. pap. 2.95 (ISBN 0-345-33143-5). Ballantine.

Tanglewood Murder. 1980. 11.95 (ISBN 0-671-61018-X, Wyndham). S&S.

Tanglewood Tales. Nathaniel Hawthorne. (Airmont Classics Ser.). (Illus.). (gr. 7 up). 1968. pap. 1.25 (ISBN 0-8049-0175-9, CL-175). Airmont.

Tanglewood Tales. Nathaniel Hawthorne. (Bambi Classics Ser.). (Illus.). 240p. (Orig.). (YA) (gr. 9-12). 1981. pap. 3.95 (ISBN 0-89531-024-4, 0221-48). Sharon Pubns.

Tanglewood Tales. Nathaniel Hawthorne. (Dent's Illustrated Children's Classics Ser.). (Illus.). 256p. (gr. 4 up). 1974. Repr. of 1950 ed. 11.00x (ISBN 0-460-05010-9, BKA 01601, Pub. by J. M. Dent, England). Biblio Dist.

Tanglewood Tales see Tales & Sketches.

Tanglewood's Secret. Patricia M. St. John. (gr. 5-8). 1951. pap. 4.50 (ISBN 0-8024-0007-8). Moody.

Tango. Earl Atkinson. (Ballroom Dancing Ser.). 1983. lib. bdg. 79.95 (ISBN 0-87700-490-0). Revisionist Pr.

Tango. Earl Atkinson. (Ballroom Dance Ser.). 1986. lib. bdg. 79.95 (ISBN 0-8490-3634-8). Gordon Pr.

Tango. Daniel Halpern. 96p. 1987. 17.95 (ISBN 0-670-81544-6). Viking.

Tango. Daniel Halpern. 96p. 1988. pap. 10.95 (ISBN 0-14-058588-5). Penguin.

Tango. Slawomir Mrozek. Tr. by Ralph Manheim & Teresa Dzieduszycka. (Orig.). 1969. pap. 3.95 (ISBN 0-394-17264-7, E433, Ever). Grove.

Tango & How to Dance It. Gladys B. Crozier. (Ballroom Dancing Ser.). 1986. lib. bdg. 79.95 (ISBN 0-8490-3476-0). Gordon Pr.

Tango & Other up to Date Dances. J. S. Hopkins. (Ballroom Dance Ser.). 1985. lib. bdg. 79.95 (ISBN 0-87700-659-8). Revisionist Pr.

Tango & Other Up to Date Dances. J. S. Hopkins. (Ballroom Dance Ser.). 1986. lib. bdg. 79.95 (ISBN 0-8490-3331-4). Gordon Pr.

Tango & Rumba. Frank Veloz & Yolanda Veloz. (Ballroom Dance Ser.). 1986. lib. bdg. 79.95 (ISBN 0-8490-3383-7). Gordon Pr.

Tango & Rumba. Yolanda Veloz & Frank Veloz. (Ballroom Dance Ser.). 1985. lib. bdg. 79.50 (ISBN 0-87700-718-7). Revisionist Pr.

Tango Argentino: A History of the Tango. Lucy Gordon. (Ballroom Dance Ser.). 1986. lib. bdg. 39.95 (ISBN 0-8490-3471-X). Gordon Pr.

Tango Attitude. (Ballroom Dance Ser.). 1985. lib. bdg. 74.50 (ISBN 0-87700-798-5). Revisionist Pr.

Tango Attitude. (Ballroom Dance Ser.). 1986. lib. bdg. 79.95 (ISBN 0-8490-3403-5). Gordon Pr.

Tango Charlie & Foxtrot Romeo. John Varley. Bd. with Star Pits. Samuel R. Delany. 1989. 2.95. Tor Bks.

Tango Key. Alison Drake. 352p. 1988. pap. 3.50 (ISBN 0-345-34774-9). Ballantine.

Tango Made Easy. (Ballroom Dance Ser.). 1985. lib. bdg. 79.95 (ISBN 0-87700-674-1). Revisionist Pr.

Tango Mejor! Un Enfoque Communicativo, Estructural & Cultural. Thomas A. Lathrop. 1987. pap. write for info. (ISBN 0-471-84921-9); workbook avail. (ISBN 0-471-81804-6); cassette avail. (ISBN 0-471-84919-7). Wiley.

Tango Rond De Jambe for Intermediate Classes. 1985. lib. bdg. 74.00 (ISBN 0-87700-797-7). Revisionist Pr.

Tango Rond de Jambe for Intermediate Classes. (Ballroom Dance Ser.). 1986. lib. bdg. 79.95 (ISBN 0-8490-3402-7). Gordon Pr.

Tangram Diary. Clara E. Clark. (Illus.). 64p. (Orig.). (gr. 3-6). 1980. pap. 6.95 (ISBN 0-934734-05-4). Construct Educ.

Tangram Geometry in Metric. Juanita Brownlee. (Illus., Orig.). (gr. 5-10). 1976. pap. 6.95 (ISBN 0-918932-43-2, 0140701407). Activity Resources.

Tangram: The Ancient Chinese Shapes Game. Joost Elffers. Tr. by R. J. Hollingdale. 1977. pap. 8.95 (ISBN 0-14-004181-8). Penguin.

Tangrams. Peter Van Note. (Illus.). 1966. pap. 3.25 (ISBN 0-8048-0567-9). C E Tuttle.

Tangrams: Three Hundred & Thirty Puzzles. Ronald C. Read. 1978. pap. 3.50 (ISBN 0-486-21483-4). Dover.

Tangut (Hsi Hsia) Studies: A Bibliography. Luc Kwanten & Susan Hesse. Ed. by Denis Sinor. LC 80-51975. (Indiana University Uralic & Altaic Ser.: Vol. 137). 125p. 1980. pap. text ed. 9.00 (ISBN 0-933070-05-5). Ind U Res Inst.

Tania: A Biography & Memoir of Isak Dinesen. M. Parmenia. LC 87-1682. 384p. 1987. pap. text ed. 8.95 (ISBN 0-07-041909-4). McGraw.

Tania-Concert Band Score. Edward Weiss. pap. 34.00 (ISBN 0-317-10078-5, 2002892). Bks Demand UMI.

Tania: Memories of a Lost World. Tania Alexander. LC 87-28825. (Illus.). 168p. 1988. 16.95 (ISBN 0-917561-55-4). Adler & Adler.

Tanjore Maharatta: Principality in Southern India, The Land of Chola, The Eden of the South. William Hickey. 1988. Repr. 25.00x (ISBN 81-206-0302-8, Pub. by Asian Educ Servs India). South Asia Bks.

Tank & AFV Crew Uniforms since 1916. (Illus.). 1984. pap. 6.95 (ISBN 0-89747-103-2, 6027). Squad Sig Pubns.

Tank Battalions of the U. S. Army. James A. Sawicki. LC 82-6069. (Illus.). 427p. 1983. 25.00 (ISBN 0-9602404-5-4). Wyvern.

Tank Corps Honours & Awards, 1916-1919. enl. ed. 402p. 1987. 42.00x (Pub. by Picton UK). State Mutual Bk.

Tank Engine Thomas Again. Reverend W. Awdry. (Railway Ser.). (Illus.). 64p. (gr. k-2). 1985. Repr. of 1949 ed. 6.95 (ISBN 0-7182-0003-9, Pub. by Kaye & Ward). David & Charles.

Tank Sergeant. Ralph Zumbro. (Illus.). 224p. 1986. 16.95 (ISBN 0-89141-265-4). Presidio Pr.

Tank Sergeant. Ralph Zumbro. (Illus.). 264p. pap. 3.95 (ISBN 0-671-63945-5). Archway.

Tank Sergeant. Ralph Zumbro. 1988. pap. 3.95 (ISBN 0-317-67551-6). PB.

Tank Vehicles for Flammable & Combustible Liquids. National Fire Protection Association Staff. 1985. 10.50 (ISBN 0-317-63417-8, 385-85). Natl Fire Prot.

Tank Vehicles for Flammable & Combustible Liquids. (Thirty Ser). 1974. pap. 2.50 (ISBN 0-685-58035-0, 385). Natl Fire Prot.

Tank vs. Tank: The Illustrated Story of Armored Battlefield Conflict in the 20th Century. Kenneth Macksey. (Illus.). 192p. 1988. 24.95 (ISBN 0-88162-282-6). Salem Hse Pubs.

Tank War Nineteen Thirty-Nine to Nineteen Forty-Five. Janusz Piekalkiewicz. (Illus.). 332p. 1986. 24.95 (ISBN 0-7137-1666-5, Pub. by Blandford Pr England). Sterling.

Tank War Vietnam. Simon Dunstan. (Tanks Illustrated Ser.: Vol. 6). (Illus.). 68p. (Orig.). 1985. pap. 9.95 (ISBN 0-85368-603-3, Pub. by Arms & Armour). Sterling.

Tank War: 1939-1945. Janusz Piekalkiewicz. Tr. by Jan Van Heurck from Ger. (Illus.). 332p. 1986. 19.95 (ISBN 0-918678-08-0). Historical Times.

Tank Warfare: The Story of the Tanks in the Great War. F. Mitchell. 336p. 1987. 70.00x (ISBN 0-907590-22-5, Pub. by S P A Bks Ltd). State Mutual Bk.

Tankas from the Koelz Collection: Museum of Anthropology, University of Michigan. rev. ed. Carolyn Copeland. (Michigan Papers on South & Southeast Asia: No. 18). (Illus.). 100p. (Orig.). 1986. pap. 15.95 (ISBN 0-89148-018-8). Ctr S&SE Asian.

Tanker Cargo Handling: A Practical Handbook. D. Rutherford. (Illus.). 111p. 1980. text ed. 19.95x (ISBN 0-85264-256-3). Lubrecht & Cramer.

Tanker Derbent. Krymov. 298p. (Rus.). 1985. 39.00x (ISBN 0-317-42787-3, Pub by Collets (UK)). State Mutual Bk.

Tanker Derbent. Iurii S. Krymov, pseud. Tr. by B. Kagan. LC 74-10086. (China Studies: from Confucius to Mao Ser). 184p. 1975. Repr. of 1940 ed. 18.15 (ISBN 0-88355-173-X). Hyperion Conn.

Tanker Derbent. Y. Krymov. 297p. 1985. pap. 4.00 (ISBN 0-8285-2986-8, Pub. by Raduga Pubs USSR). Imported Pubns.

Tanker Handbook for Deck Officers. 6th rev. ed. C. Baptist. (Illus.). 1980. 40.00. Heinman.

Tanker Handbook for Desk Officers. 6th ed. C. Baptist. 298p. 1988. 48.00x (ISBN 0-85174-386-2). Sheridan.

Tanker Operations: A Handbook for the Ship's Officer. 2nd ed. G. S. Marton. LC 84-45260. (Illus.). xiv, 242p. 1984. text ed. 18.00x (ISBN 0-87033-316-X). Cornell Maritime.

Tanker Performance & Cost: Measurement, Analysis & Management. Ernest Gannett. LC 73-80638. 117p. 1969. 8.50x (ISBN 0-87033-122-1). Cornell Maritime.

Tanker Register, 1986. 26th ed. 1986. 275.00x (ISBN 0-8002-3998-9). Intl Pubns Serv.

Tanker Safety Guide (Liquefield Gas) ICS Staff. 1978. 765.00 (ISBN 0-317-61497-5, Pub. by Witherby & Co England). State Mutual Bk.

Tao of Symbols. James N. Powell. 1982. pap. 9.95 (ISBN 0-688-01354-6, Quill NY). Morrow.
Tao of Tai-Chi Chuan: Way to Rejuvenation. Tsung H. Jou. Ed. by Shoshana Shapiro. (Illus.). 280p. (Orig.). 1981. pap. 17.00 (ISBN 0-8048-1357-4, Pub. by Tai Chi Foun.). C E Tuttle.
Tao of the Loving Couple: True Liberation Through the Tao. Jolan Chang. (Illus.). 129p. 1983. pap. 9.95 (ISBN 0-525-48042-0). Dutton.
Tao of Wing Chun Do, 2 pts, Vol. 1, pt. 1. 4th ed. James W. DeMile. (Illus.). 1983. 6.95 ea. (ISBN 0-918642-01-9); Pt. 1. Pt. 2. Tao of Wing.
Tao Shuo (Discussions on Porcelain) Zhu Yan. 105p. 1938. 25.00x (ISBN 0-317-46364-0, Pub. by Han-Shan Tang Ltd). State Mutual Bk.
Tao Te Ching. Lao Tsu. (Classics Ser.). (Orig.). 1964. pap. 3.95 (ISBN 0-14-044131-X). Penguin.
Tao Te Ching. Lao Tsu. Ed. by Gia-Fu Feng. Tr. by Jane English. 1972. pap. 12.95 (ISBN 0-394-71833-X, V-833, Vin). Random.
Tao Te Ching. Lao Tsu. (Sacred Texts Ser.). Orig. Title: Chinese. viii, 88p. 1983. pap. 8.75 (ISBN 0-88695-007-4). Concord Grove.
Tao Te Ching. Lao Tsu. Tr. by Richard Wilhelm. 224p. 1985. pap. 10.95 (ISBN 1-85063-011-9). Routledge Chapman & Hall.
Tao Te Ching. Tr. by Ch'u Ta-Kao. (Unwin Paperbacks Ser.). (Illus.). 128p. 1982. pap. 9.95 (ISBN 0-04-299011-4). Unwin Hyman.
Tao Te Ching: A New English Version. Tr. by Stephen Mitchell from Chinese. LC 88-45123. 128p. 1988. 14.95 (HarpT). Har-Row.
Tao Teh King. Tr. by Mears. 5.25 (ISBN 0-8356-5123-1). Theos Pub Hse.
Tao-Teh-King see Inner Life.
Tao Teh King: Nature & Intelligence. Lao Tzu. LC 58-9331. (Orig.). 1958. pap. 6.95 (ISBN 0-8044-6387-5). Ungar.
Tao-Teh King: Sayings of Lao-Tzu. rev. ed. Tr. by C. Spurgeon Medhurst from Chinese. LC 72-83648. 180p. (Orig.). 1972. pap. 2.25 (ISBN 0-8356-0430-6, Quest). Theos Pub Hse.
Tao: The Chinese Philosophy of Time & Change. Philip Rawson & Laszlo Legeza. (Art & Imagination Ser.). (Illus.). 1984. pap. 11.95f (ISBN 0-500-81002-8). Thames Hudson.
Tao: The Golden Gate, Vol. 1. Bhagwan Shree Rajneesh. Ed. by Ma Prem Asha. LC 84-42615. (Tao Ser.). 336p. (Orig.). 1984. pap. 4.95 (ISBN 0-88050-646-6). Chidvilas Inc.
Tao: The Golden Gate, Vol. 2. Bhagwan Shree Rajneesh. Ed. by Swami Krishna Prabhu. LC 84-42615. (Tao Ser.). 304p. (Orig.). 1985. pap. 4.95 (ISBN 0-88050-647-4). Chidvilas Inc.
Tao: The Three Treasures, 4 vols. Bhagwan Shree Rajneesh. Ed. by Ma Prema Veena & Swami Anand Somendra. LC 76-905202. (Tao Ser.). (Illus., Orig.). 1977. Vol. II, 346 pgs., 1976. 15.95 ea. (ISBN 0-88050-151-0). Vol. III, 404 pgs. 1976 (ISBN 0-88050-152-9). Vol. IV, 422 pgs. 1977 (ISBN 0-88050-153-7). Chidvilas Inc.
Tao: The Three Treasures, Vol. I. 2nd ed ed. Bhagwan Shree Rajneesh. Ed. by Ma Prem Veena. LC 83-10910. (Tao Ser.). 336p. 1983. pap. 4.95 (ISBN 0-88050-650-4). Chidvilas Inc.
Tao: The Watercourse Way. Alan Watts & Al Chung-Liang Huang. LC 76-4762. 1977. pap. 6.95 (ISBN 0-394-73311-8). Pantheon.
T'ao Ya Or Pottery Refinements. Geoffrey R. Sayer. 163p. 1959. 225.00x (ISBN 0-317-45287-8, Pub. by Han-Shan Tang Ltd). State Mutual Bk.
Tao Ya: Pottery Refinements. Chen Liangba. 244p. 1910. Repr. of 1906 ed. 225.00x (ISBN 0-317-43948-0, Pub. by Han-Shan Tang Ltd.). State Mutual Bk.
T'ao Yuan-ming: His Works & Their Meaning, 2 Vols. A. R. Davis. LC 82-22092. (Cambridge Studies in Chinese History, Literature & Institutions). 320p. 1984. Set. 127.50 (ISBN 0-521-25347-0). Cambridge U Pr.
TaOci Nineteen Forty-Nine to Nineteen Fifty-Nine: Pottery & Porcelain 1949-1959. 1961. 125.00x (ISBN 0-317-45284-3, Pub. by Han-Shan Tang Ltd). State Mutual Bk.
Taoci Xiaoshi-Short History of Ceramics. Zhu Jiequin. 52p. 1936. 50.00x (ISBN 0-317-46365-9, Pub. by Han-Shan Tang Ltd). State Mutual Bk.
Taoism & the Rite of Cosmic Renewal. Michael R. Saso. (Illus.). 1972. pap. 8.00x (ISBN 0-87422-011-4). Wash St U Pr.
Taoism: The Parting of the Way. Holmes Welch. Orig. Title: Parting of the Way. 1966. pap. 7.95 (ISBN 0-8070-5973-0, BP224). Beacon Pr.
Taoism: The Road to Immortality. John Blofeld. LC 77-90882. 195p. 1979. pap. 9.95 (ISBN 0-87773-116-0, 73582-X). Shambhala Pubns.
Taoism: The Road to Immortality. John Blofeld. pap. 13.95 (ISBN 0-394-73582-X). Shambhala Pubns.
Taoism: The Way of the Mystic. J. C. Cooper. 1973. pap. 10.50 (ISBN 0-85030-096-7, Pub. by Thorsons UK). Weiser.
Taoist Health Exercise Book. 3rd ed. Da Liu. (Illus.). 172p. 1983. pap. 5.95 (ISBN 0-399-50745-0, Perigee). Putnam Pub Group.
Taoist I Ching. Tr. by Thomas Cleary from Chinese. LC 85-27890. 332p. 1986. pap. 9.95 (ISBN 0-87773-352-X, 74387-3). Shambhala Pubns.
Taoist I Ching. Liu I-Ming. Tr. by Thomas Cleary. 333p. 1988. pap. 12.95 (ISBN 0-394-74387-3, 352). Shambhala Pubns.
Taoist Secrets of Love: Cultivating Male Sexual Energy. Mantak Chia. 1984. pap. 14.00 (ISBN 0-943358-19-1). Aurora Press.
Taoist Tales. Raymond Van Over. 1973. pap. 3.50 (ISBN 0-452-00701-1, Mer). NAL.
Taoist Texts. Frederic H. Balfour. lib. bdg. 79.95 (ISBN 0-87968-191-8). Krishna Pr.
Taoist Vision. Ed. by William McNaughton. LC 70-143183. (Illus.). 1971. 7.95 (ISBN 0-472-09174-3). U of Mich Pr.
Taoist Ways to Transform Stress into Vitality: The Inner Smile - Six Healing Sounds. Mantak Chia. LC 85-81656. (Illus.). 146p. (Orig.). 1986. pap. 9.95 (ISBN 0-935621-00-8). Heal Tao Bks.
Taoist Yoga. Charles Luk. 1970. pap. 6.95 (ISBN 0-87728-067-3). Weiser.
Taoist Yoga: The Chinese Art of K'ai Men. Chee Soo. (Illus.). 160p. (Orig.). 1983. pap. 6.99 (ISBN 0-85030-332-X, Pub. by Aquarian Pr England). Sterling.
Taormina. Photos by Wilhelm Von Gloeden. (Illus.). 112p. 1986. 50.00 (ISBN 0-942642-22-8). Twelvetrees Pr.
Taos: A Painter's Dream. Patricia J. Broder. (Illus.). 368p. 1980. 59.00 (ISBN 0-8212-1103-X, 831670). NYGS.
Taos: A Pictorial History. John Sherman. 1985. 35.00 (ISBN 0-88307-668-3); pap. 19.95 (ISBN 0-88307-667-5). Gannon.
Taos Eighteen Forty-Seven: The Revolt in Contemporary Accounts. Ed. by Michael McNierney. 102p. 1980. pap. 4.95 (ISBN 0-933472-07-2). Johnson Bks.
Taos Guide. Kathryn Johnson. LC 83-4900. (Illus.). 64p. (Orig.). 1983. pap. 5.95 (ISBN 0-86534-026-9). Sunstone Pr.
Taos Indians. Blanche C. Grant. (Beautiful Rio Grande Classic Ser.). (Illus.). 198p. 1984. pap. 10.00 (ISBN 0-87380-141-5). Rio Grande.
Taos Mosaic: Portrait of a New Mexico Village. Claire Morrill. LC 73-82778. (Illus.). 189p. 1982. pap. 15.95 (ISBN 0-8263-0618-7). U of NM Pr.
Taos Pueblo. George Alpert. LC 83-63106. (Illus.). 160p. 1984. 60.00 (ISBN 0-87358-350-7). Paradise Hse.
Taos Pueblo: A Walk Through Time. John J. Bodine. LC 77-73460. 1977. pap. 2.95 (ISBN 0-89016-038-4). Lightning Tree.
Taos: Station Number Thirty-Two. Hank Mitchum. (Stagecoach Ser.). 192p. (Orig.). 1987. pap. 2.95 (ISBN 0-553-26856-2). Bantam.
Taos Tales. Ed. by Elsie W. Parsons. LC 41-4069. (AFS Memoirs). Repr. of 1940 ed. 26.00 (ISBN 0-527-01086-3). Kraus Repr.
Taos to Tome: True Rates of Hispania New Mexico. Marc Simmons. (Illus.). vi, 90p. (Orig.). 1986. pap. 5.95 (ISBN 0-941270-26-2). Ancient City Pr.
Taos Trappers: The Fur Trade in the Far Southwest, 1540-1846. David J. Weber. LC 75-145508. (Illus.). 280p. 1980. pap. 8.95 (ISBN 0-8061-1702-8). U of Okla Pr.
Taoye Tongshi: The Process of Porcelain Manufacture. Tan-chung T'an. 23p. 1971. 10.00x (ISBN 0-317-45289-4, Pub. by Han-Shan Tang Ltd). State Mutual Bk.
Taoyong: Pottery Images. Chen Wanli. 1957. 150.00x (ISBN 0-317-43943-X, Pub. by Han-Shan Tang Ltd.). State Mutual Bk.
Taozhen: Porcelain Pillows. Chen Wanli. 1954. 100.00x (ISBN 0-317-43942-1, Pub. by Han-Shan Tang Ltd.). State Mutual Bk.
Tap along with Tommy, 3 vols. Tommy Sutton. Ed. by Georgia Dreger. LC 86-90550. (Illus.). 486p. 1986. Set. 49.95 (ISBN 0-9617568-0-2); Vol. 1. write for info. (ISBN 0-9617568-1-0); Vol. 2. write for info. (ISBN 0-9617568-2-9); Vol. 3. write for info. (ISBN 0-9617568-3-7). T Sutton.
Tap, Clap & Sing. Peggy Wise. (Illus.). 52p. (Orig.). (gr. 1-5). 1986. pap. text ed. 4.50 (ISBN 0-9616794-1-7). Plum Apple Pub.
Tap Dance (A Dictionary in Labanotation) Sheila Marion. Ed. by Cook et al. (Illus.). 60p. (Orig.). 1986. pap. text ed. 20.00 (ISBN 0-9602002-5-8). Ray Cook.
Tap Dancing for Big Mom. Roseann Lloyd. Date not set. pap. 4.50 (ISBN 0-89823-073-X). New Rivers Pr.
Tap Dancing for the Relatives. Richard Michelson. LC 85-9166. (Contemporary Poetry Ser.). 69p. 1985. 8.95 (ISBN 0-8130-0827-1). U Presses Fla.
Tap Dancing: Techniques, Routines, Terminology. Constance Atwater. LC 75-158799. (Illus.). (YA) (gr. 9 up). 1971. 13.50 (ISBN 0-8048-0671-3). C E Tuttle.
Tap Techique: Graded Exercises from Beginning Through Advanced Levels. Dean Diggins. LC 88-40201. 128p. 1988. pap. 12.50 (ISBN 0-913793-07-8). Teal Pr.
Tap the Deck. Tanis Knight & Larry Lewin. Ed. by Herbert J. Hrebic. (Writing Program Ser.). (Illus., Orig.). (gr. 5-6). 1985. text ed. 9.10 (ISBN 0-933282-18-4); pap. text ed. 6.00 (ISBN 0-933282-17-6). Stack the Deck.
Tap Water & the Dynamics of Good Health. Robert A. Gegan. 84p. (Orig.). 1986. pap. text ed. 3.50 (ISBN 0-940062-03-8). Consumer Info Pubns.
Tapa in Polynesia. Simon Kooijman. LC 77-178296. (Bulletin Ser: No. 234). (Illus.). 500p. 1972. pap. 24.00 (ISBN 0-910240-13-2). Bishop Mus.
Tapa Samples from Polynesia. Robert D. Craig & Vernice W. Pera. softcover 3.50 (ISBN 0-939154-06-4). Inst Polynesian.
Tapas & Appetizers. Jose Sarrau. Tr. by Francesca P. Slesinger. pap. 7.95 (ISBN 0-671-62555-1, Fireside). S&S.
Tapas: The Little Dishes of Spain. Penelope Casas. LC 85-40160. (Illus.). 256p. (Orig.). 1985. 22.45 (ISBN 0-394-54086-7); pap. 12.95 (ISBN 0-394-74235-4). Knopf.
Tapas, Wines & Good Times. Don Foster & Marge Foster. (Illus.). 192p. (Orig.). 1986. pap. 12.95 (ISBN 0-8092-4877-8). Contemp Bks.
Tape. 3rd ed. F. Gifford. (Illus.). 224p. 1987. pap. text ed. 12.95X (ISBN 0-89582-163-X). Morton Pub.
Tape: a Radio News Handbook. F. Gifford. (Communication Arts Bks.). 1977. 14.00x (ISBN 0-8038-7161-9). Hastings.
Tape & Disk Files, COBOL 3. Ruth Ashley & Judi N. Fernandez. LC 84-11943. (Data Processing Training Ser.). 250p. 1985. pap. text ed. 59.95x spiral bd. (ISBN 0-471-87184-2). Wiley.
Tape Automated Bonding. Business Communications Staff. 154p. 1987. pap. 1950.00 (ISBN 0-89336-615-3, GB-104). BCC.
Tape Codes & Indexes for 1968-1972 Interviewing Years see Panel Study of Income Dynamics: Complete Documentation for Interviewing Years 1968-1981.
Tape Drywall Like a Pro... No Sanding Needed. Terrence J. Moore. (Illus.). 64p. 1987. pap. write for info. (ISBN 0-9618679-0-6). Raha Pr.
Tape Music Composition. David Keane. (Illus., Orig.). 1980. pap. 18.95x (ISBN 0-19-311919-6). Oxford U Pr.
Tape Reading & Its Maximal Interpretation for Stock Market Profits. Richard D. Wyckoff. (Library of the Great Stock Market Classics). (Illus.). 175p. 1983. 175.75x (ISBN 0-89266-412-6). Am Classical Coll Pr.
Tape Reading & Market Tactics. Humphrey B. Neill. LC 73-115001. 1984. Repr. of 1931 ed. flexible cover 10.00 (ISBN 0-87034-074-3). Fraser Pub Co.
Tape-Recorded Interview: A Manual for Field Workers in Folklore & Oral History. Edward D. Ives. LC 79-20527. 1980. lib. bdg. 11.95x (ISBN 0-87049-257-8); pap. text ed. 5.50x (ISBN 0-87049-291-8). U of Tenn Pr.
Tape Recorder. rev. ed. Robert Sloan & Claude Sanders. (Bridges for Ideas Handbook Ser.). 1973. pap. text ed. 6.00x (ISBN 0-913648-09-4). U Tex Austin Film Lib.
Tape Recording Local History. David Haines. 2.50 (ISBN 0-913714-17-8). Legacy Bks.
Tape Recording Made Easy: A Programmed Primer. 1983. 3.75 (ISBN 0-9601006-3-6). G T Yeamans.
Tape-Recording Your Church's History. Ronald A. Tonks. Ed. by Charles W. Deweese. (Resource Kit for Your Church's History ser.). 7p. 1984. pap. 0.50 (ISBN 0-939804-17-4). Hist Comm S Baptist.
Taped Story of Virginia. Robert Fields & Henry D. McCoy, II. Ed. by Lewis P. Wilkinson. (American Heroes & Heroines Ser.). (Illus.). 32p. (gr. 6-12). 1984. pap. 30.00 (ISBN 0-935525-01-7); audio cassette version 7.95 (ISBN 0-935525-00-9). Cassette Concepts.
Tapestries in Sand: The Spirit of Indian Sandpainting. rev. ed. David Villasenor. (Illus.). 112p. (gr. 4 up). 1966. 12.95 (ISBN 0-911010-23-8); pap. 6.95 (ISBN 0-911010-22-X). Naturegraph.
Tapestries of Europe & Colonial Peru in the Museum of Fine Arts, Boston. Adolph S. Cavallo. LC 67-17672. 1968p. 1968. boxed set 17.50 (ISBN 0-87846-015-2). Mus Fine Arts Boston.
Tapestries of Life: Women's Work, Women's Consciousness, & the Meaning of Daily Experience. Bettina Aptheker. 272p. 1989. 35.00x (ISBN 0-87023-658-X); pap. 12.95 (ISBN 0-87023-659-8). U of Mass Pr.
Tapestries of the Lowlands. Heinrich Gobel. Tr. by Robert West. LC 73-79046. (Illus.). 1974. Repr. of 1924 ed. lib. bdg. 75.00 (ISBN 0-87817-132-0). Hacker.
Tapestry. Ed. by Wilfred Bockelman. 128p. (Orig.). 1985. pap. 4.95 (ISBN 0-8066-2177-X, 10-6201). Augsburg.
Tapestry. Arthur Moore. (Orig.). 1979. pap. 2.50 (ISBN 0-89083-523-3). Zebra.
Tapestry. Belva Plain. 448p. 1988. large print 19.95 (ISBN 0-385-29656-8); pap. 18.95 (ISBN 0-385-29630-4). Delacorte.
Tapestry. Belva Plain. 1989. pap. price not set. Dell.
Tapestry. James M. Rose & Barbara W. Brown. (Illus.). 163p. (Orig.). 1979. pap. 4.95x (ISBN 0-9607744-2-4). New London County.
Tapestry. Edith Schaeffer. 640p. 1985. pap. 10.95 (ISBN 0-8499-3016-2, 3016-2). Word Bks.
Tapestry & Embroidery in the Collection of the National Palace Museum, Taipei. (Illus.). 1986. 500.00 (ISBN 0-89659-672-9). Abbeville Pr.
Tapestry: Contemporary Imagery-Ancient Tradition. Valerie Clausen. 52p. pap. 7.50 (ISBN 0-910524-09-2). Eastern Wash.
Tapestry: Henry Moore & West Dean. Edwin Mullins. (Illus.). 49p. (Orig.). 1980. pap. 5.00 (ISBN 0-88397-032-5). Intl Exhibitions.
Tapestry Loom Techniques: A Guide to Exploration on the Two Harness Loom. Jules Kliot. 1974. pap. 2.95 (ISBN 0-916896-04-8). Lacis Pubns.
Tapestry Maker: Poems by Ted Malone. E. T. Malone. LC 73-179907. 96p. 1971. 1.98 (ISBN 0-910244-64-2). Blair.
Tapestry: Monographs. Mary Vance. (Architecture Ser.: A 1358). 37p. 1985. 5.25 (ISBN 0-89028-348-6). Vance Biblios.
Tapestry of Animals. Augustus Young. (Illus.). 1977. saddlestitched 1.50 (ISBN 0-685-04215-4, Pub. by Menard Pr). Small Pr Dist.
Tapestry of Childhood. Bettye V. Colburn. (Illus.). 230p. 1979. 9.00 (ISBN 0-682-49297-3). Exposition-Phoenix.
Tapestry of Culture. 2nd ed. Abraham Rosman & Paula G. Rubel. 352p. 1984. pap. text ed. write for info (ISBN 0-394-33999-1, RanC). Random.
Tapestry of Dreams. Roberta Gellis. 480p. 1986. pap. 6.95 (ISBN 0-425-07627-X). Berkley Pub.
Tapestry of Dreams. Roberta Gellis. 496p. 1986. pap. 3.95 (ISBN 0-515-08600-2). Jove Pubns.
Tapestry of Love. Cathryn Ladd. (Adventures in Love Ser.: No. 32). 1982. pap. 1.75 (ISBN 0-451-11786-7, AE1786, Sig). NAL.
Tapestry of Magics. Brian Daley. 304p. 1983. pap. 2.95 (ISBN 0-345-29682-6, Del Rey). Ballantine.
Tapestry of Mathematics. new ed. Mary Laycock & Connie Johnson. (Illus.). 1978. pap. text ed. 18.95 (ISBN 0-918932-51-3). Activity Resources.
Tapestry of Pride. Catherine Lyndell. 1987. pap. 3.95 (ISBN 0-671-62328-1). PB.
Tapestry of the North. Amelia B. Kesling. 159p. 1986. 8.75 (ISBN 0-8062-2628-5). Carlton.
Tapestry of Time. Richard Cowper. pap. 2.95 (ISBN 0-671-62500-4). PB.
Tapestry, the Mirror of Civilization. Phyllis Ackerman. LC 74-108123. Repr. of 1933 ed. 31.50 (ISBN 0-404-00279-X). AMS Pr.
Tapestry Two. Archer M. Huntington. 1952. 2.00 (ISBN 0-87535-070-4). Hispanic Soc.
Tapestry Warriors. Cherry Wilder. LC 82-16279. 276p. (gr. 8up). 1983. pap. 12.95 (ISBN 0-689-30966-X, Argo). Atheneum.
Taphonomy & Paleoecology of the Christensen Bog Mastodon Bone Bed, Hancock County, Indiana. Russell W. Graham et al. (Reports of Investigations Ser.: No. 38). (Illus.). 29p. (Orig.). 1983. pap. 4.00x (ISBN 0-89792-097-X). Ill St Museum.
Taphonomy of Rampithecus Wickeri at Fort Ternan, Kenya. Pat Shipman. (Museum Briefs Ser.: No. 26). (Illus.). v, 37p. 1982. pap. 2.00 (ISBN 0-913134-26-0). Mus Anthro MO.
Tapies & the New Culture. Lluis Permanyer. LC 86-6510. (Illus.). 216p. 75.00 (ISBN 0-8478-0724-X). Rizzoli Intl.
Tapies: The Complete Works Nineteen Forty-Three to Nineteen Sixty. Anna Agusti. LC 88-42714. (Vol. I). (Illus.). 550p. 1988. 175.00 (ISBN 0-8478-0980-3). Rizzoli Intl.
Tapis De Bruyere Rose. Margaret Mayo. (Collection Harlequin Ser.). 192p. 1983. pap. 1.95 (ISBN 0-373-49368-1). Harlequin Bks.
Tapisseries. Charles Peguy. (Poesie Ser.). pap. 6.95 (ISBN 0-685-37042-9). Schoenhof.
Tappan Creative Cookbook for Microwave Ovens & Ranges. Sylvia Schur. 1977. pap. 6.95 (ISBN 0-452-25312-8, Z5312, Plume). NAL.
Tappan on Survival. Mel Tappan. LC 81-82264. 1982. 7.95 (ISBN 0-916172-04-X). Janus Pr.
Tappan Zee Dress: Plain & Fancy, 1780-1930. Anne R. Adams. (Illus.). 40p. 1981. pap. 2.00 (ISBN 0-911183-20-5). Rockland County Hist.
Tappan's Burrow. Zane Grey. pap. 2.50 (ISBN 0-671-83592-0). PB.
TAPPI Career Planning Manual: Career Development for Technical Professionals in the Pulp, Paper, & Allied Industries. Technical Association of the Pulp & Paper Industry. pap. 28.80 (ISBN 0-317-30113-6, 2025298). Bks Demand UMI.
TAPPI High Barrier Packaging Seminar, 1985: Marriott Hilton Head Hotel, Hilton Head, SC, April 1. Technical Association of the Pulp & Paper Industry. pap. 20.00 (ISBN 0-317-26880-5, 2025296). Bks Demand UMI.
Tapping Earth's Heat. Patricia Lauber. LC 78-6283. (Good Earth Ser.). (Illus.). (gr. 2-6). 1978. PLB 7.22 (ISBN 0-8116-6110-5). Garrard.
Tapping in to the NEC. Richard W. Osborn & George W. Flach. Ed. by Richard W. Osborn. LC 82-82124. (Illus.). 178p. 1982. pap. text ed. 8.50 (ISBN 0-87765-226-0, NEC-QUE). Natl Fire Prot.
Tapping Reeve & the Litchfield Law School. Marian C. McKenna. LC 85-18901. 224p. 1986. lib. bdg. 30.00 (ISBN 0-379-20220-4). Oceana.
Tapping the Government Grapevine: The User-Friendly Guide to U. S. Government Information Sources. Judith S. Robinson. 192p. 1988. 36.00 (ISBN 0-89774-179-X); pap. 24.50 (ISBN 0-89774-520-5). Oryx Pr.
Tapping the Small-Business Market. Stuart R. Veale. LC 87-7732. 320p. 1987. 35.00 (ISBN 0-13-884420-8). NY Inst Finance.
Tapping the Source. Kem Nunn. LC 83-7544. 310p. 1984. 14.95 (ISBN 0-385-29272-4). Delacorte.
Tapping the Source. Kem Nunn. 1988. pap. 7.95 (ISBN 0-440-20078-4). Dell.
Taproots of Falconhurst. Ashley Carter. 1983. pap. 2.95 (ISBN 0-449-12600-5, GM). Fawcett.

Targeting of Drugs. Ed. by Gregory Gregoriadis et al. LC 82-3822. (NATO ASI Series A, Life Sciences: Vol. 47). 440p. 1982. 75.00x (ISBN 0-306-41001-X, Plenum Pr). Plenum Pub.

Targeting of Drugs with Synthetic Systems, Vol. 113. Ed. by Gregory Gregoriadis et al. LC 86-16891. (NATO ASI Series: Series A: Life Sciences). 308p. 1986. 55.00x (ISBN 0-306-42377-4, Plenum Pr). Plenum Pub.

Targeting the Computer: Government Support & International Competition. Kenneth Flamm. LC 87-11706. 266p. 1987. 31.95 (ISBN 0-8157-2852-2); pap. 11.95t (ISBN 0-8157-2851-4). Brookings.

Targeting the Top. Nancy Lee. 352p. 1981. pap. 2.95 (ISBN 0-345-29643-5). Ballantine.

Targets. Donald McQuinn. 512p. 1983. pap. 3.75 (ISBN 0-523-48060-1, Dist. by Warner Pub. Services & Saint Martin's Press). Tor Bks.

Targets & Indicators: A Blueprint for the International Coordination of Economic Policy. Marcus Miller & John Williamson. LC 87-22724. (Policy Analyses in International Economics: No. 22). 118p. (Orig.). 1987. pap. 10.00 (ISBN 0-88132-051-X). Inst Intl Eco.

Targets & Syntactic Change. John Haiman. LC 73-87535. (Janua Linguarum, Ser. Minor: No. 186). 156p. (Orig.). 1974. pap. text ed. 18.50x (ISBN 90-2792-703-0). Mouton.

Targets for Health for All Two Thousand: Targets in Support of the European Regional Strategy for Health for All. 201p. 1985. pap. 12.00 (ISBN 92-890-1034-7). World Health.

Targets for Research in Library Education. Ed. by Harold Borko. LC 72-9923. pap. 63.30 (ISBN 0-317-26362-5, 2024223). Bks Demand UMI.

Targets for the Design of Antiviral Agents. Ed. by E. De Clercq & R. T. Walker. LC 83-24627. (NATO ASI Series A, Life Sciences: Vol. 73). 390p. 1984. 69.50x (ISBN 0-306-41618-2, Plenum Pr). Plenum Pub.

Targets: Media Guide. Howard Hirshman. 1986. write for info. Robinson Pr.

Targets of Satire in the Comedies of Etherege, Wycherley, & Congreve. Ursula Jantz. Ed. by James Hogg. (Poetic Drama & Poetic Theory Ser.). 242p. (Orig.). 1978. pap. 15.00 (ISBN 3-7052-0874-8, Pub. by Salzburg Studies). Longwood Pub Group.

Targetted Counties & Municipalities in the South. Richard Hudlin & K. Farouk Brimah. 1983. pap. 1.00 (ISBN 0-318-00969-2). Voter Ed Proj.

Targilon for Sefer Bamidbar, Vol. I. Israel Rosenfeld. text ed. 4.00 (ISBN 0-914131-64-8, A23). Torah Umesorah.

Targilon for Sefer Bemidbar, Vol. II. Israel Rosenfeld. text ed. 4.00 (ISBN 0-914131-65-6, A24). Torah Umesorah.

Targilon Shmuel Aleph. Solomon Skaist. 53p. (gr. 5-6). pap. 1.50 (ISBN 0-318-13639-2). Board Jewish Educ.

Targum & Testament: Aramaic Paraphrases of the Hebrew Bible: a Light on the New Testament. Martin McNamara. 226p. 1972. 17.50x (ISBN 0-7165-0619-X, BBA 02203, Pub. by Irish Academic Pr Ireland). Biblio Dist.

Targum Jonathan of the Former Prophets. Daniel Harrington & Anthony J. Saldarini. (The Aramaic Bible (The Targums) Ser.: Vol. 10). (Orig.). 1987. 49.00 (ISBN 0-89453-479-3). M Glazier.

Targum Jonathan to the Prophets. Pinkos Churgin. LC 78-63558. (Yale Oriental Ser. Researches: No. 14). Repr. of 1927 ed. 32.50 (ISBN 0-404-60284-3). AMS Pr.

Targum Neophyti One: A Textual Study: Leviticus, Numbers, Deuteronomy, Vol. 2. B. Barry Levy. LC 86-11117. (Brown Studies in Judaism). 396p. (Orig.). 1987. lib. bdg. 31.75 (ISBN 0-8191-6313-9, Pub. by Studies in Judaism); pap. text ed. 19.50 (ISBN 0-8191-6314-7). U Pr of Amer.

Targum of Ezekiel. Samson H. Levey. (The Aramaic Bible (The Targums) Series: Vol, 13). (Orig.). 1987. 37.95 (ISBN 0-89453-482-3). M Glazier.

Targum of Jeremiah. Robert Hayward. (The Aramaic Bible (The Targums) Ser.: Vol. 12). 1987. 47.95 (ISBN 0-89453-481-5). M Glazier.

Targum Onkelos on Deuteronomy. Israel Drazin. 1981. 45.00x (ISBN 0-87068-755-7). Ktav.

Targum Onkelos to Genesis. M. Aberbach & B. Grossfeld. 45.00x (ISBN 0-87068-339-X). Ktav.

Targum Onqelos to Deuteronomy. Tr. by Bernard Grossfeld. LC 86-45349. (Aramaic Bible Ser.: Vol. 9). 1988. text ed. 45.95X. M Glazier.

Targum Onqelos to Exodus. Tr. by Bernard Grossfeld. LC 88-45083. (Aramaic Bible Ser.: Vol. 7). 1988. text ed. 45.95X (ISBN 0-89453-486-6). M Glazier.

Targum Onqelos to Genesis. Tr. by Bernard Grossfeld. LC 86-45349. (Aramaic Bible Ser.: Vol. 6). 1988. text ed. 49.95X. M Glazier.

Targum Onqelos to Leviticus & Numbers. Tr. by Bernard Grossfeld. LC 88-45359. (Aramaic Bible Ser.: Vol. 8). 1988. text ed. 47.95X (ISBN 0-89453-487-4). M Glazier.

Targum Pseudo-Jonathan of the Pentateuch. E. G. Clarke. 1983. 150.00x (ISBN 0-88125-015-5). Ktav.

Targumic Approaches to the Gospels: Essays in the Mutual Definition of Judaism & Christianity. Bruce Chilton. 200p. (Orig.). 1987. lib. bdg. 24.75 (ISBN 0-8191-5731-7, Pub. by Studies in Judaism); pap. text ed. 12.25 (ISBN 0-8191-5732-5). U Pr of Amer.

Targumic Traditions. J. T. Forestell. LC 79-19293. (Society of Biblical Literature Aramaic Studies: No. 4). 151p. 1984. pap. 12.00 (ISBN 0-89130-352-9, 06-13-04). Scholars Pr GA.

Targums & Rabbinic Literature. John Bowker. LC 71-80817. 1969. 70.00 (ISBN 0-521-07415-0). Cambridge U Pr.

Targums of Onkelos & Jonathan Ben Uzziel on the Pentateuch with the Fragments of the Jerusalem Targum from the Chaldee. J. W. Etheridge. 1969. Repr. of 1865 ed. 59.50x (ISBN 0-87068-045-5). Ktav.

Targun Neophyti One: A Textual Study: Introduction, Genesis, Exodus. B. B. Levy. LC 86-11117. (Studies in Judaism). 470p. (Orig.). 1986. lib. bdg. 38.50 (ISBN 0-8191-5464-4, Pub. by Studies in Judaism); pap. text ed. 23.00 (ISBN 0-8191-5465-2). U Pr of Amer.

Tarheel Talk: An Historical Study of the English Language in North Carolina to 1860. Norman E. Eliason. x, 324p. 1980. Repr. of 1956 ed. lib. bdg. 23.00x (ISBN 0-374-92528-3, Octagon). Hippocrene Bks.

Tarhumara: Middle America. Ed. by Frank W. Porter, III. (Indians of North America Ser.). (Illus.). (gr. 5 up). 1989. 16.95 (ISBN 1-55546-730-X). Chelsea Hse.

Tariff & Competition in Canada. H. C. Eastman & S. Stykolt. (Illus.). 1969. 27.50 (ISBN 0-312-78540-2). St Martin.

Tariff & the Development of the Cotton Industry in China, 1842-1937. Shou-Eng Koo. Ed. by Ramon H. Myers. LC 80-8831. (China During the Interregnum 1911-1949, The Economy & Society Ser.). 269p. 1982. lib. bdg. 36.00 (ISBN 0-8240-4687-0). Garland Pub.

Tariff Commission: Its History, Activities & Organization. Joshua Bernhardt. LC 72-3018. (Brookings Institution. Institute for Government Research. Service Monographs of the U. S. Government: No. 5). Repr. of 1922 ed. 21.50 (ISBN 0-404-57105-0). AMS Pr.

Tariff Examiner. Jack Rudman. (Career Examination Ser.: C-828). (Cloth bdg. avail. on request). pap. 12.00 (ISBN 0-8373-0828-3). Natl Learning.

Tariff History of the United States. 8th ed. Frank W. Taussig. Repr. of 1931 ed. 24.00 (ISBN 0-384-59570-7). Johnson Repr.

Tariff in the Days of Henry Clay & since, An Exhaustive Review of Our Tariff Legislation from 1812 to 1895. W. McKinley. Repr. of 1896 ed. 21.00 (ISBN 0-527-59900-X). Kraus Repr.

Tariff Levels & the Economic Unity of Europe: An Examination of Tariff Policy Export Movements & the Economic Integration of Europe 1913-1931. Heinrich Liepmann. Tr. by H. Stenning from Ger. LC 79-12741. (Studies in International Economics: No. 3). (Illus.). 424p. 1980. Repr. of 1938 ed. lib. bdg. 39.50x (ISBN 0-87991-852-7). Porcupine Pr.

Tariff of Syria, 1919 to 1932. Norman Burns. LC 76-180328. (Mid-East Studies Ser.). Repr. of 1933 ed. 24.00 (ISBN 0-404-56234-5). AMS Pr.

Tariff on Iron & Steel. Abraham Berglund & Phillip G. Wright. (Brookings Institution Reprint Ser). Repr. of 1929 ed. lib. bdg. 36.50x (ISBN 0-697-00151-2). Irvington.

Tariff, Politics, & American Foreign Policy, 1874-1901. Tom E. Terrill. LC 72-140921. (Contributions in American History Ser.: No. 31). 1973. lib. bdg. 46.95x (ISBN 0-8371-5819-2, TTP/). Greenwood.

Tariff Politics: Australian Policy-Making 1960-1980. Leon Glezer. 360p. 1982. 35.00x (ISBN 0-522-84190-2, Pub. by Melbourne U Pr). Intl Spec Bk.

Tariff Preferences in Mediterranean Diplomacy. Alfred Tovias. LC 77-12265. 1978. 20.00x (ISBN 0-312-78550-X). St Martin.

Tariff Problem. 4th ed. William J. Ashley. LC 68-30515. 1968. Repr. of 1920 ed. 35.00x (ISBN 0-678-00433-1). Kelley.

Tariff Problem in China. Chin Chu. LC 68-56650. (Columbia University Studies in the Social Sciences: No. 169). Repr. of 1916 ed. 17.50 (ISBN 0-404-51169-4). AMS Pr.

Tariff Problem in Great Britain, 1918-1923. Rixford K. Snyder. LC 70-155604. (Stanford University. Stanford Studies in History, Economics, & Political Science: Vol. 5, Pt. 2). Repr. of 1944 ed. 20.00 (ISBN 0-404-50970-3). AMS Pr.

Tariff Reform in British Politics, Nineteen Hundred Three to Nineteen Thirteen. Alan Sykes. 1979. text ed. 47.50x (ISBN 0-19-822483-4). Oxford U Pr.

Tariff Reform in France, 1860-1900: The Politics of Economic Interest. Michael S. Smith. LC 79-25272. 288p. 1980. 32.50x (ISBN 0-8014-1257-9). Cornell U Pr.

Tariff Reform Movement in Great Britain, 1881-1895. Benjamin H. Brown. Repr. of 1943 ed. 8.00 (ISBN 0-404-01119-5). AMS Pr.

Tariff Retaliation: Repercussions of the Hawley-Smoot Bill. Joseph Jones. LC 82-48312. (World Economy Ser.). 352p. 1983. lib. bdg. 44.00 (ISBN 0-8240-5367-2). Garland Pub.

Tariffs: A Study in Method. Theodore E. Gregory. LC 68-20038. 1968. Repr. of 1921 ed. 45.00x (ISBN 0-678-00420-X). Kelley.

Tariffs, Quotas, & Trade: The Politics of Protectionism. Walter Adams et al. LC 78-66267. 330p. 1979. pap. text ed. 7.95 (ISBN 0-917616-34-0). ICS Pr.

Tariffs: The Case for Protectionism. Lewis E. Lloyd. 9.50 (ISBN 0-8159-6902-3). Devin.

Tarification Ferroviaire dans un Marche Concurrentiel de Transports Interieurs de Marchandises: Communications et Debats du Colloque International de Nice - Octobre, 1961. (Economies et Societes Ser. K: No. 6). 1962. pap. 26.00 (ISBN 0-8115-0725-4). Kraus Repr.

Tarifs Douaniers et Echanges Commerciaux en Europe Occidentale: Une Enquete par P.E.P (Political & Economic Planning) (Economies et Societes Ser. R.: No. 5). 1960. pap. 19.00 (ISBN 0-8115-0785-8). Kraus Repr.

Tarikh Al-Ridda: Gleaned from al-Iktifa of al-Balansi with Notes & An Introduction. Khurshid A. Fariq. 183p. (Arabic.). 1981. text ed. 20.00x (ISBN 0-7069-1334-5, Pub. by Vikas India). Advent NY.

Tarjaman-ul-Quran, 3 vols. A. K. Azad. Vol. 1. 16.50 (ISBN 0-686-18512-9); Vol. 2. 20.00 (ISBN 0-686-67787-0); Vol. 3. 20.00. Kazi Pubns.

Tarjei Vesaas. Kenneth C. Chapman. LC 78-110715. (World Authors Ser.). 1970. lib. bdg. 17.95 (ISBN 0-8057-2948-8). Irvington.

Tarjuma'n Al-Ashwa'q. Ibn Arabi. 14.25 (ISBN 0-8356-5505-9). Theos Pub Hse.

Tarjuman Al-Qura'n: A Critical Analysis of Maulana Abul Kalam Azad's Approach to the Understanding of the Qura'n. I. Azad Faruqi. 128p. 1983. text ed. 15.95x (ISBN 0-7069-1342-6, Pub. by Vikas India). Advent NY.

Tark & the Golden Tide. Colum MacDonnell. 1977. pap. 1.25 (ISBN 0-8439-0470-4, Leisure Bks). Leisure NY.

Tark: College Basketball's WinningestCoach. Jerry Tarkanian & Terry Pluto. (Illus.). 1988. 17.95 (ISBN 0-07-062802-5). McGraw.

Tark! The Sports Career of Francis Tarkenton. James Hahn & Lynn Hahn. Ed. by Howard Schroeder. LC 80-28881. (Sports Legends Ser.). (Illus.). 48p. (Orig.). (gr. 3-5). 1981. PLB 8.95 (ISBN 0-89686-121-X). Crestwood Hse.

Tarkanian: Countdown of a Rebel. Richard Harp & Joseph McCullough. LC 84-940. (Illus.). 224p. (Orig.). 1984. pap. 11.95 (ISBN 0-88011-229-8, PHAR0229). Leisure Pr.

Tarlov Ciper, No. 207. Nick Carter. 208p. 1985. pap. 2.50 (ISBN 0-441-79831-4). Ace Bks.

Tarlton's Jests & News Out of Purgatory, with a Life by J. O. Halliwell. Tarlton. LC 71-131503. Repr. of 1844 ed. 16.50 (ISBN 0-404-07943-1). AMS Pr.

Tarnished Angel. Elaine Barbieri. 1988. pap. 4.50 (ISBN 0-515-09748-9). Jove Pubns.

Tarnished Badge. facsimile ed. Ralph L. Smith. LC 74-3852. (Criminal Justice in America Ser.). 1974. Repr. of 1965 ed. 21.00x (ISBN 0-405-06167-6). Ayer Co Pubs.

Tarnished Expansion: The Alaska Scandal, the Press, & Congress, 1867-1871. Paul S. Holbo. LC 82-17513. (Illus.). 164p. 1983. text ed. 14.95x (ISBN 0-87049-380-9). U of Tenn Pr.

Tarnished Gold: The Record Industry Revisited. R. Serge Denisoff. 350p. 1986. pap. 16.95 (ISBN 0-88738-618-0); 34.95 (ISBN 0-88738-068-9). Transaction Bks.

Tarnished Hero: A Sam Sharpstein Novel. Steve W. Berman. LC 87-92175. 1988. 17.95 (ISBN 0-87212-214-X). Libra.

Tarnished Knight. William C. Stump. (Illus.). 346p. 1984. 14.95 (ISBN 0-9613487-0-4). W C Stump.

Tarnished Victory. Created by Rosemary Joyce. (Dream Girls Ser.: No. 3). (YA) (gr. 7 up). pap. 2.50 (ISBN 0-671-62112-2). Archway.

Tarnished Warrior, Major General James Wilkinson. James R. Jacobs. 33.00 (ISBN 0-8369-6943-X, 7824). Ayer Co Pubs.

Tarnschriften Der Kpd Aus Dem Antifaschistischen Widerstandskampf: Original-getreue Reproduktion Von 12 Heften Aus Den Jahren 1935-1936. Institut fur Marxismus-Leninismus beim ZK Der Sed. Ed. by Gerhard Nitzsche & Margot Pikarski. 996p. (Ger.). 1986. lib. bdg. 49.00 (ISBN 3-598-07229-5). K G Saur.

Taro: A Review of "Colocasia Esculenta" & Its Potentials. Ed. by Jaw-Kai Wang. LC 82-21903. (Illus.). 418p. 1983. text ed. 35.00x (ISBN 0-8248-0841-X). UH Pr.

Taro Classico. Stuart R. Kaplan. Tr. by Maio Miranda from Eng. (Illus.). 224p. (Orig., Port.). pap. 9.95 (ISBN 0-88079-251-5). US Games Syst.

Taroleywick: A Century of Iowa Farming. Henry C. Taylor. LC 70-103840. pap. 36.00 (ISBN 0-317-55556-1, 2029623). Bks Demand UMI.

Tarot. Piers Anthony. 1987. 8.95 (ISBN 0-441-79841-1, Pub. by Ace Science Fiction). Ace Bks.

Tarot. Stuart R. Kaplan. Tr. by Burkhardt Kiegeland from Eng. (Illus.). 256p. (Orig., Ger.). 1984. pap. 9.95 (ISBN 3-88034-224-5). US Games Syst.

Tarot. S. L. Mathers. 1973. 59.95 (ISBN 0-8490-1177-9). Gordon Pr.

Tarot. S. L. Mathers. LC 71-17150. 1969. pap. 1.25 (ISBN 0-87728-100-9). Weiser.

Tarot. Mouni Sadhu. pap. 10.00 (ISBN 0-87980-157-3). Wilshire.

Tarot: A Guide to Reading Your Own Cards. Nancy Shavick. 144p. (Orig.). 1985. pap. 8.95 (ISBN 0-9615315-0-9). Prima Materia.

Tarot: A New Handbook for the Apprentice. Eileen Connolly. LC 80-22271. 244p. 1980. Repr. of 1979 ed. lib. bdg. 25.95x (ISBN 0-89370-645-0). Borgo Pr.

Tarot: A New Handbook for the Apprentice. Eileen Connolly. LC 79-15303. (Illus.). 1979. pap. 10.95 (ISBN 0-87877-045-3). Newcastle Pub.

Tarot: An Essay. Manly P. Hall. pap. 2.95 (ISBN 0-89314-382-0). Philos Res.

Tarot & Astrology. Muriel B. Hasbrouck. 304p. (Orig.). 1987. pap. 6.95 (ISBN 0-89281-121-8, Destiny Bks). Inner Tradit.

Tarot & Transformation. Lynn M. Buess. LC 73-77608. (Illus.). 1977. pap. 7.95 (ISBN 0-87516-238-X). DeVorss.

Tarot Card Symbology. 3rd, rev. ed. Max F. Long. Ed. by E. Otha Wingo. (Illus.). 1983. pap. 10.00 (ISBN 0-910764-07-7). Huna Res Inc.

Tarot Cards for Fun & Fortune Telling. Stuart R. Kaplan. LC 71-119490. (Illus.). 96p. 1970. 5.95 (ISBN 0-913866-02-4). US Games Syst.

Tarot Cards Painted by Bonifacio Bembo for the Visconti-Sforza Family. Gertrude Moakley. (Illus.). 124p. 1966. 15.00 (ISBN 0-87104-175-8). NY Pub Lib.

Tarot Classic. Stuart R. Kaplan. LC 74-183028. (Illus.). 240p. 1972. pap. 6.95 (ISBN 0-913866-17-2). US Games Syst.

Tarot Classic Gift Set. Stuart R. Kaplan. LC 74-183028. (Illus.). 240p. 1972. pap. 15.00 card deck incl. (ISBN 0-913866-55-5). US Games Syst.

Tarot Constellations: Patterns of Personal Destiny. Mary K. Greer. LC 88-2906. 210p. 1988. lib. bdg. 28.95x (ISBN 0-8095-6128-X). Borgo Pr.

Tarot Constellations: Patterns of Personal Destiny. Mary K. Greer. 192p. (Orig.). 1987. pap. 12.95 (ISBN 0-87877-128-X). Newcastle Pub.

Tarot Design Book. Caren Caraway. (International Design Library). (Illus.). 48p. 1980. pap. 5.95 (ISBN 0-916144-56-9). Stemmer Hse.

Tarot Divination. Aleister Crowley. 68p. 1976. pap. 3.95 (ISBN 0-87728-347-8). Weiser.

Tarot for Lovers. E. W. Neville. Ed. by Julie Lockhart. (Illus.). 252p. (Orig.). 1987. pap. 14.95 (ISBN 0-914918-75-3, Pub. by Whitford Pr). Schiffer.

Tarot for Tomorrow: An Advanced Handbook of Tarot Prediction. Emily Peach. (Illus.). 192p. (Orig.). 1988. pap. 12.95 (ISBN 0-85030-466-0, Pub. by Aquarian Pr England). Sterling.

Tarot for Your Self: A Workbook for Personal Transformation. Mary K. Greer. LC 84-21620. (Illus.). 253p. 1984. Repr. of 1984 ed. lib. bdg. 28.95x (ISBN 0-89370-677-9). Borgo Pr.

Tarot for Your Self: A Workbook for Personal Transformation. Mary K. Greer. (Illus.). 256p. (Orig.). 1984. pap. 12.95 (ISBN 0-87877-077-1). Newcastle Pub.

Tarot Handbook: Practical Applications of Ancient Visual Symbols. Angeles Arrien. LC 87-19461. (Illus.). 320p. (Orig.). 1987. pap. 25.00 (ISBN 0-916955-02-8). Arcus Pub.

Tarot II: The Handbook for the Journeyman. Eileen Connolly. 300p. (Orig.). 1988. pap. 12.95 (ISBN 0-87877-124-7). Newcastle Pub.

Tarot in Action: An Introduction to Simple & More Complex Tarot Spreads. Sasha Fenton. (Illus.). 240p. (Orig.). 1987. pap. 7.99 (ISBN 0-85030-525-X, Pub. by Aquarian Pr). Sterling.

Tarot: In Art, Mysticism & Divination. Sylvie Simon. 1988. 24.95 (ISBN 0-89281-216-8). Inner Tradit.

Tarot: Love Is in the Cards. Nancy F. Sussan. (Love Life Guides Ser.: No. 4). 128p. (Orig.). 1988. pap. 2.95 (ISBN 1-55802-044-6). Lynx Bks.

Tarot Made Easy. Nancy Garen. 1989. 11.95 (ISBN 0-671-67087-5, Fireside). S&S.

Tarot: Mirror of the Soul. Gerd Ziegler. (Illus.). 168p. (Orig.). 1988. pap. 8.95 (ISBN 0-87728-683-3). Weiser.

Tarot Mirrors: Reflections of Personal Meaning. Mary K. Greer. (Illus.). 206p. 1988. Repr. lib. bdg. 28.95x (ISBN 0-8095-6131-X). Borgo Pr.

Tarot Mirrors: Reflections of Personal Meaning. Mary K. Greer. 206p. (Orig.). 1988. pap. 12.95 (ISBN 0-87877-131-X). Newcastle Pub.

Tarot of Cornelius Agrippa. Frederick Morgan. LC 77-94782. (Illus.). 50p. (Orig.). 1978. pap. 10.00 (ISBN 0-915298-11-2). Hudson Rev.

Tarot of the Bohemians. Papus. pap. 7.00 (ISBN 0-87980-158-1). Wilshire.

Tarot of the Magicians. Oswald Wirth. LC 85-51592. 224p. (Orig.). 1985. pap. 12.50 (ISBN 0-87728-656-6). Weiser.

Tarot of the Witches Book. Stuart R. Kaplan. LC 73-80526. (Illus.). 96p. 1981. pap. 4.95 (ISBN 0-913866-40-7). US Games Syst.

Tarot Path to Self-Development. Micheline Stuart. LC 77-6016. (Illus.). 57p. 1977. pap. 5.95 (ISBN 0-87773-110-1). Shambhala Pubns.

Tarot Poems. Stephen Dunstan. 56p. 1980. pap. 5.95 (ISBN 0-906427-10-X, Pub. by Bloodaxe Bks). Dufour.

Tarot Revealed: A Modern Guide to Reading the Tarot Cards. Eden Gray. 1971. pap. 3.95 (ISBN 0-451-13700-0, AE1965, Sig). NAL.

TITLE INDEX

TASKS AHEAD: SPEECHES OF

Tarot Revelations. 2nd ed. Joseph Campbell & Richard Roberts. LC 81-86684. (Illus.). 304p. 1982. pap. 8.95 (ISBN 0-942380-00-2). Vernal Equinox.

Tarot: Spanish Language Edition of Tarot Classic. Stuart R. Kaplan. (Illus.). 256p. 1982. pap. 4.95 (ISBN 84-01-47101-X). US Games Syst.

Tarot: The Handbook for the Journeyman. Eileen Connolly. LC 87-31995. 193p. 1987. lib. bdg. 28.95x (ISBN 0-8095-6124-7). Borgo Pr.

Tarot: The Open Labyrinth. Rachel Pollack. pap. 8.99 (ISBN 0-85030-465-2, Pub. by Aquarian Pr England). Sterling.

Tarot: The Open Labyrinth. Rachel Pollack. (Illus.). 159p. 1988. Repr. lib. bdg. 22.95x (ISBN 0-8095-7060-2). Borgo Pr.

Tarot: The Origins, Meaning & Uses of the Cards. Alfred Douglas. 1973. pap. 6.95 (ISBN 0-14-003737-3). Penguin.

Tarot, the Royal Path to Wisdom. Joseph D. D'Agostino. 1976. pap. 3.50 (ISBN 0-87728-329-X). Weiser.

Tarot Therapy: A New Approach to Self Explorations. Jan Woudhuysen. (Illus.). 216p. 1988. pap. 8.95 (ISBN 0-87477-470-5). J P Tarcher.

Tarot Trumps: Cosmos in Miniature. Date not set. price not set (ISBN 0-85030-450-4, Pub. by Thorsons UK). Weiser.

Tarot Unveiled: The Method to Its Magic. Laura E. Clarson. Ed. by Phyllis B. Moore. (Illus.). vii, 117p. (Orig.). 1988. pap. 11.95 (ISBN 0-945766-11-4). Visionary Ents.

Tarot Workbook: Understanding & Using Tarot Symbolism. Emily Peach. (Illus.). 160p. (Orig.). 1985. pap. 14.95 spiral (ISBN 0-85030-390-7, Pub. by Aquarian Pr England). Sterling.

Tarpaulin Muster. facs. ed. John Masefield. LC 73-132120. (Short Story Index Reprint Ser). 1907. 14.00 (ISBN 0-8369-3677-9). Ayer Co Pubs.

Tarquin Star Globe: To Cut Out & Make Yourself. Gerald Jenkins & Magdalen Bear. (Illus.). 32p. (gr. 4 up). 1988. pap. 6.95 (ISBN 0-906212-60-X, Tarquin). Parkwest Pubns.

Tarquinia, Villanovans & Early Etruscans. Hugh Hencken. LC 67-24729. (American School of Prehistoric Research Bulletins: No. 23). 1968. pap. 50.00x (ISBN 0-87365-524-9). Peabody Harvard.

Tarr. Wyndham Lewis. 336p. 1983. pap. 5.95 (ISBN 0-14-006289-0). Penguin.

Tarrano the Conqueror. Ray Cummings. Ed. by Lester Del Ray. LC 75-400. (Library of Science Fiction). 1975. lib. bdg. 21.00 (ISBN 0-8240-1406-5). Garland Pub.

Tarrington Chase. Sylvia Thorpe. 1980. pap. 1.75 (ISBN 0-449-50055-1, Coventry). Fawcett.

Tarry Flynn. Patrick Kavanagh. 12.50 (ISBN 0-8159-6903-1). Devin.

Tarry Flynn. Patrick Kavanagh & P. J. O'Connor. Ed. by John Nemo. (Abbey Theatre Ser.). 1977. pap. 2.50x (ISBN 0-912262-40-0). Proscenium.

Tars, Turks & Tankers: The Role of the United States Navy in the Middle East, Eighteen Hundred to Nineteen Seventy-Nine. Thomas A. Bryson. LC 80-12281. 283p. 1980. lib. bdg. 22.50 (ISBN 0-8108-1306-8). Scarecrow.

Tarski Symposium: Proceedings of the Symposium in Pure Mathematics, University of California, Berkeley, June 1971. Symposium in Pure Mathematics Staff. Ed. by L. Henkin. LC 74-8666. (Vol. 25). 498p. 1979. pap. 49.00 (ISBN 0-8218-1425-7, PSPUM-25). Am Math.

Tarsos under Alexander. Edward T. Newell. (Alexander the Great Ser.). (Illus.). 68p. 1981. 25.00 (ISBN 0-916710-87-4). Obol Intl.

Tart, with a Silken Finish. Peter Barthelme. 192p. 1988. 13.95 (ISBN 0-312-01832-0). St Martin.

Tartan for Me! 3rd ed. Philip D. Smith, Jr. 101p. (Orig.). 1986. pap. 7.95 (ISBN 0-9616643-2-0). P D Smith.

Tartan Sell. Jonathan Gash. 240p. 1986. 14.95 (ISBN 0-312-78614-X, J Kahn). St Martin.

Tartan Sell. Jonathan Gash. 240p. 1987. pap. 3.50 (ISBN 0-14-009745-7). Penguin.

Tartan Tiger. Jean B. Smith. (Illus., Orig.). (gr. 7 up). 1986. pap. 10.00 (ISBN 0-935827-00-5). Tartan Tiger.

Tartan Weavers' Guide. Will Scarlett. 1985. 9.95 (ISBN 0-318-04591-5). Robin & Russ.

Tartans. Ed. by Wolfgang Hageney. (Illus.). 256p. (Eng., Fr., Span., Ital., Ger.). 1988. 59.95 (ISBN 88-7070-080-1, Pub. by Editions Belveder). R Silver.

Tartans: Their Art & History. Ann Sutton & Richard Carr. LC 84-6488. (Illus.). 192p. 1984. 19.95 (ISBN 0-668-06189-8, 6189-8). Arco.

Tartar Steppe. Dino Buzzati. 214p. 1986. pap. 7.50 (ISBN 0-85635-576-3, 50252-6). Carcanet.

Tartarin de Tarascon. Alphonse Daudet. (Coll. Prestige). 1965. 27.95 (ISBN 0-685-11580-1). French & Eur.

Tartarin de Tarascon. Alphonse Daudet. (Folio Ser.: No. 1824). pap. 6.95 (ISBN 0-685-34887-3). Schoenhof.

Tartarin de Tarascon. Alphonse Daudet. (Illus.). 159p. 1977. 8.95 (ISBN 0-686-55600-3). French & Eur.

Tartarin de Tarascon. Alphonse Daudet. write for info. French & Eur.

Tartarin of Tarascon. Alphonse Daudet. Bd. with Tartarin on the Alps. 1969. Repr. of 1910 ed. 12.95x (ISBN 0-460-00423-9, Evman). Biblio Dist.

Tartarin on the Alps see Tartarin of Tarascon.

Tartarin sur les Alpes. Alphonse Daudet. 8.95 (ISBN 0-686-55601-1). French & Eur.

Tartini: His Life & Times. Lev Ginsberg. Ed. by Herbert R. Axelrod. Tr. by I. Levin from Rus. (Illus.). 384p. 1981. 19.95 (ISBN 0-87666-590-3, Z-58). Paganiniana Pubns.

Tartuffe. Moliere, pseud. Tr. by Renee Waldinger from Fr. 1959. pap. text ed. 4.95 (ISBN 0-8120-0166-4). Barron.

Tartuffe. Moliere, pseud. (Fr. & Eng.). pap. 7.95 (ISBN 0-685-34238-7). French & Eur.

Tartuffe. Moliere, pseud. Tr. by Richard Wilbur. LC 63-17778. 164p. 1968. pap. 3.95 (ISBN 0-15-688180-2, Harv). HarBraceJ.

Tartuffe. Moliere, pseud. Ed. by Haskell M. Block. LC 58-13149. (Crofts Classics Ser.). 1988. pap. text ed. 4.50x (ISBN 0-88295-059-2). Harlan Davidson.

Tartuffe. Date not set. pap. price not set (ISBN 0-413-53410-3). Heinemann Ed.

Tartuffe see Misanthrope & Tartuffe.

Tartuffe & Other Plays: Ridiculous Precieuses, School for Husbands, School for Wives, Critique for the School for Wives, Versailles Impromptu, Don Juan. Moliere, pseud. Tr. by Donald M. Frame. 1967. pap. 3.50 (ISBN 0-451-52011-4, CE1566, Sig Classics). NAL.

Tartuffe Notes, Misanthrope Notes & Bourgeois Gentleman Notes. James L. Roberts & Denis M. Calandra. (Orig.). 1968. pap. 3.75 (ISBN 0-8220-1265-0). Cliffs.

Tarumba: The Selected Poems of Jaime Sabines. Jaime Sabines. Tr. by Philip Levine & Ernesto Trejo. 88p. 1979. pap. 6.00 (ISBN 0-918786-21-5). Twin Peaks Pr.

Taruru: Aboriginal Song Poetry from the Pilbara. Tr. by C. von Brandenstein & A. P. Thomas. 150p. 1975. 9.00x (ISBN 0-8248-0363-9). UH Pr.

Taryag: The Six Hundred Thirteen Mitzvos. Rabbi Alon I. Tolwin. 106p. 1983. pap. 5.95 (ISBN 0-87306-378-3). Feldheim.

Taryn Goes to the Dentist. Jill Krementz. LC 85-25510. (Illus.). 16p. (ps). 1986. 3.95 (ISBN 0-517-56168-9). Crown.

Tarzan. Illus. by Jon Townley & Bill Selby. (Pop-up Bks). (Illus.). 12p. (ps-3). 1984. 10.95 (ISBN 0-394-86594-4, Pub. by BYR). Random.

Tarzan & Shane Meet the Toad. limited ed. Gerald Locklin et al. 1975. 2.50 (ISBN 0-917554-01-9). Maelstrom.

Tarzan & the Ant Men, No. 10. Edgar Rice Burroughs. 1985. pap. 2.25 (ISBN 0-345-32393-9). Ballantine.

Tarzan & the Castaways. Edgar Rice Burroughs. 1980. pap. 2.50 (ISBN 0-345-35255-6). Ballantine.

Tarzan & the Castaways. Edgar Rice Burroughs. LC 64-25826. (Illus.). 1975. Repr. 14.95 (ISBN 0-940724-10-3). A E Ryter Bks.

Tarzan & the Forbidden City. Edgar Rice Burroughs. 1980. pap. 1.95 (ISBN 0-345-29106-9). Ballantine.

Tarzan & the Foreign Legion. Edgar Rice Burroughs. 1984. pap. 2.50 (ISBN 0-345-34750-1). Ballantine.

Tarzan & the Golden Lion, No. 9. Edgar Rice Burroughs. 1980. pap. 2.50 (ISBN 0-345-34237-2). Ballantine.

Tarzan & the Jewels of Opar, No. 5. Edgar Rice Burroughs. (Tarzan Ser.). 160p. 1984. pap. 2.50 (ISBN 0-345-32161-8). Ballantine.

Tarzan & the Leopard Man. Edgar Rice Burroughs. 1980. pap. 2.25 (ISBN 0-345-33828-6). Ballantine.

Tarzan & the Lion Men. Edgar Rice Burroughs. 1980. pap. 1.95 (ISBN 0-345-28988-9). Ballantine.

Tarzan & the Lost Empire, No. 12. Edgar Rice Burroughs. 1985. pap. 2.50 (ISBN 0-345-32957-0). Ballantine.

Tarzan & the Madman. Edgar Rice Burroughs. LC 64-15789. (Illus.). 1975. Repr. 14.95 (ISBN 0-940724-11-1). A E Ryter Bks.

Tarzan & the Tarzan Twins. Edgar Rice Burroughs. LC 63-10779. (Illus.). 14.95 (ISBN 0-940724-12-X). A E Ryter Bks.

Tarzan & the Well of Slaves. Douglas Niles. LC 84-91355. (Endless Quest Books Ser.). (Illus.). 160p. (gr. 4-7). 1985. pap. 2.25 (ISBN 0-394-73968-X). Random.

Tarzan & Tradition: Classical Myth in Popular Literature. Erling B. Holtsmark. LC 80-1023. (Contributions to the Study of Popular Culture: No. 1). (Illus.). xv, 196p. 1981. lib. bdg. 35.00 (ISBN 0-313-22530-3, HOT/). Greenwood.

Tarzan at Mars' Core. Edward Hirschman. (Tarzan Science-Fiction Ser.). 152p. 1977. pap. 39.95x. DeLethein Pr.

Tarzan at the Earth's Core. Edgar Rice Burroughs. 1985. pap. 2.25 (ISBN 0-345-32822-1). Ballantine.

Tarzan at the Earth's Core. Edgar Rice Burroughs. LC 62-21543. (Illus.). 14.95 (ISBN 0-940724-13-8). A E Ryter Bks.

Tarzan, Jane, & Jungle Lust. Edward Hirschman. (Tarzan Ser.). 226p. 1983. pap. 45.00x. DeLethein Pr.

Tarzan, King of the Apes. Joan D. Vinge. LC 83-42826. (Illus.). 128p. (gr. 5-9). 1983. lib. bdg. 4.99 (ISBN 0-394-96212-5). Random.

Tarzan Lord of the Jungle, No. 11. Edgar Rice Burroughs. 1984. pap. 2.50 (ISBN 0-345-32455-2). Ballantine.

Tarzan of Athens: A Biographical Study of G. Wilson Knight. John E. Van Domelen. 172p. 1987. 14.95 (ISBN 0-948265-31-0, Pub. by Redcliffe Pr Ltd). Intl Spec Bk.

Tarzan of the Apes. Edgar Rice Burroughs. 1976. Repr. of 1906 ed. lib. bdg. 17.95x (ISBN 0-89966-046-0). Buccaneer Bks.

Tarzan of the Apes. Harold Woods & Geraldine Woods. LC 81-19873. (Step-up Adventures Ser.: No. 4). (Illus.). 96p. (gr. 2-5). 1982. lib. bdg. 4.99 (ISBN 0-394-95089-5); pap. 2.95 (ISBN 0-394-85089-0). Random.

Tarzan of the Apes, No. 1. Edgar Rice Burroughs. (Tarzan Ser.). 256p. 1984. pap. 2.95 (ISBN 0-345-31977-X). Ballantine.

Tarzan of the Movies. Gabe Essoe. (Illus.). 224p. 1972. (Pub. by Citadel Pr); pap. 7.95 (ISBN 0-8065-0295-9). Lyle Stuart.

Tarzan the Invincible. Edgar Rice Burroughs. 1980. pap. 2.50 (ISBN 0-345-35163-0). Ballantine.

Tarzan the Magnificent. Edgar Rice Burroughs. 1980. pap. 1.95 (ISBN 0-345-28980-3). Ballantine.

Tarzan the Terrible, No. 8. Edgar Rice Burroughs. 1985. pap. 2.25 (ISBN 0-345-32392-0). Ballantine.

Tarzan the Triumphant. Edgar Rice Burroughs. 1979. pap. 2.50 (ISBN 0-345-35274-2). Ballantine.

Tarzan the Untamed, No. 7. Edgar Rice Burroughs. 1985. pap. 2.25 (ISBN 0-345-32391-2). Ballantine.

Taschenbuch Der Geholzverwendung see Pocket Guide to Choosing Woody Ornamentals.

Taschenbuch der Vornamen. 144p. (Ger.). 1978. pap. 2.95 (ISBN 0-686-40186-7). Langenscheidt.

Taschenlexikon Elektronik, Funktechnik. 320p. (Ger.). 1974. 24.95 (ISBN 3-87144-176-7, M-7630, Pub. by Verlag Harri Deutsch). French & Eur.

Taschenwoerterbuch der Botanischen Pflanzennamem. 2nd ed. F. Boerner. 435p. (Ger.). 1966. 45.00 (ISBN 3-489-56322-0, M-7631, Pub. by P. Parey). French & Eur.

Taschenwoerterbuch des Fremdenverkehrs. W. Friedrich. 187p. (Ger & Eng., Dictionary of Tourism). 1970. 24.95 (ISBN 3-19-006281-1, M-7632, Pub. by M. Hueber). French & Eur.

Taschenwoerterbuch Eisen und Stahl. H. Freeman. 600p. (Ger. & Eng., Dictionary of Iron and Steel). 1966. 24.95 (ISBN 3-19-006215-3, M-7634, Pub. by M. Hueber). French & Eur.

Taschenwoerterbuch Kraftfahrzeugtechnik. H. Freeman. 377p. (Ger. & Eng., Dictionary of Automotive Engineering). 1968. 49.95 (ISBN 3-19-006270-6, M-7635, Pub. by M. Hueber). French & Eur.

Taschenworterbuch: Deutsch-Englisch. Johannes Haase & Hedwig Hansel. 282p. (Ger. & Eng.). 1981. 35.00x (ISBN 0-317-59411-7, Pub. by Collets (UK)). State Mutual Bk.

Taschenworterbuch: Englisch-Deutsch. Jurgen Schroder. 452p. (Eng. & Ger.). 1981. 40.00x (ISBN 0-317-59413-3, Pub. by Collets (UK)). State Mutual Bk.

Tascosa: Historic Site in the Texas Panhandle. Pauline D. Robertson & R. L. Robertson. (Illus.). 72p. 1977. pap. 3.50 (ISBN 0-942376-01-3). Paramount TX.

Tasek Bera: The Ecology of a Freshwater Swamp. J. I. Furtado & S. Mori. 1982. text ed. 79.00 (ISBN 90-6193-100-2, Pub. by Junk Pubs Netherlands). Kluwer Academic.

Tasha: Her Middle Name Is Mischief. Louise Kantenwein. (Illus.). (gr. k-5). 1981. 5.00. Exposition-Phoenix.

Tasha Tudor Book of Fairy Tales. Tasha Tudor. (Illus.). (ps-2). 1961. 8.95 (ISBN 0-448-44200-0, G&D). Putnam Pub Group.

Tasha Tudor's Bedtime Book. Ed. by Kate Klimo. LC 77-853. (Illus.). 48p. (gr. 1-7). 1978. 6.95 (ISBN 0-448-47217-1, G&D); PLB 5.99 (ISBN 0-448-13038-6). Putnam Pub Group.

Tasha Tudor's Bedtime Stories. Illus. & selected by Tasha Tudor. (Illus.). 48p. (ps-5). 1988. 10.95 (ISBN 0-448-09328-6, G&D). Putnam Pub Group.

Tasha Tudor's Book of Fairy Tales. Illus. & selected by Tasha Tudor. (Illus.). 48p. (ps-5). 1988. 10.95 (ISBN 0-448-09329-4, G&D). Putnam Pub Group.

Tasha Tudor's Old-Fashioned Gifts, Presents & Favors for All Occasions. Tasha Tudor & Linda Allen. (Illus.). 1981. pap. 8.95 (ISBN 0-679-20984-0). McKay.

Tasha Tudor's Sampler: A Tale for Easter Pumpkin Moonshine the Dolls' Christmas. Tasha Tudor. (Illus.). (gr. k-3). 1977. 9.95 (ISBN 0-679-20412-1). McKay.

Tasha Tudor's Treasure, 3 vols. Tasha Tudor. (Tasha Tudor Ser.). 144p. (gr. k-4). 1981. 13.95 (ISBN 0-679-20983-2). McKay.

Tashlich. Avrohom C. Feuer. (Art Scroll Mesorah Ser.). 64p. 1979. 6.95 (ISBN 0-89906-158-3); pap. 4.95 (ISBN 0-89906-159-1). Mesorah Pubns.

Tasi Fe Tasi Eighty-Seven - Proc. R. Slansky. 1000p. 1988. 98.00 (ISBN 9971-50-438-3); pap. 48.00 (ISBN 9971-50-439-1). World Scientific Pub.

TASI Lectures in Elementary Particle Physics: Proceedings of the Theoretical Advanced Study Institute, Ann Arbor, Michigan, June 4-29, 1984. Ed. by D. Williams. 657p. 1986. 67.00 (ISBN 9971-50-270-4). World Scientific Pub.

Task Ahead. Indira Gandhi. 137p. 1984. 24.95. Asia Bk Corp.

Task Analysis. Center for Occupational Research & Development Staff. (Robotics-Automated Systems Technology Ser.). (Illus.). 206p. 1981. pap. text ed. 22.00 (ISBN 1-55502-175-1). Ctr Res & Dev.

Task Analysis. Ellsworth Community College Staff. Ed. by Michael Davis. (RATES Ser.: No. 2). (Illus.). 56p. (Orig.). 1984. pap. 3.00x (ISBN 0-916671-51-8). Material Dev.

Task Analysis for the Sheetfed Offset Press. Date not set. text ed. write for info. (ISBN 0-88362-115-0). Graphic Arts Tech Found.

Task Analysis in Instructional Design: Some Cases from Mathematics. Lauren B. Resnick. 49p. 1975. 1.00 (ISBN 0-318-14742-4, ED 115 486). Learn Res Dev.

Task & Organization. Ed. by Eric J. Miller. LC 75-12606. (Wiley Series on Individuals, Groups, & Organizations). pap. 103.30 (2030928). Bks Demand UMI.

Task-Centered Casework. William J. Reid & Laura Epstein. LC 72-4931. 350p. 1972. 23.50x (ISBN 0-231-03466-0). Columbia U Pr.

Task-Centered Management in Human Services. Bageshwari Parihar. (Illus.). 190p. 1984. 21.75 (ISBN 0-398-04920-3). C C Thomas.

Task-Centered Practice. William J. Reid & Laura Epstein. LC 76-28177. 1977. 24.00x (ISBN 0-231-04072-5). Columbia U Pr.

Task-Centered Practice with Families & Groups. Anne Fortune. (Springer Series on Social Work: Vol. 6). 272p. 1985. text ed. 23.95 (ISBN 0-8261-4460-8). Springer Pub.

Task-Centered System. William J. Reid. 1978. 25.50x (ISBN 0-231-03797-X). Columbia U Pr.

Task Design: An Integrative Approach. Ricky W. Griffin. (Scott, Foresman Series in Management & Organizations). 1982. pap. text ed. write for info. (ISBN 0-673-16544-2). Scott F.

Task Design & Employee Motivation. Ramon J. Aldag & Arthur P. Brief. 179p. 1979. pap. text ed. write for info. (ISBN 0-673-15146-8). Scott F.

Task for Diogenes: A Satire. Francis Neilson. 59.95 (ISBN 0-87700-017-4). Revisionist Pr.

Task Force on Concerns of Physically Disabled Women: Toward Intimacy-Family Planning & Sexuality Concerns of Physically Disabled Women. 63p. 1978. pap. text ed. 4.95 (ISBN 0-87705-337-5). Human Sci Pr.

Task Force on Concerns of Physically Disabled Women Within Reach: Providing Family Planning Services to Physically Disabled. 47p. 1978. pap. text ed. 4.95 (ISBN 0-87705-338-3). Human Sci Pr.

Task Force on Governance of New Towns: New Towns-Laboratories for Democracy Report. Twentieth Century Fund. (Twentieth Century Fund Ser.). pap. 14.00 (ISBN 0-527-02807-X). Kraus Repr.

Task Force Report: The Police. President's Commission on Law Enforcement & Administration of Justice. LC 73-154585. (Police in America Ser). 1971. Repr. of 1967 ed. 23.50 (ISBN 0-405-03383-4). Ayer Co Pubs.

Task Force: The Falklands War, 1982. Martin Middlebrook. 448p. 1988. pap. 7.95 (ISBN 0-14-008035-X). Penguin.

Task of Adam. John Leax. 1985. 7.95 (ISBN 0-310-45490-5, 9374). Zondervan.

Task of Gestalt Psychology. Wolfgang Kohler. LC 69-17397. (Illus.). 1969. 26.50x (ISBN 0-691-08614-1); pap. 8.50x (ISBN 0-691-02452-9). Princeton U Pr.

Task of Social Hygiene. Havelock Ellis. 414p. 1980. Repr. lib. bdg. 45.00 (ISBN 0-8495-1340-5). Arden Lib.

Task of Universities in a Changing World. Ed. by Stephen D. Kertesz. LC 71-148191. 1971. pap. 6.95x (ISBN 0-268-00486-2). U of Notre Dame Pr.

Task-Oriented Performance: The Top Management System. Craig M. Watson. 200p. Date not set. cancelled (ISBN 0-88730-096-0). Ballinger Pub.

Task-Oriented Team Development. Irwin M. Rubin et al. (Illus.). 1978. text ed. 80.00 3-ring binder (ISBN 0-07-054196-5). McGraw.

Task-Related Norms in a State Legislature: The Case of Oklahoma. Lelan E. McLemore. (Legislative Research Ser.: No. 5). 1973. pap. 2.00 (ISBN 0-686-18647-8). Univ OK Gov Res.

Task-Specific Problem Solving Architectures. B. Chandrasekaran & Tom Bylander. (Illus.). 100p. 1988. pap. text ed. 5.00x (ISBN 0-929280-10-5). Amer Artificial.

Task, Talk & Text in the Operating Room. Catherine J. Pettinari. Ed. by Roy O. Freedle. (Advances in Discourse Processes Ser.: Vol. 33). 208p. 1988. text ed. 32.50 (ISBN 0-89391-459-2). Ablex Pub.

Task Variables in Mathematical Problem Solving. Ed. by Gerald A. Goldin & Edwin C. McClintok. (Problem Solving Ser.). 495p. 1984. pap. text ed. 18.00 (ISBN 0-89859-727-7). L Erlbaum Assocs.

Task Worthy of Travail. Mercer H. Parks. LC 74-11835. 527p. 1975. 19.00x (ISBN 0-88415-784-9, Pub. by Pacesetter Pr). Gulf Pub.

Tasks Ahead: Speeches of Mrs. Ghandi. Indira Ghandi. 1984. text ed. 17.50x. Coronet Bks.

Tasks & Masks: Themes & Styles of African Literature. Lewis Nkosi. LC 82-107343. 212p. pap. 55.20 (2030350). Bks Demand UMI.
Tasks, Errors & Mental Models. Ed. by L. P. Goodstein et al. 300p. 1987. 77.00x (ISBN 0-85066-401-2). Taylor & Francis.
Tasks of Business Credit Personnel. Credit Research Foundation. 14p. 1985. 40.00 (ISBN 0-939050-40-4). Credit Res NYS.
Tasks of Contemporary Philosophy: Proceedings of the International Wittgenstein Symposium, 10th, 1985, Pt. I. Ed. by Werner Leinfellner & Franz M. Wuketits. 1987. pap. text ed. 89.00 (ISBN 90-277-9151-1, Pub. by Reidel Holland). Kluwer Academic.
Tasks of Emotional Development. Haskel Cohen & Geraldine R. Weil. LC 75-42572. 359p. 1975. 28.00 (ISBN 0-916598-02-0); pap. 12.00 manual (ISBN 0-317-00903-6); 49 pictures 25.00 (ISBN 0-317-00904-4). T E D Assocs.
Tasks of Residential Workers: A Study of Western Australia. Patricia Hansen. 1988. text ed. 37.00 (ISBN 0-566-05667-4, Pub. by Gower Pub England). Gower Pub Co.
Tasks of Tantalon: A PuzzleQuest Book. Steve Jackson. (Illus.). 36p. (ps-6). 1987. 12.95 (ISBN 0-19-279792-1). Oxford U Pr.
Tasks of the Youth Leagues. V. I. Lenin. 22p. 1976. pap. 0.75 (ISBN 0-8285-1943-9, Pub. by Progress Pubs USSR). Imported Pubns.
Tasks to Jobs: Developing a Modular System of Training for Hotel Occupations. 5th ed. (Hotel & Tourism Management Ser.: No. 3). 1985. text ed. 21.00. Intl Labour Office.
Taslim Na Pazir. Ashraf Pahlavi. 232p. (Orig., Persian, Modern.). 1984. pap. 9.50x (ISBN 0-318-18459-1). Iran Bks.
Tasmania: A Wildlife Journey. Joyce Powzyk. LC 86-7288. (Illus.). 32p. (gr. 3-6). 1987. 11.75 (ISBN 0-688-06459-0); PLB 11.88 (ISBN 0-688-06460-4). Lothrop.
Tass Is Authorized to Announce... Julian Semyonov. Tr. by Charles Buxton from Rus. LC 87-4903. 448p. 1987. 17.95 (ISBN 0-7145-4120-6). Riverrun NY.
Tass Is Authorized to Announce... Julian Semyonov. 384p. (Orig.). 1988. pap. 4.50 (ISBN 0-380-70569-9). Avon.
Tassajara Bread Book. Edward Brown. 16.75 (ISBN 0-8446-6266-6). Peter Smith.
Tassajara Bread Book. Edward E. Brown. LC 75-143877. (Illus.). 145p. (Orig.). 1977. pap. 5.95 (ISBN 0-87773-025-3, 73003-8). Shambhala Pubns.
Tassajara Bread Book. rev. & updated ed. Edward E. Brown. LC 85-2462. (Illus.). 146p. 1986. pap. 8.95 (ISBN 0-87773-343-0, 74196-X). Shambhala Pubns.
Tassajara Bread Book. rev. ed. Edward E. Brown. pap. 8.95 (ISBN 0-394-74196-X). Shambhala Pubns.
Tassajara Cooking. Edward E. Brown. LC 85-8185. (Illus.). 252p. 1986. pap. 9.95 (ISBN 0-87773-344-9, 74193-5). Shambhala Pubns.
Tassajara Cooking. Edward E. Brown. pap. 9.95 (ISBN 0-394-74193-5). Shambhala Pubns.
Tassajara Cooking: A Vegetarian Cooking Book. Edward E. Brown. LC 73-86144. (Illus.). 256p. 1974. pap. 8.95 (ISBN 0-87773-047-4, 70949-7). Shambhala Pubns.
Tassajara Recipe Book: Favorites of the Guest Season. Edward E. Brown. LC 84-23576. (Illus.). 160p. (Orig.). 1985. pap. 8.95 (ISBN 0-87773-308-2, 73520-X). Shambhala Pubns.
Tassajara Recipe Book: Favorites of the Guest Season. Edward E. Brown. pap. 8.95 (ISBN 0-394-73520-X). Shambhala Pubns.
Tasse Cassee see Breakfast Time, Ernest & Celestine.
Tasso: Aminta. Ed. by Sarah D'Alberti. 1967. pap. 4.95x (ISBN 0-913298-21-2). S F Vanni.
Tasso & His Times. William Boulting. LC 68-24953. (World History Ser., No. 48). 1969. Repr. of 1907 ed. lib. bdg. 54.95x (ISBN 0-8383-0915-1). Haskell.
Tasso & Milton: The Problem of the Christian Epic. Judith A. Kates. LC 82-71268. 184p. 1983. 24.50 (ISBN 0-8387-5046-X). Bucknell U Pr.
Tasso's Dialogues: A Selection, with the Discourse on the Art of the Dialogue. Torquato Tasso. Tr. by Carnes Lord & Dain A. Trafton. LC 81-12937. (Biblioteca Italiana: No. 4). 288p. 1983. 25.00x (ISBN 0-520-04464-9); pap. 10.95x (ISBN 0-520-04985-3). U of Cal Pr.
Taste. Roald Dahl. (Perfect Presents Story-Gifts Ser.). (Illus.). 44p. 1986. pap. 4.95 (ISBN 1-55628-004-1). Redpath Pr.
Taste. J. M. Parramon & J. J. Puig. (Child's Guide to the Five Senses Ser.). (Illus.). 32p. (ps). 1985. pap. 3.95 (ISBN 0-8120-3566-6); Span. ed. pap. 3.95 (ISBN 0-8120-3608-5). Barron.
Taste & Odor Control Experiences Handbook. American Water Works Association Staff. (AWWA Handbooks-General Ser.). (Illus.). 118p. 1976. pap. text ed. 8.00 (ISBN 0-89867-011-X). Am Water Wks Assn.
Taste & Odour in Waters & Aquatic Organisms. Ed. by P. E. Persson et al. (Water Science & Technology Ser.: No. 15). (Illus.). 340p. 1983. pap. 91.00 (ISBN 0-08-029713-7). Pergamon.
Taste & See. Penny King. 160p. (Orig.). 1986. cancelled (ISBN 0-912145-09-9). MMI Pr.
Taste & See. William O. Paulsell. LC 76-5634. 1976. pap. 2.50x (ISBN 0-8358-0347-3). Upper Room.
Taste & Smell. John Allen. LC 86-6658. (Let's Look Up Ser.). (Illus.). 32p. (gr. 3-6). 1986. PLB 9.96 (ISBN 0-382-09175-2). Silver Burdett Pr.
Taste & Smell. Ed Catherall. LC 82-50140. (Fun with Science Ser.). 12.68 (ISBN 0-382-06647-2). Silver.
Taste & Temperament: A Brief Study of Psychological Types in Their Relation to the Visual Arts. Joan Evans. LC 78-13857. (Illus.). 1980. Repr. of 1939 ed. 21.45 (ISBN 0-88355-790-8). Hyperion Conn.
Taste & the Antique: The Lure of Classical Sculpture 1500-1900. Francis Haskell & Nicholas Penny. LC 80-24951. (Illus.). 1982. 65.00x (ISBN 0-300-02641-2); pap. 16.95x (ISBN 0-300-02913-6, Y-438). Yale U Pr.
Taste & Tour of Dallas. Candy Coleman. (Illus.). 112p. (Orig.). 1986. spiral bdg. 7.95 (ISBN 0-943768-08-X). C Coleman.
Taste for Death. P. D. James. LC 86-45273. 480p. 1986. 18.95 (ISBN 0-394-55583-X). Knopf.
Taste for Death. P. D. James. 713p. 1987. lib. bdg. 20.95x (ISBN 0-8161-4265-3, Large Print Bks); pap. 12.95 (ISBN 0-8161-4266-1, Large Print Bks). G K Hall.
Taste for Death. P. D. James. 512p. 1987. pap. 4.95 (ISBN 0-446-32352-7). Warner Bks.
Taste for Death. Peter O'Donnell. LC 84-60553. (Modesty Blaise Ser.). 256p. 1984. pap. 3.95 (ISBN 0-89296-094-9). Mysterious Pr.
Taste for Health: Delicious Low-Fat Low Cholesterol Recipes. rev. ed. Lipid Research Clinic. LC 84-80259. (Illus.). 88p. 1984. pap. 4.95 (ISBN 0-941016-16-1). Penfield.
Taste for Quiet: And Other Disquieting Tales. Judith Gorog. (Illus.). 124p. (gr. 4 up). 1982. 9.95 (ISBN 0-399-20922-0, Philomel). Putnam Pub Group.
Taste from Back Home. Barbara Wortham. LC 82-62529. (Illus.). 330p. 1983. pap. 12.95 (ISBN 0-915216-79-5). Marathon Intl Pub Co.
Taste of a Rain Forest. Pranab Chatterjee. (Redbird Bk.). 1976. lib. bdg. 10.00 (ISBN 0-89253-121-5); flexible bdg. 4.80 (ISBN 0-89253-137-1). Ind-US Inc.
Taste of Adirondack Restaurants. Sue Schildge. (Illus.). 1986. spiral bdg. 12.95 (ISBN 0-317-39324-3, Dist. by North Country). Schildge Pub.
Taste of America. Jane Stern & Michael Stern. (Illus.). 304p. 1988. 16.95 (ISBN 0-8362-2125-7); pap. 9.95 (ISBN 0-8362-2126-5). Andrews & McMeel.
Taste of Appalachia: A Collection of Traditional Mountain Recipes Still in Use Today. Lyn Kellner. LC 87-61712. (Illus.). 64p. (Orig.). 1987. pap. 5.95 (ISBN 0-944010-00-8). Simmer Pot Pr.
Taste of Ashes. Howard Browne. (Modern Hard-Boiled Detective Ser.). 224p. 1988. pap. 7.95 (ISBN 0-939767-13-9). D McMillan.
Taste of Astrology: A Cookbook. Lucy Ash. LC 88-45209. (Illus.). 352p. 1988. 19.95 (ISBN 0-394-55667-4). Knopf.
Taste of Blackberries. Doris B. Smith. LC 72-7558. (Illus.). (gr. 2-5). 1973. 12.89 (ISBN 0-690-80511-X, Crowell Jr Bks); PLB 12.89 (ISBN 0-690-80512-8). HarpJ.
Taste of Blackberries. Doris B. Smith. (gr. 4-6). 1976. pap. 2.25 (ISBN 0-590-33784-X, Apple Paperbacks). Scholastic Inc.
Taste of Blackberries. Doris B. Smith. LC 88-45077. (Trophy Bk.). (Illus.). 96p. (gr. 2-5). 1988. pap. 2.95 (ISBN 0-06-440238-X, Trophy). HarpJ.
Taste of Blood. Todd Moore. (Dillinger Ser.: Vol. 5). (Illus.). 40p. (Orig.). 1988. pap. 5.95 (ISBN 0-940381-15-X). Kangaroo Ct Pub.
Taste of China. James Ballingall. (Illus.). 208p. 1984. 13.95 (ISBN 0-531-09768-4). Watts.
Taste of College: Summer Programs for High School Students on Campus 1988 Guide. Ed. by David A. Nowitz. xii, 205p. 1988. pap. 12.95 (ISBN 0-944714-00-5). College Bound.
Taste of Columbus II. Beth Chilcoat & David Chilcoat. (Illus.). 128p. (Orig.). 1982. pap. 8.95 (ISBN 0-9608710-1-2). Corban Prods.
Taste of Country Cooking. Edna Lewis. 1976. 16.45 (ISBN 0-394-48311-1); pap. 12.95 (ISBN 0-394-73215-4). Knopf.
Taste of Daylight. Crystal Thrasher. LC 84-2967. 228p. (gr. 7 up). 1984. 12.95 (ISBN 0-689-50313-X, M K McElderry). Macmillan.
Taste of Eden. Abra Taylor. (Superromances Ser.). 384p. 1982. pap. 2.50 (ISBN 0-373-70012-1, Pub. by Worldwide). Harlequin Bks.
Taste of France. Robert Freson. LC 83-6709. (Illus.). 288p. 1983. 45.00 (ISBN 0-941434-36-2). Stewart Tabori & Chang.
Taste of Freedom: The ICU in Rural South Africa 1924-1930. Helen Bradford. LC 87-10451. 448p. 1988. text ed. 40.00 (ISBN 0-300-03873-9). Yale U Pr.
Taste of Grace, Vol. 1. Gerald Twombly & Timothy Kennedy. (Illus.). 182p. 1982. pap. 7.50 (ISBN 0-910219-04-4). Little People.
Taste of Hate. Lisa Muro. LC 85-90224. 98p. 1985. 7.95 (ISBN 0-533-06722-7). Vantage.
Taste of Heaven: Adventures in Food & Faith. new ed. Lionel Blue & June Rose. (Orig.). 1978. pap. 4.50 (ISBN 0-87243-077-4). Templegate.
Taste of Honey. Shelagh Delaney. (Orig.). 1959. pap. 6.95 (ISBN 0-394-17480-1, E159, Ever). Grove.
Taste of Honey & Notes. Date not set. pap. price not set (ISBN 0-413-49250-8). Heinemann Ed.
Taste of India. Madhur Jaffrey. LC 85-72598. (Illus.). 256p. 1986. 29.95 (ISBN 0-689-11615-2). Atheneum.
Taste of India. Madhur Jaffrey. (Illus.). 256p. 1988. pap. 17.95 (ISBN 0-689-70726-6). Atheneum.
Taste of India: Delicious Vegetarian Recipes for Body, Mind & Spirit. Inderjit Kaur. LC 85-21262. 216p. 1985. Repr. lib. bdg. 24.95x (ISBN 0-89370-898-4). Borgo Pr.
Taste of Ireland: In Food & in Pictures. Theodora Fitzgibbon. (Illus.). 122p. 1970. pap. 14.95 (ISBN 0-330-02458-2). Bks Britain.
Taste of Italy. Antonio Carluccio. 1986. 24.95 (ISBN 0-316-12858-9). Little.
Taste of Japan: Food Fact & Fable; What the People Eat; Customs & Etiquette. Donald Richie. LC 84-48696. (Illus.). 116p. 1985. 18.95 (ISBN 0-87011-675-4). Kodansha.
Taste of Joy: Recovering the Lost Glow of Discipleship. Calvin Miller. LC 83-7839. Orig. Title: Illusive Thing Called Joy. 144p. 1983. pap. 4.95 (ISBN 0-87784-831-9). Inter-Varsity.
Taste of Kentucky. Janet A. Anderson. LC 86-9197. (Illus.). 112p. 1986. 12.00 (ISBN 0-8131-1580-9). U pr of Ky.
Taste of Lebanon. rev. ed. Mary Salloum. LC 88-596. (Illus.). 200p. 1988. Repr. of 1983 ed. text ed. 17.95 (ISBN 0-940793-08-3). Interlink Pub.
Taste of Liberty. Bulat Okudzhava. Tr. by L. Gruliow from Rus. Orig. Title: Bednyi Avrosimov. 250p. 1986. 29.50 (ISBN 0-88233-981-8); pap. 9.95 (ISBN 0-88233-982-6). Ardis Pubs.
Taste of Life. Julie Stafford. 1984. 9.95 (ISBN 0-89815-137-6). Ten Speed Pr.
Taste of Love. Elizabeth Glenn. (Harlequin American Romance Ser.). 256p. 1983. pap. 2.25 (ISBN 0-373-16036-4). Harlequin Bks.
Taste of Maryland. Ed. by C. Strohecker. (Illus.). 96p. 1984. pap. 10.00 (ISBN 0-911886-28-1). Walters Art.
Taste of Mexico. Patricia Quintana & William A. Orme, Jr. Ed. by Marilyn Wilkinson. LC 86-5817. (Illus.). 304p. 1986. 40.00 (ISBN 0-941434-89-3). Stewart Tabori & Chang.
Taste of Mexico: A Primer of Mexican Cooking. Esther G. Davis. Ed. by Elizabeth Rand. LC 76-43616. (Illus.). 1976. plastic comb bdg. 5.95 (ISBN 0-914488-11-2). Rand-Tofua.
Taste of Milwaukee. Friends of the Museum, Inc. Staff. Ed. by Mary Garity. (Illus.). 200p. 1983. 9.95 (ISBN 0-913965-00-6). Friends Mus Inc.
Taste of Morocco: A Culinary Journey with Recipes. Robert Carrier. (Illus.). 244p. 1987. 30.00 (ISBN 0-517-56559-5, 565595, C N Potter). Crown.
Taste of Murder. Joanna Cannan. (Mystery Classics Ser.). 192p. 1987. pap. 4.50 (ISBN 0-486-25296-5). Dover.
Taste of My Own Medicine: When the Doctor Is the Patient. Edward E. Rosenbaum. LC 87-43218. 192p. 1988. 16.95 (ISBN 0-394-56282-8). Random.
Taste of New Hampshire. American Cancer Society Staff. 192p. 1981. pap. 5.00 (ISBN 0-686-31484-0). Am Cancer NH.
Taste of New Wine. Keith Miller. 1982. pap. 10.95 (ISBN 0-8499-0151-0, 4111-3). Word Bks.
Taste of Olde York. Yorkville Historical Society Staff. Intro. by Anne T. Allison & Jo R. Owens. (Illus.). 255p. (Orig.). 1986. pap. 7.00 (ISBN 0-912081-03-1). Delmar Co.
Taste of Oregon. Ed. by Junior League of Eugene. (Illus.). 382p. 1980. Repr. of 1982 ed. spiral bound 12.95 (ISBN 0-9607976-0-2). Jr League Eugene.
Taste of Paradise. Margaret Mayo. (Lythway Ser.). 232p. 1988. lib. bdg. 18.50x (ISBN 0-7451-0687-0, Pub. by Chivers Pr UK). G K Hall.
Taste of Philippines. K. Mitchell. (Illus.). 40p. 1979. 5.95. Asia Bk Corp.
Taste of Provence. Leslie Forbes. 1987. 19.95 (ISBN 0-316-28877-2). Little.
Taste of Provence. Julian Moore. (Illus.). 1988. 22.95 (ISBN 0-8050-0660-5). H Holt & Co.
Taste of Quality: Favorite Recipes from the Merillat Kitchens of America. Ruth Seighman. 1980. write for info. (ISBN 0-937304-01-8). Rand Partners.
Taste of Rabbit Tracks: Expedition into a Frozen Wilderness. Mike Shields. 1978. 10.50 (ISBN 0-682-49082-2, Banner). Exposition-Phoenix.
Taste of Russia. Darra Goldstein. 240p. 1985. 24.95x (ISBN 0-7090-2053-8, Pub. by R Hale Ltd UK). State Mutual Bk.
Taste of Scotland: In Food & in Pictures. Theodora Fitzgibbon. (Illus.). 122p. 1971. pap. 14.95 (ISBN 0-330-02872-3). Bks Britain.
Taste of Shabbos, The Complete Cookbook. Compiled by Aish Hatorah Women's Organization Staff. 1987. 16.95 (ISBN 0-87306-426-7); deluxe ed. 18.95 (ISBN 0-317-57131-1). Feldheim.
Taste of Smalltalk. Ted Kaehler & Dave Patterson. 160p. (Orig.). 1986. pap. 15.50x (ISBN 0-393-95505-2). Norton.
Taste of South Carolina. The Palmetto Cabinet. (Illus.). 345p. 1985. Repr. of 1983 ed. spiral bd. 11.95 (ISBN 0-87844-064-X). Sandlapper Pub Co.
Taste of Steel. Robert W. March. 224p. pap. 2.50 (ISBN 0-8439-2022-X, Leisure Bks). Leisure NY.
Taste of Summer. Charles B. Dickson. 20p. 1988. 5.00 (ISBN 0-943825-03-2). Skyefield Pr.
Taste of Summer. Beverly Sutherland. (Illus.). 152p. 1987. 15.95 (ISBN 0-88162-233-8). Salem Hse Pubs.
Taste of Summer. Diane R. Worthington. (Illus.). 352p. 1988. 19.95 (ISBN 0-553-05273-X). Bantam.
Taste of Tahoe III. Sonnie Imes. (Orig.). 1985. pap. 8.95 (ISBN 0-934181-00-4, TX1-694-525). Tastes of Tahoe.
Taste of Texas. Jane Trahey. 1949. 14.95 (ISBN 0-394-40176-X). Random.
Taste of Texas Cookbook. Joy M. Angel. Ed. by Edwin M. Eakin. (Illus.). 160p. 1987. 10.95 (ISBN 0-89015-621-2); pap. text ed. 4.95 (ISBN 0-89015-623-9). Eakin Pr.
Taste of Thailand. Vatcharin Bhumichitr. (Illus.). 224p. 1988. 29.95 (ISBN 0-689-11994-1). Atheneum.
Taste of Thailand. David Scott & Kristiaan Inwood. (Illus.). 138p. 1987. pap. 15.95 (ISBN 0-7126-1291-2, Pub. by Century Hutchinson). David & Charles.
Taste of the Bayou: Creole & Cajun Recipes. Ann Diamond. 156p. 1984. 5.95 (ISBN 0-89896-082-7). Larksdale.
Taste of the Country: A Collection of Calvin Beale's Writings. Calvin Beale. Ed. by Peter A. Morrison. LC 87-43183. 320p. 1988. lib. bdg. 28.50x (ISBN 0-271-00631-5). Pa St U Pr.
Taste of the Holidays. Dot Gibson. 96p. 1988. pap. 3.95 (ISBN 0-941162-07-9). D Gibson.
Taste of the Knife. 3rd ed. Marnie Walsh. Ed. by Tom Trusky. LC 76-15877. (Modern & Contemporary Poets of the West). (Orig.). 1976. pap. 4.50 (ISBN 0-916272-03-6). Ahsahta Pr.
Taste of the Mountains Cooking School Cookbook. Steven Raichlen. 1986. 16.95 (ISBN 0-671-54429-2, Poseidon). PB.
Taste of the Pineapple: Essays on C.S. Lewis as Reader, Critic, & Imaginative Writer. Ed. by Bruce L. Edwards. 264p. 1988. text ed. 33.95 (ISBN 0-87972-407-2); pap. text ed. 16.95 (ISBN 0-87972-406-4). Bowling Green Univ.
Taste of the South. Terry Thompson. (Illus.). 208p. 1988. pap. 9.95. Price Stern.
Taste of the South. Ed. by Mrs. J. Baldwin Wakeland et al. (Illus.). 430p. 1984. 17.95 (ISBN 0-317-07201-3). Sym League.
Taste of Time. Ferol Egan. LC 76-48209. 1977. text ed. 9.95 (ISBN 0-07-019050-X). McGraw.
Taste of Treason. Laura Pender. (Intrigue Ser.: No. 62). Date not set. pap. 2.25 (ISBN 0-317-63668-5). Harlequin Bks.
Taste of Tuscany: Classic Recipes from the Heart of Italy. Compiled by & illus. by Leslie Forbes. (Illus.). 1985. 16.95 (ISBN 0-316-28876-4). Little.
Taste of War. Margaret Bourke-White. Ed. by Jonathan Silverman. (Century Travellers Ser.). (Illus.). 320p. 1986. pap. 13.95 (ISBN 0-7126-1030-8, Pub. by Century Hutchinson). David & Charles.
Taste of Wine: The Art & Science of Wine Appreciation. Emile Peynaud. Tr. by Michael Schuster from Fr. (Illus.). 258p. 1987. 27.50x (ISBN 0-356-14911-0, Pub. by MacD & Co). Trans-Atl Phila.
Taste of Yiddish. Lillian M Feinsilver. LC 70-88260. 480p. 1980. 14.95 (ISBN 0-498-02427-X); pap. 6.95 (ISBN 0-498-02515-2). A S Barnes.
Taste, Olfaction & the Central Nervous System: A Festschrift in Honor of Carl Pfaffmann. Ed. by Donald Pfaff. LC 84-43054. 346p. 1985. cloth 29.95 (ISBN 0-87470-039-6). Rockefeller.
Taste Organ in the Bullhead (Teleostei) K. Reutter. (Advances in Anatomy, Embryology & Cell Biology: Vol. 55, Pt. 1). (Illus.). 1978. pap. 32.00 (ISBN 0-387-08880-6). Springer-Verlag.
Taste the Difference. Muriel Wall. 50p. 1982. pap. text ed. 6.00 (ISBN 0-941472-03-5, 525). ICA Pubs.
Taste the Raindrops. Anna G. Hines. LC 82-9251. (Illus.). 24p. (gr. k-3). 1983. 10.25 (ISBN 0-688-01422-4); PLB 10.88 (ISBN 0-688-01423-2). Greenwillow.
Taste the Seasons. Ed. by Linda Brandt. LC 85-51259. (Illus.). 136p. 1985. 18.95x (ISBN 0-9615260-0-9). Woodside-Atherton.
Tastebuds. Jean Winslow et al. (Illus.). 260p. (Orig.). 1985. pap. 12.95 (ISBN 0-9614874-0-2). Winslow Wolverton.
Tastee Company Express Cookbook: Low Calorie, Low Sodium, Low Cholesterol Cooking. 3rd, rev. ed. Shellie H. Blumenfield. 176p. 1988. pap. 8.95 (ISBN 0-9620347-1-1). Tastee Co Inc.
Tastemakers. Russell Lynes. LC 82-25116. (Illus.). xiv, 362p. 1983. Repr. of 1955 ed. lib. bdg. 48.50x (ISBN 0-313-23843-X, LYTA). Greenwood.
Tastemakers: The Development of American Popular Taste. Russell Lynes. (Illus.). 384p. 1980. pap. 6.95 (ISBN 0-486-23993-4). Dover.
Tastemakers: The Shaping of American Popular Taste. Russell Lynes. 16.25 (ISBN 0-8446-5786-7). Peter Smith.
Tastes & Tales: Jewish Cookery for Young People with Tales from Around the World. Malvina W. Liebman. (Illus.). 200p. (Orig.). 1986. spiral bdg. 8.95 (ISBN 0-930029-02-X). Central Agency.
Tastes of Aspen. Jill Sheeley. (Illus.). 200p. 1988. perfect bound 12.95 (ISBN 0-9609108-1-6). Courtney Pr.

Tastes of California Wine Country Napa Sonoma. Sonnie Imes. (Orig.). 1986. pap. 9.95 (ISBN 0-934181-03-9, TX1-813-253). Tastes of Tahoe.

Tastes of California Wine Country: North Coast. Sonnie Ames. (Orig.). 1987. pap. 9.95 (ISBN 0-934181-04-7). Tastes of Tahoe.

Tastes of Liberty: A Celebration of Our Great Ethnic Cooking. Chateau Ste. Michelle Staff. LC 85-4675. (Illus.). 256p. 1987. 30.00 (ISBN 0-941434-75-3). Stewart Tabori & Chang.

Tastes of Marin. Sonnie Imes. (Orig.). 1984. pap. 7.95 (ISBN 0-934181-01-2, TX1-469-552). Tastes of Tahoe.

Tastes of Reno. Sonnie Imes. (Orig.). 1983. pap. 6.95 (ISBN 0-934181-02-0, TX1-337-599). Tastes of Tahoe.

Tastes of Tahoe. Sonnie Imes. (Orig.). 1979. pap. 6.95 (ISBN 0-934181-98-5, TX1-394-072). Tastes of Tahoe.

Tastes of Tahoe II. Sonnie Imes. (Orig.). 1983. pap. 7.95 (ISBN 0-934181-97-7, TX1-267-260). Tastes of Tahoe.

Tastes of the Adirondack Restaurants. Sue Schildge. Ed. by Vernon Taylor. (Illus.). 250p. 1985. spiral bound 12.95 (ISBN 0-9615595-1-9). Schildge Pub.

Tastes of the Pacific Northwest: Traditional & Innovative Recipes from America's Newest Regional Cuisine. Fred Brack & Tina Bell. LC 88-422. 1988. pap. 16.95 (ISBN 0-385-24387-1). Doubleday.

Tastes of Washington. Fred Brack & Tina Bell. 160p. 1986. pap. 16.95 (ISBN 0-937627-00-3). Evergreen Pub WA.

TASTEX: Tokai Advanced Safeguards Technology Exercise. (Technical Reports Ser.: No. 213). (Illus.). 227p. 1982. pap. 34.00 (ISBN 92-0-175082-X, IDC213, IAEA). UNIPUB.

Tasting. Richard L. Allington. LC 79-29662. (Begininng to Learn about Ser.). (Illus.). 32p. (ps-2). 1985. pap. 9.27 (ISBN 0-8172-2493-9). Raintree Pubs.

Tasting. Richard L. Allington & Kathleen Krull. LC 79-29662. (Beginning to Learn about Ser.). (Illus.). 32p. (ps-2). 1980. PLB 15.33 (ISBN 0-8172-1292-2). Raintree Pubs.

Tasting. Henry Pluckrose. (Think About Ser.). 32p. (gr. k-3). 1986. lib. bdg. 10.90 (ISBN 0-531-10173-8). Watts.

Tasting. Kathie B. Smith & Victoria Crenson. LC 87-5884. (Troll Question Bk.). (Illus.). 24p. (gr. k-3). 1987. PLB 8.59 (ISBN 0-8167-1014-7); pap. text ed. 1.95 (ISBN 0-8167-1015-5). Troll Assocs.

Tasting & Touring: The Northwest Winery Guide. Chuck Hill. (Illus.). 288p. (Orig.). 1987. pap. 11.95 (ISBN 0-9617699-1-2, 4526). Speed Graphics.

Tasting Good: The International Salt-Free Diet Cookbook. Merle Schell. LC 82-8276. 432p. 1982. pap. 7.95 (ISBN 0-452-25364-0, Z5364, Plume). NAL.

Tasting It. David MacArthur. (Illus.). 104p. (Orig.). 1984. pap. 9.95 (ISBN 0-9612674-0-2). Wine Country.

Tasting Party. Jane B. Moncure. LC 82-4411. (Five Senses Ser.). (Illus.). 32p. (ps-3). 1982. PLB 11.93 (ISBN 0-516-03253-4); pap. 2.95 (ISBN 0-516-43253-2). Childrens.

Tastings: The Best from Ketchup to Caviar. Jenifer H. Lang. (Illus.). 352p. 1986. pap. 14.95. Crown.

Tasty Adventures in Science. Sally Fox. (Illus.). (gr. 3-6). 1962. PLB 6.19 (ISBN 0-8313-0037-X). Lantern.

Tasty Economical Cookbook, Vol. 2. M. R. Bawa Muhaiyaddeen. (Illus.). 166p. 1983. spiral 9.95 (ISBN 0-914390-22-8). Fellowship Pr Pa.

Tasty Imitations: A Practical Guide to Meat Substitutes: (TVP Recipes) Barbara G. Salsbury. LC 74-78024. (Illus.). 76p. 1973. pap. 5.50 (ISBN 0-88290-025-0). Horizon Utah.

Tasty Side of New England. Beth Hillson. 1989. 11.95 (ISBN 0-8289-0664-5). Greene.

Tasty Timesaving Cooking. Better Homes & Gardens Editors. 240p. 1988. 24.95 (ISBN 0-696-01750-4). BH&G.

Tasty Treats. Zokeisha. (Puffies Ser.). (Illus.). 8p. (ps). 1982. 3.50 (ISBN 0-671-44847-1, Little Simon). S&S.

Tat. Schnurre. (EMC Easy Readers: Series C). pap. 4.95 (ISBN 0-88436-040-7, 45272). EMC.

TAT-8 Fiber Optics Undersea Cable. 1984. 75.00 (ISBN 0-317-11964-8). Info Gatekeepers.

Tata Casehaua y Otros Cuentos. Miguel Mendez. LC 77-89980. 1978. pap. 6.00 (ISBN 0-915808-28-5). Editorial Justa.

Tata Era. Pierre Dessureault. (Illus.). 100p. 1988. pap. 24.95 (ISBN 0-88884-554-5, Pub. by Natl Gallery Canada). U of Chicago Pr.

Tata Lecture Notes on Theta Functions. David Mumford. (Progress in Mathematics Ser.: Vol.43). 1983. Vol. 1, 220pp. text ed. 28.50x (ISBN 0-8176-3109-7); Vol. 2, 200pp. text ed. 24.95 (ISBN 0-8176-3110-0). Birkhauser.

Tatar Yoke. Charles J. Halperin. 231p. (Orig.). 1986. pap. 15.95 (ISBN 0-89357-161-X). Slavica.

Tatars of Crimea: Their Struggle for Survival. Ed. by Edward Allworth. (Central Asia Book Ser.). (Illus.). xii, 396p. 1988. lib. bdg. 52.50 (ISBN 0-8223-0758-8). Duke.

Tate. Dale Oldham. 1978. pap. 1.50 (ISBN 0-505-51306-4, Pub. by Tower Bks). Leisure NY.

Tate Gallery: An Illustrated Companion. (Illus.). 152p. 1985. pap. 14.95 (ISBN 0-946590-03-6). Salem Hse Pubs.

Tate Gallery Constable Collection. Leslie Parris. (Illus.). 208p. 24.95 (ISBN 0-905005-92-9). Salem Hse Pubs.

Tate Gallery: Illustrated Biennial Report 1982-84. (Illus.). 150p. pap. 12.95 (ISBN 0-946590-10-9). Salem Hse Pubs.

Tate Gallery: Illustrated Biennial Report 1984-86. Tate Gallery Staff. (Illus.). 164p. (Orig.). 1987. pap. 9.95 (ISBN 0-946590-48-6, Pub. by Tate Gall Pubns). Salem Hse Pubs.

Tate Gallery: Illustrated Catalogue of Acquisitions 1980-82. (Illus.). 304p. pap. 14.95 (ISBN 0-318-04087-5). Salem Hse Pubs.

Tate Gallery: Illustrated Catalogue of Aquisitions 1982-84. (Illus.). 456p. 1987. pap. 16.95 (ISBN 0-946590-49-4, Pub. by Tate Gall Pubns). Salem Hse Pubs.

Tatemae & Honne: Good Form & Real Intention in Japanese Business Culture. Mitsubishi Corporation Staff. 225p. 1988. 19.95 (ISBN 0-02-921591-9). Free Pr.

Tatiana: Five Passports in a Shifting Europe. Tatiana Metternich. (Century Classic Ser.). (Illus.). 360p. 1988. pap. 13.95 (ISBN 0-7126-1877-5, Pub. by Century Hutchinson). David & Charles.

Tatja Grimm's World. Vernor Vinge. 1987. pap. 3.50 (ISBN 0-671-65336-9). Baen Bks.

Tatl'ahwt'aenn Nenn' The Headwaters People's Country. Ed. by James Kari et al. LC 85-72828. (Illus.). x, 219p. 1986. pap. 10.00 (ISBN 1-55500-000-2). Alaska Native.

Tatler. Richard Steele. 1968. Repr. of 1953 ed. 12.95x (ISBN 0-460-00993-1, Evman). Biblio Dist.

Tatler, 3 vols. Richard Steele. Ed. by Donald F. Bond. 1987. Vol. 1: 632pgs. 120.00 (ISBN 0-19-812484-8); Vol. 2: 560pgs. 115.00 (ISBN 0-19-818533-2); Vol. 3: 584pgs. 115.00 (ISBN 0-19-818534-0). Oxford U Pr.

Tatler: The Making of a Literary Journal. Richmond P. Bond. (Illus.). 288p. 1971. text ed. 20.00x (ISBN 0-674-86830-7). Harvard U Pr.

Tatlin. Guy Davenport. LC 81-48197. (Poetry & Fiction Ser.). 272p. 1982. text ed. 8.95 (ISBN 0-8018-2800-7). Johns Hopkins.

Tatlin. Ed. by Larissa A. Zhadova & Eva Korner. LC 86-31605. (Illus.). 540p. 1988. 75.00 (ISBN 0-8478-0827-0). Rizzoli Intl.

Tatlong Dula. M. R. Avena. 198p. (Orig., Tagalog.). 1983. pap. 8.50x (ISBN 971-10-0062-8, Pub. by New Day Phillipines). Cellar.

Tatoo. Jeff Jaguer. (Illus.). 192p. 1988. 30.00 (ISBN 1-85265-100-8, Pub. by Milestone Pubns UK). Seven Hills Bks.

Tatoosh. Martha Hardy. LC 80-81574. (Illus.). 252p. 1980. pap. 6.95 (ISBN 0-89886-005-9). Mountaineers.

Tatsuo Takayama. Tatsuo Takayama. LC 87-81683. (Illus.). 182p. 1988. 150.00 (ISBN 0-87011-846-3). Kodansha.

Tatted Hearts. Jacquelyn Smyers. (Illus., Orig.). Date not set. pap. price not set (ISBN 0-9615130-1-2). Very Idea.

Tattered China Card. Robert L. Downen. (Journal of Social Political & Economic Studies Monograph: No. 11). 128p. pap. text ed. 20.00 (ISBN 0-930690-16-8). Coun Soc Econ.

Tattered Coat. 2nd ed. Nash Buckingham. (Nash Buckingham Collection Ser.). (Illus.). 210p. Date not set. Repr. of 1972 ed. 20.00 (ISBN 0-318-20035-X). Buckingham Mint.

Tattered Tallis. Carol K. Hubner. (Judaica Youth Series: Devorah Doresh Mysteries). (Illus.). 128p. (gr. 3-8). 1979. 6.95 (ISBN 0-910818-19-3). Judaica Pr.

Tatterhood & Other Tales. Ed. by Ethel J. Phelps. (Illus.). 192p. (Orig.). (gr. 1up). 1978. o. p. 11.95 (ISBN 0-912670-49-5); pap. 8.95 (ISBN 0-912670-50-9). Feminist Pr.

Tattie's River Journey. Shirley R. Murphy. LC 82-45508. (Illus.). 32p. (ps-3). 1983. 11.95 (ISBN 0-8037-8767-7, 01160-350); PLB 11.89 (ISBN 0-8037-8770-7). Dial Bks Young.

Tatting. Elgiva Nicholls. (Knitting, Crocheting, Tatting Ser.). 144p. 1984. pap. 3.95 (ISBN 0-486-24612-4). Dover.

Tatting: Designs from Victorian Lace Craft. Ed. by Jules Kliot & Kaethe Kliot. (Illus.). 1978. pap. text ed. 5.95 (ISBN 0-916896-13-7). Lacis Pubns.

Tatting Doilies & Edgings. Rita Weiss. (Illus.). 50p. (Orig.) 1980. pap. 2.50 (ISBN 0-486-24051-7). Dover.

Tatting Patterns. Julia E. Sanders. 1978. pap. 2.50 (ISBN 0-486-23554-8). Dover.

Tattletale Sparkie. Lucy A. Conley. (gr. 3 up). 1983. 7.50 (ISBN 0-318-01337-1). Rod & Staff.

Tattletales of Cupid. Paul L. Ford. LC 70-94720. (Short Story Index Reprint Ser.). 1898. 17.00 (ISBN 0-8369-3099-1). Ayer Co Pubs.

Tattoo. Jack Cady. 1978. pap. 6.25 (ISBN 0-931594-01-4). Circinatum Pr.

Tattoo. Stefan Richter. (Illus.). 1986. 60.00 (ISBN 0-318-19367-1, Pub. by Quartet). Salem Hse Pubs.

Tattoo. Earl Thompson. 1975. pap. 3.95 (ISBN 0-451-11157-5, AE1157, Sig). NAL.

Tattoo the Wicked Cross. Floyd Salas. LC 81-80895. 352p. 1982. 15.95 (ISBN 0-933256-26-4); pap. text ed. 8.95 (ISBN 0-933256-27-2). Second Chance.

Tattooed Countess. Carl Van Vechten. LC 77-78307. 296p. Repr. of 1924 ed. 23.50 (ISBN 0-404-15127-2). AMS Pr.

Tattooed Countess. Carl Van Vechten. LC 87-19237. (Bur Oak Bks.). 320p. 1987. pap. 9.95 (ISBN 0-87745-186-9). U of Iowa Pr.

Tattooed Desert. Richard Shelton. LC 76-134489. (Pitt Poetry Ser). pap. 15.60 (ISBN 0-8357-9761-9, 2015446). Bks Demand UMI.

Tattooed Heart of the Drunken Sailor. Ivan Arguelles. 26p. (Orig.). 1983. pap. 4.00 (ISBN 0-941160-07-6). Ghost Pony Pr.

Tattooed Innocent & the Raunchy Grandmother: An Adult Fairy Tale, Quite Grim. Robert F. Cline. LC 81-69430. 192p. (Orig.). 1983. pap. 7.95 (ISBN 0-9607082-0-0). Argos House.

Tattooed Lady in the Garden. Pattiann Rogers. (Poetry Ser.). viii, 120p. 1986. 20.00x (ISBN 0-8195-5145-7); pap. 12.95 (ISBN 0-8195-6149-5). Wesleyan U Pr.

Tattooed Potato & Other Clues. Ellen Raskin. (Illus.). 172p. (gr. 4-7). 1981. pap. 2.25 (ISBN 0-380-55558-1, 63875-4, Camelot). Avon.

Tattooed Potato & Other Clues. Ellen Raskin. (gr. 4-7). 1975. 14.95 (ISBN 0-525-40805-3, 01451-440). Dutton.

Tattooing in the Marquesas. Willowdean C. Handy. (BMB). Repr. of 1922 ed. 13.00 (ISBN 0-527-02104-0). Kraus Repr.

Tattooists. Albert L. Morse. Ed. by John A. Walsh. (Illus.). 1977. 59.95x (ISBN 0-918320-01-1). A L Morse.

Tattoos. Art Homer. Ed. by Craig Goad & William Trowbridge. 36p. (Orig.). 1986. pap. 3.00 (ISBN 0-9616467-0-5). GreenTower Pr.

Tattoos: Poems. Art Homer et al. Ed. by Craig Goad. 32p. pap. 3.50 (ISBN 0-317-61674-9). GreenTower Pr.

Tattva-Sangraha of Santaraksita with Commentary of Kamalasila. Shantaraksita. Tr. by Ganganath Jha. 1593p. 1986. Repr. of 1937 ed. Set. 85.00 (ISBN 81-208-0058-3, Pub. by Motilal Banarsidass India); Vol. 1. 50.00 (ISBN 81-208-0059-1); Vol. 2. 50.00 (ISBN 81-208-0060-5). Orient Bk Dist.

Tattvarthadhigama Sutra (A Treatise on the Essential Principles of Jainism) Umasvati. Ed. & intro. by J. L. Jaini. LC 73-3836. (Sacred Books of the Jainas: No. 2). Repr. of 1920 ed. 27.50 (ISBN 0-404-57702-4). AMS Pr.

Tatum's Favorite Shape. Dorothy Thole. (Illus.). 32p. (gr. k-3). pap. 2.50 (ISBN 0-590-11905-2). Scholastic Inc.

Taube, Dove of War. John A. Devries. LC 77-91439. (World War I Aircraft Ser.). (Illus.). 84p. 1978. pap. 7.95 (ISBN 0-911852-82-4). Hist Aviation.

Tauberian Reminder Theorems. T. H. Ganelius. (Lecture Notes in Mathematics: Vol. 232). 75p. 1971. pap. 13.00 (ISBN 0-387-05657-2). Springer-Verlag.

Tauberian Theorems for Generalized Functions. V. S. Vladimirov et al. 1987. lib. bdg. 89.00 (ISBN 90-277-2383-4, Pub. by Reidel Holland). Kluwer Academic.

Tauberian Theory & Its Applications. Ed. by A. G. Postnikov. LC 80-23821. (Proceedings of the Steklov Institute of Mathematics: No. 144). 1980. 38.00 (ISBN 0-8218-3048-1). Am Math.

Tauferaktenband Osterreich III. Grete Mecenseffy. (TAK Ser.: Vol. XIV). 795p. (Ger.). 1982. 105.00 (ISBN 0-8361-1265-2). Herald Pr.

Taufertum Und Reformation Im Gesprach. John H. Yoder. 221p. 1969. 29.00x (ISBN 0-8361-1164-8). Herald Pr.

Taunton & Mason: Cotton Machinery & Locomotive Manufacture in Taunton, Massachusetts, 1811-1861. John W. Lozier. Ed. by Stuart Bruchey. (American Business History Ser.). 559p. 1986. lib. bdg. 65.00 (ISBN 0-8240-8359-8). Garland Pub.

Taureau Blanc. Voltaire. Ed. by R. Pomeau. 171p. 1957. 8.95 (ISBN 0-686-55760-3). French & Eur.

Taures: Astro-Numerology. Michael J. Kurban. (Illus.). 50p. (Orig.). 1986. pap. 8.00 (ISBN 0-938863-10-X). Libra Press Chi.

Taurine & Neurological Disorders. Ed. by Andre Barbeau & Ryan Huxtable. LC 77-85076. 482p. 1978. 81.00 (ISBN 0-89004-202-0). Raven.

Taurine: Biological Actions & Clinical Perspectives. Simo S. Oja et al. LC 85-4303. (Progress in Clinical & Biological Research Ser.: Vol. 179). 500p. 1985. 68.00 (ISBN 0-8451-5029-4). A R Liss.

Taurine In Nutrition & Neurology. Ed. by Ryan J. Huxtable & Herminia Pasantes-Morales. LC 81-15699. (Advances in Experimental Medicine & Biology: Vol. 139). 564p. 1981. 89.50x (ISBN 0-306-40839-2, Plenum Pr). Plenum Pub.

Tauromaquia & the Bulls of Bordeaux. Francisco Goya. LC 69-15666. (Illus.). 1969. pap. 7.95 (ISBN 0-486-22342-6). Dover.

Taurus. (Day by Day Horoscopes 1988 Ser.). 192p. 1987. pap. 2.95 (ISBN 0-425-10119-3). Berkley Pub.

Taurus. (Super Horoscopes 1986 Ser.). 256p. 1985. pap. 3.95 (ISBN 0-441-79331-2). Ace Bks.

Taurus. (Total Horoscopes 1986 Ser.). 256p. 1985. pap. 2.95 (ISBN 0-441-82031-X) (ISBN 0-317-31695-8). Ace Bks.

Taurus. (Astroanalysis Ser.). 360p. 1985. pap. 8.95. Ace Bks.

Taurus. (Your 1986 Caprice Horoscopes Ser.). 96p. 1985. pap. 2.25 (ISBN 0-441-09473-2). Ace Bks.

Taurus. (Super Horoscope 1987 Ser.). 1987. pap. 3.95 (ISBN 0-441-79313-4, Pub. by Charter Bks). Ace Bks.

Taurus. (Astroanalysis Ser.). 1987. pap. 8.95 (ISBN 0-317-63301-5, Charter Pub). Berkley Pub.

Taurus. pap. 3.50 (ISBN 0-515-09122-7). Jove Pubns.

Taurus. 1987. pap. 3.95 (ISBN 0-441-79359-2, Pub. by Charter Bks). Ace Bks.

Taurus. 1988. pap. 8.95 (ISBN 0-425-11207-1). Berkley Pub.

Taurus see Astroanalysis.

Taurus Method. 2nd ed. Michael Chisholm. 1985. 75.00 (ISBN 0-930233-08-5). Windsor.

Taurus: Through the Numbers. Paul Rice & Valeta Rice. 40p. 1983. pap. 2.50 (ISBN 0-87728-566-7). Weiser.

Taurus Trouble. (Zodiac Club Ser.). 1984. pap. 1.95 (ISBN 0-399-21109-8). Putnam Pub Group.

Taurus 1987. Sydney Omarr. 1987. pap. 2.95 (ISBN 0-451-14403-1, Pub. by Sig). NAL.

Tausend Redensarten Deutsch. Heinz Griesbach & Dora Schulz. 248p. 10.95 (ISBN 3-468-43112-0). Langenscheidt.

Tausug: Violence & Law in a Philippine Moslem Society. Thomas M. Kiefer. (Illus.). 150p. 1986. pap. text ed. 7.95x (ISBN 0-88133-242-9). Waveland Pr.

Tautomerism of Heterocycles: Supplement I to Advances in Heterocyclic Chemistry. J. Elguero et al. (Serial Publication). 1976. 124.50 (ISBN 0-12-020651-X). Acad Pr.

Taux de Croissance du Revenu National Sovietique. J. M. Collette. (Economies et Societes Series G: No. 12). 1961. pap. 19.00 (ISBN 0-8115-0703-3). Kraus Repr.

Tavern at the Ferry. Edwin Tunis. LC 73-4488. (Illus.). 128p. (gr. 5 up). 1973. 19.70 (ISBN 0-690-00099-5, Crowell Jr Bks). HarpJ.

Tavern Cartoons. 2nd ed. William Armstrong. (Armstrong Cartoon Ser.). (Illus.). 48p. (Orig.). (ps up). 1972. pap. 1.00 (ISBN 0-913452-09-2). Jesuit Bks.

Tavern Days in the Hawkeye State. Inez E. Kirkpatrick. (Illus.). 370p. (Orig.). (gr. 7 up). Date not set. pap. cancelled (ISBN 0-916170-15-2). J B Pub.

Tavern in a Box. Dale Zaklad. (Illus.). 118p. 1986. teaching module 250.00 (ISBN 0-9616415-3-3). Fraunces Tavern.

Tavern Knight. Rafael Sabatini. 1977. pap. 1.75 (ISBN 0-505-51128-2, Pub. by Tower Bks). Leisure NY.

Taverners' Place. Joanna Trollope. 560p. 1987. 19.95 (ISBN 0-312-00068-5). St Martin.

Tavistock Abbey. H. P. Finberg. LC 69-10850. (Illus.). 1969. Repr. of 1951 ed. 37.50x (ISBN 0-678-05597-1). Kelley.

Tavola Italiana: A Regional Guide to the Classic Cuisines of Italy with over 235 Recipes & Recommendations for the Traditional Wines to Go with Them. Tom Maresca & Diane Darrow. (Illus.). 352p. 1988. 22.95 (ISBN 0-688-06629-1). Morrow.

Tawache & the Legend of Sacred Mountain. William James. Ed. by Sharon Tittle. LC 84-90509. (Journey to Ishta Ser.: Bk. 1). (Illus.). (ps-3). 1984. 6.95 (ISBN 0-931903-00-9). James Pub Inc.

Tawheed, Its Relevance for Thought & Life. I. Al-Faruqi. 1988. 15.95. Kazi Pubns.

Tawhid: Its Implications for Thought & Life. Ismail Raji al Faruqi. (Muslim Training Manual Ser.: Vol. 2). 367p. (Orig.). Date not set. price not set. IIIT VA.

Tawi Tales: Folktales from Jammu. Noriko Mayeda & W. Norman Brown. (American Oriental Ser.: Vol. 57). 1974. pap. 10.00x (ISBN 0-940490-57-9). Am Orient Soc.

Tawney, Galbraith & Adam Smith. David Reisman. 1982. 27.50x (ISBN 0-312-78639-5). St Martin.

Tawny Gold Man. Amii Lorin. (Candlelight Ecstasy Ser.: No. 1). 1980. pap. 1.50 (ISBN 0-440-18978-0). Dell.

Tawny Rose. Katherine Kent. LC 83-40426. 192p. 1984. 12.95 (ISBN 0-8027-0775-0). Walker & Co.

Tax Accounting, 2 vols. Durkwood L. Alkire. 1982. looseleaf 155.00 (703); Update 1985 45.00; 1986 59.00. Bender.

Tax Accounting Methods: Characteristics, Adoptions, Changes. Davenport. 312p. 1988. 45.00 (5260). Commerce.

Tax Action Coordinator, 9 vols. ann. subscr. 507.00, single payment; quarterly payment 135.00; 2 year subscr. 447.00, annually; quarterly payment 127.50. Res Inst Am.

Tax Advantaged Investment for Educators see Educators Financial Kit.

Tax-Advantaged Investments. Ed. by Personal Finance Magazine Staff. (Sylvia Porter Ser.: No. 6). 1987. 7.95 (ISBN 0-553-45086-7). Bantam.

Tax-Advantaged Investments. David F. Windish. Date not set. write for info. S&S.

Tax-Advantaged Investments. 3rd ed. David F. Windish. (Illus.). 256p. 1987. 37.50 (ISBN 0-13-884693-6). NY Inst Finance.

Tax Analysis & Forms: 1977, 6 vols. Jere McGaffey. LC 77-12085. 350.00 (ISBN 0-317-11955-9). Callaghan.

Tax & Business Organization Aspects of Small Business. 4th ed. Jonathan Sobeloff. 234p. 1974. Incl. 1977 suppl. pap. 12.00 (ISBN 0-317-30802-5, B298); Suppl. only. pap. 2.00 (ISBN 0-317-30803-3, B299). Am Law Inst.
Tax & Contractual Arrangements for the Exploitation of Natural Resources. Arvind Virmani. (Working Paper: No. 752). 156p. 1985. 8.00 (ISBN 0-8213-0599-9, WP 0752). World Bank.
Tax & Estate Planning for Divorce & Separation. Waldo G. Rothenberg. LC 85-80745. 1985. 79.50 (ISBN 0-318-19873-8); Suppl. 1987. 24.00. Lawyers Co-Op.
Tax & Estate Planning with Closely Held Corporations, Vol. I. Waldo G. Rothenberg. 1981. 89.50 (ISBN 0-686-31141-8); Suppl. 1987. 25.00; Suppl. 1988. 27.00. Lawyers Co Op.
Tax & Expenditure Limitation: A Policy Perspective. W. Ward Wright. 48p. (Orig.). 1981. pap. 5.00 (ISBN 0-87292-019-4). Coun State Govts.
Tax & Financial Aspects of Divorce. Frank E. Sander. Date not set. 15.00 (ISBN 0-318-23982-5, 5327); audiotapes 50.00 (ISBN 0-318-23983-3); videotape 325.00 (ISBN 0-318-23984-1). Natl Prac Inst.
Tax & Financial Planning for the Family. Burns. (Tax & Business Guides for Professionals Ser.). 1988. write for info. (ISBN 0-471-81564-0). Wiley.
Tax & Investment Policies for Hard Minerals: Public & Multinational Enterprise in Indonesia. Ed. by S. Malcolm Gillis. Beals. LC 70-23352. 320p. 1980. prof ref 35.00x (ISBN 0-88410-488-5). Ballinger Pub.
Tax Angles in Patents, Trademarks, & Copyrights. 88p. 1978. pap. 3.00 (ISBN 0-685-39499-9, 5329). Commerce.
Tax Anxiety Xperience, Vol. 1: The Tax Planning Guide, 1985. Eva Rosenberg. (Tax Anxiety Xperience Ser.). 240p. 1985. pap. 9.95 (ISBN 0-932669-01-8); Videotape (VHS) & Book Package 65.00 (ISBN 0-932669-02-6). Ind Res Servs Irvine.
Tax Anxiety Xperience, Vol. 2: Tax Reduction for Entrepreneurs & Home-Based Businesses, 1985. Eva Rosenberg. (Tax Anxiety Xperience Ser.). 175p. (Orig.). 1988. pap. 16.95 (ISBN 0-932669-03-4). Ind Res Servs Irvine.
Tax Aspects of Acquisition & Mergers. 2nd ed. Philip Cooke & Jan M. Van der Beek. (Orig.). 1983. pap. text ed. 31.00 (ISBN 90-654-4151-4, Pub. by Kluwer Law & Taxation). Kluwer Academic.
Tax Aspects of Acquisitions & Mergers. Ed. by Philip Cooke & Jan M. Van der Beek. 148p. 1982. pap. 35.00 cancelled (ISBN 90-200-0629-0, Pub. by Kluwer Law Netherlands). Kluwer Academic.
Tax Aspects of Buying & Selling Corporate Businesses. J. Clifton Fleming, Jr. LC 83-20291. (Tax & Estate Planning Ser.). 612p. 1984. text ed. 90.00 (ISBN 0-07-021298-8). Shepards-McGraw.
Tax Aspects of California Partnerships. LC 83-72279. 250p. 1983. 65.00 (ISBN 0-88124-119-9). Cal Cont Ed Bar.
Tax Aspects of California Partnerships. 251p. 1987. 65.00 (TX-37740); November '85 supp. 17.00; May '87 supp. 19.00. Cal Cont Ed Bar.
Tax Aspects of Charitable Giving. 48p. pap. 3.00 (ISBN 0-317-04223-8, 5497). Commerce.
Tax Aspects of Divorce & Separation. Robert S. Taft. LC 83-26825. 1984. looseleaf 70.00 (ISBN 0-318-01110-7). NY Law Pub.
Tax Aspects of Four Hundred & One (K) Plans: Information for Employers & Employees. 48p. 1983. pap. 2.00 (ISBN 0-317-04224-6, 4895). Commerce.
Tax Aspects of High Technology Operations. Deloitte, Haskins & Sells Staff & High Technology Industry Group Staff. LC 85-3306. (Tax & Business Guides for Professionals Ser.). 403p. 1985. text ed. 65.00x (ISBN 0-471-88874-5, Pub. by Ronald Pr). Wiley.
Tax Aspects of Marital Dissolution. Harold G. Wren et al. 1986. 85.00. Callaghan.
Tax Aspects of Marital Dissolutions: A Basic Guide for General Practioners. 204p. 1987. pap. 35.00 (TX-33350); September '83 supp. pap. 15.00; June '87 supp. pap. 25.00. Cal Cont Ed Bar.
Tax Aspects of Marital Dissolutions: A Basic Guide for General Practitioners. John R. Walker & California Continuing Education of the Bar. LC 79-51367. x, 204p. 1979. 35.00 (ISBN 0-88124-063-X). Cal Cont Ed Bar.
Tax Aspects of Municipal Finance. Practising Law Institute. 298p. 1985. pap. 45.00 (ISBN 0-317-27690-5, #N4-4434). PLI.
Tax Aspects of Property & Casualty Risk Management. Kakacek & Adams. 128p. (Orig.). 1987. pap. 15.00 (5268). Commerce.
Tax Aspects of Real Estate Investments: A Practical Guide for Structuring Real Estate Transactions. Peter M. Fass et al. (Taxation Ser.). 1987. looseleaf 95.00 (ISBN 0-87632-576-2, RC). Clark Boardman.
Tax Aspects of Real Estate Transactions. Massachusetts Continuing Legal Education Inc. LC 84-61750. 258p. 1985. 35.00. Mass CLE.
Tax Aspects of Vacation Homes. Price Waterhouse. 14p. 1987. write for info. Am Inst CPA.
Tax, Attacks, & Counterattacks: Your Indispensable Guide to Long-Range Tax Strategy. Richard A. Westin & Alan H. Neff. LC 83-4353. 153p. 1983. 8.95 (ISBN 0-15-188082-4). HarBraceJ.
Tax Audit Answer Book. Panel Publishers, Inc. 1985. 45.00 (ISBN 0-916592-56-1). Panel Pubs.
Tax Audit Guidelines for Internal Revenue Examiners: As Issued by the Internal Revenue Service, April 23, 1985. United States Internal Revenue Service. LC 85-236068. (Illus.). 1985. 8.00 (ISBN 0-13-884768-1). P-H.
Tax Auditor. Jack Rudman. (Career Examination Ser.: C-2313). (Cloth bdg. avail. on request). 1988. pap. 14.00 (ISBN 0-8373-2313-4). Natl Learning.
Tax Aversion: The Economic Legal & Moral Inter-Relationships Between Avoidance & Evasion. A. Seldon et al. (Institute of Economic Affairs Readings Ser.: No. 22). 1979. technical 9.25 (ISBN 0-255-36126-2). Transatl Arts.
Tax Avoidance-Tax Evasion, Vol. LXVIIIa. 1983. write for info. Kluwer Academic.
Tax Avoidance thru Interest-Free Loans see Tax Savings thru Interest-Free Loans.
Tax Benefit Position of a Typical Worker in Member Countries 1981. 55p. (Orig.). 1983. pap. 7.00x (ISBN 92-64-02358-5). OECD.
Tax Benefit Position of Production Workers 1979-1983. OECD. 234p. (Orig.). 1984. pap. 28.00x (ISBN 92-64-02663-0). OECD.
Tax-Benefit Position of Production Workers, 1979-1984. OECD. 248p. (Orig.). 1986. pap. 28.00x (ISBN 92-64-02792-0). OECD.
Tax-Benefit Position of Production Workers, 1983-1986. OECD. 253p. (Orig., Eng. & Fr.). 1987. pap. 26.00x (ISBN 92-64-02968-0). OECD.
Tax Benefit Position of Production Workers 1981-1985. OECD Staff. 256p. (Orig., Eng. & Fr.). 1986. pap. 27.00x (ISBN 92-64-02839-0). OECD.
Tax Benefits for Homeowners. 32p. 1985. pap. 2.00 (ISBN 0-317-04226-2, 4722). Commerce.
Tax Benefits for Homeowners. 32p. (Orig.). 1987. pap. 3.00 (5275). Commerce.
Tax Breaks: An Introduction to Tax Expenditures. National League of Cities Staff. LC 85-196052. (Policy Working Paper of National League of Cities). iii, 70p. Date not set. price not set (ISBN 0-933729-04-9). Natl League Cities.
Tax Burden on Indian Agriculture. Ved P. Gandhi. LC 66-15721. (Illus.). 260p. 1966. pap. 5.00x (ISBN 0-915506-06-8). Harvard Law Intl Tax.
Tax Burdens in American Agriculture: An Intersectoral Comparison. Charles A. Sisson. 1982. 18.50x (ISBN 0-8138-1680-7). Iowa St U Pr.
Tax Cashier. Jack Rudman. (Career Examination Ser.: C-2573). (Cloth bdg. avail. on request). pap. 12.00 (ISBN 0-8373-2573-0). Natl Learning.
Tax Cheating: Hide & Seek with the IRS. Mark Siegel & Barry Wolfson. 162p. (Orig.). 1988. pap. 7.95 (ISBN 0-945165-01-3). Blue Sky Pr Inc.
Tax Collector. Jack Rudman. (Career Examination Ser.: C-801). (Cloth bdg. avail. on request). pap. 12.00 (ISBN 0-8373-0801-1). Natl Learning.
Tax Companion, 1986. LC 80-65410. 656p. 1986. pap. 12.95 (ISBN 0-88462-643-1, 5606-01, Longman Fin Serv Pub). Longman Finan.
Tax Companion, 1987. 1987. write for info (ISBN 0-88462-686-5, 5606-01, Real Estate Ed). Longman Finan.
Tax Companion, 1988. Longman Financial Services Institute Staff. 1988. pap. 11.95 (ISBN 0-88462-743-8). Longman Finan.
Tax Compliance Agent. Jack Rudman. (Career Examination Ser.: C-2122). (Cloth bdg. avail. on request). 1988. pap. 14.00 (ISBN 0-8373-2122-0). Natl Learning.
Tax Compliance Agent (Spanish Speaking) Jack Rudman. (Career Examination Ser.: C-2123). (Cloth bdg. avail. on request). 1988. pap. 16.00 (ISBN 0-8373-2123-9). Natl Learning.
Tax Compliance Representative. Jack Rudman. (Career Examination Ser.: C-2997). (Cloth bdg. avail. on request). 1988. pap. 14.00 (ISBN 0-8373-2997-3). Natl Learning.
Tax Concepts for Decision Making. William A. Raabe & James E. Parker. (Illus.). 766p. 1985. text ed. 45.50 (ISBN 0-314-85289-1). West Pub.
Tax Consequences of Agriculture Liquidations & Bankruptcies. Hamline University, Advanced Legal Education Staff. 192p. 1985. 47.70. Hamline Law.
Tax Consequences of Marriage, Separation, & Divorce. 3rd ed. Lowell S. Thomas, Jr. 224p. 1986. 60.00 (ISBN 0-317-65918-9, B452). Am Law Inst.
Tax Consequences of Marriage, Separation & Divorce 1987 Supplement. Lowell S. Thomas, Sr. 30p. 1987. pap. 85.00 incl. suppl. (ISBN 0-8318-0579-X, B452/B579). Am Law Inst.
Tax Consequences of Oil & Gas Exploration & Development Under Tax Reform. Lewis G. Mosburg, Jr. 30p. (Orig.). 1986. pap. text ed. 4.95 (ISBN 0-910649-50-2). Energy Textbks.
Tax Consequences Upon Conversion of Property's Use: A Comparative Study. Yaakov Neeman. LC 79-115426. 270p. 1970. 15.00 (ISBN 0-379-00461-5). Oceana.
Tax Considerations in the Organization of a Small Business. 32p. 1983. 2.00x (ISBN 0-686-89047-7, 88470-0). P-H.
Tax Coordination in the European Community. Sijbren Cnossen & Erasmus Universiteit Rotterdam, Faculteit der Ecinomische Wetenschappen. LC 86-18526. (International Taxation: No. 7). 387p. 1987. 99.00 (ISBN 9-06-544272-3, Pub. by Kluwer Law Netherlands). Kluwer Academic.
Tax Counseling Financially Distressed Businesses Under the New Laws. 161p. 1987. pap. 22.00 (TX-49010). Cal Cont Ed Bar.
Tax Court. (Information Services Ser.). Date not set. price not set ring bound looseleaf. P-H.
Tax Court Decisions Reports. write for info. (146). Commerce.
Tax Court Declaratory Judgement Proceedings. Murray H. Falk. (Procedural Law Affecting Qualified Plans Ser.). 13p. 1978. pap. 1.50 (ISBN 0-317-31255-3, B375). Am Law Inst.
Tax Court Memorandum Decisions. write for info. (145). Commerce.
Tax Court Practice. 6th ed. Loyal E. Keir, Jr. et al. 319p. 1981. pap. 5.00 (ISBN 0-686-31971-0, B264). Am Law Inst.
Tax Court Reports. write for info. (144). Commerce.
Tax Credits & Intergovernmental Fiscal Relations. James A. Maxwell. LC 86-22731. 216p. 1986. Repr. of 1962 ed. lib. bdg. 39.75x (ISBN 0-313-25279-3, MATX). Greenwood.
Tax Credits for Low Income Housing. 1987 ed. Joseph Guggenheim. 22.00 (ISBN 0-317-67629-6, 18812). US League Savi Inst.
Tax Credits for Low Income Housing: New Opportunities for Developers, Non-Profits, & Communities under the 1986 Tax Reform Act. 3rd. rev. ed. Ed. by Joseph Guggenheim. (Illus.). 148p. 1987. pap. 25.95 (ISBN 0-941239-01-2). Simon Pubns.
Tax Deduction Checklist: Songwriters, Musicians, Performers. Robert A. Livingston. 1982. 7.95 (ISBN 0-9607558-4-5). GLGLC Music.
Tax Deductions for Job-Related Moving Expenses. 32p. 1984. pap. 2.00 (ISBN 0-317-19217-5, 4826). Commerce.
Tax Deductions for Job-Related Moving Expense. 32p. 1988. pap. 3.00 (5212). Commerce.
Tax-Deferred Annuities - Section 403(b) 3rd ed. David E. Kenty & Jeffrey L. London. (Tax Management Portfolio Ser.: No. 388). 1987. looseleaf 50.00. BNA.
Tax-Deferred Annuities for Employees of Exempt Organizations. William F. Heller. (Kinds of Qualified Plans Ser.). 40p. 1979. pap. 2.00 (ISBN 0-317-31075-5, B335). Am Law Inst.
Tax-Deferred Real Property Exchanges. 240p. 1987. pap. 28.00 (RE-49085). Cal Cont Ed Bar.
Tax Dilemma. Donald D. Kaufman. LC 78-11279. (Christian Peace Shelf Ser.). 1978. pap. 3.95 (ISBN 0-8361-1872-3). Herald Pr.
Tax Division Administration Manual 1987-1988: Appointed Members of the AICPA Tax Division. AICPA Tax Division. 68p. 1987. write for info. Am Inst CPA.
Tax Elasticities of Central Government Personal Income Tax Systems. (OECD Studies in Taxation). 50p. (Orig.). 1984. pap. 7.50X (ISBN 92-64-12571-X). OECD.
Tax Equity Act of Nineteen Eighty-Two: TEFRA. Ed. by Law & Business Inc. Staff & Legal Times Seminars Staff. (Seminar Course Handbooks). 1983. pap. 30.00 (C01449, Law & Business). HarBraceJ.
Tax, Estate & Financial Planning for the Elderly. John J. Regan. 1985. Updates avail. looseleaf 90.00 (289); Updates 1986 35.00. Bender.
Tax Ethics, Unaccounted Income-Some Tax Reforms: Or Black Money-the Norm of the Day. O. P. Chopra. (Illus.). vi, 119p. 1985. text ed. 30.00x (ISBN 0-86590-602-5, Pub. by B R Pub Corp Delhi). Apt Bks.
Tax Examiner. Jack Rudman. (Career Examination Ser.: C-802). (Cloth bdg. avail. on request). pap. 14.00 (ISBN 0-8373-0802-X). Natl Learning.
Tax Examiner Trainee. Jack Rudman. (Career Examination Ser.: C-803). (Cloth bdg. avail. on request). pap. 12.00 (ISBN 0-8373-0803-8). Natl Learning.
Tax Executive: 1951-1986, Vols. 4-38. Bound set. 1050.00x (ISBN 0-686-90051-0). Rothman.
Tax Exempt Bonds after the Tax Reform Act of 1986. Ballard et al. 32p. (Orig.). 1986. pap. text ed. 15.00 (ISBN 0-936093-43-9). Packard Pr Fin.
Tax Exempt Charitable Organizations. 2nd ed. Paul E. Treusch & Norman A. Sugarman. LC 83-70067. 726p. 1983. 95.00 (ISBN 0-8318-0429-7, B429). Am Law Inst.
Tax Exempt Charitable Organizations: ALI-ABA Course of Study Materials. 2nd ed. Paul E. Treusch & Norman A. Sugarman. LC 83-70067. 726p. 1983. 95.00 (B429). Am Law Inst.
Tax-Exempt Finance in Minnesota. Advanced Legal Education, Hamline University School of Law Staff. LC 85-152766. 528p. 1985. 47.40. Hamline Law.
Tax-Exempt Financing, 4 vols. Ed. by Kenneth B. Frank & Joseph B. Langhirt. 3500p. 1983. looseleaf 595.00 (ISBN 0-932500-23-4). Natl Hlth Pub.
Tax-Exempt Financing of Housing Investment. George E. Peterson. 196p. 1979. pap. text ed. 11.75 (ISBN 0-87766-251-7). Urban Inst.
Tax-Exempt Financing under the Tax Reform Act. LC 86-62571. (Tax Law & Estate Planning Ser.: No. 245). 112p. 1986. 45.00 (ISBN 0-317-58245-3, J43588). PLI.
Tax Exempt Financing, 1988. Neil P. Arkuss & Henry S. Klaiman. 432p. 1988. pap. 45.00 (J4-3615). PLI.
Tax-Exempt Industrial Development Financing. Pennsylvania Bar Institute. 320p. 1985. 55.00 (ISBN 0-318-19075-3, 290). PA Bar Inst.
Tax-Exempt Organizations. E. C. Lashbrooke, Jr. LC 84-22253. xi, 364p. 1985. lib. bdg. 56.95 (ISBN 0-89930-083-9, LTE/, Quorum). Greenwood.
Tax-Exempt Organizations. (Information Services Ser.). Date not set. price not set ring bound looseleaf. P-H.
Tax-Exempt Property: A Case Study of Hartford, Connecticut. Gregory H. Wassall. 1974. pap. 3.00 (ISBN 0-686-17297-3). Lincoln Inst Land.
Tax-Exempt Securities & the Surtax. Charles O. Hardy. (Brookings Institution Reprint Ser). Repr. of 1926 ed. lib. bdg. 34.00x (ISBN 0-697-00158-X). Irvington.
Tax Exile. Jonathan Gems. (Playwright's Press Ser.). 60p. 1987. pap. 6.95 (ISBN 0-948553-02-2, 1166). Routledge Chapman & Hall.
Tax Expenditure Limitations: How to Implement & Live Within Them. Jerome G. Rose. 275p. 1982. 20.00x (ISBN 0-88285-078-4). Transaction Bks.
Tax Expenditures. Stanley S. Surrey & Paul R. McDaniel. (Illus.). 368p. 1985. text ed. 29.50x (ISBN 0-674-86832-3). Harvard U Pr.
Tax Expenditures: A Review of the Issues & Country Practices. OECD Staff. 87p. (Orig.). 1984. pap. 12.00x (ISBN 92-64-12589-2). OECD.
Tax Facts on Investments, No. 2. Advanced Sales Reference Service Department Editorial Staff. 448p. 1988. pap. 10.75 (ISBN 0-87218-456-0). Natl Underwriter.
Tax Facts on Life Insurance, No. 1. Advanced Sales Reference Service Department Staff. 675p. 1988. pap. 10.75 (ISBN 0-87218-455-2). Natl Underwriter.
Tax Facts, 1986 Tax Reform & Beyond: A Home Study Program. Dianne M. Rankin. (Illus.). 40p. 1987. wkbk. 28.00 (ISBN 0-939926-32-6); incl Cass. 0.00 (ISBN 0-939926-31-8). Fruition Pubns.
Tax Fraud & Evasion. 5th ed. Harry G. Balter. 1983. Cumulative Suppls., annual. 115.00 (ISBN 0-88262-796-1, TFE); Suppl. 1987. 45.25; 29.75. Warren Gorham & Lamont.
Tax Fraud: Audits, Investigations, Prosecutions, 2 vols. Robert S. Fink. Ed. by Stuart E. Abrams et al. 1980. Set, updates avail. looseleaf 150.00 (305); Updates 1985 95.00; Update 1986 95.00. Bender.
Tax-Free Trade Zones of the World, 3 vols. Walter H. Diamond & Dorothy B. Diamond. 1977. Set. looseleaf 235.00 (716); Updates 1985. 146.50; Updates 1986. 206.00. Bender.
Tax Guide for Buying & Selling a Business. 6th ed. Stanley Hagendorf. LC 85-25667. 289p. 1986. 39.95 (ISBN 0-13-885005-4, Pub. by Busn). P-H.
Tax Guide for College Teachers, 1985. Allen Bernstein. 400p. 1984. pap. 18.95 (ISBN 0-916018-27-X). Acad Info Serv.
Tax Guide for College Teachers, 1986. Allen Bernstein. 416p. 1985. pap. 19.95 (ISBN 0-916018-30-X). Acad Info Serv.
Tax Guide for College Teachers 1988. Allen Bernstein. 21.95 (ISBN 0-916018-36-9). Acad Info Serv.
Tax Guide for Patents, Trademarks & Copyrights. 5th ed. Ed. by Taxation Committee of the Patent Law Association of Chicago. LC 83-27520. 1984. pap. 37.50 (ISBN 0-87632-433-2). Clark Boardman.
Tax Guide: Going Through Divorce. Date not set. price not set (ISBN 0-944817-01-7). Allyear Tax.
Tax Guide: Investor Gains & Losses. Date not set. price not set (ISBN 0-944817-03-3). Allyear Tax.
Tax Guide: Selling Your Home. Date not set. price not set (ISBN 0-944817-00-9). Allyear Tax.
Tax Guide: Winning Your Audit. Date not set. price not set (ISBN 0-944817-04-1). Allyear Tax.
Tax Guide: Writing Your Will. Date not set. price not set (ISBN 0-944817-02-5). Allyear Tax.
Tax Handbook for Small Business Owners. Steven A. Hopfenmuller. 375p. 1987. 39.95 (ISBN 0-941949-02-8). Hooksett Pub.
Tax Haven Investing: A Guide to Offshore Banking Investment Opportunities. Richard B. Miller. 275p. 1988. 27.50 (ISBN 1-55738-015-5). Probus Pub Co.
Tax Havens & Measures Against Tax Evasion & Avoidance in the EEC. Ed. by J. F. Avery Jones. xiv, 144p. 1974. text ed. 25.00x (ISBN 0-85227-027-5). Rothman.
Tax Havens & Offshore Finance: A Study of Transnational Economic Development. Richard A. Johns. LC 82-10755. 270p. 1983. 35.00x (ISBN 0-312-78641-7). St Martin.
Tax Havens & Their Uses. Richard Gordon. 240p. 1983. text ed. cancelled (ISBN 0-8290-1490-X). Irvington.
Tax Havens for Corporations. Adam Starchild. LC 79-9325. 176p. 1979. 29.00x (ISBN 0-87201-818-0). Gulf Pub.
Tax Havens in the Caribbean. 1986. lib. bdg. 79.95 (ISBN 0-8490-3563-5). Gordon Pr.
Tax Havens in the Caribbean. U. S. Department of the Treasury Staff. 62p. 1985. pap. 8.00 (ISBN 0-87364-325-9). Paladin Pr.
Tax Havens of the World, 3 vols. Walter H. Diamond & Dorothy B. Diamond. 1974. Updating service for one year avail. looseleaf set 210.00 (722); Annual Renewal. 160.00. Bender.
Tax Help for the Self-Employed. LC 83-106289. Date not set. price not set. P-H.
Tax Ideas, 3 vols. LC 65-254. write for info. P-H.

Tax Reform Act of 1986: Manual. 160p. 1986. 11.95 (ISBN 0-88462-585-0, 5606-06, Pub. by Longman Fin Serv Pub). Longman Finan.

Tax Reform Act of 1986: Special Update. Robert J. Haft et al. (Securities Law Ser.). 1986. pap. 85.00 (ISBN 0-87632-533-9). Clark Boardman.

Tax Reform & Real Estate. Ed. by James R. Follain. (Orig.). 1986. pap. text ed. 20.00 (ISBN 0-87766-396-3). Addendum, The Impact of the Senate Finance Committee Plan, (July, 1986), 15p. Urban Inst.

Tax Reform & the U. S. Economy. Joseph A. Pechman. LC 87-70178. (Dialogues on Public Policy Ser.). 108p. 1987. pap. 10.95t (ISBN 0-8157-6959-8). Brookings.

Tax Reform for a Productive Economy: CED Statement on National Policy. (CED Statement on National Policy Ser.). 24p. 1985. pap. 5.00 (ISBN 0-87186-081-3). Comm Econ Dev.

Tax Reform in Disequilibrium Economies. Serge Wibaut. (Illus.). 150p. Date not set. price not set (ISBN 0-521-35588-5). Cambridge U Pr.

Tax Reform in Eighteenth-Century Lombardy. Daniel M. Klang. (East European Monographs: No. 27). 110p. 1977. 20.00x (ISBN 0-914710-20-6). East Eur Quarterly.

Tax Reform Update Including Technical Corrections. (Tax Law & Estate Planning Ser.). 698p. 1987. 45.00 (J4-3610). PLI.

Tax Reform 1984: The Law, Reports, Hearings, Debates & Related Documents, 20 vols. Bernard D. Reams, Jr. LC 85-45437. Set. lib. bdg. 945.00 (ISBN 0-89941-430-3). W S Hein.

Tax Reform 1986: Analysis & Planning. LC 86-226364. 316p. Date not set. price not set. Bender.

Tax Reforms & Asset Markets. Jonas Agell. 182p. (Orig.). 1985. pap. text ed. 34.00x (ISBN 91-7204-248-6, Pub. by Almqvist & Wiksell). Coronet Bks.

Tax Refund Litigation. Marvin J. Garbis & Allen L. Schwait. 264p. 1971. Incl. 1977 suppl. pap. 5.00 (ISBN 0-317-30821-1, B323); Suppl. 1977 only. pap. 1.00 (ISBN 0-317-30822-X, B324). Am Law Inst.

Tax Relations Among Governmental Units. Tax Policy League. LC 77-74959. (American Federalism-the Urban Dimension). 1978. Repr. of 1938 ed. lib. bdg. 19.00x (ISBN 0-405-10502-9). Ayer Co Pubs.

Tax Research. Raabe. 622p. 1987. 47.00. West Pub.

Tax Research Techniques. 2nd ed. Ray M. Sommerfeld & G. Fred Streuling. (Study in Federal Taxation Ser.: No. 5). 237p. 1981. 16.00 (ISBN 0-685-65552-0). Am Inst CPA.

Tax Return Preparer's Liability. Jules Ritholz & Barry London. LC 85-147123. 25.00 (ISBN 0-13-885252-9). P-H.

Tax Return Preparer's Liability Handbook. Shafiroff. 1986. write for info. (ISBN 0-471-82664-2). Wiley.

Tax Revolt. Alvin Rabushka & Pauline Ryan. (Publication Ser.: No. 270). 288p. 1982. 16.95t (ISBN 0-8179-7701-5). Hoover Inst Pr.

Tax Revolt: Something for Nothing in California. David O. Sears & Jack Citrin. LC 81-20049. (Illus.). 304p. 1982. text ed. 27.00x (ISBN 0-674-86835-8). Harvard U Pr.

Tax Revolt: Something for Nothing in California. enl. ed. David O. Sears & Jack Citrin. LC 84-25233. 1984. pap. 10.95x (ISBN 0-674-86836-6). Harvard U Pr.

Tax Revolt: The Battle for the Constitution. Martin A. Larson. LC 84-14219. 304p. 1985. 16.95 (ISBN 0-8159-6922-8). Devin.

Tax Rulings. write for info. BNA.

Tax Sales Manual 1983-84. Russell A. Morse, Jr. (Mining District Record Ser.). 8p. 1983. pap. 25,00 (ISBN 0-943714-00-1). Cmdrs-Rusty's.

Tax Sales Manual, 1984-85. Russell A. Morse, Jr. 32p. 1984. pap. 17.50 (ISBN 0-943714-01-X). Cmdrs-Rusty's.

Tax Savers. Sunset Editors. Incl. Automobile. LC 86-80874. 5.95; Itemized Deductions. LC 86-80877. 5.95; Home Office. LC 86-80875. 5.95; Homeowners. LC 86-80876. 5.95. 1986. write for info. (Sunset Bks). Sunset-Lane.

Tax Saving Ideas for Retirees. 48p. 1982. 3.50x (88670-5). P-H.

Tax-saving Plans for Self-employed. 72p. 1985. 6.00 (22); members 3.00. Am Consul Eng.

Tax Saving Plans for Self-Employed after Tax Reform. 72p. (Orig.). 1987. pap. 5.00 (5348). Commerce.

Tax Savings Strategies for Every Professional. William H. Newton. 225p. 1988. write for info. (ISBN 0-471-62758-5). Wiley.

Tax Savings thru Interest-Free Loans. rev. ed. Harry G. Gordon. Orig. Title: Tax Avoidance thru Interest-Free Loans. 162p. (Orig.). 1981. pap. 19.95 (ISBN 0-9612184-0-1). H G Gordon.

Tax Shelter Answer Book. Jonathan W. Skiba & Joseph P. Sullivan. LC 84-22653. 1984. 39.95 (ISBN 0-916592-51-0). Panel Pubs.

Tax Shelter Controversies. Ed. by Law & Business Inc. Staff & Legal Times Seminars Staff. (Seminar Course Handbooks). 1983. pap. 35.00 (ISBN 0-686-89375-1, C01384, Law & Business). HarBraceJ.

Tax Shelter Guidebook. Emil Sebetic. 1984. pap. cancelled (ISBN 0-87760-002-3). R Gallen & Co.

Tax Shelter Legislation: ALI-ABA & ABA Section of Taxation Course of Study Materials. ALI-ABA Committee on Continuing Professional Education & American Bar Association Section of Law Staff. write for info. Amer Bar Assn.

Tax Shelter Opportunities in Real Estate. Executive Reports Corporation Editorial Staff. 1978. 89.50 (ISBN 0-13-885269-3). Exec Reports.

Tax Shelter Revenue Rulings. Compiled by Stephen B. Meister. 850p. 1981. 150.00looseleaf (ISBN 0-932500-07-2). Natl Hlth Pub.

Tax Sheltered Opportunities for the Owner of a Closely-Held Business. Executive Reports Corporation Editorial Staff. 1981. 119.50 (ISBN 0-13-886507-8). Exec Reports.

Tax Shelters after Tax Reform. 32p. (Orig.). 1986. pap. 4.00 (5381). Commerce.

Tax Shelters & Tax-Free Income for Everyone. Special Edition ed. William C. Drollinger. LC 81-125456. 1981. 14.95 (ISBN 0-914244-08-6). Epic Pubns.

Tax Shelters & Tax-Free Income for Everyone, Vol II. 4th ed. William C. Drollinger & William C. Jr. Drollinger. LC 81-125456. 1981. 24.95 (ISBN 0-914244-06-X). Epic Pubns.

Tax Shelters & Tax-Free Income for Everyone, Vol. 1. 4th ed. William C. Drollinger. LC 81-125456. 1981. 21.95 (ISBN 0-914244-04-3). Epic Pubns.

Tax Shelters for the Middle Class. R. Westin. 1983. text ed. 85.00 (ISBN 0-07-069484-2). McGraw.

Tax Shelters in Canada: Choose with Care. 12th ed. William E. McLeod. 144p. 1987. 6.95 (ISBN 0-88908-678-8). ISC Pr.

Tax Shelters in Executive Compensation. Executive Reports Corporation Editorial Staff. 1979. 89.50 (ISBN 0-13-886721-6). Exec Reports.

Tax Shelters in Plain English. Robert D. Fierro. 1983. pap. 6.95 (ISBN 0-14-006362-5). Penguin.

Tax Shelters: The Basics. Andersen, Arthur & Co. Staff. LC 82-74373. (Illus.). iii, 147p. 1985. 15.95 (ISBN 0-318-11685-5). A Andersen.

Tax Shelters: The Bottom Line. Robert A. Stanger. LC 82-60132. 238p. 1982. 24.50 (ISBN 0-943570-01-8). R A Stanger.

Tax Slants on Self-Employment & Estimated Taxes. Commerce Clearing House Staff. LC 86-198027. (Tax Angles & Tax Savings Ser.). 32p. Date not set. price not set. Commerce.

Tax Smart: The Touche Ross Guide to Total Tax Strategy. Robert Wool & Touche Ross & Company. 320p. 1988. pap. 16.95 (ISBN 0-385-29618-5). Delacorte.

Tax Strategies for Corporate Financings & Refinancings: The New Financial Products. Louis S. Freeman. 586p. 1987. pap. 45.00 (J4-3605). PLI.

Tax Strategies for Leveraged Buyouts & Other Corporate Acquisitions & Restructurings, 1987, 2 vols. Louis S. Freeman. 1486p. 1987. pap. 45.00 (J4-3604). PLI.

Tax Strategies for Leveraged Buyouts & Other Corporate Acquisitions 1986. (Tax Law & Estate Planning Ser.). 818p. 1986. 15.00 (J4-3581). PLI.

Tax Strategies for Separation & Divorce. W. J. Brown. (Family Law Publications). 526p. 1984. text ed. 90.00 (ISBN 0-07-043038-1). Shepards-McGraw.

Tax Strategies in Divorce. Allan R. Koritzinsky et al. 400p. 1987. loose-leaf 65.00 (ISBN 0-941161-17-X). PES Inc WI.

Tax Strategies: Making the Right Decision. 2nd ed. Auster. 312p. (Orig.). 1988. pap. 37.50 (5273). Commerce.

Tax Strategies: Making the Right Decision. Rolf Auster. 300p. 1983. pap. 27.50 (ISBN 0-317-04234-3, 4935). Commerce.

Tax Strategy for Physicians. 3rd ed. Lawrence Farber. 300p. 1986. 29.95 (ISBN 0-87489-387-9). Med Economics.

Tax Systems of Africa, Asia & the Middle East: A Guide for the Business & the Professions. C. J. Platt. 264p. 1982. pap. text ed. 37.50x (ISBN 0-566-02335-0). Gower Pub Co.

Tax Systems of Western Europe: A Guide for Business & the Professions. 3rd Ed. ed. C. J. Platt. LC 84-18705. 198p. 1985. pap. text ed. 36.50 (ISBN 0-566-02534-5). Gower Pub Co.

Tax Tactics for Small Business: Pay Less Taxes Legally. Ed. by Dale L. Flesher. 100p. (Orig.). 1980. pap. 4.00 (ISBN 0-938004-06-9). U MS Bus Econ.

Tax Target: Washington. Gary Allen. 1979. 10.00 (ISBN 0-89245-015-0). Concord Bks.

Tax Technician. Jack Rudman. (Career Examination Ser.: C-2370). (Cloth bdg. avail. on request). pap. 14.00 (ISBN 0-8373-2370-3). Natl Learning.

Tax Technician Trainee. Jack Rudman. (Career Examination Ser.: C-214). (Cloth bdg. avail. on request). pap. 12.00 (ISBN 0-8373-0214-5). Natl Learning.

Tax That Shook the Street: Wall Street's War with the State of New York. Stephen Shedrowitz. (Illus.). 23p. (Orig.). 1973. pap. 2.00 (ISBN 0-934939-04-7). State Revenue Soc.

Tax Tips for Professionals. Prentice-Hall Editorial Staff. LC 85-154863. Date not set. 4.25 (ISBN 0-13-884973-0). P-H.

Tax Tips for Small Business, 1988-89. General Business Services Staff. (Successful Business Library). 150p. 1988. pap. 12.95 (ISBN 1-55571-042-5). PSI Res.

Tax Treaties. (Information Services Ser.). Date not set. price not set ring bound looseleaf. P-H.

Tax Treaties Between Developed & Developing Countries: Eighth Report. 2.00 (ISBN 92-1-159025-6, E.80.XVI.1). UN.

Tax Treaties Between Developed & Developing Countries: Fourth Report. 9.50 (E.73.XVI.1). UN.

Tax Treaties Between Developed & Developing Countries: Fifth Report. 11.00 (E.75.XVI.1). UN.

Tax Treaties Between Developed & Developing Countries: Second Report. 3.00 (E.71.XVI.2). UN.

Tax Treaties Between Developed & Developing Countries: Sixth Report. 12.00 (E.76.XVI.3). UN.

Tax Treaties Between Developed & Developing Countries: Seventh Report. 4.00 (E.78.XVI.1). UN.

Tax Treaties Between Developed & Developing Countries: Third Report. Repr. 4.50 (E.72.XVI.4). UN.

Tax Treatment of Commodity Futures & Futures Options. rev. ed. Terence A. Faircloth et al. 36p. (Orig.). 1988. pap. 3.95 (ISBN 0-915513-19-6). Ctr Futures Ed.

Tax Treatment of Interest in International Economic Transactions, Vol. LXVIIa. 661p. pap. 42.00 (ISBN 0-686-41006-8). Kluwer Academic.

Tax Treatment of Plans & Participants. William L. Sollee. (Tax & Estate Planning Considerations for Qualified Plans Ser.). 23p. 1978. pap. 2.00 (ISBN 0-317-31199-9, B366). Am Law Inst.

Tax Treatment of Social Security. Mickey D. Levy. 1980. pap. 7.00 (ISBN 0-8447-3370-9). Am Enterprise.

Tax Treatment of Transfer Pricing. Ed. by Hubert Hamaekers & Maurice H. Collins. write for info. Human Serv Pr.

Tax Views. Ed. by Sidney Kess. write for info. Commerce.

Tax We Need. 2nd ed. Tertius Chandler. 100p. 1984. pap. 5.00 (ISBN 0-9603872-3-4). Gutenberg.

Tax We Need. Tertius Chandler. 110p. 1987. pap. 5.00 (ISBN 0-317-61637-4). Schalkenbach.

Tax-Wise Ways to Handle Retirement Benefits in Marital Split-Ups. 32p. 1983. 2.30x. P-H.

Tax-Wise Ways to Sell Your House. Prentice-Hall Editorial Staff. 30p. 1984. 2.75x (88679-6). P-H.

Tax Workbook 1987. Tom Copeland. (Family Day Care Business Ser.). 48p. (Orig.). (ps). 1987. pap. text ed. 5.50 (ISBN 0-934140-43-X). Toys 'n Things.

Taxable Sales in Virginia, 1985. (Statistical Ser.). 1986. 3.14 (ISBN 0-317-69891-5). U Va Ctr Pub Serv.

Taxation see Taxes.

Taxation, a Radical Approach. Vito Tanzi et al. (Institute of Economic Affairs, Readings in Political Economy Ser.: No. 4). 1970. pap. 4.25 technical (ISBN 0-255-35981-0). Transatl Arts.

Taxation: Adaptable to Courses Utilizing to Bittker & Clark's Casenotes on Estate & Gift Taxation. Casebooks Publishing Co., Inc. Staff. Ed. by Norman S. Goldenberg et al. (Legal Briefs Ser.). 1984. pap. write for info. (ISBN 0-87457-128-6, 1217). Casenotes Pub.

Taxation: Adaptable to Courses Utilizing Andrew's Casebook on Basic Federal Income Taxation. Casenotes Publishing Co., Inc. Staff. Ed. by Norman S. Goldenberg et al. (Legal Briefs Ser.). 1984. pap. write for info. (ISBN 0-87457-126-X, 1215). Casenotes Pub.

Taxation: Adaptable to Courses Utilizing Bittker, Stone & Klein's Casebook on Federal Income, Estate & Gift Tax ation. Casenotes Publishing Co., Inc. Staff. Ed. by Norman S. Goldenberg et al. (Legal Briefs Ser.). 1983. pap. write for info. (ISBN 0-87457-127-8, 1210). Casenotes Pub.

Taxation: Adaptable to Courses Utilizing Freeland, Lind & Stephens' Casebook on Fundamentals of Federal Income Taxation. Casenotes Publishing Co., Inc. Staff. Ed. by Norman S. Goldenberg et al. (Legal Briefs Ser.). 1985. pap. write for info. (ISBN 0-87457-129-4, 1212). Casenotes Pub.

Taxation: Adaptable to Courses Utilizing Graetz's Casebook on Federal Income Taxation. Casenotes Publishing Co., Inc. Staff. Ed. by Norman S. Goldenberg et al. (Legal Briefs Ser.). 1985. pap. write for info. (ISBN 0-87457-130-8, 1211). Casenotes Pub.

Taxation: Adaptable to Courses Utilizing Kragen & McNulty's Casebook on Federal Income Taxation, Vol. 1. Casenotes Publishing Co., Inc. Staff. Ed. by Peter Tenen. (Legal Briefs Ser.). 1985. pap. write for info. (ISBN 0-87457-132-4, 1216). Casenotes Pub.

Taxation: Adaptable to Courses Utilizing Kahn & Waggoner's Casebook on Basic Federal Taxation of Gifts, Trusts, & Estates. Casenotes Publishing Co., Inc. Staff. Ed. by Norman S. Goldenberg et al. (Legal Briefs Ser.). 1982. pap. write for info. (ISBN 0-87457-131-6, 1214). Casenotes Pub.

Taxation: Adaptable to Courses Utilizing Lind, Schwarz, Lathrope & Rosenberg's Casebook on Fundamentals of Corporate Taxation. Casenotes Publishing Co., Inc. Staff. Ed. by Norman S. Goldenberg et al. (Legal Briefs Ser.). (Orig.). 1987. pap. text ed. write for info. (ISBN 0-87457-150-2, 1218). Casenotes Pub.

Taxation: Adaptable to Courses Utilizing Surrey, McDaniel & Gutman's Casebook on Federal Wealth Transfer Taxation. Casenotes Publishing Co., Inc. Staff. Ed. by Peter Tenen et al. (Legal Briefs Ser.). 1982. pap. write for info. (ISBN 0-87457-133-2, 1213). Casenotes Pub.

Taxation & Democracy in America. Sidney Ratner. LC 79-17325. 600p. 1980. Repr. of 1942 ed. lib. bdg. 40.00x (ISBN 0-374-96717-2, Octagon). Hippocrene Bks.

Taxation & Economic Development: A Conference in Hungary. Michael Wasylenko et al. (International Socioeconomic Research Ser.). 321p. (Hungarian.). 1988. pap. text ed. 20.00 (ISBN 0-940191-10-5). Univ TN Ctr Bus Econ.

Taxation & Economic Development: Twelve Critical Studies. Ed. by J. F. Toye. (Twelve Critical Studies Ser.). 299p. 1978. 29.50x (ISBN 0-7146-3016-0, F Cass Co); pap. 12.00x (ISBN 0-7146-4028-X, F Cass Co). Biblio Dist.

Taxation & Fiscal Federalism: Essays in Honour of Russell Mathews. G. Brennan et al. 320p. 1988. 18.00 (ISBN 0-08-034401-1). Pergamon.

Taxation & Foreign Currency: Supplement One, 1973-1981. Donald R. Ravenscroft. LC 81-19391. 233p. 1982. pap. 30.00x (ISBN 0-915506-25-4). Harvard Law Intl Tax.

Taxation & Foreign Currency: The Income Tax Consequences of Foreign Exchange Transactions & Exchange Rate Fluctuations. Donald R. Ravenscroft. LC 72-81277. (Illus.). 888p. 1973. 50.00x (ISBN 0-915506-15-7). Harvard Law Intl Tax.

Taxation & Mining: Nonfuel Minerals in Bolivia & Other Countries. Malcolm Gillis et al. LC 77-23806. 384p. 1978. prof ref 50.00x (ISBN 0-88410-458-3). Ballinger Pub.

Taxation & Political Change in the Young Nation 1781-1833. Dall W. Forsythe. LC 77-822. 167p. 1977. 25.00x (ISBN 0-231-04192-6). Columbia U Pr.

Taxation & Social Policy. Cedric Sandford. 1981. text ed. 30.50x (ISBN 0-435-82789-8). Gower Pub Co.

Taxation & the Deficit Economy: Fiscal Policy & Capital Formation in the United States. Ed. by Dwight R. Lee. LC 85-63549. (Illus.). 554p. 1986. 34.95 (ISBN 0-936488-13-1); pap. 14.95 (ISBN 0-936488-03-4). PRIPP.

Taxation & the Incentive to Work. 2nd ed. C. V. Brown. (Illus.). 1983. 34.00x (ISBN 0-19-877213-0); pap. 16.95x (ISBN 0-19-877212-2). Oxford U Pr.

Taxation & Welfare. Arnold C. Harberger. LC 77-99171. (Midway Reprint Ser.). 1978. pap. text ed. 17.00x (ISBN 0-226-31595-9). U of Chicago Pr.

Taxation as a Professional Career. write for info. Am Inst CPA.

Taxation Aspects of Acquisitions & Mergers of Corporations. Ed. by Ernest & Whinney. 192p. 1980. pap. 34.00 (ISBN 90-2000-629-0, Pub. by Kluwer Law Netherlands). Kluwer Academic.

Taxation by Political Inertia: Financing the Growth of Government in Britain. Richard Rose & Terence Karran. LC 87-11478. 256p. 1987. text ed. 39.95x (ISBN 0-04-320197-0); pap. text ed. 16.95x (ISBN 0-04-320198-9). Unwin Hyman.

Taxation During the War. Josiah Stamp. (Economic & Social History of the World War, British Ser.). 1932. 80.00x (ISBN 0-317-27603-4). Elliots Bks.

Taxation for Accountants: 1966-1986, 37 vols. Bound set. 1295.00x (ISBN 0-686-90055-3). Rothman.

Taxation for Development: Principles & Applications. Stephen R. Lewis. LC 83-19308. 1984. 29.95x (ISBN 0-19-503052-4); pap. 12.95x (ISBN 0-19-503053-2). Oxford U Pr.

Taxation for Engineering & Technical Consultants. Marc J. Lane. LC 80-12065. pap. 45.50 (ISBN 0-317-07941-7, 2055530). Bks Demand UMI.

Taxation for Financial Planning. National Underwriter Company, Advanced Sales Reference Service Department Editorial Staff. 676p. 1986. looseleaf 100.00 (ISBN 0-87218-450-1). Natl Underwriter.

Taxation for Lawyers: 1972-1987, 15 vols. Bound set. 600.00x (ISBN 0-686-90056-1). Rothman.

Taxation for Small Manufacturers. Marc J. Lane. LC 80-11621. pap. 42.50 (ISBN 0-317-07945-X, 2055532). Bks Demand UMI.

Taxation for the Computer Industry. Marc J. Lane. LC 80-12070. pap. 47.30 (ISBN 0-317-07943-3, 2055531). Bks Demand UMI.

Taxation for the General Practitioner. 195p. 1983. 5.00 (ISBN 0-318-02445-4). ICLE Georgia.

Taxation, Housing Markets & the Markets for Building Land. B. Gutting. (Microeconomic Studies). viii, 138p. 1987. 35.80 (ISBN 0-387-18381-7). Springer-Verlag.

Taxation in Ancient India. Kunwar Prasad. 1987. 21.00 (Pub. by Mittal). South Asia Bks.

Taxation in Canada. Nathan Boidman & Bruno Ducharme. 300p. 1983. 62.00 (ISBN 0-686-41019-X). Kluwer Academic.

Taxing Insurers: The Revolution Ahead. Carolyn Bowers. Ed. by Richard D. Hadley. 508p. 1983. pap. text ed. 63.00 1-5 copies (ISBN 0-914176-24-2); pap. text ed. 57.00 6-15 copies. Wash Busn Info.

Taxing the Family. Ed. by Rudolph G. Penner. LC 83-9929. (No. 83A). 174p. 1983. 23.00 (ISBN 0-8447-2244-8); pap. 12.50 (ISBN 0-8447-2243-X). Am Enterprise.

Taxis & Behavior see Queues: Receptors & Recognition Series B.

Taxonomia de Suelos. 2nd ed. Soil Survey Staff. Tr. by Walter L. Leighton from Eng. (SMSS Technical Monograph: No. 5). (Span.). 1986. pap. text ed. 8.00 (ISBN 0-932865-04-6). Cornell U Dept.

Taxonomia y la Revolucion En las Ciencias Biologicas. rev. ed. (Serie De Biologia: No. 3). (Span.). 1980. pap. 3.50 (ISBN 0-8270-6050-5). OAS.

Taxonomic Analysis in Biology: Computers, Models & Databases. Lois A. Abbott et al. LC 85-4188. 320p. 1985. 45.00x (ISBN 0-231-04926-9); pap. 17.50x (ISBN 0-231-04927-7). Columbia U Pr.

Taxonomic & Nomenclatural Study of the Genus Amanita Section Amanita for North America. D. T. Jenkins. (Bibliotheca Mycologica Ser.: No. 57). (Illus.). 1977. lib. bdg. 36.00x (ISBN 3-7682-1132-0). Lubrecht & Cramer.

Taxonomic Investigations in the Genera Perityle & Laphamia (Compositae) W. E. Niles. (Memoirs of the New York Botanical Garden Ser.: Vol. 21 (1)). 82p. 1970. 10.00x (ISBN 0-89327-070-9). NY Botanical.

Taxonomic Investigations of Stigeoclonium. E. R. Cox & H. C. Bold. (Phycological Studies: No. 7). (Illus.). 1979. pap. text ed. 33.00x (ISBN 3-87429-130-8). Lubrecht & Cramer.

Taxonomic Investigations on the Ascomycetous Genus Cucurbitaria S. F. Gray. F. Mirza. (From Nova Hedwigia Ser.: No. 16). (Illus.). 54p. 1968. pap. text ed. 12.00x (ISBN 3-7682-0614-9). Lubrecht & Cramer.

Taxonomic Keys to the Common Animals of the North Central States. 4th. ed. Samuel Eddy et al. 1982. write for info. (ISBN 0-8087-2210-7). Burgess MN Intl.

Taxonomic Literature: A Selective Guide to Botanical Publications & Collections with Dates, Commentaries & Types. F. A. Stafleu & R. S. Cowan. (Sti-Vuy Ser.: Vol. 6). 926p. 1986. lib. bdg. 205.20x (ISBN 90-313-0714-9). Lubrecht & Cramer.

Taxonomic Literature: A Selective Guide to Botanical Publications & Collections with Dates, Commentaries & Types, Vol. 1-5. F. A. Stafleu & R. S. Cowan. 1985. Repr. of 1976 ed. lib. bdg. 1053.00x (ISBN 90-313-0224-4). Lubrecht & Cramer.

Taxonomic Literature: LH-O, Vol. 3. Stafleu & R. S. Cowan. 1982. 135.00 (ISBN 90-313-0444-1, Pub. by Junk Pubs Netherlands). Kluwer Academic.

Taxonomic Literature, Volume Four: P-Sack. Ed. by F. A. Stafleu & R. S. Cowan. (Regnum Vegetabile: No. 110). 1984. pap. text ed. 155.00 (ISBN 90-3130-549-9, Pub. by Junk Pubs Netherlands). Kluwer Academic.

Taxonomic Notes on the Species, Figured by H. B. Brady in His Report on the Foraminifera...During the Years 1873-1876. Reginald W. Barker. LC 62-6771. (Society of Economic Paleontologists & Mineralogists, Special Publication: No. 9). pap. 65.50 (ISBN 0-317-27163-6, 2024735). Bks Demand UMI.

Taxonomic Relationships of Diomma Engler ex Harms. see Memoirs of the New York Botanical Garden.

Taxonomic Review of the Genus Origanum (Labiatae) J. H. Ietswaart. (Leiden Botanical Ser.: No. 4). (Illus.). 1980. pap. 31.50 (ISBN 90-6021-463-3, Pub. by Leiden Univ. Holland). Kluwer Academic.

Taxonomic Review of the Pallid Bat: Antrozous Pallidus (Le Conte) Chester O. Martin & David J. Schmidly. (Special Publications of the Museum Ser.: No. 18). (Illus.). 48p. 1982. pap. 7.00 (ISBN 0-89672-097-7). Tex Tech Univ Pr.

Taxonomic Review of the Southern Andean Marsupial Frogs (Hylidae Gastrotheca) William E. Duellman & Thomas H. Fritts. (Occasional Papers: No. 9). 37p. 1972. pap. 2.00 (ISBN 0-686-80344-2). U of KS Mus Nat Hist.

Taxonomic Revision of the American Species of Cladophora (Chlorophyceae) in the North Atlantic. C. Van den Hoek. (Oceans & Their Geographic Distribution Ser.). Date not set. price not set (ISBN 0-444-85541-6). Elsevier.

Taxonomic Revision of the Castilleja Viscidula Group. N. H. Holmgren. (Memoirs of the New York Botanical Garden Series: Vol. 21 (4)). 63p. 1971. 8.50x (ISBN 0-89327-073-3). NY Botanical.

Taxonomic Revision of the Genus Entorrhiza C. Weber (Ustilaginales) J. M. Fineran. (Nova Hedwigia Ser.). (Illus.). 1979. pap. text ed. 15.00x (ISBN 3-7682-1211-4). Lubrecht & Cramer.

Taxonomic Revision of the Genus Macrolobium (Leguminosae-Caesalpinioideae) see Memoirs of the New York Botanical Garden.

Taxonomic Revision of the Genus Persea (Lauraceae) in the Western Hemisphere. L. E. Kopp. (Memoirs of the New York Botanical Garden Ser.: Vol. 14 (1)). 117p. 1966. 10.00x (ISBN 0-89327-049-0). NY Botanical.

Taxonomic Revision of the Liophis Lineatus Complex (Reptilia: Colubridae) of Central & South America. Edward J. Michaud & James R. Dixon. (Contributions in Biology & Geology Ser.: No. 71). 24p. 1987. 4.95 (ISBN 0-89326-151-3). Milwaukee Pub Mus.

Taxonomic Revision of the Superspecific Groups of the Cretaceous & Cenozoic Tellinidae. Freydoun Afshar. LC 72-98019. (Geological Society of America Memoir Ser.: No. 119). pap. 57.80 (ISBN 0-317-28386-3, 2025467). Bks Demand UMI.

Taxonomic Studies of the Encyrtidae with the Descriptions of New Species & a New Genus: Hymenoptera: Chalcidoidea. Gordon Gordh & V. Trjapitzin. (Publications in Entomology: Vol. 93). 1982. pap. 11.00x (ISBN 0-520-09629-0). U of Cal Pr.

Taxonomic Studies on Lac Insects of India. R. K. Varshney. 1976. 30.00 (ISBN 0-318-18590-3). Oriental Insects.

Taxonomic Study of the Ranunculus Hispidus: Complex in the Western Hemisphere. Thomas Duncan. (U. C. Publications in Botany: Vol. 77). 1980. pap. 20.00x (ISBN 0-520-09617-7). U of Cal Pr.

Taxonomical Revision of the Garovaglioideae (Pterobryaceae, Musci) H. J. During. (Bryophytorum Bibliotheca Ser.: No. 12). (Illus.). 1977. lib. bdg. 36.00x (ISBN 3-7682-1161-4). Lubrecht & Cramer.

Taxonomies of Human Performance: The Description of Human Tasks. Edwin A. Fleishman & Marilyn A. Quaintance. 1984. 39.95 (ISBN 0-12-260450-4). Acad Pr.

Taxonomies of the School Library Media Program. David V. Loertscher. xvi, 336p. 1988. lib. bdg. 23.50 (ISBN 0-87287-662-4). Libs Unl.

Taxonomisch-Pflanzengeographische Monographie der Gattung Bovista. H. Kreisel. 1967. 60.00x (ISBN 3-7682-5425-9). Lubrecht & Cramer.

Taxonomist's Glossary of Genitalia in Insects. Ed. by S. L. Tuxen. 1970. text ed. 27.50x (ISBN 0-934454-76-0). Lubrecht & Cramer.

Taxonomists' Glossary of Mosquito Anatomy. R. E. Harbach & Kenneth L. Knight. LC 80-83112. (Illus.). 430p. 1980. 24.95. Plexus Pub.

Taxonomy & Behavioral Science: Comparative Performance of Grouping Methods. Juan Mezzich & Herbert Solomon. (Quantitative Studies in Social Relations). 1980. 42.00 (ISBN 0-12-493340-8). Acad Pr.

Taxonomy & Classification of the Subfamily Lamiinae: Tribes Parmenini Through Acanthoderini. E. Gordon Linsley & John A. Chemsak. (UC Publications in Entomology: Vol. 102). 1985. pap. 21.00x (ISBN 0-520-09690-8). U of Cal Pr.

Taxonomy & Distribution of the Stomioid Fish Genus Eustomias (Melanostomiidae) Pt. 2: Biradiostamies, New Subgenus. Janet R. Gomon & Robert H. Gibbs, Jr. LC 84-600383. (Smithsonian Contributions to Zoology: No. 409). pap. 20.00 (ISBN 0-317-42008-9, 2025685). Bks Demand UMI.

Taxonomy & Distribution of the Stomioid Fish Genus Eustomias (Melanostomiidae), I: Subgenus Nominostomias. LC 83-600023. (Smithsonian Contributions to Zoology: No. 380). pap. 36.00 (ISBN 0-317-29925-5, 2021730). Bks Demand UMI.

Taxonomy & Pathology of Venturia Species. A. Sivanesan. (Bibliotheca Mycologica Ser.: No. 59). 1977. lib. bdg. 24.00x (ISBN 3-7682-1167-3). Lubrecht & Cramer.

Taxonomy, Distribution, & Phylogeny of the Cymatiid Gastropods Argobuccinum, Fusitriton, Mediargo, & Priene see Bulletins of American Paleontology.

Taxonomy in Europe: Final Report of the European Science Research Council's Ad Hoc Group on Biological Recording Systematics & Taxonomy. Ed. by V. H. Heywood & R. B. Clark. (European Science Research Council Review Ser.: Vol. 17). 170p. 1982. pap. 16.50 (ISBN 0-444-86363-X, North Holland). Elsevier.

Taxonomy, Morphology & Ecology of Recent Ostracoda. J. W. Neale. 1969. 45.00x (ISBN 0-934454-77-9). Lubrecht & Cramer.

Taxonomy of Agastache Section Brittonastrum (Lamiaceae-Nepeteae) Roger W. Sanders. Ed. by Christiane Anderson. LC 86-22278. (Systematic Botany Monographs: Vol. 15). (Illus.). 92p. (Orig.). 1987. lib. bdg. 11.00 (ISBN 0-912861-15-0). Am Soc Plant.

Taxonomy of Amauroderma (Basidiomycetes, Polyporaceae) Joao S. Furtado. (Memoirs of the New York Botanical Garden: Vol. 34). (Illus.). 1981. pap. 17.50x (ISBN 0-89327-234-5). NY Botanical.

Taxonomy of Communication Media. Rudy Bretz. LC 72-125874. (Illus.). 192p. 1971. 29.95 (ISBN 0-87778-012-9). Educ Tech Pubns.

Taxonomy of Computer Science & Engineering. AFIPS Taxonomy Committee & Robert L. Ashenhurst. LC 79-57474. ix, 462p. 1980. 40.25 (ISBN 0-88283-008-2). AFIPS Pr.

Taxonomy of Concepts in Communication. Reed H. Blake & Edwin O. Haroldsen. (Humanistic Studies in the Communication Arts). (Illus.). 176p. 1975. pap. text ed. 8.00x (ISBN 0-8038-7155-4). Hastings.

Taxonomy of Critical Tasks for Evaluating Student Teaching. Kuehl. 1979. 2.50 (ISBN 0-686-38070-3). Assn Tchr Ed.

Taxonomy of Cyperus (Cyperaceae) in Costa Rica & Panama. Gordon C. Tucker. Ed. by Christiane Anderson. LC 83-7144. (Systematic Botany Monographs: Vol. 2). (Illus.). 85p. 1983. 9.00 (ISBN 0-912861-02-9). Am Soc Plant.

Taxonomy of Educational Objectives: Handbook 1: Cognitive Domain. Benjamin S. Bloom et al. LC 64-12369. 1977. pap. text ed. 16.95 (ISBN 0-582-28010-9). Longman.

Taxonomy of Educational Objectives: Handbook 2: Affective Domain. David R. Krathwohl et al. 1969. pap. text ed. 16.95 (ISBN 0-582-28239-X). Longman.

Taxonomy of Flowering Plants. 2nd ed. Cedric L. Porter. LC 66-19914. (Illus.). 472p. 1967. 34.95x (ISBN 0-7167-0709-8). W H Freeman.

Taxonomy of North American Flies of the Genus Limnia (Diptera: Sciomyzidae) G. C. Steyskal et al. (UC Publications in Entomology: No. 83). 1978. pap. 16.50x (ISBN 0-520-09577-4). U of Cal Pr.

Taxonomy of Porifera. Ed. by J. Vacelet & N. Boury Esnault. (NATO ASI Ser.: No. G13). viii, 332p. 1987. 89.00 (ISBN 0-387-16091-4). Springer-Verlag.

Taxonomy of Saxifraga (Saxifragaceae) Section Boraphila Subsection Integrifoliae in Western North America: Patrick E. Elvander Revision of The Genus Heuchera (Saxifragaceae) in Eastern North America. Elizabeth F. Wells. LC 84-393. (Systematic Botany Monographs: Vol. 3). (Illus.). 121p. (Orig.). 1984. pap. 16.00 (ISBN 0-912861-03-7). Am Soc Plant.

Taxonomy of Specimens of the Pennsylvanian-Age Marattialean Fern Psaronius from Ohio & Illinois. James E. Mickle. (Scientific Papers: Vol. XIX). (Illus.). vii, 64p. (Orig.). 1984. pap. 5.00x (ISBN 0-89792-101-1). Ill St Museum.

Taxonomy of Survey Errors. Lessler et al. (Probability & Mathematical Statistics Ser.). 1988. write for info. (ISBN 0-471-86908-2). Wiley.

Taxonomy of the Bruchidae (Coleoptera) of Northwest India, Part II: Larvae. G. L. Arora. 1978. 30.00 (ISBN 0-318-18593-8). Oriental Insects.

Taxonomy of the Flowering Plants. A. M. Johnson. (Illus.). 1977. Repr. of 1931 ed. lib. bdg. 90.00x (ISBN 3-7682-1169-X). Lubrecht & Cramer.

Taxonomy of the Genus Phytophtora. C. M. Tucker. (Illus.). 36.00x (ISBN 3-7682-0515-0). Lubrecht & Cramer.

Taxonomy of the Indian Myxomycetes. T. N. Lakhanpal & K. G. Mukerji. (Bibliotheca Mycologica: No. 78). (Illus.). 532p. 1981. lib. bdg. 72.00x (ISBN 3-7682-1287-4). Lubrecht & Cramer.

Taxonomy of the Psychomotor Domain: A Guide for Developing Behavioral Objectives. Anita J. Harrow. LC 74-185136. 1979. pap. text ed. 14.95 (ISBN 0-582-28128-8, Pub. by MacKay). Longman.

Taxonomy of the Subgenus Pterodes, Genus Luzula see Memoirs of the New York Botanical Garden.

Taxonomy of Thelypteris Subgenus Steiropteris (Including Glaphyropteris) Alan R. Smith. (UC Publications in Botany: Vol. 76). 1980. pap. 15.95x (ISBN 0-520-09602-9). U of Cal Pr.

Taxonomy of Viruses. (Illus.). 20p. 1980. pap. 10.25 (ISBN 90-220-0719-7, PDC149, PUDOC). UNIPUB.

Taxonomy of Visual Processes. William R. Uttal. LC 80-18262. 1120p. 1981. text ed. 100.00x (ISBN 0-89859-075-2). L Erlbaum Assocs.

Taxonomy of Water Mite Larvae. Vikram Prasad & David Cook. (Memoir Ser.: No. 18). (Illus.). 326p. 1972. 30.00x (ISBN 0-686-08727-5). Am Entom Inst.

Taxonomy of West African Flowering Plants. Omotoye Olorode. (Illus.). 176p. 1984. text ed. 25.95 (ISBN 0-582-64429-1). Longman.

Taxonomy, Phylogeny & Zoogeography of Beetles & Ants. Ed. by George E. Ball. (Entomologica Ser.). 1985. lib. bdg. 105.00 (ISBN 90-6193-511-3, Pub. by Junk Pubs Netherlands). Kluwer Academic.

Taxpayer Revolt in Perspective: A Primer on Paying for Government. Donald Phares. 192p. Date not set. 30.00 (ISBN 0-89946-025-9). Oelgeschlager.

Taxpayer Service Representative. Jack Rudman. (Career Examination Ser.: C-833). (Cloth bdg. avail. on request). pap. 14.00 (ISBN 0-8373-0833-X). Natl Learning.

Taxpayers Message to Congress: Repeal the Federal Reserve Act. Casimir F. Gierut. 288p. 10.50 (ISBN 0-318-17465-0). Natl Comm Repeal.

Taxpayer's New Clothes. Tom Toles. (Illus., Orig.). 1985. pap. 6.95 (ISBN 0-8362-1256-8). Andrews & McMeel.

Taxpayers, Payers Guide to Revolt: Perspectives on the Taxpayers Revolt. Robert J. Dworak. LC 80-135. 272p. 1980. 44.95 (ISBN 0-275-90473-3, C0473); pap. 18.95 (ISBN 0-275-91490-9, B1490). Praeger.

Taxpayers Survival Manual. Howard Fishkin. 1979. pap. 2.95 (ISBN 0-933586-06-X). Book Promo Pr.

Taxpayer's Vehicle Log. Ed. by W. J. Turner & Assoc., Inc. 64p. (Orig.). 1984. pap. text ed. 2.95 (ISBN 0-936537-01-9). Metro WI.

Taxscam: How the Internal Revenue Service Swindles You & What You Can Do about It. Alan Stang. LC 88-60843. 312p. (Orig.). 1988. pap. 9.95 (ISBN 0-9620089-0-7). Mt Sinai Pr.

Tay-Sachs Disease: Screening & Prevention, Papers. International Conference on Tay-Sachs Disease - Screening & Prevention, 1st, Palm Springs, Calif., Dec. 1975. Ed. by Michael M. Kaback et al. LC 77-12734. (Progress in Clinical & Biological Research: Vol. 18). 450p. 1977. 75.00 (ISBN 0-8451-0018-1). A R Liss.

Tayeb Salih's "Season of Migration to the North" A Casebook. Mona T. Amyuni. 174p. (Orig.). 1986. pap. text ed. 18.00x (ISBN 0-8156-6075-8, Am U Beirut). Syracuse U Pr.

Taylor Act Amendments of 1969: A Supplemental Primer for School Personnel & Others Interested in Collective Negotiations. Walter E. Oberer et al. (ILR Bulletin Ser.: No. 62). 56p. 1970. pap. 2.00 (ISBN 0-87546-236-7). ILR Pr.

Taylor Hay Technique. Taylor Hay. LC 86-82486. 118p. 1986. 12.95 (ISBN 0-939285-02-9). HayMaker Bk Co.

Taylor Made a Trilogy of One Act Plays. George Taylor. 1982. 15.00x (ISBN 0-903653-31-1, Pub. by New Playwrights Network). State Mutual Bk.

Taylor Made: The Best of Bee Talk. Richard Taylor. Ed. by Kim Flottum. (Illus.). 200p. 1988. 17.95 (ISBN 0-936028-00-9). A I Root.

Taylor-Moore Lodge. Suzanne Taylor-Moore. 1981. pap. 3.50x (ISBN 0-938758-10-1). MTM Pub Co.

Taylor System in Franklin Management. 2nd ed. George D. Babcock. (Management History Ser.: No. 7). (Illus.). 271p. 1972. Repr. of 1918 ed. 25.00 (ISBN 0-87960-008-X). Hive Pub.

Taylor System of Scientific Management. C. Bertrand Thompson. LC 73-6566. (Management History Ser.: No. 25). (Illus.). 183p. 1973. Repr. of 1917 ed. 25.00 (ISBN 0-87960-062-4). Hive Pub.

Taylorism in France, 1904-1920: The Impact of Scientific Management on Factory Relations & Society. George G. Humphreys. Ed. by Stuart Bruchey. (American Business History Ser.). 275p. 1986. lib. bdg. 35.00 (ISBN 0-8240-8355-5). Garland Pub.

Taylor's Guide to Annuals. rev. ed. Norman Taylor. Ed. by Gordon P. DeWolf, Jr. LC 85-30496. (Taylor's Guides to Gardening Ser.). 479p. 1986. 14.95 (ISBN 0-395-40447-9). HM.

Taylor's Guide to Annuals. Norman Taylor & Gordon P. De Wolf, Jr. 1985. pap. write for info. HM.

Taylor's Guide to Bulbs. rev. ed. Norman Taylor. Ed. by Gordon P. DeWolf, Jr. LC 85-30508. (Taylor's Guides to Gardening Ser.). 463p. 1986. 14.95 (ISBN 0-395-40449-5). HM.

Taylor's Guide to Bulbs. Norman Taylor & Gordon P. De Wolf, Jr. 1985. pap. write for info. HM.

Taylor's Guide to Garden Design. (Taylor's Gardening Guides). (Illus.). 480p. 1988. pap. 16.95 (ISBN 0-395-46784-5). HM.

Taylor's Guide to Ground Covers, Vines & Grasses. Taylor's Guide Staff. (Illus.). 496p. (Orig.). 1987. pap. 14.95 (ISBN 0-395-43094-1). HM.

Taylor's Guide To Houseplants. Gordon P. DeWolf, Jr. (Illus.). 480p. 1987. pap. 14.95 (ISBN 0-317-53568-4). HM.

Taylor's Guide to Perennials. rev. ed. Norman Taylor. Ed. by Gordon P. DeWolf, Jr. LC 85-30495. (Taylor's Guides to Gardening Ser.). 479p. 1986. pap. 14.95 (ISBN 0-395-40448-7). HM.

Taylor's Guide to Perennials. Norman Taylor & Gordon P. De Wolf, Jr. 1985. pap. write for info. HM.

Taylor's Guide to Roses. rev. ed. Norman Taylor. Ed. by Gordon P. DeWolf, Jr. LC 85-30492. (Taylor's Guides to Gardening Ser.). 495p. 1986. pap. 14.95 (ISBN 0-395-40450-9). HM.

Taylor's Guide to Roses. Norman Taylor & Gordon P. De Wolf, Jr. 1985. pap. write for info. HM.

Taylor's Guide to Shrubs. Taylor's Guide Staff. (Illus.). 480p. 1987. pap. 14.95 (ISBN 0-395-43093-3). HM.

Taylor's Guide to Trees. (Taylor's Gardening Guides). (Illus.). 1988. pap. 14.95 (ISBN 0-395-46783-7). HM.

Taylor's Guide To Vegetables & Herbs. Gordon P. DeWolf. (Illus.). 480p. (Orig.). pap. 14.95 (ISBN 0-395-43092-5). HM.

Taylors Gut: In the Delaware State. Dudley C. Lunt. (Illus.). 320p. 1986. pap. 8.95 (ISBN 0-912608-30-7). Mid Atlantic.

Taylors of Ongar: An Analytical Bio-Bibliography. Christina D. Stewart. LC 74-23641. (Reference Library of the Humanities: No. 7). (Illus.). 1200p. 1975. lib. bdg. 152.00 (ISBN 0-8240-1063-9). Garland Pub.

Taylorvision. Edmund E. Taylor. LC 84-51960. (Illus.). 64p. (Orig.). 1984. pap. text ed. 3.98 (ISBN 0-9613839-0-9). Tel Pr.

Teach Soul-Winning. C. S. Lovett. 1962. pap. 2.95 tchr's. guide (ISBN 0-938148-12-5). Personal Christianity.
Teach Speech. Loretta Minn. (gr. 3-7). 1982. 6.95 (ISBN 0-86653-058-4, GA 418). Good Apple.
Teach, Teacher. Abridged ed. Luanna C. Blagrove. (Illus.). 1988. 24.95 (ISBN 0-939776-42-1). Blagrove Pubns.
Teach the Freeman: The Correspondence of Rutherford B. Hayes & the Slater Fund for Negro Education 1881-1887, 2 vols. in 1. R. B. Hayes. Repr. of 1959 ed. 42.00 (ISBN 0-527-38930-7). Kraus Repr.
Teach the Grown-Ups Where Babies Come from. Lisbeth H. Naber. (Illus.). 32p. (ps-2). 1986. 6.95 (ISBN 0-8059-3012-4). Dorrance.
Teach the Mind, Touch the Spirit: A Guide to Focused Field Trips. Helen H. Voris et al. (Illus.). 90p. (Orig.). 1986. pap. write for info. (ISBN 0-914868-09-8). Field Mus.
Teach the Word. Paul F. Henson. 1972. 5.25 (ISBN 0-87148-826-4); pap. 4.25 (ISBN 0-87148-827-2). Pathway Pr.
Teach Them About Satan. C. S. Lovett. 1970. pap. 5.45 tchr's guide (ISBN 0-938148-26-5). Personal Christianity.
Teach Them Diligently. Arthur Nazigian. 1986. pap. 2.95 (ISBN 0-8010-6747-2). Baker Bk.
Teach Them Good Customs: Colonial Indian Education & Acculturation in the Andes. Robert D. Wood. LC 85-50096. 142p. (Orig.). 1986. pap. 15.00X. Labyrinthos.
Teach Us, Amelia Bedelia. Peggy Parish. LC 76-22663. (Greenwillow Read-Alone Bks.). (Illus.). 56p. (gr. 1-4). 1977. 10.25 (ISBN 0-688-80069-6); PLB 10.88 (ISBN 0-688-84069-8). Greenwillow.
Teach Us, Amelia Bedelia. Peggy Parish. (ps-3). 1980. pap. 2.50 (ISBN 0-590-33362-3). Scholastic Inc.
Teach Us, Amelia Bedelia. Peggy Parish. (Hello Reader Ser.). (Illus.). 64p. (gr. k-3). 1987. pap. 2.50 (ISBN 0-590-40940-9, Hello Reader). Scholastic Inc.
Teach Us To Outgrow Our Madness. Kenzaburo Oe. Tr. & intro. by John Nathan. LC 76-54582. 1977. 10.00 (ISBN 0-394-41338-5). Grove.
Teach Us To Outgrow Our Madness. Kenzaburo Oe. Tr. & intro. by John Nathan. LC 76-54582. 1977. pap. 9.95 (ISBN 0-394-17002-4, E687, Ever). Grove.
Teach Us to Pray. Elaine Dull & Jo Anne Sekowsky. (Aglow Bible Study Book Enrichment). 64p. 1980. pap. 2.95 (ISBN 0-930756-49-5, 522002). Aglow Pubns.
Teach Us to Pray. Charles Fillmore & Cora Fillmore. 1976. 5.95 (ISBN 0-87159-152-9). Unity School.
Teach Us to Pray. Dawn Tullis. 2.25 (ISBN 0-686-13717-5). Crusade Pubs.
Teach Us To Pray: The Disciples Request Cast Anew. Fred C. Lofton. 96p. 1983. pap. 4.00 (ISBN 0-89191-751-9). Prog Bapt Pub.
Teach What You Preach. Anderson. 1982. pap. 8.95 (ISBN 0-8298-0481-1). Pilgrim NY.
Teach with Success. rev. ed. Guy P. Leavitt. Rev. by Eleanor Daniel. LC 78-63285. (Illus.). 160p. (Orig.). 1978. pap. 7.95 (ISBN 0-87239-231-7, 3232). Standard Pub.
Teach Witnessing. C. S. Lovett. 1966. pap. 5.95 tchr's. guide (ISBN 0-938148-09-5). Personal Christianity.
Teach Ye Diligently. Boyd K. Packer. LC 75-22704. (Illus.). 329p. 1975. 14.95 (ISBN 0-87747-558-X). Deseret Bk.
Teach Your Baby Math. Glenn Doman. 112p. 1982. pap. 2.95 (ISBN 0-671-55444-1). PB.
Teach Your Baby to Sleep Through the Night. Charles E. Schaefer & Michael R. Petronko. 144p. 1987. 13.95 (ISBN 0-399-13270-8, Putnam). Putnam Pub Group.
Teach Your Baby to Swim. Bonnie Prudden. LC 73-79534. (Illus.). 1978. pap. text ed. 12.95 (ISBN 0-9602146-0-7). Bonnie Prudden.
Teach Your Child Decision Making: An Effective 8-Step Program for Parents of Children of All Ages to Solve Everyday Problems & Make Sound Decisions. John Clabby. LC 85-10123. (Illus.). 360p. 1987. pap. 8.95 (ISBN 0-385-19390-4). Doubleday.
Teach Your Child the Consequences of Crime. Clifton M. Kelly & Sherman P. Wantz. LC 82-81035. (Illus.). 200p. (Orig.). 1982. pap. 6.95 (ISBN 0-943328-00-4). Highlands Pub.
Teach your Child the Value of Money. Harold Moe & Sandy Moe. Ed. by Margaret Larson. (Illus.). 128p. (Orig.). 1987. pap. 7.95x (ISBN 0-9612310-4-1). Harsand Pr.
Teach Your Child to Read in Sixty Days. Sidney Ledson. 100p. 1987. pap. 3.95 (ISBN 0-425-09340-9). Berkley Pub.
Teach Your Child to Read in Twenty Minutes A Day. Barbara J. Fox. (Orig.). 1986. pap. 9.95 (ISBN 0-446-38346-5). Warner Bks.
Teach Your Child with Games. Gretchen Buchenholz. Ed. by Manon Tingue. 128p. 1984. pap. 8.95 (Fireside). S&S.
Teach Your Computer to Think in BASIC. David P. Kressen. Ed. by Russell Jacobs. (Illus.). 88p. (gr. 5 up). 1983. pap. text ed. 7.50 (ISBN 0-918272-10-6). Jacobs.
Teach Your Computer to Think in BASIC: Teacher's Resource Book. David P. Kressen. 1983. 5.95 (ISBN 0-918272-11-4). Jacobs.
Teach Your Dad How to Fish. Burr Smidt. (Illus.). 222p. 1977. 19.95 (ISBN 0-912588-43-8). Greycliff Pub.
Teach Your Own: New & Hopeful Path for Parents & Educators. John Holt. 384p. 1982. pap. 8.95 (ISBN 0-385-29006-3, Delta). Dell.
Teach Your Tot to Swim. Pauline Petsel. (Orig.). pap. 1.00 (ISBN 0-8200-0607-6). Great Outdoors.
Teach Yourself Apple BASIC. Peter Mears. 192p. 1983. write for info., spiral bound incl. disk. Addison-Wesley.
Teach Yourself Arabic. S. Ali. 9.50 (ISBN 0-686-83575-1). Kazi Pubns.
Teach Yourself Arabic. Arthur S. Ritton. (Teach Yourself Ser.). 1979. pap. 9.95 (ISBN 0-679-10164-0). McKay.
Teach Yourself Arabic Phrase Book. 1980. pap. 5.95 (ISBN 0-679-10550-6). McKay.
Teach Yourself Arithmetic: Decimalized & Metricated. L. C. Pascoe. (Teach Yourself Ser.). 1972. pap. 5.95 (ISBN 0-679-10452-6). McKay.
Teach Yourself Astrology. Jeff Mayo. (Teach Yourself Ser.). (Orig.). 1980. pap. 6.95 (ISBN 0-679-12001-7). McKay.
Teach Yourself Astronomy. D. S. Evans. (Teach Yourself Ser.). 1978. pap. 6.95 (ISBN 0-679-10416-X). McKay.
Teach Yourself Backgammon. Robin Clay. (Teach Yourself Ser.). (Illus.). 1978. pap. 3.95 (ISBN 0-679-10241-8). McKay.
Teach Yourself Ballet. Woodward. (Teach Yourself Ser.). 1977. pap. 7.95 (ISBN 0-679-10518-2). McKay.
Teach Yourself Biblical Hebrew. Roland K. Harrison. (Teach Yourself Ser.). 1979. pap. 6.95 (ISBN 0-679-10180-2). McKay.
Teach Yourself Biology. J. R. Hall. (Teach Yourself Ser.). 1980. pap. 6.95 (ISBN 0-679-10388-0). McKay.
Teach Yourself Book-Keeping. D. Cousins. (Teach Yourself Ser.). 1978. pap. 7.95 (ISBN 0-679-10455-0). McKay.
Teach Yourself Botany. J. H. Elliott. (Teach Yourself Ser.). 1978. pap. 4.95 (ISBN 0-679-10390-2). McKay.
Teach Yourself Calligraphy: For Beginners from Eight to Eighty. Ed. by Ellen Korn. (Illus.). 96p. (gr. 8 up). 1982. pap. 6.95 comb binding (ISBN 0-688-01994-3). Morrow.
Teach Yourself Cantonese. R. Bruce. (Teach Yourself Ser). 1979. pap. 8.95 (ISBN 0-679-10208-6). McKay.
Teach Yourself Card Games for One. (Teach Yourself Bks.). 1980. pap. 6.95 (ISBN 0-679-10352-X). McKay.
Teach Yourself Card Games for Two. K. Parlett. (Teach Yourself Ser.). 1980. pap. 7.95 (ISBN 0-679-12054-8). McKay.
Teach Yourself Catalan. Alan Yates. (Teach Yourself Bks.). 1979. pap. 9.95 (ISBN 0-679-10231-0). McKay.
Teach Yourself Chemistry. John S. Clarke. 1979. pap. 5.95 (ISBN 0-679-12055-6). McKay.
Teach Yourself Chess. G. Abrahams. (Teach Yourself Ser.). 1980. pap. 7.95 (ISBN 0-679-10354-6). McKay.
Teach Yourself Chinese. H. R. Williamson. (Teach Yourself Ser.). 1979. pap. 6.95 (ISBN 0-679-10209-4). McKay.
Teach Yourself Codes & Ciphers. F. Higenbottam. (Teach Yourself Ser.). 1980. pap. 3.95 (ISBN 0-679-10356-2). McKay.
Teach Yourself Colloquial Arabic. T. F. Mitchell. (Teach Yourself Ser.). 1979. pap. 6.95 (ISBN 0-679-10165-9). McKay.
Teach Yourself Computer Based Systems. Race. (Teach Yourself Ser.). pap. 7.95. McKay.
Teach Yourself Computer Based Systems. 1983. pap. 5.95. Macmillan.
Teach Yourself Computer Programming - FORTRAN. A. S. Radford. (Teach Yourself Ser.). 1975. pap. 5.95. McKay.
Teach Yourself Computer Programming: FORTRAN. 1983. pap. 5.95. Macmillan.
Teach Yourself Computer Programming in BASIC. L. R. Carter & E. Huzan. (Teach Yourself Ser.). 174p. 1981. pap. 5.95 (ISBN 0-679-10535-2). McKay.
Teach Yourself Computer Programming in COBOL. 1983. pap. 7.95 (ISBN 0-679-10259-0). McKay.
Teach Yourself Computer Programming in Pascal. D. Lightfood. 1984. pap. 8.95 (ISBN 0-679-10539-5). McKay.
Teach Yourself Computer Programming: MSX Basic. (Teach Yourself Bks.). Date not set. pap. 6.95 (ISBN 0-679-10540-9). McKay.
Teach Yourself Computer Programming with the Commodore 64. L. R. Carter & E Huzan. 192p. 1983. pap. 6.95 (ISBN 0-679-10538-7). McKay.
Teach Yourself Creative Writing. (Teach Yourself Bks.). Date not set. pap. 6.95 (ISBN 0-679-10260-4). McKay.
Teach Yourself Critical Path Analysis. Lang. (Teach Yourself Ser.). 1977. pap. 6.95 (ISBN 0-679-10504-2). McKay.
Teach Yourself Crochet. Jean Kinmond. (Teach Yourself Bks.). (Orig.). 1980. pap. 4.95 (ISBN 0-679-12057-2). McKay.
Teach Yourself Czech. W. R. Lee & Z. Lee. (Teach Yourself Ser.). 1979. pap. 9.95 (ISBN 0-679-10211-6). McKay.
Teach Yourself Dancing. Imperial Society of Teachers of Dancing. (Teach Yourself Ser.). 1978. pap. 6.95 (ISBN 0-679-10244-2). McKay.
Teach Yourself Dancing. Imperial Society of Teachers of Dancing Staff. (Ballroom Dance Ser.). 1985. lib. bdg. 74.95 (ISBN 0-87700-852-3). Revisionist Pr.
Teach Yourself Dancing. Imperial Society of Teachers of Dancing Staff. (Ballroom Dance Ser.). 1986. lib. bdg. 79.95 (ISBN 0-8490-3260-1). Gordon Pr.
Teach Yourself Danish. H. A. Koefoed. (Teach Yourself Ser.). 1979. pap. 7.95 (ISBN 0-679-10212-4). McKay.
Teach Yourself Dart Player's Handbook. George Hakim. 1979. pap. 3.50 (ISBN 0-679-12076-9). McKay.
Teach Yourself dBASE III Plus. Pierre-Jean Charra & Marie-Jose Meys. Tr. by EDIDACOM Staff. 171p. binder with book and diskette 69.95. Tutorland.
Teach Yourself Dutch. H. Koolhoven. (Teach Yourself Ser.). pap. 6.95 (ISBN 0-679-10213-2). McKay.
Teach Yourself Electricity. C. W. Wilman. (Teach Yourself Ser.). 1980. pap. 4.95 (ISBN 0-679-10395-3). McKay.
Teach Yourself Electronic Computers. F. L. Westwater & D. H. Joyce. (Teach Yourself Ser.). 1979. pap. 3.50 (ISBN 0-679-10382-1). McKay.
Teach Yourself Electronics. (Teach Yourself Bks.). 1979. pap. 6.95 (ISBN 0-679-10396-1). McKay.
Teach Yourself Elementary Logic. (Teach Yourself Bks.). Date not set. pap. 5.95 (ISBN 0-679-10534-4). McKay.
Teach Yourself English Grammar. Gordon Humphries. (Teach Yourself Ser.). 1980. pap. 8.95 (ISBN 0-679-10166-7). McKay.
Teach Yourself English: Self Preparation for English Proficiency Examinations. rev. ed. William L. Young. LC 68-8682. (Orig.). (gr. 8-12). 1977. pap. 6.95 (ISBN 0-8120-0373-X). Barron.
Teach Yourself Esperanto. John Cresswell & John Hartley. (Teach Yourself Ser.). 1980. pap. 9.95 (ISBN 0-679-10167-5). McKay.
Teach Yourself Esperanto Dictionary. J. C. Wells. (Teach Yourself Ser.). (Esperanto.). 1974. pap. 9.95 (ISBN 0-679-10205-1). McKay.
Teach Yourself Essentials of Accounting on the IBM PC. Robert N. Anthony. 80p. 1983. write for info. incl. disk (ISBN 0-201-15328-9). Addison-Wesley.
Teach Yourself Everyday French. N. Scarlyn Wilson. (Teach Yourself Ser.). 1979. pap. 6.95 (ISBN 0-679-10168-3). McKay.
Teach Yourself Everyday Spanish. L. D. Collier. (Teach Yourself Ser.). 1979. pap. 6.95 (ISBN 0-679-10169-1). McKay.
Teach Yourself Finnish. A. H. Whitney. (Teach Yourself Ser.). pap. 7.95 (ISBN 0-679-10170-5). McKay.
Teach Yourself First French. N. Scarlyn Wilson. (Teach Yourself Ser.). 1969. pap. 4.95 (ISBN 0-679-10215-9). McKay.
Teach Yourself First German. L. Stringer. (Teach Yourself Ser.). 1966. pap. 4.95 (ISBN 0-679-10171-3). McKay.
Teach Yourself Fortune Telling: Palmistry, the Crystal Ball, Tea Leaves, the Tarot. Rachel Pollack. (Illus.). 144p. 1986. pap. 10.95 (ISBN 0-8050-0125-5). H Holt & Co.
Teach Yourself French. J. Adams & N. S. Wilson. (Teach Yourself Ser.). pap. 7.95 (ISBN 0-679-10172-1). McKay.
Teach Yourself French Grammar. Edward S. Jenkins. (Teach Yourself Ser.). pap. 5.95 (ISBN 0-679-10173-X). McKay.
Teach Yourself Gaelic. Roderick Mackinnon. (Teach Yourself Ser.). 1979. pap. 8.95 (ISBN 0-679-10217-5). McKay.
Teach Yourself Geometry. P. Abbott. (Teach Yourself Ser.). 1976. pap. 9.95 (ISBN 0-679-10398-8). McKay.
Teach Yourself German. J. Adams et al. (Teach Yourself Ser.). 1978. pap. 8.95 (ISBN 0-679-10174-8). McKay.
Teach Yourself German Dictionary. (Teach Yourself Bks.). Date not set. pap. 6.95 (ISBN 0-679-10246-9). McKay.
Teach Yourself German Grammar. P. G. Wilson. (Teach Yourself Ser.). 1979. pap. 7.95 (ISBN 0-679-10175-6). McKay.
Teach Yourself German Phrase Book. Hamilton. (Teach Yourself Ser.). 1980. pap. 3.95 (ISBN 0-679-10176-4). McKay.
Teach Yourself Good English. G. H. Thornton & Katheleen Baron. (Teach Yourself Ser.). pap. 3.95 (ISBN 0-679-10177-2). McKay.
Teach Yourself Greek. F. K. Smith & T. W. Melluish. (Teach Yourself Ser.). pap. 7.95 (ISBN 0-679-10178-0). McKay.
Teach Yourself Greek Phrase Book. 1980. pap. 3.95 (ISBN 0-679-10700-2). McKay.
Teach Yourself Guitar. Dale Fradd. (Teach Yourself Ser.). 1975. pap. 7.95 (ISBN 0-679-10365-1). McKay.
Teach Yourself Guitar. Harry Taussig. (Illus.). 150p. pap. 9.95 (ISBN 0-8256-0010-3, Pub. by Oak). Music Sales.
Teach Yourself Hausa. Charles H. Kraft & A. H. Kirk-Greene. (Teach Yourself Ser). 1973. pap. 9.95 (ISBN 0-679-10179-9). McKay.
Teach Yourself House Repairs. T. Wilkins. (Teach Yourself Ser.). 1978. pap. 3.95 (ISBN 0-679-10471-2). McKay.
Teach Yourself Human Anatomy & Physiology. David Le Vay. (Teach Yourself Ser.). 1978. pap. 10.95 (ISBN 0-679-10399-6). McKay.
Teach Yourself Icelandic. P. J. Glendening. (Teach Yourself Ser.). 1979. pap. 6.95 (ISBN 0-679-10181-0). McKay.
Teach Yourself Indonesian. John B. Kwee. (Teach Yourself Ser.). 1980. pap. 7.95 (ISBN 0-679-10182-9). McKay.
Teach Yourself Inventing at the Professional Level. Joseph Spiteri. pap. text ed. 49.95 (ISBN 0-942661-01-X). Discovry Enterp.
Teach Yourself Irish. Myles Dillon & D. O. Croinin. (Teach Yourself Ser.). 1979. pap. 5.95 (ISBN 0-679-10183-7). McKay.
Teach Yourself Italian. K. Speight. (Teach Yourself Ser.). 1978. pap. 8.95 (ISBN 0-679-10184-5). McKay.
Teach Yourself Italian Phrase Book. (Teach Yourself Ser.). 1976. pap. 3.95 (ISBN 0-679-10236-1). McKay.
Teach Yourself Japanese. C. J. Dunn & S. Yanoda. (Teach Yourself Ser.). 1979. pap. 7.95 (ISBN 0-679-10185-3). McKay.
Teach Yourself Jazz. John Chilton. 1979. pap. 6.95 (ISBN 0-679-12225-7). McKay.
Teach Yourself Keyboard Playing & Improvisation, Vol. 1. Jack Weaton & Peter Alexander. Orig. Title: Touch Sensitivity. 126p. 1987. pap. 21.95 (ISBN 0-939067-33-1). Alexander Pub.
Teach Yourself Latin. F. K. Smith. (Teach Yourself Ser.). 1979. pap. 10.95 (ISBN 0-679-10186-1). McKay.
Teach Yourself Latin Dictionary. A. Wilson. (Teach Yourself Ser.). (Lat.). 1974. pap. 6.95 (ISBN 0-679-10204-3). McKay.
Teach Yourself Lead Guitar. Steve Tarshis. 64p. pap. 7.95 (ISBN 0-8256-2200-X). Music Sales.
Teach Yourself Linguistics. (Teach Yourself Bks.). Date not set. pap. 8.95 (ISBN 0-679-10258-2). McKay.
Teach Yourself Lip Reading. Olive M. Wyatt. (Illus.). 172p. 1974. 21.75 (ISBN 0-398-02128-7). C C Thomas.
Teach Yourself Living Welsh. John T. Bowan & P. Jones. (Teach Yourself Ser). 1978. pap. 7.95 (ISBN 0-679-10825-4). McKay.
Teach Yourself Malay. Lewis. (Teach Yourself Ser.). 1980. pap. 6.95 (ISBN 0-679-10187-X). McKay.
Teach Yourself Management Accounting. Brian Murphy. (Teach Yourself Ser.). 1978. pap. 3.95 (ISBN 0-679-10477-1). McKay.
Teach Yourself Manual for Drawing & Painting. (Teach Yourself Bks.). 1978. pap. 9.95 (ISBN 0-679-12300-8). McKay.
Teach Yourself Mechanical Engineering: Hand Tools, No. 1. A. E. Peatfield. (Teach Yourself Ser.). 1950. 1.00 (ISBN 0-486-21724-8). Dover.
Teach Yourself Micro-Electronics & Micro-Computers. 1983. pap. 5.95 (ISBN 0-679-10254-X). Macmillan.
Teach Yourself Microsoft Word 4 for IBM PC, Ps - Compatibles. Pierre-Jean Charra. Tr. by EDIDACOM Staff. 252p. Date not set. binder with book and diskette 89.95. Tutorland.
Teach Yourself Modern Dancing. Bernard Stetson. (Ballroom Dance Ser.). 1985. lib. bdg. 79.95 (ISBN 0-8490-3251-2). Gordon Pr.
Teach Yourself Modern Greek. S. A. Sofronious. (Teach Yourself Ser.). pap. 6.95 (ISBN 0-679-10189-6). McKay.
Teach Yourself Modern Persian. J. Male. (Teach Yourself Ser.). 1979. pap. 8.95 (ISBN 0-679-10220-5). McKay.
Teach Yourself More German. Sydney W. Wells. (Teach Yourself Ser.). 1979. pap. 4.95 (ISBN 0-679-10190-X). McKay.
Teach Yourself New Era Shorthand. (Teach Yourself Bks.). Date not set. pap. 7.95 (ISBN 0-679-12325-3). McKay.
Teach Yourself New Testament Greek. D. F. Hudson. 1979. pap. 6.95. McKay.
Teach Yourself Norwegian. A. Sommerfelt & I. Marm. (Teach Yourself Ser.). pap. 7.95 (ISBN 0-679-10221-3). McKay.
Teach Yourself Office Management. P. W. Betts. (Teach Yourself Ser.). 1980. pap. 4.95 (ISBN 0-679-10383-X). McKay.
Teach Yourself Organization & Methods. R. G. Breadmore. (Teach Yourself Ser.). 1976. pap. 4.95 (ISBN 0-679-10509-3). McKay.
Teach Yourself Painting & Drawing. Carole Vincent. (Illus.). 176p. 1985. pap. 12.95 (ISBN 0-7137-1580-4, Pub. by Blandford Pr England). Sterling.
Teach Yourself Physics. D. Bryant. (Teach Yourself Ser.). 1979. pap. 8.95 (ISBN 0-679-10406-2). McKay.
Teach Yourself Piano. King C. Palmer. (Teach Yourself Ser.). 1974. pap. 7.95 (ISBN 0-679-10256-6). McKay.
Teach Yourself Polish. M. Corbridge-Patkaniowska. (Teach Yourself Ser.). 1974. pap. 7.95 (ISBN 0-679-10232-9). McKay.
Teach Yourself Portuguese. J. W. Barker. (Teach Yourself Ser.). pap. 6.95 (ISBN 0-679-10193-4). McKay.
Teach Yourself Rhythm Guitar. Mark Michaels. 64p. pap. 7.95 (ISBN 0-8256-2201-8). Music Sales.
Teach Yourself Rock Bass. David Gross. 64p. pap. 7.95 (ISBN 0-8256-2202-6). Music Sales.

Teach Yourself Rock Drums. Mike Finkelstein. 80p. pap. 7.95 (ISBN 0-8256-2211-5). Music Sales.
Teach Yourself Rock Piano. Jeff Gutcheon. 72p. pap. 7.95 (ISBN 0-8256-2207-7). Music Sales.
Teach Yourself Rock Theory. Steve Tarshis. 72p. pap. 7.95 (ISBN 0-8256-2204-2). Music Sales.
Teach Yourself Romanian. M. Murrell. (Teach Yourself Ser.). 1972. pap. 8.95 (ISBN 0-679-10222-1). McKay.
Teach Yourself Russian. M. Fourman. (Teach Yourself Ser.). pap. 8.95 (ISBN 0-679-10223-X). McKay.
Teach Yourself Sanskrit. (Teach Yourself Ser). 1976. pap. 10.95 (ISBN 0-679-10238-8). McKay.
Teach Yourself Self-Defense. Eric Dominy. (Illus.). 1963. 10.95 (ISBN 0-87523-150-0). Emerson.
Teach Yourself Serbo-Croat. Vera Javarek & Miroslava Sudjic. (Teach Yourself Ser.). pap. 6.95 (ISBN 0-679-10195-0). McKay.
Teach Yourself Spanish. N. Scarlyn Wilson. (Teach Yourself Ser.). 1980. pap. 7.95 (ISBN 0-679-10197-7). McKay.
Teach Yourself Spanish Dictionary. M. H. Raventos. (Teach Yourself Ser.). (Span.). 1974. pap. 9.95 (ISBN 0-679-10230-2). McKay.
Teach Yourself Spanish Phrase Book. Coleman & Newton. (Teach Yourself Ser.). 1976. pap. 3.95 (ISBN 0-679-10237-X). McKay.
Teach Yourself Swahili. D. V. Perrott. (Teach Yourself Ser.). 1979. pap. 6.95 (ISBN 0-679-10225-6). McKay.
Teach Yourself Swahili Dictionary. D. V. Perrot. (Teach Yourself Ser.). (Swahili.). 1978. pap. 6.95 (ISBN 0-679-10015-6). McKay.
Teach Yourself Swedish. R. J. McClean. (Teach Yourself Ser.). 1978. pap. 8.95 (ISBN 0-679-10226-4). McKay.
Teach Yourself Technical Drawing. 1980. pap. 8.95 (ISBN 0-679-12476-4). McKay.
Teach Yourself the Cinema. Keith Reader. 1979. pap. 4.95 (ISBN 0-679-12056-4). McKay.
Teach Yourself the Pocket Calculator. L. R. Carter & E. Huzan. 1979. pap. 4.95 (ISBN 0-679-12375-X). McKay.
Teach Yourself to Cook. Evelyn White & Jessie R. Watson. 1974. lib. bdg. 69.95 (ISBN 0-685-51371-8). Revisionist Pr.
Teach Yourself to Play the Folk Harp. Sylvia Woods. 80p. 1982. pap. 8.95 (ISBN 0-9602990-3-3). Woods Mus Bks Pub.
Teach Yourself to Read Hebrew. 2nd rev. ed. Ethelyn Simon & Joseph Anderson. 104p. 1985. pap. 7.95 (ISBN 0-939144-11-5). EKS Pub Co.
Teach Yourself to Swim: The Racing Strokes. Lucille Griffin. (Illus.). 73p. (Orig.). 1985. pap. 10.00x (ISBN 0-9615520-0-X). Gap Mountain.
Teach Yourself Torchon Lace: Six Basic Lessons in Bobbin Lace with Workcards. Eunice Arnold. 1980. 9.95 (ISBN 0-686-27276-5). Robin & Russ.
Teach Yourself Transatlantic. Robert Hobbs. 238p. 1986. text ed. 9.95 (ISBN 0-87484-689-7). Mayfield Pub.
Teach Yourself Trigonometry. P. Abbott. (Teach Yourself Ser.). 1979. pap. 6.95 (ISBN 0-679-10409-7). McKay.
Teach Yourself Turkish. G. L. Lewis. (Teach Yourself Ser). 1979. pap. 5.95 (ISBN 0-679-10200-0). McKay.
Teach Yourself Typing. (Teach Yourself Bks.). 1979. pap. 6.95 (ISBN 0-679-12475-6). Mckay.
Teach Yourself Welding. C. G. Brainbridge. (Teach Yourself Ser.). 192p. 1981. pap. 6.95 (ISBN 0-679-10495-X). McKay.
Teach Yourself Yoruba. E. C. Rowlands. (Teach Yourself Ser). 1979. pap. 9.95 (ISBN 0-679-10224-8). McKay.
Teachability of Language. Mabel L. Rice & Richard L. Schiefelbusch. Ed. by Robert K. Hoyt, Jr. 416p. 1988. text ed. price not set (ISBN 1-55766-011-5). P H Brookes.
Teachable Moments. Kay K. Berg & Donald B. Rogers. LC 85-71827. 52p. (Orig.). 1985. pap. 3.95 (ISBN 0-88177-019-1, DR019B). Discipleship Res.
Teachable Spirit. Paulette Woods. 76p. 1984. pap. 3.50 (ISBN 0-8341-0904-2). Beacon Hill.
Teachables from Trashables: Home-Made Toys That Teach. Toys 'n Things Press. LC 79-64910. (Illus., Orig.). 1979. pap. 12.95 (ISBN 0-934140-00-6). Toys 'n Things.
Teachables II. Rhoda Redleaf. Ed. by Jill Hix. (Illus.). 224p. (Orig.). 1987. pap. 12.95 (ISBN 0-934140-41-3). Toys 'n Things.
Teacher. Sylvia Ashton-Warner. 234p. 1986. pap. 7.95 (ISBN 0-671-61768-0, Touchstone). S&S.
Teacher. Kira Daniel. LC 88-10041. (What's It Like to Be a... Ser.). (Illus.). 32p. (gr. k-2). 1988. PLB 9.89 (ISBN 0-8167-1430-4); pap. text ed. 1.95 (ISBN 0-8167-1431-2). Troll Assocs.
Teacher. Jack Rudman. (Career Examination Ser.: C-2267). (Cloth bdg. avail. on request). 1988. pap. 16.00 (ISBN 0-8373-2267-7). Natl Learning.
Teacher--Counselor Guide to Adolescent Enrichment. Monte Elchoness. 286p. (Orig.). 1987. wkbk. 14.95 (ISBN 0-936781-02-5). Monroe Pr.
Teacher! A Christlike Model for Students. Neal F. McBride. (Complete Teacher Training Meeting Ser.). 48p. 1986. 9.95 (ISBN 0-89191-313-0). Cook.
Teacher Absence & Leave Regulations: Some Basic Facts & Principles Related to Temporary Absence of Teachers for Use in Formulating Valid Absence Regulations. William D. Kuhlmann. LC 70-176939. (Columbia University. Teachers College. Contributions to Education: No. 564). Repr. of 1933 ed. 22.50 (ISBN 0-404-55564-0). AMS Pr.
Teacher Aide in the Instructional Team. Don A. Welty & Dorothy R. Welty. (Illus.). 1976. pap. 29.95 (ISBN 0-07-069263-7). McGraw.
Teacher & Child. Haim G. Ginott. 256p. 1975. pap. 3.95 (ISBN 0-380-00323-6). Avon.
Teacher & Christian Belief. Ninian Smart. 208p. 1966. 8.00 (ISBN 0-227-67703-X). Attic Pr.
Teacher & Education in Emerging Indian Society. C. L. Anand et al. 358p. 1983. 6.95. Asia Bk Corp.
Teacher & Religion. F. H. Hilliard. 191p. 1963. 8.50 (ISBN 0-227-67675-0). Attic Pr.
Teacher & Student Perceptions: Implications for Learning. J. M. Levine & M. C. Wang. (Illus.). 432p. 1983. text ed. 39.95 o. (ISBN 0-89859-206-2). L Erlbaum Assocs.
Teacher & the Drug Scene. John Eddy. (Fastback Ser.: No. 26). (Orig.). 1973. pap. 0.90 (ISBN 0-87367-026-4). Phi Delta Kappa.
Teacher & the Machine. Philip W. Jackson. LC 68-12729. (Horace Mann Lecture Ser.). Repr. of 1968 ed. 25.50 (ISBN 0-8357-9762-7, 2017870). Bks Demand UMI.
Teacher & the World's Religions. D. W. Gundry. 160p. 1968. 6.50 (ISBN 0-227-67456-1). Attic Pr.
Teacher: Anne Sullivan Macy. Helen Keller. LC 84-25274. (Illus.). vi, 247p. 1985. Repr. of 1955 ed. lib. bdg. 39.75x (ISBN 0-313-24738-2, KETE). Greenwood.
Teacher As Gift. Gertrude A. Sullivan. 64p. 1979. wire coil 5.95 (ISBN 0-697-01729-X). Wm C Brown.
Teacher as Minister Weekly Plan Book. 208p. 1979. 4.80 (ISBN 0-686-39948-X). Natl Cath Educ.
Teacher As World Citizen: A Scenario of the 21st Century. Theodore Brawick. (Education Futures Ser.: No. 5). 1976. 9.95 (ISBN 0-88280-042-6); pap. 5.95 (ISBN 0-88280-043-4). ETC Pubns.
Teacher at Work: Professional Development & the Early Childhood Educator. Margaret Yonemura. (Early Childhood Education Ser.). 176p. 1986. text ed. 19.95x (ISBN 0-8077-2832-2); pap. text ed. 10.95x (ISBN 0-8077-2815-2). Tchrs Coll.
Teacher Attitudes: An Annotated Bibliography & Guide. Marjorie Powell & Joseph W. Beard. LC 83-48213. 350p. 1985. lib. bdg. 66.00 (ISBN 0-8240-9053-5). Garland Pub.
Teacher Burnout. Alfred S. Alschuler. 96p. 1984. 7.95 (ISBN 0-8106-1680-7). NEA.
Teacher Burnout. Steve Truch. 152p. 1980. pap. text ed. 9.00 (ISBN 0-87879-242-2). Acad Therapy.
Teacher Burnout in the Public Schools: Structural Causes & Consequences for Children. Anthony G. Dworkin. LC 86-5713. (Educational Leadership Ser.). 241p. 1986. 49.50 (ISBN 0-88706-348-9); pap. 16.95x (ISBN 0-88706-349-7). State U NY Pr.
Teacher Career Stages: Implications for Staff Development. Peter J. Burke et al. LC 84-61200. (Fastback Ser.: No. 214). 50p. (Orig.). 1984. pap. 0.90 (ISBN 0-87367-214-3). Phi Delta Kappa.
Teacher Careers: Crisis & Continuities. Patricia Sikes et al. (Issues in Education & Training Ser.: Vol. 5). 225p. 1985. 33.00x (ISBN 1-85000-066-2, Falmer Pr); pap. 18.00x (ISBN 1-85000-067-0, Falmer Pr). Taylor & Francis.
Teacher-Centered In-Service Education: Planning & Products. Robert A. Luke. 72p. 1980. 9.95 (ISBN 0-8106-1624-6). NEA.
Teacher Centers: What Place in Education. Ed. by Sharon Feiman. (Orig.). 1980. pap. 1.50 (ISBN 0-686-29035-6). U Chi Ctr Policy.
Teacher Centers: Where, What, Why? Roy A. Edelfelt & Tamar Orvell. LC 78-61321. (Fastback Ser.: No. 117). 1978. pap. 0.90 (ISBN 0-87367-117-1). Phi Delta Kappa.
Teacher Certification in Ohio & a Proposed Plan of Reconstruction. Frank B. Dilley. LC 73-176720. (Columbia University. Teachers College. Contributions to Education: No. 630). Repr. of 1935 ed. 22.50 (ISBN 0-404-55630-2). AMS Pr.
Teacher Certification Tests. 2nd ed. Elna Dimock. (Professional Certification & Licensing Teacher Competency Tests). 1987. pap. 12.95 (ISBN 0-13-891011-1). P-H.
Teacher, Child & Waldorf Education. Willi Aeppli. Tr. by Angelika V. Ritscher from Ger. 1987. pap. 3.50 (ISBN 0-88010-166-0). Anthroposophic.
Teacher-Clinician Planbook & Guide to the Development of Speech Skills. Daniel Ling. LC 77-93949. 1978. pap. text ed. 8.00 (ISBN 0-88200-116-7, A2092). Alexander Graham.
Teacher Competency: Problems & Solutions. 8.95 (ISBN 0-686-36516-X, 021-00332). Am Assn Sch Admin.
Teacher Competency Testing & the Teacher Educator. Medley. 1982. 2.25 (ISBN 0-686-38078-9). Assn Tchr Ed.
Teacher Competency Tests. Elna M. Dimock. 160p. 1985. pap. 7.95 (ISBN 0-668-06231-2). Arco.
Teacher Constructed Tests. Louis Wildman. 1977. 7.00 (ISBN 0-939630-06-0). Inst Qual Hum Life.
Teacher Contracts see Encyclopedia of Public School Collective Bargaining Clauses.
Teacher-Designed Student Feedback: A Strategy for Improving Classroom Instruction. Gerald D. Bailey. 64p. 1983. 7.95 (ISBN 0-8106-1689-0). NEA.
Teacher Development for Better Pupil Achievement: Report of Regional Technical Working Group Cum Training Workshop on In-Service Training of Educational Personnel. (APEID Ser.). 85p. (Orig.). 1986. pap. text ed. 10.00 (ISBN 0-318-21536-5, UB214, UB). UNIPUB.
Teacher Development in Schools. Intro. by Edward J. Meade, Jr. 63p. (Orig.). pap. 3.50 (ISBN 0-317-63093-8). Acad Educ Dev.
Teacher Development: Induction, Renewal & Redirection. Peter Burke. LC 86-29357. 225p. 1987. 42.00x (ISBN 1-85000-143-X, Falmer Pr); pap. 22.00x (ISBN 1-85000-144-8, Falmer Pr). Taylor & Francis.
Teacher: Economic Growth & Society. Ed. by Mary I. Frank. LC 84-6621. (Journal of Children in Contemporary Society Ser.: Vol. 16, Nos. 3-4). 185p. 1984. text ed. 29.95 (ISBN 0-86656-286-9). Haworth Pr.
Teacher Education. Ed. by Kevin Ryan. LC 6-16938. (National Society for the Study of Education Yearbooks Ser: 74th Yearbook, Pt. 2). xvi, 336p. 1975. 10.00x (ISBN 0-226-60118-8). U of Chicago Pr.
Teacher Education & Curriculum for Development. (Illus.). 72p. 1977. pap. 5.00 (ISBN 0-685-76010-3, UB56, UB). UNIPUB.
Teacher Education & Educational Technology see Educational Technology Reviews Ser.
Teacher Education & Professional Development. Gordon Kirk. (Professional Issues in Education Ser.: Vol. 2). 1987. pap. 7.95 (ISBN 0-7073-0522-5, Pub. by Scot Acad Pr). Longwood Pub Group.
Teacher Education & the New Profession of Teaching. Martin Haberman & T. M. Stinnett. LC 73-7238. 1973. 24.00x (ISBN 0-8211-0751-8); text ed. 21.50x 10 or more copies (ISBN 0-685-42633-5). McCutchan.
Teacher Education & the Revival of Civic Learning. R. Freeman Butts. (Seventh Annual DeGarmo Lecture). 1982. 4.00 (ISBN 0-933669-31-3). Soc Profs Ed.
Teacher Education As Actor Training. Ed. by Ayers Bagley. (Occasional Paper: No. 3). 1974. pap. 4.00 (ISBN 0-933669-06-2). Soc Profs Ed.
Teacher Education at DePauw University. Ed. by Clifton J. Phillips. (Sesquicentennial Ser.: No. 4). (Illus.). 32p. (Orig.). 1986. pap. write for info. (ISBN 0-936631-03-1). DePauw Univ.
Teacher Education: Current Prospects. Arun K. Gupta. 227p. 1984. text ed. 25.00x (ISBN 0-86590-268-2, Sterling Pubs India). Apt Bks.
Teacher Education Evaluation. Ed. by William J. Gephart & Jerry B. Ayers. 1988. lib. bdg. 35.95 (ISBN 0-89838-270-X). Kluwer Academic.
Teacher Education for the Future. William Van Til et al. (NSCTE Monographs). 1968. 3.00 (ISBN 0-933669-01-1). Soc Profs Ed.
Teacher Education in Agriculture. 2nd ed. Ed. by Arthur L. Berkey. (Illus.). 350p. 1982. text ed. 15.95x (ISBN 0-8134-2217-5). Inter Print Pubs.
Teacher Education in America: A Documentary History. Ed. by Merle L. Borrowman. LC 65-17004. Repr. of 1965 ed. 66.00 (ISBN 0-8357-9609-4, 2016925). Bks Demand UMI.
Teacher Education in Nepal: Historical & Comprehensive. Kedar N. Shrestha. 55p. 1980. 6.00 (ISBN 0-318-12886-1, 34). Am-Nepal Ed.
Teacher Education in the Classroom: Initial & In-Service. Patricia M. E. Ashton et al. 144p. 1983. 22.50 (ISBN 0-7099-1248-X, Pub. by Croom Helm Ltd). Routledge Chapman & Hall.
Teacher Education in the Sixth Five-Year Plan. Kedar N. Shrestha. 57p. 1979. 6.00 (ISBN 0-318-12887-X, 32). Am-Nepal Ed.
Teacher Education in the Sixth-Five-Year Plan: Planning, Implementing, Evaluating. Kedar N. Shrestha. 57p. 1979. 6.00 (ISBN 0-318-04177-4). Am-Nepal Ed.
Teacher Education in the United States: The Responsibility Gap. Study Commission on Undergraduate Education & the Education of Teachers. LC 75-34710. xxxviii, 224p. 1976. 21.50x (ISBN 0-8032-0875-8); pap. 5.95x (ISBN 0-8032-5839-9, BB 621, Bison). U of Nebr Pr.
Teacher Education: Issues, Needs & Plans for Action. 88p. (Orig.). 1987. pap. text ed. 15.00 (ISBN 0-317-67235-5, UB355, UB). UNIPUB.
Teacher Education: Role-Playing & Analogies to Art. Ed. by Ayers Bagley. (Occasional Paper: No. 7). 1975. pap. 2.50 (ISBN 0-933669-10-0). Soc Profs Ed.
Teacher Effectiveness: An Annotated Bibliography & Guide to Research Education. Marjorie Powell. LC 81-48423. 780p. 1986. lib. bdg. 55.00 (ISBN 0-8240-9388-7). Garland Pub.
Teacher Effectiveness & Teacher Education: The Search for a Scientific Basis. N. L. Gage. LC 71-134225. (Illus.). 1972. 14.95x (ISBN 0-87015-190-8). Pacific Bks.
Teacher Effectiveness Training. Thomas Gordon. 1975. 13.95 (ISBN 0-88326-080-8, Wyden). McKay.
Teacher Evaluation: A Color & Activity Book. Bill Allen & Lamont Lyons. LC 76-21433. (Mandala Ser. in Education). (Illus.). Date not set. pap. price not set (ISBN 0-8290-2148-5). Irvington.
Teacher Evaluation & Development: Positive & Constructive, Vol. 3. Fredric H. Genck. (School Management Model Ser.). 90p. (Orig.). 1984. pap. 38.00 (ISBN 0-318-04003-4). Inst Pub Mgmt.
Teacher Evaluation & Merit Pay: An Annotated Bibliography. Elizabeth L. Karnes & Donald D. Black. LC 85-27226. (Bibliographies & Indexes in Education: No. 2). 403p. 1986. lib. bdg. 46.95 (ISBN 0-313-24557-6, KTE/). Greenwood.
Teacher Evaluation: Five Keys to Growth. Daniel L. Duke & Richard J. Stiggins. 48p. 1986. 6.95 (ISBN 0-8106-1536-3). NEA.
Teacher Evaluation Handbook. Renfro C. Manning. 224p. 1988. 27.95 (ISBN 0-13-888389-0). P-H.
Teacher Evaluation: Improvement, Accountability, & Effective Learning. Milbrey McLaughlin & R. Scott Pfeiffer. 176p. 1988. text ed. 25.95x (ISBN 0-8077-2891-8); pap. text ed. 13.95x (ISBN 0-8077-2890-X). Tchrs Coll.
Teacher Evaluation...Five Keys to Growth. 60p. 1986. 6.95 (ISBN 0-317-61145-3, 021-00179). Am Assn Sch Admin.
Teacher Evaluative Standards & Student Effort. Natriello & Dornbusch. (Research on Teaching Monograph). (Illus.). 320p. 1983. text ed. 33.95 (ISBN 0-582-28431-7). Longman.
Teacher Expectancies. Ed. by Jerome B. Dusek et al. (Psychology of Teaching & Instruction Ser.). 408p. 1985. 39.95 (ISBN 0-89859-443-X). L Erlbaum Assocs.
Teacher Fairs: Counterpoint to Criticism. Sara Ingrassia & Sue Foley. LC 83-83086. (Fastback Ser.: No. 204). 50p. 1984. pap. 0.90 (ISBN 0-87367-204-6). Phi Delta Kappa.
Teacher Friendly: A BASIC Programming Course Just for Classroom Teachers. Mark J. Hallenbeck & Donald F. Boetel. LC 84-62179. 1985. pap. 11.95 (ISBN 0-8224-6757-7). D S Lake Pubs.
Teacher-Friendly Computer Book. Murray Suid. 96p. (gr. 2-6). 1984. 7.95 (ISBN 0-912107-19-7). Monday Morning Bks.
Teacher Growth Notebook. Ed. by Greg D. Cook & Julie Schmitz. 193p. 1984. tchr's. ed. 19.95 (ISBN 0-89191-213-4). Cook.
Teacher Handbook for Sequencing Math Skills: Grades K-4. (Illus.). 1979. pap. 3.95 (ISBN 0-934734-03-8). Construct Educ.
Teacher Handbook for Symbol Communications Technique (SCT) rev. ed. Alfred W. Munzert. 8p. pap. write for info. (ISBN 0-917292-30-8). H U Public.
Teacher Immortal: The Enduring Influence Of Wilson C. Morris. 120p. 1985. pap. 10.00 (ISBN 0-318-17674-2). Sigma Tau Gamma.
Teacher Improvement Through Clinical Supervision. Charles A. Reavis. LC 78-50395. (Fastback Ser.: No. 111). 1978. pap. 0.90 (ISBN 0-87367-111-2). Phi Delta Kappa.
Teacher in America. Jacques Barzun. LC 80-82370. 496p. 1981. 9.00 (ISBN 0-913966-78-9, Liberty Clas); pap. 4.00 (ISBN 0-913966-79-7). Liberty Fund.
Teacher in America. Jacques Barzun. 328p. 1986. pap. text ed. 10.25 (ISBN 0-8191-5447-4). U Pr of Amer.
Teacher in Fiction, Non-Fiction, Films & Drama: An Annotated Bibliography. Mariann P. Winick. (Reference Library of the Humanities: Vol. 69). (LC 76-024749). 1984. lib. bdg. 21.00 (ISBN 0-8240-9928-1). Garland Pub.
Teacher in International Law. Manfred Lachs. 1982. lib. bdg. 47.50 (ISBN 90-247-2566-6, Pub. by Martinus Nijhoff Netherlands). Kluwer Academic.
Teacher in International Law: Teachings & Teaching. 2nd, rev. ed. Manfred Lachs. LC 86-2540. 1986. 43.50 (ISBN 9-02-473313-8, Pub. by Kluwer-Nijhoff (Netherlands)). Kluwer Academic.
Teacher in the Catholic School. Francis Raftery. 61p. 1986. 6.60 (ISBN 0-318-20567-X). Natl Cath Educ.
Teacher in the Urban Community. Leonard Covello & Guido D'Agnostino. (Quality Paperback Ser.: No. 242). 275p. 1970. pap. 5.95 (ISBN 0-8226-0242-3). Littlefield.
Teacher Incentives. Cresap et al. Ed. by Thomas F. Koerner. 56p. (Orig.). pap. text ed. 6.00 (ISBN 0-88210-160-9, NASSP). Natl Assn Principals.
Teacher Incentives: A Tool for Effective Management. 1984. 5.00 (ISBN 0-317-61144-5, 021-00125). Am Assn Sch Admin.
Teacher Induction: A New Beginning. Ed. by Douglass M. Brooks. LC 87-70080. (Papers from the National Commission on the Induction Process). 1987. 9.00 (ISBN 0-317-60476-7). Assn Tchr Ed.
Teacher, Kids, & LOGO. Carolyn Green & Christi Jaeger. (Illus.). 160p. 1984. pap. 19.95 (ISBN 0-9612226-0-3). Educomp Pubns.
Teacher Learning. Ed. by Gwyneth Dow. (Routledge Education Bks.). 110p. 1982. pap. 12.95x (ISBN 0-7100-9020-X). Routledge Chapman & Hall.
Teacher Liability in School-Shop Accidents. rev. ed. Denis J. Kigin. LC 82-61688. 1983. pap. 7.50x (ISBN 0-911168-51-6). Prakken.

Teacher-Made Aids for Elementary School Mathematics: Readings from the Arithmetic Teacher. Ed. by Seaton E. Smith, Jr. & Carl A. Backman. LC 73-21581. (Illus.). 186p. 1974. pap. 9.00 (ISBN 0-87353-093-4). NCTM.

Teacher-Made Aids for Elementary School Mathematics: Readings from the Arithmetic Teacher, Vol. 2. Ed. by Carole J. Reesink. LC 73-21581. (Illus.). 185p. 1985. pap. 10.00 (ISBN 0-87353-225-2). NCTM.

Teacher-Made Games. 1980. 14.50 (ISBN 0-939418-00-2). Ferguson-Florissant.

Teacher-Made Tests. 2nd ed. John A. Green. 224p. 1975. pap. text ed. 14.50 scp (ISBN 0-06-042489-3, HarpC). Har-Row.

Teacher Merit Pay: Promises & Pitfalls, Vol. 8. Fredric H. Genck. (School Management Model Ser.). 30p. (Orig.). 1984. pap. 22.00 (ISBN 0-318-04008-5). Inst Pub Mgmt.

Teacher Militancy: A History of Teacher Strikes 1896-1987. Roger V. Seifert. 200p. 1987. 42.00x (ISBN 1-85000-247-9, Falmer Pr); pap. 21.00x (ISBN 1-85000-248-7, Falmer Pr). Taylor & Francis.

Teacher My Stomach Hurts! A Guide to Student Health Complaints. Daniel D. Stuhlman & Arnold G. Brody. (Teacher Education Ser.: No. 1). (Orig.). 1980. pap. 1.25 (ISBN 0-934402-04-3). BYLS Pr.

Teacher: Neither Savior nor Stooge. James Henderson. 1985. 10.00x (ISBN 0-317-62202-1, Guild of Pastoral Psych). State Mutual Bk.

Teacher of Advertising & Lettering. D. M. Campana. (Illus.). 8.00 (ISBN 0-939608-29-4). Campana Art.

Teacher of Animal Painting. D. M. Campana. (Illus.). 6.95 (ISBN 0-939608-14-6). Campana Art.

Teacher of Brain Injured Children: A Discussion of the Bases for Competency. Ed. by William M. Cruickshank. LC 66-20050. (Special Education & Rehabilitation Monograph: No. 7). 1966. 10.95x (ISBN 0-8156-2096-9). Syracuse U Pr.

Teacher of China Painting. A. M. Campana. (Illus.). 1959. 9.95 (ISBN 0-939608-00-6). Campana Art.

Teacher of Dante, & Other Studies in Italian Literature. facs. ed. Nathan H. Dole. LC 67-26733. (Essay Index Reprint Ser). 1908. 16.00 (ISBN 0-8369-0383-8). Ayer Co Pubs.

Teacher of Drawing. A. M. Campana. (Illus.). 1954. 12.00 (ISBN 0-939608-13-8). Campana Art.

Teacher of Firing China & Glass. A. M. Campana. (Illus.). 1961. 3.50 (ISBN 0-939608-02-2). Campana Art.

Teacher of Flower & Fruit Painting. A. M. Campana. (Illus.). 1961. 14.95 (ISBN 0-939608-03-0). Campana Art.

Teacher of Geometrical Drawing. D. M. Campana. 6.95 (ISBN 0-939608-26-X). Campana Art.

Teacher of Jesso-Craft. D. M. Campana. (Illus.). 5.50 (ISBN 0-939608-21-9). Campana Art.

Teacher of Linoleum Block Painting. D. M. Campana. 3.50 (ISBN 0-939608-25-1). Campana Art.

Teacher of Nations & Our Era. Libor Brom. (Czech.). 1982. pap. 15.00 (ISBN 0-916824-03-9). Comenius World.

Teacher of Oil Painting. A. M. Campana. (Illus.). 1965. 6.60 (ISBN 0-939608-07-3). Campana Art.

Teacher of Pastel Painting. D. M. Campana. (Illus.). 8.45 (ISBN 0-939608-09-X). Campana Art.

Teacher of Picture Frame Finishing. A. M. Campana. (Illus.). 1962. 12.95 (ISBN 0-939608-12-X). Campana Art.

Teacher of Pottery, Clay Modeling, Casting, Sculpturing, Wood Carving. A. M. Campana. (Illus.). 1962. 5.40 (ISBN 0-939608-10-3). Campana Art.

Teacher of Pottery Made at Home. D. M. Campana. (Illus.). 6.00 (ISBN 0-939608-11-1). Campana Art.

Teacher of Rose Painting. A. M. Campana. (Illus.). 1959. 10.95 (ISBN 0-939608-01-4). Campana Art.

Teacher of Textile Painting. A. M. Campana. (Illus.). 3.50 (ISBN 0-939608-15-4). Campana Art.

Teacher of Water Color Painting. A. M. Campana. (Illus.). 1955. 7.60 (ISBN 0-939608-08-1). Campana Art.

Teacher Politics: The Influence of Unions. Maurice R. Berube. LC 87-29546. (Contributions to the Study of Education Ser.: No. 26). 192p. 1988. lib. bdg. 37.95 (ISBN 0-313-25685-3, BTH/). Greenwood.

Teacher Practitioner in Nursing, Midwifery & Health Visiting. Peter Jarvis & Sheila Gibson. LC 85-5950. 119p. (Orig.). 1985. pap. 13.50 (ISBN 0-7099-1437-7, Pub. by Croom Helm Ltd). Routledge Chapman & Hall.

Teacher Preparation & Certification: The Call for Reform. John P. Sikula & Robert A. Roth. LC 83-83084. (Fastback Ser.: No. 202). 50p. 1984. pap. 0.90 (ISBN 0-87367-202-X). Phi Delta Kappa.

Teacher-Pupil Conflict in Secondary Schools: An Educational Approach. K. A. Cronk. 250p. 1987. 40.00x (ISBN 1-85000-263-0, Falmer Pr); pap. 22.00x (ISBN 1-85000-264-9, Falmer Pr). Taylor & Francis.

Teacher Rebellion. David Selden. LC 83-4403. 256p. 1985. 16.95 (ISBN 0-88258-099-X). Howard U Pr.

Teacher Renewal: Professional Issues, Personal Choices. Ed. by Francis S. Bolin & Judith McConnell-Falk. 240p. 1986. text ed. 26.95x; pap. 16.95x (ISBN 0-8077-2822-5). Tchrs Coll.

Teacher Renewal: Revitalization of Classroom Teachers. Patricia E. Hanely & Kevin J. Swick. (What Research Says to the Teacher Ser.). 32p. 1983. 2.50 (ISBN 0-8106-1059-0). NEA.

Teacher-Researcher: How to Study Writing in the Classroom. Miles Myers. 177p. 1985. pap. 14.00 (ISBN 0-8141-5012-8). NCTE.

Teacher Retirement System of Texas. (Policy Research Project Reports: No. 79). 73p. 1987. 8.00 (ISBN 0-89940-683-1). LBJ Sch Pub Aff.

Teacher Self-Assessment: A Means for Improving Classroom Instruction. Gerald D. Bailey. 72p. 1985. 7.95 (ISBN 0-8106-1687-4). NEA.

Teacher Strategies: Explorations in the Sociology of the School. Peter Woods. 288p. 1980. 28.00 (ISBN 0-7099-0115-1, Pub. by Croom Helm Ltd); pap. 13.50 (ISBN 0-7099-0178-X). Routledge Chapman & Hall.

Teacher Strikes: Boon or Bane? A Bibliographic Review. Alva W. Stewart. (Public Administration Ser.: P 1679). 10p. 1985. 2.00 (ISBN 0-89028-409-1). Vance Biblios.

Teacher-Student Work Manual: A Model for Evaluating Traditional U. S. History Textbooks. Mack B. Morant. Ed. by Billy R. Dixon et al. LC 81-52187. 52p. 1982. student work manual 7.95 (ISBN 0-936026-15-4). R&M Pub Co.

Teacher Study Group Leader's Manual. Cheryl Asselin et al. 1975. pap. 5.00x (ISBN 0-918560-10-1). A Adler Inst.

Teacher Survey NEA Report: Computers in the Classroom. National Education Association of the United States Staff. pap. 24.50 (ISBN 0-317-55509-X, 2029543). Bks Demand UMI.

Teacher Talk: And What it Really Means. Chick Moorman & Nancy Moorman. (Illus.). 180p. 1988. pap. 9.95 (ISBN 0-9616046-2-X). Prsnl Power Pr.

Teacher, Teacher, I Done It! I Done It! I Done It! Grace B. Ferrier. 290p. 18.95. Bonus Books.

Teacher, Teacher, I Done It! I Done It! I Done Done It! Grace B. Ferrier. Ed. & intro. by Bill Nunn. (Illus.). 288p. (Orig.). 1986. 18.95; pap. 12.95 (ISBN 0-915637-02-2). Westphalia Pr.

Teacher, the Child, & Music. Phyllis Irwin & Joy Nelson. 285p. 1986. Spiralbound. pap. write for info. (ISBN 0-534-05346-7). Wadsworth Pub.

Teacher, The Children Are Here: A Guide for Teachers of the Elementary Grades. Diane Appleman & Johanna McClear. 1988. pap. 9.95 (ISBN 0-673-38001-7). Scott F.

Teacher, The Free Choice of the Will, Grace & Free Will. St. Augustine. Bd. with Two Works on Free Will. LC 67-30350. (Fathers of the Church Ser.: Vol. 59). 232p. 1968. 17.95x (ISBN 0-8132-0059-8). Cath U Pr.

Teacher Thinking: A New Perspective on Persisting Problems in Education. Ed. by R. Halkes & J. K. Olsen. 236p. 1984. pap. text ed. 22.00 (ISBN 90-265-0558-2, Pub. by Swets Zeitlinger Netherlands). Hogrefe Intl.

Teacher Thinking: A Study of Practical Knowledge. Freema Elbaz. LC 82-14418. 224p. 1983. 25.00 (ISBN 0-89397-144-8). Nichols Pub.

Teacher Time Savers. Charlie Daniel. (gr. k-3). 1978. 6.95 (ISBN 0-916456-20-X, GA76). Good Apple.

Teacher to Teacher. Nancy Doda. 63p. 1981. 5.95 (ISBN 0-318-15787-X, NMSA007). Natl Middle Schl.

Teacher-Trainer Chairman - Language Arts & Social Studies - I.S. & Jr. H.S. Jack Rudman. (Teachers License Examination Ser.: CH-30). (Cloth bdg. avail. on request). pap. 15.95 (ISBN 0-8373-8180-0). Natl Learning.

Teacher-Trainer Chairman - Math & Science - I.S. & Jr. H.S. Jack Rudman. (Teachers License Examination Ser.: CH-29). (Cloth bdg. avail. on request). pap. 15.95 (ISBN 0-8373-8179-7). Natl Learning.

Teacher Training & Special Educational Needs. Ed. by John Sayer & Neville Jones. LC 85-21340. 208p. 1985. 29.00 (ISBN 0-7099-3379-7, Pub. by Croom Helm Ltd). Routledge Chapman & Hall.

Teacher Training & Student Achievement in Less Developed Countries. Torsten Husen & Lawrence J. Saha. (Working Paper: No. 310). ii, 133p. 1978. 8.00 (ISBN 0-686-36043-5, WP-0310). World Bank.

Teacher-Training Program for Ohio. Alonzo F. Myers. LC 70-177049. (Columbia University. Teachers College. Contributions to Education: No. 266). Repr. of 1927 ed. 22.50 (ISBN 0-404-55266-8). AMS Pr.

Teacher Tune-Ups. Donna Goodrich. LC 84-80655. 80p. (Orig.). 1985. pap. 2.25 (ISBN 0-88243-754-2, 02-0754). Gospel Pub.

Teacher Turnover in the Cities & Villages of New York State. Willard S. Elsbree. LC 75-176750. (Columbia University. Teachers College. Contributions to Education: No. 300). Repr. of 1928 ed. 22.50 (ISBN 0-404-55300-1). AMS Pr.

Teacher: Twenty-Five Years Later. Lawrence J. Babin. 1981. pap. 1.00x (ISBN 0-912492-26-0). Pyquag.

Teacher, Twist Your Head Around! Gertrude M. Clark. 32p. 1986. 5.75 (ISBN 0-8062-2857-1). Carlton.

Teacher Unions & the Power Structure. Charles W. Cheng. LC 81-82467. (Fastback Ser.: No. 165). 50p. 1981. pap. 0.90 (ISBN 0-87367-165-1). Phi Delta Kappa.

Teacher Unions in Schools. Susan M. Johnson. 262p. 1984. lib. bdg. 29.95 (ISBN 0-87722-327-0). Temple U Pr.

Teacher-Written Tests. Patrick W. Miller & Harley E. Erickson. 64p. 1985. 7.95 (ISBN 0-8106-1529-0). NEA.

Teachers: A Survival Guide for the Grown-up in the Classroom. Peterson. 144p. 1986. pap. 6.95 (ISBN 0-452-25741-7, Plume). NAL.

Teachers: A to Z. (gr. 1-3). 1987. 11.95 (ISBN 0-8027-6676-5); PLB 12.85 (ISBN 0-8027-6677-3). Walker & Co.

Teacher's Almanac 1987-88. Sherwood Harris & Lorna B. Harris. (Illus.). 320p. 1987. 29.95x (ISBN 0-8160-1807-3). Facts on File.

Teacher's Almanac, 1988-89. Sherwood Harris & Lorna B. Harris. (Teacher's Almanac Ser.). (Illus.). 320p. 1988. 29.95x (ISBN 0-8160-1986-X). Facts on File.

Teachers & Classes. Kevin Harris. (Education Bks.). 190p. 1982. pap. 10.95x (ISBN 0-7100-0865-1). Routledge Chapman & Hall.

Teachers & Machines: The Classroom Use of Technology Since 1920. Larry Cuban. 144p. 1985. pap. text ed. 10.95x (ISBN 0-8077-2792-X). Tchrs Coll.

Teachers & Parents: An Adult-to-Adult Approach. Dorothy Rich. 112p. 1987. 9.95 (ISBN 0-8106-0277-6). NEA.

Teachers & Politics in France: A Pressure Group Study of the Federation de l'Education Nationale. James M. Clark. LC 67-13494. 1967. 12.00x (ISBN 0-8156-2103-5). Syracuse U Pr.

Teachers & Politics in Japan. Donald R. Thurston. LC 72-6525. (Studies of the East Asian Institute, Columbia University). 352p. 1973. 28.00x (ISBN 0-691-07553-0). Princeton U Pr.

Teachers & Teacher Education in Developing Countries. Linda A. Dove. 320p. 1986. 34.50 (ISBN 0-7099-0886-5, Pub. by Croom Helm Ltd). Routledge Chapman & Hall.

Teachers & Teaching. Peter Dawson. 176p. 1984. pap. 9.95x (ISBN 0-631-13175-2). Basil Blackwell.

Teachers & Television. Ernest Chaot et al. 256p. 1986. 31.00 (ISBN 0-7099-4819-0, Pub. by Croom Helm UK). Routledge Chapman & Hall.

Teachers & Television. Ernest Choat et al. 1987. lib. bdg. 45.00x (Pub. by Croom Helm UK). Routledge Chapman & Hall.

Teachers & Testing. David A. Goslin. LC 67-25912. 202p. 1967. 17.50x (ISBN 0-87154-358-3). Russell Sage.

Teachers & Texts. Michael W. Apple. 224p. 1987. 19.95 (ISBN 0-7102-0774-3, Pub. by Routledge UK). Routledge Chapman & Hall.

Teachers & Texts: A Political Economy of Class & Gender Relations in Education. Michael W. Apple. 259p. 1988. text ed. 12.95 (ISBN 0-415-90074-3). Routledge Chapman & Hall.

Teachers & the Law. 2nd ed. Louis Fischer et al. 395p. 1987. 38.95 (ISBN 0-582-28449-X); pap. text ed. 21.95 (ISBN 0-582-28448-1). Longman.

Teachers & Their Use of Educational Technology (Report of a Regional Training Workshop) (Illus.). 52p. (Orig.). 1987. pap. text ed. 7.50 (ISBN 0-317-59393-5, UB234, UB). UNIPUB.

Teachers & Writers Handbook of Poetic Forms. Ed. by Ron Padgett. 230p. 1987. pap. 11.95 (ISBN 0-915924-23-4). Tchrs & Writers Coll.

Teachers As Curriculm Planners: Narratives of Experience. F. Michael Connelly & Jean D. Clandinin. 240p. 1988. text ed. 26.95x (ISBN 0-8077-2907-8); pap. text ed. 15.95x (ISBN 0-8077-2906-X). Tchrs Coll.

Teachers As Inquirers: Strategies for Learning with & about Early Adolescents. Chris Stevenson. 45p. 1986. 6.00 (ISBN 0-318-23122-0). Natl Middle Schl.

Teachers As Intellectuals: Toward a Critical Pedagogy of Learning. Henry A. Giroux. (Critical Studies in Education). 288p. 1988. text ed. 39.95 (ISBN 0-89789-157-0); pap. text ed. 14.95 (ISBN 0-89789-156-2). Bergin & Garvey.

Teacher's Bag of Tricks. Patty Nelson. (Illus.). 80p. (gr. 2-6). 1986. pap. text ed. 6.95 (ISBN 0-86530-132-8). Incentive Pubns.

Teacher's Bible Commentary. Ed. by Hobbs & Paschall. LC 75-189505. 26.95 (ISBN 0-8054-1116-X). Broadman.

Teacher's Book of Affective Instruction: A Competency Based Approach. Richard B. Smith. (Orig.). 1987. wkbk., 184pgs. 22.50 (ISBN 0-8191-6483-6); lab manual, 94pgs. 5.00 (ISBN 0-8191-6484-4). U Pr of Amer.

Teacher's Book of Lists. Sheila Madsen & Bette Gould. LC 79-11230. 1979. pap. 12.95 (ISBN 0-673-16446-2). Scott F.

Teachers Catalog of Creative Program Ideas. Compiled by Ellen Meyers. (Illus.). 128p. 1986. pap. 10.00 (ISBN 0-939229-00-5). Impact II.

Teachers, Catholic Schools, & Faith Community: A Program of Spirituality. Ted Wojcicki & Kevin Convey. 135p. (Orig.). 1982. pap. 14.00. Jesuit Educ Ctr Human Dev.

Teacher's Choice: Ideas & Activities for Teaching Basic Skills. Sandra Kaplan et al. 1978. 12.95 (ISBN 0-673-16447-0). Scott F.

Teachers College Follow-up Service: Its Factors & Development in an Unsupervised Service Area. Effie G. Bathhurst. LC 79-176542. (Columbia University. Teachers College. Contributions to Education: No. 478). Repr. of 1931 ed. 22.50 (ISBN 0-404-55478-4). AMS Pr.

Teacher's Commentary. Lawrence O. Richards. 1200p. 1987. text ed. 27.95 (ISBN 0-89693-810-7). Victor Bks.

Teacher's Communication Resource Book. P. Susan Mamchak & Steven R. Mamchak. LC 85-16730. 233p. 1985. pap. 18.95x (ISBN 0-13-888355-6, Busn). P-H.

Teachers' Companion to Microcomputers. John Niman. LC 83-49527. (Illus.). 208p. 1984. pap. 16.95x (ISBN 0-669-08267-8); solutions manual avail. Lexington Bks.

Teacher's Computer Activities Book: Forty Student Projects to Use with Your Classroom Software. Patricia Shillingburg et al. (Computers & Education Ser.). 192p. 1987. pap. 15.95x (ISBN 0-8077-2824-1). Tchrs Coll.

Teacher's Contract & Other Legal Phases of Teacher Status. Earl W. Anderson. LC 78-176515. (Columbia University. Teachers College. Contributions to Education: No. 246). Repr. of 1927 ed. 22.50 (ISBN 0-404-55246-3). AMS Pr.

Teacher's Contractual Status As Revealed by an Analysis of American Court Decisions. Ira M. Allen. LC 77-176512. (Columbia University. Teachers College. Contributions to Education: No. 304). Repr. of 1928 ed. 22.50 (ISBN 0-404-55304-4). AMS Pr.

Teacher's CopeBook: End the Year Better Than You Started. Kay Winters. LC 80-81682. (gr. k-6). 1980. pap. 9.95 (ISBN 0-8224-6767-4). D S Lake Pubs.

Teacher's Craft. John Powell. (SCRE Publications Ser.: No. 85). 264p. 1985. text ed. 28.50x (ISBN 0-901116-98-X, Pub. by Scot Council Research); pap. text ed. 19.95x (ISBN 0-901116-99-8). Humanities.

Teachers' Curriculum Guide & Student Worksheet for America's 400th Anniversary Handbook. H. B. Rogers. 350p. 1984. pap. 24.50x (ISBN 0-912367-09-1). Storie McOwen.

Teacher's Dependency Load. Theresa P. Pyle. LC 79-177172. (Columbia University. Teachers College. Contributions to Education: No. 782). Repr. of 1939 ed. 22.50 (ISBN 0-404-55782-1). AMS Pr.

Teacher's Dictation Library, 2 pts. Roberta Thomas. 1974. pap. text ed. 21.95 ea. Pt. 1 (ISBN 0-89420-064-X, 139555). Pt. 2 (ISBN 0-89420-065-8, 139666). pt. 1 Optional cassette recordings 229.95 (ISBN 0-89420-212-X, 139000); pt. 2 Optional cassette recordings 289.95 (ISBN 0-89420-213-8, 139300). Natl Book.

Teachers Dictation Manual. Allen I. McHose. (Eastman School of Music Ser.). 26.95x (ISBN 0-89197-437-7); pap. text ed. 12.95x (ISBN 0-89197-960-3). Irvington.

Teacher's Dilemma: Essays of School Law & School Discipline. Thomas R. McDaniel. LC 82-21743. (Illus.). 158p. (Orig.). 1983. lib. bdg. 26.25 (ISBN 0-8191-2944-5); pap. text ed. 11.75 (ISBN 0-8191-2945-3). U Pr of Amer.

Teacher's Enrichment Activities Guide, 1 bk. Sullivan Assoc. pap. text ed. 5.00 (ISBN 0-8449-1980-2). Learning Line.

Teacher's Expectations & Teaching Reality. Ed. by A. Adams & W. Tulasiewicz. 256p. 1988. lib. bdg. 55.00 (ISBN 0-415-00552-3). Routledge Chapman & Hall.

Teacher's Experience. S. Shatsky. 342p. 1981. 8.00 (ISBN 0-8285-2158-1, Pub. by Progress Pubs USSR). Imported Pubns.

Teacher's Friend. Ella J. Anderson. 1970. pap. 3.85x (ISBN 0-87813-905-2). Christian Light.

Teacher's Gold Mine. Dorothy Michener & Beverly Muschlitz. LC 79-89646. (Illus.). 224p. 1979. pap. text ed. 10.95 (ISBN 0-913916-83-8, IP 83-8). Incentive Pubns.

Teacher's Guide. Edmondson et al. (Junior & Senior High Ser.). 111p. 1984. 9.95 (ISBN 0-911655-23-9, LWTG). Learning Wks.

Teachers Guide. (Crayola Creativity Ser.). (Illus.). 32p. Date not set. 25.00 (ISBN 0-86696-213-1). Binney & Smith.

Teacher's Guide for Melachim I: A Teacher's Guide. C. D. Rabinowitz. 5.00 (ISBN 0-914131-66-4, B45). Torah Umesorah.

Teacher's Guide for Sefer Shoftim. (Hebrew.). 4.00 (ISBN 0-914131-67-2, B42). Torah Umesorah.

Teacher's Guide for Sefer Yehoshua. C. D. Rabinowitz. (Hebrew.). 4.00 (ISBN 0-914131-68-0, B41). Torah Umesorah.

Teacher's Guide for Shmuel I-II. Rev. ed. C. D. Rabinowitz. (Hebrew.). 5.00 (ISBN 0-914131-69-9). Torah Umesorah.

Teacher's Guide to Action Research: Evaluation, Enquiry & Development in the Classroom. Ed. by Jon Nixon. 209p. 1981. pap. 10.95 (ISBN 0-86216-041-3). Basil Blackwell.

Teacher's Guide to Beyond O.K. Win Wenger. (Psychegenics Library of Experiential Protocols). 36p. (Orig.). 1985. pap. 2.00. Psychegenics.

Teacher's Guide to Classroom Management. Daniel L. Duke & Adrienne M. Meckel. 160p. 1983. pap. text ed. write for info (ISBN 0-394-32690-3, RanC). Random.

Teaching about Aids: A Teachers Guide. Danek S. Kaus & Robert D. Reed. LC 86-63523. 75p. (Orig.). 1987. 6.50x (ISBN 0-88247-766-8). R & E Pubs.

Teaching about Aids: Lesson Plans for Elementary & High School. Eileen P. Flynn. LC 87-63005. (Illus.). 88p. 1988. tchr's ed. 8.95 (ISBN 1-55612-113-X). Sheed & Ward MO.

Teaching about Alcohol: Concepts, Methods, & Classroom Activities. Peter Finn & Patricia O'Gorman. 241p. 1981. text ed. write for info. (ISBN 0-205-07195-3, Pub. by Longwood Div). Wm C Brown.

Teaching about American Indians in Connecticut. (Ethnic Studies Bulletins: No. 7). 17p. 1982. 2.00. I N Thut World Educ Ctr.

Teaching about Colorado & Community History. Gary R. Smith. (Illus.). 91p. (Orig.). (gr. 4-12). 1978. pap. 12.95 (ISBN 0-943804-05-1). U of Denver Teach.

Teaching about Conflict: Nothern Ireland. Jacquelyn S. Johnson. (Illus.). 145p. (gr. 7-12). 1983. pap. 14.95 (ISBN 0-943804-36-1). U of Denver Teach.

Teaching about Cultural Awareness. rev. ed. Gary R. Smith & George G. Otero. (Illus.). 225p. (gr. 4-12). 1982. pap. 14.95 (ISBN 0-943804-18-3). U of Denver Teach.

Teaching about Cultural Awareness with Student Handouts in Spanish. George G. Otero & Gary R. Smith. Tr. by Ann L. Espinosa & Ismael E. Espinosa. (Illus.). 235p. (gr. 4-12). pap. 15.95 (ISBN 0-943804-26-4). U of Denver Teach.

Teaching about Diversity: Latin America. rev. ed. Kenneth A. Switzer & Charlotte A. Redden. (Cultural Studies Ser.). (Illus.). 165p. (gr. 9-12). 1982. pap. 15.95 (ISBN 0-943804-19-1). U of Denver Teach.

Teaching about Diversity: Latin America; with Student Handouts in Spanish. Kenneth A. Switzer & Charlotte A. Redden. Tr. by Ann L. Espinosa & Ismael E. Jacome. (Illus.). 175p. (Orig.). (gr. 9-12). 1982. pap. 15.95 (ISBN 0-943804-27-2). U of Denver Teach.

Teaching about Drugs. 3rd ed. American School Health Association & the Pharmaceutical Manufacturers Association Curriculum Guide Rewrite Committee. 213p. 1985. pap. text ed. 13.95 (ISBN 0-89917-447-7). Tichenor Pub.

Teaching about Drugs: A Curriculum Guide, K-12. 3rd ed. Curriculum Guide Rewrite Committee. 205p. 1985. 13.95 (ISBN 0-317-37219-X). Am Sch Health.

Teaching about Energy: Nineteen Eighty-Four to Nineteen Eighty-Five Supplement. John Lord et al. (Energy Eighty Ser.). 280p. 1985. pap. 10.00 (ISBN 0-934653-05-4). Enterprise Educ.

Teaching about Ethnic Conflict. Steven L. Lamy. (Illus.). 223p. (Orig.). pap. 15.95 (ISBN 0-943804-07-8). U of Denver Teach.

Teaching about Ethnic Heritage. rev. ed. George G. Otero & Gary R. Smith. Rev. by Edith King. (Illus.). 147p. (Orig.). (gr. k-12). 1977. pap. 16.95 (ISBN 0-943804-06-X). U of Denver Teach.

Teaching About Families: Text Book Evaluations & Recommendations for Secondary Schools. Hyman Rodman. LC 79-136300. 1970. 4.50x (ISBN 0-87299-013-3). Howard Doyle.

Teaching about Food & Hunger. George G. Otero & Gary R. Smith. (Illus.). 227p. (Orig.). (gr. 6-12). 1978. pap. 14.95 (ISBN 0-943804-35-3). U of Denver Teach.

Teaching about Korea: Elementary & Secondary Activities. Ed. by Yong-Sook Lee et al. 226p. (Orig.). 1986. pap. 15.95 (ISBN 0-89994-309-8). Soc Sci Ed.

Teaching about Latin America: Curriculum Projects for Grades 6-12. Ed. by Robert J. Knowlton. 75p. 1984. pap. 5.00 (ISBN 0-317-43429-2). Tulane Lat Am Lib.

Teaching about New Mexico History & Culture. George G. Otero. (Illus.). 108p. (gr. 1-8). 1978. pap. 12.95 (ISBN 0-943804-04-3). U of Denver Teach.

Teaching about Nuclear Disarmament. James M. Becker. LC 85-61792. (Fastback Ser.: No. 229). 50p. 1985. pap. 0.90 (ISBN 0-87367-229-1). Phi Delta Kappa.

Teaching about Nuclear War. (Illus.). 72p. (Orig.). 1985. pap. text ed. 6.00 (ISBN 0-87355-053-6). Natl Sci Tchrs.

Teaching about Peace & Nuclear War: A Balanced Approach. John Zola & Jaye Zola. 114p. (Orig.). 1985. pap. 10.95 (ISBN 0-89994-305-5). Soc Sci Ed.

Teaching about Perception: The Arabs. George G. Otero, Jr. (Orig.). (gr. 5-12). 1978. pap. 15.95 (ISBN 0-943804-20-5). U of Denver Teach.

Teaching about Population Growth. updated ed. George G. Otero. (Illus.). (gr. 6-12). 1983. pap. 14.95 (ISBN 0-943804-01-9). U of Denver Teach.

Teaching about Population Issues. updated ed. George G. Otero. (Illus.). 81p. (gr. 6-12). 1983. pap. 14.95 (ISBN 0-943804-02-7). U of Denver Teach.

Teaching About Race Relations: Problems & Effects. Lawrence Stenhouse & Verna K. Gajendra. (Routledge Education Books). 260p. 1982. 26.95x (ISBN 0-7100-9036-6). Routledge Chapman & Hall.

Teaching about Religion in the Public Schools. Charles R. Kniker. LC 84-62994. (Fastback Ser.: No. 224). 50p. (Orig.). 1985. pap. 0.90 (ISBN 0-87367-224-0). Phi Delta Kappa.

Teaching about Spaceship Earth: A Role-Playing Experience for the Middle Grades. (Illus.). 1972. 1.95 (ISBN 0-685-84002-6). ACEI.

Teaching about the Constitution. Ed. by Clair W. Keller & Denny L. Schillings. LC 87-61298. (Bulletin Ser.: No. 80). (Orig.). 1987. pap. text ed. 10.95 (ISBN 0-87986-055-3). Nat Coun Soc Studies.

Teaching about the Consumer & the Global Marketplace. Ed. by Bruce Koranski. (Illus.). 219p. (Orig.). (gr. 4-12). 1981. pap. 15.95 (ISBN 0-943804-17-5). U of Denver Teach.

Teaching about the Future: Tools, Topics, & Issues. John D. Haas et al. (Illus.). 176p. (Orig.). 1987. pap. 21.95 (ISBN 0-89994-311-X). Soc Sci Ed.

Teaching about the Law. Ronald Gerlach & Lynn Lamprecht. 345p. 1975. pap. 15.75 (ISBN 0-87084-834-8). Anderson Pub Co.

Teaching about the Other Americans: Minorities in United States History. Ann Curry. 9.95 (ISBN 0-86548-028-1). R & E Pubs.

Teaching about the United Nations & the Specialized Agencies: A Selected Bibliography, (UNESCO) (Education Studies & Documents: No. 29). pap. 13.00 (ISBN 0-8115-1353-X). Kraus Repr.

Teaching about United States History. rev. ed. Gary R. Smith. (Illus.). (gr. 6-12). 1979. pap. 16.95 (ISBN 0-943804-03-5). U of Denver Teach.

Teaching About Vision. rev. & enl. ed. (Illus.). 72p. 2.00 (ISBN 0-318-15870-1, P619). Natl Soc Prevent Blindness.

Teaching about Women in the Social Studies: Concepts, Methods & Materials. Ed. by Jean D. Grambs. LC 75-43431. (Bulletin Ser.: No. 48). 119p. 1976. pap. text ed. 8.35 (ISBN 0-87986-005-7, 498-15254). Nat Coun Soc Studies.

Teaching about World Cultures. Michelle Sanborn et al. (Illus.). 237p. (gr. 7-12). 1986. pap. 16.95 (ISBN 0-943804-41-8). U of Denver Teach.

Teaching Abroad. Ed. by Barbara C. Connotillo. 160p. 1984. pap. text ed. 11.95 (ISBN 0-87206-124-8). Inst Intl Educ.

Teaching Abroad 1988-91. 250p. 1988. pap. 21.95 (ISBN 0-87206-158-2, 1582E). Inst Intl Educ.

Teaching Across Cultures in the Univesity ESL Program (1986) Patricia Byrd. 149p. 1986. pap. text ed. write for info. (ISBN 0-912207-17-5). NAFSA Washington.

Teaching Activities for Defensive Living: Films & Support Materials for Teaching Defensive Living or Any Outdoor Activity. Grit Peterson & Skip Stoffel. 1978. pap. 6.00 (ISBN 0-913724-22-X). Emerg Response Inst.

Teaching Adults. Alan Roger. 224p. 1986. 59.00x (ISBN 0-335-15235-X, Open Univ Pr); pap. 19.00x (ISBN 0-335-15234-1). Taylor & Francis.

Teaching Adults: An Active Learning Approach. Elizabeth Jones. LC 85-63557. 155p. 1986. 6.00 (ISBN 0-912674-96-2, NAEYC #205). Natl Assn Child Ed.

Teaching Adults Through Discussion. Ed. by Ed Stewart. 32p. 1978. pap. 1.50 (ISBN 0-8307-0508-2, 9970401). Regal.

Teaching Adults with Confidence. Paul E. Loth. 48p. 1984. pap. 3.95 (ISBN 0-910566-43-7); seminar planbook 3.95 (ISBN 0-910566-44-5). Evang Tchr.

Teaching Afro-American History. Robert L. Harris, Jr. LC 85-71550. 66p. Date not set. pap. 5.00 (ISBN 0-87229-033-6). Am Hist Assn.

Teaching Agriculture Through Problem Solving. 3rd ed. John R. Crunkilton & Al H. Krebs. 1981. text ed. 14.95x (ISBN 0-8134-2199-3). Inter Print Pubs.

Teaching AIDS. rev. ed. Marcia Quackenbush & Pamela Sargent. 164p. (YA) 1988. pap. text ed. 19.95 (ISBN 0-941816-41-9). Network Pubns.

Teaching Aids & Techniques see Language Classroom.

Teaching Aids & Techniques: Principle Demonstrations see Culture, Literature, & Articulation.

Teaching Aids & Techniques: The Secondary School Language Laboratory see Language Learner.

Teaching Aids for Blind & Visually Limited Children. Barbara Dorward & Natalie Barraga. 139p. 1968. 3.00 (ISBN 0-89128-062-6, PEP062). Am Foun Blind.

Teaching All Children to Read. Michael Wallach & Lise Wallach. LC 75-19503. (Illus.). 1979. pap. 5.50X (ISBN 0-226-87167-3, P849). U of Chicago Pr.

Teaching All Children to Read. Michael A. Wallach & Lisa Wallach. LC 75-19503. (Illus.). 352p. 1976. kit 30.00x (ISBN 0-226-87168-1). U of Chicago Pr.

Teaching All the Children to Write. Ed. by James L. Collins. 100p. 1983. pap. text ed. 7.00 (ISBN 0-930348-10-9). NY St Eng Coun.

Teaching American History: New Directions. Ed. by Matthew T. Downey. LC 81-86080. (Bulletin Ser.: No. 67). (Illus.). 115p. (Orig.). 1982. pap. text ed. 8.75 (ISBN 0-87986-043-X, 498-15306). Nat Coun Soc Studies.

Teaching American History: Structured Inquiry Approaches. Ed. by Glenn M. Linden & Matthew T. Downey. 110p. 1976. 12.95 (ISBN 0-89994-185-0). Soc Sci Ed.

Teaching American History: The Quest for Relevancy. Ed. by Allan O. Kownslar. LC 74-81013. (Yearbook Ser.: No. 44). (Illus.). 237p. 1974. pap. text ed. 3.50 (ISBN 0-87986-035-9, 490-15280). Nat Coun Soc Studies.

Teaching American Indian History: An Interdisciplinary Approach. Larry L. Vantine. LC 78-62223. 1978. soft cover 11.95 (ISBN 0-88247-546-0). R & E Pubs.

Teaching an Infant to Swim. Virginia H. Newman. LC 82-23395. (Illus.). 128p. 1983. pap. 7.95 (ISBN 0-15-688242-6, Harv, Harv). HarBraceJ.

Teaching & Applying Mathematical Modelling. Ed. by J. S. Berry et al. LC 84-4561. (Mathematics & Its Applications Ser.: 1-176). 491p. 1984. text ed. 88.95x (ISBN 0-470-20079-0). Halsted Pr.

Teaching & Assessing Writing: Recent Advances in Understanding, Evaluating & Improving Student Performance. Edward M. White. LC 84-43036. (Higher Education Ser.). 1985. text ed. 25.95x (ISBN 0-87589-641-3). Jossey-Bass.

Teaching & Celebrating Advent. rev. ed. Donald Griggs & Patricia Griggs. (Griggs Educational Resources Ser.). (Illus.). 1980. pap. 6.95 (ISBN 0-687-41080-0). Abingdon.

Teaching & Celebrating Lent-Easter. Patricia Griggs & Donald Griggs. (Griggs Educational Resources Ser.). 1980. pap. 6.95 (ISBN 0-687-41081-9). Abingdon.

Teaching & Coaching Tennis. 4th ed. John F. Kenfield, Jr. 152p. 1982. pap. text ed. write for info. (ISBN 0-697-07184-7). Wm C Brown.

Teaching & Development: A Soviet Investigation. L. V. Zankov et al. Ed. by Beatrice B. Szekely. Tr. by Arlo Schultz. LC 77-82338. (Illus.). 296p. (Orig., Rus.). 1977. 40.00 (ISBN 0-87332-109-X). M E Sharpe.

Teaching & Learning. Ed. by Donald Vandenberg. LC 69-17365. (Reading in the Philosophy of Education Ser.). 308p. 1969. 24.95 (ISBN 0-252-00009-9); pap. 9.95 (ISBN 0-252-00008-0). U of Ill Pr.

Teaching & Learning. Ed. by Donald Vandenberg. LC 69-17365. (Readings in the Philosophy of Education Ser.). pap. 77.30 (ISBN 0-317-41924-2, 2025920). Bks Demand UMI.

Teaching & Learning: A Problem-Solving Focus. Ed. by Frances R. Curcio. (Illus.). 114p. 1987. pap. 13.50 (ISBN 0-87353-240-6). NCTM.

Teaching & Learning about Aging. Richard O. Ulin. 92p. 1982. 7.95 (ISBN 0-8106-1826-5). NEA.

Teaching & Learning About Science & Society. John M. Ziman. LC 80-40326. (Illus.). 148p. 1980. 27.95 (ISBN 0-521-23221-X). Cambridge U Pr.

Teaching & Learning About Science & Social Policy. Kenneth D. Benne & Max Birnbaum. 132p. 1978. 9.95 (ISBN 0-89994-233-4). Soc Sci Ed.

Teaching & Learning America's Christian Historу. Rosalie J. Slater. LC 65-26334. 1965. lib. bdg. 12.50 (ISBN 0-912498-02-1). Found Am Christ.

Teaching & Learning Basic Skills: A Guide for Adult Basic Education & Developmental Education Programs. Mark H. Rossman & Elizabeth C. Fisk. LC 83-9118. 1984. pap. text ed. 15.95x (ISBN 0-8077-2746-6). Tchrs Coll.

Teaching & Learning English As a Foreign Language. Charles C. Fries. (Orig.). 1945. pap. 9.95x (ISBN 0-472-08347-3). U of Mich Pr.

Teaching & Learning for Practice. Barbara Butler & Doreen Elliott. 130p. 1985. pap. text ed. 8.95 (ISBN 0-566-00869-6). Gower Pub Co.

Teaching & Learning in a Diverse World: Multicultural Education for Young Children. Patricia G. Ramsey. (Early Childhood Education Ser.). 1986. text ed. 26.95x (ISBN 0-8077-2830-6); pap. text ed. 15.95x (ISBN 0-8077-2828-4). Tchrs Coll.

Teaching & Learning in a Microelectronic Age. Harold G. Shane. LC 86-63343. 90p. (Orig.). 1987. pap. 4.00 (ISBN 0-87367-434-0). Phi Delta Kappa.

Teaching & Learning in Social Work Education. Date not set. 3.10. Coun Soc Wk Ed.

Teaching & Learning in the Elementary School. 3rd ed. John Jarolimek & Clifford D. Foster. 416p. 1985. text ed. write for info. (ISBN 0-02-360340-2). Macmillan.

Teaching & Learning Languages. Earl W. Stevick. 21.95 (ISBN 0-521-24818-3); pap. 9.95 (ISBN 0-521-28201-2). Cambridge U Pr.

Teaching & Learning Math in Secondary Schools. Frederick H. Bell. 576p. 1978. pap. text ed. write for info. (ISBN 0-697-06017-9). Wm C Brown.

Teaching & Learning Mathematical Problem Solving: Multiple Research Perspectives. Ed. by Edward S. Silver. (Problem Solving Ser.). 469p. 1985. pap. text ed. 49.95 (ISBN 0-89859-681-5); pap. 14.95 (ISBN 0-89859-759-5). L Erlbaum Assocs.

Teaching & Learning Mathematics. Peter G. Dean. (Woburn Education Ser.). (Illus.). 280p. 1982. 22.50x (ISBN 0-7130-0168-2, Pub. by Woburn Pr England); pap. text ed. 12.50x (ISBN 0-7130-4007-6). Biblio Dist.

Teaching & Learning of Psychoanalysis: Selected Papers of Joan Fleming, M.D. Ed. by Stanley Weiss. LC 86-14910. (Guilford Psychoanalysis Ser.). 216p. 1986. lib. bdg. 25.00 (ISBN 0-89862-326-X). Guilford Pr.

Teaching & Learning of Psychotherapy. rev. ed. Rudolf Ekstein & Robert S. Wallerstein. LC 70-184442. 277p. 1972. text ed. 37.50 (ISBN 0-8236-6363-9). Intl Univs Pr.

Teaching & Learning Primary Science. Wynne Harlen. 256p. 1985. pap. text ed. 15.95x (ISBN 0-8077-2865-9). Tchrs Coll.

Teaching & Learning Process. Terry W. Blue. 72p. 1981. 7.95 (ISBN 0-8106-1684-X, 1684-X-06). NEA.

Teaching & Learning Psychiatry & Behavioral Science. Ed. by Joel Yager. 560p. 1982. 59.50 (ISBN 0-8089-1457-X, 794943). Grune.

Teaching & Learning Reading: A Pragmatic Approach. Barbara E. Swaby. 1984. text ed. write for info. (ISBN 0-673-39181-7). Scott F.

Teaching & Learning Signing Exact English: An Idea Book. Gerilee Gustason. 470p. (Orig.). 1983. pap. 39.95 (ISBN 0-916708-08-X); 37.50. Modern Signs.

Teaching & Learning the Language Arts. 2nd ed. Edna P. DeHaven. 1983. text ed. write for info. (ISBN 0-673-39148-5). Scott F.

Teaching & Learning the Language Arts. 3rd ed. Edna P DeHaven. 1988. text ed. write for info. (ISBN 0-673-39715-7). Scott F.

Teaching & Learning with Computers: A Guide for College Faculty & Administrators. Barry Heermann. LC 87-46331. (Higher Education Ser.). 1988. 22.95x (ISBN 1-55542-084-2). Jossey-Bass.

Teaching & Learning with LOGO. Allan Martin. 246p. 1986. pap. text ed. 15.95x (ISBN 0-8077-2799-7). Tchrs Coll.

Teaching & Learning with Magic. Windley. (ps-6). Date not set. pap. 9.95 (ISBN 0-317-63416-X). Acropolis.

Teaching & Learning with Robots. Ed. by Colin Terry & Peter Thomas. 256p. 1988. lib. bdg. 50.00x (ISBN 0-7099-4318-0, Pub. by Croom Helm UK). Routledge Chapman & Hall.

Teaching & Loving the Elderly. Martha T. John. 274p. 1983. spiral bdg. 23.00x (ISBN 0-398-04812-6). C C Thomas.

Teaching & Mainstreaming Autistic Children. Peter Knoblock. 360p. pap. text ed. 19.95 (ISBN 0-89108-111-9). Love Pub Co.

Teaching & Managing: Inseparable Activities in Schools. Cyril Wilkinson & Ernie Cave. 224p. 1988. lib. bdg. 49.95x (ISBN 0-7099-3693-1, Pub. by Croom Helm UK). Routledge Chapman & Hall.

Teaching & Mastery of Language. Aelita K. Markova. Ed. by Beatrice B. Szekely. Tr. by Michel Vale. LC 78-65595. pap. 73.30 (ISBN 0-317-41987-0, 2026124). Bks Demand UMI.

Teaching & Mastery of Language. Aelita K. Markova. Ed. by Beatrice B. Szekely. LC 78-65595. Repr. of 1979 ed. 73.30 (2027621). Bks Demand UMI.

Teaching & Media: A Systematic Approach. 2nd ed. Vernon S. Gerlach & Donald P. Ely. (Illus.). 1980. text ed. write for info. (ISBN 0-13-891358-7). P-H.

Teaching & Morality. Francis C. Wade. LC 63-17962. 1963. 2.95 (ISBN 0-8294-0080-X). Loyola.

Teaching & Personality. David Fontana. 208p. 1986. text ed. 34.95 (ISBN 0-631-14913-9); pap. text ed. 14.95 (ISBN 0-631-14914-7). Basil Blackwell.

Teaching & Practice of Art at DePauw. Ed. by Clifton J. Phillips. (Sesquicentennial Ser.: No. 3). (Illus.). 32p. (Orig.). 1986. pap. write for info (ISBN 0-936631-02-3). DePauw Univ.

Teaching & Reaching. Sally E. Stuart. 1980. pap. 9.95 (ISBN 0-87162-243-2, D7790). Warner Pr.

Teaching & Reaching: Junior Resources. Sally E. Stuart. 1983. pap. 7.95 (ISBN 0-87162-285-8, D5702). Warner Pr.

Teaching & Reaching: Kindergarten Resources. Sally E. Stuart. 1983. pap. 7.95 (ISBN 0-87162-283-1, D5700). Warner Pr.

Teaching & Reaching: Primary Resources. Sally E. Stuart. 1983. pap. 7.95 (ISBN 0-87162-284-X, D5701). Warner Pr.

Teaching & Research in International Law in Asia & the Pacific: Report of a Regional Consultation Meeting Including Nine Country Status Surveys, Seoul, Republic of Korea, 10-13 October 1984. (Occasional Monographs & Papers Ser.: No. 11). 264p. 1986. pap. 12.75 (UB183 6011, UNESCO). UNIPUB.

Teaching & Research in Philosophy: Asia & the Pacific. (Studies on Teaching & Research in Philosophy Throughout the World: No. II). (Illus.). 423p. (Orig.). 1987. pap. text ed. 25.50 (ISBN 92-3-102389-6, U1569, UNESCO). UNIPUB.

Teaching & Research in Philosophy: Africa. (Studies on Teaching & Research in Philosophy Throughout the World Ser.: No. 1). 287p. 1985. pap. 15.75 (ISBN 92-3-102124-9, U1447, UNESCO). UNIPUB.

Teaching & Talking with Deaf Children. David Wood et al. LC 85-26553. 199p. 1986. 35.95 (ISBN 0-471-90827-4). Wiley.

Teaching & Teacher Education: Implementing Reform. Robert A. Roth. LC 85-63695. (Fastback Ser.: No. 240). 50p. (Orig.). 1986. pap. 0.90 (ISBN 0-87367-240-2). Phi Delta Kappa.

Teaching & the Art of Questioning. J. T. Dillon. LC 83-61781. (Fastback Ser.: No. 194). 50p. 1983. pap. 0.90 (ISBN 0-87367-194-5). Phi Delta Kappa.

Teaching & the Case Method. rev. ed. C. Roland Christensen et al. LC 86-22732. (Illus.). 304p. 1987. 29.95 (ISBN 0-87584-178-3, 9-387-001); instr's guide 14.95 (ISBN 0-87584-181-3, 5-387-010). Harvard Busn.

Teaching & the Unconscious Mind. J. C. Hill. LC 78-141661. 176p. 1971. text ed. 20.00x (ISBN 0-8236-6365-5). Intl Univs Pr.

Teaching & Worship of the Liberal Catholic Church. Edmund W. Sheehan. Ed. by William H. Pitkin. (Illus.). 1978. pap. 2.25 (ISBN 0-918980-07-0). St Alban Pr.

Teaching & Writing Popular Fiction: Horror, Adventure, Mystery & Romance in the American Classroom. new ed. Karen M. Hubert. (Illus.). 236p. (Orig.). 1976. pap. 8.95. Tchrs & Writers Coll.

Teaching Anthropology. Ed. by P. C. Rice. (Special Issues of the Anthropology & Education Quarterly Ser.: Vol. 16, No. 4). 1985. 7.50 (ISBN 0-317-66347-X). Am Anthro Assn.

Teaching Aphasic Children: The Instructional Methods of Barry & McGinnis. Hortense Barry & Mildred A. McGinnis. LC 87-29799. (Classics Ser.). (Illus.). 244p. 1988. text ed. 24.00x (ISBN 0-89079-171-6, 1433). Pro Ed.

Teaching Aphasics & Other Language Deficient Children: Theory & Application of the Association Method. rev. ed. Etoile Dubard. LC 83-1284. (Illus.). 1983. 20.00x (ISBN 0-87805-182-1). U Pr of Miss.

Teaching Apprentice Program in Language & Literature. Ed. by Joseph Gibaldi & James V. Mirollo. LC 81-1159. (Options for Teaching Ser.: No. 4). ix, 138p. (Orig.). 1981. pap. 17.50x (ISBN 0-87352-303-2, J203). Modern Lang.

Teaching Approaches in Music Theory: An Overview of Pedagogical Philosophies. Michael R. Rogers. LC 83-10167. 236p. 1984. 24.50x (ISBN 0-8093-1147-X). S Ill U Pr.

Teaching Archery: Steps to Success. Kathleen M. Haywood & Catherine F. Lewis. (Steps to Success Activity Ser.). (Illus., Orig.). 1988. pap. text ed. write for info. (ISBN 0-88011-334-0). Leisure Pr.

Teaching Art as a Career. rev. ed. 1971. pap. 2.00 (ISBN 0-937652-25-3). Natl Art Ed.

Teaching Art in the Elementary School: Enhancing Visual Perception. Phil H. Rueschoff & M. Evelyn Swartz. LC 78-75641. (Illus.). pap. 86.30 (ISBN 0-317-10362-8, 2055518). Bks Demand UMI.

Teaching Art to the Deaf. Linda K. Kingsley. 1974. lib. bdg. 69.95 (ISBN 0-8490-1179-5). Gordon Pr.

Teaching Art to Young Children Four to Nine. Rob Barnes. (Illus.). 176p. 1987. text ed. 34.95x (ISBN 0-04-371096-4); pap. text ed. 14.95x (ISBN 0-04-371097-2). Unwin Hyman.

Teaching As a Conserving Activity. Neil Postman. 1987. pap. 4.95 (ISBN 0-440-38486-9, LE). Dell.

Teaching As a Lively Art. rev. ed. Margorie Spock. 145p. 1986. pap. 8.95 (ISBN 0-88010-127-X). Anthroposophic.

Teaching As a Moral Craft. Alan R. Tom. LC 83-17520. 256p. 1984. pap. text ed. 15.95 (ISBN 0-582-28307-8). Longman.

Teaching As a Subversive Activity. Neil Postman & Charles Weingartner. 1987. pap. 4.95 (ISBN 0-440-38485-0, LE). Dell.

Teaching as Jesus Taught. Georgianna Summers. LC 83-70161. 96p. (Orig.). 1983. pap. 4.50 (ISBN 0-88177-000-0, DR000B). Discipleship Res.

Teaching As Though Students Mattered. Ed. by Joseph Katz. LC 84-82380. (Teaching & Learning Ser.: No. 21). (Orig.). 1985. pap. text ed. 12.95x (ISBN 0-87589-771-1). Jossey-Bass.

Teaching As Treatment. Robert R. Carkhuff & Bernard G. Bernson. LC 75-40865. (Support Ser.). (Illus.). 150p. 1976. pap. text ed. 15.00x (ISBN 0-914234-84-6). Human Res Dev Pr.

Teaching Asian Musics in Elementary & Secondary Schools. rev. ed. William M. Anderson. (Illus.). 107p. 1986. pap. 7.95 (ISBN 0-937203-13-0); cassette 6.00 (ISBN 0-937203-14-9). World Music Pr.

Teaching ASL as a Second-Foreign Language: Proceedings of National Symposium on Sign Language Research & Teaching. Ed. by Frank Caccamise & Mervin Garretson. 240p. (Orig.). 1982. pap. text ed. 16.95 (ISBN 0-913072-49-4). Natl Assn Deaf.

Teaching Assistant. Jack Rudman. (Career Examination Ser.: C-2845). (Cloth bdg. avail. on request). 1988. pap. 16.00 (ISBN 0-8373-2845-4). Natl Learning.

Teaching Atlas of Mammography. 2nd rev. ed. Lazzlo Tabar & Peter B. Dean. (Illus.). 328p. 1985. 110.00 (ISBN 0-86577-198-7). Thieme Med Pubs.

Teaching Authority & Infallibility in the Church, No. 6. Ed. by Paul C. Empie et al. LC 79-54109. (Lutherans & Catholics in Dialogue). 368p. (Orig.). 1978. pap. 9.95 (ISBN 0-8066-1733-0, 10-6222). Augsburg.

Teaching Authority in the Early Church. Robert B. Eno. LC 83-83253. (Message of the Fathers of the Church Ser.: Vol. 14). 1984. 15.95 (ISBN 0-89453-354-1); pap. 9.95 (ISBN 0-89453-325-8). M Glazier.

Teaching Authority of the Believers. Ed. by Johannes-Baptist Metz & Edward Schillebeeckx. (Concilium Ser.). 128p. 1985. pap. 14.95 (Pub. by T & T Clark Ltd UK). Fortress.

Teaching Basic Aquatics...Especially to Those Who Have Difficulty Learning. Marlene M. Donahue-Gandy. LC 84-71097. (Illus.). 104p. (Orig.). 1984. pap. 10.00 (ISBN 0-9613514-0-3). M M Donahue Gandy.

Teaching Basic Behavioural Principles: A Manual for Course Tutors Using "Helping the Retarded". A. C. Capie et al. 88p. 1985. tchr's manual 25.00x (ISBN 0-906054-20-6, Pub. by British Inst Mental). State Mutual Bk.

Teaching Basic Burn Care. Irving Feller & Claudella A. Jones. LC 75-15373. (Illus.). 1975. plastic 3-ring binder 120.00 (ISBN 0-917478-27-4). Natl Inst Burn.

Teaching Basic Business, Marketing, Enterpreneurial Skills. Calfrey C. Calhoun. LC 87-71589. 224p. 1988. pap. text ed. 20.00 (ISBN 0-938991-15-9). Colonial Pr AL.

Teaching Basic Guitar Skills to Special Learners: A Data-Based Approach. 2nd, rev. ed. Robert Krout. 1983. pap. 13.25 spiral binding (ISBN 0-918812-31-3). MMB Music.

Teaching Basic Gymnastics: A Coeducational Approach. 2nd ed. Phyllis S. Cooper. 217p. 1989. write for info. (ISBN 0-02-324691-X). Macmillan.

Teaching Basic Skills in College: A Guide to Objectives, Skills Assessment, Course Content, Teaching Methods, Support Services, & Administration. Alice S. Trillin et al. LC 79-92469. (Higher Education Ser.). 1980. text ed. 29.95x (ISBN 0-87589-456-9). Jossey-Bass.

Teaching Basic Skills in Reading. Leslie A. Perry & Cynthia C. Woodington. (Illus.). 178p. 1985. 21.75 (ISBN 0-398-05091-0). C C Thomas.

Teaching BASIC: Thirty Lesson Plans, Activities, & Quizzes, Applesoft, 2 Vols. John A. Vonk & Fritz J. Erickson. LC 83-80815. 152p. (Orig.). 1983. Vol. 1, Applesoft. pap. 19.95 (ISBN 0-918452-45-7); Vol. 2, TRS-80. pap. 19.95 (ISBN 0-918452-48-1). Learning Pubns.

Teaching Basics: Adult. Daryl Dale. (Illus.). 80p. (Orig.). 1985. pap. 2.00 (ISBN 0-87509-369-8). Chr Pubns.

Teaching Basics: Junior. Daryl Dale. (Illus.). 73p. (Orig.). 1985. pap. 2.00 (ISBN 0-87509-359-0). Chr Pubns.

Teaching Basics: Preschool. Mavis Weisman. Ed. by Daryl Dale. (Illus.). 78p. (Orig.). 1985. pap. 2.00 (ISBN 0-87509-370-1). Chr Pubns.

Teaching Basics: Primary. Daryl Dale. (Illus.). 77p. (Orig.). 1985. pap. 2.00 (ISBN 0-87509-363-9). Chr Pubns.

Teaching Basics: Youth. Daryl Dale. (Illus.). 80p. (Orig.). 1985. pap. 2.00 (ISBN 0-87509-364-7). Chr Pubns.

Teaching Behavioral Self-Control to Students. Edward Workman. LC 82-435. (Illus.). 120p. (Orig.). 1982. pap. text ed. 16.00x (ISBN 0-936104-23-6, 0071). Pro Ed.

Teaching Behaviorally Disordered Students: Preferred Practices. Daniel P. Morgan & William R. Jenson. 480p. 1988. case bound 27.95 (ISBN 0-675-20543-3); supplements avail. Merrill.

Teaching Bible Stories More Effectively with Puppets. Roland Sylwester. (Illus.). 64p. 1976. pap. 4.50 (ISBN 0-570-03731-X, 12-2633). Concordia.

Teaching Bible Truths with Single Objects. Lindgren. 1979. 3.50 (ISBN 0-88207-036-3). Victor Bks.

Teaching Bilingual Children: Anthology Dealing with Key Issues & Practical Problems in Bilingual Education. Ed. by Arthur Tobier. 54p. 1974. pap. 2.00 (ISBN 0-918374-17-0). City Coll Wk.

Teaching Children. C. H. Spurgen. 1983. pap. 0.95 (ISBN 0-686-40816-0). Pilgrim Pubns.

Teaching Children about Science: Ideas & Activities Every Teacher & Parent Can Use. Elaine Levenson. (Illus.). 272p. 1985. pap. 15.95 (ISBN 0-13-891730-2). P-H.

Teaching Children & Youth with Behavior Disorders. 2nd ed. Thomas M. Shea & Anne M. Bauer. (Illus.). 400p. 1987. text ed. 31.95 (ISBN 0-13-891888-0). P-H.

Teaching Children Basic Skills: A Curriculum Handbook. 2nd ed. Thomas M. Stephens et al. 512p. 1983. pap. text ed. 29.95 (ISBN 0-675-20013-X). Merrill.

Teaching Children Charity. Linda Eyre & Richard Eyre. LC 85-27468. (Illus.). 280p. 1986. 9.95 (ISBN 0-87579-024-0). Deseret Bk.

Teaching Children in the Laboratory. Joan Solomon. 156p. 1980. 25.00 (ISBN 0-7099-2304-X, Pub. by Croom Helm Ltd); pap. 9.00 (ISBN 0-7099-2305-8). Routledge Chapman & Hall.

Teaching Children Joy. Linda Eyre & Richard Eyre. (Illus.). 202p. 1980. 9.95 (ISBN 0-87747-816-3). Deseret Bk.

Teaching Children Joy. Linda Eyre & Richard Eyre. 203p. pap. 9.95 (ISBN 0-87747-888-0, Pub. by Shadow Mountain). Deseret Bk.

Teaching Children Joy. Linda Eyre & Richard Eyre. LC 84-201498. 240p. 1988. pap. 3.50 (ISBN 0-345-00674-7). Ballantine.

Teaching Children Music: Fundamentals of Music & Method. 2nd ed. Grant Newman. 424p. 1984. write for info. plastic comb binding (ISBN 0-697-03616-2); study guide avail. (ISBN 0-697-03620-0); instr's. manual avail. (ISBN 0-697-03632-4). Wm C Brown.

Teaching Children of the Poor: An Ethnographic Study in Latin America. Beatrice Avalos. (Illus.). 175p. (Orig.). 1987. pap. text ed. 10.00 (ISBN 0-88936-484-2, IDRC253, Pub. by IDRC). UNIPUB.

Teaching Children Responsibility. Linda Eyre & Richard Eyre. LC 82-12842. (Illus.). 253p. 1982. 9.95 (ISBN 0-87747-918-6). Deseret Bk.

Teaching Children Responsibility. Linda Eyre & Richard Eyre. 240p. 1988. pap. 3.50 (ISBN 0-345-32703-9). Ballantine.

Teaching Children Science. Joseph Abruscato. (Illus.). 544p. 1982. write for info. (ISBN 0-13-891754-X). P-H.

Teaching Children Science. 2nd ed. Joseph Abruscato. (Illus.). 432p. 1988. text ed. price not set (ISBN 0-13-891763-9). P-H.

Teaching Children Sensitivity. Linda Eyre & Richard Eyre. (Teaching Children Ser.: No. 3). 1988. pap. 3.95 (ISBN 0-345-34078-7). Ballantine.

Teaching Children Tennis the Vic Braden Way. Vic Braden & Bill Bruns. (Sports Illustrated Bk). (Illus.). 1980. pap. 12.95 (ISBN 0-316-10513-9). Little.

Teaching Children the Bible: New Models in Christian Education. Marion Pardy. LC 87-45193. 224p. (Orig.). 1988. pap. 12.95 (ISBN 0-06-254829-8, RD 721, HarpR). Har-Row.

Teaching Children Through the Environment. Pamela Mays. 256p. 1985. pap. text ed. 19.95 (ISBN 0-340-35902-1). Princeton Bk Co.

Teaching Children to Become Independent Readers. Margaret La Pray. 1972. 16.50x (ISBN 0-87628-102-1). Ctr Appl Res.

Teaching Children to Read. 3rd ed. Lillian Gray. LC 63-11837. pap. 114.50 (ISBN 0-317-07747-3, 2012543). Bks Demand UMI.

Teaching Children to Read. 2nd ed. Richard J. Smith & Dale Johnson. LC 79-26387. (Education Ser.). 1980. text ed. write for info. (ISBN 0-201-07006-5). Addison-Wesley.

Teaching Children to Summarize in Fifth Grade History. Chester O. Newlun. LC 75-177120. (Columbia University. Teachers College. Contributions to Education: No. 404). Repr. of 1930 ed. 22.50 (ISBN 0-404-55404-0). AMS Pr.

Teaching Children to Use Computers: A Friendly Guide. Stephen D. Savas & E. S. Savas. (Computers & Education Ser.). 112p. 1985. pap. text ed. 7.95x (ISBN 0-8077-2791-1). Tchrs Coll.

Teaching Children to Write: Its Connection with the Development of Spatial Consciousness in the Child. Audrey E. McAllen. (Illus.). 80p. 1977. pap. 7.00 (ISBN 0-85440-317-5, Pub. by Steinerbooks). Anthroposophic.

Teaching Children to Write K-8. Robert Hillerich. LC 85-3588. 290p. 1985. 18.95x (ISBN 0-13-891805-8, Busn). P-H.

Teaching Children with Confidence. David Jenkins. 48p. 1983. pap. 3.95 (ISBN 0-910566-39-9); seminar planbook 3.95 (ISBN 0-910566-40-2). Evang Tchr.

Teaching Children with Severe Difficulties: A Radical Reappraisal. Barbara Shears & Susan Wood. Ed. by Len Barton. (Series on Special Education Needs: Policy, Practice & Social Issues). 200p. 1986. 25.50 (ISBN 0-7099-4446-2, Pub. by Croom Helm UK); pap. 11.95 (ISBN 0-7099-4450-0, Pub. by Croom Helm UK). Routledge Chapman & Hall.

Teaching China's Lost Generation. Barlow & Lowe. Date not set. 9.95 (ISBN 0-8351-1818-5). China Bks.

Teaching Choral. Duane S. Crowther. 300p. (Orig.). 1987. tchr's. guide 29.95 (ISBN 0-317-57607-0). Horizon Utah.

Teaching Choral Concepts: Simple Lesson Plans & Teaching Aids for In-Rehearsal Choir Instruction. Duane S. Crowther. LC 79-89356. (Illus.). 447p. 1979. 29.95 (ISBN 0-88290-119-2). Horizon Utah.

Teaching Choral Sight Reading. Jack Boyd. LC 75-12658. 210p. 1981. pap. text ed. 12.95 (ISBN 0-916656-17-9). Mark Foster Mus.

Teaching Christian Values. Lucie W. Barber. LC 83-22981. 250p. (Orig.). 1984. pap. 12.95 (ISBN 0-89135-041-1). Religious Educ.

Teaching Christian Values in the Family. Jim Larson. (Illus.). 48p. 1982. pap. text ed. 19.95 (ISBN 0-89191-649-0). Cook.

Teaching Church. 2nd ed. L. T. Johnson & Edward A. Buchanan. (Enabling Ser.). (Illus.). 95p. (Orig.). 1984. pap. 5.95 (ISBN 0-935597-00-9). Harvest IL.

Teaching Church: Active in Mission. Paul Gehris & Kathy Gehris. 80p. 1987. pap. 5.95 (ISBN 0-8170-1080-7). Judson.

Teaching Church at Work. Ed. by Kenneth D. Blazier. 64p. 1980. pap. 3.50 (ISBN 0-8170-0879-9). Judson.

Teaching Church in Our Time. Ed. by George A. Kelly. 1978. 6.00 (ISBN 0-8198-0523-8); pap. 4.50 (ISBN 0-8198-0524-6). Dghtrs St Paul.

Teaching Clinical Decison Making: A Handbook for Instructors. Ed. by Randall D. Cebul & Lawrence H. Beck. LC 85-3532. 192p. 1985. 35.00 (ISBN 0-275-91333-3, C1333). Praeger.

Teaching Clinical Nursing. 2nd ed. Ed. by Susan J. Hinchliff. LC 85-32550. (Illus.). 282p. (Orig.). 1986. pap. 16.95 (ISBN 0-443-02845-1). Churchill.

Teaching College Students to Read Analytically: An Individualized Approach. Jan Cooper et al. LC 85-5081. 58p. (Orig.). 1985. pap. 6.50 (ISBN 0-8141-5059-4). NCTE.

Teaching Communication & Reading Skills in the Content Areas. Dorothy G. Hennings. 125p. (Orig.). 1982. pap. 5.00 (ISBN 0-87367-780-3). Phi Delta Kappa.

Teaching Communication-Related Business Skills. LC 87-71590. 224p. 1987. pap. text ed. 20.00 (ISBN 0-938991-14-0). Colonial Pr AL.

Teaching Communication Skills. Ed. by P. J. Hills & Margaret McLaren. (Communication Ser.). 240p. 1986. 39.00 (ISBN 0-7099-4761-5, Pub. by Croom Helm UK). Routledge Chapman & Hall.

Teaching Composition: Twelve Bibliographical Essays. 2nd, rev. ed. Ed. by Gary Tate. LC 86-40376. 432p. 1987. pap. text ed. 16.95x (ISBN 0-87565-069-4). Tex Christian.

Teaching Comprehensive Medical Care: A Psychological Study of a Change in Medical Education. Kenneth Hammond. (Commonwealth Fund Ser.). 664p. 1959. text ed. 37.00x (ISBN 0-674-86910-9). Harvard U Pr.

Teaching Computation-Related Business Skills. Calfrey C. Calhoun. LC 87-71588. 224p. 1987. pap. text ed. 20.00 (ISBN 0-938991-16-7). Colonial Pr AL.

Teaching Computer Programming to Kids & Other Beginners: A Teacher's Manual. Royal Van Horn. (YA) 1982. ringbinder 10.95 (ISBN 0-88408-154-0, Sterling Swift). Heath.

Teaching Computer Studies. Eleanor Bujea & Stanley Voyce. (Illus.). 352p. 1988. text ed. 32.00 (ISBN 0-13-891953-4). P-H.

Teaching Computers to Teach. Esther R. Steinberg. 200p. 1984. text ed. 24.95xT (ISBN 0-89859-368-9); pap. text ed. 14.95xT (ISBN 0-89859-453-7). L Erlbaum Assocs.

Teaching Concepts: An Instructional Design Guide. M. David Merrill & Robert D. Tennyson. LC 76-28182. (Illus.). 240p. 1977. 34.95 (ISBN 0-87778-093-5). Educ Tech Pubns.

Teaching Conflict, Nuclear War & the Future. John Zola & Reny Sieck. (Teaching about Conflict & Related Issues Ser.). (Illus.). 219p. (Orig.). 1984. pap. 18.95 (ISBN 0-943804-55-8). U of Denver Teach.

Teaching Conflict Resolution & Peace Education. rev. ed. Ed. by Frank A. Stone. 56p. 1982. 5.00 (ISBN 0-317-65387-3). I N Thut World Educ Ctr.

Teaching Consumer Skills & How to Survive in America. Farren Webb. (Illus., Orig.). (gr. 6-12). 1978. pap. 12.95 (ISBN 0-943804-32-9). U of Denver Teach.

Teaching Content Area Reading Skills. 3rd ed. Harry W. Forgan & Charles T. Mangrum, II. 328p. 1985. pap. 23.95 (ISBN 0-675-20308-2). Merrill.

Teaching Content Through Reading: A Human Experience. E. C. Frederick. (Illus.). 214p. 1984. Spiral 20.75x (ISBN 0-398-04901-7). C C Thomas.

Teaching Craft, Design & Technology Five to Thirteen. Peter H. Williams. LC 84-72700. (Teaching 5-13 Ser.). 152p. 1985. 26.00 (ISBN 0-7099-2775-4, Pub. by Croom Helm Ltd); pap. 12.00 (ISBN 0-7099-2776-2). Routledge Chapman & Hall.

Teaching Creative Behavior. Doris J. Shallcross. 168p. 1985. pap. 9.50 (ISBN 0-943456-07-X). Bearly Ltd.

Teaching Creatively: Learning Through Discovery. Byron G. Massialas & Jack Zevin. LC 81-19375. 270p. 1983. pap. 14.95 (ISBN 0-89874-437-7). Krieger.

Teaching Creativity Through Metaphor. Judith A. Sanders & Donald A. Sanders. 1982. pap. text ed. 17.95 (ISBN 0-582-28185-7). Longman.

Teaching Critical Television Viewing Skills: An Integrated Approach. Milton E. Ploghoft & James A. Anderson. (Illus.). 208p. 1982. 23.00 (ISBN 0-398-04616-6). C C Thomas.

Teaching Critical Thinking. Jamesa. Drake. LC 75-30309. 1976. pap. 8.75x (ISBN 0-8134-1774-0, 1774). Inter Print Pubs.

Teaching Critical Thinking. Grace E. Grant. 148p. 1988. lib. bdg. 38.95 (ISBN 0-275-92749-0, C2749). Praeger.

Teaching Culture. Seelye. 1984. pap. text ed. 19.95 (ISBN 0-8442-9328-8). Natl Textbk.

Teaching Dance to Senior Adults. Liz Lerman. (Illus.). 190p. 1984. photocopy ed. 21.50x (ISBN 0-398-04903-3). C C Thomas.

Teaching Deaf Children: Techniques & Methods. Danielle M. Sanders. (Orig.). 1988. pap. text ed. 17.50 (ISBN 0-316-77015-9, 770159). College-Hill.

Teaching Demography: A Summary Handlist of Universities & Other Institutions, Vol. I. 97p. 1986. 14.50 (ISBN 92-1-123101-9, E.85.II.H.2). UN.

Teaching Demography: Details of Curricula & Related Matters in Universities & Other Institutions Teaching Demography, Vol. II. 99p. 1986. 13.00 (ISBN 92-1-123102-7, E.85.II.H.3). UN.

Teaching Design for Mainstreaming the Handicapped. Uriel Cohen & John Hunter. (Publications in Architecture & Urban Planning Ser.: R81-1). (Illus.). v, 87p. 1981. 6.00 (ISBN 0-938744-17-8). U of Wis Ctr Arch-Urban.

Teaching Developmentally Disabled Children: The Me Book. O. Ivar Lovaas. LC 80-26047. 264p. 1981. pap. 21.00x (ISBN 0-936104-78-3, 1213). Pro-Ed.

Teaching Discipline: A Positive Approach for Educational Development. Clifford Madsen & Charles Madsen. 318p. 1983. pap. 18.95x (ISBN 0-89892-053-1). Contemp Pub Co of Raleigh.

Teaching Disturbed & Disturbing Students. Paul Zionts. LC 84-22328. 281p. 1985. pap. 19.00x (ISBN 0-936104-48-1, 1291). Pro Ed.

Teaching Dog Obedience Classes: The Manual for Instructors. Joachim Volhard & Gail T. Fisher. LC 85-27172. (Illus.). 384p. 1986. 24.95 (ISBN 0-87605-765-2). Howell Bk.

Teaching Drama. Norah Morgan & Juliana Saxton. x, 230p. (Orig.). 1987. pap. text ed. 17.50x (ISBN 0-435-08458-5). Heinemann Ed.

Teaching Drama to Young Children. Mem Fox. LC 86-14858. 126p. 1987. pap. text ed. 15.00 (ISBN 0-435-08265-5). Heinemann Ed.

Teaching Drawing from Art. Brent Wilson et al. LC 86-72605. (Illus.). 192p. 1987. 19.95 (ISBN 0-87192-188-X). Davis Mass.

Teaching Driver Education to the Physically Disabled: A Sample Course. Edward C. Colverd & Menahem Less. LC 78-62053. (Driver Education Ser.). (Illus.). 54p. 1978. 5.00x (ISBN 0-686-38805-4). Human Res Ctr.

Teaching Early Adolescents Creatively: A Manual for Church School Teachers. Edward D. Seely. 222p. 1971. Westminster John Knox.

Teaching Early Primary Thinking see Just Think Program Series.

Teaching-Earth Science in the Secondary School. John Tomikel. LC 72-78361. 1972. 6.00 (ISBN 0-910042-09-8); pap. 3.00 (ISBN 0-910042-12-8). Allegheny.

Teaching Eating Skills: A Handbook for Teachers. Susan B. Stainback & Harriet A. Healy. 110p. 1982. 17.50 (ISBN 0-398-04742-1). C C Thomas.

Teaching, Education, Culture & Information As Means of Eliminating Racial Discrimination. Implementation of the International Convention on the Elimination of All Forms of Racial Discrimination Article 7. 18p. 1986. 5.00 (ISBN 92-1-154045-3, E.85.XIV.3). UN.

Teaching Effectiveness: Its Meaning, Assessment & Improvement. Ed. by Madan Mohan & Ronald E. Hull. LC 75-14090. 326p. 1975. 34.95 (ISBN 0-87778-084-6). Educ Tech Pubns.

Teaching Eighteenth-Century Poetry. Ed. by Christopher Fox. LC 86-47851. (Studies in the Eighteenth Century: No. 12). 1987. write for info. (ISBN 0-404-63512-1). AMS Pr.

Teaching Elementary Health Science. 2nd ed. Walter D. Sorochan & Stephen J. Bender. LC 78-62551. (Health Education Ser.). (Illus.). 1979. text ed. write for info. (ISBN 0-201-07492-3). Addison-Wesley.

Teaching Elementary Language Arts. 3rd ed. Dorothy Rubin. LC 84-25200. 424p. 1985. text ed. 28.95 (ISBN 0-03-071042-1, HoltC). HR&W.

Teaching Elementary Language Arts: A Literature Approach. Betty Coody & David Nelson. (Illus.). 390p. 1986. Repr. of 1982 ed. text ed. 24.95x (ISBN 0-88133-187-2). Waveland Pr.

Teaching Elementary Mathematics in a Technological Age. James Wiebe. (Orig.). 1988. pap. text ed. 28.00 (ISBN 0-89787-520-6). Gorsuch Scarisbrick.

Teaching Elementary Mathematics: Research Based Material. Tom Post. 496p. 1988. text ed. 37.00 scp. (ISBN 0-205-11076-2). Allyn.

Teaching Elementary Reading: Principles & Strategies. 4th ed. Robert Karlin & Andrea R. Karlin. 480p. 1987. text ed. 24.00 net (ISBN 0-15-588004-7, HC). HarBraceJ.

Teaching Elementary Reading Today. Wilma H. Miller. 1984. text ed. 31.95 (ISBN 0-03-059342-5). HR&W.

Teaching Elementary School Mathematics. 4th ed. C. Alan Riedesel. (Illus.). 416p. 1985. text ed. write for info. (ISBN 0-13-892621-2). P-H.

Teaching Elementary School Mathematics. 3rd ed. Robert G. Underhill. 1981. text ed. 32.95 (ISBN 0-675-09998-6). Merrill.

Teaching Elementary School Mathematics for Understanding. 4th ed. John L. Marks. (Illus.). 512p. 1975. text ed. 38.95 (ISBN 0-07-040422-4). McGraw.

Teaching Elementary School Mathematics for Understanding. 5th ed. John L. Marks & A. A. Hiatt. 416p. 1985. text ed. 38.95 (ISBN 0-07-040423-2). McGraw.

Teaching Elementary School Science: A Competency-Based Approach. Clifford H. Edwards & Robert L. Fisher. 1977. text ed. 29.95 (ISBN 0-275-22510-0). HR&W.

Teaching Elementary Science. 4th ed. William K. Esler & Mary K. Esler. 540p. 1984. text ed. write for info. (ISBN 0-534-03408-X). Wadsworth Pub.

Teaching Elementary Science. 5th ed. William K. Esler & Mary K. Esler. Date not set. text ed. write for info. (ISBN 0-534-09528-3). Wadsworth Pub.

Teaching Elementary Science: Who's Afraid of Spiders? Selma Wasserman & George Ivany. 320p. 1988. text ed. 28.50 (ISBN 0-06-043243-8, HarpC). Har-Row.

Teaching Elementary Social Studies: A Rational & Humanistic Approach. Pearl Oliner. (Illus.). 381p. 1976. text ed. 24.00 net (ISBN 0-15-588052-7, HC). HarBraceJ.

Teaching Emotionally Disturbed. (National Teachers Examination Ser.: NT-43). Date not set. pap. 13.95 (ISBN 0-8373-8453-2). Natl Learning.

Teaching Emotionally Disturbed Children. Peter Knoblock. LC 82-83370. 448p. 1983. text ed. 31.95 (ISBN 0-395-29708-7); instr's. manual 2.00 (ISBN 0-395-29709-5). HM.

Teaching Emotionally Disturbed Children. Richard L. McDowell & Gary W. Adamson. 1982. text ed. write for info. (ISBN 0-673-39166-3). Scott F.

Teaching Energy Awareness. rev. ed. Patrick D. Gore & John E. Masoncup. (Illus.). 309p. (gr. 6-12). pap. 16.95 (ISBN 0-943804-00-0). U of Denver Teach.

Teaching Engineering: A Beginner's Guide. Madhu S. Gupta. LC 87-22543. 288p. 1987. 52.50 (ISBN 0-87942-234-3, PCO2238). Inst Electrical.

Teaching-Engineering, Science, Mathematics. abr. ed. Hugh Skilling. LC 76-47476. 128p. 1977. pap. text ed. 7.50 (ISBN 0-88275-461-0). Krieger.

Teaching English. Tricia Evans. (Illus.). 212p. 1982. pap. 11.95 (ISBN 0-7099-0902-0, Pub. by Croom Helm Ltd). Routledge Chapman & Hall.

Teaching English. David Martin. pap. 1.75 (ISBN 0-686-32333-5). Rod & Staff.

Teaching English As a Foreign Language. 2nd ed. Ed. by Geoffrey Broughtn et al. (Routledge Education Bks.). 256p. 1980. 21.95x (ISBN 0-7100-0642-X); pap. 9.95x (ISBN 0-7100-8951-1). Routledge Chapman & Hall.

Teaching English As a Second Language: An Annotated Bibliography. Wallace L. Goldstein. LC 75-17987. (Reference Library of the Humanities Ser.: Vol. 23). 218p. 1975. lib. bdg. 41.00 (ISBN 0-8240-9991-5). Garland Pub.

Teaching English as a Second Language: An Annotated Bibliography, Vol. 2. Wallace L. Goldstein. LC 83-48197. 334p. 1983. lib. bdg. 41.00 (ISBN 0-8240-9097-7). Garland Pub.

Teaching English As a Second Language: A Guide for the Volunteer Teacher. M. Christine Hjelt & Georgia E. Stewart. 89p. 1986. pap. text ed. 8.00 (ISBN 0-912207-20-5). NAFSA Washington.

Teaching English As a Second Language. John Bright & Gordon McGregor. (English As a Second Language Bk.). 1975. text ed. 13.95x (ISBN 0-582-54003-8). Longman.

Teaching English As a Second Language. Robert L. Politzer & Frieda N. Politzer. LC 79-27293. 256p. 1981. Repr. of 1972 ed. lib. bdg. 18.50 (ISBN 0-89874-068-1). Krieger.

Teaching English As a Second Language: Techniques & Procedures. Christina B. Paulson & Mary N. Bruder. (Orig.). 1976. pap. text ed. write for info. (ISBN 0-673-39289-9). Scott F.

Teaching English As a Second or Foreign Language. Ed. by Marianne Celce-Murcia & Lois McIntosh. 408p. 1979. pap. text ed. 18.95 (ISBN 0-88377-125-X). Newbury Hse.

Teaching English Creatively. John H. Bushman & Kay P. Bushman. (Illus.). 222p. 1986. 27.25x (ISBN 0-398-05263-8). C C Thomas.

Teaching English in the Secondary School. Robert P. Parker, Jr. & Maxine E. Daly. LC 72-88812. (Orig.). 1973. pap. text ed. 7.95 (ISBN 0-02-923870-6). Free Pr.

Teaching English: Reflections on the State of the Art. Stephen Judy. LC 79-17965. 120p. 1979. pap. text ed. 7.50x (ISBN 0-8104-6041-6). Boynton Cook Pubs.

Teaching English: Speaking, Reading, Writing, Pt. 2. 4th ed. Bertha E. Segal. 105p. 1983. tchr's ed. 11.50 (ISBN 0-938395-06-8). B Segal.

Teaching English Through Action. 5th ed. Bertha E. Segal. 153p. 1987. tchr's ed. 14.95 (ISBN 0-938395-00-9). B Segal.

Teaching English Through Action: Student Profile Cards (Continuum) Bertha E. Segal. 2p. 1985. Repr. of 1984 ed. tchr's ed. 7.50 (ISBN 0-938395-01-7). B Segal.

Teaching English Through English. Jane Willis. (Handbooks for Language Teachers). (Illus.). 192p. 1981. pap. text ed. 13.95 (ISBN 0-582-74608-6). Longman.

Teaching English to Japanese. 2nd ed. Sumako Kimizuka. (Illus.). 1977. pap. 8.25 (ISBN 0-911756-06-X, Neptune Bks). Tail Feather.

Teaching English to Speakers of Other Languages: Substance & Technique. Betty W. Robinett. LC 78-11448. (Illus.). 1979. 16.95x (ISBN 0-8166-0840-7); pap. text ed. 9.95x (ISBN 0-8166-0868-7). U of Minn Pr.

Teaching English to Speakers of Other Languages: Substance & Technique. Betty W. Robinett. 1979. pap. text ed. 8.95 (ISBN 0-07-053179-X). McGraw.

Teaching English with Video. Margaret Allan. (English As a Second Language Bk.). (Orig.). 1985. pap. 13.95 (ISBN 0-582-74616-7). Longman.

Teaching Environmental Literature: Materials, Methods, Resources. Ed. by Frederick O. Waage. LC 84-27179. (Option for Teaching Ser.: No. 7). 191p. 1985. 32.50x (ISBN 0-87352-308-3); pap. 18.00x (ISBN 0-87352-309-1). Modern Lang.

Teaching ESL Composition: Principles & Techniques. Jane B. Hughey et al. LC 82-8255. (English Composition Program). 272p. 1983. pap. text ed. 15.50 (ISBN 0-88377-256-6). Newbury Hse.

Teaching Ethics in Journalism Education. Clifford G. Christians & Catherine L. Covert. LC 80-10426. (Teaching of Ethics Ser.). 71p. 1980. pap. 4.00 (ISBN 0-916558-08-8). Hastings Ctr.

Teaching Ethics in Nursing: A Handbook for Use of the Case Study Approach. Minerva Applegate & Nina Entrekin. 88p. (Orig.). 1984. pap. text ed. 14.95 (ISBN 0-88737-094-2, 41-1963). Natl League Nurse.

Teaching Ethnic Studies: Concepts & Strategies, 43rd Yearbook. Ed. by James A. Banks. LC 73-75298. (Illus.). 297p. 1973. 8.25 (ISBN 0-87986-000-6, 490-15278); pap. 4.00 (ISBN 0-87986-036-7, 490-15276). Nat Coun Soc Studies.

Teaching Exceptional Children & Youth in the Regular Classroom. Terry Cicchelli & Claire Ashby-Davis. 368p. (Orig.). 1986. text ed. 29.95x (ISBN 0-8156-2341-0); pap. text ed. 12.95 (ISBN 0-8156-2342-9). Syracuse U Pr.

Teaching Exceptional Children: Assessing & Modifying Social Behavior. Phillip S. Strain et al. (Educational Psychology Ser.). 1976. 19.95 (ISBN 0-12-673450-X). Acad Pr.

Teaching Exceptional Students. Ted Gloeckler & Carol Simpson. 448p. 1988. text ed. 29.95 (ISBN 0-87484-793-1). Mayfield Pub.

Teaching Exceptional Students in the Regular Classroom. Raymond M. Glass et al. 1982. text ed. write for info. (ISBN 0-673-39147-7). Scott F.

Teaching Expressive & Receptive Language to Students with Moderate & Severe Handicaps. Linda M. Makahon et al. LC 85-3522. 224p. 1985. pap. 26.00x (ISBN 0-936104-68-6, 1296). Pro Ed.

Teaching Faculty in Black Colleges & Universities: A Survey of Selected Social Science Disciplines, 1977-1978. James E. Newby. LC 82-17620. (Illus.). 112p. (Orig.). 1983. pap. text ed. 10.00 (ISBN 0-8191-2788-4). U Pr of Amer.

Teaching Faith & Morals. Suzanne M. De Benedittis. 200p. (Orig.). 1981. pap. 8.95 (ISBN 0-86683-621-7, HarpR). Har-Row.

Teaching Fieldwork to Educational Researchers: A Symposium. (Special Issues of the Anthropology & Education Quarterly Ser.: Vol. 14, No. 3). 1983. 7.50 (ISBN 0-317-66342-9). Am Anthro Assn.

Teaching First Aid & Emergency Care. Glen G. Gilbert. 248p. 1981. pap. 18.95 (ISBN 0-8403-2536-3). Kendall-Hunt.

Teaching First Aid & Emergency Care. Alton Thygerson. 96p. (Orig.). 1987. pap. text ed. write for info. (ISBN 0-86720-096-0). Jones & Bartlett.

Teaching Five to Eight Year Olds. Ed. by Maurice Chazan et al. 1987. text ed. 45.00 (ISBN 0-631-14004-2); pap. text ed. 15.95 (ISBN 0-631-14005-0). Basil Blackwell.

Teaching for Changed Attitudes & Values. J. Ruud. LC 71-187577. 1972. pap. 1.50 (ISBN 0-911365-00-1, A261-08378). Home Econ Educ.

Teaching for Christian Maturity. George M. Flattery. 124p. 1968. 1.50 (ISBN 0-88243-618-X, 02-0618). Gospel Pub.

Teaching for Competence. Norman Higgins & Howard J. Sullivan. LC 82-19584. 112p. 1983. pap. 8.95x (ISBN 0-8077-2725-3). Tchrs Coll.

Teaching for Competence in the Delivery of Direct Services. Date not set. 3.50. Coun Soc Wk Ed.

Teaching for Craft Retailers. Florence Nelson. 8p. 1984. 3.50 (ISBN 0-918328-12-8). Carma.

Teaching for Creative Endeavor: Bold New Venture. Ed. by William B. Michael. LC 76-6603. Repr. of 1968 ed. 30.00 (ISBN 0-404-15292-9). AMS Pr.

Teaching for Decision. Richard L. Dresselhaus. LC 73-75502. 124p. 1973. pap. 1.25 (ISBN 0-88243-616-3, 02-0616). Gospel Pub.

Teaching for Effective Study. Bernard Chibnall. Ed. by P. J. Hills. (New Patterns of Learning Ser.). 160p. 1986. 29.95 (ISBN 0-7099-3457-2, Pub. by Croom Helm UK). Routledge Chapman & Hall.

Teaching for Employability. P. Murphy. 1973. pap. 1.00 (ISBN 0-911365-01-X, A261-08414). Home Econ Educ.

Teaching for Health: The Nurse As Health Educator. Lyn C. Coutts & Leslie K. Hardy. LC 84-11365. (Illus.). 225p. 1985. pap. text ed. 17.50 (ISBN 0-443-02751-X). Churchill.

Teaching for Learning. 2nd ed. Myron Dembo. 1981. pap. text ed. write for info. (ISBN 0-673-16450-0). Scott F.

Teaching for Life-Changing Learning. Peggy Payne. (C. E. Ministries Ser.). 94p. (Orig.). 1984. pap. 3.50 (ISBN 0-89367-092-8). Light & Life.

Teaching for Life Response. Dean Merril. (Complete Teacher Training Meeting Ser.). 48p. 1986. 9.95 (ISBN 0-89191-316-5). Cook.

Teaching for Results. Findley B. Edge. 1956. 11.95 (ISBN 0-8054-3401-1). Broadman.

Teaching for Talent. Starr Cline. (Illus.). 56p. (Orig.). (gr. k-6). 1984. 5.95 (ISBN 0-88047-040-2, 8406). DOK Pubs.

Teaching for the Two-Sided Mind: A Guide to Right Brain-Left Brain Education. Linda V. Williams. 1986. pap. 8.95 (ISBN 0-671-62239-0, Touchstone Bks). S&S.

Teaching for Thinking. Leif Fearn. 193p. (Orig.). 1980. pap. text ed. 9.85 (ISBN 0-940444-04-6). Kabyn.

Teaching for Thinking: Theory, Strategies, & Activities for the Classroom. 2nd ed. Louis Raths et al. 240p. 1986. pap. 14.95x (ISBN 0-8077-2814-4). Tchrs Coll.

Teaching for Transfer: A Perspective. Nina Selz & William L. Ashley. 19p. 1978. 2.35 (ISBN 0-318-22210-8, IN141). Natl Ctr Res Voc Ed.

Teaching for Wholeness. Carolyn DiPaolo. 112p. (Orig.). 1985. pap. 5.95 (ISBN 0-87604-178-0). ARE Pr.

Teaching for Workplace Success. Audrey Champagne. 22p. 1986. 3.00 (ISBN 0-318-22211-6, OC113). Natl Ctr Res Voc Ed.

Teaching Foreign Language Skills. 2nd, rev. ed. Wilga M. Rivers. LC 80-24993. 1981. pap. 18.00x (ISBN 0-226-72097-7). U of Chicago Pr.

Teaching Foreign Language: Speaking, Reading, Writing. 3rd ed. Bertha E. Segal. 102p. tchr's. ed. 11.50 (ISBN 0-938395-09-2). B Segal.

Teaching Foreign Language: Speaking, Reading, Writing. 5th ed. Bertha E. Segal. 1988. 11.50 (ISBN 0-938395-24-6). B Segal.

Teaching Foreign Languages in Schools: The Silent Way. Caleb Gattegno. 144p. 1972. pap. text ed. 5.95 (ISBN 0-87825-046-8). Ed Solutions.

Teaching: From Command to Discovery. Muska Mosston. 189p. 1972. pap. text ed. write for info. (ISBN 0-534-00165-3). Wadsworth Pub.

Teaching from the Tabernacle. Roy L. De Witt. LC 86-60046. (Illus.). 168p. (Orig.). pap. 8.95 (ISBN 0-9616360-0-9). Revival Teach.

Teaching from the Tabernacle. Roy L. DeWitt. 176p. 1988. pap. 9.95 (ISBN 0-8010-2987-2). Baker Bk.

Teaching Function of the Nursing Practitioner. 4th ed. Margaret Pohl. (Foundations of Nursing Ser.). 176p. 1981. pap. text ed. write for info. (ISBN 0-697-05546-9). Wm C Brown.

Teaching Functional Academics: A Curriculum Guide for Adolescents & Adults with Learning Problems. Michael Bender & Peter J. Valletutti. LC 81-11477. (Illus.). 296p. 1981. pap. 21.00x (ISBN 0-89079-139-2, 1198). Pro-Ed.

Teaching Functional Language. Steven F. Warren & Ann Rogers-Warren. LC 84-20998. (Illus.). 368p. 1985. text ed. 25.00x (ISBN 0-936104-87-2, 1319). Pro Ed.

Teaching General Music: Action Learning for Middle & Secondary Schools. Thomas A. Regelski. LC 80-5561. (Illus.). 448p. 1981. text ed. 26.60 (ISBN 0-02-872070-9). Schirmer Bks.

Teaching General Semantics. 2nd ed. Ed. by Mary Morain. LC 75-108193. 142p. 1977. pap. text ed. 7.00x (ISBN 0-918970-04-0). Intl Gen Semantics.

Teaching Genocide Awareness in Multicultural Education. (Ethnic Studies Bulletins: No. 6). 24p. 1982. 2.00 (ISBN 0-918158-65-6). I N Thut World Educ Ctr.

Teaching German in America: Prolegomena to a History. Ed. by David Benseler et al. (Monatshefte Occasional Ser.: Vol. 7). 1988. text ed. 25.00x (ISBN 0-299-97022-1); pap. text ed. 14.00x (ISBN 0-299-97023-X). U of Wis Pr.

Teaching Gifted Children & Adolescents. Raymond H. Swassing. 464p. 1985. 32.95 (ISBN 0-675-20131-4). Merrill.

Teaching Gifted Children: Principles & Strategies. Aimee Howley et al. 1986. text ed. write for info. (ISBN 0-673-39159-0). Scott F.

Teaching Gifted Children Through Motor Learning. James H. Humphrey. (Illus.). 140p. 1985. 21.50x (ISBN 0-398-05098-8). C C Thomas.

Teaching Gifts. Irene V. Grindall. LC 85-71784. 64p. (Orig.). 1985. pap. 3.50 (ISBN 0-88177-020-5, DR020B). Discipleship Res.

Teaching Global Awareness: An Approach for Grades 1-6. Junelle P. Barrett et al. (Illus.). 217p. (Orig.). (gr. 1-6). pap. 19.95 (ISBN 0-943804-13-2). U of Denver Teach.

Teaching Global Awareness Using the Media. Steven L. Lamy et al. (Illus.). 157p. (Orig.). (gr. 6-12). 1981. pap. 15.95 (ISBN 0-943804-16-7). U of Denver Teach.

Teaching Global Awareness with Simulations & Games. updated ed. Steven L. Lamy et al. (Illus.). 245p. (Orig.). (gr. 6-12). 1983. pap. text ed. 15.95 (ISBN 0-943804-15-9). U of Denver Teach.

Teaching God's Word to Children. 266p. 1985. 6.95 (ISBN 0-910068-71-2). Am Christian.

Teaching Golf: Steps to Success. DeDe Owens & Linda K. Bunker. (Steps to Success Activity Ser.). (Illus., Orig.). 1988. pap. text ed. price not set (ISBN 0-88011-322-7). Leisure Pr.

Teaching Golf to Special Populations. Ed. by Dede Owens. LC 84-5772. (Illus.). 160p. 1984. pap. 10.95 (ISBN 0-88011-036-8, POWE0036). Leisure Pr.

Teaching Good Behavior. Time-Life Books Editors. (Successful Parenting Ser.). 144p. 1987. 17.27; lib. bdg. 21.17. Time-Life.

Teaching Good Behavior. Ed. by Time-Life Books Staff. (Successful Parenting Ser.). 144p. 1987. 12.95 (ISBN 0-8094-5933-7); lib. bdg. 12.95 (ISBN 0-8094-5934-5). Time Life.

Teaching Grammar of Thai. William Kuo. LC 82-13519. (Illus.). 500p. 1983. lib. bdg. 38.75 (ISBN 0-8191-2678-0); pap. text ed. 20.50 (ISBN 0-8191-2679-9). U Pr of Amer.

Teaching Guide for Indian Literature, Vol. I. Diana Campbell. 110p. (gr. 4-8). 1983. 4.50x (ISBN 0-936008-14-8). Navajo Curr.

Teaching Guide for Indian Literature, Vol. II. Diana Campbell. 69p. (gr. 6 up). 1983. 4.50 (ISBN 0-936008-20-2). Navajo Curr.

Teaching Mathematics to Young Children. Dennis Thyer & John Maggs. 246p. 1981. pap. 12.00x (ISBN 0-03-910292-0, Pub. by Cassell UK). Taylor & Francis.

Teaching Mathematics, Vol. 1: Culture, Motivation, History & Classroom Management. Edwin J. Nichols et al. Ed. by Oswald M. Ratteray. (Illus.). 48p. (Orig.). 1986. pap. 3.50 (ISBN 0-941001-00-8). Inst Indep Educ.

Teaching Medical Anthropology. Ed. by Harry F. Todd & Julio L. Ruffini. (Society for Medical Anthropology Special Publications). 1979. pap. 5.00 members (ISBN 0-686-36582-8); pap. 3.50. Am Anthro Assn.

Teaching Medical Sociology. Ed. by Y Nuyens & J. Vansteenkiste. 1978. pap. 22.50 (ISBN 90-207-0719-1, Martinus Nijhoff Pubs). Kluwer Academic.

Teaching Mentally Handicapped Children: A Handbook of Practical Activities. Barbara Brooks. 238p. 25.00x (ISBN 0-7062-3634-3, Pub. by Ward Lock Educ Co Ltd). State Mutual Bk.

Teaching Mentally Retarded Children Through Music. M. K. Hoshizaki. (Illus.). 172p. 1983. 20.75x (ISBN 0-398-04739-1). C C Thomas.

Teaching Method for Brain-Injured & Hyperactive Children: A Demonstration-Pilot Study. William Cruickshank. LC 81-6255. (Syracuse University Special Education & Rehabilitation Monograph: No. 6). (Illus.). xxi, 576p. 1981. Repr. of 1961 ed. lib. bdg. 48.50x (ISBN 0-313-23071-4, CRTC). Greenwood.

Teaching Methodologies for Population Education: Inquiry-Discovery Approach Values Clarification. 1986. 5.00 (UB332, UB). UNIPUB.

Teaching Methods & Applied Techniques. Anthony B. Colletti. write for info. (ISBN 0-912126-82-5). Keystone Pubns.

Teaching Methods for the Bibliographic Instruction Librarian. Marilla D. Svinicki. 54p. 1981. 15.00x (ISBN 0-8389-6751-5); members 10.00x (ISBN 0-317-37027-8). ALA.

Teaching Methods in the Soviet School. I. D. Zverev. (Educational Sciences Ser.). 116p. (Orig.). 1984. pap. 6.50 (ISBN 92-3-102126-5, U1381, UNESCO). UNIPUB.

Teaching Mildly & Moderately Handicapped Students. Bill R. Gearheart & James DeRuiter. (Illus.). 384p. 1986. text ed. write for info. (ISBN 0-13-893900-4). P-H.

Teaching Mildly Handicapped Children: Methods & Materials. George Marsh, II et al. (A Generic Approach to Comprehensive Teaching Ser.). 448p. 1983. 31.95 (ISBN 0-675-20590-5). Merrill.

Teaching Mildly Handicapped Children: Methods & Materials-A Generic Approach. Harold D. Love. 180p. 1984. 21.75x (ISBN 0-398-04942-4). C C Thomas.

Teaching Mildly Retarded Children in the Regular Classroom. Martin Henley. LC 84-62990. (Fastback Ser.: No. 220). 50p. (Orig.). 1985. pap. 0.90 (ISBN 0-87367-220-8). Phi Delta Kappa.

Teaching Ministry of the Church: An Examination of Basic Principles of Christian Education. James D. Smart. LC 54-10569. 208p. 1971. pap. 6.95 (ISBN 0-664-24910-8). Westminster John Knox.

Teaching Minorities More Effectively: A Model for Educators. Thomas J. Brown. 82p. (Orig.). 1987. lib. bdg. 18.50 (ISBN 0-8191-5662-0); pap. text ed. 8.50 (ISBN 0-8191-5663-9). U Pr of Amer.

Teaching Models in Education of the Gifted. C. June Maker. LC 82-1692. 484p. 1982. 36.50 (ISBN 0-89443-682-1). Aspen Pub.

Teaching Modern Educational Dance. Wendy Slater. 109p. 1987. pap. text ed. 16.95 (ISBN 0-7463-0372-6). Princeton Bk Co.

Teaching Modern Ideas of Biology. O. Roger Anderson. LC 73-185961. (Studies in Science Education Ser.). pap. 62.80 (ISBN 0-317-41944-7, 2025987). Bks Demand UMI.

Teaching Modern Languages. Ed. by G. Richardson. 300p. 1983. pap. 16.95 (ISBN 0-89397-158-8). Nichols Pub.

Teaching Modern Science. 4th ed. Arthur Carin & Robert Sund. 336p. 1985. pap. 24.95 (ISBN 0-675-20221-3). Merrill.

Teaching Modern Science. 5th ed. Arthur Carin & Robert Sund. 352p. 1988. pap. 24.95 (ISBN 0-675-20973-0). Merrill.

Teaching Montessori in the Home: The Pre-School Years. Elizabeth G. Hainstock. 1976. pap. 4.50 (ISBN 0-452-25418-3, Z5418, Plume). NAL.

Teaching Montessori in the Home: The Preschool Years. Elizabeth G. Hainstock. 1968. 14.95 (ISBN 0-394-41018-1). Random.

Teaching Montessori in the Home: The School Years. Elizabeth G. Hainstock. 1978. pap. 6.95 (ISBN 0-452-25794-8, Z5420, Plume). NAL.

Teaching Morality & Religion. Alan Harris. 104p. 1975. 14.95x (ISBN 0-8464-1274-8). Beekman Pubs.

Teaching Morphology Developmentally: Methods & Materials for Teaching Bound Morphology. Kenneth G. Shipley & Carolyn S. Banis. 1981. 99.00 (ISBN 0-88450-728-9, 3137-B). Communication Skill.

Teaching Movement & Dance. Phyllis Weikart. LC 82-6239. (Illus.). 359p. (Orig.). 1982. pap. 18.00 (ISBN 0-931114-16-0). High-Scope.

Teaching Movement & Dance: Intermediate Folk Dance. Phyllis Weikart. 300p. (Orig.). 1984. pap. 18.00 (ISBN 0-931114-30-6). High Scope.

Teaching Music in Primary Schools. D. Maxwell-Timmins. 1987. 49.00x (ISBN 0-7217-2539-2, Pub. by Schofield & Sims). State Mutual Bk.

Teaching Music in the Elementary Classroom. 2nd ed. Charles R. Hoffer & Marjorie L. Hoffer. 325p. 1987. text ed. 18.00 (Pub. by HC). HarBraceJ.

Teaching Music in the Secondary Schools. 3rd ed. Charles R. Hoffer. 432p. 1983. text ed. write for info. (ISBN 0-534-01348-1). Wadsworth Pub.

Teaching Music in Today's Secondary Schools: A Creative Approach to Contemporary Music Education. 2nd ed. Malcolm E. Bessom et al. 1980. text ed. 21.95 (ISBN 0-03-021556-0). HR&W.

Teaching Music in Twentieth-Century America. Lois Choksy et al. (Illus.). 400p. 1985. text ed. 30.00 (ISBN 0-13-892662-X). P-H.

Teaching Music in Urban Schools. Otis D. Simmons. LC 75-2549. 1975. pap. 6.50 (ISBN 0-8008-7554-0, Crescendo). Taplinger.

Teaching Music: The Human Experience. Shirley S. Mullins. 115p. (Orig.). 1985. pap. text ed. 9.95 (ISBN 0-9616262-0-8). Media Servs.

Teaching Musical Appreciation. Terence Dwyer. 1967. 6.75 (ISBN 0-19-317409-X). Oxford U Pr.

Teaching Nature in Cities & Towns. Sonia W. Vogl & Robert L. Vogl. (Illus.). 102p. 1985. pap. text ed. 9.95x (ISBN 0-8134-2458-5, 2458). Inter Print Pubs.

Teaching New Behavior. Ellsworth Community College Staff. Ed. by Michael Davis. (RATES Ser.: No. 7). (Illus.). 62p. (Orig.). 1983. pap. 3.00x (ISBN 0-916671-43-7). Material Dev.

Teaching Non-Western Studies: A Handbook of Materials & Methods. Stephen Guild et al. 139p. (Orig.). 1972. pap. 4.00 (ISBN 0-932288-02-2). Ctr Intl Ed U of MA.

Teaching Nursing: A Self-Instructional Handbook. Christine Ewan & Ruth White. LC 84-16980. 250p. (Orig.). 1984. pap. 15.00 (ISBN 0-7099-0936-5, Pub. by Croom Helm Ltd). Routledge Chapman & Hall.

Teaching Nursing Home: A New Approach to Geriatric Research, Education & Clinical Care. Ed. by Edward L. Schneider et al. (Illus.). 384p. 1985. text ed. 49.50 (ISBN 0-88167-060-X); pap. text ed. 33.50 (ISBN 0-88167-061-8). Raven.

Teaching Nursing Homes: Myths & Realities. Mary Walsh & Norma Small. 400p. 1988. text ed. 35.00 (ISBN 0-932500-94-3). Natl Hlth Pub.

Teaching Nutrition. 2nd ed. Ercel S. Eppright et al. LC 63-24032. pap. 89.30 (ISBN 0-317-28207-7, 2022764). Bks Demand UMI.

Teaching Nutrition: A Review of Programs & Research. Ed. by Joanne P. Nestor & Judith A. Glotzer. 302p. 1984. pap. text ed. 16.50 (ISBN 0-8191-4115-1). U Pr of Amer.

Teaching Nutrition & Food Science. Margaret Knight. 1976. pap. 20.95 (ISBN 0-7134-3099-0, Pub. by Batsford England). David & Charles.

Teaching Nutrition, Exercise & Weight Control to the Moderately-Mildly Handicapped. Anthony F. Rotatori et al. (Illus.). 198p. 1985. spiral bdg. 21.75 (ISBN 0-398-05080-5). C C Thomas.

Teaching Nutrition in Biology Classes: An Experimental Investigation of High School Biology Pupils in Their Study of the Relation of Food to Physical Well-Being. Nelson E. Bingham. LC 74-176565. (Columbia University. Teachers College. Contributions to Education: No. 772). Repr. of 1939 ed. 22.50 (ISBN 0-404-55772-4). AMS Pr.

Teaching Occupational Home Economics. Terrass & Comfort. 1979. 18.20 (ISBN 0-02-665800-3). Bennett IL.

Teaching of Addai. George Howard. LC 81-5802. (SBL Texts & Translations Ser.). 1981. pap. 13.50 (ISBN 0-89130-490-8, 060216). Scholars Pr GA.

Teaching of African Literature. rev. ed. Ed. by Thomas Hale & Richard Priebe. LC 85-50380. (African Literature Association Annuals Ser.: No. 2). 200p. 1989. 24.00 (ISBN 0-89410-472-1); pap. 14.00 (ISBN 0-89410-473-X). Three Continents.

Teaching of Arabic As a Foreign Language. Raja Nasr. 15.00x (ISBN 0-86685-047-3); pap. text ed. 10.00x (ISBN 0-686-86195-7). Intl Bk Ctr.

Teaching of Arithmetic & the Waldorf School Plan. Hermann Von Baravalle. 1967. pap. 3.95 (ISBN 0-916786-12-9, Pub by Waldorf School Monographs). St George Bk Serv.

Teaching of Art: The Roots of Self Deception. 81p. 1982. pap. 3.50x (ISBN 0-905171-91-8, Pub. by Welsh Arts Wales). Intl Spec Bk.

Teaching of Braille Reading. Randall K. Harley et al. (Illus.). 200p. 1979. photocopy ed. 23.00x (ISBN 0-398-03836-8). C C Thomas.

Teaching of Business Communication II. Ed. by G. A. Douglas. 292p. 1987. pap. 9.95 (ISBN 0-931874-18-1). Assn Busn Comm.

Teaching of Calvin: A Modern Interpretation. Adam M. Hunter. LC 83-45618. Repr. of 1950 ed. 37.50 (ISBN 0-404-19836-8). AMS Pr.

Teaching of Christ. 2nd ed. Ronald Lawler et al. LC 75-34852. 640p. 1983. pap. 9.95 (ISBN 0-87973-850-2, 850). Our Sunday Visitor.

Teaching of Christ. G. Campbell Morgan. 352p. 1984. 16.95 (ISBN 0-8007-0395-2). Revell.

Teaching of Classical & Modern Foreign Languages: Common Areas & Problems see Language Learner.

Teaching of Classical Ballet. Joan Lawson. LC 73-83997. (Illus.). 1974. 19.95 (ISBN 0-87830-143-7). Theatre Arts.

Teaching of Classical Cultures see Culture in Language & Learning.

Teaching of Classical Subjects in English. Ed. by Clarence A. Forbes. 98p. (Gr., Lat. & Eng.). 4.50 (ISBN 0-318-12463-7, B20). Amer Classical.

Teaching of Computer Appreciation & Library Automation. A. J. Oulton et al. (R&D Report 5647). 136p. (Orig.). 1981. pap. 12.00 (ISBN 0-905984-75-7, Pub. by British Lib). Longwood Pub Group.

Teaching of Contemporary World Issues. Ed. by Robert Harris. 198p. (Orig.). 1987. pap. text ed. 10.50 (ISBN 92-3-102356-X, U1565, UNESCO). UNIPUB.

Teaching of Development Economics. Kurt Martin. Ed. by John Knapp. 238p. 1967. 30.00x (ISBN 0-7146-1014-3, F Cass Co). Biblio Dist.

Teaching of Dynamic Psychiatry: A Reappraisal of the Goals & Techniques in the Teaching of Psychoanalytic Psychiatry. Ed. by Grete L. Bibring. LC 67-27426. 277p. 1968. text ed. 30.00x (ISBN 0-8236-6380-9). Intl Univs Pr.

Teaching of Economics. Harvard University, Faculty of Art Staff & Sciences. (Harvard Studies in Education: Vol. 3). 1917. 19.00 (ISBN 0-384-21660-9). Johnson Repr.

Teaching of Economics in Africa. I. Livingston et al. 1973. 10.00x (ISBN 0-85621-011-0, Pub. by Scot Acad Pr). Longwood Pub Group.

Teaching of Economics in Secondary Schools. Association Of Assistant Masters In Secondary Schools. (Illus.). 1971. 15.95 (ISBN 0-521-08010-X). Cambridge U Pr.

Teaching of Elementary Problem Solving in Engineering & Related Fields. Ed. by James L. Lubkin. 198p. 1980. 10.00 (ISBN 0-318-13172-2). Am Soc Eng Ed.

Teaching of Employability Skills: Who's Responsible? Nina Selz. 31p. 1980. 2.80 (ISBN 0-318-22212-4, SN29). Natl Ctr Res Voc Ed.

Teaching of English. 3rd ed. M. R. Panchal. 194p. 1984. pap. text ed. 10.00x (ISBN 0-7069-2621-8, Pub. by Vikas India). Advent NY.

Teaching of English as a Foreign Language in Ten Countries. E. G. Lewis & C. E. Massad. 300p. (Orig.). 1975. pap. text ed. 15.75x (ISBN 91-22-00020-8, Pub. by Almqvist & Wiksell). Coronet Bks.

Teaching of English: From the Sixteenth Century to 1870. Ian Michael. (Illus.). 600p. 1987. 69.50 (ISBN 0-521-24196-0). Cambridge U Pr.

Teaching of English in the Secondary School. Charles S. Thomas. 1978. Repr. of 1927 ed. 25.00 (ISBN 0-8492-2640-6). R West.

Teaching of English in the Universities of England. Raymond W. Chambers. 1922. lib. bdg. 19.50 (ISBN 0-8414-3359-3). Folcroft.

Teaching of English Suffixes. Edward L. Thorndike. LC 78-177713. (Columbia University. Teachers College. Contributions to Education: No. 847). Repr. of 1941 ed. 22.50 (ISBN 0-404-55847-X). AMS Pr.

Teaching of English Usage. 2nd ed. Robert C. Pooley. LC 73-91939. 241p. (Orig.). 1974. pap. 9.75 (ISBN 0-8141-5134-5). NCTE.

Teaching of English: 76th Yearbook, Part I. Ed. by James R. Squire. LC 76-44918. (National Society for the Study of Education). (Illus.). 1977. lib. bdg. 12.00x (ISBN 0-226-60122-6). U of Chicago Pr.

Teaching of Ethics in Higher Education: A Report by the Hastings Center. Ed. by Daniel Callahan. LC 80-10294. (Teaching of Ethics Ser.). 103p. 1980. pap. 5.00 xerox form only (ISBN 0-916558-09-6). Hastings Ctr.

Teaching of Ethics in the Military. Peter L. Stromberg et al. LC 81-86583. (Teaching of Ethics in Higher Education Ser.: Vol. XII). 85p. (Orig.). 1982. pap. 5.00 (ISBN 0-916558-16-9). Hastings Ctr.

Teaching of Ethnic Dance. Anatol M. Joukowsky. LC 79-7768. (Dance Ser.). (Illus.). 1980. Repr. of 1965 ed. lib. bdg. 19.00x (ISBN 0-8369-9296-2). Ayer Co Pubs.

Teaching of Evaluation Across the Disciplines. Ed. by Barbara G. Davis. LC 85-60837. (Program Evaluation Ser.: No. 29). (Orig.). 1986. pap. text ed. 14.95x (ISBN 0-87589-727-4). Jossey-Bass.

Teaching of General Mathematics in the Secondary Schools of the United States: A Study of the Development & Present Status of General Mathematics. Clarence McCormick. LC 70-178806. (Columbia University. Teachers College. Contributions to Education: No. 386). Repr. of 1929 ed. 22.50 (ISBN 0-404-55386-9). AMS Pr.

Teaching of Geography. Zoe A. Thralls. LC 58-6701. (Illus.). 1958. 24.00x (ISBN 0-89197-442-3); pap. text ed. 12.95x (ISBN 0-89197-443-1). Irvington.

Teaching of George Eliot. William Myers. LC 83-26615. 272p. 1984. 28.50x (ISBN 0-389-20450-1, 08010). B&N Imports.

Teaching of High School English. 5th ed. J. N. Hook & William H. Evans. LC 81-19682. 521p. 1982. write for info. (ISBN 0-02-355780-X). Macmillan.

Teaching of History. J. C. Aggarwal. 279p. 1983. text ed. 27.50x o. p. (ISBN 0-7069-2163-1, Pub. by Vikas India); pap. text ed. 8.95x (ISBN 0-7069-2164-X, Pub. by Vikas India). Advent NY.

Teaching of History. Dennis Gunning. 197p. 1978. pap. 11.50 (ISBN 0-85664-762-4, Pub. by Croom Helm Ltd); 22.00 (ISBN 0-85664-326-2). Routledge Chapman & Hall.

Teaching of History. 2nd. rev. ed. S. K. Kochhar. xiii, 386p. 1984. text ed. 25.00x (ISBN 0-86590-425-1, Pub. by Sterling Pubs India). Apt Bks.

Teaching of History: A Manual of Method for Elementary & Junior High Schools. Paul Klapper. 1979. Repr. of 1926 ed. lib. bdg. 30.00 (ISBN 0-8492-1484-X). R West.

Teaching of History in English Schools. Olive E. Shropshire. LC 70-177789. (Columbia University. Teachers College. Contributions to Education: No. 617). Repr. of 1936 ed. 22.50 (ISBN 0-404-55671-X). AMS Pr.

Teaching of Home Science. 2nd ed. R. R. Das et al. 146p. 1984. text ed. 13.95x (ISBN 0-86590-184-8, Pub. by Sterling India). Apt bks.

Teaching of Human Sexuality in Schools for Health Professionals. D. R. Mace & R. H. Bannermann. (Public Health Paper: No. 57). 1974. pap. 2.00 (ISBN 92-4-130057-4). World Health.

Teaching of Instrumental Music. Richard J. Colwell. (Illus.). 1969. 33.00 (ISBN 0-13-893131-3). P-H.

Teaching of Islam. M. Ahmad. 208p. 1984. 150.00x (ISBN 1-85077-020-4, Pub. by Darf Pubs Ltd). State Mutual Bk.

Teaching of Italian in the United States: A Documentary History. Joseph G. Fucilla. LC 74-17929. 304p. 1975. Repr. 19.00x (ISBN 0-405-06401-2). Ayer Co Pubs.

Teaching of Judaica in American Universities: Proceedings. Leon A. Jick. 1970. 15.00x (ISBN 0-87068-127-3). Ktav.

Teaching of Legal Research. Christopher G. Wren & Jill R. Wren. 54p. 1988. tchr's ed. 3.00 (ISBN 0-916951-19-7). Adams & Ambrose.

Teaching of Literature see Foreign Language Teachers & Tests.

Teaching of Mathematics. 3rd. ed. Kulbir S. Sidhu. xi, 382p. 1984. text ed. 35.00x (ISBN 0-86590-429-4, Pub. by Sterling Pubs India). Apt Bks.

Teaching of Mathematics from Intermediate Algebra Through First Year Calculus. Dubisch. LC 74-23520. 136p. 1975. Repr. of 1963 ed. 10.50 (ISBN 0-88275-198-0). Krieger.

Teaching of Modern Greek in the English Speaking World. Ed. by Anne Farmakides et al. (Modern Greek Language Ser.: No. 1). 140p. (Orig.). 1984. pap. text ed. 15.00 (ISBN 0-917653-01-7). Hellenic Coll Pr.

Teaching of Music. Gowri Kuppuswamy & H. Hariharan. 88p. 1980. 13.95 (ISBN 0-940500-57-4, Pub. by Sterling India). Asia Bk Corp.

Teaching of On-Line Cataloguing & Searching & the Use of New Technology in U. K. Schools of Librarianship & Information Science. Lucy A. Tedd. (R&D Report 5616). 126p. (Orig.). 1981. pap. 12.75 (ISBN 0-905984-67-6, Pub. by British Lib). Longwood Pub Group.

Teaching of Personality Development, Pt. 1. (Sociological Review Monographs: No. 1). pap. 15.00 (ISBN 0-8115-3307-7). Kraus Repr.

Teaching of Personality Development, Pt. 2. (Sociological Review Monographs: No. 2). pap. 11.00 (ISBN 0-8115-3308-5). Kraus Repr.

Teaching of Physical Sciences in the Secondary Schools of the United States, France & Soviet Russia. Alexander Efron. LC 75-176742. (Columbia University. Teachers College. Contributions to Education: No. 725). Repr. of 1937 ed. 22.50 (ISBN 0-404-55725-2). AMS Pr.

Teaching of Political Economy: A Critique of Non-Marxian Theories. Ed. by A. Smirnov et al. Tr. by H. C. Creighton. 334p. 1984. 8.95 (ISBN 0-8285-2831-4, Pub. by Progress Pubs USSR). Imported Pubns.

Teaching of Political Economy: A Critique of Non-Marxian Theories. A. D. Smirnov. 334p. 1981. 18.75 (ISBN 0-317-53794-6, Pub. by Collets (UK)). State Mutual Bk.

Teaching of Practical Statistics. C. W. Anderson & R. M. Loynes. LC 87-8238. (Probability & Mathematical Ser.). 199p. 1987. 52.95 (ISBN 0-471-91572-6). Wiley.

Teaching of Practice Skills in Undergraduate Programs in Social Welfare & Other Helping Services. Frank Loewenberg & Ralph Dolgoff. Date not set. 3.00 (70-310-70). Coun Soc WK Ed.

Teaching of Prayer: A Teacher's Guide. C. D. Rabinowitz. 2.25 (ISBN 0-914131-71-0, B50). Torah Umesorah.

Teaching of Primary Science: Policy & Practice. Ed. by Colin Richards & Derek Holford. 275p. 1983. 36.00x (ISBN 0-905273-35-4, Falmer Pr); pap. 19.00x (ISBN 0-905273-34-6). Taylor & Francis.

Teaching of Psychology: Method, Content, & Context. Ed. by John Radford & David Rose. LC 79-40824. 362p. 1980. 77.95 (ISBN 0-471-27665-0, Pub. by Wiley-Interscience). Wiley.

Teaching of Psychosomatic Medicine & Consultation-Liaison Psychiatry. Ed. by C. P. Kimball & A. J. Krakowski. (Bibliotheca Psychiatrica Ser.: No. 159). 1979. pap. 55.50 (ISBN 3-8055-2955-4). S Karger.

Teaching Reading Skills Through the Newspaper. 2nd ed. Arnold B. Cheyney. LC 84-10884. (Reading Aids Ser.). 1984. 4.50 (ISBN 0-87207-210-X). Intl Reading.

Teaching Reading, Thinking, Study Skills in Content Classrooms. 2nd ed. Marian J. Tonjes & Miles V. Zintz. 512p. 1987. pap. text ed. write for info. (ISBN 0-697-00974-2). WM C Brown.

Teaching Reading through the Arts. Ed. by John E. Cowen. 118p. 1983. pap. 7.00 (ISBN 0-87207-733-0). Intl Reading.

Teaching Reading to Bilingual Children: A Step-by-Step Guide That Guarantees Reading Success. Ellen C. Henderson. LC 78-186481. 1972. pap. text ed. 5.00 (ISBN 0-682-47437-1, University). Exposition-Phoenix.

Teaching Reading to Deaf Children. Beatrice O. Hart. LC 78-50668. 1978. pap. text ed. 12.95 (ISBN 0-88200-117-5, C1119). Alexander Graham.

Teaching Reading to Every Child. 2nd ed. David Lapp & James Flood. 704p. 1983. text ed. write for info. (ISBN 0-02-367640-X). Macmillan.

Teaching Reading to Handicapped Children. Charles H. Hargis. 272p. 1982. text ed. 18.95 (ISBN 0-89108-113-5). Love Pub Co.

Teaching Reading to Mentally Handicapped Children. James Thatcher. (Special Education Ser.). 64p. 1984. pap. 15.00 (ISBN 0-7099-2408-9, Pub. by Croom Helm Ltd). Routledge Chapman & Hall.

Teaching Reading to Slow & Disabled Learners. Samuel A. Kirk et al. 304p. 1988. pap. text ed. 14.95x (ISBN 0-88133-334-4). Waveland Pr.

Teaching Reading to Students with Limited English Proficiencies. Betty Anderson & Rosie W. Joels. (Illus.). 98p. 1986. 18.50x (ISBN 0-398-05179-8). C C Thomas.

Teaching Reading Using Microcomputers. Robert T. Rude. (Illus.). 272p. 1986. pap. text ed. 22.00 (ISBN 0-13-895285-X). P-H.

Teaching Reading with the Other Language Arts. Ed. by Ulrich H. Hardt. (IRA Bks.: N0. 734). 188p. 1983. 10.00 (ISBN 0-87207-734-9). Intl Reading.

Teaching Record: Integrative Learning. Date not set. 4.40. Coun Soc Wk Ed.

Teaching Religion Effectively Program. Mary Cove & Jane Regan. 96p. 1982. pap. 3.50 (ISBN 0-697-01825-3); program manual 24.95 (ISBN 0-697-01826-1). Wm C Brown.

Teaching Religion: The Secularization of Religion Instruction in a West German School System. W. Clinton Terry, III. LC 80-5569. 208p. 1981. pap. text ed. 13.00 (ISBN 0-8191-1367-0). U Pr of Amer.

Teaching Religion with Confidence & Joy. Greg Dues. LC 87-51568. 80p. (Orig.). 1988. pap. 4.95 (ISBN 0-89622-359-0). Twenty-Third.

Teaching Research Curriculum for Moderately & Severely Handicapped. H. D. Fredericks et al. (Illus.). 340p. 1978. photocopy ed. spiral 27.25x (ISBN 0-398-03330-7). C C Thomas.

Teaching Research Curriculum for Moderately & Severely Handicapped: Gross & Fine Motor. H. D. Fredericks et al. (Illus.). 264p. 1980. pap. 23.75x (ISBN 0-398-04035-4); developmental chart 4.00x. C C Thomas.

Teaching Research Curriculum for Moderately & Severely Handicapped: Self-Help & Cognitive. H. D. Fredericks et al. (Illus.). 280p. 1980. pap. 24.75x (ISBN 0-398-04034-6); developmental chart 4.00x. C C Thomas.

Teaching Research Motor-Development Scale: For Moderately & Severely Retarded Children. photocopy ed. H. D. Fredericks et al. (Illus.). 80p. 1972. 13.00 (ISBN 0-398-02284-4). C C Thomas.

Teaching Riding: Step-by-Step Schooling for Horse & Rider. Diane S. Solomon. LC 81-40281. (Illus.). 321p. 1986. 18.95 (ISBN 0-8061-1580-7). U of Okla Pr.

Teaching Role of the School Media Specialist. Kay E. Vandergrift. LC 78-27401. (School Media Centers Focus on Trend & Issues Ser.: No. 3). pap. 20.00 (ISBN 0-317-27977-7, 2025607). Bks Demand UMI.

Teaching Sacraments. Patricia Smith. LC 86-54328. (Theology & Life Ser.: Vol. 17). (Orig.). pap. 8.95 (ISBN 0-89453-599-4). M Glazier.

Teaching School. rev. ed. Eric W. Johnson. 1987. pap. 13.50 (ISBN 0-934338-62-0). NAIS.

Teaching School Chemistry. UNESCO Staff. 302p. 1987. text ed. 35.00x (ISBN 81-207-0595-5, Pub. by Sterling Pubs India). Apt Bks.

Teaching School Mathematics. Ed. by W. Servais & T. Varga. (Source Books on Curricula & Methods). (Illus.). 308p. (Orig., Co-published with Penguin Books Ltd., London). 1971. pap. 5.00 (ISBN 92-3-100884-6, U661, UNESCO). UNIPUB.

Teaching School Physics. Ed. by John L. Lewis. (Source Books on Curricula & Methods). (Illus.). 416p. (Orig., Co-published with Penguin Books Ltd., London). 1972. pap. 6.50 (ISBN 92-3-100937-0, U662, UNESCO). UNIPUB.

Teaching Science As a Decision Making Process. Cohen et al. 296p. 1984. pap. text ed. 16.50 (ISBN 0-8403-3402-8). Kendall-Hunt.

Teaching Science as a Second Culture. Francis Dart. Ed. by Kenneth Ives. (Illus.). 60p. 1983. pap. 4.00 (ISBN 0-89670-009-7). Progresiv Pub.

Teaching Science As Inquiry. Steven J. Rakow. LC 86-61751. (Fastback Ser.: No. 246). 50p. (Orig.). 1986. pap. 0.90 (ISBN 0-87367-246-1). Phi Delta Kappa.

Teaching Science in an Outdoor Environment: Handbook for Students, Parents, Teachers, & Camp Leaders. Phyllis P. Gross & Esther P. Railton. LC 73-173903. (California Natural History Guides: No. 30). (Illus.). 175p. 1972. pap. 5.95 (ISBN 0-520-02148-7). U of Cal Pr.

Teaching Science in Australian Schools. Kwong Lee Dow. Ed. by R. J. Selleck. (Second Century in Australian Education Ser.). (Illus.). 120p. 1971. pap. 8.50x (ISBN 0-522-84014-0, Pub. by Melbourne U Pr). Intl Spec Bk.

Teaching Science in the Elementary School. David P. Butts. LC 72-86790. (Orig.). 1973. pap. text ed. 7.95 (ISBN 0-02-905060-X). Free Pr.

Teaching Science in the Elementary School: Content, Process & Attitude. Donna M. Wolfinger. 1984. text ed. write for info. (ISBN 0-673-39186-8). Scott F.

Teaching Science Through Discovery. 5th ed. Arthur Carin & Robert Sund. 512p. 1985. 32.95 (ISBN 0-675-20387-2). Merrill.

Teaching Science Through Discovery. 6th ed. Arthur Carin & Robert Sund. 576p. 1988. 32.95 (ISBN 0-675-20972-2). Merrill.

Teaching Science to Children: An Integrated Approach. Alfred E. Friedl. 301p. 1986. pap. text ed. write for info (ISBN 0-394-35641-1, RanC). Random.

Teaching Science to Infants. Romola Showell. (Ward Lock Educational Ser.). 29.00x (ISBN 0-7062-3847-8, Pub. by Ward Lock Educ Co Ltd). State Mutual Bk.

Teaching Science to Young Children: A Resource Book. Mary D. Iatridis. LC 84-48879. (Garland Reference Library of Social Science: Vol. 304). 150p. 1986. lib. bdg. 28.00 (ISBN 0-8240-8747-X). Garland Pub.

Teaching Science with Every Day Things. 2nd ed. Victor E. Schmidt & Verne N. Rockcastle. (Illus.). 224p. 1982. pap. 19.95 (ISBN 0-07-055355-6). McGraw.

Teaching Second Language Reading for Academic Purposes. David Eskey & Fraida Dubin. (A-W Second Language Professional Library). 1986. pap. text ed. 16.95 (ISBN 0-201-11668-5). Addison-Wesley.

Teaching Secondary English. John J. De Boer. LC 76-100155. 1970. Repr. of 1951 ed. lib. bdg. 25.00x (ISBN 0-8371-3426-9, DETS). Greenwood.

Teaching Secondary School Art: Discovering Art Objectives, Art Skills, Art History, Art Ideas. 2nd ed. Earl W. Linderman. 272p. 1980. pap. text ed. write for info (ISBN 0-697-03301-5). Wm C Brown.

Teaching Secondary School Mathematics. 2nd ed. Alfred S. Posamentier & Jay Stepelman. 416p. 1986. pap. text ed. 29.95 (ISBN 0-675-20422-4). Merrill.

Teaching Self-Hypnosis: An Introductory Guide for Clinicians. David A. Soskis. (Professional Bks.). 1986. text ed. 19.95 (ISBN 0-393-70010-0). Norton.

Teaching Seminar with Milton H. Erickson, M.D. Ed. by Jeffrey K. Zeig. LC 80-23804. 340p. 1980. 30.00 (ISBN 0-87630-247-9). Brunner-Mazel.

Teaching Shakespeare. W. Edens et al. 1977. 26.00x (ISBN 0-691-06339-7). Princeton U Pr.

Teaching Shira is More Than Clapping Hands see Kadima Kesher Series.

Teaching Singing. John C. Burgin. LC 72-10594. 290p. 1973. 19.50 (ISBN 0-8108-0565-0). Scarecrow.

Teaching Skillful Thinking. 25.00 (611-86018). Assn Supervision.

Teaching Slow Learners Through Active Games. J. H. Humphrey & Dorothy D. Sullivan. 192p. 1973. 21.75x (ISBN 0-398-00886-8). C C Thomas.

Teaching Soccer: Tactics, Skills & Drills of the Most Popular Ball Game in the World. John Hayward. LC 76-24434. (Illus.). 1976. pap. 2.95 (ISBN 0-917252-01-2). Per Ardua.

Teaching Social Change: A Group Approach. Norman E. Zinberg & Harold N. Boris. LC 75-26746. pap. 66.00 (ISBN 0-317-42064-X, 2025884). Bks Demand UMI.

Teaching Social Skills to Children: Innovative Approaches. Ed. by Gwendolyn Cartledge & JoAnne F. Milburn. (Pergamon General Psychology Ser.). 400p. 1986. text ed. 38.50 (ISBN 0-08-031591-7, J115, M117, Pub. by PPI); pap. text ed. 15.95 (ISBN 0-08-031590-9). Pergamon.

Teaching Social Studies in Other Nations. Ed. by Howard D. Mehlinger & Jan L. Tucker. LC 79-53231. (Bulletin Ser.: No. 60). (Illus.). 104p. (Orig.). 1979. pap. text ed. 8.75 (ISBN 0-87986-024-3, 498-15280). Nat Coun Soc Studies.

Teaching Social Studies in the Elementary School. John R. Lee. LC 73-14017. (Illus.). 1974. 14.95 (ISBN 0-02-918360-X); pap. text ed. 12.95 (ISBN 0-02-918370-7). Free Pr.

Teaching Social Studies in the Elementary School: Issues & Practices. Mark Schug & R. Beery. 1987. text ed. write for info. (ISBN 0-673-15978-7). Scott F.

Teaching Social Studies in the Elementary School: The Basis for Citizenship. 2nd ed. Theodore Kaltsounis. (Illus.). 384p. 1987. text ed. write for info. (ISBN 0-13-895657-X). P-H.

Teaching Social Studies in the Secondary School. John R. Lee et al. LC 72-91998. (Orig.). 1973. pap. text ed. 7.95 (ISBN 0-02-918380-4). Free Pr.

Teaching Social Work Research. Date not set. 6.60. Coun Soc Wk Ed.

Teaching Sociology of Aging: Syllabi and Materials. D. Harris. 300p. 1986. 16.00 (ISBN 0-317-36344-1). Am Sociological.

Teaching Sociology: The Quest for Excellence. Ed. by Frederick L. Campbell et al. LC 84-1107. 256p. 1984. lib. bdg. 24.95x (ISBN 0-8304-1097-X). Nelson-Hall.

Teaching Spanish in the Secondary School in Trinidad, West Indies: A Curriculum Perspective. Venus E. Deonanan & Carlton R. Deonanan. LC 79-6199. 373p. 1980. pap. text ed. 16.50 (ISBN 0-8191-1005-1). U Pr of Amer.

Teaching Spanish-Speaking Children. L. S. Tireman. Ed. by Carlos E. Cortes. LC 76-1591. (Chciago Heritage Ser.). 1976. Repr. of 1948 ed. 12.00x (ISBN 0-405-09526-0). Ayer Co Pubs.

Teaching Spanish Speech Sounds: Drills for Articulation Therapy. Larry J. Mattes & George Santiago. (Illus.). 122p. 1985. pap. text ed. 18.50 (ISBN 0-930951-02-6). Acad Comm.

Teaching Spanish to the Hispanic Bilingual: Issues, Aims, & Methods. Guadalupe Valdes-Fallis et al. LC 80-20707. (Bilingual Education Ser.). 272p. 1981. text ed. 18.95x (ISBN 0-8077-2629-X). Tchrs Coll.

Teaching Spanish to the Native Spanish Speaker see Sensitivity in the Foreign Language Classroom.

Teaching Special Needs Students in Regular Classrooms. Catherine V. Morsink. 1984. text ed. write for info. (ISBN 0-673-39173-6). Scott F.

Teaching Special Students in the Mainstream. 2nd ed. Rena B. Lewis & Donald H. Doorlag. 1987. Additional supplements may be obtained from publisher. text ed. 27.95 (ISBN 0-675-20472-0). Merrill.

Teaching Speech for the Stage: A Manual for Classroom Instruction. Evangeline Machlin. 1980. pap. 4.95 (ISBN 0-87830-573-4). Theatre Arts.

Teaching Speech Handicapped. Jack Rudman. (Teachers License Examination Ser.: NT-26). (Cloth bdg. avail. on request). pap. 13.95 (ISBN 0-8373-8436-2). Natl Learning.

Teaching Speech in the Elementary School: A Comparative Study of Speech Education in the Elementary Schools of England & of the United States. Emma B. Meader. LC 70-177064. (Columbia University. Teachers College. Contributions to Education: No. 317). Repr. of 1928 ed. 22.50 (ISBN 0-404-55317-6). AMS Pr.

Teaching Speech to Hearing-Impaired Infants & Children: Zero to Three Years. Dene Stovall. (Illus.). 102p. 1982. spiral bdg. 15.25 (ISBN 0-398-04680-8). C C Thomas.

Teaching Spelling. Edmund Henderson. LC 84-81010. 256p. 1985. pap. text ed. 22.75 (ISBN 0-395-35771-3). HM.

Teaching Spelling. Mike Torbe. 1985. 15.00x (ISBN 0-7062-3663-7, Pub. by Ward Lock Educ Co Ltd). State Mutual Bk.

Teaching Spontaneous Communication to Autistic & Developmentally Handicapped Children. Eric Schopler & Linda R. Watson. (Diagnosis & Teaching Curricula for Autisim & Developmental Disabilities Ser.). (Illus.). 200p. 1988. Includes reproducible evaluation forms. text ed. 39.95x (ISBN 0-8290-2227-9). Irvington.

Teaching Sports Medicine & Recreation to Family Practice Residents. Ed. by STFM Task Force on Teaching Sports Medicine & Recreation. 122p. 1981. 5.00 (ISBN 0-942295-15-3). Soc Tchrs Fam Med.

Teaching Standard English As a Second Dialect: Issues & Perspectives. Orlando L. Taylor. (Orig.). 1989. price not set. College-Hill.

Teaching State Government. Allan D. Kownslar. 1980. text ed. 12.00 (ISBN 0-07-035411-1). McGraw.

Teaching Statistics & Probability: 1981 Yearbook. National Council of Teachers of Mathematics. LC 81-1679. (Illus.). 256p. 1981. 18.00 (ISBN 0-87353-170-1). NCTM.

Teaching Strategies: A Guide to Better Instruction. 2nd ed. Donald C. Orlich et al. LC 84-81085. 379p. 1985. pap. text ed. 19.50 (ISBN 0-669-06746-6). Heath.

Teaching Strategies & Techniques for Adjunct Faculty. Donald E. Greive. 32p. 1986. pap. 3.95x (ISBN 0-940017-02-4). Info Tec OH.

Teaching Strategies for Children in Conflict: Curriculum Methods & Materials. 2nd ed. H. Swanson & Henry R. Reinert. 1984. pap. text ed. 27.95 (ISBN 0-675-20591-3). Merrill.

Teaching Strategies for Developing Intellectual Abilities. You-Yuh Kuo. 1976. pap. 7.00 (ISBN 0-9601274-1-0). East West Cult.

Teaching Strategies for Ethnic Studies. 4th ed. Banks. 1986. 31.00 (ISBN 0-205-10344-8). Allyn.

Teaching Strategies for Language Development. Jane Rieke et al. 119p. 1977. 22.50 (ISBN 0-8089-0996-7, 793540). Grune.

Teaching Strategies for Parents & Professionals, Vol. II. Eric Schopler et al. LC 78-13415. (Individualized Assessment & Treatment for Autistic & Developmentally Disabled Children Ser.). (Illus.). 256p. 1980. pap. 21.00x (1170). Pro Ed.

Teaching Strategies for the Social Studies: Inquiry, Valuing & Decision Making. 3rd ed. James A. Banks. LC 84-14388. 544p. 1985. text ed. 26.95x (ISBN 0-582-28570-4). Longman.

Teaching Stress Management & Relaxation Skills: An Instructor's Guide. John D. Curtis et al. (Illus.). 280p. 1985. text ed. 26.50 (ISBN 0-9611456-2-5). Coulee Pr.

Teaching Stress Management Skills: A Manual for Beginning & Experienced Teachers. Frances K. Wiggins & Suni Petersen. (Illus.). 167p. (Orig.). 1986. pap. text ed. 16.95 (ISBN 0-942937-01-5). Rivijon Pr.

Teaching Stringed Instruments in Classes. Elizabeth Green. 1987. 14.75 (ISBN 0-89917-507-4). Am String Tchrs.

Teaching Students Through Their Individual Learning Styles: A Practical Approach. Kenneth Dunn & Rita Dunn. (Illus.). 1978. pap. 30.00 (ISBN 0-87909-808-2, Reston). P-H.

Teaching Students to Learn. Graham Gibbs. 111p. 1981. (Pub. by Open Univ Pr); pap. 21.00x (ISBN 0-335-10033-3). Taylor & Francis.

Teaching Students To Read. James Flood & Diane Lapp. xxiv, 642p. 1986. pap. write for info. (ISBN 0-02-338450-6). Macmillan.

Teaching Students to Read. Diane Lapp & James Flood. 64p. 1986. pap. text ed. write for info. (ISBN 0-02-367670-1). Macmillan.

Teaching Students to Read Through Their Individual Learning Styles. rev. ed. Marie Carbo et al. (Illus.). 384p. 1986. text ed. 30.00 (ISBN 0-8359-7517-7, Reston). P-H.

Teaching Students to Teach Themselves. Crawford W. Lindsey, Jr. 148p. 1988. pap. 21.50 (ISBN 0-89397-315-7). Nichols Pub.

Teaching Students to Think Critically: A Guide for Faculty in All Disciplines. Chet Meyers. LC 86-45627. (Higher Education Ser.). 1986. text ed. 19.95x (ISBN 1-55542-011-7). Jossey-Bass.

Teaching Students with Behavior Disorders: Techniques for Classroom Instruction. Patricia A. Gallagher. 300p. 1979. text ed. 22.95 (ISBN 0-89108-091-0). Love Pub Co.

Teaching Students with Learning & Behavior Problems. 4th ed. Donald D. Hammill & Nettie Bartel. LC 85-30803. (Illus.). 432p. 1986. 24.00x (ISBN 0-89079-116-3, 1398). Pro Ed.

Teaching Students with Learning & Behavior Problems. 3rd ed. Gerald Wallace & James Kauffman. 384p. (Additional supplements may be obtained from publisher). 1986. text ed. 32.95 (ISBN 0-675-20534-4). Merrill.

Teaching Students with Learning Problems. 2nd ed. Cecil Mercer & Ann Mercer. 544p. 1985. 28.95 (ISBN 0-675-20355-4). Merrill.

Teaching Students with Learning Problems. Cecil D. Mercer & Ann Mercer. 560p. 1988. pap. 28.95 (ISBN 0-675-21027-5). Merrill.

Teaching Students with Severe Emotional & Learning Impairments. Ellen Browning. 331p. 1985. 32.95x (ISBN 0-205-07677-7, 247677, Pub. by Longwood Div). Allyn.

Teaching Study Skills: A Guide for Teachers. 2nd ed. Devine. 384p. 1987. 32.95 (ISBN 0-205-18984-9, Pub. by Longwood Div). Allyn.

Teaching Styles & Pupil Progress. Neville Bennett. 1976. 16.00x (ISBN 0-674-87095-6). Harvard U Pr.

Teaching Styles As Related to Student Achievement. 2nd ed. David L. Silvernail. 40p. 1986. 2.50 (ISBN 0-8106-1069-8). NEA.

Teaching Sunday School. Brian Freer. 1984. pap. 4.95 (ISBN 0-87552-972-0, Evangel Pr UK). Presby & Reformed.

Teaching Suzuki Cello: A Manual for Teachers & Parents. Charlene Wilson. (Illus.). 128p. 1980. pap. 5.95 (ISBN 0-87297-052-3). Diablo.

Teaching Swimming: Steps to Success. David G. Thomas. (Steps to Success Activity Ser.). (Illus., Orig.). 1988. pap. text ed. write for info. (ISBN 0-88011-310-3). Leisure Pr.

Teaching Tactics for Japan's English Classrooms. John Wharton. 140p. (Orig.). 1986. pap. 6.95 (ISBN 0-911285-02-4). Global Pr Co.

Teaching Tactics for Japan's English Classrooms. Ed. by John Wharton. (Illus.). 140p. 1986. pap. 6.95. Global Pr Co.

Teaching Talk: Strategies for Production & Assessment. Gillian Brown et al. (Illus.). 192p. 1985. 21.95 (ISBN 0-521-26528-2); pap. 9.95 (ISBN 0-521-31942-0). Cambridge U Pr.

Teaching Teachers about Law: A Guide to Law-Related Teacher Education Programs. 225p. 1976. pap. 2.00 (ISBN 0-686-47951-3). Amer Bar Assn.

Teaching Teachers, Teaching Students. Ed. by D. J. Albers & L. A. Steen. 152p. 1981. 16.95x (ISBN 0-8176-3043-0). Birkhauser.

Teaching Teachers to Teach: A Basic Manual for Church Teachers. Donald L. Griggs. (Griggs Educational Resources Ser.). 1983. pap. 7.95 (ISBN 0-687-41120-3). Abingdon.

Teaching Through Radio & Television. rev. ed. William B. Levenson & Edward Stasheff. Repr. of 1952 ed. lib. bdg. 35.00x (ISBN 0-8371-2414-X, LERT). Greenwood.
Teaching Through Self-Instruction: A Practical Handbook for Course Developers. Derek Rountree. 386p. 1986. 28.50 (ISBN 0-89397-250-9). Nichols Pub.
Teaching Tips: A Guidebook for the Beginning College Teacher. 8th ed. Wilbert J. McKeachie. LC 85-60982. 353p. 1986. pap. text ed. 12.50 (ISBN 0-669-06752-0). Heath.
Teaching Tips for Cosmetology. Linnea Lindquist. 24p. 1981. pap. text ed. 13.75 (ISBN 0-314-63395-2). West Pub.
Teaching to Change Lives. Howard G. Hendricks. Ed. by Tom Womack. 1987. 9.95 (ISBN 0-88070-198-6). Multnomah.
Teaching to Meet Crisis Needs. Billie Davis. LC 83-82815. (Sunday School Staff Training Ser.). 128p. (Orig.). 1984. pap. 2.95 (ISBN 0-88243-609-0, 02-0609). Gospel Pub.
Teaching to Meet Crisis Needs see Ensenando a Enfrentar...Crisis.
Teaching to Read: Historically Considered. Mitford M. Mathews. LC 75-20588. 1976. pap. 3.95x (ISBN 0-226-51013-1, P678, Phoen). U of Chicago Pr.
Teaching to the Heart: An Affective Approach to Reading Instruction. Nancy L. Cecil. 151p. (Orig.). 1987. pap. text ed. 8.95 (ISBN 0-88133-274-7). Sheffield Wisc.
Teaching Today & Tomorrow. Charles R. Kniker & Natalie A. Naylor. 1981. pap. text ed. 30.95 (ISBN 0-675-08034-7). Merrill.
Teaching Today's Health. 2nd ed. David Anspaugh & Gene Ezell. 576p. 1987. text ed. 31.95 (ISBN 0-675-20542-5). Merrill.
Teaching Toddlers. Carol E. Miller. 1971. pap. 2.50 (ISBN 0-915374-22-6, 22-6). Rapids Christian.
Teaching Toddlers: How to Share God's Love with One-Year-Olds. rev. ed. Betty Aldridge et al. (Illus.). 64p. 1988. pap. text ed. 5.95 (ISBN 0-87403-365-9, 3189). Standard Pub.
Teaching Tomorrow's Nurse: A Nurse Educator Reader. Ed. by Susan K. Mirin. LC 79-90378. 224p. 1980. pap. 34.25 (ISBN 0-913654-59-0). Aspen Pub.
Teaching Torah: A Treasury of Activities & Insights. Sorel G. Loeb & Barbara B. Kadden. LC 84-70318. 300p. 1984. pap. text ed. 15.00 (ISBN 0-86705-013-6). AIRE.
Teaching under Attack. Walter Roy. (Illus.). 130p. 1983. 29.00 (ISBN 0-7099-2212-4, Pub. by Croom Helm Ltd); pap. 11.50 (ISBN 0-7099-2213-2). Routledge Chapman & Hall.
Teaching Undergraduates: Essays from the Lilly Endowment Workshop on the Liberal Arts. Ed. by Bruce A. Kimball. (Contemporary Issues in Philosophy Ser.). 220p. 1988. text ed. 23.95 (ISBN 0-87975-489-3). Prometheus Bks.
Teaching Vermont's Heritage: Proceedings of the Second Working Conference on Vermont's Heritage for Teachers. Intro. by Marshall True et al. (Illus.). 160p. (Orig.). 1984. pap. text ed. 5.00x (ISBN 0-944277-11-X). U VT Ctr Rsch VT.
Teaching Visually Handicapped. Jack Rudman. (Teachers License Examination Ser.: NT-27). (Cloth bdg. avail. on request). pap. 13.95 (ISBN 0-8373-8437-0). Natl Learning.
Teaching Visuals from Willmington's Guide to the Bible. 298p. 1981. pap. 16.95 three-ring notebook (ISBN 0-8423-6939-2). Tyndale.
Teaching Vocabulary. Michael Wallace. Ed. by Marion Geddes & Gillian Sturtridge. (Practical Language Teaching Ser.: No. 10). 144p. (Orig.). 1983. pap. text ed. 10.00x (ISBN 0-435-28974-8). Heinemann Ed.
Teaching Vocational Agriculture-Agribusiness. Harold R. Binkley & Rodney W. Tulloch. (Illus.). 250p. 1981. pap. 13.95x (ISBN 0-8134-2153-5). Inter Print Pubs.
Teaching Volleyball: Steps to Success. Barbara L. Viera & Bonnie J. Ferguson. (Steps to Success Activity Ser.). (Illus., Orig.). 1988. pap. text ed. price not set (ISBN 0-88011-316-2). Leisure Pr.
Teaching: What It's All About. Leo W. Anglin, Jr. et al. 372p. 1982. text ed. 27.50 scp (ISBN 0-397-47399-0, HarpC). Har-Row.
Teaching: Why Not Try Psychology? John A. Glover et al. (Orig.). 1979. pap. text ed. 8.95 (ISBN 0-8403-1772-7). Kendall-Hunt.
Teaching with Charisma. Duck. 364p. 1980. text ed. 29.00 (ISBN 0-205-07256-9, 2372568). Allyn.
Teaching with Confidence: How to Get off the Classroom Wall. Bill W. Hillman. (Illus.). 296p. 1981. 32.75x (ISBN 0-398-04103-2). C C Thomas.
Teaching with Eggs. Alfred De Vito. (Illus.). 70p. (Orig.). (gr. 3-8). 1982. pap. 6.95 (ISBN 0-686-32839-6). Creat Ventures IN.
Teaching with Feeling: Compassion & Self-Awareness in the Classroom Today. Herbert M. Greenberg. LC 69-13393. 1969. pap. 7.87scp (ISBN 0-672-63601-8). Pegasus.
Teaching with Flannelgraph. Helen Sizemore. (Illus.). 48p. 1976. pap. 1.95 (ISBN 0-87239-074-8, 3280). Standard Pub.
Teaching with LOGO. Daniel Watt & Molly Watt. 1985. write for info. Addison-Wesley.
Teaching with Music Through the Church Year. Judy G. Smith. 1979. pap. 7.95 (ISBN 0-687-41133-5). Abingdon.
Teaching with Newspapers: The Living Curriculum. Lynn Rhoades & George Rhoades. LC 80-82682. (Fastback Ser.: No. 149). 1980. pap. 0.90 (ISBN 0-87367-149-X). Phi Delta Kappa.
Teaching with Object Talks. Cara Roberts. (Illus.). 48p. (Orig.). 1982. pap. 2.95 (ISBN 0-87239-533-2, 2889). Standard Pub.
Teaching with Power: A Guide for Missionaries. Grant Von Harrison. 19p. (Orig.). (YA) (gr. 11 up). 1983. pap. 1.95 (ISBN 0-942241-07-X, 8724). Pubs Bk Sales.
Teaching with Quotes. Alfred De Vito. (Illus.). 162p. (Orig.). 1983. pap. 10.95 (ISBN 0-942034-01-5). Creat Ventures IN.
Teaching with Student Math Notes. Ed. by Evan Maletsky. (Illus.). 128p. 1987. pap. 13.50 (ISBN 0-87353-244-9). NCTM.
Teaching with Survival Graphics: Illustrated Visuals on Survival Philosophy, No. 1. rev. ed. Eugene H. Fear. (A B C Ser.). 1979. pap. 3.00 (ISBN 0-913724-08-4). Emerg Response Inst.
Teaching with Survival Graphics No. 2. Gene Fear. (D.E.F. Ser). (Illus.). 1975. pap. 3.00 (ISBN 0-913724-12-2). Emerg Response Inst.
Teaching with Survival Graphics No. 3. Gene Fear. (G.I.J. Ser). (Illus.). 1975. pap. 3.00 (ISBN 0-913724-13-0). Emerg Response Inst.
Teaching with the Flannelboard. Diane M. Kohl. (Teaching Aids Early Childhood Ser.). 70p. (gr. 3-7). 1984. 6.95 (ISBN 0-513-01771-2). Denison.
Teaching with Toys: Making Your Own Educational Toys. Sally Goldberg. 96p. 1981. pap. 8.95 (ISBN 0-472-06334-0). U of Mich Pr.
Teaching with Writing: An Interdisciplinary Workshop Approach. Toby Fulwiler. 176p. (Orig.). 1987. pap. text ed. 13.50x (ISBN 0-86709-055-3). Boynton CooK Pubs.
Teaching Without Grades. Max S. Marshall. LC 68-56417. 158p. 1968. pap. 6.95x (ISBN 0-87071-317-5). Oreg St U Pr.
Teaching Without Tears. R. L. Bowley. 204p. 1973. pap. 9.95 (ISBN 0-8464-0909-7). Beekman Pubs.
Teaching Without Tears. R. L. Bowley. 1968. 6.95 (ISBN 0-8022-0165-2). Philos Lib.
Teaching Without Tears: The Classroom Teachers Survival Book. Charles O. Preece. 124p. 1988. 14.95 (ISBN 0-9619349-2-1). C O Preece.
Teaching Without Tears: The Classroom Teachers Survival Book. rev. ed. Charles O. Preece. 124p. 1988. pap. 12.95 (ISBN 0-9619349-3-X). C O Preece.
Teaching Without Tears: Your First Year in the Secondary School. Jenny Gray. LC 67-29159. (Illus.). (gr. 9-12). 1968. pap. 6.95 (ISBN 0-8224-6920-0). D S Lake Pubs.
Teaching Women's History. Gerda Lerner. LC 80-71043. 88p. (Orig.). 1981. pap. text ed. 5.00 (ISBN 0-87229-023-9). Am Hist Assn.
Teaching Women's Literature from a Regional Perspective. Ed. by Leonore Hoffman & Deborah Rosenfelt. LC 82-211. 224p. 1982. 30.00x (ISBN 0-87352-334-2); pap. 16.50x (ISBN 0-87352-335-0). Modern Lang.
Teaching Word Attack Skills. 4th, rev. ed. Lee A. Rinsky. 1988. pap. text ed. write for info. (ISBN 0-89787-524-9). Gorsuch Scarisbrick.
Teaching Word Attack Skills. 3rd ed. Lee-Ann Rinsky. 203p. 1984. pap. text ed. 16.00x (ISBN 0-89787-512-5). Gorsuch Scarisbrick.
Teaching Word Processing: First Steps. Linda Firth. (Orig.). 1987. ring binder 57.50 (ISBN 0-273-02749-2, Pub. by Pitman Pub Ltd London). Trans-Atl Phila.
Teaching Word Processing in the Elementary School. John T. Riley & Judie L. Hurtz. 38p. 1985. pap. 7.95 (ISBN 0-912007-03-6). Computer Direct.
Teaching World History: Structured Inquiry Through a Historical-Anthropological Approach. Ed. by Douglas D. Alder & Glenn M. Linden. 164p. 1976. 9.95 (ISBN 0-89994-195-8). Soc Sci Ed.
Teaching Writing. Eugene Hammond. 212p. 1983. text ed. 19.95 (ISBN 0-07-025893-7). McGraw.
Teaching Writing: A Systematic Approach. Colin Peacock. 160p. (Orig.). 1986. pap. 17.00 (ISBN 0-7099-4028-9, Pub. by Croom Helm Ltd). Routledge Chapman & Hall.
Teaching Writing As a Second Language. Alice S. Horning. (Studies in Writing & Rhetoric). 80p. (Orig.). 1986. pap. text ed. 8.50x (ISBN 0-8093-1327-8). S Ill U Pr.
Teaching Writing: Essays from the Bay Area Writing Project. Ed. by Gerald Camp. 336p. (Orig.). 1983. pap. text ed. 15.00x (ISBN 0-86709-081-2). Boynton Cook Pubs.
Teaching Writing in All Disciplines. Ed. by C. Williams Griffin. LC 81-48585. (Teaching & Learning Ser.: No. 12). 1982. 12.95x (ISBN 0-87589-926-9). Jossey-Bass.
Teaching Writing in Every Class: A Guide for Grades 6-12. Hollingsworth & Eastman. 256p. 1987. pap. text ed. 35.95 scp. (ISBN 0-205-11134-3, Pub. by Longwood Div); pap. text ed. 26.21 net. Allyn.
Teaching Writing in K-8 Classrooms: The Time Has Come. Iris M. Tiedt & S. Suzanne Bruemmer. (Illus.). 1983. pap. write for info. (ISBN 0-13-896290-1). P-H.
Teaching Writing in the Content Areas: Elementary School. Stephen N. Tchudi & Susan J. Tchudi. 64p. 1983. 5.95 (ISBN 0-8106-0776-X). NEA.
Teaching Writing in the Content Areas: Middle School-Junior High School. Stephen N. Tchudi & Margie C. Huerta. 64p. 1983. 5.95 (ISBN 0-8106-0777-8). NEA.
Teaching Writing in the Content Areas: Middle School-Junior High. Stephen N. Tchudi & Margie C. Huerts. 64p. 1983. 7.25 (ISBN 0-8141-3157-3). NCTE.
Teaching Writing in the Content Areas: College. Stephen N. Tchudi. 128p. 1986. pap. 8.50 (ISBN 0-8141-0728-1). NCTE.
Teaching Writing in the Content Areas: Elementary. Stephen N. Tchudi & Susan J. Tchudi. 64p. 1983. 7.00 (ISBN 0-8141-1314-1). NCTE.
Teaching Writing in the Content Areas: Senior High School. Stephen N. Tchudi & Joanne Yates. 64p. 1983. 8.50 (ISBN 0-8141-2116-0). NCTE.
Teaching Writing in the Content Areas: Senior High School. Stephen N. Tchudi & Joanne M. Yates. 80p. 1983. 6.95 (ISBN 0-8106-0778-6). NEA.
Teaching Writing: Making Theory Practice Connections. JoAnn Sipple. 160p. 1984. pap. text ed. 13.95 (ISBN 0-675-20254-X). Merrill.
Teaching Writing Manual. rev. ed. Evelyn Rothstein & Diane Gess. (Illus.). 170p. 1987. pap. text ed. 17.95 (ISBN 0-913935-39-5). ERA-CCR.
Teaching Writing: Pedagogy, Gender, & Equity. Ed. by Cynthia L. Caywood & Gillian R. Overing. LC 86-14520. 238p. 1986. 54.50 (ISBN 0-88706-352-7); pap. 18.95 (ISBN 0-88706-353-5). State U NY Pr.
Teaching Writing: Problems & Solutions. American Association of School Administrators Staff. 11.95 (ISBN 0-318-01772-5, 021-00901). Am Assn Sch Admin.
Teaching Writing Skills. Donn Byrne. (Handbooks for Language Teachers). (Illus.). 1980. pap. text ed. 13.95 (ISBN 0-582-74602-7). Longman.
Teaching Writing Skills: A Global Approach. rev. ed. John Benegar. (Illus.). 189p. (Orig.). (gr. 6-12). 1985. pap. 16.95 (ISBN 0-943804-31-0). U of Denver Teach.
Teaching Writing with a Word Processor, Grades 7-13. Dawn Rodrigues & Raymond J. Rodrigues. 83p. 1986. pap. text ed. 6.25 (ISBN 0-8141-5241-4). NCTE.
Teaching Writing with Computers: The Power Process. Owen Solomon. (Illus.). 176p. 1986. text ed. 20.00 (ISBN 0-13-896366-5); pap. text ed. write for info (ISBN 0-13-896358-4). P-H.
Teaching Writing with the Computer as Helper. J. Terence Kelly & Kamala Anandam. (Pocket Reader Ser.: No. 2). 56p. 1982. pap. 5.00 ea. (ISBN 0-87117-115-5); pap. 25.00 12 copies. Am Assn Comm Jr Coll.
Teaching Writing with the Microcomputer. E. Marilyn Schaeffer. LC 86-63877. (Fastback Ser.: No. 254). 50p. pap. 0.90 (ISBN 0-87367-254-2). Phi Delta Kappa.
Teaching Written English. Ronald White. (Practical Language Teaching Ser.). (Orig.). 1980. pap. text ed. 9.00x (ISBN 0-435-28968-3). Heinemann Ed.
Teaching Written Expression: The Phelps Sentence Guide Program. Diana Phelps-Tersaki & Tricia Phelps. 112p. 1980. pap. text ed. 9.00 (ISBN 0-87879-248-1); Phelps Guides, 25-pkg. 8.00 (ISBN 0-87879-290-2). Acad Therapy.
Teaching Young Children. Carol Seefeldt. (Illus.). 1980. text ed. write for info. (ISBN 0-13-896423-8). P-H.
Teaching Young Children at School & Home. Edythe Margolin. 448p. 1982. text ed. write for info. (ISBN 0-02-375980-1). Macmillan.
Teaching Young Children to Read. 4th ed. Durkin. 1986. 38.00 (ISBN 0-205-10265-4). Allyn.
Teaching Young Dancers: Muscular Coordination in Classical Ballet. Joan Lawson. LC 75-15369. (Illus.). 1975. 19.95 (ISBN 0-87830-144-5). Theatre Arts.
Teaching Your Child About God. Wes Haystead. LC 68-29315. 1983. pap. 5.95 (ISBN 0-8307-0896-0, 5418029). Regal.
Teaching Your Child about Sex. Terrance Drake & Marvia Drake. LC 83-71726. 60p. 1983. 6.95 (ISBN 0-87747-951-8). Deseret Bk.
Teaching Your Child Money Management: A Complete Step-by-Step Workbook for the Parent. James L. Wagner. Ed. by Teri H. Vito & Kathleen Aldenbrook. (Illus.). 1987. wkbk. 10.00 (ISBN 0-944043-00-3). Insight Comns.
Teaching Your Child to Handle Peer Pressure. Penelope Grenoble et al. (Parentbooks That Work Ser.). 128p. (Orig.). 1988. pap. 5.95 (ISBN 0-8092-4671-6). Contemp Bks.
Teaching Your Child to Lead: A Parents Guide. Ernest Y. Flores. LC 81-51217. (Illus.). 60p. 1981. perfect bound 5.95 (ISBN 0-88247-592-4). R & E Pubs.
Teaching Your Child to Listen. 1979. 6.00 (ISBN 0-939418-19-3). Ferguson-Florissant.
Teaching Your Child to Read. Ann Fusco & Anne Russo. (Illus.). 116p. (Orig.). 1982. pap. 12.00 (ISBN 0-9607368-0-8). Leprechaun Pr.
Teaching Your Child to Read. 1980. 4.00 (ISBN 0-939418-13-4). Ferguson-Florissant.
Teaching Your Children about Sex. John C. Howell. LC 72-90038. 1973. pap. 4.95 (ISBN 0-8054-5607-4). Broadman.
Teaching Your Computer to Talk: A Manual of Command & Response. Edward R. Teja. (Illus.). 208p. pap. 8.95 (ISBN 0-8306-1330-7, 1330). TAB Bks.
Teaching Your Down's Syndrome Infant see Teaching the Infant with Down Syndrome.
Teaching Your Horse to Jump. W. J. Froud. pap. 5.00 (ISBN 0-87980-227-8). Wilshire.
Teaching Your Horse Tricks for Fun & Profit. Jonnie Stinson. (Illus.). 96p. 1978. text ed. 15.00. J Stinson.
Teaching Your Occupation to Others: A Guide to Surviving the First Year. Paul A. Bott. (Orig.). 1986. pap. text ed. 9.95x (ISBN 0-935920-40-4). Natl Pub Black Hills.
Teaching Yourself in Libraries: A Guide to the High School Media Center & Other Libraries. Lillian L. Shapiro. LC 78-16616. 180p. (gr. 7-12). 1978. 10.00 (ISBN 0-8242-0628-2). Wilson.
Teaching Yourself to Teach. Howard E. Walker. 1983. kit 15.70 (ISBN 0-687-41137-8); wkbk. 1.60 (ISBN 0-687-41138-6). Abingdon.
Teaching Youth. Larry Richards. 155p. 1982. pap. 4.95 (ISBN 0-8341-0776-7). Beacon Hill.
Teaching Youth about Conflict & War. William A. Nesbitt & Norman Abramowitz. Ed. by Charles Bloomstein. LC 73-75291. (Teaching Social Studies in an Age of Crisis: No. 5). pap. 28.00 (ISBN 0-317-08320-1, 2005099). Bks Demand UMI.
Teaching Youth with Confidence. Bill Bynum. 48p. 1983. pap. 3.95 (ISBN 0-910566-41-0); seminar planbook 3.95 (ISBN 0-910566-42-9). Evang Tchr.
Teaching 1: Classroom Management. Wesley C. Becker et al. LC 74-31012. (Illus.). 1975. pap. text ed. write for info. (ISBN 0-574-18025-7, 13-6025); instr's. guide avail. (ISBN 0-574-18026-5, 13-6026). SRA.
Teachings. David Fisher. (Illus.). 40p. lib. bdg. 8.95 (ISBN 0-918510-02-3); pap. 2.95 (ISBN 0-918510-01-5); signed cloth ed. 10.95 (ISBN 0-686-96877-8). Monday Bks.
Teachings & Miracles of Jesus. Daughters of St. Paul. 1981. 5.00 (ISBN 0-686-73821-7); pap. 4.00 (ISBN 0-8198-7302-0). Dghtrs St Paul.
Teachings from the American Earth: Indian Religion & Philosophy. Ed. by Dennis Tedlock & Barbara Tedlock. (Illus.). 304p. 1976. pap. 8.95 (ISBN 0-87140-097-9). Liveright.
Teachings of Christ Story-N-Puzzle Book. Ruby Maschke. 48p. (Orig.). (gr. 4 up). 1981. pap. 2.50 (ISBN 0-87239-451-4, 2842). Standard Pub.
Teachings of Christ Ungame Cards. 1.50 (ISBN 0-317-15786-8). Chr Marriage.
Teachings of Dante. facs. ed. Charles A. Dinsmore. (Select Bibliographies Reprint Ser.). 1901. 17.00 (ISBN 0-8369-5521-8). Ayer Co Pubs.
Teachings of Don Juan. Carlos Castaneda. 1982. pap. 4.95 (ISBN 0-671-60041-9). WSP.
Teachings of Don Juan: A Yaqui Way of Knowledge. Carlos Castaneda. LC 68-17303. 1968. 22.50x (ISBN 0-520-00217-2); pap. 8.95 (ISBN 0-520-02258-0). U of Cal Pr.
Teachings of Grandfather Fox. Leonard Nathan. LC 76-57990. 49p. 1976. 3.50 (ISBN 0-87886-079-7). Greenfld Rev Pr.
Teachings of Hafiz. Gertrude Bell. 1979. 14.95 (ISBN 0-900860-63-4, Pub. by Octagon Pr England). Ins Study Human.
Teachings of Hasidism. Ed. by Joseph Dan. (Orig.). 1983. pap. text ed. 10.95x (ISBN 0-87441-346-X). Behrman.
Teachings of Islam: A Solution of Five Fundamental Religious Problems from the Muslim Point of View. M. G. Atemed. 208p. 1984. text ed. 23.00. Coronet Bks.
Teachings of Islam (Tablighi Nisab) M. Zakeriyya. 1987. 25.00 (ISBN 0-933511-09-4). Kazi Pubns.
Teachings of Jehovah's Witnesses. John H. Gerstner. pap. 1.95 (ISBN 0-8010-3718-2). Baker Bk.
Teachings of Jesus. Norman Anderson. LC 83-4312. (Jesus Library). 216p. 1983. pap. 8.95 (ISBN 0-87784-926-9). Inter-Varsity.
Teachings of Kirpal Singh, 3 vols. Ed. by Ruth Seader. Vol. I, The Holy Path, 104 pp. 3.00 (ISBN 0-318-03046-2); Vol. III, The New Life, 200 pp. 3.50 (ISBN 0-318-03047-0); One-Volume Ed., 474 pp. 7.95 (ISBN 0-318-03048-9). Sant Bani Ash.
Teachings of Kirpal Singh: Three Volumes Complete in One Book. 2nd ed. Kirpal Singh. LC 81-51513. (Illus.). 506p. (Orig.). 1982. pap. 9.95 (ISBN 0-918224-13-6). Sawan Kirpal Pubns.
Teachings of Maimonides. Jacob Minkin. LC 87-70737. 450p. 1987. Repr. of 1957 ed. 40.00 (ISBN 0-87668-953-5). Aronson.
Teachings of Mormonism. John H. Gerstner. pap. 1.95 (ISBN 0-8010-3719-0). Baker Bk.
Teachings of Nature in the Kingdom of Grace. C. H. Spurgeon. 1976. pap. 4.95 (ISBN 0-686-18094-1). Pilgrim Pubns.
Teachings of Old Testament. John Job. (Bible Study Commentaries Ser.). 128p. 1984. pap. 4.95 (ISBN 0-317-43392-X). Chr Lit.

Teatro de Max Aub. Estela R. Lopez. LC 76-46372. (Coleccion Uprex; Serie Teatro y Cine: No. 52). (Orig.). 1977. pap. text ed. 1.85 (ISBN 0-8477-0052-6). U of PR Pr.

Teatro en Puerto Rico: Notas Para Su Historia. 2nd ed. Antonio Saez. (UPREX, Teatro y Cine: No.6). pap. 1.85 (ISBN 0-8477-0006-2). U of PR Pr.

Teatro Hispanoamericano: Una Bibliografia Anotada. Richard F. Allen. (Reference Bks). 683p. 1987. lib. bdg. 45.00x (ISBN 0-8161-8395-3). G K Hall.

Teatro, Prosa, Poesia. Althea C. Reynolds & Argentina Brunetti. (Illus.). 160p. 1982. pap. text ed. 18.50 (ISBN 0-915838-12-5). Anma Libri.

Teatro Rioplatense. (Ayacucho Library Collection Ser.: Vol. 8). (Span.). 1986. 35.00 (ISBN 0-317-56253-3, Pub. by Biblioteca Ayacucho); pap. 15.00 (ISBN 0-317-56254-1, Pub. by Biblioteca Ayacucho). Humanities.

Teatro y Censura en la Espana Franquista. Hilde F. Cramsie. LC 83-49363. (American University Studies II - Romance Languages & Literature: Vol. 9). 213p. 1985. text ed. 25.60 (ISBN 0-8204-0092-0). P Lang Pubs.

Teatro y Practicas Escenicas II: La Comedia. Ed. by Jose L. Valles. 1986. pap. 24.00 (ISBN 0-7293-0242-3, Pub. by Tamesis Bks Ltd). Longwood Pub Group.

Teatros y Comedias en Madrid: Sixteen Eighty-Seven to Sixteen Ninety-Nine, Estudio y Documentos. Ed. by N. D. Shergold & J. E. Varey. (Serie C: Fuentes para la Historia del Teatro en Espana, VI). 319p. (Orig., Span.). 1979. pap. 22.50 (ISBN 0-7293-0064-1, Pub. by Tamesis Bks Ltd). Longwood Pub Group.

Teatros y Comedias en Madrid: Sixteen Fifty-One to Sixteen Sixty-Five, Estudio y Documentos. Ed. by J. E. Varey & N. D. Shergold. (Serie C: Fuentes para la Historia del Teatro en Espana, IV). 258p. (Orig., Span.). 1973. pap. 18.00 (ISBN 0-900411-55-4, Pub. by Tamesis Bks Ltd). Longwood Pub Group.

Teatros y Comedias en Madrid: Sixteen Hundred to Sixteen Fifty, Estudio y Documentos. Ed. by J. E. Varey & N. D. Shergold. (Serie C: Fuentes para la Historia del Teatro en Espana, III). 195p. (Orig., Span.). 1971. pap. 18.00 (ISBN 0-900411-21-X, Pub. by Tamesis Bks Ltd). Longwood Pub Group.

Teatros y Comedias en Madrid: Sixteen Sixty-Six to Sixteen Eighty-Seven, Estudio y Documentos. Ed. by J. E. Varey & N. D. Shergold. (Serie C: Fuentes para la Historia del Teatro en Espana, V). 206p. (Orig., Span.). 1974. pap. 18.00 (ISBN 0-900411-89-9, Pub. by Tamesis Bks Ltd). Longwood Pub Group.

Teatros Y Comedias en Madrid: 1699-1719. N. D. Shergold & J. E. Varey. (Series C: Vol. XI). 222p. (Span.). 1986. pap. 18.00 (ISBN 0-7293-0241-5, Pub. by Tamesis Bks Ltd). Longwood Pub Group.

Teays-Age Drainage Effects on Present Distributional Patterns of Ohio Biota. Ed. by Charles C. King. 1983. pap. 2.00 (ISBN 0-86727-093-4). Ohio Bio Survey.

Tebaldo ed Isolina. Francesco Morlacchi. Ed. by Philip Gossett. (Italian Opera Ser., 1810-1840). 85.00 (ISBN 0-8240-6573-5). Garland Pub.

Tebb's Art of Bobbin Lace, Including the Supplement. 1980. 18.95 (ISBN 0-686-27274-9). Robin & Russ.

Tebe Sonati Iran: Traditional Medicine of Iran. Sadegh M. Angha. LC 83-80800. 519p. (Persian.). 1983. 75.00 (ISBN 0-910735-45-X). MTO Printing & Pubn Ctr.

Tech-General License Manual. 1988. 5.00 (ISBN 0-87259-014-3). Am Radio.

Tech Law. Kevin Barrett & Terry K. Amthor. (Illus.). 96p. (gr. 10-12). 12.00 (ISBN 0-915795-38-8). Iron Crown Ent Inc.

Tech Speak: How to Tell High-Tech. Edward Tenner. 1986. pap. 8.95 (ISBN 0-517-56220-0). Crown.

Tech Tran Special REport: Machine Vision Systems. 2nd ed. Tech Tran Consultants Staff. 224p. 1986. text ed. 53.95 (ISBN 0-07-063243-X). McGraw.

Tech Trans - 1988: The International Technology Transfer Directory. Ed. by John Cronin & Christa Gandenberger. 432p. 1988. 400.00 (ISBN 0-9619976-0-5). DirecTech Pub Inc.

Tech War. (Able Team Ser.: No. 18). Date not set. pap. 2.25 (ISBN 0-317-63981-1, Pub. by Worldwide). Harlequin Bks.

Technetium in Chemistry & Nuclear Medicine. Ed. by Marino Nicolini et al. 384p. 1986. text ed. 111.50 (ISBN 8-87749-010-1). Raven.

Technetium in the Environment: Proceedings of a Seminar Organized by the CEC Radiation Protection Programme & the Service d'Etudes et de Recherches sur l'Environnement du Commissariat a l'Energie Atomique, France, in Collaboration with the Office of Health & Environmental Research of the Dept. of Energy, U. S. A., held in 1986. Ed. by G. Desmet & C. Muttenaere. 384p. 1986. 106.25 (ISBN 0-85334-421-3). Elsevier.

Technic of the Bow Op. 50 for Violin. Casorti. (Carl Fischer Music Library Ser.: No. L-345). (Ger. & Fr.). pap. 6.00 (ISBN 0-8258-0042-0, L-345). Fischer Inc NY.

Technic Time, Pt. A. Louise Goss & Marion McArtot. (Frances Clark Library for Piano Students). 48p. (Orig.). (gr. k-6). 1974. pap. text ed. 7.95 (ISBN 0-87487-189-1). Birch Tree Gr.

Technical Advances. Ed. by J. Gybels et al. (Journal: Applied Neurophysiology Ser.: Vol. 45, No. 4-5). (Illus.). iv, 208p. 1981. pap. 52.00 (ISBN 3-8055-3499-X). S Karger.

Technical Advances in Biomedical Physics. Ed. by Philip P. Dendy. 1984. lib. bdg. 57.00 (ISBN 90-247-2934-3, Pub. by Martinus Nijhoff Netherlands). Kluwer Academic.

Technical Aide. Jack Rudman. (Career Examination Ser.: C-1514). (Cloth bdg. avail. on request). pap. 16.00 (ISBN 0-8373-1514-X). Natl Learning.

Technical Aide in Science & Engineering. Jack Rudman. (Career Examination Ser.: C-829). (Cloth bdg. avail. on request). pap. 18.00 (ISBN 0-8373-0829-1). Natl Learning.

Technical Aids. Lloyd S. Nelson. 51p. 8.50 (ISBN 0-318-13256-7, 1201); members 17.95 (ISBN 0-318-13257-5); LP 19.95. Am Soc QC.

Technical Aids to Teaching Higher Education. 3rd ed. Collin F. Page & John Kitching. 92p. 1981. pap. 29.00x (ISBN 0-900868-49-X, Open Univ Pr). Taylor & Francis.

Technical Americana: A Checklist of Technical Publications Printed Before 1831. Evald Rink. LC 81-4036. 1981. lib. bdg. 80.00 (ISBN 0-527-75447-1). Kraus Intl.

Technical Analysis Explained: An Illustrated Guide for the Investor. Martin J. Pring. 1980. text ed. 39.95 (ISBN 0-07-050871-2). McGraw.

Technical Analysis Explained: The Successful Investor's Guide to Spotting Investment Trends & Turning Points. 2nd ed. Martin J. Pring. 384p. 1985. text ed. 44.95 (ISBN 0-07-050885-2). McGraw.

Technical Analysis in Commodities. P. J. Kaufman. LC 79-19513. 227p. 1980. 52.50 (ISBN 0-471-05627-8). Wiley.

Technical Analysis of Common Stocks for Immediate Profits, 2 vols. Carlo M. Flumiani. (Illus.). 238p. 1986. Set. 237.50 (ISBN 0-86654-191-8). Inst Econ Finan.

Technical Analysis of Stock Trends. 5th ed. Robert D. Edwards & John Magee. (Illus.). 75.00 (ISBN 0-910944-00-8). Magee.

Technical Analysis of Stocks & Commodities: Investment Techniques, Vol. 2. Ed. by Jack K Hutson. LC 86-50575. (Illus.). 224p. (Orig.). 1987. pap. 45.00 (ISBN 0-938773-01-1). Tech Analysis.

Technical Analysis of Stocks & Commodities: Intelligent Trading, Vol. 4. Ed. by Jack K. Hutson. LC 86-50575. (Illus.). 484p. (Orig.). 1988. pap. 55.95 (ISBN 0-938773-03-8). Tech Analysis.

Technical Analysis of Stocks & Commodities: Profitable Trading Methods, Vol. 1. Ed. by Jack K. Hutson. LC 86-50575. (Illus.). 192p. (Orig.). 1986. pap. 39.00 (ISBN 0-938773-00-3). Tech Analysis.

Technical Analysis of Stocks & Commodities: Successful Speculation, Vol. 3. Ed. by Jack K. Hutson. LC 86-50575. (Illus.). 272p. (Orig.). 1988. pap. 49.95 (ISBN 0-938773-02-X). Tech Analysis.

Technical Analysis of Stocks & Commodities: Trading Strategies, Vol. 5. Ed. by Jack K. Hutson. LC 86-50575. (Illus.). 384p. (Orig.). 1988. pap. 59.95 (ISBN 0-938773-04-6). Tech Analysis.

Technical Analysis of Stocks, Options & Futures: Advanced Trading Systems & Techniques. William F. Eng. 475p. 1988. 49.50 (ISBN 1-55738-003-1). Probus Pub Co.

Technical Analysis of the Futures Markets: A Comprehensive Guide to Trading Methods & Applications. John J. Murphy. 1986. 45.00 (ISBN 0-13-898008-X). P-H.

Technical Analysis of the Futures Markets: Study Guide. John J. Murphy. LC 87-10991. (Illus.). 160p. (Orig.). 1987. pap. text ed. 24.95 (ISBN 0-13-858747-7). NY Inst Finance.

Technical & Business Revolution: American Woolens to 1832. Elizabeth Hitz. Ed. by Stuart Bruchey. (American Business History Ser.). 363p. 1986. lib. bdg. 45.00 (ISBN 0-8240-8378-4). Garland Pub.

Technical & Economic Criteria for Media Selection & Planning in Educational Institutions. (Educational Studies & Documents: No. 48). 81p. 1985. pap. 5.00 (ISBN 92-3-102234-2, U1444, UNESCO). UNIPUB.

Technical & Market Survey of Fluidic Applications. D. C. Bain & P. J. Baker. 1969. text ed. 32.00x (ISBN 0-900983-02-7, Dist. by Air Science Co.). BHRA Fluid.

Technical & Professional Assistant. Jack Rudman. (Career Examination Ser.: C-805). (Cloth bdg. avail. on request). pap. 16.00 (ISBN 0-8373-0805-4). Natl Learning.

Technical & Realistic Illustrations of Japan. (Graphic-Sha Bks.). (Illus.). 1984. 32.95 (ISBN 4-7661-0245-2). Bks Nippan.

Technical & Realistic Illustrations of Japan. (Illus.). 160p. 1986. pap. 25.00 (ISBN 0-8161-8809-2, Pub. by Graphic-Sha Pub Co Ltd Japan). G K Hall.

Technical & Scientific Abbreviations & Acronyms: English-German. Ed. by Wuster. 200p. 1968. cancelled 27.00 (ISBN 0-87015-051-0, Pub. by O Brandstetter WG). IPS.

Technical & Scientific Reader in English. Howard H. Hirschhorn. (gr. 9-12). 1970. pap. text ed. 7.00 (ISBN 0-13-898404-2, 17430). Prentice ESL.

Technical & Scientific Writing. Sarah H. Collins & Frederick B. Tuttle, Jr. 127p. 1979. pap. 7.95 (ISBN 0-8106-1718-8). NEA.

Technical & Vocational Education: Country Studies. UNESCO Regional Office for Education in Asia & the Pacific. 670p. 1985. pap. 62.50 (UB174, UNESCO). UNIPUB.

Technical & Vocational Education in Asia & Oceania. 35p. 1980. pap. 6.50 (ISBN 0-686-63037-8, UB85, UNESCO). UNIPUB.

Technical & Vocational Education in the United Kingdom: A Bibliographical Survey (UNESCO) R. C. Benge. (Education Studies & Documents: No. 27). pap. 16.00 (ISBN 0-8115-1351-3). Kraus Repr.

Technical & Vocational Education in the U. S. A. A Bibliographical Survey (UNESCO) (Education Studies & Documents: No. 36). pap. 16.00 (ISBN 0-8115-1360-2). Kraus Repr.

Technical & Vocational Education in the U. S. S. R. A Bibliographical Survey (UNESCO) M. I. Movsovic. (Education Studies & Documents: No. 30). pap. 16.00 (ISBN 0-8115-1354-8). Kraus Repr.

Technical & Vocational Teacher Education & Training. (Monographs on Education: No. 8). (Illus.). 240p. (Orig.). 1973. pap. 5.00 (ISBN 92-3-101097-2, U663, UNESCO). UNIPUB.

Technical Arabic: A Language Reader Incorporating Technical & Scientific Terms. Vernon Daykin. 132p. (Eng. & Arabic.). 1972. pap. text ed. 17.50 (ISBN 0-85331-330-X, Pub. Lund Humphries Pubs UK). Humanities.

Technical Arithmetic for Mechanics. 1983. 1.25 (ISBN 0-471-63878-1). Wiley.

Technical Aspects of Data Communication. John E. McNamara. 387p. 1982. 39.95 (ISBN 0-686-98097-2). Telecom Lib.

Technical Aspects of Data Communication. 3rd ed. John E. McNamara. (Illus.). 400p. 1988. text ed. 42.00 (ISBN 0-317-65728-3). Digital Pr.

Technical Aspects of Health Care Administration. Fischer. 1988. price not set (ISBN 0-471-62746-1). Wiley.

Technical Assessment of Nuclear Power & Its Alternatives: Proceedings, American Nuclear Society Topical Meeting, Los Angeles, 27-29 February 1980. 374p. pap. 46.00 (ISBN 0-89448-107-X, 700045). Am Nuclear Soc.

Technical Assessment of Specific Aspects of EPA Proposed Environmental Radiation Standard for the Uranium Fuel Cycle (40CFR 190) & Its Association Documentation (AIF-NESP-011) NUS Corporation. (National Environmental Studies Project: NESP Reports). 150p. 1976. 10.00 (ISBN 0-318-13598-1); NESP sponsors 5.00 (ISBN 0-318-13599-X). US Coun Energy Awareness.

Technical Assistance Advisements Sales Tax on Services, June-December 1987. Florida Department of Revenue. 443p. 1988. write for info. Am Inst CPA.

Technical Assistance & Aid Agency Staff: Alternative Techniques for Greater Effectiveness. Jerry M. Silverman. (Technical Paper: No. 28). 48p. 1984. 5.00 (ISBN 0-8213-0409-7, BK 0409). World Bank.

Technical Assistance Guide: A Directory of Resources for New York Non-Profit Organizations. Ed. by Technical Assistance Clearinghouse Staff. LC 88-141103. 83p. 1986. pap. text ed. 7.50 (ISBN 0-88156-067-7). Comm Serv Soc NY.

Technical Assistance Packet: Legal Service Provider Agreements. 1986. 14.50 (ISBN 0-317-65827-1, 2-018). Am Prepaid.

Technical Assistance Packet: Prepaid Legal Service Plan Description. 1987. 14.50 (ISBN 0-317-65829-8, 2-019). Am Prepaid.

Technical Assistance: Theory & Guidelines. Sidney C. Sufrin. LC 66-29623. pap. 31.50 (2022379). Bks Demand UMI.

Technical Assistant. Jack Rudman. (Career Examination Ser.: C-1515). (Cloth bdg. avail. on request). pap. 16.00 (ISBN 0-8373-1515-8). Natl Learning.

Technical Automotive Dictionary: Russian-English-German-French-Bulgarian. G. Sikora. 624p. (Rus., Eng., Ger., Fr. & Bulgarian.). 1977. leatherette 95.00 (ISBN 0-686-92472-X, M-9828). French & Eur.

Technical BASIC. Vincent Kassab. (Illus.). 320p. 1984. pap. 26.00 (ISBN 0-13-898114-0). P-H.

Technical Basis for Legislation on Irradiated Food: A Report. Joint FAO-IAEA-WHO Expert Committee, Rome, 1964. (Technical Report Ser: No. 316). 56p. (Eng., Fr., Rus. & Span.). 1966. pap. 2.00 (ISBN 92-4-120316-1). World Health.

Technical Bulletins of Dianetics & Scientology, 12 vols. L. Ron Hubbard. Incl. Vol. 1. 1950-53 (ISBN 0-88404-041-0); Vol. 2. 1954-56 (ISBN 0-88404-042-9); Vol. 3. 1957-59 (ISBN 0-88404-043-7); Vol. 4. 1960-61 (ISBN 0-88404-044-5); Vol. 5. 1962-64 (ISBN 0-88404-045-3); Vol. 6. 1965-69 (ISBN 0-88404-046-1); Vol. 7. 1970-71 (ISBN 0-88404-047-X); Vol. 8. 1972-76 (ISBN 0-88404-048-8); Vol. 9. Auditing Ser., 1965-75 (ISBN 0-88404-049-6); Vol. 10. Case Supervisor Ser. & Cumulative Index, 1970-75 (ISBN 0-88404-050-X); Vol. 11. 1976-78 (ISBN 0-88404-065-8); Vol. 12. 1979-80 (ISBN 0-88404-074-7). 1980. 1382.63 set; 124.33 ea. Bridge Pubns Inc.

Technical Bulletins: 1944-1974, Vol. 3. Association of Operative Millers. 1975. 25.00 (ISBN 0-686-00376-4). AG Pr.

Technical Bulletins: 1944-1975, Vol. 4. Association of Operative Millers. 1977. 25.00 (ISBN 0-686-00375-6). AG Pr.

Technical Calculus. Paul Calter. 432p. 1988. text ed. 35.00 (ISBN 0-13-898149-3). P-H.

Technical Calculus. 2nd ed. Dale Ewen & Michael A. Topper. (Illus.). 656p. 1986. text ed. write for info (ISBN 0-13-898164-7). P-H.

Technical Calculus with Analytic Geometry. Judith L. Gersting. 501p. 1984. text ed. write for info. (ISBN 0-534-02893-4). Wadsworth Pub.

Technical Calculus with Analytic Geometry. Peter Kuhfittig. LC 82-9714. (Mathematics Ser.). 512p. 1982. text ed. 26.00 pub net (ISBN 0-534-01191-8). Brooks-Cole.

Technical Calculus with Analytic Geometry. 3rd ed. Allyn J. Washington. (Illus.). 450p. 1986. text ed. 35.95 (ISBN 0-8053-9512-1); instr's. guide 6.95 (ISBN 0-8053-9513-X); student solutions manual 9.95 (ISBN 0-8053-9514-8). Benjamin-Cummings.

Technical Careers Test. Jack Rudman. (Career Examination Ser.: C-804). (Cloth bdg. avail. on request). pap. 16.00 (ISBN 0-8373-0804-6). Natl Learning.

Technical Ceramics (U. S.) 255p. 1985. 1800.00 (ISBN 0-86621-398-8, A1473). Frost & Sullivan.

Technical Change & American Enterprise. J. Herbert Holloman. LC 74-19049. 52p. 1974. 1.50 (ISBN 0-89068-013-2). Natl Planning.

Technical Change & Economic Policy: Science & Technology in the New Economic & Social Context. 117p. 1980. 12.50 (ISBN 92-64-12102-1). OECD.

Technical Change & Economic Theory. Ed. by Giovanni Dosi et al. 550p. 1988. 59.00x (ISBN 0-86187-274-6, Pub. by Pinter Pubs UK). Columbia U Pr.

Technical Change & Employment. Roy Rothwell & Walter Zegveld. 1980. 12.95x (ISBN 0-312-78770-7). St Martin.

Technical Change & Full Employment. Christopher Freeman & Luc Soete. (Illus.). 280p. Date not set. text ed. 55.00 (ISBN 0-631-14099-9). Basil Blackwell.

Technical Change & Industrial Policy, Vol. 19. Chapman & Humphrys. 288p. 1987. text ed. 49.95 (ISBN 0-631-15215-6). Basil Blackwell.

Technical Change & Industrial Transformation. Giovanni Dosi. LC 83-16017. 338p. 1984. 29.95 (ISBN 0-312-78775-8). St Martin.

Technical Change & Social Conflict in Agriculture: Latin American Perspectives. Ed. by Martin E. Pineiro & Eduardo J. Trigo. 266p. 1983. pap. 46.00x (ISBN 0-86531-802-6). Westview.

Technical Change, Relative Prices, & Environmental Resource Evaluation. Vincent K. Smith. LC 74-6840. pap. 29.30 (ISBN 0-317-26482-6, 2023816). Bks Demand UMI.

Technical Choice Innovation & Economic Growth: Essays on American & British Experience in the Nineteenth Century. Paul A. David. LC 74-76583. pap. 86.00 (ISBN 0-317-26014-6, 2024448). Bks Demand UMI.

Technical Co-operation in Industry. (Monographs on Industrialization of Developing Countries: Problems & Prospects). pap. 4.00 (ISBN 92-1-106048-6, E.69.II.B.39 VOL.21). UN.

Technical Co-Operation in Latin-American Agriculture. Arthur T. Mosher. LC 75-26310. (World Food Supply Ser). (Illus.). 1976. Repr. of 1957 ed. 36.50x (ISBN 0-405-07788-2). Ayer Co Pubs.

Technical College Physics. Jerry Wilson. 1982. (CBS C); instr's. manual 21.50 (ISBN 0-03-058491-4); study guide o.p. 12.95 (ISBN 0-03-058492-2). SCP.

Technical College Physics. 2nd ed. Jerry D. Wilson. 640p. 1987. text ed. 44.00 (ISBN 0-03-008494-6). SCP.

Technical Communication. Rebecca B. Carosso. 622p. 1986. pap. text ed. write for info. (ISBN 0-534-06180-X). Wadsworth Pub.

Technical Communication. A. Eisenberg. 1982. text ed. 33.95 (ISBN 0-07-019096-8); pap. text ed. 26.95 (ISBN 0-07-019097-6). McGraw.

Technical Communication: A Practical Guide. Joseph P. Dagher. (Illus.). 1978. pap. text ed. write for info (ISBN 0-13-898247-3). P-H.

Technical Communication: An Outline. Thomas L. Warren. (Quality Paperback Ser: No. 332). 148p. 1978. pap. 4.95 (ISBN 0-8226-0332-2). Littlefield.

Technical Communications. Center for Occupational Research & Development Staff. (High Technology Ser.). (Illus.). 228p. 1985. pap. text ed. 23.00 (ISBN 1-55502-164-6). Ctr Res & Dev.

Technical Communicator's Handbook of Technology Transfer. Hyman Olken. 144p. 1980. pap. 12.50x (ISBN 0-934818-01-0). Olken Pubns.

Technical Conference on Dry Bean Research: Proceedings. Food Processors Institute Staff. (Orig.). 1985. pap. text ed. 10.00 (ISBN 0-937774-14-6). Food Processors.

Technical Conference 1984: Proceedings. 214p. 1985. 15.00. Irrigation.

Technical Consultation on Methods of Evaluating Small-Scale Fisheries in the Western Mediterranean. (FAO Fisheries Report Ser.: No. 362). (Illus.). 155p. (Orig.). 1986. pap. text ed. 14.50 (ISBN 92-5-002458-4, F2967, FAO). UNIPUB.

Technical Control for the Modern Pianist: Finger Exercises Used by Members of the Piano Teachers Congress of N.Y., Inc. Piano Teachers Congress Members. Ed. by Albert De Vito. LC 78-95128. 1978. 8.95 (ISBN 0-934286-11-6). Kenyon.

Technical Correspondence: A Handbook & Reference Source for the Technical Professional. Herman M. Weisman. LC 67-30919. 265p. 1968. 17.50 (ISBN 0-471-92640-X, Pub. by Wiley). Krieger.

Technical Data on Telephone Security Devices & Equipment. abr. ed. Ed. by Michael P. Jones. (Illus.). 38p. 1984. pap. text ed. 6.00 (ISBN 0-89904-080-2). Crumb Elbow Pub.

Technical Demography. 1986. 4.50 (ISBN 0-471-63960-5). Wiley.

Technical Descriptive Geometry. 2nd ed. B. Leighton Wellman. 1957. text ed. 42.95 (ISBN 0-07-069234-3). McGraw.

Technical Design Graphics Problem Solver. rev. ed. Ed. by Research & Education Association Staff. LC 81-86648. (Illus.). 960p. (Orig.). 1986. 19.85 (ISBN 0-87891-534-6). Res & Educ.

Technical Development in Malting. D. F. Ball & K. A. Marsden. 200p. 1987. text ed. 37.00x (ISBN 0-566-05377-2, Pub. by Gower Pub England). Gower Pub Co.

Technical Development of Modern Aviation. Ronald E. Miller & David Sawers. (Airlines History Project Ser.). Date not set. Repr. of 1968 ed. 42.50 (ISBN 0-404-19328-5). AMS Pr.

Technical Development of Television. Ed. by Christopher H. Sterling & George Shiers. LC 75-23902. (Historical Studies in Telecommunications Ser.). 1976. Repr. 54.00x (ISBN 0-405-07761-0). Ayer Co Pubs.

Technical Dictionary: Archtiecture & Building. Tawfik Abd-El-Gawad. 1319p. (Eng., Fr., Ger. & Arabic.). 1976. 35.00x (ISBN 0-686-44745-X, Pub. by Collets (UK)). State Mutual Bk.

Technical Dictionary English-Slovene. 1137p. (Eng. & Slovene.). 1975. 150.00 (ISBN 0-686-92318-9, M-9891). French & Eur.

Technical Dictionary for Automotive Engineering, 2 vols. Ed. by R. Bosch. (Eng. & Ger.). 1976. 68.00 (Pub. by VDI W Germany). IPS.

Technical Dictionary for Batteries & Direct Energy Conservation. Ed. by Bogenschutz. 200p. 1968. cancelled 11.00 (ISBN 3-87097-002-2, Pub. by O Brandstetter WG). IPS.

Technical Dictionary for Civil Engineers. Research & Education Association. 1408p. cancelled (ISBN 0-87891-531-1). Res & Educ.

Technical Dictionary for the Shoe Industry. Gerhard Knebel. (Eng. & Ger.). 1966. pap. 75.00 (ISBN 3-7785-0040-6, M-7641, Pub. by Huethig). French & Eur.

Technical Dictionary for Weaponry. Gustav Sybertz. (Ger. & Eng.). 1969. pap. 24.95 (ISBN 3-7888-0081-X, M-7642, Pub. by Neumann-Neudamm). French & Eur.

Technical Dictionary of Aeronautical Engineering. Muhammad Zimaity. 370p. (Eng., Fr., Ger. & Arabic.). 1976. 40.00x (Pub. by Collets (UK)). State Mutual Bk.

Technical Dictionary of Crystallography. 132p. 1980. 40.00x (ISBN 0-686-72093-8, Pub. by Collets (UK)). State Mutual Bk.

Technical Dictionary of Data Processing, Computers & Office Machines, English, German, French, Russian. E. Burger. (Eng., Ger., Fr & Rus.). 1970. 190.00 (ISBN 0-08-006425-6). Pergamon.

Technical Dictionary of Data Processing& English, French, German, Russian, Slovene, 2 vol. Ed. by E. Burger. 960p. (Eng., Fr., Ger., Rus. & Slovene.). Set. 195.00 (ISBN 0-686-92330-8, M-9889). French & Eur.

Technical Dictionary of High Polymers: English, French, German, Russian. W. Dawydoff. 1969. 185.00 (ISBN 0-08-013112-3). Pergamon.

Technical Dictionary of Hydraulics & Pneumatics. Ed. by Gunter Neubert. 1973. 55.00 (ISBN 0-08-016958-9). Pergamon.

Technical Dictionary of Petrochemistry. W. Leipnitz. 240p. (Eng., Ger., Fr. & Rus.). 1976. 75.00 (ISBN 0-686-56469-3, M-7640, Pub. by Vlg. Technik). French & Eur.

Technical Dictionary of Printing. Wolfgang Muller. 1020p. (Eng., Ger., Fr., Rus., Hungarian, Span., Pol. & Slovak.). 1981. 150.00x (ISBN 0-317-59451-6, Pub. by Collets (UK)). State Mutual Bk.

Technical Dictionary of Printing Technique. Ismail Shawki & Rashwan A. Mahmoud. 420p. (Eng., Fr., Ger. & Arabic.). 1981. 50.00x (ISBN 0-317-59453-2, Pub. by Collets (UK)). State Mutual Bk.

Technical Dictionary of Spectroscopy & Spectral Analysis: English, German, French, Russian. H. Moritz & T. Torok. 1971. 93.00 (ISBN 0-08-015864-1). Pergamon.

Technical Dictionary on Irrigation Drainage. (Port.). write for info. US Comm Irrigation.

Technical Dictionary: Refrigeration & Air Conditioning. (Eng., Fr., Ger. & Arabic.). 1979. 35.00x (ISBN 0-686-44746-8, Pub. by Collets (UK)). State Mutual Bk.

Technical Dictionary: The Textile Industry. (Eng., FR., Ger. & Arabic.). 1975. 30.00x (ISBN 0-686-44748-4, Pub. by Collets (UK)). State Mutual Bk.

Technical Digest-Symposium on Optical Fiber Measurements. U. S. Department of Commerce. 1980. pap. 50.00. Info Gatekeepers.

Technical Division Four of the Organization Executive Course see Organization Executive Course: An Encyclopedia of Scientology Policy (1950-1951, 1953-1974,.

Technical Drafting. Spence & Atkins. (gr. 9-12). 1980. text ed. 26.40 (ISBN 0-02-665810-0); Inst. Resource Guide 80 12.68 (ISBN 0-02-665820-8). Bennett IL.

Technical Drawing. 4th ed. W. Abbott. (Illus.). 1976. pap. 23.50x (ISBN 0-216-90210-X). Trans-Atl Phila.

Technical Drawing. 8th ed. Frederick E. Giesecke et al. 780p. 1986. write for info. (ISBN 0-02-342600-4). Macmillan.

Technical Drawing & Design. David L. Goetsch & John A. Nelson. 950p. 1986. text ed. 42.95 (ISBN 0-8273-2223-2); instr's. guide 12.00 (ISBN 0-8273-2222-4); wkbk. 17.50 (ISBN 0-8273-2224-0); solutions manual 8.00 (ISBN 0-8273-2230-5). Delmar.

Technical Drawing & Graphics. Jack Rudman. (DANTES Ser.: No. 36). 1988. 25.95 (ISBN 0-8373-6686-0); pap. 13.95 (ISBN 0-8373-6636-4). Natl Learning.

Technical Drawing Problems. 6th ed. F. H. Giesecke et al. (Series I). 1981. pap. text ed. write for info. (ISBN 0-02-342740-X). Macmillan.

Technical Drawing Problems. Henry Spencer et al. 1989. pap. text ed. write for info.; answer key avail. Macmillan.

Technical Drawing Problems. George Stegman & Jerry Jenkins. 224p. 1986. write for info. (ISBN 0-02-416330-9). Macmillan.

Technical Drawing Problems, No. 4. George Stegman & Jerry Jenkins. 97p. 1986. write for info.; write for info. instr's. manual (ISBN 0-02-416340-6). Macmillan.

Technical Drawing Problems: Series Three. 3rd ed. Henry C. Spencer et al. (Illus.). 1980. pap. text ed. write for info. (ISBN 0-02-414360-X); answer key avail. (ISBN 0-02-414660-9). Macmillan.

Technical Drawing Problems: Series Two. 5th ed. Henry C. Spencer et al. (Illus.). 1989. pap. text ed. write for info. (ISBN 0-02-414670-6); answer key avail. (ISBN 0-02-414680-3). Macmillan.

Technical Drawing with AutoCAD. Leendert Kersten. 334p. 1987. pap. text ed. 27.95x (ISBN 0-912855-75-4). E Bowers Pub.

Technical-Economical Dictionary for Business Purposes. B. Bajic et al. 1700p. (Eng., Fr., Ger., Serbian & Croatian.). 1973. 95.00 (ISBN 0-686-92638-2, M-9689). French & Eur.

Technical Editing: Principles & Practices. Ed. by Lola M. Zook. (Anthology Ser., No. 4). 1975. pap. 25.00x (ISBN 0-914548-15-8). Soc Tech Comm.

Technical Editor's & Secretary's Desk Guide. George Freedman & Deborah A. Freedman. 1985. text ed. 32.50 (ISBN 0-07-021918-4). McGraw.

Technical Education Curriculum. National Center for Research in Vocational Education Staff. 57p. 1985. 5.50 (ISBN 0-318-22213-2, BB77). Natl Ctr Res Voc Ed.

Technical Education for Development. C. Sanders. 1966. 13.50x (ISBN 0-85564-023-5, Pub by U of W Austral Pr). Intl Spec Bk.

Technical Education in the Arab States (UNESCO) Mohammed K. Harby et al. (Education Studies & Documents: No. 53). pap. 15.00 (ISBN 0-8115-1377-7). Kraus Repr.

Technical Electricity & Electronics. 2nd ed. Peter Buban & Marshall L. Schmitt. (Illus.). (gr. 11-12). 1976. text ed. 32.40 (ISBN 0-07-008643-5). McGraw.

Technical Electronic Publishing: Pre-Press & Paper-Based. International Resource Development, Inc. Staff. 170p. 1986. 1650.00x (ISBN 0-88694-717-0). Intl Res Dev.

Technical Elite. Jay M. Gould. LC 66-15566. (Illus.). 1966. 19.50x (ISBN 0-678-00131-6). Kelley.

Technical English: Writing, Reading, & Speaking. 5th ed. Nell A. Pickett & Ann A. Laster. 757p. 1988. pap. text ed. 26.95 (ISBN 0-06-045204-8, HarpC). Har-Row.

Technical Enterprise: Present & Future Patterns. Herbert I. Fusfeld. LC 86-3340. 328p. 1987. Prof. ref. 34.95x (ISBN 0-88730-033-2). Ballinger Pub.

Technical Environmental Guidelines for Offshore Oil & Gas Development. Ed. by John T. Gilbert. 330p. 1983. 49.95 (ISBN 0-87814-208-8, P-4317). Pennwell Bks.

Technical Evaluation of Bids for Nuclear Power Plants: A Guidebook. (Technical Reports Ser.: No. 204). (Illus.). 98p. 1981. pap. 18.00 (ISBN 92-0-155081-2, IDC204, IAEA). UNIPUB.

Technical Excellence in America: Incentives for Investment in Human Capital. Debra Van Opstal. 47p. 1984. 6.00 (ISBN 0-89206-063-8). CSI Studies.

Technical Excellence in America: Incentives for Investment in Human Capital. Ed. by Debra Van Opstal. 56p. (Orig.). 1984. pap. text ed. 6.95 (ISBN 0-8191-6070-9, Pub. by CSIS). U Pr of Amer.

Technical Factors see Building in Use Study.

Technical Factors in the Treatment of the Severely Disturbed Patient. Ed. by Peter Giovacchini & L. Bryce Boyer. LC 81-20587. 544p. 1982. 40.00x (ISBN 0-87668-630-7). Aronson.

Technical Foundations in Nursing. Janet-Beth M. Flynn & Ritva Hackel. 1988. pap. 32.95 (ISBN 0-8385-8840-9). Appleton & Lange.

Technical Freehand Drawing & Sketching. K. Knowlton et al. 1976. text ed. 36.95 (ISBN 0-07-035207-0). McGraw.

Technical Glossary of Horticultural & Landscape Terminology. Ed. by Edward B. Ballard et al. LC 78-165521. 1971. text ed. 5.50 (ISBN 0-935336-00-1); tchr's. ed. 4.00 (ISBN 0-935336-00-1). Horticult Research.

Technical Graphics: Electronics Worktext. E. A. Maruggi. 288p. 1986. pap. text ed. 26.95 (ISBN 0-675-20311-2). Merrill.

Technical Guide for Reviewing Prime Farmland Restoration Plans in the Midwest. Russell Boulding. (Illus.). 1984. pap. 5.00 (ISBN 0-943724-07-4). Illinois South.

Technical Guide to Thermal Processes. J. Gosse. Tr. by W. A. Gray. (Illus.). 200p. 1985. 42.50 (ISBN 0-521-25263-6); pap. 14.95 (ISBN 0-521-31741-X). Cambridge U Pr.

Technical Guideline for Sorghum & Millet: Seed Production. Kuldip R. Chopra. 110p. 1982. pap. text ed. 8.25 (ISBN 92-5-101259-8, F2377, FAO). UNIPUB.

Technical Guideline on Seed Potato Micro-Propagation & Multiplication. Ed. by Raymond A George. (FAO Plant Production & Protesction Paper: No. 71). (Illus.). 55p. (Orig.). 1986. pap. text ed. 7.50 (ISBN 92-5-102368-9, F2941, FAO). UNIPUB.

Technical Guidelines for Pharmaceuticals in the European Economic Community. Ed. by Duilio Poggiolini. LC 83-9580. 74p. 1983. 27.00 (ISBN 0-89004-851-7). Raven.

Technical Guidelines for Vegetable Seed Technology. 170p. 1980. pap. 11.25 (ISBN 92-5-101024-2, F2146, FAO). UNIPUB.

Technical Handbook on Symbiotic Nitrogen Fixation. 105p. (Orig.). 1984. pap. 13.75 (ISBN 92-5-101440-X, F2572, FAO). UNIPUB.

Technical History of the Beginnings of Radar. S. S. Swords. Ed. by S. Bowers. (History Ser.). 300p. 1986. casebound 68.00 (ISBN 0-86341-043-X, HT006). Inst Elect Eng.

Technical History of the Rio Tinto Mines. Leonard Salkield. (Illus.). 114p. 1987. text ed. 27.00 (ISBN 0-318-24008-4). IMM-North Am.

Technical History of the Tinto Mines: Some Notes on Exploitation from Pre-Phoenician to the 1950's. Leonard U. Salkied. 1987. text ed. 27.00 (ISBN 0-900488-95-6). Imm-North Am.

Technical Illustration. James D. Bethune. LC 82-8529. 237p. 1983. write for info. (ISBN 0-471-05308-2). Wiley.

Technical Illustration. James H. Earle. (gr. 12 up). 1978. 6.50 (ISBN 0-932702-65-1). Creative Texas.

Technical Illustration. 3rd ed. T. A. Thomas. (Illus.). 1978. text ed. 39.95 (ISBN 0-07-064228-1). McGraw.

Technical Illustration & Graphics. Jan Mracek. (Illus.). 352p. 1983. 34.00. P-H.

Technical Instruction. Dale Crane. 209p. 1981. pap. 13.95 (ISBN 0-89100-183-2, EA-183-2). IAP.

Technical Instructions for the Safe Transport of Dangerous Goods by Air, 1987-88. Dangerous Goods Panel of Air Navigations Staff & Commission of ICAO Staff. 535p. 1986. fabric cover 40.00 (ISBN 0-940394-21-9). Intereg.

Technical Instructions for the Safe Transport of Dangerous Goods by Air 1989-90. Dangerous Goods Panel of Air Navigations Commission of ICAO. (Illus.). 535p. 1988. 42.00 (ISBN 0-940394-28-6). Intereg.

Technical: Instructor Resource Guide. Center for Occupational Research & Development Staff. (Job Safety & Health Instructional Materials Ser.). 82p. 1981. pap. text ed. 20.00 (ISBN 1-55502-038-0). Ctr Res & Dev.

Technical Intelligentsia & the East German Elite: Legitimacy & Social Change in Mature Communism. Thomas A. Baylis. LC 72-95306. (Illus.). 1974. 41.00x (ISBN 0-520-02395-1). U of Cal Pr.

Technical Intelligentsia & the Soviet State. Nicholas Lampert. LC 79-15419. 190p. 1979. 37.50 (ISBN 0-8419-0534-7). Holmes & Meier.

Technical Introduction to the Apple IIgs. Apple Computer, Inc. Staff. 160p. 1987. pap. 9.95 (ISBN 0-201-17742-0). Addison-Wesley.

Technical Introduction to the Macintosh Family. Apple Computer, Incorporated Staff. (Illus.). 160p. 1987. pap. 19.95 (ISBN 0-201-17765-X). Addison-Wesley.

Technical Manager: How to Manage People & Make Decisions. Baird. 26.95 (ISBN 0-317-64298-7). Van Nos Reinhold.

Technical Manager: How to Manage People & Make Decisions. Bruce F. Baird. (Illus.). 168p. 1983. 22.50 (ISBN 0-534-97925-4, Lifetime Learn). Van Nos Reinhold.

Technical Manager's Survival Book. Melvin Silverman. 300p. 1983. text ed. 39.50 (ISBN 0-07-057515-0). McGraw.

Technical Manual. American Association of Textile Chemists & Colorists. 362p. 1987. 63.00 (ISBN 0-318-12171-9). Am Assn Text.

Technical Manual. 9th ed. Frances K. Widmann. LC 85-1346. (Illus.). 544p. 1985. text ed. 35.00 (ISBN 0-915355-06-X). Am Assn Blood.

Technical Manual & Dictionary of Classical Ballet. 3rd, rev. ed. Gail Grant. (Illus.). 160p. 1982. pap. 2.95 (ISBN 0-486-21843-0). Dover.

Technical Manual for ELSA: English Language Skills Assessment in a Reading Context. Cecelia Doherty & Donna Ilyin. (ELSA Tests Ser.). 1981. pap. 4.50 (ISBN 0-88377-226-4). Newbury Hse.

Technical Manual of Deep Wholistic Bodywork: Postural Integration. Jack W. Painter. 203p. 1987. pap. 22.00 (ISBN 0-317-60439-2). Bodymind Bks.

Technical Math. Bernard J. Rice & Jerry D. Strange. 672p. 1982. text ed. 23.00 (ISBN 0-87150-327-1, 2611, Prindle). PWS Kent Pub.

Technical Math with Calculus. Bernard Rice & Jerry Strange. LC 82-20445. 1983. text ed. 29.00 (ISBN 0-87150-376-X, 2801, Prindle). PWS Kent Pub.

Technical Mathematics. 3rd ed. Jacqueline Austin & Margarita S. Isern. LC 82-60533. 1983. pap. text ed. 25.95 (ISBN 0-03-061234-9); instr's manual 20.00 (ISBN 0-03-061236-5). HR&W.

Technical Mathematics. Paul Calter. (Illus.). 688p. 1983. write for info. (ISBN 0-13-598714-8). P-H.

Technical Mathematics. Linda Davis. 736p. 1988. 36.95 (ISBN 0-675-20338-4). Merrill.

Technical Mathematics. Philip M. Jaffe & Rodolfo Maglio. 1979. text ed. write for info. (ISBN 0-673-15111-5). Scott F.

Technical Mathematics. Harry Lewis. 800p. 1986. text ed. 36.95 (ISBN 0-8273-2212-7); cancelled instr's. guide (ISBN 0-8273-2213-5). Delmar.

Technical Mathematics. Rudolph E. Lynn. LC 84-7343. 712p. 1985. write for info. (ISBN 0-471-88743-9). Wiley.

Technical Mathematics. 3rd ed. Harold S. Rice & Raymond M. Knight. 1972. text ed. 34.95 (ISBN 0-07-052200-6). McGraw.

Technical Mathematics. Jack Rudman. (DANTES Ser.: No. 37). 1988. 25.95 (ISBN 0-8373-6687-9); pap. 13.95 (ISBN 0-8373-6637-2). Natl Learning.

Technical Mathematics & Calculus. Rudolph E. Lynn. LC 84-27037. 963p. 1985. write for info. (ISBN 0-471-87902-9); wkbk. avail. (ISBN 0-471-81667-1). Wiley.

Technical Mathematics I. Thomas J. McHale & Paul T. Witzke. 704p. 1987. pap. text ed. 29.95x (ISBN 0-201-15408-0). Addison-Wesley.

Technical Mathematics II. Thomas J. McHaLe & Paul T. Witzke. (Illus.). 704p. 1987. pap. text ed. 29.95x (ISBN 0-201-15409-9). Addison-Wesley.

Technical Mathematics with Applications. 2nd ed. Carole E. Goodson & S. L. Miertschin. LC 85-20168. 806p. 1986. write for info. (ISBN 0-471-83725-3); pap. 15.95 study guide 03/1985 450p. (ISBN 0-471-88508-8). Wiley.

Technical Mathematics with Calculus. Paul Calter. (Illus.). 1008p. 1984. write for info (ISBN 0-13-898312-7). P-H.

Technical Mathematics with Calculus. C. E. Goodson & S. L. Miertschin. LC 84-21926. 1152p. 1985. write for info. (ISBN 0-471-86639-3). Wiley.

Technical Mathematics with Calculus. Carole E. Goodson & Susan L. Miertschin. LC 82-17618. 1002p. 1983. 31.95x (ISBN 0-471-08244-9); tchr's. ed. avail. (ISBN 0-471-89075-8); study guide avail. (ISBN 0-471-87578-3); student manual 21.95 (ISBN 0-471-88515-0); student solutions manual avail. (ISBN 0-471-89290-4). Wiley.

Technical Mathematics with Calculus. 3rd ed. Harold S. Rice & Raymond M. Knight. (Illus.). 704p. 1974. text ed. 41.95 (ISBN 0-07-052205-7). McGraw.

Technical Mechanics: Applied Statics & Dynamics. Irving Granet. 1984p. text ed. 28.95 (ISBN 0-03-061708-1). HR&W.

Technical, Medical, & Educational Problems of Acute Care: Proceedings. International Symposium on Acute Care, 4th, Rio de Janeiro, November 1975. Ed. by B. M. Tavares. (Current Topics in Critical Care Medicine Ser.: Vol 2). (Illus.). 200p. 1977. 32.75 (ISBN 3-8055-2374-2). S Karger.

Technical Metals. Harold V. Johnson. (gr. 9-12). 1981. text ed. 26.00 (ISBN 0-02-665850-X); student guide 7.60 (ISBN 0-02-665870-4); student gd., ans. key 2.00 (ISBN 0-02-665880-1); teachers guide 2.64 (ISBN 0-02-665860-7). Bennett IL.

Technical Mineralogy & Petrography: An Introduction to Materials Technology, 2 vols. A. Szymanski. (Materials Science Technology: No. 43). 950p. 1988. Set. 352.75 (ISBN 0-444-98991-9, North Holland). Elsevier.

Technical Nursing of the Adult: Medical, Surgical & Psychiatric Approaches. 2nd ed. Sandra B. Fielo & Sylviac. Edge. 1974. write for info. (ISBN 0-02-337280-X, 33728). Macmillan.

Technical Papers. Symposium on Measurement, Mapping, and Management in the Coastal Zone from Virginia to Maine, New York, 1979. 272p. 1980. cancelled 11.00 (ISBN 0-317-32496-9, G420); members 6.00 (ISBN 0-317-32497-7). Am Congrs Survey.

Technical Papers. 470p. cancelled 6.00 (ISBN 0-317-32490-X, T651); members 3.00 (ISBN 0-317-32491-8). Am Congrs Survey.

Technical Papers: Forty-Ninth Meeting of the Americal Society of Photogrammetry. 411p. 1983. pap. 15.00 (ISBN 0-937294-47-0). ASP & RS.

Technical Papers of the ASP Fall Technical Meeting: October 1980. 7.00 (ISBN 0-937294-32-2); pap. 5.00 member. ASP & RS.

Technical Papers: Proceedings of the ACSM-ASP Fall Convention, September 1982. ACSM-ASP Fall Convention Staff. pap. 15.00 (ISBN 0-937294-39-X); pap. 7.00 members. ASP & RS.

Technical Papers, 1984: ASP-ACSM Fall Convention. 848p. 1984. Members 12.00. pap. 17.00 (ISBN 0-937294-59-4). ASP & RS.

Technical Papers, 1985: ASP 51st Annual Meeting, March 1985, 2 vols. ASP. 899p. 1985. pap. 17.00 (ISBN 0-937294-62-4). ASP & RS.

Technical Pascal. Andrew C. Staugaard. 384p. 1988. pap. text ed. 21.75 (ISBN 0-317-62009-6). P-H.

Technical Petroleum Dictionary of Well-Logging Drilling, & Production Terms. Ed. by S. Ketchian et al. 366p. 1965. 144.00 (ISBN 0-677-61140-4). Gordon & Breach.

Technical Physics. Bigliano & Ferrigno. 1988. text ed. 31.50 (ISBN 0-534-07686-6, 36G0160, PWS-Kent Ser Tech). PWS Kent Pub.

Technical Physics. 3rd ed. Frederick Bueche. 1984. write for info. (ISBN 0-471-60384-8). Wiley.

Technical Physics. Debuvitz. 1988. write for info. (ISBN 0-471-81487-3). Wiley.

Technical Physics. Clarence R. Green. (Illus.). 832p. 1984. write for info (ISBN 0-13-898387-9). P-H.

Technical Physics. 2nd ed. P. J. Ouseph. LC 86-5568. 680p. 1986. write for info. (ISBN 0-471-80579-3). Wiley.

Technical Physics. James F. Sullivan. 750p. 1986. 31.50 (ISBN 0-471-04796-1); 12.30 (ISBN 0-471-88509-6). Wiley.

Technical Physics Laboratory Manual. Olan E. Kruse et al. 1971. pap. 10.50x wkbk. (ISBN 0-934786-07-0). G Davis.

Technical Pocket Dictionary, English-German, German-English, 2 vols. 2nd ed. Henry G. Freeman. (Eng. & Ger.). 18.00x ea. Ger.-Eng. Eng.-Ger (ISBN 3-19-006213-7). Adlers Foreign Bks.

Technical Presentation Skills. Steve Mandel. Ed. by Michael Crisp. (Fifty-Minute Ser.). (Illus.). 74p. (Orig.). 1988. pap. 7.95 (ISBN 0-931961-55-6). Crisp Pubns.

Technical Procedure for City Surveys. (Manual & Report on Engineering Practice Ser.: No. 10). 189p. 1963. pap. 4.00x (ISBN 0-87262-205-3). Am Soc Civil Eng.

Technical Program Abstracts & Bibiographies, 1987. 923p. (Orig.). 1987. pap. text ed. 45.00 (ISBN 0-317-67222-3). Soc Expl Geophys.

Technical Program Abstracts & Biographies, 1986. (Illus.). 640p. (Orig.). pap. text ed. 60.00 (ISBN 0-931830-44-3). Soc Expl Geophys.

Technical Progress & Industrial Growth in the U. S. S. R. & Eastern Europe: An Empirical Study, 1961-75. Erkin I. Bairam. 230p. 1988. text ed. 47.00 (ISBN 0-566-05621-6, Pub. by Gower Pub England). Gower Pub Co.

Technical Progress & Soviet Economic Development. Ed. by Ronald Amann & Julian Cooper. 256p. 1986. text ed. 45.00x (ISBN 0-631-14572-9). Basil Blackwell.

Technical Rationale Behind CSC-STD-003-85: Computer Security Requirements, Guidance for Applying the Department of Defense Trusted Computer System Evaluation Criteria in Specific Environments. Intro. by Robert L. Bortzman. (CSC-STD Ser.: No. 004-85). 45p. (Orig.). 1985. pap. 2.00 (ISBN 0-318-20153-4, S/N 008-000-00441-2). USGPO.

Technical Reference Handbook. E. P. Rasis. (Illus.). 220p. 1984. 14.96 (ISBN 0-8269-3450-1). Am Technical.

Technical Report, No. 5. Y. John Wang & Yie W. Chien. (Sterile Pharmaceutical Packaging Compatibility & Stability). 137p. 1984. pap. 35.00 (ISBN 0-939459-04-3). PDA.

Technical Report, No. 7. PDA Task Force on Depyrogenation. (Depyrogenation Ser.). 116p. 1985. pap. 35.00 (ISBN 0-939459-06-X). PDA.

Technical Report Form. rev. ed. John A. Walter. 35p. 1973. pap. 2.15x (ISBN 0-88408-000-5). Univ Co-Op Soc.

Technical Report on a Study of the Agroclimatology of the Humid Tropics of Southeast Asia. 259p. 1982. pap. 19.50 (ISBN 92-5-101174-5, F2273, FAO). UNIPUB.

Technical Report on the IDMS-R Systems Desk Reference. Robert Husband. 209p. 1986. pap. 125.00 (ISBN 0-471-85236-8). Wiley.

Technical Report Standards: How to Prepare & Write Effective Technical Reports. Lawrence R. Harvill & Thomas L. Kraft. LC 77-70964. (Illus.). 1979. pap. 5.95 (ISBN 0-930206-01-0). Weber Systems.

Technical Report Writing. 2nd ed. James W. Souther & Myron L. White. LC 84-15474. 104p. 1984. Repr. of 1977 ed. lib. bdg. 24.50 (ISBN 0-89874-786-4). Krieger.

Technical Report Writing Today. 3rd ed. Steven E. Pauley & Daniel Riordan. LC 86-81305. 388p. 1987. pap. text ed. 28.76 (ISBN 0-395-34251-1); instr's manual 2.36 (ISBN 0-395-34252-X); transparencies 13.96 (ISBN 0-395-42727-4). HM.

Technical Secretary: Terminology & Transcription. Dorothy Adams & Margaret A. Kurtz. (Diamond Jubilee Ser.). 1967. text ed. 37.80 (ISBN 0-07-000320-3). McGraw.

Technical Service Development. Rex P. Gatto. (Illus.). 120p. 1985. teacher's ed. 45.00 (ISBN 0-945997-19-1); wrkbk. 35.00 (ISBN 0-945997-18-3). GATTO Training Assocs.

Technical Services in Libraries. Maurice F. Tauber. LC 54-10328. (Columbia Library Service Studies, No. 7). 1954. 52.00x (ISBN 0-231-02054-6). Columbia U Pr.

Technical Services in the Small Library. Harvey Hahn. (LAMA Small Libraries Publications). 12p. 1987. pap. 2.50x (ISBN 0-8389-5689-0). ALA.

Technical Services Manual for Small Libraries. John B. Corbin. LC 70-156885. 206p. 1971. 16.50 (ISBN 0-8108-0388-7). Scarecrow.

Technical Shop Mathematics. 2nd ed. John G. Anderson. LC 82-11847. (Illus.). 500p. 1983. 23.95x (ISBN 0-8311-1145-3); ans. manual avail. Indus Pr.

Technical Sketching for Engineers, Technologists & Technicians. Besterfield & O'Hagan. 1983. text ed. 31.00 (ISBN 0-8359-7540-1, Reston). P-H.

Technical Specifications of the NRPB Radon Personal Dosemeter. 7p. (Orig.). pap. text ed. 8.10 (ISBN 0-85951-285-1, HM242, HMSO). UNIPUB.

Technical Statics & Strength of Materials. 2nd ed. Thrower. 1986. 34.00 (ISBN 0-534-06384-5, 77F6071, PWS-Kent Ser Tech). PWS Kent Pub.

Technical Studies for the Cornet. Herbert L. Clarke. 53p. 1934. pap. 7.50 (ISBN 0-8258-0158-3, 02280). Fischer Inc NY.

Technical Studies for Violin, Op. 92, Pt. 1. Hans Sitt. (Carl Fischer Music Library: No. 500). 1932. pap. 4.95 (ISBN 0-8258-0151-6, L500). Fischer Inc NY.

Technical Study of European Romanesque Architecture with Innumerable Illustrations. Karl B. Halibrand. (Illus.). 156p. 1984. 137.75 (ISBN 0-86650-133-9). Gloucester Art.

Technical Support Aide. Jack Rudman. (Career Examination Ser.: C-2476). (Cloth bdg. avail. on request). pap. 14.00 (ISBN 0-8373-2476-9). Natl Learning.

Technical Talk. Judy M. Eddy & Sydney S. Gingrow. 112p. 1984. pap. text ed. 14.95 (ISBN 0-8403-3956-9). Kendall-Hunt.

Technical Terms in Plastics Engineering. A. M. Wittfoht. 324p. (Eng., Ger., Fr., Span. & Dutch.). 1976. 94.75 (ISBN 0-444-99846-2). Elsevier.

Technical Terms, Symbols & Definitions in English, French, German, Italian, Portuguese, Russian, Spanish & Swedish Used in Soil Mechanics & Foundation. 5th ed. 256p. 1981. text ed. 82.00 (ISBN 0-317-65974-X, Pub. by A A Balkema). Brookfield Pub Co.

Technical Terms Used in Bibliographies & by the Book & Printing Trades. Axel Moth. LC 77-6172. 1977. Repr. of 1917 ed. lib. bdg. 30.00 (ISBN 0-89341-153-1). Longwood Pub Group.

Technical Thermodynamics. V. V. Sushkov. (Russian Monographs Ser). 392p. 1965. 124.00 (ISBN 0-677-20520-1). Gordon & Breach.

Technical, Trade & Business School Data Handbook: 1988-90 Edition, 2 vols. 3rd biennial ed. Ed. by Louis Mazzari & Deborah Otaguro. 1800p. 1988. Set. pap. 85.00 national ed. (ISBN 0-317-60560-7); pap. 45.00 northeast-southeast ed. (ISBN 0-317-60561-5); pap. 50.00 midwest-west ed. (ISBN 0-317-60562-3). Orchard Hse MA.

Technical Transformation of Agriculture in Communist China. Leslie T. Kuo. LC 73-181867. (Special Studies in International Economics & Development). 1971. 39.50x (ISBN 0-275-28276-7). Irvington.

Technical Trends & Strategic Policy. Sidney D. Drell & Thomas H. Johnson. (Occasional Paper of Center for International Security & Arms Control Ser.). 41p. (Orig.). 1988. pap. 9.00 (ISBN 0-935371-18-4). ISIS.

Technical Variants. Hanon & Lindquist. 32p. (Orig.). (gr. k-12). 1929. pap. text ed. 5.95 (ISBN 0-87487-657-5). Birch Tree Gr.

Technical Veterinary Dictionary. Wolfgang Lindeke. 185p. (Eng., Ger., Slovene & Rus.). 1972. 95.00 (ISBN 0-686-92494-0, M-9894). French & Eur.

Technical-Vocational Mathematics. L. Mrachek & C. Kromschlies. LC 76-48917. 1978. pap. 31.00 (ISBN 0-13-898569-3). P-H.

Technical Wall Street Encyclopedia. Carlo M. Flumiani. (Library). 198p. 1982. 155.50 (ISBN 0-86654-041-5). Inst Econ Finan.

Technical Woodworking. 2nd ed. Chris H. Groneman & E. R. Glazener. 1975. text ed. 34.44 (ISBN 0-07-024964-4). McGraw.

Technical Workshop to Work Out a System of Documentation. Seameo Project in Archaeology & Fine Arts Staff. 217p. 1983. 60.00x (Pub. by Han-Shan Tang Ltd). State Mutual Bk.

Technical Writer. Ann Stuart. (Illus.). 400p. 1988. text ed. 18.50 (ISBN 0-03-004579-7). HR&W.

Technical Writers' Guide: 1500 Verbs & Usages. 1140p. 1985. Set. pap. 170.00 cardboard slipcase (Inter Am U Pr). Taylor & Francis.

Technical Writer's Handbook. Ed. by Harry E. Chandler. 1983. 54.00 (ISBN 0-87170-151-0). ASM.

Technical Writing. Francis B. Emerson. LC 85-80764. 560p. 1987. pap. text ed. 29.56; instr's. manual 2.36; transparencies 27.56 (ISBN 0-395-43755-5). HM.

Technical Writing. 2nd ed. David E. Fear. 1978. pap. text ed. write for info (ISBN 0-394-32100-6, RanC). Random.

Technical Writing. Koenigsec. Date not set. price not set. Macmillan.

Technical Writing. 4th ed. John Lannon. 1988. pap. text ed. write for info. (ISBN 0-673-39734-3). Scott F.

Technical Writing. 3rd ed. John M. Lannon. 1984. pap. text ed. write for info. (ISBN 0-673-39274-0). Scott F.

Technical Writing. 5th ed. Gordon Mills et al. 576p. 1986. pap. text ed. 21.95 (ISBN 0-03-062019-8, HoltC). HR&W.

Technical Writing - Leader Guide. Kelly M. Cowser. 702p. 1988. wkbk. 60.00 (ISBN 0-933427-15-8). Shipley.

Technical Writing: A Bibliography. Sarojini Balachandran. 1977. pap. 4.60 (ISBN 0-931874-07-6). Assn Busn Comm.

Technical Writing: A Guide with Models. Bonnie C. Brinegar & Craig B. Skates. 1983. pap. write for info. (ISBN 0-673-15410-6). Scott F.

Technical Writing: A Practical Approach. Turner. 1983. text ed. write for info. (ISBN 0-8359-7546-0, Reston); instr's. manual avail. (ISBN 0-8359-7547-9). P-H.

Technical Writing: A Reader-Centered Approach. Paul V. Anderson. 823p. 1987. pap. text ed. 20.00 net (ISBN 0-15-589680-6, HC); instr's. manual net 3.50 (ISBN 0-15-589681-4). HarBraceJ.

Technical Writing & Communication. Contrib. by Helen E. Plotkin & Carole M. Mablekos. Date not set. audio course, incl. 6 cass. & 180p. manual 465.00 (A3); addtl. manual 35.00. Am Chemical.

Technical Writing Casebook. Thomas N. Trzyna & Margaret W. Batschelet. 200p. 1988. pap. text ed. write for info. (ISBN 0-534-08658-6). Wadsworth Pub.

Technical Writing Essentials. Michael H. Markel. LC 87-60508. 224p. 1987. pap. text ed. write for info. (ISBN 0-312-00736-1); write for info. instr's. manual (ISBN 0-312-01288-8); write for info. instr's. ed. (ISBN 0-312-01287-X). St Martin.

Technical Writing for Social Scientists. John S. Harris & Reed H. Blake. LC 75-20129. 128p. 1976. 18.95x (ISBN 0-911012-39-7); pap. 8.95x (ISBN 0-88229-362-1). Nelson-Hall.

Technical Writing for the Future. Levy. 1988. price not set (ISBN 0-471-86030-1). Wiley.

Technical Writing: Forms & Formats. 2nd ed. Raymond MacKenzie et al. (Illus.). 184p. 1983. pap. text ed. 14.95 (ISBN 0-8403-3217-3, 40321701). Kendall-Hunt.

Technical Writing Mechanics. Roberta M. Humble. (Illus.). 288p. 1987. pap. text ed. 18.30 (ISBN 0-940139-00-6). Tot Lot Child Care.

Technical Writing: Principles & Forms. 2nd ed. Deborah C. Andrews & Margaret D. Blickle. 1982. text ed. write for info. (ISBN 0-02-303470-X). Macmillan.

Technical Writing: Principles & Practice. James L. Miles et al. 352p. 1982. pap. text ed. write for info. (ISBN 0-574-22065-8, 13-5065); instr's. guide avail. (ISBN 0-574-22066-6, 13-5066). SRA.

Technical Writing Process. Marilyn S. Samuels. (Illus.). 320p. 1988. pap. text ed. 16.95 (ISBN 0-19-503679-4). Oxford U Pr.

Technical Writing: Process & Product. Charles R. Stratton. 480p. 1984. pap. text ed. 22.95 (ISBN 0-03-056733-5). HR&W.

Technical Writing: Situations & Strategies. 2nd ed. Michael H. Markel. LC 87-60517. 596p. 1987. pap. text ed. write for info. (ISBN 0-312-00269-6); write for info. instr's manual (ISBN 0-312-00270-X). St Martin.

Technical Writing Strategies: Complete Management Guide. Maus. 1988. price not set (ISBN 0-471-84266-4). Wiley.

Technical Writing: Structure, Standards & Style. Robert W. Bly & Gary Blake. LC 82-15223. 160p. 1982. text ed. 11.95 (ISBN 0-07-006174-2); pap. text ed. 6.95 (ISBN 0-07-006173-4). McGraw.

Technical Writing: The Easy Way. Harley Bjelland. LC 81-90026. (Illus.). 116p. (Orig.). 1981. pap. 10.00 (ISBN 0-939648-00-8). Norway Bks.

Technical Writing (Various Modules) Terry R. Bacon et al. 196p. 1987. wkbk. 60.00 (ISBN 0-933427-22-0). Shipley.

Technical Writing with Word Processing. Linda Duttlinger. 324p. 1987. pap. text ed. 23.95 (ISBN 0-8403-4384-1). Kendall-Hunt.

Technical Writing Workbook. Sally T. Taylor. 256p. 1985. pap. text ed. 10.95 (ISBN 0-8403-3680-2). Kendall-Hunt.

Technically Write! Communicating in a Technological Era. 3rd ed. Ron S. Blicq. (Illus.). 416p. 1986. pap. text ed. write for info (ISBN 0-13-898750-5). P H.

Technically Write! Communicating in a Technological Era. 2nd ed. Ron S. Bricq. (Illus.). 448p. 1981. P-H.

Technician As Writer: Preparing Technical Reports. Ingrid Brunner & J. C. Mathes. 240p. 1980. pap. text ed. write for info. (ISBN 0-02-315950-2). Macmillan.

Technician As Writer: Preparing Technical Reports. Ingrid Brunner et al. 1980. pap. 18.76 scp (ISBN 0-672-61523-1); scp tchrs manual 3.67 (ISBN 0-672-61524-X). Bobbs.

Technician Education Directory, 1986. 12th ed. Ed. by Lawrence Prakken et al. LC 63-22652. 1986. 45.00 (ISBN 0-911168-61-3). Prakken.

Technician Education Yearbook, 1963-64. Ed. by Lawrence W. Prakken & Jerome C. Patterson. LC 63-22652. 1963. 10.00 (ISBN 0-911168-01-X). Prakken.

Technician Education Yearbook, 1965-66. 2nd ed. Ed. by Lawrence W. Prakken & Jerome C. Patterson. LC 63-22652. 1965. 10.00 (ISBN 0-911168-02-8). Prakken.

Technician Education Yearbook, 1967-68. 3rd ed. Ed. by Lawrence W. Prakken & Jerome C. Patterson. LC 63-22652. 1967. 10.00 (ISBN 0-911168-03-6). Prakken.

Technician Education Yearbook, 1969-70. 4th ed. Ed. by Lawrence W. Prakken & Jerome C. Patterson. LC 63-22652. 1969. 10.00 (ISBN 0-911168-04-4). Prakken.

Technician Education Yearbook, 1975-76. 7th ed. Ed. by Lawrence W. Prakken & Jerome C. Patterson. LC 63-22652. 1975. 16.00 (ISBN 0-911168-33-8). Prakken.

Technician Education Yearbook, 1977-78. 8th ed. Ed. by Lawrence W. Prakken & Jerome C. Patterson. LC 63-22652. 1977. 18.00 (ISBN 0-911168-36-2). Prakken.

Technician Education Yearbook, 1980. 9th ed. Ed. by Lawrence W. Prakken et al. LC 63-22652. (Illus.). 1979. 25.00 (ISBN 0-911168-44-3). Prakken.

Technician Education Yearbook, 1982. 10th ed. Ed. by Lawrence Prakken et al. LC 63-22652. (Illus.). 376p. 1982. 35.00 (ISBN 0-911168-49-4). Prakken.

Technician Education Yearbook, 1984. 11th ed. Ed. by Lawrence Prakken et al. LC 63-22652. (Illus.). 360p. 1984. 45.00 (ISBN 0-911168-54-0). Prakken.

Technician's Guide to Fiber Optics. Donald J. Sterling, Jr. LC 86-32988. 288p. 1987. text ed. 27.95 (ISBN 0-8273-2612-2); instr's guide 8.00 (ISBN 0-8273-2613-0). Delmar.

Technicians Guide To Programmable Controllers. Richard A. Cox. LC 84-7715. 160p. 1984. pap. text ed. 18.50 (ISBN 0-8273-2420-0); instr's. guide 6.00 (ISBN 0-8273-2421-9). Delmar.

Technicians Guide to Servicing Two-Way FM Radio. Daniel K. Neely. (Illus.). 1978. 14.95 (ISBN 0-13-898635-5, Parker). P-H.

Technician's Handbook. Chris Christensen. Ed. by Tim Weidner. (Illus.). 210p. 1983. pap. 4.75 (ISBN 0-942588-01-0). Franzak & Foster.

Technician's Handbook of Plastics. Peter A. Grandilli. 272p. 1981. 27.95 (ISBN 0-442-23870-3). Van Nos Reinhold.

Technician's Handbook of Plastics. Peter A. Grandilli. 246p. 1981. 33.00 (ISBN 0-686-48117-8, B327). T-C Pubns CA.

Technicians of the Finite: The Rise & Decline of the Schizophrenic in American Thought, 1840-1960. S. P. Fullinwider. LC 81-23771. (Contributions in Medical History Ser.: No. 9). ix, 253p. 1982. lib. bdg. 35.00 (ISBN 0-313-23021-8, FFI/). Greenwood.

Technicians of the Sacred: A Range of Poetries from Africa, America, Asia, Europe & Oceania. 2nd, rev. ed. Ed. by Jerome Rothenberg. LC 84-16276. 1985. 47.50x (ISBN 0-520-04900-4); pap. 15.95 (ISBN 0-520-04912-8). U of Cal Pr.

Technicolor Time Machine. Harry Harrison. 256p. 1985. pap. 2.95 (ISBN 0-8125-3970-2, Dist. by Warner Pub. Services & Saint Martin's Press). Tor Bks.

Technics & Civilization. Lewis Mumford. LC 63-19641. (Illus.). 495p. 1963. pap. 8.95 (ISBN 0-15-688254-X, Harv). HarBraceJ.

Technics & Human Development see Myth of the Machine.

Technics & Praxis. (Boston Studies in the Philosophy of Science XXIV Synthesis Library: No. 130). 1978. lib. bdg. 24.00 (ISBN 9-0277-0953-X, Pub. by Reidel Holland); pap. 8.50 (ISBN 9-0277-0954-8). Kluwer Academic.

Technics for the Crime Investigator. 2nd ed. William Dienstein. 272p. 1974. 31.50x (ISBN 0-398-03112-6). C C Thomas.

Technics of the Organ. Edwin Evans. LC 78-13905. 1978. Repr. of 1938 ed. lib. bdg. 15.00 (ISBN 0-89341-437-9). Longwood Pub Group.

Technics of Violin Playing. Karl Courvoisier. LC 77-94555. 1978. Repr. of 1899 ed. lib. bdg. 10.00 (ISBN 0-89341-403-4). Longwood Pub Group.

Technics of Violin Playing. Karl Courvoisier. Repr. lib. bdg. 19.00 (ISBN 0-403-03861-8). Scholarly.

Technik Des Englischen Gegenwartsromanes. Margarete Blumenthal. pap. 9.00 (ISBN 0-384-04775-0). Johnson Repr.

Technik und Handhabung der Funktionsregler. R. Fraenkel. (Illus.). 124p. 1984. 27.50 (ISBN 3-8055-3924-X). S Karger.

Technik-Worterbuch: Chemie & Chemische Technik. 720p. (Ger.). 1980. vinyl 90.00x (ISBN 0-569-07861-X, Pub. by Collets (UK)). State Mutual Bk.

Technik-Worterbuch: Elektronik, Elektrotechnik. 1980. 120.00x (ISBN 0-686-72091-1, Pub. by Collets (UK)). State Mutual Bk.

Technique: The Fundamental Techniques of Cooking - an Illustrated Guide. Jacques Pepin. LC 76-9733. (Illus.). 1976. 24.50 (ISBN 0-8129-0610-1). Times Bks.

Techniques & Applications of Fast Reactions in Solution. Ed. by W. J. Gettins & E. Wyn-Jones. (Nato Advanced Study Institutes Series: Math & Physical Sciences: No. C50). 1979. lib. bdg. 58.00 (ISBN 90-277-1022-8, Pub. by Reidel Holland). Kluwer Academic.

Techniques & Applications of Path Integration. L. S. Schulman. LC 80-19129. 359p. 1981. 45.95 (ISBN 0-471-76450-7, Pub. by Wiley-Interscience). Wiley.

Techniques & Applications of Plasma Chemistry. Ed. by John R. Hollahan & Alexis T. Bell. LC 74-5122. 403p. 1974. 67.50 (ISBN 0-471-40628-7, Pub. by Wiley-Interscience). Wiley.

Techniques & Applications of Thin Layer Chromatography. Ed. by Joseph C. Touchstone & Joseph Sherma. LC 84-11924. 395p. 1985. text ed. 84.00 (ISBN 0-471-88017-5, Pub. by Wiley-Interscience). Wiley.

Techniques & Basic Experiments for the Study of Brain & Behavior. Jan Bures et al. 1976. 51.00 (ISBN 0-444-41502-5, North Holland). Elsevier.

Techniques & Basic Experiments for the Study of Brain & Behavior. 2nd, rev. ed. Jan Bures et al. 1983. 113.25 (ISBN 0-444-80448-X, I-351-83); pap. 36.50 (ISBN 0-444-80535-4). Elsevier.

Techniques & Concepts of High-Energy Physics IV. Ed. by T. Ferbel. LC 87-21293. (NATO ASI Series B, Physics: Vol. 164). (Illus.). 600p. 1987. 115.00x (ISBN 0-306-42688-9, Plenum Pr). Plenum Pub.

Techniques & Concepts of High-Energy Physics I. Ed. by Thomas Ferbel. LC 81-13767. (NATO ASI Series B, Physics: Vol. 66). 554p. 1981. 89.50x (ISBN 0-306-40721-3, Plenum Pr). Plenum Pub.

Techniques & Concepts of High-Energy Physics II. Ed. by Thomas Ferbel. (NATO ASI Series B, Physics: Vol. 99). 350p. 1983. 59.50x (ISBN 0-306-41385-X, Plenum Pr). Plenum Pub.

Techniques & Concepts of High-Energy Physics III. Ed. by Thomas Ferbel. (Nato ASI Series B, Physics: Vol. 128). 460p. 1986. 72.50x (ISBN 0-306-42106-2, Plenum Pr). Plenum Pub.

Techniques & Decision Making in the Assessment of Off-Site Consequences of an Accident in a Nuclear Facility. (Safety Guides Ser.: No. 86). 185p. (Orig.). 1987. pap. 42.00 (ISBN 92-0-123687-5, ISP743, IAEA). UNIPUB.

Techniques & Experiments for Organic Chemistry. Ralph J. Fessenden & Joan S. Fessenden. 480p. 1983. text ed. 24.00 pub net (ISBN 0-87150-755-2). Brooks-Cole.

Techniques & Experiments in Organic Chemistry. 5th ed. Ault. 1987. 40.00 (ISBN 0-205-08752-3). Allyn.

Techniques & Experiments in Organic Chemistry. 2nd ed. Ed. by Leon B. Gortler & Robert C. Tripp. (Illus.). 1978. lab manual 12.95 (ISBN 0-89529-016-2). Avery Pub.

Techniques & Guidelines for Social Work Practice. Bradford Sheafor et al. 464p. 1988. text ed. 34.00 scp. (ISBN 0-205-10583-1). Allyn.

Techniques & Indications in Radiology Kidney & Urinary Tract. S. Lange. (Thiemeflexi Book Ser.). (Illus.). 233p. 1987. pap. text ed. 17.00 (ISBN 0-317-58781-1). Thieme Med Pubs.

Techniques & Materials in Biology. Marjorie P. Behringer. LC 80-12458. 602p. 1982. Repr. of 1973 ed. lib. bdg. 41.50 (ISBN 0-89874-175-0). Krieger.

Techniques & Materials of Tonal Music: With an Introduction to Twentiethth Century Techniques. 3rd ed. Thomas E. Benjamin et al. LC 85-80651. 320p. 1985. text ed. 32.76 (ISBN 0-395-35917-1). HM.

Techniques & Methods of Organic & Organometallic Chemistry, Vol. 1. Ed. by Donald B. Denney. LC 69-20008. pap. 60.50 (2027123). Bks Demand UMI.

Techniques & Methods of Polymer Evaluation. Ed. by Philip E. Slade & Lloyd T. Jenkins. LC 66-19038. Vol. 1: Thermal Analysis. pap. 65.80 (2027110). Bks Demand UMI.

Techniques & Practice for Pretreatment of Low & Intermediate Level Solid & Liquid Radioactive Wastes. (Technical Reports Ser.: No. 272). (Illus.). 106p. (Orig.). 1987. pap. text ed. 28.00 (ISBN 92-0-125087-8, IDC272, IAEA). UNIPUB.

Techniques & Principles in Language Teaching. Diane Larsen-Freeman. (Techniques in Teaching English As a Second Language Ser.). 142p. 1986. pap. 5.95x (ISBN 0-19-434133-X). Oxford U Pr.

Techniques & Problems of Assessment for Teachers. Ed. by H. G. Macintosh. 1974. pap. 18.95x (ISBN 0-7131-1816-4). Trans-Atl Phila.

Techniques & Problems of Theory Construction in Sociology. Jerald Hage. LC 72-6447. (Illus.). pap. 63.80 (ISBN 0-317-08645-6, 2020263). Bks Demand UMI.

Techniques du Test 1 - Test Techniques 1. Network Staff. 1984. 95.00x (ISBN 0-907634-42-7, Pub. by Network Events Ltd). State Mutual Bk.

Techniques du Test 11 - Test Techniques 11. Network Staff. 1984. 95.00x (ISBN 0-907634-43-5, Pub. by Network Events Ltd). State Mutual Bk.

Techniques for Articulatory Disorders. Elizabeth C. Bosley. 166p. 1981. 20.50x (ISBN 0-398-04139-3). C C Thomas.

Techniques for Assessing Industrial Hazards: A Manual. Technica, Ltd. Staff. (World Bank Technical Paper Ser.: No. 55). 182p. 1988. 10.00 (ISBN 0-8213-0779-7, BK0779). World Bank.

Techniques for Behavior Change: Applications of Adlerian Theory. Ed. by Arthur G. Nikelly. 224p. 1979. 28.25 (ISBN 0-398-01401-9). C C Thomas.

Techniques for Computer Graphics. Ed. by D. F. Rogers & R. A. Earnshaw. (Illus.). 590p. 1987. 59.50 (ISBN 0-387-96492-4). Springer-Verlag.

Techniques for Construction Network Scheduling. James D. Stevens. (Illus.). 256p. 1988. 39.50 (ISBN 0-07-061291-9). McGraw.

Techniques for Controlling Air Pollution from the Operation of Nuclear Facilities. (Safety Ser.: No. 17). (Illus.). 118p. 1966. pap. 9.75 (ISBN 92-0-123166-0, ISP121, IAEA). UNIPUB.

Techniques for Dealing with Child Abuse. Arlene Baxter. (Illus.). 118p. 1985. 21.50x (ISBN 0-398-05110-0). C C Thomas.

Techniques for Dealing with Child Sexual Abuse. Arlene Baxter. (Illus.). 158p. 1986. 23.00x (ISBN 0-398-05220-4). C C Thomas.

Techniques for Dealing with Family Violence. Arlene Baxter. (Illus.). 158p. 1987. 24.75x (ISBN 0-398-05369-3). C C Thomas.

Techniques for High Temperature Fatigue Testing: Based on th Edited Proceedings of the Springfield Symposium, Preston, U. K., 13-14 September 1983. Ed. by G. Sumner & V. B. Livesey. (Illus.). 224p. 1985. 54.00 (ISBN 0-85334-314-4, Pub. by Elsevier Applied Sci England). Elsevier.

Techniques for Identifying Transuranic Speciation in Aquatic Environments: Proceedings of a Technical Committee Meeting, Italy, 24-28 March 1980, Jointly Organized by IAEA and the Commission of European Communities. (Panel Proceedings Ser.). 290p. 1982. pap. 35.25 (ISBN 92-0-021081-3, ISP613, IAEA). UNIPUB.

Techniques for Image Processing & Classification in Remote Sensing. Robert A. Schowengerdt. LC 83-11769. 272p. 1983. 34.50 (ISBN 0-12-628980-8). Acad Pr.

Techniques for Including Musical Examples in Theses & Dissertations: A Handbook. Dwight D. Gatwood. LC 70-18258. (Illus.). 37p. (Orig.). 1970. pap. 3.95 (ISBN 0-934082-09-X, Pub. by Nashville Res Pubns TN). Theodore Front.

Techniques for Industrial Pollution Prevention. Michael Overcash. LC 86-2722. (Illus.). 200p. 1986. 44.95 (ISBN 0-87371-071-1). Lewis Pubs Inc.

Techniques for Making Functional Population Projections. Donald J. Bogue & Susan Biehler. LC 79-53201. (Orig.). 1979. pap. text ed. 4.00 (ISBN 0-89836-013-7). Comm & Family.

Techniques for Meeting Nutrition Education Needs. Wendy L. Way & Susan A. Nitzke. 1981. 4.00 (ISBN 0-911365-18-4, A261-08450). Home Econ Educ.

Techniques for Multiaxial Creep Testing. Ed. by D. J. Gooch & I. M. How. 366p. 1986. 74.25 (ISBN 1-85166-033-X, Pub. by Elsevier Applied Sci England). Elsevier.

Techniques for Multiobjective Decision Making in Systems Management: Advances in Industrial Engineering, No. 2. F. Szidarovsky et al. 506p. 1986. 131.75 (ISBN 0-444-42592-6). Elsevier.

Techniques for Nuclear & Particle Physics Experiments. W. R. Leo. (Illus.). 380p. 1987. pap. 49.50 (ISBN 0-387-17386-2). Springer-Verlag.

Techniques for Nurses: A Comprehensive Clinical Approach. B. Kozier & G. Erb. 1982. text ed. write for info. (ISBN 0-201-03911-7). Addison-Wesley.

Techniques for Observing Normal Child Behavior. Nancy T. Carbonara. LC 61-9991. 1961. pap. 2.95x (ISBN 0-8229-5043-X). U of Pittsburgh Pr.

Techniques for Organizational Effectiveness. Claire Fulcher & Mary Grefe. 90p. 1978. 4.00 (ISBN 0-318-12415-7); members 3.00 (ISBN 0-318-12416-5). Am Assn Univ Women.

Techniques for Police Instructors. John C. Klotter. 180p. 1978. 21.75x (ISBN 0-398-01029-3). C C Thomas.

Techniques for Project Appraisal under Uncertainty. Shlomo Reutlinger. LC 74-94827. (Occasional Paper No. 10, World Bank Ser). 95p. (Orig.). 1970. pap. 7.95x (ISBN 0-8018-1154-6). Johns Hopkins.

Techniques for Radar Speed Detection. LC 82-109905. (Traffic Patrol & Direction Ser.). (Illus.). 14p. 5.00. Traffic Inst.

Techniques for Rapid Assessment of Seismic Vulnerability. Ed. by Charles Scawthorn. (Sessions Proceedings Ser.). 116p. 1986. 15.00x (ISBN 0-87262-552-4). Am Soc Civil Eng.

Techniques for Reducing Roadway Occupancy During Routine Maintenance Activities. (National Cooperative Highway Research Project Report). 55p. 1975. 4.40 (ISBN 0-309-02340-8). Transport Res Bd.

Techniques for Separation & Selection of Specific Lymphocytes. W. Haas & H. Von Boehmer. (Current Topics in Microbiology & Immunology Ser.: Vol. 84). (Illus.). 1978. 35.00 (ISBN 0-387-09029-0). Springer-Verlag.

Techniques for Starting & Maintaining an FHA-HERO Chapter. V. L. Clark et al. pap. 5.00 (ISBN 0-911365-28-1, A261-08472). Home Econ Educ.

Techniques for Studying Semiconducting Materials see Semiconductors & Semimetals.

Techniques for Success in College: Reading & Study Skills. Selma Wilf. (Illus.). 352p. 1986. pap. text ed. write for info (ISBN 0-13-901851-4). P H.

Techniques for Teaching Conservation Education. Robert E. Brown & G. W. Mouser. LC 64-24115. Repr. of 1964 ed. 30.00 (ISBN 0-8357-9054-1, 2013323). Bks Demand UMI.

Techniques for the Analysis & Modeling of Enzyme Kinetic Mechanisms. Cham F. Lam. (Medical Computing Ser.). 396p. 1981. 121.00 (ISBN 0-471-09981-3, Pub. by Res Stud Pr). Wiley.

Techniques for the Analysis of Membrane Proteins. Ed. by C. I. Ragan & R. J. Cherry. 450p. 1986. text ed. 99.00 (ISBN 0-412-24970-7, 9969, Pub. by Chapman & Hall England). Routledge Chapman & Hall.

Techniques for the Automated Optimisation of High-Performance Liquid Chromatography Separations. John C. Berridge. LC 85-12485. 1986. 49.95 (ISBN 0-471-90861-4, Pub. by Wiley-Interscience). Wiley.

Techniques for the Collection & Reporting of Data on Community Water Supply: Report. WHO Scientific Group. Geneva, 1971. (Technical Report Ser.: No. 490). (Also avail. in French & Spanish). 1972. pap. 1.20 (ISBN 92-4-120490-7). World Health.

Techniques for the Retrieval of Chemical Information. Ed. by A. Kent. 1978. 51.00 (ISBN 0-08-021193-3). Pergamon.

Techniques for the Solidification of High-Level Waste. (Technical Reports Ser.: No. 176). (Illus.). 1978. pap. 23.00 (ISBN 92-0-125077-0, IDC176, IAEA). UNIPUB.

Techniques for the Study of Ion-Molecule Reactions. Ed. by James M. Farrar & William F. Saunders. (Weissberger Techniques of Chemistry Ser.). 752p. 1988. write for info. (ISBN 0-471-84812-3). Wiley.

Techniques for the Study of Mixed Populations. Ed. by D. W. Lovelock & R. Davies. (Society for Applied Bacteriology Technical Ser.). 1979. 55.50 (ISBN 0-12-456650-2). Acad Pr.

Techniques for Three D Machine Perception: Machine Intelligence & Pattern Recognition, Vol. 3. Ed. by A. Rosenfeld. 320p. 1985. 50.00 (ISBN 0-444-87901-3, North Holland). Elsevier.

Techniques for Writing: Composition. Rev. ed. Milton Wohl. LC 78-646. 1985. pap. text ed. 11.50 (ISBN 0-317-57098-6). Newbury Hse.

Techniques in Abdominal Surgery. Philippe Detrie. Tr. by Richard R. Pryer from Fr. LC 73-593870. pap. 31.80 (ISBN 0-317-26196-7, 2052070). Bks Demand UMI.

Techniques in Bedside Hemodynamic Monitoring. 3rd ed. Daily. 1984. 20.95 (ISBN 0-8016-4375-9). Mosby.

Techniques in Biocompatibility Testing, Vols. I-II. David F. Williams. 1986. Vol. I, 216 pgs. 2 vol. set 270.00 (ISBN 0-8493-6627-5). Vol. II, 240 pgs. CRC Pr.

Techniques in Bioproductivity & Photosynthesis. 2nd ed. Ed. by J. Coombs et al. (Illus.). 200p. 1985. text ed. 47.00 (ISBN 0-08-031999-8, Pub. by PPL); pap. text ed. 26.00 (ISBN 0-08-031998-X). Pergamon.

Techniques in Business Credit Management. R. D. Rutherford. Ed. by James J. Andover. LC 84-18965. 96p. 1984. pap. 16.95 (ISBN 0-934914-58-3). NACM.

Techniques in Calcium Research. M. V. Thomas. (Biological Techniques Ser.). 1982. 42.50 (ISBN 0-12-688680-6). Acad Pr.

Techniques in Cardiac Surgery. 2nd ed. Denton A. Cooley. (Illus.). 245p. 1984. 105.00 (ISBN 0-7216-2701-3). Saunders.

Techniques in Cell Cycle Analysis. Ed. by Joe W. Gray & Zbigniew Darzynkiewicz. LC 86-16114. (Biological Methods Ser.). 304p. 1987. 64.50 (ISBN 0-89603-097-0). Humana.

Techniques in Cleft Lip, Nose & Palate Reconstruction. Kapetansky. LC 65-73299. 1987. text ed. 79.00 (ISBN 0-397-58302-8, Lippincott Medical). Lippincott.

Techniques in Clinical Capillary Microscopy. Ed. by F. Mahler et al. (Mikrozirkulation in Forschung und Klinik, Progress in Applied Microcirculation Ser.: Vol. 11). (Illus.). xii, 152p. 1986. pap. 52.75 (ISBN 3-8055-4327-1). S Karger.

Techniques in Clinical Electrophysiology of Vision. G. Niemeyer & Charles Huber. 1982. lib. bdg. 99.00 (ISBN 90-6193-727-2, Pub. by Junk Pubs Netherlands). Kluwer Academic.

Techniques in Clinical Endodontics. Ed. by Harold Gerstein. (Illus.). 416p. 1983. 57.95 (ISBN 0-7216-4087-7). Saunders.

Techniques in Clinical Nursing: A Nursing Process Approach. 2nd ed. Barbara Kozier & Glenora Erb. (Illus.). 1000p. 1986. pap. text ed. 37.75 (ISBN 0-201-11755-X, Hlth-Sci); write for info. student wkbk. (ISBN 0-201-11759-2, Hlth-Sci). Addison-Wesley.

Techniques in College Reading. James Schiavone. 224p. 1985. pap. text ed. 19.95 (ISBN 0-8403-3978-X). Kendall-Hunt.

Techniques in Condensed Matter Physics at Low Temperatures. R. C. Richardson & E. Smith. 450p. 1988. 45.25 (ISBN 0-201-15002-6, Adv Bk Prog MSP). Addison-Wesley.

Techniques in Corporate Manpower Planning. C. Verhoeven. (International Ser. in Management Science-Operations Research). 192p. 1982. lib. bdg. 30.00 (ISBN 0-89838-072-3, Pub. by Kluwer-Nijhoff (Netherlands)). Kluwer Academic.

Techniques in Craniofacial Surgery. Kenneth E. Salyer. LC 65-40389. (Gower Bk.). (Illus.). 250p. 1989. write for info. (Lippincott Medical). Lippincott.

Techniques in Data Communications. Ralph Glasgal. 200p. 1983. text ed. 44.00 (ISBN 0-89006-122-X). Artech Hse.

Techniques in Electrochemistry, Corrosion & Metal Finishing: A Handbook. A. T. Kuhn. LC 86-26769. 567p. 1987. 130.00 (ISBN 0-471-91407-X). Wiley.

Techniques in Experimental High Energy Physics. T. Ferbel. 608p. 1986. 45.25 (ISBN 0-201-11487-9, Adv Bk Prog MSP). Addison-Wesley.

Techniques in Extracorporeal Circulation. 2nd ed. Marion I. Ionescu. 1981. text ed. 140.00 (ISBN 0-407-00173-5). Butterworth.

Techniques in Fast Reactor Critical Experiments. W. G. Davey & W. C. Redman. LC 79-119375. 314p. 1970. 23.00 (ISBN 0-677-02680-3, 450006). Am Nuclear Soc.

Techniques in General Thoracic Surgery. Maurice Hood. (Illus.). 378p. 1984. 58.00 (ISBN 0-7216-1137-0). Saunders.

Techniques in Immunocytochemistry, Vol. 1. Ed. by G. R. Bullock & P. Petrusz. 1982. 60.00 (ISBN 0-12-140401-3). Acad Pr.

Techniques in Immunocytochemistry, Vol. 1. Ed. by G. R. Bullock & P. Petrusz. 306p. 1986. pap. 25.00 (ISBN 0-12-140404-8). Acad Pr.

Techniques in Immunocytochemistry, Vol. 2. Ed. by G. R. Bullock & P. Petrusz. 1983. 51.50 (ISBN 0-12-140402-1). Acad Pr.

Techniques in Immunocytochemistry, Vol. 2. Ed. by G. R. Bullock & P. Petrusz. 290p. 1986. pap. 25.00 (ISBN 0-12-140405-6). Acad Pr.

Techniques in Immunocytochemistry, Vol. 3. Ed. by G. R. Bullock & P. Petrusz. 241p. 1988. pap. 29.50 (ISBN 0-12-140406-4). Acad Pr.

Techniques in Immunocytochemistry, Vol. 3. Gillian R. Bullock & Peter Petrusz. 1985. 52.50 (ISBN 0-12-140403-X). Acad Pr.

Techniques in Interviewing for Law Enforcement & Corrections Personnel: A Programmed Text. Robert J. Wicks & Ernest H. Josephs, Jr. 152p. 1977. spiral bdg. 21.50x (ISBN 0-398-03677-2). C C Thomas.

Techniques in Large Animal Surgery. A. Simon Turner & Wayne McIlwraith. (Illus.). 350p. 1988. pap. text ed. price not set (ISBN 0-8121-1177-X). Lea & Febiger.

Techniques in Machine Knitting. Kathleen Kinder. (Illus.). 144p. 1985. 14.95 (ISBN 0-668-06285-1). Arco.

Techniques in Mineral Exploration. J. H. Reedman. (Illus.). 526p. 1979. 120.75 (ISBN 0-85334-817-0, Pub. by Elsevier Applied Sci England); pap. 75.75 (ISBN 0-85334-851-0, Pub. by Elsevier Applied Sci England). Elsevier.

Techniques in Molecular Biology. John M. Walker & Wim Gaastra. LC 83-9419. (Illus.). 1983. 32.00x (ISBN 0-02-949830-9). Macmillan.

Techniques in Molecular Biology, Vol. 2. Ed. by John M. Walker & Wim Gaastra. 300p. 1987. 35.00x (ISBN 0-02-948791-9). Macmillan.

Techniques in Neuroanatomical Research. Ed. by C. Heym & W. G. Forssmann. (Illus.). 410p. 1981. 61.00 (ISBN 0-387-10686-3). Springer-Verlag.

Techniques in Operational Research: Models, Search & Randomization, Vol. 2. B. Conolly. LC 80-41741. (Mathematics & Its Applications Ser.). 340p. 1981. 95.00x (ISBN 0-470-27130-2). Halsted Pr.

Techniques in Organic Reaction Kinetics. Petr Zuman & Ramesh C. Patel. LC 84-7450. 352p. 1984. text ed. 51.95 (ISBN 0-471-03556-4, Wiley-Interscience). Wiley.

Techniques in Pheremone Research. Ed. by H. E. Hummel & T. A. Miller. (Springer Series in Expereimental Entomology). (Illus.). 450p. 1984. 75.10 (ISBN 0-387-90919-2). Springer-Verlag.

Techniques in Photomorphogenesis. Ed. by Harold Smith & Martin G. Holmes. (Biological Techniques Ser.). 1984. 78.00 (ISBN 0-12-652990-6). Acad Pr.

Techniques in Psychophysiology. Ed. by Irene Martin & Peter H. Venables. LC 78-4925. 699p. 1980. 107.00 (ISBN 0-471-27637-5, Pub. by Wiley-Interscience). Wiley.

Techniques in Somatic Cell Genetics. Ed. by Jerry W. Shay. LC 82-9848. (Illus.). 568p. 1982. 65.00x (ISBN 0-306-41040-0, Plenum Pr). Plenum Pub.

Techniques in Surgical Casting & Splinting. Kent K. Wu. LC 87-2894. (Illus.). 273p. 1987. pap. text ed. 24.95 (ISBN 0-8121-1076-5). Lea & Febiger.

Techniques in Teaching Vocabulary. Virginia F. Allen. (Teaching Techniques in English as a Second or Foreign Language Ser.). (Illus., Orig.). 1983. pap. 5.95x (ISBN 0-19-434130-5). Oxford U Pr.

Techniques of Twentieth-Century Composition: A Guide to the Materials of Modern Music. 3rd ed. Leon Dallin. 304p. 1974. text ed. write for info. (ISBN 0-697-03614-6). Wm C Brown.

Techniques of Typography. Cal Swann. (Illus.). 96p. 1982. pap. 14.95 (ISBN 0-913720-40-2). Beil.

Techniques of Upholstery: Easy Chairs, Settees & Occasional Chairs. Robert J. McDonald. (Illus.). 128p. 1988. 19.95 (ISBN 0-7134-5631-0, Pub. by Batsford England). David & Charles.

Techniques of Vacuum Ultraviolet Spectroscopy. James A. Samson. LC 67-19780. 1980. Repr. of 1967 ed. 35.00 (ISBN 0-918626-15-3). VUV Assocs.

Techniques of Veterinary Radiography. Joe P. Morgan & Sam Silverman. (Venture Series in Veterinary Medicine). (Illus.). 334p. 1984. pap. text ed. 39.95x (ISBN 0-8138-1728-5). Iowa St U Pr.

Techniques of Vigilance: A Textbook for Police Self-Defense. Kevin Parsons. LC 79-63190. (Illus.). 1980. 35.00 (ISBN 0-8048-1214-4). C E Tuttle.

Techniques of Wedding Photography. Sheila Hurth & Robert Hurth. Ed. by Vernon Gorter. LC 87-31237. 160p. (Orig.). 1988. pap. 14.95 (ISBN 0-89586-632-3, HP Bks). Price Stern.

Techniques of Wood Sculpture. David Orchard. LC 84-27327. (Illus.). 144p. 1985. 14.95 (ISBN 0-89134-121-8). North Light Bks.

Techniques of Wood Surface Decoration. David Hawkins. (Illus.). 168p. (Orig.). 1987. pap. 12.95 (ISBN 0-8069-6472-3). Sterling.

Techniques of Working with Resistance. Ed. by Donald Milman & George Goldman. LC 85-18653. 417p. 1986. 37.50x (ISBN 0-87668-616-1). Aronson.

Techniques of Working with the Working Press. Hal Golden & Kitty Hanson. LC 62-11972. 232p. 1962. 10.00 (ISBN 0-379-00056-3). Oceana.

Techniques of Writing. 4th ed. Paul L. Kinsella. 471p. 1985. pap. text ed. 13.00 net (ISBN 0-15-589730-6, HC); answer key avail. (ISBN 0-15-589731-4). HarBraceJ.

Techniques of Writing Business Letters, Memos & Reports. rev. ed. Courtland L. Bovee. (Illus.). 90p. 1978. 8.95x (ISBN 0-935732-02-0); pap. 7.95x (ISBN 0-935732-03-9). Roxbury Pub Co.

Techniques, Technology & Training in the Manufacture of Men's Clothing. 51p. 1970. 20.00 (ISBN 0-318-13705-4). Clothing Mfrs.

Techniques with a Thirty-Six Inch Baton: Modern Methods Made Easy. George M. Pekar & Timothy N. Oettmeier. (Illus.). 82p. 1983. 10.75 (ISBN 0-398-04751-0). C C Thomas.

Technisch Wissenschaftliches Taschenwoerterbuch. 408p. (Ger., Technical Scientific Dictionary). 75.00 (ISBN 3-87749-014-X, M-7643, Pub. by Georg Siemens Verlagsbuchhandlung). French & Eur.

Technisches Deutschfuer Auslaender. Jaroslav Strasak. (Ger., Technical German for Foreigners). 1969. 29.95 (ISBN 3-87097-041-3, M-7644). French & Eur.

Technisches Englisch. 7th ed. Henry G. Freeman. (Ger. & Eng.). 1975. 48.00 (ISBN 3-7736-5011-6, M-7647, Pub. by Girardet). French & Eur.

Technisches Taschenwoerterbuch. 3rd ed. H. Freeman. 584p. (Ger. & Eng., German-English Technical Dictionary). 1972. 39.95 (ISBN 3-19-006212-9, M-7648, Pub. by M. Hueber). French & Eur.

Technisches Taschenwoerterbuch. A. Grunwald-Beyer. 533p. (Ger. & Fr.). 25.00 (ISBN 3-87749-013-1, M-7646, Pub. by Georg Siemens Verlagsbuchhandlung). French & Eur.

Technisches Taschenwoerterbuch. A. Kroeger-Jannetti. 804p. (Ger. & Span.). 75.00 (ISBN 3-87749-012-3, M-7645, Pub. by Georg Siemens Verlagsbuchhandlung). French & Eur.

Technisches Woerterbuch, 2 vols. Ulatko Dabac. (Croatian. & Ger.). 1969. 195.00 (ISBN 3-7625-0550-0, M-7653, Pub. by Bauverlag). French & Eur.

Technisches Woerterbuch, Vol. 1. Antonin Kucera. (Rus. & Ger.). 1966. 75.00 (ISBN 3-87097-025-1, M-7654, Pub. by Brandstetter). French & Eur.

Technisches Woerterbuch, Vol. 1. A. Naxerova. (Czech. & Ger.). 1970. 89.95 (ISBN 3-87097-049-9, M-7649, Pub. by Brandstetter). French & Eur.

Technisches Woerterbuch, Vol. 1. 2nd ed. Salvatore Orlando-Meyer. (Ital. & Ger.). 1977. 95.00 (ISBN 3-87097-079-0, M-7651, Pub. by Brandstetter). French & Eur.

Technisches Woerterbuch, Vol. 2. Antonin Kucera. (Rus. & Ger.). 1966. 85.00 (ISBN 3-87097-026-X, M-7655, Pub. by Brandstetter). French & Eur.

Technisches Woerterbuch, Vol. 2. A. Naxerova. (Czech. & Ger.). 1972. 89.95 (ISBN 3-87097-056-1, M-7650, Pub. by Brandstetter). French & Eur.

Technisches Woerterbuch, Vol. 2. 2nd ed. Salvatore Orlando-Meyer. (Ital. & Ger.). 1977. 95.00 (ISBN 3-87097-080-4, M-7652, Pub. by Brandstetter). French & Eur.

Techniseasonal Commodity Trading. Everet Beckner. 1984. 65.00 (ISBN 0-318-04207-X). Windsor.

Techno-Bandits: How the Soviets Are Stealing America's High-Tech Future. Linda Melvern et al. 305p. 1984. 15.95 (ISBN 0-395-36066-8). HM.

Techno-Economic Aspects of the International Division of Labour in the Automotive Industry. 246p. (Orig.). pap. 23.00 (ISBN 92-1-116304-8, E.83.II.E.14). UN.

Techno-Economic Trends in Airborne Equipment for Agriculture & Other Selected Areas: Proceedings of a Seminar Organized by the United Nations Economic Commission for Europe, Warsaw, Poland, 18-22 September 1978. (ECE Seminars & Symposia). (Illus.). 294p. 1980. 89.00 (ISBN 0-08-022425-3). Pergamon.

Technocracy: Technological Social Design. Ed. by Technocracy Inc. (Illus.). 76p. (Orig.). 1975. pap. 2.00 (ISBN 0-686-28500-X). Technocracy.

Technocracy vs. Democracy: The Comparative Politics of International Airports. Elliot J. Feldman & Jerome Milch. (Illus.). 299p. 1982. 26.95 (ISBN 0-86569-063-4). Auburn Hse.

Technocratic Illusion: A Study of Managerial Power in Italy. Flavia Derossi. Tr. by Susan LoBello from Ital. LC 81-14341. 284p. 1982. 40.00 (ISBN 0-87332-185-5). M E Sharpe.

Technocratic Socialism: The Soviet Union in the Advanced Industrial Era. Erik P. Hoffmann & Robbin F. Laird. LC 85-4553. (Policy Studies). (Illus.). ix, 229p. 1985. 37.50 (ISBN 0-8223-0644-1); pap. text ed. 12.95 (ISBN 0-8223-0692-1). Duke.

Technocrats. Forrest W. Horton, Jr. 320p. 1986. pap. 3.50 (ISBN 0-8439-2381-4, Leisure Bks). Leisure NY.

Technocrats & Nuclear Politics: The Influence of Professional Experts in Policy-Making. Andrew Massey. 200p. 1988. text ed. 39.00 (ISBN 0-566-05644-5, Pub. by Gower Pub England). Gower Pub Co.

Technocrats: Prophets of Automation. Henry Elsner. LC 67-14522. (Men & Movements Ser.). pap. 67.50 (ISBN 0-317-52019-9, 2027413). Bks Demand UMI.

Technocrimes. August Bequai. LC 85-45801. 208p. 1986. 25.00X (ISBN 0-669-12342-0); pap. 12.95 (ISBN 0-669-13842-8). Lexington Bks.

Technoeconomics: Concepts & Cases. J. C. Wright. 178p. 1983. pap. text ed. 29.00 (ISBN 0-686-88185-0, APO133, APO). UNIPUB.

Technolgy Explosion in Medical Science: Implications for the Health Care Industry & the Public (1981-2001) Ed. by James Gay & Barbara S. Jacobs. (Health Care Administration Monographs: Vol. 2). 176p. 1983. text ed. 14.95 (ISBN 0-88331-205-0). Luce.

Technologcal Transformation: Strategic Issues & Options. Ed. by Rustam Lalkaka & Wu Mingyu. (Illus.). 350p. 1987. text ed. 50.00x (ISBN 0-89891-020-X). Advent NY.

Technological Acceleration & the Great Depression. Joseph P. Waters. Ed. by Stuart Bruchey. LC 76-45122. (Nineteen Seventy-Seven Dissertations Ser.). (Illus.). 1977. lib. bdg. 25.50x (ISBN 0-405-09933-9). Ayer Co Pubs.

Technological Advances & Consequent Dangers: Growing Threats to Civilization. Robert H. Kupperman. LC 84-1815. (Significant Issues Ser.: Vol. 6, No. 1). 11p. 1984. 5.95 (ISBN 0-89206-053-0). CSI Studies.

Technological Advances & Consequent Dangers: Growing Threats to Civilization. Robert H. Kupperman. (Siginificant Issues Ser.: Vol. VI, No. 1). 16p. (Orig.). 1984. pap. text ed. 6.95 (ISBN 0-8191-5925-5, Pub. by CSIS). U Pr of Amer.

Technological & Social Change: A Transdisciplinary Model. Jacob Fried & Paul Molnar. 1979. text ed. 20.00 (ISBN 0-89433-074-8). Petrocelli.

Technological Aspects of the Mechanical Behavior of Polymers. Ed. by Raymond F. Boyer. LC 74-181576. (Applied Polymer Symposia: No. 24). Repr. of 1974 ed. 23.00 (ISBN 0-8357-9378-8, 2007371). Bks Demand UMI.

Technological Basis of Radiation Therapy: Practical Clinical Applications. Ed. by Seymour H. Levitt & Norah Tapley. LC 83-9889. (Illus.). 336p. 1984. text ed. 45.00 (ISBN 0-8121-0898-1). Lea & Febiger.

Technological Breakthrough in Agriculture. K. Siva Prasad. 1987. 17.50x (ISBN 81-85076-15-4, Pub. by Chugh Pubns India). South Asia Bks.

Technological Capability in the Third World. Ed. by Martin Fransman & Kenneth King. LC 83-13737. 256p. 1984. 30.00 (ISBN 0-312-78792-8). St Martin.

Technological Challenge for Social Changes see Science & Future Choice.

Technological Change & Agrarian Structure: A Study of Bangladesh. Iftikhar Ahmed. (WEP Study Ser.). xvi, 136p. (Orig.). 1981. pap. 10.50 (ISBN 92-2-102543-8). Intl Labour Office.

Technological Change & Agrarian Structure: A Study of Bangladesh. Ahmed Iftikhar. (WEP Study Ser.). xiii, 136p. 1981. pap. 10.50 (ISBN 92-2-102543-8, ILO169, ILO). UNIPUB.

Technological Change & Economic Growth: Proceedings, C. I. C. Conference, 1964. Ed. by Floyd A. Bond. (Michigan Business Papers: No. 41). 1965. pap. 1.00 (ISBN 0-87712-090-0). UMI Div Res GSBA.

Technological Change & Human Development: An International Conference. Theodore W. Kheel et al. Ed. by Wayne L. Hodges & Matthew A. Kelly. LC 78-629733. 404p. 1970. pap. 8.00 (ISBN 0-87546-043-7). ILR Pr.

Technological Change & Industrial Development: Issues & Opportunities. Frederick T. Moore. (Working Paper: No. 613). 96p. 1983. 5.00 (ISBN 0-8213-0257-4, WP 0613). World Bank.

Technological Change & Industrial Relations: An International Symposium. Roger Blanpain. 1983. pap. text ed. 32.00 (ISBN 90-312-0205-3, Pub. by Kluwer Law Netherlands). Kluwer Academic.

Technological Change & Industry. C. P. Thakur. LC 72-924275. (Illus.). 348p. 1974. 15.00x (ISBN 0-89684-505-2). Orient Bk Dist.

Technological Change & Management. Ed. by David W. Ewing. LC 78-125645. 1970. 10.00x (ISBN 0-674-87230-4, Pub. by Harvard Busn. School). Harvard U Pr.

Technological Change & Productivity Growth. Albert N. Link. (Fundamentals of Pure & Applied Economics Ser.: Vol. 13). 90p. 1987. pap. text ed. 26.00 (ISBN 3-7186-0347-0). Harwood Academic.

Technological Change & Regional Development. Ed. by A. Gillespie. (Pion London Papers in Regional Science Ser.: No. 12). (Illus.). 171p. 1984. pap. 15.00x (ISBN 0-85086-107-1, NO. 5072). Routledge Chapman & Hall.

Technological Change & the British Iron Industry, 1700-1870. Charles K. Hyde. LC 76-45901. 1977. text ed. 38.50x (ISBN 0-691-05246-8). Princeton U Pr.

Technological Change & the Transformation of America. Ed. by Steven E. Goldberg & Charles R. Strain. 240p. 1987. text ed. 22.50x (ISBN 0-8093-1351-0). S Ill U Pr.

Technological Change & United States Energy Consumption, 1939-1954. Alan M. Strout. Ed. by Stuart Bruchey. LC 78-22753. (Energy in the American Economy Ser.). (Illus.). 1979. lib. bdg. 25.50x (ISBN 0-405-12017-6). Ayer Co Pubs.

Technological Change & Worker's Movements. Ed. by Melvyn Dubofsky. (Explorations in the World-System Ser.: Vol. 4). 320p. 1985. text ed. 29.95 (ISBN 0-8039-2465-8). Sage.

Technological Change at Work. Ian McLoughlin & Jon Clark. 224p. 1988. 65.00x (ISBN 0-335-15417-4, Open Univ Pr); pap. 21.00x (ISBN 0-335-15416-6, Open Univ Pr). Taylor & Francis.

Technological Change, Collective Bargaining, & Industrial Efficiency. Paul Willman. (Illus.). 264p. 1986. 29.95x (ISBN 0-19-827262-6). Oxford U Pr.

Technological Change, Development & the Environment: Socio-Economic Perspectives. Ed. by Clem Tisdell & P. Maitra. 288p. 1988. lib. bdg. 60.00 (ISBN 0-415-00447-0). Routledge Chapman & Hall.

Technological Change: Economics, Management & Environment. Ed. by Bela Gold. LC 74-17112. 1975. 44.00 (ISBN 0-08-018012-4). Pergamon.

Technological Change, Employment & Spatial Dynamics. Ed. by P. Nijkamp. (Lecture Notes in Economics & Mathematical Systems Ser.: Vol. 270). vii, 466p. 1986. 38.50 (ISBN 0-387-16478-2). Springer-Verlag.

Technological Change, Employment Generation & Multinationals: A Case Study of a Foreign Firm & a Local Multinational in India. Sanjaya Lall. (Working Paper Ser.: No. 27). 72p. (Orig.). 1984. pap. 10.50 (ISBN 92-2-103425-9, ILO313, ILO). UNIPUB.

Technological Change for Rural Development in India. V. G. Asari. 236p. 1985. 29.95x (ISBN 0-317-39864-4, Pub. by B R Pubs Delhi). Asia Bk Corp.

Technological Change for Rural Development in India. V. Gopalakrishnan Asari. ix, 236p. 1985. text ed. 37.50x (ISBN 0-86590-600-9, Pub. by B R Pub Corp Delhi). Apt Bks.

Technological Change in Japan's Beef Industry. James Simpson et al. (Westview Replica Edition Ser.). 225p. 1985. soft cover 35.00x (ISBN 0-86531-876-X). Westview.

Technological Change in Postharvest Handling & Transportation of Grains. Ed. by B. R. Champ et al. 208p. (Orig.). 1987. pap. text ed. 27.00x (ISBN 0-949511-29-3, Pub. by ACIAR Australia). Agribookstore.

Technological Change in Printing & Publishing. Lowell H. Hattery & George P. Bush. LC 77-176224. 275p. 1973. 23.75 (ISBN 0-87671-503-X). Lomond.

Technological Change in the American Cotton Spinning Industry, 1790-1836. Robert R. MacMurray. Ed. by Stuart Bruchey. LC 76-39835. (Nineteen Seventy-Seven Dissertations Ser.). (Illus.). 1977. lib. bdg. 42.00x (ISBN 0-405-09915-0). Ayer Co Pubs.

Technological Change in the German Democratic Republic. Raymond Bentley. 340p. 1984. 39.50x (ISBN 0-86531-812-3). Westview.

Technological Change, Industrial Restructuring & Regional Development. Ash Amin & John Goddard. 192p. 1986. text ed. 39.95x (ISBN 0-04-338131-6). Unwin Hyman.

Technological Change: Its Impact on Man & Society. Emanuel G. Mesthene. LC 76-106960. (Studies in Technology & Society). 1970. 11.00 (ISBN 0-674-87235-5). Harvard U Pr.

Technological Change, Rationalisation & Industrial Relations. Ed. by Otto Jacobi et al. LC 85-2166. 320p. 1986. 35.00x (ISBN 0-312-78878-9). St Martin.

Technological Change: The Tripartite Response, 1982-1985. Intro. by Hadv Sarafati. 355p. 1985. pap. 21.00. Intl Labour Office.

Technological Change, Work Organisation & Pay: Lessons from Asia. International Labour Office Staff. (Labour-Management Relations Ser.: No. 68). v, 218p. (Orig.). 1988. pap. 17.50 (ISBN 92-2-106324-0). Intl Labour Office.

Technological Changes & the Law: A Reader. Otto G. Gara & Bruce A. Naegeli. LC 79-92276. 925p. 1980. 40.00 (ISBN 0-89941-037-5). W S Hein.

Technological Choice in the Indian Environment. Ed. by Vinod Vyasulu. 351p. 1980. 44.95x (ISBN 0-940500-59-0, Pub. by Sterling India). Asia Bk Corp.

Technological Choices in the Indian Environment. Ed. by V. Vyasulu. 351p. 1980. 44.95. Asia Bk Corp.

Technological Competition & Trade in the Experimentally Organized Economy. Gunnar Eliasson. 118p. (Orig.). 1987. pap. text ed. 23.50x (ISBN 91-7204-294-X, Pub. by Industriens Sweden). Coronet Bks.

Technological Conscience: Survival & Dignity in an Age of Expertise. Manfred Stanley. LC 78-428. 1978. 17.95 (ISBN 0-02-930610-8). Free Pr.

Technological Conscience: Survival & Dignity in an Age of Expertise. Manfred Stanley. LC 81-8199. 1981. pap. 9.95X (ISBN 0-226-77096-6). U of Chicago Pr.

Technological Decisions & Democracy: European Experiments in Public Participation. Dorothy Welkin. LC 77-9133. pap. 28.00 (ISBN 0-317-10754-2, 2021937). Bks Demand UMI.

Technological Dependence, Monopoly & Growth. M. Merhav. 1969. 27.00 (ISBN 0-08-012754-1). Pergamon.

Technological Development. Dale Littler. 224p. 1988. 38.50x (ISBN 0-86003-530-1, Pub. by Philip Allan); pap. 15.00x (ISBN 0-86003-632-4, Pub. by Philip Allan). Humanities.

Technological Development in China, India & Japan: Cross-Cultural Perspectives. Erik Baark & Andrew Jamison. LC 85-22199. 172p. 1986. 32.50 (ISBN 0-312-78794-4). St Martin.

Technological Development Strategies for Developing Countries: A Review for Policy Makers. Maximo Halty-Carrere. 155p. 1979. pap. text ed. 12.95x (ISBN 0-920380-24-7, Pub. by Inst Res Pub Canada). Brookfield Pub Co.

Technological Developments & Their Implications for Employment in the Printing & Allied Trade, with Particular Reference to Developing Countries, Report III: Second Tripartite Technical Meeting for the Printing & Allied Trades, Geneva, 1981. 46p. (Orig.). 1981. pap. 7.00 (ISBN 92-2-102693-0). Intl Labour Office.

Technological Developments & Trends in Pediatric Radiology. Ed. by H. J. Kaufmann. (Progress in Pediatric Radiology Ser.: Vol. 7). (Illus.). 1979. 110.75 (ISBN 3-8055-2953-8). S Karger.

Technological Developments in Drugs & Pharmaceutical Industry in India. Husain Ahmad. 1988. 32.00x (ISBN 81-7013-004-2, Pub. by Navrang). South Asia Bks.

Technological Dictionary: Mechanics, Metallurgy, Hydraulics & Related Industries. Ed. by Michel Feutry et al. (In 4 languages). 1976. lib. bdg. 55.00x (ISBN 2-85608-000-6). Marlin.

Technological Diffusion & Industrialization Before 1914. A. G. Kenwood & A. L. Lougheed. LC 81-14332. 224p. 1982. 32.50x (ISBN 0-312-78795-2). St Martin.

Technological Diffusion & the Computer Revolution: The UK Experience. Paul Stoneman. LC 75-12136. (University of Cambridge, Dept. of Applied Economics, Monographs: No. 25). (Illus.). 231p. pap. 60.10 (2030623). Bks Demand UMI.

Technological Diffusion in the Hospital Sector. Louise B. Russell & Carol S. Burke. LC 75-37308. 240p. 1976. 8.00 (ISBN 0-89068-007-8). Natl Planning.

Technological Education-Technological Style. Ed. by Melvin Kranzberg. 1986. 15.00 (ISBN 0-911302-59-X). San Francisco Pr.

Technological Engineering Dictionary German-Serbocroatian. Ed. by S. Radic. 495p. (Ger., Serbian & Croatian.). 1981. 95.00 (ISBN 0-686-92294-8, M-9687). French & Eur.

Technological Entrepreneurship: The Allocation of Money & Effort in Technology-Based Firms. Patricia L. Braden. (Michigan Business Reports: No. 62). (Illus.). 1977. pap. 5.00 (ISBN 0-87712-187-7). UMI Div Res GSBA.

Technological Exchange - the US-Japanese Experience: Proceedings of a Japan-America Society of Washington Symposium, Washington, D.C., 1981. 132p. 1982. pap. 8.00. Japan-Am Soc.

Technological Forecasting: A Practical Approach. Marvin J. Cetron. 372p. 1969. 99.00 (ISBN 0-677-02140-2). Gordon & Breach.

Technological Forecasting for Decision-Making. 2nd ed. J. P. Martino. 384p. 1983. pap. 36.25 (ISBN 0-444-00722-9, North Holland). Elsevier.

Technological Frontiers & Foreign Relations. National Academy of Sciences et al. 320p. 1985. pap. text ed. 19.95x (ISBN 0-309-03541-4). Natl Acad Pr.

Technological Hazards. Ed. by Donald J. Zeigler et al. LC 83-22356. (Resource Publications in Geography). 90p. 1983. pap. 6.00 (ISBN 0-89291-173-5). Assn Am Geographers.

Technology & Education: Policy Implementation - Evaluation. LC 81-81832. 372p. 1981. 20.00 (ISBN 0-317-36894-X); 18.00 (ISBN 0-317-36895-8). Assn Ed Comm Tech.

Technology & Education: Policy, Implementation, Evaluation-Proceedings. National Conference on Technology & Education, January 26-28, 1981. 340p./1981. lib. bdg. 20.00 (ISBN 0-318-03015-2). Inst Educ Lead.

Technology & Empire: Perspectives on North America. George Grant. 143p. 1969. 16.95 (ISBN 0-88784-705-6, Pub. by Hse Anansi Pr Canada); pap. 8.95 (ISBN 0-88784-605-X). U of Toronto Pr.

Technology & Employment: Concepts & Clarifications. Eli Ginzberg et al. (CHR Studies in the New Economy Ser.). (Illus.). 118p. 1986. 27.50 (ISBN 0-8133-0399-0). Westview.

Technology & Employment in Footwear Manufacturing: A Study Prepared for the Int'l Labour Office Within the Framework of the World Employment Programme. Gerard K. Boon. LC 80-50458. 232p. 1980. 45.00x (ISBN 90-286-0170-8, Pub. by Sijthoff & Noordhoff). Kluwer Academic.

Technology & Employment in Industry: A Case Study Approach. 3rd, rev. & enl. ed. Ed. by A. A. Bhalla. v, 436p. 1985. pap. 26.25 (ISBN 92-2-103970-6). Intl Labour Office.

Technology & Employment in the Electronics Industry. Luc Soete & Giovanni Dosi. LC 83-43165. 90p. 1984. pap. 60.00 large format (ISBN 0-86187-378-5, Pub. by Frances Pinter). Longwood Pub Group.

Technology & Employment: Innovation & Growth in the U. S. Economy. National Academy of Science & National Academy of Engineering. Ed. by Richard M. Cyert & David M. Mowery. 288p. 1987. 34.95x (ISBN 0-309-03782-4); pap. 19.95x (ISBN 0-309-03744-1). Natl Acad Pr.

Technology & Employment Practices in Developing Countries. Hubert Schmitz. LC 85-6640. 254p. 1985. 32.50 (ISBN 0-7099-3301-0, Pub. by Croom Helm Ltd). Routledge Chapman & Hall.

Technology & Enterprise: Issac Holden & the Mechanisation of Woolcombing in France, 1848-1914. Katrina Honeyman & Jordon Goodman. (Pasold Studies in Textile History). 180p. 1986. text ed. 42.00 (ISBN 0-85967-727-3, Pub. by Gower Pub England). Gower Pub Co.

Technology & Global Industry: Companies & Nations in the World Economy. National Academy of Engineering Staff. 208p. 1987. pap. text ed. 19.95x (ISBN 0-309-03736-0). Natl Acad Pr.

Technology & Handicapped People. Office of Technology Assessment, Congress of the U. S. 224p. 1983. text ed. 29.50 (ISBN 0-8261-4510-8). Springer Pub.

Technology & Human Fulfillment. George W. Thompson, Jr. LC 85-6039. (Orig.). 1985. lib. bdg. 26.25 (ISBN 0-8191-4678-1); pap. text ed. 11.50 (ISBN 0-8191-4679-X). U Pr of Amer.

Technology & Human Productivity: Challanges for the Future. Ed. by John W. Murphy & John T. Pardeck. LC 85-23237. 256p. 1986. 38.95 (ISBN 0-89930-194-0, PTH/, Quorum Bks). Greenwood.

Technology & Human Service Delivery: Challenges & a Critical Perspective. Intros. by John W. Murphy & John T. Pardeck. LC 82-2794. (Computers in Human Services Ser.: Vol. 3, Nos. 1-2). (Illus.). 160p. 1988. text ed. 22.95 (ISBN 0-86656-731-3). Haworth Pr.

Technology & Human Values in American Civilization: A Guide to Information Sources. Ed. by Stephen H. Cutcliffe et al. (American Information Guide Ser.: Vol. 9). 728p. 1980. 68.00x (ISBN 0-8103-1475-4). Gale.

Technology & Humanism: Some Exploratory Essays for Our Times. William G. Carleton. LC 70-112601. 1970. 17.95x (ISBN 0-8265-1154-6). Vanderbilt U Pr.

Technology & Industry in Tanzania see African Industrialisation: Technology & Change in Tanzania.

Technology & Information Transfer: A Survey of Practice in Industrial Organizations. Richard S. Rosenbloom & Francis W. Wolek. LC 70-119550. pap. 47.50 (ISBN 0-317-10820-4, 2002225). Bks Demand UMI.

Technology & Institutional Response: Papers Presented to a Joint Session of the American Military Institute at the Duquesne History Forum, Pittsburgh, Pennsylvania, 1 November 1972. 132p. 1975. pap. text ed. 13.50x (ISBN 0-89126-007-2). MA-AH Pub.

Technology & International Affairs. Joseph S. Szyliowicz. LC 81-13985. 302p. 1981. 44.95 (ISBN 0-275-90727-9, C0727). Praeger.

Technology & International Relations. Ed. by Otto Hieronymi. 200p. 1987. 32.50 (ISBN 0-312-78933-5). St Martin.

Technology & Justice. George P. Grant. 128p. (Orig.). 1986. pap. 8.95 (ISBN 0-88784-152-X, Pub. by Hse Anansi Pr Cananda). U of Toronto Pr.

Technology & Labor: Study of the Human Problems of Labor Saving. Elliot D. Smith & Richmond C. Nyman. Ed. by Leon Stein. LC 77-70533. (Work Ser.). 1977. Repr. of 1939 ed. lib. bdg. 24.50x (ISBN 0-405-10201-1). Ayer Co Pubs.

Technology & Labour in Japanese Coal Mining. 65p. 1980. pap. 5.00 (ISBN 92-808-0082-5, TUNU090, UNU). UNIPUB.

Technology & Language Testing. Ed. by Charles W. Stansfield. 185p. 1986. 12.50. Tchrs Eng Spkrs.

Technology & Management in Court Reporting Systems. National Center for State Courts Staff. 34p. (On loan through the NCSC Library). 1973. write for info. (MAB-121). Natl Ctr St Courts.

Technology & Manufacture of Ammonia. Samuel Strelzoff. LC 87-21385. 308p. 1988. Repr. of 1981 ed. lib. bdg. 99.50 (ISBN 0-89464-250-2). Krieger.

Technology & Physics of Molecular Beam Epitaxy. Ed. by M. G. Dowsett & E. H. Parker. 680p. 1985. 89.50x (ISBN 0-306-41860-6, Plenum Pr). Plenum Pub.

Technology & Planned Organizational Change. James C. Taylor. LC 78-161549. 151p. 1971. 12.00x (ISBN 0-87944-003-1). Inst Soc Res.

Technology & Politics. Ed. by Michael E. Kraft & Norman J. Vig. 400p. 1988. lib. bdg. 59.75 (ISBN 0-8223-0838-X); pap. text ed. 17.95 (ISBN 0-8223-0846-0). Duke.

Technology & Production. G. Clews & R. Leonard. (Industrial Studies). 192p. 1985. text ed. 29.95x (ISBN 0-86003-527-1, Pub. by Philip Allan UK); pap. text ed. 9.95x (ISBN 0-86003-629-4). Humanities.

Technology & Reality. James Feibleman. 250p. 1982. 25.00 (ISBN 90-247-2519-4, Pub. by Martinus Nijhoff Netherlands). Kluwer Academic.

Technology & Responsibility. Ed. by Paul T. Durbin. 1987. lib. bdg. 69.00 (ISBN 90-277-2415-6, Pub. by Reidel Holland). KLuwer Academic.

Technology & Rural Women: Conceptual & Empirical Issues. Iftikhar Ahmed. (Illus.). 384p. 1985. text ed. 39.95x (ISBN 0-04-382043-3). Unwin Hyman.

Technology & Science in World Bank Operations. Ed. by Paul S. Shapiro. 292p. 1980. 8.00 (ISBN 0-8213-0058-X, BK 0058). World Bank.

Technology & Science of Informatics. 1987. write for info. Wiley.

Technology & Sector Choice in Economic Development. G. K. Boon. 324p. 1978. 40.00x (ISBN 90-286-0068-X, Pub. by Sijthoff & Noordhoff). Kluwer Academic.

Technology & Skills in ASEAN: An Overview. Ed. by C. Y Ng et al. 164p. 1987. pap. text ed. 21.50x (ISBN 9971-988-27-5, Pub. by Gower Pub England). Gower Pub Co.

Technology & Skills in Malaysia. H. Osman-Rani et al. 80p. 1987. pap. text ed. 13.95x (ISBN 9971-988-34-8, Pub. by Gower Pub England). Gower Pub Co.

Technology & Skills in Singapore. Chng Meng Kng et al. 124p. 1987. pap. text ed. 16.50x (ISBN 9971-988-32-1, Pub. by Gower Pub England). Gower Pub Co.

Technology & Social Change. 2nd ed. Ed. by H. Russell Bernard & Pertti Pelto. (Illus.). 393p. 1987. pap. text ed. 10.95x (ISBN 0-88133-261-5). Waveland Pr.

Technology & Social Change in Rural Areas. Ed. by Gene F. Summers. (Rural Studies Ser.). 400p. 1984. pap. 36.00x (ISBN 0-86531-600-7). Westview.

Technology & Social Complexity. Maurice N. Richter, Jr. LC 82-5683. 120p. 1983. 52.50 (ISBN 0-87395-644-3); pap. 17.95 (ISBN 0-87395-645-1). State U NY Pr.

Technology & Social Institutions. Ed. by Kan Chen. LC 74-77658. 224p. 1974. 23.05 (ISBN 0-87942-035-9, PC00315). Inst Electrical.

Technology & Social Progress. Ed. by Philip K. Eckman. (Science & Technology Ser.: Vol. 18). (Illus.). 1969. 20.00x (ISBN 0-87703-046-4, Pub. by Am Astronaut). Univelt Inc.

Technology & Social Shock. Edward W. Lawless. 1977. pap. 15.00x (ISBN 0-8135-0781-2). Rutgers U Pr.

Technology & Social Structure. Thomas P. Flack. 240p. 1986. 16.95. Enquiry Pr.

Technology & Society, 53 bks. Ed. by Daniel J. Boorstin. 1972. Repr. set. 1502.50 (ISBN 0-405-04680-4). Ayer Co Pubs.

Technology & Society. 11p. 1980. pap. 5.00 (ISBN 92-808-0171-6, TUNU185, UNU). UNIPUB.

Technology & Society under Lenin & Stalin. Kendall E. Bailes. LC 77-85558. (Studies of the Russian Institute, Columbia University). 1978. 58.50x (ISBN 0-691-05260-3); pap. 19.95x LPE (ISBN 0-691-10063-2). Princeton U Pr.

Technology & State: Monographs. Mary Vance. (Public Administration Ser., Bibliography: P 1808). 68p. 1985. pap. 10.50 (ISBN 0-89028-638-8). Vance Biblios.

Technology & Style. Ed. by W. D. Kingery. (Ceramics & Civilization Ser.: Vol. II). 350p. 1986. 60.00 (ISBN 0-916094-76-6). Am Ceramic.

Technology & the American Economic Transition: Choices for the Future. LC 87-61982. (Illus.). 509p. (Orig.). 1988. pap. 20.00 (S/N 052-003-01096-8). USGPO.

Technology & the Canadian Mind: Innis, McLuhan, Grant. Arthur Kroker. LC 85-14575. (New World Perspectives Ser.). 144p. (Orig.). 1985. 22.50 (ISBN 0-312-78831-2); pap. 8.95 (ISBN 0-312-78832-0). St Martin.

Technology & the Character of Contemporary Life: A Philosophical Inquiry. Albert Borgmann. LC 84-8639. viii, 302p. 1987. pap. 12.95 (ISBN 0-226-06629-0). U of Chicago Pr.

Technology & the Courts: An Update. National Center for State Courts Staff. (Research Essay Ser.). 10p. 1978. manuscript 0.60 (E-008). Natl Ctr St Courts.

Technology & the Future. 4th ed. Albert Teich. LC 85-61254. 224p. 1986. pap. text ed. write for info. (ISBN 0-312-78998-X). St Martin.

Technology & the Future: A Philosophical Challenge. Schuurman & Egbert. 1980. 19.95x (ISBN 0-88906-111-4). Radix Bks.

Technology & the Future of Health Care. Ed. by John B. McKinlay. (Milbank Readers Ser.: No. 8). 496p. 1982. pap. text ed. 13.95x (ISBN 0-262-63084-2). MIT Pr.

Technology & the Future of the U. S. Construction Industry. American Institute of Architects Staff. 1986. 33.95 (ISBN 0-913962-81-3). Am Inst Arch.

Technology & the Healing of the Earth. Thomas Berry. (Teilhard Studies). 1985. 3.00 (ISBN 0-89012-043-9). Anima Pubns.

Technology & the Human Condition. Bernard Gendron. LC 76-28120. 1977. write for info. (ISBN 0-312-78890-8); pap. text ed. 11.50 (ISBN 0-312-78925-4). St Martin.

Technology & the Human Prospect. Ed. by Roy MacLeod. 300p. 1986. 43.00 (ISBN 0-86187-530-3, Pub. by Frances Pinter). Longwood Pub Group.

Technology & the Quality of Health Care. Richard H. Egdahl & Paul M. Gertman. LC 78-7307. 336p. 1978. text ed. 43.95 (ISBN 0-89443-025-4). Aspen Pub.

Technology & the Regulation of Financial Markets. Ed. by Anthony Saunders & Lawrence J. White. LC 85-45050. (Salomon Brothers Center Bk.). 208p. 1986. 33.00x (ISBN 0-669-11143-0). Lexington Bks.

Technology & the Rise of the Networked City in Europe & America. Ed. by Joel A. Tarr & Gabriel Dupuy. (Technology & Urban Growth Ser.). (Illus.). 1988. 34.95 (ISBN 0-87722-540-0). Temple U Pr.

Technology & the Rural Community: The Social Impact. Ed. by M. J. Campbell. Orig. Title: New Technology & Rural Development. 432p. 1988. lib. bdg. 55.00x (ISBN 0-7099-4864-6, Pub. by Croom Helm UK). Routledge Chapman & Hall.

Technology & the Transformation of White Color Work. Ed. by Robert E. Kraut. 296p. 1987. text ed. 32.50 (ISBN 0-89859-633-5). L Erlbaum Assocs.

Technology & Union Survival: A Study of the Printing Industry. Daniel T. Scott. LC 87-2334. 204p. 1987. lib. bdg. 34.95 (ISBN 0-275-92680-X, C2680). Praeger.

Technology & Utopian Thought. Mulford Q. Sibley. LC 72-88752. (Critical Issues in Political Science Ser.). pap. 15.00 (ISBN 0-8357-9055-X, 2013326). Bks Demand UMI.

Technology & War. Martin Van Creveld. (Illus.). 304p. 1988. 22.95 (ISBN 0-02-933151-X). Free Pr.

Technology & Women's Voices Keeping in Touch. Ed. by Cheris Kramarae. 256p. 1988. pap. 13.95 (ISBN 0-7102-0679-8, Pub. by Routledge UK). Routledge Chapman & Hall.

Technology & Work: East West Comparisons. Ed. by Peter Grootings. 256p. 1986. 39.00 (ISBN 0-7099-3801-2, Pub. by Croom Helm Ltd). Routledge Chapman & Hall.

Technology & You. David L. Goetsch & John A. Nelson. LC 86-19751. 384p. 1987. text ed. 23.95 (ISBN 0-8273-2662-9); instr's. guide 8.00 (ISBN 0-8273-2663-7). Delmar.

Technology Applications GAP: Overcoming Constraints to Small-Farm Development. Deborah M. Sands. (FAO Research & Technology Paper Ser.: No. 1). 125p. (Orig.). 1986. pap. text ed. 13.50 (ISBN 92-5-102450-2, F2964, FAO). UNIPUB.

Technology As a Social & Political Phenomenon. Philip L. Bereano. LC 76-18723. pap. 144.10 (2032004). Bks Demand UMI.

Technology As Institutionally Related to Human Values. Ed. by Philip C. Ritterbush & Martin Green. LC 74-10037. 1974. 10.00 (ISBN 0-87491-511-2). Acropolis.

Technology Assessment: A Historical Approach. Illinois Institute of Technology Staff. 48p. 1985. pap. text ed. 4.95 saddle stitch (ISBN 0-8403-3730-2). Kendall-Hunt.

Technology Assessment & Development. Ed. by Mangalam Srinivisan. LC 82-3795. 288p. 1982. 38.95 (ISBN 0-275-90908-5, C0908). Praeger.

Technology Assessment & New Kidney Stone Treatment Methods. Ed. by Finn Kamper-Jorgensen et al. (Commission of the European Communities Health Services Research Ser.: No. 4). (Illus.). 208p. 1988. 49.95 (ISBN 0-19-261649-8). Oxford U Pr.

Technology Assessment: Creative Futures. Ed. by M. A. Boroush et al. (Systems Science & Engineering Ser.: Vol. 5). 406p. 1980. 74.00 (ISBN 0-444-00328-2, North-Holland). Elsevier.

Technology Assessment for Development. 166p. 1980. pap. 13.00 (ISBN 92-1-104084-1, E.80.II.A.1). UN.

Technology Assessment for State & Local Government: A Guide to Decision Making. Lawrence P. O'Keefe. LC 82-71314. pap. 55.50 (ISBN 0-317-26718-3, 2023520). Bks Demand UMI.

Technology Assessment for Water Supplies. Evan Vlachos & David W. Hendricks. LC 76-19871. 1977. 21.00 (ISBN 0-918334-13-6). WRP.

Technology Assessment in a Dynamic Environment. Ed. by Marvin J. Cetron & Bodo Bartocha. LC 72-75869. 1050p. 1973. 264.00 (ISBN 0-677-13150-X). Gordon & Breach.

Technology Assessment: Methods for Measuring the Level of Computer Security. William Neugent et al. LC 85-600600. (Computer Science & Technology Ser.). (Illus.). 216p. (Orig.). 1985. pap. 8.00 (ISBN 0-318-18852-X, S/N 003-003-02686-7). USGPO.

Technology Assessment Process: A Strategic Framework for Managing Technical Innovation. Blake L. White. 1988. lib. bdg. 39.95 (ISBN 0-89930-318-8, WTA/, Quorum Bks). Greenwood.

Technology Assimilation & Adaptation. 379p. 1986. pap. 19.00 (ISBN 0-317-59557-1, U-APO186, Pub. by APO). UNIPUB-Kraus Intl.

Technology Based Learning: Selected Readings. Nick Rushby. 250p. 1987. 37.50 (ISBN 0-89397-270-3). Nichols Pub.

Technology-Based Training: State of the Art Report, No. 8. Ed. by M. Labinger & P. J. Finch. (Infotech Ser.: No. 14). 368p. 1987. 428.00 (ISBN 0-08-034097-0). Pergamon.

Technology, Bureaucracy, & Healing in America. Roger J. Bulger. LC 88-14281. 138p. 1988. text ed. 14.50x (ISBN 0-87745-219-9). U of Iowa Pr.

Technology, Change & Society. rev. ed. Edward C. Pytlik et al. Ed. by Paul DeVore. LC 85-72427. (Illus.). 312p. 1985. text ed. 19.95 (ISBN 0-87192-170-7). Davis Mass.

Technology, Characterization & Properties of Epitaxial Electronic Materials: Proceedings of the Winter School, ICTP, Trieste, 13-24 January, 1986. Ed. by A. Baldereschi & C. Paorici. 340p. 1988. 58.00 (ISBN 9971-50-506-1). World Scientific Pub.

Technology Choice & Employment Generation by Multinational Enterprises in Developing Countries. viii, 91p. 1984. pap. 12.25 (ISBN 92-2-103718-5). Intl Labour Office.

Technology Choice in Developing Countries: The Textile & Pulp & Paper Industries. Michel A. Amsalem. (Illus.). 224p. 1983. 32.50x (ISBN 0-262-01072-0). MIT Pr.

Technology Common to Aero & Marine Engineering. Ed. by Society for Underwater Technology. 1988. lib. bdg. 118.00 (ISBN 1-85333-054-X, Pub. by Graham & Trotman UK). Kluwer Academic.

Technology, Competition, & the Soviet Bloc in the World Market. Kazimierz Z. Poznanski. LC 87-35050. (Research Ser.: No. 70). (Illus.). x, 226p. 1987. pap. 13.95x (ISBN 0-87725-170-3). U of Cal Intl St.

Technology Connection. Marc S. Gerstein. (A-W Organization Development Ser.). (Illus.). 144p. 1987. pap. text ed. write for info. (ISBN 0-201-12188-3). Addison-Wesley.

Technology Control, Competition & National Security: Conflict & Consensus. Ed. by Bernard L. Seward. LC 86-24999. 334p. (Orig.). 1987. lib. bdg. 29.75 (ISBN 0-8191-5735-X, Pub. by Ctr for Law & Natl Security); pap. text ed. 16.50 (ISBN 0-8191-5736-8). U Pr of Amer.

Technology Crossing Borders: The Choice, Transfer, & Management of International Technology Flows. Ed. by Robert Stobaugh & Louis T. Wells, Jr. LC 83-26591. 340p. 1984. 29.50 (ISBN 0-87584-158-9). Harvard Busn.

Technology, Culture & Communication: A Report to the French Minister of Research & Industry. A. Mattelart & Y. Stourdze. (Information Research & Resource Reports Ser.: Vol. 6). 244p. 1985. 66.00 (ISBN 0-444-87606-5, North-Holland). Elsevier.

Technology-Dependent Children: Hospital vs. Home Care. Office of Technology Assessment Task Force Staff. LC 65-20068. (SIRC Bk.). (Illus.). 1987. 27.50 (ISBN 0-397-53006-4, Lippincott Medical). Lippincott.

Technology, Development & the Environment: A Re-Appraisal. A. K. Reddy. (Illus.). 60p. 1980. pap. 9.75 (ISBN 0-08-025693-7). Pergamon.

Technology Development in Developing Countries. Hyung S. Choi. 301p. 1986. 22.75 (ISBN 92-833-1085-3, U-APO184, Pub. by APO); pap. 18.50 (ISBN 92-833-1086-1, U-APO172, Pub. by APO). UNIPUB-Kraus Intl.

Technology Diffusion: Federal Programs & Procedures. Granville W. Hough. LC 73-88035. 406p. 1975. 44.00 (ISBN 0-912338-05-9); microfiche 12.50 (ISBN 0-912338-06-7). Lomond.

Technology, Economic Growth & the Labour Process. Phil Blackburn et al. LC 84-22849. 272p. 1985. 29.95 (ISBN 0-312-79001-5). St Martin.

Technology Edge: Opportunities for America in World Competition. Gerard K. O'Neill. 256p. 1984. 16.95 (ISBN 0-671-44766-1). S&S.

Technology, Education, & the Measurement of Productivity: Early Papers with Notes to Subsequent Literature. Zvi Griliches. (Illus.). 288p. 1988. text ed. price not set (ISBN 0-631-15614-3). Basil Blackwell.

Technology Policy & Economic Performance: Lessons from Japan. Christopher Freeman. 150p. 1987. 25.00 (ISBN 0-86187-928-7, Pub. by Pinter Pubs UK). Columbia U Pr.

Technology, Politics, & Society in China. Rudi Volti. (Special Studies on China & East Asia). 350p. 1982. lib. bdg. 39.00 (ISBN 0-89158-951-1). Westview.

Technology, Power & Social Change. Ed. by Charles A. Thrall & Jerold M. Starr. LC 74-4213. (Arcturus Books Paperbacks). 179p. 1974. pap. 2.45x (ISBN 0-8093-0688-3). S Ill U Pr.

Technology, Public Policy, & the Changing Structure of American Agriculture. (OTA-F Ser.: No. 285). (Illus.). 380p. (Orig.). 1986. pap. 13.00 (ISBN 0-318-20154-2, S/N 052-003-01018-6). USGPO.

Technology, Regions, & Policy. Ed. by John Rees. 336p. 1986. 36.95x (ISBN 0-8476-7409-6, Rowman & Littlefield). Rowman.

Technology, Strategy, & Arms Control. Ed. by Wolfram F. Hanrieder. 162p. 1985. 39.00 (ISBN 0-8133-0177-7). Westview.

Technology, Strategy & National Security. Ed. by Franklin D. Margiotta & Ralph Sanders. LC 85-600557. 209p. (Orig.). 1985. pap. 3.75 (ISBN 0-318-18853-8, S/N 008-020-01027-8). USGPO.

Technology, Strategy & Politics of SDI. Stephen J. Cimbala. (Special Studies in National Security & Defense Policy). 238p. 1987. pap. 34.50 (ISBN 0-8133-7116-3). Westview.

Technology, the Economy, & Society: The American Experience. Ed. by Joel Colton & Stuart Bruchey. LC 86-24475. 304p. 1987. 35.00 (ISBN 0-231-05964-7). Columbia U Pr.

Technology, the University, & the Community. Ed. by George Bugliarello & H. A. Simon. 1976. 65.00 (ISBN 0-08-017872-3). Pergamon.

Technology to Payoff: Managing the New Product from Creation to Customer. Frederick J. Buttrell. LC 84-7673. 200p. 1985. 37.50x (ISBN 0-915601-00-1). Swansea Pr.

Technology Trade with the Middle East: Policy Issues & Economic Trends. James J. Emery et al. (Special Studies in International Economics & Business). 350p. 1985. pap. 31.00x (ISBN 0-8133-7043-4). Westview.

Technology, Tradition, & the State in Africa. John R. Goody. LC 79-24375. 96p. pap. 25.00 (2030597). Bks Demand UMI.

Technology Transfer, 3 vols. Sagafi-Nejad. (Pergamon Policy Studies on International Development). 1983. Set. 145.00 (ISBN 0-08-028070-6). Pergamon.

Technology Transfer: A Project Guide for International HRD. Ed. by Angus Reynolds. LC 83-12865. (Illus.). 145p. 1984. 21.00 (ISBN 0-934634-68-8). Intl Human Res.

Technology Transfer: A Realistic Approach. Silvere Seurat. LC 78-62608. 174p. 1979. 19.00x (ISBN 0-87201-822-9). Gulf Pub.

Technology Transfer: A Unit Report from the Energy Task Force of the Urban Cosortium. 80p. 1981. 15.00 (ISBN 0-318-17348-4, DG/81-305). Pub Tech Inc.

Technology Transfer: An Executive Guide. R. Duane Hall. LC 87-4954. Date not set. price not set (ISBN 0-394-55325-X). Random.

Technology Transfer & Change in the Arab World: Proceedings of a Seminar, Beirut, Oct. 1977. United Nations Economic Commission for Western Asia, Natural Resources, Science & Technology Division. Ed. by A. B. Zahlan. 1979. 110.00 (ISBN 0-08-022435-0). Pergamon.

Technology Transfer & Development: India's Hindustan Machine Tools Company. R. C. Mascarenhas. 235p. 1982. pap. 30.50x (ISBN 0-86531-934-0). Westview.

Technology Transfer & East-West Relations. Mark E. Schaffer. 288p. write for info. (ISBN 0-7099-3416-5). St Martin.

Technology Transfer & East-West Relations. Ed. by Mark E. Schaffer. LC 84-40373. 384p. 1985. 39.95 (ISBN 0-312-79016-3). St Martin.

Technology Transfer & Economic Development. Ed. by Robert G. Hawkins. (Research in International Business & Finance Ser.: Vol. 2). 350p. 1981. 56.50 (ISBN 0-89232-140-7). Jai Pr.

Technology Transfer & Foreign Trade: The Case of Japan, 1950 to 1966. rev. ed. Yoshihiro Tsurumi. Ed. by Stuart Bruchey. LC 80-600. (Multinational Corporations Ser.). (Illus.). 1980. lib. bdg. 28.50x (ISBN 0-405-13390-1). Ayer Co Pubs.

Technology Transfer & Human Factors. Charles T. Stewart, Jr. & Yasumitsu Nihei. 224p. 1986. 33.00x (ISBN 0-669-14251-4). Lexington Bks.

Technology Transfer & Human Values: Concepts, Applications, Cases. Peter B. Heller. (Illus.). 380p. (Orig.). 1985. lib. bdg. 31.50 (ISBN 0-8191-4548-3); pap. text ed. 16.50 (ISBN 0-8191-4549-1). U Pr of Amer.

Technology Transfer & Nationalization in Ghana. Stephen Adei. (Technology Transfer & Nationalization Ser.). 113p. (Orig.). 1987. pap. text ed. 12.00 (ISBN 0-317-67087-5, IDRCTS55, Pub. by IDRC). UNIPUB.

Technology Transfer & U. S. Security Assistance: The Impact of Licensed Production. David J. Louscher & Michael D. Salomone. (Westview Special Studies in National Security & Defense Policy). 192p. 1986. pap. 24.50 (ISBN 0-8133-7302-6). Westview.

Technology Transfer Between East & West. Eugene Zaleski & Helgard Wienert. 435p. 1980. 50.00 (ISBN 92-64-12125-0). OECD.

Technology Transfer by Multinationals, Vol. 2. Ed. by H. W. Singer. 1987. 32.00x (ISBN 81-7024-160-X, Pub. by Ashish India). South Asia Bks.

Technology Transfer by State & Local Government. Samuel I. Doctors. LC 81-11194. 280p. 1981. text ed. 35.00 (ISBN 0-89946-050-X). Oelgeschlager.

Technology Transfer Directory. 330p. 1986. 55.00 (ISBN 0-318-21243-9). GRQ Inc.

Technology Transfer: Geographic, Economic, Cultural & Technical Dimensions. Ed. by A. Coskun Samli. LC 84-16113. (Illus.). xviii, 296p. 1985. lib. bdg. 40.95 (ISBN 0-89930-057-X, SBK/, Quorum). Greenwood.

Technology Transfer: How to Make It Work, a Management Handbook. Hyman Olken. 92p. 1972. pap. 7.00 (ISBN 0-934818-00-2). Olken Pubns.

Technology Transfer in Export Processing Zones the Semiconductor Industry in Malaysia. Ed. by Mark Lester. (Contemporary Studies in Economic & Financial Analysis: Vol. 47). 1988. 52.50 (ISBN 0-89232-429-5). Jai Pr.

Technology Transfer in Fibres, Textile & Apparel. Gerard K. Boon. 600p. 1981. 166.25 (ISBN 90-286-0520-7, Pub. by Sijthoff & Noordhoff). Kluwer Academic.

Technology Transfer in Industrialized Countries. Ed. by S. Gee. 464p. 1979. 35.00x (ISBN 90-286-0038-8, Pub. by Sijthoff & Noordhoff). Kluwer Academic.

Technology Transfer in Rural Industries: Cases & Analysis. T. K. Moulik & P. Purushotham. 1986. 18.50 (ISBN 0-86132-124-3, Pub. by Popular Prakashan). South Asia Bks.

Technology Transfer in the Developing World: The Case of the Chile Foundation. Frank Meissner. LC 87-36127. 192p. 1988. lib. bdg. 37.95 (ISBN 0-275-92926-4, C2926). Praeger.

Technology Transfer in the Peoples' Republic of China: Law & Practice. Richard J. Goossen. LC 86-33343. 1987. 62.50 (ISBN 9-02-473442-8, Pub. by Kluwer-Nijhoff (Netherlands)). Kluwer Academic.

Technology Transfer: Law & Practice in Latin America. International Law & Practice Section. 360p. 1980. 12.00. Amer Bar Assn.

Technology Transfer Law: The Export Administrative Acts of the United States, 1969-1985 Federal Laws, Legislative Histories, &.., 15 vols. in 33 bks. Bernard D. Reams, Jr. 1986. Repr. Set 1495.00 (ISBN 0-89941-437-0). W S Hein.

Technology Transfer: New Issues, New Analysis. Ed. by Alan W. Heston & Howard Pack. (Annals of the American Academy of Political & Social Science: Vol. 458). 322p. 1981. 15.00 (ISBN 0-8039-1707-4). Sage.

Technology Transfer Practice on International Firms. Ed. by F. Bradbury. 324p. 1978. 37.50x (ISBN 9-0286-0377-8, Pub. by Sijthoff & Noordhoff). Kluwer Academic.

Technology Transfer, Productivity, & Economic Policy. Edwin Mansfield et al. 1983. 35.50 (ISBN 0-393-95222-3). Norton.

Technology Transfer: Survey of an Emerging Service Industry. Justin A. Bereny. 130p. 1986. pap. 49.50x (ISBN 0-89934-231-0, Pub. by Busn-Tech Info). Busn Tech Info Serv.

Technology Transfer, the Research Process, & Creating a Productive Environment. (Record). 51p. 1979. 3.00 (ISBN 0-309-02993-7). Transport Res Bd.

Technology Transfer to & from the Soviet Bloc: A Bibliography. Ben Silverstein. (Public Administration Ser.: P 1986). 5p. 1986. 3.00 (ISBN 0-89028-966-2). Vance Biblios.

Technology Transfer to China. LC 87-619823. (OTA-ISC-340). (Illus.). 251p. (Orig.). 1987. pap. 10.00 (S/N 052-003-01069-1). USGPO.

Technology Transfer to Developing Countries: The Case of the Fertilizer Industry. Subrata Ghatak. Ed. by Edward I. Altman & Ingo Walter. LC 80-82478. (Contemporary Studies in Economic & Financial Analysis: Vol. 27). 200p. 1981. 52.50 (ISBN 0-89232-160-1). Jai Pr.

Technology Trap. Leo J. Moser. LC 78-26034. 288p. 1979. 23.95x (ISBN 0-88229-419-9); pap. 11.95 (ISBN 0-88229-669-8). Nelson-Hall.

Technology Two Thousand. Peter Evans. (Your World 2000 Ser.). (Illus.). 64p. (YA) (gr. 7 up). 1986. 12.95 (ISBN 0-8160-1155-9). Facts on File.

Technology Utilization Ideas for the 70's & Beyond: Proceedings of the Governor Rockefeller Symposium, Winrock, Arkansas, October 1970. Ed. by Fred W. Forbes & Paul Dergarabedian. (Science & Technology Ser.: Vol. 26). 1971. lib. bdg. 30.00x (ISBN 0-87703-057-X, Pub. by Am Astronaut). Univelt Inc.

Technology Vectors: Science of Advanced Material & Process Engineering Ser, Vol. 29. (Illus.). 1611p. 1984. 60.00 (ISBN 0-938994-24-7). Soc Adv Material.

Technology Venturing: American Innovation & Risk-Taking. Ed. by Eugene B. Konecci & Robert L. Kuhn. LC 85-12192. 272p. 1985. 38.95 (ISBN 0-275-90211-0, C0211). Praeger.

Technology, Vol. 2 (incl. 1983-1987 Supplements) Ed. by Eleanor C. Goldstein. (Social Issues Resources Ser.). 1987. 75.00 (ISBN 0-89777-060-9). Soc Issues.

Technology War: A Case for Competitiveness. David H. Brandin & Michael A. Harrison. LC 87-6167. 244p. 1987. 24.95 (ISBN 0-471-83455-6, Pub. by Wiley-Interscience). Wiley.

Technology, Women & Farming Systems. Heather Baser. (Studies in Technology & Social Change: No. 5). 26p. (Orig.). 1988. pap. text ed. 4.00 (ISBN 0-945271-08-5). ISU-TSCP.

Technology, World Politics, & American Policy. Victor Basiuk. LC 76-51841. (Institute of War & Peace Studies). 409p. 1977. 40.00x. Columbia U Pr.

Technology's Crucible. James Martin. (Illus.). 192p. 1986. pap. 15.95 (ISBN 0-13-902024-1). P-H.

Technology's Future: The Hague Congress Technology Assessment. Thomas J. Knight. LC 80-22193. 264p. 1982. text ed. 14.50 (ISBN 0-89874-283-8). Krieger.

Technology's Storytellers: Reweaving the Human Fabric. John M. Staudenmaier. 350p. 1985. text ed. 37.50x (ISBN 0-262-19237-3). MIT Pr.

Technomics: The Economics of Technology & the Computer Industry. William H. Inmon. 200p. 1985. 35.00 (ISBN 0-87094-688-9). Dow Jones-Irwin.

Technophobia: Getting Out of the Technology Trap. Hal Hellman. LC 75-44372. 324p. 1976. 8.95 (ISBN 0-87131-206-9). M Evans.

Technopolis Strategy: Japan, High Technology & the Control of the 21st Century. Sheridan M. Tatsuno. (Illus.). 320p. 1985. pap. 19.95 (ISBN 0-89303-885-7). Brady Comp Bks.

Technostress: The Human Cost of the Computer Revolution. Craig Brod & Wes St. John. 288p. canceled (ISBN 0-201-11211-6). Addison-Wesley.

Teckla. Steven Brust. 224p. 1987. pap. 2.95 (ISBN 0-441-79977-9, Pub. by Ace Science Fiction). Ace Bks.

Tecnica. J. A. Lopez. (Span.). 7.95 (ISBN 84-241-5628-5). E Torres & Sons.

Tecnica de Navegacion y Pilotaje Marino. 2nd ed. Antonio Marquez. Ed. by USAmerica Publishing. LC 84-52183. (Illus.). 152p. (Span.). 1985. 12.50 (ISBN 0-934763-00-3). Usamerica.

Tecnica del Maestro. Raymund Andrea. 173p. (Orig., Span.). 1984. pap. 7.00 (ISBN 0-912057-85-8, GS-513). AMORC.

Tecnica Edilizia Romana, 2 Vols. Giuseppe Lugli. (It). Repr. of 1957 ed. Set. 225.00 (ISBN 0-384-34180-2). Johnson Repr.

Tecnicas Mecanograficas Modernas. 3rd ed. J. Q. Gorbea. 240p. 1979. text ed. 20.88 (ISBN 0-07-023791-3). McGraw.

Tecnologia Farmaceutica Industrial. Rodolfo S. Escabi. LC 76-46412. (Orig., Span.). 1977. pap. 10.00 (ISBN 0-8477-2321-6). U of PR Pr.

Teco Art Pottery. Ars Ceramica, Ltd. Staff. (Illus.). 1.50 (ISBN 0-89344-029-9). Ars Ceramica.

Tectomagnetics & Local Geomagnetic Field Variations. Ed. by M. Fuller et al. (Advances in Earth & Planetary Sciences Ser.: No. 5). 140p. 1979. 22.50x (ISBN 0-89955-212-9, Pub. by Japan Sci Soc Japan). Intl Spec Bk.

Tectonic & Geologic Evolution of Southeast Asian Seas & Islands, Pt. 1. Ed. by D. E. Hayes. (Geophysical Monograph Ser.: Vol. 23). 334p. 1980. 32.00 (ISBN 0-87590-023-2). Am Geophysical.

Tectonic & Geologic Evolution of Southeast Asian Seas & Islands, Pt. 2. Ed. by D. E. Hayes. (Geophysical Monograph: Vol. 27). 396p. 1983. 42.00 (ISBN 0-87590-053-4). Am Geophysical.

Tectonic Controls on Magma Chemistry. Ed. by S. D. Weaver & R. W. Johnson. 286p. 1987. 109.75 (ISBN 0-444-42862-3). Elsevier.

Tectonic Essays, Mainly Alpine. E. B. Bailey. 1935. 39.50x (ISBN 0-19-854368-9). Oxford U Pr.

Tectonic Evolution of a Forearc Terrane, Southern Scotia Ridge, Antarctica. Ian W. Dalziel. (Special Paper Ser.: No. 200). (Illus.). 1984. 9.00 (ISBN 0-8137-2200-4). Geol Soc.

Tectonic Evolution of the Caledonide-Appalachian Orogen. Ed. by R. A. Gayer. 194p. 1985. pap. 39.50 (ISBN 3-528-08596-7, Pub. by Vieweg & Sohn). IPS.

Tectonic Geology of the Himalaya. Ed. by P. S. Saklani. (Current Trends in Geology Ser.: Vol. I). 340p. 1978. 50.00 (ISBN 0-88065-187-3, Pub. by Messers Today & Tomorrows Printers & Publishers India). Scholarly Pubns.

Tectonic Geomorphology. Ed. by J. T. Hack & M. Morisawa. (Binghamton Symposia in Geomorphology International Ser.: No. 15). 400p. 1985. text ed. 50.00 (ISBN 0-04-551098-9). Unwin Hyman.

Tectonic Influence on Sedimentation, Early Cretaceous, East Flank Powder River Basin, Wyoming & South Dakota. R. J. Weimer et al. Ed. by Jon Raese & J. H. Goldberg. LC 82-17894. (Colorado School of Mines Quarterly: Vol. 77, No. 4). (Illus.). 61p. 1983. pap. text ed. 12.00 (ISBN 0-686-82131-9). Colo Sch Mines.

Tectonic Processes. Darrell Weyman. (Process in Physical Geography Ser.: No. 4). (Illus.). 128p. (Orig.). 1981. pap. text ed. 12.95x (ISBN 0-04-551044-X). Unwin Hyman.

Tectonic Settings of Regional Metamorphism. Ed. by E. R. Oxburgh et al. (Philosophical Transactions of Royal Society, Series A: Vol. 321, 1987). (Illus.). 276p. 1987. lib. bdg. 107.00x (ISBN 0-85403-290-8, Pub. by Royal Soc London). Scholium Intl.

Tectonic Stresses in the Alpine-Mediterranean Region: Proceedings. Ed. by A. E. Scheidegger. (Rock Mechanics Supplementum: Vol. 9). (Illus.). 270p. 1980. pap. 75.60 (ISBN 0-387-81578-3). Springer-Verlag.

Tectonics & Geophysics of Continental Rifts. Ed. by Ivar B. Ramberg & Else-Ragnhild Neumann. (NATO Advanced Study Institute Ser.: No. 37). 1978. lib. bdg. 42.00 (ISBN 90-277-0867-3, Pub. by Reidel Holland). Kluwer Academic.

Tectonics & Sedimentation. Ed. by W. M. Dickinson. (Special Publication Ser.: No. 22). 204p. 1974. 16.00 (ISBN 0-918985-03-X); members 13.00. SEPM.

Tectonics of Africa: Explanatory Memoir on International Tectonic Map of Africa. 29.00 (ISBN 92-3-000872-9, U666, UNESCO). UNIPUB.

Tectonics of Asia. Emile Argand. Ed. by Albert V. Carozzi. LC 76-14288. 1977. 23.95x (ISBN 0-02-840390-8). Hafner.

Tectonics of Middle North America: Middle North America East of the Cordilleran Systems. Philip B. King. (Illus.). 1969. Repr. 19.95x (ISBN 0-02-847920-3). Hafner.

Tectonics: Proceedings of the 27th International Geological Congress, Vol. 7. International Geological Congress Staff. 392p. 1984. lib. bdg. 97.50 (ISBN 90-6764-016-6). Coronet Bks.

Tectonics, Sedimentation, & Petroleum Potential, Northern Denver Basin, Colorado, Wyoming, and Nebraska. Stephen A. Sonnenberg & Robert J. Weimer. Ed. by Jon W. Raese. LC 81-17980. (Colorado School of Mines Quarterly Ser.: Vol. 76, No. 2). (Illus.). 45p. 1981. pap. text ed. 10.00 (ISBN 0-686-46973-9). Colo Sch Mines.

Tecumseh: An Indian Moses. William H. Van Hoose. LC 84-17557. 244p. (gr. 8 up). 1984. lib. bdg. 18.95 (ISBN 0-938936-24-7); pap. 6.95 (ISBN 0-938936-25-5). Daring Bks.

Tecumseh & the Quest for Indian Leadership. R. David Edmunds. (Library of American Biographers). 1984. pap. text ed. write for info. (ISBN 0-673-39336-4). Scott F.

Tecumseh & the Quest for Indian Leadership. R. David Edmunds. 256p. 1984. 14.95 (ISBN 0-316-21151-6). Little.

Tecumseh & the Shawnee Prophet. Edward Eggleston & Lillie E. Seeyle. 327p. 1981. Repr. of 1878 ed. lib. bdg. 50.00 (ISBN 0-89987-211-5). Darby Bks.

Tecumseh, Past & Present. 56p. 1957. 5.50 (ISBN 0-686-46439-7). Shawnee County Hist.

Tecumseh, Shawnee War Chief. new ed. Jane Fleischer. LC 78-18046. (Illus.). 48p. (gr. 4-6). 1979. PLB 9.59 (ISBN 0-89375-153-7); pap. 1.95 (ISBN 0-89375-143-X). Troll Assocs.

Tecumseh: Shawnee Warrior-Statesman. James McCague. LC 73-83167. (Indians Ser.). (Illus.). 80p. (gr. 2-5). 1970. PLB 6.69 (ISBN 0-8116-6607-7). Garrard.

Tecumseh: Vision of Glory. Glenn Tucker. LC 72-85011. (Illus.). 399p. 1973. Repr. of 1956 ed. 25.00x (ISBN 0-8462-1698-1). Russell.

Tecumseh's Last Stand. John Sugden. LC 85-40480. (Illus.). 288p. 1985. 19.95 (ISBN 0-8061-1944-6). U of Okla Pr.

Ted & Dolly Fairytale Flight. Richard Fowler. (Slot Books). (Illus.). 24p. (ps-3). 1984. 8.95 (ISBN 0-88110-190-7). EDC.

Ted & Dolly's Magic Carpet Ride. Richard Fowler. (Slot Bks.). 24p. (ps-1). 1984. 8.95 (ISBN 0-88110-155-9). EDC.

Ted & Dottie in a Day of Fun. Wade Davis. (Illus.). (gr. 1-2). 1967. text ed. 6.84 (ISBN 0-87443-032-1). Benson.

Ted Brewer Explains Sailboat Design. Ted Brewer. LC 84-48686. (Illus.). 240p. 1985. 17.95 (ISBN 0-87742-193-5). Intl Marine.

Ted Bundy: The Deliberate Stranger. Richard Larsen. Date not set. pap. 3.95 (ISBN 0-671-63032-6). PB.

Ted E. Bear Finds Christmas. Diane Mayfield. 32p. (ps-2). 1988. 4.95 (ISBN 0-8249-8251-7). Ideals.

Ted E. Bear Finds Christmas: Sound Classics. 32p. (ps-2). 1988. 9.95 (ISBN 0-8249-7277-5). Ideals.

Ted E. Bear Rescues Santa Claus. (gr. k-5). 1985. 2.95 (ISBN 0-8249-8115-4). Ideals.

Ted Hughes. Dennis Walder. (Open Guides to Literature Ser.). 128p. 1987. 42.00x (ISBN 0-335-15113-2, Open Univ Pr); pap. 13.00x (ISBN 0-335-15112-4, Open Univ Pr). Taylor & Francis.

Ted Hughes. Thomas West. 96p. 1985. pap. 5.95 (ISBN 0-416-35400-9, NO. 9032). Routledge Chapman & Hall.

Ted Hughes: A Bibliography, 1946-1980. Keith Sagar & Stephen Tabor. 274p. 1982. 47.00x (ISBN 0-7201-1654-6). Mansell.

Ted Hughes: A Critical Study. Terry Gifford & Neil Roberts. 288p. 1986. pap. 17.95 (ISBN 0-571-13932-9). Faber & Faber.

Ted Hughes: A Critical Study. Neil Roberts & Terry Gifford. 288p. 1981. 25.00 (ISBN 0-571-11701-5); pap. 17.95. Faber & Faber.

Teddy's Best Toys. (Cuddle Doll Bks.). (Illus.). 12p. (ps). 1985. 3.95 (ISBN 0-394-87111-1, BYR). Random.
Teddy's Birthday Party. Michelle Cartlidge. (Picture Puffins Activity Book Ser.). (Illus.). 8p. (Orig.). (ps up). 1986. pap. 3.95 (ISBN 0-14-032068-7, Puffin). Penguin.
Teddy's Birthday Party. Arthur L. Farnham & Lorraine J. Farnham. (gr. 3-5). 1984. 5.95 (ISBN 0-533-05944-5). Vantage.
Teddy's Christmas. Michelle Cartlidge. (Illus.). 32p. (ps). 1986. pap. 9.95 (ISBN 0-671-62912-3, Little Simon). S&S.
Teddy's Christmas Cutout Book. Amanda Davidson. (Illus.). 10p. (gr. k-2). 1987. 3.95 (ISBN 0-8050-0560-9). H Holt & Co.
Teddy's Christmas Gift. Jan Mogensen. LC 82-26095. (Teddy Tales Ser.). (Illus.). 29p. (ps-2). 1985. PLB 9.95 (ISBN 1-55532-004-X). Stevens Inc.
Teddy's Dinner. Michelle Cartlidge. (Teddy Bear Board Bks.). (Illus.). (ps). 1986. bds. 2.95 (ISBN 0-671-61347-2, Little Simon). S&S.
Teddy's Ear. Niki Daly. (Illus.). 24p. (ps-1). 1985. 4.95 (ISBN 0-670-80808-3). Viking.
Teddy's Favorite. Thomas L. Hakes. (gr. k). 1985. pap. 2.75x (ISBN 0-915020-50-5). Bardic.
Teddy's Favorite Food. Amanda Davidson. LC 85-60280. (Illus.). 12p. (ps-k). 1985. 3.95 (ISBN 0-03-005002-2). H Holt & Co.
Teddy's First Christmas. Amanda Davidson. LC 82-82092. (Illus.). 24p. (ps-2). 1982. 7.95 (ISBN 0-03-062616-1). H Holt & Co.
Teddy's Garden. Michelle Cartlidge. (Teddy Bear Board Bks.). (Illus.). (ps). 1986. bds. 2.95 (ISBN 0-671-61346-4, Little Simon). S&S.
Teddy's Holiday. Michelle Cartlidge. (Puffin Activity Bks.). (ps up). 1987. pap. 3.95 (ISBN 0-317-52434-8, Puffin Bks). Penguin.
Teddy's House. Michelle Cartlidge. (Teddy Bear Board Bks.). (Illus.). (ps). 1986. bds. 2.95 (ISBN 0-671-61345-6, Little Simon). S&S.
Teddy's Toys. Michelle Cartlidge. (Teddy Bear Board Bks.). (Illus.). (ps). 1986. bds. 2.95 (ISBN 0-671-61348-0, Little Simon). S&S.
Teddy's Toys. Amye Rosenberg. (Golden Sturdy Shape Bks.). (Illus.). 14p. (ps-k). 1986. 2.95 (ISBN 0-307-12315-4, Pub. by Golden Bks). Western Pub.
Teddy's Trip to Africa. Arthur L. Farnham & Lorraine J. Farnham. (Illus.). (gr. 3-5). 1982. 5.95 (ISBN 0-533-05288-2). Vantage.
Teddy's Winter Adventure. Ken Forsse. (Teddy Ruxpin Adventure Ser.). (Illus.). 26p. (ps). 1985. incl. audio-cassette 9.95 (ISBN 0-934323-12-7). Alchemy Comms.
Ted's Stroke: The Caregiver's Story. Ellen Paullin. Ed. by Calvin Kytle & Jane Gold. LC 88-1872. 160p. 1988. 14.95 (ISBN 0-932020-54-2). Seven Locks Pr.
Tee-Ga's Story: A Cougar's Autobiography. Jim Swayne & Ot-Ne-We Swayne. (Illus.). 105p. 1986. pap. 10.00 (ISBN 0-9608008-3-2). Legacy Hse.
TEE in Japan: A Realistic Vision: the Feasibility of Theological Education by Extension for Churches in Japan. W. Frederic Sprunger. LC 81-7739. (Illus.). 472p. (Orig.). 1981. pap. 15.95x (ISBN 0-87808-434-7). William Carey Lib.
Tee Time. Charlie Achuff. (Illus.). 66p. (Orig.). 1988. pap. 5.95 (ISBN 1-55618-050-0). Brunswick Pub.
Tee Time Toddler. Ted Lynn & Mary Lynn. Ed. by Kathryn Marcouiller. (Toddler Ser). 48p. (Orig.). 1987. pap. 2.95 (ISBN 0-944009-00-X). Compupress.
Teen-Age Buddy. Milton Bowser. Ed. by Mary M. MacLean. (Illus.). 100p. (Orig.). 1984. pap. 5.00 (ISBN 0-940178-28-1). Sitare Inc.
Teen-Age Dance Book. B. White. (Ballroom Dance Ser.). 1985. lib. bdg. 79.95 (ISBN 0-87700-711-X). Revisionist Pr.
Teen-Age Dance Book. B. White. (Ballroom Dance Ser.). 1986. lib. bdg. 79.95 (ISBN 0-8490-3379-9). Gordon Pr.
Teen-Age Detective Stories. Ed. by Abraham L. Furman. LC 68-23983. (gr. 6-10). 1968. 4.25 (ISBN 0-8313-0044-2). Lantern.
Teen-Age Great Rescue Stories. Ed. by Abraham L. Furman. (gr. 6-10). PLB 6.19 (ISBN 0-8313-0050-7). Lantern.
Teen-Age Party Time Stories. Ed. by Abraham L. Furman. (gr. 6-10). 1966. PLB 6.19 (ISBN 0-8313-0039-6). Lantern.
Teen-age Pregnancies: Can We Afford Not to Prevent Them? Patrick D. Bustos. (State Legislative Reports: Vol. 12, No. 10). 1987. pap. 5.00 (ISBN 1-55516-183-9). Natl Conf State Legis.
Teen-Age Secret Agent Stories. Ed. by Abraham L. Furman. (Teen-Age Library). (gr. 5-10). PLB 6.19 (ISBN 0-8313-0042-6). Lantern.
Teen-Age Space Adventures. Ed. by Abraham L. Furman. 192p. (YA) (gr. 7 up). 1972. PLB 6.19 (ISBN 0-8313-1595-4). Lantern.
Teen-Age Spy Stories. Ed. by Abraham L. Furman. (gr. 6-10). 4.25 (ISBN 0-8313-0041-8); PLB 6.19. Lantern.
Teen-Age Suspense Stories. Ed. by Richard M. Elam. (gr. 6-10). 1963. PLB 6.19 (ISBN 0-8313-0047-7). Lantern.
Teen-Age Underwater Adventure. Ed. by Thomas. (Illus.). (gr. 6-10). 1962. PLB 6.19 (ISBN 0-8313-0091-4). Lantern.
Teen-Ager, the Bible Speaks to You. W. Riess. 104p. 1987. pap. 3.95 (ISBN 0-570-06610-7, 12HH2102). Concordia.
Teen-Ager You're Dating. Walter Riess. LC 12-2650. (Orig.). 1964. pap. 3.95 (ISBN 0-570-06615-8, 12-2650). Concordia.
Teen-Agers at Work. rev. ed. Yvette Dogin. 1983. pap. 3.75 (ISBN 0-88323-184-0, 164). Richards Pub.
Teen-Agers at Work. Yvette Dogin. 64p. (YA) (gr. 8 up). Date not set. pap. text ed. 3.75 (ISBN 0-88323-244-8, 164); tchr's. key 1.25 (277). Richards Pub.
Teen-Agers' Treasure Chest. Floyd D. Carey, Jr. 100p. 1963. pap. 1.25 (ISBN 0-87148-830-2). Pathway Pr.
Teen Angel: And Other Stories of Young Love. Marianne Gingher. 224p. 1988. 17.95 (ISBN 0-689-11967-4). Atheneum.
Teen Conflicts. Ed. by Evelyn Bachelor et al. (Illus.). 240p. (Orig.). (YA) (gr. 8 up). 1972. pap. 7.95 (ISBN 0-87297-007-8). Diablo.
Teen Dating Guide. Marjabelle Y. Stewart. (gr. 5-9). 1984. pap. 2.25 (ISBN 0-451-13123-1, Sig). NAL.
Teen Drug Use. George M. Beschner & Alfred S. Friedman. LC 85-45378. 256p. 1986. 25.00x (ISBN 0-669-11602-5); pap. 14.95x (ISBN 0-669-13834-7). Lexington Bks.
Teen Girl Talk: A Guide to Beauty, Fashion & Health. Molly Douglas. (Illus.). 1980. pap. 4.95 (ISBN 0-87491-412-4). Acropolis.
Teen Girl's Beauty Guide to Total Color Success. Marjabelle Y. Stewart. 160p. (YA) (gr. 7-12). 1986. pap. 2.50 (ISBN 0-451-14453-8, Sig Vista). NAL.
Teen Girls Guide to Social Success. Marjabelle Y. Stewart. 224p. (YA) (gr. 7 up). 1982. pap. 2.50 (ISBN 0-451-11886-3, Sig Vista). NAL.
Teen Guide. 6th ed. Valerie M. Chamberlain & Peyton B. Buddinger. Ed. by Martha O'Neill. (Illus.). 528p. (YA) 1985. text ed. 28.04 (ISBN 0-07-007842-4); pap. text ed. 10.92 (ISBN 0-07-007831-9). McGraw.
Teen Guide to Homemaking. 4th ed. J. H. Brinkley et al. 1976. text ed. 31.64 (ISBN 0-07-007840-8). McGraw.
Teen Guide to Homemaking. 5th ed. Valerie M. Chamberlain. 1982. text ed. 29.04 (ISBN 0-07-007843-2). McGraw.
Teen I Want to Be. Mary A. Green. LC 85-21722. 224p. (gr. 7-11). 1986. 12.95 (ISBN 0-8407-9040-6); pap. 8.95 (ISBN 0-8407-9544-0). Oliver-Nelson.
Teen is a Four-Letter Word: A Survival Kit for Parents. Joan W. Anderson. LC 82-25114. 140p. 1983. pap. 5.95 (ISBN 0-932620-19-1). Betterway Pubns.
Teen Manners--Why Bother: Showing You Care Helps Others to Like you. Sarah Fletcher. (Illus.). 64p. (YA) (gr. 7-12). 1987. pap. 3.95 (ISBN 0-570-04449-9, 12-3060). Concordia.
Teen Model Book. Judith Lasch. LC 85-2983. (Illus.). 192p. (gr. 7 up). 1985. 9.29 (ISBN 0-671-52614-6). Messner.
Teen Pregnancy. Sonia Bowe-Gutman. (Coping with Modern Problems Ser.). 72p. (YA) (gr. 7 up). 1987. PLB 9.95 (ISBN 0-8225-0039-6). Lerner Pubns.
Teen Pregnancy. Roger Ewy & Donna Ewy. LC 83-17809. (Illus., Orig.). 1984. pap. 14.95 (ISBN 0-87108-652-2). Pruett.
Teen Pregnancy: Impact on the Schools. Ed. by Roberta Weiner. LC 86-83248. 94p. (Orig.). 1987. pap. text ed. 29.95 (ISBN 0-937925-03-9, TEEN-BIP). Capitol VA.
Teen Pregnancy: The Challenges We Faced, the Choices We Made. Donna Ewy & Roger Ewy. 1985. pap. 3.95 (ISBN 0-451-13915-1, Sig). NAL.
Teen Scene: Personal Stories for Students Who Are Beginning to Read. Kamla D. Koch et al. (Illus.). 139p. 1987. pap. text ed. 6.95 (ISBN 0-916591-07-7); tchr's. ed. 5.00 (ISBN 0-916591-08-5). Linmore pub.
Teen Sex. Margaret O. Hyde. LC 88-101. 120p. (gr. 7-12). 1988. 9.95 (ISBN 0-664-32726-5). Westminster John Knox.
Teen Sex Survival Manual: How to Cope in an R-Rated World. James Watkins. LC 87-71391. 176p. (Orig.). 1987. pap. 6.95 (ISBN 0-88270-634-9). Bridge Pub.
Teen Sexuality: Decisions & Choices. Janice E. Rench. (Coping with Modern Problems Ser.). (Illus.). 72p. (YA) (gr. 7 up). 1988. lib. bdg. 9.95 (ISBN 0-8225-0041-8). Lerner Pubns.
Teen Skin. Jerome Z. Litt. (Orig.). 1986. pap. 3.50 (ISBN 0-345-32462-5). Ballantine.
Teen Star Yearbook. Grace Catalano. Ed. by Jennifer Weis. (Illus.). 176p. (Orig.). 1988. pap. 3.50 (ISBN 0-7701-0937-3). PaperJacks US.
Teen Suicide: A Book for Friends, Family, & Classmates. Janet Kolehmainen & Sandra Handwerk. (Coping with Modern Problems Ser.). 72p. (gr. 7 up). 1986. PLB 9.95 (ISBN 0-8225-0037-X); pap. 4.95 (ISBN 0-8225-9514-1). Lerner Pubns.
Teen Talent: Creative Writing Manual. Carolyn Dirkson. LC 77-77026. 1977. pap. 1.00 (ISBN 0-87148-838-8). Pathway Pr.
Teen Talk. George B. Eager. 48p. (Orig.). (gr. 7-12). 1981. pap. 1.00 (ISBN 0-9603752-1-X). Mailbox.
Teen Talks with God. Robert Boden. (YA) (gr. 7-12). 1980. pap. 3.95 (ISBN 0-570-03812-X, 12-2921). Concordia.
Teen Teacher Survival Kit. Robert Klausmeier. 80p. 1986. tchr's ed 9.95 (ISBN 0-89191-364-5). Cook.
Teen to Teen. Ruth H. Smith. pap. 2.70 (ISBN 0-89137-813-8). Quality Pubns.
Teen Trouble Zones: A Parent's Helpbook. David P. Givens. 224p. 1988. 18.95 (ISBN 0-936389-09-5); pap. 10.95 (ISBN 0-936389-10-9). Tudor Pubs.
Teen Troubles: How to Keep Them from Becoming Tragedies. Carolyn M. Wesson. 1988. 17.95 (ISBN 0-8027-1011-5). Walker & Co.
Teenage Alcoholism & Substance Abuse: Causes, Cures & Consequences. John Bartimole & Carmella Bartimole. (Illus.). 160p. (Orig.). 1986. pap. 6.95 (ISBN 0-936320-18-4, Pub. by Compact Bks). Fell.
Teenage & Pregnant: What You Can Do. Herma Silverstein. (Illus.). (YA) (gr. 7 up). Date not set. pap. 5.95. Messner.
Teenage Behavior in Shopping Centers. Martin B. Millison. 1976. 14.00 (ISBN 0-685-82622-8); members. 7.00. Intl Coun Shop.
Teenage Body Book Guide. Kathy McCoy & Charles Wibbelsman. Date not set. pap. 9.95 (ISBN 0-671-50637-4). PB.
Teenage Body Book Guide to Dating. Kathy McCoy. (Orig.). (gr. 8-12). 1983. pap. 6.95 (ISBN 0-671-45580-X, Wallaby). S&S.
Teenage Body Book Guide to Sexuality. Kathy McCoy. pap. 8.95 (ISBN 0-671-54681-3). PB.
Teenage Competition: A Survival Guide. Susan Cohen & Daniel Cohen. LC 86-24307. 156p. (gr. 7 up). 1987. 11.95 (ISBN 0-87131-487-8). M Evans.
Teenage Connection: A Tool for Effective Teenage Communication. Carla Crutsinger. LC 87-73063. 225p. (YA) (gr. 7-12). pap. 13.95x (ISBN 0-944662-00-5). Brainworks Inc.
Teenage Depression & Suicide. John Chiles. (Encyclopedia of Psychoactive Drugs Ser.). (Illus.). 1986. PLB 17.95 (ISBN 0-87754-771-8). Chelsea Hse.
Teenage Distance Running. Kim Valentine. LC 73-76250. (Illus.). 96p. (Orig.). 1973. pap. 3.50 (ISBN 0-911520-50-3, Swallow). Tafnews.
Teenage Employment Guide. Rev. ed. Allan B. Goldenthal. (Illus.). 208p. (Orig.). (gr. 9-12). 1983. pap. 9.95 (ISBN 0-671-43542-6). Monarch Pr.
Teenage Entrepreneur's Guide: 50 Money-Making Business Ideas. Sarah L. Riehm. LC 87-1904. (Illus.). 250p. (Orig.). (YA) (gr. 7-12). 1987. pap. 8.95 (ISBN 0-940625-00-8). Surrey Bks.
Teenage Fathers. Bryan E. Robinson. LC 86-45896. 192p. 1987. 25.00x (ISBN 0-669-14586-6); pap. 14.95x (ISBN 0-669-14587-4). Lexington Bks.
Teenage Fitness. Bonnie Prudden. LC 63-10628. (Illus.). 1965. 13.45i (ISBN 0-06-111380-8, HarpT). Har-Row.
Teenage Fitness. Bonnie Prudden. 1988. pap. 10.95 (ISBN 0-345-33303-9). Ballantine.
Teenage Fitness. Bonnie Prudden. (YA) (gr. 7 up). 1988. pap. 10.95 (ISBN 0-317-69501-0). Fawcett.
Teenage Guide to Healthy Skin & Hair. Irwin I. LuBowe & Barbara Huss. 224p. 1983. pap. cancelled (ISBN 0-8290-1159-5). Irvington.
Teenage Mambo. (Ballroom Dance Ser.). 1985. lib. bdg. 44.00 (ISBN 0-87700-794-2). Revisionist Pr.
Teenage Mambo. (Ballroom Dance Ser.). 1986. lib. bdg. 79.95 (ISBN 0-8490-3400-0). Gordon Pr.
Teenage Mambo, No. 2. (Ballroom Dance Ser.). 1985. lib. bdg. 74.00 (ISBN 0-87700-792-6). Revisionist Pr.
Teenage Mambo, No. 2. (Ballroom Dance Ser.). 1986. lib. bdg. 79.95 (ISBN 0-8490-3404-3). Gordon Pr.
Teenage Marriage & Divorce: Nineteen Seventy to Nineteen Eighty-One. Barbara F. Wilson. Ed. by Mary Olmsted. (Series 21: No. 43). 33p. 1985. pap. 1.25 (ISBN 0-8406-0319-3). Natl Ctr Health Stats.
Teenage Marriage: Coping with Reality. Jeanne W. Lindsay. LC 83-19638. (Illus.). 208p. 1984. 14.95 (ISBN 0-930934-12-1); pap. 9.95 (ISBN 0-930934-11-3); tchr's. guide 5.95 (ISBN 0-930934-19-9); study guide 2.50 (ISBN 0-930934-13-X). Morning Glory.
Teenage Marriage: Coping with Reality. 2nd, rev. ed. Jeanne W. Lindsay. (Illus.). 208p. 1988. 15.95 (ISBN 0-930934-31-8); pap. 9.95 (ISBN 0-930934-30-X). Morning Glory.
Teenage Money Making Guide. Ed. by Allan H. Smith. LC 84-90126. (Illus.). 281p. (Orig.). (gr. 6-12). 1984. pap. 10.00 (ISBN 0-931113-00-8). Success Publ.
Teenage Motherhood: Social & Economic Consequences. Kristin A. Moore et al. 50p. 1979. pap. 7.95x (ISBN 0-87766-243-6, 24300). Urban Inst.
Teenage Mutant Ninja Turtles Adventures. Erick Wujcik. Ed. by Alex Marciniszyn. (Illus.). 48p. (Orig.). 1985. pap. 6.95 (ISBN 0-916211-16-9). Palladium Bks.
Teenage Mutant Ninja Turtles & Other Strangeness. Erick Wujcik. Ed. by Alex Marciniszyn & Kevin Siembieda. (Illus.). 110p. (Orig.). 1985. pap. 9.95 (ISBN 0-916211-14-2). Palladium Bks.
Teenage Parents & Their Offspring. Ed. by Keith G. Scott et al. (Illus.). 328p. 1980. 42.50 (ISBN 0-8089-1314-X, 793946). Grune.
Teenage Parent's Child Support Guide. Barry T. Schnell. Ed. by Randall Aungst. LC 88-81534. (First Edition Ser.). 96p. (Orig.). 1988. pap. 14.95 (ISBN 0-910599-26-2). Consumer Aware.
Teenage Patients of Family Planning Clinics: United States, 1978. Eugenia Eckard. Ed. by Klaudia Cox. (Series Thirteen: No,. 57). 50p. 1981. pap. 1.75 (ISBN 0-686-73365-7). Natl Ctr Health Stats.
Teenage Pregnancy: A New Beginning. Linda Barr & Catherine Monserrat. (Illus.). 100p. Date not set. spiral bdg. 10.00; study guide 2.00. Morning Glory.
Teenage Pregnancy: A Research Guide to Programs & Services. Patrick A. Gilloti. (Legal Research Guides Ser.: Vol. 4). 44p. 1988. lib. bdg. 25.00 (ISBN 0-89941-586-5). W S Hein.
Teenage Pregnancy: Developing Life Options. Kristen Amundson. 24p. (Orig.). 1988. pap. text ed. write for info. (ISBN 0-87652-134-0, 021-00242). Am Assn Sch Admin.
Teenage Pregnancy in a Family Context: Implications for Policy. Ed. by Theodora Ooms. (Family Impact Seminar Ser.). 425p. 1982. pap. 12.95x (ISBN 0-87722-205-3). Temple U Pr.
Teenage Pregnancy in a Family Context: Implications for Policy. Ed. by Theodora Ooms. (Family Impact Seminar Ser.). 456p. 1981. 34.95 (ISBN 0-87722-204-5). Temple U Pr.
Teenage Pregnancy in Industrialized Countries. Elise F. Jones. LC 86-9237. 304p. 1988. pap. 12.95 (ISBN 0-300-04362-7). Yale U Pr.
Teenage Pregnancy in Industrialized Countries. Elise F. Jones et al. LC 86-9237. 304p. 1987. 32.50x (ISBN 0-300-03705-8). Yale U Pr.
Teenage Pregnancy: Research Related to Clients & Services. Jean E. Bedger. 224p. 1980. 26.00x (ISBN 0-398-03923-2). C C Thomas.
Teenage Pressure Molds a Poet. Gregory Moore. 32p. 1987. cancelled (ISBN 0-8062-3035-5). Carlton.
Teenage Reading. Ed. by Peter Kennerley. 180p. 1985. 20.00x (ISBN 0-7062-3889-3, Pub. by Ward Lock Educ Co Ltd). State Mutual Bk.
Teenage Romance: Or, How to Die of Embarrassment. Delia Ephron. LC 81-411. (Illus.). 144p. 1981. 10.95 (ISBN 0-670-69503-3). Viking.
Teenage Romance: Or, How to Die of Embarrassment. Delia Ephron. 1982. pap. 5.95 (ISBN 0-345-30457-8). Ballantine.
Teenage Sexual Health: A Guide for Counselors, Nurses, Teachers, Sex Educators, Physicians, Parents & Teachers. Amelia Withington & Robert A. Hatcher. LC 83-8456. (Illus.). 226p. 1983. pap. 12.95x (ISBN 0-8290-1271-0). Irvington.
Teenage Sexuality. Ed. by Neal Bernards et al. (Opposing Viewpoints Ser.). (Illus.). 1988. lib. bdg. 13.95 (ISBN 0-89908-430-3); pap. 6.95 (ISBN 0-89908-405-2). Greenhaven.
Teenage Sexuality. Stewart Meikle et al. (Illus.). 180p. 1985. pap. 20.50. College-Hill.
Teenage Stress: How to Cope in a Complex World. Eileen Van Wie. LC 87-7742. (Illus.). 224p. (gr. 6 up). 1987. 11.29 (ISBN 0-671-63824-6); pap. 5.95 (ISBN 0-671-65980-4). Messner.
Teenage Stress: Understanding the Tensions You Feel at Home, at School & among Your Friends. Daniel Cohen & Susan Cohen. LC 83-16477. 160p. (gr. 5 up). 1984. PLB 10.95 (ISBN 0-87131-423-1). M Evans.
Teenage Suicide. Sandra Gardner & Gary Rosenberg. LC 85-14277. 160p. (gr. 7 up). 1985. 11.29 (ISBN 0-671-49975-0); pap. 4.95 (ISBN 0-671-63241-8). Messner.
Teenage Suicide: What Can the Schools Do? Jerilyn K. Pfeifer. LC 85-63689. (Fastback Ser.: No. 234). 50p. (Orig.). 1986. pap. 0.75 (ISBN 0-87367-234-8). Phi Delta Kappa.
Teenage Survival Book: The Complete Revised, Updated Edition of You. Sol Gordon. 150p. 1981. pap. 12.95 (ISBN 0-8129-0972-0). Times Bks.
Teenage Survival Manual: How to Enjoy the Trip to Twenty. H. Samm Coombs. (Illus.). 1978. pap. 5.95 (ISBN 0-87516-277-0). DeVorss.
Teenage World: Adolescents' Self-Image in Ten Countries. Daniel Offer et al. LC 88-4127. (Illus.). 288p. 1988. 35.00x (ISBN 0-306-42747-8, Plenum Med Bk). Plenum Pub.
Teenager & the Law. Albert L. Ayars & John M. Ryan. 1978. pap. 8.95 (ISBN 0-8158-0369-9). Chris Mass.
Teenagers. J. M. Parramon et al. (Barron's Family Ser.). 32p. (gr. 3-5). pap. 3.95 ea. Eng. ed (ISBN 0-8120-3851-7). Span. ed.: Los Jovenes (ISBN 0-8120-3855-X). Barron.
Teenager's (Absolutely Basic) Introduction to the New Testament. Jim Auer. 96p. 1986. pap. 2.95 (ISBN 0-89243-257-8). Liguori Pubns.
Teenagers Ahead. David F. Slonaker. LC 79-16999. (Illus.). 128p. 1980. 17.95x (ISBN 0-88229-314-1). Nelson-Hall.
Teenagers & Peer Pressure. Stephen D. Willeford & Ruth H. Smith. 1984. pap. 2.70 (ISBN 0-89137-809-X). Quality Pubns.
Teenagers & Purity, Teenagers & Going Steady, Teenagers & Looking Ahead to Marriage. Robert Fox. 1978. pap. 0.75 (ISBN 0-8198-0370-7). Dghtrs St Paul.

Teenagers & Teenpics: The Juvenilization of American Movies in the 1950s. Thomas P. Doherty. (Media & Popular Culture Ser.: No. 3). (Illus.). 1988. 34.95 (ISBN 0-04-445139-3); pap. 12.95 (ISBN 0-04-445140-7). Unwin Hyman.

Teenagers & Their Problems. Gerardo Castillo. 1986. pap. 8.95 (ISBN 1-85182-012-4). Lumen Christi.

Teenager's Ask & Answer Book. Lawrence Graham & Betty J. Graham. LC 86-702. 160p. (YA) (gr. 7 up). 1986. 11.29 (ISBN 0-671-60167-9). Messner.

Teenagers at Risk: How Exploitation Leads to Running Away, Violence, Substance Abuse & Suicide. Edsel Erickson & Alan McEvoy. Date not set. pap. 14.95 (ISBN 1-55691-010-X). Learning Pubns.

Teenagers Face-to-Face with Cancer. Karen Gravelle & John Bertram. LC 86-8608. 96p. (YA) (gr. 7 up). 1987. 11.29 (ISBN 0-671-54549-3). Messner.

Teenagers from Outer Space. Michael Pondsmith. (Illus.). 77p. (YA) (gr. 5-12). 1987. wkbk. 10.00 (ISBN 0-937279-98-6, TS 2001). R Talsorian.

Teenagers from Outer Space. Mike Pondsmith. 96p. 1988. pap. 9.95 (ISBN 0-312-93110-7). Tor Bks.

Teenagers, Graybeards & 4-F's. Harrington E. Crissey, Jr. Incl. Vol. 1. The National League. (Illus.). 150p. 1981; Vol. 2. The American League. (Illus.). 179p. 1982. pap. 9.00 (ISBN 0-9608878-1-4). H E Crissey.

Teenager's Guide to Breaking into TV Commercials. Cortland Jessup. LC 86-30671. 48p. (Orig.). 1987. pap. 4.95 (ISBN 0-87576-129-1). Pilot Bks.

Teenager's Guide to Economics & Finance, 2 vols. in one. C. M. Flumiani. LC 72-91789. (Illus.). 70p. (gr. 10-12). 1973. Set. 97.75 (ISBN 0-913314-16-1). Am Classical Coll Pr.

Teenager's Guide to Economics & Finance. C. M. Flumiani. 93p. 1987. pap. 27.75 (ISBN 0-86654-234-5). Inst Econ Finan.

Teenager's Guide to Living with an Alcoholic Parent. Edith L. Hornik-Beer. 96p. (Orig.). 1984. pap. 4.95 (ISBN 0-89486-239-1). Hazelden.

Teenagers Guide to Money, Banking & Finance. David Spiselman. LC 87-11059. 128p. (YA) (gr. 6 up). 1988. 11.29 (ISBN 0-671-64345-2); pap. 5.95 (ISBN 0-671-65979-0). Messner.

Teenager's Guide to Study, Travel, & Adventure Abroad. Council on International Educational Exchange Staff. 288p. 1988. pap. 9.95 (ISBN 0-312-02296-4). St Martin.

Teenager's Guide to Study, Travel, & Adventure Abroad, 1987-1988: Council on International Educational Exchange (CIEE) CIEE Staff. 256p. 1986. pap. 8.95 (ISBN 0-312-00194-0). St Martin.

Teenager's Guide to the Best Summer Opportunities. Jan Greenberg. LC 84-19717. 208p. 1985. 16.95 (ISBN 0-916782-59-X); pap. 9.95 (ISBN 0-916782-58-1). Harvard Common Pr.

Teenager's Guidebook to Wall Street & the Stock Market. Carlo M. Flumiani. (Illus.). 143p. 1984. 57.75x (ISBN 0-89266-433-9). Am Classical Coll Pr.

Teenagers: Parental Guidance Suggested. Rich Wilkerson. LC 82-83838. 196p. (Orig.). 1983. pap. 5.95 (ISBN 0-89081-370-1). Harvest Hse.

Teenagers Pocket Companion, No. 2. Floyd D. Carey. 1962. pap. 0.25 (ISBN 0-87148-828-0). Pathway Pr.

Teenagers Pocket Companion, No. 3. Floyd D. Carey. 1962. pap. 0.25 (ISBN 0-87148-829-9). Pathway Pr.

Teenagers Pray. William A. Kramer. LC 55-12193. (gr. 8-12). 1956. 4.95 (ISBN 0-570-03018-8, 6-1054). Concordia.

Teenager's Survival Guide to Moving. Patricia C. Nida & Wendy M. Heller. LC 84-21543. 164p. (gr. 7 up). 1985. 10.95 (ISBN 0-689-31077-3, Atheneum Childrens Bks). Macmillan.

Teenager's Survival Guide to Moving. Patricia C. Nida & Wendy M. Heller. 144p. (YA) 1987. pap. 2.95 (ISBN 0-02-044510-5, Collier). Macmillan.

Teenagers Talk about Suicide. Marion Crook. (Teenagers Talk About...Ser.). 128p. (YA) (gr. 7-12). 1988. pap. 12.95 (ISBN 1-55021-013-0, Pub. by NC Press Ltd). U of Toronto Pr.

Teenagers: The Continuing Challenge. Shirley Gould. 174p. 1987. pap. 7.95 (ISBN 0-525-48310-1, 0772-230). Dutton.

Teenagers Themselves. Compiled by Glenbard East Echo Staff. Ed. by Howard Spanogla. LC 83-26568. (Illus.). 272p. (gr. 9-12). 1985. 16.95 (ISBN 0-915361-04-3, Dist. by Watts); pap. 9.95 (ISBN 0-915361-33-7, 09734-X). Adama Pubs Inc.

Teenagers Themselves. (Illus.). 320p. 1984. 16.95 (ISBN 0-531-09842-7). Watts.

Teenagers Today. Daughters of St. Paul. 1981. 4.00 (ISBN 0-8198-7303-9); pap. 3.00 (ISBN 0-8198-7304-7). Dghtrs St Paul.

Teenagers' Turn see Parents Perspective.

Teenagers: When to Worry & What to Do. Douglas H. Powell. LC 85-16214. 336p. 1987. pap. 8.95 (ISBN 0-385-19341-6). Doubleday.

Teenagers Who Use Organized Family Planning Services: United States, 1978. (Series 13: No. 57). 18p. 2.50. Natl Ctr Health Stats.

Teendreams & Our Own People. David Edgar. (Methuen Modern Play Ser.). 160p. 1988. pap. 10.95 (ISBN 0-413-16890-5). Heinemann Ed.

Teenie Weenies Book: The Life & Art of William Donahey. Joseph M. Cahn. LC 84-80569. (Illus.). 128p. (Orig.). (YA) (gr. 7-12). 1986. 16.95 (ISBN 0-88138-035-0). Green Tiger Pr.

Teens & Self Esteem: Helping Christian Youth Discover Their Worth. Jerry McCant. 152p. (Orig.). 1985. pap. 5.95 (ISBN 0-8341-1055-5). Beacon Hill.

Teens Can Make a Difference. Kathleen M. Zaffore. 160p. 1987. pap. 5.95 (ISBN 0-87403-233-4, 3233). Standard Pub.

Teens: Giving Youth the Grow-ahead. Lawrence O. Richards. LC 87-63568. (Successful Teaching Ser.). 112p. (Orig.). 1988. pap. 4.95 (ISBN 1-55513-167-0, 60301). Cook.

Teen's Guide to Ministry: You Can Make It Happen. Joseph Moore. 128p. 1988. pap. 3.95 (ISBN 0-89243-284-5). Liguori Pubns.

Teens in Action. Patricia J. Thompson & Judy Jax. 1988. text ed. 17.95 (ISBN 0-8219-0303-9, 40452); tchr's. ed. 20.00 (ISBN 0-8219-0304-7, TE-50809); wkbk. 5.95 (ISBN 0-8219-0305-5, WK-50654). EMC.

Teens Look at Marriage: Rainbows, Roles & Reality. Jeanne W. Lindsay. LC 84-18954. (Illus.). 256p. (Orig.). 1985. 15.95 (ISBN 0-930934-16-4); pap. 9.95 (ISBN 0-930934-15-6); study guide 2.50 (ISBN 0-930934-20-2). Morning Glory.

Teens Parenting: The Challenge of Babies & Toddlers. Jeanne W. Lindsay. LC 80-84900. (Illus.). 320p. 1981. 14.95 (ISBN 0-930934-07-5); pap. 9.95 (ISBN 0-930934-06-7); tchr's. guide 5.95 (ISBN 0-930934-09-1); wkbk. 2.50 (ISBN 0-930934-08-3). Morning Glory.

Teens Speak Out: A Report from Today's Teens on Their Most Intimate Thoughts, Feelings & Hopes for the Future. Jane Rinzler. LC 85-80629. 171p. 1986. pap. 7.95 (ISBN 0-917657-50-0). D I Fine.

Teens Talk about Alcohol & Alcoholism. Ed. by Paul Dolmetsch & Gail Mauriette. LC 86-16616. 144p. (YA) 1987. pap. 6.95 (ISBN 0-385-23084-2). Doubleday.

Teens, Temple Marriage & Eternity. Allan Burgess. LC 87-36581. 125p. (gr. 7-12). 1988. 8.95 (ISBN 0-87579-116-6). Deseret Bk.

Teeny Tiny. Jill Bennett. LC 85-12347. (Illus.). 32p. (ps-1). 1986. 8.95 (ISBN 0-399-21293-0, G&D). Putnam Pub Group.

Teeny-Tiny. Leland B. Jacobs. LC 75-6550. (Easy Venture Ser.). (Illus.). 32p. (gr. k-2). 1976. PLB 6.69 (ISBN 0-8116-6070-2). Garrard.

Teeny-Tiny Folktales: Simple Folktales for Young Children Plus Flannelboard Patterns. Ed. by Elizabeth S. McKinnon & Jean Warren. LC 86-51510. (Totline Teaching Tales Ser.). (Illus.). 80p. (Orig.). (ps). 1987. pap. 6.95 (ISBN 0-911019-12-X). Warren Pub Hse.

Teeny Tiny Tots. pap. 4.98 (ISBN 0-317-38605-0). Gick.

Teeny-Tiny Woman. Paul Galdone. LC 84-4311. (Illus.). 32p. (ps-3). 1984. PLB 11.95 (ISBN 0-89919-270-X, Clarion). HM.

Teeny-Tiny Woman. Paul Galdone. LC 84-4311. (Illus.). 32p. (ps-3). 1986. pap. 4.95 (ISBN 0-89919-463-X, Pub. by Clarion). Ticknor & Fields.

Teeny Tiny Woman. Retold by Jane O'Connor. LC 86-485. (Step into Reading Bks.). (Illus.). 32p. (ps-1). 1986. lib. bdg. 6.99 (ISBN 0-394-98320-3, BYR); pap. 2.95 (ISBN 0-394-88320-9, BYR). Random.

Teeny Tiny Woman: An Old English Ghost Tale. Barbara Seuling. (Illus.). (gr. k-3). 1978. pap. 3.95 (ISBN 0-14-050266-1, Puffin). Penguin.

Teepee. Francis H. Wise & Joyce M. Wise. (Phonetic Reader Ser: No. 2). (Illus.). 20p. (Dr. Wise Learn to Read Ser.). (ps). 1973. pap. text ed. 1.50 (ISBN 0-915766-36-1). Wise Pub.

Teepee Neighbors. Grace Coolidge. LC 83-40487. 200p. 1984. pap. 7.95 (ISBN 0-8061-1889-X). U of Okla Pr.

Teetering on the Tightrope. Carol Amen. LC 79-18718. (Orion Ser.). 1979. pap. 3.95 (ISBN 0-8127-0250-6). Review & Herald.

Teeth. John Gaskin. LC 83-50855. (Your Body Ser.). (Illus.). 32p. (gr. 2-4). 1984. PLB 11.90 (ISBN 0-531-03769-X). Watts.

Teeth. Simon Hillson. (Cambridge Manuals in Archaeology). (Illus.). 350p. 1986. 47.50 (ISBN 0-521-30405-9). Cambridge U Pr.

Teeth. Henry Pluckrose. Ed. by FS Staff. (Look at Ser.). (Illus.). 32p. (gr. 1-3). 1988. 10.40 (ISBN 0-531-10550-4). Watts.

Teeth: Form, Function & Evolution. Ed. by Bjorn Kurten. LC 81-10210. 456p. 1982. 60.00x (ISBN 0-231-05202-2). Columbia U Pr.

Teeth 'n' Smiles. David Hare. 92p. 1976. pap. 5.95 (ISBN 0-571-10995-0). Faber & Faber.

Teeth of Mordor. Terry K. Amthor. Ed. by Peter C. Fenlon. (Fortresses of Middle-Earth Ser.). 32p. (YA) (gr. 10-12). 1988. pap. 6.00 (ISBN 0-915795-96-5). Iron Crown Ent Inc.

Teeth of the Gale. Joan Aiken. LC 87-35050. 320p. (YA) (gr. 7 up). 1988. 14.95i (ISBN 0-06-020044-8); PLB 14.89 (ISBN 0-06-020045-6). HarpJ.

Teeth of the Horse. Ed. by William E. Jones. (Horse Health & Care Ser.). (Illus.). 1973. pap. 4.95 (ISBN 0-912830-15-8). Printed Horse.

Teeth of the Tiger. Maurice LeBlanc. 490p. 1980. Repr. of 1914 ed. lib. bdg. 17.95x (ISBN 0-89968-204-9). Lightyear.

Teeth of the Wolf. Alain Paris. Tr. by Martin Sokolinsky. 252p. 1983. 15.95 (ISBN 0-03-059899-0). H Holt & Co.

Teeth, Teeth, Teeth. Sidney Garfield. 35.00 (ISBN 0-685-07412-9). Borden.

Teetoncey. Theodore Taylor. (Illus.). (gr. 3-7). 1984. pap. 1.95 (ISBN 0-380-00346-5, 52118-0, Camelot). Avon.

Teetoncey & Ben O'Neal. Theodore Taylor. (Illus.). 154p. (gr. 3-7). 1984. pap. 1.25 (ISBN 0-380-00764-9, 30536-4, Camelot). Avon.

Teetotalism, Eighteen Forty-Two. 25p. 1984. pap. text ed. 12.50 (ISBN 0-87556-380-5). Saifer.

Tefillin Handbook. David Rosoff. (Orig.). 1984. pap. 4.95 (ISBN 0-87306-373-2). Feldheim.

Tefuga. Peter Dickinson. 1986. pap. 14.95 (ISBN 0-394-55180-X). Pantheon.

Tegafur-Ftorafur. Ed. by N. I. Perevodchikova & W. Queisser. (Beitraege zur Onkologie-Contributions to Oncology Ser.: Vol. 14). (Illus.). viii, 146p. 1983. pap. 30.75 (ISBN 3-8055-3653-4). S Karger.

Teged. Aron Kibedi Varga. LC 73-88423. (Hungarian.). 1973. pap. 4.00 (ISBN 0-911050-42-6). Occidental.

Tegotomono: Music for Japanese Koto. Bonnie C. Wade. LC 75-5265. (Contributions in Intercultural & Comparative Studies: No. 2). 1976. lib. bdg. 36.95 (ISBN 0-8371-8908-X, WAT/). Greenwood.

TEG's Nineteen Ninety-Four: An Anticipation of the Near Future. Robert Theobald & J. M. Scott. LC 70-150754. 210p. 1972. 8.95x (ISBN 0-8040-0509-5, 8, Pub by Swallow); (Pub by Swallow). Ohio U Pr.

Tehachapi. John R. Signor. LC 83-20490. (Illus.). 278p. 44.95 (ISBN 0-87095-088-6). Gldn West Bks.

Teheran Wipeout. (Executioner Ser.: No. 76). Date not set. pap. 2.25 (ISBN 0-317-63945-5, Pub. by Worldwide). Harlequin Bks.

Tehidy & the Bassets. Michael Tangye. 1985. 8.00x (ISBN 0-907566-97-9, Pub. by Dyllansow & Truran). State Mutual Bk.

Tehillim: Psalms, 2 vols. A. C. Feuer. 1985. 46.95 (ISBN 0-89906-064-1); pap. 36.95 (ISBN 0-89906-065-X); slipcased gift ed. 49.95 (ISBN 0-89906-066-8). Mesorah Pubns.

Tehillim (Psalms, 3 vols. Avrohom C. Fever. Incl. Vol. 1. Psalms 1-30. 368p. 1977. (ISBN 0-89906-050-1); pap. (ISBN 0-89906-051-X); Vol. 2. Psalms 31-55. 352p. 1978. (ISBN 0-89906-052-8); pap. (ISBN 0-89906-053-6); Vol. 3. Psalms 56-85. 384p. 1979. (ISBN 0-89906-054-4); pap. (ISBN 0-89906-055-2). (Art Scroll Tanach Ser.). 15.95 ea.; pap. 12.95 ea. Mesorah Pubns.

Tehran-Yalta-Potsdam: The Soviet Protocols. Ed. by Robert Beitzell. (Russian Ser.: Vol. 17). 30.00 (ISBN 0-87569-013-0). Academic Intl.

Teilhard & Mandel: Contrasts & Parallels. Edward O. Dodson. (Teilhard Studies). 1984. pap. 3.00 (ISBN 0-89012-039-0). Anima Pubns.

Teilhard & Prigogine. James F. Salmon. (Teilhard Studies). 1986. 3.00 (ISBN 0-89012-045-5). Anima Pubns.

Teilhard & the Unity of Knowledge. Ed. by Thomas M. King & James F. Salmon. LC 82-60590. 1983. pap. 6.95 (ISBN 0-8091-2491-2). Paulist Pr.

Teilhard de Chardin: A Short Biography. John Grim & Mary E. Grim. (Teilhard Studies). 1984. pap. 3.00 (ISBN 0-89012-038-2). Anima Pubns.

Teilhard de Chardin: An Analysis & Assessment. David G. Jones. LC 70-127933. pap. 20.00 (ISBN 0-317-08998-6, 2012937). Bks Demand UMI.

Teilhard de Chardin: In Quest of the Perfection of Man. Ed. by Joseph L. Alioto et al. LC 72-9596. 290p. 1973. 24.50 (ISBN 0-8386-1258-X). Fairleigh Dickinson.

Teilhard de Chardin's Biological Ideas. Alexander Wolsky. (Teilhard Studies). 1981. 3.00 (ISBN 0-89012-024-2). Anima Pubns.

Teilhard de Chardin's Vision of the Future. Francis Neilson. 1979. lib. bdg. 39.50 (ISBN 0-685-96640-2). Revisionist Pr.

Teilhard in the Ecological Age. Thomas Berry. (Teilhard Studies). 1982. 3.00 (ISBN 0-89012-032-3). Anima Pubns.

Teilhard, Scripture, & Revelation: Teilhard de Chardin's Reinterpretation of Pauline Themes. Richard W. Kropf. LC 73-20907. 352p. 1980. 29.50 (ISBN 0-8386-1481-7). Fairleigh Dickinson.

Teilhard, Taoism, & Western Thought. Allerd Stikker. (Teilhard Studies). 1986. 3.00 (ISBN 0-89012-044-7). Anima Pubns.

Teilhardism & the New Religion: A Thorough Analysis of the Teachings of Pierre Teilhard de Chardin. Wolfgang Smith. LC 87-50749. 248p. (Orig.). 1988. pap. 8.00. TAN Bks Pubs.

Teilhard's Mysticism of Knowing. Thomas M. King. 192p. 1981. 14.95 (ISBN 0-8164-0491-7, HarpR). Har-Row.

Teilhards Unity of Knowledge. Thomas M. King. (Teilhards Studies). 1983. pap. 3.00 (ISBN 0-89012-035-8). Anima Pubns.

Teilhard's Vision of the Past: The Making of a Method. Robert J. O'Connell. LC 82-71279. x, 205p. 1982. 25.00 (ISBN 0-8232-1090-1); pap. 10.00 (ISBN 0-8232-1091-X). Fordham.

Teilhard's Way. Thomas H. King. (Way of the Christian Mystics Ser.: Vol. 12). 1988. pap. 9.95 (ISBN 0-89453-631-1). M Glazier.

Teilnahme und Spiegelung: Festschrift fuer Horst Ruediger. Ed. by Erwin Koppen & Beda Allemann. viii, 680p. (Ger.). 1975. 118.00x (ISBN 3-11-004013-1). De Gruyter.

Tejano Community: Eighteen Thirty-Six to Nineteen Hundred. Arnoldo De Leon. LC 81-52053. (Illus.). 297p. 1985. pap. 10.95x (ISBN 0-8263-0822-8). U of NM Pr.

Tejanos: A Texas-Mexican Anthology. Ed. by Nicolas Kanellos. 128p. (Span.). 1980. 7.50 (ISBN 0-934770-21-2). Arte Publico.

Tejanos & the Numbers Game: A Socio-Historical Interpretation from the Federal Censuses, 1850-1900. Arnoldo De Leon & Kenneth L. Stewart. (Illus.). 128p. Date not set. 22.50x (ISBN 0-8263-1118-0). U of NM Pr.

Tejidos Hechos en Telares Manuales. (Productos Latinoamericanos Incluidos En el Sistema Generalizado De Preferencias De los Estados Unidos Ser.). 9p. 1977. pap. text ed. 3.00 (ISBN 0-8270-3480-6). OAS.

Teka Stone. George B. Markle, IV. 128p. (Orig.). 1982. pap. 3.95 (ISBN 0-9606262-1-2). Yesnaby Inc.

Tekhnika Komicheskogo U Gogolia. Aleksandr L. Slonimskii. LC 63-7523. (Slavic Reprint Ser., No. 2). 71p. (Rus.). 1963. pap. 6.00x (ISBN 0-87057-070-6). U Pr of New Eng.

Tekhnologiia Konstruktsionnykh: Materialov. P. A. Averchenko. 112p. 30.00x (ISBN 0-317-42709-1, Pub. by Collets (UK)). State Mutual Bk.

Teknologi Kampungan: A Compendium of Indonesian Indigenous Technologies. Craig Thorburn. Ed. by Ken Darrow & Bill Stanley. (Illus.). 154p. 1982. pap. 5.00 (ISBN 0-917704-16-9). Volunteers Asia Pr.

Tekst en Uitleg: Een Inleiding in de Tekstweten-Schap. J. Renkema. xiv, 333p. 1986. pap. write for info. (ISBN 90-6765-308-X). Foris Pubns.

Tekst-Sociologische Analyse. T. Hak. (Studies over Taalgebruik). x, 374p. 1988. pap. write for info. (ISBN 90-6765-369-1). Foris Pubns.

Teksty, Nineteen Fifty-Five to Nineteen Seventy-Seven. Vladimir Ufliand. (Rus.). 1979. 12.00 (ISBN 0-88233-379-8); pap. 3.00 (ISBN 0-88233-380-1). Ardis Pubs.

Tektite. Forrest B. Johnson. Ed. by Fred Zuber. 384p. (Orig.). 1988. pap. 7.95 (ISBN 0-89896-249-8). Larksdale.

Tel Quel, 2 vols. Paul Valery. (Idees Ser.). Set. pap. 7.90 (ISBN 0-685-36627-8); pap. 7.95 ea. Schoenhof.

Tel quel see Oeuvres.

Tel Qu'en Lui-Meme. Georges Duhamel. 1973. 8.95 (ISBN 0-686-55197-4). French & Eur.

Tele-Robotics: The New Medium for Marketing, Sales, & Politics. Richard L. Corbeil, Sr. (Illus.). 112p. 1984. 10.00 (ISBN 0-682-40137-4). Exposition-Phoenix.

Tele-Shopping: A Guide to Television's Home Shopping Networks. Daniel Paisner. 160p. (Orig.). 1987. pap. 3.95 (ISBN 0-446-34539-3, Pub. by Popular Lib). Warner Bks.

Telecare Ministry: Using the Telephone in a Care Ministry. Harald Grindal. 32p. 1984. pap. 4.95 (ISBN 0-8066-2099-4, 23-1899). Augsburg.

Telecom Basics. Jack L. Dempsey. 104p. 1988. 20.00 (ISBN 0-917845-07-2). Intertec IL.

Telecom Deregulation. Andrew D. Lipman. 260p. 1987. 60.00 (ISBN 0-917845-06-4). Intertec IL.

Telecom Factbook, 1985. 1985. 59.00 (ISBN 0-911486-17-8). Warren Pub Inc.

Telecom Factbook, 1986. rev. ed. 1986. 95.00 (ISBN 0-911486-22-4). Warren Pub Inc.

Telecom Integrated Circuits. 157p. 1985. 1650.00x (ISBN 0-88694-659-X). Intl Res Dev.

Telecom Mosaic: Piecing Together the New International Structure. Robert R. Bruce et al. 456p. 1988. text ed. price not set (ISBN 0-408-02670-7). Butterworth.

Telecom Pacific. Ed. by Syed A. Rahim & Dan J. Wedemeyer. 200p. 1983. pap. text ed. 12.50x (ISBN 0-8248-0918-1). Pac Telecom.

Telecom Report. Ed. by A. G. Siemens. 500p. 1988. 290.00 (ISBN 0-471-91823-7). Wiley.

Telecom Resale Markets. 160p. 1984. 1650.00x (ISBN 0-88694-617-4). Intl Res Dev.

Telecommunicating Typesetters. Michael L. Kleper. (Illus.). 1982. pap. 10.00 (ISBN 0-930904-02-8). Graphic Dimensions.

Telecommunication & Control - TELECON '84: Proceedings, IASTED Symposium, Halkidiki, Greece, August 27-30, 1984. Ed. by G. V. Bafas. 498p. 1984. 120.00 (ISBN 0-88986-072-6, 075). Acta Pr.

Telecommunication & Control - TELECON '85: Proceedings, IASTED Symposium, Rio de Janeiro, Brazil, December 10-13, 1985. Ed. by J. A. Felippe de Souza. 361p. 1985. 70.00 (ISBN 0-318-22565-4, 095). Acta Pr.

Telecommunication & Data Communication System Design with Troubleshooting. Harold B. Killen. (Illus.). 336p. 1986. text ed. 43.00 (ISBN 0-13-902545-6). P-H.

Telecommunication Economics & International Regulatory Policy: An Annotated Bibliography. Marcellus S. Snow. LC 86-12130. (Bibliographies & Indexes in Economics & Economic History: No. 4). 230p. 1986. 40.95 (ISBN 0-313-25370-6, SWT/). Greenwood.

Telecommunication Engineering. 2nd ed. J. Dunlop & D. G. Smith. 560p. Date not set. text ed. 32.95. Van Nos Reinhold.
Telecommunication Equipment: Equipment Fundamentals & Network Structures. Vincent J. Coughlin. (Illus.). 144p. 1984. 30.95 (ISBN 0-442-21737-4). Van Nos Reinhold.
Telecommunication Equipment Maintenance. (Market Research Reports). 1987. write for info. (ISBN 0-86621-857-2, A1678). Frost & Sullivan.
Telecommunication for the Executive. Ronald R. Thomas. 180p. 1984. 22.50 (ISBN 0-89433-233-3). Petrocelli.
Telecommunication in Alaska. Ed. by Robert M. Walp. 133p. 1982. pap. text ed. 7.50x (ISBN 0-8248-0926-2). Pac Telecom.
Telecommunication Industry: Growth & Structural Change. 292p. 1988. pap. 50.00 (ISBN 92-1-116409-5, E.87.II.E.35). UN.
Telecommunication Market Opportunities. 622p. 1985. 4500.00x (ISBN 0-88694-676-X). Intl Res Dev.
Telecommunication Networks: Protocols, Modeling & Analysis. Mischa Schwartz. (Illus.). 575p. 1987. text ed. 49.50 (ISBN 0-201-16423-X). Addison-Wesley.
Telecommunication Principles. J. O'Reilly. 1984. pap. 20.95 (ISBN 0-442-30592-3). Van Nos Reinhold.
Telecommunication Project Management. James B. Pruitt. 1987. 50.00 (ISBN 0-917845-05-6). Intertec IL.
Telecommunication Switching: State of the Art Impact on Networks & Services, 2 pts. Ed. by AEI Staff. 1410p. 1984. Set. 316.00 (ISBN 0-444-86860-7, North-Holland). Elsevier.
Telecommunication System Engineering. Roger L. Freeman. 480p. 1980. 56.95 (ISBN 0-686-91743-X). Telecom Lib.
Telecommunication System Engineering: Analog & Digital Network Design. Roger L. Freeman. LC 79-26661. 480p. 1980. 55.95 (ISBN 0-471-02955-6). Wiley.
Telecommunication Systems. Pierre-Gerard Fontolliet. 450p. 1986. text ed. 66.00 (ISBN 0-89006-184-X). Artech Hse.
Telecommunication Technologies. H. Inose. 1984. 95.00 (ISBN 0-444-87565-4). Elsevier.
Telecommunication Technologies: 1983. Ed. by H. Inose. (Japan Annual Reviews of Electronics, Computers & Telecommunications (JARECT): Vol. 9). 340p. 1983. 95.00 (ISBN 0-444-86655-8, I-161-83). Elsevier.
Telecommunication Traffic Engineering. rev. ed. Ed. by D. Bear. 244p. 1980. pap. 33.00 (ISBN 0-906048-36-2, TE002). Inst Elect Eng.
Telecommunication Transmission. (IEE Conference Ser.: No. 246). 301p. 1985. pap. 86.00 (ISBN 0-85296-307-6, IC246). Inst Elect Eng.
Telecommunication Transmission Handbook. 2nd ed. Roger L. Freeman. LC 81-7499. 706p. 1981. 66.95 (ISBN 0-471-08029-2). Wiley.
Telecommunications. 2nd ed. W. Fraser. 812p. 1969. 158.00 (ISBN 0-677-61240-0). Gordon & Breach.
Telecommunications. Arnold Rosen. 304p. 1987. text ed. 23.00 (ISBN 0-15-589815-9); instr's. manual 6.75 (ISBN 0-317-56571-0). HarBraceJ.
Telecommunications. John Stevenson. LC 84-50817. (Visual Science Ser.). 48p. (gr. 6 up). 1985. 14.96 (ISBN 0-382-06834-3); pap. 6.75 (ISBN 0-382-09003-9). Silver.
Telecommunications, 33 vols. (Illus.). 14902p. 1974. Set. 805.00 (ISBN 0-405-06030-0). Ayer Co Pubs.
Telecommunications. (SPEC Kit & Flyer Ser.: No. 98). 129p. 1983. 20.00 (ISBN 0-318-03458-1). OMS.
Telecommunications: A Management Perspective. Cross. 1988. pap. write for info. (ISBN 0-471-85353-4). Wiley.
Telecommunications Abstracts 1985-1986 Index. write for info. (EIC Intell). Bowker.
Telecommunications Access & Public Policy. Allan Baughcum & Gerald Faulhaber. Ed. by Melvin J. Voigt. LC 84-6233. (Telecommunications & Information Science Ser.). 300p. 1984. text ed. 45.00 (ISBN 0-89391-259-X). Ablex Pub.
Telecommunications Aide. Jack Rudman. (Career Examination Ser.: C-2877). (Cloth bdg. avail. on request). pap. 14.00 (ISBN 0-8373-2877-2). Natl Learning.
Telecommunications America: Markets Without Boundaries. Manley R. Irwin. LC 83-9448. (Illus.). xiv, 147p. 1984. lib. bdg. 36.95 (ISBN 0-89930-029-4, IIS/, Quorum). Greenwood.
Telecommunications: An Interdisciplinary Text. Leonard Lewin. 687p. 1984. text ed. 70.00 (ISBN 0-89006-140-8). Artech Hse.
Telecommunications: An Interdisciplinary Survey. Ed. by Leonard Lewin. LC 78-26665. pap. 160.00 (ISBN 0-317-27673-5, 2025056). Bks Demand UMI.
Telecommunications: An Introduction. Cross. 1988. pap. write for info. (ISBN 0-471-85286-4). Wiley.
Telecommunications: An Introduction to Radio, Television & other Electronic Media. 2nd ed. Lynne S. Gross. 504p. 1986. pap. text ed. write for info. (ISBN 0-697-00479-1); write for info. instr's. manual (ISBN 0-697-00906-8). Wm C Brown.
Telecommunications Analyst. Jack Rudman. (Career Examination Ser.: C-3000). (Cloth bdg. avail. on request). 1988. pap. 14.00 (ISBN 0-8373-3000-9). Natl Learning.
Telecommunications Analyst Trainee. (Career Examination Ser.: C-3483). Date not set. pap. 14.00 (ISBN 0-8373-3483-7). Natl Learning.
Telecommunications & Developmentally Disabled People: Evaluations of Audio Conferencing, Personal Computers, Computers Conferencing, & Electronic Mail. Robert Johansen et al. 235p. 1981. 15.00 (ISBN 0-318-19195-4, R-50). Inst Future.
Telecommunications & Economic Development. Robert J. Saunders et al. LC 82-49065. (World Bank Ser.). 384p. 1983. pap. 16.95x (ISBN 0-8018-2829-5). Johns Hopkins.
Telecommunications & Equity--Policy Research Issues: Proceedings of the Thirteenth Annual Telecommunications Policy Research Conference, Airlie House, Airlie, VA, 21-24 April 1985. Ed. by J. Miller. 348p. 1986. 105.25 (ISBN 0-444-70013-7). Elsevier.
Telecommunications & State Development. Karl Case et al. 10.00. CSPA.
Telecommunications & the Computer. 2nd ed. James Martin. 1976. 59.00 (ISBN 0-13-902494-8). P-H.
Telecommunications & the Computer. James Martin. 670p. 1976. 60.00 (ISBN 0-686-98073-5). Telecom Lib.
Telecommunications & the Law, Vol. I. Ed. by Walter Sapronov. 464p. 1988. 50.00 (ISBN 0-7167-8155-7). W H Freeman.
Telecommunications & the Law: An Anthology. Ed. by Walter Sapronov. (Advances in Telecommunication Networks Ser.). (Illus.). 1988. text ed. 50.00 (ISBN 0-88175-153-7, Computer Sci Pr). W H Freeman.
Telecommunications Annual Index 1987. 1988. pap. text ed. 155.00 (ISBN 0-89947-059-9, EIC Intell). Bowker.
Telecommunications Careers. James L. Schefter. Ed. by James Rasof. (High-Tech Careers Ser.). (Illus.). 112p. (YA) (gr. 7-12). 1988. 11.90 (ISBN 0-531-10426-5). Watts.
Telecommunications Circuits Data Book. Ed. by Texas Instruments Engineering Staff. (Illus., Orig.). 1986. pap. 9.95 (ISBN 0-89512-194-8). Tex Instr Inc.
Telecommunications: Concepts, Development & Management. Mary M. Blyth & W. John Blyth. 352p. 1985. text ed. 30.08 scp (ISBN 0-672-97991-8); scp instr's. guide 7.33 (ISBN 0-672-97992-6). Bobbs.
Telecommunications Cost & Call Management. (Illus.). 516p. 1982. looseleaf 397.00 (ISBN 0-318-23151-4). Faulkner Tech Reports.
Telecommunications Deregulation Sourcebook. Stuart Brotman. 1987. text ed. 66.00 (ISBN 0-89006-205-6). Artech Hse.
Telecommunications Digest. Herbert A. Pairitz. 288p. 1985. text ed. 24.95 (ISBN 0-07-048102-4); pap. text ed. 12.95 (ISBN 0-07-048097-4). McGraw.
Telecommunications: Economics & Regulations. James M. Herring & Gerald C. Gross. LC 74-4686. (Telecommunications Ser.). 558p. 1974. Repr. of 1936 ed. 35.00x (ISBN 0-405-06050-5). Ayer Co Pubs.
Telecommunications for Information Management & Transfer: Proceedings of the First International Conference Held at Leicester Polytechnic, April 1987. Ed. by Mel Collier. 200p. 1988. text ed. 42.00 (ISBN 0-566-05551-1, Pub. by Gower Pub England). Gower Pub Co.
Telecommunications for Local Government. Ed. by Fred S. Knight et al. LC 82-15617. (Practical Management Ser.). (Illus.). 217p. (Orig.). 1982. 21.00 (ISBN 0-87326-036-8). Intl City Mgt.
Telecommunications for Management. C. T. Meadow & A. S. Tedesco. 400p. 1985. text ed. 42.95 (ISBN 0-07-041198-0). McGraw.
Telecommunications Function of the British Post Office. Douglas C. Pitt. 208p. 1980. text ed. 37.95 (ISBN 0-566-00273-6). Gower Pub Co.
Telecommunications in China. 130.00 (ISBN 0-686-33028-5). Info Gatekeepers.
Telecommunications in Crisis: The First Amendment, Technology, & Deregulation. Edwin Diamond et al. 1983. pap. 6.00 (ISBN 0-932790-39-9). Cato Inst.
Telecommunications in Health Care. H. U. Brown. 112p. 1982. 49.50 (ISBN 0-8493-5588-5). CRC Pr.
Telecommunications in Ports: Conference Proceedings. 118p. 1971. 14.75 (ISBN 0-317-59743-4, Pub. by T Telford UK). Am Soc Civil Eng.
Telecommunications in the Information Age: A Nontechnical Primer on the New Technologies. 2nd ed. Loy A. Singleton. LC 85-28793. 373p. 1986. prof. ref. 19.95x (ISBN 0-88730-098-7). Ballinger Pub.
Telecommunications in the Post-Divestiture Era. Ed. by Albert L. Danielsen & David R. Kamerschen. LC 86-45505. 272p. 29.00x (ISBN 0-669-13445-7). Lexington Bks.
Telecommunications in the U. S. Trends & Policies. Ed. by Leonard Lewin. LC 81-67809. (Artech Telecom-Computer Library). (Illus.). 449p. 1981. 60.00x (ISBN 0-89006-104-1). Artech Hse.
Telecommunications in the Year Two Thousand. Ed. by Indu Singh. LC 82-13800. (Communication & Information Science Ser.). 224p. 1983. text ed. 42.50 (ISBN 0-89391-137-2). Ablex Pub.
Telecommunications in the 1980's & After. Ed. by Sir James Lighthill et al. LC 79-670286. (Philosophical Transactions of the Royal Society). 1978. text ed. 50.00x (ISBN 0-85403-097-2, Pub. by Royal Soc London). Scholium Intl.
Telecommunications in Turmoil: Technology & Public Policy. Gerald R. Faulhaber. LC 87-1377. 200p. 1987. 29.95x (ISBN 0-88730-157-6). Ballinger Pub.
Telecommunications Industry. E. Sciberras & B. D. Payne. 1987. 60.00 (ISBN 0-912289-71-6). St James Pr.
Telecommunications Industry in Japan. Business Communications Staff. 120p. 1986. pap. 1950.00 (ISBN 0-89336-469-X, G-099). BCC.
Telecommunications Industry: The Challenge of Structural Change. OECD. (Information Computer Communications Policy Ser.: No. 14). 113p. (Orig.). 1988. pap. 18.00x (ISBN 92-64-13092-6). OECD.
Telecommunications Industry: The Dynamics of Market Structure. Gerald W. Brock. LC 80-25299. (Harvard Economic Studies: No. 151). (Illus.). 384p. 1981. text ed. 25.00x (ISBN 0-674-87285-1). Harvard U Pr.
Telecommunications Law Reform: Legislative Analysis. 64p. 1980. 6.00 (ISBN 0-8447-0227-7). Am Enterprise.
Telecommunications Making Sense out of New Technology & New Legislation: Proceedings of the 21st Annual Clinic on Library Applications of Data Processing, 1984. Deborah K. Conrad & Michael Flavin. 1985. text ed. 15.00 (ISBN 0-87845-072-6). U of Ill Lib Info Sci.
Telecommunications Management. B. L. Sherman. 432p. 1987. text ed. 31.95 (ISBN 0-07-056581-3). McGraw.
Telecommunications Management, Control, & Audit. Bernard K. Plagman & Anne O'Loughlin. 207p. 1988. pap. text ed. 45.00 (ISBN 0-89413-181-8). Inst Inter Aud.
Telecommunications Management for Business & Government. Larry A. Arredondo. Ed. by Harry Newton. 280p. 1980. 15.00 (ISBN 0-936648-07-4). Telecom Lib.
Telecommunications Management for the Data Processing Executive: A Decision-Maker's Guide to Systems Planning & Implementation. Milburn D. Smith, III. LC 87-2520. 208p. 1987. lib. bdg. 37.95 (ISBN 0-89930-110-X, LOT/, Quorum Bks). Greenwood.
Telecommunications Management Planning: ISDN Networks, Products & Services. Robert K. Heldman. (Illus.). 544p. 1987. 49.95 (ISBN 0-8306-2864-9, 2864, TAB-TPR). TAB Bks.
Telecommunications Measurements, Analysis, & Instrumentation. Kamilo Feher. (Illus.). 448p. 1987. text ed. 56.00 (ISBN 0-13-902404-2). P-H.
Telecommunications Networks: A Technical Introduction. Robert Murphy. LC 87-61013. 336p. 1987. 29.95 (ISBN 0-672-22588-3). Sams.
Telecommunications Networks: Issues & Trends. Ed. by M. E. Jacob. 179p. 1986. lib. bdg. 38.95 (ISBN 0-313-25782-5); pap. 28.50 (ISBN 0-313-25783-3). Greenwood.
Telecommunications on the Apple IIe & IIc. Russell Holt & Gary Little. 1986. pap. 14.95 (ISBN 0-89303-887-3). P-H.
Telecommunications Outlook. Thomas B. Cross. (Illus.). 300p. 1985. 300.00 (ISBN 0-923426-04-3). Cross Info.
Telecommunications Planning. Chantico-QED Staff. (Chantico Technical Management Ser.). 364p. 1988. 39.94 (ISBN 0-89435-254-7). Qed Info Sci.
Telecommunications Policies in Ten Countries: Prospects for Future Competitive Access. Martin J. Kalin. (NTIA Contractor Report Ser.: No. 85-33). 172p. (Orig.). 1986. pap. 5.50 (ISBN 0-318-21648-5, S/N 003-000-00639-5). USGPO.
Telecommunications Policy & the Citizen: Public Interest Perspectives on the Communications Act Rewrite. Ed. by Timothy R. Haight. 296p. 1981. 44.95 (ISBN 0-275-90359-1, C0359); pap. 19.95 (ISBN 0-03-054136-0). Praeger.
Telecommunications Policy Yearbook 1981. Ed. by Jorge R. Schement et al. LC 81-22648. 332p. 1982. 44.95 (ISBN 0-275-90897-6, C0897). Praeger.
Telecommunications: Pressures & Policies for Change. OECD Staff. 142p. (Orig.). 1983. pap. 14.00x (ISBN 92-64-12428-4). OECD.
Telecommunications Principles. 2nd ed. J. J. O'Reilly. 176p. 1988. text ed. 24.95. Van Nos Reinhold.
Telecommunications, Radio & Information Technology (Communications 84) (IEE Conference Publications Ser.: No. 235). 179p. 1984. pap. 76.00 (ISBN 0-85296-292-4, IC235). Inst Elect Eng.
Telecommunications Regulation & Deregulation in Industrialized Democracies. Ed. by M. S. Snow. 346p. 1986. 92.75 (ISBN 0-444-87926-9, North-Holland). Elsevier.
Telecommunications Regulation & the Constitution. Robert J. Buchan & C. Christopher Johnston. 276p. (Orig.). 1982. pap. text ed. 18.95x (ISBN 0-920380-69-7, Pub. by Inst Res Pub Canada). Brookfield Pub Co.
Telecommunications Regulation Today & Tomorrow. Ed. by Eli M. Noam. 1984. 45.00 (ISBN 0-15-004294-9, Law & Business). HarBraceJ.
Telecommunications Regulatory Monitor. David A. Irwin. LC 87-114898. 1984. 3.97 (ISBN 0-934960-19-4). Phillips Pub Inc.
Telecommunications Revolution. Graham Storrs. LC 84-73582. (Tomorrow's World Ser.). (Illus.). 48p. (gr. 5-8). 1985. lib. bdg. 12.40 (ISBN 0-531-18015-8, Pub. by Bookwright Pr). Watts.
Telecommunications Sourcebook, 1988. North American Telecommunications Association Staff. Ed. by Mary Lou Coffman et al. (Illus.). 250p. (Orig.). 1987. pap. text ed. 35.00 (ISBN 0-940919-02-8). NA Telecomm Assn.
Telecommunications Specialist. (Career Examination Ser.: C-3410). Date not set. pap. 16.00 (ISBN 0-8373-3410-1). Natl Learning.
Telecommunications Survival Guide for Retailers. 65p. 1985. 28.00 (ISBN 0-317-65514-0, 30-5070). Natl Ret Merch.
Telecommunications Switching. J. Gordon Pearce. LC 80-20586. (Applications of Communications Theory Ser.). 348p. 1981. 42.50x (ISBN 0-306-40584-9, Plenum Pr). Plenum Pub.
Telecommunications Switching Principles. Michael T. Hills. (Illus.). 1979. text ed. 40.00x (ISBN 0-262-08092-3). MIT Pr.
Telecommunications System Giude. (Illus.). 720p. 1982. looseleaf 397.00. Faulkner Tech Reports.
Telecommunications Systems. (Illus.). 1975. pap. 3.50 (ISBN 0-685-54122-3). Natl Fire Prot.
Telecommunications Systems & Equipment Market in the Middle East Arab Countries. 399p. 1984. 1750.00 (ISBN 0-86621-620-0, W692). Frost & Sullivan.
Telecommunications Systems & Services Directory. 3nd ed. Ed. by John Krol. LC 83-11628. 1987. 285.00x (ISBN 0-8103-2345-1). Gale.
Telecommunications Systems: Principles & Practices for Rural & Forestry Fire Services. National Fire Protection Association Staff. (Illus.). 31p. 1986. 12.00 (ISBN 0-317-63400-3, 297-86). Natl Fire Prot.
Telecommunications Technician. (Career Examination Ser.: C-3411). Date not set. pap. 14.00 (ISBN 0-8373-3411-X). Natl Learning.
Telecommunications Technologies, 1985-1986: Japan Annual Reviews in Electronics Computers & Telecommunications, Vol. 20. Ed. by H. Inose. 378p. 1985. 86.00 (ISBN 0-444-87862-9, North-Holland). Elsevier.
Telecommunications Technology. R. L. Brewster. LC 85-27347. (Electrical & Electronic Engineering Ser.). 200p. 1986. 34.95 (ISBN 0-470-20270-X). Halsted Pr.
Telecommunications Test Equipment. Market Intelligence Research Company Staff. Ed. by W. Hammersley. 317p. (Orig.). 1986. pap. text ed. 995.00x (ISBN 0-916483-04-5, A054). Market Res Co.
Telecommunications Test Equipment. 137p. 1985. 1650.00x (ISBN 0-88694-662-X). Intl Res Dev.
Telecommunications: The Complete Guide to Business Communications with the Personal Computer. Jerry Willis. 256p. 1986. pap. cancelled (ISBN 0-915391-22-8, Pub. by Microtrend). Slawson Comm.
Telecommunications Transmission Engineering: Facilities, Vol. 2. Ed. by Robert H. Klie. (Illus.). 739p. 1977. text ed. 25.00 (350-052). AT&T Customer Info.
Telecommunications Transmission Engineering: Networks & Services, Vol. 3. 2nd ed. Ed. by Robert H. Klie. (Illus.). 625p. 1977. text ed. 25.00 (350-053). AT&T Customer Info.
Telecommunications Transmission Engineering: Principles, Vol. 1. 2nd ed. Ed. by Robert H. Klie. (Illus.). 665p. 1977. text ed. 25.00 (350-051). AT&T Customer Info.
Telecommunications Transmission Handbook. Roger L. Freeman. 700p. 1981. 67.95 (ISBN 0-686-98109-X). Telecom Lib.
Telecommunications-Transportation Tradeoff: Options for Tomorrow. Jack M. Nilles et al. LC 76-18107. 208p. 1976. text ed. 44.50 (ISBN 0-471-01507-5, JW). Krieger.
Telecommunications: Voice-Data with Fiber Optic Applications. Wayne Tomasi & Vincent Alisousksas. (Illus.). 400p. 1988. text ed. 40.00 (ISBN 0-13-902602-9). P-H.
Telecommunications, 1987: Current Developments in Policy & Regulation. (Patents, Copyrights, Trademarks, & Literary Property Ser.). 984p. 1987. 45.00 (G4-3804). PLI.
Telecommuters. Francis Kinsman. LC 87-25413. 238p. 1987. 42.95 (ISBN 0-471-91789-3). Wiley.
Telecommuting: A Selective, Annotated Bibliography. James J. Sanchez. (Public Administration Ser.: P 2263). 15p. 1987. 3.75 (ISBN 1-55590-523-4). Vance Biblios.
Telecommuting: How to Make It Work for You & Your Company. Gil E. Gordon & Marcia M. Kelly. 233p. 1986. 29.95 (ISBN 0-13-902339-9, Busn). P-H.
Telecommuting: The Organizational & Behavioral Effects of Working at Home. Reagan M. Ramsower. Ed. by Richard Farmer. LC 84-28095. (Research for Business Decisions Ser.: No. 75). 208p. 1985. 39.95 (ISBN 0-8357-1628-7). UMI Res Pr.

Telephony's Dictionary. 2nd ed. Graham Langley. 416p. 1986. 40.00 (ISBN 0-917845-04-8). Intertec IL.
Telepolitics. Frederick D. Wilhelmsen & Jane Bret. LC 73-187493. 254p. 10.00 (ISBN 0-912766-04-2). Tundra Bks.
Teleports & the Intelligent City. Ed. by Andrew D. Lipman et al. 450p. 1986. 55.00 (ISBN 0-87094-706-0). Dow Jones-Irwin.
Teleports in the Information Age: Proceedings of the Teleports '86 Congress, Amsterdam, The Netherlands, May 21-23, 1986. Ed. by J. M. Noothoven van Goor & G. Lefcoe. 350p. 1987. 105.25 (ISBN 0-444-70183-4, North Holland). Elsevier.
Teleports Market. 233p. 1985. 1700.00 (ISBN 0-86621-308-2, A1388). Frost & Sullivan.
Teleprinting & Electronic Mail. 185p. 1985. 1650.00x (ISBN 0-88694-651-4). Intl Res Dev.
Teleprocessing Network Organization. reference ed. James Martin. 1969. 38.00 (ISBN 0-13-902452-2). P-H.
Telepsychics: The Magic Power of Perfect Living. Joseph Murphy. LC 73-6775. 230p. 1988. pap. 8.95 (ISBN 0-87516-598-2). DeVorss.
Teles: The Cynic Teacher. Ed. by Edward N. O'Neil. LC 76-41800. (Society of Biblical Literature. Texts & Translantion - Graeco-Roman Religion Ser.). 1979. pap. 8.95 (ISBN 0-89130-092-9, 060211). Scholars Pr GA.
Telescope. Louis Bell. 287p. 1981. pap. 6.95 (ISBN 0-486-24151-3). Dover.
Telescope. Louis Bell. (Illus.). 13.25 (ISBN 0-8446-5877-4). Peter Smith.
Telescope Making for Beginners. Roy Worvill. 79p. 1984. 20.00x (ISBN 0-900707-80-1, Pub. by Kahn & Averill). State Mutual Bk.
Telescope Making (1905) Paul N. Hasluck. (Illus.). 160p. 1983. pap. 12.50 (ISBN 0-87556-498-4). Saifer.
Telescopes & Islands. Charles L. Black. LC 76-179826. (New Poetry Ser.). Repr. of 1963 ed. 16.00 (ISBN 0-404-56026-1). AMS Pr.
Telescopes & Observatories. Heather Couper & Nigel Henbest. (Space Scientist Ser.). (Illus.). 32p. (gr. 4-6). 1987. PLB 10.90 (ISBN 0-531-10361-7). Watts.
Telescopes for the Nineteen Eighties. Ed. by G. Burbidge & A. Hewitt. (Illus.). 1981. text ed. 27.00 (ISBN 0-8243-2902-3). Annual Reviews.
Telescopes: Stars & Stellar Systems, Vol. I. Ed. by Gerald P. Kuiper & Barbara Middlehurst. LC 60-14356. (Midway Reprint Ser.). (Illus.). 1977. pap. text ed. 21.00x (ISBN 0-226-45962-4). U of Chicago Pr.
Telescopes, Tides, & Tactics: A Galilean Dialogue about the "Starry Messenger" & Systems of the World. Stillman Drake. LC 82-24790. 256p. 1983. lib. bdg. 22.50x (ISBN 0-226-16231-1). U of Chicago Pr.
Telescopic Prosthetic Therapy: Peridontal Prosthesis - Fixed & Removable. I. L. Yalisove & J. B. Dietz, Jr. (Illus.). 367p. 1977. text ed. 48.50x (ISBN 0-89313-005-2). G F Stickley Co.
Telescreen & Radiographic Examination of Urinary Transport. Hajos. 1978. cancelled 12.00 (ISBN 963-05-1507-5, Pub. by Akademiai Kaido Hungary). IPS.
Telescreen & Radiographic Examination of Urinary Transport. Endre Hajos. 118p. 1978. 56.00x (ISBN 0-569-08455-5, Pub. by Collets (UK)). State Mutual Bk.
Telesearch: Direct Dial the Best Job of Your Life. John Truitt. LC 82-15714. 118p. 1983. 11.95x (ISBN 0-87196-900-9). Facts on File.
Telesearch: Direct Dial the Best Job of Your Life. John Truitt. Ed. by B. Lippman. 128p. 1985. pap. 5.95 (ISBN 0-02-008850-7, Collier). Macmillan.
Teleshock: How to Survive the Break-up of Ma Bell. William J. Cook & Christopher Ma. Date not set. pap. 5.95 (ISBN 0-671-55400-X). PB.
Teleshopping. 314p. 1983. 1285.00x (ISBN 0-88694-547-X). Intl Res Dev.
Teleshopping, Telebanking & Telesoftware - Services & Systems: A Selective, Annotated Bibliography. James J. Sanchez. (Public Administration Ser.: P 2261). 12p. 1987. 3.75 (ISBN 1-55590-521-8). Vance Biblios.
Telesoftware. National Computing Centre. 30p. 1983. pap. 8.50 (ISBN 0-471-88587-8). Wiley.
Teletechniques: An Instructional Model for Interactive Teleconferencing. Lorne A. Parker & Mavis K. Monson. Ed. by Danny G. Langdon. LC 79-24442. (Instructional Design Library). 108p. 1980. 23.95 (ISBN 0-87778-158-3). Educ Tech Pubns.
Teletext & Videotex in the United States: Market Potential, Technology, & Public Policy Issues. John Tydeman & Hubert Lipinski. (Illus.). 314p. 1982. text ed. 43.50 (ISBN 0-07-000427-7). McGraw.
Teletext: Display Systems. Ed. by Network Staff. 1985. 95.00x (ISBN 0-904999-86-6, Pub. by Network Events Ltd). State Mutual Bk.
Teletext Systems: A Selective, Annotated Bibliography. James J. Sanchez. (Public Administration Ser.: P 2265). 9p. 1987. 3.00 (ISBN 1-55590-525-0). Vance Biblios.
Teletraffic Analysis & Computer Performance Evaluation: Proceedings of the International Seminar, Centre for Mathematics & Computer Science, Amsterdam, The Netherlands, June 2-6, 1986. International Seminar, Centre for Mathematics & Computer Science, Staff. Ed. by O. J. Boxma et al. (North Holland Studies in Telecommunication: No. 7). 530p. 1986. 118.50 (ISBN 0-444-70025-0, North Holland). Elsevier.
Teletraffic Issues in an Advanced Information Society, ITC 11, 2 pts. Ed. by M. Akiyama. 1200p. 1986. Set. 125.00 (ISBN 0-444-87919-6, North Holland). Elsevier.
Teletypist. Jack Rudman. (Career Examination Ser.: C-831). (Cloth bdg. avail. on request). pap. 12.00 (ISBN 0-8373-0831-3). Natl Learning.
Televangelism: Power & Politics on God's Frontier. Jeffrey K. Hadden & Anson Shupe. LC 87-30556. 1988. 19.95 (ISBN 0-8050-0778-4). H Holt & Co.
Televangelism: The Marketing of Popular Religion. Razelle Frankl. LC 86-6584. (Illus.). 224p. 1987. 22.50 (ISBN 0-8093-1299-9). S Ill U Pr.
Televised Legislatures: Political Information Technology & Public Choice. W. Mark Crain. 1988. lib. bdg. 34.00 (ISBN 0-89838-262-9). Kluwer Academic.
Televised Medicine Advertising & Children. Thomas S. Robertson et al. LC 79-4280. 192p. 1979. 38.95 (ISBN 0-275-90413-X, C0413). Praeger.
Television see also T V.
Television. Karen Jacobson. LC 82-4456. (New True Bks.). (Illus.). (gr. k-4). 1982. PLB 12.60 (ISBN 0-516-01659-8). Childrens.
Television. Jacques Lacan. Tr. by Denis Hollier & Rosalind Kraus. (Illus.). Date not set. 19.95 (ISBN 0-393-02496-2). Norton.
Television. David Lachenbruch. LC 84-9914. (Look Inside Ser.). (Illus.). 48p. (gr. 4-12). 1984. PLB 15.99 (ISBN 0-8172-1408-9); pap. 9.27 (ISBN 0-8172-1435-6). Raintree Pubs.
Television. Andrew Langley. (Topics Ser.). 32p. (gr. 4-6). 1987. lib. bdg. 11.90 (ISBN 0-531-18118-9, Pub. by Bookwright Pr). Watts.
Television. (Illus., Arabic.). (gr. 5-12). 3.50x (ISBN 0-86685-237-9). Intl Bk Ctr.
Television. Michael Winship. LC 87-42662. (Illus.). 416p. 1988. 24.45 (ISBN 0-394-56401-4). Random.
Television, a Danger for the Individual. J. Schootemeijer. Ed. by De Rozekruis Pevs Staff. (Orig.). 1986. pap. 1.75 (ISBN 90-70196-44-1). Rozekruis Pr.
Television: A Guide to the Literature. Mary B. Cassata & Thomas D. Skill. LC 83-43236. 160p. 1985. lib. bdg. 36.00 (ISBN 0-89774-140-4). Oryx Pr.
Television: A Struggle for Power. Frank Waldrop & Joseph Borkin. LC 72-161140. (History of Broadcasting: Radio to Television Ser.). 1971. Repr. of 1938 ed. 22.00 (ISBN 0-405-03561-6). Ayer Co Pubs.
Television: A World Survey. UNESCO. LC 72-4684. (International Propaganda & Communications Ser.). 235p. 1972. Repr. of 1955 ed. 15.00 (ISBN 0-405-04768-1). Ayer Co Pubs.
Television Advertising & Televangelism: Discourse Analysis of Persuasive Language. Rosemarie Schmidt & Joseph F. Kess. LC 87-15812. (Pragmatics & Beyond Ser.: No. VII-5). vi, 88p. 1986. 21.95x (ISBN 1-55619-006-9). Benjamins North Am.
Television & Adult Education. Ed. by Robert Hilliard. 160p. 1985. 18.95 (ISBN 0-87073-241-2). Schenkman Bks Inc.
Television & Aggression: An Experimental Field Study. Seymour Feshbach & Roger D. Singer. LC 70-138457. (Jossey-Bass Behavioral Science Ser.). pap. 51.00 (ISBN 0-317-26063-4, 2023777). Bks Demand UMI.
Television & Aggression: Results of a Panel Study. J. Ronald Milavsky et al. (Quantitative Studies in Social Relations). 493p. 1982. 29.95 (ISBN 0-12-495980-6). Acad Pr.
Television & America's Children: A Crisis of Neglect. Edward L. Palmer. Ed. by George Gerbner & Marsha Siefert. (Communications & Society Ser.). 208p. 1988. 19.95 (ISBN 0-19-505540-3). Oxford U Pr.
Television & Antisocial Behavior: Field Experiments. Stanley Milgram & R. Lance Shotland. 1973. 19.95 (ISBN 0-12-496350-1). Acad Pr.
Television & Cable Factbook, 2 vols, No. 53. rev. ed. 1985. 173.00 (ISBN 0-911486-20-8). Stations Vol (ISBN 0-911486-18-6). Cable & Services Vol (ISBN 0-911486-19-4). Warren Pub Inc.
Television & Cable Factbook, 2 vols, No. 54. rev. ed. 1986. Set. 225.00 (ISBN 0-911486-25-9). Stations Vol (ISBN 0-911486-23-2). Cable & Services Vol (ISBN 0-911486-24-0). Warren Pub Inc.
Television & Children. David A. England. LC 83-83089. (Fastback Ser.: No. 207). 50p. (Orig.). 1984. pap. 0.90 (ISBN 0-87367-207-0). Phi Delta Kappa.
Television & Children. Michael J. Howe. LC 76-28991. 157p. 1977. 19.50 (ISBN 0-208-01537-X, Linnet). Shoe String.
Television & Children: A Special Medium for a Special Audience. Aimee Dorr. LC 85-19675. (CommText Ser.: Vol. 14). 160p. 1986. text ed. 19.95 (ISBN 0-8039-2568-9); pap. text ed. 9.95 (ISBN 0-8039-2565-4). Sage.
Television & Delinquency. James D. Halloran et al. LC 71-517136. (Great Britain Television Research Committee Working Paper Ser.: No. 3). pap. 55.50 (ISBN 0-317-28256-5, 2022636). Bks Demand UMI.
Television & Education. Ed. by Chester M. Pierce. LC 77-94473. (Sage Contemporary Social Science Issues Ser.: No. 44). pap. 26.00 (ISBN 0-317-08983-8, 2021940). Bks Demand UMI.
Television & Ethics: A Bibliography. Thomas Cooper. 300p. 1988. lib. bdg. 45.00x (ISBN 0-8161-8966-8, Hall Reference). G K Hall.
Television & History. Colin McArthur. (Television Monograph: No. 8). 60p. 1978. pap. 6.95 (ISBN 0-85170-073-X, Pub. by British Film Inst England). U of Ill Pr.
Television & Law Enforcement. Joseph Missonellie & James S. D'Angelo. (Illus.). 180p. 1984. 21.75 (ISBN 0-398-05007-4). C C Thomas.
Television & National Sport: The U. S. & Britain. Joan M. Chandler. (Sport & Society Ser.). 256p. 1988. 24.95 (ISBN 0-252-01516-9). U of Ill Pr.
Television & Radio. 5th, ref. ed. Giraud Chester et al. (Illus.). 1978. write for info. (ISBN 0-13-902981-8). P-H.
Television & Radio. Louis Sabin. LC 84-8446. (Illus.). 32p. (gr. 3-6). 1985. PLB 8.45 (ISBN 0-8167-0310-8); pap. text ed. 1.95 (ISBN 0-8167-0311-6). Troll Assocs.
Television & Radio Announcing. 5th ed. Stuart W. Hyde. LC 86-81341. 544p. 1987. pap. text ed. 36.76 (ISBN 0-395-35939-2); instr's. manual 2.36 (ISBN 0-395-42468-2). HM.
Television & Radio in the United Kingdom. Burton Paulu. 1981. 39.50x (ISBN 0-8166-0941-1). U of Minn Pr.
Television & Radio: 1973 & 1974 Supplement: Forms Bk. II. Joseph Taubman. LC 74-189328. 60.00 (ISBN 0-318-00775-4). Law-Arts.
Television & Religion: The Shaping of Faith & Value. William F. Fore. LC 87-1214. 224p. (Orig.). 1987. pap. 11.95 (ISBN 0-8066-2268-7, 10-6229). Augsburg.
Television & Social Behavior: Beyond Violence & Children. Ed. by Stephen B. Withey & Ronald P. Abeles. LC 79-29684. 356p. 1980. text ed. 36.00x (ISBN 0-89859-014-0). L Erlbaum Assocs.
Television & Social Control. Mallory Wober & Barrie Gunter. LC 87-18763. 250p. 1988. 29.95 (ISBN 0-312-01305-1). St Martin.
Television & Technology: Alternative Communication Systems. William E. McCavitt. LC 83-10428. (Illus.). 152p. (Orig.). 1983. lib. bdg. 27.25 (ISBN 0-8191-3329-9); pap. text ed. 12.00 (ISBN 0-8191-3330-2). U Pr of Amer.
Television & the Aggressive Child: A Cross National Comparison. Ed. by L. R. Huesmann & L. D. Eron. (Zillman-Bryant Ser.). 326p. 1986. text ed. 36.00 (ISBN 0-89859-754-4). L Erlbaum Assocs.
Television & the Aging Audience. Richard H. Davis. LC 80-68093. (Illus.). 107p. (Orig.). 1980. 12.00x (ISBN 0-88474-096-X, 05731-2); pap. 8.00x (05732-0). Lexington Bks.
Television & the Child: An Empirical Study of the Effect of Television on the Young. Hilde T. Himmelweit et al. LC 59-197. pap. 135.80 (ISBN 0-317-29717-1, 2019716). Bks Demand UMI.
Television & the Classroom. Don Kaplan. LC 86-7321. (Video Bookshelf Ser.). 165p. 1986. pap. 32.95 (ISBN 0-86729-138-9). Knowledge Indus.
Television & the Classroom Reading Program: If You Can't Beat 'em Join 'em. George J. Becker. LC 73-89304. (Reading Aids Ser.). pap. 20.00 (2026792). Bks Demand UMI.
Television & the News: A Critical Appraisal. Harry J. Skornia. LC 68-8629. (Pacific Books Paperbounds, PB-13). 1974. pap. 3.95 (ISBN 0-87015-209-2). Pacific Bks.
Television & the Performing Arts: A Handbook & Reference Guide to American Cultural Programming. Brian G. Rose. LC 85-14655. 291p. 1986. lib. bdg. 36.95 (ISBN 0-313-24159-7, RTV/). Greenwood.
Television & the Preschool Child: A Psychological Theory of Instruction & Curriculum Development. Ed. by H. Lesser. (Educational Psychology Ser.). 1977. 24.95 (ISBN 0-12-444250-1). Acad Pr.
Television & the Presidential Elections: Self-Interest & the Public Interest. Ed. by Martin Linsky. LC 82-49010. 160p. 1983. 21.50x (ISBN 0-669-06397-5); pap. 12.95x (ISBN 0-669-06947-7). Lexington Bks.
Television & the Red Menace: The Video Road to Vietnam. J. Fred MacDonald. 256p. 1985. 35.00 (ISBN 0-275-90141-6, C0141); pap. 14.95 (ISBN 0-275-91807-6, B1807). Praeger.
Television & the School. Joseph R. Amatuzzi. LC 82-60522. 125p. 1983. pap. 14.95 (ISBN 0-88247-676-9). R & E Pubs.
Television & the Socialization of the Minority Child. Ed. by Gordon Berry & C. Mitchell-Kernan. LC 81-22795. 1982. 39.50 (ISBN 0-12-093220-2). Acad Pr.
Television & Video in Libraries & Schools. Helen M. Gothberg. LC 82-23957. 246p. 1983. 27.50 (ISBN 0-208-01859-X, Lib Prof Pubns). Shoe String.
Television & Youth: Twenty-Five Years of Research & Controversy. John P. Murray. 278p. (Orig.). 1980. pap. text ed. 10.00 (ISBN 0-938510-00-2, 010-TV). Boys Town Ctr.
Television As a Social Issue. Ed. by Stuart Oskamp. (Applied Social Psychology Annual Ser.: Vol. 8). 320p. 1988. text ed. 39.95 (ISBN 0-8039-3069-0); pap. text ed. 17.95 (ISBN 0-8039-3070-4). Sage.
Television As an Instrument of Terror. Arthur A. Berger. LC 78-55942. 214p. 1979. 12.95 (ISBN 0-87855-708-3). Transaction Bks.
Television Audience: Patterns of Viewing. A. Ehrenberg et al. 250p. 1986. text ed. 47.50 (ISBN 0-566-05083-8, Pub. by Gower Pub England). Gower Pub Co.
Television by Satellite: Legal Aspects. Stephen De B. Bate. 1987. 150.00x (ISBN 0-906214-43-2, Pub. by ESC Ltd UK). State Mutual Bk.
Television Censorship & the Law. Colin R. Munro. 187p. 1979. text ed. 37.95x (ISBN 0-566-00176-4). Gower Pub Co.
Television Comedy Series: An Episode Guide to 153 TV Sitcoms in Syndication. Joel Eisner & David Krinsky. LC 83-42901. (Illus.). 880p. 1984. lib. bdg. 55.00x (ISBN 0-89950-088-9). McFarland & Co.
Television Contacts Directory, 1988. Ed. by Bob Del Pazzo. 1988. 233.00 (ISBN 0-935224-34-3). Larimi Comm.
Television Coverage of International Affairs. Ed. by William C. Adams. LC 81-15054. (Communication & Information Science Ser.). 1982. 37.50 (ISBN 0-89391-103-8). Ablex Pub.
Television Coverage of the Middle East. William C. Adams. LC 81-15049. (Communications & Information Sciences Ser.). 176p. 1981. text ed. 32.50x (ISBN 0-89391-083-8X). Ablex Pub.
Television Coverage of the Nineteen Eighty Presidential Campaign. Ed. by William C. Adams. LC 83-3768. (Communication & Information Science Ser.). 1983. 35.00 (ISBN 0-89391-104-6). Ablex Pub.
Television Coverage of the Nineteen Eighty-Three General Election. Barrie Gunter et al. 142p. 1986. text ed. 37.95 (ISBN 0-566-00861-0, Pub. by Gower Pub England). Gower Pub Co.
Television Culture: Popular Pleasures & Politics. John Fiske. (Studies in Communication). 400p. 1988. 49.95x (ISBN 0-416-92440-9); pap. text ed. 12.95x (ISBN 0-416-92430-1). Routledge Chapman & Hall.
Television Deregulation. Linda K. Lewis. (Public Administration Ser.: P 1895). 47p. 1986. 12.50 (ISBN 0-89028-805-4). Vance Biblios.
Television Diagrams, 1948. 144p. 1987. 17.00 (ISBN 0-938630-59-8, TV-2). ARS Enterprises.
Television Digest's Cable & Station Coverage Atlas. rev. ed. LC 67-118025. 1981-82. 115.50 (ISBN 0-911486-05-4). Warren Pub Inc.
Television Digest's Cable & Station Coverage Atlas, 1983. rev. ed. 1983. 121.00 (ISBN 0-911486-09-7). Warren Pub Inc.
Television Digest's Cable & Station Coverage Atlas, 1986. rev. ed. 1986. 195.00 (ISBN 0-911486-26-7). Warren Pub Inc.
Television Drama Programming: A Comprehensive Chronicle, 1975-1980. Larry J. Gianakos. LC 81-5319. 471p. 1981. 27.50 (ISBN 0-8108-1438-2). Scarecrow.
Television Drama Series Programming: A Comprehensive Chronicle, 1947-1959. Larry J. Gianakos. LC 80-17023. 581p. 1980. 35.00 (ISBN 0-8108-1330-0). Scarecrow.
Television Drama Series Programming: A Comprehensive Chronicle, 1959-1975. Larry J. Gianakos. LC 78-650. 806p. 1978. 37.50 (ISBN 0-8108-1116-2). Scarecrow.
Television Drama Series Programming: A Comprehensive Chronicle, 1980-1982. Larry J. Gianakos. LC 83-3388. 686p. 1983. 45.00 (ISBN 0-8108-1626-1). Scarecrow.
Television Drama Series Programming: A Comprehensive Chronicle, 1982-1984. Larry J. Gianakos. LC 85-30428. 838p. 1987. 62.50 (ISBN 0-8108-1876-0). Scarecrow.
Television Electronics: Theory & Servicing. 8th ed. M. Kiver & M. Kaufman. 768p. 1983. text ed. 33.95 (ISBN 0-8273-1328-4). Delmar.
Television Electronics: Theory & Service. 8th ed. Milton Kiver & Milton Kaufman. 974p. 1983. 45.95 (ISBN 0-442-24871-7). Van Nos Reinhold.
Television Engineering Handbook. K. B. Benson. 1472p. 1985. text ed. 95.50 (ISBN 0-07-004779-0). McGraw.
Television Engineering: Report. International Television Conference, London, 1962. LC 65-56108. (Institution of Electrical Engineers Conference Report Ser.: No. 5). pap. 148.00 (ISBN 0-317-10164-1, 2050325). Bks Demand UMI.
Television Evening News Covers Inflation: 1978-79. Tom Bethell. Ed. by Media Institute Staff. (Illus.). 52p. (Orig.). 1980. pap. 5.00 (ISBN 0-937790-00-1). Media Inst.
Television Evening News Covers Nuclear Energy: A Ten Year Perspective. Media Institute Staff. (Illus.). 140p. (Orig.). 1979. pap. 35.00 (ISBN 0-937790-03-6). Media Inst.
Television Experience: What Children See. sagemark ed. Mariann P. Winick & Charles Winick. LC 78-19670. (People & Communication Ser.: Vol. 6). (Illus.). 215p. 1979. 35.00 (ISBN 0-8039-1142-4). Sage.

Tell Me about Yourself: How to Interview Anyone from Your Friends to Famous People. D. L. Mabery. LC 85-7001. 80p. (gr. 4 up). 1985. PLB 9.95 (ISBN 0-8225-1604-7). Lerner Pubns.
Tell Me Africa: An Approach to African Literature. James Olney. LC 72-12111. 304p. 1973. 41.00x (ISBN 0-691-06254-4); pap. 12.50x (ISBN 0-691-01310-1). Princeton U Pr.
Tell Me Again, Lord, I Forget. Ruth H. Calkin. (Living Bks.). 160p. (Orig.). 1986. 3.50 (ISBN 0-8423-6990-2). Tyndale.
Tell Me Another. Bob Barton. LC 86-18406. 160p. (Orig.). 1986. pap. text ed. 12.50x (ISBN 0-435-08231-0). Heinemann Ed.
Tell Me How Long the Train's Been Gone. James Baldwin. 1986. pap. 1.95 (ISBN 0-440-38581-4, LE). Dell.
Tell Me How to Please God: 16 Lessons, Vol. 4. Lois J. Haas. (Tiny Steps of Faith Ser.). (ps). 1974. complete kit 14.95 (ISBN 0-86508-020-8); text only 3.45 (ISBN 0-86508-021-6); color & action book o.p. 0.90 (ISBN 0-86508-022-4). BCM Pubn.
Tell Me How to Trust God: 16 Lessons, Vol. 3. Lois J. Haas. (Tiny Steps of Faith Ser.). (ps). 1970. complete kit 14.95 (ISBN 0-86508-017-8); text only 3.45 (ISBN 0-86508-018-6); color & action book o.p. 0.90 (ISBN 0-86508-019-4). BCM Pubn.
Tell Me If the Lovers Are Losers. Cynthia Voigt. LC 81-8079. 252p. (gr. 7 up). 1982. 11.95 (ISBN 0-689-30911-2, Atheneum Childrens Bks). Macmillan.
Tell Me I'm Allowed to Love. J. Henry. 1979. 5.50 (ISBN 0-682-49500-X). Exposition-Phoenix.
Tell Me More: An ESL Conversation Text. Sandra Elbaum & Judi Peman. 1988. pap. text ed. price not set (ISBN 0-673-38003-3). Scott F.
Tell Me No Lies. Mira Lederer. 1982. pap. 2.50 (ISBN 0-89083-945-X). Zebra.
Tell Me No Lies. Mira Lederer. 304p. 1988. pap. 3.95 (ISBN 0-8217-2435-5). Zebra.
Tell Me No Lies. Elizabeth Lowell. 400p. 1986. pap. 3.95 (ISBN 0-373-97029-3, Pub. by Worldwide). Harlequin Bks.
Tell Me of a Land That's Fair. James V. Hutton, Jr. 52p. 1988. Repr. lib. bdg. 19.95x (ISBN 0-8095-8217-1). Borgo Pr.
Tell Me of a Land That's Fair. James V. Hutton, Jr. 52p. (Orig.). 1987. pap. 5.00 (ISBN 0-935931-37-6). Iberian Pub.
Tell Me Papa. Joy Johnson & Marvin Johnson. 1980. pap. 7.95 boards (ISBN 0-930194-02-0). Ctr Thanatology.
Tell Me, Sean O'Farrell. Padraic O'Farrell. 98p. (Orig.). 1986. pap. 9.95 (ISBN 0-85342-789-5, Pub. by Mercier Pr Ireland). Irish Bks Media.
Tell Me Some More. Crosby N. Bonsall. LC 61-5773. (Harper I Can Read Bks.). (Illus.). 64p. (gr. k-3). 1961. PLB 10.89 (ISBN 0-06-020601-2). HarpJ.
Tell Me that You Love Me, Junie Moon. Marjorie Kellogg. LC 68-24600. 216p. (YA) (gr. 9 up). 1984. pap. 3.95 (ISBN 0-374-51825-4). FS&G.
Tell Me Who I Am. Adrian Van Kaam & Susan Muto. 4.95 (ISBN 0-87193-145-1). Dimension Bks.
Tell Me Who I Am: James Agee's Search for Selfhood. Mark A. Doty. LC 80-22440. xvi, 144p. 1981. 20.00 (ISBN 0-8071-0758-1). La State U Pr.
Tell Me Why. rev. ed. Arkady Leokum. (Tell Me Why Bks.). (Illus.). 208p. (gr. 2-9). 1986. No. 1. 9.95 ea. (ISBN 0-448-22501-8, G&D). No. 2 (ISBN 0-448-22502-6). No. 3 (ISBN 0-448-22503-4). No. 4 (ISBN 0-448-22504-2). Putnam Pub Group.
Tell Me Why, No. 5. Arkady Leokum. (Illus.). 176p. (gr. 2-9). 1988. 9.95 (ISBN 0-448-19069-9, G&D). Putnam Pub Group.
Tell Me Why: A Beatles Commentary. Tim Riley. LC 87-40492. 1988. 19.95 (ISBN 0-394-55061-7). Knopf.
Tell Me Why: A Guide to Children's Questions about Faith & Life. Marilyn F. Holm. LC 85-7355. 144p. (Orig.). 1985. pap. 7.95 (ISBN 0-8066-2160-5, 10-6230). Augsburg.
Tell My Priests: Words of Our Lord to Priests about His Mercy as Revealed to Sister Faustina Kowalska. Compiled by George W. Kosicki & Marians of the immaculate Conception. LC 87-62982. 112p. 1988. pap. text ed. write for info. (ISBN 0-944203-08-6). Marian Pr.
Tell Rubeidheh: An Uruk Village in the Jebel Hamrin. Ed. by R. G. Killick. (Iraq Archaeological Reports). (Illus.). 180p. 1988. pap. text ed. 70.00 (ISBN 0-85668-431-7, Pub. by Aris & Phillips UK). Humanities.
Tell-Tale Article: A Critical Approach to Modern Poetry. G. Rostrevor Hamilton. LC 75-20458. 1950. lib. bdg. 27.00 (ISBN 0-8414-4827-2). Folcroft.
Tell-Tale Article: A Critical Approach to Modern Poetry. George R. Hamilton. LC 72-3494. (Essay Index Reprint Ser.). Repr. of 1949 ed. 12.50 (ISBN 0-8369-2906-3). Ayer Co Pubs.
Tell Tale Connection. George Vandeman. 1985. pap. 2.95 (ISBN 0-8163-0581-1). Pacific Pr Pub Assn.
Tell-Tale Heart. Edgar Allan Poe. (Creative's Classics Ser.). (Illus.). 32p. (YA) (gr. 9 up). 1980. PLB 8.95 (ISBN 0-87191-772-6). Creative Ed.
Tell-Tale Heart. Edgar Allan Poe. Ed. by Raymond Harris. (Classics Ser.). (Illus.). 48p. (Orig.). (gr. 6-12). 1982. text ed. 3.00x (ISBN 0-89061-262-5, 467); tchr's. ed. 4.00x (ISBN 0-89061-263-3, 469); cassette 12.00 (468). Jamestown Pubs.
Tell-Tale Heart & Other Writings. Edgar Allan Poe. 432p. (gr. 7-12). 1983. pap. 3.50 (ISBN 0-553-21228-1, Bantam Classics). Bantam.
Tell the Next Generation: Homilies & Near Homilies. Walter J. Burghardt. LC 79-91895. 240p. 1980. pap. 8.95 (ISBN 0-8091-2252-9). Paulist Pr.
Tell the People: Talks with James Yen About the Mass Education Movement. Pearl S. Buck. 141p. 1959. 7.50 (ISBN 0-942717-16-3); pap. 4.00 (ISBN 0-318-14582-0). Intl Inst Rural.
Tell the Rock I'm Alive. 1973. pap. 1.50 (ISBN 0-913862-02-9, Co-Pub Successful Living). Aragorn Bks.
Tell the Time. (Teddies Ser.). (Illus.). 32p. (gr. k-3). 1987. PLB 13.31 (ISBN 0-8172-2744-X); pap. 9.27 (ISBN 0-8172-2746-6). Raintree Pubs.
Tell the Time. (Play & Learn Sticker Bks.). 24p. (ps-k). 1988. pap. 2.95 (ISBN 0-8249-8280-0). Ideals.
Tell the Time with Benji. (ps). bds. 5.50 (ISBN 0-904494-49-7). Borden.
Tell the Truth. 2nd ed. Will Metzger. LC 83-25304. 187p. (Orig.). 1981. pap. 7.95 (ISBN 0-87784-934-X). Inter Varsity.
Tell the Truth, Marly Dee. Barbara Williams. 128p. (gr. 4-6). 1982. 9.95 (ISBN 0-525-44020-8). Dutton.
Tell the World! Heather. (Orig.). 1988. pap. 7.00 (ISBN 0-915541-32-7). Star Bks Inc.
Tell the World. Eric Wright. 1981. pap. 3.95 (ISBN 0-87552-947-X, Evangel Pr UK). Presby & Reformed.
Tell Them Everything: A Sojourn in the Prison of HM Queen Elizabeth II at Ard Macha (Armagh) Margaretta D'Arcy. 127p. (Orig.). 1981. pap. 5.95 (ISBN 0-86104-349-9, Pub by Pluto Pr). Longwood Pub Group.
Tell Them from Me. Lesley Gow & Andrew McPherson. 137p. 1980. text ed. 17.25 (ISBN 0-08-025738-0); pap. text ed. 11.00 (ISBN 0-08-025739-9). Pergamon.
Tell Them I Am Coming. Richard E. Eby. 1980. pap. 5.95 (ISBN 0-8007-5045-4, Power Bks). Revell.
Tell Them I Am Coming. Richard E. Eby. 160p. 1984. pap. 3.50 (ISBN 0-8007-8496-0, Spire Bks). Revell.
Tell Them I Love Them. Joyce Meyer. 52p. (Orig.). 1988. pap. 3.00 (ISBN 0-944834-00-0). Life Word-Meyer Ministries.
Tell Them It Was Wonderful. Ludwig Bemelmans. 336p. 1987. pap. text ed. 7.95 (ISBN 0-07-004453-8). McGraw.
Tell Them It Was Wonderful: Selected Writings. Ludwig Bemelmans. Intro. by Madeleine Bemelmans. (Illus.). 336p. 1985. 19.95 (ISBN 0-670-80391-X). Viking.
Tell Them, Such Is God. Rose Mathias. LC 87-72435. 266p. (Orig.). 1988. pap. 5.95 (ISBN 0-87029-210-2, 20256-4). Abbey.
Tell Toqaan: A Syrian Village. Louise E. Sweet. (Anthropological Papers Ser.: No. 14). (Illus.). 1960. pap. 2.50x (ISBN 0-932206-20-4). U Mich Mus Anthro.
Tell-Trothes New Yeares Gift, & the Passionate Morrice, 1593; John Lane's Tom Tell-Trothe's Message, & His Pens Complaint, 1600; Thomas Powell's Tom of All Trades, 1631; The Glass of Godly Love (by John Rogers?), 1596. Ed. by F. J. Furnivall. (New Shakespeare Soc., London, Ser.: Ser. 6, Nos. 2-3). 1876. pap. 52.00 (ISBN 0-8115-0243-0). Kraus Repr.
Tell Us Our Names: Story Theology from an Asian Perspective. C. S. Song. LC 84-5139. (Illus.). 224p. (Orig.). 1984. pap. 12.95 (ISBN 0-88344-512-3). Orbis Bks.
Tell Us the Reason Why. Dorothy Gilliham. 96p. 1986. 8.50 (ISBN 0-8062-2892-X). Carlton.
Tell Your Secret. Fran Lance & Pat King. 128p. 1986. pap. 5.95 (ISBN 0-89221-142-3). New Leaf.
Teller & Tale in Joyce's Fiction: Oscillating Perspectives. John P. Riquelme. LC 82-7805. 288p. 1983. text ed. 29.50x (ISBN 0-8018-2854-6). Johns Hopkins.
Teller & the Tale: Aspects of the Short Story. Ed. by Wendell M. Aycock. LC 81-52254. (Proceedings Comparative Literature Symposium Ser.: Vol. 13). 156p. 1982. pap. 12.00 (ISBN 0-89672-100-0). Tex Tech Univ Pr.
Teller County Colorado. Claude Wiatrowski & Margaret Wiatrowski. (Illus.). 24p. (Orig.). 1987. pap. 3.00 (ISBN 0-936206-19-5). Mntn Automation.
Teller Difference Rates: A Study of Factors Affecting Teller Performance. 18p. 1976. 15.00 (700). Bank Admin Inst.
Teller of Tales. Eric Knudsen. 288p. 1987. pap. 3.95 (ISBN 0-935180-33-8). Mutual Pub HI.
Teller Operations. 9th ed. 120p. 1987. pap. 19.95 (ISBN 0-912857-41-2). Inst Finan Educ.
Teller Operations Manual. 124p. 1981. 60.00 (ISBN 0-317-33828-5, 701). Bank Admin Inst.
Teller World. 2nd ed. Paul F. Jannott. LC 82-18497. 124p. 1983. pap. 26.00 (ISBN 0-87267-040-6). Bank Admin Inst.
Tellers & Listeners: The Narrative Imagination. Barbara Hardy. 279p. 1975. 38.50 (ISBN 0-485-11153-5, Pub. by Athlone Pr UK). Humanities.
Tellers of the Word. John Navone & Thomas Cooper. 1981. 23.00; pap. 14.00. Haymkt Doyma.
Tellers of the Word. John Navone & Thomas Cooper. 341p. 1981. 23.00; pap. 14.00. Jesuit Educ Ctr Human Dev.
Teller's Tales: Short Stories. Sherwood Anderson. Intro. by Frank Gado. LC 83-80751. (Signature Ser.). 229p. (Orig.). 1983. pap. 14.75 (ISBN 0-912756-09-8); pap. text ed. 4.95 (ISBN 0-912756-08-X). Union Coll.
Tellico Archaeology: Twelve Thousand Years of Native American History. Jefferson Chapman. LC 85-15080. (Illus.). 142p. (Orig.). 1985. lib. bdg. 16.95x (ISBN 0-87049-480-5, Pub. by U of TN Dept of Anthropology); pap. 8.95 (ISBN 0-87049-481-3). U of Tenn Pr.
Telling: A Loving Hagadah for Passover (Non-Sexist, Yet Traditional) rev. ed. Dov ben Khayyim. (Illus.). 48p. 1984. pap. 4.00 (ISBN 0-9612500-0-3). Rakhamim Pubns.
Telling & Retelling: Quotation in Biblical Narrative. George Savran. LC 85-45315. (Indiana Studies in Biblical Literature). 192p. 1988. 39.95x (ISBN 0-253-35928-7). Ind U Pr.
Telling Classical Tales: Chaucer & the "Legend of Good Women". Lisa J. Kiser. LC 83-45135. 184p. 1983. 22.50x (ISBN 0-8014-1601-9). Cornell U Pr.
Telling Each Other the Truth. William Backus. 250p. (Orig.). 1985. pap. 5.95 (ISBN 0-87123-852-7, 210852). Bethany Hse.
Telling Educator's Lives: Intellectual Biography in Educational Studies. Frank A. Stone. (Multicultural Research Guides Ser.). 18p. 1983. 2.00. I N Thut World Educ Ctr.
Telling Fortunes by Cards. Cecily Kent. LC 83-3906. 192p. 1983. lib. bdg. 19.95x (ISBN 0-89370-655-8). Borgo Pr.
Telling Fortunes by Cards. Cecily Kent. 1982. pap. 6.95 (ISBN 0-87877-055-0). Newcastle Pub.
Telling Fortunes: Love Magic, Dream Signs, & Other Ways to Learn the Future. Alvin Schwartz. LC 85-45174. (Illus.). 128p. (gr. 4 up). 1987. 11.75i (ISBN 0-397-32132-5, Lipp Jr Bks); PLB 11.89 (ISBN 0-397-32133-3). HarpJ.
Telling How Texts Talk: Essays on Reading & Ethnomethodology. A. W. McHoul. (International Library of Phenomenology & Moral Sciences). 1982. 21.95x (ISBN 0-7100-9047-1). Routledge Chapman & Hall.
Telling Lies. Paul Ekman. 320p. 1986. pap. 3.95 (ISBN 0-425-09298-4). Berkley Pub.
Telling Lies. Lisa Norby. (Cheerleaders Ser.: No. 43). 160p. (Orig.). (gr. 6-10). 1988. pap. 2.50 (ISBN 0-590-41629-4). Scholastic Inc.
Telling Lies: Clues to Deceit in the Marketplace, Politics & Marriage. Paul Ekman. 320p. 1985. 17.95 (ISBN 0-393-01931-4). Norton.
Telling Lives: The Biographer's Art. Ed. by Marc Pachter. LC 81-10312. 151p. 1981. pap. 12.95 (ISBN 0-8122-1118-9). U of Pa Pr.
Telling Memories among Southern Women: Domestic Workers & Their Employers in the Segregated South. Susan Tucker. (Illus.). 320p. 1988. 24.95 (ISBN 0-8071-1440-5). La State U Pr.
Telling of Lies. Timothy Findley. 1988. pap. 7.95 (ISBN 0-440-55001-7, Delta). Dell.
Telling Right from Wrong: What Is Moral, What Is Immoral & What Is Neither One Nor the Other. Timothy J. Cooney. 158p. 1985. 20.95 (ISBN 0-87975-297-1). Prometheus Bks.
Telling Secrets. Wendy Lichtman. LC 85-45271. 256p. (YA) (gr. 7 up). 1986. 13.25i (ISBN 0-06-023884-4); PLB 12.89 (ISBN 0-06-023885-2). HarpJ.
Telling Stories: A Theoretical Analysis of Narrative Fiction. Steven Cohan & Linda M. Shires. (New Accent Ser.). 224p. 1988. text ed. 37.50 (ISBN 0-415-01386-0); pap. text ed. 11.95 (ISBN 0-415-01387-9). Routledge Chapman & Hall.
Telling Stories Like Jesus Did: Creative Parables for Teachers. Christelle L. Estrada. LC 86-62626. 92p. 1987. pap. 8.95 (ISBN 0-89390-097-4). Resource Pubns.
Telling Stories to Children. Sylvia Ziskind. LC 75-42003. 162p. 1976. 20.00 (ISBN 0-8242-0588-X). Wilson.
Telling Tales. Sara Maitland. 200p. 1985. 17.95 (ISBN 0-904526-87-9, Journeyman Pr England); pap. 7.95 (ISBN 0-904526-86-0). Riverrun NY.
Telling the American Story: A Structural & Cultural Analysis of Conversational Storytelling. Livia Polanyi. 158p. 1988. pap. text ed. 9.95x (ISBN 0-262-66062-8, Pub. by Bradford). MIT Pr.
Telling the American Story: From the Structure of Linguistic Texts to the Grammar of a Culture. Livia Polanyi. LC 84-24196. (Language & Being Ser.). 168p. 1985. 34.50 (ISBN 0-89391-041-4). Ablex Pub.
Telling the Company's Financial Story. Opinion Research Corporation Staff. LC 64-24874. 1964. 8.00 (ISBN 0-317-20196-4). Finan Exec.
Telling the Next Generation: The Educational Development in North American Calvinist Christian Schools. Harro W. Van Brummelen. (Illus.). 332p. (Orig.). 1986. lib. bdg. 29.00 (ISBN 0-8191-5307-9, Pub. by Inst Christ Stud); pap. text ed. 15.50 (ISBN 0-8191-5308-7). U Pr of Amer.
Telling the Story: Evangelism in Black Churches. James O. Stallings. 128p. 1988. pap. 7.95 (ISBN 0-8170-1124-2). Judson.
Telling the Story of the Local Church: The Who, What, When, Where & Why of Communication. Velma Sumrall & Lucille Germany. (Orig.). 1979. pap. 5.00 (ISBN 0-8164-2193-5, HarpR). Har-Row.
Telling the Story: Variety & Imagination in Preaching. Richard A. Jensen. LC 79-54113. 190p. (Orig.). 1979. pap. 10.95 (ISBN 0-8066-1766-7, 10-6232). Augsburg.
Telling the Truth. Sonia Johnson. (Crossing Press Pamphlet Ser.). 28p. 1987. pap. 3.00 (ISBN 0-89594-241-0). Crossing Pr.
Telling the Truth about Jerusalem: A Collection of Essays & Poems. Ann Oakley. 288p. 1986. text ed. 24.95 (ISBN 0-631-14773-X); pap. 9.95 (ISBN 0-631-14951-1). Basil Blackwell.
Telling the Truth: The Gospel As Tragedy, Comedy, & Fairy Tale. Frederick Buechner. LC 77-7839. 1977. 13.95 (ISBN 0-06-061156-1, HarpR). Har-Row.
Telling the Truth: The Theory & Practice of Documentary Fiction. Barbara Foley. LC 85-48198. 280p. 1986. 24.95x (ISBN 0-8014-1877-1). Cornell U Pr.
Telling the Truth to Troubled People. William Backus. 256p. (Orig.). 1985. pap. 6.95 (ISBN 0-87123-811-X, 210811). Bethany Hse.
Telling the U. N. Story: New Approaches to Teaching About the U. N. & Its Related Agencies. Leonard S. Kenworthy. LC 63-21937. 166p. (Orig.). 1963. 6.00 (ISBN 0-379-00207-8). Oceana.
Telling the Whole Story. George M. Bass. 1983. 6.95 (ISBN 0-89536-642-8, 2007). CSS of Ohio.
Telling Time. Watson. (Simple Facts Ser.). (Illus.). 28p. (ps-2). 1985. 3.95 (ISBN 0-86020-778-1). EDC.
Telling Triple: Essays, Poems, & Stories. Antonio Allego. 136p. (Orig.). 1986. pap. 6.75x (ISBN 971-10-0281-7, Pub. by New Day Philippines). Cellar.
Telling Writing. 4th ed. Ken Macrorie. (gr. 10 up). 1985. pap. 14.00x. Boynton Cook Pubs.
Telling Your Story, Exploring Your Faith. B. J. Hateley. Ed. by Herbert Lambert. LC 85-13307. 120p. (Orig.). 1985. pap. 8.95 (ISBN 0-8272-3626-3). CBP.
Telling Yourself the Truth. William Backus & Marie Chapian. LC 80-10136. 41p. (Orig.). 1980. pap. 5.95 (ISBN 0-87123-562-5, 210562); study guide 2.50 (ISBN 0-87123-567-6, 210567). Bethany Hse.
Telltale. Ed. by R. A. Foakes & J. C. Gibson. LC 82-45711. (Malone Society Reprint Ser.: No. 110). 1959. 40.00 (ISBN 0-404-63111-8). AMS Pr.
Telltale Kiss. Ruth Burnett. (YA) (gr. 7 up). 1984. 9.95 (ISBN 0-8034-8402-X, Avalon). Bouregy.
Telltale Lilac Bush & Other West Virginia Ghost Tales. Ruth A. Musick. LC 64-14000. (Illus.). 208p. 1965. pap. 7.00 (ISBN 0-8131-0136-0). U Pr of Ky.
Telltale Summer of Tina C. Lila Perl. (Illus.). 208p. (gr. 4-6). 1984. pap. 2.50 (ISBN 0-590-41324-4, Apple Paperbacks). Scholastic Inc.
Telluride. Rose Weber. (Illus.). pap. 3.95 (ISBN 0-936564-10-5). Little London.
Telluride: From Pick to Powder. Richard L. Fetter. LC 77-87369. (Illus.). 1979. pap. 7.95 (ISBN 0-87004-265-3). Caxton.
Telluride Smile: A Henry Dyer Novel. Raymond H. Ring. 256p. 1988. 15.95 (ISBN 0-396-09222-5). Dodd.
Telluride Story. David Lavender. 68p. (Orig.). 1987. pap. 14.95 (ISBN 0-9608764-6-4). Wayfinder Pr.
Telo Dzhona Brauna. Stephen V. Benet. Tr. by Ivan Elagin from Eng. (Rus.). 1980. 15.00 (ISBN 0-88233-266-X); pap. 9.00 (ISBN 0-88233-267-8). Ardis Pubs.
TeloFacts IBM PC Software. Deborrah Smithy-Willis et al. TeloFacts 1. 49.95 (ISBN 0-317-00073-X); TeloFacts 2. 199.95 (ISBN 0-88056-177-7). Dilithium Pr.
Teltech CICS-VS Application Design Guide. Teltech. 1988. write for info. (ISBN 0-471-85706-8). Wiley.
Telugu English Dictionary. C. P. Brown. 1424p. 1986. Repr. of 1903 ed. 32.00X (ISBN 0-8364-1690-2, Pub. by Usha). South Asia Bks.
Telugu English Dictionary. P. Sankaranarayana. 1380p. 1986. Repr. 20.00X (ISBN 0-8364-1695-3, Pub. By Usha). South Asia Bks.
Telugu Verbal Bases. Bhadriraju Krishnamurti. 1972. 27.00 (ISBN 0-89684-328-9). Orient Bk Dist.
Telugu Verbal Bases: A Comparative & Descriptive Study. Bhadriraju Krishnamurti. LC 61-63422. (California University Publications in Linguistics Ser.: Vol. 24). pap. 133.30 (ISBN 0-317-10155-2, 2011682). Bks Demand UMI.
Telzey Toy. James H. Schmitz. 192p. 1982. pap. 2.50 (ISBN 0-441-80035-1). Ace Bks.
Temalpakh: Cahuilla Indian Knowledge & Usage of Plants. Lowell J. Bean & Katherine S. Saubel. LC 72-85815. 1972. pap. 12.00 (ISBN 0-939046-24-5). Malki Mus Pr.
Temas de Isaias. Ronald Youngblood. Orig. Title: Themes from Isaiah. (Span.). 1986. write for info. (ISBN 0-8297-0896-0). Life Pubs Intl.
Temas Martianos. Cintio Vitier & Fina Garcia. LC 81-68709. (Nave y el Puerto Ser.). 345p. (Span.). 1982. pap. 10.95 (ISBN 0-940238-44-6). Ediciones Huracan.
Temas y Dialogos. 4th ed. David F. Altabe. LC 83-22669. 232p. (Span.). 1984. pap. 14.95 (ISBN 0-03-063564-0). HR&W.

Temas y Dialogos. 5th ed. David F. Altabe. (Illus.). 288p. (Span.). 1987. pap. text ed. 11.95 (ISBN 0-03-007543-2). HR&W.

Tematica E Struttura Dell'Eneide di Virgilio. E. Coleiro. 148p. (Orig., Ital.). 1983. pap. 22.00x (ISBN 90-6032-245-2, Pub. by B R Gruener Netherlands). Benjamins North Am.

Tematica Narrativa de Severo Sarduy: De Donde Son Los Cantantes. Jose Sanchez-Boudy. LC 77-78252. (Coleccion Polymita Ser.). 102p. (Orig., Span.). 1985. pap. 10.00 (ISBN 0-89729-257-X). Ediciones.

Temenos & Topophilia. John Nicholas. 1985. 10.00x (ISBN 0-317-62206-4, Guild of Pastoral Psych). State Mutual Bk.

Temistocle. Ed. by Ernest Warburton. (Johann Christian Bach Ser., 1735-1782). 1988. lib. bdg. 125.00 (ISBN 0-8240-6056-3). Garland Pub.

Temmoku: A Study of Pottery & Tea Aesthetics. F. Bleicher & W. C. Hu. 1984. write for info (ISBN 0-89344-032-9). Ars Ceramica.

Temmoku: A Study of the Ware of Chien. James M. Plumer. 126p. 1972. 125.00x (ISBN 0-317-45294-0, Pub. by Han-Shan Tang Ltd). State Mutual Bk.

Temoignage sur la Culture Arabo-Musulmane see Cahiers de L'Institut de Science Economique Appliquee.

Temoins de l Homme: La Condition Humaine dans la Litterature Contemporaine. Pierre-Henri Simon. (Cahiers de la Fondat. Nat. Sc. Polit.). pap. 8.75 (ISBN 0-685-36580-8). French & Eur.

Temoins du Monde Francais. Ed. by Adrien Therio & James F. Burks. LC 68-12127. (Illus., Orig., Fr.). (YA) (gr. 9 up). 1968. pap. text ed. 9.95x (ISBN 0-89197-446-6). Irvington.

Temp Worker's Handbook. William Lewis & Nancy Schuman. 176p. 1988. 10.95 (ISBN 0-8144-7681-3). AMACOM.

Tempeh Cookery. Ed. by Coleen Pride. LC 83-73651. (Illus.). 128p. (Orig.). 1984. pap. 10.95 (ISBN 0-913990-39-6). Book Pub Co.

Tempeh Production: A Craft & Technical Manual. William Shurtleff & Akiko Aoyagi. LC 85-304441. (Soyfoods Production Ser.: No. 3). (Illus.). 176p. 1985. pap. 24.95 (ISBN 0-933332-23-8). Soyfoods Center.

Tempel und Heiligtuemer im alten Mesopotamien: Typologie, Morphologie und Geschichte. Ernst Heinrich. (Illus.). 1982. 112.00 (ISBN 3-11-008531-3). De Gruyter.

Tempel Von Jerusalem. Konrad Rupprecht. (Beihefte 144 Zur Zeitschrift Fuer die Alttestamentliche Wissenschaft). 1976. text ed. 22.80x (ISBN 3-11-006619-X). De Gruyter.

Tempel von Paestum, 2 pts. Friedrich Krauss. (Denkmaeler Antiker Architektur, Vol. 9, Pt. 1, Fascicule 1). (Illus.). 97p. (Ger.). 1978. Repr. of 1959 ed. 70.0000169042x (ISBN 3-110022-37-0). De Gruyter.

Temper. Lawrence H. Conrad. LC 74-22774. (Labor Movement in Fiction & Non-Fiction). Repr. of 1924 ed. 24.00 (ISBN 0-404-58414-4). AMS Pr.

Temper Embrittlement of Alloy Steels: A Symposium Presented at the Seventy-Fourth Annual Meeting, American Society for Testing & Materials. American Society for Testing & Materials, Committee A-1 on Steel. LC 73-185535. (American Society for Testing & Materials Ser.: No. 499). pap. 35.30 (ISBN 0-317-10341-5, 2015504). Bks Demand UMI.

Temper of the Night. Lisa Keller. 48p. 1982. 6.95 (ISBN 0-89962-230-5). Todd & Honeywell.

Temper of the Seventeenth Century in English Literature. Barrett Wendell. 1978. Repr. of 1904 ed. lib. bdg. 30.00 (ISBN 0-8414-9571-8). Folcroft.

Temper of the Seventeenth Century in English Literature. Clark Lectures, 1902-1903. facs. ed. Barrett Wendell. LC 67-26794. (Essay Index Reprint Ser). 1904. 19.00 (ISBN 0-8369-0980-1). Ayer Co Pubs.

Temper of Victorian Belief: Studies in the Religious Novels of Pater, Kingsley, & Newman. David A. Downes. LC 76-147189. 159p. 1972. 29.50 (ISBN 0-8290-0209-X). Irvington.

Temper of Western Europe. Clarence C. Brinton. LC 70-97339. Repr. of 1953 ed. lib. bdg. 25.00x (ISBN 0-8371-2799-8, BRWE). Greenwood.

Temper Tantrum Book. Edna M. Preston & Rainey Bennett. (Picture Puffins Ser). (Illus.). (ps-3). 1976. pap. 4.95 (ISBN 0-14-050181-9, Puffin). Penguin.

Temper Your Child's Tantrums. abr. ed. James Dobson. (Pocket Guides). 80p. 1986. pocket guide 2.25 (ISBN 0-8423-6994-5). Tyndale.

Temperament. Arnold H. Buss & Robert Plomin. 200p. 1984. text ed. 24.95 (ISBN 0-89859-415-4). L Erlbaum Assocs.

Temperament & Behavior Disorders in Children. Alexander Thomas et al. LC 68-13025. 309p. 1968. 35.00x (ISBN 0-8147-0415-8). NYU Pr.

Temperament & Character of the Arabs. Sania Hamady. LC 60-9942. 285p. 1960. 29.50x (ISBN 0-8290-0210-3). Irvington.

Temperament & Child Psychopathology. William T. Garrison & Felton J. Earls. (Developmental Clinical Psychology & Psychiatry Ser.: Vol. 12). 160p. 1987. text ed. 19.95 (ISBN 0-8039-2296-5); pap. text ed. 12.95 (ISBN 0-8039-2297-3). Sage.

Temperament & Development. Alexander Thomas & Stella Chess. LC 76-49428. 1977. 32.50 (ISBN 0-87630-139-1). Brunner-Mazel.

Temperament & Eating Characteristics. A. Mehrabian. (Illus.). 150p. 1987. 38.00 (ISBN 0-387-96510-6). Springer-Verlag.

Temperament & Social Interaction in Infants & Children. Ed. by Jacqueline V. Lerner & Richard M. Lerner. LC 85-60824. (Child Development Ser.: No. 31). (Orig.). 1986. pap. text ed. 14.95x (ISBN 0-87589-798-3). Jossey-Bass.

Temperament & the Christian Faith. O. Hallesby. LC 62-9093. 106p. 1978. pap. 4.50 (ISBN 0-8066-1660-1, 10-6237). Augsburg.

Temperament Discussed: Temperament & Development in Infancy & Childhood. Ed. by Geldolph Kohnstamm. 180p. 1987. pap. text ed. 15.30 (ISBN 90-265-0783-6, Pub. by Swets & Zeitlinger (Netherlands)). Hogrefe Intl.

Temperament in Clinical Practice. Stella Chess & Alexander Thomas. LC 85-17733. 315p. 1986. text ed. 30.00 (ISBN 0-89862-669-2). Guilford Pr.

Temperament-Personality-Activity. Jan Strelau. 1984. 53.00 (ISBN 0-12-673280-9). Acad Pr.

Temperamental Bases of Behavior: Warsaw Studies on Individual Differences. Ed. by Jan Strelau. 220p. 1985. pap. text ed. 22.25 (ISBN 90-265-0598-1, Pub. by Swets Zeitlinger Netherlands). Hogrefe Intl.

Temperamental Differences in Infants & Young Children: Symposium No. 89. CIBA Foundation Symposium. 320p. 1986. 54.95 (ISBN 0-471-91058-9). Wiley.

Temperaments & the Arts: Their Relation & Function in Waldorf Pedagogy. Magda Lissau. 1984. pap. 9.95 (ISBN 0-916786-74-9). St George Bk Serv.

Temperance. Ellen G. White. 1949. pap. 9.95 deluxe ed. (ISBN 0-8163-0151-4, 20100-4). Pacific Pr Pub Assn.

Temperance Selections. facsimile ed. Ed. by John H. Bechtel. LC 71-116393. (Granger Index Reprint Ser). 1893. 14.00 (ISBN 0-8369-6134-X). Ayer Co Pubs.

Temperate & Subtropical Fruit Production. D. Jackson. 250p. 1986. text ed. 39.95 (ISBN 0-409-70149-1). Butterworth.

Temperate Broad-Leaved Evergreen Forests. Ed. by J. D. Ovington. (Ecosystems of the World Ser.: Vol. 10). 242p. 1983. 108.00 (ISBN 0-444-42091-6, I-399-83). Elsevier.

Temperate Chile: A Progressive Spain. W. Anderson Smith. 1976. lib. bdg. 59.95 (ISBN 0-8490-2732-2). Gordon Pr.

Temperate Deserts & Semi-Deserts. Ed. by N. E. West. (Ecosystems of the World Ser.: Vol. 5). 522p. 1983. 221.00 (ISBN 0-444-41931-4, I-483-82). Elsevier.

Temperate Zone Pomology. rev. ed. Melvin N. Westwood. (Illus.). 448p. 1988. Repr. of 1978 ed. text ed. 39.95 (ISBN 0-88192-113-0). Timber.

Temperature, 2 pts. Ed. by Theodore H. Benziger. Incl. Pt. 1. Arts & Concept. 66.00 (ISBN 0-12-786141-6); Pt. 2. Thermal Homeostasis. 73.00 (ISBN 0-12-786142-4). (Benchmark Papers in Human Physiology: Vols. 9 & 10). 1977. Acad Pr.

Temperature. T. J. Quinn. (Monographs in Physical Measurement). 1983. 69.00 (ISBN 0-12-569680-9). Acad Pr.

Temperature. Y. A. Smorodinsky. 263p. 1985. 4.95 (ISBN 0-8285-2898-5, Pub by Mir Pubs USSR). Imported Pubns.

Temperature & Animal Cells. Ed. by K. Bowler & B. J. Fuller. (Society for Experimental Biology Symposia Ser.: No. 41). 460p. 1987. 70.00x (ISBN 0-948601-08-6, Biochemical Society). Rsrch Bks CT.

Temperature & Life. H. Precht et al. LC 73-13495. (Illus.). 779p. 1973. 88.00 (ISBN 0-387-06441-9). Springer-Verlag.

Temperature & Velocity Measurements. Ed. by Network Staff. 1985. 100.00x (ISBN 0-904999-95-5, Pub. by Network Events Ltd). State Mutual Bk.

Temperature Biology of Animals. A. R. Cossins & K. Bowler. 300p. 1987. text ed. 57.50 (ISBN 0-412-15900-7, Pub. by Chapman & Hall). Routledge Chapman & Hall.

Temperature Control. Myer Kutz. LC 74-32302. 230p. 1975. Repr. of 1968 ed. 15.00 (ISBN 0-88275-264-2). Krieger.

Temperature Controlled Storage & Distribution Buyers Guide, 1988. Ed. by Portcullis Press Ltd. Staff. 1985. 150.00x (Pub. by Portcullis Pr UK). State Mutual Bk.

Temperature Dependent Thomas-Fermi Theory, Vol. 147. J. Messer. (Lecture Notes in Physics Ser.). 131p. 1981. pap. 12.00 (ISBN 0-387-10875-0). Springer-Verlag.

Temperature Effect on Concrete - STP 858. Ed. by Tarun R. Naik. LC 84-70335. (Illus.). 180p. 1985. text ed. 28.00 (ISBN 0-8031-0435-9, 04-858000-07). ASTM.

Temperature: Its Measurement & Control in Science & Industry, Proceedings of the Sixth International Symposium, Washington, DC, March 15, 1982. Ed. by James F. Schooley. LC 62-19138. 1472p. 1982. 110.00 (ISBN 0-88318-403-6). Am Inst Physics.

Temperature: Its Measurement & Control in Science & Industry: Temperature, Vol. 3, Pts. 1-3. American Institute of Physics Staff. 864p. 1972. Repr. of 1962 ed. Pt. 1. 56.00 (ISBN 0-88275-057-7). Krieger.

Temperature: Its Measurement & Control in Science & Industry, Vol. 3. American Institute of Physics Staff. Ed. by Charles M. Herzfeld. LC 62-19138. 1108p. (Orig.). 1972. Repr. of 1962 ed. Pt. 2 Applied Methods & Instruments. 72.50 (ISBN 0-88275-059-3, (K)VN). Krieger.

Temperature: Its Measurement & Control in Science & Industry, Vol. 3. American Institute of Physics Staff. Ed. by Charles M. Herzfeld. LC 62-19138. 696p. 1972. Repr. of 1963 ed. Pt. 3 Biology & Medicine. 44.50 (ISBN 0-88275-058-5, (K)VN, K). Krieger.

Temperature: Its Measurement & Control in Science & Industry, 3 pts, Vol. 4. Symposium on Temperature, 5th, 1971, Washington D. C. Ed. by Harmon H. Plumb. Incl. Pt. 1. Basic Methods, Scales & Fixed Points, Radiation. Ed. by H. Preston-Thomas et al; Pt. 2. Resistance, Electronic & Magnetic Thermometry; Controls & Calibration; Bridges. Ed. by L. G. Rubin et al; Pt. 3. Thermocouples, Biology & Medicine, Geophysics & Space. Ed. by D. I. Finch et al. LC 62-19138. pap. 160.00 ea. (2052133). Bks Demand UMI.

Temperature Measurement & Control. J. R. Leigh. (IEE Control Engineering Ser.: No. 34). 1987. write for info. (CE034). Inst Elect Eng.

Temperature Measurement & Control Temperature. 110p. 1978. pap. text ed. 19.20x (ISBN 0-318-20353-7, Pub. by Inst Metals). Brookfield Pub Co.

Temperature Measurement Thermocouples: An ANSI Approved Standard MC96.1. rev. ed. 48p. 1982. pap. text ed. 20.00X (ISBN 0-87664-708-5). Instru Soc.

Temperature Measurements in Seeded Air & Nitrogen Plasmas. H. N. Olsen et al. LC 79-131016. 133p. 1970. 19.00 (ISBN 0-403-04524-X). Scholarly.

Temperature Monitoring & Recording in Blood Bank: Proposed Guideline, Vol. 4. National Committee for Clinical Laboratory Standards. 1984. 20.00 (ISBN 0-318-03282-1, I16-P). Natl Comm Clin Lab Stds.

Temperature of History, Phases of Science & Culture in the Nineteeth Century. Stephen G. Brush. LC 77-11999. (Studies in the History of Science). (Illus.). 1978. lib. bdg. 18.95 (ISBN 0-89102-073-X). B Franklin.

Temperature-Programmed Reduction for Solid Materials. Jones & McNichol. 208p. 1986. 59.75 (ISBN 0-8247-7583-X). Dekker.

Temperature Regulation. S. A. Richards & P. S. Fielden. LC 73-77794. (Wykeham Science Ser.: No. 27). 212p. 1973. pap. 18.00x (ISBN 0-8448-1335-4, Pub. by Crane Russak & Co). Taylor & Francis.

Temperature Regulation & Drug Action: Proceedings. Pharmacology of Thermoregulation Symposium, 2nd, Paris, 1974. Ed. by P. Lommax & E. Schonbaum. 450p. 1975. 99.50 (ISBN 3-8055-1756-4). S Karger.

Temperature Regulation & Energy Metabolism in the Newborn. Ed. by John C. Sinclair. (Monographs in Neonatology). 272p. 1978. 49.50 (ISBN 0-8089-1090-6, 794085). Grune.

Temperature Relations in Animals & Man. Helmut Laudien. (BIONA Report Ser.: No. 4). 229p. 1986. pap. 18.00 (Pub. by Gustav Fischer Verlag). VCH Pubs.

Temperature-Salinity Analysis of World Ocean Waters. O. I. Mamayev. (Oceanography Ser.: Vol. 11). 374p. 1975. 129.00 (ISBN 0-444-41251-4). Elsevier.

Temperature Sensing Markets. Market Intelligence Research Company Staff. Ed. by W. Hammersley. 425p. (Orig.). 1986. pap. text ed. 1495.00x (ISBN 0-916483-14-2, A075). Market Res Co.

Temperatures Very Low & Very High. Mark W. Zemansky. 144p. 1981. pap. 4.50 (ISBN 0-486-24072-X). Dover.

Tempered by Fire. Emma Goldrick. (Romances Ser.: No. 2846). 192p. Date not set. pap. 1.95 (ISBN 0-317-63903-X). Harlequin Bks.

Tempered Wind. Jeanne Dixon. LC 87-1379. 224p. (gr. 7 up). 1987. 13.95 (ISBN 0-689-31339-X, Atheneum Childrens Bks). Macmillan.

Tempered Zeal: A Columbia Law Professor's Year on the Streets with the New York City Police. Richard H. Uviller. 224p. 1988. 19.95 (ISBN 0-8092-4607-4). Contemp Bks.

Tempering. Howard S. Buck. LC 70-144708. (Yale Ser. of Younger Poets: No. 1). Repr. of 1919 ed. 18.00 (ISBN 0-404-53801-0). AMS Pr.

Tempering. Gloria Skurzynski. 192p. (gr. 6 up). 1983. 10.95 (ISBN 0-89919-152-5, Clarion). HM.

Temperlines in Japanese Swords. 1986. Repr. of 1974 ed. 3.50 (ISBN 0-910704-50-3). Hawley.

Tempest. Aime Cesaire. Tr. by Richard Miller from Fr. (Ubu Repertory Theater Publications Ser.: No. 14). 88p. (Orig.). 1986. pap. text ed. 6.25 (ISBN 0-913745-15-4). Ubu Repertory.

Tempest. Ed. by Alan Durband. (Shakespeare Made Easy Ser.). 288p. 1985. pap. 4.95 (ISBN 0-8120-3603-4). Barron.

Tempest. Michael Fleck. 1979. pap. 4.95 (ISBN 0-87613-054-6). New Age.

Tempest. Forman. (Book Note Ser.). 1986. pap. 2.50 (ISBN 0-8120-3545-3). Barron.

Tempest. David Hirst. (Text & Performance Ser.). 80p. 1984. pap. text ed. 8.50x (ISBN 0-333-34465-0, Pub. by Macmillan UK). Humanities.

Tempest. Arthur Moore. (Orig.). 1979. pap. 2.50 (ISBN 0-89083-521-7). Zebra.

Tempest. Fyre Northrop. 1981. pap. 3.75 (ISBN 0-14-070713-1). Penguin.

Tempest. Ed. by A. L. Rowse. LC 84-5070. (Contemporary Shakespeare Ser.: Vol. I). 104p. (Orig.). 1984. pap. text ed. 3.45 (ISBN 0-8191-3899-1). U Pr of Amer.

Tempest. Christina Savage. (Orig.). 1982. pap. 3.50 (ISBN 0-440-18895-4). Dell.

Tempest. William Shakespeare. (Airmont Shakespeare Ser.). (gr. 11 up). pap. 1.25 (ISBN 0-8049-1007-3, S7). Airmont.

Tempest. William Shakespeare. Ed. by Arthur Quiller-Couch et al. (New Shakespeare Ser). 1969. pap. 5.95x (ISBN 0-521-09500-X). Cambridge U Pr.

Tempest. 6th ed. William Shakespeare. Ed. by Frank Kermode. (Arden Shakespeare Ser.). 1966. 37.00x (ISBN 0-416-47360-1, NO. 2490); pap. 7.95 (ISBN 0-416-10190-9, NO. 2491). Routledge Chapman & Hall.

Tempest. William Shakespeare. Ed. by Robert Langbaum. pap. 2.25 (ISBN 0-451-52125-0, Sig Classics). NAL.

Tempest. William Shakespeare. Ed. by Louis B. Wright & Virginia A. LaMar. (Folger Library). (Illus.). (gr. 10 up). 1961. pap. text ed. 2.95. PB.

Tempest. William Shakespeare. Ed. by Northrop Frye. (Shakespeare Ser.). 1959. pap. 2.25 (ISBN 0-14-071415-4, Pelican). Penguin.

Tempest. William Shakespeare. Ed. by J. H. Walter. (Players' Shakespeare Ser). (gr. 9 up). 1967. 3.50 (ISBN 0-8238-0117-9). Plays.

Tempest. William Shakespeare. (BBC-TV Shakespeare Ser.). (Illus.). 88p. 1980. pap. 2.95 (ISBN 0-8317-8681-7, Mayflower Bks). Smith Pubs.

Tempest. William Shakespeare. Ed. by Louis B. Wright & Virginia A. La Mar. (Folger Library Ser.). 216p. pap. 2.95 (ISBN 0-671-49618-2). WSP.

Tempest. William Shakespeare. (Classics Ser.). 1988. pap. 2.95 (ISBN 0-553-21307-5, Bantam Classsics). Bantam.

Tempest. William Shakespeare. Ed. by Stephen Orgel. (Oxford Shakespeare Ser.). 264p. 1987. 34.00 (ISBN 0-19-812917-3); pap. 8.50 (ISBN 0-19-281450-8). Oxford U Pr.

Tempest: A Screenplay. Paul Mazursky & Leon Capetanos. LC 82-81975. (Illus.). 1982. 11.95 (ISBN 0-933826-40-0); pap. 4.95 (ISBN 0-933826-41-9). PAJ Pubns.

Tempest & Shipwreck in Dutch & Flemish Art: Convention, Rhetoric, & Interpretation. Lawrence O. Goedde. LC 86-43030. (Illus.). 300p. 1988. 42.50x (ISBN 0-271-00487-8). Pa St U Pr.

Tempest & Tenderness. Ann M. Wills. (Superromance Ser.). 295p. 1983. pap. 2.95 (ISBN 0-373-70062-8, Pub. by Worldwide). Harlequin Bks.

Tempest: Complete Study Edition. William Shakespeare. Ed. by Sidney Lamb. (Illus., Orig.). pap. 3.95 (ISBN 0-8220-1440-8). Cliffs.

Tempest in a Teapot: The Falkland Islands War. R. Reginald & Jeffrey M. Elliot. LC 83-8807. (Stokvis Studies in Historical Chronology & Thought: Vol. 3). (Illus.). 173p. 1983. lib. bdg. 19.95x (ISBN 0-89370-167-X); pap. text ed. 9.95x (ISBN 0-89370-267-6). Borgo Pr.

Tempest in Venice. John Sampson. 268p. 1986. 8.95 (ISBN 0-9613075-2-8). Thornfield Pr.

Tempest Notes. L. L. Hillegass. (Orig.). 1971. pap. 3.25 (ISBN 0-8220-0083-0). Cliffs.

Tempest of the Heart. Nancy Moulton. (Avon Romance Ser.). 384p. 1987. pap. 3.95 (ISBN 0-380-89957-4). Avon.

Tempest over Mexico: A Personal Chronicle. Rosa E. King. LC 71-111721. (American Imperialism: Viewpoints of United States Foreign Policy, 1898-1941). 1970. Repr. of 1935 ed. 18.00 (ISBN 0-405-02031-7). Ayer Co Pubs.

TEMPEST Secure Computing Equipment & Markets. International Resource Development Inc. Staff. 183p. 1987. 2100.00x (ISBN 0-88694-738-3). Intl Res Dev.

Tempest Tost. Robertson Davies. 1980. pap. 4.95 (ISBN 0-14-005431-6). Penguin.

Tempest Valley. Vince Taylor. LC 75-16567. 1976. 12.95 (ISBN 0-87949-045-4). Ashley Bks.

Tempest: What Sort of Play? H. F. Brooks. (Shakepeare Lectures). 1978. pap. 5.50 (ISBN 0-85672-175-1, Pub. by British Acad). Longwood Pub Group.

Tempest Within: Account of East Pakistan. D. Moraes. 102p. 1971. 5.95. Asia Bk Corp.

Tempestuous Heights. Kamala Sanders. 176p. 1981. 8.50 (ISBN 0-682-49741-X). Exposition-Phoenix.

Tempestuous Lovers. Suzanne Simmons. (Candlelight Ecstacy Ser.: No. 12). (Orig.). 1981. pap. 1.50 (ISBN 0-440-18551-3). Dell.

Tempestuous Petticoat: The Story of an Invinciible Edwardian. Claire Leighton. 272p. pap. 7.95 (ISBN 0-89733-099-4). Academy Chi Pubs.

Tempestuous Voyage: The Diary of Annah Maud Gould's Trip Abroad the Ship Berlin. Annah M. Gould. Ed. by Laura Penny. (Illus.). xii, 84p. (Orig.). 1987. pap. 9.50 (ISBN 1-55613-030-9). Heritage Bk.

Tempete. Aime Cesaire. 1975. pap. 3.95 (ISBN 0-686-51959-0). French & Eur.

Tempi Moderni. Anna C. Burney. (Ital.). 1982. pap. text ed. 15.95 (ISBN 0-03-059557-6). HR&W.

Tempio Malatestiano, Leone Battista Alberti, & the Malatesta Family: A Bibliography. Carole Cable. (Architecture Ser.: A 1679). 7p. 1986. 3.00 (ISBN 1-55590-029-1). Vance Biblios.
Templar Tradition in the Age of Aquarius. Gaetan Delaforge. (Illus.). 175p. (Orig.). 1987. pap. 10.00 (ISBN 0-939660-20-2). Threshold VT.
Templario & Excerpts from Other Operas. Otto Nicolai. Ed. by Philip Gosset. (Italian Opera Ser., 1810-1840). 85.00 (ISBN 0-8240-6575-1). Garland Pub.
Templars: Knights of God. Edward Burman. (Crucible Ser.). 208p. 1987. pap. 9.95 (ISBN 0-85030-396-6). Inner Tradit.
Template-Free Quiltmaking. Trudie Hughes. LC 86-50462. (Illus.). 96p. 1986. pap. 12.95 (ISBN 0-943574-37-4). That Patchwork.
Temple. Robert Greenfield. 480p. 1983. 15.95 (ISBN 0-671-44735-1). Summit Bks.
Temple. Janet Hamill. Ed. by Maureen Owen. LC 80-16515. (Illus.). 33p. (Orig.). 1981. pap. 2.50 (ISBN 0-916382-22-2). Telephone Bks.
Temple. Stephen Spender. 1988. 15.95 (ISBN 0-8021-1057-6). Grove.
Temple & Contemplation. Henry Corbin. Tr. by Philip Sherrard & Liaddain Sherrard. (Illus.). 390p. 1986. text ed. 49.95 (ISBN 0-7103-0129-4); pap. text ed. 17.95 (ISBN 0-7103-0130-8). Routledge Chapman & Hall.
Temple, & Other Poems. Tr. by Arthur Waley. LC 78-70137. Repr. of 1923 ed. 25.00 (ISBN 0-404-17407-8). AMS Pr.
Temple & the Teahouse in Japan. Werner Blaser. 180p. (Eng. & Ger.). 1988. 109.50 (ISBN 0-8176-1963-1). Birkhauser.
Temple Arts of Kerala. Ronald M. Bernier. (Illus.). 258p. 1982. 99.00x (ISBN 0-940500-79-5, Pub by S Chand India). Asia Bk Corp.
Temple Arts of Kerala: A South Indian Tradition. Ronald M. Berner. 272p. 100.00 (ISBN 0-317-52158-6, Pub. by S Chand India). State Mutual Bk.
Temple aux Miroirs. Alain Robbe-Grillet & I. Ionesco. 50.00 (ISBN 0-686-54740-3). French & Eur.
Temple-Beau; or, the Town Coquets: A Novel, 1754. Ed. by Michael F. Shugrue. (Flowering of the Novel, 1740-1775 Ser: Vol. 42). 1975. lib. bdg. 61.00 (ISBN 0-8240-1141-4). Garland Pub.
Temple Beyond Time: Mount Moriah - From Solomon's Temple to Christian & Islamic Shrines. rev. ed. Herbert A. Klein. Ed. by Joseph Simon. LC 86-90357. (Illus.). 192p. (ps-12). 1986. Repr. of 1970 ed. 27.50 (ISBN 0-934710-14-7). J Simon.
Temple Culture of South India. V. Parameswaran Pillai. 1986. 40.00X (ISBN 0-317-53516-1, Pub. by Manohar India). South Asia Bks.
Temple Culture of South India. V. R. Pillai. (Illus.). xii, 201p. 1986. text ed. 37.50x (ISBN 81-210-0168-4, Pub. by Inter India Pubns N Delhi). Apt Bks.
Temple de la gloire see Oeuvres Completes De Jean-Philippe Rameau.
Temple Documents of the Third Dynasty of Ur from Umma. Ed. by George G. Hackman. LC 78-63524. (Babylonian Inscriptions in the Collection of James B. Nies: No. 5). Repr. of 1937 ed. 28.50 (ISBN 0-404-60135-9). AMS Pr.
Temple Documents of the Third Dynasty of Ur From Umma. Ed. by George G. Hackman. 1937. 27.50x (ISBN 0-686-83806-8). Elliots Bks.
Temple du Gout. Voltaire. 203p. 1953. 7.50 (ISBN 0-686-55761-1). French & Eur.
Temple du Soleil. Herge. (Illus., Fr.). (gr. 7-9). looseleaf bdg. 15.95 (ISBN 0-685-28412-3). French & Eur.
Temple Entry Movement & the Sivakasi Riots. B. Sobhanan. 1986. 11.00X (ISBN 0-8364-1856-5, Pub. by Heritage India). South Asia Bks.
Temple Flowers. J. P. Vaswani & Jyoti Mirchandani. 182p. 1986. text ed. 25.00x (ISBN 0-317-43153-6, Pub. by Chopmen Pubs Singapore). Advent NY.
Temple Gateways of South India: The Architecture & Iconography of the Cidammaram Gopuras. J. C. Harle. (Illus.). 179p. 1963. 65.00x (ISBN 0-317-39167-4, Pub. by Luzac & Co Ltd). State Mutual Bk.
Temple Greek & Latin Classics, 5 Vols. Ed. by G. Lowes Dickinson & H. O. Meredith. Repr. of 1907 ed. Set. 120.00 (ISBN 0-404-07900-8). AMS Pr.
Temple House: A Novel. Elizabeth D. Stoddard. LC 8-15672. (Avail. in set with the morgesons & two men. 55.00). Repr. of 1901 ed. 19.00 (ISBN 0-384-58315-6). Johnson Repr.
Temple Household Horseback: Rugs of the Tibetan Plateau. Diana K. Myers et al. LC 84-52139. (Illus.). 112p. 1984. pap. 27.50 (ISBN 0-87405-024-3). Textile Mus.
Temple Houston: Lawyer with a Gun. Glenn Shirley. LC 79-24049. 1980. 19.95 (ISBN 0-8061-1627-7). U of Okla Pr.
Temple in Man: Sacred Architecture & the Perfect Man. R. A. Schwaller De Lubicz. Tr. by Robert Lawlor & Deborah Lawlor. LC 81-13374. (Illus.). 132p. 1981. pap. 6.95 (ISBN 0-89281-021-1). Inner Tradit.
Temple in Nimes. James Wright. (Metacom Limited Edition Ser.: No. 5). 28p. 1982. ltd. 25.00 (ISBN 0-911381-04-X). Metacom Pr.
Temple in Society. Ed. by Michael V. Fox. LC 88-3979. vi, 138p. 1988. text ed. 15.00x (ISBN 0-931464-38-2). Eisenbrauns.
Temple Israel of Tallahassee, Florida: 1937-1987. Claire B. Levenson. 96p. 1987. text ed. 6.95 (ISBN 0-9616000-1-2). Peninsular Pub Co.
Temple, Its Ministry & Services. Alfred Edersheim. 1950. 5.95 (ISBN 0-8028-8133-5). Eerdmans.
Temple Kent. D. G. Devon. 288p. 1982. pap. 2.75 (ISBN 0-345-29848-9). Ballantine.
Temple Lea Houston. Bernice Tune. (Illus.). 192p. 1981. 12.95 (ISBN 0-89015-282-9). Eakin Pr.
Temple Legend. Rudolf Steiner. Tr. by John Wood from Ger. 1986. pap. 21.50 (ISBN 0-85440-540-2, Pub. by Steinerbooks). Anthroposophic.
Temple Legend. Rudolf Steiner. Tr. by John Wood from Ger. 1986. 33.50 (ISBN 0-85440-780-4, Pub by Steinerbooks). Anthroposophic.
Temple Magick. William Gray. Ed. by Anne Holm. LC 88-45184. (High Magick Ser.). 250p. (Orig.). 1988. pap. 9.95 (ISBN 0-87542-274-8). Llewellyn Pubns.
Temple Messages. Ed. by Temple of the People Publications Staff. (Illus.). 183p. 1983. 10.50 (ISBN 0-933797-07-9). Halcyon Bk.
Temple, Monarchy & Word of God. John Endres. (Message Biblical Spirituality Ser.: Vol. 2). 1988. 12.95 (ISBN 0-89453-552-8); pap. 9.95 (ISBN 0-89453-568-4). M Glazier.
Temple of Baseball. Ed. by Richard Grossinger. (Io Ser.: No. 34). (Illus.). 268p. (Orig.). 1985. deluxe ed. 27.50 (ISBN 0-938190-44-X); pap. 12.95 (ISBN 0-938190-43-1). North Atlantic.
Temple of Chausatha-Yogini at Bheraghat. R. K. Sharma. (Illus.). 184p. 1978. 60.00. Asia Bk Corp.
Temple of Dawn. Yukio Mishima. 1973. 13.45 (ISBN 0-394-46614-4). Knopf.
Temple of Eternity: Thomas Traherne's Philosophy of Time. Richard D. Jordan. LC 70-189560. (National University Publications). 1972. 17.50 (ISBN 0-8046-9019-7, Pub by Kennikat). Assoc Faculty Pr.
Temple of Flame. Dave Morris & Oliver Johnson. (Golden Dragon Ser.: No. 2). 192p. (YA) 1986. pap. 2.50 (ISBN 0-425-08762-X, Pub by Berkley-Pacer). Berkley Pub.
Temple of God. Annalee Skarin. 224p. 1979. pap. 5.95 (ISBN 0-87516-093-X). DeVorss.
Temple of God & Other Poems. Pearl Weaver. 48p. 1988. 6.95 (ISBN 0-89962-712-9). Todd & Honeywell.
Temple of Hibis in el Khargeh Oasis: Metropolitan Museum of Art Egyptian Expedition Publications, 2 vols. in 1. Herbert E. Winlock et al. LC 76-168414. (Vol. 13 & 14). (Illus.). 298p. 1972. Repr. of 1938 ed. 38.50 (ISBN 0-405-02252-2). Ayer Co Pubs.
Temple of Jerusalem. Andre Parrot. Tr. by Beatrice E. Hooke from Fr. LC 85-8037. (Studies in Biblical Archaeology: No. 5). (Illus.). 112p. 1985. Repr. of 1957 ed. lib. bdg. 38.50x (ISBN 0-313-24224-0, PATJ). Greenwood.
Temple of Khonsu, Vol. 1: Scenes of King Herihor in the Court with Translations of Texts. Epigraphic Survey Staff. LC 78-59119. (Oriental Institute Publications: No. 100). (Illus.). 1979. 90.00x (ISBN 0-918986-20-6). Oriental Inst.
Temple of Khonsu: Vol. 2, Scenes & Inscriptions in the Court & the First Hypostyle Hall. Epigraphic Survey Staff. LC 80-82999. (Oriental Institute Publications Ser.: Vol. 103). 1981. pap. 95.00x incl. 96 plates in portfolio (ISBN 0-918986-29-X). Oriental Inst.
Temple of Mentuhotep at Dier El Bahari. Dieter Arnold. (Publications of the Metropolitan Museum of Art Egyptian Expedition: Vol. XXI). (Illus.). 1977. 60.00 (ISBN 0-87099-163-9). Metro Mus Art.
Temple of Momus: Mitchell's Olympic Theatre. David L. Rinear. LC 85-22077. (Illus.). 237p. 1987. 27.50 (ISBN 0-8108-1850-7). Scarecrow.
Temple of Oblivion. Serge Le Tendre & Regis Loisel. (Roxanna & the Quest for the Time Bird Ser.). 48p. 1987. pap. 7.95x (ISBN 0-918348-34-X). NBM.
Temple of Poseidon. Oscar Broneer. LC 73-61010. (Isthmia Ser: Vol. 1). (Illus.). 1971. 25.00x (ISBN 0-87661-931-6). Am Sch Athens.
Temple of Rameses One at Abydos see Bas-Reliefs from the Temple of Rameses One at Abydos.
Temple of Solomon: Archaeological Fact & Medieval Tradition in Christian, Islamic & Jewish Art. Ed. by Joseph Gutmann. LC 75-19120. 1976. 9.00 (ISBN 0-89130-013-9, 090103). Scholars Pr GA.
Temple of the Dawn. Yukio Mishima. (Sea of Fertility Tetralogy Ser.). 320p. 1975. pap. 4.95 (ISBN 0-671-54063-7). WSP.
Temple of the Golden Pavilion. Yukio Mishima. Tr. by Ivan Morris. (The Perigee Japanese Library). (Illus.). 288p. 1981. pap. 7.95 (ISBN 0-399-50488-5, Perigee). Putnam Pub Group.
Temple of the Holy Spirit. Matthew J. O'Connell. 345p. 1983. pap. 17.50 (ISBN 0-916134-64-4). Pueblo Pub Co.
Temple of the Mind: Education & Literary Taste in Seventeenth-Century England. John R. Mulder. LC 79-79059. 1969. 27.50x (ISBN 0-672-53602-1). Irvington.
Temple of the Warriors at Chichen Itza, Yucatan, 2 vols. Earl H. Morris et al. LC 77-11511. (Carnegie Institution of Washington. Publication: No. 406). Repr. of 1931 ed. Set. 104.50 (ISBN 0-404-16280-0). AMS Pr.
Temple of the Warriors: The Adventure of Exploring & Restoring a Masterpiece of Native American Architecture in the Ruined City of Chichen Itza, Yucatan. Earl H. Morris. LC 76-44764. (Illus.). Repr. of 1931 ed. 41.50 (ISBN 0-404-15871-4). AMS Pr.
Temple of Tone. George A. Audsley. LC 79-108119. (BCL Ser.: No. 1). (Illus.). 1970. Repr. of 1925 ed. lib. bdg. 19.50 (ISBN 0-404-00417-2). AMS Pr.
Temple of Your Being. S. King. 1985. Book & Cassette Pack. 25.00x (ISBN 0-317-54328-8, Pub. by J Richardson UK); pap. 49.00x. State Mutual Bk.
Temple of Zeus at Nemea. rev., suppl. ed. Bert H. Hill. Ed. by Charles Williams. LC 67-102135. (Illus.). 1966. portfolio 22.00x (ISBN 0-87661-921-9). Am Sch Athens.
Temple on the River. Jacques Hebert. LC 67-30119. pap. 43.80 (ISBN 0-317-28419-3, 2022301). Bks Demand UMI.
Temple Organization in a Chinese Village. Gary Seaman. (Asian Folklore & Social Life Monographs: Vol. 101). 173p. 1981. 16.00x (ISBN 0-89986-332-9). Oriental Bk Store.
Temple Poems. Richard O'Connell. 1985. pap. 6.00 (ISBN 0-317-38870-3). Atlantis Edns.
Temple Propaganda: The Purpose & Character of 2 Maccabees. Robert Doran. LC 81-10084. (Catholic Biblical Quarterly Monographs). ix, 156p. 1981. pap. 4.50 (ISBN 0-915170-11-6). Catholic Biblical.
Temple Reflections. Paul F. Schmidt. LC 80-80346. (Illus.). 112p. 1980. 16.00 (ISBN 0-912998-04-0); pap. 6.00 (ISBN 0-912998-05-9). Hummingbird.
Temple: Sacred Poems & Private Ejaculations. 6th ed. George Herbert. LC 72-5489. (Select Bibliographies Reprint Ser.). 1972. Repr. of 1882 ed. 18.00 (ISBN 0-8369-6915-4). Ayer Co Pubs.
Temple Scroll: The Hidden Law of the Dead Sea Sect. Yigael Yadin. 1985. 24.45 (ISBN 0-394-54498-6). Random.
Temple Talks: On Willingness to Be Wrong. 56p. 1978. pap. 2.95 (ISBN 0-933740-02-6). Mindbody Inc.
Temple Talks: On Willingness to Be Wrong. 2nd ed. 93p. 1983. pap. 6.95. Mindbody Inc.
Temple Talks: Transcendental Aim. 163p. 1983. 7.95x (ISBN 0-933740-03-4). Mindbody Inc.
Temple Teachings Book I: Cosmogenesis & the Nine Laws. Gloria R. Rivers. Ed. by Owen Cramer. Date not set. pap. text ed. 12.00 (ISBN 0-918341-03-5). Temple Pubns.
Temple Teachings Book II: Realms of Creation & Being. Gloria R. Rivers. Ed. by Owen Cramer. LC 86-50300. Date not set. pap. text ed. 12.00 (ISBN 0-918341-04-3); tape cassette 12.00. Temple Pubns.
Templeman on Marine Insurance: Its Principles & Practice. 6th ed. R. J. Lambeth. 628p. 1986. 89.50x (ISBN 0-273-02537-6). Sheridan.
Templer: Tiger of Malaya. J. Cloake. 1986. 74.75X (ISBN 0-245-54204-3, Pub. by Harrap Ltd England). State Mutual Bk.
Temples. M. Winslow Chapman. 1979. 6.00 (ISBN 0-8233-0303-9). Golden Quill.
Temples & Elephants: Travels in Siam in 1881-1882. Carl Bock. (Oxford in Asia Paperbacks Ser.). (Illus.). 472p. 1985. pap. 8.95 (ISBN 0-19-582623-X). Oxford U Pr.
Temples & Fields. Phillis Levin. LC 88-4822. 96p. 1988. 13.95x (ISBN 0-8203-1052-2); pap. 6.95 (ISBN 0-8203-1053-0). U of Ga Pr.
Temples & Idol Worship. Panduranga R. Malyala. Date not set. 4.99 (ISBN 0-938924-02-8). Sri Shirdi Sai.
Temples & Temple-Service in Ancient Israel. Menahem Haran. 416p. 1985. Repr. of 1978 ed. text ed. 20.00x (ISBN 0-931464-18-8). Eisenbrauns.
Temples & Tombs of Ancient Nubia: The International Rescue Campaign at Abu Simbel, Philae & Other Sites. Ed. by Torgny Save-Soderbergh. LC 86-50517. (Illus.). 1987. 29.95 (ISBN 0-500-01392-6). Thames Hudson.
Temples, Churches & Mosques: A Guide to the Appreciation of Religious Architecture. J. G. Davies. LC 82-13130. (Illus.). 256p. 1982. 27.50 (ISBN 0-8298-0634-2). Pilgrim NY.
Temples, Kings & Peasants: Perceptions of South India's Past. George Spencer. 1987. 27.00x (ISBN 0-8364-2277-5, Pub. by New Era Bks). South Asia Bks.
Temples of Bankura District. David McCutchion. 12.00 (ISBN 0-89253-673-X); flexible cloth 6.75 (ISBN 0-89253-674-8). Ind-US Inc.
Temples of Bhitargaon. Mohammad Zaheer. (Illus.). 184p. 1981. 75.00. Asia Bk Corp.
Temples of Birbhum. Sukhamay Bandyopadhyay. (Illus.). 180p. 1984. text ed. 75.00x (ISBN 0-86590-255-0, Pub. by B R Pub Corp India). Apt Bks.
Temples of Convenience. Lucinda Lambton. 60p. 1983. 39.00x (ISBN 0-86092-010-0, Pub. by Fraser Bks). State Mutual Bk.
Temples of Midnapur. G. Santra. 1980. 24.00x (ISBN 0-8364-0595-1, Pub. by Mukhopadhyay India). South Asia Bks.
Temples of Mukhalingam. B. Masthanaiah. (Illus.). 136p. 1978. 28.00 (ISBN 0-89684-136-7, Pub. by Cosmo Pubns India). Orient Bk Dist.
Temples of Nara & Their Art. Minoru Ooka. LC 72-78601. (Heibonsha Survey of Japanese Art Ser.: Vol. 7). Orig. Title: Nara No Tera. (Illus.). 192p. 1973. 20.00 (ISBN 0-8348-1010-7). Weatherhill.
Temples of Nepal. Ronald M. Bernier. 204p. 25.00X (ISBN 0-317-52159-4, Pub. by S Chand India). State Mutual Bk.
Temples of Nepal: An Introductory Survey. Ronald M. Bernier. (Illus.). 247p. 1970. text ed. 27.50x. Coronet Bks.
Temples of Per Ramesses. E. Uphill. (Illus.). 300p. 1984. pap. text ed. 45.00x (ISBN 0-85668-265-9, Pub. by Aris & Phillips UK). Humanities.
Templet Development for the Pipe Trades. Raymond P. Jones. LC 63-22021. (Illus.). 166p. 1963. pap. 16.95 (ISBN 0-8273-0077-8). Delmar.
Templets & the Explanation of Complex Patterns. Michael J. Katz. (Illus.). 128p. 1986. 24.95 (ISBN 0-521-30673-6). Cambridge U Pr.
Templo del Sol. Herge. (Illus.). 62p. (Span.). 15.95 (ISBN 0-686-54340-8). French & Eur.
Templo del Sol. Herge. (Illus.). 62p. (Ital.). pap. 15.95 (ISBN 0-686-54358-0). French & Eur.
Templus Financial Planning Models for 1-2-3. Daniel Sueltz & Bruce Kinder. 1984. pap. 79.95 (ISBN 0-13-903063-8). P-H.
Tempo. Al Geiberger & Larry Dennis. LC 79-52550. (Illus.). 160p. 1986. pap. 8.95 (ISBN 0-394-75406-9, Dist. by Random House). Golf Digest.
TEMPO: A Unified Treatment of Binding Time & Parameter Passing Concepts in Programming Languages. N. D. Jones & S. S. Muchnick. (Lecture Notes in Computer Science Ser.: Vol. 66). 1978. pap. 14.00 (ISBN 0-387-09085-1). Springer-Verlag.
Tempo: An Office-Procedures Simulation. Nancy Wolff. 1983. write for info. Client Co. Manual (ISBN 0-574-20708-2, 13-3708); write for info. Employment Handbook (ISBN 0-574-20705-8, 13-3705); write for info. Working Papers (ISBN 0-574-20707-4, 13-3707); write for info.Model Answers (ISBN 0-574-20674-4, 13-3674); write for info. Office Manager's Handbook (ISBN 0-574-20706-6, 13-3706). SRA.
Tempo & Mode in Evolution. George G. Simpson. LC 83-23132. (Columbia University Biological Ser.). 256p. 1984. pap. 19.00 (ISBN 0-231-05847-0). Columbia U Pr.
Tempo: Golf's Master Key: How to Find It, How to Keep It. Al Geiberger & Larry Dennis. (Illus.). 160p. Date not set. 8.95 (ISBN 0-671-63532-8). S&S.
Tempo: Life, Work & Leisure. Ed. by Donald W. Cummings & John Herum. (Illus.). 336p. 1974. pap. text ed. 18.95 (ISBN 0-395-17839-8); instr's. guide 3.00 (ISBN 0-395-17867-3). HM.
Tempo Notation in Renaissance Spain. Charles Jacobs. (Wissenschaftliche Abhandlungen-Musicological Studies Ser.: Vol. 8). 121p. 1966. lib. bdg. 20.00 (ISBN 0-912024-78-X). Inst Mediaeval Mus.
Tempo of Modern Life. facs. ed. James T. Adams. LC 74-121444. (Essay Index Reprint Ser). 1931. 20.00 (ISBN 0-8369-1691-3). Ayer Co Pubs.
Tempo-Patterns of Shakespeare's Plays. John W. Draper. 163p. 1957. 33.50x (ISBN 3-533-00958-0). Adlers Foreign Bks.
Tempo Word Find Puzzles, No. 4. Linda Doherty. 1982. pap. 1.50 (ISBN 0-448-05572-4, Pub. by Tempo). Ace Bks.
Tempomatic IV: A Management Simulation. 3rd ed. Charles R. Scott, Jr. & Alonzo J. Strickland. LC 83-82340. 128p. 1983. pap. text ed. 21.56 (ISBN 0-395-34299-6); instr's. manual 1.96 (ISBN 0-395-34300-3); write for info computer center manual & computer systems for various types of computers avail. HM.
Temporal. Jose M. Garcia. 58p. (Orig.). 1986. pap. 3.50 (ISBN 0-943722-13-6). Gavea-Brown.
Temporal & Spiritual Conquest of Ceylon, 6 bks. in 2 vols. Fernao De Queyroz. LC 71-153629. Repr. of 1930 ed. 105.00 (ISBN 0-404-09630-1). AMS Pr.
Temporal Aspects in Information Systems: Proceedings of the IFIP TC8 WG8.1 Working Conference, Sophia-Antipolis, France, 13-15 May, 1987. Ed. by C. Rolland et al. 265p. 1988. 66.00 (ISBN 0-444-70373-X, North Holland). Elsevier.
Temporal Aspects of Speech Production & Perception. Ed. by K. Kohler. (Journal: Phonetica: Vol. 38, No. 1-3). (Illus.). 212p. 1981. pap. 86.00 (ISBN 3-8055-3415-9). S Karger.
Temporal Codes for Memories: Issues & Problems. B. J. Underwood. 176p. 1977. 19.95x (ISBN 0-89859-142-2). L Erlbaum Assocs.
Temporal Dimensions of Development Administration. Ed. by Dwight Waldo et al. LC 73-97215. (Comparative Administration Group Ser.). pap. 82.00 (ISBN 0-317-27297-7, 2023465). Bks Demand UMI.
Temporal Disorder in Human Oscillatory Systems. Ed. by L. Rensing & M. C. Mackey. (Synergetics Ser.: Vol. 36). (Illus.). 270p. 1987. 62.30 (ISBN 0-387-17765-5). Springer-Verlag.

Ten Commandments. J. I. Packer. 1982. pap. 3.95 (ISBN 0-8423-7004-8); leader's guide 2.95 (ISBN 0-8423-7005-6). Tyndale.
Ten Commandments. Thomas Watson. 245p. pap. 10.95 (ISBN 0-85151-146-5). Banner of Truth.
Ten Commandments & Human Rights. Walter Harrelson. Ed. by Walter Brueggemann & John R. Donahue. LC 77-15234. (Overtures to Biblical Theology Ser.). 240p. 1980. pap. 10.95 (ISBN 0-8006-1527-1, 1-1527). Fortress.
Ten Commandments & the Sermon on the Mount. Rudolf Steiner. Tr. by Frieda Solomon from Ger. 44p. 1978. pap. 2.00 (ISBN 0-910142-79-3). Anthroposophic.
Ten Commandments & Today's Christian. Finbarr Connolly & Peter Burns. 48p. 1985. pap. 1.50 (ISBN 0-89243-233-0). Liguori Pubns.
Ten Commandments for Husband. Benny Bristow. 1986. pap. 4.95 (ISBN 0-89137-623-2). Quality Pubns.
Ten Commandments for Now. Stephen M. Crotts. LC 87-62893. 1988. pap. text ed. 2.50 (ISBN 0-932050-34-4). New Puritan.
Ten Commandments for Today. William Barclay. LC 83-6103. 208p. (Orig.). 1983. pap. 8.95 (ISBN 0-06-060417-4, RD 476, HarpR). Har-Row.
Ten Commandments for Wives. Benny Bristow. pap. 4.95 (ISBN 0-89137-430-2). Quality Pubns.
Ten Commandments in Today's World. George Drew. 48p. (Orig.). 1979. pap. 6.95 (ISBN 0-940754-00-2). Ed Ministries.
Ten Commandments: Learning about God's Law. G. A. Truitt. LC 56-1398. (Concept Books for Children). (gr. 1 up). 1983. pap. 3.95 (ISBN 0-570-08527-6). Concordia.
Ten Commandments, Revelation at Sinai see Torah Anthology: Mem Lo'ez.
Ten Commandments: Text & Activity Book. Nancy Karkowsky. (gr. 3-4). 4.95 (ISBN 0-317-70145-2). Behrman.
Ten Commandments: Then & Now. Jim Lewis. LC 84-50912. 95p. (Orig.). 1984. pap. 5.95 (ISBN 0-942482-07-7). Unity Church Denver.
Ten Commandments Yesterday & Today. James B. Coffman. pap. 4.50 (ISBN 0-88027-094-2). Firm Foun Pub.
Ten Commandments: Youth & Adult Student. Carol E. Miller. 1971. pap. 0.95 (ISBN 0-915374-45-5). Rapids Christian.
Ten Common Inferences: Oscar-The Big Escape for Use with Apple II. California State University Staff. 1984. 49.95 (ISBN 0-07-831014-8). McGraw.
Ten Common Inferences: Oscar-The Big Escape for Use with IBM-PC, Pt. 2. California State University Staff. 1984. 49.95 (ISBN 0-07-831015-6). McGraw.
Ten Contemporaries, Notes Towards Their Definitive Bibliography. John Gawsworth. LC 72-192872. 1932. lib. bdg. 30.00 (ISBN 0-8414-1050-X). Folcroft.
Ten Contemporaries, Second Series. John Gawsworth. LC 72-193506. 1933. lib. bdg. 30.00. Folcroft.
Ten Contemporary Polish Stories. Ed. by Edmund Ordon. LC 74-2842. 252p. 1974. Repr. of 1958 ed. lib. bdg. 35.00x (ISBN 0-8371-7436-8, ORPS). Greenwood.
Ten Coptic Legal Texts: Metropolitan Museum of Art, Department of Egyptian Art Publications, Vol. 2. A. Arthur Schiller. LC 71-168410. (Metropolitan Museum of Art Publications in Reprint). (Illus.). 126p. 1972. Repr. of 1932 ed. 22.00 (ISBN 0-405-02246-8). Ayer Co Pubs.
Ten Copycats in a Boat & Other Riddles. Alvin Schwartz. LC 79-2811. (Harper I Can Read Bks.). (Illus.). 64p. (gr. k-3). 1980. 8.70i (ISBN 0-06-025237-5); PLB 9.89 (ISBN 0-06-025238-3). HarpJ.
Ten Copycats in a Boat & Other Riddles. Alvin Schwartz. LC 79-2811. (Trophy I Can Read Bks.). (Illus.). 64p. (gr. k-3). 1985. pap. 3.50 (ISBN 0-06-444076-1, Trophy). HarpJ.
Ten Cupcake Romance. M. L. Kennedy. 176p. (Orig.). (gr. 7 up). 1986. pap. 2.25 (ISBN 0-590-33932-X, Wildfire). Scholastic Inc.
Ten Dates for Mates. Dave Arp & Claudia Arp. LC 83-3954. 176p. 1983. pap. 9.95 (ISBN 0-8407-5845-6). Nelson.
Ten Day Fully Financed Wealth System Guide. Tyler G. Hicks. 100p. 1987. pap. 10.00 (ISBN 0-934311-38-2). Intl Wealth.
Ten Day Pure Body Plan. Leslie Kenton. 1987. pap. 4.95 (ISBN 0-671-63438-0). PB.
Ten Days. Connie Vanderwerff. (Destiny Ser.). 96p. 1986. pap. 6.95 (ISBN 0-8163-0630-3). Pacific Pr Pub Assn.
Ten Days in the Light of 'Akka. rev. ed. Julia M. Grundy. LC 79-12177. 1979. pap. 6.95 (ISBN 0-87743-131-0, 332-040). Baha'i.
Ten Days of Infamy. Malcolm Decker. LC 68-20204. (Illus.). 1968. Repr. of 1968 ed. 17.00 (ISBN 0-405-00053-7). Ayer Co Pubs.
Ten Days on the Plains. Ed. by Paul A. Hutton. LC 85-10915. (DeGolyer Library Publications: No. 2). (Illus.). 200p. 1985. 21.95 (ISBN 0-87074-207-8). SMU Press.
Ten Days That Shook the World. John Reed. 1982. lib. bdg. 75.00 (ISBN 0-8490-3225-3). Gordon Pr.
Ten Days That Shook the World. John Reed. LC 67-27252. (Illus.). 445p. (Orig.). 1967. pap. 3.50 (ISBN 0-7178-0200-0). Intl Pubs Co.
Ten Days That Shook the World. John Reed. 1979. pap. 3.95 (ISBN 0-14-002433-6). Penguin.
Ten Days That Shook the World. John Reed. Ed. by Bertam D. Wolfe. 1960. pap. 4.95 (ISBN 0-394-70719-2, V719, Vin). Random.
Ten Days That Shook the World. John Reed. 1982. pap. 3.95 (ISBN 0-451-62417-3, Ment). NAL.
Ten Days That Shook the World. John Reed. (Classics Ser.). 301p. (Orig.). 1987. pap. 4.50 (ISBN 0-553-21268-0, Bantam Classics). Bantam.
Ten Days to a Great New Life. William E. Edwards. pap. 3.00 (ISBN 0-87980-159-X). Wilshire.
Ten Days to a New You. Guy B. Giovanni. 40p. (Orig.). 1983. pap. 3.00 (ISBN 0-912981-02-4). Hse Bon Giovanni.
Ten Days to a Successful Memory. Joyce Brothers & Edward P. Eagen. 256p. 1984. 16.95 (ISBN 0-13-903600-8). P-H.
Ten Days to Destiny. G. C. Kiriakopoulos. 352p. 1986. pap. 3.95 (ISBN 0-380-70102-2). Avon.
Ten Days to Destiny: The Battle for Crete 1941. G. C. Kiriakopoulos. 464p. 1985. 18.95 (ISBN 0-531-09785-4). Watts.
Ten Decisive Battles of Christianity. Frank S. Mead. LC 72-117823. (Essay Index Reprint Ser). 1937. 15.00 (ISBN 0-8369-1812-6). Ayer Co Pubs.
Ten-Dollar Bill. Dougald B. MacEachen. (Illus.). 128p. 1984. pap. 8.00 (ISBN 0-682-40181-1). Exposition-Phoenix.
Ten Dollar Book That Can Make You Rich. Joe Bart. 1976. 10.00 (ISBN 0-8184-0232-6); lib. bdg. 10.00 (ISBN 0-685-69538-7). Lyle Stuart.
Ten, Ekrane Suzibus: Amerikos Lietuviu Kinematografija, 1909-1979. Raimundas M. Lapas. LC 81-69029. (Illus.). 386p. (Eng. & Lithuanian.). 19.95 (ISBN 0-941618-00-5). Baltic Cinema.
Ten English Farces. facs. ed. Ed. by Leo Hughes & A. H. Scouten. LC 79-132135. (Play Anthology Reprint Ser). 1948. 14.25 (ISBN 0-8369-8212-6). Ayer Co Pubs.
Ten Essays on Zionism & Judaism. Achad Ha-am, pseud. LC 73-2202. (Jewish People; History, Religion, Literature Ser.). Repr. of 1922 ed. 26.50 (ISBN 0-405-05267-7). Ayer Co Pubs.
Ten Essential Points for Creating a Successful Relationship. Joanne Tangedahl. 24p. pap. 2.50 (ISBN 0-942494-46-6). Coleman Pub.
Ten European Elections: Campaigns & Results of the 1979-81 First Direct Elections to the European Parliament. Ed. by Karlheinz Reif. LC 84-18874. 232p. 1985. text ed. 34.95 (ISBN 0-566-00694-4). Gower Pub Co.
Ten Ever-Lovin' Blue-Eyed Years. Walt Kelly. 11.95 (ISBN 0-671-21428-4, Fireside). S&S.
Ten Famous Plays. John Galsworthy. LC 75-41108. (BCL Ser.: II). 1976. Repr. of 1952 ed. 41.75 (ISBN 0-404-14749-6). AMS Pr.
Ten Favorite French Stories. Joseph S. Galland. (Fr.). 1985. pap. text ed. 9.95x (ISBN 0-89197-962-X). Irvington.
Ten Fifteenth Century Comic Poets. Ed. by Melissa Furrow. LC 83-48231. (Medieval Texts Ser.). 330p. 1985. lib. bdg. 60.00 (ISBN 0-8240-9428-X). Garland Pub.
Ten First Little Golden Books. (ps). 1981. Set. write for info (ISBN 0-307-93614-7, Golden Bks). Western Pub.
Ten First Street, Southeast: Congress Builds a Library, 1886-1897. Helen-Anne Hilker. LC 80-60780. (Illus.). iv, 102p. 1980. pap. 5.50 (ISBN 0-8444-0351-2). Lib Congress.
Ten Flemish Poems. Tr. by Manfred Wolf. 1972. pap. 2.25 (ISBN 0-685-27793-3). Twowindows Pr.
Ten Folk Dances in Labanotation. Fred Berk & Lucy Venable. i, 32p. 1959. pap. text ed. 7.95 (ISBN 0-932582-09-5). Dance Notation.
Ten-Foot Chain. facs. ed. Achmed Abdullah et al. LC 73-116924. (Short Story Index Reprint Ser). 1920. 13.00 (ISBN 0-8369-3426-1). Ayer Co Pubs.
Ten Foot Square Hut & Tales of Heike. Tr. by A. L. Sadler. LC 72-157261. (Illus.). 1971. pap. 7.50 (ISBN 0-8048-0879-1). C E Tuttle.
Ten Foot Square Hut & Tales of the Heike. Chomei Kamo. Ed. by Arthur L. Sadler. Repr. of 1928 ed. lib. bdg. 35.00x (ISBN 0-8371-3114-6, KATF). Greenwood.
Ten for Our Time. Lowell Erdahl. 1986. 5.50 (ISBN 0-89536-786-6, 6804). CSS of Ohio.
Ten Forty Handbook. Julian Block. 550p. 1989. pap. 23.50 (ISBN 0-13-903535-4, Busn). P-H.
Ten-Forty Handbook, 1985: How to Prepare Income Tax Returns. Martin E. Holbrook. 538p. 1984. 21.00 (ISBN 0-13-903659-8). P-H.
Ten-Forty Handbook: 1988 Special New Tax Law Edition. Julian Block & Alan S. Robinson. 550p. 1987. pap. 27.00 (ISBN 0-13-903709-8). P-H.
Ten Forty Preparation 1986. Sidney Kess & Ben Eisenberg. 760p. 1986. 24.50 (ISBN 0-317-44575-8, 5486). Commerce.
Ten Forty Preparation, 1988. Kess & Eisenberg. 728p. (Orig.). 1988. pap. 27.50 (5282). Commerce.
Ten Four-Part Motets for the Church's Year. Giovanni P. Palestrina. Tr. by Alec Harman. (Lat. & Eng.). 1964. 9.95 (ISBN 0-19-353332-4). Oxford U Pr.
Ten Furry Monsters. Stephanie Calmenson. LC 84-4998. (Illus.). 48p. (ps-3). 1984. 5.95 (ISBN 0-8193-1128-6). Parents.
Ten Gates: The Kong-An Teaching of Zen Master Seung Sahn. Ed. by Stan Lombardo & Dennis Duermeier. (Illus.). 148p. (Orig.). 1987. pap. 7.95 (ISBN 0-942795-01-6). Primary Point Pr.
Ten Georgian Glees for Mixed Voices. David Johnson. 64p. 1981. pap. 9.00 (ISBN 0-19-343658-2). Oxford U Pr.
Ten Go Hopping. Viv Allbright. LC 85-13010. (Illus.). 29p. (gr. 2-5). 1985. 6.95 (ISBN 0-571-13473-4). Faber & Faber.
Ten Good Reasons to be a Catholic: A Teenager's Guide to the Church. Jim Auer. LC 87-80988. (YA) (gr. 7-12). 1987. pap. 1.95 (ISBN 0-89243-271-3). Liguori Pubns.
Ten Good Things I Know about Retirement. J. Winston Pearce. LC 82-71668. 1982. 8.95 (ISBN 0-8054-5429-2). Broadman.
Ten Grandmothers. Alice Marriott. LC 45-1584. (Civilization of the American Indians Ser.: Vol. 26). 306p. 1985. pap. 9.95 (ISBN 0-8061-1825-3). U of Okla Pr.
Ten Great & Good Men. Henry M. Butler. Repr. of 1912 ed. 25.00 (ISBN 0-686-19868-9). Ridgeway Bks.
Ten Great & Good Men. Henry M. Butler. Repr. of 1909 ed. 25.00 (ISBN 0-686-18791-1). Scholars Ref Lib.
Ten Great Mysteries. Howard Haycraft. Repr. of 1959 ed. 55.00. Darby Bks.
Ten Great Mysteries by Edgar Allan Poe. Edgar Allan Poe. Ed. by Groff Conklin. 218p. (gr. 7 up). 1968. pap. 2.25 (ISBN 0-590-08595-6, Schol Pap). Scholastic Inc.
Ten Great Works of Philosophy. Robert P. Wolff. 480p. 1973. pap. 5.95 (ISBN 0-451-62577-3, Ment). NAL.
Ten Great Years: Statistics of the Economic & Cultural Achievements of the People's Republic of China. Peoples Republic of China. Repr. of 1960 ed. 21.00 (ISBN 0-404-56908-0). AMS Pr.
Ten Greatest Salespersons. Robert L. Shook. 196p. 1980. pap. 4.95 (ISBN 0-06-465104-5, P BN 5104, B&N Bks). Har-Row.
Ten Greek Plays in Contemporary Translations. Ed. by Levi R. Lind. Incl. Prometheus Bound. Aeschylus; Agamemnon. Aeschylus; Antigone. Sophocles; Oedipus Rex. Sophocles; Philoctetes. Sophocles; Alcestis. Euripides; Suppliants. Euripides; Andromache. Euripides; Bacchae. Euripides; Lysistrata. Aristophanes. LC 57-59175. (YA) (gr. 9up). 1957. pap. 6.95 (ISBN 0-395-05117-7, RivEd). HM.
Ten Greek Popes. Dennis Michelis. 1987. pap. 5.95 (ISBN 0-937032-54-9). Light&Life Pub Co MN.
Ten Guidelines for Written Communication. 11p. 8.95 (ISBN 0-911703-07-1). CDS Assocs.
Ten Heavy Facts about Sex. Sol Gordon. (Illus.). 20p. (Orig.). (gr. 9-12). 1983. pap. 1.95 (ISBN 0-934978-32-8). Ed-U Pr.
Ten-Hour Job Search Training Mini Course for Vocational-Occupational Skills Program. Lawrence E. Barlow. 14p. (Orig.). 1985. 1.50x (ISBN 0-940150-03-4). Voc Career Assess.
Ten Hours Movement in Eighteen Thirty-One & Eighteen Thirty-Two. 21.00 (ISBN 0-405-04439-9). Ayer Co Pubs.
Ten Ideas That Make a Difference. Ernest Holmes. Ed. by Willis H. Kinnear. 96p. 1966. pap. 4.50 (ISBN 0-911336-32-X). Sci of Mind.
Ten in a Bed. Adapted by & illus. by Mary Rees. (Illus.). (ps-1). 1988. 12.95 (ISBN 0-316-73708-9, Joy St Bks). Little.
Ten Independent Contractor Case Studies. James R. Urquhart, III. 1988. 49.95. Fidelity Pub.
Ten Introductions: A Collection of Modern Verse. Genevieve Taggard & Dudley Fitts. Repr. of 1934 ed. lib. bdg. 25.00 (ISBN 0-8495-5325-3). Arden Lib.
Ten Introductions: A Collection of Modern Verse. Genevieve Taggard & Dudley Fitts. 1977. Repr. of 1934 ed. 20.00. Century Bookbindery.
Ten Japanese Paintings. Robert T. Paine. 72p. 1939. 315.00x (ISBN 0-317-68511-2, Pub. by Han-Shan Tang Ltd). State Mutual Bk.
Ten Japanese Poets. Tr. by Hiroaki Sato. LC 73-86247. (Illus.). 136p. 1974. pap. 3.00 (ISBN 0-914102-00-1). Bluefish.
Ten-Key Adding Machine: Student Guide. Marvin W. Hempel. 1970. pap. text ed. 5.55 (ISBN 0-89420-056-9, 126600); cassette recordings 142.40 (ISBN 0-89420-187-5, 156700). Natl Book.
Ten-Key Touch System on Electronic Calculators: With Business & Industry Applications. Gilbert Eckern & Walt Hardin. (Illus.). 240p. 1983. pap. text ed. 14.95 (ISBN 0-89863-074-6). Star Pub CA.
Ten Keys to Latin America. Frank Tannenbaum. 1966. pap. 4.95 (ISBN 0-394-70312-X, Vin). Random.
Ten Keys to Understanding People. Henry C. Smith & James J. Mullin. LC 87-80562. (Self-Paced Program for Improving Relationships). (Orig.). 1987. pap. 8.95 (ISBN 0-942027-00-0). Lantern Hill Pr.
Ten Keys to Writing Success. Donald E. Bower. LC 87-60072. 160p. (Orig.). 1987. pap. 10.95 (ISBN 0-88100-057-4). Natl Writ Pr.
Ten Kids, No Pets. Ann M. Martin. LC 87-25206. 184p. (gr. 3-7). 1988. 12.95 (ISBN 0-8234-0691-1). Holiday.
Ten Late Breakfast. Alexandria Carlier. (Illus.). 128p. 1989. 19.95. Interlink Pub.
Ten Late Breakfasts. Alexandra Carlier. (Cookery Book Ser.). (Illus.). 128p. 1989. 19.95 (ISBN 0-940793-24-5). Interlink Pub.
Ten Leading Causes of Death in Selected Countries. 1959-67. Vol. 12, Nos. 5-6. pap. 2.00 (ISBN 0-686-09170-1); Vol. 15, No. 1. pap. 3.60 (ISBN 0-686-09171-X); Vol. 17, Nos. 1-2. pap. 3.60 (ISBN 0-686-09172-8); Vol. 20, No. 1. pap. 3.60 (ISBN 0-686-09173-6); Vol. 20, No. 2. pap. 2.80 (ISBN 0-686-09174-4). World Health.
Ten Lectures on Art. Edward J Poynter. 14.00 (ISBN 0-8369-7325-9, 8118). Ayer Co Pubs.
Ten Lectures on Operator Algebras. William Arveson. LC 84-9222. (CBMS Regional Conference Series in Mathematics: Vol. 55). 93p. 1984. pap. 16.00 (ISBN 0-8218-0705-6). Am Math.
Ten Lectures on the Probabilistic Method. Joel Spencer. LC 87-60539. (CBMS-NSF Regional Conference Ser.: No. 52). vi, 78p. 1987. pap. text ed. 14.00 (ISBN 0-89871-213-0). Soc Indus-Appl Math.
Ten Lessons in Seven Universal Rays. M. R. Wilson-Ludlam. 75p. 1984. 7.00 (ISBN 0-86690-275-9, 2534-01). Am Fed Astrologers.
Ten Lessons of the Energy Crisis. Morris Goran. LC 80-130511. 1980. 19.80x (ISBN 0-915250-35-7). Environ Design.
Ten Letter-Writers. facs. ed. Lyn L. Irvine. LC 68-16942. (Essay Index Reprint Ser). 1932. 17.00 (ISBN 0-8369-0560-1). Ayer Co Pubs.
Ten Letter-Writers. Lyn L. Irvine. 1932. Repr. 30.00 (ISBN 0-8274-2856-1). R West.
Ten Little Babies Counts. Janet Martin. (Ten Little Babies Bks.). (Illus.). (ps). 1986. bds. 3.95 (ISBN 0-312-79112-7). St Martin.
Ten Little Babies Dress. Janet Martin. (Ten Little Babies Bks.). 14p. 1986. bds. 3.95 (ISBN 0-312-79113-5). St Martin.
Ten Little Babies Eat. Janet Martin. (Ten Little Babies Bks.). (Illus.). 14p. (ps). 1986. bds. 3.95 (ISBN 0-312-79114-3). St Martin.
Ten Little Babies Play: A Book of Colors. Janet Martin. (Ten Little Babies Bks.). (Illus.). 14p. (ps). 1986. bds. 3.95 (ISBN 0-312-79115-1). St Martin.
Ten Little Bunnies. Marlene E. Gawron. (Cut & Paste Ser.). (Illus.). (ps-1). 1981. 3.50 (ISBN 0-913545-06-6). Moonlight FL.
Ten Little Care Bears Counting Book. Bobbi Katz. LC 83-60084. (Care Bear Bks.). (Illus.). 14p. (ps-k). 1983. 4.95 (ISBN 0-394-86088-8). Random.
Ten Little Chicks in the Farmyard. 5.50 (ISBN 0-904494-07-1, Brimax Bks). Borden.
Ten Little Crocodiles. Colin West. (Counting Bks.). (Illus.). 32p. (ps). 1988. 8.95 (ISBN 0-8120-5884-4). Barron.
Ten Little Dogs. 5.50 (ISBN 0-86112-044-2, Brimax Bks). Borden.
Ten Little Fingers. Monica Stuart & Gill Soper. 96p. (gr. 4-7). 1975. 9.95 (ISBN 0-571-10828-8). Faber & Faber.
Ten Little Friends. Hideo Kiso. (Fun Time Ser.). (Illus.). 22p. (ps-1). 1981. 3.50 (ISBN 0-89346-199-7). Heian Intl.
Ten Little Indians. Agatha Christie. 176p. 1983. pap. 3.95 (ISBN 0-671-55222-8). PB.
Ten Little Indians. Agatha Christie. pap. 3.95 (ISBN 0-671-49949-1). WSP.
Ten Little Indians. E. Patrick Murray, pseud. 432p. 1988. pap. 3.95 (ISBN 0-8217-2452-5). Zebra.
Ten Little Kittens. 5.50 (ISBN 0-900195-04-5, Brimax Bks). Borden.
Ten Little Lambs. Dick Dudley. (Pop-Up-Counting Story Books). (Illus.). 12p. (ps-k). 1988. 8.95 (ISBN 0-8120-5953-0). Barron.
Ten Little Motor Cars. 5.50 (ISBN 0-904494-80-2, Brimax Bks). Borden.
Ten Little Puppy Dogs. Illus. by Lisa McCue. LC 86-63577. (Chunky Bks.). (Illus.). 28p. (ps). 1987. 2.95 (ISBN 0-394-89149-X, BYR). Random.
Ten Little Rabbits. Maurice Sendak. pap. 3.50 (ISBN 0-939084-09-0, Pub. by Rosenbach Mus & Lib). U Pr of Va.
Ten Little Rabbits. 5.50 (ISBN 0-686-85729-1, Brimax Bks). Borden.
Ten Lives of the Buddha: Siamese Temple Paintings & Jataka Tales. Elizabeth Wray et al. LC 73-179982. (Illus.). 156p. 1972. 20.00 (ISBN 0-8348-0067-5). Weatherhill.
Ten Love Poems. Ed. by Robert Bly. 1981. pap. 3.50 (ISBN 0-915408-24-4). Ally Pr.
Ten Luminous Emanations, Vol. 1. Yehuda Ashlag. 160p. 1970. 12.95 (ISBN 0-943688-08-6); pap. 9.95 (ISBN 0-943688-29-9). Res Ctr Kabbalah.
Ten Luminous Emanations, Vol. 2. Yehuda Ashlag. Ed. by Philip S. Berg. 208p. 1972. 13.95 (ISBN 0-943688-09-4); pap. 9.95 (ISBN 0-943688-25-6). Res Ctr Kabbalah.
Ten Madrigals. Orlandus Lassus. Ed. by Denis Arnold. 1977. 11.95 (ISBN 0-19-343668-X). Oxford U Pr.
Ten Madrigals. Claudio Monteverdi. Ed. by Denis Stevens. 1979. pap. 12.95x (ISBN 0-19-343676-0). Oxford U Pr.

Ten Madrigals for Mixed Voices. Andrea Gabrieli. Ed. by Denis Arnold. 84p. 1970. pap. 9.95 (ISBN 0-19-343591-8). Oxford U Pr.

Ten Madrigals for Mixed Voices. Luca Marenzio. Ed. by Denis Arnold. 1966. 9.95 (ISBN 0-19-343675-2). Oxford U Pr.

Ten Masses: Personal Impressions. Vincent G. Dethier. LC 88-14523. 102p. 1988. pap. 4.95 (ISBN 0-8189-0537-9). Alba.

Ten Master Historians. facs. ed. Lionel M. Angus-Butterworth. LC 69-18919. (Essay Index Reprint Ser). 1961. 16.00 (ISBN 0-8369-0000-6). Ayer Co Pubs.

Ten Men Dead: The Story of the 1981 Irish Hunger Strike. David Beresford. 1989. 18.95 (ISBN 0-87113-269-9). Atlantic Monthly.

Ten Men of Minnesota & American Foreign Policy, 1898-1968. Barbara Stuhler. LC 73-15967. (Public Affairs Center Publications Ser.). (Illus.). 263p. 1973. 8.95 (ISBN 0-87351-080-1). Minn Hist.

Ten-Meter FM for the Radio Amateur. Dave Ingram. (Illus.). 140p. (Orig.). 1980. 9.95 (ISBN 0-8306-9933-3, 1189H). TAB Bks.

Ten Mile Treasure. Andre Norton. (Illus.). (gr. 4-6). 1981. pap. 1.95 (ISBN 0-671-56102-2). Archway.

Ten Million Acres of Timber: The Remarkable Story of Forest Protection in the Maine Forestry District 1909-1972. Austin H. Wilkins. LC 78-60181. (Illus.). xxiv, 312p. 1978. pap. 8.95 (ISBN 0-931474-03-5). TBW Bks.

Ten Million Bayonets: Inside the Armies of the Soviet Union. David C. Isby. (Illus.). 128p. 1988. 19.95 (ISBN 0-85368-774-9, Pub. by Arms & Armour). Sterling.

Ten Million Dollar Golf Ball. Albert E. Killeen. LC 85-13760. 128p. 1986. 11.95 (ISBN 0-688-06096-X). Morrow.

Ten Million Photoplay Plots. W. Aber Hill. Ed. by Bruce S. Kupelnick. LC 76-52108. (Classics of Film Literature Ser.). 1978. lib. bdg. 18.00 (ISBN 0-8240-2879-1). Garland Pub.

Ten Minute Cure for the Common Cold: A Natural Approach. James F. Dorobiala. Ed. by Kerry A. Martinez. LC 87-18114. 160p. (Orig.). 1988. 24.95 (ISBN 0-944346-01-4); pap. 9.95 (ISBN 0-944346-02-2); VHS. videotape 49.95 (ISBN 0-944346-03-0); 59.90 set (ISBN 0-944346-04-9); Beta. videotape 49.95 (ISBN 0-944346-05-7); 59.90 set (ISBN 0-944346-06-5). Sun Eagle Pub.

Ten-Minute Entrepreneur. Mark Stevens. 272p. (Orig.). 1985. pap. text ed. 7.95 (ISBN 0-446-38069-5). Warner Bks.

Ten-Minute Gourmet Diet Cookbook. Yvonne Y. Tarr. (Illus.). 1967. 5.95 (ISBN 0-8184-0125-7). Lyle Stuart.

Ten Minute Stories. facsimile ed. Algernon Blackwood. LC 72-103495. (Short Story Index Reprint Ser.). 1914. 18.00 (ISBN 0-8369-3237-4). Ayer Co Pubs.

Ten Minutes with Me. 3rd ed. Joanne Cohn-Gilletly. (Illus., Orig.). (gr. k-3). 1980. pap. 2.00 (ISBN 0-916634-05-1). Double M Pr.

Ten Miracles of Jesus Workbook. Jamie Buckingham. 72p. (Orig.). 1988. wkbk. 5.95 (ISBN 0-941478-96-3); videocassette 29.95x (ISBN 0-317-67588-5). Paraclete Pr.

Ten Mistakes Parents Make with Teenagers & How to Avoid Them. Jay Kesler. 1988. 14.95 (ISBN 0-317-68191-5). Wolgemuth & Hyatt.

Ten Modern American Playwrights: An Annotated Bibliography. Kimball King. LC 80-8498. (American Literature Catalogue Ser.). 251p. 1982. lib. bdg. 40.00 (ISBN 0-8240-9489-1). Garland Pub.

Ten Modern Irish Playwrights: A Comprehensive Annotated Bibliography. Kimball King. LC 78-68289. (Reference Library of Humanities). 1979. lib. bdg. 22.00 (ISBN 0-8240-9789-0). Garland Pub.

Ten Modern Masters. 3rd ed. Robert G. Davis. 583p. 1972. pap. text ed. 12.00 net (ISBN 0-15-590281-4, HC); instr's. manual avail. (ISBN 0-15-590282-2). HarBraceJ.

Ten Modern Poets. facs. ed. Rica Brenner. LC 68-22091. (Essay Index Reprint Ser). 1930. 18.00 (ISBN 0-8369-0249-1). Ayer Co Pubs.

Ten Modern Scottish Novels. I. Murray & B. Tait. 252p. 1984. text ed. 25.00x (Pub. by Aberdeen U Scotland). Humanities.

Ten Months among the Tents of the Tuski. William H. Hooper. LC 74-5847. (Illus.). Repr. of 1853 ed. 31.00 (ISBN 0-404-11652-3). AMS Pr.

Ten Months in Treblinka: Memoirs of Oskar Strawczynski see Elegy for My People: A Nation Torn Asunder.

Ten More Aesthetic Realism Essays. Eli Siegel. 1979. pap. 2.95 (ISBN 0-911492-23-2). Aesthetic Realism.

Ten Motets. Olandus Lassus. Ed. by Clive Wearing. 1981. 12.00 (ISBN 0-19-353238-7). Oxford U Pr.

Ten Myths about Christianity. Michael Green & Gordon Carkner. (Illus.). 80p. (Orig.). 1988. pap. 2.50 (ISBN 0-7459-1441-1). Lion USA.

Ten Nequdoth of the Torah. Butin. Date not set. 15.00. Ktav.

Ten New England Leaders. Williston Walker. LC 76-83445. (Religion in America Ser). 1969. Repr. of 1901 ed. 28.00 (ISBN 0-405-00278-5). Ayer Co Pubs.

Ten Nigerian Tone Systems. John Bendor-Samuel. (Language Data, African Ser.: No. 4). 129p. 1974. microfiche (2) 4.00x (ISBN 0-88312-704-0). Summer Inst Ling.

Ten Nights of Dream, Hearing Things, the Heredity of Taste. Soseki Natsume. Tr. by Aiko Ito & Graeme Wilson. LC 73-86136. 1974. 6.95 (ISBN 0-8048-1136-9). C E Tuttle.

Ten, Nine, Eight. Molly Bang. LC 81-20106. (Illus.). 24p. (ps-1). 1983. 12.95 (ISBN 0-688-00906-9); PLB 12.88 (ISBN 0-688-00907-7). Greenwillow.

Ten, Nine, Eight. Molly G. Bang. (ps-3). 1985. pap. 3.95 (ISBN 0-14-050543-1). Penguin.

Ten North-East Poets. Ed. by Neil Astley. 104p. 1980. pap. 8.95 (ISBN 0-906427-13-4, Pub. by Bloodaxe Bks). Dufour.

Ten North Frederick. John O'Hara. 1955. 14.95 (ISBN 0-394-44814-6). Random.

Ten North Frederick. John O'Hara. 408p. 1985. pap. 4.50 (ISBN 0-88184-173-0). Carroll & Graf.

Ten Northeast Poets: An Anthology. Ed. by L. W. Wheeler. 184p. 1985. text ed. 16.80 (ISBN 0-08-032430-4, Pub. by AUP); pap. text ed. 9.50 (ISBN 0-08-032431-2). Pergamon.

Ten Notable Women of Latin America. James D. Henderson & Linda R. Henderson. LC 78-15253. (Illus.). 1978. 22.95x (ISBN 0-88229-426-1). Nelson-Hall.

Ten O'Clock Club. Carol B. York. (Illus.). 112p. (gr. 2-5). 1985. pap. 2.50 (ISBN 0-590-41084-9, Lucky Star). Scholastic Inc.

Ten of the Best. Ed. by Reader's Digest Editors. LC 84-27591. (Illus.). 608p. 1985. 18.99 (ISBN 0-89577-207-8). RD Assn.

Ten of the Best New Zealand Trout Flies. Mike Weddell. (Illus.). 64p. (Orig.). 1987. pap. 12.95 (ISBN 0-86868-097-4, Pub. by J McIndoe Ltd New Zealand). Intl Spec Bk.

Ten One-Act Plays. Ed. by Cosmo Pieterse. (African Writers Ser.). 1968. pap. text ed. 7.50 (ISBN 0-435-90034-X). Heinemann Ed.

Ten Paintings. D. H. Lawrence. (Illus.). 64p. 1981. 20.00 (ISBN 0-933806-13-2). Black Swan CT.

Ten Papers in Analysis. M. S. Budjanu et al. LC 73-16013. (Translations Ser.: No. 2, Vol. 102). 1973. 46.00 (ISBN 0-8218-3052-X, TRANS 2-102). Am Math.

Ten Papers in Analysis. LC 86-20550. (TRANS2 Ser.: Vol. 131). 120p. 1986. text ed. 45.00 (ISBN 0-8218-3106-2). Am Math.

Ten Papers in Complex Analysis, Vol. 122. Incl. Vol. 123. Seven Papers on Elliptic Boundary Value Problems. LC 84-15750. 83.00 (ISBN 0-8218-3082-1); Vol. 124. Fifteen Papers on Functional Analysis. 67.00 (ISBN 0-8218-3085-6). (Translations Ser.: No. 2). 1984. text ed. 60.00. Am Math.

Ten Papers on Algebra & Functional Analysis. N. D. Filippov et al. LC 51-5559. (Translations Ser.: No. 2, Vol. 96). 1970. 35.00 (ISBN 0-8218-1796-5, TRANS 2-96). Am Math.

Ten Papers on Analysis. B. F. Bylov et al. LC 51-5559. (Translations Ser.: No. 2, Vol. 74). 1968. 39.00 (ISBN 0-8218-1774-4, TRANS 2-74). Am Math.

Ten Papers on Differential Equations & Functional Analysis. A. D. Aleksandrov et al. LC 51-5559. (Translations Ser.: No. 2, Vol. 68). 1968. 39.00 (ISBN 0-8218-1768-X, TRANS 2-68). Am Math.

Ten Papers on Functional Analysis & Measure Theory. L. M. Abramov et al. LC 51-5559. (Translations Ser.: No. 2, Vol. 49). 1966. 27.00 (ISBN 0-8218-1749-3, TRANS 2-49). Am Math.

Ten Papers on Topology. P. S. Aleksandrov et al. LC 51-5559. (Translatons Ser.: No. 2, Vol. 30). 1963. 33.00 (ISBN 0-8218-1730-2, TRANS 2-30). Am Math.

Ten Parables of Jesus Workbook. Jamie Buckingham. 72p. (Orig.). 1988. wkbk. 5.95 (ISBN 0-941478-97-1); videocassette 29.95x (ISBN 0-317-67590-7). Paraclete Pr.

Ten Pennies for Jesus. Alton Ward. (Illus.). 24p. (Orig.). (ps-1). 1986. pap. 3.50 (ISBN 0-570-04132-5, 56-1560). Concordia.

Ten Per Cent & No Surrender: The Preston Strike, 1853-1854. H. I. Dutton & J. E. King. (Illus.). 288p. 1981. o. p. 44.50 (ISBN 0-521-23620-7). Cambridge U Pr.

Ten Percent of Life. Hiber Conteris. 288p. 1987. 15.95 (ISBN 0-671-64589-7, Fireside); pap. 6.95 (ISBN 0-671-63419-4). S&S.

Ten Percent Solution: Your Key to Financial Security. Ed Blitz. 180p. 1988. pap. 12.95 (ISBN 0-8306-3023-6, 30023, Liberty Hse). TAB Bks.

Ten Personal Studies. Wilfrid P. Ward. LC 73-107742. (Essay Index Reprint Ser.). 1908. 21.00 (ISBN 0-8369-1584-4). Ayer Co Pubs.

Ten Plagues of Egypt. Shoshana Lepon. Ed. by Neva Goldstein-Alpern. (Illus.). 32p. (gr. 4-8). 1988. 8.95 (ISBN 0-910818-77-0); pap. 6.95 (ISBN 0-910818-76-2). Judaica Pr.

Ten Plays. Alfred de Musset. Tr. by R. Pellissier & M. Dey. LC 87-7426. 506p. 1987. Repr. of 1907 ed. lib. bdg. 49.50X (ISBN 0-86527-358-8). Fertig.

Ten Plays. David Pinski. Tr. by Isaac Goldberg from Yiddish. LC 77-70360. (One-Act Plays in Reprint Ser.). 1977. Repr. of 1920 ed. 16.50x (ISBN 0-8486-2021-6). Roth Pub Inc.

Ten Plays of Euripides. Euripides. Tr. by Moses Hadas & John H. McLean. Incl. Alcestis; Andromache; Bacchants; Electra; Hippolytus; Ion; Iphigenia among the Taurians; Iphigenia at Aulis; Medea; Trojan Women. (Orig., Incl. introduction to each play & glossary). (gr. 11-12). 1981. pap. 2.95 (ISBN 0-553-21160-9, Bantam Classics). Bantam.

Ten Plus One. Ed McBain. 176p. 1987. pap. 2.95 (ISBN 0-451-14598-4, Sig). NAL.

Ten Plus One Bible Stories from Creation to Samson, Retold in Everyday Language for Today's Children. John Behnke. LC 83-82022. (Orig.). (gr. k up). 1984. pap. 2.95 (ISBN 0-8091-6552-X). Paulist Pr.

Ten Poems & Lyrics by Mao Tse-tung. Mao Tse-tung. Tr. & illus. by Wang Hui-Ming. LC 74-21248. (Illus.). 72p. 1975. 9.00x (ISBN 0-87023-178-2); pap. 5.95 (ISBN 0-87023-182-0). U of Mass Pr.

Ten-Point Plan for College Acceptance. Lawrence Graham. (Illus.). 144p. 1981. pap. 6.95 (ISBN 0-399-50678-0, Perigee). Putnam Pub Group.

Ten Pound Immigrants. Reg Appleyard. 192p. 1988. 60.00x (ISBN 1-85283-220-7, Pub. by Boxtree Ltd UK). State Mutual Bk.

Ten Presidents & the Press. Ed. by Kenneth W. Thompson. LC 82-20293. (American Presidents & the Press Ser.). 128p. (Orig.). 1983. lib. bdg. 23.25 (ISBN 0-8191-2877-5); pap. text ed. 9.00 (ISBN 0-8191-2878-3). U Pr of Amer.

Ten Principal Upanishads. Swami S. Patanjali. Tr. by William B. Yeats. (Orig.). 1970. pap. 5.95 (ISBN 0-571-09363-9). Faber & Faber.

Ten Principal Upanishads. A. Wade. 75.00 (ISBN 0-8490-1183-3). Gordon Pr.

Ten Principal Upanishads. William B. Yeats & Swami Shree. 1975. pap. 6.95 (ISBN 0-02-071550-1, Collier). Macmillan.

Ten Questions on Prayer. Gerald Heard. LC 51-10133. (Orig.). 1951. pap. 2.50x (ISBN 0-87574-058-8, 058). Pendle Hill.

Ten Questions to the Zionists or, Zionist Complicity in Nazi War Atrocities. Michael B. Weismandel. 1980. lib. bdg. 59.95 (ISBN 0-686-68886-4). Revisionist Pr.

Ten Red Rods. Timothy J. Thompson. LC 80-83135. (Illus.). 16p. (Orig.). (ps-1). 1980. pap. text ed. 3.50 (ISBN 0-915676-02-8). Ed Sys Pub.

Ten Rillington Place. Ludovic Kennedy. 1985. pap. 0.95 (ISBN 0-685-03264-7, 06759). Avon.

Ten Roads to the Top. William E. Bates & La Donna G. Bates. LC 81-82937. 203p. 1981. pap. 8.75 (ISBN 0-87218-019-0). Natl Underwriter.

Ten Rules for Investing. James L. Fraser. LC 64-20192. 1964. 2.00 (ISBN 0-87034-030-1). Fraser Pub Co.

Ten Rungs: Hasidic Sayings. Martin Buber. LC 62-13135. 1962. pap. 4.95 (ISBN 0-8052-0018-5). Schocken.

Ten Sacred Songs see Music of the Moravians in America from the Archives of the Moravian Church at Bethlehem Pa,.

Ten Sails in the Sunrise. Allan Campbell. 200p. 1986. 14.95 (ISBN 0-317-39595-5). C I L Inc.

Ten Sales from One Article Idea: The Process & Correspondence. Gordon Burgett. LC 81-13060. (Illus.). 108p. (Orig.). 1982. pap. 7.95 (ISBN 0-9605078-2-5). Write to Sell.

Ten SATs. 3rd ed. The College Board Staff. 298p. 1988. pap. 9.95 (ISBN 0-87447-303-9). College Bd.

Ten SATs. 2nd ed. 304p. (Orig.). 1986. pap. 8.95 (ISBN 0-87447-246-6). College Bd.

Ten SATs: Scholastic Aptitude Tests of the College Board. 304p. (Orig.). (gr. 11-12). 1983. pap. 8.95 (ISBN 0-87447-161-3, 001613). College Bd.

Ten Seasons: New York Theatre in the Seventies. Samuel L. Leiter. LC 86-369. (Contributions in Drama & Theatre Studies). 257p. 1986. 36.95 (ISBN 0-313-24994-6, LTS/). Greenwood.

Ten-Second Business Forms. Robert L. Adams. 208p. 1987. pap. 12.95 (ISBN 0-937860-78-6). Adams Inc MA.

Ten Seconds to Clear Your Brain: Discover How Your Mind Works. J. O. Johnson. LC 86-91801. (Illus.). 152p. 1987. 14.95 (ISBN 0-9617712-1-6, Dist. by Slawson Comm); softcover 9.95 (ISBN 0-9617712-2-4); wire-o bdg. 19.95 (ISBN 0-9617712-3-2); pocket size 4.95 (ISBN 0-9617712-4-0). J O Johnson.

Ten Secrets for Taking Dynamic Photographs. Gary Bernstein. (Illus.). 160p. 1988. pap. 14.95 (ISBN 0-89586-541-6). Price Stern.

Ten Series of Meditations on the Mysteries of the Rosary. John Ferraro. (Illus., Orig.). 1964. 5.00 (ISBN 0-8198-0157-7); pap. 4.00 (ISBN 0-8198-0158-5). Dghtrs St Paul.

Ten Sermons from the Gospel of John see Tozer Pulpit.

Ten Sermons on the Ministry of the Holy Spirit see Tozer Pulpit.

Ten Sermons on the Voices of God Calling Man see Tozer Pulpit.

Ten Sevens. Charles Lee. LC 82-15771. 80p. 1983. 12.50 (ISBN 0-915180-23-5). Harrowood Bks.

Ten Signs of Faith. Hassan Kazemi. Ed. by Helen Graves. LC 85-51959. 154p. 1986. 8.95 (ISBN 1-55523-012-1). Winston-Derek.

Ten Sixty-Six: The Year of the Conquest. David Howarth. 208p. 1981. pap. 5.95 (ISBN 0-14-005850-8). Penguin.

Ten Sleepy Sheep. Holly Keller. LC 83-1477. (Illus.). 32p. (gr. k-3). 1983. 10.25 (ISBN 0-688-02306-1); PLB 10.88 (ISBN 0-688-02307-X). Greenwillow.

Ten Speed Babysitter. Alison C. Herzig & Jane L. Mali. LC 87-13425. 144p. (gr. 4-7). 1987. 11.95 (ISBN 0-525-44340-1, 01160-350). Dutton.

Ten-Speed Babysitter. Alison C. Herzig & Jane L. Mali. (gr. 2-9). Date not set. pap. 2.95. Troll Assocs.

Ten Speed Commandments: An Irreverent Guide to the Complete Sport of Cycling. Mike Keefe. LC 86-29233. (Illus.). 144p. 1987. pap. 5.95 (ISBN 0-385-23803-7, Dolp). Doubleday.

Ten-Speed Summer. Deborah Kent. (Sweet Dreams Ser.: No. 77). 192p. 1985. pap. 2.25 (ISBN 0-553-24387-X). Bantam.

Ten Spikes to the Rail. John R. Twohy. (Illus.). 211p. (Orig.). Date not set. 17.50 (ISBN 0-9610240-0-3); pap. 10.00 (ISBN 0-9610240-1-1). Goat Rock.

Ten Standard Turns: Cross Turns, Spot Turns, Pivots, Twinkles. 1985. lib. bdg. 76.00 (ISBN 0-87700-796-9). Revisionist Pr.

Ten Statement FORTRAN Plus FORTRAN IV. 2nd ed. Michael Kennedy & Martin B. Solomon. (Illus.). 400p. 1975. pap. text ed. write for info (ISBN 0-13-903385-8). P-H.

Ten Steps: Controlled Composition for Beginning & Intermediate Language Development. 2nd, rev. ed. Gay Brookes & Jean Withrow. Ed. by Helen Munch. 72p. (gr. 7-12). 1988. pap. text ed. 4.95 (ISBN 0-88084-253-9); tchr's. manual 2.25 (ISBN 0-88084-254-7). Alemany Pr.

Ten Steps for Church Growth. Donald A. McGavran & Winfield C. Arn. LC 76-62950. 1977. pap. 6.95 (ISBN 0-06-065352-3, RD 215, HarpR). Har-Row.

Ten Steps for Disciplining Difficult Students. Susan Hawley & Robert C. Hawley. 48p. 1985. pap. text ed. 4.95 (ISBN 0-913636-16-9). Educ Res MA.

Ten Steps for Motivating Reluctant Learners. Robert C. Hawley. 42p. (Orig.). pap. 4.95 (ISBN 0-913636-14-2). Educ Res MA.

Ten Steps in the Land of Life. Lena Allen-Shore. LC 82-61165. 1983. 13.95 (ISBN 0-88400-088-5); pap. 6.95 (ISBN 0-88400-089-3). Shengold.

Ten Steps in Writing the Research Paper. rev. ed. Roberta H. Markman & Marie L. Waddell. LC 70-140138. (Orig.). (gr. 9 up). 1982. text ed. 6.95 o.p (ISBN 0-8120-5406-7); pap. text ed. 6.95 (ISBN 0-8120-2023-5). Barron.

Ten Steps to Advancing Reading Skills. John Langan. 1988. pap. text ed. 15.00, 450p. (ISBN 0-944210-93-7); instr's. manual & test bank, 100p. 10.00 (ISBN 0-944210-94-5). Townsend NJ.

Ten Steps to Breaking the Two Hundred Barrier. Bill Sullivan. 99p. 1988. pap. 5.95 (ISBN 0-8341-1223-X). Beacon Hill.

Ten Steps to Building Reading Skills. John Langan. 1988. pap. text ed. 15.00, 425p. (ISBN 0-944210-91-0); instr's. manual & test bank, 100p. 10.00 (ISBN 0-944210-92-9). Townsend NJ.

Ten Steps to Improving Reading Skills. John Langan. 496p. 1988. pap. text ed. 15.00 (ISBN 0-944210-88-0, LB2395-3-L36); instr's. manual, 75p 10.00 (ISBN 0-944210-89-9). Townsend NJ.

Ten Steps to Service Success. Ronald A. Nykiel. 1989. 16.95 (ISBN 0-87212-220-4). Libra.

Ten Steps to the Good Life. Harold J. Brokke. LC 75-44926. 160p. 1976. pap. 1.95 (ISBN 0-87123-332-0, 200332). Bethany Hse.

Ten Steps to Victory over Depression. Tim LaHaye. 1974. pap. 2.75 (ISBN 0-310-27002-2, 18074P). Zondervan.

Ten Stories for Children. Nelle A. Hardegrove. (Illus.). 10p. (Orig.). (gr. 1-5). 1987. pap. text ed. 7.95 (ISBN 0-9619227-3-7). N A Hardegrove.

Ten Studies in Anglo-Dutch Relations. J. A. Dorsten. (Publications of Sir Thomas Browne Institute Ser: No. 5). 1974. lib. bdg. 34.00 (ISBN 90-6021-217-7, Pub. by Leiden Univ. Holland). Kluwer Academic.

Ten Super Sunday Schools in the Black Community. Sidney Smith. LC 86-926. 1986. pap. 5.95 (ISBN 0-8054-6252-X). Broadman.

Ten Talents in the American Theatre. Ed. by David H. Stevens. LC 76-20514. 299p. 1976. Repr. of 1957 ed. lib. bdg. 35.00x (ISBN 0-8371-8996-9, STTA). Greenwood.

Ten Talents Vegetarian Natural Foods Cookbook. rev. ed. Frank J. Hurd & Rosalie Hurd. 1985. spiral bdg. 16.95 (ISBN 0-9603532-4-0); 3 copies 11.02 ea.; 30 copies 9.32 ea.; 100 copies 8.98 ea.; 200 copies 8.56 ea.; looseleaf binder 6.95, 3 binders 4.50 ea. (ISBN 0-9603532-1-6); chart 4.95; 3 charts 3.20 ea. Ten Talents.

Ten Tales. facs. ed. Francois Coppee. Ed. by Walter Learned. LC 76-86140. (Short Story Index Reprint Ser.). (Illus.). 1891. 17.00 (ISBN 0-8369-3044-4). Ayer Co Pubs.

Ten Tales of Christmas. Ed. by Lynne Miller. 112p. (gr. 4-6). 1987. pap. 2.50 (ISBN 0-590-41447-X). Scholastic Inc.

Ten Tall Tales. E. J. Bird. LC 84-12086. (Carolrhoda Good Time Library). (Illus.). 96p. (gr. 2-6). 1984. PLB 8.95 (ISBN 0-87614-267-6). Carolrhoda Bks.

Ten Tests of Abraham. Shoshana Lepon. (Judaica Bible Series for Young Children). (Illus.). 32p. (Orig.). (gr. k-4). 1986. 7.95 (ISBN 0-317-52412-7); pap. 5.95 (ISBN 0-910818-67-3). Judaica Pr.

Ten Theologians Respond to the Unification Church. Herbert Richardson. LC 81-70679. 199p. 1981. pap. 10.95. Rose Sharon Pr.
Ten-Thirty on a Summer Night see Four Novels.
Ten Thousand a Year, 3 vols. in 2. Samuel Warren. LC 79-8215. Repr. of 1841 ed. Set. 84.50 (ISBN 0-404-62163-5). AMS Pr.
Ten Thousand Baby Names. Bruce Lansky. (Orig.). 1985. pap. write for info. Meadowbrook.
Ten Thousand Characters. G. Hugh Casey. 421p. 1980. 105.00x (ISBN 0-317-69239-9, Pub. by Han-Shan Tang Ltd). State Mutual Bk.
Ten Thousand Commandments: A Story of the Antitrust Laws. Harold M. Fleming. LC 75-172211. (Right Wing Individualist Tradition in America Ser). 1972. Repr. of 1951 ed. 16.00 (ISBN 0-405-00420-6). Ayer Co Pubs.
Ten Thousand Day War: Vietnam 1945-1975. Peter Arnett & Michael MacLear. LC 81-8841. (Illus.). 368p. 1981. 16.95 (ISBN 0-312-79094-5). St Martin.
Ten Thousand Days. Kenneth Royce. 256p. 1984. pap. 3.50 (ISBN 0-88184-082-3). Carroll & Graf.
Ten Thousand Days Has Our Youth, Vol. 1. Stephen McNamee. LC 86-42964. 328p. 1987. 19.75 (ISBN 0-930950-03-8); pap. 11.75 (ISBN 0-930950-04-6). Nopoly Pr.
Ten Thousand Dreams Interpreted. Gustavus H. Miller. LC 72-95999. 640p. 1931. pap. 8.95 (ISBN 0-528-88582-0). Rand McNally.
Ten Thousand Famous Freemasons, 4 vols. William R. Denslow. 1979. Repr. Set. soft cover, slip cover 29.95 (ISBN 0-88053-072-3, M-664). Macoy Pub.
Ten Thousand Garden Questions Answered by Twenty Experts. 4th ed. Ed. by Marjorie J. Dietz. LC 80-2738. (Illus.). 1440p. 1982. pap. 19.95 (ISBN 0-385-18509-X). Doubleday.
Ten Thousand Goddam Cattle: A History of the American Cowboy in Song, Story & Verse. rev. ltd. ed. Katie Lee. (Illus.). 247p. 1985. pap. 12.95 (ISBN 0-934573-68-9). Katyd Bks & Recds.
Ten Thousand Ideas for Term Papers, Projects & Reports. Kathryn Lamm. LC 83-5982. 441p. (Orig.). 1984. pap. 6.95 (ISBN 0-668-05598-7, 5598). Arco.
Ten Thousand Ideas for Term Papers, Projects, Reports, & Speeches. 2nd, rev. ed. Kathryn Lamm. (Education & Guidance Ser.). 500p. (YA) (gr. 9-12). 1987. pap. 7.95 (ISBN 0-13-905209-7). Arco.
Ten Thousand Jokes, Toasts & Stories. Ed. by Lewis Copeland. LC 66-737. 1956. pap. 19.95 (ISBN 0-385-00163-0). Doubleday.
Ten Thousand Leaves: A Translation of Man'yoshu, Japan's Premier Anthology of Classical Poetry, Vol. 1. Tr. by Ian H. Levy from Japanese. LC 80-8561. (Princeton Library of Asian Translations). (Illus.). 280p. 1981. 39.00x (ISBN 0-691-06452-0); pap. 12.95 (ISBN 0-691-00029-8). Princeton U Pr.
Ten Thousand Leaves: Love Poems from the Manyoshu. Tr. by Harold Wright from Japanese. LC 78-65436. (Illus.). 96p. 1986. 14.95 (ISBN 0-87951-214-8). Overlook Pr.
Ten Thousand Leaves: Love Poems from the Manyoshu. Tr. by Harold Wright. 96p. 1988. pap. 8.95 (ISBN 0-87951-240-7). Overlook Pr.
Ten Thousand Legal Words. Margaret A. Kurtz et al. 1971. text ed. 10.68 (ISBN 0-07-035669-6). McGraw.
Ten Thousand Legal Words: Spelled & Divided for Quick Reference. Margaret A. Kurtz & Dorothy Adams. 128p. 1984. text ed. 8.95 (ISBN 0-07-035645-9). McGraw.
Ten Thousand Lines Across Europe. John Heading. 1986. 52.00x (ISBN 0-86332-067-8, Pub. by Book Guild Ltd). State Mutual Bk.
Ten Thousand Medical Words, Spelled & Divided for Quick Reference. Edward E. Byers. 128p. 1972. text ed. 10.00 (ISBN 0-07-009503-5). McGraw.
Ten Thousand Miles on a Bicycle. rev. ed. Karl Kron, pseud. LC 82-23120. 911p. 1982. 21.95 (ISBN 0-9610060-0-5). E Rosenblatt.
Ten Thousand Miles with a Dog Sled. Hudson Stuck. LC 87-35192. (Illus.). xxxii, 516p. 1988. 32.50x (ISBN 0-8032-4192-5, Pub. by Bison); pap. 11.95 (ISBN 0-8032-9185-X, Bison). U of Nebr Pr.
Ten Thousand Miles with a Dog Sled. (Illus.). 452p. 1988. pap. 14.95 (ISBN 0-935632-66-2). Wolfe Pub Co.
Ten Thousand Seeds. Linda Ty-Casper. 191p. (Orig.). 1987. pap. 9.50x (ISBN 971-113-055-6, Pub. by Ateneo de Manila U Pr Philippines). Cellar.
Ten Thousand Things. Maria Dermout. Ed. by E. M. Beekman. Tr. by Hans Koning from Dutch. LC 82-21867. (Library of the Indies). 320p. 1983. Repr. of 1958 ed. lib. bdg. 20.00x (ISBN 0-87023-384-X). U of Mass Pr.
Ten Thousand Things. Maria Dermout. 1984. pap. 7.95 (ISBN 0-394-72443-7, Vin). Random.
Ten Thousand Tons by Christmas: A Comprehensive Story of Flying the Hump in W. W. II by an Officer Who Was There. Edwin L. White. LC 77-72751. (Illus.). 1977. 7.95 (ISBN 0-912760-05-2). Valkyrie Pub Hse.
Ten Thousand Two Hundred Dollars in 14 Days: How to Buy & Sell Cars & Trucks for Profit. Tom Carter. LC 87-91429. (Illus.). 200p. 1987. pap. 10.00 (ISBN 0-945162-00-6). T Carter Pub Co.
Ten Thousand Vital Records of Eastern New York, 1777-1834. Fred Q. Bowman. 356p. 1987. 22.50 (642). Genealog Pub.
Ten Thousand Vital Records of Western New York, 1809-1850. Fred Q. Bowman. LC 84-81870. 318p. 1985. 22.50 (ISBN 0-8063-1099-5). Genealog Pub.
Ten Thousand Wonderful Things. Edmund F. King. 59.95 (ISBN 0-8490-1184-1). Gordon Pr.
Ten Thousand Wonderful Things. Ed. by Edmund F. King. LC 75-124587. 700p. 1970. Repr. of 1860 ed. 44.00x (ISBN 0-8103-3009-1). Gale.
Ten Thousand Working Days. Robert Schrank. LC 77-14521. 1978. 25.00 (ISBN 0-262-19169-5); pap. 7.95x (ISBN 0-262-69064-0). MIT Pr.
Ten Timely Truths. Don DeWelt. 1949. pap. 2.50 (ISBN 0-89900-135-1). College Pr Pub.
Ten Times More Beautiful: The Rebuilding of Vietnam. Kathleen Gough. LC 78-14890. 277p. 1978. 12.50 (ISBN 0-85345-464-7). Monthly Rev.
Ten Times One Is Ten - the Possible Reformation: A Story in Nine Chapters. Edward E. Hale. LC 76-42803. Repr. of 1871 ed. 15.50 (ISBN 0-404-60069-7). AMS Pr.
Ten to Seventeen February Afternoons. Lawrence E. Keith. (Orig.). 1977. pap. 4.00 (ISBN 0-932222-00-5). Sunrise Tortoise.
Ten-Ton Monster. R. G. Austin. (Which Way Bks.: No. 21). (Illus.). (gr. 3-6). pap. 2.25 (ISBN 0-671-55820-X). Archway.
Ten Tools of Language-Written. 2nd ed. Ann N. Black & Jo R. Smith. (Illus.). 166p. (gr. 11-12). 1982. pap. text ed. 12.60x (ISBN 0-910513-00-7). Mayfield Printing.
Ten Tools of Language-Written: Revised Edition II, Form B. rev. ed. Ann N. Black & Jo R. Smith. (Illus.). 166p. 1983. pap. text ed. 12.60x (ISBN 0-910513-01-5). Mayfield Printing.
Ten Top Stories. Ed. by David A. Sohn. Bd. with Flowers for Algernon. Keyes; So Much Unfairness of Things. Bryan; Backward Boy. Coghlan; Denton's Daughter. Lowenberg; Hoods I Have Known. Spatt; Planet of the Condemned. Murphy; Test. Thomas; See How They Run. Coxe; Polar Night. Burke; Turtle. Vukelich. (Orig.). (gr. 6-12). pap. 2.95 (ISBN 0-553-25326-3). Bantam.
Ten Top Stories. Ed. by David A. Sohn. 176p. (Orig.). 1985. pap. 3.50 (ISBN 0-553-26979-8). Bantam.
Ten Tough Issues for Teenagers. Jim Auer. 64p. 1988. pap. 1.95 (ISBN 0-89243-287-X). Liguori Pubns.
Ten Trail Trips in Yosemite National Park. William R. Jores. (Illus.). 1980. pap. 4.95 (ISBN 0-89646-064-9). Outbooks.
Ten Trends: Dentistry's Emerging Directions. J. E. Dunlap. 125p. 1986. 34.95 (ISBN 0-87814-312-2). Pennwell Bks.
Ten Tudor Statesmen. Arthur D. Innes. LC 79-118479. 1971. Repr. of 1934 ed. 24.50x (ISBN 0-8046-1228-5, Pub by Kennikat). Assoc Faculty Pr.
Ten Venetian Motets. Ed. by Denis Arnold. 1981. text ed. 10.75x (ISBN 0-19-353035-X). Oxford U Pr.
Ten Victorian Poets. F. L. Lucas. LC 66-13343. xx, 202p. 1966. Repr. of 1948 ed. 21.00 (ISBN 0-208-00568-4, Archon). Shoe String.
Ten Vineyard Lunches. Richard Olney. (Cookery Book Ser.). (Illus.). 128p. 1988. 19.95 (ISBN 0-940793-23-7). Interlink Pub.
Ten Ways to Become Rich. James L. Fraser. LC 67-18101. (Illus.). 1967. flexible cover 2.00 (ISBN 0-87034-031-X). Fraser Pub Co.
Ten Ways to Lobby Your Representatives from Home. Daniel P. Moriarty. 1979. pap. 2.00 (ISBN 0-933968-03-5). D Moriarty.
Ten Ways to Lose Ten Pounds in Two Weeks. Susie Tompkins. 64p. 1984. pap. 2.95 (ISBN 0-553-26343-9). Bantam.
Ten Ways to Meditate. Paul Reps. LC 70-83639. (Illus.). 64p. 1981. 9.95 (ISBN 0-8348-0163-9). Weatherhill.
Ten Ways to Strengthen Your Family. David W. Cochran. 1980. 1.00 (ISBN 0-939926-00-8). Fruition Pubns.
Ten Ways You Can Earn One Million Dollars This Year. Charles R. Whitlock & R. Dwane Krumme. Date not set. pap. 8.95 (ISBN 0-943631-01-7). Princeton Pr Pub.
Ten Week Garden. Cary Scher. LC 73-76848. (Illus.). 407p. 1973. pap. 10.00 (ISBN 0-87110-101-7). Ultramarine Pub.
Ten Weeks to a Better Marriage. Randall Cirner & Therese Cirner. 132p. (Orig.). 1985. pap. 7.95 (ISBN 0-89283-237-1). Servant.
Ten Women of Mystery. Earl Bargainnier. LC 80-85393. 1981. 21.95 (ISBN 0-87972-172-3); pap. 10.95 (ISBN 0-87972-173-1). Bowling Green Univ.
Ten Women Poets of Greece. Dino Siotis. 1982. pap. 6.00 (ISBN 0-918034-11-6, Pub. by Wire Pr). Small Pr Dist.
Ten Word Books, 10 bks. Bob Reese et al. Ed. by Dan Wasserman. (Illus.). (gr. k-6). Set. PLB 59.50 (ISBN 0-89868-066-2); Set. pap. 19.50 (ISBN 0-89868-077-8). ARO Pub.
Ten Words of Freedom: An Introduction to the Faith of Israel. LC 75-139344. pap. 60.00 (2026879). Bks Demand UMI.
Ten Words That Will Change Your Life. Ervin Seale. 192p. 1972. pap. 6.95 (ISBN 0-911336-38-9). Sci of Mind.
Ten Year Cumulative Index to the Journal of Recreational Mathematics. Ed. by Joseph S. Madachy. 160p. 1982. pap. 10.00x (ISBN 0-89503-020-9). Baywood Pub.
Ten Year Harvest: Third Decennial Reader 1966-1976. Ed. by Louis Harap. 286p. (Orig.). 1977. 3.50 (ISBN 0-9618122-1-4). AFPOJS.
Ten Year Index: Mental & Physical Disability Law Reporter. ABA, Commission on the Mentally Disabled. 1987. pap. write for info. Amer Bar Assn.
Ten Year Index to Periodical Articles Related to Law (1959-1968) Ed. by Roy M. Mersky & J. Myron Jacobstein. LC 65-29677. 1970. 35.00 (ISBN 0-87802-050-0). Glanville.
Ten-Year Index to the Geological Society of America Bulletin, Vols. 81-90. Geological Society of America Staff. LC 1-23380. 1980. pap. 6.25 (ISBN 0-8137-9081-6). Geol Soc.
Ten Year Index to 'The White Light' Magazine, 1973-1983. Nelson White & Anne White. LC 83-91461. 50p. (Orig.). 1984. pap. 7.00 (ISBN 0-939856-37-9). Tech Group.
Ten-Year Review of Collaboration in Energy RD & D 1976-1986. OECD. 244p. (Orig.). 1987. pap. 35.00x (ISBN 92-64-12917-0). OECD.
Ten-Year Supplement to Abridged UDC Editions: 1958-1968. 1969. pap. 7.50 (ISBN 92-3-000797-8, U672, UNESCO). UNIPUB.
Ten Years. Grandin Conover. LC 72-77578. 76p. 1971. 9.00x (ISBN 0-87023-116-2); pap. 4.95 (ISBN 0-87023-117-0). U of Mass Pr.
Ten Years after. Gerard Malanga. LC 77-7032. 160p. 1977. pap. 4.00 (ISBN 0-87685-286-X). Black Sparrow.
Ten Years after Helsinki: The Making of the European Security Regime. Ed. by Kari Mottola. 200p. 1986. 25.00 (ISBN 0-8133-7192-9). Westview.
Ten Years After: Vietnam Today. Tim Page. LC 87-45353. (Illus.). 128p. 1987. 30.00 (ISBN 0-394-56464-2); pap. 18.95 (ISBN 0-394-75654-1). Knopf.
Ten Years Behind the Iron Curtain: Notes of a Victim of Yalta 1945-1955 see Desiat' Let Za Zheleznym Zanavesom: Zapiski Zhertvy Yalty 1945-1955.
Ten Years Beyond Baker Street. Cay Van Ash. LC 82-48687. 448p. 1988. pap. 4.95 (ISBN 0-06-080947-7, P 947, PL). Har-Row.
Ten Years' Captivity in the Mahdi's Camp. J. F. Wingate. 482p. 1986. 350.00x (ISBN 1-85077-120-0, Pub. by Darf Pubs Ltd). State Mutual Bk.
Ten Years Digging in Egypt. Flinders Petrie. (Illus.). 204p. 1976. pap. 10.00 (ISBN 0-89005-107-0). Ares.
Ten Years Exile. De Stael. 434p. 1969. 25.00x (ISBN 0-87556-075-X). Saifer.
Ten Years' Exile. Madame DeStael. 1985. 65.00x (ISBN 0-900000-07-4, Pub. by Centaur Bks). State Mutual Bk.
Ten Years in Equatoria & the Return with Emin Pasha, 2 Vols. Gaetano Casati. Tr. by J. Randolph Clay. LC 73-76854. (Illus.). 1970. Repr. of 1891 ed. Vol. 1. 24.75 (ISBN 0-8371-1513-2, CER&); Vol. 2. 24.75 (ISBN 0-8371-1514-0, CES&). Greenwood.
Ten Years in Japan: A Contemporary Record. Joseph C. Grew. LC 72-4275. (World Affairs Ser.: National & International Viewpoints). (Illus.). 578p. 1972. Repr. of 1944 ed. 36.50 (ISBN 0-405-04600-6). Ayer Co Pubs.
Ten Years in Nevada; or, Life on the Pacific Coast. Mary M. Mathews. LC 84-20813. (Illus.). vi, 343p. 1985. 28.95x (ISBN 0-8032-3089-3); pap. 7.50 (ISBN 0-8032-8124-2, BB 870, Bison). U of Nebr Pr.
Ten Years in Oregon. Daniel Lee & Joseph H. Frost. LC 72-9457. (Far Western Frontier Ser.). (Illus.). 348p. 1973. Repr. of 1844 ed. 24.50 (ISBN 0-405-04985-4). Ayer Co Pubs.
Ten Years in Oregon. Daniel Lee & Joseph H. Frost. 344p. 1968. Repr. of 1844 ed. 19.95 (ISBN 0-87770-017-6). Ye Galleon.
Ten Years in the Ranks U. S. Army. Augustus Meyers. Ed. by Richard H. Kohn. LC 78-22387. (American Military Experience Ser.). 1979. Repr. of 1914 ed. lib. bdg. 24.50x (ISBN 0-405-11864-3). Ayer Co Pubs.
Ten Years in Wall Street: Or, Revelations of Inside Life & Experience on Change. William W. Fowler. (Illus.). 1870. 26.00 (ISBN 0-8337-4643-X). B Franklin.
Ten Years Later. 72p. 1979. pap. 5.50 (ISBN 0-686-74543-4, SSC161, SSC). UNIPUB.
Ten Years Later: Violations of the Helsinki Accords. Helsinki Watch Staff. 329p. 1985. 10.00 (ISBN 0-938579-91-6, Helsinki Watch). Fund Free Expression.
Ten Years of Activities, 1971-1981. Inter-American Commission on Human Rights. LC 83-122693. xix, 403p. 1982. 50.00 (ISBN 0-8270-1456-2). OAS.
Ten Years of Championship Bicycle Racing. write for info. Countryman.
Ten Years of Championship Bicycle Racing. Velo-news Editors. LC 83-80418. (Illus.). 128p. (Orig.). 1983. specialty trade 14.95 (ISBN 0-941950-03-4). Velo-News.
Ten Years of Collecting: Denver Art Museum. Denver Art Museum Staff. LC 81-67724. (Illus.). 64p. (Orig.). 1981. pap. 2.25 (ISBN 0-914738-24-0). Denver Art Mus.
Ten Years of Experience in Precast Segmental Construction. (PCI Journal Reprints Ser.). 36p. 1985. pap. 6.00 (ISBN 0-318-19747-2, JR152). Prestressed Concrete.
Ten Years of Multinational Business. Ed. by Malcolm Crawford & James Poole. LC 82-13821. (Economist Intelligence Ser.). 184p. 1982. 32.00x. Ballinger Pub.
Ten Years of Multinational Business. (Economist Intelligence Unit Ser.). (Illus.). 1982. 25.00. Abt Bks.
Ten Years of Training: Developments in France, Federal Republic of Germany & United Kingdom, 1968-1978. 263p. (Orig.). 1980. pap. 12.25 (ISBN 92-2-102254-4). Intl Labour Office.
Ten Years of Wall Street. Barnie F. Winkelman. LC 87-80055. 381p. pap. 15.00 (ISBN 0-87034-082-4). Fraser Pub Co.
Ten Years of Wanderings among the Ethiopians. Thomas J. Hutchinson. 329p. 1967. Repr. of 1861 ed. 35.00x (ISBN 0-7146-1817-9, BHA-01817, F Cass Co). Biblio Dist.
Ten Years of World Food Programme Development Aid: 1963-72. pap. 11.25 (F1215, FAO). UNIPUB.
Ten Years on a Georgian Plantation. Frances B. Leigh. 1973. Repr. lib. bdg. 59.95 (ISBN 0-8490-1185-X). Gordon Pr.
Ten Years on in Northern Ireland. Kevin Boyle et al. 1980. 20.00x (ISBN 0-900137-16-9, Pub. by NCCL England). State Mutual Bk.
Ten Years on the Pacific Coast. Francis X. Blanchet. 96p. 1982. 12.00 (ISBN 0-87770-281-0). Ye Galleon.
Ten Years under the Earth. Norbert Casteret. Tr. by Burrows Massey. LC 75-26892. (Illus.). 255p. 1975. 10.95 (ISBN 0-914264-06-0); pap. 6.50 (ISBN 0-914264-07-9). Cave Bks MO.
Ten Years' War: An Account of the Battle with the Slum in New York. facsimile ed. Jacob A. Riis. LC 70-103655. (Select Bibliographies Reprint Ser). 1900. 26.50 (ISBN 0-8369-5155-7). Ayer Co Pubs.
Ten Years Women in Design - Chicago: Anniversary Exhibit. Ed. by Mary J. Krysinski. (Illus.). 75p. (Orig.). 1988. pap. write for info. (ISBN 0-9620348-0-0). Women Design.
Ten'a Texts & Tales from Anvik, Alaska...with Vocabulary by Pliny Earle Goddard. John W. Chapman. LC 73-3541. (American Ethnological Society. Publications: No. 6). Repr. of 1914 ed. 30.00 (ISBN 0-404-58156-0). AMS Pr.
Tenacity of Prejudice: Anti-Semitism in Contemporary America. Gertude J. Selznick & Stephen Steinberg. LC 78-31365. (Univ of California Five-Year Study of Anti-Semitism). (Illus.). 1979. Repr. of 1969 ed. lib. bdg. 35.00x (ISBN 0-313-20965-0, SETP). Greenwood.
Tenancy & Resource Use Efficiency in Agriculture. M. M. Islam & B. N. Banerjee. 1987. 21.00 (ISBN 81-7099-020-3, Pub. by Mittal). South Asia Bks.
Tenant. John Gill. 160p. 1985. 14.95 (ISBN 0-89733-142-7); pap. 3.95 (ISBN 0-89733-141-9). Academy Chi Pubs.
Tenant for Death. Cyril Hare. 200p. 1981. pap. 3.95 (ISBN 0-486-24103-3). Dover.
Tenant Information Handbook: Apartment Renting in Washington, D.C. Ruth E. Evans. LC 87-288836. (Illus.). (YA) Date not set. pap. price not set (ISBN 0-9620084-5-1). Essence Creations.
Tenant-Landlord. Kenneth Meiser. (Illus.). 90p. 1983. pap. 20.00. NJ Inst CLE.
Tenant-Landlord Law in New Jersey. Kenneth Meiser. 358p. 1978. looseleaf bdg. 45.00. NJ Inst CLE.
Tenant-Landlord Law in New Jersey: 1983 Supplement. Kenneth Meiser. 101p. 1983. looseleaf bdg. 20.00. NJ Inst CLE.
Tenant Movement in New York City, 1904-1984. Ed. by Ronald Lawson & Mark Naison. (Illus.). 300p. 1986. text ed. 35.00 (ISBN 0-8135-1158-5); pap. text ed. 15.00 (ISBN 0-8135-1203-4). Rutgers U Pr.
Tenant of Wildfell Hall. Anne Bronte. 339p. 1979. pap. 5.95 (ISBN 0-586-02657-6, Pub. by Granada England). Academy Chi Pubs.
Tenant of Wildfell Hall. Anne Bronte. Bd. with Agnes Grey. 1978. Repr. of 1914 ed. 14.95x (ISBN 0-460-00685-1, Evman). Biblio Dist.
Tenant of Wildfell Hall. Anne Bronte. 1982. pap. 4.75x (ISBN 0-460-11685-1, Evman). Biblio Dist.
Tenant of Wildfell Hall. Anne Bronte. Ed. by G. D. Hargreaves. (Penguin English Library). 1980. pap. 4.95 (ISBN 0-14-043137-3). Penguin.
Tenant of Wildfell Hall. Anne Bronte. LC 79-4122. (Banquo Bks). 1979. pap. 4.95 (ISBN 0-912800-70-4). Woodbridge Pr.
Tenant Resource & Advocacy Center. Maier Spielberg & Danielson Spielberg. 57p. pap. 5.00 (ISBN 0-686-36543-7). Ctr Responsive Law.
Tenant Supervisor. Jack Rudman. (Career Examination Ser.: C-543). (Cloth bdg. avail. on request). pap. 14.00 (ISBN 0-8373-0543-8). Natl Learning.
Tenants. Bernard Malamud. 230p. 1971. 10.00 (ISBN 0-374-27290-5). FS&G.
Tenants. Bernard Malamud. 230p. 1988. pap. 8.95 (ISBN 0-374-52102-6). FS&G.

Teneriffe Lace. Ed. by Jules Kliot & Kaethe Kliot. (Illus.). 96p. 1986. pap. 9.00 (ISBN 0-916896-22-6). Lacis Pubns.

Tenetehara Indians of Brazil. Charles Wagley & Eduardo Galvao. LC 79-82359. (Columbia Univ. Contributions to Anthropology Ser.: Vol. 35). 1969. Repr. of 1949 ed. 24.50 (ISBN 0-404-50585-6). AMS Pr.

Tenets of Islam. A. M. Muhajir. 1969. 7.25x (ISBN 0-87902-107-1). Orientalia.

Tenets of Islam. 14.50 (ISBN 0-686-18485-8). Kazi Pubns.

Tenets of Stoicism Assembled & Systematized from the Works of L. A. Seneca. H. B. Timothy. 118p. (Orig.). 1973. pap. text ed. 28.50x (ISBN 0-317-57965-7, Pub. by A M Hakkert). Coronet Bks.

Tengo. Nicholas Guillen. Tr. by Richard Carr. 1974. 5.00 (ISBN 0-910296-28-6). Broadside Pr.

Tengo Prisa. Olga Rosado. (Coleccion Espejo De Paciencia). 1978. pap. 5.00 (ISBN 0-89729-197-2). Ediciones.

Tengu. Graham Masterton. 384p. (Orig.). 1983. pap. 3.50 (ISBN 0-523-48061-X, Dist. by Warner Pub. Services & Saint Martin's Press). Tor Bks.

Tengu Child: Stories by Kikuo Itaya. Kikuo Itaya. Tr. by John Gardner. LC 82-5876. (Illus.). 243p. 1983. 15.95 (ISBN 0-8093-1081-3). S Ill U Pr.

Tenkiller. L. Jay Martin. 256p. 1988. pap. 2.95 (ISBN 0-8217-2415-0). Zebra.

Tenmoku. Koyama Fujio. 22p. 1962. 60.00x (ISBN 0-317-44223-6, Pub. by Han-Shan Tang Ltd). State Mutual Bk.

Tenn-Tom Country: The Upper Tombigbee Valley in History & Geography. James Doster & David C. Weaver. LC 85-13974. (Illus.). 311p. 1987. 49.95 (ISBN 0-8173-0279-4). U of Ala Pr.

Tenne Tragedies of Seneca, 2 pts in 1 vol. Lucius Annaeus Seneca. 1966. Repr. of 1887 ed. 45.00 (ISBN 0-8337-3231-5). B Franklin.

Tennessee: A Guide to the State see WPA Guide to Tennessee.

Tennessee John Stoltzfus: Amish Church-Related Documents & Family Letters. Ed. by Paton Yoder. Tr. by Noah G. Good et al from Gr. LC 86-80085. (Mennonite Sources & Documents Ser.: No. 1). (Illus.). 296p. 1987. 24.95 (ISBN 0-9614479-5-8). Lancaster Mennonite.

Tennessean. Anne Royall. LC 78-64092. Repr. of 1827 ed. 37.50 (ISBN 0-404-17166-4). AMS Pr.

Tennesseans in the Civil War: A Military History of Confederate & Union Units with Available Rosters of Personnel, Pt. 1, Military History. Tennessee Historical Commission. 1964. 32.50x (ISBN 0-87402-017-4). U of Tenn Pr.

Tennesseans in the Civil War, Part II: Rosters. Tennessee Historical Commission. 612p. Repr. of 1965 ed. 42.50x (ISBN 0-87402-018-2). U of Tenn Pr.

Tennessee. Allan Carpenter. LC 78-11522. (New Enchantment of America State Bks). (Illus.). 96p. (gr. 4 up). 1979. PLB 15.93 (ISBN 0-516-04142-8). Childrens.

Tennessee. Wilma Dykeman. (States & the Nation). (Illus.). 224p. 1975. 14.95 (ISBN 0-393-05555-8, Co-Pub by AASLH). Norton.

Tennessee. Wilma Dykeman. (States & the Nation Ser.). (Illus.). 1984. 7.95 (ISBN 0-393-30144-3). Norton.

Tennessee! Dana F. Ross. (Wagons West Ser.: No. 17). 320p. 1986. pap. 4.50 (ISBN 0-553-25622-X). Bantam.

Tennessee! Dana F. Ross. 384p. 1987. lib. bdg. 16.95x (ISBN 0-8161-4193-2, Large Print Bks). G K Hall.

Tennessee. Illus. by Edward Schell. (Illus.). 128p. 1986. Repr. of 1979 ed. 35.00 (ISBN 0-9613859-3-6). Wakestone Bks.

Tennessee. Turner Program Services, Inc. Staff & James I. Clark. (Portrait of America Library). 48p. (gr. 4 up). 1985. PLB 15.33 (ISBN 0-86514-444-3); pap. text ed. 9.27 (ISBN 0-86514-519-9); Beta video 113.33 (ISBN 0-86514-069-3); VHS video 113.33 (ISBN 0-86514-144-4); 3/4" video 136.00 (ISBN 0-86514-219-X); tchr's guide 13.27 (ISBN 0-86514-294-7); student activity bk. 6.60 (ISBN 0-86514-369-2); index 13.27. Raintree Pubs.

Tennessee: A Guide to the State. Federal Writers' Project Staff. 558p. 1939. Repr. 59.00x (ISBN 0-403-02191-X). Somerset Pub.

Tennessee: A Short History. 2nd ed. Robert E. Corlew. LC 80-13553. (Illus.). 652p. 1981. 29.95x (ISBN 0-87049-258-6); pap. text ed. 14.50x (ISBN 0-87049-302-7). U of Tenn Pr.

Tennessee Adventures. Christine Snyder. 32p. 1988. 6.95 (ISBN 0-8062-3235-8). Carlton.

Tennessee Almanac & Book of Facts. James Crutchfield. 1988. 10.95 (ISBN 0-934395-59-4). Rutledge Hill Pr.

Tennessee Almanac & Book of Facts. Ed. by James A. Crutchfield. LC 86-1746. 336p. 1986. 14.95 (ISBN 0-934395-26-8); pap. 9.95 (ISBN 0-934395-06-3). Rutledge Hill Pr.

Tennessee Automotive Directory. Ed. by T. L. Spelman. 1985. 24.95 (ISBN 1-55527-030-1). Auto Contact Inc.

Tennessee Beginnings. new ed. Intro. by John Dobson. Bd. with A Short Description of the Tennessee Government (1793) Daniel Smith; The Constitution of the State of Tennessee, (1796; A Catechetical Exposition of the Constitution of the State of Tennessee, (1803) Willie Blount. LC 74-583. (Illus.). 144p. 1974. 16.50 (ISBN 0-87152-152-0). Reprint.

Tennessee Blue. Patricia Griffith. 10.95 (ISBN 0-931848-75-X, Pub. by Crown). Dryad Pr.

Tennessee Bride. F. Rosanne Bittner. 384p. (Orig.). 1988. pap. 3.95 (ISBN 0-445-20634-9, Pub. by Popular Lib). Warner Bks.

Tennessee Business Directory, 1988-89. rev. ed. American Directory Publishing Co., Inc. Staff. 1386p. 1988. pap. 95.00 (ISBN 0-944316-21-2). Amer Directory.

Tennessee Census Index 1810, Vol. 1. Ronald V. Jackson. (Illus.). lib. bdg. 20.00 (ISBN 0-317-17072-4). Accelerated Index.

Tennessee Census Index 1820. Ronald V. Jackson. LC 77-86083. (Illus.). lib. bdg. 26.00 (ISBN 0-89593-135-4). Accelerated Index.

Tennessee Census Index 1830. Ronald V. Jackson. LC 77-86073. (Illus.). lib. bdg. 43.00 (ISBN 0-89593-136-2). Accelerated Index.

Tennessee Census Index 1840. Ronald V. Jackson. LC 77-86074. (Illus.). lib. bdg. 55.00 (ISBN 0-89593-137-0). Accelerated Index.

Tennessee Census Index 1850. Ronald V. Jackson. LC 77-86075. (Illus.). lib. bdg. 60.00 (ISBN 0-89593-138-9). Accelerated Index.

Tennessee Census Index 1860 A-K. Ronald V. Jackson. (Illus.). lib. bdg. 110.00 (ISBN 0-317-17073-2). Accelerated Index.

Tennessee Census Index 1860 L-Z. Ronald V. Jackson. (Illus.). lib. bdg. 110.00 (ISBN 0-317-17074-0). Accelerated Index.

Tennessee Chronology & Factbook, Vol. 42. Robert I. Vexler. LC 78-26261. (Chronologies & Documentary Handbook of the States). 145p. 1978. 8.50 (ISBN 0-379-16167-2). Oceana.

Tennessee Civil War Questionnaires, 5 vols. Ed. by John T. Moore & Colleen M. Elliott. 1985. Set. 250.00t (ISBN 0-89308-221-X); Vol. 1. 60.00t (ISBN 0-89308-216-3); Vol. 2. 60.00t (ISBN 0-89308-217-1); Vol. 3. 60.00t (ISBN 0-89308-218-X); Vol. 4. 60.00t (ISBN 0-89308-219-8); Vol. 5. 60.00t (ISBN 0-89308-220-1). Southern Hist Pr.

Tennessee Code Annotated, 30 vols. write for info (ISBN 0-672-83239-9, Bobbs-Merrill Law). Michie Co.

Tennessee: Conflict of Laws. 6.00 (ISBN 0-686-90905-4). Am Law Inst.

Tennessee Corporations: Tennessee Practice Systems Library Selection. Ronald L. Gilman. LC 79-91162. looseleaf bdg. 94.50; Suppl. 1986. 35.00; Suppl. 1987. 47.50. Lawyers Co-Op.

Tennessee County Maps. rev. ed. Ed. by C. J. Puetz. (Illus.). 144p. Date not set. pap. 11.90 (ISBN 0-916514-15-3). Cnty Maps.

Tennessee Courthouse Facilities, Profile & Evaluation, Vol. II. National Center for State Courts Staff. 127p. 1977. manuscript 7.62 (SRO-001). Natl Ctr St Courts.

Tennessee Cousins: A History of Tennessee People. Worth S. Ray. LC 68-24685. (Illus.). 811p. 1984. Repr. of 1950 ed. 27.50 (ISBN 0-8063-0289-5). Genealog Pub.

Tennessee: Cry of the Heart. Dotson Radar. 368p. 1986. pap. 8.95 (ISBN 0-452-25801-4, Plume). NAL.

Tennessee Digest. 2nd ed. (Key Number Digests). 1986. write for info. West Pub.

Tennessee Directory of Manufacturers, 1988. 576p. 1988. pap. 75.00 (ISBN 0-318-02872-7). Manufacturers.

Tennessee Folk Culture: An Annotated Bibliography. Eleanor E. Goehring. LC 81-16036. (Illus.). 152p. 1982. text ed. 16.50x (ISBN 0-87049-344-2). U of Tenn Pr.

Tennessee Football: A Brief Photo-History. cancelled (ISBN 0-916242-43-9). Yoknapatawpha.

Tennessee Genealogical Research. 138p. 1986. pap. 8.00 (ISBN 0-913857-05-X). Genealog Sources.

Tennessee Guide to Real Estate Licensing Examinations. 2nd ed. Robert A. Sigafoos et al. LC 86-11076. 129p. 1986. pap. 14.95 (ISBN 0-471-85095-0). Wiley.

Tennessee Guide to Real Estate Licensing Examinations for Salespersons & Brokers. Robert A. Sigafoos et al. LC 81-11540. 120p. 1982. pap. text ed. write for info. (ISBN 0-471-87759-X). Wiley.

Tennessee Hiking Guide. Sierra Club, Tennesse Chapter. Ed. by Robert S. Brandt. LC 81-19664. (Illus.). 32p. (Orig.). 1982. pap. 2.50 (ISBN 0-87049-343-4). U of Tenn Pr.

Tennessee Hill Folk. Joe Clark. LC 72-2880. (Illus.). 96p. 1972. 10.95 (ISBN 0-8265-1183-X). Vanderbilt U Pr.

Tennessee Historical & Biographical Index, Vol. 1. Ronald V. Jackson. LC 78-53717. (Illus.). 1984. lib. bdg. 30.00 (ISBN 0-89593-200-8). Accelerated Index.

Tennessee History: A Bibliography. Ed. by Sam B. Smith. LC 74-8504. pap. 135.00 (ISBN 0-317-10296-6, 2019703). Bks Demand UMI.

Tennessee Homecoming Cookbook: Famous Parties, People, Places. Phila Hach. 1986. 9.95 (ISBN 0-9606192-6-7). Hach.

Tennessee: In Words & Pictures. Dennis Fradin. LC 79-19218. (Young People's Stories of Our States Ser.). (Illus.). 48p. (gr. 2-5). 1980. PLB 13.27 (ISBN 0-516-03942-3). Childrens.

Tennessee Jurisprudence, 29 vols. Michie Compnay Editorial Staff. Set. 1800.00x (ISBN 0-87215-503-X, 77370); Nineteen Eighty-six suppl. only. 1987 suppl. only 125.00x (ISBN 0-87215-874-8). Michie Co.

Tennessee Law of Evidence. Donald F. Paine. 303p. 1974. with 1981 cum. suppl. 45.00x (ISBN 0-672-81876-0, Bobb-Merrill Law); 1981 cum. suppl. only 15.00x (ISBN 0-87215-437-8). Michie Co.

Tennessee Legal Research Handbook. Lewis L. Laska. LC 77-71305. x, 203p. 1977. lib. bdg. 30.00 (ISBN 0-930342-04-6); pap. 18.00 (ISBN 0-89941-264-5). W S Hein.

Tennessee Letters: From Carson Valley, 1857-1860. David Thompson. LC 82-61696. (Historical Ser.). (Illus.). 189p. 1983. 15.50 (ISBN 0-913205-02-8). Grace Dangberg.

Tennessee Life & Health. 3rd ed. 1980. 18.00 (ISBN 0-930868-38-2). Merritt Co.

Tennessee Municipal Handbook. Victor C. Hobday. LC 85-620867. Date not set. price not set. Tenn Muni League.

Tennessee Politics: A Program for Research. Richard L. Wilson. 224p. 1976. pap. text ed. 16.95 (ISBN 0-8403-1573-2). Kendall-Hunt.

Tennessee Private Acts Index. Michie Company Editorial Staff. 652p. 1984. Incl. 1986 Suppl. 75.00x (ISBN 0-87215-812-8); Suppl. 1987 8.00x, (ISBN 0-87215-870-5). Michie Co.

Tennessee Probate: Tennessee Practice Systems Library Selection, 2 vols. Albert W. Secor. LC 79-91164. 179.00; Suppl. 1987. 56.00; Suppl. 1988. 56.00. Lawyers Co-Op.

Tennessee Property & Casualty. 3rd ed. 1987. write for info. (ISBN 0-930868-37-4). Merritt Co.

Tennessee Puzzle Book. Donna L. Pape et al. 71p. 1984. pap. 1.95 (ISBN 0-938232-54-1). Winston-Derek.

Tennessee Records: Bible Records & Marriage Bonds. Jeannette T. Acklen et al. LC 67-28618. (Illus.). 521p. 1980. Repr. of 1933 ed. 22.50 (ISBN 0-8063-0000-0). Genealog Pub.

Tennessee Red Berry Tales. Bob Galbreath. Ed. by Deborah G. Garrett. 97p. (Orig.). (gr. 3 up). 1986. pap. 7.95 (ISBN 0-9616918-0-8). Whites Creek Pr.

Tennessee Sketches. facsimile ed. Louisa P. Looney. (Short Story Index Reprint Ser.). Repr. of 1901 ed. 20.00 (ISBN 0-8369-4020-2). Ayer Co Pubs.

Tennessee Smithology. Emma B. Reeves. (Illus.). 153p. 1975. pap. 12.50 (ISBN 0-317-05109-1). E B Reeves.

Tennessee Soldiers in the Revolution: A Roster of Soldiers Living During the Revolutionary War in the Counties of Washington & Sullivan. Penelope J. Allen. LC 75-970. 71p. 1982. pap. 5.00 (ISBN 0-8063-0666-1). Genealog Pub.

Tennessee Statistical Abstract, 1988. Ed. by Betty B. Vickers. 740p. (Orig.). 1988. pap. text ed. 27.95 (ISBN 0-940191-11-3). Univ TN Ctr Bus Econ.

Tennessee Studies in Literature, Vol. 24. Ed. by Allison R. Ensor & Thomas J. Heffernan. LC 58-63252. 1979. text ed. 13.95x (ISBN 0-87049-271-3). U of Tenn Pr.

Tennessee Supplement for Modern Real Estate Practice. William M. Emerson. 130p. (Orig.). 1981. pap. 9.95 (ISBN 0-88462-338-6, 1510-46, Real Estate Ed). Longman Finan.

Tennessee Survival. Betty L. Hall & Ronald E. Galbraith. 160p. (Orig.). (gr. 10-12). 1979. pap. text ed. 5.84 (ISBN 0-03-055531-0). Westwood Pr.

Tennessee Tidbits, Seventeen Seventy-Eight to Nineteen Fourteen, Vol. I. Marjorie H. Fischer. 350p. 1985. 32.50 (ISBN 0-89308-534-0). Southern Hist Pr.

Tennessee Towns: From Adams to Yorkville. Tom Siler. (Illus.). 108p. 1985. pap. 5.00 (ISBN 0-941199-03-7). ETHS.

Tennessee Trails. 3rd ed. Evans Means. LC 84-1650. (Pak-Bks.). (Illus.). 208p. 1988. pap. 9.95 (ISBN 0-87106-730-7). Globe Pequot.

Tennessee Trivia. Jill Couch & Ernie Couch. LC 85-28313. 192p. (Orig.). 1986. pap. 5.95 (ISBN 0-934395-07-1). Rutledge Hill Pr.

Tennessee Truckers Roundup. John L. LeMay. 374p. (Orig.). 1988. pap. 4.50 (ISBN 0-945696-00-0). Roadrunner TX.

Tennessee Valley Authority. Alanson Van Fleet. (Know Your Government Ser.). (Illus.). 96p. 1987. lib. bdg. 12.95 (ISBN 1-55546-123-9). Chelsea Hse.

Tennessee: Vol. 1: the Old River-Frontier to Secession. Donald Davidson. LC 78-15103. (Tennesseeannna Editions Ser.). 1979. 18.95 (ISBN 0-87049-265-9). U of Tenn Pr.

Tennessee Votes: 1799-1976: Studies in Tennessee Politics. Anne H. Hopkins & William Lyons. 393p. (Orig.). 1978. pap. 8.50 (ISBN 0-914079-02-6). Bureau Pub Admin U Tenn.

Tennessee Waltz: The Making of a Political Prisoner. James E. Ray. (Illus.). 325p. 1987. 19.95 (ISBN 0-911805-07-9). S Judd Pubs.

Tennessee Williams. Intro. by Harold Bloom. (Modern Critical Views Ser.). 168p. 1987. 19.95 (ISBN 0-87754-636-3). Chelsea Hse.

Tennessee Williams. Roger Boxill. LC 86-20337. 182p. 1987. 19.95 (ISBN 0-312-00209-2). St Martin.

Tennessee Williams. 2nd ed. Signi L. Falk. (United States Authors Ser.). 1978. lib. bdg. 15.95 (ISBN 0-8057-7202-2, Twayne). G K Hall.

Tennessee Williams. Signi L. Falk. (United States Authors Ser.). 1985. pap. 7.95 (ISBN 0-8057-7445-9, Twayne). G K Hall.

Tennessee Williams. Felicia H. Londre. LC 79-4830. (Literature and Life Ser.). (Illus.). 219p. 1980. 16.95x (ISBN 0-8044-2539-6). Ungar.

Tennessee Williams. Benjamin Nelson. 1961. 20.00 (ISBN 0-8392-1111-2). Astor-Honor.

Tennessee Williams: A Bibliography. Drewey W. Gunn. LC 80-12714. (Scarecrow Author Bibliographies: No. 48). 270p. 1980. 22.50 (ISBN 0-8108-1310-6). Scarecrow.

Tennessee Williams: A Moralist's Answer to the Perils of Life. Ingrid Rogers. (European University Studies, Anglo-Saxon Language & Literature: Ser. 14, Vol. 44). x, 268p. 1976. pap. 28.70 (ISBN 3-261-02056-3). P Lang Pubs.

Tennessee Williams: A Portrait in Laughter & Lamentation. Harry Rasky. (Illus.). 240p. 1986. 19.95 (ISBN 0-396-08775-2). Dodd.

Tennessee Williams: A Study of Short Fiction. Dennis Vannatta. 168p. 1988. lib. bdg. 18.95x (ISBN 0-8057-8304-0, Twayne). G K Hall.

Tennessee Williams' Letters to Donald Windham: 1940-1965. Tennessee Williams. Ed. by Donald Winham. LC 77-73863. 1977. 10.00 (ISBN 0-03-022636-8). H Holt & Co.

Tennessee Williams' Letters to Donald Windham: 1940-1965. Tennessee Williams. (Illus.). 1976. ltd. ed. 110.00x (ISBN 0-917366-01-8). S Campbell.

Tennessee Williams on File. Compiled by Catherine M. Arnott & Simon Trussler. (Writers on File Ser.). 96p. 1985. pap. 6.50 (ISBN 0-413-54280-7, 9388). Heinemann Ed.

Tennessee Williams on the Soviet Stage. Irene Shaland. LC 86-32506. 100p. 1987. lib. bdg. 18.75 (ISBN 0-8191-6109-8). U Pr of Amer.

Tennessee Williams' Plays: Memory, Myth & Symbol. Judith Thompson. (University of Kansas Humanistic Studies: Vol. 54). 253p. 1988. text ed. 46.90 (ISBN 0-8204-0476-4). P Lang Pubs.

Tennessee Williams' The Glass Menagerie. Intro. by Harold Bloom. (Modern Critical Interpretations Ser.). 160p. 1988. lib. bdg. 19.95 (ISBN 1-55546-052-6). Chelsea Hse.

Tennessee Williams's Streetcar Named Desire. Intro. by Harold Bloom. (Modern Critical Interpretations Ser.). 1987. 19.95 (ISBN 1-55546-053-4). Chelsea Hse.

Tennessee Yeomen, 1840-1860. Blanche H. Clark. LC 76-154662. xiii, 200p. 1971. Repr. of 1942 ed. lib. bdg. 18.50x (ISBN 0-374-91669-1, Octagon). Hippocrene Bks.

Tennesseeans at War: Volunteers & Patriots in Defense of Liberty. James Crutchfield. LC 87-9898. 192p. 1988. 19.95 (ISBN 0-934395-38-1). Rutledge Hill Pr.

Tennessee's Indian Peoples: From White Contact to Removal, 1540-1840. Ronald N. Satz. LC 77-21634. (Tennessee Three Star Ser.). (Illus.). 1979. lib. bdg. 9.95x (ISBN 0-87049-285-3); pap. 3.50 (ISBN 0-87049-231-4). U of Tenn Pr.

Tennessee's Presidents. Frank B. Williams, Jr. LC 81-3391. (Tennessee Three Star Ser.). (Illus.). 124p. 1981. pap. 3.50 (ISBN 0-87049-322-1). U of Tenn Pr.

Tennessee's War, 1861-1865: Described by Participants. Ed. by Stanley F. Horn. LC 65-64988. 364p. 1965. 26.95x (ISBN 0-87402-019-0). U of Tenn Pr.

Tenney Committee: Legislative Investigation of Subversive Activities in California. Edward L. Barrett, Jr. Repr. of 1951 ed. 37.00 (ISBN 0-384-03445-4). Johnson Repr.

Tenniel Illustrations to the "Alice" Books. Michael Hancher. LC 84-11842. (Illus.). 176p. 1985. pap. 17.50 (ISBN 0-8142-0408-2). Ohio St U Pr.

Tennis. 2nd ed. Joel R. Barton, III & William A. Grice. (Illus.). 88p. 1981. pap. text ed. 3.95x (ISBN 0-89641-065-X). American Pr.

Tennis. 3rd ed. Joel R. Barton, III & William A. Grice. (Illus.). 118p. 1984. pap. text ed. 4.95x (ISBN 0-89641-147-8). American Pr.

Tennis. David Claxton & John Faribault. (Orig.). 1987. pap. text ed. 5.75 (ISBN 0-89787-606-7). Gorsuch Scarisbrick.

Tennis. 3rd ed. Robert E. Gensemer. 100p. 1982. pap. text ed. write for info. (ISBN 0-697-05999-5). Wm C Brown.

Tennis. Dewayne J. Johnson et al. (Illus.). 67p. (Orig.). 1980. pap. text ed. 3.95x (ISBN 0-89641-040-4). American Pr.

Tennis. 4th ed. Joan D. Johnson & Paul Xanthos. (Pysical Education Activities Ser.). 144p. 1980. pap. text ed. write for info. (ISBN 0-697-07174-X). Wm C Brown.

Tennis. Joan D. Johnson & Paul J. Xanthos. 176p. 1988. pap. text ed. write for info. (ISBN 0-697-00363-9). Wm C Brown.

Tennyson in France. Marjorie Bowden. LC 72-192406. 1930. lib. bdg. 20.00 (ISBN 0-8414-2536-1). Folcroft.

Tennyson: Interviews & Recollections. Ed. by Norman Page. (Interviews & Recollections Ser.). 218p. 1983. 28.50x (ISBN 0-389-20066-2). B&N Imports.

Tennyson, Lord Alfred: Idylls of the King. Alfred Tennyson. Ed. by J. M. Gray. LC 82-62851. (Yale English Poets Ser.: No. 16). 371p. 1983. 30.00t (ISBN 0-300-03059-2); pap. 11.95x (ISBN 0-300-03060-6, YEP-16). Yale U Pr.

Tennyson Number. Bookman Staff. 1902. Repr. 32.00 (ISBN 0-8274-3584-3). R West.

Tennyson: Poems. Alfred Tennyson. (Poetry Library). 248p. 1985. pap. 3.95 (ISBN 0-14-058502-8). Penguin.

Tennyson, Poet, Philosopher, Idealist. J. Cummings Walters. 370p. 1980. Repr. of 1893 ed. lib. bdg. 40.00 (ISBN 0-89984-505-3). Century Bookbindery.

Tennyson: Poet, Philosopher, Idealist. John C. Walters. LC 70-153481. (Studies in Tennyson, No. 27). 1971. Repr. of 1893 ed. lib. bdg. 53.95x (ISBN 0-8383-1238-1). Haskell.

Tennyson, Ruskin, Mill & Other Literary Estimates. Frederic Harrison. LC 71-111835. (Essay Index Reprint Ser.). 1900. 20.00 (ISBN 0-8369-1612-3). Ayer Co Pubs.

Tennyson Sixty Years after. Paul F. Baum. 331p. 1976. Repr. of 1948 ed. lib. bdg. 26.00 (ISBN 0-374-90467-7, Octagon). Hippocrene Bks.

Tennyson: The Critical Heritage. John D. Jump. 1967. 65.00 (ISBN 0-7100-2941-1). Routledge Chapman & Hall.

Tennyson: The Muses' Tug-of-War. Daniel Albright. LC 86-1546. (Virginia Victorian Studies). xi, 257p. 1986. text ed. 24.95x (ISBN 0-8139-1100-1). U Pr of VA.

Tennyson, the Story of His Life. Evan J. Cuthbertson. LC 73-14566. Repr. of 1898 ed. lib. bdg. 20.50 (ISBN 0-8414-3472-7). Folcroft.

Tennyson: The Story of His Life. Evan J. Cuthertson. 1978. lib. bdg. 20.00 (ISBN 0-8495-0745-6). Arden Lib.

Tennyson: The Unquiet Heart. Robert B. Martin. (Illus.). 1980. 39.95x (ISBN 0-19-812072-9). Oxford U Pr.

Tennyson: The Unquiet Heart. Robert B. Martin. LC 83-1655. (Illus.). 656p. 1983. pap. 12.95 (ISBN 0-571-11842-9). Faber & Faber.

Tennysoniana. 2nd. & rev. ed. Richard H. Shepherd. LC 70-148302. Repr. of 1879 ed. 10.00 (ISBN 0-404-08899-6). AMS Pr.

Tennyson's Camelot: The Idylls of the King & Its Medieval Sources. David Staines. 252p. 1982. text ed. 22.95x (ISBN 0-88920-115-3, Pub. by Wilfrid Laurier Canada). Humanities.

Tennyson's Debt to Environment. William G. Ward. LC 78-27085. 1974. Repr. of 1898 ed. lib. bdg. 17.00 (ISBN 0-8414-9711-7). Folcroft.

Tennyson's Dramas: A Critical Study. Dennis M. Organ. (Graduate Studies: No. 17). 125p. 1979. 7.00 (ISBN 0-89672-066-7). Tex Tech Univ Pr.

Tennyson's Idylls of the King. Arthur W. Fox. LC 79-113334. 1970. Repr. of 1909 ed. 17.00x (ISBN 0-8046-1017-7, Pub by Kennikat). Assoc Faculty Pr.

Tennyson's Idylls of the King & Arthurian Story from the Sixteenth Century. facsimile ed. Mungo W. Maccallum. LC 73-154159. (Select Bibliographies Reprint Ser). Repr. of 1894 ed. 24.50 (ISBN 0-8369-5775-X). Ayer Co Pubs.

Tennyson's in Memoriam. J. F. Genung. LC 76-129342. (Studies in Tennyson, No. 27). 1970. Repr. of 1883 ed. lib. bdg. 45.95x (ISBN 0-8383-1146-6). Haskell.

Tennyson's in Memoriam. John F. Genung. LC 74-14525. 1974. Repr. of 1884 ed. lib. bdg. 22.00 (ISBN 0-8414-4545-1). Folcroft.

Tennyson's "In Memoriam" Its Message to the Bereaved & Sorrowful. Thomas A. Moxon. LC 76-46488. 1977. Repr. of 1917 ed. lib. bdg. 17.50 (ISBN 0-8414-6185-6). Folcroft.

Tennyson's Locksley Hall & Thomas Carlyle in Booker Memorial Studies. W. D. Templeman. 1950. Repr. 25.00 (ISBN 0-8274-3924-5). R West.

Tennyson's Maud: A Definitive Edition. Ed. by Susan Shatto. LC 85-26431. (Illus.). 320p. 1986. 39.50x (ISBN 0-8061-1986-1). U of Okla Pr.

Tennyson's Maud: The Biographical Genesis. Ralph W. Rader. 1978. Repr. of 1963 ed. 37.50x (ISBN 0-520-03617-4). U of Cal Pr.

Tennyson's "Maud" Vindicated: An Explanatory Essay. Robert J. Mann. Ed. by Fredeman et al. (Victorian Muse Ser.). 78p. 1986. lib. bdg. 25.00 (ISBN 0-8240-8611-2). Garland Pub.

Tennyson's Methods of Composition. C. Ricks. (Chatterton Lectures on An English Poet). 1966. pap. 5.50 (ISBN 0-902732-88-9, Pub. by British Acad). Longwood Pub Group.

Tennyson's Poetry. Alfred Tennyson. Ed. by Robert W. Hill, Jr. (Critical Edition Ser). 1972. pap. 13.95x (ISBN 0-393-09953-9). Norton.

Tennysons Sprache und Stil. Roman Dyboski. 1907. pap. 25.00 (ISBN 0-384-13620-6). Johnson Repr.

Tennyson's Style. W. David Shaw. LC 76-12814. 328p. 1976. 29.95x (ISBN 0-8014-1021-5). Cornell U Pr.

Tennyson's Two Brothers. Harold Nicolson. 1947. Repr. lib. bdg. 20.50 (ISBN 0-8414-6256-9). Folcroft.

Tennyson's Use of the Bible. Edna M. Robinson. 119p. 1968. Repr. of 1917 ed. 17.50x (ISBN 0-87752-093-3). Gordian.

Tenor of Justice: Criminal Courts & the Guilty Plea Process. Peter F. Nardulli et al. 464p. 1988. 39.95 (ISBN 0-252-01463-4). U of Ill Pr.

Tenor Voice. Anthony Frissell. 1971. 10.00 (ISBN 0-8283-1387-3). Branden Pub Co.

Tense. Bernard Comrie. (Cambridge Textbooks in Linguistics Ser.). 175p. 1985. 29.95 (ISBN 0-521-23652-5); pap. 10.95 (ISBN 0-521-28138-5). Cambridge U Pr.

Tense & Aspect Systems. Osten Dahl. 240p. 1985. 45.00x (ISBN 0-631-14114-6). Basil Blackwell.

Tense & Tense Logic. John E. Clifford. (Janua Linguarum, Ser. Minor: No. 215). 173p. (Orig.). 1975. pap. text ed. 24.25x (ISBN 90-2793-453-3). Mouton.

Tense-Aspect & the Development of Auxiliaries in Kru Languages. Lynell Marchese. LC 86-60586. (Publications in Linguistics Ser.: No. 78). (Illus.). 200p. (Orig.). 1986. pap. text ed. 20.00x (ISBN 0-88312-097-6); microfiche (6) 10.80 (ISBN 0-88312-407-6). Summer Inst Ling.

Tense-Aspect: Between Semantics & Pragmatics. Ed. by Paul J. Hopper. (Typological Studies in Language: 1). x, 350p. 1982. 48.00x (ISBN 90-272-2865-5); pap. 31.95 (ISBN 90-272-2861-2). Benjamins North Am.

Tense Aspect System of the Spanish Verb As Used in Cultivated Bogata Spanish. Charles Rallides. LC 73-147933. (Janua Linguarum, Ser. Practica: No. 119). 66p. 1971. pap. text ed. 7.20x (ISBN 0-686-22488-4). Mouton.

Tense Logic. Robert P. McArthur. 1976. lib. bdg. 21.00 (ISBN 90-277-0697-2, Pub. by Reidel Holland). Kluwer Academic.

Tense Significance As the Time of the Action. Oscar E. Johnson. (LD). 1936. pap. 13.00 (ISBN 0-527-00767-6). Kraus Repr.

Tense Situations. Pamela Hartmann et al. 192p. 1985. pap. text ed. 10.95 (ISBN 0-03-069902-9, HoltC). HR&W.

Tensile Structures. Frei Otto. 490p. 1973. pap. 25.00x (ISBN 0-262-65005-3). MIT Pr.

Tension & Harmony: The Navajo Rug, Vol. 52, No. 4. 32p. 1982. pap. 4.00 (ISBN 0-686-46247-5). Mus Northern Ariz.

Tension Areas of the World: A Problem Oriented World Regional Geography. Ed. by D. Gordon Bennett. LC 81-82632. (Illus.). 342p. 1982. text ed. 19.95 (ISBN 0-941226-01-8). Park Pr Co.

Tension Between East & West. Rudolf Steiner. Tr. by B. A. Rowley from Ger. 188p. 1983. pap. 8.95 (ISBN 0-88010-071-0). Anthroposophic.

Tension-Free India. Sudarshan Kumar. 1986. 50.00x (Pub. by Archives Pubs). State Mutual Bk.

Tension Getters. Ed. by Mike Yaconelli & David Lynn. 128p. (Orig.). (YA) (gr. 8-12). 1985. pap. 8.95 (ISBN 0-310-45241-4, 11371P). Zondervan.

Tension Getters II. rev. ed. Ed. by Mike Yaconelli & David Lynn. (Orig.). (gr. 8-12). 1985. pap. 8.95 (ISBN 0-310-34931-1, 10774P). Zondervan.

Tension in Boccaccio: Boccaccio & the Fine Arts. Patricia M. Gathercole. LC 74-28151. (Romance Monographs: No. 14). 1975. 18.00x (ISBN 84-399-3503-X). Romance.

Tension in Palestine-Peacemaking in Paris, 1919. Ed. by Isaiah Friedman & Howard M. Sachar. (Rise of Israel Ser.). 370p. 1987. lib. bdg. 80.00 (ISBN 0-8240-4909-8). Garland Pub.

Tension-in-Repose: A Basic Home Series Course. Millicent Linden. (Illus.). 100p. (A 248465). 1971. 4.95 (ISBN 0-912628-08-1). M Linden NY.

Tension-in-Repose: An Introduction to Living in a State of Orgasm, Vol. 1. Millicent Linden. LC 62-22285. (Illus.). 1975. 5.00 (ISBN 0-912628-09-X). M Linden NY.

Tension of Popular Participation. National Center for State Courts Staff. (Research Essay Ser.). 12p. 1977. manuscript 0.72 (E-004). Natl Ctr St Courts.

Tension of the Lyre: Poetry in Shakespeare's Sonnets. Hallett Smith. LC 80-39610. (Illus.). 192p. 1981. 29.95 (ISBN 0-87328-114-4). Huntington Lib.

Tension over the Farakka Barrage: A Techno-Political Tangle in South Asia. Khurshida Begum. 1988. 34.00x (ISBN 0-8364-2271-6, Pub. by KP Bagchi India). South Asia Bks.

Tension: Slowing Down Your Life. Lura J. Geiger. (Orig.). 1987. pap. 34.50 (ISBN 0-931055-34-2); cassettes incl. LuraMedia.

Tension Structures: Behavior & Analysis. John W. Leonard. LC 87-3950. 416p. 1988. text ed. 49.95 (ISBN 0-07-037226-8). McGraw.

Tensioning of Tendons: Force-Elongation Relationship. (FIP State of the Art Report). 18p. 1986. 25.00 (ISBN 0-7277-0260-2, Pub. by T Telford UK). Am Soc Civil Eng.

Tensions. 15.00x (ISBN 0-317-58014-0, Pub. by New Playwrights Network). State Mutual Bk.

Tensions Between the Churches of the First World & the Third World, Vol. 144. Ed. by Virgil Elizondo & Norbert Greinacher. (Concilium 1981). 128p. (Orig.). 1981. pap. 6.95 (ISBN 0-8164-2311-3, HarpR). Har-Row.

Tensions Can Be Reduced to Nuisances. Edmund Bergler. 1979. 12.95 (ISBN 0-87140-976-3); pap. 3.95 (ISBN 0-87140-123-1). Liveright.

Tensions in American Puritanism. R. Reinitz. LC 70-100325. (Problems in American History Ser.). pap. 52.00 (ISBN 0-8357-9991-3, 2019292). Bks Demand UMI.

Tensions in Moral Theology. Charles E. Curran. LC 87-40622. 256p. 1988. text ed. 19.95x (ISBN 0-268-01866-9). U of Notre Dame Pr.

Tensions in the Connection. R. Sheldon Dueuker. 128p. 1983. pap. 4.95 (ISBN 0-687-41243-9). Abingdon.

Tensions in the Middle East. Philip W. Thayer. LC 78-6231. 1978. Repr. of 1958 ed. lib. bdg. 35.00x (ISBN 0-313-20505-1, THTE). Greenwood.

Tensions: Necessary Conflicts in Life & Love. H. A. Williams. 1976. 6.95 (ISBN 0-87243-070-7). Templegate.

Tensions of Economic Development in Southeast Asia. Ed. by J. C. Daruvala. LC 73-19306. (Illus.). 163p. 1974. Repr. of 1962 ed. lib. bdg. 35.00x (ISBN 0-8371-7321-3, DAED). Greenwood.

Tensor Analysis & Continuum Mechanics. W. Fluegge. LC 74-183541. (Illus.). vii, 207p. 1972. 39.00 (ISBN 0-387-05697-1). Springer-Verlag.

Tensor Analysis for Physicists. J. A. Schouten. 289p. 1988. pap. text ed. 7.95t (ISBN 0-486-65582-2). Dover.

Tensor Analysis: Fundamentals & Applications. Wasley S. Krogdahl. LC 78-62755. 1978. 24.50 (ISBN 0-8191-0594-5). U Pr of Amer.

Tensor Analysis on Manifolds. Richard Bishop & Samuel Goldberg. (Illus.). 1980. pap. 5.95 (ISBN 0-486-64039-6). Dover.

Tensor Analysis: Theory & Applications to Geometry & Mechanics of Continua. 2nd ed. Ivan S. Sokolnikoff. LC 64-13223. (Applied Mathematics Ser.). pap. 93.30 (ISBN 0-317-08559-X, 2055264). Bks Demand UMI.

Tensor Calculus. Ed. by Stanislaw Golab. 371p. 1974. 116.00 (ISBN 0-444-41124-0). Elsevier.

Tensor Calculus. Synge & Schild. 1978. pap. text ed. 7.00 (ISBN 0-486-63612-7). Dover.

Tensor Calculus. John L. Synge & A. Schild. LC 75-323720. (Mathematical Expositions Ser.: No. 5). pap. 83.50 (ISBN 0-317-09117-4, 2014430). Bks Demand UMI.

Tensor Geometry: The Geometric Viewpoint & Its Uses. C. T. Dodson. 516p. 1979. pap. 34.95 (ISBN 0-470-20468-0, Co-Pub. with Longman). Wiley.

Tensor Methods in Statistics. Peter McCullagh. (Monographs on Statistics & Applied Probability). 304p. 1987. text ed. 35.00 (ISBN 0-412-27480-9, Pub. by Chapman & Hall). Routledge chapman & Hall.

Tensor Products of Principal Series Representations, Reduction of Tensor Products of Principal Series Representations of Complex Semisimple Lie Groups. F. L. Williams. LC 73-19546. (Lecture Notes in Mathematics: Vol. 358). 132p. 1973. pap. 17.00 (ISBN 0-387-06567-9). Springer-Verlag.

Tent & Testament: Camping Tour in Palestine with Some Notes on Scriptural Sites. Herbert Rix. Ed. by Moshe Davis. LC 77-70737. (America & the Holy Land Ser.). (Illus.). 1977. Repr. of 1907 ed. lib. bdg. 30.00x (ISBN 0-405-10280-1). Ayer Co Pubs.

Tent & Town: Rugs & Embroideries from Central Asia. Cathryn Cootner. LC 82-49068. (H. McCoy Jones Collection). (Illus.). 16p. 1982. pap. 2.95x (ISBN 0-88401-043-0). Fine Arts Mus.

Tent in the Notch. Edward A. Rand. LC 72-2040. (Black Heritage Library Collection Ser.). Repr. of 1881 ed. 15.50 (ISBN 0-8369-9054-4). Ayer Co Pubs.

Tent in Which to Pass a Summer Night. George Trevelyan & Belle Gaunt. LC 85-62286. 130p. 1985. 9.95 (ISBN 0-913299-23-5, Dist. by NAL). Stillpoint.

Tent Life in Siberia. George Kennan. 448p. 1986. pap. 14.95 (ISBN 0-87905-254-6, Peregrine Smith). Gibbs Smith Pub.

Tent Life in Siberia: A New Account of an Old Undertaking Adventures among the Koraks & Other Tribes in Kamchatka & Northern Asia. George Kennan. LC 79-115572. (Russia Observed, Series I). 1970. Repr. of 1910 ed. 31.00 (ISBN 0-405-03037-1). Ayer Co Pubs.

Tent Life in the Holy Land. William C. Prime. Ed. by Moshe Davis. LC 77-70734. (America & the Holy Land Ser.). (Illus.). 1977. Repr. of 1857 ed. lib. bdg. 38.50x (ISBN 0-405-10278-X). Ayer Co Pubs.

Tent Life with English Gypsies in Norway. 2nd ed. Hubert F. Smith. LC 75-3464. (Illus.). Repr. of 1874 ed. 39.00 (ISBN 0-404-16894-9). AMS Pr.

Tent of Meeting Catalogue & Guide. Ed. by Anna Walton. 40p. (Orig.). 1985. 5.00 (ISBN 0-9615531-1-1). Tent Meeting.

Tent of Meeting Texts. Ed. by John Menken. (Illus.). 134p. (Orig.). 1985. pap. 8.00 (ISBN 0-9615531-0-3). Tent Meeting.

Tent of Miracles. Jorge Amado. 1988. pap. 7.95 (ISBN 0-380-75472-X, 54916-6, Bard). Avon.

Tentacles of Progress: Technology Transfer in the Age of Imperialism, 1850-1940. Daniel R. Headrick. (Illus.). 416p. 1988. 32.50 (ISBN 0-19-505115-7); pap. text ed. 11.95 (ISBN 0-19-505116-5). Oxford U Pr.

Tentacles of Unreason: Stories. Joan Givner. LC 84-24154. (Illinois Short Fiction Ser.). 144p. 1985. 11.95 (ISBN 0-252-01203-8). U of Ill Pr.

Tentamina Semiologica, Sive Quaedam Generalem Theoriam Signorum Spectantia: Semiologische Versuche mit dem Ziel der Begruendung einer allgemeinen Zeichentheorie (1789) Johannes C. Hoffbauer. Tr. by A. Eschbach from Lat. (Foundation of Semiotics Ser.: No. 4). xv, 120p. (Eng.). 1988. 26.00 (ISBN 90-272-3274-1). Benjamins North Am.

Tentatio et Consolatio: Studien zu Bugenhagens Interpretatio in Librum Psalmorum. Hans H. Holfelder. LC 73-80563. (Arbeiten Zur Kirchengeschichte, Vol. 46). 132p. (Ger.). 1974. 35.60 (ISBN 3-11-004327-0). De Gruyter.

Tentation de l'Occident. Andre Malraux. pap. 6.95 (ISBN 0-685-34271-9). French & Eur.

Tentation de Saint Antoine. Gustave Flaubert. Ed. by Maynial. (Class. Garnier). pap. 29.95 (ISBN 0-685-34903-9). French & Eur.

Tentative & Other Preliminary Drafts: Tentative Draft, No. 1. xix, 247p. 1973. 9.00 (ISBN 0-686-91054-0). Am Law Inst.

Tentative & Other Preliminary Drafts: Tentative Draft, No. 2, Pt. II. xxi, 284p. 1974. 10.00 (ISBN 0-686-91055-9). Am Law Inst.

Tentative & Other Preliminary Drafts: Tenetative Draft, No. 3, Pt. IV. xxiv, 233p. 1975. 8.00 (ISBN 0-317-01011-5). Am Law Inst.

Tentative & Other Preliminary Drafts: Tentative Draft, No. 4, Pt. V, VI, VII. 328p. 1976. 12.00 (ISBN 0-686-91056-7). Am Law Inst.

Tentative & Other Preliminary Drafts: Tentative Draft, No. 11. 145p. 1965. 5.00 (ISBN 0-686-91042-7). Am Law Inst.

Tentative & Other Preliminary Drafts: Tentative Draft, No. 12. 158p. 1966. 5.00 (ISBN 0-686-91043-5). Am Law Inst.

Tentative & Other Preliminary Drafts: Tentative Draft, No. 13. 172p. 1967. 6.50 (ISBN 0-686-91044-3). Am Law Inst.

Tentative & Other Preliminary Drafts: Tentative Draft, No. 16. xi, 215p. 1970. 7.50 (ISBN 0-686-91045-1). Am Law Inst.

Tentative & Other Preliminary Drafts: Tentative Draft, No. 17. xiv, 180p. 1971. 7.50 (ISBN 0-686-91046-X). Am Law Inst.

Tentative & Other Preliminary Drafts: Tentative Draft, No. 18. ix, 102p. 1972. 6.50 (ISBN 0-686-91047-8). Am Law Inst.

Tentative & Other Preliminary Drafts: Tentative Draft, No. 19. xii, 354p. 1972. 10.00 (ISBN 0-686-91048-6). Am Law Inst.

Tentative & Other Preliminary Drafts: Tentative Draft, No. 20. xv, 321p. 1974. 10.50 (ISBN 0-686-91049-4). Am Law Inst.

Tentative & Other Preliminary Drafts: Tentative Draft, No. 21. xi, 91p. 1975. 5.00 (ISBN 0-686-91050-8). Am Law Inst.

Tentative & Other Preliminary Drafts: Tentative Draft, No. 23. x, 75p. 1977. 5.00 (ISBN 0-686-91051-6). Am Law Inst.

Tentative Bibliography of Kentucky Speech see Minor Dialect Areas of the Upper Midwest.

Tentative Guide for Plastics in Building Construction. 52p. 1973. pap. 2.00 (ISBN 0-685-44143-1, 205M-T). Natl Fire Prot.

Tentative Guide to Historical Materials of the Spanish Borderlands. Francis B. Steck. LC 71-143659. (Research & Source Works Ser: No. 676). 1971. Repr. of 1943 ed. 19.00 (ISBN 0-8337-3379-6). B Franklin.

Tentative Inventory of the Habits of Children from Two to Four Years of Age. Ruth Andrus. LC 77-176520. (Columbia University. Teachers College. Contributions to Edution: No. 160). Repr. of 1924 ed. 22.50 (ISBN 0-404-55160-2). AMS Pr.

Tentative Pregnancy: Prenatal Diagnosis & the Future of Motherhood. Barbara K. Rothman. 288p. 1986. 17.95 (ISBN 0-670-80841-5). Viking.

Tentative Pregnancy: Prenatal Diagnosis & the Future of Motherhood. Barbara K. Rothman. 288p. 1987. pap. 6.95 (ISBN 0-14-009486-5). Penguin.

Tentative Service Requirements for Bridge Rail Systems. (National Cooperative Highway Research Program Report). 62p. 1970. 3.20 (ISBN 0-309-01784-X). Transport Res Bd.

Tentative Skid-Resistance Requirements for Main Rural Highways. (National Cooperative Highway Research Program Report). 96p. 1967. 3.60 (ISBN 0-317-36107-4, 1541). Transport Res Bd.

Tentative Standard for Evaluating Fire Protection at a New Facility. 1970. pap. 2.00 (ISBN 0-685-58200-0, 5A-T). Natl Fire Prot.

Tentative Standard for Legally Required Emergency & Standby Power Systems: 1983. 1983. 8.00 (ISBN 0-317-07386-9, NFPA 110-T). Natl Fire Prot.

Tentative Standard for Protective Clothing for Fire Fighters. 1973. pap. 2.00 (ISBN 0-685-58201-9, 19A-T). Natl Fire Prot.

Tentative Standard for the Safe Use of Electricity in Patient Care Areas of Health Care Facilities. 96p. 1973. pap. 2.00t (ISBN 0-685-44142-3, 76B-T). Natl Fire Prot.

Tentative Standard for the Use of Inhalation Anesthetics in Ambulatory Care Facilities. 1973. pap. 2.00 (ISBN 0-685-58205-1, 56G-T). Natl Fire Prot.

Terence: The Brothers (Adelphoi) Ed. & tr. by A. S. Gratwick. (BC-AP Classical Texts). 250p. (Orig., Lat. & Eng.). 1986. text ed. 49.00 (ISBN 0-86516-134-8); pap. 16.50 (ISBN 0-86516-133-X). Bolchazy-Carducci.

Terence: The Comedies. Terence. Tr. by Betty Radice. (Classics Ser.). 1976. pap. 6.95 (ISBN 0-14-044324-X). Penguin.

Terence: The Mother in Law. Ed. by S. Ireland. (Classical Texts-Latin Texts Ser.). 200p. 1988. text ed. 49.95 (ISBN 0-85668-373-6, Pub. by Aris & Phillips UK); pap. text ed. 16.50 (ISBN 0-85668-374-4). Humanities.

Terence: The Self-Tormentor. Ed. by A. J. Brothers. (Classical Texts-Latin Texts Ser.). 200p. 1987. text ed. 49.95 (ISBN 0-85668-302-7, Pub. by Aris & Phillips UK); pap. text ed. 16.50 (ISBN 0-85668-303-5, Pub. by Aris & Phillips UK). Humanities.

Terence: The Self-Tormentor (Heaton Timoroumenos) Ed. & tr. by A. J. Brothers. (BC-AP Classical Texts). 250p. (Orig., Lat. & Eng.). 1986. 49.00 (ISBN 0-86516-132-1); pap. 16.50 (ISBN 0-86516-131-3). Bolchazy-Carducci.

Terence's Bembine Phormio: A Palaeographic Examination. Elaine Coury. (Illus.). 150p. 30.00. Bolchazy-Carducci.

Teresa: A Woman; A Biography of Teresa of Avila. Victoria Lincoln. Ed. by Elias Rivers & Antonio T. De Nicolas. LC 84-8561. (Series in Cultural Perspectives). 440p. 1985. 49.50 (ISBN 0-87395-936-1); pap. 16.95 (ISBN 0-87395-937-X). State U NY Pr.

Teresa, a Woman: A Biography of Teresa of Avila. Victoria Lincoln. LC 84-8561. 440p. 1985. 14.95 (ISBN 0-913729-11-6). Paragon Hse.

Teresa Carreno "By the Grace of God". Marta Milinowski. LC 76-58931. (Music Reprint Ser.). 1977. Repr. of 1940 ed. lib. bdg. 45.00 (ISBN 0-306-70870-1). Da Capo.

Teresa of Avila: The Interior Castle. Tr. by Kieran Kavanaugh & Otilio Rodrigues. LC 79-66484. (Classics of Western Spirituality Ser.). 256p. 1979. 12.95 (ISBN 0-8091-0303-6); pap. 9.95 (ISBN 0-8091-2254-5). Paulist Pr.

Teresa of Calcutta. D. Jeanene Watson. LC 84-60313. (Sower Ser.). (gr. 3-6). 1984. 8.95 (ISBN 0-88062-013-7); pap. 4.95 (ISBN 0-88062-012-9). Mott Media.

Teresa of Watling Street. Arnold Bennett. LC 74-17051. (Collected Works of Arnold Bennett: Vol. 78). 1976. Repr. of 1904 ed. 18.75 (ISBN 0-518-19159-1). Ayer Co Pubs.

Teresa Tendon, Podiatrist: Computerized Accounting Practice Set. Christine Sprenger et al. 1986. Apple. pap. 17.95x (ISBN 0-256-03532-6); IBM. pap. 17.95x (ISBN 0-256-03533-4). Irwin.

Teresa: The Story of Byron's Last Mistress. Austin K. Gray. 1948. 25.00 (ISBN 0-8274-3586-X). R West.

Teresina in America, 2 vols. in 1. Maria T. Longworth. LC 73-13158. (Foreign Travelers in America, 1810-1935 Ser.). 734p. 1974. Repr. 52.00x (ISBN 0-405-05478-5). Ayer Co Pubs.

Teresita. William C. Holden. LC 78-2321. (Illus.). 256p. 1978. 14.95 (ISBN 0-916144-24-0); pap. 5.95 (ISBN 0-916144-25-9). Stemmer Hse.

Tereza Batista: Home from the Wars. Jorge Amado. Tr. by Barbara S. Merello. 576p. 1988. pap. 9.95 (ISBN 0-380-75468-1). Avon.

Terezin Requiem. Josef Bor. 1978. pap. 1.95 (ISBN 0-380-01673-7, 33449-6, Bard). Avon.

Terina. R. Ross Holloway & G. Kenneth Jenkins. 1983. 55.00 (ISBN 0-318-19611-5). Numismatic Fine Arts.

Terina: Diary of a Hostage in Ethiopia. Terina Kelly. (Illus.). 112p. 1984. 9.95 (ISBN 0-86327-033-6, Pub. by Wolfhound Pr Ireland); pap. 5.25 (ISBN 0-86327-032-8, Pub. by Wolfhound Pr Ireland). Irish Bks Media.

Terlingua Teacher: Where the Rainbows Wait. Trent Janes & Carlton Stowers. 192p. 1983. pap. 8.95 (ISBN 0-89015-376-0). Eakin Pr.

Terlullianus, De Idololatria: Critical Text, Translation & Commentary. J. H. Waszink & J. Van Winden. (Vigilae Christianae Ser.: Suppl. 1). xii, 317p. 1987. 67.25 (ISBN 90-04-08105-4, Pub. by E J Brill). Heinman.

Term Banks for Tomorrow's World: Translating & the Computer 4. Ed. by Barbara Snell. 212p. 1983. 29.00 (ISBN 0-85142-172-5). Learned Info.

Term Loan Handbook. ABA, Committee on Development in Business Financing, Corporation, Banking & Business Law Section. Ed. by John J. McCann. 300p. 1983. 55.00 (H4285X, Pub. by Law & Business). HarBraceJ.

Term Logic with Choice Operator. rev. ed. Hans Hermes. LC 79-125498. (Lecture Notes in Mathematics: Vol. 6). 1970. pap. 10.70 (ISBN 0-387-04899-5). Springer-Verlag.

Term One All Done. Ronald J. St. Cyr. 33p. 1986. 5.95 (ISBN 0-8059-3011-6). Dorrance.

Term Paper: A Manual & Model. 4th ed. Charles W. Cooper & Edmund J. Robins. 1967. pap. 1.25x (ISBN 0-8047-0348-5). Stanford U Pr.

Term Paper Study Aids. John Moran et al. 1986. pap. 2.25 (ISBN 0-87738-025-2). Youth Ed.

Term Paper Writing: The Fastest Easiest Legitimate Method Known to Man. rev ed. L. Michael Tompkins. 1980. pap. 6.00 (ISBN 0-931324-01-7). La Grange.

Term Structure of Interest Rates: Expectations & Behavior Patterns. Burton G. Malkiel. LC 66-21836. (Illus.). pap. 73.30 (ISBN 0-317-08743-6, 2051944). Bks Demand UMI.

Term Structure of Interest Rates in the United States, 1884-1914. Jean M. Gray. LC 77-14785. (Dissertations in American Economic History Ser.). 1978. 23.50 (ISBN 0-405-11037-5). Ayer Co Pubs.

Terminal. Colin Forbes. LC 85-47601. 320p. 1985. 14.95 (ISBN 0-689-11589-X). Atheneum.

Terminal. Colin Forbes. 432p. 1987. pap. 3.95 (ISBN 0-8217-1968-8). Zebra.

Terminal Aleph. Pamela Edwards. (Illus.). 80p. 1986. pap. 6.00 (ISBN 0-915572-40-0). Panjandrum.

Terminal & Life-Threating Illness: An Occupational-Behavioral Perspective. Kent N. Tigges & William M. Marcil. LC 87-43327. 304p. 1988. pap. 29.95 (ISBN 1-55642-022-6). Slack Inc.

Terminal Bar. Larry Mitchell. 220p. (Orig.). 1982. pap. 6.00 (ISBN 0-930762-05-3). Calamus Bks.

Terminal Beach. J. G. Ballard. 1987. pap. 3.50 (ISBN 0-88184-370-9). Carroll & Graf.

Terminal Care. Ed. by Richard Turnbull. LC 84-4522. (Death Education, Aging, & Health Care Ser.). 400p. 1985. 39.95 (ISBN 0-89116-317-4). Hemisphere Pub.

Terminal Care at Home. Ed. by Roy Spilling. (General Practice Ser.: No. 10). (Illus.). 200p. 1986. pap. 19.95 (ISBN 0-19-261508-4). Oxford U Pr.

Terminal Care: Friendship Contracts with Dying Patients. Loma Feigenberg. LC 79-25904. 1980. 30.00 (ISBN 0-87630-224-X). Brunner-Mazel.

Terminal Degrees: The Job Crisis in Higher Education. Emily K. Abel. LC 83-26876. 240p. 1984. 35.00 (ISBN 0-275-91108-X, C1108). Praeger.

Terminal Eocene Events. Ed. by C. Pomerol & I. Premoli Silva. (Developments in Palaeontology & Stratigraphy Ser.: Vol. 9). 414p. 1986. 81.75 (ISBN 0-444-42623-X). Elsevier.

Terminal Justice. Victor Wartofsky. Ed. by Damaris Rowland. 320p. 1988. pap. 3.95 (ISBN 0-425-10750-7). Berkley Pub.

Terminal Man. Michael Crichton. 1972. 13.00 (ISBN 0-394-44768-9). Knopf.

Terminal Marketing of Tientsin Cotton: An Analysis of the Accounts of the Principal Chinese Banks, 1932-1934. H. D. Fong. Ed. by Ramon H. Myers. LC 80-8821. (China During the Interregnum 1911-1949, The Economy & Society Ser.). 142p. 1982. lib. bdg. 24.00 (ISBN 0-8240-4676-5). Garland Pub.

Terminal Nerve (Nervus Terminalis) Structure, Function & Evolution. Ed. by Leo S. Demski & Marlene Schwanzel-Fukuda. (Annals of the New York Academy of Sciences: Vol. 519). 469p. 1987. 117.00 (ISBN 0-89766-433-7). NY Acad Sci.

Terminal Operations, Vol. II. Cargo Systems Staff. 1980. 195.00x (ISBN 0-907499-12-0, Pub. by Cargo Systs UK). State Mutual Bk.

Terminal Operations, Vol. III. Ed. by Cargo Systems Staff. 1983. 195.00x (ISBN 0-907499-39-2, Pub. by Cargo Systs UK). State Mutual Bk.

Terminal Operations & Text Editing on the Vax with VMS. Lyle Langlois & Shirley J. Petras. 100p. (Orig.). 1986. pap. text ed. 14.00 (ISBN 0-89787-419-6). Gorsuch Scarisbrick.

Terminal Patient: Oral Care. Ed. by Bernard Schoenberg et al. LC 72-9892. 1973. 34.00x (ISBN 0-88238-701-4). Columbia U Pr.

Terminal Placebos. James Bertolino. (Illus.). 1975. saddlestitched in wrappers 2.00 (ISBN 0-912284-67-6). New Rivers Pr.

Terminal Tower Complex. Jim Toman & Dan Cook. Ed. by Tom Luckay. LC 80-81212. (Cleveland Landmarks Ser.: Vol. 1). (Illus.). 82p. (Orig.). 1980. pap. 8.50 (ISBN 0-936760-01-X). Cleveland Landmarks.

Terminal Transferase In Immunobiology & Leukemia. Ed. by Umberto Bertazzoni & Fred J. Bollum. LC 82-3691. (Advances in Experimental Medicine & Biology: Vol. 145). 406p. 1982. 69.50x (ISBN 0-306-40989-5, Plenum Pr). Plenum Pub.

Terminal Vision: The Educational Elite's Plan for Your Children. Eric Buehrer. LC 87-83576. 200p. (Orig.). 1988. pap. 5.95 (ISBN 0-945072-01-5, Gldn Apple Bks). NACE.

Terminal Visions: The Literature of Last Things. W. Warren Wagar. LC 81-48625. 256p. 1982. 24.50x (ISBN 0-253-35847-7). Ind U Pr.

Terminals & Data Communications Equipment in the Insurance Industry. 190p. 1984. 1475.00 (ISBN 0-86621-057-1, A1066). Frost & Sullivan.

Terminals & Network Products for the 3270 Environment. International Resource Development Staff. 192p. 1986. 2300.00x (ISBN 0-88694-692-1). Intl Res Dev.

Terminals & Printers Buyer's Guide. Tony Webster. LC 84-883. (Illus.). 345p. 1984. pap. text ed. 19.95 (ISBN 0-07-068968-7, BYTE Bks). McGraw.

Terminating Life. Ed. by Gary E. McCuen & Therese Boucher. LC 88-2692. (Ideas in Conflict Ser.). (Illus.). 144p. 1985. lib. bdg. 11.95 (ISBN 0-86596-051-8). G E McCuen Pubns.

Terminating Litigation Without Trial. 147p. 1986. pap. 28.00 (CP-49021). Cal Cont Ed Bar.

Termination & Relocation: Federal Indian Policy, 1945-1960. Donald L. Fixico. LC 86-16057. (Illus.). 286p. 1986. 27.50x (ISBN 0-8263-0908-9). U of NM Pr.

Termination Handbook. Robert Coulson. LC 81-66988. 235p. 1981. 17.95 (ISBN 0-02-906700-6). Free Pr.

Termination Handbook: A Book for Those on Both Sides of the "Firing Line". Robert Coulson. 240p. 1986. pap. 9.95 (ISBN 0-02-906470-8). Free Pr.

Termination Interview. Lynne Murray. LC 87-29925. 288p. 1988. 16.95x (ISBN 0-312-01518-6). St Martin.

Termination of Employment, 1 vol. Kenneth McColluch. LC 85-157641. 1987. 390.00; 360.00; write for info. P-H.

Termination of Employment at the Initiative of the Employer, Report VIII, No. 2: International Labour Conference, 67th Session, 1981. International Labour Conference, 67th Session, 1981. 147p. (Orig.). 1981. pap. 15.75 (ISBN 92-2-102412-1). Intl Labour Office.

Termination of Employment at the Initiative of the Employer, Report V (1) International Labour Conference, 68th Session, 1982. 80p. (Orig.). 1982. pap. 10.50 (ISBN 92-2-102795-3). Intl Labour Office.

Termination of Employment at the Initiative of the Employer, Report V (2) International Labour Conference, 68th Session, 1982. 87p. (Orig.). 1982. pap. 12.25 (ISBN 92-2-102796-1). Intl Labour Office.

Termination of Hostilities in the Early Arab Conquests, A.D. 34-56. D. R. Hill. 188p. 1985. 49.00x (ISBN 0-317-39169-0, Pub. by Luzac & Co Ltd). State Mutual Bk.

Termination of Multipartite Treaties. Harold J. Tobin. LC 33-34572. (Columbia University. Studies in the Social Sciences: No. 388). Repr. of 1933 ed. 24.50 (ISBN 0-404-51388-3). AMS Pr.

Termination of Treaties in International Law: The Doctrine of Rebus Sic Stantibus & Desuetude. Athanassios Vamvoukos. 396p. 1985. 59.00x (ISBN 0-19-876179-1). Oxford U Pr.

Termination: The Closing at Baker Plant. Alfred Slote. LC 69-13100. 360p. 1977. Repr. of 1969 ed. 12.00x (ISBN 0-87944-219-0). Inst Soc Res.

Termination Trap: Best Strategies for a Job Going Sour. Stephen Cohen. (Illus.). 224p. (Orig.). 1984. pap. 9.95 (ISBN 0-913589-00-4). Williamson Pub Co.

Terminations. facs. ed. Henry James. LC 71-134966. (Short Story Index Reprint Ser). 1895. 14.50 (ISBN 0-8369-3696-5). Ayer Co Pubs.

Terminations. Henry James. 1973. lib. bdg. 40.00 (ISBN 0-8414-5366-7). Folcroft.

Terminations in Psychoanalysis. Stephen K. Firestein. LC 76-46811. 261p. 1978. text ed. 30.00x (ISBN 0-8236-6450-3). Intl Univs Pr.

Terminators. Donald Hamilton. (Matt Helm Ser.). 224p. 1980. pap. 1.95 (ISBN 0-449-14035-0, GM). Fawcett.

Terminological Data Banks: Proceedings of the First Conference Convened 2 & 3 April, 1979 by Infoterm. Ed. by Christian Galiuski. 207p. 1980. pap. 20.00 (ISBN 3-598-21365-4). K G Saur.

Terminological Dictionary of Automatic Control. 641p. 1977. leatherette 39.95 (ISBN 0-686-92164-X, M-9059). French & Eur.

Terminologie de la Documentation. Ed. by Gernot Wersig. Ulrich Neveling. 274p. (Eng., Fr., Ger., Rus. & Span.). 1976. pap. 32.50 (ISBN 0-686-67750-1, M-6529). French & Eur.

Terminologie de la Gestion: Les Organigrammes. L. Larouche & J. Pilon. Ed. by M. Cote. 223p. 1974. pap. 12.95 (ISBN 0-686-92153-4, M-9220). French & Eur.

Terminologie de la Geston des Imprimes Administratifs. M. Viller & A. Drollet. Ed. by J. Corbeil. 92p. 1975. pap. 7.95 (ISBN 0-7754-2334-3, M-9221). French & Eur.

Terminologie de l'Etiquetage: Anglais-Francais. M. Villers. 42p. 1974. pap. 7.95 (ISBN 0-7754-3243-1, M-9233). French & Eur.

Terminologie et Lexicographie Medicales. 60p. (Fr.). 1967. pap. 29.95 (ISBN 0-686-57229-7, M-6530). French & Eur.

Terminologie Fondamentale en Odonto-Stomatologie et Lexique: Francais-Anglais, Anglais-Francais. 259p. (Fr. & Eng.). 1977. 35.95 (ISBN 0-686-57210-6, M-6492). French & Eur.

Terminologie van het Crediet-Wezen in het Grieksch. Jan Korver. Ed. by Moses Finley. LC 79-4987. (Ancient Economic History Ser.). (Dutch.). 1980. Repr. of 1934 ed. lib. bdg. 16.00x (ISBN 0-405-12372-8). Ayer Co Pubs.

Terminologies of the Eighties: With a Special Section: 10 Years of Infoterm, Convened by Helmut Felber & Others. (Infoterm Ser.: No. 7). 412p. 1982. pap. 35.00 (ISBN 3-598-21367-0). K G Saur.

Terminology & Communication Skills in the Health Sciences. J. Lea. 1975. pap. 17.95 (ISBN 0-87909-821-X, Reston). P-H.

Terminology & Concepts in Mental Retardation. Joel R. Davitz et al. LC 61-62621. (TC Series in Special Education). 135p. pap. 35.10 (2030145). Bks Demand UMI.

Terminology & Definitions of Speech Defects. Mardel Ogilvie. LC 70-177132. (Columbia University. Teachers College. Contributions to Education: No. 859). Repr. of 1942 ed. 22.50 (ISBN 0-404-55859-3). AMS Pr.

Terminology Bulletin: Disarmament, No. 335. 315p. 1986. 3.00 (ISBN 92-1-002047-2, MULT.86.I.14). UN.

Terminology Bulletin: Names of Countries & Adjectives of Nationality, No. 333. 61p. 1985. 7.00 (ISBN 92-1-002046-4, EFS.85.I.25). UN.

Terminology Bulletin: No. 311-Rev. 1. 405p. 1981. pap. 26.00 (ISBN 0-686-97591-X, MULT.81.I.26). UN.

Terminology for Allied Health Professionals. Carolee Sormunen. 550p. 1985. write for info. (ISBN 0-538-11190-9, K19). SW Pub.

Terminology for the Devil & Evil Spirits in the Apostolic Fathers. Francis X. Gokey. LC 79-8100. 224p. Repr. of 1961 ed. 29.00 (ISBN 0-404-18412-X). AMS Pr.

Terminology for the Health Professions. Eugene M. Wroble. (Illus.). 704p. 1982. pap. text ed. 19.95 (ISBN 0-397-54259-3, 64-02259, Lippincott Nursing). Lippincott.

Terminology of Adult Education. Colin Titmus. (IBEDATA Ser.). 88p. (Eng., Fr. & Span., 2nd Printing 1981). 1979. pap. 6.00 (ISBN 92-3-001683-7, U950, UNESCO). UNIPUB.

Terminology of Anatomy & Physiology: A Programmed Approach. Dale P. Layman. LC 82-13448. 293p. 1983. pap. 15.95 (ISBN 0-471-86262-2). Wiley.

Terminology of Communication Disorders: Speech, Language, & Hearing. 2nd ed. Lucille Nicolosi. (Illus.). 338p. 1982. 22.95 (ISBN 0-683-06499-1). Williams & Wilkins.

Terminology of Forest Science, Technology, Practice & Products. rev. ed. Ed. by F. C. Ford-Robertson & Robert K. Winters. LC 82-61327. (Multilingual Forestry Terminology Ser.: No. 1). 370p. 1983. pap. 10.00 (ISBN 0-939970-16-3, SAF 83-01). Soc Am Foresters.

Terminology of Forestry & Related Subjects. Jean E. Gorse. (Eng. & Fr.). 1988. 7.50 (BK0966). World Bank.

Terminology of Heating, Ventilation, Air-Conditioning & Refrigeration. 180p. 1986. 30.00. Am Heat Ref & Air Eng.

Terminology of Malaria & of Malaria Eradication: Report of a Drafting Committee. 127p. (Eng., Fr., Rus. & Span.). 1963. pap. 6.40 (ISBN 92-4-154014-1). World Health.

Terminology of Technical & Vocational Education: Revised Edition 1984. (IBEDATA Ser.). 103p. 1985. pap. 9.50 (ISBN 92-3-002191-1, U1437, UNESCO). UNIPUB.

Terminology of Technical & Vocational Education. (IBEDATA Ser.). 88p. (3rd Printing 1981). 1978. pap. 5.00 (U884, UNESCO). UNIPUB.

Terminology of Water Supply & Environmental Sanitation. Paul J. Biron. (Eng., Fr. & Span.). 1988. 23.00 (BK0585). World Bank.

Terminology of Waters Supply & Environmental Sanitation: A World Bank-UNICEF Glossary. Paul J. Biron. 176p. 1987. 23.00 (ISBN 0-8213-0585-9, BK-0585). World Bank.

Terminology: Special Education. 1978. pap. 15.75 (ISBN 92-3-001564-4, U844, UNESCO). UNIPUB.

Termite Life & Termite Control in Tropical South Asia. M. L. Roonwal. 177p. 1979. 32.00x (ISBN 81-85046-02-6, Pub. by Scientific). State Mutual Bk.

Termite Repair. 2nd, rev. ed. George T. Demaree. (Illus.). 128p. (Orig.). 1987. pap. 16.95 (ISBN 0-935831-00-2). Tradesman Pub.

Termite Report: The Homeowner & Buyer's Guide to Structural Pest Control. Donald V. Pearman. (Illus.). 140p. (Orig.). 1988. pap. 16.95 (ISBN 0-943743-00-1). Pear Pub.

Termites & Soils. T. G. Wood. 1971. 45.00 (ISBN 0-12-440850-8). Acad Pr.

Termites & Termite Control. 2nd rev. ed. Ed. by Charles A. Kofoid. (Illus.). Repr. of 1934 ed. 46.00 (ISBN 0-384-30050-2). Johnson Repr.

Termites et Champignons: Les Champignons termitophiles d'Afrique Noire et d'Asie Meridionale. Roger Heim. (Collection "Flores et Faunes Acruelles"). (Illus.). 207p. (Fr.). 1977. lib. bdg. 62.50x (ISBN 2-85004-004-5). Lubrecht & Cramer.

Termodinamica para Muchos. I. R. Krichevski & I. V. Petrianov. 173p. (Span.). 1980. pap. 3.25 (ISBN 0-8285-1863-7, Pub. by Mir Pubs USSR). Imported Pubns.

Terms & Conditions of Contract. R. W. Oliver & A. D. Allwright. 125p. 20.00 (ISBN 0-317-43795-X, Pub. by Inst Purchasing Supp). State Mutual Bk.

Terms & Definitions for the Weighing Industry. 4th ed. 75p. 1981. 5.00 (ISBN 0-318-16449-3, S-M-2). Scale Mfrs.

Terms & Renewals. Peter Wild. (Orig.). 1970. 10.00x (ISBN 0-685-04868-3); pap. 4.25 (ISBN 0-912136-20-0). Twowindows Pr.

Terms & Sentences: Theophrastus on Hypothetical Syllogisms. Jonathan Barnes. (Dawes Hicks Lectures on Philosophy). (Illus.). 1985. pap. 5.50 (ISBN 0-85672-494-7, Pub. by British Acad). Longwood Pub Group.

Terrible Tales of the Happy Days School. Lois Duncan. LC 82-82623. (Illus.). 32p. (gr. 3-6). 1983. PLB 10.95 (ISBN 0-316-19541-3). Little.
Terrible, Terrible Tiger. Colin Hawkins & Jacqui Hawkins. LC 87-40675. (Early Reader Ser.). (Illus.). 32p. (ps-3). 1988. bds. 5.95 (ISBN 1-55782-043-0). Warner Bks.
Terrible Thing That Happened at Our House. Marge Blaine. LC 86-4827. (Illus.). 40p. (ps-3). 1980. Repr. of 1975 ed. 12.95 (ISBN 0-02-710720-5, Four Winds). Macmillan.
Terrible Thing That Happened at Our House. Mary Blaine. 32p. (gr. k-3). 1983. pap. 2.95 (ISBN 0-590-40355-9). Scholastic Inc.
Terrible Threes. Ishmael Reed. 224p. 1989. 16.95 (ISBN 0-689-11893-7). Atheneum.
Terrible Tide. Alisa Craig, pseud. 192p. 1987. pap. 2.95 (ISBN 0-380-70336-X). Avon.
Terrible Tide. Alisa Craig. 1985. 24.95x (ISBN 0-7090-1839-8, Pub. by R Hale Ltd UK). State Mutual Bk.
Terrible Tragadabas: El Terrible Tragadabas. Joe Hayes. (Illus.). 32p. (Orig.). (ps-4). 1987. pap. 3.95 (ISBN 0-939729-02-4); bk. & cassette 7.95, (ISBN 0-939729-03-2). Trails West Pub.
Terrible Troll. Mercer Mayer. LC 68-28730. (Illus.). (gr. k-3). 1968. PLB 11.89 (ISBN 0-8037-8621-2). Dial Bks Young.
Terrible Troll. Mercer Mayer. LC 68-28730. (Pied Piper Bk.). (Illus.). 32p. (ps-2). 1981. pap. 4.95 (ISBN 0-8037-8636-0). Dial Bks Young.
Terrible Truth about Lawyers. Mark McCormack. 1988. pap. 4.95. Avon.
Terrible Truth about Lawyers: What They Didn't Teach Me at Yale Law School. Mark H. McCormack. LC 87-11491. 256p. 1987. 17.95 (ISBN 0-688-06621-6, Pub. by Beech Tree Bks). Morrow.
Terrible Truth: Secrets of a Sixth-Grader. Stephen Roos. LC 83-5253. (Illus.). 128p. (gr. 4-6). 1983. 12.95 (ISBN 0-385-29306-2). Delacorte.
Terrible Truth: Secrets of a Sixth-Grader. Stephen Roos. (Illus.). 128p. (gr. 4-7). 1984. pap. 2.50 (ISBN 0-440-48578-9, YB). Dell.
Terrible Tuesday. Hazel Townson. LC 85-71978. (Illus.). 32p. (ps-3). 1986. 11.75 (ISBN 0-688-06243-1, Morrow Junior Books); lib. bdg. 11.88 (ISBN 0-688-06244-X). Morrow.
Terrible Tuesday see Black History Series 1.
Terrible Twos. Ishmael Reed. 192p. 1983. pap. 3.50 (ISBN 0-380-64949-7, 64949, Bard). Avon.
Terrible Twos. Ishmael Reed. 192p. 1988. pap. 8.95 (ISBN 0-689-70727-4). Atheneum.
Terrible Wonderful Day. Yaffa Ganz. (Illus.). 1986. 7.95 (ISBN 0-87306-423-2). Feldheim.
Terribly Wonderful. Valiska Gregory. LC 85-24003. (Mr. Poggle & Scamp Bks.). (Illus.). 24p. (ps-k). 1986. 8.95 (ISBN 0-02-738110-2, Four Winds); bds. 3.95 (ISBN 0-02-738120-X). Macmillan.
Terrier Lovers Cookbook. Ed. by Sandra G. Allen. 1977. 10.00 (ISBN 0-9600722-2-5). Skye Terrier.
Terrier of Fleete, Lincolnshire. Ed. by N. Neilson. Bd. with Eleventh Century Inquisition of St. Augustine's Canterbury. Ed. by A. Ballard. (British Academy, London, Record of the Social & Economic History of England & Wales Ser.: Vol. 4). pap. 36.00 (ISBN 0-8115-1244-4). Kraus Repr.
Terriers in the Trenches: The Post Office Rifles at War, 1914-1918. Ed. by Charles Messenger. 170p. 1987. 91.00x (Pub. by Picton UK). State Mutual Bk.
Terriers of the World: Their History & Characteristics. Tom Horner. LC 83-20745. (Illus.). 352p. 1984. 32.00 (ISBN 0-571-13145-X). Faber & Faber.
Terriers Vocation. Geoffrey Sparrow. (Illus.). pap. 2.95 (ISBN 0-85131-111-3, NL51, Pub. by J A Allen U K). S R Smith Sporting Bks.
Terrific Sex in Fearful Times. Brooks Peters. LC 87-27522. 192p. 1988. 14.95 (ISBN 0-312-01519-4). St Martin.
Terrific Tips for Parents. Paul Lewis. 80p. 1988. pap. 2.25 (ISBN 0-8423-7010-2). Tyndale.
Terrific Toys You Can Make. Joan E. Trill. LC 87-15904. (Illus.). 132p. (Orig.). 1987. pap. 9.95 (ISBN 0-8069-6592-4). Sterling.
Terrified Heart. Alicia Grace. 1976. pap. 1.25 (ISBN 0-685-72357-7, LB383ZK, Leisure Bks). Leisure NY.
Terrifying Goal of the Ecumenical Movement. Dr. G. Wasserzug. 1.45 (ISBN 0-937422-77-0). Midnight Call.
Terrigenous Elastic Depositional Systems. W. E. Galloway. (Illus.). 420p. 1983. 49.50 (ISBN 0-387-90827-7). Springer-Verlag.
Terrines, Pates, & Galantines. LC 81-21310. (Good Cook Ser.). (gr. 7 up). 22.60 (ISBN 0-8094-2926-8, Pub. by Time-Life). Silver.
Terrines, Pates & Galantines. Ed. by Time Life Books. LC 81-21310. (Illus.). 176p. 1982. 14.95 (ISBN 0-8094-2925-X). Time-Life.
Terri's Dream. Margaret Garland. (Caprice Romance Ser.). 144p. (YA) (gr. 7 up). 1984. pap. 2.25 (ISBN 0-441-80104-8, Pub. by Tempo). Ace Bks.
Territorial Allocation by Imperial Rivalry: The Human Legacy in the Near East. Joshua C. Baylson. LC 86-25013. (Research Papers Ser.: No. 221). 138p. 1987. pap. 12.00 (ISBN 0-89065-125-6). U Chicago Comm Geo.
Territorial Antelope: The Ugnad Waterbuck. C. A. Spinage. 1982. 76.00 (ISBN 0-12-657720-X). Acad Pr.
Territorial Army, Nineteen Hundred-Seven to Nineteen Forty. Peter Dennis. (Royal Historical Society Studies in History: No. 51). 160p. 1987. 45.00 (ISBN 0-86193-208-0, Pub. by Boydell & Brewer). Longwood Pub Group.
Territorial Asylum. Atle Grahl-Madsen. LC 80-10498. (Studies in International Law: Vol. 1). 231p. 1980. lib. bdg. 39.00 (ISBN 0-379-20706-0). Oceana.
Territorial Basis of Government under the State Constitutions. Alfred Z. Reed. LC 68-56685. (Columbia University. Studies in the Social Sciences: No. 106). Repr. of 1911 ed. 25.00 (ISBN 0-404-51106-6). AMS Pr.
Territorial Batallions: A Pictorial History. Ray Westlake. (Illus.). 264p. 1986. 45.00 (ISBN 0-87052-309-0). Hippocrene Bks.
Territorial Dimension in Government: Understanding the United Kingdom. Richard Rose. LC 82-9680. 1982. pap. 14.95x (ISBN 0-934540-16-0). Chatham Hse Pubs.
Territorial Dimension of Judaism. W. D. Davies. LC 81-53. (Quantum Book: No. 23). 160p. 1982. 20.00x (ISBN 0-520-04331-6). U of Cal Pr.
Territorial Dimension of Politics: Within, among, & Across Nations. Ivo D. Duchacek. LC 85-52109. 1986. 38.50 (ISBN 0-8133-7112-0). Westview.
Territorial Experience: Human Ecology as Symbolic Interaction. E. Gordon Ericksen. LC 80-14861. (Illus.). 224p. 1980. text ed. 20.00x (ISBN 0-292-78038-9). U of Tex Pr.
Territorial History of Socorro, New Mexico. Bruce Ashcroft. (Southwestern Studies: No. 85). (Orig.). 1988. 10.00 (ISBN 0-87404-170-8); pap. 5.00 (ISBN 0-87404-169-4). Tex Western.
Territorial Organisation of the Soviet Economy: The Regional Aspects of Economic Development. N. Nekrasov. 286p. 1975. 16.95 (ISBN 0-8464-0912-7). Beekman Pubs.
Territorial Papers of the United States, 26 vols. in 25. Ed. by Clarence E. Carter. LC 76-38840. Repr. of 1962 ed. Set. lib. bdg. 3465.00 (ISBN 0-404-01450-X); lib. bdg. 138.60 ea. AMS Pr.
Territorial Power Domains, Southeast Asia, & China: The Geo-Strategy of an Overarching Massif. Lim Joo-Jock. 252p. 1985. text ed. 28.50x (ISBN 9-971902-85-0, Pub. by Inst Southeast Asian Stud). Gower Pub Co.
Territorial Rights. Muriel Spark. 248p. 1984. pap. 6.95 (ISBN 0-399-50930-5, Wideview). Putnam Pub Group.
Territorial Subdivisions & Boundaries of the Wampanoag, Massachusett, & Nauset Indians. Frank G. Speck. LC 76-43847. (MAI. Indian Notes & Monographs. Miscellaneous: No. 44). Repr. of 1928 ed. 15.00 (ISBN 0-404-15701-7). AMS Pr.
Territorial Trademark Rights & the Antitrust Laws. Richard F. Dole, Jr. LC 66-63307. (Michigan Legal Publications). vi, 150p. 1985. Repr. of 1965 ed. lib. bdg. 35.00 (ISBN 0-89941-381-1). W S Hein.
Territorial Use Rights & Economic Efficiency: The Case of the Philippine Fishing Concessions. Ian R. Smith & Theodore Panayotou. (Fisheries Technical Papers: No. 245). 17p. 1985. pap. 7.50 (ISBN 92-5-102137-6, F2710, FAO). UNIPUB.
Territorial Use Rights in Marine Fisheries: Definitions & Conditions. Francis T. Christy, Jr. (Fisheries Technical Papers: No. 227). 16p. (Eng., Fr. & Span.). 1982. pap. 7.50 (ISBN 92-5-101269-5, F2371, FAO). UNIPUB.
Territories. Kathleen Thompson. (Portrait of America Ser.). (gr. 4 up). 1988. tchr.' study guide 11.93 (ISBN 0-86514-617-9); Beta video 113.33 (ISBN 0-86514-110-X); VHS video 113.33 (ISBN 0-86514-111-8); 3 quarter inch video 136.00 (ISBN 0-86514-112-6). Raintree Pubs.
Territory. O. Kuvayev. 390p. 1982. pap. 4.00 (ISBN 0-8285-2522-6, Pub. by Progress Pubs USSR). Imported Pubns.
Territory Ahead. Wright Morris. LC 77-27989. xvi, 245p. 1978. 21.00x (ISBN 0-8032-3050-8); pap. 5.50 (ISBN 0-8032-8100-5, BB 666, Bison). U of Nebr Pr.
Territory & Function. John Friedmann & Clyde Weaver. 1979. 45.00x (ISBN 0-520-03928-9); pap. 10.95x (ISBN 0-520-04105-4). U of Cal Pr.
Territory in Bird Life. Eliot Howard. LC 64-20247. 1964. pap. 1.75 (ISBN 0-689-70100-4, 62). Atheneum.
Territory in Bird Life. Henry E. Howard. Ed. by Keir B. Sterling. LC 77-84443. (Biologists & Their World Ser.). (Illus.). 1978. Repr. of 1920 ed. lib. bdg. 25.50x (ISBN 0-405-10696-3). Ayer Co Pubs.
Territory Northwest of the River Ohio, 1787-1803. Ed. by Clarence E. Carter. (Territorial Papers of the United States: Vol. 3). Repr. of 1934 ed. 69.50 (ISBN 0-404-01453-4). AMS Pr.
Territory Northwest of the River Ohio, 1787-1803 see General Introduction to the Series.
Territory of Alabama, 1817-1819. Ed. by Clarence E. Carter. (Territorial Papers of the United States: Vol. 18). Repr. of 1952 ed. 69.50 (ISBN 0-404-01468-2). AMS Pr.
Territory of Arkansas, 1819-1825. Ed. by Clarence E. Carter. (Territorial Papers of the United States: Vol. 19). Repr. of 1953 ed. 69.50 (ISBN 0-404-01469-0). AMS Pr.
Territory of Arkansas, 1825-1829. Ed. by Clarence E. Carter. (Territorial Papers of the United States: Vol. 20). Repr. of 1954 ed. 69.50 (ISBN 0-404-01470-4). AMS Pr.
Territory of Arkansas, 1829-1836. Ed. by Clarence E. Carter. (Territorial Papers of the United States: Vol. 21). Repr. of 1954 ed. 69.50 (ISBN 0-404-01471-2). AMS Pr.
Territory of Florida, 1821-1825. Ed. by Clarence E. Carter. (Territorial Papers of the United States: Vol. 22). Repr. of 1956 ed. 69.50 (ISBN 0-404-01472-0). AMS Pr.
Territory of Florida, 1824-1828. Ed. by Clarence E. Carter. (Territorial Papers of the United States: Vol. 23). Repr. of 1958 ed. 69.50 (ISBN 0-404-01473-9). AMS Pr.
Territory of Florida, 1828-1834. Ed. by Clarence E. Carter. (Territorial Papers of the United States: Vol. 24). Repr. of 1959 ed. 69.50 (ISBN 0-404-01474-7). AMS Pr.
Territory of Florida, 1834-1839. Ed. by Clarence E. Carter. (Territorial Papers of the United States: Vol. 25). Repr. of 1960 ed. 69.50 (ISBN 0-404-01475-5). AMS Pr.
Territory of Florida, 1839-1845. Ed. by Clarence E. Carter. (Territorial Papers of the United States: Vol. 26). Repr. of 1962 ed. 69.50 (ISBN 0-404-01476-3). AMS Pr.
Territory of Illinois, 1809-1814. Ed. by Clarence E. Carter. (Territorial Papers of the United States: Vol. 16). Repr. of 1948 ed. 69.50 (ISBN 0-404-01466-6). AMS Pr.
Territory of Illinois, 1814-1818. Ed. by Clarence E. Carter. (Territorial Papers of the United States: Vol. 17). Repr. of 1950 ed. 69.50 (ISBN 0-404-01467-4). AMS Pr.
Territory of Indiana, 1800-1810. Ed. by Clarence E. Carter. (Territorial Papers of the United States: Vol. 7). Repr. of 1939 ed. 69.50 (ISBN 0-404-01457-7). AMS Pr.
Territory of Indiana, 1810-1816. Ed. by Clarence E. Carter. (Territorial Papers of the United States: Vol. 8). Repr. of 1939 ed. 69.50 (ISBN 0-404-01458-5). AMS Pr.
Territory of Language: Linguistics, Stylistics, & the Teaching of Composition. Ed. by Donald A. McQuade. 376p. (Orig.). 1986. text ed. 24.95x (ISBN 0-8093-1217-4); pap. text ed. 17.95x (ISBN 0-8093-1215-8). S Ill U Pr.
Territory of Louisiana-Missouri, 1803-1806. Ed. by Clarence E. Carter. (Territorial Papers of the United States: Vol. 13). Repr. of 1948 ed. 69.50 (ISBN 0-404-01463-1). AMS Pr.
Territory of Louisiana-Missouri, 1806-1814. Ed. by Clarence E. Carter. (Territorial Papers of the United States: Vol. 14). Repr. of 1949 ed. 69.50 (ISBN 0-404-01464-X). AMS Pr.
Territory of Louisiana-Missouri, 1815-1821. Ed. by Clarence E. Carter. (Territorial Papers of the United States: Vol. 15). Repr. of 1951 ed. 69.50 (ISBN 0-404-01465-8). AMS Pr.
Territory of Michigan, 1805-1820. Ed. by Clarence E. Carter. (Territorial Papers of the United States: Vol. 10). Repr. of 1942 ed. 69.50 (ISBN 0-404-01460-7). AMS Pr.
Territory of Michigan, 1805-1837. Alec R. Gilpin. 230p. 1970. 8.00 (ISBN 0-87013-155-9). Mich St U Pr.
Territory of Michigan, 1820-1829. Ed. by Clarence E. Carter. (Territorial Papers of the United States: Vol. 11). Repr. of 1943 ed. 69.50 (ISBN 0-404-01461-5). AMS Pr.
Territory of Michigan, 1829-1837. Ed. by Clarence E. Carter. (Territorial Papers of the United States: Vol. 12). Repr. of 1945 ed. 69.50 (ISBN 0-404-01462-3). AMS Pr.
Territory of Mississippi, 1798-1817. Ed. by Clarence E. Carter. (Territorial Papers of the United States: Vol. 5). Repr. of 1937 ed. 69.50 (ISBN 0-404-01455-0). AMS Pr.
Territory of Mississippi, 1809-1817. Ed. by Clarence E. Carter. (Territorial Papers of the United States: Vol. 6). Repr. of 1938 ed. 69.50 (ISBN 0-404-01456-9). AMS Pr.
Territory of Orleans, 1803-1812. Ed. by Clarence E. Carter. (Territorial Papers of the United States: Vol. 9). Repr. of 1940 ed. 69.50 (ISBN 0-404-01459-3). AMS Pr.
Territory of the Historian. Emmanuel Le Roy-Ladurie. LC 78-31362. 1979. Repr. of 1973 ed. lib. bdg. 26.00x (ISBN 0-226-47327-9). U of Chicago Pr.
Territory of the Historian. Emmanuel Le Roy-Ladurie. Tr. by Ben Reynolds & Sian Reynolds. LC 78-31362. viii, 346p. 1982. pap. 11.95 (ISBN 0-226-47328-7). U of Chicago Pr.
Territory of Washington in 1879. Francis H. Cook. Ed. by J. Orin Oliphant. 39p. 1972. pap. 3.95. Ye Galleon.
Territory South of the River Ohio, 1790-1796. Ed. by Clarence E. Carter. (Territorial Papers of the United States: Vol. 4). Repr. of 1936 ed. 69.50 (ISBN 0-404-01454-2). AMS Pr.
Terroist. Maxwell Taylor. (Illus.). 272p. 1988. 36.00 (ISBN 0-08-033603-5). Pergamon.
Terror. Frederick Pohl. 100p. 1987. pap. 2.95 (ISBN 0-425-09106-6). Berkley Pub.
Terror Alliance. Jack D. Hunter. 320p. 1984. pap. 3.50 (ISBN 0-8439-2154-4, Leisure Bks). Leisure NY.
Terror & Communist Politics: The Role of the Secret Police in Communist States. Ed. by Jonathan R. Adelman. (Special Study). 300p. 1984. 33.00x (ISBN 0-86531-293-1). Westview.
Terror & Decorum: Poems, Nineteen Forty to Nineteen Forty-Eight. Peter R. Viereck. LC 78-178796. 110p. 1973. Repr. lib. bdg. 35.00 (ISBN 0-8371-6296-3, VTDE). Greenwood.
Terror & Progress U. S. S. R. Barrington Moore, Jr. LC 54-5995. (Russian Research Center Studies: No. 12). 1954. 20.00x (ISBN 0-674-87450-1). Harvard U Pr.
Terror & Resistance: A Study of Political Violence. Eugene V. Walter. 1969. pap. 5.95 (ISBN 0-19-501562-2). Oxford U Pr.
Terror & Urban Guerillas: A Study of Tactics & Documents. Ed. by Jay Mallin. LC 79-163842. 1983. 10.95x (ISBN 0-87024-223-7). U of Miami Pr.
Terror at Play. Seth McEvoy. (Not Quite Human Ser.: No. 5). (gr. 5 up). 1987. pap. 2.50 (ISBN 0-671-62562-4). Archway.
Terror at Thor Mountain. Junita T. Osborne. (YA) (gr. 7 up). 1984. 9.95 (ISBN 0-8034-8459-3, Avalon). Bouregy.
Terror at Tolliver Hall. Juanita T. Osborne. (YA) (gr. 7 up). 1981. 9.95 (ISBN 0-686-73960-4, Avalon). Bouregy.
Terror at Twilight. Teddy Keller. 1984. pap. 1.75 (ISBN 0-912963-02-6). Eldridge Pub.
Terror by Gaslight: More Victorian Tales of Terror. Ed. by Hugh Lamb. LC 75-27980. 222p. 1976. 8.95 (ISBN 0-8008-7559-1). Taplinger.
Terror Code. Nick Carter. (Killmaster Ser.: No. 224). 208p. 1987. pap. 2.75 (ISBN 0-441-57293-6, Pub. by Charter Bks). Ace Bks.
Terror in Australia. Shannon Gillian, pseud. (Choose Your Own Adventure Ser.: No. 81). 128p. (Orig.). 1988. pap. 2.50 (ISBN 0-553-27277-2). Bantam.
Terror in Room Two-O-One. Tom Mitcheltree. (Orig.). 1980. pap. 1.75 (ISBN 0-505-51475-3, Pub. by Tower Bks). Leisure NY.
Terror in the Dark. (Phoenix Force Ser.: No. 31). Date not set. pap. 2.25 (Pub. by Worldwide). Harlequin Bks.
Terror in the Night. Bea Carlton. LC 84-72788. 1986. pap. 6.95 (ISBN 0-89636-153-5). Accent Bks.
Terror in the Skies: The Inside Story of the World's Worst Air Crashes. (Illus.). 256p. (YA) 1988. 16.95 (ISBN 0-8065-1091-9, Citadel Pr). Lyle Stuart.
Terror in the Streets. Gordon McLean. LC 77-74159. (Illus.). 192p. 1977. pap. 2.95 (ISBN 0-87123-558-7, 200558). Bethany Hse.
Terror in the Tropics: The Army Ants. Tom Lisker. LC 77-10765. (Great Unsolved Mysteries Ser.). (Illus.). 48p. (gr. 4-5). 1977. PLB 15.33 (ISBN 0-8172-1060-1). Raintree Pubs.
Terror in the Tropics: The Army Ants. Tom Lisker. LC 77-10765. (Great Unsolved Mysteries Ser.). (Illus.). 48p. (gr. 4up). 1983. pap. 9.27 (ISBN 0-8172-2168-9). Raintree Pubs.
Terror Island. Tony Koltz. (Choose Your Own Adventure Ser.: No. 59). 128p. (gr. 4). 1986. pap. 2.25 (ISBN 0-553-25885-0). Bantam.
Terror Network. Claire Sterling. 1984. pap. 3.95 (ISBN 0-425-09153-8). Berkley Pub.
Terror of Heartbreak House. Dorien K. Miles. (YA) (gr. 7 up). 1979. 9.95 (ISBN 0-686-52555-8, Avalon). Bouregy.
Terror of Tellico Plains: The Memoirs of Ray H. Jenkins. Ray H. Jenkins. LC 78-11623. (Illus.). 199p. 1978. 6.00 (ISBN 0-941199-05-3). ETHS.
Terror on Kabran. Richard Brightfield. (Escape from Tenopia Ser.: No. 3). 144p. (Orig.). 1986. pap. 2.50 (ISBN 0-553-25636-X). Bantam.
Terror on the Rebound. Elizabeth Van Steenwyk. LC 83-7313. (Sports Mysteries Ser.). (Illus.). 64p. (gr. 3-7). 1983. PLB 11.93 (ISBN 0-516-04479-6). Childrens.
Terror Out of Zion: Irgun Zvai Leumi, Lehi & the Palestine Underground, 1929-1949. J. Bowyer Bell. 1985. pap. 2.95 (ISBN 0-380-39396-4, Discus). Avon.
Terror out of Zion: The Fight for Israeli Independence 1929-1949. Rev. ed. J. Bowyer Bell. (Illus.). 400p. 1984. Repr. of 1979 ed. 17.95 (ISBN 0-906187-11-7, Pub. by Univ Pr of Ireland). Longwood Pub Group.
Terror Tales for Teenagers. David J. Gerrick. (gr. 5 up). 1979. pap. text ed. 4.95 (ISBN 0-916750-65-5). Dayton Labs.
Terror That Comes in the Night: An Experience Centered Study of Supernatural Assault Traditions. David J. Hufford. LC 82-40350. 352p. 1982. 31.95x (ISBN 0-8122-7851-8). U of Pa Pr.
Terror Times Two. Nick Carter. 1987. pap. 2.50 (ISBN 0-441-57285-5, Pub. by Charter Bks). Ace Bks.
Terror Train. Gilbert B. Cross. LC 86-17253. 128p. (gr. 3-7). 1987. 11.95 (ISBN 0-689-31323-3, Atheneum Childrens Bks). Macmillan.
Terror under the Tent. Mary Anderson. (Mostly Ghosts Ser.: No. 3). (gr. k-6). 1987. pap. 2.50 (ISBN 0-440-48633-5, YB). Dell.

Tertiary & Pleistocene Coralline Algae from Lau, Fiji. H. H. Johnson & B. J. Ferris. (BMB). 1950. pap. 10.00 (ISBN 0-527-02309-4). Kraus Repr.

Tertiary Cheilostomatous Polyzoa of New Zealand. David A. Brown. (Illus.). 406p. 1952. 47.00x (ISBN 0-565-00064-0, Pub. by Brit Mus Nat Hist England). Sabbot-Natural Hist Bks.

Tertiary College: Assuring Our Future. David Terry. 172p. 1987. 65.00 (ISBN 0-335-10286-7, Open Univ Pr); pap. 24.00 (ISBN 0-335-10285-9). Taylor & Francis.

Tertiary Entomostraca. T. R. Jones. (Illus.). 1855. pap. 10.00 (ISBN 0-384-27850-7). Johnson Repr.

Tertiary Stratigraphy of Western Washington & Northwestern Oregon. Charles E. Weaver. (Publications in Geology: No. 4). 266p. 1937. pap. 17.50x (ISBN 0-295-73962-2). U of Wash Pr.

Tertium Organum: A Key to the Enigmas of the World. P. D. Ouspensky. Tr. by P. D. Ouspensky & E. Kadloubovsky. LC 81-52264. 320p. pap. 8.95 (ISBN 0-394-75168-X, Vin). Random.

Tertulia: Conversacion, Composicion & Repaso Gramatical. William W. Cressey & Edward E. Borsoi. (Span.). 1972. P-H.

Tertullian: A Historical & Literary Study. Timothy D. Barnes. 1985. 49.95x (ISBN 0-19-814362-1). Oxford U Pr.

Tertullian, the Treatise Against Hermogenes. Ed. by W. J. Burghardt et al. LC 56-13257. (Ancient Christian Writers Ser.: No. 24). 179p. 1956. 10.95 (ISBN 0-8091-0148-3). Paulist Pr.

Tertullian, Treatise on Marriage & Remarriage: To His Wife, an Exhortation to Chastity Monogamy. Ed. by W. J. Burghardt et al. LC 78-62462. (Ancient Christian Writers Ser.: No. 13). 103p. 1951. 10.95 (ISBN 0-8091-0149-1). Paulist Pr.

Tertullian, Treatise on Penance: On Penitence & on Purity. Ed. by W. J. Burghardt et al. LC 58-10746. (Ancient Christian Writers Ser.: No. 28). 138p. 1959. 12.95 (ISBN 0-8091-0150-5). Paulist Pr.

Tertullien: Etude sur les sentiments a l'egard de l'empire et de la societe civile. Charles A. Guinebert. LC 82-45819. Date not set. Repr. of 1902 ed. 57.50 (ISBN 0-404-62386-7). AMS Pr.

Terumat Zvi. Samson R. Hirsch. 1088p. 1986. 35.00 (ISBN 0-910818-66-5). Judaica Pr.

Teryosha. A. Tolstoy. 24p. 1976. pap. 0.99 (ISBN 0-8285-1242-6, Pub. by Progress Pubs USSR). Imported Pubns.

Terytoria Ukrainy. Omelian Terlets'Kyi. (Ukrainian.). 1970. pap. text ed. 3.00 (ISBN 0-918884-27-6). Slavia Lib.

Terzaghi Lectures, Nineteen Seventy-Four to Nineteen Eighty-Two. (Geotechnical Special Publication: No. 1). 435p. 1986. 40.00x (ISBN 0-87262-532-X). Am Soc Civil Eng.

Terzaghi Lectures: 1963-1972. Karl Terzaghi. (Terzaghi Lecture Ser.: Nos. 1-9). (Illus.). pap. 107.30 (ISBN 0-317-09410-6, 2017761). Bks Demand UMI.

Terzo Libro del Corpus Tibullianum; 'Originalita e Sentimento Letterario in Claudiano"; "L Cantica di Terenzio"; 'Analisi Ritmica di Alcuni Luoghi dei Comici Latini' Various Essays. G. Baligan et al. (Studi Pubblicati Dall'Istituto di Filologia Classica (Universita di Bologna): No. 1). 132p. 1948. pap. text ed. 8.25 (ISBN 0-905205-38-3, Pub. by F Cairns). Longwood Pub Group.

Teshuvah: A Guide for the Newly Observant Jew. Adin Steinsaltz. 192p. 1987. 19.95 (ISBN 0-02-931150-0). Free Pr.

Tesla Coil Secrets. Richard A. Ford. 1985. pap. 6.95 (ISBN 0-917914-31-7). Lindsay Pubns.

Tesla: Complete Patents. Ed. by J. T. Ratzlaff. (Nikola Tesla Ser.). 1986. lib. bdg. 125.00 (ISBN 0-8490-3838-3). Gordon Pr.

Tesla Experiments with Alternate Currents. 1986. pap. 8.95 (ISBN 0-917914-39-2). Lindsay Pubns.

Tesla: Man out of Time. Margaret Cheney. (Illus.). 336p. 1983. pap. 4.95 (ISBN 0-440-39077-X, LE). Dell.

Tesla Said. John T. Ratzlaff. LC 83-72252. (Illus.). 292p. (Orig.). 1984. pap. text ed. 28.00 (ISBN 0-914119-00-1). Tesla Bk Co.

Tesla Speaks, 3 vols. Ruth E. Norman et al. Incl. Vol. 1. Scientists. 324p (ISBN 0-932642-20-9); Vol. 2. Philosophers. 451p (ISBN 0-932642-21-7); Vol. 3. Presidents (ISBN 0-932642-22-5). (Illus.). 1973. 9.95 ea. Unarius Pubns.

Teso in Transformation: Peasantry & Class in Colonial Uganda, 1890-1927. Joan Vincent. LC 80-28813. 320p. 1982. 40.00x (ISBN 0-520-04163-1). U of Cal Pr.

TESOL Techniques & Procedures. J. Donald Bowen et al. 1985. pap. text ed. 18.95 (ISBN 0-88377-291-4). Newbury Hse.

Tesoretto: The Little Treasure. Brunetto Latini. Ed. by Julia B. Holloway. LC 80-8956. (Garland Library of Medieval Literature). 1981. lib. bdg. 36.00 (ISBN 0-8240-9376-3). Garland Pub.

Tesoro de la Lengua Castellana, O Espanola. Sebastian De Covarrubias Horozco. (Span., Microphoto Reprod). 1927. 7.50 (ISBN 0-87535-020-8). Hispanic Soc.

Tesoro de los Modocs. new ed. John Benteen. Tr. by John T. Diaz from Eng. (Compadre Collection, Sundance Ser: No. 5). (Illus.). 160p. (Span.). 1975. pap. 0.95 (ISBN 0-88473-535-4). Fiesta Pub.

Tesoro de Rackham. Herge. (Illus.). 62p. (Span.). 15.95 (ISBN 0-686-54338-6). French & Eur.

Tesoro di Rakam. Herge. (Illus.). 62p. (Ital.). pap. 15.95 (ISBN 0-686-54356-4). French & Eur.

Tesoro Hispanico. 2nd ed. Robert Lado et al. 1982. text ed. 35.44 (ISBN 0-07-035756-0). McGraw.

Tesoros de la Cocina Mexicana. Hoteles Camiro Real Chefs. (Illus.). 176p. 1985. 19.95 (ISBN 0-914373-03-X). Wieser & Wieser.

Tesoros Del Firmamento. F. Ziguel. 280p. (Span.). 1973. pap. 4.95 (ISBN 0-8285-1471-2, Pub. by Mir Pubs USSR). Imported Pubns.

Tess D'Urbevilles. Thomas Hardy. (Study Texts Ser.). (YA) (gr. 7 up). Date not set. pap. 5.95. Longman Trade.

Tess Jaray: Prints & Drawings, 1964-1984. Compiled by Deana Petherbridge. (Illus.). 32p. (Orig.). pap. 20.00x (ISBN 0-907849-06-7, Pub. by Ashmolean Museum). State Mutual Bk.

Tess Jaray: Prints & Drawings, 1964-1984. Intro. by Deana Petherbridge. (Illus.). 32p. (Orig.). 1984. pap. 5.75 (ISBN 0-317-58670-X, Pub. by Ashmolean Mus). Longwood Pub Group.

Tess of the D'Urbervilles. Thomas Hardy. (Airmont Classics Ser.). (gr. 11 up). pap. 2.95 (ISBN 0-8049-0082-5, CL-82). Airmont.

Tess of the D'Urbervilles. Thomas Hardy. (Literature Ser). (gr. 7-12). 1969. pap. text ed. 7.25 (ISBN 0-87720-717-8). AMSCO Sch.

Tess of the D'Urbervilles. Thomas Hardy. (Classics Ser.). 448p. (gr. 9-12). 1984. pap. 2.95 (ISBN 0-553-21168-4, Bantam Classics). Bantam.

Tess of the D'Urbervilles. Thomas Hardy. Ed. by William E. Buckler. LC 60-707. (YA) (gr. 9 up). 1960. pap. 5.95 (ISBN 0-395-05144-4, RivEd). HM.

Tess of the D'Urbervilles. Thomas Hardy. (Modern Library College Editions Ser.). 1951. pap. 3.50 (ISBN 0-394-30946-4, T46). Random.

Tess of the D'Urbervilles. Thomas Hardy. (Movie tie-in ed.). 1981. pap. 2.95 (ISBN 0-451-51924-8, CE1686, Sig Classics). NAL.

Tess of the D'Urbervilles. 2nd ed. Thomas Hardy. Ed. by Scott Elledge. (Critical Editions). (Illus.). 1978. pap. text ed. 7.95x (ISBN 0-393-09044-2). Norton.

Tess of the D'Urbervilles. Thomas Hardy. Ed. by A. Alvarez & David Skilton. (English Library Ser). 1978. pap. 2.95 (ISBN 0-14-043135-7). Penguin.

Tess of the D'Urbervilles. Thomas Hardy. Ed. by Juliet Grindle & Simon Gatrell. 1983. 98.00x (ISBN 0-19-812495-3). Oxford U Pr.

Tess of the D'Urbervilles. Thomas Hardy. LC 51-2271. 8.95 (ISBN 0-394-60484-9). Modern Lib.

Tess of the D'Urbervilles. Thomas Hardy. 302p. 1988. pap. 4.95. Running Pr.

Tess of the D'Urbervilles. Thomas Hardy et al. Ed. by Simon Gatrell & Nancy Barrineau. (World's Classics Ser.). 456p. 1988. pap. 2.95 (ISBN 0-19-281826-0). Oxford U Pr.

Tess of the D'Urbervilles: A Pure Woman. Thomas Hardy. 448p. 1984. pap. 2.95x (ISBN 0-460-01056-5, DEL-05220, Pub. by Evman England). Biblio Dist.

Tess of the D'Urbervilles (Hardy) Berc. (Book Notes Ser.). 1984. pap. 2.50 (ISBN 0-8120-3445-7). Barron.

Tess of the D'Urbervilles Notes. Lorraine M. Force. (Orig.). 1966. pap. 3.50 (ISBN 0-8220-1273-1). Cliffs.

Tess of the D'Urbervilles With Reader's Guide. Thomas Hardy. (Amsco Literature Program). (gr. 9-12). 1972. text ed. 13.17 (ISBN 0-87720-825-5); pap. text ed. 9.42 (ISBN 0-87720-815-8); tchr's. ed. 8.33 (ISBN 0-87720-915-4). AMSCO Sch.

Tess of the D'Urbevilles. Thomas Hardy. (Study Texts Ser.). 1988. pap. 5.95 (ISBN 0-582-01978-8). Longman.

Tess of the D'Uvbervilles. Terence Wright. LC 86-10261. (Critics Debate Ser.). 1987. text ed. 22.50 (ISBN 0-391-03450-2); pap. text ed. 7.95 (ISBN 0-391-03451-0). Humanities.

Tess: The Extended Simulation Support System. Charles R. Standridge & A. A. B. Pritsker. LC 87-29469. 368p. 1987. pap. 34.95 (ISBN 0-470-20876-7, Pub. by Halsted Press). Wiley.

Tessa. Jean Giraudoux. pap. 9.95 (ISBN 0-685-33931-9). French & Eur.

Tessa. Barbara Steiner. LC 87-31524. 224p. (gr. 7 up). 1988. 11.95 (ISBN 0-688-07232-1). Morrow.

Tessa see Theatre.

Tessarae: A Mosaic of Twentieth Century Brazilian Poetry. Charles R. Carlisle. 1983. pap. 8.00 (ISBN 0-317-60614-X). Latitudes Pr.

Tesse, Are You Really a Cat? D. C. Harrold. (Illus.). 102p. 1986. 19.95 (ISBN 0-317-64554-4). Tesse Enter.

Tesselator: An Interactive Tesselation Design Program. A. Hallam. 1984. 75.00x (ISBN 0-201-14434-4, Pub. by Addison-Wesley Pubs Ltd). State Mutual Bk.

Tessellations File. Chris De Cordova. 32p. (Orig.). 1986. pap. 4.25 (ISBN 0-906212-35-9, Pub. by Tarquin). Parkwest Pubns.

Tesseract. Joseph Addison. 1988. pap. 3.50 (ISBN 0-345-34744-7, Del Rey). Ballantine.

Test. Pierre Boulle. LC 57-12252. 12.95 (ISBN 0-8149-0069-0). Vanguard.

Test. Shahar Yonay & Rina Yonay. (gr. 7-12). 1988. 14.95 (ISBN 0-9616783-4-8). S Yonay.

Test see Holocaust: A History of Courage & Resistance.

Test see Ten Top Stories.

Test & Measurement. Paul W. Cates. 30.00 (ISBN 0-686-22193-1). Freedom Univ-FSP.

Test & Measurement Instrumentation Industry: Yearbook of Market Information 1985. Market Intelligence Research Company Staff. 377p. 1985. pap. text ed. 695.00 (ISBN 0-317-19568-9). Market Res Co.

Test & Protest: The Influence of Consumers Union. Norman I. Silber. (Illus.). 172p. 1983. 34.50 (ISBN 0-8419-0749-8); pap. 16.75x (ISBN 0-8419-0877-X). Holmes & Meier.

Test-Answers for FCC General Radio-Telephone Operator License. 12th ed. Ed. by Warren Weagant. 192p. 1987. pap. write for info. Command Prods.

Test Anxiety: Theory, Research, & Applications. Ed. by Irwin G. Sarason. LC 79-28344. (Illus.). 432p. 1980. text ed. 45.00x (ISBN 0-89859-022-1). L Erlbaum Assocs.

Test Bank for an American Portrait. 2nd ed. David Burner et al. 96p. 1985. write for info (ISBN 0-02-371290-2). Macmillan.

Test Bank for College Algebra. 2nd ed. Bernard Kolman & Arnold Shapiro. 1985. text ed. 10.00 (ISBN 0-12-417899-5). Acad Pr.

Test Bank to Accompany General Chemistry. Robert Balahura. Ed. by LC LW & GLH. 214p. 1984. W H Freeman.

Test Buster Pep Rally. Robert P. Bowman. Ed. by Don L. Sorenson. Tr. by Merle. 180p. 3-ring 79.95 (ISBN 0-932796-21-4). Ed Media Corp.

Test Chart for Rotary Microfilm Cameras: ANSI-AIIM MS17-1983. Association for Information & Image Management Staff. (Standards & Recommended Practices Ser.). 10p. 1983. pap. 30.00 (ISBN 0-317-06197-6, M017). Assn Inform & Image Mgmt.

Test Construction: A Bibliography of Selected Resources. Nancy P. O'Brien. LC 87-25119. 320p. 1988. lib. bdg. 39.95 (ISBN 0-313-23435-3, CTC/). Greenwood.

Test Construction: Development & Interpretation of Achievement Tests. 2nd ed. Dorothy C. Adkins. 1974. pap. 14.95 (ISBN 0-675-08845-3). Merrill.

Test Critiques, Vol. I. Ed. by Daniel J. Keyser & Richard C. Sweetland. LC 84-26895. (Illus.). 800p. 1985. 85.00x (ISBN 0-9611286-6-6, Test Corp America). Westport Pubs.

Test Critiques, Vol. II. Ed. by Daniel J. Keyser & Richard C. Sweetland. LC 84-26895. (Illus.). 872p. 1985. 85.00x (ISBN 0-9611286-7-4, Test Corp America). Westport Pubs.

Test Critiques, Vol. III. Ed. by Daniel J. Keyser & Richard C. Sweetland. LC 84-26895. (Illus.). 784p. 1985. 85.00x (ISBN 0-9611286-8-2, Test Corp America). Westport Pubs.

Test Critiques, Vol. IV. Ed. by Daniel J. Keyser & Richard C. Sweetland. LC 84-26895. (Illus.). 768p. 1986. 85.00x (ISBN 0-933701-02-0, Test Corp America). Westport Pubs.

Test Critiques, Vol. V. Ed. by Daniel J. Keyser & Richard C. Sweetland. LC 84-26895. (Illus.). 624p. 1987. 85.00x (ISBN 0-933701-04-7, Test Corp America). Westport Pubs.

Test Critiques, Vol. VI. Ed. by Daniel J. Keyser & Richard C. Sweetland. LC 84-26895. (Illus.). 800p. 1987. 85.00x (ISBN 0-933701-10-1, Test Corp America). Westport Pubs.

Test Critiques, Vol. I. Ed. by Daniel J. Keyser & Richard C. Sweetland. LC 84-26895. (Illus.). 800p. 1987. pap. text ed. 30.00 (ISBN 0-933701-14-4, Test Corp America). Westport Pubs.

Test Critiques, Vol. II. Ed. by Daniel J. Keyser & Richard C. Sweetland. LC 84-26895. (Illus.). 872p. 1987. pap. text ed. 30.00 (ISBN 0-933701-15-2, Test Corp America). Westport Pubs.

Test Critiques, Vol. III. Ed. by Daniel J. Keyser & Richard C. Sweetland. (Illus.). 784p. 1987. pap. text ed. 30.00 (ISBN 0-933701-16-0, Test Corp America). Westport Pubs.

Test Critiques, Vol. IV. Ed. by Daniel J. Keyser & Richard C. Sweetland. LC 84-26895. (Illus.). 768p. 1987. pap. text ed. 30.00 (ISBN 0-933701-17-9, Test Corp America). Westport Pubs.

Test Critiques, Vol. V. Ed. by Daniel J. Keyser & Richard C. Sweetland. LC 84-26895. (Illus.). 624p. 1987. pap. text ed. 30.00 (ISBN 0-933701-18-7, Test Corp America). Westport Pubs.

Test Critiques, Vol. VI. Ed. by Daniel J. Keyser & Richard C. Sweetland. LC 84-26895. (Illus.). 800p. 1987. pap. text ed. 30.00 (ISBN 0-933701-19-5, Test Corp America). Westport Pubs.

Test Critiques Compendium: Reviews of Major Tests from the Test Critiques Series. Ed. by Daniel J. Keyser & Richard C. Sweetland. LC 87-10247. (Illus.). 640p. (Orig.). 1987. text ed. 49.00x (ISBN 0-933701-08-X, Test Corp America); pap. text ed. 29.00x (ISBN 0-933701-09-8, Test Corp America). Westport Pubs.

Test Critiques: Softcover Set. Ed. by Daniel J. Keyser & Richard C. Sweetland. LC 84-25895. (Illus.). 1987. pap. text ed. write for info. (ISBN 0-933701-13-6, Test Corp America). Westport Pubs.

Test Data Analysis: To Improve Student Learning & Board Support, Vol. 5. Fredric H. Genck. (School Management Model Ser.). 90p. (Orig.). 1984. pap. 38.00 (ISBN 0-318-04005-0). Inst Pub Mgmt.

Test des Composants - Component Testing. Network Staff. 1984. 95.00x (ISBN 0-907634-41-9, Pub. by Network Events Ltd). State Mutual Bk.

Test des Systemes - Systems Testing. Network Staff. 1984. 95.00x (ISBN 0-907634-44-3, Pub. by Network Events Ltd). State Mutual Bk.

Test Design: Contributions from Psychology & Psychometrics. Susan Embretson. 1985. 33.00 (ISBN 0-12-238180-7). Acad Pr.

Test Design Handbook. Carol Copperud. LC 79-361. (Illus.). 168p. 1979. 33.95 (ISBN 0-87778-136-2). Educ Tech Pubns.

Test Equating. Ed. by Paul Holland. 1982. 62.50 (ISBN 0-12-352520-9). Acad Pr.

Test Examples for Nonlinear Programming Codes. W. Hock & K. Schittkowski. (Lecture Notes in Economics & Mathematical Systems Ser.: Vol. 187). 177p. 1981. pap. 17.00 (ISBN 0-387-10561-1). Springer-Verlag.

Test Excavations in the Mangum Reservoir Area of Southwestern Oklahoma. Frank C. Leonhardy. (Contributions of the Museum of the Great Plains Ser.: No. 2). (Illus.). 1966. 2.50 (ISBN 0-685-85507-4). Mus Great Plains.

Test for Examining Expressive Morphology. Kenneth G. Shipley & Terry A. Stone. 36p. 1983. pap. 24.95 (ISBN 0-88450-847-1, 4644-B). Communication Skill.

Test for Homoscedasticity: The B-H Critical Values. V. Shvyrkov & A. C. Davis, III. LC 84-50865. (Illus.). 83p. (Orig.). 1984. text ed. 21.19 (ISBN 0-942004-10-8). Throwkoff Pr.

Test Images for Printing: An International Reference for Print Standardization, Quality Control, & Troubleshooting. 2 ed. George W. Jorgensen. LC 84-81307. (Illus.). 210p. 1984. 104.00 (ISBN 0-88362-071-5, 1514). Graphic Arts Tech Found.

Test Item Construction in the Cognitive Domain. K. B. Green. 1979. 2.00 (ISBN 0-911365-15-X, A261-08442). Home Econ Educ.

Test Item File see Business.

Test Items in Education. G. J. Mouly. 1962. pap. text ed. 7.95 (ISBN 0-07-043540-5). McGraw.

Test Lessons in Primary Reading. 2nd ed. William A. McCall & Mary L. Harby. 1980. pap. text ed. 3.50x (ISBN 0-8077-5965-1); manual 1.25x (ISBN 0-8077-5966-X). Tchrs Coll.

Test Lessons in Reading Figurative Language. William A. McCall et al. (gr. 9-12). 1980. pap. text ed. 6.00x (ISBN 0-8077-5970-8); manual 1.75x (ISBN 0-8077-5971-6). Tchrs Coll.

Test Match Career of Geoffrey Boycott. C. D. Clark. 176p. 1986. 65.00x (ISBN 0-946771-07-3, Pub. by Spellmount Ltd Pubs). State Mutual Bk.

Test Methods & Design Allowables for Fibrous Composites - STP 734. Ed. by C. Chamis. 429p. 1981. 44.00 (ISBN 0-8031-0700-5, 04-734000-33). ASTM.

Test Methods for Vertebrate Pest Control & Management Materials - STP 625. Ed. by W. B. Jackson & R. E. Marsh. 256p. 1977. 26.00 (04-625000-48). ASTM.

Test Methods, Specifications, & Standards. National Academy of Sciences. LC 77-79218. (Fire Safety Aspects of Polymeric Materials Ser.: Vol. 2). 99p. 1979. 18.00 (ISBN 0-87762-223-X). Technomic.

Test: Numbers 1-35. Nov. 6, 1756-July 9, 1757, 2 vols. in 1. Bd. with Con-Test: Numbers 1-38. Nov. 23, 1756-Aug. 6, 1757. LC 73-176144. Repr. 70.00 (ISBN 0-686-76933-3). AMS Pr.

Test of a Tenderfoot. Date not set. price not set (ISBN 0-914565-35-4). Capstan Pubns.

Test of Auditory Comprehension. Los Angeles County Schools. (Auditory Skills Instructional Planning System Ser.: 2nd Component). (Illus.). 330p. 1981. easel-case 75.00x (ISBN 0-943292-08-5). Foreworks.

Test of Battle: The American Expeditionary Forces in the Meuse-Argonne Campaign. Paul Braim. LC 85-40991. (Illus.). 240p. 1987. 34.50 (ISBN 0-87413-301-7). U Delaware Pr.

Test of Components & Microprocessors. Ed. by Network Staff. 1982. 95.00x (ISBN 0-904999-36-X, Pub. by Network Events Ltd). State Mutual Bk.

Test of Courage & All Things Come of Age. Liam O'Flaherty. (Illus.). 48p. (ps-5). 1984. write for info. (ISBN 0-86327-048-4, Pub. by Wolfhound Pr Ireland); pap. 4.95 (ISBN 0-86327-044-1). Irish Bks Media.

Test of English As a Foreign Language. 4th ed. Babin et al. 384p. 1987. pap. 8.95 (ISBN 0-13-924515-4). Arco.

Test of English As a Foreign Language (TOEFL) rev. ed. Edward C. Gruber. (Exam Preparation Ser.). 528p. (gr. 12). 1981. pap. text ed. 7.95 (ISBN 0-671-18987-5). Monarch Pr.

Test of English As a Foreign Language (TOEFL) Jack Rudman. (Admission Test Ser.: ATS-30). 29.95 (ISBN 0-8373-5130-8); pap. 17.95 (ISBN 0-8373-5030-1). Natl Learning.

Test of Fire. Ben Bova. 320p. 2.95 (ISBN 0-8125-3208-2, Dist. by Warner Pub. Services & Saint Martin's Press). Tor Bks.

Test of General Educational Development (GED) Jack Rudman. (Admission Test Ser.: ATS-61). 25.95 (ISBN 0-8373-5161-8); pap. 13.95 (ISBN 0-8373-5061-1). Natl Learning.

Testaments of Love: A Study of Love in the Bible. Leon Morris. (Orig.). 1981. 13.95 (ISBN 0-8028-3502-3). Eerdmans.
Testaments of the Twelve Patriarchs: A Critical History of Research. H. Dixon Slingerland. LC 75-34233. (Society of Biblical Literature. Monograph). 1977. 13.50 (060021); pap. 9.95 (ISBN 0-89130-062-7). Scholars Pr GA.
Testaments of the Twelve Patriarchs: A Study of Their Text, Composition, & Origin. M. De Jonge. 184p. 1976. pap. text ed. 29.50x (ISBN 90-232-1339-4, Pub. by Van Gorcum Holland). Coronet Bks.
Teste Dein Deutsch! Stufe 1. Marianne Zingel. 175p. pap. 6.95 (ISBN 3-468-38525-0). Langenscheidt.
Teste Dein Deutsch! Stufe 2. Marianne Zingel. 191p. pap. 6.95. Langenscheidt.
Teste Dein Wirtschaftsdeutsch. Charlotte Lissok. 112p. (Ger.). 1973. pap. 6.95 (ISBN 3-468-38527-7). Langenscheidt.
Tested Advertising Methods. 4th ed. John Caples. 318p. 1974. 14.95 (ISBN 0-13-906909-7, Busn); pap. 8.95 (ISBN 0-13-906891-0). P-H.
Tested by Temptation. W. Graham Scroggie. LC 79-2559. (W. Graham Scroggie Library). 76p. 1980. pap. 4.50 (ISBN 0-8254-3732-6). Kregel.
Tested Demonstrations in Chemistry. 6th ed. Journal of Chemical Education. Ed. by Hubert N. Alyea & Frederic B. Dutton. LC 65-22683. pap. 59.30 (ISBN 0-317-42018-6, 2025968). Bks Demand UMI.
Tested Electronic Troubleshooting Methods. 2nd ed. Walter H. Buchsbaum. LC 82-13167. 272p. 1982. 24.95 (ISBN 0-13-906966-6). P-H.
Tested Electronic Troubleshooting Methods. 2nd ed. Walter H. Buchsbaum. (Illus.). 272p. 1987. pap. 12.95 (ISBN 0-13-906942-9, Busn). P-H.
Tested Practices: Organizing a School Counseling Program - the Priority: Career Counseling Program. James Wiggins. (NVGA Bk.). 80p. 1974. pap. 3.60 nonmembers (ISBN 0-911547-76-2, 72208W34); pap. 2.75 members. Am Assn Coun Dev.
Tested Studies for Laboratory Teaching: Proceedings of the First Workshop of the Association for Biology Laboratory Education. Ed. by Jon C. Glase. LC 80-82832. 288p. 1980. text ed. 19.95 (ISBN 0-8403-2271-2). Kendall-Hunt.
Tested Studies for Laboratory Teaching: Proceedings of the Fourth Workshop Conference. Able Harris. 144p. 1984. text ed. 20.95 (ISBN 0-8403-3296-3). Kendall-Hunt.
Tested Studies for Laboratory Teaching: Proceedings of the Second Workshop-Conference of the Association of Biology-Laboratory Education (ABLE) Jon C. Glase. LC 81-81747. 288p. 1981. text ed. 20.95 (ISBN 0-8403-2471-5). Kendall-Hunt.
Tested Studies for Laboratory Teaching: Proceedings of the Third Workshop-Conference of Association for Biology Laboratory Education. Association for Biology Laboratory Education Staff. 240p. 1984. text ed. 20.95 (ISBN 0-8403-3178-9). Kendall-Hunt.
Tested Ways to Successful Fund Raising. George A. Brakeley. LC 79-54828. pap. 46.30 (ISBN 0-317-27059-1, 2023544). Bks Demand UMI.
Tested Ways to Successful Fund Raising. George A. Brakeley, Jr. 1982. pap. 8.95 (ISBN 0-8144-7568-X). AMACOM.
Tested Ways to Successful Fund Raising. George A. Brakely, Jr. 1981. pap. 19.95 (ISBN 0-686-31961-3). Public Serv Materials.
Testfact 2. Douglas T. Wilson & Robert Wood. write for info. (ISBN 0-89498-018-1). Sci Ware.
Testicular & Epididymal Pathology. Manuel Nistal & Ricardo Paniagua. (Illus.). 368p. 1984. text ed. 57.00 (ISBN 0-86577-112-X). Thieme Med Pubs.
Testicular Cancer. Saad Khoury et al. LC 85-19915. (Progress in Clinical & Biological Research Ser.: Vol. 203). 776p. 1985. 98.00 (ISBN 0-8451-5053-7). A R Liss.
Testicular Cancer & Other Tumors of the Genitourinary Tract. Ed. by M. Pavone-Macaluso et al. LC 84-26493. (Ettore Majorana International Sciences Ser.: Life Sciences: Vol. 18). 550p. 1985. 105.00x (ISBN 0-306-41906-8, Plenum Pr). Plenum Pub.
Testicular Development: Structure & Function. Ed. by Anna Steinberger & Emil Steinberger. 556p. 1980. text ed. 100.50 (ISBN 0-89004-397-3). Raven.
Testifying in Court. 2nd ed. Jack E. Horsley & John Carlova. LC 83-863. 154p. 1983. casebound 29.50 (ISBN 0-87489-315-1). Med Economics.
Testifying in Court: A Guide for Physicians. 3rd ed. Jack E. Horsley & John Carlova. 200p. 1988. 31.95 (ISBN 0-87489-455-7). Med Economics.
Testigo de la Esperanza. Francisco Matos-Paoli. (UPREX, Poesia: No. 29). pap. 1.85 (ISBN 0-8477-0029-1). U of PR Pr.
Testigos de Jehova. updated ed. Walter Martin. 144p. 1988. 3.95 (ISBN 0-88113-285-3). Edit Betania.
Testigos de Jehova. M. W. Nelson. 130p. 1984. pap. 2.95 (ISBN 0-311-06352-7). Casa Bautista.
Testimonial Privileges. Scott N. Stone & Ronald S. Liebman. 684p. 1983. 85.00 (ISBN 0-317-38897-5). Shepards-McGraw.
Testimonie of Antique. Abbot Aelfric. LC 73-36208. (English Experience Ser.: No. 214). Repr. of 1567 ed. 35.00 (ISBN 90-221-0214-9). Walter J Johnson.
Testimonies: A Collection of Lesbian Coming Out Stories. Ed. by Sarah Holmes. 200p. (Orig.). 1988. pap. 7.95 (ISBN 1-55583-142-7). Alyson Pubns.
Testimonies Concerning Slavery. Moncure D. Conway. LC 77-82187. (Anti-Slavery Crusade in America Ser). 1969. Repr. of 1865 ed. 13.00 (ISBN 0-405-00625-X). Ayer Co Pubs.
Testimonies for the Church, 9 vols. Ellen G. White. 1948. 8.95 ea. (ISBN 0-8163-0152-2); Set. 79.95 (ISBN 0-8163-0153-0, 20140-0). Pacific Pr Pub Assn.
Testimonies in the Life, Character, Revelations, & Doctrines of Mother Ann Lee. 2nd ed. Shakers. LC 72-2994. Repr. of 1888 ed. 32.50 (ISBN 0-404-10756-7). AMS Pr.
Testimonies to Ministers. Ellen G. White. 10.95 (ISBN 0-317-28268-9). Pacific pr Pub Assn.
Testimonios de una Gestion Universitaria. Arturo Morales-Carrion. LC 77-11056. (Illus.). 1978. pap. 3.75 (ISBN 0-8477-2740-8). U of PR Pr.
Testimony. Adriana Dardan. 1986. 13.95 (ISBN 0-533-06599-2). Vantage.
Testimony. Jean R. Matthew. LC 86-16126. 80p. 1987. pap. 7.95 (ISBN 0-8262-0623-9, 83-36315). U of Mo Pr.
Testimony: An Introduction to Christian Doctrine. Morton H. Smith. (Orig.). 1986. pap. text ed. 5.95 (ISBN 0-934688-25-7); leader's guide 3.95 (ISBN 0-934688-26-5). Great Comm Pubns.
Testimony & Demeanor: Stories. John Casey. (Shoreline Bks.). 1986. pap. 6.95 (ISBN 0-393-30393-4). Norton.
Testimony Before the Joint Commission to Consider the Present Organizations of the Signal Service, Geological Survey, Coast & Geodetic Survey, & the Hydrographic Office of the Navy Department: With a View to Secure Greater Efficiency & Economy of Administration of the Public in Said Bureaus, 2 vols. U. S. Senate (49th Congress, 1st Session, Mis. Doc. No. 82) Ed. by I. Bernard Cohen. LC 79-7946. (Three Centuries of Science in America Ser.). 1980. Repr. of 1866 ed. Set. lib. bdg. 98.00x (ISBN 0-405-12527-5). Ayer Co Pubs.
Testimony Before the Joint Commission to Consider the Present Organizations of the Signal Service, Geological Survey, Coast & Geodetic Survey, & the Hydrographic Office of the Navy Department: With a View to Secure Greater Efficiency, Vol. 1. United States Commission to Consider the Present, Organizations of the Signal Service, Geological Survey, Coast, & Geodetic Survey, & Hydrographic Office. 49.00 (ISBN 0-405-12518-6). Ayer Co Pubs.
Testimony: Death of a Guatemalan Village. Victor Montejo. Tr. by Victor Perera. LC 86-7163. 144p. 1987. 16.95 (ISBN 0-915306-61-1); pap. 8.95 (ISBN 0-915306-65-4). Curbstone.
Testimony in Stone. J. Bernard Nicklin. 1961. 6.00 (ISBN 0-685-08818-9). Destiny.
Testimony: Memoirs of Dmitri Shostakovich. Ed. by Solomon Volkov. Tr. by Antonia W. Bouis from Rus. LC 84-4399. (Illus.). 336p. 1984. pap. 9.95 (ISBN 0-87910-021-4). Limelight Edns.
Testimony of God. Watchman Nee. Tr. by Stephen Kaung. 1979. pap. 2.75 (ISBN 0-935008-44-6). Christian Fellow Pubs.
Testimony of God Against Slavery, or a Collection of Passages from the Bible, Which Show the Sin Holding Property in Man. La Roy Sunderland. LC 73-92444. 1970. Repr. of 1835 ed. 17.00x (ISBN 0-403-03707-7, 403-00183-8). Scholarly.
Testimony of Justin Martyr to Early Christianity. George T. Purves. 1977. lib. bdg. 59.95 (ISBN 0-8490-2735-7). Gordon Pr.
Testimony of Leon Fraser on the Bretton Woods Agreement Act. Leon Fraser. LC 84-80692. 84p. pap. 8.00 (ISBN 0-87034-073-5). Fraser Pub Co.
Testimony of Richard V. Secord, Joint Hearings, May 5-8, 1987. 701p. 1987. pap. 19.00 (S/N 052-070-06331-9). USGPO.
Testimony of Teeth: Forensic Aspects of Human Dentition. Spencer L. Rogers. (Illus.). 134p. 1988. text ed. 27.50x (ISBN 0-398-05450-9). C C Thomas.
Testimony of the Rocks: Or, Geology in Its Bearings on Two Theologies, Natural & Revealed. Hugh Miller. Ed. by Stephen J. Gould. LC 79-8336. (History of Paleontology Ser.). (Illus.). 1980. Repr. of 1857 ed. lib. bdg. 42.00x (ISBN 0-405-12720-0). Ayer Co Pubs.
Testimony of Two. Mary Youmans & Roger Youmans. pap. 7.95 (ISBN 0-910924-91-0). Macalester.
Testimony of Two Men. Taylor Caldwell. 704p. 1984. pap. 3.95 (ISBN 0-449-20572-X, Crest). Fawcett.
Testimony of Two Men. Taylor Caldwell. 24.95 (ISBN 0-88411-171-7, Pub. by Aeonian Pr). Amereon Ltd.
Testimony: Selected Poems, Nineteen Fifty-Four to Nineteen Eighty-Six. Hans Juergesen. Date not set. pap. price not set. U Presses Fla.
Testimony, the United States 1885-1890, Recitative. Charles Reznikoff. LC 65-15675. 1965. 3.75 (ISBN 0-685-79043-6); sewn in wrappers 1.95 (ISBN 0-685-79044-4). Small Pr Dist.
Testimony: The United States, 1885-1915, Vol. 1. Charles Reznikoff. Ed. by Seamus Cooney. LC 78-7618. 250p. 1978. 20.00 (ISBN 0-87685-322-X); pap. 7.50 (ISBN 0-87685-321-1). Black Sparrow.
Testimony: The United States, 1885-1915, Vol. 2. Charles Reznikoff. Ed. by Seamus Cooney. LC 78-7618. 250p. 1979. 20.00 (ISBN 0-87685-333-5); pap. 7.50 (ISBN 0-87685-332-7). Black Sparrow.
Testimony to Hilaire Belloc. Eleanor Jebb & Reginald Jebb. 1956. 25.00 (ISBN 0-8274-3587-8). R West.
Testimony to Music. Music Eudcators National Conference Staff. 136p. 1986. 18.50 (ISBN 0-317-60252-7, 1049A). Music Ed Natl.
Testing, Vol. I. Ed. by Shirley C. Seal. (Fluid Power Standards 1987 Ser.). (Illus.). 404p. 1987. 120.00 (ISBN 0-942220-90-0). Natl Fluid Power.
Testing Active & Passive Electronic Components. Powell. (Electrical Engineering Ser.). 232p. 1987. 55.00 (ISBN 0-8247-7705-0). Dekker.
Testing Adolescents: A Reference Guide for Comprehensive Psychological Assessments. Ed. by Robert G. Harrington. LC 87-1938. (Illus.). 464p. 1987. 40.00x (ISBN 0-933701-01-2, Test Corp America). Westport Pubs.
Testing Adults: A Reference Guide for Special Psychodiagnostic Assessments. Ed. by Dennis P. Swiercinsky. LC 85-17341. (Illus.). 288p. 1985. 40.00x (ISBN 0-9611286-9-0, Test Corp America). Westport Pubs.
Testing & Characterization of Powders & Fire Particles. Ed. by J. K. Beddow & T. P. Meloy. (Powder Advisory Centre Publication Ser. (POWTECH)). 176p. 1979. 75.00 (ISBN 0-471-25602-1, Wiley Heyden). Wiley.
Testing & Completing. 2nd ed. Ed. by Mark Longley. (Rotary Drilling Ser.: Unit II, Lesson 5). (Illus.). 72p. 1983. pap. text ed. 6.95 (ISBN 0-88698-120-4, 2.20520). PETEX.
Testing & Control in the Wool Industry. Ed. by Wira Staff. 1955. 60.00x (ISBN 0-317-43609-0, Pub. by Wira Tech Group). State MutuaL Bk.
Testing & Ethnic Minority Students: An Annotated Bibliography. James A. Vasquez et al. 34p. 1981. 3.90 (ISBN 0-317-15115-0). Natl Clearinghse Bilingual Ed.
Testing & Evaluation: New Views. 2nd, 1980 ed. Ed. by Monroe D. Cohen. LC 74-34211. 64p. 1980. Repr. of 1975 ed. 4.55 (ISBN 0-87173-000-6). ACEI.
Testing & Evaluation of Solidified High-Level Radioactive Waste. Ed. by A. R. Hall. 1987. pap. text ed. 88.00 (ISBN 0-86010-893-7, Pub. by Graham & Trotman UK). Kluwer Academic.
Testing & Inspection & Listed Product Manual. HPMA. 159p. 1987. 5.00 (ISBN 0-318-18921-6). Hardwd Ply.
Testing & Maintenance of Complex Systems. Ed. by Network Staff. 1982. 69.00x (ISBN 0-904999-43-2, Pub. by Network Events Ltd). State Mutual Bk.
Testing & Measurement in the Classroom. Dale P. Scannell & Dick Tracy. 1975. pap. text ed. 23.16 (ISBN 0-395-18608-0). HM.
Testing & Monitoring of Off-Gas Clean-up Systems at Nuclear Facilities. (Technical Reports Ser.: No. 243). 66p. 1985. pap. 15.50 (ISBN 92-0-125284-6, IDC243, IAEA). UNIPUB.
Testing & Quality Control: The Lodz Textile Seminars. (Training for Industry Ser.). pap. 2.00 (ISBN 92-1-106040-0, E.70.II.B.6/VOL.7). UN.
Testing & Servicing Microprocessors. Dean L. Smith. (Illus.). 325p. (Orig.). 1983. pap. text ed. 35.00x (ISBN 0-918699-04-5). D L Smith.
Testing & Teaching for Oral Proficiency. Lisken-Gasparro. 171p. 1987. pap. text ed. 12.50 (ISBN 0-8384-1505-9). Heinle & Heinle.
Testing & Test Methods of Fibre Cement Composites: RILEM Symposium held April 5-7, 1978. RILEM International Symposium. Ed. by R. N. Swamy. (Illus.). pap. 138.80 (ISBN 0-317-08289-2, 2019629). Bks Demand UMI.
Testing & Test Modification in Vocational Evaluation. Karl F. Botterbusch & Nancy Michaels. 170p. (Orig.). 1985. pap. 16.50x (ISBN 0-916671-54-2). Material Dev.
Testing: Behind the Scenes at Consumer Reports, 1936-1986. Consumer Reports Book Editors & Monte Florman. 184p. (Orig.). 1986. 20.00 (ISBN 0-89043-064-0); pap. 13.00 (ISBN 0-89043-056-X). Consumer Reports.
Testing Children: A Reference Guide for Effective Clinical & Psychoeducational Assessments. Ed. by S. Joseph Weaver. LC 84-8882. (Illus.). 320p. 1984. 40.00x (ISBN 0-9611286-2-3, Test Corp America). Westport Pubs.
Testing Children: Standardized Testing in Local Education Authorities & Schools. Caroline Gipps et al. iv, 188p. 1984. text ed. 30.00x (ISBN 0-435-82323-X). Heinemann Ed.
Testing Computer Software. Cem Kaner. 256p. 1988. 27.50. TAB BKS.
Testing: Concepts, Policy, Practice, & Research. Ed. by Robert Glaser & Lloyd Bond. (Special Issues, American Psychologist: Vol. 36, No. 10). 1981. pap. 16.00 (ISBN 1-55798-001-2, 4013610); members 12.00. Am Psychol.
Testing, Counseling & Supportive Services for Disadvantaged Youth. Jesse E. Gordon. (Orig.). 1969. pap. 4.95x (ISBN 0-87736-309-9). U of Mich Inst Labor.
Testing Democracy: Electoral Behavior & Progressive Reform in New Jersey, 1880-1920. John F. Reynolds. LC 87-31947. (Illus.). xvii, 245p. 1988. 39.95x (ISBN 0-8078-1789-9). U of NC Pr.
Testing Democratic Theories in Korea. Sung M. Pae. 318p. 1986. lib. bdg. 29.00 (ISBN 0-8191-5379-6); pap. text ed. 15.25 (ISBN 0-8191-5380-X). U Pr of Amer.
Testing Digital Circuits. Wilkins. 1986. pap. 30.95 (ISBN 0-442-31748-4). Van Nos Reinhold.
Testing Drugs for the Ageing Brain. (Journal: Gerontology: Vol. 28, Suppl. 2). (Illus.). xiv, 58p. 1983. pap. 36.75 (ISBN 3-8055-3659-3). S Karger.
Testing English As a Second Language. David P. Harris. 1969. text ed. 5.95 (ISBN 0-07-026795-2). McGraw.
Testing ESL Composition: A Practical Approach. Holly Jacobs et al. 152p. 1981. pap. 14.50 (ISBN 0-88377-225-6). Newbury Hse.
Testing, Evaluation & Measurements in Metal Casting. Sarat C. Panigrahi. 304p. 1987. 15.00x (ISBN 81-204-0171-9, Pub. by Oxford IBH). South Asia Bks.
Testing, Evaluation & Shallow Land Burial of Low & Medium Radioactive Waste Forms. Ed. by W. Krissher & R. A. Simon. (Radioactive Waste Management Ser.: Vol. 13). 239p. 1984. 49.00 (ISBN 3-7186-0206-7). Harwood Academic.
Testing Fire Apparatus: Acceptance & Service Tests for Aerial Ladders, Pt. II. Paul R. Lyons. LC 78-59790. (Illus.). 50p. (Orig.). 1979. pap. text ed. 65.00 (ISBN 0-87765-136-1, SL-31). Natl Fire Prot.
Testing Fire Apparatus: Acceptance & Service Tests for Elevating Platforms, Pt. III. Paul R. Lyons. LC 78-59790. (Illus.). 54p. (Orig.). 1979. pap. text ed. 65.00 (ISBN 0-87765-137-X). Natl Fire Prot.
Testing Fire Apparatus: Acceptance & Service Tests for Pumpers, Pt. 1. Paul R. Lyons. LC 78-59790. 1979. pap. text ed. 65.00 (ISBN 0-87765-129-9). Natl Fire Prot.
Testing Fire Department Aerial Ladders & Elevating Platforms. National Fire Protection Association Staff. 23p. 1980. 12.00 (ISBN 0-317-63555-7, 1904-80). Natl Fire Prot.
Testing for Control of Hot Mix Quality. (Training Aids Ser.: No. 13). 1978. Package: instr's. manual, student wkbk., slides, tape. 400.00 (ISBN 0-317-58496-0); Instr's. manual, 45 pg. 14.00 (ISBN 0-317-58497-9); Student wkbk., 40 pg. 14.00 (ISBN 0-317-58498-7). Natl Asphalt Pavement.
Testing for Effects of Chemicals on Ecosystems. National Research Council Commission on Natural Resources. 128p. 1981. pap. 8.50x (ISBN 0-309-03142-7). Natl Acad Pr.
Testing for Electrical Safety in Hospitals. Noel L. Mhyre. (Illus.). 27p. 1975. 2.00 ea. (ISBN 0-917054-03-2). Med Communications.
Testing for Oral Proficiency: Familiarization Kits. Liskin-Gasparro. 1987. French Kit. (text & tape) 50.00 (ISBN 0-8384-1500-8); German Kit. (text & tape) 50.00 (ISBN 0-8384-1501-6); Spanish Kit. (text & tape) 50.00 (ISBN 0-8384-1502-4); English as a Second Language Kit. (text & tape) 50.00 (ISBN 0-8384-1503-2); Four Lang. Prepack. (complete pack. text & tape) 175.00 (ISBN 0-8384-1504-0). Heinle & Heinle.
Testing for Prediction of Material Performance in Structures & Components: A Symposium. Presented at the Annual Meeting, American Society & Materials. American Society for Testing & Materials Staff. LC 72-79572. (American Society for Testing & Materials. Special Technical Publication: No.515). pap. 79.80 (ISBN 0-317-08194-2, 2015505). Bks Demand UMI.
Testing for Teacher Certification. Ed. by National Evaluation Systems Inc, Staff et al. 288p. 1985. text ed. 24.95 (ISBN 0-89859-758-7). L Erlbaum Assocs.
Testing For Teachers. 2nd ed. Bruce W. Tuckman. 248p. 1988. pap. text ed. 12.00 (ISBN 0-15-591435-9, HC). HarBraceJ.
Testing for the Direction of Exports: India's Exports of Manufactures in the 1970s. Ashok Khanna. (Working Paper: No. 538). 41p. 1983. 5.00 (ISBN 0-8213-0132-2, WP 0538). World Bank.
Testing for Toxicity. Ed. by J. W. Gorrod. 366p. 1981. 53.00x (ISBN 0-85066-218-4). Taylor & Francis.
Testing Ground. G. F. Newman. 346p. 1988. 19.95 (ISBN 0-7181-2868-0, Pub. by Michael Joseph). David & Charles.
Testing Handicapped People. Willingham. 256p. 1988. text ed. 28.00 scp. (ISBN 0-205-11388-5). Allyn.
Testing Hardened Concrete: Nondestructive Methods. V. M. Malhotra. (Monograph: No. 9). 1976. 35.50 (ISBN 0-685-85144-3, M-9) (ISBN 0-685-85145-1). ACI.
Testing in Counseling, Uses & Misuses. Harley D. Christiansen. (Illus.). 96p. (Orig.). 1981. pap. text ed. 11.95 (ISBN 0-915456-03-6). P Juul Pr.
Testing in Employment & Training Programs: An Action Planning Guidebook. National Center for Research in Vocational Education. 144p. 1983. 8.75 (ISBN 0-318-22215-9, RD220). Natl Ctr Res Voc Ed.

Tetrahedrally-Bonded Amorphous Semiconductors. Ed. by David Adler & Hellmut Fritzsche. (Institute for Amorphous Studies). 580p. 1985. 79.50x (ISBN 0-306-42076-7, Plenum Pr). Plenum Pub.

Tetrahedrally Bonded Amorphous Semiconductors: Proceedings of the AIP Conference, No. 20, Yorktown Heights, No. 20. AIP Conference. Ed. by M. Brodsky et al. LC 74-80145. 369p. 1974. 16.00 (ISBN 0-88318-119-3). Am Inst Physics.

Tetralin. (American Petroleum Institute Monograph Ser.). 50p. 1978. 8.00 (ISBN 0-317-33102-7, 82270500). Am Petroleum.

Tetraphenylborates. Popouych. (IUPAC Solubility Data Ser.). 260p. 1981. 110.00 (ISBN 0-08-023928-5). Pergamon.

Tetraplegia & Paraplegia. 3rd ed. Ida Bromley. LC 85-7786. (Illus.). 261p. 1985. pap. text ed. 26.00 (ISBN 0-443-03233-5). Churchill.

Tetrascroll: A Cosmic Fairytale. R. Buckminster Fuller. 128p. 1983. pap. 7.95 (ISBN 0-312-79364-2). St Martin.

Tetum Ghosts & Kin: Fieldwork in an Indonesian Community. David Hicks. (Illus.). 143p. 1988. pap. text ed. 8.50x (ISBN 0-88133-320-4). Waveland Pr.

Tetum Ghosts & Kin: Fieldwork in an Indonesian Community. David B. Hicks. Ed. by Robert B. Edgerton & L. L. Langness. LC 76-28114. (Illus.). 143p. 1976. pap. text ed. 9.95 (ISBN 0-87484-368-5). Mayfield Pub.

Teudar: A King of Cornwall. W. H. Pascoe. 1985. 25.00x (ISBN 1-85022-001-8, Pub. by Dyllansow & Truran). State Mutual Bk.

Teufelbuecher in Auswahl, 3 vols. Ed. by Ria Stambaugh. (Ausgaben Deutscher Literatur des 15. bis 18. Jahrh). (Ger). Vol. 1, 1970. write for info (ISBN 3-11-006388-3); Vol. 2, 1972. 112.00x (ISBN 3-11-003924-9); Vol. 3, 1973. 141.00x (ISBN 3-11-004127-8). De Gruyter.

Teufelbuecher in Auswahl, Vol. 4. Ed. by Ria Stambaugh. (Ausgaben Detuscher Literatur Des XV. Bix XVIII, Jahrhunderts). 1978. 96.00x (ISBN 3-11-007331-5). De Gruyter.

Teuffel's History of Roman Literature, 2 Vols. Wilhelm S. Teuffel. Ed. by Ludwig Schwabe. Tr. by George C. Warr. (Research & Source Works Ser.: No. 168). 1968. Set. 55.50 (ISBN 0-8337-3494-6). B Franklin.

Teutonic Antiquities: Historical & Geographical Sketches of Roman & Barbarian History. C. Chatfield. LC 77-6984. 1977. Repr. of 1828 ed. lib. bdg. 30.00 (ISBN 0-89341-210-4). Longwood Pub Group.

Teutonic Legends in the Nibelungen Lied & the Nibelungen Ring. W. C. Sawyer. 1976. lib. bdg. 59.95 (ISBN 0-8490-2736-5). Gordon Pr.

Teutonic Myth & Legend. Donald A. MacKenzie. LC 77-91530. 1978. Repr. of 1912 ed. lib. bdg. 50.00 (ISBN 0-89341-313-5). Longwood Pub Group.

Teutonic Mythology, 4 Vols. 4th ed. Jacob Grimm. Tr. by James S. Stallybrass. Set. 60.00 (ISBN 0-8446-2168-4). Peter Smith.

TeV Physics & Beyond: Proceedings of the 8th & Nuclear Particle Physics Summer School. Ed. by R. Delbourgo & J. Fox. 324p. 1987. 78.00x (ISBN 9971-50-301-8); pap. 55.00 (ISBN 9971-50-304-2). World Scientific Pub.

Teverton Hall. Jane Gillespie. 1988. pap. 2.95 (ISBN 0-312-90674-9). St Martin.

Teville Obsession. Caroline Stafford. 1979. pap. 1.75 (ISBN 0-449-24077-0, Crest). Fawcett.

Tevye the Dairyman & the Railroad Stories. Scholem Aleichem. Ed. by Ruth R. Wisse. Tr. by Hillel Halkin from Yiddish. LC 86-24835. (Library of Yiddish Classics). 352p. 1987. 19.95 (ISBN 0-8052-4026-8). Schocken.

Tevye the Dairyman & the Railroad Stories. Scholem Aleichem. LC 86-24835. 352p. 1988. pap. 10.95 (ISBN 0-8052-0905-0). Schocken.

Tewa Tales. Ed. by Elsie W. Parsons. LC 29-6325. (AFS M). Repr. of 1926 ed. 26.00 (ISBN 0-527-01071-5). Kraus Repr.

Tewa World: Space, Time, Being, & Becoming in a Pueblo Society. Alfonso Ortiz. LC 72-94079. 1972. pap. 9.00x (ISBN 0-226-63307-1, P447, Phoen). U of Chicago Pr.

Tex. S. E. Hinton. LC 78-50448. 224p. (gr. 7 up). 1979. pap. 13.95 (ISBN 0-385-29020-9). Delacorte.

Tex. S. E. Hinton. 192p. (gr. 7 up). 1980. pap. 2.95 (ISBN 0-440-97850-5, LFL). Dell.

Tex. Donald Knuth. LC 86-1232. (Computers & Typesetting Ser.: Vol. B). 608p. 1986. text ed. write for info. (ISBN 0-201-13437-3). Addison-Wesley.

Tex. Donald E. Knuth. (Computer Science Ser.). 512p. 1985. text ed. write for info. Addison-Wesley.

Tex. Clarence Mulford. (Hopalong Cassidy Ser). 1976. Repr. of 1922 ed. lib. bdg. 18.95x (ISBN 0-88411-226-8, Pub. by Aeonian Pr). Amereon Ltd.

TEX & Metafont, New Directions in Typesetting. Donald E. Knuth. LC 79-25891. 355p. 1979. write for info. Am Math.

Tex Arcana. John Findley. (Illus.). 80p. (Orig.). 1987. pap. 10.95 (ISBN 0-87416-036-7). Catalan Communs.

Tex Avery: King of Cartoons. Joe Adamson. (Quality Paperbacks Ser.). (Illus.). 238p. 1985. pap. 14.95 (ISBN 0-306-80248-1). Da Capo.

TEX for Scientific Documentation. Ed. by J. Desarmenien. (Lecture Notes in Computer Science Ser.: Vol. 236). vi, 204p. 1986. pap. 19.80 (ISBN 0-387-16807-9). Springer-Verlag.

Tex for Scientific Documentation of the First European Conference Como, Italy. Ed. by Dario Lucarella. 224p. 1986. pap. write for info. (ISBN 0-201-13399-7). Addison-Wesley.

Tex-Mex Food. Robert Fischer. Ed. by FS Staff. (Illus.). 72p. (gr. 4-9). 1988. 9.90 (ISBN 0-531-10505-9). Watts.

Tex! The Man Who Built the Texas Cowboys. Bob St. John. 336p. 1988. 18.95 (ISBN 0-13-911975-2). P-H.

Tex Thorne Comes out of the West. Zane Grey. 300p. Repr. of 1937 ed. lib. bdg. 18.95x (ISBN 0-89190-761-0, Pub. by River City Pr). Amereon Ltd.

Texaco & the Ten Billion Dollar Jury. James Shannon. (Illus.). 384p. 1988. 19.95 (ISBN 0-13-911959-0). P-H.

Texan. William C. Knott. 368p. (Orig.). 1987. pap. 3.95 (ISBN 0-445-20241-6, Pub. by Popular Lib). Warner Bks.

Texan Came Riding. Frank O'Rourke. 1984. pap. 2.25 (ISBN 0-451-13224-6, Sig). NAL.

Texan in England. J. Frank Dobie. (Illus.). 301p. 1980. pap. 7.95 (ISBN 0-292-78034-6). U of Tex Pr.

Texan Scouts. Joseph A. Altsheler. (Texan Ser.). 1985. 20.95 (ISBN 0-8488-0202-0, Pub. by American Hse.). Amereon Ltd.

Texan Star. Joseph A. Altsheler. (Texan Ser.). 1985. 20.95 (ISBN 0-8488-0201-2, Pub. by American Hse.). Amereon Ltd.

Texan Triumph. Joseph A. Altsheler. (Texan Ser.). 1985. 20.95 (ISBN 0-8488-0203-9, Pub. by American Hse.). Amereon Ltd.

Texana at the University of Texas. Compiled by Walter P. Webb. LC 62-63428. (Illus.). 1962. pap. 5.00 (ISBN 0-87959-025-4). U of Tex H Ransom Ctr.

Texans. David Nevin. LC 75-15450. (Old West Ser.). (Illus.). (gr. 7 up). 1975. 19.94 (ISBN 0-8094-1502-X, Pub. by Time-Life). Silver.

Texans. David Nevin. (Old West Ser.). (Illus.). 1976. 14.95 (ISBN 0-8094-1500-3). Time-Life.

Texans. Bill Pronzini & Martin H. Greenberg. 1988. pap. 3.50 (ISBN 0-449-13470-9, GM). Fawcett.

Texans & Government: What Citizens Want. 30p. 1987. 5.00 (ISBN 0-89940-684-X). LBJ Sch Pub Aff.

Texan's Garden of Trivia. June R. Welch. 200p. 1984. pap. 7.95 (ISBN 0-912854-15-4). Yellow Rose Pr.

Texan's Guide to Consumer Protection. John L. Hill. LC 79-16767. 222p. (Orig.). 1979. pap. 9.95x (ISBN 0-87201-132-1). Gulf Pub.

Texan's Lady. Lauren Wilde. 480p. 1984. pap. 3.50 (ISBN 0-8217-1420-1). Zebra.

Texans, Politics & the New Deal. Lionel V. Patenaude. Ed. by Robert E. Burke & Frank Freidel. LC 82-49075. (Modern American History Ser.). 1983. 33.00 (ISBN 0-8240-5659-0). Garland Pub.

Texar the Southerner. Jules Verne. 4.95 (ISBN 0-87497-041-5). Assoc Bk.

Texas. Allan Carpenter. LC 78-18430. (New Enchantment of America State Bks). (Illus.). 96p. (gr. 4 up). 1979. PLB 15.93 (ISBN 0-516-04143-6). Childrens.

Texas. rev. ed. Jerry Flemmons. (Illus.). 128p. 1986. Repr. 29.95 (ISBN 0-938379-02-X). Tradewinds Pub.

Texas. Joe B. Frantz. (States & the Nation). (Illus.). 1976. 14.95 (ISBN 0-393-05580-9, Co-Pub by AASLH). Norton.

Texas. Ed. by Harrap Limited Staff. 1986. pap. 49.75X (ISBN 0-245-54293-0, Pub. by Harrap Ltd England). State Mutual Bk.

Texas. Phil Hollenbeck & Billy Porterfield. (Illus.). 1985. 16.95 (ISBN 0-19-540615-X). Skyline Press.

Texas. Mary A. Holley. LC 85-51947. (Illus.). 434p. 1985. ltd. ed. 50.00 (ISBN 0-87611-076-6); pap. 9.95 (ISBN 0-87611-074-X). Tex St Hist Assn.

Texas. Insight Guides Staff. (Illus.). 384p. 1985. pap. 15.95 (ISBN 0-13-912122-6). P-H.

Texas, 2 vols. James A. Michener. (Illus.). 943p. 1986. 125.00 (ISBN 0-292-78071-0). U of Tex Pr.

Texas. James A. Michener. 1987. pap. 5.95 (ISBN 0-449-21092-8, Crest). Fawcett.

Texas. James A. Michener. 1986. 21.95 (ISBN 0-394-54154-5). Random.

Texas. Ed. by Betty L. Phillips & Bryce Phillips. (First Book Ser.). (Illus.). 96p. (gr. 4-9). PLB 10.40 (ISBN 0-531-10395-1). Watts.

Texas! Dana F. Ross. (Wagons West Ser.). 368p. (Orig.). 1984. pap. 4.50 (ISBN 0-553-26070-7). Bantam.

Texas. Turner Program Services, Inc. Staff & James I. Clark. LC 85-9980. (Portrait of America Library). 48p. (gr. 4 up). 1985. PLB 15.33 (ISBN 0-86514-445-1); pap. text ed. 9.27 (ISBN 0-86514-520-2); Beta video 113.33 (ISBN 0-86514-070-7); VHS video 113.33 (ISBN 0-86514-145-2); 3/4" video 136.00 (ISBN 0-86514-220-3); tchr's guide 13.27 (ISBN 0-86514-295-5); student activity bk. 6.60 (ISBN 0-86514-370-6); index 13.27. Raintree Pubs.

Texas: A Brief Account. William H. Wharton. pap. 4.50 wrappers (ISBN 0-8363-0093-9). Jenkins.

Texas: A Conquest of Civilizations. George Pierce Garrison. LC 72-3753. (American Commonwealths: No. 15). Repr. of 1903 ed. 34.00 (ISBN 0-404-57215-4). AMS Pr.

Texas: A Geography. Terry G. Jordan & John L. Bean, Jr. LC 83-6642. (Geographies of the United States Ser.). 450p. 1983. text ed. 47.00x o. p. (ISBN 0-86531-088-2); pap. text ed. 26.00x (ISBN 0-86531-481-0). Westview.

Texas: A Guide to the Lone Star State. Federal Writers' Project Staff. LC 40-10658. 717p. 89.00x (ISBN 0-403-02192-8). Somerset Pub.

Texas: A History. Seymour V. Connor. LC 71-136037. (Illus., Orig.). 1971. text ed. 25.95x (ISBN 0-88295-724-4). Harlan Davidson.

Texas: A History. Joe B. Frantz. (States & the Nation Ser.). (Illus.). 1984. pap. 7.95 (ISBN 0-393-30173-7). Norton.

Texas: A Literary Portrait. Don Graham. LC 85-71202. (Illus.). 250p. 1985. 45.00x (ISBN 0-931722-40-3); pap. 16.95 (ISBN 0-931722-41-1). Corona Pub.

Texas: A Picture Tour. Intro. by Lon Tinkle. 160p. 1986. pap. 17.95 (ISBN 0-684-18631-4). Scribner.

Texas: A Salute from Above. T. R. Fehrenbach. 280p. 1985. 34.95. Texas World Bks.

Texas: A Salute from Above. T. R. Fehrenbach. 280p. 1985. 34.95 (ISBN 0-940672-28-6). Shearer Pub.

Texas: A Sesquicentennial Celebration. Ed. by Donald W. Whisenhunt. 440p. 1984. 19.95 (ISBN 0-89015-441-4); pap. 12.95 (ISBN 0-89015-488-0). Eakin Pr.

Texas: A World in Itself. George S. Perry & Arthur Fuller. (Illus.). 293p. 1975. Repr. of 1941 ed. 7.95 (ISBN 0-88289-094-8). Pelican.

Texas: A Year with the Boys. William Hoffman. LC 83-51251. 216p. 1983. 15.95 (ISBN 0-87833-337-1). Taylor Pub.

Texas Agricultural Law Handbook. Ed. by Lon R. Vinion. LC 84-43233. (Agricultural Law Handbook Ser.: Vol. II). 143p. 1986. pap. 19.95x (ISBN 0-89950-165-6). McFarland & Co.

Texas Alcoholic Beverage Code: With Tables & Index: As Amended Through the 1983 Regular & First Called Sessions of the 68th Legislature. Texas Legislature. LC 85-134413. (Texas Statutes & Codes Ser.). 147p. write for info. West Pub.

Texas: All Hail the Mighty State. Archie P. McDonald. 288p. 1983. 14.95 (ISBN 0-89015-388-4); pap. 9.95 (ISBN 0-89015-389-2). Eakin Pr.

Texas Almanac & State Industrial Guide, 1986-1987. 53rd ed. Ed. by Mike Kingston. (Illus.). 768p. 1985. 14.95 (ISBN 0-914511-02-5); pap. 8.95 (ISBN 0-914511-03-3). Dallas Morning.

Texas Almanac 1988-89: State Industrial Guide. Ed. by Mike Kingston. 640p. 14.95 (ISBN 0-914511-04-1); pap. 8.95 (ISBN 0-914511-05-X). Dallas Morning.

Texas Almanac, 1988-89: Teacher's Guide. Ed. by Dennis Campbell. 40p. 1987. 2.50 (ISBN 0-914511-06-8). Dallas Morning.

Texas Alphabet. James Rice. (Illus.). 132p. (gr. k-5). 1988. 10.95 (ISBN 0-88289-692-X). Pelican.

Texas: Amazing but True. Jack Maguire. (Illus.). 1984. 9.95 (ISBN 0-89015-487-2). Eakin Pr.

Texas: An Album of History. James L. Haley. LC 84-10202. (Illus.). 320p. 1985. pap. 24.95 (ISBN 0-385-17307-5). Doubleday.

Texas: An Educational Coloring Book. Spizzirri Publishing Company Staff. Ed. by Linda Spizzirri. (Illus.). 32p. (gr. 1-8). 1985. pap. 1.49 (ISBN 0-86545-070-6). Spizzirri.

Texas & Christmas: A Collection of Traditions, Memories & Folklore. Ed. by Judy Alter & Joyce G. Roach. LC 83-4717. (Illus.). 86p. 1983. pap. 6.50 (ISBN 0-912646-81-0). Tex Christian.

Texas & Germany: Crosscurrents. Francis Abernethy et al. Ed. by Joseph Wilson. (Rice University Studies: Vol. 63, No. 3). (Illus.). 139p. 1977. pap. 10.00x (ISBN 0-89263-233-X). Rice Univ.

Texas & Southwestern Lore. Ed. by J. Frank Dobie. LC 33-1131. (Texas Folklore Society Publications Ser.: No. 6). 246p. 1982. Repr. of 1927 ed. 13.95 (ISBN 0-87074-044-X). SMU Press.

Texas & the American Revolution. (Illus.). 72p. 1975. pap. text ed. 2.95 (ISBN 0-933164-23-8). U of Tex Inst Tex Culture.

Texas & the Mexican Revolution: A Study in State & National Border Policy 1910-1920. Don M. Coerver & Linda B. Hall. LC 84-2510. (Illus.). 181p. 1984. text ed. 15.95 (ISBN 0-939980-05-3); pap. text ed. 9.95x (ISBN 0-939980-06-1). Trinity U Pr.

Texas & the Mexican War. Nathaniel W. Stephenson. 1919. 8.50x (ISBN 0-686-83810-6). Elliots Bks.

Texas & the Mexican War see Chronicles of America.

Texas & the Southwest Historical & Sightseeing Guide. Anthony Hitchcock & Jean Lindgren. (Compleat Traveler's Guides Ser.). (Illus.). 1981. pap. 4.95 (ISBN 0-89102-200-7). B Franklin.

Texas & the Southwest, 1985. Connie Sherley. Ed. by Robert C. Fisher. (Fisher Annotated Travel Guides Ser.). (Illus.). 1984. pap. 12.95 (ISBN 0-8116-0016-5). NAL.

Texas Annotated Penal Statutes with Forms Branch's, 5 vols. 3rd ed. LC 74-81698. incl 1985 Suppl 262.50. Suppl. 1986. 36.50. Lawyers Co-Op.

Texas Anthem, No. 1. James Reno. 352p. 1986. pap. 3.50 (ISBN 0-451-14377-9, Sig). NAL.

Texas Appellate Courts, 2 vols. National Center for State Courts Staff. 1980. Vol. I, 103 pgs. manuscript 6.18 (SRO-004); Vol. II, 162 pgs. manuscript 9.72 (SRO-005). Natl Ctr St Courts.

Texas Appellate Courts II Project: A Study for the Court of Appeals Fifth Supreme Judicial District, Dallas, Texas. National Center for State Courts Staff. 244p. (On loan through the NCSC Library). 1981. write for info. (SRO-010). Natl Ctr St Courts.

Texas Appellate Courts III Project: A Continuation Study on the Implementation of S. J. R. 36. National Center for State Courts Staff. 167p. 1982. manuscript 10.02 (SRO-018). Natl Ctr St Courts.

Texas Appellate Practice Manual. Ed. by Donald M. Hunt. 376p. 1974. incl. supplement 45.00 (ISBN 0-938160-04-4, 6320). State Bar TX.

Texas Appellate Practice Manual-1982 Cumulative Supplement. Ed. by Yvonne M. Faulks. 153p. 1982. pap. 20.00 (ISBN 0-938160-05-2, 6230). State Bar TX.

Texas Archeology: Essays Honoring R. King Harris. Ed. by Kurt House. LC 78-10491. (Institute for the Study of Earth & Man Reports of Investigations: No. 3). (Illus.). 192p. 1978. 12.50 (ISBN 0-87074-170-5). SMU Press.

Texas Architecture of the '80s: A Bibliography. Carole Cable. (Architecture Ser.: A 1526). 12p. 1986. 3.75 (ISBN 0-89028-696-5). Vance Biblios.

Texas Art Review. Les Krantz. LC 82-83197. (Illus.). 190p. 1982. 35.00x (ISBN 0-87201-018-X); pap. 15.95x (ISBN 0-88415-019-4, Lone Star Bks). Gulf Pub.

Texas Arts Journal. pap. 10.00 (ISBN 0-686-78140-6). New London Pr.

Texas Assassin. J. T. Edson. 192p. (Orig.). 1986. pap. 2.50 (ISBN 0-425-09348-4). Berkley Pub.

Texas at the Crossroads: People, Politics, Policy. Ed. by Anthony Champagne & Edward J. Harpham. LC 87-9959. 416p. 1987. pap. 14.95 (ISBN 0-89096-317-7). Tex A&M Univ Pr.

Texas Atlas of Higher Education. 208p. 1974. pap. 5.00 (ISBN 0-89940-803-6). LBJ Sch Pub Aff.

Texas Attorney's-Secretary's Handbook, 1987. Ed. by Julie Welborn. looseleaf 40.00 (ISBN 0-409-25273-5). Butterworth TX.

Texas Auto Trails: The Northeast. Myra H. McIlvain. (Illus.). 277p. 1984. pap. 9.95 (ISBN 0-292-78055-9). U of Tex Pr.

Texas Auto Trails: The South & the Rio Grande Valley. Myra H. McIlvain. (Illus.). 256p. 1985. pap. 9.95 (ISBN 0-292-78064-8). U of Tex Pr.

Texas Auto Trails: The Southeast. Myra H. McIlvain. (Illus.). 293p. 1982. pap. 8.95 (ISBN 0-292-78050-8). U of Tex Pr.

Texas Automotive Directory. Ed. by T. L. Spelman. 1985. 24.95 (ISBN 1-55527-031-X). Auto Contact Inc.

Texas Baptist Leadership & Social Christianity, 1900-1980. John W. Storey. LC 85-40747. (Texas A&M Southwestern Studies: No. 5). (Illus.). 237p. 1986. 22.50x (ISBN 0-89096-251-0). Tex A&M Univ Pr.

Texas Baptist Orphanage: My Heritage of Dreams & Happiness. Georgia D. Edwards. (Illus.). 120p. 1987. 17.95 (ISBN 0-943639-00-X). Anchor Pub Co.

Texas Bed & Breakfast. Ann Ruff et al. (Guidebook Ser.). (Illus.). 250p. 1985. pap. 9.95 (ISBN 0-87719-020-8). Texas Month Pr.

Texas Bibliography. Gilbert R. Cruz & James A. Irby. 1982. 15.95 (ISBN 0-89015-307-8). Eakin Pr.

Texas Bill of Rights: A Commentary & Litigation Manual. James C. Harrington. 330p. 1988. perfect bdg. with pocketpart 85.00 (ISBN 0-409-25202-6). Butterworth TX.

Texas Birds from A to Z. Glenna Grimmer. (Stories for Young Americans Ser.). (Illus.). 40p. (gr. 4-6). 1985. 9.95 (ISBN 0-89015-533-X). Eakin Pr.

Texas Birds: Where They Are & How to Find Them. Edward A. Kutac. LC 82-9880. (Illus.). 110p. (Orig.). 1982. pap. 9.95x (ISBN 0-88415-063-1, Lone Star Bks). Gulf Pub.

Texas, Blood Red. Shepard Rifkin. Ed. by Chris Kingsley. 208p. 1987. pap. 2.95 (ISBN 0-7701-0686-2). Paperjacks US.

Texas Blossom. Kathleen Drymon. 1984. pap. 3.75 (ISBN 0-8217-1305-1). Zebra.

Texas Bluebonnet. Jean Andrews. (Illus.). 64p. 1986. 9.95 (ISBN 0-292-70758-4). U of Tex Pr.

Texas Bluebonnet Trails. Jay Woodard. 24p. (Orig.). 1988. pap. 9.95 (ISBN 0-9618888-0-6). Anglo-Am TX.

Texas Born. James Reno. (Texas Anthem Ser.: No. 2). 352p. 1986. pap. 3.50 (ISBN 0-451-14560-7, Sig). NAL.

Texas Brazos. G. Clifton Wisler. 448p. 1987. pap. 3.95 (ISBN 0-8217-1969-6). Zebra.

Texas Brazos: Caddo Creek. G. Clifton Wisler. 432p. 1988. pap. 3.95 (ISBN 0-8217-2257-3). Zebra.

Texas Brazos: Fortune Bend. G. Clifton Wisler. 432p. 1987. pap. 3.95 (ISBN 0-8217-2069-4). Zebra.

Texas Bred. Michael French. 352p. (Orig.). 1986. pap. 3.95 (ISBN 0-553-26164-9). Bantam.

Texas Bride. F. Rosanne Bittner. 352p. (Orig.). Date not set. pap. 4.50 (ISBN 0-445-20636-5, Pub. by Popular Lib). Warner Bks.

Texas Bride. Catherine Creel. (Orig.). 1982. pap. 3.50 (ISBN 0-8217-1050-8). Zebra.

Texas Hill Country: Interpretations by Thirteen Artists. Intro. by A. C. Greene. LC 81-40400. (Joe & Betty Moore Texas Art Ser.: No. 5). (Illus.). 122p. (Orig.). 1981. pap. 29.95 (ISBN 0-89096-116-6) (ISBN 0-89096-359-2). Tex A&M Univ Pr.
Texas Historic Inns Cookbook. Ann Ruff & Gail Drago. Ed. by Scott Lubeck. (Illus.). 224p. 1984. 16.95 (ISBN 0-932012-45-0). Texas Month Pr.
Texas Historical & Biographical Index, Vol. 1. Ronald V. Jackson. LC 78-53718. (Illus.). 1984. lib. bdg. 30.00 (ISBN 0-89593-201-6). Accelerated Index.
Texas History. 2nd ed. Ed. by Walter L. Buenger. (Texas History Ser.). (Illus.). 546p. 1983. pap. text ed. 20.95x (ISBN 0-89641-138-9). American Pr.
Texas History. 2nd ed. Ed. by Frank H. Smyrl. (Texas History Ser.). (Illus.). 474p. 1985. pap. text ed. 16.95x (ISBN 0-89641-159-1). American Pr.
Texas History Classroom Plays, Vol. 1. Jan E. Seale. (Texas History Classroom Plays Kit Ser.). (Illus.). 56p. (gr. 4-8). 1986. PLB 4.25. Knowing Pr.
Texas History Fun Skits. Niles Rutherford. 48p. 1987. 5.95 (ISBN 0-89962-600-9). Todd & Honeywell.
Texas History Movies. 65p. 1986. pap. 2.00 (ISBN 0-87611-080-4). Tex St Hist Assn.
Texas History Plays Series. Jan E. Seale. (Illus.). (ps-8). 1986. PLB 89.95. Knowing Pr.
Texas History Stories. E. G. Littlejohn. LC 86-62880. (Illus.). 288p. 1986. pap. 9.95 (ISBN 0-938349-07-4); wkbk. 6.95 (ISBN 0-938349-10-4). State House Pr.
Texas Homebuyer's Manual. The State Bar of Texas, Real Estate, Probate & Trust Law Section Staff. Ed. by Michael Graham. LC 86-3084. 80p. (Orig.). 1986. pap. 6.95 (ISBN 0-87201-836-9). Gulf Pub.
Texas Homes of the Nineteenth Century. Drury B. Alexander & Todd Webb. (Illus.). 290p. 1966. 39.95 (ISBN 0-292-73634-7). U of Tex Pr.
Texas Honky-Tonk Music. James Rice. (Illus.). 64p. 1985. 4.95 (ISBN 0-89015-528-3). Eakin Pr.
Texas, Images of the Landscape. Jim Bones. LC 86-50062. (Illus.). 192p. 1986. 34.95 (ISBN 0-942394-16-X). Westcliffe Pubs Inc.
Texas in Bloom: Photographs from Texas Highways Magazine. Intro. by Glen Evans. (Louise Lindsey Merrick Texas Environment Ser.: No. 7). (Illus.). 148p. 1984. 24.95 (ISBN 0-89096-180-8). Tex A&M Univ Pr.
Texas in Children's Books: An Annotated Bibliography. Barbara Immroth. LC 86-10361. xx, 187p. (Orig.). 1986. lib. bdg. 26.00 (ISBN 0-208-02116-7, Lib Prof Pubns); pap. 19.50x (ISBN 0-208-02117-5, Lib Prof Pubns). Shoe String.
Texas in Color. Evelyn Oppenheimer. (Profiles of America Ser.). 9.95 (ISBN 0-8038-7108-2). Hastings.
Texas in Eighteen Forty; Or, the Emigrant's Guide to the New Republic. 20.00 (ISBN 0-405-04997-8). Ayer Co Pubs.
Texas in Gray: The Civil War Years, 1861-1865. Frank H. Smyrl. (Texas History Ser.). (Illus.). 55p. (Orig.). 1983. pap. text ed. 2.95x (ISBN 0-89641-130-3). American Pr.
Texas in Historic Sites & Symbols. Betsy Warren. (Illus.). 28p. (gr. k-3). 1982. pap. 4.50 (ISBN 0-937460-05-2). Hendrick-Long.
Texas in Seventeen Seventy-Six. Seymour V. Connor. LC 75-37049. 1975. 15.00 (ISBN 0-8363-0136-6). Jenkins.
Texas in the Middle Eighteenth Century: Studies in Spanish Colonial History & Administration. Herbert E. Bolton. (California Univ. Publications in History: Vol. 3). 1977. Repr. of 1915 ed. 48.00 (ISBN 0-527-00941-5). Kraus Repr.
Texas in the Middle Eighteenth Century: Studies in Spanish Colonial History & Administration. Herbert E. Bolton. (Texas History Paperbacks Ser.: No. 8). 511p. 1970. pap. 10.95 (ISBN 0-292-70034-2). U of Tex Pr.
Texas in the War, Eighteen Sixty-One to Eighteen Sixty-Five. Compiled by Harold B. Simpson. 1984. 15.00 (ISBN 0-912172-29-0). Hill Coll Pr.
Texas in Transition. Larry McMurty et al. (Symposium Ser.). (Illus.). 254p. 1986. 10.00 (ISBN 0-89940-419-7). LBJ Sch Pub Aff.
Texas: In Words & Pictures. Dennis Fradin. LC 80-27497. (Young People's Stories of Our States Ser.). (Illus.). 48p. (gr. 2-5). 1981. PLB 13.27 (ISBN 0-516-03943-1); pap. 3.95 (ISBN 0-516-43943-X). Childrens.
Texas in 1837. Ed. by Andrew F. Muir. (Illus.). 264p. 1988. pap. 9.95 (ISBN 0-292-78099-0). U of Tex Pr.
Texas Incorporation System. Bender's Editorial Staff. 1985. looseleaf incl. disks 500.00 (ISBN 0-317-37661-6, 776). Bender.
Texas: Insight Guide. Date not set. write for info. S&S.
Texas Instrument User's Encyclopedia: TI 99, 2, 4, 4a & 8. Gary Phillips & David Reese. Ed. by Michael F. Mellin & Robert Sandberg. 300p. (Orig.). 1983. pap. 14.95 (ISBN 0-912003-15-4). Bk Co.
Texas Instruments Computer Program Writing Workbook. Len Turner. 96p. 1983. 4.95 (ISBN 0-86668-812-9). ARCsoft.
Texas Instruments Home Computer Games Programs. Len Turner. 96p. 1983. 8.95 (ISBN 0-86668-032-2). ARCsoft.
Texas Instruments Home Computer Graphics Programs. Len Turner. 112p. 1983. 9.95 (ISBN 0-86668-031-4). ARCsoft.
Texas Insurance Code: With Tables & Index, As Amended Through the 1983 Regular & First Called Sessions of the 68th Legislature. Texas Legislature. LC 85-134807. (Texas Statutes & Codes Ser.). 600p. write for info. West Pub.
Texas Is the Place for Me. Carl Urbantke. Ed. by Robert C. Cotner. (Illus.). 8.50 (ISBN 0-8363-0094-7). Jenkins.
Texas Is...(the Sesquicentennial Remembered) Mark Holbrook. (Illus.). 200p. 1986. 50.00 (ISBN 0-9617487-0-2). Ringtail Prod.
Texas-Israeli War, 1999. Howard Waldrop & Jake Saunders. 1978. 2.95 (ISBN 0-345-33994-0, Del Rey Bks). Ballantine.
Texas Job Bank. 2nd ed. (Job Bank Ser.). 276p. 1987. pap. 9.95 (ISBN 0-937860-48-4). Adams Inc MA.
Texas Jurisprudence, 85 Vol. set. 3rd ed. LC 79-51183. write for info. Lawyers Co-Op.
Texas Jurisprudence Pleading & Practice Forms 2d, 13 Vols. LC 72-88069. write for info. Lawyers Co-Op.
Texas Labor Laws. 3rd ed. Joan McCrea. LC 77-90788. 90p. (Orig.). 1978. pap. 6.95x (ISBN 0-87201-414-2). Gulf Pub.
Texas Land Grab. Johnny Nelson. 1979. pap. 1.25 (ISBN 0-8439-0671-5, Leisure Bks). Leisure NY.
Texas Land Title Abstracts. Ed. by Skipper Steely. (Illus.). 450p. 1984. 25.00 (ISBN 0-915263-01-7). Wright Pr.
Texas' Last Frontier: Fort Stockton & the Trans-Pecos, 1861-1895. Clayton W. Williams. Ed. by Ernest Wallace. LC 81-48379. (Centennial Series of the Association of Former Students: No. 10). (Illus.). 480p. 1982. 19.50 (ISBN 0-89096-126-3). Tex A&M Univ Pr.
Texas Law Finder: A New Topical Reference Guide for Coordinated Research Providing Comprehensive References to the Following West Publications, Vernon's Texas Statutes & Codes Annotated, Vernon's Texas Rules Annotated, Texas Practice Series, West's Texas Forms, Texas Digest, United States Code Annotated, Corpus Juris Secundum, Federal Publications, Key Number Publications, Texts & Treatises, 1982. West Publishing Company. LC 82-830775. vi, 1201p. 1985. 26.00. West Pub.
Texas Law in Layman's Language. 3rd ed. Ralph Walton & Charles Turner. LC 75-18201. 250p. (Orig.). 1982. pap. 9.95x (ISBN 0-87201-828-8). Gulf Pub.
Texas Law Locator, 14 vols. Shepard's Citation, Inc. Editorial Staff. (Law Locators Ser.). Set. 970.00 (ISBN 0-317-38905-X). Shepards-McGraw.
Texas Law Office Handbook: Texas Association of Legal Secretaries. 2nd ed. LC 76-142446. 710p. 55.00; Suppl. 1986. 12.00. Lawyers Co-Op.
Texas Law Review: 1922-1986, 64 vols. Bound set, with index. 2676.00x (ISBN 0-686-90057-X). Rothman.
Texas Lawyer: The Life of W. H. Burges. J. F. Hulse. LC 81-84678. (Illus.). 390p. 1982. 29.95 (ISBN 0-930208-12-9). Mangan Bks.
Texas Lawyer's Guide, 1980, 2 vols. Jeremy Wicker & Daniel Benson. LC 80-18753. Set. 145.00 (ISBN 0-317-12213-4); Suppl., 1982. 25.00; Suppl., 1983. 30.00. Callaghan.
Texas Lawyers' Professional Ethics. 2nd ed. Texas Young Lawyers Association Staff. LC 86-61559. 310p. 1986. 63.00 (ISBN 0-938160-44-3, 6334). State Bar TX.
Texas League: A Century of Baseball. Bill O'Neal. Ed. by Melissa Roberts. (Illus.). 332p. 1987. 17.95 (ISBN 0-89015-596-8); pap. 12.95 (ISBN 0-89015-609-3). Eakin Pr.
Texas Legal Practice Forms, 2 vols. Dennis Taylor & S. Stevenson. LC 82-20673. 1020p. 1982. 135.00 (ISBN 0-317-12215-0). Callaghan.
Texas Legislative Handbook 1987-1988. Scott Sayers. Ed. by Julie Sayers. 44p. (Orig.). 2.10 (ISBN 0-934367-05-1). TX St Direct.
Texas Legislature Manual. Scott Sayers. Ed. by Julie Sayers. 120p. (Orig.). 4.75 (ISBN 0-934367-02-7). TX St Direct.
Texas-Legislature Pre-Session Conference, 66th: Proceedings. 138p. 1979. pap. 3.50 (ISBN 0-89940-075-2). LBJ Sch Pub Aff.
Texas Library History: A Bibliography. Compiled by A. E. Skinner. LC 83-4234. 96p. 1983. pap. 22.00x (ISBN 0-89774-106-4). Oryx Pr.
Texas Life & Health Insurance. 2nd ed. Ed. by The Merritt Co Staff. 202p. 1985. write for info. Merritt Co.
Texas Lignite: Near-Surface & Deep-Basin Resources. W. R. Kaiser. (Report of Investigations Ser.: RI 79). (Illus.). 70p. 1979. Repr. of 1974 ed. 3.00 (ISBN 0-318-03203-1). Bur Econ Geology.
Texas Lily. Stephanie Blake. 336p. Date not set. pap. 3.95 (ISBN 0-441-80926-X, Pub by Charter Bks). Ace Bks.
Texas Limitations Manual. Jennifer Mellett. 306p. 1987. looseleaf 70.00 (ISBN 0-318-21797-X). Butterworth TX.
Texas Litigation Guide, 19 vols. William V. Dorsaneo et al. 1977. looseleaf set 1100.00 (719); Updates. 1985 380.00; 1986 473.00. Bender.
Texas Liveoak. Paul Foreman. LC 78-17104. 1977. o.s. 7.50 (ISBN 0-914476-67-X); pap. 5.00x (ISBN 0-914476-66-1). Thorp Springs.
Texas Local Recording Agent's Licensing Course. 3rd ed. 1985. write for info. correspondence course (ISBN 0-930868-34-X). Merritt Co.
Texas Log Buildings: A Folk Architecture. Terry G. Jordan. LC 77-24559. (Illus.). 240p. 1978. pap. 11.95 (ISBN 0-292-78051-6). U of Tex Pr.
Texas Longhorn Baseball: Kings of the Diamond. Wilbur Evans & Bill Little. LC 82-50032. (College Sports Series: Baseball). 490p. 1983. 17.95 (ISBN 0-87397-234-1). Strode.
Texas Longhorn: Relic of the Past, Asset for the Future. Don Worcester. LC 86-6025. (Essays on the American West Ser.: No. 8). (Illus.). 112p. 1987. 12.95 (ISBN 0-89096-285-5). Tex A&M Univ Pr.
Texas Looks Ahead, Vol. 1. The Resources Of Texas. facs. ed. Texas University. Ed. by Lorena Drummond. LC 68-58814. (Essay Index Reprint Ser). 1944. 24.50 (ISBN 0-8369-0093-6). Ayer Co Pubs.
Texas Lore, Vol. 1. Patrick M. Reynolds. (Texas Lore Ser.). (Illus.). 56p. (Orig.). 1983. pap. 3.25 (ISBN 0-932514-07-3). Red Rose Studio.
Texas Lore, Vol. 2. Patrick M. Reynolds. (Illus.). 56p. (Orig.). 1984. pap. 3.25 (ISBN 0-932514-09-X). Red Rose Studio.
Texas Lore, Vol. 3. Patrick M. Reynolds. (Illus.). 56p. 1985. pap. 3.25 (ISBN 0-932514-11-1). Red Rose Studio.
Texas Lore, Vol. 4. Patrick M. Reynold. (Illus.). 56p. (Orig.). 1986. pap. 3.25 (ISBN 0-932514-13-8). Red Rose Studio.
Texas Lore, Vol. 5. Patrick M. Reynolds. (Illus.). 56p. (Orig.). pap. 3.25 (ISBN 0-932514-15-4). Red Rose Studio.
Texas Mammals East of the Balcones Fault Zone. David J. Schmidly. LC 83-45098. (W. L. Moody, Jr., Natural History Ser.: No. 6). (Illus.). 408p. 1983. 19.95 (ISBN 0-89096-158-1); pap. 12.95 (ISBN 0-89096-171-9). Tex A&M Univ Pr.
Texas Manhunter, Jack Duncan. Rick Miller. 175p. 1986. 19.95 (ISBN 0-932702-41-4). Creative Texas.
Texas Manufacturers Register, 1988. 1040p. 1988. 114.00 (ISBN 0-318-04034-4). Manufacturers.
Texas Marital Property Rights. J. Thomas Oldham. LC 87-60920. 498p. (Orig.). 1987. pap. text ed. 35.00 (ISBN 0-916081-05-2). J Marshall Pub Co.
Texas Marvel. Rita Kerr. Ed. by Melissa Roberts. 120p. (gr. 4-7). 1987. 7.95 (ISBN 0-89015-597-6). Eakin Pr.
Texas Matrimonial Property Law. Joseph W. McKnight & William A. Reppy. 376p. 1983. 30.00x (ISBN 0-87215-551-X). Michie Co.
Texas Media Directory. 2nd ed. Ed. by Martin Pollack. LC 87-71097. 1987. pap. 50.00 (ISBN 0-936836-10-5). Alliance Pubs.
Texas Medical Malpractice: A Guide for the Health Sciences. Rapp. 476p. 1988. pap. text ed. 29.95 (ISBN 0-8016-4095-4). Mosby.
Texas-Mexican Cancionero: Folksongs of the Lower Border. Americo Paredes. LC 75-16393. (Music in American Life Ser.). (Illus.). 218p. 1981. pap. 9.95 (ISBN 0-252-00894-4). U of Ill Pr.
Texas-Mexican Conjunto: History of a Working-Class Music. Manuel Pena. (Mexican American Monograph: No. 9). (Illus.). 238p. 1985. text ed. 19.95x (ISBN 0-292-78068-0); pap. 8.95 (ISBN 0-292-78080-X). U of Tex Pr.
Texas Microwave Cookbook. Carolyn H. White. LC 81-83423. (Illus.). 176p. 1981. 9.95 (ISBN 0-941294-00-5). Home Ec Consult.
Texas Missions & Landmarks. rev., 2nd ed. Jack Harmon. (Illus.). 68p. 1978. pap. 7.95 (ISBN 0-933164-17-3). U of Tex Inst Tex Culture.
Texas Monthly Guidebooks: Texas. Ed. by Patricia Sharpe & Robert S. Weddle. 724p. (Orig.). 1982. pap. 13.95 (ISBN 0-932012-25-6). Texas Month Pr.
Texas Monthly's Political Reader. 3rd ed. David F. Prindle. 256p. 1985. pap. text ed. 11.95 (ISBN 0-87719-003-8). Texas Month Pr.
Texas Motorway Company & Adastra. 350p. 1978. pap. 20.00. K G Wilks.
Texas Municipal Zoning Law. John Mixon. LC 85-389. 556p. 1985. Looseleaf 100.00 (ISBN 0-409-25019-8). Butterworth TX.
Texas Museums: A Guidebook. Paula E. Tyler & Ron Tyler. (Illus.). 327p. 1983. 16.95 (ISBN 0-292-78062-1); pap. 8.95 (ISBN 0-292-78063-X). U of Tex Pr.
Texas Myths. Ed. by Robert F. O'Connor. LC 85-40743. (Published for the Texas Committee for the Humanities). 264p. 1986. 17.95 (ISBN 0-89096-264-2). Tex A&M Univ Pr.
Texas National Energy Modeling Project: An Experience in Large-Scale Model Transfer & Evaluation. Ed. by Milton L. Holloway. 1980. 29.00 (ISBN 0-12-352950-6). Acad Pr.
Texas Natural Resources Code: With Tables & Index, As Amended Through the 1983 Regular & First Called Sessions of the 68th Legislature. Texas Legislature. LC 85-121064. (Texas Statutes & Codes Ser.). 315p. write for info. West Pub.
Texas Navy: Freedom Fighters for the Republic of Texas. Linda E. Devereaux. Ed. by Joe Ericson. LC 83-81716. (Illus.). 1983. pap. 14.50 (ISBN 0-911317-21-X). Ericson Bks.
Texas Navy: Its Forgotten Battles & Shirtsleeve Diplomacy. Jim D. Hill. LC 87-10017. (Illus.). 224p. 1987. 19.95 (ISBN 0-938349-17-1); pap. 12.95 (ISBN 0-938349-18-X); Limited ed. deluxe ed. 50.00 (ISBN 0-938349-19-8). State House Pr.
Texas Night Before Christmas. James Rice. (Illus.). 32p. (gr. 1-6). 1986. 10.95 (ISBN 0-88289-603-2). Pelican.
Texas Night Riders. Ray Slater. 176p. pap. 1.95 (ISBN 0-8439-2023-8, Leisure Bks). Leisure NY.
Texas Noon. Leonard Sanders. 1989. price not set. Delacorte.
Texas Notary Law Primer. 3rd ed. The National Notary Magazine Editors. 1988. pap. 8.75 (ISBN 0-933134-51-7). Natl Notary.
Texas: Observations, Historical, Geographical & Descriptive. Mary A. Holley. LC 72-9451. (Far Western Frontier Ser.). (Illus.). 172p. 1973. Repr. of 1833 ed. 14.00 (ISBN 0-405-04979-X). Ayer Co Pubs.
Texas Oil Directory. Ed. by Lalla Howell. (Illus.). 1985. pap. 90.00 (ISBN 0-317-40908-5). Tradex Pubns.
Texas Oil Register. Ed. by Lalla Howell. (Illus.). 1985. pap. 90.00 (ISBN 0-317-40909-3). Tradex Pubns.
Texas on Paper. Linda Cathcart & Cheryl A. Brutvan. (Illus.). 37p. 1982. 6.00 (ISBN 0-916365-05-0). Ind Curators.
Texas on the Halfshell. Joe Daniel & Phil Britton. LC 81-43408. (Illus.). 240p. 1982. pap. 12.95 (ISBN 0-385-17904-9, Dolp). Doubleday.
Texas on the Rocks. Daniel Da Cruz. 304p. (Orig.). 1986. pap. 3.50 (ISBN 0-345-31659-2, Del Rey). Ballantine.
Texas: One Hundred Years Ago. new ed. Compiled by Skip Whitson. (Sun Historical Ser). (Illus., Orig.). 1976. pap. 3.50 (ISBN 0-89540-030-8, SB-030). Sun Pub.
Texas, Our Texas. Paul Burka. LC 85-28890. (Illus.). 171p. 10.95 (ISBN 0-87719-051-8). Texas Month Pr.
Texas, Our Texas. Ed. by Paul Burka. 182p. 1988. pap. 7.95 (ISBN 0-87719-106-9). Texas Month Pr.
Texas Out Back. Leon Hale & Harry A. DeYoung. LC 73-89806. (Illus.). 68p. 1974. 7.95 (ISBN 0-89052-002-X, 102P). Madrona Pr.
Texas Outback. Caleb Pirtle, III. Ed. by Shirley D. Ratisseau. LC 86-62065. (Illus.). 162p. 1986. 19.95 (ISBN 0-918865-05-0). McLennan Hse.
Texas Outdoors. Tony Elliott. (This is America Ser.). (Illus.). (gr. 1-8). 1986. pap. 4.95 (ISBN 0-914565-24-9, 24-9). Capstan Pubns.
Texas Panhandle Forefathers, Vol. I. Ed. by Amarillo Genealogical Society Staff. (Illus.). 388p. 1983. 50.00 (ISBN 0-88107-011-4). Curtis Media.
Texas Panhandle Frontier. Fredrick W. Rathjen. (M. K. Brown Range Life Ser.: No. 12). (Illus.). 302p. 1985. pap. 9.95 (ISBN 0-292-78082-6). U of Tex Pr.
Texas Parks & Campgrounds: A Vacation Guide to Central, South & West Texas. George O. Miller & Delena Tull. Ed. by Scott Lubeck. (Guidebook Ser.). 200p. 1984. pap. 7.95 (ISBN 0-932012-89-2). Texas Month Pr.
Texas Parks & Campgrounds: A Vacation Guide to North, East & the Coastal Texas. George Miller & Delen a Tull. Ed. by Scott Lubeck. 200p. 1984. pap. 7.95 (ISBN 0-932012-70-1). Texas Month Pr.
Texas Parks Guide. Barbara McCaig. Ed. by Chris Boyce. 100p. (Orig.). 1988. pap. text ed. 5.95 (ISBN 0-935201-40-8). Affordable Adven.
Texas Passion. Leah Guild. (Orig.). 1983. pap. 1.95 (ISBN 0-317-02747-6, BH064). Holloway.
Texas Patriot Ancestor Album. Ed. by Heritage Publishers Services Staff. LC 86-82963. 250p. 1987. 49.95 (ISBN 0-939379-05-8). Herit Pubs Servs.
Texas Pattern Jury Charges, Vol. 1. 2nd ed. Committee on Pattern Jury Charges of the State Bar of Texas. LC 87-62226. 144p. 1987. 85.00 (ISBN 0-938160-47-8, 6281). State Bar TX.
Texas Pattern Jury Charges, Vol. 3. State Bar of Texas, Committee on Pattern Jury Charges. LC 78-13954. 380p. 1982. 65.00 (ISBN 0-938160-28-1, 6315). State Bar TX.
Texas Pattern Jury Charges: (General, Motor Vehicles, Damages, Vol. 1. 2nd ed. Committee on Pattern Jury Charges. LC 87-62226. 144p. 1987. loose-leaf 85.00 (ISBN 0-938160-49-4, 6281). State Bar TX.
Texas Pattern Jury Charges: (Workmen's Compensation), 1976 Cumulative Supplement, Vol. 2. Committee on Pattern Jury Charges. LC 78-13954. 45p. 1976. pap. 5.00 (ISBN 0-938160-03-6, 6306). State Bar TX.
Texas Pattern Jury Charges: 1984 Cumulative Supplement, Vol. 3. State Bar of Texas, Committee on Pattern Jury Charges. LC 78-13954. 45p. 1985. pap. 20.00 (ISBN 0-938160-39-7, 6286). State Bar TX.
Texas Peace Officer. Ray K. Robbins et al. LC 85-63434. 465p. 1986. 31.00 (ISBN 0-8211-1716-5); text ed. 24.80 (ISBN 0-317-46845-6). McCutchan.

Texas Weather. George W. Bomar. (Illus.). 277p. 1983. 24.95 (ISBN 0-292-78052-4); pap. 12.95 (ISBN 0-292-78053-2). U of Tex Pr.

Texas West of the Pecos. Jim Bones, Jr. LC 81-40397. (Louise Lindsey Merrick Texas Environment Ser.: No. 4). (Illus.). 138p. 1981. 29.95 (ISBN 0-89096-117-4). Tex A&M Univ Pr.

Texas Wildfire. Wanda Oewn. 1984. pap. 3.75 (ISBN 0-8217-1337-X). Zebra.

Texas Wildfire. Eleanor Woods. (Candlelight Supreme Ser.: No. 163). (Orig.). 1987. pap. 2.75 (ISBN 0-440-18780-X). Dell.

Texas Wildflower: Laurian Kane. Kitt Brown. (Frontier Woman Saga Ser.: No. 3). 1982. pap. 2.95 (ISBN 0-686-87387-4, GM). Fawcett.

Texas Wildflower Portraits. Lou-Ellen Okennon & Bob Okennon. (Illus.). 270p. 1987. 55.00 (ISBN 0-87719-098-4). Texas Month Pr.

Texas Wildflowers: A Field Guide. Campbell Loughmiller & Lynn Loughmiller. (Illus.). 287p. 1984. 22.95 (ISBN 0-292-78059-1); pap. 11.95 (ISBN 0-292-78060-5). U of Tex Pr.

Texas Wildlife Coloring Book. Illus. by John Carter. (Illus.). 40p. 1984. 2.95 (ISBN 0-89015-483-X). Eakin Pr.

Texas Wildlife: Photographs from Texas Parks & Wildlife Magazine. Intro. by David Baxter. LC 77-99281. (Louise Lindsey Merrick Texas Environment Ser.: No. 1). (Illus.). 196p. 1978. 24.95 (ISBN 0-89096-047-X). Tex A&M Univ Pr.

Texas Wills & Estates: Cases & Materials. Gerry W. Beyer. 468p. 1987. perfect bdg. 24.00 (ISBN 0-409-25203-4). Butterworth TX.

Texas Wills & Trusts System. Ed. by Fred C. Weekley. 1984. looseleaf incl. disks cancelled 1595.00 (ISBN 0-317-37655-1, 773). Bender.

Texas Women: A Celebration of History. 2nd ed. Mary B. Rogers. LC 81-51413. (Illus.). 80p. (Orig.). 1986. pap. 15.00 (ISBN 0-9606256-0-7). Tex Foun Womens Res.

Texas Women: A Pictorial History. Ruthe Winegarten. (Illus.). 180p. 1986. 24.95 (ISBN 0-89015-532-1). Eakin Pr.

Texas Woollybacks: The Range Sheep & Goat Industry. Paul H. Carlson. LC 82-40311. (Illus.). 256p. 1982. 19.50 (ISBN 0-89096-133-6). Tex A&M Univ Pr.

Texas Workers Compensation Trial Manual: 1986 Revision. rev. ed. P. Hardberger. LC 82-62103. 1984. looseleaf 70.00 (ISBN 0-911110-42-9). Parker & Son.

Texas: Yesterday & Today. Sibyl Hancock & Fay Venable. 1981. 7.95 (ISBN 0-89015-304-3). Eakin Pr.

Texas Yesterday, Today & Tomorrow. Ed. by S. Charles Maurice & Svetozar Pejovich. (Public Issues Ser.: No. 22). 1986. pap. 2.00 (ISBN 0-86599-026-3). Ctr Educ Res.

Texastat '74 & '76. Ed. by Douglas S. Harlan. LC 78-52839. 224p. 1978. pap. 15.00 (ISBN 0-911536-75-2). Trinity U Pr.

TexaStats Seventy-Two: Compilation of Voting Data on the Major Campaigns in Texas. 244p. 1974. pap. 7.50 (ISBN 0-89940-304-2). LBJ Sch Pub Aff.

Texasville. Larry McMurtry. 512p. 1987. 18.95 (ISBN 0-671-62533-0). S&S.

Texasville. Larry McMurtry. pap. 3.95 (ISBN 0-671-64878-0, Touchstone Bks.). S&S.

Texasville. Larry McMurtry. 576p. 1988. pap. 4.95 (ISBN 0-671-65764-X). PB.

Texian Stomping Grounds. Ed. by J. Frank Dobie et al. LC 41-4871. (Texas Folklore Society Publications: No. 17). 1967. Repr. of 1941 ed. 11.95 (ISBN 0-87074-048-2). SMU Press.

Texians. David L. Hicks & Dan Parkinson. LC 79-91599. 272p. 1981. 8.95 (ISBN 0-89896-000-2). Larksdale.

Texians & Texans. Incl. Afro-American Texans. 2nd, rev. ed. (Texians & Texans). (Illus.). 31p. 1987. 3.50 (ISBN 0-86701-036-3); Anglo-American Texans. 2nd ed. (Texians & the Texans Ser.). (Illus.). 24p. 1985. Repr. of 1985 ed. 3.50 (ISBN 0-86701-028-2); Belgian Texans (ISBN 0-933164-97-1); Chinese Texans (ISBN 0-933164-91-2); Czech Texans (ISBN 0-86701-011-8); French Texans; Greek Texans (ISBN 0-86701-007-X); Indian Texans; Italian Texans. rev. ed. (Texians & the Texans). (Illus.). 1987. 3.50 (ISBN 0-86701-033-9); Jewish Texans (ISBN 0-86701-024-X); Mexican Texans. rev.,2nd ed. (Illus.). 23p. 1986. 3.50 (ISBN 0-86701-030-4); Los Tejanos Mexicanos. (Span.) (ISBN 0-933164-89-0); Norwegian Texans. rev., 2nd ed. (Texians & the Texans). (Illus.). 20p. 1985. 3.50 (ISBN 0-86701-029-0); Spanish Texans (ISBN 0-933164-32-7); Syrian & Lebanese Texans (ISBN 0-933164-15-7); Swiss Texans (ISBN 0-933164-92-0); German-Texans. rev., 2nd ed. (Texians & Texans ser.). (Illus.). 1987. 3.50 (ISBN 0-86701-037-1). (Texians & Texans Ser.). pap. 36.90 set (ISBN 0-317-04135-5); pap. 3.50 ea. U of Tex Inst Tex Culture.

Texican. Dane Coolidge. 1975. lib. bdg. 16.30x (ISBN 0-89966-065-7). Buccaneer Bks.

Text & Concordance of Biblioteca Nacional Manuscript Res. 270-217: Libro Que Es Hecho de las Animalias Que Cacan: The Book of Moamin. Anthony J. Cardenas. (Spanish Ser.: No. 38). 26p. 1987. pap. 10.00x (ISBN 0-942260-99-6); 4 microfiches avail. Hispanic Seminary.

Text & Concordance of Biblioteca Nacional Manuscript 18052, Visita y consejo de medicos. Ed. by Cynthia M. Wasick. (Medieval Spanish Medical Texts Ser.: No. 3). 1986. 10.00x (ISBN 0-942260-54-6). Hispanic Seminary.

Text & Concordance of Biblioteca Nacional Manuscript 2153 Cirugia Rimada. Ed. by Victoria G. Serrano & Michael R. Solomon. (Medieval Spanish Medical Tests Ser.: No. 6). 1986. 10.00x (ISBN 0-942260-72-4). Hispanic Seminary.

Text & Concordance of Biblioteca Nacional Manuscript 3356: Speculum al Foderi. Ed. by Michael Solomon. (Medieval Spanish Medical Texts Ser.: No. 4). 1985. 10.00x (ISBN 0-942260-60-0). Hispanic Seminary.

Text & Concordance of Biblioteca Nacional Manuscript 9218 Historia del gran Tamerlan. Ed. by Juan L. Rodriguez et al. (Spanish Ser.: No. 20). 1986. 10.00x (ISBN 0-942260-62-7). Hispanic Seminary.

Text & Concordance of Escorial Manuscript F. iv. l. Arte Cisoria. Enrique De Villena. Ed. by John O'Neill. (Spanish Ser.: No. 37). 10p. 1987. pap. 10.00 (ISBN 0-942260-98-8); 2 microfiches avail. Hispanic Seminary.

Text & Concordance of Escorial Manuscript M.III 7: Viajes de John of Mandeville. Ed. by Maria Del Mar Martinez Rodriguez & Juan Luis Rodriguez Bravo. (Dialect Ser.: No. 7). 8p. text ed. 10.00x & 3 Microfiches (ISBN 0-942260-46-5). Hispanic Seminary.

Text & Concordance of the British Library Manuscript IB42463: Historia de la linda Melusina. Ed. by Ivy M. Corfis. (Spanish Ser.: No.27). 12p. text ed. 10.00x & 10 Microfiches (ISBN 0-317-47051-5). Hispanic Seminary.

Text & Concordance of the Suma de la Flor di Cirugia: Biblioteca Nacional Madrid,3383. Maria C. Villar. (Spanish Medical Texts Ser.: No. 10). 4p. 1987. microfiche avail. 10.00 (ISBN 0-940639-06-8). Hispanic Seminary.

Text & Concordance of the Tratado de la Generacion de la Criatura: I-51 Biblioteca Nacional, Madrid. Maria J. Mancho. (Spanish Medical Texts Ser.: No. 11). 10p. 1987. microfiche avail. 10.00 (ISBN 0-940639-07-6). Hispanic Seminary.

Text & Concordance of the Tratado de Patologia General: Biblioteca Nacional Madrid, 10.051. Maria T. Herrera. (Spanish Medical Texts Ser.: No. 15). 4p. 1987. microfiches avail 10.00 (ISBN 0-940639-11-4). Hispanic Seminary.

Text & Concordance of the Vatican Manuscript 6428 Cuento de Tristan de Leonis. Ed. by Ivy A. Corfis. (Spanish Ser.: No. 26). 1986. 10.00x (ISBN 0-942260-69-4). Hispanic Seminary.

Text & Concordances of Biblioteca Nacional Manuscript 3384 Espejo de Medicina. Alfonso Chirino. Ed. by Cynthia M. Wasick. (Medieval Spanish Medical Texts Ser.: No. 5). 1986. 10.00x (ISBN 0-942260-56-2). Hispanic Seminary.

Text & Concordances of Escorial Manuscript M.I.28: Tratado de las Fiebres. 2nd ed. Isaac Israeli & Ruth M. Richards. (Medieval Spanish Medical Texts Ser.: No. 1). 13p. incl. 14 microfiches 1984 10.00x (ISBN 0-942260-44-9). Hispanic Seminary.

Text & Concordances of Fernando del Pulgar - Claros Varones de Castilla & Letras, Seville, 1500. Ed. by Michael L. Dangerfield. (Spanish Ser.: No. 29). 6p. 1986. 10.00x (ISBN 0-942260-71-6); microfiche incl. Hispanic Seminary.

Text & Concordances of Seville Colombina Manuscript 7-6-27. Macer Herbolario. Ed. by Porter Conerly & Enrica J. Ardemagni. (Medieval Spanish Medical Texts Ser.: No. 7). 10p. 1986. 10.00x (ISBN 0-942260-78-3); microfiche incl. Hispanic Seminary.

Text & Concordances of the Escorial Manuscript of the Arcipreste de Talavera of Alfonso Martinez de Toledo. Ed. by Eric W. Naylor. (Spanish Ser.: No. 12). 6p. incl. 3 microfiches 1983 10.00x (ISBN 0-942260-38-4). Hispanic Seminary.

Text & Context: Essays to Honor Nils Ake Nilsson. Ed. by Peter A. Jenson et al. (Stockholm Studies in Russian Literature: No. 23). 202p. (Orig.). 1987. pap. 32.00x (ISBN 91-22-00879-9, Pub. by Almqvist & Wiksell). Coronet Bks.

Text & Context Folksong in a Bosnian Muslim Village. Yvonne R. Lockwood. (Illus.). 220p. (Orig.). 1983. pap. 12.95 (ISBN 0-89357-120-2). Slavica.

Text & Context: The Social Anthropology of Tradition. Ed. by Ravindra K. Jain. LC 77-842. (ASA Essays in Social Anthropology Ser.: Vol. 2). (Illus.). 256p. 1977. text ed. 16.50 (ISBN 0-915980-03-7). ISHI PA.

Text & Discourse Constitution: Empirical Aspects, Theoretical Approaches. Ed. by Janos S. Petofi. (Research in Text Theory Ser.: Vol. 4). 516p. 1987. lib. bdg. 154.00x (ISBN 0-89925-326-1). De Gruyter.

Text & Document Processing in Science & Technology. Robert Ransom. 239p. 1988. pap. 24.95 (ISBN 0-470-20981-X). Wiley.

Text & Epistemology. William Frawley. Ed. by Roy O. Freedle. LC 87-1847. (Advances in Discourse Processes Ser.: Vol. 24). 208p. 1987. text ed. 36.50 (ISBN 0-89391-397-9). Ablex Pub.

Text & Iconography of Joinville's Credo. Lionel J. Friedman. LC 58-7918. 1958. 12.00x (ISBN 0-910956-42-1). Medieval Acad.

Text & Interpretation: A Practical Commentary, Revelation. L. Van Hartingsveld. Ed. by A. S. Van Der Woude. (Text & Interpretation Ser.). 128p. (Orig., Dutch.). 1985. pap. 7.95 (ISBN 0-8028-0100-5). Eerdmans.

Text & Interpretation: Studies in the New Testament. Ed. by Ernest Best & R. McL. Wilson. LC 78-2962. pap. 71.50 (ISBN 0-317-26088-X, 2024416). Bks Demand UMI.

Text & Its Margins. M. Alexiou & V. Lambropoulos. LC 85-62596. 288p. 1985. 25.00 (ISBN 0-918618-30-4); pap. 12.00 (ISBN 0-918618-29-0). Pella Pub.

Text & Presentation. Ed. by Karelisa Hartigan. LC 88-3536. (University of Florida Comparative Drama Conference Papers: Vol. VIII). (Illus.). 232p. 1988. lib. bdg. 24.75 (ISBN 0-8191-6907-2). U Pr of Amer.

Text & Readings on Jurisprudence: The Philosophy of Law. George C. Christie. 1056p. 1973. write for info. West Pub.

Text & Reality: Aspects of Reference in Biblical Texts. Bernard C. Lategan & Willem S. Vorster. LC 85-47735. 144p. 1985. pap. 1.95 (ISBN 0-8006-1514-X). Fortress.

Text & Reality: Aspects of Reference in Biblical Texts. Bernard C. Lategan & Willem S. Vorster. 1975. 14.95 (ISBN 0-89130-822-9, 06 06 14); pap. 9.95 (ISBN 0-89130-823-7). Scholars Pr GA.

Text & Tagmeme. Kenneth Pike & Evelyn Pike. 284p. 1983. text ed. 32.50 (ISBN 0-89391-210-7). Ablex Pub.

Text & Texture: Close Readings of Selected Biblical Texts. Michael Fishbane. LC 79-14083. 154p. 1979. pap. 7.95 (ISBN 0-8052-0726-0). Schocken.

Text & Transmission: Survey of Latin Classics. Ed. by Leighton. D. Reynolds. 1983. 59.00x (ISBN 0-19-814456-3). Oxford U Pr.

Text As Contract: The Nature & Function of Narrative Discourse in the Erzahlungen of Heinrich von Kleist. Timothy J. Mehigan. (European University Studies: Series 1, German Language & Literature: Vol. 985). 450p. 1987. 40.00 (ISBN 3-8204-9872-9). P Lang Pubs.

Text-Atlas of Cat Anatomy. James E. Crouch. LC 68-25206. pap. 103.80 (ISBN 0-317-27963-7, 2056016). Bks Demand UMI.

Text-Atlas of Histology. C. Roland Leeson et al. (Illus.). 768p. 1988. 49.00 (ISBN 0-7216-2386-7). Saunders.

Text Book: An Introduction to Literary Language. Robert Scholes et al. LC 87-60579. 320p. 1988. pap. text ed. write for info. (ISBN 0-312-00251-3); write for info. instr's. manual (ISBN 0-312-00256-4); write for info. instr's. ed. (ISBN 0-312-01311-6). St Martin.

Text-Book in the History of Education. Paul Monroe. 772p. 1981. Repr. of 1928 ed. lib. bdg. 50.00 (ISBN 0-89760-555-1). Telegraph Bks.

Text Book of English Legal History. V. D. Kulshreshtha. 296p. 1983. pap. text ed. 36.00x (ISBN 0-317-54606-6, Pub. by Eastern Bk India). State Mutual Bk.

Text Book of Irish Literature, 2 Vols. Eleanor Hull. LC 70-153595. Repr. of 1908 ed. Set. 49.50 (ISBN 0-404-09244-6). AMS Pr.

Text-Book of Palaeontology, 3 vols. K. A. Von Zittel. Ed. by C. R. Eastmann & A. Smith Woodward. Incl. Vol. 2. Vertebrates I: Pisces, Amphibia, Reptile, Aves. 25.00x (ISBN 3-7682-7100-5); Vol. 3. Mammalia. 25.00x (ISBN 3-7682-7103-X). 1964. Set. 98.00x (ISBN 3-7682-7100-5). Lubrecht & Cramer.

Text, Cases & Materials on Sex-Based Discrimination. 3rd ed. Herma H. Kay. (American Casebook Ser.). 1050p. 1988. text ed. write for info. (ISBN 0-314-39751-5). West Pub.

Text-Cassette see Zimmerfrei.

Text, Context, & Hypertext: Writing with & for the Computer. Ed. by Edward Barrett. (Information Systems Ser.). 250p. 1988. text ed. 35.00x (ISBN 0-262-02275-3). MIT Pr.

Text der Aristotelischen Rhetorik: Prolegomena zu einer kritischen Ausgabe. R. Kassel. (Peripatoi, Vol. 3). 151p. 1971. 38.80 (ISBN 3-11-003740-8). De Gruyter.

Text, Discourse, & Process: Toward a Multidisciplinary Science of Texts. Robert De Beaugrande. (Advances in Discourse Processes Ser.: Vol. 4). 1980. text ed. 47.50x (ISBN 0-89391-033-3). Ablex Pub.

Text Editing: Keyboarding, Applications & Exercises. Arnold Rosen & William Hubbard. LC 84-27090. 231p. 1985. pap. write for info. (ISBN 0-471-81068-1). Wiley.

Text Generation: Using Discourse Strategies & Focus Constraints to Generate Natural Language Text. Kathleen R. McKeown. (Studies in Natural Language Processing). (Illus.). 248p. 1985. 34.50 (ISBN 0-521-30116-5). Cambridge U Pr.

Text, Interpretation, Theory. Michael Payne & James M. Heath. LC 85-5893. (Bucknell Review Ser.: Vol. 29. No. 2). 176p. 1985. 16.50 (ISBN 0-8387-5097-4). Bucknell U Pr.

Text, Literature, & Aesthetics: In Honor of Monroe C. Beardsley. Ed. by L. Aagaard-Mogensen & L. DeVos. (Elementa Ser.: Vol. 45). 232p. 1986. pap. text ed. 35.00 (ISBN 90-6203-998-7). Humanities.

Text-Manual for Remedial Handwriting. Warren H. Gardner. 1966. pap. 4.95 (ISBN 0-8134-0847-4, 847). Inter Print Pubs.

Text of Chaucer's Legend of Good Women. Ernest F. Amy. LC 65-21088. (Studies in Chaucer, No. 6). 1969. Repr. of 1918 ed. lib. bdg. 39.95 (ISBN 0-8383-0502-4). Haskell.

Text of Chinese Military Terms. Ed. by P. K. Li. 390p. (Chinese & Eng.). 1972. pap. 12.95 (ISBN 0-686-92268-9, M-9577). French & Eur.

Text of Gulliver's Travels. Harold Williams. LC 74-31475. 1952. lib. bdg. 20.00 (ISBN 0-8414-9351-0). Folcroft.

Text of Henry Fifth. Hereward T. Price. LC 72-190332. Repr. of 1920 ed. lib. bdg. 19.00 (ISBN 0-8414-1096-8). Folcroft.

Text of King Lear. Madeleine Doran. LC 74-164775. (Stanford University. Stanford Studies in Language & Literature: Vol. 4, Pt. 2). 1931. 21.00 (ISBN 0-404-51807-9). AMS Pr.

Text of King Lear. Madeleine Doran. LC 74-7224. 1931. lib. bdg. 16.50 (ISBN 0-8414-3758-0). Folcroft.

Text of Paradise Lost: A Study in Editorial Procedure. R. G. Moyles. 198p. 1985. 25.00x (ISBN 0-8020-5634-2). U of Toronto Pr.

Text of Piers Plowman. R. W. Chambers. LC 72-195253. lib. bdg. 15.00 (ISBN 0-8414-3015-2). Folcroft.

Text of Piers Plowman. R. W. Chambers & J. H. Grattan. 1978. Repr. of 1931 ed. lib. bdg. 16.50 (ISBN 0-8495-0825-8). Arden Lib.

Text of Shakespeare. Thomas R. Lounsbury. LC 74-130240. Repr. of 1906 ed. 29.50 (ISBN 0-404-04035-7). AMS Pr.

Text of Shakespeare's Lear. B. A. Van Dam. (Materials for the Study of the Old English Drama Series 2: Vol. 10). pap. 11.00 (ISBN 0-8115-0303-8). Kraus Repr.

Text of the Book of Llan Dav. Ed. by John G. Evans & J. Rhys. LC 78-72667. (Series of Old Welsh Texts: Vol. 4). Repr. of 1893 ed. 62.50 (ISBN 0-404-60584-2). AMS Pr.

Text of the Bruts from the Red Book of Hergest. Ed. by John Rhys & John G. Evans. LC 78-72662. (Series of Old Welsh Texts: Vol. 2). Repr. of 1890 ed. 62.50 (ISBN 0-404-60582-6). AMS Pr.

Text of the Epistles: A Disquisition upon the Corpus Paulinum. G. Zuntz. (Schweich Lectures on Biblical Archaeology). 306p. 1946. 8.25 (ISBN 0-85672-715-6, Pub. by British Acad). Longwood Pub Group.

Text of the GATT: Analytical Index. 3rd Rev. ed. 1970. pap. 18.00 (G97, GATT). UNIPUB.

Text of the General Agreement on Tariffs & Trade. (Illus.). 96p. (Orig.). 1987. pap. text ed. 7.50 (ISBN 0-317-55611-8, G181, GATT). UNIPUB.

Text of the Greek Bible. 3rd, rev. ed. F. G. Kenyon. 1975. 40.50 (ISBN 0-7156-0641-7, Pub. by Duckworth London); pap. 13.50 (ISBN 0-7156-0652-2). Longwood Pub Group.

Text of the Holocaust: A Documentation of the Nazis' Extermination Propaganda from 1919-45. C. C. Aronsfeld. LC 85-351. 1985. 16.00 (ISBN 0-916288-17-X); pap. 10.00 (ISBN 0-916288-18-8). Micah Pubns.

Text of the Mabinogion from the Red Book of Hergest. Ed. by John Rhys & John G. Evans. LC 78-72663. (Series of Old Welsh Texts: Vol. 1). Repr. of 1887 ed. 52.50 (ISBN 0-404-60581-8). AMS Pr.

Text of the New Testament. Kurt Aland & Barbara Aland. Tr. by Erroll F. Rhodes from Ger. (Illus.). 344p. 1987. 29.95 (ISBN 0-8028-3620-8). Eerdmans.

Text of the New Testament: Its Transmission, Corruption, & Restoration. 2nd ed. Bruce M. Metzger. 1968. 14.95x (ISBN 0-19-500391-8). Oxford U Pr.

Text of the Old Testament. E. Naville. (British Academy, London, Schweich Lectures in Biblical Archaeology Series, 1915). pap. 19.00 (ISBN 0-8115-1257-6). Kraus Repr.

Text of the Old Testament. Ernst Wurthwein. Tr. by Erroll F. Rhodes. LC 79-15492. (Illus.). 1980. text ed. 18.95 (ISBN 0-8028-3530-9). Eerdmans.

Text of the Septuagint: Its Corruptions & Their Emendation. Peter Katz. Ed. by D. W. Gooding. LC 74-161292. pap. 110.00 (ISBN 0-317-28405-3, 2022451). Bks Demand UMI.

Text of the Talmud: Misnah, 3 vols. Hyman E. Goldin. 1933. Set. 10.00 (ISBN 0-88482-838-7). Hebrew Pub.

Text Processing. Ed. by Wolfgang Burghardt & Klaus Hoelker. (Research in Text Theory Ser.). 466p. 1979. text ed. 82.00x (ISBN 3-11-007565-2). De Gruyter.

Text Processing. A. Colin Day. (Computer Science Text Ser.: No. 20). 150p. 1984. o. p. 32.50 (ISBN 0-521-24432-3); pap. 13.95 (ISBN 0-521-28683-2). Cambridge U Pr.

Text Processing: Algorithms, Languages, & Applications. Allen B. Tucker, Jr. LC 79-23130. (Computer Science & Applied Mathematics Ser.). 1979. 30.00 (ISBN 0-12-702550-2). Acad Pr.

Text Processing & Document Manipulation: Proceedings of the International Conference Nottingham, April 1986. Ed. by J. C. Van Vliet. (British Computer Society Workshop Ser.). 250p. 1986. 42.50 (ISBN 0-521-32592-7). Cambridge U Pr.

Text Processing: Text Analysis & Generation. Sture Allen. (Data Linguistica ser.). 653p. (Orig.). 1982. pap. text ed. 57.50x (ISBN 91-22-00594-3). Coronet Bks.

Text Processing with UNIX. David W. Barron & Michael J. Rees. 240p. 1987. pap. text ed. 26.95 (ISBN 0-201-14219-8). Addison-Wesley.

Text Production. Robert de Beaugrande. Ed. by Roy O. Freedle. LC 83-25756. (Advances in Discourse Processes Ser.: Vol. 11). 400p. 1983. text ed. 49.50 (ISBN 0-89391-158-5); pap. text ed. 29.50 (ISBN 0-89391-159-3). Ablex Pub.

Text Production. Michael Riffaterre. Tr. by Therese Lyons. LC 82-25509. 336p. 1983. 29.00x (ISBN 0-231-05334-7); pap. 15.00 (ISBN 0-231-05335-5). Columbia U Pr.

Text Ray. Floyd Bergman. pap. 5.10 (ISBN 0-317-20153-0). Campus.

Text Retrieval: A Directory of Software. Ed. by Catherine D. Hamilton et al. LC 84-22284. 180p. 1985. text ed. 34.50 (ISBN 0-566-03527-8). Gower Pub Co.

Text Retrieval: A Directory of Software. Robert Kimberley. 200p. 1986. text ed. 95.50 (ISBN 0-566-05372-1, Pub. by Gower Pub England). Gower Pub Co.

Text Searching Algorithms for Parallel Processors. C. A. Pogue & O. Willett. (British Library Reseach Paper: No. 11). 1987. pap. 7.50 (ISBN 0-7123-3101-8, Pub. by British Lib). Longwood Pub Group.

Text-Sound Texts. Ed. by Richard Kostelanetz. LC 78-72281. 10.00 (ISBN 0-932360-60-2); pap. 5.00. RK Edns.

Text to Reader: A Communicative Approach to Fowles, Barth, Cortazar & Boon. Theo D'Haen. (Utrecht Publications in Comparative Literature: 16). x, 162p. 1983. 36.00x (ISBN 90-272-2191-X); pap. 24.00x (ISBN 90-272-2201-0). Benjamins North Am.

Text: Transactions of the Society for Textual Scholarship, Vol. 3. Ed. by D. C. Greetham & W. Speed Hill. LC 83-45281. (Illus.). 1987. 45.00 (ISBN 0-404-62553-3). AMS Pr.

Text: Transactions of the Society for Textual Scholarship, Vol. 4. Ed. by D. C. Greetham & W. Speed Hill. LC 83-45281. 1988. 45.00 (ISBN 0-404-62554-1). AMS Pr.

Text und Variantenkonkordanz zu Schillers "Kabale und Liebe". Peter M. Daly & Claus O. Lappe. 1976. 182.00x (ISBN 3-11-002225-7). De Gruyter.

Text, Vol. 3: Transactions of the Society for Textual Scholarship. Ed. by D. C. Greetham & W. Speed Hill. LC 83-45281. (Illus.). 1987. 45.00 (ISBN 0-404-62550-9). AMS Pr.

Text 1 see Orientation in American English.

Textaufbau in den Erzahlungen Dostoevskijs. Wolf Schmid. (Beihefte zu Poetic: No. 10). 318p. 1986. 47.00x (ISBN 90-6032-253-3, Pub. by B R Gruner Netherlands). Benjamins North Am.

Textband see Opicinus de Canistris: Weltbild & Bekenntnisse Eines Avignonesischen Klerikers des 14 Jahrhunderts.

Textbank Systems. E. Mergenthaler. (Lecture Notes in Medical Informatics: Vol. 27). vi, 177p. 1985. pap. 17.00 (ISBN 0-387-15974-6). Springer-Verlag.

Textbook. Donald Knuth. (Computers & Typesetting Ser.: Vol. A). 496p. 1986. text ed. write for info. Addison-Wesley.

Textbook & Guide to the Standard Nomenclature of Diseases & Operations. Thompson & Hayden. 1967. 14.50 (ISBN 0-917036-07-7). Physicians Rec.

Textbook for Childbirth Educators. 2nd ed. Patricia Hassid. (Illus.). 1983. pap. text ed. 19.50 (ISBN 0-397-54469-3, 64-04107, Lippincott Nursing). Lippincott.

Textbook for Dental Assistants. Virginia Park et al. LC 73-80978. pap. 158.30 (ISBN 0-317-26118-5, 2025170). Bks Demand UMI.

Textbook for Dental Nurses. 6th ed. Levison. (Illus.). 316p. 1985. 16.50 (ISBN 0-632-01282-X, B29764). Mosby.

Textbook for Pressman Training. 2nd ed. Frank Drazan. (Illus.). 106p. 1986. pap. 20.00 (ISBN 0-318-21789-9). F Drazan.

Textbook for the Clinical Application of Therapeutic Drug Monitoring. Ed. by William J. Taylor & Mary H. Diers-Caviness. LC 85-71233. (Illus.). 500p. text ed. 55.00 (ISBN 0-9614903-0-6, 9520-55). Abbott Laboratories.

Textbook in Analytic Group Psychotherapy. S. R. Slavson. LC 64-15375. 563p. 1964. text ed. 57.50x (ISBN 0-8236-6460-0). Intl Univs Pr.

Textbook in Methods of Instruction see Methods of Instruction.

Textbook in Oral Pathology. 4th ed. William G. Shafer et al. (Illus.). 944p. 1983. 44.95 (ISBN 0-7216-8128-X). Saunders.

Textbook in the History of Education. Paul Monroe. LC 77-109914. Repr. of 1905 ed. 28.50 (ISBN 0-404-04357-7). AMS Pr.

Textbook National Medicine. 600p. 1986. 150.00 (ISBN 0-318-23858-6). John Bastyr.

Textbook of Acute Internal Medicine. Lawrence B. Gardner. (Concise Textbook Ser.: Vol. 17). 1016p. 1985. 36.50 (ISBN 0-87488-689-9). Elsevier.

Textbook of Adverse Drug Reactions. Ed. by D. M. Davies. (Illus.). 1985. 95.00x (ISBN 0-19-261479-7). Oxford U Pr.

Textbook of Algebra, 2 Vols. 7th ed. George Chrystal. LC 64-21987. (gr. 9-12). text ed. 15.95 ea. (ISBN 0-8284-0084-9). Chelsea Pub.

Textbook of Analytical Chemistry. S. P. Banerjee. 1985. text ed. 79.00x (ISBN 0-317-38800-2, Pub. by Current Dist). State Mutual Bk.

Textbook of Analytical Geometry of Three Dimensions. 1985. 2.50 (ISBN 0-471-63876-5). Wiley.

Textbook of Analytical Geometry of Two Dimensions. 2nd ed. 1986. 2.50 (ISBN 0-471-63875-7). Wiley.

Textbook of Anatomy. 4th ed. W. Henry Hollinshead & Cornelius Rosse. (Illus.). 954p. 1985. text ed. 41.50 (ISBN 0-06-141263-5, Lippincott Medical). Lippincott.

Textbook of Anatomy & Physiology. 12th ed. Anthony & Thibodeau. (Illus.). 900p. 1987. student ed. 27.50 (ISBN 0-8016-0284-X). Mosby.

Textbook of Applied Thermodynamics: Steam & Thermal Engineering. S. K. Kulshrestha. (Illus.). xi, 443p. 1983. text ed. 37.50x (ISBN 0-7069-2158-5, Pub. by Vikas India). Advent NY.

Textbook of Astrology. A. J. Pearce. 500p. 1970. 10.00 (ISBN 0-86690-142-6, 1371-01). Am Fed Astrologers.

Textbook of Basic Nursing. 4th ed. Caroline B. Rosdahl. LC 64-4040. (Illus.). 1985. pap. text ed. 36.95 (ISBN 0-397-54463-4); 10.95 (ISBN 0-397-54462-6). Lippincott.

Textbook of Behavioral Science. Wedding. Date not set. price not set (ISBN 0-8016-5509-9). Mosby.

Textbook of Biochemistry, Vol. 2. Thomas M. Devlin. 400p. (Japanese.). 1984. write for info. (ISBN 0-471-88695-5). Wiley.

Textbook of Biochemistry: With Clinical Correlations. Thomas M. Devlin. LC 81-13063. 1265p. 1982. 39.95x (ISBN 0-471-05039-3, Pub. by Wiley Med); Japanese Ed. pap. text ed. 37.05 (ISBN 0-471-88696-3). Wiley.

Textbook of Biochemistry with Clinical Correlations. 2nd ed. Ed. by Thomas M. Devlin. LC 85-26318. 1016p. 1986. 39.95 (ISBN 0-471-81462-8, Pub. by Wiley Medical). Wiley.

Textbook of Biological Feedback. Mariella Fischer-Williams et al. LC 80-15235. 511p. 1981. 49.95 (ISBN 0-89885-014-2); pap. 24.95 (ISBN 0-89885-261-7). Human Sci Pr.

Textbook of Biopharmaceutic Analysis: A Description of Methods for the Determination of Drugs in Biologic Fluids. Robert V. Smith & James T. Stewart. LC 80-39872. (Illus.). 308p. 1981. text ed. 25.00 (ISBN 0-8121-0770-5). Lea & Febiger.

Textbook of Botany, Vol. I. 6th rev. ed. S. N. Pandey & P. S. Trivedi. 531p. 1983. (Pub. by Vikas India); 40.00x (ISBN 0-7069-0511-3). Advent NY.

Textbook of Botany: Algae, Fungi, Bacteria, Virus, Lichens, Mycoplasma & Elementary Plant Pathology, Vol. I. 1977. 12.00x. Intl Bk Dist.

Textbook of Botany: Vol. II. 9th ed. S. N. Pandey et al. viii, 531p. 1981. text ed. 40.00x (ISBN 0-7069-2397-9, Pub. by Vikas India). Advent NY.

Textbook of Botany: Vol. II (Bryophyta, Pteridophyta, Gymnosperms & Paleobotany) S. N. Pandey et al. (Illus.). 1974. 10.50 (ISBN 0-686-20315-1). Intl Bk Dist.

Textbook of Breast Cancer. Ed. by M. P. Vaidya & H. S. Shukla. (Illus.). xx, 420p. 1983. text ed. 37.50x (ISBN 0-7069-2161-5, Pub. by Vikas India); pap. text ed. 18.95x (Pub. by Vikas India). Advent NY.

Textbook of Bunion Surgery. Ed. by Joshua Gerbert. LC 80-68895. (Illus.). 356p. 1981. monograph 34.50 (ISBN 0-87993-153-1). Futura Pub.

Textbook of Cardiovascular Technology. Lunn Bronson. LC 65-8907. (Illus.). 416p. 1988. 29.95 (ISBN 0-397-50726-7, Lippincott Medical). Lippincott.

Textbook of Chemical Knetics. Sanzone. 1987. write for info. (ISBN 0-471-09195-2). Wiley.

Textbook of Chemical Technology. S. D. Shukla & G. N. Pandey. Vol. 1, 1976. text ed. 20.00x (ISBN 0-7069-0463-X, Pub. by Vikas India); Vol. 2, 1979. text ed. 27.50x (ISBN 0-7069-0755-8, Pub. by Vikas India). Advent NY.

Textbook of Chemistry, 2 pts. 1983. Pt. 1. 3.00 (ISBN 0-471-63865-X); Pt. 2. 2.25 (ISBN 0-471-63866-8). Wiley.

Textbook of Child Behavior & Development. 2nd & rev. ed. B. Kuppuswamy. xii, 288p. 1980. text ed. 27.50x (ISBN 0-317-17266-2, Pub. by Vikas India). Advent NY.

Textbook of Child Neurology. 3rd ed. John H. Menkes. LC 84-26100. (Illus.). 827p. 1985. text ed. 58.50 (ISBN 0-8121-0946-5). Lea & Febiger.

Textbook of Christian Ethics. Robin Gill. 571p. 1986. pap. 24.95 (ISBN 0-567-29127-8, Pub. by T & T Clark Ltd UK). Fortress.

Textbook of Clinical Cardioplegia. Ed. by Richard M. Engelman & Sidney Levitsky. LC 81-69558. (Illus.). 512p. 1982. 59.50 (ISBN 0-87993-167-1). Futura Pub.

Textbook of Clinical Chemistry. Norbert W. Tietz. (Illus.). 1919p. 1986. 75.00 (ISBN 0-7216-8886-1). Saunders.

Textbook of Clinical Electrocardiography. A. B. De Luna. 1987. lib. bdg. 118.00 (ISBN 0-89838-826-0, Pub. by Martinus Nijhoff Netherlands); pap. text ed. 60.00 (ISBN 0-89838-835-X). Kluwer Academic.

Textbook of Clinical Laboratory Supervision. Ed. by Kathleen Becan-McBride. (Illus.). 352p. 1982. 26.50 (ISBN 0-8385-8871-9). Appleton & Lange.

Textbook of Clinical Neuropharmacology. Harold L. Klawans et al. 382p. 1981. text ed. 56.50 (ISBN 0-89004-430-9). Raven.

Textbook of Clinical Ophthalmology, Vol. 1. R. P. Dhanda & V. Kalevar. 800p. 1986. text ed. 45.00x (ISBN 0-7069-2705-2, Pub. by Vikas India). Advent NY.

Textbook of Clinical Otology. Gordon H. Hughes. (Illus.). 448p. 1985. text ed. 89.95 (ISBN 0-86577-183-9). Thieme Med Pubs.

Textbook of Clinical Periodontology. Jan Lindhe. (Illus.). 549p. 1984. 75.00 (ISBN 0-7216-1315-2). Saunders.

Textbook of Coal Petrology. 3rd, rev. & enl. ed. E. Stach et al. Ed. by D. G. Murchison et al. Tr. by D. G. Murchison. (Illus.). 536p. 1982. lib. bdg. 80.50x (ISBN 3-443-01018-0). Lubrecht & Cramer.

Textbook of Commerce. 3rd ed. Henry G. Hughes & John W. Loveridge. 1981. pap. 13.75 (ISBN 0-408-70928-6). Butterworth.

Textbook of Comparative Education. 3rd ed. T. S. Sodhi. ix, 416p. 1983. text ed. 32.50x o. p. (ISBN 0-7069-2224-7, Pub. by Vikas India); pap. text ed. 15.95x (ISBN 0-7069-2225-5, Pub. by Vikas India). Advent NY.

Textbook of Contraceptive Practice. 2nd ed. Malcolm Potts & Peter Diggory. LC 83-5295. 350p. 1984. 62.50 (ISBN 0-521-24934-1); pap. 27.95 (ISBN 0-521-27085-5). Cambridge U Pr.

Textbook of Convergence. W. L. Ferrar. (Illus.). 1980. Repr. of 1938 ed. 19.95x (ISBN 0-19-853176-1). Oxford U Pr.

Textbook of Cost Accountancy. M. N. Arora. 750p. 1984. text ed. 45.00x (ISBN 0-7069-2538-6, Pub. by Vikas India); (Pub. by Vikas India). Advent NY.

Textbook of Cystic Fibrosis. J. Lloyd-Still. (Illus.). 520p. 1983. 75.00 (ISBN 0-7236-7026-9). PSG Pub Co.

Textbook of Demography. O. S. Shrivastava. 500p. 1983. (Pub. by Vikas India); pap. text ed. 15.95x (ISBN 0-7069-2136-4, Pub. by Vikas India). Advent NY.

Textbook of Dendrology. 6th ed. William M. Harlow. (Illus.). 1979. text ed. 46.95 (ISBN 0-07-026570-4). McGraw.

Textbook of Dental Radiology. 2nd ed. Olaf E. Langland et al. (Illus.). 684p. 1984. 49.25x (ISBN 0-398-04910-6). C C Thomas.

Textbook of Dermatology. 4th ed. A. Rook. (Illus.). 2700p. 1986. 395.00 (ISBN 0-632-00949-7). Year Bk Med.

Textbook of Developmental Pediatrics. Ed. by Marvin I. Gottlieb & John E. Williams. LC 83-30411. 568p. 1987. 59.50x (ISBN 0-306-42334-0, Plenum Med). Plenum Pub.

Textbook of Diagnostic Medicine. Ed. by A. H. Samiy. LC 85-23966. (Illus.). 900p. 1987. text ed. 69.50 (ISBN 0-8121-1006-4). Lea & Febiger.

Textbook of Diagnostic Ultrasonography. Hagen & Ansert. (Illus.). 800p. 1988. text ed. 71.50 (ISBN 0-8016-2446-0). Mosby.

Textbook of Diagnostic Ultrasonography. 2nd ed. Sandra L. Hagen-Ansert. LC 82-8190. (Illus.). 800p. 1983. text ed. 68.00 (ISBN 0-8016-2016-3). Mosby.

Textbook of Disorders & Injuries of Musculoskeletal Structure. 2nd ed. Robert B. Salter. (Illus.). 597p. 1983. text ed. 43.95 (ISBN 0-683-07500-4). Williams & wilkins.

Textbook of Disturbances of Mental Life: Disturbances of the Soul & Their Treatment. Johann Heinroth. Vol. 1 Theory. pap. 76.80 (ISBN 0-317-19872-6, 2023102); Vol. 2 Practice. pap. 61.00 (ISBN 0-317-19873-4). Bks Demand UMI.

Textbook of Disturbances of the Mental Life, or Disturbances of the Psyche & Their Treatment. Johann C. Heinroth. 235p. 1975. text ed. 69.00x (Pub. by Keter Pub Jerusalem). Coronet Bks.

Textbook of Dynamics. 2nd ed. Frank Chorlton. LC 82-25484. (Mathematics & Its Applications Ser.). 271p. 1983. 56.00x (ISBN 0-470-27407-7); pap. 34.95x (ISBN 0-470-27408-5). Halsted Pr.

Textbook of Echocardiography. Vincent E. Friedewald. LC 76-4247. pap. 62.60 (ISBN 0-317-07788-0, 2016663). Bks Demand UMI.

Textbook of Echocardiography. Ed. by Martin S. Sutton & Paul Oldershaw. (Illus.). 1988. 90.00 (ISBN 0-86542-032-7). Blackwell Sci.

Textbook of Economic Botany. 1987. 9.00 (ISBN 0-471-63921-4). Wiley.

Textbook of Economic Geography. 2nd ed. S. P. Chatterjee. 142p. 1988. pap. 8.95x (ISBN 0-86131-842-0, Pub. by Orient Longman LTD India). Apt Bks.

Textbook of Economics. Murray Wolfson. 1978. pap. 15.95x (ISBN 0-416-77090-8, NO. 2856). Routledge Chapman & Hall.

Textbook of Elementary Physics, 3 vols. Ed. by G. S. Landsberg. Tr. by MIR Publishers. Incl. Vol. 1. Mechanics, Heat & Molecular Physics; Vol. 2. Electricity & Magnetism; Vol. 3. Oscillations, Waves, Optics & Structure of the Atom. (Illus.). 1485p. 1975. text ed. 59.00 set (ISBN 0-8464-0913-5). Beekman Pubs.

Textbook of Endocrine Physiology. Ed. by James E. Griffin & Sergio R. Ojeda. (Illus.). 368p. 1988. 35.00 (ISBN 0-19-505442-3); pap. 18.95 (ISBN 0-19-505443-1). Oxford U Pr.

Textbook of Endocrine Physiology. Constance R. Martin. (Illus.). 1976. 26.95x (ISBN 0-19-502295-5). Oxford U Pr.

Textbook of Entomology. 4th ed. Herbert H. Ross et al. LC 81-16097. 696p. 1982. text ed. 41.45 (ISBN 0-471-73694-5, Pub. by John Wiley & Sons, inc.). Wiley.

Textbook of Environmental Physiology. 2nd ed. George E. Folk. LC 73-8683. pap. 120.50 (ISBN 0-317-28604-8, 2055425). Bks Demand UMI.

Textbook of Epilepsy. 3rd ed. Ed. by John P. Laidlaw & Alan Richens. LC 85-7786. (Illus.). 261p. 1988. text ed. 135.00 (ISBN 0-443-03667-5). Churchill.

Textbook of European Musical Instruments. Frances W. Galpin. LC 75-36509. (Illus.). 256p. 1976. Repr. of 1956 ed. lib. bdg. 35.00x (ISBN 0-8371-8648-X, GAEM). Greenwood.

Textbook of European Musical Instruments. Francis W. Galpin. 1977. lib. bdg. 59.95 (ISBN 0-8490-2737-3). Gordon Pr.

Textbook of Family Practice. 3rd ed. Robert F. Rakel. (Illus.). 1584p. 1984. 99.00 (ISBN 0-7216-7429-1). Saunders.

Textbook of Fire Assaying. 3rd ed. Edward E. Bugbee. Ed. by Jon W. Raese. LC 81-17021. (Illus.). 314p. 1981. Repr. of 1940 ed. text ed. 21.00 (ISBN 0-918062-47-0). Colo Sch Mines.

Textbook of Fish Culture: Breeding & Cultivation of Fish. 2nd ed. Marcel Huet. Tr. by Henry Kahn from Fr. (Illus.). 456p. text ed. 60.00 (ISBN 0-85238-140-9, Pub. by Fishing News Ltd). Scholium Intl.

Textbook of Fish Culture: Breeding & Cultivation of Fish. 2nd ed. Marcel Huet. (Illus.). 438p. 1986. text ed. 55.95 (FN 116, FNB). UNIPUB.

Textbook of Fish Culture: Breeding & Cultivation of Fish. 1978. 40.00x (ISBN 0-685-63460-4). State Mutual Bk.

Textbook of Fish Health. George Post. (Illus.). 256p. 1983. 29.95 (ISBN 0-87666-599-7, H-1043). TFH Pubns.

Textbook of Foreign Exchange. Paul Einzig. 1969. 25.95 (ISBN 0-312-79380-4). St Martin.

Textbook of Fungi, Bacteria & Viruses. H C. Dube. 240p. 1986. text ed. 27.50x (ISBN 0-7069-2885-7, Pub. by Vikas India); pap. text ed. 10.95x (Pub. by Vikas India). Advent NY.

Textbook of Gastroenterology. Ian A. Bouchier et al. (Illus.). 1600p. 1984. 79.00 (ISBN 0-7216-0956-2, Bailliere-Tindall). Saunders.

Textbook of Gastroenterology & Nutrition in Infancy, 2 vols. Ed. by Emanuel Lebenthal. (Illus.). 1182p. 1981. Set. text ed. 148.00 (ISBN 0-686-77542-2). Vol. 1: Gastrointestinal Development & Perinatal Nutrition (ISBN 0-89004-526-7). Vol. 2: Gastrointestinal Disease & Nutritional Inadequacies (ISBN 0-89004-533-X). Raven.

Textbook of General Chemistry. Boris Nekrasov. Tr. by MIR Publishers. (Illus.). 472p. 1975. text ed. 22.95 (ISBN 0-8464-0914-3). Beekman Pubs.

Textbook of General Medicine & Primary Care. Ed. by John Noble. 2320p. 1987. text ed. 85.00 (ISBN 0-317-53603-6, Little Med Div). Little.

Textbook of Genito-Urinary Surgery, 2 vols. Ed. by H. N. Whitfield & W. F. Hendry. (Illus.). 1437p. 1985. Set. text ed. 250.00 (ISBN 0-443-02657-2). Churchill.

Textbook of Geriatric Medicine & Gerontology. 3rd ed. Ed. by J. C. Brocklehurst. LC 83-27277. (Illus.). 1079p. 1985. text ed. 150.00 (ISBN 0-443-02696-3). Churchill.

Textbook of Glaucoma. 2nd ed. M. Bruce Shields. (Illus.). 550p. 1986. 96.95 (ISBN 0-683-07694-9). Williams & Wilkins.

Textbook of Gynaecology. Ajoy K. Ghosh. 552p. 1983. text ed. 69.00x (ISBN 0-317-38799-5, Pub. by Current Dist). State Mutual Bk.

Textbook of Gynaecology. Kumud P. Tamaskar. (Illus.). 650p. Date not set. pap. cancelled (ISBN 0-7069-2464-9, Pub. by Vikas India). Advent NY.

Textbook of Gynecology. Ed. by Russell R. De Alvarez. LC 76-10816. pap. 140.50 (ISBN 0-317-28609-9, 2055418). Bks Demand UMI.

Textbook of Head & Neck Anatomy. 2nd ed. James L. Hiatt. (Illus.). 384p. 1987. text ed. 27.95 (ISBN 0-683-03975-X). Williams & Wilkins.

Textbook of Health Education. L. Ramachandran & T. Dharmalingam. 278p. 1983. o. p. 20.00x (ISBN 0-7069-2327-8, Pub. by Vikas India); pap. text ed. 8.95x (ISBN 0-7069-2328-6, Pub. by Vikas India). Advent NY.

Textbook of Hematology. Shirlyn B. McKenzie. LC 87-3834. (Illus.). 507p. 1988. text ed. 38.50 (ISBN 0-8121-1096-X). Lea & Febiger.

Textbook of Histology. Finn Geneser. (Illus.). 831p. 1986. text ed. 49.50 (ISBN 0-8121-1051-X). Lea & Febiger.

Textbook of Histology. 5th ed. C. Roland Leeson et al. (Illus.). 605p. 1985. 34.95 (ISBN 0-7216-1201-6). Saunders.
Textbook of Histology. N. N. Majumdar. 450p. 1980. text ed. 30.00x (ISBN 0-7069-1012-5, Vikas India). Advent NY.
Textbook of Home Economics. Kamal Mehta. 1983. text ed. 15.00x o. p. (ISBN 0-7069-2317-0, Pub. by Vikas India); pap. text ed. 7.95x (ISBN 0-7069-2318-9, Pub. by Vikas India). Advent NY.
Textbook of Horseshoeing for Horseshoers & Veterinarians. Anton Lungwitz. Tr. by John W. Adams. LC 66-28443. (Illus.). 216p. 1966. 14.95 (ISBN 0-87071-308-6); soft cover o.p. 6.00 (ISBN 0-87071-329-9). Oreg St U Pr.
Textbook of Human Biology. 3rd ed. J. K. Inglis. (Illus.). 416p. 1986. text ed. 40.00 (ISBN 0-08-029807-9, Pub. by PPL); pap. text ed. 22.95 (ISBN 0-08-029806-0). Pergamon.
Textbook of Human Genetics. 3rd ed. Max Levitan. (Illus.). 456p. 1988. 37.50 (ISBN 0-19-504935-7). Oxford U Pr.
Textbook of Human Genetics. 2nd ed. Max Levitan & Ashley Montagu. (Illus.). 1977. text ed. 32.50x (ISBN 0-19-502101-0). Oxford U Pr.
Textbook of Human Virology. Robert B. Belshe. (Illus.). 1088p. 1984. 95.00 (ISBN 0-88416-458-6). PSG Pub Co.
Textbook of Immunology. 5th ed. Barrett. (Illus.). 496p. 1987. International Edition. pap. text ed. 29.95. Mosby.
Textbook of Immunology. 2nd ed. Emil R. Unanue & Baruj Benacerraf. (Illus.). 324p. 1984. pap. 19.50 (ISBN 0-683-08504-2, 8504-2). Williams & Wilkins.
Textbook of Immunopathology, 2 vols. 2nd ed. Ed. by Peter A. Miescher & Hans J. Mueller-Eberhard. LC 76-155406. (Illus.). 544p. 1976. Vol. I. 107.00 (ISBN 0-8089-0931-2, 792911). Grune.
Textbook of Infectious Diseases. Waldman. (Textbook Ser.: Vol. 4). 1984. 47.50 (ISBN 0-87488-668-6). Med Exam.
Textbook of Inorganic Chemistry. 1985. 5.00 (ISBN 0-471-63856-0). Wiley.
Textbook of Inorganic Chemistry: General Principles, Vol. 1. K. N. Upadhyaya. (Illus.). 262p. 1985. text ed. 25.00x (ISBN 0-7069-2613-7, Pub. by Vikas India). Advent NY.
Textbook of Inorganic Chemistry: The Representative Elements, Vol. 2. K. N. Upadhyaya. 256p. 1985. text ed. 25.00x (ISBN 0-7069-2666-8, Pub. by Vikas India). Advent NY.
Textbook of Inorganic Chemistry: The Transition Elements, Vol. 3. K. N. Upadhyaya. 264p. 1986. text ed. 25.00x (Pub. by Vikas India). Advent NY.
Textbook of Insurance Broking. Roderick Clews. 1987. 37.50 (ISBN 0-85941-386-1, Pub. by Woodhead-Faulkner). Longwood Pub Group.
Textbook of Insurance Broking. Ed. by Roderick Clews. 209p. 1980. 24.75 (ISBN 0-85941-121-4, Pub. by Woodhead-Faulkner). Longwood Pub Group.
Textbook of Internal Medicine. Ed. by William N. Kelley et al. (Illus.). 2400p. 1988. text ed. 95.00 one vol. ed. (ISBN 0-397-50795-X, Lippincott Medical); text ed. 115.00 two vol. ed. (ISBN 0-397-50945-6). Lippincott.
Textbook of Internal Medicine. Stein. Date not set. write for info. (ISBN 0-444-00600-1). Elsevier.
Textbook of Israeli Hebrew: With an Introduction to the Classical Language. nd ed. Haiim B. Rosen. LC 62-9116. 1976. pap. text ed. 16.00x (ISBN 0-226-72603-7, P689, Phoen, P684). U of Chicago Pr.
Textbook of Jurisprudence. 4th ed. George Whitecross Paton. Ed. by G. W. Paton & David P. Dorham. 1972. text ed. 34.95x (ISBN 0-19-825314-1). Oxford U Pr.
Textbook of Labour & Industrial Laws. V. N. Pandey. 416p. 1980. 90.00x (ISBN 0-317-54680-5, Pub. by Eastern Bk India). State Mutual Bk.
Textbook of Laparoscopy. Jaroslav F. Hulka. 194p. 1985. 53.50 (ISBN 0-8089-1730-7, 792082). Grune.
Textbook of Large Animal Surgery. 2nd ed. Oehme. 660p. 1987. 64.95 (ISBN 0-683-06635-8). Williams & Wilkins.
Textbook of Limnology. 3rd ed. Gerald A. Cole. (Illus.). 402p. 1988. Repr. of 1983 ed. text ed. 28.95x (ISBN 0-88133-378-6). Waveland Pr.
Textbook of Liquid Chromatography. Snyder et al. 1987. write for info. (ISBN 0-471-85149-3). Wiley.
Textbook of Lithology. K. C. Jackson. 1970. text ed. 50.95 (ISBN 0-07-032143-4). McGraw.
Textbook of Macro & Semimicro Qualitative Inorganic Analysis. 5th ed. A. I. Vogel. 680p. 1979. 41.95 (ISBN 0-470-20606-3, Co-Pub. with Longman). Wiley.
Textbook of Materials Technology. Lawrence H. Van Vlack. LC 70-190614. 1973. text ed. write for info. (ISBN 0-201-08066-4); write for info. instructor's manual (ISBN 0-201-08067-2). Addison-Wesley.
Textbook of Mathematics for Pre University Students, Vol. 2. 1983. 2.00 (ISBN 0-471-63882-X). Wiley.
Textbook of Medical Physiology. 7th ed. Arthur C. Guyton. (Illus.). 1056p. 1986. 55.00 (ISBN 0-7216-1260-1). Saunders.
Textbook of Medical Record Linkage. Ed. by J. A. Baldwin et al. (Illus.). 364p. 1987. 79.00 (ISBN 0-19-261319-7). Oxford U Pr.
Textbook of Medical-Surgical Nursing. 6th ed. Lillian S. Brunner & Doris S. Suddarth. LC 64-5500. 1800p. 1987. text ed. 56.50 (ISBN 0-397-54641-6, Lippincott Nursing). Lippincott.
Textbook of Medical Treatment. 15th ed. Ed. by Ronald H. Girdwood & J. C. Petrie. LC 87-10282. (Illus.). 593p. 1987. pap. text ed. 46.00 (ISBN 0-443-03211-4). Churchill.
Textbook of Medical Virology. Ed. by Erik Lycke & Erling Norrby. 369p. 1983. text ed. 39.95 (ISBN 0-407-00253-7). Butterworth.
Textbook of Medicine. 2nd, rev. & enl. ed. 848p. 1983. 69.00x (ISBN 0-317-38797-9, Pub. by Current Dist). State Mutual Bk.
Textbook of Microbiology. 2nd ed. R. Ananthanarayan & Jayaram Paniker. (Illus.). 618p. 1982. pap. text ed. 25.00x (ISBN 0-86131-293-7, Pub. by Orient Longman Ltd India). Apt Bks.
Textbook of Microbiology. S. K. Sarkar. 1985. 45.00x (ISBN 0-317-39562-9, Pub. by Current Dist). State Mutual Bk.
Textbook of Microscopic Anatomy. Kurt E. Johnson. 1988. write for info. (ISBN 0-471-88247-X). Churchill.
Textbook of Mineralogy. 4th ed. Edward S. Dana & William E. Ford. 851p. 1932. write for info. (ISBN 0-471-19305-4). Wiley.
Textbook of Modern Algebra. R. Balakrishnan & N. Ramabhadran. 1986. text ed. 22.50x (ISBN 0-7069-2965-9, Pub. by Vikas India). Advent NY.
Textbook of Modern Karate. Teruyuki Okazaki & Milorand V. Stricevic. LC 80-84418. (Illus.). 352p. 1984. 34.95 (ISBN 0-87011-461-1). Kodansha.
Textbook of Modern Plant Pathology. K. S. Bilgrami & H. C. Dube. 1976. 13.50 (ISBN 0-7069-0421-4). Intl Bk Dist.
Textbook of Modern Plant Pathology. 6th ed. K. S. Bilgrami & R. C. Dube. 1985. text ed. 35.00x (ISBN 0-7069-2879-2, Pub. by Vikas India). Advent NY.
Textbook of Modern Toxicology. E. Hodgson & P. E. Levi. 500p. 1987. 41.75 (ISBN 0-444-01131-5). Elsevier.
Textbook of Modern Western Armenian. Kevok B. Bardakjian & Robert W. Thomson. LC 77-1774. 1985. pap. 15.00x (ISBN 0-88206-504-1). Caravan Bks.
Textbook of Modern Western Armenian. Kevork B. Bardakjian & Robert W. Thomson. LC 77-1774. 1977. pap. text ed. 15.00x. Caravan Bks.
Textbook of Motor Development. 2nd ed. Charles B. Corbin. 336p. 1980. pap. text ed. write for info. (ISBN 0-697-07266-5). Wm C Brown.
Textbook of Neonatal Surgery: Care of Surgical Neonates in Developing Countries. K. Yadav. 500p. 1983. text ed. 45.00x (ISBN 0-7069-2066-X, Pub. by Vikas India). Advent NY.
Textbook of Neonatology. Ed. by N. R. Roberton. (Illus.). 962p. 1986. text ed. 165.00 (ISBN 0-443-02716-1). Churchill.
Textbook of Neonatology. D. Vidyasagar. (Illus.). 450p. 1987. 55.00 (ISBN 81-85017-38-7). PSG Pub Co.
Textbook of Nephrology, 2 vols. Shaul G. Massry & Richard J. Glassock. 1600p. 1988. Set. 140.00 (ISBN 0-683-05620-4). Williams & Wilkins.
Textbook of Neurological Nursing. Phyllis J. Pallett & Mary T. O'Brien. 1984. text ed. write for info. (ISBN 0-673-39367-4). Scott F.
Textbook of Neuropathology. Richard L. Davis & David M. Robertson. 976p. 1985. 139.95 (ISBN 0-683-02343-8). Williams & Wilkins.
Textbook of Nuclear Medicine, Vol. 1: Basic Science. 2nd ed. Ed. by John Harbert et al. LC 83-25594. (Illus.). 526p. 1984. text ed. 85.00 (ISBN 0-8121-0891-4). Lea & Febiger.
Textbook of Nuclear Medicine, Vol. 2: Clinical Applications. 2nd ed. Ed. by John Harbert et al. LC 83-25594. (Illus.). 724p. 1984. text ed. 98.50 (ISBN 0-8121-0928-7). Lea & Febiger.
Textbook of Nursing for the Use of Training Schools, Families & Private Students. Clara S. Weeks-Shaw. Ed. by Susan Reverby. LC 83-49123. (History of American Nursing Ser.). 396p. 1984. Repr. of 1885 ed. lib. bdg. 50.00 (ISBN 0-8240-6527-1). Garland Pub.
Textbook of Obstetrics. V. I. Bodyazhina. 400p. 1984. 12.00 (ISBN 0-8285-2574-9, Pub. by Mir Pubs USSR). Imported Pubns.
Textbook of Occlusion. Ed. by Mohl et al. (Illus.). 408p. 1988. text ed. 48.00 (ISBN 0-86715-167-6, 1676). Quint Pub Co.
Textbook of Operative Dentistry. 2nd ed. Lloyd Baum et al. (Illus.). 603p. 1985. 52.50 (ISBN 0-7216-1432-9). Saunders.
Textbook of Ophthalmic Photography. Don Wong. LC 82-84064. (Illus.). 120p. (Orig.). 1982. 49.50 (ISBN 0-935726-02-0). Inter-Optics Pubns.
Textbook of Ophthalmic Plastic & Reconstructive Surgery. Roger Kohn. LC 87-26042. (Illus.). 344p. 1988. text ed. 95.00 (ISBN 0-8121-1112-5). Lea & Febiger.
Textbook of Ophthalmology. 9th ed. Harold G. Scheie & Daniel M. Alert. LC 75-19856. (Illus.). 1977. text ed. write for info. (ISBN 0-7216-7951-X). Saunders.
Textbook of Ophthalmology. 2nd ed. G. M. Seal. 512p. 1982. 69.00x (ISBN 0-317-39563-7, Pub. by Current Dist). State Mutual Bk.
Textbook of Oral & Maxillofacial Surgery. 6th ed. Gustav O. Kruger. (Illus.). 896p. 1983. 55.95 (ISBN 0-8016-2793-1). Mosby.
Textbook of Oral Biology. James H. Shaw et al. LC 76-14687. pap. 160.00 (ISBN 0-317-26105-3, 2025172). Bks Demand UMI.
Textbook of Oral Surgery. Gordon W. Pedersen. (Illus.). 528p. 1988. 34.95 (ISBN 0-7216-2426-X). Saunders.
Textbook of Ore Dressing. 3rd, rev. ed. Robert H. Richards et al. LC 40-10540. pap. 156.00 (ISBN 0-317-29998-0, 2051848). Bks Demand UMI.
Textbook of Organic Chemistry, Vol. I. K. S. Tewari. 1977. 13.50x (ISBN 0-7069-0442-7). Intl Bk Dist.
Textbook of Organic Chemistry, Vol. II. K. S. Tewari. 1977. 10.50x (ISBN 0-686-12060-4). Intl Bk Dist.
Textbook of Organic Chemistry. K S Tewari et al. 1394p. 1986. text ed. 60.00x (ISBN 0-7069-2876-8, Pub. by Vikas India). Advent NY.
Textbook of Organic Chemistry. 1985. 6.00 (ISBN 0-471-63853-6). Wiley.
Textbook of Orthodontics. W. Houston & W. Tulley. 336p. 1986. pap. text ed. 32.00 (ISBN 0-7236-0747-8). PSG Pub Co.
Textbook of Orthopaedic Medicine: Diagnosis of Soft Tissue Lesions, Vol. 1. 8th ed. J. Cyriax. (Illus.). 1983. text ed. 70.00 (ISBN 0-7216-0777-2, Bailliere-Tindall). Saunders.
Textbook of Orthopaedic Medicine: Treatment by Manipulation, Massage & Injection, Vol. 2. 11th ed. James Cyriax & Margaret Coldham. (Illus.). 288p. 1984. 39.95 (ISBN 0-7216-0960-0, Bailliere-Tindall). Saunders.
Textbook of Otolaryngology. 7th ed. De Weese et al. (Illus.). 550p. 1987. 45.95 (ISBN 0-8016-1274-8). Mosby.
Textbook of Otolaryngology. Collin S. Karmody. LC 83-14868. (Illus.). 269p. 1983. text ed. 24.50 (ISBN 0-8121-0887-6). Lea & Febiger.
Textbook of Paediatrics, 2 vols. 3rd ed. John O. Forfar & Gavin C. Arneil. (Illus.). 1984. text ed. 194.25 (ISBN 0-443-02426-X). Churchill.
Textbook of Pain. Ed. by Patrick D. Wall & Ronald Melzack. (Illus.). 888p. 1984. text ed. 130.00 (ISBN 0-443-02715-3). Churchill.
Textbook of Pediatric Allergy. R. Michael Sly. (Textbook Ser.: Vol. 7). 1984. pap. text ed. 39.25 (ISBN 0-87488-365-2). Med Exam.
Textbook of Pediatric Clinical Pharmacology. Stuart M. MacLeod & Ingeborg C. Radde. (Illus.). 480p. 1985. 56.50 (ISBN 0-88416-456-X). PSG Pub Co.
Textbook of Pediatric Dermatology. Ed. by Lawrence Parish et al. Date not set. write for info. (ISBN 0-8089-1863-X, 793249). Grune.
Textbook of Pediatric Emergency Medicine. 2nd ed. Gary Fleisher. 1584p. 1988. 112.50 (ISBN 0-683-03254-2). Williams & Wilkins.
Textbook of Pediatric Infectious Diseases. 2nd ed. Ralph D. Feigin & James D. Cherry. (Illus.). 1872p. 1987. Set. 195.00 (ISBN 0-7216-1372-1); Vol. I. 105.00 (ISBN 0-7216-1370-5); Vol. II. 99.00 (ISBN 0-7216-1371-3). Saunders.
Textbook of Pediatric Intensive Care. Mark C. Rogers. (Illus.). 1500p. 1987. 154.95 (ISBN 0-683-07320-6). Williams & Wilkins.
Textbook of Pediatric Neurology. Gerald S. Golden. LC 86-30432. (Topics in Pediatrics Ser.). 346p. 1987. 49.50x (ISBN 0-306-42359-6, Plenum Med). Plenum Pub.
Textbook of Pediatric Nursing. 6th ed. Dorothy R. Marlow. (Illus.). 1358p. 1988. 47.95 (ISBN 0-7216-6100-9). Saunders.
Textbook of Pediatric Nutrition. Ed. by Robert M. Suskind. 680p. 1981. text ed. 103.00 (ISBN 0-89004-253-5). Raven.
Textbook of Pediatrics. Russo. (Textbook Ser.). Date not set. price not set (ISBN 0-444-01009-2). Elsevier.
Textbook of Phacoemulsification. Maloney & Grindle. LC 87-28607. (Illus.). 1988. 68.00 (ISBN 0-918916-06-2). Lasenda.
Textbook of Pharmaceutical Analysis. 3rd ed. Kenneth A. Connors. LC 81-19742. 664p. 1982. 57.95x (ISBN 0-471-09034-4, Pub. by Wiley-Interscience). Wiley.
Textbook of Pharmacology. G. Kuschinsky & H. Lullman. 1973. 52.50 (ISBN 0-12-430050-2). Acad Pr.
Textbook of Pharmacology & Nursing Care: Using the Nursing Process. Malseed & Harrigan. LC 64-3737. 1988. write for info. (ISBN 0-397-54432-4). Lippincott.
Textbook of Physical Chemistry. 2nd rev. ed. K. K. Sharma & L K. Sharma. 1980. text ed. 25.00x (Pub. by Vikas India). Advent NY.
Textbook of Physical Chemistry. K. K. Sharma & L. K. Sharma. 1977. 12.00x. Intl Bk Dist.
Textbook of Physical Chemistry. 1985. 5.00 (ISBN 0-471-63864-1). Wiley.
Textbook of Physical Diagnosis. Mark H. Swartz. (Illus.). 704p. 1988. 39.95 (ISBN 0-7216-2475-8). Saunders.
Textbook of Physics, 2 vols. Alok Chakrabarty. 1985. text ed. 82.00x (ISBN 0-317-38802-9, Pub. by Current Dist). State Mutual Bk.
Textbook of Physics. Patitpaban Misra. 630p. 1986. text ed. 40.00x (ISBN 0-7069-3017-7, Pub. by Vikas India). Advent NY.
Textbook of Physiology. 2nd ed. Ed. by Sarada Subrahmanyam & K. Madhaven Kutty. 818p. 1979. 30.00x (ISBN 0-86125-415-5, Pub. by Orient Longman India). Apt Bks.
Textbook of Plant Virus Diseases. 3rd ed. K. M. Smith. 1973. 68.50 (ISBN 0-12-651350-3). Acad Pr.
Textbook of Plantation Crops. K. M. Pillai. 168p. 1986. pap. text ed. 8.95x (ISBN 0-7069-2544-0, Pub. by Vikas India). Advent NY.
Textbook of Polymer Science. 3rd ed. Fred W. Billmeyer, Jr. LC 83-19870. 578p. 1984. 39.50 (ISBN 0-471-03196-8, Pub. by Wiley-Interscience). Wiley.
Textbook of Practical Oral & Maxillofacial Surgery. 3rd ed. Ed. by Daniel E. Waite. LC 85-23973. (Illus.). 570p. 1987. text ed. 55.00 (ISBN 0-8121-1028-5). Lea & Febiger.
Textbook of Pre University Algebra. 1983. 1.75 (ISBN 0-471-63886-2). Wiley.
Textbook of Pressman Training Classroom Guide. 100p. spiral 25.00 (ISBN 0-318-23318-5). F Drazan.
Textbook of Pressman's Training. Date not set. 25.00. F Drazan.
Textbook of Psoriasis. Ed. by Paul D. Mier & Peter C. Van de Kerkhof. LC 85-16669. (Illus.). 292p. 1986. text ed. 96.00 (ISBN 0-443-03210-6). Churchill.
Textbook of Psychiatry. Eugen Bleuler. LC 75-16685. (Classics in Psychiatry Ser.). (Illus.). 1976. Repr. of 1924 ed. 49.50x (ISBN 0-405-07417-4). Ayer Co Pubs.
Textbook of Psychiatry. 5th ed. Merrill T. Eaton, Jr. et al. (Textbook Ser.: Vol. 11). 1985. pap. text ed. 33.75 (ISBN 0-87488-838-7). Med Exam.
Textbook of Psychology. 4th ed. D. O. Hebb & D. C. Donderi. 400p. 1987. text ed. 24.95 (ISBN 0-89859-934-2); instr.'s manual incl. (ISBN 0-89859-988-1). L Erlbaum Assocs.
Textbook of Psychology. Edward B. Titchener. LC 80-14831. (Hist. of Psych. Ser.). Repr. of 1910 ed. 75.00x (ISBN 0-8201-1354-9). Schol Facsimiles.
Textbook of Psychology & the Study of Psychology **see Outlines of Psychology.**
Textbook of Psychotherapy. Vimala Veeraraghavan. 1986. text ed. 27.95x (ISBN 81-207-0030-9, Pub. by Sterling Pubs India). Apt Bks.
Textbook of Pulmonary Diseases. 3rd ed. Ed. by Gerald L. Baum. 1983. 99.00 (ISBN 0-316-08386-0). Little.
Textbook of Radiographic Positioning & Related Anatomy. 2nd ed. Bontrager. 1987. text ed. 71.95 (ISBN 0-8016-0698-5). Mosby.
Textbook of Radiographic Science. Ed. by H. Brian Bentley. LC 85-19507. (Illus.). 216p. (Orig.). 1987. pap. text ed. 24.00 (ISBN 0-443-02550-9). Churchill.
Textbook of Radiologic Diagnosis, 2 Vols. 5th ed. Royal College of Radiologists. (Illus.). 1050p. 1985. Vol.1; The Central Nervous System. 130.00 (ISBN 0-7216-1523-6); Vol. 2; The Cardiovascular System. 130.00 (ISBN 0-7216-1621-6). Saunders.
Textbook of Radiology. Charles E. Putman & Carl E. Ravin. (Illus.). 2592p. 1988. Set. 295.00 (ISBN 0-7216-1334-9); Vol. I. 95.00 (ISBN 0-7216-1335-7); Vol. II. 99.00 (ISBN 0-7216-1336-5); Vol. III. 99.00 (ISBN 0-7216-2529-0). Saunders.
Textbook of Radiology & Imaging, 2 vols. 4th ed. David Sutton. (Illus.). 1857p. 1987. Set. text ed. 295.00 (ISBN 0-443-03329-3). Churchill.
Textbook of Radiotherapy. 3rd ed. Ed. by Gilbert H. Fletcher. LC 80-10523. (Illus.). 959p. 1980. text ed. 60.00 (ISBN 0-8121-0674-1). Lea & Febiger.
Textbook of Refrigeration & Air Conditioning Engineering. L N Misra. 715p. 1986. pap. text ed. 25.00x (ISBN 0-7069-2778-8, Pub. by Vikas India). Advent NY.
Textbook of Renal Disease. Ed. by Judith A. Whitworth. LC 86-26925. (Illus.). 408p. 1987. pap. text ed. 46.00 (ISBN 0-443-02853-2). Churchill.
Textbook of Respiratory Medicine, 2 vols. John F. Murray & Jay A. Nadel. (Illus.). 2400p. 1988. Set. 210.00 (ISBN 0-7216-1439-6); Vol. 1. 105.00 (ISBN 0-7216-1440-X); Vol. 2. 105.00 (ISBN 0-7216-1441-8). Saunders.
Textbook of Rheumatology, 2 vols. 2nd ed. William N. Kelley et al. (Illus.). 2121p. 1985. Set. 210.00 (ISBN 0-7216-5365-0); Vol. 1. 115.00 (ISBN 0-7216-5363-4); Vol. 2. 105.00 (ISBN 0-7216-5362-6). Saunders.
Textbook of Rheumatology. Robert A. Turner & Christopher M. Wise. (Textbook Ser.: Vol. 14). 1985. pap. text ed. 39.25 (ISBN 0-87488-041-6). Med Exam.
Textbook of Roman Law. J. A. Thomas. 1976. 52.75 (ISBN 0-7204-0513-0, North-Holland); pap. 21.00 (ISBN 0-7204-0517-3). Elsevier.
Textbook of Secretarial Practice. Ashok A. Bagrial. 629p. 1986. text ed. 45.00x (ISBN 0-7069-2578-5, Pub. by Vikas India). Advent NY.
Textbook of Sexual Medicine. Robert C. Kolodny et al. 1979. text ed. 28.00 (ISBN 0-316-50154-9). Little.

Textiles in Daily Life in the Middle Ages. Rebecca Martin. LC 84-28492. (Illus.). 70p. 1985. pap. 7.95x (ISBN 0-910386-80-3, Pub. by Cleveland Museum of Art). Ind U Pr.

Textiles in Perspective. Betty Smith & Ira Block. (Illus.). 512p. 1982. text ed. write for info (ISBN 0-13-912808-5). P-H.

Textiles in Transition: Technology, Wages, & Industry Relocation in the U. S. Textile Industry, Eighteen Eighty to Nineteen Thirty. Nancy F. Kane. LC 87-24950. 208p. 1988. lib. bdg. 37.95 (ISBN 0-313-25529-6, KIW/). Greenwood.

Textiles of Ancient Mesopotamia, Persia, & Egypt. Florence E. Petzel. LC 87-90471. 226p. 1987. pap. text ed. 11.00 (ISBN 0-9618476-0-3). F E Petzel.

Textiles of Ancient Peru & Their Techniques. Raoul D'Harcourt. Ed. by Grace G. Denny & Carolyn M. Osborne. Tr. by Sadie Brown from Fr. LC 62-17150. (Illus.). 320p. 1987. pap. 19.95 (ISBN 0-295-95331-4). U of Wash Pr.

Textiles of Baluchistan. M. G. Konieczny. (Illus.). 77p. 1979. 21.50 (ISBN 0-7141-1557-6, Pub. by Brit Mus); pap. 12.50 (ISBN 0-7141-1549-5). Textile Mus.

Textiles of the Arts & Crafts Movement. Linda Parry. LC 87-51290. (Illus.). 200p. 1988. pap. 24.95 (ISBN 0-500-27497-5). Thames Hudson.

Textiles: Properties & Behavior. Edward Miller. (Illus.). 192p. 1984. pap. 22.95 (ISBN 0-7134-2545-8, Pub. by Batsford England). David & Charles.

Textiles: Volume 07.01, Textiles - Yarns, Fabrics, & General Test Methods. 1282p. 1986. 73.00 (ISBN 0-8031-0885-0). ASTM.

Textiles: Volume 07.02, Textiles - Fibers, Zippers. 906p. 1986. 59.00 (ISBN 0-8031-0886-9). ASTM.

Texto e Ideologia en la Narrativa Chilena. Lucia G. Cunningham. LC 87-20006. (Towards a Social History of Hispanic & Luso-Brazilian Literature Ser.). 256p. (Orig., Span.). 1988. pap. 9.95 (ISBN 0-910235-28-7). Prisma Bks.

Texto General de Cosmetologia. Milady Editors. (Span.). 1986. 20.25 (ISBN 0-318-22641-3). Milady Pub.

Texto Libre de Prejuicios Sexuales y Raciales: Guia para la Preparacion de Materiales de Ensenanza. Isabel Pico & Idsa Alegria. 56p. (Span.). 1983. pap. 6.50 (ISBN 0-8477-2470-0). U of PR Pr.

Texto Trejos. J. M. Trejos & Charlotte M. Trejos. 14p. (Eng. & Span.). 1986. pap. 1.95 (ISBN 0-939551-01-2). Trejos Lit Agy.

Texto y Concordancia: Fabula de Polyfemo y Galathea, y las Soledades. Alfonso Callejo & Maria T. Pajares. (Spanish Ser.: No. 25). 1985. 15.00x. Hispanic Seminary.

Textos de Ayer y de Hoy. Frank Vecchio. 196p. 1985. pap. text ed. 15.95x (ISBN 0-471-80607-2). Wiley.

Textos Encogidoes de la Reforma Radical. Ed. by John H. Yoder. 500p. (Orig., Span.). 1984. pap. 25.00 (ISBN 0-8361-1237-7). Herald Pr.

Textos Folkloricos de los Bora. Eva Thiesen. (Comunidades y Culturas Peruanas: No. 2). 96p. 1975. pap. write for info. (ISBN 0-88312-648-6); microfiche 2.00 (ISBN 0-88312-498-X). Summer Inst Ling.

Textos Hixkaryana. Desmond Derbyshire. 206p. 1965. microfiche (3) 6.00 (ISBN 0-88312-499-8). Summer Inst Ling.

Textos y Concordancia de la obra completa de Juan Manuel. Ed. by Reinaldo Ayerbe-Chaux. (Spanish Ser.: No. 28). 12p. 1986. incl. 32 microfiches 15.00x (ISBN 0-942260-70-8). Hispanic Seminary.

Textos y Pretextos. Rafael C. Pereda. LC 85-14137. (Span.). 1985. 6.00 (ISBN 0-8477-3516-8). U of PR Pr.

Texts & Calendars I: An Analytical Guide to Serial Publications. E. L. Mullins. (Royal Historical Society Guides & Handbooks Ser.: No. 7). 674p. 1958. 15.00 (ISBN 0-901050-14-8, Pub. by Boydell & Brewer). Longwood Pub Group.

Texts & Calendars II: An Analytical Guide to Serial Publications, 1957-1982. E. L. Mullins. (Royal Historical Society Guides & Handbooks: No.12). 324p. 1983. 27.00 (ISBN 0-86193-100-9, Pub. by Boydell & Brewer). Longwood Pub Group.

Texts & Concordances of Escorial Manuscript: Menor dano de la Medicina. Alfonso Chirino. Ed. by Enrica J. Ardemagni. Ruth M. Richards & Michael R. Solomon. (Medieval Spanish Medical Texts Ser.: No. 2). 11p. incl. 11 microfiches 1984 10.00x (ISBN 0-942260-41-4). Hispanic Seminary.

Texts & Concordances of Manuscript Esp. 226 of the Bibliotheque Nationale, Paris: Cancionero Castellano Y Catalan de Paris. Ed. by Robert G. Black. (Spanish Ser.: No. 23). 16p. text ed. 10.00x & 7 Microfiches (ISBN 0-942260-65-1). HIspanic Seminary.

Texts & Concordances of the Works of Caterina da Siena: Il Dialogo, Le Orazioni' L'Epistolario. Ed. by Suzanne Noffke. 10p. 1987. text ed. 10.00x incl. 13 microfiches (ISBN 0-940639-02-5). Hispanic Seminary.

Texts & Contexts. Geoffery Summerfield & Judith Fishman. 1986. write for info (ISBN 0-394-35159-2, RanC). Random.

Texts & Pretexts. Aldous L. Huxley. LC 76-16523. 1976. Repr. of 1933 ed. lib. bdg. 35.00x (ISBN 0-8371-8851-2, HUTP). Greenwood.

Texts & Studies. Saul Lieberman. 1973. 35.00x (ISBN 0-87068-210-5). Ktav.

Texts & Studies in Jewish History & Literature, 2 Vols. rev. ed. Jacob Mann. 1970. Set. 99.50x (ISBN 0-87068-085-4). Ktav.

Texts & Testaments: Critical Essays on the Bible & Early Church Fathers. Ed. by W. Eugene March. LC 79-92585. 321p. 1980. 15.00 (ISBN 0-911536-80-9). Trinity U Pr.

Texts & Their Traditions in the Medieval Library of Rochester Cathedral Priory. Mary P. Richards. LC 87-72869. (Transactions Ser.: Vol. 78). (Illus.). 212p. 1988. pap. 20.00 (ISBN 0-317-67283-5). Am Philos.

Text's Boyfriend. Harrison Fisher. (Burning Deck Poetry Ser.). 24p. (Orig.). 1980. pap. 10.00 signed ed (ISBN 0-930900-85-5). Burning Deck.

Texts from Hellenistic Babylonia in the Ashmolean Museum. Ed. by Gilbert J. McEwan. (Oxford Editions of Cuneiform Texts Ser.). (Illus.). 1982. pap. 48.00x (ISBN 0-19-815457-7). Oxford U Pr.

Texts from Tall-i Malyan No. 1: Elamite Administrative Texts. Matthew W. Stolper. (Occasional Publications of the Babylonian Fund: Vol. 6 OPBF 6). xix, 208p. 1984. 30.00x (ISBN 0-934718-61-X). Univ Mus of U PA.

Texts from the Buddhist Canon. Dhammapada. Tr. by Samuel Beal from Chinese. LC 78-72420. Repr. of 1878 ed. 22.50 (ISBN 0-404-17284-9). AMS Pr.

Texts from the Time of Nebuchadnezzar. David B. Weisberg. LC 79-16038. (Yale Oriental Ser. Babylonian Texts: Vol. XVII). 288p. 1980. text ed. 50.00t (ISBN 0-300-02338-3). Yale U Pr.

Texts in the Mastabeh of Se'n-Wosret-Ankh at Lisht: Metropolitan Museum of Art Egyptian Expedition Publications, Vol. 12. William C. Hayes. LC 70-168407. (Metropolitan Museum of Art Publications in Reprint). (Illus.). 64p. 1972. Repr. of 1937 ed. 17.00 (ISBN 0-405-02240-9). Ayer Co Pubs.

Texts in Transit. Graydon Snyder & Kenneth Shaffer. (Orig.). 1976. pap. 3.95 (ISBN 0-685-61334-8). Brethren.

Texts of Keats's Poems. John Keats. Ed. by Jack Stillinger. LC 73-86940. 320p. 1974. text ed. 22.50x (ISBN 0-674-87511-7). Harvard U Pr.

Texts of King Lear & Their Origins, Vol. 1: Nicholas Okes & the First Quarto. Peter W. Blayney. LC 77-82485. (New Cambridge Shakespeare Studies & Supplementary Text Ser.). (Illus.). 1983. 99.00 (ISBN 0-521-22634-1). Cambridge U Pr.

Texts of Taoism, 2 vols. Tr. by James Legge. Ed. by F. Max Muller. 396p. 1891. Vol. 1. pap. 6.95 (ISBN 0-486-20990-3); Vol. 2. pap. 6.95 (ISBN 0-486-20991-1). Dover.

Texts of Terror: Literary-Feminist Readings of Biblical Narratives. Phyllis Trible. LC 83-48906. (Overtures to Biblical Theology Ser.). 144p. 1984. pap. 8.95 (ISBN 0-8006-1537-9, 1-1537). Fortress.

Texts of the Kaibab Paiutes & Uintah Utes see **Southern Paiute.**

Texts of the Peace Conference at the Hague, 1899 & 1907 with English Translation & Appendix of Related Documents. Ed. by James B. Scott. 24.00 (ISBN 0-8369-7168-X, 8000). Ayer Co Pubs.

Texts of the Songs. Ed. by Elise B. Jorgens. (English Song Ser.: 1600-1675). 300p. 1987. lib. bdg. 75.00 (ISBN 0-8240-8242-7). Garland Pub.

Texts of the Tokyo Round Agreements. 208p. (Orig.). 1987. pap. text ed. 22.00 (ISBN 0-317-55603-7, G182, GATT). UNIPUB.

Texts of the Ukraine "Peace" with Maps. Ed. by Paul R. Magocsi. (Revolution & Nationalism in the Modern World: No. 3). 184p. pap. 12.00x (ISBN 0-686-30403-9). Zubal inc.

Texts of the White Yajurveda. Tr. by Ralph T. Griffith. xi, 388p. 1987. 31.00x (ISBN 81-2150-047-8, Pub. by Munshiram Manoharial India). South Asia Bks.

Texts on Zulu Religion: Traditional Zulu Ideas about God. Ed. by Irving Hexham. LC 87-10992. (African Studies: Vol. 6). 496p. 1987. lib. bdg. 69.95x (ISBN 0-88946-181-3). E Mellen.

Texts Pertaining to the Invention of the Balloon in 1782. Ed. & tr. by Paul Maravelas. (Illus.). 28p. text ed. 75.00x (ISBN 0-318-19997-1). P Maravelas.

Textual Analysis: Some Readers Reading. Ed. by Mary A. Caws. LC 85-18808. 350p. 1986. 32.00x (ISBN 0-87352-140-4); pap. text ed. 17.50x (ISBN 0-87352-141-2). Modern Lang.

Textual & Historical Studies in the Book of Jubilees. James Vander Kam. LC 76-45388. (Harvard Semitic Monograph). 1976. text ed. 10.50 (ISBN 0-89130-118-6, 040014). Scholars Pr GA.

Textual & Literary Criticism. Fredson T. Bowers. (Sanders Lectures in Bibliography: 1957-58). pap. 49.00 (ISBN 0-317-26059-6, 2024423). Bks Demand UMI.

Textual & Stylistic Commentary on Theocritus' Idyll XXV. G. Chryssafis. (London Studies in Classical Philology: Vol. I). 289p. (Orig.). 1981. pap. 69.00x (ISBN 90-70265-21-4, Pub. by Gieben Amsterdam). Benjamins North Am.

Textual & Subject Indexes of C. H. Spurgeon's Sermons. C. H. Spurgeon. (Key to the Metropolitan Tabernacle Pulpit set). 1971. 2.95 (ISBN 0-686-09095-0). Pilgrim Pubns.

Textual Commentary on the Greek New Testament. Ed. by Bruce M. Metzger. 776p. 1975. 6.50x (ISBN 3-438-06010-8, 08515, Pub. by United Bible). Am Bible.

Textual Concordance of the Holy Scriptures: (Bible Passages Taken from the Douay-Rheims Bible) Ed. by Thomas D. Williams. LC 85-52025. 848p. (Orig.). 1985. pap. 30.00 (ISBN 0-89555-286-8). Tan Bks Pubs.

Textual Confrontations: Comparative Readings in Latin American Literature. Alfred J. MacAdam. LC 86-24913. 216p. 1987. lib. bdg. 19.95x (ISBN 0-226-49990-1). U of Chicago Pr.

Textual Connections in Acts. Stephen H. Levinsohn. LC 86-20238. (SBL Monograph). 197p. 1987. 18.95 (ISBN 1-55540-060-4, 06-00-31); pap. 13.95 (ISBN 1-55540-061-2). Scholars Pr GA.

Textual Criticism & Editorial Technique. M. L. West. 150p. 1973. 33.75x (ISBN 3-519-07402-8); pap. 24.00x (ISBN 3-519-07401-X). Adlers Foreign Bks.

Textual Criticism & Jehan le Venelais. Jean Le Nevelon & E. B. Ham. LC 47-5589. Repr. of 1946 ed. 20.00 (ISBN 0-527-45750-7). Kraus Repr.

Textual Criticism & Literary Interpretation. Jerome J. McGann. LC 84-16174. (Illus.). 240p. 1985. lib. bdg. 22.00x (ISBN 0-226-55842-8); pap. 10.95x (ISBN 0-226-55843-6). U of Chicago Pr.

Textual Criticism of Inscriptions. Roland G. Kent. (LM). 1926. pap. 16.00 (ISBN 0-527-00806-0). Kraus Repr.

Textual Criticism of the Old Testament: The Septuagint After Qumran. Ralph W. Klein. Ed. by Gene M. Tucker. LC 74-80420. (Guides to Biblical Scholarship: Old Testament Ser.). 96p. (Orig.). 1974. pap. 4.95 (ISBN 0-8006-1087-3, 1-1087). Fortress.

Textual Criticism: Recovering the Text of the Hebrew Bible. P. Kyle McCarter, Jr. LC 86-4388. (Guides to Biblical Scholarship, Old Testament Ser.). 96p. 1986. pap. 4.95 (ISBN 0-8006-0471-7, 1-471). Fortress.

Textual Criticism since Greg: A Chronicle, 1950-1985. G. Thomas Tanselle. LC 87-23758. 150p. 1988. pap. 9.95x (ISBN 0-8139-1166-4). U Pr of Va.

Textual Exile: The Reader in Sterne & Foscolo. Sante Matteo. (American University Studies III: Comparitive Literature: Vol. 15). 292p. 1985. text ed. 35.00 (ISBN 0-8204-0168-4). P Lang Pubs.

Textual History of King Lear. P. W. Stone. 1980. 60.00 (ISBN 0-85967-536-X). Scolar.

Textual History of Richard Third. David L. Patrick. LC 36-30683. (Stanford University. Stanford Studies in Languages & Literature: No. 1). Repr. of 1936 ed. 22.75 (ISBN 0-404-51810-9). AMS Pr.

Textual Notes on the New American Bible. 124p. 1.30 (ISBN 0-318-13671-6); members 1.00 (ISBN 0-318-13672-4). Catholic Biblical.

Textual Power: Literary Theory & the Teaching of English. Robert Scholes. LC 84-19628. (Illus.). 192p. 1985. 20.00 (ISBN 0-300-03350-8). Yale U Pr.

Textual Power: Literary Theory & the Teaching of English. Robert Scholes. LC 84-19628. 192p. 1986. pap. 8.95x (ISBN 0-300-03726-0). Yale U Pr.

Textual Problems of the First Folio. Alice Walker. LC 78-8342. 1979. Repr. of 1953 ed. lib. bdg. 29.00 (ISBN 0-8495-5736-4). Arden Lib.

Textual Strategies: Perspectives in Post-Structuralist Criticism. Intro. by Josue V. Harari. LC 79-7617. (Paperback Ser.). 464p. 1979. 44.50x (ISBN 0-8014-1218-8); pap. 12.95x (ISBN 0-8014-9180-0). Cornell U Pr.

Textual Studies in Ancient & Medieval Geometry. Wilbur R. Knorr. 640p. 1988. 89.00 (ISBN 0-8176-3387-1). Birkhauser.

Textual Studies in Hinduism. Arvind Sharma. 1980. lib. bdg. 14.95x (ISBN 0-914914-15-4). New Horizons.

Textual Studies in Hinduism. Arvind Sharma. 1985. 12.50x (ISBN 0-8364-1291-5, Pub. by Manohar India). South Asia Bks.

Textual Studies in Hinduism. Arvind Sharma. 183p. 1980. 12.95. Asia Bk Corp.

Textual Studies in the Book of Joshua. Leonard Greenspoon. LC 83-3434. (Harvard Semitic Monographs). 412p. 1983. 21.75 (ISBN 0-89130-622-6, 04 00 28). Scholars Pr GA.

Textual Studies of Goethe's Faust. H. G. Fiedler. LC 73-20371. (Studies in Goethe, No. 61). 1974. lib. bdg. 75.00x (ISBN 0-8383-1809-6). Haskell.

Textual Studies of Goethe's Faust. Hermann G. Fiedler. 92p. 1980. Repr. of 1946 ed. lib. bdg. 20.00 (ISBN 0-8492-4705-5). R West.

Textual Tradition of Strabo's Geography. A. Diller. iv, 222p. (Orig.). 1975. pap. text ed. 64.50x (ISBN 0-317-57966-5, Pub. by A M Hakkert). Coronet Bks.

Textuality & Legitimacy in the Printed Constitution. Michael Warner. (Illus.). 30p. 1987. pap. 4.50 (ISBN 0-912296-96-8, Dist. by Univ Pr of Va.). Am Antiquarian.

Textural Tradition of Euripides' Phoinissai. Donald J. Mastronarde & Jan M. Bremer. LC 82-13492. (UC Publications in Classical Studies: Vol. 27). 464p. 1983. pap. text ed. 35.95x (ISBN 0-520-09664-9). U of Cal Pr.

Texture: A Design Element. George F. Horn. LC 74-82683. (Concepts of Design Ser). (Illus.). 72p. (gr. 7 up). 1974. 10.95 (ISBN 0-87192-066-2). Davis Mass.

Texture Analysis in Materials Science: Mathematical Methods. 2nd ed. Hans Bunge. Tr. by Peter Morris from Ger. LC 79-40054. 1982. text ed. 110.00 (ISBN 0-408-10642-5). Butterworth.

Texture Measurement of Foods: Psychophysical Fundamentals-Sensory, Mechanical & Chemical Procedures & Their Interrelationships. Ed. by A. Kramer et al. LC 72-93271. 175p. 1973. lib. bdg. 34.00 (ISBN 90-277-0307-8, Pub. by Reidel Holland). Kluwer Academic.

Texture of Knowledge: An Essay on Religion & Science. James W. Jones. LC 80-69036. 112p. 1981. lib. bdg. 24.25 (ISBN 0-8191-1360-3); pap. text ed. 9.00 (ISBN 0-8191-1361-1). U Pr of Amer.

Texture of My Days. Marva Weigelt. 85p. (Orig.). 1981. pap. 2.50 (ISBN 0-8341-0690-6). Beacon Hill.

Texture...A Closer Look. Lois Ericson. Ed. by Lennart Ericson. (Illus.). 224p. (Orig.). 1987. pap. 21.95 (ISBN 0-911985-04-2). Eric's Pr.

Textured Patterns for Machine Knitting. Shelia Sharp. (Illus.). 144p. 1987. 24.95 (ISBN 0-7134-4811-3, Pub. by Batsford England). David & Charles.

Textured Protein Products. M. Gutcho. LC 77-85662. (Food Technology Review Ser.: No. 44). (Illus.). 1978. 39.00 (ISBN 0-8155-0681-3). Noyes.

Texturen: Essays und Anderes zu Hans Magnus Enzenberger. Reinhold Grimm. LC 83-48820. (New York University Ottendorfer Ser.: Vol. 19). 224p. 1985. text ed. 19.50 (ISBN 0-8204-0059-9). P Lang Pubs.

Textures. Ed. by Wolfgang Hageney. (Illus.). 112p. 1986. pap. 26.95 (ISBN 88-7070-065-8). R Silver.

Textures: A Photographic Album for Artists & Designers. Phil Brodatz. (Illus., Orig.). 1966. pap. 7.95 (ISBN 0-486-21669-1). Dover.

Textures in Non-Ferrous Metals & Alloys. Ed. by H. D. Merchant & J. G. Morris. LC 85-11569. (Illus.). 231p. 1985. 54.00 (ISBN 0-87339-001-6). Metal Soc.

Textures of Liquid Crystals. D. Demus & L. Richter. (Illus.). 228p. 1978. 118.00 (ISBN 0-89573-015-4). VCH Pubs.

Textus Roffensis see **Early English Manuscripts in Facsimile.**

Textus Roffensis: Part 1 see **Early English Manuscripts in Facsimile.**

Teyku: The Unsolved Problem in the Babylonian Talmus. Louis Jacobs. LC 80-70887. 312p. 1981. 20.00 (ISBN 0-8453-4501-X, Cornwall Bks). Assoc Univ Prs.

Teyr-al Nader dar Sharhe Seyr-al Saer va Teyr-al Nader. Nader S. Angha. LC 85-80048. 81p. (Persian.). 1985. 55.00 (ISBN 0-910735-39-5); pap. 25.00 (ISBN 0-910735-37-9). MTO Printing & Pubn Ctr.

TFB: Typewriting for Business. Leger Morrison. 208p. 1985. pap. text ed. 11.50x (ISBN 0-935920-34-X); wkbk. 5.00x (ISBN 0-935920-35-8). Natl Pub Black Hills.

T.F.H. Book of Budgerigars. Evelyn Miller. (Illus.). 80p. 6.95 (ISBN 0-87666-849-X, HP-004). TFH Pubns.

T.F.H. Book of Gerbils. Marshall Ostrow. (Illus.). 64p. 1981. 6.95 (ISBN 0-87666-824-4, HP-009). TFH Pubns.

T.F.H. Book of Guinea Pigs. William Ritter. (Illus.). 80p. 1982. 6.95 (ISBN 0-87666-823-6, HP-008). TFH Pubns.

T.F.H. Book of Hamsters. Mervin F. Roberts. (Illus.). 80p. 1981. 6.95 (ISBN 0-87666-848-1, HP-003). TFH Pubns.

T.F.H. Book of Kittens. Marjorie F. Schrody. (Illus.). 96p. 6.95 (ISBN 0-87666-817-1, HP-012). TFH Pubns.

T.F.H. Book of Lovebirds. Georg A. Radtke. Tr. by Annemarie Lambrich from Ger. (Illus.). 80p. 6.95 (ISBN 0-87666-846-5, HP-001). TFH Pubns.

T.F.H. Book of Puppies. Herbert Richards. (Illus.). 96p. 6.95 (ISBN 0-87666-816-3, HP-013). TFH Pubns.

Th. Nast: His Period & His Pictures. Albert B. Paine. LC 78-177504. (Illus.). Repr. of 1904 ed. 27.50 (ISBN 0-405-08831-0). Ayer Co Pubs.

Thachers: Island of the Twin Lights. Eleanor C. Parsons. LC 85-9544. (Illus.). 160p. (Orig.). 1985. pap. 9.95 (ISBN 0-914659-14-6). Phoenix Pub.

Thackerary in the United States, 1852-3, 1855-6, Including a Record of a Variety of Thackerayana, 2 vols. in 1. James G. Wilson. LC 4-31633. (Illus.). 1969. Repr. of 1904 ed. 54.00 (ISBN 0-527-97120-0). Kraus Repr.

Thackeray. G. K. Chesterton & Lewis Melville. LC 72-12906. 1973. lib. bdg. 15.00 (ISBN 0-8414-1025-9). Folcroft.

Thackeray. Geoffrey U. Ellis. LC 79-160465. (English Literature Ser., No. 33). 1971. Repr. of 1933 ed. lib. bdg. 33.95x (ISBN 0-8383-1300-0). Haskell.

Thackeray. M. Elqin. 59.95 (ISBN 0-8490-1187-6). Gordon Pr.

Thackeray. Anthony Trollope. Ed. by John Morley. LC 68-58404. (English Men of Letters). Repr. of 1879 ed. lib. bdg. 7.80 (ISBN 0-404-51736-6). AMS Pr.

Thackeray. Anthony Trollope. 1977. Repr. of 1887 ed. lib. bdg. 25.50 (ISBN 0-8414-8644-1). Folcroft.

Thackeray. Anthony Trollope. LC 67-23880. 224p. 1968. Repr. of 1879 ed. 34.00x (ISBN 0-8103-3060-1). Gale.

Thackeray: A Study. Adolphus A. Jack. LC 74-103194. 1970. Repr. of 1895 ed. 21.50x (ISBN 0-8046-0831-8, Pub by Kennikat). Assoc Faculty Pr.

Thackeray: A Study in Technique. S. K. Sinha. Ed. by James Hogg. (Romantic Reassessment Ser.). 176p. (Orig.). 1979. pap. 15.00 (ISBN 3-7052-0550-1, Pub. by Salzburg Studies). Longwood Pub Group.

Thackeray Als Historischer Romanschriftsteller. Gudrun Vogel. pap. 8.00 (ISBN 0-384-64800-2). Johnson Repr.

Thackeray & Form of Fiction. John Loofbourow. LC 75-42172. 224p. 1976. Repr. of 1964 ed. 27.50x (ISBN 0-87752-177-8). Gordian.

Thackeray & His Twentieth Century Critics: An Annotated Bibliography of British & American Criticism, 1900-1975. John C. Olmsted. LC 76-24394. (Reference Library of the Humanities Ser.: Vol. 62). 1977. lib. bdg. 43.00 (ISBN 0-8240-9915-X). Garland Pub.

Thackeray at Work. John Sutherland. (Illus.). 165p. 1979. 36.50 (ISBN 0-485-11146-2, Pub. by Athlone Pr UK). Humanities.

Thackeray in the United States. James Wilson. LC 70-119439. (Studies in Comparative Literature, No. 35). 1970. Repr. of 1905 ed. lib. bdg. 79.95x (ISBN 0-8383-1067-2). Haskell.

Thackeray: Interviews & Recollections, 2 Vols. Ed. by Phillip Collins. LC 81-21327. 394p. 1983. Vol. 1. 22.50 (ISBN 0-312-79488-6); Vol. 2. 22.50 (ISBN 0-312-79489-4). St Martin.

Thackeray Library. Henry S. Van Duzer. 1971. Repr. of 1919 ed. lib. bdg. 18.00 (ISBN 0-8337-3615-9). B Franklin.

Thackeray the Humourist & the Man of Letters. Theodore Taylor. LC 72-174687. (English Literature Ser., No 33). 1971. Repr. of 1864 ed. lib. bdg. 49.95x (ISBN 0-8383-1339-6). Haskell.

Thackeray: The Major Novels. Juliet McMaster. LC 76-151380. 1971. pap. 7.50 (ISBN 0-8020-6309-8). U of Toronto Pr.

Thackeray: The Sentimental Cynic. Lambert Ennis. (Nortwestern University. Humanities Ser.: No. 25). Repr. of 1950 ed. 28.00 (ISBN 0-404-50725-5). AMS Pr.

Thackerayana (1901) William Makepeace Thackeray. LC 71-137436. (English Literature Ser., No. 33). 1970. Repr. of 1901 ed. lib. bdg. 55.95x (ISBN 0-8383-1191-1). Haskell.

Thackeray's Canvass of Humanity: An Author & His Public. Robert A. Colby. LC 78-27465. (Illus.). 1979. 30.00x (ISBN 0-8142-0282-9). Ohio St U Pr.

Thackeray's "English Humourists". Edgar F. Harden. LC 84-40411. 280p. 1985. 34.50 (ISBN 0-87413-274-6). U Delaware Pr.

Thackeray's Haunts & Homes. Eyre Crowe. LC 74-2069. 1897. lib. bdg. 17.00. Folcroft.

Thackeray's Letters to an American Family. Lucy W. Baxter. (Illus.). 1904. 25.00 (ISBN 0-8274-3590-8). R West.

Thackeray's Literary Apprenticeship. Harold S. Gulliver. 1979. Repr. of 1934 ed. lib. bdg. 33.00 (ISBN 0-8414-4631-8). Folcroft.

Thackeray's Novels: A Fiction That Is True. Jack P. Rawlins. 1974. 37.50x (ISBN 0-520-02562-8). U of Cal Pr.

Thackeray's Universe: Shifting Worlds of Imagination & Reality. Catherine Peters. (Illus.). 304p. 1987. 29.95 (ISBN 0-19-504855-5). Oxford U Pr.

Thaddeus. Joyce Alexander & Dorsey Alexander. (Illus., Calligraphy & Illus.). 1972. pap. 5.00 (ISBN 0-912020-20-2). Turtles Quill.

Thaddeus Jones & the Dragon. J. Hjelm. LC 68-56830. (Illus.). 64p. (gr. 2-5). 1968. PLB 10.95 (ISBN 0-87783-039-8); pap. 3.94 deluxe ed. (ISBN 0-87783-110-6). Oddo.

Thaddeus of Warsaw. rev. ed. Jane Porter. LC 70-162883. (Bentley's Standard Novels: No. 4). (Illus.). Repr. of 1831 ed. 17.50 (ISBN 0-404-54404-5). AMS Pr.

Thaddeus Q. Jeannette Picraux. 279p. 1988. 4.95 (ISBN 0-533-07437-1). Vantage.

Thaddeus Stevens. Ralph Korngold. LC 74-12629. 460p. 1974. Repr. of 1955 ed. lib. bdg. 35.00x (ISBN 0-8371-7733-2, KOTS). Greenwood.

Thaddeus Stevens. Samuel W. McCall. Ed. by John T. Morse, Jr. LC 78-128951. (American Statesmen: No. 31). Repr. of 1899 ed. 29.00 (ISBN 0-404-50881-2). AMS Pr.

Thaddeus Stevens. Samuel W. McCall. 1899. 20.00 (ISBN 0-8414-6386-7). Folcroft.

Thaddeus Stevens, Commoner. Edward B. Callender. LC 70-39881. Repr. of 1882 ed. 18.00 (ISBN 0-404-00011-8). AMS Pr.

Thaddeus Stevens, Scourge of the South. Fawn M. Brodie. (Illus.). 17.75 (ISBN 0-8446-0329-5). Peter Smith.

Thai American Friendship Patterns. Manu Maniwatana. (Monograph Ser.: No. 5). (Orig.). 1987. pap. cancelled (ISBN 0-934584-18-4). Pacific Asian.

Thai Boxing Dynamite: The Explosive Art of Muay Thai. Rebac Zoran. (Illus.). 120p. 1987. pap. text ed. 14.00 (ISBN 0-87364-426-3). Paladin Pr.

Thai Buddhism: Its Rites & Activities. Kenneth E. Wells. LC 77-87081. (Illus.). viii, 320p. Repr. of 1960 ed. 34.50 (ISBN 0-404-16876-0). AMS Pr.

Thai Cultural Reader, Bk. I. Robert B. Jones et al. 517p. 1976. Repr. of 1970 ed. 7.50 (ISBN 0-87727-503-3). Cornell SE Asia.

Thai-English & English-Thai Dictionary. 1974. 22.50 (ISBN 0-87557-087-9, 087-9). Saphrograph.

Thai-English Dictionary. George B. McFarland. 1944. 35.00x (ISBN 0-8047-0383-3). Stanford U Pr.

Thai-English Student's Dictionary. Ed. by Mary R. Haas. 1964. 28.50x (ISBN 0-8047-0567-4). Stanford U Pr.

Thai Forms. Jean-Michel Beurdeley. (Illus.). 128p. 1980. 47.50 (ISBN 0-8348-0150-7, 28518). Weatherhill.

Thai Home-Cooking from Kamolmal's Kitchen. William Crawford & Kamolmal Pookarakso. 1986. pap. 8.95 (ISBN 0-452-25834-0, Plume). NAL.

Thai Home Cooking from Kamolmal's Kitchen. William Crawford & Kamolmal Pootaraksa. 315p. 1985. 16.95 (ISBN 0-453-00493-8). NAL.

Thai Horse. William Diehl. LC 86-40345. 464p. 1988. 18.95 (ISBN 0-394-54628-8, Pub. by Villard Bks). Random.

Thai Insurgency: Contemporary Developments. R. Sean Randolph & W. Scott Thompson. (Washington Papers: Vol. IX, No. 81). 88p. (Orig.). 1981. pap. text ed. 7.95 (ISBN 0-8191-6025-3, Pub. by CSIS). U Pr of Amer.

Thai Peasant Social Structure. Jack M. Potter. 1976. 22.00x (ISBN 0-226-67635-8). U of Chicago Pr.

Thai Radical Discourse: The Real Face of Thai Feudalism Today. Craig J. Reynolds. (Studies on Southeast Asia: No. 3). 186p. (Orig.). 1987. pap. text ed. 16.50 (ISBN 0-87727-702-8). Cornell SE Asia.

Thai Reader. Mary Haas. LC 79-92824. 216p. (Thai.). 1978. pap. 10.00x (ISBN 0-87950-264-9). Spoken Lang Serv.

Thai Reading. 6.50 (ISBN 0-87727-511-4). Cornell SE Asia.

Thai Syntax: An Outline. Udom Warotamasikkhadit. LC 71-159472. (Janua Linguarum, Ser. Practica: No. 68). 77p. (Orig.). 1972. pap. text ed. 12.00x (ISBN 90-2792-095-8). Mouton.

Thai System of Writing. Mary R. Haas. LC 79-92825. 130p. 1979. pap. 5.00x (ISBN 0-87950-266-5). Spoken Lang Serv.

Thai Titles & Ranks: Including a Translation of Traditions of Royal Lineage in Siam by King Chulalongkorn. Robert B. Jones. LC 79-30150. (Cornell University Southeast Asia Program Ser.: Data Paper No. 81). pap. 43.50 (ISBN 0-317-08926-9, 2010482). Bks Demand UMI.

Thai Values & Behavior Patterns. Robert L. Mole. LC 71-130419. (Illus.). 1971. 4.75 (ISBN 0-8048-0947-X). C E Tuttle.

Thai Vocabulary. Mary R. Haas. LC 79-92827. 373p. (Thai.). 1980. pap. 10.00x (ISBN 0-87950-265-7). Spoken Lang Serv.

Thai Writing. 6.50 (ISBN 0-87727-512-2). Cornell SE Asia.

Thai Young Turks. Chai-Anan Samudavanija. 120p. (Orig.). 1982. pap. text ed. 17.00x (ISBN 9971-902-39-7, Pub. by Inst Southeast Asian Stud). Gower Pub Co.

THAID: A Sequential Analysis Program for the Analysis of Nominal Scale Dependent Variables. James N. Morgan & Robert C. Messenger. LC 72-619720. 98p. 1973. 12.00x (ISBN 0-87944-137-2). Inst Soc Res.

Thailand. Ed. by Harrap Limited Staff. 1986. pap. 49.75X (ISBN 0-245-54117-9, Pub. by Harrap Ltd England). State Mutual Bk.

Thailand. Sylvia McNair. LC 86-29933. (Enchantment of the World Ser.). (Illus.). 128p. (gr. 5-9). 1987. PLB 22.60 (ISBN 0-516-02792-1). Childrens.

Thailand. 2nd ed. (Post Guides). (Illus.). 144p. (Orig.). 1988. pap. 8.95 (ISBN 1-55650-063-7). Hunter Pub NY.

Thailand. (Hildebrand Travel Guides). 300p. 1988. 10.95 (ISBN 3-88989-076-8). Hunter Pub NY.

Thailand. (Insiders Guides Ser.). (Illus.). 224p. (Orig.). 1988. pap. 13.95 (ISBN 1-55650-054-8). Hunter Pub NY.

Thailand. (Let's Visit Places & Peoples - - Nations, Dependencies, & Sovereignties of the World Ser.). (Illus.). (gr. 5 up). 1988. 12.95 (ISBN 0-222-00982-9). Chelsea Hse.

Thailand. Michael S. Watts. (World Bibliographical Ser.: No. 65). 275p. 1986. lib. bdg. 47.85 (ISBN 1-85109-008-8). ABC-Clio.

Thailand - U. S. Relations: Changing Political, Strategic, & Economic Factors. Ed. by Ansil Ramsay & Wiwat Mungkandi. LC 88-8027. (Research Papers & Policy Studies: No. 23). 330p. (Orig.). 1988. pap. 20.00 (ISBN 1-55729-001-6). IEAS.

Thailand: A Handbook of Historical Statistics. Constance M. Wilson. 360p. (gr. 10-12). 1983. lib. bdg. 80.00 (ISBN 0-8161-8115-2, Hall Reference). G K Hall.

Thailand: A Rice-Growing Society. Ed. by Yoneo Ishii. LC 78-3839. (Center for Southeast Asian Studies, Kyoto University Monograph). 347p. 1978. pap. text ed. 13.00x (ISBN 0-8248-0626-3). UH Pr.

Thailand: A Short History. David K. Wyatt. LC 83-25953. (Illus.). 368p. 1986. 32.50x (ISBN 0-300-03054-1); pap. 13.95 (ISBN 0-300-03582-9, Y-565). Yale U PR.

Thailand: A Travel Survival Kit. 3rd ed. Joe Cummings. (Illus.). 288p. (Orig.). 1987. pap. 8.95 (ISBN 0-908086-95-4). Lonely Planet.

Thailand: An Analysis of Structural & Non-Structural Adjustments. Arne Drud & Wafik Grais. LC 82-10890. (World Bank Staff Working Papers: No. 513). 93p. (Orig.). 1982. pap. 5.00 (ISBN 0-8213-0023-7, WP0513). World Bank.

Thailand: An Annotated Bibliography of Bibliographies. Donn V. Hart. (Northern Illinois University Center for SEA Studies - Occasional Papers Ser.: No. 5). 1977. wrps. 4.00x (ISBN 0-686-09453-0). Cellar.

Thailand: An Annotated Bibliography of Local & Regional Development. (Country Bibliography Ser.: No. 6). 168p. 1982. pap. 10.00 (ISBN 0-686-43304-1, CRD148, UNCRD). UNIPUB.

Thailand: An Assessment of Alternative Foreign Borrowing Strategies. Homi J. Kharas & Hisanobu Shishido. (Working Paper: No. 781). 156p. 1985. 8.00 (ISBN 0-8213-0666-9, WP 0781). World Bank.

Thailand & Burma. Frank Kusy & Frances Capel. (Cadogan Guides). 1988. pap. 14.95 (ISBN 0-87106-798-6). Globe Pequot.

Thailand & the CGIAR Centers: A Study of Their Collaboration in Agricultural Research. Rungruang Isarangkura. (CGIAR Study Paper: No. 16). 103p. 1986. 5.00 (ISBN 0-317-59167-3, BK 0825). World Bank.

Thailand & the Fall of Singapore: The Frustrating of an Asian Revolution. Nigel Brailey. (Special Studies Ser.). 1985. 28.00x (ISBN 0-8133-0301-X). Westview.

Thailand & the United States. Frank C. Darling. 1965. 12.00 (ISBN 0-8183-0212-7). Pub Aff Pr.

Thailand Bibliography. John B. Mason & H. Carroll Parish. LC 73-1839. 247p. 1973. Repr. of 1958 ed. lib. bdg. 22.50 (ISBN 0-8371-6804-X, MATB). Greenwood.

Thailand: Buddhist Kingdom As Modern Nation State. Charles F. Keyes. (Profiles-Nations of Contemporary Asia Ser.). 240p. 1987. 32.50 (ISBN 0-86531-138-2). Westview.

Thailand: Case Study of Agricultural Input & Output Pricing. Trent Bertrand. (Working Paper: No. 385). ix, 134p. 1980. 8.00 (ISBN 0-686-36080-X, WP-0385). World Bank.

Thailand: Guide to Business & Investment. C Cordier et al. 155p. 1986. text ed. 53.95 (ISBN 0-566-02634-1, Pub. by Gower Pub England). Gower Pub Co.

Thailand in Transition: The Role of Oppositional Forces. Ross Prizzia. (Asian Studies at Hawaii: No. 32). 144p. 1985. pap. text ed. 9.00x (ISBN 0-8248-0977-7). UH Pr.

Thailand: Industrial Development Strategy in Thailand. Bela Balassa. x, 59p. 1980. pap. 5.00 (ISBN 0-686-39672-3, BK-9155). World Bank.

Thailand: Its People, Its Society, Its Culture. Frank J. Moore et al. LC 74-79218. (Survey of World Cultures Ser.: No. 15). pap. 157.30 (ISBN 0-317-11189-2, 2010454). Bks Demand UMI.

Thailand: Managing Public Resources for Structural Adjustment. Johannes Linn et al. 352p. 1984. 20.00 (ISBN 0-8213-0377-5, BK 0377). World Bank.

Thailand: Natural Resources Profile. Ed. by Anat Arbhabhirama et al. (Natural Resources of South-East Asia Ser.). (Illus.). 300p. 1988. 45.00 (ISBN 0-19-588887-1). Oxford U Pr.

Thailand: Origins of Military Rule. David Elliott. 190p. 1978. 26.25x (ISBN 0-905762-10-X, Pub. by Zed Pr England); pap. 8.75x (ISBN 0-905762-11-8, Pub. by Zed Pr England). Humanities.

Thailand Phrasebook. Joe Cummings. 96p. (Orig.). 1984. pap. 3.95 (ISBN 0-908086-57-1). Lonely Planet.

Thailand: Politics, Economy, & Socio-Cultural Setting. Woodworth G. Thrombley & William J. Siffin. LC 76-6602. Repr. of 1972 ed. 24.50 (ISBN 0-404-15297-X). AMS Pr.

Thailand: Pricing & Marketing Policy for Intensification of Rice Agriculture. 184p. 1984. 8.00 (ISBN 0-8213-0556-5, BK 0556). World Bank.

Thailand: Society & Politics. John L. Girling. LC 80-69822. (Politics & International Relations of Southeast Asia Ser.). 312p. (Orig.). 1985. pap. 9.95x (ISBN 0-8014-9328-5). Cornell U Pr.

Thailand Strategy for Fertilizer Development a Prefeasibility Study. E. C. Kapusta et al. (Technical Bulletin Ser.: T-17). (Illus.). 36p. (Orig.). 1980. pap. 4.00 (ISBN 0-88090-016-4). Intl Fertilizer.

Thailand, the Kingdom of Siam. (Asian Guides Ser.). 1988. 9.95 (ISBN 0-8442-9717-8). Natl Textbk.

Thailand: The Modernization of a Bureaucratic Polity. Fred W. Riggs. (Illus.). 484p. 1966. text ed. 20.00x (ISBN 0-8248-0034-6, Eastwest Ctr). UH Pr.

Thailand: Toward a Development Strategy of Full Participation. E. R. Lim & John Shilling. xiv, 232p. 1980. pap. 10.00 (ISBN 0-686-36122-9, BK-9125). World Bank.

Thailand Travel Guide. (Berlitz Travel Guides). (Illus.). 1982. pap. 4.95 (ISBN 0-02-969030-7, Berlitz). Macmillan.

Thailand's Agriculture. F. E. O'Riley & P. I. McDonald. 98p. 1983. 61.00x (ISBN 0-569-08779-1, Pub. by Collets (UK)). State Mutual Bk.

Thailand's Foreign Relations, Nineteen Sixty-Four to Nineteen Eighty. Corrine Phuangkasem. 56p. 1984. pap. 13.95 (ISBN 9971-902-71-0, Pub. by Inst Southeast Asian Stud). Gower Pub Co.

Thailand's Reproductive Revolution: Rapid Fertility Decline in a Third World Setting. John Knodel et al. LC 87-8172. (Social Demography Ser.). (Illus.). 272p. 1987. text ed. 45.00x (ISBN 0-299-11050-8); pap. text ed. 19.95x (ISBN 0-299-11054-0). U of Wis Pr.

Thais. Anatole France. (Coll. Bleue). 1960. pap. 14.95 (ISBN 0-685-11585-2). French & Eur.

Thais. Anatole France. Tr. by Basia Gulati from Fr. LC 75-20893. pap. 3.95 (ISBN 0-226-25989-7, P711, Phoen). U of Chicago Pr.

Thais & North Americans. John Fieg. Ed. by George W. Renwick. LC 80-83909. (Country Orientation Ser.). 82p. 1980. pap. text ed. 10.00x (ISBN 0-933662-15-7). Intercult Pr.

Thak Vehicle Fire Fighting. NFPA. Ed. by Paul R. Lyons. LC 75-24677. (Slide Script Ser.: No. SL-1). 52p. 1975. pap. text ed. 25.00 (ISBN 0-87765-048-9); 34 slides incl. (ISBN 0-685-62584-2). Natl Fire Prot.

Thalamocortical Organization of the Auditory System in the Cat: Studied by Retrograde Axonal Transport of Horseradish Peroxidase. (Advances in Anatomy, Embryology, & Cell Biology Ser.: Vol. 57). (Illus.). 1979. pap. 24.00 (ISBN 0-387-09449-0). Springer-Verlag.

Thalamus. Edward G. Jones. 918p. 1985. 135.00x (ISBN 0-306-41856-8, Plenum Pr). Plenum Pub.

Thalamus & Basal Telencephalon of the Cat. Alvin Berman & Edward G. Jones. (Illus.). 180p. 1982. text ed. 250.00x (ISBN 0-299-08440-X). U of Wis Pr.

Thalamus & Midbrain of Man: A Physiological Atlas Using Electrical Stimulation. Ronald R. Tasker et al. (Illus.). 528p. 1982. 60.25 (ISBN 0-398-04475-9). C C Thomas.

Thalamus & Pain. J. Besson et al. (International Congress Ser.: Vol. 770). 1987. 88.00 (ISBN 0-444-80928-7). Elsevier.

Thalassemia: An Interdisciplinary Approach. Ed. by John T. Chirban. (Illus.). 106p. 1987. lib. bdg. 19.75 (ISBN 0-8191-5675-2); pap. text ed. 9.75 (ISBN 0-8191-5676-0). U Pr of Amer.

Thalassemia: Pathophysiology & Management, Part A, Part A. Ed. by Suthat Fucharoen et al. LC 87-22836. (Birth Defects - Original Article Ser., 1987: Vol. 23, No. 5A). 628p. 1987. 170.00 (ISBN 0-8451-1066-7, 1066). A R Liss.

Thalassemia: Pathophysiology & Management, Pt. B: Ed. by Suthat Fucharoen et al. LC 87-22836. (Birth Defects: Original Article Ser.: Vol. 23, No. 5B). 500p. 1988. 160.00 (ISBN 0-8451-1067-5, 1067). A R Liss.

Thalassemia Pathophysiology & Management, Pt. B. Rowley et al. 1988. write for info. (ISBN 0-471-61043-7). Wiley.

Thalassemia: Recent Advances in Detection & Treatment. Ed. by Antonio Cao & Ugo Carcassi. LC 82-16179. (Birth Defects: Original Article Ser.: Vol. 18, No. 7). 400p. 1982. 82.00 (ISBN 0-8451-1051-9). A R Liss.

Thalassemia Recent Advances in Detection & Treatment. Liss et al. 400p. 1988. write for info. (ISBN 0-471-61395-9). Wiley.

Thalassius & on the Cliffs: The Composition of a Poet. Margot K. Louis. (Edwin H. Land Prize Essays). 1976. pap. 2.00 (ISBN 0-87391-014-1). Smith Coll.

Thalassocracies, Studies in Chronography 2. Molly B. Miller. LC 77-91204. 185p. 1971. 59.50 (ISBN 0-87395-062-3). State U NY Pr.

Thalatta: Der Weg der Griechen Zum Meer. Albin Lesky. LC 72-7899. (Greek History Ser.). (Ger.). Repr. of 1947 ed. 29.00 (ISBN 0-405-04798-3). Ayer Co Pubs.

Thalberg: Life & Legend. Bob Thomas. LC 82-49236. (Cinema Classics Ser.). 416p. 1985. lib. bdg. 66.00 (ISBN 0-8240-5779-1). Garland Pub.

Thallium. I. M. Korenman. (Analytical Chemistry of the Elements Ser.). 171p. 1970. text ed. 39.00x (ISBN 0-7065-0744-4, Pub. by Keter Pub Jerusalem). Coronet Bks.

Thallium-201 & Technettium-99m-Pyrophosphate Nyocardial Imaging in the Coronary Care Unit. Ed. by Frans J. Wackers. (Developments in Cardiovascular Medicine Ser.: No. 9). (Illus.). 255p. 1981. PLB 42.00 (ISBN 90-247-2396-5, Pub. by Martinus Nijhoff Netherlands). Kluwer Academic.

Thallium-201 Myocardial Imaging. Ed. by James L. Ritchie. LC 78-3004. 166p. 1978. 34.00 (ISBN 0-89004-274-8). Raven.

Thames. Charles Lyte. LC 80-50936. (Rivers of the World Ser.). (Illus.). 68p. (gr. 4 up). PLB 14.96 (ISBN 0-382-06369-4). Silver.

Thames & Hudson Dictionary Art Terms. Edward Lucie-Smith. LC 83-51331. (World Art Ser.). (Illus.). 208p. 1988. pap. 11.95 (ISBN 0-500-20222-2). Thames Hudson.

Thames & Hudson Dictionary of Art & Artists. Ed. by Herbert Read & Nikos Stangos. LC 84-50342. (Illus.). 1985. 19.95f. Thames Hudson.

Thames & Hudson Dictionary of Art & Artists. rev. ed. Ed. by Herbert Read & Nikos Stangos. LC 87-50342. (World of Art Ser.). (Illus.). 1988. pap. 11.95 (ISBN 0-500-20223-0). Thames Hudson.

Thames & Hudson Dictionary of Art Terms. Edward Lucie-Smith. LC 83-51331. (Illus.). 216p. 1984. text ed. 19.95f (ISBN 0-500-23389-6). Thames Hudson.

Thames & Hudson Encyclopaedia of 20th-Century Music. Paul Griffiths. LC 85-51468. (Illus.). 208p. 1986. 19.95 (ISBN 0-500-23449-3). Thames Hudson.

Thames & Hudson Encyclopedia of British Art. Ed. by David Bindman. LC 84-51499. (Illus.). 320p. 1985. 24.95f (ISBN 0-500-23420-5). Thames Hudson.

Thames & Hudson Manual of Architectural Ceramics. David Hamilton. (Illus.). 1978. 18.95 (ISBN 0-500-68014-0). Thames Hudson.

Thames & Hudson Manual of Bookbinding. Arthur W. Johnson. (Illus.). 224p. 1981. pap. 10.95f (ISBN 0-500-68011-6). Thames Hudson.

Thames & Hudson Manual of Direct Metal Sculpture. Trevor Faulkner. (Illus.). 1980. pap. 10.95 (ISBN 0-500-68015-9). Thames Hudson.

Thames & Hudson Manual of Dyes & Fabrics. Joyce Storey. (Manuals Ser.). (Illus.). 1986. pap. 10.95f (ISBN 0-500-68016-7). Thames Hudson.

Thames & Hudson Manual of Etching & Engraving. Walter Chamberlain. (Illus.). 1978. pap. 10.95f (ISBN 0-500-68001-9). Thames Hudson.

Thames & Hudson Manual of Pottery & Ceramics. David Hamilton. (Manual Ser.). (Illus.). 1982. pap. 10.95 (ISBN 0-500-68007-8). Thames Hudson.

Thames & Hudson Manual of Professional Photography. John Constantine & Julia Wallis. LC 82-50814. (Thames & Hudson Manual Ser.). (Illus.). 1983. pap. 10.95 (ISBN 0-500-68025-6). Thames Hudson.

Thames & Hudson Manual of Screen Printing. Tim Mara. (Illus.). 1979. 18.95 (ISBN 0-500-67019-6). Thames Hudson.

Thames & Hudson Manual of Silversmithing: The Constructional Processes. Frances Loyen. (Illus.). 1980. pap. 10.95 (ISBN 0-500-68021-3). Thames Hudson.

Thames & Hudson Manual of Stoneware & Porcelain. David Hamilton. LC 81-53054. (Thames & Hudson Manuals Ser.). (Illus., Orig.). 1982. pap. 12.95 (ISBN 0-500-68024-8). Thames Hudson.

Thames & Hudson Manual of Textile Printing. Joyce Storey. (Manuals Ser.). (Illus.). 1985. pap. 10.95f (ISBN 0-500-68008-6). Thames Hudson.

Thames & Hudson Manual of Typography. Ruari McLean. LC 80-50803. (Illus.). 1988. pap. 11.95 (ISBN 0-500-68022-1). Thames Hudson.

Thames & Severn Canal. Humphrey W. Household. LC 70-77877. (Illus.). 1969. 19.95x (ISBN 0-678-05508-4). Kelley.

Thames Barrier. Stuart Gilbert & Ray Horner. 216p. 1984. 24.00 (ISBN 0-7277-0182-7, Pub. by T Telford UK). Am Soc Civil Eng.

Thames Barrier Design: Conference Proceedings. 208p. 1978. 36.50 (ISBN 0-7277-0057-X, Pub. by T Telford UK). Am Soc Civil Eng.

Thames Groundwater Scheme: Conference Proceedings. 245p. 1978. 35.00 (ISBN 0-7277-0060-X, Pub. by T Telford UK). Am Soc Civil Eng.

Thames: Record of a Working Waterway. D. Wilson. (Illus.). 120p. 1988. 29.95 (ISBN 0-7134-5298-6, Pub. by Batsford England). David & Charles.

Thames-Side in the Past. F. C. Hodgson. 1973. Repr. of 1913 ed. 25.00 (ISBN 0-8274-0174-4). R West.

Thames Tunnel to Channel Tunnel: One Hundred & Fifty Years of Civil Engineering. Ed. by Will Howie & Mike Chrimes. 308p. 1987. 27.00 (ISBN 0-7277-0396-X, Pub. by T Telford UK). Am Soc Civil Eng.

Thamyris: Is There a Future for Poetry? R. C. Trevelyan. lib. bdg. 15.50 (ISBN 0-8495-5329-6). Arden Lib.

Thamyris or Is There a Future for Poetry? R. C. Trevelyan. 1973. lib. bdg. 18.50 (ISBN 0-8414-8407-4). Folcroft.

Thanatochemistry: A Survey of General, Organic & Biochemistry for Funeral Service Professionals. James M. Dorn & Barbara Hopkins. 1985. text ed. 46.00 (ISBN 0-8359-7640-8, Reston). P-H.

Thanatologic Aspects of Aging. Ed. by Margot Tallmer et al. (Thantology Service Ser.). 190p. 1980. pap. 9.95x (ISBN 0-930194-25-X). Ctr Thanatology.

Thanatology Abstracts, 1977. Otto S. Margolis & Daniel J. Cherico. 17.00 (ISBN 0-405-12503-8). Ayer Co Pubs.

Thanatology Abstracts 1979. Otto S. Margolis & Daniel J. Cherico. 15.00 (ISBN 0-405-14222-6, 19702). Ayer Co Pubs.

Thanatology Course Outlines, Vol. 2. Daniel J. Cherico & Otto S. Margolis. 16.50 (ISBN 0-405-12514-3). Ayer Co Pubs.

Thanatology Curriculum-Medicine. Ed. by Robert De Bellis et al. LC 88-2934. (Loss, Grief & Care Ser.: Vol. 2, Nos. 1 & 2). (Illus.). 130p. 1988. text ed. 22.95 (ISBN 0-86656-738-0). Haworth Pr.

Thanatology Library with Updates. Roberta Halporn. (Illus.). 50p. 1982. pap. 5.75 (ISBN 0-930194-07-1). Ctr Thanatology.

Thanatology Thesaurus. Ed. by Roberta Halporn. (Thanatology Service Ser.). 50p. 1989. pap. 15.95 (ISBN 0-930194-17-9). Ctr Thanatology.

Thanatopsis Wings, No. 48. Ed. by Jackson Wilcox. (Wings Ser.). (Illus.). 36p. (Orig.). 1988. pap. 3.50 (ISBN 0-944231-02-0). Slvr Wings CA.

Thanatos: Earth Poems. Thomas Parkinson. 1976. pap. 2.00 (ISBN 0-685-79271-4). Oyez.

Thanatos Syndrome. Walker Percy. 1987. limited, signed, slipcased 75.00 (ISBN 0-374-27355-3); 17.95 (ISBN 0-374-27354-5). FS&G.

Thanatos Syndrome. Walker Percy. 1988. pap. 4.95 (ISBN 0-317-67165-0). Ivy Books.

Thanatos Syndrore. Walker Percy. 384p. 1988. pap. 4.95 (ISBN 0-8041-0220-1, Pub. by Ivy). Ballantine.

Thangam Philip Book of Banking. Thangam Philip. 122p. 1982. pap. 3.50x (ISBN 0-86131-285-6). Apt Bks.

Thangs Yankee Don't Know. 1.95 (ISBN 0-936672-31-5). Aerial Photo.

Thank a Bored Angel: Selected Poems. Samuel Hazo. LC 83-4129. 128p. 1983. 14.00 (ISBN 0-8112-0869-9); pap. 6.25 (ISBN 0-8112-0868-0, NDP555). New Directions.

Thank God Ahead of Time: The Life & Spirituality of Solanus Casey. Michael H. Crosby. 1985. 9.50 (ISBN 0-8199-0879-7). Franciscan Herald.

Thank God for Black Power. James H. Boykin. LC 83-90000. 172p. 1983. pap. 10.00x (ISBN 0-9603342-2-X). Boykin.

Thank God for Everything. Frederick K. Price. 31p. pap. 0.75 mini-bk. (ISBN 0-89274-056-6). Harrison Hse.

Thank God for Good & Bad Times. Monica Desir. (Anchor Ser.). 91p. 1985. pap. 5.95 (ISBN 0-8163-0612-5). Pacific Pr Pub Assn.

Thank God for My Breakdown. Walter Reiss. 1980. 4.95 (ISBN 0-8100-0114-4, 12N1717). Northwest Pub.

Thank God for New Churches! Church Planting: Source of New Life. James H. Lehman. 108p. (Orig.). 1984. pap. 6.95 (ISBN 0-87178-840-3). Brethren.

Thank God for Prayer. Russell W. Lake. LC 83-50397. 293p. 1983. 5.95 (ISBN 0-87159-159-6). Unity School.

Thank God for the Atom Bomb & Other Essays. Paul Fussell. LC 88-2234. 1988. 17.95 (ISBN 0-671-63866-1). Summit Bks.

Thank God for the Crumbs. Bonnie Kotter. Ed. by Gerald Wheeler. (Banner Bks.). 96p. (Orig.). 1986. pap. 6.95 (ISBN 0-8280-0315-7). Review & Herald.

Thank God I Have a Teenager. Charles S. Mueller. LC 84-24363. 128p. (Orig.). 1985. pap. 6.95 (ISBN 0-8066-2126-5, 10-6239). Augsburg.

Thank God, I'm a Teenager. rev. ed. Charles S. Mueller & Donald R. Bardill. LC 88-6215. (Illus.). 144p. (YA) (gr. 7-12). 1988. pap. 7.95 (ISBN 0-8066-2351-9, 10-6242). Augsburg.

Thank God I'm Free. James Robison. 1988. 14.95 (ISBN 0-8407-7610-1). Nelson.

Thank God It's Friday: Meditations For Hard-Working Catholics. Andrew Costello. 1987. 12.95 (ISBN 0-88347-213-9). Thomas More.

Thank God, It's Monday! William E. Diehl. LC 81-71390. 192p. 1982. pap. 6.95 (ISBN 0-8006-1656-1, 1-1656). Fortress.

Thank Goodness for People. Charles M. Schulz. pap. 3.95 (ISBN 0-03-018121-6). H Holt & Co.

Thank Gutenberg for Shakespeare & Ben Franklin. John M. Fontana. 24p. 1964. pap. 1.25 (ISBN 0-685-26780-6). J M Fontana.

Thank You. Colleen Reece. LC 82-9560. (What Does it Mean? Ser.). (Illus.). 32p. (gr. 1-2). 1982. PLB 5.95 (ISBN 0-89565-239-0, 4899, Pub. by Childs World). Standard Pub.

Thank You. Illus. by Tony Tallarico. (Mind Your Manners Ser.). (Illus.). (ps-1). 1985. text ed. 3.95 (ISBN 0-89828-151-2, 81512). Tuffy Bks.

Thank You, Amelia Bedelia. Peggy Parish. LC 64-11835. (Illus.). (gr. k-3). 1964. 8.70i (ISBN 0-06-024665-0); PLB 9.89 (ISBN 0-06-024652-9). HarpJ.

Thank You, Amelia Bedelia. Peggy Parish. LC 64-11835. (Trophy Picture Bks.). (Illus.). 32p. (gr. k-3). 1983. pap. 3.50 (ISBN 0-06-443037-5, Trophy). HarpJ.

Thank You, Dad. Richard Haffey. (Greeting Book Line Ser.). 24p. (Orig.). 1986. pap. 1.50 (ISBN 0-89622-305-1). Twenty-Third.

Thank You, Dr. Lamaze. Marjorie Karmel. LC 80-8372. 192p. 1983. pap. 7.95 (ISBN 0-06-090996-X, CN 996, PL). Har-Row.

Thank You, Fog: Last Poems. W. H. Auden. LC 74-9049. 1974. 8.95 (ISBN 0-394-49496-2). Random.

Thank You for a Book to Read. Patricia Smeltzer & Victor Smeltzer. (Illus.). 24p. (gr. k-6). 1983. pap. 2.50 (ISBN 0-86683-719-1, AY8319, HarpR). Har-Row.

Thank You for a Drink of Water. Patricia Smeltzer & Victor Smeltzer. (Illus.). 24p. (gr. k-6). 1983. pap. 2.50 (ISBN 0-86683-721-3, AY8317, HarpR). Har-Row.

Thank You for a Loaf of Bread. Patricia Smeltzer & Victor Smeltzer. (Illus.). 24p. (gr. k-6). 1983. pap. 2.50 (ISBN 0-86683-720-5, AY8318, HarpR). Har-Row.

Thank You for a Pair of Jeans. Patricia Smeltzer & Victor Smeltzer. (Illus.). 24p. (gr. k-6). 1983. pap. 2.50 (ISBN 0-86683-718-3, AY8320, HarpR). Har-Row.

Thank You for Being. Clinton Weyand. (Illus.). 104p. (Orig.). 1978. 5.95 (ISBN 0-938292-07-2). Being Bks.

Thank You for Being a Friend. Jill Briscoe. 192p. (Orig.). 1981. pap. 6.95 (ISBN 0-310-21851-9, 9261P). Zondervan.

Thank You for My Grandchild. Betty Isler. 1983. pap. 2.08 (ISBN 0-570-03915-0, 12-2850). Concordia.

Thank You for My Spouse. Jeanette Groth. LC 12-2826. 1983. pap. 2.75 (ISBN 0-570-03885-5). Concordia.

Thank You for Our Day on the Beach. Eira Reeves. (Thank You God Ser.). (Illus.). 24p. (Orig.). (ps). 1988. pap. 2.95 (ISBN 0-8170-1134-X). Judson.

Thank You for the Tadpole. Photos by Mary Raynor. (Share-a-Story Bks.). (gr. k-2). 1988. 8.95 (ISBN 0-385-29604-5); pap. 2.50 (ISBN 0-317-69488-X). Delacorte.

Thank You for the Tadpole. Pat Thomson. (Share-a-Story Ser.: No. 5). (gr. k-6). 1988. pap. 2.50 (ISBN 0-440-40027-9, YB). Dell.

Thank You for the World. (Illus.). 16p. 1982. pap. 0.99 (ISBN 0-86683-655-1, AY8234, HarpR). Har-Row.

Thank You for This Child. Jeanette Groth. (Illus.). 1980. pap. 2.50 (ISBN 0-570-03797-2, 12-2906). Concordia.

Thank You, God. Debby Anderson. (Sparklers Ser.). (Illus.). (ps up). 1986. plastic comb bdg. 2.95 (ISBN 0-89191-931-7, 59311, Chariot Bks). Cook.

Thank You, God. Marian Bennett. (My Surprise Bks.). (Illus.). 10p. (ps-2). 1985. 4.95 (ISBN 0-87239-906-0, 2730). Standard Pub.

Thank You, God. Lucille E. Hein. (Illus.). 32p. (ps up). 1981. pap. 3.50 (ISBN 0-8170-0912-4). Judson.

Thank You, God. Laurel Rooney. Ed. by Carl Fisher. 1986. dupl. masterbk. 9.95 (ISBN 0-89837-113-9). Pflaum Pr.

Thank You, God. Anne Smith. 24p. (Orig.). (ps). 1988. pap. text ed. 1.75 (ISBN 0-936625-44-9). Womans Mission Union.

Thank You God. Gordon Stowell. (Little Fish Books About You & Me Ser.: III). 14p. (YA) (gr. 1-7). 1984. mini-bk 0.59 (ISBN 0-8307-0960-6, 5608436). Regal.

Thank You God. (First Prayer Ser.). (ps). 2.95 (ISBN 0-86112-196-1, Pub. by Brimax Bks). Borden.

Thank You, God, for Christmas. Henrietta Gambill. (Little Happy Day Bks.). (Illus.). 24p. (ps-2). 1986. pap. 0.49 (ISBN 0-87403-159-1, 2119). Standard Pub.

Thank You, God, for Christmas. Henrietta D. Gambill. LC 87-91997. (Happy Day Bks.). (Illus.). 32p. (gr. k-2). 1988. 1.75 (ISBN 0-87403-402-7, 24-03812). Standard Pub.

Thank You, God, for Me. Marybeth Hageman. (Christian Self-Discovery Ser.). (Illus.). (ps). 1987. pap. 2.25 (ISBN 0-570-09114-4, 56-1589). Concordia.

Thank You God for Our Day in the Country. Eira Reeves. (Thank You God Ser.). 24p. (Orig.). (ps). 1988. pap. 2.95 (ISBN 0-8170-1135-8). Judson.

Thank You God for Our Day in the Town. Eira Reeves. (Thank You God Ser.). (Illus.). 24p. (Orig.). (ps). 1988. pap. 2.95 (ISBN 0-8170-1136-6). Judson.

Thank You God for Our Day Indoors. Eira Reeves. (Thank You God Ser.). (Illus.). 24p. (Orig.). (ps). 1988. pap. 2.95 (ISBN 0-8170-1137-4). Judson.

Thank You, God, for Water. Dorothy Mock. (Happy Day Bks.). (Illus.). 24p. (ps-2). 1985. 1.59 (ISBN 0-87239-880-3, 3680). Standard Pub.

Thank You, God, for Winter. Jane B. Moncure. (Child's World Books of the Seasons). (Illus.). (ps-2). 1985. PLB 4.95 (ISBN 0-89565-082-7, R4905). Standard Pub.

Thank You, God: Prayers for Young Children. Ron Klug & Lyn Klug. LC 80-67800. 32p. (Orig.). (ps-1). 1980. pap. 4.95 (ISBN 0-8066-1862-0, 10-6243). Augsburg.

Thank You Hashem. Yaffa Rosenthal. (ArtScroll Youth Ser.). (Illus.). 32p. (gr. 1-8). 1983. 8.95 (ISBN 0-89906-777-8); pap. 5.95 (ISBN 0-89906-778-6). Mesorah Pubns.

Thank You Henrietta. Niki Daly. LC 86-40020. (Viking Kestrel Picture Bks.). (Illus.). 24p. (ps-1). 1986. 4.95 (ISBN 0-670-81254-4, Viking Kestrel). Viking.

Thank You, Jackie Robinson. Barbara Cohen. LC 87-29341. (Illus.). (gr. 3-6). 1988. PLB 11.95 (ISBN 0-688-07909-1). Lothrop.

Thank You, Jeeves. P. G. Wodehouse. Repr. lib. bdg. 18.95x (ISBN 0-89190-294-5, Pub. by River City Pr). Amereon Ltd.

Thank You, Jeeves. P. G. Wodehouse. LC 82-48821. 192p. 1983. pap. 3.95 (ISBN 0-06-080657-5, P 657, PL). Har-Row.

Thank You Lord. Jane B. Moncure. (Child's World Books of Values). (Illus.). (ps-2). 1985. PLB 4.95 (ISBN 0-89565-077-0, R4912). Standard Pub.

Thank You Lord. Louise Reece. (Illus.). 164p. (Orig.). 1983. pap. 3.95x (ISBN 0-9614264-0-3). Lovejoy Pr.

Thank You Mr. Moto. John P. Marquand. Repr. lib. bdg. 18.95x (ISBN 0-88411-142-3, Pub. by Aeonian Pr). Amereon Ltd.

Thank You, Mr. Moto. John P. Marquand. 288p. 1985. pap. 3.95 (ISBN 0-316-54698-4). Little.

Thank You Mr. President. Merriman Smith. LC 75-31769. (FDR & the Era of the New Deal Ser.). 1975. Repr. of 1946 ed. lib. bdg. 32.50 (ISBN 0-306-70740-3). Da Capo.

Thank You, Mom. Richard Haffey. (Greeting Book Line Ser.). 24p. (Orig.). 1986. pap. 1.50 (ISBN 0-89622-306-X). Twenty-Third.

Thank You Music Lovers: A Bio-Discography of Spike Jones & His City Slickers, 1941-1965. Compiled by Jack Mirtle. LC 85-27128. (Discographies Ser.: No. 20). 448p. 1986. lib. bdg. 56.95 (ISBN 0-313-24814-1, MSN/). Greenwood.

Thank You, Nicky! Harriet Ziefert. (Illus.). (ps-1). 1988. pap. 4.95 (ISBN 0-317-69640-8, Puffin Bks). Penguin.

Thank You Prayers. (Illus.). 16p. 1982. pap. 0.99 (ISBN 0-86683-654-3, AY8233, HarpR). Har-Row.

Thank You, Queen Isabella. John Works. LC 85-40750. (Tarleton State University Southwestern Studies in the Humanities: No. 2). 118p. 1986. 12.95 (ISBN 0-89096-245-6). Tex A&M Univ Pr.

Thank You, Queen Isabella. John Works. 192p. 1987. pap. 3.95 (ISBN 0-345-34107-4). Ballantine.

Thank You Saint Jude. John W. Spencer. 224p. 1986. 12.95 (ISBN 0-941219-01-1). Phillips Pub MA.

Thank You, Uncle Sam: Letters of a World War II Army Nurse from North Africa & Italy. Eugenia M. Kielar. 264p. 1987. 16.95 (ISBN 0-317-59674-8). Dorrance.

Thankful Blossom, & Other Eastern Tales & Sketches. facsimile ed. Bret Harte. LC 72-37546. (Short Story Index Reprint Ser.). Repr. of 1896 ed. 25.00 (ISBN 0-8369-4105-5). Ayer Co Pubs.

Thankful Days: Verses for Children, No. 2. Merna B. Shank. (ps-9). 1982. pap. 1.95 (ISBN 0-87813-212-0). Park View.

Thankful Praise. Keith Watkins. LC 86-24514. 192p. (Orig.). 1987. pap. 9.95 (ISBN 0-8272-3650-6). CBP.

Thankful Praise: A Studyguide. Cy Rowell. 24p. (Orig.). 1987. pap. 2.50 (ISBN 0-8272-3651-4). CBP.

Thankfulness. Janet McDonnell. LC 88-2657. (What Is It?--A Values Ser.). (Illus.). 32p. (gr. k-3). 1988. PLB 7.95 (ISBN 0-89565-375-3). Childs World.

Thanks. Ruth S. Odor. LC 79-23926. (What Does It Mean Ser.). (Illus.). 32p. (ps-2). 1980. 10.33 (ISBN 0-516-06449-5). Childrens.

Thanks. Ruth S. Odor. LC 79-23926. (What Does It Mean? Ser.). (Illus.). (ps-2). 1980. PLB 6.75 (ISBN 0-89565-113-0). Childs World.

Thanks a Lot, Triceratot: A Tiny Dinos Story about Helping Others. Guy Gilchrist. LC 87-40686. (Tiny Dinos Ser.). (Illus.). 24p. (ps-2). 1988. bds. 4.95 (ISBN 1-55782-070-8). Warner Bks.

Thanks Be to God. Robert N. Rodenmayer. 126p. 1960. 7.50 (ISBN 0-227-67615-7). Attic Pr.

Thanks Doctor. Robert D. Carpenter. LC 72-78231. 200p. 1972. pap. text ed. 5.95 (ISBN 0-9600576-1-7). RDC Pubs.

Thanks for Asking, Mr. President. Caroline H. Babington. LC 86-10006. 145p. (Orig.). 1986. pap. 9.95 (ISBN 0-88247-754-4). R & E Pubs.

Thanks for Listening! Jack Brickhouse et al. LC 86-2103. (Illus.). 224p. 1986. 15.95 (ISBN 0-912083-16-6). Diamond Communications.

Thanks for the Dance. Lorna Madsen & Theodore W. Clymer. (Chapman Puzzle Bks.). (Orig.). (gr. k-2). 1985. pap. 2.00 (ISBN 0-930687-24-8). Chapman Brook.

Thanks for the Memories. Perry Tanksley. 4.50 (ISBN 0-686-15451-7). Allgood Bks.

Thanks Giving: Stewardship Sermons out of the Ethnic Minority Experience. Ed. by J. LaVon Kincaid, Sr. LC 83-73266. 88p. 1984. pap. text ed. 6.95 (ISBN 0-88177-007-8, DR007B). Discipleship Res.

Thanks Lord, I Needed That! Charlene Potterbaum. LC 77-86470. 155p. 1979. pocket size 3.95 (ISBN 0-88270-411-7, P411-7). Bridge Pub.

Thanks Songbook. Gary L. Johnson. 32p. 1980. pap. 2.50 (ISBN 0-87123-776-8, 280776). Bethany Hse.

Thanks to God & the Revolution: Popular Religion & Class Consciousness in the New Nicaragua. Roger N. Lancaster. 280p. 1988. 25.00x (ISBN 0-231-06730-5). Columbia U Pr.

Thanksgiving. Margaret Baldwin. (First Bks.). (Illus.). 72p. (gr. 4 up). 1983. PLB 10.40 (ISBN 0-531-04532-3). Watts.

Thanksgiving. Judy Beach & Kathleen Spencer. (Teachers' Holiday Helpers Ser.). (gr. 1-3). 1987. pap. 4.95 (ISBN 0-8224-6772-0). D S Lake Pubs.

Thanksgiving. Janet Evanovich. (Loveswept Ser.: No. 289). 192p. (Orig.). 1988. pap. 2.50 (ISBN 0-553-21941-3). Bantam.

Thanksgiving. Robert Schauffler. Repr. of 1925 ed. 35.00 (ISBN 0-686-18792-X). Scholars Ref Lib.

Thanksgiving. Alana Willoughby. Ed. by Alton Jordan. (ARO Holidays Ser.). (Illus.). (gr. k-3). PLB 3.95 (ISBN 0-89868-024-7, Read Res); pap. text ed. 1.75 (ISBN 0-89868-057-3). ARO Pub.

Thanksgiving. Lee Wyndham. LC 63-13890. (Holiday Bks.). (Illus.). (gr. 2-5). 1963. PLB 7.56 (ISBN 0-8116-6551-8). Garrard.

Thanksgiving Activity Book. Gail Aemmer. (Stick-Out-Your-Neck Ser.). (Illus.). 32p. (gr. 3-6). 1982. pap. 1.98 (ISBN 0-88724-042-9, CD-8016). Carson-Dellos.

That Spanish Woman. F. W. Kenyon. 1978. pap. 1.75 (ISBN 0-505-51301-3, Pub. by Tower Bks). Leisure NY.

That Special Kiss. Elsie W. Strother. (YA) (gr. 7 up). 1982. 9.95 (ISBN 0-686-84744-X, Avalon). Bouregy.

That Special Magic. Elizabeth S. Montfort. LC 87-71719. (Illus.). 53p. (Orig.). (gr. 2-3). 1988. pap. 5.00 (ISBN 0-916383-37-7). Aegina Pr.

That Strange Divine Sea: Reflections on Being a Catholic. Christopher Derrick. LC 83-80190. 189p. (Orig.). 1983. pap. 8.95 (ISBN 0-89870-029-9). Ignatius Pr.

That Strange Feeling. J. H. Rhodes. 1985. 9.95 (ISBN 0-8034-8528-X, Avalon). Bouregy.

That Summer. David Edgar. 80p. 1988. pap. text ed. 9.95 (ISBN 0-413-17450-6). Heinemann Ed.

That Tantalus. William Bronk. 1971. pap. 8.00 (ISBN 0-685-00987-4). Elizabeth Pr.

That Terrible Halloween Night. James Stevenson. LC 79-27775. (Illus.). 32p. (ps). 1980. 10.95 (ISBN 0-688-80281-8); PLB 11.88 (ISBN 0-688-84281-X). Greenwillow.

That Terrible Halloween Night. James Stevenson. 32p. (gr. k-3). pap. 2.95 (ISBN 0-590-33365-8). Scholastic Inc.

That Terrible Night Santa Got Lost in the Woods. Larry L. King. (Illus.). 29p. 1981. 15.00 (ISBN 0-88426-060-7). Encino Pr.

That the World May Believe: The Acts of the Apostles. Helen S. Thomsen. (gr. 7 up). 1978. pap. 2.25x (ISBN 0-8192-4085-0); tchrs guide 2.25x (ISBN 0-8192-4084-2). Morehouse.

That the World May Know. Earl Paulk. 189p. (Orig.). 1987. pap. 7.95 (ISBN 0-917595-15-7). K-Dimension.

That They All May Be One. National Conference of Directors of Religious Education. 1977. 3.60 (ISBN 0-318-00800-9). Natl Cath Educ.

That They All May Be One. 26p. 1977. 3.60 (ISBN 0-318-20611-0). Natl Cath Educ.

That They May All Be One. Elbridge B. Linn. 1969. 4.50 (ISBN 0-88027-020-9). Firm Foun Pub.

That They May Have Life: The Story of the American University of Beirut, 1866-1941. Stephen B. Penrose, Jr. 1970. 17.95x (ISBN 0-8156-6000-6, Am U Beirut). Syracuse U Pr.

That They May Know You. Andrew Thompson. 112p. 1982. 10.55 (ISBN 0-318-00801-7). Natl Cath Educ.

That They May Live: Theological Reflections on the Quality of Life. Ed. by George Devine. 314p. 1984. pap. text ed. 11.25 (ISBN 0-8191-3852-5, College Theo Soc). U Pr of Amer.

That They Were at the Beach. Leslie Scalapino. LC 85-60854. 128p. (Orig.). 1985. pap. 9.50 (ISBN 0-86547-211-4). N Point Pr.

That Time o' Day. John Booth. 1988. 30.00x (Pub. by Ian Henry Pubns England). State Mutual Bk.

That Time of Year: A Chronicle of Life in a Nursing Home. Joyce Horner. LC 81-23128. 224p. (Orig.). 1982. pap. 9.95 (ISBN 0-87023-367-X). U of Mass Pr.

That Tragic Queen: The Deirdre Legend in Anglo-Irish Literature. Herbert V. Fackler. 1978. pap. 15.00 (ISBN 3-7052-0916-7, Pub. by Salzburg Studies). Longwood Pub Group.

That Unforgettable Encounter. David S. McCarthy. 108p. (Orig.). 1983. pap. 2.95 (ISBN 0-8341-0834-8). Beacon Hill.

That Unknown Day. Carlos E. Portillo. LC 85-52117. (Illus.). 400p. (Orig.). 1986. 14.95 (ISBN 0-937365-00-9); pap. 9.95 (ISBN 0-937365-01-7). WCP Pubns.

That Voice. Robert Pinget. Tr. by Barbara Wright. LC 82-60910. 114p. 1983. 10.95 (ISBN 0-87376-041-7). Red Dust.

That Was Balzac. George Middeton. 1973. Repr. of 1933 ed. 30.00 (ISBN 0-8274-0707-6). R West.

That Was the Life. Dora J. Hamblin. (Illus.). 1978. pap. 5.95 (ISBN 0-393-08824-3). Norton.

That Was the Life. Dora J. Hamblin. (Illus.). 1977. 10.00 (ISBN 0-393-08764-6). Norton.

That Was Then, This Is Now. S. E. Hinton. 224p. (gr. 7 up). 1972. pap. 2.95 (ISBN 0-440-98652-4, LFL). Dell.

That Was Then, This Is Now. Susie E. Hinton. (Illus.). (gr. 7 up). 1971. 12.95 (ISBN 0-670-69798-2). Viking.

That We May Be Willing to Receive. Elise N. Morgan. (Meditation Ser.). 1938. 4.50 (ISBN 0-87516-331-9). DeVorss.

That We May Have Fellowship: Studies in First John. John Lineberry. 112p. 1986. pap. 4.95 (ISBN 0-87227-115-3). Reg Baptist.

That We Might Have Life. Martha Popson. LC 80-2080. 128p. (gr. 6 up). 1981. pap. 2.75 (ISBN 0-385-17438-1, Im). Doubleday.

That We Might Live. Grace C. Nash. Ed. by Boye De Mente. LC 84-62031. (Illus.). 255p. 1985. pap. 9.95 (ISBN 0-914778-58-7). Shano Pubs.

That Which Concerneth Me. facs. ed. J. Baxter & L. Harvey. LC 79-178468. (Black Heritage Library Collection). Repr. of 1934 ed. 12.00 (ISBN 0-8369-8911-2). Ayer Co Pubs.

That Which Is. 2nd ed. (Illus.). 232p. 1988. pap. 4.95 (ISBN 0-940267-08-X). Knoll Pub.

That Wild Fellow John Neal & the American Literary Revolution. Benjamin Lease. LC 72-81630. pap. 63.80 (ISBN 0-317-26518-0, 2024054). Bks Demand UMI.

That Winter. Pamela Gillilan. 1986. pap. 10.95 (ISBN 1-85224-005-9, Pub. by Bloodaxe Bks). Dufour.

That Woman I Married. Melvin R. Miller. 104p. 1986. pap. 3.95 (ISBN 0-88144-061-2). Christian Pub.

That Woman: Indira Gandhi's Seven Years in Power. K. A. Abbas. 1973. 11.25 (ISBN 0-89684-553-2). Orient Bk Dist.

That Woman Must Be on Drugs. Nicole Hollander. (Illus.). 128p. 1981. pap. 5.95 (ISBN 0-312-79510-6). St Martin.

That Wonderful Night. (Illus.). (ps-3). plastic bdg. 2.00 (ISBN 0-8198-0189-5); pap. 1.25 (ISBN 0-8198-0190-9). Dghtrs St Paul.

That Yankee Cat: The Maine Coon. Marilis Hornidge. LC 80-67660. (Illus., Orig.). 1981. 12.95 (ISBN 0-911764-22-4). Durrell.

That Yankee Cat: The Maine Coon. Marilis Hornidge. LC 85-82198. (Illus.). 114p. 1986. pap. 8.95 (ISBN 0-88448-026-7). Harpswell Pr.

That Ye May Abound. Mrs. Charles Walker. (Illus.). 80p. (Orig.). 1980. pap. 3.00 (ISBN 0-89114-096-4). Baptist Pub Hse.

That Ye May Heal: A Manual for Individual & Group Study of Meditation for Healing, from the Edgar Cayce Records. rev. ed. Compiled by Mary A. Woodward. 53p. 1970. pap. 3.50 (ISBN 0-87604-075-X). ARE Pr.

That You May Believe (John) Leader's Guide. (New Horizons Bible Study). 48p. 1983. pap. 1.95 (ISBN 0-89367-082-0). Light & Life.

That You May Believe (John) Student Guide. (New Horizons Bible Study). 64p. 1983. pap. 2.50 (ISBN 0-89367-081-2). Light & Life.

That You May Believe: Miracles & Faith-Then & Now. Colin Brown. 224p. (Orig.). 1985. pap. 9.95 (ISBN 0-8028-0086-6). Eerdmans.

That You May Believe: Studies in the Gospel of John. Homer Hailey. (Illus.). 1982. 9.95 (ISBN 0-913814-51-2). Nevada Pubns.

That You May Know. 1987. pap. 2.95 (ISBN 1-55513-279-0, Life Journey). Cook.

That You May Prosper: Dominion by Covenant. Ray Sutton. 347p. 1987. 16.95 (ISBN 0-930464-11-7). Inst Christian.

That You May Prosper: Dominion by Covenant. Ray R. Sutton. write for info. (ISBN 0-930462-50-5). Am Bur Eco Res.

That Your Joy May Be Full. 3.50 (ISBN 0-318-02211-7). Chrstphrs NY.

That Your Joy Might Be Full. Joseph L. Palotta. 247p. 1981. pap. 6.95 (ISBN 0-9604852-1-X). Revelation Hse.

Thatch: A Complete Guide to the Ancient Craft of Thatching. Robert West. LC 87-15377. (Illus.). 160p. 1988. 20.00 (ISBN 1-55562-044-2). Main Street.

Thatched Kitchen: Harvest & Holiday Cookbook. Patricia Collier. LC 72-87655. 1972. 5.95 (ISBN 0-88351-008-1). Test Recipe.

Thatched Roofs: A Comprehensive Bibliography. Mary E. Huls. (Architecture Ser.: A 1857). 5p. 1987. 3.00 (ISBN 1-55590-387-8). Vance Biblios.

Thatcher & Friends: The Anatomy of the Tory Party. John Ross. 122p. (Orig.). 1983. pap. 6.75 (ISBN 0-86104-512-2, Pub by Pluto Pr). Longwood Pub Group.

Thatcher Government. 2nd ed. Peter Riddell. 270p. 1986. pap. text ed. 14.95 (ISBN 0-631-14519-2). Basil Blackwell.

Thatcher Payne-in-the-Neck. Betty Bates. LC 85-42879. (Illus.). 144p. (gr. 3-7). 1985. 12.95 (ISBN 0-8234-0584-2). Holiday.

Thatcher Payne-in-the-Neck. Betty Bates. (gr. k-6). 1987. pap. 2.75 (ISBN 0-440-48598-3, YB). Dell.

Thatcherism & British Politics: The End of Consensus? Dennis A. Kavanagh. 256p. 1987. 44.00 (ISBN 0-19-827522-6); pap. 11.95 (ISBN 0-19-827521-8). Oxford U Pr.

Thatcherism at Work: Industrial Relations & Economic Change. John MacInnes. 192p. 1987. 59.00x (ISBN 0-335-15517-0, Open Univ Pr); pap. 19.00x (ISBN 0-335-15516-2, Open Univ Pr). Taylor & Francis.

Thatcherism: Personality & Politics. Ed. by Kenneth Minogue & Michael Biddiss. LC 87-3495. 208p. 1987. 35.00 (ISBN 0-312-00940-2). St Martin.

Thatcher's Craft. Ed. by CoSIRA Staff. 60.00x (ISBN 0-317-44794-7, Pub. by CoSIRA UK). State Mutual Bk.

Thatcher's Reign: A Bad Case of the Blues. Melanie McFadyean et al. (Illus.). 144p. 1985. pap. 7.95 (ISBN 0-7011-2857-7, Pub. by Chatto & Windus-Hogarth Pr). Salem Hse Pubs.

Thatching & Thatched Buildings. Michael Billet. (Illus.). 208p. 1979. 18.50 (ISBN 0-7091-7205-2). Transatl Arts.

That's a Fact! Three-Two-One Magazine Staff. LC 83-72644. (Three-Two-One Contact Bks). (Illus.). 96p. (ps-5). 1984. pap. 2.95 (ISBN 0-394-86486-7, BYR). Random.

That's a Fact, Too! Three-Two-One Magazine Staff. LC 83-72645. (Three-Two-One Contact Bks.). (Illus.). 96p. (ps-5). 1984. pap. 2.95 (ISBN 0-394-86487-5, BYR). Random.

That's a Good Question. 2nd ed. Roger Forster & Paul Marston. Tr. by Hugo S. Sun & Silas Chan. 204p. (Chinese.). 1982. pap. write for info (ISBN 0-941598-01-2). Living Spring Pubns.

That's a Great Idea: How to Get, Evaluate, Protect, Develop, & Sell New Product Ideas. Tony Husch & Linda Foust. LC 87-13891. 256p. (Orig.). 1987. pap. 8.95 (ISBN 0-89815-218-6). Ten Speed Pr.

That's All, Folks: The Art of the Warner Brothers Animation. Stephen Schneider. 1988. 39.95 (ISBN 0-8050-0889-6). H Holt & Co.

That's All They're Good For. Tim Jackson. (What Are Friends For? Ser.: No. 3). (Illus.). 20p. (gr. 5-9). 1986. pap. 1.00 (ISBN 0-942675-02-9). Creative License.

That's Doctor Sinatra, You Little Bimbo! G. B. Trudeau. LC 85-82193. 128p. 1986. pap. 5.95 (ISBN 0-03-008537-3, Owl Bks). H Holt & Co.

That's Easy For You to Say: An Assault on Stuttering. Lon L. Emerick & Lawrence Jupin. LC 85-417. 264p. 1985. pap. 8.95 (ISBN 0-932620-43-4). Betterway Pubns.

That's Entertaining. Yvonne Y. Tarr. (Illus.). 320p. 1987. 29.95 (ISBN 0-671-52320-1). S&S.

That's How It Was. Kevin Danaher. 128p. (Orig.). 1984. pap. 9.95 (ISBN 0-85342-714-3, Pub. by Mercier Pr Ireland). Irish Bks Media.

That's How It Was. Sheila White. 88p. 1986. 29.00x (ISBN 0-7212-0702-2, Pub. by Regency Pr). State Mutual Bk.

That's It, Folks! Mark O'Donnell. pap. 3.50x (ISBN 0-317-04375-7). Dramatists Play.

That's Jazz! Stephanie R. Sorine. LC 81-15639. (Illus.). 48p. 1982. Knopf.

That's Just Fine & Who-O-O Did It. Joan M. Lexau. LC 70-155568. (Garrard Venture Ser.). (Illus.). 40p. (gr. k-3). 1971. PLB 6.69 (ISBN 0-685-00127-X); pap. 1.19 (9027). Garrard.

That's Life. Fred B. Chernow & Carol Chernow. (Illus.). 36p. (gr. 1-7). Date not set. pap. 2.49 (ISBN 0-9610742-2-1). Purcell Prods.

That's Life. Ruthann Hall. 1974. pap. 2.25 (ISBN 0-89265-020-6). Randall Hse.

That's Life. William Herrick. LC 84-27378. 256p. 1985. 17.50 (ISBN 0-8112-0946-6); pap. 9.95 (ISBN 0-8112-0947-4, NDP596). New Directions.

That's Life: Jokes & Anecdotes. Ellen Nixon. 1987. 6.95 (ISBN 0-533-07271-9). Vantage.

That's Life, Snoopy. Charles M. Schulz. 1987. pap. 2.25 (ISBN 0-449-21398-6, Crest). Fawcett.

That's Me, Sloppy Stanley! Helene Chirinian. (Me & My Family Ser.). (Illus.). 32p. (ps-2). 1988. pap. 2.95. Price Stern.

That's Muscle Control. Ed Jubinville. 150p. 1986. 19.95 (ISBN 0-935783-08-3). Fitness Ctr Info.

That's My Baby. Norma Klein. LC 87-40442. (YA) (gr. 12 up). 1988. 16.95 (ISBN 0-670-81730-9). Viking.

That's My Boy. Jose L. Cortes. Tr. by John Medcalf. (Illus.). 192p. (YA) (gr. 4-9). 1986. pap. 6.95 (ISBN 0-00-599796-8, Collins Liturgical). HarpR.

That's My Brother. Ruth O. Szittya. LC 82-70603. (Illus.). 32p. (Orig.). (gr. 3). 1982. pap. 3.95 (ISBN 0-913408-74-3). Friends United.

That's My Dad. Ralph Steadman. (Illus.). 32p. (gr. k-2). 1987. 11.95 (ISBN 0-86264-133-0, Pub. by Century Hutchinson). David & Charles.

That's My Opinion. Michael A. Musmanno. Ed. by Wilmore Brown. 512p. 1967. 17.50x (ISBN 0-87215-035-6). Michie Co.

That's Not All! Rex Schneider. Ed. by Barbara Gregorich. (Start to Read! Ser.). (Illus.). 16p. (Orig.). (gr. k-2). 1985. pap. 1.95 (ISBN 0-88743-019-8, 06019). Sch Zone Pub Co.

That's Not All Folks: My Life in the Golden Age of Cartoons & Radio. Mel Blanc. LC 87-40401. 1988. 17.95 (ISBN 0-446-51244-3). Warner Bks.

That's Not Chester! Carol Nicklaus. (Illus.). 32p. (ps-3). 1983. pap. 2.25 (ISBN 0-380-63073-7, 63073-7, Camelot). Avon.

That's not Entirely True: An Album of Fotoverigraphs. Macduff Everton. (Artists Books: Vol 1). (Illus.). 56p. (Orig.). 1986. 28.00 (ISBN 0-938531-00-X); pap. 15.00 (ISBN 0-938531-01-8). Tixcacalcupul.

That's Not Fair. Gyo Fujikawa. (Illus.). 32p. (ps-2). 1983. pap. 3.95 (ISBN 0-448-16466-3, G&D). Putnam Pub Group.

That's Not Fair. Elspeth C. Murphy. LC 87-35458. (Proverbs to Grow on Ser.). 24p. (gr. 4-7). 1988. pap. 2.95 (ISBN 1-55513-354-1, Chariot Bks). Cook.

That's Not My Style. Mary Anderson. LC 82-13772. 168p. (gr. 7 up). 1983. 11.95 (ISBN 0-689-30968-6, Atheneum Childrens Bks). Macmillan.

That's Not Santa. Leonard Kessler. (gr. k-3). 1981. pap. 1.95 (ISBN 0-590-32263-X). Scholastic Inc.

That's Not What I Meant. Deborah Tannen. LC 85-13885. 224p. 1986. 12.95 (ISBN 0-688-04812-9). Morrow.

That's Not What I Meant: How Conservational Style Makes or Breaks Relationships. Deborah Tannen. 1987. pap. 2.95 (ISBN 0-345-34090-6). Ballantine.

That's Our New Ad Campaign...? A Handy Guide for C.E.O.s, Presidents, Ad Managers, Account Executives, Art Directors, Copywriters, Students, & Anybody Else Who Wants to Learn How to Create Better Ads. Dick Wasserman. 288p. 1988. 21.95 (ISBN 0-669-16974-9). Lexington Bks.

That's That. Dwight Bolinger. (Janua Linguarum, Ser. Minor: No. 155). 79p. (Orig.). 1972. pap. text ed. 11.50x (ISBN 90-2792-319-1). Mouton.

That's the Lawyer. Stephen G. E. Burrows. 256p. 1980. 10.00 (ISBN 0-682-49594-8). Exposition-Phoenix.

That's the Way It Is, Amigo. Hila Colman. LC 74-30398. (Illus.). 96p. (gr. 6 up). 1975. 11.70i (ISBN 0-690-00750-7, Crowell Jr Bks). HarpJ.

That's the Way the Kingdom Crumbles. Stan Campbell. (BibleLog Ser.: Bk. 2). 144p. (YA) (gr. 8 up). 1988. pap. text ed. 4.95 (ISBN 0-89693-658-9). Victor Bks.

That's Tough: Four Simulation Games on Christian Commitment for Junior High Youth Groups. Paul Boostrom. (Best of Young Teen Action Ser.). 32p. 1985. pap. 4.95 (ISBN 0-317-39454-1). Cook.

That's What a Friend Is. P. K. Hallinan. LC 76-27744. (Illus.). 32p. (gr. k-3). 1977. PLB 11.93 (ISBN 0-516-03628-9); pap. 2.95 (ISBN 0-516-43628-7). Childrens.

That's What a Friend Is. P. K. Hallinan. (Illus.). 32p. (gr. k-6). 1981. pap. 2.95 (ISBN 0-8249-8006-9). Ideals.

That's What Counts. Jane Weinberger. LC 87-50549. (Illus.). 40p. (gr. k-4). 1988. pap. 5.95 (ISBN 0-932433-33-2). Windswept Hse.

That's What Happens When It's Spring. Elaine W. Good. (Illus.). (ps-1). 1987. 12.95 (ISBN 0-934672-53-9). Good Bks PA.

That's What She Said: Contemporary Poetry & Fiction by Native American Women. Ed. by Rayna Green. LC 83-49002. (Midland Bks: 338). (Illus.). 352p. 1984. 29.95x (ISBN 0-253-35855-8); pap. 12.50x (ISBN 0-253-20338-4). Ind U Pr.

That's What T. J. Says. Betty Bates. LC 82-80815. 160p. (gr. 5-7). 1982. 10.95 (ISBN 0-8234-0465-X). Holiday.

That's Work! Barbara Gregorich. Ed. by Joan Hoffman. (Get Ready! Bk.). (Illus.). 32p. (ps). 1983. pap. 1.95 wkbk. (ISBN 0-938256-69-6). Sch Zone Pub Co.

Thaw in Bulgarian Literature. Atanas Slavov. (East European Monographs: No. 84). 190p. 1981. 20.00x (ISBN 0-914710-78-8). East Eur Quarterly.

Thawing Out. Philip K. Jason. LC 79-15901. pap. 4.27 (ISBN 0-931848-27-X). Dryad Pr.

Thayer Catalog Instruction Sheets, Vol. 1. Glenn Gravatt. Ed. by Theron Fox. (Illus.). xiv, 322p. 1980. 20.00 (ISBN 0-915926-27-X). Magic Ltd.

Thayer Catalog Instruction Sheets, Vol. 2. Glenn Gravattt. Ed. by Theron Fox & Barbara Walker. (Illus.). xii, 324p. 1979. 20.00 (ISBN 0-915926-28-8). Magic Ltd.

Thayer Catalog Instruction Sheets, Vol. 3. Glenn Gravatt. Ed. by Theron Fox & Barbara Walker. (Illus.). xi, 312p. 1980. 22.50 (ISBN 0-915926-29-6). Magic Ltd.

Thayer Catalog Instruction Sheets, Vol. 4. Glenn Gravatt. Ed. by Theron Fox. 324p. 1981. 25.00 (ISBN 0-915926-30-X). Magic Ltd.

Thayer's Greek-English Lexicon of the New Testament. Ed. by Joseph Thayer. 1984. 24.95 (ISBN 0-8010-8872-0). Baker Bk.

Thayer's Greek-English Lexicon of the New Testament. Joseph H. Thayer. LC 78-67264. (Gr. & Eng.). 1978. pap. 17.95 (ISBN 0-8054-1376-6). Broadman.

Thayer's Life of Beethoven, 2 Vols. rev ed. Ed. by Elliot Forbes. 1967. Set. 102.00x (ISBN 0-691-09103-X); pap. 19.95 1 vol. ed. (ISBN 0-691-02702-1). Princeton U Pr.

The Caudills: Courageous Missionaries see Caudill: Misoneros Audaces.

The Christian's Sacrifice & Service of Praise see Romans Twelve: Christain Life & Service.

The Extent of Dominance of Tenochtitlan During the Reign of Mocteuczoma Ilhuicamina see Studies in Middle American Anthropology.

The Ghost of S. W. I. see Sara's Ghost.

The Hasinai Indians of East Texas As Seen by Europeans, 1687-1772 see Philological & Documentary Studies.

The Identification of Lienzo A: A Tracing in the Latin American Library of Tulane University see Philological & Documentary Studies.

The Index-A Guide to Washington Film, Video, Multi-Image, Sound & Talent Services see Index 1989: A Directory of Pacific Northwest Film, Video, & Audio Production Resources.

The Letter. Donald M. Smith. Ed. by Diane Parker et al. LC 83-91201. (Illus.). 217p. 20.00 (ISBN 0-914731-00-9). DMS Publishing Co.

The Orrs: Missionary Duet see Orr: Duo Misonero.

The Personal Archive of Francisco Morazan see Philological & Documentary Studies.

The Promise of His Coming see Welcome Back Jesus.

The Rest: Poetry. Aram Saroyan. 105p. (Do not slash article). 1986. Signed edit. 20.00 (ISBN 0-9606772-4-0); lib. bdg. 10.00 (ISBN 0-9606772-3-2); pap. 5.00 (ISBN 0-9606772-2-4). Blackberry Bks.

The Sexual Addiction see Out of the Shadows: Understanding Sexual Addiction.

The Tao of Sexology see Best Way to Make Love Work.

Thea at Sixteen. Susan B. Pfeffer. (Sebastian Sisters Ser.: No. 2). 176p. (YA) (gr. 6 up). 1988. pap. 13.95 (ISBN 0-553-05498-8, Starfire). Bantam.

Theatre Arts: 1925, IX. 1971. 77.00 (ISBN 0-405-03455-5, 586). Ayer Co Pubs.
Theatre Arts: 1926, X. 1971. pap. 55.00 (ISBN 0-405-03482-2, 613). Ayer Co Pubs.
Theatre Arts: 1926, X. 1971. 77.00 (ISBN 0-405-03456-3, 587). Ayer Co Pubs.
Theatre Arts: 1927, XI. 1971. pap. 55.00 cancelled (ISBN 0-405-03483-0, 614). Ayer Co Pubs.
Theatre Arts: 1927, XI. 1971. 77.00 (ISBN 0-405-03457-1, 588). Ayer Co Pubs.
Theatre Arts: 1928, XII. 1971. pap. 55.00 (ISBN 0-405-03484-9, 615). Ayer Co Pubs.
Theatre Arts: 1929, XIII. 1971. pap. 55.00 (ISBN 0-405-03485-7, 616). Ayer Co Pubs.
Theatre Arts: 1929, XIII. 1971. 77.00 (ISBN 0-405-03459-8, 590). Ayer Co Pubs.
Theatre Arts: 1930, XIV. 1971. pap. 55.00 (ISBN 0-405-03486-5, 617). Ayer Co Pubs.
Theatre Arts: 1930, XIV. 1971. 77.00 (ISBN 0-405-03460-1, 591). Ayer Co Pubs.
Theatre Arts: 1931, XV. 1971. pap. 55.00 (ISBN 0-405-03487-3, 618). Ayer Co Pubs.
Theatre Arts: 1931, XV. 1971. 77.00 (ISBN 0-405-03461-X, 592). Ayer Co Pubs.
Theatre Arts: 1932, XVI. 1971. pap. 55.00 cancelled (ISBN 0-405-03488-1, 619). Ayer Co Pubs.
Theatre Arts: 1932, XVI. 1971. 77.00 (ISBN 0-405-03462-8, 593). Ayer Co Pubs.
Theatre Arts: 1933, XVII. 1971. cancelled 77.00 (ISBN 0-405-03463-6, 594). Ayer Co Pubs.
Theatre Arts: 1934, XVII. 1971. pap. 55.00 (ISBN 0-405-03490-3, 621). Ayer Co Pubs.
Theatre Arts: 1934, XVIII. 1971. 77.00 (ISBN 0-405-03464-4, 595). Ayer Co Pubs.
Theatre Arts: 1935, XIX. 1971. pap. 55.00 (ISBN 0-405-03491-1, 622). Ayer Co Pubs.
Theatre Arts: 1935, XIX. 1971. 77.00 (ISBN 0-405-03465-2, 596). Ayer Co Pubs.
Theatre Arts: 1936, XX. 1971. pap. 55.00 (ISBN 0-405-03492-X, 623). Ayer Co Pubs.
Theatre Arts: 1936, XX. 1971. 77.00 (ISBN 0-405-03466-0, 597). Ayer Co Pubs.
Theatre Arts: 1937, XXI. 1971. pap. 55.00 (ISBN 0-405-03493-8, 624). Ayer Co Pubs.
Theatre Arts: 1937, XXI. 1971. 77.00 (ISBN 0-405-03467-9, 598). Ayer Co Pubs.
Theatre Arts: 1938, XXII. 1971. pap. 55.00 (ISBN 0-405-03494-6, 625). Ayer Co Pubs.
Theatre Arts: 1938, XXII. 1971. 77.00 (ISBN 0-405-03468-7, 599). Ayer Co Pubs.
Theatre Arts: 1939, XXIII. 1971. pap. 55.00 (ISBN 0-405-03495-4, 626). Ayer Co Pubs.
Theatre Arts: 1939, XXIII. 1971. 77.00 (ISBN 0-405-03469-5, 600). Ayer Co Pubs.
Theatre Arts: 1940, XXIV. 1971. pap. 55.00 (ISBN 0-405-03496-2, 627). Ayer Co Pubs.
Theatre Arts: 1940, XXIV. 1971. 77.00 (ISBN 0-405-03470-9, 601). Ayer Co Pubs.
Theatre Arts: 1941, XXV. 1971. pap. 55.00 (ISBN 0-405-03497-0, 628). Ayer Co Pubs.
Theatre Arts: 1941, XXV. 1971. 77.00 (ISBN 0-405-03471-7, 602). Ayer Co Pubs.
Theatre As a Weapon: Workers' Theatre in the Soviet Union, Germany & Britain, 1917-1934. Richard Stourac & Kathleen McCreery. (Illus.). 384p. 1986. lib. bdg. 55.00 (ISBN 0-317-40573-X). Routledge Chapman & Hall.
Theatre. Asmodee: Avec: Les Mal Aimes. Francois Mauriac. (Illus.). 12.50 (ISBN 0-686-55478-7). French & Eur.
Theatre at Stratford-Upon-Avon: A Catalogue-Index to Productions of the Shakespeare Memorial-Royal Shakespeare Theatre, 1879 to 1978, 2 vols. Compiled by Michael Mullin. LC 79-8578. 1980. Vol. 1. lib. bdg. 45.00 (ISBN 0-313-22169-3, MSH/1); Vol. 2. lib. bdg. 45.00 (ISBN 0-313-22170-7, MSH/2). Greenwood.
Theatre at Work. Jim Hiley. (Illus.). 220p. 1981. 26.95x (ISBN 0-7100-0815-5). Routledge Chapman & Hall.
Theatre Au College Du Moyen Age a Nos Jours, Avec Bibliographie Et Appendices. L. V. Gofflot. 1907. 23.50 (ISBN 0-8337-1365-5). B Franklin.
Theatre: Avec: Atlas-Hotel, Vol. 2. Armand Salacrou. 278p. 1944. 4.95 (ISBN 0-686-55442-6). French & Eur.
Theatre: Avec: Boubouroche, La Peur des Coups. Georges Courteline. 253p. 1965. 8.95 (ISBN 0-686-54637-7). French & Eur.
Theatre: Avec: Guernica, Le Labyrinthe, Le Tricycle,Pique-Nique en Campagne, La Bicyclette du Condamne, Vol. 2. 221p. 1968. 9.95 (ISBN 0-686-54464-1). French & Eur.
Theatre: Avec: Jeux de Massacre, Macbeth, La Vase, Exercises de Conversation et de Diction Francaise pour Etudiants Americains, Vol. 5. Eugene Ionesco. (Blanche Ser.). 344p. 18.95 (ISBN 0-686-54201-0). Schoenhof.
Theatre: Avec: La Logeuse, Opera Parle, Le Oullou, Aetanima, Vol. 3. Jacques Audiberti. 264p. 1956. 9.95 (ISBN 0-686-54506-0). French & Eur.
Theatre: Avec: La Querre de Mil Ans, Bella Ciao, Vol. 10. 5.95 (ISBN 0-686-54469-2). French & Eur.
Theatre: Avec: La Terre est Ronde, Vol. 4. Armand Salacrou. 284p. 1945. 7.95 (ISBN 0-686-55444-2). French & Eur.
Theatre: Avec: L'Archipel Lenoir, Vol. 6. Armand Salacrou. 320p. 1954. 5.95 (ISBN 0-686-55446-9). French & Eur.
Theatre: Avec: Le Barbier de Seville, Le Marriage de Figaro, La Mere Coupable. Pierre de Beaumarchais & Rene Pomeau. 320p. 1965. 9.95 (ISBN 0-686-54086-7). French & Eur.
Theatre: Avec: Le Ciel et la Mer, La Grande Revue du 20e Siecle, Vol. 9. Fernando Arrabal. 261p. 1969. 15.95 (ISBN 0-686-54468-4). French & Eur.
Theatre: Avec: Le Grand Ceremonial, Ceremonie Pour un Noir Assassine, Dieu est-il Devenu Fou, Vol. 3. Fernando Arrabal. 221p. 1968. 19.95 (ISBN 0-686-54465-X). French & Eur.
Theatre: Avec: Le Jardin des Delices, Bestialite Erotique, Une Torture Nommee Dostoievsky, Vol. 6. Fernando Arrabal. 192p. 1969. 9.95 (ISBN 0-686-54466-8). French & Eur.
Theatre: Avec: Le Quenouille de Barberine, Le Chandelier, Il ne faut Jurer de Rein, Un Caprice, Il Faut qu'une port soit Ouverte ou Fermee, Vol. 2. Alfred de Musset. Ed. by Maurice Rat. 448p. 1964. 9.95 (ISBN 0-686-55559-7). French & Eur.
Theatre: Avec: Les Batisseurs d'Empire, Le Gouter des Generaux, L'Equarrissage Pour Tous, Le Dernier des Metiers. Boris Vian. 361p. 1972. 14.95 (ISBN 0-686-55706-9). French & Eur.
Theatre: Avec: Les Eaux et Forets, Le Square, La Musica, Vol. 1. Marguerite Duras. (Blanche Ser.). 176p. 1956. 17.95 (ISBN 0-686-55852-9). Schoenhof.
Theatre: Avec: Les Fiances du Havre, Vol. 5. Armand Salacrou. 366p. 1947. 6.95 (ISBN 0-686-55445-0). French & Eur.
Theatre: Avec: Les Marrons de feu, La Nuit Ventienne, La Coup et les Levres, A quoi revent les Jeunes Filles, Andre del Sorto, Les Caprices de Marianne, Vol. 1. Alfred de Musset. Ed. by Maurice Rat. 448p. 1964. 9.95 (ISBN 0-686-55558-9). French & Eur.
Theatre: Avec: Michel Auclair, Le Pelerin, L'Air du Temps, Vol. 2. Charles Vildrac. 356p. 1948. 4.95 (ISBN 0-686-55719-0). French & Eur.
Theatre: Avec: Operas Paniques, Ars Amandi, Dieu Tente par le Mathematiques, Vol. 8. Fernando Arrabal. 192p. 1970. 9.95 (ISBN 0-686-54467-6). French & Eur.
Theatre: Avec: Pomme, Pomme, Pomme, Baton et Ruban, Boutique Fermee, La Brigitta, Vol. 5. 264p. 1962. 5.95 (ISBN 0-686-54508-7). French & Eur.
Theatre: Avec: Pourquoi pas moi, Vol. 7. Armand Salacrou. 288p. 1957. 5.95 (ISBN 0-686-55447-7). French & Eur.
Theatre: Avec: Pucelle, La Fete Noire, Les Naturels du Borelais, Vol. 2. Jacques Audiberti. 312p. 1970. 9.95 (ISBN 0-686-54505-2). French & Eur.
Theatre: Avec: Quoat-Quoat, L'Ampelour, Les Femmes de Boeuf, La Mal Court, Vol. 1. Jacques Audiberti. 200p. 1970. 9.95 (ISBN 0-686-54504-4). French & Eur.
Theatre: Avec: Sodome et Gommorrhe, L'Appollon de Bellac, La Folle de Chaillot, Pour Lucrece, Vol. 4. Jean Giraudoux. 340p. 1959. 13.95 (ISBN 0-686-54014-X). French & Eur.
Theatre: Avec: Suzanne Andler, Des Journees Entieres dans les Arbres, Yes Peut-Etre?, Le Shape, et, Vol. 2. Marguerite Duras. (Blanche Ser.). 298p. 1968. 18.95 (ISBN 0-686-55853-7). Schoenhof.
Theatre: Avec: Une Femme Libre, Vol. 3. Armand Salacrou. 336p. 1942. 10.95 (ISBN 0-686-55443-4). French & Eur.
Theatre Backstage from A to Z. rev. ed. Warren C. Lounsbury. LC 59-2246. (Illus.). 200p. 1972. pap. text ed. 14.95x (ISBN 0-295-95264-4). U of Wash Pr.
Theatre Book of the Year, 1942-1943. George J. Nathan. LC 75-120099. (Illus.). 350p. 1971. 22.50 (ISBN 0-8386-7946-3). Fairleigh Dickinson.
Theatre Book of the Year, 1943-1944. George J. Nathan. LC 75-120099. 350p. 1972. 22.50 (ISBN 0-8386-7962-5). Fairleigh Dickinson.
Theatre Book of the Year, 1944-1945. George J. Nathan. LC 75-120099. 350p. 1972. 22.50 (ISBN 0-8386-7961-7). Fairleigh Dickinson.
Theatre Book of the Year 1945-1946. George J. Nathan. LC 75-120099. (Theatre World of George Jean Nathan Ser.). 350p. 1974. 22.50 (ISBN 0-8386-1174-5). Fairleigh Dickinson.
Theatre Book of the Year 1946-1947. George J. Nathan. LC 75-120099. (Theatre World of George Jean Nathan Ser.). 350p. 1975. 22.50 (ISBN 0-8386-1175-3). Fairleigh Dickinson.
Theatre Bouffe, Vol. 12. Fernando Arrabal. 240p. 1978. 19.95 (ISBN 0-686-54470-6). French & Eur.
Theatre Business: The Correspondence of the First Abbey Theatre Directors-William Butler Yeats, Lady Gregory, & J. M. Synge. Ed. by Ann Saddlemyer. LC 82-466. (Illus.). 360p. 1982. 24.95x (ISBN 0-271-00309-X). Pa St U Pr.
Theatre Cat. Maureen Potter. (Illus.). 64p. (gr. 4-8). 1986. 11.95 (ISBN 0-86278-085-3, Pub. by O'Brien Pr Ireland). Irish Bks Media.
Theatre Check List: A Guide to the Planning & Construction of Proscenium & Open Stage Theatres. rev ed. American Theatre Planning Board Staff. LC 69-19619. (Illus.). 1983. pap. 14.95x (ISBN 0-8195-6005-7). Wesleyan U Pr.
Theatre, Childern & Youth. rev. ed. Jed H. Davis & Mary J. Evans. (Illus.). 360p. 1987. pap. text ed. 28.00 (ISBN 0-87602-026-0). Anchorage.
Theatre Choisi. Eugene Labiche. (Club des Classiques). 474p. 1971. 9.95 (ISBN 0-686-54255-X). French & Eur.
Theatre Collections in Libraries & Museums, an International Handbook. Rosamond Gilder & George Freedley. (Library of Literature, Drama & Criticism). 1970. Repr. of 1936 ed. 18.00 (ISBN 0-384-18487-1). Johnson Repr.
Theatre Companies of the World, 2 vols. Ed. by Colby H. Kullman & William C. Young. LC 84-539. 1024p. 1985. Set. lib. bdg. 95.00 (ISBN 0-313-21456-5, YTC/); Vol. 1. lib. bdg. 65.00 (ISBN 0-313-25667-5, YTC/01); Vol. 2. lib. bdg. 65.00 (ISBN 0-313-25668-3, YTC/02). Greenwood.
Theatre Complet, 9 tomes. Jean Anouilh. Set. 175.00 (ISBN 0-685-11593-3). French & Eur.
Theatre Complet. Pierre de Beaumarchais. 45.00 (ISBN 0-686-54088-3). French & Eur.
Theatre Complet, 2 tomes. Pierre Corneille. Ed. by Lievre & Callois. (Bibl. de la Pleiade). 1934. Set. 159.95 (ISBN 0-685-11592-5). French & Eur.
Theatre Complet. Goethe. 1376p. write for info. French & Eur.
Theatre Complet. Pierre C. Marivaux. Ed. by Arland. (Bibl. de la Pleiade). 1950. lea. 46.95 (ISBN 0-685-11591-7). French & Eur.
Theatre Complet, 3 vols. Jean Racine. (Illus.). Set. 200.00 (ISBN 0-686-54715-2). French & Eur.
Theatre Complet, Vol. 1. Alexandre Dumas. (Illus.). 588p. 1974. 42.00 (ISBN 0-686-55211-3). French & Eur.
Theatre Complet, Vol. 1. Pirandello. 1536p. 45.00 (ISBN 0-686-56547-9). French & Eur.
Theatre Complet: Avec: Bajazet, Mithridate, Iphigenie, Phedre, Esther, Athalie, Vol. 2. Jean Racine. Ed. by Andre Stegmann. 378p. 5.95 (ISBN 0-686-54714-4). French & Eur.
Theatre Complet: Avec: Cromwell, Vol. 1. Victor Hugo. 1836p. 1963. 45.00 (ISBN 0-686-54043-3). French & Eur.
Theatre Complet: Avec: La Thebaide, Alexandre le Grand, Andromaque, Les Plaideurs, Britannicus, Berenice, Vol. 1. Jean Racine. Ed. by Andre Stegmann. 436p. 5.95 (ISBN 0-686-54713-6). French & Eur.
Theatre Complet: Avec: Les Burgraves, Vol. 2. Victor Hugo. 1936p. 1964. 49.95 (ISBN 0-686-54044-1). French & Eur.
Theatre Complet: Christine ou Stockholm, Fontainebleau et Rome, Vol. 1, Pt. 6. Alexandre Dumas. 186p. 1976. 15.00 (ISBN 0-686-55210-5). French & Eur.
Theatre Complet: Comment je devins Auteur Dramatique. Ivanhoe, Vol. 1, Pt. 1. Alexandre Dumas & Fernande Bassan. 144p. 1976. 12.50 (ISBN 0-686-55206-7). French & Eur.
Theatre Complet: Flesque de Lavagna, Vol. 1, Pt. 4. Alexandre Dumas. 166p. 1976. 12.50 (ISBN 0-686-55208-3). French & Eur.
Theatre Complet: Henry III et sa Cour, Vol. 1, Pt. 5. Alexandre Dumas. 152p. 1976. 12.50 (ISBN 0-686-55209-1). French & Eur.
Theatre Complet: La Chasse et l'Amour, La Noce et l'Enterrement, Vol. 1, Pt. 2. Alexandre Dumas. 126p. 1976. 12.50 (ISBN 0-686-55207-5). French & Eur.
Theatre Complet, Parades, Lettres Relatives a son Theatre. Pierre A. De Beaumarchais. Ed. by Allem & Courant. (Bibl de la Pleiade). 1954. 85.00 (ISBN 0-685-11590-9). French & Eur.
Theatre Complete see Oeuvres Completes.
Theatre Crafts How-To, Vol. 1. Compiled by Theatre Crafts Magazine Staff. (Illus.). 176p. 1986. pap. text ed. 9.95x (ISBN 0-317-59044-8). Drama Bk.
Theatre Crafts How-To: Glues, Adhesives, Wood, Metalworking, Plastics, Plastic Safety, Plastic-Working Tools, Carpentry Tips & Tricks, Vol. 1. Theatre Crafts Magazine Editors. (Illus.). 173p. (Orig.). 1984. pap. 9.95x (ISBN 0-916477-01-0). Theatre Crfts Mag.
Theatre de Clara Gazul. Prosper Merimee. 1968. 8.95 (ISBN 0-686-54762-4). French & Eur.
Theatre de la Gaite. Victor Hugo. 1961. 15.00 (ISBN 0-686-54045-X). French & Eur.
Theatre de la Revolution: Avec: Quatorza Juillet, Danton, Les Loups. Romain Rolland. 366p. 1927. 4.95 (ISBN 0-686-55275-X). French & Eur.
Theatre de Pagnol: Personnages et Themes Dans les Oeuvres de Jeunesse. P. Gounelle Kline. (American University Studies II-Romance Languages & Literature: Vol. 46). 170p. 1987. text ed. 20.00 (ISBN 0-8204-0320-2). P Lang Pubs.
Theatre de Situations. Jean-Paul Sartre. Ed. by Michel Contat & Michel Rybalka. (Idees Ser.). 384p. 1973. 8.95 (ISBN 0-686-55004-8). Schoenhof.
Theatre Des Bons Engins, Fifteen Thirty-Nine. Guillaume de La Perriere. LC 63-7783. 1963. Repr. of 1539 ed. 40.00x (ISBN 0-8201-1036-1). Schol Facsimiles.
Theatre des Varietes. Joseph Long. (Theatre in Focus Ser.). (Illus.). 120p. (Orig.). 1980. pap. text ed. 70.00x incl. slides (ISBN 0-85964-063-9). Chadwyck-Healey.
Theatre Directory of the San Francisco Bay Area 1987-88. 5th ed. Ed. by Jean Schiffman. 150p. 1987. pap. 13.50 (ISBN 0-9605896-4-3). Theatre Bay Area.
Theatre Directory 1987-88. Ed. by John Istel. 70p. 1987. pap. 4.95 (ISBN 0-930452-75-5). Theatre Comm.
Theatre Directory, 1988-89. Ed. by John Istel. 1988. pap. 4.95 (ISBN 0-930452-91-7, Pub. by Theatre Comm). Pub Ctr Cult Res.
Theatre, Drama, & Audience in Goethe's Germany. Walter H. Bruford. LC 73-10579. 388p. 1974. Repr. of 1950 ed. lib. bdg. 35.00x (ISBN 0-8371-7016-8, BRTD). Greenwood.
Theatre du Peuple: Avec: Essai d'Esthetique d'un Theatre Nouveau. Romain Rolland. 244p. 1926. 3.95 (ISBN 0-686-55276-8). French & Eur.
Theatre Du XVII Siecle: Montchrestien, Hardy, Tabarin, Theophile De Viau, Racan, Mairet, Rotrou, Vol. 1. (Pleiade Ser.). 1432p. 48.95 (ISBN 0-686-56582-7). Schoenhof.
Theatre Du XVIII Siecle: Crebillon, Le Sage, Voltaire, Piron, Destouches, Fagan, Gresset, Theatre des Boulevards, etc, Vol. 1. (Pleiade Ser.). 1568p. 39.95 (ISBN 0-686-56583-5). Schoenhof.
Theatre Du XVIII Siecle: Diderot, Palissot, Favart, Sedaine, Colle, Carmontelle, La Harpe, M. J. Chenier, Sade, etc, Vol. 2. (Pleiade Ser.). 1584p. 40.95 (ISBN 0-686-56584-3). Schoenhof.
Theatre: Edition Definitive. Armand Salacrou. 279p. 1977. 17.95 (ISBN 0-686-55441-8). French & Eur.
Theatre Education: Mandate for Tomorrow. Ed. by Jed H. Davis. 60p. 1985. pap. 6.00 (ISBN 0-87602-023-6). Anchorage.
Theatre: Essays on the Arts of the Theatre. facs. ed. Ed. by Edith J. Isaacs. LC 68-22919. (Essay Index Reprint Ser). 1927. 21.50 (ISBN 0-8369-0561-X). Ayer Co Pubs.
Theatre et Son Double. Antonin Artaud. (Folio Essay Ser.: No. 14). 256p. 1971. 7.95 (ISBN 0-686-53839-0). Schoenhof.
Theatre Experience. 3rd ed. Edwin Wilson. (Illus.). 448p. 1985. pap. text ed. 29.95 softcover (ISBN 0-07-070671-9). McGraw.
Theatre Festivals of the Medici, 1539-1637. A. M. Nagler. LC 76-8447. (Music Reprint Ser.). 190p. 1976. Repr. of 1964 ed. lib. bdg. 32.50 (ISBN 0-306-70779-9). Da Capo.
Theatre for Everybody: The Story of the Old Vic & Sadler's Wells. Edward J. Dent. LC 78-59017. (Illus.). 1979. Repr. of 1945 ed. 25.75 (ISBN 0-88355-691-X). Hyperion Conn.
Theatre for the Ninety-Eight Percent. Maxine Klein. LC 77-86334. (Illus.). 176p. 1978. 20.00 (ISBN 0-89608-001-3); pap. 7.50 (ISBN 0-89608-000-5). South End Pr.
Theatre for the People: The Story of the Volksbuhne. Cecil W. Davies. LC 77-73794. 191p. 1977. text ed. 12.50x (ISBN 0-292-78021-4). U of Tex Pr.
Theatre for Voluptuous Worldlings. Jan Van Der Noot. LC 43-1514. 1978. Repr. of 1569 ed. 45.00x (ISBN 0-8201-1179-1). Schol Facsimiles.
Theatre for Working-Class Audiences in the United States, 1830-1980. Ed. by Bruce A. McConachie & Daniel Friedman. LC 84-19773. (Contributions in Drama & Theatre Studies: No. 14). (Illus.). viii, 264p. 1985. lib. bdg. 36.95 (ISBN 0-313-24629-7, MTU/). Greenwood.
Theatre for Youth: Twelve Plays with Mature Themes. Ed. by Coleman A. Jennings & Gretta Berghammer. 524p. (gr. 8 up). 1986. 30.00 (ISBN 0-292-78081-8); pap. 15.95 (ISBN 0-292-78085-0). U of Tex Pr.
Theatre Francais Avant La Renaissance, 1430-1550. Ed. by Edouard Fournier. 1965. Repr. of 1872 ed. 32.00 (ISBN 0-8337-1225-X). B Franklin.
Theatre francophone dans un milieu franco-americain. Ernest B. Guillet. (Illus.). 52p. (Fr.). 1981. pap. text ed. 1.50 (ISBN 0-911409-37-8). Natl Mat Dev.
Theatre from Nigeria. Sebastian S. Bondy et al. 1967. Five works in one unit. 20.00 (ISBN 0-8115-3040-X). Kraus Repr.
Theatre Games. Fred Owens. (Illus.). 220p. (Orig.). 1979. pap. 12.00 (ISBN 0-936182-00-8). Diamond Heights.
Theatre Games: A New Approach to Drama Training. Clive Barker. 226p. 1988. pap. text ed. 12.95 (ISBN 0-413-45380-4). Heinemann Ed.
Theatre Games for Young Performers. Maria C. Novelly et al. Ed. by Kathy Pijanowski & Arthur L. Zapel. LC 85-60572. (Illus.). 160p. (Orig.). (gr. 6-10). 1985. pap. text ed. 7.95 (ISBN 0-916260-31-3). Meriwether Pub.
Theatre Guild. Walter P. Eaton. 1988. Repr. lib. bdg. 75.00x. Am Biog Serv.
Theatre Guild, the First Ten Years. Walter P. Eaton. 1971. Repr. of 1929 ed. 25.00x (ISBN 0-403-00922-7). Scholarly.
Theatre Guild, the First Ten Years, with Articles by the Directors. Walter P. Eaton. LC 75-107799. (Select Bibliographies Reprint Ser). 1929. 26.50 (ISBN 0-8369-5180-8). Ayer Co Pubs.
Theatre in a Tent: The Development of a Provincial Entertainment. William Slout. LC 72-188635. 153p. 14.00 (ISBN 0-87972-028-X). Bowling Green Univ.
Theatre in Action. Geoffrey Whitworth. LC 77-173186. (Illus.). Repr. of 1938 ed. 29.00 (ISBN 0-405-09074-9). Ayer Co Pubs.
Theatre in Crisis: Sophocles' Reconstruction of Genre & Politics in Philoctetes. C. Greengard. 120p. (Orig.). 1987. pap. text ed. 23.50x (ISBN 0-317-57967-3, Pub. by A M Hakkert). Coronet Bks.
Theatre in Education. Lowell Swortzell & Nancy Sowrtzell. text ed. 14.95 (ISBN 0-582-28237-3). Longman.

Theatre Student: Practical Stage Lighting. Emmet Bongar. LC 70-125194. (Theatre Student Ser.). (Illus.). (gr. 9 up). 1971. PLB 11.95 (ISBN 0-8239-0224-2). Rosen Group.

Theatre Student: Properties & Dressing the Stage. Karl Bruder. Ed. by Paul Kozelka. LC 68-21661. (Theatre Student Ser.). (Illus.). (gr. 9 up). 1969. PLB 11.95 (ISBN 0-8239-0150-5). Rosen Group.

Theatre Student: Scenery. W. Joseph Stell. LC 70-75264. (Theatre Student Ser.). (Illus.). 256p. (gr. 9 up). 1970. PLB 11.95 (ISBN 0-8239-0152-1). Rosen Group.

Theatre Student: Techniques of Group Theatre. Jan Kubicki. LC 73-86317. (Theatre Student Ser.). (Illus.). 142p. (YA) (gr. 7-12). 1975. PLB 14.95 (ISBN 0-8239-0292-7). Rosen Group.

Theatre Student: You Can Write a Play. Milton Polsky. (Theatre Stucent Ser.). (Illus.). 170p. 1983. lib. bdg. 14.95 (ISBN 0-8239-0558-6). Rosen Group.

Theatre Subject Headings, Vol. 1. 2nd enlarged ed. New York Public Library, Research Libraries. 1966. lib. bdg. 68.00 (ISBN 0-8161-0740-8, Hall Library). G K Hall.

Theatre Technique. 5th ed. Eileen Dixon. (Illus.). 304p. 1983. pap. 11.95 (ISBN 0-7216-0804-3, Bailliere-Tindall). Saunders.

Theatre: The Dynamics of the Art. Brian Hansen. (Illus.). 304p. 1986. pap. text ed. write for info. (ISBN 0-13-912676-7). P H.

Theatre: The Human Art. Sam Smiley. 576p. text ed. 33.95t scp (ISBN 0-06-046292-2, HarpC). Har-Row.

Theatre: The Rediscovery of Style. Michel Saint-Denis. LC 60-10492. 1968. pap. 7.95 (ISBN 0-87830-523-8). Theatre Arts.

Theatre: The Search for Style. John D. Mitchell. LC 81-85193. 350p. 1982. 25.00 (ISBN 0-87359-028-7); pap. 17.50. Northwood Inst Pr.

Theatre Through Its Stage Door. David Belasco. Ed. by Louis V. Defoe. LC 69-56534. (Illus.). 1968. Repr. of 1919 ed. 22.00 (ISBN 0-405-08261-4, Blom Pubns). Ayer Co Pubs.

Theatre Unbound. Alexander Bakshy. LC 68-56535. 1968. Repr. of 1923 ed. 20.00 (ISBN 0-405-08232-0, Pub. by Blom). Ayer Co Pubs.

Theatre We Worked for: The Letters of Eugene O'Neill to Kenneth Macgowan. Eugene O'Neill. Ed. by Jackson R. Bryer. LC 81-299. (Illus.). 292p. 1982. 32.50x (ISBN 0-300-02583-1). Yale U Pr.

Theatre Workshop Story. Howard Goorney. Ed. by M. Hay & P. Roberts. 226p. 1981. pap. 11.95 (ISBN 0-413-48760-1, NO. 3454). Heinemann Ed.

Theatre Workshops. Dario Fo & Franca Rame. (Illus.). 1987. pap. 9.95 (ISBN 0-936839-89-9). Applause Theatre Bk Pubs.

Theatre World, Vol. 37. John Willis. (Illus.). 288p. 1982. 30.00 (ISBN 0-517-54344-3). Crown.

Theatre World, Vol. 43, 1986-87. John Willis. (Illus.). 256p. 1988. 35.00 (ISBN 0-517-56828-4). Crown.

Theatre World: 1972-1973, Vol. 29. 1973. 9.95 (ISBN 0-517-50618-1). Crown.

Theatre World: 1973-1974, Vol. 30. John Willis. (Illus.). 288p. 1974. 10.95 (ISBN 0-517-51651-9). Crown.

Theatre World: 1974-1975, Vol. 31. Ed. by John Willis. (Illus.). 288p. 1975. 12.95 (ISBN 0-517-52322-1). Crown.

Theatre World: 1978-1979, Vol. 35. rev. ed. John Willis. (Illus.). 18.95 (ISBN 0-517-53997-7). Crown.

Theatre World: 1979-1980, Vol. 36. John Willis. Ed. by Brandt Aymar. (Illus.). 288p. 1981. 25.00 (ISBN 0-517-54264-1). Crown.

Theatre World: 1981-1982, Vol. 38. John Willis. 1983. 25.00 (ISBN 0-517-54945-X). Crown.

Theatre World: 1983-84, Vol. 40. John Willis. 256p. 1985. 24.95 (ISBN 0-517-55681-2). Crown.

Theatre World, 1984-1985, Vol. 41. John Willis. 1986. 27.50 (ISBN 0-517-56117-4). Crown.

Theatre World, 1985-1986, Vol. 42. John Willis. 1987. 35.00 (ISBN 0-517-56530-7). Crown.

Theatre Year. 4th ed. Photos by Donald Cooper. (Illus.). 129p. 1984. pap. 11.95 (ISBN 0-9507578-3-7, NO. 3996). Routledge Chapman & Hall.

Theatre 1969: La Contestation, Vol. 1. 288p. 1969. 8.95 (ISBN 0-686-54471-4). French & Eur.

Theatre 1969: Le Grand Guignol, Vol. 2. 304p. 1969. 9.95 (ISBN 0-686-54472-2). French & Eur.

Theatre 1970: Theatre en Mange. Fernando Arrabal. 208p. 1970. 19.95 (ISBN 0-686-54473-0). French & Eur.

Theatre 1971: Les Monstres. Fernando Arrabal. 19.95 (ISBN 0-686-54474-9). French & Eur.

Theatre 1972: Bob Wilson. Fernando Arrabal. 19.95 (ISBN 0-686-54475-7). French & Eur.

Theatres. Ham. 1988. 67.95 (ISBN 0-442-20497-3). Van Nos Reinhold.

Theatres de la foire, Sixteen Sixty to Seventeen Eighty-Nine. Maurice Albert. LC 78-135169. (Drama Ser.). 1971. Repr. of 1900 ed. 21.00 (ISBN 0-8337-0030-8). B Franklin.

Theatres for Drama Performance: Recent Experiences in Acoustical Design. Ed. by R. H. Talaske & C. E. Boner. LC 86-72934. 122p. 1987. pap. 15.00 prepaid (ISBN 0-88318-516-4); pap. 12.50 ea. on prepaid orders of 5 or more. Acoustical Soc Am.

Theatres for Literature. Marion L. Kleinau & Janet L. McHughes. 314p. 1980. pap. text ed. 16.95 (ISBN 0-87484-623-4). Mayfield Pub.

Theatres of Accumulation: Studies in Asian & Latin America Urbanization. Warwick Armstrong & Terence McGee. 320p. 1985. text ed. 40.00 (ISBN 0-416-78570-0, 9706); pap. text ed. 14.95 (ISBN 0-416-39800-6, 9528). Routledge Chapman & Hall.

Theatres of Europe: West & East. Henry Popkin. (Illus.). 330p. 18.95 (ISBN 0-8180-0508-4). Horizon.

Theatres of Inigo Jones & John Webb. John Orrell. (Illus.). 240p. 1985. 44.50 (ISBN 0-521-25546-5). Cambridge U Pr.

Theatres of London. Raymond Mander & Joe Mitchenson. LC 78-11808. 1979. Repr. of 1961 ed. lib. bdg. 35.00x (ISBN 0-313-21227-9, MATL). Greenwood.

Theatres of Memory. Raphael Samuel. 220p. 1988. text ed. 27.95 (ISBN 0-86091-209-4, Pub. by Verso). Routledge Chapman & Hall.

Theatres of Portsmouth. John Offord. (Down Memory Lane, Old Hampshire Ser.). (Illus.). 72p. (Orig.). 1987. pap. 4.95 (ISBN 0-903852-47-0, Pub. by Milestone Pubns UK). Seven Hills Bks.

Theatres of the Left, Eighteen Eighty to Nineteen Thirty-Five. Ed. by Raphael Samuel. (History Workshop Ser.). 288p. (Orig.). 1985. pap. 17.95x (ISBN 0-7100-0901-1). Routledge Chapman & Hall.

Theatrewritings. Bonnie Marranca. 1984. 19.95 (ISBN 0-933826-67-2); pap. 8.95 (ISBN 0-933826-68-0). PAJ Pubns.

Theatric Aspects of Sanskrit Drama. G. K. Bhat. 1985. 12.50x (ISBN 0-8364-1365-2, Pub. by Bhanarkar Oriental Inst). South Asia Bks.

Theatrical Anecdotes. Peter Hay. 406p. 1987. 19.95 (ISBN 0-19-503818-5). Oxford U Pr.

Theatrical Cavalcade. Ernest Short. LC 70-102851. (Illus.). 1970. Repr. of 1942 ed. 24.00x (ISBN 0-8046-0764-8, Pub by Kennikat). Assoc Faculty Pr.

Theatrical Companion to Shaw: A Pictorial Record of the First Performance of the Plays of Bernard Shaw. Raymond Mander & Joe Mitchenson. LC 72-189962. lib. bdg. 49.00 (ISBN 0-8414-1100-X). Folcroft.

Theatrical Compositions of the Major English Romantic Poets. Joan Mandell Baum. Ed. by James Hogg. (Poetic Drama & Poetic Theory Ser.). 257p. (Orig.). 1980. pap. 15.00 (ISBN 3-7052-0890-X, Pub. by Salzburg Studies). Longwood Pub Group.

Theatrical Costume: A Guide to Information Sources. Ed. by Jackson Kesler. LC 79-22881. (Performing Arts Information Guide Ser.: Vol. 6). 320p. 1979. 68.00x (ISBN 0-8103-1455-X). Gale.

Theatrical Craftsmanship of Richard Brinsley Sheridan's 'School for Scandal' Thomas H. Jordan. 1974. 69.95 (ISBN 0-87700-209-6). Revisionist Pr.

Theatrical Criticism in London to Seventeen Ninety-Five. Charles H. Gray. LC 64-14708. 1931. 18.00 (ISBN 0-405-08574-5). Ayer Co Pubs.

Theatrical Design & Production: An Introduction to Scene Design & Construction, Lighting, Sound, Costume, & Makeup. Michael Gillette. 592p. 1987. text ed. 29.95 (ISBN 0-87484-578-5). Mayfield Pub.

Theatrical Designs from Baroque Through Neoclassicism. Janos Scholz. 1976. Repr. of 1940 ed. lib. bdg. write for info. (ISBN 0-87817-179-7). Hacker.

Theatrical Designs of Charles Ricketts. Eric Binnie. Ed. by Bernard Beckerman. LC 84-23921. (Theater & Dramatic Studies: No. 23). 200p. 1985. 39.95 (ISBN 0-8357-1584-1). UMI Res Pr.

Theatrical Digs: Tales from the Green Room. Lord Taverners' Company. (Illus.). 128p. 1988. 15.95 (ISBN 0-7153-8982-3). David & Charles.

Theatrical Entertainments in Rural Missouri Before the Civil War. Elbert R. Bowen. LC 71-78861. 156p. 1960. 15.00x (ISBN 0-8262-0541-0). U of Mo Pr.

Theatrical Event: A "Mythos," a Vocabulary, a Perspective. David Cole. LC 74-21922. (Illus.). 1975. 16.00x (ISBN 0-8195-4078-1); pap. 9.95x (ISBN 0-8195-6047-2). Wesleyan U Pr.

Theatrical Evolution: Seventeen Seventy-Six to Nineteen Seventy-Six. Kenneth Spritz. LC 76-9774. (Illus.). 120p. cancelled (ISBN 0-89062-021-0, Pub. by Hudson River Mus); pap. 6.95 (ISBN 0-89062-143-8). Pub Ctr Cult Res.

Theatrical Image. James H. Clay & Daniel Krempel. LC 85-91268. (Illus.). 314p. 1985. pap. text ed. 14.50 (ISBN 0-8191-4978-0). U Pr of Amer.

Theatrical Impressions. Jules Lemaitre. LC 75-102847. 1970. Repr. of 1924 ed. 24.00x (ISBN 0-8046-0757-5, Pub by Kennikat). Assoc Faculty Pr.

Theatrical Impressions. Julius Lemaitre. 1975. Repr. of 1924 ed. 25.00 (ISBN 0-8274-4137-1). R West.

Theatrical Legitimation: Allegories of Genius in 17th-Century England & France. Timothy Murray. (Illus.). 304p. 1987. 29.95 (ISBN 0-19-504268-9). Oxford U Pr.

Theatrical Makeup. Bert Broe. (Illus.). 96p. 1985. 13.95 (ISBN 0-8253-0295-1). Beaufort Bks NY.

Theatrical Management in the West & South for Thirty Years. Sol Smith. LC 67-13343. (Illus.). 1968. Repr. of 1868 ed. 20.00 (ISBN 0-405-08983-X). Ayer Co Pubs.

Theatrical Movement: A Bibliographical Anthology. Ed. by Bob Fleshman. LC 85-1795. 756p. 1986. 57.50 (ISBN 0-8108-1789-6). Scarecrow.

Theatrical Notes. Joseph Knight. LC 70-82835. 1893. 18.00 (ISBN 0-405-08712-8, Blom Pubns). Ayer Co Pubs.

Theatrical Performances in the Ancient World: Hellenistic & Early Roman Theatre. Bruno Gentili. (London Studies in Classical Philology: Vol. 2). 117p. (Orig.). 1979. pap. 27.00 (ISBN 0-317-67329-7, Pub. by Gieben Amsterdam). Benjamins North Am.

Theatrical Prints of the Torii Masters: Exhibition Catalogue. (Illus.). 1978. 18.95 (ISBN 0-8048-1300-0). C E Tuttle.

Theatrical Public in the Time of Garrick. Harry W. Pedicord. LC 53-12030. (Arcturus Books Paperbacks). 281p. 1966. pap. 2.65x (ISBN 0-8093-0222-5). S Ill U Pr.

Theatrical Rambles of Mr. & Mrs. John Greene. Charles Durang. Ed. by William L. Slout. LC 84-11165. (Clipper Studies in the American Theater: No. 1). 142p. (Orig.). 1987. lib. bdg. 19.95x (ISBN 0-89370-360-5); pap. text ed. 9.95x (ISBN 0-89370-460-1). Borgo Pr.

Theatrical Recorder, 2 Vols. Thomas Holcroft. (Research & Source Works Ser.: No. 233). (Illus.). 1968. Repr. of 1806 ed. 52.00 (ISBN 0-8337-1723-5). B Franklin.

Theatrical Scene Painting: A Lesson Guide. William H. Pinnell. (Illus.). 160p. (Orig.). 1987. pap. 24.95x (ISBN 0-8093-1332-4). S Ill U Pr.

Theatrical Seasonings-Encore! Ed. by Joan M. Good et al. LC 83-50926. (Illus.). 336p. (Orig.). 1983. pap. 11.95 comb. binding (ISBN 0-9612330-0-1). Stage Guild.

Theatrical Space in Ibsen, Chekhov & Strindberg: Public Forms of Privacy. Freddie Rokem. Ed. by Oscar Brockett. LC 85-16415. (Theater & Dramatics Studies: No. 32). (Illus.). 106p. 1985. 39.95 (ISBN 0-8357-1707-0). UMI Res Pr.

Theatrical Touring & Founding in North America. Ed. by L. W. Conolly. LC 81-23766. (Contributions in Drama & Theatre Studies: No. 5). (Illus.). xiv, 245p. 1982. lib. bdg. 35.00 (ISBN 0-313-22595-8, CTH/). Greenwood.

Theatrical Trip for a Wager. Horton Rhys. LC 73-81217. 1861. 22.00 (ISBN 0-405-08884-1, Blom Pubns). Ayer Co Pubs.

Theatrical World of Eighteen Ninety-Seven. William Archer. LC 77-82818. Repr. of 1898 ed. 22.00 (ISBN 0-405-08211-8, Pub. by Blom). Ayer Co Pubs.

Theatrical World of Eighteen Ninety-Three. William Archer. LC 77-82818. Repr. of 1894 ed. 22.00 (ISBN 0-405-08210-X, Pub. by Blom). Ayer Co Pubs.

Theatrical Writings of Fabrizio Carini Motta. Ed. by Orville K. Larson. (Illus.). 160p. 1987. text ed. 19.95x (ISBN 0-8093-1337-5). S Ill U Pr.

Theatricals: Two Comedies. Henry James. 1971. Repr. of 1894 ed. 39.00x (ISBN 0-403-01043-8). Scholarly.

Theatro de los Theatros de los Passados Y Presentes Siglos. Francisco B. Candamo. Ed. by Duncan W. Moir. (Serie B: Textos, III). 191p. (Orig., Span.). 1970. pap. 14.50 (ISBN 0-900411-09-0, Pub. by Tamesis Bks Ltd). Longwood Pub Group.

Theatrum Majorum, the Cambridge of 1776: Diary of Dorothy Dudley. Dorothy Dudley. LC 73-140861. (Eyewitness Accounts of the American Revolution Ser., No. 3). (Illus.). 1970. Repr. of 1876 ed. 13.00 (ISBN 0-405-01228-4). Ayer Co Pubs.

Theatrum Mundi: The History of an Idea. Lynda G. Christian. Ed. by James J. Wilhelm & Richard Saez. (Harvard Dissertations in Comparative Literature Ser.). 294p. 1987. lib. bdg. 45.00 (ISBN 0-8240-8425-X). Garland Pub.

Theatrum Redivivum. Richard Baker. 154p. 25.00 (ISBN 0-384-03109-9). Johnson Repr.

Theatrum Redivivum, 17 vols. Ed. by Peter Davison. Repr. 535.00 (ISBN 0-384-59985-0). Johnson Repr.

Theatrum Redivivum: In Answer to Mr. Pryn's Histrio-Mastix see Mr. William Prynn-His Defence of Stage-Plays: Retraction of a Former Book of His Called 'Histrio-Mastix'.

Theban Hegemony, 371 - 362 B. C. John Buckler. (Harvard Historical Studies: No. 98). (Illus.). 355p. 1980. text ed. 25.00x (ISBN 0-674-87645-8). Harvard U Pr.

Theban Mysteries. Amanda Cross. 1979. pap. 2.95 (ISBN 0-380-45021-6, 60176-1). Avon.

Theban Necropolis Volume One, Part Two: Royal Tombs & Smaller Cemeteries. 2nd, rev ed. Bertha Porter & Rosalind Moss. (Topographical Bibliography of Ancient Egyptian Hieroglyphic Texts, Reliefs & Paintings Ser). 440p. 1964. text ed. 49.95x (ISBN 0-900416-15-7, Pub. by Aris & Phillips UK). Humanities.

Theban Necropolis: Volume 1, Pt. 1, Private Tombs. 2nd rev. ed. Bertha Porter & Rosalind Moss. (Topographical Bibliography of Ancient Egyptian Hieroglyphic Texts, Reliefs & Paintings Ser.). 493p. 1970. text ed. 60.00x (ISBN 0-900416-10-6, Pub. by Aris & Phillips UK). Humanities.

Theban Plays. Sophocles. Tr. by E. F. Watling. Incl. King Oedipus; Oedipus at Colonus; Antigone. (Classics Ser.). (Orig.). (YA) (gr. 9 up). 1950. pap. 2.95 (ISBN 0-14-044003-8). Penguin.

Theban Temples, Vol. 2. rev ed. Bertha Porter & Rosalind Moss. (Topographical Bibliography of Ancient Egyptian Hieroglyphic Texts, Reliefs & Paintings Ser.). 586p. 1972. text ed. 60.00 (ISBN 0-900416-18-1, Pub. by Aris & Phillips UK). Humanities.

Thebes in the Fifth Century. Nancy H. Demand. (States & Cities of Ancient Greece Ser.). 208p. 1983. 21.95x (ISBN 0-7100-9288-1). Routledge Chapman & Hall.

Theft by Employees. Richard C. Hollinger & John P. Clark. LC 82-48028. 176p. 1983. 29.00x (ISBN 0-669-05887-4). Lexington Bks.

Theft in the Market. R. L. Carter. (Institute of Economic Affairs, Hobart Papers Ser.: No. 60). 1975. technical 4.25 (ISBN 0-255-36060-6). Transatl Arts.

Theft of a Nation. William W. Baker. 164p. (Orig.). 1982. pap. 7.95 (ISBN 0-910643-00-8). Defenders Pubns.

Thefts of Nick Velvet. Edward D. Hoch. LC 77-20721. 1978. 10.00 (ISBN 0-89296-036-1). Mysterious Pr.

Their Adventures Will: Profiles of Memorable Louisiana Women. Diane M. Moore. (Illus.). 256p. 1984. 24.00 (ISBN 0-937614-07-6). Acadiana Pr.

Their Blood Runs Cold: Adventures with Reptiles & Amphibians. Whit Gibbons. LC 82-17395. (Illus.). 158p. (Orig.). 1983. pap. 9.95 (ISBN 0-8173-0133-X). U of Ala Pr.

Their Brothers' Keepers. Philip Friedman. LC 57-8773. 232p. 1978. pap. 12.95 (ISBN 0-89604-002-X). Holocaust Pubns.

Their Brother's Keepers: American Jewry & the Holocaust. Seymour M. Finger. 336p. 1988. 34.50 (ISBN 0-8419-1036-7). Holmes & Meier.

Their Brothers' Keepers: Moral Stewardship in the United States, 1800 to 1865. Clifford S. Griffin. LC 83-8563. xv, 332p. 1983. Repr. of 1960 ed. lib. bdg. 48.50 (ISBN 0-313-24059-0, GRTB). Greenwood.

Their Brothers' Keepers: The Christian Heroes & Heroines Who Helped the Oppressed Escaper the Nazi Terror. Philip Friedman. 232p. Repr. 4.95 (ISBN 0-686-95090-9). ADL.

Their Child. Robert Herrick. (Collected Works of Robert Herrick). 1988. Repr. of 1903 ed. lib. bdg. 59.00x. Am Biog Serv.

Their Child see Collected Works.

Their Day in Court. Percival Pollard. (American Studies). 1970. Repr. of 1909 ed. 32.00 (ISBN 0-384-47170-6). Johnson Repr.

Their Eyes on the Stars: Four Black Writers. Margaret G. Clark. LC 73-3499. (Toward Freedom Ser.). (Illus.). (gr. 5-9). 1973. PLB 3.98 (ISBN 0-8116-4804-4). Garrard.

Their Eyes Were Watching God. Zora N. Hurston. LC 70-88437. 1970. Repr. of 1937 ed. 29.75x (ISBN 0-8371-1885-9, HUE&). Greenwood.

Their Eyes Were Watching God. Zora N. Hurston. LC 77-18230. 296p. 1978. 6.95 (ISBN 0-252-00686-0). U of Ill Pr.

Their Fathers' God. O. E. Rolvaag. Tr. by Trygve M. Ager. LC 82-17636. x, 338p. 1983. pap. 7.95 (ISBN 0-8032-8911-1, BB 824, Bison). U of Nebr Pr.

Their Fathers' God. Ole E. Rolvaag. Tr. by Trygve M. Ager. LC 73-11847. 338p. 1973. Repr. of 1931 ed. lib. bdg. 35.00 (ISBN 0-8371-7068-0, ROFG). Greenwood.

Their Finest Hour. Winston S. Churchill. 1986. pap. 9.95 (ISBN 0-395-41056-8). HM.

Their Finest Hour see Second World War.

Their Finest Hour: Saga of India's Dec Victory. G. S. Bhargava. 1972. 7.50 (ISBN 0-89684-559-1). Orient Bk Dist.

Their Finest Hour: The War in the First Person. Ed. by Allan A. Michie & Walter Graebner. LC 41-2009. pap. 53.30 (ISBN 0-317-28769-9, 2051682). Bks Demand UMI.

Their Finest Hours: Narratives of the RAF & Luftwaffe in WW II. Jerome Klinkowitz. 176p. 1988. text ed. 18.95xt (ISBN 0-8138-0122-2). Iowa St U Pr.

Their Future Is Now: Today Is for Children. Ed. by Laura L. Dittmann & Marjorie Ramsey. LC 82-22716. (Illus.). 48p. 1982. pap. 7.50 (ISBN 0-87173-102-9). ACEI.

Their Gracious Pleasure. Claude Manceron. LC 80-36724. (French Revolution Ser.: Vol. 3). (Illus.). 480p. 1981. 19.95 (ISBN 0-394-50155-1). Knopf.

Their Heads Are Green & Their Hands Are Blue. Paul Bowles. LC 83-16577. 208p. 1984. pap. 8.50 (ISBN 0-88001-043-6). Ecco Pr.

Their Immortal Hearts. x ed. Ed. by Bruce McAllister. 1980. pap. 5.00 (ISBN 0-915596-24-5). West Coast.

Their Japan. Frederic De Garis. 204p. 1936. 420.00x (ISBN 0-317-69166-X, Pub. by Han-Shan Tang Ltd). State Mutual Bk.

Their Last Lap at Indy: A Book of Tributes. DeNonie Barber. (Illus.). 1980. 8.95 (ISBN 0-916620-49-2). Portals Pr.

Their Lawful Occasions. Rudyard Kipling. 1987. pap. 2.95 (ISBN 0-940561-01-8). White Rose Pr.

Their Majesties' Servants: Or Annals of the English Stage, 3 Vols. John Doran. Ed. by R. W. Lowe. LC 68-58985. Repr. of 1888 ed. Set. 125.00 (ISBN 0-404-02170-0). AMS Pr.

Their Master's War. Mick Farren. 304p. 1988. pap. 3.50 (ISBN 0-345-34554-1, Del Rey). Ballantine.

Their Morals & Ours. new ed. Leon Trotsky et al. Ed. by House. LC 73-82168. 96p. 1974. 14.00 (ISBN 0-87348-318-9); pap. 4.95 (ISBN 0-87348-319-7). Path Pr NY.

Their Music Is Mary. Clifford J. Laube. 3.50 (ISBN 0-910984-11-5). Montfort Pubns.

Their Name Is Pius. Lillian Olf. LC 74-107729. (Essay Index Reprint Ser). 1941. 27.50 (ISBN 0-8369-1768-5). Ayer Co Pubs.

Their Number Become Thinned: Native American Population Dynamics in Eastern North America. Henry F. Dobyns. LC 83-5952. (Native American Historic Demography Ser.). 396p. 1983. text ed. 34.95x (ISBN 0-87049-400-7); pap. text ed. 16.95x (ISBN 0-87049-401-5). U of Tenn Pr.

Their Own Voices. 1985. 8.95 (ISBN 0-932334-60-1, Dist. by North Country). Heart of the Lakes.

Their Own Voices: Oral Accounts of Early Settlers in Washington County, New York. Asa Fitch. Ed. by Winston Adler. 160p. 1983. 15.00 (ISBN 0-932334-59-8); pap. 8.95. Heart of the Lakes.

Their Pilgrimage. Charles D. Warner. 1973. Repr. of 1866 ed. 17.50 (ISBN 0-8274-0792-0). R West.

Their Place on Stage: Black Women Playwrights in America. Elizabeth Brown-Guillory. (Contributions in Afro-American & African Studies: No. 117). 1988. 37.85 (ISBN 0-313-25985-2, BGY/). Greenwood.

Their Pride & Joy. Paul Buttenwieser. LC 86-23958. 432p. 1987. pap. 18.95 (ISBN 0-385-29567-7). Delacorte.

Their Pride & Joy. Paul Buttenwieser. (YA) (gr. 6 up). 1988. pap. 8.95 (ISBN 0-440-50073-7, LE). Dell.

Their Religion. facs. ed. Arthur J. Russell. LC 78-128308. (Essay Index Reprint Ser). 1935. 20.00 (ISBN 0-8369-2131-3). Ayer Co Pubs.

Their Revolution or Ours. Helen Bugbee. 103p. 1985. 4.70 (ISBN 0-89697-263-1). Intl Univ Pr.

Their Rights & Liberties. Thomas O. Hanley. 160p. 1984. 9.95 (ISBN 0-8294-0471-6). Loyola.

Their Royal Highnesses the Duke & Duchess of York. Christopher Warwick & Valerie Garner. (Illus.). 192p. 1986. 22.95 (ISBN 0-283-99386-3). Salem Hse Pubs.

Their Ruling Passions. facs. ed. Percy Colson. LC 70-136645. (Biography Index Reprint Ser.). 1949. 21.00 (ISBN 0-8369-8040-9). Ayer Co Pubs.

Their Shadows Before: A Story of the Southampton Insurrection. facs. ed. Pauline C. Bouve. LC 72-39078. (Black Heritage Library Collection). Repr. of 1899 ed. 16.50 (ISBN 0-8369-9016-1). Ayer Co Pubs.

Their Sister's Keepers: Women's Prison Reform in America, 1830-1930. Estelle B. Freedman. LC 80-24918. (Women & Culture Ser.). 272p. 1981. text ed. 22.95x (ISBN 0-472-10008-4); pap. 12.95x (ISBN 0-472-08052-0). U of Mich Pr.

Their Solitary Way: The Puritan Social Ethic in the First Century of Settlement in New England. Stephen Foster. LC 76-151573. (Yale Historical Publications Miscellany Ser.: No. 94). pap. 59.50 (ISBN 0-317-29587-X, 2021997). Bks Demand UMI.

Their Story-Our Story. Forrest W. Jackson. LC 85-6623. (YA) (gr. 7-12). 1985. pap. 4.95 (ISBN 0-8054-3618-9, 4236-18). Broadman.

Their Story: Twentieth Century Pentecostals. Fred J. Foster. Ed. by Mary H. Wallace. LC 86-26718. (Illus.). 192p. 1983. pap. 4.95 (ISBN 0-912315-05-9). Word Aflame.

Their Tattered Flags: The Epic of the Confederacy. Frank E. Vandiver. LC 87-6520. (Texas A&M University Military History Ser.: No. 5). 376p. (Orig.). 1987. pap. 12.95 (ISBN 0-89096-355-X). Tex A&M Univ Pr.

Their Universe: A Look into Children's Hearts & Minds. Arlene Uslander et al. LC 72-6164. 1973. pap. 6.95 (ISBN 0-440-08684-1). Delacorte.

Their Wedding Journey. William D. Howells. 240p. 1976. Repr. of 1872 ed. lib. bdg. 16.95x (ISBN 0-89190-457-3, Pub. by Queens Hse). Amereon Ltd.

Their Words, My Thoughts. 1981. full music ed. 18.95 (ISBN 0-19-917035-5); student's ed. 8.75 (ISBN 0-19-917034-7). Oxford U Pr.

Their Words Were Bullets: The Southern Press in War, Reconstruction & Peace. Hodding Carter. LC 73-90553. (Mercer University Lamar Lecture Ser.: No. 12). 88p. 1969. 6.50 (ISBN 0-8203-0236-8). U of Ga Pr.

Their Yesterdays. Harold B. Wright. 1975. lib. bdg. 17.85x (ISBN 0-89966-207-2). Buccaneer Bks.

Theirs Be the Power: The Moguls of Eastern Kentucky. Harry M. Caudill. LC 83-5771. (Illus.). 198p. 1983. 15.95 (ISBN 0-252-01029-9). U of Ill Pr.

Theirs Is the Kingdom. Lowell Hagan & Jack Westerhof. LC 86-11679. (Illus.). 336p. (gr. 3 up). 1986. 16.95 (ISBN 0-8028-5013-8). Eerdmans.

Theirs Is the Kingdom. Mairin Healy. (Short Play Ser.). 1969. pap. 0.50 (ISBN 0-912262-17-6). Proscenium.

Theirs Was the Kingdom. R. F. Delderfield. Date not set. pap. 4.95 (ISBN 0-671-63734-7). PB.

Theism. Clement Dore. 1984. lib. bdg. 34.50 (ISBN 0-318-00886-6, Pub. by Reidel Holland). Kluwer Academic.

Theism & Cosmology. facs. ed. John Laird. LC 74-84317. (Essay Index Reprint Ser). 1942. 21.50 (ISBN 0-8369-1147-4). Ayer Co Pubs.

Theism & Humanism. A. J. Balfour. Repr. of 1915 ed. 32.00 (ISBN 0-527-04810-0). Kraus Repr.

Theism & Thought: A Study in Familiar Beliefs. Arthur J. Balfour. LC 77-27208. (Gifford Lectures: 1922-23). Repr. of 1923 ed. 22.50 (ISBN 0-404-60469-2). AMS Pr.

Theism, Atheism & the Doctrine of the Trinity. W. Waite Willis, Jr. LC 86-6640. (American Academy of Religion Academy Ser.). 200p. 1987. 15.95 (ISBN 1-55540-020-5, 01-01-53); pap. 11.95 (ISBN 1-55540-021-3). Scholars Pr GA.

Theism... Comprising the Deems Lectures for 1902. Borden P. Bowne. LC 75-3075. (Philosophy in America Ser.). Repr. of 1902 ed. 37.50 (ISBN 0-404-59076-4). AMS Pr.

Theism in an Age of Science. Phillip H. Wiebe. 188p. (Orig.). 1988. lib. bdg. 22.50 (ISBN 0-8191-6819-X); pap. text ed. 11.75 (ISBN 0-8191-6820-3). U Pr of Amer.

Theism in Medieval India. J. Estlin Carpenter. 1977. Repr. of 1921 ed. 22.50x (ISBN 0-89684-457-9). Orient Bk Dist.

Theism in Medieval India. J. Estlin Carpenter. 564p. Repr. of 1921 ed. text ed. 37.50x. Coronet Bks.

Theism in Medieval India. Joseph E. Carpenter. LC 77-27152. (Hibbert Lectures: 1919). Repr. of 1921 ed. 48.00 (ISBN 0-404-60419-6). AMS Pr.

Theism in Medieval India. K. Carpenter. 1977. 22.50x (ISBN 0-8364-0100-X). South Asia Bks.

Theism in the Discourse of Jonathan Edwards. R. C. De Prospo. LC 84-40406. 296p. 1985. 37.50 (ISBN 0-87413-281-9). U Delaware Pr.

Theism of Edgar Sheffied Brightman. James J. McLarney. LC 75-3089. Repr. of 1936 ed. 11.50 (ISBN 0-404-59087-X). AMS Pr.

Theism: The Implication of Experience. William W. Fenn. 1969. 10.00 (ISBN 0-87233-005-2). Bauhan.

Theismann. Joe Theismann & Dave Kindred. 1987. 17.95 (ISBN 0-8092-4843-3). Contemp Bks.

Theist & Atheist: A Typology of Non-Belief. Thomas Molnar. 1979. text ed. 30.00x (ISBN 90-279-7788-7). Mouton.

Theistic Evolution. Bert Thompson. pap. 5.50 (ISBN 0-89315-300-1). Lambert Bk.

Theistic Evolution. Bert Thompson. 235p. (Orig.). 1977. pap. 5.50 (ISBN 0-932859-08-9). Apologetic Pr.

Thekla. D. Lucinda Wicke. 104p. 1987. 12.75 (ISBN 0-8062-3088-6). Carlton.

Thelephoraceae of North America. Edward A. Burt. (Illus.). 1966. 45.00x. Hafner.

Thelephoraceae of North America, 15 Pts. Edward A. Burt. (Illus.). 900p. 1966. Repr. of 1926 ed. lib. bdg. 45.00x (ISBN 0-945345-04-6). Lubrecht & Cramer.

Thelma. Marie Corelli. lib. bdg. 47.00 (ISBN 0-8414-2391-1). Folcroft.

Thelma D. Sullivan's Compendium of Nahuatl Grammar. Thelma D. Sullivan. Ed. by Wick R. Miller & Karen Dakin. Tr. by Neville Stiles from Span. LC 88-17082. 352p. 1988. 25.00x (ISBN 0-87480-282-2). U of Utah Pr.

Thelonious Monk. Stuart Isacoff. 64p. pap. 9.95 (ISBN 0-8256-4080-6). Music Sales.

Them. Joyce Carol Oates. 1984. pap. 3.95 (ISBN 0-449-20692-0, Crest). Fawcett.

Them & Us. James Downey. (Illus.). 258p. 1983. pap. 8.95 (ISBN 0-907085-57-1, Pub. by Ward River Pr Ireland). Irish Bks Media.

Them & Us. 1987. 7.95 (ISBN 0-317-55308-9). United Elec R&M.

Them Bones. Howard Waldrop. (Ace Special Ser.: No. 5). 224p. 1984. pap. 2.95 (ISBN 0-441-80557-4, Pub. by Ace Science Fiction). Ace Bks.

Them Children: A Study in Language Learning. Martha C. Ward. Ed. by George Spindler & Louise Spindler. (Case Studies in Education & Culture). 112p. 1982. pap. text ed. 6.95x (ISBN 0-8290-0323-1). Irvington.

Them Children: A Study in Language Learning. Martha C. Ward. (Illus.). 99p. 1986. pap. text ed. 6.95x (ISBN 0-88133-213-5). Waveland Pr.

Them Cow Pokes. 64p. 1962. 3.95 (ISBN 0-917207-03-3). Reid Ent.

Them or Us: Archetypal Interpretations of Fifties Alien Invasion Films. Patrick Lucanio. LC 86-43049. 106p. 1987. 27.50 (ISBN 0-253-35871-X); pap. 12.50 (ISBN 0-253-20435-6). Ind U Pr.

Them: Stalin's Polish Puppet. Teresa Toranska. Tr. by Agnieszka Kolakowska. LC 86-45364. 256p. 1987. 22.45i (ISBN 0-06-015657-0, HarpT). Har-Row.

Them: Stalin's Polish Puppets. Teresa Toranska. Tr. by Agnieszka Kolakowska from Polish. LC 86-45364. 384p. 1988. pap. 9.95 (ISBN 0-06-091493-9, PL-1493, PL). Har-Row.

Them That Glitter & Them That Don't. Bette Greene. LC 92-13020. 224p. (YA) (gr. 7-12). 1983. lib. bdg. 10.99 (ISBN 0-394-94692-8). Knopf.

Them Was the Days: An American Saga of the '70's. Martha F. McKeown. LC 50-7450. (Illus.). xvi, 282p. 1961. pap. 5.95 (ISBN 0-8032-5131-9, BB 117, Bison). U of Nebr Pr.

Thematic Analysis of Francois Mauriac's "Genitrix, le Desert De L'amour, & le Noeud De Viperes". Ruth B. Paine. LC 76-8024. (Romance Monographs: No. 20). 1976. 22.00x (ISBN 84-399-4950-2). Romance.

Thematic Analysis of Mme. D'Aulnoy's "Contes De Fees". Jane T. Mitchell. LC 78-6947. (Romance Monographs: No. 30). 1978. 20.00x (ISBN 84-399-8448-0). Romance.

Thematic Apperception Test. Henry A. Murray. LC 43-3797. 1943. manual with cards 15.00x (ISBN 0-674-87720-9); pap. 2.50x manual only (ISBN 0-674-87721-7). Harvard U Pr.

Thematic Apperception Test. 2nd ed. M. I. Stein. 386p. 1981. 43.75 (ISBN 0-398-04480-5). C C Thomas.

Thematic Apperception Test. Silvan S. Tomkins. 308p. 1947. 39.50 (ISBN 0-8089-0506-6, 794615). Grune.

Thematic Approach to the Works of F. G. Junger. Anton H. Richter. (American University Studies I (Germanic Languages & Literature): Vol. 5). 121p. 1982. pap. text ed. 14.20 (ISBN 3-261-04944-8). P Lang Pubs.

Thematic Catalog of the Instrumental Music of Florian Leopold Gassmann. George R. Hill. (Music Indexes & Bibliographies: No. 12). 1976. 28.00 (ISBN 0-913574-12-0). Eur-Am Music.

Thematic Catalog of the Works of Jeremiah Clarke. Thomas F. Taylor. LC 75-23551. (Detroit Studies in Music Bibliography Ser.: No. 35). 1977. 12.00 (ISBN 0-911772-84-7). Harmonie Pk Pr.

Thematic Catalogue. Ed. by Ernest Warburton. (Johann Christian Bach Ser., 1735-1782). 75.00 (ISBN 0-8240-6097-0). Garland Pub.

Thematic Catalogue of the Works of Giovanni Battista Sammartini. Ed. by Newell Jenkins & Bathia Churgin. 1977. 40.00x (ISBN 0-674-87735-7). Harvard U Pr.

Thematic Catalogues in Music: An Annotated Bibliography. Barry S. Brook. LC 72-7517. (RILM Retrospectives Ser.: No. 1). 1972. lib. bdg. 32.00 (ISBN 0-918728-02-9). Pendragon NY.

Thematic Index of the Works of Francois Couperin. Maurice Cauchie. LC 74-24057. Repr. of 1949 ed. 14.50 (ISBN 0-404-12879-3). AMS Pr.

Thematic Index to the Works of Benedetto Pallavicino. Peter Flanders. (Music Indexes & Bibliographies: No. 11). 1974. pap. 9.00 (ISBN 0-913574-11-2). Eur-Am Music.

Thematic Index to the Works of Salamon Rossi. Joel Newman & Fritz Rikko. (Music Indexes & Bibliographies: No. 6). 1972. pap. 12.50 (ISBN 0-913574-06-6). Eur-Am Music.

Thematic Journal: A Diary for Self-Observation & Self-Revelation. Alan K. White. 100p. (Orig.). 1984. pap. 8.95 (ISBN 0-914865-00-5). Av Text Corp.

Thematic Language Stimulation: A Workbook for Aphasics & Their Clinicians. Shirley Morganstein & Marilyn C. Smith. 360p. 1982. wkbk. 23.00 (ISBN 0-88450-829-3, 4600-B). Communication Skill.

Thematic Maps. David J. Cuff & Mark T. Mattson. (Illus.). 176p. 1982. 15.95x (ISBN 0-416-60221-5, NO. 2893); tchr's. manual 3.95 (ISBN 0-416-34320-1, NO. 3731). Routledge Chapman & Hall.

Thematic Origins of Scientific Thought: Kepler to Einstein. Gerald Holton. LC 72-83467. 300p. 1973. 19.50x (ISBN 0-674-87745-4); pap. 10.95 (ISBN 0-674-87746-2). Harvard U Pr.

Thematic Origins of Scientific Thought: Kepler to Einstein. rev. ed. Gerald Holton. LC 87-34163. 504p. 1988. 25.00x (ISBN 0-674-87747-0); pap. 12.95 (ISBN 0-674-87748-9). Harvard U Pr.

Thematic Patterns in Sonatas of Beethoven. Rudolph Reti. (Music Reprint Ser.). 1989. 27.50 (ISBN 0-306-79714-3). Da Capo.

Thematic Process in Music. Rudolph R. Reti. LC 77-13622. 1978. Repr. of 1951 ed. lib. bdg. 29.75x (ISBN 0-8371-9875-5, RETH). Greenwood.

Thematic Studies in Phenomenology & Pragmatism. Patrick L. Bourgeois & Sandra B. Rosenthal. viii, 206p. (Orig.). 1983. pap. 22.00x (ISBN 90-6032-238-X). Benjamins North Am.

Thematics of Commitment. P. M. Cryle. LC 84-42590. 456p. 1984. text ed. 44.50x (ISBN 0-691-06610-8). Princeton U Pr.

Theme a Week. E. M. Hardwick. 256p. 1976. 32.00x (ISBN 0-7217-3017-5, Pub. by Schofield & Sims UK). State Mutual Bk.

Theme & Form: An Introduction to Literature. 4th ed. Ed. by Monroe C. Beardsley et al. 704p. 1975. text ed. write for info. (ISBN 0-13-912972-3). P-H.

Theme & Image in the Poetry of Sa de Miranda. T. F. Earle. (Oxford Modern Languages & Literature Monograph). 1980. 29.95x (ISBN 0-19-815754-1). Oxford U Pr.

Theme & Paragraph. Phillip Burnham & Richard Lederer. Orig. Title: Basic Composition. (Illus.). 1976. pap. text ed. 4.25x (ISBN 0-88334-078-X). Ind Sch Pr.

Theme & Structure in Swift's Tale of a Tub. Ronald Paulson. LC 72-6570. (Yale Studies in English Ser.: No. 143). x, 259p. 1972. Repr. of 1960 ed. 26.00 (ISBN 0-208-01133-1, Archon). Shoe String.

Theme & Variation. Ray Cook. 59p. (Orig.). 1981. pap. text ed. 15.00 (ISBN 0-9602002-3-1). Ray Cook.

Theme & Variation in the Short Story. facsimile ed. Ed. by John D. Ferguson et al. LC 74-37541. (Short Story Index Reprint Ser.). Repr. of 1938 ed. 25.00 (ISBN 0-8369-4100-4). Ayer Co Pubs.

Theme & Variations: A Study of Linear Twelve Tone Composition. Robert Kelly. LC 58-12777. 113p. 1969. pap. 7.95 (ISBN 0-252-00029-3). U of Ill Pr.

Theme & Variations: The Impact of Great Ideas. Laurence Behrens & Leonard J. Rosen. (Orig.). 1988. pap. text ed. write for info. (ISBN 0-673-39707-6). Scott F.

Theme Communications for the Eighties, Getting to the Point: Proceedings. International Technical Communication Conference, 28th, Pittsburgh, Pennsylvania, May 20-23, 1981. Ed. by Della A. Whittaker. 450p. 45.00x (ISBN 0-914548-34-4, Pub. by Soc Tech Comm). Univelt Inc.

Theme, Embodiment & Structure in the Poetry of George Crabbe. Rodney S. Edgecombe. Ed. by James Hogg. (Romantic Reassessment Ser.). 285p. (Orig.). 1983. pap. 15.00 (ISBN 0-317-40108-4, Pub. by Salzburg Studies). Longwood Pub Group.

Theme et Variations. 3rd ed. M. Peter Hagiwara & Francoise De Rocher. LC 84-15170. 620p. 1985. write for info. (ISBN 0-471-88264-X). Wiley.

Theme for Reason. Elizabeth Ogilvie. 22.95 (ISBN 0-89190-394-1, Pub. by Am Repr). Amereon Ltd.

Theme Gardens. Barbara Damrosch. LC 82-60062. (Illus.). 224p. 1982. 22.50 (ISBN 0-89480-218-6, 351); pap. 14.95 (ISBN 0-89480-217-8, 487). Workman Pub.

Theme in English Expository Discourse. 2nd rev ed. Linda K. Jones. LC 78-100090. (Edward Sapir Monograph Series in Language, Culture, & Cognition: No. 2). xiv, 241p. 1980. pap. 8.00x (ISBN 0-933104-10-3). Jupiter Pr.

Theme Is Freedom. facsimile ed. John Dos Passos. LC 71-99632. (Essay Index Reprint Ser). 1956. 22.00 (ISBN 0-8369-1460-0). Ayer Co Pubs.

Theme of Alienation in the Prose of Peter Weiss. Kathleen Vance. (American University Studies I (German Language & Literature): Vol. 4). 228p. 1981. pap. text ed. 28.35 (ISBN 3-261-04971-5). P Lang Pubs.

Theme of Enclosure in Selected Works of Doris Lessing. Shirley Budhos. LC 86-50290. 128p. 1987. 15.00 (ISBN 0-87875-314-1). Whitston Pub.

Theme of Government in Piers Plowman. Anna P. Baldwin. (Piers Plowman Studies: No. I). 107p. 1987. 41.00 (ISBN 0-85991-073-3, Pub. by Boydell & Brewer). Longwood Pub Group.

Theme of Honour's Tongue. C. Barber. 171p. 1985. pap. text ed. 19.95x (ISBN 91-7346-138-5, Pub. by Acta Universitat Sweden). Humanities.

Theme of Identity in the Essays of James Baldwin. Jarub Mokkem. 196p. (Orig.). 1975. pap. text ed. 25.00x (ISBN 91-7346-008-7, Pub. by Almqvist & Wiksell). Coronet Bks.

Theme of Patriotism in the Poetry of the Early Eighteenth Century. Bonamy Dobree. 1949. lib. bdg. 16.00 (ISBN 0-8414-2478-0). Folcroft.

Theme of Revenge in Elizabethan Tragedy. Percy Simpson. LC 76-25856. 1935. lib. bdg. 17.50 (ISBN 0-8414-7584-9). Folcroft.

Theme of Spenser's "Foure Hymnes". J. W. Bennett. LC 76-100731. 1970. pap. 39.95x (ISBN 0-8383-0003-0). Haskell.

Theme of the Nazi Concentration Camp in French Literature. Cynthia Haft. (New Babylon Studies in the Social Sciences: No. 12). 1973. 14.40x (ISBN 90-2797-190-0). Mouton.

Theme on a Pipedream. F. H. Sasse. 4.95 (ISBN 0-85131-027-3, NL51, Pub. by J A Allen U K). S R Smith Sporting Bks.

Themes & Conclusions. Igor Stravinsky. 328p. 1982. pap. 9.95 (ISBN 0-520-04652-8). U of Cal Pr.

Themes & Conventions in the Comedy of Manners. R. C. Sharma. LC 77-3414. Repr. of 1965 ed. lib. bdg. 39.00 (ISBN 0-8414-7828-7). Folcroft.

Themes & Conventions of Elizabethan Tragedy. 2nd ed. Muriel C. Bradbrook. (History of Elizabethan Drama Ser.). 270p. 1980. 52.50 (ISBN 0-521-22770-4); pap. 17.95 (ISBN 0-521-29695-1). Cambridge U Pr.

Themes & Schemes. Beverly Armstrong. (Teacher Timesavers Ser.). (Illus.). 40p. (gr. 1-4). 1986. 4.95 (ISBN 0-88160-128-4, LW 126). Learning Wks.

Themes & Texts: Toward a Poetics of Expressivenes. Alexander Zholkovsky. Ed. by Kathleen Parthe. LC 83-45152. 304p. 1983. 39.95x (ISBN 0-8014-1505-5). Cornell U Pr.

Themes & Theories in Modern Japanese History: Essays in Memory of Richard Storry. Ed. by Sue Henny & Jean-Pierre Lehmann. 320p. 1987. 65.00 (ISBN 0-485-11242-6, Pub. by Athlone Pr UK). Humanities.

Themes & Theses of Six Recent Papal Documents: A Commentary. Robert F. Morneau. 160p. (Orig.). 1985. pap. 5.95 (ISBN 0-8189-0482-8). Alba.

Themes & Variations. John Cage. LC 81-13626. (Illus.). 150p. 25.00 (ISBN 0-930794-22-2); pap. 9.95 (ISBN 0-930794-23-0). Station Hill Pr.

Themes & Variations. Aldous L. Huxley. LC 79-128264. (Essay Index Reprint Ser). 1950. 19.00 (ISBN 0-8369-1883-5). Ayer Co Pubs.

Themes & Variations: A College Reader. W. Ross Winterowd & Charlotte Preston. 425p. 1985. pap. text ed. 12.00 net (ISBN 0-15-591470-7, HC); instr's. manual avail. (ISBN 0-15-591471-5). HarBraceJ.

Themes & Variations: Classics to Moderns. (Music for Millions Ser.: Vol. 77). 1974. pap. 8.95 (ISBN 0-8256-4077-6). Music Sales.

Themes & Variations in English Poetry of the Renaissance. Douglas Bush. LC 74-3413. lib. bdg. 15.50 (ISBN 0-8414-3104-3). Folcroft.
Themes & Variations in European Psychiatry: An Anthology. Ed. by Steven R. Hirsh & Michael Shepherd. LC 73-86374. 450p. 1974. 30.00x (ISBN 0-8139-0511-7). U Pr of Va.
Themes Col Writ. John Brereton & Jane Dobija. 432p. 1986. pap. text ed. write for info (ISBN 0-394-34082-5, RanC). Random.
Themes et Discussions. Thomas H. Brown. 240p. 1982. pap. text ed. 15.00 (ISBN 0-669-02844-4). Heath.
Themes for Teaching U. S. History: Conflict & Change. David C. King & Cathryn J. Long. 72p. 5.00 (ISBN 0-318-14213-9, GPH 102). Amer Forum.
Themes for Writers: A College Reader. Joyce S. Steward. 1983. pap. text ed. write for info. (ISBN 0-673-15575-7). Scott F.
Themes from Acts. Paul E. Pierson. LC 82-80153. (Bible Commentary for Laymen Ser.). (Orig.). 1982. pap. 3.95 (ISBN 0-8307-0819-7, S361107). Regal.
Themes from Isaiah. Ronald Youngblood. LC 83-19128. (Bible Commentary for Laymen Ser.). 1983. pap. text ed. 3.95 (ISBN 0-8307-0906-1, S373106). Regal.
Themes from Isaiah see Temas de Isaias.
Themes from Kaplan. Ed. by Joseph Almog et al. 560p. 1988. 39.95 (ISBN 0-19-505217-X). Oxford U Pr.
Themes from Masterworks, 3 bks. Ed. by Louise Goss. (Frances Clark Library for Piano Students). 16p. (Orig.). (gr. k-12). 1970. pap. text ed. 5.95 Bk. 1 (ISBN 0-87487-191-3); pap. text ed. 5.95 Bk. 2 (ISBN 0-87487-192-1); pap. text ed. 5.95 Bk. 3 (ISBN 0-87487-193-X). Birch Tree Gr.
Themes from Northern Sudan. Ahmed Al-Shahi. (Brismes-British Society for Middle Eastern Studies: Vol. 1). (Illus.). 156p. 1986. 29.95 (ISBN 0-86372-064-1, Pub. by Ithaca Pr UK). Humanities.
Themes I. A. L. Staveley. 1984. 20.00 (ISBN 0-89756-005-1). Two Rivers.
Themes II. A. L. Staveley et al. 112p. 1982. 20.00 (ISBN 0-89756-010-8). Two Rivers.
Themes III. A. L. Staveley et al. 1984. 20.00 (ISBN 0-89756-013-2). Two Rivers.
Themes in African & World History: A Schema for Integrating Africa into World History; Tropical Africa: The Colonial Heritage; The African Heritage & the Slave Trade. rev. ed. George E. Brooks, Jr. (African Humanities Ser.). 59p. 1983. pap. text ed. 5.00 (ISBN 0-941934-06-3). Indiana Africa.
Themes in American Literature. Philip J. McFarland et al. (Literature Ser.). (Illus.). (gr. 11). 1975. text ed. 24.48 (ISBN 0-395-20083-0); tchr's resource bk. 11.16 (ISBN 0-395-20081-4). HM.
Themes in Cultural Psychiatry: An Annotated Bibliography 1975-1980. Armando R. Favazza & Ahmed D. Faheem. LC 82-2738. 208p. 1982. 30.00x (ISBN 0-8262-0377-9). U of MO Pr.
Themes in Economic Anthropology. Ed. by Raymond Firth. (Illus.). 1970. pap. 13.95x (ISBN 0-422-72540-4, NO. 2198, Pub by Tavistock England). Routledge Chapman & Hall.
Themes in Linguistics: The Nineteen Seventies. Ed. by Eric P. Hamp. LC 72-94473. (Janua Linguarum, Ser. Minor: No. 172). (Illus.). 129p. 1973. pap. text ed. 10.00x (ISBN 90-2792-365-5). Mouton.
Themes in Modern Social History. Linda W. Rosenzweig & Peter N. Stearns. LC 85-71853. 1985. pap. 8.95 (ISBN 0-88748-059-4). Carnegie Mellon.
Themes in Motor Development. Ed. by H. T. Whiting & M. G. Wade. 1986. lib. bdg. 79.00 (ISBN 90-247-3390-1, Pub. by Martinus Nijoff Netherlands). Kluwer Academic.
Themes in Old Testament Theology. William A. Dyrness. LC 79-2380. 1979. pap. 10.95 (ISBN 0-87784-726-6). Inter-Varsity.
Themes in Roman Satire. Niall Rudd. LC 85-29544. 248p. 1986. 27.50x (ISBN 0-8061-1994-2). U of Okla Pr.
Themes in Science Fiction. Leo P. Kelley. (Patterns in Literary Art Ser.). 432p. (gr. 10-12). 1972. pap. 13.80 (ISBN 0-07-033504-4). McGraw.
Themes in Soviet Marxist Philosophy: Selected Articles from the Sovetskaja Enciklopedija. Ed. by T. J. Blakeley. (Sovietica: No. 37). 230p. 1975. lib. bdg. 39.50 (ISBN 90-277-0637-9, Pub. by Reidel Holland). Kluwer Academic.
Themes in the Christian History of Central Africa. Ed. by T. O. Ranger & John Weller. 1974. 48.00x (ISBN 0-520-02536-9). U of Cal Pr.
Themes in the Historical Geography of France. H. C. Clout. 1977. 99.00 (ISBN 0-12-175850-8). Acad Pr.
Themes in the History of the Family. Ed. by Tamara K. Hareven. LC 78-53938. 1978. pap. 7.50 (ISBN 0-912296-15-1, Dist. by U Pr of Va). Am Antiquarian.
Themes in Theology: The Three-Fold Cord. Donald M. MacKinnon. 256p. 1988. 29.95 (ISBN 0-567-09446-4, Pub. By T & T Clark Ltd Uk). Fortress.
Themes in World Literature. Philip J. McFarland et al. (Literature Ser.). (Illus.). 1975. text ed. 28.80 (ISBN 0-395-20156-X); tchr's resource bk 11.60 (ISBN 0-395-20157-8). HM.
Themes of Adulthood Through Literature. Sharan B. Merriam. 1983. pap. text ed. 19.95x (ISBN 0-8077-2731-8). Tchrs Coll.
Themes of Elizabeth Gaskell. Enid L. Duthie. 217p. 1980. 29.50x (ISBN 0-8476-6224-1). Rowman.
Themes of Indigenous Acculturation in Northwest Mexico. Ed. by Thomas B. Hinton & Phil C. Weigand. LC 80-39646. (Anthropological Papers: No. 38). 76p. 1981. pap. 7.95x (ISBN 0-8165-0324-9). U of Ariz Pr.
Themes of Islamic Civilization. Ed. by John A. Williams. 392p. 1971. 43.00x (ISBN 0-520-01685-8); pap. 11.95x (ISBN 0-520-04514-9). U of Cal Pr.
Themes of Magic in Nineteenth Century French Fiction. Emile Caillet. 59.95 (ISBN 0-8490-1188-4). Gordon Pr.
Themes of Magic in Nineteenth Century French Fiction. Emile Cailliet. LC 80-22976. (Studies in Comparative Literature: No. 2). 228p. 1981. Repr. of 1932 ed. lib. bdg. 27.50x (ISBN 0-87991-501-3). Porcupine Pr.
Themes of Peace in Renaissance Poetry. James Hutton. Ed. by Rita Guerlac. LC 84-7631. (Illus.). 280p. 1984. 39.95x (ISBN 0-8014-1613-2). Cornell U Pr.
Themes of Work & Love in Adulthood. Ed. by Neil J. Smelser & Erik H. Erikson. LC 79-26130. (Harvard Paperbacks Ser.). 312p. 1981. pap. 10.95 (ISBN 0-674-87751-9). Harvard U Pr.
Themes of Work & Love in Adulthood. Ed. by Neil J. Smelser & Erik H. Erikson. (Illus.). 307p. 1980. 21.00x (ISBN 0-674-87750-0). Harvard U Pr.
Themes Out of School: Effects & Causes. Stanley Cavell. LC 83-63126. 288p. 1984. 20.00 (ISBN 0-86547-146-0). N Point Pr.
Themes out of School: Effects & Causes. Stanley Cavell. xiv, 268p. 1988. pap. 12.95 (ISBN 0-226-09788-9). U of Chicago Pr.
Themes, Scenes & Taste in the History of Japanese Garden Art. Wybe Kuitert. (Japonica Neerlandica Ser.: Vol. 3). (Illus.). xiii, 348p. 1988. 46.00x (ISBN 90-5063-021-9, Pub. by Gieben Amsterdam). Benjamins North Am.
Themes, Thoughts & Treasures, Vols. I & II. Ed. by Jimmy L. Gravely. 90p. (Orig.). 1986. Set. pap. 9.95 (ISBN 0-936903-00-7). Certified Feelings.
Themis: A Study of the Social Origins of Greek Religion. Jane Harrison. 559p. 1963. 25.00 (ISBN 0-85036-057-9, Pub. by Merlin Pr UK). Longwood Pub Group.
Then. Carroll Arnett. 1965. pap. 3.00 (ISBN 0-685-00981-5). Elizabeth Pr.
Then Again. Sue McCauley. 352p. 1988. 22.95 (ISBN 0-340-40101-X, Pub. by Hodder & Stoughton UK). David & Charles.
Then Again, Maybe I Won't. Judy Blume. LC 77-156548. 176p. (gr. 5-7). 1971. 12.95 (ISBN 0-02-711090-7). Bradbury Pr.
Then Again, Maybe I Won't. Judy Blume. 128p. (gr. 6 up). 1976. pap. 2.95 (ISBN 0-440-98659-1, LFL). Dell.
Then Again, Maybe I Won't. Judy Blume. 164p. (gr. 5-8). 1986. pap. 3.25 (ISBN 0-440-48659-9, YB). Dell.
Then Again, Maybe I Won't. Judy Blume. (Children's Ser.). (gr. 5-7). 1988. lib. bdg. 13.95x (ISBN 0-8161-4417-6, Large Print Bks). G K Hall.
Then Am I Strong. Francena H. Arnold. 1969. pap. 3.95 (ISBN 0-8024-0060-4). Moody.
Then & Now. facs. ed. Ed. by Anna Brinton. LC 72-128214. (Essay Index Reprint Ser). 1960. 21.50 (ISBN 0-8369-1905-X). Ayer Co Pubs.
Then & Now. Kathleen Campbell. 1985. pap. 5.00 (ISBN 0-941150-29-1). Barth.
Then & Now. Illus. by Peter Firmin. (What's the Difference Ser.). (Illus.). 16p. (ps-1). 1986. 2.95 (ISBN 0-86020-965-2). EDC.
Then & Now. W. Somerset Maugham. LC 75-25364. (Works of W. Somerset Maugham Ser.). 1977. Repr. of 1946 ed. 20.00x (ISBN 0-405-07822-6). Ayer Co Pubs.
Then & Now: A Photographic History of Vegetation Change in the Central Great Basin Desert. Garry F. Rogers. (Illus.). 159p. (Orig.). 1982. pap. 10.00x (ISBN 0-87480-206-7). U of Utah Pr.
Then & Now: Cartoons about Airline Pilots. Michael J. Ray. 96p. (Orig.). 1986. pap. 6.95 (ISBN 0-936283-00-9). U Temecula Pr.
Then & Now in Education, Eighteen Forty-Five to Nineteen Twenty-Three. Otis W. Caldwell & Stuart A. Courtis. LC 77-165711. (American Education Ser, No. 2). 1971. Repr. of 1923 ed. 19.00 (ISBN 0-405-03700-7). Ayer Co Pubs.
Then & Now: On the One Hundreth Anniversary of the First General Strike in the U. S. Terry Moon & Ron Brokmeyer. (Illus.). 50p. 1977. pap. 1.00x (ISBN 0-914441-17-5). News & Letters.
Then & Now: The Personal Past in the Poetry of Robert Penn Warren. Floyd C. Watkins. LC 81-51016. 200p. 1982. 15.00 (ISBN 0-8131-1456-X). U Pr of Ky.
Then & Then & Now. Wade F. Waunting. LC 86-90328. 94p. 1987. 8.95 (ISBN 0-533-07256-5). Vantage.
Then Badger Said This. Elizabeth Cook-Lynn. (Illus.). 42p. 1983. 2.95 (ISBN 0-87770-307-8). Ye Galleon.
Then Came Oil. C. B. Glasscock. LC 75-6474. (History & Politics of Oil Ser.). (Illus.). 349p. 1976. Repr. of 1938 ed. 25.85 (ISBN 0-88355-292-2). Hyperion Conn.
Then Came Violence: A Virgil Tibbs Mystery. John Ball. LC 87-45595. 216p. 1988. pap. 3.95 (ISBN 0-06-080883-7, P-883, PL). Har-Row.
Then I'll Be Home Free. Phyllis A. Wood. (YA) (gr. 6 up). 1988. pap. 2.75 (ISBN 0-451-15373-1, Sig). NAL.
Then King Down Came. Richard Johnson. (Orig.). 1970. pap. 2.00 (ISBN 0-932264-14-X). Trask Hse Bks.
Then Ninth Vibration, & Other Stories. Lily Moresby & Adams Beck. Ed. by R. Reginald & Douglas Menville. LC 75-46251. (Supernatural & Occult Fiction Ser.). 1976. Repr. of 1922 ed. lib. bdg. 24.50x (ISBN 0-405-08111-1). Ayer Co Pubs.
Then the Moon Began to Sing. Alice S. Newton. 1981. 6.00 (ISBN 0-8233-0335-7). Golden Quill.
Then the Sun Came Up. Helen Tucker. (Orig.). 1986. pap. 7.00 (ISBN 0-915541-10-6). Star Bks Inc.
Then, the Toaster Said... Bill Harvey. (Illus.). 144p. (Orig.). 1985. pap. 5.95 (ISBN 0-930297-18-0, 84-081379). Ike & Dudatt Pubns.
Then There Were Five. Elizabeth Enright. (Illus.). (gr. k-6). 1987. pap. 2.95 (ISBN 0-440-48806-0, YB). Dell.
Then Truth Will Out. Leonard E. Read. 177p. 1971. 3.00 (ISBN 0-910614-27-X). Foun Econ Ed.
Thence Round Cape Horn. Robert E. Johnson. LC 79-6111. (Navies & Men Ser.). (Illus.). 1980. Repr. of 1963 ed. lib. bdg. 28.50x (ISBN 0-405-13040-6). Ayer Co Pubs.
Thendara House. Marion Zimmer Bradley. 416p. 1988. pap. 3.95 (ISBN 0-88677-240-0). DAW Bks.
Theo & Me: Growing Up Okay. Malcolm-Jamal Warner & Daniel Paisner. 160p. (gr. 5 up). 1988. 14.95 (ISBN 0-525-24694-0, 01451-440). Dutton.
Theo Hios: Fifty-Two Years of Painting: A Letter to the World. Lawrence Campbell. (Illus.). 154p. (Orig.). 1987. pap. 22.50x (ISBN 0-8390-0383-8). Abner Schram Ltd.
Theo, the Indian Fighter. Wells Teague. Ed. by Edwin M. Eakin. (Illus.). 112p. (gr. 4-7). 1987. 8.95 (ISBN 0-89015-614-X). Eakin Pr.
Theo Tobiasse: Artist in Exile. Chaim Potok. (Illus.). 200p. 1986. 50.00 (ISBN 0-8478-0778-9). Rizzoli Intl.
Theo van Doesburg: Painting into Architecture, Theory into Practice. Allan Doig. (Cambridge Urban & Architectural Studies: No. 10). 328p. 1987. 59.50 (ISBN 0-521-32213-8). Cambridge U Pr.
Theo Van Doesburg: Propagandist & Practitioner of the Avant-Garde, 1909-1923. Hannah L. Hedrick. LC 79-24699. (Studies in the Fine Arts: Avant-Garde: No. 5). pap. 45.00 (2070086). Bks Demand UMI.
Theo Zephyr. Dean Hughes. LC 86-28885. 128p. (gr. 4-8). 1987. 11.95 (ISBN 0-689-31345-4, Atheneum Childrens Bks). Macmillan.
Theocratic Kingdom, 3 vols. George N. H. Peters. LC 88-12845. (Kregel Limited Edition Library). 2180p. 1988. Set. 99.95 (ISBN 0-8254-3502-1). Kregel.
Theocritan Element in the Works of William Wordsworth. Leslie Broughton. LC 74-8708. 1920. lib. bdg. 25.00 (ISBN 0-8414-3198-1). Folcroft.
Theocritus, 2 vols. 2nd ed. Ed. by A. S. Gow. 332p. 1987. Repr. of 1952 ed. 150.00. Cambridge U Pr.
Theocritus. Theocritus. Tr. by Charles S. Calverley. LC 73-39212. (Select Bibliographies Reprint Ser.). Repr. of 1869 ed. 17.00 (ISBN 0-8369-6814-X). Ayer Co Pubs.
Theocritus' Coan Pastorals: A Poetry Book. Gilbert Lawall. 156p. 1986. Repr. of 1967 ed. lib. bdg. 24.25 (ISBN 0-8191-5527-6, Pub. by Ctr for Hellenic Studies). U Pr of Amer.
Theocritus' Coan Pastorals: A Poetry Book. Theocritus. Ed. by Gilbert W. Lawall. LC 67-14343. (Center for Hellenic Studies Ser). (Illus.). 144p. 1967. 10.00 (ISBN 0-674-87765-9). Harvard U Pr.
Theocritus: Idylls & Epigrams. Daryl Hine. LC 82-71256. 144p. 1983. 17.95 (ISBN 0-689-11320-X); pap. 10.95 (ISBN 0-689-11321-8). Atheneum.
Theocritus in English Literature. Robert T. Kerlin. LC 72-188488. Repr. of 1910 ed. lib. bdg. 39.50 (ISBN 0-8414-5568-6). Folcroft.
Theoderich Und Iustinian. Berthold Rubin. pap. 8.00 (ISBN 0-384-52465-6). Johnson Repr.
Theodicies in Conflict: A Dilemma in Puritan Ethics & Nineteenth-Century American Literature. Richard Forrer. LC 85-27220. (Contributions to the Study of Religion: No. 17). 302p. 1986. lib. bdg. 38.95 (ISBN 0-313-25191-6, FTS/). Greenwood.
Theodicy. Leibniz. LC 85-8833. 400p. 1985. pap. 10.95 (ISBN 0-87548-437-9). Open Court.
Theodicy in Baroque Literature. Richard Saez. Ed. by James Wilhelm. LC 84-48375. (Comparative Literature Ser.). 300p. 1985. lib. bdg. 39.00 (ISBN 0-8240-6700-2). Garland Pub.
Theodicy in Islamic Thought. Eric Ormsby. LC 84-3396. 320p. 1984. text ed. 33.50x (ISBN 0-691-07278-7). Princeton U pr.
Theodicy in the Old Testament. Ed. by James L. Crenshaw. LC 83-8885. (Issues in Religion & Theology Ser.). 176p. 1983. pap. 2.50 (ISBN 0-8006-1764-9). Fortress.
Theodontia. A. J. Charig & B. Krebs. (Encyclopedia of Paleoherpetology Ser.: Pt. 13). (Illus.). 137p. 1976. lib. bdg. 75.90x (ISBN 3-437-30184-5). Lubrecht & Cramer.
Theodor Adorno: A Bibliography. Ed. by Joan Nordquist. (Social Theory: A Bibliographic Ser.: No. 10). 60p. (Orig.). 1988. pap. 15.00 (ISBN 0-937855-18-9). Ref Rsch Serv.
Theodor & Mr. Balbini. Petra Mathers. LC 87-45860. (Illus.). 32p. (gr. k-3). 1988. 11.95i (ISBN 0-06-024122-5); PLB 11.89 (ISBN 0-06-024144-6). HarpJ.
Theodor Billroth Privat: Die Billroth Seegen Briefe. Ed. by K. B. Absolon & Ernst Kern. (Illus.). 291p. 1987. 39.50 (ISBN 0-930329-07-4). Kabel Pubs.
Theodor Boveri: Life & Work of a Great Biologist, 1862-1915. Friedrich Baltzer. LC 67-21996. (Illus.). 187p. pap. 48.70 (2029943). Bks Demand UMI.
Theodor Fontane As a Critic of the Drama. Bertha E. Trebein. LC 16-14031. (Columbia University. Germanic Studies, Old Ser.: No. 21). Repr. of 1916 ed. 21.50 (ISBN 0-404-50421-3). AMS Pr.
Theodor Fontane: The Major Novels. Alan Bance. LC 81-21688. (Anglica Germanica Ser.: No. 2). 250p. 1982. 47.50 (ISBN 0-521-24532-X). Cambridge U Pr.
Theodor Fontane und der Roman Vom Markischen Junker. Hans G. Wegner. (Ger). pap. 13.00. Johnson Repr.
Theodor Fontanes Irrungen, Wirrungen, Die 'Erste Seite' als Schlussel zum WWerk. G. H. Hertling. (Germanic Studies in America, Band 54). 1985. text ed. 15.00 (ISBN 0-8204-0314-8). P Lang Pubs.
Theodor Fontanes Roman "Der Stechlin". E. Behrend. pap. 9.00 (ISBN 0-384-03770-4). Johnson Repr.
Theodor Geiger on Social Order & Mass Society. Theodor Geiger. Ed. by Renate Mayntz. LC 69-19157. (Heritage of Sociology Ser). 1969. pap. 2.95x (ISBN 0-226-51388-2, P333, Phoen). U of Chicago Pr.
Theodor Gomperz & John Stuart Mill. A. Weinberg. 64p. (Orig.). 1963. pap. text ed. 12.50x (ISBN 0-317-56051-4, Pub. by Droz Switzerland). Coronet Bks.
Theodor Herzl. Norman H. Finkelstein. (Impact Biography Ser.). (Illus.). 128p. 1987. lib. bdg. 11.90 (ISBN 0-531-10421-4). Watts.
Theodor Herzl: The Road to Israel. Miriam Gurko. 1988. 12.95. JPS Phila.
Theodor Mundt und Seine Beziehungen Zum Jungen Deutschland. O. Draeger. 1909. pap. 9.00 (ISBN 0-384-12605-7). Johnson Repr.
Theodor Storm. A. Tilo Alt. LC 72-2793. (Twayne's World Authors Ser.). 157p. 1973. text ed. 17.95 (ISBN 0-8290-1757-7). Irvington.
Theodor Storm: Studies in Ambivalence. David Artiss. (German Language & Literature Monographs: No. 5). xix, 215p. 1978. 32.00x (ISBN 90-272-0965-0). Benjamins North Am.
Theodor Storm's Craft of Fiction: The Torment of a Narrator. Clifford A. Bernd. LC 67-64644. (North Carolina University. Studies in the Germanic Languages & Literature: No. 43). Repr. of 1963 ed. 27.00 (ISBN 0-404-50943-6). AMS Pr.
Theodor Storms Erzahlung "Aquis Submersus". T. Muller. pap. 9.00 (ISBN 0-384-40430-8). Johnson Repr.
Theodor Storms Erzahlungskunst in Ihrer Entwicklung. H. Eichentopf. 1908. pap. 9.00 (ISBN 0-384-14020-3). Johnson Repr.
Theodor Storm's Novellen: Essays on Literary Technique. E. Allen McCormick. LC 64-64253. (North Carolina. University. Studies in the Germanic Languages & Literatures: No. 47). Repr. of 1966 ed. 27.00 (ISBN 0-404-50947-9). AMS Pr.
Theodora: Portrait in a Byzantine Landscape. Antony Bridge. (Illus.). 194p. 1984. Repr. of 1978 ed. 13.95 (ISBN 0-89733-102-8). Academy Chi Pubs.
Theodore. David Melton. 1978. 3.99 (ISBN 0-8309-0196-5). Ind Pr MO.
Theodore. Edward Ormondroyd. LC 66-10352. (Illus.). (ps-3). 1966. 5.95 (ISBN 0-395-27717-5, Pub. by Parnassus). HM.
Theodore. Edward Ormondroyd. LC 66-10352. (Illus.). 40p. (ps-3). 1984. pap. 4.95 (ISBN 0-395-36610-0). HM.
Theodore Beza, The Counsellor of the French Reformation, 1519-1605. Henry M. Baird. LC 76-121596. 1970. Repr. of 1899 ed. 25.50 (ISBN 0-8337-0151-7). B Franklin.
Theodore Blegen. John T. Flanagan. 181p. 1977. 8.00 (ISBN 0-87732-060-8). Norwegian-Am Hist Assn.
Theodore Bump: What's in Your Trunk. Craig Lovik. Incl. You're Late for Church. 6.95 (ISBN 0-570-04124-4, 56-1535). (Theodore Bump Ser.). (Illus.). 32p. (gr. 6-8). 1985. 6.95 (ISBN 0-570-04123-6, 56-1534). Concordia.
Theodore Chasseriau: Illustrations for Othello. Jay M. Fisher. LC 79-67570. 1980. pap. 6.98 (ISBN 0-912298-50-2). Baltimore Mus.
Theodore de Banville. Alvin Harms. (World Authors Ser.). 1983. lib. bdg. 21.95 (ISBN 0-8057-6547-6, Twayne). G K Hall.

Theologians of Our Time. Ed. by Leonhard Reinisch. 1964. pap. 8.95x (ISBN 0-268-00378-5). U of Notre Dame Pr.

Theologians under Hitler. Robert P. Erickson. LC 84-40731. 256p. 1987. pap. 9.95 (ISBN 0-300-03889-5, Y-618). Yale U Pr.

Theologians under Hitler: Gerhard Kittel, Paul Althaus, & Emanuel Hirsch. Robert P. Ericksen. LC 84-40731. (Illus.). 256p. 1985. 25.00x (ISBN 0-300-02926-8). Yale U Pr.

Theologians under Hitler: Gerhard Kittel, Paul Althaus, & Emmanuel Hirsch. Robert P. Ericksen. 1987. pap. 8.95 (ISBN 0-317-59962-3). Yale U Pr.

Theologic Principle of Universalism: A Way of Life. Joe Jenkins. (Orig.). 1984. pap. 4.00 (ISBN 0-916801-00-4). Inst Univ.

Theological Aesthetics of Hans Urs von Balthasar. Louis Roberts. 1987. 36.95x (ISBN 0-8132-0634-0). Cath U Pr.

Theological Aesthetics: Theology. Jeffrey A. Kay. (European University Studies: Ser. 23, Vol. 60). 115p. 1976. pap. 12.90 (ISBN 3-261-01893-3). P Lang Pubs.

Theological & Dogmatic Works. St. Ambrose. (Fathers of the Church Ser.: Vol. 44). 343p. 1963. 34.95x (ISBN 0-8132-0044-X). Cath U Pr.

Theological & Miscellaneous Works, 25 vols. in 26. Joseph Priestley. Set. pap. 1352.00 (ISBN 0-527-72751-2). Kraus Repr.

Theological & Religious Reference Materials: General Resources & Biblical Studies. G. E. Gorman & Lyn Gorman. LC 83-22759. (Bibliographies & Indexes in Religious Studies: No. 1). xvi, 526p. 1984. 58.95 (ISBN 0-313-20924-3, GRM/). Greenwood.

Theological & Religious Reference Materials: Practical Theology. Compiled by G. E. Gorman et al. LC 86-380. (Bibliographies & Indexes in Religious Studies: No. 7). 402p. 1986. lib. bdg. 50.95 (ISBN 0-313-25397-8, GPA/). Greenwood.

Theological & Religious Reference Materials: Systematic Theology & Church History. G. E. Gorman & Lyn Gorman. LC 83-22759. (Bibliographies & Indexes in Religious Studies: No. 2). xiv, 401p. 1985. lib. bdg. 48.95 (ISBN 0-313-24779-X, GOS/). Greenwood.

Theological Anthropology. Ed. by J. Patout Burns. LC 81-43080. (Sources of Early Christian Thought Ser.). 1981. pap. 7.95 (ISBN 0-8006-1412-7). Fortress.

Theological Approach to Art. Roger Hazelton. LC 67-221000065. pap. 39.50 (ISBN 0-317-10384-9, 2001852). Bks Demand UMI.

Theological Cautions. Paul Toinet. Tr. by Michael J. Wrenn. 1982. 12.00 (ISBN 0-8199-0835-5). Franciscan Herald.

Theological Department in Yale College, 1822-1858. John T. Wayland. Ed. by Bruce Kuklick. (American Religious Thought of the 18th & 19th Centuries Ser.). 500p. 1987. lib. bdg. 70.00 (ISBN 0-8240-6962-5). Garland Pub.

Theological Development of Edwards Amasa Park: Last of the "Consistent Calvinists". Anthony C. Cecil, Jr. LC 74-83338. (American Academy of Religion. Dissertation Ser.). 1974. pap. 9.95 (ISBN 0-88420-118-X, 010101). Scholars Pr GA.

Theological Dictionary of the New Testament, 10 vols. Ed. by Gerhard Kittel & Gerhard Friedrich. Incl. Vol. 1. 1964. 39.95 (ISBN 0-8028-2243-6); Vol. 2. 1965. 39.95 (ISBN 0-8028-2244-4); Vol. 3. 1966. 39.95 (ISBN 0-8028-2245-2); Vol. 4. 1967. 39.95 (ISBN 0-8028-2246-0); Vol. 5. 1968. 39.95 (ISBN 0-8028-2247-9); Vol. 6. 1969. 39.95 (ISBN 0-8028-2248-7); Vol. 7. 1970. 39.95 (ISBN 0-8028-2249-5); Vol. 8. 1972. 39.95 (ISBN 0-8028-2250-9); Vol. 9. 1973. 39.95 (ISBN 0-8028-2322-X); Vol; Vol. 10. 1976. 29.95 (ISBN 0-8028-2323-8). Set. 399.50 (ISBN 0-8028-2324-6). Eerdmans.

Theological Dictionary of the New Testament. abridged ed. Ed. by Gerhard Kittel & Gerhard Friedrich. Tr. by Geoffrey Bromiley from Ger. 1300p. 1985. pap. 49.95 cloth (ISBN 0-8028-2404-8). Eerdmans.

Theological Dictionary of the Old Testament, 5 vols. Ed. by G. Johannes Botterweck & Helmer Ringgren. 560p. 1978. Set. 149.75 (ISBN 0-8028-2338-6); Vol. I. 29.95 ea. (ISBN 0-8028-2325-4). Vol. II (ISBN 0-8028-2326-2). Vol. III (ISBN 0-8028-2327-0). Vol. IV (ISBN 0-8028-2328-9). Vol. V (ISBN 0-8028-2329-7). Eerdmans.

Theological Diversity & the Authority of the Old Testament. John Goldingay. 240p. (Orig.). 1987. pap. 14.95 (ISBN 0-8028-0229-X). Eerdmans.

Theological Education for Social Ministry. Ed. by Dieter T. Hessel. 192p. 1988. pap. 10.95 (ISBN 0-8298-0773-X). Pilgrim NY.

Theological Essays. Frederick D. Maurice. 436p. (Orig.). Date not set. pap. write for info. (ISBN 0-87921-048-6). Attic Pr.

Theological Essays of the Later Benjamin Jowett. Benjamin Jowett. 1906. 20.00 (ISBN 0-932062-91-1). Sharon Hill.

Theological Ethics, Vol. 1. Helmut Thielicke. LC 78-31858. Repr. of 1979 ed. 160.00 (2027550). Bks Demand UMI.

Theological-Exegetical Approach to Glossolalia. Watson E. Mills. 192p. (Orig.). 1985. lib. bdg. 26.25 (ISBN 0-8191-4526-2); pap. text ed. 11.50 (ISBN 0-8191-4527-0). U Pr of Amer.

Theological Ferment: Personal Reflections. Paul Clasper. 226p. (Orig.). 1982. pap. 6.75 (ISBN 0-686-37687-0, Pub. by New Day Philippines). Cellar.

Theological Foundations for Ministry. Ray S. Anderson. LC 78-13613. 1978. pap. 9.95 (ISBN 0-8028-1776-9). Eerdmans.

Theological Foundations of the Mormon Religion. Sterling M. McMurrin. LC 65-26131. 1965. pap. 9.95 (ISBN 0-87480-051-X). U of Utah Pr.

Theological German. Helmut W. Ziefle. 256p. 1986. pap. 14.95 (ISBN 0-8010-9931-5). Baker Bk.

Theological Imagination: Constructing the Concept of God. Gordon D. Kaufman. LC 81-12960. 310p. 1981. pap. 13.95 (ISBN 0-664-24393-2). Westminster John Knox.

Theological Interpretation of American History. rev. ed. C Gregg Singer. LC 64-13205. 1981. pap. 10.95 (ISBN 0-87552-426-5). Presby & Reformed.

Theological Investigations, Vols. 1-17, 20. Karl Rahner. Incl. Vol. 1. 22.50x (ISBN 0-8245-0377-5); Vol. 2. Man & the Church. 22.50x (ISBN 0-8245-0378-3); Vol. 3. Theology of the Spiritual Life. 24.50x (ISBN 0-8245-0379-1); Vol. 4. More Recent Writings. 24.50x (ISBN 0-8245-0380-5); Vol. 5. Later Writings. 27.50x (ISBN 0-8245-0381-3); Vol. 6. Concerning Vatican Council II. 24.50x (ISBN 0-8245-0382-1); Vol. 7. Further Theology of the Spiritual Life I. 19.50x (ISBN 0-8245-0383-X); Vol. 8. Further Theology of the Spiritual Life II. 19.50x (ISBN 0-8245-0384-8); Vol. 9. Writings of 1965-1967, I. 19.50x (ISBN 0-8245-0385-6); Vol. 10. Writings of 1965-1967, II. 22.50x (ISBN 0-8245-0386-4); Vol. 11. Confrontation I. 22.50 (ISBN 0-8245-0387-2); Vol. 12. Confrontations II. 22.50x (ISBN 0-8245-0388-0); Vol. 13. Theology Anthropology, Christology. 22.50x (ISBN 0-8245-0389-9); Vol. 14. In Dialogue with the Future. 22.50 (ISBN 0-8245-0390-2); Penance in the Early Church. 500p. 29.50x (ISBN 0-8245-0025-3); Vol. 16. Experience of the Spirit: Source of Theology. 1979. 19.50x (ISBN 0-8245-0392-9); Vol. 17. Jesus, Man & the Church. 19.50x (ISBN 0-8245-0026-1); Vol. 20. Concern for the Church. 14.50x. Crossroad NY.

Theological Investigations, Vol. 22: Humane Society & the Church of Tomorrow. Karl Rahner. 288p. 1987. 24.50x (ISBN 0-8245-0802-5). Crossroad NY.

Theological Libraries at Oxford. Thomas P. Slavens. 197p. 1984. pap. text ed. 32.50 (ISBN 3-598-10563-0). K G Saur.

Theological Method in Jacques Ellul. Daniel B. Clendenin. LC 87-10506. 184p. (Orig.). 1987. lib. bdg. 24.50 (ISBN 0-8191-6427-5); pap. text ed. 11.75 (ISBN 0-8191-6428-3). U Pr of Amer.

Theological Method in Luther & Tillich: Law-Gospel & Correlation. Wayne G. Johnson. LC 80-5691. 204p. 1982. lib. bdg. 29.00 (ISBN 0-8191-1895-8). U Pr of Amer.

Theological Method of Karl Rahner. Anne Carr. LC 76-51639. (American Academy of Religion, Dissertation Ser.: No. 19). pap. 72.30 (ISBN 0-317-08410-0, 2017556). Bks Demand UMI.

Theological Methodology of Hans Kung. Catherine M. LaCugna. LC 81-16654. (American Academy of Religion Academy Ser.). 1982. 12.95 (ISBN 0-89130-546-7, 01 01 39). Scholars Pr GA.

Theological Models for the Parish. Sabbas Kilian. LC 76-42986. 1977. 5.95 (ISBN 0-8189-0337-6). Alba.

Theological Papers of John Henry Newman: On Biblical Inspiration & on Infallibility, Vol. 2. John H. Newman. Ed. by J. Derek Holmes. 1979. text ed. 22.50x (ISBN 0-19-920081-5). Oxford U Pr.

Theological Papers of John Henry Newman: On Faith & Certainty, Vol. 1. John H. Newman. Ed. by Derek Holmes. 1976. 22.50x (ISBN 0-19-920071-8). Oxford U Pr.

Theological Questions: Analysis & Argument. Owen C. Thomas. LC 83-60658. 134p. (Orig.). 1983. pap. 8.95 (ISBN 0-8192-1328-4). Morehouse.

Theological Reflections: Essays on Related Themes. Henry Stob. LC 81-1472. pap. 69.30 (ISBN 0-317-20015-1, 2023223). Bks Demand UMI.

Theological Roots of Pentecostalism. Donald W. Dayton. LC 87-10522. (Studies in Evangelicalism: No. 5). (Illus.). 201p. 1987. 22.50 (ISBN 0-8108-2037-4). Scarecrow.

Theological Roots of Pentecostalism. Donald W. Dayton. 208p. 1987. pap. 19.95 (ISBN 0-310-39371-X, 10386P). Zondervan.

Theological Science. Thomas F. Torrance. 1969. pap. 7.95 (ISBN 0-19-520083-7). Oxford U Pr.

Theological Themes of Youth Ministry. William Myers. 128p. 1987. pap. 8.95 (ISBN 0-8298-0756-X). Pilgrim NY.

Theological Thinking. Carl Raschke. LC 87-26604. (Studies in Religion). 169p. 1988. 19.95 (ISBN 1-55540-187-2, 01-00-53); pap. 12.95 (ISBN 1-55540-188-0). Scholars Pr GA.

Theological Tractates. Boethius. Bd. with Consolation of Philosophy. (Loeb Classical Library: No. 74). 13.95x (ISBN 0-674-99083-8). Harvard U Pr.

Theological Transition in American Methodism, 1790-1935. Robert E. Chiles. LC 83-16666. 238p. 1983. pap. text ed. 12.00 (ISBN 0-8191-3551-8). U Pr of Amer.

Theological Treatises on the Trinity. Marius Victorinus. (Fathers of the Church Ser.: Vol. 69). 357p. 1981. 29.95x (ISBN 0-8132-0069-5). Cath U Pr.

Theological Wordbook of the Bible. Alan Richardson. 1962. pap. 8.95 (ISBN 0-02-089090-7, Collier). Macmillan.

Theological Wordbook of the Old Testament, 2 Vols. Ed. by R. Laird Harris et al. LC 80-28047. 1800p. 1980. text ed. 49.95 (ISBN 0-8024-8631-2). Moody.

Theological Works of Isaac Barrow, 9 Vols. Isaac Barrow. Ed. by Alexander Napier. LC 72-161751. Repr. of 1859 ed. Set. lib. bdg. 215.00 (ISBN 0-404-00670-1); lib. bdg. 25.00 ea. AMS Pr.

Theologico-Political Treatise: Political Treatise. Benedict Spinoza. Tr. by R. H. Elwes. pap. text ed. 6.95 (ISBN 0-486-20249-6). Dover.

Theologies of the Body: Humanist & Christian. Benedict M. Ashley. (Illus.). 770p. (Orig.). 1985. pap. 20.95 (ISBN 0-935372-15-6). Pope John Ctr.

Theologies of the Eucharist in the Early Scholastic Period. Gary Macy. (Illus.). 1984. 32.00x (ISBN 0-19-826669-3). Oxford U Pr.

Theologische Enzyklopadie (1831-32) Kurt-Victor Selge et al. Ed. by Friedrich Schleiermacher. (SchleiermacherArchiv Ser.: Band 4). 256p. 1987. lib. bdg. 70.00x (ISBN 3-11-010894-1). De Gruyter.

Theologische Grundstrukturen des Alten Testaments. Georg Fohrer. (Theologische Bibliothek Toepelmann, 24). 1972. pap. 23.20x (ISBN 3-11-003874-9). De Gruyter.

Theologische Lebenswerk Johannes Oekolampads. Ernst Staehelin. pap. 55.00 (ISBN 0-384-57418-1). Johnson Repr.

Theologische Realenzyklopaedie: Agende-Anselm Von Cantebury, Vol. 2. Ed. by Michael Wolter. (Illus.). 1978. 128.00x (ISBN 3-11-007379-X). De Gruyter.

Theologische Realeuzyklopaedie, 25 vols. Ed. by G. Krause & G. Mueller. (Ger.). write for info. De Gruyter.

Theology, 5 vols. Timothy Dwight. LC 75-3132. Repr. of 1819 ed. 200.00 set (ISBN 0-404-59136-1). AMS Pr.

Theology - The Quintessence of Science. William B. Turner. LC 80-82649. 306p. 1981. 17.50 (ISBN 0-8022-2375-3). Philos Lib.

Theology After Freud: An Interpretive Inquiry. Peter Homans. LC 76-84162. 1970. 29.50x (ISBN 0-672-51245-9); pap. text ed. 16.95x (ISBN 0-8290-1399-7). Irvington.

Theology after Wittgenstein. Fergus Kerr. 224p. 1986. text ed. 45.00 (ISBN 0-631-14688-1). Basil Blackwell.

Theology: An Assessment of Current Trends Report. Lutheran Church in America Task Group for Long-Range Planning. LC 68-55757. pap. 43.50 (2026880). Bks Demand UMI.

Theology: An Orthodox Standpoint. Apostolos Makrakis. Ed. by Orthodox Christian Educational Society. Tr. by Denver Cummings from Hellenic. (Logos & Holy Spirit in the Unity of Christian Thought Ser.: Vol. 4). 216p. 1977. pap. 5.00x (ISBN 0-938366-03-3). Orthodox Chr.

Theology & Bioethics: Exploring the Foundation & Frontiers. Earl E. Shelp. 1985. lib. bdg. 39.50 (ISBN 90-277-1857-1, Pub. by Reidel Holland). Kluwer Academic.

Theology & Black Experience: The Lutheran Heritage Interpreted by Aprican & African-American Theologians. Ed. by Albert Pero & Ambrose Moyo. 272p. (Orig.). Date not set. pap. 14.95 (ISBN 0-8066-2353-5, 10-6284). Augsburg.

Theology & Ethics in Paul. Victor P. Furnish. LC 68-17445. 1978. pap. 12.95 (ISBN 0-687-41499-7). Abingdon.

Theology & Ethics of Behavior Modification. Clyde J. Steckel. LC 79-62910. 1979. pap. text ed. 12.00 (ISBN 0-8191-0718-2). U Pr of Amer.

Theology & Ethics of Sex. Sakae Kubo. (Horizon Ser.). 1980. pap. 5.95 (ISBN 0-8127-0288-3). Review & Herald.

Theology & Integration: Four Essays in Philosophical Theology. Anders Jeffner. (Acta Universitatis Upsakiebsis). 73p. (Orig.). 1987. pap. 20.00x (ISBN 91-554-2087-7, Pub. by Uppsala Univ Acta Univ Uppsliensis (Uppsala Sweden)). Coronet BKs.

Theology & Literature. T. R. Wright. (Signposts Ser.). 224p. text ed. 49.95 (ISBN 0-631-14848-5); pap. text ed. 24.95 (ISBN 0-631-14849-3). Basil Blackwell.

Theology & Meaning: A Critique of Metatheological Scepticism. Raeburne S. Heimbeck. LC 68-13146. 1969. 27.50x (ISBN 0-8047-0704-9). Stanford U Pr.

Theology & Ministry in Context & Crisis: A South African Perspective. John W. DeGruchy. 182p. (Orig.). 1987. pap. 9.95 (ISBN 0-8028-0290-7). Eerdmans.

Theology & Modern Life. Ed. by Paul Schilpp. LC 70-117852. (Essay Index Reprint Ser). 1940. 19.00 (ISBN 0-8369-1727-8). Ayer Co Pubs.

Theology & Modern Life: Essays in Honor of Harris Franklin Rall. Ed. by Paul A. Schilpp. (Essay Index Reprint Ser.). 307p. 1982. Repr. of 1940 ed. lib. bdg. 18.00 (ISBN 0-686-79705-1). Irvington.

Theology & Modern Literature. Amos N. Wilder. LC 58-11556. pap. 39.30 (ISBN 0-317-10086-6, 2003002). Bks Demand UMI.

Theology & Narrative: A Critical Introduction. Michael Goldberg. 304p. (Orig.). 1982. pap. 11.95 (ISBN 0-687-41503-9). Abingdon.

Theology & Philosophical Inquiry: An Introduction. Vincent Brummer. LC 81-11557. 320p. (Orig.). 1982. pap. 16.95 (ISBN 0-664-24398-3). Westminster John Knox.

Theology & Philosophy. Ingolf U. Dalferth. 192p. 1988. text ed. 39.95x (ISBN 0-631-15354-3). Basil Blackwell.

Theology & Poetry Studies in the Medieval Piyyut. Ed. & tr. by Jacob J. Petuchowski. (Littman Library of Jewish Civilization). 1978. 18.50x (ISBN 0-19-710014-7). Oxford U Pr.

Theology & Political Society. Charles Davis. LC 80-40014. 180p. 1980. 29.95 (ISBN 0-521-22538-8). Cambridge U Pr.

Theology & Politics. Duncan B. Forrester. (Signposts in Theology Ser.). 176p. Date not set. text ed. 50.00 (ISBN 0-631-15282-2); pap. text ed. 17.00 (ISBN 0-631-15283-0). Basil Blackwell.

Theology & Practice. Duncan B. Forrester. 1986. 32.00x (ISBN 0-317-54395-4, Pub. by Hesketh UK). State Mutual Bk.

Theology & Praxis: Epistemological Foundations. Clodovis Boff. Tr. by Robert R. Barr. LC 86-21671. 416p. (Orig., Port.). 1987. pap. 19.95 (ISBN 0-88344-416-X). Orbis Bks.

Theology & Religious Pluralism: The Challenge of Other Religions. Gavin D'Costa. (Signposts in Theology Ser.). 160p. 1986. text ed. 39.95 (ISBN 0-631-14517-6); pap. text ed. 14.95 (ISBN 0-631-14518-4). Basil Blackwell.

Theology & Sanity. rev. ed. F. J. Sheed. LC 78-62340. 1978. pap. 6.95 (ISBN 0-87973-854-5). Our Sunday Visitor.

Theology & Science in Mutual Modification. Harold Nebelsick. 1981. text ed. 19.95x (ISBN 0-19-520273-2). Oxford U Pr.

Theology & Science Today. Parker L. Johnstone. 208p. 1983. 7.95 (ISBN 0-917802-08-X). Theoscience Found.

Theology & Setting of Discipleship in the Gospel of Mark. John R. Donahue. LC 83-60749. (Pere Marquette Lecture Ser.). 1983. 7.95 (ISBN 0-87462-538-6). Marquette.

Theology & Society. Gregory Baum. 312p. 1988. pap. 12.95 (ISBN 0-8091-2931-0). Paulist Pr.

Theology & Sociology: A Reader. Ed. by Robin Gill. 1988. pap. 14.95 (ISBN 0-8091-2978-7). Paulist Pr.

Theology & Technology: Essays in Christian Analysis & Exegesis. Ed. by Carl Mitcham & Jim Grote. LC 84-2183. 534p. (Orig.). 1984. lib. bdg. 38.00 (ISBN 0-8191-3808-8); pap. text ed. 21.75 (ISBN 0-8191-3809-6). U Pr of Amer.

Theology & the Cain Complex. Richard Hughes. LC 81-43698. 148p. (Orig.). 1982. lib. bdg. 26.00 (ISBN 0-8191-2357-9); pap. text ed. 10.00 (ISBN 0-8191-2358-7). U Pr of Amer.

Theology & the Church. Juan L. Segundo. LC 85-51459. (Illus.). 208p. 1987. pap. 8.95 (ISBN 0-06-254704-6, HarpR). Har-Row.

Theology & the Church. Dumitru Staniloae. Tr. by Robert Barringer from Romanian. LC 80-19313. 240p. 1980. pap. 8.95 (ISBN 0-913836-69-9). St Vladimirs.

Theology & the Church: A Response to Cardinal Ratzinger. Juan L. Segundo. LC 85-51459. 175p. 1985. 14.95 (ISBN 0-86683-491-5, HarpR). Har-Row.

Theology & the Dialectics of Otherness: On Reading Bonhoeffer & Adorno. Wayne W. Floyd, Jr. LC 88-5428. 368p. (Orig.). 1988. lib. bdg. 29.75 (ISBN 0-8191-6974-9); pap. text ed. 17.50 (ISBN 0-8191-6975-7). U Pr of Amer.

Theology & the Justification of Faith: Constructing Theories in Systematic Theology. Wentzel Van Huyssteen. 1988. pap. 18.95 (ISBN 0-8028-0366-0). Eerdmans.

Theology & the Kingdom of God. Wolfhart Pannenberg. LC 69-12668. 144p. 1969. pap. 5.95 (ISBN 0-664-24842-X). Westminster John Knox.

Theology & the Philosophy of Science. Wolfhart Pannenberg. Tr. by Francis McDonagh. LC 76-20763. 464p. 1976. 17.50 (ISBN 0-664-21337-5). Westminster John Knox.

Theology & the Problem of Evil. Kenneth Surin. (Signposts in Theology Ser.). 192p. 1986. text ed. 39.95 (ISBN 0-631-14663-6); pap. text ed. 14.95 (ISBN 0-631-14664-4). Basil Blackwell.

Theology & the Scientific Imagination from the Middle Ages to the Seventeenth Century. Amos Funkenstein. LC 85-43281. 368p. 1986. text ed. 47.50x (ISBN 0-691-08408-4). Princeton U Pr.

Theology & the Third World Church. J. Andrew Kirk. LC 83-8560. (Outreach & Identity: Evangelical Theological Monographs). 64p. (Orig.). 1983. pap. 4.95 (ISBN 0-87784-892-0). Inter-Varsity.

Theology Anthropology, Christology see Theological Investigations.

Theology As an Empirical Science. Douglas C. Macintosh. Ed. by Edwin S. Gaustad. LC 79-52601. (Baptist Tradition Ser.). 1980. Repr. of 1919 ed. lib. bdg. 23.00x (ISBN 0-405-12466-X). Ayer Co Pubs.

Theology As Thanksgiving: From Israel's Psalms to the Church's Eucharist. Harvey H. Guthrie, Jr. 1981. 15.95 (ISBN 0-8164-0486-0, HarpR). Har-Row.

Theophile Gautier & the Fantastic. Albert B. Smith. LC 76-56455. (Romance Monographs: No. 23). 1977. 18.00x (ISBN 84-399-6137-5). Romance.

Theophile Gautier's Short Stories. Theophile Gautier. Tr. by George B. Ives. LC 73-122710. (Short Story Index Reprint Ser). 1903. 15.00 (ISBN 0-8369-3543-8). Ayer Co Pubs.

Theophilus North. Thornton Wilder. 352p. 1984. pap. 3.95 (ISBN 0-380-00160-8, 53108-9, Bard). Avon.

Theophilus North. Thornton Wilder. 372p. 1987. pap. 4.95 (ISBN 0-88184-314-8). Carroll & Graf.

Theophrastaceae. (Flora del Paraguay Ser.). Date not set. price not set (ISBN 0-915279-06-1). Miss Botan.

Theophrastan "Character" The History of a Literary Genre. J. W. Smeed. 1985. 47.50x (ISBN 0-19-815805-X). Oxford U Pr.

Theophrastean Studies: On Natural Science, Physics & Metaphysics, Ethics, Religion & Rhetoric, Vol. III. Ed. by William W. Fortenbaugh. 384p. 1987. 49.95 (ISBN 0-88738-171-5). Transaction Bks.

Theophrasts Methode in Seinen Botanischen Schriften. George Wohrle. (Studien Zur Antiken Philosophie: Band 13). 192p. 1985. 37.00x (ISBN 90-6032-257-6, Pub by B R Gruner Netherlands). Benjamins North Am.

Theophrastus & the Greek Physiological Psychology Before Aristotle. G. M. Stratton. (Classical Studies Ser.). (Eng. & Gr.). Repr. of 1917 ed. lib. bdg. 52.00 (ISBN 0-697-00017-6). Irvington.

Theophrastus Bombastus von Hohenheim Called Paracelsus. John M. Stillman. LC 79-8625. (Illus.). viii, 184p. Repr. of 1920 ed. 34.50 (ISBN 0-404-18491-X). AMS Pr.

Theophrastus de Ventis. Theophrastus. Tr. by Victor Coutant & Val L. Eichenlaub. LC 75-17766. 168p. 1975. text ed. 9.95x (ISBN 0-268-01829-4). U of Notre Dame Pr.

Theophrastus of Eresus: On His Life & Work. Ed. by William W. Fortenbaugh. (Studies in Classical Humanities: Vol. II). 350p. 1985. text ed. 49.95x (ISBN 0-88738-009-3). Transaction Bks.

Theophylline & Other Methylxanthines. Ed. by N. Rietbrock et al. (Methods in Clinical Pharmacology Ser.: Vol. 3). 318p. 1982. write for info (Pub. by Vieweg & Sohn). IPS.

Theophysical Glossary. Helene Blavatsky. lib. bdg. 69.95 (ISBN 0-87968-487-9). Krishna Pr.

Theopompus & Fifth-Century Athens. Walter R. Connor. LC 68-14253. (Center for Hellenic Studies Ser.). Repr. of 1968 ed. 62.20 (ISBN 0-8357-9180-7, 2016543). Bks Demand UMI.

Theoreme de Picard-Borel. R. Nevanlinna. LC 73-14779. 179p. 1974. Repr. of 1970 ed. text ed. 13.95 (ISBN 0-8284-0272-8). Chelsea Pub.

Theoremes de Bertini et Applications. Jean-Pierre Jouanolou. (Progress in Mathematics Ser.: Vol. 42). 170p. 1983. text ed. 16.95 (ISBN 0-8176-3164-X). Birkhauser.

Theoremes d'indices Gevrey pour les equations differentielles ordinaires. Jean-Pierre Ramis. LC 83-27157. (Memoirs: No. 296). 96p. 1984. pap. 12.00 (ISBN 0-8218-2296-9, MEMO 296). Am Math.

Theorems & Problems in Functional Analysis. A. A. Kirillov & A. D. Gvishiani. (Problem Books in Mathematics Ser.). (Illus.). 352p. 1982. 51.00 (ISBN 0-387-90638-X). Springer-Verlag.

Theoretic Arithmetic of the Pythagoreans. Thomas Taylor. 248p. (Orig.). 1983. pap. 12.50 (ISBN 0-87728-558-6). Weiser.

Theoretic Arithmetic of the Pythagoreans. Thomas Taylor. pap. 12.50 (ISBN 0-686-43261-4). Philos Res.

Theoretical Acoustics. Philip M. Morse & K. Uno Ingard. 960p. 1987. text ed. 83.00x (ISBN 0-691-08425-4); pap. text ed. 25.00 (ISBN 0-691-02401-4). Princeton U Pr.

Theoretical Acoustics & Numerical Techniques. Ed. by P. Filippi. (CISM International Centre for Mechanical Sciences, Courses & Lectures Ser.: No. 277). xiv, 348p. 1983. pap. 31.00 (ISBN 0-387-81786-7). Springer-Verlag.

Theoretical Advances in Behavior Genetics, No. 2. Ed. by J. R. Royce & L. P. Mos. (NATO Advanced Study Institute Ser.). 722p. 1980. 75.00x (ISBN 90-286-0569-X, Pub. by Sijthoff & Noordhoff). Kluwer Academic.

Theoretical Aerodynamics. L. M. Milne-Thompson. 430p. 1973. pap. text ed. 8.95 (ISBN 0-486-61980-X). Dover.

Theoretical Alchemy. A. Cockren. 1987. pap. 4.95 (ISBN 0-916411-67-2). Alchemical Pr.

Theoretical Analysis of Growth & Cycles. J. J. Paunio. (Illus.). 122p. 1974. 117.75 (ISBN 0-913314-38-2). Am Classical Coll Pr.

Theoretical & Applied Aspects of Eye Movement Research: Proceedings of the European Conference on Eye Movements, 2nd, Nottingham, U. K., Sept. 19-23, 1983. Ed. by A. G. Gale & E. Johnson. (Advances in Psychology Ser.: Vol. 22). 566p. 1984. 102.75 (ISBN 0-444-87557-3, North Holland). Elsevier.

Theoretical & Applied Mechanics, Vol. 28,29,30. Hideo Takami. 500p. 1981. Vol. 28. 112.50 (ISBN 0-86008-264-4, Pub. by U of Tokyo Japan); Vol. 29. 112.50 (ISBN 0-86008-282-2); Vol. 30. 112.50 (ISBN 0-86008-300-4). Columbia U Pr.

Theoretical & Applied Mechanics, Vol. 31. Ed. by Hideo Takami. 500p. 1983. 112.50 (ISBN 0-86008-323-3, Pub. by U of Tokyo Japan). Columbia U Pr.

Theoretical & Applied Mechanics, Vol. 32. Ed. by Kozo Kawata. 537p. 1984. 112.50 (ISBN 0-86008-344-6, Pub. by U of Tokyo Japan). Columbia U Pr.

Theoretical & Applied Mechanics, Vol. 34. Ed. by Kozo Kawata. 530p. 1986. 112.50 (ISBN 0-86008-393-4, Pub. by U of Tokyo Japan). Columbia U Pr.

Theoretical & Applied Mechanics, Vol. 35. Ed. by Jumpei Shioiri. (Theoretical & Applied Mechanics Ser.). 500p. 1987. 127.50 (ISBN 0-86008-410-8, Pub. by U of Tokyp Japan). Columbia U Pr.

Theoretical & Applied Mechanics, Vol. 36. Ed. by Jumpei Shiori. 450p. 1988. 142.50 (ISBN 0-86008-421-3, Pub. by U of Tokyo Japan). Columbia U Pr.

Theoretical & Applied Mechanics: Proceedings. IUTAM International Congress, 14th. Ed. by W. T. Koiter. 492p. 1977. 126.50 (ISBN 0-7204-0549-1, North-Holland). Elsevier.

Theoretical & Applied Mechanics: Proceedings of the Japan National Congress for Applied Mechanics, Vol. 21. Ed. by Tomo-o Ishihara. 550p. 1973. 57.50 (ISBN 0-86008-080-3, Pub. by U of Tokyo Japan). Columbia U Pr.

Theoretical & Applied Mechanics: Proceedings of the Japan National Congress for Applied Mechanics, Vol. 22. Ed. by Toshie Okumura. 528p. 1974. 54.50 (ISBN 0-86008-117-6, Pub. by U of Tokyo Japan). Columbia U Pr.

Theoretical & Applied Mechanics: Proceedings of the Japan National Congress for Applied Mechanics, Vol. 23. Ed. by Toshie Okumura. 560p. 1975. 57.50 (ISBN 0-86008-138-9, Pub. by U of Tokyo Japan). Columbia U Pr.

Theoretical & Applied Mechanics: Proceedings of the Japan National Congress for Applied Mechanics, Vol. 25. Ed. by Yoshikatsu Tsuboi. 727p. 1977. 97.50 (ISBN 0-86008-181-8, Pub. by U of Tokyo Japan). Columbia U Pr.

Theoretical & Applied Mechanics: Proceedings of the Japan National Congress for Applied Mechanics, Vol. 26. Ed. by Yoshiyuki Yamamoto. 579p. 1978. 97.50 (ISBN 0-86008-200-8, Pub. by U of Tokyo Japan). Columbia U Pr.

Theoretical & Applied Mechanics: Proceedings of the Japan National Congress for Applied Mechanics, Vol. 27. Ed. by Yoshiyuki Yamamoto. 579p. 1979. 112.50 (ISBN 0-86008-245-8, Pub. by U of Tokyo Japan). Columbia U Pr.

Theoretical & Applied Mechanics: Proceedings of the 15th International Congress, Toronto, August, 1980. Ed. by F. P. Rimrott & B. Tabarrok. 458p. 1981. 126.50 (ISBN 0-444-85411-8, North-Holland). Elsevier.

Theoretical & Applied Mechanics: Proceedings of 16th International Congress, August, 1984, Lingby, Denmark. Niordson & Olhoff. 1985. 118.50 (ISBN 0-444-87707-X, North-Holland). Elsevier.

Theoretical & Clinical Aspects of Allergic Diseases. Ed. by H. Bostrom & N. Ljungstedt. (Illus.). 302p. 1983. text ed. 49.50x (ISBN 91-22-00595-1, Pub. by Almqvist & Wiksell). Coronet Bks.

Theoretical & Computational Plasma Physics. (Proceedings Ser.). (Illus.). 516p. 1978. pap. 58.50 (ISBN 92-0-130078-6, ISP474, IAEA). UNIPUB.

Theoretical & Computational Radiation Hydrodynamics: Vol. 1, Radiation-Hydrodynamics Theoretical Considerations. G. C. Pomraning et al. LC 70-135085. 228p. 1969. 20.00 (ISBN 0-403-04529-0). Scholarly.

Theoretical & Conceptual Bases of Instructional Design. Rita Richey. 228p. 1986. 33.50 (ISBN 0-89397-248-7). Nichols Pub.

Theoretical & Empirical Advances in Community Mental Health. Ed. by Edward M. Bennett & Bruce Tefft. LC 85-21371. (Studies in Health & Human Services: Vol. 5). 280p. 1985. lib. bdg. 59.95x (ISBN 0-88946-131-7). E Mellen.

Theoretical & Empirical Aspects of Corporate Taxation. OECD. 76p. 1974. 3.75x (ISBN 92-64-11237-5). OECD.

Theoretical & Empirical Foundations of Rational-Emitive Therapy. Albert Ellis & John M. Whiteley. 1979. 8.95 (ISBN 1-55620-031-5, 71002C). Am Assn Coun Dev.

Theoretical & Experimental Analysis of Members of Earthquake Proof Frame Panel Buildings. M. A. Mardzhanishvili. 1987. 28.50x (ISBN 0-8364-2121-3, Pub. by Oxford IBH). South Asia Bks.

Theoretical & Experimental Analysis of Members of Earthquake-Proof Frame Panel Buildings. M. Mardzhanishvilli & L. Mardzhanishvilli. Tr. by K. Dhillon from Rus. 180p. 1986. text ed. 41.00 (ISBN 90-6191-472-8, Pub. by A A Balkema). Brookfield Pub Co.

Theoretical & Experimental Aspects of Valence Fluctuations & Heavy Fermions. Ed. by L. C. Gupta & S. K. Malik. LC 87-25816. 776p. 1987. 125.00x (ISBN 0-306-42763-X, Plenum Pr). Plenum Pub.

Theoretical & Experimental Base for Teaching Reading. Richard L. Venezky. (Janua Linguarum, Series Didactica: No. 9). (Illus.). 48p. 1976. pap. text ed. 6.80x (ISBN 0-686-22608-9). Mouton.

Theoretical & Experimental Bases of the Behaviour Therapies. Ed. by M. Philip Feldman & Anne Broadhurst. LC 75-20000. pap. 118.80 (ISBN 0-317-07802-X, 2020430). Bks Demand UMI.

Theoretical & Experimental Biophysics. Ed. by Arthur Cole. LC 66-29484. Vol. 1. pap. 102.30 (2027124); Vol. 2. pap. 89.30. Bks Demand UMI.

Theoretical & Experimental Investigations of Hadronic Few-Body Systems. Ed. by C. Ciofi degli Atti et al. (Few-Body Systems, Supplement 1). (Illus.). 640p. 1986. 84.70 (ISBN 0-387-81983-5). Springer-Verlag.

Theoretical & Mathematical Physics: A Collection of Survey Articles, Part 3, on the 50th Anniversary of the Institute. Vladimirov et al. (STEKLO Ser.: Vol. 175). 270p. Date not set. pap. text ed. price not set. Am Math.

Theoretical & Operational Aspects of Intramural Sports. Ed. by Thomas P. Sattler et al. 368p. 1978. pap. text ed. 17.95x (ISBN 0-918438-44-6, PSAT0044). Leisure Pr.

Theoretical & Philosophical Aspects of Psychical Research. Alan J. Mayne. 15.00x (ISBN 0-317-43552-3, Pub. by Soc of Metaphysicians). State Mutual Bk.

Theoretical & Practical Aspects of Allergic Disorders: Proceedings of the Collegium Internationale Allergologicum, 9th, London, Sept. 1972. Collegium Internationale Allergologicum Staff. Ed. by D. Parker et al. (International Archives of Allergy & Applied Immunology: Vol. 45, Nos. 1-2). (Illus.). 1973. pap. 52.00 (ISBN 3-8055-1605-3). S Karger.

Theoretical & Practical Aspects of Uranium Geology. Royal Society of London et al. Ed. by S. H. Bowie & W. S. Fyfe. (Illus.). 1979. lib. bdg. 46.00x (ISBN 0-85403-106-5, Pub. by Royal Soc London). Scholium Intl.

Theoretical Anthropology. David Bidney. LC 53-12098. 506p. 1953. 48.00x (ISBN 0-231-01910-6). Columbia U Pr.

Theoretical Approach see Explaining the Vote: Presidential Choices in the Nation & the States, 1968.

Theoretical Approach to Inorganic Chemistry. A. F. Williams. (Illus.). 1979. 60.00 (ISBN 0-387-09073-8). Springer-Verlag.

Theoretical Approach to Preselection of Carcinogens & Chemical Carcinogenesis. Veljko Veljkovic. 124p. 1981. 64.00 (ISBN 0-677-05490-4). Gordon & Breach.

Theoretical Approaches. (Structure & Bonding Ser.: Vol. 68). 190p. 1987. 77.50 (ISBN 0-387-18058-3). Springer-Verlag.

Theoretical Approaches in Dance-Movement Therapy, Vol. II. Penny L. Bernstein. 224p. 1984. pap. text ed. 20.95 (ISBN 0-8403-3463-X). Kendall Hunt.

Theoretical Approaches in Neurobiology. Ed. by Werner E. Reichardt & Tomaso Poggio. (Illus.). 208p. 1980. text ed. 35.00x (ISBN 0-262-18100-2). MIT Pr.

Theoretical Approaches to Complex Systems: Proceedings, Tuebingen, Germany, June 11-12, 1977. Ed. by R. Heim & G. Palm. (Lecture Notes in Biomathematics: Vol. 21). 1978. pap. 16.00 (ISBN 0-387-08757-5). Springer-Verlag.

Theoretical Approaches to Personality. Barry D. Smith & Harold J. Vetter. (Illus.). 416p. 1982. write for info (ISBN 0-13-913491-3). P-H.

Theoretical Approaches to Turbulence. Ed. by D. L. Dwoyer et al. LC 85-14765. (Applied Mathematical Sciences Ser.: Vol. 58). (Illus.). xii, 373p. 1985. pap. 39.50 (ISBN 0-387-96191-7). Springer-Verlag.

Theoretical Aspects & the New Developments in Magneto-Optics. Ed. by J. T. Devreese. LC 80-18871. (NATO ASI Series B, Physics: Vol. 60). 636p. 1981. 95.00x (ISBN 0-306-40555-5, Plenum Pr). Plenum Pub.

Theoretical Aspects of Band Structures & Electronic Properties of Psuedo-One-Dimensional Solids. Ed. by Hiroshi Kamimura. 1985. lib. bdg. 54.00 (ISBN 90-277-1927-6, Pub. by Reidel Holland). Kluwer Academic.

Theoretical Aspects of International Relations. Ed. by William T. Fox. (International Studies Ser). 1959. 9.95x (ISBN 0-268-00273-8). U of Notre Dame Pr.

Theoretical Aspects of Mainly Low Dimensional Magnetic Systems. Hans C. Fogedby. (Lecture Notes in Physics Ser.: Vol. 131). 163p. 1980. pap. 15.00 (ISBN 0-387-10238-8). Springer Verlag.

Theoretical Aspects of Passivization in the Framework of Applicative Grammar. Jean-Pierre Descles et al. LC 85-26794. (Pragmatics & Beyond Ser.: VI-1). viii, 115p. (Orig.). 1986. pap. 28.00x (ISBN 0-915027-67-4). Benjamins North Am.

Theoretical Aspects of Reasoning about Knowledge: Proceedings of the 1986 Conference. Ed. by Joseph Y. Halpern. LC 86-2755. (Illus.). 407p. (Orig.). 1986. 22.95 (ISBN 0-934613-04-4). Morgan Kaufmann.

Theoretical Aspects of the Design of Fund-Supported Adjustment Programs: A Study by the Research Department of the IMF. (Occasional Papers: No. 55). v, 51p. 1987. pap. 7.50 (ISBN 0-939934-99-X). Intl Monetary.

Theoretical Aspects of the Design of Fund-Supported Adjustment Programs: A Study by the Research Department of the International Monetary Fund. (International Monetary Fund Occasional Paper: No. 55). 51p. 1987. pap. text ed. 7.50 (ISBN 0-317-68040-4, IMF88, Pub. by Internat Monet Fund). UNIPUB.

Theoretical Aspects of the Localized Corrosion of Metals. Jaromir Tousek Institute of Physical Metallurgy Czechoslovakian Academy of Sciences, Brno, CSSR. (Materials Science Surveys Ser.: Vol. 3). 180p. 1985. 32.00 (ISBN 0-87849-526-6). Trans Tech.

Theoretical Aspects of the Localized Corrosion of Metals. J. Tousek. 180p. 1986. text ed. 42.00x (ISBN 0-317-65492-6). Trans Tech.

Theoretical Basis of the Living System. Jorge Macedo. LC 75-17399. (Illus.). 84p. 1979. 10.50 (ISBN 0-87527-158-8). Fireside Bks.

Theoretical Biology. E. S. Bauer. 294p. 1983. text ed. 22.50x (ISBN 963-05-3014-7, Pub. by Akademiai Kiado Hungary). Humanities.

Theoretical Biology. E. S. Bauer. 296p. 1982. 89.00x (Pub. by Collets (UK)). State Mutual Bk.

Theoretical Biology & Complexity. Ed. by Robert Rosen. 1985. 62.00 (ISBN 0-12-597280-6). Acad Pr.

Theoretical Chemistry, Vols. 1-3. Ed. by R. N. Dixon & C. Thomson. LC 73-92911. Vol. 1 1974. 1973 literature 29.00 (ISBN 0-85186-754-5); Vol. 2 1975. 32.00 (ISBN 0-85186-764-2); Vol. 3 1978. 34.00 (ISBN 0-85186-774-X). Am Chemical.

Theoretical Chemistry: Advances & Perspectives, Vol. 5. Ed. by A. R. Katritzky & A. J. Boulton. LC 75-21963. 1980. 71.00 (ISBN 0-12-681905-X). Acad Pr.

Theoretical Chemistry: Advances & Perspectives, Vol. 4: Periodicities in Chemistry & Biology. Ed. by Henry Eyring & Douglas Henderson. 1978. 85.50 (ISBN 0-12-681904-1). Acad Pr.

Theoretical Chemistry of Biological Systems. Ed. by G. Naray-Szabo. (Studies in Physical & Theoretical Chemistry: No. 41). 504p. 1986. 155.25 (ISBN 0-444-42597-7). Elsevier.

Theoretical Chemistry: Theory of Scattering-Papers in Honor of Henry Eyring, Vol. 6a. Ed. by Douglas Henderson. (Serial Publication). 1981. 70.50 (ISBN 0-12-681906-8). Acad Pr.

Theoretical Chemistry: Theory of Scattering: Papers in Honor of Henry Eyring, Vol. 6B. Ed. by Douglas Henderson. (Serial Publications). 1981. 69.50 (ISBN 0-12-681907-6). Acad Pr.

Theoretical Climatology. Ghil. (Nonequilibrium Problems in the Physical Sciences & Biology Ser.). 1986. write for info. (ISBN 0-471-09748-9). Wiley.

Theoretical Computations of Fuel Used & the Exhaust Produced in Drying Aggregates. (Information Series). 86p. 10.00 (ISBN 0-317-34980-5, 61). Natl Asphalt Pavement.

Theoretical Computer Science Fifth Conference. Ed. by P. Deussen. (Lecture Notes in Computer Science Ser.: Vol. 104). 261p. 1981. pap. 19.00 (ISBN 0-387-10576-X). Springer-Verlag.

Theoretical Computer Science: GI Conference, 4th Conference, Aachen, March 26-28, 1979. Ed. by K. Weihrauch. (Lecture Notes in Computer Science: Vol. 67). 1979. pap. 20.00 (ISBN 0-387-09118-1). Springer-Verlag.

Theoretical Computer Science: Proceedings, Dortmund, FRG, 1983. Ed. by A. B. Cremers & H. P. Kriegel. (Lecture Notes in Computer Science Ser.: Vol. 145). 367p. 1983. pap. 20.00 (ISBN 0-387-11973-6). Springer-Verlag.

Theoretical Computer Science: Proceedings of the GI Conference on Theoretical Computer Science, 3rd, Darmstadt, March 1977. Ed. by H. Tzschach & K. G. Waldshchimdt. (Lecture Notes in Computer Science: Vol. 48). 1977. pap. 25.00 (ISBN 3-540-08138-0). Springer-Verlag.

Theoretical Concepts. R. Tuomela. LC 73-80989. (Library of Exact Philosophy: Vol. 10). xiv, 254p. 1973. 46.00 (ISBN 0-387-81119-2). Springer-Verlag.

Theoretical Concepts & Hypothetico-Inductive Inference. I. Niiniluoto & R. Tuomela. LC 73-83567. (Synthese Library: No. 53). 1973. lib. bdg. 39.50 (ISBN 90-277-0343-4, Pub. by Reidel Holland). Kluwer Academic.

Theoretical Concepts in Physics: An Alternative View of Theoretical Reasoning in Physics. Malcolm S. Longair. 320p. 1984. pap. 19.95 (ISBN 0-521-27553-9). Cambridge U Pr.

Theoretical Controversy & Social Significance. G. C. Harcourt. (Edward Shann Memorial Lecture in Economics Ser.). 29p. 1977. pap. 3.00x (ISBN 0-85564-117-7, Pub. by U of W Austral Pr). Intl Spec Bk.

Theoretical Cosmology. A. K. Raychauduri. (Oxford Studies in Physics). (Illus.). 1979. 29.95x (ISBN 0-19-851462-X). Oxford U Pr.

Theoretical Criminology. 3rd ed. George B. Vold & Thomas J. Bernard. 1985. 19.95x (ISBN 0-19-503616-6). Oxford U Pr.

Theoretical Dimensions of Henry James. John C. Rowe. LC 84-40158. (Wisconsin Project on American Writers Ser.: No. 2). 304p. 1984. 21.50x (ISBN 0-299-09970-9); pap. 10.95x (ISBN 0-299-09974-1). U of Wis Pr.

Theorie Analytique de le Societe dans l'Oeuvre de Talcott Parsons Societe, Mouvements Sociaux et Ideologies. Francois Chazel. (Premiere Serie Etudes: No. 16). 1974. pap. 14.00x (ISBN 90-2797-306-7). Mouton.

Theorie De la Connaissance et Philosophie De la Parole Dans le Brahmanisme Classique. Madeleine Biardeau. (Le Monde D'outre-Mer Passe et Present, Etudes: No. 23). 1963. pap. 34.80x (ISBN 90-2796-178-6). Mouton.

Theorie de la Deuxieme Microlocalisation dans le Domaine Complex. Yves Laurent. (Progress in Mathematics Ser.: No. 53). 311p. 1985. text ed. 39.95x (ISBN 0-8176-3287-5). Birkhauser.

Theorie de la valeur. 2nd ed. Christian Cornelissen. LC 77-147839. (Research & Source Works Ser.: No. 649). 1971. Repr. of 1913 ed. 29.50 (ISBN 0-8337-0681-0). B Franklin.

Theorie De L'elasticite Des Corps Solides. Alfred Clebsch. 1883. 60.00 (ISBN 0-384-09285-3). Johnson Repr.

Theorie der Congruenzen. 2nd ed. Pafnuti L. Chebyshev. LC 71-113123. xvii, 366p. (Ger.). 1972. text ed. 17.50 (ISBN 0-8284-0254-X). Chelsea Pub.

Theorie der Funktionen Mehrerer Komplexer Veranderlicher. A. Cazacu. (Mathematische Reihe Ser.: No. 51). 360p. (Ger.). 1975. 74.95x (ISBN 0-8176-0770-6). Birkhauser.

Theorie der Geometrishen Konstruktionen. L. Bierberbach. (Mathematische Rehihe Ser.: No. 13). (Illus.). 162p. (Ger.). 1952. 23.95x (ISBN 0-8176-0030-2). Birkhauser.

Theorie der Gruppen Von Endlicher Ordnung. A. Speiser. (MA Ser.: No. 22). 272p. (Ger.). 1980. 38.95x (ISBN 0-8176-1151-7). Birkhauser.

Theorie der Konvexen Koerper. T. Bonnesen & W. Fenchel. LC 49-29452. (Ger). 6.95 (ISBN 0-8284-0054-7). Chelsea Pub.

Theorie der Poesie, 2 vols. Christian H. Schmid. Repr. of 1767 ed. Set. 175.00 (ISBN 0-384-54010-4). Johnson Repr.

Theorie der Theologie: Enzyklopaedie als Methodenlehre. Friedrich Mildenberger. 164p. (Ger.). 1972. 19.95 (ISBN 3-7668-0384-0, M-7094). French & Eur.

Theorie des Fonctions Algebriques de Deux Variables Independantes, 2 vols. in 1. Emile Picard & G. Simart. LC 67-31156. (Fr). 1971. 29.50 (ISBN 0-8284-0248-5). Chelsea Pub.

Theorie Des Fonctions Algebriques et Leurs Integrales, Vol. 1. 3rd ed. Paul Appell et al. LC 72-114210. 1977. text ed. 29.50 (ISBN 0-8284-0285-X). Chelsea Pub.

Theorie Des Fonctions Algebriques et Leurs Integrales: Volume II. Paul Appell et al. LC 72-114210. text ed. 29.50 (ISBN 0-8284-0299-X). Chelsea Pub.

Theorie Des Graphes et Structures Sociales. Claude Flament. (Mathematiques et Sciences De L'homme: No. 2). 1968. pap. 10.80x (ISBN 90-2796-312-6). Mouton.

Theorie des Kommunikativen Handelns see Theory of Communicative Action, Vol. I: Reason & the Rationalization of Society.

Theorie Des Operations Lineaires. 2nd ed. Stefan Banach. LC 63-21849. (Fr). 12.95 (ISBN 0-8284-0110-1). Chelsea Pub.

Theorie des Semi-Groupes de Markov. Jacques Neveu. LC 58-9788. (California University Publications in Statistics Ser.: Vol. 2 No. 14). pap. 20.00 (ISBN 0-317-08330-9, 2021185). Bks Demand UMI.

Theorie Economique Du Systeme Feodal: Pour un Modele De L'economie Polonaise 16e-18e Siecles. Witold Kula. (Civilisations et Societes: No. 15). 1970. pap. 9.60 (ISBN 90-2796-284-7). Mouton.

Theorie et Politique see Saint-Simonisme et Pari pour l'Industrie, XIXe et XXe Siecles.

Theorie Generale Des Surfaces, 4 Vols. 2nd ed. Gaston Darboux. LC 67-16997. (Fr). 1968. Set. 95.00 (ISBN 0-8284-0216-7). Chelsea Pub.

Theorie, la Pratique et L'art En Photographie Avec le Procede Au Gelatino Bromure D'argent. Frederic Dillaye. Ed. by Peter C. Bunnell & Robert A. Sobieszek. LC 76-23053. (Sources of Modern Photography Ser.). (Illus., Fr.). 1979. Repr. of 1891 ed. lib. bdg. 44.00x (ISBN 0-405-09618-6). Ayer Co Pubs.

Theorie Leibnizienne de la Sustance. Jacques Jalabert. Ed. by R. C. Sleigh, Jr. LC 84-48420. (Philosophy of Lebniz Ser.). 282p. 1985. lib. bdg. 45.00 (ISBN 0-8240-6533-6). Garland Pub.

Theorie Marxienne de L'Evolution Sociale: Livres et Articles. Bibliographie Marxologique Historie et Societe 1893-1918 see Cahiers de l'Institut de Science Economique Appliquee.

Theorie Nouvelle d'Economie Sociale et Politique, Ou Etudes Sur L'organization Des Societes. Constantin Pecqueur. 1971. Repr. of 1842 ed. lib. bdg. 46.50 (ISBN 0-8337-2703-6). B Franklin.

Theorie Probabiliste du Controle des Diffusions. Jean-Michel Bismut. LC 75-41602. (Memoirs: No. 167). 130p. 1976. pap. 16.00 (ISBN 0-8218-1867-8, MEMO-167). Am Math.

Theorie Quantique De la Liaison Chimique see Quantum Theory of the Chemical Bond.

Theorie und Geschichte Des Photographischen Objecktivs. Moritz Von Rohr. Ed. by Peter C. Bunnell & Robert A. Sobieszek. LC 78-19592. (Sources of Modern Photography Ser.). (Ger.). 1979. Repr. of 1899 ed. lib. bdg. 32.50x (ISBN 0-405-09869-3). Ayer Co Pubs.

Theorie und Praxis der Linearen Integralgleichungen: Vol. I. S. Fenyo & H. Stolle. (LMW - MA Ser.: 74). 250p. (Ger.). 1982. text ed. 50.95x (ISBN 0-8176-1164-9). Birkhauser.

Theorie und Praxis der Linearen Integralgleichungen: Vol. 2. S. Fenyo & H. Stolle. 304p. (Ger.). 1982. text ed. 44.95x (ISBN 0-8176-1165-7). Birkhauser.

Theorie und Praxis der Linearen Integralaleichungen 4. Stefan Fenyo & Hans W. Stolle. 370p. (Ger.). 1984. text ed. 44.95 (ISBN 3-7643-1167-3). Birkhauser.

Theorie Zufaelliger Prozesse. A. Wentzell. (Mathematische Reihe: No. 65). 264p. (Ger.). 1979. 50.95 (ISBN 0-8176-1021-9). Birkhauser.

Theories & Applications of Counseling: Systems & Techniques of Counseling & Psychotherapy. Donald J. Tosi & Steven W. Leclair. (Illus.). 380p. 1987. 39.50x (ISBN 0-398-05345-6). C C Thomas.

Theories & Approaches to International Politics. 3rd ed. Patrick M Morgan. LC 79-66439. 304p. 1981. text ed. 24.95 (ISBN 0-686-68062-6); pap. 9.95 (ISBN 0-87855-791-1). Transaction Bks.

Theories & Approaches to International Politics. 4th ed. Patrick M. Morgan. 314p. (Orig.). 1986. 24.95 (ISBN 0-88738-093-X); pap. text ed. 16.95x (ISBN 0-88738-630-X). Transaction Bks.

Theories & Concepts in Comparative Industrial Relations. Intro. by Jack Barbash. 264p. 1988. text ed. 29.95x (ISBN 0-87249-580-9). U of SC Pr.

Theories & Criticisms of Sir Henry Maine. Morgan O. Evans. viii, 93p. 1981. Repr. of 1896 ed. lib. bdg. 18.50x (ISBN 0-8377-0540-1). Rothman.

Theories & Methods in Rural Community Studies. Ed. by H. Mendras & I. Mihailescu. LC 82-16508. (Vienna Centre Ser.: No. 9). 304p. 1982. 57.00 (ISBN 0-08-025813-1, PBL). Pergamon.

Theories & Methods of Group Counseling in the Schools. 2nd ed. George M. Gazda (Illus.). 384p. 1976. 27.25 (ISBN 0-398-03547-4). C C Thomas.

Theories & Models in Cellular Transformation. Ed. by L. Santi & Luciano Zardi. 1985. 35.00 (ISBN 0-12-619080-1). Acad Pr.

Theories & Observation in Science. Ed. by Richard E. Grandy. vii, 184p. 1980. lib. bdg. 27.00 (ISBN 0-917930-39-8); pap. 9.40 (ISBN 0-917930-19-3). Ridgeview.

Theories & Strategies in Counseling & Psychotherapy. Burl E. Gilliland et al. (Illus.). 384p. 1984. text ed. write for info. (ISBN 0-13-913574-X). P-H.

Theories & Systems of Psychology. 3rd ed. Robert W. Lundin. LC 84-81195. 400p. 1985. text ed. 25.50 (ISBN 0-669-06744-X); test item file 2.00 (ISBN 0-669-09444-7). Heath.

Theories & Things. W. V. Quine. LC 81-4517. 216p. 1981. text ed. 16.00x (ISBN 0-674-87925-2, Belknap Pr). Harvard U Pr.

Theories & Things. W. V. Quine. 232p. 1986. pap. text ed. 7.95x (ISBN 0-674-87926-0, Belknap Pr). Harvard U Pr.

Theories at Work: On the Structure & Functioning of Theories in Science, in Particular During the Copernican Revolution. Marinus Dirk Stafleu. (Christian Studies Today). 310p. (Orig.). 1987. lib. bdg. 28.75 (ISBN 0-8191-6570-0, Pub. by Inst Christ Stud); pap. text ed. 16.50 (ISBN 0-8191-6571-9). U Pr of Amer.

Theories de Boisguilbert et Leur Place dans l'Histoire des Doctrines Economiques. Albert Talbot. LC 76-143660. (Research & Reference Ser: No. 889). 156p. (Selected Essays in History, Economics, & Social Science, No. 322). 1972. Repr. of 1903 ed. lib. bdg. 21.00 (ISBN 0-8337-3467-9). B Franklin.

Theories des Mehrfach-Schusses. H Braendli. (Illus.). 200p. (Ger.). 1950. 29.95x (ISBN 0-8176-0042-6). Birkhauser.

Theories Economiques et Sociales De Thorstein Veblen: Contribution a L'histoire Des Doctrines Economiques. William Jaffe. LC 78-153147. (Research & Source Works Ser.: No. 147). (Illus.). 1971. lib. bdg. 18.50 (ISBN 0-8337-1819-3). B Franklin.

Theories En Psychologie Sociale. Morton Deutsch & Robert M. Krauss. (Oeuvre Sociologique: No. 3). (Illus.). 1972. pap. 12.80x (ISBN 90-2797-136-6). Mouton.

Theories for Admissible Sets: A Unifying Approach to Proof Theory. Gerhard Jager. (Studies in Proof Theory: Lecture Notes: Vol. 2). 176p. 1986. pap. text ed. 35.00 (ISBN 88-7088-149-0, Pub. by Bibliopolis Italy). Humanities.

Theories for Social Work with Groups. Robert W. Roberts & Helen Northen. LC 76-4967. 400p. 1976. 24.00x (ISBN 0-231-03885-2). Columbia U Pr.

Theories in Intercultural Communication. Ed. by Young Y. Kim & William B. Gudykunst. (International & Intercultural Communication Annual Ser.: Vol. 12). 320p. 1988. text ed. 35.00 (ISBN 0-8039-3149-2); pap. text ed. 16.95 (ISBN 0-8039-3150-6). Sage.

Theories in Social Psychology. Morton Deutsch & Robert M. Krauss. LC 65-25230. (Basic Topics in Psychology Ser). 1965. text ed. 13.95x (ISBN 0-465-08435-4). Basic.

Theories, Models & Simulations in International Relations: Essays & Research in Honor of Harold Guetzkow. Ed. by Michael D. Ward. (Special Studies Ser.). 1985. 49.00x (ISBN 0-8133-0026-6). Westview.

Theories of Action in Conrad. Francis A. Hubbard. Ed. by A. Walton Litz. LC 84-8769. (Studies in Modern Literature: No. 40). 126p. 1984. 27.95 (ISBN 0-8357-1588-4). UMI Res Pr.

Theories of Adolescence. 4th ed. Rolf E. Muuss. 336p. 1982. pap. text ed. 9.00 (ISBN 0-394-32424-2, RanC). Random.

Theories of Adolescence. 5th ed. Rolf E. Muuss. 512p. 1988. pap. text ed. 18.50 (ISBN 0-394-37517-3, RanC). Random.

Theories of Adolescence. 2nd ed. Rolfe Muuss. 19.00 (ISBN 0-8446-2635-X). Peter Smith.

Theories of Americanization: A Critical Study. Isaac B. Berkson. LC 77-87743. (American Education: Its Men, Institutions & Ideas, Ser. 1). 1969. Repr. of 1920 ed. 15.00 (ISBN 0-405-01387-6). Ayer Co Pubs.

Theories of Americanization: A Critical Study, with Special Reference to the Jewish Group. Isaac B. Berkson. LC 78-176558. (Columbia University. Teachers College. Contributions to Education: No. 109). Repr. of 1920 ed. 22.50 (ISBN 0-404-55109-2). AMS Pr.

Theories of Animal Memory: Animal Cognition. Ed. by Donald F. Kendrick et al. (Comparitive Cognition & Neuroscience Bever-Alton Roeblatt). 224p. 1986. text ed. 32.50 (ISBN 0-89859-636-X); pap. 17.95 (ISBN 0-89859-697-1). L Erlbaum Assocs.

Theories of Art: From Plato to Winckelman. Moshe Barasch. 352p. 1985. 47.50x (ISBN 0-8147-1060-3); pap. 17.50 (ISBN 0-8147-1061-1). NYU Pr.

Theories of Authorship. Ed. by John Caughie. (B. F. I. Readers in Film Studies). (Illus.). 320p. 1981. 29.95x (ISBN 0-7100-0649-7); pap. 14.95x (ISBN 0-7100-0650-0). Routledge Chapman & Hall.

Theories of Bibliographic Education: Designs for Teaching. Ed. by Cerise Oberman & Katina Strauch. 233p. 1982. 44.95 (ISBN 0-8352-1506-7). Bowker.

Theories of Biological Pattern Formation: Proceedings. Ed. by S. Brenner & J. D. Murray. (Royal Society of London). (Illus.). 191p. 1982. Repr. text ed. 62.00x (ISBN 0-85403-176-6, Pub. by Royal Soc London). Scholium Intl.

Theories of Business Behavior. Joseph W. McGuire. LC 82-15550. xix, 268p. 1982. Repr. of 1964 ed. lib. bdg. 38.50x (ISBN 0-313-23567-8, MCTH). Greenwood.

Theories of Carcinogenesis: Facts, Fashion or Fiction? Olav H. Iversen. 327p. 1987. 59.95 (ISBN 0-89116-579-7). Hemisphere Pub.

Theories of Career Development. 3rd ed. Samuel H. Osipow. (Illus.). 320p. 1983. write for info. (ISBN 0-13-913640-1). P-H.

Theories of Charges: A Study of Finitely Additive Measures. Bhaskara K. Rao. (Pure & Applied Mathmatics Ser.). 1983. 69.00 (ISBN 0-12-095780-9). Acad Pr.

Theories of Chemical Reaction Rates. Keith J. Laidler. LC 78-26387. 244p. 1979. Repr. of 1969 ed. text ed. 21.50 (ISBN 0-88275-819-5). Krieger.

Theories of Child Development. 2nd ed. Alfred L. Baldwin. LC 80-24517. 582p. 1980. text ed. write for info. (ISBN 0-471-04583-7). Wiley.

Theories of Chromatic & Enharmonic Music in Late Sixteenth Century Italy. Karol Berger. LC 79-24734. (Studies in Musicology: No. 10). pap. 48.70 (2070037). Bks Demand UMI.

Theories of Claude Debussy. Leon Vallas. LC 78-66922. (Encore Music Editions Ser.). 1986. Repr. of 1929 ed. 19.95 (ISBN 0-88355-766-5). Hyperion Conn.

Theories of Coalition Formation. James P. Kahan & Amnon Rapoport. (Basic Studies in Human Behavior). 384p. 1984. text ed. 39.95x (ISBN 0-89859-298-4). L Erlbaum Assocs.

Theories of Cognitive Development: Implications for the Mentally Retarded. Robert M. Allen et al. LC 72-92899. (Illus.). 1973. 10.95x (ISBN 0-87024-249-0). U of Miami Pr.

Theories of Comparative Economic Growth. Kwang Choi. (Illus.). 298p. 1983. pap. text ed. 13.95x (ISBN 0-8138-1771-4). Iowa St U Pr.

Theories of Comparative Politics: The Search for a Paradigm. Ronald H. Chilcote. LC 80-19762. 480p. (Orig.). 1981. pap. 19.95x (ISBN 0-89158-971-6). Westview.

Theories of Competition. L. G. Telser. 397p. 1988. 43.00 (ISBN 0-444-01248-6, North Holland). Elsevier.

Theories of Computational Complexity. C. Claude. (Annals of Discrete Mathematics Ser.: No. 35). 488p. 1988. 105.25 (ISBN 0-444-70356-X, North-Holland). Elsevier.

Theories of Concepts: A History of the Major Philosophical Tradition. Morris Weltz. 344p. 1988. pap. text ed. 47.50 (ISBN 0-415-00180-3, Pub. by Kegan Paul). Routledge Chapman & Hall.

Theories of Contemporary Art. Richard Hertz. (Illus.). 320p. 1985. pap. text ed. 23.00 (ISBN 0-13-913666-5). P-H.

Theories of Convention in Contemporary American Criticism. Robert M. Browne. 120p. 1986. Repr. of 1955 ed. lib. bdg. 30.00 (ISBN 0-8492-9623-4). R West.

Theories of Convention in Contemporary American Criticism. Robert M. Browne. 120p. 1987. Repr. of 1956 ed. lib. bdg. 35.00 (ISBN 0-89987-998-5). Darby Bks.

Theories of Counseling. 3rd. ed. Herbert M. Burks, Jr. & Buford Stefflre. (Illus.). 1979. text ed. 39.95 (ISBN 0-07-009061-0). McGraw.

Theories of Counseling & Psychotherapy. 4th ed. C. H. Patterson. 608p. 1985. pap. text ed. 35.95 scp (ISBN 0-06-045053-3, HarpC). Har-Row.

Theories of Criticism: Essays in Literature & Art. 1985. write for info. Lib Congress.

Theories of Delinquency: An Examination of the Explanations of Delinquent Behavior. Donald J. Shoemaker. 1984. pap. 9.95x (ISBN 0-19-503391-4). Oxford U Pr.

Theories of Development. 2nd ed. William C. Crain. (Illus.). 320p. 1985. pap. text ed. 27.00 (ISBN 0-13-913617-7). P-H.

Theories of Development. P. W. Preston. (International Library of Sociology). 300p. 1982. 27.95x (ISBN 0-7100-9055-2). Routledge Chapman & Hall.

Theories of Development & Underdevelopment. Ronald H. Chilcote. 135p. 1984. lib. bdg. 33.00 (ISBN 0-8133-0036-3); pap. text ed. 14.95 (ISBN 0-8133-0037-1). Westview.

Theories of Development: Mode of Production or Dependency? Ed. by Ronald H. Chilcote & Dale L. Johnson. (Class, State & Development Ser.: Vol. 2). (Illus.). 272p. 1983. 29.95 (ISBN 0-8039-1925-5); pap. 14.00 (ISBN 0-8039-1926-3). Sage.

Theories of Developmental Psychology. Patricia H. Miller. LC 82-17482. (Illus.). 350p. 1983. text ed. 26.95 (ISBN 0-7167-1431-0); pap. text ed. 15.95 (ISBN 0-7167-1432-9). W H Freeman.

Theories of Deviance. 3rd, rev. ed. Ed. by Stuart H. Traub & Craig B. Little. LC 84-61603. 400p. 1985. pap. text ed. 18.50 (ISBN 0-87581-309-7). Peacock Pubs.

Theories of Discourse: An Introduction. Diane Macdonell. 160p. 1986. text ed. 34.95x (ISBN 0-631-14838-8); pap. text ed. 12.95x (ISBN 0-631-14839-6). Basil Blackwell.

Theories of Economic Growth. Ed. by Bert F. Hoselitz et al. LC 60-10898. 1965. pap. text ed. 5.95 (ISBN 0-02-915220-8). Free Pr.

Theories of Economic Growth & Development. Irma Adelman. 1961. 15.00x (ISBN 0-8047-0083-4); pap. 6.95x (ISBN 0-8047-0084-2). Stanford U Pr.

Theories of Elastic Plates. V. Panc. (Mechanics of Surface Structures Ser.: No. 2). 736p. 1975. 80.00x (ISBN 90-286-0104-X, Pub. by Sijthoff & Noordhoff). Kluwer Academic.

Theories of Engineering Experimentation. Schenck. 302p. 1979. 37.50 (ISBN 0-89116-504-5). Hemisphere Pub.

Theories of Error in Indian Philosophy. Bijayananda Kar. 1978. 11.00x (ISBN 0-8364-0304-5). South Asia Bks.

Theories of Ethics. Ed. by Philippa Foot. (Oxford Readings in Philosophy Ser.). 1967. pap. 8.95x (ISBN 0-19-875005-6). Oxford U Pr.

Theories of Evidence: Bentham & Wigmore. William Twining. LC 85-50306. (Jurists: Profiles in Legal Theory Ser.). 272p. 1986. 29.50x (ISBN 0-8047-1285-9). Stanford U Pr.

Theories of Evidence: Bentham & Wigmore. William Twining. 352p. 1986. 27.95x (ISBN 0-297-78668-7, Pub. by Weidenfeld & Nicolson England). Biblio Dist.

Theories of Evolution. H. James Birx. (Illus.). 432p. 1984. 43.50x (ISBN 0-398-04902-5). C C Thomas.

Theories of Existence. Timothy L. Sprigge. 192p. 1985. pap. 6.95 (ISBN 0-14-022167-0). Penguin.

Theories of Explanation. Joseph C. Pitt. (Illus.). 234p. 1988. 32.00 (ISBN 0-19-504970-5); pap. text ed. 11.95 (ISBN 0-19-504971-3). Oxford U Pr.

Theories of Fluids with Microstructure: An Introduction. V. K. Stokes. (Illus.). 230p. 1984. 46.50 (ISBN 0-387-13708-4). Springer-Verlag.

Theories of Group Behavior. Ed. by B. Mullen & G. R. Geothals. (Social Psychology Ser.). (Illus.). 255p. 1986. 40.00 (ISBN 0-387-96351-0). Springer-Verlag.

Theories of Group Processes. Cary L. Cooper. LC 74-28089. (Individuals, Groups & Organizations Ser.). 275p. 1975. 59.95 (ISBN 0-471-17117-4, Pub. by Wiley-Interscience); pap. text ed. 22.00 (ISBN 0-471-99452-9). Wiley.

Theories of Group Processes. Ed. by Cary L. Cooper. LC 74-28089. pap. 55.00 (ISBN 0-317-09544-7, 2051855). Bks Demand UMI.

Theories of Heavy-Electron Systems. Ed. by P. A. Lee et al. (Journal Comments on Condensed Matter Physics). 65p. 1986. pap. text ed. 18.00 (ISBN 0-677-21460-X). Gordon & Breach.

Theories of High Temperature Superconductivity. J. Woods Halley. 256p. 1988. 53.75 (ISBN 0-201-12008-9, 12008). Addison-Wesley.

Theories of History. Ed. by Patrick Gardiner. LC 58-6481. 1959. text ed. 19.95 (ISBN 0-02-911210-9). Free Pr.

Theory & Application of Digital Signal Processing. Lawrence R. Rabiner & Bernard Gold. (Illus.). 720p. 1975. ref. ed. 51.00 (ISBN 0-13-914101-4). P-H.

Theory & Application of Environmental Economics. P. Nijkamp. (Studies in Regional Science & Urban Economics: Vol. 1). 332p. 1977. 73.75 (ISBN 0-7204-0763-X, North-Holland). Elsevier.

Theory & Application of Mathematical Programming. G. Mitra. 1977. 57.00 (ISBN 0-12-500450-8). Acad Pr.

Theory & Application of Microbiological Assay. Willam Hewitt & Stephen Vincent. 350p. 1988. price not set (ISBN 0-12-346445-5). Acad Pr.

Theory & Application of Random Fields: Proceedings, Bangalore, India, 1982. Ed. by G. Kallianpur. (Lecture Notes in Control & Information Sciences Ser.: Vol. 49). 290p. 1983. pap. 16.80 (ISBN 0-387-12232-X). Springer-Verlag.

Theory & Application of Reliability: With Emphasis on Bayesian & Nonparametric Methods, 2 vols. Ed. by C. P. Tsokos & I. N. Shimi. 1977. Vol. 1. 79.50 (ISBN 0-12-702101-9); Vol. 2. 79.50 (ISBN 0-12-702102-7). Acad Pr.

Theory & Application of Special Functions: Proceedings of the Advanced Seminar, University of Wisconsin, Madison, March-April, 1975. University of Wisconsin, Madison, Advanced Seminar Staff. Ed. by Richard A. Askey. (University of Wisconsin Mathematics Research Center Publications: No. 35). 1975. 29.50 (ISBN 0-12-064850-4). Acad Pr.

Theory & Application of the Z-Transform Method. Eliahu I. Jury. LC 64-17145. 344p. 1973. Repr. of 1964 ed. 25.50 (ISBN 0-88275-122-0). Krieger.

Theory & Applications of Boundary Element Methods: Proceedings of the 1st Japan-China Symposium, 1-6 June 1987, Karuizawa, Japan. Ed. by M. Tanaka & Du Quinghua. (Illus.). 400p. 1987. 110.00 (ISBN 0-08-035902-7). Pergamon.

Theory & Applications of Correspondence Analysis. Michael Greenacre. 1984. 64.50 (ISBN 0-12-299050-1). Acad Pr.

Theory & Applications of Differentiable Functions of Several Variables. M. Berkolaiko et al. LC 84-24501. (Proceedings of the Steklov Institute of Mathematics Ser.: Vol. 161). 253p. 1985. text ed. 65.00 (ISBN 0-8218-3083-X). Am Math.

Theory & Applications of Differentiable Functions of Several Variables, 4. Ed. by S. M. Nikol'ski. LC 68-1677. (Proceedings of the Steklov Institute: No. 117). 1974. 88.00 (ISBN 0-8218-3017-1, STEKLO-117). Am Math.

Theory & Applications of Differentiable Functions of Several Variables, 6. Ed. by S. M. Nikol'Skii. (Proceedings of the Steklov Institute of Mathematics: No. 140). 1979. 93.00 (ISBN 0-8218-3039-2). Am Math.

Theory & Applications of Differentiable Functions of Several Variables: Proceedings. Steklov Institute of Mathematics, Academy of Sciences, U. S. S. R. Ed. by S. M. Nikol'skii. (Proceedings of the Steklov Institute of Mathematics: No. 77). 1967. 50.00 (ISBN 0-8218-1877-5, STEKLO-77). Am Math.

Theory & Applications of Differentiable Functions of Several Variables, 2: Proceedings. Steklov Institute of Mathematics, Academy of Sciences, U. S. S. R. Ed. by S. M. Nikol'skii. (Proceedings of the Steklov Institute of Mathematics: No. 89). 1968. 74.00 (ISBN 0-8218-1889-9, STEKLO-89). Am Math.

Theory & Applications of Differentiable Functions of Several Variables, 3: Proceedings. Steklov Institute of Mathematics, Academy of Sciences, U. S. S. R. Ed. by S. M. Nikol'skii. (Proceedings of the Steklov Institute of Mathematics: No. 105). 1971. 50.00 (ISBN 0-8218-3005-8, STEKLO-105). Am Math.

Theory & Applications of Differentiable Functions of Several Variables, 5: Proceedings. Steklov Institute of Mathematics, Academy of Sciences, U. S. S. R. Ed. by S. M. Nikol'skii. (Proceedings of the Steklov Institute of Mathematics: No. 131). 252p. 1975. 67.00 (ISBN 0-8218-3031-7, STEKLO-131). Am Math.

Theory & Applications of Differentiable Functions of Several Variables. (Proceedings of the Steklov Institute of Mathematics Ser.: Vol. 170). 300p. 1987. pap. text ed. 120.00 (ISBN 0-8218-3101-1). Am Math.

Theory & Applications of Differentiable Functions of Several Variables. (STEKLO Ser.: Vol. 173). 296p. 1988. pap. text ed. 116.00 (ISBN 0-8218-3117-8). Am Math.

Theory & Applications of Distance Geometry. 2nd ed. Leonard M. Blumenthal. LC 79-113117. 1970. text ed. 18.95 (ISBN 0-8284-0242-6). Chelsea Pub.

Theory & Applications of Drilling Fluid Hydraulics. EXLOG Staff. LC 84-25172. (EXLOG Series of Petroleum Geology & Engineering Handbooks). (Illus.). 203p. 1985. text ed. 27.00 (ISBN 0-88746-045-3). Intl Human Res.

Theory & Applications of Fourier Analysis. Ed. by C. Rees et al. (Pure & Applied Mathematics Ser.: Vol. 59). 1980. 45.00 (ISBN 0-8247-6903-1). Dekker.

Theory & Applications of Harmonic Integrals. W. V. Hodge. (Cambridge Mathematical Library). 281p. Date not set. pap. 19.95 (ISBN 0-521-35881-7). Cambridge U Pr.

Theory & Applications of Holomorphic Functions on Algebraic Varieties over Arbitrary Ground Fields. Oscar Zariski. LC 52-42839. (Memoirs: No. 5). 90p. 1972. pap. 13.00 (ISBN 0-8218-1205-X, MEMO-5). Am Math.

Theory & Applications of Inverse Problems. Haario. (Research Notes in Mathematics Ser.). 152p. 1988. pap. 46.95 (ISBN 0-470-21004-4). Wiley.

Theory & Applications of Inverse Problems. Ed. by Heikki Haario. 350p. 1988. 31.95 (ISBN 0-470-21044-3). Wiley.

Theory & Applications of Linear Differential & Difference Equations: A Systems Approach in Engineering. R. M. Johnson. (Mathematics & Its Applications Ser.). 183p. 1984. 29.95 (ISBN 0-470-20106-1). Halsted Pr.

Theory & Applications of Liquid Crystals. Ed. by D. Kinderlehrer & J. Ericksen. (IMA Ser.: Vol. 5). (Illus.). 375p. 1987. 37.00 (ISBN 0-387-96546-7). Springer-Verlag.

Theory & Applications of Mathematics for Elementary School Teachers. Joseph Hashisaki. 402p. 1984. write for info. (ISBN 0-471-09637-7); tchr's. manual avail. (ISBN 0-471-87234-2). Wiley.

Theory & Applications of Moment Methods in Many-Fermion Systems. Ed. by B. J. Dalton et al. LC 80-21054. 520p. 1980. 85.00x (ISBN 0-306-40463-X, Plenum Pr). Plenum Pub.

Theory & Applications of Nonlinear Control Systems. Ed. by C. I. Byrnes & A. Lindquist. 592p. 1986. 142.00 (ISBN 0-444-70055-2, North-Holland). Elsevier.

Theory & Applications of Sequential Nonparametrics. Pranab K. Sen. LC 84-52332. (CBMS-NSF Regional Conference Ser.: No. 49). vi, 100p. 1985. pap. text ed. 17.00 (ISBN 0-89871-051-0). Soc Indus-Appl Math.

Theory & Applications of Singular Perturbations, Oberwolfach, Germany 1981: Proceedings. Ed. by W. Eckhaus & E. M. De Jager. (Lecture Note in Mathematics: Vol. 942). 372p. 1982. pap. 23.00 (ISBN 0-387-11584-6). Springer-Verlag.

Theory & Applications of Some New Classes of Integral Equations. A. Ramm. 344p. 1980. pap. 31.50. Springer-Verlag.

Theory & Applications of Statistical Inference Functions. D. L. McLeish & C. S. Small. (Lecture Notes in Statistics Ser.: Vol. 44). (Illus.). vi, 124p. 1988. pap. 25.00 (ISBN 0-387-96720-6). Springer-Verlag.

Theory & Applications of Statistical Wave-Period Processing, 3 vols. Albert A. Gerlach. 1434p. 1970. 435.00 (ISBN 0-677-02510-6). Gordon & Breach.

Theory & Applications of Stochastic Differential Equations. Zeev Schuss. LC 80-14767. (Probability & Mathematical Statistics: Applied Probability & Statistics Ser.00741629x). 321p. 1980. 46.95 (ISBN 0-471-04394-X). Wiley.

Theory & Applications of the Linear Model. Franklin A. Graybill. LC 75-41970. 1976. text ed. 37.00 (ISBN 0-87872-108-8, Duxbury Pr). PWS Kent Pub.

Theory & Applications of the Poincare Group. Y. S. Kim & Marilyn E. Noz. 1986. text ed. 73.00 (ISBN 90-277-2141-6, Pub. by Reidel Holland). Kluwer-Academic.

Theory & Applications of Volterra Operators in Hilbert Space. I. C. Gohberg & M. G. Krein. LC 71-120134. (Translations of Mathematical Monographs: Vol. 24). 1970. 71.00 (ISBN 0-8218-1574-1, MMONO-24). Am Math.

Theory & Computation of Ocean Currents. A. S. Sarkisyan. 104p. 1968. text ed. 26.00x (ISBN 0-7065-0636-7, Pub. by Keter Pub Jerusalem). Coronet Bks.

Theory & Craft of American Law-Elements. Soia Mentschikoff & Irwin P. Stotzky. LC 80-70678. 1981. 33.50. Bender.

Theory & Craft of the Scenographic Model. rev. ed. Darwin R. Payne. (Illus.). 192p. 1985. 19.95x (ISBN 0-8093-1193-3); pap. 14.95x (ISBN 0-8093-1194-1). S Ill U Pr.

Theory & Decision: Essays in Honor of Werner Leinfellner. Ed. by Gerald L. Eberlein & Hal Berghel. 1987. lib. bdg. 74.00 (ISBN 90-277-2519-5, Pub. by Reidel Holland). Kluwer Academic.

Theory & Design in the First Machine Age. Reyner Banham. 340p. 1980. pap. 10.95 (ISBN 0-262-52058-3). MIT Pr.

Theory & Design of Adaptive Filters. John R. Treichler et al. LC 87-6062. (Topics in Digital Signal Processing Ser.). 342p. 1987. 34.95 (ISBN 0-471-83220-0, Pub. by Wiley-Interscience). Wiley.

Theory & Design of Concrete Shells. B. K. Chatterjee. 256p. 1971. 95.00 (ISBN 0-677-61740-2). Gordon & Breach.

Theory & Design of Concrete Shells. B. K. Chatterjee. 320p. 1988. lib. bdg. 75.00 (ISBN 0-412-31660-9, Pub. by Chapman & Hall England). Routledge Chapman & Hall.

Theory & Design of Cryogenic Systems. A. Arkharov. 430p. 1981. 11.60 (ISBN 0-8285-1974-9, Pub. by Mir Pubs USSR). Imported Pubns.

Theory & Design of Digital Computer Systems. Lewin. 1980. pap. 31.95 (ISBN 0-442-30761-6). Van Nos Reinhold.

Theory & Design of Digital Computer System. Lewin. pap. 29.95 (ISBN 0-317-64299-5). Van Nos Reinhold.

Theory & Design of Digital Computer Systems. 2nd ed. Douglas Lewin. 472p. 1980. pap. text ed. 34.95 (ISBN 0-470-26959-6). Halsted Pr.

Theory & Design of Linear Active Networks. Sundaram Natarajan. 464p. 1987. 46.95x (ISBN 0-317-53615-X). Macmillan.

Theory & Design of Microwave Filters & Circuits see Advances in Microwaves.

Theory & Design of Pressure Vessels. 3rd ed. John F. Harvey. (Illus.). 640p. 1985. 54.95 (ISBN 0-442-23248-9). Van Nos Reinhold.

Theory & Design of Steel Structures. Giulio Ballio & Federico Mazzolani. 664p. 1983. 66.00x (ISBN 0-412-23660-5, NO. 6886, Pub. by Chapman & Hall England). Routledge Chapman & Hall.

Theory & Design of Surface Structures Slabs & Plates. Gustav Florin. (Structural Engineering Ser.: Vol. 2). (Illus.). 222p. 1980. 38.00x (ISBN 0-87849-034-5); pap. 24.00 (ISBN 0-87849-035-3). Trans Tech.

Theory & Design of Switching Circuits. Arthur Friedman & Premachandran R. Menon. LC 75-15888. (Digital Systems Design Ser.). (Illus.). 581p. 1975. 42.95 (ISBN 0-914894-52-8, Computer Sci Pr). W H Freeman.

Theory & Design of Wood & Fiber Composite Materials. Ed. by Benjamin A. Jayne. LC 72-1998. (Wood Science Ser.: No. 3). (Illus.). 464p. 1972. text ed. 25.00x (ISBN 0-8156-5031-0). Syracuse U Pr.

Theory & Detection of Magnetic Monopoles in Gauge Theories: A Collected Set of Lecture Notes. Ed. by N. S. Craigie et al. 700p. 1986. 83.00 (ISBN 9971-966-94-8); pap. 41.00 (ISBN 9971-966-95-6). World Scientific Pub.

Theory & Estimation of Macroeconomic Rationing Models. H. R. Sneessens. (Lecture Notes in Economics & Mathematical Systems Ser.: Vol. 191). (Illus.). 138p. 1981. pap. 14.00 (ISBN 0-387-10837-8). Springer-Verlag.

Theory & Evaluation of Formation Pressures: A Pressure Detection Reference Handbook. EXLOG Staff. Ed. by Alun Whittaker. LC 85-2287. (EXLOG Series of Petroleum Geology & Engineering Handbooks). (Illus.). 231p. 1985. text ed. 34.95 (ISBN 0-88746-052-6). Intl Human Res.

Theory & Evidence. Clark Glymour. LC 79-3209. 352p. 1980. 44.50x (ISBN 0-691-07240-X). Princeton U Pr.

Theory & Experience of Economic Development: Essays in Honor of Sir W. Arthur Lewis. Ed. by Mark Gersovitz et al. 416p. 1982. text ed. 45.00x (ISBN 0-04-330323-4). Unwin Hyman.

Theory & Experiment in Gravitational Physics. Clifford M. Will. LC 80-39642. pap. 91.60 (2031743). Bks Demand UMI.

Theory & Experiment in Psychical Research. new ed. William G. Roll. LC 75-7398. (Perspectives in Psychical Research Ser.). (Illus.). 1975. 38.50x (ISBN 0-405-07047-0). Ayer Co Pubs.

Theory & Experiment: Recent Insights & New Perspectives on Their Relation. Ed. by Diderik Batens & Jean P. Van Dendegem. 1988. lib. bdg. 64.00 (ISBN 90-277-2645-0, Pub. by Reidel Holland). Kluwer Academic.

Theory & Experimental Investigation of Social Structures. David Willer. 288p. 1987. text ed. 38.00 (ISBN 2-88124-156-5). Gordon & Breach.

Theory & Experiments in Basic Electric Circuits. Sidney N. Sonsky. (Illus.). 1978. lab manual 14.95x (ISBN 0-89529-050-2). Avery Pub.

Theory & Explanation in Archaeology: The Southampton Conference. Colin Renfrew et al. 1982. 29.95 (ISBN 0-12-586960-6). Acad Pr.

Theory & History. Ludwig von Mises. Ed. by Robin W. Wicks. LC 83-49147. (History & Historiography Ser.). 384p. 1985. lib. bdg. 40.00 (ISBN 0-8240-6380-5). Garland Pub.

Theory & History of Architecture. Manfredo Tafuri. LC 79-2638. (Icon Editions Ser.). (Illus.). 320p. 1980. 20.00i (ISBN 0-06-438580-9, HarpT); pap. 10.95 (ISBN 0-06-430108-7, IN-108). Har-Row.

Theory & History of Bibliography. Georg Schneider. 1977. lib. bdg. 69.95 (ISBN 0-8490-2741-1). Gordon Pr.

Theory & History of Folklore. Vladimir Propp. Ed. by Anatoly Liberman. Tr. by Ariadna Y. Martin & Richard P. Martin. LC 83-14840. (Theory & History of Literature Ser.: Vol. 5). (Illus.). 288p. (Rus.). 1984. pap. 14.95 (ISBN 0-8166-1182-3). U of Minn Pr.

Theory & Management of Tropical Fisheries. Ed. by D. Pauly & G. I. Murphy. (ICLARM Conference Proceedings: No. 9). (Illus.). 360p. 1983. 32.50x (ISBN 971-04-0021-5, Pub. by ICLARM Philippines); pap. 28.50x (ISBN 971-04-0022-3, Pub. by ICLARM Philippines). Intl Spec Bk.

Theory & Management of Tropical Multispecies Stock: A Review, with Emphasis on the Southeast Asian Demersal Fisheries. Daniel Pauly. (ICLARM Studies & Reviews: No. 1). (Illus.). 35p. 1983. pap. text ed. 6.50x (ISBN 0-89955-398-2, Pub. by ICLARM Philippines). Intl Spec Bk.

Theory & Meaning. David Papineau. 1979. text ed. 45.00x (ISBN 0-19-824585-8). Oxford U Pr.

Theory & Meaning of the Line of the Heart, the Line of Fate & the Lines of Union in the Hand. St. Germain. (Illus.). 121p. 1980. Repr. of 1888 ed. deluxe ed. 127.75 (ISBN 0-89901-021-0). Found Class Reprints.

Theory & Measurement. Henry E. Kyburg. LC 82-17905. (Studies in Philosophy). (Illus.). 280p. 1984. 44.50 (ISBN 0-521-24878-7). Cambridge U Pr.

Theory & Measurement in Sociology. Chester A. Winton. LC 74-9539. 124p. 1974. text ed. 6.95x (ISBN 0-470-95515-5). Halsted Pr.

Theory & Measurement of Demand. Henry Schultz. LC 38-19565. (Illus.). 1957. Repr. of 1938 ed. 22.00x (ISBN 0-226-74083-8). U of Chicago Pr.

Theory & Measurement of Economic Externalities. Ed. by Steven A. Lin. 1976. 24.95 (ISBN 0-12-450450-7). Acad Pr.

Theory & Measurement of Social Interest. James E. Crandall. LC 81-9973. 224p. 1981. 30.00x (ISBN 0-231-05256-1). Columbia U Pr.

Theory & Method in Ethnomusicology. Bruno Nettl. LC 64-16964. (Illus.). 1964. text ed. 19.95 (ISBN 0-02-922860-3). Free Pr.

Theory & Method in Lexicography. Ed. by Ladislav Zgusta. 1980. pap. text ed. 11.50 (ISBN 0-917496-14-0). Hornbeam Pr.

Theory & Method in Urban & Regional Analysis. P. W. Batey. (London Papers in Regional Science). 184p. 1978. pap. 16.00x (ISBN 0-85086-066-0, NO. 2928, Pub. by Pion England). Routledge Chapman & Hall.

Theory & Methodology of Training: The Key to Athletic Performance. Tudor O. Bompa. 304p. 1983. pap. text ed. 24.95 (ISBN 0-8403-4058-3). Kendall-Hunt.

Theory & Methods in Dance Movement Therapy: A Manual for Therapists, Students & Educators. 2nd ed. Penny L. Bernstein. 1980. perfect bdg. 17.95 (ISBN 0-8403-2378-6). Kendall-Hunt.

Theory & Methods in Migration & Ethnic Research. (IMR Special Issues Ser.). Date not set. pap. 14.95 (A7). Ctr Migration.

Theory & Methods of Calculations of Molecular Spectra. L. A. Gribov & W. J. Orville-Thomas. LC 88-181. 720p. 1988. price not set (ISBN 0-471-91882-2). Wiley.

Theory & Methods of Scaling. Warren S. Torgerson. LC 83-23852. 474p. 1985. Repr. of 1958 ed. 36.50 (ISBN 0-89874-722-8). Krieger.

Theory & Methods of Scaling. Warren S. Torgerson. LC 58-10812. 1958. pap. 118.50 (ISBN 0-317-08170-5, 2020339). Bks Demand UMI.

Theory & Methods of Social Research. 2nd ed. Johan Galtung. LC 67-26343. (Illus.). 534p. 1969. 40.00x (ISBN 0-231-03088-6). Columbia U Pr.

Theory & Methods of Structural Analysis. Ziad M. Elias. LC 85-13765. 669p. 1986. 59.95 (ISBN 0-471-89768-X). Wiley.

Theory & Models in Vegetation Science: Abstracts. Ed. by Rik Leemans et al. (Illus.). 112p. (Orig.). 1985. pap. text ed. 26.50x (Pub. by Almqvist & Wiksell). Coronet Bks.

Theory & Models in Vegetation Science. Ed. by I. C. Prentice & E. Van Der Maarel. (Advances in Vegetation Science Ser.). 1987. lib. bdg. 122.50 (ISBN 90-6193-646-2, Pub. by Junk Pubs Netherlands). Kluwer Academic.

Theory & Musicianship: Lessons with Worksheets & Supplements, Bk. 2, Pt. 2. Edith McIntosh. 62p. 1957. pap. 4.95 (ISBN -08258-0160-5, 04012). Fischer Inc NY.

Theory & Nonneutral Plasmas. Ronald C. Davidson. 1988. write for info. (ISBN 0-201-09529-7). Addison-Wesley.

Theory & Nursing: A Systematic Approach. Chinn & Jacobs. 1986. 23.95 (ISBN 0-8016-0983-6). Mosby.

Theory & Observations of Normal Stellar Atmospheres: Proceedings of the Third Harvard-Smithsonian Conference on Stellar Atmosphere. Ed. by Owen Gingerich. 1970. 45.00x (ISBN 0-262-07035-9). MIT Pr.

Theory & Personality: The Significance of T. S. Eliot's Criticism. Brian Lee. 148p. 1979. 36.50 (ISBN 0-485-11185-3, Pub. by Athlone Pr UK). Humanities.

Theory & Policy Design for Basic Needs Planning: A Case Study of Ecuador. Rudolf Teekens. 730p. 1988. text ed. 45.00 (ISBN 0-566-05538-4, Pub. by Gower Pub England). Gower Pub Co.

Theory & Politics: Studies in the Development of Critical Theory. Hulmet Dubiel. Tr. by Benjamin Gregg from Ger. (German Social Thought Ser.). (Illus.). 188p. 1985. text ed. 20.00x (ISBN 0-262-04080-8). MIT Pr.

Theory & Practice. Jurgen Habermas. Tr. by John Viertel from Ger. LC 72-6227. 310p. 1973. 35.00x (ISBN 0-8070-1526-1); pap. 10.95x (BPA 21). Beacon Pr.

Theory & Practice. Rosa Luxemburg. Tr. by David Wolff from Ger. (Illus.). 67p. (Orig.). 1980. pap. 2.00x (ISBN 0-914441-22-1). News & Letters.

Theory & Practice. Rotenstreich. (Van Leer Jerusalem Foundation Series). 1977. lib. bdg. 24.00 (ISBN 90-247-2004-4, Spub. by Martinus Nijhoff Netherlands). Kluwer Academic.

Theory & Practice: An Introduction to Philosophy. Gerald Runkle. 480p. 1985. text ed. 27.95 (ISBN 0-03-061757-X, HoltC). HR&W.

Theory & Practice: Basic College Writing. Randy DeVillez & Susan R. Schreiber. 448p. 1986. pap. text ed. 23.95 (ISBN 0-8403-3828-7). Kendall-Hunt.

Theory & Practice: Essays Presented to Gene Weltfish. Ed. by Stanley Diamond. (Studies in Anthropology). 1979. text ed. 44.25 (ISBN 90-279-7958-8). Mouton.

Theory & Practice for Ceramo Metal Restorations. Masahiro Kuwata. (Illus.). 150p. 1980. 72.00 (ISBN 0-931386-15-2). Quint Pub Co.

Theory & Practice Formation in the U. S. S. R. Bella Feygin. Ed. by Cynthia Corell. (Illus., Orig.). Date not set. pap. text ed. 35.00 (ISBN 1-55831-008-8). Delphic Associates.

Theory & Practice: History of a Concept from Aristotle to Marx. Nicholas Lobkowicz. 454p. 1983. pap. text ed. 17.75 (ISBN 0-8191-3335-3). U Pr of Amer.

Theory & Practice in Affinity Techniques. Ed. by P. V. Sundaram & F. Eckstein. 1979. 87.50 (ISBN 0-12-677150-2). Acad Pr.

Theory & Practice in American Politics. Ed. by William H. Nelson. LC 64-15813. 1967. pap. 1.95X (ISBN 0-226-57187-4, P254, Phoen). U of Chicago Pr.

Theory & Practice in Behavior Therapy. Aubrey J. Yates. LC 74-30018. (Wiley-Interscience Publication Ser.). pap. 65.30 (ISBN 0-317-26094-4, 2025176). Bks Demand UMI.

Theory & Practice in Defence Decision Making. M. Blunden & O. Greene. (Illus.). 240p. 1988. 33.71 (ISBN 0-08-033621-3, BDP). Pergamon.

Theory & Practice in Education. R. F. Dearden. 192p. 1984. 19.95x (ISBN 0-7100-9910-X). Routledge Chapman & Hall.

Theory & Practice in Experimental Bacteriology. 2nd ed. G. G. Meynell & Elinor Meynell. LC 72-85729. (Illus.). 1970. 65.00 (ISBN 0-521-07682-X). Cambridge U Pr.

Theory & Practice in Finite Element Structural Analysis: Proceedings of the 1973 Tokyo Seminar on Finite Element Analysis. Ed. by Yoshiaki Yamada & Richard H. Gallagher. 733p. 1973. 60.00x (ISBN 0-86008-097-8, Pub. by U of Tokyo Japan). Columbia U Pr.

Theory & Practice in Health Education. Helen S. Ross & Paul Mico. LC 80-82564. (Illus.). 338p. 1980. text ed. 23.95 (ISBN 0-87484-406-1). Mayfield Pub.

Theory & Practice in Henry James. Herbert L. Hughes. LC 76-26959. 1926. lib. bdg. 37.50 (ISBN 0-8414-4818-3). Folcroft.

Theory & Practice in Historical Study. Social Science Research Council - Committee on Historiography. LC 46-3597. 1946. pap. 18.00 (ISBN 0-527-03283-2). Kraus Repr.

Theory & Practice in Interpersonal Attraction. Ed. by Steve Duck. 1977. 105.50 (ISBN 0-12-222850-2). Acad Pr.

Theory & Practice in Regional Science. I. Masser. (London Papers in Regional Science). 166p. 1976. pap. 12.50x (ISBN 0-85086-051-2, NO. 2947, Pub. by Pion England). Routledge Chapman & Hall.

Theory & Practice in Renaissance Textual Criticism: Beatus Rhenanus Between Conjecture & History. John F. D'Amico. 1988. 38.00 (ISBN 0-520-06199-3). U of Cal Pr.

Theory & Practice in the Human Services. Earl Hollander. 85p. 1985. pap. text ed. 25.00 (ISBN 0-933195-10-9). CA College Health Sci.

Theory & Practice in the Organic Laboratory. 3rd ed. John A. Landgrebe. 576p. 1982. pap. text ed. 33.00 (ISBN 0-669-04494-6). Heath.

Theory & Practice in the Teaching of Composition: Processing, Distancing, & Modeling. Ed. by Miles Myers & James Gray. LC 83-2288. 256p. 1983. pap. 13.75 (ISBN 0-8141-5399-2). NCTE.

Theory & Practice of African Politics. Christian P. Potholm. (Illus.). 302p. 1985. pap. text ed. 15.50 (ISBN 0-8191-4734-6). U Pr of Amer.

Theory & Practice of African Politics. 2nd ed. Christian P. Potholm. LC 87-14747. 272p. 1988. pap. text ed. 14.75 (ISBN 0-8191-7001-1). U Pr of Amer.

Theory & Practice of American Marxism, Nineteen Fifty-Seven to Nineteen Seventy. Richard Guarasci. LC 80-1376. 170p. 1980. pap. text ed. 13.50 (ISBN 0-8191-1149-X). U Pr of Amer.

Theory & Practice of Archaeology: A Workbook. Thomas C. Patterson. (Illus.). 192p. 1983. pap. write for info. (ISBN 0-13-913350-X). P-H.

Theory & Practice of Autonomy. Gerald Dworkin. (Cambridge Studies in Philosophy). 176p. Date not set. 34.50 (ISBN 0-521-34452-2); pap. 11.95 (ISBN 0-521-35767-5). Cambridge U Pr.

Theory & Practice of Bank Book-Keeping & Joint Stock Accounts: Exemplified & Elucidated in a Complete Set of Bank Account Books. Christopher C. Marsh. Ed. by Richard P. Brief. LC 77-87278. (Development of Contemporary Accounting Thought Ser). 1978. Repr. of 1856 ed. lib. bdg. 27.50x (ISBN 0-405-10906-7). Ayer Co Pubs.

Theory & Practice of Biological Control. Ed. by C. B. Huffaker & P. S. Messenger. 1977. 98.50 (ISBN 0-12-360350-1). Acad Pr.

Theory & Practice of Biological Wastewater Treatment. Ed. by K. Curi. W. Wesley Eckenfelder. (NATO, Advanced Study Institute Series Applied Science: No. 35). 548p. 1980. 49.50x (ISBN 90-286-0510-X, Pub. by Sijthoff & Noordhoff). Kluwer Academic.

Theory & Practice of Body Massage. Frank Nichols. 1979. 11.35 (ISBN 0-87350-088-1). Milady Pub.

Theory & Practice of Brief Therapy. Simon H. Budman & Alan S. Gurman. 402p. 1988. lib. bdg. 30.00 (ISBN 0-89862-716-8). Guilford Pr.

Theory & Practice of Central Banking, 1797-1913. Edward V. Morgan. 252p. 1965. 29.00x (ISBN 0-7146-1237-5, F Cass Co). Biblio Dist.

Theory & Practice of Combinatorics. A. Rosa & G. Sabidussi. (Mathematics Studies Ser.: Vol. 60). 264p. 1982. 105.25 (ISBN 0-444-86318-4, North Holland). Elsevier.

Theory & Practice of Community Social Work. Ed. by Samuel H. Taylor & Robert W. Roberts. 464p. 1985. 25.00x (ISBN 0-231-05368-1). Columbia U Pr.

Theory & Practice of Compiler Writing. Jean-Paul Tremblay & Paul G. Sorenson. 816p. 1985. text ed. 46.95 (ISBN 0-07-065161-2). McGraw.

Theory & Practice of Controllable Pitch Propellors. E. R. May. (Marine Engineering Practice Ser.: Vol. 2, Pt. 13). 1979. pap. 6.00x (ISBN 0-900976-62-4, Pub. by. Inst Marine Eng). Intl Spec Bk.

Theory & Practice of Counseling & Psychotherapy. 3rd ed. Ed. by Gerald Corey. LC 85-6676. (Counseling Ser.). 400p. 1985. pap. 21.25 (ISBN 0-534-05076-X); student manual, 192p 8.50. Brooks Cole.

Theory & Practice of Direct Methods in Crystallography. Ed. by M. F. Ladd & R. A. Palmer. LC 79-10566. (Illus.). 436p. 1980. 55.00x (ISBN 0-306-40223-8, Plenum Pr). Plenum Pub.

Theory & Practice of Early Reading, Vol. 1. Ed. by Lauren B. Resnick & Phyllis A. Weaver. LC 79-22322. 416p. 1980. text ed. 39.95x (ISBN 0-89859-003-5). L Erlbaum Assocs.

Theory & Practice of Early Reading, Vol. 2. Lauren B. Resnick & Phyllis A. Weaver. LC 79-23784. 368p. 1980. text ed. 39.95x (ISBN 0-89859-010-8). L Erlbaum Assocs.

Theory & Practice of Early Reading, Vol. 3. Ed. by Lauren B. Resnick & Phyllis A. Weaver. 400p. 1980. text ed. 39.95 (ISBN 0-89859-011-6). L Erlbaum Assocs.

Theory & Practice of Econometrics. 2nd ed. George G. Judge et al. LC 84-7254. (Probability & Mathematical Statistics Ser.). 1019p. 1985. write for info. (ISBN 0-471-89530-X). Wiley.

Theory & Practice of Eel Culture. Isao Matsui. Tr. by Alamelu Gopal from Japanese. 141p. 1980. text ed. 28.00 (ISBN 90-6191-036-6, Pub. by A A Balkema). Brookfield Pub Co.

Theory & Practice of Encounter Group Leadership see Personal Growth Through Interaction.

Theory & Practice of Engineering with Rubber. P. K. Freakley & A. R. Payne. (Illus.). 666p. 1978. 133.25 (ISBN 0-85334-772-7, Pub. by Elsevier Applied Sci England). Elsevier.

Theory & Practice of English Narrative Verse. William Van Doorn. LC 72-195910. 1932. lib. bdg. 27.00 (ISBN 0-8414-8875-4). Folcroft.

Theory & Practice of English Narrative Verse since Eighteen Thirty-Three. Willem V. Doorn. 253p. 1980. Repr. of 1833 ed. lib. bdg. 27.00 (ISBN 0-8492-4220-7). R West.

Theory & Practice of Environmental Quality Analysis. Eric Hyman et al. (CPL Bibliographies Ser.: 27). 103p. 15.00. Coun Plan Librarians.

Theory & Practice of Environmental Quality Analysis: Water Resources Management, Land Suitability Analysis, Economics & Aesthetics, No. 27. Eric Hyman et al. 103p. 1980. 15.00. CPL Biblios.

Theory & Practice of Error Control Codes. Richard E. Blahut. LC 82-11441. (Illus.). 512p. 1983. text ed. write for info. (ISBN 0-201-10102-5). Addison-Wesley.

Theory & Practice of Evaluation. Michael Scriven. 400p. 1987. pap. 12.50 (ISBN 0-918528-13-5). Edgepress.

Theory & Practice of Events Research. Edward E. Azar & Joseph Ben-Dak. 328p. 1975. 88.00 (ISBN 0-677-15550-6). Gordon & Breach.

Theory & Practice of Exchange in Germany. Frank C. Child. Ed. by Mira Wilkins. LC 78-3904. (International Finance Ser.). 1978. Repr. of 1958 ed. lib. bdg. 23.50x (ISBN 0-405-11209-2). Ayer Co Pubs.

Theory & Practice of Feminist Literary Criticism. Ed. by Gabriela Mora & Karen S. Van Hooft. LC 81-67051. (Studies in Literary Analysis). 291p. 1982. lib. bdg. 25.00x (ISBN 0-916950-23-9); pap. 15.00x (ISBN 0-916950-22-0). Biling Rev-Pr.

Theory & Practice of Finance. Thomas J. Hindelang & Michael M. Holland. LC 82-24279. (Illus.). 848p. 1986. cancelled (ISBN 0-201-04086-7). Addison-Wesley.

Theory & Practice of Foundation Engineering. Louis J. Goodman & R. H. Karol. LC 68-12070. (Macmillan Series in Civil Engineering). (Illus.). pap. 111.80 (ISBN 0-317-10610-4, 2010517). Bks Demand UMI.

Theory & Practice of Go. O. Korschelt. Tr. by George Leckie & Samuel P. King. LC 65-22637. (Illus.). 1965. 10.95 (ISBN 0-8048-0572-5). C E Tuttle.

Theory & Practice of Group Counseling. 2nd ed. Gerald Corey. Incl. Student Manual for Theory & Practice of Counseling & Psychotherapy. 192p. pap. 8.50. LC 84-5026. (Psychology-Counseling Ser.). 600p. 1984. text ed. 22.75 pub net (ISBN 0-534-03223-0). Brooks-Cole.

Theory & Practice of Group Psychotherapy. 3rd ed. Irvin D. Yalom. LC 85-47566. 608p. 1985. 24.95x (ISBN 0-465-08447-8). Basic.

Theory & Practice of Histological Techniques. 2nd ed. Ed. by John D. Bancroft & Alan Stevens. (Illus.). 662p. 1982. text ed. 96.00 (ISBN 0-443-02006-X). Churchill.

Theory & Practice of History. Leopold Von Ranke. Ed. by Georg G. Iggers & Konrad Von Moltke. Tr. by Wilma Iggers from Ger. LC 79-167691. 500p. 1983. pap. text ed. 19.95x (ISBN 0-8290-1315-6). Irvington.

Theory & Practice of Histotechnology. 2nd ed. Dezna C. Sheehan & Barbara B. Hrapchak. LC 87-17446. 493p. 1987. text ed. 52.50 (ISBN 0-935470-39-5). Battelle.

Theory & Practice of Human Rights. L. J. Macfarlane. LC 84-27743. 185p. 1985. 25.00 (ISBN 0-312-79716-8). St Martin.

Theory & Practice of Husserl's Phenomenology. Harry P. Reeder. 200p. (Orig.). 1986. lib. bdg. 22.75 (ISBN 0-8191-5478-4); pap. text ed. 12.50 (ISBN 0-8191-5479-2). U Pr of Amer.

Theory & Practice of Industrial Pharmacy. 3rd ed. Ed. by Leon Lachman et al. LC 84-27806. (Illus.). 902p. 1986. text ed. 85.00 (ISBN 0-8121-0977-5). Lea & Febiger.

Theory & Practice of Infection Control. Inge Gurevich et al. 444p. 1984. 44.95 (ISBN 0-275-91432-1, C1432). Praeger.

Theory & Practice of International Organization. 2nd ed. Samuel S. Chen. 133p. 1974. text ed. 29.75x (ISBN 0-8422-5139-1); pap. text ed. 9.75x (ISBN 0-8422-0362-1). Irvington.

Theory & Practice of International Organization. rev. ed. Samuel Shih-Tsai Chen. 1979. text ed. 17.95 (ISBN 0-8403-1946-0, 40194601). Kendall-Hunt.

Theory & Practice of International Relations. 7th ed. William C. Olson. (Illus.). 416p. 1987. pap. text ed. write for info. (ISBN 0-13-914573-7). P-H.

Theory & Practice of International Trade Linkage Models. A. Italianer. 1987. lib. bdg. 73.50 (ISBN 90-247-3407-X, Pub. by Martinus Nijhoff Netherlands). Kluwer Academic.

Theory & Practice of Italian Communism. Alastair Davidson. 302p. (Orig.). 1982. pap. 9.95 (ISBN 0-85036-265-2, Pub. by Merlin Pr UK). Longwood Pub Group.

Theory & Practice of Literacy Work: Policies, Strategies & Examples. Daniel Hamadache & Ali Martin. (Illus.). 232p. (Orig.). 1987. pap. text ed. 15.00 (ISBN 92-3-102397-7, U1573, UNESCO). UNIPUB.

Theory & Practice of Livestock Breeding. N. F. Rostovtsev. 216p. 1961. text ed. 43.00x (ISBN 0-7065-0355-4, Pub. by Keter Pub Jerusalem). Coronet Bks.

Theory & Practice of Lubrication for Engineers. 2nd ed. Dudley D. Fuller. LC 83-27394. 682p. 1984. text ed. 64.95x (ISBN 0-471-04703-1, Pub. by Wiley-Interscience). Wiley.

Theory & Practice of Meditation. 2nd ed. Himalayan Institute. 150p. (Orig.). 1986. pap. 5.95 (ISBN 0-89389-075-8). Himalayan Pubs.

Theory & Practice of Microelectronics. Sorab K. Ghandhi. LC 68-28501. (Illus.). 1968. 50.95x (ISBN 0-471-29718-6, Pub. by Wiley-Interscience). Wiley.

Theory & Practice of Microelectronics. Sorab K. Ghandhi. LC 83-19994. 504p. 1984. Repr. of 1968 ed. 49.50 (ISBN 0-89874-702-3). Krieger.

Theory & Practice of Modem Design. John A. Bingham. LC 87-37262. 453p. 1988. 49.95 (ISBN 0-471-85108-6). Wiley.

Theory & Practice of Money. Jennie Hawthrone. (Illus.). 272p. 1984. pap. 17.95 (ISBN 0-434-90717-0, Pub. by W Heinemann Ltd). David & Charles.

Theory & Practice of Motor Insurance. K Cannar. 399p. 1978. text ed. 135.00x (ISBN 0-900886-24-2, Pub. by Witherby & Co England). State Mutual Bk.

Theory & Practice of Multiple Criteria Decision Making: Collection of Papers Presented at a Workshop, Moscow, May 1981. Ed. by C. Carisson & Y. Kochetkov. x, 170p. 1983. 63.25 (ISBN 0-444-86579-9, I-004-83, North-Holland). Elsevier.

Theory & Practice of Mysticism. Charles M. Addison. 1977. lib. bdg. 59.95 (ISBN 0-8490-2742-X). Gordon Pr.

Theory & Practice of Observing Behavior. C. Fassnacht. (Behavioural Development Monographs). 1982. 56.00 (ISBN 0-12-249780-5). Acad Pr.

Theory & Practice of Organizational Psychology: A Collection of Original Essays. Ed. by Nigel Nicholson & Toby Wall. (Organizational & Occupational Psychology Ser.). 1982. 61.00 (ISBN 0-12-518040-3). Acad Pr.

Theory & Practice of Peacekeeping. Indar J. Rikhye. LC 83-40193. (Illus.). 250p. 1984. 25.00 (ISBN 0-312-79718-4). St Martin.

Theory & Practice of Perspective. G. A. Storey. LC 74-174406. (Illus.). Repr. of 1910 ed. 16.00 (ISBN 0-405-09004-8, Pub. by Blom). Ayer Co Pubs.

Theory & Practice of Physical Activity. March L. Krotee & Frederick C. Hatfield. 112p. 1979. pap. text ed. 15.95 (ISBN 0-8403-2009-4). Kendall-Hunt.

Theory & Practice of Piano Construction. William B. White. LC 74-78811. 160p. 1975. pap. 3.50 (ISBN 0-486-23139-9). Dover.

Theory & Practice of Poster Art. Duke Wellington. 1986. Repr. of 1934 ed. 29.95 (ISBN 0-911380-70-1). Signs of Times.

Theory & Practice of Psychiatric Rehabilitation. Ed. by Fraser N. Watts & Douglas H. Bennett. LC 83-1055. 370p. 1984. 54.95 (ISBN 0-471-90147-4). Wiley.

Theory & Practice of Public Health. 5th ed. Ed. by William Hobson. (Illus.). 1979. text ed. 145.00x (ISBN 0-19-264227-8). Oxford U Pr.

Theory & Practice of Pulse Plating. Jean-Claude Puippe & Frank Leaman. (Illus.). 250p. Date not set. 52.00 (ISBN 0-936569-02-6); pap. 37.00 (ISBN 0-936569-01-8). Am Electro Surface.

Theory & Practice of Radiation Thermometry. Dewitt. 1988. price not set (ISBN 0-471-61018-6). Wiley.

Theory & Practice of Recursive Identification. Lennart Ljung & Tonsten Soderstom. Ed. by Alan S. Willsky. (MIT Press Signal Processing, Optimization, & Control Ser.). (Illus.). 544p. 1983. 60.00x (ISBN 0-262-12095-X). MIT Pr.

Theory & Practice of Recursive Identification. Lennart Ljung & Torsten Suderstrom. (Signal Processing Ser.). 552p. 1987. pap. text ed. 19.95x (ISBN 0-262-62058-8). MIT Pr.

Theory & Practice of Regional Geochemical Exploration. Maria V. Foldvar. 1978. cancelled 26.50 (ISBN 963-05-1442-7, Pub. by Akademiai Kaido Hungary). IPS.

Theory & Practice of Reliable System Design. Daniel Siewiorek & Robert Swarz. 772p. 1982. pap. 47.00 (ISBN 0-932376-17-7, EY-AX016-DP). Digital Pr.

Theory & Practice of Rivers & Other Poems. Jim Harrison. (Illus.). 64p. 1986. Signed Ltd. ed. write for info. (ISBN 0-916947-05-X); pap. 7.95 (ISBN 0-916947-06-8). Winn Bks.

Theory & Practice of Robots & Manipulators, III: Proceedings of the 3rd Symposium. Ed. by A. Morecki & G. Bianchi. 596p. 1980. 155.25 (ISBN 0-444-99772-5). Elsevier.

Theory & Practice of Robots & Manipulators: Proceedings of Ro Man Sy - 1986 Sixth CISMIFTOMM Symposium. A. Morecki. 650p. 1987. 65.00x (ISBN 0-262-13226-5). MIT Pr.

Theory & Practice of Robots & Manipulators: Proceedings of RoManSy '84--the Fifth CISM-IFToMM Symposium. Ed. by A. Morecki et al. 448p. 1985. text ed. 47.50x (ISBN 0-262-13208-7). MIT Pr.

Theory & Practice of Running GPM's. 100p. 1987. 10.00 (ISBN 0-87916-014-4). UPSTAT.

Theory & Practice of Scanning Optical Microscopy. Tony C. Wilson & J. R. Sheppard. 1984. 43.50 (ISBN 0-12-757760-2). Acad Pr.

Theory & Practice of School Consultation. Michael J. Curtis & Joseph E. Zins. (Illus.). 384p. 1981. 45.00x (ISBN 0-398-04171-7). C C Thomas.

Theory & Practice of Scientific Management. C. Bertrand Thompson. LC 72-80596. (Management History Ser.: No. 15). vii, 319p. 1972. Repr. of 1917 ed. 23.50 (ISBN 0-87960-015-2). Hive Pub.

Theory & Practice of Self Psychology. Majorie T. White & Marcella B. Weiner. LC 86-919. 240p. 1986. 25.00 (ISBN 0-87630-425-0). Brunner-Mazel.

Theory & Practice of Shell Structures. L. Fischer. (Illus.). 1968. cancelled (ISBN 3-4330-0127-8). Adlers Foreign Bks.

Theory & Practice of Silvicultural Systems. Ram Prakash & L. S. Khanna. 263p. 1979. text ed. 16.25x (ISBN 0-89955-401-6, Pub. by Intl Bk Dist). Intl Spec Bk.

Theory & Practice of Social Case Work. 2nd ed. Gordon Hamilton. LC 51-12493. 328p. 1951. 22.50 (ISBN 0-231-01862-2). Columbia U Pr.

Theory & Practice of Social Planning. Alfred J. Kahn. LC 79-81406. 360p. 1969. 29.95x (ISBN 0-87154-430-X). Russell Sage.

Theory & Practice of Social Welfare Policy: Analysis, Processes, & Current Issues. Bruce S. Jansson. 470p. 1984. text ed. write for info. (ISBN 0-534-01469-0). Wadsworth Pub.

Theory & Practice of Sociocriticism. Edmond Cros. LC 87-21167. (Theory & History of Literature Ser.: Vol. 53). (Illus.). 1988. 35.00x (ISBN 0-8166-1579-9); pap. 14.95 (ISBN 0-8166-1580-2). U of Minn Pr.

Theory & Practice of Teaching. David P. Page. LC 77-89216. (American Education: Its Men, Institutions & Ideas, Ser. 1). 1969. Repr. of 1847 ed. 15.00 (ISBN 0-405-01455-4). Ayer Co Pubs.

Theory & Practice of the Cine-Roman. W. F. Van Wert. LC 77-22912. 1978. lib. bdg. 32.00x (ISBN 0-405-10756-0). Ayer Co Pubs.

Theory & Practice of the European Convention. P. van Dijk & F. van Hoof. 1984. pap. 54.00 (ISBN 90-654-4079-8, Pub. by Kluwer Law Netherlands). Kluwer Academic.

Theory & Practice of the Photographic Art. W. Sparling. LC 72-9237. (Literature of Photography Ser.). Repr. of 1856 ed. 18.00 (ISBN 0-405-04942-0). Ayer Co Pubs.
Theory & Practice of Translation. Ed. by Lillebill Grahs & Gustav Korlen. 356p. 1978. pap. 31.60 (ISBN 3-261-03072-0). P Lang Pubs.
Theory & Practice of Translation. Ed. by Eugene A. Nida & C. R. Taber. 220p. 1969. 8.00x (ISBN 90-04-03857-4, 08510, Pub. by United Bible). Am Bible.
Theory & Practice of Transport. David Stewart-David. 1980. pap. 13.95 (ISBN 0-434-91864-4, Pub. by W Heinemann Ltd). David & Charles.
Theory & Practice of Virtue. Gilbert C. Meilaender. LC 83-40598. 202p. 1984. pap. text ed. 8.95 (ISBN 0-268-01858-8). U of Notre Dame Pr.
Theory & Practice of Virtue. Gilbert C. Meilaender, Jr. LC 83-40598. 208p. 1984. text ed. 18.95 (ISBN 0-268-01852-9). U of Notre Dame Pr.
Theory & Practice of War. Ed. by Michael Howard. LC 74-20502. (Midland Bks: No. 177). 384p. 1984. 22.50x (ISBN 0-253-35950-3); pap. 8.95x (ISBN 0-253-20177-2). Ind U Pr.
Theory & Practice of Wave Propagation & Diffraction in the U. S. S. R. Augustin Tuzhilin. Ed. by Maureen Young. 157p. (Orig.). Date not set. pap. text ed. 35.00 (ISBN 1-55831-053-3). Delphic Associates.
Theory & Practice: The Great Composers As Teachers & Students. Alfred Mann. (Illus.). 1987. 29.95 (ISBN 0-393-02352-4). Norton.
Theory & Principles of Education: Philosophical & Sociological Bases of Education. J. C. Aggarwal. 361p. 1986. (Pub. by Vikas India); pap. text ed. 13.95x (ISBN 0-7069-2805-9, Pub. by Vikas India). Advent NY.
Theory & Principles of Electrode Processes. B. E. Conway. LC 65-17090. 302p. 1965. 22.50 (JW). Krieger.
Theory & Principles of Tort see Foundations of Legal Liability: A Presentation of the Theory & Development of the Common Law.
Theory & Problems of Child Development. 3rd ed. David P. Ausubel et al. LC 79-93284. 688p. 1980. 42.50 (ISBN 0-8089-1183-X, 790280). Grune.
Theory & Problems of Industrial Psychology. Willard A. Kerr & Florence W. Dunbar. 411p. 1966. text ed. 10.00 (ISBN 0-317-11979-6, Pub. by William James). Psychometric.
Theory & Procedure of Scale Analysis with Applications in Political Research. R. J. Mokken. (Methods & Models in the Social Sciences Ser). 353p. 1971. text ed. 26.40x (ISBN 90-2796-882-9). Mouton.
Theory & Processes of History. Frederick J. Teggart. 11.25 (ISBN 0-8446-3057-8). Peter Smith.
Theory & Processes of History. Frederick J. Teggart. 1976. pap. 11.95x (ISBN 0-520-03176-8). U of Cal Pr.
Theory & Processes of History. Frederick J. Teggart. 323p. Repr. of 1941 ed. lib. bdg. 75.00 (ISBN 0-918377-95-1). Russell Pr.
Theory & Reality in Development: Essays in Honour of Paul Streeton. Ed. by Sanjaya Lall & Frances Stewart. LC 85-11868. 256p. 1986. 29.95 (ISBN 0-312-79726-5). St Martin.
Theory & Reality in Foreign Policy Making: Nigeria after the Second Republic. Ibraham A. Gambari. LC 88-15884. 1989. text ed. 39.95 (ISBN 0-391-03603-3). Humanities.
Theory & Reality in Public International Law. rev. ed. Charles De Visscher. Tr. by P. E. Corbett. LC 67-21020. (Center of International Studies Ser). 1968. 57.00x (ISBN 0-691-09210-9). Princeton U Pr.
Theory & Reality in World Politics. Carey B. Joynt & Percy E. Corbett. LC 77-14693. 1978. 15.95x (ISBN 0-8229-1132-9). U of Pittsburgh Pr.
Theory & Religious Understanding: A Critique of the Hermeneutics of Joachim Wach. Charles M. Wood. LC 75-26839. (American Academy of Religion. Dissertation Ser.). 1975. pap. 9.95 (ISBN 0-89130-026-0, 010112). Scholars Pr GA.
Theory & Research in Behavioral Pediatrics, Vol. 1. Ed. by Hiram E. Fitzgerald et al. 308p. 1982. 42.50x (Plenum Pr). Plenum Pub.
Theory & Research in Behavioral Pediatrics, Vol. 2. Ed. by Hiram E. Fitzgerald et al. 266p. 1984. 42.50x (ISBN 0-306-41566-6, Plenum Pr). Plenum Pub.
Theory & Research in Behavioral Pediatrics, Vol. 3. Ed. by Hiram E. Fitzgerald & Barry M. Lester. 226p. 1986. 39.50x (ISBN 0-306-42328-6, Plenum Pr). Plenum Pub.
Theory & Research in Behavioral Pediatrics, Vol. 4. Ed. by H. E. Fitzgerald et al. (Illus.). 248p. 1988. 45.00x (ISBN 0-306-42882-2, Plenum Pr). Plenum Pub.
Theory & Research in Learning Disabilities. Ed. by J. P. Das & R. Mulcaby. LC 82-112219. 296p. 1982. 50.00x (ISBN 0-306-41112-1, Plenum Pr). Plenum Pub.
Theory & Research in Lubrication: Foundations for Future Developments. Mayo D. Hersey. LC 66-21058. 504p. 1966. text ed. 32.50 (ISBN 0-471-37346-X, Pub. by Wiley). Krieger.
Theory & Resistance in Education: A Pedagogy for the Opposition. Henry A. Giroux. Frwd. by Paulo Freire. 304p. 1983. text ed. 29.95 (ISBN 0-89789-031-0); pap. 12.95 (ISBN 0-89789-032-9). Bergin & Garvey.
Theory & Skill Building, Bk. 1. Charles R. Hopkins & Margaret A. Morton. LC 77-80674. (Hedman Stenotype System Ser.). (Illus.). 372p. text ed. 18.00x (ISBN 0-939056-00-3). Hedman Steno.
Theory & Structures of International Political Economy. Ed. by Todd Sandler. (Westview Special Studies in International Economics & Business). 280p. 1980. lib. bdg. 41.50x (ISBN 0-89158-765-9); pap. 13.00x o. p. (ISBN 0-86531-330-X). Westview.
Theory & Taste: Four Studies in Aesthetics. Teddy Brunius. 119p. (Orig.). 1969. pap. text ed. 15.95x (Pub. by Almqvist & Wiksell). Coronet Bks.
Theory & Technique of Family Therapy. Charles P. Barnard & Ramon G. Corrales. (Illus.). 352p. 1981. 21.75x (ISBN 0-398-03859-7). C C Thomas.
Theory & Technique of Latin-American Dancing. F. Borrows. (Ballroom Dance Ser.). 1985. lib. bdg. 66.00. Revisionist Pr.
Theory & Technique of Latin-American Dancing. F. Borrows. (Ballroom Dance Ser.). 1986. lib. bdg. 79.95 (ISBN 0-8490-3389-6). Gordon Pr.
Theory & Technique of Playwriting & Screenwriting. John H. Lawson. LC 82-47511. (Cinema Classics Ser.). 478p. 1984. lib. bdg. 50.00 (ISBN 0-8240-5768-6). Garland Pub.
Theory & Technique of Twelve Tone Composition. Larry Fotine. 1967. 12.50 (ISBN 0-933830-00-9). Poly Tone.
Theory & the Meaning of the Lines of the Hand with Special Emphasis on the Life & the Anticipation of One's Life Span. D. Saint Germain. (Illus.). 136p. 1983. 117.85 (ISBN 0-89901-124-1). Found Class Reprints.
Theory & the Meaning of the Lines of the Hand with Special Emphasis on the Line of Life & the Anticipation of One's Life Span. D. St. Germain. (Illus.). 126p. 1980. Repr. of 1876 ed. deluxe ed. 127.75 (ISBN 0-89901-020-2). Found Class Reprints.
Theory & Treatment of Anorexia Nervosa & Bulimia: Biomedical, Sociocultural, & Psychological Perspectives. Ed. by Steven W. Emmett. LC 84-29267. 352p. 1985. 35.00 (ISBN 0-87630-384-X). Brunner-Mazel.
Theory & Understanding: A Critique of Interpretive Social Science. Finn Collin. 340p. 1985. 45.00 (ISBN 0-631-14256-8). Basil Blackwell.
Theory & Use of Color. Luigina De Grandis. (Illus.). 160p. (Orig.). 1986. pap. 16.95 (ISBN 0-8109-2317-3). Abrams.
Theory & Use of Color. Luiginia De Grandis. (Illus.). 120p. 1987. pap. text ed. 13.95 (ISBN 0-13-914441-2). P-H.
Theory, Application & Practice of the Dow Method of Stock Market Trading. Robert Rhea. (Illus.). 137p. 1985. 227.50 (ISBN 0-86654-143-8). Inst Econ Finan.
Theory, Application & Practice of the Point & Figure Method of Stock Market Chart Analysis. William De La Vallieres. (New Stock Market Library). (Illus.). 1978. 197.50 (ISBN 0-89266-126-7). Am Classical Coll Pr.
Theory Building. rev. ed. Robert Dubin. LC 77-90010. (Illus.). 1978. text ed. 24.95 (ISBN 0-02-907620-X). Free Pr.
Theory Building & Data Analysis in the Social Sciences. Ed. by Herbert B. Asher et al. LC 83-3458. 464p. 1984. text ed. 34.95x (ISBN 0-87049-398-1); pap. text ed. 14.95x (ISBN 0-87049-399-X). U of Tenn Pr.
Theory Building for Basic Institutional Change. James E. Herrick. LC 76-55963. 1977. soft bdg. 11.95 (ISBN 0-88247-437-5). R & E Pubs.
Theory Building for Learning How to Learn. Ed. by Robert M. Smith. 150p. 1988. 24.95 (ISBN 0-934328-07-2); pap. 12.95 (ISBN 0-934328-08-0). Educ Studies Pr.
Theory Building in Developmental Psychology. P. Van Geert. 500p. 1986. 108.00 (ISBN 0-444-70042-0, North-Holland). Elsevier.
Theory, Construction & Calculations of Agricultural Machines, Vol. 1. E. S. Bosoi et al. (Russian Translation Ser.: No. 66). 325p. 1988. text ed. 55.00 (ISBN 90-6191-914-2, Pub. by A A Balkema). Brookfield Pub Co.
Theory Construction & Data Analysis in the Behavioral Sciences. Ed. by Samuel Shye. LC 78-62554. (Social & Behavioral Science Ser.). (Illus.). 1978. text ed. 49.95x (ISBN 0-87589-379-1). Jossey-Bass.
Theory Control & Research Design. Schrieshe. write for info. (ISBN 0-275-90017-7, C0017). Praeger.
Theory, Design & Application of Electronic Devices & Circuits. Leslie E. Worden. (Illus.). 700p. text ed. write for info. (ISBN 0-89894-014-1). Advocate Pub Group.
Theory, Determination & Control of Physical Properties of Food Materials. Ed. by Chokyun Rha. LC 74-76481. (Food Material Science Ser: No. 1). xi, 315p. 1975. lib. bdg. 68.50 (ISBN 90-277-0468-6, Pub. by Reidel Holland). Kluwer Academic.
Theory Development & Educational Administration. Ed. by Eddy J. Van Meter. 1973. pap. text ed. 12.95x (ISBN 0-8422-0297-8). Irvington.
Theory Development: What, Why, How? Dorothy E. Johnson & Imogene M. King. 86p. 1978. 11.95 (ISBN 0-88737-219-8, 15-1708). Natl League Nurse.
Theory for All Music: Problems & Solutions in the Analysis of Non-Western Forms. Jay Rahn. 288p. 1983. 35.00x (ISBN 0-8020-5538-9). U of Toronto Pr.
Theory for Economic Efficiency: Essays in Honor of Abba P. Lerner. Ed. by Harry Greenfield. 1979. text ed. 40.00x (ISBN 0-262-07074-X). MIT Pr.
Theory for Nursing: Systems, Concepts & Process. Imogene M. King. LC 81-1996. 181p. 1981. 17.50 (ISBN 0-471-07795-X). Wiley.
Theory for Social Work Practice. Ruth E. Smalley. LC 67-14290. 1967. 32.00x (ISBN 0-231-02769-9); pap. 16.00x (ISBN 0-231-08327-0). Columbia U Pr.
Theory Formulations. Ed. by Williard E. Stone. (University of Florida Accounting Ser.: No. 6). 1970. pap. 6.00x (ISBN 0-8130-0341-5). U Presses Fla.
Theory I: End Your One-Minute Search for Excellence. Richard E. Thompson & David R. Thompson. LC 86-90531. (Illus.). 105p. (Orig.). pap. 5.95 (ISBN 0-940555-00-X). Senss Pubns.
Theory in Anthropology: A Sourcebook. Ed. by Robert A. Manners & David Kaplan. LC 67-17606. 1968. lib. bdg. 41.95x (ISBN 0-202-01041-4). Aldine de Gruyter.
Theory in Nonparametic: Asymptotic Distribution. Manfred Denker. Ed. by Gerd Fischer. 210p. 1985. pap. 18.00 (ISBN 3-528-08905-9, Pub. by Vieweg & Sohn Germany). IPS.
Theory in Practice: Increasing Professional Effectiveness. Chris Argyris & Donald A. Schon. LC 74-3606. (Higher Education Ser.). 218p. 1974. 23.95x (ISBN 0-87589-230-2). Jossey-Bass.
Theory in Psychopharmacology, Vol. 2. Ed. by Steven J. Cooper. 1983. 66.00 (ISBN 0-12-188002-8). Acad Pr.
Theory in Retailing: Traditional & Nontraditional Sources. Ronald W. Stampfl & Elizabeth C. Hirschman. LC 80-23919. (American Marketing Association, Proceedings Ser.). pap. 49.80 (ISBN 0-317-20072-0, 20233354). Bks Demand UMI.
Theory in the Classroom. Ed. by Cary Nelson. LC 85-16531. 248p. 1986. 19.95 (ISBN 0-252-01265-8); pap. 10.95 (ISBN 0-252-01471-5). U of Ill Pr.
Theory, Law, & Policy of Contemporary Japanese Treaties. Louis J. Adams. LC 73-11245. 288p. 1974. lib. bdg. 21.00 (ISBN 0-379-00021-0). Oceana.
Theory, Law & Policy of Soviet Treaties. Jan F. Triska & Robert M. Slusser. 1962. 50.00x (ISBN 0-8047-0122-9). Stanford U Pr.
Theory, Methods, & Processes of Counseling & Psychotherapy. Rickey L. George & Therese S. Cristiani. (Counseling & Human Development Ser.). (Illus.). 400p. 1981. P-H.
Theory Notebook Complete. John Brimhall. 96p. (Orig.). 1985. pap. text ed. 8.95 (ISBN 0-8494-0028-7, M465). Hansen Ed Mus.
Theory of A. R. Luria. Donna R. Vocate. (Functions of Spoken Language in the Development of Higher Mental Processes Ser.). 208p. 1986. text ed. 27.50 (ISBN 0-89859-709-9). L Erlbaum Assocs.
Theory of Accounting Measurement, Vol. 10. Yuji Ijiri. (Studies in Accounting Research). 210p. 1975. 6.00 (ISBN 0-86539-022-3). Am Accounting.
Theory of Accounts. Scott. LC 75-18482. (History of Accounting Ser.). (Illus.). 1976. Repr. 20.00x (ISBN 0-405-07564-2). Ayer Co Pubs.
Theory of Achievement Motivation. Ed. by J. W. Atkinson & Norman T. Feather. LC 74-7064. 404p. 1974. Repr. of 1966 ed. 27.50 (ISBN 0-88275-166-2). Krieger.
Theory of Action. Lawrence Davis. (Foundations of Philosophy Ser.). 1979. ref. o.p. 17.95 (ISBN 0-13-913152-3). P-H.
Theory of Action-at-a-Distance in Relativistic Particle Dynamics. Edward H. Kerner. (International Science Review Ser.). 232p. 1972. 88.00 (ISBN 0-677-13990-X). Gordon & Breach.
Theory of Action Identification. Robin R. Vallacher & Daniel M. Wegner. (Basic Studies in Human Behavior). 272p. 1985. text ed. 29.95 (ISBN 0-89859-617-3). L Erlbaum Assocs.
Theory of Action: Towards a New Synthesis Going Beyond Parsons. Richard Munch. 358p. 1988. text ed. 59.95 (ISBN 0-7102-1218-6, Pub. by Routledge UK). Routledge Chapman & Hall.
Theory of Adaptive Economic Behaviour. John G. Cross. LC 83-7563. 199p. 1983. 39.50 (ISBN 0-521-25110-9). Cambridge U Pr.
Theory of Advanced First Aid. J. A. Wood. 1985. lib. bdg. 14.50 (ISBN 0-85200-892-9, Pub. by MTP England). Kluwer Academic.
Theory of Advertising: A Simple Exposition of the Principles of Psychology in Their Relation to Successful Advertising. Walter D. Scott. Ed. by Henry Assael & Samuel Craig. LC 84-46036. 252p. 1985. lib. bdg. 30.00 (ISBN 0-8240-6730-4). Garland Pub.
Theory of African Literature: Implications for Practical Criticism. Chidi Amuta. 224p. 1988. text ed. 39.95 (ISBN 0-86232-546-3, Pub. by Zed Pr UK); pap. text ed. 12.50 (ISBN 0-86232-547-1, Pub. by Zed Pr UK). Humanities.
Theory of Algebraic Numbers. 2nd ed. Harry Pollard & H. G. Diamond. LC 75-27003. (Carus Mathematical Monographs: No. 9). xii, 162p. 1975. 21.00 (ISBN 0-88385-018-4). Math Assn.
Theory of Algorithms: Colloquia Mathematica Societatis Janos Bolyai Ser. Ed. by L. Lovasz & E. Szemeredi. (Vol. 44). 430p. 1986. 94.75 (ISBN 0-444-87760-6). Elsevier.
Theory of Alloy Phase Formation: Proceedings of a Symposium-Sponsored by the TMS-AIME Alloy Phases Committee & the Chemistry & Physics of Metals Committee at the 10th AIME Annual Meeting, New Orleans, La., February 19-20, 1979. Metallurgical Society of AIME Staff. Ed. by L. H. Bennett. LC 80-80305. pap. 133.80 (ISBN 0-317-26178-9, 2024264). Bks Demand UMI.
Theory of American Film: The Films & Techniques of George Stevens. Bruce Petri. Ed. by Stephen Orgel. (Harvard Dissertations in American & English Literature). 401p. 1987. lib. bdg. 65.00 (ISBN 0-8240-0070-6). Garland Pub.
Theory of Analytic Functions: A Brief Course. A. I. Markushevich. 432p. 1983. 10.95 (ISBN 0-8285-2389-4, Pub. by Mir Pubs USSR). Imported Pubns.
Theory of Approximate Methods & Their Application to the Numerical Solution of Singular Integral Equations, No. 2. V. V. Ivanov. (Mechanics Analysis Ser.). 348p. 1976. 40.00x (ISBN 90-286-0036-1, Pub. by Sijthoff & Noordhoff). Kluwer Academic.
Theory of Approximation. Dunham Jackson. LC 30-32147. (Colloquium Pbns. Ser.: Vol. 11). 178p. 1982. Repr. of 1930 ed. 30.00 (ISBN 0-8218-1011-1, COLL-11). Am Math.
Theory of Arithmetic Functions. Ed. by A. A. Gioia & D. L. Goldsmith. (Lecture Notes in Mathematics: Vol. 251). 287p. 1972. pap. 18.00 (ISBN 0-387-05723-4). Springer-Verlag.
Theory of Art in the "Encyclopedie". Amy C. Simowitz. Ed. by Donald Kuspit. LC 83-4999. (Studies in the Fine Arts: Art Theory: No. 9). 148p. 1983. 37.95 (ISBN 0-8357-1433-0). UMI Res Pr.
Theory of Art: Inexhaustibility by Contrast. Stephen D. Ross. LC 81-9027. (SUNY Series in Systematic Philosophy). 246p. 1982. 44.50x (ISBN 0-87395-554-4); pap. 18.95x (ISBN 0-87395-555-2). State U NY Pr.
Theory of Art, Tragedy & Culture: The Philosophy of Eliseo Vivas. Hugh Curtler. (World of Art Ser.). 224p. 1983. pap. text ed. 11.00 (ISBN 0-930586-15-8). Haven Pubns.
Theory of Asymmetrical Elasticity. 2nd ed. W. Nowaki. 1986. 95.00 (ISBN 0-08-027584-2). Pergamon.
Theory of Atomic Collisions, Vol. II. 3rd ed. N. F. Mott & O. S. Massey. (International Series of Monographs on Physics). (Illus.). 558p. 1987. 31.95 (ISBN 0-19-852031-X). Oxford U Pr.
Theory of Atomic Collisions, Vol. I. 3rd ed. N. F. Mott & O. S. Massey. (International Series on Monographs on Physics). (Illus.). 362p. 1987. pap. 26.95 (ISBN 0-19-852030-1). Oxford U Pr.
Theory of Atomic Spectra. Edward U. Condon & George H. Shortley. (Orig.). 1935. pap. 37.50 (ISBN 0-521-09209-4). Cambridge U Pr.
Theory of Atomic Structure & Spectra. Robert D. Cowan. LC 81-4578. (Los Alamos Ser. in Basic & Applied Sciences: No. 3). 650p. 1981. 50.00x (ISBN 0-520-03821-5). U of Cal Pr.
Theory of Auditing. Charles W. Schandl. LC 78-17862. 1978. text ed. 13.00 (ISBN 0-914348-23-X). Scholars Bk.
Theory of Automatic Control. Ed. by A. Netushil. 806p. 1978. 15.00 (ISBN 0-8285-0698-1, Pub. by Mir Pubs USSR). Imported Pubns.
Theory of Backmixing: The Design of Continuous Flow Chemical Plant with Backmixing. J. C. Mecklenburgh & S. Hartland. LC 74-32190. pap. 132.30 (ISBN 0-317-41980-3, 2025977). Bks Demand UMI.
Theory of Bases & Cones. P. K. Kamthan. 272p. 1985. pap. 28.95 (ISBN 0-470-20509-1, Co-Pub. with Longman). Wiley.
Theory of Beam Columns, Vol. 2: Space Behavior & Design. Chen Wai-Fah & Toshio Atsuta. 1977. text ed. 81.95x (ISBN 0-07-010759-9). McGraw.
Theory of Beauty & of Human Beauty, 2 vols. John Ruskin. (Illus.). 287p. 1986. 217.55 (ISBN 0-89901-268-X). Found Class Reprints.
Theory of Beauty in the Classical Aesthetics of Japan. Toshihiko Izutsu & Toyo Izutsu. 172p. 1981. 31.50 (ISBN 90-247-2381-7, Pub. by Martinus Nijhoff Netherlands). Kluwer Academic.
Theory of Behavior in Organizations. James C. Naylor et al. LC 79-6798. 1980. 24.95 (ISBN 0-12-514450-4). Acad Pr.
Theory of Bessel Functions. George N. Watson. pap. text ed. 42.50 (ISBN 0-521-09382-1). Cambridge U Pr.
Theory of Best Approximation & Functional Analysis. Ivan Singer. (CBMS-NSF Regional Conference Ser.: No. 13). vii, 95p. (Orig.). 1974. pap. text ed. 15.50 (ISBN 0-89871-010-3). Soc Indus-Appl Math.

Theory of Electromagnetic Flow Measurement. J. A. Shercliff. (Cambridge Science Classics Ser.). (Illus.). 160p. 1987. pap. 14.95 (ISBN 0-521-33554-X). Cambridge U Pr.

Theory of Electromagnetic Flow-Measurement. John A. Shercliffe. (Cambridge Engineering Ser.). pap. 39.50 (ISBN 0-317-09192-1, 2050749). Bks Demand UMI.

Theory of Electromagnetic Wave Propagation. Charles H. Papas. 257p. 1988. pap. 6.95t (ISBN 0-486-65678-0). Dover.

Theory of Electromagnetic Waves: A Coordinate Free Approach. Hollis C. Chen. (McGraw-Hill Series in Electrical Engineering). (Illus.). 464p. 1983. text ed. 49.95 (ISBN 0-07-010688-6). McGraw.

Theory of Energy Transfers & Conversions. Federico Grabiel. LC 67-23440. (Illus.). pap. 57.80 (ISBN 0-317-07883-6, 2006350). Bks Demand UMI.

Theory of English Lexicography 1530-1791. Tetsuro Hayashi. (Studies in the History of Linguistics Ser.: No. 18). xii, 168p. 1978. 26.00x (ISBN 90-272-0959-6). Benjamins North Am.

Theory of Environmental Policy. 2nd. ed. William J. Baumol & Wallace E. Oates. 288p. 1988. 49.50 (ISBN 0-521-32224-3); pap. 17.95 (ISBN 0-521-31112-8). Cambridge U Pr.

Theory of Epistemic Rationality. Richard Foley. LC 86-31963. 352p. 1987. text ed. 35.00x (ISBN 0-674-88276-8). Harvard U Pr.

Theory of Equilibrium Growth. Avinash Dixit. (Illus.). 1976. text ed. 19.95x (ISBN 0-19-877080-4); pap. text ed. 11.95x (ISBN 0-19-877081-2). Oxford U Pr.

Theory of Error Correcting Codes, 2 Pts. in 1 vol. F. J. MacWilliams & N. J. Sloane. (Mathematical Library: Vol. 16). 762p. 1978. 56.25 (ISBN 0-444-85193-3, North-Holland). Elsevier.

Theory of Ethnicity: An Anthropologist's Perspective. Ronald A. Reminick. LC 83-1161. 80p. (Orig.). 1983. lib. bdg. 22.75 (ISBN 0-8191-3075-3); pap. text ed. 8.75 (ISBN 0-8191-3076-1). U Pr of Amer.

Theory of Evolution & Dynamical Systems: Mathematical Aspects of Selection. J. Hofbauer & K. Sigmund. (London Mathematical Society Students Texts Ser.: No. 7). (Illus.). 350p. Date not set. price not set (ISBN 0-521-35288-6); pap. price not set (ISBN 0-521-35838-8). Cambridge U Pr.

Theory of Evolving Tonality. Joseph Yasser. (Illus.). 1932. 15.00x (ISBN 0-8450-2599-6, Pub. by Am. Library of Musicology). Broude.

Theory of Evolving Tonality. Joseph Yasser. LC 74-34376. (Music Reprint Ser.). (Illus.). x, 381p. 1975. Repr. of 1932 ed. lib. bdg. 47.50 (ISBN 0-306-70729-2). Da Capo.

Theory of Excitable Media. V. S. Markin et al. LC 87-13373. (Nonequilibrium Problems in the Physical Sciences & Biology Ser.). 303p. 1987. 79.95 (ISBN 0-471-81676-0, Pub. by Wiley-Interscience). Wiley.

Theory of Excitons. Robert S. Knox. (Solid State Physics: Advances in Research & Applications Suppl. 5). 1964. 56.50 (ISBN 0-12-607765-7). Acad Pr.

Theory of Experiential Education. 15.00 (ISBN 0-318-19112-1). Assn Exper Ed.

Theory of Externalities, Public Goods & Club Goods. Richard Cornes & Todd Sandler. (Illus.). 320p. 1986. 37.50 (ISBN 0-521-30184-X); pap. 13.95 (ISBN 0-521-31774-6). Cambridge U Pr.

Theory of Extremal Problems. A. D. Ioffe & V. M. Tihomirov. (Studies in Mathematics & Its Applications: Vol. 6). 460p. 1979. 85.00 (ISBN 0-444-85167-4, North Holland). Elsevier.

Theory of Family Systems. Norman Ackerman. 225p. 1984. 26.95 (ISBN 0-89876-032-1). Gardner Pr.

Theory of Feeding & Growth of Animals. J. R. Parks. (Advanced Series in Agriculture: Vol. 11). (Illus.). 322p. 1982. 71.50 (ISBN 0-387-11122-0). Springer-Verlag.

Theory of Feelings. Agnes Heller. (Dialectic & Society Ser.: No. 7). 252p. 1979. pap. text ed. 20.00 (ISBN 90-232-1699-7, Pub. by Van Gorcum Holland). Longwood Pub Group.

Theory of Fertility Decline. J. C. Caldwell. LC 81-68983. (Population & Social Structure Ser.). 1982. 34.00 (ISBN 0-12-155080-X). Acad Pr.

Theory of Fiction: Henry James. Henry James. Ed. by James E. Miller, Jr. LC 78-147168. xx, 367p. 1972. pap. 8.95x (ISBN 0-8032-5747-3, BB 542, Bison). U of Nebr Pr.

Theory of Film Language. Jerry L. Salvaggio. Ed. by Garth S. Jowett. LC 79-6684. (Dissertations on Film, 1980 Ser.). 1980. lib. bdg. 22.00x (ISBN 0-405-12916-5). Ayer Co Pubs.

Theory of Film Practice. Noel Burch. Tr. by Helen R. Lane from Fr. LC 80-8676. (Illus.). 172p. 1981. pap. 8.95x (ISBN 0-691-00329-7). Princeton U Pr.

Theory of Film: The Redemption of Physical Reality. Siegfried Kracauer. (Illus.). 1960. pap. 10.95 (ISBN 0-19-500721-2). Oxford U Pr.

Theory of Finance. Eugene F. Fama & Merton H. Miller. 346p. 1972. 30.95x (ISBN 0-03-086732-0). Dryden Pr.

Theory of Finance: Being a Short Treatise on the Doctrine of Interest & Annuities-Certain. George King. Ed. by Richard P. Brief. LC 80-1506. (Dimensions of Accounting Theory & Practice Ser.). 1981. Repr. of 1882 ed. lib. bdg. 14.00x (ISBN 0-405-13531-9). Ayer Co Pubs.

Theory of Finance: Evidence & Applications. John D. Martin & Samuel H. Cox. (Illus.). 736p. 1988. text ed. price not set (ISBN 0-03-063854-2). Dryden Pr.

Theory of Financial Decision Making. Jonathan E. Ingersoll, Jr. LC 86-1907. (Studies in Financial Economics). 400p. 1987. 39.50x (ISBN 0-8476-7359-6, Rowman & Littlefield). Rowman.

Theory of Financial Decisions. 2nd ed. Charles W. Haley & Lawrence D. Schall. (Illus.). 1979. text ed. 42.95 (ISBN 0-07-025568-7). McGraw.

Theory of Financial Management. Ezra Solomon. LC 63-8405. (Illus.). 1963. 24.00x (ISBN 0-231-02604-8). Columbia U Pr.

Theory of Financial Markets & Information. J. A. Ohlson. 362p. 1987. 38.95 (ISBN 0-444-01161-7, North Holland). Elsevier.

Theory of Fish Population Dynamics As the Biological Background for Rational Exploitation & Management of Fishery Resources. G. V. Nikolskii. Ed. by R. Jones. Tr. by J. E. Bradley from Rus. (Illus.). 323p. 1980. Repr. of 1969 ed. lib. bdg. 48.00x (ISBN 3-87429-171-5). Lubrecht & Cramer.

Theory of Flexible Shells. E. L. Axelrad. (North-Holland Series in Applied Mathematics & Mechanics: No. 28). 300p. 1986. 80.00 (ISBN 0-444-87954-4, North-Holland). Elsevier.

Theory of Flight. Richard Von Mises. pap. 10.95 (ISBN 0-486-60541-8). Dover.

Theory of Flight. Muriel Rukeyser. LC 74-144741. (Yale Series of Younger Poets: No. 34). Repr. of 1935 ed. 18.00 (ISBN 0-404-53834-7). AMS Pr.

Theory of Flight. Richard Von Mises. 17.00 (ISBN 0-8446-2599-X). Peter Smith.

Theory of Fluctuations in Contemporary Economic Thought. Sidney D. Merlin. LC 68-54286. (Columbia University. Studies in the Social Sciences: No. 556). Repr. of 1949 ed. 16.50 (ISBN 0-404-51556-8). AMS Pr.

Theory of Fluid Flow in Undeformable Porous Media. V. I. Aravin & S. N. Numerov. 528p. 1965. text ed. 100.00 (ISBN 0-7065-0522-0, Pub. by Keter Pub Jerusalem). Coronet Bks.

Theory of Fog Condensation. A. G. Amelin. 248p. 1967. text ed. 50.00x (ISBN 0-7065-0593-X, Pub. by Keter Pub Jerusalem). Coronet Bks.

Theory of Forest Dynamics: The Ecological Implications of Forest Succession Models. H. H. Shugart. (Illus.). 305p. 1984. 47.90 (ISBN 0-387-96000-7). Springer-Verlag.

Theory of Formal Deducibility. Haskell B. Curry. (Orig.). 1957. pap. 5.95x (ISBN 0-268-00274-6). U of Notre Dame Pr.

Theory of Fourier Series & Integrals. P. L. Walker. LC 85-17931. 192p. 1986. 34.95 (ISBN 0-471-90112-1). Wiley.

Theory of Free Banking: A Study of the Supply of Money under Competitive Note Issue. George A. Selgin. 232p. 1988. 33.50 (ISBN 0-8476-7578-5). Rowman.

Theory of Free Radical Polymerization. K. S. Bagdasar'yan. 328p. 1968. text ed. 64.00x (ISBN 0-7065-0604-9, Pub. by Keter Pub Jerusalem). Coronet Bks.

Theory of Free Will. St. Augustine. (Illus.). 117p. 1984. 97.75 (ISBN 0-89266-466-5). Am Classical Coll Pr.

Theory of Freedom. Stanley I. Benn. 448p. Date not set. 49.50 (ISBN 0-521-34260-0); pap. 17.95 (ISBN 0-521-34802-1). Cambridge U Pr.

Theory of Freedom in Hegel's Conception of the Universe. Hugo W. Wastermarck. (Essential Library of the Great Philosophers). (Illus.). 99p. 1984. pap. 117.75 (ISBN 0-89266-446-0). Am Classical Coll Pr.

Theory of Fully Ionized Plasmas. Gunter Ecker. 1972. 99.50 (ISBN 0-12-229750-4). Acad Pr.

Theory of Functions. 2nd ed. Constantin Caratheodory. LC 60-16838. Vol. 1. 14.95 (ISBN 0-8284-0097-0); Vol. 2. 14.95 (ISBN 0-8284-0106-3). Chelsea Pub.

Theory of Functions, 2 vols. Konrad Knopp. (Illus.). Vol. 1. pap. 4.50 (ISBN 0-486-60156-0); Vol. 2. pap. text ed. 3.95 (ISBN 0-486-60157-9). Dover.

Theory of Functions. 2nd ed. Edward C. Titchmarsh. 1939. 24.95x (ISBN 0-19-853349-7). Oxford U Pr.

Theory of Functions & Its Applications. Ed. by L. S. Pontrjagin & E. A. Voltov. LC 77-10017. (Steklov Institute of Mathematics, Proceedings: No. 134). 1977. 92.00 (ISBN 0-8218-3034-1, STEKLO 134). Am Math.

Theory of Functions of a Complex Variable, 3 vols. in 1. 2nd ed. A. I. Markushevich. Tr. by Richard A. Silverman from Rus. LC 77-8515. 1977. text ed. 35.00 (ISBN 0-8284-0296-5). Chelsea Pub.

Theory of Functions of a Complex Variable. George Yankovsky. 311p. 1973. 22.50 (ISBN 0-8464-1275-6). Beekman Pubs.

Theory of Functions of a Real Variable. R. L. Jeffery. (Mathematics Ser.). 256p. 1985. pap. 6.00 (ISBN 0-486-64781-1). Dover.

Theory of Functions on Complex Manifolds. Ed. by Collet's Holdings, Ltd. Staff. 1986. 98.00x (ISBN 0-317-46748-4, Pub. by Collets (UK)). State Mutual Bk.

Theory of Functions on Complex Manifolds. Gennadi M. Henkin & Jurgen Leiterer. (Monographs in Mathematics). 240p. 1983. text ed. 37.00 (ISBN 3-7643-1477-X). Birkhauser.

Theory of Fundamental Interactions: Proceedings of the International School of Physics, Enrico Fermi Course LXXXI, Varenna, Italy, July 21 - August 2, 1980. Ed. by G. Costa & R. R. Gatto. (Enrico Fermi International Summer School of Physics Ser.: Vol. 81). 300p. 1982. 102.75 (ISBN 0-444-86156-4, I-324-82, North Holland). Elsevier.

Theory of Fundamental Processes. Richard P. Feynman. (Frontiers in Physics Ser.: No. 4). (Illus.). 1961. pap. 37.75 (ISBN 0-8053-2507-7, Adv Bk Prog MSP). Addison-Wesley.

Theory of Gambling & Statistical Logic. rev. ed. Richard A. Epstein. 1977. 39.50 (ISBN 0-12-240760-1). Acad Pr.

Theory of Games. Jianhua Wang. (Mathematical Monographs). (Illus.). 224p. 1988. 55.00 (ISBN 0-19-853560-0). Oxford U Pr.

Theory of Games & Economic Behavior. John Von Neumann & Oskar Morgenstern. LC 53-4426. 664p. 1980. 69.00x (ISBN 0-691-04183-0); pap. 22.50x (ISBN 0-691-00362-9). Princeton U Pr.

Theory of Games & Markets: An Introduction to Game Theory & Related Topics. J. Rosenmuller. 554p. 1981. 105.25 (ISBN 0-444-85482-7, North-Holland). Elsevier.

Theory of Games & Statistical Decisions. David A. Blackwell & M. A. Girshick. 368p. 1980. pap. 7.95 (ISBN 0-486-63831-6). Dover.

Theory of Gauge Fields in Four Dimensions. H. Blaine Lawson, Jr. LC 85-441. (Regional Conference Series in Mathematics). 101p. 1985. pap. text ed. 18.00 (ISBN 0-8218-0708-0, CBMS-58). Am Math.

Theory of Gene Frequencies see Evolution & the Genetics of Populations.

Theory of General Economic Equilibrium. Trout Rader. 1972. 29.95 (ISBN 0-12-575040-4). Acad Pr.

Theory of General Economic Equilibruim. Andreu Mas-Collel. (Econometric Society Monograph). 369p. 1985. 42.50 (ISBN 0-521-26514-2). Cambridge U Pr.

Theory of General Static Equilibrium. Eraldo Fossati. Ed. by G. L. Shackle. 1957. lib. bdg. 29.50 (ISBN 0-678-08076-3). Kelley.

Theory of Generalised Functions. 2nd ed. D. S. Jones. LC 80-41830. 500p. 1982. 87.50 (ISBN 0-521-23723-8). Cambridge U Pr.

Theory of Generalized Spectral Operators. I. Colojoara & C. Foias. LC 68-24488. (Mathematics & Its Applications Ser.). 248p. 1968. 94.00 (ISBN 0-677-01480-5). Gordon & Breach.

Theory of German Word Order from the Renaissance to the Present. Aldo Scaglione. LC 80-16619. 275p. 1981. 22.50x (ISBN 0-8166-0980-2); pap. 10.95 (ISBN 0-8166-0983-7). U of Minn Pr.

Theory of Grammatical Agreement. Steven G. Lapointe. Ed. by Jorge Hankamer. (Outstanding Dissertations in Linguistics Ser.). 375p. 1985. 47.00 (ISBN 0-8240-5433-4). Garland Pub.

Theory of Grammatical Relations. John S. Bowers. LC 80-21018. 304p. 1981. 37.50x. Cornell U Pr.

Theory of Graphs. International Computation Centre. 434p. 1967. 165.00 (ISBN 0-677-11780-9). Gordon & Breach.

Theory of Graphs. Oystein Ore. LC 61-15687. (Colloquium Pbns. Ser.: Vol. 38). 270p. 1983. pap. 29.00 (ISBN 0-8218-1038-3, COLL-38). Am Math.

Theory of Graphs: A Basis for Network Theory. Lee M. Maxwell & Myril B. Reed. LC 77-106387. 181p. 1975. text ed. 25.00 (ISBN 0-08-016321-1). Pergamon.

Theory of Graphs & Its Applications. Claude Berg. Tr. by Alison Doig from Fr. LC 81-23719. x, 247p. 1982. Repr. of 1962 ed. lib. bdg. 35.00x (ISBN 0-313-23351-9, BETG). Greenwood.

Theory of Graphs in Linguistics. Ernesto Zierer. LC 71-129294. (Janua Linguarum, Ser. Minor: No. 94). 1970. pap. text ed. 7.20x (ISBN 90-2791-277-7). Mouton.

Theory of Ground Vehicles. J. Y. Wong. LC 78-16714. 330p. 1978. 63.00 (ISBN 0-471-03470-3, Pub. by Wiley-Interscience). Wiley.

Theory of Ground Water Movement. P. Polubarinova-Kochina. Tr. by R. De Wiest. 1962. 73.00x (ISBN 0-691-08048-8). Princeton U Pr.

Theory of Groundwater Flow. A. Verruijt. 200p. 1970. 77.00 (ISBN 0-677-61660-0). Gordon & Breach.

Theory of Group Representations. M. A. Naimark. (Illus.). 576p. 1982. 82.50 (ISBN 0-387-90602-9). Springer-Verlag.

Theory of Group Representations & Applications. A. Barut & R. Raczka. 740p. 1986. 75.00 (ISBN 9971-50-216-X, Z0352M-B); pap. 41.00 (ISBN 9971-50-217-8). World Scientific Pub.

Theory of Group Structures, 2 vols. Mackenzie. 550p. 1976. Set. 70.00 (ISBN 0-677-05330-4). Gordon & Breach.

Theory of Groups. 2nd ed. Marshall Hall, Jr. LC 75-42306. xiii, 434p. text ed. 14.95 (ISBN 0-8284-0288-4). Chelsea Pub.

Theory of Groups. Ian D. MacDonald. 1968. pap. 19.95x (ISBN 0-19-853138-9). Oxford U Pr.

Theory of Groups. Ian D. MacDonald. LC 88-578. 262p. 1988. Repr. of 1968 ed. lib. bdg. 19.95 (ISBN 0-89464-287-1). Krieger.

Theory of Groups & Its Application to Physical Problems. S. Bhagavantam & T. Venkatarayudu. 1969. 38.50 (ISBN 0-12-095460-5). Acad Pr.

Theory of Groups & Quantum Mechanics. Hermann Weyl. 1950. pap. text ed. 8.00 (ISBN 0-486-60269-9). Dover.

Theory of Growth & the Tradition of Ricardian Dynamics. Badal Mukherji. (Illus.). 1984. text ed. 10.95x (ISBN 0-19-561490-9). Oxford U Pr.

Theory of Growth in a Corporate Economy: Management Preference, Research & Development & Economic Growth. Hiroyuki Odagiri. LC 80-23494. (Illus.). 256p. 1981. 47.50 (ISBN 0-521-23132-9). Cambridge U Pr.

Theory of Harmony. Ernst Levy. Ed. by Siegmund Levarie. LC 85-12604. (Series in Cultural Perspectives). (Illus.). 99p. 1985. 39.50x (ISBN 0-87395-993-0); pap. 12.95x (ISBN 0-87395-992-2). State U NY Pr.

Theory of Harmony. Arnold Schoenberg. Tr. by Roy E. Carter. 1983. 57.50x (ISBN 0-520-04945-4); pap. 14.95 (ISBN 0-520-04944-6). U of Cal Pr.

Theory of Harmony. Matthew Shirlaw. LC 72-87348. (Music Reprint Ser.). 1969. Repr. of 1917 ed. lib. bdg. 49.50 (ISBN 0-306-71658-5). Da Capo.

Theory of Harmony in the Romantic Poetry by Ludovico Ariosto. Benedetto Croce. (Illus.). 111p. 1983. 127.75 (ISBN 0-89266-413-4). Am Classical Coll Pr.

Theory of Heat. 3rd ed. James C. Maxwell. LC 77-173064. Repr. of 1872 ed. 11.25 (ISBN 0-404-04277-5). AMS Pr.

Theory of Heat. 3rd ed. James C. Maxwell. 1970. Repr. of 1872 ed. lib. bdg. 35.00x (ISBN 0-8371-4097-8, MATH). Greenwood.

Theory of Heat & Mass Transfer. A. V. Lykov et al. 568p. 1965. text ed. 115.00x (ISBN 0-7065-0561-1, Pub. by Keter Pub Jerusalem). Coronet Bks.

Theory of Heavy Fermions & Valence Fluctuations. T. Kasuya & T. Saso. (Series in Solid-State Sciences: Vol. 62). (Illus.). xii, 287p. 1985. 32.00 (ISBN 0-387-15922-3). Springer-Verlag.

Theory of Hedge Investment. Brendan Brown. LC 82-5651. 240p. 1982. 25.00 (ISBN 0-312-79783-4). St Martin.

Theory of Heuristic Information in Game-Tree Searches. C. H. Tzeng. (Symbolic Computation - Artificial Intelligence Ser.). (Illus.). 120p. 1988. 39.50 (ISBN 0-387-18665-4). Springer-Verlag.

Theory of History & Society, with Special Reference to the Chronographia of Michael Psellus: Eleventh Century Byzantium. 2nd ed. A. A. Gadolin. (Illus.). 244p. 1986. lib. bdg. 45.00x (ISBN 90-256-0906-6, Pub. by A M Hakkert). Coronet Bks.

Theory of Holors: A Generalization of Tensors. Parry Moon & Domina E. Spencer. (Illus.). 330p. 1986. 72.50 (ISBN 0-521-24585-0). Cambridge U Pr.

Theory of HP Spaces. Peter L. Duren. LC 74-117092. (Pure & Applied Mathematics Ser.: Vol. 38). 1970. 59.50 (ISBN 0-12-225150-4). Acad Pr.

Theory of Hydromagnetic Stability. Bhimsen K. Shivamoggi. 284p. 1986. text ed. 110.00 (ISBN 2-88124-049-6). Gordon & Breach.

Theory of Imperfect Competition: A Radical Reconstruction. Donald Dewey. LC 73-79190. (Studies in Economics). (Illus.). 205p. 1969. 32.50x (ISBN 0-231-03164-5). Columbia U Pr.

Theory of Imperfect Crystalline Solids: Trieste Lectures, 1970. 608p. (Orig.). 1972. pap. 49.00 (ISBN 92-0-130071-9, ISP270, IAEA). UNIPUB.

Theory of Imperialism & the Inevitability of the Revolutionary Upheaval. Vladimir I. Lenin. 107p. 1987. 127.45 (ISBN 0-86722-166-6). Inst Econ Pol.

Theory of Income & Wealth Distribution. Ed. by Y. S. Brenner et al. LC 87-35308. 340p. 1988. 45.00 (ISBN 0-312-01965-3). St Martin.

Theory of Income Distribution. Harold Lydall. (Illus.). 1979. 42.00x (ISBN 0-19-828415-2). Oxford U Pr.

Theory of Incommensurate Crystals. V. L. Pokrovsky & A. L. Talapov. (Soviet Scientific Reviews Section A Physics Reviews Supplement Ser.: Vol. 1). 171p. 1982. text ed. 94.00 (ISBN 3-7186-0134-6). Harwood Academic.

Theory of Incomplete Cylindrical Functions & Their Applications. M. M. Agrest & M. S. Maksimov. Tr. by H. E. Fettis et al from Rus. LC 78-139673. (Grundlehren der Mathematischen Wissenschaften: Vol. 160). (Illus.). 1971. 65.00 (ISBN 0-387-05111-2). Springer-Verlag.

Theory of Indexing. Gerard Salton. (CBMS-NSF Regional Conference Ser.: No. 18). v, 56p. (Orig.). 1975. pap. text ed. 11.00 (ISBN 0-89871-015-4). Soc Indus-Appl Math.

Theory of Indian Music. Ram Avatar. (Illus.). 160p. 1980. 39.95 (ISBN 0-940500-13-2, Pub. by Punkaj India). Asia Bk Corp.

Theory of Indian Music. Swarup Bishan. 233p. 1987. 21.00x (ISBN 0-8364-2081-0, Pub. by Mittal). South Asia Bks.

TITLE INDEX

THEORY OF MOLECULAR INTERACTIONS.

Theory of Indigenous Southeast Asian Urbanism. Richard A. O'Connor. (Research Notes & Discussions). 142p. (Orig.). 1984. pap. text ed. 13.00x (ISBN 9971-902-61-3, Pub. by Inst Southeast Asian Stud). Gower Pub Co.

Theory of Indistinguishables: A Search for Explanatory Principles Below the Level of Physics. A. F. Parker-Rhodes. 248p. 1981. 39.50 (ISBN 90-277-1214-X, Pub. by Reidel Holland). Kluwer Academic.

Theory of Industrialism: Causal Analysis & Economic Plans. Johan Akerman. LC 80-21155. (Illus.). 332p. 1981. Repr. of 1960 ed. lib. bdg. 39.50x (ISBN 0-87991-859-4). Porcupine Pr.

Theory of Inequality among Men & the Collision of the Cultures. Jean-Jacques Rousseau. (Illus.). 137p. 1987. 149.75 (ISBN 0-89266-606-4). Am Classical Coll Pr.

Theory of Inertial Inflation: The Foundation of Successful Economic Reforms in Argentina & Brazil. Luiz C. Pereira & Yoshiaki Nakano. LC 86-29832. 225p. 1987. lib. bdg. 32.00 (ISBN 1-55587-007-4). Lynne Rienner.

Theory of Inertial Navigation: Aided Systems. V. D. Andreev. 424p. 1970. text ed. 85.00 (ISBN 0-7065-0708-8, Pub. by Keter Pub Jerusalem). Coronet Bks.

Theory of Inflation. J. I. Laliwala. 304p. 1983. 30.00x (ISBN 0-7069-2445-2, Pub. by Vikas India). Advent NY.

Theory of Innovation & Economic Evolution. Joseph A. Schumpeter. 138p. 1986. 147.55 (ISBN 0-86654-204-3). Inst Econ Finan.

Theory of Instruction: Principles & Applications. Siegfried Engelmann & Douglas Carnine. (Illus.). 385p. 1982. text ed. 49.50x (ISBN 0-8290-0977-9); pap. text ed. 29.95x (ISBN 0-8290-2040-3). Irvington.

Theory of Insurrection & Revolution, 2 vols. Nikolai I. Lenin. 275p. 1986. Set. 287.50 (ISBN 0-86722-139-9). Inst Econ Pol.

Theory of Integration. R. Henstock. 220p. 1988. 53.00 (ISBN 9971-50-450-2); pap. 28.00 (ISBN 9971-50-451-0). World Scientific Pub.

Theory of Inter-Sectoral Money Flows & Income Formation. John S. Chipman. LC 78-64212. (Johns Hopkins University. Studies in the Social Sciences. Sixty-Eighth Ser. 1950: 2). 160p. 1982. Repr. of 1851 ed. 24.50 (ISBN 0-404-61317-9). AMS Pr.

Theory of Interest. Irving Fisher. LC 86-7451. Repr. of 1930 ed. 45.00x (ISBN 0-678-00003-4). Kelley.

Theory of Interest. Stephen G. Kellison. 1971. Repr. of 1970 ed. 19.95x (ISBN 0-256-00283-5). Irwin.

Theory of Interest. F. A. Lutz. Tr. by Claus Witlich from Ger. 336p. 1967. lib. bdg. 37.00 (ISBN 90-277-0099-0, Pub. by Reidel Holland). Kluwer Academic.

Theory of Interest: As Determined by Impatience to Spend Income & Opportunity to Invest It. Irving Fisher. LC 77-22591. (Illus.). 1977. pap. 17.95x (ISBN 0-87991-864-0). Porcupine Pr.

Theory of Intermolecular Forces. 2nd ed. H. Margenau & N. Kestner. LC 79-142172. 1971. text ed. 83.00 (ISBN 0-08-016502-8). Pergamon.

Theory of International Law. G. I. Tunkin. Tr. by William E. Butler from Rus. LC 73-92258. 480p. 1974. text ed. 29.50x (ISBN 0-674-88001-3). Harvard U Pr.

Theory of International Politics. Kenneth N. Waltz. (Illus.). 250p. 1979. text ed. write for info (ISBN 0-394-34942-3, RanC). Random.

Theory of International Prices. James W. Angell. LC 65-19644. 1965. Repr. of 1926 ed. 49.50x (ISBN 0-678-00094-8). Kelley.

Theory of International Trade. A. Dixit & V. D. Norman. (Cambridge Economic Handbooks). 250p. 1980. 49.50 (ISBN 0-521-23481-6); pap. 19.95 (ISBN 0-521-29969-1). Cambridge U Pr.

Theory of International Trade. Ali M. El-Agraa. LC 83-3395, 208p. 1983. 35.00x (ISBN 0-312-79850-4). St Martin.

Theory of International Trade. James R. Markusen & James R. Melvin. 342p. 1988. text ed. 43.50 (ISBN 0-06-044212-3, HarpC). Har-Row.

Theory of International Trade under Uncertainty. Elhanan Helpman & Assaf Razin. (Economic Theory, Econometrics & Mathematical Economics Ser.). 1979. 47.00 (ISBN 0-12-339650-6). Acad Pr.

Theory of Intuition & Expression in Art. Benedetto Croce. (Illus.). 142p. 1983. 83.55x (ISBN 0-86650-070-7). Gloucester Art.

Theory of Intuition As an Analytical Instrument of Prediction Supplanting Both the Statistical & the Technical Approach in the Anticipation of Stock Market Price Movements & the Capturing of Speculative Profits. Spencer Fleming. (Illus.). 117p. 1988. 117.50 (ISBN 0-86654-263-9). Inst Econ Finan.

Theory of Intuition in Husserl's Phenomenology. Emmanuel Levinas. Tr. by Andre Orianne from Fr. (Studies in Phenomenology & Existential Philosophy). 165p. 1973. 29.95x (ISBN 0-8101-0413-X). Northwestern U Pr.

Theory of Intuition in Husserl's Phenomenology. Emmanuel Levinas. Tr. by Andre Orianne from Fr. (Studies in Phenomenology & Existential Philosophy). 207p. 1985. pap. 12.95 (ISBN 0-8101-0708-2). Northwestern U Pr.

Theory of Inventiveness. C. M. Flumiani. LC 68-23100. (Illus.). 32p. 1972. 117.75 (ISBN 0-913314-15-3). Am Classical Coll Pr.

Theory of Inventiveness in Schematic Representations. Carlo M. Flumiani. (Illus.). 141p. 1982. 127.75 (ISBN 0-86654-027-X). Inst Econ Finan.

Theory of Investment Cycles in a Socialist Economy. Nikola Cobeljic & Radmila Stojanovic. Ed. by Jerzy Karcz. LC 68-14431. pap. 43.50 (ISBN 0-317-41932-3, 2026140). Bks Demand UMI.

Theory of Investment of the Firm. Friedrich A. Lutz & Vera C. Lutz. 1970. Repr. of 1951 ed. lib. bdg. 35.00 (ISBN 0-8371-1108-0, LUTI). Greenwood.

Theory of Ionization of Atoms by Electron Impact. Raimonds Peterkops. Ed. by D. G. Hummer. Tr. by Elliot Aronson. LC 77-81310. (Illus.). pap. 68.30 (ISBN 0-317-09233-2, 2012203). Bks Demand UMI.

Theory of Ionospheric Waves. K. C. Yeh & C. H. Liv. (International Geophysics Ser., Vol. 17). 1972. 83.00 (ISBN 0-12-770450-7). Acad Pr.

Theory of Irrationalities of the Third Degree. B. N. Delone & D. K. Faddeev. LC 63-21548. (Translations of Mathematical Monographs: Vol. 10). 509p. 1978. pap. 55.00 (ISBN 0-8218-1560-1, MMONO-10). Am Math.

Theory of Island Biogeography. Roger H. MacArthur & Edward O. Wilson. (Monographs in Population Biology: Vol. 1). (Illus.). 1967. 26.50x (ISBN 0-691-08049-6); pap. 11.50x (ISBN 0-691-08050-X). Princeton U Pr.

Theory of Jacobi Forms. Martin Eichler & Don Zagier. (Progress in Mathematics Ser.: No. 55). 154p. 1985. 16.95 (ISBN 0-8176-3180-1). Birkhauser.

Theory of Jets in Electron: Position Annihilation. G. Kramer. (Springer Tracts in Modern Physics: Vol. 102). (Illus.). 106p. 1984. 39.30 (ISBN 0-387-13068-3). Springer-Verlag.

Theory of Join Spaces: A Contemporary Approach to Convex Sets & Linear Geometry. W. Prenowitz & J. Jantosciak. (Undergraduate Texts in Mathematics). (Illus.). 1979. 36.00 (ISBN 0-387-90340-2). Springer-Verlag.

Theory of Joint Maximization. P. Dixon. LC 74-24348. (Contributions to Economic Analysis: Vol. 91). 212p. 1975. 63.25 (ISBN 0-444-10792-4, North-Holland). Elsevier.

Theory of Justice. John Rawls. LC 73-168432. (Illus.). 1971. 27.00x (ISBN 0-674-88010-2, Belknap Pr); pap. 11.95 (ISBN 0-674-88014-5). Harvard U Pr.

Theory of Knowledge. D. W. Hamlyn. (Modern Introductions to Philosophy Ser.). 308p. 1980. pap. text ed. 15.00x (ISBN 0-333-11548-1). Humanities.

Theory of Knowledge. Leonard T. Hobhouse. LC 74-101094. Repr. of 1896 ed. 28.00 (ISBN 0-404-03278-8). AMS Pr.

Theory of Knowledge. Charles A. Strong. LC 75-3405. Repr. of 1923 ed. 20.00 (ISBN 0-404-59399-2). AMS Pr.

Theory of Knowledge & Existence. Walter T. Stace. 1970. Repr. of 1932 ed. lib. bdg. 25.00x (ISBN 0-8371-4343-8, STTK). Greenwood.

Theory of Knowledge Implicit in Goethe's World Conception. 2nd ed. Rudolf Steiner. Tr. by Olin D. Wannamaker from Ger. LC 70-76994. Orig. Title: Grundlinien Einer Erkenntnistheorie der Goetheschen Weltanschauung. 133p. 1978. 14.00 (ISBN 0-910142-94-7); pap. 7.95 (ISBN 0-910142-85-8). Anthroposophic.

Theory of Knowledge of Giambattista Vico: On the Method of the New Science Concerning the Common Nature of the Nations. Richard Manson. xiii, 84p. 1969. 16.50 (ISBN 0-208-00899-3, Archon). Shoe String.

Theory of Knowledge of Vital Du Four. John E. Lynch. (Philosophy Ser). 1972. 17.00 (ISBN 0-686-11546-5). Franciscan Inst.

Theory of Laminar Flames. J. D. Buckmaster & G. S. S. Ludford. LC 81-21573. (Cambridge Monographs on Mechanics & Applied Mathematics Ser.). (Illus.). 250p. 1982. 59.50 (ISBN 0-521-23929-X). Cambridge U Pr.

Theory of Laminar Flows. Ed. by Franklin K. Moore. (High Speed Aerodynamics & Jet Propulsion Ser.: Vol. 4). 1964. 100.00x (ISBN 0-691-08051-8). Princeton U Pr.

Theory of Laminated Spacetime. Barbara Dewey. LC 85-70368. (Illus.). 120p. 1985. 16.95 (ISBN 0-933123-02-7). Bartholomew Bks.

Theory of Language, Pts. 1 & 2. James Beattie. LC 78-147953. Repr. of 1788 ed. 36.50 (ISBN 0-404-08201-7). AMS Pr.

Theory of Language, Culture & Human Behavior. Joe E. Pierce. 160p. 1972. 9.95 (ISBN 0-913244-03-1). Hapi Pr.

Theory of Latice Dynamics in the Harmonic Approximation. 2nd ed. Ed. by A. A. Maradudin et al. (Solid State Physics: Suppl. 3). 1971. 98.00 (ISBN 0-12-607783-5). Acad Pr.

Theory of Laughter. V. K. Menon. LC 78-21711. 1972. Repr. of 1931 ed. lib. bdg. 39.50 (ISBN 0-8414-6329-8). Folcroft.

Theory of Law. Philip Soper. 208p. 1984. text ed. 18.95x (ISBN 0-674-88025-0). Harvard U Pr.

Theory of Law & Civil Society. Agost Pulszky. LC 79-1616. 1980. Repr. of 1888 ed. 35.00 (ISBN 0-88355-919-6). Hyperion Conn.

Theory of Legal Argumentation. Robert W. Alexy. Tr. by Ruth Adler & Neil MacCormick. 320p. 1989. 65.00 (ISBN 0-19-825503-9). Oxford U Pr.

Theory of Legal Science. Huntington Cairns. vii, 155p. 1969. Repr. of 1941 ed. 17.50x (ISBN 0-8377-2000-1). Rothman.

Theory of Legal Science. Aleksander Peczenik et al. 1984. lib. bdg. 74.00 (ISBN 90-277-1834-2, Pub. by Reidel Holland). Kluwer Academic.

Theory of Legislation. Jeremy Bentham. (Illus.). lii, 555p. 1987. Repr. of 1931 ed. 47.50x (ISBN 0-8377-1947-X). Rothman.

Theory of Legislation: An Essay on the Dynamics of Public Mind. Elijah Jordan. LC 30-20688. pap. 121.50 (ISBN 0-317-09406-8, 2011230). Bks Demand UMI.

Theory of Lexical Phonology. K. P. Mohanan. 1987. lib. bdg. 63.00 (ISBN 0-317-56506-0, Pub. by Reidel Holland); pap. text ed. 23.00 (ISBN 0-317-56507-9, Pub. by Reidel Holland). Kluwer Academic.

Theory of Liberty, Legitimacy & Power: New Directions in the Intellectual & Scientific Legacy of Max Weber. Ed. by Vatro Murvar. (International Library of Sociology). 224p. 1985. 39.95x (ISBN 0-7102-0355-1). Routledge Chapman & Hall.

Theory of Library Classification. Brian Buchanan. (Outlines of Modern Librarianship Ser.). 141p. 1980. text ed. 17.50 (ISBN 0-85157-270-7, Pub. by Bingley England). ALA.

Theory of Lie Groups. Claude Chevalley. (Mathematical Ser.: Vol. 8). 1946. 34.50x (ISBN 0-691-08052-6). Princeton U Pr.

Theory of Limit Cycles. Yan-Qian et al. LC 86-14070. (Translations of Mathematical Monographs: Vol. 66). 440p. 1986. text ed. 144.00 (ISBN 0-8218-4518-7). Am Math.

Theory of Linear Accelerators. A. D. Vlasov. 256p. 1968. text ed. 53.00x (ISBN 0-7065-0468-2, Pub. by Keter Pub Jerusalem). Coronet Bks.

Theory of Linear & Integer Programming. Alexander Shrijver. LC 85-12314. (Discrete Mathematics Ser.). 471p. 1986. 71.95 (ISBN 0-471-90854-1, Pub. by Wiley-Interscience). Wiley.

Theory of Linear Induction Machinery. Michel Poloujadoff. (Monographs in Electrical & Electronic Engineering). (Illus.). 1980. text ed. 49.00x (ISBN 0-19-859322-8). Oxford U Pr.

Theory of Linear Models & Multivariate Analysis. Steven F. Arnold. LC 80-23017. (Probability & Mathematical Statistics Ser.). 475p. 1981. 54.95 (ISBN 0-471-05065-2). Wiley.

Theory of Linear Operations. S. Banach. (Mathematical Library: No. 38). 238p. 1987. 89.50 (ISBN 0-444-70184-2, North Holland). Elsevier.

Theory of Linear Resonance Accelerators. I. M. Kapchinskiy. Tr. by S. J. Amoretty from Rus. (Accelerators & Storage Rings Ser.: Vol. 5). 398p. 1985. text ed. 180.00 (ISBN 3-7186-0233-4). Harwood Academic.

Theory of Linear Systems. Research & Education Association Staff. LC 82-80746. (Illus.). 224p. (Orig.). 1982. pap. text ed. 10.60 (ISBN 0-87891-539-7). Res & Educ.

Theory of Linear Systems. J. E. Rubio. (Electrical Science Ser). 1971. 71.00 (ISBN 0-12-601650-X). Acad Pr.

Theory of Liquids. John G. Kirkwood. Ed. by B. Alder. (Documents on Modern Physics Ser.). (Illus.). 166p. (Orig.). 1968. 59.00 (ISBN 0-677-00350-1). Gordon & Breach.

Theory of Literary Criticism: A Logical Analysis. John M. Ellis. LC 73-83055. 1974. pap. 10.95x (ISBN 0-520-03413-9). U of Cal Pr.

Theory of Literary Production. Pierre Macherey. Tr. by Geoffrey Wall from Fr. 1978. pap. 11.50x (ISBN 0-7100-0087-1). Routledge Chapman & Hall.

Theory of Literature. rev. ed. Rene Wellek & Austin Warren. 375p. 1956. pap. 7.95 (ISBN 0-15-689084-4, Harv). HarBraceJ.

Theory of Lubrication: With Applications to Liquid & Gas-Film Lubrication. Nicolae Tipei. Ed. by William A. Gross. 1962. 40.00x (ISBN 0-8047-0028-1). Stanford U Pr.

Theory of Luminescence. B. I. Stepanov & V. P. Gribkovskii. 506p. 1969. 157.00 (ISBN 0-677-61530-2). Gordon & Breach.

Theory of Machines & Mechanisms, 2 Vols. American Society of Mechanical Engineers Staff. 1979. Set. 75.00 (ISBN 0-317-06827-X). Vol. 1, 1607p (G00148). Vol. 2, 1654p (G00149). ASME.

Theory of Machines & Mechanisms. Joseph E. Shigley & John J. Uiker. (Mechanical Engineering Ser.). (Illus.). 576p. 1980. text ed. 51.95x (ISBN 0-07-056884-7). McGraw.

Theory of Machines & Mechanisms: Proceedings of the 7th World Congress, Seville, Spain, 17-22 September 1987. Ed. by E. Bautista et al. (Illus.). 15000p. 1987. 655.00 (ISBN 0-08-034815-7). Pergamon.

Theory of Macroeconomic Policy. M. H. Peston. 279p. 1982. text ed. 38.50x (ISBN 0-86003-038-5, Pub. by Philip Allan UK); pap. text ed. 19.95 (ISBN 0-86003-136-5). Humanities.

Theory of Magnetic Resonance. 2nd ed. Charles P. Poole & Horacio A. Farach. LC 86-11013. 359p. 1987. 59.95 (ISBN 0-471-81530-6). Wiley.

Theory of Magnetism I. D. C. Mattis. (Solid-State Sciences Ser.: Vol. 17). (Illus.). xv, 300p. 1988. pap. 39.50 (ISBN 0-387-18425-2). Springer-Verlag.

Theory of Magnetism II. D. C. Mattis. (Springer Series in Solid-State Sciences: Vol. 55). (Illus.). 190p. 1985. 36.00 (ISBN 0-387-15025-0). Springer-Verlag.

Theory of Magnetism One: Statistics & Dynamics. (Springer Series in Solid-State Sciences: Vol. 17). (Illus.). 320p. 1981. 39.50 (ISBN 0-387-10611-1). Springer-Verlag.

Theory of Market Failure: A Critical Examination. Ed. by Tyler Cowen. 410p. 1988. lib. bdg. 21.75 (ISBN 0-913969-13-3, Pub. by G Mason Univ Pr). Univ Pub Assocs.

Theory of Markets. Tun Thin. LC 60-5398. (Economic Studies: No. 114). (Illus.). 1960. 8.95x (ISBN 0-674-88080-3). Harvard U Pr.

Theory of Mathematical Structures. Jiri Adamek. 1983. lib. bdg. 59.50 (ISBN 90-277-1459-2, Pub. by Reidel Holland). Kluwer Academic.

Theory of Matrices, 2 Vols. Felix R. Gantmacher. LC 59-11779. Vol. 1. 19.95 (ISBN 0-8284-0131-4); Vol. 2. 17.95 (ISBN 0-8284-0133-0). Chelsea Pub.

Theory of Matrices. Peter Lancaster & Miron Tismenetsky. (Computer Science & Applied Mathematics Ser.). 1985. 59.00 (ISBN 0-12-435560-9). Acad Pr.

Theory of Matrices in Numerical Analysis. Alston S. Householder. LC 74-83763. 288p. 1975. pap. text ed. 6.00 (ISBN 0-486-61781-5). Dover.

Theory of Matrix Structural Analysis. J. S. Przemieniecki. 480p. 1985. pap. 10.00 (ISBN 0-486-64948-2). Dover.

Theory of Max-Min, & Its Application to Weapons Allocation Problems. J. M. Danskin. (Econometrics & Operation Research: Vol. 5). (Illus.). 1967. 28.00 (ISBN 0-387-03943-0). Springer-Verlag.

Theory of Meaning. G. H. Parkinson. (Oxford Readings in Philosophy). 1968. pap. 9.95x (ISBN 0-19-875007-2). Oxford U Pr.

Theory of Measurements. Lucius Tuttle & John Satterly. pap. 86.80 (ISBN 0-317-09118-2, 2014443). Bks Demand UMI.

Theory of Medical Ethics. Robert M. Veatch. LC 81-66106. 448p. 1981. 20.95 (ISBN 0-465-08437-0). Basic.

Theory of Medical Ethics. Robert M. Veatch. LC 81-66106. 387p. 1983. pap. 9.95 (ISBN 0-465-08439-7, CN-5100). Basic.

Theory of Melody: A Complete General Presentation of the Practical Materials, Resources, & Phenomena. Paul R. Narveson. (Illus.). 380p. 1984. lib. bdg. 33.00 (ISBN 0-8191-3833-9); pap. text ed. 16.25 (ISBN 0-8191-3834-7). U Pr of Amer.

Theory of Mental Tests. Harold Gulliksen. 512p. 1987. Repr. of 1950 ed. text ed. 49.95 (ISBN 0-8058-0024-7). L Erlbaum Assocs.

Theory of Metal Corrosion. V. V. Skorchelletti. 248p. 1976. text ed. 44.00x (ISBN 0-7065-1564-1, Pub. by Keter Pub Jerusalem). Coronet Bks.

Theory of Metal Oxidation, Vol. 1: Fundamentals. A. T Fromhold. LC 75-23121. (Defects in Crystalline Solids: Vol. 9). (Illus.). 548p. 1976. 171.00 (ISBN 0-444-10957-9, North-Holland). Elsevier.

Theory of Metal Oxidation Vol. 2: Space Charge. A. T. Fromhold. (Defects in Crystalline Solids Ser.: Vol. 12). 332p. 1980. 116.00 (ISBN 0-444-85381-2, North-Holland). Elsevier.

Theory of Meter. Seymour Chatman. (Janua Linguarum, Ser. Minor: No. 36). (Orig.). 1964. pap. text ed. 19.20x (ISBN 0-686-22469-8). Mouton.

Theory of Method. Husain Sarkar. LC 82-45911. 192p. 1983. text ed. 32.50x (ISBN 0-520-04730-3). U of Cal Pr.

Theory of Microwave Remote Sensing. 2nd ed. Jin A. Kong et al. LC 84-17397. (Remote Sensing & Image Processing Ser.). 613p. 1985. text ed. 47.50 (ISBN 0-471-88860-5, Pub. by Wiley Medical). Wiley.

Theory of Middle English Alliterative Meter with Critical Applications. Robert W. Sapora, Jr. LC 77-89927. 1977. 11.00x (ISBN 0-910956-75-8, SAM1); pap. 5.00x (ISBN 0-910956-61-8). Medieval Acad.

Theory of Modelling & Simulation. Bernard P. Zeigler. LC 84-19443. 460p. 1984. Repr. of 1976 ed. lib. bdg. 32.50 (ISBN 0-89874-808-9). Krieger.

Theory of Modern Literature: Browning, G. Eliot, Hardy, Meredith. S. Law Wilson. 1973. Repr. of 1899 ed. 30.00 (ISBN 0-8274-0675-4). R West.

Theory of Modulation. Thorvald Otterstrom. LC 74-34379. (Music Reprint Ser). (Illus.). viii, 162p. (Ger. & Eng.). 1975. Repr. of 1935 ed. lib. bdg. 29.50 (ISBN 0-306-70721-7). Da Capo.

Theory of Molecular Excitations. A. S. Davydov. LC 72-75767. 314p. 1971. 55.00x (ISBN 0-306-30440-6, Plenum Pr). Plenum Pub.

Theory of Molecular Fluids: Fundamentals, Vol. 1. C. G. Gray & K. E. Gubbins. (International Series of Monographs on Chemistry). (Illus.). 1984. 95.00x (ISBN 0-19-855602-0). Oxford U Pr.

Theory of Molecular Interactions. I. G. Kaplan. (Studies in Physical & Theoretical Chemistry: No. 42). 416p. 1986. 142.00 (ISBN 0-444-42696-5). Elsevier.

Theory of Molecular Relaxation: Applications in Chemistry & Biology. Francis K. Fong. LC 75-17814. (Illus.). pap. 83.00 (ISBN 0-317-09104-2, 2017400). Bks Demand UMI.

Theory of Molecular Spectroscopy - Vol. 1: The Quantum Mechanics & Group Theory of Vibrating & Rotating Molecules. C. J. Schutte. 512p. 1976. 106.50 (ISBN 0-7204-0291-3, North-Holland). Elsevier.

Theory of Monads. Herbert W. Carr. LC 75-3101. Repr. of 1922 ed. 24.00 (ISBN 0-404-59098-5). AMS Pr.

Theory of Money. 3rd. ed. Walter T. Newlyn. (Illus.). 1978. pap. 34.50x (ISBN 0-19-877099-5). Oxford U Pr.

Theory of Money. Jurg Niehans. LC 77-17247. (Illus.). 1980. text ed. 34.50x (ISBN 0-8018-2055-3); pap. text ed. 12.95x (ISBN 0-8018-2372-2). Johns Hopkins.

Theory of Money. Jacob T. Schwartz. (Mathematics & Its Applications Ser.). 102p. 1965. 39.00 (ISBN 0-677-01020-6). Gordon & Breach.

Theory of Money & Banks Investigated. George Tucker. LC 63-23038. 1964. Repr. of 1839 ed. 45.00x (ISBN 0-678-00032-8). Kelley.

Theory of Money & Credit. Ludwig Von Mises. 493p. 1971. 6.00 (ISBN 0-910614-34-2). Foun Econ Ed.

Theory of Money & Credit. Ludwig Von Mises. Tr. by H. E. Batson from Ger. LC 79-25752. 544p. 1981. 12.00 (ISBN 0-913966-70-3, Liberty Clas); pap. 6.00 (ISBN 0-913966-71-1). Liberty Fund.

Theory of Monopolistic Competition: A Re-Orientation of the Theory of Value. 8th ed. Edward H. Chamberlin. LC 63-649. (Economic Studies: No. 38). 1962. 27.50x (ISBN 0-674-88125-7). Harvard U Pr.

Theory of Monopoly Capitalism: An Elaboration of Marxian Political Economy. John B. Foster. 288p. (Orig.). 1986. 26.00 (ISBN 0-85345-688-7); pap. 10.00 (ISBN 0-85345-689-5). Monthly Rev.

Theory of Moral Sentiments. Adam Smith. LC 76-9430. 1977. 9.95 (ISBN 0-913966-12-6, Liberty Clas). Liberty Fund.

Theory of Moral Sentiments. Adam Smith. (Glasgow Edition of the Works & Correspondence of Adam Smith Ser.). (Illus.). 1976. 54.00x (ISBN 0-19-828189-7). Oxford U Pr.

Theory of Moral Sentiments. 6th ed. Adam Smith. 1986. lib. bdg. 30.00X (ISBN 0-935005-66-8); pap. text ed. 15.00X (ISBN 0-935005-67-6). Ibis Pub VA.

Theory of Moral Sentiments: Glasgow Edition. Adam Smith. LC 81-23693. 422p. 1984. pap. 5.50 (ISBN 0-86597-012-2, Liberty Clas). Liberty Fund.

Theory of Morality. Alan Donagan. LC 76-25634. 1979. pap. 10.00x (ISBN 0-226-15567-6, P838, Phoen); 20.00x (ISBN 0-226-15566-8). U of Chicago Pr.

Theory of Morals. Edgar F. Carritt. LC 73-3021. 144p. 1974. Repr. of 1928 ed. lib. bdg. 22.50 (ISBN 0-8371-6827-9, CATM). Greenwood.

Theory of Morals. Richard Hildreth. LC 69-16311. 1969. Repr. of 1844 ed. 37.50x (ISBN 0-678-00827-2). Kelley.

Theory of Morals. M. Timur. 695p. 1965. 8.95 (ISBN 0-8022-1724-9). Philos Lib.

Theory of Morals: An Introduction to Ethical Philosophy. E. F. Carritt. 144p. 1982. Repr. of 1928 ed. lib. bdg. 30.00 (ISBN 0-89984-118-X). Century Bookbindery.

Theory of Mordell-Weil. J. P. Serre. (Aspects of Mathematics Ser.). 250p. 1987. pap. price not set (ISBN 3-528-08968-7, Pub. by Vieweg & Sohn). IPS.

Theory of Motion in Plato's Later Dialogues. J. B. Skemp. 213p. Repr. of 1942 ed. lib. bdg. 33.00x (Pub. by A M Hakkert). Coronet Bks.

Theory of Multinational Enterprise. Jean-Francois Hennart. 208p. text ed. 19.95x (ISBN 0-472-10017-3). U of Mich Pr.

Theory of Multiobjective Optimization. Monograph ed. Yoshikazu Sawaragi et al. (Mathematics in Science & Engineering Ser.). 1985. 54.00 (ISBN 0-12-620370-9). Acad Pr.

Theory of Multiphoton Processes. Farhad H. Faisal. (Physics of Atoms & Molecules Ser.). 410p. 1986. 65.00x (ISBN 0-306-42317-0, Plenum Pr). Plenum Pub.

Theory of Multipliers in Spaces of Differentiable Functions. V. G. Maz'ya & T. O. Shaposhnikova. 354p. 1986. 111.00 (ISBN 0-470-20542-3, Co-Pub. with Longman). Wiley.

Theory of Narrative. F. K. Stanzel. 328p. 1986. pap. 16.95 (ISBN 0-521-31063-6). Cambridge U Pr.

Theory of Natural Monopoly. William W. Sharkey. LC 82-1136. (Illus.). 1982. 39.50 (ISBN 0-521-24394-7); pap. 16.95 (ISBN 0-521-27194-0). Cambridge U Pr.

Theory of Natural Philosophy. Roger J. Boscovich. (Illus.). 1966. pap. 8.95x (ISBN 0-262-52003-6). MIT Pr.

Theory of Need in Marx. Agnes Heller. LC 76-19162. 1976. 19.95x (ISBN 0-312-79800-8). St Martin.

Theory of Nets. Chen. 1988. write for info. (ISBN 0-471-85148-5). Wiley.

Theory of Neutralization & the Archiphoneme in Functional Phonology. Tsutomu Akamatsu. LC 87-28723. (Current Issues in Linguistic Theory Ser.: No. 43). xix, 501p. 1988. 88.00x. Benjamins North Am.

Theory of Neutron Scattering from Condensed Matter, Vol. 1. Stephen W. Lovesey. (International Series of Monographs on Physics). (Illus.). 1986. 75.00x (ISBN 0-19-852015-8); pap. 32.50x (ISBN 0-19-852028-X). Oxford U Pr.

Theory of Neutron Scattering from Condensed Matter, Vol. 2. Stephen W. Lovesey. (International Series of Monographs on Physics). (Illus.). 1986. 59.00x (ISBN 0-19-852017-4); pap. 32.50x (ISBN 0-19-852029-8). Oxford U Pr.

Theory of NMR Parameters. Isal Ando & Graham A. Webb. 1984. 63.50 (ISBN 0-12-056820-9). Acad Pr.

Theory of Non-Linear & Parametric Circuits. Frantisek Kouril & Kamil Verba. (Mathematics & Its Applications-Ellis Horwood Ser.: 1-176). 350p. 1985. 74.95x (ISBN 0-470-20014-6). Halsted Pr.

Theory of Nonlinear Age-Dependent Population Dynamics. Webb. (Pure & Applied Mathematics: A Series of Monographs & Textbooks). 456p. 1985. 69.75 (ISBN 0-8247-7290-3). Dekker.

Theory of Nonlinear Lattices. M. Toda. (Springer Series in Solid-State Sciences: Vol. 20). (Illus.). 220p. 1981. 42.00 (ISBN 0-387-10224-8). Springer-Verlag.

Theory of Northern Athapaskan Prehistory. John W. Ives. (Investigations in American Archaeology Ser.). 300p. 1988. pap. 30.00 (ISBN 0-8133-7517-7). Westview.

Theory of Nuclear Magnetic Relaxation in Liquids. J. R. McConnell. (Illus.). 200p. 1987. 49.50 (ISBN 0-521-32112-3). Cambridge U Pr.

Theory of Nuclear Reactions. Ed. by O. K. Kocherga. 712p. 1988. 78.00 (ISBN 9971-50-481-2); pap. 44.00 (ISBN 9971-50-482-0). World Scientific Pub.

Theory of Nuclear Structure. M. Pal. 1983. 41.95 (ISBN 0-442-27524-2). Van Nos Reinhold.

Theory of Nuclear Structure & Reactions: Proceedings of the Second La Rabida International Summer School on Nuclear Physics, Huelva, Spain, June 23-July 6, 1985. Ed. by M. Lozano & G. Madurga. 650p. 1986. 79.00 (ISBN 9971-50-074-4). World Scientific Pub.

Theory of Nuclear Structure: Trieste Lectures, 1969. (Illus.). 961p. (Orig.). 1970. pap. 56.00 (ISBN 92-0-130070-0, ISP249, IAEA). UNIPUB.

Theory of Numbers. S. Iyanaga. (Mathematical Library: Vol. 8). 542p. 1976. 144.75 (ISBN 0-444-10678-2, North-Holland). Elsevier.

Theory of Numbers. 2nd ed. George B. Mathews. LC 61-17958. 14.95 (ISBN 0-8284-0156-X). Chelsea Pub.

Theory of Numbers, Mathematical Analysis & Their Applications. N. N. Bogolyubov & K. K. Mardzhanishvili. LC 83-22405. (Proceedings of the Steklov Institute of Mathematics: Vol. 157). 248p. 1983. pap. 78.00 (ISBN 0-8218-3076-7, STEKL 157). Am Math.

Theory of Numbers, Mathematical Analysis & Their Applications. Ed. by N. N. Bogolyubov et al. LC 79-20552. (Proceedings of the Steklov Institute: No. 142). 1979. 93.00 (ISBN 0-8218-3042-2, STEKLO 142). Am Math.

Theory of Numbers: Proceedings. Symposium in Pure Mathematics - Pasadena - 1963. Ed. by A. L. Whiteman. LC 65-17382. (Proceedings of Symposia in Pure Mathematics: Vol. 8). 216p. 1979. pap. 30.00 (ISBN 0-8218-1408-7, PSPUM-8). Am Math.

Theory of Operator Algebras One. M. Takesaki. LC 79-13655. 1979. 66.00 (ISBN 0-387-90391-7). Springer-Verlag.

Theory of Oral Composition: History & Methodology. John M. Foley. LC 87-45402. 192p. 1988. 35.00x (ISBN 0-253-34260-0); pap. 9.95x (ISBN 0-253-20465-8). Ind U Pr.

Theory of Orbits in the Restricted Problem of Three Bodies. Victor G. Szebehely. 1967. 59.00 (ISBN 0-12-680650-0). Acad Pr.

Theory of Ordinary Differential Equations. John Charles Burkhill. LC 76-369325. (Longman Mathematical Ser.). pap. 32.50 (ISBN 0-317-08520-4, 2013563). Bks Demand UMI.

Theory of Ordinary Differential Equations. Earl A. Coddington & Norman Levinson. LC 84-4438. 444p. 1984. Repr. of 1955 ed. lib. bdg. 33.50 (ISBN 0-89874-755-4). Krieger.

Theory of Organic Reactions. N. D. Epiotis. LC 77-17405. (Reactivity & Structure Ser.: Vol. 5). (Illus.). 1978. 63.00 (ISBN 0-387-08551-3). Springer-Verlag.

Theory of Organizations. David Silverman. LC 72-150812. 1971. text ed. 14.95x (ISBN 0-465-08438-9). Basic.

Theory of Orientation & Stereoselection. K. Fukui. LC 75-25597. (Reactivity & Structure: Vol. 2). (Illus.). 120p. 1975. 27.00 (ISBN 0-387-07426-0). Springer-Verlag.

Theory of Oscillators. A. A. Andronov et al. xxxii, 815p. 1987. pap. 17.95 (ISBN 0-486-65508-3). Dover.

Theory of Parody: The Teachings of Twentieth-Century Art Forms. Linda Hutcheon. (Illus.). 192p. 1985. text ed. 25.00 (ISBN 0-416-37080-2, NO. 4090); pap. 10.95 (ISBN 0-416-37090-X, NO. 4091). Routledge Chapman & Hall.

Theory of Parsing, Translation, & Compiling, Vol. 2 Compiling. Alfred V. Aho & Jeffrey D. Ullman. (Illus.). 471p. 1973. ref. ed. 58.00 (ISBN 0-13-914564-8). P-H.

Theory of Parsing, Translation & Compiling: Vol. 1, Parsing. Alfred V. Aho & Jeffrey D. Ullman. (Illus.). 592p. 1972. ref. ed. 58.00 (ISBN 0-13-914556-7). P-H.

Theory of Partial Coherence. Mark J. Beran & George B. Parrent. pap. 51.80 (ISBN 0-317-08514-X, 2010137). Bks Demand UMI.

Theory of Partial Differential Equations. H. Melvin Lieberstein. (Mathematics in Science & Engineering Ser.: Vol. 93). 1972. 77.00 (ISBN 0-12-449550-8). Acad Pr.

Theory of Partial Differential Equations. Sigeru Mizohata. LC 72-83593. 350p. 1973. 79.95 (ISBN 0-521-08727-9). Cambridge U Pr.

Theory of Particulate Processes. Alan D. Randolph & Maurice A. Larson. 1971. 68.00 (ISBN 0-12-579650-1). Acad Pr.

Theory of Particulate Processes: Analysis & Techniques of Continuous Crystallization. 2nd ed. Ed. by Alan D. Randolph & Maurice A. Larsen. 369p. 1988. 55.00 (ISBN 0-12-579652-8). Acad Pr.

Theory of Parties & Electoral Systems. Richard S. Katz. LC 80-8019. 176p. 1981. text ed. 18.50x (ISBN 0-8018-2435-4). Johns Hopkins.

Theory of Party Competition. David B. Robertson. LC 74-23542. 220p. pap. 57.20 (2030394). Bks Demand UMI.

Theory of Pay. Adrian Wood. LC 78-1038. 261p. pap. 67.90 (2030630). Bks Demand UMI.

Theory of Peasant Economy. A. V. Chayanov. LC 85-40758. 400p. 1986. 32.50x (ISBN 0-299-10570-9); pap. text ed. 14.95x (ISBN 0-299-10574-1). U of Wis Pr.

Theory of Perceptions. George Pitcher. LC 73-120759. pap. 47.50 (ISBN 0-317-10596-5, 2011399). Bks Demand UMI.

Theory of Performing Arts. Andre Helbo. LC 87-14584. (Critical Theory Ser.: No. 5). viii, 153p. 1987. 30.00x (ISBN 1-55619-014-X). Benjamins North Am.

Theory of Personality & Individual Differences: Factors, Systems, & Processes. Joseph R. Royce & D. Arnold Powell. (Illus.). 272p. 1983. 41.00 (ISBN 0-13-914473-0). P-H.

Theory of Personality: The Psychology of Personal Constructs. George A. Kelly. 1963. pap. 6.95 (ISBN 0-393-00152-0, Norton Lib). Norton.

Theory of Pharmaceutical Systems, 2 vols. Jens T. Carstensen. 1972. 75.00 ea. Vol. 1 (ISBN 0-12-161101-9). Vol. 2, 1973 (ISBN 0-12-161102-7). Acad Pr.

Theory of Phase Transition. Ya G. Sinai. 164p. 1983. 36.00 (ISBN 0-08-026469-7, C111, D125). Pergamon.

Theory of Phonological Weight. Larry M. Hyman. (Language Science Ser.: No. 19). 136p. 1985. 35.00 (ISBN 9-067-65106-0); pap. 23.90 (ISBN 9-067-65107-9). Foris Pubns.

Theory of Photons & Electrons: Second Corrected Printing. 2nd rev. ed. J. M. Jauch & F. Rohrlich. LC 75-8890. (Texts & Monographs in Physics). (Illus.). 533p. 1976. 37.00 (ISBN 0-387-07295-0). Springer-Verlag.

Theory of Planetary Atmospheres. 2nd ed. Joseph W. Chamberlain & Donald M. Hunten. (International Geophysics Ser.). 1987. 49.50 (ISBN 0-12-167251-4). Acad Pr.

Theory of Planetary Atmospheres: An Introduction to Their Physics & Chemistry. Joseph W. Chamberlain. (International Geophysics Ser.). 1978. 35.00 (ISBN 0-12-167250-6). Acad Pr.

Theory of Planning. John Sillince. 230p. 1986. text ed. 42.00 (ISBN 0-566-05231-8, Pub. by Gower Pub England). Gower Pub Co.

Theory of Plant Breeding. Oliver Mayo. (Illus.). 1980. text ed. 76.00x (ISBN 0-19-854536-3). Oxford U Pr.

Theory of Plasma Instabilities, 2 vols. A. B. Mikhailovskii. Incl. Vol. 1. Instabilities of a Homogeneous Plasma. 308p. 1974 (ISBN 0-306-17181-3, Consultants); Vol. 2. Instabilities of an Inhomogeneous Plasma. 332p. 1974 (ISBN 0-306-17182-1, Consultants). LC 73-83899. (Studies in Soviet Science - Physical Sciences Ser.). 1974. 59.50x ea. (Consultants). Plenum Pub.

Theory of Plasticity. J. Chakrabarty. 548p. 1987. text ed. 52.95 (ISBN 0-07-010392-5). McGraw.

Theory of Plates & Shells. 2nd ed. Stephen P. Timoshenko & S. Woinowsky-Krieger. (Engineering Societies Monographs). (Illus.). 1959. text ed. 59.95 (ISBN 0-07-064779-8). McGraw.

Theory of Poetry. Lascell Abercrombie. 1988. Repr. of 1924 ed. lib. bdg. 49.00x. Am Biog Serv.

Theory of Poetry. Lascelles Abercrombie. LC 69-17712. 1969. Repr. of 1926 ed. 18.00 (ISBN 0-8196-0223-X). Biblo.

Theory of Poetry. Lascelles Abercrombie. LC 76-131602. 222p. 1924. Repr. 11.00x (ISBN 0-403-00489-6). Scholarly.

Theory of Poetry. John James. 1977. saddlestitched 3.00 (ISBN 0-685-50387-9, Pub by St Edns). Small Pr Dist.

Theory of Poetry in England from the 16th to the 19th Century. Richard P. Cowl. 59.95 (ISBN 0-8490-1190-6). Gordon Pr.

Theory of Poetry in England: Its Development in Doctrines & Ideas from the 16th to the 19th Century. R. R. Cowl. LC 75-90366. 334p. 1970. Repr. of 1914 ed. 35.00x (ISBN 0-87753-009-2). Phaeton.

Theory of Point Estimation. Erich L. Lehmann. LC 82-21881. (Probability & Mathematical Statistics Ser.). 506p. 1983. 42.95 (ISBN 0-471-05849-1, Pub. by Wiley-Interscience). Wiley.

Theory of Political Choice Behavior. Bruce I. Newman & Jagdish N. Sheth. (Praeger Series in Public & Nonprofit Sector Marketing). 199p. 1986. 33.95 (ISBN 0-275-92187-5, C2187). Praeger.

Theory of Political Coalitions. William H. Riker. LC 84-684. xii, 300p. 1984. Repr. of 1962 ed. lib. bdg. 41.50x (ISBN 0-313-24299-2, RITH). Greenwood.

Theory of Political Decision Modes: Intraparty Decision Making in Switzerland. Jurg Steiner & Robert H. Dorff. LC 79-16390. (Illus.). xii, 239p. 1980. 25.00x (ISBN 0-8078-1406-7). U of NC Pr.

Theory of Political Economy. W. Stanley Jevons. 278p. Repr. of 1871 ed. 15.25 (ISBN 0-935005-74-9). Ibis Pub VA.

Theory of Politics. Richard Hildreth. LC 69-16312. Repr. of 1853 ed. 37.50x (ISBN 0-678-00518-4). Kelley.

Theory of Politics. Ed. by Richard Hildreth. LC 70-153031. (Research & Source Works Ser.: No. 673). 1971. Repr. of 1854 ed. lib. bdg. 19.00 (ISBN 0-8337-1704-9). B Franklin.

Theory of Polymer Dynamics. M. Doi & S. F. Edwards. (Illus.). 400p. 1986. 78.50 (ISBN 0-19-851976-1). Oxford U Pr.

Theory of Polymer Dynamics. M. Doi & S. F. Edwards. (International Series of Monographs on Physics). (Illus.). 408p. 1988. pap. 35.00 (ISBN 0-19-852033-6). Oxford U Pr.

Theory of Popular Elasticity: Proceedings of the CISM, Department of Mechanics of Deformable Bodies, 1970. CISM (International Center for Mechanical Sciences), Department for Mechanics of Deformable Bodies Staff. Ed. by W. Nowacki. (CISM Pubns. Ser.: No. 25). (Illus.). 286p. 1974. pap. 27.20 (ISBN 0-387-81078-1). Springer-Verlag.

Theory of Population: Essay in Marxist Research. D. I. Valentey. 408p. 19.75x (ISBN 0-317-53796-2, Pub. by Collets (UK)). State Mutual Bk.

Theory of Population Genetics & Evolutionary Ecology: An Introduction. rev. ed. Jonathan Roughgarden. 656p. 1987. Repr. 24.96x (ISBN 0-02-948851-6). Macmillan.

Theory of Positonal Games: With Applications in Economics. Ed. by Iosif Krass & Shawkat Hammoudeh. LC 81-10922. (Economic Theory, Econometrics & Mathematical Economics Ser.). 1981. 56.50 (ISBN 0-12-425920-0). Acad Pr.

Theory of Possibility: A Constructivistic & Conceptualistic Account of Possible Individuals & Possible Worlds. Nicholas Rescher. LC 75-10540. 1975. 25.95x (ISBN 0-8229-1122-1). U of Pittsburgh Pr.

Theory of Potential & Spherical Harmonics. Wolfgang Sternberg & Turner L. Smith. LC 44-9717. (Mathematical Expositions: No. 3). pap. 80.50 (ISBN 0-317-09115-8, 2014421). Bks Demand UMI.

Theory of Price. 4th ed. George J. Stigler. (Illus.). 384p. 1987. text ed. write for info. (ISBN 0-02-417400-9). Macmillan.

Theory of Price Control: The Classic Account. John Kenneth Galbraith. 1952. text ed. 9.95x (ISBN 0-674-88170-2); pap. 3.95 (ISBN 0-674-88175-3). Harvard U Pr.

Theory of Price Uncertainty, Production, & Profit. Clement A. Tisdell. LC 68-20881. 1968. 28.00x (ISBN 0-691-04191-1). Princeton U Pr.

Theory of Probability. B. Gnedenko. 392p. 1978. 8.45 (ISBN 0-8285-0748-1, Pub. by Mir Pubs USSR). Imported Pubns.

Theory of Probability. 3rd ed. Harold Jeffreys. 1983. pap. 29.95x (ISBN 0-19-853193-1). Oxford U Pr.

Theory of Probability: A Critical Introductory Treatment. Bruno De Finetti. LC 73-10744. (Probability & Mathematical Statistics Ser.: Vol. 1). 300p. 1974. 69.95 (ISBN 0-471-20141-3, Pub. by Wiley-Interscience). Wiley.

Theory of Probability & the Elements of Statistics. 5th ed. B. V. Gnedenko. Tr. by Bernard Seckler from Rus. LC 61-13496. 529p. 1987. pap. text ed. write for info. (ISBN 0-8284-1132-8, 132). Chelsea Pub.

Theory of Profit. Zubair Hasan. 1974. 10.50 (ISBN 0-7069-0353-6). Intl Bk Dist.

Theory of Profit. Donald M. Lamberton. LC 70-1657. 1965. 25.00x (ISBN 0-678-06259-5). Kelley.

Theory of Program Structures: Schemes, Semantics, Verification. S. A. Greibach. (Lecture Notes in Computer Science: Vol. 36). xvi, 364p. 1985. pap. 18.00 (ISBN 0-387-07415-5). Springer-Verlag.

Theory of Programming Language Semantics, 2 vols. R. Milne & C. Strachey. 1976. Set. 88.00x (ISBN 0-412-14260-0, NO. 6320, Pub. by Chapman & Hall). Routledge Chapman & Hall.

Theory of Property Rights-With Application to the California Gold Rush. John R. Umbeck. (Illus.). 158p. 1981. text ed. 17.95x (ISBN 0-8138-1675-0). Iowa St U Pr.

Theory of Protection. W. M. Corden. (Illus.). 1971. 19.95x (ISBN 0-19-828413-6). Oxford U Pr.

Theory of Pseudo-Rigid Bodies. H. Cohen & R. G. Muncaster. (Tracts in Natural Philosophy Ser.: Vol. 33). (Illus.). 210p. 1988. 69.80 (ISBN 0-387-96635-8). Springer-Verlag.

Theory of Psychological Dispositions see Yale Psychological Studies, N.S.

Theory of Psychopharmacology, Vol. I. Ed. by S. J. Cooper. 1982. 66.00 (ISBN 0-12-188001-X). Acad Pr.

Theory of Public Bureaucracy: Politics, Personality, & Organization in the State Department. Donald P. Warwick et al. LC 75-4907. 264p. 1975. text ed. 18.50x (ISBN 0-674-88181-8); pap. 7.95x (ISBN 0-674-88195-8). Harvard U Pr.

Theory of Public Choice, II. James M. Buchanan & Robert D. Tollison. 512p. 1984. text ed. 30.00x (ISBN 0-472-10040-8); pap. text ed. 18.95x (ISBN 0-472-08041-5). U of Mich Pr.

Theory of Public Utility Pricing. Stephen Brown & David Sibley. 216p. 1986. 39.50 (ISBN 0-521-30626-4); pap. 13.95 (ISBN 0-521-31400-3). Cambridge U Pr.

Theory of Quantitative Economic Policy: With Applications to Economic Growth, Stabilization & Planning. 2nd rev. ed. K. A. Fox et al. (Studies in Mathematical & Managerial Economics: Vol. 5). (Illus.). 290p. 1974. 52.75 (ISBN 0-444-10544-1, North-Holland). Elsevier.

Theory of Quantum Fluids. E. Feenberg. (Pure & Applied Physics Ser.: Vol. 31). 1969. 69.50 (ISBN 0-12-250850-5). Acad Pr.

Theory of Random Functions, 2 Vols. Andre Blanc-LaPierre & R. Fortet. LC 65-16343. (Illus.). 810p. 1968. Set. 186.00 (ISBN 0-677-04250-7). Gordon & Breach.

Theory of Rank Tests. Jaroslav Hajek & Zbynek Sidak. 1967. 66.50 (ISBN 0-12-317250-0). Acad Pr.

Theory of Rate Processes in Condensed Media. B. Fain. (Lecture Notes in Chemistry Ser.: Vol. 20). (Illus.). 166p. 1980. 21.00 (ISBN 0-387-10249-3). Springer Verlag.

Theory of Reading. Ed. by Frank Gloversmith. LC 84-280. 264p. 1984. 27.50x (ISBN 0-389-20467-6, 08028). B&N Imports.

Theory of Reasons for Action. David A. Richards. 1971. 29.00x (ISBN 0-19-824362-6). Oxford U Pr.

Theory of Recursive Functions & Effective Computability. Hartley Rogers, Jr. 504p. (Orig.). 1987. pap. text ed. 15.00x (ISBN 0-262-68052-1). MIT Pr.

Theory of Reflection & Cybernetics: The Concepts of Reflection & Their Significance for Materialist Monism. J. Zeman. 256p. 1988. 95.25 (ISBN 0-444-98953-6, North-Holland). Elsevier.

Theory of Reflection of Electromagnetic & Particle Waves. John Lekner. 1987. lib. bdg. 78.50 (ISBN 90-247-3418-5, Pub. by Martinus Nijhoff Netherlands). Kluwer Academic.

Theory of Relational Databases. David Maier. LC 82-2518. (Principles of Computer Science Ser.). 637p. 1983. text ed. 42.95 (ISBN 0-914894-42-0, Computer Sci Pr). W H Freeman.

Theory of Relations. R. Fraisse. (Studies in Logic & the Foundations of Mathematics: Vol. 118). 398p. 1986. 89.50 (ISBN 0-444-87865-3, North Holland). Elsevier.

Theory of Relativity. 2nd ed. C. Moller. (International Series of Monographs on Physics). (Illus.). 1972. pap. text ed. 18.95x (ISBN 0-19-560539-X). Oxford U Pr.

Theory of Relativity. 2nd ed. R. K. Pathria. 1974. pap. text ed. 35.00 (ISBN 0-08-018995-4). Pergamon.

Theory of Relativity. Wolfgang Pauli. xiv, 241p. 1981. pap. 6.00 (ISBN 0-486-64152-X). Dover.

Theory of Relativity & A Priori Knowledge. Hans Reichenbach. 1965. 34.00x (ISBN 0-520-01059-0). U of Cal Pr.

Theory of Reliability. Ed. by A. Serra & R. E. Barlow. (Enrico Fermi International Summer School of Physics Ser.: Vol. 94). 492p. 1986. 118.50 (ISBN 0-444-86991-3, North-Holland). Elsevier.

Theory of Religion. William S. Bainbridge & Rodney Stark. (Toronto Studies in Religion: Vol. 2). 500p. 1987. text ed. 52.50 (ISBN 0-8204-0356-3). P Lang Pubs.

Theory of Religion. Georges Bataille. Tr. by Robert Hurley. 110p. 1989. 17.95 (ISBN 0-942299-08-6). Zone Bks.

Theory of Religious Liberty in England, 1603-1639. Thomas Lyon. 1972. lib. bdg. 20.00x (ISBN 0-374-95212-4, Octagon). Hippocrene Bks.

Theory of Reproduction & Accumulation. Oskar Lange & A. Banasinski. 1969. 42.00 (ISBN 0-08-012256-6). Pergamon.

Theory of Retracts. Sze-Tsen Hu. LC 64-25182. Repr. of 1965 ed. 58.50 (2027597). Bks Demand UMI.

Theory of Rights: Persons under Laws, Institutions, & Morals. Carl Wellman. LC 84-22299. 234p. 1985. 34.95x (ISBN 0-8476-7397-9, Rowman & Allanheld). Rowman.

Theory of Rings. Nathan Jacobson. LC 43-15310. (Mathematical Surveys Ser.: No. 2). 151p. 1986. pap. 33.00 (ISBN 0-8218-1502-4, SURV-2). Am Math.

Theory of Rings. Neal H. McCoy. LC 72-11558. xxi, 161p. 1972. Repr. of 1964 ed. text ed. 12.50 (ISBN 0-8284-0266-3). Chelsea Pub.

Theory of Robots: Proceedings of the IFAC-IFIP-IMACS Symposium, Vienna, Austria, 3-5 December 1986. Ed. by P. Kopacek & I. Troch. (IFAC Proceedings Ser.). (Illus.). 366p. 1988. 117.00 (ISBN 0-08-034803-3). Pergamon.

Theory of Rotating Diatomic Molecules. Masataka Mizushima. LC 74-34080. 543p. 1975. 39.50 (ISBN 0-471-61187-5, Pub. by Wiley). Krieger.

Theory of Rotating Fluids. H. P. Greenspan. (Cambridge Monographs on Mechanics & Applied Mathematics). (Illus.). 328p. 1980. pap. 27.95 (ISBN 0-521-29956-X). Cambridge U Pr.

Theory of Rotating Stars. Jean-Louis Tassoul. LC 78-51198. (Astrophysics Ser: No. 1). (Illus.). 1978. 73.00 (ISBN 0-691-08211-1); pap. 22.00 (ISBN 0-691-08214-6). Princeton U Pr.

Theory of Science. George Gale. (Illus.). 1979. text ed. 32.95 (ISBN 0-07-022680-6). McGraw.

Theory of Science, (Die Wissenschaftslehre Oder Versuch Einer Neuen Darstellung der Logik) Bernhard Bolzano. Ed. & tr. by Rolf George. LC 71-126765. 1972. 48.50x (ISBN 0-520-01787-0). U of Cal Pr.

Theory of Seismic Prospecting Instruments. 2nd ed rev ed. V. P. Nomokov & D. K. Ganguli. 150p. 1967. 45.00 (ISBN 0-677-60980-9). Gordon & Breach.

Theory of Semigroup Valued Measures. M. Sion. LC 73-17935. (Lecture Notes in Mathematics: Vol. 355). v, 140p. 1973. pap. 17.00 (ISBN 0-387-06542-3). Springer-Verlag.

Theory of Semiotics. Umberto Eco. LC 74-22833. (Advances in Semiotics: Midland Bks: No. 217). 368p. 1976. 25.00x (ISBN 0-253-35955-4); pap. 10.95x (ISBN 0-253-20217-5). Ind U Pr.

Theory of Sets. E. Kamke. Tr. by Frederick Bagemihl. 1950. pap. 4.00 (ISBN 0-486-60141-2). Dover.

Theory of Sets: Monographs. 2nd ed. A. P. Morse. (Pure & Applied Mathematics Ser.). 1986. 59.00 (ISBN 0-12-507952-4). Acad Pr.

Theory of Sets of Points. 2nd ed. William H. Young & Grace C. Young. LC 75-184793. 330p. 1972. text ed. 19.50 (ISBN 0-8284-0259-0). Chelsea Pub.

Theory of Sex Allocation: MPB. E. L. Charnov. 1982. 55.00x (ISBN 0-691-08311-8); pap. 17.50 (ISBN 0-691-08312-6). Princeton U Pr.

Theory of Share Tenancy. Steven N. Cheung. LC 70-80862. 1969. 17.00x (ISBN 0-226-10358-7). U of Chicago Pr.

Theory of Sheaves. Richard G. Swan. LC 64-24979. (Chicago Lectures in Mathematics Ser). (Orig.). 1964. 8.00x (ISBN 0-226-78329-4). U of Chicago Pr.

Theory of Shell Structures. C. R. Calladine. (Illus.). 780p. Date not set. pap. 39.50 (ISBN 0-521-36945-2). Cambridge U Pr.

Theory of Shell Structures. Christopher R. Calladine. LC 82-4255. 700p. 1983. 160.00 (ISBN 0-521-23835-8). Cambridge U Pr.

Theory of Shells: Proceedings of the IUTAM Symposium on Shell Theory, 3rd Symposium, Russia, August 1978. Ed. by W. T. Koiter & G. K. Mikhailov. 704p. 1980. 137.00 (ISBN 0-444-85338-3, North-Holland). Elsevier.

Theory of Ship Wave Resistance for Unsteady Motion in Still Water. A. N. Shebalov. (University of Michigan Dept. of Naval Architecture & Marine Engineering Report Ser.: No. 67). pap. 20.00 (ISBN 0-317-28264-6, 2022628). Bks Demand UMI.

Theory of Simple Liquids. 2nd ed. Jean P. Hansen & Ian R. McDonald. 547p. 1987. 95.00 (ISBN 0-12-323851-X). Acad Pr.

Theory of Slow Atomic Collisions. E. E. Nikitin & S. Y. Umanskii. (Series in Chemical Physics: Vol. 30). (Illus.). 440p. 1984. 65.00 (ISBN 0-387-12414-4). Springer-Verlag.

Theory of Social Action. Raimo Tuomela. 1984. lib. bdg. 64.00 (ISBN 90-277-1703-6, Pub. by Reidel Holland). Kluwer Academic.

Theory of Social Action: The Correspondence of Alfred Schutz & Talcott Parsons. Ed. by Alfred Schutz. LC 77-15761. (Indiana University Studies in Phenomenology & Existenatial Philosophy). pap. 42.80 (ISBN 0-317-27818-5, 2056036). Bks Demand UMI.

Theory of Social & Economic Organization. Max Weber. Tr. by Talcott Parsons. 1947. pap. 17.95 (ISBN 0-02-934920-6). Free Pr.

Theory of Social & Economic Organization. Max Weber. 1964. pap. 16.95x (ISBN 0-02-934930-3). Free Pr.

Theory of Social Economy. rev. ed. Gustav Cassel. Tr. by S. L. Barron. LC 67-19584. 1967. Repr. of 1932 ed. 49.50x (ISBN 0-678-00241-X). Kelley.

Theory of Social Interaction. Jonathan H. Turner. LC 87-32531. 240p. 1988. text ed. 35.00x (ISBN 0-8047-1463-0); pap. text ed. 10.95x (ISBN 0-8047-1479-7). Stanford U Pr.

Theory of Social Intercourse. Arthur Schopenhauer. (Illus.). 151p. 1985. 117.50 (ISBN 0-89266-504-1). Am Classical Coll Pr.

Theory of Social Intercourse. Arthur Schopenhauer. (Illus.). 167p. 1988. 137.75 (ISBN 0-89920-193-8). Am Inst Psych.

Theory of Social Psychology, 2 vols. John Dewey. (Illus.). 327p. 1987. Set. 195.25 (ISBN 0-89266-584-X). Am Classical Coll Pr.

Theory of Soil Consolidation. Y. K. Zaretskii. 324p. 1972. text ed. 64.00x (ISBN 0-7065-1138-7, Pub. by Keter Pub Jerusalem). Coronet Bks.

Theory of Solitons: The Inverse Scattering Method. S. Novikov et al. Ed. by V. E. Zakharov. (Contemporary Soviet Mathematics Ser.). 272p. 1984. 59.50x (ISBN 0-306-10977-8, Consultants). Plenum Pub.

Theory of Solutions. John G. Kirkwood. Ed. by Z. W. Salsburg & J. Poirier. (Documents on Modern Physics Ser.). 316p. (Orig.). 1968. 92.00 (ISBN 0-677-01030-3). Gordon & Breach.

Theory of Solutions & Stereo-Chemistry. Ed. by I. Bernard Cohen. LC 80-2103. (Development of Science Ser.). (Illus.). 1981. lib. bdg. 35.00x (ISBN 0-405-13868-7). Ayer Co Pubs.

Theory of Sound, Vols. I & II. Strutt Rayleigh. Vol. 1. pap. 9.95 (ISBN 0-486-60292-3); Vol. 2. pap. 9.95 (ISBN 0-486-60293-1). Dover.

Theory of Space, Time & Gravitation. 2nd ed. V. A. Fock. 1964. text ed. 83.00 (ISBN 0-08-010061-9). Pergamon.

Theory of Spatial Pricing & Market Areas. Melvin L. Greenhut & Hiroshi Ohta. LC 74-83786. x, 265p. 1975. 31.50 (ISBN 0-8223-0333-7). Duke.

Theory of Spectrochemical Excitation. Paul W. Boumans. LC 66-27686. pap. 98.50 (ISBN 0-317-27891-6, 2055791). Bks Demand UMI.

Theory of Speech & Language. Alan H. Gardiner. LC 79-4125. 1979. Repr. of 1951 ed. lib. bdg. 35.00x (ISBN 0-313-20987-1, GATS). Greenwood.

Theory of Spinors. Elie Cartan. 160p. 1981. pap. 5.00 (ISBN 0-486-64070-1). Dover.

Theory of Splines & Their Applications. J. Harold Ahlberg et al. (Mathematics in Science & Engineering Ser.: Vol. 38). 1967. 69.50 (ISBN 0-12-044750-9). Acad Pr.

Theory of Static Converter Systems: Mathematical Analysis & Interpretation: Part A: Steady State Processes. M. A. Slonim & J. K. Delson. (Studies in Electrical & Electronic Engineering: Vol. 10). 316p. 1984. 108.00 (ISBN 0-444-42255-2). Elsevier.

Theory of Statistical Experiments. H. Heyer. (Springer Series in Statistics). (Illus.). 289p. 1982. 29.00 (ISBN 0-387-90785-8). Springer-Verlag.

Theory of Statistical Inference. Shelemyahu Zacks. LC 77-132227. (Probability & Mathematical Statistics Ser.). 609p. 1971. 71.95x (ISBN 0-471-98103-6, Pub. by Wiley-Interscience). Wiley.

Theory of Statistical Inference. Shelemyahu Zacks. LC 77-132227. (Wiley Probability & Mathematical Statistics Ser.). pap. 155.50 (2056297). Bks Demand UMI.

Theory of Stein Spaces. H. Grauert & R. Remmert. LC 79-1430. (Grundlehren der Mathematischen Wissenschaften: Vol. 236). (Illus.). 1979. 67.00 (ISBN 0-387-90388-7). Springer-Verlag.

Theory of Stellar Pulsation. J. P. Cox. LC 79-3198. (Ser. in Astrophysics: No. 2). (Illus.). 1980. 67.50x (ISBN 0-691-08252-9); pap. 19.50x (ISBN 0-691-08253-7). Princeton U Pr.

Theory of Stellar Spectra. Charles R. Cowley. (Topics in Astrophysics & Space Physics Ser.). 272p. 1970. 84.00 (ISBN 0-677-02400-2). Gordon & Breach.

Theory of Stochastic Processes. D. R. Fox. 1965. 22.00x (ISBN 0-412-15170-7, NO. 6430, Pub. by Chapman & Hall). Routledge Chapman & Hall.

Theory of Stochastic Processes III. I. I. Giehman & A. V. Skorohod. (Grundlehren der Mathematischen Wissenschften: Vol. 232). 1979. 79.50 (ISBN 0-387-90375-5). Springer-Verlag.

Theory of Stochastic Processes in Hydrology & River Runoff Regulation. N. A. Kartvelishvili. 232p. 1968. text ed. 48.00x (ISBN 0-7065-0683-9, Pub. by Keter Pub Jerusalem). Coronet Bks.

Theory of Stock Speculation. Arthur Crump. LC 83-80982. 1983. pap. 8.00 (ISBN 0-87034-068-9). Fraser Pub Co.

Theory of Strict Liability: Toward a Reformulation of Tort Law. Richard A. Epstein. (Cato Papers Ser.: No. 8). 141p. 1979. pap. 4.00x (ISBN 0-932790-08-9). Cato Inst.

Theory of Structural Semantics. Samuel Abraham & Ferenc Kiefer. (Janua Linguarum, Ser. Minor: No. 49). 1966. 11.20x (ISBN 90-2790-581-9). Mouton.

Theory of Structural Transformations in Solids. A. G. Khachaturyan. LC 82-21957. 574p. 1983. 69.95x (ISBN 0-471-07873-5, Pub. by Wiley-Interscience). Wiley.

Theory of Structures. 2nd ed. Stephen P. Timoshenko & D. H. Young. (Illus.). 1965. text ed. 59.95 (ISBN 0-07-064868-9). McGraw.

Theory of Stylistic Rules in English. Michael S. Rochemont. Ed. by Jorge Hankamer. (Outstanding Dissertations in Linguistics Ser.). 120p. 1985. 26.00 (ISBN 0-8240-5438-5). Garland Pub.

Theory of Subject Analysis: A Source Book. Ed. by Lois M. Chan et al. 450p. 1985. lib. bdg. 36.00 (ISBN 0-87287-489-3). Libs Unl.

Theory of Suboptimal Decisions: Decomposition & Aggregation. A. A. Pervozvanskii & V. G. Gaitsgori. 1988. lib. bdg. 99.00 (ISBN 90-277-2401-6, Pub. by Reidel Holland). Kluwer Academic.

Theory of Subsonic Plane Flow. Leslie C. Woods. LC 61-4283. (Cambridge Aeronautical Ser.: No. 3). pap. 154.00 (ISBN 0-317-08679-0, 2051464). Bks Demand UMI.

Theory of Substitutions. 2nd ed. Eugen Netto. LC 64-10289. 1964. 14.95 (ISBN 0-8284-0165-9). Chelsea Pub.

Theory of Suicide. Maurice L. Farber. Ed. by Robert Kastenbaum. LC 76-19568. (Death & Dying Ser.). 1977. Repr. of 1968 ed. lib. bdg. 17.00x (ISBN 0-405-09564-3). Ayer Co Pubs.

Theory of Superconductivity. John M. Blatt. (Pure and Applied Physics Ser.: Vol. 17). 1964. 82.50 (ISBN 0-12-104950-7). Acad Pr.

Theory of Superconductivity. Ed. by N. N. Bogoliubov. (International Science Review Ser.). (Illus.). 370p. 1968. 78.00 (ISBN 0-677-00080-4). Gordon & Breach.

Theory of Superconductivity. M. Crisan. 330p. 1988. 48.00 (ISBN 9971-50-569-X). World Scientific Pub.

Theory of Superconductivity. J. Robert Schrieffer. 1988. pap. text ed. 28.95 (ISBN 0-317-69750-1). Addison-Wesley.

Theory of Superconductivity: Frontiers in Physics, Vol. 20. Schrieffer. 296p. 1964. 44.25; pap. 28.95. Addison-Wesley.

Theory of Support & Money Bargaining. Patrick Spread. LC 83-40615. 320p. 1984. 25.00 (ISBN 0-312-79858-X). St Martin.

Theory of Surfaces of Plow Bottoms. Ed. by L. V. Gyachev. Tr. by C. B. Malvadkar from Rus. 310p. 1986. text ed. 46.00 (ISBN 90-6191-459-0, Pub. by A A Balkema). Brookfield Pub Co.

Theory of Symbolic Transformations: A Humanistic Scientific Psychology. Louis Carini. LC 83-1049. (Illus.). 176p. (Orig.). 1983. lib. bdg. 27.50 (ISBN 0-8191-3053-2); pap. text ed. 12.25 (ISBN 0-8191-3054-0). U Pr of Amer.

Theory of Symmetric Lattices. F. Maeda & S. Maeda. LC 73-128138. (Grundlehren der Mathematischen Wissenschaften: Vol. 173). (Illus.). 1971. 39.50 (ISBN 0-387-05118-X). Springer-Verlag.

Theory of Symmetry Changes at Continuous Phase Transitions. J. Kocinski. (Phase Transition Phenomena Ser.: Vol. 2). 1984. 94.75 (ISBN 0-444-99658-3, I-393-83). Elsevier.

Theory of Syntactic Recognition for Natural Languages. Mitchell P. Marcus. (Artificial Intelligence Ser.). 335p. 1979. text ed. 35.00x (ISBN 0-262-13149-8). MIT Pr.

Theory of Syntax in Modern Linguistics. Olga Akhmanova & Galina Mikael'An. LC 69-13300. (Janua Linguarum, Ser. Minor: No. 68). (Orig.). 1969. pap. text ed. 17.60x (ISBN 90-2790-683-1). Mouton.

Theory of Target Compression by Longwave Laser Emission. Ed. by G. V. Sklizkov. (Proceedings of the Lebedev Physics Institute of the Academy of Sciences of the U. S. S. R. Ser.: Vol. 170). 167p. 1987. text ed. 73.00 (ISBN 0-941743-05-5). Nova Sci Pubs.

Theory of Taxation for Developing Countries. Ed. by David Newberry & Nicholas Stern. (World Bank Publication). 710p. 1987. 59.00 (ISBN 0-19-520498-0); pap. 29.95 (ISBN 0-19-520541-3). Oxford U Pr.

Theory of Technical Change & Economic Invariance: Application of Lie Groups. Ryuzo Sato. LC 80-68563. (Economic, Econometrics & Mathematical Economic Ser.). 1981. 39.95 (ISBN 0-12-619460-2). Acad Pr.

Theory of Technology: Continuity & Change in Human Development. Thomas R. DeGregori. 264p. (Orig.). 1985. pap. text ed. 19.50x (ISBN 0-8138-1778-1). Iowa St U Pr.

Theory of the Absolute & of the Relative Ethnics. Herbert Spencer. 345p. 1988. Repr. 198.75 (ISBN 0-89901-352-X). Found Class Reprints.

Theory of the Arts. Francis Sparshott. LC 81-47952. 720p. 1982. 61.00 (ISBN 0-691-07266-3). Princeton U Pr.

Theory of the Avant-Garde. Peter Burger. Tr. by Michael Shaw from Ger. LC 83-10549. (Theory & History of Literature Ser.: Vol. 4). 190p. 1984. 25.00x (ISBN 0-8166-1067-3); pap. 12.95 (ISBN 0-8166-1068-1). U of Minn Pr.

Theory of the Avant-Garde. Renato Poggioli. (Belknap Ser.). 256p. 1981. pap. 8.95 (ISBN 0-674-88216-4). Harvard U Pr.

Theory of the Balance of Trade in England. Bruno Suviranta. LC 67-28342. 1967. Repr. of 1923 ed. 27.50x (ISBN 0-678-00328-9). Kelley.

Theory of the Consumption Function. Milton Friedman. (General Ser.: No. 63). 259p. 1957. 30.50 (ISBN 0-691-04182-2, Dist. by Princeton U Pr). Natl Bur Econ Res.

Theory of the Earth, 2 vols. James Hutton. 1960. Repr. of 1795 ed. 87.00x (ISBN 3-7682-0025-6). Lubrecht & Cramer.

Theory of the Earth-Seventeen Eighty-Five James Hutton's Abstract. James Hutton. facsimile 5.75 (ISBN 0-317-64728-8, Pub. by Scot Acad Pr). Longwood Pub Group.

Theory of the Earth, 1788 see System of the Earth, 1785.

Theory of the Earth's Gravity Field. M. Pick et al. 538p. 1973. 147.50 (ISBN 0-444-40939-4). Elsevier.

Theory of the Earth's Shape. V. C. Dragomir et al. (Developments in Solid Earth Geophysics Ser.: Vol. 13). 694p. 1982. 152.75 (ISBN 0-444-99705-9). Elsevier.

Theory of the Economic & Political Elites in the Historical Scenario of the 20th Century. Vilfredo Pareto. 181p. 1984. 147.75 (ISBN 0-89901-220-5). Found Class Reprints.

Theory of the Electromagnetic Field. David M. Cook. (Illus.). 560p. 1975. write for info. (ISBN 0-13-913293-7). P-H.

Theory of the Evolution of Development. W. Arthur. LC 88-5628. 150p. 1988. 44.95 (ISBN 0-471-91974-8). Wiley.

Theory of the Expenditure Budgetary Process. D. G. Hartle. LC 76-25827. (Ontario Economic Council Research Studies). 1976. pap. 4.95x (ISBN 0-8020-3341-5). U of Toronto Pr.

Theory of the Film: Character & Growth of a New Art. Bela Balazs. LC 71-169347. (Arno Press Cinema Program). (Illus.). 312p. 1972. Repr. of 1952 ed. 24.50 (ISBN 0-405-03910-7). Ayer Co Pubs.

Theory of the Firm: Resource Allocation in a Market Economy. 2nd ed. Kalman J. Cohen & Richard M. Cyert. (Illus.). 640p. 1975. write for info. (ISBN 0-13-913798-X). P-H.

Theory of the Foreign Exchanges. George J. Goschen. Ed. by Mira Wilkins. LC 78-3918. (International Finance Ser.). 1978. Repr. of 1892 ed. lib. bdg. 17.00x (ISBN 0-405-11221-1). Ayer Co Pubs.

Theory of the Functions of the Human Passions. Albert Brisbane. LC 75-304. (Radical Tradition in America Ser). (Illus.). 166p. 1975. Repr. of 1856 ed. 18.70 (ISBN 0-88355-209-4). Hyperion Conn.

Theory of the Gene. Thomas H. Morgan. (Illus.). 343p. 1985. Repr. of 1926 ed. lib. bdg. 100.00 (ISBN 0-8492-6843-5). R West.

Theory of the General Strike from the French Revolution to Poland. Phil H. Goodstein. 337p. 1984. 35.00x (ISBN 0-88033-050-3). East Eur Quarterly.

Theory of the Good & the Right. Richard B. Brandt. 1979. 39.95x (ISBN 0-19-824550-5); pap. 16.95x (ISBN 0-19-824744-3). Oxford U Pr.

Theory of the Growth of the Firm. Edith T. Penrose. LC 79-91109. Repr. of 1980 ed. 76.00 (2027623). Bks Demand UMI.

Theory of the Holy Roman Empire. James Bryce. (Illus.). 157p. 1984. Repr. of 1866 ed. 127.75 (ISBN 0-89901-145-4). Found Class Reprints.

Theory of the Inhomogeneous Electron Gas. Ed. by S. Lundqvist & N. H. March. (Physics of Solids & Liquids Ser.). 426p. 1983. 69.50x (ISBN 0-306-41207-1, Plenum Pr). Plenum Pub.

Theory of the Innate Ideas & Their Correlation with Eternity of the Being. V. M Mathieson. (Illus.). 107p. 1987. 117.75 (ISBN 0-89266-579-3). Am Classical Coll Pr.

Theory of the Innate Ideas in the Writings by Descartes, Spinoza, Pascal & Others. Francis Bowen. 1987. 137.45 (ISBN 0-89266-601-3). Am Classical Coll Pr.

Theory of the Just Price: A Historical & Critical Study of the Problem of Economic Value. Rudolph Kaulla. Tr. by Robert D. Hogg from Ger. LC 78-20473. 1980. Repr. of 1940 ed. text ed. 20.75 (ISBN 0-88355-851-3). Hyperion Conn.

Theory of the Knowable & of the Unknowable. Herbert Spencer. (Illus.). 137p. 1984. 157.50 (ISBN 0-89266-456-8). Am Classical Coll Pr.

Theory of the Labor Movement. Selig Perlman. LC 66-18323. 1966. Repr. of 1928 ed. 27.50x (ISBN 0-678-00025-5). Kelley.

Theory of the Labor Movement. Selig Perlman. LC 79-9092. 1979. pap. 12.95x (ISBN 0-87991-818-7). Porcupine Pr.

Theory of the Law of Evidence as Established in the United States & of the Conduct of the Examination of Witnesses. 3rd ed. William Reynolds. xix, 206p. 1983. Repr. of 1897 ed. lib. bdg. 22.50x (ISBN 0-8377-1039-1). Rothman.

Theory of the Leisure Class. Thorstein Veblen. 1954. pap. 4.95 (ISBN 0-451-62591-9, ME2345, Ment). NAL.

Theory of the Leisure Class. Thorstein Veblen. 1979. pap. 4.95 (ISBN 0-14-005363-8). Penguin.

Theory of the Leisure Class. Thorstein B. Veblen. LC 65-15958. 1975. Repr. of 1899 ed. 37.50x (ISBN 0-678-00057-3). Kelley.

Theory of the Linguistic Sign. J. W. Mulder & S. G. Hervey. (Janua Linguarum, Ser. Minor: No. 136). 70p. (Orig.). 1972. pap. text ed. 8.80x (ISBN 90-2792-187-3). Mouton.

Theory of the Location of Industries. Alfred Weber. Tr. by Carl J. Friedrich. LC 77-102554. (Illus.). 1971. Repr. of 1929 ed. 13.50x (ISBN 0-8462-1521-7). Russell.

Theory of the Measurement of Enterprise Income. Robert R. Sterling. LC 79-11417. 1979. Repr. of 1970 ed. text ed. 20.00 (ISBN 0-914348-26-4). Scholars Bk.

Theory of the Mixed Constitution in Antiquity: A Critical Analysis of Polybuis Political Ideas. Kurt Von Fritz. LC 75-7318. (Roman History Ser.). 1975. Repr. 40.00x (ISBN 0-405-07082-9). Ayer Co Pubs.

Theory of the Modern Drama. Peter Szondi. Ed. by Michael Hays. LC 86-19302. (Theory & History of Literature Ser.: Vol. 29). 146p. (Orig.). 1987. 19.50x (ISBN 0-8166-1284-6); pap. 10.95 (ISBN 0-8166-1285-4). U of Minn Pr.

Theory of the Modern Stage. Ed. by Eric Bentley. 496p. 1976. pap. 7.95 (ISBN 0-14-020947-6, Pelican). Penguin.

Theory of the Moral Emotions. Edward Westermarck. (Illus.). 161p. 1984. 137.75 (ISBN 0-89266-464-9). Am Classical Coll Pr.

Theory of the Moral Life. John Dewey. LC 60-9060. 1980. pap. text ed. 9.95x (ISBN 0-8290-0263-4). Irvington.

Theory of the Mounts of the Hand & the Message They Convey to the Future of Man. Count de St. Germain. (Illus.). 131p. 1983. Repr. of 1898 ed. 115.45 (ISBN 0-89901-110-1). Found Class Reprints.

Theory of the Multi-Product Firm. K. Laitinen. (Studies in Mathematical & Managerial Economics Ser.: Vol. 28). 228p. 1981. 73.75 (ISBN 0-444-85495-9, North-Holland). Elsevier.

Theory of the Multinational Enterprise. Peter J. Buckley. (Studia Oeconomiae Negotiorum: No. 26). 64p. (Orig.). 1987. pap. 18.00x (ISBN 91-554-2025-7, Pub. by Uppsala Univ Acta Univ Uppsaliensis (Uppsala Sweden)). Coronet Bks.

Theory of the Novel. Georg Lukacs. Tr. by Anna Bostock from Ger. 1971. pap. 7.95 (ISBN 0-262-62027-8). MIT Pr.

Theory of the Novel. Ed. by Philip Stevick. LC 67-25335. 1967. pap. text ed. 13.95 (ISBN 0-02-931490-9). Free Pr.

Theory of the Novel in Early German Romanticism. Diana Behler. (Utah Studies in Literature & Linguistics: Vol. 11). 162p. 1978. pap. 18.95 (ISBN 3-261-03027-5). P Lang Pubs.

Theory of the Nuclear Shell Model. R. D. Lawson. (OSNP). (Illus.). 1980. text ed. 98.00x (ISBN 0-19-851516-2). Oxford U Pr.

Theory of the Origin & Development of the Heroic Hexameter. FitzGerald Tisdall. Repr. of 1889 ed. 25.00 (ISBN 0-686-20112-4). Quality Lib.

Theory of the Origins & Development of the Heroic Hexameter. Fitzgerald Tisdall. 1889. 27.50 (ISBN 0-8274-3982-2). R West.

Theory of the Political Oligarchy As Applied to the Growth & Decline of the Venetian Empire. George B. McClellan. (Illus.). 217p. 1987. 127.45 (ISBN 0-89901-328-7). Inst Econ Pol.

Theory of the Price Index: Fisher's Test Approach & Generalizations. W. Eichhorn & J. Voeller. (Lecture Notes in Economics & Mathematical Systems: Vol. 140). 1976. soft cover 13.00 (ISBN 0-387-08059-7). Springer-Verlag.

Theory of the Properties of Metals & Alloys. Nevill F. Mott & H. Jones. 1936. pap. 7.95 (ISBN 0-486-60456-X). Dover.

Theory of the Riemann Zeta-Function. 2nd ed. E. C. Titchmarsh. 380p. 1987. pap. 49.95 (ISBN 0-19-853369-1). Oxford U Pr.

Theory of the Roman & of the Medieval Empires: A Critical Evaluation. James Bryce. 256p. 1987. Set. 187.85 (ISBN 0-86722-155-0). Inst Econ Pol.

Theory of the Ruling Class in Germany & Its Responsibility for the Historical & Politcal Collapse of the Country. Maurice Millioud. 187p. 1985. 117.95 (ISBN 0-86722-099-6). Inst Econ Pol.

Theory of the Social Revolutions, 2 vols. A. F. Pollard. (Illus.). 247p. 1985. Repr. of 1907 ed. Set. 247.55 (ISBN 0-89901-238-8). Found Class Reprints.

Theory of the Soul, 2 vols. Emmanuel Swedenborg. (Illus.). 245p. 1986. Set. 187.45 (ISBN 0-89901-261-2). Found Class Reprints.

Theory of the Spirit & the Egocentric Propensities of Man, 2 vols. Giovanni Gentile. (Illus.). 311p. 1986. 237.45 (ISBN 0-89901-264-7). Found Class Reprints.

Theory of the State. J. K. Bluntschli. 1979. Repr. of 1892 ed. lib. bdg. 65.00 (ISBN 0-8495-0543-7). Arden Lib.

Theory of the State. facsimile ed. Johann K. Bluntschli. LC 77-152975. (Select Bibliographies Reprint Ser). Repr. of 1895 ed. 29.00 (ISBN 0-8369-5727-X). Ayer Co Pubs.

Theory of the State, 2 vols. Woodrow Wilson. (Illus.). 291p. 1984. Repr. of 1885 ed. Set. 225.75 (ISBN 0-89901-188-8). Found Class Reprints.

Theory of the State & the Conflicts of History with Emphasis upon Contemporary Political Rivalries for World Leadership, 2 vols. Cornelius J. Merrymount. (Illus.). 221p. 1986. 237.15 (ISBN 0-89266-553-X). Am Classical Coll Pr.

Theory of the Steady State see Mathematical Theory of Diffusion & Reaction in Permeable Catalysts.

Theory of the Theater & Other Principles of Dramatic Criticism. Clayton Hamilton. 481p. 1976. Repr. of 1939 ed. lib. bdg. 34.50x (ISBN 0-374-93422-3, Octagon). Hippocrene Bks.

Theory of the Theatre. Clayton Hamilton. 1975. Repr. of 1915 ed. 20.00 (ISBN 0-8274-4124-X). R West.

Theory of the Two Charismas. Michael A. Toth. LC 81-40054. 204p. (Orig.). 1982. pap. text ed. 13.00 (ISBN 0-8191-2012-X). U Pr of Amer.

Theory of the Unmagnetized Plasma. David C. Montgomery. (Illus.). 412p. 1971. 102.00 (ISBN 0-677-03350-8). Gordon & Breach.

Theory of the Word. H. Christian Bock. 1988. 10.00 (ISBN 0-533-07831-8). Vantage.

Theory of the World Soul. A. Fielding-Hall. (Illus.). 161p. 1985. Repr. of 1910 ed. 127.75 (ISBN 0-89901-235-3). Found Class Reprints.

Theory of Thermal-Neutron Nuclear Reactors, Pt. 2. A. D. Galanin. LC 58-22338. (Soviet Journal of Atomic Energy Supplement Ser.: Nos. 2-3, 1957). (Illus.). pap. 27.00 (ISBN 0-317-09426-2, 2020663). Bks Demand UMI.

Theory of Thermal Stresses. Bruno A. Boley & Jerome H. Weiner. LC 84-19404. 602p. 1985. Repr. of 1960 ed. lib. bdg. 52.50 (ISBN 0-89874-806-2). Krieger.

Theory of Thermally Induced Gas Phase Reactions. Evengii Nikitin. Tr. by E. W. Schlag. LC 66-12733. pap. 41.80 (ISBN 0-317-09605-2, 2050961). Bks Demand UMI.

Theory of Thermodynamics. J. R. Waldram. (Illus.). 1985. 67.50 (ISBN 0-521-24575-3); pap. 24.95 (ISBN 0-521-28796-0). Cambridge U Pr.

Theory of Thin Shells: Proceedings. International Union of Theoretical & Applied Mechanics Symposium, 2nd Copenhagen, 1967. Ed. by F. I. Niordson. LC 68-26458. (Illus.). 1969. 67.90 (ISBN 0-387-04735-2). Springer-Verlag.

Theory of Thin Walled Bars. Atle Gjelsvik. LC 80-26501. 260p. 1981. 42.95 (ISBN 0-471-08594-4). Krieger.

Theory of Thought & Knowledge. B. P. Bowne. 1897. 29.00 (ISBN 0-527-10460-4). Kraus Repr.

Theory of Thought Process. Robert O. Jones. LC 68-13395. 1969. 8.95 (ISBN 0-8022-2283-8). Philos Lib.

Theory of Tikhonov Regularization for Fredholm Equations of the First Kind. C. W. Groetsch. 128p. 1984. pap. 16.95 (ISBN 0-470-20485-0, Co-Pub. with Longman). Wiley.

Theory of Toleration under the Later Stuarts. Alexander A. Seaton. 1972. lib. bdg. 23.00x (ISBN 0-374-97233-8, Octagon). Hippocrene Bks.

Theory of Topological Semigroups. Carruth & Hildebrandt. (Monographs & Textbooks in Pure & Applied Mathematics). 408p. 1983. 55.00 (ISBN 0-8247-1795-3). Dekker.

Theory of Topological Structures: An Approach to Categorical Topology. Gehard Preuss. 1988. lib. bdg. 69.00 (ISBN 90-277-2627-2, Pub. by Reidel Holland). Kluwer Academic.

Theory of Total Consonance. Paul Rosberger. LC 71-92560. (Illus.). 108p. 1970. 16.50 (ISBN 0-8386-7570-0). Fairleigh Dickinson.

Theory of Trade & Protection. William P. Travis. LC 64-16070. (Economic Studies: No. 121). (Illus.). 1964. 20.00x (ISBN 0-674-88305-5). Harvard U Pr.

Theory of Transcendentalism & the Tests of Truth. Joseph Cook. (Illus.). 301p. 1988. 157.50 (ISBN 0-89266-628-5). Am Classical Coll Pr.

Theory of Transformations in Metals & Alloys., Part 1: Equilibrium & General Kinetic Theory. 2nd ed. J. W. Christian. LC 74-22470. 564p. 1975. text ed. 89.00 (ISBN 0-08-018031-0). Pergamon.

Theory of Turbulent Plasma. A. A. Vedenov. 104p. 1966. text ed. 23.50x (ISBN 0-7065-0465-8, Pub. by Keter Pub Jerusalem). Coronet Bks.

Theory of Twenty-One: Finding the Power to Succeed. Chuck Reeves. LC 83-14119. (Illus.). 128p. 1983. 9.95 (ISBN 0-87131-421-5). M Evans.

Theory of Ultra Filters. W. W. Comfort & S. Negrepontis. (Grundlehren der Mathematischen Wissenschaften Ser.: Vol. 211). 480p. 1974. 67.00 (ISBN 0-387-06604-7). Springer-Verlag.

Theory of Ultraspherical Multipliers. W. C. Connett & Alan Lee Schwartz. LC 76-58958. (Memoirs: No. 183). 92p. 1977. pap. 15.00 (ISBN 0-8218-2183-0, MEMO-183). Am Math.

Theory of Unemployment Reconsidered. Edmond Malinvaud. LC 77-1117. 128p. 1979. pap. 19.95x (ISBN 0-470-26883-2). Halsted Pr.

Theory of Unemployment Reconsidered. 2nd ed. Edmond Malinvaud. 140p. 1985. 45.00 (ISBN 0-631-14475-7); pap. 11.95x (ISBN 0-631-14371-8). Basil Blackwell.

Theory of Unimolecular Reactions. Wendell Forst. (Physical Chemistry Ser.). 1973. 106.50 (ISBN 0-12-262350-9). Acad Pr.

Theory of Union Bargaining Goals. Wallace N. Atherton. LC 72-14017. 160p. 1973. 26.00x (ISBN 0-691-04199-7). Princeton U Pr.

Theory of Unitary Group Representation. G. W. Mackey. Ed. by Irving Kaplansky. LC 76-17697. (Lectures in Mathematics Ser.). 1976. pap. 10.00x (ISBN 0-226-50052-7). U of Chicago Pr.

Theory of Valency in Progress. Ed. by V. I. Kuznetsov. 262p. 1980. 8.95 (ISBN 0-8285-1707-X, Pub. by Mir Pubs USSR). Imported Pubns.

Theory of Valuation. Dewey Neurath. (Foundations of the Unity of Science Ser: Vol. 2, No. 4). 1939. pap. 6.00x (ISBN 0-226-57594-2). U of Chicago Pr.

Theory of Valuation: Frontiers of Modern Financial Theory. Bhattacharya & Constantinides. (Studies in Financial Economics). 1988. text ed. 37.50 (ISBN 0-8476-7486-X); pap. text ed. 18.50 (ISBN 0-8476-7487-8). Rowman.

Theory of Valuations. O. F. Schilling. LC 50-12178. (Mathematical Surveys Ser.: No. 4). 253p. 1982. pap. 39.00 (ISBN 0-8218-1504-0, SURV-4). Am Math.

Theory of Value. Carl Menger. (Illus.). 131p. 1984. 137.75 (ISBN 0-89901-133-0). Found Class Reprints.

Theory of Value: An Axiomatic Analysis of Economic Equilibrium. Gerard Debreu. (Cowles Foundation Mongraph: No. 17). 128p. 1972. pap. 7.95 (ISBN 0-300-01559-3, Y-251). Yale U Pr.

Theory of Value & Obligaiton. Robin Attfield. 272p. 1987. lib. bdg. 45.00x (ISBN 0-7099-0572-6, Pub. by Croom Helm UK). Routledge Chapman & Hall.

Theory of Value Before Adam Smith. Hannah R. Sewall. LC 65-26382. 1968. Repr. of 1901 ed. 22.50x (ISBN 0-678-00279-7). Kelley.

Theory of Value, Distribution & Welfare Economics. J. M. Joshi. 1980. text ed. 25.00x (ISBN 0-7069-0689-6, Pub. by Vikas India). Advent NY.

Theory of Van der Waals Attraction. D. Langbein. LC 25-9130. (Springer Tracts in Modern Physics: Vol. 72). (Illus.). 150p. 1974. 46.10 (ISBN 0-387-06742-6). Springer-Verlag.

Theory of Verse. James Routh. LC 76-26077. 1948. lib. bdg. 25.50 (ISBN 0-8414-7243-2). Folcroft.

Theory of Vibration with Applications. 3rd ed. William Thompson. (Illus.). 496p. 1988. text ed. 49.33 (ISBN 0-13-914532-X). P-H.

Theory of Vibrational Spectroscopy & Its Applications to Polymeric Materials. Paul C. Painter et al. LC 81-12969. 530p. 1982. 93.50 (ISBN 0-471-09346-7, Pub. by Wiley-Interscience). Wiley.

Theory of Vibrations with Applications. 2nd ed. William Thomson. (Illus.). 608p. 1981. text ed. 54.00 (ISBN 0-13-914523-0). P-H.

Theory of Viscoelasticity: An Introduction. 2nd ed. R. M. Christensen. 357p. 1982. 59.00 (ISBN 0-12-174252-0). Acad Pr.

Theory of Voting. Robin Farquharson. LC 70-81417. 1969. 20.00x (ISBN 0-300-01121-0). Yale U Pr.

Theory of Wages. Paul H. Douglas. LC 64-22237. 1964. Repr. of 1934 ed. 49.50x (ISBN 0-678-00062-X). Kelley.

Theory of Wages & Employment. Allan M. Cartter. LC 75-31357. (Illus.). 193p. 1976. Repr. of 1959 ed. lib. bdg. 35.00x (ISBN 0-8371-8512-2, CATW). Greenwood.

Theory of Wages & Its Application to the Eight Hour Question & Other Laboure Problems. Herbert M. Thompson. LC 79-51868. 1981. Repr. of 1892 ed. 17.15 (ISBN 0-88355-960-9). Hyperion Conn.

Theory of War & Revolution, 2 vols. V. I. Lenin. (Illus.). 227p. 1987. 176.55 (ISBN 0-86722-148-8). Inst Econ Pol.

Theory of Waveguides & Cavities. R. A. Waldron. 134p. 1969. 50.00 (ISBN 0-677-61480-2). Gordon & Breach.

Theory of Wealth, Value & Exchange, 2 vols. Frank W. Taussig. 386p. 1988. Repr. of 1911 ed. 247.75 (ISBN 0-86654-244-2). Inst Econ Pol.

Theory of Will in Classical Antiquity. Albrecht Dihle. LC 81-7472. (Sather Classical Lectures: No. 48). 288p. 1982. 37.50x (ISBN 0-520-04059-7). U of Cal Pr.

Theory of Wing Sections: Including a Summary of Airfoil Data. Ira H. Abbott & Albert E. Von Doenhoff. (Illus.). 1949. pap. 10.95 (ISBN 0-486-60586-8). Dover.

Theory of Wit & Humour. F. R. Fleet. LC 71-105785. 1970. Repr. of 1890 ed. 21.50x (ISBN 0-8046-0951-9, Pub by Kennikat). Assoc Faculty Pr.

Theory on the Nature of Humanity. James B. Thomas. LC 86-90039. 168p. (gr. 11 up). 1986. 14.95 (ISBN 0-9616285-0-2). J B Thomas.

Theory, Policy, Institutions: Papers from the Carnegie-Rochester Conference on Public Policy. Ed. by K Brunner & A. H. Meltzer. 446p. 1983. 22.00 (ISBN 0-444-86809-7, I-415-83, North-Holland). Elsevier.

Theory, Practice & Process Principles for Physical Separation. Ed. by Mark P. Freeman & Joseph A. FitzPatrick. LC 81-68949. 750p. 1981. pap. 50.00 (ISBN 0-8169-0204-6, P-32). Am Inst Chem Eng.

Theory, Principles & Techniques of Phase Diagrams see Phase Diagrams: Materials Science & Technology.

Theory, Technology & Public Policy on Bilingual Education. Ed. by Raymond V. Padilla. LC 83-60508. 425p. (Orig.). 1983. pap. 10.00 (ISBN 0-89763-066-1). Natl Clearinghse Bilingual Ed.

Theory Why: In Which the Boss Solves the Riddle of Quality. John Guaspari. LC 86-47593. 128p. 1986. 9.95 (ISBN 0-8144-5876-9). AMACOM.

Theory Z Hospital Management: Lessons from Japan. Seth B. Goldsmith. LC 83-15574. 149p. 1983. 33.95 (ISBN 0-89443-949-9). Aspen Pub.

Theory Z: How American Business Can Meet the Japanese Challenge. William G. Ouchi. 1982. pap. 4.50 (ISBN 0-380-59451-X). Avon.

Theory Z School: Beyond Effectiveness. Paul S. George. 106p. 1983. 5.95 (ISBN 0-318-17879-6). Natl Middle Schl.

THEOS-OASIS User's Handbook. Walter Stagner. 300p. (Orig.). pap. 19.95 (ISBN 0-938862-00-6). Weber Systems.

THEOS User's Handbook. Walter Stagner. 300p. (Orig.). pap. cancelled (ISBN 0-317-66561-8). Weber Systems.

Theosophia: An Introduction. Lydia Ross & Charles J. Ryan. 1974. pap. 1.75 (ISBN 0-913004-13-8). Point Loma Pub.

Theosophic Correspondence Between Louis Claude de Saint-Martin & Kirchberger, Baron de Liebistorf. Louis Claude de Saint-Martin. Tr. by Edward B. Penny from Fr. LC 82-61304. xxxii, 326p. Repr. of 1863 ed. 15.00 (ISBN 0-911500-62-6). Theos U Pr.

Theosophical Articles & Notes. H. P. Blavatsky et al. 300p. 1985. Repr. 10.50 (ISBN 0-938998-29-3). Theosophy.

Therapeutic Selectivity & Risk-Benefit Assessment of Hypolipidemic Drugs. Ed. by Giorgio Ricci et al. 352p. 1982. text ed. 71.50 (ISBN 0-89004-649-2). Raven.

Therapeutic Self: Developing Resonance-Key to Effective Relationships. John G. Watkins. LC 77-27633. 543p. 1978. text ed. 39.95 (ISBN 0-87705-306-5). Human Sci Pr.

Therapeutic State: Psychiatry in the Mirror of Current Events. Thomas Szasz. LC 83-63057. 360p. 1984. 23.95 (ISBN 0-87975-239-4); pap. 14.95 (ISBN 0-87975-242-4). Prometheus Bks.

Therapeutic Strategies in Primary & Metastatic Liver Cancer. Ed. by C. Herfarth et al. (Recent Results in Cancer Research Ser.: Vol. 100). (Illus.). 370p. 1986. 85.00 (ISBN 0-387-16011-6). Springer-Verlag.

Therapeutic Studies. Kenneth L. Artiss. 1986. text ed. 22.50 (ISBN 0-9615865-0-8). Psych Bks.

Therapeutic Systems: Rate-Controlled Drug Delivery: Concept & Development. 2nd, rev. ed. Klaus Heilman. (Illus.). 147p. 1984. 37.95 (ISBN 0-86577-119-7). Thieme Med Pubs.

Therapeutic Touch: A Book of Readings. Marianne Borelli & Patricia Heidt. 220p. 1981. pap. text ed. 16.95 (ISBN 0-8261-3111-5). Springer Pub.

Therapeutic Touch: A Practical Guide. Janet Macrae. LC 87-45444. (Illus.). 112p. 1988. pap. 5.95 (ISBN 0-394-75588-X). Knopf.

Therapeutic Touch: How to Use Your Hands to Help or to Heal. Dolores Krieger. (Illus.). 1979. 14.95 (ISBN 0-13-914820-5, Spec); pap. 7.95 (ISBN 0-13-914812-4, Spec). P-H.

Therapeutic Trances: The Cooperation Principle in Ericksonian Psychotherapy. Stephen G. Gilligan. LC 86-20706. 384p. 1986. 37.50 (ISBN 0-87630-442-0). Brunner-Mazel.

Therapeutic Use of Child's Play. Charles Schaefer. LC 75-9556. 688p. 1977. 50.00x (ISBN 0-87668-209-3). Aronson.

Therapeutic Value of Music. Manly P. Hall. pap. 2.95 (ISBN 0-89314-815-6). Philos Res.

Therapeutic Voice of Olga Silverstein. Bradford P Keeney & Olga Silverstein. (Guilford Systemic Family Therapy in Practice Ser.). 193p. 1986. lib. bdg. 19.95 (ISBN 0-89862-350-2). Guilford Pr.

Therapeutics for Aggression: Psychological-Physical Crisis Intervention. Michael Thackrey. 227p. 1987. 29.95 (ISBN 0-89885-305-2). Human Sci Pr.

Therapeutics: From the Primitives to the 20th Century. Erwin H. Ackerknecht. LC 72-88252. 1973. 18.95x (ISBN 0-02-840060-7). Hafner.

Therapeutics in Rheumatology. Ed. by J. M. Moll et al. 606p. 1986. text ed. 71.00 (ISBN 0-88167-258-0). Raven.

Therapeutics in the Elderly: Scientific Foundations & Clinical Practice. Ed. by K. O'Malley & J. L. Waddington. (International Congress Ser.: No. 677). 236p. 1985. 103.75 (ISBN 0-444-80711-X, Excerpta Medica). Elsevier.

Therapeutics in the Elderly. Jeffrey Delafuente & Ronald Stewart. 352p. 1987. 33.95 (ISBN 0-683-02600-3). Williams & Wilkins.

Therapeutics of Hypertension. Ed. by J. I. Robertson et al. (International Congress & Symposium Ser.: No. 26). 264p. 1980. pap. 28.00 (ISBN 1-85315-026-6, Pub. by Royal Society of Medicine Services Ltd). Longwood Pub Group.

Therapeutics Through Exercise. Ed. by David Lowenthal et al. (Hahnemann Symposia Ser.). 240p. 1979. 42.50 (ISBN 0-8089-1209-7, 792591). Grune.

Therapie der Zweierbeziehung see Dynamics of Couples Therapy.

Therapies for Adolescents: Current Treatments for Problem Behaviors. Michael D. Stein & J. Kent Davis. LC 81-20761. (Social & Behavioral Science Ser.). 1982. text ed. 29.95x (ISBN 0-87589-513-1). Jossey-Bass.

Therapies for Adults: Depressive, Anxiety, & Personality Disorders. Howard L. Millman et al. LC 82-48064. (Social & Behavioral Science Ser.). 1982. text ed. 29.95x (ISBN 0-87589-537-9). Jossey-Bass.

Therapies for Children: A Handbook of Effective Treatments for Problem Behaviors. Charles E. Schaefer & Howard L. Millman. LC 77-79481. (Social & Behavioral Science Ser). 1977. text ed. 29.95x (ISBN 0-87589-337-6). Jossey-Bass.

Therapies for School Behavior Problems. Howard L. Millman et al. LC 80-8318. (Social & Behavioral Science Ser.). 1980. text ed. 29.95x (ISBN 0-87589-483-6). Jossey-Bass.

Therapies, Myths & Cosmic Powers. Cyril A. Brathwaite. 1985. 6.95 (ISBN 0-533-06522-4). Vantage.

Therapist. Ellen Plasil. 224p. 1986. pap. 3.95 (ISBN 0-312-90363-4). St Martin.

Therapist. Ellen Plasil. 1988. pap. 3.95 (ISBN 0-317-65539-6). St Martin.

Therapist Responds. Clifton E. Kew & Clinton J. Kew. LC 79-171467. 1972. 6.95 (ISBN 0-8022-2070-3). Philos Lib.

Therapist: The Shocking True Story of a Woman Sexually Exploited by Her Analyst. Ellen Plasil. 1985. 13.95 (ISBN 0-312-79912-8, Pub. by Marek). St Martin.

Therapists' Dilemmas. Ed. by Wendy Dryden. 192p. 1987. 29.95 (ISBN 0-89116-775-7). Hemisphere Pub.

Therapist's Guide to Pediatric Assessment. Linda King-Thomas. Ed. by Bonnie J. Hacker. 304p. 1987. pap. 25.00 (ISBN 0-316-49372-4, Little Med Div). Little.

Therapist's Handbook: Treatment Methods of Mental Disorders. 2nd ed. Ed. by Benjamin B. Wolman. 480p. 1982. 41.95 (ISBN 0-442-25616-7). Van Nos Reinhold.

Therapists, Lawyers, & Divorcing Spouses. Ed. by Esther O. Fisher. Mitchell S. Fisher. LC 82-15515. (Journal of Divorce Ser.: Vol. 6, Nos. 1-2). 138p. 1982. text ed. 32.95 (ISBN 0-86656-169-2, B169). Haworth Pr.

Therapist's Manual for Cognitive Behavior Therapy in Groups. Lawrence I. Sank & Carolyn S. Shaffer. 230p. 1984. 35.00x (ISBN 0-306-41229-2, Plenum Pr). Plenum Pub.

Therapist's Notebook. Bob Goodkin. LC 81-90025. 127p. (Orig.). 1981. pap. 3.95 (ISBN 0-9605872-0-9). Lenox Bks.

Therapist's Own Family: Toward the Differentiation of Self. Peter Titelman. LC 87-17128. 352p. 1987. 30.00x (ISBN 0-87668-921-7). Aronson.

Therapist's Pregnancy: Intrusion in the Analytic Space. Sheri Fenster et al. 160p. 1986. text ed. 19.95 (ISBN 0-88163-044-6). Analytic Pr.

Therapist's Thesaurus: A Cartoon Guide. Robert Wilkins & Penny Loudon. LC 86-61879. (Illus.). 88p. (Orig.). 1987. pap. 6.95 (ISBN 0-914783-17-3). Charles.

Therapist's View of Personal Goals. Carl R. Rogers. LC 60-11607. (Orig.). 1960. pap. 2.50x (ISBN 0-87574-108-8). Pendle Hill.

Theraplay: A New Treatment Using Structured Play for Problem Children & Their Families. Ann M. Jernberg. LC 79-88769. (Social & Behavioral Science Ser.). 1979. text ed. 34.95x (ISBN 0-87589-432-1). Jossey-Bass.

Therapy: A Clinical Introduction. Richard I. Lanyon & Barbara P. Lanyon. 192p. 1978. pap. text ed. write for info (ISBN 0-394-34770-6, RanC). Random.

Therapy: A Method of Teaching Sector Psychotherapy see Clinical Interview.

Therapy American Style: Person Power Through Self-Help. Kenneth B. Matheny & Richard J. Riordan. LC 79-4283. (Illus.). 276p. 1979. 21.95x (ISBN 0-88229-417-2). Nelson-Hall.

Therapy & Ethics: The Courtship of Law & Psychology. Norman J. Finkel. (Current Issues in Behavioral Psychology Ser.). 208p. 1980. 39.50 (ISBN 0-8089-1222-4, 791262). Grune.

Therapy & Prevention of Infections in Cancer Patients: Proceedings, Lausanne, 1978. European Organization for Research & Treatment of Cancer Staff & International Antimicrobial Therapy Group Staff. Ed. by M. Glauser & J. Klastersky. (Illus.). 1979. pap. 34.00 (ISBN 0-08-024434-3). Pergamon.

Therapy & Technique. Sigmund Freud. 1963. pap. 5.95 (ISBN 0-02-076600-9, Collier). Macmillan.

Therapy Book Locator Guide. Harold Pallatz. LC 75-29787. 1975. 1.50 (ISBN 0-915068-00-1). Ideal World.

Therapy for Couples: A Clinician's Guide for Effective Treatment. Billie S. Ables & Jeffrey M. Brandsma. LC 76-50698. (Social & Behavioral Science Ser.). 1977. text ed. 24.95x (ISBN 0-87589-312-0). Jossey-Bass.

Therapy for Stutterers, No. 10. Ed. by C. Woodruff Starkweather. LC 74-17097. 120p. 1974. pap. 1.50 (ISBN 0-933388-08-X). Speech Found Am.

Therapy, Ideology, & Social Change: Mental Healing in Urban Ghana. Leith Mullings. Ed. by Charles Leslie. LC 83-18072. (Comparative Studies of Health Systems & Medical Care: Vol. 10). 260p. 1984. 37.50x (ISBN 0-520-04712-5). U of Cal Pr.

Therapy in Andrology. G. F. Menchini-Fabris et al. (International Congress Ser.: Vol. 596). 296p. 1983. 102.00 (ISBN 0-444-90284-8, Excerpta Medica). Elsevier.

Therapy in Motion. Ed. by Maureen N. Costonis. LC 77-9077. 298p. 1977. 22.95 (ISBN 0-252-00586-4). U of Ill Pr.

Therapy in Nuclear Medicine. Ed. by Richard P. Spencer. 416p. 1978. 79.50 (ISBN 0-8089-1070-1, 794235). Grune.

Therapy in the Ghetto: Political Impotence & Personal Disintegration. Barbara Lerner. LC 74-186606. 256p. 1972. 28.50x (ISBN 0-8018-1373-5). Johns Hopkins.

Therapy Made Fun! Set 2. Linda Newton. 1982. text ed. 18.95x (ISBN 0-8134-2232-9). Inter Print Pubs.

Therapy of Alcoholism: Medical Research Reference Analysis with Bibliography. Kathleen U. Langstrom. LC 84-45986. 150p. 1987. 34.50 (ISBN 0-88164-294-0); pap. 26.50 (ISBN 0-88164-295-9). ABBE Pubs Assn.

Therapy of Angina Pectoris. Weiner & Frishman. 376p. 1986. 59.75 (ISBN 0-8247-7536-8). Dekker.

Therapy of Love. Julie Luedtke. (YA) (gr. 7 up). 1981. 9.95 (ISBN 0-686-84695-8, Avalon). Bouregy.

Therapy of Lung Metastases. Ed. by P. Drings & I. Vogt-Moykopf. (Contributions to Oncology Ser.: Vol. 30). (Illus.). viii, 222p. 1988. 44.75 (ISBN 3-8055-4749-8). S Karger.

Therapy of Malignant Brain Tumors. K. Jellinger. (Illus.). 500p. 1987. 132.00 (ISBN 0-387-81946-0). Springer-Verlag.

Therapy of Mental Disorders: Medical Analysis Index with Research Bibliography. Tana Oshimata. LC 85-47868. 150p. 1987. 34.50 (ISBN 0-88164-410-2); pap. 26.50 (ISBN 0-88164-411-0). ABBE Pubs Assn.

Therapy of Poetry. Molly Harrower. 128p. 1972. 14.25x (ISBN 0-398-02311-5). C C Thomas.

Therapy of Renal Diseases & Related Disorders. Ed. by Wadi N. Suki & Shaul G. Massry. 1984. lib. bdg. 119.50 (ISBN 0-89838-652-7, Pub. by Martinus Nijhoff Netherlands). Kluwer Academic.

Therapy-Resistant Depressions. World Congress of Psychiatry, 6th, Honolulu, Hawaii, August-September 1977. Ed. by Cesar P. De Francisco. (International Pharmacopsychiatry Ser.: Vol. 14, No. 2). (Illus.). 1979. pap. 16.00 (ISBN 3-8055-3055-2). S Karger.

Therapy Through Hypnosis. Ed. by Raphael H. Rhoades. pap. 5.00 (ISBN 0-87980-162-X). Wilshire.

Therapy Under Analysis. Ed. by Allen Hammond. 52p. 1986. pap. 2.25. AAAS.

Therapy with Women: A Feminist Philosophy of Treatment. Susan Sturdivant. (Springer Series: Focus on Women: Vol. 2). 224p. 1980. text ed. 18.95 (ISBN 0-8261-2881-5). Springer Pub.

Theravada Buddhism: A Social History from Ancient Benares to Modern Colombo. Richard F. Gombrich. 240p. 1988. text ed. 49.95 (ISBN 0-7100-9678-X, Pub. by Kegan Pual); pap. text ed. 14.95 (ISBN 0-7102-1319-0, Pub. by Kegan Paul). Routledge Chapman & Hall.

Theravada Buddhism in Southeast Asia. Robert C. Lester. LC 71-185154. 1973. 8.95 (ISBN 0-472-06184-4). U of Mich Pr.

Theravada Meditation: The Buddhist Transformation of Yoga. Winston L. King. LC 79-25856. 192p. 1980. 22.75x (ISBN 0-271-00254-9). Pa St U Pr.

There Ain't No Such Animal & Other East Texas Tales. Bill Brett. LC 78-21777. (Illus.). 128p. 1979. 12.95 (ISBN 0-89096-068-2). Tex A&M Univ Pr.

There & Back. Abraham Morevski. LC 67-27245. 256p. 1967. 6.95 (ISBN 0-87527-057-3). Fireside Bks.

There & Back Again. Joanne Sandstrom. LC 83-48925. (Illus.). 208p. 1984. pap. 12.95 (ISBN 0-914577-07-7). Earendil Pr.

There & Back Again. Diane Wilmer. LC 88-16659. (Step by Step Bks.). (Illus.). 32p. (ps-2). Date not set. bds. 4.95 (ISBN 0-689-71250-2, Aladdin Bks). Macmillan.

There & Back: Memories & Thoughts of a Jewish Actor - Moreuski. LC 67-27245. 256p. 1967. 6.95. Green.

There Are Babies to Adopt: A Resource Guide for Prospective Parents. Christine A. Adamec. LC 87-14012. (Orig.). 1987. 16.95 (ISBN 0-938179-08-X); pap. 9.95 (ISBN 0-938179-04-7). Mills Sanderson.

There Are Doors. Gene Wolfe. 320p. 1988. 17.95. Tor Bks.

There Are Doors. Gene Wolfe. 320p. 1989. pap. price not set. Tor Bks.

There are Hundreds of Reasons Why You Might Need a Lawyer. Standing Committee on Lawyer Referral & Information Service. 1980. 100 copies 12.00. Amer Bar Assn.

There Are Men Too Gentle to Live among Wolves. James Kavanaugh. 1970. 9.95 (ISBN 0-87690-165-8). Dutton.

There Are Men Too Gentle to Live among Wolves. James Kavanaugh. (Illus.). 1984. pap. 5.95 (PL-4105, Torch). Har-Row.

There Are No Dragons Out There: The Miracle of You & What You Can Become. A. David Thomas. LC 86-18205. 150p. (Orig.). 1986. pap. 7.95 (ISBN 0-913420-21-2). Olympus Pub Co.

There Are No Ghosts in the Soviet Union. Reginald Hill. 230p. 1988. 16.95 (ISBN 0-88150-119-0, Foul Play). Countryman.

There Are No Mysteries in Project Analysis. Egil M. Lomeland. 1986. 10.95 (ISBN 0-317-38090-7). Vantage.

There Are No Problem Horses, Only Problem Riders. Mary Twelveponies. 1982. 13.95 (ISBN 0-395-32053-4); pap. 9.95 (ISBN 0-395-33194-3). HM.

There Are No Spies. Bill Granger. LC 86-40040. 272p. 1986. 16.95 (ISBN 0-446-51283-4). Warner Bks.

There Are No Spies. Bill Granger. 384p. (Orig.). 1987. pap. 3.95 (ISBN 0-446-34705-1). Warner Bks.

There Are No Tomorrows. Kris King. Ed. by Sylvia Ashton. LC 78-53082. 1979. 13.95 (ISBN 0-87949-097-7). Ashley Bks.

There Are No Trees in the Prison. Joseph Bruchac. 1978. pap. 2.50 (ISBN 0-942396-24-3). Blackberry ME.

There Are No Victors Here: A Local Perspective on the Treaty of Portsmouth. Peter E. Randall. LC 85-16986. (Portsmouth Marine Society Ser.: No. 8). (Illus.). 96p. 1985. 19.95 (ISBN 0-915819-07-4). Portsmouth Marine Soc.

There Are Still Kings: The Ten Reigning Royal Families of Europe. Francoise Jaudel & Laure Boulay. 288p. 1984. 17.95 (ISBN 0-517-54838-0, C N Potter Bks). Crown.

There Are Those. Nathan Levy & Janet Levy. LC 82-81111. (Illus.). 32p. (ps up). 1982. 14.95 (ISBN 0-9608240-0-6). NL Assoc Inc.

There Are Two Kinds of Terrible. Peggy Mann. (gr. 5 up). 1979. pap. 1.50 (ISBN 0-380-45823-3, 45823, Camelot). Avon.

There Came a Proud Beggar. Mark Linder. 486p. (Orig.). 1986. 18.95 (ISBN 0-88184-198-6). Carroll & Graf.

There Comes A Time: A Challenge to the Two-Party System. Gerald J. Fresia. LC 86-12190. 225p. 1986. lib. bdg. 40.95 (ISBN 0-275-92095-X, C2095). Praeger.

There Goes Herschel: Countdown to the Pros. Bill Cromartie. LC 83-80722. (Illus.). 224p. (Orig.). 1983. pap. 11.95 (ISBN 0-88011-159-3). Scribner.

There Goes My Aching Back. John Burak. LC 74-21437. 1975. 8.50 (ISBN 0-682-48134-3, Banner). Exposition-Phoenix.

There Goes the Ghost. Victoria Sherrow. LC 83-49485. (Illus.). 32p. (gr. k-3). 1985. 11.25i (ISBN 0-06-025509-9); PLB 10.89g (ISBN 0-06-025510-2). HarpJ.

There Goes the Shutout. Charles M. Schulz. LC 76-43499. (Peanuts Parade Books: No. 13). 1977. pap. 4.95 (ISBN 0-03-020676-6). H Holt & Co.

There Hangs the Knife. Marcia Muller. LC 88-1009. 240p. 1988. 15.95 (ISBN 0-312-01833-9, Pub. by Thomas Dunne Bks). St Martin.

There I Was...Flat on My Back. Bob Stevens. LC 75-25247. 1975. 11.95 (ISBN 0-8168-8954-6, 28954, TAB-Aero). TAB Bks.

There Is a Better Way. R. E. McMaster, Jr. Date not set. price not set. Reaper Pub.

There Is a Better Way to Manage. Malcolm Bird. 128p. 1985. pap. 19.95 (ISBN 0-89397-207-X). Nichols Pub.

There is a Better Way to Manage. Hugh A. McLean. 336p. 1982. 19.95 (ISBN 0-8144-5713-4). AMACOM.

There Is a Carrot in My Ear & Other Noodle Tales. Alvin Schwartz. LC 80-8442. (Harper I Can Read Bks.). (Illus.). 64p. (gr. k-3). 1982. 8.70i (ISBN 0-06-025233-2); PLB 10.89 (ISBN 0-06-025234-0). HarpJ.

There Is a Carrot in My Ear & Other Noodle Tales. Alvin Schwartz. LC 80-8442. (Trophy I Can Read Bks.). (Illus.). 64p. (gr. k-3). 1986. pap. 3.50 (ISBN 0-06-444103-2, Trophy). HarpJ.

There Is a Cure for Arthritis. Paavo O. Airola. pap. 5.95 (ISBN 0-13-914671-7, Reward). P-H.

There Is a Cure for Arthritis. Paavo O. Airola. 224p. 1988. pap. 6.95 (ISBN 0-13-914698-9). P-H.

There Is a Fortune to be Made in Software Maintenance: Opportunities in the 30 Billion Dollar Software AfterMarket. Girish Parikh. LC 84-51942. (Illus.). 402p. (Orig.). 1985. pap. 500.00 (ISBN 0-932888-00-3, TFSM). Shetal Ent.

There Is a Method to This Madness, No. 1. Steve Skinner. Ed. by Executype. (Illus.). 74p. 1983. 12.95 (ISBN 0-317-03270-4). Saddle Sore.

There Is a Place Where You Are Not Alone. Hugh Prather. LC 80-912. 224p. 1980. pap. 7.95 (ISBN 0-385-14778-3, Dolp). Doubleday.

There Is a Rainbow. Louis Gittner. (Illus.). 65p. (Orig.). 1981. pap. 5.95 (ISBN 0-9605492-1-8). Touch Heart.

There Is a Rainbow Behind Every Dark Cloud. Center for Attitudinal Healing Staff. 1979. pap. 7.95 (ISBN 0-89087-253-8). Celestial Arts.

There Is a Rainbow in the Moon. Lauren. 80p. 1985. 8.95 (ISBN 0-911051-24-4). Plain View.

There Is a River: The Black Struggle for Freedom in America. Vincent Harding. LC 81-47304. (Illus.). 448p. 1981. 19.95 (ISBN 0-15-189342-X). HarBraceJ.

There Is a River: The Black Struggle for Freedom in American. Vincent Harding. LC 82-40024. 480p. 1983. pap. 6.95 (ISBN 0-394-71148-3, Vin). Random.

There Is a Safe Place to Hide. C. Anthony & R. Anthony. 1950. pap. 2.95 (ISBN 0-910140-01-4). C & R Anthony.

There Is a Season. Search Institute Staff. Ed. by Dorothy Williams. 1985. program manual 24.95 (ISBN 0-697-02047-9); pap. 4.95 parent book (ISBN 0-697-02046-0); video cassettes avail. Wm C Brown.

There Is a Serpent in Eden. Robert Bloch. (Orig.). 1979. pap. 2.25 (ISBN 0-89083-514-4). Zebra.

There Is a Singing Underneath: Meditations in Central Park. Thomas P. Coffey. 128p. 1985. pap. 4.95 (ISBN 0-87193-217-2). Dimension Bks.

There Is a Song, We Shall Sing It. Kofi Awoonor et al. (African Poetry Ser.). cancelled. Greenfld Rev Pr.

There Is a Tide. Agatha Christie. 1970. pap. 1.95 (ISBN 0-440-18692-7). Dell.

There Is a Tide. Agatha Christie. 240p. 1987. pap. 3.50 (ISBN 0-425-06803-X). Berkley Pub.

There Is a Tide. Agatha Christie. 1987. 9.95 (ISBN 0-553-35066-8). Bantam.

There Is a Tree More Ancient Than Eden. rev. ed. Leon Forrest. 210p. 1988. pap. 8.95 (ISBN 0-9614644-5-3). Another Chicago Pr.

There Is a Way. Stefan Nadzo. 129p. 1981. pap. 4.75. Coleman Pub.

There Is a Way: Meditations for a Seeker. Stefan C. Nadzo. LC 80-66831. (Illus.). 129p. (Orig.). 1980. pap. 5.95. Eden's Work.

There Is a Way Out. Vernon Howard. LC 75-11137. 173p. 1982. pap. 7.00 (ISBN 0-87516-472-2). DeVorss.

TITLE INDEX THERE'S NOTHING NEAT ABOUT

There Is Always Love. Emilie Loring. 1976. Repr. of 1940 ed. lib. bdg. 17.95x (ISBN 0-88411-363-9, Pub. by Aeonian Pr). Amereon Ltd.
There Is Always Time to Die. Adam Starkopf. 256p. 1981. 16.95 (ISBN 0-89604-027-5); pap. 10.95 (ISBN 0-89604-028-3). Holocaust Pubns.
There Is Always Time to Die. Adam Starkopf. 256p. 10.95 (ISBN 0-686-95091-7); pap. 5.95 (ISBN 0-686-99462-0). ADL.
There Is Confusion. Jessie R. Fauset. LC 73-18575. Repr. of 1924 ed. 23.50 (ISBN 0-404-11386-9). AMS Pr.
There Is Help for Your Church. Howard Ball. LC 81-65669. 40p. (Orig.). 1981. pap. text ed. 1.50 (ISBN 0-934396-14-0). Churches Alive.
There Is Hope. Oswald C. Hoffman. 104p. 1985. 9.95 (ISBN 0-570-03979-7, 15-2184). Concordia.
There Is No Asia. Dwight Cooke. LC 79-118487. (Essay & General Literature Index Reprint Ser). 1971. Repr. of 1954 ed. 29.50x (ISBN 0-8046-1404-0, Pub by Kennikat). Assoc Faculty Pr.
There Is No Balm in Birmingham. Ann Deagon. LC 75-41623. (Third Godine Poetry Chapbook Ser.). 1978. 5.00 (ISBN 0-87923-177-7). Godine.
There Is No Darkness. Joe Haldeman & Jack C. Haldeman, II. 256p. 1984. pap. 2.95 (ISBN 0-441-80567-1, Pub. by Ace Science Fiction). Ace Bks.
There Is No Death. Florence Marryat. 69.95 (ISBN 0-8490-1192-2). Gordon Pr.
There Is No Empty Space. Jan Van Rijckenborgh. (Orig.). 1986. pap. 4.00 (ISBN 90-70196-50-6). Rozekruis Pr.
There Is No Gene for Good Teaching: A Handbook on Lecture Skills for Medical Teachers. 3rd ed. Neal A. Whitman. 24p. 1986. pap. text ed. 6.00 (ISBN 0-940193-00-0). Univ UT Sch Med.
There Is No Happiness Without a Feeling. Edward J. Smith. 119p. 1984. 20.00 (ISBN 0-682-40130-7). Exposition-Phoenix.
There Is No Male & Female: The Fate of a Dominical Saying in Paul & Gnosticism. Dennis R. MacDonald. LC 86-45200. (Harvard Dissertations in Religion Ser.). 160p. 1987. pap. 14.95 (ISBN 0-8006-7076-0, 1-7076). Fortress.
There Is No Mistaking a Pierce Arrow. Brooks T. Brierley. (Illus.). 160p. 1986. 39.00 (ISBN 0-9615791-0-2). Garrett & String.
There Is No Truce. facs. ed. Rudolph W. Chamberlain. LC 74-124229. (Select Bibliographies Reprint Ser). 1935. 23.50 (ISBN 0-8369-5418-1). Ayer Co Pubs.
There Is No Zoo in Zoology. Charles H. Elster. 1988. pap. 6.95 (ISBN 0-02-031830-8, Collier). Macmillan.
There Is No Zoo in Zoology: And Other Beastly Mispronunciations. Charles H. Elster. 1988. 16.95 (ISBN 0-02-535280-6). Macmillan.
There Is Nothing More. 368p. 1974. pap. 5.95 (ISBN 0-911988-40-8). AMI Pr.
There Is Only One Me. Julie Gibbons. 20p. (gr. 1-4). 1974. pap. 3.50 (ISBN 0-911336-56-7). Sci of Mind.
There Is Only One Nigeria. Peggy Watt. 203p. 1987. 49.00x (ISBN 0-7223-1913-4, Pub. by A H Stockwell England). State Mutual Bk.
There Is Something Else. Chuck Patterson. Ed. by Mary H. Wallace. (Illus., Orig.). 1982. pap. 5.95 (ISBN 0-912315-23-7). Word Aflame.
There Is Still Love. Malachi Martin. 208p. 1985. pap. 2.95 (ISBN 0-345-30406-3). Ballantine.
There Lies a Fair Land. Ed. by John Solensten. Date not set. pap. 7.50 (ISBN 0-89823-067-5). New Rivers Pr.
There May Be Heaven. Elizabeth Ogilvie. Repr. lib. bdg. 17.95x (ISBN 0-88411-338-8, Pub. by Aeonian Pr). Amereon Ltd.
There Might Have Been An Insane Heart: Selected Poems In Armenian Language. Sonia Balassanian. 80p. (Orig., Armenian.). 1982. pap. 5.00 (ISBN 0-9608388-0-5). S Balassanian.
There Must Be a Lone Ranger: The American West in Film & in Reality. Jenni Calder. LC 74-20216. (Illus.). 256p. 1975. 8.95 (ISBN 0-8008-7636-9). Taplinger.
There Must Be a Pony. James Kirkwood. (YA) 1989. pap. price not set (ISBN 0-440-20238-8). Dell.
There Must Be a Way. Robert Bonazzi. 1988. pap. 7.00 (ISBN 0-941179-18-4). Latitudes Pr.
There Must Be Heresies. J. C. Metcalfe. 1963. pap. 2.25 (ISBN 0-87508-922-4). Chr Lit.
There Must Be More to Love Than Death: Three Short Novels. Charles Newman. LC 76-17743. 217p. 1976. 12.95 (Pub by Swallow). Ohio U Pr.
There Must Be More to Love Than Death: Three Short Novels. LC 76-17743. 217p. 1976. 12.95. Ultramarine Pub.
There Must Be Some Mistake. Marian Babson. 192p. 1987. 13.95 (ISBN 0-312-00693-4, Pub. by Thomas Dunne Bks). St Martin.
There Once Was a Cook. Lora T. Spence et al. (Illus.). (gr. k up). 1985. pap. 12.95 (ISBN 0-9614501-0-X). Wesley Inst.
There Once Was a Time. Piero Ventura. (Illus.). 160p. (gr. 5 up). 1987. pap. 19.95 (ISBN 0-399-21356-2, Putnam). Putnam Pub Group.
There Really Was a Hollywood. Janet Leigh. 320p. 1985. pap. 3.95 (ISBN 0-515-09080-8). Jove Pubns.
There Shall Be One Christ. Ed. by Michael Meilach. (Spirit and Life Ser). 1968. 2.50 (ISBN 0-686-11576-7). Franciscan Inst.
There Shall Be Retribution: Nazi War Criminals & Their Protectors. Vladimir Molchanov. 200p. 1984. 12.50x (ISBN 0-317-53824-1, Pub. by Collets (UK)). State Mutual Bk.
There Shall Be Signs from 1948 to 1982. Wim Malgo. 1980. 2.95 (ISBN 0-937422-00-2). Midnight Call.
There She Blows: A Narrative of a Whaling Voyage, in the Indian & South Atlantic Oceans. Ben-Ezra S. Ely. Ed. by Curtis Dahl. LC 76-142726. (American Maritime Library: Vol. 3). (Illus.). xxxiii, 208p. 1971. ltd. ed. 15.00 (ISBN 0-8195-4033-1). Mystic Seaport.
There Shines Forth Christ. Julian Stead. 1983. pap. 8.95 (ISBN 0-932506-29-1). St Bedes Pubns.
There was a Carpenter who Loved the Lord. Betty R. Carter. 1988. 6.95 (ISBN 0-533-07599-8). Vantage.
There Was a Hill... Lark Carrier. LC 84-25536. (Illus.). 40p. (ps up). 1985. 14.95 (ISBN 0-907234-70-4). Picture Bk Studio.
There Was a Little Boy. Barbara K. Davidson. 1968. 2.00 (ISBN 0-936426-03-9). Play Schs.
There Was a Man: The Saga of Gordon Kahl. Capstan Turner & A. J. Lowery. 264p. (Orig.). 1986. pap. 5.95 (ISBN 0-9614465-0-1). Sozo Pub Co.
There Was a Place. Myra C. Livingston. 40p. (gr. 3-7). Date not set. 9.95 (ISBN 0-689-50464-0, M K McElderry). Macmillan.
There Was a Time. Taylor Caldwell. 1974. Repr. of 1947 ed. lib. bdg. 25.95x (ISBN 0-88411-157-1, Pub. by Aeonian Pr). Amereon Ltd.
There Was an Old Lady. Illus. by Pam Adams. (Books with Holes). (Illus.). 16p. (ps-2). 1975. 8.00 (ISBN 0-85953-021-3, Pub. by Child's Play England). Playspaces.
There Was an Old Lady Who Swallowed a Fly. Illus. by Pam Adams. (Books with Holes Ser.). (Illus.). 16p. (ps-2). 1973. pap. 5.00 (ISBN 0-85953-018-3, Pub. by Child's Play England). Playspaces.
There Was an Old Woman. Ellery Queen. Bd. with Origin of Evil. 1980. pap. 3.50 (ISBN 0-451-12683-1, AE2683, Sig). NAL.
There Was an Old Woman. Stephen Wyllie. LC 85-42639. (Illus.). 32p. (ps-3). 1985. 7.95 (ISBN 0-694-00050-7). HarpJ.
There Was Once an Elephant. G. Tsyferov. 12p. 1974. pap. 0.99 (ISBN 0-8285-1243-4, Pub. by Progress Pubs USSR). Imported Pubns.
There Was So Much Laughter. Gary Morgan. 50p. 1984. pap. 2.95x (ISBN 0-942424-03-4). W Anglia Pubns.
There We Sat Down: Talmudic Judaism in the Making. Jacob Neusner. pap. 9.95x (ISBN 0-87068-676-3). Ktav.
There Were Also Strangers. Borden Deal. 280p. 1986. 15.95 (ISBN 0-88282-018-4). New Horizon NJ.
There Were Days Like That. Harold P. Levy. Ed. by Beverley J. DeWitt. (Illus.). 164p. (Orig.). 1985. pap. 9.95 (ISBN 0-9615303-0-8). Blue Whale Pr.
There Were Giants in those Days. Gerald Eskenazi. 1987. pap. 9.95 (ISBN 0-13-914680-6). P-H.
There Were Ten in the Bed. Illus by Pam Adams. (Illus.). 24p. (ps-2). 1979. 5.50 (ISBN 0-85953-095-7, Pub. by Childs Play England). Playspaces.
There Were These Two Guys. Jonathan Litter. (Orig.). 1988. pap. 3.50 (ISBN 0-945926-01-4). Paradigm RI.
There Were Zulus at the Bottom of Our Garden. Margaret Heard. 204p. 1987. 29.00x (ISBN 0-7223-1910-X, Pub. by A H Stockwell England). State Mutual Bk.
There Will Always Be a Day That the Creator Will Bless Me. A. C. Doyle. 16p. 1985. pap. text ed. 0.75 (ISBN 0-917593-06-5, Pub. by Intl Partners). Prosperity & Profits.
There Will Be No Time. William L. Borden. LC 46-8052. 1946. 2.50 (ISBN 0-911090-03-7). Pacific Bk Supply.
There Will be Time. Poul Anderson. Bd. with Dancer From Atlantis. 1988. pap. 2.95 (ISBN 0-451-15412-6, AE1752, Sig). NAL.
There Will Be War. J. E. Pournelle. 352p. 1983. pap. 2.95 (ISBN 0-8125-4951-1, Dist. by Warner Pub. Services & Saint Martin's Press). Tor Bks.
There Will Be War: Blood & Iron, Vol. III. J. E. Pournelle. 384p. (Orig.). 1984. pap. 2.95 (ISBN 0-8125-4955-4). Tor Bks.
There Will Be War: Day of the Tyrant, Vol. IV. J. E. Pournelle. 352p. 1985. pap. 2.95 (ISBN 0-8125-4957-0, Dist. by Warner Pub. Services & Saint Martin's Press). Tor Bks.
There Will Be War: Guns of Darkness, No. 6. J. E. Pournelle. 192p. (Orig.). 1987. pap. 3.95 (ISBN 0-8125-4961-9, Dist. by St Martin's Pr & Warner Pub Servs). Tor Bks.
There Will Be War: Men of War, Vol. II. J. E. Pournelle. 320p. (Orig.). 1984. pap. 2.95 (ISBN 0-8125-4953-8, Dist. by Warner Pub Services & Saint Martin's Press). Tor Bks.
There Will Be War, Number 5: Warrior. J. E. Pournelle. 352p. (Orig.). 1986. pap. 2.95 (ISBN 0-8125-4959-7, Dist. by Warner Pub Services & St. Martin's Press). Tor Bks.
There Will Never Be Another You. Dan Zadra. (Adventures in Human Potential Ser.). (Illus.). 32p. (gr. 6 up). PLB 8.95 (ISBN 0-88682-015-4). Creative Ed.
There You Go Again. George Fisher. LC 87-10747. (Illus.). 250p. 1987. 15.95 (ISBN 1-55728-013-4); pap. 9.95 (ISBN 1-55728-014-2). U of Ark Pr.
Thereby Hangs a Tale: Stories of Curious Word Origins. Charles E. Funk. LC 84-48645. 320p. 1985. pap. 5.95 (ISBN 0-06-091260-X, CN 1260, PL). Har-Row.
Therefore. J. Glenn Harvey. (Orig.). 1984. pap. 3.95 (ISBN 0-915059-02-9). Ind Christ Pubns.
There'll Be a Hot Time in the Old Town Tonight: The Great Chicago Fire of 1871 Told with Song and Pictures. Reissue. ed. Robert Quackenbush. LC 74-4283. (Illus.). 32p. (ps up). 1988. Repr. of 1974 ed. PLB 12.89 (ISBN 0-397-32267-4, Lipp Jr Bks). HarpJ.
There's a Bat in Bunk Five. Paula Danziger. LC 80-64833. 160p. (gr. 7 up). 1980. pap. 10.95 (ISBN 0-385-29013-6); pap. 13.95 (ISBN 0-385-29015-2). Delacorte.
There's a Bat in Bunk Five. Paula Danziger. 160p. (gr. 5-9). 1988. pap. 2.95 (ISBN 0-440-40098-8, LE). Dell.
There's a Bat Wing in My Lunchbox. Ann Hodgman. 96p. 1987. pap. 2.50 (ISBN 0-380-75426-6, Camelot). Avon.
There's a Boy in the Girl's Bathroom. Louis Sachar. Ed. by Frances Foster. LC 86-20100. 224p. (gr. 5 up). 1987. 11.95 (ISBN 0-394-88570-8); lib. bdg. 11.99 (ISBN 0-394-98570-2). Knopf.
There's a Boy in the Girls' Bathroom. Louis Sachar. LC 86-20100. 208p. (gr. 3-7). 1988. pap. 2.95 (ISBN 0-394-80572-0). Knopf.
There's a Caterpillar in My Lemonade. Diana Gregory. LC 84-40794. (Illus.). 1980. 9.70i (ISBN 0-201-03603-7, Lipp Jr Bks). HarpJ.
There's a Dinosaur in the Park! Rodney Martin. 1985. 16.00x (ISBN 0-907349-65-X, Pub by Spindlewood). State Mutual Bk.
There's a Dinosaur in the Park! Rodney Martin. LC 86-42811. (Illus.). 31p. (gr. 2-3). 1987. PLB 11.25 (ISBN 1-55532-151-8). Stevens Inc.
There's a Drunk in the Pulpit. Joseph W. Wise. 128p. 1987. 9.95 (ISBN 0-8062-3161-0). Carlton.
There's a Hand in the Sky. Oscar De Mejo. LC 83-2320. (Illus.). 64p. (gr. 4 up). 1983. (Pant Bks Young). Pantheon.
There's a Hippopotamus on Our Roof Eating Cake. Hazel Edwards. LC 85-16386. (Illus.). 32p. (ps-1). 1986. 12.95 (ISBN 0-8234-0592-3). Holiday.
There's a Hippopotamus under My Bed. Mike Thaler. (Illus.). 32p. (gr. k-3). 1978. pap. 2.50 (ISBN 0-380-40238-6, Camelot). Avon.
There's a Light in the Gardibee House & Other Stories. Eugene J. Mahoney. 117p. (Orig.). 1985. pap. 2.95 (ISBN 0-9615994-0-5). E J Mahoney.
There's a Little Ambiguity over There among the Bluebells & Other Theater Poems. Ruth Krauss. LC 68-19709. (Illus.). 1968. 10.00 (ISBN 0-89366-062-0). Ultramarine Pub.
There's a Little Bit of Me in Jamey. Diana Amadeo. Ed. by Ann Fay. (Illus.). (gr. 1-4). 1988. 10.50g (ISBN 0-8075-7854-1). A Whitman.
There's a Lot More to Health Than Not Being Sick. Bruce Larson. (QP Proven Word Ser.). 144p. 1984. pap. 7.99 (ISBN 0-8499-2997-0). Word Bks.
There's a Monster in Your Closet! Understanding Phobias. Brent Filson. (Illus.). 64p. 1986. 9.29 (ISBN 0-671-55496-4). Messner.
There's a Monster under My Bed. James Howe. LC 85-20026. (Illus.). 32p. (ps-3). 1986. 11.95 (ISBN 0-689-31178-8, Atheneum Childrens Bks). Macmillan.
There's a New World Coming. Hal Lindsey. 320p. 1984. pap. 3.95 (ISBN 0-553-24555-4). Bantam.
There's a New World Coming: An In-Depth Analysis of the Book of Revelation. updated ed. Hal Lindsey. 288p. 1984. pap. 7.95 (ISBN 0-89081-440-6). Harvest Hse.
There's a Nightmare in My Closet. Mercer Mayer. LC 68-15250. (Pied Piper Bk.). (Illus.). 32p. (gr. k-3). 1976. pap. 3.95 (ISBN 0-8037-8574-7, 0383-120). Dial Bks Young.
There's a Nightmare in My Closet. Mercer Mayer. LC 68-15250. (Illus.). (gr. k-3). 1968. 11.95 (ISBN 0-8037-8682-4, 01063-320); PLB 11.89 (ISBN 0-8037-8683-2). Dial Bks Young.
There's a One-Armed Bandit in My Kitchen. Candy Coleman. (Illus.). 48p. (Orig.). 1980. pap. text ed. 3.00 (ISBN 0-943768-03-9). C Coleman.
There's a Party at Mona's Tonight. Harry Allard. (Snuggle & Read Story Bks.). (Illus.). 32p. (ps-3). 1985. pap. 2.50 (ISBN 0-380-69920-6, Camelot). Avon.
There's a Rainbow in My Paintbox. Jackie Shaw. (Illus., Orig.). 1977. pap. 5.95 (ISBN 0-941284-05-0). Deco Design Studio.
There's a Sheep in My Mirror. Susie Shellenberger. 108p. 1985. pap. 4.50 (ISBN 0-8341-1054-7). Beacon Hill.
There's a Skunk in My Trunk. Donald W. Kruse. Ed. by May Davenport. Bd. with Spotty the Goat. Robert W. Walker; Christopher C. Cat. Edith Cutting; Night Dancers. Jan Pendleton. LC 81-71555. 58p. (Orig.). (gr. 3-5). 1984. pap. 3.50x (ISBN 0-943864-32-1). Davenport.
There's a Song in My Heart & Other Poems & Lyrics. Carole McCune. 76p. 1987. 7.95 (ISBN 0-533-07684-6). Vantage.
There's a Time & a Place: Prayers for the Christian Year. Jamie Wallace. (Illus.). 159p. 1986. pap. 4.95 (ISBN 0-00-599697-X, Collins Liturgical). HarpR.
There's a Trick with a Knife I'm Learning to Do: Poems 1962-1978. Michael Ondaatje. 1979. 12.95 (ISBN 0-393-01191-7). Norton.
There's a Vulture Outside. Charles M. Schulz. 1976. pap. 4.95 (ISBN 0-03-017481-3). H Holt & Co.
There's a Way Back to God. William MacDonald. 1986. pap. 2.25 (ISBN 0-937396-42-7). Walterick Pubs.
There's a Wocket in My Pocket! Dr. Seuss. LC 74-5516. (Bright & Early Book Ser). (Illus.). 36p. (ps-1). 1974. 5.95 (ISBN 0-394-82920-4, BYR); lib. bdg. 6.99 (ISBN 0-394-92920-9). Random.
There's Always Been a Women's Movement This Century. Dale Spender. (Illus.). 200p. (Orig.). 1983. pap. 5.95 (ISBN 0-86358-002-5, Pandora Pr). Routledge Chapman & Hall.
There's an Alligator under My Bed. Mercer Mayer. LC 86-19944. (Illus.). 32p. (ps-3). 1987. 11.95 (ISBN 0-8037-0374-0, 01160-350); PLB 11.89 (ISBN 0-8037-0375-9). Dial Bks Young.
There's an Angel in My Locker. Mary L. Carney. 112p. (Orig.). (gr. 7-9). 1985. pap. 5.95 (ISBN 0-310-28471-6, 11341P). Zondervan.
There's an Ant in Anthony. Bernard Most. LC 79-23089. (Illus.). 32p. (gr. k-3). 1980. 10.25 (ISBN 0-688-22226-9); PLB 10.88 (ISBN 0-688-32226-3). Morrow.
There's an Awful Lot of Weirdos in Our Neighborhood. Colin McNaughton. (gr. 1-5). Date not set. 14.95 (ISBN 0-671-64641-9). S&S.
There's an Iguana in My Plumbing. Elenore C. Bierman. Ed. by Sylvia Ashton. LC 75-777. 1976. 13.95 (ISBN 0-87949-050-0). Ashley Bks.
There's an Owl in our Belfry. William L. Bates. (Illus.). 112p. (Orig.). 1985. pap. 7.95 (ISBN 0-9615781-0-6). Periwinkle.
There's More... Much More. Sue Alexander. LC 86-33632. (Illus.). 32p. (ps-3). 1987. 12.95 (ISBN 0-15-200605-2, Gulliver Bks). HarBraceJ.
There's More to Being Thin Than Being Thin. Neva Coyle & Marie Chapian. 170p. (Orig.). 1984. pap. 5.95 (ISBN 0-87123-443-2, 210443). Bethany Hse.
There's More to Life Than Pumpkins, Drugs & Other False Gods. Kenneth G. Reiners. LC 80-50424. 64p. (Orig.). 1980. pap. 4.25 (ISBN 0-934104-03-4). Woodland.
There's More to Musicals Than Music. Martha Eddins et al. (Illus.). 72p. 1980. pap. 5.95 (ISBN 0-916642-13-5, 566). Somerset Pr IL.
There's More...Much More. Sue Alexander. (Illus.). (ps-3). 12.95 (ISBN 0-317-62359-1, Gulliver Bks). HarBraceJ.
There's Music in the Air. Malvina Reynolds. LC 76-19261. (Illus.). 96p. (gr. 1-12). 1976. pap. 5.00 (ISBN 0-915620-05-7). Schroder Music.
There's New Life in the Small Congregation: Why It Happens & How. Ronald Crandall & Ray Sells. LC 83-71697. 120p. (Orig.). 1983. pap. 7.50 (ISBN 0-88177-001-9, DR001B). Discipleship Res.
There's No Business. Charles Bukowski. LC 84-2977. (Illus.). 24p. (Orig.). 1984. 10.00 (ISBN 0-87685-623-7); pap. 4.00 (ISBN 0-87685-622-9). Black Sparrow.
There's No Business Like Soul Business. Doug Marlette. (Illus.). 128p. (Orig.). 1987. pap. 6.95 (ISBN 0-934601-20-8). Peachtree Pubs.
There's No One Like You, Snoopy: Selected Cartoons from "You're You, Charlie Brown, Vol. I. Charles M. Schulz. (Peanuts Ser.). (Illus.). (gr. 1-5). 1985. pap. 2.25 (ISBN 0-449-20776-5, Crest). Fawcett.
There's No Place Like a Home. Mary I. Hulse. 72p. 1986. 6.95. Carlton.
There's No Place Like Home. Marc Brown. LC 84-4229. (Illus.). 48p. (ps-3). 1984. 5.95 (ISBN 0-8193-1125-1). Parents.
There's No Place Like Home: Confessions of an Interior Designer. Carleton Varney. LC 80-1020. 228p. 1980. 12.95 (ISBN 0-672-51872-4). Bobbs.
There's No Place to Cry at the Ritz. Nancy Winters. 336p. 1988. 18.95 (ISBN 0-525-24658-4). Dutton.
There's No Such Place As Far Away. Richard Bach. (Illus.). 1979. pap. 14.95 (ISBN 0-385-29038-1, E Friede). Delacorte.
There's No Such Thing As a Chanukah Bush, Sandy Goldstein. Susan Sussman. Ed. by Kathleen Tucker. (Illus.). 40p. (gr. 3-7). 1983. PLB 7.50 (ISBN 0-8075-7862-2). A Whitman.
There's No Such Thing As a Dragon. Jack Kent. (Golden Look-Look Bks.). (Illus.). 24p. (gr. k-3). 1975. pap. write for info (ISBN 0-307-11841-X, Golden Bks). Western Pub.
There's No Time for Love, Charlie Brown. Charles M. Schulz. (Charlie Brown Ser.). (gr. 3 up). 1974. 4.95 (ISBN 0-394-83048-2, BYR). Random.
There's Not a Bathing Suit in Russia & Other Bare Facts. Will Rogers. Ed. by Joseph A. Stout, Jr. LC 73-89307. (The Writings of Will Rogers Ser., Series I: Vol. 2). (Illus.). 95p. 1973. 9.25 (ISBN 0-914956-03-5). Okla State Univ Pr.
There's Nothing Going Wrong with Your Head. Al Hall. LC 87-82367. 40p. (YA). (gr. 9 up). 1988. 14.95 (ISBN 0-944637-00-0). E Pubns.
There's Nothing Neat about Seeing Your Feet: The Life & Times of a Fat American. Ludlow Porch. LC 84-60923. 157p. 1984. 9.95 (ISBN 0-931948-65-7). Peachtree Pubs.

There's Nothing That I Wouldn't Do If You Would Be My POSSLQ. Charles Osgood. LC 81-47460. 204p. 1981. 10.95 (ISBN 0-03-057667-9). H Holt & Co.

There's Nothing to Do! James Stevenson. LC 85-8104. (Illus.). 32p. (gr. k-3). 1986. 11.75 (ISBN 0-688-04698-3); PLB 11.88 (ISBN 0-688-04699-1). Greenwillow.

There's One Born Every Minute. Harry Blackstone. (Illus.). 150p. (Orig.). 1984. pap. 5.95 (ISBN 0-87477-329-6). J P Tarcher.

There's One Born Every Minute: A Blank Book. P. T. Barnum. 60p. 1982. pap. 1.50 (ISBN 0-86541-011-9). Filter.

There's Plenty of Money for Nonprofit Groups Willing to Earn Their Shares: How to Do It Successfully. J. H. Pritchard. LC 83-72188. (Illus.). 472p. 1984. 57.00 (ISBN 0-914207-01-6, 84-1116); 6 ring binder 57.00 (ISBN 0-914207-00-8). Cornucopia Pubns.

There's Plenty of Room at the Top: A Practical Guide to Success in Business. Loire Brophy. 1946. 12.50 (ISBN 0-932062-18-0). Sharon Hill.

There's Someone I Want You to Meet. Shirley Lord. 1989. 18.95 (ISBN 0-517-57158-7). Crown.

There's Something in a Sunday. Marcia Muller. 1989. 16.95 (ISBN 0-89296-270-4). Mysterious Pr.

There's Something in My Attic. Mercer Mayer. LC 86-32875. (Illus.). 32p. (ps-3). 1988. 11.95 (ISBN 0-8037-0414-3, 01160-350); PLB 11.89 (ISBN 0-8037-0415-1). Dial Bks Young.

There's Something Wrong with Our Money. Wainwright Tuttle. (Illus.). 160p. (Orig.). 1982. pap. 7.00 (ISBN 0-9609494-0-2). Jebco Bks.

There's the Sea. Eben M. Anderson. LC 84-90214. (Illus.). 61p. 1985. 6.95 (ISBN 0-533-06265-9). Vantage.

Theresa. Iris Rowland. 1985. 24.95x (ISBN 0-7090-1837-1, Pub. by R Hale Ltd UK). State Mutual Bk.

Theresa. Arthur Schnitzler. Tr. by William A. Drake. LC 70-175445. 460p. 1972. Repr. of 1928 ed. 27.50 (ISBN 0-404-05617-2). AMS Pr.

Theresa Pollak: European Drawings. Marilyn A. Zeitlin. (Illus.). 48p. (Orig.). 1986. pap. text ed. write for info. (ISBN 0-935519-05-X). Anderson Gal.

Therese. Dorothy Day. 1979. pap. 7.95 (ISBN 0-87243-090-1). Templegate.

Therese. Gerard Manley Hopkins. Tr. by Francois Mauriac from Fr. 383p. 1951. pap. 8.95 (ISBN 0-374-50333-8). FS&G.

Therese Desqueyroux. Francois Mauriac. (Coll. Diamant). 1955. 11.50 (ISBN 0-685-11594-1). French & Eur.

Therese Desqueyroux. Francois Mauriac. 9.95 (ISBN 0-686-55479-5). French & Eur.

Therese Neumann. Johannes Steiner. LC 66-27536. (Illus.). 1967. pap. 5.95 (ISBN 0-8189-0144-6). Alba.

Therese of Lisieux. Monica Furlong. LC 87-43048. (Virago Pioneers Ser.). (Illus.). 160p. 1987. 12.95 (ISBN 0-394-53706-8); pap. 7.95 (ISBN 0-394-75360-7). Pantheon.

Therese of Lisieux: A Biography. Patricia O'Connor. LC 83-63169. 168p. 1984. pap. 5.95 (ISBN 0-87973-607-0, 607). Our Sunday Visitor.

Therese of Lisieux: A Vocation of Love. Marie-Pascale Ducrocq. LC 81-20512. 77p. (Orig.). 1982. pap. 3.95 (ISBN 0-8189-0431-3). Alba.

Therese Raquin. Emile Zola. (Folio Ser.: No. 1116). 256p. 1970. 7.95 (ISBN 0-686-55805-7). Schoenhof.

Therese Raquin. Emile Zola. Tr. by Leonard W. Tancock. (Classics Ser.). (Orig.). 1962. pap. 4.95 (ISBN 0-14-044120-4). Penguin.

Therese Raquin. Emile Zola. 256p. 1970. write for info. French & Eur.

Therese, the Little Flower of Lisieux. Dorothy Smith. 1988. pap. 2.95. Paulist Pr.

Thermal Accommodation & Adsorption Coefficients of Gases, Vol. II-1. 1st ed. Y. S. Touloukian & C. Y. Ho. (McGraw-Hill-CINDAS Data Ser. on Material Properties). 448p. (Orig.). 1981. text ed. 59.95 (ISBN 0-07-065031-4). McGraw.

Thermal Agents in Rehabilitation. Ed. by Susan L. Michlovitz. LC 85-16122. (Contemporary Perspectives in Rehabiliation Ser.: Vol. 1). (Illus.). 317p. 1986. text ed. 29.00 (ISBN 0-8036-6164-9). Davis Co.

Thermal Analysis, 3 vols. International Conference on Thermal Analysis, 4th, Budapest, 1974. Ed. by I. Buzas. LC 76-373658. Vol. 1- Theory Inorganic Chemistry. pap. 160.00 ea. (2024032). Vol. 2- Organic & Macromolecular Chemistry. Earth Sciences. Vol. 3- Applied Sciences, Methodics, & Instrumentation. Bks Demand UMI.

Thermal Analysis. International Conference on Thermal Analysis, 5th, Kyoto, 1977. Ed. by H. Chihara. LC 78-323070. pap. 148.80 (ISBN 0-317-29341-9, 2024033). Bks Demand UMI.

Thermal Analysis. Ed. by W. W. Wendlandt & L. W. Collins. (Benchmark Papers in Analytical Chemistry: Vol. 2). 1976. 83.00 (ISBN 0-12-787750-9). Acad Pr.

Thermal Analysis. 3rd ed. Wesley W. Wendlandt. LC 85-12419. (Chemical Analysis Ser.). 814p. 1986. 95.00 (ISBN 0-471-88477-4, Pub. by Wiley-Interscience). Wiley.

Thermal Analysis Abstracts. 1987. write for info. Wiley.

Thermal Analysis & Control of Electronic Equipment. Allan D. Kraus & A. Bar-Cohen. 680p. 1983. text ed. 66.50 (ISBN 0-07-035416-2). McGraw.

Thermal Analysis: European Symposium 2nd, Proceedings. Ed. by David Dollimore. 1981. 91.95 (ISBN 0-471-25661-7, Pub. by Wiley Heyden). Wiley.

Thermal Analysis in Polymer Characterization. Ed. by Edith A. Turi. 168p. 1982. 57.95 (ISBN 0-471-26192-0, Pub. by Wiley Heyden). Wiley.

Thermal Analysis of Liquid-Metal Fast Breeder. Tang et al. Ed. by Diane Wojciechowski. LC 77-14646. (Nuclear Science Technology Monograph). (Illus.). 1978. 46.00 (ISBN 0-89448-011-1, 300013). Am Nuclear Soc.

Thermal Analysis of Minerals. D. N. Todor. 256p. 1976. 33.00. Abacus Pr.

Thermal Analysis of Pressurized Water Reactors. 2nd, rev., reprint ed. L. S. Tong & Joel Weisman. Ed. by Diane Wallin. LC 79-54237. (Monograph). 1979. 45.00 (ISBN 0-89448-019-7, 300015). Am Nuclear Soc.

Thermal Analysis: Proceedings. European Symposium on Thermal Analysis Staff & Dollimore. 1981. 61.95 (Wiley Heyden). Wiley.

Thermal Analysis: Proceedings of the ICTA Conference, Kyoto, 1977. ICTA Conference Staff & Chihara. 1975. 125.00 (ISBN 0-471-25628-5, Wiley Heyden). Wiley.

Thermal Analysis: Proceedings of the Seventh International Conference on Thermal Analysis, 2 vols. Bernard Miller. 1530p. 1982. 135.00 (ISBN 0-471-26243-9). Wiley.

Thermal Analysis. Vol. I: Theory Instrumentation-Applied Sciences Industrial-Applications. Hans G. Wiedemann. 628p. 1980. 99.95x (ISBN 0-8176-1085-5). Birkhauser.

Thermal Analysis. Vol. 2: Organic Chemistry, Melallurgy, Earth Sciences, Organic Chemistry, Polymers, Biological Sciences, Medicine, Pharmacy. Wolfgang Hemminger. 606p. 1980. 99.95 (ISBN 0-8176-1086-3). Birkhauser.

Thermal & Acoustic Insulation. R. M. Diamant. (Illus.). 424p. 1986. text ed. 95.00 (ISBN 0-408-01394-X). Butterworth.

Thermal & Chemical Welding of Plastics. EEMUA Staff. 1976. 75.00x (ISBN 0-85931-030-2, Pub. by EEMUA). State Mutual Bk.

Thermal & Cryogenic Insulating Materials; Building Seals & Sealants; Fire Tests; Building Constructions; Environmental Acoustics (215 Standards) sec ASTM Annual Book of Standards, 1986.

Thermal & Energetic Studies of Cellular Biological Systems. Arthur James et al. (Illus.). 232p. 1987. 88.00 (ISBN 0-7236-0909-8). PSG Pub Co.

Thermal & Environmental Effects in Fatigue: Research-Design Interface. Ed. by C. E. Taske et al. (PVP Ser.: Vol. 71). 256p. 1983. pap. text ed. 50.00 (ISBN 0-317-02651-8, H00257). ASME.

Thermal & Flow Design of Helium-Cooled Reactors. Melese & Katz. 432p. 1985. 59.00 (ISBN 0-89448-027-8, 300019). Am Nuclear Soc.

Thermal Assessment of Breast Health. Ed. by Michael Gautherie et al. 350p. 1984. 55.00 (ISBN 0-85200-791-4, Pub. by MTP Pr England). Kluwer Academic.

Thermal Characteristics of the Moon, PAAS28. Ed. by John W. Lucas. LC 79-39803. (Illus.). 340p. 1972. 39.95 (ISBN 0-262-12058-5). AIAA.

Thermal Characteristics of Tumors: Applications in Detection & Treatment. Ed. by Rakesh K. Jain & Pietro M. Gullino. LC 80-13379. (N.Y. Academy of Sciences Annals: Vol. 335). 542p. 1980. 97.00x (ISBN 0-89766-046-3); pap. write for info. (ISBN 0-89766-047-1). NY Acad Sci.

Thermal Characterization of Polymeric Materials. Ed. by Edith A. Turi. LC 81-17578. 1981. 112.00 (ISBN 0-12-703780-2). Acad Pr.

Thermal Characterization Techniques. Ed. by P. Slade, Jr. & L. T. Jenkins. LC 79-114993. (Techniques & Methods of Polymer Evaluation Ser: Vol. 2). 384p. 1970. 85.00 (ISBN 0-8247-1638-8). Dekker.

Thermal Comfort: Analysis & Applications in Environmental Engineering. P. O. Fanger. LC 81-20935. 244p. 1982. Repr. of 1970 ed. 24.50 (ISBN 0-89874-446-6). Krieger.

Thermal Computation for Electrical Equipment. Gordon N. Ellison. 1984. 40.95 (ISBN 0-442-21923-7). Van Nos Reinhold.

Thermal Conditions in Freezing Lakes & Rivers. A. A. Pivovarov. LC 73-12269. 136p. 1973. 21.95 (ISBN 0-470-69103-4, Pub. by Wiley). Krieger.

Thermal Conditions in Freezing Lakes & Rivers. A. A. Pivovarov. 144p. 1974. text ed. 37.50x (ISBN 0-7065-1350-9, Pub. by Keter Pub Jerusalem). Coronet Bks.

Thermal Conduction in Semiconductors. Bhandari. 250p. 1988. 24.95 (ISBN 0-470-21049-4). Wiley.

Thermal Conductions in Solids. R. Berman. (Oxford Studies in Physics). (Illus.). 1976. 55.00x (ISBN 0-19-851429-8); pap. 26.95x (ISBN 0-19-851430-1). Oxford U Pr.

Thermal Conductivity, No. 19. Ed. by D. W. Yarbrough. (Illus.). 570p. 1988. 115.00x (ISBN 0-306-42787-7, Plenum Pr). Plenum Pub.

Thermal Conductivity of Building Materials. Frank B. Rowley & Axel B. Algren. LC 37-27901. (University of Minnesota Engineering Experimentation Bulletin Ser.: No. 12). pap. 36.00 (ISBN 0-317-29494-6, 2055907). Bks Demand UMI.

Thermal Conductivity of Solids. J. E. Parrott & Audrey D. Stuckes. 1975. 17.95x (ISBN 0-85086-047-4, NO. 2942, Pub. by Pion England). Routledge Chapman & Hall.

Thermal Conductivity of Uranium Dioxide. (Technical Reports Ser.: No. 59). 1966. pap. 10.00 (ISBN 92-0-145166-0, IDC59, IAEA). UNIPUB.

Thermal Conductivity 16. Ed. by David C. Larsen. 644p. 1982. 97.50x (ISBN 0-306-41032-X, Plenum Pr). Plenum Pub.

Thermal Conductivity 17. Ed. by J. G. Hust. 794p. 1983. 120.00x (ISBN 0-306-41177-6, Plenum Press). Plenum Pub.

Thermal Conductivity, 18. Ed. by David R. Ashworth & David R. Smith. 764p. 1985. 125.00x (ISBN 0-306-41918-1, Plenum Pr). Plenum Pub.

Thermal Continentaligy of India: A Climatic Study. A. Sachi Devi. (Illus.). 128p. 1987. text ed. 27.50x (ISBN 81-210-0178-1, Pub. by Inter India Pubns N. Delhi). Apt Bks.

Thermal Control & Radiation, PAAS31. Ed. by C. L. Tien. LC 72-10480. (Illus.). 523p. 1973. 49.50 (ISBN 0-262-20023-6); members 24.50 (ISBN 0-317-32199-4). AIAA.

Thermal Conversion of Solid Waste & Biomass. Ed. by Jerry L. Jones & Shirley B. Radding. LC 80-14754. (ACS Symposium Ser.: No. 130). 1980. 69.95 (ISBN 0-8412-0565-5, Pub. by Royal Soc Chem London). Am Chemical.

Thermal Conversion Systems for Municipal Solid Waste. H. L. Hickman, Jr. et al. LC 84-16496. (Pollution Technology Review Ser.: No. 113). (Illus.). 746p. 1985. 56.00 (ISBN 0-8155-1001-2). Noyes.

Thermal Cutting-360 Terms in 17 Languages see Terms for Welding & Allied-Processes in Different Languages (11W): WT.

Thermal Degradation of Cellulose. (Bibliographic Ser.: No. S45). 55p. 1969. 8.00 (ISBN 0-317-34461-7). Inst Paper Chem.

Thermal Delight in Architecture. Lisa Heschong. 1979. pap. 5.95x (ISBN 0-262-58039-X). MIT Pr.

Thermal Design Considerations in Frozen Ground Engineering. Ed. by Thomas G. Krzewinski & Rupert G. Tart, Jr. 277p. 1985. 28.00x (ISBN 0-87262-500-1). Am Soc Civil Eng.

Thermal Design of Aeroassisted Orbital Transfer Vehicles, PAAS 96. Ed. by H. F. Nelson. LC 85-3853. (Illus.). 566p. 1985. 74.50 (ISBN 0-915928-94-9). AIAA.

Thermal Design of Nuclear Reactors. R. H. Winterton. LC 80-41187. (Illus.). 200p. 1981. text ed. 44.00 (ISBN 0-08-024215-4); pap. text ed. 24.00 (ISBN 0-08-024214-6). Pergamon.

Thermal Design of Precast Concrete Buildings. 51p. 1985. pap. 8.00 (ISBN 0-318-19727-8, JR-306). Prestressed Concrete.

Thermal Design Principles of Spacecraft & Entry Bodies. Ed. by Jerry T. Bevans. (Progress in Astronautics & Aeronautics Ser.: Vol. 21). 1969. 28.00 (ISBN 0-12-535121-6). Acad Pr.

Thermal Design Principles, PAAS21. Ed. by Jerry T. Bevans. LC 64-103. (Illus.). 855p. 1969. 79.50 (ISBN 0-317-36814-1). AIAA.

Thermal Discharges: A Guide to Power & Process Plant Cooling Water Discharges into Rivers, Lakes & Seas. Donald S. Miller & B. A. Brighouse. 221p. 1984. softcover 53.00 (ISBN 0-906085-93-4, Dist. by Air Science Co.). BHRA Fluid.

Thermal Discharges at Nuclear Power Stations. (Technical Reports Ser.: No. 155). (Illus.). 155p. (Orig.). 1974. pap. 19.00 (ISBN 92-0-125274-9, IDC155, IAEA). UNIPUB.

Thermal Dissociation of Chemical Compounds. I. S. Kulikov. 208p. 1967. text ed. 43.00x (ISBN 0-7065-0595-6, Pub. by Keter Pub Jerusalem). Coronet Bks.

Thermal Ecology II: Proceedings. Ed. by Gerald W. Esch & Robert W. McFarlane. LC 76-28206. (ERDA Symposium Ser.). 414p. 1976. pap. 18.25 (ISBN 0-87079-223-7, CONF-750425); microfiche 6.50 (ISBN 0-87079-224-5, CONF-750425). DOE.

Thermal Ecology: Proceedings. Ed. by J. Whitfield Gibbons & Rebecca R. Sharitz. LC 74-600136. (AEC Symposium Ser.). 687p. 1974. 25.25 (CONF-730505); microfiche 6.50 (ISBN 0-87079-225-3, CONF-730505). DOE.

Thermal Efficiency Construction. Richard P. Bentley. 1988. 15.75 (ISBN 0-317-68200-8). R P Bentley.

Thermal Effluent Disposal from Power Generation: Proceedings. International Advanced Course & Workshop on Thermal Effluent Disposal from Power Generation, Aug. 23-28, 1976, Dubrovnik, Yugoslavia. Ed. by Z. Zaric. LC 77-28808. (Thermal & Fluids Engineering, International Centre for Heat & Mass Transfer Ser.). (Illus.). 375p. 1978. text ed. 89.95 (ISBN 0-89116-093-0). Hemisphere Pub.

Thermal Electrocyclic Reactions. Elliot N. Marvel. (Organic Chemistry Ser.). 1980. 77.00 (ISBN 0-12-476250-6). Acad Pr.

Thermal Energy Conservation: Building & Services Design. J. W. Weller & A. Youle. (Illus.). vii, 266p. 1981. 63.00 (ISBN 0-85334-938-X, Pub. by Elsevier Applied Sci England). Elsevier.

Thermal Energy Storage. G. Beckmann & P. V. Gilli. (Topics in Energy Ser.). (Illus.). 240p. 1984. 43.00 (ISBN 0-387-81764-6). Springer Verlag.

Thermal Energy Storage. Ed. by G. Beghi. 1982. 59.50 (ISBN 90-277-1428-2, Pub. by Reidel Holland). Kluwer Academic.

Thermal Energy Storage. Ed. by E. G. Kovach. LC 77-71233. 1977. pap. 14.75 (ISBN 0-08-021724-9). Pergamon.

Thermal Energy Storage in Aquifiers. Schaetzle. (Design & Applications). 275p. 1980. 40.00 (ISBN 0-08-025977-4). Pergamon.

Thermal Engineering Joint Conference: Proceedings of the ASME-JSME, 4. Ed. by Y. Mori & W. Yang. 2005p. 1983. pap. text ed. 150.00 set (ISBN 0-317-02652-6, I00158); Vol. 1. pap. text ed. 50.00 (ISBN 0-317-02653-4, I00158A); Vol. 2. pap. text ed. 40.00 (ISBN 0-317-02654-2, I00158B); Vol. 3. pap. text ed. 50.00 (ISBN 0-317-02655-0, I00158C); Vol. 4. pap. text ed. 50.00 (ISBN 0-317-02656-9, I00158D). ASME.

Thermal Environmental Conditions for Human Occupancy, 1981. (ASHRAE Standards Ser.: No. 55). 36.00 (ISBN 0-317-58697-1). Am Heat Ref & Air Eng.

Thermal Environmental Engineering. 2nd ed. James L. Threlkeld. 1970. 54.00 (ISBN 0-13-914721-7). P-H.

Thermal Expansion of Crystals. R. S. Krishnan et al. LC 77-30620. (International Ser. in the Science of the Solid State: Vol. 12). 1980. 63.00 (ISBN 0-08-021405-3). Pergamon.

Thermal Expansion: Proceedings, No. 17. American Institute of Physics. Ed. by R. E. Taylor & G. L. Denman. LC 73-94415. 1974. pap. 14.00 (ISBN 0-88318-116-9). Am Inst Physics.

Thermal Expansion 1971: Proceedings of the AIP Conference, Corning, NY, 1971, No. 3. American Institute of Physics. Ed. by M. G. Graham & H. E. Hagy. LC 72-76970. 311p. 1972. 13.00 (ISBN 0-88318-102-9). Am Inst Physics.

Thermal Expansion 7. Ed. by David C. Larsen. LC 82-9083. 224p. 1982. 59.50x (ISBN 0-306-41031-1, Plenum Pr). Plenum Pub.

Thermal Expansion 8. Ed. by Thomas H. Hahn. 294p. 1984. 85.00x (ISBN 0-306-41825-8, Plenum Pr). Plenum Pub.

Thermal Fatigue in Heat Exchangers for Domestic Gas Furnaces. L. E. Hulbert et al. 180p. 1975. softcover 20.00 (ISBN 0-318-12722-9, M60016). Am Gas Assn.

Thermal Fatigue of Materials & Components - STP 612. Ed. by D. A. Spera & D. F. Mowbray. 271p. 1976. 27.00 (ISBN 0-8031-0586-X, 04-612000-30). ASTM.

Thermal Flow in Porous Media. Horia I. Ene & Dan Polisevski. 1987. lib. bdg. 64.00 (ISBN 90-277-2225-0, Pub. by Reidel Holland). Kluwer Academic.

Thermal Geotechnics. Alfred R. Jumikis. 1977. 50.00x (ISBN 0-8135-0824-X). Rutgers U Pr.

Thermal Hydraulics, 2 vols. Maurizio Cumo & Antonio Naviglio. 1988. Vol. I, Physical Properties & Characteristic Dimensionless Groups, 176 pgs. 99.00 (ISBN 0-8493-6789-1, 6789); Vol. II, Nucleate Boiling Heat Transfer, 160 pgs. 95.00 (ISBN 0-8493-6790-5, 6790). CRC Pr.

Thermal Hydraulics of a Boiling Water Nuclear Reactor. R. T. Lahey & Frederick J. Moody. LC 76-45712. (Nuclear Science Technology Ser.). (Illus.). 1977. 48.00 (ISBN 0-89448-010-3, 300011). Am Nuclear Soc.

Thermal Hydraulics of Nuclear Reactors: Proceedings, 2 vols. 1525p. 1983. 110.00 (ISBN 0-89448-110-X, 700081). Am Nuclear Soc.

Thermal Imaging. Ed. by Abel. 143p. 1986. 43.00 (ISBN 0-89252-671-8, 636). SPIE.

Thermal Imaging Systems. Ed. by J. M. Lloyd. LC 75-9635. (Optical Physics & Engineering Ser.). 456p. 1975. 69.50x (ISBN 0-306-30848-7, Plenum Pr). Plenum Pub.

Thermal Infrared Sensing for Diagnostics & Control: Thermosense, No. 8. Ed. by H. Kaplan. 168p. 1985. 50.00 (ISBN 0-89252-616-5, 581). SPIE.

Thermal Infrared Sensing for Diagnostics & Control: Thermosense, No. 9. Ed. by Madding. 274p. 1987. 57.00 (ISBN 0-89252-815-X, 780). SPIE.

Thermal Injury. Dressler et al. (Illus.). 256p. 1988. pap. 31.95 (ISBN 0-8016-2456-8). Mosby.

Thermal Insulation. Michael R. Harrison. Ed. by Elias P. Gyftopoulos & Karen C. Cohen. (Industrial Energy-Conservation Manuals: No. 11). 112p. 1982. loose-leaf 20.00x (ISBN 0-262-08112-1). MIT Pr.

Thermal Insulation. S. D. Probert & D. R. Hub. (Illus.). 121p. 1968. 34.25 (ISBN 0-444-20025-8, Pub. by Elsevier Applied Sci England). Elsevier.

Thermal Insulation Building Guide. William C. Turner. LC 82-16232. 1988. 49.50 (ISBN 0-88275-985-X). Krieger.

Thermal Insulation Handbook. William C. Turner. LC 76-52962. 640p. (Orig.). 1981. 72.50 (ISBN 0-88275-510-2). Krieger.

Thermal Insulation Handbook. William C. Turner & John F. Malloy. 624p. 1981. text ed. 79.00 (ISBN 0-07-039805-4). McGraw.

Thermodynamic Properties of Ethylene. Ed. by V. V. Sychev et al. Tr. by Vladimir D. Azbel from Rus. (National Standard Reference Data Service of the U. S. S. R.: A Series of Property Tables). 1987. 120.00 (ISBN 0-89116-612-2). Hemisphere Pub.

Thermodynamic Properties of Gases: A Handbook. C. L. Rivkin. 286p. 1988. 77.50 (ISBN 0-89116-750-1). Hemisphere Pub.

Thermodynamic Properties of Helium. Ed. by V. V. Sychev. Tr. by G. E. Slark from Rus. (National Standard Reference Data Service of the U. S. S. R.). 316p. 1987. 120.00 (ISBN 0-89116-613-0). Hemisphere Pub.

Thermodynamic Properties of Individual Substances, 2 vols, Pt. I. 3rd, rev. & enl. ed. Ed. by L. V. Gurvich. (Illus.). 830p. 1988. Set. 135.01 (ISBN 0-08-027585-0). Pergamon.

Thermodynamic Properties of Materials, Vol. 2. Ed. by V. P. Glushko. Tr. by Henri Bronstein from Rus. Date not set. 100.00 (ISBN 0-89116-533-9). Hemisphere Pub.

Thermodynamic Properties of Methane. Ed. by V. V. Sychev et al. Tr. by Dov B. Lederman from Rus. (National Standard Reference Data Service of the U. S. S. R.: A Series of Property Tables). 342p. 1987. 120.00 (ISBN 0-89116-614-9). Hemisphere Pub.

Thermodynamic Properties of Methane-Nitrogen Mixtures. O T. Bloomer & B E. Eakin. (Research Bulletin Ser.: No.21). iv, 51p. (B). 1955. 3.50; supplement 3.50. Inst Gas Tech.

Thermodynamic Properties of Multicomponent Systems, Multicomponent Phase Equilibria & Chemical Equilibria. Ed. by B. M. Goodwin. (AIChEMI Modular Instruction D Ser.: Vol. 3: Thermodynamics). 46p. 1983. pap. 30.00 (ISBN 0-8169-0211-9, J-16). Am Inst Chem Eng.

Thermodynamic Properties of Nitrogen. O. T. Bloomer & K. N. Rao. (Research Bulletin Ser.: No. 18). iv, 28p. 1952. 3.50 (ISBN 0-317-56857-4); Supplement 3.50 (ISBN 0-317-56858-2). Inst Gas Tech.

Thermodynamic Properties of Nitrogen. Ed. by V. V. Sychev et al. Tr. by Dov B. Lederman from Rus. (National Standard Reference Data Service of the U. S. S. R.: A Series of Property Tables). 342p. 1987. 120.00 (ISBN 0-89116-615-7). Hemisphere Pub.

Thermodynamic Properties of Nonelectro-Lyte Solutions. William E. Acree, Jr. LC 83-9998. (Monograph). 1984. 82.50 (ISBN 0-12-043020-7). Acad Pr.

Thermodynamic Properties of Organic Compounds. rev. ed. George J. Janz. (Physical Chemistry Ser.: Vol. 6). 1967. 77.00 (ISBN 0-12-380451-5). Acad Pr.

Thermodynamic Properties of Oxygen. Ed. by V. V. Sychev et al. Tr. by Dimitri Gokhman. (National Standard Reference Data Service of the U. S. S. R.: A Series of Property Tables). 308p. 1987. 120.00 (ISBN 0-89116-616-5). Hemisphere Pub.

Thermodynamic Properties of Sulfides. L. B. Pankratz et al. LC 87-600243. (Mines Bureau Bulletin Ser.: 689). 431p. 1987. 21.00 (ISBN 0-318-23849-7, S/N 024-004-02173-0). USGPO.

Thermodynamic Properties of the Elements. Ed. by Daniel R. Stull & Gerard C. Sinke. LC 57-1340. (Advances in Chemistry Ser: No. 18). 1956. 24.95 (ISBN 0-8412-0019-X). Am Chemical.

Thermodynamic Properties of Water to 1,000 C & 10,000 Bars. C. Wayne Burnham et al. LC 73-96715. (Geological Society of America. Special Paper Ser.: No. 132). pap. 27.10 (2031866). Bks Demand UMI.

Thermodynamic Relations in Open Systems. George Tunell. LC 77-80609. (Carnegie Institution of Washington Publication Ser.: No. 408a). pap. 21.30 (ISBN 0-317-27755-3, 2015542). Bks Demand UMI.

Thermodynamic Theory. Ed. by G. A. Mansoori. LC 80-25560. (AIChEMI Modular Instruction D Ser.: Vol. 5: Thermodynamics). 74p. 1985. pap. 30.00 (ISBN 0-8169-0258-5, J-27). Am Inst Chem Eng.

Thermodynamic Theory of Domain Structures. I. Privorotskii. 129p. 1975. text ed. 39.50 (ISBN 0-7065-1520-X, Pub. by Keter Pub Jerusalem). Coronet Bks.

Thermodynamic Values at Low Temperature for Natural Inorganic Materials. Terri Woods. 1986. 18.95 (ISBN 0-317-58325-5). Oxford U Pr.

Thermodynamics. M. M. Abbott & H. C. VanNess. (Schaum Outline Ser). 1972. pap. text ed. 10.95 (ISBN 0-07-000040-9). McGraw.

Thermodynamics. William Z. Black & James G. Hartley. 755p. 1984. text ed. 57.50 scp (ISBN 0-06-040732-8, HarpC). Har-Row.

Thermodynamics. 6th ed. Virgil M. Faires & Clifford M. Simmang. (Illus.). 1978. text ed. write for info. (ISBN 0-02-335530-1, 33553). Macmillan.

Thermodynamics. Enrico Fermi. 1937. pap. 4.50 (ISBN 0-486-60361-X). Dover.

Thermodynamics. N. A. Gokcen. LC 75-332953. 460p. 1975. text ed. 29.90x (ISBN 0-918910-01-3). Techscience Inc.

Thermodynamics. 3rd ed. Jack P. Holman. (Illus.). 1980. text ed. 49.95 (ISBN 0-07-029625-1). McGraw.

Thermodynamics. 4th, rev. ed. Jack P. Holman. 832p. 1987. text ed. 45.95 (ISBN 0-07-029633-2). McGraw.

Thermodynamics. I. Muller. 496p. 1985. 130.00 (ISBN 0-470-20549-0, Co-Pub. with Longman). Wiley.

Thermodynamics. 2nd ed. Pitzer & Brewer. (Advanced Chemistry Ser.). 1961. text ed. 60.95 (ISBN 0-07-037622-0). McGraw.

Thermodynamics. P. C. Rakshit. 1985. 79.00x (ISBN 0-317-38807-X, Pub. by Current Dist). State Mutual Bk.

Thermodynamics, 2 Vols. 1966. Vol. 1. 32.25 (ISBN 92-0-040066-3, ISP109-1, IAEA); Vol. 2. 39.50 (ISBN 92-0-040166-X, ISP109-2). UNIPUB.

Thermodynamics. 4th ed. Kenneth Wark. LC 82-10031. (Illus.). 1249p. 1983. text ed. 49.95 (ISBN 0-07-068284-4). McGraw.

Thermodynamics. Kenneth Wark. 976p. 1988. text ed. 45.95 (ISBN 0-07-068286-0). McGraw.

Thermodynamics see Physical Chemistry: An Advanced Treatise in Eleven Volumes.

Thermodynamics: A Generalized Approach. A. I. Veinik. 272p. 1964. text ed. 56.00 (ISBN 0-7065-0283-3, Pub. by Keter Pub Jerusalem). Coronet Bks.

Thermodynamics: A Rigorous Postulatory Approach. S. H. Chue. LC 76-44878. 286p. pap. 74.40 (2029857). Bks Demand UMI.

Thermodynamics: An Advanced Textbook for Chemical Engineers. G. Astarita. (Illus.). 425p. Date not set. price not set (ISBN 0-306-43048-7, Plenum Pr). Plenum Pub.

Thermodynamics: An Advanced Treatment for Chemists & Physicists. E. A. Guggenheim. (Personal Library). 390p. 1985. pap. 24.95 (ISBN 0-444-86951-4, North-Holland). Elsevier.

Thermodynamics & an Introduction to Thermostatistics. 2nd ed. Herbert B. Callen. LC 85-6387. 493p. 1985. write for info. (ISBN 0-471-86256-8). Wiley.

Thermodynamics & an Introduction to Thermostatistics. 2nd ed. 493p. 1987. pap. write for info. (ISBN 0-471-61056-9). Wiley.

Thermodynamics & Constitutive Equations. Ed. by G. Grioli. (Lecture Notes in Physics Ser.: Vol. 228). (Illus.). v, 257p. 1985. pap. 19.00 (ISBN 0-387-15228-8). Springer-Verlag.

Thermodynamics & Control of Biological Free-Energy Transduction. N. V. Westerhoff & K. Van Dam. 576p. 1987. 237.50 (ISBN 0-444-80783-7). Elsevier.

Thermodynamics & Electrode Processes in Solid State Electronics see Physics of Electrolytes.

Thermodynamics & Electrodynamics of Superconductors. Ed. by V. L. Ginzburg. (Proceedings of the Lebedev Physics Institute of the Academy of Sciences of the U. S. S. R. Ser.: Vol. 174, Supplemental Volume 1). 291p. 1988. text ed. 96.00 (ISBN 0-941743-18-7). Nova Sci Pubs.

Thermodynamics & Fluid Mechanics of Turbomachinary, Vols. I & II. Ed. by A. S. Ucer et al. 1985. Set. lib. bdg. 148.00 (ISBN 90-247-3223-9, Pub. by Martinus Nijhoff Netherlands). Kluwer Academic.

Thermodynamics & Gas Dynamics of Internal-Combustion Engines, Vol. II. Ed. by J. H. Horlock & D. E. Winterbone. (Illus.). 668p. 1987. 135.00 (ISBN 0-19-856212-8). Oxford U Pr.

Thermodynamics & Gas Dynamics of Internal Combustion Engines, Vol. 1. Rowland S. Benson. Ed. by J. H. Horlock & D. Winterbone. (Illus.). 1982. text ed. 145.00x (ISBN 0-19-856210-1). Oxford U Pr.

Thermodynamics & Heat Power. 3rd ed. Irving Granet. 1985. text ed. write for info. (ISBN 0-8359-7674-2, Reston); instr's. manual avail. P-H.

Thermodynamics & Its Applications. 2nd ed. Michael Modell & Robert C. Reid. (Illus.). 512p. 1983. text ed. 56.00 (ISBN 0-13-915017-X). P-H.

Thermodynamics & Kinetics of Diffusion of Solids. B. S. Bokshtein. 1985. 37.50x (ISBN 81-205-0027-X, Pub. by Oxford IBH). South Asia Bks.

Thermodynamics & Regulation of Biological Processes. Ed. by I. Lamprecht & A. I. Zotin. LC 84-23302. (Illus.). xiv, 573p. 1984. 175.00 (ISBN 3-11-009789-3). De Gruyter.

Thermodynamics & the Development of Order. Emmett L. Williams. (Creation Research Society Monograph: No. 1). (Illus.). 141p. (Orig.). 1981. pap. 7.95 (ISBN 0-940384-01-9). Creation Research.

Thermodynamics Exam File. Ed. by Stuart T. McComas. LC 84-24688. (Exam File Ser.). 250p. (Orig.). 1985. pap. 9.95 (ISBN 0-910554-49-8). Engineering.

Thermodynamics for Chemical Engineers. K. E. Bett et al. LC 75-24573. 504p. 1975. text ed. 32.50x (ISBN 0-262-02119-6). MIT Pr.

Thermodynamics for Chemists. Samuel Glasstone. LC 72-189791. 528p. 1972. Repr. of 1947 ed. 41.50 (ISBN 0-88275-021-6). Krieger.

Thermodynamics for Engineering Technologists. Ed. by R. Will. (Engineering Technology: Vol. 1). 1980. 45.00 (ISBN 0-8247-6864-7). Dekker.

Thermodynamics for Engineers. B. V. Karlekar. (Illus.). 544p. 1983. write for info (ISBN 0-13-914986-4). P-H.

Thermodynamics for Geologists. Raymond Kern & Alain Weisbrod. Tr. by Duncan McKie from Fr. LC 67-22353. 304p. 1967. pap. 14.75x (ISBN 0-87735-306-9). Freeman Cooper.

Thermodynamics: Fundamentals, Applications. Otto Redlich. 278p. 1976. 89.50 (ISBN 0-444-41487-8). Elsevier.

Thermodynamics in Geology. Ed. by Donald Fraser. (Nato Adv. Study Inst. Ser. C: No. 30). 1977. lib. bdg. 50.00 (ISBN 90-277-0794-4, Pub. by Reidel Holland); pap. 16.00 (ISBN 90-277-0834-7). Kluwer Academic.

Thermodynamics of Aqueous Systems with Industrial Applications. Ed. by Stephen A. Newman. LC 80-16044. (ACS Symposium Ser.: No. 133). 1980. 69.95 (ISBN 0-8412-0569-8); supplement 9.95 (ISBN 0-8412-0590-6). Am Chemical.

Thermodynamics of Biological Processes. Ed. by A. I. Zotin & I. Lamprecht. 1978. 100.00x (ISBN 3-11-007312-9). De Gruyter.

Thermodynamics of Crystals. Duane C. Wallace. LC 71-161495. (Illus.). pap. 95.80 (ISBN 0-317-09102-6, 2017402). Bks Demand UMI.

Thermodynamics of Electrical Phenomena in Metals & a Condensed Collection of Thermodynamic Formulas. P. W. Bridgman. (Illus.). 12.00 (ISBN 0-8446-1737-7). Peter Smith.

Thermodynamics of Electrical Processes. Malcolm McChesney. LC 75-166417. pap. 71.50 (ISBN 0-317-10940-5, 2016147). Bks Demand UMI.

Thermodynamics of Fluid Systems. L. C. Woods. (Oxford Engineering Science Ser). (Illus.). 1975. 65.00x (ISBN 0-19-856125-3); pap. 24.95x (ISBN 0-19-856180-6). Oxford U Pr.

Thermodynamics of Fluids: An Introduction to Equilibrium Theory. K. C. Chao & R. A. Greenkorn. (Chemical Processing & Engineering Ser.: Vol. 4). 1975. soft cover 75.00 (ISBN 0-8247-7035-8). Dekker.

Thermodynamics of Gases see Encyclopedia of Physics.

Thermodynamics of Hot Nuclear Matter. Ed. by Collet's Holdings, Ltd. Staff. 1986. 70.00x (ISBN 0-317-52966-8, Pub. by Collets (UK)). State Mutual Bk.

Thermodynamics of Irreversible Processes in Many-Component Fluids. Collet's Holdings, Ltd. Staff. 1986. 49.00x (ISBN 0-317-52967-6, Pub. by Collets (UK)). State Mutual Bk.

Thermodynamics of Nonequilbrium Processes. S. Wisniewski & B. Staniszewski. LC 75-41486. 1976. lib. bdg. 53.00 (ISBN 90-277-0331-0, Pub. by Reidel Holland). Kluwer Academic.

Thermodynamics of Nuclear Materials: 1962. 1962. 33.00 (ISBN 92-0-040062-0, ISP58, IAEA). UNIPUB.

Thermodynamics of Nuclear Materials: 1967. 890p. (Eng., Fr. & Rus.). 1968. pap. 50.25 (ISBN 92-0-040068-X, ISP162, IAEA). UNIPUB.

Thermodynamics of Nuclear Materials: 1974, 2 Vols. (Proceedings Ser.). (Illus.). 484p. 1975. Vol. 1. pap. 46.50 (ISBN 92-0-040175-9, ISP380-1, IAEA); Vol. 2. pap. 53.75 (ISBN 0-685-54200-9, ISP380-2). UNIPUB.

Thermodynamics of Nuclear Materials, 1979, Vol. 1. (Illus.). 600p. 1980. pap. 81.50 (ISBN 92-0-040080-9, ISP520 1, IAEA); pap. 60.00 (ISBN 92-0-040180-5, ISP520). UNIPUB.

Thermodynamics of Point Defects & Thier Connection to Bulk Properties. P. A. Varatsos & K. D. Alexopoulos. (Defeats in Solids Ser.: Vol. 14). 459p. 1985. 137.00 (ISBN 0-444-86944-1, North Holland). Elsevier.

Thermodynamics of Polymer Solutions. Michio Kurata. Tr. by Hiroshi Fujita from Japanese. (MMI Press Polymer Monographs: Vol. 1). 306p. 1982. 108.00 (ISBN 3-7186-0023-4). Harwood Academic.

Thermodynamics of Polymerization. Hideo Sawada. 1976. 95.00 (ISBN 0-8247-6470-6). Dekker.

Thermodynamics of Rock-Forming Crystalline Solutions. S. K. Saxena. (Minerals, Rocks & Inorganic Materials Ser.: Vol. 8). (Illus.). xii, 188p. 1973. 37.00 (ISBN 0-387-06175-4). Springer-Verlag.

Thermodynamics of Silicates. V. I. Babushkin et al. Tr. by B. N. Frenkel & V. A. Terentyev. (Illus.). 470p. 1985. 132.50 (ISBN 0-387-12750-X). Springer Verlag.

Thermodynamics of Simple Materials with Fading Memory. W. A. Day. LC 77-183992. (Springer Tracts in Natural Philosophy: Vol. 22). (Illus.). 152p. 1972. 29.00 (ISBN 0-387-05704-8). Springer-Verlag.

Thermodynamics of Soil Solutions. Garrison Sposito. (Illus.). 1981. 53.50x (ISBN 0-19-857568-8). Oxford U Pr.

Thermodynamics of Solids. 2nd ed. Richard A. Swalin. LC 72-6334. (Wiley Series on the Science & Technology of Materials). 387p. 1972. 54.95 (ISBN 0-471-83854-3, Pub. by Wiley-Interscience). Wiley.

Thermodynamics of the Polymerization of Protein. Fumio Oosawa & Sho Asakura. 1976. 54.50 (ISBN 0-12-527050-X). Acad Pr.

Thermodynamics: Principles & Applications. Frank C. Andrews. LC 77-150607. Repr. of 1971 ed. 75.00 (ISBN 0-8357-9993-X, 2055278). Bks Demand UMI.

Thermodynamics: Principles Characterizing Physical & Chemical Processes. J. M. Honig. (Studies in Modern Thermodynamics: Vol. 4). 442p. 1982. 131.75 (ISBN 0-444-42092-4, I-267-82). Elsevier.

Thermodynamics Problem Solver. Research & Education Association Staff. LC 84-61810. (Illus.). 992p. 1986. pap. text ed. 23.85 (ISBN 0-87891-555-9). Res & Educ.

Thermodynamics: Second Law Analysis. Ed. by Richard A. Gaggioli. LC 80-10486. (ACS Symposium Ser.: No. 122). 1980. 34.95 (ISBN 0-8412-0541-8). Am Chemical.

Thermodynamics, Solutions Manual. L. R. Martin & N. A. Gokcen. (Illus.). 1978. pap. 6.95x (ISBN 0-918910-02-1). Techscience Inc.

Thermodynamics, Statistical Physics & Kinetics. Y. B. Rumer & M. S. Ryvkin. 1980. 12.00 (ISBN 0-8285-1853-X, Pub. by Mir Pubs USSR). Imported Pubns.

Thermodynamics Tables in SI Units. 2nd ed. R. W. Haywood. 1972. 12.95 (ISBN 0-521-09714-2). Cambridge U Pr.

Thermodynamics, the Kinetic Theory of Gases & Statistical Mechanics. 3rd ed. Francis W. Sears & Gerhard L. Salinger. 464p. 1975. text ed. write for info. (ISBN 0-201-06894-X). Addison-Wesley.

ThermodynamicsData for Biochemistry & Biotechnology. Ed. by H. J. Hinz. (Illus.). 480p. 1986. 142.00 (ISBN 0-387-16368-9). Springer-Verlag.

Thermodynamique Macroscopique, 2 Vols. F. Fer. (Fr). 1971. Vol. 1, 300p. 108.00 (ISBN 0-677-50300-8); Vol. 2, 248p. 92.00 (ISBN 0-677-50310-5). Gordon & Breach.

Thermodynamique Structurale Des Alliages see Structural Thermodynamics of Alloys.

Thermoelasticity. 2nd ed. W. K. Nowacki. 580p. 1986. 120.00 (ISBN 0-08-024767-9, PBL). Pergamon.

Thermoelasticity. 2nd rev. & enl. ed. H. Parkus. 1976. soft cover 28.40 (ISBN 0-387-81375-6). Springer-Verlag.

Thermoelectricity: Theory, Thermometry, Tool - STP 852. Daniel D. Pollock. LC 84-70046. (Illus.). 300p. 1985. text ed. 45.00 (ISBN 0-8031-0409-X, 04-852000-40). ASTM.

Thermoforming. James L. Throne. (Hanser Publications). (Illus.). 300p. 1987. 65.00 (ISBN 0-19-520749-1). Oxford U Pr.

Thermoforming--a Plastics Processing Guide. G. Gruenwald. LC 87-50432. 224p. 1987. pap. 49.00 (ISBN 0-87762-526-3). Technomic.

Thermographic Investigations into the Physiological Basis of Regional Anaesthesia. G. Sprotte. (Anaesthesiology & Intensive Care Medicine Ser.: Vol. 159). (Illus.). 65p. 1984. pap. 32.00 (ISBN 0-387-12638-4). Springer-Verlag.

Thermographic Papers. (Bibliographic Ser.: No. 221). 67p. 1965. 8.00 (ISBN 0-317-34462-5). Inst Paper Chem.

Thermography & Personal Injury Litigation. Samuel Hodge. LC 86-19090. (Trial Practice Library). 364p. 1987. 85.00 (ISBN 0-471-84469-1). Wiley.

Thermography & Personal Injury Litigation: 1987 Supplement. Samuel D. Hodge. (Medico-Legal Library Ser.). 64p. 1987. pap. 30.00 (ISBN 0-471-63606-1, Pub. by Wiley Law Pub.). Wiley.

Thermography: Proceedings of the European Congress on Thermography, 1st, Amsterdam, June 1974. European Congress on Thermography Staff. Ed. by N. J. Aarts. (Bibliotheca Radiologica Ser.: Vol. 6). (Illus.). xiv, 262p. 1975. pap. 65.50 (ISBN 3-8055-2134-0). S Karger.

Thermohaline Finestructure of the Ocean. Ed. by K. N. Fedorov. Tr. by D. A. Brown & J. S. Turner. 1978. text ed. 65.00 (ISBN 0-08-021673-0). Pergamon.

Thermohydraulics of Two-Phase Systems for Industrial Design & Nuclear Engineering. Delhaye. 525p. 1981. 54.95 (ISBN 0-89116-481-2). Hemisphere Pub.

Thermoinelasticity: Proceedings. International Union of Theoretical & Applied Mechanics Symposium, Glasgow, 1968. Ed. by B. A. Boley. LC 75-94050. (Illus.). 1970. 79.70 (ISBN 0-387-80961-9). Springer-Verlag.

Thermological Methods. Ed. by J. M. Engel et al. LC 85-17827. (Applied Thermology Ser.). 326p. 1985. lib. bdg. 70.00 (ISBN 0-89573-410-9). VCH Pubs.

Thermoluminescence & Thermoluminescent Dosimetry, Vols. II & III. Ed. by Yigal S. Horowitz. 1984. 99.00. Vol. II, 232p (ISBN 0-8493-5665-2). Vol. III, 216p. 89.00 (ISBN 0-8493-5666-0). CRC Pr.

Thermoluminescence & Thermoluminescent Dosimetry, Vol. I. Ed. by Yigal S. Horowitz. 200p. 1984. 85.00 (ISBN 0-8493-5664-4). CRC Pr.

Thermoluminescence Dating. M. J. Aitken. (Studies in Archaeological Science). 1985. 69.00 (ISBN 0-12-046380-6); pap. 40.50 (ISBN 0-12-046381-4). Acad Pr.

Thermoluminescence Dosimetry. A. F. McKinlay. (Medical Physics Handbook: No. 5). 180p. 1981. 40.00x (ISBN 0-85274-520-6, Pub. by A Hilger UK). Taylor & Francis.

Thermoluminescence of Solids. S. W. McKeever. (Cambridge Solid State Science Ser.). (Illus.). 400p. 1985. 72.50 (ISBN 0-521-24520-6). Cambridge U Pr.

Thermoluminescence of Solids. S. W. McKeever. (Cambridge Solid State Science Ser.). (Illus.). 376p. Date not set. pap. price not set (ISBN 0-521-36811-1). Cambridge U Pr.

Thermoluminescence Techniques in Archaeology. S. J. Fleming. (Illus.). 1979. 55.00x (ISBN 0-19-859929-3). Oxford U Pr.

Thermoluminescent Dosimetry. John R. Cameron & N. Suntharalingam. LC 68-16061. pap. 48.70 (ISBN 0-317-11063-2, 2012631). Bks Demand UMI.

Thermomagnetic Effects in Semiconductors. I. M. Tsidil'Kovskii. Ed. by H. J. Goldsmid et al. Tr. by A. Tybulewicz. 1963. 68.50 (ISBN 0-12-701850-6). Acad Pr.

Thermomechanical Behavior of High Temperature Composites. Ed. by J. Jortner. (AD-04 Ser.). 1982. 30.00 (H00248). ASME.

Thermomechanical Couplings in Solids: Proceedings of the Internat. Union of Theoretical & Applied Mechanics Jean Mandel Memorial Symp.. Paris, France, 1-5 Sept., 1986. Ed. by H. D. Bui & Q. S. Nguyen. 426p. 1987. 116.00 (ISBN 0-444-70236-9, North Holland). Elsevier.

Thermomechanical Processing & Transformation-Induced Plasticity: The Possible Achievement of Ultra-High Strength, Ductile Copper-Base Alloys. Stanford Research Institute. 92p. 1972. 13.80 (ISBN 0-317-34554-0, 135). Intl Copper.

Thermomechanical Processing of Aluminum Alloys: Processings of a Symposium Sponsored by the TMS-AIME Heat Treatment Committee at the TMS Fall Meeting in St. Louis, MO, October 18, 1978. The Metallurgical Society of AIME. Ed. by James G. Morris. LC 79-88848. pap. 58.30 (2056148). Bks Demand UMI.

Thermomechanical Processing of High Strength Low Alloy Steels. Imao Tamura et al. (Illus.). 256p. 1988. text ed. 120.00 (ISBN 0-408-11034-1). Butterworth.

Thermomechanics in Solids. Ed. by W. Nowacki & I. N. Sneddon. (CISM-International Center for Mechanical Sciences: Vol. 223). 1977. pap. 15.40 (ISBN 0-387-81343-8). Springer-Verlag.

Thermomechanics of Magnetic Fluids: Theory & Applications, Proceedings. new ed. International Advanced Course & Workshop on Thermomechanics of Magnetic Fluids, Udine, Italy, Oct. 3-7, 1977. Ed. by Boris Berkovsky. LC 78-15126. 318p. 1978. text ed. 95.00 (ISBN 0-89116-143-0). Hemisphere Pub.

Thermometry. James F. Schooley. 336p. 1986. 129.00 (ISBN 0-8493-5833-7). CRC Pr.

Thermophiles: General, Molecular, & Applied Microbiology. Ed. by Thomas D. Brock. LC 86-7785. 400p. 1986. 45.00 (ISBN 0-471-82001-6). Wiley.

Thermophilic Microbes in Ethanol Production. Gary E. Slapack et al. 224p. 1987. 93.00 (ISBN 0-8493-5299-1). CRC Pr.

Thermophilic Microorganisms & Life at High Temperatures. Thomas D. Brock. LC 78-6110. (Springer Ser. in Microbiology). (Illus.). 1978. 49.00 (ISBN 0-387-90309-7). Springer-Verlag.

Thermophysical Aspects of Re-Entry Flows, PAAS 103. Ed. by Carl D. Scott & James N. Moss. LC 86-10807. (Illus.). 626p. 1986. 79.50 (ISBN 0-930403-10-X). AIAA.

Thermophysical Properties of Freon-22. A. V. Kletskii. 72p. 1971. text ed. 23.00x (ISBN 0-7065-1168-9, Pub. by Keter Pub Jerusalem). Coronet Bks.

Thermophysical Properties of Freons, Vol. 1. Ed. by V. V. Altunin. Tr. by Jamil Ghojel from Rus. (National Standard Reference Data Service of the U. S. S. R.: A Series of Property Tables). 200p. 1987. 120.00 (ISBN 0-89116-600-9). Hemisphere Pub.

Thermophysical Properties of Freons, Vol. 2. Ed. by V. V. Altunin. Tr. by Jamil Ghojel from Rus. (National Standard Reference Data Service of the U. S. S. R.: A Series of Property Tables). 243p. 1987. 120.00 (ISBN 0-89116-601-7). Hemisphere Pub.

Thermophysical Properties of Gaseous & Liquid Methane. V. A. Zagoruchenko & A. M. Zhuravlev. 252p. 1971. text ed. 53.00x (ISBN 0-7065-1031-3, Pub. by Keter Pub Jerusalem). Coronet Bks.

Thermophysical Properties of Gases & Liquids. Viktor Abramovich Rabinovich. (Physical Constants & Properties of Substances No.1). pap. 53.80 (ISBN 0-317-08438-0, 2004605). Bks Demand UMI.

Thermophysical Properties of High Temperature Solid Materials, Vols. 1-6. Purdue University, Thermophysical Properties Research Center Staff. LC 67-15295. pap. 160.00 ea. (2056565). Bks Demand UMI.

Thermophysical Properties of Liquid Air & Its Components. A. A. Vasserman & V. A. Rabinovich. 244p. 1970. text ed. 53.00x (ISBN 0-7065-0730-4, Pub. by Keter Pub Jerusalem). Coronet Bks.

Thermophysical Properties of Lithium Hydride, Deuteride, & Tritide & to Their Solutions with Lithium. E. E. Spil'rain et al. Tr. by Stephen J. Amoretty from Rus. LC 87-12601. (Translation Ser.). (Illus.). 213p. 1987. 45.00. Am Inst Physics.

Thermophysical Properties of Materials. G. Grimvall. (Selected Topics in Solid State Physics Ser.: Vol. 18). 400p. 1986. 105.25 (ISBN 0-444-86985-9). Elsevier.

Thermophysical Properties of Matter: Specific Heat - Metallic Elements & Alloys. Purdue University, Thermophysical Properties Research Center. LC 73-129616. (TPRC Data Series: Vol. 4). pap. 160.00 (ISBN 0-317-26282-3, 2055697). Bks Demand UMI.

Thermophysical Properties of Matter: Specific Heat Nonmetallic Liquids & Gases. Purdue University, Thermophysical Properties Research Center. LC 73-129616. (Vol. 6). pap. 95.80 (ISBN 0-317-27798-7, 2055953). Bks Demand UMI.

Thermophysical Properties of Matter: Thermal Conductivity - Nonmetallic Liquids & Gases. Purdue University, Thermophysical Properties Research Center. LC 73-129616. (TPRC Data Ser: Vol. 3). pap. 160.00 (ISBN 0-317-26375-7, 2055696). Bks Demand UMI.

Thermophysical Properties of Matter: Thermal Expansion-Nonmetallic Solids. Purdue University, Thermophysical Properties Research Center Staff & Y. S. Touloukian. LC 73-129616. (TPRC Data Ser.: Vol. 13). pap. 160.00 (ISBN 0-317-26280-7, 2055698). Bks Demand UMI.

Thermophysical Properties of Matter: The TPRC Data Series, Vol 12: Thermal Expansion: Metallic Elements & Alloys. Purdue University, Thermophysical Properties Research Center. LC 73-129616. pap. 160.00 (ISBN 0-317-07898-4, 2022726). Bks Demand UMI.

Thermophysical Properties of Matter: The TPRC Data Series, Vol. 1: Thermal Conductivity; Metallic Elements & Alloys. Purdue University, Thermophysical Properties Research Center. LC 73-129616. pap. 160.00 (ISBN 0-317-28047-3, 2055777). Bks Demand UMI.

Thermophysical Properties of Matter: The TPRC Data Series, Vol. 6 Supplement: Specific Heat: Nonmetallic Liquids & Gases. Purdue University, Thermophysical Properties Research Center. LC 73-129616. pap. 42.30 (ISBN 0-317-28042-2, 2055778). Bks Demand UMI.

Thermophysical Properties of Matter: The TPRC Data Series, 5 vols, Vols. 7-11. Purdue University, Thermophysical Properties Research Center & Y. S. Touloukian. Incl. Vol. 7. Thermal Radiative Properties: Metallic Elements & Alloys. pap. 160.00 (ISBN 0-317-10946-4); Vol. 8. Thermal Radiative Properties: Nonmetallic Solids. pap. 160.00 (ISBN 0-317-10947-2); Vol. 9. Thermal Radiative Properties: Coatings. pap. 160.00 (ISBN 0-317-10948-0); Vol. 10. Thermal Diffusivity. pap. 160.00 (ISBN 0-317-10949-9); Vol. 11. Viscosity. pap. 160.00 (ISBN 0-317-10950-2). LC 73-129616. pap. (2019412). Bks Demand UMI.

Thermophysical Properties of Neon, Argon, Krypton & Xenon. Ed. by V. A. Rabinovich & V. A. Vasserman. (National Standard Reference Data Service of the U. S. S. R. Ser.: Vol. 10). 635p. 1987. 150.00 (ISBN 0-89116-675-0). Hemisphere Pub.

Thermophysical Properties of Refrigerants. 237p. 1976. 24.00 (ISBN 0-910110-25-5, LSPTH2); members 16.00 (ISBN 0-318-12775-X). Am Heat Ref & Air Eng.

Thermophysical Properties of Solids & of Selected Fluids for Energy Technology: Proceedings, 2 Vols, Vol. 2. Symposium on Thermophysical Properties, 8th. 1981. 65.00 (I00152). ASME.

Thermophysical Properties: Proceedings of the Fourth Symposium, University of Maryland, College Park, Maryland, 1968. American Society of Mechanical Engineers Staff. Ed. by Jerzy R. Moszynski. LC 59-1391. pap. 121.50 (ISBN 0-317-29841-0, 2051923). Bks Demand UMI.

Thermophysical Properties: Proceedings of the Fifth Symposium, Newton MA, September 30-October 2, 1970, (Sponsored by Standing Committee on Thermophysical Properties, Heat Transfer Division, The American Society of Mechanical Engineers) 5th ed. Symposium on Thermophysical Properties. Ed. by C. F. Bonilla. LC 59-1391. pap. 128.30 (2056158). Bks Demand UMI.

Thermophysical Properties: Proceedings of the Seventh Symposium. (Bk. No. G00133). 1978. 90.00 (ISBN 0-685-37587-0). ASME.

Thermophysical Properties: Proceedings of the 6th Symposium. Sponsored by Standing Committee on Thermophysical Properties, Heat Transfer Division, ASME,...Atlanta, Georgia, Augaut 6-8, 1973. Symposium on Thermophysical Properties (6th: 1973: Atlanta). Ed. by P. E. Liley. LC 59-1391. pap. 103.80 (ISBN 0-317-08104-7, 2016833). Bks Demand UMI.

Thermophysical Properties Research Literature Retrieval Guide. 2nd ed. Purdue University, Thermophysical Properties Research Center. Ed. by Y. S. Touloukian et al. LC 60-14226. Bk. 1. pap. 160.00 (ISBN 0-317-10668-6, 2022724); Bk. 2. pap. 158.00 (ISBN 0-317-10669-4); Bk. 3. pap. 160.00 (ISBN 0-317-10670-8). Bks Demand UMI.

Thermophysical Properties Research Literature Retrieval Guide 1900-1980, Vol. 5: Oxide Mixtures & Minerals. Ed. by J. F. Chaney & V. Ramdas. LC 81-15776. 414p. 1982. 95.00x (ISBN 0-306-67225-1, IFI-Plenum). Plenum Pub.

Thermophysical Properties Research Literature Retrieval Guide 1900-1980, Vol. 4: Alloys, Intermetallic Compounds & Ceramics. Ed. by J. F. Chaney & V. Ramdas. LC 81-15776. 736p. 1982. 140.00x (ISBN 0-306-67224-3, IFI-Plenum). Plenum Pub.

Thermophysical Properties Research Literature Retrieval Guide 1900-1980, Vol. 7: Coatings, Systems, Composites, Foods, Animal & Vegetable Products. Ed. by J. F. Chaney & V. Ramdas. LC 81-15776. 642p. 1982. 125.00x (ISBN 0-306-67227-8, IFI-Plenum); Set of 7 Vols. 850.00 (ISBN 0-686-97458-1). Plenum Pub.

Thermophysical Properties Research Literature Retrieval Guide 1900-1980, Vol. 6: Mixtures & Solutions. Ed. by J. F. Chaney & V. Ramdas. LC 81-15776. 498p. 1982. 110.00x (ISBN 0-306-67226-X, IFI-Plenum). Plenum Pub.

Thermophysical Properties Research Literature Retrieval Guide 1900-1980, Vol. 2: Inorganic Compounds. Ed. by J. F. Chaney & V. Ramdas. LC 81-15776. 1094p. 1982. 215.00x (ISBN 0-306-67222-7, IFI-Plenum). Plenum Pub.

Thermophysical Properties Research Literature Retrieval Guide 1900-1980, Vol. 3: Organic Compounds & Polymeric Materials. 2nd ed. Ed. by J. F. Chaney & V. Ramdas. LC 81-15776. 630p. 1982. 125.00x (ISBN 0-306-67223-5, IFI-Plenum). Plenum Pub.

Thermophysical Properties Research Literature Retrieval Guide 1900-1980, Vol. 1: Elements. Ed. by J. F. Chaney & V. Ramdas. LC 81-15776. 804p. 1982. 150.00x (ISBN 0-306-67221-9, IFI-Plenum). Plenum Pub.

Thermophysical Properties Symposium, 7th: Proceedings, 7th, American Society of Mechanical Engineers. 980p. 1978. 90.00 (ISBN 0-317-33595-2, G00133); members 60.00 (ISBN 0-317-33596-0). ASME.

Thermophysics & Spacecraft Thermal Control, PAAS35. Ed. by Robert C. Hering. LC 74-4417. (Illus.). 551p. 1974. 59.50 (ISBN 0-262-08075-3). AIAA.

Thermophysics & Temperature Control of Spacecraft & Entry Vehicles, PAAS18. Ed. by Gerhard B. Heller. LC 66-26844. (Illus.). 865p. (J). 1966. 79.50 (ISBN 0-317-36818-4). AIAA.

Thermophysics & Thermal Control, PAAS65, 2 vols. Ed. by Raymond Viskanta. LC 78-31972. (Illus.). 447p. 1979. 59.50 (ISBN 0-915928-30-2). AIAA.

Thermophysics: Applications to Thermal Design of Spacecraft, PAAS23. Ed. by Jerry T. Bevans. LC 64-103. (Illus.). 580p. 1970. 49.50 (ISBN 0-317-36810-9). AIAA.

Thermophysics of Atmospheric Entry, PAAS82. Ed. by T. E. Horton. LC 82-6686. (Illus.). 521p. 1982. 59.50 (ISBN 0-915928-66-3). AIAA.

Thermophysics of Glaciers. I. A. Zotikov. 1986. lib. bdg. 109.00 (ISBN 90-277-2163-7, Pub. by Reidel Holland). Kluwer Academic.

Thermophysics of Spacecraft & Outer Planet Entry Probes, PAAS56. Ed. by Allie M. Smith. LC 77-24090. (Illus.). 449p. 1977. 59.50 (ISBN 0-915928-20-5). AIAA.

Thermophysics of Spacecraft & Planetary Bodies, PAAS20. Ed. by Gerhard B. Heller. LC 67-30649. (Illus.). 975p. 1967. 89.50 (ISBN 0-317-36816-8). AIAA.

Thermoplastic Elastomers, P-026N. Business Communications Staff. 144p. 1985. 1750.00 (ISBN 0-89336-431-2). BCC.

Thermoplastic Elastomers: A Comprehensive Review. Ed. by N. R. Legge et al. (Hanser Publications). (Illus.). 600p. 1987. 95.00 (ISBN 0-19-520719-X). Oxford U Pr.

Thermoplastic Polymer Additives. Lutz. (Plasatics Engineering Ser.). 552p. 1988. 149.75 (ISBN 0-8247-7901-0). Dekker.

Thermoplastics: Materials Engineering. L. Mascia. (Illus.). xiii, 446p. 1983. 102.75 (ISBN 0-85334-146-X, I-432-82, Pub. by Elsevier Applied Sci England). Elsevier.

Thermoplastics Pipework & Ducting in Unplasticised Polyvinyl Chloride & Polythene. EEMUA Staff. 1965. 75.00x (ISBN 0-85931-046-9, Pub. by EEMUA). State Mutual Bk.

Thermoregulation & Temperature Regulation. H. Hensel. (Physiological Society Monographs Ser.). 1981. 91.00 (ISBN 0-12-341260-9). Acad Pr.

Thermoregulatory Mechanisms & Their Therapeutic Implications: Symposium, 4th, Oxford, July-August, 1979. Ed. by B. Cox et al. (Illus.). 1979. 43.50 (ISBN 3-8055-0277-X). S Karger.

Thermoset Powder Coatings. Portcullis Press, Ltd. Staff. 140p. 1986. 110.00x (ISBN 0-317-54374-1, Pub. by Portcullis Pr UK). State Mutual Bk.

Thermoset Technology 86' Regional Technical Conference, March 19-21, 1986, Ramada Hotel O'Hare, Rosemont, IL. Society of Plastics Engineers Staff. pap. 28.10 (ISBN 0-317-58182-1, 2029709). Bks Demand UMI.

Thermosets by Design: Regional Technical Conference Sponsored by the Chicago Section & the Thermose Division of SPE, March 7-9, 1984, Ramada, the O'Hare Inn, Des Plaines, Ill. Society of Plastics Engineers. pap. 20.00 (ISBN 0-317-30375-9, 2024724). Bks Demand UMI.

Thermosetting Plastics. J. F. Monk. 224p. 1981. 41.95 (ISBN 0-470-20547-4, Co-Pub. with Longman). Wiley.

Thermospheric Circulation, PAAS27. Ed. by W. Webb. LC 79-37738. (Illus.). 372p. 1972. 49.50 (ISBN 0-262-23053-4). AIAA.

Thermostat Metals. G. Vacuumschmelze. LC 83-1376. 144p. 1984. 18.95 (ISBN 0-471-26262-5). Wiley.

Thermostat Repairer. (Career Examination Ser.: C-3408). Date not set. pap. 14.00 (ISBN 0-8373-3408-X). Natl Learning.

Thermothropic Liquid Crystals, Fundamentals. G. Vertegon & W. H. De Jeu. (Chemicals Physics Ser.: Vol. 45). (Illus.). 330p. 1988. 76.50 (ISBN 0-387-17946-1). Springer-Verlag.

Thermotropic Liquid Crystals. Ed. by G. W. Gray. (Critical Reports on Applied Chemistry). 1987. 74.95 (ISBN 0-471-91504-1). Wiley.

Theron Came Later. Patricia L. Pilot. 210p. 1984. 7.45 (ISBN 0-89697-137-6). Intl Univ Pr.

Thersites. John Heywood. LC 72-133744. (Tudor Facsimile Texts. Old English Plays: No. 31). Repr. of 1912 ed. 49.50 (ISBN 0-404-53331-0). AMS Pr.

Thesauri Used in Online Databases: An Analytical Guide. Lois M. Chan & Richard Pollard. LC 88-10985. 288p. 1988. lib. bdg. 45.00 (ISBN 0-313-25788-4, CTI/). Greenwood.

Thesaurus Construction: A Practical Manual. 2nd ed. Jean Aitchison & Alan Gilchrist. 160p. 1987. pap. 45.00 (ISBN 0-85142-197-0). Learned Info.

Thesaurus for Information Processing in Sociology. Jean Viet. 1971. pap. text ed. 16.00x (ISBN 90-2796-941-8). Mouton.

Thesaurus for SoyaScan: Computerized Bibliographic Database on Soybeans & Soyfoods. rev., 2nd ed. William Shurtleff & Akiko Aoyagi. 34p. 1986. pap. 9.95 spiral bound (ISBN 0-933332-24-6). Soyfoods Center.

Thesaurus fur Parlamentsmaterialien. Ed. by Deutscher Bundestag & Gruppe Datenverarbeitung. 180p. 1985. lib. bdg. 36.00 (ISBN 3-598-10584-3). K G Saur.

Thesaurus Guide: Analytical Directory of Selected Vocabularies for Information Retrieval, 1985. 748p. 1985. 105.25 (ISBN 0-444-87736-3, North-Holland). Elsevier.

Thesaurus: Index Terms for SAE Electronic Database. 1986. 34.00 (ISBN 0-89883-515-1, B-THES). Soc Auto Engineers.

Thesaurus-Leitfaden. 2nd ed. Gernaot Wersig & Petra Schuck-Wersig. (DGD-Schriftenreihe Ser.: Vol. 8). 400p. 1985. lib. bdg. 38.00 (ISBN 3-598-21252-6). K G Saur.

Thesaurus Linguae Graecae-Canon of Greek Authors & Works: From Homer to A.D. 400. 2nd ed. Luci Berkowitz & Karl A. Squitter. 1985. text ed. 24.95x (ISBN 0-19-503720-0). Oxford U Pr.

Thesaurus Linguae Tschuvaschorum, Vol. 2. Nikolaj I. Ashmarin. LC 68-64532. (Uralic & Altaic Ser: Vol. 70, Bk. 1). 335p. 1968. pap. text ed. 9.00x (ISBN 0-87750-070-3). Res Ctr Lang Semiotic.

Thesaurus Linguae Tschuvaschorum, Vol. 4. 2nd ed. Nikolaj I. Ashmarin. (Uralic & Altaic Ser). 352p. (Rus. & Chuvash.). 1969. pap. text ed. 9.00x (ISBN 0-87750-073-8). Res Ctr Lang Semiotic.

Thesaurus Literature Botanicae. 2nd ed. G. A. Pritzel. 1972. 120.00x (ISBN 3-87429-035-2). Lubrecht & Cramer.

Thesaurus Litteraturae Mycologicae et Lichenologicae, 5 Vols. Gustav Lindau. pap. 275.00 (ISBN 0-384-32707-9). Johnson Repr.

Thesaurus Nineteen Eighty-Five, 2 vols. OECD Staff. 469p. (Orig.). 1985. Set. pap. 50.00x (ISBN 92-64-12628-7). OECD.

Thesaurus Novus Ancecdotorum, 5 vols. Edmond Martene & Ursin Durand. 5142p. 1717. text ed. 1035.00x (ISBN 0-576-72815-2, Pub. by Gregg Intl Pubs England). Gregg Intl.

Thesaurus Novus Anecdotorum Seu Collectio Monumentorum, 5 Vols. folio ed. Ed. by Edmund Martene & Ursin Durand. LC 68-56785. (Research & Source Works Ser: No. 274). (Lat). 1969. Repr. of 1717 ed. Set. 450.00 (ISBN 0-8337-2253-0). B Franklin.

Thesaurus of African Languages: A Classified & Annotated Inventory of the Spoken Languages of Africa, with an Appendix on their Orthographic Representation. Ed. by Michael Mann & David Dalby. 400p. 1987. lib. bdg. 76.00 (ISBN 3-598-10638-6). K G Saur.

Thesaurus of Book Digests: Nineteen Fifty to Nineteen Eighty. Irving Weiss & Anne D. Weiss. 608p. 1980. 14.95 (ISBN 0-517-54175-0, Michelman Bks). Crown.

Thesaurus of British Archaeology. Lesley Adkins & Roy A. Adkins. LC 81-12898. (Illus.). 320p. 1982. 28.50x (ISBN 0-389-20245-2). B&N Imports.

Thesaurus of Chemical Products, Vol. 1: Generic-to-Tradename. M. Ash & I. Ash. 1986. 145.00 (ISBN 0-8206-0315-5). Chem Pub.

Thesaurus of Chemical Products, Vol. 2: Tradename-to-Generic. M. Ash & I. Ash. 1986. 145.00 (ISBN 0-8206-0316-3). Chem Pub.

Thesaurus of Engineering & Scientific Terms. rev. ed. Engineers Joint Council Editors. LC 68-6569. 1969. flexible cover 125.00x (ISBN 0-87615-163-2). AAES.

Thesaurus of English Words & Phrases. rev. ed. Peter M. Roget. Ed. by John L. Roget & Samuel R. Roget. 42.50 (ISBN 0-87559-049-7); thumb indexed 47.50 (ISBN 0-87559-050-0). Shalom.

Thesaurus of ERIC Descriptors, 1986. 11th ed. Compiled by Educational Resources Information Center (ERIC) Staff. LC 86-42555. 640p. 1987. 65.00 (ISBN 0-89774-159-5). Oryx Pr.

Thesaurus of Forest Products Terms. 167p. 1980. 30.00 (ISBN 0-317-34177-4, 65T1). Forest Prod.

Thesaurus of Forest Products Terms (1986 Edition) 146p. 1986. 30.00 (ISBN 0-317-64567-6). Forest Prod.

Thesaurus of Medieval Hebrew Poetry, 4 Vols. rev. ed. Israel Davidson. (Library of Jewish Classics). 1970. Set. 150.00x (ISBN 0-87068-003-X). Ktav.

Thesaurus of Photographic Science & Engineering Terms. Society of Photographic Scientists & Engineers. LC 68-3006. pap. 34.30 (ISBN 0-317-10422-5, 2003621). Bks Demand UMI.

Thesaurus of Psychological Index Terms. 5th ed. 1988. text ed. 65.00 (3100050); members 49.00. Am Psychol.

Thesaurus of Rock & Soil Mechanics Terms. Ed. by J. P. Jenkins & A. M. Smith. 72p. 1984. pap. 21.00 (ISBN 0-08-031632-8). Pergamon.

Thesaurus of Scientific, Technical & Engineering Terms. Hemisphere Staff. 1217p. 1988. 125.00 (ISBN 0-89116-794-3, 66-65020). Hemisphere Pub.

Thesaurus of Slang. Esther Lewin & Albert Lewin. 432p. 1988. 40.00x (ISBN 0-8160-1742-5). Facts on File.

Thesaurus of Sociological Indexing Terms. Ed. by Sociological Abstracts Staff et al. LC 86-63220. 236p. 1986. spiral bdg. 51.50 (ISBN 0-930710-03-7). Soc Abstracts.

Thesaurus of Spanish Idioms & Everyday Language. Lawrence K. Brown. 165p. (Span.). 1975. pap. 8.95x (ISBN 0-8044-6059-0). Ungar.

Thesaurus of Terms on Copper Technology. 407p. 40.00 (ISBN 0-318-17324-7, 110/0). Copper Devel Assn.

Thesaurus of University Terms. Jill M. Tatem & Jeffrey Rollison. 46p. (Orig.). 1986. pap. 8.00 (ISBN 0-931828-69-4). Soc Am Archivists.

Thesaurus on Resource Recovery Terminology - STP 832. Ed. by H. I. Hollander. LC 83-72052. 279p. 1984. pap. 24.00 (ISBN 0-8031-0256-9, 04-832000-16). ASTM.

Thesaurus Palaeohibernicus, 3 vols. Ed. by Whitley Stokes & John Strachan. LC 78-72646. (Celtic Language & Literature: Goidelic & Brythonic). Repr. of 1910 ed. Set. 150.00 (ISBN 0-404-17593-7). AMS Pr.

These. Charles Peguy. pap. 4.95 (ISBN 0-685-37043-7). French & Eur.

These American Lands: Parks, Wilderness, & the Public Lands. The Wilderness Society Staff & Dvan Zaslowsky. LC 86-3156. (Illus.). 384p. 1986. 22.95 (ISBN 0-8050-0084-4). H Holt & co.

These & Other Lands: Fiction from the Heartland. Ed. by Heartlands Fiction Collective. 176p. 1987. 16.95 (ISBN 0-915637-03-0); pap. 8.95 (ISBN 0-915637-04-9). Westphalia Pr.

These & Those. Simon Schwab. 3.50 (ISBN 0-87306-076-8). Feldheim.

These Are Gifts: A Study Guide for Understanding Spiritual Gifts. Skip Bell. 72p. 1985. pap. write for info. (ISBN 0-910347-03-4). Chatham Comm Inc.

These Are My Children. Alberta Murray. 116p. 1977. 14.95 (ISBN 0-87770-194-6). Ye Galleon.

These Are My People. Mildred T. Howard. (Illus.). 152p. (Orig.). (gr. 3). 1984. pap. 6.28 (ISBN 0-89084-242-6). Bob Jones Univ Pr.

These Are My Pets. Mercer Mayer. LC 87-83016. (Golden Easy Readers Ser.). (Illus.). 40p. (gr. k-2). 1988. 3.95 (ISBN 0-307-11664-6). Western Pub.

These Are My Rites: A Brief History of the Eastern Rites of Christianity. Edward E. Finn. LC 79-24937. (Illus.). 104p. 1980. pap. 4.95 (ISBN 0-8146-1058-7). Liturgical Pr.

These Are Our Lives. Federal Writers Project. 448p. 1975. pap. 9.95 (ISBN 0-393-00763-4, Norton Lib). Norton.

These Are Our Lives. WPA Writers' Project Editors. LC 69-18578. (American Negro: His History & Literature Ser., No. 2). 1969. Repr. of 1939 ed. 17.50 (ISBN 0-405-01911-4). Ayer Co Pubs.

These Are Our Voices: The Story of Oak Ridge, 1942-1970. Ed. by Jim Overholt. (Illus.). 535p. 1987. 19.95 (ISBN 0-9606832-4-0). Children's Mus.

These Are the Endangered. Charles Cadieux. LC 80-54448. (Illus.). 240p. 1981. 16.95 (ISBN 0-913276-35-9). Stone Wall Pr.

These Are the Garments. Charles W. Slemming. 1963. pap. 3.25 (ISBN 0-87508-507-5). Chr Lit.

These Are the Sacraments. A. M. Coniaris. 1981. pap. 6.95 (ISBN 0-937032-22-0). Light&Life Pub Co MN.

These Are the Words of the Covenant. Eleh D. Ha-Berit. 150p. Repr. of 1819 ed. text ed. 41.40x (ISBN 0-576-80124-0, Pub. by Gregg Intl Pubs England). Gregg Intl.

These Are Your Children. 4th ed. Gladys G. Jenkins & Helen S. Shacter. 366p. 1975. pap. write for info. (ISBN 0-673-07931-7). Scott F.

These Are Your Neighbors. Barbara Kerewsky-Halpern. (Literacy Volunteers of America Readers Ser.). 48p. (Orig.). 1983. pap. 1.95 (ISBN 0-8428-9614-7). Cambridge Bk.

These Beautiful Hills: A Natural History of the U. S. Air Force Academy. Thomas N. James. (Illus.). 56p. (Orig.). 1972. pap. 1.50 (ISBN 0-910584-30-3). Filter.

These Branching Moments: Forty Odes. Jelaluddin Rumi. Tr. by Coleman Barks & John Moyne. LC 87-36429. 52p. (Orig.). 1988. pap. 6.95 (ISBN 0-914278-50-9). Copper Beech.

These Earthen Vessels. W. T. Purkiser. 118p. 1985. pap. 4.95 (ISBN 0-8341-0977-8). Beacon Hill.

These Foolish Things. Michael Sadleir. Ed. by Michael Levien. LC 87-60485. (Modern Romance Classics Ser.). 264p. 1987. Repr. of 1937 ed. 18.95 (ISBN 0-7206-0670-5, Pub. by P Owen Ltd). Dufour.

These Forty Days: Lenten Exercises. John P. Henry. LC 87-73061. 112p. (Orig.). 1988. pap. 4.95 (ISBN 0-87793-377-4). Ave Maria.

These Fragile Outposts. Barbara B. Chamberlain. 327p. 1981. pap. 9.95 (ISBN 0-940160-12-9). Parnassus Imprints.

These Fragments I Have Shored: Collage & Montage in Early Modernist Poetry. Andrew M. Clearfield. Ed. by A. Walton Litz. LC 84-57. (Studies in Modern Literature: No. 36). 162p. 1984. 37.95 (ISBN 0-8357-1539-6). UMI Res Pr.

These Gentle Hills. rev. ed. John Kollock. LC 76-16599. (Illus.). 95p. 1985. pap. 8.95 (ISBN 0-931948-49-5). Peachtree Pubs.

These Golden Pleasures. Valerie Sherwood. 512p. (Orig.). 1977. pap. 3.95 (ISBN 0-446-30761-0). Warner Bks.

These Green-Going-to-Yellow. Marvin Bell. LC 81-66013. 1981. 10.95 (ISBN 0-689-11228-9); pap. 6.95 (ISBN 0-689-11227-0). Atheneum.

These Hallowed Hills. Ana Leigh. (Kirkland Chronicles Ser.: Vol. I). 480p. (Orig.). 1986. pap. 3.95 (ISBN 0-8439-2340-7, Leisure Bks). Leisure NY.

These Happy Golden Years. rev. ed. Laura I. Wilder. LC 52-7532. (Illus.). (gr. 5 up). 1953. 13.70i (ISBN 0-06-026480-2); PLB 13.89 (ISBN 0-06-026481-0). HarpJ.

These Happy Golden Years. Laura I. Wilder. (Nine Little House Bks.). (ps up). 1986. pap. 3.50 (ISBN 0-317-53657-5, Trophy). HarpJ.

These Happy Golden Years see Little House Books.

These Harvest Years. facsimile ed. Ed. by Janet H. Baird. LC 74-167308. (Essay Index Reprint Ser). Repr. of 1951 ed. 18.00 (ISBN 0-8369-2581-5). Ayer Co Pubs.

These Hills, My Home: A Buffalo River Story. Billie T. Hardaway. (Illus.). 179p. 1980. 8.95 (ISBN 0-941186-01-6); pap. 5.95 (ISBN 0-941186-02-4). J & B Bks.

These Honored Dead: The Union Casualties at Gettysburg. John W. Busey. LC 87-82810. (Illus.). 404p. 1988. 24.00 (ISBN 0-944413-07-2). Longstreet Hse.

These I Do Remember: Fragments from the Holocaust. Gerda S. Haas. LC 82-71674. 300p. 1982. 16.95 (ISBN 0-87027-203-9). Cumberland Pr.

These Kingdoms. Kenneth McKenny. 464p. (Orig.). 1987. pap. 4.95 (ISBN 0-345-34109-0). Ballantine.

These Last Four Centuries: A Romp Through Intellectual History. Christopher C. Faille. LC 88-1297. 404p. (Orig.). 1988. lib. bdg. 34.50 (ISBN 0-8191-6909-9); pap. text ed. 12.50 (ISBN 0-8191-6910-2). U Pr of Amer.

These Latter Days. Laura Kalpakian. pap. 3.95 (ISBN 0-671-61272-7). PB.

These Little Worlds. Fred Asnes. Ed. by Chuck Taylor. (Illus.). 82p. (Orig.). 1985. 10.95 (ISBN 0-941720-23-3); pap. 4.95 (ISBN 0-941720-22-5). Slough Pr Tx.

These Live Tomorrow. Clinton L. Scott. 1964. pap. write for info. (ISBN 0-933840-06-3). Unitarian Univ.

These Live Tomorrow. 2nd ed. Clinton L. Scott. (Illus.). 230p. 1987. pap. 10.95 (ISBN 0-933840-32-2, Skinner House Bks). Unitarian Univ.

These Men are Dangerous: The Early Years of the S. A. S. Dereck Harrison. (Illus.). 256p. 1988. 24.95 (ISBN 0-7137-2049-2, Pub. by Blandford Pr England). Sterling.

These Men Shall Never Die. facsimile ed. Lowell J. Thomas. LC 73-152217. (Essay Index Reprint Ser). Repr. of 1943 ed. 35.00 (ISBN 0-8369-2379-0). Ayer Co Pubs.

These Men She Gave: Civil War Diary of Athens, Georgia. John F. Stegeman. LC 64-14674. (Illus.). 188p. 1964. 14.00 (ISBN 0-8203-0179-5). U of Ga Pr.

These Modern Nights: Poems. Richard Lyons. LC 87-26355. 80p. (Orig.). 1988. pap. 6.95 (ISBN 0-8262-0672-7). U of Mo Pr.

These Modern Women: Autobiographical Essays from the Twenties. Ed. by Elaine Showalter. 160p. (Orig.). 1978. pap. 8.95 (ISBN 0-912670-46-0). Feminist Pr.

These Moderns: Some Parisian Closeups. Francois Dumas Ribadeau. LC 71-113308. 1971. Repr. of 1932 ed. 27.00x (ISBN 0-8046-1357-5, Pub by Kennikat). Assoc Faculty Pr.

These, My Singing Words: A Collection of Poems. Marvin E. Girard. LC 76-1233. 119p. 1976. 6.00 (ISBN 0-8233-0240-7). Golden Quill.

These Old Shades. Georgette Heyer. 1980. pap. 1.75 (ISBN 0-449-24000-2, Crest). Fawcett.

These Old Shades. Georgette Heyer. 224p. 1988. pap. 2.95 (ISBN 0-451-15135-6, Sig). NAL.

These Our Actors: Theatre Acting of Peggy Ashcroft, John Gielgud, Laurence Olivier, Ralph Richardson. Richard Findlater. (Illus.). 192p. 1984. 29.95 (ISBN 0-241-11060-2, Pub. by Hamish Hamilton England). David & Charles.

These People. Lloyd Schwartz. LC 81-13151. (Wesleyan Poetry Program Ser.: Vol.103). 64p. 1981. 17.00 (ISBN 0-8195-2103-5); pap. 8.95 (ISBN 0-8195-1103-X). Wesleyan U Pr.

These Perspicuous Verses. Robert McLaughlin. 112p. 11.95 (ISBN 0-85398-118-3); pap. 6.50 (ISBN 0-85398-119-1). G Ronald Pub.

These Primal Years. John Bowen. 213p. 1981. 10.00 (ISBN 0-682-49719-3). Exposition-Phoenix.

These Rooms. Suzanne E. Berger. Ed. by Joan Norris & Michael Peich. LC 79-83711. 1979. 12.00 (ISBN 0-915778-38-6); pap. 4.25x (ISBN 0-915778-39-4). Penmaen Pr.

These Small Stones. Ed. by Norma Farber & Myra C. Livingston. LC 87-264. (Charlotte Zolotow Bks.). 128p. (gr. 3-7). 1987. 11.95i (ISBN 0-06-024013-X); PLB 11.89 (ISBN 0-06-024014-8). HarpJ.

These Sought a Country. Robert L. Cate. LC 84-23909. 1985. pap. 10.95 (ISBN 0-8054-1232-8). Broadman.

These Special Children: The Ostomy Book for Parents of Children with Colostomies, Ileostomies, & Urostomies. Katherine Jeter. (Illus.). 300p. 1982. 19.95 (ISBN 0-915950-51-0); pap. 13.95 (ISBN 0-915950-53-7). Bull Pub.

These Splendid Priests. facs. ed. Compiled by James J. Walsh. LC 68-29252. (Essay Index Reprint Ser). 1968. Repr. of 1926 ed. 17.00 (ISBN 0-8369-0973-9). Ayer Co Pubs.

These Splendid Sisters. Compiled by James J. Walsh. LC 75-128326. (Essay Index Reprint Ser.). 1927. 18.00 (ISBN 0-8369-1856-8). Ayer Co Pubs.

These Stones Speak. P. E. Gillum. 1974. 7.95 (ISBN 0-934942-14-5). White Wing Pub.

These Stones Will Shout. Mark Link. 297p. (YA) (gr. 9-12). 1975. 16.95 (ISBN 0-89505-046-3). Tabor Pub.

These Stones Will Shout: A New Voice for the Old Testament. Mark Link. LC 82-74383. (Illus.). 300p. (gr. 9-12). 1983. pap. 9.95 (ISBN 0-89505-117-6). Tabor Pub.

These Strange Ashes. Elisabeth Elliot. LC 74-25684. 132p. 1979. pap. 7.95 (ISBN 0-06-062234-2, RD 488, HarpR). Har-Row.

These Things Are Written: An Introduction to the Religious Ideas of the Bible. James M. Efird. LC 77-15749. (Biblical Foundations Ser.). 1978. pap. 8.95 (ISBN 0-8042-0073-4, John Knox). Westminster John Knox.

These Things Happen. Marian Thurm. 200p. 1988. 16.95 (ISBN 0-671-64924-8, Poseidon Pr). PB.

These Things I've Loved. Perry Tanksley. 5.95 (ISBN 0-686-21184-7). Allgood Bks.

These Thirteen. William Faulkner. Ed. by Noel Polk. (William Faulkner Manuscripts Ser.). 1987. lib. bdg. 100.00 (ISBN 0-8240-6812-2). Garland Pub.

These, Too, Shall Be Loved. Flower A. Newhouse. LC 76-49246. 1976. pap. 6.00 (ISBN 0-910378-11-8). Christward.

These Too Were Here (Willa Cather) Elizabeth M. Vermorcken. LC 76-30901. 1977. lib. bdg. 29.00 (ISBN 0-8414-6061-2). Folcroft.

These Truths Can Change Your Life. Joseph Murphy. 280p. 1982. pap. 7.50 (ISBN 0-87516-476-5). DeVorss.

These Twain. Arnold Bennett. LC 74-17052. (Collected Works of Arnold Bennett: Vol. 79). 1976. Repr. of 1915 ed. 41.25 (ISBN 0-518-19160-5). Ayer Co Pubs.

These Two Commandments. 2nd ed. Boyce Mouton. (Orig.). 1978. pap. 3.95 (ISBN 0-89900-138-6). College Pr Pub.

These Unalienable Rights. 3rd ed. 106p. 1975. 1.00 (ISBN 0-318-14099-3). Federal Bar.

These United States, Vol. II. 3rd ed. Irwin Unger. (Illus.). 448p. 1986. pap. text ed. write for info (ISBN 0-13-915133-8). P-H.

These United States, First Series. facs. ed. Ed. by Ernest H. Gruening. LC 70-134088. (Essay Index Reprint Ser). 1923. 22.00 (ISBN 0-8369-2109-7). Ayer Co Pubs.

These United States, Second Series. facs. ed. Ed. by Ernest H. Gruening. LC 70-134088. (Essay Index Reprint Ser). 1924. 24.50 (ISBN 0-8369-2140-2). Ayer Co Pubs.

These United States: The Questions of Our Past, Vols. I & II. 3rd ed. Irwin Unger. 960p. 1986. text ed. write for info. (ISBN 0-13-915190-7). P-H.

These United States: To 1877, Vol. 1. 3rd ed. Irwin Unger. (Illus.). 448p. 1986. pap. text ed. write for info (ISBN 0-13-915109-5). P-H.

These Were Actors: Extracts from a Newspaper Cutting Book, 1811-1833. James Agate. LC 72-91889. Repr. of 1943 ed. 14.00 (ISBN 0-405-08195-2, Pub. by Blom). Ayer Co Pubs.

These Were Muses. Mona Wilson. LC 78-95336. 1970. Repr. of 1924 ed. 20.50x (ISBN 0-8046-1349-4, Pub. by Kennikat). Assoc Faculty Pr.

These Were the Greeks. H. D. Amos & A. G. Lang. LC 81-71846. (Illus.). 224p. (Orig.). 1982. pap. 13.95 (ISBN 0-8023-1275-6). Dufour.

These Were the Romans. G. I. Tingay & J. Badcock. LC 86-11654. (Illus.). 196p. (gr. 10-12). 1986. pap. 13.95 (ISBN 0-8023-1280-2). Dufour.

These Were the Sioux. Mari Sandoz. LC 85-8914. (Illus.). 118p. (gr. 6-12). 1985. pap. 4.95 (ISBN 0-8032-9151-5, BB 920, Bison). U of Nebr Pr.

These Women Walked With God: The Saga of Citeaux Third Epoch. M. Raymond. 255p. Date not set. price not set (ISBN 0-8198-7341-1); pap. price not set (ISBN 0-8198-7342-X). Dghtrs St Paul.

These Wonderful Old Things. Ed. by Sandra Callaway. (Illus., Orig.). Date not set. pap. price not set (ISBN 0-9615130-2-0). Very Idea.

These Words: Weddings & After an Essay & Poetry. William McIlvanney. 1986. 34.75x (ISBN 0-906391-61-X, Pub. by Mainstream Scotland). State Mutual Bk.

Thesee. Andre Gide. (Folio Ser.: No. 1334). 116p. 1946. 5.95 (ISBN 0-686-56059-0). Schoenhof.

Thesee. Jean-Baptiste Lully. Ed. by Theodore De Lajarte. (Chefs-d'oeuvre classiques de l'opera francais Ser.: Vol. 26). (Illus.). 262p. (Fr.). 1972. pap. 27.50x (ISBN 0-8450-1126-X). Broude.

Theses & Dissertations on Black American Music. Eddie S. Meadows. LC 80-128580. (Front Music Publications: No. 1). ii, 19p. (Orig.). 1980. pap. 5.00 (ISBN 0-934082-01-4). Theodore Front.

Theses & Dissertations on Virginia History: A Bibliography. Compiled by Richard R. Duncan. 1986. 10.00; pap. (ISBN 0-88490-136-X). VA State Lib.

Theses in Germanic Studies, 1903-1961. Ed. by F. Norman. (Publications of the Institute of Germanic Studies: Vol. 4). 46p. 1962. pap. text ed. 6.95x (ISBN 0-85457-015-2, Pub. by Inst Germanic UK). Humanities.

Theses in Germanic Studies, 1962-1967. Ed. by S. S. Prawer & V. J. Riley. (Publications of the Institute of Germanic Studies: Vol. 10). 18p. 1968. pap. text ed. 6.95x (ISBN 0-85457-032-2, Pub. by Inst Germanic UK). Humanities.

Theses in Germanic Studies, 1967-1972. Ed. by W. D. Robson-Scott & V. J. Riley. (Publications of the Institute of Germanic Studies: Vol. 17). 18p. 1973. pap. text ed. 6.95x (ISBN 0-85457-055-1, Pub. by Inst Germanic UK). Humanities.

Theses in Germanic Studies, 1972-1977. Ed. by C. V. Bock & V. J. Riley. (Publications of the Institute of Germanic Studies: Vol. 27). 57p. 1980. pap. text ed. 10.50x (ISBN 0-85457-081-0, Pub. by Inst Germanic UK). Humanities.

Theses on Africa 1963-1975: Accepted by Universities in the United Kingdom & Ireland. Compiled by J. H. McIlwaine. 140p. 1978. lib. bdg. 33.00x (ISBN 0-7201-0728-8). Mansell.

Theses on Asia Accepted by Universities in the United Kingdom & Ireland: 1877-1964. Ed. by B. C. Bloomfield. 127p. 1967. 25.00x (ISBN 0-7146-1093-3, F Cass Co). Biblio Dist.

Theses on Caribbean Topics, Seventeen Seventy-Eight to Nineteen Sixty-Eight. Ed. by Enid M. Baa. pap. 3.10 (ISBN 0-8477-2000-4). U of PR Pr.

Theses on Islam, Middle East, & Northwest Africa, 1880-1978. Compiled by Peter Sluglett. 160p. 1983. 27.00x (ISBN 0-7201-1651-1). Mansell.

Theses: Resolutions & Manifestos of the First Four Congresses of the Third International. Alan Adler. Tr. by Alix Holt & Barbara Holland. Orig. Title: Kommunisticheskii internatsional Dolumentakh. 481p. 1980. 34.95 (Pub. by Ink Links Ltd); pap. 13.95 (Pub. by Ink Links Ltd). Longwood Pub Group.

Theseus & Other Poems. Frederick Buell. LC 73-24550. 89p. 1971. 2.95 (ISBN 0-87886-003-7). Greenfld Rev Pr.

Theseus & the Minotaur. Retold by & illus. by Leonard E. Fisher. LC 88-1970. (Illus.). 32p. (gr. 1-4). 1988. PLB 14.95 (ISBN 0-8234-0703-9). Holiday.

Theseus & the Minotaur. Adapted by C. J. Naden. LC 80-50067. (Illus.). 32p. (gr. 4-8). 1980. PLB 10.79 (ISBN 0-89375-363-7); pap. 2.50 (ISBN 0-89375-367-X). Troll Assocs.

Theseus & the Minotaur. As told by Catherine Storr. (Stories Clippers Ser.). (Illus.). 32p. (gr. k-5). 1985. PLB 15.33 (ISBN 0-8172-2506-4); pap. 9.27 (ISBN 0-8172-2514-5). Raintree Pubs.

Theseus & the Road to Athens. Pamela Espeland. LC 80-27713. (Myths for Modern Children Ser.). (Illus.). 32p. (gr. 1-4). 1981. PLB 7.95 (ISBN 0-87614-141-6). Carolrhoda Bks.

Thesis & the Book. Ed. by Eleanor Harman & Ian Montagnes. LC 76-10704. 1976. pap. 9.95 (ISBN 0-8020-6293-8). U of Toronto Pr.

Thesis of Paradise Lost. Gerald A. Wilkes. LC 76-28374. 1976. Repr. of 1961 ed. lib. bdg. 30.00 (ISBN 0-8414-9514-9). Folcroft.

Thesis Projects in Science & Engineering. Richard M. Davis. LC 78-65255. (Illus.). 1979. pap. text ed. 8.95 (ISBN 0-312-79963-2). St Martin.

Thesis Writer's Handbook: A Complete One-Source Guide for Writers of Research Papers. Joan I. Miller & Bruce J. Taylor. (Illus.). 322p. 1987. pap. 10.95 (ISBN 0-937473-12-X). Alcove Pub Co OR.

Thespis: Ritual, Myth, & Drama in the Ancient Near East. 2nd rev. ed. Theodor H. Gaster. LC 75-15735. 515p. 1975. 40.00x (ISBN 0-87752-188-3). Gordian.

Thess. I, II; Tim. I, II; Titus; Philomen see Commentaries on the New Testament.

Thessalonian Correspondence: Pauline Rhetoric & Millenarian Piety. Robert Jewett. LC 86-45204. (Foundations & Facets Ser.). 256p. 1986. text ed. 17.95 (ISBN 0-8006-2111-5, 1-2111). Fortress.

Thessalonian Epistles. John F. Walvoord. 1958. pap. 4.95 (ISBN 0-310-34071-3, 6392P). Zondervan.

Thessalonians. David P. Kuske. (People's Bible Ser.). 1984. pap. 4.95 (ISBN 0-8100-0193-4, 15N0406). Northwest Pub.

Thessalonians. (Erdmans Commentaries Ser.). pap. 2.95 (ISBN 0-8010-3408-6). Baker Bk.

Thessalonians. D. E. Whiteley. (New Clarendon Bible Ser). (Illus.). 1969. 8.95x (ISBN 0-19-836906-9). Oxford U Pr.

Thessalonians see Practical Truth Series.

Thessalonians & Galations. Stephen Doyle. (Read & Pray Ser.). 1980. 1.75 (ISBN 0-8199-0635-2). Franciscan Herald.

Thessalonians: Critical & Exegetical Commentary. James E. Frame. Ed. by Samuel R. Driver & Charles A. Briggs. (International Critical Commentary Ser.). 336p. 1912. 29.95 (ISBN 0-567-05032-7, Pub. by T & T Clark Ltd UK). Fortress.

Thessalonians, Philippians, & Philemon One & Two. Ernest W. Saunders. Ed. by John Hayes. (Knox Preaching Guides Ser.). 1983. pap. 4.95 (John Knox). Westminster John Knox.

Thessalonians, Timothy & Titus. William Hendriksen. 404p. 1979. 21.95 (ISBN 0-8010-4213-5). Baker Bk.

Thessalonians, Titus, Vol. X. Beacon Bible ExpositionsStaff. 6.95 (ISBN 0-8010-0743-7). Baker Bk.

Thessalonians 1 & 2. F. F. Bruce. (Word Biblical Commentary Ser.: Vol. 45). 275p. 1982. 22.95 (ISBN 0-8499-0244-4). Word Bks.

Thessalonica Eiusque Agro Dissertatio Geographica. T. L. Tafel. 688p. 1972. 50.00x (ISBN 0-902089-36-6). State Mutual Bk.

Thessalonike see Greek Museums.

Thessalonike Archaeological Museum. Manolis Andronikos. Tr. by Kay Cicellis. (Greek Museums Ser). (Illus.). 32p. (Orig.). 1975. pap. 9.50 (ISBN 0-89241-013-2). Caratzas.

Theta Functions. J. Igusa. LC 74-183900. (Grundlehren der Mathematischen Wissenschaften: Vol. 194). 232p. 1972. 46.00 (ISBN 0-387-05699-8). Springer-Verlag.

Theta Functions, Kernel Functions, & Abelian Integrals. Dennis A. Hejhal. LC 72-6824. (Memoirs: No. 129). 112p. 1972. pap. 12.00 (MEMO-129). Am Math.

Theta Molecular Model Sets for Organic Chemistry. Ronald Starkey. 1982. pap. write for info. (ISBN 0-471-86604-0). Wiley.

Thetis et Pelee. Pascal Collasse. Ed. by Louis Soumis. (Chefs-d'oeuvre classiques de l'opera francais Ser.: Vol. 9). (Illus.). 320p. (Fr.). 1972. pap. 27.50x. Broude.

Thetis et Pelee Pascal Collasse see Chefs-D'oeuvres Classiques De L'opera Francais Ser.

They All Come to Geneva & Other Tales of a Public Diplomat. Max W. Kraus. (Illus.). 136p. 1988. 14.95 (ISBN 0-932020-52-6). Seven Locks Pr.

They All Laughed at Christopher Columbus: Tales of Medicine & the Art of Discovery. Gerald Weissmann. 1987. 17.95 (ISBN 0-8129-1618-2). Times Bks.

They All Laughed When I Sat Down at the Computer: And Other True Tales of One Man's Struggle With Personal Computing. Erik Sandberg-Diment. 256p. 1986. pap. 7.95 (ISBN 0-13-917014-6). P-H.

They All Laughed When I Sat Down at the Computer. Erik Sandberg-Diment. Ed. by Marnie Hagmann. LC 85-5275. 256p. 1985. 16.95 (ISBN 0-671-52750-9). S&S.

They All Played Ragtime. rev. ed. Rudi Blesh & Harriet Janis. LC 66-19054. (Illus.). 347p. pap. 9.95 (ISBN 0-8256-0091-X, 000091, Oak). Music Sales.

They All Sang on the Corner: A Second Look at New York City's Rhythm & Blues Vocal Groups. Philip Groia. LC 83-61960. Orig. Title: They All Sang on the Corner: New York City's R&B Vocal Groups of the 1950's. (Illus.). 192p. 1986. pap. 20.00x (ISBN 0-9612058-0-6). Phillie Dee Ent.

They All Sang on the Corner: New York City's R&B Vocal Groups of the 1950's see They All Sang on the Corner: A Second Look at New York City's Rhythm & Blues Vocal Groups.

They All Sat Down: Pianists in Profile. Leonice T. Kidd. (Illus.). 149p. (Orig.). (YA) (gr. 8-12). 1986. pap. 9.95 (ISBN 0-9619974-0-0). Chrlstn SC.

They All Want to Write: Written English in the Elementary School. 4th ed. Alvina T. Burrows et al. LC 84-15470. 238p. 1984. lib. bdg. 27.50 (ISBN 0-208-02042-X, Lib Prof Pubns); pap. 20.00x (ISBN 0-208-02043-8, Lib Prof Pubns). Shoe String.

They Always Call Us Ladies: Stories from Prison. Jean Harris. 288p. 1988. 18.95 (ISBN 0-684-18963-1). Scribner.

They & We. Peter J. Rose. 190p. pap. 7.95 (ISBN 0-686-95008-9). ADL.

They & We: Racial & Ethnic Relations in the United States. 3rd ed. Peter I. Rose. 252p. 1981. pap. text ed. write for info (ISBN 0-394-32402-1, RanC). Random.

They Are All Gone Now: And So Are You. Ric Masten. 112p. (Orig.). 1985. pap. 6.00 (ISBN 0-931104-15-7). Sunflower Ink.

They Are My Friends: A History of the Joseph Knight Family, 1825-1850. William G. Hartley. 1986. 18.50 (ISBN 0-910523-23-1). Grandin Bk Co.

They Became Part of Us: Experiences of Families Adopting Children Everywhere. Ed. by Laurel Strassberger & Barb Holtan. LC 85-62549. (Illus.). 202p. (Orig.). 1985. pap. 7.95 (ISBN 0-931323-05-3). Mini-World Pubns.

They Blew Our Weather. Frederick Clare. (Illus.). 192p. 1982. 20.00 (ISBN 0-682-49824-6). Exposition-Phoenix.

They Broke the Prairie: Being Some Account of the Settlement of the Upper Mississippi Valley by Religious & Educational Pioneers, Told in Terms of One City, Galesburg, & of One College, Knox. Earnest E. Calkins. LC 75-138103. 1971. Repr. of 1937 ed. lib. bdg. 35.00x (ISBN 0-8371-5679-3, CABP). Greenwood.

They Brought Their Women. Edna Ferber. LC 70-110188. (Short Story Index Reprint Ser.). 1936. 17.00 (ISBN 0-8369-3339-7). Ayer Co Pubs.

They Builded Better Than They Knew. facsimile ed. Julius H. Cohen. LC 70-156633. (Essay Index Reprint Ser). Repr. of 1946 ed. 21.50 (ISBN 0-8369-2350-2). Ayer Co Pubs.

They Built for Eternity. facsimile ed. Gustav-Adolf Gedat. Tr. by Roland H. Bainton. LC 72-167345. (Essay Index Reprint Ser). Repr. of 1953 ed. 36.00 (ISBN 0-8369-2451-7). Ayer Co Pubs.

They Built on Rock: The Story of the Celtic Christian Church. Diana Leathem. 1977. lib. bdg. 59.95 (ISBN 0-8490-2743-8). Gordon Pr.

They Built the Capitol. Ihna T. Frary. LC 76-99660. (Select Bibliographies Reprint Ser). 1940. 33.00 (ISBN 0-8369-5089-5). Ayer Co Pubs.

They Built with Faith: True Tales of God's Guidance in L.D.S. Chapel Building World-Wide. H. Dyke Walton. LC 79-89353. 125p. 1979. 5.95 (ISBN 0-88290-122-2). Horizon Utah.

They Burn the Thistles: Memed My Hawk, Part II. Yashar Kemal. pap. 4.95 (ISBN 0-906495-47-4). Writers & Readers.

They Cage the Animals at Night. Jennings M. Burch. LC 84-6809. 304p. 1984. 14.95 (ISBN 0-453-00469-5). NAL.

They Cage the Animals at Night. Jennings M. Burch. 1985. pap. 3.95 (ISBN 0-451-13853-8, Sig). NAL.

They Call Him the Buffalo Doctor. Jean Cummings. LC 73-147172. 320p. 1980. Repr. of 1971 ed. 7.00 (ISBN 0-8187-0035-1). Harlo Pr.

They Call Him Tommie. Bill Tremper. (Illus.). 50p. (Orig.). 1980. pap. 6.95 (ISBN 0-9604166-0-9). Tremper.

They Call It Wrestling: A Pictorial Anthology of the American Wrestler. Wade Schalles. LC 82-81800. (Illus.). 288p. 1983. 29.95 (ISBN 0-88011-074-0, PSCH0074). Leisure Pr.

They Call Me Coach. John Wooden & Jack Tobin. (Illus.). 272p. (Orig.). 1988. pap. 9.95 (ISBN 0-8092-4591-4). Contemp Bks.

They Call Me Dirty. Conrad Dobler & Vic Carucci. 288p. 1988. 17.95 (ISBN 0-399-13399-2, Putnam). Putnam Pub Group.

They Call Me Hunter. Hunter Wells. (Illus.). 241p. 1984. 16.50 (ISBN 0-942078-09-8). R Tanner Assocs Inc.

They Call Me Moses Masaoka. Mike Masaoka & Bill Hosokawa. Ed. by Howard Cady. LC 87-11120. (Illus.). 352p. 1987. 18.95 (ISBN 0-688-06236-9). Morrow.

They Call Me Super Mex. Lee Trevino & Sam Blair. 200p. 1983. 13.45 (ISBN 0-394-52336-9). Random.

They Call Me the Mercenary: Bush Warfare, No. 10. Axel Kilgore. (They Call Me the Mercenary Ser.). (Orig.). 1982. pap. 2.50 (ISBN 0-8217-1023-0). Zebra.

They Call Me the Mercenary: Death Lust, No. 11. (Orig.). 1982. pap. 2.50 (ISBN 0-8217-1056-7). Zebra.

They Call Me the Mercenary, No. 13: Naked Blade, Naked Gunn. Axel Kilgore. 1983. pap. 2.50 (ISBN 0-686-43977-5). Zebra.

They Call Me the Mercenary, No. 14: The Siberian Alternative. Axel Kilgore. (Orig.). 1983. pap. 2.50 (ISBN 0-8217-1194-6). Zebra.

They Call Me the Mercenary, No. 18: The Hard Men. Axel Kilgore. 192p. 1984. pap. 2.50 (ISBN 0-8217-1429-5). Zebra.

They Call Me the Mercenary, No. 5: Canadian Killing Ground. Axel Kilgore. (Orig.). pap. 2.50 (ISBN 0-89083-829-1). Zebra.

They Call Me the Mercenary: The Terror Contract, No. 9. Axel Kilgore. (They Call Me the Mercenary Ser.). 1982. pap. 2.50 (ISBN 0-89083-985-9). Zebra.

They Call Us the Screamers: The History of a Radical Primal Commune. Jenny James. LC 83-62664. 194p. 1983. 11.50 (ISBN 0-904573-27-3, Pub. by Caliban Bks); pap. 5.75 (ISBN 0-904573-55-9). Longwood Pub Group.

They Called Him Wild Bill. Joseph G. Rosa. (Illus.). 1982. pap. 15.95 (ISBN 0-8061-1538-6). U of Okla Pr.

They Called Me Cassandra. Genevieve Tabouis. LC 76-172178. (Europe 1815-1945 Ser.). (Illus.). 448p. 1973. Repr. of 1942 ed. lib. bdg. 45.00 (ISBN 0-306-70298-3). Da Capo.

They Called Them Greasers: Anglo Attitudes toward Mexicans in Texas, 1821-1900. Arnoldo De Leon. 167p. 1983. 19.95 (ISBN 0-292-70363-5); pap. 8.95 (ISBN 0-292-78054-0). U of Tex Pr.

They Came Before Columbus: The African Presence in Ancient America. Irvan Van Sertima. 1977. 18.95 (ISBN 0-394-40245-6). Random.

They Came for Sandalwood: A Study of the Sandalwood Trade in the South-West Pacific, 1830-1865. D. Shineberg. 1967. 19.00x (ISBN 0-522-83828-6, Pub by Melbourne U Pr). Intl Spec Bk.

They Came from Dubuque. John Tigges. 144p. 1983. pap. 12.95 (ISBN 0-8403-3094-4). Kendall-Hunt.

They Came Like Swallows. William Maxwell. LC 86-46249. 192p. 1988. pap. 9.95 (ISBN 0-87923-677-9). Godine.

They Came This Way: The Humboldt Valley, Highroad to the Gold Rush. ltd. ed. Don Chase. (Illus.). 1973. velo-bind 3.50 (ISBN 0-918634-31-8); pap. 3.00 limited ed. (ISBN 0-918634-15-6). D M Chase.

They Came to Baghdad. Agatha Christie. 1974. pap. 1.95 (ISBN 0-440-18700-1). Dell.

They Came to Baghdad. Agatha Christie. 240p. 1986. pap. 2.95 (ISBN 0-425-06804-8). Berkley Pub.

They Came to Japan. Michael Cooper. 439p. 1965. write for info. (Pub. by Han-Shan Tang Ltd). State Mutual Bk.

They Came to Japan: An Anthology of European Reports on Japan, 1543-1640. Compiled by Michael Cooper. (Center for Japanese & Korean Studies, UC Berkley). 447p. pap. 11.95x (ISBN 0-520-04509-2). U of Cal Pr.

They Came to Kill. (Able Team Ser.: No. 15). Date not set. pap. 2.25 (ISBN 0-317-63978-1, Pub. by Worldwide). Harlequin Bks.

They Came to Louisiana: Letters of a Catholic Mission, 1854-1882. Ed. by Sr. Dorothea O. McCants. LC 72-96258. (Illus.). Repr. of 1970 ed. 72.80 (ISBN 0-8357-9392-3, 2020997). Bks Demand UMI.

They Came to Pennsylvania Workshop. Lucille Wallower & Ellen J. Wholey. LC 76-14140. (gr. 4-5). 1984. pap. 4.65 (ISBN 0-931992-02-8). Penns Valley.

They Came to Praise I. C. C. Englebert D. Schnotzelhorst. 74.98 (ISBN 0-317-58499-5). Schirmer Bks.

They Came to Stay: North Americans in the U. S. S. R. Paula Garb. 195p. 1987. 7.95 (ISBN 0-8285-3579-5, Pub. by Progress Pubs USSR). Imported Pubns.

They Came to the Hill. M. Joyce Jones. 1985. 18.95 (ISBN 0-901976-55-5, Pub. by United Writers Pubns England). State Mutual Bk.

They Came to the Mountain. Platt Cline. 364p. 1988. 24.95 (ISBN 0-87358-153-9). Northland.

They Came to the Smoky Hill: History of Three Generations. Frank Z. Glick. 1987. pap. 29.95 (ISBN 0-89745-092-2). Sunflower U Pr.

They Can Make Music. Phillip Bailey. (Illus.). 1973. 9.95x (ISBN 0-19-311913-7). Oxford U Pr.

They Can Only Kill You Once. Dan Brennan. 1977. pap. 1.50 (ISBN 0-8439-0455-0, Leisure Bks). Leisure NY.

They Can Sue Me? Jonathan Stevenson. 1987. pap. 24.95 (ISBN 1-55645-502-X). Busn Legal Reports.

They Cannot Kill Us All: An Eyewitness Account of South Africa Today. Richard Manning. (Illus.). 288p. 1987. 16.95 (ISBN 0-395-43781-4). HM.

They Changed Their Worlds: Nine Women of Asia - Based on Biographies Published by Ramon Magsaysay Award Foundation, Manila, Philippines. Ed. by Mae H. Esterline. LC 87-8208. (Illus.). 188p. (Orig.). 1987. lib. bdg. 24.75 (ISBN 0-8191-6309-0); pap. text ed. 12.50 (ISBN 0-8191-6310-4). U Pr of Amer.

They Chose Life: Jewish Resistance in the Holocaust. Yehuda Bauer. LC 73-89085. (Illus.). 64p. (Orig.). 1973. pap. 2.00 (ISBN 0-87495-000-7). Am Jewish Comm.

They Chose Minnesota: A Survey of the State's Ethnic Groups. Ed. by June D. Holmquist. LC 81-14124. (Illus.). 614p. (Orig.). 1988. pap. 24.95 (ISBN 0-87351-231-6). Minn Hist.

They Chose to Live: The Racial Agony of an American Church. J. Herbert Gilmore. LC 72-75577. pap. 51.50 (ISBN 0-317-07872-0, 2012911). Bks Demand UMI.

They Come Out on Halloween Night. Michael P. Jones. (Illus.). 1984. write for info. Crumb Elbow Pub.

They Conquered AIDS! Scott J. Gregory & Bianca Leonardo. (Illus.). 360p. 1989. 24.95 (ISBN 0-930852-03-6). Tree Life Pubns.

They Could Not Talk & So They Drew: Children's Styles of Coping & Thinking. Myra F. Levick. (Illus.). 240p. 1983. 38.00x (ISBN 0-398-04800-2). C C Thomas.

They Counted Not the Cost: A History of the Memorial Union Corporation, 1919-1929. John J. Zimmerman. Ed. by Larry E. Anderson. (Illus.). 48p. 1982. pap. 5.00 (ISBN 0-934068-01-1). Memorial Union.

They Cry, Too. Lucille Lavender. 176p. 1986. pap. 7.95 (ISBN 0-310-41651-5, 9970P). Zondervan.

They Dance in the Sky. Jean Guard & Ray A. Williamson. (Illus.). (gr. 6 up). 1987. 12.95 (ISBN 0-395-39970-X). HM.

They Dare to Speak Out: People & Institutions Confront Israel's Lobby. Paul Findley. LC 84-28977. 372p. 1985. 16.95 (ISBN 0-88208-179-9); pap. 8.95 (ISBN 0-88208-180-2). Chicago Review.

They Dared to Cross Frontiers. Faye D. Flynt. (Orig.). (gr. 4-6). 1975. pap. 1.95 (ISBN 0-377-00029-9). Friendship Pr.

They Dared to Live. facs. ed. Robert M. Bartlett. LC 76-90606. (Essay Index Reprint Ser.). 1937. 20.00 (ISBN 0-8369-1273-X). Ayer Co Pubs.

They Did Something about It. facsimile ed. Robert M. Bartlett. LC 70-90607. (Essay Index Reprint Ser). 1939. 17.00 (ISBN 0-8369-1243-8). Ayer Co Pubs.

They Didn't Know It Couldn't Be Done (Jack Johnson) Salvatore Fradella. (Illus.). 64p. 1986. 7.95 (ISBN 0-89962-543-6). Todd & Honeywell.

They Do It with Mirrors. Jim Conaway. 1977. pap. 1.50 (ISBN 0-505-51190-8, Pub. by Tower Bks). Leisure NY.

They Don't Dance Much. J. Rose. 1986. pap. 25.75x (ISBN 0-245-54378-3, Pub. by Harrap Ltd England). State Mutual Bk.

They Don't Dance Much. James Ross. LC 74-23650. (Lost American Fiction Ser.). 308p. 1975. Repr. of 1940 ed. 8.95 (ISBN 0-8093-0714-6). S Ill U Pr.

They Dwell in Monasteries. Frank Monaco. (Illus.). 80p. (Orig.). 1982. pap. 7.95 (ISBN 0-8164-2409-8, HarpR). Har-Row.

They Enriched Humanity: Adveventurers of the Nineteenth Century. David Wren. Repr. of 1948 ed. lib. bdg. 20.00 (ISBN 0-8495-5907-3). Arden Lib.

They Feed They Lion. Philip Levine. LC 74-183612. 1972. pap. 4.95 (ISBN 0-689-10490-1). Atheneum.

They Felled the Redwoods: A Saga of Rails & Flumes in the High Sierra. 3rd rev. ed. Hank Johnston. LC 78-104874. (Illus.). 1966. 21.95 (ISBN 0-87046-003-X, Pub. by Trans-Anglo). Interurban.

They Followed His Call. Adrienne Von Speyr. Tr. by Erasmo Leiva-Merikakis from Ger. LC 86-80294. 137p. (Orig.). 1986. pap. 6.95 (ISBN 0-89870-100-7). Ignatius Pr.

They Followed Jesus: Word Search Puzzles. John H. Tiner. 48p. (gr. 6 up). pap. 2.50 (ISBN 0-87239-586-3, 2784). Standard Pub.

They Followed The Rivers. Floyd Conn & Sadie Conn. (Illus.). 241p. 1981. 14.50x (ISBN 0-9607602-0-2). Kiowa Pr.

They Fought Back: The Story of Jewish Resistance in Nazi Europe. Yuri Suhl. 316p. Repr. 7.95 (ISBN 0-686-95093-3). ADL.

They Fought Back: The Story of the Jewish Resistance in Nazi Europe. Ed. & tr. by Yuri Suhl. LC 74-26766. (Illus.). 351p. 1975. pap. 11.95 (ISBN 0-8052-0479-2). Schocken.

They Fought for the Union. Francis A. Lord. LC 81-6579. (Illus.). x, 375p. 1981. Repr. of 1960 ed. lib. bdg. 52.50x (ISBN 0-313-22740-3, LOTF). Greenwood.

They Fought with What They Had: The Story of the Army Air Forces in the Southwest Pacific, Nineteen Forty-One to Nineteen Forty-Two. Walter D. Edmonds. Repr. of 1951 ed. 29.95 (ISBN 0-89201-068-1). Zenger Pub.

They Found Him Dead. Georgette Heyer. Repr. lib. bdg. 19.95 (ISBN 0-89190-647-9, Pub. by River City Pr). Amereon Ltd.

They Found Him Dead. Georgette Heyer. 240p. 1987. pap. 2.95 (ISBN 0-425-09565-7). Berkley Pub.

They Found the Buried Cities: Exploration & Excavation in the American Tropics. Robert Wauchope. LC 65-24433. (Illus.). Repr. of 1965 ed. 74.10 (ISBN 0-8357-9658-2, 2016986). Bks Demand UMI.

They Found the Secret: Twenty Lives That Reveal a Touch of Eternity. V. Raymond Edman. 176p. 1984. pap. 6.95 (ISBN 0-310-24051-4, 9564P). Zondervan.

They Gave Us Shakespeare: John Heminge & Henry Condell. Charles Connell. (Illus.). 110p. 1982. 15.95x (ISBN 0-85362-193-4, Oriel). Routledge Chapman & Hall.

They Grow in Silence: Understanding Deaf Children & Adults. 2nd ed. Ed. by Eugene D. Mindel & McCay Vernon. LC 86-21638. (Illus.). 224p. 1986. pap. text ed. 25.00 (ISBN 0-316-57422-8, 574228). College-Hill.

They Had Faces Then. John Springer & Jack Hamilton. (Illus.). 1978. pap. 9.95 (ISBN 0-8065-0657-1, Pub. by Citadel Pr). Lyle Stuart.

They Had Faces Then: Annabella to Zorina: the Superstars, Stars & Starlets of the 1930s. John Springer & Jack Hamilton. (Illus.). 384p. 1974. 19.95 (ISBN 0-8065-0300-9, Pub. by Citadel Pr). Lyle Stuart.

They Had Faces Then: Hollywood in the 30's - The Legendary Ladies. John Springer & Jack Hamilton. (Illus.). 352p. Date not set. pap. 15.95 (ISBN 0-8065-1108-7, Citadel Pr). Lyle Stuart.

They Had Their Hour: Benjamin Franklin, Thomas Jefferson. Marquis James. 324p. 1982. Repr. of 1926 ed. lib. bdg. 40.00 (ISBN 0-8495-2802-X). Arden Lib.

They Had to Die: New Light on the Deaths of Calvo Sotelo, Sanjurjo & Mola in the Spanish Civil War. Jenaro Artiles. 98p. 1971. pap. text ed. 3.75x (ISBN 0-8093-0539-9). S Ill U Pr.

They Hanged My Saintly Billy. Robert Graves. (Illus.). 267p. 1980. 14.95 (ISBN 0-89733-030-7); pap. 6.95 (ISBN 0-89733-029-3). Academy Chi Pubs.

They Have a Word for It. Howard Rheingold. 224p. (Orig.). 1988. pap. 7.95 (ISBN 0-87477-464-0). J P Tarcher.

They Have Found a Faith. facsimile ed. Marcus L. Bach. LC 74-134049. (Essay Index Reprint Ser). Repr. of 1946 ed. 18.00 (ISBN 0-8369-2481-9). Ayer Co Pubs.

They Have No Rights. Walter Ehrlich. 266p. 1979. pap. 7.95 (ISBN 0-686-95751-2). Jefferson Natl.

They Have No Rights: Dred Scott's Struggle for Freedom. Walter Ehrlich. LC 78-22135. (Contributions in Legal Studies Ser.: No. 9). (Illus.). xvi, 266p. 1979. lib. bdg. 35.00 (ISBN 0-313-20819-0, ETH/). Greenwood.

They Have Sought Out Many Inventions. Edith Lanning. 192p. 1987. 10.95 (ISBN 0-8062-3097-5). Carlton.

They Have to Be Carefully Taught. 161p. 1981. 8.10x (ISBN 0-88314-191-4). AAHPERD.

They Heard Georgia Singing. Zell Miller. (Illus.). 256p. 1984. 9.95 (ISBN 0-87797-110-2); pap. 5.95 (ISBN 0-87797-111-0). Cherokee.

They Knew Billy the Kid: Interviews with Old Time New Mexicans. Ed. by Robert F. Kadlec. LC 87-70295. (Illus.). 136p. (Orig.). 1987. 18.95 (ISBN 0-941270-37-8); pap. 9.95 (ISBN 0-941270-36-X). Ancient City Pr.

They Knew Franklin Pierce. Carl I. Bell. 1980. 8.95 (ISBN 0-917780-01-9). April Hill.

They Knew Paul Bunyan. E. C. Beck. Ed. by Richard M. Dorson. LC 80-789. (Folklore of the World Ser.). 1980. Repr. of 1956 ed. lib. bdg. 26.50x (ISBN 0-405-13328-6). Ayer Co Pubs.

They Led a Nation. Virginia Sneve. Ed. by N. Jane Hunt. LC 75-254. (Illus.). 1975. pap. 4.95 (ISBN 0-88498-027-8). Brevet Pr.

They Led the Way: Fourteen American Women. Johana Johnston. (Scholastic Biography Ser.). (Illus.). 128p. (Orig.). (gr. 4-6). 1987. pap. 2.50 (ISBN 0-590-41342-2). Scholastic Inc.

They Left Their Mark: William Austin Burt & His Sons, Surveyors of the Public Domain. John S. Burt. (Illus.). 188p. 1987. 35.00 (ISBN 0-910845-31-X, 977). Landmark Ent.

They Lived in Tubac. Elizabeth R. Brownell. LC 85-51587. 1987. 14.95 (ISBN 0-87026-061-8). Westernlore.

They Lived Their Lives. Eda Howink. 1981. 5.50 (ISBN 0-8233-0329-2). Golden Quill.

They Looked for a City. Lydia Buksbazen. 1977. pap. 3.95 (ISBN 0-87508-041-3). Chr Lit.

They Looked for a City. LC 58-17705. 1955. pap. 3.95 (ISBN 0-915540-15-0). Frnds Israel.

They Love Me, They Love Me Not: A Worldwide Study of the Effects of Parental Acceptance & Rejection. Ronald P. Rohner. LC 75-17092. (Comparative Studies Ser.). 312p. 1975. 19.00x (ISBN 0-87536-331-8). HRAFP.

They Loved the Land. Ed. & commentary by Bennett Wayne. LC 74-915. (Garrard Target Ser.). (Illus.). 168p. (gr. 5 up). 1974. PLB 7.99 (ISBN 0-8116-4908-3). Garrard.

They Loved Their Enemies: True Stories of African Christians. Marian Hostetler. LC 87-29696. (Peace & Justice Ser.: Vol. 3). 104p. (Orig.). 1988. pap. 4.95 (ISBN 0-8361-3456-7). Herald Pr.

They Met at Gettysburg. 3rd ed. Edward J. Stackpole. LC 56-13070. (Illus.). 344p. 1982. pap. 10.95 (ISBN 0-8117-2089-6). Stackpole.

They Met God: A Number of Conversion Accounts & Personal Testimonies of God's Presence & Leading in the Lives of Children. Ed. by J. C. Wenger. LC 64-15344. pap. 48.00 (ISBN 0-317-26611-X, 2025422). Bks Demand UMI.

They Met Jesus, Neighborhood Bible Study. Marilyn Kunz & Catherine Schell. 1971. pap. 2.95 (ISBN 0-8423-7080-3). Tyndale.

They Met the Master: Sermons on Contemporary Saints. Carroll R. Gunkel. 1980. 4.50 (ISBN 0-89536-388-7, 2035). CSS of Ohio.

They Never Came Home. Lois Duncan. 192p. 1980. pap. 2.50 (ISBN 0-380-50229-1, 60045-5, Flare). Avon.

They Never Said It: A Book of Fake Quotes, Misquotes, & Curious Citations. Paul F. Boller, Jr. & John George. 160p. 1989. 16.95 (ISBN 0-19-505541-1). Oxford U Pr.

They Never Stopped Teaching. Richard Spindle. 96p. 1982. pap. 2.50 (ISBN 0-8341-0735-X). Beacon Hill.

They of Rome. Lois Parker. 128p. 1980. pap. 6.95 (ISBN 0-8127-0308-1). Review & Herald.

They of the High Trails. Hamlin Garland. (Collected Works of Hamlin Garland). 1988. lib. bdg. 59.00x. Am Biog Serv.

They of the High Trails see Collected Works.

They Overcame: An Exposition of the First Three Chapters of Revelation. Marcus L. Loane. (Canterbury Books). 144p. 1981. pap. 3.95 (ISBN 0-8010-5609-8). Baker Bk.

They Paved the Way: A History of N. H. Women. Olive Tardiff. (Illus.). vi, 98p. (Orig.). (gr. 9-12). 1980. pap. text ed. 3.95 (ISBN 0-917890-22-1). Heritage Bk.

They Played the Game: The Story of Baseball Greats. Harry Grayson. LC 77-167349. (Essay Index Reprint Ser.). Repr. of 1944 ed. 25.00 (ISBN 0-8369-2692-7). Ayer Co Pubs.

They Preached Liberty. Franklin P. Cole. LC 76-26327. 1976. 5.95 (ISBN 0-913966-16-9, Liberty Pr); pap. 1.25 (ISBN 0-913966-20-7). Liberty Fund.

They Pushed Back the Forest: A Century in Del Norte Country, Cal. Doris Chase. (Illus.). 1959. pap. 3.00 (ISBN 0-918634-14-8). D M Chase.

They Really Taught Us How to Write. Ed. by Patricia Geuder et al. LC 74-16760. 140p. 1974. pap. 7.50 (ISBN 0-8141-5422-0). NCTE.

They Refused to Die. Lionel Wilson. LC 83-60117. (Strange but True Ser.). (Illus.). 1983. 10.96 (ISBN 0-382-06681-2). Silver.

They Represent You, 1987. 1988. pap. 3.00x (ISBN 0-686-64779-3). LWV NYC.

They Rest among the Known Black Defenders of America Who Have Responded to the Call of Taps. Robert E. Greene. LC 80-67671. (Illus.). 62p. 1982. write for info. (ISBN 0-9603320-1-4). R E Greene.

They Rose above It. Bob Considine. 1977. pap. 1.75 (ISBN 0-449-23417-7, Crest). Fawcett.

They Said It Couldn't Be Done! Wallene T. Dockery & Steve Williford. LC 86-61416. (Motivational Ser.). 96p. 1987. 11.95 (ISBN 0-936169-03-6). Sports Market.

They Said It Couldn't Be Done. Mary Wilkes & Barbara Morrison. LC 76-24056. (Illus.). (gr. 5). 1976. pap. 2.95 (ISBN 0-87970-140-4). North Plains.

They Sang for Horses: The Impact of the Horse on Navajo & Apache Folklore. LaVerne H. Clark. LC 66-18527. (Illus.). 225p. 1966. pap. 14.95 (ISBN 0-8165-0810-0). U of Ariz Pr.

They Sang with the Spirit. Frank Eifert & Evelyn Stenbock. 104p. 1983. pap. 3.95 (ISBN 0-8341-0824-0). Beacon Hill.

They Sank the Red Dragon. Bernard Edwards. (Illus.). 228p. 1987. text ed. 19.95 (ISBN 0-7083-0966-6, Pub. by U of Wales). Humanities.

They Saw His Glory: Stories of Conversion & Service. Ed. by Byron Burkholder. 186p. (Orig.). 1984. pap. 5.95 (ISBN 0-919797-40-7). Kindred Pr.

They Saw It Happen. Gordon Lindsay. 1.75 (ISBN 0-89985-010-3). Christ Nations.

They Saw It Happen: An Anthology of Eye-Witnesses' Accounts of Events in British History, 1465-1688. Frwd. by C. R. Routh. LC 84-6585. xvi, 220p. 1984. Repr. of 1956 ed. lib. bdg. 38.50x (ISBN 0-313-24301-8, ROTH). Greenwood.

They Saw Nessie...or They Thought They Did! Picton Publishing Staff. (Illus.). 1987. 7.00x (Pub. by Picton UK). State Mutual Bk.

They Saw the Lord: The Resurrection Appearances. Bonnell Spencer. LC 83-61765. 235p. 1983. pap. 8.95 (ISBN 0-8192-1332-2). Morehouse.

They Say You Can't Have a Baby: The Dilemma of Infertility. Madeleine Blais. 1979. 12.95 (ISBN 0-393-01260-3). Norton.

They Serve Fugitively. Ruth Kittson, pseud. 45p. 1959. pap. 3.95. Orphan Voyage.

They Served with Honor. David E. Hays. 220p. (Orig.). 1985. pap. text ed. 16.95 perfect bdg. (ISBN 0-933227-45-0). Closson Pr.

They Shall Be Mine. John Tallach. 128p. (gr. 9-12). 1981. pap. 5.95 (ISBN 0-85151-320-4). Banner of Truth.

They Shall Be My People. John Timmer. LC 83-15380. 200p. 1983. pap. 7.55 (ISBN 0-933140-82-7); pap. 6.50 leader's guide (ISBN 0-933140-83-5). CRC Pubns.

They Shall Cast Out Demons. Bill Burke. 1983. 12.00 (ISBN 0-932526-05-5). Nexus Pr.

They Shall Not Pass: The Autobiography of La Pasionaria. Dolores Ibarruri. LC 66-25065. 360p. 1976. pap. 4.25 (ISBN 0-7178-0468-2). Intl PubS Co.

They Shoot Canoes, Don't They? Patrick McManus. LC 80-24131. 228p. 1981. 12.95 (ISBN 0-03-058646-1). H Holt & Co.

They Shoot Canoes, Don't They. Patrick McManus. 1982. pap. 6.25 (ISBN 0-03-062377-4, Owl Bks). H Holt & Co.

They Shoot Canoes, Don't They? Patrick E. McManus. 14.95 (ISBN 0-8050-0165-4). H Holt & Co.

They Shoot Canoes, Don't They? Patrick E. McManus. pap. 6.50 (ISBN 0-8050-0030-5). H Holt & Co.

They Shoot Canoes, Don't They? Patrick F. McManus. (Large Print Bks.). 323p. 1988. lib. bdg. 17.95x (ISBN 0-8161-4390-0, Large Print Bks). G K Hall.

They Shoot to Slay. Leonard Gribble. (Lythway Ser.). 232p. 1988. lib. bdg. 18.50x (ISBN 0-7451-0674-9, Pub. by Chivers Pr UK). G K Hall.

They Should Have Served That Cup of Coffee. Ed. by Dick Cluster. LC 78-68476. (Illus.). 270p. 1979. 20.00 (ISBN 0-89608-083-8); pap. 9.00 (ISBN 0-89608-082-X). South End Pr.

They Showed the Way: Forty American Negro Leaders. Charlemae H. Rollins. LC 64-20692. (gr. 4 up). 1964. 12.70 (ISBN 0-690-81612-X, Crowell Jr Bks). HarpJ.

They Sought a New World: The Story of European Immigration to North America. William Kurelek & Margaret S. Engelhart. (Illus.). 48p. (gr. 4 up). 1985. 14.95 (ISBN 0-88776-172-0, Dist. by U of Toronto Pr); pap. 6.95 (ISBN 0-88776-213-1). Tundra Bks.

They Speak with Other Tongues. John L. Sherril. 1982. pap. 2.50 (ISBN 0-515-08154-X). Jove Pubns.

They Speak with Other Tongues. John Sherrill. 144p. 1966. pap. 3.50 (Chosen). Revell.

They Stay for Death. Sara Woods. 192p. 1988. pap. 3.50 (ISBN 0-380-70587-7). Avon.

They Stood in the Door. Don MacNaughtton. 413p. 1985. 24.00x (ISBN 0-7223-1752-2, Pub. by A H Stockwell England). State Mutual Bk.

They Stooped to Folly: A Comedy of Morals. Ellen Glasgow. 351p. Repr. of 1929 ed. lib. bdg. 45.00 (ISBN 0-918377-38-2). Russell Pr.

They Stopped to Folly: A Comedy of Morals. Ellen Glasgow. 351p. 1986. Repr. of 1929 ed. lib. bdg. 45.00 (ISBN 0-89984-670-X). Century Bookbindery.

They Taught Themselves: American Primitive Painters of the 20th Century. Sidney Janis. LC 83-45880. Repr. of 1942 ed. 72.50 (ISBN 0-404-20134-2). AMS Pr.

They Tell a Story. Martha Lupton. LC 74-167052. vi, 560p. 1972. Repr. of 1940 ed. 43.00x (ISBN 0-8103-3112-8). Gale.

They That See the Sun. Lloyd W. Kline. 112p. (Orig.). 1985. pap. 9.00 (ISBN 0-931733-01-4). Peninsula United Homes.

They That Take the Sword. Esme Wingfield-Stratford. LC 72-89273. 440p. 1973. Repr. of 1932 ed. 31.00x (ISBN 0-8046-1764-3, Pub by Kennikat). Assoc Faculty Pr.

They That Walk in Darkness: Ghetto Tragedies. Israel Zangwill. LC 70-116969. (Short Story Index Reprint Ser). 1899. 27.50 (ISBN 0-8369-3473-3). Ayer Co Pubs.

They Thought They Were Free: The Germans 1933-45. 2nd ed. Milton Mayer. LC 55-5137. 1966. pap. 9.95 (ISBN 0-226-51192-8, P222, Phoen). U of Chicago Pr.

They: Three Parodies of H. Rider Haggard's She. Ed. by R. Reginald & Douglas Melville. LC 77-84277. (Lost Race & Adult Fantasy Ser.). (Illus.). 1978. lib. bdg. 49.50x (ISBN 0-405-11015-4). Ayer Co Pubs.

They, Too, Were Flesh & Blood. Evelyn Stough. 80p. 1987. 6.75 (ISBN 0-8062-2812-1). Carlton.

They Took a Stand. Brian Blandford. LC 86-13878. 227p. 1986. pap. 4.95 (S183217). Regal.

They Took the Challenge: The Story of Rolling Meadows. Esther Perica. LC 79-14803. (Illus.). 167p. 1980. 9.75 (ISBN 0-9602782-0-6). Rolling Meadows.

They Tore out My Heart & Stomped That Sucker Flat. Lewis Grizzard. 140p. (ps-k). 1982. 9.95 (ISBN 0-931948-38-X). Peachtree Pubs.

They Tore Out My Heart & Stomped That Sucker Flat. Lewis Grizzard. 144p. 1986. pap. 5.95 (ISBN 0-446-37039-8). Warner Bks.

They Tried to Cut It All. Edwin Van Syckle. LC 81-4526. (Illus.). 308p. 1981. pap. 11.95 (ISBN 0-914718-60-6). Pacific Search.

They Voted for Roosevelt: The Presidential Vote, 1932-1944. Edgar E. Robinson. LC 75-120659. 1970. Repr. of 1947 ed. lib. bdg. 20.00x (ISBN 0-374-96884-5, Octagon). Hippocrene Bks.

They Walked Like Men. Clifford D. Simak. 1979. pap. 3.50 (ISBN 0-380-42861-X, 42861-X). Avon.

They Watched Him Die. Roger J. Green. (Illus.). 208p. (gr. 6 up). 1988. 13.95 (ISBN 0-19-271573-9). Oxford U Pr.

They Went Thataway, 3 Vols. in 1. Charles H. Hamlin. LC 64-4203. 440p. 1985. Repr. of 1966 ed. 25.00 (ISBN 0-8063-0588-6). Genealog Pub.

They Went to Bush. W. B. Collins. 231p. 10.00 (ISBN 0-685-26801-2). Univ Place.

They Were Defeated. Rose Macaulay. (Twentieth-Century Classics Ser.). 445p. 1986. pap. 6.95 (ISBN 0-19-281316-1). Oxford U Pr.

They Were Giants. facs. ed. Charles R. Brown. LC 68-54332. (Essay Index Reprint Ser). 1934. 18.00 (ISBN 0-8369-0257-2). Ayer Co Pubs.

They Were Giants. facsimile ed. Charles R. Brown. LC 68-54332. (Essay Index Reprint Ser.). 285p. 1982. Repr. of 1934 ed. lib. bdg. 17.00 (ISBN 0-8290-0835-7). Irvington.

They Were San Franciscans. facs. ed. Miriam A. De Ford. LC 70-117781. (Essay Index Reprint Ser). 1941. 22.00 (ISBN 0-8369-1914-9). Ayer Co Pubs.

They Were Strong & Good. Robert Lawson. (Illus.). (gr. 4-6). 1940. lib. bdg. 13.95 (ISBN 0-670-69949-7). Viking.

They Were There. R. Andersen & R. Barlag. 1977. pap. 1.75 (ISBN 0-570-03769-7, 12-2704). Concordia.

They Were There. facs. ed. Ed. by Curt Riess. LC 70-134127. (Essay Index Reprint Ser). 1944. 34.50 (ISBN 0-8369-2029-5). Ayer Co Pubs.

They Were Women Like Me: Women of the New Testament in Devotions for Today. Joy Jacobs. 216p. 1985. 14.95 (ISBN 0-13-917048-0); pap. 7.95 (ISBN 0-13-917030-8). P-H.

They Were Women, Too. Joy Jacobs. LC 1-67319. 375p. 1981. pap. 8.95 (ISBN 0-87509-304-3). Chr Pubns.

They Won the War. facs. ed. Frank H. Simonds. LC 68-58813. (Essay Index Reprint Ser). 1931. 14.00 (ISBN 0-8369-0126-6). Ayer Co Pubs.

They Won't Demolish Me! Roch Carrier. Tr. by Sheila Fischman from Fr. (Anansi Fiction Ser.: No. 30). 134p. (Orig.). 1974. pap. 7.95 (ISBN 0-88784-328-X, Pub. by Hse Anansi Pr Canada). U of Toronto Pr.

They Wore Garnet & Black. Don Barton. (Illus.). 330p. 1986. 14.95 (ISBN 0-9615503-0-9). Spur Pubs.

They Work for Tomorrow. facsimile ed. Robert M. Bartlett. LC 70-111813. (Essay Index Reprint Ser.). 1943. 17.00 (ISBN 0-8369-1592-5). Ayer Co Pubs.

They Work with Wildlife: Jobs for People Who Want to Work with Animals. Edward R. Ricciuti. LC 80-7918. 160p. (YA) (gr. 7 up). 1983. 11.70i (ISBN 0-06-025003-8); PLB 11.89g (ISBN 0-06-025004-6). HarpJ.

They Worked All Their Lives: Women of the Urban Poor in England 1880-1939. Carl Chinn. LC 87-36701. 208p. 1988. 39.95 (ISBN 0-7190-2436-6, Pub. by Manchester Univ Pr). St Martin.

They Wouldn't Be Chessmen. A. E. Mason. 256p. 1985. pap. 3.50 (ISBN 0-88184-158-7). Carroll & Graf.

They Wouldn't Let Us Die: The Prisoners of War Tell Their Story. Stephen A. Rowan. LC 73-80413. 1973. 12.95 (ISBN 0-8246-0157-2). Jonathan David.

They Write Their Own Sentences: The FBI Handwriting Analysis Manual. (Illus.). 56p. 1987. pap. 8.00 (ISBN 0-87364-446-8). Paladin Pr.

They Wrote on Clay: The Babylonian Tablets Speak Today. Edward Chiera. Ed. by George G. Cameron. LC 38-27631. (Illus.). 1956. pap. 9.95 (ISBN 0-226-10425-7, P2, Phoen). U of Chicago Pr.

They'll Never Make a Movie Starring Me. Alice Bach. LC 72-12240. 208p. (gr. 7 up). 1973. 12.89 (ISBN 0-06-020323-4). HarpJ.

They'll Outgrow It & Other Myths. Leah Yarrow. LC 86-50458. (Illus.). 104p. 1986. pap. 7.95 (ISBN 0-933149-07-7). Woodbine House.

They're All Dead Aren't They. Joy Swift. 217p. 1987. 13.95 (ISBN 0-8163-0684-2). Pacific Pr Pub Assn.

They're Never Too Young for Books: Literature for Pre-Schoolers. Edythe M. McGovern. LC 80-80216. 294p. (Orig.). 1980. pap. 10.00 (ISBN 0-9604064-0-9). Mar Vista.

They're Not Heavy - They're Our Future. Ted Stetzinger. LC 87-42913. 170p. 1988. 10.95 (ISBN 1-55523-120-9). Winston-Derek.

They're Off. Anne Alcock. (Illus.). 1979. 18.95 (ISBN 0-85131-299-3, BL187, Pub. by J A Allen U K). S R Smith Sporting Bks.

They're Playing My Game. Hank Stramm & Lou Sahadi. 1987. pap. 3.50 (ISBN 0-312-90748-6). St Martin.

They're Playing My Game: An Autobiography of NFL Coach Hank Stram. Hank Stram & Lou Sahadi. LC 86-12527. 224p. 1986. 14.95 (ISBN 0-688-06080-3). Morrow.

They're Playing Our Secret. Dianna Booher. (YA) (gr. 7 up). 1988. pap. 5.95 (ISBN 0-317-68096-X). Revell.

They're Playing Our Song. Neil Simon. 1980. 9.95 (ISBN 0-394-51069-0). Random.

They're Playing Our Song. Max Wilk. (Illus.). 320p. 1986. 24.95 (ISBN 0-918432-79-0). NY Zoetrope.

They're Rioting in Room Thirty-Two. Janice Harrell. (Crosswinds Ser.). pap. 2.25 (ISBN 0-373-88009-X). Harlequin Bks.

They've Discovered a Head in the Box for the Bread & Other Laughable Limericks. Ed. by John E. Brewton & Lorraine A. Blackburn. LC 77-26598. (Illus.). (gr. 3-7). 1978. (Crowell Jr Bks); PLB 12.89 (ISBN 0-690-03883-6). HarpJ.

Thiagaraja: A Great Musician Saint. M. S. Aiyar. 238p. 1986. Repr. 20.00X (ISBN 0-8364-1766-6, Pub. by Usha). South Asia Bks.

Thiamin Pyrophosphate Biochemistry, 2 vols. Ed. by A. Schellenberger & R. L. Showen. 1988. Vol. I, 176 pgs. 95.00 (ISBN 0-8493-4682-7, 4682); Vol. II, 192 pgs. 99.50 (ISBN 0-8493-4683-5, 4683). CRC Pr.

Thiamin: Twenty Years of Progress, Vol. 378. Ed. by Henry Z. Sable & Clark J. Gubler. 472p. 1982. 102.00x (ISBN 0-89766-145-1); pap. 102.00x (ISBN 0-89766-146-X). NY Acad Sci.

Thiamine. Ed. by Clark J. Gubler et al. LC 75-29485. pap. 100.80 (ISBN 0-317-28657-9, 2055087). Bks Demand UMI.

Thian Ti Hwui: The Hung-League. Gustave Schlegel. LC 73-12558. (Illus.). Repr. of 1866 ed. 26.00. AMS Pr.

Thin Layer Chromatography. R. J. Hamilton. (Analytical Chemistry by Open Learning Ser.). 200p. 1987. pap. 19.95 (ISBN 0-471-91377-4). Wiley.

Thin Layer Chromatography: A Practical Laboratory Handbook. A. A. Akhrem & A. I. Kuznetsova. 136p. 1965. text ed. 29.00x (ISBN 0-7065-0585-9, Pub. by Keter Pub Jerusalem). Coronet Bks.

Thin Layer Chromatography: Quantitative Environmental & Clinical Applications. Ed. by Joseph C. Touchstone & Dexter Rogers. LC 80-36871. 561p. 1980. 78.00x (ISBN 0-471-07958-8, Pub. by Wiley-Interscience). Wiley.

Thin-Layer Chromatography with Flame Ionization Detection. M. Ranny. 1986. lib. bdg. 54.00 (ISBN 90-277-1973-X, Pub. by Reidel Holland). Kluwer Academic.

Thin Liquid Film Phenomena. Ed. by William B. Krantz et al. LC 86-32069. (Symposium Ser.: Vol. 82, No. 252). 194p. 1986. pap. 46.00 (ISBN 0-8169-0394-8). Am Inst Chem Eng.

Thin Liquid Films. Ivanov. (Surfactant Science Ser.). 1160p. 1987. 195.00 (ISBN 0-8247-7763-8). Dekker.

Thin Man. Dashiell Hammett. 192p. 1972. pap. 2.95 (ISBN 0-394-71774-0, Vin). Random.

Thin Metal Films & Gas Chemisorption. Ed. by P. Wissman. (Studies in Surface Science & Catalysis: No. 32). 538p. 1987. 173.75 (ISBN 0-444-42800-3). Elsevier.

Thin Mountain Air. Paul Horgan. 336p. 1977. 10.00 (ISBN 0-374-27466-5). FS&G.

Thin Needle Aspiration Biopsy. William J. Frable. (Major Problems in Pathology: Vol. 14). (Illus.). 384p. 1983. 73.00 (ISBN 0-7216-3835-X). Saunders.

Thin Plan. Michael D. LeBow. LC 87-35282. (Illus.). 184p. (Orig.). 1988. pap. 9.95 (ISBN 0-87322-927-4, LLEB9027, Pub. by Life Enhancement). Human Kinetics.

Thin Plate Design for In-Plane Loading. D. G. Williams & B. Aalami. LC 79-17855. (Constrado Monographs). 210p. 1980. 62.95x (ISBN 0-470-26834-4). Halsted Pr.

Thin Plate Working, Vol. 1. 2nd ed. Ed. by H. Dickson et al. (Illus.). 1977. 37.50x (ISBN 0-686-65561-3) (ISBN 0-85083-387-6). Trans-Atl Phila.

Thin Plate Working, Vol. 2. Ed. by H. Dickson et al. (Engineering Craftsmen: No. D22). (Illus.). 1969. spiral bdg. 37.50x. Trans-Atl Phila.

Thin Plate Working One. 50.00x (ISBN 0-85083-156-3, Pub. by Engineering Ind). State Mutual Bk.

Thin Plate Working Two. 50.00x (Pub. by Engineering Ind). State Mutual Bk.

Thin Red Line. James Jones. 1962. lib. bdg. 30.00x (ISBN 0-684-15555-9, ScribT). Scribner.

Thin Reinforced Concrete Shells: Special Analysis Problems. Victor Gioncu. LC 78-10388. 500p. 1980. 96.95x (ISBN 0-471-99735-8). Wiley.

Thin Scars - Purple Leaves. Lise Couchot. (Rockbook Ser.: No. 10). 24p. (Orig.). 1981. pap. 3.00 (ISBN 0-930012-40-2). J Mudfoot.

Thin Seam Coal Mining Technology. J. Clark et al. LC 82-7968. (Energy Tech. Rev. 80). (Illus.). 385p. 1983. 36.00 (ISBN 0-8155-0909-X). Noyes.

Thin Sets in Harmonic Analysis. L. A. Lindahl & F. Poulsen. (Lecture Notes in Pure & Applied Mathematics Ser.: Vol. 2). 1971. 45.00 (ISBN 0-8247-1317-6). Dekker.

Thin Shell Theory: New Trends & Applications. Ed. by W. Olszak. (CISM Courses & Lectures Ser.: Vol. 240). (Illus.). 301p. 1980. pap. 28.00 (ISBN 0-387-81602-X). Springer-Verlag.

Thin Shells: Computing & Theory. J. E. Gibson. (International Series in Structure & Solid Body Mechanics). (Illus.). 1980. 63.00 (ISBN 0-08-023275-2); pap. 22.00 (ISBN 0-08-024204-9). Pergamon.

Thin Thighs in Thirty Days. Wendy Stehling. 1982. pap. 3.50 (ISBN 0-553-34309-2). Bantam.

Thin Thighs in Thirty Years. Cathy Guisewite. (Illus.). 128p. (Orig.). 1986. pap. 6.95 (ISBN 0-8362-2081-1). Andrews & McMeel.

Thin Volume of Hate. Leslie Bottorff. 1973. pap. 2.95 (ISBN 0-913270-15-6). Sunstone Pr.

Thin Walled Steel Structures. Ed. by K. C. Rockey & H. V. Hill. 608p. 1969. 205.00 (ISBN 0-677-61270-2). Gordon & Breach.

Thin-Walled Structures. Ed. by J. Rhodes & A. C. Walker. 796p. 1980. 74.95x (ISBN 0-470-26906-5). Halsted Pr.

Thin White Line. Rayanne Moore. (American Romance Ser.). 192p. 1983. pap. 2.25 (ISBN 0-373-16008-9). Harlequin Bks.

Thin Wing in a Compressible Flow. E. A. Krasilshchikova. Tr. by G. Leib from Rus. 248p. 1983. 55.00x (ISBN 0-306-10972-7, Consultants). Plenum Pub.

Thin Within. Judy Wardwell. 1986. pap. 4.50 (ISBN 0-671-61906-3). PB.

Thin Within: How to Eat & Live Like a Thin Person. Judy Wardell & Barbara Austin. 272p. 1985. 14.95 (ISBN 0-517-55687-1, Harmony). Crown.

Thin Woman. Dorothy Cannell. (Crime Monthly Ser.). 256p. 1985. pap. 3.95 (ISBN 0-14-007947-5). Penguin.

Thine Enemy. Ralph W. Neighbour, Sr. 1986. pap. 5.95 (ISBN 0-937931-06-3). Global TN.

Thine Health. Nicholas C. Eliopoulos. Ed. by Nicholas G. Phystiklakis. (Orig.). 1980. 18.00x (ISBN 0-9605396-2-X). Eliopoulos.

Thine Is the Kingdom. Heini Arnold. 36p. 1985. pap. 1.50 (ISBN 0-87486-182-9). Plough.

Thine Is the Kingdom. Paul Marshall. 160p. 1986. pap. 7.95 (ISBN 0-8028-0174-9). Eerdmans.

Thing. Robin Klein. (Illus.). 32p. (ps-6). 1987. 10.95 (ISBN 0-19-554330-0); pap. 4.95 (ISBN 0-19-554549-4). Oxford U Pr.

Thing & the Fantastic Four in One Thing after Another. Warren Spector. LC 86-91540. (Marvel Super Heores Adventure Gamebook: No. 5). 192p. (Orig.). 1987. pap. 2.95 (ISBN 0-88038-436-0). TSR Inc.

Thing at the Foot of the Bed. Maria Leach. 112p. (gr. 4-5). 1981. pap. 2.75 (ISBN 0-440-48773-0, YB). Dell.

Thing at the Foot of the Bed. Maria Leach. LC 59-6658. (Illus.). 128p. (gr. 3-5). 1987. PLB 12.95 (ISBN 0-399-21496-8, Philomel). Putnam Pub Group.

Thing from the Lake. Eleanor M. Ingram. Ed. by R. Reginald & Douglas Menville. LC 75-46281. (Supernatural & Occult Fiction Ser.). 1976. Repr. of 1921 ed. lib. bdg. 24.50x (ISBN 0-405-08140-5). Ayer Co Pubs.

Thing in Kat's Attic. Charlotte T. Graeber. LC 84-8117. (Illus.). 80p. (gr. 1-4). 1984. 9.95 (ISBN 0-525-44146-8). Dutton.

Thing in the Swamp & More Not-So-Scary. William E. Warren & Edward Frascino. LC 84-6769. (Illus.). 96p. (gr. 3-7). 1984. 10.95 (ISBN 0-13-917196-7). P-H.

Thing King. Charles E. Eaton. 104p. 1982. 9.95 (ISBN 0-8453-4743-8, Cornwall Bks). Assoc Univ Prs.

Thing of Beauty: Art Nouveau, Art Deco, Arts & Crafts Movement, & Aesthetic Movement Objects in Atlanta Collections. Roy Frangiamore & James Grady. Ed. by Kelly Morris. (Illus.). 91p. 1980. pap. 10.50 (ISBN 0-939802-04-X). High Mus Art.

Thing You Love Most. Wade G. Harding. 192p. 1987. 11.95 (ISBN 0-8062-3084-3). Carlton.

Thingnapped! Robin Klein. (Illus.). 32p. (ps-6). 1987. 10.95 (ISBN 0-19-554574-5); pap. 4.95 (ISBN 0-19-554784-5). Oxford U Pr.

Things. Sandy Larsen. 144p. 1984. pap. 4.50 (ISBN 0-88207-109-2). Victor Bks.

Things. (Learning Science Program Ser.). (gr. 1). 4.80 (ISBN 0-02-656250-2); tchr's annotated ed. 8.25 (ISBN 0-02-656260-X). Benziger Pub Co.

Thing's Ain't What They Used to Be. Al Young. LC 87-71146. 256p. (Orig.). 1987. pap. 8.95 (ISBN 0-88739-024-2). Creative Arts Bk.

Things & Ideals. Max C. Otto. 1924. 18.00 (ISBN 0-527-68800-2). Kraus Repr.

Things & Words. Fred Justus. (Early Education Ser.). 24p. (ps-1). 1978. wkbk. 5.00 (ISBN 0-8209-0203-9, K-5). ESP.

Things Are Seldom What They Seem. Sandy Asher. LC 82-72819. 144p. (gr. 7up). 1983. pap. 11.95 (ISBN 0-385-29250-3). Delacorte.

Things Are Seldom What They Seem or Local Sculptors - Found Materials. Katy Kline. (Illus.). 10p. (Orig.). 1986. pap. 1.00 (ISBN 0-938437-16-X). MIT List Visual Arts.

Things Around Us. Fred Justus. (Science Ser.). 24p. (ps). 1975. wkbk. 5.00 (ISBN 0-8209-0138-5, S-R). ESP.

Things at Home. Humberstone. (Let's Find Out about... Ser.). (gr. 2-5). 1981. 6.95 (ISBN 0-86020-502-9, Usborne-Hayes); PLB 11.96 (ISBN 0-88110-021-8); pap. 2.95 (ISBN 0-86020-501-0). EDC.

Things Change. David Mamet & Shel Silverstein. (Illus.). 64p. 1988. pap. 7.95 (ISBN 0-8021-3047-X). Grove.

Things Chinese: Or Notes Connected with China. rev. 5th ed. J. Dyer Ball. Ed. by Chalmers Werner. LC 74-164085. (Tower Bks). 772p. 1971. Repr. of 1926 ed. 56.00x (ISBN 0-8103-3917-X). Gale.

Things Chinese: Or Notes Connected with China. James D. Ball. lib. bdg. 79.95 (ISBN 0-87968-476-3). Krishna Pr.

Things Common, Properly: Selected Poems, 1942 to 1982. Peter Whigham. Ed. by Peter Jay. (Literary Ser.). 220p. 1984. 20.00 (ISBN 0-933806-21-3). Black Swan CT.

Things Divine & Supernatural Conceived by Analogy with Things Natural & Human. Peter Browne. Ed. by Rene Wellek. LC 75-11203. (British Philosophers & Theologians of the 17th & 18th Centuries: Vol. 9). 1976. Repr. of 1733 ed. lib. bdg. 51.00 (ISBN 0-8240-1758-7). Garland Pub.

Things Fall Apart. Chinua Achebe. LC 59-7114. 1959. 12.95 (ISBN 0-8392-1113-9); pap. 7.95 (ISBN 0-8392-5006-1). Astor-Honor.

Things Fall Apart. Chinua Achebe. 1985. pap. 2.95 (ISBN 0-449-20810-9, Crest). Fawcett.

Things Fall Apart. Chinua Achebe. (African Writers Ser.). pap. 4.00 (ISBN 0-435-90001-3). Heinemann Ed.

Things for Kids to Do. Thelma Griffhorn. 132p. 1985. pap. 6.95 (ISBN 0-89693-525-6). Victor Bks.

Things: Four Metabletic Reflections. J. H. Vandenberg. LC 74-125033. 140p. 1970. pap. text ed. 10.00 (ISBN 0-8207-0192-0). Duquesne.

Things Hidden since the Foundation of the World. Rene Girard. Tr. by Stephen Bann & Michael Metteer. LC 86-63637. 448p. (Eng.). 1987. text ed. 30.00x (ISBN 0-8047-1403-7). Stanford U Pr.

Things Hunting Men. Ed. by David Drake. (Starhunters Ser.: Vol. II). 320p. (Orig.). 1988. pap. 3.50 (ISBN 0-671-65412-8). Baen Bks.

Things I Can Do. Patricia Mahany. (Little Happy Day Bks.). (Illus.). 24p. (ps-2). 1985. 0.49 (ISBN 0-87239-938-9, 2194). Standard Pub.

Things I Can Do Myself. Craig J. Lovik. (Christian Self-Discovery Ser.). (Illus.). (ps). 1987. pap. 2.25 (ISBN 0-570-09111-X, 56-1586). Concordia.

Things I Did... & Things I Think I Did. Jean Negulesco. 305p. 1984. 18.95 (ISBN 0-671-50734-6, Linden Pr). S&S.

Things I Did for Love. Ellen Conford. 160p. (YA) (gr. 7-12). 1987. 13.95 (ISBN 0-553-05431-7). Bantam.

Things I Did for Love. Ellen Conford. 144p. (YA) 1988. pap. 2.95 (ISBN 0-553-27374-4, Starfire). Bantam.

Things I Hate! Harriet Wittels & Joan Greisman. LC 73-11053. (Illus.). 32p. (ps-3). 1973. 13.95 (ISBN 0-87705-096-1). Human Sci Pr.

Things I Have Learned: Chapel Talks. Bob Jones, Sr. 224p. 1944. pap. 4.95 (ISBN 0-89084-022-9). Bob Jones Univ Pr.

Things I Learned After It Was Too Late: (& Other Minor Truths) Charles M. Schulz. (Illus.). 1981. pap. 6.95 (ISBN 0-03-059264-X). H Holt & Co.

Things I Like to Do. Harry Bornstein. (Signed English Ser.). 18p. 1974. pap. 3.50 (ISBN 0-913580-41-4, Clerc Bks). Gallaudet Univ Pr.

Things I Like to Do. (Super Chubby Board Bks.). (ps-1). 1985. 4.95 (ISBN 0-671-54735-6, Little Simon). S&S.

Things I Like to Eat. Zokeisha. (Chubby Board Bks.). (Illus.). 16p. (ps-k). 1981. 2.95 (ISBN 0-671-44449-2, Little Simon). S&S.

Things I Like to Look At. Zokeisha. (Chubby Board Bks.). (Illus.). 16p. (ps-k). 1981. 2.95 (ISBN 0-671-44451-4, Little Simon). S&S.

Things I Like to Play With. Zokeisha. (Chubby Board Bks.). (Illus.). 16p. (ps-k). 1981. 2.95 (ISBN 0-671-44450-6, Little Simon). S&S.

Things I Like to Wear. Zokeisha. (Chubby Board Bks.). (Illus.). 16p. (ps-k). 1981. board 2.95 (ISBN 0-671-44452-2, Little Simon). S&S.

Things I Love the Most. B. Rosenkrans. (Poke & Look Bks.). (Illus.). 24p. (gr. k-1). 1985. 6.95 (ISBN 0-448-01458-0, G&D). Putnam Pub Group.

Things I Meant to Say to You When We Were Old. Merrit Malloy. LC 76-26353. 144p. 1977. pap. 8.95 (ISBN 0-385-12326-4, Dolp). Doubleday.

Things I Remember. facsimile ed. Frederick T. Martin. LC 75-1859. (Leisure Class in America Ser.). (Illus.). 1975. Repr. of 1913 ed. 19.00x (ISBN 0-405-06925-1). Ayer Co Pubs.

Things I Want, Poems for Two Children. John M. Shaw. 1967. 5.00 (ISBN 0-9607778-7-3). Friends Fla St.

Things in Loops & Knots I Pick from the Ground Become a Small Italian Opera. Coco Gordon. (Intimate Ser.: No. 1). (Illus.). 88p. (Orig.). 1987. pap. 25.00 (ISBN 0-943375-00-2). W Space.

Things in Mouldy Manor. Keith Moseley. (Spooky Pop-Ups Ser.). (gr. 2 up). 1988. 7.95 (ISBN 0-448-09289-1, G&D). Putnam Pub Group.

Things in My House. Elisabeth Ivanovsky. (Picture-Word Boards Bks.). (Illus.). (ps). 1985. bds. 3.98 (ISBN 0-517-47341-0). Outlet Bk Co.

Things in Place. Jerry Bumpus. LC 75-10744. 141p. 1975. pap. 5.95 (ISBN 0-914590-15-4). Fiction Coll.

Things in Revolt. Lev Lunts. Intro. by & tr. by Gary Kern. 228p. 1987. 25.00 (ISBN 0-88233-924-9). Ardis Pubs.

Things in the Saddle. facs. ed. George Norlin. LC 74-80393. (Essay Index Reprint Ser). 1940. 17.50 (ISBN 0-8369-1047-8). Ayer Co Pubs.

Things in This Mirror Are Closer Than They Seem. Charles W. Darling. LC 86-5127. 20p. (Orig.). 1986. pap. 4.00 (ISBN 0-916897-08-7). Andrew Mtn Pr.

Things Invisible to See. Nancy Willard. LC 84-47892. 263p. 1985. 16.45 (ISBN 0-394-54058-1). Knopf.

Things I've Had to Learn Over & Over & Over (Plus a Few Minor Discoveries) Charles M. Schulz. (Illus.). 128p. 1984. 7.95 (ISBN 0-03-000742-9). H Holt & Co.

Things Japanese in Hawaii. John DeFrancis. (Illus.). 224p. 1973. pap. 9.50 (ISBN 0-8248-0233-0). UH Pr.

Things Not Generally Known. J. Timbs. lib. bdg. 59.95 (ISBN 0-8490-1193-0). Gordon Pr.

Things Not Generally Known. John Timbs. Ed. by David A. Wells. LC 68-30584. 432p. 1968. Repr. of 1857 ed. 48.00x (ISBN 0-8103-3101-2). Gale.

Things of the Mind: Dialogues with J. Krishnamurti. Ed. by Brij B. Khare. LC 84-11334. 199p. 1985. 14.95 (ISBN 0-8022-2470-9). Philos Lib.

Things of Worth. Edward C. Spruill. Compiled by Jean Harrison. (Illus.). 102p. (Orig.). 1983. pap. 4.95 (ISBN 0-937594-04-0). Bunkhouse.

Things Outdoors. Eliot Humberstone. (Let's Find Out about... Ser.). (gr. 2-5). 1981. 6.95 (ISBN 0-86020-465-0, Usborne-Hayes); PLB 11.96 (ISBN 0-88110-019-6); pap. 2.95 (ISBN 0-86020-464-2). EDC.

Things Past. Michael Sadleir. 1973. Repr. of 1944 ed. 25.00 (ISBN 0-8274-0929-X). R West.

Things People Do. Anne Civardi. (Illus.). 38p. (ps-4). 1986. 10.95 (ISBN 0-86020-864-8, Pub. by Usborne); PLB 12.96 (ISBN 0-88110-236-9). EDC.

Things Seen & Heard. facs. ed. Edgar J. Goodspeed. LC 68-29208. (Essay Index Reprint Ser). 1968. Repr. of 1925 ed. 17.00 (ISBN 0-8369-0484-2). Ayer Co Pubs.

Things Seen & Unseen: Discourse & Ideology in Tokugawa Nativism. Harry Harootunian. 488p. 1988. 40.00x (ISBN 0-226-31706-4); pap. 14.95x (ISBN 0-226-31707-2, Chicago Original Paperback). U of Chicago Pr.

Things Seen on the Riviera. Leslie Richardson. Repr. of 1924 ed. 20.00. Darby Bks.

Things: Selected Writings of Francis Ponge. Francis Ponge. Tr. by Cid Corman from Fr. 1986. 7.50 (ISBN 0-934834-70-9). White Pine.

Things Stirring Together or Far Away. Larry Eigner. LC 73-23121. 120p. (Orig.). 1974. pap. 5.00 (ISBN 0-87685-187-1). Black Sparrow.

Things That Accompany Salvation. R. K. Campbell. 40p. pap. 0.45 (ISBN 0-88172-013-5). Believers Bkshelf.

Things That Are: Poems. Alice Raphael. 1969. 4.95 (ISBN 0-8079-0155-5); pap. 1.95 (ISBN 0-8079-0156-3). October.

Things That Divide Us. Ed. by Faith Conlon et al. LC 85-8290. 191p. (Orig.). 1985. pap. 8.95 (ISBN 0-931188-32-6). Seal Pr Feminist.

Things That Fly. Myron Turner. LC 77-88694. vi, 61p. 1978. 7.95 (ISBN 0-8040-0783-7, Pub by Swallow); pap. 4.95 (ISBN 0-8040-0826-4). Ohio U Pr.

Things That Go. Humberstone. (Let's Find out about... Ser.). (gr. 2-5). 1981. 6.95 (ISBN 0-86020-500-2, Usborne-Hayes); PLB 11.96 (ISBN 0-88110-020-X); pap. 2.95 (ISBN 0-86020-493-6). EDC.

Things That Go. Illus. by Tadasu Izawa. (My First Puppet Picture Bks.). (Illus.). 48p. (ps-1). 1984. 4.95 (ISBN 0-448-09776-1, G&D). Putnam Pub Group.

Things That Go. Anne Rockwell. LC 86-6199. (ps-1). 1986. 10.95 (ISBN 0-525-44266-9). Dutton.

Things That Go. Huck Scarry. (ps-1). 1986. 3.98 (616556). Outlet Bk Co.

Things That Go. Richard Scarry. (Golden Look-Look Bks.). (Illus.). 24p. (ps-3). 1987. 1.50 (ISBN 0-307-11817-7, Pub. by Golden Bks). Western Pub.

Things That Go. Richard Scarry. (Golden Story Book 'n' Tape Ser.). (Illus.). 24p. (Orig.). (ps-3). 1988. pap. 5.45 (ISBN 0-307-13965-4). Western Pub.

Things That Go. (Platt & Munk Peggy Cloth Bks.). (Illus.). 8p. (ps). 1978. 2.50 (ISBN 0-448-46809-3, G&D). Putnam Pub Group.

Things That Go: A First-Look-It-Up Book. (Learning Curves Bks.). (Illus.). 12p. (ps-1). 1987. 5.95 (ISBN 0-553-18358-3). Bantam.

Things That Go Board Shape Book. (Board Shape Bks.). (Illus.). (ps). 1985. bds. 1.69 (ISBN 0-517-46322-9). Outlet Bk Co.

Things That Go Bump in the Flight: A Reassuring Guide to Air Travel. Robert Welch. LC 87-1418. (Illus.). 156p. (Orig.). 1987. pap. 5.95 (ISBN 0-932620-75-2). Betterway Pubns.

Things That Go "Bump" in the Night. A. E. Florence. LC 87-80367. (Illus.). 64p. 1987. pap. 3.95 (ISBN 0-943512-11-5, FL/67). Linwood Pub.

Things That Go Bump in the Night. Louis C. Jones. (York State Bks.). (Illus.). 220p. 1983. pap. 9.95 (ISBN 0-8156-0184-0). Syracuse U Pr.

Things That Go Bump in the Night. Louis C. Jones. 16.95 (ISBN 0-89190-627-4, Pub. by Am Repr). Amereon Ltd.

Things That Go Bump in the Night, & Other Fears. Bob Donahue & Marilyn Donahue. (YA) (gr. 7 up). 1983. pap. 3.95 (ISBN 0-8423-7083-8). Tyndale.

Things That Go Fast. Elizabeth Spires. (Illus.). 12p. (ps-3). 1982. pap. 2.95 (ISBN 0-89954-201-8). Antioch Pub Co.

Things That Go! How to Make Toy Boats, Cars, & Planes. Judith Conaway. LC 86-7130. (Illus.). 48p. (gr. 1-5). 1987. PLB 9.49 (ISBN 0-8167-0838-X); pap. text ed. 1.95 (ISBN 0-8167-0839-8). Troll Assocs.

Things That Happen. J. E. Tiles. Ed. by Andrew Brennan & William E. Lyons. (Scots Philosophical Monograph: Vol. 1). (Illus.). 157p. 1981. 12.50 (ISBN 0-08-025724-0). Pergamon.

Things That Happen. J. E. Tiles. (Scots Philosophical Monographs). 132p. 1981. text ed. 25.00x (Pub by Aberdeen U Scotland). Humanities.

Things That Happen Where There Aren't Any People. William Stafford. (American Poets Continuum Ser.: No. 6). 10.00 (ISBN 0-918526-19-1); pap. 6.95 (ISBN 0-918526-20-5). Boa Edns.

Things That Have Interested Me: First Series. Arnold Bennett. LC 74-17049. (Collected Works of Arnold Bennett: Vol. 80). 1976. Repr. of 1921 ed. 27.50 (ISBN 0-518-19161-3, 19161). Ayer Co Pubs.

Things That Have Interested Me: Second Series. Arnold Bennett. LC 74-17091. (Collected Works of Arnold Bennett: Vol. 81). 1976. Repr. of 1923 ed. 24.25 (ISBN 0-518-19162-1). Ayer Co Pubs.

TITLE INDEX THINK TANK.

Things That Have Interested Me: Third Series. Arnold Bennett. LC 74-17074. (Collected Works of Arnold Bennett: Vol. 82). 1976. Repr. of 1926 ed. 22.75 (ISBN 0-518-19163-X). Ayer Co Pubs.

Things That Make for Peace: Biblical Meditations. Barbara Gerlach. (Illus.). 64p. (Orig.). 1983. pap. 4.95 (ISBN 0-8298-0664-4). Pilgrim NY.

Things That Matter. Hiasaura Rubenstein & Mary H. Block. 1982. text ed. write for info. (ISBN 0-02-404180-7). Macmillan.

Things That Move. (First Words Sticker Bks.). 24p. (ps-k). 1988. pap. 2.95 (ISBN 0-8249-8285-1). Ideals.

Things That Sail. Huck Scarry. (ps-1). 1986. 3.98 (616564). Outlet Bk Co.

Things That Stings. Catherine A. Kirsch. (Illus.). 1978. 20.00 (ISBN 0-916750-66-3). Dayton Labs.

Things That Surround Us. Muska Nagel. Ed. by Constance Hunting. 68p. (Orig.). 1987. pap. 8.95 (ISBN 0-913006-39-4). Puckerbrush.

Things the Baptism in the Holy Spirit Will Do for You. Alice Shevkenek. 1976. pap. 1.00 (ISBN 0-89350-005-4). Fountain Pr.

Things the Manual Never Told You: Tips, Techniques, & Shortcuts from the Nation's Largest User Group. Compiled by Boston Computer Society Staff. Date not set. write for info. Addison-Wesley.

Things They Say Behind Your Back: Stereotypes & the Myths Behind Them. William B. Helmreich. 276p. 1983. pap. 14.95 (ISBN 0-87855-953-1). Transaction Bks.

Things to Come. Foster Bailey. 1974. pap. 6.00 (ISBN 0-85330-129-8). Lucis.

Things to Come. John M. Murry. LC 70-93364. (Essay Index Reprint Ser). 1928. 19.00 (ISBN 0-8369-1337-X). Ayer Co Pubs.

Things to Come. John M. Murry. 318p. 1984. Repr. of 1938 ed. lib. bdg. 35.00 (ISBN 0-89984-751-X). Century Bookbindery.

Things to Come. J. Dwight Pentecost. 1958. 20.95 (ISBN 0-310-30890-9, 6355, Pub by Dunhan). Zondervan.

Things to Come: An Illustrated History of the Science Fiction Film. Douglas A. Menville & R. Reginald. LC 83-8789. 212p. 1983. Repr. of 1977 ed. lib. bdg. 19.95x (ISBN 0-89370-019-3). Borgo Pr.

Things to Come & Go: Three Stories. Bette Howland. LC 82-48724. 192p. 1983. 11.45 (ISBN 0-394-53032-2). Knopf.

Things to Come: The World Food Crisis. 47p. 1974. pap. 5.75 (ISBN 0-686-92721-4, F460, FAO). UNIPUB.

Things to Count. (Platt & Munk Peggy Cloth Bks.). (Illus.). 8p. (ps). 1978. 2.50 (ISBN 0-448-46808-5, G&D). Putnam Pub Group.

Things to Do in Fort Wayne. Robert Novak. 1973. 1.00 (ISBN 0-685-67934-9). Windless Orchard.

Things to Do in Zoobilee Zoo. Jan Carr. (Zoobilee Zoo Ser.). (Illus.). 32p. (ps-3). 1988. pap. 1.95 (ISBN 0-590-42116-6). Scholastic Inc.

Things to Do with Toddlers & Twos. Karen Miller. 9.95 (ISBN 0-910287-04-X). Telshare Pub Co.

Things to Do with Your Apple IIe Computer. Jerry Willis et al. 1983. pap. 3.95 (ISBN 0-451-12848-6, Sig). NAL.

Things to Do with Your Atari Computer. Jerry Willis et al. 1983. pap. 3.95 (ISBN 0-451-12850-8, Sig). NAL.

Things to Do with Your Colecovision Adam. Jerry Willis et al. pap. cancelled (ISBN 0-451-13182-7). Dilithium Pr.

Things to Do with Your Commodore VIC-20 Computer. Jerry Willis et al. pap. 3.95 (ISBN 0-451-12844-3, Sig). NAL.

Things to Do with Your Commodore 64 Computer. Jerry Willis et al. pap. 3.95 (ISBN 0-451-12843-5, Sig). NAL.

Things to Do with Your IBM-PCjr. Jerry Willis et al. pap. cancelled (ISBN 0-451-13183-5). Dilithium Pr.

Things to Do with Your IBM Personal Computer. Jerry Willis et al. 1983. pap. 3.95 (ISBN 0-451-12849-4, Sig). NAL.

Things to Do with Your Osborne Computers. Jerry Willis et al. 1983. pap. 3.95 (ISBN 0-451-12852-4, Sig). NAL.

Things to Do with Your TI 99-4A Computer. Jerry Willis et al. pap. 3.95 (ISBN 0-451-12842-7, Sig). NAL.

Things to Do with Your TRS-80 Color Computer. Jerry Willis et al. 1984. pap. 3.95 (ISBN 0-451-12854-0, Sig). NAL.

Things to Do with Your TRS-80 Model IV Computer. Jerry Willis et al. 1983. pap. 3.95 (ISBN 0-451-12845-1, Sig). NAL.

Things to Do with Your TRS-80 Model 100 Computer. Jerry Willis et al. 1983. pap. 3.95 (ISBN 0-451-12847-8, Sig). NAL.

Things to Know about Death & Dying. LC 84-40835. (Look Before You Leap Ser.). (Illus.). 48p. (gr. 4 up). 1985. 8.96 (ISBN 0-382-06780-0); pap. 4.75 (ISBN 0-382-06969-2). Silver.

Things to Know about Going to the Dentist. Lisa A. Marsoli. LC 84-50439. (Look Before You Leap Ser.). (Illus.). 48p. (gr. 4 up). 1985. 8.96 (ISBN 0-382-06781-9); pap. 4.75 (ISBN 0-382-06961-7). Silver.

Things to Know about Going to the Doctor. Lisa A. Marsoli. LC 84-50447. (Look Before You Leap Ser.). (Illus.). 48p. (gr. 4 up). 1985. 8.96 (ISBN 0-382-06788-6); pap. 4.75 (ISBN 0-382-06967-6). Silver.

Things to Know Before Buying a Bicycle. Joanne Fink. LC 84-50443. (Look Before You Leap Ser.). (Illus.). 48p. (gr. 4 up). 1985. 8.96 (ISBN 0-382-06785-1); pap. 4.75 (ISBN 0-382-06964-1). Silver.

Things to Know Before Going to Camp. Lisa A. Marsoli. LC 84-50446. (Look Before You Leap Ser.). (Illus.). 48p. (gr. 4 up). 1985. 8.96 (ISBN 0-382-06787-8); pap. 4.75 (ISBN 0-382-06966-8). Silver.

Things to Know Before You Babysit. Lisa A. Marsoli. LC 84-50444. (Look Before You Leap Ser.). (Illus.). 48p. (gr. 4 up). 1985. 8.96 (ISBN 0-382-06778-9); pap. 4.75 (ISBN 0-382-06959-5). Silver.

Things to Know Before You Get a Pet. Lisa A. Marsoli. LC 84-50442. (Look Before You Leap Ser.). (Illus.). 48p. (gr. 4 up). 1985. 8.96 (ISBN 0-382-06784-3); pap. 4.75 (ISBN 0-382-06968-4). Silver.

Things to Know Before You Go to the Hospital. Lisa A. Marsoli. LC 84-50440. (Look Before You Leap Ser.). (Illus.). 48p. (gr. 4 up). 1985. 8.96 (ISBN 0-382-06782-7); pap. 4.75 (ISBN 0-382-06962-5). Silver.

Things to Know Before You Move. Lisa A. Marsoli. LC 84-50441. (Look Before You Leap Ser.). (Illus.). 48p. (gr. 4 up). 1985. 8.96 (ISBN 0-382-06783-5); pap. 4.75 (ISBN 0-382-06963-3). Silver.

Things to Know Before You Take a Plane Trip. Lisa A. Marsoli. LC 84-50445. (Look Before You Leap Ser.). (Illus.). 48p. (gr. 4 up). 1985. 8.96 (ISBN 0-382-06779-7); pap. 4.75 (ISBN 0-382-06960-9). Silver.

Things to Love. Richard Scarry. (Golden Look-Look Bks.). (Illus.). 24p. (ps-3). 1987. 1.50 (ISBN 0-307-11818-5, Pub. by Golden Bks). Western Pub.

Things to Make. Peggy R. Greene. LC 77-91652. (Picturebacks Ser.). (Illus.). 32p. (ps-3). 1981. Random.

Things to Make & Do see Child Horizons.

Things to Make & Do for Christmas. Ellen Weiss. (Things to Make & Do Bks.). (gr. k-3). 1980. PLB 10.90 (ISBN 0-531-02293-5, C02); pap. 3.95 (ISBN 0-531-02145-9). Watts.

Things to Make & Do for Halloween. Gail Gibbons. LC 75-19396. (Things to Make & Do Ser.). (Illus.). 48p. (gr. k-2). 1976. PLB 10.90 (ISBN 0-531-01103-8). Watts.

Things to Make & Do for Thanksgiving. (Things to Make & Do Ser.). (gr. 1-3). 1977. lib. bdg. 10.90 (ISBN 0-531-01324-3). Watts.

Things to Make & Do for Valentine's Day. Tomie De Paola. (Illus.). 48p. (gr. k-4). 1985. pap. 1.50 (ISBN 0-590-11821-8). Scholastic Inc.

Things to Make & Do for Valentine's Day. Tomie De Paola. (Things to Make & Do Ser.). (Illus.). 48p. (gr. k-3). 1976. PLB 10.90 (ISBN 0-531-01187-9). Watts.

Things to Make: Arabic. (Ladybird Stories Ser.). (Illus.). 3.50x (ISBN 0-86685-238-7). Intl Bk Ctr.

Things to Play With. Anne Rockwell. LC 87-33399. (Illus.). 24p. (ps-1). 1988. 11.95 (ISBN 0-525-44409-2, 01160-350). Dutton.

Things to Remember, Things to Forget. Susie E. Odor. 168p. 1981. 7.95 (ISBN 0-8059-2809-X). Dorrance.

Things to Think About. Robert A. Logan. 180p. 1982. 10.95 (ISBN 0-8059-2837-5). Dorrance.

Things Unutterable: Paul's Ascent to Paradise in Its Greco-Roman, Judaic & Early Christian Contexts. James Tabor. LC 86-18924. (Studies in Judaism Ser.). 166p. (Orig.). 1986. lib. bdg. 23.50 (ISBN 0-8191-5643-4, Pub. by Studies in Judaism); pap. text ed. 12.25 (ISBN 0-8191-5644-2, Pub. by Studies in Judaism). U Pr of Amer.

Things We Believe. Edwin R. Rodgers. LC 68-27391. 1968. pap. text ed. 1.00 (ISBN 0-910812-02-0). Johnny Reads.

Things We Do for Love. Benjamin M. Schutz. 224p. 1989. 16.95 (ISBN 0-684-18990-9). Scribner.

Things We Know: Fourteen Essays on Problems of Knowledge. Frank B. Ebersole. LC 68-63599. 1968. 7.50 (ISBN 0-87114-016-0). U of Oreg Bks.

Things We Said Today: The Complete Lyrics & a Concordance to the Beatles' Songs, 1960-1970. Colin Campbell & Allan Murphy. LC 80-83203. (Rock & Roll Reference Ser.: No. 4). (Illus.). 430p. 1980. 39.50 (ISBN 0-87650-104-8). Pierian.

Things Which Are Done in Secret. Marlene Dixon. 296p. 1976. 19.95 (ISBN 0-919618-68-5, Dist by U of Toronto Pr); pap. 9.95 (ISBN 0-919618-92-8, Dist. by U of Toronto Pr). Black Rose Bks.

Things Which Become Sound Doctrine. J. Dwight Pentecost. 1970. Repr. 7.95 (ISBN 0-310-30901-8, 6504P). Zondervan.

Things Which Son Must Come to Pass: Commentary on Revelation. Philip Mauro. 1984. Repr. 16.95 (ISBN 0-317-11813-7). Reiner.

Things You Can Make for Children. Sunset Editors. LC 86-80872. 1986. 14.95 (ISBN 0-376-01681-7, Sunset Bks). Sunset-Lane.

Thingumajig Book of Do's & Don'ts. Irene Keller. (Illus.). 32p. (Orig.). (gr. k-6). 1983. 3.95 (ISBN 0-8249-8050-6). Ideals.

Thingumajig Book of Do's & Don'ts. Irene Keller. (Ideals Read Aloud Storybks). (Illus.). 32p. (gr. k-4). 1983. PLB 11.93 (ISBN 0-516-09158-1). Childrens.

Thingumajig Book of Health & Safety. Irene Keller. (Ideals Read Aloud Storybooks Ser.). (Illus.). (gr. k-4). 1982. PLB 11.93 (ISBN 0-516-09156-5). Childrens.

Thingumajig Book of Health & Safety. 32p. (gr. k-6). 1982. pap. 3.95 (ISBN 0-8249-8031-X). Ideals.

Thingumajig Book of Manners. Irene Keller. (Ideals Read Aloud Storybooks Ser.). (Illus.). 32p. (gr. k-4). 1981. PLB 11.93 (ISBN 0-516-09155-7). Childrens.

Thingumajig Book of Manners. Irene Keller. (Illus.). 32p. (gr. k-6). 1981. 3.95 (ISBN 0-8249-8010-7). Ideals.

Thingumajig Christmas. Irene Keeler. (Illus.). (gr. k-4). 1982. PLB 11.93 (ISBN 0-516-09157-3). Childrens.

Thinis. Patricia. (Illus.). 330p. (Orig.). 1980. sprial bdg. 7.95 (ISBN 0-935146-12-1). Morningland.

Think. Robert Anthony. 480p. 1987. pap. 2.95 (ISBN 0-425-08747-6). Berkley Pub.

Think. 2nd ed. Gerard P. Weber et al. (Word Is Life Ser.). (gr. 7). 1979. 3.60 (ISBN 0-02-658700-9); tchrs. ed. 8.00 (ISBN 0-02-658710-6); family handbook 0.64 (ISBN 0-02-658750-5). Benziger Pub Co.

Think about Floating & Sinking. Henry Pluckrose. (Think about Ser.). (Illus.). (gr. k-3). 1987. PLB 10.90 (ISBN 0-531-10294-7). Watts.

Think about It! Ruth I. Dowell. (Illus.). 36p. (Orig.). (ps-6). 1986. pap. text ed. 3.00 (ISBN 0-945842-04-X). Pollyanna Prodns.

Think about It! Kindergarten. Imogene Forte. (Illus.). 80p. (ps-k). 1981. pap. text ed. 6.95 (ISBN 0-913916-96-X, IP-96X). Incentive Pubn.

Think about It! Middle Grades. Imogene Forte. (Illus.). 80p. (gr. 4-6). 1981. pap. text ed. 6.95 (ISBN 0-913916-98-6, IP 98-6). Incentive Pubn.

Think about It! Primary. Imogene Forte. (Illus.). 80p. (gr. 1-3). 1981. pap. text ed. 6.95 (ISBN 0-913916-97-8, IP 97-8). Incentive Pubn.

Think about It Tomorrow, Snoopy. Charles M. Schulz. 1983. pap. 1.95 (ISBN 0-449-20454-5, Crest). Fawcett.

Think about It, You Might Learn Something. Robyn Supraner. LC 73-8752. (Illus.). 112p. (gr. 3-7). 1973. 9.95 (ISBN 0-395-17707-3). HM.

Think About Nuclear Arms Control: Understanding the Arms Race. Richard Smoke. (Think Ser.). (Illus.). 178p. 1988. PLB 14.85 (ISBN 0-8027-6761-3); pap. 5.95 (ISBN 0-8027-6762-1). Walker & Co.

Think Again. Robert Anthony. 480p. 1987. pap. 2.95 (ISBN 0-425-09572-X). Berkley Pub.

Think Aloud: Increasing Social & Cognitive Skills--A Problem-Solving Program for Children (Primary Level) Bonnie W. Camp & Mary A. Bash. LC 81-51871. (Illus.). 296p. 1981. 3-ring binder 49.95 (ISBN 0-87822-254-5, 2545). Res Press.

Think Aloud: Increasing Social & Cognitive Skills-A Problem-Solving Program for Children, Classroom Program, Grades 5 & 6. Mary Ann S. Bash & Bonnie W. Camp. LC 85-61577. (Illus.). 285p. 1985. pap. 35.95 (ISBN 0-87822-242-1). Res Press.

Think Aloud: Increasing Social & Cognitive Skills-A Problem-Solving Program for Children, Classroom Program, Grades 3 & 4. Mary Ann S. Bash & Bonnie W. Camp. LC 85-61576. (Illus.). 277p. 1985. pap. 35.95 (ISBN 0-87822-241-3). Res Press.

Think Aloud: Increasing Social & Cognitive Skills-A Problem-Solving Program for Children, Classroom Program, Grades 1 & 2. Bonnie W. Camp & Mary Ann S. Bash. LC 85-61575. (Illus.). 307p. 1985. pap. 35.95 (ISBN 0-87822-240-5). Res Press.

Think & Act: A Series of Articles Pertaining to Men & Women, Work & Wages. Virginia Penny. LC 75-156420. (American Labor Ser., No. 2). 1971. Repr. of 1869 ed. 24.50 (ISBN 0-405-02938-1). Ayer Co Pubs.

Think & Explain with Statistics. Lincoln E. Moses. 400p. 1986. text ed. write for info. (ISBN 0-201-15619-9). Addison-Wesley.

Think & Grow Rich. Napoleon Hill. 1983. pap. 2.95 (ISBN 0-449-20365-4, Crest). Fawcett.

Think & Grow Rich. Napoleon Hill. pap. 7.00 (ISBN 0-87980-163-8). Wilshire.

Think & Grow Rich Action Pack. Napoleon Hill. (Illus.). 352p. 1988. 8.95 (ISBN 0-525-48349-7). Dutton.

Think & Thank: A Tale. facsimile ed. Samuel W. Cooper. LC 74-27975. (Modern Jewish Experience Ser.). 1975. Repr. of 1890 ed. 14.00x (ISBN 0-405-06704-6). Ayer Co Pubs.

Think & Write. Fred Justus. (Early Education Ser.). 24p. (gr. 1). 1982. wkbk. 5.00 (ISBN 0-8209-0220-9, K-22). ESP.

Think Back on Us. A Contemporary Chronicle of the 1930s: The Literary Record. Malcolm Cowley. Ed. by Henry D. Piper. LC 72-5606. (Arcturus Books Paperbacks). 210p. (Pt. 2 of the hardbound ed. of Think Back On Us). 1972. pap. 7.95x (ISBN 0-8093-0599-2). S Ill U Pr.

Think Back on Us. A Contemporary Chronicle of the 1930s: The Social Record. Malcolm Cowley. Ed. by Henry D. Piper. LC 72-5606. (Arcturus Books Paperbacks). 213p. (Pt. 1 of the hardbound ed. of Think Back On Us). 1972. pap. 7.95x (ISBN 0-8093-0598-4). S Ill U Pr.

Think Big. Martha Symonds. (Gifted & Talented Ser.). 76p. (gr. 4-6). 1977. 6.95 (ISBN 0-88160-024-5, LW 209). Learning Wks.

Think Black. 3rd ed. Don L. Lee. 1969. pap. 3.00 (ISBN 0-910296-03-0). Broadside Pr.

Think Chinese, Speak Chinese. Allan B. Goldenthal. (Illus.). (gr. 10-12). 1978. write for info.; pap. text ed. 14.95 (ISBN 0-88345-358-4, 18602); cassettes 45.00 (ISBN 0-686-67814-1, 58687). Prentice ESL.

Think Chinese, Speak Chinese. 1981. 50.00x (ISBN 0-686-75661-4, Pub. by European Schoolbks England). State Mutual Bk.

Think! Draw! Write, 2 levels. Jean Marzollo & Katherine Martin-Widmer. Incl. Level I. (gr. 1-3) (ISBN 0-8224-6946-4); Level II. (gr. 4-6). 1981. pap. 5.95 ea. D S Lake Pubs.

Think Fast America. Lambert Schuyler. 1982. lib. bdg. 69.95 (ISBN 0-87700-443-9). Revisionist Pr.

Think Fast, Mr. Moto. John P. Marquand. LC 85-7044. 1986. pap. 3.95 (ISBN 0-316-54703-4). Little.

Think Fast, Mr. Peters. Stuart Kaminsky. 224p. 1988. 15.95x (ISBN 0-317-64892-6, Pub. by Thomas Dunne Bks). St Martin.

Think First, Read Later! Piagetian Prerequisites for Reading. T. Gary Waller. Ed. by Frank B. Murray. (Ira Series on the Development of the Reading Process Ser.). 1978. pap. text ed. 3.00 (ISBN 0-87207-522-2). Intl Reading.

Think for Yourself. Robert P. Crawford. LC 64-8498. 1979. Repr. of 1937 ed. 10.00 (ISBN 0-87034-011-5). Fraser Pub Co.

Think Harmony with Horses. Ray Hunt. 100p. 1987. Repr. 12.95 (ISBN 0-914330-15-2). Panorama West.

Think Home. 2nd ed. Lisa Espineli-Chinn. 45p. Date not set. pap. write for info. (ISBN 0-910796-12-2). Intl Students Inc.

Think It Through. George Howard. 48p. (Orig.). 1984. pap. 2.95 (ISBN 0-89109-163-7). NavPress.

Think Jewish: A Contemporary View of Judaism, a Jewish View of Today's World. Zalman I. Posner. LC 78-71323. 1979. 8.95 (ISBN 0-9602394-0-5); pap. 4.95 (ISBN 0-9602394-1-3). Kesher.

Think Like a Grandmaster. Alexander Kotov. 1976. pap. 16.95 (ISBN 0-7134-3160-1, Pub. by Batsford England). David & Charles.

Think Like a Lawyer: How to Get What You Want by Using Advocacy Skills. Robert J. Dudley. LC 79-26488. 234p. 1980. 19.95x (ISBN 0-88229-571-3). Nelson-Hall.

Think Like a President: A Managers Guide to Making It Happen. J. Keith Louden. (Illus.). 212p. 1982. P-H.

Think Like a Tycoon. 4th ed. Bill Greene. (Illus.). 253p. 1980. 19.95 (ISBN 0-936602-07-4); pap. 14.95 wkbk. J C Print.

Think Like a Tycoon. Bill Greene. 1982. pap. 5.95 (ISBN 0-449-90068-1, Columbine). Fawcett.

Think Metric! Franklyn M. Branley. LC 72-78279. (Illus.). (gr. 3-6). 1973. 12.89 (ISBN 0-690-81861-0, Crowell Jr Bks). HarpJ.

Think of England. Frederic Raphael. 192p. 1988. 15.95 (ISBN 0-684-18972-0). Scribner.

Think of One. P. Inman. 96p. (Orig.). 1986. pap. 7.50 (ISBN 0-937013-17-X). Potes Poets.

Think of Something Quiet. Clare Cherry. LC 80-82981. (Early Childhood Library). (ps-4). 1981. pap. 8.95 (ISBN 0-8224-6949-9). D S Lake Pubs.

Think of Your Future. William MacDonald. pap. 1.95 (ISBN 0-937396-44-3). Walterick Pubs.

Think of Your Future: Retirement Planning Workbook. AARP's Worker Equity Department Staff. 304p. 1988. 24.95 (ISBN 0-673-24893-3, 826). Am Assn Retire.

Think on New Levels. Robert G. Chaney. (Adventures in Esoteric Learning Ser.). 56p. 1963. pap. 4.25 (ISBN 0-918936-16-0). Astara.

Think on These Things. Jiddu Krishnamurti. 1970. pap. 5.50 (ISBN 0-06-080192-1, P192, PL). Har-Row.

Think on These Things. John Maxwell. 128p. 1979. pap. 2.95 (ISBN 0-8341-0600-0). Beacon Hill.

Think on These Things. Date not set. price not set. ARE Pr.

Think on These Things see Piensa Estas Cosas.

Think on Your Feet: The Art of Thinking & Speaking under Pressure. Kenneth Wydro. 192p. 1981. (Spec); pap. text ed. 6.95 (ISBN 0-13-917807-4, Spec). P-H.

Think Persian. 2nd ed. John Kollock. LC 83-51800. (Illus.). 96p. 1985. pap. 4.95 (ISBN 0-931948-71-1). Peachtree Pubs.

Think Slim-Be Slim. rev. ed. Elsye Birkinshaw. LC 80-7115. (Illus.). 144p. (Orig.). 1981. pap. 7.95 (ISBN 0-912800-91-7). Woodbridge Pr.

Think Smart, Move Fast: Decision Making-Problem Solving for Super Executives. Charles H. Ford. LC 82-71321. 272p. 1984. pap. 9.95 (ISBN 0-8144-7624-4). AMACOM.

Think Tank. Dianne Draze. (Illus.). (gr. 5-12). 1978. tchrs'. ed. 7.50 (ISBN 0-931724-09-0). Dandy Lion.

Think Tank Theatre: Decision Making Applied. Donald A. Borchardt. 350p. (Orig.). 1985. pap. text ed. 19.75 (ISBN 0-8191-4337-5, Co-pub by Am Theat Assn). U Pr of Amer.

Think Tanks: Their Role in Our Society, a Checklist. Alva W. Stewart. (Public Administration Ser.: P 2091). 10p. 1987. 3.00 (ISBN 1-55590-171-9). Vance Biblios.

Think Thin. Murray J. Siegel & Dolores Van Keuren. LC 76-151435. 288p. 1981. pap. 15.95 (ISBN 0-8397-7993-3). Eriksson.

Think Thin Today. Timoux Thomas. 1983. pap. 3.95 (ISBN 0-938936-08-5). Daring Bks.

Think Thinner, Snoopy. Charles M. Schulz. 1983. pap. 1.95 (ISBN 0-449-20322-0, Crest). Fawcett.

Think Twice Before You Accept That Job. Richard J. Thain. 150p. 1986. pap. 15.00 (ISBN 0-87094-898-9). Dow Jones-Irwin.

Think Twice: Communication Activities for Beginning to Intermediate Students. David Hover. (Illus.). 1986. pap. text ed. 7.50 student's handbook, 96p. (ISBN 0-521-27385-4); pap. 9.95 tchr's. guide, 128p. (ISBN 0-521-27386-2). Cambridge U Pr.

Think Twice: Medical Effects of Physical Punishment. Leslie Taylor & Adah Maurer. (Illus.). 80p. 1985. 5.95 (ISBN 0-932141-05-6). End Violence.

Think: Why You Were Born. Olson & Hanratty. LC 81-68336. 80p. 1981. 5.50 (ISBN 0-86690-007-1, 1360-01). Am Fed Astrologers.

Think-Write: A Guide to Research Writing Across the Curriculm. Linda Shamoon. 128p. 1986. pap. text ed. 13.95 (ISBN 0-8403-3835-X). Kendall-Hunt.

Think Young-Be Young! rev ed. Elsye Birkinshaw. LC 86-28240. Orig. Title: Turn Off Your Age. 160p. (Orig.). 1987. pap. 7.95x (ISBN 0-88007-157-5). Woodbridge Pr.

Think Your Troubles Away. Ernest Holmes. Ed. by Willis H. Kinnear. 96p. 1963. pap. 4.50 (ISBN 0-911336-29-X). Sci of Mind.

Think Your Way to Success. Lewis Losoncy. 1982. pap. 5.00 (ISBN 0-87980-396-7). Wilshire.

Think Yourself Thin. Frank J. Bruno. 272p. 1975. pap. 6.95 (ISBN 0-06-463348-9, EH 348, B&N Bks). Har-Row.

Thinker Sheets. Becky Daniel & Charlie Daniel. (gr. 2-6). 1978. 6.95 (ISBN 0-916456-23-4, GA78). Good Apple.

Thinkers & Tinkers: Early American Men of Science. Silvio A. Bedini. (Illus.). 519p. 1983. Repr. of 1975 ed. 24.00 (ISBN 0-910845-19-0, 901). Landmark Ent.

Thinker's Guide to Management Action. William P. Fisher. 126p. 1978. pap. 5.95 (ISBN 0-317-57848-0, MG891). Natl Restaurant Assn.

Thinker's Guide to Ultrasonic Imaging. Raymond L. Powis & Windy J. Powis. (Illus.). 430p. 1984. 49.50 (ISBN 0-8067-1581-2). Urban & S.

Thinkers of Indian Renaissance. Ed. by D. H. Bishop. 420p. 1986. 36.95. Asia Bk Corp.

Thinkers of the East. Idries Shah. 1971. 18.95 (ISBN 0-900860-46-4, Pub. by Octagon Pr England). Ins Study Human.

Thinkers of the East. Idries Shah. 208p. 1972. pap. 5.95 (ISBN 0-14-003410-2). Penguin.

Thinkers of the Indian Renaissance. 1983. 10.00 (ISBN 0-471-63985-0). Wiley.

Thinkers of the Twentieth Century. 2nd ed. 650p. 1987. 85.00x (Pub. by St James). Gale.

Thinkers of the Twentieth Century. 2nd ed. Ed. by Roland Turner. 1987. 85.00 (ISBN 0-912289-83-X); Standing Order. 76.50. St James Pr.

Thinker's Tool Chest. Ralph V. Alday. 1988. 10.00 (ISBN 0-533-07994-2). Vantage.

Thinking. Richard L. Allington. Kathleen Krull. LC 80-15390. (E. G. Beginning to Learn about... Ser.). (Illus.). 32p. (ps-2). 1985. pap. 9.27 (ISBN 0-8172-2494-7). Raintree Pubs.

Thinking. Richard L. Allington & Kathleen Krull. LC 80-15390. (Beginning to Learn about Ser.). (Illus.). 32p. (ps-2). 1980. PLB 15.33 (ISBN 0-8172-1319-8). Raintree Pubs.

Thinking. Kathie B. Smith & Victoria Crenson. LC 87-5886. (Troll Question Bk.). (Illus.). 24p. (gr. k-3). PLB 8.59 (ISBN 0-8167-1016-3); pap. text ed. 1.95 (ISBN 0-8167-1017-1). Troll Assocs.

Thinking A. I. D. S. Mary C. Bateson & Richard Goldsby. 1988. 12.95 (ISBN 0-201-15594-X). Addison-Wesley.

Thinking about America: The United States in the 1990s. Ed. by Annelise Anderson & Dennis L. Bark. 680p. 1988. 24.95 (ISBN 0-8179-8751-7); pap. 14.95 (ISBN 0-8179-8752-5). Hoover Inst Pr.

Thinking About an M.B.A.? Charles J. Shields. 16p. (Orig.). 1988. pap. 1.95 (ISBN 0-87866-588-9). Petersons Guides.

Thinking about Art. Edmund B. Feldman. (Illus.). 480p. 1985. write for info (ISBN 0-13-917493-1). P-H.

Thinking about Art. Lucie-Smith. 1985. 11.95. Riverrun NY.

Thinking about Art. Edward Lucie-Smith. 237p. 1968. 13.95 (ISBN 0-7145-0552-8). Dufour.

Thinking about Basic Beliefs: An Introduction to Philosophy. Howard Kahane. 238p. 1983. pap. text ed. write for info. (ISBN 0-534-01318-X). Wadsworth Pub.

Thinking about Being: Aspects of Heidegger's Thought. Robert W. Shahan & J. N. Mohanty. LC 81-40297. 208p. 1985. 19.95X (ISBN 0-8061-1780-X). U of Okla Pr.

Thinking about Children: Sociology & Fertility in Post-War England. Joan Busfield & Michael Paddon. LC 76-22986. pap. 84.30 (2031625). Bks Demand UMI.

Thinking about Crime. James Q. Wilson. 1977. pap. 3.95 (ISBN 0-394-72185-3, Vin). Random.

Thinking about Crime. rev. ed. James Q. Wilson. 1985. pap. 7.95 (ISBN 0-394-72917-X, Vin). Random.

Thinking about Development. Lisa Peattie. LC 81-15858. (Environment, Development, & Public Policy-Cities & Development Ser.). 208p. 1981. 29.50x (ISBN 0-306-40761-2, Plenum Pr). Plenum Pub.

Thinking about Education. Krister Ottosson. 72p. 7.95 (ISBN 0-7188-2301-X, Pub. by Lutterwrth). Attic Pr.

Thinking About Engineering? Charles J. Shields. 16p. (Orig.). 1988. pap. 1.95 (ISBN 0-87866-587-0). Petersons Guides.

Thinking about Ethics. Richard L. Purtill. 160p. 1976. pap. text ed. write for info. (ISBN 0-13-917716-7). P-H.

Thinking about Faith: An Introductory Guide to Philosophy & Religion. David Cook. 1986. pap. 9.95 (ISBN 0-310-44131-5, 18401P). Zondervan.

Thinking about God. Brian Davies. 1986. pap. 15.75 (ISBN 0-225-66476-3, HarpR). Har-Row.

Thinking about God. Fisher Humphreys. LC 74-81556. 228p. (Orig.). 1974. pap. 12.00 (ISBN 0-914520-00-8). Insight Pr.

Thinking about Human Rights: Contending Approaches to Human Rights in U. S. Foreign Policy. Michael R. Fowler. Ed. by Kenneth W. Thompson. (Exxon Education Foundation Series on Rhetoric & Political Discourse: Vol. 6). (Orig.). 1987. lib. bdg. 24.75 (ISBN 0-8191-5818-6, Pub. by White Miller Center); pap. text ed. 12.50 (ISBN 0-8191-5819-4). U Pr of Amer.

Thinking about Knowing. Alan Howard. 1985. pap. 5.95 (ISBN 0-916786-81-1). St George Bk Serv.

Thinking About Law? Charles J. Shields. 16p. (Orig.). 1988. pap. 1.95 (ISBN 0-87866-586-2). Petersons Guides.

Thinking About Medicine? Charles J. Shields. 16p. (Orig.). 1988. pap. 1.95 (ISBN 0-87866-585-4). Petersons Guides.

Thinking about Morality. William K. Frankena. (Michigan Faculty Ser.). 112p. 1980. pap. 4.95 (ISBN 0-472-06316-2). U of Mich Pr.

Thinking about Music: An Introduction to the Philosophy of Music. Lewis Rowell. LC 82-21979. (Illus.). 304p. 1984. lib. bdg. 25.00x (ISBN 0-87023-386-6); pap. text ed. 12.95. U of Mass Pr.

Thinking about National Security: Defense & Foreign Policy in a Dangerous World. Harold Brown. LC 82-23859. 278p. 1983. 26.50x (ISBN 0-86531-548-5); pap. text ed. 16.95x (ISBN 0-86531-702-X). Westview.

Thinking about Nuclear Weapons: Analyses & Prescriptions. Ed. by Fred Holroyd. 432p. (Orig.). 1985. pap. 15.00 (ISBN 0-86569-130-4). Auburn Hse.

Thinking about Peace & War. Martin Ceadel. 232p. 1987. 29.95 (ISBN 0-19-219200-0). Oxford U Pr.

Thinking about Peace: The Conceptualization & Conduct of U. S. - Soviet Detente. Paul F. Herman, Jr. LC 86-32520. (Illus.). 250p. (Orig.). 1987. lib. bdg. 26.75 (ISBN 0-8191-6105-5); pap. text ed. 12.75 (ISBN 0-8191-6106-3). U Pr of Amer.

Thinking about Police: Contemporary Readings. C. B. Klockars. (Criminology & Criminal Justice Ser.). 592p. 1983. text ed. 28.95 (ISBN 0-07-035054-X). McGraw.

Thinking about Politics: Two Political Sciences. Mark E. Kann. 229p. 1980. pap. text ed. 21.00 (ISBN 0-8299-0314-3). West Pub.

Thinking about Psychology. John L. Vogel. LC 84-15662. 550p. 1986. 27.95x (ISBN 0-8304-1153-4); study guide 8.95 (ISBN 0-8304-1154-2); write for info. instr's. resource manual (ISBN 0-8304-1155-0). Nelson-Hall.

Thinking about Religion: A Philosophical Introduction to Religion. Richard L. Purtill. 1978. pap. text ed. write for info (ISBN 0-13-917724-8). P-H.

Thinking about Rural Development. Ralph Whitlock. 6.50 (ISBN 0-7188-2299-4, Pub. by Lutterwrth). Attic Pr.

Thinking about Science: Max Delbruck & the Origins of Molecular Biology. Ernst P. Fischer & Carol Lipson. (Illus.). 1988. 19.95 (ISBN 0-393-02508-X). Norton.

Thinking about SDI. Stephen J. Hadley. 32p. (Orig.). 1986. pap. text ed. 8.00 (ISBN 0-941700-21-6). JH FPI SAIS.

Thinking about Sex & Love: A Philosophical Inquiry. J. F. Hunter. LC 79-27352. 172p. 1981. 21.95 (ISBN 0-312-80018-5). St Martin.

Thinking about Sikhism. Owen W. Cole. 192p. 11.00 (ISBN 0-7188-2421-0, Pub. by Lutterwrth). Attic Pr.

Thinking about Social Thinking. Antony Flew. 200p. 1985. 34.95x (ISBN 0-631-14189-8); pap. 12.95x (ISBN 0-631-14191-X). Basil Blackwell.

Thinking about Society: Theory & Practice. I. C. Jarvie. 1986. lib. bdg. 68.00 (ISBN 90-277-2068-1, Pub. by Reidel Holland). Kluwer-Academic.

Thinking about the American People. John McClymer. 98p. 3.95 (ISBN 0-686-68744-2). Stony Brook Pr.

Thinking about the Family: Views of the Parents of Children. Ed. by Richard D. Ashmore & David M. Brodzinsky. 336p. 1986. text ed. 39.95 (ISBN 0-89859-693-9). L Erlbaum Assocs.

Thinking about the Next War. Thomas Powers. LC 82-47930. 1982. 10.45 (ISBN 0-394-52831-X). Knopf.

Thinking about the Playwright. Eric Bentley. 369p. 1987. 38.95x (ISBN 0-8101-0732-5); pap. 14.95 (ISBN 0-8101-0733-3). Northwestern U Pr.

Thinking about the Unthinkable in the 1980's. Herman Kahn. LC 84-1432. 229p. 1984. 16.95 (ISBN 0-671-47544-4). S&S.

Thinking about the Unthinkable in the Nineteen Eighties. Herman Kahn. 1985. 8.95. S&S.

Thinking about the Work Experience. Bruce Dollar & Peter Kleinbard. 65p. 1981. pap. 5.00 (ISBN 0-912041-11-0). Natl Comm Res Youth.

Thinking about Things. Brenda Judge. 248p. 1985. 24.00x (ISBN 0-7073-0456-3, Pub. by Scot Acad Pr); pap. 15.00. Longwood Pub Group.

Thinking about Thinking. Alan Howard. 1981. pap. 4.50 (ISBN 0-916786-51-X). St George Bk Serv.

Thinking about Thinking. Clark McKowen. (Illus.). 320p. (Orig.). 1986. pap. 14.95 (ISBN 0-86576-097-7). W Kaufmann.

Thinking about Thinking. Merl R. Wolfare. 1955. 6.95 (ISBN 0-8022-1917-9). Philos Lib.

Thinking about Thinking with NLP. LC 85-63154: 1985. pap. 10.95 (ISBN 0-916990-16-8). Meta Pubns.

Thinking about TLC LOGO. 2nd ed. John R. Allen et al. 236p. 1984. pap. 17.45 (ISBN 0-03-064116-0). HR&W.

Thinking about TLC LOGO: For Mattel Aquarius. John R. Allen et al. LC 83-10771. 220p. 1983. pap. 14.95 (ISBN 0-03-064114-4). HR&W.

Thinking about Women. Mary Ellmann. LC 67-20309. 1970. pap. 4.95 (ISBN 0-15-689900-0, Harv). HarBraceJ.

Thinking about Women: Sociological Perspectives on Sex & Gender. 2nd ed ed. Margaret L. Andersen. 551p. 1988. text ed. write for info. (ISBN 0-02-303350-9). Macmillan.

Thinking Across Cultures. Ed. by Donald M. Topping et al. (Third International Conference on Thinking Ser.). 552p. 1988. text ed. 69.95 (ISBN 0-89859-913-X). L Erlbaum Assocs.

Thinking Ahead: UNESCO & the Challenge of Today & Tomorrow. (Illus.). 363p. 1977. pap. 7.50 (ISBN 92-3-101525-7, U802, UNESCO). UNIPUB.

Thinking: An Experimental & Social Study. Frederic C. Bartlett. LC 82-983. 203p. 1982. Repr. of 1964 ed. lib. bdg. 35.00x (ISBN 0-313-23412-4, BART). Greenwood.

Thinking & Deciding. Jonathan Baron. (Illus.). 500p. Date not set. 54.50 (ISBN 0-521-34253-8); pap. 19.95 (ISBN 0-521-34800-5). Cambridge U Pr.

Thinking & Destiny. 9th ed. Harold W. Percival. LC 47-1811. (Illus.). 1000p. 1982. deluxe ed. 22.95 (ISBN 0-911650-09-1, 091); pap. 12.95 (ISBN 0-911650-06-7). Word Foun.

Thinking & Doing. Philosophical Foundations of Institutions & H. N. Castaneda. LC 75-16169. (Philosophical Studies: No. 7). 396p. 1975. lib. bdg. 58.00 (ISBN 90-277-0610-7, Pub. by Reidel Holland). Kluwer Academic.

Thinking & Doing: Youth and a New International Economic Order. Barbara B. Day. (Illus.). 96p. 1980. pap. 5.00 (ISBN 92-3-101841-8, U1075, UNESCO). UNIPUB.

Thinking & Language. Judith Greene. (Essential Psychology Ser.). 1975. pap. 4.95x (ISBN 0-416-81880-3, NO. 2736). Routledge Chapman & Hall.

Thinking & Learning Skills, Vol. I: Relating Instruction to Research. Ed. by Judith W. Segal et al. 568p. 1985. text ed. 55.00 (ISBN 0-89859-165-1). L Erlbaum Assocs.

Thinking & Learning Skills, Vol. II: Research & Open Questions. Ed. by Judith W. Segal et al. 640p. 1985. text ed. 59.95 (ISBN 0-89859-166-X). L Erlbaum Assocs.

Thinking & Perceiving. John W. Yolton. LC 61-11288. 175p. 1962. pap. 4.95 (ISBN 0-87548-067-5). Open Court.

Thinking & Problem Solving: An Introduction to Human Cognition & Learning. Richard E. Mayer. 1977. pap. write for info. (ISBN 0-673-15055-0). Scott F.

Thinking & Reasoning: Psychological Approaches. Ed. by Jonathan Evans. (International Library of Psychology). 300p. 1983. 21.95x (ISBN 0-7100-9460-4). Routledge Chapman & Hall.

Thinking & Representation. H. H. Price. (Studies in Philosophy, No. 40). 1977. lib. bdg. 24.95x (ISBN 0-8383-0117-7). Haskell.

Thinking & Speaking: A Guide to Intelligent Oral Communication. 5th ed. Otis M. Walter & Robert L. Scott. 320p. 1984. pap. text ed. write for info. (ISBN 0-02-424370-1). Macmillan.

Thinking & Writing in College. Thomas Anselmo et al. 1986. pap. text ed. write for info. (ISBN 0-673-39245-7); instr's. manual avail. (ISBN 0-316-04336-2). Scott F.

Thinking Back: The Perils of Writing History. C. Vann Woodward. LC 85-19692. x, 158p. 1986. 12.95 (ISBN 0-8071-1304-2). LA State U Pr.

Thinking Back: The Perils of Writing History. C. Vann Woodward. LC 85-19692. x, 158p. 1987. pap. 6.95 (ISBN 0-8071-1377-8). La State U Pr.

Thinking Better. David Lewis & James Greene. 1983. pap. 7.95 (ISBN 0-03-064167-5). H Holt & Co.

Thinking Big in Small Places. Charles Nieman. 43p. (Orig.). 1986. wkbk. 4.95 (ISBN 0-914307-53-3). Word Faith.

Thinking Big: The Story of a Young Dwarf. Susan Kuklin. LC 85-10425. (Illus.). 48p. (ps-1). 1986. 11.75 (ISBN 0-688-05826-4); PLB 11.88 (ISBN 0-688-05827-2). Lothrop.

Thinking Black: An Introduction to Black Political Power. Frank McQuilkin. 1970. pap. 2.95 (ISBN 0-02-805100-9, 80510). Macmillan.

Thinking Body: A Study of Balancing Forces of Dynamic Man. Mabel E. Todd. LC 68-28048. (Illus.). 314p. 1968. pap. 15.95 (ISBN 0-87127-014-5, Pub. by Dance Horiz). Princeton Bk Co.

Thinking, Changing, Rearranging. Jill Anderson. 1985. 7.00 (ISBN 0-9608284-0-0); pap. text ed. 17.00 instr's. guide (ISBN 0-9608284-1-9). Timberline Pr.

Thinking, Changing, Rearranging: Skill Builder. Jill Anderson. (Illus.). 80p. (gr. 2). pap. 6.95 (ISBN 0-943920-30-2). Metamorphous Pr.

Thinking Christian Woman. Helen Hosier. LC 87-81656. 192p. (Orig.). 1988. pap. 5.95 (ISBN 0-89081-612-3). Harvest Hse.

Thinking Clearly about Death. Jay F. Rosenberg. 256p. 1983. pap. write for info. (ISBN 0-13-917559-8). P-H.

Thinking Computer: Mind Inside Matter. Bertram Raphael. LC 75-30839. (Psychology Ser.). (Illus.). 322p. 1976. pap. text ed. 16.95x (ISBN 0-7167-0723-3). W H Freeman.

Thinking Creatively: A New Approach to Psychology & Individual Lives. Leona E. Tyler. LC 83-48166. (Social & Behavioral Science Ser.). 1983. text ed. 26.95x (ISBN 0-87589-585-9). Jossey-Bass.

Thinking Critically. John Chaffee. 352p. 1985. pap. text ed. 15.50 (ISBN 0-395-34105-1); 2.00 (ISBN 0-395-34106-X). HM.

Thinking Critically. 2nd. ed. John Chaffee. LC 87-80616. 450p. 1988. pap. text ed. 19.16 (ISBN 0-395-43248-0); handbook 2.36 (ISBN 0-395-45038-1). Hm.

Thinking Development. Fred Justus. (Early Education Ser.). 24p. (gr. k). 1981. wkbk. 5.00 (ISBN 0-8209-0213-6, K-15). ESP.

Thinking: Directed, Undirected & Creative. K. J. Gilhooly. 1982. 33.00 (ISBN 0-12-283480-1); pap. 18.00 (ISBN 0-12-283482-8). Acad Pr.

Thinking: Directed, Undirected & Creative. 2nd ed. K. J. Gilhooly. 340p. 1988. price not set (ISBN 0-12-283483-6); pap. price not set (ISBN 0-12-283484-4). Acad Pr.

Thinking Divorce? Consider the Shocking Personal & Financial Realities. Daniel Z. Shapiro. 108p. (Orig.). 1983. pap. 7.95 (ISBN 0-930256-11-5). Almar.

Thinking Economically: How Economic Principles Can Contribute to Clear Thinking. Maurice Levi. LC 83-46090. 304p. 1987. pap. 7.95 (ISBN 0-465-08554-7, PL 5178). Basic.

Thinking English. Michael Thorn et al. 1984. pap. text ed. 11.95 (ISBN 0-03-062981-0). HR&W.

Thinking Faith Through: Twenty-Four Topics for Christians for Individual Reading & Group Discussions, with Notes for Leaders. Leigh Pope. (Illus.). 80p. (Orig.). 1983. pap. text ed. 6.95 (ISBN 0-85819-413-9, Pub. by JBCE). ANZ Religious Pubns.

Thinking, Feeling & Being. Ignatio Matte-Blanco. 300p. 1988. text ed. 35.00 (ISBN 0-415-00677-5, Pub. by Routledge UK). Routledge Chapman & Hall.

Thinking for Orchestra: Practical Exercises in Orchestration. Rene Leibowitz. 240p. Repr. of 1960 ed. lib. bdg. 39.00 (Pub. by Am Repr Serv). Am Biog Serv.

Thinking for Yourself: Developing Critical Thinking Skills Through Writing. Marlys Mayfield. 304p. 1987. pap. text ed. write for info. (ISBN 0-534-07308-5). Wadsworth Pub.

Thinking FORTH: A Language & Philosophy for Solving Problems. Leo Brodie. (Illus.). 224p. 1984. pap. 16.95 (ISBN 0-13-917568-7). P-H.

Thinking: From Association to Gestalt. Jean M. Mandler & George Mandler. LC 81-13347. (Perspectives in Psychology Ser.). x, 300p. 1982. Repr. of 1964 ed. lib. bdg. 35.00x (ISBN 0-313-23261-X, MATK). Greenwood.

Thinking Game: A Guide to Effective Study. Eugene J. Meehan. LC 88-4335. (Studies in Political Thinking). (Illus.). 256p. (Orig.). 1988. pap. text ed. 12.95x (ISBN 0-934540-64-0). Chatham Hse Pubs.

Thinking Games, 2 bks. Anderson & Bereitner. Incl. Bk. 1. LC 79-57429. (gr. k-3) (ISBN 0-8224-6941-3); Bk. 2. LC 80-65124. (gr. 4-7) (ISBN 0-8224-6942-1). 1980. pap. 6.95 ea. D S Lake Pubs.

Thinking Globally...Acting Locally. League of Women Voters Education Fund Staff. 87p. 1988. pap. 5.00 (ISBN 0-89959-406-9, 849). LWV US.

Third & Long. Neil Lomax. (Illus.). 192p. 1986. 12.95 (ISBN 0-8007-1497-0). Revell.

Third & Possibly the Best Six Hundred & Thirty-Seven Best Things Anybody Ever Said. Robert Byrne. LC 86-47657. (Illus.). 192p. 1986. 10.95 (ISBN 0-689-11822-8). Atheneum.

Third & Possibly the Best Six Hundred & Thirty-Seven Things Anyone Ever Said. Robert Byrne. 192p. 1987. pap. 2.95 (ISBN 0-449-21337-4, Crest). Fawcett.

Third Annual Bankruptcy Litigation Institute. 35.00 (ISBN 0-317-29479-2, #CO1465, Law & Business). HarBraceJ.

Third Annual Conference on African Linguistics. Ed. by Erhard Voeltz. (African Ser.: No. 7). 265p. 1974. pap. text ed. 25.00x (ISBN 0-87750-181-5). Res Ctr Lang Semiotic.

Third Annual Educational Conference on Prepaid Legal Services: November Nineteen Eighty-Three. 800p. 1983. 55.00 (ISBN 0-317-40260-9, 3-014). Am Prepaid.

Third Annual Expert Systems in Government Conference: Proceedings. 298p. 1987. 60.00 (ISBN 0-8186-0809-9, EZ809). IEEE Comp Soc.

Third Annual Immigration Law Conference: Proceedings, Federal Bar Association, 1982. 434p. 40.00 (ISBN 0-318-14100-0). Federal Bar.

Third Annual Internships for College Students Interested in Law, Medicine & Politics. 125p. 1988. pap. 25.00 (ISBN 0-317-58989-X). Graduate Group.

Third Annual Internships for Two-Year College Students. 125p. 1988. pap. 25.00 (ISBN 0-317-58991-1). Graduate Group.

Third Annual Internships in New York City & Washington, D. C. 125p. 1988. pap. 25.00 (ISBN 0-317-58990-3). Graduate Group.

Third Annual Labor & Employment Law Institute: Labor & Employment Relations in the Age of the Robot, Computer & Foreign Competion. Ed. by Marlin M. Volz. LC 87-9725. (Illus.). viii, 352p. 1987. lib. bdg. 57.50x (ISBN 0-8377-1237-8). Rothman.

Third Annual National Directory of Art Internships: 1988-89 New Internships for Artists. rev. ed. Warren Christensen. (Illus.). 300p. 1988. pap. text ed. 30.00 perfect bdg. (ISBN 0-945941-00-5). NNAP.

Third Annual Securities Law. 35.00 (ISBN 0-317-29543-8, #CO2763, Law & Business). HarBraceJ.

Third Annual Securities Law & Enforcement Institute. John M. Fedders & Theodore A. Levine. LC 85-136460. 786p. write for info. (Pub. by Law & Business). HarBraceJ.

Third Annual Seminar on Grant Law. 199p. 30.00 (ISBN 0-318-14101-9). Federal Bar.

Third Annual Structuring Partnership Agreements. 35.00 (ISBN 0-317-29544-6, #CO3611, Law & Business). HarBraceJ.

Third Annual Tax Shelter Controversies: The IRS, Justice & SEC Crack Down. Maxwell Mortimer & Cono Namorato. LC 84-13116. Date not set. price not set (Law & Business). HarBraceJ.

Third Anti-Coloring Book. Susan Striker & Edward Kimmel. (Illus.). 96p. (Orig.). (gr. 2 up). 1980. pap. 3.95 (ISBN 0-03-056814-5, Owl Bks.). H Holt & Co.

Third Apple: Personal Computers & the Cultural Revolution. Jean-Louis Gassee. 208p. 1987. 14.95 (ISBN 0-15-189850-2). HarBraceJ.

Third Arab-Israeli War. Edgar O'Ballance. LC 72-1059. 288p. 1972. 25.00 (ISBN 0-208-01292-3, Archon). Shoe String.

Third Arm. Kenneth Royce. 224p. 1983. pap. 3.50 (ISBN 0-88184-051-3). Carroll & Graf.

Third Arm. Ed. by Kenneth Royce. 300p. 1980. text ed. 9.95 (ISBN 0-07-054169-8). McGraw.

Third Asia Pacific Physics Conference. Ed. by C. N. Yang et al. 800p. 1989. 84.00 (ISBN 9971-50-651-3). World Scientific Pub.

Third Asian-Pacific Regional Meeting of the International Astronomical Union, Kyoto, Japan, September 30 - October 6, 1984, 2 pts. Ed. by M. Kitamura & E. Budding. 1986. Pt. 1. lib. bdg. 98.00 (ISBN 90-277-1867-9, Pub. by Reidel Holland); Pt. 2. lib. bdg. 49.00 (ISBN 90-277-2210-2, Pub. by Reidel Holland). Kluwer-Academic.

Third Assembling: An Annual of Otherwise Unpublishable Imaginative Work, No. 3. annual Ed. by Richard Kostelanetz et al. (Illus.). 300p. (Orig.). 1972. pap. 10.00 (ISBN 0-685-27997-9). Assembling Pr.

Third Attidudinal Survey of Honolulu Residents, 1983. Research Committee on the Study of Honolulu Residents Staff. 170p. 1986. pap. text ed. 19.50x (ISBN 0-8248-1054-6, Pub. by Inst Stat Tokyo). UH Pr.

Third Betrayal. Michael Hartland. 208p. 1987. 16.95 (ISBN 0-02-548610-1). Macmillan.

Third Blonde. M. S. Craig. 204p. 1987. pap. 2.95 (ISBN 1-55547-140-4). Critics Choice Paper.

Third Book of Criticism. Randall Jarrell. 334p. 1969. 7.50 (ISBN 0-374-27504-1). FS&G.

Third Book of Horace's Odes. Horace. Tr. by Gordon Williams. 1969. pap. 11.95x (ISBN 0-19-912001-3). Oxford U Pr.

Third Book of Individual Open Salts Illustrated. Allan B. Smith & Helen B. Smith. (Illus.). 1976. pap. 7.50 (ISBN 0-940554-06-2). Country Hse.

Third Book of Junior Authors. Ed. by Doris De Montreville & Donna Hill. LC 75-149381. (Illus.). 320p. 1972. 30.00 (ISBN 0-8242-0408-5). Wilson.

Third Book of Lost Swords. Fred Saberhagen. 304p. 1989. pap. price not set. Tor Bks.

Third Book of Modern Verse. facs. ed. Ed. by Jessie B. Rittenhouse. LC 79-149114. (Granger Index Reprint Ser). 1927. 21.00 (ISBN 0-8369-6239-7). Ayer Co Pubs.

Third Book of Swords. Fred Saberhagen. 320p. 1985. pap. 3.50 (ISBN 0-8125-5333-0, Dist. by Warner Pub. Services & Saint Martin's Press). Tor Bks.

Third Branch: Administrative Office of the U. S. Courts, 11 Vols. in 2 Bks, 1968-79. LC 76-39614. 1980. Repr. of 1968 ed. lib. bdg. 90.00 (ISBN 0-930342-35-6). W S Hein.

Third Breeders' Cup: Annual Supplement. The Blood Horse Staff. (Illus.). 115p. 1986. pap. 6.00 (ISBN 0-939049-03-1). Blood Horse.

Third British Empire. 3rd ed. Alfred E. Zimmern. LC 79-4333. 1979. Repr. of 1934 ed. lib. bdg. 35.00 (ISBN 0-313-20990-1, ZITB). Greenwood.

Third British National Conference on Databases (BNCOD 3) held July 11-12, 1984. Ed. by J. Longstaff. (British Computer Society Workshop Ser.). 250p. 1984. 49.50 (ISBN 0-521-26841-9). Cambridge U Pr.

Third Caldecott Collection: The Queen of Hearts, The Farmer's Boy. Randolph Caldecott. (Picture Bk.). (Illus.). 64p. 1986. 4.95 (ISBN 0-7232-3434-5). Warne.

Third Census of Finnegans Wake: An Index to the Characters & Their Roles. Adaline Glasheen. LC 75-3770. 1977. 40.00x (ISBN 0-520-02980-1). U of Cal Pr.

Third Century: America As a Post-Industrial Society. Seymour M. Lipset. 1980. pap. 7.95x (ISBN 0-226-48458-0, P884, Phoen). U of Chicago Pr.

Third Century: America's Renaissance in the Asian Era. Joel Kotkin & Yoriko Kishimoto. 1988. 19.95 (ISBN 0-517-56984-1). Crown.

Third Century Hoard of Tetradrachms from Gordion. D. H. Cox. (University Museum Monographs: No. 9). (Illus.). v, 20p. 1953. pap. 6.00 (ISBN 0-934718-01-6). Univ Mus of U PA.

Third Century in American Education. Ed. by D. N. Aspy et al. 158p. 1984. pap. text ed. 25.00x (ISBN 0-914234-67-6). Human Res Dev Pr.

Third Century Iran see Persepolis, Third: The Royal Tombs & Other Monuments.

Third Child: A Study in the Prediction of Fertility. Charles F. Westoff et al. (Office of Population Research Ser). 1963. 38.50x (ISBN 0-691-09339-3). Princeton U Pr.

Third Choice. Robert Gregory. LC 78-54131. 1979. 16.95 (ISBN 0-87949-117-5). Ashley Bks.

Third City: Philosophy at War with Positivism. Borna Bebek. 352p. 1983. 29.95x (ISBN 0-7100-9042-0). Routledge Chapman & Hall.

Third Class City Code. Pennsylvania State Legislature Staff. 225p. (Orig.). 1982. text ed. 3.45 (ISBN 0-8182-0002-2). Commonweal PA.

Third Coast: Contemporary Michigan Fiction. Ed. by James Tipton & Robert E. Wegner. LC 81-15936. (Illus.). 336p. 1982. 27.50x (ISBN 0-8143-1694-8); pap. 8.50x (ISBN 0-8143-1695-6). Wayne St U Pr.

Third Cold War. Walter LaFeber. LC 81-80739. (Charles Edmondson Historical Lectures Ser.). 42p. (Orig.). 1981. pap. 4.50 (ISBN 0-918954-25-8). Baylor Univ Pr.

Third Collection: Papers by Bernard J. F. Longergan, S. J. Ed. by Frederick E. Crowe. LC 84-61028. 272p. 1985. pap. 12.95 (ISBN 0-8091-0363-X); pap. 9.95 (ISBN 0-8091-2650-8). Paulist Pr.

Third Colloquium in Biological Sciences: Cellular Signal Transduction. Pref. by Fleur L. Strand. (Annals of the New York Academy of Sciences: Vol. 594). 455p. 1987. 114.00 (ISBN 0-89766-383-7). NY Acad Sci.

Third Conference on Integrated Online Library Systems, September 23 & 24, 1986, St. Louis, Missouri: Proceedings. Ed. by David C. Genaway. vi, 460p. 1987. pap. 39.95 (ISBN 0-943970-05-9). Genaway.

Third Conference on Vitamin C. Ed. by John J. Burns et al. (Annals of the New York Academy of Sciences: Vol. 498). (Illus.). 537p. 1987. 134.00 (ISBN 0-89766-391-8). NY Acad Sci.

Third Congress of Lao People's Revolutionary Party. 117p. 1985. pap. 2.95 (Pub. by Progress Pubs USSR). Imported Pubns.

Third Congress of the Lao People's Revolutionary Party: Documents & Materials Vietiane, April 27-30, 1982. Ed. by Collet's Holdings, Ltd. Staff. 116p. 1984. 25.00x (ISBN 0-317-42841-1, Pub by Collets (UK)). State Mutual Bk.

Third Continuation see Continuations of the Old French Perceval of Chretien De Troyes.

Third Crossword Puzzle Book. Leslie A. Hill & P. R. Popkin. (Illus.). 1970. pap. text ed. 2.95x (ISBN 0-19-432553-9). Oxford U Pr.

Third Crystal. Ken Forsse & Bill Angelos. (Teddy Ruxpin Adventure Ser.). (Illus.). 34p. (ps). 1987. incl. cassettes 9.95 (ISBN 0-934323-43-7). Alchemy Comms.

Third Cuckoo. Kenneth Gregory. 282p. 1985. 14.95 (ISBN 0-04-808054-3). Unwin Hyman.

Third Deadly Sin. Lawrence Sanders. 416p. 1985. pap. 4.95. Berkley Pub.

Third Decade of Cardiac Pacing: Advances in Technology & Clinical Applications. Ed. by Serge S. Barold & Jacques Mugica. LC 81-67066. (Illus.). 480p. 1982. 47.50 (ISBN 0-87993-159-0). Futura Pub.

Third Degree. Zechariah Chafee, Jr. et al. LC 70-90169. (Mass Violence in America Ser). Repr. of 1931 ed. 14.00 (ISBN 0-405-01304-3). Ayer Co Pubs.

Third Degree: A Detailed Account of Police Brutality. Emanuel H. Lavine. LC 74-676. (Civil Liberties in American History Ser.). 248p. 1974. Repr. of 1930 ed. lib. bdg. 32.50 (ISBN 0-306-70601-6). Da Capo.

Third Department: The Establishment & Practices of the Political Police in the Russia of Nicholas I. Peter S. Squire. LC 69-10198. pap. 72.00 (2027272). Bks Demand UMI.

Third Department: The Political Police in the Russia of Nicholas First. P. S. Squire. LC 69-10198. (Illus.). 1968. Cambridge U Pr.

Third Dictionary of Acronyms & Abbreviations: More Abbreviations in Management, Technology, & Information Science. Eric Pugh. LC 76-29722. 208p. 1977. 25.00 (ISBN 0-208-01535-3, Linnet). Shoe String.

Third "Did I Ever Tell You...?". Iris Grender. (Did I Ever Tell You? Ser.). (Illus.). 64p. (gr. 1-3). 1987. 12.95 (ISBN 0-09-140370-7, Pub. by Century Hutchinson). David & Charles.

Third Digest of Investigations in the Teaching of Science. Francis D. Curtis. LC 74-153694. pap. 109.80 (ISBN 0-317-42006-2, 2026002). Bks Demand UMI.

Third Dimension in Organic Chemistry. Alan Bassindale. 242p. 1984. pap. 24.95x (ISBN 0-471-90189-X, Pub. by Wiley Interscience). Wiley.

Third Discourse - Criticism of Sectarian Doctrines; Fourth Discourse - Methods of Construction & Interpretation of Law see Kitab Al-Anwar Wal-Maraoib: Code of Karaite Law.

Third Door. Ellen Tarry. LC 70-135613. 1971. Repr. of 1955 ed. 35.00x (ISBN 0-8371-5200-3, TTD&). Greenwood.

Third Duma, Election & Profile. Alfred Levin. LC 73-633. x, 210p. 1973. 25.00 (ISBN 0-208-01325-3, Archon). Shoe String.

Third E. C. Photovoltaic Solar Energy Conference. Wolfgang Palz. 1982. 81.50 (ISBN 90-277-1230-1, Pub. by Reidel Holland). Kluwer Academic.

Third Eagle. R. A. Macavoy. 1988. 18.95 (ISBN 0-385-24919-5, Foundation Bks). Doubleday.

Third Earl of Shaftesbury, 1671-1713. Robert Voitle. LC 83-20365. xiii, 428p. 1984. text ed. 37.50 (ISBN 0-8071-1139-2). La State U Pr.

Third Eastern Regional Ground Water Conference, 1986: Proceedings. LC 86-23602. 1986. 43.75 (ISBN 0-318-23036-4). Natl Water Well.

Third Electoral System, 1853-1892: Parties, Voters, & Political Cultures. Paul Kleppner. LC 78-7949. xxi, 424p. 1979. 32.50x (ISBN 0-8078-1328-1). U of NC Pr.

Third Encounter. Sara Woods. 1986. pap. 3.50 (ISBN 0-380-69863-3). Avon.

Third European Bioenergetics Conference. Ed. by G. Schafer. (ICSU Short Reports Ser.). 793p. 1985. 87.50 (ISBN 0-521-30813-5). Cambridge U Pr.

Third European Bioenergetics Conference. Ed. by Gunter Schafer. (ICSU Press Short Reports Ser.: No. 3). 1985. 74.50. ICSU Pr.

Third European Meeting on Ferroelectricity (Zurich, 1975) Proceedings, 3 Vols. Ed. by I. Lefkowitz & G. Taylor. 762p. 1976. pap. 589.00x (ISBN 0-677-40205-8). Gordon & Breach.

Third Experiment: Is There Life on Mars? David E. Fisher. LC 84-21548. 192p. (gr. 7 up). 1985. 12.95 (ISBN 0-689-31080-3, Atheneum Childrens Bks). Macmillan.

Third Eye. Douglas Baker. 1987. 40.00x (ISBN 0-906006-59-7, Pub. by Claregate Coll UK). State Mutual Bk.

Third Eye. Lois Duncan. (gr. 7up). 1984. 14.95 (ISBN 0-316-19553-7). Little.

Third Eye. Lois Duncan. 224p. (gr. 6-12). 1985. pap. 2.95 (ISBN 0-440-98720-2, LFL). Dell.

Third Eye. Mollie Hunter. LC 78-22159. (YA) (gr. 8 up). 1979. PLB 12.89 (ISBN 0-06-022677-3). HarpJ.

Third Eye. T. Lobsang Rampa. 1988. pap. 3.95 (ISBN 0-345-00754-9). Ballantine.

Third Eye Centre, Glasgow: The First Ten Years 1975-1985. 40p. 1985. 25.00x (Pub. by Third Eye Centre). State Mutual Bk.

Third Eye Philosophy: Essays in East-West Thought. Troy W. Organ. LC 86-12597. 200p. 1986. text ed. 26.95x (ISBN 0-8214-0851-8). Ohio U Pr.

Third-Eye Theology: Theology in Formation in Asian Settings. Choan-Seng Song. LC 79-4208. pap. 72.00 (ISBN 0-317-26666-7, 2025121). Bks Demand UMI.

Third Eyelid. Frona Lane. LC 78-179805. (New Poetry Ser.). Repr. of 1951 ed. 16.00 (ISBN 0-404-56005-9). AMS Pr.

Third Face of War. Gene Schulze. LC 76-94463. (Illus.). 1969. 9.50 (ISBN 0-8363-0097-1). Jenkins.

Third Factory. Viktor Shklovsky. Ed. & tr. by Richard Sheldon. 1977. 12.95 (ISBN 0-88233-132-9). Ardis Pubs.

Third Fiber Optics & Communications Exposition: FOC '80, San Francisco. 125.00 (ISBN 0-686-33022-6). Info Gatekeepers.

Third Five-Year Annotated Index to Media Report to Women: 1982-1986. 54p. 1987. 5.00 (ISBN 0-930470-10-9). Womens Inst Free Press.

Third Flight of the Starfire. Edwin Mumford. 1972. 4.00 (ISBN 0-682-47503-3). Exposition-Phoenix.

Third Force in Missions. Paul Pomerville. 196p. 1986. pap. 9.95 (ISBN 0-913573-15-9). Hendrickson MA.

Third Force Psychology & the Study of Literature. Ed. by Bernard J. Paris. LC 85-47629. 344p. 1986. 39.50x (ISBN 0-8386-3263-7). Fairleigh Dickinson.

Third Force: The Psychology of Abraham Maslow. Frank G. Goble. 1984. pap. 3.95 (ISBN 0-671-50983-7). PB.

Third French Republic, Eighteen-Seventy to Nineteen-Forty. Leslie Derfler. LC 82-177. (Anvil Ser.). 192p. 1982. pap. text ed. 7.50 (ISBN 0-89874-480-6). Krieger.

Third Friday: A Novel of Suspense. George Bellak. LC 87-31251. 384p. 1988. 18.95 (ISBN 0-688-04399-2). Morrow.

Third from the Sun. Guy De Marco. 265p. 1981. 10.00 (ISBN 0-682-49670-7, Banner). Exposition-Phoenix.

Third Garfield Treasury. Jim Davis. 1985. pap. 8.95 (ISBN 0-345-32635-0). Ballantine.

Third Generation Greek Americans: A Study of Religious Attitudes. Alice Scourby. Ed. by Francesco Cordasco. LC 80-893. (American Ethnic Groups Ser.). lib. bdg. 16.00x (ISBN 0-405-13454-1). Ayer Co Pubs.

Third Generation: Young Conservatives Look to the Future. Intro. by Benjamin Hart. LC 87-4540. 240p. (Orig.). 1987. 17.95 (ISBN 0-89526-572-9); pap. 9.95 (ISBN 0-89526-791-8). Regnery Gateway.

Third George. Jean Plaidy. (Georgian Saga Ser.: Vol. 5). 352p. 1987. 17.95 (ISBN 0-399-13245-7, Putnam). Putnam Pub Group.

Third Girl. Agatha Christie. 1984. pap. 3.50 (ISBN 0-671-54212-5). PB.

Third Girl from the Left. Ann Turner. LC 85-30028. 153p. (gr. 7 up). 1986. 12.95 (ISBN 0-02-789510-6). Macmillan.

Third Globe: Symposium for the Reconstruction of the Globe Playhouse, Wayne State University. LC 81-3362. (Illus.). 268p. 1981. 25.00x (ISBN 0-8143-1680-8). Wayne St. U Pr.

Third Grade Is Terrible. Barbara Baker. LC 88-3631. (Illus.). 80p. (gr. 2-5). 1988. 10.95 (ISBN 0-525-44425-4, 01063-320). Dutton.

Third Grave. David Case. (Illus.). 192p. 1981. 10.95 (ISBN 0-87054-089-0). Arkham.

Third Helpings. Calvin Trillin. 192p. 1984. pap. 5.95 (ISBN 0-14-007314-0). Penguin.

Third Herman Treasury. Jim Unger. LC 82-72416. (Illus.). 208p. 1982. 7.95. Andrews & McMeel.

Third Horizon. Frank Dossetor. 1985. 10.00x (ISBN 0-317-62218-8, Guild of Pastoral Psych). State Mutual Bk.

Third IMA Conference on Control Theory. Ed. by J. E. Marshall et al. LC 81-67923. 1982. 99.00 (ISBN 0-12-473960-1). Acad Pr.

Third Indochina Conflict. Ed. by David W. Elliott. (Westview Replica Edition Ser.). 250p. 1981. pap. 39.00x (ISBN 0-89158-739-X). Westview.

Third Intermediate Period in Egypt, 1100-650 B.C. 2nd. ed. K. A. Kitchen. (Illus.). 628p. 1986. pap. text ed. 40.00 (ISBN 0-85668-298-5, Pub. by Aris & Phillips UK). Humanities.

Third International after Lenin. Leon Trotsky. LC 70-130578. 1970. pap. 8.95 (ISBN 0-87348-185-2). Path Pr NY.

Third International & Its Place in History. Vladimir I. Lenin. 51p. 1976. pap. 0.75 (ISBN 0-8285-0175-0, Pub. by Progress Pubs USSR). Imported Pubns.

Third International Conference on AIDS: Abstracts, Washington, D. C. Ed. by U. S. Public Health Services & World Health Organization Staff. (Special Studies on AIDS). 248p. 1988. 35.00 (ISBN 0-317-66265-1). Univ Pub Group.

Third International Conference on Facility Operations-Safeguards Interface: American Nuclear Society, San Diego, CA, November 29 to December 4, 1987. Date not set. price not set (ISBN 0-89448-138-X, 700132). Am Nuclear Soc.

Third International Conference on Geotextiles, 5 vols. Date not set. 140.00. Indus Fabrics.

Third International Conference on Logic Programming. Ed. by E. Shapiro. (Lecture Notes in Computer Science: Vol. 225). ix, 720p. 1986. pap. 39.00 (ISBN 0-387-16492-8). Springer-Verlag.

Third International Conference on Minority Languages: Celtic Papers. Ed. by E. Mac Oein et al. 1987. 41.00 (ISBN 0-905028-64-3, Pub. by Multilingual Matters). Taylor & Francis.

Third International Conference on Occupant Protection. Incl. 420p. 1974. 30.00 (ISBN 0-89883-029-X, P-53); members 25.00 (ISBN 0-317-37268-8); 344p. 1966. 8.00 (ISBN 0-89883-012-5, P-12); 488p. 1967. 10.00 (P-20); 462p. 35.00 (ISBN 0-89883-018-4, P-28); 835p. 1971. 35.00 (ISBN 0-89883-025-7, P-39). Soc Auto Engineers.

Third International Conference on Picture Archiving & Communication Systems (PACS III) for Medical Applications. Ed. by R. H. Schneider & S. J. Dwyer, III. 249p. 1985. 43.00 (ISBN 0-89252-571-1, 536). SPIE.

Third International Conference on Space Structures. Ed. by Nooshin. 1056p. 1984. 210.75 (ISBN 0-85334-309-8, Pub. by Elsevier Applied Sci England). Elsevier.

Third International Conference on System Science in Health Care. Ed. by W. Van Eimeren et al. (Health Systems Research Ser.). xxxiii, 1452p. 1984. 74.00 (ISBN 0-387-13692-4). Springer-Verlag.

Third International Conference on the Study of Shamanism & Alternate Modes of Healing, 1986: Proceedings. Ed. by Ruth-Inge Heinze et al. 349p. (Orig.). 1987. pap. 21.00 (ISBN 0-945875-00-2). Independent Scholars Asia Inc.

Third International Coral Reef Symposium: Proceedings, 1977, 2 Vols. 1300p. 1977. 60.00 set (ISBN 0-930050-03-7). Vol. 1 (ISBN 0-930050-01-0). Vol. 2 (ISBN 0-930050-02-9). Univ Miami A R C.

Third International Directory of Private Presses (Letterpress) Ed. by Budd Westreich. (Illus.). 160p. 1982. 25.00 (ISBN 0-936300-04-3); pap. 15.00 (ISBN 0-936300-03-5). Pr Arden Park.

Third International Meeting on Ferroelectricity, (Edinburgh, 1973) Proceedings, 2 Vols. Ed. by I. Lefkowitz & G. Taylor. 620p. 1974. 355.00 (ISBN 0-677-40215-5). Gordon & Breach.

Third International Meeting on Lithium Batteries. Electrochemical Society of Japan Staff. 1987. 117.00 (ISBN 1-85166-149-2). Elsevier.

Third International Meeting on Reactor Thermal Hydraulics: Proceedings in Newport, RI October 10-15, 1985. 1200p. Date not set. 105.00 (ISBN 0-89448-122-3, 700103). Am Nuclear Soc.

Third International Pacific Conference Proceedings. 1985. 95.00 (ISBN 0-89883-733-2, P 169). Soc Auto Engineers.

Third Jewish Catalog: Creating Community. Ed. by Sharon Strassfeld & Michael Strassfeld. LC 80-19818. (Illus.). 416p. 1980. 9.95 (ISBN 0-8276-0183-2, 466). JPS Phila.

Third Judicial Circuit Court of Michigan: Technical Assistance Report. National Center for State Courts Staff. 216p. 1979. manuscript 12.96 (NCRO-012). Natl Ctr St Courts.

Third Lady. Shizuko Natsuki. 256p. (Orig.). 1987. pap. text ed. 2.95 (ISBN 0-345-33765-4). Ballantine.

Third Leaders, Reprinted from the Times. facs. ed. London Times. LC 68-16980. (Essay Index Reprint Ser). 1928. 15.00 (ISBN 0-8369-0946-1). Ayer Co Pubs.

Third Leaf: The Birth of a Vineyard. Betty Williams. (Illus.). 80p. (Orig.). 1986. pap. 10.00 (ISBN 0-936784-05-9). J Daniel.

Third Level see Competency Tests for Basic Reading Skills.

Third Life of Grange Copeland. Alice Walker. LC 77-3427. 247p. 1977. pap. 4.95 (ISBN 0-15-689960-4, Harv). HarBraceJ.

Third Life of Grange Copeland. Alice Walker. 1988. pap. 3.95 (ISBN 0-671-66142-6). PB.

Third Life of Per Smevik. Ole Rolvaag. Tr. by Ella V. Tweet & Solweig Zempel. LC 86-45764. 144p. 1987. pap. 6.95 (ISBN 0-06-097076-6, PL 7076, PL). Har-Row.

Third Line Medicine: Modern Treatment for Persistent Systems. Melvyn R. Werbach. 232p. 1986. pap. 8.95 (ISBN 1-85063-041-0, 30410). Routledge Chapman & Hall.

Third Man. Graham Greene. 1988. pap. 9.95 (ISBN 0-571-12634-0). Faber & Faber.

Third Man & the Fallen Idol. Graham Greene. 1981. pap. 3.95 (ISBN 0-14-003278-9). Penguin.

Third Man, Loser Takes All. Graham Greene. 208p. 1983. 20.95 (ISBN 0-670-70084-3). Viking.

Third Math Helper. Eva Pollack. (Math Tutorial Program Ser.). 64p. (gr. k-2). 1975. 3.95 (ISBN 0-87594-142-7). Book-Lab.

Third Millenium: A History of the World A. D. 2000-3000. Brian Stableford & David Langford. LC 85-156. (Illus.). 224p. (Orig.). 1985. 19.50 (ISBN 0-394-53980-X); pap. 13.95 (ISBN 0-394-74151-X). Knopf.

Third Mind. William S. Burroughs. (Illus.). 194p. 1982. pap. 7.95 (ISBN 0-8050-0184-0). Seaver Bks.

Third Mind. Williams S. Burroughs. pap. 7.95 (ISBN 0-317-62779-1). Seaver Bks.

Third Miss Symons. F. M. Mayor. 288p. 1988. pap. 6.95 (ISBN 0-14-016179-1). Penguin.

Third Music. Ann R. Colton. LC 82-71249. (Illus.). 432p. 1982. 15.95 (ISBN 0-917187-00-8). A R C Pub.

Third National Cone Box Show Catalog. William Bracker & James J. Nabors. (Illus.). 64p. (Orig.). 1979. pap. text ed. 11.95 saddle stitch (ISBN 0-8403-2181-3). Kendall-Hunt.

Third National Symposium on Aquifer Restoration & Ground: Proceedings. 1983. 43.75 (ISBN 0-318-23017-8). Natl Water Well.

Third Notch & Other Stories. Shahnon Ahmad. Tr. by Harry Aveling from Malay. (Writing in Asia Ser.). 1981. pap. text ed. 5.50x (ISBN 0-686-72743-6, 00238). Heinemann Ed.

Third of a Century with George Way Harley in Liberia. Winifred J. Harley. (Liberian Studies Monograph Ser: No. 2). 1973. 5.00 (ISBN 0-916712-00-1). Liberian Studies.

Third Omni Book of Science Fiction. Ed. by Ellen Datlow. 1985. pap. 3.95 (ISBN 0-8217-1575-5). Zebra.

Third Omnibus of Crime. Ed. by Dorothy L. Sayers. 808p. 1985. Repr. of 1935 ed. lib. bdg. 49.50 (ISBN 0-8495-5070-X). Arden Lib.

Third Opinion: An International Guide to Alternative Therapy Centers for the Treatment & Prevention of Cancer. John M. Fink. 196p. pap. 9.95 (ISBN 0-89529-382-X). Avery Pub.

Third Option. Theodore Shackley. 1988. pap. 3.95 (ISBN 0-440-20219-1). Dell.

Third or Eighteen-Twenty Land Lotteries of Georgia. Silas E. Lucas, Jr. (Seven Land Lotteries of Georgia & Other Land Records Ser.). 412p. 1984. Repr. of 1973 ed. 35.00 (ISBN 0-89308-021-7, GA 26). Southern Hist Pr.

Third-Order Linear Differential Equations. Michal Gregus. (Mathematics & Its Applications (East European Ser.)). 1986. lib. bdg. 59.00 (ISBN 90-277-2193-9, Pub. by Reidel Holland). Kluwer-Academic.

Third Pagoda & Other Legends of China. J. Frank Bucher. 176p. 1984. 9.00 (ISBN 0-682-40129-3, Banner). Exposition-Phoenix.

Third Palenque Round Table, 1978, Pt. 1. Ed. by Merle Greene Robertson & Donnan C. Jeffers. LC 79-64960. (Palenque Round Table Ser.: Vol. IV). (Illus.). 232p. (Orig.). 1979. pap. text ed. 25.00x (ISBN 0-292-78036-2, Pub. by Pre-Columbian Mexico). U of Tex Pr.

Third Palenque Round Table, 1978, Pt. 2. Ed. by Merle Greene Robertson. (Palenque Round Table Ser.: Vol. V). (Illus.). 244p. 1980. text ed. 35.00x (ISBN 0-292-78037-0). U of Tex Pr.

Third Part of the Countess of Pembroke's Yvychurch see Golden Booke of the Leaden Gods.

Third Parties in America. Steven J. Rosenstone et al. LC 83-43091. 266p. 1984. 28.00x (ISBN 0-691-02225-9); pap. 9.95 (ISBN 0-691-07673-1). Princeton U Pr.

Third Parties in American Politics. Howard P. Nash, Jr. 1958. 9.00 (ISBN 0-8183-0213-5). Pub Aff Pr.

Third Party Computer Maintenance (Europe) 262p. 1985. 1950.00 (ISBN 0-86621-677-4, E749). Frost & Sullivan.

Third Party Financing for Energy Savings. Ed. by Derek Fee. 672p. 1988. write for info. (ISBN 1-85302-012-5, Pub. by J Kingsley Pubs UK). UNIPUB.

Third-Party Financing: Increasing Investment in Energy Efficient Industrial Projects. 122p. executive summary 4.00. Alliance Save Ener.

Third Party Footprints. James Youngdale. (Illus.). 10.00 (ISBN 0-87018-064-9). Ross.

Third Party Maintenance. (Marketing Research Reports). Date not set. write for info. (ISBN 0-86621-865-3, A1686). Frost & Sullivan.

Third-Party Maintenance of Computer & Datacom Equipment. International Resource Development, Inc. Staff. 175p. 1987. 1650.00x (ISBN 0-88694-724-3). Intl Res Dev.

Third Party Protection of Software & Firmware: Direct Protection of Zeros & Ones. John J. Borking. LC 84-24752. 522p. 1985. 110.75 (ISBN 0-444-87677-4, North-Holland). Elsevier.

Third-Party Settlement of Disputes in Theory & Practice. Lillian L. Randolph. LC 73-8942. 464p. 1973. lib. bdg. 24.00 (ISBN 0-379-00017-2). Oceana.

Third Passenger. Caroline Crane. 1985. 24.95x (ISBN 0-7090-1772-3, Pub. by R Hale Ltd UK). State Mutual Bk.

Third Peacock. Robert F. Capon. 108p. (Orig.). 1986. pap. 7.95 (ISBN 0-86683-497-4, HarpR). Har-Row.

Third Person. Lehman Strauss. 1954. 7.95 (ISBN 0-87213-827-5). Loizeaux.

Third Person Rural. Noel Perrin. (Penguin Nonfiction Ser.). 192p. 1985. pap. 6.95 (ISBN 0-14-007685-9). Penguin.

Third Person Rural: Further Essays of a Sometime Farmer. Noel Perrin. LC 82-49337. (Illus.). 208p. 1983. 13.95 (ISBN 0-87923-467-9). Godine.

Third Planet. Paul D. Lowman, Jr. LC 77-128348. (Illus.). 170p. 1972. 45.00x (ISBN 0-8139-0577-X). U Pr of Va.

Third Planet: An Invitation to Geology. Konrad B. Krauskopf. LC 74-77823. (Illus.). 528p. 1974. text ed. 18.00x (ISBN 0-87735-359-X); pap. text ed. 12.00 (ISBN 0-87735-360-3). Freeman Cooper.

Third Planet from Altair. Edward Packard. (Choose Your Own Adventure Ser.: No. 7). 128p. (Orig.). (gr. 5 up). 1981. pap. 1.95 (ISBN 0-553-23185-5). Bantam.

Third Planet from Altair. Edward Packard. LC 78-23998. (Illus.). (gr. 4-6). 1979. 11.70 (ISBN 0-397-31827-8); text ed. 11.89 (ISBN 0-397-31884-7). Har-Row.

Third Policeman. Flann O'Brien. 1976. pap. 7.95 (ISBN 0-452-25912-6, Plume). NAL.

Third Portuguese Empire: A Study in Economic Imperialism, 1826-1975. Gervase Clarence-Smith. 256p. (Orig.). 1986. pap. 14.00 (ISBN 0-7190-1805-6, Pub. by Manchester Univ Pr). St Martin.

Third Power: Farmers to the Front (Fourth Edition) facsimile ed. James A. Everitt. LC 74-30630. (American Farmers & the Rise of Agribusiness Ser.). (Illus.). 1975. Repr. of 1907 ed. 29.00x (ISBN 0-405-06799-2). Ayer Co Pubs.

Third-Prize Surprise. Susan Saunders. (Bad News Bunny Ser.: No. 1). (gr. 2-5). 1987. pap. 2.50 (ISBN 0-671-62713-9, Minstrel Bks). S&S.

Third Rainbow Book of Adventures. Ed. by Jutta Kapphammer & Philip S. Helm. (Illus.). 235p. (Orig.). 1987. pap. 11.95 (ISBN 0-932471-07-2). Falsoft.

Third Reading Helper. rev. ed. Gloria Orlick. (Reading Tutorial Program). (Illus.). (gr. 1 up). 1983. pap. 3.45 programmed bk (ISBN 0-87594-004-8). Book-Lab.

Third Reformation: Charismatic Movements & the Lutheran Tradition. Carter Lindberg. LC 83-11371. x, 346p. 1983. 24.95 (ISBN 0-86554-075-6, MUP/H83). Mercer Univ Pr.

Third Regional Symposium on the Development of Deltaic Areas: Proceedings. Regional Symposium on the Development of Deltaic Areas, 3rd. (Water Resources Development Ser.: No. 50). pap. 17.00 (ISBN 92-1-119156-4, E.78.II.F.10). UN.

Third Reich. Klaus Hildebrand. Tr. by P. S. Falla from Ger. (Illus.). 168p. 1984. 34.95x (ISBN 0-04-943033-5); pap. 11.95x (ISBN 0-04-943032-7). Unwin Hyman.

Third Reich. Henri Lichtenberger. Tr. by Koppel S. Pinson. LC 73-102249. (Select Bibliographies Reprint Ser). 1937. 32.00 (ISBN 0-8369-5134-4). Ayer Co Pubs.

Third Reich - Weimar Trilogy, 3 vols. Date not set. Set. 86.70 (ISBN 0-87436-424-8). ABC-Clio.

Third Reich Almanac. James Taylor & Warren Shaw. (Illus.). 400p. 1988. text ed. 24.95 (ISBN 0-88687-363-0, World Almanac). Pharos Bks NY.

Third Reich & the Christian Churches. Ed. by Peter Matheson. 128p. Date not set. pap. 11.95 (ISBN 0-567-29105-7, Pub. by T & T Clark Ltd UK). Fortress.

Third Reich & the Palestine Question. Francis R. Nicosia. 335p. 1986. text ed. 35.00x (ISBN 0-292-72731-3). U of Tex Pr.

Third Reich at War: A Historical Bibliography. LC 83-27168. (ABC-Clio Research Guides Ser.: No. 11). 270p. 1984. lib. bdg. 34.00 (ISBN 0-87436-393-4). ABC-Clio.

Third Reich, 1933-1945: A Bibliographical Guide to German National Socialism. Louis L. Snyder. Ed. by Thomas Spira. (Canadian Review of Studies in Nationalism vol. 7, Reference Library of Social Science). 1987. lib. bdg. 42.00 (ISBN 0-8240-8463-2). Garland Pub.

Third Reich, 1933-39: A Historical Bibliography. LC 83-21527. (Research Guides: No. 10). 239p. 1984. lib. bdg. 34.00 (ISBN 0-87436-379-9). ABC-Clio.

Third Republic. Raymond Recouly. Tr. by E. F. Buckley. LC 28-23849. (National History of France: No. 10). Repr. of 1928 ed. 45.00 (ISBN 0-404-50800-6). AMS Pr.

Third Republic & the Centennial of 1789. Brenda Nelms. Ed. by William H. McNeill & David H. Pinkney. (Modern European History Ser.). 304p. 1987. lib. bdg. 45.00 (ISBN 0-8240-8039-4). Garland Pub.

Third Republic Defended: Bourgeois Reform in France, 1880-1914. Sanford Elwitt. LC 86-2914. 304p. 1986. text ed. 27.50 (ISBN 0-8071-1294-1). La State U Pr.

Third Republic from Its Origins to the Great War, 1871-1914. Jean-Marie Mayeur & Madeleine Reberioux. Tr. by J. R. Foster. LC 83-15084. (Cambridge History of Modern France Ser.: No. 4). (Illus.). 414p. 1984. 67.50 (ISBN 0-521-24931-7). Cambridge U Pr.

Third Republic from Its Origins to the Great War, 1871-1914. Jean-Marie Mayeur & Madeleine Reberioux. (Cambridge History of Modern France Ser.: No. 4). (Illus.). 412p. 1988. pap. 14.95 (ISBN 0-521-35857-4). Cambridge U Pr.

Third Review of Special Education. Ed. by Lester Mann & David A. Sabatino. (Journal of Special Education Press Series in Special Education). (Illus.). 288p. 1976. 60.00 (ISBN 0-8089-0979-7, 792673). Grune.

Third Rib Knife. Philip Kienholz. 32p. 1966. pap. 1.50 (ISBN 0-911042-12-1). N Dak Inst.

Third Rider. Barry Cord. 1978. pap. 1.25 (ISBN 0-505-51318-8, Pub. by Tower Bks). Leisure NY.

Third River Basin Management Conference: Proceedings of a Conference Held in York, 4-8 July 1983 & Incorporating the Workshop on Advances in the Application of Mathematical Modelling to Water Quality Management Held in London, July 11-12 1983. Ed. by D. H. Newsome & A. M. Edwards. (Illus.). 670p. 1984. pap. 130.00 (ISBN 0-08-031505-4). Pergamon.

Third Rome: National Bolshevism in the U. S. S. R. Mikhail Agursky. LC 86-9264. 350p. 1985. 45.00x (ISBN 0-8133-0139-4). Westview.

Third Rose: Gertrude Stein & Her World. John M. Brinnin. 464p. 1987. pap. 14.95 (ISBN 0-201-05880-4). Addison-Wesley.

Third Saturday in October. Al Browning. LC 87-18949. (Illus.). 352p. 1987. 16.95 (ISBN 0-934395-58-6). Rutledge Hill Pr.

Third SCI-RSC Medical Chemistry Symposium. Ed. by R. W. Lambert. (Royal Society of Chemistry Special Publication Ser.: No. 55). (Illus.). 396p. 1986. pap. 63.00x flex-text (ISBN 0-85186-616-6, Pub. by Royal Soc Chem). Scholium Intl.

Third Selections from Modern Poets. John Squire. Repr. of 1948 ed. lib. bdg. 15.00 (ISBN 0-8495-5009-2). Arden Lib.

Third Selections from Modern Poets. Ed. by John Squire. 1978. Repr. of 1948 ed. lib. bdg. 12.50 (ISBN 0-8492-2578-7). R West.

Third Seminar on Advanced Vehicle System Dynamics: Proceedings of the Third ICTS Seminar Held at Amalfi, Italy, May 5-10, 1986. A. D. De Pater & H. B. Pacejka. (Supplement to Vehicle System Dynamics Ser.: Vol. 16). 366p. 1987. pap. 34.00 (ISBN 90-265-0676-7, Pub. by Swets Pub Serv Holland). Taylor & Francis.

Third September Nineteen Thirty-Nine. Sheila Gordon. (Day That Made History Ser.). (Illus.). 64p. (YA) (gr. 7-9). 1988. 17.95 (ISBN 0-85219-757-8, Pub. by Batsford England). David & Charles.

Third Series see Contemporary Portraits.

Third Sikh War - Towards or Away from Khalistan. D. H. Bhutani. 137p. 1986. 22.95. Asia Bk Corp.

Third Sikh War? Towards or Away from Khalistan? D. H. Butani. 137p. 1986. 25.00x (ISBN 81-85002-02-9, Pub. by Promilla). South Asia Bks.

Third Soviet Generation. M. Davidow. 221p. 1983. 6.95 (ISBN 0-8285-2685-0, Pub. by Progress Pubs USSR). Imported Pubns.

Third Soviet-Japanese Symposium on Ferroelectricity: Akademgorodok, Novosibirsk, U. S. S. R., September 9-14, 1984. Ed. by K. S. Aleksandrov & J. Kobayashi. 530p. 1985. pap. text ed. 240.00 (ISBN 0-677-21270-4). Gordon & Breach.

Third Statistical Account of Scotland: The County of Kincardine. Ed. by Dennis Smith. (Illus.). 288p. 1987. 33.75 (ISBN 0-7073-0503-9, Pub. by Scot Acad Pr). Longwood Pub Group.

Third Statistical Account of Scotland: The County of Ross & Cromarty. Ed. by A. S. Mather. (Illus.). 500p. 1987. 56.25 (ISBN 0-7073-0506-3, Pub. by Scot Acad Pr). Longwood Pub Group.

Third Steps in Ballet: Basic Allegro Steps. Thalia Mara. (Illus.). 64p. (Orig.). (YA) (gr. 6-9). 1987. pap. 6.95 (ISBN 0-916622-55-X). Princeton Bk Co.

Third Story. Carole Taylor. LC 86-10306. (Orig.). 1986. pap. 7.95 (ISBN 0-917597-06-0). Lace Pubns.

Third-Story Cat. Leslie Baker. (Illus.). 32p. (ps-3). 1987. 12.95 (ISBN 0-316-07832-8). Little.

Third Strike: A Father's Story of His Son's Struggle with Cancer. Robert L Semel. (Human Condition Ser.). (Illus.). 224p. (Orig.). 1985. 17.95 (ISBN 0-943920-60-4); pap. 9.95 (ISBN 0-943920-61-2). Metamorphous Pr.

Third Supplement see Children's Literature: A Guide to Reference Sources.

Third Supplement to the Cumulation of the Library Catalog Supplements of the New York State School of Industrial & Labor Relations. Cornell University Staff. 1979. lib. bdg. 190.00 (ISBN 0-8161-0260-0, Hall Library). G K Hall.

Third Supplementary Catalogue of Arabic Books, 1958-1969, 4 vols. Martin Lings & Yasin H. Safadi. 1976. Set. 375.00 (Pub. by British Lib). Vol. 1: Authors A-KHULI. Vol. 2: Authors KHULUSI-Z. Vol. 3: Title Index. Vol. 4: Subject Index. Longwood Pub Group.

Third Teddy Bear & Friends Price Guide. Helen Sieverling. (Illus.). 200p. (Orig.). 1988. pap. 9.95 (ISBN 0-87588-311-7). Hobby Hse.

Third Testament. Malcolm Muggeridge. 192p. 1983. pap. 2.95 (ISBN 0-345-30516-7). Ballantine.

Third Testament of the Holy Bible. S. Joseph Iannarelli. 1985. 5.95 (ISBN 0-533-06645-X). Vantage.

Third Testament, Vol. One: Tales on the Evolution of God in Consciousness. John M. Fitzgerald. LC 88-70629. 145p. 1988. 25.00 (ISBN 0-9620390-2-0); pap. 15.00 (ISBN 0-9620390-0-4). Closet Pr.

Third Thousand Years. W. Cleon Skousen. 1964. 12.95 (ISBN 0-88494-122-1). Bookcraft Inc.

Third Treasury of Kahlil Gibran. Kahlil Gibran. LC 73-90950. 484p. 1974. 9.95 (ISBN 0-8065-0403-X, Pub. by Citadel Pr). Lyle Stuart.

Third Treasury of Kahlil Gibran. Kahlil Gibran. Ed. by Andrew D. Sherfan. 1978. pap. 5.95 (ISBN 0-8065-0648-2, Pub. by Citadel Pr). Lyle Stuart.

Third Tripartite Technical Meeting for the Timber Industry, Geneva, 1-10 December 1981: Note on the Proceedings. iii, 78p. 1982. 10.50 (ISBN 92-2-102767-8). Intl Labour Office.

Third Truth. Michael Hastings. (Spymaster Ser.). 1988. pap. 4.50 (ISBN 0-02-043560-6, Collier). Macmillan.

Third Try at World Order. Harlan Cleveland. 3.95 (ISBN 0-686-25998-X). Aspen Inst Human.

Third Try at World Order. Harlan Cleveland. 140p. (Orig.). 1977. pap. text ed. 8.00 (ISBN 0-8191-5901-8, Pub. by Aspen Inst for Humanistic Studies). U Pr of Amer.

Third Underground Shopper. Sue Goldstein. 480p. (Orig.). 1987. pap. 8.95 (ISBN 0-8362-7937-9). Andrews & McMeel.

Third United Nations Conference of the Law of the Sea: Summary Records of Meetings, Vol. IV. 12.00 (ISBN 92-1-133228-1, E.75.V.10). UN.

Third United Nations Conference on the Law of the Sea, 18 vols. Ed. by Renate Platzoder. 1982. 100.00 ea. Vol. 1 (ISBN 0-379-20724-9). Vol. 2 (ISBN 0-379-20804-0). Vol. 3 (ISBN 0-379-20805-9). Vol. 4. Set 1200.00 (ISBN 0-379-20806-7). Vol. 5 (ISBN 0-379-20807-5). Vol. 6 (ISBN 0-379-20808-3). Vol. 7 (ISBN 0-379-20809-1). Vol. 8 (ISBN 0-379-20810-5), Vol. 9 (ISBN 0-379-20811-3), Vol. 10 (ISBN 0-379-20812-1), Vol. 11 (ISBN 0-379-20813-X) Oceana.

Third United Nations Conference on the Law of the Sea: Official Records: Plenary Meetings: Summary Records of Meetings, 183rd & 184th Meetings & Verbatim Records of Meetings, 185th to 193rd Meetings & Documents, Vol. XVII. Resumed Eleventh Session, New York, 22-24 September 1982 & Final Part of the Eleventh Session & Conclusion of the Conference, Montego Bay, 6-10 December 1982. 245p. 1985. pap. 23.00 (E.84.V.3). UN.

Third United Nations Conference on the Law of the Sea: Summary Records of Meetings, Vol. I. 12.00 (ISBN 92-1-133205-2, E.75.V.3). UN.

Third United Nations Conference on the Law of the Sea: Summary Records of Meetings, Vol. II. 19.00 (ISBN 92-1-133218-4, E.75.V.4). UN.

Third United Nations Conference on the Law of the Sea: Documents of the Conference, Vol. III. 14.00 (ISBN 92-1-133230-3, E.75.V.5). UN.

Third United Nations Conference on the Law of the Sea: Summary Records of Meetings, Vol. V. 14.00 (ISBN 92-1-133227-3, E.76.V.8). UN.

Third United Nations Conference on the Law of the Sea: Documents of the Conference, Vol. VI. 13.00 (ISBN 92-1-133225-7, E.77.V.2). UN.

Third United Nations Conference on the Law of the Sea: Summary Records of Meetings, Vol. VII. 7.00 (ISBN 92-1-133226-5, E.78.V.3). UN.

Third United Nations Conference on the Law of the Sea: Summary Records of Meetings, Vol. IX. 14.00 (ISBN 92-1-133224-9, E.79.V.3). UN.

Third United Nations Conference on the Law of the Sea: Official Records, Seventh Session, Vol. X. 11.00 (ISBN 92-1-133223-0, E.79.V.4). UN.

Third United Nations Conference on the Law of the Sea: Official Records, Eighth Session, Vol. XI. 10.00 (ISBN 92-1-133222-2, E.80.V.6). UN.

Third United Nations Conference on the Law of the Sea: Official Records, Summary of Meetings, Resumed Eighth Session, Vol. XII. 9.00 (ISBN 92-1-133221-4, E.80.V.12). UN.

Third United Nations Conference on the Law of the Sea: Official Records, Summary Records of Meetings, Ninth Session, Vol. XIII. 12.00 (ISBN 92-1-133220-6, E.81.V.5). UN.

Third United Nations Conference on the Law of the Sea: Summary Records of Meetings & Documents, Resumed Ninth Session; Geneva, 28 July- 29 August 1980, Vol. XIV. 15.00 (ISBN 92-1-133219-2, E.82.V.2). UN.

Third United Nations Conference on the Law of the Sea Offical Records: Summary Records of Meetings & Documents, Eleventh Session; New York, 8 March- 30 April 1982, Vol. XVI. 281p. 27.00 (ISBN 92-1-133244-3, E.84.V.2). UN.

Third United Nations Conference on the Law of the Sea: Summary Records of Meetings & Documents, Resumed Eleventh Session; New York 22 & 24 September 1982, Vol. XVII. 245p. 23.00 (ISBN 92-1-133333-4, E.84.V.3). UN.

Third United Nations Conference on the Law of the Sea, Vol XV. 243p. 1983. pap. text ed. 23.00 (E.83.V.4). UN.

Third United Nations Conference on the Law of the Sea: Official Records: Summary Records of Meetings: Plenary Meetings - 156th to 182nd Meetings, First Committee's 55th & 56th Meetings, & Second Committee's 59th Meeting & Documents, 11th Session, New York, March 8 - April 30, 1982, Vol. XVI. United Nations Conference Staff. 281p. 1985. pap. 27.00 (E.84.V.2). UN.

Third United Nations Conference on the Law of the Sea: Official Records, Vol. 14. 187p. 1980. pap. 15.00 (E.82.V.2). UN.

Third Victim. Lilla M. Waltch. (Lisa Davis Mystery Ser.). 1987. 15.95 (ISBN 0-396-08942-9). Dodd.

Third Violet see Prose & Poetry.

Third Virginia Infantry. Lee Wallace. (Virginia Regimental Histories Ser.). (Illus.). 117p. 1986. 16.45 (ISBN 0-317-64927-2). H E Howard.

Third Vow & Other Stories. Phanishwar N. Renu. Tr. by Kathryn Hansen. 1986. 18.50X (ISBN 81-7001-013-6, Pub. by Chanakya India). South Asia Bks.

Third Voyage of Captain Cook. Heinrich Zimmerman. 1988. 29.95 (ISBN 0-87770-165-2). Ye Galleon.

Third Voyage of Captain Cooke. Heinrich Zimmermann. 1988. Repr. of 1781 ed. ltd. ed. 29.95. Ye Galleon.

Third Wave. Alvin Toffler. 576p. (Orig.). 1984. pap. 4.95 (ISBN 0-553-24698-4). Bantam.

Third Wave & Education's Futures. William C. Miller. LC 81-80013. (Fastback Ser.: No. 155). 1981. pap. 0.90 (ISBN 0-87367-155-4). Phi Delta Kappa.

Third Wave & the Local Church. Dennis M. Davis & Steve Clapp. 175p. (Orig.). 1983. pap. 8.00 (ISBN 0-914527-54-1). C-Four Res.

Third Wave Images. Andrew Dazz. 61p. 1988. 6.95 (ISBN 0-533-07538-6). Vantage.

Third Wave of the Holy Spirit: Encountering the Power of Signs & Wonders Today. C. Peter Wagner. 160p. (Orig.). 1988. pap. text ed. 6.95 (ISBN 0-89283-601-6). Servant.

Third Wave: Russian Literature in Emigration. Olga Matich & Michael Heim. 300p. 1983. pap. 25.00 (ISBN 0-88233-782-3); pap. 13.50 (ISBN 0-88233-783-1). Ardis Pubs.

Third Way. Paul M. Lederach. LC 80-26280. 152p. 1980. pap. 6.95 (ISBN 0-8361-1934-7). Herald Pr.

Third Way: A Journal of Life in the West Bank. Raja Shehadeh. 1982. 12.95 (ISBN 0-7043-2354-0, Pub. by Quartet Bks). Salem Hse Pubs.

Third Way: Marxist-Leninist Theory & Modern Industrial Society. Ota Sik. Tr. by Marian Sling from Ger. LC 76-8032. 512p. 1976. 40.00 (ISBN 0-87332-084-0). M E Sharpe.

Third Wedding. Costas Taktsis. Tr. by Leslie Finer. pap. 8.95 (ISBN 0-317-43349-0). Red Dust.

Third Western States Exhibition Catalog. Charlotta Kotik et al. Ed. by Cheryl A. Jamison. (Illus.). 128p. 1986. deluxed 49.95 (ISBN 0-9611710-3-0); pap. 24.95 (ISBN 0-9611710-2-2). Western States.

Third Woman: Minority Woman Writers of the United States. Dexter Fisher. LC 79-87863. 1980. pap. text ed. 25.56 (ISBN 0-395-27707-8). HM.

Third Workshop on Grand Unification. Ed. by P. H. Frampton & H. Van Dam. (Progress in Physics Ser.: Vol. 6). 384p. 1982. text ed. 34.50 (ISBN 0-8176-3105-4). Birkhauser.

Third World. Christopher Barlow. 1979. 17.95 (ISBN 0-7134-1878-8, Pub. by Batsford England). David & Charles.

Third World. Ed. by Naton Leslie & Jim Villani. LC 88-60726. (Pig Iron Ser.: No. 14). (Illus.). 96p. (Orig.). 1988. pap. 7.95 (ISBN 0-917530-23-3). Pig Iron Pr.

Third World. Peter Worsley. LC 74-124639. (Nature of Human Society Ser). 374p. 1973. pap. 10.00x (ISBN 0-226-90753-8). U of Chicago Pr.

Third World, Vol. 1 (incl. 1980 & 1982 Supplements) Ed. by Eleanor C. Goldstein. (Social Issues Resources Ser.). 1983. 75.00 (ISBN 0-89777-031-5). Soc Issues.

Third World: A Vital New Force in International Affairs. 2nd ed. Peter Worsley. LC 74-124639. (Nature of Human Society Ser.). 1970. 20.00x (ISBN 0-226-90751-1). U of Chicago Pr.

Third World Affairs, 1985. Third World Foundation Staff. 436p. 1985. pap. 39.50x (ISBN 0-8133-0289-7). Westview.

Third World Affairs 1986. Third World Foundation Staff. 476p. 1986. pap. 41.50 (ISBN 0-8133-0385-0). Westview.

Third World & Decision-Making in the International Monetary Fund: The Quest for Full & Effective Participation. Tyrone Ferguson. 1988. 45.00 (ISBN 0-86187-957-0, Pub. by Pinter Pubs UK). Columbia U Pr.

Third World & International Relations. Ed. by Philipe Braillard & Mohammad-Reza Djalili. LC 85-28280. 300p. 1986. lib. bdg. 38.50x (ISBN 0-931477-70-0). Lynne Rienner.

Third World & Peace: Some Aspects of Problems of the Inter-Relationship of Interdevelopment & International Security. Marion Mushkat. LC 82-774. 356p. 1983. 27.50x (ISBN 0-312-80039-8). St Martin.

Third World & the Rich Countries: Prospects for the Year 2000. Angelos Angelopoulos. LC 72-75694. (Special Studies in International Economics & Development). 1972. text ed. 46.50x (ISBN 0-275-28608-8). Irvington.

Third World & the Soviet Union. Zaki Laidi. 192p. 1988. text ed. 45.00 (ISBN 0-86232-730-X, Pub. by Zed Pr UK); pap. text ed. 15.00 (ISBN 0-86232-731-8, Pub. by Zed Pr UK). Humanities.

Third World Atlas. Ben Crow et al. 76p. 1984. 65.00x (ISBN 0-335-15015-2, Pub. by Open Univ Pr); pap. 24.00x (ISBN 0-335-10259-X, Pub. by Open Univ Pr). Taylor & Francis.

Third World Attitudes Toward International Law: An Introduction. Frederick Snyder & Surakiart Sathirathai. LC 86-5383. 1987. 185.00 (ISBN 0-89838-914-3, Pub. by Kluwer-Nijhoff (Netherlands)). Kluwer Academic.

Third World Challenge to Psychiatry: Culture Accomodation & Mental Health Care. Howard N. Higginbotham. LC 83-24259. 314p. 1984. pap. text ed. 25.00x (ISBN 0-8248-0894-0, Pub. by Eastwest Ctr). UH Pr.

Third World Cinema: Film, Politics & Aesthetics. Ed. by John D. Downing. 1986. 29.95 (ISBN 0-275-92049-6, C2049). Praeger.

Third World City. David Drakakis-Smith. (Introductions to Development Ser.). 160p. 1987. pap. text ed. 9.95 (ISBN 0-416-91970-7). Routledge Chapman & Hall.

Third World Coalition in International Politics. 2nd ed. Robert A. Mortimer. 165p. 1984. lib. bdg. 39.00x (ISBN 0-86531-773-9); pap. text ed. 16.95x (ISBN 0-86531-774-7). Westview.

Third-World Conflict & International Security. Ed. by Christoph Bertram. LC 81-19036. 121p. 1982. 19.50 (ISBN 0-208-01957-X, Archon). Shoe String.

Third World Conflicts & Refugeeism: Dimensions, Dynamics, & Trends of the World Refugee Problem. H. Hakovirta. (Commentationes Scientarium Socialium Ser.: No. 32). 160p. (Orig.). 1986. pap. 42.50x (ISBN 951-653-140-7). Coronet Bks.

Third World Conundrum: A Call to Christian Partnership. Max Peberdy. 188p. pap. 7.50 (ISBN 0-85364-463-2, Pub. by Paternoster UK). Attic Pr.

Third World Coups D'Etat & International Security. Steven R. David. LC 86-45451. 192p. 1986. text ed. 22.50x (ISBN 0-8018-3307-8). Johns Hopkins.

Third World Development: A Basic Needs Approach. Ed. by Pradip K. Ghosh. LC 83-26681. (International Development Resource Bks.: No. 13). (Illus.). xv, 436p. 1984. lib. bdg. 46.95 (ISBN 0-313-24149-X, GTW/). Greenwood.

Third World Development: Problems & Prospects. Edward G. Stockwell & Karen A. Laidlaw. LC 79-24088. 362p. 1981. text ed. 24.95x (ISBN 0-88229-532-2); pap. text ed. 12.95x (ISBN 0-88229-751-1). Nelson-Hall.

Third World Diplomats in Dialogue with the First World. Robert J. Moore. (Studies in International Development Research). 256p. 1984. text ed. 39.95x (ISBN 0-333-36341-8, Pub. by Macmillan England); pap. text ed. 15.00x (ISBN 0-333-36342-6). Humanities.

Third World Economic Handbook. Stuart Sinclair. 224p. 1985. 137.00x (ISBN 0-686-83129-2, Pub. by Euromonitor). State Mutual Bk.

Third World Economic Handbook. 198p. 1983. 80.00x (ISBN 0-903706-85-7, Pub. by Euromonitor Pubns). Gale.

Third World: Exploring U. S. Interests. John W. Sewell & John A. Mathieson. (Headline Series 259). (Illus.). 64p. (gr. 11-12). 1982. pap. 4.00 (ISBN 0-87124-076-9). Foreign Policy.

Third World Film Making & the West. Roy Armes. (Orig.). 1987. 49.95x (ISBN 0-520-05667-1); pap. 17.95 (ISBN 0-520-05690-6). U of Cal Pr.

Third World Guide: Nineteen Eighty-Six to Nineteen Eighty-Seven. Third World Publications Staff. (Illus.). 632p. 1986. pap. 22.50 (ISBN 0-394-62330-4, Ever). Grove.

Third World Ideology & Western Reality: Manufacturing Political Myth. Carlos Rangel. 180p. 1986. pap. 19.95 (ISBN 0-88738-601-6). Transaction Bks.

Third World in Global Development. A. Hoogvetl. 240p. 1982. (Pub. by Macmillan UK); pap. text ed. 15.00 (ISBN 0-333-27682-5). Humanities.

Third World in Perspective. H. A. Reitsma & J. M. Kleinpenning. LC 85-14507. (Illus.). 444p. 1985. 37.50x (ISBN 0-8476-7450-9, Rowman & Allanheld). Rowman.

Third World in Perspective. H. A. Reitsma & J. M. Kleinpenning. (Illus.). 444p. 1986. pap. 22.95x (ISBN 0-8476-7481-9, Rowman & Allanhelp). Rowman.

Third World in Transition: The Case of the Peasantry in Botswana. Jan Hesselberg. 256p. 1988. pap. 29.50 (ISBN 0-8419-9788-8). Holmes & Meier.

Third World in World Economy. Pierre Jalee. Tr. by Mary Klopper from Fr. LC 70-81791. 224p. 1969. pap. 4.50 (ISBN 0-85345-177-X). Monthly Rev.

Third World Industrialisation in the 1980's: Open Economies in a Closing World. Ed. by Raphael Kaplinsky. 142p. 1984. 29.50x (ISBN 0-7146-3240-6, Pub. by F Cass Co). Biblio Dist.

Third World Instability: Central America As a European-American Issue. Ed. by Andrew J. Pierre. 168p. 1985. pap. 5.95 (ISBN 0-87609-005-6). Coun Foreign.

Third World Instability: The Case of Central America. Ed. by Andrew J. Pierre. 128p. 1985. 20.00x (ISBN 0-8147-6594-7). NYU Pr.

Third World: Latin America. 2nd ed. Philip Evanson. LC 84-93314. 128p. 1984. pap. text ed. 6.95 (ISBN 0-87967-499-7). Dushkin Pub.

Third World Legal Studies: Law in Alternative Strategies of Rural Development. Ed. by M. L. Marasinghe. 313p. 1982. pap. 15.00 (ISBN 0-686-37983-7). Intl Ctr Law.

Third World Legal Studies Nineteen Eighty-Five: Developing Legal Resources with the Third World's Poor. Ed. by M. L. Marasinghe et al. 210p. 1987. pap. 20.00 (ISBN 0-318-23293-6). Intl Ctr Law.

Third World Liberation Theologies: A Reader. Ed. by Deane W. Ferm. LC 85-15302. 400p. (Orig.). 1986. pap. 16.95 (ISBN 0-88344-516-6). Orbis Bks.

Third World Liberation Theologies: An Introductory Survey. Deane W. Ferm. LC 85-15534. pap. 10.95 (ISBN 0-88344-515-8). Orbis Bks.

Third World Lives of Struggle. Ed. by Hazel Johnson & Henry Bernstein. xiv, 271p. (Orig.). 1983. pap. text ed. 18.50 (ISBN 0-435-96130-6). Heinemann Ed.

Third World Marxist-Leninist Regimes: Strengths, Vulnerabilities & U. S. Policies. Uri Ra'anan et al. (IFPA Special Reports Ser.: No. 3). 96p. 1985. pap. 9.95 (ISBN 0-08-033160-2, Pub by P-B). Pergamon.

Third World Mass Media & Their Search for Modernity: The Case of Commonwealth Caribbean, 1717-1976. John A. Lent. LC 75-39110. 405p. 1978. 32.50 (ISBN 0-8387-1896-5). Bucknell U Pr.

Third World: Middle East. 2nd ed. Henry Bucher. LC 84-93316. (Illus.). 160p. 1984. pap. text ed. 6.95 (ISBN 0-87967-498-9). Dushkin Pub.

Third World Militarization: A Challenge to Third World Diplomacy. Ed. by Jagat S. Mehta. LC 85-50860. (Symposia Ser.). 250p. 1985. 10.50 (ISBN 0-89940-006-X). LBJ Sch Pub Aff.

Third-World Military Expenditure & Arms Production. Robert E. Looney. LC 88-4465. 242p. 1988. 55.00 (ISBN 0-312-02034-1). St Martin.

Third World Minerals & Global Pricing: A New Theory. Chibuzo Nwoke. LC 87-12621. 244p. 1987. 45.00x (ISBN 0-86232-441-6, Pub. by Zed Pr); pap. 15.00 (ISBN 0-86232-442-4). Humanities.

Third World Multinationals: Technology Choice & Employment Generation in Nigeria. C. N. S. Nambudiri. (Working Paper Ser.: No. 25). 41p. (Orig.). 1984. pap. 8.55 (ISBN 92-2-103386-4, ILO311, ILO). UNIPUB.

Third World Multinationals: The Rise of Foreign Investment from Developing Countries. Louis T. Wells, Jr. 272p. 1983. 27.50x (ISBN 0-262-23113-1). MIT Pr.

Third World Opera: Poems. Simeon Dumdum, Jr. 48p. (Orig.). 1988. pap. 4.50x (ISBN 971-10-0335-X, Pub. by New Day Philippines). Cellar.

Third World Out! Tim Adams. Ed. by A. L. Hardy. LC 78-74429. 1978. pap. 14.00 (ISBN 0-686-23919-9). Central FL Voters.

Third World Peasantry: A Continuing Saga of Deprivation, 2 vols. R. P. Misra. 1986. text ed. 75.00x (ISBN 81-207-0158-5, Pub. by Sterling Pubs India). Apt Bks.

Third World Policies of Industrialized Nations. Ed. by Phillip Taylor & Gregory A. Raymond. LC 81-13308. (Contributions in Political Science Ser.: No. 76). (Illus.). xix, 282p. 1982. lib. bdg. 36.95 (ISBN 0-313-22730-6, TTW/). Greenwood.

Third-World Political Organizations. Gwyenth Williams. LC 81-2029. 147p. 1981. text ed. 32.50x (ISBN 0-86598-052-7, Pub. by Allanheld). Rowman.

Third-World Political Organizations: A Review of Developments. 2nd ed. Gwyneth Williams. LC 86-18541. (Illus.). 168p. 1987. text ed. 25.00 (ISBN 0-391-03481-2); pap. text ed. 12.50 (ISBN 0-391-03483-9). Humanities.

Third World Politics: A Comparative Introduction. Paul Cammack et al. LC 87-31140. 320p. 1988. text ed. 38.50x (ISBN 0-8018-3649-2); pap. text ed. 14.95x (ISBN 0-8018-3661-1). Johns Hopkins.

Third World Politics: An Introduction. Christopher Clapham. 256p. 1985. 25.00x (ISBN 0-299-10330-7); pap. text ed. 12.50x (ISBN 0-299-10334-X). U of Wis Pr.

Third World Politics: China & the Afro-Asian People's Solidarity Organization, 1957-1967. Charles Neuhauser. LC 76-2492. (East Asian Monographs Ser: No. 27). 1968. pap. 11.00x (ISBN 0-674-88455-8). Harvard U Pr.

Third-World Poverty: New Strategies for Measuring Development Progress. Ed. by William P. McGreevey. LC 78-75318. (Human Affairs Research Center Ser.). 240p. 1980. 29.00x (ISBN 0-669-02839-8). Lexington Bks.

Third World: Premises of U. S. Policy. 2nd rev. ed. Ed. by W. Scott Thompson. LC 83-8426. 319p. 1983. text ed. 22.95 (ISBN 0-917616-58-8); pap. text ed. 8.95 (ISBN 0-917616-57-X). ICS Pr.

Third World: Problems & Perspectives. Ed. by Alan B. Mountjoy. (Illus.). 1979. 25.00x (ISBN 0-312-80036-3). St Martin.

Third World Proletariat? Peter Lloyd. (Controversies in Sociology Ser.: No. 11). 144p. 1982. text ed. 22.50 (ISBN 0-04-301140-3); pap. text ed. 11.95x (ISBN 0-04-301141-1). Unwin Hyman.

Third World Radical Regimes: U. S. Policy Under Carter & Reagan. Anthony Lake. LC 85-81057. (Headline Ser.: No. 272). (Illus.). 56p. (Orig.). 1985. pap. 4.00 (ISBN 0-87124-099-8). Foreign Policy.

Third World Reassessed. Elbaki Hermassi. LC 78-62848. 1980. 25.00x (ISBN 0-520-03764-2). U of Cal Pr.

Third World Resource Directory: A Guide to Organizations & Publications. Ed. by Thomas P. Fenton & Mary J. Heffron. LC 83-6783. 304p. (Orig.). 1984. pap. 17.95 (ISBN 0-88344-509-3). Orbis Bks.

Third World, Second Sex, Vol. 2. Ed. by Miranda Davies. 304p. text ed. 49.95 (ISBN 0-317-70048-0, Pub. by Zed Pr UK); pap. text ed. 15.00 (ISBN 0-86232-753-9, Pub by Zed Pr UK). Humanities.

Third World-Second Sex: Women's Struggles & National Liberation. Ed. by Miranda Davies. (Illus.). 1983. 32.50x (ISBN 0-86232-017-8, Pub. by Zed Pr); pap. 11.50 (ISBN 0-86232-029-1). Humanities.

Third World: South Asia. 2nd ed. James Norton. LC 84-92907. (Illus.). 128p. 1984. pap. text ed. 6.95 (ISBN 0-87967-502-0). Dushkin Pub.

Third World: Southeast Asia. 2nd ed. Donald K. Swearer. LC 84-92909. (Illus.). 128p. 1984. pap. text ed. 6.95 (ISBN 0-87967-501-2). Dushkin Pub.

Third World: States of Mind & Being. Ed. by Jim Norwine & Alfonso Gonzalez. (Illus.). 320p. 1988. text ed. 39.95 (ISBN 0-04-910106-4); pap. text ed. 17.95. Unwin Hyman.

Thirteen Treatises on T'ai Chi Ch'uan. Cheng Man-Ching et al. Tr. by Benjamin P. Jeng & Martin Inn. (Illus.). 226p. (Orig.). 1985. 16.95 (ISBN 0-938190-46-6). North Atlantic.
Thirteen Uncanny Stories. Hans H. Jahnn. Tr. by Gerda Jordan from Ger. LC 84-47544. (American University Studies I (Germanic Languages & Literature: Vol. 20). 168p. (Orig.). 1984. pap. text ed. 23.15 (ISBN 0-8204-0113-7). P Lang Pubs.
Thirteen Ways of Looking at a Blackbird. Lukas Foss. 1979. pap. 7.50 (ISBN -08258-0064-1, PCB114). Fischer Inc NY.
Thirteen Ways to Sink a Sub. Jamie Gilson. (Illus.). (gr. 3-7). 1982. 11.95 (ISBN 0-688-01304-X). Lothrop.
Thirteen Ways to Sink a Sub. Jamie Gilson. (Illus.). 128p. (gr. 3-6). 1983. pap. 2.50 (ISBN 0-671-62567-5). Archway.
Thirteen Ways to Survive the Squash Season. David Wilson & Liana Wilson. 12p. (Orig.). 1982. pap. 1.50 (ISBN 0-934852-25-1). Lorien Hse.
Thirteen Worthies. facs. ed. Llewelyn Powys. LC 67-22112. (Essay Index Reprint Ser). 1923. 15.00 (ISBN 0-8369-0799-X). Ayer Co Pubs.
Thirteen Worthies. Llewelyn Powys. 1985. 29.00x (ISBN 0-317-38814-2, Pub. by Redcliffe Pr Ltd). State Mutual Bk.
Thirteen Worthies. Llewelyn Powys. 192p. 1983. pap. 4.95 (ISBN 0-905459-59-8, Pub. by Redcliffe Pr Ltd). Intl Spec Bk.
Thirteen Years at the Russian Court a Personal Record of the Last Years & Death of the Czar Nicholas Second & His Family. Pierre Gilliard. LC 75-115539. (Russia Observed, Series I). 1970. Repr. of 1921 ed. 18.00 (ISBN 0-405-03029-0). Ayer Co Pubs.
Thirteen Years of Travel & Exploration in Alaska: 1877-1889. W. H. Pierce. Ed. by Robert N. De Armond. LC 77-2893. (Northern History Library). (Illus.). 1977. pap. 3.95 (ISBN 0-88240-076-2). Alaska Northwest.
Thirteenth Apostle. Eugene Vale. 352p. 1983. pap. 7.95 (ISBN 0-9609674-0-0). Jubilee Pr.
Thirteenth Assembling Annual. Ed. by Charles Doria et al. (Illus.). 100p. (Orig.). 1987. pap. 10.00 (ISBN 0-317-59200-9). Assembling Pr.
Thirteenth Caesar & Other Poems. Sacheverell Sitwell. LC 77-29071. lib. bdg. 29.00 (ISBN 0-8414-7881-3). Folcroft.
Thirteenth Census of the United States Taken in the Year 1910. U.S. Bureau of the Census, 1910. LC 75-22857. (America in Two Centuries Ser). 1976. Repr. of 1913 ed. 42.00x (ISBN 0-405-07724-6). Ayer Co Pubs.
Thirteenth-Century Church at St. Denis. Caroline A. Bruzelius. LC 85-3354. 256p. 1986. 32.50t (ISBN 0-300-03190-4). Yale U Pr.
Thirteenth-Century England I: Proceedings of the Newcastle-Upon-Tyne Conference 1985. Ed. by P. R. Ross & S. D. Lloyd. (Thirteenth-Century England Ser.). 1986. 54.00 (ISBN 0-85115-452-2, Pub. by Boydell & Brewer). Longwood Pub Group.
Thirteenth-Century Tomb Near Fuzhou. Fujian Sheng Museum Staff. 145p. 1982. 100.00x (ISBN 0-317-43751-8, Pub. by Han-Shan Tang Ltd). State Mutual Bk.
Thirteenth Century, 1216-1307. 2nd ed. Frederick M. Powicke. (Illus.). 1962. 45.00x (ISBN 0-19-821708-0). Oxford U Pr.
Thirteenth Chief Directorate. Chubin. 1988. price not set (Putnam). Putnam Pub Group.
Thirteenth Directorate. Barry Chubin. 352p. 1988. 18.95 (ISBN 0-399-13400-X, Putnam). Putnam Pub Group.
Thirteenth Gate: Travels among the Lost Tribes of Israel. Tudor Parfitt. LC 87-1295. 167p. 1987. 17.95 (ISBN 0-917561-43-0). Adler & Adler.
Thirteenth, Greatest of Centuries. 12th ed. James J. Walsh. LC 71-112004. (Illus.). Repr. of 1952 ed. 28.00 (ISBN 0-404-06818-9). AMS Pr.
Thirteenth Gun. A. L. Cahill. (Orig.). 1981. pap. 1.75 (ISBN 0-505-51587-3, Pub. by Tower Bks). Leisure NY.
Thirteenth International Conference on Defects in Semiconductors. Ed. by L. C. Kimerling & J. M. Parsey, Jr. LC 85-62228. (Illus.). 1252p. 1985. 10.00 (ISBN 0-89520-485-1). Metal Soc.
Thirteenth Juror: The Story of the Nineteen Twenty Nine Loray Strike. Robert L. Williams & Elizabeth W. Williams. 1984. 13.95 (ISBN 0-318-01452-1); pap. 7.95 (ISBN 0-318-01453-X). Herald NC.
Thirteenth Labor. Belluomini Ronald. LC 85-70532. (Living Poets Ser.). 1985. pap. 5.00 (ISBN 0-934218-32-3). Dragons Teeth.
Thirteenth Majestral. Hayford Peirce. 288p. 1989. pap. price not set (ISBN 0-8125-4892-2). Tor Bks.
Thirteenth Man: A Reagan Cabinet Memoir. Terrel H. Bell. 300p. 1988. 19.95 (ISBN 0-02-902351-3). Free Pr.
Thirteenth Member. Molly Hunter. (gr. 6-9). 1988. 17.25 (ISBN 0-8446-6362-X). Peter Smith.
Thirteenth Night & A Short Sharp Shock. Howard Brenton. Incl. (New Theatrescripts Ser.). 76p. 1981. pap. 4.95 (ISBN 0-413-48500-5, O. 3500). Heinemann Ed.
Thirteenth Party Congress & China's Reform. (Illus.). 113p. (Orig.). 1987. pap. 3.95 (ISBN 0-8351-1835-5). China Bks.
Thirteenth Pearl. Carolyn Keene. LC 78-57931. (Nancy Drew Ser.: Vol. 56). (Illus.). (gr. 3-7). 1979. 4.50 (ISBN 0-448-09556-4, G&D). Putnam Pub Group.
Thirteenth Session. Supplement No.1: Report of the Preparatory Committee of the Whole for Special Session of the General Assembly on the Critical Economic Situation in Africa, Official Records. 35p. 1986. pap. 5.00 (ISBN 0-317-56952-X). UN.
Thirteenth Special Session. 2-6 April 1984. Annexes: (Official Record) 37p. 1986. 6.00. UN.
Thirteenth Summer. Stephen Roos. LC 87-11382. (Illus.). 112p. (gr. 3-6). 1987. PLB 12.95 (ISBN 0-689-31299-7, Atheneum Childrens Bks). Macmillan.
Thirteenth Tribe. Arthur Koestler. 255p. 1986. pap. 6.00. Noontide.
Thirteenth Tribe: The Khazar Empire & Its Heritage. Arthur Koestler. 1976. 14.95 (ISBN 0-394-40284-7). Random.
Thirteenth Trick. Russell Braddon. LC 73-665. 168p. 1973. 5.95 (ISBN 0-393-08375-6). Norton.
Thirteenth Valley. John M. Del Vecchio. 688p. 1984. pap. 4.95 (ISBN 0-553-26020-0). Bantam.
Thirteenth Virginia Cavalry. Daniel T. Balfour. (Virginia Regimental Histories Ser.). (Illus.). 115p. 1986. 16.45 (ISBN 0-930919-29-7). H E Howard.
Thirties. Edmund Wilson. 800p. 1982. pap. 6.95 (ISBN 0-671-43193-5). WSP.
Thirties Floral Fabrics. 1988. 10.95 ea. (ISBN 0-8109-1742-4); slipcased set 40.00 (ISBN 0-8109-1738-6). Abrams.
Thirties: From Notebooks & Diaries of the Period. Edmund Wilson. Ed. by Leon Edel. LC 79-28700. 800p. 1980. 15.00 (ISBN 0-374-27572-6). FS&G.
Thirties in Vogue. Carolyn Hall. (Illus.). 1984. 25.00 (ISBN 0-517-55442-9). Crown.
Thirtieth Annual International Conference Proceedings. 704p. Date not set. pap. text ed. price not set (ISBN 0-935406-97-2). Am Prod & Inventory.
Thirtieth Institute for City & County Attorneys. 343p. 1983. 12.50 (ISBN 0-318-02417-9). ICLE Georgia.
Thirtieth Midwest Symposium on Circuits & Systems. Ed. by G. Glasford & K. Jabbour. 1460p. 1988. 245.00 (ISBN 0-444-01303-2, North Holland). Elsevier.
Thirtieth Piece of Silver. Lilian Hayes. LC 70-125217. (Short Story Index Reprint Ser). 1924. 29.00 (ISBN 0-8369-3584-5). Ayer Co Pubs.
Thirtieth Report. Organization of Peace Commission. LC 82-219541. Date not set. price not set. Comm Peace.
Thirtieth Session Supplement Four: Report of the Committee on Invisibles & Financing Related to Trade on Its Eleventh Session. 1986. pap. 4.00 (ISBN 0-317-52481-X). UN.
Thirtieth Session Supplement I: Resolutions & Decisions. 1986. pap. 4.00 (ISBN 0-317-52480-1). UN.
Thirtieth Session. Supplement No. 5: Report of the Committee on Invesibles & Financing Related to Trade on Its 11th Session, 25 February - 8 March, 1985, Official Records, 2nd Pt. 32p. 1986. pap. 6.00 (ISBN 0-317-56964-3). UN.
Thirtieth Session Supplement Six: Report of the Working Party on the Medium-Term Plan & the Programme Budget on its Ninth Session. 1986. pap. 5.00 (ISBN 0-317-52482-8). UN.
Thirtieth Stapp Car Crash Conference Proceedings. 1986. 45.00 (ISBN 0-89883-451-1, P189). Soc Auto Engineers.
Thirtieth Virginia Infantry. Robert K. Krick. (Virginia Regimental Histories Ser.). (Illus.). 143p. 1983. 16.45 (ISBN 0-930919-03-3). H E Howard.
Thirtieth Year. Ingeborg Bachmann. (Modern German Voices Ser.). 200p. 1987. 19.95 (ISBN 0-8419-1068-5). Holmes & Meier.
Thirtieth Year to Heaven: New American Poets. LC 80-22063. (Bree Bks.: No. 2). 1980. 12.95 (ISBN 0-917492-09-9). Jackpine Pr.
Thirty. Bert E. Grove. 64p. 1988. 7.95 (ISBN 0-8062-3255-2). Carlton.
Thirty an' Seen a Lot. Evangelina Vigil. LC 81-68073. 88p. (Orig.). 1982. pap. 5.00 (ISBN 0-934770-13-1). Arte Publico.
Thirty at Athens. Peter Krentz. LC 81-70697. (Illus.). 168p. 1982. 22.50x (ISBN 0-8014-1450-4). Cornell U Pr.
Thirty Bible Reasons Why Christ Heals Today. Gordon Lindsay. (Divine Healing & Health Ser.). 1.50 (ISBN 0-89985-031-6). Christ Nations.
Thirty Birds That Will Build in Bird Houses. Illus. by R. B. Layton. LC 77-81805. (Illus.). 1977. pap. 10.95x (ISBN 0-912542-05-5). Nature Bks Pubs.
Thirty Caprices for the Clarinet. Ernesto Cavallini. 64p. 1909. pap. 8.00 (ISBN 0-8258-0238-5, 0106). Fischer Inc NY.
Thirty Card Mysteries. Charles T. Jordan. (Illus.). 1974. pap. 5.00 (ISBN 0-915926-41-5). Magic Ltd.
Thirty Changing Meter Duets for Treble Clef Instruments. James Meyer. 41p. 1984. pap. 9.95 (ISBN 0-938170-05-8). Wimbledon Music.
Thirty Corpses Every Thursday. Fredric Brown. (Fredric Brown in the Detective Pulps Ser.: Vol. 6). 193p. 1986. pap. 5.95 (ISBN 0-9609986-5-9). D McMillan.
Thirty Customized Microprocessor Projects. Delton T. Horn. (Illus.). 322p. 1986. pap. 14.95 (ISBN 0-8306-2705-7, NO. 2705). TAB Bks.
Thirty Day Action Guide to Big Money Selling. William E. Edwards. 1972. 49.50 (ISBN 0-13-918698-0). Exec Reports.
Thirty Day Mental Diet. Willis Kinnear. 144p. 1965. pap. 7.95 (ISBN 0-911336-20-6). Sci of Mind.
Thirty Day Peace Diet: A Way to Unconditional Love. Bob Cranmer & Judy Cranmer. Ed. by John Willis. LC 88-60626. (Illus.). 128p. (Orig.). 1988. pap. 8.95 (ISBN 0-929009-17-7). Rt Brain Unltd Pubns.
Thirty Days to a Better Life. John W. Adams. 1988. pap. 7.95 (ISBN 0-9602166-4-2). Golden Key.
Thirty Days to a Flatter Stomach for Men. Roy Matthews & Nancy Burstein. 1983. pap. 3.50 (ISBN 0-553-34337-8). Bantam.
Thirty Days to a Flatter Stomach for Women. Nancy Burstein. 1983. pap. 3.50 (ISBN 0-553-34345-9). Bantam.
Thirty Days to a More Powerful Vocabulary. Wilfred Funk & Norman Lewis. 256p. 1988. pap. 3.50 (ISBN 0-671-53031-3, 80003). PB.
Thirty Days to a More Powerful Vocabulary. Norman Lewis & Wilfred Funk. pap. 3.50 (ISBN 0-317-56682-2). PB.
Thirty Days to Beautiful Legs. Marc Selner. 1985. pap. 3.00 (ISBN 0-87980-407-6). Wilshire.
Thirty Days to Beautiful Nails. Patricia Bozic. 64p. (Orig.). 1984. pap. 3.50 (ISBN 0-446-38028-8). Warner Bks.
Thirty Days to Better English. Norman Lewis. 208p. 1985. pap. 3.95 (ISBN 0-451-13538-5, Sig). NAL.
Thirty Days to Better Nutrition. Virginia Aronson. 240p. 1987. pap. text ed. write for info. (ISBN 0-13-918731-6). P-H.
Thirty Days to Happiness: Setting Yourself up to Win in Life. Liah Kraft-Macoy. 156p. 1987. pap. 8.95 (ISBN 0-913299-53-7, Dist. by NAL). Stillpoint.
Thirty Days to Metric Mastery: For People Who Hate Math. Don C. Steinke. (Illus., Orig.). 1981. pap. 6.95x (ISBN 0-9605344-0-7). Hse of Charles.
Thirty Days to More Powerful Writing. Jonathan Price. 1988. pap. 6.95 (ISBN 0-449-90137-8, Columbine). Fawcett.
Thirty Days to Understanding Your Bible. Max E. Anders. 1988. pap. 8.95 (ISBN 0-317-68190-7). Wolgemuth & Hyatt.
Thirty Days to Victorious Living: A Devotional Workbook. Joanna S. Seaman. 84p. (Orig.). 1986. pap. write for info. (ISBN 0-939113-00-7). Ansley Pubns.
Thirty Eight - Twenty Two - Thirty Six Conceptual Statistics for Beginners. 4th ed. Isadore Newman & Carole Newman. 207p. 1977. pap. text ed. 5.50 (ISBN 0-917180-06-2). I Newman.
Thirty Eight Basic Speech Experiences. 7th ed. Clark S. Carlile. 235p. 1982. pap. text ed. 8.85 (ISBN 0-931054-07-9). Clark Pub.
Thirty-Eight Latin Stories Deisgned to Accompany Frederick M. Wheelock's Latin: An Introductory Course Based on Ancient Authors. Anne H. Groton & James M. May. Tr. by Anne H. Groton & James M. May. 110p. (Orig., Lat. & Eng.). 1986. pap. 10.00 (ISBN 0-86516-171-2). Bolchazy-Carducci.
Thirty-Eight Recipes for Bulletin Boards & Art Projects That Christian Kids Can Make. Jean Staffeld et al. (Illus.). 1978. pap. 5.50 (ISBN 0-570-03774-3, 12-2721). Concordia.
Thirty-Eight Short Stories: An Introductory Anthology. 2nd ed. Ed. by Michael Timko. 1978. pap. text ed. 9.00 (ISBN 0-394-32182-0, KnopfC). Knopf.
Thirty-Eight State U. S. A. G. Etzel Pearcy. LC 73-83685. (Monograph: No.2). (Illus.). 1973. 4.95x (ISBN 0-916434-09-5). Plycon Pr.
Thirty-Eighth Session, Supplement: Report of the Economic & Social Council for the Year 1983, No. 3. (Official Record Ser.). 104p. 12.50. UN.
Thirty-Eighth Session, Supplement: Reports of the Security Council June 16, 1982 to June 15, 1983. (Official Record Ser.: No. 2). 70p. 8.50. UN.
Thirty-Eighth Western New York Exhibition. LC 80-50571. (Illus.). 43p. 1980. pap. 5.50 (ISBN 0-914782-33-9). Buffalo Acad.
Thirty Epigrams. Illus. by Richard O'Connell. (Illus.). 1971. pap. 6.00 (ISBN 0-685-62619-9). Atlantis Edns.
Thirty Exercises for Better Golf. Frank W. Jobe et al. LC 85-73724. (Illus.). 110p. (Orig.). 1986. pap. 7.95 (ISBN 0-936691-00-X). Champ Pr Inglewood.
Thirty Famous One-Act Plays. Ed. by Bennett Cerf & Van H. Cartmell. LC 49-9032. 1943. 9.95 (ISBN 0-394-60473-3). Modern Lib.
Thirty Favorite Bible Stories with Discussion Questions. John C. Reid. LC 81-21514. (Illus.). 192p. (Orig.). (gr. k-5). 1982. pap. 4.95 (ISBN 0-87239-498-0, 3373). Standard Pub.
Thirty Favorite Novenas. 31p. 1975. pap. 0.40 (ISBN 0-89555-105-5). TAN Bks Pubs.
Thirty-Fifth Battalion Cavalry. John E. Divine. (Virginia Regimental Histories Ser.). (Illus.). 112p. 1985. 16.45 (ISBN 0-930919-19-X). H E Howard.
Thirty Fifth Biennial of American Painting. (Illus.). 1977. 5.00 (ISBN 0-686-20555-3). Corcoran.
Thirty Fifth Dell Crossword Puzzles. Ed. by Kathleen Rafferty. 1978. pap. 1.25 (ISBN 0-440-18544-0). Dell.
Thirty-First Annual of Advertising Art in Japan. 1988. 79.95 (ISBN 4-568-53087-3). Rockport Pubs.
Thirty-First of February. facs. ed. Nelson S. Bond. LC 78-121524. (Short Story Index Reprint Ser). 1949. 19.00 (ISBN 0-8369-3480-6). Ayer Co Pubs.
Thirty-First of February. Julian Symons. 190p. 1987. pap. 3.50 (ISBN 0-88184-317-2). Carroll & Graf.
Thirty-First Session, Supplement No. 3: Report of the Special Committee on Preferences on its 13th Session 10-19 April 1985, Official Records. 28p. 1986. pap. 5.00 (ISBN 0-317-54449-7). UN.
Thirty First Session. Supplement No. 5: Report of the Committee on Commodities on Its 2nd Special Session 21-25 January 1985, Official Records. 1986. pap. 4.00 (ISBN 0-317-56965-1). UN.
Thirty First Staff Car Crash Conference Proceedings. 1987. 30.00 (ISBN 0-89883-462-7, P202). Soc Auto Engineers.
Thirty-Five Amazing Games for Your Commodore 128. John Mihalik. LC 85-81856. 112p. pap. 9.95 (ISBN 0-89586-398-7). Price Stern.
Thirty-Five & Counting. James C. Schaap. 300p. 1986. pap. 7.95 (ISBN 0-932914-11-X). Dordt Coll Pr.
Thirty-Five & Holding: Complete Conditioning for the Adult Male. Pete Broccoletti. (Illus.). 192p. 1982. wire bdg. 10.95 (ISBN 0-89651-779-9). B L Pub.
Thirty-Five Easy Ways to Lose Fat. Dirk Tousley & Rick Guyton. LC 85-51720. 160p. 1985. pap. 8.95 (ISBN 0-914541-25-0). White Dove Pub Co.
Thirty Five Handicraft Projects for Children. LC 12-2957. 1982. pap. 5.50 (ISBN 0-570-03864-2). Concordia.
Thirty-Five Letters of Cicero. Cicero. Ed. by David Stockton. 1969. pap. 8.95x (ISBN 0-19-912005-6). Oxford U Pr.
Thirty-Five Millimeter Dreams. Sue Mathews. (Penguin Nonfiction Ser.). 304p. 1985. pap. 8.95 (ISBN 0-14-006709-4). Penguin.
Thirty-Five Millimeter Handbook: A Complete Course from Basic Techniques to Professional Applications. rev. ed. Michael Freeman. LC 84-27705. 320p. 1985. 14.98 (ISBN 0-89471-339-6, Pub. by Courage Bks). Running Pr.
Thirty-Five Millimeter Photographer's Handbook. rev. ed. Julian Calder & John Garrett. 1986. 14.95 (ISBN 0-517-56122-0). Crown.
Thirty-Five Miniatures & Other Pieces for Organ. Flor Peeters. 64p. (Orig.). (gr. 7-12). 1975. pap. text ed. 10.95 (ISBN 0-87487-602-8). Birch Tree Gr.
Thirty-Five mm Microfilming for Drawing Offices. W. J. Barrett. (Illus.). 135p. 1970. 8.95 (ISBN 0-240-50698-7). Focal Pr.
Thirty-five MM Panorama. Roger Hicks. (Illus.). 176p. 1988. pap. 12.95 (ISBN 0-7153-9292-1, Pub. by David & Charles Pub England). Sterling.
Thirty-Five MM Panorama. Roger W. Hicks. (Illus.). 176p. 1987. 24.95 (ISBN 0-7153-8930-0, Pub. by David & Charles Pub England). Sterling.
Thirty-Five Papers on Statistics & Probability. G. A. Ambarcumjan et al. LC 61-9803. (Selected Translations in Mathematical Statistics & Probability Ser.: Vol. 4). 1963. 35.00 (ISBN 0-8218-1454-0, STAPRO-4). Am Math.
Thirty-Five-Plus Diet for Women. Jean P. Spodnik & Barbara Gibbons. 240p. 1988. pap. 4.50 (ISBN 0-671-66181-7). PB.
Thirty-Five Plus Diet for Women: Kaiser Permanente Clinic's Breakthrough Metabolism Diet. Jean Spodnik & Barbara Gibbons. LC 86-45745. 192p. 1987. 15.95i (ISBN 0-06-015718-6, HarpT). Har-Row.
Thirty-Five Practical Programs for the Casio Pocket Computer. Jim Cole. (Illus.). 96p. 1982. 8.95 (ISBN 0-86668-014-4). ARCsoft.
Thirty-Five Receipts from the "The Larder Invaded". William W. Weaver. 91p. 1986. pap. 8.95 (ISBN 0-914076-69-8). Lib Co Phila.
Thirty-Five Scientific Communications from the All-Union Conference on Functional Analysis & Its Applications & Five Papers on Analysis. LC 51-5559. (Translations Ser.: No. 2, Vol. 16). 1960. 40.00 (ISBN 0-8218-1716-7, TRANS 2-16). Am Math.
Thirty-Five Simple Studies on the Book of Revelation. M. R. De Hann. 304p. 1988. pap. 10.95 (ISBN 0-310-23441-7, 9500P). Zondervan.
Thirty-Five Sundays. Lyn Lifshin. (Offset Offshoot Ser.: No. 3). 56p. 1979. pap. 4.00 (ISBN 0-317-06439-8). Ommation Pr.
Thirty-Five Thousand Tennessee Marriage Records & Bonds, 3 vols. Ed. by Silas E. Lucas, Jr. 1981. Set. 135.00 (ISBN 0-89308-226-0). Vol. 1, (a-f), 604pp (ISBN 0-89308-223-6). Vol. 2, (g-n), 610pp (ISBN 0-89308-224-4). Vol. 3, (o-z), 580pp (ISBN 0-89308-225-2). Southern Hist Pr.
Thirty-Five Thousands Palabras. M. Villamizar & G. E. Franco. 1985. text ed. 8.84 (ISBN 0-07-067456-6). McGraw.
Thirty-Five Years in Russia. George Hume. LC 79-115548. (Russia Observed Ser). (Illus.). 1971. Repr. of 1914 ed. 21.00 (ISBN 0-405-03082-7). Ayer Co Pubs.

Thirty Songs, for High Voice. Franz Liszt. Ed. by Carl Armbruster. 11.25 (ISBN 0-8446-5502-3). Peter Smith.

Thirty Strange Stories. H. G. Wells. LC 72-103531. (Short Story Index Reprint Ser.). 1897. 27.50 (ISBN 0-8369-3274-9). Ayer Co Pubs.

Thirty Tales & Sketches. Edward Garnett. 354p. Repr. of 1929 ed. lib. bdg. 30.00 (ISBN 0-89987-325-1). Darby Bks.

Thirty Tales & Sketches. facs. ed. Robert B. Graham. LC 76-125213. (Short Story Reprint Ser.). Repr. of 1929 ed. 20.00 (ISBN 0-8369-3580-2). Ayer Co Pubs.

Thirty-Third Biennial Exhibition of Art, Venice, 1966. American Federation of Arts Staff. (Illus.). 1966. 5.00 (ISBN 0-8079-0123-7); pap. 2.00 (ISBN 0-8079-0124-5). October.

Thirty-Third Virginia Infantry. Robert K. Krick. (Virginia Regimental Histories Ser.). (Illus.). 151p. 1987. 16.45 (ISBN 0-930919-37-8). H E Howard.

Thirty-Thirty Three. Ed. by Fran Ringold. 146p. 1987. pap. 5.50. Art & Human Council Tulsa.

Thirty Thousand Bequest. Samuel L. Clemens. (Works of Mark Twain). 1988. Repr. of 1902 ed. lib. bdg. 59.00x. Am Biog Serv.

Thirty Thousand Bequest see Writings of Mark Twain.

Thirty Thousand Kicks: What's It Like to Be a Rockette? Judith Anne Love. (Illus.). 1980. 7.50 (ISBN 0-682-49456-9, Banner). Exposition-Phoenix.

Thirty Thousand Miles with John Heckewelder see Travels of John Heckewelder in Frontier America.

Thirty Thousand on the Hoof. Zane Grey. 240p. 1982. pap. 2.95 (ISBN 0-671-63170-5). PB.

Thirty-Three. Marjorie Fletcher. LC 75-32642. 72p. 1976. pap. 7.95 (ISBN 0-914086-12-X). Alicejamesbooks.

Thirty-Three Adult Computer Games in BASIC for the IBM PC, Apple II, IIe & TRS-80. David W. Chance. (Illus.). 378p. 1983. 18.95 (ISBN 0-8306-0627-0, 1627); pap. 13.50 (ISBN 0-8306-1627-6). TAB Bks.

Thirty-Three by Arthur Conan Doyle. Arthur Conan Doyle. 1986. 6.98 (625431). Outlet Bk Co.

Thirty-Three Challenging Computer Games for the TRS-80, Apple & Pet. David Chance. (Illus.). 252p. 15.95 (ISBN 0-8306-9703-9, 1275). TAB Bks.

Thirty-Three Fun & Easy Weekend Electronics Project. Andres Guzman. LC 87-13883. (Illus.). 140p. 1987. 14.95 (ISBN 0-8306-0261-5, 2861); pap. 8.95 (ISBN 0-8306-2861-4). TAB Bks.

Thirty-Three Games of Skill & Chance for the IBM PC. Robert J. Traister. (Illus.). 256p. 1983. 18.95 (ISBN 0-8306-0126-0, 1526HB). TAB Bks.

Thirty-Three Hiking Trails: Southern Washington Cascades. Don Lowe & Roberta Lowe. Ed. by Thomas K. Worcester. (Illus.). 80p. (Orig.). 1985. pap. 7.95 (ISBN 0-911518-68-1). Touchstone Oregon.

Thirty-Three New Apple Computer Programs for Home, School & Office. Fred White. (Illus.). 96p. (Orig.). 1982. pap. 8.95 (ISBN 0-86668-016-0). ARCsoft.

Thirty Three Photovoltaic Projects. Homer L. Davidson. (Illus.). 272p. (Orig.). 1982. 16.95 (ISBN 0-8306-2467-8, 1467); pap. 10.95 (ISBN 0-8306-1467-2). TAB Bks.

Thirty-Three Poems. Robert Lax. 210p. 1988. 19.95 (ISBN 0-8112-1049-9); pap. 12.95 (ISBN 0-8112-1085-5). New Directions.

Thirty-Three Prayers. Gi-Gi Grant. 1986. 6.95 (ISBN 0-533-05468-0). Vantage.

Thirty-Three Useful Projects for the Woodworker. School Shop Magazine Staff. (Illus.). 160p. 1986. pap. 12.95 (ISBN 0-8306-2783-9, NO. 2783). TAB Bks.

Thirty-Three Ways to Ease Work - Family Tensions: An Employer's Checklist. (National Report on Work & Family Ser.: Special Report No. 2). 32p. 1988. 35.00 (ISBN 0-87179-958-8). BNA.

Thirty-Two BASIC Programs for the Apple Computer. Tom Rugg & Phil Feldman. LC 80-68533. (Illus.). 280p. 1983. pap. 14.95 (ISBN 0-918398-34-7); pap. 19.95 incl. disk. Weber Systems.

Thirty-Two BASIC Programs for the Apple Computer. Tom Rugg & Phil Feldman. (Thirty-Two Programs Ser.). (Illus.). 304p. pap. 19.95 (ISBN 0-517-56364-9); pap. 39.95 (ISBN 0-517-56365-7); software pkg. incl. Crown.

Thirty-Two BASIC Programs for the Atari Computer. Tom Rugg & Phil Feldman. (Illus.). 288p. 1983. pap. 14.95 (ISBN 0-88056-084-3); incl. disk 19.95 (ISBN 0-88056-172-6). Weber Systems.

Thirty-Two Basic Programs for the Atari Computer. Tom Rugg et al. (Thirty-Two Programs Ser.). (Illus.). 288p. pap. 19.95 (ISBN 0-517-56366-5); software pkg. 39.95 (ISBN 0-517-56367-3). Crown.

Thirty-Two BASIC Programs for the Coleco Adam. Tom Rugg & Phil Feldman. 288p. 1984. pap. 19.95 (ISBN 0-88056-141-6); write for info. Dilithium Pr.

Thirty-Two BASIC Programs for the Coleco Adam. Tom Rugg & Phil Feldman. (Illus.). 288p. pap. 19.95 (ISBN 0-517-56368-1); pap. 39.95 (ISBN 0-517-56369-X); software pkg. incl. Crown.

Thirty Two Basic Programs for the IBM-PC Jr. Tom Rugg. 5.95 (ISBN 0-88056-306-0). Weber Systems.

Thirty-Two BASIC Programs for the IBM PCjr. Tom Rugg & Phil Feldman. (Thirty-Two Programs Ser.). (Illus.). 354p. pap. 19.95 (ISBN 0-517-56370-3); pap. 39.95 (ISBN 0-517-56371-1). Crown.

Thirty-Two BASIC Programs for the TI 99-4A. Tom Rugg & Phil Feldman. (Illus.). 288p. 1983. pap. 5.95 (ISBN 0-88056-136-X); incl. cassette 9.95 (ISBN 0-88056-188-2); incl. disk 9.95 (ISBN 0-88056-203-X). Weber Systems.

Thirty-Two BASIC Programs for the TRS-80 (Level II) Computer. Tom Rugg & Phil Feldman. LC 79-56399. 270p. 1983. pap. 14.95 (ISBN 0-918398-27-4); incl. disk 19.95; incl. cassette 9.95. Weber Systems.

Thirty-Two Basic Steps into Hindi Vocubulary: A Vocabulary Workbook. Harinder J. Dhillon. (Illus.). 143p. (Orig., Hindi.). 1986. 14.95 (ISBN 0-9617188-0-3); cass. 14.95. H J Dhillon.

Thirty Two Basic Steps into Panjabi Vocabulary: A Vocabulary Workbook. Harinder J. Dhillon. (Illus.). 143p. (Orig., Panjabi.). 1986. Gurmukhi Script. pap. 14.95 (ISBN 0-9617188-1-1); cassette 14.95 (ISBN 0-317-54405-5). H J Dhillon.

Thirty Two Basic Steps into Panjabi Vocabulary: A Vocabulary Workbook. Harinder J. Dhillon. (Illus.). 143p. (Orig., Panjabi.). 1986. Persian Script. pap. 14.95 (ISBN 0-9617188-2-X); cassette 14.95 (ISBN 0-317-54403-9). H J Dhillon.

Thirty Two Basic Steps into Urdu Vocabulary: A Vocabulary Workbook. Harinder J. Dhillon. (Illus.). 143p. (Orig., Urdu.). 1986. pap. 14.95 (ISBN 0-9617188-3-8); cassette 14.95 (ISBN 0-317-54404-7). H J Dhillon.

Thirty Two Canons for Keyboard Instruments. Robert Donahue. 1975. pap. 3.25 (ISBN 0-934286-57-4). Kenyon.

Thirty-Two Cantigas d'Amigo of Dom Diniz: Typology of a Portuguese Renunciation. Rip Cohen. (Portuguese Ser.: No. 1). 1987. 12.50 (ISBN 0-942260-55-4). Hispanic Seminary.

Thirty-Two Earth Worlds Speak to Planet Earth, 3 parts. Ruth E. Norman. (Tesla Speaks Ser.: Vol. IV). (Illus.). 1974. 9.95 ea.; Part 1. (ISBN 0-932642-23-3); Part 2. (ISBN 0-932642-24-1); Part 3. (ISBN 0-932642-25-X). Unarius Pubns.

Thirty-Two Elephant Reminders: A Book of Healthy Rules. Mary M. McKee. (Illus.). 72p. (Orig.). 1987. pap. 3.95 (ISBN 0-932194-59-1). Health Comm.

Thirty-Two Gun Frigate Essex: Building A Plank-On-Frame Model. Portia Takakjian. (Illus.). 80p. (Orig.). 1985. 9.95 (ISBN 0-9615021-0-X). Phoen Pubns.

Thirty Two Million Judges: Analysis of 1977 Lok Sabha & State Elections in India. G. G. Mirchandani. 1977. 12.00x (ISBN 0-8364-0052-6). South Asia Bks.

Thirty-Two Papers on Statistics & Probability. M. Arato et al. LC 61-9803. (Selected Translations in Mathematical Statistics & Probability Ser.: Vol. 10). 1972. 40.00 (ISBN 0-8218-1460-5, STAPRO-10). Am Math.

Thirty-Two Piano Sonatas of Ludvig Van Beethoven, 2 Vols. Ed. by Artur Schnabel. 1983. pap. 24.95 ea.; Vol. I. 27.95 (ISBN 0-671-49198-9). Vol. II (ISBN 0-671-49199-7). S&S.

Thirty-Two Picture Postcards of Old Philadelphia. Ed. by Robert F. Looney. (Dover Postcard Ser). (Illus., Orig.). 1977. pap. 3.50 (ISBN 0-486-23421-5). Dover.

Thirty Two President's Square. Roland Carr. 12.50 (ISBN 0-87491-079-X). Acropolis.

Thirty-Two Sonatas for the Pianoforte, 2 Vols. Ludwig Van Beethoven. Ed. by Arthur Schnabel. 1935. Set. pap. 15.00 (ISBN 0-686-66528-7, Fireside); pap. 7.50 ea.; Vol. 1. pap. (07100); Vol. 2. pap. (07110). S&S.

Thirty-Two VisiCalc Worksheets. T. G. Lewis. (Illus.). 192p. 1983. 26.95 (ISBN 0-8306-1637-3, 1637). TAB BKS.

Thirty-Two Visicalc Worksheets. Ted Lewis. (Thirty-Two Programs Ser.). (Illus.). 192p. pap. 19.95 (ISBN 0-517-56372-X); Incl. disk for IBM. pap. 39.95 (ISBN 0-517-56373-8); Incl. disk for Apple. pap. 39.95 (ISBN 0-517-56374-6). Crown.

Thirty Velocity Studies for Trumpet. Claude Gordon. (Ger., Fr. & Span.). 1981. pap. 6.95 (ISBN 0-8258-0213-X, 05092). Fischer Inc NY.

Thirty Ways to Conserve Energy in Apartments, Condominiums, & Other Multihousing Properties. Fifty copies. 27.50 (ISBN 0-686-46418-4). Inst Real Estate.

Thirty Ways to Dump a Sister. Janet A. Bloss. (Illus.) 144p. (gr. 3-6). 1986. 2.25 (ISBN 0-87406-057-5). Willowisp Pr.

Thirty Ways to Improve Your Grades. Harry Shaw. LC 75-42468. 192p. (Orig.). 1976. pap. text ed. 4.95 (ISBN 0-07-056510-4). McGraw.

Thirty-Year History of Programs Carried on National Radio Networks in the United States, 1926-1956. Ed. by Harrison B. Summers. LC 78-161155. (History of Broadcasting: Radio to Television Ser). 1971. Repr. of 1958 ed. 18.00 (ISBN 0-405-03572-1). Ayer Co Pubs.

Thirty Years a Detective: A Thorough & Comprehensive Expose of Criminal Practices of All Grades & Classes. Alan Pinkerton. (Criminology, Law Enforcement, & Social Problems Ser.: No. 154). (Illus.). 1975. Repr. of 1884 ed. Witn Intro. Essay & Index Added. 20.00x (ISBN 0-87585-154-1). Patterson Smith.

Thirty Years a Slave. facs. ed. Louis Hughes. LC 79-89404. (Black Heritage Library Collection Ser). 1896. 15.50 (ISBN 0-8369-8607-5). Ayer Co Pubs.

Thirty Years a Slave: From Bondage to Freedom. Louis Hughes. LC 75-92431. 1896. 14.00x (ISBN 0-403-00164-1). Scholarly.

Thirty Years a Watchtower Slave. William J. Schnell. (Direction Bks). pap. 3.95 (ISBN 0-8010-7933-0). Baker Bk.

Thirty Years after Brown. Jennifer L. Hochschild. LC 84-29739. 55p. (Orig.). 1985. pap. 4.95 (ISBN 0-941410-49-8). Jt Ctr Pol Studies.

Thirty Years Ago, or the Memoirs of a Water Drinker, 2 Vols. William Dunlap. Repr. of 1836 ed. 28.00 (ISBN 0-384-13324-X). Johnson Repr.

Thirty Years among the Dead. condensed ed. Carl A. Wickland. 1924. pap. 3.95 (ISBN 0-910122-08-3). Amherst Pr.

Thirty Years among the Dead. Carl A. Wickland. LC 80-19669. 390p. 1980. Repr. of 1974 ed. lib. bdg. 19.95x (ISBN 0-89370-625-6). Borgo Pr.

Thirty Years among the Dead. Carl A. Wickland. 390p. 1974. pap. 6.95 (ISBN 0-87877-025-9, P-25). Newcastle Pub.

Thirty Years & Still Training for Safety: Proceedings of the 30th Annual Meeting Corporate Aviation Safety Seminar, April 14-16,1985, AMFAC Hotel & Resort, Dallas - Fort Worth International Airport. Corporate Aviation Safety Seminar Staff. pap. 56.00 (ISBN 0-317-42279-0, 2025797). Bks Demand UMI.

Thirty Years at Sea. Edward Shippen. Ed. by Richard H. Kohn. LC 78-22396. (American Military Experience Ser.). 1979. Repr. of 1879 ed. lib. bdg. 25.50x (ISBN 0-405-11872-4). Ayer Co Pubs.

Thirty Years at the Mansion. Liza Ashley. LC 84-73313. (Illus.). 176p. 1985. 18.95 (ISBN 0-935304-88-6). August Hse.

Thirty Years' Battle with Crime: Or, the Crying Shame of New York, As Seen under the Broad Glare of an Old Detective's Lantern. John H. Warren, Jr. LC 73-112582. (Rise of Urban America). (Illus.). 1970. Repr. of 1875 ed. 25.50 (ISBN 0-405-02484-3). Ayer Co Pubs.

Thirty Years Experience of a Medical Officer in the English Convict Service. John Campbell. LC 83-49236. (Crime & Punishment in England, 1850-1922 Ser.). 139p. 1984. lib. bdg. 30.00 (ISBN 0-8240-6211-6). Garland Pub.

Thirty Years in Hell: Or, the Confessions of a Drug Fiend. D. F. Macmartin. Ed. by Gerald N. Grob. LC 80-1256. (Addiction in America Ser.). 1981. Repr. of 1921 ed. lib. bdg. 25.00x (ISBN 0-405-13606-4). Ayer Co Pubs.

Thirty Years in the Arctic Regions. John Franklin. LC 88-14329. xiv, 480p. 1988. 29.95x (ISBN 0-8032-1975-X); pap. 10.95 (ISBN 0-8032-6867-X, Bison). U of Nebr Pr.

Thirty Years Later: The Shore Line. Ed. by Norman Carlson. LC 85-72307. (NS-300 Ser.). (Illus.). 32p. (Orig.). 1985. pap. 6.00 (ISBN 0-915348-00-4, NS-300). Central Electric.

Thirty Years' Musical Recollections. Henry F. Chorley. LC 77-183330. 436p. 1972. Repr. of 1926 ed. 40.00x (ISBN 0-8443-0026-8). Vienna Hse.

Thirty Year's Musical Recollections. Henry F. Chorley. Ed. by Ernest Newman. LC 77-183330. 411p. Date not set. Repr. of 1926 ed. 75.00. Vienna Hse.

Thirty Years' Musical Recollections, 2 vols. Henry F. Chorley. LC 83-7558. (Music Reprint Ser.). 1983. Repr. of 1862 ed. Set. lib. bdg. 65.00 (ISBN 0-306-76216-1); Vol. I: 312 pp. lib. bdg. Vol. II: 323 pp. lib. bdg. Da Capo.

Thirty Years of American Zionism, Vol.1. Louis Lipsky. Ed. by Moshe Davis. LC 77-70718. (America & the Holy Land Ser.). 1977. Repr. of 1927 ed. lib. bdg. 26.50x (ISBN 0-405-10263-1). Ayer Co Pubs.

Thirty Years of Buddhist Studies. Edward Conze. 274p. 1967. 40.00x (ISBN 0-317-39172-0, Pub. by Luzac & Co Ltd). State Mutual Bk.

Thirty Years of Championship Golf. Gene Sarazen & Herbert W. Wind. Date not set. 17.95x (ISBN 0-940889-13-7). Classics Golf.

Thirty Years of J. L. Steg: Nineteen Forty-Eight to Nineteen Seventy-Eight. Intro. by Alan Fern. LC 78-71034. (Illus.). 1978. pap. 3.95 (ISBN 0-89494-007-4). New Orleans Mus Art.

Thirty Years of Life & Labor, 1859-1889. rev. ed. Terence V. Powderly. LC 66-21692. 1967. Repr. of 1890 ed. 45.00x (ISBN 0-678-00249-5). Kelley.

Thirty Years of Liturgical Renewal. Ed. by Frederick McManus. 500p. (Orig.). 1987. pap. 16.95 (ISBN 1-55586-154-7). US Catholic.

Thirty Years of Lynching in the United States, 1889-1918. National Association For The Advancement Of Colored People. LC 73-94142. (American Negro: His History & Literature, Ser. No. 3). 1970. Repr. of 1919 ed. 11.00 (ISBN 0-405-01932-7). Ayer Co Pubs.

Thirty Years of Musical Life in London. Hermann Klein. LC 78-2565. (Music Reprint Ser., 1978). (Illus.). 1978. Repr. of 1903 ed. lib. bdg. 49.50 (ISBN 0-306-77586-7). Da Capo.

Thirty Years of Musical Life in London 1870-1900. Hermann Klein. 1980. Repr. of 1903 ed. lib. bdg. 50.00 (ISBN 0-89341-442-5). Longwood Pub Group.

Thirty Years of New York Politics, Up-to-Date. Matthew P. Breen. LC 73-19132. (Politics & People Ser.). (Illus.). 918p. 1974. Repr. 64.00x (ISBN 0-405-05857-8). Ayer Co Pubs.

Thirty Years of Parity Nonconservation: A Symposium Honoring T. D. Lee. Ed. by Robert Novick. 220p. 1987. 25.00 (ISBN 0-8176-3375-8). Birkhauser.

Thirty Years of Prestressed Concrete Railroad Bridges. (PCI Journal Reprints Ser.). 36p. pap. 9.00 (ISBN 0-318-19796-0, JR285). Prestressed Concrete.

Thirty Years of Psychical Research: Being a Treatise on Metaphysics. Charles Richet. Tr. by Stanley De Brath from Fr. LC 75-7397. (Perspectives in Psychical Research Ser.). (Illus.). 1975. Repr. of 1923 ed. 49.50x (ISBN 0-405-07046-2). Ayer Co Pubs.

Thirty Years of Rock & Roll Trivia. Fred L. Worth. 288p. (Orig.). 1980. pap. 2.50 (ISBN 0-446-91494-0). Warner Bks.

Thirty Years of State Constitution Making: 1938-1968. Albert L. Sturm. 173p. 1970. 1.00 (ISBN 0-318-15816-7). Citizens Forum Gov.

Thirty Years of the American Neptune. Ed. by Ernest S. Dodge. LC 72-82988. 1972. 24.50x (ISBN 0-674-88465-5). Harvard U Pr.

Thirty Years of the Communist Party of China: An Outline History. Hu Ch'lao-Mu. LC 73-877. (China Studies: from Confucius to Mao Ser.). (Illus.). 95p. 1973. Repr. of 1951 ed. 15.00 (ISBN 0-88355-071-7). Hyperion Conn.

Thirty Years of the Communist Party of China. Chi'Iai-Mu Hu. 1976. lib. bdg. 59.95 (ISBN 0-8490-2744-6). Gordon Pr.

Thirty Years of the Freedom Charter. Ed. by Jeremy Cronin & Raymond Suttner. (Illus.). 266p. 1987. pap. text ed. 15.95 (ISBN 0-86975-299-5, Pub. by Ravan Pr). Ohio U Pr.

Thirty Years of Yugoslav Literature: 1945-1975. Thomas Eekman. LC 78-53535. (Joint Committee on Eastern Europe Publication Ser.: No. 5). 1978. 15.00 (ISBN 0-930042-21-2). Mich Slavic Pubns.

Thirty Years on the Force. John Woods. (Juniper Bk.: No. 21). 1977. 5.00 (ISBN 1-55780-020-0). Juniper Pr WI.

Thirty Years on the Line. Leo D. Stapleton. 272p. 1987. pap. 3.95 (ISBN 0-380-70327-0). Avon.

Thirty Years Passed among the Players in England & America. Joe Cowell. Ed. by Arthur Saxon. LC 78-26796. (Archon Books on Popular Entertainments). (Illus.). viii, 103p. 1979. Repr. of 1844 ed. 19.50 (ISBN 0-208-01778-X, Archon). Shoe String.

Thirty Years' Review of China's Science & Technology, 1949-1979. Ed. by World Sci Singapore. viii, 314p. 1982. 76.00 (ISBN 9971-950-48-0). World Scientific Pub.

Thirty Years That Shook Physics: The Story of Quantum Theory. George Gamow. 240p. 1985. pap. 4.95 (ISBN 0-486-24895-X). Dover.

Thirty Years: The New York City Ballet. Lincoln Kirstein. LC 78-7132. 1978. 15.00 (ISBN 0-394-50257-4); pap. 6.95 (ISBN 0-394-73615-X). Knopf.

Thirty Years' View, or, a History of the Working of the American Government for Thirty Years, from 1820-1850, 2 vols. Thomas H. Benton. LC 68-28617. 1968. Repr. of 1856 ed. Vol. 1. Vol. 2. lib. bdg. 40.00 (ISBN 0-8371-0782-2, BETB). Greenwood.

Thirty Year's War. Geoffrey Parker. (Illus.). 320p. 1985. 32.95x (ISBN 0-7100-9788-3). Routledge Chapman & Hall.

Thirty Years War. Geoffrey Parker. (Illus.). 320p. 44.00 (ISBN 0-317-53180-8). Routledge Chapman & Hall.

Thirty Years' War. Ed. by Geoffrey Parker. 384p. 1988. pap. text ed. 15.95 (ISBN 0-7102-1181-3, Pub. by Routledge UK). Routledge Chapman & Hall.

Thirty Years War. J. V. Polisensky. Tr. by Robert Evans. 1971. 42.50x (ISBN 0-520-01868-0). U of Cal Pr.

Thirty Years' War. 2nd ed. Ed. by Theodore K. Rabb. LC 80-6215. (Illus.). 190p. 1981. lib. bdg. 26.25 (ISBN 0-8191-1746-3); pap. text ed. 8.50 (ISBN 0-8191-1747-1). U Pr of Amer.

Thirty Years' War. Henrik Tikkanen. Tr. by George Blecher & Lone T. Blecher. LC 86-8740. (Modern Scandinavian Literature in Translation Ser.). (Illus.). vi, 158p. 1987. pap. 8.95 (ISBN 0-8032-9407-7, Bison). U of Nebr Pr.

Thirty Years War. C. V. Wedgewood. 542p. 1981. pap. 13.95 (ISBN 0-416-32020-1, NO. 3578). Routledge Chapman & Hall.

Thirty Years War for Wild Life. William T. Hornaday. LC 71-125768. (American Environmental Studies). 1970. Repr. of 1931 ed. 14.00 (ISBN 0-405-02675-7). Ayer Co Pubs.

This House of Sky: Landscapes of a Western Mind. Ivan Doig. 15.75 (ISBN 0-8446-6218-6). Peter Smith.

This I Believe. Charles T. Crabtree. LC 81-84913. 160p. (Orig.). 1982. pap. 2.95 (ISBN 0-88243-758-5, 02-0758). Gospel Pub.

This I Believe. Donald D. Day. 224p. 1972. pap. 1.95 (ISBN 0-9600500-1-9). Three D Pubs.

This I Believe. 52p. (Eng. & Span.). 5.00 ea. Life Ins Mktg Res.

This I Can Believe. facs. ed. Alfred G. Walton. LC 79-142708. (Essay Index Reprint Ser). 1935. 18.00 (ISBN 0-8369-2207-7). Ayer Co Pubs.

This I Can Leave You: A Woman's Days on the Pitchfork Ranch. Mamie S. Burns. LC 86-5933. (Centennial Ser. of the Association of Former Students, Texas A & M University: No. 21). (Illus.). 324p. 1986. 16.95 (ISBN 0-89096-286-3). Tex A&M Univ Pr.

This If Anything of Mine: Poems, Nineteen Thirty to Nineteen Seventy-Five. Elizabeth W. Watson. 1976. 5.00 (ISBN 0-8233-0248-2). Golden Quill.

This Immortal People: A Short History of the Jewish People. Emil B. Cohn. LC 84-62563. 180p. (Orig.). 1985. pap. 5.95 (ISBN 0-8091-2693-1). Paulist Pr.

This in Which. George Oppen. LC 65-15674. (Orig.). 1965. 3.50 (ISBN 0-8112-0337-9). New Directions.

This Inch of Time: Memoirs of Politics & Diplomacy. Howard Beale. 1978. 25.00x (ISBN 0-522-84127-9, Pub. by Melbourne U Pr). Intl Spec Bk.

This Insults Women, No. I. Robert Watt. 1973. pap. 4.00 (ISBN 0-912518-05-7). Druid Bks.

This Insults Women, No. II. Robert Watt. 1973. pap. 4.00 (ISBN 0-912518-04-9). Druid Bks.

This Is. Gloria Patrick. LC 70-84092. (Illus.). (gr. k-3). 1970. PLB 4.95g (ISBN 0-87614-003-7). Carolrhoda Bks.

This Is a Crocodile. Evhy Constable. LC 86-12910. (Illus.). 24p. (ps-2). 1986. 12.95 (ISBN 0-02-724320-6). Bradbury Pr.

This Is a Printing Office: Broadsheet. Beatrice Warde & Albert Sperisen. (Broadsheet Ser.: No. 1). 1984. 85.00 (ISBN 0-520-05360-5). U of Cal Pr.

This Is a Recording: Listening with a Purpose. Barbara F. Swartz & Richard L. Smith. (Illus.). 136p. 1986. pap. text ed. write for info (ISBN 0-13-919200-X). P H.

This Is a Strange Country: Letters of a Westering Family, 1880-1906. Ed. by Byrd Gibbens. (Illus.). 576p. 1988. 29.95 (ISBN 0-8263-1107-5). U of NM Pr.

This Is a Test. Mimi Smith. LC 82-51221. (Artists' Bk.). 48p. (Orig.). 1983. pap. 10.00 (ISBN 0-89822-031-9). Visual Studies.

This Is About Incest. Margaret Randall. 72p. 1987. 16.95 (ISBN 0-932379-30-3); pap. 7.95 (ISBN 0-932379-29-X). Firebrand Bks.

This Is Adam. Brainard Cheney. 1958. 12.95 (ISBN 0-8392-1116-3). Astor-Honor.

This Is an Orchestra. rev. ed. Elsa Z. Posell. (Illus.). 96p. (gr. 2-5). 1973. 11.95 (ISBN 0-395-17712-X). HM.

This Is Apartheid: A Pictorial Introduction. International Defense & Aid Fund, Research & Information Department Staff. (Illus.). 40p. 1984. pap. 2.00 (ISBN 0-904759-55-5). Intl Defense & Aid.

This Is Astronomy. Lloyd Motz. LC 56-12016. (Illus.). 279p. (Orig.). 1958. pap. 14.00x (ISBN 0-231-08549-4). Columbia U Pr.

This Is Ballroom Dance. L. Ellfeldt. (Ballroom Dance Ser.). 1985. lib. bdg. 79.00 (ISBN 0-87700-825-6). Revisionist Pr.

This Is Ballroom Dance. L. Ellfeldt. (Ballroom Dance Ser.). 1986. lib. bdg. 79.95 (ISBN 0-8490-3281-4). Gordon Pr.

This Is BASIC: An Introduction to Computer Programming. Robert F. Sutherland. (Illus.). 384p. 1984. pap. text ed. write for info. (ISBN 0-02-418370-9). Macmillan.

This Is Birmingham: The Founding & Growth of an American City. John C. Henley, Jr. (Illus.). 1960. cloth 9.95 (ISBN 0-87651-008-X); pap. 6.95 (ISBN 0-87651-009-8). Southern U Pr.

This Is Boat Handling at Close Quarters. Dick Everitt & Rodger Witt. LC 85-81014. (This Is... (Sailing Ser.)). (Illus.). 160p. 1986. Repr. 18.95 (ISBN 0-688-06237-7, Pub. by Hearst Marine Bks). Morrow.

This Is Cape Breton. Alice Seward. LC 83-91474. 112p. 1985. 8.95 (ISBN 0-533-06063-X). Vantage.

This Is Carbon: A Defense of D. H. Lawrence's "The Rainbow" Against His Admirers. Gerald J. Butler. LC 85-30232. 151p. (Orig.). 1986. pap. 7.95x (ISBN 0-915781-02-6). Genitron Press.

This Is Catamaran Sailing. Ernst W. Barth & Klaus J. Enzmann. Tr. by John Powell from Ger. (Illus.). 144p. 1986. 24.95 (ISBN 0-85177-388-5, Pub. by Nautical Bks England). Sheridan.

This Is Charleston. rev. ed. Samuel G. Stoney. 139p. (Orig.). pap. text ed. 6.95 (ISBN 0-910326-04-5). Carolina Art.

This Is Child Health in the Home. A. Gullensward. 1986. 14.75X (ISBN 0-245-53914-X, Pub. by Harrap Ltd England). State Mutual Bk.

This Is Data Processing: Systems & Concepts. J. R. Verzello & J. Reutter. 560p. 1982. text ed. 34.95x (ISBN 0-07-067325-X). McGraw.

This Is Dinosaur: Echo Park Country & Its Magic Rivers. Ed. by Wallace Stegner. (Illus.). 128p. 1985. 25.00 (ISBN 0-911797-11-4); pap. 8.95 (ISBN 0-911797-12-2). R Rinehart Inc.

This Is Electronics, 2 bks. ITT Educational Services Inc. Incl. Bk. 1. Basic Principles (ISBN 0-672-97619-6); Bk. 2. Circuits & Applications (ISBN 0-672-97620-X). LC 74-105093. 1978. text ed. 32.60 scp ea. Set. Bobbs.

This Is Fairfield County. 2nd ed. Ed. by Donna M. Keane. (Connecticut in Profile Ser.). (Illus.). 168p. 1983. pap. 9.95 (ISBN 0-912733-01-2). Profiles Pub.

This Is for You. facs. ed. Compiled by William S. Lord. LC 78-121926. (Granger Index Reprint Ser.). 1902. 17.00 (ISBN 0-8369-6167-6). Ayer Co Pubs.

This Is Germany. C. Domville-Fife. 59.95 (ISBN 0-8490-1195-7). Gordon Pr.

This Is Germany. Emmanuel Y. Punay. 1987. cancelled (ISBN 0-8062-2998-5). Carlton.

This Is Germany. facsimile ed. Ed. by Arthur Settel. LC 70-156715. (Essay Index Reprint Ser). Repr. of 1950 ed. 25.00 (ISBN 0-8369-2427-4). Ayer Co Pubs.

This Is God Speaking: Twenty-Six Lessons for Children's Church. Jessie Sullivan. LC 81-18476. (Illus.). 112p. (Orig.). (gr. 1-6). 1982. pap. 7.95 (ISBN 0-87239-496-4, 3371). Standard Pub.

This Is God's Home. Sri Chinmoy. 50p. (Orig.). pap. 2.00 (ISBN 0-88497-233-X). Aum Pubns.

This Is Gold Country. Bob Utecht. LC 77-91022. (Illus.). 1977. pap. 10.00 (ISBN 0-87832-041-5). Piper.

This Is Grand Canyon. Elizabeth F. McFarland. (Illus.). 32p. 1986. pap. 2.00 (ISBN 0-9615359-1-1). Crest Pr Inc.

This Is Grant Wood Country. 2nd ed. Compiled by Joan Liffring-Zug. LC 77-88038. (Illus.). 64p. 1977. pap. 9.95 (ISBN 0-9603858-2-7). Penfield.

This Is Home Now. Floyd A. Robinson. 230p. 1983. 14.95 (ISBN 0-8138-1776-5). Iowa St U Pr.

This Is How It Was. William J. Laubenstein. (Illus.). vi, 132p. 1971. pap. 2.95 (ISBN 0-913228-03-6). Dillon-Liederbach.

This Is How My Body Works. Edith Heuser. (gr. 6-10). 1981. pap. 5.95 (ISBN 0-8120-2412-5). Barron.

This Is Iowa. Marquis Childs & Paul Engel. Ed. by Clarence A. Andrews. LC 82-61137. (Illus.). 320p. 1982. lib. bdg. 14.95 (ISBN 0-934582-04-1). Midwest Heritage.

This Is Ireland. Brendan O'Heithir. (Illus.). 128p. (Orig.). 1987. pap. 9.95 (ISBN 0-937702-07-2). Irish Bks Media.

This Is It. Bhagwan Shree Rajneesh. Ed. by ma Prem Maneesha. LC 82-230731. (Initiation Talks Ser.). (Illus.). 672p. (Orig.). 1979. 8.95 (ISBN 0-88050-156-1). Chidvilas Inc.

This Is It. Alan W. Watts. 1972. pap. 3.95 (ISBN 0-394-71904-2, Vin). Random.

This Is It: A Manager's Guide to Information Technology. 2nd ed. S. Curran et al. 345p. 1988. text ed. 55.00x (ISBN 0-86003-560-3, Pub. by Philip Allan UK); pap. text ed. 25.00 (ISBN 0-86003-660-X). Humanities.

This Is It: It's How You Live It Now, the Endless Meditation. Bhagavan Jivananda. (Orig.). pap. cancelled (ISBN 0-941404-27-7). Falcon Pr AZ.

This Is Jest for You. Skip Wilson. LC 85-1399. (Orig.). 1986. pap. 9.95 (ISBN 0-87949-261-9). Ashley Bks.

This Is Just to Say. bilingual ed. Bill Deemer. Tr. by Stefan Hyner from Eng. (Orig., Ger.). 1981. pap. 4.00 (ISBN 0-940556-03-0). Coyote.

This Is Karate. Mas Oyama. 34.95x (ISBN 0-685-22138-5). Wehman.

This Is Karate. rev. ed. Masutatsu Oyama. LC 65-17218. (Illus.). 368p. 1973. boxed 33.50 (ISBN 0-87040-254-4). Japan Pubns USA.

This Is Kendo. Sasamori & Warner. 16.50x (ISBN 0-685-22139-3). Wehman.

This Is Kendo: The Art of Japanese Fencing. Gordon Warner & Junzo Sasamori. LC 64-22900. 1964. 17.95 (ISBN 0-8048-0574-1). C E Tuttle.

This Is Liquid Sugar (Including Supplement) P. X. Hoynak & G. N. Bollenback. 1966. text ed. 14.50x (ISBN 0-934636-04-4). Key Bk Serv.

This Is Living: An Inspirational Guide to Freedom from the Fat Ogre. Lynn Redgrave. 1988. pap. price not set. NAL.

This Is Luther. Ewald Plass. 1984. pap. 4.95 (ISBN 0-570-03942-8, 12-2875). Concordia.

This Is Me. Keith Faulkner. (Tug-a-Tab Bks.). (Illus.). 10p. (ps-k). 1987. 5.95 (ISBN 0-312-00967-4). St Martin.

This Is Me. LC 85-61671. (Chunky Books Ser.). (Illus.). 28p. (ps-k). 1986. bds. 2.95 (ISBN 0-394-87816-7). Random.

This Is Me & My Two Families. Marla D. Evans. (Illus.). 88p. 1988. pap. 12.95 (ISBN 0-945354-06-1). Magination Pr.

This Is Me & My Two Families: A Self-Awareness Scrapbook Journal for Children Living with Two Families. M. D. Evans. 1986. write for info. (ISBN 0-9617474-0-4). M Evans.

This Is Michael Jackson. D. L. Mabery. LC 84-10043. (Illus.). 48p. (gr. 4-9). 1984. PLB 8.95 (ISBN 0-8225-1600-4). Lerner Pubns.

This Is Milwaukee. Robert Wells. LC 78-71508. 1978. Repr. of 1970 ed. 12.50 (ISBN 0-932476-00-7). Renaissance Bks.

This Is My Apple, Go Get Your Own. Elysabeth N. Faslund. (Herland Ser.: No. 4). 30p. 1983. pap. 3.50 (ISBN 0-934996-23-7). American Studies Pr.

This Is My Beloved. Walter Benton. 1943. 9.95 (ISBN 0-394-40458-0); pocket ed. o.p. 5.00 (ISBN 0-394-40459-9). Knopf.

This Is My Beloved: Psalms of Communion. Lucy Brown. 180p. (Orig.). Date not set. pap. price not set. Cedargarden.

This Is My Beloved Son - Listen to Him, Vol. 1. Anthony Coniaris. 1987. pap. 9.95 (ISBN 0-937032-55-7). Light&Life Pub Co MN.

This Is My God. Herman Wouk. 1983. pap. 4.95 (ISBN 0-671-49353-1). PB.

This Is My God: The Jewish Way of Life. Herman Wouk. 1986. pap. 8.95 (ISBN 0-671-62258-7, Touchstone Bks). S&S.

This Is My God: The Jewish Way of Life. Herman Wouk. (Illus.). 358p. 1988. 17.95 (ISBN 0-316-95507-8); ltd. ed. 100.00 (ISBN 0-316-95508-6). Little.

This Is My Home. Douglas & McIntyre. (Illus.). 128p. 1986. 24.95 (ISBN 0-88894-517-5). Salem Hse Pubs.

This Is My Home, Lord. Helen Lee. 128p. 1983. pap. 4.95 (ISBN 0-86683-683-7, HarpR). Har-Row.

This Is My House. Mercer Mayer. LC 87-116603. (Golden Easy Readers Ser.). (Illus.). 40p. (gr. k-2). 1988. 3.95 (ISBN 0-307-11660-3). Western Pub.

This Is My Land. Lirrel Starling. 1976. 6.00 (ISBN 0-685-73155-3). Byzantine Pr.

This Is My Life. Agnes Hunt. Ed. by William R. Phillips & Janet Rosenberg. LC 79-6013. (Physically Handicapped in Society Ser.). 1980. Repr. of 1942 ed. lib. bdg. 22.00x (ISBN 0-405-13116-X). Ayer Co Pubs.

This Is My Opinion about... Linda P. Silbert & Alvin J. Silbert. (Little Twirps Creative Thinking Workbooks). (Illus.). (gr. 5-12). 1977. 2.98 (ISBN 0-89544-020-2, 020). Silbert Bress.

This Is My Song. Mae L. Higgins. (Illus.). 16p. (Orig.). (ps-3). 1986. pap. 3.95 saddlestiched (ISBN 0-9616410-0-2). M L Higgins.

This Is My Story. W. K. Wilson. Date not set. price not set (ISBN 0-933959-04-4). Merton Pr.

This Is My Story, This Is My Song. Mary Bramer. 1984. pap. 2.25 (ISBN 0-570-03923-1, 12-2857). Concordia.

This Is My Trunk. Steven M. Harris. LC 85-7462. (Illus.). 32p. (gr. 4). 1985. 11.95 (ISBN 0-689-31128-1, Atheneum Childrens Bks). Macmillan.

This Is Namibia: A Pictorial Introduction. International Defense & Aid Fund, Research & Information Department Staff. (Illus.). 40p. 1984. pap. 2.00 (ISBN 0-904759-56-3). Intl Defense & Aid.

This Is New Jersey. 3rd ed. John T. Cunningham. 1978. pap. 14.95 (ISBN 0-8135-0862-2). Rutgers U Pr.

This Is New York City: Facts & Trends for Social Planning. 1980. 2.00 (ISBN 0-86671-066-3). Comm Coun Great NY.

This Is Not a Letter & Other Poems. Kay Boyle. 1985. 9.95 (ISBN 0-940650-61-4). Sun & Moon CA.

This Is Not a Photograph: Twenty Years of Photography, 1966-1986. Joseph Jacobs. LC 87-80681. 110p. 1987. pap. 19.95 (ISBN 0-317-62953-0). Ringling Mus Art.

This Is Not a Pipe: Illustrations & Letters by Rene Magritte. Michel Foucault. Tr. by James Harkness. LC 80-26627. (Quantum Books: No. 24). (Illus.). 112p. 1982. 22.00x (ISBN 0-520-04232-8); pap. 6.95 (ISBN 0-520-04916-0). U of Cal Pr.

This Is Not a Place to Sing. Christina Pacosz. 48p. (Orig.). 1987. pap. 4.95 (ISBN 0-931122-47-3). West End.

This Is Not for You. Jane Rule. 302p. 1982. pap. 7.95 (ISBN 0-930044-25-8). Naiad Pr.

This Is Our Hope. R. E. Orchard. 150p. 1966. 3.95 (ISBN 0-88243-617-1, 02-0617). Gospel Pub.

This Is Our Land, Vol. 1. Val J. McClellan. LC 77-151749. (Illus.). 1977. 12.50x (ISBN 0-533-02248-7). Western Pubs FL.

This Is Our Land, Vol. 2. Val J. McClellan. LC 77-151749. (Illus.). 1979. 13.95x (ISBN 0-9602218-0-8). Western Pubs FL.

This Is Our Mass. Thomas Coyle. LC 85-50691. 144p. 1985. pap. 3.50 (ISBN 0-89622-233-0). Twenty-Third.

This Is Our St. Rose Church in Proctor Minnesota. Claire W. Schumacher. (Illus.). 100p. 1976. pap. 3.00 (ISBN 0-917378-02-4). Schumacher Pubns.

This Is Our World. Paul B. Sears. (Illus.). 1971. 16.50x (ISBN 0-8061-0932-7); pap. 8.95x (ISBN 0-8061-0933-5). U of Okla Pr.

This Is Pearl: The United States & Japan, 1941. Walter Millis. LC 77-138594. (Illus.). 1971. Repr. of 1947 ed. lib. bdg. 35.00x (ISBN 0-8371-5795-1, MITP). Greenwood.

This Is PR: The Realities of Public Relations. 3rd ed. Doug Newsom & Alan Scott. 518p. 1985. text ed. write for info. (ISBN 0-534-04287-2). Wadsworth Pub.

This Is PR: The Realities of Public Relations. 4th ed. Doug Newsom et al. Date not set. text ed. write for info. (ISBN 0-534-10140-2). Wadsworth Pub.

This Is Progress. 48p. 1977. 2.00x (ISBN 0-904393-13-5, Pub. by CIIR). State Mutual Bk.

This Is Psychotherapy: For Those Considering It, for Those Involved in It, & for the Curious. Phineas Kadushin. LC 82-61943. 320p. 1983. 16.95 (ISBN 0-9610000-0-7). Tip-Top.

This Is Ragtime. Terry Waldo. (Roots of Jazz Ser.). 244p. 1984. Repr. of 1976 ed. lib. bdg. 29.50 (ISBN 0-306-76229-3). Da Capo.

This Is Reading. Frank G. Jennings. LC 82-361. 210p. 1982. 29.50x (ISBN 0-306-40990-9, Plenum Pr); pap. 14.95x (ISBN 0-306-40992-5). Plenum Pub.

This Is Reality. Roy E. Davis. 160p. 1983. pap. 3.95 (ISBN 0-317-20863-2). CSA Pr.

This is Riding. Gunnar Hedlund. 1988. 50.00x (ISBN 0-901366-85-4, Pub. by Harrap Ltd England). State Mutual Bk.

This Is Riding: Dressage, Jumping, Eventing in Words & Pictures. Gunnar Hedlund. Tr. by Sigrid Young from Swedish. LC 88-11979. (Illus.). 144p. 1988. 22.95 (ISBN 0-939481-09-X). Half Halt Pr.

This Is Sailing. Richard Creagh-Osborne. LC 84-62460. 1985. 17.95 (ISBN 0-688-05429-3, Pub. by Hearst Marine Bks). Morrow.

This Is School. David Aspy. 100p. 1986. pap. 10.00 (ISBN 0-87425-036-6). Human Res Dev Pr.

This Is Southeast Asia Today. Addison Eastman. (Orig.). (YA) (gr. 9 up). 1968. pap. 0.85 (ISBN 0-377-83101-8). Friendship Pr.

This Is That: Personal Experiences, Sermons & Writings. Aimee S. McPherson. Ed. by Daonald W. Dayton. (Higher Christian Life Ser.). 685p. 1985. 85.00 (ISBN 0-8240-6428-3). Garland Pub.

This Is That-That Is This. Kenneth K. Buzby. 1987. 7.95 (ISBN 0-533-07134-8). Vantage.

This Is the ABC: Australian Broadcasting Commission, 1932-1983. K. S. Inglis. (Illus.). 521p. 1983. 21.95x (ISBN 0-522-84258-5, Pub. by Melbourne U Pr). Intl Spec Bk.

This Is the Abyssinian Cat. Kate Faler. (Illus.). 192p. 1983. 16.95 (ISBN 0-87666-866-X, PS-783). TFH Pubns.

This Is the Afghan Hound. Joan M. Brearley. (Illus.). 1965. 12.95 (ISBN 0-87666-231-9, PS-639). TFH Pubns.

This Is the Alaskan Malamute. Joan M. Brearley. (Illus.). 415p. 1975. 19.95 (ISBN 0-87666-650-0, PS-737). TFH Pubns.

This Is the American Pit Bull Terrier. Richard F. Stratton. (Illus.). 1976. 14.95 (ISBN 0-87666-660-8, PS-613). TFH Pubns.

This Is the Bear. Sarah Hayes. LC 85-45749. (Trophy Picture Bks.). (Illus.). 32p. (ps-2). 1986. pap. 2.95 (ISBN 0-06-443103-7, Trophy). HarpJ.

This Is the Bear. Sarah Hayes. LC 85-45752. (Illus.). 32p. (ps-2). 1986. PLB 11.89 (ISBN 0-397-32171-6, Lipp Jr Bks). HarpJ.

This Is the Best Time of Day, Charlie Brown. Charles M. Schulz. (Peanuts Ser.). 1987. pap. 2.25 (ISBN 0-317-57101-X, Juniper). Fawcett.

This Is the Best Time of Day, Charlie Brown: Selected Cartoons from "And a Woodstock in a Birch". Charles M. Schulz. 128p. 1982. pap. 1.75 (ISBN 0-449-24485-7, Crest). Fawcett.

This Is the Bichon Frise. Joan McD. Brearly & Anna K. Nicholas. (Illus.). 1973. 14.95 (ISBN 0-87666-247-5, PS-700). TFH Pubns.

This Is the Child. Terry Pringle. LC 82-48876. 1983. 13.45 (ISBN 0-394-52921-9). Knopf.

This Is the Day. Nona Freeman. Ed. by Charles Clanton. 256p. (Orig.). 1978. pap. 4.95 (ISBN 0-912315-36-9). Word Aflame.

This Is the Day. Sue M. Kidd. (Illus.). 60p. 1987. 7.95 (ISBN 0-8378-1828-1). Gibson.

This Is the Day. Gene Markey. (Illus.). 1978. 5.00 (ISBN 0-87482-099-5). Wake-Brook.

This Is the Day: The Biblical Doctrine of the Christian Sunday in it's Jewish & Early Church Setting. Roger T. Beckwith & Wilfrid Scott. 192p. 1978. 12.00 (ISBN 0-551-05568-5). Attic Pr.

This Is the Faith. Francis J. Ripley. 317p. 1973. pap. 5.95 (ISBN 0-903348-02-0). Lumen Christi.

This Is the House That Jack Built. Illus. by Pam Adams. (Books with Holes Ser.). (Illus.). 16p. (Orig.). (ps-2). 1977. pap. 5.00 (ISBN 0-85953-075-2, Pub. by Child's Play England). Playspaces.

This Is the House That Jack Built. Illus. by Liz Underhill. LC 86-26999. (Illus.). 32p. 1987. 12.95 (ISBN 0-8050-0339-8). H Holt & Co.

This Is the House Where Jack Lives. Joan Heilbroner. LC 62-7311. (Harper I Can Read Bks.). (Illus.). (gr. k-3). PLB 9.89 (ISBN 0-06-022286-7). HarpJ.

This Is the Irish Setter. Joan McD. Brearley. (Illus.). 480p. 1975. 19.95 (ISBN 0-87666-655-1, H-952). TFH Pubns.

This Is the Life. Goodspeed. (gr. 7-12). 1981. text ed. 15.40 (ISBN 0-02-665910-7). Bennett IL.

This Is the Maine Coon Cat. Sharyn P. Bass. (Illus.). 160p. 1983. 19.95 (ISBN 0-87666-867-8, H-1057). TFH Pubns.

This Is the Newfoundland. K. Drury. 17.95 (ISBN 0-87666-340-4, PS-666). TFH Pubns.

This Is the One I Want. Linda Richman. (Illus.). 172p. 1987. spiral bdg. 24.00. Mayer-Johnson.

This is the One I Want. Linda G. Richman. (Illus.). 172p. 1987. spiral bdg. 24.00. Mayer-Johnson.

TITLE INDEX THIS QUARTER: THE SURREALIST

This Is the Place for Me. Joanna Cole. (Illus.). 32p. (Orig.). (gr. k-3). 1986. pap. 1.95 (ISBN 0-590-33996-6). Scholastic Inc.
This Is the Prophet Jesus. Fred Howes. LC 82-72741. 276p. 1983. pap. 8.95 (ISBN 0-87516-497-8). DeVorss.
This Is the Puzzle of Poverty. Jeanette Struchen. (Illus.). (gr. 9 up). 1966. pap. 0.85 (ISBN 0-377-83081-X). Friendship Pr.
This Is the Russian Blue. Ingeborg Urcia. (Illus.). 160p. 1983. 19.95 (ISBN 0-87666-864-3, PS-784). TFH Pubns.
This Is the Saint Bernard. Marlene Anderson & Joan McD. Brearley. (Illus.). 1973. 17.95 (ISBN 0-87666-376-5, PS-698). TFH Pubns.
This Is the Samoyed. Joan McD. Brearley. (Illus.). 384p. 1975. 17.95 (ISBN 0-87666-379-X, H-954). TFH Pubns.
This Is the Scottish Terrier. T. Allen Kirk, Jr. 1966. 12.95 (ISBN 0-87666-385-4, PS-626). TFH Pubns.
This Is the Shih Tzu. rev. ed. Allan Easton. 1969. 12.95 (ISBN 0-87666-389-7, PS661). TFH Pubns.
This Is the Siberian Husky. Joan McD. Brearly. (Illus.). 543p. 1974. 17.95 (ISBN 0-87666-392-7, PS-707). TFH Pubns.
This Is the South. facsimile ed. Ed. by Robert W. Howard. LC 77-167357. (Essay Index Reprint Ser.). Repr. of 1959 ed. 29.00 (ISBN 0-8369-2507-6). Ayer Co Pubs.
This Is the Torah. A. J. Kolatch. LC 87-33624. 364p. 1988. 16.95 (ISBN 0-8246-0330-3). Jonathan David.
This Is the Way. Donald Gee. Orig. Title: Studies in Guidance. 64p. 1975. pap. 0.95 (ISBN 0-88243-630-9, 02-0630). Gospel Pub.
This Is the Way I Pass My Time. Ellen J. Gehret et al. LC 84-62851. (Pennsylvania German Society Ser.: Vol. XVIII). (Illus.). 292p. 1985. 45.00 (ISBN 0-911122-48-6). Penn German Soc.
This Is the Way I See Aesthetic Realism. Chaim Koppelman. (Illus.). 1969. pap. 1.95x (ISBN 0-911492-11-9). Aesthetic Realism.
This Is the Way My Garden Grows: And Comes Into My Kitchen. Barbara D. Borland. (Illus.). 158p. 1986. 13.95 (ISBN 0-393-02298-6). Norton.
This Is the Word of the Lord. rev. ed. William Freburger. LC 83-72480. 176p. 1984. spiral bound 6.95 (ISBN 0-87793-309-X). Ave Maria.
This Is the Word of the Lord: Year A: The Year of Matthew. Ed. by Robin Duckworth. 1980. pap. 9.95 (ISBN 0-19-213248-2). Oxford U Pr.
This Is the Word of the Lord: Year B., the Year of the Mark. Robin Duckworth. 1981. pap. 9.95 (ISBN 0-19-826662-6). Oxford U Pr.
This Is the Word of the Lord: Year C. the Year of Luke. Robin Duckworth. (Orig.). 1982. pap. 9.95 (ISBN 0-19-826666-9). Oxford U Pr.
This Is Truth about the Self. 3rd ed. Ann Davies. 1984. 4.50 (ISBN 0-938002-03-1). Builders of Adytum.
This Is Tucson: Guidebook to the Old Pueblo. 2nd ed. Peggy H. Lockard. (Illus.). 308p. 1985. pap. 8.95 (ISBN 0-914468-09-X). Pepper Pub.
This Is Tucson: Guidebook to the Old Pueblo. 3rd ed. Peggy H. Lockard. LC 87-60321. (Illus.). 316p. 1988. pap. 9.95 (ISBN 0-914468-23-5). Pepper Pub.
This Is Vermont. Merkle & Vermont Historical Society. (Illus.). 1965. pap. 1.98 (ISBN 0-911868-14-3). Carstens Pubns.
This Is Washington, D.C. abr. ed. M. Sasek. LC 72-90997. (Illus.). 48p. (gr. 3-6). 1973. pap. 3.95 (ISBN 0-02-045180-6, Collier). Macmillan.
This Is Weird. Patty Wolcott. (Illus.). 32p. (Orig.). (gr. k-3). 1986. pap. 2.50 (ISBN 0-590-33934-6). Scholastic Inc.
This Is Wisdom. Satguru S. Keshavadas. (Illus.). 96p. (Orig.). 1975. pap. 3.50 (ISBN 0-942508-07-6). Vishwa.
This Is Women's Work: An Anthology of Women's Poetry, Prose & Graphics. Ed. by Susan Efros. LC 74-19118. (Illus.). 160p. 1974. pap. 6.95 (ISBN 0-915572-02-8). Panjandrum.
This Is Your Body. rev. ed. James B. Olsen. 64p. 1982. 3.75 (ISBN 0-88336-537-5). New Readers.
This Is Your Captain Speaking. Ivy Ruckman. (gr. 5 up). 1987. 13.95 (ISBN 0-8027-6734-6). Walker & Co.
This Is Your Day. Edward Newhouse. LC 74-2800. (Labor Movement in Fiction & Non-Fiction). Repr. of 1937 ed. 28.50 (ISBN 0-404-58456-X). AMS Pr.
This Is Your Law. 2nd ed. Communications Library Staff. 70p. 1987. pap. text ed. 25.00x (ISBN 0-934339-87-2). Comm Lib.
This Is Your Life. 1986. pap. 2.70 (ISBN 0-89137-815-4). Quality Pubns.
This Is Your Life. Meg Wolitzer. 1988. 17.95 (ISBN 0-517-56929-9). Crown.
This Is Your Life, Bhodi Li, No. IV. David Peters. (Photon Adventure Novel Ser.). 1987. pap. 2.50 (ISBN 0-425-10185-1, Pub by Berkley-Pacer). Berkley Pub.
This Is Your Life, Charlie Brown: Selected Cartoons from "It's a Dog's Life, Charlie Brown", Vol. 1. Charles M. Schulz. (Peanuts Series). (Illus.). 1982. pap. 2.25 (ISBN 0-449-23918-7, Crest). Fawcett.
This Is Your Life Story: How to Write It, How to Teach It. Velma Krauch. LC 87-82424. 192p. (Orig.). 1988. pap. 11.95 (ISBN 0-9619408-5-9). Encore Pub.
This Is Zion. Allen R. Hagood. (Illus.). 73p. 1982. pap. 2.95 (ISBN 0-915630-06-0). Zion.
This Island Earth. Ed. by Oran W. Nicks. LC 78-608969. (NASA Ser.: SP-250). (Illus.). 192p. 1987. 12.00 (ISBN 0-318-23531-5, S/N 033-000-00321-8). USGPO.
This Island Isn't Big Enough for the Four of Us. Gery Greer & Bob Ruddick. LC 86-47750. 160p. (gr. 3-7). 1987. 11.95i (ISBN 0-690-04612-X, Crowell Jr Bks); PLB 11.89 (ISBN 0-690-04614-6). HarpJ.
This Island Now. Peter Abrahams. 256p. 1985. pap. 8.95 (ISBN 0-571-13439-4). Faber & Faber.
This Issue Commemorating the 70th Birthday of Dr. Josiah L. Lowe. Ed. by Dr. Clark T. Rogerson. LC 66-6394. (Memoirs of the New York Botanical Garden Ser.: Vol. 28, No. 1). 1976. pap. 20.00x (ISBN 0-89327-004-0). NY Botanical.
This Jockey Drives Late Nights. Henry Livings. 1981. pap. 6.95 (ISBN 0-413-29490-0, NO. 6478). Heinemann Ed.
This Journey. James Wright. LC 81-70280. 100p. 1982. pap. 5.95 (ISBN 0-394-70825-3, Vin). Random.
This Journey. James Wright. 91p. 1982. 10.00 (ISBN 0-394-52365-2). Random.
This Kind of Woman: Ten Stories by Japanese Women Writers, 1960-1976. Yukiko Tanaka & Elizabeth Hanson. 320p. 1984. pap. 9.95 (ISBN 0-399-51090-7, Perigee). Putnam Pub Group.
This Kind of Woman: Ten Stories by Japanese Women Writers, 1960-1976. Ed. by Yukiko Tanaka & Elizabeth Hanson. LC 81-51332. 320p. 1982. 25.00x (ISBN 0-8047-1130-5). Stanford U Pr.
This Land Is Mine. Jesse Stuart. 12.95 (ISBN 0-89190-893-5, Pub. by Am Repr). Amereon Ltd.
This Land Is Our Land: The West Bank under Israeli Occupation. Jan Metzger et al. (Illus.). 278p. 1983. 24.75x (ISBN 0-86232-086-0, Pub. by Zed Pr England); pap. 10.25 (ISBN 0-86232-073-9, Pub. by Zed Pr England). Humanities.
This Land Is Your Land: The Struggle to Save America's Public Lands. Bernard Shanks. LC 84-5359. (Illus.). 320p. 1984. 19.95 (ISBN 0-87156-822-5). Sierra.
This Land of Liberty. Ernest Bates. LC 73-19817. (Civil Liberties in American History Ser.). 383p. 1974. Repr. of 1930 ed. lib. bdg. 42.50 (ISBN 0-306-70597-4). Da Capo.
This Land of Liberty: A History of America's Jews. Helene Kenvin. 216p. (gr. 7-9). 1986. pap. text ed. 7.95x (ISBN 0-87441-421-0). Behrman.
This Land, This South: An Environmental History. Albert E. Cowdrey. LC 82-20154. (New Perspectives on the South Ser.). 256p. 1983. 23.00 (ISBN 0-8131-0302-9). U Pr of Ky.
This Land, This Time, 4 vols. Dobrica Cosic. Tr. by Muriel Heppell. Incl. Into the Battle. 8.95 (ISBN 0-15-644991-9); Reach to Eternity. 7.95 (ISBN 0-15-676012-6); South to Destiny. 7.95 (ISBN 0-15-683913-X); Time of Death. 7.95 (ISBN 0-15-690445-4). 1983. Repr. of 1978 ed. Set. write for info. (ISBN 0-15-690026-2, Harv). HarBraceJ.
This Land Turns Evil Slowly. Mary L. Roby. Bd. with Dig a Narrow Grave. 1978. pap. 2.50 (ISBN 0-451-11696-8, AE1696, Sig). NAL.
This Land Was Theirs. 4th ed. Wendell H. Oswalt. 496p. 1987. pap. text ed. 24.95 (ISBN 0-87484-815-6). Mayfield Pub.
This Land Was Theirs: A Study of the North American Indian. 3rd ed. Wendell H. Oswalt. 569p. 1978. pap. text ed. write for info (ISBN 0-394-34413-8, RandC). Random.
This Land...This Beauty. Shinzo Maeda. 96p. 1987. 36.95 (ISBN 4-766-10420-X, Pub. by Graphic Sha Japan). Bks Nippan.
This Leaving We Cannot Live Without. Judith McPheron. LC 84-46169. 64p. 1985. pap. 6.95 (ISBN 0-931722-34-9). Corona Pub.
This Life. Sidney Poitier. 416p. 1981. pap. 2.95 (ISBN 0-345-29407-6). Ballantine.
This Life. Sidney Poitier. LC 79-3488. 1980. 15.45 (ISBN 0-394-50549-2). Knopf.
This Life I've Loved-Stevenson. Isobel Field. 1973. Repr. of 1938 ed. 30.00 (ISBN 0-8274-0532-4). R West.
This Light Will Spread: Selected Poems Nineteen Sixty to Nineteen Seventy-Five. Paul Mariah. 15.00 (ISBN 0-686-25740-5); pap. 6.95 (ISBN 0-686-25741-3). Man-Root.
This Little Measure. Sara Woods. (Anthony Maitland Detective Ser.). 192p. 1986. pap. 2.95 (ISBN 0-380-69862-5). Avon.
This Little Nose. Jan Ormerod. LC 87-2605. (Illus.). 24p. (ps). 1987. 5.95 (ISBN 0-688-07276-3). Lothrop.
This Little Pig. Colin Hawkins & Jacqui Hawkins. LC 85-40640. (Jollypops Ser.). (Illus.). 12p. (ps-1). 1986. 2.95 (ISBN 0-670-80316-2, Viking Kestrel). Viking.
This Little Pig... Nancy Southerland-Holmes. (Illus.). 42p. 1982. pap. 6.00 (ISBN 0-943574-10-2). That Patchwork.
This Little Pig. Illus. by Eleanor Wasmuth. (Illus.). (ps). 1986. bds. 2.95 (ISBN 0-671-61727-3, Little Simon). S&S.
This Little Pig: A Mother Goose Favorite. Illus. by Leonard B. Lubin. LC 84-10021. (Illus.). 32p. (ps-2). 1985. 11.75 (ISBN 0-688-04088-8); PLB 11.88 (ISBN 0-688-04089-6). Lothrop.
This Little Pig Had a Riddle. Richard Latta. Ed. by Anne Fay. LC 83-26112. (Illus.). 32p. (gr. 1-5). 1984. PLB 7.95 (ISBN 0-8075-7893-2). A Whitman.
This Little Pig Stayed Home. Donna Guthrie. (Storybook Special). (Illus.). 32p. (ps-7). 1987. 8.95 (ISBN 0-8431-1820-2); cassette & bk. 12.95 (ISBN 0-8431-1788-5). Price Stern.
This Little Pig Went to Market. LC 84-61284. (Baby Fingers Ser.). (Illus.). 14p. (ps). 1985. bds. 2.95 (ISBN 0-394-87030-1, BYR). Random.
This Little Room & Other Poems, 1945-1975. Clinton Williams. LC 75-25134. 1975. 5.00 (ISBN 0-934614-01-6); pap. 3.95 (ISBN 0-686-14928-9). Talisman Research.
This Longing (Rumi) Tr. by Cokman Barks & Jhon Moyne. 96p. (Orig.). 1988. pap. 8.00 (ISBN 0-939660-29-6). Threshold VT.
This Loving Darkness: Silent Films & Spanish Writers 1920 - 1936. C. B. Morris. 1980. 39.50x (ISBN 0-19-713440-8). Oxford U Pr.
This Loving Promise. Matthew Braun. 1984. pap. 3.75 (ISBN 0-8217-1404-X). Zebra.
This Loving Torment. Valerie Sherwood. 528p. (Orig.). 1977. pap. 3.95 (ISBN 0-446-32831-6). Warner Bks.
This Magic Moment. Gregg Easterbrook. 300p. 1986. 17.95 (ISBN 0-312-80054-1, Pub. by Thomas Dunne Bks). St Martin.
This Man & Music. Anthony Burgess. 240p. 1983. text ed. 14.95 (ISBN 0-07-008964-7). McGraw.
This Man & Music. Anthony Burgess. 192p. 1985. pap. 3.95 (ISBN 0-380-69852-8, Discus). Avon.
This Man from Lebanon. Barbara Young. (Illus.). 1950. 18.45 (ISBN 0-394-44848-0). Knopf.
This Man Is My Brother. Myron Brinig. LC 78-63980. (Gay Experience). Repr. of 1932 ed. 37.50 (ISBN 0-404-61501-5). AMS Pr.
This Man Jesus: The Gospel Narrative of His Life & Ministry. Irene B. Harrel & Alie H. Benson. 224p. 1988. pap. 6.95 (ISBN 0-310-27701-9). Zondervan.
This Mess We're In! Fred J. Wall. 112p. 1985. pap. 4.95 (ISBN 0-682-40176-5). Exposition-Phoenix.
This Mighty Dream: Social Protest Movements in the United States. Madeleine Adamson & Seth Borgos. (Illus.). 128p. 1984. 19.95x (ISBN 0-7102-0040-4); pap. 9.95 (ISBN 0-7102-0042-0). Routledge Chapman & Hall.
This Mighty Sum of Things: Wordsworth's Theme of Benevolent Necessity. Thomas J. Rountree. LC 65-12244. Repr. of 1965 ed. 27.00 (ISBN 0-8357-9621-3, 2103214). Bks Demand UMI.
This Migrant Earth. Tomas Rivera. Tr. by Rolando Hinojosa from Span. LC 85-73354. 160p. (Orig.). 1986. pap. 8.00 (ISBN 0-934770-55-7). Arte Publico.
This Misery of Boots. H. G. Wells. 1907. lib. bdg. 29.50 (ISBN 0-8414-9416-9). Folcroft.
This Misery of Boots. H. G. Wells. 48p. 1987. pap. text ed. 2.50 (ISBN 0-930997-01-8, W-01). East Bay Bks.
This Modern Music. facs. ed. John T. Howard. LC 68-58796. (Essay Index Reprint Ser). 1942. 16.00 (ISBN 0-8369-0018-9). Ayer Co Pubs.
This Modern World. 2nd ed. Derek Wood. (gr. 7-12). 1980. pap. text ed. 10.00x (ISBN 0-435-31951-5). Heinemann Ed.
This Morning with God. Ed. by Carol Adeney. LC 68-28080. 1978. pap. 11.95 (ISBN 0-87784-870-X). Inter-Varsity.
This Morning's Mockingbird. George Swede. 16p. 1980. 7.00 (ISBN 0-913719-46-3); pap. 2.00 (ISBN 0-913719-45-5). High-Coo Pr.
This Music Crept by Me upon the Waters see One Act: Eleven Short Plays of the Modern Theater.
This My Island. Lisl Beer. 3.75 (ISBN 0-8283-1103-X). Branden Pub Co.
This 'n That. Bette Davis & Michael Herskowitz. (Illus.). 208p. 1987. 17.95 (ISBN 0-399-13246-5, Putnam). Putnam Pub Group.
This 'n' That. Bette Davis & Michael Herskowitz. 1988. pap. 3.95 (ISBN 0-317-67131-6). Berkley Pub.
This Nation Shall Endure. Ezra T. Benson. LC 77-21466. 1977. 9.95 (ISBN 0-87747-658-6). Deseret Bk.
This New Day. (Gifts of Growth Ser.). 386p. (Orig.). 1985. pap. 6.95 (ISBN 0-934391-02-5). Quotidian.
This New Land. G. Clifton Wisler. LC 87-17749. (gr. 5 up). 1987. 13.95 (ISBN 0-8027-6726-5); PLB 14.85 (ISBN 0-8027-6727-3). Walker & Co.
This New Yet Unapproachable America: Essays after Emerson after Wittgenstein. Stanley Cavell. 108p. 1989. 19.95x (ISBN 0-945953-01-1); pap. 9.95 (ISBN 0-945953-00-3). Living Batch Bks.
This Old Bill. Loren D. Estleman. LC 83-20766. 203p. (gr. 7 up). 1984. 15.00 (ISBN 0-385-19165-0). Ultramarine Pub.
This Old House Guide to Building & Remodeling Materials. Bob Vila et al. 496p. (Orig.). 1988. pap. 16.95 (ISBN 0-446-38246-9). Warner Bks.
This Old House: Restoring, Rehabilitating & Renovating. Bob Vila & Jane Davison. (Illus.). 336p. 1980. pap. 19.95 (ISBN 0-316-17702-4). Little.
This Old House: The Story of Clara Rust, Alaska Pioneer. Jo A. Wold. LC 76-22728. (Illus.). 262p. (Orig.). pap. 6.95 (ISBN 0-88240-069-X, 062). Alaska Northwest.
This Old Man. Illus. by Pam Adams. (Books with Holes Ser.). (Illus.). 16p. (Orig.). (ps-2). pap. 5.00 (ISBN 0-85953-026-4, Pub. by Childs Play England). Playspaces.
This Old Man. Illus. by Pam Adams. (Books with Holes). (Illus.). 16p. (ps-2). 8.00 (ISBN 0-85953-027-2, Pub. by Child's Play England). Playspaces.
This Old Man. Lois Ruby. LC 84-14258. 192p. (gr. 7 up). 1984. 11.95 (ISBN 0-395-36563-5). HM.
This Old Man. Lois Ruby. 1987. pap. 2.50 (ISBN 0-317-57105-2, Juniper). Fawcett.
This Old Man: The Counting Song. Illus. by Robin M. Koontz. (ps-1). 1988. 12.95 (ISBN 0-396-09120-2). Putnam Pub Group.
This Old Monmouth of Ours. William S. Hornor. LC 73-89903. 1974. 24.00 (ISBN 0-686-11780-8). Morris Genealog Lib.
This Once: New & Selected Poems, 1965-1978. David Gitin. LC 79-1108. (Selected Works Ser.: No. 3). 1979. 17.95 (ISBN 0-912652-48-9); signed & numbered 29.95x (ISBN 0-912652-50-0); pap. 7.95 (ISBN 0-912652-49-7). Blue Wind.
This One's about the ACC. Lyndon Fuller. LC 82-70558. 96p. 1982. pap. 4.95 (ISBN 0-89089-027-7). Carolina Acad Pr.
This One's on Me. Donald Jack. Ed. by Colleen Dimson. 448p. 1988. pap. 4.95 (ISBN 0-7701-0975-6). PaperJacks US.
This One's on Me. Donald L. Jack. LC 87-15739. 320p. 1988. 16.95 (ISBN 0-385-25064-9). Doubleday.
This Our Caesar: A Study of Bernard Shaw's "Ceasar & Cleopatra". Gordon W. Couchman. 1973. pap. text ed. 19.20 (ISBN 90-2792-601-8). Mouton.
This Our Church: The People and Events That Shaped It. William A. Herr. (Basics of Christian Thought Ser.). 1986. 17.95 (ISBN 0-88347-193-0). Thomas More.
This Outcast Generation & Luminous Moss. Taijun Takeda. Tr. by Yusaburo Shibuya & Sanford Goldstein. LC 67-20951. 1967. pap. 4.25 (ISBN 0-8048-1501-1). C E Tuttle.
This Pair of Hands. Dallas Mucci. 150p. (Orig.). 1988. pap. 5.95. Beacon Hill.
This Paradox Shadow. Jane Morrel. 112p. 1982. pap. 11.95 (ISBN 0-933180-33-0). Spoon Riv Poetry.
This Passover Or the Next I Will Never Be in Jerusalem. Hilton Obenzinger. LC 80-20986. 1980. lib. bdg. 12.50x (ISBN 0-917672-13-5); pap. 5.95x (ISBN 0-917672-12-7). Momos.
This Pendent World. Pauline Petran. 84p. 1987. 7.95 (ISBN 0-533-07496-7). Vantage.
This People, This Parish. Robert K. Hudnut. 192p. 1986. pap. 7.95 (ISBN 0-310-38241-6, 12329P). Zondervan.
This Perfect Day. Ira Levin. 1979. pap. 2.25 (ISBN 0-440-18704-4). Dell.
This Person Is You. Christopher Markert. LC 68-28486. (Illus., Orig.). (YA) (gr. 10 up). 1968. pap. 2.50 (ISBN 0-8283-1016-5). Branden Pub Co.
This Place. Andrea Freud-Loewenstein. 544p. 1984. 14.95 (ISBN 0-86358-039-4). Routledge Chapman & Hall.
This Place Called Kansas. Charles C. Howes. LC 83-51177. (Illus.). 264p. 1984. pap. 9.95 (ISBN 0-8061-1859-8). U of Okla Pr.
This Place Has No Atmosphere. Paula Danziger. LC 85-46070. 176p. (gr. 5-8). 1986. pap. 14.95 (ISBN 0-385-29489-1). Delacorte.
This Place Has No Atmosphere. Paula Danziger. (gr. k-12). 1987. pap. 2.95 (ISBN 0-440-98726-1, LFL). Dell.
This Planted Vine: A Narrative History of the Episcopal Diocese of New York. James Elliott Lindsley. LC 84-47588. (Illus.). 320p. 1984. 24.50i (ISBN 0-06-015347-4, HarpT). Har-Row.
This Poetick Liturgie: Robert Herrick's Ceremonial Mode. Leigh De Neef. LC 74-75910. vii, 200p. 1974. 21.95 (ISBN 0-8223-0323-X). Duke.
This Precipice Garden. James DePriest. 60p. 1987. 15.00 (ISBN 0-940869-00-4); pap. 8.00 (ISBN 0-940869-01-2). Univ Portland Pr.
This Present Darkness. Frank E. Peretti. LC 86-70282. 416p. (Orig.). 1986. pap. 8.95 (ISBN 0-89107-390-6, Crossway Bks). Good News.
This Promised Land. Robert Easton. (Saga of California Trilogy: Vol. I). 328p. (Orig.). 1982. pap. 9.95 (ISBN 0-88496-183-4). Capra Pr.
This Promised Land: The Saga of California, Vol. 1. Robert Easton. 328p. 1988. Repr. lib. bdg. 24.95x (ISBN 0-8095-4050-9). Borgo Pr.
This Proud Place. B. A. King. LC 82-12425. (Illus.). 1982. 24.95. Black Ice.
This Proud Place: An Affectionate Look at New England in Words & Photos. B. A. King. LC 82-12425. (Illus.). 96p. 1982. 24.95 (ISBN 0-914378-91-0). Countryman.
This Quarter: The Surrealist Number. Ed. by Edward Titus. LC 71-88578. Repr. of 1932 ed. 12.00 (ISBN 0-405-00740-X). Ayer Co Pubs.

This Quiet Dust: And Other Writings. William Styron. 304p. 1982. 17.00 (ISBN 0-394-50934-X). Random.
This Real Night. Rebecca West. (Fiction Ser.). 272p. 1985. 16.95 (ISBN 0-670-80432-0). Viking.
This Real Night. Rebecca West. (Penguin Fiction Ser.). 272p. 1986. pap. 6.95 (ISBN 0-14-008684-6). Penguin.
This Realm of England. facsimile ed. John Marriott. LC 78-140368. (Select Bibliographies Reprint Ser). Repr. of 1938 ed. 21.50 (ISBN 0-8369-5611-7). Ayer Co Pubs.
This Realm of England: 1399 to 1688. 5th ed. Lacey B. Smith. LC 87-81185. (History of England Ser.: Vol. II). 384p. 1987. pap. text ed. 11.00 (ISBN 0-669-13422-8). Heath.
This Realm, This England. Samuel Chamberlain. 1941. 13.95 (ISBN 0-8038-7063-9). Hastings.
This Religion of Islam. Sayyid Qutb. 104p. (Orig.). 1977. pap. 2.95x (ISBN 0-939830-08-6, Pub. by IIFSO Kuwait). New Era Pubns MI.
This River Is in the South. Philip Mead. LC 83-21634. 50p. 1984. 10.95 (ISBN 0-7022-1695-X). U of Queensland Pr.
This Room Is Mine! As told by Mary C. Olson. (Step Ahead Beginning Readers Ser.). (Illus.). 32p. (gr. 4-8). 1987. pap. write for info. (ISBN 0-307-03681-2, Pub. by Golden Bks). Western Pub.
This Rough Magic. Mary Stewart. 1964. 9.95 (ISBN 0-688-02614-1). Morrow.
This Rough New Land. rev. ed. Kenneth Sollitt. LC 85-63052. (Ann of the Prairie Ser.: Vol. 1). Orig. Title: Remember the Days. 190p. 1985. pap. 4.95 (ISBN 0-940652-03-X). Sunrise Bks.
This Running Life. George A. Sheehan. 1981. 8.95 (ISBN 0-671-25609-2, Fireside). S&S.
This Sceptred Isle. G. Wilson Knight. 1940. lib. bdg. 20.00 (ISBN 0-8414-5490-6). Folcroft.
This Scheming World. Saikaku Ihara. Tr. by Masanori Takatsuka & David Stubbs. LC 65-17850. 1965. pap. 4.25 (ISBN 0-8048-1115-6). C E Tuttle.
This School Is Driving Me Crazy. Nat Hentoff. 160p. (gr. 7 up). 1978. pap. 2.95 (ISBN 0-440-98702-4, LFL). Dell.
This Sculptured Earth: The Landscape of America. John A. Shimer. LC 59-10628. (Illus.). 255p. 1959. 38.00x (ISBN 0-231-02331-6). Columbia U Pr.
This Season's People: A Book of Spiritual Teachings. Stephen Gaskin. LC 86-159636. (Illus.). 1976. 5.95 (ISBN 0-913990-05-1). Book Pub Co.
This Sentient Earth. Trevor Hoyle. (Orig.). 1979. pap. 1.95 (ISBN 0-89083-473-3). Zebra.
This Sex Which Is Not One. Luce Irigaray. Tr. by Catherine Porter & Carolyn Burke. LC 84-23013. (Paperback Ser.). 208p. 1985. 29.95x (ISBN 0-8014-1546-2); pap. 12.95x (ISBN 0-8014-9331-5). Cornell U Pr.
This Shakespeare Industry. Ivor Brown & George Fearon. LC 70-92951. (Studies in Shakespeare, No. 24). 1970. Repr. of 1939 ed. lib. bdg. 52.95x (ISBN 0-8383-1063-X). Haskell.
This Shakespeare Industry: Amazing Monument. Ivor J. Brown & George Fearon. LC 77-98824. Repr. of 1939 ed. lib. bdg. 35.00x (ISBN 0-8371-2850-1, BRSI). Greenwood.
This Sheba, Self: The Conceptualization of Economic Life in Eighteenth-Century America. J. E. Crowley. LC 73-19334. (Studies in Historical & Political Science, 92nd Ser: Ninety-Second Series (1974)). 174p. 1974. 20.00x (ISBN 0-8018-1579-7). Johns Hopkins.
This Shining Woman: Mary Wollstonecraft. M. Bowen. 1972. lib. bdg. 59.95 (ISBN 0-8490-1196-5). Gordon Pr.
This Side of Evil. Carolyn Keene. (Nancy Drew Files Ser.: No. 14). 160p. (Orig.). (YA) (gr. 7 up). 1987. pap. 2.95 (ISBN 0-671-64139-5). Archway.
This Side of Glory. Gwen Bristow. 278p. 1979. Repr. lib. bdg. 19.95x (ISBN 0-89966-026-6). Buccaneer Bks.
This Side of Heaven. Alexandra Scott. (Harlequin Romances Ser.). 192p. 1982. pap. 1.50 (ISBN 0-373-02514-9). Harlequin Bks.
This Side of Innocence. Taylor Caldwell. 1976. Repr. of 1946 ed. lib. bdg. 26.95x (ISBN 0-88411-164-4, Pub. by Aeonian Pr). Amereon Ltd.
This Side of Innocence. Taylor Caldwell. 512p. 1984. pap. 3.95 (ISBN 0-446-31248-7). Warner Bks.
This Side of Love. Paula Christian. LC 78-54181. 144p. 1978. pap. 7.50 (ISBN 0-931328-01-2). Timely Bks.
This Side of Oregon. Ralph Friedman. LC 79-57241. (Illus., Orig.). 1983. pap. 9.95 (ISBN 0-87004-284-X). Caxton.
This Side of Paradise. F. Scott Fitzgerald. 1920. lib. rep. ed. 20.00x (ISBN 0-684-15601-6, ScribT); pap. 9.95 (ISBN 0-684-71765-4, SL60, ScribT); pap. 5.95 rack size (ISBN 0-684-17468-5). Scribner.
This Side of Paradise. F. Scott Fitzgerald. (Scribner Classics Ser.). 1987. pap. 9.95 (ISBN 0-317-56224-X). Scribner.
This Side of Paradise. F. Scott Fitzgerald. 7288p. pap. 4.95 (ISBN 0-02-019920-1, Collier). Macmillan.
This Side of Paradise. Fitzgerald F. Scott. 18.95 (ISBN 0-89190-603-7, Pub. by Am Repr). Amereon Ltd.
This Side of Tomorrow. rev. ed. Ruth L. Hill. 192p. (Orig.). 1987. pap. 5.95 (ISBN 0-89081-594-1). Harvest Hse.
This Side of Tomorrow. Janet C. Woolridge. LC 87-51042. 200p. 1988. 13.95 (ISBN 1-55523-122-5). Winston-Derek.
This Side the Other Side. Minh D. Trinh. LC 80-81781. (Illus.). 1980. 10.00 (ISBN 0-911050-48-5). Occidental.
This Side Up: Days in the Life of Michael Kip. Michael Kip. (Illus.). 144p. (Orig.). 1975. pap. 5.95 (ISBN 0-914378-08-2). Countryman.
This Soil of Sand. Mark Raney. (Illus.). 26p. 1978. 20.00 (ISBN 0-933272-01-4). Hurricane Co.
This Solemn Mockery. John Whitehead. (Illus.). Date not set. 22.50 (ISBN 0-89979-044-5). British Am Bks.
This Song Is for You. Sandy Miller. (Heart to Heart Ser.: No. 5). 176p. 1985. pap. 2.25 (ISBN 0-345-31634-7). Ballantine.
This Species of Property: Slave Life & Culture in the Old South. Leslie H. Owens. LC 75-38110. 1976. pap. 9.95 (ISBN 0-19-502245-9). Oxford U Pr.
This Sporting Life. Ron Brown. (Down Memory Lane, Old Hampshire Ser.). (Illus.). 64p. (Orig.). Date not set. pap. 4.95 (ISBN 0-903852-23-3, Pub. by Milestone Pubns UK). Seven Hills Bks.
This Sporting Life. Ed. by Emilie Buchwald & Ruth Roston. LC 86-60749. 176p. 1987. pap. 8.50 (ISBN 0-915943-14-X). Milkweed Ed.
This Sporting Life. David Storey. 256p. 1986. pap. 2.95 (ISBN 0-380-00254-X, 58024-1, Bard). Avon.
This Stage Play World: English Literature & Its Background, 1580-1625. Julia Briggs. LC 82-22473. 1983. pap. 8.95x (ISBN 0-19-289134-0). Oxford U Pr.
This Star Shall Abide. Sylvia L. Engdahl. (Illus.). 256p. (gr. 5-9). 1979. pap. 2.50 (ISBN 0-689-70458-5, Aladdin). Macmillan.
This State of Wonders: The Letters of an Iowa Frontier Family, 1858-1861. Ed. by John K. Folmar. LC 86-7012. (Illus.). 186p. 1986. text ed. 16.95x (ISBN 0-87745-154-0). U of Iowa Pr.
This Stinging Exultation. Mary B. Treudley. (Asian Folklore & Social Life Monograph: No.42). 310p. 1972. 16.00x (ISBN 0-89986-041-9). Oriental Bk Store.
This Strange Joy: Selected Poems of Sandro Penna. Sandro Penna. Tr. by W. S. Di Piero from Ital. LC 81-22288. 154p. 1982. 15.00 (ISBN 0-8142-0328-0). Ohio St U Pr.
This Strange New Feeling. Julius Lester. LC 81-68782. 160p. (gr. 7 up). 1982. 14.95 (ISBN 0-8037-8491-0, 01451-440). Dial Bks Young.
This Strange New Feeling. Julius Lester. 164p. (gr. 7 up). 1985. pap. 2.50 (ISBN 0-590-41061-X, Point); tchr's. guide 1.25 (ISBN 0-590-40681-7). Scholastic Inc.
This Stranger, My Father. Robert Hawks. LC 87-26245. 228p. (gr. 5-9). 1988. 13.95 (ISBN 0-395-44089-0). HM.
This Stranger, My Son. Louise Wilson. 1987. pap. 3.95 (ISBN 0-451-14748-0, Sig). NAL.
This Stream of Dreams. Roberta Latow. 304p. 1988. pap. 3.95 (ISBN 0-553-26404-4). Bantam.
This Stubborn Quantum: Sixty Poems. Jeremy Ingalls. LC 82-74424. 100p. 1983. 10.00 (ISBN 0-9610662-0-2). Capstone Edns.
This Stubborn Soil. William Owens. 320p. 1986. 17.95 (ISBN 0-941130-19-3). N Lyons Bks.
This Summer. Mary B. Crabtree. 84p. (Orig.). 1985. pap. 2.95 (ISBN 0-88120-730-6). SRA.
This Sweet Sickness. Patricia Highsmith. 250p. 1982. pap. 4.95 (ISBN 0-14-003469-2). Penguin.
This Tender & Delicate Business: The Public Trust Doctrine in American Law & Economic Policy, 1789-1920. Molly Selvin. Ed. by Harold Hyman & Stuart Bruchey. (American Legal & Constitutional History Ser.). 498p. 1987. lib. bdg. 60.00 (ISBN 0-8240-8292-3). Garland Pub.
This, That & the Other Thing. facs. ed. Reginald T. Townsend. LC 75-84344. (Essay Index Reprint Ser). 1929. 14.50 (ISBN 0-8369-1112-1). Ayer Co Pubs.
This, the House We Live In. Eleanor T. Lincoln & John A. Pinto. (Illus.). 188p. (Orig.). 1983. pap. 9.50 (ISBN 0-87391-030-3). Smith Coll.
This Time & Place. Martin F. Bridges. 1979. 10.95 (ISBN 0-87881-077-3). Mojave Bks.
This Time Called Life. rev. ed. Walter Rinder. LC 75-174240. (Illus., Orig.). 1984. pap. 6.95 (ISBN 0-912310-05-7). Celestial Arts.
This Time Count Me In. Phyllis A. Wood. LC 80-15068. (Hiway Book: A High Interest - Low Reading Level Book). 120p. 1980. 8.95 (ISBN 0-664-32665-X). Westminster John Knox.
This Time for Keeps. John P. MacCormac. LC 72-4584. (Essay Index Reprint Ser.). Repr. of 1943 ed. 18.00 (ISBN 0-8369-2962-4). Ayer Co Pubs.
This Time for Real. Susan Gorman. (Sweet Dreams Ser.: No. 145). 192p. (Orig.). (YA) (gr. 7 up). 1988. pap. 2.50 (ISBN 0-553-27175-X). Bantam.
This Time for Us. Elaine K. Stirling. (Superromance Ser.: No. 261). 308p. Date not set. pap. 2.75 (ISBN 0-317-63879-3). Harlequin Bks.
This Time Next Year. Anne N. Stallworth. LC 74-155672. 288p. 1972. 14.95 (ISBN 0-8149-0704-0). Vanguard.
This Time of Darkness. H. M. Hoover. 192p. (gr. 7 up). 1980. 10.95 (ISBN 0-670-50026-7). Viking.
This Time of Darkness. H. M. Hoover. (YA) (gr. 7 up). 1985. pap. 3.95 (ISBN 0-14-031872-0, Puffin). Penguin.
This Time of Morning. Nayantara Sahgal. 221p. 1969. pap. cancelled (ISBN 0-88253-079-8). Ind-US Inc.
This Time, Tempe Wick? Patricia L. Gauch. LC 74-79706. (Illus.). 48p. (gr. 2-6). 1974. 6.95 (ISBN 0-698-20300-3, Coward). Putnam Pub Group.
This Time, Tempe Wick? Patricia L. Gauch. LC 86-61791. (Illus.). 48p. (gr. 2-4). 1986. Repr. of 1974 ed. 11.95 (ISBN 0-936915-04-8). McDonald Shoe Tree Pr.
This Time Yesterday. Antonio M. Allego. 109p. (Orig.). 1984. pap. 6.25x (ISBN 971-10-0152-7, Pub. by New Day Philippines). Cellar.
This Too Shall Pass: The Story of an Alcoholic. E. Valentine Joyce. 1986. 55.00x (ISBN 0-86332-089-9, Pub. by Book Guild Ltd.). State Mutual Bk.
This Torch of Freedom: Speeches & Addresses. facsimile ed. Stanley Baldwin. LC 73-157962. (Essay Index Reprint Ser). Repr. of 1935 ed. 20.00 (ISBN 0-8369-2213-1). Ayer Co Pubs.
This Towering Passion. Valerie Sherwood. 512p. (Orig.). 1978. pap. 3.95 (ISBN 0-446-30770-X). Warner Bks.
This Treatise Concernynge the Fruytfull Saynges of Davyd..Was Made & Compyled by..John Fyssher..Bysshop of Rochester. John Fisher. LC 79-84106. (English Experience Ser.: No. 925). 296p. 1979. Repr. of 1509 ed. lib. bdg. 28.00 (ISBN 90-221-0925-9). Walter J Johnson.
This Tremendous Lover. M. Eugene Boylan. 396p. 1987. pap. 7.95 (ISBN 0-87061-138-0). Chr Classics.
This Troubled World. John Drinkwater. 14.00 (ISBN 0-8369-0392-7). Ayer Co Pubs.
This Ugly Civilization. Ralph Borsodi. LC 74-2668. (American Utopian Adventure Ser.). (Illus.). 468p. Repr. of 1929 ed. lib. bdg. 37.50x (ISBN 0-87991-025-9). Porcupine Pr.
This Unchanging Mask. Frances Mason. LC 74-144733. (Yale Series of Younger Poets: No. 26). Repr. of 1928 ed. 18.00 (ISBN 0-404-53826-6). AMS Pr.
This Unfriendly Soil: The Loyalist Experience in Nova Scotia, 1783-1791. Neil MacKinnon. 244p. 1986. 29.95x (ISBN 0-7735-0596-2). McGill-Queens U Pr.
This Vast Pollution. Thomas F. Bastow. LC 86-80697. 211p. 1986. 16.95 (ISBN 0-937715-01-8). Green Fields Bks.
This Very Earth. Erskine Caldwell. 12.95 (ISBN 0-89190-164-7, Pub. by Am Repr). Amereon Ltd.
This Very Madness. Gloria Alley. LC 77-86737. 95p. 1977. 6.00 (ISBN 0-8233-0270-9). Golden Quill.
This Very Place the Lotus Paradise. Bhagwan Shree Rajneesh. Ed. by Swami Anand Madyapa. LC 84-42805. (Photobiography Ser.). 568p. (Orig.). 1984. 100.00x (ISBN 0-88050-705-5). Chidvilas Inc.
This Wanting to Sing: Asian in South America. Ed. by Jaime Jacinto et al. (Illus.). 40p. (Orig.). 1988. pap. 4.00 (ISBN 0-936556-17-X). Contact Two.
This War Called Peace. Brian Crozier et al. LC 84-24137. 315p. 1985. 17.95 (ISBN 0-87663-463-3). Universe.
This Was a Poet: A Critical Biography of Emily Dickinson. George F. Whicher. LC 80-22989. 337p. 1980. 27.50 (ISBN 0-208-01903-0, Archon). Shoe String.
This Was America: True Accounts of People & Places, Manners & Customs, As Recorded by European Travelers to the Western Shore in the 18th, 19th & 20th Centuries. Ed. by Oscar Handlin. LC 49-7940. 1969. 37.00x (ISBN 0-674-88470-1). Harvard U Pr.
This Was Andersonville. John McElroy. (Illus.). 1957. 29.95 (ISBN 0-8392-1117-1). Astor-Honor.
This Was Chesapeake Bay. Robert H. Burgess. LC 63-20545. (Illus.). 223p. 1963. 24.95 (ISBN 0-87033-125-6). Tidewater.
This Was Corporate America. Chauncey Hare. 1984. 15.00 (ISBN 0-910663-40-8). ICA Inc.
This Was Harlem: A Cultural Portrait, 1900-1950. Jervis Anderson. (Illus.). 400p. 1982. pap. 13.95 (ISBN 0-374-51757-6). FS&G.
This Was Logging: Drama in the Northwest Timber Country. Ralph W. Andrews. (Illus.). 157p. 1985. pap. 9.95 (ISBN 0-88740-035-3). Schiffer.
This Was My Daddy. Walter G. Slappey. 5.00 (ISBN 0-930061-02-0). Interspace Bks.
This Was My Life. Joseph C. Smith. 1985. 8.95 (ISBN 0-533-06505-4). Vantage.
This Was My Newport. facsimile ed. Maud H. Elliott. LC 75-1842. (Leisure Class in America Ser.). (Illus.). 1975. Repr. of 1944 ed. 20.00x (ISBN 0-405-06911-1). Ayer Co Pubs.
This Was New York: The Nation's Capital in 1789. facsimile ed. Frank Monaghan & Marvin Lowenthal. LC 70-117884. (Select Bibliographies Reprint Ser). Repr. of 1943 ed. 26.50 (ISBN 0-8369-5337-1). Ayer Co Pubs.
This Was Our Land. Russell Baehr. Ed. by Verne Reaves. (Illus.). 250p. (Orig.). 1985. 15.95x (ISBN 0-89288-113-5); pap. 8.95x (ISBN 0-89288-108-9). Maverick.
This Was the Life - Excerpts from the Judgment Records of Frederick County, Maryland, 1748-1765. Millard M. Rice. LC 79-84276. 1979. 12.00 (ISBN 0-913186-08-2). Monocacy.
This Was the Life: Excerpts from the Judgment Records of Frederick County, Maryland, 1748-1765. Millard M. Rice. LC 84-80270. 308p. 1984. Repr. of 1979 ed. 20.00 (ISBN 0-8063-1077-4). Genealog Pub.
This Was Their Time. Florence E. Sherfey. (Illus.). 206p. 1975. Ye Galleon.
This Was Tomorrow. Elswyth Thane. 1976. Repr. of 1951 ed. lib. bdg. 19.95x (ISBN 0-88411-962-9, Pub. by Aeonian Pr). Amereon Ltd.
This Was Toscanini. Samuel Antek & Robert Hupka. LC 63-15196. (Illus.). 196p. 1963. 35.00 (ISBN 0-8149-0018-6). Vanguard.
This Wasn't Supposed to Happen: Single Women over Thirty Talk Frankly about Their Lives. Susan C. Bakos. 224p. 1985. 15.95 (ISBN 0-8264-0360-3). Continuum.
This Way Daybreak Comes: Women's Values & the Future. Annie Cheatham & Mary C. Powell. (Illus.). 288p. 1986. lib. bdg. 34.95 (ISBN 0-86571-070-8); pap. 12.95 (ISBN 0-86571-069-4). New Soc Pubs.
This Way Down. Phylliss Adams et al. (BTR Ser.). (Illus.). 32p. (gr. k-3). 1982. PLB 4.95 (ISBN 0-8136-5404-1, Dist. by Caroline Hse); pap. 2.25 (ISBN 0-8136-5904-3). Modern Curr.
This Way for the Gas, Ladies & Gentlemen. Tadeusz Borowski. 1976. pap. 6.95 (ISBN 0-14-004114-1). Penguin.
This Way to Better Teaching. Clyne W. Buxton. 1974. 5.25 (ISBN 0-87148-835-3); pap. 4.25 (ISBN 0-87148-836-1). Pathway Pr.
This Way to Better Teaching Instructor's Guide. 1974. pap. 4.95 (ISBN 0-87148-837-X). Pathway Pr.
This Way to Books. Caroline F. Bauer. LC 82-19985. 376p. 1983. 40.00 (ISBN 0-8242-0678-9). Wilson.
This Way to Foster Parenting. Barbara Kendrick & Carol Ertl. 292p. (Orig.). 1979. pap. 9.00 (ISBN 1-55719-109-3). U NE Ctr Applied Urban Rsch.
This Way to the Apocalypse: The Politics of the 1960's. Sidney Bernard. LC 77-94632. (Illus.). 252p. 1969. 7.00 (ISBN 0-912292-09-1). The Smith.
This Way Up. Charles Hunter & Frances Hunter. 1978. pap. 5.95 (ISBN 0-917726-23-5). Hunter Bks.
This Way Up: The Local Official's Handbook for Privatization & Contracting Out. Ed. by R. Q. Armington & William D. Ellis. LC 84-14371. 168p. (Orig.). 1985. pap. 6.95 (ISBN 0-89526-824-8). Regnery Gateway.
This We Believe. NMSA Committee. 1982. 3.25 (ISBN 0-318-18690-X). Natl Middle Schl.
This We Believe. 2nd ed. Arnold T. Olson. LC 61-18801. 1965. Repr. of 1961 ed. 6.95 (ISBN 0-911802-01-0). Free Church Pubns.
This We Believe. James L. Slay. 1963. pap. 4.95 (ISBN 0-87148-832-9). Pathway Pr.
This We Believe. Mrs. Z. W. Swafford. (Illus.). 109p. (Orig.). 1983. pap. 2.50 (ISBN 0-89114-115-4). Baptist Pub Hse.
This We Believe. (Eng. & Ger.). pap. 0.60 (ISBN 0-8100-0004-0, 04-0622). Northwest Pub.
This We Believe. James Waltner. LC 68-20281. 1968. pap. 5.95 (ISBN 0-87303-845-2). Faith & Life.
This We Believe, Leader's Guide. Herman Enns. LC 78-130643. 1970. pap. 1.75 (ISBN 0-87303-846-0). Faith & Life.
This Well-Wooded Land: Americans & Their Forest from Colonial Times to the Present. Thomas R. Cox et al. LC 85-1141. (Illus.). xviii, 347p. 1985. 27.95x (ISBN 0-8032-1426-X). U of Nebr Pr.
This Whole Human Rights Business. V. Bolshakov. 327p. 1985. pap. 2.95 (ISBN 0-8285-2973-6, Pub. by Progress Pubs USSR). Imported Pubns.
This Wild Abyss: The Story of the Men Who Made Modern Astronomy. Gale E. Christianson. LC 77-81428. (Illus.). 1979. pap. text ed. 9.95 (ISBN 0-02-905660-8). Free Pr.
This Wild Abyss: The Story of the Men Who Made Modern Astronomy. Gale E. Christianson. LC 77-81428. (Illus.). 1978. 14.95 (ISBN 0-02-905380-3). Free Pr.
This Wild Abyss: The Story of the Men Who Made Modern Astronomy. Gale E. Christianson. 1979. pap. 9.95x (ISBN 0-317-30517-4). Free Pr.
This Wildfire Magic. Sara Chance. (Silhouette Desire Ser.: No. 107). 1983. pap. 1.95 (ISBN 0-671-49860-6). Harlequin Bks.
This Will Drive You Sane. Bill L. Little. LC 77-86452. 1980. pap. 6.50 (ISBN 0-89638-047-5). CompCare.
This Will Kill That. Gerard Malanga. LC 83-8731. 166p. 1983. pap. 8.50 (ISBN 0-87685-495-1); signed ed. 25.00 (ISBN 0-87685-496-X). Black Sparrow.
This-Will-Kill-You, Cookbook. Roland A. Mulhauser. LC 72-130403. 1970. pap. 2.50 (ISBN 0-8048-0945-3). C E Tuttle.
This Woman: Poetry of Love & Change. Barbara O'Mary. LC 72-95283. (Illus.). 64p. (Orig.). 1973. pap. 2.95 (ISBN 0-87810-024-5). Times Change.
This World. Harvey Shapiro. LC 72-142725. (Wesleyan Poetry Program: Vol. 57). 1971. pap. 17.00x (ISBN 0-8195-2057-8); pap. 12.95 (ISBN 0-8195-1057-2). Wesleyan U Pr.

Thomas Chatterton. Charles E. Russell. LC 70-130258. (English Literature Ser., No. 33). 1970. Repr. of 1908 ed. lib. bdg. 52.95x (ISBN 0-8383-1162-8). Haskell.

Thomas Chatterton the Marvelous Boy. Esther Ellinger. LC 74-13489. 1930. lib. bdg. 16.50 (ISBN 0-8414-3974-5). Folcroft.

Thomas Chatterton: The Marvelous Boy. Esther P. Ellinger. 75p. 1980. Repr. of 1930 ed. lib. bdg. 17.50 (ISBN 0-8492-4408-0). R West.

Thomas Chaucer. Martin B. Ruud. LC 78-174797. Repr. of 1926 ed. 15.50 (ISBN 0-404-05469-2). AMS Pr.

Thomas Chippendale, 1718-1779: A Bibliography. Mary Vance. (Architecture Ser.: A 1398). 11p. 1985. 2.00 (ISBN 0-89028-428-8). Vance Biblios.

Thomas Christy's Road Across the Plains. Ed. by Robert H. Becker. 1969. limited ed 35.00 (ISBN 0-912094-13-3). Old West.

Thomas Clarkson: A Monograph: Being a Contribution Towards the History of the Abolition of the Slave Trade & Slavery. facs. ed. James Elmes. LC 76-89414. (Black Heritage Library Collection Ser). 1854. 16.00 (ISBN 0-8369-8569-9). Ayer Co Pubs.

Thomas Cole. Matthew Baigell. (Illus.). 84p. 1985. pap. 16.95 (ISBN 0-8230-0648-4). Watson-Guptill.

Thomas Cole & Victorian Clockmaking. J. B. Hawkins. (Illus.). 1975. 39.50 (ISBN 0-686-30713-5). Apollo.

Thomas Cole & Victorian Clockmaking. J. B. Hawkins. (Illus.). 253p. 1975. Repr. of 1975 ed. 39.50 (ISBN 0-9598503-0-9). Antique Collect.

Thomas Cole's Poetry: The Collected Poems of America's Foremost Painter of the Hudson River School, Reflecting His Feelings for Nature & the Romantic Spirit of the 19th Century. Thomas Cole. Ed. by Marshall B. Tymn. LC 72-7843. (Illus.). 1972. casebound 15.00 (ISBN 0-87387-057-3). Shumway.

Thomas Cole's Voyage of Life. Paul D. Schweizer & Dan Kushel. (Illus.). 80p. (Orig.). 1985. pap. text ed. 12.95 (ISBN 0-915895-03-X). Munson Williams.

Thomas Condon: Pioneer Geologist of Oregon. Ellen C. McCornack. (Illus.). 372p. 1928. 19.95x (ISBN 0-87071-331-0). Oreg St U Pr.

Thomas Couture & the Eclectic Vision. Albert Boime. LC 79-23507. (Illus.). 704p. 1980. 105.00x (ISBN 0-300-02158-5). Yale U Pr.

Thomas Cranmer & the English Reformation, 1849-1556. Albert F. Pollard. LC 83-45587. Date not set. Repr. of 1927 ed. 42.50 (ISBN 0-404-19905-4). AMS Pr.

Thomas Cranmer of Canterbury. Charles Williams. 75p. Repr. of 1936 ed. lib. bdg. 35.00 (ISBN 0-8495-5916-2). Arden Lib.

Thomas Cranner. Jasper Ridley. 450p. 1983. Repr. of 1962 ed. lib. bdg. 65.00 (ISBN 0-89987-737-0). Darby Bks.

Thomas Davis. Eileen Sullivan. Ed. by James F. Carens. LC 72-482. (Irish Writers Ser.). 90p. 1979. 4.50 (ISBN 0-8387-1234-7); pap. 1.95 (ISBN 0-8387-1237-1). Bucknell U Pr.

Thomas Davis, Selections from His Prose & Poetry. Thomas Davis. LC 75-28810. (Illus.). 392p. Repr. of 1914 ed. 48.00 (ISBN 0-404-13803-9). AMS Pr.

Thomas De Quincey. Horace A. Eaton. LC 74-159182. 1971. Repr. of 1936 ed. lib. bdg. 40.00x (ISBN 0-374-92459-7, Octagon). Hippocrene Bks.

Thomas De Quincey. Ripley Hitchcock. LC 77-4066. 1899. lib. bdg. 20.00 (ISBN 0-685-10811-2). Folcroft.

Thomas De Quincey. Alexander H. Japp. 1890. 27.50 (ISBN 0-8274-3608-4). R West.

Thomas De Quincey: A Bibliography Based Upon the De Quincey Collection in the Moss Side Library. Manchester, England. Public Libraries, Moss Side Branch. 1908. 20.50 (ISBN 0-8337-1442-2). B Franklin.

Thomas De Quincey: A Biography. Horace A. Eaton. 542p. 1983. Repr. of 1936 ed. lib. bdg. 50.00 (ISBN 0-89987-221-2). Darby Bks.

Thomas De Quincey: A Reference Guide. Ed. by H. O. Dendurent. 1978. lib. bdg. 24.00 (ISBN 0-8161-7840-2, Hall Reference). G K Hall.

Thomas De Quincey: Bicentenary Studies. Ed. & intro. by Robert L. Snyder. LC 85-40487. (Illus.). 416p. 1986. 29.50x (ISBN 0-8061-1849-0). U of Okla Pr.

Thomas De Quincey, Literary Critic. John E. Jordan. LC 70-189248. 301p. 1973. Repr. of 1952 ed. 32.50x (ISBN 0-87752-160-3). Gordian.

Thomas De Quincey: The Prose of Vision. V. A. De Luca. 184p. 1980. 20.00x (ISBN 0-8020-5480-3). U of Toronto Pr.

Thomas De Quincey's Reluctant Autobiography. John C. Whale. LC 83-27511. 254p. 1984. 27.50x (ISBN 0-389-20461-7, BNB 08022). B&N Imports.

Thomas De Quincey's Theory of Literature. Sigmund K. Proctor. 1967. lib. bdg. 20.50x (ISBN 0-374-96688-5, Octagon). Hippocrene Bks.

Thomas Dekker. Mary L. Hunt. LC 73-8949. 1911. Repr. lib. bdg. 30.00 (ISBN 0-8414-4706-3). Folcroft.

Thomas Dekker. George R. Price. LC 68-17241. (Twayne's English Authors Ser.). 1969. lib. bdg. 17.95 (ISBN 0-8057-1148-1); pap. text ed. 5.95x (ISBN 0-8290-2006-3). Irvington.

Thomas Dekker. Ernest Rhys. 1949. 20.00 (ISBN 0-8274-3607-6). R West.

Thomas Dekker: A Reference Guide. Doris R. Adler. 330p. 1983. lib. bdg. 57.00 (ISBN 0-8161-8384-8, Hall Reference). G K Hall.

Thomas Dekker: A Study. Mary L. Hunt. 1978. Repr. of 1911 ed. lib. bdg. 30.50 (ISBN 0-8495-2305-2). Arden Lib.

Thomas Dekker: A Study in Economic & Social Backgrounds. Kate L. Gregg. LC 77-3181. 1924. Repr. lib. bdg. 20.00 (ISBN 0-8414-4425-0). Folcroft.

Thomas Dekker & the Traditions of English Drama. Larry S. Champion. (American University Studies IV, (English Language & Literature): Vol. 27). 260p. 1985. text ed. 25.15 (ISBN 0-8204-0214-1). P Lang Pubs.

Thomas Dekker: The Wonderful Year, the Gull's Horn-Book, Penny Wise, Pound Foolish, English Villainies Discovered by Lantern & Candlelight & Selected Writing. Thomas Dekker. Ed. by Eric D. Pendry. LC 68-88991. (Stratford-Upon-Avon Library). (Illus.). 1968. 27.00x (ISBN 0-674-88486-8). Harvard U Pr.

Thomas Dekker's Pamphlets, & Jacobean Popular Literature, 1603-1609, 2 vols. Frederick O. Waage. Ed. by James Hogg. (Elizabethan & Renaissance Studies). 563p. (Orig.). 1977. pap. 30.00 (ISBN 3-7052-0698-2, Pub. by Salzburg Studies). Longwood Pub Group.

Thomas Dewey: The Upset Presidential Candidate of 1948. Gerald Kurland. Ed. by D. Steve Rahmas. LC 70-185659. (Outstanding Personalities Ser.: No. 3). 32p. 1972. lib. bdg. 3.75incl. catalog cards (ISBN 0-87157-503-5); pap. 2.50 vinyl laminated covers (ISBN 0-87157-003-3). SamHar Pr.

Thomas Dongan, Governor of New York (1682-1688) John H. Kennedy. LC 73-3564. (Catholic University of America. Studies in American Church History: No. 9). Repr. of 1930 ed. 20.00 (ISBN 0-404-57759-8). AMS Pr.

Thomas D'urfey's - The Richmond Heiress, 1693: An Edition with Introduction & Notes. Ed. by Stephen Orgel. (Satire & Sense Ser.). 289p. 1987. lib. bdg. 45.00 (ISBN 0-8240-6017-2). Garland Pub.

Thomas D'urfey's - The Virtuous Wife: A Critical Edition. Ed. by Stephen Orgel. (Satire & Sense Ser.). 300p. 1987. lib. bdg. 45.00 (ISBN 0-8240-6018-0). Garland Pub.

Thomas E. Dewey & His Times. Richard N. Smith. 720p. 1984. pap. 11.95 (ISBN 0-671-41742-8, Touchstone Bks). S&S.

Thomas E. Dewey & His Times. Richard N. Smith. 22.50 (ISBN 0-317-12800-0). S&S.

Thomas E. Dewey, Nineteen Thirty-Seven to Nineteen Forty-Seven: A Study in Political Leadership. Barry K. Beyer. Ed. by Frank Freidel. LC 78-62375. (Modern American History Ser.: Vol. 2). 1979. lib. bdg. 43.00 (ISBN 0-8240-3626-3). Garland Pub.

Thomas E. Watson Revisited: The Saga of a Great Southern Populist. Thomas H. Irwin. 1984. lib. bdg. 79.95 (ISBN 0-87700-601-6). Revisionist Pr.

Thomas Eakins, 2 vols. Lloyd Goodrich. (Ailsa Mellon Bruce Studies in American Art). (Illus.). 1983. 90.00 (ISBN 0-674-88490-6). Vol. I: 368p. Vol. II: 384p. Harvard U Pr.

Thomas Eakins Collection. Theodor Siegl. LC 76-58647. (Handbooks in American Art: No. 1). (Illus.). 178p. (Orig.). 1978. pap. 11.95 (ISBN 0-87633-031-6). Phila Mus Art.

Thomas Eakins Collection of the Hirshhorn Museum & Sculpture Garden. Phyllis D. Rosenzweig. LC 77-608029. (Illus.). 240p. 1977. 39.95x (ISBN 0-87474-812-7, ROTE). Smithsonian.

Thomas Eakins Collection of the Hirshhorn Museum & Sculpture Garden. Smithsonian Institution Staff. LC 79-10081. 1979. 32.50 (ISBN 0-226-69102-0, Chicago Visual Lib); 2 colorfiches incl. U of Chicago Pr.

Thomas Eakins: The Heroism of Modern Life. Elizabeth Johns. LC 83-42606. (Illus.). 207p. 1984. 50.00 (ISBN 0-691-04022-2). Princeton U Pr.

Thomas Edison. Josephine Ross. (Profiles Ser.). (Illus.). 64p. (gr. 3-6). 1982. 9.95 (ISBN 0-241-10713-X, Pub. by Hamish Hamilton England). David & Charles.

Thomas Edison - Alexander Graham Bell. Naunerle C. Farr. (Pendulum Illustrated Biography Ser.). (Illus.). (gr. 4-12). 1979. text ed. 7.50 (ISBN 0-88301-369-X); pap. text ed. 2.95 (ISBN 0-88301-357-6); wkbk. 1.25 (ISBN 0-88301-381-9). Pendulum Pr.

Thomas Edison: A Study. Elbert Hubbard. 1979. pap. 2.00 (ISBN 0-932282-45-8). Caledonia Pr.

Thomas Edison Book of Easy & Incredible Experiments. Cook. (Science Editions Ser.). 1988. 22.95 (ISBN 0-471-62089-0); pap. 11.95 (ISBN 0-471-62090-4). Wiley.

Thomas Edison, Chemist. Byron M. Vanderbilt. LC 75-172526. 1971. 12.95 (ISBN 0-8412-0129-3); pap. 8.95 (ISBN 0-8412-0534-5). Am Chemical.

Thomas Edison: Father of Electricity & Master Inventor of Our Modern Age. Gerald Kurland. Ed. by D. Steve Rahmas. LC 72-89210. (Outstanding Personalities Ser.: No. 46). 32p. 1972. lib. bdg. 3.75 incl. catalog cards (ISBN 0-87157-542-6); pap. 2.50 vinyl laminated covers (ISBN 0-87157-042-4). SamHar Pr.

Thomas Ellwood & Other Worthies of the Olden Time. Frances A. Budge. 1891. Repr. 20.00 (ISBN 0-8274-3609-2). R West.

Thomas Florschuetz: Bodily Images. John P. Jacob. 32p. (Orig.). 1988. catalogue 4.00 (ISBN 0-935519-08-4). Anderson Gal.

Thomas Francis Meagher: An Irish Revolutionary in America. Robert G. Athearn. LC 76-6321. (Irish Americans Ser.). (Illus.). 1976. Repr. of 1949 ed. 15.00 (ISBN 0-405-09318-7). Ayer Co Pubs.

Thomas Francis Roberts 1860-1919. David Williams. 48p. 1961. pap. text ed. 6.95x (ISBN 0-7083-0167-3, Pub. by U of Wales). Humanities.

Thomas Frognall Dibdin: Selections. Ed. by Victor E. Neuburg. LC 77-18012. (Great Bibliographers Ser.: No. 3). 253p. 1978. 17.50 (ISBN 0-8108-1077-8). Scarecrow.

Thomas Fuller, Selections: With Essays by Charles Lamb, Leslie Stephen & Co. E. K. Broadus. 1979. Repr. of 1928 ed. lib. bdg. 20.00 (ISBN 0-8492-3742-4). R West.

Thomas Gage's Travels in the New World. Thomas Gage. Ed. & intro. by J. Eric Thompson. LC 58-6856. (American Exploration & Travel Ser.: Vol. 58). (Illus.). 430p. (Orig.). 1985. pap. 11.95 (ISBN 0-8061-1904-7). U of Okla Pr.

Thomas Gainsborough. John Hayes. (Illus.). 158p. 14.95 (ISBN 0-905005-77-5); pap. 8.95 (ISBN 0-905005-72-4). Salem Hse Pubs.

Thomas George-A Retrospective: Paintings & Works on Paper. Intro. by Churchill Lathrop. (Illus.). 32p. (Orig.). 1987. pap. 7.50 (ISBN 0-938766-04-X). NJ State Mus.

Thomas George Lawson: African Historian & Administrator in Sierra Leone. David E. Skinner. LC 78-70393. (Publications Ser., No. 222: Hoover Colonial Studies). 254p. 1980. pap. 10.95x (ISBN 0-8179-7221-8). Hoover Inst Pr.

Thomas Gray. Morris Golden. (Twayne English Author Ser.: Vol. 6). 160p. 1988. lib. bdg. 19.95 (ISBN 0-8057-6961-7, Twayne). G K Hall.

Thomas Gray: A Reference Guide. Alan T. McKenzie. 1982. lib. bdg. 40.50 (ISBN 0-8161-8451-8, Hall Reference). G K Hall.

Thomas Gray of Pembroke. Sydney C. Roberts. LC 73-11384. Repr. of 1955 ed. lib. bdg. 20.00 (ISBN 0-8414-2593-0). Folcroft.

Thomas Gray, Philosopher Cat. Philip J. Davis. (HBJ-Boston Bk.). (Illus.). 144p. 1988. 9.95 (ISBN 0-15-188100-6). HarBraceJ.

Thomas Gray's Elegy Written in a Country Churchyard. Intro. by Harold Bloom. (Modern Critical Interpretations Ser.). 1987. 19.95 (ISBN 0-87754-420-4). Chelsea Hse.

Thomas Grocery Register, 3 vols. 2431p. 1988. Set. 125.00 (ISBN 0-937200-44-1). Vol. 1 (ISBN 0-937200-45-X). Vol. 2 (ISBN 0-937200-46-8). Vol. 3 (ISBN 0-937200-47-6). Thomas Intl Pub.

Thomas H. Benton. Theodore Roosevelt. Ed. by John T. Morse, Jr. LC 79-128972. (American Statesmen: No. 23). Repr. of 1899 ed. 32.00 (ISBN 0-404-50873-1). AMS Pr.

Thomas H. Huxley. James R. Ainsworth-Davis. LC 70-158236. (English Men of Science: No. 2). Repr. of 1907 ed. 21.50 (ISBN 0-404-07892-3). AMS Pr.

Thomas H. Mawson, 1861-1933: A Selected Bibliography. Jo N. Beglo. (Architecture Ser.: A 1427). 12p. 1985. 2.00 (ISBN 0-89028-477-6). Vance Biblios.

Thomas Halsey & His Descendants in America. 2nd ed. Jacob L. Halsey & Edmund D. Halsey. 549p. 1972. Repr. of 1895 ed. 37.00 (ISBN 0-911660-11-9). Yankee Peddler.

Thomas Hardy. Intro. by Harold Bloom. (Modern Critical Views Ser.). 247p. 1986. 24.50 (ISBN 0-87754-645-2). Chelsea Hse.

Thomas Hardy. L. J. Butler. LC 77-23532. (British Authors Ser.). 1978. pap. 11.95 (ISBN 0-521-29271-9). Cambridge U Pr.

Thomas Hardy. Richard C. Carpenter. (English Authors Ser.). 1964. lib. bdg. 16.95 (ISBN 0-8057-1244-5, Twayne). G K Hall.

Thomas Hardy. H. Child. LC 72-3631. (Studies in Thomas Hardy, No. 14). 1972. Repr. of 1916 ed. lib. bdg. 35.95x (ISBN 0-8383-1584-4). Haskell.

Thomas Hardy. Harold Child. LC 78-8740. 1916. lib. bdg. 15.00 (ISBN 0-8414-3366-6). Folcroft.

Thomas Hardy. John Goode. (Rereading Literature Ser.). 192p. 1988. text ed. 34.95x (ISBN 0-631-13954-0); pap. text ed. 9.95x (ISBN 0-631-13953-2). Basil Blackwell.

Thomas Hardy. Desmond Hawkins. LC 76-9790. 1950. lib. bdg. 25.00 (ISBN 0-8414-4745-4). Folcroft.

Thomas Hardy. Irving Howe. Ed. by Alexia Dorszynski. 224p. 1985. pap. 6.95 (ISBN 0-02-052010-7, Collier). Macmillan.

Thomas Hardy. Patricia Ingham. (Feminist Readings Ser.). 1989. text ed. 29.95 (ISBN 0-391-03554-1); pap. text ed. 12.50 (ISBN 0-391-03555-X). Humanities.

Thomas Hardy. Annie Macdonell. LC 77-148276. Repr. of 1895 ed. 19.45 (ISBN 0-404-08885-6). AMS Pr.

Thomas Hardy. Annie Macdonell. LC 72-4841. 1895. lib. bdg. 35.50 (ISBN 0-8414-0000-8). Folcroft.

Thomas Hardy. McDowall. 59.95 (ISBN 0-8490-1197-3). Gordon Pr.

Thomas Hardy. Henry Nevinson. LC 72-2084. (Studies in Thomas Hardy, No. 14). 1972. Repr. of 1941 ed. lib. bdg. 29.95x (ISBN 0-8383-1466-X). Haskell.

Thomas Hardy. Henry W. Nevinson. LC 74-23622. 1974. Repr. of 1941 ed. lib. bdg. 15.50 (ISBN 0-8414-6283-6). Folcroft.

Thomas Hardy, Novelist Or Poet. A. Edward Newton. LC 76-41673. 1929. lib. bdg. 25.50 (ISBN 0-8414-6294-1). Folcroft.

Thomas Hardy. Norman Page. 212p. (Orig.). 1981. pap. 10.00 (ISBN 0-7100-8615-6). Routledge Chapman & Hall.

Thomas Hardy. Henry Tomlinson. LC 70-160129. (Studies in Thomas Hardy, No. 14). 1971. lib. bdg. 40.95x (ISBN 0-8383-1283-7). Haskell.

Thomas Hardy. Henry J. Tomlinson. 1979. Repr. of 1929 ed. lib. bdg. 17.00 (ISBN 0-8492-8425-2). R West.

Thomas Hardy. Henry M. Tomlinson. LC 73-11383. 74. Repr. of 1929 ed. lib. bdg. 17.00 (ISBN 0-8414-2691-0). Folcroft.

Thomas Hardy. A. Stanton Whitfield. 1921. lib. bdg. 25.00 (ISBN 0-8414-9715-X). Folcroft.

Thomas Hardy, 2 vols. R. E. Zachrisson. 200.00 (ISBN 0-8490-1198-1). Gordon Pr.

Thomas Hardy: A Bibliographical Study. Richard L. Purdy. (Illus.). 1978. Repr. of 1954 ed. text ed. 39.95x (ISBN 0-19-818131-0). Oxford U Pr.

Thomas Hardy: A Biography. Michael Millgate. (Illus.). 688p. 1985. pap. 13.95 (ISBN 0-19-281472-9). Oxford U Pr.

Thomas Hardy, a Critical Biography. Evelyn Hardy. LC 73-12879. 1953. lib. bdg. 37.00 (ISBN 0-8414-4748-9). Folcroft.

Thomas Hardy: A Critical Biography. Evelyn Hardy. LC 75-83860. (Illus.). 1970. Repr. of 1954 ed. 20.00x (ISBN 0-8462-1411-3). Russell.

Thomas Hardy, a Critical Study. Lascelles Abercrombie. LC 64-8920. 1964. Repr. of 1912 ed. 11.00x (ISBN 0-8462-0117-8). Russell.

Thomas Hardy: A Study of His Writings & Their Background. William R. Rutland. LC 62-13851. (Illus.). 1962. Repr. of 1938 ed. 23.00x (ISBN 0-8462-0268-9). Russell.

Thomas Hardy: An Annotated Bibliography of Writings about Him, Vol. II. Ed. by W. Eugene Davis & Helmut E. Gerber. LC 72-7514. (Annotated Secondary Bibliography Series on English Literature in Transition, 1880-1920). 735p. 1983. 45.00 (ISBN 0-87580-091-2). N Ill U Pr.

Thomas Hardy: An Annotated Bibliography of Writings about Him. Ed. by Helmut E. Gerber & W. Eugene Davis. LC 72-7514. (Annotated Secondary Bibliography Ser. on English Literature in Transition, 1880-1920). 841p. 1973. 35.00 (ISBN 0-87580-039-4). N Ill U Pr.

Thomas Hardy: An Illustration of the Philosophy of Schopenhauer. Helen Garwood. LC 74-10776. 1911. lib. bdg. 22.00 (ISBN 0-8414-4521-4). Folcroft.

Thomas Hardy & British Poetry. Donald Davie. LC 70-188291. 1972. 18.95x (ISBN 0-19-501572-X). Oxford U Pr.

Thomas Hardy & the Cosmic Mind: A New Reading of "the Dynasts". J. O. Bailey. LC 77-24118. 1977. Repr. of 1956 ed. lib. bdg. 35.00x (ISBN 0-8371-9743-0, BATH). Greenwood.

Thomas Hardy & Women: Sexual Ideology & Narrative Form. Penny Boumelha. LC 81-22903. 188p. 1982. text ed. 28.50x (ISBN 0-389-20259-2, 07077). B&N Imports.

Thomas Hardy & Women: Sexual Ideology & Narrative Form. Penny Boumelha. LC 84-49663. 192p. 1985. pap. 10.95X (ISBN 0-299-10244-0). U of Wis Pr.

Thomas Hardy Annual, No. 5. Ed. by Norman Page. 236p. 1987. text ed. 55.00 (ISBN 0-333-38666-3, Pub. by Macmillan England). Humanities.

Thomas Hardy Annual, No. 4. Ed. by Norman Page. (Literary Annual Ser: Hardy: No. 4). 228p. 1986. text ed. 45.00x (ISBN 0-333-38665-5, Pub. by Macmillan UK). Humanities.

Thomas Hardy As a Man, Writer & Philosopher. R. E. Zachrisson. (Studies in Thomas Hardy, No. 14). 1970. pap. 39.95x (ISBN 0-8383-0104-5). Haskell.

Thomas Hardy Calendar. Cecil Palmer. LC 73-557. 1973. lib. bdg. 27.50 (ISBN 0-8414-1518-8). Folcroft.

Thomas Hardy Calendar. Cecil Palmer. 133p. 1980. Repr. lib. bdg. 32.00 (ISBN 0-8492-2172-2). R West.

Thomas Hardy: Distance & Desire. J. Hillis Miller. LC 75-102670. 1970. 21.95x (ISBN 0-674-88505-8, Belknap Pr). Harvard U Pr.

Thomas Hardy: His British & American Critics. D. J. Winslow. 59.95 (ISBN 0-8490-1199-X). Gordon Pr.

Thomas Hardy in Maine. Carl Weber. LC 75-22203. (Studies in Thomas Hardy, No. 14). 1975. lib. bdg. 40.95x (ISBN 0-8383-2077-5). Haskell.

Thomas Hardy in Maine. Carl Weber. 1942. Repr. 17.00 (ISBN 0-8274-3610-6). R West.

Thomas Hardy: Materials for a Study of His Life, Times, & Works. Ed. by James S. Cox. (Illus.). 728p. 1968. 65.00x (ISBN 0-900749-85-7, Pub. by Toucan Pr UK). Spoon River.

Thomas Hardy: More Materials for a Study of His Life, Times, & Works. Ed. by James S. Cox. (Illus.). 564p. 1971. 65.00x (ISBN 0-900749-65-2, Pub. by Toucan Pr UK). Spoon River.

Thomas Hardy: Notes on His Life & Work. Henry S. Canby. LC 74-11144. 1925. lib. bdg. 15.00 (ISBN 0-8414-3515-4). Folcroft.

Thomas Hardy: Notes on His Life & Work. Henry S. Canby et al. 1978. Repr. lib. bdg. 15.00 (ISBN 0-8495-0812-6). Arden Lib.

Thomas Hardy: Novelist or Poet. Alfred E. Newton. LC 70-160428. (Studies in Thomas Hardy, No. 14). 1971. Repr. of 1929 ed. lib. bdg. 22.95x (ISBN 0-8383-1298-5). Haskell.

Thomas Hardy of the Wessex Novels. J. G. Sime. LC 74-10581. Repr. of 1928 ed. lib. bdg. 29.00 (ISBN 0-8414-7504-0). Folcroft.

Thomas Hardy, O.M. C. Holland. LC 68-952. (Studies in Thomas Hardy, No. 14). 1969. Repr. of 1933 ed. lib. bdg. 49.95x (ISBN 0-8383-0570-9). Haskell.

Thomas Hardy Omnibus. Thomas Hardy. 42.95 (ISBN 0-88411-688-3, Pub. by Aeonian Pr). Amereon Ltd.

Thomas Hardy: Poet & Novelist. S. C. Chew. 59.95 (ISBN 0-8490-1200-7). Gordon Pr.

Thomas Hardy, Poet in Modern Writers at Work. Mark Van Doren. Ed. by J. K. Piercy. 1973. Repr. of 1930 ed. 45.00 (ISBN 0-8274-0432-8). R West.

Thomas Hardy Selected Stories. Thomas Hardy. 1980. pap. 3.95 (ISBN 0-312-71119-0). St Martin.

Thomas Hardy: The "Dream-Country" of His Fiction. Anne Alexander. (Critical Studies). 262p. 1987. 27.50 (ISBN 0-389-20712-8). B&N Imports.

Thomas Hardy: The Forms of Tragedy. Dale Kramer. LC 74-17084. 184p. 1975. text ed. 22.50x (ISBN 0-8143-1530-5). Wayne St U Pr.

Thomas Hardy: The Poetry of Necessity. James Richardson. LC 76-8100. 1977. lib. bdg. 12.00x (ISBN 0-226-71237-0). U of Chicago Pr.

Thomas Hardy: The Will & the Way. Roy Morrell. LC 78-27475. 1978. lib. bdg. 39.00 (ISBN 0-8414-6332-8). Folcroft.

Thomas Hardy: The Writer & His Background. Norman Page. LC 80-5188. 1980. 27.50 (ISBN 0-312-80132-7). St Martin.

Thomas Hardy: Towards a Materialist Criticism. George Wotton. LC 85-749. 246p. 1985. 28.75x (ISBN 0-389-20564-8). B&N Imports.

Thomas Hardy's English. Ralph W. Elliott. Ed. by David Crystal. (Language Library). 384p. 1984. 34.95x (ISBN 0-631-13659-2). Basil Blackwell.

Thomas Hardy's English. Ralph W. Elliott. 388p. 1986. pap. text ed. 15.95x (ISBN 0-631-14922-8). Basil Blackwell.

Thomas Hardy's Epic-Drama: A Study of the Dynasts. Harold Orel. Repr. of 1963 ed. lib. bdg. 35.00x (ISBN 0-8371-0602-8, ORTD). Greenwood.

Thomas Hardy's Heroines: A Chorus of Priorities. Pamela L. Jekel. LC 85-51934. 233p. 1986. 22.50x (ISBN 0-87875-309-5). Whitston Pub.

Thomas Hardy's Jude the Obscure. Intro. by Harold Bloom. (Modern Critical Interpretations Ser.). 152p. 1987. 24.50 (ISBN 0-87754-741-6). Chelsea Hse.

Thomas Hardy's Tess of the D'Urbervilles: A Facsimile of the Manuscript, with Related Materials. Ed. by Gatrell. (Thomas Hardy Archive Ser.). 720p. 1986. lib. bdg. 150.00 (ISBN 0-8240-7476-9). Garland Pub.

Thomas Hardy's Tess of the D'Urbervilles. Intro. by Harold Bloom. (Modern Critical Interpretations Sr.). 136p. 1986. 19.95 (ISBN 0-87754-744-0). Chelsea Hse.

Thomas Hardy's The Return of the Native: Facsimile of the Manuscript, with Related Materials. Gatrell. (Thomas Hardy Archives Ser.). 512p. 1986. lib. bdg. 100.00 (ISBN 0-8240-7475-0). Garland Pub.

Thomas Hardy's Twilight View of Life. R. E. Zachrisson. (Studies in Thomas Hardy, No. 14). 1970. pap. 39.95x (ISBN 0-8383-0105-3). Haskell.

Thomas Hardy's Universe. Ernest Brennecke. LC 73-15715. 1974. Repr. of 1924 ed. lib. bdg. 15.00 (ISBN 0-8414-3318-6). Folcroft.

Thomas Hardy's Universe: A Study of a Poet's Mind. E. Brennecke. LC 68-689. (Studies in Thomas Hardy, No. 14). 1969. Repr. of 1924 ed. lib. bdg. 75.00x (ISBN 0-8383-0651-9). Haskell.

Thomas Hardy's Wessex. H. Lea. 35.00 (ISBN 0-8490-1201-5). Gordon Pr.

Thomas Hardy's Wessex. Hermann Lea. 1979. Repr. of 1913 ed. lib. bdg. 45.50 (ISBN 0-8495-3326-0). Arden Lib.

Thomas Hardy's Wessex. Hermann Lea. LC 76-58449. 1977. Repr. of 1913 ed. lib. bdg. 42.00 (ISBN 0-8414-5736-0). Folcroft.

Thomas Hariot, the Mathematician, the Philosopher & the Scholar. Henry Stevens. LC 72-82433. 213p. 1972. Repr. of 1900 ed. 19.50 (ISBN 0-8337-3399-0). B Franklin.

Thomas Harriot: A Biography. John W. Shirley. LC 83-3961. (Illus.). 1983. 55.00x (ISBN 0-19-822901-1). Oxford U Pr.

Thomas Harriott: Renaissance Scientist. John W. Shirley. (Illus.). 1974. 59.00x (ISBN 0-19-858140-8). Oxford U Pr.

Thomas Hart Benton. Theodore Roosevelt. LC 68-24995. (American Biography Ser., No. 32). 1969. Repr. of 1903 ed. lib. bdg. 52.95x (ISBN 0-8383-0275-0). Haskell.

Thomas Haweis. Arthur S. Wood. LC 57-3828. (Church Historical Society Ser.: No. 70). 1957. 15.00x (ISBN 0-8401-5070-9). A R Allenson.

Thomas Henry Huxley. Edward Clodd. LC 75-30018. Repr. of 1902 ed. 20.00 (ISBN 0-404-14023-8). AMS Pr.

Thomas Henry Huxley. Edward Clodd. LC 74-2491. 1902. lib. bdg. 20.00 (ISBN 0-685-45595-5). Folcroft.

Thomas Henry Huxley. Leonard Huxley. LC 76-102247. (Select Bibliographies Reprint Ser). 1920. 18.00 (ISBN 0-8369-5132-8). Ayer Co Pubs.

Thomas Heywood. Frederich S. Boas. LC 75-15587. 159p. 1974. Repr. of 1950 ed. 20.00x (ISBN 0-87753-056-4). Phaeton.

Thomas Heywood. Frederick S. Boas. LC 74-5032. 1973. lib. bdg. 15.00. Folcroft.

Thomas Heywood. Frederick S. Boas. Repr. of 1950 ed. 19.00 (ISBN 0-403-02292-4). Somerset Pub.

Thomas Heywood. Thomas Heywood. text ed. 20.00 (ISBN 0-8369-8185-5, 8323). Ayer Co Pubs.

Thomas Heywood: A Study in the Elizabethan Drama of Everyday Life. Otelia Cromwell. LC 69-15681. (Yale Studies in English Ser.: No. 78). viii, 227p. 1969. Repr. of 1928 ed. 25.00 (ISBN 0-208-00767-9, Archon). Shoe String.

Thomas Heywood, Dramatic Works, with a Life & Remarks on His Writing by J. P. Collier, 2 vols. Thomas Heywood. Incl. The First & Second Parts of King Edward IV; The Fair Maid of the Exchange; Fortune by Land & Sea; The First & Second Parts of the Fair Maid of the West. Repr. of 1851 ed; The Royal King & Loyal Subject; A Woman Skilled with Kindness; Two Historical Plays on the Life & Reign of Queen Elizabeth; The Golden & Silver Ages; An Apology for Actors. (Shakespeare Society of London Publications Ser.: Vol. 5). Set. pap. 59.00 (ISBN 0-8115-0165-5). Kraus Repr.

Thomas Heywood et la Drama Domestique Elizabethan. Michel Grivelet. 1957. Repr. 50.00 (ISBN 0-8274-3612-2). R West.

Thomas Heywood: Playwright & Miscellanist. Arthur M. Clark. 356p. 1985. Repr. of 1931 ed. lib. bdg. 65.00 (ISBN 0-89984-138-4). Century Bookbindery.

Thomas Heywood: Reference Guide to Literature. Michael Wentworth. (Reference Guides to Literature Ser.). 367p. 1986. lib. bdg. 55.00x (ISBN 0-8161-8575-1). G K Hall.

Thomas Heywood's Pagenats: A Critical Edition. David M. Bergeron. LC 86-12156. (Renaissance Imagination Ser.: Vol. 16). 156p. 1986. lib. bdg. 45.00 (ISBN 0-8240-5464-4). Garland Pub.

Thomas Heywood's "The Fair Maid of the West" A Critical Edition, Pt. 1. Brownell Salomon. Ed. by James Hogg. (Jacobean Drama Studies). 209p. (Orig.). 1975. pap. 15.00 (ISBN 0-317-40109-2, Pub. by Salzburg Studies). Longwood Pub Group.

Thomas Hill & Rebecca Miles: Ancestors & Descendants. rev. ed. Mary L. Donnelly. LC 84-247052. (Illus.). 911p. 1984. 45.00 (ISBN 0-939142-09-0). Donnelly.

Thomas Hobbes: A Reference Guide. Charles H. Hinnant. 1980. lib. bdg. 31.50 (ISBN 0-8161-8173-X, Hall Reference). G K Hall.

Thomas Hobbes: Radical in the Service of Reaction. Arnold A. Rogow. LC 85-15592. 287p. 1986. 19.95 (ISBN 0-393-02288-9). Norton.

Thomas Hobbes: The Natural & the Artifacted Good. Martin A. Bertman. (European University Studies: Ser. 20, Philosophy: Vol. 48). 158p. 1981. 16.20 (ISBN 3-261-04770-4). P Lang Pubs.

Thomas Hoccleve: A Study in Early Fifteenth-Century English Poetic. Jerome Mitchell. LC 67-21855. (Illus.). Repr. of 1968 ed. 31.40 (2014938). Bks Demand UMI.

Thomas Holcroft's - Seduction: A Critical Edition with Annotations. Ed. by Stephen Orgel. (Satire & Sense Ser.). 320p. 1987. lib. bdg. 50.00 (ISBN 0-8240-6021-0). Garland Pub.

Thomas Hood: His Life & Times. Walter Jerrold. LC 68-24911. (English Biography Ser., No. 31). (Illus.). 1969. Repr. of 1907 ed. lib. bdg. 49.95x (ISBN 0-8383-0209-2). Haskell.

Thomas Hood und Die Soziale Tendenzdichtung Seiner Zeit. Emil Oswald. Repr. of 1904 ed. 25.00 (ISBN 0-384-43870-9). Johnson Repr.

Thomas Hooker: Preacher, Founder, Democrat. George L. Walker. 1972. Repr. of 1891 ed. lib. bdg. 19.00 (ISBN 0-8422-8120-7). Irvington.

Thomas Hooker, 1586-1647. Frank Shuffelton. LC 76-45912. 1977. 42.00x (ISBN 0-691-05249-2). Princeton U Pr.

Thomas Hornsby Ferril. A. Thomas Trusky. LC 73-8335. (Western Writers Ser: No. 6). 1973. pap. 2.95x (ISBN 0-88430-005-6). Boise St Univ.

Thomas Howard Earl of Arundel: Patronage & Collecting in the Seventeenth Century. David Howarth. (Illus.). 82p. 1985. pap. 14.95 (Pub. by Ashmolean Mus). Longwood Pub Group.

Thomas Hunt Morgan: A Scientific Biography. Garland Allen. LC 77-85526. (Illus.). 1978. text ed. 54.00x (ISBN 0-691-08200-6). Princeton U Pr.

Thomas Hunt Morgan: Pioneer of Genetics. Ian B. Shine & Sylvia Wrobel. LC 76-9519. (Kentucky Bicentennial Bookshelf Ser.). (Illus.). 176p. 1976. pap. 6.95 (ISBN 0-8131-0219-7). U Pr of Ky.

Thomas Hunt Morgan: Pioneer of Genetics. Ian B. Shine & Sylvia Wrobel. LC 76-40551. (Illus.). 188p. 1976. 15.00 (ISBN 0-8131-0095-X). U Pr of Ky.

Thomas Hutchinson Papers, 2 vols. Compiled by Thomas Hutchinson & W. H. Whitmore. (Prince Soc.: Nos. 1 & 2). 1967. 47.50 (ISBN 0-8337-1779-0). B Franklin.

Thomas in Trouble. Andrea Da Rif. LC 86-10591. (Illus.). 32p. (ps-3). 1987. 10.95 (ISBN 0-689-50395-4, M K McElderry). Macmillan.

Thomas International Photo Directory of Antique Cameras. Douglas B. Thomas. (Illus.). 356p. 1983. 39.75x (ISBN 0-9612128-0-2). Thomas Intl DC.

Thomas J. Collins. Ed. by William S. Peterson. LC 73-80684. (Browning Institute Studies: Vol. 4). (Illus.). 224p. 1976. 30.00x (ISBN 0-930252-07-1). Browning Inst.

Thomas J. Comber, Missionary Pioneer to the Congo. John B. Myers. LC 74-98739. (Illus.). Repr. of 1888 ed. lib. bdg. cancelled (ISBN 0-8371-2769-6, MYC&, Pub. by Negro U Pr). Greenwood.

Thomas J. Rusk: Soldier, Statesman, Jurist. Mary W. Clarke. LC 79-157043. (Illus.). 1971. 9.50 (ISBN 0-685-00320-5). Jenkins.

Thomas Jackson, Weaver. Harriet Tidball. LC 76-24005. (Shuttle Craft Guild Monograph: No. 13). (Illus.). 37p. 1964. pap. 7.45 (ISBN 0-916658-13-9). Shuttle Craft.

Thomas Jefferson. Roger Bruns. (World Leaders: Past & Present Ser.). (Illus.). 112p. 1986. lib. bdg. 16.95x (ISBN 0-87754-583-9). Chelsea Hse.

Thomas Jefferson, 2 vols. Ed. by Carol B. Fitzgerald. (Meckler's Bibliographies of the Presidents of the United States, 1789-1989 Ser.: No. 3). (Illus.). 1988. lib. bdg. 90.00x (ISBN 0-88736-117-X). Meckler Corp.

Thomas Jefferson. Jim Hargrove. LC 86-9658. (Encyclopedia of Presidents Ser.). (Illus.). 100p. (gr. 3 up). 1986. PLB 15.93 (ISBN 0-516-01385-8). Childrens.

Thomas Jefferson. John T. Morse, Jr. LC 77-128975. (American Statesmen: No. 11). Repr. of 1898 ed. 29.00 (ISBN 0-404-50861-8). AMS Pr.

Thomas Jefferson. John T. Morse, Jr. LC 80-23357. (American Statesmen Ser.). 330p. 1981. pap. 5.95 (ISBN 0-87754-183-3). Chelsea Hse.

Thomas Jefferson. David S. Muzzey. 319p. 1982. Repr. of 1918 ed. lib. bdg. 45.00 (ISBN 0-89987-590-4). Darby Bks.

Thomas Jefferson. Charles Patterson. LC 86-23361. (First Books: Biographies of Great Americans). (Illus.). 96p. (gr. 4-8). 1987. lib. bdg. 10.40 (ISBN 0-531-10306-4). Watts.

Thomas Jefferson. Laurence Santrey. LC 84-2579. (Illus.). 32p. (gr. 3-6). 1985. PLB 8.45 (ISBN 0-8167-0176-8); pap. text ed. 1.95 (ISBN 0-8167-0177-6). Troll Assocs.

Thomas Jefferson. John S. Williams. LC 13-9744. Repr. of 1913 ed. 18.50 (ISBN 0-404-06985-1). AMS Pr.

Thomas Jefferson: A Comprehensive, Annotated Bibliography of Writings about Him, 1826-1980. Frank Shuffelton. LC 83-48200. (Reference Library of Social Science: Vol. 184). 508p. 1984. lib. bdg. 54.00 (ISBN 0-8240-9078-0). Garland Pub.

Thomas Jefferson: A Reference Biography. Ed. by Merrill Peterson. LC 86-6736. 1986. lib. bdg. 70.00 (ISBN 0-684-18069-3). Scribner.

Thomas Jefferson: A Reference Guide. Eugene L. Huddleston. 1982. lib. bdg. 34.50 (ISBN 0-8161-8141-1, Hall Reference). G K Hall.

Thomas Jefferson: A Strange Case of Mistaken Identity. Alf J. Mapp, Jr. (Illus.). 512p. 1987. lib. bdg. 22.95 (ISBN 0-8191-5782-1, Pub. by Madison Bks). U Pr of Amer.

Thomas Jefferson, American Humanist. Karl Lehmann. LC 85-13479. xviii, 273p. 1985. 25.00x (ISBN 0-8139-1078-1); pap. 12.95. U Pr of Va.

Thomas Jefferson, American Tourist. Edward H. Dumbauld. (American Exploration & Travel Ser.: No. 9). (Pap. ed. 1978 reprint of 1946 ed.). 1976. 19.95x (ISBN 0-8061-1345-6); pap. 9.95 (ISBN 0-8061-1353-7). U of Okla Pr.

Thomas Jefferson: An Intimate History. Fawn M. Brodie. 832p. 1975. pap. 5.95 (ISBN 0-553-25443-X). Bantam.

Thomas Jefferson: An Intimate History. Fawn M. Brodie. (Illus.). 800p. 1974. 24.95 (ISBN 0-393-07480-3). Norton.

Thomas Jefferson & Education in a Republic. Charles F. Arrowood. (Works of Charles Flinn Arrowood). vii, 184p. 1985. Repr. of 1930 ed. lib. bdg. 39.00 (Pub. by Am Repr Serv). Am Biog Serv.

Thomas Jefferson & Education in a Republic. Charles F. Arrowood. 1988. Repr. of 1930 ed. lib. bdg. 49.00x. Am Biog Serv.

Thomas Jefferson & Education in a Republic. Ed. by Charles F. Arrowood. LC 79-136406. (BCL Ser.: No. 1). Repr. of 1930 ed. 12.00 (ISBN 0-404-00406-7). AMS Pr.

Thomas Jefferson & Education in a Republic. Ed. by Charles F. Arrowood. LC 70-131611. 1970. Repr. of 1930 ed. 11.00 (ISBN 0-403-00498-5). Scholarly.

Thomas Jefferson & His Copying Machines. Silvio A. Bedini. LC 81-7288. (Illus.). 233p. 1984. text ed. 20.00x (ISBN 0-8139-1025-0). U Pr of Va.

Thomas Jefferson & His Unknown Brother. Ed. by Bernard Mayo & James A. Bear. LC 80-25272. 59p. 1981. 7.95 (ISBN 0-8139-0890-6); pap. 3.95 (ISBN 0-8139-0911-2). U Pr of Va.

Thomas Jefferson & Music. Helen Cripe. LC 73-81099. (Thomas Jefferson Memorial Foundation Series). (Illus.). viii, 157p. 1974. 9.95x (ISBN 0-8139-0504-4); pap. 4.95x (ISBN 0-8139-0547-8). U Pr of Va.

Thomas Jefferson & the American Ideal. Russell Shorto. (Henry Steele Commager's Americans Ser.). (Illus.). 144p. (gr. 3-6). 1987. pap. 4.95 (ISBN 0-8120-3918-1). Barron.

Thomas Jefferson & the Law. Edward Dumbauld. LC 78-5742. (Illus.). 1978. 32.50x (ISBN 0-8061-1441-X). U of Okla Pr.

Thomas Jefferson & the National Capital. Thomas Jefferson. Ed. by Saul Padover. LC 83-45441. Repr. of 1946 ed. 76.00 (ISBN 0-404-20135-0). AMS Pr.

Thomas Jefferson & the New Nation: A Biography. Merrill D. Peterson. LC 70-110394. 1970. 39.95x (ISBN 0-19-500054-4). Oxford U Pr.

Thomas Jefferson & the New Nation: A Biography. Merrill D. Peterson. LC 70-110394. (Illus.). 1104p. 1986. pap. 16.95 (ISBN 0-19-501909-1). Oxford U Pr.

Thomas Jefferson & the Sciences: An Original Anthology. Ed. by I. Bernard Cohen. LC 79-7970. (Three Centuries of Science in America Ser.). (Illus.). 1980. 57.50x (ISBN 0-405-12552-6). Ayer Co Pubs.

Thomas Jefferson & the Stony Mountains: Exploring the West from Monticello. Donald Jackson. LC 80-10546. (Illus.). 351p. 1981. 22.95 (ISBN 0-252-00823-5). U of Ill Pr.

Thomas Jefferson: Architect. 2nd ed. Fiske Kimball. LC 67-27459. (Architecture & Decorative Art Ser). 1968. lib. bdg. 85.00 (ISBN 0-306-70965-1). Da Capo.

Thomas Jefferson As Social Scientist. Randolph Benson. LC 70-118124. 333p. 1971. 27.50 (ISBN 0-8386-7705-3). Fairleigh Dickinson.

Thomas Jefferson: Father of Our Democracy. David A. Adler. LC 87-45336. (Illus.). (gr. 1-4). 1987. PLB 12.95 (ISBN 0-8234-0667-9). Holiday.

Thomas Jefferson: His Life & Words. Ed. by Nick Beilenson. (Illus.). 64p. 1986. 5.95 (ISBN 0-88088-347-2, 883472). Peter Pauper.

Thomas Jefferson, Landscape Architect. Frederick D. Nichols & Ralph E. Griswold. LC 77-10601. (Illus.). ix, 196p. 1981. pap. 6.95x (ISBN 0-8139-0899-X). U Pr of Va.

Thomas Jefferson, Lawyer. Frank L. Dewey. LC 85-26571. 200p. 1986. 20.00 (ISBN 0-8139-1079-X). U Pr of VA.

Thomas Jefferson: Magnificent Populist. Martin A. Larson. 318p. 1985. pap. 11.95 (ISBN 0-8159-5902-8). Devin.

Thomas Jefferson: Man on a Mountain. Natalie Bober. LC 87-37462. (Illus.). 288p. (YA) (gr. 7 up). 1988. 14.95 (ISBN 0-689-31154-0, Atheneum Childrens Bks). Macmillan.

Thomas Jefferson: Mini-Play & Activities. (Presidents Ser.). (gr. 7 up). 1979. 6.50 (ISBN 0-89550-338-7). Stevens & Shea.

Thomas Jefferson: Selected Writings. Ed. by Harvey C. Mansfield, Jr. LC 77-86039. (Crofts Classics Ser.). 1979. pap. text ed. 3.95x (ISBN 0-88295-120-3). Harlan Davidson.

Thomas Jefferson: The Apostle of Americanism. Gilbert Chinard. 1957. pap. 9.95 (ISBN 0-472-06013-9, 13, AA). U of Mich Pr.

Thomas Jefferson 1743-1826: Chronology, Documents, Bibliographical Aids. Ed. by A. Bishop. LC 70-140619. (Presidential Chronology Ser). 122p. 1971. 8.00 (ISBN 0-379-12082-8). Oceana.

Thomas Jefferson: 3rd President of the United States. Rebecca Stefoff. LC 87-35953. (Presidents of the United States Ser.). (Illus.). 128p. (gr. 5-9). 1988. PLB 12.95 (ISBN 0-944483-07-0). Garrett Ed Corp.

Thomas Jefferson's Architectural Drawings. 2nd ed. Ed. by Frederick D. Nichols. LC 76-163982. (Illus.). 48p. (Orig.). 1961. pap. 4.95 (ISBN 0-8139-0328-9). U Pr of Va.

Thomas Jefferson's Architectural Drawings. 3rd ed. (Massachusetts Historical Society Picture Books Ser.). 49p. 1960. pap. 2.00 (ISBN 0-934909-17-2). Mass Hist Soc.

Thomas Jefferson's Cook Book. 2nd ed. Marie Kimball. LC 76-22698. 1987. Repr. of 1976 ed. 8.95 (ISBN 0-8139-0706-3). U Pr of Va.

Thomas Jefferson's European Travel Diaries. Thomas Jefferson. Ed. by James M. Morris & Persephone Weene. (Illus.). 144p. 1987. pap. 7.95 (ISBN 0-9615964-3-0). I Stephanus Pub.

Thomas Jefferson's Farm Book: With Commentary & Relevant Extracts from Other Writings. Ed. by Edwin M. Betts. LC 52-13160. (Illus.). 552p. 1987. Repr. of 1953 ed. 30.00 (ISBN 0-8139-0705-5). U Pr of Va.

Thomas Jefferson's Flower Garden at Monticello. 3rd ed. Edwin M. Betts & Hazlehurst B. Perkins. Rev. by Peter J. Hatch. LC 86-5613. (Illus.). xiv, 64p. 1986. pap. 7.95 (ISBN 0-8139-1087-0). U Pr of VA.

Thomas Jefferson's Garden Book. Ed. by Edwin M. Betts. (Memoirs Ser.: Vol. 22). (Illus.). 1981. Repr. of 1944 ed. 25.00 (ISBN 0-87169-022-5). Am Philos.
Thomas Jefferson's Life of Jesus. Thomas Jefferson. 1976. 2.95 (ISBN 0-87243-056-1). Templegate.
Thomas Jefferson's Paris. Ed. by Howard C. Rice, Jr. LC 75-30203. (Illus.). 160p. 1976. 38.00x (ISBN 0-691-05232-8). Princeton U Pr.
Thomas Jefferson's Rotunda Restored, 1973-1976: A Pictorial Review with Commentary. Joseph L. Vaughan & Omer A. Gianniny, Jr. LC 80-27087. (Illus.). 1981. 27.50 (ISBN 0-8139-0888-4). U Pr of Va.
Thomas Jefferson's Views on Public Education. John C. Henderson. LC 76-137239. Repr. of 1890 ed. 28.00 (ISBN 0-404-03236-2). AMS Pr.
Thomas Jewett Goree Letters Vol. 1: The Civil War Correspondence. Ed. by Langston J. Goree. LC 81-67136. (Illus.). 338p. Date not set. Repr. lib. bdg. 65.00 (ISBN 0-943162-00-9). Family History.
Thomas Jonathan Jackson...Eccentric Genius. Allen Carpenter. (Mighty Warriors Ser.). (Illus.). 112p. (gr. 4-8). 1987. PLB 66.64 4 bk. set (ISBN 0-317-60501-1); PLB 16.66 (ISBN 0-86625-326-2). Rourke Corp.
Thomas Keith's Scotland. John Hannavy. (Illus.). 96p. 1981. pap. 19.95 (ISBN 0-86241-006-1, Pub. by Canongate Pub Scotland). Pelican.
Thomas Ken & Izaak Walton: A Sketch of Their Lives & Family Connection. E. Marston. 1908. Repr. 35.00 (ISBN 0-8274-3613-0). R West.
Thomas Ken: Bishop & Non-Juror. Hugh A. L. Rice. LC 58-4172. 1958. 10.00x (ISBN 0-8401-2008-7). A R Allenson.
Thomas Killigrew, Cavalier Dramatist. Alfred Harbage. LC 67-23854. 1967. Repr. of 1930 ed. 19.00 (ISBN 0-405-08597-4). Ayer Co Pubs.
Thomas Kyd's Mystery Play: Myth & Ritual in the Spanish Tragedy. Frank Ardolino. (American University Studies IV (English Language & Literature): Vol. 29). 194p. text ed. 24.60 (ISBN 0-8204-0232-X). P Lang Pubs.
Thomas L. McKenney, Architect of America's Early Indian Policy: 1816-1830. Herman J. Viola. LC 74-18075. (Illus.). 365p. (Orig.). 1974. pap. 8.95 (ISBN 0-8040-0669-5, Swallow); 15.00. Ohio U Pr.
Thomas Lange & Charles Ryskamp: American Literary Autographs from Washington Irving to Henry James. Herbert Cahoon. 19.00 (ISBN 0-8446-5655-0). Peter Smith.
Thomas Lester: His Lace & the East Midlands Industry. Anne Buck. 29.95 (ISBN 0-903585-09-X). Robin & Russ.
Thomas L'Imposteur: Roman. Jean Cocteau. (Folio Ser.: No. 480). 1971. 3.95 (ISBN 0-685-11596-8). Schoenhof.
Thomas L'Imposteur: Roman. Jean Costeau. 1971. write for info. French & Eur.
Thomas Lodge. Wesley D. Rae. LC 67-25185. (Twayne's English Authors Ser.). 1967. lib. bdg. 17.95 (ISBN 0-89197-964-6); pap. text ed. 5.95x (ISBN 0-8290-2007-1). Irvington.
Thomas Lodge & Other Elizabethans. Charles J. Sisson. 1966. lib. bdg. 37.00x (ISBN 0-374-97467-5, Octagon). Hippocrene Bks.
Thomas Lord Cromwell. LC 76-133745. (Tudor Facsimile Texts. Old English Plays: No. 97). Repr. of 1911 ed. 49.50 (ISBN 0-404-53397-3). AMS Pr.
Thomas Love Peacock. Olwen Campbell. 104p. 1983. Repr. of 1953 ed. lib. bdg. 30.00 (ISBN 0-89987-143-7). Darby Bks.
Thomas Love Peacock. Olwen W. Campbell. LC 73-157327. (Select Bibliographies Reprint Ser.). 1972. Repr. of 1953 ed. 14.00 (ISBN 0-8369-5787-3). Ayer Co Pubs.
Thomas Love Peacock. W. H. Helm. 1973. 20.00 (ISBN 0-8274-0275-9). R West.
Thomas Love Peacock. James Mulvihill. (Twayne English Author Ser.). 152p. 1987. lib. bdg. 24.95x (ISBN 0-8057-6957-9, Twayne). G K Hall.
Thomas Love Peacock. John B. Priestly. LC 74-131808. 1970. Repr. of 1927 ed. 39.00x (ISBN 0-403-00695-3). Scholarly.
Thomas Love Peacock: A Critical Study. A. Martin Freeman. LC 74-11329. 1911. lib. bdg. 27.00 (ISBN 0-8414-4226-6). Folcroft.
Thomas Love Peacock: Letters to Edward Hookham & Percy B. Shelley with Fragments of Unpublished MSS. Percy Bysshe Shelley. Ed. by Garnett Richard. 1974. Repr. of 1910 ed. lib. bdg. 45.00 (ISBN 0-8414-8093-1). Folcroft.
Thomas Lovell Beddoes. R. Snow. 59.95 (ISBN 0-8490-1202-3). Gordon Pr.
Thomas Lovell Beddoes. James R. Thompson. (English Authors Ser.). 1985. lib. bdg. 20.95 (ISBN 0-8057-6892-0, Twayne). G K Hall.
Thomas Lovell Beddoes: Eccentric & Poet. Royall H. Snow. 1928. lib. bdg. 45.00 (ISBN 0-8414-1554-4). Folcroft.
Thomas Lyster. David Wurtzel. 224p. 1987. pap. 3.95 (ISBN 0-380-70180-4). Avon.
Thomas Macaulay: Sculptural Views on Perceptual Ambiguity, 1968-1986. Betty Collings & Donald Kuspit. LC 86-61901. 71p. (Orig.). 1986. pap. text ed. 14.95 (ISBN 0-937809-00-4). Dayton Art.
Thomas MacDonagh: A Critical Biography. Johann A. Norstedt. LC 78-31320. (Illus.). 175p. 1980. 14.95x (ISBN 0-8139-0786-1). U Pr of Va.
Thomas McKean. John M. Coleman. LC 74-19952. 1975. 16.95 (ISBN 0-912834-07-2). Am Faculty Pr.
Thomas McKean: The Shaping of an American Republicanism. G. S. Rowe. LC 77-94085. (Illus.). 1978. text ed. 25.00x (ISBN 0-87081-100-2). Colo Assoc.
Thomas McKnight. (Illus.). 120p. 1984. 30.00 (ISBN 0-88363-484-8). H L Levin.
Thomas McKnight's World: A Vision of Earthly Happiness. Thomas McKnight. (Illus.). 200p. 1987. 75.00 (ISBN 0-89659-781-4). Abbeville Pr.
Thomas Mann. Intro. by Harold Bloom. (Modern Critical Views Ser.). 358p. 1986. 29.50 (ISBN 0-87754-725-4). Chelsea Hse.
Thomas Mann. Ignace Feuerlicht. (World Authors Ser.). 1968. lib. bdg. 17.95 (ISBN 0-8057-2584-9, Twayne). G K Hall.
Thomas Mann. Joseph P. Stern. LC 67-16891. (Columbia Essays on Modern Writers Ser.: No. 24). 1967. pap. 5.00 (ISBN 0-231-02847-4, MW24). Columbia U Pr.
Thomas Mann: A Critical Study. R. J. Hollingdale. LC 79-161509. 204p. 1971. 20.00 (ISBN 0-8387-1004-2). Bucknell U Pr.
Thomas Mann: A Study. Martin Swales. 117p. 1980. 13.50x (ISBN 0-8476-6270-5). Rowman.
Thomas Mann & Italy. Ilsedore B. Jonas. Tr. by Betty Crouse. LC 79-9779. 208p. 1979. 17.75 (ISBN 0-8173-8063-9). U of Ala Pr.
Thomas Mann in Context: Proceedings of the Centennial Colloquium on Thomas Mann, Clark University, 1975. Centennial Colloquim on Thomas Mann Staff. Ed. by Kenneth Hughes. LC 77-26366. pap. 34.50 (ISBN 0-317-27753-7, 2015545). Bks Demand UMI.
Thomas Mann Pro & Contra Wagner. Thomas Mann. Tr. by Allan Blunden. LC 85-20819. 240p. (Ger.). 1986. lib. bdg. 25.00x (ISBN 0-226-50334-8); pap. 10.95 (ISBN 0-226-50335-6). U of Chicago Pr.
Thomas Mann: The Ironic German. Erich Heller. LC 79-63046. 314p. 1979. pap. 7.50 (ISBN 0-89526-906-6). Regnery Gateway.
Thomas Mann: The Ironic German, a Study. Erich Heller. 1958. 12.00x (ISBN 0-911858-29-6). Appel.
Thomas Mann: The Making of an Artist, 1875 to 1911. Richard Winston. LC 81-47515. 352p. 1981. 17.45 (ISBN 0-394-47171-7). Knopf.
Thomas Mann: The Uses of Tradition. T. J. Reed. 1974. pap. 11.95x (ISBN 0-19-815747-9). Oxford U Pr.
Thomas Mann: The World As Will & Representation. Fritz Kaufmann. LC 73-75847. xiii, 322p. 1973. Repr. of 1957 ed. lib. bdg. 22.50x (ISBN 0-8154-0480-8). Cooper Sq.
Thomas Mann, 1875-1955. Stanley Corngold et al. (Illus.). 62p. 1975. pap. 3.00 (ISBN 0-87811-021-6). Princeton Lib.
Thomas Mann's Doctor Faustus: The Sources & Structure of the Novel. Gunilla U. Bergsten. LC 69-14483. pap. 63.50 (ISBN 0-317-29848-8, 2020031). Bks Demand UMI.
Thomas Mann's "Goethe & Tolstoy" Notes & Sources. Ed. by Clayton Koelb. Tr. by Alcyone Scott & Clayton Koelb. LC 82-13497. x, 255p. 1984. text ed. 23.75 (ISBN 0-8173-0138-0). U of Ala Pr.
Thomas Mann's Magic Mountain. Intro. by Harold Bloom. (Modern Critical Interpretations Ser.). 123p. 1986. 19.95 (ISBN 0-87754-902-8). Chelsea Hse.
Thomas Mann's Novel, "Der Zauberberg" A Study. Hermann J. Weigand. LC 78-149678. Repr. of 1933 ed. 18.50 (ISBN 0-404-06889-8). AMS Pr.
Thomas Mayhew, Patriarch to the Indians, 1593-1682. Lloyd C. Hare. LC 76-104347. (Illus.). Repr. of 1932 ed. 20.00 (ISBN 0-404-03108-0). AMS Pr.
Thomas Mayhew, Patriarch to the Indians 1593 to 1682. Lloyd C. Hare. LC 76-145070. 231p. 1932. Repr. 12.00 (ISBN 0-403-01012-8). Scholarly.
Thomas Mellon & His Times. Thomas Mellon. 1885. 39.00 (ISBN 0-527-62950-2). Kraus Repr.
Thomas Merton: A Bibliography. rev. ed. Frank Dell'Isola. LC 74-79148. (Serif Ser.: No. 31). 200p. 1975. 13.50x (ISBN 0-87338-156-4). Kent St U Pr.
Thomas Merton: A Pictorial Biography. James H. Forest. LC 80-82249. (Illus.). 112p. (Orig.). 1980. pap. 5.95 (ISBN 0-8091-2284-7). Paulist Pr.
Thomas Merton & Asia: His Quest for Utopia. Alexander Lipski. (Cistercian Studies: No. 74). 1983. 17.95 (ISBN 0-87907-874-X); pap. 7.95 (ISBN 0-87907-974-6). Cistercian Pubns.
Thomas Merton, Brother Monk. M. Basil Pennington. LC 86-43016. 224p. 1987. 15.95 (ISBN 0-06-066497-5, HarpR). Har-Row.
Thomas Merton: Contemplative Critic. Henri J. Nouwen. LC 80-8896. 176p. 1981. pap. 6.95 (ISBN 0-06-066324-3, RD 357, HarpR). Har-Row.
Thomas Merton Monk. rev., enl. ed. Patrick Hart. pap. 7.95 (ISBN 0-87907-752-2). Cistercian Pubns.
Thomas Merton: Monk & Artist. Victor A. Kramer. 1988. pap. 11.95 (ISBN 0-317-68103-6). Cistercian Pubns.
Thomas Merton Monk & Poet: A Critical Study. George Woodcock. 200p. 1978. 7.95 (ISBN 0-374-27635-8); pap. 3.95 (ISBN 0-374-51487-9). FS&G.
Thomas Merton on Mysticism. Raymond Bailey. 280p. 1987. pap. 5.95 (ISBN 0-385-24015-5, Im). Doubleday.
Thomas Merton on Nuclear Weapons. Ronald Powaski. 1988. pap. 7.95 (ISBN 0-8294-0586-0). Loyola.
Thomas Merton on Prayer. John J. Higgins. 200p. 1975. pap. 4.95 (ISBN 0-385-02813-X, Im). Doubleday.
Thomas Merton on St. Bernard. Intro. by Jean Leclercq. (Cistercian Studies: No. 9). 1980. 13.95 (ISBN 0-87907-809-X); pap. 4.95 (ISBN 0-87907-909-6). Cistercian Pubns.
Thomas Merton Reader. Ed. by Thomas P. McDonnell. LC 74-29. 600p. 1974. pap. 6.50 (ISBN 0-385-03292-7, Im). Doubleday.
Thomas Merton, Social Critic: A Study. James T. Baker. LC 76-132827. 183p. pap. 47.60 (2030047). Bks Demand UMI.
Thomas Merton Studies Center: Three Essays. Thomas Merton & John H. Griffin. 1969. 12.00 (ISBN 0-87775-022-X). Unicorn Pr.
Thomas Merton: The Development of a Spiritual Theologian. Donald Grayston. LC 84-27299. (Toronto Studies in Theology: Vol. 20). 225p. 1985. lib. bdg. 49.95x (ISBN 0-88946-758-7). E Mellen.
Thomas Merton's Dark Path. rev. ed. William H. Shannon. 260p. 1987. pap. 8.95 (ISBN 0-374-52019-4). FS&G.
Thomas Merton's Dark Path: The Inner Experience of a Contemplative. William H. Shannon. LC 80-28091. 256p. 1981. 15.00 (ISBN 0-374-27636-6). FS&G.
Thomas Merton's Rewriting: The Five Versions of Seeds-New Seeds of Contemplation as A Key to the Development of His Thought. Donald Grayston. (Studies in Art & Religious Interpretation: Vol. 8). 1987. lib. bdg. 69.95x (ISBN 0-88946-559-2). E Mellen.
Thomas Merton's Shared Contemplation: A Protestant Perspective. Daniel J. Adams. Ed. by Teresa A. Doyle. (Cistercian Studies: No. 62). 1979. 8.00 (ISBN 0-87907-862-6). Cistercian Pubns.
Thomas Middelton's-A Trick to Catch the Old One, A Mad World, My Masters', & Aphra Behn's City Heiress. Marston S. Balch. Ed. by JAmes Hogg. (Jacobean Drama Studies). 84p. (Orig.). 1981. pap. 15.00 (ISBN 3-7052-0387-8, Salzburg Studies). Longwood Pub Group.
Thomas Middelton's-No Wit, No Help Like a Woman's & The Counterfeit Bridegroom (1677), & Further Adaptations. Marston S. Balch. Ed. by James Hogg. (Jacobean Drama Studies). 129p. (Orig.). 1980. pap. 15.00 (ISBN 3-7052-0385-1, Salzburg Studies). Longwood Pub Group.
Thomas Middleton, 2 vols. Havelock Ellis. 1988. Repr. Set. lib. bdg. 75.00x. Am Biog Serv.
Thomas Middleton: A Reference Guide. Sara J. Steene. (Reference Guides to Literature Ser.). 1984. lib. bdg. 61.00 (ISBN 0-8161-8340-6, Hall Reference). G K Hall.
Thomas Middleton: An Annotated Bibliography. Dorothy Wolff. LC 84-45367. (Reference Library of the Humanities). 100p. 1985. lib. bdg. 25.00 (ISBN 0-8240-8819-0). Garland Pub.
Thomas Middleton & the New Comedy Tradition. George E. Rowe, Jr. LC 79-4289. xii, 240p. 1979. 22.00x (ISBN 0-8032-3853-3). U of Nebr Pr.
Thomas Middleton: Michaelmas Term & a Trick to Catch the Old One. George R. Price. (Studies in English Literature: No. 91). 227p. 1976. pap. text ed. 27.20x (ISBN 0-686-22606-2). Mouton.
Thomas Middleton's City Comedies. Anthony Covatta. LC 72-3261. 187p. 1974. 18.00 (ISBN 0-8387-1196-0). Bucknell U Pr.
Thomas Moore. Stephen Gwynn. LC 73-13838. 1905. Repr. lib. bdg. 19.00 (ISBN 0-8414-4448-X). Folcroft.
Thomas Moore. Seamus Maccall. 1973. Repr. of 1935 ed. 20.00 (ISBN 0-8274-0109-4). R West.
Thomas Moore Anecdotes, Being Anectodes, Bon-Mots, & Epigrams. Thomas Moore. LC 74-13039. (Raconteur Ser: Vol. 1). 1974. Repr. of 1899 ed. lib. bdg. 30.50 (ISBN 0-8414-4848-5). Folcroft.
Thomas Moore the Poet: His Life & Works. Andrew J. Symington. 1880. lib. bdg. 17.00 (ISBN 0-8414-8011-7). Folcroft.
Thomas Moran, Artist of the Mountains. Thurman Wilkins. LC 65-11235. (Illus.). pap. 96.80 (ISBN 0-317-10416-0, 2005062). Bks Demand UMI.
Thomas Moran: Drawings, Oils & Watercolors from the Thomas Gilcrease Institute of American History & Art. James K. Ballinger. LC 86-60332. (Illus.). 32p. (Orig.). 1986. 9.00 (ISBN 0-910407-18-5). Phoenix Art.
Thomas Moran: Watercolors of the American West. Carol Clark. LC 80-13459. (Illus.). 192p. 1980. 27.50 (ISBN 0-292-75059-5). U of Tex Pr.
Thomas Moran's Journey to the Tetons in 1879. Fritiof Fryxell. 12p. 1988. lib. bdg. 19.95x (ISBN 0-8095-6108-5). Borgo Pr.
Thomas More. Stephen L. Gywnn. 204p. 1980. Repr. of 1905 ed. lib. bdg. 27.00 (ISBN 0-8495-2045-2). Arden Lib.
Thomas More. Christopher Hollis. 1934. Repr. 20.00 (ISBN 0-8274-3614-9). R West.
Thomas More. Anthony Kenny. (Past Master Ser.). 1983. pap. 4.95 (ISBN 0-19-287573-6). Oxford U Pr.
Thomas More. Seamus MacCall. 1978. Repr. of 1935 ed. lib. bdg. 20.00 (ISBN 0-8495-3748-7). Arden Lib.
Thomas More. facs. ed. Daniel Sargent. LC 71-119963. (Select Bibliographies Reprint Ser). 1933. 19.00 (ISBN 0-8369-5406-8). Ayer Co Pubs.
Thomas More. Daniel Sargent. 299p. 1980. Repr. of 1933 ed. lib. bdg. 30.00 (ISBN 0-89984-412-X). Century Bookbindery.
Thomas More: A Biography. Richard Marius. LC 84-47645. (Illus.). 543p. 1984. 22.45 (ISBN 0-394-45982-2). Knopf.
Thomas More & Erasmus. Ernest E. Reynolds. LC 65-26739. x, 260p. 1966. 25.00 (ISBN 0-8232-0670-X). Fordham.
Thomas More: History & Providence. Alistair Fox. LC 82-11178. 288p. 1983. text ed. 32.00x (ISBN 0-300-02951-9). Yale U Pr.
Thomas More: History & Providence. Alistair Fox. LC 82-11178. 288p. 1985. pap. text ed. 11.95x (ISBN 0-300-03415-6, Y-536). Yale U Pr.
Thomas More's Prayer Book: A Facsimile Reproduction of the Annotated Pages. St. Thomas More. Tr. by Louis L. Martz & Richard S. Sylvester. LC 69-15454. (Elizabethan Club Ser.: No. 4). (Illus., Lat. & Eng.). 1969. 29.95x (ISBN 0-300-00179-7). Yale U Pr.
Thomas Morley's First Book of Consort Lessons, 6 vols. Ed. by William Casey. LC 81-80729. 1982. pap. 45.00x spiral bdg. (ISBN 0-918954-27-4). Baylor Univ Pr.
Thomas Munro & the Development of Administrative Policy in Madras, 1792-1818: The Origins of the Munro System. T. H. Beaglehole. LC 65-17209. pap. 48.30 (ISBN 0-317-26048-0, 2024419). Bks Demand UMI.
Thomas My Brother. Sandy Michel. 1981. pap. 4.00 (ISBN 0-917178-15-7). Lenape Pub.
Thomas N. Page: A Memoir of a Virginia Gentleman. Rosewell Page. LC 68-8238. 1969. Repr. of 1923 ed. 23.00x (ISBN 0-8046-0343-X, Pub by Kennikat). Assoc Faculty Pr.
Thomas N. Page: A Memoir of a Virginia Gentleman. Rosewell Page. 1923. Repr. 7.95 (ISBN 0-8274-3615-7). R West.
Thomas, Naogeorg, Werke, Vol. 1: Tragoedia Nova Pammachius, Mit der Deutschen Uebersetzung des Johann Tyrolff. Ed. by Hans-Gert Roloff. (Ausgaben Deutscher Literatur des 15th bis 18th Jahrhunderts). 1974. 112.00x (ISBN 3-11-004074-3). De Gruyter.
Thomas Nast: His Period & His Pictures. Albert B. Paine. LC 80-20105. (American Men & Women of Letters Ser.). (Illus.). 624p. 1981. pap. 8.95 (ISBN 0-87754-169-8). Chelsea Hse.
Thomas Nast: His Period & Pictures. Albert B. Paine. (Illus.). 1904. 13.25 (ISBN 0-8446-1339-8). Peter Smith.
Thomas Nast's Christmas Drawings. Thomas Nast. (Illus.). 1978. pap. 5.00 (ISBN 0-486-23660-9). Dover.
Thomas Nelson Page. Theodore L. Gross. (Twayne's United States Authors Ser). 1967. pap. 8.95x (ISBN 0-8084-0298-6, T111, Twayne). New Coll U Pr.
Thomas of Britain: Tristan. Valerie Roberts. 150p. 1986. lib. bdg. 20.00 (ISBN 0-8240-8777-1). Garland Pub.
Thomas of Erceldoune. Ed. by James A. Murray. (EETS, OS Ser.: No. 61). Repr. of 1875 ed. 29.00 (ISBN 0-527-00055-8). Kraus Repr.
Thomas Onetwo. Ernest Robson. (Illus.). 1971. 6.95. Primary Pr.
Thomas Onetwo. Ernest M. Robson. (Illus.). 1971. 10.00. Ultramarine Pub.
Thomas Osborne Davis: Ein Irischer Freiheitssanger. Johannes Schiller. Repr. of 1915 ed. 25.00 (ISBN 0-384-53865-7). Johnson Repr.
Thomas Otway. Edgar Schumacher. LC 74-131457. 1970. Repr. of 1924 ed. lib. bdg. 18.50 (ISBN 0-8337-3176-9). B Franklin.
Thomas Paine. A. J. Ayer. (Illus.). 256p. 1989. 19.95 (ISBN 0-689-11996-8). Atheneum.
Thomas Paine. Harry H. Clark. 436p. 1980. Repr. lib. bdg. 35.00 (ISBN 0-8495-0794-4). Arden Lib.
Thomas Paine. Moncure D. Conway. LC 80-24838. (American Men & Women of Letters Ser.: 2 vols.). 896p. 1982. Set. pap. 17.90 (ISBN 0-87754-172-8). Chelsea Hse.
Thomas Paine. Ellery Sedgwick. LC 78-10619. 1978. Repr. of 1899 ed. lib. bdg. 25.50 (ISBN 0-8414-7910-0). Folcroft.
Thomas Paine: American Revolutionary Writer. John G. Buchanan. Ed. by D. Steve Rahmas. (Outstanding Personalities Ser.: No. 85). (YA) (gr. 7-12). 1976. lib. bdg. 3.75 incl. catalog cards (ISBN 0-87157-585-X); pap. 2.50 vinyl laminated covers (ISBN 0-87157-085-8). SamHar Pr.
Thomas Paine Collection of Richard Gimbel in the Library of the American Philosophical Society. Compiled by Hildegard Stephans. LC 76-49800. 1976. lib. bdg. 60.00 (ISBN 0-8420-2108-6). Scholarly Res Inc.
Thomas Paine Portfolio. Carl Shapiro et al. 1976. 5.00x (ISBN 0-914937-05-7). Ind Pubns.
Thomas Paine, Prophet & Martyr of Democracy. Mary A. Best. 59.95 (ISBN 0-8490-1203-1). Gordon Pr.

Thonet Bentwood & Other Furniture: The 1904 Illustrated Catalogue & Supplements. Thonet Company Staff. (Illus.). 154p. 1980. pap. 9.95 (ISBN 0-486-24024-X). Dover.
Thonner's Analytical Key to the Families of Flowering Plants. Ed. by R. Geesink et al. (Leiden Botanical Ser.: Vol. 5). 200p. 37.00 (ISBN 90-6021-461-7, Pub. by Junk Pubs Netherlands). Kluwer Academic.
Thonner's Analytical Key to the Families of Flowering Plants, Vol. 5. R. Geesink et al. (Leiden Botanical Ser.). (Illus.). 253p. 1981. 29.50 (ISBN 90-220-0744-8, PDC225, PUDOC); pap. 37.50 (ISBN 90-220-0730-8, PDC224). UNIPUB.
Thoor Ballylee: Home of William Butler Yeats. Mary Hanley & Liam Miller. 1977. pap. 6.95 (ISBN 0-85105-300-9, Pub. by Colin Smythe Ltd Britain). Dufour.
Thor Heyerdahl: Across the Seas of Time. Paul Westman. LC 82-1431. (Taking Part Ser.). (Illus.). 48p. (gr. 3 up). 1982. PLB 9.95 (ISBN 0-87518-225-9). Dillon.
Thor, the Last of the Sperm Whales. Robert M. McClung. LC 87-26090. 64p. (gr. 3-7). 1988. Repr. of 1971 ed. PLB 14.50 (ISBN 0-208-02186-8, Linnet). Shoe String.
Thoracic & Cardiovascular Surgery. 4th ed. Ed. by William Glenn et al. (Illus.). 1695p. 1983. 150.00 (ISBN 0-8385-8956-1). Appleton & Lange.
Thoracic Anesthesia. Ed. by Joel A. Kaplan. (Illus.). 736p. 1982. text ed. 79.00 (ISBN 0-443-08166-2). Churchill.
Thoracic Cirripedia of the Gulf of California. Dora P. Henry. (Publications in Oceanography Ser.: No. 4-4). (Illus.). 23p. 1960. pap. 7.50x (ISBN 0-295-73968-1). U of Wash Pr.
Thoracic Drainage: Manual of Procedures. N. H. Fishman. 1983. 26.50 (ISBN 0-8151-3259-X). Year Bk Med.
Thoracic Lumbar Spine & Spinal Cord Injuries. Ed. by P. Harris. (Advances in Neurotraumatology Ser.: Vol. 2). (Illus.). 230p. 1987. 61.00 (ISBN 0-387-81928-2). Springer-Verlag.
Thoracic Medicine. Ed. by Peter Emerson. 1981. text ed. 110.00 (ISBN 0-407-00210-3). Butterworth.
Thoracic Oncology. Ed. by Noah C. Choi & Hermes C. Grillo. (Illus.). 384p. 1983. text ed. 60.50 (ISBN 0-89004-434-1, 494). Raven.
Thoracic Oncology. Roth et al. 944p. 1988. 85.00 (ISBN 0-7216-1950-9). Saunders.
Thoracic Outlet Syndrome. Erich W. Pollak. (Illus.). 240p. 1986. monograph 39.50 (ISBN 0-87993-246-5). Fairleigh Dickinson.
Thoracic Surgery. 3rd ed. H. Bolooki. (Specialty Board Review Ser.: Vol. 18). 1981. 33.75 (ISBN 0-87488-118-8). Med Exam.
Thoracic Trauma. Hood & Boyd. 448p. 1989. price not set (ISBN 0-7216-2353-0). Saunders.
Thoracotomy Exercise Manual. 1983. 5.00 (ISBN 0-940876-07-8). City Hope.
Thora's Saga: A Tale of Old Iceland. J. Russell Boulding. LC 85-73124. (Illus.). 184p. (Orig.). (gr. 6-12). 1986. pap. 4.95 (ISBN 0-936001-00-3). Peaceable Kingdom.
Thorburn's Birds & Mammals. John Southern. (Illus.). 96p. 1986. 60.00 (ISBN 0-7153-8830-4). Salem Hse Pubs.
Thore-Buerger & the Art of the Past. Frances S. Jowell. LC 76-23632. (Outstanding Dissertations in the Fine Arts - 19th Century). (Illus.). 1977. Repr. of 1971 ed. lib. bdg. 76.00 (ISBN 0-8240-2701-9). Garland Pub.
Thoreau. Elbert Hubbard. 1930. 15.00 (ISBN 0-8274-3616-5). R West.
Thoreau. H. A. Page. 1979. 42.50 (0-911156-32-9). Bern Porter.
Thoreau: A Century of Criticism. Walter R. Harding. LC 55-116. pap. 54.30 (ISBN 0-317-28189-5, 2022784). Bks Demand UMI.
Thoreau: A Chronology. V. Munoz. Tr. by W. Scott Johnson. (Libertarian & Anarchist Chronology Ser.). 1979. lib. bdg. 59.95 (ISBN 0-8490-3021-8). Gordon Pr.
Thoreau: A Glimpse. Samuel A. Jones. LC 72-3174. (American Literature Ser., No. 49). (Illus.). 1972. Repr. of 1903 ed. lib. bdg. 29.95x (ISBN 0-8383-1516-X). Haskell.
Thoreau: A Naturalist's Liberty. John Hildebidle. 192p. 1983. text ed. 16.00x (ISBN 0-674-88640-2). Harvard U Pr.
Thoreau Abroad: Twelve Bibliographical Essays. Ed. by Eugene F. Timpe. LC 71-146512. 203p. 1971. 23.50 (ISBN 0-208-00401-7, Archon). Shoe String.
Thoreau Amongst Friends & Philistines & Other Thoreauviana. Samuel A. Jones. Ed. by George Hendrick. LC 82-6444. xxvi, 241p. 1983. 24.95x (ISBN 0-8214-0675-2). Ohio U Pr.
Thoreau & Indian Thought: A Study of the Impact of Indian Thought on the Life of Henry David Thoreau. D. G. Deshmukh. LC 80-2505. Repr. of 1974 ed. 19.50 (ISBN 0-404-19053-7). AMS Pr.
Thoreau & the American Indians. Robert F. Sayre. LC 76-45910. 1977. 29.50x (ISBN 0-691-06330-3); pap. text ed. 13.50x (ISBN 0-691-10226-0). Princeton U Pr.
Thoreau & the Wild Appetite. Kenneth A. Robinson. LC 80-2682. (Thoreau Ser.). (Illus.). Repr. of 1957 ed. 18.50 (ISBN 0-404-19079-0). AMS Pr.
Thoreau & Whitman: A Study of Their Esthetics. Charles R. Metzger. LC 68-26925. v, 113p. 1968. Repr. of 1961 ed. 17.50 (ISBN 0-208-00691-5, Archon). Shoe String.
Thoreau As World Traveler. John A. Christie. LC 65-24586. (Illus.). 358p. 1966. 35.00x (ISBN 0-231-02833-4). Columbia U Pr.
Thoreau As World Traveler. John A. Christie. (Special Publication Ser.: No. 37). (Illus.). 358p. 1965. 9.50 (ISBN 0-318-12736-9). Am Geographical.
Thoreau Calender. E. M. Evors. LC 73-563. 1973. lib. bdg. 25.00 (ISBN 0-8414-1503-X). Folcroft.
Thoreau Centennial. Ed. by Walter Harding. LC 65-19729. 119p. 1964. 16.95x (ISBN 0-87395-015-1). State U NY Pr.
Thoreau: Centennial Appreciations. Frederick W. Roman et al. 1946. Repr. lib. bdg. 22.00 (ISBN 0-8414-7473-7). Folcroft.
Thoreau Chronology. Leonard F. Kleinfeld. 1980. lib. bdg. 69.95 (ISBN 0-87700-306-8). Revisionist Pr.
Thoreau Gazetteer. Robert F. Stowell. Ed. by William Howarth. 1970. 29.00x (ISBN 0-691-06156-4); pap. 9.95x (ISBN 0-691-01315-2). Princeton U Pr.
Thoreau: His Home, Friends & Books. Annie R. Marble. LC 73-85906. Repr. of 1902 ed. 34.50 (ISBN 0-404-04185-X). AMS Pr.
Thoreau: His Home, Friends & Books. Annie R. Marble. 59.95 (ISBN 0-8490-1204-X). Gordon Pr.
Thoreau: His Life & Aims. H. Page. 59.95 (ISBN 0-8490-1205-8). Gordon Pr.
Thoreau: His Life & Aims. H. Page. LC 72-3653. (American Literature Ser., No. 49). 1972. Repr. of 1878 ed. lib. bdg. 49.95x (ISBN 0-8383-1585-2). Haskell.
Thoreau: His Life & Aims. H. A. Page. LC 76-28372. 1901. lib. bdg. 30.50 (ISBN 0-8414-6778-1). Folcroft.
Thoreau in the Human Community. Mary E. Moller. LC 79-22549. (New England Writers Ser.). 224p. 1980. lib. bdg. 17.50x (ISBN 0-87023-293-2). U of Mass Pr.
Thoreau in the Mountains. Henry David Thoreau. Ed. by William Howarth. (Illus.). 384p. 1982. 17.95 (ISBN 0-374-27643-9); pap. 8.95 (ISBN 0-374-51761-4). FS&G.
Thoreau Library: A Catalogue. Raymond Adams. LC 73-16257. lib. bdg. 15.00 1936 (ISBN 0-8414-2941-3); lib. bdg. 15.00 1937 suppl. (ISBN 0-8414-2939-1). Folcroft.
Thoreau Library of Raymond Adams. Raymond Adams. LC 80-2502. Repr. of 1937 ed. AMS Pr.
Thoreau Library of Raymond Adams. Raymond Adams. 80p. 1980. Repr. of 1936 ed. lib. bdg. 20.00 (ISBN 0-8495-0063-X). Arden Lib.
Thoreau Library of Raymond Adams: A Catalogue Supplement. 1978. Repr. of 1936 ed. lib. bdg. 20.50 (ISBN 0-8492-0073-3). R West.
Thoreau: Mystic, Prophet, Ecologist. William J. Wolf. LC 73-22368. 224p. 1974. 6.95 (ISBN 0-8298-0269-X). Pilgrim NY.
Thoreau on the Art of Writing. Franklin W. Hamilton. 1967. pap. 2.00 (ISBN 0-911938-01-X). Walden Pr.
Thoreau on the Lecture Platform. Walter R. Harding. LC 80-2681. Repr. of 1982 ed. 18.00 (ISBN 0-404-19077-4). AMS Pr.
Thoreau, Poet-Naturalist. new & enl. ed. William E. Channing. Ed. by F. B. Sanborn. LC 65-27095. (Illus.). 1902. 20.00 (ISBN 0-8196-0173-X). Biblo.
Thoreau Profile. Milton Meltzer & Walter Harding. 1969. pap. 4.00 sewn (ISBN 0-912130-01-6). Thoreau Found.
Thoreau Profile. Milton Meltzer & Walter A. Harding. (Illus.). 13.25 (ISBN 0-8446-0797-5). Peter Smith.
Thoreau: Selected Writings. Henry David Thoreau. Ed. by Lewis Leary. LC 58-5337. (Crofts Classics Ser.). 1958. pap. text ed. 3.95x (ISBN 0-88295-099-1). Harlan Davidson.
Thoreau Stalks the Land Disguised As a Father. Barry Targan. 1975. 2.00 (ISBN 0-912678-20-8). Greenfld Rev Pr.
Thoreau, the Cosmic Yankee. Frederick Roman. LC 77-9275. 1977. lib. bdg. 25.00 (ISBN 0-8414-7385-4). Folcroft.
Thoreau the Platonist. Daniel A. Dombrowski. (American University Studies V - Philosophy: Vol. 10). 219p. 1986. text ed. 29.00 (ISBN 0-8204-0364-4). P Lang Pubs.
Thoreau the Poet-Naturalist: With Memorial Verses. William E. Channing. LC 80-2680. Repr. of 1873 ed. 37.50 (ISBN 0-404-19073-1). AMS Pr.
Thoreau's Alternative History: Changing Perpectives on Nature, Culture, & Language. Joan Burbick. 192p. 1987. text ed. 26.95x (ISBN 0-8122-8058-X). U of Pa Pr.
Thoreau's Cape Cod with the Early Photographs of H. W. Gleason. Thea Wheelwright & Katharine Knowles. LC 79-163877. (Illus.). 1974. pap. 3.95 (ISBN 0-517-51707-8). Barre.
Thoreau's Comments on the Art of Writing. Richard Dillman. 66p. (Orig.). 1987. lib. bdg. 15.25 (ISBN 0-8191-6600-6); pap. text ed. 8.25 (ISBN 0-8191-6601-4). U Pr of Amer.
Thoreau's Complex Weave: The Writing of "A Week on the Concord & Merrimack Rivers", with the Text of the First Draft. Linck C. Johnson. LC 85-17859. xxii, 490p. 1986. 37.50x (ISBN 0-8139-1063-3). U Pr of Va.
Thoreau's Guide to Cape Cod. Henry David Thoreau. Ed. by Alexander B. Adams. (Illus.). 1962. 14.50 (ISBN 0-8159-6904-X). Devin.
Thoreau's Library. Walter R. Harding. LC 80-2507. Repr. of 1957 ed. 21.50 (ISBN 0-404-19055-3). AMS Pr.
Thoreau's Method: A Handbook for Nature Study. David Pepi. (Illus.). 204p. 1985. 13.95 (ISBN 0-13-919887-3); pap. 5.95 (ISBN 0-13-919879-2). P-H.
Thoreau's Minnesota Journey: Two Documents. Henry David Thoreau. Ed. by Walter Harding. LC 80-2524. (Thoreau Ser.). (Illus.). 80p. 1981. Repr. of 1962 ed. 18.50 (ISBN 0-404-19072-3). AMS Pr.
Thoreau's Philosophy of Life, with Special Consideration of the Influence of Hindoo Philosophy. Helena A. Snyder. LC 80-2518. (Thoreau Ser.). 104p. Repr. of 1902 ed. 22.50 (ISBN 0-404-19066-9). AMS Pr.
Thoreau's Reading: A Study in Intellectual History with Bibliographical Catalogue. Robert Sattelmeyer. 400p. 1988. 39.50 (ISBN 0-691-06745-7). Princeton U Pr.
Thoreau's Redemptive Imagination. Frederick Garber. LC 77-73031. (Gotham Library). 229p. 1977. pap. 40.00x (ISBN 0-8147-2965-7); pap. 17.50x (ISBN 0-8147-2966-5). NYU Pr.
Thoreau's Seasons. Richard Lebeaux. LC 83-17982. (New England Writers Ser.). 432p. 1984. 28.50 (ISBN 0-87023-401-3). U of Mass Pr.
Thoresby Society Publications, Vols. 16-18, 32. Thoresby Society - Leeds. 34.00 ea. (ISBN 0-384-60340-8). Johnson Repr.
Thorgal - The Archers. Jean Van Hamme & Grzegorz Rosinski. Tr. by Chris Tanz. (Illus.). 48p. 1987. pap. 6.95 (ISBN 0-9617885-0-X, Starblaze). Donning Co.
Thorgal: Child of the Stars. Jean Van Hamme. Tr. by Chris Tanz from Fr. (Illus.). 48p. 1986. pap. 6.95. Ink Pub AZ.
Thorgal: Child of the Stars. Jean Van Hamme. (Illus.). 48p. pap. 6.95 (ISBN 0-89865-501-3, Starblaze). Donning Co.
Thorgal: The Archers. Jean Van Hamme. Tr. by Chris Tanz & Jean-Paul Bierny. (Illus.). 48p. 1987. 6.95 (ISBN 0-317-57529-5). Ink Pub Az.
Thorgal: The Archers. Jean Van Hamme. Tr. by Chris Tanz & Jean-Paul Bierny. (Illus.). 48p. 1988. pap. 5.95 (ISBN 0-9617885-2-6). Ink Pub AZ.
Thorgal: The Sorceress Betrayed. Jean Van Hamme. Tr. by Chris Tanz & Jean-Paul Bierny. (Thorgal). Orig. Title: Magicienne Trahie & L'ile des mers gelees. (Illus.). 104p. 1988. pap. 12.95 (ISBN 0-9617885-1-8). Ink Pub AZ.
Thorgal: The Sorceress Betrayed. Jean Van Hamme. 48p. 1988. 12.95 (ISBN 0-89865-620-6, Starblaze). Donning Co.
Thorium. R. I. Ryabchikov & E. K. Gol'braikh. (Analytical Chemistry of the Elements Ser.). 300p. 1970. text ed. 59.00x (ISBN 0-7065-0747-9, Pub. by Keter Pub Jerusalem). Coronet Bks.
Thorium Fuel Cycle. Compiled by E. Roth. (Bibliographical Ser.: No. 39). 462p. 1972. pap. 40.00 (ISBN 92-0-054070-8, ISP21 39, IAEA). UNIPUB.
Thorium Fuel Cycle: Proceedings. Ed. by Ray G. Wymer. LC 67-62083. (AEC Symposium Ser.). 847p. 1968. pap. 29.25 (ISBN 0-87079-228-8, CONF-660524); microfiche 6.50 (ISBN 0-87079-229-6, CONF-660524). DOE.
Thorium: Its Industrial Hygiene Aspects. Roy E. Albert. (U. S. Atomic Energy Commission Monographs). 1966. 25.00 (ISBN 0-12-048656-3). Acad Pr.
Thorkelin Transcripts of Beowulf see Early English Manuscripts in Facsimile.
Thorn Bird Country. Photos by Jo Daniell. (Illus.). 128p. 1983. pap. 12.95 (ISBN 0-446-37573-X). Warner Bks.
Thorn Birds. Colleen McCullough. 540p. 1981. pap. 6.95 (ISBN 0-380-56390-8, 56390-8). Avon.
Thorn Birds. Colleen McCullough. 1978. pap. 4.95 (ISBN 0-380-01817-9). Avon.
Thorn Birds. Colleen McCullough. LC 76-26271. 1977. 19.95i (ISBN 0-06-012956-5, HarpT). Har-Row.
Thorn Bush Blooms. Rosalyn Alsobrook. 304p. (Orig.). 1981. pap. 2.95 (ISBN 0-505-51753-1, Pub. by Tower Bks). Leisure NY.
Thorn-Fruit. Clifford Lanier. 1973. Repr. of 1867 ed. lib. bdg. 35.00 (ISBN 0-8490-1206-6). Gordon Pr.
Thorn in My Side. Heather Lang. (Harlequin American Romance Ser.). 256p. 1983. pap. 2.25 (ISBN 0-373-16031-3). Harlequin Bks.
Thorn in the Chrysanthemum: Suicide & Economic Success in Modern Japan. Mamoru Iga. 286p. 25.00x (ISBN 0-520-05648-5). U of Cal Pr.
Thorn in the Starfish: The Immune System & How It Works. Robert S. Desowitz. LC 86-23675. 1987. 16.95 (ISBN 0-393-02435-0). Norton.
Thorn in the Starfish: The Immune System & How It Works. Robert S. Desowitz. (Illus.). 1988. pap. 7.95 (ISBN 0-393-30556-2). Norton.
Thorn of a Rose: Amy Lowell Reconsidered. Glenn R. Ruihley. LC 74-13542. (Illus.). 191p. 1975. 23.50 (ISBN 0-208-01458-6, Archon). Shoe String.
Thorn of Arimithia. Frank G. Slaughter. 1976. Repr. of 1959 ed. lib. bdg. 19.95x (ISBN 0-89190-288-0, Pub. by River City Pr). Amereon Ltd.
Thorn of Love. Robin L. Hatcher. 480p. (Orig.). 1985. pap. 3.95 (ISBN 0-8439-2194-3, Leisure Bks). Leisure NY.
Thorn of Love. Robin L. Hatcher. 480p. 1988. pap. 3.95 (ISBN 0-8439-2653-8, Pub. by Leisure Bks CT). Leisure NY.
Thorn Rose. Errol Le Cain. (Illus.). (ps-3). 1978. pap. 3.95 (ISBN 0-14-050222-X, Puffin). Penguin.
Thorn Witch. E. J. Taylor. LC 84-12533. (Biscuit, Buttons & Pickles Ser.). (Illus.). 204p. (ps-3). 1985. PLB 7.95 (ISBN 0-394-86833-1). Knopf.
Thorndike Barnhart Handy Dictionary. Ed. by Clarence L. Barnhart. 1971. pap. 3.50 (ISBN 0-553-25664-5). Bantam.
Thorndike Encyclopedia of Banking & Financial Tables. rev. 3rd ed. David Thorndike. 1987. 84.00 (ISBN 0-88712-883-1). Warren Gorham & Lamont.
Thorndike Encyclopedia of Banking & Financial Tables. rev. ed. Ed. by David Thorndike. 1700p. 1980. 84.00 (ISBN 0-88262-472-5, 80-51347). Warren Gorham & Lamont.
Thorndike's Compound Interest & Annuity Tables. 1982. 96.00 (ISBN 0-88262-836-4). Warren Gorham & Lamont.
Thorns among the Sagebrush. Elaine V. Bercik. 189p. 1984. 7.95 (ISBN 0-89697-161-9). Intl Univ Pr.
Thorns & Arabesques: Contexts for Conrad's Fiction. William W. Bonney. LC 80-13308. 272p. 1980. text ed. 28.50x (ISBN 0-8018-2345-5). Johns Hopkins.
Thorns & Blossoms. Marian F. Winkelman. 1980. 6.50 (ISBN 0-533-04213-5). Vantage.
Thorns & Thistles: Juvenile Delinquents in the United States, 1825-1940. Robert M. Mennel. LC 72-95187. 259p. 1973. 20.00x (ISBN 0-87451-070-8). U Pr of New Eng.
Thorns & Thistles: Juvenile Delinquents in the United States, 1825-1940. Robert M. Mennel. LC 72-95187. pap. 64.80 (ISBN 0-317-41775-4, 2025640). Bks Demand UMI.
Thorns Thistles & Chrome. Joe E. Pierce. 160p. (Orig.). pap. 5.95 (ISBN 0-913244-63-5). Hapi Pr.
Thornton Cox Guide to Portugal. 2nd ed. Ed. by Thornton Cox. (Thorton Cox Guides Ser.). (Illus.). 140p. 1987. pap. 8.95 (ISBN 0-87052-367-8). Hippocrene Bks.
Thornton Romances. James O. Halliwell. LC 74-16120. 1973. lib. bdg. 27.00 (ISBN 0-8414-4862-0). Folcroft.
Thornton Romances. Ed. by James O. Halliwell-Phillipps. 1844. 37.00 (ISBN 0-384-21090-2). Johnson Repr.
Thornton Romances: The Early English Metrical Romances of Perceval, Isumbras, Eglamour & Degravant. Ed. by James O. Halliwell-Phillipps. LC 73-177456. Repr. of 1844 ed. 37.00 (ISBN 0-404-50130-3). AMS Pr.
Thornton the Worrier. Marjorie W. Sharmat. LC 78-1286. (Illus.). 32p. (gr. k-3). 1978. reinforced bdg. 9.95 (ISBN 0-8234-0328-9). Holiday.
Thornton W. Burgess, a Descriptive Book Bibliography. Wayne W. Wright. LC 78-64641. (Illus.). 159p. 15.00 (ISBN 0-88492-028-3). W S Sullwold.
Thornton Wilder. Rex Burbank. (Twayne's United States Authors Ser.). 1961. pap. 8.95x (ISBN 0-8084-0300-1, T5, Twayne). New Coll U Pr.
Thornton Wilder. 2nd ed. Rex J. Burbank. (United States Authors Ser.). 1978. lib. bdg. 16.95 (ISBN 0-8057-7223-5, Twayne). G K Hall.
Thornton Wilder. David Castronovo. (Literature & Life Ser.). 185p. 1986. 16.95x (ISBN 0-8044-2119-6). Ungar.
Thornton Wilder. Hermann Stresau. Tr. by Frieda Schutze. LC 71-149478. (Literature & Life Ser.). 1971. 11.95 (ISBN 0-8044-2844-1). Ungar.
Thornton Wilder: A Bibliographical Checklist of Work by & about Thornton Wilder. Compiled by Richard H. Goldstone. LC 79-6273. (Studies in Modern Literature: No. 7). 120p. 1982. 34.50 (ISBN 0-404-18046-9). AMS Pr.
Thorny Gates of Learning in Sung China: A Social History of Examinations (960-1279 AD) John W. Chaffee. (Cambridge Studies in Chinese History, Literature & Institutions). 250p. 1985. 44.50 (ISBN 0-521-30207-2). Cambridge U Pr.
Thornyhold. Mary Stewart. 1988. 15.45. Morrow.
Thorold Dickinson: The Man & His Films. Jeffrey Richards. 224p. 1986. 39.00 (ISBN 0-7099-2293-0, Pub. by Croom Helm Ltd). Routledge Chapman & Hall.
Thorough-Bass Accompaniment according to Johann David Heinichen. rev. ed. George J. Buelow. LC 85-21005. (Studies in Musicology: No. 84). 490p. 1986. 69.95 (ISBN 0-8357-1648-1). UMI Res Pr.
Thoroughbred. Carole E. Welker. LC 73-77061. (Breed Ser.). 64p. 1974. pap. 2.95 (ISBN 0-88376-002-9). Dreenan Pr.
Thoroughbred Broodmare Records, 1982: Annual Edition. Ed. by Blood-Horse, Inc. Staff. 2724p. 1983. o. p. 87.50 (ISBN 0-936032-59-6); leather binding 50.00 (ISBN 0-936032-60-X). Blood-Horse.
Thoroughbred Broodmare Records, 1983. Ed. by Blood-Horse, Inc. Staff. 2800p. 40.00 (ISBN 0-936032-72-3); leather 50.00 (ISBN 0-936032-73-1). Blood Horse.
Thoroughbred Business. Jocelyn de Moubray. (Illus.). 192p. 1988. 29.95 (ISBN 0-241-12379-8, Pub. by Hamish Hamilton). David & Charles.

Thoroughbred Field Hunter. Christian T Goeldner. LC 75-20593. (Illus.). 184p. 1976. 9.95 (ISBN 0-498-01767-2). A S Barnes.

Thoroughbred Handicapping. William L. Quirin. LC 84-60211. 320p. 1984. 19.95 (ISBN 0-688-03064-5). Morrow.

Thoroughbred Handicapping As an Investment. Dick Mitchell. 300p. 1986. text ed. 39.95 (ISBN 0-9614168-3-1). Cynthia Pub Co.

Thoroughbred Horses. Dorothy H. Patent. LC 84-48742. (Illus.). 87p. (gr. 3-7). 1985. reinforced bdg. 12.95 (ISBN 0-8234-0558-3). Holiday.

Thoroughbred Pedigrees Simplified. Miles Napier. 7.95 (ISBN 0-85131-191-1, BL175, Pub. by J A Allen U K). S R Smith Sporting Bks.

Thoroughbred Stallion Records, 1983. Ed. by Blood-Horse, Inc. Staff. 747p. 1984. 42.50 (ISBN 0-936032-71-5). Blood Horse.

Thoroughbred Stallion Records, 1984. 750p. 1985. 42.50 (ISBN 0-936032-84-7). Blood-Horse.

Thoroughbred Stallion Records, 1985. 800p. 1986. 42.50 (ISBN 0-936032-93-6); pap. 30.00 (ISBN 0-936032-97-9). Blood-Horse.

Thoroughbred Stallion Records, 1986. The Blood-Horse Inc. Staff. 800p. 1987. pap. 60.00 (ISBN 0-939049-08-2). Blood Horse.

Thoroughbred Style: Racing Dynasties-The Horses, the Owners, the Studs. Anne Lambton & John Offen. (Illus.). 256p. 1986. 35.00 (ISBN 0-88162-196-X). Salem Hse Pubs.

Thoroughbreds. Michael Geller. 352p. 1984. pap. 3.50 (ISBN 0-8439-2165-X, Leisure Bks). Leisure NY.

Thoroughbreds. Alvin F. Staufer & Edward May. LC 74-75354. (Illus.). 352p. 1975. 35.00 (ISBN 0-944513-03-4). Staufer Bks.

Thoroughly Efficient Navy. William W. Kaufmann. LC 87-11596. (Studies in Defense Policy). 123p. 1987. pap. 8.95t (ISBN 0-8157-4845-0). Brookings.

Thoroughly Married. Dennis Guernsey. 145p. 1984. pap. text ed. 5.95 (ISBN 0-8499-3000-6, 3000-6). Word Bks.

Thoroughly Modern Millie. Richard Morris & Hila Colman. 12.95 (ISBN 0-88411-449-X, Pub. by Aeonian Pr). Amereon Ltd.

Thorpe! the Sports Career of James Thorpe. James Hahn & Lynn Hahn. Ed. by Howard Schroeder. LC 80-28405. (Sports Legends Ser.). (Illus.). 48p. (Orig.). (gr. 3-5). 1981. PLB 9.95 (ISBN 0-89686-123-6). Crestwood Hse.

Thorpe's Dictionary of Applied Chemistry, 11 vols. 4th, rev. & enl. ed. Jocelyn F. Thorpe & M. A. Whiteley. Incl. Vol. 1. A - Bl. pap. 160.00 (ISBN 0-317-10765-8); Vol. 2. Bl - Chemical Analysis. pap. 160.00 (ISBN 0-317-10766-6); Vol. 3. Chemical Calculations - Diffusion. pap. 158.00 (ISBN 0-317-10767-4); Vol. 4. Digallic Acid - Feeding Stuffs. Repr. of 1940 ed. pap. 156.80 (ISBN 0-317-10768-2); Vol. 5. Feh - Glass. Repr. of 1941 ed. pap. 156.00 (ISBN 0-317-10769-0); Vol. 6. Glau - Inv (Index to Vols. I-VI) Repr. of 1950 ed. pap. 155.80 (ISBN 0-317-10770-4); Vol. 7. Iodazide - Metegallic Acid. Repr. of 1946 ed. pap. 160.00 (ISBN 0-317-10771-2); Vol. 8. LC 47-129. Repr. of 1946 ed. pap. 160.00 (ISBN 0-317-10772-0); Vol. 9. Oils, Fatty -Pituitary Body. Repr. of 1949 ed. pap. 160.00 (ISBN 0-317-10773-9); Vol. 10. Plagioclase - Sodium. LC 37-28650. Repr. of 1937 ed. pap. 160.00 (ISBN 0-317-10774-7); Vol. 12. General Index. LC 47-129. Repr. of 1946 ed. pap. 47.80 (ISBN 0-317-10775-5, 2005892). LC 37-28650. pap. (2004549). Bks Demand UMI.

Thor's Goats & Other Crazy Ways to Ride Around. Slim Goatsend. (Odd Books for Odd Moments Ser.). (Illus.). 72p. (Orig.). pap. cancelled (ISBN 0-938338-07-2). Winds World Pr.

Thor's Hammer. Ed. by Reginald Bretnor. (Future at War Ser.: Bk. I). 1987. 3.95 (ISBN 0-671-65342-3). Baen Bks.

Thor's Hammer: Essays on John Gardner. Ed. by Jeff Henderson. (Illus.). 208p. (Orig.). 1988. lib. bdg. 28.50 (ISBN 0-944436-01-3); pap. text ed. 14.50 (ISBN 0-944436-02-1). Univ Central AR Pr.

Thor's Home. Rodney Nelson. (Kestrel Ser.: No. 8). 28p. 1983. pap. 3.00 (ISBN 0-914974-40-8). Holmgangers.

Thorsby. Joan Hessayon. 208p. 1989. 24.95 (ISBN 0-7126-1828-7, Pub. by Century Hutchinson). David & Charles.

Thorson's Guide to Campus-Free College Degrees. Marcie K. Thorson. 136p. 1986. pap. 15.00 (ISBN 0-916277-03-8). Careers Unltd.

Thorstein Veblen: A Reference Guide. Jerry L. Simich & Rick Tillman. (R G L Se.). 1985. lib. bdg. 43.50 (ISBN 0-8161-8358-9). G K Hall.

Thorstein Veblen & His America. Joseph Dorfman. LC 64-7662. (Illus.). 1972. Repr. of 1934 ed. 45.00x (ISBN 0-678-00007-7). Kelley.

Thorstein Veblen & the Institutionalists: A Study in the Philosophy of Economics. David Seckler. LC 73-91642. 175p. 1975. text ed. 15.00x (ISBN 0-87081-055-3). Colo Assoc.

Thorstein Veblen: The Carleton College Veblen Seminar Essays. Ed. by Carlton C. Qualey. LC 68-28400. 170p. 1968. 26.50x (ISBN 0-231-03111-4). Columbia U Pr.

Thorstein Veblen's Social Theory. Arthur K. Davis. Ed. by Harriet Zuckerman & Robert K. Merton. LC 79-8989. (Dissertations on Sociology). 1980. lib. bdg. 42.00x (ISBN 0-405-12961-0). Ayer Co Pubs.

Those Amazing Americans. Walter E. Hempstead, Jr. (Illus.). 48p. 1981. 2.95 (ISBN 0-940094-00-2). Hempstead House.

Those Amazing Prophecies That Prove the Bible. Gordon Lindsay. (Prophecy Ser.). 1.25 (ISBN 0-89985-053-7). Christ Nations.

Those Bicentennials...from American Rails. G. R. Cockle. LC 78-50294. (Illus.). 1986. 35.00 (ISBN 0-916160-04-1). G R Cockle.

Those Black Diamond Men. William F. Gibbons. LC 74-22785. (Labor Movement in Fiction & Non-Fiction). Repr. of 1902 ed. 34.00 (ISBN 0-404-58431-4). AMS Pr.

Those Bloomin' Books: A Handbook for Extending Thinking Skills. Carol S. Kruise. 150p. 1986. lib. bdg. 17.50 (ISBN 0-87287-548-2). Libs Unl.

Those Born at Koona. John Smyly & Carolyn Smyly. (Illus.). 120p. pap. 9.95 (ISBN 0-88839-101-3). Hancock House.

Those Buried Texans, No Stone Unturned. Tom Allen. LC 80-82288. (Illus.). 172p. (Orig.). 1980. pap. 6.95 (ISBN 0-937460-00-1). Hendrick-Long.

Those Celadon Blues. rev. ed. Robert Tichane. LC 83-62553. (Oriental Glaze Ser.). (Illus.). 214p. 1983. 22.00x (ISBN 0-914267-03-5). NYS Inst Glaze.

Those Crazy Class Pictures: Junior High, No. 7. Kate Kenyon. 160p. (Orig.). (YA) (gr. 7 up). 1987. pap. 2.50 (ISBN 0-590-41160-8). Scholastic Inc.

Those Crazy Wonderful Years: When We Ran Warner Brothers. Stuart Jerome. (Illus.). 256p. 1983. 14.95 (ISBN 0-8184-0343-8). Lyle Stuart.

Those Curious New Cults in the Eighties. rev. ed. Bill Petersen. LC 72-93700. 1982. pap. text ed. 3.95 (ISBN 0-87983-317-3). Keats.

Those Days: An American Album. Richard Critchfield. 1987. pap. 8.95 (ISBN 0-317-59955-0, LE). Dell.

Those Drinking Days. Donald Newlove. 176p. 1989. pap. price not set (ISBN 0-07-046416-2). McGraw.

Those Drinking Days: Myself & Other Writers. Donald Newlove. LC 80-84518. 176p. 1981. 9.95 (ISBN 0-8180-0250-6). Horizon.

Those Earnest Victorians. Esme Wingfield-Stratford. 11.75 (ISBN 0-8446-0966-8). Peter Smith.

Those Elegant Decorums: The Concept of Propriety in Jane Austen's Novels. Jane Nardin. LC 73-4821. 168p. 1973. 34.50x (ISBN 0-87395-236-7). State U NY Pr.

Those Europeans. Sisley Huddleston. LC 79-90647. (Essay Index Reprint Ser). 1924. 19.00 (ISBN 0-8369-1218-7). Ayer Co Pubs.

Those Extra Chances in Bridge. Terence Reese & Roger Trezel. (Master Class Ser.). (Illus.). 128p. 1987. pap. 7.95 (ISBN 0-575-02634-0, Pub. by Gollancz England). David & Charles.

Those Fabulous Flying Machines: A History of Flight in Three Dimensions with Punch-Out Plane Model. Seymour Reit. (Illus.). 12p. (gr. 4-7). 1985. 17.95 (ISBN 0-02-776020-0). Macmillan.

Those Fallacies by Slight of Reason. Francis Schwanauer. 1978. pap. text ed. 9.75 (ISBN 0-8191-0619-4). U Pr of Amer.

Those Fascinating Little Lamps. John Solverson. 19.95 (ISBN 0-915410-43-5); pap. 15.95 (ISBN 0-317-65839-5). Antique Pubns.

Those Fascinating Paper Dolls: An Illustrated Handbook for Collectors. Marion Howard. (Illus.). 320p. 1981. pap. 10.00 (ISBN 0-486-24055-X). Dover.

Those Fatal Generals. E. V. Westrate. LC 68-16300. 1968. Repr. of 1936 ed. 25.00x (ISBN 0-8046-0497-5, Pub by Kennikat). Assoc Faculty Pr.

Those Four & Plenty More. Eleanor Dewees. Ed. by Bobbie J. Van Dolson. (gr. 2-5). 1981. pap. 6.95 (ISBN 0-8280-0092-1). Review & Herald.

Those Gasoline Lines & How They Got There. Helmut Merklein & William Murchison. LC 79-55245. 150p. 1980. lib. bdg. 10.95 (ISBN 0-933028-10-5); pap. 5.95 (ISBN 0-933028-09-1). Fisher Inst.

Those Giants: Let Them Rise! Erika Duncan. LC 85-8197. 176p. 1986. 14.95 (ISBN 0-8052-4000-4). Schocken.

Those Glittering Years. Alida Harvie. (Illus.). 232p. 1984. 30.00x (ISBN 0-317-43632-5, Pub. by Regency Pr). State Mutual Bk.

Those Glorious Glamour Years. Margaret Bailey. (Illus.). 384p. 1983. pap. 12.95 (ISBN 0-8065-0860-4, Pub. by Citadel Pr). Lyle Stuart.

Those Glorious Glamour Years: Classic Hollywood Costume Design of the 1930's. Margaret J. Bailey. (Illus.). 352p. Date not set. pap. 15.95 (ISBN 0-8065-1065-X, Citadel Pr). Lyle Stuart.

Those Glorious Glamour Years: The Great Hollywood Costume Designs of the Thirties. Margaret J. Bailey. (Illus.). 352p. 1982. 25.00 (ISBN 0-8065-0784-5, Pub. by Citadel Pr). Lyle Stuart.

Those Great Cowboy Sidekicks. David Rothel. LC 84-10513. 338p. 1984. 29.50 (ISBN 0-8108-1707-1). Scarecrow.

Those Happy Golden Years. Miriam Wood. 1980. 6.95 (ISBN 0-8280-0062-X, 20380-2). Review & Herald.

Those Harper Women. Stephen Birmingham. 352p. 1985. pap. 3.95 (ISBN 0-425-10649-7). Berkley Pub.

Those Having Torches. facs. ed. Mount Holyoke College. LC 68-57335. (Essay Index Reprint Ser). 1954. 14.50 (ISBN 0-8369-0716-7). Ayer Co Pubs.

Those He Came to Save. Roy C. Putnam. LC 77-13764. Repr. of 1978 ed. 35.50 (ISBN 0-8357-9029-0, 2016414). Bks Demand UMI.

Those Hours Spent Outdoors: Reflections on Hunting & Fishing. William G. Tapply. 224p. 1988. 17.95 (ISBN 0-684-18776-0). Scribner.

Those in Bondage. Victor DeKock. LC 76-122865. 1971. Repr. of 1950 ed. 23.50x (ISBN 0-8046-1368-0, Pub by Kennikat). Assoc Faculty Pr.

Those Incredible B2FDC-B2J4C's! see Bicentennial Two Dollar Bill Cancellations.

Those Incredible Jackson Boys. Ed. by R-O Magazine Editors. (Star Bks.). (Illus.). 192p. 1984. pap. 2.95 (ISBN 0-89531-086-4). Sharon Pubns.

Those Incredible Jackson Boys. Ed. by Sharon Starbooks. 1984. pap. 2.95 (ISBN 0-451-13307-2, Sig). NAL.

Those Kings & Queens of Old Hawaii: A Mele to Their Memory. Paul Bailey. LC 75-259. (Illus.). 381p. 1975. 20.00 (ISBN 0-87026-035-9). Westernlore.

Those Magnificent Clydesdales: The Gentle Giants. Karen C. Flanigan. 1977. 6.95 (ISBN 0-517-53426-6). Crown.

Those Magnificent Cowgirls. Milt Riske. LC 83-71805. (Illus.). 130p. 1984. pap. 15.00 (ISBN 0-913701-00-9). Wyoming Pub.

Those Many-Splendored Faraway Places. J. Paul Werner. (Illus.). 304p. 1976. lib. bdg. 8.95x (ISBN 0-9601368-1-9, 3455). J P Werner.

Those Mysterious Priests. Fulton J. Sheen. 1979. pap. 10.00 (ISBN 0-385-08102-2). Lumen Christi.

Those Nut-Cracking Elizabethans. W. J. Lawrence. LC 74-98684. (Studies in Drama, No. 39). 1970. Repr. of 1935 ed. lib. bdg. 49.95x (ISBN 0-8383-0988-7). Haskell.

Those of My Blood. Jacqueline Lichtenberg. 416p. 1988. 19.95 (ISBN 0-312-02298-0). St Martin.

Those of the Gray Wind: The Sandhill Cranes. Paul A. Johnsgard. LC 86-4292. (Illus.). xii, 116p. 1986. pap. 5.50 (ISBN 0-8032-7566-8, Bison). U of Nebr Pr.

Those of the Street: The Catholic-Jews of Mallorca. Kenneth Moore. LC 76-636. 1979. pap. text ed. 8.95x (ISBN 0-268-01836-7). U of Notre Dame Pr.

Those of the Street: The Catholic Jews of Mallorca. Kenneth Moore. LC 76-636. 224p. 1977. text ed. 19.95 (ISBN 0-268-01830-8). U of Notre Dame Pr.

Those Other People. Alice Childress. 144p. (gr. 8 up). 1989. 13.95 (ISBN 0-399-21510-7, Putnam). Putnam Pub Group.

Those People: The Subculture of a Housing Project. Colette Petonnet. Tr. by Rita Smidt from Fr. LC 72-825. (Contributions in Sociology: No. 10). 1973. lib. bdg. 35.00 (ISBN 0-8371-6393-5, PTP/). Greenwood.

Those Powerful Years: The South Coast & Los Angeles 1887-1917. Joseph S. O'Flaherty. (Illus.). 1978. 12.00 (ISBN 0-682-49103-9, Lochinvar). Exposition-Phoenix.

Those Preachin' Women. Ed. by Ella P. Mitchell. 128p. 1985. pap. 7.95 (ISBN 0-8170-1073-4). Judson.

Those Preaching Women, Vol 2: (More Sermons by Black Women Preachers) Ed. by Ella P. Mitchell. 112p. 1988. pap. 7.95 (ISBN 0-8170-1131-5). Judson.

Those Proposed by the Central Committee of the Sed for Karl Marx Year 1983. Collets Staff. 40p. 1983. pap. 5.00x (ISBN 0-317-53852-7, Pub. by Collets (UK)). State Mutual Bk.

Those Puzzling Parables. Jack B. Scott. (Orig.). 1987. pap. text ed. 5.95 (ISBN 0-934688-27-3); leader's guide 3.95 (ISBN 0-934688-28-1). Great Comm Pubns.

Those Radio Commentators! Irving E. Fang. (Illus.). 1977. 14.95x (ISBN 0-8138-1500-2); 2 records incl. Iowa St U Pr.

Those Six-Gun Heroes: Twenty-Five Great Movie Cowboys. Douglas E. Nye. LC 82-8338. (Illus.). 152p. (Orig.). 1982. pap. 11.95 (ISBN 0-943274-01-X). SC Ed Comm Inc.

Those Southern Milners: A Collection of Record Abstracts for the Southern States Between 1606 & 1850 with Biographical & Historical Sketches, Family Records, & Genealogies up to 1900. Virginia S. Hershey. (Illus.). 426p. 1980. 40.00x (ISBN 0-9605320-0-5, TX-578-128). Hershey.

Those Strange Louisiana Names. Codman Parkerson. 1969. pap. 1.50 (ISBN 0-685-08223-7). Claitors.

Those Strenuous Dames of the Colorado Prairie. Nell Propst. LC 82-12304. (Illus.). 1982. 18.95 (ISBN 0-87108-627-1). Pruett.

Those Summer Girls I Never Met. Richard Peck. Date not set. price not set. Delacorte.

Those Superstitions. Charles Igglesden. LC 73-12798. 237p. 1974. Repr. of 1932 ed. 40.00x (ISBN 0-8103-3621-9). Gale.

Those Swinging Years: Autobiography of Luise King Rey. Luise K. Rey. LC 83-61978. (Illus.). 1983. 10.95 (ISBN 0-913420-23-9); pap. 8.95 (ISBN 0-913420-24-7). Olympus Pub Co.

Those Swinging Years: The Autobiography of Charlie Barnet. Charlie Barnet & Stanley Dance. LC 83-14923. (Illus.). 226p. 1984. 19.95 (ISBN 0-8071-1128-7). La State U Pr.

Those Ten Months: President's Rule in Gujrat. Narayan Shriman. 1973. 9.00 (ISBN 0-686-20319-4). Intl Bk Dist.

Those Terrible Carpetbaggers. Richard N. Current. (Illus.). 494p. 1988. 24.95 (ISBN 0-19-504872-5). Oxford U Pr.

Those Terrible Terwilliger Twins. Marilyn J. Walton. LC 84-17732. (Family Bks.). (Illus.). 32p. (ps-3). 1985. PLB 14.65 (ISBN 0-940742-39-X). Raintree Pubs.

Those Terrible Toy-Breakers. David McPhail. LC 80-10450. (Illus.). 48p. (ps-3). 1980. 5.95 (ISBN 0-686-86574-X); PLB 5.95 (ISBN 0-686-91535-6). Parents.

Those Terrible Toy-Breakers. David McPhail. (Read Aloud Bks.). (Illus.). 48p. (ps-2). 1988. pap. 2.95 (ISBN 0-517-56851-9). Crown.

Those That Won't Break. Mark Delk. 560p. 1987. 19.95 (ISBN 0-8062-3171-8). Carlton.

Those Times & These. Irvin S. Cobb. LC 72-5862. (Short Story Index Reprint Ser). Repr. of 1917 ed. 21.00 (ISBN 0-8369-4201-9). Ayer Co Pubs.

Those Tremendous Mountains: The Story of the Lewis & Clark Expeditions. David F. Hawke. (Illus.). 288p. 1985. pap. 7.95 (ISBN 0-393-30289-X). Norton.

Those Warm, Fuzzy Cleveland Kids. 2nd ed. Dave Cockley. 32p. 1986. pap. 2.95 (ISBN 0-86551-015-6). Corinthian.

Those Were the Days: Landmarks of Old Goleta. Gary B. Coombs et al. LC 86-81698. (Illus.). 1986. 15.00x (ISBN 0-911773-08-8); pap. 8.50x (ISBN 0-911773-09-6). Inst Am Res.

Those Were the Nights. James Agate. LC 77-91890. Repr. of 1947 ed. 18.00 (ISBN 0-405-08196-0, Pub. by Blom). Ayer Co Pubs.

Those Who Blink. William Mills. LC 85-24160. 176p. 1986. 14.95 (ISBN 0-8071-1270-4). La State U Pr.

Those Who Came Before: Southwestern Archeology in the National Park System. 2nd ed. Robert H. Lister & Florence C. Lister. Ed. by Rose Houk et al. LC 83-60100. 184p. 1983. pap. 12.95 (ISBN 0-911408-62-2). SW Pks Mnmts.

Those Who Came Before: Southwestern Archeology in the National Park System. Robert H. Lister & Florence C. Lister. LC 83-60100. (Illus.). 184p. 1984. 37.50 (ISBN 0-8165-0851-8). U of Ariz Pr.

Those Who Can, Teach. 4th ed. Kevin Ryan & James M. Cooper. LC 83-82566. 480p. 1983. text ed. 28.95 (ISBN 0-395-34257-0); instr's manual 2.00 (ISBN 0-395-34258-9). HM.

Those Who Can, Teach. 5th ed. Kevin Ryan & James M. Cooper. LC 87-80431. 496p. 1988. text ed. 34.76 (ISBN 0-395-35808-6); instr's manual with test items 2.36 (ISBN 0-395-44724-0). HM.

Those Who Fall. John Muirhead. LC 86-5411. (Illus.). 291p. 1987. 18.95 (ISBN 0-394-54983-X). Random.

Those Who Fall. John Muirhead. 304p. 1988. pap. 4.50 (ISBN 0-671-64944-2). PB.

Those Who Go Against the Current. Shirley Seifert. 1976. Repr. of 1943 ed. lib. bdg. 11.95 (ISBN 0-89190-141-8, Pub. by River City Pr). Amereon Ltd.

Those Who Have Vanished. Ronald L. Wallace. 541p. 1983. 25.00x (ISBN 0-256-06735-X). Dorsey.

Those Who Hunt the Night. Barbara Hambly. LC 88-47803. 304p. 1988. 16.95 (ISBN 0-345-34380-8, Del Rey Bks). Ballantine.

Those Who Love: Biographical Novel of Abigail & John Adams. Irving Stone. LC 65-19900. 1965. 15.95 (ISBN 0-385-00157-6). Doubleday.

Those Who Move with God. Elbert Willis. 1977. 1.25 (ISBN 0-89858-006-4). Fill the Gap.

Those Who Perish. Edward Dahlberg. LC 75-41070. Repr. of 1934 ed. 15.00 (ISBN 0-404-14528-0). AMS Pr.

Those Who Ponder Proverbs: Aphoristic Thinking & Biblical Literature. James G. Williams. (Bible & Literature Ser.: No. 2). text ed. 24.05 (ISBN 0-907459-02-1, Pub. by Almond Pr England); pap. text ed. 10.95x (ISBN 0-907459-03-X, Pub. by Almond Pr England). Eisenbrauns.

Those Who Remain. Charles R. Taylor. (Illus.). 104p. (Orig.). 1980. pap. 2.95 (ISBN 0-937682-02-0). Today Bible.

Those Who Ride the Night Winds. Nikki Giovanni. LC 82-20811. 121p. 1983. 9.95 (ISBN 0-688-01906-4). Morrow.

Those Who Ride the Night Winds. Nikki Giovanni. 64p. (Orig.). 1984. pap. 5.70 (ISBN 0-688-02653-2, Quill NY). Morrow.

Those Who Saw Her: The Apparitions of Mary. Catherine M. Odell. LC 85-63143. 200p. (Orig.). 1986. pap. 6.95 (ISBN 0-87973-720-4, 720). Our Sunday Visitor.

Those Who Served. Twentieth Century Fund of Task Force on Policies Toward Veterans. Ed. by M. K. Taussig. 1974. pap. 10.00 (ISBN 0-527-02854-1). Kraus Repr.

Those Who Stayed Behind: Rural Society in Nineteenth-Century New England. Hal S. Barron. LC 83-26354. (Illus.). 212p. 1984. 29.95 (ISBN 0-521-25784-0). Cambridge U Pr.

Those Who Stayed Behind: Rural Society in Nineteenth Century New England. Hal S. Barron. (Interdisciplinary Perspectives on Modern History Ser.). (Illus.). 192p. 1988. pap. 8.95 (ISBN 0-521-34777-7). Cambridge U Pr.

Those Who Trespass. Dan Masterson. LC 84-28075. 80p. 1985. pap. 5.95 (ISBN 0-938626-43-4). U of Ark Pr.
Those Who Walk Away. Patricia Highsmith. Ed. by Gary Fisketjon. 240p. 1988. pap. 7.95 (ISBN 0-87113-259-1). Atlantic Monthly.
Those Who Watch. Robert Silverberg. 144p. 1987. pap. 2.95 (ISBN 0-451-15019-8, Sig). NAL.
Those Who Were There: Eyewitness Accounts of the War in Southeast Asia, 1956-1975, & Aftermath; Annotated Bibliography of Books, Articles, & Topic-Related Magazines, Covering Writings Both Factual & Imaginative. Ed. by Merritt Clifton et al. LC 83-25434. (American Dust Ser.: No. 15). 297p. 1984. 12.95 (ISBN 0-913218-97-9). Dustbooks.
Those Who Won't & Those Who Will. Darlene Loomis. (Illus.). 12p. (Orig.). 1977. pap. 1.00 (ISBN 0-686-36278-0). Drain Enterprise.
Those Whose Names Were Terrible. Carole Marsh. (Lost Colony Collection). (Illus.). 75p. (Orig.). (gr. 4-8). 1983. pap. 7.95 (ISBN 0-935326-48-0). Gallopade Pub Group.
Those Women. Nor Hall. LC 88-4676. 96p. (Orig.). 1988. pap. 12.50 (ISBN 0-88214-333-6). Spring Pubns.
Those Wonderful Unauthorized Accessories for Model A Ford. Ed. by Murray Fahnestock. LC 73-164930. (Illus.). 256p. 1971. pap. 12.95 (ISBN 0-911160-27-2). Post-Era.
Those Wonderful Years. Harry A. Reed. 1987. 15.95 (ISBN 0-533-06994-7). Vantage.
Those Words! Sally Jordan. (Weathering Storms Ser.). (Illus.). 32p. (gr. 5-9). 1986. saddle stitch 0.79 (ISBN 0-87403-042-0, 3540). Standard Pub.
Thoth Deck. Aleister Crowley. 12.00 (ISBN 0-685-47277-9). Weiser.
Thoth System: Multi-Process Structuring & Probability. David R. Cheriton. (Operating & Programming Systems Ser.: Vol. 8). 191p. 1982. 62.75 (ISBN 0-444-00701-6, North-Holland). Elsevier.
Thoth: The Hermes of Egypt. P. Boylan. 215p. 1979. 12.50 (ISBN 0-89005-280-8). Ares.
Thou Art Consecrated Unto Me. Stavsky. 1.50 (ISBN 0-87306-101-2). Feldheim.
Thou Art the Vine. Heini Arnold. 36p. 1985. pap. 1.50 (ISBN 0-87486-178-0). Plough.
Thou Dost Open up My Life. Rufus M. Jones. LC 63-11819. (Orig.). 1963. pap. 2.50x (ISBN 0-87574-127-4). Pendle Hill.
Thou Givest...They Gather. Amy Carmichael. 1970. pap. 3.95 (ISBN 0-87508-083-9). Chr Lit.
Thou Shalt Call His Name. (Illus.). 102p. 1975. pap. 2.50 (ISBN 0-915952-00-9). Lord's Line.
Thou Shalt Not Be Aware: Psychoanalysis & Society's Betrayal of the Child. Alice Miller. Tr. by Hunter Hannum & Hildegarde Hannum. 320p. 1984. 16.95 (ISBN 0-374-27646-3). FS&G.
Thou Shalt Not Be Aware! Society's Betrayal of the Child. Alice Miller. 1986. pap. 8.95 (ISBN 0-452-00801-8, Mer). NAL.
Thou Shalt Not Be Aware: Society's Betrayal of the Child. Alice Miller. LC 85-32084. 336p. 1988. pap. 9.95 (ISBN 0-452-00929-4, Mer). NAL.
Thou Shalt Not Kill. Robert W. Meals. LC 84-90002. 131p. 1985. 10.00 (ISBN 0-533-06098-2). Vantage.
Thou Shalt Not Kill. Antoine Reboul. Tr. by Stephanie Craig. LC 77-77312. Orig. Title: Tu Ne Tueras Point. (gr. 5-8). 1969. 14.95 (ISBN 0-87599-161-0). S G Phillips.
Thou Shalt Remember: Lessons of a Lifetime. Hannah Hurnard. LC 87-46212. 176p. (Orig.). 1988. pap. 8.95 (ISBN 0-06-064094-4, RD-737, HarpR). Har-Row.
Thou Shalt Worship the Lord Thy God. Andy T. Ritchie, Jr. 1969. 5.95 (ISBN 0-88027-021-7). Firm Foun Pub.
Thou Shell of Death. Nicholas Blake. 1977. pap. 1.95i (ISBN 0-06-080428-9, P428, PL). Har-Row.
Thou When Thou Prayest. 2nd ed. William O. Carver. 1987. 5.95 (ISBN 0-8054-6946-X). Broadman.
Though Hearts Resist. Meg Hudson. (Superromance Ser.). 295p. 1983. pap. 2.95 (ISBN 0-373-70064-4, Pub. by Worldwide). Harlequin Bks.
Though I Be Crushed. LC 85-61194. 130p. 1985. pap. 9.95 (ISBN 0-912624-04-3). Nembutsu Pr.
Though We Are Apart, Love Unites Us. Ed. by Susan P. Schutz. (Illus.). 64p. (Orig.). 1985. pap. 4.95 (ISBN 0-88396-235-7). Blue Mtn Pr CO.
Thought. Gilbert H. Harman. LC 72-4044. 232p. 1973. 28.00x (ISBN 0-691-07188-8); pap. 11.95x (ISBN 0-691-01986-X). Princeton U Pr.
Thought. Julian J. Joyce. 106p. (Orig.). 1987. pap. 5.00 (ISBN 0-944851-00-2). Earth Star.
Thought-A-Week Guide to a Better Relationship. Judith Saly. 1987. pap. 2.95 (ISBN 0-345-33340-3). Ballantine.
Thought-A-Week Guide to Better Parenting. Hope Holiner & Arlene Shulman. (Orig.). 1987. pap. 2.95 (ISBN 0-345-33338-1). Ballantine.
Thought-A-Week Guide to Living with Your Teenager. Jack Clark. (Orig.). 1987. pap. 2.95 (ISBN 0-345-33345-4). Ballantine.
Thought, Action, & Passion. Richard McKeon. LC 54-9579. (Midway Reprint Ser). x, 305p. 1974. pap. 16.00x (ISBN 0-226-56031-7). U of Chicago Pr.
Thought & Action. Stuart Hampshire. LC 83-6559. 304p. 1983. text ed. 24.95x (ISBN 0-268-01846-4); pap. text ed. 10.95 (ISBN 0-268-01847-2). U of Notre Dame Pr.
Thought & Character of William James, 2 vols. Ralph B. Perry. LC 74-5778. (Illus.). 1974. Repr. of 1935 ed. Greenwood.
Thought & Character: The Rhetoric of Democratic Education. Frederick J. Antczak. 242p. 1985. text ed. 27.50x (ISBN 0-8138-1781-1). Iowa St U Pr.
Thought & Choice in Chess. 2nd ed. Adriaan D. De Groot. (Psychological Studies: No. 4). 1978. text ed. 33.60x (ISBN 0-686-27037-1). Mouton.
Thought & Emotion: Developmental Perspectives. Ed. by David J. Bearison & Herbert Zimiles. (Jean Paget Society Ser.). 256p. 1985. text ed. 29.95 (ISBN 0-89859-530-4). L Erlbaum Assocs.
Thought & Experience. Peter H. Hess. 220p. Date not set. text ed. 25.00x (ISBN 0-8020-5788-8). U of Toronto Pr.
Thought & Knowledge: An Introduction to Critical Thinking. Diane F. Halpern. 424p. 1984. 39.95 (ISBN 0-89859-381-6); pap. text ed. 19.95 (ISBN 0-89859-514-2). L Erlbaum Assocs.
Thought & Knowledge: Essays. Norman Malcolm. LC 76-25647. 208p. 1977. 28.50x (ISBN 0-8014-1074-6). Cornell U Pr.
Thought & Language. Philip B. Ballard. 1973. Repr. of 1934 ed. 14.50 (ISBN 0-8274-1291-6). R West.
Thought & Language. rev. ed. Lev S. Vygotsky. Ed. by Alexey Kozulin. 256p. 1986. text ed. 27.50x (ISBN 0-262-22029-6); pap. text ed. 9.95 (ISBN 0-262-72010-8). MIT Pr.
Thought & Language - Language & Reading. Ed. by Maryanne Wolf et al. (Reprint Ser.: No. 14). 732p. 1980. 14.95x (ISBN 0-916690-15-6). Harvard Educ Rev.
Thought & Letters in Western Europe, A.D. 500 to 900. 2nd ed. Max L. Laistner & H. H. King. (Paperback Ser.). 416p. 1966. pap. 12.95x (ISBN 0-8014-9037-5). Cornell U Pr.
Thought & Letters in Western Europe, A. D. 500-900. Max Laistner. 59.95 (ISBN 0-8490-1207-4). Gordon Pr.
Thought & Nature: Studies in Rationalist Philosophy. Arthur W. Collins. LC 84-4023. 272p. 1985. text ed. 24.95 (ISBN 0-268-01856-1). U of Notre Dame Pr.
Thought & Nature: Studies in Rationalist Philosophy. Arthur W. Collins. LC 84-40823. 256p. 1986. pap. 10.95 (ISBN 0-268-01857-X). U of Notre Dame Pr.
Thought & Object: Essays on Intentionality. Andrew Woodfield. 1982. 37.50x (ISBN 0-19-824606-4); pap. 13.95x (ISBN 0-19-824677-3). Oxford U Pr.
Thought & Place: The Architecture of Eternal Places in the Philosophy of Giambattista Vico. Donald Kunze. (Emory Vico Studies: Vol. 2). 235p. 1987. text ed. 39.50 (ISBN 0-8204-0477-2). P Lang Pubs.
Thought & Reality in Hegel's System. Gustavus W. Cunningham. LC 83-48505. (Philosophy of Hegel Ser.). 151p. 1984. lib. bdg. 25.00 (ISBN 0-8240-5628-0). Garland Pub.
Thought & Reference. Kent Bach. 320p. 1988. 59.00 (ISBN 0-19-824983-7). Oxford U Pr.
Thought & Style in the Works of Leon Bloy. Sr. M. Rosalie Brady. LC 70-94176. (Catholic Universtiy of America Studies in Romance Languages & Literatures Ser: No. 30). Repr. of 1945 ed. 19.00 (ISBN 0-404-50330-6). AMS Pr.
Thought & the Brain. Henri Pieron. LC 73-2981. (Classics in Psychology Ser.). Repr. of 1927 ed. 23.50 (ISBN 0-405-05153-0). Ayer Co Pubs.
Thought & Things: A Study of the Development & Meaning of Thought or Genetic Logic, 3 vols. James M. Baldwin. LC 75-3029. (Philosopy in America Ser.). Repr. of 1911 ed. 97.00 set (ISBN 0-404-59025-X). AMS Pr.
Thought & Things: Study of the Development & Meaning of Thought or Genetic Logic, 4 vols. in 2. James M. Baldwin. LC 74-21397. (Classics in Child Development Ser). 1975. Repr. 94.00x (ISBN 0-405-06451-9). Ayer Co Pubs.
Thought & Vision: A Critical Reading of H. D.'s Poetry. Angela DiPace Fritz. LC 87-13173. 1988. 34.95x (ISBN 0-8132-0642-1). Cath U Pr.
Thought & Wisdom. C. West Churchman. (Systems Inquiry Ser.). 150p. 1982. pap. text ed. 10.95x (ISBN 0-914105-03-5). Intersystems Pubns.
Thought As Energy: Exploring the Spiritual Nature of Man. Ed. by Willis H. Kinnear. (Illus.). 92p. 1975. pap. 4.50 (ISBN 0-911336-62-1). Sci of Mind.
Thought Brigade. Roger W. Stuart. 1963. 10.95 (ISBN 0-8392-1118-X). Astor-Honor.
Thought, Consciousness, & Reality: Psychiatry & the Humanities, Vol. 2. Ed. by Joseph H. Smith. LC 77-77350. 1977. 40.00x (ISBN 0-300-02138-0). Yale U Pr.
Thought Control & Technological Slavery in America. (Analysis Ser.: No. 1). 1982. pap. 10.00 (ISBN 0-686-42834-X). Inst Analysis.
Thought Control & Technological Slavery in America: Illustration & Selected Correspondence. (Analysis Ser.). 75p. 1983. pap. 20.00 (ISBN 0-686-42852-8). Inst Analysis.
Thought Control in America: A New Technology Analysis. Charles W. Lachenmeyer. 140p. 1982. pap. 10.00 (ISBN 0-938526-04-9). Inst Analysis.
Thought Control in Prewar Japan. Richard H. Mitchell. LC 75-39566. 240p. 1976. 28.50x (ISBN 0-8014-1002-9). Cornell U Pr.
Thought Control in the U. S. A. Hollywood Arts Science & Professions Council. Ed. by Bruce S. Kupelnick. LC 76-52131. (Classics of Film Literature Ser.). 1978. lib. bdg. 31.00 (ISBN 0-8240-2895-3). Garland Pub.
Thought Dial. Sydney Omar. pap. 4.00 (ISBN 0-87980-164-6). Wilshire.
Thought, Fact, & Reference: The Origins & Ontology of Logical Atomism. Herbert Hochberg. 1978. 29.50x (ISBN 0-8166-0867-9). U of Minn Pr.
Thought for Rosh Hashonoh. C. B. Chavel. 64p. 1980. pap. 3.50 (ISBN 0-88328-029-9). Shilo Pub Hse.
Thought for the Day. M. K. Gandhi. 595p. 1982. 24.95. Asia Bk Corp.
Thought for Yom Kippur. C. B. Chavel. 64p. 1980. pap. 3.50 (ISBN 0-88328-028-0). Shilo Pub Hse.
Thought Forces. Prentice Mulford. 172p. 1984. pap. 9.50 (ISBN 0-89540-144-4, SB-144). Sun Pub.
Thought Forms. Besant & Leadbeater. 8.75 (ISBN 0-8356-7187-9). Theos Pub Hse.
Thought Forms. abr. ed. Annie Besant & Charles W. Leadbeater. (Illus.). 1969. pap. 5.50 (ISBN 0-8356-0008-4, Quest). Theos Pub Hse.
Thought Forms. Frank Chilcote. 1987. write for info. Scriptorium Pr.
Thought I Heard a Baby Cry. Don Gates. LC 83-820226. 54p. 1983. pap. 4.25 (ISBN 0-940248-13-1). Guild Pr.
Thought Images. rev. ed. Frank Chilcote. Ed. by Margery Weierbach. 50p. 1987. pap. 7.95 (ISBN 0-931485-23-1). Scriptorium Pr.
Thought in the Young Child. Ed. by W. Kessen & Clementina Kuhlmann. (SRCD M). 1962. 20.00 (ISBN 0-527-01593-8). Kraus Repr.
Thought into Speech: The Psychology of a Language. James Deese. (Century Psychology Ser.). (Illus.). 160p. 1984. text ed. 30.00 (ISBN 0-13-919944-6). P-H.
Thought Objects. Barbara Ess. (Illus.). 142p. 1987. pap. 12.00 (ISBN 0-939784-17-3). CEPA Gall.
Thought Objects: Just Another Asshole No. 7. Ed. by Barbara Ess & Glenn Branca. 11.95 (ISBN 0-317-59114-2). Just Another.
Thought of Chang Tsai. Ira E. Kasoff. (Cambridge Studies in Chinese History Literature, & Institutions). 250p. 1984. 62.50 (ISBN 0-521-25549-X). Cambridge U Pr.
Thought of Gregory the Great. G. R. Evans. (Cambridge Studies in Medieval Life & Thought: Fourth Series: No. 2). 160p. 1986. 42.50 (ISBN 0-521-30904-2). Cambridge U Pr.
Thought of Gregory the Great. G. R. Evans. 175p. Date not set. pap. 10.95 (ISBN 0-521-36826-X). Cambridge U Pr.
Thought of Jacques Ellul: A Systematic Exposition. Darrell J. Fasching. LC 81-22529. (Toronto Studies in Theology: Vol. 7). 272p. 1982. lib. bdg. 49.95x (ISBN 0-88946-961-X). E Mellen.
Thought of John Austin: Jurisprudence, Colonial Reform, & the British Constitution. Wilfrid E. Rumble. LC 84-28302. 278p. 1985. 40.00 (ISBN 0-485-11292-2, Pub. by Athlone Pr UK). Humanities.
Thought of Mao Tse-Tung. Stuart R. Schram. (Contemporary China Institute Publications). 275p. Date not set. price not set (ISBN 0-521-32549-8); pap. 12.95 (ISBN 0-521-31062-8). Cambridge U Pr.
Thought of Paul Tillich. Ed. by James L. Adams et al. 1985. 24.45 (ISBN 0-06-060072-1). Har-Row.
Thought of the Evangelical Leaders: John Newton, Thomas Scott, Charles Simeon, Etc. Ed. by Josiah Pratt. 1978. 23.95 (ISBN 0-85151-270-4). Banner of Truth.
Thought of the Heart. James Hillman. LC 84-5462. (Eranos Lectures: No. 2). 50p. (Orig.). 1981. pap. 8.00 (ISBN 0-88214-402-2). Spring Pubns.
Thought Patterns in Poetry & Prose. Kathryn G. Hansen. (Illus.). 37p. 1986. pap. 3.75 (ISBN 0-318-19334-5). K Hansen.
Thought Power. Besant. 4.95 (ISBN 0-8356-7460-6). Theos Pub Hse.
Thought Power: Its Control & Culture. Annie Besant. LC 73-7644. 1967. pap. 3.50 (ISBN 0-8356-0312-1, Quest). Theos Pub Hse.
Thought Probes: Philosophy Through Science Fiction. Ed. by Fred D. Miller & Nicholas D. Smith. (Illus.). 368p. 1981. text ed. write for info. (ISBN 0-13-920041-X). P-H.
Thought-Processing. Felton J. Koch. 1988. 13.95 (ISBN 0-533-07592-0). Vantage.
Thought-Reader's Thoughts: Being the Impressions & Confessions of Stuart Cumberland. Stuart Cumberland. LC 75-7373. (Perspectives in Psychical Research Ser.). 1975. Repr. of 1888 ed. 25.50x (ISBN 0-405-07024-1). Ayer Co Pubs.
Thought Reform of the Chinese Intellectuals. Theodore H. Chen, pseud. LC 78-2821. 247p. 1984. Repr. of 1960 ed. 23.00 (ISBN 0-8305-0001-4). Hyperion Conn.
Thought Starters. Richard C. Anderson. (Illus.). 105p. 12.95 (ISBN 0-913842-04-4). Correlan Pubns.
Thought Structure of Romans with Special Reference to Chapter Six. Bruce N. Kaye. 203p. (Orig.). 1979. pap. 5.95 (ISBN 0-931016-03-7). Schola Pr TX.
Thought to be Rehearsed: Aphorism in Wallace Stevens's Poetry. Beverly Coyle. Ed. by A. Walton Litz. LC 83-5778. (Studies in Modern Literature: No. 9). 130p. 1983. 37.95 (ISBN 0-8357-1414-4). UMI Res Pr.
Thought Tracking Level 1: Simple Phrases. Reusable ed. Kitty Wehrli. (gr. 2). 1976. wkbk. 6.50 (ISBN 0-89039-186-6). Ann Arbor FL.
Thought Tracking Level 2: Sequential Phrases. Reusable ed. Kitty Wehrli. (gr. 2). wkbk. 6.50 (ISBN 0-89039-188-2). Ann Arbor FL.
Thought Tracking Level 3: Simple Sentences. Reusable ed. Kitty Wehrli. (gr. 2). 1976. wkbk. 6.50 (ISBN 0-89039-190-4). Ann Arbor FL.
Thought Tracking Level 4: Questions & Answers. Reusable ed. Kitty Wehrli. (gr. 2 up). 1976. wkbk. 6.50 (ISBN 0-89039-192-0). Ann Arbor FL.
Thought Transference. Edmund Shaftesbury. 20.50x (ISBN 0-685-22141-5). Wehman.
Thought Vibrations: The Amazing Law of Mentalism. A. Victor Segno. 208p. 1973. pap. 6.95 (ISBN 0-87877-020-8, G-20). Newcastle Pub.
Thought Without Language. Ed. by L. Weiskrantz. (Illus.). 450p. 1988. 80.00 (ISBN 0-19-852180-4); pap. 49.95 (ISBN 0-19-852177-4). Oxford U pr.
Thought You'd Never Ask. Bob Collins. 226p. 1984. pap. 6.95 (ISBN 0-89651-782-9). B L Pub.
Thoughtful Faith: Essays on Belief by Mormon Scholars. Ed. by Philip L. Barlow. LC 86-71882. 275p. 1986. 14.95 (ISBN 0-939651-00-9). Canon Pr.
Thoughtful Roads. Darrin S. Bush. 1979. 7.95 (ISBN 0-87881-084-6). Mojave Bks.
Thoughtology. Thomas A. Hughes. (Illus.). 32p. (Orig.). 1985. pap. 2.35 (ISBN 0-9614866-0-0, 866-0). TA Hughes Pubns.
Thoughts. James Alberione. 1973. 3.00 (ISBN 0-8198-0332-4). Dghtrs St Paul.
Thoughts. Billie Hill. 32p. 1986. 5.95 (ISBN 0-89962-547-9). Todd & Honeywell.
Thoughts-a-Fleeting. W. Kacy. LC 84-90051. 43p. 1985. 6.95 (ISBN 0-533-06131-8). Vantage.
Thoughts about Architecture. J. B. Bakema. Ed. by Marianne Grey. (Academy Architecture Ser.). (Illus.). 160p. 1982. pap. 14.95 (ISBN 0-312-80190-4). St Martin.
Thoughts about Children. Johann C. Blumhardt & Christopher F. Blumhardt. Tr. by Hutterian Society of Brothers. LC 79-24844. 77p. 1980. pap. 3.50 (ISBN 0-87486-224-8). Plough.
Thoughts among the Ruins: Collected Essays on Europe & Beyond. George Lichtheim. 524p. 1986. pap. 24.95 (ISBN 0-88738-657-1). Transaction Bks.
Thoughts: An Essay on Content. Christopher Peacocke. (Aristotelian Society Ser.). 200p. 1986. text ed. 24.95x (ISBN 0-631-14674-1). Basil Blackwell.
Thoughts & Aphorisms. Sri Aurobindo. 1979. pap. 6.00 (ISBN 0-89744-927-4). Auromere.
Thoughts & Feelings from the Heart. Joseph M. Archie. 1987. 6.95 (ISBN 0-533-06989-0). Vantage.
Thoughts & Feelings: The Art of Cognitive Stress Intervention. Matthew McKay et al. 224p. 1981. 22.50 (ISBN 0-934986-09-6); pap. 12.50 (ISBN 0-934986-03-7). New Harbinger.
Thoughts & Glimpses. Sri Aurobindo. 30p. 1973. pap. 1.00 (ISBN 0-89071-308-1, Pub. by Sri Aurobindo Ashram India). Aurobindo Assn.
Thoughts & Meditations. Kahlil Gibran. Tr. by Anthony R. Ferris. 128p. 1984. pap. 3.95 (ISBN 0-8065-0916-3, 240, Pub. by Citadel Pr). Lyle Stuart.
Thoughts & Reflections for a Busy Christian. Mary J. Marshall. (Illus.). 88p. (Orig.). 1987. pap. 3.95 (ISBN 0-914544-68-3). Living Flame Pr.
Thoughts & Sayings of St. Margaret Mary. St. Margaret Mary Alacoque. LC 86-50852. 109p. 1986. pap. 2.50 (ISBN 0-89555-302-3). TAN Bks Pubs.
Thoughts & Their Subjects: A Study of Wittgenstein's Tractatus. H. Kannisto. (Acta Philosophica Fennica Ser.: Vol. No. 40). 184p. (Orig.). 1986. pap. 24.00x. Coronet Bks.
Thoughts & Things. Matanah. Ed. by Delores F. Ridge. LC 76-29534. 58p. (Orig.). 1976. pap. text ed. 4.00 (ISBN 0-9600978-2-1). Knees Pbk.
Thoughts & Thinkers. Anthony Quinton. 350p. 1982. 54.50 (ISBN 0-8419-0772-2); pap. 29.50 (ISBN 0-8419-0773-0). Holmes & Meier.
Thoughts Are Free: A Quaker Youth in Nazi Germany. Anna S. Halle. LC 85-61843. (Orig.). 1985. pap. 2.50 (ISBN 0-87574-265-3). Pendle Hill.
Thoughts Are Things. Ernest Holmes. Ed. by Willis H. Kinnear. 96p. 1967. pap. 4.50 (ISBN 0-911336-33-8). Sci of Mind.
Thoughts Are Things. Edward Walker. leatherette 3.00 (ISBN 0-911662-18-9). Yoga.
Thoughts: Education for Peace & One World. Irene Taafaki. (Illus.). 336p. 1986. 25.00 (ISBN 0-85398-221-X); pap. text ed. 14.50 (ISBN 0-85398-222-8). G Ronald Pub.
Thoughts for Aspirants. Sri Ram. Series II. 3.95 (ISBN 0-8356-7449-5). Theos Pub Hse.
Thoughts for Aspirants. 7th ed. N. Sri Ram. (Series 2). 1969. 4.25 (ISBN 0-8356-7195-X). Theos Pub Hse.

Th'overthrow of Stage-Players. John Rainoldes et al. LC 70-170414. (English Stage Ser.: Vol. 11). lib. bdg. 61.00 (ISBN 0-8240-0594-5). Garland Pub.

Thracian Art Treasures. Ivan Venedikov & Todor Gerassimov. 388p. 1979. 69.00x (ISBN 0-686-97596-0, Pub. by Collets (UK)). State Mutual Bk.

Thracians. R. F. Hoddinott. LC 80-51906. (Ancient Peoples & Places Ser.). (Illus.). 192p. 1981. 19.95 (ISBN 0-500-02099-X). Thames Hudson.

Thrales of Streatham Park. Mary Hyde. (Illus.). 1977. 24.50x (ISBN 0-674-88746-8). Harvard U Pr.

Thralls of the Dragon's Heart. Elizabeth H. Boyer. 304p. 1982. pap. 3.50 (ISBN 0-345-33749-2, Del Rey). Ballantine.

Thrasherville: An Old Plymouth Settlement. Ellis W. Brewster. (Pilgrim Society Notes Ser.: No. 10). 1960. 2.00 (ISBN 0-940628-40-6). Pilgrim Soc.

Thrasymachus: New Greek Course. C. W. Peckett & A. R. Munday. 344p. 1984. Repr. of 1965 ed. 16.00 (ISBN 0-86292-139-2, Pub. by Bristol Classical UK). Focus Info Gr.

Thread of Ariadne: A Study of Ancient Greek Dress. Elsa Gullberg & Paul Astrom. (Studies in Mediterranean Archaeology Ser.: No. XXI). (Illus.). 1970. pap. text ed. 19.95x (ISBN 91-85058-34-3). Humanities.

Thread of Blue Denim: A Farm Woman's Celebration of Country Living. Patricia P. Leimbach. LC 87-45063. (Illus.). 256p. 1987. pap. 6.95 (ISBN 0-06-097092-8, PL/7092, PL). Har-Row.

Thread of Deceit: Espionage Myths of World War II. Nigel West. LC 84-22346. 1985. 16.45 (ISBN 0-394-53941-9). Random.

Thread of Discourse. 3rd ed. Roy E. Grimes. LC 74-78506. (Janua Linguarum Series Minor: No. 207). 408p. (Orig.). 1984. pap. text ed. 19.95x (ISBN 90-2793-164-X). Mouton.

Thread of Gold, an Anthology of Poetry. Ed. by Eleanor Graham. LC 75-99030. (Granger Index Reprint Ser). 1964. 13.00 (ISBN 0-8369-6104-8). Ayer Co Pubs.

Thread of Life. Richard Wollheim. (William James Lectures Ser.). 304p. 1986. pap. 8.95x (ISBN 0-674-88758-1). Harvard U Pr.

Thread of Life: Symbolism of Miniature Art from Ecuador. Johannes Wilbert. Bd. with Further Exploration of the Rowe Chavin Seriation & Its Implications for North Central Coast Chronology. Peter Roe; Man & a Feline in Mochica Art. Elizabeth P. Benson. (Studies in Pre-Columbian Art & Archaeology: Nos. 12-14). (Illus.). 1974. 20.00x (ISBN 0-88402-061-4). Dumbarton Oaks.

Thread of Life: The Smithsonian Looks at Evolution. Roger Lewin. LC 82-16834. (Illus.). 256p. 1982. 27.50 (ISBN 0-89599-010-5, Dist. by Norton). Smithsonian Bks.

Thread of Love. Robert J. Schlomann. (Illus.). 144p. (Orig.). 1985. pap. 3.95x (ISBN 0-935237-00-3). Rowillan Pub.

Thread Painting. Liz Hubbard. (Illus.). 160p. 1988. 19.95 (ISBN 0-7153-9000-7, Pub. by David & Charles Pub England). Sterling.

Thread That Runs So True. Jesse Stuart. 1958. lib. bdg. 30.00 (ISBN 0-684-15160-X, ScribT); pap. 8.95 (ISBN 0-684-71904-5, ScribT). Scribner.

Thread Winding in the Loom of Eternity: California Poets in the Schools Statewide Anthology, 1987. Eva Poole-Gilson et al. LC 86-71766. 91p. 1987. pap. 6.95 (ISBN 0-939927-03-9). Calif Poets Schls.

Threaded Interpretive Languages. Ronald Loeliger. 272p. 1981. text ed. 27.95 (ISBN 0-07-038360-X, BYTE Bks). McGraw.

Threading My Way: Twenty-Seven Years of Autobiography. Robert D. Owen. LC 67-18582. 1967. Repr. of 1874 ed. 39.50x (ISBN 0-678-00261-4). Kelley.

Threads. Marie Landowska. 64p. 1985. 5.95 (ISBN 0-89015-499-6). Eakin Pr.

Threads: A Tapestry of Self & Career Exploration. 3rd ed. Robert S. Barkhaus & Charles W. Bolyard. 176p. 1985. pap. 11.95 (ISBN 0-8403-3610-1). Kendall-Hunt.

Threads Cable-Strong: William Faulkner's Go Down, Moses. Dirk Kuyk, Jr. LC 81-72030. 192p. 1982. 22.50 (ISBN 0-8387-5037-0). Bucknell U Pr.

Threads of Circumstance. Ruby Dymond. 206p. 1987. 23.00x (ISBN 0-7212-0733-2, Pub. by Regency Pr). State Mutual Bk.

Threads of Fate: A Collection of Short Stories. Jacob Sallo. 160p. 1988. 9.95 (ISBN 0-8059-3140-6). Dorrance.

Threads of History: Americana Recorded on Cloth, 1775 to the Present. Herbert R. Collins. LC 79-16166. (Illus.). 566p. 1979. 65.00x (ISBN 0-87474-326-5, COTH). Smithsonian.

Threads of Light. David Kherdian. (Farm Poems: Bks. III & IV). (Illus.). 76p. 1985. 10.00 (ISBN 0-89756-014-0). Two Rivers.

Threads of Public Policy: A Study in Political Leadership. Robert Eyestone. 216p. pap. text ed. 14.95x (ISBN 0-8290-0325-8). Irvington.

Threads of Time. Gregory Benford et al. 16.95 (ISBN 0-88411-847-9, Pub. by Aeonian Pr). Amereon Ltd.

Threads of Tradition & Culture along the Gulf Coast (1986) Ed. by Ronald V. Evans. (Gulf Coast History & Humanities Conference Publications Ser.: Vol. X). Date not set. text ed. 15.00 (ISBN 0-940836-18-1). U of W Fla.

Threads That Bind the Heart. Glenna Luschei & William K. Murphy. 1987. Handoriented artist bk. 50.00 (ISBN 0-318-22920-X). Solo Pr.

Threat from Within: Unethical Politics & Politicians. Michael Kronenwetter. (Illus.). 128p. (gr. 7-12). 1986. PLB 11.40 (ISBN 0-531-10252-1). Watts.

Threat: Inside the Soviet Military Machine. Andrew Cockborn. 333p. 1983. 16.45 (ISBN 0-394-52402-0). Random.

Threat: Inside the Soviet Military Machine. Andrew Cockburn. 1984. pap. 4.95 (ISBN 0-394-72379-1, Vin). Random.

Threat of False Doctrine. Gerald F. Mundfrom. (Orig.). 1988. pap. 5.00x (ISBN 0-9615494-2-4). Mercy & Truth.

Threat of Falsehood: A Study in Jeremiah. Thomas Overholt. LC 71-131589. (Studies in Biblical Theology, 2nd Ser: No. 16). pap. 10.00x (ISBN 0-8401-3066-X). A R Allenson.

Threat of Impending Disaster: Contributions to the Psychology of Stress. Ed. by George H. Grosser et al. 1965. pap. 6.95x (ISBN 0-262-57027-0). MIT Pr.

Threat of International Chaos. Francis Neilson. 1979. lib. bdg. 39.95 (ISBN 0-685-96641-0). Revisionist Pr.

Threat of International Terrorism. Contrib. by Dacor Bacon House Staff. 500p. 1988. lib. bdg. price not set (ISBN 0-379-20787-7). Oceana.

Threat of Modern Warfare to Man & His Environment: An Annotated Bibliography Prepared Under the Auspices of the International Peace Research Association (IPRA) (Reports & Papers in the Social Sciences: No. 40). 25p. 1979. pap. 5.00 (ISBN 92-3-101608-3, U927, UNESCO). UNIPUB.

Threat of Peace: James F. Byrnes & the Council of Foreign Ministers, 1945-46. Patricia D. Ward. LC 79-88604. 237p. 1979. 15.50x (ISBN 0-87338-233-1). Kent St U Pr.

Threat of Soviet Imperialism. Ed. by Charles G. Haines. LC 70-122866. (Essay & General Literature Index Reprint Ser). 1971. Repr. of 1954 ed. 32.00x (ISBN 0-8046-1409-1, Pub by Kennikat). Assoc Faculty Pr.

Threat of Terrorism: Combating Political Violence in Europe. Ed. by Juliet Lodge. 256p. 1987. 33.50 (ISBN 0-8133-0642-6). Westview.

Threat of the Pirate Ship. Kate Chambers. (Diana Winthrop Ser.: No. 6). 1984. pap. 2.25 (ISBN 0-451-13066-9, Sig Vista). NAL.

Threat Perception in International Crisis. Raymond Cohen. LC 79-3964. 214p. 1979. 29.50x (ISBN 0-299-08000-5). U of Wis Pr.

Threat to Development: Pitfalls of the NIE. William Loehr & John P. Powelson. LC 82-4777. (Special Study in Social, Political, & Economic Developmen). 170p. 1982. pap. text ed. 16.95x (ISBN 0-86531-129-3). Westview.

Threat to Genesis. Rudolf Wittenberg. LC 76-15750. (Living Poets' Library Ser.). 1976. pap. 3.50 (ISBN 0-686-17002-4). Dragons Teeth.

Threatened & Endangered Plants & Animals of Maryland. Ed. by Arnold W. Norden et al. (Maryland Natural Heritage Program Special Publication Ser.). 475p. 1984. pap. 13.00 (ISBN 0-317-30118-7). MD Dept Natural Res.

Threatened Birds of Africa & Related Islands. N. J. Collar & S. N. Stuart. (Illus.). 797p. Date not set. text ed. 63.00 (ISBN 2-88032-604-4). Princeton U Pr.

Threatened Identities. Ed. by Glynis M. Breakwell. LC 82-8451. 269p. 1983. 63.95x (ISBN 0-471-10233-4, Pub. by Wiley-Interscience). Wiley.

Threatened with Resurrection: Amenazado de Resurreccion. Julia Esquivel. 128p. (Eng. & Span.). 1982. pap. 5.95 (ISBN 0-87178-844-6). Brethren.

Threatening Youth: State Policy & the Containment of the Young. Bernard Davies. LC 86-12588. 192p. 1986. 59.00x (ISBN 0-335-15392-5, Open Univ Pr); pap. 21.00x (ISBN 0-335-15391-7). Taylor & Francis.

Threats & Other Promises. Vernor Vinge. 320p. (Orig.). 1988. pap. 3.50 (ISBN 0-671-69790-0). Baen Bks.

Threats Instead of Trees. Michael Ryan. LC 73-87737. (Younger Poets Ser.: No. 69). 96p. 1974. Repr. 14.95t (ISBN 0-300-01738-3). Yale U Pr.

Threats of Quotas in International Trade: Their Effect on the Exporting Country. Gerard L. Stockhausen. LC 87-23682. (Contributions in Economics & Economic History Ser.: No. 78). 192p. 1988. lib. bdg. 37.95 (ISBN 0-313-25785-X, SQT/). Greenwood.

Threats of Revolution in Britain, 1789-1848. Malcolm I. Thomis & Peter Holt. LC 76-52416. viii, 147p. 1977. 23.50 (ISBN 0-208-01657-0, Archon). Shoe String.

Threats to International Financial Stability. Ed. by R. Portes & A. K. Swoboda. LC 87-10310. 326p. 42.50 (ISBN 0-521-34556-1); pap. 16.95 (ISBN 0-521-34789-0). Cambridge U Pr.

Threats to Security in East Asia-Pacific: National & Regional Perspectives. Charles E. Morrison. LC 82-48632. 256p. 1983. 32.00x (ISBN 0-669-06369-X). Lexington Bks.

Threats to the International Civil Service: Past Pressures & New Trends. Yves Beigbeder. 220p. 1988. 39.00x (ISBN 0-86187-953-8, Pub. by Pinter Pubs UK). Columbia U Pr.

Three. Donna D. Guyer. 176p. 1987. text ed. 16.95 (ISBN 0-682-40340-7). Exposition-Phoenix.

Three. Ira Levin. 1985. 12.45 (ISBN 0-394-54512-5). Random.

Three A. M. Meditations for the Middle of the Night. Richard A. Wing. LC 21-786068. 144p. (Orig.). 1985. pap. 9.95 (ISBN 0-934849-00-5). Arthur Pub.

Three Across Kansas. Jack P. Jones. 192p. 1986. 14.95 (ISBN 0-8027-4059-6). Walker & Co.

Three Adventures of Sherlock Holmes. (Classics Ser.). (gr. 4 up). 1988. pap. 3.95 (ISBN 0-582-52286-2). Longman.

Three Adventures of Sherlock Holmes see New Method Supplementary Readers.

Three Adventures of Sherlock Holmes see New Method Supplementary Readers: Bestseller Pack.

Three Aesop Fox Fables. Paul Galdone. LC 79-133061. (Illus.). 32p. (ps-2). 1971. 13.95 (ISBN 0-395-28810-X, Clarion). HM.

Three African Tribes in Transition. 1972 see Contemporary Change in Traditional Societies.

Three Against the Third Republic: Sorel, Barres & Maurras. Michael Curtis. LC 76-26140. 1976. Repr. of 1959 ed. lib. bdg. 35.00x (ISBN 0-8371-9048-7, CUTR). Greenwood.

Three Ages of Musical Thought: Essays on Ethics & Aesthetics. Eric Werner. LC 80-28330. (Music Reprint Ser.). iv, 368p. 1981. Repr. of 1965 ed. 45.00 (ISBN 0-306-76032-0). Da Capo.

Three Ages of the Italian Renaissance. Robert S. Lopez. LC 75-94759. Repr. of 1970 ed. 34.30 (ISBN 0-8357-9819-4, 2011465). Bks Demand UMI.

Three Alexander Calders: A Family Memoir. Margaret C. Hayes. (Illus.). 320p. 1987. pap. 14.95 (ISBN 0-87663-506-0). Universe.

Three American Composers. Edith Borroff. (Illus.). 310p. (Orig.). 1986. lib. bdg. 28.00 (ISBN 0-8191-5371-0); pap. text ed. 15.25 (ISBN 0-8191-5372-9). U Pr of Amer.

Three American Literatures: Essays in Chicano, Native American, & Asian-American Literature for Teachers of American Literature. Ed. by Houston A. Baker, Jr. LC 82-63420. iii, 265p. 1982. 32.00x (ISBN 0-87352-353-9); pap. 17.50x (ISBN 0-87352-352-0). Modern Lang.

Three American Modernist Painters. Incl. Max Weber. Alfred H. Barr, Jr; Maurice Stern. H. M. Kallen; Stuart Davis. James J. Sweeney. LC 70-86440. (Museum of Modern Art Publications in Reprint Ser). (Illus.). 152p. 1970. Repr. of 1945 ed. 13.00 (ISBN 0-685-22839-8). Ayer Co Pubs.

Three American Modernist Painters: Max Weber, with an Introduction by Alfred H. Barr, Jr.; Maurice Sterne by H. M. Kallen, with a Note by the Artist; Stuart Davis by James Johnson Sweeney. James J. Sweeney & New York City Museum of Modern Art Max Weber, Retrospective Exhibition, 1907-1930, 1969. 1969. Repr. of 1933 ed. 21.00 (ISBN 0-405-01528-3, 15554). Ayer Co Pubs.

Three American Moralists-Mailer, Bellow, & Trilling. Nathan A. Scott, Jr. LC 73-11558. 192p. 1973. pap. text ed. 7.95x (ISBN 0-268-00507-9). U of Notre Dame Pr.

Three American Originals. Joseph Reed et al. xxvi, 232p. 1987. 25.00; pap. 12.95 (ISBN 0-8195-6187-8). Wesleyan U Pr.

Three American Originals: John Ford, William Faulkner, & Charles Ives. Joseph W. Reed. LC 83-23349. (Illus.). 236p. 1984. 25.00 (ISBN 0-8195-5101-5); pap. 12.95. Wesleyan U Pr.

Three American Painters: Kenneth Noland, Jules Olitski, Frank Stella see Exhibition Catalogues from the Fogg Art Museum.

Three American Romantic Painters. Incl. Charles Burchfield, Early Watercolor. Alfred H. Barr, Jr; Florine Stettheimer. Henry McBridge; Franklin Watkins. Andrew C. Ritchie. LC 74-86441. (Museum of Modern Art Publications in Reprint Ser). 132p. 1970. Repr. of 1950 ed. 13.00 (ISBN 0-685-22840-1). Ayer Co Pubs.

Three American Romantic Painters: Burchfield, Stettheimer, Watkins. Henry McBride & New York City Museum of Modern Art Charles Burchfield, Early Water Colors 1970. 1969. 18.00 (ISBN 0-405-01538-0, 15564). Ayer Co Pubs.

Three American Sculptors & the Female Nude. Jeanne L. Wasserman & James B. Cuno. Ed. by Peter L. Walsh. (Illus.). 72p. (Orig.). pap. 7.50 (ISBN 0-916724-41-7). Harvard Art Mus.

Three Americans & Three Englishmen. Charles F. Johnson. LC 73-12885. 1886. Repr. lib. bdg. 37.50 (ISBN 0-8414-5260-1). Folcroft.

Three: An Unfinished Woman, Pentimento, Scoundrel Time. Lillian Hellman. (The complete text, with new commentaries by the author). 1979. 19.95 (ISBN 0-316-35514-3); pap. 14.95 (ISBN 0-316-35511-9). Little.

Three & Half Powers: The New Balance in Asia. Harold C. Hinton. LC 74-23956. pap. 80.00 (ISBN 0-317-11160-4, 2055230). Bks Demand UMI.

Three & Many Wishes of Jason Reid. Hazel Hutchins. (Illus.). (gr. 1-4). 1988. 10.95 (ISBN 0-317-69255-0). Viking.

Three & One Make Five: An Inspector Alvarez Novel. Roderic Jeffries. 188p. 1984. 11.95 (ISBN 0-312-80240-4). St Martin.

Three Anglican Divines on Prayer: Jewel, Andrewes & Hooker. John E. Booty. LC 80-+013. vii, 48p. (Orig.). 1978. pap. 3.00 (ISBN 0-936384-00-X). Cowley Pubns.

Three Apples from Heaven: Armenian Folk Tales. O. Sheohmelian. Ed. by Arra Avakian & Harold Bond. Tr. by O. Sheohmelian from Armenian. (Illus.). 150p. (Orig.). 1982. pap. 6.95 (ISBN 0-933706-23-5). Ararat Pr.

Three Approaches to Classroom Management: Views From a Psychological Perspective. Jerry D. Lehman. LC 81-43843. 130p. (Orig.). 1982. lib. bdg. 25.50 (ISBN 0-8191-2572-5); pap. 10.00 (ISBN 0-8191-2573-3). U Pr of Amer.

Three Approaches to Electron Correlation in Atoms. Oktay Sinanogly & Keith A. Brueckner. LC 76-89666. (Yale Series in the Sciences). (Illus.). pap. 99.50 (ISBN 0-317-09328-2, 2022039). Bks Demand UMI.

Three Archaic Poets: Archilochus, Alcaeus, Sappho. Anne P. Burnett. 336p. 1983. text ed. 27.00x (ISBN 0-674-88820-0). Harvard U Pr.

Three Are One. Stuart Olyott. 1979. pap. 4.95 (ISBN 0-87552-935-6, Evangel Pr UK). Presby & Reformed.

Three Argentina Thinkers. Solomon Lipp. xii, 177p. 1969. text ed. 9.95x (ISBN 0-88920-101-3, Pub. by Wilfrid Laurier Canada). Humanities.

Three Aspects of the Cross see Cross & Sanctification.

Three Aspects of the Late Alfred Lord Tennyson. John M. Moore. LC 79-185968. (Studies in Tennyson, No. 27). vi, 144p. 1972. Repr. of 1901 ed. lib. bdg. 45.95x (ISBN 0-8383-1387-6). Haskell.

Three Augustan Women Playwrights. Constance Clark. (American University Studies IV - English Language & Literature: Vol. 40). 364p. 1986. text ed. 35.00 (ISBN 0-8204-0309-1). P Lang Pubs.

Three Autobiographical Fragments. Isaiah Thomas. 1962. pap. 4.50x (ISBN 0-912296-32-1, Dist. by U Pr of Va). Am Antiquarian.

Three Axioms for a Theory of Conduct: Philosophy, & the Humanistic Science of Psychology. Louis Carini. 108p. (Orig.). 1984. pap. text ed. 8.00 (ISBN 0-8191-3971-8). U Pr of Amer.

Three Babies: Biographies of Cognitive Development. Ed. by Joseph Church. LC 78-14252. 1978. Repr. lib. bdg. 32.50x (ISBN 0-313-21029-2, CHTB). Greenwood.

Three Battles of Winchester. Brandon Beck & Charles Grunder. Ed. by Mary Light & Georgia Caldwell. (Illus.). 50p. 1988. pap. 4.95 (ISBN 0-939685-07-8). Country Pub Inc.

Three Beams of Light: Chronicles of a Lighthouse Keeper's Family. Norma Engel. LC 86-50408. (Illus.). 276p. (Orig.). 1986. pap. 8.95 (ISBN 0-938711-00-8). Tecolote Pubns.

Three Bears. Paul Galdone. (Illus.). (gr. k-3). 1973. pap. 2.50 (ISBN 0-590-33825-0). Scholastic Inc.

Three Bears. Paul Galdone. LC 78-158833. (Illus.). 32p. (ps-3). 1985. pap. 4.95 (ISBN 0-89919-401-X, Pub. by Clarion). Ticknor & Fields.

Three Bears. Ed. & illus. by Paul Galdone. LC 78-158833. (Illus.). 32p. (ps-3). 1972. 11.95 (ISBN 0-395-28811-8, Clarion). HM.

Three Bears. Illus. by Sally M. Hardy. (Cut & Paste Ser.). (Illus.). (ps-3). 1982. 3.50 (ISBN 0-913545-08-2). Moonlight FL.

Three Bears. Margaret Hillert. (Beginning-to-Read Ser.). (Illus.). (ps). 1963. (Dist. by Caroline Hse); PLB 4.39 (ISBN 0-8136-5515-3); pap. 1.95 (ISBN 0-695-38710-3). Modern Curr.

Three Bears. Anne McGill-Franzen. LC 79-62977. (Learn-a-Tale Ser.). (Illus.). (gr. k-2). 1979. PLB 12.51 (ISBN 0-8393-0182-0). Raintree Pubs.

Three Bears. Illus. by Yuri Salzman. (Super Shape Bks.). (Illus.). 24p. (gr. 2-5). 1987. pap. write for info. (ISBN 0-307-10050-2, Pub. by Golden Bks). Western Pub.

Three Bears. Kevin Scally. (Magic Road Bk.). (Illus.). 32p. (ps-3). 1984. 3.95 (ISBN 0-448-11129-2, G&D). Putnam Pub Group.

Three Bears. Illus. by Robin Spowart. LC 86-27322. (Illus.). 32p. (ps-1). 1987. 4.95 (ISBN 0-394-88862-6); lib. bdg. 7.99 (ISBN 0-394-98862-0). Knopf.

Three Bears. (Fr.). (gr. k-3). 4.25 (ISBN 0-685-28449-2). French & Eur.

Three Bears. (Picture Tales Ser.). (Illus.). 32p. (ps-1). 1985. 2.49 (ISBN 0-517-46239-7). Outlet Bk Co.

Three Bears. (Illus.). 24p. (ps-k). 1.29 (ISBN 0-317-68239-3, Checkerboard Pr). Macmillan.

Three Bears. Leo Tolstoy. (Illus.). 16p. 1976. pap. 1.99 (ISBN 0-8285-1244-2, Pub. by Progress Pubs USSR). Imported Pubns.

Three Bears & Fifteen Other Stories. Anne Rockwell. LC 74-5381. (Illus.). 128p. (gr. k-5). 1975. 13.95 (ISBN 0-690-00597-0, Crowell Jr Bks); PLB 13.89 (ISBN 0-690-00598-9). HarpJ.

Three Bears & Fifteen Other Stories. Anne Rockwell. LC 74-5381. (Trophy Bks.). (Illus.). 128p. (ps-3). 1984. pap. 7.95 flexi-bind (ISBN 0-06-440142-1, Trophy). HarpJ.

Three Bears & Other Plays. Dyan Cassie. LC 76-48596. (gr. 1-6). 1977. pap. text ed. 3.95x (ISBN 0-8134-1886-0, 1886). Inter Print Pubs.

Three Bears & The Little Match Girl. Tolstoy & Hans Christian Andersen. (Upside Down Books). (Illus.). 48p. (ps-3). 1985. 4.95 (ISBN 0-88110-250-4). EDC.

Three Bears Get in Shape. Shirleyann Costigan. (Three Bears Ser.). (Illus.). (gr. 2-4). 1984. pap. 3.95 (ISBN 0-8224-6929-4). D S Lake Pubs.

Three Bears Go to Camp. Shirleyann Costigan. (Three Bears Ser.). (Illus.). (gr. 1-3). 1984. pap. 3.95 (ISBN 0-8224-6933-2). D S Lake Pubs.

Three Bears Go to Town. Shirleyann Costigan. (Three Bears Ser.). (Illus.). (gr. 2-4). 1984. pap. 3.95 (ISBN 0-8224-6931-6). D S Lake Pubs.

Three Bears Go West. Shirleyann Costigan. (Three Bears Ser.). (Illus.). (gr. 1-3). 1984. pap. 3.95 (ISBN 0-8224-6932-4). D S Lake Pubs.

Three Bears in the Ministry. Beverly Burgess. 32p. (Orig.). (ps). 1982. pap. 3.98 (ISBN 0-89274-252-6). Harrison Hse.

Three Bears Join the Circus. Shirleyann Costigan. (Three Bears Ser.). (Illus.). (gr. 2-4). 1984. pap. 3.95 (ISBN 0-8224-6934-0). D S Lake Pubs.

Three Bears, (Lots of Bees,) & One Pot of Honey. Karla F. Stouse. LC 87-70530. (Learn a Value Ser.). (Illus.). 16p. (Orig.). (gr. 2 up). 1987. pap. 7.95 incl. cassette (ISBN 0-87029-206-4). Abbey.

Three Bears Rhyme Book. Jane Yolen. LC 86-19514. (Illus.). 32p. (ps-3). 1987. 14.95 (ISBN 0-15-286386-9, HJ). HarBraceJ.

Three Bears Spot the Clues. Shirleyann Costigan. (Three Bears Ser.). (Illus.). (gr. 2-4). 1984. pap. 3.95 (ISBN 0-8224-6935-9). D S Lake Pubs.

Three Bears Upstairs. Jane B. Moncure. LC 87-11715. (Magic Castle Reader's Ser.). (Illus.). 32p. (ps-2). 1987. PLB 7.75 (ISBN 0-89565-373-7). Childs World.

Three Bedtime Stories. (Illus.). (ps-1). 1985. 2.98 (ISBN 0-517-46989-8). Outlet Bk Co.

Three Bells Told Again. Wayne Cargile. 1973. 2.00 (ISBN 0-87012-155-3). McClain.

Three Big Words. Kenneth E. Hagin. 1983. pap. 0.50 mini bk. (ISBN 0-89276-258-6). Hagin Ministries.

Three Billionaires. James M. Bryant. 1977. pap. 7.00 (ISBN 0-686-19545-0). J M Bryant.

Three Billionaires. James M. Bryant. pap. 7.00 (ISBN 0-318-18290-4). Rocket Pub Co.

Three Billy-Goats Gruff. Ellen Appleby. (Easy to Read FolkTales Ser.). (Illus.). 32p. (gr. k-2). 1985. pap. 2.50 (ISBN 0-590-41121-7); incl. cassette 5.95 (ISBN 0-590-63068-7). Scholastic Inc.

Three Billy Goats Gruff. Paul Galdone. (Illus.). 32p. (ps-3). 1981. pap. 4.95 (ISBN 0-89919-035-9, Pub. by Clarion). Ticknor & Fields.

Three Billy Goats Gruff. Retold by & illus. by Paul Galdone. LC 72-85338. (Illus.). 32p. (ps-3). 1973. 12.95 (ISBN 0-395-28812-6, Clarion). HM.

Three Billy Goats Gruff. Patricia McKissack & Fredrick McKissack. LC 86-33450. (Start-off Stories Ser.). (Illus.). 32p. (ps-2). 1987. PLB 10.60 (ISBN 0-516-02366-7); pap. 2.95 (ISBN 0-516-42366-5). Childrens.

Three Billy Goats Gruff. Illus. by Ed Parker. LC 78-18068. (Illus.). 32p. (gr. k-3). 1979. PLB 9.79 (ISBN 0-89375-121-9); pap. 1.95 (ISBN 0-89375-099-9); cassette 9.95. Troll Assocs.

Three Billy Goats Gruff. Illus. by Jacqueline B. Smith. (Pudgy Pal Board Bks.). (Illus.). 18p. (ps). 1988. bds. 3.95 (ISBN 0-448-10230-7, G&D). Putnam Pub Group.

Three Billy Goats Gruff. Janet Stevens. LC 86-33512. (Illus.). 40p. (ps-3). 1987. 12.95 (ISBN 0-15-286396-6, HJ). HarBraceJ.

Three Billy-Goats Gruff. (Ladybird Stories Ser.). (Illus., Arabic.). (gr. 5-8). 3.50x (ISBN 0-86685-239-5). Intl Bk Ctr.

Three Billy-Goats-Gruff. (Picture Tales Ser.). (Illus.). 32p. (ps-1). 1985. 2.49 (ISBN 0-517-46241-9). Outlet Bk Co.

Three Billy Goats Gruff. (Book & Cassette Favorites Ser.). (gr. 3-4). 1987. incl. cass. 6.95 (ISBN 0-317-64578-1). HM.

Three Billy Goats Gruff. (Square Format Fairy Tales Ser.). (Illus.). 28p. (ps up). 1987. 3.95 (ISBN 0-7214-5031-8). Ladybird Bks.

Three Billy Goats Gruff. (Golden Story Book 'n' Tape Classics Ser.). (Illus.). 24p. (Orig.). (gr. k-3). 1988. pap. 5.45 (ISBN 0-307-13968-9). Western Pub.

Three Billy Goats Gruff. (Illus.). (gr. k-9). 1988. pap. 2.50. Scholastic Inc.

Three-Bladed Doom. Robert E. Howard. 1987. pap. 2.95 (ISBN 0-441-80781-X, Pub. by Ace Science Fiction). Ace Bks.

Three Blind Mice. Stephen Cosgrove. (Favorite Fairy Tales Ser.). (Illus.). 24p. (ps-1). 1988. 5.95 (ISBN 0-8249-8272-X). Ideals.

Three Blind Mice & Other Stories. Agatha Christie. 1980. pap. 2.50 (ISBN 0-440-15867-2). Dell.

Three Blind Mice & Other Stories. Agatha Christie. 224p. 1986. pap. 3.50 (ISBN 0-425-06806-4). Berkley Pub.

Three Blind Mice & Other Stories. Agatha Christie. (Popular Author Ser.). 338p. 1988. lib. bdg. 16.95 (ISBN 0-8161-4461-3, Large Print Bks). G K Hall.

Three Blue Suits. Aline Bernstein. 72p. 1988. lib. bdg. 17.95x (ISBN 0-8214-0898-4); pap. 8.95x (ISBN 0-8214-0899-2). Ohio U Pr.

Three Bob Day see Stichus.

Three-Body Force in the Three-Nucleon System. Ed. by B. Berman & B. Gibson. (Lecture Notes in Physics Ser.: Vol. 260). xi, 530p. 1986. 48.40 (ISBN 0-387-16805-2). Springer-Verlag.

Three Body Physics. Redish. 1988. write for info. (ISBN 0-471-04556-6). Wiley.

Three Books of Dog. Roger Stutter. 1986. 39.00x (ISBN 0-86332-053-8, Pub. by Book Guild Ltd). State Mutual Bk.

Three Books of Occult Philosophy or Magic. Heinrich C. Agrippa von Nettesheim. LC 79-8222. (Illus.). Repr. of 1898 ed. 39.50 (ISBN 0-404-18401-4). AMS Pr.

Three Books of Polydore Vergil's English History, Comprising the Reigns of Henry Sixth, Edward Fourth, & Richard Third. Polydorus Vergilius. Ed. by Henry Ellis. (Camden Society, London. Publications, First Ser.: No. 29). Repr. of 1844 ed. 28.00 (ISBN 0-404-50129-X). AMS Pr.

Three Books of Polydore Vergil's English History: Comprising the Reigns of Henry VI, Edward IV, & Richard III. Polydorus Vergilius. Repr. of 1844 ed. 28.00 (ISBN 0-384-64245-4). Johnson Repr.

Three Books of the Potter's Art. Cipriano Piccolpasso. 1980. 210.00 (ISBN 0-85967-452-5). Scolar.

Three Books on Fishing: Associated with the Complete Angler by Izaac Walton. LC 62-7054. 1962. Repr. of 1659 ed. 35.00x (ISBN 0-8201-1017-5). Schol Facsimiles.

Three Boulevard Farces: A Little Hotel on the Side, a Flea in Her Ear, the Lady from Maxim's Plays. Georges Feydeau. Tr. by John Mortimer. 288p. 1985. pap. 5.95 (ISBN 0-14-048191-5). Penguin.

Three Bournonville Barres & Music for the Three Bournonville Barres. Valerie J. Sutton. (Illus.). 72p. (Orig.). 1975. pap. text ed. 25.00x (ISBN 0-914336-16-9). Ctr Sutton Movement.

Three Bowls of Rice, India & Japan: A Century of Effort. Kusum Nair. 1973. 8.50. Mich St U Pr.

Three Boxes of Life: And How to Get Out of Them. Richard N. Bolles. LC 78-17000. (Illus.). 480p. 1981. 14.95 (ISBN 0-913668-52-4); pap. 9.95 (ISBN 0-913668-58-3). Ten Speed Pr.

Three Boys of New Almaden & Other Stories of Early California. Elizabeth Alston. 120p. (Orig.). (gr. 5-6). Date not set. pap. 8.95 (ISBN 0-9603674-0-3). M Dorian.

Three Brass Monkeys. Bonnie Pike. (Orig.). 1988. pap. 5.95 (ISBN 0-932419-11-9). Susan Hunter.

Three British Revolutions: 1641, 1688, 1776. Ed. by J. G. Pocock. LC 79-27572. (Folger Institute Essays, Published for the Folger Shakespeare Library). 456p. 1980. pap. 18.95x L.P.E. (ISBN 0-691-10087-X). Princeton U Pr.

Three Bullets Sealed His Lips. Bruce A. Rubenstein & Lawrence E. Ziewacz. (Illus.). 200p. 1987. pap. 13.00 (ISBN 0-87013-252-0). Mich St U Pr.

Three Burlesque Plays of Thomas Duffett. Ed. by Ronald E. Dilorenzo. LC 72-81173. 319p. 1973. 30.00x (ISBN 0-87745-033-1). U of Iowa Pr.

Three by Ben Jonson. Ed. by Jonathan Price. (Illus., Orig.). 1980. pap. 2.95 (ISBN 0-451-51368-1, CE1368, Sig Classics). NAL.

Three by Finney. Jack Finney. 1987. 10.95 (ISBN 0-671-64048-8, Fireside). S&S.

Three by Flannery O'Connor: Wise Blood, the Violent Bear It Away, a Good Man Is Hard to Find. Flannery O'Connor. 1980. pap. 4.95 (ISBN 0-451-52101-3, Sig Classics). NAL.

Three by Harry Barba. Harry Barba. LC 67-27073. (Orig.). 1967. pap. 15.00 (ISBN 0-911906-00-2). Harian Creative.

Three by Irving. John Irving. Bd. with Water-Method Man; One Hundred & Fifty-Eight Pound Marriage. 784p. 1980. 15.95 (ISBN 0-394-50983-8). Random.

Three by Peter Handke. Peter Handke. 1985. pap. 3.95 (ISBN 0-380-00968-4, 60303-9, Bard). Avon.

Three By Szekely: Three Books in One Volume, Book of Vitamins, Book of Minerals & Book of Herbs. Edmond B. Szekely. LC 83-47674. 200p. (Orig.). 1983. pap. 7.95 (ISBN 0-87983-342-4). Keats.

Three by Tennessee Williams. Tennessee Williams. Incl. Bird of Youth; The Rose Tattoo; Night of the Iguana. 1976. pap. 4.50 (ISBN 0-451-52149-8, Sig Classics). NAL.

Three by the Sea. Edward Marshall. (Easy-to-Read Bks.). (Illus.). 48p. (ps-3). 1981. PLB 9.89 (ISBN 0-8037-8687-5); pap. 4.95 (ISBN 0-8037-8671-9, 0383-120). Dial Bks Young.

Three by Three: Barba, Bond, Hamalian. Incl. Love, in the Persian Way. Harry Barba; Poems. Harold Bond; The Secret Careers of Samuel Roth. Leo Hamalian. LC 77-78963. 115p. (Orig.). 1969. pap. 15.00 (ISBN 0-911906-01-0). Harian Creative.

Three by Three: Bloom Blood. Joe Napora. Ed. by Larry Smith. Bd. with After Uelsmann. Michael Cole; Edge of Heaven. Roy Bentley. (Ohio Writers Ser.: Nos. 9, 10, & 11). (Illus.). 108p. (Orig.). 1988. pap. 7.95 (ISBN 0-933087-11-X). Bottom Dog Pr.

Three by Three: Masterworks of the Southern Gothic. Doris Betts et al. LC 85-61992. 568p. (Orig.). 1985. 22.95 (ISBN 0-931948-80-0); pap. 14.95 (ISBN 0-931948-84-3). Peachtree Pubs.

Three by Truman Capote. Truman Capote. 1985. 12.45 (ISBN 0-394-54513-3). Random.

Three Byzantine Literatures: A Layman's Guide. Ihor Sevcenko. (Nichola E. Kulukundis Lectures in History of Hellenism Ser.). 26p. 1985. pap. 2.50 (ISBN 0-917653-13-0). Holy Cross Orthodox.

Three Byzantine Military Treatises. Ed. by George T. Dennis. LC 84-26053. (Dumbarton Oaks Texts Ser.: Vol. 9). (Illus.). 400p. (Eng. & Gr.). 1985. 28.00x (ISBN 0-88402-140-8). Dumbarton Oaks.

Three Byzantine Saints. Tr. by Elizabeth Dawes & Norman H. Baynes. 275p. 1977. pap. 9.95 (ISBN 0-913836-44-3). St Vladimirs.

Three Capitals: A Book About the First Three Capitals of Alabama-St. Stephens, Huntsville, & Cahawba, 1818-1826. William H. Brantley. LC 76-28483. (Bicentennial Bk.). (Illus.). 256p. 1976. Repr. of 1947 ed. 15.95 (ISBN 0-8173-5231-7). U of Ala Pr.

Three Case Histories. Sigmund Freud. 1963. pap. 5.95 (ISBN 0-02-076650-5, Collier). Macmillan.

Three Catholic Afro-American Congresses. Congress of Colored Catholics of the United States. 14.00 (ISBN 0-405-10863-X, 11829). Ayer Co Pubs.

Three Catholic Reformers of the Fifteenth Century. facsimile ed. Mary H. Allies. LC 73-38755. (Essay Index Reprint Ser). Repr. of 1878 ed. 13.00 (ISBN 0-8369-2633-1). Ayer Co Pubs.

Three Catholic Writers of the Modern South. Robert H. Brinkmeyer, Jr. LC 84-19641. 1985. 20.00x (ISBN 0-87805-246-1). U Pr of Miss.

Three-Cent Stamp of the United States, 1851-1857 Issue. Carroll Chase. LC 75-18277. (Illus.). 384p. 1976. Repr. 35.00x (ISBN 0-88000-070-8). Quarterman.

Three Centuries & the Island: A Historical Geography of Settlement & Agriculture in Prince Edward Island, Cananda. Andrew H. Clark. LC 59-2157. pap. 75.00 (ISBN 0-317-27978-5, 2055817). Bks Demand UMI.

Three Centuries of Accounting in Massachusetts. new ed. William Holmes & Linda H. Kistler. Ed. by Richard P. Brief. LC 77-87295. (Development of Contemporary Accounting Thought Ser). 1978. lib. bdg. 27.50x (ISBN 0-405-10922-9). Ayer Co Pubs.

Three Centuries of American Rhetorical Discourse: An Anthology & a Review. Ed. by Ronald F. Reid. 758p. 1988. text ed. 29.95x (ISBN 0-88133-313-1); pap. text ed. 19.95x (ISBN 0-88133-310-7). Waveland Pr.

Three Centuries of Architect Craftsman. Amery. pap. 37.95 (ISBN 0-317-64300-2). Van Nos Reinhold.

Three Centuries of Ballingers in America. Emma B. Reeves. LC 75-27993. (Illus.). 614p. 1977. lib. bdg. 20.00 (ISBN 0-911013-02-4). E B Reeves.

Three Centuries of English & American Plays: A Check List - England 1500-1800 & United States 1714-1830. Ed. by G. William Bergquist. 1963. 37.50x (ISBN 0-02-841230-3). Hafner.

Three Centuries of English Church Music. W. H. Parry. 1977. lib. bdg. 59.95 (ISBN 0-8490-2745-4). Gordon Pr.

Three Centuries of English Essays: From Francis Bacon to Max Beerbohm. facs. ed. Ed. by Vere H. Collins. LC 67-26727. (Essay Index Reprint Ser). 1931. 11.00 (ISBN 0-8369-0327-7). Ayer Co Pubs.

Three Centuries of English Poetry. Rosaline Masson. Repr. of 1887 ed. lib. bdg. 25.50 (ISBN 0-8414-6452-9). Folcroft.

Three Centuries of German Life in America. Rudolf Cronau. 59.95 (ISBN 0-8490-1210-4). Gordon Pr.

Three Centuries of German Painting & Drawing: From the Collections of the Wallraf-Richartz Musuem, Cologne. Ekkehard Mai et al. LC 85-14261. (Illus.). 224p. 1985. pap. 24.95 (ISBN 0-295-96437-5, Pub. by Smithsonian Traveling). U of Wash Pr.

Three Centuries of Harpsichord Making. Frank T. Hubbard. LC 65-12784. (Illus.). 1965. 27.95x (ISBN 0-674-88845-6). Harvard U Pr.

Three Centuries of Harvard. Samuel E. Morison. 520p. 1986. pap. text ed. 10.95x (ISBN 0-674-88891-X, Belknap Pr). Harvard U Pr.

Three Centuries of Harvard, 1636-1936. facsim. ed. Samuel E. Morison. LC 36-14160. 1936. 27.00x (ISBN 0-674-88890-1, Belknap Pr). Harvard U Pr.

Three Centuries of Peace Treaties & Their Teachings, 1582-1913. Walter G. Phillimore. LC 73-147602. (Library of War & Peace; International Law). 1975. lib. bdg. 46.00 (ISBN 0-8240-0363-2). Garland Pub.

Three Centuries of Poor Law Administration: A Study of Legislation in Rhode Island. Margaret Creech. 19.00 (ISBN 0-405-19031-X). Ayer Co Pubs.

Three Centuries of Science in America Series, 66 bks. Ed. by I. Bernard Cohen. (Illus.). 1980. Set. lib. bdg. 2939.000.00x (ISBN 0-405-12525-9). Ayer Co Pubs.

Three Centuries of Scottish Literature, 2 vols. Hugh Walker. 1982. Repr. of 1893 ed. lib. bdg. 150.00 set (ISBN 0-89984-522-3). Vol. 1, 219p. Vol. 2, 254p. Century Bookbindery.

Three Centuries of Southern Poetry. Carl Holliday. 1977. Repr. of 1908 ed. 27.50. Century Bookbindery.

Three Centuries of Southern Poetry: 1607-1907. Carl Holliday. 267p. 1982. Repr. of 1908 ed. lib. bdg. 50.00 (ISBN 0-8495-2432-6). Arden Lib.

Three Centuries of Thumb Bibles. Ruth Adomeit. LC 78-68238. (Garland Reference Library of Humanities). (Illus.). 435p. 1980. 73.00 (ISBN 0-8240-9818-8). Garland Pub.

Three Centuries to Concorde. Charles Burnet. 288p. 1979. casebound 22.00 (ISBN 0-85298-412-X, MEP-113, Pub. by Institution of Mechanical Engineers). Soc Auto Engineers.

Three Centuries-Two Continents: Essays on the Arts in America & Their European Background in Honor of Robert C. Smith. Ed. by Nancy H. Schless & Kenneth L. Ames. (Illus.). 1983. pap. text ed. cancelled (ISBN 0-89257-028-8). Am Life Foun.

Three Chapters from the Samadhirajasutra. Tr. by Constantin Regamey from Sanskrit & Tibetan. 112p. 1984. Repr. of 1938 ed. lib. bdg. 17.50x (ISBN 0-88181-003-7). Canon Pubns.

Three Chapters of Letters Relating to the Suppression of Monasteries. Thomas Wright. 37.00 (ISBN 0-384-69545-0). Johnson Repr.

Three Chapters of Letters Relating to the Suppression of Monasteries. Ed. by Thomas Wright. LC 72-74268. (Camden Society, London. Publications First Ser.: No. 26). Repr. of 1843 ed. 37.00 (ISBN 0-404-50126-5). AMS Pr.

Three Chapters on Courtly Love in Arthurian France & Germany. Hermann J. Weigand. LC 56-58693. (North Carolina. University. Studies in the Germanic Languages & Literatures: No. 17). Repr. of 1956 ed. 27.00 (ISBN 0-404-50917-7). AMS Pr.

Three Chapters on the Nature of Mind. Bernard Bosanquet. Ed. by Helen Bosanquet. LC 23-2356. 1968. Repr. of 1923 ed. 18.00 (ISBN 0-527-10054-4). Kraus Repr.

Three Cheers for Hippo! John Stadler. LC 87-497. (Illus.). 32p. (ps-3). 1987. 11.95i (ISBN 0-690-04668-5, Crowell Jr Bks). HarpJ.

Three Cheers for Kneesaa! An Ewok Adventure. Jane E. Gerver. LC 83-62250. (Ewok Mini-Storybooks). (Illus.). 32p. (ps-3). 1983. pap. 1.25 (ISBN 0-394-86354-2, BYR). Random.

Three Cheers for the Paraclete. Thomas Keneally. 304p. 1984. pap. 5.95 (ISBN 0-14-003099-9). Penguin.

Three Children's Plays: The Poet & the Rent; The Frog Prince & the Revenge of the Space Pandas or Binky Rudich & the Two-Speed Clock. David Mamet. 144p. (gr. 3-7). 1986. 18.95 (ISBN 0-394-55302-0). Grove.

Three Children's Plays: The Poet & the Rent; The Frog Prince & the Revenge of the Space Pandas or Binky Rudich & the Two-Speed Clock. David Mamet. 144p. (gr. 3-7). pap. 8.95 (ISBN 0-394-62167-0, Ever). Grove.

Three Chilean Thinkers. Solomon Lipp. 164p. 1975. text ed. 11.50x (ISBN 0-88920-018-1, Pub. by Wilfred Lawrier Canada); pap. text ed. 5.75x (ISBN 0-88920-017-3). Humanities.

Three Christian Capitals: Topography & Politics. Richard Krautheimer. (Una's Lectures: No. 4). 168p. 1983. 35.00x (ISBN 0-520-04541-6); pap. 10.95x (ISBN 0-520-06034-2). U of Cal Pr.

Three Christian Transcendentalists: James Marsh, Caleb Sprague Henry, Frederic Henry Hedge. Ronald V. Wells. LC 75-159256. xxxii, 290p. 1971. Repr. of 1943 ed. lib. bdg. 20.00x (ISBN 0-374-98345-3, Octagon). Hippocrene Bks.

Three Christmas Plays. Dorothy J. Goulding. 20p. (gr. 3-6). Repr. of 1955 ed. 3.00 (ISBN 0-88020-103-7). Coach Hse.

Three Christs of Ypsilanti: A Psychological Study. Milton Rokeach. LC 81-404. (Morningside Book). 360p. 1981. pap. 13.00x (ISBN 0-231-05271-5). Columbia U Pr.

Three Cities. Sholem Asch. 899p. pap. 10.50 (ISBN 0-88184-009-2). Carroll & Graf.

Three Civilizations, Two Cultures, & One State: Canada's Political Traditions. Douglas V. Verney. LC 85-25313. (Duke University Center for International Studies Publication). (Illus.). xiii, 454p. 1986. 36.50 (ISBN 0-8223-0654-9). Duke.

Three Classic Don Juan Plays. Ed. by Oscar Mandel. LC 73-149071. xii, 133p. 1971. pap. 5.50x (ISBN 0-8032-5739-2, BB 537, Bison). U of Nebr Pr.

Three Classic Silent Screen Comedies Starring Harold Lloyd. Donald W. McCaffrey. LC 74-4993. (Illus.). 264p. 1976. 25.00 (ISBN 0-8386-1455-8). Fairleigh Dickinson.

Three Classical Poets: Sappho, Catullus & Juvenal. Richard Jenkyns. 256p. 1982. text ed. 24.95x (ISBN 0-674-88895-2). Harvard U Pr.

Three Classical Tragedies: Coriolanus, Timon of Athens, Titus Andronicus. William Shakespeare. (Classics Ser.). 1988. pap. 4.95 (ISBN 0-553-21284-2, Bantam Classics). Bantam.

Three Classics in the Aesthetic of Music. Claude Debussy et al. pap. 4.50 (ISBN 0-486-20320-4). Dover.

Three Classics of Italian Calligraphy: The Writing Books of Arrighi, Tagliente, Palatino. Oscar Ogg. (Illus.). 15.00 (ISBN 0-8446-0829-7). Peter Smith.

Three Classics of Italian Calligraphy. Ed. by Oscar Ogg. 1953. pap. 6.50 (ISBN 0-486-20212-7). Dover.

Three Clean Fuels from Coal-Technology & Economics: Synthetic Natural Gas, Methanol, & Medium Btu Gas. Ed. by A. Kasem. 1979. 495.00 (ISBN 0-8247-6923-6). Dekker.

Three Clerks, 3 vols. Anthony Trollope. Ed. by N. John Hall. LC 80-1876. (Selected Works of Anthony Trollope Ser.). 1981. Repr. of 1858 ed. lib. bdg. 105.00 (ISBN 0-405-14126-2). Ayer Co Pubs.

Three Clerks. Anthony Trollope. 497p. 1981. pap. 8.95 (ISBN 0-486-24099-1). Dover.

Three Clicks Left. Katerina Gogou. Tr. by Jack Hirschman from Gr. LC 82-63186. (Literature Ser.: No. 2). 64p. 1983. pap. 4.50 (ISBN 0-941842-01-0). Night Horn Books.

Three Club Juggling: An Introduction. Dick Franco. Ed. by Brian Dube & Ann Zemaitis. LC 87-30370. (Illus.). 128p. 1987. 16.95 (ISBN 0-917643-03-8); pap. 12.95 (ISBN 0-917643-02-X). B Dube.

Three Coffins. John D. Carr. lib. bdg. 11.50x (ISBN 0-89966-048-7). Buccaneer Bks.

Three Coffins. John D. Carr. 256p. 1986. pap. 4.95 (ISBN 0-930330-39-0). Intl Polygonics.

Three Coffins. John D. Carr. LC 79-690. 306p. 1979. Repr. of 1936 ed. 15.00 (ISBN 0-8398-2533-1). Ultramarine Pub.

Three: Collection of Poetry. 84p. 1981. pap. 9.00 (ISBN 0-935090-06-1). Almanac Pr.

Three Comedies. Ben Jonson. Ed. by Michael Jamieson. (English Library). 1966. pap. 4.95 (ISBN 0-14-043013-X). Penguin.

Three Comedies. Johann Nestroy. Tr. by Max Knight & Joseph Fabry. Incl. Man Full of Nothing; Talisman; Love Affairs & Wedding Bells. LC 66-28138. (Illus.). xiii, 258p. pap. 6.95x (ISBN 0-8044-6583-5). Ungar.

Three Comedies by Pedro Calderon de la Barca. Pedro Calderon de la Barca. Tr. by Kenneth Muir & Ann L. MacKenzie. LC 85-5369. (Studies in Romance Languages: No. 31). 256p. 1985. 25.00 (ISBN 0-8131-1546-9); pap. 9.00 (ISBN 0-8131-0166-2). U Pr of Ky.

Three Comedies: Mine Hostess, the Boors, & the Fan. Carlo Goldoni. Tr. by Clifford Bax & I. M. Rawson. LC 79-4666. 1979. Repr. of 1961 ed. lib. bdg. 35.00x (ISBN 0-313-21259-7, GOTC). Greenwood.

Three Comedies of American Family Life. Ed. by Joseph E. Mersand. Incl. Life with Father. Howard Lindsay & Russell Crouse; I Remember Mama. John Van Druten; You Can't Take It with You. Moss Hart & George S. Kaufman. 320p. pap. 3.95 (ISBN 0-671-42886-1). WSP.

Three Comedies: The Birds, the Clouds, the Wasps. Aristophanes. Ed. by William Arrowsmith. (Illus.). 400p. 1969. pap. 9.95 (ISBN 0-472-06153-4, 153, AA). U of Mich Pr.

Three Complete Novels. Frederick Forsyth. 33.95 (ISBN 0-88411-564-X, Pub. by Aeonian Pr). Amereon Ltd.

Three Concepts of Time. Kenneth G. Denbigh. 160p. 1981. pap. 26.50 (ISBN 0-387-10757-6). Springer-Verlag.

Three Contemporary Chinese Painters: Chang Da-chien, Ting Yin-yung, Ch'eng Shih-fa. T. C. Lai. LC 75-27182. 1975. 12.50x (ISBN 0-295-95463-9). U of Wash Pr.

Three Contemporary Novelists: An Annotated Bibliography of Works by & About John Hawkes, Joseph Heller & Thomas Pynchon. Robert M. Scotto. LC 75-42889. (Reference Library of the Humanities Ser.: Vol. 52). 1977. lib. bdg. 25.00 (ISBN 0-8240-9948-6). Garland Pub.

Three Contemporary Poets of New England. Guy Rotella. (United States Authors Ser.). 1983. lib. bdg. 19.95 (ISBN 0-8057-7377-0, Twayne). G K Hall.

Three Continents. Ruth P. Jhabvala. LC 87-7880. 416p. 1987. 18.95 (ISBN 0-688-07184-8). Morrow.

Three Continents. Ruth P. Jhabvala. 1988. 7.95 (ISBN 0-671-66362-3, Fireside). S&S.

Three Contributions to the Development of Accounting Thought. Ed. by Maurice Moonitz & Richard P. Brief. LC 77-87315. (Development of Contemporary Accounting Thought Ser). 1978. lib. bdg. 34.50x (ISBN 0-405-10928-8). Ayer Co Pubs.

Three Contributions to the Theory of Sex. Sigmund Freud. Tr. by A. A. Brill from Ger. 118p. 1982. Repr. of 1925 ed. lib. bdg. 40.00 (ISBN 0-89984-211-9). Century Bookbindery.

Three Cornered Sun: A Historical Novel. Linda Ty-Casper. 1979. pap. 6.75x (ISBN 0-686-26800-8, Pub. by New Day Pub Phillipines). Cellar.

Three Corners: Exploring Marriage & the Self. Stephen R. Marks. LC 85-45461. 272p. 1985. 28.00x (ISBN 0-669-11769-2); pap. text ed. 14.95x (ISBN 0-669-11768-4). Lexington Bks.

Three Corners to Nowhere. Martin Caidin. 1988. pap. 2.95 (ISBN 0-671-65401-2). Baen Bks.

Three Corvettes. Nicholas Monsarrat. 223p. 1982. pap. 4.95 (ISBN 0-583-12085-7, Pub. by Granada England). Academy Chi Pubs.

Three Costume Plays for Women. 1985. 20.00x (ISBN 0-86025-830-0, Pub. by Ian Henry Pubns England). State Mutual Bk.

Three Count Hustle. Earl Atkinson. (Ballroom Dance Ser.). 1986. lib. bdg. 79.95 (ISBN 0-8490-3642-9). Gordon Pr.

Three Count Hustle. (Ballroom Dance Ser.). 1985. lib. bdg. 70.00 (ISBN 0-87700-724-1). Revisionist Pr.

Three Court Dances of the Early Renaissance. Ingrid Brainard & Ray Cook. (Illus.). ix, 23p. 1977. pap. text ed. 9.95 (ISBN 0-932582-10-9). Dance Notation.

Three Criminal Law Reformers: Beccaria, Bentham, Romilly. Coleman Phillipson. LC 77-17157. (Criminology, Law Enforcement, & Social Problems Ser.: No. 113). 1970. 20.00x (ISBN 0-87585-113-4); pap. 8.50x (ISBN 0-87585-904-6). Patterson Smith.

Three Crises in American Foreign Affairs & a Continuing Revolution. Howard Trivers. LC 73-188703. 232p. 1972. 7.95x (ISBN 0-8093-0574-7). S Ill U Pr.

Three Critical Essays on Modern English Poetry. T. S. Eliot & Aldous Huxley. LC 74-34435. 1973. lib. bdg. 12.50 (ISBN 0-8414-3957-5). Folcroft.

Three Critical Years, 1904-05-06. Maurice Paleologue. 12.95 (ISBN 0-8315-0015-8). Speller.

Three Cross & Deputy of Violence. Ray Hogan. (Orig.). 1978. pap. 2.50 (ISBN 0-451-11604-6, AE1604, Sig). NAL.

Three Crosses. Leonard Peusch. 1978. 0.75 (ISBN 0-8199-0723-5). Franciscan Herald.

Three C's: Children, Computers & Communication. Tom Stonier & Cathy Conlin. LC 85-16937. 218p. 1985. pap. 14.95 (ISBN 0-471-90828-2). Wiley.

Three Cubic Meter Biogas Plant. (Illus.). 28p. 1979. write for info (ISBN 0-86619-069-4). Vols Tech Asst.

Three Cuckolds. Leon Katz. (Commedia in Performance Ser.: Vol. 1). 96p. (Orig.). 1986. pap. 5.95 (ISBN 0-936839-06-6). Applause Theatre Bk Pubs.

Three Cultures: Science, the Humanities & Religious Values. Joseph M. Zycinski. (Philosophy in Science Library). 96p. (Orig.). pap. 9.95 (ISBN 0-88126-727-9). Pachart Pub Hse.

Three-D & the MAFIA Club. Kenneth L. Lindsay. viii, 228p. (Orig.). 1981. pap. 10.00 (ISBN 0-943980-00-3). AIGA Pubns.

Three-D Animated Apple. Phil Cohen. 1984. 23.95 (ISBN 0-13-920224-2). P-H.

Three-D Computer Graphics. Mark A. Willis. 140p. 1983. pap. text ed. 16.95 (ISBN 0-87567-041-5). Entelek.

Three-D Constructions. James Rizzi. (Illus.). 119p. 1988. 50.00 (ISBN 0-936598-02-6). J Szoke Graphics.

Three D Cookbook. LC 81-52188. 224p. 1982. 14.95 (ISBN 0-941478-01-7). Paraclete Pr.

Three D Graphics & Geometric Modelling see Geometric Modelling & Computer Graphics: Techniques & Applications.

Three-D-Light: A Handbook Laboratory in the Rendering of the Universal Mesh. David R. Wheeler. LC 76-21441. (Illus.). 1976. pap. 12.95 (ISBN 0-918562-01-5). Biohydrant.

Three-D Machine Vision. Richard K. Miller. 272p. 1986. spiral bdg. 190.00 (ISBN 0-89671-101-3). SEAI Tech Pubns.

Three-D Machine Vision. Technical Insights, Inc. 215p. 1984. 190.00 (ISBN 0-317-14659-9). Tech Insights.

Three-D Machine Vision. 215p. 190.00 (ISBN 0-317-65581-7). TBC Inc.

Three-D Maze Art. Larry Evans. LC 80-16987. (Illus.). (gr. 1-12). 1980. pap. 4.95 (ISBN 0-89844-012-2). Troubador Pr.

Three-D Mazes, Vol. 1. Larry Evans. (Illus.). 40p. 1976. pap. 2.95 (ISBN 0-8431-1744-3). Troubador Pr.

Three-D Monster Mazes. Larry Evans. (Illus.). 40p. 1976. pap. 2.95 (ISBN 0-8431-1745-1). Troubador Pr.

Three-D Optical Illusions. Larry Evans. 32p. 1977. pap. 4.95 (ISBN 0-8431-1739-7). Troubador Pr.

Three-D Oscilloscope: A Practical Manual & Guide. Homer B. Tilton. 288p. 1987. 27.95 (ISBN 0-13-920240-4, Busn). P-H.

Three-D Paper Ornaments & Calendars. Bennett Arnstein. 1988. pap. 9.95 (ISBN 0-9620058-0-0). B Arnstein.

Three D: The Story of the Christian Group Diet Program That Is Sweeping the Country. Carol Showalter. LC 77-90947. 144p. 5.95 (ISBN 0-941478-05-X). Paraclete Pr.

Three-D, Two-D, One-D. David A. Adler. LC 74-5156. (Young Math Ser.). (Illus.). 40p. (gr. k-3). 1974. (Crowell Jr Bks); PLB 12.89 (ISBN 0-690-00543-1). HarpJ.

Three-D Vision Applications for Industry. Richard K. Miller. (Illus.). 160p. 1984. pap. text ed. 190.00 (ISBN 0-89671-060-2). SEAI Tech Pubns.

Three Daughters. Waltraud A. Mitgutsch. Tr. by Lisel Mueller. (Helen & Kurt Wolff Book Ser.). 1987. 15.95 (ISBN 0-15-175298-2). HarBraceJ.

Three Daughters of Madame Liang. Pearl S. Buck. (John Day Bk.). 1969. o.s.i 10.00i (ISBN 0-381-98055-3, A79000). T Y Crowell.

Three-Day Collision Course. Lachlan Patterson. 1985. 7.95 (ISBN 0-533-06026-5). Vantage.

Three-Day Enchantment. Mollie Hunter. LC 84-48350. (Charlotte Zolotow Bks.). (Illus.). 64p. (gr. k-4). 1985. 11.70i (ISBN 0-06-022691-9); PLB 11.89g (ISBN 0-06-022693-5). HarpJ.

Three-Day Week-Offshoot of an EDP Operation. M. C. Dobelis. (Illus.). 1976. pap. 0.50 (ISBN 0-918230-04-7). Barnstable.

Three Days. Clayton E. Krug. 1981. pap. 0.79 (ISBN 0-8100-0138-1, 15N0381). Northwest Pub.

Three Days at Gettysburg. Henry J. Hunt. Ed. by William R. Jones. (Illus.). 1978. pap. 4.95 (ISBN 0-89646-036-3). Outbooks.

Three Days for Emeralds. Mignon G. Eberhart. LC 87-42668. 272p. 1988. 14.95 (ISBN 0-394-56108-2). Random.

Three Days for Emeralds. Mignon G. Eberhart. LC 88-14726. 382p. 1988. Repr. of 1988 ed. lib. bdg. 17.95 (ISBN 0-89621-167-3). Thorndike Pr.

Three Days in Downtown Honolulu. Milly Singletary. (Illus.). 48p. (Orig.). 1982. pap. 4.95 (ISBN 0-941244-02-4). Sunset Phoenix.

Three Days of Judgement. Stanley J. Marks & Ethel M. Marks. 1981. 10.95 (ISBN 0-938780-02-6); pap. 7.95 (ISBN 0-938780-01-8). Bur Intl Aff.

Three Days on a River in a Red Canoe. Vera B. Williams. LC 80-23893. (Illus.). 32p. (gr. k-3). 1981. 11.75 (ISBN 0-688-80307-5); PLB 11.88 (ISBN 0-688-84307-7). Greenwillow.

Three Days on a River in a Red Canoe. Vera B. Williams. LC 80-23893. (Illus.). 32p. (gr. k-3). 1984. pap. 3.95 (ISBN 0-688-04072-1). Greenwillow.

Three Days Scene at the Temple in Jerusalem. 2nd ed. Jakob Lorber. Tr. by Dr. Nordewin & Hildegard Von Koerber. LC 82-83492. 128p. 1982. pap. 6.00 (ISBN 0-934616-10-8). Valkyrie Pub Hse.

Three Days' Terror. John Creasey. (Black Dagger Crime Ser.). 136p. 1987. text ed. 14.95x (ISBN 0-86220-707-X, Pub. by Firecrest Pub Ltd). Prescott Pr Nh.

Three Days to Tucson. Erle Adkins. 1981. pap. 1.95 (ISBN 0-89083-744-9). Zebra.

Three Days' Tournament, a Study in Romance & Folklore. Jessie L. Weston. LC 76-144538. Repr. of 1902 ed. 5.00 (ISBN 0-404-53558-5). AMS Pr.

Three Days Tournament: Study in Romance & Folk-Lore. Jessie L. Weston. LC 65-26456. (Studies in Comparative Literature, No. 35). 1969. Repr. of 1902 ed. lib. bdg. 42.95x (ISBN 0-8383-0643-8). Haskell.

Three Days with Johnny Two-Suits. Gary Class. 56p. (Orig.). 1981. pap. 1.95 (ISBN 0-943530-00-8). Pro Libris Pr.

Three Days with Joyce. Gisele Freund. Tr. by Peter St. J. Ginna from Fr. (Illus.). 80p. 1985. 17.95 (ISBN 0-89255-096-1). Persea Bks.

Three Deaths for Buck Duane. Romer Z. Grey. 1988. 30.00x (ISBN 0-86025-200-0, Pub. by Ian Henry Pubns England). State Mutual Bk.

Three Decades in Shiwa: Economic Development & Social Change in a Japanese Farming Community. Mitsuru Shimpo. 160p. 1987. 80.00x (ISBN 0-317-39124-0, Pub. by Norbury Pubns Ltd). State Mutual Bk.

Three Decades of British Art, 1740-1770. Ellis K. Waterhouse. LC 65-23431. (American Philosophical Society, Philadelphia. Memoirs Ser.: Vol. 63). (Illus.). pap. 22.80 (ISBN 0-317-10474-8, 2015020). Bks Demand UMI.

Three Decades of Exploration: Homage to Leo Castelli. Ed. by Ruth A. Matinko-Wald. LC 87-62753. 16p. (Orig.). 1987. pap. write for info. (ISBN 0-942461-02-9). Mus Art Fl.

Three Decades of Federal Legislation 1855 to 1885. facsimile ed. Samuel S. Cox. LC 75-114870. (Select Bibliographies Reprint Ser). 1885. 33.00 (ISBN 0-8369-5275-8). Ayer Co Pubs.

Three Decades of Max. Peter Max & Gerrit Henry. 256p. cancelled (ISBN 0-88282-016-8). New Horizon NJ.

Three Decades of Palestine: Speeches & Papers on the Upbuilding of the Jewish National Home. Arthur Ruppin. LC 70-97301. (Illus.). 342p. 1975. Repr. of 1936 ed. lib. bdg. 35.00x (ISBN 0-8371-2629-0, RUPA). Greenwood.

Three Decades of the French New Novel. Ed. by Lois Oppenheim. 224p. 1986. 28.95 (ISBN 0-252-01158-9). U of Ill Pr.

Three Decades to Doom. David A. Oxley. 1985. 12.95 (ISBN 0-533-06552-6). Vantage.

Three-Dee Mouse Mazes. Dan Nevins. (Illus.). 48p. (gr. 8-11). 1987. pap. 1.95 (ISBN 0-8431-1883-0). Price Stern.

Three Degrees above Zero: Bell Labs in the Information Age. Jeremy Bernstein. (Illus.). 320p. 1984. 19.95 (ISBN 0-684-18170-3). Scribner.

Three Degrees above Zero: Bell Labs in the Information Age. Jeremy Bernstein. 1986. pap. 4.50 (ISBN 0-451-62529-3, Ment). NAL.

Three Detective Stories. English Language Services Staff. (Collier-Macmillan English Readers). pap. 3.73 (ISBN 0-02-971440-0). Macmillan.

Three Detectives & the Knight in Armor. Simon Brett. 176p. (gr. 5-9). 1987. 12.95 (ISBN 0-684-18895-3, Pub. by Scribner). Macmillan.

Three Detectives & the Missing Superstar. Simon Brett. LC 86-15556. 192p. (gr. 5-9). 1986. 12.95 (ISBN 0-684-18708-6, Pub. by Scribner). Macmillan.

Three Determinants of Attention-Seeking in Young Children. J. L. Gewirtz. (Society for Research in Child Development). 1954. pap. 14.00 (ISBN 0-527-01561-X). Kraus Repr.

Three Devils: Luther's, Milton's & Goethe's. David Masson. LC 78-128340. Repr. of 1874 ed. 18.45 (ISBN 0-404-04247-3). AMS Pr.

Three Devils: Luther's, Milton's & Goethe's. David Masson. LC 72-193946. 1874. lib. bdg. 32.50 (ISBN 0-8414-6495-2). Folcroft.

Three Diagnostic Scorings for the Thurstone Personality Schedule. Edmund S. Conklin. LC 37-28256. (Science Ser.: No. 6). 1937. pap. 20.00 (ISBN 0-317-08001-6, 2055229). Bks Demand UMI.

Three Dialogues see Empiricists.

Three Dialogues Between Hylas & Philonous: Berkeley. Ed. by Colin M. Turbayne. 1954. pap. text ed. write for info. (ISBN 0-02-421670-4). Macmillan.

Three Dialogues Between Hylas & Philonous. George Berkeley. Ed. by Colin M. Turbayne. 1954. pap. 5.99 scp (ISBN 0-672-60206-7, LLA39). Bobbs.

Three Dialogues Between Hylas & Philonous. George Berkeley. Ed. by Robert M. Adams. LC 79-65276. (HPC Philosophical Classics Ser.). 138p. 1979. lib. bdg. 17.50 (ISBN 0-915144-62-X); pap. text ed. 3.95 (ISBN 0-915144-61-1). Hackett Pub.

Three Dialogues Between Hylas & Philonous. George Berkeley. (Great Books in Philosophy). 110p. 1988. pap. text ed. 3.95 (ISBN 0-87975-485-0). Prometheus Bks.

Three Different Worlds: Women, Men, & Children in an Industrializing Community. Frances A. Rothstein. LC 82-6216. (Contributions in Family Studies: No. 7). (Illus.). xii, 148p. 1982. lib. bdg. 35.00 (ISBN 0-313-22594-X, RTW/). Greenwood.

Three Dimension Models of Basic Crystal Forms: 111 Crystal Models. Construction Kit. A. J. Gude. 1948. pap. 11.50 (ISBN 0-686-47211-X). Polycrystal Bk Serv.

Three Dimension Models of Simple Crystal Forms: Construction Kit. A. J. Gude. 1957. pap. 4.50x (ISBN 0-686-47218-7). Polycrystal Bk Serv.

Three-Dimensional Biomedical Imaging. Robert A. Robb. 1985. Vol. I, 184 p. 75.00 (ISBN 0-8493-5264-9); Vol. II, 160 p. 75.00 (ISBN 0-8493-5265-7). CRC Pr.

Three-Dimensional Bulletin Boards. Lynn Brisson. Ed. by Sally Sharpe. (Illus.). 80p. 1988. pap. text ed. 6.95 (ISBN 0-86530-164-6, IP 28-4). Incentive Pubns.

Three-Dimensional Coastal Ocean Models. Ed. by Norman S. Heaps. (Coastal & Estuarine Sciences Ser.: Vol. 4). (Illus.). 224p. 1987. 30.00 (ISBN 0-87590-253-7). Am Geophysical.

Three-Dimensional Computer Vision. Y. Shirai. (Symbolic Computation, Computer Graphics Ser.). 375p. 1987. 98.00 (ISBN 0-387-15119-2). Springer-Verlag.

Three Dimensional Constitutive Relationships & Ductile Fracture. Ed. by S. Nemat-Nasser. 440p. 1981. 110.75 (ISBN 0-444-86108-4, North Holland). Elsevier.

Three-Dimensional Continuum Computer Programs for Structural Analysis: Presented at the Winter Annual Meeting of the American Society of Mechanical Engineers, New York, NY, November 26-30, 1972. Ed. by Thomas A. Cruse & Donald S. Griffin. LC 72-92593. pap. 20.00 (ISBN 0-317-10641-4, 2022061). Bks Demand UMI.

Three-Dimensional Design. Katie Pasquini. LC 88-70657. (Illus.). 80p. (Orig.). 1988. pap. text ed. 13.95 (ISBN 0-914881-19-1). C & T Pub.

Three-Dimensional Graphics. Ed. by Rikuyo-sha. 144p. 1988. 34.95 (ISBN 4-897-37067-1). Bks Nippan.

Three-Dimensional Ground-Water Modeling in Depositional Systems, Wilcox Group, Oakwood Salt Dome Area, East Texas. G. E. Fogg et al. (Report of Investigations Ser.: RI 133). (Illus.). 55p. 1983. 3.25 (ISBN 0-318-03289-9). Bur Econ Geology.

Three-Dimensional Imaginary Techniques. T. Okoshi. 1976. 56.50 (ISBN 0-12-525250-1). Acad Pr.

Three-Dimensional Imaging & Remote Sensing Imaging. Ed. by Robbins & Bernstein. 1988. 50.00 (ISBN 0-89252-937-7, 902). SPIE.

Three-Dimensional Link Theory & Invariants of Plane Curve Singularities. David Eisenbud & Walter D. Neumann. (Annals of Mathematics Studies: No. 110). 185p. 1985. text ed. 44.00x (ISBN 0-691-08380-0); pap. text ed. 14.95x (ISBN 0-691-08381-9). Princeton U Pr.

Three-Dimensional Lunar Trajectories. V. A. Egorov. 160p. 1969. text ed. 37.50 (ISBN 0-7065-0640-5, Pub. by Keter Pub Jerusalem). Coronet Bks.

Three-Dimensional Machine Vision. Takeo Kanade. 1987. lib. bdg. 85.00 (ISBN 0-89838-188-6). Kluwer Academic.

Three-Dimensional Microanatomy of Cells & Tissue Surfaces. Ed. by D. J. Allen et al. 1981. 90.00 (ISBN 0-444-00607-9). Elsevier.

Three-Dimensional Models of Marine & Estuarine Dyanmics. Ed. by J. C. Nihoul & B. M. Jamart. 360p. 1987. 142.00 (ISBN 0-444-42794-5). Elsevier.

Three Dimensional Needlepoint. Gale Litvak. (Illus.). 1984. 15.95 (ISBN 0-399-12926-X, Putnam). Putnam Pub Group.

Three Dimensional Poe. Haldeen Braddy. LC 73-75915. 1973. 10.00 (ISBN 0-87404-045-0). Tex Western.

Three-Dimensional Problems of Elasticity & Thermoelasticity. V. D. Kupradze et al. 930p. 1979. 197.50 (ISBN 0-444-85148-8, North-Holland). Elsevier.

Three Golden Pearls on a String. Thomas White. (Illus.). 120p. 1987. pap. 8.95 (ISBN 1-55643-034-5). North Atlantic.
Three Good Events. Ilyon. Tr. by Edward B. Adams from Korean. (Children's Stories from Korean History: Vol. 4). (Illus.). 28p. (gr. 5). 1986. 6.50 (ISBN 0-317-52116-0, Pub. by Seoul Intl Pub Hse Korea). C E Tuttle.
Three Gothic Novels. Ed. by Peter Fairclough. Incl. Castle of Otronto. Horace Walpole; Vathek. William Bockford; Frankenstein. Mary Wollstonecraft Shelley. (English Library Ser.). (Orig.). 1968. pap. 4.95 (ISBN 0-14-043036-9). Penguin.
Three Great Friday Sermons & Other Theological Discourses. Apostolos Makrakis. Ed. by Orthodox Christian Educational Society. Tr. by Denver Cummings from Hellenic. 107p. (Orig.). 1952. pap. 3.00x (ISBN 0-938366-48-3). Orthodox Chr.
Three Great Gothic Novels. E. F. Bieler. 20.95 (ISBN 0-8488-0060-5, Pub. by Amereon Hse). Amereon Ltd.
Three Great Irishmen: Shaw, Yeats, Joyce. Arland Ussher. LC 68-54235. 1953. 15.00 (ISBN 0-8196-0222-1). Biblo.
Three Great Jewish Plays. Ed. & tr. by Joseph C. Landis. 272p. 1986. pap. 8.95 (ISBN 0-936839-04-X). Applause Theatre Bk Pubs.
Three Great Plays of Euripides. R. Ware. pap. 2.50 (ISBN 0-452-00672-4, Mer). NAL.
Three Great Tales. Joseph Conrad. Incl. Nigger of the Narcissus; Heart of Darkness; Typhoon. 1958. pap. 3.95 (ISBN 0-394-70155-0, V-155, Vin). Random.
Three Great Teachers of Our Own Time. Alexander H. Japp. 255p. 1980. Repr. of 1865 ed. lib. bdg. 30.00 (ISBN 0-8492-1281-2). R West.
Three Great Teachers of Our Time: Carlyle, Tennyson, & Ruskin. Alexander H. Japp. LC 77-567. 1977. Repr. of 1865 ed. lib. bdg. 42.00 (ISBN 0-8414-5303-9). Folcroft.
Three Greatest Italian Poets of the Nineteenth Century. William D. Howells. (Illus.). 144p. 1983. Repr. of 1887 ed. 127.75. Found Class Reprints.
Three Greatest Prayers: Commentaries on the Lord's Prayer, the Hail Mary & the Apostles' Creed. St. Thomas Aquinas. Tr. by Laurence Shapcote from Lat. 160p. 1988. Repr. of 1937 ed. text ed. price not set (ISBN 0-918477-05-0). Sophia Inst Pr.
Three Greek Plays: The Trojan Women of Euripedes & Prometheus Bound & Aggamemnon of Aeschylus. Tr. by Edith Hamilton. 1958. pap. 6.95 (ISBN 0-393-00203-9, Norton Lib). Norton.
Three Greek Romances. Ed. & tr. by Moses Hadas. LC 53-10378. 1964. text ed. 29.50x (ISBN 0-8290-2405-0). Irvington.
Three Greek Romances. Tr. by Moses Hadas. Incl. Daphnis & Chloe. Longus; Ephesian Tale. Xenophon; Hunters of Euboia. Dio Chrysoston. LC 53-10378. 1964. pap. 6.65 scp (ISBN 0-672-60442-6, LLA201). Bobbs.
Three Guineas. Virginia Woolf. LC 38-27681. 188p. 1963. pap. 4.95 (ISBN 0-15-690177-3, Harv). HarBraceJ.
Three Guns North. Burt Arthur & Budd Arthur. 1979. pap. 1.25 (ISBN 0-505-51349-8, Pub. by Tower Bks). Leisure NY.
Three Hat Day. Laura Geringer. LC 85-42640. (Illus.). 32p. (ps-3). 1985. 12.70i (ISBN 0-06-021988-2); PLB 12.89 (ISBN 0-06-021989-0). HarpJ.
Three Hat Day. Laura Geringer. LC 85-42640. (Trophy Picture Bks.). (Illus.). 32p. (ps-3). 1987. pap. 3.95 (ISBN 0-06-443157-6, Trophy). HarpJ.
Three Hearts & Three Lions. Paul Anderson. 176p. 1984. pap. 2.50 (ISBN 0-441-80822-0). Ace Bks.
Three Heroines of New England Romance. Louise Guiney. 1894. Repr. 25.00 (ISBN 0-8274-3622-X). R West.
Three Heroines of New England Romance. H. P. Spofford. 1973. Repr. of 1894 ed. 35.00 (ISBN 0-8274-0877-3). R West.
Three Hinged-Arch Storage Building in Precast Prestressed Concrete. (PCI Journal Reprints Ser.). 8p. pap. 4.00 (ISBN 0-686-40022-4, JR81). Prestressed Concrete.
Three Historians of Alexander the Great. N. G. Hammond. LC 83-7630. (Cambridge Classical Studies). 208p. 1984. 47.50 (ISBN 0-521-25451-5). Cambridge U Pr.
Three Honest Men: Edmund Wilson, F. R. Leavis, Lionel Trilling. Ed. by Philip French. 120p. 1984. 16.50 (ISBN 0-85635-299-3). Carcanet.
Three Hostages. John Buchan. 284p. Repr. of 1924 ed. lib. bdg. 18.95x (Pub. by River City Pr). Amereon Ltd.
Three Hours for Lunch: The Life & Times of Christopher Morley. Helen McK. Oakley. LC 75-39492. 1976. 12.00 (ISBN 0-88370-005-0). Watermill Pubs.
Three Houses. Angela Thirkell. 134p. 1987. 11.95 (ISBN 0-86072-103-5, Pub. by Quartet Bks). Salem Hse Pubs.
Three Hulas from Hawaii. Carol Roes & M. Loke. (Hula Book Ser.: Bk. 6). 1968. pap. 5.50 (ISBN 0-930932-11-0); record incl. M Loke.
Three Hundered Best Rated Stocks. Ed. by Consumer Guide Editors. 1987. pap. 6.95 (ISBN 0-451-82159-9, Sig). NAL.
Three Hundred & Fifty Secondary Diseases-Disorders to Alcoholism. LC 85-73319. 45p. 1985. pap. 2.25 (ISBN 0-88270-610-1). Bridge Pub.
Three Hundred & Sixty Degrees of the Zodiac. Adriano Carelli. 208p. 1982. 9.00 (ISBN 0-86690-063-2, 1032-01). Am Fed Astrologers.
Three Hundred & Sixty Five Day Simple Interest Savings Factor Tables. Ed. by Financial Publishing Co. Staff. (Illus.). 272p. 1985. pap. 27.00 (ISBN 0-87600-720-5). Finan Pub.
Three Hundred & Sixty Five Days of Christmas. R. Smith Kiliper. Ed. by Nancy Pearson. (Illus.). 28p. 1987. 14.95x (ISBN 0-944509-01-0). Antler Pr.
Three Hundred & Sixty-Five Devotions (1988-89) Ed. by Eileen Wilmoth. 1988. pap. 5.95 large print ed. (ISBN 0-87403-377-2); pap. 3.95 pocket ed. (ISBN 0-87403-376-4). Standard Pub.
Three Hundred & Three Mini-Lessons for Social Studies. Mary Ann Williamson. (Illus.). 200p. 1976. pap. 6.95 (ISBN 0-87491-037-4). Acropolis.
Three Hundred Art Nouveau Designs & Motifs in Full Color. Ed. by Carol B. Grafton. (Illus.). 48p. pap. 6.95 (ISBN 0-486-24354-0). Dover.
Three Hundred Best Hotels in the World. Rene Lecler. (Illus.). 224p. (Orig.). 1981. pap. 11.95 (ISBN 0-8317-8745-7, Pub. by Mayflower Bks). Smith Pubs.
Three Hundred Best Hotels in the World. Rene Lecler. LC 82-10778. (Illus.). 240p. 1983. pap. 9.95 (ISBN 0-89919-160-6). Ticknor & Fields.
Three Hundred Best Hotels in the World. Rene Lecler. 220p. 1985. pap. 7.95 (ISBN 0-13-920216-1). P H.
Three Hundred Best Selling Home Plans. Ed. by L. F. Garlinghouse Co Staff. LC 85-90952. (Illus.). 224p. (Orig.). 1985. pap. 6.95 (ISBN 0-938708-15-5). L F Garlinghouse Co.
Three Hundred Charts You Can Use in Preaching, Teaching & Studying on Divorce & Remarriage. Thomas B. Warren. 1978. pap. 11.00looseleaf (ISBN 0-934916-29-2). Natl Christian Pr.
Three Hundred Classic Blocks for Crochet Projects. Linda P. Schapper. LC 87-14370. (Illus.). 256p. 1987. 19.95 (ISBN 0-8069-6578-9); pap. 12.95 (ISBN 0-8069-6580-0). Sterling.
Three Hundred English Words Using Medical Word Components. Verlee E. Gross. 40p. (Orig.). 1972. pap. 3.00x (ISBN 0-912256-04-4). Halls of Ivy.
Three Hundred Fifteen Group. W. L. Brinson. write for info. (ISBN 0-932298-40-0). Copple Hse.
Three Hundred Five Authentic Art Nouveau Jewelry Designs. Maurice Dufrene. 48p. 1985. pap. 4.95 (ISBN 0-486-24904-2). Dover.
Three Hundred Most Abused Drugs. rev. ed. E. G. Bludworth. (Illus.). 29p. 1985. 3.50 (ISBN 0-9606732-1-0). MAD Hse.
Three Hundred Ninety-Seven Chairs. Ed. by Arthur C. Danto. 1988. 24.95 (ISBN 0-8109-1698-3). Abrams.
Three Hundred One French Verbs. 1981. 5.50 (ISBN 0-8120-2496-6). Barron.
Three Hundred One German Verbs. 1981. 5.50 (ISBN 0-8120-2498-2). Barron.
Three Hundred One Spanish Verbs. 1981. 5.50 (ISBN 0-8120-2497-4). Barron.
Three Hundred Pound Cat. Rosamond Dauer. (Illus.). 32p. (gr. k-3). 1983. pap. 2.25 (ISBN 0-380-62745-0, 62745-0, Camelot). Avon.
Three Hundred Seed Thoughts: Illustrative Stories for Speakers. Herb Miller & Douglas V. Moore. 157p. (Orig.). 1986. pap. 9.95 (ISBN 0-937462-01-2). Net Pr.
Three Hundred Sermon Outlines From the New Testament. William H. Smitty. LC 81-86666. (Orig.). 1983. pap. 4.50 (ISBN 0-8054-2246-3). Broadman.
Three-Hundred Sermon Outlines from the Old Testament. Ed. by William H. Smitty. LC 81-67996. 1982. pap. 4.75 (ISBN 0-8054-2242-0). Broadman.
Three Hundred Sixty Brilliant & Instructive End Games. Aleksei A. Troitzky. LC 68-12938. Orig. Title: Chess Handbook of Three Hundred Sixty Brilliant & Instructive End Games. (Illus.). 1968. pap. 3.95 (ISBN 0-486-21959-3). Dover.
Three Hundred Sixty Day Simple Interest Savings Factor Tables. Ed. by Financial Publishing Co. Staff. 272p. 1986. pap. 27.00 (ISBN 0-87600-620-9). Finan Pub.
Three Hundred Sixty-Five Days. Ronald J. Glasser. LC 77-156599. 1971. pap. 7.95 (ISBN 0-8076-0995-1). Braziller.
Three Hundred Sixty-Five Days of Black History. 2nd ed. Catherine Gaynell. (Illus.). 14p. 1983. 7.15 (ISBN 0-911249-01-X). Clover Intl.
Three Hundred Sixty-Five Days of Creative Play for Children 2-6 Years. Sheila Ellison & Judith Gray. (Illus.). 400p. (Orig.). pap. 14.95 spiral bdg. (ISBN 0-9620467-0-1). Fantashe Inc.
Three Hundred Sixty-Five Days with Baba. Dominga L. Reyes. 1987. 7.50 (ISBN 0-939375-01-X). World Univ Amer.
Three Hundred Sixty-Five Devotions: 1987-1988. Ed. by Eileen Wilmoth. 1987. pap. 5.95 large print (ISBN 0-87403-230-X, 4088); pap. 3.95 pocket ed. (ISBN 0-87403-228-8, 3088). Standard Pub.
Three Hundred Sixty-Five Diet Tips. Julie Davis. 208p. 1985. pap. 3.50 (ISBN 0-345-31848-X). Ballantine.
Three Hundred Sixty-Five Reasons Not to Have Another War: 1989 Peace Calendar. Grace Paley & Vera B. Williams. (Illus.). 128p. (Orig.). 1988. wire bdg. 8.75 (ISBN 0-86571-142-9). New Soc Pubs.
Three Hundred Sixty-Five Starry Nights: An Introduction to Astronomy for Every Night of the Year. Chet Raymo. (Illus.). 225p. 1982. pap. 12.95 (ISBN 0-13-920512-8). P-H.
Three Hundred Sixty-Five Stories for Bedtime. (Illus.). (ps-1). 1985. 5.98 (ISBN 0-517-46715-1). Outlet Bk Co.
Three Hundred Sixty-Five Ways to Cook Chicken. Cheryl Sedeker. LC 85-45231. 240p. 1986. 14.95i (ISBN 0-06-015539-6, HarpT). Har-Row.
Three Hundred Sixty-Five Ways to Cook Pasta. Marie Simmons. LC 87-46171. (Illus.). 224p. 1988. 14.95 (ISBN 0-06-015865-4). Har-Row.
Three Hundred Sixty-Seventh Fighter Group in World War II. Peter R. Moody. (Illus.). 75p. (Orig.). 1979. pap. 13.00x (ISBN 0-89126-080-3). MA-AH Pub.
Three Hundred Sixty-Six Stories for Bedtime. Stefanie Harwood. (Illus.). 236p. Date not set. 8.95 (ISBN 0-8317-8500-4, 785004). Smith Pubs.
Three Hundred Thirty-Five Crucial Questions on Christian Unity. Thomas B. Warren. 48p. 1984. pap. 1.50 (ISBN 0-934916-06-3). Natl Christian Pr.
Three Hundred Thirty-Three: A Bibliography of the Science Fantasy Novel. Joseph H. Crawford et al. LC 74-15959. (Science Fiction Ser). 82p. 1965. Repr. 14.00x (ISBN 0-405-06324-5). Ayer Co Pubs.
Three Hundred Thirty-Three More Science Tricks & Experiments. Robert J. Brown. (Illus.). 208p. 1984. 15.95 (ISBN 0-8306-0835-4); pap. 10.95 (ISBN 0-8306-1835-X, 1835). TAB Bks.
Three Hundred Thirty-Three Science Tricks & Experiments. Robert J. Brown. (Illus.). 208p. (Orig.). 1984. 15.95 (ISBN 0-8306-0825-7); pap. 9.95 (ISBN 0-8306-1825-2, 1825). TAB Bks.
Three Hundred Twenty Desert Watering Places in Southeastern California & Southwestern Nevada. W. C. Mendenhall. 104p. 14.95 (ISBN 0-913814-62-8). Nevada Pubns.
Three Hundred Twenty-Ninth Friend. Marjorie W. Sharmat. LC 76-6454. (Illus.). 48p. (gr. k-3). 1979. 9.95 (ISBN 0-02-782260-5, Four Winds). Macmillan.
Three Hundred Ways to Make Your Business Even More Successful. Allan Smith. 24p. 1988. write for info. (ISBN 0-931113-13-X). Success Publ.
Three Hundred Ways to Say No to Your Man. Erica Heller & Vicki Levites. 64p. 1983. 4.95 (ISBN 0-671-49534-8, Fireside). S&S.
Three Hundred Years at the Keyboard: A Piano Sourcebook from Bach to the Moderns. Patricia Fallows-Hammond. LC 83-23056. 312p. 1984. 21.95; pap. 15.95 (ISBN 0-89496-043-1). Ross Bks.
Three Hundred Years of American Drama & Theatre. 2nd ed. Garff B. Wilson. 1982. write for info.ref. ed. (ISBN 0-13-920330-3). P-H.
Three Hundred Years of American Seating Furniture: Garvan & Other Colls., Yale U. P. E. Kane. (Illus.). 319p. 25.00 (ISBN 0-686-47005-2). Apollo.
Three Hundred Years of Carolina Cooking. LC 76-124563. (Illus.). 318p. 1970. 9.95 (ISBN 0-9608172-0-4). Greenville SC Jr League.
Three Hundred Years of Education in South Africa. Edward G. Pells. Repr. of 1954 ed. lib. bdg. 25.00x (ISBN 0-8371-2217-1, PEEA). Greenwood.
Three Hundred Years of French Architecture, 1494-1794. facs. ed. Reginald Blomfield. LC 70-124233. (Select Bibliographies Reprint Ser). 1936. 16.00 (ISBN 0-8369-5414-9). Ayer Co Pubs.
Three Hundred Years of Gravitation. Ed. by S. W. Hawking & W. Israel. (Illus.). 704p. 1987. 69.50 (ISBN 0-521-34312-7). Cambridge U Pr.
Three Hundred Years of Kitchen Collectibles. 2nd ed. Linda C. Franklin. (Illus.). 578p. (Orig.). 1984. pap. 10.95 (ISBN 0-89689-041-4, 1454). Bks Americana.
Three Hundred Years of Psychiatry, 1535-1860. Richard Hunter & Ida Macalpine. LC 82-73004. xxvi, 1107p. 1982. Repr. of 1963 ed. 95.00 (ISBN 0-910177-00-7). Carlisle Pub.
Three-Hydroxy-Three-Methylglutaryl Coenzyms a Reductase. John R. Sabine. 288p. 1984. 125.00 (ISBN 0-8493-6551-1). CRC Pr.
Three Icelandic Sagas. 1950. Repr. 17.50 (ISBN 0-8274-3623-8). R West.
Three Imperial Mathematicians. Edward Rosen. 120p. 1986. 20.00 (ISBN 0-89835-242-8). Abaris Bks.
Three in One Pioneer Family Adventure Series. Sandy Dengler. (gr. 6). 1985. pap. 5.95 (ISBN 0-8024-6365-7). Moody.
Three Incredible Weeks with Meher Baba. Malcolm Schloss & Charles Purdom. Ed. by Filis Frederick. LC 80-109542. (Illus.). 165p. 1979. pap. 5.95 (ISBN 0-913078-36-0). Sheriar Pr.
Three Indian Campaigns. Wesley Merritt. 24p. pap. 3.95 (ISBN 0-8466-4037-6, I37). Shorey.
Three Indo-Anglian Poets: Henry Derozio, Toru Dutt & Sarojini Naidu. K. R. Nair. 128p. 1988. text ed. 18.95x (ISBN 81-207-0740-0, Pub. by Sterling Pubs India). Apt Bks.
Three-Ingredient Cookbook. Phyllis S. Prokop. LC 81-66561. 1981. 9.95 (ISBN 0-8054-7909-0). Broadman.
Three-Ingredient Cookbook. Sondra J. Stang. 1985. pap. 8.95 (ISBN 0-452-25668-2, Plume). NAL.
Three Ingredient Cookbook. Sondra J. Stang. 304p. 1987. pap. 3.95 (ISBN 0-451-14868-1, Sig). NAL.
Three Intellectual Plays: Jack Ruby, Mariana Alcoforado, Pocahontas. Edward W. Pearlstien. 146p. 1979. pap. 1.95 (ISBN 0-917636-02-3). Edit Consult.
Three International Episodes. 1985. 1.85 (ISBN 0-393-00351-5). Norton.
Three Investigator's Book of Mystery Puzzles. Barbara McCall. (Three Investigators Mystery Ser.). (Illus.). 64p. (gr. 3-7). 1982. pap. 1.50 (ISBN 0-394-85107-2). Random.
Three Investigators in the Case of the Weeping Coffin. Stine. (Find Your Fate Mysteries). 1985. pap. 1.95 (ISBN 0-394-86725-4). Random.
Three Irish Bardic Tales: Being Metrical Versions of the Three Tales Known As the Three Sorrows of Story-Telling. John Todhunter. LC 75-28845. Repr. of 1896 ed. 20.00 (ISBN 0-404-13829-2). AMS Pr.
Three Irish Glossaries. Ed. by Whitley Stokes. LC 78-72647. (Celtic Language & Literature: Goidelic & Brythonic). Repr. of 1862 ed. 27.50 (ISBN 0-404-17597-X). AMS Pr.
Three Irish Plays. Ed. by Harrison H. Schaff. Incl. Land of Heart's Desire. William B. Yeats; Twisting of the Rope. Douglas Hyde; Riders to the Sea. John M. Synge. 1962. pap. 3.00 (ISBN 0-8283-1457-8, IPL). Branden Pub Co.
Three Iron Mining Towns: A Study in Cultural Change. Paul H. Landis. LC 72-112555. (Rise of Urban America). 1970. Repr. of 1938 ed. 13.00 (ISBN 0-405-02462-2). Ayer Co Pubs.
Three Ivans Choreography Nijinska. Ray G. Cook. (Illus.). 30p. (Orig.). 1988. pap. text ed. 20.00 looseleaf (ISBN 0-9602002-8-2). Ray Cook.
Three Jacobean Tragedies. Ed. by Garmini Salgado. Incl. White Devil. John Webster; Revenger's Tragedy. Cyril Tourneur; Changeling. Thomas Middleton. (English Library Ser.). 1965. pap. 5.95 (ISBN 0-14-043006-7). Penguin.
Three Jacobean Witchcraft Plays. Ed. by Peter Corbin & Douglas Sedge. (Revels Plays Companion Library). 272p. 1986. 50.00 (ISBN 0-7190-1949-4, Pub. by Manchester Univ Pr). St Martin.
Three Japanese Plays from the Traditional Theatre. Ed. by Earle Ernst. LC 75-31473. (Illus.). 200p. 1976. Repr. of 1959 ed. lib. bdg. 35.00x (ISBN 0-8371-8532-7, ERTJ). Greenwood.
Three Jesuits Speak. Yves De Montcheuil & Charles Nicolet. Ed. by Henri De Lubac. LC 87-82017. 212p. (Orig.). 1987. pap. 12.95 (ISBN 0-89870-093-0). Ignatius Pr.
Three Jewels: A Study & Translation of Minamoto Tamenori's Sanboe. Edward Kamens. LC 87-30940. (Michigan Monograph Series in Japanese Studies: No. 2). 1988. text ed. 29.95 (ISBN 0-939512-34-3). U Mi Japan.
Three Jewish Philosophers: Philo, Saadya, Gaon, Jehuda, Halevi. Ed. by Hans Lewy et al. LC 60-9081. 1969. pap. text ed. 7.95x (ISBN 0-689-70126-8, T6). Atheneum.
Three Jolly Fellows. E. Raud. 126p. 1985. 5.95 (ISBN 0-8285-3133-1, Pub. by Perioodika Tallinn). Imported Pubns.
Three Jollys, Jollys Visit L. A., Jolly Gets Mugged: An ESL Adult-Child Reader. Valerie H. Weisberg. (Jolly Ser.). (Illus.). 76p. (Orig.). 1985. pap. text ed. 6.95x (ISBN 0-9610912-4-X). V H Pub.
Three Kentucky Artists: Hart, Price, & Troye. J. Winston Coleman, Jr. LC 74-7873. (Kentucky Bicentennial Bookshelf Ser.). (Illus.). 96p. 1974. 6.95 (ISBN 0-8131-0202-2). U Pr of Ky.
Three Kentucky Presidents: Lincoln, Taylor, Davis. Holman Hamilton. LC 77-92922. (Kentucky Bicentennial Bookshelf Ser.). (Illus.). 96p. 1978. 6.95 (ISBN 0-8131-0246-4). U Pr of Ky.
Three Keys to Spiritual Renewal. Clark Pinnock. 112p. 1986. pap. 4.95 (ISBN 0-87123-656-7). Bethany Hse.
Three Keys to the Kingdom. Mother M. Angelica. 116p. (Orig.). 1975. pap. text ed. 5.00 (ISBN 1-55794-017-7, B50). Eternal Wrd TV.
Three Kinds of Love. M. Toyotome. pap. 0.75 (ISBN 0-87784-132-2). Inter-Varsity.
Three Kingdoms: Russian Folktales from Alexander Afanasiev's Collection. Ed. by A. Kurkin. 152p. 1985. 10.95 (Pub. by Raduga Pubs USSR). Imported Pubns.
Three Kings. Hyman E. Goldin. 144p. 1929. 4.95 (ISBN 0-88482-737-2). Hebrew Pub.
Three Kings of Cologne. Joannes Of Hildesheim. Ed. by C. Horstmann. (EETS, OS Ser.: No. 85). Repr. of 1886 ed. 45.00 (ISBN 0-527-00083-3). Kraus Repr.
Three Kings of Israel. Mark E. Petersen. LC 80-36697. 179p. 1980. 6.95 (ISBN 0-87747-829-5). Deseret Bk.
Three Kittens. V. Suteyev. Tr. by Mirra Ginsburg. (Illus.). (gr. k-3). 1987. pap. 3.50 (ISBN 0-517-56551-X). Crown.
Three Ladies of London. Robert Wilson. LC 78-133767. (Tudor Facsimile Texts. Old English Plays: No. 55). Repr. of 1911 ed. 49.50 (ISBN 0-404-53355-8). AMS Pr.

Three Miseries of Barbary: Plague, Famine, Civill Warre. George Wilkins. LC 77-26339. (English Experience Ser.: No. 178). 32p. 1969. Repr. of 1606 ed. 20.00 (ISBN 90-221-0178-9). Walter J Johnson.

Three Miss Kings. Ada Cambridge. 352p. 1987. pap. 6.95 (ISBN 0-14-016164-3). Penguin.

Three Models of Independent Living in the Netherlands, No. 27. Gerben DeJong. (International Exchange of Experts & Information in Rehabilitation Ser.). pap. 3.00 (ISBN 0-939986-40-X). World Rehab Fund.

Three Models of Learning Disabilities. Ed. by Robert Piazza. (Special Education Ser.). (Illus., Orig.). 1978. pap. text ed. 16.00 (ISBN 0-89568-089-0). Spec Learn Corp.

Three Modern Japanese Plays. Ed. by Yozant Iwaski & Glenn Hughes. LC 76-40387. (One-Act Plays in Reprint Ser.). 1976. Repr. of 1923 ed. 15.00x (ISBN 0-8486-2003-8). Roth Pub Inc.

Three Modern Kyogen. Donald Richie. LC 77-188014. 96p. 1972. pap. 2.25 (ISBN 0-8048-1038-9). C E Tuttle.

Three Modern Plays for Women. Joan Lesse. 1978. 20.00 (ISBN 0-86025-831-9, Pub. by Ian Henry Pubns England). State Mutual Bk.

Three Modern Seers. Havelock Ellis. 227p. 1980. Repr. lib. bdg. 35.00 (ISBN 0-8495-1335-9). Arden Lib.

Three Modern Seers. Havelock Ellis. 59.95 (ISBN 0-8490-1211-2). Gordon Pr.

Three Modes of Criticism: The Literary Theories of Scherer, Walzel, & Staiger. Peter Salm. 1968. 15.00 (ISBN 0-8295-0128-2). UPB.

Three Modes of Modern Southern Fiction: Ellen Glasgow, William Faulkner, Thomas Wolfe. C. Hugh Holman. LC 66-19490. (Mercer University Lamar Lecture Ser: No. 9). 110p. 1966. 9.00x (ISBN 0-8203-0185-X). U of Ga Pr.

Three Months in a Workshop: A Practical Study. Paul Gohre. LC 74-38277. (Evolution of Capitalism Ser.). 236p. 1972. Repr. of 1895 ed. 25.50 (ISBN 0-405-04121-7). Ayer Co Pubs.

Three Months in the Southern States. Arthur J. Fremantle. LC 84-2701. (Collector's Library of the Civil War Ser.). 1984. kivar binding 26.60 (ISBN 0-8094-4454-2, Pub. by Time-Life). Silver.

Three Months' Residence at Nablus: And an Account of the Modern Samaritans. John Mills. LC 77-87610. Repr. of 1864 ed. 25.50 (ISBN 0-404-16434-X). AMS Pr.

Three More Novels: Vainglory, Inclinations, & Caprice. Ronald Firbank. LC 86-2363. (Revived Modern Classics Ser.). 448p. 1986. pap. 9.95 (ISBN 0-8112-0975-X, NDP614). New Directions.

Three More Plays for Reading. Tom Bowie. 1988. 16.95 (ISBN 0-932508-08-1). Seven Oaks.

Three Motets. Giaches De Wert. Ed. by Bernard B. De Surcy. LC 68-8191. (Penn State Music Series, No. 19). 64p. pap. 5.75x (ISBN 0-271-09119-3). Pa St U Pr.

Three Mountains Press Anthology of Poetry. (Orig.). 1976. pap. text ed. 2.00 (ISBN 0-930986-01-6). Three Mtn Pr.

Three Mughal Poets: Mir, Sauda, Mir Hasan. Ralph Russell & Khurshidul Islam. LC 68-15643. 1968. 21.00x (ISBN 0-674-88980-0). Harvard U Pr.

Three Musicians. Rod Townley. LC 77-826861. (Illus.). 96p. (Orig.). 1978. pap. 3.50 (ISBN 0-912292-43-1). The Smith.

Three Musketeers. Alexandre Dumas. (Airmont Classics Ser.). (gr. 8 up). pap. 3.95 (ISBN 0-8049-0127-9, CL-127). Airmont.

Three Musketeers. Alexandre Dumas. (Illustrated Junior Library). (Illus.). (gr. 4-6). 1953-59. pap. 6.95 (ISBN 0-448-11024-5, G&D); deluxe ed. 11.95 (ISBN 0-448-06024-8). Putnam Pub Group.

Three Musketeers. Alexandre Dumas. 1976. lib. bdg. 20.95 (ISBN 0-89968-148-4). Lightyear.

Three Musketeers. Alexandre Dumas. Ed. by Naunerle Farr. (Now Age Illustrated Ser., No. 2). (Illus.). 64p. (Orig.). (gr. 5-10). 1974. 7.50 (ISBN 0-88301-218-9); pap. text ed. 2.95 (ISBN 0-88301-133-6). Pendulum Pr.

Three Musketeers. Alexandre Dumas. 1982. pap. 5.95 (ISBN 0-14-044025-9). Penguin.

Three Musketeers. Alexandre Dumas. (Regents Illustrated Classics Ser.). 62p. (gr. 7-12). 1982. pap. text ed. 3.50 (ISBN 0-13-920463-6, 20533). Prentice ESL.

Three Musketeers. Alexandre Dumas. 1984. Repr. lib. bdg. 20.95x (ISBN 0-89966-486-5). Buccaneer Bks.

Three Musketeers. Alexandre Dumas. (Illus.). 608p. 1984. 14.95 (ISBN 0-396-08355-2). Dodd.

Three Musketeers. unabridged ed. Alexandre Dumas. Tr. by Lowell Bair from Fr. 560p. 1984. pap. 4.95 (ISBN 0-553-21337-7, Bantam Classics). Bantam.

Three Musketeers. Alexandre Dumas. LC 84-50433. (Silver Burdett Classics for Kids Ser.). (Illus.). 37p. (gr. 3 up). 1984. 5.96 (ISBN 0-382-06812-2). Silver.

Three Musketeers. Alexandre Dumas. LC 84-50433. (Silver Burdett Classics for Kids Ser.). (Illus.). 32p. (gr. 3 up). 1985. pap. 3.60 (ISBN 0-382-06955-2). Silver.

Three Musketeers. Alexandre Dumas. (Puffin Classics Ser.). 1987. pap. 2.25 (ISBN 0-14-035054-3, Puffin Bks). Penguin.

Three Musketeers. As told by Catherine Storr. (Stories Clippers Ser.). (Illus.). 32p. (gr. k-5). 1985. PLB 15.33 (ISBN 0-8172-2500-5); pap. 9.27 (ISBN 0-8172-2508-0). Raintree Pubs.

Three Musketeers. (Classics Ser.). (gr. 4 up). 1988. pap. 3.95 (ISBN 0-582-01384-4). Longman.

Three Musketeers: Student Activity Book. Marcia Sohl & Gerald Dackerman. (Now Age Illustrated). (Illus.). (gr. 4-10). 1976. wkbk 1.25 (ISBN 0-88301-197-2). Pendulum Pr.

Three Muslim Sages. Seyyed H. Nasr. LC 75-14430. 192p. 1976. pap. text ed. 10.00x (ISBN 0-88206-500-9). Caravan Bks.

Three Mysteries of Jesus. Glenn Clark. 1978. 0.95 (ISBN 0-910924-85-6). Macalester.

Three Mystic Poets: A Study of W. B. Yeats, A. E. & Rabindrath Tagore. Abinash C. Bose. LC 72-187263. 1945. lib. bdg. 15.00 (ISBN 0-8414-2534-5). Folcroft.

Three Napoleonic Battles. Harold T. Parker. LC 82-21082. (Illus.). xxiii, 235p. 1983. pap. text ed. 12.75 (ISBN 0-8223-0547-X). Duke.

Three Negro Classics. Ed. by John H. Franklin. Incl. Up from Slavery. Booker T. Washington; Souls of Black Folk. William E. Du Bois; Autobiography of an Ex-Colored Man. James Weldon Johnson. (YA) (gr. 7 up). 1965. pap. 4.95 (ISBN 0-380-01581-1, 60260-1, Discus). Avon.

Three Neo-Tech Papers. Frank R. Wallace. 1986. 17.50 (ISBN 0-911752-50-1). I & O Pub.

Three Nephites: Substance & Significance of the Legend in Folklore. Lee H. Hector. Ed. by Richard Dorson. LC 77-70608. (International Folklore Ser.). 1977. Repr. of 1949 ed. lib. bdg. 14.00x (ISBN 0-405-10105-8). Ayer Co Pubs.

Three New England Watercolor Painters. Gail Savage et al. LC 74-21601. (Illus.). 72p. (Orig.). 1974. pap. 1.50x (ISBN 0-86559-016-8). Art Inst Chi.

Three New Mexico Chronicles. Ed. by H. Bailey Carroll & J. Villasana Haggard. Incl. Exposicion. Pedro B Pino; Ojeada. Antonio Barreiro; Addition. Jose A. De Escudero. LC 67-24722. (Quivira Society Publications Ser). 342p. 1967. Repr. of 1942 ed. 17.00 (ISBN 0-405-00085-5). Ayer Co Pubs.

Three New Species of Centrolenid Frogs from the Pacific Versant of Ecuador & Colombia. William E. Duellman. (Occasional Papers: No. 88). 9p. 1981. 1.25 (ISBN 0-317-04856-2). U of KS Mus Nat Hist.

Three New Species of Darters (Percidae, Etheostoma) of the Subgenus Nanostoma from Kentucky & Tennessee. Lawrence M. Page & Brooks M. Burr. (Occasional Papers: No. 101). (Illus.). 20p. 1982. 4.00 (ISBN 0-317-04835-X). U of KS Mus Nat Hist.

Three Nigerian Emirates: A Study in Oral History. Victor N. Low. LC 74-176163. pap. 82.00 (ISBN 0-317-27770-7, 2015424). Bks Demand UMI.

Three Nights in the Heart of the Earth. Brett Laidlaw. 1988. 15.95 (ISBN 0-393-02510-1). Norton.

Three Northumbrian Poems. Ed. by A. H. Smith. (Old English Ser.). 1968. pap. text ed. 4.95x (ISBN 0-89197-571-3). Irvington.

Three Notelets on Shakespeare. W. J. Thoms. LC 72-3737. (Studies in Shakespeare, No. 24). 1972. Repr. of 1865 ed. lib. bdg. 39.95x (ISBN 0-8383-1570-4). Haskell.

Three Notes on Longfellow. Carl L. Johnson. (American Literature Ser., No. 49). 1970. pap. 39.95x (ISBN 0-8383-0047-2). Haskell.

Three Notes on Thomas Hardy. Benton L. Hatch & Walter Peirce. 1978. Repr. of 1966 ed. 15.00 (ISBN 0-8492-5310-1). R West.

Three Novellas. John Herdman. 1988. pap. 8.95 (ISBN 0-948275-37-5). Polygon Assoc.

Three Novellas. Ivan S. Turgenev. 15.95 (ISBN 0-89190-476-X, Pub. by Am Repr). Amereon Ltd.

Three Novels. Samuel Beckett. Incl. Molloy; Malone Dies; Unnamable. 1965. pap. 7.95 (ISBN 0-394-17299-X, B78, BC). Grove.

Three Novels. F. Scott Fitzgerald. Ed. by Malcolm Cowley & Edmund Wilson. 1970. pap. text ed. 11.95 (ISBN 0-684-16245-8, SL248, ScribT). Scribner.

Three Novels. Ernest Hemingway. Bd. with Sun Also Rises; Farewell to Arms; Old Man & the Sea. 650p. 1978. pap. text ed. write for info. (ISBN 0-02-353550-4, Pub. by Scribner). Macmillan.

Three Novels. V. S. Naipaul. LC 82-47819. 1982. 18.45 (ISBN 0-394-52847-6). Knopf.

Three Novels. Robert Silverberg. 1988. pap. 4.95 (ISBN 0-553-27287-X, Spectra). Bantam.

Three Novels. Harriet Beecher Stowe. Ed. by Kathryn K. Sklar. Incl. Uncle Tom's Cabin; Minister's Wooing; Oldtown Folks. LC 81-18629. 1478p. 1982. 27.50 (ISBN 0-940450-01-1). Library of America.

Three Novels by Mariano Azuela. Mariano Azuela. Tr. by Frances K. Hendricks & Beatrice Berler. LC 78-68663. 373p. 1979. 15.00 (ISBN 0-911536-78-7). Trinity U Pr.

Three Novels: Ferdydurke, Pornografia, & Cosmos. Witold Gombrowicz. Tr. by Eric Mosbacher & Alastair Hamilton. 1978. pap. 9.95 (ISBN 0-394-17067-9, E720, Ever). Grove.

Three Novels of F. Scott Fitzgerald. F. Scott Fitzgerald. Bd. with Great Gatsby; Tender is the Night; Last Tycoon. 634p. 1979. pap. text ed. write for info. (ISBN 0-02-337980-4, Pub. by Scribner). Macmillan.

Three Novels of Madame De Duras: Ourika, Edouard, Olivier. Grant Crichfield. (De Proprietatibus Litterarum, Series Practica: No. 114). 67p. (Orig.). 1975. pap. text ed. 11.20x (ISBN 90-2793-316-2). Mouton.

Three Novels: The Blackmailer, A Man of Power, The Great Occasion. Isabel Colegate. 536p. 1984. 25.00 (ISBN 0-670-52409-3); pap. 9.95 (ISBN 0-14-006975-5). Viking.

Three Number Author Tables. G. C. Makkar. 200p. 1974. 6.00 (ISBN 0-88065-153-9, Pub. by Messers Today & Tomorrows Printers & Publishers India). Scholarly Pubns.

Three Odes of Keats. E. L. Marilla. LC 74-2320. 1962. Repr. lib. bdg. 18.00 (ISBN 0-8414-6121-X). Folcroft.

Three Odes of Keats. E. L. Marilla. (Essays & Studies on English Language & Literature: Vol. 24). (Orig.). 1962. pap. 15.00 (ISBN 0-8115-0222-8). Kraus Repr.

Three of a Kind. Emily Chase. (Girls of Canby Hall Ser.: No. 16). (Illus.). 176p. (Orig.). (gr. 6 up). 1985. pap. 1.95 (ISBN 0-590-33706-8). Scholastic Inc.

Three of a Kind. Merritt Clifton. 20p. 1979. pap. 1.00 (ISBN 0-686-27927-1). Samisdat.

Three of a Kind. Robert Shaw. LC 77-7591. 1978. 14.95 (ISBN 0-87949-104-3). Ashley Bks.

Three of a Kind: Are We Constitutional Christians? Wilfred T. Adderley. LC 86-91708. 59p. 1988. 5.95 (ISBN 0-533-07365-0). Vantage.

Three of China's Mighty Men. Leslie T. Lyall. pap. 3.95 (ISBN 0-340-25561-7). OMF Bks.

Three of Us. Cynthia Blair. 368p. 1988. pap. 3.95 (ISBN 0-345-32927-9). Ballantine.

Three Old English Prose Texts. Ed. by S. Rypins. (EETS OS: No. 161). Repr. of 1924 ed. 34.00 (ISBN 0-527-00158-9). Kraus Repr.

Three Old Timers of Cape Cod. Edward Darling. (Illus.). 1974. 5.00 (ISBN 0-87482-034-0). Wake-Brook.

Three on the Trail. Max Brand. 208p. 1985. pap. 2.50 (ISBN 0-446-32688-7). Warner Bks.

Three on the Trail. Max Brand. (Large Print Books (General Ser.)). 1985. lib. bdg. 13.95 (ISBN 0-8161-3851-6). G K Hall.

Three One Act Plays for Radio see Behan: The Complete Plays.

Three or Four Hills & a Cloud: Wesleyan Poetry, Vol. 106. Robert Farnsworth. LC 82-4932. 64p. 1982. pap. 8.95 (ISBN 0-8195-1108-0). Wesleyan U Pr.

Three Orations in Favour of the Olynthians with Fower Orations Against King Philip. Demosthenes. Tr. by Thomas Wilson. LC 68-54637. (English Experience Ser.: No. 54). 200p. 1968. Repr. of 1570 ed. 27.50 (ISBN 90-221-0054-5). Walter J Johnson.

Three Orders: Feudal Society Imagined. Georges Duby. Tr. by Arthur Goldhammer. LC 80-13158. 432p. 1980. lib. bdg. 32.00x (ISBN 0-226-16771-2, PHOEN); pap. 12.95 (ISBN 0-226-16772-0). U of Chicago Pr.

Three Othellos. Daniel Amneus. 1986. 15.00 (ISBN 0-9610864-2-4); pap. 10.00 (ISBN 0-9610864-3-2). Primrose Pr.

Three Outsiders: Pascal, Kierkegaard, Simone Weil. Diogenes Allen. LC 82-83552. 143p. (Orig.). 1983. pap. 6.50 (ISBN 0-936384-08-5). Cowley Pubns.

Three Ovidian Tales. Ed. by Raymond J. Cormier. LC 84-48061. 130p. 1985. lib. bdg. 20.00 (ISBN 0-8240-8956-1). Garland Pub.

Three Pacific Northwest Poets: William Stafford, Richard Hugo, & David Wagoner. Sanford Pinsker. (United States Authors Ser.). 160p. 1987. 19.95 (ISBN 0-8057-7500-5, Twayne). G K Hall.

Three Pairs of Silk Stockings. Panteleimon S. Romanov. Ed. by Stephen Graham. Tr. by Leonide Zarine from Rus. LC 72-90308. (Soviet Literature in English Translation Ser.). 344p. 1973. Repr. of 1931 ed. 22.50 (ISBN 0-88355-019-9). Hyperion Conn.

Three Pakistan Villages. John J. Honigmann. 95p. 1958. pap. text ed. 4.00 (ISBN 0-89143-057-1). U NC Inst Res Soc Sci.

Three Palladins. Harold Lamb. 12.00 (ISBN 0-686-27901-8). D M Grant.

Three Pamphlets on the Jacobean Antifeminist Controversy. LC 78-5847. 1978. Repr. of 1620 ed. 35.00x (ISBN 0-8201-1307-7). Schol Facsimiles.

Three Panics: An Historical Episode. 3rd ed. R. Cobden. Repr. of 1862 ed. 20.00 (ISBN 0-527-18230-3). Kraus Repr.

Three Papers on Dynamical Systems. LC 81-4981. (Translations Series Two: Vol. 116). 1981. 41.00 (ISBN 0-8218-3066-X, TRANS2-116). Am Math.

Three Papers on Hardy. Benton L. Hatch et al. 1966. lib. bdg. 17.50 (ISBN 0-8414-5018-8). Folcroft.

Three Papers on Quality of Urban Environment. Gary L. Ault et al. 55p. 1967. pap. 2.00 (ISBN 0-318-00016-4, EDA 5). Inst for Urban & Regional.

Three Papers on the History & Language of the Hittites see Mediterranean Studies.

Three Part Conductus in Related Sources. Ed. by Gordon Anderson. (Gesamtausgaben: Vol. X-9). 160p. 1986. lib. bdg. write for info. (ISBN 0-931902-24-X). Inst Mediaeval Mus.

Three Partners, & Other Tales. facsimile ed. Bret Harte. LC 76-37547. (Short Story Index Reprint Ser.). Repr. of 1900 ed. 23.50 (ISBN 0-8369-4106-3). Ayer Co Pubs.

Three Passions of Countess Natalya. Alan Fisher. Ed. by Black & Boegehold. 352p. 1985. lib. bdg. 15.95 (ISBN 0-02-538460-0). Macmillan.

Three Paths to the Lake. Ingeborg Bachmann. (Modern German Voices Ser.). Orig. Title: Simultaneous. 243p. 1988. 24.50 (ISBN 0-8419-1070-7). Holmes & Meier.

Three Pearls of Number Theory. Aleksander Y. Khinchin. LC 52-2385. 1952. 9.00x (ISBN 0-910670-04-8). Graylock.

Three Penny Lane. Fielding Dawson. LC 80-27344. 150p. (Orig.). 1981. signed ed. 20.00 (ISBN 0-87685-447-1); pap. 5.00 (ISBN 0-87685-446-3). Black Sparrow.

Three Percent of Mankind Suffers from Psoriasis but Are Not Acquainted with It's Workings. Silvio Gaetti. 1988. 12.95 (ISBN 0-533-07202-6). Vantage.

Three Percent Solution & the Future of NATO. Foreign Policy Research Institute Staff. LC 80-27824. 118p. (Orig.). 1981. pap. 6.95 (ISBN 0-910191-02-6). For Policy Res.

Three Perfect Ideas. Roy J. Rackley. LC 81-51549. 574p. (Orig.). 1981. pap. 18.95 (ISBN 0-940470-00-4). Santiago Pr.

Three "Perfect Novels" - & What They Have in Common. Louis Auchincloss. 1981. ltd. ed. 10.00 (ISBN 0-89723-025-6). Bruccoli.

Three Perfections: Chinese Painting, Poetry & Calligraphy. Michael Sullivan. LC 80-18189. (Illus.). 64p. pap. 6.95 (ISBN 0-8076-0997-8). Braziller.

Three Perfections: Chinese Painting, Poetry & Calligraphy. Michael Sullivan. 64p. 1980. 70.00x (Pub. by Han-Shan Tang Ltd). State Mutual Bk.

Three Perils of Man: War, Women & Witchcraft. James Hogg. (Scottish Classics Ser.: Vol. 6). 528p. (Orig.). 1987. pap. 9.50 (ISBN 0-7073-0511-X, Pub. by Scot Acad Pr). Longwood Pub Group.

Three-Personed God: The Trinity As a Mystery of Salvation. William J. Hill. LC 81-18012. 354p. 1982. pap. 15.95x (ISBN 0-8132-0676-6). Cath U Pr.

Three Persons from the Bible: Or Babylon. Thomas H. Weisser. (Illus.). 44p. pap. 2.00 (ISBN 0-317-17477-0). Tom Weisser.

Three Perspectives of Biology. Donald B. Pribor. 82p. 1986. pap. text ed. 7.95 (ISBN 0-89917-471-X, Pub. by College Town Pr). Tichenor Pub.

Three-Phase Cage Induction Motors. EEMUA Staff. 1981. 75.00x (ISBN 0-85931-137-6, Pub. by EEMUA). State Mutual Bk.

Three-Phase Catalytic Reactors. P. A. Ramachandran & R. V. Chaudhari. LC 81-23521. (Topics in Chemical Engineering Ser.: Vol. 2). (Illus.). 440p. 1983. 96.00 (ISBN 0-677-05650-8). Gordon & Breach.

Three-Phase Electricity. Wolfgang Weiske. (Siemens Programmed Instruction Ser.: 15). pap. 20.00 (ISBN 0-317-27748-0, 2052091). Bks Demand UMI.

Three-Phase Motor Winding Data from Simple Measurements. 3rd ed. Samuel Heller. (Illus., Orig.). 1961. pap. 32.00 (ISBN 0-911740-00-7). Datarule.

Three-Phase Power & Its Measurements. Hans-Joachim Gaus. (Siemens Programmed Instruction Ser.: 16). pap. 20.00 (ISBN 0-317-27745-6, 2052092). Bks Demand UMI.

Three Phases of Cooperation in the West. Amos G. Warner. LC 78-63783. (Johns Hopkins University. Studies in the Social Sciences. Sixth Ser. 1888: 7-8). Repr. of 1888 ed. 11.50 (ISBN 0-404-61048-X). AMS Pr.

Three Phases of Cooperation in the West. Amos G. Warner. (Johns Hopkins University Studies in Historical & Political Science, Ser. 6: Nos. 7, 8). 79p. pap. 9.00 (ISBN 0-384-66803-8). Johnson Repr.

Three Phases of Eve. Eve Arden. LC 85-1692. (Illus.). 288p. 1985. 17.95 (ISBN 0-312-80267-6). St Martin.

Three Phases of Eve: An Autobiography. Eve Arden. (Illus.). 288p. 1988. pap. 9.95x (ISBN 0-312-01521-6, Pub. by Thomas Dunne Bks). St Martin.

Three Phases of Matter. 2nd ed. Alan J. Walton. (Illus.). 1983. 49.50x (ISBN 0-19-851957-5); pap. 24.95x (ISBN 0-19-851953-2). Oxford U Pr.

Three Phillipines Epic Plays: Lam-ang, Labaw Donggon & Bantugan. Mig A. Enriquez. 198p. 1983. (Pub. by New Day Phillipines); pap. 10.00 (ISBN 0-686-39823-8). Cellar.

Three Philosophers: Lavoisier, Priestley & Cavendish. Wallace R. Aykroyd. LC 77-98808. Repr. of 1935 ed. lib. bdg. 35.00 (ISBN 0-8371-2890-0, AYTB). Greenwood.

Three Physico-Theological Discourses: Primitive Chaos, & Creation of the World, the General Deluge, Its Causes & Effects. John Ray. Ed. by Claude C. Albritton, Jr. LC 77-6538. (History of Geology Ser.). 1978. Repr. of 1713 ed. lib. bdg. 34.50x (ISBN 0-405-10457-X). Ayer Co Pubs.

Three Piano Works. Cecile Chaminade. Incl. Sonata in C Minor, Opus 21; Etude Symphonique, Opus 28; Six Concert Etudes, Opus 35. LC 79-1501. (Women Composers Ser.: No. 2). 1979. Repr. of 1895 ed. 27.50 (ISBN 0-306-79551-5). Da Capo.
Three Pieces. Ntozake Shange. 1982. pap. 5.95 (ISBN 0-14-048170-2). Penguin.
Three Pigs. Tony Ross. LC 83-2356. (Illus.). 32p. (gr. 2-4). 1983. 10.95 (ISBN 0-394-86143-4, Pant Bks Young); lib. bdg. 10.99 (ISBN 0-394-96143-9). Pantheon.
Three Pillars of Zen: Teaching, Practice, Enlightenment. Philip Kapleau. LC 78-22794. (Illus.). 1980. pap. 10.95 (ISBN 0-385-14786-4, Anch). Doubleday.
Three Pioneer Rapides Families. G. M. Stafford. 1968. 22.50 (ISBN 0-87511-631-0). Claitors.
Three Pioneer Tennessee Documents: Donelson's Journal, Cumberland Compact, Minutes of Cumberland Court. Three Pioneer Tennessee Documents. LC 64-64789. pap. 20.00 (ISBN 0-317-26104-5, 2024382). Bks Demand UMI.
Three Places in New Inkland. David Cole et al. LC 77-72826. 1977. pap. 5.95 (ISBN 0-9605610-1-3). Zartscorp.
Three Plays. John Ashbery. 1978. 15.00 (ISBN 0-915990-12-1); pap. 7.50 (ISBN 0-915990-13-X). Z Pr.
Three Plays. Bjornstjerne Bjornson. Tr. by Edwin Bjorkman from Norwegian. LC 87-38139. vi, 280p. 1988. Repr. of 1913 ed. lib. bdg. 35.00x (ISBN 0-86527-383-9). Fertig.
Three Plays. Noel Coward. Incl. Blithe Spirit; Hay Fever; Private Lives. 1979. pap. 7.95 (ISBN 0-394-17535-2, E742, Ever). Grove.
Three Plays. Nissim Ezekiel. (Writers Workshop Bluebird Ser.). 95p. 1975. cancelled (ISBN 0-88253-660-5); pap. text ed. 4.00 (ISBN 0-88253-659-1). Ind-US Inc.
Three Plays. Ford. (Classics Ser.). 1971. pap. 6.95 (ISBN 0-14-043059-8). Penguin.
Three Plays. Eugene Ionesco. Tr. by Donald Watson from Fr. Incl. Amedee; New Tenant; Victims of Duty. 1958. pap. 3.95 (ISBN 0-394-17212-4, E119, Ever). Grove.
Three Plays. Nikos Kazantzakis. Incl. Kouros; Melissa; Christopher Columbus. 1969. S&S.
Three Plays. D. H. Lawrence. 1982. pap. 5.95 (ISBN 0-14-048086-2). Penguin.
Three Plays. Noel Leslie. LC 79-50026. (One-Act Plays in Reprint Ser.). 1980. Repr. of 1920 ed. 15.00x (ISBN 0-8486-2050-X). Roth Pub Inc.
Three Plays. Thomas Middleton. Ed. by Kenneth Muir. (Rowman & Littlefield University Library). 217p. 1975. pap. 4.75x (ISBN 0-87471-556-3). Rowman.
Three Plays. Thomas Middleton. Ed. by Kenneth Muir. 238p. 1984. pap. 6.95x (ISBN 0-460-11368-2, DEL-05077, Pub. by Evman England). Biblio Dist.
Three Plays. M. J. Molloy. 1975. 10.00x (ISBN 0-912262-30-3). Proscenium.
Three Plays. Joyce Carol Oates. LC 80-20210. 157p. 1980. 12.95 (ISBN 0-86538-001-5); pap. 7.95 (ISBN 0-86538-002-3). Ontario Rev NJ.
Three Plays. Eugene O'Neill. Incl. Desire Under the Elms; Strange Interlude; Mourning Becomes Electra. 1959. pap. 5.95 (ISBN 0-394-70165-8, Vin). Random.
Three Plays. facsimile ed. David Pinski. Tr. by Isaac Goldberg from Yiddish. LC 74-29513. (Modern Jewish Experience Ser.). (Eng.). 1975. Repr. of 1918 ed. 21.00x (ISBN 0-405-06739-9). Ayer Co Pubs.
Three Plays. Harold Pinter. Incl. Collection; Slight Ache; Dwarfs. 1962. pap. 4.95 (ISBN 0-394-17240-X, E350, Ever). Grove.
Three Plays. Alexander Solzhenitsyn. Incl. Victory Celebrations; Prisoners; Love-Girl & the Innocent. 365p. 1986. 20.00 (ISBN 0-374-28356-7); pap. 10.95 (ISBN 0-374-51924-2). FS&G.
Three Plays. August Strindberg. Incl. Miss Julie; Outlaw; Stronger. pap. 3.00 (ISBN 0-8283-1458-6, IPL). Branden Pub Co.
Three Plays. August Strindberg. Tr. by Peter Watts. Incl. Father; Miss Julie; Easter. (Classics Ser.). (Orig.). 1958. pap. 3.95 (ISBN 0-14-044082-8). Penguin.
Three Plays. Thornton Wilder. Bd. with Our Town; The Skin of Our Teeth; The Matchmaker. LC 85-42603. 416p. 1985. pap. 8.95 (ISBN 0-06-091293-6, PL 1293, PL). Har-Row.
Three Plays about Crime & Criminals. Ed. by George Freedley. Incl. Arsenic & Old Lace. Joseph Kesselring; Detective Story. Sidney Kingsley; Kind Lady. Edward Chodorov. 279p. pap. 3.95 (ISBN 0-671-47229-1). WSP.
Three Plays: Absurd Person Singular, Absent Friends, & Bedroom Farce. Alan Ayckbourn. LC 78-20339. 1979. pap. 6.95 (ISBN 0-394-17083-0, B423, BC). Grove.
Three Plays: All Mine, the Row, the Partners. Francis Pollini. 1967. 7.50 (ISBN 0-685-79045-2). Small Pr Dist.
Three Plays by Armand Salacrou: The World Is Round, When the Music Stops, Marguerite. Armand Salacrou. LC 67-28877. (Minnesota Drama Editions Ser.: No. 4). pap. 57.30 (ISBN 0-317-29491-1, 2055909). Bks Demand UMI.
Three Plays by David Garrick. David Garrick. Ed. by Elizabeth P. Stein. LC 67-23858. 1967. Repr. of 1926 ed. 14.00 (ISBN 0-405-08556-7). Ayer Co Pubs.
Three Plays by Emmanuel Robles: Plaidoyer Pour un Rebelle (Case for a Rebel), L'Horloge (the Clock), & Porfirio. Emmanuel Robles. Tr. by James A. Kilker from Fr. LC 77-24662. (Illus.). 223p. 1977. 17.50x (ISBN 0-8093-0822-3). S Ill U Pr.
Three Plays by George Bernard Shaw. Intro. by Sylvan Barnet. 1985. pap. 4.95 (ISBN 0-451-51903-5, Sig Classics). NAL.
Three Plays by Hebbel. Ed. & tr. by Marion W. Sonnenfeld. LC 72-3531. 271p. 1974. 24.50 (ISBN 0-8387-1239-8). Bucknell U Pr.
Three Plays by John Cromwell. John Cromwell. 1988. 13.95 (ISBN 0-533-07842-3). Vantage.
Three Plays by Louisiana Playwrights. Ed. by Cj Stevens. LC 82-80740. (Illus.). 229p. (Orig.). 1982. pap. 13.50 (ISBN 0-88127-006-7). Oracle Pr LA.
Three Plays by Plautus. Paul Roche. 1984. pap. 6.00x (ISBN 0-86516-035-X). Bolchazy Carducci.
Three Plays by Thornton Wilder. Thornton Wilder. 1984. pap. 2.95 (ISBN 0-380-00527-1, 69005-5, Bard). Avon.
Three Plays by Tina Howe. Tina Howe. 256p. (Orig.). 1984. pap. 4.95 (ISBN 0-380-85001-X, 85001-X, Bard). Avon.
Three Plays: 'Enrico IV', 'Sei personaggi in cerca d'autore', 'La giara' Luigi Pirandello. Ed. by F. Firth. (Italian Texts). 308p. (Ital.). 1969. pap. 11.00 (ISBN 0-7190-0346-6, Pub. by Manchester Univ Pr). St Martin.
Three Plays for a Gay Theater. Richard Hall. LC 82-12099. 188p. (Orig.). 1983. pap. 6.95 (ISBN 0-912516-73-9). Grey Fox.
Three Plays for Church. Bill Mabry. 1976. pap. 2.95 (ISBN 0-8054-7512-5). Broadman.
Three Plays for Reading. Tom Bowie. LC 79-64092. 1979. pap. 16.95 (ISBN 0-932508-04-9). Seven Oaks.
Three Plays: Juno & the Paycock, The Shadow of a Gunman, & The Plough & the Stars. Sean O'Casey. 218p. 1969. pap. 3.95 (ISBN 0-312-80290-0, Papermac). St Martin.
Three Plays: Norm & Ahmed, Rooted, The Roy Murphy Show. Alexander Buzo. 19p. Date not set. pap. 7.95. Applause Theatre Bk Pubs.
Three Plays of Adventure. Charlotte B. Chorpenning & Anne Nicholson. 1972. 5.00x (ISBN 0-85343-504-9). Coach Hse.
Three Plays of Euripides. Euripides. Tr. & intro. by Paul Roche. Incl. Alcestis; Medea; Bacchae. 126p. 1974. pap. 4.95x (ISBN 0-393-09312-3). Norton.
Three Plays: Phaedra, Andromache, Britannicus. Jean Racine. Tr. by George Dillon. LC 61-15938. 1961. pap. text ed. 8.00X (ISBN 0-226-15077-1, P76, Phoen). U of Chicago Pr.
Three Plays: Piaf. Pam Gems. 1986. pap. 6.95 (ISBN 0-14-048203-2). Penguin.
Three Plays: Procession, Bhoma, Stale News. Badal Sircar. 1983. pap. 8.00x (ISBN 0-8364-0964-7, Pub. by Seagull Bks India). South Asia Bks.
Three Plays: Striptease, Repeat Performance, the Prophets. Slawomir Mrozek. Tr. by Lola Gruenthal et al from Pol. 168p. (Orig.). 1986. pap. 5.95 (ISBN 0-936839-49-X). Applause Theatre Bk Pubs.
Three Plays: The Last Carnival; Beef, No Chicken; A Branch of the Blue Nile. Derek Walcott. LC 85-30774. 312p. 1986. 22.50 (ISBN 0-374-28618-3); pap. 9.95 (ISBN 0-374-51883-1). FS&G.
Three Plays: The Weavers, Hannele, the Beaver Coat. Gerhart Hauptmann. Tr. by Horst Frenz & Miles Waggoner. LC 77-6945. 1978. pap. 7.95x (ISBN 0-8044-6254-2). Ungar.
Three Plays: To Anchor a Cloud; Apply, No Reply; A Clean Break. Dilip Hiro. 176p. (Orig.). 1985. pap. 10.00 (ISBN 0-946013-01-2, Pub. by Madison Bks UK). Three Continents.
Three Plus One Equals Billions: The Bendix-Martin Marietta War. Allan Sloan. 272p. 1984. pap. 8.95 (ISBN 0-88184-025-4). Carroll & Graf.
Three Poems. John Ashbery. 120p. 1986. pap. 7.95 (ISBN 0-14-058585-0). Penguin.
Three Poems. Jon Silkin. 8p. 1969. signed 7.50 (ISBN 0-913219-09-6). Pym-Rand Pr.
Three Poems for Now. facsimile of 1953 ed. Gordden Link. LC 53-12585. 42p. 1972. 4.95 (ISBN 0-87419-043-6, U Pr of Wash). Larlin Corp.
Three Poetical Prayer-Makers of the Island of Britain. Gwyn Jones. (Warton Lectures on English Peotry). 9p. 1981. pap. 5.50 (ISBN 0-85672-356-8, Pub. by British Acad). Longwood Pub Group.
Three Poets & Reality. Ruth Hofrichter. LC 78-86024. (Essay & General Literature Index Reprint Ser). 1969. Repr. of 1942 ed. 23.00x (ISBN 0-8046-0564-5, Pub by Kennikat). Assoc Faculty Pr.
Three Poets & Reality. Ruth Hofrichter. 1942. 21.50x (ISBN 0-686-83821-1). Elliots Bks.
Three Poets at Yuyama. Steven D. Carter. LC 83-81286. (Japan Research Monograph: No. 4). 126p. pap. 6.00x (ISBN 0-912966-61-0). IEAS.
Three Poets of the Rhymers' Club. Ed. by Derek Stanford. (Fyfield Ser.). 177p. 1974. 7.50 (ISBN 0-85635-089-3). Carcanet.
Three Point One Four One Six & All That. Philip J. Davis & William G. Chinn. 1985. pap. 16.95 (ISBN 0-8176-3304-9). Birkhauser.
Three-Pointed Star: The Story of Mercedes-Benz. David Scott-Moncrieff. 1979. 18.95 (ISBN 0-85614-058-9, Pub. by Wilton Hse England). Motorbooks Intl.
Three Pointed Star: The Story of the Mercedez-Benz. David Scott-Moncrieff. 18.95 (F407, Pub. by G T Foulis Ltd). Haynes Pubns.
Three Political Plays. Ed. by Arlene Sykes. (Contemporary Australian Plays Ser.: No. 9). 156p. 1980. 24.50x (ISBN 0-7022-1439-6). U of Queensland Pr.
Three Popular French Comedies. Ed. by Albert Bermel. LC 75-1959. x, 187p. 1975. pap. 8.95x (ISBN 0-8044-6044-2). Ungar.
Three Portraits: Hitler, Mussolini, Stalin. Emil Ludwig. LC 78-63689. (Studies in Fascism: Ideology & Practice). 128p. Repr. of 1940 ed. 19.50 (ISBN 0-404-16905-8). AMS Pr.
Three-Pound Universe. Judith Hooper & Dick Teresi. 1987. pap. 12.95 (ISBN 0-440-58507-4, LE). Dell.
Three Power Strike. Gin Foon Mark. (Orig.). Date not set. pap. price not set (ISBN 0-938045-07-5). Bubbling-Well.
Three Predatory Women. Sydney Loch. LC 70-125230. (Short Story Index Reprint Ser). 1926. 17.00 (ISBN 0-8369-3597-7). Ayer Co Pubs.
Three Prefaces on Linnaeus & Robert Brown. W. T. Stearn. (Illus.). 1962. pap. 11.50x (ISBN 3-7682-0099-X). Lubrecht & Cramer.
Three Presidents & Their Books: The Readings of Jefferson, Lincoln, & F. D. Roosevelt. Arthur E. Bestor et al. LC 54-12305. (Fifth Annual Windsor Lectures Ser.). pap. 35.30 (ISBN 0-317-28792-3, 2020219). Bks Demand UMI.
Three Press Secretaries on the Presidency: Jody Powell, George Reedy, Jerry TerHorst. Jody Powell et al. Ed. by Kenneth W. Thompson. LC 83-16804. (Presidency & the Press Ser.). 124p. (Orig.). 1984. lib. bdg. 21.00 (ISBN 0-8191-3576-3, Co-pub. by White Burkett Miller Center); pap. text ed. 8.00 (ISBN 0-8191-3577-1). U Pr of Amer.
Three Princes of Serendip. Marie Pilny. 160p. (gr. 4-10). 1987. write for info. (ISBN 0-932806-03-1). Synergy Pubns.
Three Principles of Productivity Movement in Japan. 26p. 1986. pap. 7.50 (ISBN 92-833-1808-0, APO179, APO). UNIPUB.
Three Principles of the Divine Essence. Jacob Behem. 1978. Repr. of 1909 ed. 12.00 (ISBN 0-911662-65-0). Yoga.
Three Prize Essays on American Slavery. Richard B. Thurston et al. 12.25 (ISBN 0-8369-8620-2, 8504). Ayer Co Pubs.
Three Problem Plays: All's Well That Ends Well, Measure for Measure, Troilus & Cressida. William Shakespeare. (Classics Ser.). 1988. pap. 4.95 (ISBN 0-553-21287-7, Bantam Classics). Bantam.
Three Prophecies of Queen Sondok. Ilyon. Tr. by Edward B. Adams from Korean. (Children's Stories from Korean History: Vol. 2). (Illus.). 28p. (gr. 5). 1986. 6.50 (ISBN 0-317-52112-8, Pub. by Seoul Intl Pub Hse Korea). C E Tuttle.
Three Prophetic Novels. H. G. Wells. Incl. When the Sleeper Wakes; Story of the Days to Come; Time Machine. 14.75 (ISBN 0-8446-3151-5). Peter Smith.
Three Prophetic Novels of H. G. Wells. H. G. Wells. Ed. by E. F. Bleiler. pap. 5.95 (ISBN 0-486-20605-X). Dover.
Three Prophets of Religious Liberalism. Ed. by Conrad Wright. 1961. pap. 4.00 (ISBN 0-933840-20-9). Unitarian Univ.
Three Prose Works. John Aubrey. Ed. by John Buchanan-Brown. Incl. Miscelanies; Remaines of Gentilisme & Judaisme; Observations. LC 77-183306. (Centaur Classics Ser.). 624p. 1972. 35.00x (ISBN 0-8093-0567-4). S Ill U Pr.
Three Prose Works. John Aubrey. Ed. by Buchanan & Brown. 1983. 70.00x (ISBN 0-900000-21-X, Pub. by Centaur Bks). State Mutual Bk.
Three P's in Recovery. 2nd ed. J. B. Brown. 24p. 1984. pap. write for info. H-&-H Pubs.
Three Psalm Tunes by Thomas Tallis. Ed. by Hermione Abbey. 16p. (Orig.). 1982. pap. 2.50 (ISBN 0-939400-02-2). RWS Bks.
Three Psychologies: Perspectives from Freud, Skinner & Rogers. 3rd ed. Robert D. Nye. LC 86-9663. (Psychology Ser.). 225p. 1986. pap. text ed. 10.75 pub net (ISBN 0-534-06528-7). Brooks-Cole.
Three Puerto Rican Families. Alex H. Westfried. 176p. 1985. pap. text ed. 9.95x (ISBN 0-88133-184-8). Sheffield Wisc.
Three Puple Pansies. Elizabeth Flanders. (Illus.). 19p. (ps). Date not set. pap. 7.95. Flightstream Pr.
Three-Quarter Length Portrait of Michael Arlen. Osbert Sitwell. LC 76-46487. 1976. Repr. of 1931 ed. lib. bdg. 27.50 (ISBN 0-8414-7722-1). Folcroft.
Three-Quarter Time: The Life & Music of the Strauss Family of Vienna. Jerome Pastene. LC 76-91768. (Illus.). 1971. Repr. of 1951 ed. lib. bdg. 35.00x (ISBN 0-8371-3991-0, PATQ). Greenwood.
Three Questions. Leo Tolstoy. LC 83-71787. (Creative's Classic Short Stories Ser.). 32p. (gr. 4 up). 1983. PLB 8.95 (ISBN 0-87191-962-1). Creative Ed.
Three-R Approach to Phonetics. Joseph N. Heath. (gr. 1). 1967. pap. 2.00 (ISBN 0-87505-316-5, Pub. by Lawrence). Borden.
Three Railway Engines. Reverend W. Awdry. (Railway Ser.). (Illus.). 64p. (gr. k-2). 1985. Repr. of 1945 ed. 6.95 (ISBN 0-7182-0000-4, Pub. by Kaye & Ward). David & Charles.
Three Rastell Plays. John Rastell. Ed. by Richard Axton. (Tudor Interludes Ser.: No. I). 175p. 1979. 42.00 (Pub. by Boydell & Brewer). Longwood Pub Group.
Three Reformation Catechisms: Catholic, Anabaptist, Lutheran. Ed. by Denis Janz. LC 82-20799. (Texts & Studies in Religion: Vol. 13). viii, 224p. 1982. lib. bdg. 49.95x (ISBN 0-88946-800-1). E Mellen.
Three Reformers. Jacques Maritain. LC 70-112813. 1970. pap. 16.00x (ISBN 0-8046-1080-0, Pub by Kennikat). Assoc Faculty Pr.
Three Religions of China. William E. Soothill. LC 73-899. (China Studies: from Confucius to Mao Ser.). (Illus.). 271p. 1986. Repr. of 1929 ed. 28.00 (ISBN 0-88355-093-8). Hyperion Conn.
Three Religious Rebels: The Saga of Citeaux First Epoch. M. Raymond. 300p. 1988. price not set (ISBN 0-8198-7339-X); pap. price not set (ISBN 0-8198-7340-3). Dghtrs St Paul.
Three Remarkable Women. Harold Balyoz. 285p. 1986. pap. 14.95 (ISBN 0-9609710-1-7). Altai Pub.
Three Renaissance Pacifists: Essays in the Theories of Erasmus, More, & Vives. Philip C. Dust. (American University Studies IX: History: Vol. 23). 229p. 1987. text ed. 36.50 (ISBN 0-8204-0392-X). P Lang Pubs.
Three Restoration Comedies: Etherege: The Man of Mode; Wycherley: the Country Wife; Congreve: Love for Love. Ed. by Garmini Salgago. (English Library Ser.). 368p. 1976. pap. 5.95 (ISBN 0-14-043027-X). Penguin.
Three Ring Binder see Business.
Three Ring Circus: Poems from a Life. Ruth M. Kempher. 80p. 1982. pap. 4.95 (ISBN 0-935684-04-2). Plumbers Ink Bks.
Three-Ring Inferno. Dayle Courtney. LC 82-5561. (Thorne Twins Adventure Bks.). (Illus.). 192p. (Orig.). (gr. 5 up). 1982. pap. 2.98 (ISBN 0-87239-551-0, 2892). Standard Pub.
Three-Ring Mad. Ed. by William M. Gaines. (Illus., Orig.). 1964. pap. 1.25 (ISBN 0-451-06917-X, Y6917, Sig). NAL.
Three-Ring Psychus. John Shirley. 240p. (Orig.). 1980. pap. 1.95 (ISBN 0-89083-674-4). Zebra.
Three Rivers. Walter C. Kidney. (Illus.). 80p. 1982. pap. 7.95 (ISBN 0-916670-07-4). Pitt Hist & Landmks Found.
Three Rivers. Robin Latow. 384p. 1981. pap. 3.50 (ISBN 0-345-33827-8). Ballantine.
Three Rivers. C. J. Mills. LC 87-27110. 320p. 1988. 17.95x (ISBN 0-312-01522-4). St Martin.
Three Rivers Cookbook, Vol. Two. Ed. by Carolyn S. Hammer & Doris H. Paul. (Illus.). 254p. (Orig.). 1981. pap. 9.95 (ISBN 0-9607634-1-4). T Rivers Cookbook.
Three Rivers Cookbook, Vol. One. Ed. by Norma Sproull & Ann H. Garrett. (Illus.). 254p. (Orig.). 1973. pap. 9.95 (ISBN 0-9607634-0-6). T Rivers Cookbook.
Three Rivers of France. 2nd ed. Freda White. (Illus.). 232p. 1984. pap. 9.95 (ISBN 0-571-13386-X). Faber & Faber.
Three Rivers Ten Years. Ed. by Gerald Costanzo. 1983. 14.95 (ISBN 0-915604-84-1); pap. 7.95 (ISBN 0-915604-85-X). Carnegie-Mellon.
Three Rivers to Run. Albert Butler. (Orig.). 1981. pap. 1.95 (ISBN 0-505-51672-1, Pub. by Tower Bks). Leisure NY.
Three Roads to Chihuahua. Roy Swift. Ed. by Melissa Roberts. (Illus.). 256p. 1988. 24.95 (ISBN 0-89015-640-9). Eakin Pr.
Three Robbers. Tomi Ungerer. (Illus.). (ps-3). 1975. pap. 4.95 (ISBN 0-689-70418-6, Aladdin). Macmillan.
Three Robbers. Tomi Ungerer. LC 87-11549. (Illus.). 32p. (ps-3). 1987. Repr. of 1962 ed. PLB 14.95 (ISBN 0-689-31391-8, Atheneum Childrens Bks). Macmillan.
Three Robots. LC 80-84356. (Illus.). 1983. pap. 3.95 (ISBN 0-9601334-4-5). Growth Unltd.
Three Robots & the Sandstorm. Art Fetting. LC 82-90993. (Illus.). 96p. 1983. pap. 3.95 (ISBN 0-9601334-3-7). Growth Unltd.
Three Robots Discover Their Pos-Abilities: A Lesson in Goal Setting. Art Fettig. LC 84-81461. (Illus.). (gr. k-7). 1984. pap. 3.95 (ISBN 0-916927-00-8). Growth Unltd.
Three Robots Find a Grandpa. Art Fettig. LC 84-80378. (Illus.). 96p. (Orig.). (gr. k-7). 1984. pap. 3.95 (ISBN 0-9601334-8-8); cassette incl. Growth Unltd.
Three Robots Learn about Drugs. Art Fettig. LC 86-83041. (Illus.). 96p. 1987. pap. 3.95 (ISBN 0-916927-04-0). Growth Unltd.
Three Roman Catholic Poets in The Darkling Plain. J. Heath-Stubbs. 1950. Repr. 25.00 (ISBN 0-8274-3922-9). R West.
Three Roman Poets: Plautus, Catullus, Ovid. Their Lives, Times & Works. F. A. Wright. 1928. 40.00 (ISBN 0-8274-3991-1). R West.
Three Roman Poets: Plautus, Catullus, Ovid. Frederick A. Wright. 1977. lib. bdg. 69.95 (ISBN 0-8490-2746-2). Gordon Pr.
Three Romes. Russell Fraser. LC 84-12946. 352p. 1985. 17.95 (ISBN 0-15-190186-4). HarBraceJ.

Three Ronsard Studies. I. Silver. 172p. 1978. text ed. 34.00x (ISBN 0-317-56052-2, Pub. by Droz Switzerland). Coronet Bks.
Three R's: A Handbook for Teachers, Tutors & Parents. Gary Don Hadley. LC 77-14052. (Illus.). 266p. 1977. 14.95 (ISBN 0-87491-187-7); pap. 5.95 (ISBN 0-87491-186-9). Acropolis.
Three R's at Home. Howard B. Richman & Susan P. Richman. LC 88-90813. 228p. (Orig.). 1988. pap. 7.95 (ISBN 0-929446-00-3). PA Homeschoolers.
Three R's for Children, Vol. III. Nadia Chilkovsky. 32p. pap. 9.95 (ISBN 0-932582-62-1). Princeton Bk Co.
Three R's for Dancing, Vol. II. Nadia Chilkovsky. 32p. pap. 9.95 (ISBN 0-932582-61-3). Princeton Bk Co.
Three R's for the Gifted: Reading, Writing, & Research. Nancy Polette. LC 82-31. 180p. 1982. lib. bdg. 18.50 (ISBN 0-87287-289-0). Libs Unl.
Three Rs of Investing: Return, Risk & Relativity. Austin S. Donnelly. LC 84-72830. 1985. 25.00 (ISBN 0-87094-557-2). Dow Jones-Irwin.
Three Russian Writers & the Irrational: Zamyatin, Pil'nyak, & Bulgakov. T. R. Edwards. LC 81-6148. (Cambridge Studies in Russian Literature). 250p. 1982. 44.50 (ISBN 0-521-23670-3). Cambridge U Pr.
Three Sacred Byzantine Poets. George A. Malloney et al. Ed. by Nomikos V. Vaporis. 74p. 1979. pap. 3.25. Holy Cross Orthodox.
Three Sad Races: Racial Identity & National Consciousness in Brazilian Literature. David T. Haberly. LC 82-4467. (Illus.). 198p. 1983. 32.95 (ISBN 0-521-24722-5). Cambridge U Pr.
Three Saints Lives. Ed. by M. Amelia Klenke. (History Ser). 1947. 3.50 (ISBN 0-686-17963-3). Franciscan Inst.
Three Sarahs: Documents of Antebellum Black College Women. Ellen N. Lawson. LC 84-18914. (Studies in Women in Religion: Vol. 13). (Illus.). 350p. 1985. lib. bdg. 59.95x (ISBN 0-88946-536-3). E Mellen.
Three Satirists of Snobbery: Thackeray, Meredith, Proust. Margaret M. Goodell. 59.95 (ISBN 0-8490-1212-0). Gordon Pr.
Three Satirists of Snobbery: Thackery, Meredith, Proust. Margaret M. Goodell. LC 76-25175. 1939. lib. bdg. 35.00 (ISBN 0-8414-4437-4). Folcroft.
Three Satyric Plays of Albert Tallman. Albert Tallman. LC 75-28897. (Illus.). 1975. pap. 10.00 (ISBN 0-87423-019-5). Westburg.
Three Saviours Are Here. 2nd ed. George King. 96p. 1982. 9.25 (ISBN 0-937249-06-8). Aetherius Soc.
Three Schools of Education: Approaches to Institutional History. Ed. by Ayers Bagley. (SPE Monograph Ser.). 1984. 5.50 (ISBN 0-933669-25-9). Soc Profs Ed.
Three Scientists & Their Gods: A Search for Meaning in an Age of Information. Robert Wright. 320p. 1988. 18.95 (ISBN 0-8129-1328-0). Times Bks.
Three Score Years & Ten. Ralph Whitlock. 1988. 30.00x (ISBN 0-86025-875-0, Pub. by Ian Henry Pubns England). State Mutual Bk.
Three Screen Comedies by Samson Raphaelson: Trouble in Paradise, The Shop Around the Corner, Heaven Can Wait. Samson Raphaelson. LC 81-50948. 512p. 1983. 21.50 (ISBN 0-299-08780-8). U of Wis Pr.
Three Screenplays. Robert Rossen. LC 82-49275. (Cinema Classics Ser.). 276p. 1984. lib. bdg. 35.00 (ISBN 0-8240-5774-0). Garland Pub.
Three Secret Poems. George Seferis. Tr. by Walter Kaiser. LC 69-12734. 1969. 5.95x (ISBN 0-674-89055-8). Harvard U Pr.
Three Secret Prophecies of Fatima Revealed. Arthur Crockett. (Illus.). 72p. 1982. pap. 9.95 (ISBN 0-938294-13-X). Global Comm.
Three Secret Protocols: Soviet-German Secret Diplomacy, 1939-1941. Bronis J. Kaslas. 1979. 1.25x (ISBN 0-916876-02-0). Euramerica Pr.
Three Secret Protocols: The Lithuanian Strip in Soviet-German Secret Diplomacy, 1939-1941. rev., 2nd ed. Bronis Kaslas. (History -Eastern Europe Ser.). (Illus., Orig.). 1980. pap. 1.50 (ISBN 0-916876-03-9). Euramerica Pr.
Three Secrets. Mildred W. Brown. 24p. (Orig.). 1984. pap. 6.50 (ISBN 0-939296-12-8). Bond Pub Co.
Three Sectional Staff. Kam Yuen. LC 79-87639. (Weapons Ser.). (Illus.). 1979. pap. 7.95 (ISBN 0-89750-064-4, 332). Ohara Pubns.
Three Sections. Philip Holmes. 72p. (Orig.). 1971. 5.95 (ISBN 0-900977-75-2, Pub. by Anvil Pr Poetry). Longwood Pub Group.
Three Sections of Poems. Philip Holmes. 1971. 5.95 (ISBN 0-685-27683-X, Pub. by Anvil Pr); signed ltd. ed. 15.00 (ISBN 0-685-27684-8). Small Pr Dist.
Three-Sector, Time Series Model of the Labor Market in India. Raj Krishna. (World Bank Staff Working Papers: No. 637). 52p. 1984. 5.00 (ISBN 0-8213-0351-1, WP0637). World Bank.
Three Sermons: The Benefit of Contentation, the Affinitie of the Faithful, the Lost Sheep Is Found. Henry Smith. LC 76-57418. (English Experience Ser.: No. 832). 1977. Repr. of 1599 ed. lib. bdg. 25.00 (ISBN 90-221-0832-5). Walter J Johnson.
Three Sets of Tables: Expected Size of a Selected Subset in Paired Comparison Experiments; Tables of Admissible & Optimal Balanced Tratment Incomplete Block (BTIB) Designs for Comparing Treatments with a Control; Expected Variances & Covariances of Order Statistics for a Family of Symmetric Distributions, 3 pts. B. Trawinski et al. Ed. by M Tiku & S. Kumra. LC 74-6283. (Selected Tables in Mathematical Statistics Ser.: Vol. 8). 270p. 1985. text ed. 33.00. Am Math.
Three Sevens. William Phelon & Mira M. Phelon. Ed. by R. Swinburne Clymer. 212p. 1977. 7.95 (ISBN 0-932785-47-6). Philos Pub.
Three Ships Come Sailing. Gilchrist Waring. 1948. 5.00 (ISBN 0-87517-013-7). Dietz.
Three Short Novels. Kay Boyle. 1982. pap. 6.95 (ISBN 0-14-006109-6). Penguin.
Three Short Novels. Kay Boyle. Incl. Crazy Hunter; Bridgegroom's Body; Decision. 1958. pap. 3.00 (ISBN 0-685-29882-5). Small Pr Dist.
Three Short Novels from Papua New Guinea. Ed. by Mike Greicus. Incl. Fires of Dawn. Benjamin Umba; Flight of a Villager. August Kituai; Tali. Jim Baital. 140p. 1976. 12.00x (ISBN 0-582-71437-0, Pub. by Longman Paul Zealand). Three Continents.
Three Short Novels of Dostoyevsky. Ed. by Avrahm Yarmolinsky. Tr. by Constance Garnett. Incl. Double; Notes from the Underground; Eternal Husband. LC 60-57341. 1960. pap. 3.95 (ISBN 0-385-09435-3, A193, Anch). Doubleday.
Three Short Stories. Robert Musil. Ed. by Hugh Sacker. (Clarendon German Ser). 1970. pap. 8.95x (ISBN 0-19-832467-7). Oxford U Pr.
Three Short Works on Japanese Americans. Ed. by Roger Daniels. LC 78-3223. (Asian Experience in North America Ser.). 1978. lib. bdg. 24.50 (ISBN 0-405-11291-2). Ayer Co Pubs.
Three Sillies. Illus. by Arthur Friedman. LC 80-27636. (Illus.). 32p. (gr. k-4). 1981. PLB 9.79 (ISBN 0-89375-486-2); pap. text ed. 1.95 (ISBN 0-89375-487-0). Troll Assocs.
Three Sillies. Paul Galdone. LC 80-22197. (Illus.). 40p. (ps-3). 1981. 9.95 (ISBN 0-395-30172-6, Clarion). HM.
Three Sillies. Kathryn Hewitt. LC 85-16375. (Illus.). 32p. (ps-3). 1986. 13.95 (ISBN 0-15-286855-0, HJ). Harbracej.
Three Sillies & Ten Other Stories. Anne Rockwell. LC 85-45404. (Trophy Picture Bks.). (Illus.). 96p. (ps-3). 1986. flexi-bind 7.95 (ISBN 0-06-443093-6, Trophy). HarpJ.
Three Sirens. Irving Wallace. 1971. pap. 4.50 (ISBN 0-451-13829-5, Sig). NAL.
Three Sisters. Anton Chekhov. Tr. by Michael Frayn. (Theatre Classics Ser.). 1983. pap. 7.95 (ISBN 0-413-52450-7, NO.3940). Heinemann Ed.
Three Sisters. Anton Chekhov. Tr. by Lanford Wilson. 1984. pap. 3.50x (ISBN 0-317-17221-2). Dramatists Play.
Three Sisters. Anton P. Chekhov. Ed. by J. M. C. Davidson. (Library of Russian Classics). 120p. 1984. pap. text ed. 9.95x (ISBN 0-900186-46-1). Basil Blackwell.
Three Sisters. Norma F. Mazer. 240p. (gr. 7 up). 1986. 12.95 (ISBN 0-590-33774-2, Scholastic Hardcover). Scholastic Inc.
Three Sisters. Norma F. Mazer. 240p. (gr. 7 up). 1987. pap. 2.50 (ISBN 0-590-33254-6, Point). Scholastic Inc.
Three Sisters. Audrey Wood. LC 85-29392. (Easy-to-Read Bks.). (Illus.). 48p. (ps-3). 1986. 9.95 (ISBN 0-8037-0279-5, 0966-290); PLB 9.89 (ISBN 0-8037-0280-9). Dial Bks Young.
Three Sisters see Five Major Plays.
Three Sisters of Sz. Kok Seng Tan. (Writing in Asia Ser.). 1978. pap. text ed. 5.50x (ISBN 0-686-65346-7, 00241). Heinemann Ed.
Three Sitwells: A Biographical & Critical Study. J. L. Megroz. LC 68-262145. 1969. Repr. of 1927 ed. 23.50x (ISBN 0-8046-0305-7, Pub by Kennikat). Assoc Faculty Pr.
Three Sitwells: A Biographical & Critical Study. Rodolphe L. Megroz. LC 79-145174. 1971. Repr. of 1927 ed. 29.00 (ISBN 0-403-01102-7). Scholarly.
Three-Six-Seven: Memoirs of a Very Important Man. Peter Vansittart. 236p. 1983. 18.95 (ISBN 0-7206-0602-0). Dufour.
Three Sixteenth Century Comedies: Roister Doister, Gammer Gurton's Needle & the Old Wife's Tale. Ed. by Charles Whitworth. (New Mermaids Ser.). 1984. pap. text ed. 7.95x (ISBN 0-393-90051-7). Norton.
Three Slavic Poets. Joseph Brodsky & Tymoteusz Karpowicz. pap. 3.00 (ISBN 0-318-01988-4). Elpenor.
Three Smiths in the Wind: Low Man on a Totem Pole, Life in a Putty Knife Factory, Lost in Horse Latitudes. Harry A. Smith. LC 73-112330. 1971. Repr. of 1946 ed. lib. bdg. 35.00x (ISBN 0-8371-4719-0, SMSW). Greenwood.
Three Sociological Traditions. Randall Collins. 1985. pap. 9.95x (ISBN 0-19-503519-4). Oxford U Pr.
Three Sociological Traditions: Selected Readings. Randall Collins. 1985. pap. 10.95x (ISBN 0-19-503521-6). Oxford U Pr.
Three Soldiers. John Dos Passos. 1964. pap. 12.95 (ISBN 0-395-08389-3, 40, SenEd). HM.
Three Soldiers. John Dos Passos. 433p. 1988. pap. 9.95 (ISBN 0-88184-413-6). Carroll & Graf.
Three Solid Stones. Martha Mvungi. (African Writers Ser.). 1975. pap. 6.00. Heinemann Ed.
Three Some Poems. Jeannine Dobbs et al. LC 75-23819. 88p. 1976. pap. 7.95 (ISBN 0-914086-11-1). Alicejamesbooks.
Three Songs As the Spirit Rises. Vincent D. Dempsey. 67p. (Orig.). 1987. pap. 5.95 (ISBN 0-9619897-0-X). Blue Stone Pr.
Three Sonnets by Raphael. Raphael. Rev. by G. L. Taylor. 12p. (Orig.). 1983. 2.25 (ISBN 0-907849-01-6, Pub. by Ashmolean Museum). State Mutual Bk.
Three Sonnets by Raphael. Tr. by G. L. Taylor. 12p. (Orig.). 1983. pap. 3.95 (ISBN 0-317-58668-8, Pub. by Ashmolean Mus). Longwood Pub Group.
Three Sources & Three Component Parts of Marxism. Vladimir I. Lenin. 62p. 1976. pap. 0.75 (ISBN 0-8285-0176-9, Pub. by Progress Pubs USSR). Imported Pubns.
Three Sources of National Strength. Andrew R. Cecil. (Cecil Lectures Supplement). 215p. 1987. text ed. 16.50x (ISBN 0-292-78096-6). U of Tex Pr.
Three Southwest Plays. facsimile ed. LC 70-111115. (Play Anthology Reprint Ser). 1942. 19.50 (ISBN 0-8369-8208-8). Ayer Co Pubs.
Three Spanish American Poets: Pellicer, Neruda, Andrade. Pablo Neruda et al. Ed. by Lloyd Mallan. Tr. by Mary Wicker. 1977. lib. bdg. 59.95 (ISBN 0-8490-2747-0). Gordon Pr.
Three-Speed Dad in a Ten-Speed World. Kel Groseclose. LC 83-2765. 176p. (Orig.). 1983. pap. 4.95 (ISBN 0-87123-585-4, 210585). Bethany Hse.
Three Spirits of Vandermeer Manor. Mary Anderson. (Mostly Ghosts Ser.: No. 4). (Orig.). (gr. k-6). 1987. pap. 2.50 (ISBN 0-440-48810-9, YB). Dell.
Three Spiritual Directors for Our Time: Julian of Norwich, the Cloud of Unknowing Walter Hilton. Julia Gatta. LC 86-29169. 137p. (Orig.). 1987. pap. 8.95 (ISBN 0-936384-44-1). Cowley Pubns.
Three-Stage Model of Course Design. John F. Feldhusen. Ed. by Danny G. Langdon. LC 79-26576. (Instructional Design Library). 96p. 1980. 23.95 (ISBN 0-87778-159-1). Educ Tech Pubns.
Three Steps Behind. Joyce Hardin. 320p. (Orig.). 1986. pap. 10.95 (ISBN 0-915547-91-0). Abilene Christ U.
Three Steps Forward, Two Steps Back. Charles R. Swindoll. 320p. 1985. pap. 11.95 (ISBN 0-8027-2506-6). Walker & Co.
Three Steps Forward, Two Steps Back. Charles R. Swindoll. 192p. 1985. pap. 3.50 (ISBN 0-553-25394-8). Bantam.
Three Steps Forward, Two Steps Back: Persevering Through Pressure. Charles R. Swindoll. LC 80-11892. 176p. 1980. 9.95 (ISBN 0-8407-5187-7); pap. 5.95 (ISBN 0-8407-5723-9). Nelson.
Three Steps, One Bow. Bhikshu Hung Ju & Bhikshu Hung Yo. (Illus.). 160p. (Orig.). 1976. pap. 5.00 (ISBN 0-917512-18-9). Buddhist Text.
Three Steps to Answered Prayer. Peter Popoff. Ed. by Don Tanner. LC 81-70342. 92p. 1981. pap. 2.00 (ISBN 0-938544-10-1). Faith Messenger. .
Three Steps to Chess Mastery. A. S. Suetin. Tr. by Kenneth P. Neat from Rus. (Pergamon Russian Chess Ser.). (Illus.). 204p. 1982. pap. 14.25 (ISBN 0-08-024138-7). Pergamon.
Three Steps to Revising Your Writing for Style, Grammar, Punctuation & Spelling. Barbara Walvoord. 1987. pap. text ed. write for info. (ISBN 0-673-18657-1). Scott F.
Three Steps to Success. James M. Carroll. 86p. (Orig.). 1984. pap. 4.95 (ISBN 0-89826-011-6). Natl Paperback.
Three Stooges Book of Scripts. Joan H. Maurer. LC 84-17614. (Illus.). 256p. 1984. 19.95 (ISBN 0-8065-0933-3). Lyle Stuart.
Three Stooges Book of Scripts, Vol. II. Joan H. Maurer & Norman Maurer. (Illus.). 256p. 1987. 19.95 (ISBN 0-8065-1018-8, Pub. by Citadel Pr). Lyle Stuart.
Three Stooges Scrapbook. Jeff Lenburg & Joan H. Maurer. 256p. 1982. 18.95 (ISBN 0-8065-0803-5, Pub. by Citadel Pr). Lyle Stuart.
Three Stooges Scrapbook. Joan H. Maurer et al. (Illus.). 256p. 1985. pap. 12.95 (ISBN 0-8065-0946-5, Pub. by Citadel Pr). Lyle Stuart.
Three Stories. R. V. Cassill. LC 82-82012. 75p. (Orig.). 1982. pap. 4.50 (ISBN 0-9605008-1-2). Hermes Hse.
Three Stories. Anton P. Chekhov. Ed. by L. S. Le Fleming. (Library of Russian Classics). 146p. pap. text ed. 9.95x (ISBN 0-900186-09-7). Basil Blackwell.
Three Stories. Pati Hill. 12p. (Orig.). 1979. pap. 3.00 (ISBN 0-917061-03-9). Top Stories.
Three Stories. Gordon C. Wilson. LC 80-21609. 1980. 5.00 (ISBN 0-933292-09-0); pap. 2.00 (ISBN 0-933292-06-6). Arts End.
Three Stories about Morris & Boris. Bernard Wiseman. (Illus.). (gr. k-3). 1974. pap. 1.50 (ISBN 0-590-09849-7). Scholastic Inc.
Three Stories & Ten Poems. Ernest Hemingway. 1977. 15.00 (ISBN 0-89723-005-1). Bruccoli.
Three Stories 'Die Verlobung in St Domingo', 'Das Erdbeben in Chili', & 'Michael Kohlhaas' Heinrich von Kleist. Ed. by H. B. Garland. (German Texts). 180p. (Ger.). 1953. pap. 11.00 (ISBN 0-7190-0187-0, Pub. by Manchester Univ Pr). St Martin.
Three Stories from India. Illus. by Meg Wright. (Illus.). (gr. 1-8). 1984. pap. text ed. 8.95 (ISBN 0-86508-166-2). BCM Pubn.
Three Stories of the Raj. Ved Mehta. (Illus.). 64p. 1986. 65.00 (ISBN 0-85967-722-2); deluxe ed. 350.00. Scolar.
Three Strikes & You're Out. Valjean McLenighan. (Beginning-to-Read Ser.). 32p. (gr. 2). 1980. PLB 4.39 (ISBN 0-8136-5085-2, Dist. by Caroline Hse); pap. 1.95 (ISBN 0-8136-5585-4). Modern Curr.
Three Strikes, but Not Out: Perspectives on Modern Education. Eva M. Walters. 87p. 1985. 7.95 (ISBN 0-533-06036-2). Vantage.
Three Studies in East African Criminology. R. E. Tanner. (Crime in East Africa Ser.). 67p. 1970. pap. 9.50 (ISBN 0-8419-9709-8, Africana). Holmes & Meier.
Three Studies in English Literature, Kipling, Galsworthy & Shakespeare. Andre Chevrillon. LC 67-27585. Repr. of 1923 ed. 21.50x (ISBN 0-8046-0077-5, Pub by Kennikat). Assoc Faculty Pr.
Three Studies in Literature: Jeffrey, Newman, Arnold. Lewis E. Gates. LC 72-195408. 1899. lib. bdg. 32.50 (ISBN 0-8414-4640-7). Folcroft.
Three Studies in Mineral Economics. Orris C. Herfindahl. LC 77-86399. 64p. Repr. of 1961 ed. 20.00 (ISBN 0-404-60335-1). AMS Pr.
Three Studies in Shelley & an Essay on Nature in Wordsworth & Meredith. Archibald T. Strong. LC 76-21867. 1921. lib. bdg. 37.00 (ISBN 0-8414-7737-X). Folcroft.
Three Studies in Shelley & an Essay on Nature in Wordsworth & Meredith. Archibald T. Strong. LC 68-26936. 189p. 1968. Repr. of 1921 ed. 22.50 (ISBN 0-208-00665-6, Archon). Shoe String.
Three Studies in the Renaissance: Sidney, Jonson, Milton. Richard B. Young et al. LC 69-15695. (Yale Studies in English Ser.: No. 138). vii, 282p. 1969. Repr. of 1958 ed. 28.00 (ISBN 0-208-00780-6, Archon). Shoe String.
Three Studies in Twentieth Century Obscurity. Francis Russell. 1973. lib. bdg. 69.95 (ISBN 0-87968-046-6). Gordon Pr.
Three Studies in Twentieth Century Obscurity: Joyce, Kafka, Gertrude Stein. Frances Russell. LC 68-658. (Studies in Comparative Literature, No. 35). 1969. Repr. of 1954 ed. lib. bdg. 49.95x (ISBN 0-8383-0678-0). Haskell.
Three Studies on Charles Robert Maturin. Henry W. Hinck. Ed. by Devendra P. Varma. LC 79-8458. (Gothic Studies & Dissertations Ser.). 1980. lib. bdg. 22.00x (ISBN 0-405-12647-6). Ayer Co Pubs.
Three Studies on National Integration in the Arab World. C. Farah et al. (Information Papers: No. 12). 34p. (Orig.). 1974. pap. text ed. 2.75 (ISBN 0-937694-28-2). Assn Arab-Amer U Grads.
Three Styles in the Study of Kinship. J. A. Barnes. LC 74-142057. 1972. 35.00x (ISBN 0-520-01879-6). U of Cal Pr.
Three Suitors: One Husband & Until Further Notice. Guillaume Oyono-Mbia. 1981. pap. 6.95 (ISBN 0-413-32680-2, NO. 6480). Heinemann Ed.
Three Summers. Yvonne Pepin. (Illus.). 186p. (Orig.). 1986. pap. 7.95 (ISBN 0-915288-51-6). Shameless Hussy.
Three Supernatural Novels of the Victorian Period. E. F. Bielier. 20.95 (ISBN 0-89190-697-5, Pub. by Am Repr). Amereon Ltd.
Three Supernatural Novels of the Victorian Period. Ed. by E. F. Bleiler. Bd. with Haunted Hotel. Wilkie Collins; Lost Stradivarius. J. Meade Falkner; Haunted House at Latchford. Mrs. J. H. Riddell. Set. 10.75 (ISBN 0-8446-5161-3). Peter Smith.
Three Swiss Painters: Cuno Amiet, Giovanni Giacometti, Augusto Giacometti. George Mauner. (Illus.). 166p. 1973. pap. 7.50 (ISBN 0-911209-02-6). Penn St Art.
Three Swiss Realists: Gotthelf, Keller, & Meyer. Robert Godwin-Jones & Margaret T. Peischl. LC 88-5708. 264p. 1988. lib. bdg. 26.50 (ISBN 0-8191-6965-X). U Pr of Amer.
Three Tales. Paul Bowles. LC 75-18063. 24p. (Minimum order: 3 copies). 1975. pap. 3.50 (ISBN 0-916228-10-X). Phoenix Bk Shop.
Three Tales. Gustave Flaubert. Tr. by Robert Baldick. Incl. A Simple Heart; Legend of Saint Julian Hospitator; Herodias. (Classics Ser.). (Orig.). 1961. pap. 3.95 (ISBN 0-14-044106-9). Penguin.
Three Tales. Frank O'Connor. 56p. 1971. Repr. of 1942 ed. 15.00x (ISBN 0-7165-1395-1, BBA 02074, Pub. by Cuala Press Ireland). Biblio Dist.
Three Tales from Bicol. Peria S. Intia. (Illus.). 45p. (Orig.). (gr. 4-6). 1982. pap. 3.75 (ISBN 971-10-0029-6, Pub. by New Day Philippines). Cellar.
Three Tales of My Father's Dragon. Ruth S. Gannett. (Borzoi Sprinters Ser.). (Illus.). 96p. (gr. 2-5). 1987. pap. 11.95 slipcase set (ISBN 0-394-89136-8); pap. 3.95 ea. Knopf.
Three Teachers. Gino Montenero. LC 67-11988. 102p. 1967. 5.95 (ISBN 0-8022-1141-0). Philos Lib.
Three Team Plays: Then Moses Met Maconi, Borderlands, & Jacko. Bernard Farrell et al. Intro. by Martin Drury. 256p. (Orig.). 1987. pap. 15.95 (ISBN 0-86327-107-3, Pub. by Wolfhound Pr Ireland). Irish Bks Media.
Three Tenors, One Vehicle: A Book of Songs. James Camp et al. LC 74-28757. (Open Places Poets Ser.: No. 2). 1975. pap. 2.50x (ISBN 0-913398-01-2). Open Places.

Three Texas Poets. Charles Behlen et al. (Illus.). 80p. (Orig.). 1986. lib. bdg. 12.95 (ISBN 0-317-43326-1); pap. 8.95 (ISBN 0-317-43327-X). Prickly Pear.

Three Theban Plays. Sophocles. Tr. by Theodore H. Banks. Incl. Antigone; Oedipus the King; Oedipus at Colonus. 1956. pap. 5.95x (ISBN 0-19-501059-0). Oxford U Pr.

Three Theban Plays: Antigone; Oedipus; Oedipus at Colonus. Sophocles. Tr. by Robert Fagles from Gr. LC 82-70127. 400p. 1982. 25.00 (ISBN 0-670-69805-9). Viking.

Three Theban Plays: Antigone, Oedipus the King, Oedipus at Colonus. Sophocles. Tr. by Robert Fagles. (Penguin Classics Ser.). 432p. 1984. pap. 2.95 (ISBN 0-14-044425-4). Penguin.

Three Theories of Child Development. 3rd ed. Henry W. Maier. (Illus.). 302p. 1988. pap. 14.75 (ISBN 0-8191-6765-7). U Pr of Amer.

Three Thinkers of Thay-Lee. D. L. Pape. LC 68-56828. (Oddo Sound Ser.). (Illus.). 48p. (gr. 2-5). 1968. PLB 10.95 (ISBN 0-87783-040-1). Oddo.

Three Thirty Arden. Monica Lee. LC 86-16473. (Illus.). 16p. (Orig.). 1986. pap. 5.00 (ISBN 0-935093-02-8). North Beach Pr.

Three Thirty-Four. Thomas M. Disch. 248p. 1987. pap. 3.95 (ISBN 0-88184-340-7). Carroll & Graf.

Three Thousand & One Essential Words for a Perfect Vocabulary. Prescott Evarts. LC 83-8759. 160p. (Orig.). 1983. pap. 4.95 (ISBN 0-668-05657-6, 5657-6). Arco.

Three Thousand Five Hundred Good Jokes for Speakers. Gerald F. Lieberman. LC 74-29354. 480p. 1975. pap. 6.95 (ISBN 0-385-00545-8, Dolp). Doubleday.

Three Thousand Five Hundred Good Quotes for Speakers. Gerald F. Lieberman. LC 81-43552. 288p. 1987. pap. 4.95 (ISBN 0-385-17769-0). Doubleday.

Three Thousand Futures: The Next Twenty Years for Higher Education. Carnegie Council on Policy Studies in Higher Education Staff. LC 79-9675. (Higher Education Ser.). 1980. text ed. 27.95x (ISBN 0-87589-453-4). Jossey-Bass.

Three Thousand Mice of Dr. Proctor. Hans J. Schmidt. (Children's Theatre Playscript Ser.). (gr. k-12). 1963. pap. 2.00x (ISBN 0-88020-053-7). Coach Hse.

Three Thousand Miles by Canoe. Dale E. Witmer. LC 78-65976. (Illus.). 154p. 1979. pap. 4.95 (ISBN 0-89037-201-2). Anderson World.

Three Thousand One Questions & Answers. A. R. Harding. 395p. pap. 4.50 (ISBN 0-936622-22-9). A R Harding Pub.

Three Thousand Quotations on Christian Themes. Carroll E. Simcox. 286p. 1988. pap. 9.95 (ISBN 0-8010-8286-2). Baker Bk.

Three Thousand Solved Problems in Fluid Mechanics & Hydraulics. Jack B. Evett & Cheng Liu. (Schaum's Solved Problem Ser.). 1000p. 1988. 19.95 (ISBN 0-07-019783-0). McGraw.

Three Thousand Solved Problems in Precalculus Mathematics. Philip Schmidt. (Schaum's Solved Problems Ser.). 1000p. 1988. 19.95 (ISBN 0-07-055365-3). McGraw.

Three Thousand Sound-Alikes & Look Alikes. Compiled by Mary L. Gilman. 60p. 1983. pap. 5.75 (ISBN 0-318-01718-0). Natl Shorthand Rptr.

Three Thousand Transducers Varriable of Temperature, Heat Flux, Magnetic Qualities, Humidity & Moisture, Electromagnetic & Nuclear Radiation see ISA Transducer Compendium.

Three Thousand Years in Africa: Man & His Environment in the Lake Chad Region of Nigeria. Graham Connah. LC 79-41508. (New Studies in Archaeology). (Illus.). 268p. 1981. 75.00 (ISBN 0-521-22848-4). Cambridge U Pr.

Three Thousand Years in Glass: Treasures from The Walters Art Gallery. Robert P. Bergman & Jeanny V. Canby. Ed. by Carol Strohecker. (Illus.). 16p. (Orig.). 1982. pap. 3.95 (ISBN 0-911886-24-9). Walters Art.

Three Thousand Years of Black Poetry: An Anthology. Ed. by Alan Lomax & Raoul Abdul. 288p. 1984. pap. 8.95 (ISBN 0-396-08350-1). Dodd.

Three Thousand Years of Educational Wisdom: Selections from Great Documents. 2nd enl. ed. Ed. by Robert Ulich. 1954. pap. 16.00x (ISBN 0-674-89072-8). Harvard U Pr.

Three Thousand Years of Hebrew Literature: From the Earliest Time Through the 20th Century. Nathaniel Kravitz. LC 73-150752. 586p. 1971. 20.00 (ISBN 0-8040-0505-2, Pub by Swallow); limited ed. 50.00 (ISBN 0-8040-0728-4, Pub by Swallow). Ohio U Pr.

Three Tibetan Mysteries: Tchrimekundan, Nansal, Djroazanmo, As Performed in the Tibetan Monasteries. Jacques Bacot. Tr. by H. I. Woolf from Fr. LC 78-72375. (Illus.). Repr. of 1924 ed. 28.50 (ISBN 0-404-17225-3). AMS Pr.

Three Times a Woman. 252p. 1983. pap. 3.95 (ISBN 0-88184-010-6). Carroll & Graf.

Three Times Handke. Peter Handke. 1988. pap. 8.95 (ISBN 0-02-020761-1, Collier). Macmillan.

Three Times Three. Robert Flanagan. 38p. 1977. pap. 2.50 (ISBN 0-87886-086-X). Greenfld Rev Pr.

Three to Conquer. Eric F. Russell. 224p. 1986. pap. 2.95 (ISBN 0-345-32757-8, Del Rey). Ballantine.

Three to Five Semiconductors. Ed. by H. C. Freyhardt. (Crystals. Growth, Properties & Applications Ser.: Vol. 3). (Illus.). 180p. 1980. 46.00 (ISBN 0-387-09957-3). Springer-Verlag.

Three to Get Ready. Betty Boegehold. LC 62-8042. (Harper I Can Read Bks.). (Illus.). (gr. k-3). PLB 10.89 (ISBN 0-06-020551-2). HarpJ.

Three to Win. James E. Adams. LC 77-72255. (Radiant Life Ser.). 125p. pap. 2.50 (ISBN 0-88243-906-5, 02-0906); tchr's. guide 3.95 (ISBN 0-88243-176-5, 32-0176). Gospel Pub.

Three Tomorrows: American, British & Soviet Science Fiction. John Griffiths. 217p. 1980. 28.50x (ISBN 0-389-20008-5). B&N Imports.

Three Topics in the Theory of International Trade. M. C. Kemp. (Studies in International Economics: Vol. 2). 328p. 1976. text ed. 63.25 (ISBN 0-444-10967-6, North-Holland). Elsevier.

Three Toughest on-the-Job Problems. 1974. pap. 5.95 (ISBN 0-917386-80-9). Exec Ent Pubns.

Three Tours Through London in the Years 1748, 1776, 1797. Wilmarth S. Lewis. LC 77-104252. (Illus.). 1971. Repr. of 1941 ed. lib. bdg. 35.00x (ISBN 0-8371-3977-5, LETL). Greenwood.

Three Tragedies. Federico Garcia Lorca. Tr. by Richard L. O'Connell & James Graham-Lujan. Incl. Blood Wedding; Yerma; House of Bernarda Alba. LC 77-11626. 1956. pap. 6.95 (ISBN 0-8112-0092-2, NDP52). New Directions.

Three Tragedies: Antigone, Oedipus the King, & Electra. Sophocles. Tr. by H. D. Kitto from Gr. 1962. pap. text ed. 5.95x (ISBN 0-19-500374-8). Oxford U Pr.

Three Tragedies: Blood Wedding, Yerma, Bernarda Alba. Federico Garcia Lorca. Tr. by Richard L. O'Connell & James Graham-Lujan. LC 77-3056. 1977. Repr. of 1955 ed. lib. bdg. 27.50x (ISBN 0-8371-9578-0, LOTT). Greenwood.

Three Tragedies: Trojan Women, Medea & Phaedra. Lucius Annaeus Seneca. Tr. & intro. by Frederick Ahl. LC 86-47632. (Masters of Latin Literature Ser.). 272p. 1986. 39.50x (ISBN 0-8014-1664-7). Cornell U Pr.

Three Transcendentalists: Kant, Thoreau, & Contemporary. Richard S. Hoehler. LC 71-185781. (Illus.). 432p. 1972. 20.00 (ISBN 0-930590-00-7). R Hoehler Pub.

Three Trapped Tigers. G. Cabrara Infante. 480p. (gr. 7 up). 1985. pap. 5.95 (ISBN 0-380-69964-8, Bard). Avon.

Three Treatises. rev. ed. Martin Luther. LC 73-114753. 320p. 1970. pap. 4.95 (ISBN 0-8006-1639-1, 1-1639). Fortress.

Three Treatises Concerning Wales. John Penry. 168p. 1960. text ed. 12.50x (ISBN 0-7083-0062-6, Pub. by U of Wales). Humanities.

Three Treatises on Child Rearing. Walter Harris. LC 83-48619. 234p. 1985. lib. bdg. 33.00. Garland Pub.

Three Treatises on Man: A Cistercian Anthropology. Ed. by Bernard McGinn. LC 77-184906. (Cistercian Fathers Ser.: No. 24). 1977. 13.95 (ISBN 0-87907-024-2). Cistercian Pubns.

Three Treatises on the Nature of Science. Galen. Ed. by Michael Frede & R. Walzer. LC 84-19826. (HPC Philosophical Classics Ser.). 100p. 1985. lib. bdg. 22.50 (ISBN 0-915145-91-X); pap. text ed. 6.95 (ISBN 0-915145-92-8). Hackett Pub.

Three Tudor Classical Interludes: Thersytes, Jacke Jugeler, Horestes. Ravisius Textor et al. Ed. by Marie Axton. (Tudor Interludes Ser.: No. III). 245p. 1983. 42.00 (ISBN 0-85991-096-2, Pub. by Boydell & Brewer). Longwood Pub Group.

Three Tudor Dialogues. LC 78-14887. 1979. 35.00x (ISBN 0-8201-1319-0). Schol Facsimiles.

Three Unique Suiboku-Ga Artists of Modern Japan. Ed. by Kyoto National Museum of Modern Art Staff. (Illus.). 12p. 1976. pap. 150.00x (Pub. by Han-Shan Tang Ltd). State Mutual Bk.

Three Universals. Gene Woods. 183p. 1987. 13.95 (ISBN 0-533-06897-5). Vantage.

Three Unknown Buddhist Stories in an Arabic Version. S. M. Stern & S. Walzer. 38p. 1971. 25.00x (ISBN 0-317-39173-9, Pub. by Luzac & Co Ltd). State Mutual Bk.

Three up a Tree. James Marshall. LC 86-2163. (Easy-to-Read Bks.). (Illus.). 48p. (ps-3). 1986. 9.95 (ISBN 0-8037-0328-7, 0966-290); PLB 9.89 (ISBN 0-8037-0329-5). Dial Bks Young.

Three Uses of Christian Discourse in John Henry Newman. Jouett L. Powell. LC 75-29423. (American Academy of Religion. Dissertation Ser.). 1975. pap. 9.95 (ISBN 0-89130-042-2, 010110). Scholars Pr GA.

Three Varieties of Pluralism. David Nicholls. LC 74-80654. 80p. 1974. 20.00 (ISBN 0-312-80325-7). St Martin.

Three Versions of the Story of King Lear: Anonymous ca.1594-1605; William Shakespeare 1607-1608; Nahum Tate 1681 Studies in Relation to One Another, 2 vols. Dorothy E. Nameri. Ed. by James Hogg. (Elizabethan & Renaissance Studies). 360p. (Orig.). 1976. pap. 30.00 (ISBN 3-7052-0696-6, Pub. by Salzburg Studies). Longwood Pub Group.

Three Victorian Detective Novels. Ed. by E. F. Bleiler. 1978. pap. 7.95 (ISBN 0-486-23668-4). Dover.

Three Victorian Telephone Directories. Intro. by David J. Thomas. Incl. Bk. 1. The United Telephone Company's Professions & Trades Classified Directory of 1885; Bk. 2. The United Telephone Company's Instructions for the Use of Exchange Lines & the South of England Telephone Company's (Brighton) Directory of 1885; Bk. 3. The London & Globe Telephone & Maintainance Company's Directory 1884. LC 70-101259. 1970. 24.95x (ISBN 0-678-05678-1). Kelley.

Three Victorian Travel Writers: An Annotated Bibliography of Criticism on Mrs. Frances Milton Trollope, Samuel Butler, & Robert Louis Stevenson. Frederick J. Bethke. 1978. lib. bdg. 29.00 (ISBN 0-8161-7852-6, Hall Reference). G K Hall.

Three Victorian Women Who Changed Their World: Josephine Butler, Octavia Hill, Florence Nightingale. Nancy Boyd. 1982. 29.95 (ISBN 0-19-520271-6). Oxford U Pr.

Three Viennese Comedies. Tr. by Katharina M. Wilson & Robert Harrison. LC 85-71916. (Studies in German Literature, Linguistics, & Culture: Vol. 21). (Illus.). 252p. 1986. 29.00x (ISBN 0-938100-37-8). Camden Hse.

Three Views of the Novel. Irving Stone et al. LC 77-7608. 1957. lib. bdg. 25.00 (ISBN 0-8414-7692-6). Folcroft.

Three Views-Three Philosophies of Life. Everett L. Fullam. Ed. by Patricia Lillie & Lynda Barnes. (Tips for Living Ser.). 32p. (Orig.). 1987. pap. 3.50 (ISBN 0-943525-27-6). St Pauls Ctr.

Three Virginia Frontiers. Thomas P. Abernethy. 12.00 (ISBN 0-8446-1001-1). Peter Smith.

Three Virginia Writers: A Reference Guide. Ed. by George C. Longest. 1978. lib. bdg. 31.50 (ISBN 0-8161-7841-0, Hall Reference). G K Hall.

Three Visions of Chinese Socialism. Ed. by Dorothy J. Solinger. LC 84-2260. 110p. 1984. pap. 21.50x (ISBN 0-86531-822-0). Westview.

Three Visitorian Views of the Italian Renaissance. Richard Titlebaum. Ed. by Stephen Orgel. (Harvard Dissertations in American & English Literature Ser.). 180p. 1987. lib. bdg. 25.00 (ISBN 0-8240-0080-3). Garland PUb.

Three Voices. John H. Hollands. LC 78-3793. (Orig.). 1978. pap. 6.95 (ISBN 0-89407-012-6). Strawberry Hill.

Three Voyages of Martin Frobisher: In Search of a Passage to Cathaia & India by the Northwest, A.D. 1576-78. George Best. Ed. by Richard Collinson. (Hakluyt Society, First Ser.: No. 38). (Illus.). 1964. 32.00 (ISBN 0-8337-0271-8). B Franklin.

Three Voyages of Vasco Da Gama. Gaspar Correa. 1964. 23.50 (ISBN 0-8337-3364-8). B Franklin.

Three Voyages of William Barents to the Arctic Regions, 1594, 1595, & 1596. 2nd ed. Gerrit De Veer. Ed. by K. Beynen. 1964. 32.00 (ISBN 0-8337-3622-1). B Franklin.

Three Wagner Essays. Richard Wagner. Tr. by Robert L. Jacobs. (Eulenburg Music Ser.). (Illus.). 127p. 1982. pap. text ed. 17.50 (ISBN 0-903873-56-7). Da Capo.

Three Wall Racquetball Everyone. Alan C. Moore. (Illus.). 140p. (Orig.). 1982. pap. text ed. 5.95x (ISBN 0-89459-170-3). Hunter Textbks.

Three-War Marine: The Pacific - Korea - Vietnam. Francis F. Parry. (Illus.). 336p. 1987. 22.95 (ISBN 0-935553-02-9). Pacifica Pr.

Three Wars of Roy Benavidez. Roy Benavidez & Oscar Griffin. LC 86-70715. (Illus.). 250p. 1986. 17.95 (ISBN 0-931722-58-6). Corona Pub.

Three Wars of Roy Benavidez. Roy Benavidez & Oscar Griffin. 288p. 1988. pap. 4.50 (ISBN 0-671-65236-2). PB.

Three Wartons. facsimile ed. Ed. by Eric Partridge. LC 71-128881. (Select Bibliographies Reprint Ser). Repr. of 1927 ed. 17.00 (ISBN 0-8369-5501-3). Ayer Co Pubs.

Three Waves of Change: Hospital Board Responsibilities in the New Health Care Environment. Barry S. Bader. Ed. by Barbara Shapiro. 90p. (Orig.). 1986. text ed. 15.00 (ISBN 0-915963-03-5). Bader Assoc Inc.

Three-Way Scaling & Clustering. Phipps Arabie et al. (Quantitative Applications in the Social Sciences Ser.: Vol. 65). 92p. 1987. pap. text ed. 6.50 (ISBN 0-8039-3068-2). Sage.

Three-Way Split. Rebecca Brown. LC 77-8993. (Illus.). 1978. pap. 2.00 (ISBN 0-916382-14-1). Telephone Bks.

Three Wayfarers. Thomas Hardy. LC 44-3618. 1979. Repr. of 1893 ed. lib. bdg. 30.00x (ISBN 0-8201-1206-2). Schol Facsimiles.

Three Ways for an Investor with Very Little Money to Make a Killing in the Stock Market. C. M. Flumiani. (Illus.). 210p. 1976. 88.85 (ISBN 0-913314-82-X). Am Classical Coll Pr.

Three Ways of Asian Wisdom: Hinduism, Buddhism, Zen. Nancy W. Ross. (Illus.). 1978. pap. 12.95 (ISBN 0-671-24230-X, Touchstone Bks). S&S.

Three Ways of Love. Frances P. Keyes. 1975. 6.00 (ISBN 0-8198-0477-0); pap. 5.00 (ISBN 0-8198-0478-9). Dghtrs St Paul.

Three Ways of Modern Man. Harry Slochower. LC 37-17328. 1968. Repr. of 1937 ed. 20.00 (ISBN 0-527-83656-7). Kraus Repr.

Three Ways of the Spiritual Life. R. Garrigou-Lagrange. 1977. pap. 3.00 (ISBN 0-89555-017-2). TAN Bks Pubs.

Three Ways of Thought in Ancient China. Arthur Waley. xv, 216p. 1939. pap. 7.95 (ISBN 0-8047-1169-0, SP-46). Stanford U Pr.

Three Ways to One God. Abdoldjavad Falaturi & Petuchowski. 160p. 1987. 14.95x (ISBN 0-8245-0818-1). Crossroad NY.

Three-Week Trance Diet. Jane Piirto. 240p. (Orig.). 1985. pap. 8.95 (ISBN 0-914140-14-0). Carpenter Pr.

Three Weird Animals & a Flying Monster. Reinhold W. Goll. (gr. 6-9). 1981. 4.00 (ISBN 0-686-30642-2). R W Goll.

Three West Coast Woman. Kim Addonizio et al. (Orig.). 1987. pap. 6.00 (ISBN 0-9618409-1-9). Five Fingers.

Three Who Dared: Prudence Crandall, Margaret Douglass, Myrtilla Miner-Champions of Antebellum Black Education. Philip S. Foner & Josephine F. Pacheco. LC 83-12830. (Contributions in Women's Studies: No. 47). xviii, 234p. 1984. lib. bdg. 35.00 (ISBN 0-313-23584-8, FTH/). Greenwood.

Three Windows. Abby Niebauer. (Illus.). 60p. (Orig.). 1980. deluxe ed. 140.00 (ISBN 0-940592-05-3). Heyeck Pr.

Three Winds of Death: The Saga of the 503rd Parachute Regimental Combat Team in the South Pacific. Bennett M. Guthrie. (Illus.). 272p. 1984. 13.50 (ISBN 0-682-40169-2). Exposition-Phoenix.

Three Wise Birds. Suzanne Stamler. (Jataka Tales Ser.). (Illus.). (gr. 1-6). pap. 5.95 (ISBN 0-913546-68-2). Dharma Pub.

Three Wise Men. Elizabeth Bisland. 1973. Repr. of 1930 ed. 30.00 (ISBN 0-8274-1472-2). R West.

Three Wise Men Dream Book. Zonite. pap. 4.00x (ISBN 0-685-63882-0). Wehman.

Three Wishes. M. Jean Craig. (Easy to Read Folktales Ser.). (Illus.). 48p. (Orig.). (gr. k-3). 1986. pap. 2.50 (ISBN 0-590-41744-4). Scholastic Inc.

Three Wishes. Shannon Gilligan. (Skylark Choose Your Own Adventure Ser.: No. 15). 64p. (Orig.). (gr. 1-3). 1984. pap. text ed. 2.25 (ISBN 0-553-15444-3, Skylark). Bantam.

Three Wishes. Charles Perrault. LC 78-18060. (Illus.). 32p. (gr. k-3). 1979. PLB 9.79 (ISBN 0-89375-129-4); pap. 1.95 (ISBN 0-89375-107-3). Troll Assocs.

Three Wishes: An Old Story. Margot Zemach. LC 86-80956. (Michael di Capua Bks.). (Illus.). 32p. (ps up). 1986. 13.95 (ISBN 0-374-37529-1). FS&G.

Three Wishes for Jamie. Charles O'Neal. LC 79-66116. 256p. 1980. 15.95 (ISBN 0-933256-08-6); pap. text ed. 7.95 (ISBN 0-933256-09-4). Second Chance.

Three with a Bullet. Arthur Lyons. LC 84-4598. 240p. 1986. pap. 3.95 (ISBN 0-03-008539-X, Owl Bks). H Holt & Co.

Three Women. Faith Baldwin. 1980. pap. 2.50 (ISBN 0-671-83098-8). PB.

Three Women. Marie Hanson. LC 85-71032. 190p. (Orig.). 1985. pap. 7.95 (ISBN 0-933753-01-2). Canterbury.

Three Women. Firth Haring. (Inflation Fighter Ser.). 176p. 1982. pap. 1.50 (ISBN 0-8439-1096-8, Leisure Bks). Leisure NY.

Three Women & the Lord. Adrienne Von Speyr. Tr. by Graham Harrison. LC 86-80789. (Illus.). 115p. 1986. pap. 7.95 (ISBN 0-89870-059-0). Ignatius Pr.

Three Women Black. Phyllis J. Sloan & Angela Kinamore. LC 87-81212. (Illus.). 56p. (Orig.). 1987. pap. 6.00x (ISBN 0-940248-30-1). Guild Pr.

Three Women Poets: Poems by Louise Labe, Gaspara Stampa, & Sor Juana Ines de la Cruz. Ed. by Frank J. Warnke. LC 84-46104. (Illus.). 136p. 1987. 24.50x (ISBN 0-8387-5089-3). Bucknell U Pr.

Three Women Prophets: Ellen Gould White see Millennium in America: From the Puritan Migration to the Civil War.

Three Women Prophets: Harriet Livermore see Millennium in America: From the Puritan Migration to the Civil War.

Three Women Prophets: Phoebe Palmer see Millennium in America: From the Puritan Migration to the Civil War.

Three Wonderful Beggars. Sally Scott. LC 86-22825. (Illus.). 30p. (gr. k-3). 1988. Repr. of 1987 ed. 13.00 (ISBN 0-688-06656-9); lib. bdg. 12.88 (ISBN 0-688-06657-7). Greenwillow.

Three Woonsocket Historic Walking Tours. (Illus.). 44p. (Orig.). 1980. pap. 1.95 (ISBN 0-917012-59-3). RI Pubns Soc.

Three Works by Nakano Shigeharu. Tr. by Brett DeBary. LC 79-128951. (East Asia Papers: No. 21). 166p. 1979. 7.00 (ISBN 0-939657-21-X). Cornell East Asia Pgm.

Three World Surveys by the Food & Agriculture Organization of the United Nations: An Original Anthology. LC 75-27639. (World Food Supply Ser). (Illus.). 1976. 14.00x (ISBN 0-405-07779-3). Ayer Co Pubs.

Three Worlds of Christian Marxist Encounters. Ed. by Nicolas Piediscalzi & Robert G. Thobaben. LC 84-48724. 240p. 1985. pap. 4.95 (ISBN 0-8006-1840-8, 1-1840). Fortress.

Three Worlds of Culture & World Development. Peter Worsley. LC 84-2609. 424p. 1984. lib. bdg. 30.00x o.s.i (ISBN 0-226-90754-6); pap. 15.00x (ISBN 0-226-90755-4). U of Chicago Pr.

Three Worlds of Economics. Lloyd G. Reynolds. (Studies in Comparative Economics: No. 12). (Illus.). 1971. 35.00x (ISBN 0-300-01481-3). Yale U Pr.

Three Worlds of Labor Economics. Ed. by Garth L. Mangum & Peter Philips. LC 87-26423. 392p. 1988. text ed. 39.95 (ISBN 0-87332-455-2); pap. text ed. 18.95 (ISBN 0-87332-456-0). M E Sharpe.

Three Writers in Exile: Eliot, Pound & Joyce. Doris L. Eder. LC 84-51739. 108p. 1985. 12.50x (ISBN 0-87875-292-7). Whitston Pub.

Three Writers of the Far West: A Reference Guide. Ray C. Longtin. 1980. lib. bdg. 40.50 (ISBN 0-8161-7832-1, Hall Reference). G K Hall.

Three-Year Hill see Spring of Youth.

Three-Year Longitudinal Predictive Validity Study of the Musical Aptitude Profile. Edwin Gordon. (Studies in the Psychology of Music Ser: Vol. 5). 78p. 1967. pap. 4.95s (ISBN 0-87745-009-9). U of Iowa Pr.

Three Years. George S. Friedman. (Private Library Collection). 395p. 1986. mini-bound 6.95 (ISBN 0-938422-22-7). SOS Pubns CA.

Three Years among the Indians & Mexicans. Thomas James. LC 83-23440. xvi, 182p. 1984. pap. 5.95 (ISBN 0-8032-7556-0, BB 860, Bison). U of Nebr Pr.

Three Years among the Working-Classes in the United States During the War. James D. Burn. LC 74-22735. Repr. of 1865 ed. 34.50 (ISBN 0-404-58487-X). AMS Pr.

Three Years at the East-West Divide. Max M. Kampelman. Ed. by Leonard R. Sussman. LC 83-82249. (Perspectives on Freedom Ser.: No. 2). xix, 133p. 1983. 18.00 (ISBN 0-932088-04-X); pap. 10.00 (ISBN 0-932088-05-8). Freedom Hse.

Three Years' Cruize in the Mozambique Channel: For the Suppression of the Slave Trade. facs. ed. F. L. Barnard. LC 79-149863. (Black Heritage Library Collection Ser). 1848. 19.25 (ISBN 0-8369-8745-4). Ayer Co Pubs.

Three Years in America: 1859-1862, 2 vols. in 1. facsimile ed. Israel B. Benjamin. Tr. by Charles Reznikoff from Ger. LC 74-27962. (Modern Jewish Experience Ser.). (Eng.). 1975. Repr. of 1956 ed. 52.00x (ISBN 0-405-06693-7). Ayer Co Pubs.

Three Years in Bloom: A Garden-Keeper's Journal. Intro. by Ann Lovejoy. (Illus.). 160p. 1988. 14.95 (ISBN 0-912365-17-X). Sasquatch Bks.

Three Years in California. Walter Colton. Ed. by Carlos E. Cortes. LC 76-1221. (Chicano Heritage Ser.). (Illus.). 1976. Repr. of 1854 ed. 35.50x (ISBN 0-405-09496-5). Ayer Co Pubs.

Three Years in North America, 2 vols. in 1. James Stuart. LC 73-13151. (Foreign Travelers in America, 1810-1935 Ser.). 676p. 1974. Repr. 45.50x (ISBN 0-405-05474-2). Ayer Co Pubs.

Three Years in the Army of the Cumberland. J. A. Connolly. 1959. 31.00 (ISBN 0-527-19000-4). Kraus Repr.

Three Years in the Holy City see Prince of the House of David.

Three Years in the Libyan Desert. J. C. Ewald Falls. 460p. 1985. 300.00x (ISBN 1-85077-080-8, Pub. by Darf Pubs Ltd). State Mutual Bk.

Three Years in the Rocky Mountains. David L. Brown. 28p. 1975. pap. 4.95 (ISBN 0-87770-151-2). Ye Galleon.

Three Years in the Sixth Corps. George Stevens. (Collector's Library of the Civil War). (gr. 7 up). 1983. lib. bdg. 26.60 kivar bdg (ISBN 0-8094-4266-3, Pub. by Time-Life). Silver.

Three Years in Tibet. 719p. 1909. 1600.00x (ISBN 0-317-68680-1, Pub. by Han-Shan Tang Ltd). State Mutual Bk.

Three Years of the Agricultural Adjustment Administration. E. Nourse et al. LC 79-173654. (FDR & the Era of the New Deal Ser.). 600p. 1971. Repr. of 1937 ed. lib. bdg. 75.00 (ISBN 0-306-70365-3). Da Capo.

Three Years of War in East Africa. Angus Buchanan. LC 72-90108. 1970. Repr. of 1919 ed. 35.00 (ISBN 0-8371-2026-8, BUY&). Greenwood.

Three Years on the Ocean. James I. Clark. LC 79-21873. (Quest, Adventure, Survival Ser.). (Illus.). 48p. (gr. 4-9). 1982. pap. 9.27 (ISBN 0-8172-2072-0). Raintree Pubs.

Three Years on the Ocean. James I. Clark. LC 79-21873. (Quest, Adventure, Survival Ser.). (Illus.). 48p. (gr. 4-8). 1980. PLB 15.33 (ISBN 0-8172-1572-7). Raintree Pubs.

Three Years Rings. John Perlman. 1972. 16.00 (ISBN 0-685-27715-1); pap. 8.00 (ISBN 0-685-27716-X). Elizabeth Pr.

Three Years' Wanderings in the Northern Provinces of China. Robert Fortune & Ramon H. Myers. LC 78-74307. (Modern Chinese Economy Ser.: Vol. 4). 1979. 53.00 (ISBN 0-8240-4253-0). Garland Pub.

Three Years with Company K. Ed. by Arthur A. Kent. LC 74-4989. 346p. 1976. 27.50 (ISBN 0-8386-1480-9). Fairleigh Dickinson.

Three Years with Quantrell. John McCorkle. Ed. by D. S. Barton. LC 67-6851. (American Biography Ser., No. 32). 1970. lib. bdg. 75.00x (ISBN 0-8383-1107-5). Haskell.

Three Years with the Poets. Ed. by Bertha Hazard. LC 70-108583. (Granger Index Reprint Ser). 1904. 17.00 (ISBN 0-8369-6111-0). Ayer Co Pubs.

Three Yellow Dogs. Caron L. Cohen. LC 85-24823. (Illus.). 32p. (ps-1). 1986. 11.75 (ISBN 0-688-06230-X); PLB 11.88 (ISBN 0-688-06231-8). Greenwillow.

Three Young Poets. Edmund Blunden. LC 73-10005. 1959. lib. bdg. 20.00 (ISBN 0-8414-3137-X). Folcroft.

Three Zero, Turning Thirty: An Anthology of Writers as They Turn Thirty. Ed. by Jeff Wright. (Illus.). 54p. (Orig.). 1985. pap. 5.00 (ISBN 0-938878-14-X). Hard Pr.

Threefold Garland: The World's Salvation in Mary's Prayer. Hans Urs Von Balthasar. Tr. by Erasmo Leiva-Merikakis from Ger. LC 81-83569. 146p. (Orig.). 1982. pap. 7.95 (ISBN 0-89870-015-9). Ignatius Pr.

Threefold Lotus Sutra. Tr. by Bunno Kato et al. LC 74-23158. Orig. Title: Hokke Sambu-Kyo. 404p. 1975. 19.75 (ISBN 0-8348-0105-1); pap. 10.95 (ISBN 0-8348-0106-X). Weatherhill.

Threefold Lotus Sutra: Sutra of Innumerable Meanings, Sutra of the Lotus Flower of the Wonderful Law, Sutra of Meditation on the Bodhisattva Universal Virtue. Tr. by Bunno Kato et al from Sanskrit, Chinese & Japanese. 404p. 1986. pap. 10.95 (ISBN 4-333-00208-7, Pub. by Kosei Pub Co Japan). C E Tuttle.

Threefold Method for Understanding the Seven Rays & Other Essays in Esoteric Psychology. Kurt Abraham. LC 84-81567. 120p. (Orig.). 1984. pap. 8.50 (ISBN 0-9609002-1-7). Lampus Pr.

Threefold Refuge in the Theravada Buddhist Tradition. John R. Carter & George D. Bond. LC 82-26467. 1982. 5.95x (ISBN 0-89012-030-7). Anima Pubns.

Threepenny Opera. Bertolt Brecht. Tr. by Eric Bentley & Desmond Vesey. (Orig.). 1964. pap. 3.95 (ISBN 0-394-17472-0, B333, BC). Grove.

Threepenny Opera. Bertolt Brecht. (English Book by Vesey; Lyrics by Bentley). 14.00 (ISBN 0-8446-1734-2). Peter Smith.

Threepersons Hunt. Brian Garfield. LC 73-87704. 264p. 1974. 6.95 (ISBN 0-87131-140-2). M Evans.

Three's a Crowd. Brenda Cole. (Ser.). pap. 2.25 (ISBN 0-373-88010-3). Harlequin Bks.

Three's a Crowd. Doris M. Disney. 240p. 1987. pap. 2.95 (ISBN 0-8217-2079-1). Zebra.

Three's a Crowd. Lurlene McDaniel. (Impressions Ser.). 128p. (Orig.). (gr. 6-8). 1987. pap. 2.50 (ISBN 0-87406-274-8). Willowisp Pr.

Three's a Crowd. (Orig.). 1986. pap. 2.50 (ISBN 0-449-13004-5, Pub. by Girls Only). Ballantine.

Threescore. Sarah N. Cleghorn. Ed. by Annette K. Baxter. LC 79-8783. (Signal Lives Ser.). (Illus.). 1980. Repr. of 1936 ed. lib. bdg. 34.50x (ISBN 0-405-12831-2). Ayer Co Pubs.

Threescore & Ten-Wow! Agnes D. Pylant. LC 70-151621. 1971. pap. 2.95 (ISBN 0-8054-5213-3). Broadman.

Threesomes: Studies in Sex, Power, & Intimacy. Arno Karlen. LC 87-33325. 384p. 1988. 18.95 (ISBN 0-688-06536-8, Pub. by Beech Tree Bks). Morrow.

Three...Two...One Lift Off. Thomas Buckingham. (Readers Ser.). 1984. pap. text ed. 3.00 (ISBN 0-13-920455-5). Prentice ESL.

Thresher see Krause Trio.

Thresher Sharks. S. Palmer. (Shark Discovery Library). (Illus.). 24p. (gr. k-5). Date not set. PLB 11.33 (ISBN 0-86592-460-0). Rourke Corp.

Threshing Floor. Barbara Burford. 1987. 16.95 (ISBN 0-932379-28-1); pap. 7.95 (ISBN 0-932379-27-3). Firebrand Bks.

Threshing Floor. Jennifer Russell. 408p. 1987. 16.95 (ISBN 0-8091-0394-X). Paulist Pr.

Threshing Floor. John F. Sheehan. 208p. 1982. pap. 6.95 (ISBN 0-87462-447-9). Marquette.

Threshing in the Midwest, 1820-1940: A Study of Traditional Culture & Technological Change. J. Sanford Rikoon. LC 87-45407. 224p. 1988. 35.00x (ISBN 0-253-36047-1). Ind U Pr.

Threshold. Nancy Henderson. 288p. pap. 3.95 (ISBN 0-7701-0370-7). Paperjacks US.

Threshold. Marlys Millhiser. 336p. 1984. 16.95 (ISBN 0-399-13012-8, Putnam). Putnam Pub Group.

Threshold. David R. Palmer. 288p. (Orig.). 1985. pap. 2.95 (ISBN 0-553-24878-2, Spectra). Bantam.

Threshold. Zofia Pytowska. 176p. 1982. 18.95 (ISBN 0-87073-518-7); pap. 11.25 (ISBN 0-87073-519-5). Schenkman Bks Inc.

Threshold. University of Illinois School of Architecture Staff. (Illus.). 128p. 1985. Vol. 3: Detail, 1985. 15.00 (ISBN 0-8478-5412-4); Vol. 4: Reconstructing Architectural Theory, 1988. 15.00 (ISBN 0-8478-5454-X); Vol. 5 & 6: Chicago School, 1988. 15.00 (ISBN 0-8478-5462-0). Rizzoli Intl.

Threshold Early Learning Library, 8 vols. Jean H. Orost et al. Incl. Vol. 1. Perceptual & Organizing Skills; Vol. 2. Mathematical Skills & Scientific Inquiry; Vol. 3. Language Skills & Social Concepts; Vol. 4. Music & Movement Improvisations. Miriam B. Stecher et al; Vol. 5. Art Experiences for Young Children. Naomi F. Pile; Vol. 6. Dramatizations for Young Children. Katrina Van Tassel & Milly Greimann; Vol. 7. Physical Skills. James Schoedler; Vol. 8. Health & Safety for Young Children. Dorothy D. Harrison. 1970-73. pap. text ed. 7.95 ea. Macmillan.

Threshold Is High: The Brethren in Christ in Japan. Doyle C. Book. Ed. by Ray M. Zercher & Glen A. Pierce. (Illus.). xii, 210p. (Orig.). 1986. pap. 7.95 (ISBN 0-916035-15-8). Evangel Indiana.

Threshold Level for Modern Language Learning in Schools. J. A. Van Ek. (Applied Linguistics & Language Study Ser.). 1978. pap. text ed. 11.75x (ISBN 0-582-55700-3). Longman.

Threshold Logic: A Synthesis Approach. Michael Dertouzos. (Press Research Monographs: No. 32). 1965. 27.50x (ISBN 0-262-04009-3). MIT Pr.

Threshold Logic & Its Applications. Saburo Muroga. LC 76-165830. 494p. 1971. 37.50 (ISBN 0-471-62530-2, JW). Krieger.

Threshold Models in Non-Linear Time Series Analysis. H. Tong. (Lecture Notes in Statistics: Vol. 21). (Illus.). 323p. 1983. pap. 29.50 (ISBN 0-387-90918-4). Springer-Verlag.

Threshold of a Nation: A Study in English & Irish Drama. Philip Edwards. LC 78-72085. 264p. 1983. pap. 14.95 (ISBN 0-521-27695-0). Cambridge U Pr.

Threshold of a New World: Intellectuals & the Exile Experience in Paris, 1830-1848. Lloyd S. Kramer. LC 87-19899. 320p. 1988. 31.50x (ISBN 0-8014-1939-5). Cornell U Pr.

Threshold of Anglo Saxon. Alfred J. Wyatt. LC 75-41302. Repr. of 1926 ed. 14.50 (ISBN 0-404-14634-1). AMS Pr.

Threshold of Religion. Robert R. Marett. LC 76-44755. Repr. of 1914 ed. 26.50 (ISBN 0-404-15950-8). AMS Pr.

Threshold of the Year: Poems. Mary Kinzie. LC 81-69836. (Breakthrough Ser.: No. 36). 64p. pap. 6.95 (ISBN 0-8262-0361-2). U of Mo Pr.

Threshold of War: Franklin D. Roosevelt & American Entry into World War II. Waldo Heinrichs. (Illus.). 304p. 1988. 19.95 (ISBN 0-19-504424-X). Oxford U Pr.

Threshold Pressure in Gas Storage. American Gas Association, Pipeline Research Committee et al. 309p. 1971. 6.00 (ISBN 0-318-12724-5, L20170). Am Gas Assn.

Threshold: Straight-Forward Answers to Teenager Questions about Sex. Thomas Mintz & Lorelie Mintz. LC 77-78991. 96p. 1984. pap. 6.95 (ISBN 0-8027-7259-5). Walker & Co.

Threshold to Tomorrow. Ruth Montgomery. 256p. 1983. 13.95 (ISBN 0-399-12759-3, Putnam). Putnam Pub Group.

Thresholds: A Study of Proust. Gerda Blumenthal. 112p. 1984. 13.95 (ISBN 0-917786-49-1). Summa Pubns.

Thresholds & Testimonies: Recovering Order in Literature & Criticism. Frederic Will. LC 88-145. 176p. 1988. 24.95x (ISBN 0-8143-1943-2). Wayne St U Pr.

Thresholds Between Philosophy & Psychoanalysis: Papers from the Philadelphia Association. Robin Cooper et al. 300p. Date not set. 55.00 (ISBN 1-853430-41-2, Pub. by Free Association Bks). Columbia U Pr.

Thresholds in Aging. Ed. by M. Bergener et al. 1985. pap. 39.50 (ISBN 0-12-090160-9). Acad Pr.

Thresholds in Geomorphology. Ed. by Donald R. Coates & John D. Vitek. (Binghamton Symposia in Geomorphology Ser.: Vol. 9). (Illus.). 512p. (Orig.). 1980. text ed. 60.00x (ISBN 0-04-551033-4). Unwin Hyman.

Thresholds of Initiation. Joseph L. Henderson. LC 67-24110. 1967. pap. 14.95 (ISBN 0-8195-6061-8). Wesleyan U Pr.

Thresholds of Reality: George Santayana & Modernist Poetics. Lois Hughson. (Literary Criticism Ser.). 1976. 21.95x (ISBN 0-8046-9154-1, Pub by Kennikat). Assoc Faculty Pr.

Thresholds: Studies in the Romantic Experience. Albert S. Cook. LC 85-40365. 432p. 1985. text ed. 37.50x (ISBN 0-299-10300-5). U of Wis Pr.

Thresholds to Adult Living. rev. ed. Craig. (gr. 9-12). 1982. text ed. 26.00 (ISBN 0-02-665940-9); tchr's. guide 9.32 (ISBN 0-02-665950-6). Bennett IL.

Thrice Chosen. Edouard Roditi. LC 81-9946. 135p. (Orig.). 1981. avail.; pap. 5.00 (ISBN 0-87685-350-5). Black Sparrow.

Thrice Shy: Cultural Accommodation to Blindness & Other Disasters in a Mexican Community. John L. Gwaltney. LC 71-118635. 219p. 1970. 29.50x (ISBN 0-231-03237-4). Columbia U Pr.

Thrie Tailes of the Thrie Priests of Peblis. LC 72-223. (English Experience Ser.: No. 106). 1969. Repr. of 1603 ed. 11.50 (ISBN 90-221-0106-1). Walter J Johnson.

Thrift: A Book of Domestic Counsel. Samuel Smiles. 1921. 35.00 (ISBN 0-686-19919-7). Quaker City.

Thrift Acquisitions: FDIC & FHLBB Speak. Ed. by Law & Business Inc. Staff & Legal Times Seminars Staff. (Seminar Course Handbooks). 1983. pap. 35.00 (ISBN 0-686-89353-0, C01198, Law & Business). HarBraceJ.

Thrift Book: A Directory. Ed. by Bibliotheca Press Research Division Staff. LC 80-70871. pap. text ed. 14.95 (ISBN 0-939476-09-6, Pub. by Biblio Pr GA). Prosperity & Profits.

Thrift Book Index. Bibliotheca Press Staff. LC 82-70344. 100p. 1982. pap. text ed. 8.95 (ISBN 0-939476-45-2, Pub. by Biblio Pr GA). Prosperity & Profits.

Thrift Financing Devices. C. Thomas Long & Thomas P. Vartanian. LC 85-125781. 246p. Date not set. price not set. HarBraceJ.

Thrift Industry in 1985. 1026p. 1985. 15.00 (A4-4134). PLI.

Thrift Institution Automation Survey. 247p. 1987. 150.00; members 75.00. Finan Mgrs Soc.

Thrift Institutions under Deregulation: A Bibliography, 1973-1986. Michael Stevenson. (Public Administration Ser.: P 2150). 13p. 1987. pap. 3.75 (ISBN 1-55590-290-1). Vance Biblios.

Thrift Stores & Resale Shops: An International Directory. Ed. by Alpha Pyramis Research Division Staff. 150p. 1983. text ed. 17.95 (ISBN 0-913597-13-9, Pub. by Alpha Pyramis). Prosperity & Profits.

Thrift Stores & Resale Shops: Suggestive Ideas for Specialized Thrift Stores. Center for Self-Sufficiency, Research Division Staff. 50p. 1983. pap. text ed. 4.95 (ISBN 0-910811-46-6, Pub. by Center Self Suff). Prosperity & Profits.

Thrifts Going Public. Richard T. Pratt et al. LC 83-236936. (Illus.). iv, 527p. Date not set. 35.00 (Law & Business). HarBraceJ.

Thrifts in Crisis: Structural Transformation of the Savings & Loan Industry. Frederick E. Balderston. Ed. by Kenneth T. Rosen. LC 84-18477. (Real Estate Urban Economics Ser.). 216p. 1985. 34.95x (ISBN 0-88730-018-9). Ballinger Pub.

Thrifts under Siege: Restoring Order to American Banking. Dan Brumbaugh. 240p. 1988. 39.95x (ISBN 0-88730-141-X). Ballinger Pub.

Thrifty Fifty. 33p. 1977. looseleaf 2.00 (ISBN 0-317-30779-7). Amer Bar Assn.

Thrifty Gourmet: Guide to Fine Dining in Santa Barbara for Under Seven Dollars. David Wyatt. LC 81-53014. (Illus.). 60p. (Orig.). 1981. pap. 5.95 (ISBN 0-941428-00-1). Queen Missions.

Thrifty Gourmet: 250 Great Dinners in the Bay Area for 6.95 or Less. Frank Viviano & Sharon Silva. LC 87-856. 180p. (Orig.). 1987. pap. 4.95 (ISBN 0-87701-407-8). Chronicle Bks.

Thrifty Meals for Two: Making Food Dollars Count. Mary D. Evans & Linda E. Cleveland. (Home & Garden Bulletin Ser.: No. 244). (Illus.). 69p. 1985. pap. 2.50 (ISBN 0-318-19909-2, S/N 001-000-04459-1). USGPO.

Thrill Is Gone, Bernie. G. B. Trudeau. 128p. 1983. pap. 2.25 (ISBN 0-449-20195-3, Crest). Fawcett.

Thrill Killers. Clifford Linedecker. Ed. by Colleen Dimson. (Illus.). 256p. (Orig.). 1988. pap. 3.95 (ISBN 0-7701-0650-1). Paperjacks US.

Thrill of Faith. C. S. Lovett. 1960. pap. 2.95 (ISBN 0-938148-21-4). Personal Christianity.

Thrill of the Grass. W. P. Kinsella. (Penguin Fiction Ser.). 208p. 1985. pap. 5.95 (ISBN 0-14-007386-8). Penguin.

Thrill of Victory Agony of Defeat. Donald P. Tarno. (Orig.). 1985. pap. text ed. 2.95 (ISBN 0-9616016-0-4). New Life Pubs.

Thrillers & More Thrillers. Robert Arthur. LC 68-23653. (Illus.). (gr. 7-11). 1968. 2.95 (ISBN 0-394-81561-0, BYR). Random.

Thrillers: Genesis & Structure of a Popular Genre. Jerry Palmer. 1979. 26.00x (ISBN 0-312-80347-8). St Martin.

Thrilling Adventures of Daniel Ellis. facsimile ed. Daniel Ellis. LC 76-37303. (Black Heritage Library Collection). Repr. of 1867 ed. 27.00 (ISBN 0-8369-8940-6). Ayer Co Pubs.

Thrilling Cities. Ian Fleming. 16.95 (ISBN 0-88411-874-6, Pub. by Aeonian Pr). Amereon Ltd.

Thrilling Escapes by Night. Albert Lee. 296p. 8.50 (ISBN 0-686-05596-9). Rod & Staff.

Thrilling Events: The Life of Henry Starr. Henry Starr. LC 82-2431. (Early West Ser.). (Illus.). 96p. Repr. of 1914 ed. Leather bdg. 19.95 (ISBN 0-932702-21-X). Creative Texas.

Thrilling Narrative of the Adventures, Sufferings & Starvation of Pike's Peak Gold Seekers on the Plains of the West in the Winter & Spring of 1859. Daniel Blue. 23p. 1968. pap. 4.95 (ISBN 0-87770-032-X). Ye Galleon.

Thrilling Narrative of the Sufferings of Mrs. Jane Adeline Wilson During Her Captivity Among the Comanche Indians. Jane A. Wilson. 28p. 1972. 7.50 (ISBN 0-87770-122-9); pap. 4.95 (ISBN 0-685-37707-5). Ye Galleon.

Thrills & Regressions. Michael Balint. 148p. (Orig.). 1959. text ed. 20.00x (ISBN 0-8236-6540-2). Intl Univs Pr.

Thrive on Stress. Richard Sharpe. 1978. pap. 3.50 (ISBN 0-446-30971-0). Warner Bks.

Thriving on Chaos: Handbook for a Management Revolution. Tom Peters. LC 87-45575. 561p. 1987. 19.95 (ISBN 0-394-56784-6). Knopf.

Through Masailand with Joseph Thomson. Ed. by Roland Young. 218p. 1962. 15.00x (ISBN 0-89771-010-X). State Mutual Bk.

Through Merrie England. F. L. Stevens. 1973. Repr. of 1928 ed. 25.00 (ISBN 0-8274-0869-2). R West.

Through Middle Eastern Eyes. 2nd rev. ed. Robert P. Pearson. Ed. by Leon E. Clark. (Illus.). 284p. (Orig.). (gr. 9-12). 1985. pap. 16.95x (ISBN 0-938960-26-1). CITE.

Through Moses to Jesus: The Way of the Paschal Mystery. Carlo M. Martini. Tr. by Mary T. Skerry from Ital. LC 87-73072. 128p. (Orig.). 1988. pap. 4.95 (ISBN 0-87793-375-8). Ave Maria.

Through My Day with the 'L', 'R', 'S', 'SH' Sounds, 4 bks. Linda S. Messick. (Illus.). (gr. k-6). 1975. Set. pap. text ed. 24.50x (ISBN 0-87015-218-1). Pacific Bks.

Through My Day with the 'L' Sound. Linda S. Messick. (Illus.). (gr. k-6). 1975. pap. text ed. 6.95x (ISBN 0-87015-212-2). Pacific Bks.

Through My Day with the 'R' Sound. Linda S. Messick. (Illus.). (gr. k-6). 1975. pap. text ed. 6.95x (ISBN 0-87015-213-0). Pacific Bks.

Through My Day with the 'S' Sound. Linda S. Messick. (Illus.). (gr. k-6). 1975. pap. text ed. 6.95x (ISBN 0-87015-214-9). Pacific Bks.

Through My Day with the 'Sh' Sound. Linda S. Messick. (Illus.). (gr. k-6). 1975. pap. text ed. 6.95x (ISBN 0-87015-215-7). Pacific Bks.

Through My Eyes. Lula Lamme. 48p. 1987. 6.95 (ISBN 0-89962-658-0). Todd & Honeywell.

Through My Eyes. Yvonne A. Miller. (Illus.). 48p. 1983. 5.50 (ISBN 0-682-49971-4). Exposition-Phoenix.

Through My Eyes - A Teenage Look at Life. Penny Zito. Ed. by Sherri York. LC 87-50257. (Illus.). 152p. (YA) (gr. 7 up). 1987. 7.95 (ISBN 1-55523-075-X). Winston-Derek.

Through My Eyes: The Story of a Surgeon Who Took on the Medical World & Won. Charles D. Kelman. LC 84-21446. (Illus.). 229p. 1985. 14.95 (ISBN 0-517-55600-6). Crown.

Through My Picture Window. Robert B. Phillips. LC 88-90639. (Illus.). 256p. (YA) (gr. 9-12). 1988. 9.95 (ISBN 0-9620577-1-1). R B Phillips Pub.

Through My Window. Tony Bradman. LC 86-3913. (Illus.). 26p. (gr. 3-8). 1987. 5.75 (ISBN 0-382-09258-9). Silver.

Through Nature to Eternity: Chaucer's "Legend of Good Women". Donald W. Rowe. LC 87-5993. x, 218p. 1988. 22.95x (ISBN 0-8032-3882-7). U of Nebr Pr.

Through Navajo Eyes: An Exploration in Film Communication & Anthropology. Sol Worth & John Adair. LC 78-180488. (Illus.). 320p. 1973. 20.00x (ISBN 0-253-36015-3); pap. 7.95x (ISBN 0-253-36016-1). Ind U Pr.

Through Old Rose Glasses, & Other Stories. Mary T. Earle. LC 70-128732. (Short Story Index Reprint Ser). 1900. 14.00 (ISBN 0-8369-3623-X). Ayer Co Pubs.

Through One Administration. Frances H. Burnett. LC 67-29260. lib. bdg. 16.50 (ISBN 0-8398-0181-5); pap. text ed. 6.95x (ISBN 0-89197-965-4). Irvington.

Through One Administration. Frances H. Burnett. (American Studies Ser). 1969. Repr. of 1883 ed. 18.00 (ISBN 0-384-06585-6). Johnson Repr.

Through Other Eyes: Animal Stories by Women. Ed. by Irene Zahava. 220p. (Orig.). (YA) (gr. 8-12). 1988. lib. bdg. 23.95 (ISBN 0-89594-315-8); pap. 8.95 (ISBN 0-89594-314-X). Crossing Pr.

Through Other Eyes: Essays in Understanding Conscious Models. Barbara E. Ward. 280p. 1985. 49.50x (ISBN 0-8133-0257-9). Westview.

Through Other Eyes: Vivid Narratives of Some of the Bible's Most Notable Characters. Carl E. Price. 144p. (Orig.). 1987. pap. 6.95 (ISBN 0-8358-0555-7). Upper Room.

Through Our Eyes. Ed. by Peter Putnis. 69p. 1986. pap. 8.95 (ISBN 0-949414-12-3, Pub. by Darling Downs Inst Pr Australia). Intl Spec Bk.

Through Our Eyes: The 20th Century As Seen by the San Francisco Chronicle. Intro. by Howard I. Finberg. (Illus.). 130p. 1987. pap. 8.95 (ISBN 0-87701-467-1). Chronicle Bks.

Through Our Own Eyes: Popular Art & Modern History. Guy Brett. (Illus.). 160p. 1987. 34.95 (ISBN 0-86571-092-9); pap. 16.95 (ISBN 0-86571-093-7). New Soc Pubs.

Through Paediatrics to Psychoanalysis: The Collected Papers of D. W. Winnicott. D. W. Winnicott. LC 74-84374. 23.95x (ISBN 0-465-08619-5). Basic.

Through Paphlagonia with a Donkey. David Beasley. (Adventure in the Turkish Isfendyars). (Illus.). 235p. 1984. 30.00 (ISBN 0-915317-01-X). Davus Pub.

Through Paphlagonia with a Donkey: An Adventure in the Turkish Isfendyars. David Beasley. (Illus.). 235p. 1983. pap. 9.95 (ISBN 0-915317-00-1). Davus Pub.

Through Parisian Eyes: Reflections on Contemporary French Arts & Culture. Melinda C. Porter. (Illus.). 288p. 1986. 18.95 (ISBN 0-19-504104-6). Oxford U Pr.

Through Peasant Eyes see Poet & Peasant.

Through "Poverty's Vale" A Hardscrabble Boyhood in Upstate New York, 1832-1862. Henry Conklin. Ed. by Wendell Tripp. LC 73-19980. (Illus.). 280p. 1974. 8.50 (ISBN 0-8156-0098-4); pap. 5.95 1975 (ISBN 0-8156-0117-4). Syracuse U Pr.

Through Prayer to Reality. Douglas A. Rhymes. LC 74-81813. 1976. pap. 3.95 (ISBN 0-88489-088-0). St Mary's.

Through Reconstruction see Growth of American Politics: A Modern Reader.

Through Reconstruction see Synopsis of American History.

Through Rose Colored Glasses: The Drawings & Illustrations of Rose Cecil O'Neill. Greg C. Thielen. LC 85-50464. (Illus.). 64p. (Orig.). 1985. pap. text ed. 7.00 (ISBN 0-934306-05-2). Springfield.

Through Russia: From St. Petersburg to Astrakhan & the Crimea. Katherine B. Guthrie. LC 73-115541. (Russia Observed Ser 1). 1970. Repr. of 1874 ed. 32.00 (ISBN 0-405-03030-4). Ayer Co Pubs.

Through Russia on a Mustang. Thomas Stevens. LC 78-115588. (Russia Observed, Series I). 1970. Repr. of 1891 ed. 20.00 (ISBN 0-405-03065-7). Ayer Co Pubs.

Through Russian Eyes: American-Chinese Relations. S. Sergeichuk. Ed. by Philip A. Garon. Tr. by Elizabeth M. Cody-Rutter from Rus. LC 74-75134. Orig. Title: U. S. A. & China. 1975. 15.95 (ISBN 0-914250-03-5). Intl Lib.

Through Science & Philosophy to Religion. F. R. Ansari. pap. 1.25 (ISBN 0-686-18536-6). Kazi Pubns.

Through Seasons of the Heart. John Powell. (Illus.). 384p. 1987. 13.95 (ISBN 0-89505-446-9). Tabor Pub.

Through Shen-Kan. Robert S. Clark & Arthur Sowerby. 247p. 1750.00x (ISBN 0-317-69250-X, Pub. by Han-Shan Tang Ltd). State Mutual Bk.

Through Siberia. Henry Lansdell. LC 75-115555. (Russia Observed, Series I). 1970. Repr. of 1882 ed. 42.00 (ISBN 0-405-03042-8). Ayer Co Pubs.

Through Siberia. J. Stradling. LC 76-27533. (Illus.). 1976. Repr. of 1901 ed. lib. bdg. 35.00 (ISBN 0-89341-048-9). Longwood Pub Group.

Through Siberia: The Land of the Future. Fridtjof Nansen. Tr. by Arthur G. Chater from Norwegian. LC 73-115568. (Russia Observed Ser). (Illus.). 1971. Repr. of 1914 ed. 35.00 (ISBN 0-405-03087-8). Ayer Co Pubs.

Through Space & Time. J. H. Jeans. 1940. 37.00 (ISBN 0-686-17427-5). Ridgeway Bks.

Through Space & Time. James S. Jeans. 224p. 1982. lib. bdg. 30.00 (ISBN 0-89984-911-3). Century Bookbindery.

Through Starving Russia: Being the Record of a Journey to Moscow & the Volga Provinces in August & September 1921. Carl E. Roberts. LC 75-39060. (Russian Studies: Perspectives on the Revolution Ser.). (Illus.). xv, 165p. 1977. Repr. of 1921 ed. 20.35 (ISBN 0-88355-440-2). Hyperion Conn.

Through Streets Broad & Narrow. Gabriel Fielding. LC 86-11244. (Phoenix Fiction Ser.). viii, 340p. 1986. pap. 9.95 (ISBN 0-226-24844-5). U of Chicago Pr.

Through Teacher's Eyes: Portraits of Writing Teachers' at Work. Sondra Perl & Nancy Wilson. LC 85-30242. (Illus., Orig.). 1986. pap. text ed. 16.00x (ISBN 0-435-08248-5). Heinemann Ed.

Through Tempest Trails. Denise P. Fox. LC 87-930. (Illus.). 116p. (gr. 3-7). 1987. 11.95 (ISBN 0-689-31350-0, Atheneum Childrens Bks). Macmillan.

Through the Adirondacks in Eighteen Days. Martin V. Ives. (Illus.). 176p. 1984. 17.50 (ISBN 0-916346-54-4). Harbor Hill Bks.

Through the Air: A Narrative of Forty Years' Experience As an Aeronaut. John Wise. LC 79-169444. (Literature & History of Aviation Ser). 1971. Repr. of 1873 ed. 40.00 (ISBN 0-405-03787-2). Ayer Co Pubs.

Through the Awakening Eye, Poems. Elbridge Anderson. (Illus.). 1976. pap. 4.00 (ISBN 0-915242-08-7). Pygmalion Pr.

Through the Back Door of the World in a Ship That Had Wings. William M. Masland. LC 83-90809. (Illus.). 361p. 1985. 14.50 (ISBN 0-533-05818-X). Vantage.

Through the Bering Strait: Part Two of the Fur Country. Jules Verne. 4.95 (ISBN 0-87497-042-3). Assoc Bk.

Through the Bible, Vol. I. Steve Clapp & Sue I. Mauck. (C-Four Youth Bible Materials Ser.). (Illus.). 138p. (Orig.). 1982. pap. 10.00 (ISBN 0-914527-15-0). C-Four Res.

Through the Bible Book by Book, 4 vols. Myer Pearlman. 1935. pap. 2.95 ea.; Vol. 1, 99p. (ISBN 0-88243-660-0, 02-0660); Vol. 2, 112p. (ISBN 0-88243-661-9, 02-0661); Vol. 3, 96p. (ISBN 0-88243-662-7, 02-0662); Vol. 4, 128p. (ISBN 0-88243-663-5, 02-0663). Gospel Pub.

Through the Bible in a Year: Pupil Workbook. Dana Eynon. 64p. (gr. 3-7). 1975. wkbk. 1.95 (ISBN 0-87239-011-X, 3239). Standard Pub.

Through the Bible in a Year: Teacher. Dana Eynon. LC 74-27239. 176p. 1975. tchr's manual 7.95 (ISBN 0-87239-028-4, 3237). Standard Pub.

Through the Bible Quizzes for Children. Shirley Beegle. 64p. (Orig.). (gr. 2-7). 1974. pap. 2.50 (ISBN 0-87239-324-0, 3249). Standard Pub.

Through the Bible Reading Program. McKinney et al. (Illus.). 112p. (Orig.). 1983. pap. 3.95 (ISBN 0-87239-647-9, 3076). Standard Pub.

Through the Bible Study Series, 7 vol. set. Ed. by A. L. Clanton. 2688p. 1982. text ed. 54.95 per set (ISBN 0-912315-51-2). Word Aflame.

Through the Bible Study Series, Vol. VII. Ed. by A. L. Clanton. 384p. 1982. text ed. 6.95 (ISBN 0-912315-58-X). Word Aflame.

Through the Bible Study Series, Vol. VI. Ed. by A. L. Clanton. 384p. 1981. text ed. 6.95 (ISBN 0-912315-57-1). Word Aflame.

Through the Bible Study Series, Vol. V. Ed. by A. L. Clanton. 384p. 1981. text ed. 6.95 (ISBN 0-912315-56-3). Word Aflame.

Through the Bible Study Series, Vol. IV. Ed. by A. L. Clanton. 384p. 1981. text ed. 6.95 (ISBN 0-912315-55-5). Word Aflame.

Through the Bible Study Series, Vol. III. Ed. by A. L. Clanton. 384p. 1981. text ed. 6.95 (ISBN 0-912315-54-7). Word Aflame.

Through the Bible Study Series, Vol. II. Ed. by J. L. Hall. 384p. 1981. text ed. 6.95 (ISBN 0-912315-53-9). Word Aflame.

Through the Bible Study Series, Vol. 1. Ed. by A. L. Clanton. 384p. 1981. text ed. 6.95 (ISBN 0-912315-52-0). Word Aflame.

Through the Bible with ABC's. Compiled by Patricia Mahany. (Story & Color Bks.). (Illus.). 64p. (Orig.). (ps-3). 1984. pap. 2.95 (ISBN 0-87239-798-X, 2374). Standard Pub.

Through the Bible with Preschoolers. Carole Matthews. 144p. 1985. 8.95 (ISBN 0-87239-945-1, 3330). Standard Pub.

Through the Box-Office Window. William H. Leverton. LC 79-8069. (Illus.). Repr. of 1932 ed. 26.50 (ISBN 0-404-18379-4). AMS Pr.

Through the Centuries. Iu. V. Belichko & V. O. Pidgora. 336p. 1982. 155.00x (ISBN 0-317-57469-8, Pub. by Collets UK). State Mutual Bk.

Through the Centuries: Kiev in Fine Arts of the Twelfth to Twentieth Centuries. Iu Belichko & V. Pidgora. 336p. 1982. 181.00x (ISBN 0-317-61408-8, Pub. by Collets (UK)). State Mutual Bk.

Through the Chinese Revolution. Fernand Farjenel. LC 72-79820. (China Library Ser.). 1972. Repr. of 1916 ed. 31.00 (ISBN 0-8420-1381-4). Scholarly Res Inc.

Through the Curtain. Viola P. Neal & Shafica Karagulla. LC 83-71171. 368p. 1983. 14.95 (ISBN 0-87516-517-6). DeVorss.

Through the Custom House: Nineteenth Century American Fiction & Modern Theory. John Carlos Rowe. LC 81-20866. 256p. 1982. text ed. 26.00x (ISBN 0-8018-2677-2). Johns Hopkins.

Through the Dark Continent, or, the Sources of the Nile, Around the Great Lakes of Equatorial Africa, & Down the Livingstone River to the Atlantic Ocean, 2 vols. Henry M. Stanley. LC 68-55223. (Illus.). 1970. Repr. of 1878 ed. Vol. 1. lib. bdg. 33.50 (ISBN 0-8371-1434-9, STTB); Vol. 2. lib. bdg. 33.50 (ISBN 0-8371-1435-7, STTC). Greenwood.

Through the Dark Continent: Or the Sources of the Nile Around the Great Lakes of Equatorial Africa & Down the Livingstone River to the Atlantic Ocean, 2 vols. Henry M. Stanley. (Illus.). 960p. 1988. Vol. I. pap. 9.95 (ISBN 0-486-25667-7); Vol. II. pap. 9.95 (ISBN 0-486-25668-5). Dover.

Through the Dolls' House Door. Jane Gardam. LC 87-200. (Illus.). 128p. (gr. 5 up). 1987. 10.25 (ISBN 0-688-07447-2). Greenwillow.

Through the Doors of Truth, Find Thyself. Deborah Morea. 1978. 5.50 (ISBN 0-9603022-0-4). Davida Pubns.

Through the Earth. Clement Fezandie. 12.95x (ISBN 0-913960-19-5); pap. 2.50x (ISBN 0-913960-00-4). Fax Collect.

Through the Eighties: Thinking Globally, Acting Locally. Ed. by Frank Feather. 1980. 12.50 (ISBN 0-930242-11-4). World Future.

Through the Eye of a Needle. Hal Clement. (Del Rey Bks). 1979. pap. 1.95 (ISBN 0-345-28410-0). Ballantine.

Through the Eye of a Rose Window: A Perspective on the Environment for Worship. Richard S. Vosko. 1981. pap. text ed. 7.95 (ISBN 0-89390-028-1). Resource Pubns.

Through the Eye of the Dove: One Man's Journey into Reincarnation. Hal Wolfe. Date not set. pap. price not set. Dearen Pub.

Through the Eye of the Needle: A Romance. William D. Howells. LC 78-9572. Repr. of 1907 ed. 17.50 (ISBN 0-404-11548-9). AMS Pr.

Through the Eye of the Needle: Immigrants & Enterprise in the New York Garment Trade. Roger Waldinger. LC 86-12451. 256p. 1986. 35.00x (ISBN 0-8147-9212-X). NYU Pr.

Through the Eyes of a Child. Mildred Caughey. 83p. 1979. 6.50 (ISBN 0-87770-224-1). Ye Galleon.

Through the Eyes of a Child: Introduction to Children's Literature. 2nd ed. Donna Norton. 720p. 1987. text ed. 34.95 (ISBN 0-675-20725-8). Merrill.

Through the Eyes of a Child: Introduction to Children's Literature. Donna E. Norton. 600p. 1983. text ed. 29.95 (ISBN 0-675-09832-7). Additional supplements may be obtained from publisher. Merrill.

Through the Eyes of Man. Darrin S. Bush. 76p. 1976. 6.95 (ISBN 0-87881-038-2). Mojave Bks.

Through the Eyes of Ohio's Children: A Legislative Factbook 1987-1988. CDF Ohio Staff & The Junior Leagues of Ohio Staff. (Orig.). 1987. pap. 4.95 (ISBN 0-938008-59-5). Children's Defense.

Through the Eyes of Social Science. 3rd ed. Frank Zulke. 349p. (Orig.). 1984. pap. text ed. 11.95x (ISBN 0-88133-095-7). Waveland Pr.

Through the Fire. Joseph M. Stowell. 156p. 1985. pap. 5.95 (ISBN 0-89693-601-5). Victor Bks.

Through the First Antarctic Night, Eighteen Ninety-Eight to Eighteen Ninety-Nine. Frederick A. Cook. (Illus.). 478p. 1980. 49.00x (ISBN 0-7735-0514-8). McGill-Queens U Pr.

Through the Forest: New & Selected Poems. David Wagoner. 240p. 1987. 16.95 (ISBN 0-87113-154-4); pap. 7.95 (ISBN 0-87113-153-6). Atlantic Monthly.

Through the Forest of Twisted Dreams. R. L. Stine. (Wizards, Warriors & You Ser.: Bk. 1). (Illus.). 112p. 1984. pap. 2.50 (ISBN 0-380-88047-4, 88047-4). Avon.

Through the Fourth Wall. facs. ed. William A. Darlington. LC 68-16925. (Essay Index Reprint Ser). 1922. 17.00 (ISBN 0-8369-0363-3). Ayer Co Pubs.

Through the Garden Gate. Susan Hill. (Illus.). 96p. 1988. 16.95 (ISBN 0-241-11930-8, Pub. by Hamish Hamilton). David & Charles.

Through the Gates of Death & Spiritualism in the Light of Occult Science. Dion Fortune. 240p. 1987. pap. 11.95 (ISBN 0-85030-662-0, Pub. by Thorsons UK). Weiser.

Through the Gates of Gold see Light on the Path.

Through the Gateway of Death. Hodson. 3.50 (ISBN 0-8356-7202-6). Theos Pub Hse.

Through the Gateway of the Heart. Ed. by Sophia Adamson. 205p. (Orig.). 1986. pap. 14.50 (ISBN 0-936329-00-9). Four Trees Pubns.

Through the Glass of Soviet Literature. Ernest J. Simmons. LC 53-8757. (Studies of the Russian Institute of Col. Univ.). 1963. pap. 15.00x (ISBN 0-231-08527-3). Columbia U Pr.

Through the Glass of Soviet Literature: Views, of Russian Society. Ed. & intro. by Ernest J. Simmons. LC 72-337. (Essay Index Reprint Ser.). Repr. of 1953 ed. 20.00 (ISBN 0-8369-2827-X). Ayer Co Pubs.

Through the Gospel with Dom Helder. Dom H. Camara. Tr. by Alan Neame from Fr. 160p. (Orig.). 1986. pap. 8.95 (ISBN 0-88344-266-3). Orbis Bks.

Through the Grand Canyon from Wyoming to Mexico. Ellsworth L. Kolb. cancelled (ISBN 0-8165-0835-6). U of Ariz Pr.

Through the Grecourt Gates. Eleanor T. Lincoln. (Illus.). 118p. 1978. pap. 3.50 (ISBN 0-87391-025-7). Smith Coll.

Through the Green Fuse. Michael Dudley. 32p. 1983. 10.00 (ISBN 0-913719-24-2); pap. 3.50 (ISBN 0-913719-23-4). High-Coo Pr.

Through the Green Valley. Barbara Gowdy. 288p. 1988. 16.95 (ISBN 0-312-01805-3). St. Martin.

Through the Hebrew Looking-Glass: Arab Stereotypes in Children's Literature. Fouzi El-Asmar. (Illus.). 150p. 1986. 17.95 (ISBN 0-915597-39-X); pap. 9.95 (ISBN 0-915597-37-3). Amana Bks.

Through the Hidden Door. Rosemary Wells. LC 86-24273. 256p. (gr. 5 up). 1987. 14.95 (ISBN 0-8037-0276-0, 1258-370). Dial Bks Young.

Through the Hoop. Ed. by Tema Okun & Peter Wood. (Southern Exposure Ser.). (Illus.). 128p. (Orig.). 1979. pap. 4.00 (ISBN 0-943810-07-8). Inst Southern Studies.

Through the Indian Looking-Glass. David Selbourne. 272p. (Orig.). 1982. pap. 10.25 (ISBN 0-86232-091-7, Pub. by Zed Pr England). Humanities.

Through the Kaleidoscope. Cozy Baker. LC 85-71412. (Illus.). 144p. 1985. 15.00 (ISBN 0-9608930-1-6). Beechcliff Bks.

Through the Kaleidoscope...& Beyond. Cozy Baker. LC 87-72150. (Illus.). 200p. 1987. 20.00 (ISBN 0-9608930-2-4). Beechcliff Bks.

Through the Kitchen Window. Susan Hill. (Illus.). 66p. 1980. 10.95 (ISBN 0-88045-074-6). Stemmer Hse.

Through the Landscape of Faith. Lucy Bregman. LC 85-26381. 120p. (Orig.). 1986. pap. 9.95 (ISBN 0-664-24704-0). Westminster John Knox.

Through the Legal Looking Glass, Reflections of Peoples & Cultures: A Handbook for Educators. American Bar Association Staff & Charlotte C. Anderrson. LC 82-157433. (Intercom Ser.: No. 100). (Illus.). 40p. 1981. 4.00. Amer Forum.

Through the Leper-Squint. Anthony Weymouth. LC 75-23769. (Illus.). Repr. of 1938 ed. 25.00 (ISBN 0-404-13395-9). AMS Pr.

Through the Light Continent: The United States in 1877-1878. William Saunders. LC 73-13148. (Foreign Travelers in America, 1810-1935 Ser.). 432p. 1974. Repr. 30.00x (ISBN 0-405-05472-6). Ayer Co Pubs.

Through the Loneliness: A Woman's Spiritual Journal. Antonia J. van den Beld. 144p. 1987. pap. 8.95 (ISBN 0-8091-2913-2). Paulist Pr.

Through the Looking Glass. Lewis Carroll. 1979. pap. 1.95x (ISBN 0-460-01018-2, Evman). Biblio Dist.

TITLE INDEX THUCYDIDES BOOK SIX COMMENTARY.

Through the Looking Glass. Lewis Carroll. LC 77-77325. (Illus.). (gr. 4 up). 1977. 8.95 (ISBN 0-312-80374-5). St Martin.
Through the Looking Glass. Lewis Carroll. 1981. Repr. lib. bdg. 15.95x (ISBN 0-89966-419-9). Buccaneer Bks.
Through the Looking Glass. Lewis Carroll. (Puffin Classic Ser.). 176p. (gr. 7 up). 1985. pap. 2.25 (ISBN 0-14-035039-X, Puffin). Penguin.
Through the Looking Glass see Alice's Adventures in Wonderland.
Through the Looking Glass, & What Alice Found There. Lewis Carroll. LC 84-60960. (Classics Ser.). (Illus.). 184p. (gr. 2 up). 1984. Repr. of 1941 ed. 12.95 (ISBN 0-88088-991-8, 889918). Peter Pauper.
Through the Looking Glass & What Alice Found There. Lewis Carroll. (gr. 3-8). 1986. 17.95 (ISBN 0-394-53228-7). Knopf.
Through the Looking Glass & What Alice Found There. Rosemary Nursey-Bray. (Orig.). (ps up). 1987. playscript 3.50 (ISBN 0-87602-276-X). Anchorage.
Through the Looking-Glass & What Alice Found There (California-Pennyroyal Edition) Lewis Carroll. Incl. Deluxe Edition. 198p. 225.00 (ISBN 0-520-05026-6). LC 83-47520. (Illus.). 198p. (gr. 8 up). 1983. 29.95 (ISBN 0-520-05039-8). U of Cal Pr.
Through the Looking Glass: And What Alice Found There see Alice's Adventures in Wonderland.
Through the Maze: Statistics with Computer Applications. Margaret P. Jendrek. 218p. 1985. pap. text ed. write for info. (ISBN 0-534-03921-9). Wadsworth Pub.
Through the Mental Health Maze: A Consumer's Guide to Finding a Psychotherapist. Sallie Adams & Michael Orgel. 78p. 1975. 3.25. Pub Citizen Inc.
Through the Micromaze: A Visual Guide from Ashton-Tate. Wayne Creekmore. (Through the Micromaze Ser.: Vol. 1). 250p. 1983. pap. 9.95 (ISBN 0-912677-02-3). Ashton-Tate Pub.
Through the MicroMaze: A Visual Guide to Getting Organized. W. Creekmore & S. Behasa. 1985. pap. text ed. 9.95 (ISBN 0-07-912618-9). McGraw.
Through the Micromaze: A Visual Guide to Getting Organized. Wayne Creekmore & Stephanie Behasa. (Through the Micromaze Ser.: Vol. 2). 64p. 1984. pap. 9.95 (ISBN 0-912677-18-X). Ashton-Tate Pub.
Through the Micromaze: Visual Guide to Telecommunications. Patrick Kincaid & Marlin Ouverson. 150p. 1985. pap. 9.95 (ISBN 0-912677-55-4). Ashton-Tate Pub.
Through the Microscope. Ron Taylor. (World of Science Ser.). (Illus.). 64p. (gr. 4-7). 1985. 12.95 (ISBN 0-8160-1075-7). Facts on File.
Through the Mind's Eye. Ralph M. Lewis. LC 81-84954. 371p. 1982. 12.50 (ISBN 0-912057-32-7, G-646). AMORC.
Through the Moon Gate: A Guide to China's Historical Monuments. (Illus.). 352p. 1987. 19.95 (ISBN 0-19-584077-1). Oxford U Pr.
Through the Moongate. Leonard Wolcott & Carolyn Wolcott. (Orig.). (gr. 4-6). 1978. pap. 4.00 (ISBN 0-377-00074-4). Friendship Pr.
Through the Night Raptly. Mohinder Monga. 8.00 (ISBN 0-89253-778-7); flexible cloth 4.80 (ISBN 0-89253-779-5). Ind-US Inc.
Through the Open Door: A New Look at C.S. Lewis. Dabney A. Hart. LC 83-6520. x, 164p. 1984. text ed. 15.75x (ISBN 0-8173-0187-9). U of Ala Pr.
Through the Pentateuch Chapter by Chapter. W. H. Griffith Thomas. LC 85-10076. 192p. 1985. pap. 6.95 (ISBN 0-8254-3833-0). Kregel.
Through the Port of Philadelphia: Memoirs of Charles Kurz. George H. Kurz. 152p. 1988. 15.95 (ISBN 0-317-59675-6). Dorrance.
Through the Porthole. (Illus.). 1965. pap. 2.50 (ISBN 0-914412-25-6). Inst for the Arts.
Through the Porthole: Exhibition Catalog. Intro. by Dominique De Menil. (Publication of the Rice University Institute for the Arts). (Illus.). 1965. pap. 2.50 (ISBN 0-913456-89-6). Interbk Inc.
Through the Rain Glass. Tyler Henshaw. 1980. 6.25 (ISBN 0-941490-22-X). Solo Pr.
Through the Reversal of Time. Emilio A. Jamarron. Ed. by Malvin Wald. LC 86-9644. 400p. (Orig.). 1986. pap. 18.95 (ISBN 0-317-47445-6). Blue Lagoon.
Through the Russian Revolution. Albert R. Williams. LC 75-39066. (Russian Studies: Perspectives on the Revolution Ser). (Illus.). 311p. 1977. Repr. of 1923 ed. 30.25 (ISBN 0-88355-446-1). Hyperion Conn.
Through the Safety Net. Charles Baxter. 208p. 1985. 14.95 (ISBN 0-670-80477-0). Viking.
Through the Safety Net. Charles Baxter. (Contemporary American Fiction Ser.). 224p. 1986. pap. 6.95 (ISBN 0-14-008995-0). Penguin.
Through the Scent of Water: A Neo-Pauline Discourse on the Order of Christian Assembly. Richard H. Akeroyd. 1985. pap. 5.00 (ISBN 0-916620-71-9). Portals Pr.
Through the Scriptures. A. P. Gibbs. pap. 5.95 (ISBN 0-937396-45-1). Walterick Pubs.
Through the South Seas with Jack London. Martin Johnson. (Illus.). 1976. Repr. of 1913 ed. 20.00 (ISBN 0-915046-07-5). Wolf Hse.
Through the Storm. Linda S. Judy. 64p. 1988. 7.95 (ISBN 0-89962-680-7). Todd & Honeywell.
Through the Straits of Armageddon: Arms Control Issues & Prospects. Ed. by Loch K. Johnson & Paul F. Diehl. LC 86-30813. 304p. 1987. 32.50x (ISBN 0-8203-0946-X); pap. 12.95 (ISBN 0-8203-0947-8). U of Ga Pr.
Through the Stratosphere. Maxine Davis. LC 46-4775. 1946. 2.75 (ISBN 0-911090-06-1). Pacific Bk Supply.
Through the Time Barrier: A Study in Precognition & Modern Physics. Danah Zohar. 178p. 1984. pap. 5.95 (ISBN 0-586-08431-2, Pub by Granada England). Academy Chi Pubs.
Through the Turf Smoke. facs. ed. Seumas Macmanus. LC 72-81273. (Short Story Index Reprint Ser.). 1899. 18.25 (ISBN 0-8369-3025-8). Ayer Co Pubs.
Through the Valley. Lillian Owens. 96p. 1986. pap. 3.50 (ISBN 0-89114-159-6). Baptist Pub Hse.
Through the Valley. Frances M. Swan. LC 78-73254. (Illus., Orig.). 1978. pap. 3.95 (ISBN 0-9602126-1-2). F M Swan.
Through the Valley of Death. E. M. Allison. 1985. 24.95x (ISBN 0-7090-1835-5, Pub. by R Hale Ltd UK). State Mutual Bk.
Through the Valley of Love. Shirley Cook. 224p. 1987. pap. 5.95 (ISBN 0-310-47381-0, 15584P). Zondervan.
Through the Valley of Tears. Cyril Barber & Sharalee Aspenleiter. 224p. 1987. 12.95 (ISBN 0-8007-1540-3). Revell.
Through the Valley of the Kwai. Ernest Gordon. LC 83-12967. (Illus.). 257p. 1983. Repr. of 1962 ed. lib. bdg. 38.50x (ISBN 0-313-24220-8, G0VK). Greenwood.
Through the Valley of the Shadow: A Guide for the Care of the Dying & Their Loved Ones. L. Richard Batzler. 1983. 10.95 (ISBN 0-935710-05-1). Hid Valley MD.
Through the Wall. 1909 ed. Cleveland Moffett. LC 75-32768. (Literature of Mystery & Detection). (Illus.). 1976. Repr. 31.00x (ISBN 0-405-07887-0). Ayer Co Pubs.
Through the Wall. Patricia Wentworth. 240p. 1986. pap. 2.95 (ISBN 0-553-25255-0). Bantam.
Through the Wall. Patricia Wentworth. 17.95 (ISBN 0-88411-723-5, Pub. by Aeonian Pr). Amereon Ltd.
Through the Winds Rain. rev. ed. Daniel B. Comfort, Jr. LC 80-53436. 64p. 1981. 7.95 (ISBN 0-938316-00-1). Bridges Sound.
Through the Woods. Carroll Arnett. 1971. 10.00 (ISBN 0-685-00984-X); pap. 5.00 (ISBN 0-685-00985-8). Elizabeth Pr.
Through the Wordsworth Country. Harry Goodwin & Knight. LC 78-1598. Repr. of 1887 ed. lib. bdg. 37.00x (ISBN 0-8414-4612-1). Folcroft.
Through the Wordsworth Country. Harry Goodwin & William Knight. 1887. Repr. 50.00 (ISBN 0-8274-3882-6). R West.
Through the Year in Japan. Elizabeth F. Thurley. (Through the Year Ser.). (Illus.). 72p. (gr. 7-12). 1985. 17.95 (ISBN 0-7134-4819-9, Pub. by Batsford England). David & Charles.
Through the Year in the U. S. A. Nance L. Fyson. (Through the Year Ser.). (Illus.). 72p. (YA) (gr. 7-10). 1982. 17.95 (ISBN 0-7134-4069-4, Pub. by Batsford England). David & Charles.
Through the Year in West Africa. Malcolm Green. (Through the Year Ser.). (Illus.). 72p. (gr. 7-10). 1982. 17.95 (ISBN 0-7134-3964-5, Pub. by Batsford England). David & Charles.
Through the Year with Francis of Assisi: Daily Meditations from His Words & Life. Murray Bodo. LC 87-4158. (Illus.). 240p. 1987. pap. 7.95 (ISBN 0-385-23823-1, Im). Doubleday.
Through the Year with Fulton Sheen: Inspiration Selections for Each Day of the Year. Fulton Sheen. 213p. 1985. pap. 6.95 (ISBN 0-89283-236-3). Servant.
Through the Year with Harriet. Betsy Maestro & Giulio Maestro. LC 84-29339. (Illus.). 32p. (ps-1). 1985. PLB 12.95 (ISBN 0-517-55613-8). Crown.
Through the Year with the Church Fathers. Emily Harakas. 1985. pap. 8.95 (ISBN 0-937032-37-9). Light&Life Pub Co MN.
Through the Year with the DRE: A Seasonal Guide for Christian Educators. Gail T. McKenna. 128p. (Orig.). 1987. pap. 7.95 (ISBN 0-8091-2860-8). Paulist Pr.
Through the Year with the Saints. M. Basil Pennington. 288p. 1988. pap. 7.95 (ISBN 0-385-24062-7, Im). Doubleday.
Through the Year with Thomas Merton: Daily Meditations. Ed. by Thomas P. McDonnell. LC 85-11827. (Illus.). 240p. 1985. pap. 7.95 (ISBN 0-385-23234-9, Im). Doubleday.
Through the Years in Genesee: An Illustrated History. Alice Lethbridge. 144p. 1985. 22.95 (ISBN 0-89781-161-5). Windsor Pubns Inc.
Through the Years in Old Winnsboro. Katharine T. Obear. LC 80-23314. xx, 258p. 1980. Repr. of 1940 ed. 20.00 (ISBN 0-87152-344-2). Reprint.
Through the Years: Woodward, Iowa Centennial, 1883-1893. Woodward Centennial Committee. 408p. 1983. write for info. Woodward Centennial.
Through Their Looking Glass. Rosie Seaman. LC 79-89647. (Illus.). 112p. (ps). 1979. pap. text ed. 5.95 (ISBN 0-913916-84-6, IP 84-6). Incentive Pubns.
Through These Eyes I Saw. James J. Jackson. 30p. 1985. 4.95 (ISBN 0-533-06221-7). Vantage.
Through These Men: Some Aspects of Our Passing History. John M. Brown. LC 71-167318. (Essay Index Reprint Ser.). Repr. of 1956 ed. 20.00 (ISBN 0-8369-2756-7). Ayer Co Pubs.
Through Thick & Thin "An Adventure in Whole Food Cooking". Kay Huberty. LC 81-85960. (Illus.). 300p. 1982. spiral binding 9.95 (ISBN 0-686-32819-1). Through Thick & Thin.
Through-Thickness Tension Testing of Steel- STP 794. Ed. by R. J. Glodowski. LC 82-72887. 152p. 1983. text ed. 21.00 (ISBN 0-8031-0232-1, 04-794000-02). ASTM.
Through Time & the Valley. John R. Erickson. (Illus.). 260p. 1983. pap. 7.95 (ISBN 0-9608612-1-1). Maverick Bks.
Through Trials & Triumphs: A History of Augustana College. Donald Sneen. 192p. 1985. 17.00 (ISBN 0-931170-29-X). Ctr Western Studies.
Through Troubled Waters. Marinus Nijsse. (Children's Summit Bks.). (gr. 5-8). pap. 1.95 (ISBN 0-8010-6728-6). Baker Bk.
Through Troubled Waters: A Young Father's Struggles with Grief. William H. Armstrong. 96p. (Orig.). 1983. pap. 3.35 (ISBN 0-687-41895-X, Festival). Abingdon.
Through Turkish Arabia. H. Cowper. 512p. 1987. 350.00x (ISBN 1-85077-170-7, Pub. by Darf Pubs Ltd). State Mutual Bk.
Through Twisted Thorns. J. Remy Theberge. Ed. by R. Moisan. LC 85-80145. (Illus.). 360p. (Orig.). 1985. 12.95x (ISBN 0-918862-02-7); pap. 4.50x (ISBN 0-918862-03-5). Golden Gambit.
Through Unexplores Texas. W. B. Parker. LC 84-80800. 256p. 1984. ltd. ed. 50.00 (ISBN 0-87611-073-1); pap. 8.95 (ISBN 0-87611-065-0). Tex St Hist Assn.
Through Values to Social Interpretation: Essays on Social Contexts, Actions, Types & Prospects. Howard P. Becker. LC 69-10068. 1968. Repr. of 1950 ed. lib. bdg. 35.00x (ISBN 0-8371-0014-3, BESI). Greenwood.
Through Welsh Doorways. facsimile ed. Jeannette A. Marks. LC 78-167463. (Short Story Index Reprint Ser.). Repr. of 1909 ed. 18.00 (ISBN 0-8369-3989-1). Ayer Co Pubs.
Through White Men's Eyes: A Contribution to Navajo History, 6 vols. J. Lee Correll. LC 76-49362. (Illus.). 2831p. 1979. Set. 225.00x (ISBN 0-89417-291-3). Dissemination & Assessment.
Through Wood & Nails. 1987. record 25.00x (Pub. by Wild Goose Pubns Scotland); cassette 25.00x (Pub. by Wild Goose Pubns Scotland). State Mutual Bk.
Throw a Kiss, Harry. Mary Chalmers. LC 58-5294. (Trophy Picture Bks.). (Illus.). 32p. (ps-3). 1981. pap. 1.50 (ISBN 0-06-443030-8, Trophy). HarpJ.
Throw Away Your Resume. Robert Hachheim. 1982. 8.95 (ISBN 0-8120-2520-2). Barron.
Throw Away Your Resume & Get That Job. Warren Rosaluk. (Illus.). 122p. 1983. P-H.
"Throw Down" on Drugs. William Goodman. (Illus.). 79p. (Orig.). 1987. pap. 2.95 (ISBN 0-8341-1192-6). Beacon Hill.
Throw It Out of Sight. Lawrence Abrams. LC 83-23226. (Doing & Learning Bks.). (Illus.). 120p. (gr. 5 up). 1984. lib. bdg. 10.95 (ISBN 0-87518-247-X); pap. 4.95 (ISBN 0-87518-280-1). Dillon.
Throw Out the Lifeline, Lay Out the Corse: Poems, 1965-1985. Asa Benveniste. 144p. (Orig.). 1983. pap. 9.95 (ISBN 0-85646-098-2, Pub. by Anvil Pr Poetry). Longwood Pub Group.
Throw Wide the Door. Emilie Loring. Repr. lib. bdg. 16.95x (ISBN 0-88411-372-8, Pub. by Aeonian Pr). Amereon Ltd.
Throw Your Whole Self Into Comprehension. Patti Carson et al. (Stick Out Your Neck Ser.). 104p. (Orig.). (gr. 3-6). 1977. pap. 9.95 (ISBN 0-88724-177-8, CD 0004-1). Carson-Dellos.
Throwaway Man. Paul Jarrett. 224p. 1985. 24.95x (ISBN 0-7090-2158-5, Pub. by R Hale Ltd UK). State Mutual Bk.
Throwback. Mark Manley. 256p. (Orig.). 1987. pap. 3.50 (ISBN 0-445-20277-7, Pub. by Popular Lib). Warner Bks.
Throwback. Tom Sharpe. 1984. pap. 3.95 (ISBN 0-394-72439-9, Vin). Random.
Throwing Away the Compass. Harry Humes. Ed. by Rodger Moody. 24p. 1986. 4.00 (ISBN 0-9610508-5-3). Silverfish Rev Pr.
Throwing Heat: The Autobiography of Nolan Ryan. Nolan Ryan & Harvey Frommer. LC 87-33074. 1988. 16.95 (ISBN 0-385-24438-X). Doubleday.
Throwing Madonna: From Nervous Cells to Hominid Brains. W. H. Calvin. 252p. 1983. text ed. 13.95 (ISBN 0-07-009665-1); pap. text ed. 7.95 (ISBN 0-07-009664-3). McGraw.
Throwing on the Potter's Wheel. Thomas Sellers. 4.95 (ISBN 0-934706-03-4). Prof Pubns Ohio.
Throwing Season. Michael French. LC 79-53598. (YA) (gr. 9-12). 1980. 8.95 (ISBN 0-440-08600-0). Delacorte.
Throwing Shadows. Ken Gerner. LC 84-73337. 80p. (Orig.). 1985. pap. 8.00 (ISBN 0-914742-87-6). Copper Canyon.
Throwing Shadows. E. L. Konigsburg. 160p. (gr. 7 up). 1988. pap. 3.95 (ISBN 0-02-044140-1, Collier). Macmillan.
Throwing Sticks in the National Museum - Extracts. facs. ed. Otis T. Mason. (Illus.). 31p. pap. 3.95 (ISBN 0-8466-4003-1, I3). Shorey.
Throwing the Sticks: Occult Self-Therapy - The Arts of Self-Transcendence in Post-Freudian Modes of Thought. John C. Cooper. LC 85-51340. 175p. (Orig.). 1985. pap. 9.95x (ISBN 0-932269-49-4). Wyndham Hall.
Throwing Things Away: From Middens to Resource Recovery. Laurence Pringle. LC 83-46165. (Illus.). 128p. (YA) (gr. 7 up). 1986. 12.70i (ISBN 0-690-04420-8, Crowell Jr Bks); PLB 12.89 (ISBN 0-690-04421-6). HarpJ.
Throws. 3rd ed. Ed. by Jess Jarver. (Contemporary Theory, Technique & Training Ser.). (Illus.). 160p. 1986. pap. 12.00 (ISBN 0-911521-17-8). Tafnews.
Thru the Bible, 5 vols. J. Vernon McGee. Incl. Vol. I. Genesis Through Deuteronomy. LC 81-3930. 640p. 1981. 19.95 (ISBN 0-8407-4973-2); Vol. II. Joshua Through Psalms. LC 81-3930. 896p. 1982. 22.95 (ISBN 0-8407-4974-0); Vol. III. Proverbs Through Malachi. LC 81-3930. 1024p. 1982. 22.95 (ISBN 0-8407-4975-9); Vol. IV. Matthew Through Romans. 22.95 (ISBN 0-8407-4976-7); Vol. V. Corinthians I Through Revelation. LC 81-3930. 992p. 1983. 22.95 (ISBN 0-8407-4977-5). LC 81-3930. Set. 111.75 (ISBN 0-8407-4957-0). Nelson.
Thru the Grapevine. Junior League of Elmira, Inc. Ed. by Margaret Morse. LC 82-83914. (Illus.). 368p. 1983. 14.95 (ISBN 0-9609980-1-2). Jr League Elmira.
Thrump-O-Moto. James Clavell. LC 86-4485. (Illus.). 96p. 1986. pap. 20.00 (ISBN 0-385-29504-9). Delacorte.
Thrums & the Barrie Country. John Kennedy. 1930. Repr. lib. bdg. 30.00 (ISBN 0-8414-5560-0). Folcroft.
Thrush Green. Miss Read. 1982. Repr. lib. bdg. 17.95 (ISBN 0-89966-435-0). Buccaneer Bks.
Thrush Green. Miss Read. 226p. 1987. pap. 7.95 (ISBN 0-89733-263-6). Academy Chi Pubs.
Thrust & Drag: Its Prediction & Verification, PAAS 98. Ed. by Eugene E. Covert et al. LC 85-18681. (Illus.). 346p. 1985. 59.50 (ISBN 0-930403-00-2). AIAA.
Thrust for Canada: The American Attempt on Quebec 1775-1776. Robert M. Hatch. 1979. 12.95 (ISBN 0-395-27612-8). HM.
Thrust in the Sickle & Reap. Earl Paulk. 141p. (Orig.). 1986. pap. 5.95 (ISBN 0-917595-11-4). K Dimension.
Thrust in the Sickle & Reap see Echa la Hoz y Siega.
Thrust Syphilis Down to Hell & Other Rejoyceana: Studies in the Border-lands of Literature & Medicine. J. B. Lyons. (Illus.). 204p. 1988. 29.95 (ISBN 0-907606-37-7, Pub. by Glendale Pr). Irish Bks Media.
Thryistor Design & Realization. Paul D. Taylor. LC 86-26685. (Design & Measurement in Electrical & Electronic Engineering Ser.). 250p. 1987. 54.95 (ISBN 0-471-91178-X). Wiley.
Thucydides. W. Robert Connor. LC 83-43066. 256p. 1984. 34.50 (ISBN 0-691-03569-5). Princeton U Pr.
Thucydides. W. Robert Connor. 280p. 1987. pap. 14.50 (ISBN 0-691-10239-2); 34.50. Princeton U Pr.
Thucydides. Simon Hornblower. LC 87-4213. 192p. 1987. text ed. 25.00x (ISBN 0-8018-3529-1). Johns Hopkins.
Thucydides, Bk. II. Ed. by E. C. Marchant & T. Wiedemann. 239p. Repr. of 1984 ed. 13.00x (ISBN 0-86516-041-4). Bolchazy Carducci.
Thucydides, Bk. 1. E. Marchant. 334p. 1982. Repr. of 1905 ed. 21.00 (ISBN 0-86292-027-2, Pub. by Bristol Classical UK). Focus Info Gr.
Thucydides, Bks. 1-2, Ch. 65. T. Wiedemann. 94p. 1985. 11.00 (ISBN 0-86292-170-8, Pub. by Bristol Classical UK). Focus Info Gr.
Thucydides, Bk. 4, Ch. 1-41. J. Crees & J. Wordsworth. 122p. 1982. Repr. of 1919 ed. 12.25 (Pub. by Bristol Classical UK). Focus Info Gr.
Thucydides, Bk. 4. C. E. Graves. 368p. 1982. Repr. of 1888 ed. 21.00 (ISBN 0-86292-028-0, Pub. by Bristol Classical UK). Focus Info Gr.
Thucydides, Bks. 6 & 7. Thucydides. Ed. by K. J. Dover. 1965. Bk.6. 14.95x (ISBN 0-19-831832-4). Bk. 7 (ISBN 0-19-831829-4). pap. 13.95x (ISBN 0-19-872098-X). Oxford U Pr.
Thucydides--Histories Book II. Ed. by P. J. Rhodes. (Classical Texts-Greek Texts Ser.). 200p. 1988. text ed. 49.95 (ISBN 0-85668-396-5, Pub. by Aris & Phillips UK); pap. text ed. 16.50 (ISBN 0-85668-397-3). Humanities.
Thucydides & Athenian Imperialism. Jacqueline De Romilly. Ed. by Gregory Vlastos. Tr. by Philip Thody from Eng. & Gr. LC 78-19381. (Morals & Law in Ancient Greece Ser.). 1979. Repr. of 1963 ed. lib. bdg. 30.50x (ISBN 0-405-11570-9). Ayer Co Pubs.
Thucydides & the Tradition of Funeral Speeches at Athens. rev. ed. John E. Ziolkowski. Ed. by W. R. Connor. LC 80-2674. (Monographs in Classical Studies). 1981. lib. bdg. 25.00 (ISBN 0-405-14057-6). Ayer Co Pubs.
Thucydides Book Six Commentary. Cynthia W. Shelmerdine. (Greek Commentaries Ser.). 35p. (Orig.). 1988. pap. text ed. 3.00. Bryn Mawr Commentaries.

Thucydides on the Nature of Power. A. Geoffrey Woodhead. LC 77-89973. (Martin Classical Lectures Ser: No. 24). 1970. pap. 16.50x (ISBN 0-674-89136-8). Harvard U Pr.

Thucydidis de Bello Pelopennesiaco Libri Octo, 8 vols. Ed. by I. M. Stahl & Leonardo Taran. (Ancient Greek Literature Ser.). 1929p. 1987. lib. bdg. 255.00 (ISBN 0-8240-7765-2). Garland Pub.

Thud, Republic F-105. (Illus.). 64p. 1986. pap. 6.95 (ISBN 0-89747-171-7, 5004). Squad Sig Pubns.

Thud Ridge. Jack Broughton. 288p. 1985. pap. 3.50 (ISBN 0-553-25189-9). Bantam.

Thudding Drums. facs. ed. Compiled by G. M. Miller. LC 79-76948. (Granger Index Reprint Ser.). 1942. 17.00 (ISBN 0-8369-6030-0). Ayer Co Pubs.

Thula Baba. Ntombi. (Illus.). 88p. (Orig.). 1988. pap. 7.95 (ISBN 0-86975-323-1, Pub. by Ravan Pr). Ohio U Pr.

Thule Expedition, Fifth, 1921-1924: Reports of the Danish Ethnographical Expedition to Arctic America, 27 vols, Vols. 1-10. (Illus.). Repr. Set. buckram 1440.00 (ISBN 0-404-58300-8). AMS Pr.

Thule, or Vertues Historie. Francis Rous. 1966. 54.00 (ISBN 0-8337-3072-X). B Franklin.

T.H.U.M.B.B. T. Ernesto Bethancourt. LC 83-6119. 160p. (YA) (gr. 7 up). 1983. 10.95 (ISBN 0-8234-0494-3). Holiday.

Thumbelina. Adrienne Adams & Hans Christian Andersen. LC 61-17282. (Illus.). (gr. k-4). 1961. 12.95 (ISBN 0-684-12705-9, Pub. by Scribner). Macmillan.

Thumbelina. Hans Christian Andersen. LC 79-50146. (Illus.). (ps-3). 1979. 14.95 (ISBN 0-8037-8815-0, 01451-440); PLB 14.89 (ISBN 0-8037-8814-2). Dial Bks Young.

Thumbelina. Hans Christian Andersen. LC 78-18080. (Illus.). 32p. (gr. k-4). 1979. PLB 9.79 (ISBN 0-89375-141-3); pap. 1.95 (ISBN 0-89375-119-7). Troll Assocs.

Thumbelina. Hans Christian Andersen. LC 79-50146. (Pied Piper Bk.). (Illus.). 32p. (ps-3). 1985. pap. 4.95 (ISBN 0-8037-0232-9, 0481-140). Dial Bks Young.

Thumbelina. Retold by Ellen M. Dolan & Janet L. Bolinske. (Children's Classics Ser.). (Illus.). 30p. (Orig.). (gr. 1-3). 1987. spiral bdg. 19.95 (ISBN 0-88335-546-9); text ed. 9.95 (ISBN 0-88335-556-6); pap. text ed. 4.95 (ISBN 0-88335-576-0). Milliken Pub Co.

Thumbeline. Hans Christian Andersen. LC 85-12062. (Illus.). 28p. (gr. 1 up). 1985. 13.95 (ISBN 0-88708-006-5). Picture-Bk Studio.

Thumbing down to the Riviera. Irving Stettner. (Fiction, Literature Ser.). (Illus.). 150p. (Orig.). 1986. 11.95 (ISBN 0-918154-19-7); signed by the author 25.00 (ISBN 0-317-52451-8). Stroker.

Thumblina. Margaret Davidson & Carson Davidson. (Make Believe It's You Ser.: No. 3). (Illus.). 80p. (Orig.). (gr. 4-6). 1987. pap. 2.95 (ISBN 0-590-40503-9). Scholastic Inc.

Thumbnail Sketches of Famous Arizona Desert Riders, 1538-1946. facs. ed. Frank C. Lockwood. LC 73-148224. (Biography Index Reprint Ser.). 1946. 13.00 (ISBN 0-8369-8071-9). Ayer Co Pubs.

Thumbs Up! Beginning Harp for the Adult & College-Level Student. Kathy B. Moore. LC 88-80737. (Illus., Orig.). 1988. pap. text ed. 15.00 (ISBN 0-9620436-0-5). FC Pub Co.

Thumbs Up: The Jim Brady Story. Mollie Dickenson. LC 87-17385. 322p. 1987. 19.95 (ISBN 0-688-06497-3). Morrow.

Thumbscrew & Rack. George Macdonald. (Illus.). 25p. 1983. pap. 3.00 saddle-stitched (ISBN 0-911826-72-6). Am Atheist.

Thump & Plunk. Janice M. Udry. LC 80-8443. (Illus.). 24p. (ps-3). 1981. 10.70i (ISBN 0-06-026149-8); PLB 11.89 (ISBN 0-06-026150-1). HarpJ.

Thump, Bump: Tiny the Dancing Hippo. Janet Craig. LC 87-10933. (Illus.). 32p. (gr. k-2). 1987. PLB 9.89 (ISBN 0-8167-1077-5); pap. text ed. 2.95 (ISBN 0-8167-1078-3). Troll Assocs.

Thumpity Thump Gets Dressed. Cyndy Szekeres. LC 83-83284. (Cyndy Szekeres Board Bks.). (Illus.). 16p. (ps-k). 1984. 4.95 (ISBN 0-307-12203-4, 12233, Golden Bks). Western Pub.

Thumpy's Story: A Story of Love & Grief Shared. Nancy C. Dodge. LC 84-61293. (Illus.). 24p. (gr. k-12). 1985. pap. 5.95 (ISBN 0-918533-00-7). Prairie Lark.

Thunder Alley. Mack Maloney. 432p. 1988. pap. 3.95 (ISBN 0-8217-2405-3). Zebra.

Thunder & Lightnings. Jan Mark. LC 78-4778. (Illus.). (gr. 5 up). 1979. 11.70 (ISBN 0-690-03901-8, Crowell Jr Bks). HarpJ.

Thunder & the Circus. Dick Logan et al. LC 77-74689. (Thunder the Dinosaur Ser.). 32p. (ps-7). 1987. PLB 9.95 (ISBN 0-87191-790-4). Creative Ed.

Thunder & the Dinosaur Puppet. Dick Logan et al. LC 77-74688. (Thunder the Dinosaur Ser.). 32p. (ps-7). 1987. PLB 9.95 (ISBN 0-87191-789-0). Creative Ed.

Thunder & Trumpets: The Millerite Movement & Dissenting Religion in Upstate New York, 1800-1850. David Rowe. (American Academy of Religion Studies in Religion: No. 38). 1985. 24.95 (ISBN 0-89130-770-2, 01 00 38); pap. 16.95 (ISBN 0-89130-769-9). Scholars Pr GA.

Thunder Beyond the Brazos: Mirabeau B. Lamar, A Biography. Jack C. Ramsey, Jr. 220p. 1985. 14.95 (ISBN 0-89015-462-7). Eakin Pr.

Thunder Castle. Veronica Smith. 1981. pap. 2.95 (ISBN 0-89083-795-3). Zebra.

Thunder Comes to the Rescue. Dick Logan et al. LC 77-74685. (Thunder the Dinosaur Ser.). 32p. (ps-7). 1987. PLB 9.95 (ISBN 0-87191-786-6). Creative Ed.

Thunder Disappears. Dick Logan et al. LC 77-74686. (Thunder the Dinosaur Ser.). 32p. (ps-7). 1977. PLB 9.95 (ISBN 0-87191-787-4). Creative Ed.

Thunder down the Track. Dayton O. Hyde. LC 85-20062. 180p. (gr. 5 up). 1986. 12.95 (ISBN 0-689-31203-2, Atheneum Childrens Bks). Macmillan.

Thunder Eats a Haystack. Dick Logan et al. LC 77-74680. (Thunder the Dinosaur Ser.). 32p. (ps-7). 1987. PLB 9.95 (ISBN 0-87191-782-3). Creative Ed.

Thunder Egg. Jack Little. LC 77-94288. (gr. 6 up). 1978. pap. 3.00 (ISBN 0-934768-01-3). Altair Pr.

Thunder from Above, Vol. 9. John Morrocco. Ed. by Paul Dreyfus. LC 84-70448. (Vietnam Experience Ser.). (Illus.). 192p. 1984. 16.95 (ISBN 0-939526-09-3). Boston Pub Co.

Thunder from Above: The War in the Air Through 1968. Ed. by Robert Manning. (Vietnam Experience). (Illus.). 192p. 16.95 (ISBN 0-201-11265-5). Addison-Wesley.

Thunder from Heaven: The Story of the 17th Airborne Division in WW II. Don Pay. LC 80-69273. (Airborne Ser.: No. 4). (Illus.). 179p. 1980. Repr. 25.00 (ISBN 0-89839-037-0). Battery Pr.

Thunder from the Mountain: Mau Mau Patriotic Songs. Ed. by Maina W. Kinyatti. 128p. (Orig.). 1980. 17.00x (ISBN 0-905762-83-5, Pub. by Zed Pr England). Humanities.

Thunder Gets a House. Dick Logan et al. LC 77-74681. (Thunder the Dinosaur Ser.). 32p. (ps-7). 1987. PLB 9.95 (ISBN 0-87191-783-1). Creative Ed.

Thunder Goes for a Walk. Dick Logan et al. LC 77-74683. (Thunder the Dinosaur Ser.). 32p. (ps-7). 1987. PLB 9.95 (ISBN 0-87191-785-8). Creative Ed.

Thunder Goes to a Party. Dick Logan et al. LC 77-74682. (Thunder the Dinosaur Ser.). 32p. (ps-7). 1987. PLB 9.95 (ISBN 0-87191-784-X). Creative Ed.

Thunder Heights. Phyllis Whitney. 18.95 (ISBN 0-89190-534-0, Pub. by Am Repr). Amereon Ltd.

Thunder in America. Bob Faw & Nancy Skelton. 1988. pap. 4.50 (ISBN 0-7701-0851-2). Paperjacks US.

Thunder in America: The Improbable Presidential Campaign of Jesse Jackson. Bob Faw & Nancy Skelton. LC 86-6030. 288p. 1986. 16.95 (ISBN 0-87719-052-6). Texas Month Pr.

Thunder in the Dust: Classic Images of Western Movies. John R. Hamilton. LC 87-10767. (Illus.). 160p. 1987. 29.95 (ISBN 1-55670-006-7). Stewart Tabori & Chang.

Thunder in the Mountains. Lon K. Savage. (Illus.). 160p. 1984. pap. 7.95 (ISBN 0-934750-52-1). Jalamap.

Thunder in the Southwest: Echoes from the Wild Frontier. Oren W. Arnold. LC 52-4324. pap. 61.50 (ISBN 0-317-28707-9, 2055508). Bks Demand UMI.

Thunder in the Valley. Doug Knapp et al. (Orig.). 1986. pap. 6.95 (ISBN 0-8054-6342-9). Broadman.

Thunder in the Valley: The Massabielle Saga. James H. Klien. (Illus.). 92p. 4.00 (ISBN 0-8198-7316-0, MA0135); pap. 3.00 (ISBN 0-8198-7317-9). Dghtrs St Paul.

Thunder in the Wind. June L. Shiplett. 448p. 1983. pap. 3.95 (ISBN 0-451-13599-7, Sig). NAL.

Thunder Island. James H. Kunstler. LC 87-47909. (Bantam New Fiction Ser.). 272p. (Orig.). 1988. pap. 7.95 (ISBN 0-553-34514-1). Bantam.

Thunder Lake Narrow Gauge. 2nd, rev. ed. Harvey Huston. Ed. by Ondre H. Andrews & Ondre N. Huston. LC 82-82291. 168p. pap. 14.50 (ISBN 0-9600048-3-1). Huston.

Thunder Makes a Sandcastle. Dick Logan et al. LC 77-74687. (Thunder the Dinosaur Ser.). 32p. (ps-7). 1987. PLB 9.95 (ISBN 0-87191-788-2). Creative Ed.

Thunder Monsters over Europe: A History of the 405th Fighter Group in WWII. Reginald G. Nolte. 160p. 1986. 23.50; pap. 18.95. Sunflower U Pr.

Thunder Moon. Max Brand. 160p. 1982. pap. 1.95 (ISBN 0-671-41567-0). PB.

Thunder Moon Strikes. Max Brand. 224p. 1984. pap. 2.50 (ISBN 0-446-32074-9). Warner Bks.

Thunder Moon's Challenge. Max Brand. 224p. 1984. pap. 2.50 (ISBN 0-446-32050-1). Warner Bks.

Thunder Mountain. Zane Grey. 1985. pap. 2.50 (ISBN 0-671-55814-5). PB.

Thunder Mountain. Barbara Siegel & Scott Siegel. (Firebrats Ser.: No. 3). (YA) (gr. 7 up). 1987. pap. 2.50 (ISBN 0-671-55794-7). Archway.

Thunder Mountain Massacre. J. D. Hardin. (Doc & Raider Ser.: No. 72). 192p. (Orig.). 1987. pap. 2.50 (ISBN 0-425-09784-6). Berkley Pub.

Thunder of Hell. Richard Austin. (Guardians Ser.: No. 3). 224p. 1987. pap. 2.95 (ISBN 0-515-09034-4). Jove Pubns.

Thunder of Silence. Joel S. Goldsmith. LC 61-7340. 1961. 13.45 (ISBN 0-06-063270-4, HarpR). Har-Row.

Thunder on the Gulf. C. L. Douglas. 1973. Repr. of 1936 ed. 9.95 (ISBN 0-88342-027-9). Old Army.

Thunder on the Left. Christopher D. Morley. LC 83-45821. Repr. of 1936 ed. 27.00 (ISBN 0-404-20185-7). AMS Pr.

Thunder on the Right. Mary Stewart. 224p. 1985. pap. 2.95 (ISBN 0-449-20773-0, Crest). Fawcett.

Thunder on the Right: The "New Right" & the Politics of Resentment. Alan Crawford. 1981. pap. 3.95 (ISBN 0-394-74862-X). Pantheon.

Thunder on the Right: The Protestant Fundamentalists. Gary K. Clabaugh. LC 74-9551. 283p. 1974. 19.95x (ISBN 0-88229-108-4). Nelson-Hall.

Thunder on the Tennessee. G. Clifton Wisler. LC 82-21057. 192p. (YA) (gr. 7 up). 1983. 10.95 (ISBN 0-525-67144-7, 01063-320). Lodestar Bks.

Thunder Out of China. Theodore H. White & Annalee Jacoby. LC 74-31228. (China in the Twentieth Century Ser.). vi, 331p. 1975. Repr. of 1946 ed. lib. bdg. 32.50 (ISBN 0-306-70699-7). Da Capo.

Thunder Out of China. Theodore H. White & Annalee Jacoby. (Quality Paperbacks Ser.). 345p. 1980. pap. 11.95 (ISBN 0-306-80128-0). Da Capo.

Thunder over Europe. E. Alexander Powell. 69.95 (ISBN 0-8490-1213-9). Gordon Pr.

Thunder over New England: Benjamin Bonnell, the Loyalist. Paul J. Bunnell. 1986. 12.95 (ISBN 0-8158-0436-9). Chris Mass.

Thunder over Scotland: George Wishart, Mentor of John Knox. James W. Baird. LC 82-81516. (Illus.). 1982. text ed. 7.95 (ISBN 0-938462-04-0). Green Leaf CA.

Thunder Pup. Janet Hickman. LC 81-2614. 144p. (gr. 3-7). 1981. 8.95 (ISBN 0-02-743770-1). Macmillan.

Thunder Ridge. Ben Thompson. 1978. pap. 1.50 (ISBN 0-8439-0580-8, Leisure Bks). Leisure NY.

Thunder-Root: Traditional & Contemporary N-A Verse. J. Ivaloo Volborth. (Native American Ser.). 51p. 1978. pap. 5.00 (ISBN 0-935626-24-7). U Cal AISC.

Thunder to the West. Al Cody. 1980. pap. 1.75 (ISBN 0-8439-0848-3, Leisure Bks). Leisure NY.

Thunder Waters: Experiences of Growing up in Different Indian Tribes. Frances Snow et al. (gr. 3-8). 1975. 4.75 (ISBN 0-686-26094-5); pap. 1.95 (ISBN 0-89992-072-1). Coun India Ed.

Thunderball. Ian Fleming. pap. 9.95 Fr. ed (ISBN 0-685-11597-6); pap. 9.95 Span. ed. (ISBN 0-685-11598-4). French & Eur.

Thunderball. Ian Fleming. 240p. 1985. pap. 3.50 (ISBN 0-425-08634-8). Berkley Pub.

Thunderbird. Marilyn Sachs. LC 84-21252. (Skinny Bks.). (Illus.). 88p. (gr. 7 up). 1985. 10.95 (ISBN 0-525-44163-8, 01063-320). Dutton.

Thunderbird! An Illustrated History of the Ford T-Bird. Ray Miller & Glenn Embree. LC 73-75630. (The Ford Road Ser: Vol. 4). (Illus.). 1973. 39.95 (ISBN 0-913056-04-9). Evergreen Pr.

Thunderbird: An Odyssey in Automotive Design. William P. Boyer. Ed. by Si Dunn. LC 86-50101. (Illus.). 216p. 1986. 39.95 (ISBN 0-9616289-3-6); lib. bdg. 45.00 commemorative ed. (ISBN 0-9616289-2-8); hallmark ltd. ed. 1000.00 (ISBN 0-9616289-0-1); deluxe ed. 75.00 (ISBN 0-9616289-1-X). Renn Pr NOLA.

Thunderbird Song. Carl M. Beall. 1970. 5.50 (ISBN 0-682-47055-4). Exposition-Phoenix.

Thunderbolt at Catfish Bend. Ben L. Burman. (Catfish Bend Ser.). (Illus.). 114p. (gr. 5 up). 1984. 10.95 (Dist. by Vanguard); pap. 3.95 (ISBN 0-943436-03-6). Wieser & Wieser.

Thunderbolt at Catfish Bend. Ben L. Burman. (Illus.). 128p. 1985. 12.95. Vanguard.

Thunderbolt-Champ of the Patowmack. James Percival Haynes. 288p. 1980. 11.00 (ISBN 0-682-49589-1). Exposition-Phoenix.

Thunderbolt: The History of the Eleventh Armored Division. (Divisional Ser.: No. 17). (Illus.). 1980. Repr. of 1948 ed. 22.50 (ISBN 0-89839-041-9). Battery Pr.

Thundercats & the Ghost Warrior: A Find Your Fate Fantasy. Megan Stine & H. William Stine. LC 85-60157. (Illus.). 80p. (gr. 9-12). 1985. pap. 1.95 (ISBN 0-394-87419-6, BYR). Random.

Thundercats & the Snowmen of Hook Mountain: A Find Your Fate Fantasy. Megan Stine & H. William Stine. LC 85-60502. (Illus.). 80p. (gr. 9-12). 1985. pap. 1.95 (ISBN 0-394-87420-X, BYR). Random.

Thunderers. V. Stepanov. 271p. 1986. pap. 6.95 (ISBN 0-8285-3308-3, Pub. by Progress Pubs USSR). Imported Pubns.

Thunderhawk. Jon Sharpe. (Trailsman Ser.: No. 59). 192p. 1986. pap. 2.75 (ISBN 0-451-14573-9, Sig). NAL.

Thunderhead. Mary O'Hara. 320p. (YA) (gr. 5-9). 1967. pap. 1.75 (ISBN 0-440-98875-6, LFL). Dell.

Thunderhead. Mary O'Hara. LC 87-45653. 320p. (YA) (gr. 7 up). 1988. pap. 2.95 (ISBN 0-06-080903-5, P-903, PL). Har-Row.

Thunderhoof. Syd Hoff. LC 75-129855. (Early I Can Read Bk.). (Illus.). (gr. k-3). 1971. PLB 9.89 (ISBN 0-06-022560-2). HarpJ.

Thundering Herd. Zane Grey. 1984. pap. 3.50 (ISBN 0-671-52848-3). PB.

Thundering Sneakers. Prudence Mackintosh. 200p. 1987. pap. 8.95 (ISBN 0-87719-085-2). Texas Month Pr.

Thunderland. Dan Parkinson. 368p. 1987. pap. 3.50 (ISBN 0-8217-1991-2). Zebra.

Thunderstones: A Study of Meteorites Based on Falls & Fines in Arkansas. Derek Sears. LC 87-5086. 88p. 1988. pap. 8.50 (ISBN 0-938626-94-9). U of Ark Pr.

Thunderstones & Shooting Stars. Robert T. Dodd. LC 86-7563. (Illus.). 272p. 1986. 24.95 (ISBN 0-674-89137-6). Harvard U Pr.

Thunderstones & Shooting Stars: The Meaning of Meteorites. Robert S. Dodd. (Illus.). 208p. 1988. pap. 11.95 (ISBN 0-674-89138-4). Harvard U Pr.

Thunderstorm. Mary Szilagyi. LC 84-24570. (Illus.). 32p. (ps-2). 1985. 11.95 (ISBN 0-02-788580-1). Bradbury Pr.

Thunderstorm. 3rd ed. Yu Tsao. Tr. by Tso-Liang Wang et al from Chinese. (Illus.). 151p. 1978. 6.95 (ISBN 0-917056-74-4, Pub. by Foreign Lang Pr China). Cheng & Tsui.

Thunderstorm in Church. Louise A. Vernon. LC 74-5009. (Illus.). 129p. (gr. 5-8). 1974. pap. 4.50 (ISBN 0-8361-1740-9). Herald Pr.

Thunderstorm in Human Affairs. 2nd, enl. & rev. ed. Ed. by Edwin Kessler. LC 83-47836. (Illus.). 200p. 1983. 27.95x (ISBN 0-8061-1857-1). U of Okla Pr.

Thunderstorm in Human Affairs. 2nd, rev. & enl. ed. Ed. by Edwin Kessler. LC 83-47836. (Illus.). 200p. 1988. pap. 16.95 (ISBN 0-8061-2153-X). U of Okla Pr.

Thunderstorm Morphology & Dynamics. 2nd, rev. & enl. ed. Ed. by Edwin Kessler. LC 85-8450. (Thunderstorms: A Social, Scientific, & Technological Documentary Ser.: Vol. 2). (Illus.). 432p. 1986. 68.50x (ISBN 0-8061-1936-5). U of Okla Pr.

Thunderstorms. C. Magono. (Developments in Atmospheric Science Ser.: Vol. 12). 262p. 1980. 70.25 (ISBN 0-444-15179-6). Elsevier.

Thunderstorms & Planes. Richard L. Collins. 1982. 14.95 (ISBN 0-02-527250-0). Macmillan.

Thunderstorms & Shooting Stars. Robert T. Dodd. 224p. pap. cancelled (ISBN 0-02-949220-3). Macmillan.

Thunderstruck. Pamela Toth. (Silhouette Special Edition Ser.). pap. 2.75 (ISBN 0-373-09411-6). Harlequin Bks.

Thunderweapon in Religion & Folklore. C. Blinkenberg. xii, 122p. 1985. Repr. of 1911 ed. lib. bdg. 25.00x (ISBN 0-89241-205-4). Caratzas.

Thunderweapon in Religion & Folklore. C. Blinkenberg. 1977. lib. bdg. 59.95 (ISBN 0-8490-2749-7). Gordon Pr.

Thurber Carnival. James Thurber. 1975. pap. 7.95 (ISBN 0-06-090445-3, CN445, PL). Har-Row.

Thurber Carnival. James Thurber. LC 57-11168. 1957. 10.95 (ISBN 0-394-60474-1). Modern Lib.

Thurber Country. James Thurber. 1982. (Touchstone Bks); pap. 9.95 (ISBN 0-671-45930-9, Touchstone Bks). S&S.

Thurber, Texas: The Life & Death of a Company Coal Town. John S. Spratt, Sr. Ed. by Harwood P. Hinton. (Personal Narratives of the West Ser.). (Illus.). 176p. 1986. 22.50 (ISBN 0-292-78067-2). U of Tex Pr.

Thurber's Anatomy of Confusion. Catherine M. Kenney. LC 84-465. xii, 235p. 1984. 25.00 (ISBN 0-208-02050-0, Archon Bks). Shoe-String.

Thurgarton Church. George Barker. 1969. write for info. (ISBN 0-685-01054-6, Pub. by Trigram Pr); signed ed. 100 copies 12.00 ea.; pap. 2.00 (ISBN 0-685-01056-2). Small Pr Dist.

Thurgood Marshall. Lisa Aldred. (Black Americans of Achievement Ser.). (Illus.). 112p. (gr. 5 up). Date not set. lib. bdg. 16.95x (ISBN 1-55546-601-X). Chelsea Hse.

Thuringer Porzellan. H. Scherf. 476p. (Ger.). 1980. 225.00x (ISBN 0-317-57368-3, Pub. by Collets UK). State Mutual Bk.

Thuringisch-Sachsische Kanzleisprache Bis 1325, Miteiner Neven Einleitung Von Richard K. Seymour, 2 Vols. Heinrich Bach. 40.00 (ISBN 0-384-02945-0). Johnson Repr.

Thurlow Weed. Glyndon G. Van Deusen. LC 73-87698. (American Scene Ser.). 1969. Repr. of 1947 ed. lib. bdg. 42.50 (ISBN 0-306-71693-3). Da Capo.

Thurn und Taxis: Seven Symphonies. Joseph Riepel et al. Ed. by Hugo Angerer et al. LC 84-759898. (Symphony, 1720-1840 Ser.). 1985. lib. bdg. 90.00 (ISBN 0-8240-3855-X). Garland Pub.

Thursday & the Lady. Patricia Mathews. 408p. pap. 4.50 (ISBN 0-373-97047-1, Pub by Worldwide). Harlequin Bks.

Thursday at Noon. William F. Brown. 288p. 1987. 16.95 (ISBN 0-312-00020-0, J Kahn). St Martin.

Thursday at Noon. William F. Brown. 384p. 1988. pap. 3.95 (ISBN 0-373-97080-3, Pub. by Worldwide). Harlequin Bks.

Thursday in Paris. M. Bond. 1986. 23.75 (ISBN 0-245-50647-0, Pub. by Harrap Ltd England). State Mutual Bk.

Thursday is Missing. Richard Passmore. 161p. 1984. 29.00x (ISBN 0-9506012-7-6, Pub. by T Harmsworth Pub). State Mutual Bk.

Thursday Poets: An Anthology by Members of Palo Alto Adult School. Ed. by McDonald et al. 77p. 1986. pap. 10.00 (ISBN 0-933829-09-4). Ponce Pr.

TI-Fifty-Nine Drilling Engineering Manual. Martin E. Chenevert & Reuven Hollo. LC 81-1110. 249p. 1981. 69.95 (ISBN 0-87814-161-8, P-4253). Pennwell Bks.

TI-Fifty-Nine Reservoir Engineering Manual. Reuven Hollo & Haresh Fifadara. LC 80-16295. 220p. 1980. 69.95x (ISBN 0-87814-134-0, P-4242). Pennwell Bks.

Ti Ho Sposato per Allegria. Natalia Ginzburg. (Easy Readers, Ser. A). 48p. (Ital.). 1976. pap. text ed. 3.95 (ISBN 0-88436-228-0, 55252). EMC.

Ti-keys & Mon-gers! Joyce M. Burkes. (Funny Flippin's Ser.: Bk. 2). (Illus.). 8p. (ps-6). 1987. book & cassette 4.95 (ISBN 0-931218-51-9, 4602). Joybug.

TI LOGO. Hal Abelson. (Illus.). 1984. pap. text ed. 17.95 (ISBN 0-07-038459-2, BYTE Bks). McGraw.

Ti Nv Eivai Bei Aristoteles. Curt Arpe. Bd. with Logische Regeln der Platonischen Schule in der Aristotelischen Topik. Ernst Hambruch. LC 75-13254. (History of Ideas in Ancient Greece Ser.). (Ger.). 1976. Repr. of 1974 ed. 10.00x (ISBN 0-405-07292-9). Ayer Co Pubs.

TI-59 & HP-41CV Instrument Engineering Programs. Stanley W. Thrift. LC 82-20920. 366p. 1983. 59.00x (ISBN 0-87201-387-1); 200p. Bar Code Supplement pap. (Orig.) 75.00x (ISBN 0-87201-389-8). Gulf Pub.

TI-59 Manual for Estimating Centrifugal Compressor Performance. Ronald P. Lapina. LC 83-3124. (Process Compressor Technology Ser.: Vol. 2). 334p. 1983. 59.00x (ISBN 0-87201-100-3). Gulf Pub.

TI-99: Quick Reference Guide. Gilbert Held. 80p. 1984. pap. 29.50 (ISBN 0-471-88249-6). Wiley.

TI 99-4A, Vol. 1. Tammy Buxton. (Thinking-Learning-Creating: TLC for Growing Minds Ser.). 54p. (gr. 4-12). 1983. pap. text ed. 11.95 (ISBN 0-88193-051-2). Create Learn.

TI 99-4A, Vol. 2. Tammy Buxton. (Thinking-Learning-Creating: TLC for Growing Minds Ser.). 53p. (gr. 4-12). 1983. pap. text ed. 11.95 (ISBN 0-88193-052-0). Create Learn.

TI 99-4A, Vol. 3. Marilyn Buxton & Tammy Buxton. (Thinking-Learning-Creating: TLC for Growing Minds Ser.). 65p. (gr. 5-12). 1983. pap. text ed. 11.95 (ISBN 0-88193-053-9). Create Learn.

TI 99-4A, Vol. 4. Marilyn Buxton & Tammy Buxton. (Thinking-Learning-Creating: TLC for Growing Minds Ser.). 45p. (gr. 5-12). 1983. pap. text ed. 11.95 (ISBN 0-88193-054-7). Create Learn.

TI 99-4A in Bits & Bytes. Remo A. Loreto. Ed. by Robert Wartman. (Illus., Orig.). 1983. pap. 14.99 (ISBN 0-914209-01-9). R A Loreto.

TI 99-4A Users Handbook. Weber Systems, Inc. Staff. LC 83-60591. (WSI's How to Use Your Personal Computer). 350p. 1984. pap. 14.95 (ISBN 0-938862-49-9). Weber Systems.

Tian Wen: A Chinese Book of Origins. Tr. by Stephen Field from Chinese. LC 86-12737. 128p. (Orig.). 1986. 22.95 (ISBN 0-8112-1010-3); pap. 8.95 (ISBN 0-8112-1011-1, NDP624). New Directions.

Tianitolka: Povesti. Vladimir Maramzin. 200p. (Rus.). 1981. 22.00 (ISBN 0-88233-510-3); pap. 7.50 (ISBN 0-88233-511-1). Ardis Pubs.

Tianjian Shi Yishu Bowuguan Cang Yan. Tianjin Municipal Art Museum Staff. 8p. 1979. 315.00x (ISBN 0-317-69429-4, Pub. by Han-Shan Tang Ltd). State Mutual Bk.

Tiazhelye Zvezdy. Ivan Elagin. LC 86-32761. 364p. (Rus.). 1987. text ed. 21.95 (ISBN 0-938920-86-3); pap. 12.00 (ISBN 0-938920-87-1). Hermitage.

Tibbetts Family. G. T. Ridlon. LC 71-142773. (Saco Valley Settlements Ser). 1970. pap. 2.75 (ISBN 0-8048-0843-0). C E Tuttle.

Tiber: The Roman River. Nora Nowlan. LC 67-14318. (Rivers of the World Ser.). (Illus.). 96p. (gr. 4-7). 1967. PLB 3.98 (ISBN 0-8116-6370-1). Garrard.

Tiberius & Pontius Pilate in Ethiopian Tradition & Poetry. E. Cerulli. 1965. pap. 5.50 (ISBN 0-85672-646-X, Pub. by British Acad). Longwood Pub Group.

Tiberius & the Roman Empire. Charles E. Smith. LC 42-23574. pap. 71.50 (ISBN 0-317-28662-5, 2055315). Bks Demand UMI.

Tiberius Caesar & the Roman Constitution. Olive Kuntz. 1974. lib. bdg. 75.00 (ISBN 0-87968-391-0). Gordon Pr.

Tiberius the Politician. Barbara Levick. (Classical Lives Ser.). (Illus.). 256p. 1987. pap. 14.95 (ISBN 0-7099-4132-3, Pub. by Croom Helm UK). Routledge Chapman & Hall.

Tibet. David Bonavia. LC 82-6914. (Illus.). 128p. 1982. 50.00 (ISBN 0-86565-021-7). Vendome.

Tibet. Elizabeth Booz. (Illus.). 208p. 1987. pap. 9.95 (ISBN 0-8442-9812-3, Passport Bks). Natl Textbk.

Tibet. Kevin Kling. LC 84-52067. (Illus.). 100p. 1985. 35.00 (ISBN 0-500-54105-1). Thames Hudson.

Tibet. Kevin Kling. (Illus.). 1989. pap. 16.95 (ISBN 0-500-27516-5). Thames Hudson.

Tibet. Ngapo. (Illus.). 296p. 1981. 210.00x (Pub. by Han-Shan Tang Ltd). State Mutual Bk.

Tibet: A Dreamt of Image. 1986. 20.00 (ISBN 0-471-63986-9). Wiley.

Tibet: A Political History. 3rd ed. Tsepan W. Shakabpa. 369p. 1984. pap. write for info. (ISBN 0-9611474-1-5). Potala.

Tibet-A Travel Survival Kit. Micael Buckley & Robert Strauss. (Illus.). 256p. (Orig.). 1986. pap. 7.95 (ISBN 0-908086-88-1). Lonely Planet.

Tibet & Its History. 2nd, rev. ed. Hugh E. Richardson. LC 84-5469. (Illus.). 327p. (Orig.). 1984. 19.95 (ISBN 0-87773-292-2, 54072-7). Shambhala Pubns.

Tibet & Its History. 2nd, rev. & updated ed. Hugh E. Richardson. LC 86-11836. (Illus.). 344p. 1986. pap. 10.95 (ISBN 0-87773-376-7). Shambhala Pubns.

Tibet & Its History. 2nd, rev. ed. Hugh E. Richardson. 134p. 1984. 63.00x (Pub. by Han-Shan Tang Ltd). State Mutual Bk.

Tibet & the Tibetans. Tsung-Lien Shen & Shen-Chi Liu. LC 73-7735. 200p. 1973. Repr. of 1953 ed. lib. bdg. 18.50x (ISBN 0-374-97310-5, Octagon). Hippocrene Bks.

Tibet Guide. Stephen Batchelor. (Wisdom Tibet Books - Yellow Ser.). (Illus.). 480p. (Orig.). 1987. pap. 26.95 (ISBN 0-86171-046-0). Wisdom MA.

Tibet House Museum-Catalogue Inaugural Exhibition. Tibet House Museum Staff. 88p. 1965. 80.00x (ISBN 0-317-68559-7, Pub. by Han-Shan Tang Ltd). State Mutual Bk.

Tibet in Pictures: A Journey into the Past, 2 vols. Li Gotami Govinda. LC 79-21352. 1980. Vol. I. 55.00 (ISBN 0-913546-57-7); Vol. II. 65.00 (ISBN 0-913546-58-5). Dharma Pub.

Tibet Is My Country: Autobiography of Thubten Jigme Norbu, Brother of the Dalai Lama. Thubten J. Norbu. As told to Heinrich Harrer. Tr. by Edward Fitzgerald from Ger. (Wisdom Tibet Books - Yellow Ser.). 276p. 1986. pap. 16.95 (ISBN 0-86171-045-2). Wisdom MA.

Tibet: Past & Present. Charles A Bell. lib. bdg. 79.95 (ISBN 0-87968-483-6). Krishna Pr.

Tibet Phrasebook. Melvyn Goldstein. 112p. (Orig.). 1987. pap. 2.95 (ISBN 0-86442-012-9). Lonely Planet.

Tibet: The Lost Civilization. Simon Normanton. (Illus.). 160p. 1987. 105.00x (Pub. by Han-Shan Tang Ltd). State Mutual Bk.

Tibet, the Mysterious. Thomas Holdich. (Illus.). 356p. 1983. text ed. 60.00x (ISBN 0-86590-148-1). Apt Bks.

Tibetan see Mother of Knowledge: The Enlightenment of Ye-shes Mtsho-Rgyal.

Tibetan & Buddhist Studies Commemorating the Two Hundreth Anniversary of the Birth of Alexander Csoma de Koros, 2 vols. Ed. by L. Ligeti. (Bibliotheca Orientalis Hungarica: No. 29). 827p. 1984. Set. text ed. 115.00x (ISBN 963-05-3573-4, Pub. by Akademiai Kiado Hungary). Vol. 1 (ISBN 963-05-3902-0). Vol. 2 (ISBN 963-05-3903-9). Humanities.

Tibetan & Buddhist Studies Commemorating the 200th Anniversary of the Birth of Alex-ander Csoma de Koros, 2 vols. Louis Ligeti. 388p. 1984. 350.00x (ISBN 0-569-08826-7, Pub. by Collets (UK)). State Mutual Bk.

Tibetan & Himalayan Woodblock Prints. Douglas Weiner. (Illus., Orig.). 1974. pap. 7.95 (ISBN 0-486-22988-2). Dover.

Tibetan Art & Handicrafts. Tibet House Society Staff. 53p. 1969. 90.00x (ISBN 0-317-68563-5, Pub. by Han-Shan Tang Ltd). State Mutual Bk.

Tibetan Book of the Dead. 3rd ed. Ed. by W. Y. Evans-Wentz. 1957. 24.95x (ISBN 0-19-501435-9). Oxford U Pr.

Tibetan Book of the Dead. Ed. by W. Y. Evans-Wentz. (Illus.). 1960. pap. 7.95 (ISBN 0-19-500223-7). Oxford U Pr.

Tibetan Book of the Dead. 1972. 5.95 (ISBN 0-88088-524-6). Peter Pauper.

Tibetan Book of the Dead: The Great Liberation Through Hearing in the Bardo. Tr. by Francesca Fremantle & Chogyam Trungpa. LC 74-29615. (Shambala Dragon Editions Ser.). (Illus.). 120p. 1988. pap. 9.95 (ISBN 0-87773-074-1). Shambhala Pubns.

Tibetan Book of the Great Liberation. Ed. by W. Y. Evans-Wentz. 1954. 24.95x (ISBN 0-19-501437-5). Oxford U Pr.

Tibetan Book of the Great Liberation. Ed. by W. Y. Evans-Wentz. (Illus.). 1968. pap. 9.95 (ISBN 0-19-500293-8). Oxford U Pr.

Tibetan Buddhism in Western Perspective. Herbert V. Guenther. LC 76-47758. (Illus.). 1977. pap. 12.95. Dharma Pub.

Tibetan Buddhism with Its Mystic Cults Symbolism & Mythology, & in Its Relation to Indian Buddhism. Austine Waddell. (Illus.). 598p. 1972. pap. 11.95 (ISBN 0-486-20130-9). Dover.

Tibetan Buddhist Medicine & Psychiatry: The Diamond Healing. Terry Clifford. LC 82-61872. 288p. 1984. 15.95 (ISBN 0-87728-528-4). Weiser.

Tibetan Carpet. Philip Denwood. 101p. 1977. Repr. of 1974 ed. text ed. 55.00x (ISBN 0-85668-022-2, Pub. by Aris & Phillips UK). Humanities.

Tibetan Civilization. rev. ed. R. A. Stein. Tr. by J. E. Driver. (Illus.). 1972. 32.50x (ISBN 0-8047-0806-1); pap. 9.95 (ISBN 0-8047-0901-7, SP139). Stanford U Pr.

Tibetan Dhammapada: Sayings of the Buddha - A Translation of the Tibetan Version of the Udanavarga. rev. ed. Ed. by Dharmatrata & Beth L. Simon. Tr. by Gareth Sparham et al from Tibetan. (Wisdom Basic Book - Orange Ser.). 235p. (Orig.). 1986. pap. 14.95 (ISBN 0-86171-012-6). Wisdom MA.

Tibetan Empire in Central Asia: A History of the Struggle for Great Power among Tibetans, Turks, Arabs, & Chinese during the Early Middle Ages. Christopher I. Beckwith. (Illus.). 305p. 1988. text ed. 38.00 (ISBN 0-691-05494-0). Princeton U Pr.

Tibetan-English Dictionary, 4 vols. Alexander Csoma de Koros. Incl. Vol. 1. Essay towards a Dictionary Tibetan English. 351p. text ed. 47.50x (ISBN 963-05-3819-9); Vol. 2. A Grammar of the Tibetan Language. 244p. text ed. 35.00x (ISBN 963-05-3820-2); Vol. 3. Sanskrit Tibetan-English Vocabulary. 390p. text ed. 55.00x (ISBN 963-05-3821-0); Vol. 4. Tibetan Studies. 459p. text ed. 65.00x (ISBN 963-05-3822-9). (Collected Works of Csomo de Koros). 1984. Repr. Set. text ed. 165.00x (ISBN 963-05-3818-0, Pub. by Kultura Hungary). Humanities.

Tibetan-English Dictionary. S. C. Das. (Tibetan & Eng.). Repr. of 1970 ed. 55.00x (ISBN 0-87902-125-X). Orientalia.

Tibetan-English Dictionary. rev ed. Sarat C. Das. 1353p. 1985. Repr. of 1902 ed. text ed. 40.00x (ISBN 0-86590-722-6, Pub. by Gautau Pub Hse India). Apt Bks.

Tibetan English Dictionary. Sarat C. Das. 1983. Repr. 44.00x (ISBN 0-8364-2194-9, Pub. by Motilal Banarsidass). South Asia Bks.

Tibetan-English Dictionary. S. C. Dass. (Tibetan & Eng.). 1979. 48.00 (ISBN 0-89684-329-7). Orient Bk Dist.

Tibetan English Dictionary. H. A. Jaschke. 1987. Repr. of 1881 ed. 21.00x (ISBN 81-208-0321-3, Pub. by Motilal Banarsidass). South Asia Bks.

Tibetan-English Dictionary with Supplement. Ed. by Stuart H. Buck. LC 69-16882. (Publications in the Languages of Asia: No. 1). 833p. (Tibetan & Eng.). 1969. 36.95 (ISBN 0-8132-0269-8). Cath U Pr.

Tibetan-English, English-Tibetan Dictionary, 2 vols. 3rd, rev. & enl. ed. S. C. Das & I. D. Kazi. (Tibetan & Eng.). Set. 60.00; Tibetan-English. 30.00 (ISBN 0-89581-177-4); English-Tibetan. 30.00. Heinman.

Tibetan Fantasies. Li G. Govinda. (Illus.). (gr. 1-6). 1977. 8.95 (ISBN 0-913546-48-8). Dharma Pub.

Tibetan Folk Tales. Albert L. Shelton. LC 78-63220. (Folktale). (Illus.). 192p. Repr. of 1925 ed. 24.50 (ISBN 0-404-16157-X). AMS Pr.

Tibetan Frontiers Question: From Curzon to the Colombo Conference. Frederic A. Greenhut, II. (Illus.). 178p. 1982. 24.95x (ISBN 0-940500-71-X, Pub by S Chand India). Asia Bk Corp.

Tibetan Frontiers Question from Curzon to the Colombo Conference: An Unresolved Factor in Indo-Sinic Relations. Frederic A. Greenhutt, II. 192p. 22.50 (ISBN 0-317-52160-8, Pub. by S Chand India). State Mutual Bk.

Tibetan Inroads. Stephen Lowe. 50p. 1982. pap. 4.95 (ISBN 0-413-48710-5, NO. 3611). Heinemann Ed.

Tibetan Kung Fu. M. Staples. 1976. 5.50x (ISBN 0-685-83539-1). Wehman.

Tibetan Kung-Fu: The Way of the Monk. Michael P. Staples. LC 80-106130. (Illus.). 80p. 1976. pap. 5.95 (ISBN 0-86568-004-3, 203). Unique Pubns.

Tibetan Life & Culture. Eleanor Olson. (Illus.). 1960. pap. 2.50 (ISBN 0-89013-000-0). Museum NM Pr.

Tibetan Medicine & Other Holistic Health-Care Systems. Tom Dummer. 288p. 1988. pap. 13.95 (ISBN 0-415-01278-3). Routledge Chapman & Hall.

Tibetan Medicine: Illustrated in Original Text. Ven R. Rechung. 346p. 1976. pap. 12.95 (ISBN 0-520-03048-6). U of Cal Pr.

Tibetan on Tibet. 2nd ed. G. A. Combe. (Illus.). 212p. 1988. 19.95 (ISBN 0-943389-03-8); pap. 12.95 (ISBN 0-943389-02-X). Snow Lion Graphics.

Tibetan Paintings. George N. Roerich. (Illus.). 176p. 1986. 49.95. Asia Bk Corp.

Tibetan Phrasebook. Andrew Bloomfield & Yanki Tshering. 145p. (Orig.). 1987. pap. 19.95 (ISBN 0-937938-54-8). Snow Lion.

Tibetan Pilgrimage. Peter Gold. (Illus., Orig.). 1988. pap. 14.95 (ISBN 0-937938-52-1). Snow Lion.

Tibetan Queen. David A. Riems. 109p. 1982. 25.00x (ISBN 0-901976-75-X, Pub. by United Writers Pubns England). State Mutual Bk.

Tibetan Reflections. Peter Gold. (Wisdom Tibet Books, Yellow Ser.). (Illus.). 111p. (Orig.). 1984. pap. 11.95 (ISBN 0-86171-022-3). Wisdom MA.

Tibetan Refugees: Youth & the New Generation of Meaning. Margaret Nowak. LC 82-22961. 235p. 1984. text ed. 31.00 (ISBN 0-8135-0979-3). Rutgers U Pr.

Tibetan Religious Dances. Rene De Nebesky-Wojkowitz. Ed. by Christoph Von Furer-Haimendorf. (Religion & Society: No. 2). 1976. text ed. 36.00x (ISBN 90-279-7621-X). Mouton.

Tibetan-Russian-English Dictionary. Y. N. Roerich. Ed. by Y. Parionovich & V. Dylykova. 432p. 1985. 39.00x (ISBN 0-317-42710-5, Pub. by Collets (UK)). State Mutual Bk.

Tibetan-Russian-English Dictionary with Sanskrit Parallels, Vol. 5. Y. N. Roerich. 312p. (Tibetan, Rus. & Eng.). 1985. 39.00x (ISBN 0-317-59449-4, Pub. by Collets (UK)). State Mutual Bk.

Tibetan Spaniel Champions, 1984-1986. Camino E. E. & B. Co. Staff. (Illus.). 46p. 1987. pap. 18.95 (ISBN 0-940808-41-2). Camino E E & B.

Tibetan Studies. Sarat C. Das. Ed. by Alaka Chattopadhyay. 1985. 24.00x (ISBN 0-8364-1501-9, Pub. by KP Bagchi India). South Asia Bks.

Tibetan Studies: Being a Reprint of the Articles Contributed to the Journal of the Asiatic Society of Bengal. Sandor K. Csoma. Ed. by E. Denilson. LC 78-72400. Repr. of 1912 ed. 27.50 (ISBN 0-404-17259-8). AMS Pr.

Tibetan Studies in Honour of Hugh Richardson. Ed. by M. Aris & Aung San Suu. 348p. 1981. pap. text ed. 45.00x (ISBN 0-85668-190-3, Pub. by Aris & Phillips UK). Humanities.

Tibetan Symbolic World: Psychoanalytic Explorations. Robert A. Paul. LC 81-16505. (Chicago Originals Ser.). (Illus.). 360p. 1982. lib. bdg. 14.00x (ISBN 0-226-64987-3). U of Chicago Pr.

Tibetan Tales Derived from Indian Sources. William S. Ralston. LC 76-835. 1976. Repr. of 1882 ed. lib. bdg. 42.50 (ISBN 0-8414-7229-7). Folcroft.

Tibetan Temple Paintings-Tibetaansche Templeschilderingen. W. J. Van Meurs. 44p. 1953. 100.00x (ISBN 0-317-68684-4, Pub. by Han-Shan Tang Ltd). State Mutual Bk.

Tibetan Terrier Book. Jane Reif. (Illus.). 256p. (Orig.). 1984. pap. 16.95 (ISBN 0-913337-03-X). Southfarm Pr.

Tibetan Terrier Champions, 1973-1986. Camino E. E. & B. Co. Staff. (Illus.). 119p. 1988. pap. 29.95 (ISBN 0-940808-70-6). Camino E E & B.

Tibetan Thangka Painting: Methods & Materials. David Jackson & Janice Jackson. LC 84-5565. (Illus.). 186p. 1984. 32.50 (ISBN 0-87773-301-5, 54205-3). Shambhala Pubns.

Tibetan Trek. Ronald Kaulback. 300p. 1936. 72.00x (ISBN 0-317-68686-0, Pub. by Han-Shan Tang Ltd). State Mutual Bk.

Tibetan Venture. Andre Guibaut. 239p. 1988. pap. 7.95 (ISBN 0-19-584214-6). Oxford U Pr.

Tibetan Village Communities: Structure & Change. Eva Dargyay. 112p. 1982. pap. text ed. 29.00x (ISBN 0-85668-151-2, Pub. by Aris & Phillips UK). Humanities.

Tibetan Yoga & Secret Doctrines. 2nd ed. Ed. by W. Y. Evans-Wentz. 1958. 24.95x (ISBN 0-19-501438-3). Oxford U Pr.

Tibetan Yoga & Secret Doctrines. Ed. by W. Y. Evans-Wentz. (Illus.). 1967. pap. 12.95 (ISBN 0-19-500278-4). Oxford U Pr.

Tibetan Yoga & Secret Doctrines: Or Seven Books of Wisdom of the Great Path. Ed. by Walter Y. Wentz. LC 78-70140. Repr. of 1935 ed. 49.50 (ISBN 0-404-17413-2). AMS Pr.

Tibetans on Tibet. Date not set. 5.95 (ISBN 0-8351-2042-2). China Bks.

Tibetian Studies. S. C. Das. Ed. by Alaska Chattopadhyaya. 1985. 49.00x (ISBN 0-317-20274-X, Pub. by K P Bagchi & Co). State Mutual Bk.

Tibetica: One - Three, Twenty, Twenty-Two - Twenty-Five, Twenty-Seven - Thirty-Seven. Georg G. Schoettle. 50p. 1979. pap. 1250.00x (Pub. by Han-Shan Tang Ltd). State Mutual Bk.

Tibetische Kunst. E. Stolle & Zimmermann. 94p. 1969. 72.00x (ISBN 0-317-68490-6, Pub. by Han-Shan Tang Ltd). State Mutual Bk.

Tibeto-Burman Tonology: A Comparative Analysis. Alfons Weidert. LC 87-5140. (Current Issues in Linguistics Theory Ser.: Vol. 5). xvii, 512p. 1987. 76.00x (ISBN 90-272-3548-1). Benjamins North Am.

Tibet's Great Yogi, Milarepa. 2nd ed. Ed. by W. Y. Evans-Wentz. (Illus.). 1969. pap. 9.95 (ISBN 0-19-500301-2). Oxford U Pr.

TIBs of Bill Caudill: CRSS. 206p. 1985. pap. 5.00 (ISBN 0-317-57031-5). Am Inst Arch.

Tibullus: A Commentary. Michael C. Putnam. (APA Ser.: Vol. 3). 222p. 1979. pap. 9.95x (ISBN 0-8061-1560-2). U of Okla Pr.

Tibullus: A Hellenistic Poet at Rome. Francis Cairns. LC 79-50231. 1980. pap. 18.95 (ISBN 0-521-29683-8). Cambridge U Pr.

Tibullus: Elegies: Introduction, Text, Translation & Notes. Guy Lee. (Liverpool Latin Texts (Classical & Medieval): No. 3). 157p. (Orig.). 1975. pap. text ed. 8.25 (ISBN 0-905205-09-X, Pub. by F Cairns). Longwood Pub Group.

Tibyan: Memoirs of Abd Allah b. Buluggin, Last Zirid Amir of Granada. Translated from the Emended Arabic Text & Provided with Introduction, Notes & Comments. Amin T. Tibi. (Medieval Iberian Peninsula Ser.: Vol. 5). xiii, 291p. 1986. 41.00 (ISBN 90-04-07669-7, Pub. by E J Brill). Heinman.

Tic Tac Toe. Claudia Zaslavsky. LC 82-45186. (Illus.). 96p. (gr. 4-7). 1982. 11.70 (ISBN 0-690-04316-3, Crowell Jr Bks); PLB 11.89 (ISBN 0-690-04317-1). HarpJ.

TICCIT. M. David Merrill et al. Ed. by Danny G. Langdon. LC 79-24448. (Instructional Design Library). 144p. 1980. 23.95 (ISBN 0-87778-160-5). Educ Tech Pubns.

Tichborne Case. Frederick H. Maugham. LC 74-10430. (Classics of Crime & Criminology Ser). (Illus.). 384p. 1975. Repr. of 1936 ed. 19.80 (ISBN 0-88355-197-7). Hyperion Conn.

Ticino Guide. Gerardo Brown-Manruque. (Illus.). 190p. (Orig.). 1988. pap. 17.00 (ISBN 0-910413-46-0). Princeton Arch.

Tick-Born Encephalitis & Haemorrhagic Fever with Renal Syndrome in Europe. (EURO Reports & Studies). 79p. 1986. pap. 4.80 (ISBN 92-890-1270-6). World Health.

Tied up in Tinsel. Ngaio Marsh. 1976. Repr. of 1972 ed. lib. bdg. 18.95x (ISBN 0-88411-496-1, Pub. by Aeonian Pr). Amereon Ltd.

Tied up in Tinsel. Ngaio Marsh. 288p. 1987. pap. 3.50 (ISBN 0-515-07443-8). Jove Pubns.

Tied up in Tinsel. Ngaio Marsh. 1986. 13.95 (ISBN 0-317-53158-1, Large Print Bks). G K Hall.

Tiefkuhl Lexikon. G. Doring & Rudolphi. 239p. (Ger.). 19.95 (ISBN 3-87150-020-8, M-7666, Pub. by Deutscher Fachverlag). French & Eur.

Tieh Ta Ke: Traditional Chinese Traumatology & First Aid. Rev. ed. Robert S. Flaws. (Illus.). 1985. pap. 13.95 (ISBN 0-936185-02-3). Blue Poppy.

Tiempo al Tiempo. Issac Goldemberg. 172p. (Span.). 1983. pap. 8.50 (ISBN 0-910061-18-1, 1111). Ediciones Norte.

Tiempo Artesano. Mireya Robles. 85p. (Span.). 1973. pap. 7.00 (ISBN 0-317-46767-0, 3402). Ediciones Norte.

Tiempo Congelado: Poemario De una Isla Ausente. Jose Sanchez-Boudy. LC 79-50631. (Coleccion Espejo De Paciecia Ser.). (Illus.). 131p. (Span.). 1979. pap. 6.00 (ISBN 0-89729-224-3). Ediciones.

Tiempo En Perspectiva. Georges Delacre. pap. 5.00 (ISBN 0-8477-0505-6). U of PR Pr.

Tiempo es el Diablo. Ricardo Bofill. (Biblioteca Cubana Contemporanea Ser.). 106p. (Orig., Span.). 1985. pap. 6.00 (ISBN 0-317-28601-3). Ediciones.

Tiempo Pasada De La Palabra De Dios. Kenneth Hagin, Jr. (Span.). 1983. pap. 0.50 mini bk. (ISBN 0-89276-176-8). Hagin Ministries.

Tiempo y Yo: Articulos Ensayos, Cronicas. Antonio Martinez Alvarez. (UPREX, Ensayo: No. 5). pap. 1.85 (ISBN 0-8477-0005-4). U of PR Pr.

Tiepolo: A Bicentenary Exhibition, 1770-1970 see Exhibition Catalogues from the Fogg Art Museum.

Tiepolo Drawings. George Knox. (Illus.). 316p. (Orig.). pap. 15.95 (ISBN 0-901486-63-9, Pub. by Victoria & Albert Mus UK). Faber & Faber.

Tiepolo Drawings: Forty-Four Plates. Giovanni B. Tiepolo. (Art Library). 48p. (Orig.). 1987. pap. 3.50 (ISBN 0-486-25366-X). Dover.

Tiere der Urwelt see From Dinosaurs to Fossils.

Tiergeographicshe Undokologische Beitrag Zur Okologischen Landschaftsforschung. Jurgen H. Jungbluth. (Biogeographica: No. 13). 1978. lib. bdg. 55.00 (ISBN 90-6193-214-9, Pub. by Junk Pubs Netherlands). Kluwer Academic.

Tierlexikon, 5 vols. H. Smolik. (Ger.). 1968. pap. 75.00 (ISBN 3-499-16059-5, M-7667, Pub. by Rowohlt). French & Eur.

Tierra. J. M. Parramon et al. (Four Elements Ser.). 32p. (Span.). (ps). 1985. pap. 3.95 (ISBN 0-8120-3618-2). Barron.

Tierra Amarilla Grant: A History of Chicanery. Malcolm Ebright. LC 80-69638. (Illus.). 80p. (Orig.). 1980. pap. 6.50 (ISBN 0-9605202-0-1). Ctr Land Grant.

Tierra Amarilla: Stories of New Mexico, Cuentos De Nuevo Mexico. Sabine R. Ulibarri. Tr. by Thelma C. Nason. LC 75-153942. (Illus.). 181p. (Eng. & Span.). 1971. pap. 8.95 (ISBN 0-8263-0212-2). U of NM Pr.

Tierra & Libertad! Photographs of Mexico, 1900-1935. Ed. & pref. by David Elliott. (Illus.). 104p. (Orig.). 1986. pap. 14.95 (ISBN 0-87663-891-4). Universe.

Tierra de Extranos. Jose A. Albertini. LC 82-8440. (Coleccion Caniqui Ser.). 160p. (Orig., Span.). 1983. pap. 9.95 (ISBN 0-89729-327-4). Ediciones.

Tierra Dulce: The Jesse Nusbaum Papers. Rosemary Nusbaum. LC 80-18365. (Illus.). 128p. 1980. pap. 7.95 (ISBN 0-913270-83-0). Sunstone Pr.

Tierra Metalizada (Poemas) Alberto Muller. LC 85-82279. 62p. (Orig., Span.). 1986. pap. 6.95 (ISBN 0-89729-385-1). Ediciones.

Tierra Purpurea: Alla Lejos y Hace Tiempo. Guillermo E. Hudson. (Ayacucho Library Collection Ser.: Vol. 63). (Span.). 1980. 40.00 (ISBN 0-317-56537-0, Pub. by Biblioteca Ayacucho); pap. 19.95 (ISBN 0-317-56538-9, Pub. by Biblioteca Ayacucho). Humanities.

Tierras Flacas see Lean Lands.

Tiers Livre. Francois Rabelais. Ed. by Pierre Michel. (Folio 462). 1973. 4.95 (ISBN 0-686-54704-7). French & Eur.

Tiers Livre. Francois Rabelais. Ed. by A. M. Screech. 474p. 1964. 22.50 (ISBN 0-686-54707-1). French & Eur.

Tiers Livre des Faits et Dicts Heroiques du Bon Pantagruel: Avec: Le Quart Livre et le Cinquieme Livre, 2 vols, Vol. 3. Francois Rabelais. (Illus.). 1974. 150.00 (ISBN 0-686-54705-5). French & Eur.

Tiers Monde et Commerce des Pays de L'Est. (Economies et Societes Series G: No. 13). 1962. pap. 34.00 (ISBN 0-8115-0704-1). Kraus Repr.

Tiers Monde Sovietique? Le Kazakhstan. C. Beaucourt et al. (Economies et Societes Ser. G: No. 17). 1963. pap. 34.00 (ISBN 0-8115-0708-4). Kraus Repr.

Tiers of Survival: Selected Poems. Jean Orizet. Tr. by Aletha DeWees from Fr. Orig. Title: Niveaux de Survie. 120p. (Orig.). 1984. pap. 8.00 (ISBN 0-939378-03-5). Mundus Artium.

Ties: A Play in Two Acts. Jeffrey Sweet. pap. 3.50x (ISBN 0-686-92578-5). Dramatists Play.

Ties & Tensions: The 1986 Survey of American Jewish Attitudes Toward Israel & Israelis. Steven M. Cohen. LC 87-70839. 114p. (Orig.). 1987. pap. 7.50 (ISBN 0-87495-088-0). Am Jewish Comm.

Ties of Blood. Graham Reid. 288p. 1986. pap. 11.95 (ISBN 0-571-13877-2). Faber & Faber.

Ties of Blood & Silver. Joel Rosenberg. 192p. 1984. pap. 2.75 (ISBN 0-451-14621-2, Sig). NAL.

Ties That Bind. Bonnie J. Jones. (Illus.). 153p. 1988. 24.95 (ISBN 0-9619804-0-0). B J Jones.

Ties That Bind. Jean Sutherland. 480p. (Orig.). 1986. pap. 3.95 (ISBN 0-345-32351-3). Ballantine.

Ties That Bind: African American Consciousness of Africa. Bernard Magubane. LC 86-70980. 250p. 1987. 32.00 (ISBN 0-86543-036-5); pap. 9.95 (ISBN 0-86543-037-3). Africa World.

Ties That Bind: Debts, Deficits, Demographics: Edited Conference Proceedings. 140p. (Orig.). 1988. pap. 35.00x (ISBN 0-945029-01-2). Amers Generational Equity.

Ties That Bind: Folk Art in Contemporary American Culture. Eugene Metcalf & Michael Hall. Ed. by Carolyn Krause. (Illus.). 84p. 1986. pap. 12.95 (ISBN 0-917562-45-3). Contemp Arts.

Ties That Bind: Intelligence Co-operation Between the UKUSA Countries. Jeffrey T. Richelson & Desmond Ball. (Illus.). 420p. 1986. text ed. 34.95x (ISBN 0-04-327092-1). Unwin Hyman.

Ties That Bind: Law, Marriage & the Reproduction of Patriarchal Relations. Carol Smart. 256p. (Orig.). 1984. pap. 10.95x (ISBN 0-7100-9832-4). Routledge Chapman & Hall.

Ties That Bind: Men's & Women's Social Networks. Ed. by Laura Lein & Marvin B. Sussman. LC 82-23230. (Marriage & Family Review Ser.: Vol. 5, No. 4). 111p. 1983. text ed. 28.95 (ISBN 0-86656-161-7, B161); pap. text ed. 12.95 (ISBN 0-86656-223-0). Haworth Pr.

Ties That Bind: Moorings of a Life with God. Marvin Hein. LC 80-81705. 135p. (Orig.). 1980. pap. 5.95 (ISBN 0-937364-04-5). Kindred Pr.

Ties that Bind: The Interdependence of Generations. Eric R. Kingson & Barbara A. Hirshorn. 176p. 1986. pap. 9.95. Gerontological Soc.

Ties That Bind: The Interdependence of Generations. Eric R. Kingson et al. (Illus.). 176p. (Orig.). 1986. pap. 9.95 (ISBN 0-932020-44-5). Seven Locks Pr.

Ties That Bound: Peasant Families in Medieval England. Barbara A. Hanawalt. LC 85-3112. 384p. 1986. 29.95 (ISBN 0-19-503649-2). Oxford U Pr.

Ties That Bound: Peasant Families in Medieval England. Barbara A. Hanawalt. (Illus.). 368p. 1988. pap. 8.95 (ISBN 0-19-504564-5). Oxford U Pr.

Tieta. Jorge Amado. 688p. 1980. pap. 4.95 (ISBN 0-380-50815-X, 50815-X, Bard). Avon.

Tifaifai & Quilts of Polynesia. Joyce D. Hammond. LC 86-6897. (Illus.). 114p. 1986. pap. text ed. 16.95x (ISBN 0-8248-0975-0). UH Pr.

Tiffany. Joyce Ellis. 160p. (Orig.). (gr. 9-12). 1986. pap. 3.50 (ISBN 0-87123-893-4). Bethany Hse.

Tiffany Chin: A Dream on Ice. Ray Buck. LC 86-9577. (Sports Stars Ser.). (Illus.). 48p. (gr. 2-8). 1986. PLB 11.27 (ISBN 0-516-04361-7); pap. 2.95 (ISBN 0-516-44361-5). Childrens.

Tiffany Silver. Charles H. Carpenter, Jr. 1986. 20.00 (ISBN 0-8446-6127-9). Peter Smith.

Tiffany Silver. Charles H. Carpenter, Jr. & Mary G. Carpenter. (Illus.). 296p. 1984. pap. text ed. 13.95 (ISBN 0-396-08338-2). Dodd.

Tiffany Taste. John Loring. LC 85-29211. (Illus.). 224p. 1986. pap. 50.00 (ISBN 0-385-23584-4). Doubleday.

Tiffany Wedding. John Loring. (Illus.). 1988. pap. 50.00 (ISBN 0-385-24101-1). Doubleday.

Tiffany's: One Hundred & Fifty Years. John Loring. LC 87-3319. (Illus.). 192p. 1987. 50.00 (ISBN 0-385-24252-2). Doubleday.

Tiffky Doofky. William Steig. LC 78-19657. (Michel Di Capua Bks). (Illus.). 32p. (ps-3). 1978. 10.95 (ISBN 0-374-37542-9); sunburst 3.95. FS&G.

Tiffky Doofky. William Steig. (Michael Di Capua Bks.). (Illus.). (ps up). 1987. pap. 3.95 (ISBN 0-374-47748-5, Sunburst). FS&G.

TIG & Plasma Welding: TPW. 52p. 1979. 17.00 (ISBN 0-317-37078-2). Am Welding.

Tig Welding. Richard Hunter. (Series 905). (Orig.). 1983. pap. 6.00 wkbk. (ISBN 0-8064-0377-2, 905); audio visual pkg. 399.00 (ISBN 0-317-45939-2). Bergwall.

Tiger. Witter Bynner. LC 77-70352. (One-Act Plays in Reprint Ser.). 1977. Repr. of 1913 ed. 13.50x (ISBN 0-8486-2013-5). Roth Pub Inc.

Tiger. Lisa S. De Teran. pap. 3.95 (ISBN 0-345-33680-1). Ballantine.

Tiger. Mary Hoffman. LC 84-15120. (Animals in the Wild Ser.). (Illus.). 24p. (gr. k-3). 1984. PLB 11.33 (ISBN 0-8172-2405-X). Raintree Pubs.

Tiger. Paula Hogan. LC 79-13604. (Life Cycles Clippers Ser.). (Illus.). 32p. (gr. k-3). 1981. PLB 27.99 incl. cassette (ISBN 0-8172-1841-6); cassette 14.00. Raintree Pubs.

Tiger. Paula Z. Hogan. LC 79-13604. (Life Cycles Bks.). (Illus.). (gr. k-3). 1979. PLB 14.65 (ISBN 0-8172-1506-9). Raintree Pubs.

Tiger. Angela Royston. (Animal Life Stories Ser.). (Illus.). 24p. (Orig.). (gr. 1-5). 1988. pap. 2.95 (ISBN 0-8249-8247-9). Ideals.

Tiger. Angela Royston. Ed. by JV-Warwick Press Staff. (Animal Life Stories Ser.). (Illus.). 24p. (gr. 1-3). 1988. 10.40 (ISBN 0-531-19043-9, Warwick). Watts.

Tiger. Lisa St. Aubin de Teran. 339p. 1985. 16.95 (ISBN 0-531-09706-4). Watts.

Tiger: A Hockey Story. Tiger Williams & James Lawton. (Illus.). 172p. 1986. 15.95 (ISBN 0-88894-448-9, Pub. by Douglas & McIntyre-Grounwood). Salem Hse Pubs.

Tiger & the Persimmon. Adapted by & tr. by Mark C. Setton. (Korean Folk Tales Ser.: No. 9). (Illus.). 32p. (Eng. & Korean.). (gr. 1-8). 1986. PLB write for info. (ISBN 0-87296-008-0, Pub. by Si-sa-yong-o-sa Korea); bilingual cassette incl. Si-sa-yong-o-sa.

Tiger & the Shark: Empirical Roots of Wave-Particle Dualism. Bruce R. Wheaton. LC 82-22069. (Illus.). 352p. 1983. 44.50 (ISBN 0-521-25098-6). Cambridge U Pr.

Tiger & the Shark: Empirical Roots of Wave-Particle Dualism. Bruce R. Wheaton. (Illus.). 355p. Date not set. pap. 16.95 (ISBN 0-521-35892-2). Cambridge U Pr.

Tiger Beat Hunks. Lisa Jordan. 64p. 1985. 6.95 (ISBN 0-451-82123-8). Sharon Pubns.

Tiger Beetles of the Genus Cicindela in Arizona: Coleoptera: Cicindelidae. Judy Bertholf. (Special Publications of the Museum Ser.: No. 19). (Illus.). 44p. 1983. pap. 7.00 (ISBN 0-89672-110-8). Tex Tech Univ Pr.

Tiger Book. Ed. by Tana Warren. (Drill It Handwriting Ser.). 64p. (gr. 1-2). 1983. 2.95 (ISBN 0-88037-022-X). Am Teaching.

Tiger Butte. Jack Cummings. LC 85-20288. 178p. 1986. 14.95 (ISBN 0-8027-4055-3). Walker & Co.

Tiger by the Tail: A Marionette Play. 8.00 (ISBN 0-686-23326-3). Rochester Folk Art.

Tiger by the Tail: Parenting in a Troubled Society. Kenneth R. Greenberg. LC 73-93103. 272p. 1974. 20.95x (ISBN 0-911012-77-X). Nelson-Hall.

Tiger by the Tail: The Keynesian Legacy of Inflation. Friedrich A. Hayek. (Cato Papers Ser.: No. 6). 157p. 1979. pap. 5.00x (ISBN 0-932790-06-2). Cato Inst.

Tiger Called Thomas. Charlotte Zolotow. LC 86-20878. (Illus.). 40p. (ps-3). 1988. 11.95 (ISBN 0-688-06696-8); PLB 11.88 (ISBN 0-688-06697-6). Lothrop.

Tiger Cat. Slawomir Wolski. Tr. by Elizabeth D. Crawford. LC 87-43151. (Illus.). 32p. (gr. k-3). 1988. 12.95 (ISBN 0-8050-0741-5, North South Bks). H Holt & Co.

Tiger Claws. Frank L. Packard. Repr. lib. bdg. 19.95x (ISBN 0-88411-581-X, Pub. by Aeonian Pr). Amereon Ltd.

Tiger-Crane Form of Hung Gar Kung-Fu. Bucksam Kong. LC 83-60126. (Chinese Arts Ser.). (Illus., Orig.). 1983. pap. 7.95 (ISBN 0-89750-087-3, 424). Ohara Pubns.

Tiger Eyes. Judy Blume. LC 81-6152. 256p. (gr. 7 up). 1981. 10.95 (ISBN 0-02-711080-X). Bradbury Pr.

Tiger Eyes. Judy Blume. 224p. (YA) (gr. 7 up). 1982. 3.25 (ISBN 0-440-98469-6, LFL). Dell.

Tiger Eyes. Cynthia Parker. (Superromances Ser.). 384p. 1984. pap. 2.95 (ISBN 0-373-70100-4, Pub. by Worldwide). Harlequin Bks.

Tiger Facts. Fred T. Smith. 290p. 1986. 9.95 (ISBN 0-317-42670-2). F T Smith.

Tiger Flower. Robert Vavra. LC 69-20105. (Illus.). (gr. 4 up). 1969. 9.95 (ISBN 0-688-02841-1, Reynal). Morrow.

Tiger for Malgudi. R. K. Narayan. LC 82-40444. 176p. 1983. 14.75 (ISBN 0-670-71260-4). Viking.

Tiger for Malgudi. R. K. Narayan. 176p. 1984. pap. 5.95 (ISBN 0-14-006911-9). Penguin.

Tiger Game. William E. Knight. LC 86-6223. 1987. 15.95 (ISBN 0-934878-79-X). Dembner Bks.

Tiger in His Lair. Sally Wentworth. (Harlequin Presents Ser.: No. 997). 192p. Date not set. pap. 1.95 (ISBN 0-317-63738-X). Harlequin Bks.

Tiger in the Kitchen, & Other Strange Stories. facs. ed. Villi Sorensen. Tr. by Maureen Neiiendam. LC 74-87737. (Short Story Index Reprint Ser). 1957. 17.00 (ISBN 0-8369-3060-6). Ayer Co Pubs.

Tiger in the Lake. Edward Kurkul. LC 68-11183. (Illus.). (gr. 1-3). 1968. write for info. (ISBN 0-8313-0076-0); PLB 6.19. Lantern.

Tiger in the Smoke. Margery Allingham. 223p. Repr. of 1952 ed. lib. bdg. 16.95x (ISBN 0-89190-198-1, Pub. by River City Pr). Amereon Ltd.

Tiger Is a Scaredy Cat: A Step One Book. Joan Phillips. LC 85-19673. (Step into Reading Books). (Illus.). 32p. (ps-1). 1986. lib. bdg. 6.99 (ISBN 0-394-98056-5); pap. 2.95 (ISBN 0-394-88056-0). Random.

Tiger Is Not a Man. Rita Cally. 192p. 1987. 12.95 (ISBN 0-89962-593-2). Todd & Honeywell.

Tiger Island. 2nd ed. Jack Ritchie. 1987. 4.95 (ISBN 0-932310-09-5). U of Wis-Stevens Point.

Tiger Jack. Hanson W. Baldwin. LC 78-61481. (Illus.). 1979. 12.95 (ISBN 0-88342-059-7). Old Army.

Tiger Juice: A Book About Stress for Kids (of All Ages) Stewart Bedford. LC 81-9039. 52p. (gr. 3 up). 1981. pap. 2.95 (ISBN 0-935930-02-7). A & S Pr.

Tiger Lilies: An American Childhood. Fielding Dawson. LC 84-4170. vi, 213p. 1984. 19.95 (ISBN 0-8223-0593-3). Duke.

Tiger Lilies & Other Beastly Plants. Elizabeth Ring. LC 84-7499. (Illus.). 32p. (gr. 3 up). 1985. 9.95 (ISBN 0-8027-6540-8). Walker & Co.

Tiger Lily. Shirlee Busbee. 464p. 1985. pap. 3.95 (ISBN 0-380-89499-8). Avon.

Tiger Lily & Other Stories. Julia Schayer. LC 70-98593. (Short Story Index Reprint Ser.). 1883. 17.00 (ISBN 0-8369-3167-X). Ayer Co Pubs.

Tiger Man. Penny Jordan. 192p. 1982. pap. 1.75 (ISBN 0-373-10477-4). Harlequin Bks.

Tiger Meet. Coen Van den Heuvel & Jac Van Tuyn. (Osprey Color Library). (Illus.). 128p. (Orig.). 1986. pap. 14.95 (ISBN 0-85045-703-3, Pub. by Osprey England). Motorbooks Intl.

Tiger Moon. Fiona Sunquist & Mel Sunquist. (Illus.). xii, 188p. 1988. 24.95 (ISBN 0-226-78001-5). U of Chicago Pr.

Tiger Moth. (Super Profile AC Ser.). 8.95 (ISBN 0-85429-421-X, F421, Pub. by G T Foulis LTd). Haynes Pubns.

Tiger Moth: A Tribute. Stuart McKay. (Illus.). 160p. 1988. 18.95 (ISBN 0-517-56864-0, Orion Bks). Crown.

Tiger on a String. Kassie Overend. 1985. 18.95x (ISBN 0-901976-42-3, Pub. by United Writers Pubns England). State Mutual Bk.

Tiger: Portrait of a Predator. Valmik Thapar. LC 85-27564. (Illus.). 200p. 1986. 24.95 (ISBN 0-8160-1238-5). Facts on File.

Tiger Scroll of the Koga Ninja. Jay Sensei. (Illus.). 96p. (Orig.). 1985. pap. 10.00 (ISBN 0-87364-313-5). Paladin Pr.

Tiger Sharks! Wallace H. Little & Charles Goodman. (Illus.). 246p. 1987. pap. 17.95 (ISBN 0-916693-08-2). Castle Bks.

Tiger-Skin Rug. Gerald Rose. (Illus.). 30p. (ps-1). 1984. 8.95 (ISBN 0-571-11278-1). Faber & Faber.

Tiger: Symbol of Freedom. Nicholas Courtney. (Illus.). 128p. 1981. 25.00 (ISBN 0-7043-2245-5, Pub. by Quartet England). Charles River Bks.

Tiger, Take off Your Hat. Linda P. Silbert & Alvin J. Silbert. (Little Twirps Understanding People Bks.). (Illus.). (gr. k-4). 1978. pap. 2.98 (ISBN 0-89544-051-2). Silbert Bress.

Tiger Tales. Milt Miller. (Illus.). 155p. 1984. pap. text ed. 10.00x. Sunflower U Pr.

Tiger the Lurp Dog. Kenn Miller. 256p. 1984. pap. 3.50 (ISBN 0-345-31719-X). Ballantine.

Tiger: The Making of a Sports Car. Mike Taylor. (Illus.). 19.95 (ISBN 0-85614-052-X, F406, Pub. by G T Foulis Ltd). Haynes Pubns.

Tiger! Tiger! James Gunn. (Booklet Ser.: No. 17). 55p. (Orig.). 1984. ltd. ed., signed 5.00 (ISBN 0-936055-15-4); pap. 2.25 (ISBN 0-936055-14-6). C Drumm Bks.

Tiger War. (Executioner Ser.: No. 61). 192p. 1984. pap. 2.25 (ISBN 0-373-61061-0, Pub. by Worldwide). Harlequin Bks.

Tiger Watch. Jan Wahl. LC 82-964. (Illus.). 32p. (ps-3). 1982. 12.95 (ISBN 0-15-287674-X, HJ). HarBraceJ.

Tiger Who Lost His Stripes. Anthony Paul. LC 81-83987. (Illus.). 32p. (ps-3). 1982. 11.95 (ISBN 0-15-287681-2, HJ). HarBraceJ.

Tiger Who Wore White Gloves: Or What You Are You Are. Gwendolyn Brooks. LC 74-75589. 1974. pap. 5.00 (ISBN 0-88378-031-3). Third World.

Tigerman of Terrahpur see Hombre Tigre de Terrahpur.

Tigers. L. Martin. (Wildlife in Danger Ser.). (Illus.). 24p. (gr. k-5). Date not set. PLB 11.33 (ISBN 0-86592-995-5). Rourke Corp.

Tigers. Wildlife Education, Ltd. (Illus.). 20p. (Orig.). (gr. k-12). 1985. pap. 1.95 (ISBN 0-937934-35-6). Wildlife Educ.

Tigers & Opossums: Animal Legends. Marcos Kurtycz & Ana G. Kobeh. LC 82-17949. (Illus.). (gr. k-3). 1984. 12.45i (ISBN 0-316-50718-0). Little.

Tiger's Bedtime. Stephanie Calmenson. (Golden Super Shape Bks.). (Illus.). 24p. (ps-k). 1987. pap. write for info. (ISBN 0-307-10053-7, Pub. by Golden Bks). Western Pub.

Tiger's Bedtime. Stephanie Calmenson. (Illus.). (gr. k-9). 1988. pap. 1.29. Scholastic Inc.

Tigers Brought Pink Lemonade. Patricia Hubbell. LC 87-27799. (Illus.). 32p. (gr. 3 up). 1988. 13.95 (ISBN 0-689-31417-5, Atheneum Childrens Bks). Macmillan.

Tiger's Chance. H. V. Elkin. (Cutler Ser.: No. 6). (Orig.). 1980. pap. 1.95 (ISBN 0-505-51559-8, Pub. by Tower Bks). Leisure NY.

Tiger's Daughter. Bharati Mukherjee. 224p. 1987. pap. 6.95 (ISBN 0-14-009301-X). Penguin.

Tiger's Fang. Paul Twitchell. 1979. 8.95 (ISBN 0-914766-51-1). Illum Way Pub.

Tiger's Heart. Lewis Orde. 720p. 1987. pap. 4.50 (ISBN 0-8217-2086-4). Zebra.

Tigers in a Tea Cup: Collected Haiku. rev. ed. Jane Reichhold. (Illus.). 344p. 1988. pap. 12.95 (ISBN 0-944676-07-3). AHA Bks.

Tigers in the Wood: Stories. Rebecca Kavaler. (Illinois Short Fiction Ser.). 116p. 1986. 11.95 (ISBN 0-252-01308-5). U of Ill Pr.

Tiger's Milk: Women of Nicaragua. Adriana Angel & Fiona Macintosh. LC 87-607890. 1987. 18.95 (ISBN 0-317-62071-1). Seaver Bks.

Tiger's Milk: Women of Nicaragua. Adriana Angel & Fiona Macintosh. (Illus.). 168p. 1987. 18.95 (ISBN 0-8050-0638-9). H Holt & Co.

Tilt-up Construction. 80p. 1980. 13.00 (ISBN 0-317-32094-7, C-4). ACI.

Tilt-up Load Bearing Walls: A Design Aid. 37p. 1974. pap. 4.00 (ISBN 0-89312-120-7, EB074D). Portland Cement.

Tilted Haloes. James Weekley. (Orig.). 1987. pap. 6.25 (ISBN 0-89536-871-4, 7857). CSS of Ohio.

Tilted Planet Poems: Poetry from Austin Texas. Ed. by Robin Cravey. (Illus.). 120p. (Orig.). 1986. lib. bdg. 18.00 (ISBN 0-912973-08-0); pap. text ed. 7.00 (ISBN 0-912973-09-9). Tilted Planet.

Tilted Planet Tales. Ed. by Robin Cravey. LC 84-2536. (Illus.). 138p. (Orig.). 1984. 15.00 (ISBN 0-912973-02-1); pap. 6.00 (ISBN 0-912973-01-3). Tilted Planet.

Tilted Planet Tales Number Three: Easy Orbit Fiction from Central Texas. Ed. by Jim McEnteer. (Illus.). 212p. (Orig.). 1986. lib. bdg. 21.00 (ISBN 0-912973-06-4); pap. text ed. 8.00 (ISBN 0-912973-07-2). Tilted Planet.

Tilted Planet Tales Number Two: More Fiction from Austin, Texas. Ed. by Ben Satterfield. (Tilted Planet Tales Ser.). (Illus.). 178p. (Orig.). 1985. lib. bdg. 18.00 (ISBN 0-912973-04-8); pap. text ed. 7.00 (ISBN 0-912973-05-6). Tilted Planet.

Tilting at Windmills: An Autobiography. Charles Peters. Ed. by The Washington Monthly Staff. LC 87-35903. 1988. 18.95 (ISBN 0-201-05657-7). Addison-Wesley.

Tilting Room. Ron Butlin. 136p. 1983. 13.95 (ISBN 0-86241-050-9); pap. 5.95 (ISBN 0-86241-051-7). Dufour.

Tim. Colleen McCullough. LC 73-14318. 256p. 1974. 15.45i (ISBN 0-06-012891-7, HarpT). Har-Row.

Tim. Colleen McCullough. 255p. 1988. pap. 3.50 (ISBN 0-446-31047-6). Warner Bks.

Tim: A Story of School Life. Howard O. Sturgis. LC 78-63996. (Gay Experience). Repr. of 1891 ed. 26.50 (ISBN 0-404-61514-7). AMS Pr.

Tim & Charlotte. Edward Ardizzone. (Illus.). 48p. (ps-6). 1987. pap. 4.95 (ISBN 0-19-272118-6). Oxford U Pr.

Tim & Ginger. Edward Ardizzone. (Illus.). 48p. (ps-3). 1987. pap. 4.95 (ISBN 0-19-272113-5). Oxford U Pr.

Tim & His Lamp. Fern Stubblefield. 52p. (gr. k-6). pap. 0.40 (ISBN 0-686-29170-0); pap. 1.00 3 copies (ISBN 0-686-29171-9). Faith Pub Hse.

Tim Avery's Secret. Hilda Stahl. LC 85-70271. (Wren House Mystery Ser.). 128p. (gr. 4-6). 1986. pap. 3.95 (ISBN 0-89636-213-2). Accent Bks.

Tim Bunker Paper, or Yankee Farming. facs. ed. William Clift. LC 72-137727. (American Fiction Reprint Ser). 1868. 20.00 (ISBN 0-8369-7026-8). Ayer Co Pubs.

Tim Bur-r-r. Millard Van Dien. 160p. 1986. 10.50 (ISBN 0-89962-567-3). Todd & Honeywell.

Tim Hartnell's Giant Book of Computer Games. Tim Hartnell. 400p. 1984. pap. 9.95 (ISBN 0-345-35207-6). Ballantine.

Tim Hartnell's Second Giant Book of Computer Games. Tim Hartnell & Rohan Cook. 1984. 9.95 (ISBN 0-345-32245-2). Ballantine.

Tim in Danger. Edward Ardizzone. (Illus.). 48p. (ps-3). 1987. pap. 4.95 (ISBN 0-19-272106-2). Oxford U Pr.

Tim in Tibet. Herge. (Illus.). 62p. (Ger.). pap. 15.95 (ISBN 0-686-54323-8). French & Eur.

Tim Kelley's Fishing Guide: To Colorado & Wyoming. 17th ed. Ed. by Dick Prouty. (Illus.). 386p. 1985. pap. 9.95 (ISBN 0-912553-01-4). Hart Pubns.

Tim Kitten & the Red Cupboard. Jan Wahl. (Illus.). 32p. (ps-1). 1988. 6.95 (ISBN 0-671-64153-0, Little Simon). S&S.

Tim McCoy Remembers the West. Tim McCoy & Ronald McMoy. xxiv, 306p. 1988. 26.95x (ISBN 0-8032-3113-X); pap. 8.95 (Bison). U of Nebr Pr.

Tim O'Toole & the Little People. Gerald McDermott. (Viking Kestrel Picture Bks.). (ps-3). 1987. 11.95 (ISBN 0-670-80393-6, Viking Kestrel). Viking.

Tim the Mouse. David Lloyd. (Great Escapes Ser.). (Illus.). 32p. (gr. k-3). 1985. 3.95 (ISBN 0-590-33646-0). Scholastic Inc.

Tim, the Peacemaker. Uwe Friesel. LC 72-145822. (Illus.). 32p. (ps-3). 8.95 (ISBN 0-87592-052-7). Scroll Pr.

Tim to the Lighthouse. Edward Ardizzone. (Illus.). 48p. (gr. 1-4). 1987. pap. 4.95 (ISBN 0-19-272107-0). Oxford U Pr.

Tim und der Haifschsee. Herge. (Illus.). 62p. (Ger.). pap. 15.95 (ISBN 0-686-54326-2). French & Eur.

Tim und die Picaros. Herge. (Illus.). 62p. (Ger.). pap. 15.95 (ISBN 0-686-54327-0). French & Eur.

Timachidas: The Lindian Temple-Chronicle. C. Blinkenberg. 80p. 1980. 10.00 (ISBN 0-89005-353-7). Ares.

Timaeus. Plato. Tr. by John Warrington. 1965. 10.95x (ISBN 0-460-00493-X, Evman). Biblio Dist.

Timaeus & Critias. Plato. Tr. by H. D. Lee. (Classics Ser.). 1972. pap. 4.95 (ISBN 0-14-044261-8). Penguin.

Timaeus, Critias, Cleitophon, Menexenus, Epistolae. Plato. (Loeb Classical Library: No. 234). 13.95x (ISBN 0-674-99257-1). Harvard U Pr.

Timaeus (from Plato's Cosmology) Plato. Ed. by Oskar Piest. Tr. by Francis M. Cornford. 1959. pap. 5.99 scp (ISBN 0-672-60301-2, LLA106). Bobbs.

Timaeus of Plato. Plato. Ed. by R. D. Archer-Hind. LC 72-9281. (Philosophy of Plato & Aristotle Ser.). (Gr. & Eng.). Repr. of 1888 ed. 23.50 (ISBN 0-405-04832-7). Ayer Co Pubs.

Timaeus: Plato. Benjamin Jowett. 1959. pap. text ed. write for info (ISBN 0-02-360790-4). MacMillan.

Timaios of Locri, on the Nature of the World & the Soul. Thomas H. Tobin. (Society of Biblical Literature, Texts & Translations Ser.: No. 26). 1985. 14.95 (ISBN 0-89130-767-2, 06 02 26); pap. 9.95 (ISBN 0-89130-742-7). Scholars Pr GA.

Timarion. Intro. by Barry Baldwin. LC 84-10426. 172p. 1984. 22.50x (ISBN 0-8143-1771-5). Wayne St U Pr.

Timbal Gulch Trail. Max Brand. 224p. 2.95 (ISBN 0-446-30112-4). Warner Bks.

Timber. Robert A. Davies. (Poetry Chapbook Ser.). 1979. 4.50 (ISBN 0-932191-01-0). Mr Cogito Pr.

Timber. (Spotlight on Resources Ser.). (Illus.). (gr. 5 up). Date not set. write for info. Rourke Corp.

Timber & Men: The Weyerhaeuser Story. Ralph Hidy & Allan Nevins. LC 63-7450. pap. 160.00 (ISBN 0-317-42049-6, 2056093). Bks Demand UMI.

Timber & the Forest Service. David A. Clary. LC 86-15762. (Development of Western Resources Ser.). (Illus.). xvi, 252p. 1986. 29.95x (ISBN 0-7006-0314-X). U Pr of KS.

Timber Beast. Glenn R. Duncan. (Illus.). 117p. 1979. pap. 6.95 (ISBN 0-939116-02-2). Frontier WA.

Timber Building in Britain. R. W. Brunskill. (Illus.). 256p. 1985. 35.95 (ISBN 0-575-03379-7, Pub. by Gollancz England). David & Charles.

Timber Bulkheads. Ed. by James Graham. 96p. 1987. 25.00x (ISBN 0-87262-593-1). Am Soc Civil Eng.

Timber Colony: A Historical Geography of Early Nineteenth Century New Brunswick. Graeme Wynn. 248p. 1980. o. p. 25.00x (ISBN 0-8020-5513-3); pap. 11.95c (ISBN 0-8020-6407-8). U of Toronto Pr.

Timber Construction Manual. 3rd ed. American Institute of Timber Construction Staff. LC 85-7165. 836p. 1986. 44.95 (ISBN 0-471-82758-4, Pub. by Wiley-Interscience). Wiley.

Timber Cutting Practices. 3rd ed. Steve Conway. LC 78-53017. (Forest Industries Book). (Illus.). 192p. 1978. 30.00 (ISBN 0-87930-021-3). Miller Freeman.

Timber Demand: The Future Is Now. 208p. 1981. 18.00 (ISBN 0-935018-07-7). Forest Prod.

Timber Design & Construction Sourcebook. Karl-Heintz Goetz et al. 288p. 1988. text ed. 59.95 (ISBN 0-07-023851-0). McGraw.

Timber Design for the Civil P. E. Examination. 2nd ed. Robert L. Brungraber. (Engineering Review Manual Ser.). 202p. 1987. pap. text ed. 16.95 (ISBN 0-932276-73-3). Prof Pubns CA.

Timber Designer's Manual. 2nd ed. J. A. Baird & E. C. Ozelton. (Illus.). 656p. 1984. text ed. 75.00x (ISBN 0-246-12375-3, Pub. by Granada England). Sheridan.

Timber Designer's Manual. 2nd ed. J. A. Baird & E. C. Ozelton. 464p. 1988. 84.95x (ISBN 0-8464-1303-5). Beekman Pubs.

Timber Economy of Puritan New England. Charles F. Carroll. LC 73-7122. (Illus.). 235p. 1973. pap. 25.00x (ISBN 0-87057-142-7). U Pr of New Eng.

Timber Frame Construction: All About Post-&-Beam Building. Jack Sobon & Roger Schroeder. LC 83-48972. (Illus.). 208p. 1984. 19.95 (ISBN 0-88266-366-6, Garden Way Pub); pap. 12.95 (ISBN 0-88266-365-8). Storey Comm Inc.

Timber-Frame Home: Design-Construction-Finishing. Tedd Benson. LC 87-72009. (Illus.). 240p. 1988. 24.95 (ISBN 0-918804-81-7). Taunton.

Timber-Frame House in England. Trudy West. 8.95 (ISBN 0-8038-0245-5). Architectural.

Timber-Frame Housing in Britain. Valerie J. Nurcombe. (Architecture Ser.: A 1443). 20p. 1985. 3.00 (ISBN 0-89028-513-6). Vance Biblios.

Timber-Framed Houses of Essex. Harry Forrester. 93p. 1984. 20.00x (ISBN 0-317-43708-9, Pub. by Regency Pr). State Mutual Bk.

Timber Framing Book. Elliott Wallas. 1977. pap. 13.95 (ISBN 0-918238-01-3). Housesmith's.

Timber Harvesting. 4th ed. American Pulpwood Association Staff. 300p. 1988. 26.60 (ISBN 0-8134-2775-4); text ed. 19.95x. Inter Print Pubs.

Timber in Excavations. 2nd ed. Timber Research & Development Association Staff. 76p. 1984. 26.00 (ISBN 0-7277-0869-4, Pub. by T Telford UK). Am Soc Civil Eng.

Timber in Landscape Design & Construction. David Staines & Roger Walkington. 200p. 1988. text ed. 40.00x (ISBN 0-291-39729-8, Pub. by Technical Pr England). Gower Pub Co.

Timber in North America. George Sibley. Date not set. price not set (ISBN 0-670-71322-8). Viking.

Timber: Its Nature & Behavior. Dinwoodie. 1981. pap. 15.95 (ISBN 0-442-30446-3). Van Nos Reinhold.

Timber: Its Structure, Properties & Utilization. 6th ed. H. E. Desch. 416p. (Orig.). 1980. pap. text ed. 24.95x (ISBN 0-917304-62-4). Timber.

Timber Line. Gene Fowler. 416p. 1974. pap. 2.75 (ISBN 0-89174-007-4). Comstock Edns.

Timber Line. Gene Fowler. 1981. Repr. lib. bdg. 17.95x (ISBN 0-89966-424-5). Buccaneer Bks.

Timber: Loggers Challenge the Great Northwest Forests. Ralph W. Andrews. (Illus.). 182p. 1985. pap. 11.95 (ISBN 0-88740-036-1). Schiffer.

Timber Management: A Quantitative Approach. Jerome L. Clutter et al. LC 82-25611. 333p. 1983. write for info. (ISBN 0-471-02961-0). Wiley.

Timber! Problems, Prospects, Policies. Ed. by William A. Duerr. LC 72-1160. 260p. 1973. 14.95x (ISBN 0-8138-1700-5). Iowa St U Pr.

Timber Resources for America's Future: Forest Resource Report No. 14. U. S. Dept. of Agriculture-Forest Service. LC 72-2872. (Use & Abuse of America's Natural Resources Ser). 728p. 1972. Repr. of 1958 ed. 41.00 (ISBN 0-405-04538-7). Ayer Co Pubs.

Timber Suppliers Directory. 1985. 60.00x (ISBN 0-317-43684-8, Pub. by F I R A). State Mutual Bk.

Timber Supply: Issues & Options. 218p. 1979. 18.00; members 14.00 (ISBN 0-317-17421-5). Forest Prod.

Timber Supply, Land Allocation, & Economic Efficiency. William F. Hyde. 224p. 1980. 21.00 (ISBN 0-8018-2489-5). Resources Future.

Timber Tax Journal, Vol. 15. 418p. 1979. 25.00x (ISBN 0-914272-18-7, Pub. by FICTVT). Intl Spec Bk.

Timber Tax Journal, Vol. 16. Forest Industries Committee on Timber Valuation & Taxation. 335p. 1980. 25.00x (ISBN 0-914272-19-5, Pub. by FICTVT). Intl Spec Bk.

Timber Tax Journal, Vol. 17. 1981. 27.50x (ISBN 0-914272-20-9, FICTVT). Intl Spec Bk.

Timber Tax Journal, Vol. 18. Forest Industries Committee on Timber Valuation & Taxation. 335p. 1982. 30.00 (ISBN 0-686-43165-0, Pub. by FICTVT). Intl Spec Bk.

Timber Tax Journal, Vol. 19. Forest Industries Committee on Timber Valuation & Taxation. 450p. 1983. 35.00x (ISBN 0-914272-22-5, Pub. by FICTVT). Intl Spec Bk.

Timber Tax Journal, Vol. 20. Forest Industries Committee on Timber Valuation & Taxation. 360p. 1985. 35.00x (ISBN 0-914272-23-3). Forest Ind Comm.

Timber Trade: An Introduction to Commercial Aspects. J. H. Leigh. LC 79-42776. 115p. 1980. pap. text ed. 13.75 (ISBN 0-08-024916-7). Pergamon.

Timber Trends & Prospects in Africa. 90p. 1967. pap. 19.75 (ISBN 92-5-101735-2, F462, FAO). UNIPUB.

Timber War. J. D. Hardin. Ed. by Tom Colgan. (Raider Ser.: No. 10). 192p. (Orig.). 1988. pap. 2.75 (ISBN 0-425-10757-4). Berkley Pub.

Timberdoodle: A Guide to Woodcock. Frank Woolner. (Illus.). 192p. 1987. Repr. of 1974 ed. 18.95 (ISBN 0-941130-52-5). N Lyons Bks.

Timberhill. Samantha Harte. Ed. by Jennifer Weis. 304p. (Orig.). 1988. pap. 3.95 (ISBN 0-7701-0849-0). PaperJacks US.

Timberjack & the Chief, Bk. 1. Eleanor Epperson & John Epperson. (Illus.). 148p. (gr. 6-8). 1985. 12.95 (ISBN 0-9614114-0-6). Pillar Point Pr.

Timberland Tales. B. K. Taylor. (Illus.). 96p. (Orig.). 1988. pap. 6.95 (ISBN 0-941613-06-2). Stabur Pr.

Timberline Country: The Sierra High Route. Steve Roper. LC 82-714. (Sierra Club Totebook Ser.). (Illus.). 320p. (Orig.). 1982. pap. 9.95 (ISBN 0-87156-298-7). Sierra.

Timberline Lodge: A Love Story. Ed. by Judith A. Rose. LC 86-82136. (Illus.). 128p. 1986. 29.50 (ISBN 0-932575-24-2). Gr Arts Ctr Pub.

Timberline Lodge Cookbook: The Northwest Bounty. Leif E. Benson. 1988. 29.50 (ISBN 0-932575-86-2). GR Arts Ctr Pub.

Timberline: Mountain & Arctic Forest Frontiers. Stephen F. Arno. (Illus.). 304p. (Orig.). 1984. pap. 10.95 (ISBN 0-89886-085-7). Mountaineers.

Timberline Tailings: Tales of Colorado's Ghost Town & Mining Camps. Muriel S. Wolle. LC 76-17740. (Illus.). 337p. 1977. 16.95 (ISBN 0-8040-0739-X, Pub by Swallow). Ohio U Pr.

Timbers & Gold Lace. Patricia Werner. Ed. by Nancy Parent. 400p. (Orig.). 1987. pap. 3.95 (ISBN 0-7701-0600-5). PaperJacks US.

Timbers of the New World. Samuel J. Record & Robert W. Hess. LC 73-140611. (Use & Abuse of America's Natural Resources Ser). (Illus.). 718p. 1972. Repr. of 1943 ed. 57.50 (ISBN 0-405-02806-7). Ayer Co Pubs.

Timbertoes. John Gee. (Illus.). 32p. (gr. k-2). 1967. pap. 2.50 (ISBN 0-87534-133-0). Highlights.

Timblewit. Marian Jonson. 1971. in anthology, Timblewit & Other Plays 4.50x (ISBN 0-85343-511-1). Coach Hse.

Timblewit & Other Plays. Marian Jonson. (gr. k-12). 1973. 4.50x (ISBN 0-85343-508-1). Coach Hse.

Timbuctoo the Mysterious. Felix Dubois. Tr. by Diana White. LC 70-94475. (Illus.). Repr. of 1896 ed. 35.00x (ISBN 0-8371-2372-0, DTI&). Greenwood.

Time. Richard L. Allington. Kathleen Krull. LC 82-10170. (E. G. Beginning to Learn about... Ser.). (Illus.). 32p. (gr. 1-2). 1985. pap. 9.27 (ISBN 0-8172-2495-5). Raintree Pubs.

Time. Richard L. Allington & Kathleen Krull. (Beginning to Learn about Ser.). (Illus.). 32p. (gr. 1-2). 1982. PLB 15.33 (ISBN 0-8172-1388-0). Raintree Pubs.

Time. Christopher Carrie. (Crayola Kinder Art Bks.). (Illus.). 12p. (Orig.). (gr. 3-6). 1987. pap. 4.70 (ISBN 0-86696-207-7). Binney & Smith.

Time! Jane Edmonds & Mark Sachner. LC 85-25074. (Bright Idea Bks.). (Illus.). 48p. (gr. 2-4). 1985. PLB 10.95 (ISBN 0-918831-91-1). Stevens Inc.

Time. Terry Jennings. Ed. by FS-Aladdin Staff. (Junior Science Ser.). (Illus.). 28p. (gr. 1-3). 1988. 9.90 (ISBN 0-531-17112-4, Gloucester Pr). Watts.

Time. Werner Kirst & Ulrich Diekmeyer. (Illus.). 1977. 7.95x (ISBN 0-8464-0928-3). Beekman Pubs.

Time. Al Lee. (American Poetry Ser: Vol. 3). 1975. pap. 2.95 (ISBN 0-912946-13-X). Ecco Pr.

Time. Noon. 1985. pap. 15.95 (ISBN 0-442-30642-3). Van Nos Reinhold.

Time. Jan Pienkowski. Ed. by Kate Klimo. (Pienkowski Concept Bks.). (Illus.). 32p. (ps-k). 1983. 3.95 (ISBN 0-671-46247-4, Little Simon). S&S.

Time. Henry Pluckrose. Ed. by Franklin Watts Ltd. (Knowabouts Ser.). (Illus.). 32p. (ps-6). 1988. 9.90 (ISBN 0-531-10452-4). Watts.

Time. Feenie Ziner & Elizabeth Thompson. LC 81-18080. (New True Bks.). (Illus.). 48p. (gr. k-4). 1982. PLB 12.60 (ISBN 0-516-01651-2); pap. 3.95 (ISBN 0-516-41651-0). Childrens.

Time- & Strata- Bound Ore Deposits. Ed. by D. D. Klemm & H. J. Schneider. (Illus.). 1979. 59.00 (ISBN 0-387-08502-5). Springer-Verlag.

Time a Cloud Came into the Cabin (A Mountain Tale for Boys) Jacquelyn Smyers. LC 86-50627. (Illus.). 12p. (Orig.). (ps-6). 1986. pap. 3.98 (ISBN 0-9615130-3-9). Very Idea.

Time a Cloud Came into the Cabin (A Mountain Tale for Girls) Jacquelyn Smyers. LC 86-50626. (Illus.). 12p. (Orig.). (ps-6). 1986. pap. 3.98 (ISBN 0-9615130-4-7). Very Idea.

Time: A Critical Analysis for Children. Warren Shibles. LC 77-93811. (Teaching Young People to Be Critical Ser.). (gr. 4-12). 1978. pap. 6.50 (ISBN 0-912386-17-7). Language Pr.

Time: A Philosophical Analysis. T. Chapman. 1982. 29.50 (ISBN 90-277-1465-7, Pub. by Reidel Holland). Kluwer Academic.

Time: A Philosophical Treatment. Keith Seddon. 176p. 1987. lib. bdg. 47.50x (ISBN 0-7099-5424-7, Pub. by Croom Helm UK). Routledge Chapman & Hall.

Time: A Series of the Effect of Internal Audit Activities on External Audit Fees. Wanda A. Wallace. (Illus.). 295p. 1984. pap. text ed. 33.00 (ISBN 0-89413-124-9). Inst Inter Aud.

Time after This. George Gibson. 1985. 18.95x (ISBN 0-901976-32-6, Pub. by United Writers Pubns England). State Mutual Bk.

Time after Time. Allen Appel. 420p. (Orig.). 1985. 17.95 (ISBN 0-88184-182-X). Carroll & Graf.

Time after Time. Allen Appel. 1987. pap. 6.95 (ISBN 0-440-59116-3, LE). Dell.

Time after Time. Billie Green. (Silhouette Edition Ser.). pap. 2.75 (ISBN 0-373-09415-9). Harlequin Bks.

Time after Time. Molly Keane. 256p. 1985. pap. 8.95 (ISBN 0-525-48159-1, Obelisk). Dutton.

Time: An Essay. Norbert Elias. 192p. Date not set. text ed. 40.00 (ISBN 0-631-15798-0). Basil Blackwell.

Time & a Time. Rosemary Manning. 160p. 1981. pap. 7.95 (ISBN 0-7145-2746-7, Dist by Scribner). M Boyars Pubs.

Time & a Time. Rosemary Manning. 160p. 1986. (Dist. by Kampmann & Co); pap. 9.95 (ISBN 0-317-47390-5). M Boyars Pubs.

Time & Again. Jack Finney. 400p. 1986. pap. 9.95 (ISBN 0-671-24295-4, Fireside). S&S.

Time & Again. Beverly Sommers. 256p. 1987. pap. 3.95 (ISBN 0-373-97042-0, Pub. by Worldwide). Harlequin Bks.

Time & Again: A Systematic Analysis of the Foundations of Physics. Stafleu. 1981. 19.95x (ISBN 0-88906-108-4). Radix Bks.

Time & Again: Memoirs & Letters. Helen Thomas. Ed. by Myfanwy Thomas. (Illus.). 170p. 1978. 14.50 (ISBN 0-85635-243-8). Carcanet.

Time & Aging: Conceptualization & Application in Sociological & Gerontological Research. Ephraim H. Mizruchi et al. LC 82-80240. 186p. (Orig.). 1982. lib. bdg. 26.95x (ISBN 0-930390-41-5); pap. text ed. 12.95x (ISBN 0-930390-40-7). Gen Hall.

Time & Cause: Essays Presented to Richard Taylor. Ed. by Peter Van Inwagen. (Philosophical Studies Series in Philosophy: No. 19). vii, 300p. 1980. lib. bdg. 34.00 (ISBN 90-277-1048-1, Pub. by Reidel Holland). Kluwer Academic.

Time & Chance. Brian Barnes. 336p. (Orig.). 1982. pap. 3.25 (ISBN 0-505-51815-5, Pub. by Tower Bks). Leisure NY.

Time & Change in Nature: A Laboratory Manual in General Geology. George P. Merk. 192p. 1987. pap. text ed. 15.95 (ISBN 0-8403-4602-6). Kendall-Hunt.

Time & Change in Vermont: A Human Geography. Harold A. Meeks. LC 85-29271. (Illus.). 400p. (Orig.). 1985. pap. 12.95 (ISBN 0-87106-883-4). Globe Pequot.

Time & Choice. G. L. Shackle. (Keynes & Lectures in Economics). 1976. pap. 5.50 (ISBN 0-85672-290-1, Pub. by British Acad). Longwood Pub Group.

Time & Clocks. rev. ed. Herta S. Breiter. LC 87-23229. (Read About Science Ser.). (Illus.). 48p. (gr. 3). 1987. PLB 15.33 (ISBN 0-8172-3262-1). Raintree Pubs.

Time Element & Other Stories. John O'Hara. LC 72-2694. 1972. 14.95 (ISBN 0-394-48211-5). Random.
Time Enough. Emily Kimbrough. (Illus.). 220p. 1984. pap. 7.50 (ISBN 0-910258-19-8). Book & Tackle.
Time Enough for Drums. Ann Rinaldi. LC 85-24869. 256p. (YA) (gr. 7 up). 1986. 12.95 (ISBN 0-8234-0603-2). Holiday.
Time Enough for Love. Robert A. Heinlein. 608p. 1986. pap. 4.95 (ISBN 0-425-10224-6). Berkley Pub.
Time Enough for the World, Vol. 1. Ed. by Rich Ives. 127p. (Orig.). 1986. pap. 7.00 (ISBN 0-937669-24-5). Owl Creek Pr.
Time Enough for the World, Vol. 2. Ed. by Rich Ives. 191p. (Orig.). 1987. pap. text ed. 7.00 (ISBN 0-937669-28-8). Owl Creek Pr.
Time Exposure: A Photographic Record of the Dinosaur Age. Jane Burton & Dougal Dixon. (Illus.). 96p. 1984. 14.95 (ISBN 0-8253-0217-X). Beaufort Bks NY.
Time Exposure: The Autobiography of William Henry Jackson. William H. Jackson. LC 85-21017. (Illus.). 352p. 1986. pap. 9.95 (ISBN 0-8263-0867-8). U of NM Pr.
Time Exposures: William Lyon Phelps, Carl Sandburg, Charles Chaplin, Sinclair Lewis, Theodore Dreiser, Katherine Cornell. Search-Light. 1926. Repr. 20.00 (ISBN 0-8274-3626-2). R West.
Time Factor in Transportation Processes. I. Tarski. (Developments in Civil Engineering Ser.: No. 15). 270p. 1987. 100.00 (ISBN 0-444-98994-3). Elsevier.
Time Falling Bodies Take to Light. William I. Thompson. (Illus.). 280p. 1982. pap. 9.95 (ISBN 0-312-80512-8). St Martin.
Time Flies. Bill Cosby. LC 87-13083. (Illus.). 192p. 1987. pap. 15.95 (ISBN 0-385-24040-6). Doubleday.
Time Flies. Bill Cosby. 1988. pap. 4.95 (ISBN 0-553-27724-3). Bantam.
Time Flies! Florence P. Heide. LC 84-47833. (Illus.). 112p. (gr. 3-7). 1984. 11.95 (ISBN 0-8234-0542-7). Holiday.
Time Flies! Florence P. Heide. 112p. 1985. pap. 2.50 (ISBN 0-553-15370-6, Skylark). Bantam.
Time Flowers. L. Sanina. 126p. 1984. pap. 7.00 (ISBN 0-935090-11-8). Almanac Pr.
Time for a Better Marriage. Don Dinkmeyer & Jon Carlson. 1985. 7.95 (ISBN 0-394-73394-0). Random.
Time for a Change. Marcia Cebulska. (Literacy Volunteers of America Readers Ser.). 32p. (Orig.). 1983. pap. 1.95 (ISBN 0-8428-9606-6). Cambridge Bk.
Time for a Change: A Guide to Careers for Women in Nontraditional Fields. 81p. 1981. 8.95 (ISBN 0-317-59456-7). Garrett Pk.
Time for a New Direction. Chiang. 208p. 1984. pap. text ed. 9.95 (ISBN 0-8403-3432-X). Kendall-Hunt.
Time for a New Way of Thinking. V. Kuznetsov. 282p. 1987. pap. 3.95 (ISBN 0-8285-3761-5, Pub. by Progress Pubs USSR). Imported Pubns.
Time for a Second Opinion, 1986. Kenna Farris. write for info. Port Love Intl.
Time for a Tale. (ps). 1976. 6.95 (ISBN 0-900195-21-5, Brimax Bks). Borden.
Time for Action. Robert Close. (Brassey Books). 170p. 1984. text ed. 33.00 (ISBN 0-08-028344-6); pap. text ed. 19.25 (ISBN 0-08-028345-4). Pergamon.
Time for Action. Simon. 1980. text ed. 10.00 (ISBN 0-07-057493-6). McGraw.
Time for Action. William E. Simon. 304p. 1982. pap. 2.95 (ISBN 0-425-05988-X). Berkley Pub.
Time for Anger. Franky Schaeffer. LC 82-71981. 192p. 1982. pap. 7.95 (ISBN 0-89107-263-2, Crossway Bks). Good News.
Time for Bed, Ned. Pam Zinnemann-Hope. LC 86-61429. (Illus.). 32p. (ps-2). 1987. 6.95 (ISBN 0-689-50415-2, M K McElderry). Macmillan.
Time for Bed, the Babysitter Said. Peggy P. Anderson. LC 86-27388. (ps). 1987. 12.95 (ISBN 0-395-41851-8). HM.
Time for Being Human. Eugene Kennedy. LC 86-20936. 264p. 1987. pap. 7.95 (ISBN 0-385-23538-0, Im). Doubleday.
Time for Building: Autralian Administration in Papua & New Guinea 1951-1963. Paul Hasluck. (Illus.). 1976. 25.00x (ISBN 0-522-84091-4, Pub. by Melbourne U Pr). Intl Spec Bk.
Time for Caring. William P. Lyliston. (Illus.). 25p. (Orig.). Date not set. pap. 3.35 (ISBN 0-9620078-2-X, FB-87-03). Flaming Bud Pub.
Time for Choice. Harold Bassage. (Orig.). 1970. pap. 0.95 (ISBN 0-377-80601-3). Friendship Pr.
Time for Choosing: The Speeches of Ronald Reagan. Ed. by Alfred Balitzer. Ronald Reagan. LC 83-42905. 512p. 1983. pap. 9.95 (ISBN 0-89526-838-8); pap. 15.00 (ISBN 0-89526-622-9). Regnery Gateway.
Time for Church. Donna Rathert & Lois Prahlow. 24p. (gr. 2-5). 1985. pap. 2.95 (ISBN 0-570-04129-5, 56-1540). Concordia.
Time for Commitment. Ted Engstrom & Robert C. Larson. 112p. 1987. padded gift ed. 9.95 (ISBN 0-310-51010-4, 15578P); pap. 4.95 (ISBN 0-310-51011-2, 12812P). Zondervan.
Time for Compassion. Ron L. Davis & James D. Denney. (Crucial Questions Ser.). 224p. 1986. 14.95 (ISBN 0-8007-1492-X). Revell.
Time for Consideration: A Scholarly Appraisal of the Unification Church. 2nd ed. M. Darrol Bryant & Herbert W. Richardson. LC 78-61364. (Symposium Ser.: Vol. 3). xi, 332p. 1978. pap. 19.95x (ISBN 0-88946-954-7). E Mellen.
Time for Deceit. Elsie W. Strother. 1981. 9.95 (ISBN 0-686-84697-4, Avalon). Bouregy.
Time for Decision: Sri Lankan Tamils in the West. Allen K. Jones. Ed. by Rosemary E. Tripp & Virginia Hamilton. (Illus.). 16p. 1985. pap. 2.00. US Comm Refugees.
Time for Drama. Roma Burgess & Pamela Gaudry. LC 86-12672. (English, Language & Education Ser.). 288p. 1987. pap. 21.00x (ISBN 0-335-15249-X, Open Univ Pr). Taylor & Francis.
Time for Dying. Barney G. Glaser & Anselm L. Strauss. LC 67-17601. 285p. 1968. 27.95x (ISBN 0-202-30027-7). Aldine de Gruyter.
Time for Every Purpose. Betty Isler. 80p. (Orig.). 1986. pap. 4.95 (ISBN 0-570-03986-X, 12-3013). Concordia.
Time for Faith. James Alberione. 1978. 4.00 (ISBN 0-8198-0371-5); pap. 3.00 (ISBN 0-8198-0372-3). Dghtrs St Paul.
Time for Ferrets. Lilo Hess. LC 87-9765. (Illus.). 48p. (gr. 3-6). 1987. 12.95 (ISBN 0-684-18788-4, Pub. by Scribner). Macmillan.
Time for Flowers. Dale L. Rohman. (Illus.). 140p. 1983. 50.00 (ISBN 0-935284-26-5). Patrice Pr.
Time for Giants: The Politics of the American High Command in World War II. D. Clayton James. 352p. 1987. 19.95 (ISBN 0-531-15046-1). Watts.
Time for God. Leslie D. Weatherhead. (Festival Ser.). 1981. pap. 1.75 (ISBN 0-687-42113-6). Abingdon.
Time for Hating. Taylor Lovering. 1982. 15.00x (ISBN 0-906660-62-9, Pub. by New Playwrights Network). State Mutual Bk.
Time for Heroes. Will Bryant. 288p. 1987. 17.95 (ISBN 0-312-00694-2). St Martin.
Time for Heroes. Neta Jackson et al. 150p. (Orig.). 1988. pap. 6.95 (ISBN 0-89283-395-5). Servant.
Time for Heros. Will Bryant. (Illus.). 497p. 1987. Repr. lib. bdg. write for info. (ISBN 0-89621-833-3). Thorndike Pr.
Time for Joy: Daily Affirmations. Ruth Fishel. 1988. pap. 6.95 (ISBN 0-932194-82-6). Health Comm.
Time for Learning: A Self-Instructional Handbook for Parents & Teachers of Young Children. Bernice M. Chappel. 144p. 1974. pap. text ed. 3.00 (ISBN 0-89039-059-2). Ann Arbor FL.
Time for Love. Eugene Kennedy. LC 86-23936. 160p. 1987. pap. 4.95 (ISBN 0-385-24014-7, Im). Doubleday.
Time for Me. Pat Farrell. (Everyday Ser.). (Illus.). 26p. (Orig.). 1983. pap. 3.00 (ISBN 0-915517-01-9). Everyday Ser.
Time for Murder. James Kirton. 1985. 24.95x (ISBN 0-7090-1724-3, Pub. by R Hale Ltd UK). State Mutual Bk.
Time for My Soul: A Treasury of Jewish Stories for Our Holy Days. Annette Labovitz & Eugene Labovitz. LC 86-32243. 400p. 1987. 30.00 (ISBN 0-87668-954-3). Aronson.
Time for Peace: Biblical Meditations for Advent. William F. Maestri. LC 83-22399. 94p. 1983. pap. 4.95 (ISBN 0-8189-0463-1). Alba.
Time for Peace, Mikhail Gorbachev. 304p. 1985. 15.95 (ISBN 0-931933-08-0). Richardson & Steirman.
Time for Poetry. 3rd ed. May H. Arbuthnot & Shelton L. Root, Jr. 1968. text ed. write for info. (ISBN 0-673-05549-3). Scott F.
Time for Reflection. J. Spencer Kinard. LC 86-71701. 190p. 1986. 9.95 (ISBN 0-87579-049-6). Deseret Bk.
Time for Remembering. Patricia D. Cornwell. 496p. 1985. pap. 16.95 (ISBN 0-8027-2501-5). Walker & Co.
Time for Remembering: The Ruth Graham Bell Story. Patsy D. Cornwall. LC 82-48922. 1986. pap. 5.95 (ISBN 0-06-061686-5, PL 4122, PL). Har-Row.
Time for Risking: Priorities for Women. Miriam Adeney. Ed. by Liz Heaney. LC 87-11299. 1987. pap. 7.95 (ISBN 0-88070-192-7). Multnomah.
Time for Roses. Agatha D. Anastasi. (Orig.). 1982. pap. 3.50 (ISBN 0-89083-946-8). Zebra.
Time for Snails & Painting Whales: Great Ways to Teach & Enjoy Your Young Child. Vivien Cooley. (Orig.). 1987. pap. 9.95 (ISBN 0-8024-8596-0). Moody.
Time for the Stars. Alan Garner. pap. 3.50 (ISBN 0-345-35191-6). Ballantine.
Time for the Stars. Robert A. Heinlein. (Hudson River Editions). (gr. 5-11). 1977. lib. rep. ed. 15.00x (ISBN 0-684-15163-4, ScribJ). Scribner.
Time for Trees. Joy Palmer. (Considering Conservations Ser.). 1986. 17.95 (ISBN 0-85219-646-6, Pub. by Batsford England). David & Charles.
Time for Trolls. Asbjornsen & Moe. (Tanum of Norway Tokens Ser). 1982. pap. 15.00x (ISBN 82-518-0081-1, N431). Vanous.
Time for Trumpets: The Untold Story of the Battle of the Bulge. Charles B. MacDonald. (Illus.). 640p. 1984. 19.95 (ISBN 0-688-03923-5). Morrow.
Time for Trumpets: The Untold Story of the Battle of the Bulge. Charles B. MacDonald. LC 85-6046. (Illus.). 720p. 1985. pap. 11.95 (ISBN 0-553-34226-6). Bantam.
Time for Uncle Joe. Nancy Jewell. LC 79-2695. (Illus.). 48p. (gr. k-3). 1981. PLB 11.89 (ISBN 0-06-022844-X). HarpJ.
Time for Vengeance. Giles A. Lutz. 224p. 1986. pap. 2.50 (ISBN 0-441-81134-5, Pub. by Charter Bks). Ace Bks.
Time for Winning. Shirley Sealy. (Illus.). 148p. (gr. 9-12). 1980. 5.95 (ISBN 0-934126-10-0). Randall Bk Co.
Time for Writing in the Elementary School. Eileen Tway. (Theory & Research into Practice Ser.). 32p. (Orig.). 1984. pap. 4.95 (ISBN 0-8141-5469-7). NCTE.
Time Forgotten. David Houston. (Tales of Tomorrow Ser.: No. 5). (Illus.). 208p. (Orig.). 1982. pap. 2.50 (ISBN 0-8439-1170-0, Leisure Bks). Leisure NY.
Time, Form & Style in Boswell's Life of Johnson. David L. Passler. LC 70-151585. (Yale Studies in English: No. 155). Repr. of 1971 ed. 34.20 (ISBN 0-8357-9591-8, 2013384). Bks Demand UMI.
Time Forms. Victor Gioscia. 198p. 1974. 66.00 (ISBN 0-677-04850-5). Gordon & Breach.
Time Frames. James Rush. 304p. 1988. 16.95 (ISBN 0-8065-1083-8, Pub. by Citadel Pr). Lyle Stuart.
Time Frames: The Meaning of Family Pictures. Michael Lesy. (Illus.). 1980. pap. 8.95 (ISBN 0-394-73958-2). Pantheon.
Time Frames: The Re-thinking of Darwinian Evolution & the Theory of Punctuated Equilibria. Niles Eldredge. 1985. 17.95 (ISBN 0-671-49555-0). S&S.
Time Frames: The Rethinking of Darwinian Evolution & the Theory of Punctuated Equilibria. Niles Eldridge. 1986. pap. 8.95 (ISBN 0-671-62245-5, Touchstone Bks). S&S.
Time Game: Two Views of a Prison. Anthony J. Manocchio & Jimmy Dunn. LC 72-127990. 1970. 25.00x (ISBN 0-8039-0079-1). Sage.
Time Garden. Edward Eager. LC 85-5505. (Illus.). 188p. (gr. 3-7). 1985. pap. 4.95 (ISBN 0-15-288190-5, VoyB). HarBraceJ.
Time Garden. Edward Eager. (gr. 4-6). 15.25 (ISBN 0-8446-6233-X). Peter Smith.
Time Gate: Hurtling Backward Through History. Charles R. Pellegrino. LC 84-23955. 1985. pap. 16.95 (ISBN 0-8306-1863-5, 1863P). TAB Bks.
Time Gentleman Please. Ron Brown. (Down Memory Lane, Old Hampshire Ser.). (Illus.). 64p. (Orig.). 1987. pap. 4.95 (ISBN 0-903852-20-9, Pub. by Milestone Pubns UK). Seven Hills Bks.
Time, Goods, & Well-Being. Ed. by F. Thomas Juster & Frank P. Stafford. LC 85-10818. (Illus.). 560p. 1985. 48.00x (ISBN 0-87944-293-X). Inst Soc Res.
Time-Harmonic Electromagnetic Fields. Roger F. Harrington. (Electronic & Electrical Engineering Ser.). 1961. text ed. 67.95 (ISBN 0-07-026745-6). McGraw.
Time-Honored Norwegian Recipes Adapted to the American Kitchen. rev. ed. Erna O. Xan & Sigrid Marstrander. LC 84-61063. (Illus.). 88p. 1984. pap. 5.50 (ISBN 0-941016-21-8). Penfield.
Time Hoppers. Robert Silverberg. 1977. pap. 1.50 (ISBN 0-8439-0512-3, Leisure Bks). Leisure NY.
Time in a Quantized Universe see **Time, Causality & the Quantum Theory.**
Time in a Red Coat: A Haunting Parable of War that Echoes Long in the Memory. George M. Brown. LC 84-21888. 249p. 1985. 15.95 (ISBN 0-8149-0898-5). Vanguard.
Time in Animal Behaviour. M. Richelle & H. Lejeune. (Illus.). 1980. pap. text ed. 31.00 (ISBN 0-08-025489-6). Pergamon.
Time in Dynamic Geometry. Paul H. Fejer. Ed. by Bernadette Meier. (Illus.). 70p. 1984. text ed. 60.00x (ISBN 0-9607422-2-0, TX-1-315-232). P H Fejer.
Time in Economics. George L. Shackle. LC 83-1758. (Professor Dr. F. De Vries Lectures Ser.). 111p. 1983. Repr. of 1958 ed. lib. bdg. 35.00x (ISBN 0-313-23969-X, SHTI). Greenwood.
Time in Ezra Pound's Work. William Harmon. LC 77-5958. xiii, 165p. 1977. 22.50x (ISBN 0-8078-1310-9). U of NC Pr.
Time in God's World. Beverly Beckmann. (In God's World Ser.). (Illus.). 24p. (gr. 2-5). 1985. 5.95 (ISBN 0-570-04128-7, 56-1539). Concordia.
Time in Gold, Wristwatches. Gerald Viola & GisBert Brunner. (Illus.). 256p. 1988. 79.95 (ISBN 0-88740-137-6). Schiffer.
Time in History: The Evolution of Our General Awareness of Time & Temporal Perspective. G. J. Whitrow. (Illus.). 224p. 1988. 29.95 (ISBN 0-19-215361-7). Oxford U Pr.
Time in India's Development Programmes. Robert C. Repetto. LC 71-143230. (Economic Studies: No. 137). (Illus.). 1971. 16.50x (ISBN 0-674-89180-5). Harvard U Pr.
Time in Language: Temporal Adverbial Constructions in Czech, Russian & English. Henry Kucera & Karla Trnka. LC 75-16785. (Michigan Slavic Materials: Bno. 12). 1975. pap. 10.00 (ISBN 0-930042-05-0). Mich Slavic Pubns.
Time in Many Places. Nels Olson. 218p. 1980. 9.00 (ISBN 0-87839-036-7). North Star.
Time in Medieval Literature. Richard Lock. LC 84-48370. 250p. 1985. lib. bdg. 35.00 (ISBN 0-8240-6705-3). Garland Pub.
Time in the Air. Rachel Wyatt. (AF50). 176p. 1985. pap. 9.95 (ISBN 0-88784-146-5, Pub. by Hse Anansi Pr. Canada). U of Toronto Pr.
Time In the Narrative of the Faerie Queene. Catherine Rodgers. Ed. by James Hogg. (Elizabethan & Renaissance Studies). 128p. (Orig.). 1973. pap. 15.00 (ISBN 3-7052-0654-0, Pub. by Salzburg Studies). Longwood Pub Group.
Time in the Play of "Hamlet". Edward P. Vining. Bd. with Communication. J. O. Halliwell-Phillipps; Once Used Words in Shakespeare. James D. Butler. LC 70-169825. (Shakespeare Society of New York. Publications: Nos. 5 & 6). Repr. of 1886 ed. 16.00 (ISBN 0-404-54205-0). AMS Pr.
Time in the Poetry of T. S. Eliot: A Study in Structure & Theme. Nancy K. Gish. 160p. 1981. 29.50x (ISBN 0-389-20192-8, 06957). B&N Imports.
Time Inc. The Intimate History of a Publishing Enterprise, 1923-1941. Robert T. Elson. LC 68-16868. (Illus.). 500p. 1968. 10.00 (ISBN 0-689-10077-9). Atheneum.
Time, Inflation & Growth: Some Macroeconomic Themes in an Indian Perspective. Prabhat Patnaik. (R C Dutt Lectures). 56p. 1988. pap. 8.95x (ISBN 0-86131-878-1, Pub. by Orient Longman LTD India). Apt Bks.
Time Investment Register. Josef G. Lowder. (What in the World Are You Doing with Your Life Ser.: No. 2). 32p. 1986. pap. 1.50 (ISBN 0-935597-02-6, 8507-02); diskette pckg. 29.95software (ISBN 0-935597-03-4). Comm Architects.
Time Is a Lover. Barbara Allen. 288p. 1988. pap. 3.95 (ISBN 0-317-67262-2). Bantam.
Time Is All We Have. Barnaby Conrad. (YA) 1989. pap. price not set (ISBN 0-440-20245-0). Dell.
Time Is All We Have: Four Weeks at the Betty Ford Center. Barnaby Conrad. 320p. 1986. 17.95 (ISBN 0-87795-835-1). Morrow.
Time Is an Eight Ball. Ed. by Bob H. Baber. 88p. 1984. pap. 6.00 (ISBN 0-940510-08-1). Tooth of Time.
Time Is an Illusion. Chris Griscom. 1988. pap. 7.95 (ISBN 0-671-66334-8, Fireside). S&S.
Time Is at Hand. Lillian De Waters. (Practical Demonstration Ser). pap. 0.95 (ISBN 0-686-05720-1). L De Waters.
Time Is Day. Cal Roy. (Illus.). (gr. k-3). 1968. 9.95 (ISBN 0-8392-3065-6). Astor-Honor.
Time Is Free. Roy Walker. 234p. 1980. Repr. of 1949 ed. lib. bdg. 39.50 (ISBN 0-8495-5653-8). Arden Lib.
Time Is Free: A Study of Macbeth. Roy Walker. LC 73-12893. 1949. lib. bdg. 42.50 (ISBN 0-8414-9424-X). Folcroft.
Time Is Life. Avi Shulman. (Dynamics of Personal Achievement Ser.). 96p. (Orig.). 1985. pap. 4.95 (ISBN 0-87306-927-7). Feldheim.
Time Is Money! Tested Tactics That Conserve Time for Top Executives. Ross A. Webber. LC 80-1032. (Illus.). 1980. 10.95 (ISBN 0-02-934030-6). Free Pr.
Time Is Now. Miguel Algarin. LC 83-72575. 80p. (Orig., Eng. & Span.). 1985. pap. 7.00 (ISBN 0-934770-33-6). Arte Publico.
Time Is Now. 2nd ed. Melody Sumner. (Illus.). 82p. 1983. pap. 10.00 (ISBN 0-936050-03-9). Burning Bks.
Time Is of the Essence: The DP Professional's Guide to Getting the Right Things Done. Stewart L. Stokes, Jr. LC 83-72638. 142p. 1983. pap. 24.50 (ISBN 0-89435-074-9). QED Info Sci.
Time Is on My Side: The Rolling Stones Day-By-Day, 1962-1984. Alan Stewart & Cathy Sanford. (Rock & Roll Reference Ser.: No. 24). 1988. write for info. (ISBN 0-87650-207-9, 3420). Pierian.
Time Is Out of Joint: A Study of Hamlet. Roy Walker. LC 77-24162. 1948. lib. bdg. 42.00 (ISBN 0-8414-9633-1). Folcroft.
Time Is Ripe: The Nineteen Forty Journal of Clifford Odets. Clifford Odets. 1988. 22.50 (ISBN 0-8021-1034-7). Grove.
Time Is Running Out: It's Much Later Than You Think. Leonard C. Hummel. 26p. (Orig.). 1986. pap. 1.95 (ISBN 0-940853-00-0). Power Word Pubns.
Time Is the Traveler. Gertrude M. Lutz. LC 75-22926. 80p. 1975. 5.00 (ISBN 0-8233-0225-3). Golden Quill.
Time It Never Rained. Elmer Kelton. LC 84-157. (Chisholm Trail Ser.: No. 2). 377p. 1984. 16.95 (ISBN 0-912646-91-8); pap. 9.95 (ISBN 0-912646-89-6). Tex Christian.
Time-Kept Promises. Constance O'Day Flannery. 512p. 1988. pap. 3.95 (ISBN 0-8217-2422-3). Zebra.
Time-Kissed Destiny. Constance O'Day-Flannery. 496p. 1987. pap. 3.95 (ISBN 0-8217-2223-9). Zebra.
Time-Life Book of Annuals. Time-Life Books Editors & James U. Crocket. LC 85-27287. 176p. 1986. pap. 12.95 (ISBN 0-03-008524-1, Owl Bks). H Holt & Co.
Time-Life Book of Bulbs. 1987. pap. 12.95 (ISBN 0-8050-0352-5). H Holt & Co.
Time-Life Book of Christmas. (Illus.). 256p. 1987. 24.95 (ISBN 0-13-133679-7). Prentice Hall Pr.

TITLE INDEX TIME OF YOUR LIFE.

Time-Life Book of Christmas. Time-Life Books Editors. 256p. 1987. 19.95 (ISBN 0-8094-6725-9). Time-Life.
Time-Life Book of Flowering House Plants. Time-Life Books Editors & James U. Crockett. (Illus.). 160p. 1986. pap. 12.95 (ISBN 0-8050-0122-0). H Holt & Co.
Time-Life Book of Flowering Shrubs. 1987. pap. 12.95 (ISBN 0-8050-0353-3). H Holt & Co.
Time-Life Book of Foliage House Plants. Time-Life Books Editors & James U. Crockett. (Illus.). 160p. 1986. pap. 12.95 (ISBN 0-8050-0123-9). H Holt & Co.
Time-Life Book of Perennials. Time-Life Books Editors & James U. Crocket. LC 85-27327. 160p. 1986. pap. 12.95 (ISBN 0-03-008523-3, Owl Bks). H Holt & Co.
Time-Life Book of Pruning & Grafting. Time-Life Books Editors & James U. Crocket. LC 85-27286. (Illus.). 160p. 1986. pap. 12.95 (ISBN 0-03-008528-4, Owl Bks). H Holt & Co.
Time-Life Book of Shade Gardens. Time-Life Books Editors & James U. Crocket. LC 85-27289. (Illus.). 160p. 1986. pap. 12.95 (ISBN 0-03-008519-5, Owl Bks). H Holt & Co.
Time-Life Book of Vegetables & Fruits. Time-Life Books Editors & James U. Crocket. LC 85-27326. 1986. pap. 12.95 (ISBN 0-03-008527-6, Owl Bks). H Holt & Co.
Time-Life Book of Wildflower Gardening. Time-Life Books Editors & James U. Crocket. LC 85-27290. (Illus.). 160p. 1986. pap. 12.95 (ISBN 0-03-008522-5, Owl Bks). H Holt & Co.
Time-Life Books Complete Home Repair Manual. (Illus.). 480p. 1987. 24.95 (ISBN 0-13-921636-7). Prentice Hall Pr.
Time-Life Step-by-Step Guide to the Commodore 64. 1984. pap. 12.95 (ISBN 0-394-72515-8). Random.
Time-Life Step-by-Step Guide to the IBM PC. 1984. pap. 12.95 (ISBN 0-394-72521-2). Random.
Time-Life Step-by-Step Guide to the IBM PCjr. 1984. pap. 12.95 (ISBN 0-394-72519-0). Random.
Time-Limited Psychotherapy. James Mann. LC 72-96631. (Commonwealth Fund Publications Ser). 511p. 1973. 15.00x (ISBN 0-674-89190-2); pap. 9.95x (ISBN 0-674-89191-0). Harvard U Pr.
Time Line Display of Jewish History: Mural Edition. 1981. 18.00 (ISBN 0-686-46788-4). T Black.
Time Line Display of Jewish History: Poster Edition. 1982. 10.00 (ISBN 0-686-46792-2). T Black.
Time Line Therapy. LC 87-63197. 1988. 22.95 (ISBN 0-916990-21-4). Meta Pubns.
Time Lines on File. Diagram Group Staff. 300p. 1988. 145.00 (ISBN 0-8160-1897-9). Facts on File.
Time Longer Than Rope: A History of the Black Man's Struggle for Freedom in South Africa. 2nd ed. Edward Roux. 488p. 1967. pap. 11.50x (ISBN 0-299-03204-3). U of Wis Pr.
Time Machine. H. G. Wells. (Airmont Classics Ser.). (gr. 7 up). 1964. pap. 1.75 (ISBN 0-8049-0044-2, CL-44). Airmont.
Time Machine. H. G. Wells. LC 71-183141. 128p. 1971. Repr. lib. bdg. 8.50x (ISBN 0-8376-0403-6). Bentley.
Time Machine. H. G. Wells. pap. 2.50 (ISBN 0-425-08266-0). Berkley Pub.
Time Machine. new ed. H. G. Wells. Ed. by Otto Binder. LC 73-75467. (Now Age Illustrated Ser.). (Illus.). 64p. (Orig.). (gr. 5-10). 1973. 7.50 (ISBN 0-88301-219-7); pap. 2.95 (ISBN 0-88301-102-6). Pendulum Pr.
Time Machine. H. G. Wells. Adapted by Betty R. Wright. LC 81-4097. (Short Classics Ser.). (Illus.). 48p. (gr. 4 up). 1981. PLB 15.99 (ISBN 0-8172-1675-8). Raintree Pubs.
Time Machine. H. G. Wells. 1975. pap. 2.50x (ISBN 0-460-01915-5, Evman). Biblio Dist.
Time Machine. H. G. Wells. Adapted by Betty R. Wright. LC 81-4097. (Short Classics Ser.). (Illus.). 48p. (gr. 4-12). 1983. pap. 9.27 (ISBN 0-8172-2024-0). Raintree Pubs.
Time Machine. H. G. Wells. Bd. with Invisible Man. 320p. 1984. pap. 3.50 (ISBN 0-451-51877-2, Sig Classics). NAL.
Time Machine. H. G. Wells. 11.95 (ISBN 0-89190-494-8, Pub. by Am Repr). Amereon Ltd.
Time Machine see Seven Science Fiction Novels.
Time Machine see Three Prophetic Novels.
Time Machine & the War of the Worlds: A Critical Edition. H. G. Wells. Ed. by Frank D. McConnell. (Illus.). 1977. pap. text ed. 7.95x (ISBN 0-19-502164-9). Oxford U Pr.
Time Machine: Student Activity Book. Marcia Sohl & Gerald Dackerman. (Now Age Illustrated Ser.). (Illus.). 16p. (gr. 4-10). 1976. pap. 1.25 (ISBN 0-88301-186-7). Pendulum Pr.
Time Machines: The World of Living History. Jay Anderson. (Illus.). 224p. 1984. 19.95 (ISBN 0-910050-71-6). AASLH Pr.
Time, Making It Work for You. rev. ed. Pat King. (Workbook Ser.). (Illus.). 96p. (Orig.). 1986. pap. 4.95 (ISBN 0-932305-44-X, 581002). Aglow Pubns.
Time Management. Kenneth R. Finn. (Simulation Game Ser.). 1975. pap. 24.90 (ISBN 0-89401-092-1); pap. 21.50 additional materials (ISBN 0-685-78118-6). Didactic Syst.
Time Management. Speed B. Leas. LC 78-8628. (Creative Leadership Ser.). 1978. pap. 7.95 (ISBN 0-687-42120-9). Abingdon.
Time Management & the Telephone. Dru Scott. Ed. by Michael G. Crisp. (Fifty-Minute Ser.). (Illus.). 96p. (Orig.). 1988. pap. 6.95 (ISBN 0-931961-53-X). Crisp Pubns.
Time Management for Educators. Charles E. Kozoll. LC 81-86309. (Fastback Ser.: No. 175). 50p. (Orig.). 1982. pap. 0.90 (ISBN 0-87367-175-9). Phi Delta Kappa.
Time Management for Health Care Professionals. Steven Appelbaum & Walter F. Rohrs. LC 81-3512. 260p. 1981. text ed. 41.50 (ISBN 0-89443-378-4). Aspen Pub.
Time Management for Ministers. Mark Short. (Leadership Ser.). (Orig.). 1987. pap. 5.95 (ISBN 0-8054-3114-4). Broadman.
Time Management for Teachers: Practical Techniques & Skills That Give You More to Teach. Cathy Collins. 312p. 1987. text ed. 17.50 (ISBN 0-13-921701-0). P-H.
Time Management for Writers. Ted Schwarz. 144p. 1988. 10.95 (ISBN 0-89879-309-2). Writers Digest.
Time Management Forms. (Easy-to-Make Photocopier Bks.). (Orig.). 1984. pap. 14.95 (ISBN 0-87280-032-6). Asher-Gallant.
Time Management Handbook. Pref. by James J. Messina. (Professional Handbook Ser.). 37p. (Orig.). 1982. pap. text ed. 6.00 (ISBN 0-931975-15-8). Advanced Dev Sys.
Time Management Made Easy. Peter Turla & Kathleen Hawkins. Date not set. pap. 12.95 (ISBN 0-525-48247-4). Dutton.
Time Management Skills see Productive Supervisor: A Program of Practical Managerial Skills.
Time Management Study Guide: A Manual to Accompany the Coaches Guide to Time Management. Stephen C. Jefferies. (Illus.). 1985. 3-ring notebook 18.00x (ISBN 0-931250-98-6, ACEP2021). Human Kinetics.
Time Mastery: The Beginner's Book, Vol. 5. Tisziji Munoz. (Illus., Orig.). 1987. pap. 15.00 (ISBN 0-945174-02-0). Illum Soc Pubns.
Time, Mind & Behavior. J. A. Michon & J. L. Jackson. (Illus.). 340p. 1985. 49.00 (ISBN 0-387-15444-2). Springer-Verlag.
Time Museum: An Introduction. William Andrewes & Seth Atwood. Ed. by Bruce Chandler. (Illus.). 32p. (Orig.). 1983. pap. 7.00 (ISBN 0-912947-00-4). Time Museum.
Time Museum Catalogue of the Collection; Volume I: Time Measuring Instruments, Pt. 3: Water-Clocks, Sand-Glasses, Fire-Clocks. Anthony Turner. Ed. by Bruce Chandler. (Illus.). 183p. 1984. 95.00 (ISBN 0-912947-01-2). Time Museum.
Time Museum Catalogue of the Collection; Volume I: Time Measuring Instruments, Pt. 1: Astrolabes & Related Devices. Anthony Turner. Ed. by Bruce Chandler. (Illus.). 220p. 1985. 115.00 (ISBN 0-912947-02-0). Time Museum.
Time, Narrative, & History. David Carr. LC 85-45742. (Studies in Phenomenology & Existential Philosophy). 224p. 1986. 22.50x (ISBN 0-253-36024-2). Ind U Pr.
Time No Longer. Taylor Caldwell. 1974. Repr. of 1941 ed. lib. bdg. 21.95x (ISBN 0-88411-161-X, Pub. by Aeonian Pr). Amereon Ltd.
Time of a Flower, Selected Poems. Aldo Vianello. Tr. by Richard Burns. 1968. signed ed., 50 copies 12.50 ea. (Pub. by Anvil Pr). Small Pr Dist.
Time of Agony, Time of Destiny: The Upsurge of Popular Protest in South Africa. Martin Murray. 272p. 1987. 29.95x (ISBN 0-86091-146-2, Pub. by Verso England); pap. 11.95x (ISBN 0-86091-857-2, Pub. by Verso England). Schocken.
Time of Apprenticeship: The Fiction of Young James Joyce. facsimile ed. Marvin Magalaner. LC 70-140366. (Select Bibliographies Reprint Ser). Repr. of 1959 ed. 15.00 (ISBN 0-8369-5609-5). Ayer Co Pubs.
Time of Change: A Reporter's Tale of Our Time. Harrison E. Salisbury. LC 87-45660. (Cornelia & Michael Bessie Book). (Illus.). 320p. 1988. 19.95 (ISBN 0-06-039083-2, C&M Bessie Bks). Har-Row.
Time of Change: Nineteen Eighty-Three Handbook on Women Workers. (Women's Bureau Bulletin Ser.: No. 298). (Illus.). 202p. (Orig.). 1984. pap. 6.50 (ISBN 0-318-18854-6, S/N 029-002-00065-7). USGPO.
Time of Changes. Robert Silverberg. 224p. 1986. pap. 3.95 (ISBN 0-446-34061-8). Warner Bks.
Time of Darkness: Local Legends & Volcanic Reality in Papua New Guinea. R. J. Blong. LC 81-11484. (Illus.). 270p. 1982. 27.50x (ISBN 0-295-95880-4). U of Wash Pr.
Time of Departure. Jack Boswell. 1982. 15.00x (ISBN 0-906660-16-5, Pub. by New Playwrights Network). State Mutual Bk.
Time of Desecration. Alberto Moravia. Tr. by Angus Davidson from Ital. LC 80-14438. 376p. 1980. 12.95 (ISBN 0-374-27781-8). FS&G.
Time of Destiny. Guanetta Gordon. LC 87-82474. 208p. 1987. 12.50x (ISBN 0-8233-0437-X). Golden Quill.
Time of Favor: The Story of the Catholic Family of Southern Illinois. Betty Burnett. Ed. by Gregory M. Franzwa. xvi, 305p. 1987. Sold only as a set with Profiles of Our Heritage. incl. both books 19.95 (ISBN 0-935284-48-6). Patrice Pr.
Time of Fear & Hope: The Making of the North Atlantic Treaty, 1947-1949. Escott Reid. 315p. 1981. text ed. 17.50x (ISBN 0-86598-055-1, Pub. by Allanheld). Rowman.
Time of Fine Weather. Jack C. Scott. 208p. 1985. 12.95 (ISBN 0-312-80509-8, J Kahn). St Martin.
Time of Fury. Norton Parker & Kallie Norton. 1980. pap. 2.25 (ISBN 0-8439-0791-6, Leisure Bks). Leisure NY.
Time of Gifts. Patrick L. Fermor. (Travel Library). 304p. 1984. pap. 6.95 (ISBN 0-14-009513-6). Penguin.
Time of Gifts. Patrick L. Fermor. 15.25 (ISBN 0-8446-6264-X). Peter Smith.
Time of Growing. Ed. by Jean Van Leeuwen. (gr. 8 up). 1967. 3.95 (ISBN 0-394-81895-4, BYR). Random.
Time of Her Life. Robb F. Dew. 224p. 1985. pap. 3.50 (ISBN 0-345-32542-7). Ballantine.
Time of Hope. C. P. Snow. 1961. lib. rep. ed. 20.00x (ISBN 0-684-15315-7, ScribT). Scribner.
Time of Hope: Family Celebrations & Activities for Lent & Easter. Margaret Ehlen-Miller et al. (Illus., Orig.). 1979. pap. 4.95 (ISBN 0-8192-1247-4). Morehouse.
Time of Hope, Time of Despair: Black Texans During Reconstruction. James M. Smallwood. (National University Publications, Ethnic Studies). 1981. 22.50x (ISBN 0-8046-9273-4, Pub by Kennikat). Assoc Faculty Pr.
Time of Hunting. Wayne Dodd. LC 75-4779. 128p. (gr. 6 up). 1975. 6.95 (ISBN 0-395-28903-3, Clarion). HM.
Time of Illusion. Johnathan Schell. 1976. pap. 4.76 (ISBN 0-394-72217-5, 72217, Vin). Random.
Time of Illusion. Jonathan Schell. 1976. pap. 4.76. Knopf.
Time of Innocence. Warren Burke. 192p. 1986. 15.95 (ISBN 0-8027-0888-9). Walker & Co.
Time of Man. Elizabeth M. Roberts. LC 82-40178. (Illus.). 424p. 1982. 23.00 (ISBN 0-8131-1467-5). U Pr of Ky.
Time of My Death. Alan J. Breslau. 1977. 9.95x (ISBN 0-525-21992-7). Phoenix Soc.
Time of My Life. Harry C. De Vighne. LC 84-2940. (Northern History Library). (Illus.). 64p. 1984. 6.95 (ISBN 0-88240-261-7). Alaska Northwest.
Time of My Life. Gertrude S. Legendre. LC 87-50640. (Illus.). 256p. 1987. 18.95 (ISBN 0-941711-02-1). Wyrick & Co.
Time of My Life. Audrey Willson. 1985. 18.95 (ISBN 0-901976-54-7, Pub. by United Writers Pubns England). State Mutual Bk.
Time of My Life. Bryan Woolley. 204p. 1984. 14.95 (ISBN 0-940672-17-0). Shearer Pub.
Time of My Life. Thomas Yoseloff. 8.95 (ISBN 0-8453-1761-X, Cornwall Bks). Assoc Univ Prs.
Time of My Life: An Autobiography. Willard van Orman Quine. (Illus.). 384p. 22.50x (ISBN 0-262-17003-5, Pub. by Bradford). MIT Pr.
Time of Need: Forms of Imagination in the Twentieth Century. William Barrett. write for info.; pap. 12.95 (ISBN 0-8195-6121-5). Wesleyan U Pr.
Time of Our Lives: The Story of My Father & Myself. Orrick Johns. 353p. 1973. Repr. of 1937 ed. lib. bdg. 20.00x (ISBN 0-374-94215-3, Octagon). Hippocrene Bks.
Time of Passage: SF Stories About Death & Dying. Ed. by Joseph D. Olander & Martin H. Greenberg. LC 77-76727. 1978. 9.95 (ISBN 0-8008-7733-0). Taplinger.
Time of Passion: America 1960-1980. Charles R. Morris. (Nonfiction Ser.). 288p. 1986. pap. 7.95 (ISBN 0-14-008643-9). Penguin.
Time of Personal Regeneration. Richard J. Aschwanden & Maria Aschwanden. Ed. by Charles R. Aschwanden. 60p. 1984. pap. 3.40x (ISBN 0-913071-00-5, TX1-202-40). Rama Pub Co.
Time of Predators. Joe Gores. LC 84-60551. 1984. pap. 3.95 (ISBN 0-89296-084-1). Mysterious Pr.
Time of Reckoning. Walter Wager. 288p. 1986. pap. 3.50 (ISBN 0-8125-1027-5, Dist. by Warner Pub Services & St. Martin's Press). Tor Bks.
Time of Stalin: Portrait of a Tyranny. Anton Antonov-Ovseyeneko. LC 80-8681. 376p. 1983. pap. 8.95 (ISBN 0-06-039027-1, CN1040, PL). Har-Row.
Time of Terror: The Great Dayton Flood. Allan W. Eckert. LC 65-12444. (Illus.). 341p. 1981. Repr. of 1965 ed. 9.95 (ISBN 0-913428-02-7). Landfall Pr.
Time of the Angels. Iris Murdoch. 240p. 1988. pap. 6.95 (ISBN 0-14-002848-X). Penguin.
Time of the Annihilator. John Morressy. 1985. pap. 2.95 (ISBN 0-441-81191-4, Pub. by Ace Science Fiction). Ace Bks.
Time of the Assassins. Claire Sterling. LC 83-18382. 264p. 1984. 14.95 (ISBN 0-03-063554-3). H Holt & Co.
Time of the Assassins: A Study of Rimbaud. Henry Miller. LC 55-12452. 1962. pap. 6.95 (ISBN 0-8112-0115-5, NDP115). New Directions.
Time of the Bells. Richard F. Pourade. LC 61-14059. (Illus.). 278p. 1961. 14.50 (ISBN 0-913938-01-7). Copley Bks.
Time of the Bison. Ann Turner. LC 86-23476. (Illus.). 64p. (gr. 2-6). 1987. PLB 12.95 (ISBN 0-02-789300-6). Macmillan.
Time of the Buffalo. Tom McHugh. LC 78-24261. (Illus.). xxiv, 383p. 1979. pap. 11.95 (ISBN 0-8032-8105-6, Bison). U of Nebr Pr.
Time of the Butcherbird. Alex La Guma. LC 79-670199. (African Writers Ser.). 1979. pap. text ed. 7.00 (ISBN 0-435-90212-1). Heinemann Ed.
Time of the Dark, No. 1. Barbara Hambly. 1984. pap. 3.50 (ISBN 0-345-31965-6, Del Rey). Ballantine.
Time of the Dinosaurs. Ann Packard & Shirley Stafford. (Learning Experiences for Young Children Ser.). 92p. (ps-3). 1981. write for info. (ISBN 0-9607580-1-1). S Stafford.
Time of the Doves. Merce Rodoreda. Tr. by David H. Rosenthal. 201p. (Catalan.). 1986. pap. 7.50 (ISBN 0-915308-75-4). Graywolf.
Time of the Doves. Merce Rodoreda. Tr. by David Rosenthall. LC 79-9652. 1980. 8.95 (ISBN 0-8008-7731-4). Taplinger.
Time of the Dragon. Dorothy Eden. 1981. pap. 2.75 (ISBN 0-449-23059-7, Crest). Fawcett.
Time of the Dragon: Saga Graphic Novel. Roy Thomas. LC 87-51260. (Dragonlance Novel Ser.: No. 2). (Illus.). 80p. (Orig.). 1988. pap. 9.95 (ISBN 0-88038-571-5). TSR Inc.
Time of the End. Henry J. Smith. (International Correspondence Program Ser.). 159p. (Orig.). pap. 6.95 (ISBN 0-87148-853-1). Pathway Pr.
Time of the Forest. Tom McGowen. LC 87-26191. 120p. (gr. 5-9). 12.95 (ISBN 0-395-44471-3). HM.
Time of the Great Freeze. Robert Silverberg. 224p. 1988. pap. 2.95 (ISBN 0-8125-5469-8). Tor Bks.
Time of the Gringo. Elliott Arnold. 626p. Repr. of 1970 ed. lib. bdg. 25.95x (ISBN 0-88411-180-6, Pub. by Aeonian Pr). Amereon Ltd.
Time of the Hero. Mario Vargas-Llosa. Tr. by Lysander Kemp. 409p. 1986. pap. 9.95 (ISBN 0-374-52021-6). FS&G.
Time of the Hunter's Moon. Victoria Holt. 384p. 1984. pap. 3.95 (ISBN 0-449-20511-8, Crest). Fawcett.
Time of the Leonids. Christine Bruckner. Tr. by Marlies I. Comjean from Ger. Orig. Title: Zeit Von Den Leoniden. 160p. 13.95 (ISBN 0-89182-040-X). Charles River Bks.
Time of the Peacock. Mena Abdullah & Ray Mathew. LC 83-14618. 128p. 1983. 12.95 (ISBN 0-8149-0877-2). Vanguard.
Time of the Rising Sea. Joseph Chiari. LC 74-29585. 52p. 1975. 5.00x (ISBN 0-87752-195-6). Gordian.
Time of the Singing of Birds. Grace L. Hill. 15.95 (ISBN 0-89190-072-1, Pub. by Am Repr). Amereon Ltd.
Time of the Spirit. Ed. by George Every et al. LC 84-10696. 256p. (Orig.). 1984. pap. text ed. 9.95 (ISBN 0-88141-035-7). St Vladimirs.
Time of the Thunderer: Mikhail Katkov, Russian Nationalist Extremism & the Failure of the Bimarkian System, 1871-1887. Karel Durman. 600p. 1988. 60.00 (ISBN 0-88033-134-8). East Eur Quarterly.
Time of the Toad: A Study of Inquisition in America. Dalton Trumbo. (Orig.). 1985. pap. 4.50 (ISBN 0-904526-78-X, Journey Pr England). Riverrun NY.
Time of the Transference. Alan D. Foster. (Spellsinger Ser.). 1986. 17.00 (ISBN 0-932096-43-3). Phantasia Pr.
Time of the Twins. Margaret Weis & Tracy Hickman. LC 85-52200. (Dragonlance Legends Ser.: Vol. 1). 400p. (Orig.). 1986. pap. 3.95 (ISBN 0-88038-265-1). TSR Inc.
Time of the Warlock. Larry Niven. LC 84-51291. (Illus.). 1984. 20.00 (ISBN 0-916595-01-3). SteelDragon Pr.
Time of the Witch. Mary D. Hahn. 160p. (gr. 4-8). 1982. 10.50 (ISBN 0-89919-115-0, Clarion). HM.
Time of Tigers. Elmer E. Haynes. LC 85-61329. (Illus.). 300p. (Orig.). 1986. pap. 16.00 (ISBN 0-931571-02-2). Lifetime Pr.
Time of Trains. David Plowden. (Illus.). 1987. 45.00 (ISBN 0-393-02499-7). Norton.
Time of Transition: The Growth of Families Headed by Women. Heather L. Ross & Isabel V. Sawhill. 233p. 1975. pap. 8.50 (ISBN 0-87766-148-0, 12600). Urban Inst.
Time of Triumph & of Sorrow: Spanish Politics During the Reign of Alfonso XII, 1874-1885. Earl R. Beck. LC 78-23282. 320p. 1979. 22.50x (ISBN 0-8093-0902-5). S Ill U Pr.
Time of Troubles: A Historical Study of the Internal Crisis & Social Struggles in Sixteenth & Seventeenth-Century Moscovy. S. F. Platonov. Tr. by John T. Alexander. LC 79-97029. xviii, 198p. 1970. 25.00x (ISBN 0-7006-0061-2); pap. 5.95x (ISBN 0-7006-0062-0). U Pr of KS.
Time of Troubles: The Diary of Iurii Vladimirovich Got'e. Intro. by Terence Emmons. Tr. by Terrence Emmons from Rus. (Illus.). 550p. 1988. text ed. 39.50 (ISBN 0-691-05520-3). Princeton U pr.
Time of Turmoil: Values & Voting in the 1970's. Ronald R. Stockton & Frank W. Wayman. 216p. 1983. 18.95x (ISBN 0-87013-232-6). Mich St U Pr.
Time of War: Air Force Diaries & Pentagon Memos, 1943-45. James G. Cozzens. Ed. by Matthew J. Bruccoli. 1984. 35.00 (ISBN 0-89723-043-4). Bruccoli.
Time of Wonder. Robert McCloskey. (Illus.). (gr. k-3). 1957. 14.95 (ISBN 0-670-71512-3). Viking.
Time of Wonder. Robert McClosky. (Illus.). 64p. (gr. k-3). 1977. pap. 1.95 (ISBN 0-14-050201-7, Puffin). Penguin.
Time of Your Life. Jack H. Smith. 1988. 16.95 (ISBN 0-940375-04-4). WindRiver Pub.

Time on Earth. Vilhelm Moberg. 224p. 1984. pap. 3.50 (ISBN 0-446-31127-8). Warner Bks.
Time on Task. American Association of School Administrators Staff. 6.95 (ISBN 0-318-01709-1, 021-00870). Am Assn Sch Admin.
Time on the Cross: The Economics of American Negro Slavery. Robert W. Fogel & Stanley L. Engerman. (Illus.). 304p. 1985. pap. text ed. 14.00 (ISBN 0-8191-4331-6). U Pr of Amer.
Time on Their Hands: A Report on Leisure, Recreation, & Young People. C. Gilbert Wrenn & D. L. Harley. LC 74-1718. (Children & Youth Ser.: Vol. 11). (Illus.). 1974. Repr. of 1941 ed. 25.50x (ISBN 0-405-05993-0). Ayer Co Pubs.
Time Out! Phylliss Adams et al. (BTR Ser.). (Illus.). 32p. (gr. k-3). 1982. PLB 4.95 (ISBN 0-8136-5401-7, Dist. by Caroline Hse); pap. 2.25 (ISBN 0-8136-5901-9). Modern Curr.
Time out. Al Bryant. pap. 6.95 (ISBN 0-310-22121-8, 9293P). Zondervan.
Time Out. Patt Busheister. (Loveswept Ser.: No. 292). 192p. (Orig.). 1988. pap. 2.50 (ISBN 0-553-21944-8). Bantam.
Time Out. Dawn Fergut. Date not set. 13.95 (ISBN 0-9616789-3-3). Earnest Pubns.
Time Out. Jack Vietor. 208p. 1985. pap. 11.95 (ISBN 0-8168-9025-0, 29025, TAB-Aero). TAB Bks.
Time Out. Joanna Wharton. (Campus Fever Ser.: No. 5). 192p. 1986. pap. 2.50 (ISBN 0-451-14551-8, Sig Vista). NAL.
Time Out for Coffee. Jeanette Lockerbie. (Quiet Time Bks.). 1978. pap. 3.50 (ISBN 0-8024-8759-9). Moody.
Time Out for God. Jane Sorenson. 64p. (gr. 7-9). 1985. pap. 2.50 (ISBN 0-87239-895-1, 2825). Standard Pub.
Time Out for God, No. 2. Jane Sorenson. 64p. (gr. 7-9). 1985. pap. 2.50 (ISBN 0-87239-896-X, 2826). Standard Pub.
Time Out for Grief: A Practical Guide to Passing Through Grief to Happiness. Jean G. Jones. LC 81-85051. 228p. 1982. pap. 4.50 (ISBN 0-87973-654-2, 654). Our Sunday Visitor.
Time Out for Mental Digestion. Robert Rawls, pseud. 45p. 1949. pap. 3.00x (ISBN 0-9613203-1-1). Updegraff.
Time Out for Motherhood. Lucy Scott & Meredith J. Angwin. 272p. 1988. pap. 8.95 (ISBN 0-87477-449-7). J P Tarcher.
Time Out for Motherhood: A Guide for Today's Working Woman to the Financial, Emotional, & Career Aspects of Having a Baby. Lucy Scott & Meredith J. Angwin. 272p. 1986. 15.95 (ISBN 0-87477-382-2). J P Tarcher.
Time Out for Murder. Alwyn Marston. 1986. 8.95 (ISBN 0-533-06817-7). Vantage.
Time Out: How to Take a Year (or More or Less) off Without Jeopardizing Your Job, Your Family or Your Bank Account. Bonnie M. Rubin. 1987. 18.95 (ISBN 0-393-02393-1); pap. 12.95 (ISBN 0-393-30510-4). Norton.
Time Out of Joint. Philip K. Dick. LC 84-14585. 264p. 1984. Repr. 6.95 (ISBN 0-312-94427-6). Bluejay Bks.
Time Out of Joint. Philip K. Dick. 263p. 1987. pap. 3.95 (ISBN 0-88184-352-0). Carroll & Graf.
Time Out of Joint. Benedict C. Njoku. 1983. 5.50 (ISBN 0-8233-0357-8). Golden Quill.
Time Out of Mind. Pierre Boulle. LC 66-26792. 1966. 12.95 (ISBN 0-8149-0062-3). Vanguard.
Time out of Mind. Joan M. Grant. 21.00 (ISBN 0-405-11792-2). Ayer Co Pubs.
Time Out of Mind. John R. Maxim. LC 85-21896. 502p. 1986. 17.95 (ISBN 0-395-36801-4). HM.
Time Out of Mind. John R. Maxim. 1987. pap. 4.50 (ISBN 0-8125-8569-0, Dist. by St. Martin's Pr & Warner Pub Servs). Tor Bks.
Time out of Mind. Marc Robertson. 44p. 1972. 5.00 (ISBN 0-86690-220-1). Am Fed Astrologers.
Time Out of Mind: Trekking the Hindu Kush. Lynda W. Schmidt. LC 79-90967. (Illus.). viii, 158p. (Orig.). 1979. pap. 5.95 (ISBN 0-931474-11-6). TBW Bks.
Time Out of Time: Essays on the Festival. Ed. by Alessandro Falassi. LC 86-30804. 321p. 1987. 35.00x (ISBN 0-8263-0932-1); pap. 17.50 (ISBN 0-8263-0933-X). U of NM Pr.
Time Out: Prayers for Busy People. Basil Arbour. 96p. 1984. pap. 3.95 (ISBN 0-86683-828-7, HarpR). Har-Row.
Time Outs. Nancy Holt. LC 85-51128. (Artists Ser.). (Illus.). 64p. (Orig.). 1985. pap. 10.00 (ISBN 0-89822-043-2). Visual Studies.
Time Outworn. Val Mulkerns. 9.95 (ISBN 0-8159-6905-8). Devin.
Time Past. facs. ed. Marie Scheikevitch. Tr. by Francoise Delisle. LC 70-142691. (Essay Index Reprint Ser). 1935. 20.00 (ISBN 0-8369-2073-2). Ayer Co Pubs.
Time Patrolman. Poul Anderson. 288p. (Orig.). 1983. pap. 2.95 (ISBN 0-8125-3076-4, Dist. by Warner Pub. Services & Saint Martin's Press). Tor Bks.
Time: Patterns of Flow & Return. Marie-Louise Von Franz. (Art & Imagination Ser.). (Illus.). 1979. pap. 11.95 (ISBN 0-500-81016-8). Thames Hudson.
Time Payment. Kerry Tomlinson. LC 77-93227. 60p. 1978. 10.00 (ISBN 0-930012-05-4); pap. 3.50 (ISBN 0-930012-04-6). J Mudfoot.
Time-Piece. Janice Shinebourne. 186p. (Orig.). 1986. pap. 10.00 (ISBN 0-948833-03-3, Peepal Tree UK). Three Continents.
Time Piper. Delia Huddy. (MagicQuest Ser.: No. 11). 224p. 1984. pap. 2.25 (ISBN 0-441-81205-8). Ace Bks.
Time, Place & Idea: Essays on the Novel. John H. Raleigh. LC 68-10116. (Crosscurrents-Modern Critiques Ser.). 188p. 1968. 6.95x (ISBN 0-8093-0288-8). S Ill U Pr.
Time, Place & Music: An Anthology of Ethnomusicological Observation C.1550 to 1800. Ed. by Frank Harrison. (Music Import, 1978 Ser.). (Illus.). 1978. pap. text ed. 29.50 (ISBN 0-306-77592-1). Da Capo.
Time Police, No. 2. Warren Norwood. (Orig.). 1989. pap. 3.50 mass mrkt. (ISBN 1-55802-007-1). Lynx Bks.
Time Power: The Revolutionary Time Management System That Can Change Your Professional & Personal Life. Charles Hobbs. LC 86-46072. (Illus.). 256p. 1987. 16.95i (ISBN 0-06-015589-2, HarpT). Har-Row.
Time Power: The Revolutionary Time Management System That Can Change Your Professional & Personal Life. Charles R. Hobbs. LC 86-46072. (Illus.). 256p. 1988. pap. 7.95 (ISBN 0-06-091490-4, PL-1490, PL). Har-Row.
Time Pressure. Spider Robinson. (Illus.). 224p. 1987. 16.95 (ISBN 0-441-80932-4). Ace Bks.
Time Projection Chamber: AIP Conference Proceedings, TRIUMF, Vancover, 1983, No. 108. Ed. by J. A. Macdonald. LC 83-83445. 264p. 1984. lib. bdg. 39.00 (ISBN 0-88318-307-2). Am Inst Physics.
Time-Quest Ser. Hydrabyss Red, No. 2. William Tedford. (Timequest Ser.). 240p. 1985. pap. 2.50 (ISBN 0-8439-2262-1, Leisure Bks). Leisure NY.
Time Raid. Charles Upton. LC 68-26903. (Writing Ser: No. 19). 40p. (Orig.). 1969. pap. 2.00 (ISBN 0-87704-009-5). Four Seasons Foun.
Time Raider. R. L. Stine. (Twistaplot Ser.: No. 1). (Illus.). 96p. (Orig.). (gr. 7 up). pap. 1.95 (ISBN 0-590-32637-6). Scholastic Inc.
Time Release. John M. Bennett. 1978. 2.00 (ISBN 0-686-73439-4); signed & lettered 5.00 (ISBN 0-686-73440-8). Luna Bisonte.
Time Remembered. Read. (Illus.). 112p. 1987. 14.95 (ISBN 0-395-42856-4). HM.
Time Remembered: A Journal for Survivors. Earl A. Grollman. LC 86-47753. 98p. 1987. 10.00 (ISBN 0-8070-2704-9). Beacon Pr.
Time Remembered After Pere Lachaise. Vyvyan B. Holland. LC 79-8064. Repr. of 1966 ed. 22.50 (ISBN 0-404-18375-1). AMS Pr.
Time Research: 1172 Studies. Irving Zelkind & Joseph Sprug. LC 74-14970. 253p. 1974. 19.00 (ISBN 0-8108-0768-8). Scarecrow.
Time Resolution in Auditory Systems. Ed. by A. Michelsen. (Proceedings in Life Sciences Ser.). (Illus.). 255p. 1985. 32.00 (ISBN 0-387-15637-2). Springer-Verlag.
Time-Resolved Fluorescence Spectroscopy in Biochemistry & Biology. Ed. by R. B. Cundall et al. (NATO ASI Series A, Life Sciences: Vol. 69). 800p. 1983. 120.00x (ISBN 0-306-41476-7, Plenum Pr). Plenum Pub.
Time-Resolved Laser Raman Spectroscopy. Ed. by David Phillips & George H. Atkinson. 180p. 1987. text ed. 65.00 (ISBN 3-7186-0343-8). Harwood Academic.
Time-Resolved Laser Spectroscopy in Biochemistry. Ed. by Lakowicz. 1988. 72.00 (ISBN 0-89252-944-X, 909). SPIE.
Time-Resolved Vibrational Spectroscopy: Proceedings of the JSPS-NSF Symposium Held in Honolulu, Hawaii, November 18-22, 1985. Ed. by George H. Atkinson. 436p. 1987. text ed. 89.00 (ISBN 2-88124-191-3). Gordon & Breach.
Time-Resolved Vibrational Spectroscopy. Ed. by A. Laubereau. M. Stockburger. (Proceedings in Physics Ser.: Vol. 4). (Illus.). 315p. 1985. 39.00 (ISBN 0-387-16175-9). Springer-Verlag.
Time-Resolved Vibrational Spectroscopy (Symposium) Ed. by George H. Atkinson. LC 83-9928. 1983. pap. 56.50 (ISBN 0-12-066280-9). Acad Pr.
Time, Rocks & the Rockies: The Geology of Rocky Mountain National Park. Halka Chronic. LC 84-8429. (Roadside Geology Ser.). (Illus.). 120p. (Orig.). 1984. pap. 7.95 (ISBN 0-87842-172-6). Mountain Pr.
Time, Roles & Self in Old Age. Ed. by Jaber F. Gubrium. LC 74-12131. 363p. 1976. text ed. 39.95 (ISBN 0-87705-230-1); pap. text ed. 19.95 (ISBN 0-87705-350-2). Human Sci Pr.
Time Safari. David Drake. 288p. (Orig.). 1982. pap. 2.75 (ISBN 0-523-48541-7, Dist. by Warner Pub. Services & Saint Martin's Press). Tor Bks.
Time-Sample Behavioral Checklist: Observational Assessment Instrumentation for Service & Research. Ed. by Gordon L. Paul et al. (Assessment in Residential Treatment Ser.: No. 2). 286p. 1987. pap. text ed. 18.95 (ISBN 0-87822-276-6). Res Press.
Time-Sampling Studies of Child Behavior see Differential Forecasts of Achievement & Their Use in Educational Counseling.
Time Sanctified: The Book of Hours in Medieval Art & Life. Roger S. Wieck. (Illus.). 232p. 1988. 45.00 (ISBN 0-8076-1189-1). Braziller.
Time-Saver Standard for Site Planning. Joseph DeChiara & L. E. Koppelman. (Illus.). 849p. 1984. text ed. 84.50 (ISBN 0-07-016266-2). McGraw.
Time-Saver Standards for Architectural Design Data. 6th ed. John H. Callender. 1982. text ed. 88.50 (ISBN 0-07-009663-5). McGraw.
Time-Saver Standards for Building Types. 2nd ed. Joseph De Chiara & John H. Callender. 1088p. 1980. text ed. 88.50 (ISBN 0-07-016265-4). McGraw.
Time-Saver Standards for Landscape Architecture. Cyril M. Harris. 896p. 1988. text ed. 89.50 (ISBN 0-07-026725-1). McGraw.
Time-Saver Standards for Residential Development. Ed. by J. DeChiara. (Illus.). 910p. 1984. text ed. 88.50 (ISBN 0-07-016217-4). McGraw.
Time-Saving Sermon Outlines. Russell E. Spray. (Sermon Outline Ser.). (Orig.). 1981. pap. 2.50 (ISBN 0-8010-8193-9). Baker Bk.
Time Saving Tips for Teachers. Barbara Gruber. (Instant Idea Bks.). (Illus.). 64p. 1983. 5.95 (ISBN 0-86734-047-9, FS-8301). Schaffer pubns.
Time-Scale Modeling of Dynamic Networks with Applications to Power Systems. Ed. by J. H. Chow. (Lecture Notes in Control & Information Sciences Ser.: Vol. 46). 218p. 1982. pap. 14.30 (ISBN 0-387-12106-4). Springer-Verlag.
Time, Science & Society in China & the West: The Study of Time V. Ed. by J. T. Fraser et al. LC 79-640956. (Illus.). 288p. 1986. lib. bdg. 35.00x (ISBN 0-87023-495-1). U of Mass Pr.
Time Sequence Analysis in Geophysics. 3rd ed. E. R. Kanasewich. xiv, 480p. 1981. 35.00x (ISBN 0-88864-074-9, Pub. by Univ of Alta Pr Canada). U of Nebr Pr.
Time Series. Maurice Kendall. (Charles Griffin Bk.). (Illus.). 197p. 1987. pap. 32.95 (ISBN 0-19-520571-5). Oxford U Pr.
Time-Series. 3rd, rev. ed. Maurice Kendall & J. Keith Ord. (Charles Griffin Book Ser.). 275p. 1988. 45.00 (ISBN 0-19-520706-8). Oxford U Pr.
Time Series. 2nd ed. Maurice G. Kendall. LC 76-441. 1976. 32.95x (ISBN 0-02-847780-4). Hafner.
Time Series. Norbert Wiener. 1964. pap. 9.95x (ISBN 0-262-73005-7). MIT Pr.
Time Series Analysis. E. J. Hannan. 1967. pap. 12.95x (ISBN 0-412-20480-0, NO. 6141, Pub. by Chapman & Hall). Routledge Chapman & Hall.
Time Series Analysis: A Comprehensive Introduction for Social Scientists. John M. Gottman. LC 80-25644. (Illus.). 368p. 1982. 37.50 (ISBN 0-521-23597-9). Cambridge U Pr.
Time Series Analysis & Applications. Enders A. Robinson. 612p. 1981. text ed. 35.00 (ISBN 0-934634-57-2). Intl Human Res.
Time Series Analysis & Forecasting Subroutine Library: Statlib 1, Microsoft FORTRAN Version. Physical Sciences, Inc. Staff. 270p. 1987. Book-disk pak. 295.00 (ISBN 0-471-84907-3). Wiley.
Time Series Analysis, Forecasting & Control. rev. ed. George E. Box & Gwilym Jenkins. LC 76-8713. 500p. 1976. text ed. 54.95x (ISBN 0-8162-1104-3). Holden-Day.
Time Series Analysis, Identification & Adaptive Filtering. Daniel Graupe. LC 81-20738. 402p. (Orig.). 1984. 42.00 (ISBN 0-88275-713-X). Krieger.
Time Series Analysis, Identification & Adaptive Filtering. 2nd ed. Daniel Graupe. 1989. lib. bdg. price not set (ISBN 0-89464-315-0). Krieger.
Time Series Analysis of Irregularly Observed Data: Proceedings of a Symposium Held at Texas A & M University, College Station, Texas, February 10-13, 1983. E. Parzen. (Lecture Notes in Statistics Ser.: Vol. 25). (Illus.). 370p. 1984. pap. 27.00 (ISBN 0-387-96040-6). Springer-Verlag.
Time Series Analysis: Proceedings of the International Conference, Held in Houston, Texas, August, 1980. Ed. by O. D. Anderson & M. R. Perryman. 1981. 123.75 (ISBN 0-444-86177-7). Elsevier.
Time Series Analysis: Regression Techniques. Charles W. Ostrom, Jr. LC 77-93283. (University Papers Ser.: Quantitative Applications in the Social Sciences, No. 9). 85p. 1978. pap. 6.50 (ISBN 0-8039-0942-X). Sage.
Time Series Analysis, Theory & Practice-Hydrological, Geophysical & Spatial Applications: Proceedings of the Conference, Toronto, Aug. 10-14, 1983, Vol. 6. Ed. by O. D. Anderson & J. K. Ord. 308p. 1985. 84.25 (ISBN 0-444-87683-9, North-Holland). Elsevier.
Time Series Analysis: Theory & Practice: Proceedings of International Conference, Valencia, Spain, June 22-26, 1981, No. 1. Ed. by O. D. Anderson et al. 756p. 1982. 129.00 (ISBN 0-444-86337-0). Elsevier.
Time Series Analysis, Theory & Practice: Proceedings of the Conference, Nottingham, March 1983, Vol. 5. Ed. by O. D. Anderson. 1984. 89.50 (ISBN 0-444-87568-9, I-438-84, North-Holland). Elsevier.
Time Series Analysis, Theory & Practice: Proceedings of the Conference, Toronto, Aug. 18-21, 1983, Vol. 7. Ed. by O. D. Anderson. 312p. 1985. 84.25 (ISBN 0-444-87684-7, North-Holland). Elsevier.
Time Series Analysis: Theory & Practice, No. 2. O. D. Anderson. 1983. 73.75 (ISBN 0-444-86536-5). Elsevier.
Time Series Analysis Theory & Practice, No. 3. Ed. by O. D. Anderson. 302p. 1983. 89.50 (ISBN 0-444-86625-6, I-117-83, North Holland). Elsevier.
Time Series Analysis: Theory & Practice, No. 4. Ed. by O. D. Anderson. 352p. 1983. 94.75 (ISBN 0-444-86731-7, I-253-83). Elsevier.
Time Series Analysis with Minitab. Cryer. 1986. text ed. 33.00 (ISBN 0-87150-963-6, 36G8330, Duxbury Pr). PWS Kent Pub.
Time Series & Ecological Processes. Ed. by H. H. Shugart, Jr. LC 78-5410. (SIAM-SIMS Conference Ser.: No. 5). (Illus.). xxi, 303p. (Orig.). 1978. pap. text ed. 30.00 (ISBN 0-89871-032-4). Soc Indus-Appl Math.
Time Series & Forecasting with IDA. Harry V. Roberts. (Data Analysis Ser.). 1984. text ed. 30.95 (ISBN 0-07-053136-6). McGraw.
Time Series & Forecasting with IDA. Harry V. Roberts. (Illus.). 425p. 1984. pap. text ed. 35.00 (ISBN 0-89426-059-6). Scientific Pr.
Time Series & Linear Systems. Ed. by S. Bittanti. (Lecture Notes in Control & Information Sciences Ser.: Vol. 86). xvii, 243p. 1986. pap. 26.40 (ISBN 0-387-16903-2). Springer-Verlag.
Time Series & System Analysis with Applications. S. M. Pandit & S. M. Wu. LC 88-15958. 586p. 1983. 49.95 (ISBN 0-471-86886-8); write for info solutions avail (ISBN 0-471-87392-6). Wiley.
Time Series: Data Analysis & Theory. enl. ed. David R. Brillinger. LC 80-84117. (Illus.). 552p. 1980. text ed. 49.95x (ISBN 0-8162-1150-7). Holden-Day.
Time Series Forecasting: Unified Concepts & Computer Implementation. 2nd ed. Bowerman & O'Connell. 1987. text ed. 32.50 (ISBN 0-87150-070-1, 36G0200, Duxbury Pr). PWS Kent Pub.
Time Series in Psychology. Robert A. Gregson. 456p. 1983. text ed. 49.95x (ISBN 0-89859-250-X). L Erlbaum Assocs.
Time Series in the Time Domain. Ed. by E. J. Hannan et al. (Handbook of Statistics Ser.: Vol. 5). 496p. 1985. 89.50 (ISBN 0-444-87629-4, North-Holland). Elsevier.
Time Series Methods in Hydrosciences: Proceedings of the International Conference, Burlington, Ontario, Canada, October 6-8, 1981. Ed. by A. H. El-Shaarawi. (Developments in Water Science Ser.: No. 17). 614p. 1982. 118.50 (ISBN 0-444-42102-5). Elsevier.
Time Series Models. A. C. Harvey. 240p. 1981. text ed. 39.95x (ISBN 0-86003-032-6, Pub. by Philip Allan UK). Humanities.
Time Series of Ocean Measurements, Vol. 1. (Intergovernmental Oecanographic Commission Technical Ser.: No. 24). 46p. 1983. pap. text ed. 5.00 (ISBN 92-3-102171-0, U1324, UNESCO). UNIPUB.
Time Series of Ocean Measurements, Vol. 3, 1986. J. M. Colebrook et al. (Intergovernmental Oceanographic Commission Technical Ser.: No. 31). (Illus.). 62p. (Orig.). 1987. pap. text ed. 5.00 (ISBN 0-317-58704-8, U1554, UNESCO). UNIPUB.
Time Series Package (TSPACK) F. S. Chaghaghi. (Lecture Notes in Computer Science Ser.: Vol. 187). iii, 305p. 1985. pap. 20.50 (ISBN 0-387-15202-4). Springer-Verlag.
Time Series: Proceedings of the International Conference, Held at Nottingham University, March, 1979. Ed. by O. D. Anderson. 1980. 118.50 (ISBN 0-444-85418-5). Elsevier.
Time Series: Theory & Methods. P. Brockwell & R. A. Davis. (Springer Series in Statistics). (Illus.). 520p. 1986. 48.00 (ISBN 0-387-96406-1). Springer-Verlag.
Time Sharing. Automated Education Center Staff. 1969. 15.00 (ISBN 0-403-04482-0). Scholarly.
Time Sharing. Richard Krawiec. 192p. 1986. 14.95 (ISBN 0-670-80944-6). Viking.
Time Sharing. Richard Krawiec. 192p. 1987. pap. 5.95 (ISBN 0-14-008706-0). Penguin.
Time Sharing: A New Way of Life. Larry J. Tracy. LC 76-50231. 1977. 4.95 (ISBN 0-933984-01-4). Tracy Pub.
Time Sharing: Computer Programs & Applications in Accounting. Elbert B. Greynolds, Jr. (Research Monograph: No. 57). 1974. spiral bdg. 30.00 (ISBN 0-88406-021-7). Ga St U Busn Pub.
Time Sharing Computer Systems. Wilkes. (Computer Monograph Ser.: Vol. 5). 150p. 1975. 28.00 (ISBN 0-444-19525-4). Elsevier.
Time Sharing in the U. S. 400p. 1987. write for info. D & S Pub.
Time Sharing Task Control for a Hybrid Computer Simulation Laboratory. Andrew J. Dietzler. LC 75-128003. 172p. 1969. 19.00 (ISBN 0-403-04494-4). Scholarly.
Time Slave. John Norman. (Science Fiction Ser). 1986. pap. 2.50 (ISBN 0-87997-761-2). DAW Bks.
Time, Space, & Atoms. Richard T. Cox. LC 33-6773. pap. 42.50 (ISBN 0-317-29503-9, 2055962). Bks Demand UMI.
Time: Space & Designs for Actors. Maxine Klein. 1975. pap. text ed. 30.36 (ISBN 0-395-18612-9). HM.

Time, Space & Knowledge: A New Vision of Reality. Tarthang Tulku. LC 77-19224. (Illus.). 1977. 22.95 (ISBN 0-913546-08-9); pap. 14.95 (ISBN 0-913546-09-7). Dharma Pub.

Time, Space & Life: The Probabilistic Pathways of Evolution. V. V. Nalimov. Ed. by Robert G. Colodny. (Illus.). 100p. 1985. 29.95 (ISBN 0-89495-048-7). ISI Pr.

Time, Space & Man: Essays on Microdemography. Ed. by Jan Sundin & Erik Soderland. 259p. (Orig.). 1977. pap. 22.50x (ISBN 91-22-00195-6, Pub. by Almqvist & Wiksell). Coronet Bks.

Time, Space & Mind. Irving Oyle. LC 76-11339. 128p. (Orig.). 1976. pap. 5.95 (ISBN 0-89087-122-1). Celestial Arts.

Time, Space & Pattern in Embryonic Development. William R. Jeffery & Rudolf A. Raff. LC 83-5393. (MBL Lectures in Biology: Vol. 2). 408p. 1983. 64.00 (ISBN 0-8451-2201-0). A R Liss.

Time, Space, & Structure in King Lear. Mathilda M. Millis. Ed. by JAmes Hogg. (Jacobean Drama Studies). 209p. (Orig.). 1976. pap. 15.00 (ISBN 3-7052-0356-8, Salzburg Studies). Longwood Pub Group.

Time, Space, & Transition in Anasazi Prehistory. Michael S. Berry. 112p. 1982. 20.00x (ISBN 0-87480-212-1). U of Utah Pr.

Time, Space, & Value: The Narrative Structure of the "New Arcadia". Arthur K. Amos, Jr. LC 74-30862. 203p. 1976. 20.00 (ISBN 0-8387-1614-8). Bucknell U Pr.

Time-Space Transcendence. Paul Philips. LC 84-71711. 72p. (Orig.). 1984. pap. 8.95 (ISBN 0-930149-00-9). AAP Calif.

Time Span. Ed. by Verne Powers. (Collection of 5 one-act plays: The Ultimate Weapon; Much Ado About John's Other Wife; Doctor Nostradamus; Last Directions; and The Undaunted River). (gr. k-12). 1966. pap. 3.50x (ISBN 0-88020-075-8). Coach Hse.

Time-Spirit of Matthew Arnold. R. H. Super. LC 71-107980. 1970. 6.95 (ISBN 0-472-89400-5). U of Mich Pr.

Time Steps. Charlotte V. Allen. LC 85-48138. 384p. 1986. 19.95 (ISBN 0-689-11773-6). Atheneum.

Time Stream. John Taine, pseud. Ed. by Lester Del Rey. LC 75-437. (Library of Science Fiction). 1975. lib. bdg. 21.00 (ISBN 0-8240-1439-1). Garland Pub.

Time Studies As a Basis for Rate Setting. Dwight V. Merrick. (Management History Ser.: No. 84). (Illus.). xviii, 366p. 1980. Repr. of 1919 ed. lib. bdg. 25.00 (ISBN 0-87960-100-0). Hive Pub.

Time Study Manual for the Textile Industry. 2nd ed. Norbert L. Enrick. LC 81-17159. 256p. 1982. lib. bdg. 25.50 (ISBN 0-89874-044-4). Krieger.

Time: Sweet Bandit. David A. Wilson. 40p. (Orig.). 1974. pap. 2.00 (ISBN 0-934852-12-X). Lorien Hse.

Time Table. James M. Bryant. pap. 20.00 (ISBN 0-318-18292-0). Rocket Pub Co.

Time Table. (Illus.). 1985. 20.00 (ISBN 0-318-04696-2). J M Bryant.

Time, Talents, Things: A Woman's Workshop on Christian Stewardship. Latayne C. Scott. (Woman's Workshop Ser.). 96p. (Orig.). 1987. pap. 4.50 (ISBN 0-310-38771-X, 10455P). Zondervan.

Time-Temperature Indicators. Ed. by Peter Allen. 200p. 1988. 1750.00 (ISBN 0-941285-17-0). FIND-SVP.

Time That Was: Irish Moments. Jill Freedman. LC 87-361. (Illus.). 128p. 1987. 24.95 (ISBN 0-914919-09-1). Friendly Pr NY.

Time, the Familiar Stranger. J. T. Fraser. LC 87-10865. (Illus.). 408p. 1987. 24.95 (ISBN 0-87023-576-1). U of Mass Pr.

Time, the Hour, the Solitariness of the Place. Louis Phillips. LC 85-62684. 88p. (Orig.). 1985. 13.95 (ISBN 0-930501-05-5); pap. 8.95 (ISBN 0-930501-02-0). Swallows Tale Pr.

Time: The Irretrievable Asset. Richard C. Anderson & L. R. Dobyns. LC 73-12755. (Illus.). 75p. 7.95 (ISBN 0-913842-05-2). Correlan Pubns.

Time, the Physical Magnitude. Olivier Costa de Beauregard. 1987. lib. bdg. 79.00 (ISBN 90-277-2444-X, Pub. by Reidel Holland). Kluwer Academic.

Time, Tide & Tempest: A Study of Shakespeare's Romances. Douglas L. Peterson. LC 72-94155. 280p. 1973. 29.95 (ISBN 0-87328-058-X). Huntington Lib.

Time To... Illus. by Tony Tallarico. (Tiny Bks.). (Illus.). 28p. (ps-1). 1984. bds. 3.50 (ISBN 0-89828-050-8). Tuffy Bks.

Time to Act. Archibald MacLeish. LC 71-117820. (Essay Index Reprint Ser). 1943. 18.00 (ISBN 0-8369-1713-8). Ayer Co Pubs.

Time to Be Born. Dawn Powell. LC 83-45842. Repr. of 1942 ed. 30.00 (ISBN 0-404-20206-3, PS3531). AMS Pr.

Time to Be Born, a Time to Die. Rasa Gustaitis & Ernle Young. LC 85-26804. 1986p. 1986. write for info. (ISBN 0-201-11555-7). Addison-Wesley.

Time to Be Born, A Time to Die. Robert L. Short. pap. 6.95i (ISBN 0-06-067677-9, RD 52, HarpR). Har-Row.

Time to Be Born, a Time to Die. pap. 3.50 (ISBN 0-686-96060-2); discussion Leader's guide 2.00 (ISBN 0-686-99692-5). United Syn Bk.

Time to Be Free, Vol. I. Ed. by Shirley Mikkelson. (Illus.). 164p. (Orig.). 1988. pap. 16.95 (ISBN 0-943536-35-9). Quill Bks.

Time to Be Free, Vol. II. Ed. by Shirley Mikkelson. (Illus.). 168p. (Orig.). 1988. pap. 16.95 (ISBN 0-943536-36-7). Quill Bks.

Time to Be Free, Vol. III. Ed. by Shirley Mikkelson. (Illus.). 168p. (Orig.). 1989. pap. 16.95 (ISBN 0-943536-37-5). Quill Bks.

Time to Be Free, Vol. IV. Ed. by Shirley Mikkelson. (Illus.). 168p. (Orig.). 1989. pap. 16.95 (ISBN 0-943536-38-3). Quill Bks.

Time to Be Free, Vol. V. Ed. by Shirley Mikkelson. (Illus.). 168p. (Orig.). 1989. pap. 16.95 (ISBN 0-943536-39-1). Quill Bks.

Time to Be Free, Vol. VI. Ed. by Shirley Mikkelson. (Illus.). 168p. (Orig.). 1989. pap. 16.95 (ISBN 0-943536-40-5). Quill Bks.

Time to Be Free, Vol. VII. Ed. by Shirley Mikkelson. (Illus.). 168p. (Orig.). 1989. pap. 16.95. Quill Bks.

Time to Be Re-Born. William Maestri. LC 82-24336. 147p. (Orig.). 1983. pap. 5.95 (ISBN 0-8189-0447-X). Alba.

Time to Be Renewed. Warren W. Wiersbe. Ed. by James Adair. 400p. 1986. pap. 12.95 (ISBN 0-89693-391-1). Victor Bks.

Time to Be Rich. Lacy Hunt. LC 86-42936. 1987. 19.95 (ISBN 0-89256-325-7). Rawson Assocs.

Time to Be Young. Martin Yoseloff. 4.50 (ISBN 0-8453-6445-6, Cornwall Bks). Assoc Univ Prs.

Time to Begin. Valentine Dmitriev. 248p. (Orig.). 1983. pap. 20.00 (ISBN 0-911163-01-8). Caring.

Time to Build Joseph Breuer. 1982. Vol. 2. 8.95 (ISBN 0-686-76270-3). Feldheim.

Time to Caré. Secretariat for Futures Studies, Stockholm, Sweden. LC 83-8331. (Illus.). 296p. 1984. text ed. 53.00 (ISBN 0-08-028929-0). Pergamon.

Time to Celebrate: Holiday & Seasonal Messages. Maralene Wesner & Miles Wesner. 75p. 1988. pap. 5.95 (ISBN 0-936715-10-3). Diversity Okla.

Time to Change & Other Stories. Mack Jameson & Al Nist. Ed. by Winifred H. Roderman. (Read on! Write on! Ser.). (Illus.). (gr. 7-12). 1981. pap. text ed. 3.95 (ISBN 0-915510-56-1). Janus Bks.

Time to Choose. Janine Boissard. Tr. by Mary Feeney. 196p. 1985. 15.95 (ISBN 0-316-10102-8). Little.

Time to Choose. Janine Boissard. 1986. pap. 2.50 (ISBN 0-449-70160-3, Juniper). Fawcett.

Time to Dance. Karen S. Dean. 208p. (Orig.). (gr. 7 up). 1985. pap. 2.25 (ISBN 0-590-33199-X, Point). Scholastic Inc.

Time to Dance & Other Stories. Bernard MacLaverty. 164p. 1985. pap. 5.95 (ISBN 0-8076-1135-2). Braziller.

Time to Dance, No Time to Weep: A Memoir. Rumer Godden. (Illus.). 240p. 1987. 16.95 (ISBN 0-688-07421-9, Pub. by Beech Tree Bks). Morrow.

Time to Dance: Symbolic Movement in Worship. Taylor. (Illus.). 192p. 1980. 5.95 (ISBN 0-318-16447-7). Sacred Dance Guild.

Time to Dance: Symbolic Movement in Worship. Margaret F. Taylor. Ed. by Doug Adams. 192p. 1980. 5.95 (ISBN 0-941500-17-9). Sharing Co.

Time to Dance: Twelve Practical Dances for the Non-Dance Specialist in Education, Church & Community. Martin H. Blogg. (Illus.). 72p. 1986. pap. 11.95 (ISBN 0-00-599777-1, Collins Liturgical). HarpR.

Time to Destroy-To Discover. Lawrence Fixel. 1972. regular ed 4.00 (ISBN 0-915572-09-5); ltd. signed, numbered ed 10.00 (ISBN 0-915572-58-3). Panjandrum.

Time to Die. Glenn M. Vernon. 1977. 10.00 (ISBN 0-8191-0126-5). U Pr of Amer.

Time to Die. Tom Wicker. LC 74-77947. 256p. 1975. write for info. (ISBN 0-8129-0487-7). Times Bks.

Time to Fantasize. May K. Davenport. LC 80-69294. (Illus.). 130p. (Orig.). (gr. 5-12). 1980. pap. 3.50x (ISBN 0-9603118-7-4). Davenport.

Time to Favor Zion: The Ecology of Religion & School Development on the Urban Frontier, Cincinnati, 1830-1870. F. Michael Perko. (Illus.). 276p. (Orig.). 1987. lib. bdg. 29.95; pap. 11.95 (ISBN 0-934328-05-6). Educ Studies Pr.

Time to Fly: The Memoirs of Sir Alan Cobham. Alan J. Cobham. Ed. by Christopher Derrick. LC 87-60971. (Illus.). 214p. 1987. (Pub. by Shepheard-Walwyn UK); pap. 14.95 (ISBN 0-85683-088-7, Pub. by Shepheard-Walwyn Uk). Dufour.

Time to Gather: Selected Poems. Catherine De Vinck. LC 67-28572. (Illus.). 72p. 1987. pap. 6.75 (ISBN 0-911726-02-0). Alleluia Pr.

Time to Get out of the Bath, Shirley. John Burningham. LC 76-58503. (Illus.). (gr. k-2). 1978. 13.70i (ISBN 0-690-01378-7, Crowell Jr Bks); PLB 13.89 (ISBN 0-690-01379-5). HarpJ.

Time to Go. Stephen Dixon. LC 83-22624. 192p. 1984. 16.50 (ISBN 0-8018-3234-9). Johns Hopkins.

Time to Grieve: Loss a Universal Human Experience. Bertha G. Simos. LC 75-27964. 1979. pap. 14.95 (ISBN 0-87304-153-4). Family Serv.

Time to Grow. Joanne Putnam. Ed. by Mary Wallace. LC 85-20190. (Illus.). 112p. (Orig.). 1985. pap. 4.95 (ISBN 0-912315-92-X). Word Aflame.

Time to Heal. William Goldfarb et al. LC 69-17281. 148p. 1969. text ed. 20.00x (ISBN 0-8236-6550-X). Intl Univs Pr.

Time to Heal: The Road to Recovery for Adult Children of Alcoholics. Timmen L. Cermak. 240p. 1988. 16.95 (ISBN 0-87477-454-3). J P Tarcher.

Time to Hear & Answer: Essays for the Bicentennial Season. Robert Penn Warren et al. Ed. by Taylor Littleton. LC 75-31774. (Franklin Lectures in the Sciences & Humanities Ser.: No.4). 230p. 1977. 12.95 (ISBN 0-8173-6644-X). U of Ala Pr.

Time to Keep: A History of the Christian Reformed Church. Herbert Brinks & A. James Heynen. text ed. cancelled (ISBN 0-933140-44-4); cancelled leader's guide (ISBN 0-933140-45-2). CRC Pubns.

Time to Keep & Other Stories. George M. Brown. 306p. 19.50 (ISBN 0-317-57823-5). Vanguard.

Time to Keep Silence, & Other Stores. Grace Pursglove. 1986. 40.00x (ISBN 0-86332-023-6, Pub. by Book Guild Ltd). State Mutual Bk.

Time to Keep: The Tasha Tudor Book of Holidays. Tasha Tudor. LC 77-9067. (Illus.). (gr. 4-8). 1977. 9.95 (ISBN 0-528-82019-2, Checkerboard Pr). Macmillan.

Time to Kill. M. T. Dykes. LC 82-6811. 1988. pap. 11.95 (ISBN 0-87949-223-6). Ashley Bks.

Time to Kill. Miriam Lynch. (Mystery Puzzler Ser.: No. 15). (Illus., Orig.). 1979. pap. 1.95 (ISBN 0-89083-435-0). Zebra.

Time to Laugh. Don Boys. 1980. pap. 7.50x (ISBN 0-686-40716-4). Freedom Univ-FSP.

Time to Laugh. Win Richardson. 40p. 1986. 6.50 (ISBN 0-8233-0417-5). Golden Quill.

Time to Laugh, A Time to Cry. Roy N. Tucker. 1987. 9.95 (ISBN 0-8062-3048-7). Carlton.

Time to Laugh: Funny Stories for Children. Ed. by Sara Corrin & Stephen Corrin. (Illus.). 208p. (gr. 2-4). 1985. pap. 4.95 (ISBN 0-571-13416-5). Faber & Faber.

Time to Listen: Preventing Youth Suicide. Patricia Hermes. (YA) (gr. 10 up). 1987. 12.95 (ISBN 0-15-288196-4, HJ). HarBraceJ.

Time to Live. David A. Loiry & Carol J. Loiry. LC 82-155. 1982. 12.95 (ISBN 0-9607654-2-5); pap. 7.95 (ISBN 0-9607654-0-9). Loiry Pubs Hse.

Time to Live: Graduation & Youth Messages. Maralene Wesner & Miles Wesner. 75p. 1988. pap. 5.95 (ISBN 0-936715-12-X). Diversity Okla.

Time to Love. Beryl Kingston. 480p. 1988. 19.95 (ISBN 0-312-02299-9). St Martin.

Time to Love. Helen McCullough. 272p. (Orig.). 1987. pap. 3.95 (ISBN 0-7701-0560-2). Paperjacks US.

Time to Love. Helen S. Rice. (Illus.). 128p. 1986. 13.95 (ISBN 0-8007-1496-2). Revell.

Time to Mourn. Jack Spiro. LC 67-30744. 160p. 1985. pap. text ed. 8.95 (ISBN 0-8197-0497-0). Bloch.

Time to Mourn: Expressions of Grief in Nineteenth Century America. Martha V. Pike & Janice G. Armstrong. LC 80-15105. (Illus.). 192p. (Orig.). 1980. pap. 14.95 (ISBN 0-943924-03-0, Dist. by University of Washington Press). Mus Stony Brook.

Time to Mourn: Expressions of Grief in Nineteenth Century America. Martha V. Pike & Janice G. Armstrong. LC 80-15105. (Illus.). 192p. 1980. pap. 14.95 (ISBN 0-295-96325-5, Pub. by Museums at Stony Brook). U of Wash Pr.

Time to Mourn: Judaism & Psychology of Bereavement. rev. ed. 1985. pap. 8.95x. Bloch.

Time to Mourn: Judaism & the Psychology of Bereavement. Jack D. Spiro. 1968. 8.95 (ISBN 0-8197-0185-8). Bloch.

Time to Mourn: Recovering from the Death of a Loved One. Ron DelBene et al. 24p. 1988. pap. 2.95 (ISBN 0-8358-0577-8). Upper Room.

Time to Murder & Create: The Contemporary Novel in Crisis. John W. Aldridge. LC 79-39113. (Essay Index Reprint Ser.). Repr. of 1966 ed. 26.50 (ISBN 0-8369-2682-X). Ayer Co Pubs.

Time to Pray. Rose Goldstein. LC 72-91792. 10.00 (ISBN 0-87677-141-X). Hartmore.

Time to Reap: An Emil Whippletree Mystery. Michael T. Hinkemeyer. 240p. 1984. 12.95 (ISBN 0-312-80529-2). St Martin.

Time to Reap: The Middle Age of Women in Five Israeli Subcultures. Nancy Datan et al. LC 80-26776. 208p. 1981. text ed. 22.50x (ISBN 0-8018-2516-4). Johns Hopkins.

Time to Remember. Stanley Shapiro. LC 85-30061. 224p. 1986. 16.95 (ISBN 0-394-55031-5). Random.

Time to Remember. Stanley Shapiro. 1988. pap. 3.95 (ISBN 0-451-15484-3, Sig). NAL.

Time to Remember. Maude F. Zimmer. 8.95 (ISBN 0-8315-0005-0). Speller.

Time to Remember: The Autobiography of a Chemist. Alexander Todd. LC 83-5172. 257p. 1984. 34.50 (ISBN 0-521-25593-7). Cambridge U Pr.

Time to Rend: An Essay on the Decision for American Independence. John M. Head. LC 68-63548. 1968. 7.50 (ISBN 0-87020-042-9). State Hist Soc Wis.

Time to Rhyme with Calico Cat. Donald Charles. LC 77-20994. (Calico Cat Story Bks.). (Illus.). 32p. (ps-3). 1978. PLB 11.93 (ISBN 0-516-03629-7); pap. 2.95 (ISBN 0-516-43629-5). Childrens.

Time to Spare. Lorraine H. Bailey. (Gregg-McGraw-Hill Series for Independent Living). 1978. pap. 12.00 (ISBN 0-07-003223-8). McGraw.

Time to Speak. Chinghiz Aitmatov. (Illus.). 264p. (Orig.). 1988. pap. 7.95 (ISBN 0-7178-0669-3). Intl Pubs Co.

Time to Speak: A Brief History of the Afro-Americans of Bloomington, Indiana 1865 - 1965. Frances V. Gilliam. LC 85-51626. xiii, 162p. 1985. 15.95 (ISBN 0-9615771-0-X). Pinus.

Time to Speak: A Psycholinguistic Examination of the Critical Period for Language Acquisition. Thomas Scovel. 220p. 1988. pap. text ed. 18.95 (ISBN 0-06-632532-3). Newbury Hse.

Time to Speak: The Autobiography of the Reverend Jesse Jackson. Jesse Jackson. 304p. 1988. 17.95 (ISBN 0-317-64227-8). S&S.

Time to Speak: The Evangelical-Jewish Encounter. Ed. by A. James Rudin & Marvin R. Wilson. 240p. (Orig.). 1987. pap. 11.95 (ISBN 0-8028-0281-8). Eerdmans.

Time to Stand. Walter Lord. LC 78-8708. (Illus.). 271p. 1978. pap. 5.95 (ISBN 0-8032-7902-7, BB 678, Bison). U of Nebr Pr.

Time to Stop & Think, Vol. 1. Michael Wharton. 1981. 12.00x (ISBN 0-7223-1422-1, Pub. by A H Stockwell England). State Mutual Bk.

Time to Tell. David Hacohen. Tr. by Menachem Dagut. LC 84-45243. 256p. 1985. 18.50 (ISBN 0-8453-4789-6, Cornwall Bks). Assoc Univ Prs.

Time to Think: A Cognitive Model of Delinquency, Prevention & Offender Rehabilitation. Robert R. Ross & Elizabeth A. Fabiano. LC 85-80842. 394p. 1985. pap. text ed. 24.95x (ISBN 0-915165-06-6). Inst Soc Sci.

Time to Watch: The Wrist Watch as Art, Classic, Rare, Extraordinary. Jac Zagoory & Hilda Chan. (Illus.). 200p. 1985. text ed. 88.00 (ISBN 9-622-61001-3). Chiuzac Ltd.

Time to Weep & a Time to Sing. Ed. by Mary J. Meadow & Carole A. Rayburn. 168p. 1985. pap. 8.95 (ISBN 0-86683-791-4, 8532, HarpR). Har-Row.

Time to Weep: Funeral & Grief Messages. Maralene Wesner & Miles Wesner. 75p. 1988. pap. 5.95 (ISBN 0-936715-11-1). Diversity Okla.

Time to Write: How William Sidney Porter Became O. Henry. Trueman E. O'Quinn & Jenny L. Porter. 256p. 1986. 14.95 (ISBN 0-89015-547-X). Eakin Pr.

Time Together. Sherrill Flora. (Early Childhood Ser.). 47p. (ps). 1986. stitched 5.95 (ISBN 0-513-01850-6). Denison.

Time Traders. Andre Norton. 224p. 1987. pap. 2.95 (ISBN 0-441-81255-4, Pub. by Ace Science Fiction). Ace Bks.

Time Train to Rome. G. Waters. (Puzzle Adventures Ser.). (Illus.). 48p. (gr. 3-5). 1988. PLB write for info. (ISBN 0-88110-302-0); pap. 3.95 (ISBN 0-7460-0153-3). EDC.

Time Trap. Peter H. Barnett. LC 79-57447. (Illus.). 50p. 1980. pap. 5.00 (ISBN 0-686-65258-4). Assembling Pr.

Time Trap. Jean Favors. (Micro Adventure Ser.: No. 4). 128p. (Orig.). (gr. 4-7). 1984. pap. 1.95 (ISBN 0-590-33168-X). Scholastic Inc.

Time Trap. Nicholas Fisk. 1976. 12.95 (ISBN 0-575-02195-0, Pub. by Gollancz England). David & Charles.

Time Trap. Keith Laumer. 1987. pap. 2.95 (ISBN 0-671-65340-7). Baen Bks.

Time Trap. R. Alec Mackenzie. LC 72-82874. 208p. 1972. 11.95 (ISBN 0-8144-5308-2). AMACOM.

Time Trap. R. Alec Mackenzie. LC 72-82874. (Illus.). 208p. 1975. pap. text ed. 4.95 (ISBN 0-07-044650-4). McGraw.

Time Trap of Ming. Alex Raymond. (Flash Gordon Ser). 1976. Repr. of 1974 ed. lib. bdg. 7.95 (ISBN 0-89190-111-6, Pub. by River City Pr). Amereon Ltd.

Time Travel & Other Mathematical Bewilderments. M. Gardner. 320p. 1987. 17.95 (ISBN 0-7167-1924-X); pap. 12.95 (ISBN 0-7167-1925-8). W H Freeman.

Time Travel & Papa Joe's Pipe: Essays on the Human Side of Science. Alan Lightman. 176p. 1986. pap. 5.95 (ISBN 0-14-009212-9). Penguin.

Time Travel in the Malay Crescent. Wayne Stier. (Illus.). 320p. (Orig.). 1985. pap. 10.00 (ISBN 0-911447-02-4). Meru Pub.

Time Traveler. Joyce Carol Oates. 36p. 1987. deluxe, signed ed. 50.00 (ISBN 0-935716-44-0). Lord John.

Time Traveler. Byron Preiss. (First Settlers Ser.: No. 3). 80p. 1987. pap. 2.50 (ISBN 0-553-15483-4, Skylark). Bantam.

Time Travelers: A Science Fiction Quartet. Ed. by Robert Silverberg & Martin H. Greenberg. LC 84-73521. 304p. 1985. 16.95 (ISBN 0-917657-34-9). D I Fine.

Time Travelers Strictly Cash. Spider Robinson. 100p. 1987. pap. 2.95 (ISBN 0-425-09722-6). Berkley Pub.

Time Travellers: A Science Fiction Quartet. Ed. by Robert Silverberg & Martin H. Greenberg. LC 84-73521. 284p. 1986. pap. 3.95 (ISBN 0-917657-66-7, Pub. by Primus). D I Fine.

Time Trilogy: A Wrinkle in Time; A Wind in the Door; A Swiftly Tilting Planet, 3 vols. Madeleine L'Engle. 710p. (gr. 5 up). 1979. Boxed Set. 38.85 (ISBN 0-374-37592-5). FS&G.

Time Trip. Lee Mountain. (Attention Span Ser). (Illus.). 48p. (Orig., Reading level gr. 2-3, Interest level gr. 6-9). 1978. pap. text ed. 4.80x (ISBN 0-89061-145-9, 581). Jamestown Pubs.

Time Twister. H. M. Major. (Alien Trace Ser.: No. 2). 1984. pap. 2.95 (ISBN 0-451-13283-1, Sig). NAL.
Time under Control: Efficient Self Management in & out of the Office. Ivan Fitzwater. LC 87-72603. 177p. 1988. pap. 9.00 (ISBN 0-931722-63-2). Corona Pub.
Time Unguarded. Edmund Ironside. Ed. by Roderick Macleod & Denis Kelly. LC 74-64. (Illus.). 434p. 1974. Repr. of 1963 ed. lib. bdg. 35.00x (ISBN 0-8371-7369-8, IRTG). Greenwood.
Time Use Data & the Living Standards Measurement Study. Meena Acharya. (LSMS Working Paper: No. 18). 86p. 1985. 5.00 (ISBN 0-317-59169-X, BK 0094). World Bank.
Time Value of Money. 35.00 (ISBN 0-317-29641-8, #CO3263, Law & Business). HarBraceJ.
Time Value of Money: New Regulations on Imputed Interest & OID (Original Issue Discount) 24p. 1987. pap. 20.00 (TX-49011). Cal Cont Ed Bar.
Time Value of Money Rules under the 1984 Tax Act. Mortimer M. Caplin. LC 85-136473. Date not set. 35.00. HarBraceJ.
Time Value of Money: Worked & Solved Problems. Gary E. Clayton & Christopher B. Spivey. LC 77-11332. (Illus.). 160p. 1978. pap. text ed. 13.95x (ISBN 0-7216-2602-5). Dryden Pr.
Time-Variant Discrete-Time Systems. G. Ludyk. (Advances in Control Systems & Signal Processing Ser.: Vol. 3). (Illus.). 127p. 1981. pap. 23.00 (ISBN 3-528-08496-0, Pub. by Vieweg & Sohn). IPS.
Time-Varying Image Processing & Moving Object Recognition: Proceedings of the International Workshop, Florence, Italy, 8-9 Sept. 1986. Ed. by V. Cappellini. 280p. 1987. 73.25 (ISBN 0-444-70238-5). Elsevier.
Time, Wait. Hannah Kahn. LC 83-12565. (University of Central Florida Contemporary Poetry Ser.). 76p. 1984. 8.95 (ISBN 0-8130-0775-5). U Presses Fla.
Time Wanderers. Strugatsky & Strugatsky. 1988. pap. 2.95 (ISBN 0-312-91020-7). St Martin.
Time Wanderers. Arkady Strugatsky & Boris Strugatsky. Tr. by Antonina W. Bouis. 1987. 16.95 (ISBN 0-931933-31-5). Richardson & Steirman.
Time Warp & a Time to Speak. C. D. Ingram. 1985. 7.95 (ISBN 0-533-06503-8). Vantage.
Time Warps. Isaac Asimov et al. LC 83-22888. (Science Fiction Shorts Ser.). (Illus.). 48p. (gr. 4-12). 1984. PLB 15.99 (ISBN 0-8172-1742-8). Raintree Pubs.
Time Warps, String Edits & Macromolecules: The Theory & Practice of Sequence Comparison. David Sankoff & Joseph P. Kruskal. LC 83-11874. (Illus.). 400p. 1983. write for info. (ISBN 0-201-07809-0). Addison-Wesley.
Time Wars. Poul Anderson. 384p. (Orig.). 1986. pap. 3.50 (ISBN 0-8125-3048-9, Dist. by Warner Pub Services & St. Martin's Press). Tor Bks.
Time Wars No. 7: The Argonaut Affair. Simon Hawke. 208p. 1987. pap. 2.95 (ISBN 0-441-02911-6, Pub. by Ace Science Fiction). Ace Bks.
Time Wars, No. 8: The Dracula Caper. Simon Hawke. 1988. pap. 3.50 (ISBN 0-441-16616-4). Ace Bks.
Time Wars: The Primary Conflict in Human History. Jeremy Rifkin. LC 86-25845. 1987. 18.95 (ISBN 0-8050-0377-0). H Holt & Co.
Time Wars: The Primary Conflict in Human History. Jeremy Rifkin. 1989. 7.95 (ISBN 0-671-67158-8, Touchstone Bks). S&S.
Time Was Right: A History of the Buffalo & Erie County Public Library, 1940-1975. Joseph B. Rounds. Ed. by Michael C. Mahaney. (Illus.). x, 172p. 1986. 11.95 (ISBN 0-9615896-0-4). Grosvenor Soc.
Time Was: Rossetti, Oscar Wilde, Ellen Terry. W. Graham Robertson. 1931. Repr. 30.00 (ISBN 0-8274-3628-9). R West.
Time, Water & Development. Henry D. Molumphy. (Illus.). 16p. 1986. 1.00 (ISBN 0-918397-02-2). Foster Parents.
Time Well Spent: Special Edition for Teachers. Toben L. Tobin. 248p. 1985. 12.95 (ISBN 0-935107-05-3). Jade Mist Pr.
Time Will Darken It. William Maxwell. LC 82-81311. 320p. 1983. pap. 10.95 (ISBN 0-87923-448-2, Nonpareil Bks). Godine.
Time Will Run Back: A Novel about the Rediscovery of Capitalism. Henry Hazlitt. LC 86-11175. Orig. Title: Great Idea. 384p. 1986. pap. text ed. 18.50 (ISBN 0-8191-5470-9). U Pr of Amer.
Time Winds: Poems of Uganda. Alfred Kisubi. LC 87-70809. 80p. (Orig.). 1988. pap. 9.95 (ISBN 0-933532-63-6). BKMK.
Time with Children. Elizabeth Tallent. LC 87-45100. 160p. 1987. 15.95 (ISBN 0-394-55783-2). Knopf.
Time with Children. Elizabeth Tallent. 176p. 1988. pap. 7.95 (ISBN 0-02-045540-2, Collier). Macmillan.
Time with God: Devotional Readings for Youth. Evelyn C. Foote. LC 72-97604. 1978. pap. 2.95 (ISBN 0-8054-5164-1, 4251-64). Broadman.
Time with God: How to Improve Your Daily Devotions. Graham Claydon. 48p. (Orig.). 1982. mass market 1.95 (ISBN 0-310-45202-3). Zondervan.
Time Without Bells. Horst Bienek. LC 87-17124. 352p. 1988. 19.95 (ISBN 0-689-11930-5). Atheneum.
Time Without Work: People Who Are Not Working Tell Their Stories, How They Feel, What They Do, How They Survive. Walli F. Leff & Marilyn G. Haft. LC 83-61477. 426p. 1983. 20.00 (ISBN 0-89608-186-9); pap. 9.00 (ISBN 0-89608-185-0). South End Pr.
Time, Work, & Culture in the Middle Ages. Jacques Le Goff. Tr. by Arthur Goldhammer. LC 79-25400. xvi, 384p. 1982. pap. 13.95 (ISBN 0-226-47081-4). U of Chicago Pr.
Time, Work, & Culture in the Middle Ages. Jacques Le Goff. Tr. by Arthur Goldhammer. LC 79-25400. 1980. lib. bdg. 30.00x (ISBN 0-226-47080-6). U of Chicago Pr.
Timebends: A Life. Arthur Miller. (Illus.). 640p. 1987. 25.00 (ISBN 0-8021-0015-5). Grove.
Timebends: A Life. Arthur Miller. 1988. pap. 10.95 (ISBN 0-06-097178-9). Har-Row.
Timechanges. Geoffrey Trease. (Illus.). 96p. (gr. 4-12). 1986. lib. bdg. 12.90 (ISBN 0-531-09230-5, Warwick Pr). Watts.
Timed Readings. Edward Spargo et al. (Illus., Orig.). 1979. Bk. 1, gr. 4 120p. pap. text ed. 4.00 (ISBN 0-89061-198-X, 801); Bk. 2, gr. 5 120p. pap. text ed. 4.00 (ISBN 0-89061-199-8, 802). Jamestown Pubs.
Timed Readings. Ed. by Edward Spargo et al. Incl. Book Three. (gr. 6) (ISBN 0-89061-031-2, 803); Book Four. (gr. 7) (ISBN 0-89061-032-0, 804); Book Five. (gr. 8) (ISBN 0-89061-033-9, 805); Book Six. (gr. 9) (ISBN 0-89061-034-7, 806); Book Seven. (gr. 10) (ISBN 0-89061-035-5, 807); Book Eight. (gr. 11) (ISBN 0-89061-036-3, 808); Book Nine. (gr. 12) (ISBN 0-89061-037-1, 809); Book Ten (College Level (ISBN 0-89061-038-X, 810). (Illus.). 120p. (gr. 4 up). 1975. pap. text ed. 4.80x ea.; Set. (ISBN 0-89061-099-1). Jamestown Pubs.
Timefall. Kahn. 1988. pap. 3.95 (ISBN 0-312-90878-4). St Martin.
Timefall. James Kahn. 320p. 1987. 16.95 (ISBN 0-312-00195-9). St Martin.
Timejumper. William Greenleaf. 1981. pap. 1.95 (ISBN 0-8439-0867-X, Leisure Bks). Leisure NY.
Timekeeper. (Career Examination Ser.: C-3485). Date not set. pap. 12.00 (ISBN 0-8373-3485-3). Natl Learning.
Timekeeper Conspiracy, No. 2. Time Wars Staff. 1987. pap. 2.95 (ISBN 0-317-63369-4, Pub. by Ace Science Fiction). Ace Bks.
Timelapse. Rochelle H. DuBois. LC 83-9883. (Contemporary Poetry Ser.: No. 1). 80p. (Orig.). 1983. pap. 6.50 (ISBN 0-938136-08-9). Lunchroom Pr.
Timelapse. David F. Nighbert. 320p. 1988. 17.95 (ISBN 0-312-01835-5). St Martin.
Timeless Affair: The Life of Anita McCormick Blaine. Gilbert A. Harrison. LC 79-15264. 1979. 15.00x (ISBN 0-226-31804-4). U of Chicago Pr.
Timeless Children's Tales from Around the World. Ed. by J. Clauss. (Illus.). (gr. 5-6). 1976. lib. bdg. 18.95x (ISBN 0-88411-992-0, Pub. by Aeonian Pr). Amereon Ltd.
Timeless Christian. Erik Von Kuehnelt-Leddihn. LC 73-10604. 241p. 1976. 4.50 (ISBN 0-8199-0416-3). Franciscan Herald.
Timeless Documents of the Soul. Helmuth Jacobsohn. LC 68-15329. (Studies in Jungian Thought). pap. 68.80 (ISBN 0-317-08260-4, 2010268). Bks Demand UMI.
Timeless Earth. P. Kolosimo. Ed. by Paul Stevenson. (Illus.). 270p. 1974. 7.95 (ISBN 0-8216-0209-8, Pub. by Univ Bks). Lyle Stuart.
Timeless Fashions. Ed. by Pam Aulson. (Illus.). 72p. (Orig.). 1981. pap. 2.00 (ISBN 0-918178-25-8). Simplicity.
Timeless Judaism for Our Time. Michael Kaniel. 1985. pap. 2.95 (ISBN 0-87306-944-7). Feldheim.
Timeless Passion. Constance O. Flannery. 1986. pap. 3.95 (ISBN 0-8217-1837-1). Zebra.
Timeless Sources: Rare Books in the Collection of the Cooper-Hewitt Museum. Katherine Martinez & Nancy Aakre. LC 85-71452. (Cooper-Hewitt Museum Collection Handbook Ser.). (Illus.). 32p. (Orig.). 1985. pap. 3.95x (ISBN 0-910503-49-4). Cooper-Hewitt Museum.
Timeless Spring: A Soto Zen Anthology. Tr. by Thomas Cleary. LC 79-26677. 176p. 1980. pap. 7.95 (ISBN 0-8348-0148-5). Weatherhill.
Timeless Tennesseans. James A. Crutchfield. (Illus.). 200p. 1983. 19.95 (ISBN 0-87397-186-8). Strode.
Timeless Theme: A Critical Theory Formulated & Applied. Colin Still. LC 73-1310. 1936. lib. bdg. 42.50 (ISBN 0-8414-2615-5). Folcroft.
Timeless Towns: And Haunted Places. J. R. Humphreys. (Illus.). 288p. 1988. 22.95 (ISBN 0-312-02300-6). St Martin.
Timeless Treasures: San Diego's Victorian Heritage. Karen Johl. Ed. by Elizabeth Rand. LC 81-86088. (Illus.). 160p. 1982. pap. 14.95 (ISBN 0-914488-26-0). Rand-Tofua.
Timeless Trees: The U. S. National Bonsai Collection. Photos by Peter L. Bloomer. (Illus.). 109p. 1986. 44.95 (ISBN 0-318-22508-5). Horizons West.
Timeless Trinity. Roy Lanier, Sr. pap. 9.95 (ISBN 0-89137-551-1). Quality Pubns.
Timeless Truth for Twentieth Century Times. Fred M. Barlow. 123p. 1970. 3.25 (ISBN 0-87398-838-8). Sword of Lord.
Timeless Walks in San Francisco: A Historical Walking Guide to the City. 4th rev. ed. Michelle Brant. (Illus.). 90p. 1985. pap. 5.95 (ISBN 0-9611346-0-7). Brant.
Timeless Way of Building. Christopher Alexander. 1979. 39.95 (ISBN 0-19-502402-8). Oxford U Pr.
Timelessness of Poetry. Edmund K. Chambers. 1940. lib. bdg. 17.00 (ISBN 0-8414-3582-0). Folcroft.
Timeline: Ireland. Annabel Wagner. (Weighing up the Evidence Ser.). (Illus.). 64p. (YA) (gr. 7-9). 1988. 17.95 (ISBN 0-85219-716-0, Pub. by Batsford England). David & Charles.
Timeline: South Africa. Sarah Harris. (Weighing up the Evidence Ser.). (Illus.). 64p. (YA) (gr. 7-9). 1988. 17.95 (ISBN 0-85219-724-1, Pub. by Batsford England). David & Charles.
Timeline: Women & Power. Susan Mayfield. (Weighing up the Evidence Ser.). (Illus.). 64p. (YA) (gr. 7-9). 1989. 18.95 (ISBN 0-85219-768-3, Pub. by Batsford England). David & Charles.
TimeLords. Greg Porter. (Illus.). 124p. (Orig.). 1987. pap. 12.95 (ISBN 0-943891-00-0). Blacksburg Tactical.
Timely & Profitable Help for Troubled Americans. 2nd, rev. ed. Hans J. Schneider. LC 77-89938. 288p. 1977. softcover 8.95 (ISBN 0-930294-12-2). World Wide OR.
Timely & the Timeless: Jews, Judaism & Society in a Storm-Tossed Decade. Immanuel Jakobovits. 432p. 1977. 25.00x (ISBN 0-85303-189-4, Pub. by Vallentine Mitchell England). Biblio Dist.
Timely Articles on Slavery. facs. ed. Samuel Hopkins. LC 70-81121. (Black Heritage Library Collection Ser). 1854. 14.25 (ISBN 0-8369-8603-2). Ayer Co Pubs.
Timely Pearl-A 12th Century Tangut-Chinese Glossary: Vol.I, The Chinese Glosses. Luc Kwanten. LC 82-62332. (Indiana University Uralic & Altaic Ser.: Vol. 142). 265p. 1982. 15.00 (ISBN 0-933070-10-1). Ind U Res Inst.
Timely Reading: Between Exegesis & Interpretation. Susan Noakes. LC 87-47862. 288p. 1988. 29.95x (ISBN 0-8014-2144-6). Cornell U Pr.
Timely Tips on Quantity Food Buying. Alan K. Briscoe. 27p. 1974. pap. 1.95 (ISBN 0-88290-044-7). Horizon Utah.
Timely Voices. Ed. by Roslyn Arnold. 1983. 19.95x (ISBN 0-19-554363-7). Oxford U Pr.
Timepeace. Margherita Faulkner. (W.N.J. Ser.: No. 16). 1981. pap. 6.00 (ISBN 1-55780-065-0). Juniper Pr WI.
Timepiece. Jane Flanders. LC 87-25191. (Pitt Poetry Ser.). 72p. 1988. 16.95x (ISBN 0-8229-3573-2); pap. 8.95 (ISBN 0-8229-5399-4). U of Pittsburgh Pr.
Timequake. Robert C. Lee. LC 82-13567. 152p. (gr. 5-9). 1982. 9.95 (ISBN 0-664-32698-6). Westminster John Knox.
Timequest. Ray F. Nelson. 288p. 1985. pap. 2.95 (ISBN 0-8125-4650-4, Dist. by Warner Pub Services & St. Martin's Press). Tor Bks.
Timequest: Nemydia Deep, No. 3. William Tedford. (Timequest Ser.). 288p. pap. 2.75 (ISBN 0-8439-2292-3, Leisure Bks). Leisure NY.
Timequest: Rashanyn Dark, No. 1. William Tedford. (Time Quest Ser.). 288p. 1985. pap. 2.95 (ISBN 0-8439-2232-X, Leisure Bks). Leisure NY.
Times & Places see Corridors of Time: New Haven & London, 1927-1956.
Times & Places for Literature see Foreign Languages: Reading, Literature, Requirements.
Times & Places, Home & Away: A Life of Freelancing in the Outdoors. Charles F. Waterman. LC 87-82428. (Illus.). 256p. 1988. 25.00 (ISBN 0-9609842-8-3). GSJ Press.
Times & Seasons. Mary P. Lillie. (Poetry Ser.). (Illus.). 100p. (Orig.). 1986. pap. 9.95 (ISBN 0-942996-06-2). Post Apollo Pr.
Times & Tendencies. facs. ed. Agnes Repplier. LC 71-128297. (Essay Index Reprint Ser). 1931. 19.00 (ISBN 0-8369-2028-7). Ayer Co Pubs.
Times & Triumphs of American Woman. Ed. by Elaine Scott. (Illus.). 79p. (gr. 4-9). 1986. pap. text ed. 8.00 book only (ISBN 0-9610622-1-5). Natl Wmns Hall Fame.
Times Are Never So Bad. Andre Dubus. LC 82-48703. 192p. 1983. 14.95 (ISBN 0-87923-459-8). Godine.
Times Are Never So Bad. Andre Dubus. LC 82-48703. 192p. 1986. pap. 8.95 (ISBN 0-87923-641-8). Godine.
Time's Arrow - Time's Cycle: Myth & Metaphor in the Discovery of Geological Time. Stephen J. Gould. 240p. 1988. pap. 8.95 (ISBN 0-674-89199-6). Harvard U Pr.
Time's Arrow & Evolution. 3rd ed. Harold F. Blum. LC 68-31676. (Illus.). 1968. pap. 10.50x (ISBN 0-691-02354-9). Princeton U Pr.
Time's Arrow, Time's Cycle: Myth & Metaphor in the Discovery of Geological Time. Stephen J. Gould. LC 86-29485. 240p. 1987. 17.50 (ISBN 0-674-89198-8). Harvard U Pr.
Time's Arrows: Scientific Attitudes Toward Time in Western Culture. Richard Morris. 234p. 1985. 17.95 (ISBN 0-671-50158-5). S&S.
Time's Arrows: Scientific Attitudes toward Time. Richard Morris. 288p. 1986. pap. 8.95 (ISBN 0-671-61766-4, Touchstone). S&S.
Times Atlas of China. London Times. 1983. 20.95 (ISBN 0-7230-0118-9). Van Nos Reinhold.
Times Atlas of the World. 2nd, Rev. ed. 1983. 139.95 (ISBN 0-8129-1089-3). Times Bks.
Times Atlas of the World. 7th, rev. ed. LC 85-675126. (Illus.). 520p. 1985. 149.95 (ISBN 0-8129-1298-5). Times Bks.
Times Atlas of the World. 7th, comprehensive ed. (Illus.). 139.95 (ISBN 0-317-66587-1). Times Bks.
Times Atlas of World History. rev. ed. Ed. by Geoffrey Barraclough. LC 84-675088. 360p. 85.00 (ISBN 0-7230-0261-4). Hammond Inc.
Times, Beginnings & Causes. G. E. Anscombe. (Philosophical Lectures (Henriette Hertz Trust)). 1974. pap. 5.50 (ISBN 0-85672-105-0, Pub. by British Acad). Longwood Pub Group.
Times Between. Wyatt Prunty. LC 81-13724. (Poetry & Fiction Ser.). 80p. 1982. text ed. 12.00x (ISBN 0-8018-2403-6); pap. 7.95 (ISBN 0-8018-2407-9). Johns Hopkins.
Times Book of Jumbo Crosswords. Ed. by Edward Akenhead. 126p. (Orig.). 1987. pap. 5.95 (ISBN 0-7230-0267-3). Salem Hse Pubs.
Times Books World Weather Guide. E. A. Pearce & Gordon Smith. LC 84-40112. (Illus.). 480p. 1984. 22.50 (ISBN 0-8129-1123-7). Times Bks.
Times Concise Atlas of World History. rev ed. Geoffrey Barraclough. LC 82-50111. (Illus.). 192p. 1986. pap. 24.95 (ISBN 0-8437-1133-7). Hammond Inc.
Time's Covenant: The Essays & Sermons of William Clancy. Ed. by Eugene Green. LC 86-19517. xviii, 213p. 1986. 19.95x (ISBN 0-8229-3545-7). U of Pittsburgh Pr.
Time's Dark Laughter. James Kahn. 336p. 1985. pap. 3.50 (ISBN 0-345-32701-2, Del Rey). Ballantine.
Time's Dipstick. John M. Bennett. 1976. 2.00 (ISBN 0-686-73435-1). Luna Bisonte.
Time's Distractions: A Play from the Time of Charles I. Ed. by Diane W. Strommer. LC 75-43623. 132p. 1976. 8.50x (ISBN 0-89096-008-9). Tex A&M Univ Pr.
Times Family Atlas of the World: Times Books. (Illus.). 224p. 1988. 24.95 (ISBN 0-88162-346-6). Salem Hse Pubs.
Time's Glory: Original Essays on Robert Penn Warren. Ed. by James A. Grimshaw, Jr. & Robert E. Lowrey. (Illus.). 200p. 1986. 19.95 (ISBN 0-9615143-2-9). Univ Central AR Pr.
Times in Review: New York Times Decade Books, 5 vols. Incl. Vol. 1. Nineteen Twenty-Nineteen Twenty Nine; Vol. 2. Nineteen Thirty-Nineteen Thirty Nine; Vol. 3. Nineteen Forty-Nineteen Forty Nine; Vol. 4. Nineteen Fifty-Nineteen Fifty Nine; Vol. 5. Nineteen Sixty-Nineteen Sixty Nine. (Illus.). 50.00 ea. (Co-Pub by New York Times). Ayer Co Pubs.
Times I've Seen. Ulick O'Connor. (Illus.). 1964. 19.95 (ISBN 0-8392-1119-8). Astor-Honor.
Time's Last Gift. Philip Jose Farmer. 256p. 1985. pap. 2.95 (ISBN 0-8125-3764-5, Dist. by Warner Pub Services & Saint Martin's Press). Tor Bks.
Time's Noblest Name: The Names & Titles of Jesus Christ, L-O. New rev. ed. Charles J. Rolls. pap. 5.95 (ISBN 0-87213-733-3). Loizeaux.
Times of Celebration. Ed. by David Power & Mary Collins. (Concilium 1981 Ser.: Vol. 142). 128p. (Orig.). 1981. pap. 6.95 (ISBN 0-8164-2309-1, HarpR). Har-Row.
Times of Feast, Times of Famine: A History of Climate since the Year 1000. Emmanuel L. Ladurie. Tr. by Barbara Bray. (Illus.). 1988. pap. 14.95 (ISBN 0-374-52122-0, Noonday). FS&G.
Times of Life: Prayers & Poems. Huub Oosterhuis. Tr. by N. D. Smith from Dutch. LC 79-89653. 128p. (Orig.). 1980. pap. 4.95 (ISBN 0-8091-2245-6). Paulist Pr.
Times of My Life. Betty Ford & Chris Chase. LC 78-2131. (Illus.). 1979. pap. 3.95 (ISBN 0-345-34826-5). Ballantine.
Times of Our Constitution. 2nd ed. Donald R. Haener & Janice Fry. (Illus.). 24p. (gr. 2-6). 1987. pap. 3.00 (ISBN 0-942661-03-6). Discovry Enterp.
Times of Our Lives: A Guide to the Writing of Autobiography & Memoir. X ed. Mary J. Moffat. Ed. by Thelma Shaw. LC 85-71992. 53p. (Orig.). 1985. pap. text ed. 5.95 (ISBN 0-933829-03-5). Ponce Pr.
Times of Restoration. Orville Swindoll. (Illus.). 192p. (Orig.). 1983. pap. 3.95 (ISBN 0-914903-00-4). Destiny Image.
Times of Surrender: Selected Essays. Robert Coles. LC 87-30221. 292p. 1988. 22.50 (ISBN 0-87745-188-5). U of Iowa Pr.
Times One Thousand, 1987-88. 23rd ed. 115p. 1988. 65.00x (Pub. by Times Bks UK). Taylor & Francis.
Times Past. Ed. by Glenda Hadley. (Illus., Orig.). 1982. pap. write for info. (ISBN 0-9607910-0-0). Golden Aires.
Times Remembered: Chronicles of the Towns of Bethlehem & New Scotland, N.Y. Allison P. Bennett. (Illus.). 110p. 1984. pap. 10.95 (ISBN 0-318-03966-4). Newsgraphics Delmar Inc.
Times Series Analysis & Applications. Enders A. Robinson. LC 81-81825. (Illus.). 628p. 1981. 25.00 (ISBN 0-910835-00-4). Goose Pond Pr.
Times, Space & Places: A Chronogeographic Perspective. Parkes. LC 79-40523. 1986. pap. write for info. (ISBN 0-471-27617-0). Wiley.
Times, Spaces & Places: A Chronogeographic Perspective. Don Parkes & Nigel Thrift. LC 79-40523. pap. 141.20 (2030757). Bks Demand UMI.

Times Square Bossa Nova. (Ballroom Ser.). 1985. lib. bdg. 64.00 (ISBN 0-87700-824-8). Revisionist Pr.
Times Square Bossa Nova. (Ballroom Dance Ser.). 1986. lib. bdg. 64.95 (ISBN 0-8490-3279-2). Gordon Pr.
Times Square: Forty-Five Years of Photography. Lou Stoumen. LC 84-71747. (Illus.). 160p. 1985. 25.00 (ISBN 0-89381-164-5); pap. 15.00 (ISBN 0-89381-165-3). Aperture.
Times Survey of the Foreign Ministries of the World. Ed. by Zara Steiner. (Illus.). 1982. 87.50x (ISBN 0-930466-37-3). Meckler Corp.
Times, the Man, the Company see Ford.
Times to Come. Noel Tyl. LC 73-19910. (Principles & Practice of Astrology Ser.: Vol. 12). 197p. (Orig.). 1975. pap. 3.95 (ISBN 0-87542-811-8). Llewellyn Pubns.
Time's Up! Florence P. Heide. LC 81-13240. (Illus.). 128p. (gr. 3-7). 1982. 11.95 (ISBN 0-8234-0441-2). Holiday.
Times We Had. Marion Davies. pap. 3.95 (ISBN 0-345-32739-X). Ballantine.
Times Winged Chariot. Mary N. Baldwin. 80p. 1975. 5.00 (ISBN 0-8233-0218-0). Golden Quill.
Time's Winged Chariot. Heald T. Bernard. 136p. 1985. 40.00x (ISBN 0-907033-26-1, Hutton Pr). State Mutual Bk.
Times Without Number. John Brunner. 224p. 1983. pap. 2.50 (ISBN 0-345-30679-1, Del Rey). Ballantine.
TIMES 17: The Amazing Story of the Zodiac Murders in California & Massachusetts, 1966-1981. Gareth Penn. (Orig.). 1987. pap. 17.00 (ISBN 0-9618494-0-1). Foxglove Pr.
Timesaving Aid to Virginia-West Virginia Ancestors, 3 vols. P. G. Wardell. 514p. 1988. Repr. Vol. 1. lib. bdg. 24.95x (ISBN 0-8095-8205-8); Vol. 2. lib. bdg. 24.95x (ISBN 0-8095-8206-6); Vol. 3. lib. bdg. 24.95x (ISBN 0-8095-8207-4). Borgo Pr.
Timesaving Aid to Virginia-West Virginia Ancestors, Vol. 1. P. G. Wardell. vii, 170p. (Orig.). 1985. pap. 10.00 (ISBN 0-935931-01-5). Iberian Pub.
Timesaving Aid to Virginia-West Virginia Ancestors, Vol. 2. Patrick G. Wardell. vii, 182p. (Orig.). 1986. pap. 10.00 (ISBN 0-935931-28-7). Iberian Pub.
Timesaving Aid to Virginia-West Virginia Ancestors, Vol. 3. P. G. Wardell. vi, 142p. (Orig.). 1987. pap. 10.00 (ISBN 0-935931-34-1). Iberian Pub.
Timesaving Sewing. DeCosse, Cy, Inc. Staff. LC 87-649. (Singer Sewing Reference Library). (Illus.). 128p. 1987. 14.95 (ISBN 0-86573-215-9); pap. 11.95 (ISBN 0-86573-216-7). Cy De Cosse.
Timescale. Nigel Calder. Date not set. pap. 8.95 (ISBN 0-14-006342-0). Penguin.
Timescape. Gregory Benford. 1987. pap. 3.95 (ISBN 0-671-50632-3). PB.
Timescapes of John Fowles. H. W. Fawkner. LC 82-48606. 180p. 1983. 19.50 (ISBN 0-8386-3175-4). Fairleigh Dickinson.
Timeshadow Rider. Ann Maxwell. 320p. (Orig.). 1986. pap. 2.95 (ISBN 0-8125-4560-5, Dist. by Warner Pub Service & St. Martin's Press). Tor Bks.
Timeshare Financing Manual. 1985. 38.50 (ISBN 0-318-19150-4); financial & education institutions 28.50 (ISBN 0-318-19151-2). ARRDA.
Timeshare Lenders Survey. 125.00 (ISBN 0-318-03347-X). ARRDA.
Timeshare Properties: What Every Buyer Must Know! Robert Irwin. LC 82-17185. (Illus.). 208p. 1983. text ed. 23.95 (ISBN 0-07-032082-9). McGraw.
Timeshare Property Assesment & Taxation. Kathleen Conroy & James DiChiara. Ed. by Jeanette E. Smith. (Illus., Orig.). 1983. 31.00 (ISBN 0-318-04658-X). ARRDA.
Timesharing: A Consumer's Guide to a New Vacation Concept. Rochelle H. Dubois. 32p. (Orig.). 1982. pap. 3.00 (ISBN 0-9603950-4-0). Somrie Pr.
Timesharing: Concept, Reality & Regulation. Jim Buchanan. (Public Administration Ser.: P 1756). 15p. 1985. pap. 2.25 (ISBN 0-89028-536-5). Vance Biblios.
Timesharing: The Dollars & Sense. Daniel Besser. (Condominium Guideline Ser.). 200p. 1985. 32.95 (ISBN 0-911755-03-9). Wyndham Hse.
Timesharing Two. Burlingame et al. Ed. by Stuart M. Bloch & William B. Ingersoll. LC 82-60331. (Illus.). 223p. (Orig.). 1982. 36.00 (ISBN 0-87420-611-1, TO4). Urban Land.
Timesharing: What's in It for You. Robert MacBride. LC 76-10858. pap. 20.00 (ISBN 0-317-08635-9, 2004617). Bks Demand UMI.
Timesteps. Charlotte V. Allen. 656p. 1987. pap. 4.50 (ISBN 0-425-09807-9). Berkley Pub.
Timeswept Lovers. Constance O'Day-Flannery. 496p. 1987. pap. 3.95 (ISBN 0-8217-2057-0). Zebra.
Timetable. James M. Bryant. (Illus.). 1981. 20.00 (ISBN 0-686-28942-0). J M Bryant.
Timetable of Inventions & Discoveries: From Pre-History to Present Day. Kevin Desmond. (Illus.). 246p. 1987. 16.95 (ISBN 0-87131-520-3). M Evans.
Timetables of American History. Ed. by Laurence Urdang. 480p. 1983. pap. 13.95 (ISBN 0-671-25246-1, Touchstone). S&S.
Timetables of History. rev. ed. Bernard Grun. 1982. pap. 18.95 (ISBN 0-671-24988-6). S&S.
Timetables of History: A Horizontal Linkage of People & Events. Bernard Grun. 688p. 1987. 17.95 (ISBN 0-317-63435-6, Touchstone Bks). S&S.
Timetables of Science: A Chronology of the Most Important People & Events in the History of Science. Alexander Hellemans & Bryan Bunch. 572p. 1988. 29.95 (ISBN 0-671-62130-0). S&S.
Timetrap. David Dvorkin. (Star Trek Ser.: No. 40). 288p. (Orig.). 1988. pap. 3.95 (ISBN 0-671-64870-5). PB.
Timewarps. John Gribbin. 1980. pap. 4.95 (ISBN 0-385-29078-0, Delta). Dell.
Timex Personal Computer Made Simple. Jonathan D. Siminoff et al. 1982. pap. 2.95 (ISBN 0-451-12138-4, AE2138, Sig). NAL.
Timex-Sinclair Computer Games Programs. Edward Page. 96p. 1983. 7.95 (ISBN 0-86668-026-8). ARCsoft.
Timex-Sinclair Computer Program Writing Workbook. Edward Page. 96p. 1983. 4.95 (ISBN 0-86668-810-2). ARCsoft.
Timex-Sinclair Directory 1983. 5.00 (ISBN 0-317-12960-0). E A Brown Co.
Timex-Sinclair User's Encyclopedia. Gary Phillips & James C. March. Ed. by Michael F. Mellin & Andrew Klein. 350p. (Orig.). 1983. pap. 14.95 (ISBN 0-912003-16-2). Bk Co.
Timex-Sinclair 1000: Programs, Games, & Graphics. Robin Jones & Ian Stewart. 100p. 1982. pap. 10.95 (ISBN 0-8176-3080-5). Birkhauser.
Timex TS 2000: Your Personal Computer. Ian McLean. (Illus.). 240p. 1984. pap. text ed. 12.95 (ISBN 0-13-921974-9). P-H.
Timid Pup. Robert Avrett. (Illus.). (gr. 1-3). PLB 6.19 (ISBN 0-8313-0004-3). Lantern.
Timid Timothy's Tongue Twisters. Adapted by & illus. by Dick Gackenbach. LC 85-30531. (Illus.). 32p. (ps-3). 1986. PLB 12.95 (ISBN 0-8234-0610-5); pap. 5.95 (ISBN 0-8234-0711-X). Holiday.
Timid Virgins Make Dull Company & Other Puzzles, Pitfalls & Paradoxes. Crypton. (Penguin Nonfiction Ser.). 208p. 1985. pap. 6.95 (ISBN 0-14-008043-0). Penguin.
Timid Virgins Make Dull Company & Other Puzzles, Pitfalls & Paradoxes. Paul Hoffman. (Illus.). 192p. 1984. 14.95 (ISBN 0-670-71575-1). Viking.
Timing & Patterns of Molt in Microtus Breweri. Carol Rowsemitt et al. (Occasional Papers: No. 34). 11p. 1975. pap. 1.25 (ISBN 0-317-04913-5). U of KS Mus Nat Hist.
Timing & Time Perception. Intro. by John Gibbon & Lorraine Allan. (Annals of The New York Academy of Sciences: Vol. 423). 654p. 1984. lib. bdg. 144.00x (ISBN 0-89766-240-7). NY Acad Sci.
Timing Chain. Douglas Woolf. 140p. (Orig.). 1985. limited signed 35.00 (ISBN 0-939180-37-5); pap. 7.00 (ISBN 0-939180-36-7). Tombouctou.
Timing Devices: Poems. Paul Mariani. LC 78-74253. (Illus.). 1979. 12.50x (ISBN 0-87923-277-3). Godine.
Timing for Animation. Harold Whitaker & John Halas. LC 80-41303. (Illus.). 144p. 1981. text ed. 37.95 (ISBN 0-240-50871-8). Focal Pr.
Timing Instrument Market. 247p. 1985. 1650.00 (ISBN 0-86621-299-X, A1376). Frost & Sullivan.
Timing Manipulations. James Hamilton. 1974. write for info. (ISBN 0-918845-00-9). Am Watchmakers.
Timing of Aneurysm Surgery. Ed. by L. M. Auer & N. Kassel. (Illus.). xiv, 685p. 1986. 128.00 (ISBN 3-11-010156-4). De Gruyter.
Timing of Biological Clocks. Arthur T. Winfree. LC 86-15602. (Illus.). 199p. 1986. text ed. 32.95 (ISBN 0-7167-5018-X). W H Freeman.
Timing of Economic Activities: Firms, Households, & Markets in Time-Specific Analysis. Gordon C. Winston. LC 82-1328. 303p. 1982. 37.50 (ISBN 0-521-24720-9). Cambridge U Pr.
Timing of Events: Electional Astrology. Bruce Scofield. (Illus.). 144p. (Orig.). 1986. pap. 9.95 (ISBN 0-87199-039-3). Astrolabe SW.
Timing of Motherhood: Is Later Better? Carolyn A. Walter. LC 85-45075. 160p. 1986. 14.95 (ISBN 0-669-11099-X). Lexington Bks.
Timing of Sleep & Wakefulness. J. T. Enright. (Studies of Brain Function: Vol. 3). (Illus.). 1980. pap. 31.00 (ISBN 0-387-09667-1). Springer-Verlag.
Timing Space & Spacing Time, 3 vols. Ed. by Tommy Carlstein et al. Incl. Vol. I. Making Sense of Time. 150p. 34.95x (ISBN 0-470-26511-6); Vol. II. Human Activity & Time Geography. 286p. 59.95x (ISBN 0-470-26513-2); Vol. III. Time & Regional Dynamics. 120p. 34.95x (ISBN 0-470-26512-4). 1979. Halsted Pr.
Timing the Market: How to Profit in Bull & Bear Markets with Technical Analysis. Weiss Research Staff. 250p. 1986. 25.00 (ISBN 0-917253-37-X). Probus Pub Co.
Timing the Market: How to Profit in Bull & Bear Markets with Technical Analysis. Weiss Research Staff. 210p. 1987. pap. 17.95 (ISBN 0-917253-96-5). Probus Pub Co.
Timing the Stock Market for Maximum Profits. Stanley S. G. Huang. 1987. 34.95 (ISBN 0-930233-16-6). Windsor.
Timings for Typing. Carl W. Salser. 1973. 4.85 (ISBN 0-89420-013-5, 296955). Natl Book.
Timmerman's Lectures on Catholicism. S. F. Timmerman, Jr. 1952. 3.95 (ISBN 0-88027-085-3). Firm Foun Pub.
Timmie. Mary H. Stewart. LC 85-60615. 356p. (Orig.). 1985. pap. 18.50 (ISBN 0-935834-46-X). Rainbow Books.
Timmy Learns to Draw. Paul Bermudez. (gr. 1-2). 1985. 5.95 (ISBN 0-317-18726-0). Todd & Honeywell.
Timmy O-Dowd & the Big Ditch: A Story of the Glory Days on the Old Erie Canal. Len Hilts. 144p. (gr. 3 up). 1988. 13.95 (ISBN 0-15-200606-0, Gulliver Bks). HarBraceJ.
Timmy Tiger & the Butterfly Net. Oana. LC 80-82954. (Timmy Tiger Ser.). (Illus.). 32p. (ps-4). 1981. PLB 9.95 (ISBN 0-87783-160-2). Oddo.
Timmy Tiger & the Elephant. Rae Oetting. LC 73-108730. (Timmy Tiger Ser.). (Illus.). 32p. (ps-2). 1970. PLB 9.95 (ISBN 0-87783-041-X); pap. 3.94 deluxe ed (ISBN 0-87783-111-4); cassette 7.94x (ISBN 0-87783-277-3). Oddo.
Timmy Tiger & the Masked Bandit. Oana. LC 80-82955. (Timmy Tiger Ser.). (Illus.). 32p. (ps-4). 1981. PLB 9.95x (ISBN 0-87783-161-0). Oddo.
Timmy Tiger Series, 6 vols. (Illus.). (ps-4). 1981. Set. PLB 59.70 (ISBN 0-87783-166-1); Set Of 4 Vols. pap. 15.76 deluxe ed (ISBN 0-87783-167-X); cassettes set (4) 31.76x (ISBN 0-87783-228-5). Oddo.
Timmy Tiger to the Rescue. Rae Oetting. LC 70-108733. (Timmy Tiger Ser.). (Illus.). 32p. (ps-4). 1970. PLB 9.95x (ISBN 0-87783-043-6); pap. 3.94x deluxe ed (ISBN 0-87783-112-2); cassette 7.94x (ISBN 0-87783-229-3). Oddo.
Timmy Tiger's New Coat. Rae Oetting. LC 74-108734. (Timmy Tiger Ser.). (Illus.). 32p. (ps-2). 1970. PLB 9.95 (ISBN 0-87783-044-4); pap. 3.94 deluxe ed (ISBN 0-87783-113-0); cassette 7.94x (ISBN 0-87783-230-7). Oddo.
Timmy Tiger's New Friend. Rae Oetting. LC 77-108732. (Timmy Tiger Ser.). (Illus.). (ps-2). 1970. PLB 9.95 (ISBN 0-87783-042-8); pap. 3.94 deluxe ed (ISBN 0-87783-114-9); cassette 7.94x (ISBN 0-87783-231-5). Oddo.
Timna - Azor. Edith Cutting. (Might Have Been Ser.). (Illus.). 48p. (gr. 2-7). 1985. wkbk. 2.48 (ISBN 0-86653-308-7). Good Apple.
Timoleon. Herman Melville. 70p. 1980. Repr. of 1976 ed. lib. bdg. 29.50 (ISBN 0-8495-3769-X). Arden Lib.
Timoleon. Herman Melville. LC 76-25200. 1976. lib. bdg. 29.50 (ISBN 0-8414-4833-7). Folcroft.
Timoleon. Herman Melville. 35.00 (ISBN 0-8490-1215-5). Gordon Pr.
Timoleon & the Revival of Greek Sicily, 344-317 BC. Richard J. Talbert. 248p. 1974. 27.95 (ISBN 0-521-20419-4). Cambridge U Pr.
Timoleon & the Revival of Greek Sicily, 344-317 B. C. Richard J. Talbert. LC 74-16854. (Cambridge Classical Studies). pap. 60.50 (ISBN 0-317-27982-3, 2025596). Bks Demand UMI.
Timolol Ophthalmic Solution in the Treatment of Glaucoma. D. Dausch & H. Honegger. LC 78-72505. 1978. 3.00 (ISBN 0-911910-95-6). Merck-Sharp-Dohme.
Timon. Ed. by J. C. Bulman & J. M. Nosworthy. LC 82-45735. (Malone Society Reprint Ser.: No. 139). 1978. 40.00 (ISBN 0-404-63139-8). AMS Pr.
Timon, a Play. Ed. by Alexander Dyce. LC 75-16481. Repr. of 1842 ed. 11.50 (ISBN 0-404-02229-4). AMS Pr.
Timon of Athens see also Life of Timon of Athens.
Timon of Athens. Bay Area Community College. 48p. 1981. 4.50 (ISBN 0-317-61475-4). Kendall-Hunt.
Timon of Athens. John J. Ruszkiewicz. LC 83-48274. (Shakespeare Bibliographies Ser.). 325p. 1986. lib. bdg. 42.00 (ISBN 0-8240-9195-7). Garland Pub.
Timon of Athens. 3rd ed. William Shakespeare. Ed. by H. J. Oliver. (Arden Shakespeare Ser.). 1969. 37.00x (ISBN 0-416-47250-8, NO. 2492); pap. 8.95 (ISBN 0-416-27860-4, NO. 2493). Routledge Chapman & Hall.
Timon of Athens. William Shakespeare. Ed. by G. R. Hibbard. 1981. pap. 3.75 (ISBN 0-14-070721-2). Penguin.
Timon of Athens. rev. ed. William Shakespeare. Ed. by Charlton Hinman. (Shakespeare Ser.). 1965. pap. 2.95 (ISBN 0-14-071429-4, Pelican). Penguin.
Timon of Athens. William Shakespeare. Ed. by Louis B. Wright & Virginia A. La Mar. (Folger Library Ser.). 256p. pap. 2.95 (ISBN 0-671-49117-2). WSP.
Timon of Athens see Titus Andronicus.
Timon of Athens: Modern Text with Introduction. Ed. by A. L. Rowse. LC 86-23380. 116p. (Orig.). 1987. pap. text ed. 3.45 (ISBN 0-8191-3939-4). U Pr of Amer.
Timon of Athens: Shakespeare's Pessimistic Tragedy. Rolf Soellner. LC 78-10884. (Illus.). 255p. 1979. 20.00 (ISBN 0-8142-0292-6). Ohio St U Pr.
Timor Link. CIIR Staff. 1987. 25.00 (ISBN 0-317-57998-3, Pub. by CIIR). State Mutual BK.
Timor Mortis. Will Harriss. 192p. 1986. 15.95 (ISBN 0-8027-5643-3). Walker & Co.
Timor Problem: A Geographical Interpretation of an Underdeveloped Island. Ferdinand J. Ormeling. LC 77-86997. (Illus.). 296p. Repr. of 1956 ed. 47.50 (ISBN 0-404-16769-1). AMS Pr.
Timoteo-Tito. Charles Erdman. 175p. (Span.). 1987. pap. 3.50 (ISBN 0-939125-29-3). Evangelical Lit.
Timothy & the Big Bully. Jeffrey Dinardo. (Illus.). 32p. (ps-3). 1988. bds. 5.95 (ISBN 0-671-66562-6). S&S.
Timothy & the Blanket Fairy. Nita Clarke. (gr. k-6). 1981. 6.95 (ISBN 0-933184-06-9); pap. 4.95 (ISBN 0-933184-16-6). Flame Intl.
Timothy & the Night Noises. Jeffrey Dinardo. LC 86-9383. (Illus.). 32p. (ps-2). 1986. pap. 11.95 (ISBN 0-13-922048-8). P-H.
Timothy & the Two Witches. Margaret Storey. 92p. (gr. 2-5). 1974. pap. 0.75 (ISBN 0-440-48864-8, YB). Dell.
Timothy Crump's Ward: The New Years Loan & What Became of It. Horatio Alger, Jr. 188p. 1977. Repr. of 1866 ed. 30.00 (ISBN 0-686-37023-6). G K Westgard.
Timothy Dwight: Selected Writings see Millennium in America: From the Puritan Migration to the Civil War.
Timothy Dwight, 1752-1817: A Biography. Charles E. Cuningham. LC 75-41069. Repr. of 1942 ed. 21.50 (ISBN 0-404-14746-1). AMS Pr.
Timothy Files. Lawrence Sanders. 384p. 1987. 18.95 (ISBN 0-399-13261-9, Putnam). Putnam Pub Group.
Timothy Files. Lawrence Sanders. 1988. pap. 4.95. Berkley Pub.
Timothy Flint. James K. Folsom. (Twayne's United States Authors Ser.). 1965. pap. 8.95x (ISBN 0-8084-0301-X, T83, Twayne). New Coll U Pr.
Timothy Flint: Pioneer, Missionary, Author, Editor, 1780-1840. John E. Kirkpatrick. LC 68-56780. (Research & Source Works Ser: No. 267). 1968. Repr. of 1911 ed. 21.50 (ISBN 0-8337-1930-0). B Franklin.
Timothy Goes to School. Rosemary Wells. LC 80-20785. (Illus.). 32p. (ps-2). 1981. PLB 9.89 (ISBN 0-8037-8949-1). Dial Bks Young.
Timothy Goes to School. Rosemary Wells. LC 80-20785. (Pied Piper Bk.). (Illus.). 32p. (ps-2). 1983. pap. 3.95 (ISBN 0-8037-0021-0, 0383-120). Dial Bks Young.
Timothy-James. Raymond Brown. 1983. pap. 4.95 (ISBN 0-87508-174-6). Chr Lit.
Timothy: Nez Perce Chief, Life & Times, 1800-1891. Rowena Alcorn. 1986. pap. 5.95. Ye Galleon.
Timothy-Philemon. Knofel Staion. (Standard Bible Studies). (Illus.). 1988. pap. text ed. price not set (ISBN 0-87403-172-9, 11-40112). Standard Pub.
Timothy Pickering & the Age of the American Revolution. David McLean. 55.00 (ISBN 0-405-14098-3). Ayer Co Pubs.
Timothy Pickering & the American Republic. Gerard H. Clarfield. LC 79-24326. 1980. 31.95x (ISBN 0-8229-3414-0). U of Pittsburgh Pr.
Timothy Pickering As the Leader of New England Federalism, 1800-1815. Hervey Putnam Prentiss. LC 71-124882. (American Scene Ser). (Illus.). 118p. 1972. Repr. of 1934 ed. lib. bdg. 22.50 (ISBN 0-306-71052-8). Da Capo.
Timothy Principle. Roy Robertson. 120p. 1986. pap. 4.95 (ISBN 0-89109-550-0). NavPress.
Timothy Tall Feather. Charlotte Pomerantz. LC 85-24819. (Illus.). 32p. (gr. k-3). 1986. 11.75 (ISBN 0-688-04246-5); PLB 11.88 (ISBN 0-688-04247-3). Greenwillow.
Timothy, Titus & Philemon. H. A. Ironside. 9.95 (ISBN 0-87213-391-5). Loizeaux.
Timothy, Titus & You: A Workbook for Church Leaders. George C. Scipione. 96p. 1986. pap. 3.95 (ISBN 0-87552-439-7). Presby & Reformed.
Timothy Too. Charlotte Zolotow. (ps-2). 1985. 12.95. HM.
Timothy Tuneful. Bette Distler. LC 68-11270. (Illus.). (ps-3). 1968. 3.50g (ISBN 0-685-16349-0, CCPr). Macmillan.
Timothy Turtle Learns About Love. Wendy Smith. (Illus.). (ps-4). 1977. pap. 2.50 (ISBN 0-87516-244-4). DeVorss.
Timothy: Young Pastor. Louise Caldwell. (BibLearn Ser..). (Illus.). (gr. 1-6). 1978. 5.95 (ISBN 0-8054-4239-1, 4242-39). Broadman.
Timothy's Flower. Jean Van Leeuwen. (Illus.). (ps-3). 1967. Random.
Timothy's Forest. Freya Littledale & Harold Littledale. (Illus.). (gr. k-3). 1969. PLB 6.87 (ISBN 0-87460-123-1). Lion Bks.
Timothy's Game. Lawrence Sanders. LC 87-29073. 384p. 1988. 18.95 (ISBN 0-399-13368-2). Putnam Pub Group.
Timpanogos Cave: A Window into the Earth. Stephen Trimble. Ed. by T. J. Priehs & Carolyn Dodson. LC 82-61192. (Illus.). 48p. 1983. pap. 3.50 (ISBN 0-911408-64-9). SW Pks Mnmts.
Timpetoo. Margit Raedal. LC 70-103604. (Illus.). (gr. k-3). 1971. PLB 3.95 (ISBN 0-87614-010-X). Carolrhoda Bks.
Tim's Bunnies. Ed Smith. Ed. by David Trinidad. (Illus.). 56p. (Orig.). 1988. pap. 5.95. Cold Calm Pr.
Tim's Friend Towser. Edward Ardizzone. (Illus.). 48p. (ps-3). 1987. pap. 4.95 (ISBN 0-19-272112-7). Oxford U Pr.
Timurid Architecture in Khurasan. Bernard O'Kane. LC 85-43494. (Islamic Art & Architecture Ser.: Vol. 3). (Illus.). 520p. 1987. lib. bdg. 49.95. Mazda Pubs.
Timurid Architecture of Iran & Turan, 2 vols. Lisa Golombek & Donald Wilber. (Monographs in Art & Archaeology: No. 46). (Illus.). 720p. 1988. Set. text ed. 130.00 (ISBN 0-691-03587-3). Princeton U Pr.

Tin. J. W. Price & R. Smith. (Handbook of Analytical Chemistry: Vol. 4, Pt. 3, Section A, Y). (Illus.). 1978. 86.20 (ISBN 0-387-08234-4). Springer-Verlag.

Tin & Its Alloys & Compounds. B. T. Barry & C. G. Thwaites. LC 83-12760. (Ellis Horwood Series in Industrial Metals Ser.). 268p. 1983. 74.95x (ISBN 0-470-27480-8). Halsted Pr.

Tin & Malignant Cell Growth. J. J. Zuckerman. 256p. 1988. 135.00 (ISBN 0-8493-4714-9, 4714). CRC Pr.

Tin & the Human Organism. Eugen Kolisko. pap. cancelled (ISBN 0-906492-30-0, Pub. by Kolisko Archives). St George Bk Serv.

Tin & Tin-Alloy Plating. J. W. Price. 1982. 159.00x (ISBN 0-686-81702-8, Pub. by Electrochemical Scotland). State Mutual Bk.

Tin As a Vital Nutrient: Implications in Cancer Prophylaxis & Other Physiological Processes. Ed. by Nate F. Cardarelli. 336p. 1986. 140.00 (ISBN 0-8493-6579-1). CRC Pr.

Tin Can. William J. Smith. (Chapbooks: No. 3). 1988. 30.00 (ISBN 0-937035-10-6). Stone Hse NY.

Tin Can Book. Hyla Clark. (Art Bks). (Illus., Orig.). 1977. pap. 6.95 (ISBN 0-451-79965-8, G9965, Sig). NAL.

Tin Can Factory. Una Tipper. LC 77-87411. (gr. k-6). 1978. pap. 10.00 (ISBN 0-8283-1709-7). Branden Pub Co.

Tin Can Tree. Anne Tyler. 272p. 1987. pap. 3.95 (ISBN 0-425-09903-2). Berkley Pub.

Tin Cans & Other Ships. Joseph A. Donahue. (Illus.). 1979. 7.50 (ISBN 0-8158-0378-8). Chris Mass.

Tin Cans & Trash Recovery: Saving Energy Through Utilizing Municipal Ferrous Waste. 1980. pap. 2.00 (ISBN 0-686-29241-3). Tech Info Proj.

Tin Craft of the Southwest: A Workbook. rev. ed. Fern-Rae Abraham. (Illus.). 32p. 1987. pap. 4.95 (ISBN 0-86534-098-6). Sunstone Pr.

Tin Drum. Gunter Grass. Tr. by Ralph Manheim. 1971. 10.95 (ISBN 0-394-44902-9, V-300, Vin); pap. 7.95 (ISBN 0-394-74560-4). Random.

Tin-Glaze Pottery. Alan Craiger-Smith. 1973. 45.00 (ISBN 0-571-09349-3). Faber & Faber.

Tin Horns & Calico, a Decisive Period in the Emergence of Democracy. Henry Christman. 1978. pap. 6.95 (ISBN 0-685-61130-2). Hope Farm.

Tin in Antiquity. R. D. Penhallurick. 272p. 1986. pap. 48.00 (ISBN 0-904357-81-3, Pub. by Inst Metals). Brookfield Pub Co.

Tin in Organic Synthesis. A. Rahm et al. (Illus.). 304p. 1987. text ed. 130.00 (ISBN 0-408-01435-0). Butterworth.

Tin: Its Mining, Production, Technology, & Applications. 2nd ed. Charles L. Mantell. LC 29-22211. (ACS Monograph: No. 51). 1949. 42.95 (ISBN 0-8412-0257-5). Am Chemical.

Tin: Its Production & Marketing. William Robertson. LC 82-9269. (Contributions in Economics & Economic History Ser.: No. 51). (Illus.). 212p. 1982. lib. bdg. 35.00 (ISBN 0-313-23637-2, RTN/). Greenwood.

Tin Lizzie. Peter Spier. LC 74-1510. (Illus.). 48p. (gr. 3-5). 1978. 1.95 (ISBN 0-385-13342-1); pap. 8.95 (ISBN 0-385-09470-1). Doubleday.

Tin Pan Alley. John Shepherd. (Routledge Popular Music Ser.). 154p. 1982. 14.95x (ISBN 0-7100-0904-6). Routledge Chapman & Hall.

Tin Pan Alley in Gaslight. Maxwell F. Marcuse. LC 58-59691. (Illus.). 1959. pap. 7.00 (ISBN 0-87282-084-X). Am Life Foun.

Tin Pan Alley: The Composers, the Songs, the Performers & Their Times. David Jasen. 1988. 19.95. D I Fine.

Tin-Pot Foreign General & the Old Iron Woman. Raymond Briggs. (Illus.). 48p. (gr. k up). 1985. 9.95 (ISBN 0-316-10801-4). Little.

Tin, Pt. C. Max Planck Society for the Advancement of Science, Gmelin Institute for Inorganic Chemistry. (Gmelin Handbch der Anorganischen Chemie, 8th Ed.). (Illus.). 206p. 1975. 180.50 (ISBN 0-387-93284-4). Springer-Verlag.

Tin Roofs & Palm Trees: A Report on the New South Seas. Robert Trumbull. LC 76-49164. (Illus.). 344p. 1977. 22.50x (ISBN 0-295-95544-9). U of Wash Pr.

Tin Soldier. Hans Christian Andersen. (Oxford Graded Readers). (gr. k-6). 1983. pap. 1.25x (ISBN 0-19-421742-6). Oxford U Pr.

Tin Soldier. Temple Bailey. 1975. lib. bdg. 19.10x (ISBN 0-89966-011-8). Buccaneer Bks.

Tin Stars. Ed. by Isaac Asimov et al. (Isaac Asimov's Wonderful Worlds of Science Fiction Ser.: No. 5). 1986. pap. 3.95 (ISBN 0-451-14395-7, Sig). NAL.

Tin: The Working of a Commodity Agreement. William Fox. 1977. 40.00 (ISBN 0-685-87560-1). State Mutual Bk.

Tin Toy Museum, No. 1. Toyoji Takayama. (Illus.). 128p. 1988. 24.95 (ISBN 4-7636-3040-7, Pub. by Kyoto Shoin Tokyo). Bks Nippan.

Tin Toy Museum, No. 2. Toyoji Takayama. (Illus.). 112p. 1988. 24.95 (ISBN 4-7636-3041-5, Pub. by Kyoto Shoin Tokyo). Bks Nippan.

Tin Wedding. Margaret Leech. (Shoreline Bks.). 279p. 1986. pap. 7.95 (ISBN 0-87140-141-X). Norton.

Tin Whistle Tune Book. William E. White. LC 79-26872. 1980. pap. 1.50 (ISBN 0-87935-051-2). Williamsburg.

Tin Wife. Joseph Flaherty. 256p. 1984. 16.45 (ISBN 0-671-47280-1). S&S.

Tin Woodman. David F. Bischoff & Dennis R. Bailey. 192p. 1985. pap. 2.75 (ISBN 0-441-81293-7). Ace Bks.

Tin Woodman of Oz. L. Frank Baum. (Illus.). 272p. 1985. pap. 3.50 (ISBN 0-345-33436-1, Del Rey). Ballantine.

Tina. Herman Bang. Tr. by Paul Christopherson. LC 84-12286. 224p. 1984. 18.95 (ISBN 0-485-11254-X, Pub. by Athlone Pr Ltd). Humanities.

Tina! Steven Ivory. LC 85-3649. 192p. 1985. pap. 3.95 (ISBN 0-399-51171-7). Putnam Pub Group.

Tina Gogo. Judie Angell. 160p. (gr. 5 up). 1980. pap. 1.75 (ISBN 0-440-98738-5, LFL). Dell.

Tina Turner. Laura Fissinger. 1985. pap. 2.95 (ISBN 0-345-32642-3). Ballantine.

Tina Turner. Philip Kamin. (Illus.). 32p. (gr. 4-12). 1985. pap. 4.95 (ISBN 0-88188-416-2, Pub. by Robus Bks). H Leonard Pub Corp.

Tina Turner. Terry Koenig. Ed. by Howard Schroeder. LC 86-8950. (Center Stage Ser.). (Illus.). 32p. (gr. 4-5). PLB 9.95. Crestwood Hse.

Tina Turner. D. L. Mabery. (Entertainment World Ser.). (Illus.). 40p. (gr. 4-9). 1986. lib. bdg. 8.95 (ISBN 0-8225-1609-8). Lerner Pubns.

Tina's Chance. Alison Leonard. 160p. (YA) (gr. 7 up). 1988. 11.95 (ISBN 0-670-82430-5, Viking Kestrel). Viking.

Tina's Eighteenth Summer, No. 6. Hilda Stahl. 1982. pap. 2.95 (ISBN 0-8423-7219-9). Tyndale.

Tina's Island Home. J. van Walsum-Quispel. LC 71-99920. (Illus.). 36p. (gr. k-5). 7.95 (ISBN 0-87592-053-5). Scroll Pr.

Tina's Reluctant Friend, No. 3. Hilda Stahl. (gr. 4-7). 1981. pap. 2.95 (ISBN 0-8423-7216-4). Tyndale.

Tina's Science Notebook. Tina DeCloux & Rosanne Werges. (Illus.). 70p. (gr. k-3). 1985. pap. 9.95 (ISBN 0-9615903-0-0). Symbiosis Bks.

Tina's Secret Rival, No. 5. Hilda Stahl. 1981. pap. 2.95 (ISBN 0-8423-7215-6). Tyndale.

Tinbergen Lectures in Organization Theory. 2nd, rev. ed. M. J. Beckmann. (Texts & Monographs in Economics & Mathematical Systems). 280p. 1988. 29.50 (ISBN 0-387-18515-1). Springer-Verlag.

Tincal Trail. N. J. Travis & E. J. Cocks. 1986. 24.75X (ISBN 0-245-53798-8, Pub. by Harrap Ltd England). State Mutual Bk.

Tincraft for Christmas. Lucy Sargent. (Illus.). 1969. 7.95 (ISBN 0-688-02638-9); pap. 5.95 (ISBN 0-688-07638-6). Morrow.

Tincture of the Philosophers. Paracelsus. Tr. by A. E. Waite from Lat. 1984. pap. 2.95 (ISBN 0-916411-45-1, Pub. by Alchemical). Holmes Pub.

Tincup Railroad War, No. 55. J. D. Hardin. 192p. 1985. pap. 2.50 (ISBN 0-425-08669-0). Berkley Pub.

Tinde in the Mountains: A Novel. Ken Smith. 176p. (Orig.). 1988. pap. 12.95 (ISBN 0-86975-322-3, Pub. by Ravan Pr). Ohio U Pr.

Tindel's Blue Door. 2nd ed. Beatrice Tallarico & S. C. Stone. (Weeuns Ser.). (Illus.). 19p. (gr. 2-8). 1986. pap. 2.95 (ISBN 0-936191-14-7). Tallstone Pub.

Tinderbox. Hans Christian Andersen. (Illus.). 32p. (gr. 1 up). 1988. 13.95 (ISBN 0-689-50458-6, M K McElderry). Macmillan.

Ting Hsien: A North China Rural Community. Sidney D. Gamble. LC 68-13743. (Illus.). 1954. 42.50x (ISBN 0-8047-0630-1); pap. 15.95 (ISBN 0-8047-0632-8, SP87). Stanford U Pr.

Ting Hsien Experiment in Nineteen Thirty-Four. Y. C. Yen. 64p. 1975. 6.00 (ISBN 0-942717-17-1); pap. 4.00 (ISBN 0-318-14584-7). Intl Inst Rural.

Ting Iang Mine & Other Plays. Nick Darke. (Methuen Theatrescript Ser.). 70p. 1988. pap. text ed. 9.95 (ISBN 0-413-17930-3). Heinemann Ed.

Ting-Li's Tales Told on the Devil's Mountain. Miriam Gregory. Ed. by Piequet Press Staff. (Illus.). 60p. (Orig.). (gr. 3-7). 1987. pap. write for info. (ISBN 0-914275-13-5). Piequet Pr.

Ting Ware of the Sung Dynasty, Bk. 1. Compiled by National Palace Museum Staff. 62p. 1962. 325.00x (ISBN 0-317-45304-1, Pub. by Han-Shan Tang Ltd). State Mutual Bk.

Tingambato: Archeology Today in Mexico. Iris Noble. LC 82-12443. (Illus.). 192p. (YA) (gr. 7 up). 1982. PLB 9.79 (ISBN 0-671-43014-9). Messner.

Tinies ABC Pop-Up Book. (Pop-Up Bks.). (Illus.). (ps-1). 1.49 (ISBN 0-517-43893-3). Outlet Bk Co.

Tiniest Fir Tree. Eleanor Nappa. (Illus.). 32p. (gr. 1-2). 1986. 5.95 (ISBN 0-89962-513-4). Todd & Honeywell.

Tiniest Mole. Paule Alen. LC 85-63495. (Illus.). 24p. (ps-3). 1986. 6.75 (ISBN 0-382-09209-0). Silver.

Tink in a Tangle. Dorothy Haas. Ed. by Kathleen Tucker. LC 83-16654. (Illus.). 128p. (gr. 2-5). 1984. PLB 8.95 (ISBN 0-8075-7952-1). A Whitman.

Tink in a Tangle see Too Much Trouble.

Tinker & a Poor Man: John Bunyan & His Church, 1628-1688. Christopher Hill. LC 88-45350. 432p. 1989. 22.95 (ISBN 0-394-57242-4). Knopf.

Tinker of Bedford: A Historical Fiction on the Life & Times of John Bunyan. William S. Deal. 1977. pap. 2.95 (ISBN 0-686-19330-X). Crusade Pubs.

Tinker, Tailor, & Textile Worker: Class & Politics in Egypt, 1930-1954. Ellis Goldberg. 280p. 1986. text ed. 30.00x (ISBN 0-520-05353-2). U of Cal Pr.

Tinker, Tailor, Soldier, Spy. John Le Carre. 384p. 1985. pap. 4.95 (ISBN 0-553-26778-7). Bantam.

Tinker, Tailor, Soldier, Spy. John Le Carre. 1974. 17.45 (ISBN 0-394-49219-6). Knopf.

Tinker's Journey Home. Devony Lehner. Ed. by P. Dennis Maloney. (Illus.). 34p. (ps-6). Date not set. 12.95 (ISBN 0-940305-00-3). P D Maloney.

Tinker's Leave. Maurice Baring. 1928. 25.00 (ISBN 0-8274-3630-0). R West.

Tinkler Gypsies. Andrew McCormick. LC 77-19203. 1907. 55.00 (ISBN 0-8414-6235-6). Folcroft.

Tinnitus. Jonathan W. Hazell. LC 86-9311. (Illus.). 207p. 1987. text ed. 56.00 (ISBN 0-443-02156-2). Churchill.

Tinnitus: A Guide for Sufferers & Professionals. Robert Slater et al. (Illus.). 250p. 1987. text ed. 45.00x (ISBN 0-7099-3338-X, Pub. by Croom Helm UK); pap. text ed. 17.95x (ISBN 0-7099-3339-8, Pub. by Croom Helm UK). Sheridan Med Bks.

Tinnitus & Its Management: A Clinical Text for Audiologists. John G. Clark & Paul Yanick, Jr. (Illus.). 206p. 1984. 27.25x (ISBN 0-398-05043-0). C C Thomas.

Tinnitus: Diagnosis-Treatment. Abraham Shulman et al. 400p. Date not set. price not set. Lea & Febiger.

Tinnitus: Facts, Theories, & Treatments. National Research Council. 1983. pap. text ed. 11.25x (ISBN 0-309-03328-4). Natl Acad Pr.

Tino Di Comaino, a Sienese Sculptor of the Fourteenth Century. Wilhelm R. Valentiner. Tr. by R. H. Boothroyd. LC 73-143366. (Illus.). 107p. Repr. of 1935 ed. write for info. (ISBN 0-87817-085-5). Hacker.

Tinonc: Son of the Cajun Teche. Robert L. Olivier. (Illus.). 122p. 1974. 5.95 (ISBN 0-88289-054-9). Pelican.

Tinplate. Steed. 1988. pap. 2.95 (ISBN 0-312-91076-2). St Martin.

Tinplate. Neville Steed. (Peter Marklin Mystery Ser.). 256p. 1987. 14.95 (ISBN 0-312-00196-7). St Martin.

Tinplate & Modern Canmaking Technology. E. Morgan. (Pergamon Materials Engineering Practice Ser.). (Illus.). 1985. text ed. 40.00 (ISBN 0-08-028681-X); pap. text ed. 16.75 (ISBN 0-08-028680-1). Pergamon.

Tins 'n' Bins. Robert W. Swedberg & Harriett Swedberg. LC 84-50512. (Illus.). 136p. 1985. 15.95 (ISBN 0-87069-397-2). Wallace Homestead.

Tinsel. William Goldman. 1979. pap. 10.95 (ISBN 0-385-29031-4). Delacorte.

Tinsel Town. Catherine Mann. 416p. 1986. pap. 3.95 (ISBN 0-380-70142-1). Avon.

Tinsel Town: A Novel. Catherine Mann. 1985. 19.95 (ISBN 0-671-55262-7). S&S.

Tinseltown Murders: A Mac Slade Mystery. John Blumenthal. 1985. pap. 2.95 (Fireside). S&S.

Tinseltowns U. S. A. John Kremer. (Illus.). 128p. (Orig.). 1988. 12.95 (ISBN 0-912411-21-X); pap. 6.95 (ISBN 0-912411-18-X). Ad-Lib.

Tintin & the Broken Ear. Herge. (Illus.). 62p. 15.95 (ISBN 0-416-83450-7); pap. 4.95 (ISBN 0-416-57030-5). French & Eur.

Tintin & the Golden Fleece. Herge. (gr. 3-8). looseleaf bdg. 15.95 (ISBN 0-685-11599-2). French & Eur.

Tintin & the Lake of Sharks. Herge. (Illus.). 62p. 15.95 (ISBN 0-416-78950-1); pap. 4.95 (ISBN 0-416-83630-5). French & Eur.

Tintin & the Picaros. Herge. (Illus.). 62p. 15.95 (ISBN 0-416-85170-3); pap. 4.95 (ISBN 0-416-57990-6). French & Eur.

Tintin & the Picaros. Herge. 1978. pap. 6.95 (ISBN 0-316-35849-5, Joy St Bks). Little.

Tintin au Congo. Herge. (Illus., Fr.). (gr. 7-9). looseleaf bdg. 15.95 (ISBN 0-685-28415-8). French & Eur.

Tintin au Pays de L'or Noir. Herge. (Fr.). (gr. 7-9). looseleaf bdg. 15.95 (ISBN 0-685-23420-7). French & Eur.

Tintin Au Tibet. Herge. (gr. 7-9). looseleaf bdg. 15.95 (ISBN 0-685-23422-3). French & Eur.

Tintin en America. Herge. (Illus.). 62p. (Span.). 15.95 (ISBN 0-686-54329-7). French & Eur.

Tintin en Amerique. Herge. (Illus.). 62p. (Fr.). 15.95 (ISBN 0-686-54287-8). French & Eur.

Tintin en el Congo. Herge. (Illus.). 62p. (Span.). 15.95 (ISBN 0-686-54328-9). French & Eur.

Tintin en el Pais del Oro Negro. Herge. (Illus.). 62p. (Span.). 15.95 (ISBN 0-686-54341-6). French & Eur.

Tintin en el Tibet. Herge. (Illus.). 62p. (Span.). 15.95 (ISBN 0-686-54346-7). French & Eur.

Tintin et la Mystere de la Toison d'Or. (gr. 7-9). 15.95 (ISBN 0-685-33970-X). French & Eur.

Tintin et les Picaros. Herge. (Illus.). 62p. (Fr.). 15.95 (ISBN 0-686-54304-1). French & Eur.

Tintin im Amerika. Herge. (Illus.). 62p. (Ger.). pap. 15.95 (ISBN 0-686-54306-8). French & Eur.

Tintin im Kongo. Herge. (Illus.). 62p. (Ger.). pap. 15.95 (ISBN 0-686-54305-X). French & Eur.

Tintin in America. Herge. (Illus.). 62p. 15.95 (ISBN 0-416-86120-2). French & Eur.

Tintin in America. Herge. LC 79-64865. (Adventures of Tintin Ser.). 1979. pap. 6.95 (ISBN 0-316-35852-5, Joy St Bks). Little.

Tintin in Tibet. Herge. (Illus.). 62p. 15.95 (ISBN 0-416-92600-2); pap. 4.95 (ISBN 0-416-24090-9). French & Eur.

Tintin in Tibet. Herge. LC 74-21621. (Adventures of Tintin Ser.). (gr. k up). 1975. pap. 6.95 (ISBN 0-316-35839-8, Joy St Bks). Little.

Tintin y los Picaros. Herge. (Illus.). 62p. (Span.). 15.95 (ISBN 0-686-54349-1). French & Eur.

Tintinnabulations of Boos & Applause. David Kalugin. (Illus.). 1979. pap. 4.95 (ISBN 0-933586-05-1). Book Promo Pr.

Tintoretto. Terisio Pignatti & Francesco Valcanover. (Library of Great Painters). (Illus.). 168p. 1985. 45.00 (ISBN 0-8109-1650-9). Abrams.

Tinware: Yesterday & Today. (Americana Books Ser.). (Illus.). 1974. 3.00 (ISBN 0-911410-36-8). Applied Arts.

Tiny & Tuffy the Little Koalas. (ps). 1976. 2.50 (ISBN 0-904494-31-4, Brimax Bks). Borden.

Tiny Ant Who Scared a Horned Toad. Goldie B. Despain. (Illus.). (ps-3). 1970. write for info. (ISBN 0-8313-0029-9); PLB 6.19. Lantern.

Tiny Bat & the Ball Game. Margaret Z. Searcy. LC 78-61367. (Illus.). (gr. 2-4). 1978. 7.50 (ISBN 0-916620-19-0). Portals Pr.

Tiny Christmas Elf. Sharon Peters. LC 86-30849. (Illus.). 32p. (gr. k-2). 1987. PLB 5.41 (ISBN 0-8167-0988-2); pap. text ed. 1.50 (ISBN 0-8167-0989-0). Troll Assocs.

Tiny Dinos ABC. Guy Gilchrist. LC 87-40336. (Tiny Dinos Concept Bks.). (Illus.). (ps-1). 1988. 4.95 (ISBN 1-55782-012-0). Warner Bks.

Tiny Dinos & the Best Place in the World. Guy Gilchrist. LC 87-40695. (Illus.). 48p. (ps-3). 1988. bds. 6.95 (ISBN 1-55782-101-1). Warner Bks.

Tiny Dinos Beach Party Activity Book. Guy Gilchrist. (Illus.). Date not set. 1.50 (ISBN 1-55782-030-9). Warner Bks.

Tiny Dinos Big & Small: A Book of Opposites. Guy Gilchrist. LC 87-40691. (Illus.). 24p. (ps-1). 1988. bds. 4.95 (ISBN 1-55782-106-2). Warner Bks.

Tiny Dinos Fun at the Beach: A Book of Actions. Guy Gilchrist. LC 87-40337. (Tiny Dinos Concept Bks.). (Illus.). (ps-1). 1988. 4.95 (ISBN -155782-013-9). Warner Bks.

Tiny Dinos Hide 'n' Seek. Guy Gilchrist. LC 87-40334. (Tiny Dinos Peek-a-Boo Bks.). (Illus.). (ps up). 1988. 4.95 (ISBN 1-55782-009-0). Warner Bks.

Tiny Dinos Playing Together: A Book of Everyday Feelings. Guy Gilchrist. LC 87-40338. (Tiny Dinos Concept Bks.). (Illus.). (ps-1). 1988. 4.95 (ISBN 1-55782-014-7). Warner Bks.

Tiny Dinos Silly Safari! Guy Gilchrist. LC 87-40694. (Peek-a-Boo Book Ser.). (Illus.). 12p. (ps up). 1988. bds. 4.95 (ISBN 1-55782-069-4). Warner Bks.

Tiny Dinos: Sir Waldo's Island Adventure. Corey Nash. LC 87-40332. (Illus.). 48p. (ps-2). 1988. 6.95 (ISBN 1-55782-010-4). Warner Bks.

Tiny Dinos: The Shapes We're In. Guy Gilchrist. LC 87-40690. (Illus.). 24p. (ps-1). 1988. bds. 4.95 (ISBN 1-55782-104-6). Warner Bks.

Tiny Family. Norman Bridwell. (Illus.). (gr. k-3). 1968. pap. 1.50 (ISBN 0-590-02539-2). Scholastic Inc.

Tiny Footprints. B. Kliban. LC 77-94068. (Illus.). 160p. 1978. pap. 3.95 (ISBN 0-89480-031-0, 186). Workman Pub.

Tiny Hooty & the Percher see Tommy Scott Young Spins Magical Tales.

Tiny Houses. Lester Walker. LC 86-21736. (Illus.). 208p. 1987. 19.95 (ISBN 0-87951-271-7). Overlook Pr.

Tiny Miracle. Richard M. Wainwright. 40p. 1986. text ed. 9.95 (ISBN 0-318-24006-8). Family Life.

Tiny Mouse. Gary L. Wheeler & David M. Strang. 1980. pap. 4.95 (ISBN 0-937172-10-3). JLJ Pubs.

Tiny Ptery, Come Home! A Tiny Dinos Story about Safety. Guy Gilchrist. LC 87-40688. (Tiny Dinos Ser.). (Illus.). 24p. (ps-2). 1988. bds. 4.95 (ISBN 1-55782-074-0). Warner Bks.

Tiny Seed. Eric Carle. LC 86-2534. (Illus.). 32p. (gr. k up). 1987. 14.95 (ISBN 0-88708-015-4). Picture Bk Studio.

Tiny Sheep. Bunshu Iguchi. 24p. (ps up). 1986. 9.95 (ISBN 0-8170-1108-0). Judson.

Tiny Shiny. Lloyd Funchess, Jr. 1964. 2.95 (ISBN 0-87511-052-5). Claitors.

Tiny Squash. Karean L. Sheldon. (gr. 3-5). 1987. 4.95 (ISBN 0-533-07010-4). Vantage.

Tiny Tale of Peter Rabbit. Beatrix Potter. (Peter Rabbit Board Bks.). (Illus.). 14p. (ps-k). 1982. bd 3.50 (ISBN 0-671-44518-9, Little Simon). S&S.

Tiny Tale of Peter Rabbit. 1988. pap. 2.95 (ISBN 0-671-52695-2, Little Simon). S&S.

Tiny Tales from Happywood. Marjory Arr. (gr. 1-3). 1985. pap. 4.95 (ISBN 0-533-05659-4). Vantage.

Tiny Tickle Book. McCully. (Wee Pudgy Board Bks.). (gr. 2 up). 1988. 2.50 (ISBN 0-448-09255-7, G&D). Putnam Pub Group.

Tiny Tiger Meets the Grimbles. Moira Neal. (ps). 1986. 6.95 (ISBN 0-8120-5766-X). Barron.

Tiny Tiger's Squeaky Sweater. Moira Neal. (ps). 1986. 6.95 (ISBN 0-8120-5767-8). Barron.

Tiny Tim. Illus. by Helen Oxenbury. LC 81-68916. (Illus.). 32p. (ps-3). 1982. PLB 10.95; pap. 10.95 (ISBN 0-385-29055-1). Delacorte.

Tiny Tot's Animal Talk. Illus. by Kathy Wilburn. LC 86-891488. (Golden Tiny Tot's Books). (Illus.). 12p. (ps). 1987. pap. write for info. (ISBN 0-307-06150-7, Pub. by Golden Bks). Western Pub.

Tiny Tot's Busy Day. Illus. by Kathy Wilburn. LC 86-81487. (Golden Tiny Tot's Books). (Illus.). 12p. (ps). 1987. pap. write for info. (Pub. by Golden Bks). Western Pub.

Tissue Culture Methods for Plant Pathologists: Organized by the British Plant Pathologists, Vol. 2. D. S. Ingram & J. P. Helgeson. (Federation of British Plants Pathologists Ser.). 272p. 1981. 69.95x (ISBN 0-470-27048-9). Halsted Pr.

Tissue Culture of Epithelial Cells. Ed. by Mary Taub. LC 84-13470. 310p. 1985. 52.50x (ISBN 0-306-41740-5, Plenum Pr). Plenum Pub.

Tissue Culture of Selected Tropical Fruit Plants: A Handbook on the Application of Tissue Culture to Plant Propogation. Roberto Jona. Ed. by U. G. Menini. (FAO Plant Production & Protection Paper: No. 79). (Illus.). 125p. (Orig.). 1987. pap. text ed. 8.00 (ISBN 92-5-102086-8, F3091, FAO). UNIPUB.

Tissue Culture Technique. 2nd ed. Gladys Cameron. 1950. 46.50 (ISBN 0-12-156650-1). Acad Pr.

Tissue Culture Techniques. Luccio Nuzzolo & Augusto Vellucci. LC 67-26015. (Illus.). 254p. 1983. 37.50 (ISBN 0-87527-117-0). Green.

Tissue Culture Techniques for Horticultural Crops. Kenneth C. Torres. (Illus.). 1987. text ed. write for info. (ISBN 0-87055-536-7). AVI.

Tissue Culture Techniques for Horticultural Crops. Kenneth C. Torres. (Illus.). 224p. 1988. text ed. 42.95 (ISBN 0-442-28465-9). Van Nos Reinhold.

Tissue Growth Factors. Ed. by R. Baserga. (Handbook of Experimental Pharmacology: Vol. 57). (Illus.). 500p. 1981. 176.00 (ISBN 0-387-10623-5). Springer-Verlag.

Tissue-Integrated Prostheses. Per-Ingvar Branemark et al. (Illus.). 352p. 1985. pap. text ed. 88.00 (ISBN 0-86715-129-3). Quint Pub CO.

Tissue Integration in Oral & Maxillofacial Reconstruction: Proceedings of the International Congress, Brussels, May, 1985. Ed. by D. Van Steenberghe. (Current Clinical Practice Ser.: Vol. 29). 519p. 1986. 193.75 (ISBN 0-444-90446-8). Elsevier.

Tissue Interactions & Development. Norman K. Wessells. LC 76-42696. 1977. pap. text ed. 21.95 (ISBN 0-8053-9620-9). Benjamin-Cummings.

Tissue Interactions During Organogenesis. Ed. by E. Wolff & T. Lender. (Documents in Biology Ser.: Vol. 1). 240p. 1970. 72.00 (ISBN 0-677-13010-4). Gordon & Breach.

Tissue Management in Restorative Dentistry. Ed. by William F. Malone. (Illus.). 344p. 1982. 38.00 (ISBN 0-88416-154-4). PSG Pub Co.

Tissue Nutrition & Viability. Ed. by A. R. Hargens. (Illus.). vii, 312p. 1986. 74.95 (ISBN 0-387-96202-6). Springer-Verlag.

Tissue of Lies: Eudora Welty & the Southern Romance. Jennifer L. Randisi. LC 82-45042. 198p. (Orig.). 1982. PLB 29.25 (ISBN 0-8191-2451-6); pap. text ed. 12.50 (ISBN 0-8191-2452-4). U Pr of Amer.

Tissue Plasminogen Activator in Thrombolytic Chemistry. Sobel. Ed. by Collen & Grossbard. 264p. 1987. 55.00 (ISBN 0-8247-7666-6). Dekker.

Tissue Repair & Regeneration. Ed. by L. E. Glynn. (Handbook of Inflammation: Vol. 3). 598p. 1981. 201.00 (ISBN 0-444-80278-9, Biomedical Pr). Elsevier.

Tissue Specificity & Autoimmunity. S. Shulman. (Molecular Biology, Biochemistry, & Biophysics Ser: Vol. 16). (Illus.). 250p. 1974. 37.00 (ISBN 0-387-06563-6). Springer-Verlag.

Tissue Transfers in Reconstructive Surgery. Herman T. Smet. (Illus.). 375p. 1988. text ed. price not set (ISBN 0-88167-456-7). Raven.

Tissue-Type Plasminogen Activator (t-PA) Physiological & Clinical Aspects. Cornelis Kluft. 1988. Vol. I, 256 pgs. 140.00 (ISBN 0-8493-4608-8, 4608); Vol. II, 192 pgs. 110.00 (ISBN 0-8493-4609-6, 4609). CRC Pr.

Tissue Typing Today. Ed. by Felix T. Rapaport & Jean Dausset. LC 74-170194. 160p. 1971. 64.50 (ISBN 0-8089-0738-7, 793517). Grune.

Tissues & Organs: A Text-Atlas of Scanning Electron Microscopy. Richard G. Kessel & Randy H. Kardon. LC 78-23886. (Illus.). 317p. 1979. pap. text ed. 27.95 (ISBN 0-7167-0090-5). W H Freeman.

Tista Basin: A Study in Fluvial Geomorphology. S. C. Mukkopadhyay. 308p. 1984. 49.00x (ISBN 0-317-20278-2, Pub. by K P Bagchi & Co). State Mutual Bk.

Tit for Tat. facsimile ed. M. Estes. LC 72-38649. (Black Heritage Library Collections). Repr. of 1856 ed. 22.50 (ISBN 0-8369-9007-2). Ayer Co Pubs.

Titan. Theodore Dreiser. 1965. pap. 4.95 (ISBN 0-452-00756-9, Mer). NAL.

Titan. Theodore Dreiser. LC 83-45747. Repr. of 1946 ed. 27.50 (ISBN 0-404-20084-2). AMS Pr.

Titan. Fred M. Stewart. 509p. 1985. 18.95 (ISBN 0-671-50689-7). S&S.

Titan. Fred M. Stewart. 1986. pap. 4.50 (ISBN 0-671-50692-7). PB.

Titan. John Varley. 1985. pap. 3.95 (ISBN 0-425-09846-X). Berkley Pub.

Titanic. Richard A. Boning. (Incredible Ser.). (Illus.). 48p. (gr. 5-11). 1974. PLB 7.95 (ISBN 0-87966-107-0). B Loft.

Titanic. J. Rawlinson. (Great Adventure Ser.). (Illus.). 32p. (gr. 4 up). Date not set. PLB 13.27 (ISBN 0-86592-873-8). Rourke Corp.

Titanic. Frank Sloan. (First Book Ser.). (Illus.). 96p. (gr. 4-9). 1987. PLB 9.90 (ISBN 0-531-10396-X). Watts.

Titanic & Her Era. John M. Groff & Jane E. Allen. (Illus.). 32p. 1982. pap. 2.00 (ISBN 0-913346-07-1). Phila Maritime Mus.

Titanic: Destination Disaster: The Legend & Reality. John P. Eaton & Charles A. Hass. (Illus., Orig.). 1987. pap. 10.95 (ISBN 0-393-30492-2). Norton.

Titanic: End of a Dream. Wyn C. Wade. 1980. pap. 4.95 (ISBN 0-14-005562-2). Penguin.

Titanic: End of A Dream. rev. ed. Wyn C. Wade. 488p. 1986. pap. 4.95 (ISBN 0-14-009635-3). Penguin.

Titanic Interlude. Charles E. Ziavras. LC 83-80832. (Illus.). 359p. 1983. 14.95 (ISBN 0-915940-03-5); pap. 6.95 (ISBN 0-915940-04-3). Ithaca Pr MA.

Titanic: Lost & Found. Judy Donnelly. (Step into Reading Book & Cassette Library). (Illus.). 48p. (gr. k-3). 1988. pap. 5.95 bk. & cassette pkg. (ISBN 0-394-89773-0, BYR). Random.

Titanic: Lost...& Found. Judy Donnelly. LC 86-20402. (Step into Reading Bk.). (Illus.). 48p. (gr. 1-3). 1987. lib. bdg. 6.99 (ISBN 0-394-98669-5, BYR); pap. 2.95 (ISBN 0-394-88669-0, BYR). Random.

Titanic Revisited. Leo Cohen. LC 84-60508. (Illus.). 78p. 1984. pap. 4.95 (ISBN 0-9613366-0-9). L Cohen.

Titanic: The Death & Life of a Legend. Michael Davie. LC 86-46021. 272p. 1987. 19.95 (ISBN 0-317-58565-7). Knopf.

Titanic: The Death & Life of a Legend. Micheal Davie. LC 88-13211. (Owl Bks.). (Illus.). 1988. 9.95 (ISBN 0-8050-0909-4). H Holt & Co.

Titanic, the Psychic & the Sea. Rustie Brown. LC 80-70551. (Illus.). 176p. 1981. 14.95 (ISBN 0-9605278-0-X). Blue Harbor.

Titanic: The Search for Sir Malcolm. Francois Riviere. Ed. by Bernd Metz. Tr. by Elizabeth Bell from Fr. (Illus.). 48p. (Orig.). 1988. pap. 10.95 (ISBN 0-87416-061-8). Catalan Communs.

Titanic: The Story in Pictures. John Eaton & Charles Haas. (Illus.). 1987. 45.00 (ISBN 0-393-02380-X). Norton.

Titanic: Triumph & Tragedy. John Eaton & Charles Haas. (Illus.). 1986. 45.00. Norton.

Titanic Trivia. A. F. Marshello. LC 87-90690. 104p. (Orig.). 1987. pap. 9.95 (ISBN 0-9619092-1-8). AFJ Marshello.

Titanium. Alan D. McQuillan & M. K. McQuillan. LC 56-4724. (Metallurgy of the Rarer Metals Ser.: No. 4). pap. 121.50 (ISBN 0-317-42137-9, 2025759). Bks Demand UMI.

Titanium Alloys in Surgical Implants - STP 796. Ed. by Hugh A. Luckey & Fred Kubli, Jr. LC 84-72888. 295p. 1983. text ed. 37.50 (ISBN 0-8031-0241-0, 04-796000-54). ASTM.

Titanium & Its Alloys: Investigation of Titanium Alloys. I. I. Kornilov. 392p. 1966. text ed. 79.00x (ISBN 0-7065-0395-3, Pub. by Keter Pub Jerusalem). Coronet Bks.

Titanium & Superalloys II: Battling the Economics Elements. Ed. by Brian Nolk. 188p. 1984. pap. text ed. write for info. (ISBN 0-913333-04-2). Metal Bulletin.

Titanium & Titanium Alloys: Scientific & Technological Aspects, 3 vols. Ed. by J. C. Williams & A. F. Belov. LC 79-9156. 2500p. 1982. 295.00x (ISBN 0-306-40191-6, Plenum Pr). Plenum Pub.

Titanium & Titanium Alloys: Source Book. Ed. by Matthew Donachie, Jr. 1982. 55.00 (ISBN 0-87170-140-5). ASM.

Titanium Net-Shape Technologies. Ed. by F. H. Froes & D. Eylon. LC 84-61708. 299p. 1985. 60.00 (ISBN 0-89520-482-7). Metal Soc.

Titanium, Nineteen Eighty-Seven: A Statistical Review. Ed. by Titanium Development Association. 20p. 1988. pap. 20.00 (ISBN 0-935297-08-1). Titanium.

Titanium Nineteen Eighty-Six: Products & Applications Proceedings of the Technical Program from the 1986 International Conference, 2 vols. Intro. by Titanium Development Association Staff. (Orig.). 1987. pap. 75.00x (ISBN 0-935297-04-9). Titanium.

Titanium: Physico-Chemical Properties of Its Compounds & Alloys. (Atomic Energy Review Ser.: No. 9, Special Issue). (Illus.). 460p. 1983. pap. text ed. 89.00 (ISBN 92-0-149083-6, IAER9, IAEA). UNIPUB.

Titanium Production, Processing, Handling & Storage of. (Forty Ser). 1974. pap. 2.50 (ISBN 0-685-58154-3, 481). Natl Fire Prot.

Titanium, Rapid Solidification Technology. Ed. by F. H. Froes & D. Eylon. (Illus.). 323p. 1986. 96.00 (ISBN 0-87339-050-4). Metal Soc.

Titanium Technology: Present Status & Future Trends. F. H. Froes et al. (Orig.). 1985. pap. 19.95x (ISBN 0-935297-00-6). Titanium.

Titanium the Choice... B. Bannon et al. 13p. (Orig.). 1987. pap. 2.00 (ISBN 0-935297-07-3). Titanium.

Titanium, 1986: A Statistical Review. Ed. by Titanium Development Association Staff. 1987. pap. 15.00x (ISBN 0-935297-05-7). Titanium.

Titanium '80: Science & Technology, 4 vols. LC 80-84610. 3145p. 1980. 20.00 (ISBN 0-89520-370-7). Metal Soc.

Titanotheres of Ancient Wyoming, Dakota, & Nebraska. Department of the Interior, U. S. Geologicaal Survey, Monograph & Henry F. Osborn. Ed. by Stephen J. Gould. LC 79-83341. (History of Paleontology Ser.: 55 2vols.). (Illus.). 1980. Repr. of 1929 ed. Set. lib. bdg. 224.00x (ISBN 0-405-12729-4); lib. bdg. 112.00xa. Vol. 1 (ISBN 0-405-12730-8). Vol. 2 (ISBN 0-405-12731-6). Ayer Co Pubs.

Titans. Ed. by Lorayne Ashton. (Park Avenue Ser.: No. 6). 368p. 1988. pap. 3.95 (ISBN 0-8041-0172-8, Pub. by Ivy). Ballantine.

Titans. John Jakes. 640p. 1986. pap. 4.95 (ISBN 0-515-08656-8). Jove Pubns.

Titans & Prometheans, 2 vols. Burton Rascoe. Set. 100.00 (ISBN 0-8490-1216-3). Gordon Pr.

Titans of Literature from Homer to the Present. Burton Rascoe. LC 76-121502. (Essay Index Reprint Ser). 1932. 21.50 (ISBN 0-8369-1775-8). Ayer Co Pubs.

Titans of Takeover. Robert Slater. (Illus.). 240p. 1987. 21.95 (ISBN 0-13-922055-0). P-H.

Titans ou les Trois Dumas. Andre Maurois. pap. 12.50 (ISBN 0-685-36963-3). French & Eur.

Titantic. Paul Clifford. 75p. 1988. 7.95 (ISBN 0-533-07613-7). Vantage.

Titch. Chaim Bermant. 192p. 1987. 13.95 (ISBN 0-312-01099-0). St Martin.

Titch. Pat Hutchins. LC 77-146622. (Illus.). 32p. (ps-1). 1971. 11.95 (ISBN 0-02-745880-6). Macmillan.

Tite. Clay Reynolds. 448p. 1986. 17.95a (ISBN 0-312-01170-9). St Martin.

Tite, Tragi-Comedie: A Critical Edition. Jean Magnon. 1973. pap. 14.00 (ISBN 0-384-35045-3). Johnson Repr.

Titeres y Otras Diversiones Populares de Madrid: 1758-1840, Estudio Y Documentos. Ed. by J. E. Varey. (Serie C: Fuentes para la Historia del Teatro en Espana, VII). (Illus.). 292p. (Orig., Span.). 1972. pap. 18.00 (Pub. by Tamesis Bks Ltd). Longwood Pub Group.

Tithe & Agrarian History from the Fourteenth to the Nineteenth Century: An Essay in Comparative History. Emmanuel Le Roy Ladurie & Joseph Goy. LC 81-7725. 192p. 1982. 39.50 (ISBN 0-521-23974-5). Cambridge U Pr.

Tithe: Challenge or Legalism. Douglas W. Johnson. 128p. 1984. pap. 7.95 (ISBN 0-687-42127-6). Abingdon.

Tithe Proctor: Being a Tale of the Tithe Rebellion in Ireland. William Carleton. LC 79-8246. Repr. of 1849 ed. 44.50 (ISBN 0-404-61806-5). AMS Pr.

Tithe Surveys of England & Wales. Roger J. Kain & Hugh C. Prince. (Studies in Historical Geography: No. 6). (Illus.). 344p. 1985. 54.50 (ISBN 0-521-24681-4). Cambridge U Pr.

Tithing. Karen D. Merrell. 22p. (ps-2). pap. 4.95 (ISBN 0-87747-560-1). Deseret Bk.

Tithing. A. W. Pink. pap. 0.50 (ISBN 0-686-48166-6). Reiner.

Tithing: A Call to Serious, Biblical Giving. R. T. Kendall. 128p. 1983. pap. 5.95 (ISBN 0-310-38331-5, 9279P). Zondervan.

Tithing: God's Command Or Man's Demand - Which? Tony Badillo. (Illus.). 102p. (Orig.). 1984. pap. 9.50 (ISBN 0-912977-00-0). Xavier Pr.

Tithonian (Jurassic) Ammonite Fauna & Stratigraphy of Sierra Catorce, San Luis Potosi, Mexico see Bulletins of American Paleontology.

Titian. Dario Cecchi. Tr. by Nora Wydenbruck from Ital. LC 72-13188. (Biography Index Reprint Ser). Repr. of 1958 ed. 19.50 (ISBN 0-8369-8143-X). Ayer Co Pubs.

Titian. Ugo Fasolo. (Illus.). 95p. (Orig.). 1980. pap. 13.95 (ISBN 0-935748-09-1). Scala Books.

Titian. C. Hope. LC 79-3393. (Icon Editors Ser). (Illus.). 240p. 1980. 29.95 (ISBN 0-06-433375-2); 29.45i. Har-Row.

Titian. David Rosand. (Library of Great Painters). (Illus.). 1978. 45.00 (ISBN 0-8109-1654-1). Abrams.

Titian. Tatiana Znamerovaskaya. (Masters of World Painting Ser.). 1983. pap. 26.00x (ISBN 0-317-57471-X, Pub. by Collets UK). State Mutual Bk.

Titian. T. Znamerovskaya. 32p. 1983. pap. 7.95 (ISBN 0-8285-2661-3, Pub. by Aurora Pubs USSR). Imported Pubns.

Titian & His Drawings: With Reference to Giorgione & Some Close Contemporaries. Harold E. Wethey. (Kress Foundation Studies in the History of European Art: No. 8). (Illus.). 424p. 1988. text ed. 95.00x (ISBN 0-691-04040-0). Princeton U Pr.

Titian & the Venetian Woodcut. David Rosand & Michelangelo Muraro. LC 75-25621. (Illus.). 315p. 1976. pap. 14.95 (ISBN 0-88397-067-8, Pub. by Intl Exhibit Foun). C E Tuttle.

Titian: His World & His Legacy. Ed. by David Rosand. LC 81-3823. (Bampton Lecture Series in America: No. 21). (Illus.). 312p. 1982. 64.00x (ISBN 0-231-05300-2). Columbia U Pr.

Titian Ramsay Peale, 1799-1885, & His Journals of the Wilkes Expedition: (Memoirs Ser.: Vol.52) Jessie Poesch. (Vol. 52). 214p. 1979. Repr. 20.00 (ISBN 0-87169-052-7). Am Philos.

Titian's Assistants During the Later Years. M. Roy Fisher. LC 76-23618. (Outstanding Dissertations in the Fine Arts Ser.). 1977. lib. bdg. 68.00 (ISBN 0-8240-2689-6). Garland Pub.

Titkos Tortenelmi Adatok Az 1944 Oktober 15.-I Esemenyek Sopronkohidai Kihallhatasok see Secret Historical Facts: Events of October 15, 1944; Record of Evidence of Interrogations at Sopronkohida, Hungary.

Title. Arnold Bennett. LC 74-17056. (Collected Works of Arnold Bennett: Vol. 83). 1976. Repr. of 1918 ed. 16.75 (ISBN 0-518-19164-8). Ayer Co Pubs.

Title. Christopher Franke. 32p. 1975. pap. 2.50 (ISBN 0-914946-50-1). Cleveland St Univ Poetry Ctr.

Title Derivative Indexing Techniques: A Comparative Study. Hilda Feinberg. LC 73-2671. 307p. 1973. 30.00 (ISBN 0-8108-0602-9). Scarecrow.

Title Examination in Virginia. Sidney F. Parham, Jr. 1965. pap. 17.50x (ISBN 0-87215-107-7). Michie Co.

Title Examiner. Jack Rudman. (Career Examination Ser.: C-809). (Cloth bdg. avail. on request). pap. 12.00 (ISBN 0-8373-0809-7). Natl Learning.

Title Fifty-Nine; Tort Claims Against Public Entities, Amendments to May 1, 1984: Comments & Annotations. Harry A. Margolis. LC 84-208513. (Illus.). vii, 352p. 1984. pap. 28.00 (ISBN 0-933902-10-7). Gann Law Bks.

Title Guide to the Talkies, 2 Vols. Richard B. Dimmitt. LC 65-13556. 2133p. 1965. Set. 77.50 (ISBN 0-8108-0171-X). Scarecrow.

Title Guide to the Talkies, Nineteen Sixty-Four to Nineteen Seventy-Four. Andrew A. Aros. LC 76-40451. 344p. 1977. 25.00 (ISBN 0-8108-0976-1). Scarecrow.

Title Guide to the Talkies, Nineteen Seventy-Five Through Nineteen Eighty-Four. Andrew A. Aros. LC 85-27682. 355p. 1986. 27.50 (ISBN 0-8108-1868-X). Scarecrow.

Title Index to Architecture Series: Bibliography No. A 1 to A 1000 (June 1978-July 1983) Vance Bibliographies. (Architecture Ser.: Bibliography: No. A-997). 58p. 1983. pap. 9.00 (ISBN 0-88066-567-X). Vance Biblios.

Title Index to Public Administration Series: Bibliography No. P 1001 to P 2000 (July 1982-September 1986) (Public Administration Ser.: P 2003). 60p. 1986. 14.50 (ISBN 1-55590-003-8). Vance Biblios.

Title Index to Public Administration Series: Bibliography P1 to P1000 (June 1978-July 1982) Vance Bibliographies Staff. (Public Administration Ser.: Bibliography P-1059). 57p. 1982. pap. 8.25 (ISBN 0-88066-199-2). Vance Biblios.

Title Index to the Nineteenth Century Short Title Catalogue: Series I: 1801-1815. Ed. by Gwen Averley. 850p. 1986. lib. bdg. 299.00 (ISBN 0-907977-82-0). Chadwyck-Healey.

Title Insurance & Real Estate Securities Terminology. Intro. by John R. Johnsich. (Orig.). 1980. pap. 3.95 (ISBN 0-914256-11-4). Real Estate Pub.

Title Insurance & You: What Every Lawyer Should Know. LC 79-90959. 264p. 1979. pap. 15.00 (ISBN 0-89707-013-5). Amer Bar Assn.

Title Insurance: The Lawyer's Expanding Role. American Bar Association Staff & James M. Pedowitz. LC 85-73187. 567p. 1986. 49.95. Amer Bar Assn.

Title Insurance 1984 Course Handbook. (Real Estate Law & Practice Course Handbook, 1984-85: Vol. 251). 1984. pap. 35.00 (ISBN 0-685-59706-7, N4-4432). PLI.

Title Insurance 1987: The New Policy Forms. (Real Estate Law & Practice Course Handbook Ser.: No. 289). 744p. 1987. 45.00 (N44470). PLI.

Title Insurance, 1988: Comparing the 1987 & 1970 ALTA Policies. 629p. 1988. pap. 45.00 (N4-4486). PLI.

Title IX: Evaluating Equity in Education. rev. ed. Kaye L. Willhite. LC 86-50437. 75p. 1986. 3 ring binder 39.00 (ISBN 0-937579-49-1). Willco Pub.

Title IX: Implications for Education of Women. Frank D. Aquila. LC 81-80014. (Fastback Ser.: No. 156). 1981. pap. 0.90 (ISBN 0-87367-156-2). Phi Delta Kappa.

Title Key Word & Author Index to Psychoanalytic Journals. Ed. by Paul W. Mosher. 1988. 38.00. Am Psychoanalytic.

Title Management Assertions & Aversions. S. Eilon. (Illus.). 208p. 16.25 (ISBN 0-317-66839-0); 33.00 (ISBN 0-317-66840-4). Pergamon.

Title of the Lords of Totonicapan see Annals of the Cakchiquels.

Title Page of the First Folio of Shakespeare's Plays: A Comparative Study of the Droeshout Potrait & the Stratford Monument. Marion H. Spielmann. LC 75-176001. Repr. of 1924 ed. 18.00 (ISBN 0-404-07869-9). AMS Pr.

Title Searcher. Jack Rudman. (Career Examination Ser.: C-1516). (Cloth bdg. avail. on request). pap. 12.00 (ISBN 0-8373-1516-6). Natl Learning.

Title to Territory in Africa: International Legal Issues. Malcom Shaw. 1985. 66.00x (ISBN 0-19-825379-6). Oxford U Pr.

Title VII Program Handbook. Johanna Z. Provenzano. LC 84-65559. 41p. 1984. 3.75 (ISBN 0-89763-101-3). Natl Clearinghse Bilingual Ed.

Titled Elizabethans: A Directory of Elizabethan State & Church Officers & Knights, with Peers of England, Scotland, & Ireland, 1558-1603. Ed. by Arthur F. Kinney. LC 73-5700. x, 89p. 1973. 17.50 (ISBN 0-208-01334-2, Archon). Shoe String.

To AIDS & Back: The Lord God's Way to Health. Grady L. Etheridge et al. (Illus.). 120p. (Orig.). 1988. pap. 6.00x (ISBN 0-937417-04-1). Etheridge Minist.

To Alaska for Gold. John F. Stacey. 70p. 1973. Repr. of 1896 ed. 5.50 (ISBN 0-87770-096-6). Ye Galleon.

To All Generations, a Study of Church History. Frank Roberts. 276p. (Orig.). 1981. pap. text ed. 11.95 (ISBN 0-933140-17-7); leader's guide 8.75 (ISBN 0-933140-18-5). CRC Pubns.

To All My Fans, with Love from Sylvie. Ellen Conford. 192p. (gr. 7 up). 1982. 14.95 (ISBN 0-316-15312-5). Little.

To All My Fans, with Love from Sylvie. Ellen Conford. (gr. 7 up). 1983. pap. 2.25 (ISBN 0-686-44321-7). Archway.

To All My Friends. Morris A. Mercer, Jr. (Illus.). 64p. (Orig.). 1986. pap. write for info. (ISBN 0-9617362-0-8). M A Mercer.

To All My Grandchildren: Lessons in Indonesian Cooking. Leonie Samuel-Hool. Ed. by Sherman Hool. LC 80-84766. (Illus.). 120p. 1981. 12.95 (ISBN 0-936016-50-7); pap. 7.95 (ISBN 0-936016-75-2). Goodfellow.

To All Nations: The Billy Graham Story. John Pollock. (Ruth Graham Dienert Bk.). 1985. 15.45 (ISBN 0-06-066656-0). Har-Row.

To All the Brethren: A Text-Linguistic & Rhetorical Approach to I Thessalonians. Bruce C. Johanson. (Coniectanea Biblica New Testament Ser.: No. 16). xiv, 230p. (Orig.). 1987. pap. text ed. 26.50x (ISBN 0-317-64547-1). Coronet Bks.

To All the Girls I've Loved Before: An AIDS Diary. J. W. Money. 188p. (Orig.). 1987. pap. 6.95 (ISBN 1-55583-121-4). Alyson Pubns.

To All the Islands Now. Edgar Wolfe. 105p. 1986. pap. 5.00 (ISBN 0-939391-05-8). B Woodley Pr.

To Amuse a Shrinking Sun. John Digby. (Illus.). 72p. 1984. 11.95 (ISBN 0-85646-138-5, Pub. by Anvil Pr Poetry); pap. 6.95 (ISBN 0-85646-139-3). Longwood Pub Group.

To an Aging Nation (with Occult Overtones) see Gallery Series: Poets.

To an Easy Grave. Alexander Law. 230p. 1986. 12.95 (ISBN 0-312-80623-X, Thomas Dunne Bks). St Martin.

To an Idea: A Book of Poems. David Shapiro. LC 82-22328. 96p. 1983. 14.95 (ISBN 0-87951-176-1); 50.00 (ISBN 0-87951-181-8). Overlook Pr.

To an Idea: A Book of Poems. David Shapiro. LC 82-22328. 96p. 1986. pap. 8.95 (ISBN 0-87951-255-5). Overlook Pr.

To Analyze Data. 2nd ed. Carol T. Fitz-Gibbon & Lynn L. Morris. (Program Evaluation Kit Ser.: Vol. 8). 152p. 1987. pap. text ed. 12.95 (ISBN 0-8039-3133-6). Sage.

To Analyze Delight: A Hedonist Criticism of Shakespeare. Gary Taylor. LC 84-40617. 238p. 1985. 22.50 (ISBN 0-87413-269-X). U Delaware Pr.

To Anchor a Cloud. Dilip Hiro. (Writers Workshop Bluebird Ser.). 96p. 1975. 15.00 (ISBN 0-88253-662-1); pap. text ed. 6.75 (ISBN 0-88253-661-3). Ind-US Inc.

To & Fro in Southern California: With Sketches in Arizona & New Mexico. Emma H. Adams. Ed. by Carlos E. Cortes. LC 76-1220. (Chicano Heritage Ser.). 1976. Repr. of 1887 ed. 22.00x (ISBN 0-405-09481-7). Ayer Co Pubs.

To Appomattox. Burke Davis. 444p. Repr. 3.95 (ISBN 0-915992-17-5). Eastern Acorn.

To Arm a Nation: Rebuilding America's Endangered Defenses. Richard Halloran. LC 86-8717. 396p. 1986. 21.95 (ISBN 0-02-547540-1). Macmillan.

To As Preposition of Location in Linguistic Atlas Materials see Word-List from Zora Neale Hurston.

To Ascend from a Floating Base: Shipboard Aeronautics & Aviation, 1783-1914. R. D. Layman. LC 77-89782. (Illus.). 272p. 1979. 26.50 (ISBN 0-8386-2078-7). Fairleigh Dickinson.

To Ask Again, Yes. Carolyn Thornton. (American Romance Ser.: No. 204). 245p. Date not set. pap. 2.50 (ISBN 0-317-63692-8). Harlequin Bks.

To Atlas or Not to Atlas? Ed. by Network Staff. 1985. 95.00x (ISBN 0-904999-88-2, Pub. by Network Events Ltd). State Mutual Bk.

To Attempt a Tower. Jennifer B. MacPherson. LC 85-90339. 84p. (YA) (gr. 9-12). 1985. 16.95 (ISBN 0-9614849-0-X); pap. 8.95 (ISBN 0-9614849-1-8). MacPherson Pub.

To Avoid Catastrophe: A Study in Future Nuclear Weapons Policy. Ed. by Michael P. Hamilton. LC 77-24983. pap. 60.00 (ISBN 0-317-08052-0, 2012810). Bks Demand UMI.

To Awaken a Sleeping Giant. J. Spencer Lang. Ed. by Sharon L. Goodman. (Orig.). 1986. pap. 4.00 (ISBN 0-935369-07-4). In Tradition Pub.

To Baby with Love: Your Pre-Natal Nutrition Diary. Marilyn Hanson & Robert Segura. (Illus.). 340p. (Orig.). 1982. pap. 9.95 (ISBN 0-915950-55-3). Bull Pub.

To Banbury Cross & Back: A Collection of Modern Poetry. Ed. by Louisa Persing. (Illus.). 1976. 5.95 (ISBN 0-686-17956-0). Palomar.

To Bathe a Boa. C. Imbior Kudrna. (ps-4). 1988. pap. 5.95. Lerner Pubns.

To Bathe a Boa. C. Imbiore Kudrna. (Picture Bks.). (Illus.). 32p. (gr. k-6). 1986. PLB 12.95 (ISBN 0-87614-306-0). Carolrhoda Bks.

To Battle the Gods, Bk. V. Sharon Green. (Orig.). 1986. pap. 3.50 (ISBN 0-88677-128-5). DAW Bks.

To Be a Catholic. Joseph V. Gallagher. LC 73-137884. 96p. 1970. pap. 1.95 (ISBN 0-8091-5143-X). Paulist Pr.

To Be a Child: A Book of Photographic Essays on the Psychological Rights of the Child. Ed. by P. R. Bursynski. 65p. 1979. 10.00 (ISBN 0-917668-03-0). Intl Schl Psych.

To Be a Congressman: The Promise & the Power. Sven Groennings & Jonathan P. Hawley. LC 73-7946. 250p. 1973. pap. 6.95 (ISBN 0-87491-353-5). Acropolis.

To Be a Dancer. (Satin Slippers Ser.: No. 1). 160p. 1987. pap. 2.50 (ISBN 0-449-13299-4, Juniper). Fawcett.

To Be a Doctor. Felix Marti-Ibanez. Bd. with The Young Princes; The Race & the Runner. LC 68-27688. 1968. 4.95 (ISBN 0-910922-18-7). MD Pubns.

To Be a Doctor: A Health Education Workbook. Georgette B. Skolnick. (Illus.). 215p. (Orig.). (gr. 6-9). 1982. tchr's. ed. 14.00 (ISBN 0-913855-01-4); student's wkbk. 8.00 (ISBN 0-913855-00-6). GBS CA.

To Be a Fine Lady. Della Ellis. 256p. 1988. prepub. 16.95 (ISBN 0-312-01837-1). St Martin.

To Be a Friend. Marcia A. Neese. Ed. by Marjorie Oelerich. LC 83-22342. (Boulder Gang Ser.). (Illus.). 32p. (gr. k-4). 1984. lib. bdg. 9.95 (ISBN 0-914867-01-6). Baker St Prod.

To Be a Jew. Hayim Donin. LC 72-89175. 1972. 17.95 (ISBN 0-465-08624-1). Basic.

To Be a Killer. Jay Bennett. 128p. (Orig.). (gr. 7 up). 1985. pap. 2.25 (ISBN 0-590-33208-2, Point). Scholastic Inc.

To Be a Man. William Decker. 1981. pap. 2.75 (ISBN 0-671-64936-1). PB.

To Be a Pilgrim. Joyce Cary. 20.95 (ISBN 0-88411-314-0, Pub. by Aeonian Pr). Amereon Ltd.

To Be a Pilgrim: A Spiritual Notebook. Basil Hume. LC 84-47726. 240p. 1984. 13.45 (ISBN 0-06-064081-2, HarpR). Har-Row.

To Be a Pilgrim (John Bunyan) Joyce Reason. 1961. pap. 3.50 (ISBN 0-87508-625-X). Chr Lit.

To Be a Politician. rev. ed. Stimson Bullitt. LC 75-43310. 1977. 32.50x (ISBN 0-300-02009-0). Yale U Pr.

To Be a Presbyterian. Louis Weeks. 96p. (Orig.). 1983. pap. 4.95 (ISBN 0-8042-1880-3, John Knox). Westminster John Knox.

To Be a Priest: Perspectives on Vocation & Ordination. Robert E. Terwilliger & Urban T. Holmes. 192p. (Orig.). 1975. pap. 4.95 (ISBN 0-8164-2592-2, 8164-2592-2, HarpR). Har-Row.

To Be a Revolutionary. Padre J. Carney. LC 84-42844. 230p. 1985. 15.45 (ISBN 0-06-061319-X, HarpR). Har-Row.

To Be a Slave. Julius Lester. LC 68-28738. (Illus.). (gr. 7-12). 1968. 13.95 (ISBN 0-8037-8955-6, 01354-410). Dial Bks Young.

To Be a Slave. Julius Lester. (Illus.). 160p. (gr. 7 up). 1986. pap. 2.50 (ISBN 0-590-40682-5, Point); tchr's. guide 1.25. Scholastic Inc.

To be a Slave in Brazil, Fifteen Fifty to Eighteen Eighty-Eight. Tr. by Arthur Goldhammer from Fr. 250p. pap. text ed. 12.00 (ISBN 0-8135-1155-0). Rutgers U Pr.

To Be a Slave in Brazil, Fifteen Hundred to Eighteen Eighty-Eight. Katia M. De Queiros Mattoso. Tr. by Arthur Goldhammer. 35p. text ed. 35.00 (ISBN 0-8135-1154-2). Rutgers U Pr.

To Be a Teacher: Cases, Concepts, Guided Observations. Marilyn M. Cohn et al. 448p. 1986. text ed. write for info. (ISBN 0-394-33606-2, RanC). Random.

To Be a Trial Lawyer. F. Lee Bailey. LC 84-29155. 215p. 1985. (Pub. by The Ronald Press); pap. 14.95 (ISBN 0-471-82734-7). Wiley.

To Be a Unicorn. Robert Vavra & Fleur Cowles. LC 86-8572. (Illus.). 48p. 1986. 15.95 (ISBN 0-688-06598-8). Morrow.

To Be Alive. Elroy Bode. (Illus.). 160p. 1979. 12.00 (ISBN 0-87404-064-7). Tex Western.

To Be an Arab in Israel. Fouzi El-Asmar. 247p. 1978. Repr. of 1975 ed. 6.95 (ISBN 0-88728-096-X). Inst Palestine.

To Be an Invalid: The Illness of Charles Darwin. Ralph Colp, Jr. LC 76-17698. 1977. 25.00x (ISBN 0-226-11401-5). U of Chicago Pr.

To Be & Not to Be. James L. Calderwood. LC 82-22214. 232p. 1983. 34.00x (ISBN 0-231-05628-1); pap. 17.00x (ISBN 0-231-05629-X). Columbia U Pr.

To Be & Not to Be: An Analysis of Jean-Paul Sartre's Ontology. Jacques Salvan. LC 61-12269. (Waynebooks Ser: No. 5). 197p. (Orig.). 1962. pap. 6.95x (ISBN 0-8143-1166-0). Wayne St U Pr.

To Be & Not to Be: An Analysis of Jean-Paul Sartre's Ontology. LC 61-12269. pap. 49.50 (ISBN 0-317-09002-X, 2001334). Bks Demand UMI.

To Be Born a Nation: The Liberation Struggle for Namibia. SWAPO Dept. of Information Staff. (Illus.). 360p. 1986. 39.95 (ISBN 0-86232-712-1, Pub. by Zed Pr UK); pap. 12.50. Humanities.

To Be Born a Nation: The Struggle of the Namibian People SWAPO. 384p. 1981. pap. 10.75 (ISBN 0-905762-73-8, Pub. by Zed Pr England). Humanities.

To Be Continued... Ken Weiss & Ed Goodgold. (Illus.). 351p. 1981. 17.50 (ISBN 0-940506-00-9); pap. 10.95 (ISBN 0-940506-01-7). Star Tree.

To Be Continued... An Annotated Bibliography of Science Fiction & Fantasy Series & Sequels. R. Reginald. LC 80-11206. (Borgo Reference Library: Vol. 11). 96p. Date not set. lib. bdg. 19.95x (ISBN 0-89370-808-9); pap. 9.95x (ISBN 0-89370-908-5). Borgo Pr.

To Be Farmer's Girl. L. G. Layberry. Ed. by Kathleen Morley-Clarke. 148p. 1986. 30.00x (ISBN 0-85936-289-2, Pub. by Spellmount Ltd Pubs). State Mutual Bk.

To Be Free! Ron Martin. 256p. 1986. 14.95 (ISBN 0-8149-0925-6). Vanguard.

To Be Free! Ron Martin. 224p. 1987. pap. 3.95 (ISBN 0-671-64610-9). PB.

To Be Free: Studies in American Negro History. Herbert Aptheker. LC 48-5693. pap. 64.00 (ISBN 0-317-28070-8, 2025544). Bks Demand UMI.

To Be Fully Alive. Joseph Gelberman. 89p. pap. 5.95 (ISBN 0-942494-49-0). Coleman Pub.

To Be Human: An Introduction to Cultural Anthropology. Alexander Alland, Jr. 388p. 1981. pap. text ed. write for info (ISBN 0-394-34406-5, RanC). Random.

To Be Human: An Introductory Experiment in Philosophy. Xavier O. Monasterio. 256p. (Orig.). 1985. pap. 7.95 (ISBN 0-8091-2704-0). Paulist Pr.

To Be Mature. H. L. Rutledge. LC 74-76988. 153p. 1974. pap. 5.00 (ISBN 0-914520-03-2). Insight Pr.

To Be Me. Barbara S. Hazen. LC 75-12960. (Illus.). (ps-2). 1975. 8.45 (ISBN 0-913778-09-5). Childs World.

To Be Old & Sad: Understanding Depression in the Elderly. Nathan Billig. LC 85-45736. 128p. 1986. 21.95x (ISBN 0-669-12277-7); pap. 8.95 (ISBN 0-669-12279-3). Lexington Bks.

To Be One: A Battle Against Racism. Nathan Rutstein. (Global Transformation Ser.). 160p. (Orig.). 1988. pap. price not set (ISBN 0-85398-278-3). G Ronald Pub.

To Be One Thing: Personal Unity in Kierkegaard's Thought. George Connell. LC 85-4812. xx, 198p. 1985. 17.95 (ISBN 0-86554-156-6, MUP/H146). Mercer Univ Pr.

To Be or Not to Be. Sue Byfield. (Harlequin Romances Ser.). 192p. 1983. pap. 1.50 (ISBN 0-373-02529-7). Harlequin Bks.

To Be or Not to Be. Eileen Farrell. 164p. 1964. 5.95 (ISBN 0-933932-26-X); pap. 2.50 (ISBN 0-933932-27-8). Scepter Pubs.

To Be or Not to Be: A Question of Survival. Duncan Williams. (International Library Ser.). 1975. pap. 11.75 (ISBN 0-08-019934-8). Pergamon.

To Be or Not to Be an American. (Non-Fiction Ser.). write for info. (ISBN 0-9609008-0-2). C B North.

To Be or Not to Be: An Artist's Guide to Not-for-Profit Incorporation. Volunteer Lawyers for the Arts Staff. 12p. 1986. 3.00 (ISBN 0-917103-03-3). Vol Lawyers Arts.

To Be or Not to Be: Existential-Psychological Perspectives on the Self. Ed. by Sidney M. Jourard. LC 67-65494. (University of Florida Social Sciences Monographs: No. 34). 1967. pap. 3.50 (ISBN 0-8130-0122-6). U Presses Fla.

To Be or Not To Be Human: The Nature of Human Nature. Ben Freedman. 1987. 20.00 (ISBN 0-533-06964-5). Vantage.

To Be or Not to Be in the Party. Yuri Glazov. 1988. lib. bdg. 64.00 (ISBN 90-277-2716-3); pap. 29.00 (ISBN 90-277-2717-1). Kluwer Academic.

To Be or Not to Bop: Memoirs of Dizzy Gillespie. Dizzy Gillespie & Al Fraser. (Quality Paperbacks Ser.). (Illus.). 574p. 1985. pap. 13.95 (ISBN 0-306-80236-8). Da Capo.

To Be Plain: Translations from Greek, Latin, French, & German. Raymond Oliver. 80p. 1982. 9.95 (ISBN 0-941150-01-1); pap. 4.50 (ISBN 0-941150-02-X). Barth.

To Be Seventeen In Israel: Through the Eyes of an American Teenager. Josh Clayton-Felt. LC 86-24723. (Illus.). 96p. (YA) (gr. 7-12). 1987. lib. bdg. 11.90 (ISBN 0-531-10249-1). Watts.

To Be Somebody. Evelyn Leite. 146p. 1979. pap. 6.95 (ISBN 0-89486-060-7). Hazelden.

To Be the Best. Barbara Taylor Bradford. LC 88-3813. 528p. 1988. 19.95 (ISBN 0-385-24579-3). Doubleday.

To Be the Best. Barbara Taylor Bradford. 768p. 1988. 21.50 (ISBN 0-385-24661-7, GC Large Print). Doubleday.

To Be the Bridge: A Black Perspective on White Catholicism in America. Sandra Smithson. LC 84-50080. 200p. 1984. pap. 5.95 (ISBN 0-938232-48-7). Winston-Derek.

To Be the First. William N. McElrath. LC 75-14893. (Illus.). 192p. (gr. 5up). 1976. pap. 5.95 (ISBN 0-8054-4318-5). Broadman.

To Be Worthy. Donna F. Crow. 204p. 1986. pap. 5.95 (ISBN 0-89693-512-4). Victor Bks.

To Be Young, Gifted & Black. Lorraine Hansberry. 272p. (RL 7). 1970. pap. 3.50 (ISBN 0-451-13228-9, AE3228, Sig). NAL.

To Bear Any Burden. Al Santoli. 384p. 1988. pap. 3.95 (ISBN 0-345-33188-5). Ballantine.

To Become a Fine Actor. Norman Sturgis. 93p. (Orig.). 1986. wkbk. 9.95 (ISBN 0-911455-03-5). Quartz Pr.

To Become a Racehorse Trainer. Joe Hartigan. Repr. write for info. (ISBN 0-85131-234-9, NL51, Pub. by J A Allen U K). S R Smith Sporting Bks.

To Become a Sage: The Ten Diagrams on Sage Learning by Yi T'oegye. Commentary by & tr. by Michael C. Kalton. (Neo-Confucian Studies). (Illus.). 256p. 1988. 32.50 (ISBN 0-231-06410-1). Columbia U Pr.

To Become Somebody: Growing up Against the Grain of Society. John B. Simon. 256p. 1982. 12.95 (ISBN 0-395-32052-6). HM.

To Begin With. Tom Koontz. (Illus.). 16p. (Orig.). 1983. pap. 1.00 (ISBN 0-935306-25-0). Barnwood Pr.

To Begin with Puzzles, Games & Mazes about the Book of Genesis. Zoe S. LeCours. (Illus.). 48p. (Orig.). (gr. 2-5). 1985. pap. 4.49 (ISBN 0-934661-00-6, 7077). Lions Head Pr.

To Believe in Jesus. Ruth Burrows. 6.95 (ISBN 0-87193-154-0). Dimension Bks.

To Believe Is to Exist. John R. Sheets. 1986. pap. 14.95 (ISBN 0-87193-247-4). Dimension Bks.

To Belize with Love. Hannah B. Lapp. LC 86-70999. 380p. (Orig.). (YA) (gr. 10-12). 1986. pap. 14.95 (ISBN 0-931494-94-X). Brunswick Pub.

To Bend Without Breaking. Mary E. Stuart. LC 77-6797. 1977. pap. 32.00 (ISBN 0-317-08155-1, 2021564). Bks Demand UMI.

To Bigotry, No Sanction: The Reverend Sun Myung Moon & the Unification Church. Mose Durst. LC 84-60571. (Illus.). 196p. 1984. pap. 6.95 (ISBN 0-89526-829-9). Regnery Gateway.

To Boldly Go. Eric Delve. 132p. 1986. pap. 5.50 (ISBN 0-89693-275-3). Victor Bks.

To Bread. David Duer. (Morning Coffee Chapbks. Ser.). (Illus.). 20p. 1986. pap. 10.00 (ISBN 0-918273-16-1). Coffee Hse.

To Break the Silence: Thirteen Short Stories for Young Readers. Peter Barrett. (Orig.). (gr. k-12). 1986. pap. 3.25 (ISBN 0-440-98807-1, LFL). Dell.

To Breathe Freely: Risk, Consent, & Air. Ed. by Mary Gibson. LC 84-22278. (Maryland Studies in Public Philosophy). 310p. 1985. 35.00x (ISBN 0-8476-7416-9, Rowman & Allanheld). Rowman.

To Brecht & Beyond: Soundings in Modern Dramaturgy. Darko Suvin. LC 84-252. (Studies in Contemporary Literature & Culture). 296p. 1984. 28.50x (ISBN 0-389-20463-3, 08024). B&N Imports.

To Brian...with Love. David R. Tuttle. Ed. by Robert B. Tuttle. LC 81-52343. 192p. 1981. 12.95 (ISBN 0-9606970-0-4). Brian's Hse.

To Bridge the Taiwan Strait. Robert L. Downen. (Journal of Social Political & Economic Studies Monograph: No. 13). 1982p. 1982. pap. 15.00 (ISBN 0-930690-17-6). Coun Soc Econ.

To Brighten Each Day. J. Winston Pearce. LC 83-70001. 1983. 9.95 (ISBN 0-8054-5220-6). Broadman.

To Bring Spring. George Keithley. (Kestrel Chapbooks). 36p. (Orig.). 1987. pap. 4.00 (ISBN 0-914974-46-7). Holmgangers.

To Build a Canal: Sault Ste. Marie, 1853-1854 & After. John N. Dickinson. LC 80-27693. (Illus.). 221p. 1981. 25.00 (ISBN 0-8142-0309-4). Ohio St U Pr.

To Build a Castle: My Life as a Dissenter. Vladimir Bukovsky. Tr. by Michael Scammell from Rus. 444p. 1988. pap. text ed. 17.95 (ISBN 0-89633-131-8). Ethics & Public Policy.

To Build a Fire. Jack London. (Creative's Classic Short Stories Ser.). (Illus.). 48p. (gr. 6 up). 1980. PLB 8.95 (ISBN 0-87191-769-6). Creative Ed.

To Build a Fire & Other Stories. Jack London. (Bantam Classics Ser.). 400p. 1986. pap. 4.50 (ISBN 0-553-21335-0). Bantam.

To Build a Fire: Recent Poems & a Prose Piece. Melville Cane. LC 64-14640. 80p. 1964. 9.95 (ISBN 0-15-190478-2). HarBraceJ.

To Build a Nigerian Nation. Noser Igiehon. 352p. 1985. 30.00x (ISBN 0-317-39408-8, Pub. by A H Stockwell England). State Mutual Bk.

To Build a Nigerian Nation. Noser Igiehon. 352p. 1987. 35.00x (ISBN 0-7223-0714-4, Pub. by A H Stockwell England). State Mutual Bk.

To Build a Ship. new ed. Don Berry. LC 60-5835. 1977. pap. 2.50 (ISBN 0-89174-029-5). Comstock Edns.

To Build & Be Church, Lay Ministry Resource Packet. 73p. 1979. pap. 6.50 (ISBN 1-55586-621-2). US Catholic.

To Bury Our Fathers: A Novel of Nicaragua. Sergio Ramirez. Tr. by Nick Caistor from Span. LC 84-61849. (Illus.). 250p. 1985. (Dist. by Consortium); pap. 8.95 (ISBN 0-930523-03-2). Readers Intl.

To Byzantium: Stories. Andrew Fetler. LC 76-13854. (Illinois Short Fiction Ser). 115p. 1976. pap. 8.95 (ISBN 0-252-00584-8). U of Ill Pr.

To Care for the Earth: A Call to A New Theology. Sean McDonagh. LC 87-14507. 228p. 1987. pap. 9.95 (ISBN 0-939680-42-4). Bear & Co.

To Cariboo & Back in Eighteen Sixty Two. W. Champness. 106p. 1972. 14.95 (ISBN 0-87770-109-1). Ye Galleon.

To Cassandra: Early Years. Christopher A. Anderson. LC 85-71217. 102p. 1985. pap. 10.00 (ISBN 0-931353-01-7). Andersons Pubns.

To God Be the Glory. Billy Graham & Corrie Ten Boom. 62p. 1985. pap. text ed. 4.95 large print ed. (ISBN 0-8027-2473-6). Walker & Co.
To God the Glory. Annalee Skarin. 196p. 1980. pap. 5.95 (ISBN 0-87516-094-8). DeVorss.
To God Through Faith: From Christ to Sri Ramakrishna. Sri Surath. 1978. pap. 3.00 (ISBN 0-685-58452-6). Ranney Pubns.
To Govern America. Roger Hilsman. LC 78-19177. Repr. of 1979 ed. 152.50 (2027613). Bks Demand UMI.
To Govern Evolution: Further Adventures of the Political Animal. Walter T. Anderson. LC 86-19477. 392p. 1987. 22.95 (ISBN 0-15-190483-9). HarBraceJ.
To Grill a Mockingbird & Other Tasty Titles. Ruth Young & Mitchell Rose. (Penguin Fiction Ser.). (Illus.). 96p. 1985. pap. 4.95 (ISBN 0-14-007744-8). Penguin.
To Grow in Spirit. Joe J. Christensen. 81p. 1983. 7.95 (ISBN 0-87747-968-2). Deseret Bk.
To Gwen with Love: A Tribute to Gwendolyn Brooks. Ed. by Patricia L. Brown et al. LC 76-128546. (Illus., Orig.). 1971. pap. 1.95 (ISBN 0-87485-044-4). Johnson Chi.
To H. B. Curry: Essays on Combinatory Logic, Lambda Calculus & Formalism. Ed. by J. P. Seldin & R. Hindley. 1980. 91.00 (ISBN 0-12-349050-2). Acad Pr.
To Halt Armageddon: Box No. 2. David R. Palmer. (Spectra Ser.). 288p. (Orig.). Date not set. pap. 3.50 (ISBN 0-553-25626-2). Bantam.
To Handmake a Saddle. J. H. Sheilds. (Illus.). 12.50 (ISBN 0-87556-618-9). Saifer.
To Handmake a Saddle. J. H. Shields. (Illus.). pap. 6.95 (ISBN 0-85131-222-5, NL51, Pub. by J A Allen U K). S R Smith Sporting Bks.
To Have & Have Not. Ernest Hemingway. 1937. 27.50x (ISBN 0-684-15328-9, ScribT); pap. 8.95 (ISBN 0-684-71809-X, ScribT). Scribner.
To Have & Have Not. Ernest Hemingway. 272p. 1983. pap. 4.95 rack-size (ISBN 0-684-17952-0, ScribT). Scribner.
To Have & Have Not. Ernest Hemingway. 272p. 1988. pap. 4.95 (ISBN 0-02-051880-3, Collier). Macmillan.
To Have & Have Not. Ed. by Bruce F. Kawin. LC 79-5403. (Wisconsin-Warner Brothers Screenplay Ser.). (Illus.). 232p. 1980. 18.95x (ISBN 0-299-08090-0); pap. 8.95 (ISBN 0-299-08094-3). U of Wis Pr.
To Have & to Hold. Mary Johnston. (Airmont Classics Ser.). (gr. 8 up). pap. 1.95 (ISBN 0-8049-0160-0, CL-160). Airmont.
To Have & to Hold. Mary Johnston. 403p. 1977. Repr. of 1900 ed. lib. bdg. 16.95x (ISBN 0-89966-252-8). Buccaneer Bks.
To Have & to Hold. Mary Johnston. 1899. Repr. lib. bdg. 49.00 (ISBN 0-8414-5424-8). Folcroft.
To Have & to Hold. Mary Johnston. 1969. 5.95 (ISBN 0-395-07835-0). HM.
To Have & to Hold. Mary Johnston. 1976. lib. bdg. 18.95x (ISBN 0-89968-149-2). Lightyear.
To Have & to Hold. Deborah Moggach. LC 86-19902. 1987. 17.95 (ISBN 0-525-24511-1, 01743-520). Dutton.
To Have & to Hold. Annette Reynolds. 48p. Gold edition. 12.95 (ISBN 0-85648-878-X); Silver edition. 12.95 (ISBN 0-85648-946-8). Lion USA.
To Have & to Hold: Marriage, the First Baby, & Preparing Couples for Parenthood. C. F. Clulow. 168p. 1982. text ed. 18.25 (ISBN 0-08-028470-1); pap. text ed. 10.50 (ISBN 0-08-028471-X). Pergamon.
To Have Eyes. Geoffrey Holloway. 1972. pap. 1.95 (ISBN 0-685-27681-3, Pub. by Anvil Pr); pap. 5.00 signed ltd. ed. (ISBN 0-685-27682-1). Small Pr Dist.
To Have Is to Owe. Norman A. Wingert. (Illus.). 185p. pap. 4.95 (ISBN 0-937594-00-8). Bunkhouse.
To Have or to Be? Erich Fromm. 256p. 1981. pap. 4.95 (ISBN 0-553-25437-5). Bantam.
To Have or to Be? Erich Fromm. LC 73-130449. (World Perspectives). 1976. 13.45i (ISBN 0-06-011379-0, HarpT). Har-Row.
To Have or to Be. Erich Fromm. 1987. pap. 3.95 (ISBN 0-553-24077-3). Bantam.
To Have or to Be. Erich Fromm. 1983. pap. 4.95 (ISBN 0-553-27485-6). Bantam.
To Have...to Hold: A Parents' Guide to Childbirth & Early Parenting. 3rd ed. Joyce L. Kieffer. LC 84-51100. (Illus.). 96p. 1985. 5.50 (ISBN 0-933794-04-5); inst's. manual 14.95 (ISBN 0-933794-05-3). Train Res Corp.
To Heal a Nation: The Vietnam Veterans Memorial. Jan C. Scruggs & Joel Serdlow. LC 84-48191. (Illus.). 414p. 1988. pap. 9.95 (ISBN 0-06-091354-1, PL-1354, PL). Har-Row.
To Heal a Nation: The Vietnam Veterans Memorial. Jan C. Scruggs & Joel L. Swerdlow. LC 84-48191. (Illus.). 400p. 1985. 25.95i (ISBN 0-06-015404-7, HarpT). Har-Row.
To Heal Again: Toward Serenity & the Resolution of Grief. Rusty Berkus. (Illus.). 32p. (Orig.). 1986. pap. 13.95 (ISBN 0-9609888-2-3). Red Rose Pr.
To Heal As Jesus Healed. Barbara L. Shlemon et al. LC 78-54126. 112p. 1978. pap. 2.95 (ISBN 0-87793-152-6). Ave Maria.
To Hear & Proclaim. Keifer. 1983. 4.95 (ISBN 0-912405-01-5). Pastoral Pr.
To Hear the Angels Sing. Dorothy Maclean. 217p. (Orig.). 1983. pap. text ed. 7.00 (ISBN 0-936878-01-0). Lorian Pr.
To Hear the Word: Invitation to Serious Study of the Bible. Milton P. Brown. LC 86-31082. 256p. 1987. 29.95 (ISBN 0-86554-251-1, MUP H-216); pap. 14.95 (ISBN 0-86554-252-X, MUP P-40). Mercer Univ Pr.
To Hell & Back. Audie Murphy. (Illus.). 1983. pap. 3.95 (ISBN 0-553-24297-0). Bantam.
To Hell & Back. Audie Murphy. (Military Classics Ser.). (Illus.). 304p. 1988. 14.95 (ISBN 0-8306-4002-9, 40002). TAB Bks.
To Hell with Culture: And Other Essays on Art & Society. Herbert E. Read. LC 72-3370. (Essay Index Reprint Ser.). Repr. of 1963 ed. 16.00 (ISBN 0-8369-2918-7). Ayer Co Pubs.
To Hell with Dying. Alice Walker. (Illus.). 32p. (ps-12). 1987. 13.95 (ISBN 0-15-289075-0). HarBraceJ.
To Hell with Gravy. Glenn Helgeland & Judy Helgeland. (On Target Ser.). 120p. (Orig.). 1984. pap. 8.95 (ISBN 0-913305-05-7). Target Comm.
To Hell with Male Chauvinism! Marjorie M. Booker. 1985. 7.95 (ISBN 0-533-05707-8). Vantage.
To Hell with the Kids: A View of Public Education. Gail B. Newton. (Illus.). 80p. 1984. 8.95 (ISBN 0-89962-416-2). Todd & Honeywell.
To Hell with the P.T.A. Derwin J. Jeffries. LC 65-24682. (Communications Curriculum Ser: Vol. 1). 1965. 7.95x (ISBN 0-910742-02-2). Home & Sch.
To Help Children Communicate. Frank B. May. (Elementary Education Ser.: No. C22). 472p. 1980. pap. text ed. 22.95 (ISBN 0-675-08197-1). Merrill.
To Help You Through the Hurting. Marjorie Holmes. LC 81-43571. (Illus.). 160p. 1983. 8.95 (ISBN 0-385-17842-5). Doubleday.
To Help You Through the Hurting. Marjorie Holmes. 160p. 1984. pap. 3.50 (ISBN 0-553-26384-6). Bantam.
To Helsinki: The Conference on Security & Cooperation in Europe, 1973-75. John J. Maresca. LC 85-6822. (Policy Studies). xvi, 293p. 1985. 47.50 (ISBN 0-8223-0652-2). Duke.
To Helsinki: The Conference on Security & Cooperation in Europe. 2nd ed. John J. Maresca. 310p. 1987. pap. text ed. 16.95 (ISBN 0-8223-0791-X). Duke.
To Hilda for Helping. Margot Zemach. LC 77-87584. (Illus.). 32p. (ps-3). 1977. 9.95 (ISBN 0-374-37663-8). FS&G.
To Him Who Conquers. Stephen Sanders. LC 73-111183. 210p. 1970. 50.00 (ISBN 0-385-06306-7). Fellowship Crown.
To Hold a Mirror to Nature: Dramatic Images & Reflections. Ed. by Karelisa V. Hartigan. LC 81-40310. (University of Florida Department of Classics Comparative Drama Conference Papers: Vol. 1). 176p. (Orig.). 1982. lib. bdg. 28.25 (ISBN 0-8191-2275-0); pap. text ed. 12.25 (ISBN 0-8191-2276-9). U Pr of Amer.
To Hold in My Hand: Selected Poems, 1955-1983. Hilda Morley. LC 83-40199. 213p. 1984. 13.95 (ISBN 0-935296-46-8); pap. 8.95 (ISBN 0-935296-49-2). Sheep Meadow.
To Hold This Soil. Russell Lord. LC 78-171385. (FDR & the Era of the New Deal Ser). (Illus.). 124p. 1972. Repr. of 1938 ed. lib. bdg. 22.50 (ISBN 0-306-70384-X). Da Capo.
To Honor Jernej Kopitar: Paper in Slavic Philology, No. 2. Ed. by Rado L. Lencek & Henry R. Cooper, Jr. 1982. pap. 10.00 (ISBN 0-930042-46-8). Mich Slavic Pubns.
To Honor Rene Girard: On the Occasion of His Sixtieth Birthday. (Stanford French & Italian Studies: Vol. 34). 380p. 1986. pap. 34.50 (ISBN 0-915838-03-6). Anma Libri.
To Honor Roman Jakobson: A Collection of Essays, 3 Vols. Roman Jakobson. (Janua Linguarum Ser. Major: Nos. 31-33). 1967. Vol. 1. text ed. 326.00 (ISBN 0-686-22470-1); Vol.2. 72.00 (ISBN 0-686-22471-X); Vol.3. 72.00 (ISBN 90-2790-620-3). Mouton.
To Honor the Crow People: Crow Indian Art from the Gallatin Collection. Ed. by Peter J. Powell. 1988. pap. 18.95 (ISBN 0-8032-8720-8). U of Nebr Pr.
To Honor the Sacred Trust of Civilization. Dickson A. Mungazi. 320p. 1983. 18.95 (ISBN 0-87073-454-7); pap. 11.25 (ISBN 0-87073-455-5). Schenkman Bks Inc.
To Humanity with Love. 2nd ed. J. Sig Paulson. LC 74-33594. (Illus.). 124p. 1982. pap. 4.95 (ISBN 0-87516-484-6). DeVorss.
To Hunt in the Morning. Janet Siskind. LC 73-82674. (Illus.). 1973. pap. 9.95x (ISBN 0-19-501891-5). Oxford U Pr.
To Infinity & Beyond: A Cultural History of the Infinite. Eli Maor. (Illus.). 1986. 49.50 (ISBN 0-8176-3325-1). Birkhauser.
To Insure Peace Acknowledge God. Cardinal John Krol. 1978. 5.50 (ISBN 0-8198-0561-0); pap. 3.95 (ISBN 0-8198-0562-9). Dghtrs St Paul.
To Intimate Distance. Tim Longville. 1976. signed 6.00 (ISBN 0-685-79230-7, Pub. by Grosseteste); pap. 1.00 (ISBN 0-685-79231-5). Small Pr Dist.
To Jack, with Love. Robert Bouvier. (Orig.). 1979. pap. 2.50 (ISBN 0-89083-528-4). Zebra.
To James Bond with Love. Mary W. Bond. LC 80-17134. (Illus.). 224p. 1980. 10.95 (ISBN 0-915010-28-3). Sutter House.
To Jerusalem. Folke G. Bernadotte Af Wisborg. LC 75-6424. (Rise of Jewish Nationalism & the Middle East Ser.). 280p. 1975. Repr. of 1951 ed. 23.65 (ISBN 0-88355-311-2). Hyperion Conn.
To Jerusalem & Back: A Personal Account. Saul Bellow. LC 76-42198. 192p. 1976. 11.95 (ISBN 0-670-71729-0). Viking.
To Jerusalem & Back: A Personal Account. Saul Bellow. (Nonfiction Ser.). 192p. 1985. pap. 6.95 (ISBN 0-14-007273-X). Penguin.
To Jess with Love & Memories, No. 2. Norma Johnston. (Carlisle Chronicles). 176p. (Orig.). (YA) (gr. 6-10). 1986. pap. 2.50 (ISBN 0-553-25882-6, Starfire). Bantam.
To Join Together: The Rite of Marriage, Vol. V. Kenneth Stevenson. (Studies in the Reformed Rites of the Catholic Church). 200p. (Orig.). Date not set. pap. 12.95 (ISBN 0-916134-84-9). Pueblo Pub Co.
To Judge with Justice: History & Politics of Illinois Judicial Reform. Rubin G. Cohn. LC 72-95002. (Studies in Illinois Constitution Making Ser). 180p. 1973. pap. 10.00 (ISBN 0-252-00332-2). U of Ill Pr.
To Kairwan the Holy. Alexander A. Boddy. 320p. 1985. 49.00x (ISBN 0-317-39199-2, Pub. by Luzac & Co Ltd). State Mutual Bk.
To Kairwan the Holy. Alexander A. Boddy. 320p. 1985. 250.00x (ISBN 1-85077-069-7, Pub. by Darf). State Mutual Bk.
To Keep a Promise. Fred Starr. 1969. 6.95 (ISBN 0-8158-0225-0). Chris Mass.
To Keep Art Alive: The Effort of Kenneth Hayes Miller, American Painter (1876-1952) Lincoln Rothschild. (Illus.). 208p. 1974. 30.00 (ISBN 0-87982-012-8). Art Alliance.
To Keep from Singing. Ed Ingebretsen. LC 85-60238. (Orig.). 1985. pap. 7.95 (ISBN 0-89390-061-3). Resource Pubns.
To Keep Moving: Essays Nineteen Fifty-Nine to Nineteen Sixty-Nine. Donald Hall. 1979. pap. 5.95 (ISBN 0-934888-02-7). Hobart & Wm Smith.
To Keep Our Honor Clean. Ed. by Edwin McDowell. LC 79-56025. 320p. 1980. 14.95 (ISBN 0-8149-0831-4). Vanguard.
To Keep the Blood from Drowning. Doug Flaherty. 1976. pap. 5.00 (ISBN 0-915016-07-9). Second Coming.
To Keep the House from Falling in. Richard D'Abate. 39p. 1973. 2.95 (ISBN 0-87886-028-2). Greenfld Rev Pr.
To Keep the Peace: The United Nations Condemnatory Resolution. William W. Orbach. LC 75-41989. (Illus.). 168p. 1977. 15.00 (ISBN 0-8131-1341-5). U Pr of Ky.
To Keep Them Alive: Wild Animal Breeding. Sally Tongren. LC 85-4599. (Illus.). 1985. 19.95 (ISBN 0-934878-66-8). Dembner Bks.
To Keera with Love. Kayla M. Becker & Connie K. Heckert. 170p. Date not set. pap. 7.95; study guide 1.00. Morning Glory.
To Keera with Love: Abortion, Adoption, or Keeping the Baby, The Story of One Teen's Choice. Kayla M. Becker & Connie K. Heckert. LC 87-62400. (Illus.). 170p. (Orig.). pap. 7.95 (ISBN 1-55612-072-9). Sheed & Ward MO.
To Kill a Black Man. Louis Lomax. (Orig.). 1987. pap. 3.25 (ISBN 0-87067-731-4). Holloway.
To Kill a King. Roland Cutler. 1987. pap. 3.95 (ISBN 0-425-10412-5). Berkley Pub.
To Kill a Man's Pride & Other Stories from Southern Africa. Ed. by Norman Hodge. 226p. 1984. pap. text ed. 12.95x (ISBN 0-86975-146-8, Pub. by Ravan Pr). Ohio U Pr.
To Kill a Mockingbird. Harper Lee. LC 60-7847. 1961. 17.45i (ISBN 0-397-00151-7). Har-Row.
To Kill a Mockingbird. Harper Lee. 284p. 1982. pap. 3.50 (ISBN 0-446-31049-2). Warner Bks.
To Kill a Mockingbird (Lee) Milton. (Book Notes Ser.). 1984. pap. 2.50 (ISBN 0-8120-3446-5). Barron.
To Kill a Mockingbird Notes. Eva Fitzwater. (Orig.). 1966. pap. 3.25 (ISBN 0-8220-1282-0). Cliffs.
To Kill a Mockingbird, Tender Mercies, & The Trip to Bountiful: Three Screenplays. Horton Foote. 240p. 1989. 19.95 (ISBN 0-8021-1124-6); pap. 9.95 (ISBN 0-8021-3125-5). Grove.
To Kill a Witch. Drew G. Myers. LC 84-91299. 166p. 1985. 11.95 (ISBN 0-533-06391-4). Vantage.
To Kill an Eagle: Indian Views on the Last Days of Crazy Horse. Edward Kadlecek & Mabell Kadlecek. (Illus.). 176p. (Orig.). 1981. pap. 8.95 (ISBN 0-933472-54-4). Johnson Bks.
To Kill or Not to Kill: Thoughts on Capital Punishment. William L. Clay, Sr. LC 87-812. (Great Issues of the Day Ser.: No. 4). 144p. 1988. lib. bdg. 19.95x (ISBN 0-89370-331-1); pap. text ed. 9.95x (ISBN 0-89370-431-8). Borgo Pr.
To Kill the Potemkin. Mark Joseph. LC 86-80054. 255p. 1986. 16.95 (ISBN 0-917657-80-2). D I Fine.
To Kill the Potemkin. Mark Joseph. 320p. 1987. pap. 4.50 (ISBN 0-451-40039-9, Onyx). NAL.
To Kim with Love. Lois C. Falconer. 80p. (YA) (gr. 7-10). 1987. 6.95 (ISBN 0-8059-3056-6). Dorrance.
To Kiss the Joy. Robert A. Raines. 160p. 1983. pap. 4.35 (ISBN 0-687-42185-3). Abingdon.
To Know a Fly. Vincent G. Dethier. LC 62-21838. (Illus.). 1963. pap. 9.95x (ISBN 0-8162-2240-1). Holden-Day.
To Know a Library: Essays & Annual Reports, 1970-1976. Daniel Gore. LC 77-84769. (New Directions in Librarianship: No. 1). 1978. lib. bdg. 36.95 (ISBN 0-8371-9881-X, GTK/). Greenwood.
To Know & Follow Jesus: Contemporary Christology. Thomas N. Hart. 160p. (Orig.). 1984. pap. 6.95 (ISBN 0-8091-2636-2). Paulist Pr.
To Know As We Are Known: A Spirituality of Education. Parker J. Palmer. LC 83-47731. 160p. 1983. 14.95 (ISBN 0-06-066456-8, HarpR). Har-Row.
To Know by Experience-Outward Bound North Carolina. 4th ed. Dan Meyer & Diane Meyer. LC 73-83707. 136p. 1979. Repr. of 1973 ed. 12.00 (ISBN 0-932150-03-9). MCS.
To Know Each Other & Be Known: Women's Writing Workshops. Beverly Tanenhaus. 70p. 1982. pap. 5.00 (ISBN 0-934238-06-5). Motheroot.
To Know for Real: Royce S. Pitkin & Coddard College. Ann G. Benson & Frank Adams. (Illus.). 250p. 1987. 20.00 (ISBN 0-912362-06-5). Adamant Pr.
To Know God: A Five-Day Plan. Morris Venden. Ed. by Raymond Woolsey. 125p. pap. 2.25 (ISBN 0-8280-0220-7). Review & Herald.
To Know Love. Kathleen Pieper. 1979. 9.95 (ISBN 0-686-52556-6, Avalon). Bouregy.
To Know the Knower. Swami Muktananda. 40p. 2.00. SYDA Found.
To Know the Stars. Guy Ottewell. (Illus.). 1984. pap. 7.00 (ISBN 0-934546-12-6). Astron Wkshp.
To KNow Your Self: The Essential Teachings of Swami Satchidananda. Ed. by Philip Mandelkorn. LC 77-80901. 250p. 1988. pap. 8.95 (ISBN 0-932040-34-9). Integral Yoga Pubns.
To Kokoda & Beyond: The Story of the 39th Battalion. Victor Austin. 1988. 29.95 (ISBN 0-522-84374-3); pap. 19.95 (ISBN 0-522-84379-4). Intl Spec Bk.
To Kolonos. Jascha Kessler. (TallTales Ser.). (Orig.). 1987. pap. 1.95 (ISBN 0-89807-141-0). Illuminati.
To Lead & Manage. Jules Bellaschi. LC 80-83869. 70p. (Orig.). 1980. pap. 4.95 (ISBN 0-9605144-0-6). MJ Pubns.
To Learn & to Teach. Jack D. Spiro. LC 83-13240. 128p. 1984. 7.95 (ISBN 0-8022-2429-6). Philos Lib.
To Learn & to Teach Your Life as a Rabbi. Alfred Gottschalk. (Illus.). (YA) (gr. 7-12). 1988. lib. bdg. 12.95 (ISBN 0-8239-0700-7, 0700C). Rosen Group.
To Learn with Love: A Companion for Suzuki Parents. William Starr & Constance Starr. (Illus.). 150p. 1983. pap. 10.95 (ISBN 0-914425-00-5). Kingston Ellis.
To Leave & Yet to Stay. Mother M. Angelica. 34p. Date not set. pap. text ed. 2.00 (ISBN 1-55794-018-5, B51). Eternal Wrd TV.
To Leave the Standing Grain. Michael Corr. (Illus.). 1977. pap. 5.00. Copper Canyon.
To Leave This Port. Francis J. Enright. LC 88-81198. (Illus.). 300p. Date not set. text ed. 14.95 (ISBN 0-9620291-0-6). Enright Pub Co.
To Lesbians Everywhere: Poems. Judy Greenspan. LC 75-35019. (Illus.). 1976. pap. 3.50 (ISBN 0-912968-04-4). Violet Pr.
To Lhasa & Beyond. Guiseppe Tucci. 195p. pap. 14.95 (ISBN 0-937938-57-2). Snow Lion.
To Lhasa & Beyond: Diary of the Expedition to Tibet in the Year 1947. Guiseppe Tucci. 1985. 38.50x (ISBN 0-8364-1481-0, Pub. by Oxford IBH). South Asia Bks.
To Lhasa in Disguise: A Secret Expedition Through Mysterious Tibet. William M. McGovern. 1924. 39.00 (ISBN 0-8495-3530-1). Arden Lib.
To License a Journalist? A Landmark Decision in the Schmidt Case. R. Bruce McColm. 1986. 5.00 (ISBN 0-932088-09-0). Freedom Hse.
To Life. Ruth M. Sender. LC 88-9312. 240p. (YA) (gr. 9-12). 1988. 13.95 (ISBN 0-02-781831-4). Macmillan.
To Life! Yoga with Priscilla Patrick. Priscilla Patrick. LC 82-71187. (Illus.). 76p. (Orig.). 1982. pap. 9.95 (ISBN 0-943274-00-1). SC Ed Comm Inc.
To Lift Your Heart. Maureen Arthur-Lynch. (Orig.). 1985. pap. 3.00 (ISBN 0-915541-05-X). Star Bks Inc.
To Light One Candle. 2nd ed. 161p. 1979. pap. 6.00 (ISBN 0-686-47811-8). Amer Bar Assn.
To Linger Is to Die. Lilya Wagner. LC 75-18349. (Crown Ser.). 128p. 1975. pap. 6.95 (ISBN 0-8127-0102-X). Review & Herald.
To Listen Is to Heal. Albert J. Nimeth. 1984. 5.00 (ISBN 0-8199-0874-6). Franciscan Herald.
To Listen to a Child. T. Berry Brazelton. Date not set. price not set. Addison-Wesley.
To Live Again. Catherine Marshall. 1976. pap. 3.95 (ISBN 0-380-01586-2). Avon.
To Live Again. Robert Silverberg. 224p. 1986. pap. 3.95 (ISBN 0-446-34058-8). Warner Bks.
To Live Again: Rebuilding Your Life after You've Become a Widow. Genevieve Ginsburg. 224p. 1987. 14.95 (ISBN 0-87477-426-8). J P Tarcher.

To Punish or Persuade: The Enforcement of Coal Mine Safety. John Braithwaite. LC 84-2671. 206p. 1985. 59.50 (ISBN 0-87395-931-0); pap. 19.95x (ISBN 0-87395-932-9). State U NY Pr.

To Purge This Land with Blood: A Biography of John Brown. 2nd ed. Stephen B. Oates. LC 84-2635. (Illus.). 448p. 1984. pap. 14.95x (ISBN 0-87023-458-7). U of Mass Pr.

To Pursue a Dream. Jane C. Miner. 176p. 1982. pap. 2.25 (ISBN 0-448-15690-3). Ace Bks.

To Quebec & the Stars. H. P. Lovecraft. 15.00 (ISBN 0-937986-30-5). D M Grant.

To Quench Our Thirst. David A. Franko & Robert G. Wetzel. (Illus.). 176p. 1983. text ed. 20.00x (ISBN 0-472-10032-7); pap. text ed. 9.95x (ISBN 0-472-08037-7). U of Mich Pr.

To Raise a Jewish Child: A Guide for Parents. Hayim H. Donin. LC 76-7679. 1977. 15.95 (ISBN 0-465-08626-8). Basic.

To Raise a Rainbow. Teo Savory. 1980. 15.00 (ISBN 0-87775-130-7); pap. 5.00 (ISBN 0-87775-131-5). Unicorn Pr.

To Raise an Army: The Draft Comes to Modern America. John W. Chambers, II. LC 87-15150. 448p. 1987. 24.95 (ISBN 0-02-905820-1). Free Pr.

To Raise, Destroy, & Create. Henry C. Lacey. LC 80-50078. 220p. 1981. 15.00x (ISBN 0-87875-185-8). Whitston Pub.

To Raise Myself a Little: The Diaries & Letters of Jennie, a Georgia Teacher, 1851-1886. Amelia A. Lines. Ed. by Thomas Dyer. LC 81-301. 288p. 1982. 22.00x (ISBN 0-8203-0562-6). U of Ga Pr.

To Re-Create a School Building. 1976. pap. 10.00 (ISBN 0-686-16657-4, 021-00452). Am Assn Sch Admin.

To Reach This Season: A Russians Odyssey to the West. Gregory I. Pasternak & Eugene Raleigh. LC 84-82476. 241p. 1985. pap. 12.95 (ISBN 0-943376-23-8). Magnes Mus.

To Read a Poem. Alice S. Landy. 1979. pap. text ed. 8.50 (ISBN 0-669-01535-0). Heath.

To Read Fiction. Donald Hall. 608p. 1987. pap. text ed. write for info. (ISBN 0-03-012218-X). HR&W.

To Read Literature. 2nd ed. Donald Hall. 1280p. 1987. pap. text ed. write for info. (ISBN 0-03-006207-1). HR&W.

To Read Literature: Fiction, Poetry, Drama. Ed. by Donald Hall. 1983. pap. text ed. 21.95 (ISBN 0-03-062851-2). HR&W.

To Read Poetry. Ed. by Donald Hall. 402p. 1982. pap. text ed. 15.95 (ISBN 0-03-060549-0). HR&W.

To Reason Why. Rose B. Green. 4.95 (ISBN 0-8453-1042-9, Cornwall Bks). Assoc Univ Prs.

To Recognize This Dying. Joe Napora. Ed. by John M. Gogol & Robert A. Davies. (Poetry Chapbook Ser.). 48p. (Orig.). 1987. pap. 5.00 (ISBN 0-932191-09-6). Mr Cogito Pr.

To Redeem the Soul of America: The Southern Christian Leadership Conference & Martin Luther King, Jr. Adam Fairclough. LC 86-11352. (Illus.). 514p. 1987. 35.00x (ISBN 0-8203-0898-6); pap. 17.95 (ISBN 0-8203-0938-9). U of Ga Pr.

To Reform the Nation: Theological Foundations of Wesley's Ethics. Leon O. Hynson. Ed. by Ben Chapman & Gerard Terpstra. 192p. (Orig.). 1984. pap. 4.95 (ISBN 0-310-75071-7, 17030P). Zondervan.

To Reign in Hell. Steven Brust. LC 84-50225. (Illus.). 258p. 1984. 17.00 (ISBN 0-916595-00-5). SteelDragon Pr.

To Reign in Hell. Steven Brust. 304p. 1985. pap. 2.95 (ISBN 0-441-81499-9, Pub. by Ace Science Fiction). Ace Bks.

To Remember Me. Robert Test. (Illus.). 48p. (Fr. & Eng.). 24.00 (ISBN 0-88014-017-8). Mosaic Pr OH.

To Ride a Tiger. Matthew H. Cooper. LC 85-11186. 247p. 1985. 13.95 (ISBN 0-8149-0903-5). Vanguard.

To Ride Pegasus. Anne McCaffrey. (Del Rey Bk.). 1986. pap. 3.95 (ISBN 0-345-33603-8). Ballantine.

To Rise above Principle: The Memoirs of an Unreconstructed Dean. Josef Martin. LC 87-27227. 152p. 1988. 19.95 (ISBN 0-252-01507-X). U of Ill Pr.

To Rome & Beyond (Acts B) Leader's Guide. (New Horizons Bible Study). 46p. (Orig.). 1982. pap. 1.95 (ISBN 0-89367-068-5). Light & Life.

To Rome & Beyond (Acts B) Student Guide. (New Horizons Bible Study). 68p. (Orig.). 1982. pap. 2.50 (ISBN 0-89367-069-3). Light & Life.

To Rule the Night. James B. Irwin & William A. Emerson, Jr. LC 73-11410. 1982. Repr. of 1973 ed. 9.95 (ISBN 0-8054-7227-4). Broadman.

To Run a Constitution: The Legitimacy of the Administrative State. John A. Rohr. LC 85-28867. xvi, 272p. 1986. 29.95x (ISBN 0-7006-0291-7); pap. 12.95 (ISBN 0-7006-0301-8). U Pr of KS.

To Run after Them: Cultural & Social Bases of Cooperation in a Navajo Community. Louise Lamphere. LC 77-22352. 230p. 1977. 15.95x (ISBN 0-8165-0594-2); pap. 8.95x (ISBN 0-8165-0369-9). U of Ariz Pr.

To Run & Not Be Weary. Stan Cottrell. (Illus.). 192p. 1985. 12.95 (ISBN 0-8007-1444-X). Revell.

To Sail a Ship of Treasures. Lisl Weil. LC 84-3025. (Illus.). 32p. (gr. k-4). 1984. PLB 10.95 (ISBN 0-689-31059-5, Atheneum Childrens Bks). Macmillan.

To Sail Beyond the Sunset. Robert A. Heinlein. 448p. 1987. 18.95 (ISBN 0-399-13267-8). Putnam Pub Group.

To Sail Beyond the Sunset. Robert A. Heinlein. 1988. pap. 4.95 (ISBN 0-441-74860-0). Ace Bks.

To Sail Beyond the Sunset. Robert A. Heinlein. 1988. pap. 4.95. Berkley Pub.

To Save Our Schools, to Save Our Children. ABC News Staff & Marshall Frady. LC 85-18798. (Illus.). 220p. 1986. 16.95 (ISBN 0-88282-013-3). New Horizon NJ.

To Save the Phenomena: An Essay on the Idea of Physical Theory from Plato to Galileo. Pierre Duhem. Tr. by Edmund Doland & Chaninah Maschler. LC 71-77978. (Midway Reprint Ser.). xxvi, 120p. 1985. pap. text ed. 9.95x (ISBN 0-226-16921-9). U of Chicago Pr.

To Save Their Heathen Souls: Voyage to & Life in Foochow, China, Based on Wentworth Diaries & Letters, 1854-1858. Ed. by Polly Park. LC 84-4247. (Pittsburgh Theological Monographs: New Ser. 9). (Illus., Orig.). 1984. pap. 10.00 (ISBN 0-915138-66-2). Pickwick.

To Scorch or Freeze: Poems About the Sacred. Donald Davie. (Phoenix Poetry Ser.). 56p. 1988. 20.00X (ISBN 0-226-13754-6); pap. 7.95 (ISBN 0-226-13755-4). U of Chicago Pr.

To Sea in Haste. Roland T. Carr. LC 75-13944. 1975. 12.50 (ISBN 0-87491-204-0); pap. 5.95 (ISBN 0-87491-020-X). Acropolis.

To Secure the Blessings of Liberty: American Constitutional Law & the New Religious Movements. William C. Shepherd. 128p. 1985. 12.95 (ISBN 0-8245-0664-2); pap. 8.95 (ISBN 0-8245-0670-7). Crossroad NY.

To Secure the Blessings of Liberty: Pennsylvania & the Changing U. S. Constitution. Louis M. Waddell. (Illus.). 96p. 1986. pap. 4.95 (ISBN 0-89271-035-7). Pa Hist & Mus.

To Secure These Blessings: The Great Debates of the Constitutional Convention of 1787. U. S. Constitutional Convention - 1787. Ed. by Saul K. Padover. 1962. 27.00 (ISBN 0-527-91880-6). Kraus Repr.

To See a Fine Lady. Norah Lofts. 272p. 1980. pap. 2.25 (ISBN 0-449-22890-8, Crest). Fawcett.

To See a Thing. Keith Gunderson. (Poetry Ser). (Illus.). 1975. pap. 1.00 (ISBN 0-685-79526-8). Nodin Pr.

To See a World in a Grain of Sand. Compiled by Caesar Johnson. LC 72-179257. (Illus.). 96p. 1972. 7.95 (ISBN 0-8378-1789-7). Gibson.

To See but Not to See: A Case Study of Visual Agnosia. Glyn W. Humphreys & J. Riddoch. 128p. 1987. text ed. 19.95 (ISBN 0-86377-064-9); pap. text ed. 9.95 (ISBN 0-86377-065-7). L Erlbaum Assocs.

To See His Face. Michael Wilcox. LC 84-70072. 224p. 1984. 7.95 (ISBN 0-87747-462-1). Deseret Bk.

To See Is to Think: Looking at American Art. Joshua C. Taylor. LC 74-26647. (Illus.). 118p. pap. 10.95 (ISBN 0-87474-177-7, TATSP). Smithsonian.

To See My Mother Dance. Sheila S. Klass. 160p. 1983. pap. 1.95 (ISBN 0-449-70052-6, Juniper). Fawcett.

To See or Not to See. Steve Struble. Ed. by Kathy Pohl. LC 85-15487. (Imagination Ser.). (Illus.). 32p. (gr. 2-4). 1986. PLB 14.65 (ISBN 0-8172-2700-8). Raintree Pubs.

To See Ourselves As Others See Us: Christians Jews, "Others" in Late Antiquity. Ed. by Jacob Neusner & Ernest S. Frerichs. (Scholars Press Studies in the Humanities). (Orig.). 1985. 38.95 (ISBN 0-89130-819-9, 00-01-09); pap. 25.95 (ISBN 0-89130-820-2). Scholars Pr GA.

To See Ourselves: Five Views on Canadian Women. (Illus.). 217p. 1975. pap. 14.00 (SSC79, SSC). UNIPUB.

To See the Kingdom: The Theological Vision of H. Richard Niebuhr. James W. Fowler. LC 85-17878. 304p. 1985. pap. text ed. 14.50 (ISBN 0-8191-4938-1). U Pr of Amer.

To See the Matter Clearly & Other Poems. Ruth Fainlight. 1969. 11.00 (ISBN 0-8023-1181-4). Dufour.

To See the Promised Land. Fred L. Downing. LC 86-16459. 288p. 1986. 27.50 (ISBN 0-86554-207-4, MUP-H189). Mercer Univ Pr.

To See What I See & Know What I Know: A Guide to Self-Discovery. Nathaniel Branden. LC 85-47792. 272p. 1986. pap. 8.95 (ISBN 0-553-34235-5). Bantam.

To See You Again. Alice Adams. 1982. 16.45 (ISBN 0-394-52335-0). Knopf.

To See You Again. Alice Adams. (Contemporary American Fiction Ser.). 312p. 1983. pap. 6.95 (ISBN 0-14-006483-4). Penguin.

To See Your Face Again. Eugenia Price. pap. 4.50 (ISBN 0-425-09203-8). Berkley Pub.

To See Your Face Again: A Novel, the Sequel to Savannah. Eugenia Price. LC 85-4434. 552p. 1985. 17.95 (ISBN 0-385-15275-2). Doubleday.

To Seek America: A History of Ethnic Life in the United States. Maxine S. Seller. LC 77-8248. 1977. pap. text ed. 13.95x (ISBN 0-89198-118-7). Ozer.

To Serve As Jesus Served. Clem J. Walters. LC 83-70964. 132p. 1983. pap. 3.95 (ISBN 0-943780-04-7, 8047). Charismatic Ren Servs.

To Serve Man: A Cookbook for People. Karl Wurf. (Illus.). 1976. 6.95 (ISBN 0-913896-05-5). Owlswick Pr.

To Serve the People: Congress & Constituency Service. John R. Johannes. LC 83-17050. xvi, 294p. 1984. 27.50x (ISBN 0-8032-2561-X); pap. 10.95x (ISBN 0-8032-7558-7, BB 868, Bison). U of Nebr Pr.

To Serve the Present Age. M. R. Zigler et al. Ed. by Donald F. Durnbaugh. (Illus.). 224p. 1975. pap. 4.45 (ISBN 0-87178-848-9). Brethren.

To Serve the Public Interest: Educational Broadcasting in the United States. Robert J. Blakely. 1979. 18.95x (ISBN 0-8156-2198-1); pap. 7.95x (ISBN 0-8156-0153-0). Syracuse U Pr.

To Serve Them All My Days. R. F. Delderfeld. 688p. 1984. pap. text ed. 5.95 (ISBN 0-671-55522-7). WSP.

To Serve Well & Faithfully: Labor & Indentured Servants in Pennsylvania, 1682-1800. Sharon V. Salinger. (Illus.). 224p. 1987. 29.95 (ISBN 0-521-33442-X). Cambridge U Pr.

To Serve with Honor: A Treatise on Military Ethics & the Way of the Soldier. Richard A. Gabriel. LC 81-6254. xviii, 243p. 1982. lib. bdg. 35.00 (ISBN 0-313-22545-1, GME/). Greenwood.

To Serve with Honor: A Treatise on Military Ethics & the Way of the Soldier. Richard A. Gabriel. LC 81-6254. 234p. 1987. pap. 14.95 (ISBN 0-275-92711-3, B2711). Praeger.

To Set at Liberty: Christian Faith & Human Freedom. Delwin Brown. LC 80-21783. 144p. (Orig.). 1981. pap. 6.95 (ISBN 0-88344-501-8). Orbis Bks.

To Set One's Heart: Belief & Teaching in the Church. Sara Little. LC 82-49020. 160p. 1983. pap. 8.95 (ISBN 0-8042-1442-5, John Knox). Westminster John Knox.

To Set Things Right: The Bible Speaks on Faith & Justice. Justin Vander Kolk. 48p. 1971. pap. 1.25 (ISBN 0-377-02001-X). Friendship Pr.

To Share a Dream. Willo D. Roberts. (Orig.). 1986. pap. 4.50 (ISBN 0-373-97028-5, Pub. by Worldwide). Harlequin Bks.

To Share a Moment. Monroe County Library System. (Community Anthology Ser.). 144p. (Orig.). 1987. pap. 4.00x (ISBN 0-940696-15-0). Monroe County Lib.

To Shorten the Road: Folktales From Ireland's Travelling People. George Gmelch & Ben Kroup. (Illus.). 189p. 1978. (Pub. by O'Brien Pr Ireland); pap. 7.95 (ISBN 0-86278-002-0). Irish Bks Media.

To Siberia & Russian America - Three Centuries of Russian Eastward Expansion, 1558-1867, Vol. 1: Russia's Conquest of Siberia, 1558-1700 - A Documentary Record. Ed. by Basil Dmytryshyn et al. Tr. by Basil Dmytryshyn from Rus. (North Pacific Studies: Vol. 9). (Illus.). 1986. 30.00x (ISBN 0-87595-148-1). Oregon Hist.

To Siberia & Russian America: Three Centuries of Russian Eastward Expansion, Vol. 2 see Russian Penetration of the North Pacific Ocean, 1700-1799: A Documentary Record.

To Sing in English: A Guide to Improved Diction. Dorothy Uris. LC 79-17264. 317p. (Orig.). 1971. pap. text ed. 14.95 (ISBN 0-913932-00-0). Boosey & Hawkes.

To Sing or Not to Sing. Alfred De Long. 1987. 7.95 (ISBN 0-533-07091-0). Vantage.

To Sing Our Own Songs: Cognition & Culture in Indian Education. 1985. pap. 2.50 (ISBN 0-318-19173-3). Assn Am Indian.

To Sir, with Love. E. R. Braithwaite. (gr. 9-12). 1973. pap. 2.95 (ISBN 0-515-09031-X). Jove Pubns.

To Skin a Cat. Thomas McGuane. LC 86-8916. 1986. 16.95 (ISBN 0-525-24460-3, Pub. by Seymour Lawrence). Dutton.

To Skin a Cat. Thomas McGuane. LC 87-40093. (Vintage Contemporaries Ser.). 224p. 1987. pap. 5.95 (ISBN 0-394-75521-9, Vin). Random.

To Slay the Hydra: Dutch Colonial Perspectives on the Saramaka Wars. Richard Price. (Illus.). 250p. 1984. pap. 15.50 (ISBN 0-89720-066-7). Karoma.

To Sleep No More. Dinah Lampitt. 464p. 1988. 19.95 (ISBN 0-312-01838-X). St Martin.

To Snatch an Eye. Henry Kane. Date not set. price not set. Maxim Bks.

To So Meito Ten: Exhibition of Famous Ceramics of Tang & Song. Tokyo Shirokiya Staff. 70p. 1964. 50.00x (ISBN 0-317-45308-4, Pub. by Han-Shan Tang Ltd). State Mutual Bk.

To So No Seiji: Ceramics of Tang & Song. Koyama Fujio. 24p. 1957. 60.00x (ISBN 0-317-44225-2, Pub. by Han-Shan Tang Ltd). State Mutual Bk.

To So Seika-Select Relics of the T'ang & Sung Synasties. Yamanaka Sadajiro. 1928. 3500.00x (Pub. by Han-Shan Tang Ltd). State Mutual Bk.

To Space & Back. Sally Ride & Susan Okie. LC 85-23757. (Illus.). 96p. (gr. 1 up). 1986. 16.95 (ISBN 0-688-06159-1). Lothrop.

To Speak Again. Raymond A. Berte. 196p. 1987. 19.95 (ISBN 0-941219-50-X). Phillips Pub MA.

To Speak Again: My Victory over Throat Cancer. Raymond Berte. 192p. 1988. 14.95 (ISBN 0-8159-6923-6). Devin.

To Speak in Pairs: Essays on the Ritual Languages of Eastern Indonesia. Ed. by James J. Fox. (Cambridge Studies in Oral & Literate Culture: No. 15). (Illus.). 300p. 1988. 54.50 (ISBN 0-521-34332-1). Cambridge U Pr.

To Split a Human: Mitos, Machos y la Mujer Chicana. Carmen Tafolla. (Illus.). 117p. (Orig., Eng. & Span.). 1985. pap. 9.95 (ISBN 0-932545-00-9). Mex Am Cult.

To Spoil the Sun. Joyce Rockwood. LC 86-16089. (Brown Thrasher Bk.). 180p. 1987. pap. 9.95 (ISBN 0-8203-0910-9). U of Ga Pr.

To Spoil the Sun. Joyce Rockwood. LC 76-10568. 192p. (gr. 2-6). 12.95 (ISBN 0-8050-0293-6). H Holt & Co.

To Spread the Power. George G. Hunter, III. 224p. 1987. pap. 9.95 (ISBN 0-687-42259-0). Abingdon.

To Square a Circle. Samuel Adams. Date not set. price not set (ISBN 0-393-07528-1). Norton.

To Stand the Point. Paul Burton. 28p. (Orig.). 1988. pap. text ed. 3.00 (ISBN 0-941470-19-9). Hilltop Pr CA.

To Start a New Civilization. Max Hermann. LC 76-40800. 275p. 1976. pap. 5.50 (ISBN 0-9602774-0-4). Sem Pub Hse.

To Starve the Army at Pleasure: Continental Army Administration & American Political Culture, 1775-1783. E. Wayne Carp. LC 83-19697. (Illus.). xv, 305p. 1984. 30.00x (ISBN 0-8078-1587-X). U of NC Pr.

To Stay Alive. Denise Levertov. LC 72-159739. (Orig.). 1971. 5.95 (ISBN 0-8112-0304-2). New Directions.

To Stem This Tide, a Survey of Racial Tension Areas in the United States. Charles S. Johnson. LC 74-99890. Repr. of 1943 ed. 16.00 (ISBN 0-404-00175-0). AMS Pr.

To Stretch a Plank: A Survey of Psychokinesis. Diana M. Robinson. LC 80-12335. 282p. 1981. 19.95 (ISBN 0-88229-404-0). Nelson-Hall.

To Strive, to Search, to Find. Marie Shepherd-Moore. LC 80-2367. 1979. pap. 5.95 (ISBN 0-9603948-1-8). Shepherd-Moore Ed Foun.

To Strive, to Search, to Find. (Illus.). 144p. 1976. 5.95. Shepherd-Moore Ed Foun.

To Struga with Love. Ed. by Stanley H. Barkan. LC 78-67775. (Illus., Orig.). 1978. in-folio 10.00 (ISBN 0-89304-028-2, CCC115); in-folio boxed 15.00 (ISBN 0-89304-050-9). Cross Cult.

To Study a Long Silence. V. C. Clinton-Baddeley. 192p. 1984. pap. 2.95 (ISBN 0-06-080690-7, P 690, PL). Har-Row.

To Succeed in Business, Get There, Honestly If You Can, but Get There. Frank D. Singewald. (Illus.). 64p. 1982. pap. 4.00 (ISBN 0-682-49863-7). Exposition-Phoenix.

To Suffer in Silence. Patricia Rae. 1981. pap. 2.75 (ISBN 0-89083-748-1). Zebra.

To Swallow a Toad. Peter W. Wood. LC 86-46398. 198p. 1987. 16.95 (ISBN 1-55611-019-7). D I Fine.

To Take a Dare. Crescent Dragonwagon & Paul Zindel. LC 80-8441. 256p. (YA) (gr. 7 up). 1982. 12.70i (ISBN 0-06-026858-1); PLB 12.89 (ISBN 0-06-026859-X). HarpJ.

To Take a Dare. Crescent Dragonwagon & Paul Zindel. 240p. (YA) (gr. 7-12). 1984. pap. 2.95 (ISBN 0-553-26601-2). Bantam.

To Take Place: Toward Theory in Ritual. Jonathan Z. Smith. LC 86-30869. (Chicago Studies in the History of Judaism). (Illus.). 208p. 1987. 27.50x (ISBN 0-226-76359-5). U of Chicago Pr.

To Take Your Heart Away. Jody Sorenson. (Caprice Ser.: No. 58). 160p. 1985. pap. 2.25 (ISBN 0-441-81526-X). Ace Bks.

To Talk in Time. Gene I. Namovicz. LC 86-18481. 156p. (gr. 5-9). 1987. 11.95 (ISBN 0-02-768170-X, Four Winds). Macmillan.

To Tame a Heart. Aimee Duvall. 1988. pap. 2.50. Crown.

To Tame a Land. Tex Burns, pseud. 17.95 (ISBN 0-89190-159-0, Pub. by Am Repr). Amereon Ltd.

To Tame a Land. Louis L'Amour. (HC Collection). (Orig.). 1985. pap. 2.95 (ISBN 0-553-25328-X). Bantam.

To Taste the Wine. Fern Michaels. (Orig.). 1987. pap. 4.50 (ISBN 0-345-30360-1). Ballantine.

To Teach Typing by Memory - Inductive Clues. Duk Bo Kim. 1988. 6.95 (ISBN 0-533-07530-0). Vantage.

To Teachers with Love. Ingeborg S. MacHaffie. Ed. by Margaret Nielsen. (Illus.). 90p. (Orig.). 1986. pap. 5.95 perfect bdg. (ISBN 0-9609374-2-0). Skribent.

To Tell a Free Story: The First Century of Afro-American Autobiography, 1760-1865. William L. Andrews. 1988. pap. 10.95 (ISBN 0-252-06033-4). U of Ill Pr.

To Tell of Gideon: The Art of Storytelling in the Church. John Harrell. 1975. 8.00x (ISBN 0-9615389-4-5); cassette 6.95x (ISBN 0-9615389-5-3). York Hse.

To Tell the Story. Yala Korwin. LC 87-80791. (Illus.). 130p. 1987. 13.95 (ISBN 0-89604-090-9); pap. 8.95 (ISBN 0-89604-091-7). Holocaust Pubns.

To Tell The Truth. Emily Chase. (Girls of Canby Hall Ser.: No. 15). 176p. (Orig.). (gr. 7 up). 1985. pap. 1.95 (ISBN 0-590-33759-9). Scholastic Inc.

To the Actor. Michael Chekhov. (Illus.). 208p. 1985. pap. 7.95 (ISBN 0-06-463707-7, EH 707, B&N Bks). Har-Row.

To the American Indian. Lucy Thompson. 230p. Date not set. pap. 9.95 (ISBN 0-911819-02-9). Yosemite D.

To Those Who Need It Most, Hospice Means Hope. Kenneth B. Wentzel. 1980. 9.95 (ISBN 0-89182-020-5); pap. text ed. 5.95 (ISBN 0-89182-030-2). Charles River Bks.

To Those Who Seek. Robert E. Birdsong. (Aquarian Academy Monograph, Series A: Lecture No. 2). 1974. pap. 1.25 (ISBN 0-917108-03-5). Sirius Bks.

To Toil the Livelong Day: America's Women at Work, 1780-1980. Ed. by Carol Groneman & Mary B. Norton. LC 86-47975. (Paperback Ser.). 1987. 34.95x (ISBN 0-8014-1847-X); pap. 9.95x (ISBN 0-8014-9452-4). Cornell U Pr.

To Touch a Dream. Christina Crokett. (Super Romances Ser.). 384p. 1983. pap. 2.95 (ISBN 0-373-70055-5, Pub. by Worldwide). Harlequin Bks.

To Touch a Heart. Sarah S. Weisberg. 80p. 1987. 6.95 (ISBN 0-8059-3074-4). Dorrance.

To Touch the Deer. Gus Cazzola. LC 81-10452. 130p. (gr. 5-9). 1981. 9.95 (ISBN 0-664-32684-6). Westminster John Knox.

To Touch the Hem of His Garment. Mary Drahos. 224p. (Orig.). 1983. pap. 7.95 (ISBN 0-8091-2548-X). Paulist Pr.

To Touch the Text: Biblical Studies in Honor of Joseph Fitzmeyer. M. Horgan & P. Kobelski. 480p. Date not set. text ed. 34.50x (ISBN 0-8245-0897-1). Crossroad NY.

To Touch the Water. 2nd ed. Gretel Ehrlich. Ed. by Tom Trusky. LC 80-69276. (Modern & Contemporary Poets of the West Ser.). 60p. (Orig.). 1981. pap. 4.50 (ISBN 0-916272-16-8). Ahsahta Pr.

To Treat or Not To Treat: A Working Document for Making Critical Life Decision. J. S. Showalter & Brian L. Andrew. LC 83-24018. 107p. 1984. pap. 15.00 (ISBN 0-87125-094-2); pap. 17.25. Cath Health.

To Treat or Not to Treat: Biothics & the Handicapped Newborn. Richard Sparks. 1988. pap. 9.95. Paulist Pr.

To Try Men's Souls: Loyalty Tests in American History. Harold M. Hyman. LC 81-13422. (Illus.). ix, 414p. 1982. Repr. of 1959 ed. lib. bdg. 38.50x (ISBN 0-313-23343-8, HYTM). Greenwood.

To Understand & Be Understood: A Practical Guide to Successful Relationships. Erik Blumenthal. Tr. by Nancy Benvenga from Ger. 160p. (Orig.). 1988. pap. 7.50 (ISBN 1-85168-004-7, Pub. by Oneworld Pubns). Alpha NY.

To Understand & to Help: The Life Work of Susan Isaacs (1885-1948) Lydia A. Smith. LC 83-48187. (Illus.). 352p. 1985. 39.50 (ISBN 0-8386-3211-4). Fairleigh Dickinson.

To Understand Each Other. Paul Tournier. 7.95 (ISBN 0-8042-2235-5, John Knox). Westminster John Knox.

To Understand Your Child. rev. ed. Kay Kuzma. 128p. 1985. pap. 5.95 (ISBN 0-910529-00-0). Parent Scene.

To Urania. Joseph Brodsky. 1988. 14.95 (ISBN 0-317-66200-7); ltd. ed. 60.00 (ISBN 0-317-66201-5). FS&G.

To Use the Sea. 2nd ed. Ed. by Jan Snouck-Hurgronje. LC 77-78390. 1977. 9.95x (ISBN 0-87021-707-0). Naval Inst Pr.

To Utopia & Back. Norman Horowitz. LC 85-27351. (Astronomy Ser.). (Illus.). 168p. 1986. text ed. 17.95 (ISBN 0-7167-1765-4); pap. text ed. 12.95 (ISBN 0-7167-1766-2). W H Freeman.

To Veronica 's New Lover. Marc M. Dion. (Target Midwest Poetry Ser.). 64p. 1987. 7.95 (ISBN 0-933532-60-1). BkMk.

To Vivek Then I Came. Som P. Ranchan. 111p. 1984. text ed. 18.95x (ISBN 0-7069-2488-6, Pub. by Vikas India). Advent NY.

To Wake the Dead. John D. Carr. 256p. 1984. pap. 3.50 (ISBN 0-02-018750-5). Macmillan.

To Wake the King: A Dramatic Legend. 108p. 4.00 (ISBN 0-318-13640-6). Board Jewish Educ.

To Walk & Not Grow Weary. Francis Sciacca. 84p. 1985. pap. 3.95 (ISBN 0-89109-034-7). NavPress.

To Walk As He Walked. T. B. Maston. LC 85-17173. 1985. pap. 5.95 (ISBN 0-8054-5024-6). Broadman.

To Walk in Stardust. Flavia Weedn. (Illus.). 96p. 1986. 9.95 (ISBN 0-913289-12-4). Roserich Ltd.

To Walk in the Way. Urie A. Bender. LC 79-83511. 208p. 1979. pap. 5.95 (ISBN 0-8361-1884-7). Herald Pr.

To Walk on Two Feet. Marjorie Cook. LC 77-17369. 96p. (gr. 6-9). 1978. 8.95 (ISBN 0-664-32628-5). Westminster John Knox.

To Walk Together Again: The Sacrament of Reconciliation. Richard M. Gula. LC 83-82021. (Orig.). 1984. pap. 8.95 (ISBN 0-8091-2603-6). Paulist Pr.

To Walk with a Quiet Mind: Hikes in the Woodlands, Parks & Beaches of the San Francisco Bay Area. Nancy Olmsted. LC 75-1053. (Totebook Ser.). (Illus.). 256p. 1975. pap. 8.95 (ISBN 0-87156-125-5). Sierra.

To Walk with Nature: The Drawings of Thomas Cole. Howard S. Merritt. LC 81-84873. (Illus.). 64p. (Orig.). 1981. pap. 10.00 (ISBN 0-943651-11-5). Hudson Riv.

To Wander No More. B. Russell Holt. (Bible Bookshelf). 95p. 1987. pap. 6.95 (ISBN 0-8163-0730-X). Pacific Pr Pub Assn.

To Warm Earth. David Belden. (Children of Arable Ser.: No. 2). 1988. pap. 3.95 (ISBN 0-451-15485-1, Sig). NAL.

To Warm the Earth. David Belden. (Children of Arable Ser.: No. 2). 320p. (Orig.). pap. 3.95 (Sig). NAL.

To Wear a City's Crown: The Beginnings of Urban Growth in Texas, 1836-1865. Kenneth W. Wheeler. LC 68-28698. (Illus.). 1968. 17.50x (ISBN 0-674-89340-9). Harvard U Pr.

To Wed a Doctor. Elizabeth Seifert. 1974. Repr. of 1968 ed. lib. bdg. 18.95x (ISBN 0-88411-057-5, Pub. by Aeonian Pr). Amereon Ltd.

To Wed a Doctor. Elizabeth Seifert. LC 88-20139. 389p. 1988. Repr. of 1969 ed. lib. bdg. 17.95 (ISBN 0-89621-184-3). Thorndike Pr.

To What Should We Be Loyal. William MacDonald. pap. 1.25 (ISBN 0-937396-47-8). Walterick Pubs.

To Where Streets Are Made of Gold: The Story of a Filipino Immigrant. Dorian Sikat. 1982. 7.50 (ISBN 0-682-49405-4). Exposition-Phoenix.

To Whom Else? Robert Graves. LC 77-4107. Repr. of 1931 ed. lib. bdg. 35.00 (ISBN 0-8414-4555-9). Folcroft.

To Whom Is God Betrothed? Earl Paulk. 200p. (Orig.). 1985. pap. 4.95 (ISBN 0-917595-10-6). K-Dimension.

To Whom It May Concern. Ruth Feldman. LC 86-17238. 93p. (Orig.). 1986. pap. 7.95 (ISBN 0-87233-086-9). Bauhan.

To Whom It May Concern: An Inquiry into the Art of Elephants. David Gucwa & James Ehmann. LC 85-10549. (Illus.). 1985. 14.95 (ISBN 0-393-02240-4). Norton.

To Whom Shall We Go: Christ & the Mystery of Man. Zachary Hayes. (Synthesis Ser). 96p. 1975. 1.25 (ISBN 0-8199-0702-2). Franciscan Herald.

To Whom the Land of Palestine Belongs. Christopher C. Hong. 1979. 6.50 (ISBN 0-682-49161-6). Exposition-Phoenix.

To Whom the Wilderness Speaks. Louise D. Lawrence. (Illus.). 208p. 1980. text ed. 14.95 (ISBN 0-07-092400-7). McGraw.

To Whom You Shall Go. James E. Magner, Jr. LC 78-51850. 1978. 5.00 (ISBN 0-8233-0274-1). Golden Quill.

To Will & to Do. Jacques Ellul. Tr. by C. Edward Hopkin. LC 70-91166. 1969. 12.50 (ISBN 0-8298-0137-5). Pilgrim NY.

To Will God's Will: Beginning the Journey. Ben Campbell Johnson. LC 87-14271. 126p. (Orig.). 1987. pap. 7.95 (ISBN 0-664-24086-0). Westminster John Knox.

To Will One Thing: Reflections on Kierkegaard's Purity of Heart. Jeremy D. Walker. LC 72-81506. pap. 43.80 (ISBN 0-317-26052-9, 2023841). Bks Demand UMI.

To Will One Thing: Solar Action at the Local Level. International Solar Energy Society, American Section. Ed. by Alec F. Jenkins. 1979. pap. text ed. 30.00x (ISBN 0-89553-022-8). Am Solar Energy.

To Will or Not to Will. Joseph E. Bright. xii, 72p. 1939. lib. bdg. 25.00 (ISBN 0-89941-597-0). W S Hein.

To Win a Nuclear War: The Pentagon's Secret Strategy. Michio Kaku & Daniel Axelrod. 400p. (Orig.). 1987. 30.00 (ISBN 0-89608-322-5); pap. 11.00 (ISBN 0-89608-321-7). South End Pr.

To Win or to Die: A Personal Portrait of Menachem Begin. Ned Temko. LC 87-1598. (Illus.). 320p. 1987. 18.95 (ISBN 0-688-04338-0). Morrow.

To Win the Money Game. Venita VanCaspel. 1980. pap. 1.50 (ISBN 0-8359-8692-6, Reston). P-H.

To Win the West: Missionary Reports, 1814-1815. LC 73-38467. (Religion in America, Ser. 2). 167p. 1972. Repr. 20.00 (ISBN 0-405-04091-1). Ayer Co Pubs.

To Win These Rights: A Personal Story of the CIO in the South. Lucy R. Mason. 1971. Repr. of 1952 ed. lib. bdg. 35.00x (ISBN 0-8371-3841-8, MATW). Greenwood.

To Work & to Love: A Theology of Creation. Dorothee Soelle & Shirley A. Cloyes. LC 84-47936. 160p. 1984. pap. 8.95 (ISBN 0-8006-1782-7). Fortress.

To Work & to Wed: Female Employment, Feminism, & the Great Depression. Lois Scharf. LC 79-52325. (Contributions in Women's Studies: No. 15). 1980. pap. 12.95 (ISBN 0-313-25059-6, STWPB). Greenwood.

To Write about Something. David J. Johnson. 208p. 1986. pap. text ed. 17.95 (ISBN 0-8403-4053-2). Kendall-Hunt.

To Write Paradise: Style & Error in Pound's Cantos. Christine Froula. LC 84-3649. 208p. 1985. text ed. 22.50t (ISBN 0-300-02512-2). Yale U Pr.

To Write, Write: Writing. James C. Durham. 240p. (gr. 9-12). 1981. pap. 7.25x (ISBN 0-88334-144-1). Ind Sch Pr.

To You from Me, Folk Verse. Melba Hughes. LC 86-63961. 64p. (Orig.). 1987. pap. 6.95 (ISBN 0-935834-56-7). Rainbow Books.

To Your Good Health! Charlotte A. Resnick & Gloria R. Resnick. (gr. 7-12). 1979. text ed. 18.33 (ISBN 0-87720-164-1); pap. text ed. 13.58 (ISBN 0-87720-163-3). AMSCO Sch.

To Your Scattered Bodies Go. Philip Jose Farmer. 224p. 1985. pap. 2.95 (ISBN 0-425-10334-X). Berkley Pub.

To Your Scattered Bodies Go see Philip Jose Farmer: The Complete Riverworld Novels.

To Your Wealth: How to Trade in Your Salaried Job for Your Own Small Business. 1987. lib. bdg. 76.00 (ISBN 0-8490-3893-6). Gordon Pr.

Toad at Harrow: P. G. Wodehouse in Perspective. Charles E. Gould, Jr. (Wodehouse Monograph: No. 3). 10p. (Orig.). 1982. pap. 7.50 (ISBN 0-87008-102-0). Heineman.

Toad Charts, Paper Faces, & Other Ideas for Visual Comprehension. Dorothy Z. Seymour. (gr. k-3). 1987. pap. 6.95 (ISBN 0-673-18713-6). Scott F.

Toad Food & Measle Soup. Christine McDonnell. LC 82-70204. (Illus.). 128p. (gr. 1-5). 1982. 10.95 (ISBN 0-8037-8476-7, 01063-320); PLB 10.89 (ISBN 0-8037-8488-0). Dial Bks Young.

Toad Food & Measle Soup. Christine McDonnell. (Puffin Story Bks.). (Illus.). 112p. 1984. pap. 3.95 (ISBN 0-14-031724-4, Puffin). Penguin.

Toad for Tuesday. Russell Erickson. LC 73-19900. (Illus.). 64p. (gr. k-4). 1974. PLB 10.88 (ISBN 0-688-51569-X). Lothrop.

Toad Hunt. Janet Chenery. LC 66-18653. (Science I Can Read Bks.). (Illus.). 64p. (gr. k-3). 1967. PLB 10.89 (ISBN 0-06-021263-2). HarpJ.

Toad Intruder. Lynn Luderer. (Illus.). (gr. 1-4). 1982. PLB 7.95 (ISBN 0-395-32081-X). HM.

Toad Is the Uncle of Heaven. Retold by & illus. by Jeanne M. Lee. LC 85-5639. (Illus.). 32p. (gr. k-2). 1985. 12.95 (ISBN 0-03-004652-1). H Holt & Co.

Toad of Toad Hall. A. A. Milve. (gr. k-3). 1982. pap. 2.95 (ISBN 0-380-58115-9, Bard). Avon.

Toads of War. Eddie Iroh. LC 79-670372. (African Writers Ser.). 1979. pap. text ed. 7.00 (ISBN 0-435-90213-X). Heinemann Ed.

Toady & Dr. Miracle. Mary B. Christian. LC 84-21278. (Illus.). 56p. (gr. 1-4). 1985. PLB 9.95 (ISBN 0-02-718470-6). Macmillan.

Toady & Dr. Miracle. Mary B. Christian. LC 86-22225. (Ready-to-Read Ser.). (Illus.). 56p. (gr. 1-3). 1987. pap. 3.95 (ISBN 0-689-71124-7, Aladdin Bks). Macmillan.

Toady Tales. 2nd. ed. Anna L. Carlson. LC 80-83018. 24p. (gr. k-4). 1983. pap. 1.95 (ISBN 0-939938-02-2). Karwyn Ent.

Toast to Cousin Julian. Estelle Thompson. 192p. 1987. 15.95 (ISBN 0-8027-5665-4). Walker & Co.

Toast to Sober Spirits & Joyous Juices: A Collection of Non-Alcoholic Beverage Recipes. rev. ed. Jan Blexrud. LC 76-55449. (Illus.). pap. 6.95 (ISBN 0-89638-041-6, X1979). CompCare.

Toast to the Fur Trade: A Picture Essay on Its Material Culture. Robert C. Wheeler. Ed. by Ardis H. Wheeler. LC 84-91414. (Illus.). 120p. 1985. 24.95 (ISBN 0-9614362-0-4); pap. 15.95 (ISBN 0-9614362-1-2). Wheeler Prods.

Toast to Tomorrow. Manning Coles. (Spies & Intrigues Ser.: No. 3). 310p. 1984. pap. 5.95 (ISBN 0-918172-15-2). Leetes Isl.

Toast to Wine & Spirits. Nicolas Bailly. (Illus.). 1988. pap. 16.00. Abrams.

Toasted Bagels: A Break-of-Day Book. Joyce A. Zarins. (Illus.). 48p. (gr. 1-4). 1988. PLB 9.99 (ISBN 0-698-30571-X, Coward). Putnam Pub Group.

Toasted Cheese & Cinders. Sybil Brand. 1986. 42.00x (ISBN 0-86332-113-5, Pub. by Book Guild Ltd). State Mutual Bk.

Toastmaster's Treasure Chest. 2nd ed. Herbert V. Prochnow. LC 87-46167. 640p. 1988. 25.00 (ISBN 0-06-015906-5, HarpT). Har-Row.

Toastmaster's Treasure Chest. Herbert V. Prochnow & Herbert V. Prochnow, Jr. LC 78-2161. 1979. 16.45i (ISBN 0-06-013447-X, HarpT). Har-Row.

Toba-Batak-Deutsches Worterbuch. Joh. Warneck. (Royal Institute of Linguistics & Anthropology-Leiden Ser.). 1977. lib. bdg. 40.50 (ISBN 90-247-201-84, Pub. by Martinus Nijhoff Netherlands). Kluwer Academic.

Toba Tucker: A Shinnecock Portrait. John Strong & Madeleine Burnside. LC 87-80697. (Illus.). 24p. (Orig.). 1987. pap. 7.00 (ISBN 0-933793-07-3). Guild Hall.

Tobacco. 2nd ed. B. C. Akehurst. (Tropical Agriculture Ser.). (Illus.). 1981. text ed. 110.00x (ISBN 0-582-46817-5). Wiley.

Tobacco. Rob Stepney. (Triumph Ser.). (Illus.). 64p. 1987. lib. bdg. 11.90 (ISBN 0-531-10438-9). Watts.

Tobacco - The Real Story. David Stronck. Ed. by Mary Nelson & Kay Clark. (Illus.). 30p. (gr. 5-8). 1987. pap. text ed. 2.95 (ISBN 0-941816-34-6). Network Pubns.

Tobacco: A Major International Health Hazard. Ed. by D. Zaridze & R. Peto. (IARC Scientific Ser.: No. 74). (Illus.). 350p. 1987. 46.00 (ISBN 92-832-1174-X). Oxford U Pr.

Tobacco Advertising Bans & Consumption in 16 Countries. Ed. by J. J. Boddewyn. 32p. 1986. 10.00. Intl Advertising Assn.

Tobacco Advertising Restrictions Around the World. 20p. 1983. 10.00. Intl Advertising Assn.

Tobacco, Alcohol & Cancer Prevention. Ernest H. Rosenbaum et al. Ed. by Sheila Mahoney & Nancy Wiltsek. (Illus.). 29p. 1984. pap. 2.50 (ISBN 0-933161-02-6). Better H Prog.

Tobacco: An International Perspective. David Tucker. 224p. 1985. 220.00x (ISBN 0-903706-86-5, Euromonitor). State Mutual Bk.

Tobacco & Advertising: Five Arguments Against Censorship. 29p. 1983. 10.00. Intl Advertising Assn.

Tobacco & Effects: Medical Subject Analysis with Bibliography. Scott T. Dowling. LC 87-47630. 160p. 1987. 34.50 (ISBN 0-88164-562-1); pap. 26.50 (ISBN 0-88164-563-X). ABBE Pubs Assn.

Tobacco & Marijuana. Ochsner et al. 1976. perfect bdg. 6.50 (ISBN 0-88252-048-2). Paladin Hse.

Tobacco & Shamanism in South Africa. Johannes Wilbert. LC 87-10643. 288p. 1988. text ed. 30.00 (ISBN 0-300-03879-8). Yale U Pr.

Tobacco & Slaves: The Development of Southern Cultures in the Chesapeake, 1680-1800. Allan Kulikoff. LC 85-8452. (Published for the Institute of Early American History & Culture Ser.). xviii, 449p. 1986. 30.00x (ISBN 0-8078-1671-X). U of NC Pr.

Tobacco & Slaves: The Development of Southern Cultures in the Chesapeake, 1680-1800. Allan Kulikoff. LC 85-8452. (Institute of Early American History & Culture Ser.). (Illus.). xviii, 499p. 1988. 30.00x; pap. 11.95x (ISBN 0-8078-4224-9). U of NC Pr.

Tobacco Coast. Arthur P. Middleton. LC 84-47962. (Maryland Paperback Bookshelf Ser.). 528p. 1984. pap. 14.95 (ISBN 0-8018-2534-2). Johns Hopkins.

Tobacco Colony: Life in Early Maryland, 1650-1720. G. L. Main. 1982. 38.50x (ISBN 0-691-04693-X). Princeton U Pr.

Tobacco Culture: The Mentality of the Great Tidewater Planters on the Eve of Revolution. T. H. Breen. LC 85-42676. (Illus.). 210p. 1985. 27.50 (ISBN 0-691-04729-4). Princeton U Pr.

Tobacco Culture: The Mentality of the Great Tidewater Planters on the Eve of Revolution. T. H. Breen. (Illus.). 240p. 1988. pap. text ed. 9.95 (ISBN 0-691-00596-6). Princeton U Pr.

Tobacco Diseases & Decays. Frederick A. Wolf. LC 57-6286. pap. 103.00 (ISBN 0-317-26801-5, 2023473). Bks Demand UMI.

Tobacco Habits Other than Smoking: Betel-Quid & Areca-Nut Chewing; & Some Related Nitrosamines. (IARC Monographs on the Evaluation of the Carcinogenic Risk of Chemicals to Humans: Vol. 37). 291p. 1985. pap. 42.00 (ISBN 92-832-1537-0). World Health.

Tobacco Industry in the United States. Meyer Jacobstein. LC 68-56662. (Columbia University. Studies in the Social Sciences: No. 70). Repr. of 1907 ed. 18.50 (ISBN 0-404-51070-1). AMS Pr.

Tobacco Kingdom. Joseph C. Robert. 1938. 11.75 (ISBN 0-8446-1386-X). Peter Smith.

Tobacco Lords: A Study of the Tobacco Merchants of Glasgow & Their Trading Activities. T. M. Devine. 222p. 1985. 37.00x (ISBN 0-85976-010-3, Pub. by J Donald Pubs Ltd UK). State Mutual Bk.

Tobacco Monopoly in the Philippines: Bureaucratic Enterprise & Social Change, 1766-1880. Ed. by Ed C. De Jesus. (Illus.). 244p. 1981. (Pub. by Ateneo de Manila U Pr Philippines); pap. 13.50 (ISBN 0-686-30373-3). Cellar.

Tobacco on the Periphery: A Case Study of Cuban Labour History, 1860-1958. Jean Stubbs. (Latin American Studies: No. 51). (Illus.). 224p. 1985. 44.50 (ISBN 0-521-25423-X). Cambridge U Pr.

Tobacco, Peacepipes & Indians. Louis Seig. LC 73-90817. (Wild & Woolly West Ser., No. 15). (Illus., Orig.). 1971. 8.00 (ISBN 0-910584-16-8); pap. 2.50 (ISBN 0-910584-91-5). Filter.

Tobacco Pipes of the Missouri Indians. Henry W. Hamilton. Ed. by Carl H. Chapman. (Memoir Ser.: No. 5). (Illus.). 49p. (Orig.). 1967. pap. 2.00 (ISBN 0-943414-20-2). MO Arch Soc.

Tobacco Product Liability: Affirmative & Defensive Tools, Asbestos Property Damage Litigation: Fourth Annual Toxic Tort Advocacy Institute. LC 86-183892. iv, 192p. Date not set. price not set. HarBraceJ.

Tobacco Regulations in Colonial Maryland. Vertrees J. Wyckoff. LC 78-64291. (Johns Hopkins University. Studies in the Social Sciences. Extra Volumes: 22). Repr. of 1936 ed. 24.50 (ISBN 0-404-61391-8). AMS Pr.

Tobacco Road. Erskine Caldwell. LC 78-55752. 1978. Repr. of 1932 ed. Bentley.

Tobacco Road. Erskine Caldwell. 1970. pap. 2.95 (ISBN 0-451-12156-2, AE2156, Sig). NAL.

Tobacco Smoking. (IARC Monographs on the Evaluation of the Carcinogenic Risk of Chemicals to Humans: Vol. 38). 421p. 1986. pap. 45.00 (ISBN 92-832-1538-9). World Health.

Tobacco Smoking & Nicotine: A Neurobiological Approach. Ed. by W. R. Martin et al. LC 87-18513. (Advances in Behavioral Biology Ser.: Vol. 31). (Illus.). 534p. 1987. 89.50x (ISBN 0-306-42611-0, Plenum Pr). Plenum Pub.

Tobacco, Snuff Boxes & Pipes. Lutz Libert. (Illus.). 148p. 1986. 28.50x (ISBN 0-85613-918-1, Pub. by MacD & Co). Trans-Atl Phila.

Tobacco Society of the Crow Indians. Robert H. Lowie. LC 74-7988. Repr. of 1919 ed. 13.45 (ISBN 0-404-11878-X). AMS Pr.

Tobacco Tins & Their Prices. Al Bergevin. LC 86-50132. (Illus.). 1986. pap. 15.95 (ISBN 0-87069-464-2). Wallace-Homestead.

Tobacco: What It Is, What It Does. Judith S. Seixas. LC 81-837. (Greenwillow Read-Alone Bks.). (Illus.). 56p. (gr. 1-3). 1981. 12.95 (ISBN 0-688-00769-4). Greenwillow.

Tobago. David L. Niddrie. 1981. 8.50x (ISBN 0-416-60311-4, NO. 3447). Routledge Chapman & Hall.

Todays Healthy Eating. Louise Tenney. 249p. Date not set. pap. 12.95 (ISBN 0-913923-09-5). Woodland UT.

Today's Hearing Impaired Child: Into the Mainstream of Education. Ed. by Vira J. Froehlinger. 240p. (Orig.). 1981. pap. 12.95 (ISBN 0-88200-143-4, N6184). Alexander Graham.

Today's Immigrants, Their Stories: A New Look at the Newest Americans. Thomas Kessner & Betty B. Caroli. (Illus.). 1981. 19.95x (ISBN 0-19-503000-1); pap. 8.95x (ISBN 0-19-503270-5). Oxford U Pr.

Today's Isms: Communism, Facism, Capitalism, Socialism. 9th ed. William Ebenstein & Edwin Fogelman. (Illus.). 272p. 1985. text ed. 27.67 (ISBN 0-13-924481-6); pap. text ed. 29.00 (ISBN 0-13-924473-5). P-H.

Today's Kindergarten: Exploring the Knowledge Base, Expanding the Curriculum. Bernard Spodek. (Early Childhood Education Ser.). 160p. 1986. text ed. 19.95x (ISBN 0-8077-2809-8); pap. text ed. 13.95x (ISBN 0-8077-2808-X). Tchrs Coll.

Today's Language: A Vocabulary Workbook. John T. Hiers et al. 368p. 1981. pap. text ed. 15.00 (ISBN 0-669-03078-3). Heath.

Today's Marriages & Families. Thomas P. Gullotta et al. LC 85-19051. (Psychology Ser.). 550p. 1986. text ed. 23.00 pub net (ISBN 0-534-05520-6). Brooks-Cole.

Today's Mathematics. 6th ed. James H. Heddens & William R. Spier. 688p. Date not set. pap. text ed. price not set (ISBN 0-574-23130-7, 13-6130); price not set instr's. guide (ISBN 0-574-23131-5, 13-6131). SRA.

Today's Mathematics. 5th ed. Ed. by James W. Heddens. 688p. 1984. pap. text ed. write for info. (ISBN 0-574-23110-2, 13-6110). SRA.

Today's Moral Problems. 3rd ed. Richard A. Wasserstrom. 624p. 1985. text ed. write for info. (ISBN 0-02-424840-1). Macmillan.

Today's Pastor in Tomorrow's World. Rev. ed. Carnegie S. Calian. LC 82-7114. 164p. 1982. pap. 8.95 (ISBN 0-664-24426-2). Westminster John Knox.

Today's Practical Guide to Increasing Profits for Contractors with Easy-to-Use Suggestions & Aids. Richard S. Budzik & Janet K. Budzik. LC 74-79535. (Illus.). 1974. 49.95 (ISBN 0-912914-03-3). Practical Pubns.

Today's Sects. M. C. Burrell & J. S. Wright. pap. 4.50 (ISBN 0-8010-0855-7). Baker Bk.

Today's Special: Z. A. P. & Zoe. Athena V. Lord. LC 84-9661. (Illus.). 160p. (gr. 4-7). 1984. 10.95 (ISBN 0-02-761440-9). Macmillan.

Today's Stars in Country Music. Patricia Woodward. LC 86-20127. (Illus.). 208p. (Orig.). 1987. pap. 9.95 (ISBN 0-933703-25-2). Loiry Pubs Hse.

Today's Students, Tomorrow's Future. M. Regina Auzins. LC 85-91306. 150p. 1986. 8.95 (ISBN 0-533-06819-3). Vantage.

Today's Tax & Business Law: And How to Find It. 104p. 1986. write for info. Commerce.

Today's Teen. rev. ed. Kelly & Landers. (gr. 7-9). 1981. text ed. 23.04 (ISBN 0-02-666030-X); guide 12.32tchr's (ISBN 0-02-666040-7); student guide 6.00 (ISBN 0-02-666010-5). Bennett IL.

Today's Tentmakers. J. Christy Wilson, Jr. 1979. pap. 6.95 (ISBN 0-8423-7279-2). Tyndale.

Today's Victorious Woman, Vol. I. Mrs. J. B. Livingston. pap. 4.00 (ISBN 0-89137-426-4). Quality Pubns.

Today's Victorious Woman, Vol. 2. Mrs. J. B Livingston. pap. 4.00 (ISBN 0-89137-427-2). Quality Pubns.

Today's Video: Equipment, Setup & Production. Peter Utz. (Illus.). 1216p. 1987. 49.95 (ISBN 0-13-924499-9). P-H.

Today's Waiter & Waitress. Bolt et al. (Restaurant Training Manuals Ser). (Illus., Prog. Bk.). 1979. pap. 3.50 (ISBN 0-912016-20-5, 086730220); supervisor's manual avail. (ISBN 0-912016-21-3). Lebhar Friedman.

Today's Woman in Search of Freedom. Ruthe White. 176p. (Orig.). 1985. pap. 4.95 (ISBN 0-89081-473-2). Harvest Hse.

Today's Woman, Tomorrow's Church. Kaye Ashe. 200p. 1984. pap. 9.95 (ISBN 0-88347-168-X). Thomas More.

Today's World. 2nd ed. Ella Salmi. 80p. 1985. pap. 6.50 (ISBN 0-9601542-9-9). Mentors.

Today's World Religions. M. Thomas Starkes. 1986. 10.95 (ISBN 0-937931-02-0); pap. 7.95. Global TN.

Today's Youth-Today's Librarian. Ed. by John T. Corrigan. (Catholic Library Assn. Studies in Librarianship: No. 3). 64p. 1980. pap. 5.00 (ISBN 0-87507-007-8). Cath Lib Assn.

Todd. David Melton. (Gentle Revolution Ser.). (Illus.). 266p. 1985. 13.95 (ISBN 0-936676-52-3). Better Baby.

Todd Lecture Series, Vols. 1-17. Royal Irish Academy. Repr. Set. 388.00 (ISBN 0-404-60560-5). AMS Pr.

Todd Memorial Volumes: Philological Studies, 2 Vols. facs. ed. Ed. by J. D. Fitz-Gerald & P. Taylor. LC 68-22950. (Essay Index Reprint Ser). 1968. Repr. of 1930 ed. 28.00 (ISBN 0-8369-0948-8). Ayer Co Pubs.

Todd-Sanford-Davidsohn: Clinical Diagnosis & Management by Laboratory Methods. 17th ed. John B. Henry. (Illus.). 1500p. 1984. 68.00 (ISBN 0-7216-4657-3). Saunders.

Todd Walker, Photographs. Intro. by Julia K. Nelson. LC 85-70352. (Untitled Ser.: No. 38). (Illus.). 48p. (Orig.). 1985. pap. 20.00 (ISBN 0-933286-42-2). Friends Photography.

Todd Webb Photographs: Early Western Trails & Some Ghost Towns. rev. ed. Intro. by Beaumont Newhall. LC 79-10354. (Illus.). 37p. 1979. pap. 7.95 (ISBN 0-88360-032-3, Dist. by Univ. of Texas Pr). Amon Carter.

Todd Webb: Photographs of New York & Paris, 1945-1960. Keith Davis. 116p. 1986. pap. 16.95. Hallmark.

Todd Webb: Photographs of New York & Paris, 1945-1960. Keith F. Davis. 116p. 1986. pap. 16.95 (ISBN 0-87529-620-3, Pub. by Hallmark Cards, Inc.). U of NM Pr.

Toddler & the New Baby. Sylvia Close. 128p. 1980. pap. 7.95 (ISBN 0-7100-0523-7). Routledge Chapman & Hall.

Toddler Day Care: A Guide to Responsive Caregiving. Robin L. Leavitt & Brenda K. Eheart. 192p. 1985. 20.00x (ISBN 0-669-09980-5); pap. text ed. 14.95x. Lexington Bks.

Toddler Taming. Christopher Green. 256p. 1985. pap. 6.95 (ISBN 0-449-90155-6, Columbine). Fawcett.

Toddler Years. Ed. by Dodie Schultz & Parents Magazine Editors. (Orig.). 1986. pap. 7.95 (ISBN 0-345-32172-3, Pub. by Ballantine Trade). Ballantine.

Toddlers & Parents. T. Berry Brazelton. 272p. 1976. pap. 12.95 (ISBN 0-385-29034-9, Delta). Dell.

Toddler's Behaviors with Age Mates: Issues of Interaction, Cognition & Affect. Wanda C. Bronson. LC 81-12896. (Monographs on Infancy: Vol. 1). 144p. 1981. text ed. 32.50 (ISBN 0-89391-080-5). Ablex Pub.

Toddlers Learn by Doing: Toddler Activities & Activity Log for Parents & Teachers. Rita Schrank. 144p. (Orig.). 1984. pap. 12.95 (ISBN 0-89334-085-5). Humanics Ltd.

Toddler's Potty Book. Alida Allison. 32p. (ps). 1985. softcover 3.95 (ISBN 0-8431-0673-5). Price Stern.

Todeserlebnis Des Manes see Death Experience of Manes.

Todesverstaendnis bei Simone de Beauvoir: Eine Theologische Untersuchung. Erich Schmalenberg. LC 72-77421. (Theologische Bibliothek Toepelmann, No. 25). 1972. 20.80x (ISBN 3-11-004036-0). De Gruyter.

Todo Es Armonia en la Naturaleza. L. Golovanov. 200p. (Span.). 1982. pap. 3.95 (ISBN 0-8285-2498-X, Pub. by Mir Pubs USSR). Imported Pubns.

Todo Es Bello Alrededor. Adolfo Robleto. 80p. 1983. pap. 4.95 (ISBN 0-311-08758-2, Edit Mundo). Casa Bautista.

Todos Heridos por el Norte y por el Sur. Alberto Muller. LC 80-70474. (Coleccion Caniqui Ser.). 63p. (Orig., Span.). 1982. pap. 5.00 (ISBN 0-89729-282-0). Ediciones.

Todos Santos in Rural Tlaxcala: A Syncretic, Expressive, & Symbolic Analysis of the Cult of the Dead. Hugo G. Nutini. (Illus.). 490p. 1988. text ed. 75.00 (ISBN 0-691-07755-X). Princeton U Pr.

Todos Somos Testigos. Urie A. Bender. 160p. (Span.). pap. 3.95x (ISBN 0-8361-1236-9, Pub. by Sociacion Editorial la Aurora Doblas Argentina). Herald Pr.

Toe, & Other Tales. Alexander Harvey. LC 73-125215. (Short Story Index Reprint Ser). 1913. 14.50 (ISBN 0-8369-3582-9). Ayer Co Pubs.

TOEFL Grammar Workbook. Phyllis L. Lim & Mary Kurtin. Ed. by Laurie Wellman. LC 81-17674. 256p. 1982. pap. 7.95 (ISBN 0-668-05080-2, 5080). Arco.

TOEFL Reading Comprehension & Vocabulary Workbook. 1st ed. Elizabeth Davy & Karen Davy. LC 83-3717. 256p. (Orig.). 1983. pap. 7.95 (ISBN 0-668-05594-4, 5594). Arco.

TOEFL (Test of English As a Foreign Language) 3rd ed. Edith H. Babin & Carole V. Cordes. LC 82-22809. 352p. 1983. pap. 8.95 (ISBN 0-668-05446-8); cassette 7.95 (ISBN 0-668-05743-2). Arco.

TOEFL (Test of English As a Foreign Language) Preparation Guide. Michael A. Pyle & M. Munoz. (Cliffs Test Preparation Ser.). 463p. (Orig.). 1983. pap. text ed. 14.95 (ISBN 0-8220-2018-1). Cliffs.

Toefl Test-Taking Skill Builder. Patricia N. Sullivan & Grace Q. Zhong. 256p. 1988. pap. 8.95 (ISBN 0-13-467762-5). P-H.

Toeing the Lines: Women & Party Politics in English Canada. Sylvia B. Bashevkin. 240p. 1985. 13.95 (ISBN 0-8020-2557-9); pap. 12.95 (ISBN 0-8020-6576-7). U of Toronto Pr.

Toeplitz Forms & Their Applications. 2nd ed. Ulf Grenander & Gabor Szego. LC 83-62686. ix, 245p. text ed. 16.95 (ISBN 0-8284-0321-X). Chelsea Pub.

Toff Down Pitt. Kit Fraser. 130p. 1985. 12.95 (ISBN 0-7043-2513-6, Pub. by Quartet Bks). Salem Hse Pubs.

Toffee Apple Tree. Gillian Lindsay. (Illus.). 48p. (gr. 2-5). 1984. 5.95 (ISBN 0-241-10985-X, Pub. by Hamish Hamilton England). David & Charles.

Tofu & Soymilk Production: The Book of Tofu, Vol. II. William Shurtleff & Akiko Aoyagi. LC 74-31629. (Soyfoods Production Ser.: No. 2). (Illus.). 344p. 1984. 36.95 (ISBN 0-933332-14-9); pap. 29.95 (ISBN 0-933332-13-0). Soyfoods Center.

Tofu at Center Stage. Gary Landgrebe. LC 80-69560. (Illus.). 112p. (Orig.). 1981. pap. 5.95 (ISBN 0-9601398-3-4). Fresh Pr.

Tofu Consumer Awareness & Purchasing Patterns. Ed. by Peter Allen. 87p. (Orig.). 1981. pap. 750.00 (ISBN 0-931634-20-2). FIND SVP.

Tofu Cookbook. Cathy Bauer & Juel Andersen. 1979. 9.95 (ISBN 0-87857-246-5). Rodale Pr Inc.

Tofu Cookbook: Recipes for Traditional & Modern Cooking. Junko Lampert. LC 85-25546. (Illus.). 102p. (Orig.). 1986. pap. 9.95 (ISBN 0-87701-383-7). Chronicle Bks.

Tofu Cookery. Ed. by Louise Hagler. LC 82-73003. (Illus.). 160p. (Orig.). 1982. pap. 11.95 (ISBN 0-913990-38-8). Book Pub Co.

Tofu Cookery. Fusako Holthaus. LC 82-80647. (Illus.). 159p. 1982. 18.95 (ISBN 0-87011-523-5). Kodansha.

Tofu Goes West. Gary Landgrebe. LC 78-67462. (Illus.). 114p. (Orig.). 1978. pap. 5.95 (ISBN 0-9601398-2-6). Fresh Pr.

Tofu Gourmet. Linda L. Barber & Junko Lampert. (Illus.). 128p. 1984. 14.95 (ISBN 0-87040-589-6). Japan Pubns USA.

Tofu Quick 'n Easy. Louise Hagler. LC 86-72222. (Illus.). 104p. (Orig.). 1986. pap. 5.95 (ISBN 0-913990-50-7). Book Pub Co.

Tofu, Tempeh & Other Soy Delights: Enjoying Traditional Oriental Soyfoods in American-Style Cuisine. Camille Cusumano. (Illus.). 272p. 1984. pap. 12.95 (ISBN 0-87857-489-1, 07-189-1). Rodale Pr Inc.

Tofu, Tempeh, Miso & Other Soyfoods. Richard Leviton. Ed. by Richard A. Passwater & Earl R. Mindell. (Good Health Guide Ser.). 32p. 1982. pap. 1.95 (ISBN 0-87983-284-3). Keats.

Tofutti & Other Soy Ice Creams: Non-Dairy Frozen Dessert Industry & Market, 2 vols. William Shurtleff & Akiko Aoyagi. (Soyfoods Market Studies Ser.). (Orig.). 1985. Set. pap. text ed. 135.00 spiral bdg. (ISBN 0-933332-19-X). Vol. I, 144p. Soyfoods Center.

Tog the Dog. Colin Hawkins & Jacqui Hawkins. (Illus.). 20p. (ps-1). 1986. 8.95 (ISBN 0-399-21338-4, Putnam). Putnam Pub Group.

Tog the Ribber: Or Granny's Tales. Paul Coltman. LC 84-82555. (Illus.). 32p. (ps-5). 1985. 11.95 (ISBN 0-374-37630-1). FS&G.

Togaviridae & Flaviviridae. Ed. by Sondra Schlesinger & Milton Schlesinger. LC 86-4914. (Viruses Ser.). 470p. 1986. 69.50x (ISBN 0-306-42176-3, Plenum Pr). Plenum Pub.

Togaviruses. Ed. by R. Walter Schlesinger. 1980. 87.50 (ISBN 0-12-625380-3). Acad Pr.

Togbukh Fun Vilner Geto. Herman Kruk. Ed. by Mordecai W. Bernstein. LC 62-56072. (Yivo Institute for Jewish Research, Memoirs Ser.: No. 1). (Illus.). 620p. (Yiddish.). 1961. 10.00 (ISBN 0-914512-29-3). Yivo Inst.

Togei. Koyama Fugjio. 201p. 1960. 350.00x (ISBN 0-317-68512-0, Pub. by Han-Shan Tang Ltd). State Mutual Bk.

Together. Robert Herrick. (Collected Works of Robert Herrick). 1988. Repr. of 1908 ed. lib. bdg. 59.00x. Am Biog Serv.

Together, a New People: Pastoral Statement on Migrants & Refugees. National Conference of Catholic Bishops Staff. 40p. (Orig.). 1987. pap. 3.95 (ISBN 1-55586-147-4). US Catholic.

Together: A Process for Parish Family Ministry. Joseph DiMauro & Sharon A. Tumulty. 1985. Envisioning. pap. 2.50 (ISBN 0-697-02024-X); Listening. pap. 3.50 (ISBN 0-697-02025-8); Responding. pap. 3.50 (ISBN 0-697-02026-6); Enabling. pap. 3.50 (ISBN 0-697-02027-4); Administering. pap. 3.50 (ISBN 0-697-02028-2); Administrator manual. 20.00 (ISBN 0-697-02023-1). Wm C Brown.

Together Again. Jennifer Sarasin. (Cheerleaders Ser.: No. 32). 288p. (Orig.). (gr. 7 up). 1987. pap. 2.95 (ISBN 0-590-40637-X). Scholastic Inc.

Together Alone: The Diary of an Addict's Addict. Barbara M. Youngert. (Illus.). 84p. 1985. pap. 5.00 (ISBN 0-944642-00-4, TX1741844). Hector Marie.

Together at Baptism. Joseph E. Payne et al. LC 73-144040. (Illus.). 80p. (Orig.). 1971. pap. 1.75 (ISBN 0-87793-031-7). Ave Maria.

Together at Mass: A Child's Mass Book. Gaynell B. Cronin & Joan Bellina. LC 87-70417. (Illus.). 32p. (Orig.). (ps-2). 1987. pap. 2.95 (ISBN 0-87793-357-X). Ave Maria.

Together at the Lord's Supper: Preparation for Holy Communion. Mary Montgomery & Herb Montgomery. (Illus.). (gr. 5 up). 1977. pap. text ed. 3.25 (ISBN 0-03-021291-X, 141, HarpR); parent bk. 2.25 (ISBN 0-03-021286-3, 192); leader's guide 4.95 (ISBN 0-03-021296-0, 193). Har-Row.

Together by Your Side: A Book for Comforting the Sick & Dying. Joseph M. Champlin. LC 79-51016. 80p. 1979. pap. 1.95 (ISBN 0-87793-180-1). Ave Maria.

Together: Communicating Interpersonally. 2nd ed. John Stewart & Gary A. D'Angelo. 432p. 1980. text ed. write for info (ISBN 0-394-34989-X, RanC). Random.

Together: Communicating Interpersonally. 3rd ed. John Stewart & Gary A. D'Angelo. 352p. 1988. pap. text ed. 18.50 (ISBN 0-394-35677-2, Ran C). Random.

Together Each Day. Joan W. Brown & Bill Brown. 288p. 1980. pap. 7.95 (ISBN 0-8007-5226-0). Revell.

Together for Life: Regular Edition. rev. ed. Joseph M. Champlin. (Illus.). 96p. 1970. pap. 1.75 (ISBN 0-87793-018-X). Ave Maria.

Together for Life: Special Edition for Marriage Outside Mass. rev. ed. Joseph M. Champlin. (Illus.). 96p. 1972. pap. 1.75 (ISBN 0-87793-118-6). Ave Maria.

Together Forever. Anne Kristin Carroll. 256p. (Orig.). 1982. pap. 7.95 (ISBN 0-310-45021-7, 12051P). Zondervan.

Together Forever. Francine Pascal. (Caitlin: The Forever Trilogy Ser: Bk. 3). 176p. (YA) (gr. 7 up). 1988. pap. 2.95 (ISBN 0-553-26863-5, Starfire). Bantam.

Together in Mission. Ed. by Theodore Williams. 90p. (Orig.). 1983. pap. 2.00. World Evang Fellow.

Together in Peace for Children. Joseph M. Champlin & Brian A. Haggerty. LC 76-26348. (Illus.). 72p. (gr. 2-7). 1976. 1.50 (ISBN 0-87793-119-4). Ave Maria.

Together in Peace: Penitent's Edition. Joseph M. Champlin. 104p. (Orig.). 1975. pap. 1.50 (ISBN 0-87793-095-3). Ave Maria.

Together in Solitude. rev. ed. Douglas Steere. 208p. 1985. pap. 8.95 (ISBN 0-8245-0715-0). Crossroad NY.

Together in the Dark: Mysteries of Healing. Robert H. Colfelt. LC 87-5801. 224p. 1987. 15.95 (ISBN 0-88089-021-5). Madrona Pubs.

Together: Prayers & Promises for Newlyweds. John M. Robertson. 64p. 1982. pap. 2.50 (ISBN 0-8423-7282-2). Tyndale.

Together They Built a Mountain. Patricia T. Davis. LC 74-14727. (Illus.). 196p. 1974. 6.95 (ISBN 0-915010-00-3). Sutter House.

Together... Till Death Us Do Part. John Braaten. Ed. by Michael L. Sherer. LC 86-28386. (Orig.). 1987. pap. 5.95 (ISBN 0-89536-852-8, 7811). CSS of Ohio.

Together Toward Hope: A Journey to Moral Theology. Philip Rossi. LC 83-1279. 224p. 1983. 18.95x (ISBN 0-268-01844-8). U of Notre Dame Pr.

Together We Can Deal with Life in the 80's. Ronald Jenson & Chuck MacDonald. LC 81-86296. 176p. 1982. pap. 5.95 (ISBN 0-86605-001-9). Heres Life.

Together We Communicate: Family File. Wim Saris. Tr. by Jim Gallagher et al. 128p. 1986. pap. 4.95 (ISBN 0-00-599703-8, Collins Liturgical). HarpR.

Together We Communicate: Resource File: A Living Church Project. Wim Saris. (Illus.). 88p. 1986. pap. 9.95 (ISBN 0-00-599701-1, Collins Liturgical). HarpR.

Together with God. George Douma. pap. 0.45 (ISBN 0-686-23478-2). Rose Pub MI.

Together with the Ainu: A Vanishing People. M. Inez Hilger. LC 70-145504. (Illus.). Repr. of 1971 ed. 47.90 (ISBN 0-8357-9743-0, 2016223). Bks Demand UMI.

Togetherness. Daniel R. Seagren. (Contempo Ser.). 32p. 1978. pap. 0.95 (ISBN 0-8010-8114-9). Baker Bk.

Togo. Zachery Winslow. (Places & Peoples of the World Ser.). (Illus.). 96p. (gr. 5 up). 1988. lib. bdg. 11.95x (ISBN 1-55546-190-5). Chelsea Hse.

Togo under Imperial Germany 1884-1914: A Case Study in Colonial Rule. Arthur J. Knoll. LC 77-83122. (Publications Ser.: No. 190). 1978. 10.95x (ISBN 0-8179-6901-2). Hoover Inst Pr.

Toi, qui es-tu? Paul Claudel. 1936. 8.95 (ISBN 0-686-54440-4). French & Eur.

Toil & Trouble: A History of American Labor. rev ed. Thomas R. Brooks. 402p. 1972. pap. 9.95 (ISBN 0-385-29071-3, Delta). Dell.

Toil of the Brave. Inglis Fletcher. 560p. 1986. pap. 4.50 (ISBN 0-553-25875-3). Bantam.

Toil of the Brave. Inglis Fletcher. (Albemarle Ser.). 548p. 1976. Repr. of 1946 ed. lib. bdg. 21.95x (ISBN 0-89244-010-4). Queens Hse-Focus Serv.

Toiler's Life. facsimile ed. Edward N. Harleston. LC 79-37596. (Black Heritage Library Collection). Repr. of 1907 ed. 17.50 (ISBN 0-8369-8972-4). Ayer Co Pubs.

Toilers of Land & Sea. Ralph H. Gabriel. 1926. 22.50x (ISBN 0-686-83829-7). Elliots Bks.

Toilers of Land & Sea see Pageant of America.

Toilet & Cosmetic Arts in Ancient & Modern Times: With a Review of All the Different Theories of Beauty, & Copious Allied Information Social, Hygienic, & Medical. Arnold J. Cooley. LC 78-80248. (Research & Source Ser.: No. 511). 1970. Repr. of 1866 ed. 43.00 (ISBN 0-8337-0653-5). B Franklin.

Toilet Book. rev. ed. 1977. pap. 1.75 (ISBN 0-8431-0431-7). Price Stern.

Toilet Learning: The Picture Book Technique for Children & Parents. Alison Mack. 1978. 15.95 (ISBN 0-316-54233-4); pap. 8.95 (ISBN 0-316-54237-7). Little.

Toll Collector. Jack Rudman. (Career Examination Ser.: C-810). (Cloth bdg. avail. on request). pap. 12.00 (ISBN 0-8373-0810-0). Natl Learning.
Toll Equipment Maintenance Supervisor. Jack Rudman. (Career Examination Ser.: C-2547). (Cloth bdg. avail. on request). pap. 16.00 (ISBN 0-8373-2547-1). Natl Learning.
Toll Equipment Mechanic. Jack Rudman. (Career Examination Ser.: C-2546). (Cloth bdg. avail. on request). pap. 14.00 (ISBN 0-8373-2546-3). Natl Learning.
Toll Financing & Private Sector Involvement in Road Infrastructure Development. OECD. (Road Transport Research Ser.). 150p. (Orig.). 1987. pap. 18.00x (ISBN 92-64-12943-X). OECD.
Toll for the Brave. Jack Higgins. 1984. pap. 2.95 (ISBN 0-451-13271-8, Sig). NAL.
Toll-Free Travel & Vacation Information Directory. Phil Philcox & Beverly Boe. LC 87-32774. 48p. 1988. pap. 3.95 (ISBN 0-87576-135-6). Pilot Bks.
Toll Gate. Georgette Heyer. Ed. by Joan Marlowe. 256p. 1988. pap. 3.50 (ISBN 0-425-10847-3). Berkley Pub.
Toll House Heritage Cookbook. rev. ed. 176p. pap. (ISBN 0-87469-043-9). Sammis Pub.
Toll House Tried & True Recipes. Ruth G. Wakefeld. LC 77-23560. (Cookbook Ser.). 1977. pap. 5.95 (ISBN 0-486-23560-2). Dover.
Toll House Tried & True Recipes. Ruth G. Wakefield. 13.50 (ISBN 0-8446-5684-4). Peter Smith.
Toll of Independence. Ed. by Howard H. Peckham. LC 74-75615. xvi, 176p. 1974. 17.00x (ISBN 0-226-65318-8). U of Chicago Pr.
Toll of the Twin Deficits. (CED Statement on National Policy Ser.). 88p. 1987. pap. 5.00 (ISBN 0-87186-085-6). Comm Econ Dev.
Toll of Victory. facsimile ed. Annette Reid. LC 79-144169. (Short Story Index Reprint Ser.). Repr. of 1926 ed. 17.00 (ISBN 0-8369-3784-8). Ayer Co Pubs.
Toll Section Supervisor. Jack Rudman. (Career Examination Ser.: C-1947). (Cloth bdg. avail. on request). pap. 14.00 (ISBN 0-8373-1947-1). Natl Learning.
Tollbridge. Wilma E. McDaniel. 32p. 1980. 3.00 (ISBN 0-936556-01-3). Contact Two.
Tollemache Orosius see Early English Manuscripts in Facsimile.
Tolstoi. Edward Garnett. LC 74-7035. (Studies in Tolstoy, No. 62). 1974. lib. bdg. 49.95x (ISBN 0-8383-1970-X). Haskell.
Tolstoi As Man & Artist. Dmitri S. Merezhkovsky. 1970. Repr. of 1902 ed. lib. bdg. 38.50x (ISBN 0-8371-4098-6, METO). Greenwood.
Tolstoi in the Seventies. Boris Eikhenbaum. Tr. by A. Kaspin. 1982. 32.50 (ISBN 0-88233-472-7). Ardis Pubs.
Tolstoi in the Sixties. Boris Eikhenbaum. Tr. by White from Rus. 1982. 25.00 (ISBN 0-88233-470-0). Ardis Pubs.
Tolstoi the Man. Edward A. Steiner. LC 70-92986. (Studies in Philosophy, No. 40). 1969. Repr. of 1909 ed. lib. bdg. 54.95x (ISBN 0-8383-1006-0). Haskell.
Tolstoi the Teacher. C. Baudouin. 59.95 (ISBN 0-8490-1218-X). Gordon Pr.
Tolstoi's: Ivan Ilych & Commentary. Ed. by Arthur C. Carr. 94p. 1973. pap. 1.95 (ISBN 0-930194-75-6). Ctr Thanatology.
Tolstoi's Theory of Art. H. W. Garrod. LC 74-13080. 1935. lib. bdg. 15.00 (ISBN 0-8414-4539-7). Folcroft.
Tolstoy. Gerald Abraham. LC 74-7018. (Studies in Tolstoy, No. 62). 1974. lib. bdg. 49.95x (ISBN 0-8383-1965-3). Haskell.
Tolstoy. Pietro Citati. Tr. by Raymond Rosenthal from Ital. LC 86-10141. 288p. 1986. 18.95 (ISBN 0-8052-4021-7). Schocken.
Tolstoy. Henry Gifford. (Past Masters Ser.). 1982. 12.95x (ISBN 0-19-287545-0); pap. 4.95 (ISBN 0-19-287544-2). Oxford U Pr.
Tolstoy. George R. Noyes. 1919. 20.00 (ISBN 0-8274-3633-5). R West.
Tolstoy. Romain Rolland. LC 71-147457. (Library of War & Peace; Peace Leaders: Biographies & Memoirs). 1972. lib. bdg. 46.00 (ISBN 0-8240-0316-0). Garland Pub.
Tolstoy. Romain Rolland. Tr. by Bernard Miall. LC 74-160776. 1971. Repr. of 1911 ed. 23.00x (ISBN 0-8046-1608-6, Pub by Kennikat). Assoc Faculty Pr.
Tolstoy. Henry B. Stevens. 59.95 (ISBN 0-8490-1219-8). Gordon Pr.
Tolstoy. Henri Troyat. LC 80-10745. vi, 762p. (Fr.). 1980. Repr. of 1967 ed. lib. bdg. 52.00x (ISBN 0-374-98010-1, Octagon). Hippocrene Bks.
Tolstoy. L. Winstanley. 1977. Repr. lib. bdg. 10.00 (ISBN 0-8495-5611-2). Arden Lib.
Tolstoy. Lilian Winstanley. 1982. 42.50 (ISBN 0-686-81924-1). Bern Porter.
Tolstoy: A Biography. A. N. Wilson. (Illus.). 1988. 25.00 (ISBN 0-393-02585-3). Norton.
Tolstoy: A Critical Introduction. Reginald F. Christian. LC 69-19373. 1970. pap. 17.95 (ISBN 0-521-09585-9). Cambridge U Pr.
Tolstoy: A Life of My Father. Alexandra L. Tolstoy. LC 73-3185. 543p. 1973. Repr. of 1953 ed. lib. bdg. 29.00x (ISBN 0-374-97956-1, Octagon). Hippocrene Bks.
Tolstoy & Chekhov. Logan Speirs. LC 79-120195. pap. 61.30 (ISBN 0-317-20629-X, 2024583). Bks Demand UMI.
Tolstoy & China. Derk Bodde. 12.00 (ISBN 0-384-04895-1). Johnson Repr.
Tolstoy & His Message. Ernest H. Crosby. 93p. 1980. Repr. of 1903 ed. lib. bdg. 17.00 (ISBN 0-8414-3031-4). Folcroft.
Tolstoy & His Message. Ernest H. Crosby. 1906. 25.00 (ISBN 0-8274-3636-X). R West.
Tolstoy & His Problems. Aylmer Maude. 59.95 (ISBN 0-8490-1220-1). Gordon Pr.
Tolstoy & His Problems. Aylmer Maude. LC 74-7137. (Studies in Tolstoy, No. 62). 1974. lib. bdg. 49.95x (ISBN 0-8383-1999-8). Haskell.
Tolstoy & His Wife. Tikhon Polner. 1946. 25.00 (ISBN 0-8274-3635-1). R West.
Tolstoy & India. 2nd ed. Alexander Shifman. 1978. 6.00x (ISBN 0-8364-1586-8, Pub. by National Sahitya Akademi). South Asia Bks.
Tolstoy & Nietzsche. Helen E. Davis. LC 72-119083. (Studies in Comparative Literature, No. 35). 1970. Repr. of 1929 ed. lib. bdg. 49.95x (ISBN 0-8383-1079-6). Haskell.
Tolstoy & Shakespeare. George Gibian. LC 74-11281. 1957. lib. bdg. 15.00 (ISBN 0-8414-4529-X). Folcroft.
Tolstoy & the Novel. John Bayley. iv, 316p. 1988. pap. 13.95 (ISBN 0-226-03960-9). U of Chicago Pr.
Tolstoy & the Russians: Reflections on a Relationship. Alexander Fodor. 200p. 1984. 22.50 (ISBN 0-88233-891-9). Ardis Pubs.
Tolstoy: Anna Karenina. Anthony Thorlby. (Landmarks of World Literature Ser.). 1987. 19.95 (ISBN 0-521-32819-5); pap. 5.95 (ISBN 0-521-31325-2). Cambridge U Pr.
Tolstoy: Art Time. 226p. 1981. 99.00 (ISBN 0-317-40658-2, Pub. by Collets UK). State Mutual Bk.
Tolstoy, Dostoevsky, Tourgenev. George Halperin. LC 73-13535. Repr. of 1946 ed. lib. bdg. 25.00 (ISBN 0-8414-4744-6). Folcroft.
Tolstoy Foundation, Inc: History, Aims & Achievements. Tolstoy Foundation, Inc. (Illus.). 48p. 1976. 3.00 (ISBN 0-686-16259-5). Tolstoy Found.
Tolstoy: His Life & Works. John C. Kenworthy. LC 70-155115. (Studies in European Literature, No. 56). 1971. Repr. of 1902 ed. lib. bdg. 52.95x (ISBN 0-8383-1287-X). Haskell.
Tolstoy Home. Tat'Iana L. Sukhotina. Tr. by Alec Brown. LC 51-4950. Repr. of 1951 ed. 22.50 (ISBN 0-404-06493-0). AMS Pr.
Tolstoy in Prerevolutionary Russian Criticism. Boris Sorokin. LC 78-31289. 339p. 1979. 30.00 (ISBN 0-8142-0295-0). Ohio St U Pr.
Tolstoy: Literary Fragments, Letters & Reminiscences. Leo Tolstoy. Ed. by Rene Fullop-Miller. LC 68-57229. Repr. of 1931 ed. 21.50 (ISBN 0-404-06479-5). AMS Pr.
Tolstoy on Art. Aylmer Maude. LC 72-2134. (Studies in European Literature, No. 56). 1972. Repr. of 1924 ed. lib. bdg. 55.95 (ISBN 0-8383-1459-7). Haskell.
Tolstoy on Education. Leo Tolstoy. Tr. by Leo Wiener. LC 67-25514. 1968. pap. 2.95X (ISBN 0-226-80777-0, P315, Phoen). U of Chicago Pr.
Tolstoy on Education: Tolstoy's Educational Writings, 1861-62. Ed. by Alan Pinch & Michael Armstrong. LC 81-65867. 336p. 1982. 35.00 (ISBN 0-8386-3121-5). Fairleigh Dickinson.
Tolstoy or Dostoevsky: An Essay in the Old Criticism. George Steiner. LC 85-16356. viii, 354p. 1985. pap. 12.95 (ISBN 0-226-77226-8). U of Chicago Pr.
Tolstoy: Tales of Courage & Conflict. Ed. by Charles Neider. 578p. 1985. pap. 11.95 (ISBN 0-88184-165-X). Carroll & Graf.
Tolstoy: The Critical Heritage. Ed. by A. V. Knowles. 1978. 35.00x (ISBN 0-7100-8947-3). Routledge Chapman & Hall.
Tolstoy the Rebel. Leo Hecht. (Illus.). 400p. 1975. lib. bdg. 69.95 (ISBN 0-87700-222-3). Revisionist Pr.
Tolstoy: The Ultimate Reconciliation. Martine De Courcel. 448p. 1987. 27.50 (ISBN 0-684-18569-5). Scribner.
Tolstoy's Diaries, 2 vols. Leo Tolstoy. Ed. & tr. by R. F. Christian. 768p. 1985. Set. 60.00 (ISBN 0-684-18512-1, ScribT). Scribner.
Tolstoy's Letters, 2 vols. Ed. & tr. by R. F. Christian. LC 77-90494. (Encore Editions). (Illus.). 1978. 35.00 (ISBN 0-684-15596-6, ScribT). Scribner.
Tolstoy's Major Fiction. Edward Wasiolek. LC 77-81732. 264p. 6.95X (ISBN 0-226-87398-6, Phoen). U of Chicago Pr.
Tolstoy's Message for Our Times. Francis Neilson. 1979. lib. bdg. 39.00 (ISBN 0-685-96643-7). Revisionist Pr.
Tolstoys: Twenty-Four Generations of Russian History, 1353-1983. Nikolai Tolstoy. LC 86-12456. (Illus.). 368p. 1986. pap. 10.95 (ISBN 0-688-06674-7, Quill). Morrow.
Tolstoys: Twenty Generations of Russian History 1353 to 1983. Nikolai Tolstoy. LC 83-61738. (Illus.). 352p. 1983. FPT 22.50 (ISBN 0-688-02341-X). Morrow.
Tolstoy's "What Is Art?" An Essay in the Philosophy of Art. T. J. Diffey. LC 85-16667. 240p. 1985. 29.50 (ISBN 0-7099-0891-1, Pub. by Croom Helm Ltd). Routledge Chapman & Hall.
Toltec. William Heffernan. 284p. 1989. 18.95 (ISBN 0-453-00618-3). NAL.
Toltec Heritage: From the Fall of Tula to the Rise of Tenochtitlan. Nigel Davies. LC 78-21384. (CAI Ser.: Vol. 153). (Illus.). 1980. 29.50 (ISBN 0-8061-1505-X). U of Okla Pr.
Toltecs: Until the Fall of Tula. Nigel Davies. (Civilization of the American Indian Ser.: Vol. 144). (Illus.). 552p. 1987. 16.95 (ISBN 0-8061-2071-1). U of Okla Pr.
Toluene. (Environmental Health Criteria Ser.: No. 52). 146p. 1986. pap. 8.40 (ISBN 92-4-154192-X). World Health.
Toluene, the Xylenes & Their Industrial Derivatives. Ed. by E. G. Hancock. (Chemical Engineering Monographs: Vol. 15). 552p. 1982. 163.25 (ISBN 0-444-42058-4). Elsevier.
Tom & Bear: The Training of a Guide Dog Team. Richard McPhee. LC 81-43031. (Illus.). 160p. (gr. 5 up). 1981. 12.70 (ISBN 0-690-04136-5, Crowell Jr Bks). HarpJ.
Tom & I on the Old Plantation. Archibald Rutledge. LC 72-4643. (Black Heritage Library Collections Ser.). (Illus.). Repr. of 1918 ed. 16.50 (ISBN 0-8369-9124-9). Ayer Co Pubs.
Tom & Maggie. Dorothy Horgan. (Illus.). 124p. (gr. 4 up). 1988. 13.95 (ISBN 0-19-271544-5). Oxford U Pr.
Tom & Patti Mount's Dive & Travel Haiti. Tom Mount & Patti Mount. (Illus.). 86p. Date not set. pap. 9.95x (ISBN 0-915539-03-9). Sea-Mount Pub Co.
Tom & Patti Mount's Dive & Travel Florida's Gold Coast. Tom Mount et al. (Illus.). 86p. Date not set. pap. 9.95x (ISBN 0-915539-02-0). Sea-Mount Pub Co.
Tom & Pippo & the Washing Machine. Helen Oxenbury. LC 87-37431. (Illus.). 14p. (ps-k). 1988. bds. 5.95 (ISBN 0-689-71255-3, Aladdin Bks). Macmillan.
Tom & Pippo Go for a Walk. Helen Oxenbury. LC 87-37432. (Illus.). 14p. (ps-k). 1988. bds. 5.95 (ISBN 0-689-71254-5, Aladdin Bks). Macmillan.
Tom & Pippo Make a Mess. Helen Oxenbury. LC 87-37437. (Pippo Bks). (Illus.). 14p. (ps-k). 1988. bds. 5.95 (ISBN 0-689-71253-7, Aladdin Bks). Macmillan.
Tom & Pippo Read a Story. Helen Oxenbury. LC 87-37438. (Illus.). 14p. (ps-k). 1988. bds. 5.95 (ISBN 0-689-71252-9, Aladdin Bks). Macmillan.
Tom & Ricky Map. Bob Wright. (Tom & Ricky Mystery Ser.: Nos. 1-4). (Illus.). (gr. 1-9). 1983. 2.00 (ISBN 0-87879-375-5, High Noon Books). Acad Therapy.
Tom & the Two Handles. Russell Hoban. LC 65-11459. (Harper I Can Read Bks.). (Illus.). 64p. (gr. k-3). 1965. PLB 10.89 (ISBN 0-06-022431-2). HarpJ.
Tom & Viv. Michael Hastings. (Fiction Ser.). 116p. 1985. pap 4.95 (ISBN 0-14-007594-1). Penguin.
Tom Ashley, Sam McGee, Bukka White: Tennessee Traditional Singers. Ed. by Thomas G. Burton. LC 79-19655. 250p. 1981. 22.95x (ISBN 0-87049-260-8). U of Tenn Pr.
Tom Benton & His Drawings: A Biographical Essay & Collection of His Sketches, Studies, & Mural Cartoons. Karal A. Marling. LC 85-992. (Illus.). 232p. 1985. 48.00 (ISBN 0-8262-0480-5). U of Mo Pr.
Tom Bradley: The Impossible Dream. J. Gregory Payne & Scott C. Ratzan. LC 85-52373. (Illus.). 484p. 1986. 18.95 (ISBN 0-915677-29-6). Roundtable Pub.
Tom Bradley: The Impossible Dream. J. Gregory Payne & Scott C. Ratzan. Ed. by Jim Connor. (Illus.). 384p. 1987. pap. 4.95 (ISBN 0-7701-0653-6). Paperjacks US.
Tom Brown at Oxford, 3 vols. in 2. Thomas Hughes. LC 79-8137. Repr. of 1861 ed. Set. 84.50 (ISBN 0-404-61927-4). Vol. 1 (ISBN 0-404-61928-2). Vol. 2 (ISBN 0-404-61929-0). AMS Pr.
Tom Brown's Field Guide to City & Suburban Survival, Vol. 3. Tom Brown, Jr. & Brandt Morgan. 288p. (Orig.). 1984. pap. 7.95 (ISBN 0-425-09172-4). Berkley Pub.
Tom Brown's Field Guide to Living with the Earth. Tom Brown, Jr. & Brandt Morgan. (Illus.). 288p. 1984. pap. 7.95 (ISBN 0-425-09147-3). Berkley Pub.
Tom Brown's Field Guide to Nature Observation & Tracking. Tom Brown, Jr. & Brandt Morgan. 256p. 1983. pap. 7.95 (ISBN 0-425-09966-0). Berkley Pub.
Tom Brown's Field Guide to the Forgotten Wilderness. Tom Brown, Jr. 240p. (Orig.). 1987. pap. 7.95 (ISBN 0-425-09715-3). Berkley Pub.
Tom Brown's Guide to Wild Edible & Medicinal Plants. Tom Brown, Jr. 288p. 1985. pap. 7.95 (ISBN 0-425-10063-4). Berkley Pub.
Tom Brown's Guide to Wilderness Survival. Tom Brown, Jr. & Brandt Morgan. (Illus.). 240p. (Orig.). 1984. pap. 7.95 (ISBN 0-425-10572-5). Berkley Pub.
Tom Brown's School Days. Thomas Hughes. (Airmont Classics Ser.). (gr. 7 up). 1968. pap. 1.95 (ISBN 0-8049-0174-0, CL-174). Airmont.
Tom Brown's School Days. Thomas Hughes. LC 52-8383. (YA) (gr. 7 up). 1986. pap. 2.95 (ISBN 0-451-52000-9, Sig Classics). NAL.
Tom Brown's School Days. Thomas Hughes. 1987. Repr. lib. bdg. 21.95x (ISBN 0-89966-554-3). Buccaneer Bks.
Tom Brown's Schooldays. Thomas Hughes. (Dent's Illustrated Children's Classics Ser.). (Illus.). 351p. (gr. 3 up). 1975. Repr. of 1949 ed. 11.00x (ISBN 0-460-05003-6, BKA 01604, Pub. by J. M. Dent England). Biblio Dist.
Tom Brown's Schooldays. Thomas Hughes. (Puffin Classics Ser.). 288p. (gr. 4-6). 1984. pap. 2.25 (ISBN 0-14-035022-5, Puffin). Penguin.
Tom Corkery's Dublin. Tom Corkery. (Illus.). 128p. 1980. 15.95 (ISBN 0-900068-53-1, Pub. by Anvil Bks Ireland). Irish Bks Media.
Tom Cringle's Log. Michael Scott. 1969. Repr. of 1915 ed. 8.95x (ISBN 0-460-00710-6, Evman). Biblio Dist.
Tom Disch Checklist. 2nd ed. Chris Drumm. LC 85-29953. (Drumm Bibliographies: No. 1). 64p. 1988. lib. bdg. 19.95x (ISBN 0-89370-547-0); pap. text ed. 9.95x (ISBN 0-89370-974-3). Borgo Pr.
Tom Disch Checklist. Compiled by Chris Drumm. (Booklet Ser.: No. 4). 24p. (Orig.). 1983. pap. 1.00 (ISBN 0-936055-02-2). C Drumm Bks.
Tom Dooley, Jungle Doctor. Alice H. Brown. (Stories About Christian Heroes Ser.). (Illus.). (gr. 1-3). 1979. pap. 1.95 (ISBN 0-03-049441-9, HarpR). Har-Row.
Tom Edison & the Wonderful "Why". Faye Parker. (Children's Theatre Playscript Ser.). (gr. k-12). 1961. pap. 2.25x (ISBN 0-88020-061-8). Coach Hse.
Tom Edison Finds Out. Sadyebeth Lowitz & Anson Lowitz. 1979. pap. 0.95 (ISBN 0-440-48384-0, YB). Dell.
Tom Fox & the Apple Pie. Clyde Watson. LC 74-171010. (Illus.). (ps-3). 1972. 11.70 (ISBN 0-690-82783-0, Crowell Jr Bks). HarpJ.
Tom Glazer's Treasury of Songs for Children. Tom Glazer. LC 86-753397. (Illus.). 256p. (gr. k-6). 1988. pap. 14.95 (ISBN 0-385-23693-X, Zephyr-BFYR). Doubleday.
Tom Glazer's Treasury of Songs for Children. Ed. by Tom Glazer. (Illus.). (gr. 1-6). 12.95 (ISBN 0-686-74302-4). J R Pubns.
Tom Hanks. Trakin. 1987. pap. 3.50 (ISBN 0-312-90782-6). St Martin.
Tom Horn. Tom Horn. (Orig.). 1980. pap. 1.75 (ISBN 0-505-51563-6, Pub. by Tower Bks). Leisure NY.
Tom in the Middle. Berthe Amoss. LC 86-42991. (Illus.). 32p. (gr. k-3). 1988. 12.95i (ISBN 0-06-020063-4); PLB 12.89 (ISBN 0-06-020064-2). HarpJ.
Tom Jack. John Tilley. 144p. 1985. 10.50 (ISBN 0-89962-437-5). Todd & Honeywell.
Tom Jones see also History of Tom Jones, a Foundling.
Tom Jones. Fielding. (Book Note Ser.). 1986. pap. 2.50 (ISBN 0-8120-3546-1). Barron.
Tom Jones. Henry Fielding. (Airmont Classics Ser.). (gr. 11 up). pap. 2.50 (ISBN 0-8049-0135-X, CL-135). Airmont.
Tom Jones. Henry Fielding. (Modern Library College Editions Ser.). 1950. pap. write for info (ISBN 0-394-30915-4, T15, RanC). Random.
Tom Jones. Henry Fielding. pap. 3.95 (ISBN 0-451-51977-9, CE1827, Sig Classics). NAL.
Tom Jones. Henry Fielding. Ed. by Sheridan Baker. (Critical Editions Ser.). 1973. 17.50 (ISBN 0-393-04359-2); pap. 12.95x (ISBN 0-393-09394-8). Norton.
Tom Jones. Henry Fielding. Ed. by Reg Mutter. (English Library Ser.). 1966. pap. 3.95 (ISBN 0-14-043009-1). Penguin.
Tom Jones. Henry Fielding. pap. 2.95. WSP.
Tom Jones. Henry Fielding. 1982. Repr. lib. bdg. 39.95x (ISBN 0-89966-398-2). Buccaneer Bks.
Tom Jones. Henry Fielding. LC 84-25513. 1003p. 1985. pap. 10.95 (ISBN 0-394-60519-5). Modern Lib.
Tom Jones, a Foundling, 2 vols. Henry Fielding. Ed. by Fredson Bowers. LC 73-15009. (Works of Henry Fielding). (Illus.). 1250p. 1974. Set. 50.00x (ISBN 0-8195-4068-4); pap. 14.95x (ISBN 0-8195-6048-0). Wesleyan U Pr.
Tom Jones Notes. James C. Evans. (Orig.). 1972. pap. 3.50 (ISBN 0-8220-1293-6). Cliffs.
Tom Jones Slept Here. John L. Hughes. 157p. 1985. 19.50x (ISBN 0-85088-126-9, Pub. by Gomer Pr). State Mutual Bk.
Tom Kitten's New Sweater see Peter Rabbit's First Library.
Tom Lea. Evan H. Antone. (Illus.). 192p. 1987. text ed. 20.00 (ISBN 0-87404-201-1). Tex Western.
Tom Little's Great Halloween Scare. John Peterson. (Illus.). 80p. (gr. 5-8). 1986. pap. 1.95 (ISBN 0-590-04702-7). Scholastic Inc.
Tom McCall: Maverick. Tom McCall & Steve Neal. LC 77-85394. (Illus.). 1978. 9.95 (ISBN 0-8323-0288-0); pap. 6.95 (ISBN 0-8323-0289-9). Binford-Metropolitan.
Tom MBoya: The Man Who Kenya Wanted to Forget. David Goldsworthy. LC 81-22870. 308p. 1982. 45.00 (ISBN 0-8419-0787-0, Africana). Holmes & Meier.
Tom Merton: His Life & Times. Larry Levinger. Date not set. 19.95 (ISBN 0-317-67534-6, HarpR). Har-Row.
Tom Mix & Pancho Villa. Clifford Irving. 1984. pap. 3.95 (ISBN 0-312-90367-7). St Martin.

TITLE INDEX TOMB OF NYHETEP-PTAH AT

Tom Mix Died for Your Sins. Darryl Ponicsan. 1975. pap. 8.95 (ISBN 0-440-05969-0). Delacorte.
Tom Mix: Riding up to Glory. John H. Nicholas. LC 80-81554. (Illus.). 108p. 1980. 12.95 (ISBN 0-932154-05-0). Lowell Pr.
Tom Moore's Diary. Thomas Moore. Ed. by J. B. Priestley. LC 76-131783. 1971. Repr. of 1925 ed. 39.00x (ISBN 0-403-00670-8). Scholarly.
Tom Moore's Diary. J. B. Priestly. 1988. Repr. lib. bdg. 75.00x. Am Biog Serv.
Tom Noddy's Bubble Magic. Tom Noddy. (Illus.). 128p. (Orig.). 1988. lib. bdg. 15.90 (ISBN 0-89471-660-3); pap. 8.95 (ISBN 0-89471-659-X). Running Pr.
Tom O'Bedlam. Robert Silverberg. LC 85-70754. 320p. 1985. 16.95 (ISBN 0-917657-31-4). D I Fine.
Tom O'Bedlam. Robert Silverberg. 384p. 1986. pap. 3.95 (ISBN 0-446-34002-2). Warner Bks.
Tom O'Bedlam's Night Out & Other Strange Excursions. Darrell Schweitzer. LC 85-80505. (Illus.). 192p. 1985. 20.00 (ISBN 0-932445-15-2); pap. 7.50 (ISBN 0-932445-14-4). Ganley Pub.
Tom Paine. Hesketh Pearson. 1937. Repr. 35.00 (ISBN 0-8274-3637-8). R West.
Tom Paine & the American Revolution. Eric Foner. LC 75-25456. (Illus.). 1976. pap. 9.95x (ISBN 0-19-502182-7). Oxford U Pr.
Tom Paine Friend of Mankind: Mankind. Hesketh Pearson. (Illus.). 293p. 1985. Repr. of 1937 ed. lib. bdg. 50.00 (ISBN 0-89984-535-5). Century Bookbindery.
Tom Paine Maru. L. Neil Smith. 288p. (Orig.). 1984. pap. 2.75 (ISBN 0-345-29243-X, Del Rey). Ballantine.
Tom Paine: The Greatest Exile. David Powell. LC 85-14541. 320p. 1985. 25.00 (ISBN 0-312-80886-0). St Martin.
Tom Petty & the Heartbreakers. Annene Kaye. (Orig.). Date not set. pap. 2.95 (ISBN 0-345-33886-3). Ballantine.
Tom Robbins. Mark Siegel. LC 80-69013. (Western Writers Ser.: No. 42). (Illus.). 52p. (Orig.). 1980. pap. 2.95x (ISBN 0-88430-066-8). Boise St Univ.
Tom Roberts: A Catalogue Raisonne, 1856-1931, 2 vols. Helen Topliss. (Illus.). 1985. Set. 189.00x (ISBN 0-19-554513-3). Oxford U Pr.
Tom Sawyer see also Adventures of Tom Sawyer.
Tom Sawyer. new ed. Samuel Clemens. Ed. by Irwin Shapiro. LC 73-75465. (Now Age Illustrated Ser.). (Illus.). 64p. (Orig.). (gr. 5-10). 1973. 7.50 (ISBN 0-88301-220-0); pap. 2.95 (ISBN 0-88301-103-4); student activity bk. 1.25 (ISBN 0-88301-179-4). Pendulum Pr.
Tom Sawyer. (Illustrated Junior Library). (Illus.). 320p. (gr. 3-9). 1981. pap. 7.95 (ISBN 0-448-11002-4, G&D). Putnam Pub Group.
Tom Sawyer. (Book Notes Ser.). 1985. pap. 2.50 (ISBN 0-8120-3547-X). Barron.
Tom Sawyer. rev. ed. Mark Twain. (Enriched Classics Ser.). (Illus.). (gr. 7-12). 1982. pap. 3.50 (ISBN 0-671-44135-3, RE). PB.
Tom Sawyer. Mark Twain. LC 80-22095. (Short Classics Ser.). (Illus.). 48p. (gr. 4 up). 1981. PLB 15.99 (ISBN 0-8172-1665-0). Raintree Pubs.
Tom Sawyer. Mark Twain. Adapted by June Edwards. LC 80-22095. (Short Classics Ser.). (Illus.). 48p. (gr. 4-12). 1983. pap. 9.27 (ISBN 0-8172-2025-9). Raintree Pubs.
Tom Sawyer. Mark Twain. (Dent's Illustrated Children's Classics Ser.). (Illus.). 254p. (gr. 4 up). 1974. Repr. of 1955 ed. 11.00x (ISBN 0-460-05030-3, Pub. by J M Dent England). Biblio Dist.
Tom Sawyer. Mark Twain. LC 84-50435. (Silver Burdett Classics for Kids Ser.). (Illus.). 32p. (gr. 3 up). 1984. 5.96 (ISBN 0-382-06811-4). Silver.
Tom Sawyer. Mark Twain. Date not set. price not set. S&S.
Tom Sawyer. Mark Twain. LC 84-50435. (Silver Burdett Classics for Kids Ser.). 32p. (gr. 3 up). 1985. pap. 3.67 (ISBN 0-382-06954-4). Silver.
Tom Sawyer see Good Literature for Slow Readers.
Tom Sawyer: A Comedy in Two Acts. Tim Kelly. 56p. 1983. pap. 2.50 (ISBN 0-88680-191-5). I E Clark.
Tom Sawyer: A Play. John Charlesworth & Tony Brown. 1976. pap. text ed. 5.00x (ISBN 0-435-23169-3). Heinemann Ed.
Tom Sawyer Abroad. Samuel L. Clemens. (Works of Mark Twain). 1988. Repr. of 1907 ed. lib. bdg. 59.00x. Am Biog Serv.
Tom Sawyer Abroad. Mark Twain. Bd. with Tom Sawyer Detective. (Airmont Classics Ser.). (gr. 5up). pap. 1.50 (ISBN 0-8049-0126-0, CL-126). Airmont.
Tom Sawyer Abroad see Writings of Mark Twain.
Tom Sawyer Abroad & Tom Sawyer Detective. Mark Twain. LC 81-40325. (Mark Twain Library: No. 2). (Illus.). 160p. 1981. 20.00 (ISBN 0-520-04560-2); pap. 5.95 (ISBN 0-520-04561-0). U of Cal Pr.
Tom Sawyer & Buried Treasure. Mark Twain. Adapted by I. M. Richardson. LC 83-18049. (Adventures of Tom Sawyer Ser.). (Illus.). 32p. (gr. 3-6). 1984. PLB 9.79 (ISBN 0-8167-0063-X); pap. text ed. 2.50 (ISBN 0-8167-0064-8); cassette avail. Troll Assocs.
Tom Sawyer Becomes a Pirate. Mark Twain. Adapted by I. M. Richardson. LC 83-18037: (Adventures of Tom Sawyer Ser.). (Illus.). 32p. (gr. 3-6). 1984. PLB 9.79 (ISBN 0-8167-0061-3); pap. text ed. 2.50 (ISBN 0-8167-0062-1); cassette avail. Troll Assocs.
Tom Sawyer Comes Home. Dorothy Langley. LC 73-78123. 1973. 7.95 (ISBN 0-913676-02-0). Traumwald Pr.
Tom Sawyer: Danger in the Graveyard. Mark Twain. Adapted by I. M. Richardson. LC 83-18036. (Adventures of Tom Sawyer Ser.). (Illus.). 32p. (gr. 3-6). 1984. PLB 9.79 (ISBN 0-8167-0059-1); pap. text ed. 2.50 (ISBN 0-8167-0060-5). Troll Assocs.
Tom Sawyer Detective see Tom Sawyer Abroad.
Tom Sawyer Fires. Laurence Yep. 144p. (gr. 5 up). 1984. 10.75 (ISBN 0-688-03861-1, Morrow Junior Books). Morrow.
Tom Sawyer Lost in a Cave. Mark Twain. Adapted by I. M. Richardson. LC 83-18043. (Adventures of Tom Sawyer Ser.). (Illus.). 32p. (gr. 3-6). 1984. PLB 9.79 (ISBN 0-8167-0065-6); pap. text ed. 2.50 (ISBN 0-8167-0066-4); cassette avail. Troll Assocs.
Tom Sawyer Notes. Marion P. Thayer. (Orig.). 1967. pap. 3.25 (ISBN 0-8220-1301-0). Cliffs.
Tom Seaver's Baseball Card Book. Tom Seaver & Alice Seigel. 1985. pap. 6.95 (ISBN 0-671-49525-9). Wanderer Bks.
Tom Stoppard. Ed. & intro. by Harold Bloom. (Modern Critical Views Ser.). 191p. 1986. lib. bdg. 19.95x (ISBN 0-87754-671-1). Chelsea Hse.
Tom Stoppard. 3rd ed. Ronald Hayman. (Illus.). 160p. 1979. 13.50x (ISBN 0-8476-6225-X). Rowman.
Tom Stoppard. Felicia H. Londre. LC 80-53698. (Literature & Life Ser.). 192p. 1981. 16.95x (ISBN 0-8044-2538-8). Ungar.
Tom Stoppard. Susan Rusinko. (Twayne's English Authors Ser.: 419). 184p. 1986. lib. bdg. 16.95 (ISBN 0-8057-6909-9, Twayne); pap. 6.95 (ISBN 0-8057-6927-7). G K Hall.
Tom Stoppard. Thomas Whitaker. LC 83-48296. (Modern Dramatists Ser.). (Illus.). 180p. 1984. 17.50 (ISBN 0-394-53507-3, GP-885). Grove.
Tom Stoppard. Thomas Whitaker. LC 83-48296. (Modern Dramatists Ser.). (Illus.). 180p. 1984. pap. 9.95 (ISBN 0-394-62499-8, E878, Ever). Grove.
Tom Stoppard: A Casebook. John Harty, III. (Casebook on Modern Dramatists-Garland Reference Library of the Humanities). 424p. 1988. lib. bdg. 55.00 (ISBN 0-8240-9023-3). Garland Pub.
Tom Stoppard: A Reference Guide. David Bratt. 1982. lib. bdg. 40.50 (ISBN 0-8161-8576-X, Hall Reference). G K Hall.
Tom Stoppard: An Assessment. Tim Brassell. LC 83-40126. 220p. 1985. 27.50 (ISBN 0-312-80888-7). St Martin.
Tom Stoppard: Comedy As a Moral Matrix. Joan F. Dean. LC 80-26400. (Literary Frontier Edition). 128p. 1981. text ed. 8.95x (ISBN 0-8262-0332-9). U of Mo Pr.
Tom Stoppard: The Artist As Critic. Neil Sammells. LC 87-4270. 176p. 1987. 27.50 (ISBN 0-312-00534-2). St Martin.
Tom Stoppard's Plays. Jim Hunter. LC 82-47988. 258p. 1983. pap. 12.50 (ISBN 0-394-62414-9, E825, Ever). Grove.
Tom Swift & Company: "Boys' Books" by Stratemeyer & Others. John T. Dizer, Jr. LC 81-1559. (Illus.). 192p. 1982. lib. bdg. 19.95x (ISBN 0-89950-024-2). McFarland & Co.
Tom Swift & His Electronic Electroscope. Victor Appleton, II. (gr. 5-6). 15.95 (ISBN 0-88411-462-7, Pub. by Aeonian Pr). Amereon Ltd.
Tom Swift & His Space Solatron. Victor Appleton, II. (gr. 5-6). 15.95 (ISBN 0-88411-457-0, Pub. by Aeonian Pr). Amereon Ltd.
Tom Swift & His Triphibian Atomicar. Victor Appleton, II. (gr. 5-6). 14.95 (ISBN 0-88411-459-7, Pub. by Aeonian Pr). Amereon Ltd.
Tom Swift: Ark Two. Victor Appleton. (Tom Swift Ser.: No. 7). (Illus.). 192p. (gr. 3-7). 1982. 8.95 (ISBN 0-671-43952-9); pap. 2.75 (ISBN 0-671-43953-7). Wanderer Bks.
Tom Swift: Crater of Mystery. Victor Appleton. Ed. by Wendy Barish. (Tom Swift Ser.: No. 8). 192p. (gr. 3-7). 1983. 8.95 (ISBN 0-671-43954-5); pap. 3.95 (ISBN 0-671-43955-3). Wanderer Bks.
Tom Swift: Gateway to Doom. Victor Appleton. Ed. by Wendy Barish. (Tom Swift Ser.: No. 9). 192p. (gr. 8-10). 1983. 8.95 (ISBN 0-671-43956-1); pap. 3.95 (ISBN 0-671-43957-X). Wanderer Bks.
Tom Swift Gift Set, 3 vols. Victor Appleton. Boxed Set. pap. 7.95 (ISBN 0-317-12430-7). Wanderer Bks.
Tom Swift Terror on the Moons of Jupiter. Victor Appleton, II. (gr. 5-6). 15.95 (ISBN 0-88411-460-0, Pub. by Aeonian Pr). Amereon Ltd.
Tom Swift: Terror on the Moons of Jupiter. (Tom Swift Ser.: No. 2). 192p. (gr. 3-7). 1981. 8.95 (ISBN 0-671-41182-9); pap. 2.75 (ISBN 0-671-41183-7). Wanderer Bks.
Tom Swift: The Alien Probe. Victor Appleton. (Tom Swift Ser.: No. 3). 192p. (Orig.). (gr. 3-7). 1981. 8.95 (ISBN 0-671-42538-2); pap. 2.75 (ISBN 0-671-42578-1). Wanderer Bks.
Tom Swift the Alien Probe. Victor Appleton, II. (gr. 5-6). 15.95 (ISBN 0-88411-464-3, Pub. by Aeonian Pr). Amereon Ltd.
Tom Swift the Astral Fortress. Victor Apple, II. (gr. 5-6). 15.95 (ISBN 0-88411-461-9, Pub. by Aeonian Pr). Amereon Ltd.
Tom Swift: The City in the Stars. Victor Appleton. (Tom Swift Ser.: No. 1). 192p. (Orig.). (gr. 3-7). 1981. 8.95 (ISBN 0-671-41120-9); pap. 3.50 (ISBN 0-671-41115-2). Wanderer Bks.
Tom Swift the City in the Stars. Victor Appleton, II. (gr. 5-6). 15.95 (ISBN 0-88411-463-5, Pub. by Aeonian Pr). Amereon Ltd.
Tom Swift: The Rescue Mission. Victor Appleton. (Tom Swift Ser.: No. 6). 192p. (gr. 3-7). 1981. 8.95 (ISBN 0-671-43370-9); pap. 2.50 (ISBN 0-671-43386-5). Wanderer Bks.
Tom Swift the Rescue Mission. Victor Appleton, II. (gr. 5-6). 15.95 (ISBN 0-88411-458-9, Pub. by Aeonian Pr). Amereon Ltd.
Tom Swift: The Space Fortress. Victor Appleton. (Tom Swift Ser.: No. 5). 192p. (gr. 3-7). 1981. 8.95 (ISBN 0-671-43369-5); pap. 3.95 (ISBN 0-671-43385-7). Wanderer Bks.
Tom Swift: The War in Outer Space. Victor Appleton. (Tom Swift Ser.: No. 4). 192p. (Orig.). (gr. 3-7). 1981. 8.95 (ISBN 0-671-42539-0); pap. 3.95 (ISBN 0-671-42579-X). Wanderer Bks.
Tom Swift the Water in Outer Space. Victor Appleton, II. (gr. 5-6). 14.95 (ISBN 0-88411-465-1, Pub. by Aeonian Pr). Amereon Ltd.
Tom Taylor & the Victorian Drama. Winton Tolles. LC 41-3081. Repr. of 1940 ed. 20.00 (ISBN 0-404-06474-4). AMS Pr.
Tom, the Bootblack: Or, the Road to Success. Horatio Alger. 1976. Repr. of 1878 ed. lib. bdg. 17.95x (ISBN 0-88411-812-6). Amereon Ltd.
Tom the TV Cat: A Step Two Book. Joan Heilbroner. LC 83-24600. (Step into Reading Bks.). (Illus.). 48p. (ps-2). 1984. lib. bdg. 6.99 (ISBN 0-394-96708-9, Pub. by BYR); pap. 2.95 (ISBN 0-394-86708-4). Random.
Tom Thumb. Margaret Hillert. (Just Beginning-to-Read Ser.). (Illus.). 32p. (gr. 1-6). 1981. PLB 4.39 (ISBN 0-8136-5091-7, Dist. by Caroline Hse); pap. 1.95 (ISBN 0-8136-5591-9). Modern Curr.
Tom Thumb. Charles Perrault. Ed. & illus. by Lidia Postma. LC 83-61227. (Illus.). 32p. (gr. 2 up). 1983. 10.95 (ISBN 0-8052-3855-7). Schocken.
Tom Thumb. Charles Perrault. Retold by & illus. by Mercedes Llimona. LC 85-63491. (Illus.). 24p. (ps-3). 1986. 6.75 (ISBN 0-382-09207-4, 6930421). Silver.
Tom Thumb. (Fr.). (gr. k-3). 3.50 (ISBN 0-685-28452-2). French & Eur.
Tom Thumb. (Favorite Tale Pop-Up Bks.). (Illus.). (ps-1). 1.79 (ISBN 0-517-46236-2). Outlet Bk Co.
Tom Thumb. Illus. by Marie-Laure Viney. (Musical Stories Ser.). (Illus.). 24p. (ps-2). 1988. bk & audiocassette 6.95 (ISBN 0-8120-4038-4). Barron.
Tom Thumb. Richard J. Watson. 1988. price not set (ISBN 0-15-289280-X). HarBraceJ.
Tom Thumb Book. Richard A. Boning. (gr. k-3). 1971. 5.35 (ISBN 0-87966-100-3). B Loft.
Tom Tiddler's Ground. John R. Townsend. LC 85-45859. 176p. (gr. 3-6). 1986. 11.70i (ISBN 0-397-32190-2, Lipp Jr Bks); PLB 11.89 (ISBN 0-397-32191-0). HarpJ.
Tom Tiddler's Ground. John R. Townsend. (Lythway Ser.). 168p. (gr. 3-7). 1987. PLB 12.95x (ISBN 0-7451-0591-2, Pub. by Chivers Pr UK). G K Hall.
Tom Tit Tot. Edward Clodd. LC 67-23907. 264p. 1968. Repr. of 1898 ed. 35.00x (ISBN 0-8103-3459-3). Gale.
Tom Torluemke: Images from Ultrasound. Richard H. Love. (Illus.). 16p. (Orig.). 1986. pap. 5.00 (ISBN 0-940114-20-8). Haase Mumm Pub Co.
Tom Tracy: The Trials of a New York Newsboy. Horatio Alger, Jr. (Illus.). 208p. 1978. Repr. of 1888 ed. 24.00 (ISBN 0-686-35749-3). G K Westgard.
Tom Tyler & His Wife. Ed. by G. C. Smith & W. W. Greg. LC 82-45753. (Malone Society Reprint Ser.: No. 20). 28p. Date not set. Repr. of 1661 ed. price not set (ISBN 0-404-63020-0). AMS Pr.
Tom Tyler & His Wife. LC 70-133746. (Tudor Facsimile Texts. Old English Plays: No. 144). Repr. of 1912 ed. 49.50 (ISBN 0-404-53444-9). AMS Pr.
Tom-Walker. Mari Sandoz. LC 84-5221. viii, 372p. 1984. 28.50x (ISBN 0-8032-4150-X); pap. 8.95 (ISBN 0-8032-9147-7, BB 898, Bison). U of Nebr Pr.
Tom Watson: Agrarian Rebel. C. Vann Woodward. 1963. pap. 12.95 (ISBN 0-19-500707-7). Oxford U Pr.
Tom Watson, Agrarian Rebel. C. Vann Woodward. LC 73-77845. 430p. 1982. Repr. 25.00x (ISBN 0-8139-0952-X). U Pr of Va.
Tom Wedgwood, the First Photographer. R. B. Litchfield. LC 72-9217. (Literature of Photography Ser.). Repr. of 1903 ed. 25.50 (ISBN 0-405-04924-2). Ayer Co Pubs.
Toma Tells It Straight with Love. David Toma & Irv Levy. (Orig.). 1988. pap. 3.95 (ISBN 0-440-20034-2). Dell.
Tomahawk. Buck Bradshaw. (Lythway Ser.). 168p. 1988. lib. bdg. 17.50x (ISBN 0-7451-0679-X, Pub. by Chivers Pr UK). G K Hall.
Tomahawk. Lee Deighton. 156p. 1981. pap. 1.75 (ISBN 0-345-29431-9). Ballantine.
Tomahawk. (White Indian Ser.: No. 6). 1985. pap. 3.95 (ISBN 0-553-25039-6). Bantam.
Tomahawks & Trombones. Barbara Mitchell. LC 81-21661. (Carolrhoda On My Own Bks.). (Illus.). 56p. (gr. 1-4). 1982. lib. bdg. 8.95 (ISBN 0-87614-191-2). Carolrhoda Bks.
Tomahawks to Hatpins. Catharine B. Rowles. 1975. 7.95 (ISBN 0-932052-12-6). North Country.
Tomart's Illustrated Disneyana Catalog & Price Guide, 3 vols. Tom Tumbusch. Ed. by David R. Smith et al. LC 85-51198. 144p. (Orig.). 1985. pap. 24.95 ea. Vol. 1, A-Dolls (ISBN 0-914293-01-X). Vol. 2, Dolls thru Pinback Buttons (ISBN 0-914293-02-8). Vol. 3, Pinback Buttons thru Zorro-Index (ISBN 0-914293-03-6). Tomart Pubns.
Tomart's Illustrated Disneyana Catalog & Price Guide, Vol. 4. Tom Tumbusch. Ed. by David R. Smith et al. LC 85-51198. (Illus.). 144p. (Orig.). 1987. pap. 24.95 supplement (ISBN 0-914293-04-4). Tomart Pubns.
Tomas & the Talking Birds. Ruth N. Moore. LC 78-23509. (Illus.). 120p. (gr. 3-8). 1979. pap. 3.95 (ISBN 0-8361-1874-X). Herald Pr.
Tomas Basson. J. A. Dorsten. (Publications of Sir Thomas Browne Institute Ser.: No. 1). 1961. lib. bdg. 18.00 (ISBN 90-6021-063-8, Pub. by Leiden Univ Holland). Kluwer Academic.
Tomas de Iriarte. R. Merritt Cox. LC 79-169629. (Twayne's World Authors Ser.). 161p. 1972. lib. bdg. 17.95 (ISBN 0-8290-1736-4). Irvington.
Tomas de Suria & His Voyage with Malaspina, 1791. Tomas De Suria. 91p. 1980. 12.00 (ISBN 0-87770-239-X). Ye Galleon.
Tomas, Espitas y Valvulas de Mano, Hechas de Cobre y Aleaciones de Cobre. (Productos Latinoamericanos Incluidos En el Sistema Generalizado de Preferencias de los Estados Unidos Ser.). 17p. 1978. pap. text ed. 3.00 (ISBN 0-8270-3490-3). OAS.
Tomas Masaryk: President of Czechoslovakia. Ed. by Arthur M. Schlesinger, Jr. (World Leaders - Past & Present Ser.). (Illus.). (gr. 5-12). 1989. 16.95 (ISBN 1-55546-816-0). Chelsea Hse.
Tomas Transtromer: Selected Poems. Tomas Transtromer. Ed. by Robert Hass. Tr. by Robin Fulton et al from Swedish. 160p. 1987. 18.00 (ISBN 0-88001-105-X). Ecco Pr.
Tomas y los Pajaros Parlantes. Ruth N. Moore. LC 78-70646. (Illus.). 120p. (Span.). (gr. 3-8). 1979. pap. 3.95 (ISBN 0-8361-1875-8). Herald Pr.
Tomaso da Modena: Painting in Emilia & the March of Treviso, 1340-80. Robert Gibbs. (Illus.). 520p. Date not set. price not set (ISBN 0-521-25765-4). Cambridge U Pr.
Tomaszewski's Mime Theatre. Andrzej Hausbrandt. (Theatre, Film & Literature Ser.). (Illus.). 176p. 1977. 22.50 (ISBN 0-306-77436-4). Da Capo.
Tomato & Other Colors. Ivan Chermayeff. (ps-3). 1981. 13.55 (ISBN 0-13-924753-X). P-H.
Tomato Biotechnology. Ed. by Donald Nevins & Richards A. Jones. LC 87-2867. (Plant Biology Ser.: Vol. 4). 360p. 1987. 58.00 (ISBN 0-8451-1803-X, 1803). A R Liss.
Tomatoe Crop: A Scientific Basis for Improvement. J. G. Atherton & J. Rudich. 500p. 1987. 145.00 (ISBN 0-412-25120-5, Pub. by Chapman & Hall England). Routledge Chapman & Hall.
Tomatoes. National Gardening Association Staff. 1987. pap. 4.95 (ISBN 0-317-56624-5, Villard Bks). Random.
Tomatoes in the Treetops: Collected Tales of Harry Rhine. Ben E. Kitchens. LC 82-16980. 73p. 1982. pap. 5.95 (ISBN 0-943054-39-7). Thornwood Bk.
Tomatoes in the Tropics. Ruben L. Villareal. (IADS Development-Oriented Ser.). 200p. 1980. lib. bdg. 28.50x (ISBN 0-89158-989-9). Westview.
Tomatoes Were Cheaper: Tales of the Thirties. Charles A. Jellison. 1977. 12.95x (ISBN 0-8156-0130-1). Syracuse U Pr.
Tomb. F. Paul Wilson. 1984. 19.95 (ISBN 0-918372-11-9); signed, slipcased ed. 41.00x (ISBN 0-918372-12-7). Whispers.
Tomb. F. Paul Wilson. 410p. 1986. pap. 3.95 (ISBN 0-515-08876-5). Jove Pubns.
Tomb & Other Tales. H. P. Lovecraft. 1975. pap. 2.95 (ISBN 0-345-33661-5). Ballantine.
Tomb-Builders of the Pharaohs. Morris Bierbrier. (Illus.). 160p. 1985. 15.95 (ISBN 0-684-18229-7, ScribT). Scribner.
Tomb for Anatole. Stephane Mallarme. Tr. by Paul Auster from Fr. LC 83-61395. 224p. 1983. pap. 13.50 (ISBN 0-86547-135-5). N Point Pr.
Tomb of Ken-Amun at Thebes: Metropolitan Museum of Art Egyptian Expedition Publications, 2 vols. in 1, Vol. 5. Norman De Garis Davies. LC 78-168401. (Metropolitan Museum of Art Publications in Reprint). (Illus.). 208p. 1972. Repr. of 1930 ed. 39.00. Ayer Co Pubs.
Tomb of Kheruef: Theban Tomb No. 192. Epigraphic Survey Staff. LC 79-88739. (Oriental Institute Publications Ser.: Vol. 102). (Illus.). 1980. 90.00x (ISBN 0-918986-23-0). Oriental Inst.
Tomb of Nefer-Hotep at Thebes: Metropolitan Museum of Art Egyptian Expedition Publications, 2 vols in 1, Vol. 9. Norman De Garis Davies. LC 71-168402. (Metropolitan Museum of Art Publications in Reprint). (Illus.). 192p. 1972. Repr. of 1933 ed. 39.00. Ayer Co Pubs.
Tomb of Nyhetep-Ptah at Giza & the Tomb of 'Ankhm' Ahor at Saqqara. Alexander Badawy. (U C Publications: Occasional Papers Ser.: Vol. 11). 1978. pap. 33.00x (ISBN 0-520-09575-8). U of Cal Pr.

Tomb of Queen Meryet-Amun at Thebes: Metropolitan Museum of Art Egyptian Expedition Publication, Vol. 6. Herbert E. Winlock. LC 70-168415. (Metropolitan Museum of Art Publication in Reprint). (Illus.). 204p. 1972. Repr. of 1932 ed. 32.00 (ISBN 0-405-02253-0). Ayer Co Pubs.

Tomb of Ramesses VI, 2 vols. Ed. by A. Piankoff & N. Rambova. LC 54-5646. (Bollingen Ser.: No. 40). Vol. 1- Texts. pap. 145.80 (ISBN 0-317-28638-2, 2051348); Vol. 2- Plates. pap. 53.00 (ISBN 0-317-28639-0). Bks Demand UMI.

Tomb of Rekh-Mi-Re at Thebes: Metropolitan Museum of Art Egyptian Expedition Publications, 2 vols. in 1, Vol. 11. Norman Davies. LC 75-168403. (Metropolitan Museum of Art Publications in Reprint). (Illus.). 374p. 1972. Repr. of 1943 ed. 47.50 (ISBN 0-405-02267-0). Ayer Co Pubs.

Tomb of Senebtisi at Lisht: Metropolitan Museum of Art Egyptian Expedition Publications, Vol. 1. Arthur C. Mace & Herbert E. Winlock. LC 73-168408. (Metropolitan Museum of Art Publications in Reprint). (Illus.). 228p. 1972. Repr. of 1916 ed. 32.00 (ISBN 0-405-02241-7). Ayer Co Pubs.

Tomb of the Eagles: Death & Life in a Stone Age Tribe. John W. Hedges. (Illus.). 256p. 1987. pap. 11.95 (ISBN 0-941533-05-0). New Amsterdam Bks.

Tomb of the Vizier Fe-Wer at Saqqara. Said A. El-Fikey. (Egyptology Today Ser.: No. 4). 55p. 1980. pap. text ed. 29.00x (ISBN 0-85668-158-X, Pub. by Aris & Phillips UK). Humanities.

Tomb of Tjanefer at Thebes. Keith C. Seele. LC 59-14285. (Oriental Institute Pubns. Ser: No. 86). (Illus.). 1959. 22.00x (ISBN 0-226-62187-1, OIP86). U of Chicago Pr.

Tomb of Tut-Ankh-Amen, 3 Vols. Howard Carter & A. C. Mace. LC 63-17462. (Illus.). Repr. of 1954 ed. Set. 85.00x (ISBN 0-8154-0048-9). Cooper Sq.

Tomb Robbers. Daniel Cohen. LC 79-22760. (Illus.). 96p. (gr. 5-8). 1980. text ed. 10.95 (ISBN 0-07-011566-4). McGraw.

Tomb Seven. Gene Snyder. 288p. 1985. pap. 3.50 (ISBN 0-441-81643-6). Ace Bks.

Tombeau de Charles Baudelaire. Stephane Mallarme et al. LC 77-11490. Repr. of 1896 ed. 27.50 (ISBN 0-404-16350-5). AMS Pr.

Tombeaux Ferment Mal. Jacques Audiberti. 240p. 1963. 9.95 (ISBN 0-686-54509-5). French & Eur.

Tombee: Portrait of a Cotton Planter. Theodore Rosengarten. 752p. 1988. pap. text ed. 12.95 (ISBN 0-07-053821-2). McGraw.

Tombee: Portrait of a Cotton Planter with; the Journal of Thomas Chaplin, 1822-1890. Theodore Rosengarten. LC 86-716. (Illus.). 728p. 1986. 22.95 (ISBN 0-688-05412-9). Morrow.

Tombigbee Watershed in Southeastern Prehistory. Ned J. Jenkins & Richard A. Krause. LC 85-20879. (Illus.). 220p. 1986. 18.95 (ISBN 0-8173-0281-6). U of Ala Pr.

Tombleson's Thames & the Medway. Ed. by Bishopsgate Press Ltd. Staff. 254p. 1985. 45.00x (ISBN 0-900873-30-2, Pub. by Bishopsgate Pr. Ltd.). State Mutual Bk.

Tomboy. Norma Klein. (gr. 3-5). 1980. pap. 1.95 (ISBN 0-671-45533-8). Archway.

Tomboy Bride. Harriet F. Backus. LC 79-80764. (Illus.). 1969. pap. 8.95 (ISBN 0-87108-512-7). Pruett.

Tomboy: Revelations of a Girl's Reformatory. (Grove Press Victorian Library). 224p. 1986. pap. 3.95 (ISBN 0-394-62249-9, BC). Grove.

Tombs of Anak. Frank Peretti. LC 86-73183. (Cooper Family Adventure Ser.). 144p. (Orig.). (gr. 5-8). 1987. pap. 4.95 (ISBN 0-89107-442-2, Crossway Bks). Good News.

Tombs of Atuan. Ursula K. Le Guin. LC 70-154753. (Illus.). 176p. (gr. 5-9). 1971. 15.95 (ISBN 0-689-20680-1, Atheneum Childrens Bk). Macmillan.

Tombs of Atuan. Ursula K. Le Guin. 160p. 1975. pap. 3.50 (ISBN 0-553-23903-1). Bantam.

Tombs of Atuan. Ursula K. Le Guin. (Children's Ser.). 216p. (gr. 5 up). 1988. lib. bdg. 13.95x (ISBN 0-8161-4430-3, Large Print Bks). G K Hall.

Tombs of Iteti, Sekhem ankh-Ptah, & Kaemnofert at Giza. Alexander Badawy. (University of California Publications, Occasional Papers, Archaeology: No. 9). pap. 26.30 (ISBN 0-317-29106-8, 2021386). Bks Demand UMI.

Tombstone. Matt Braun. 224p. 1981. pap. 1.95 (ISBN 0-671-82033-8). PB.

Tombstone. William Hattich. LC 80-5947. (Illus.). 64p. 1981. 14.95 (ISBN 0-8061-1753-2). U of Okla Pr.

Tombstone, Arizona Silver Camp. Robert L. Spude. (Illus.). 17p. 1979. 1.95 (ISBN 0-913814-23-7). Nevada Pubns.

Tombstone, Arizona, 1880 Business & Professional Directory. Ed. by Lonnie E. Underhill. LC 82-551. (Illus.). vi, 38p. pap. 35.00 (ISBN 0-933234-04-X, AACR2); collector's ed. 50.00 (ISBN 0-933234-05-8). Roan Horse.

Tombstone for a Trouble Shooter. William C. MacDonald. 1978. pap. 1.25 (ISBN 0-505-51308-0, Pub. by Tower Bks). Leisure NY.

Tombstone Inscriptions & Other Records of Delaware, Ohio. Esther W. Powell. 17.00 (ISBN 0-935057-50-1). OH Genealogical.

Tombstone Inscriptions of King George County, Virginia. Margaret C. Klein. LC 79-52060. 74p. 1979. pap. 7.50 (ISBN 0-8063-0845-1). Genealog Pub.

Tombstone Lode. Doyle Trent. 288p. 1986. pap. 2.95 (ISBN 0-8217-1915-7). Zebra.

Tombstone Names in Suffolk County, New York. Marjorie S. Lloyd. (Illus.). 86p. (Orig.). 1986. pap. 15.00 (ISBN 0-9617988-0-7). M Sones Lloyd.

Tombstone Records of Eighteen Cemeteries in Pound Ridge, Westchester Co., N. Y. Mable L. Jordan & Natalie M. Seth. LC 83-12997. 1983. pap. 8.50 (ISBN 0-916346-49-8). Harbor Hill Bks.

Tombstones. Dan Mckinnon. 87p. Date not set. price not set (ISBN 0-941437-03-5). House Hits.

Tomcat's Big CB Handbook: Everything They Never Told You. Tom Kneitel. (Illus.). 221p. (Orig.). 1988. pap. text ed. 13.95 (ISBN 0-939780-07-0). CRB Res.

Tome Premier. Francis Ponge. 620p. 1965. 17.50 (ISBN 0-686-54896-5). French & Eur.

Tomentelloid Fungi of North America, No. 93. 1968. 2.00 (ISBN 0-686-20703-3). SUNY Environ.

Tomfoolery: Trickery & Foolery with Words. Alvin Schwartz. LC 72-12900. (Illus.). 128p. (gr. 4 up). 1973. 12.70i (ISBN 0-397-31466-3, Lipp Jr Bks). HarpJ.

Tomie De Paola's Book of Christmas Carols. Tomie De Paola. LC 86-755157. 81p. (gr. 1 up). 1987. PLB 17.95 (ISBN 0-399-21432-1). Putnam Pub Group.

Tomie De Paola's Book of Poems. Tomie De Paola. 96p. 1988. 17.95 (ISBN 0-399-21540-9). Putnam Pub Group.

Tomie De Paola's Favorite Nursery Tales. Selected by & illus. by Tomie De Paola. (Illus.). 128p. (gr. 1 up). 1986. 17.95 (ISBN 0-399-21319-8, Putnam). Putnam Pub Group.

Tomie dePaola's Mother Goose. Illus. by Tomie De Paola. LC 84-26314. (Illus.). 127p. (ps-2). 1985. 17.95 (ISBN 0-399-21258-2, Putnam). Putnam Pub Group.

Tomiki Aikido: Book One: Randori. rev. ed. Lee A. Loi. (Illus.). 88p. 1985. pap. text ed. 12.00 (ISBN 0-87364-371-2). Paladin Pr.

Tomiki Aikido: Book Two: Koryu No Kata. rev. ed. Dr. Lee Ah Loi. (Illus.). 80p. 1986. pap. text ed. 12.00 (ISBN 0-87364-372-0). Paladin Pr.

Tomita's Theory of Modular Hilbert Algebras & Its Applications. M. Takesaki. LC 79-117719. (Lecture Notes in Mathematics: Vol. 128). 1970. pap. 10.70 (ISBN 0-387-04917-7). Springer-Verlag.

Tomlinson Papers. J. G. Bullocke. 1985. 69.00x (ISBN 0-317-44240-6, Pub. by Navy Rec Soc). State Mutual Bk.

Tommaso Campanella in America: A Critical Bibliography & a Profile. Francesco Grillo. 109p. 1954. 6.75x (ISBN 0-913298-43-3). S F Vanni.

Tommaso Campanella in America: A Supplement to the Critical Bibliography. Francesco Grillo. 48p. 1957. 5.00x (ISBN 0-913298-49-2). S F Vanni.

Tommaso Campanella: Renaissance Pioneer of Modern Thought. Bernardino M. Bonansea. LC 78-76125. 421p. 1969. 19.95x (ISBN 0-8132-0263-9). Cath U Pr.

Tommaso Landolfi's Grotesque Images. Romana Capek-Habekovic. (Studies in the Humanities-Literature Politics-Society: Vol. 3). 176p. 1987. text ed. 33.00 (ISBN 0-8204-0263-X). P Lang Pubs.

Tommaso Traetta di Bitonto (1727-1779) La Vita e le Opere. Franco Casavola. LC 80-22630. Repr. of 1957 ed. 22.50 (ISBN 0-404-18816-8). AMS Pr.

Tommorow Is Another Day: The Woman Writer in the South, 1859-1936. Anne Goodwyn Jones. LC 80-29123. (Illus.). 408p. 1981. text ed. 40.00 (ISBN 0-8071-0776-X); pap. text ed. 15.95 (ISBN 0-8071-0866-9). La State U Pr.

Tommorrow's Materials: Living in a World of Advanced Materials. K. E. Easterling. 144p. 1988. pap. 19.40 (ISBN 0-901462-40-3, Pub. by Inst Metals). Brookfield Pub Co.

Tommy & Grizel see Works of J. M. Barrie.

Tommy & Jimmy: The Dorsey Years. Herb Sanford. LC 79-27093. (Quality Paperbacks Ser.). (Illus.). 1980. pap. 6.95 (ISBN 0-306-80117-5). Da Capo.

Tommy Goes to War. Malcolm Brown. (Illus.). 272p. 1978. 17.50x (ISBN 0-460-04327-7, Pub by J M Dent England). Biblio Dist.

Tommy Hitchcock: An American Hero. Nelson W. Aldrich. 304p. 1985. 19.95 (ISBN 0-9611314-2-X). Fleet St Corp.

Tommy Knockers. Alan Leisk. 72p. 1986. 6.95. Carlton.

Tommy Learns about Time & Eternity. Peggy J. Buck. (Illus.). 68p. (Orig.). (gr. 1-3). 1980. pap. 2.50 (ISBN 0-89323-006-5, 023). Bible Memory.

Tommy Loves Tina. Janet Q. Harkin. 160p. 1984. pap. 1.95 (ISBN 0-441-81649-5). Ace Bks.

Tommy Scott Young Spins Magical Tales, 2 vols. Tommy S. Young. Ed. by Nathanial Irvin, Jr. Incl. Vol. I. Barney McCabe. LC 85-61698. 44p. 7.95; Vol. II. Tiny Hooty & the Percher. LC 85-61699. 36p. PLB 10.00. LC 85-6198. (gr. 1-8). 1985. PLB 13.95 Barney McCabe, vol. I, 44pgs. (ISBN 0-934721-01-7); PLB 13.95 Tiny Hooty & the Percher, Vol. II, 36 pgs. (ISBN 0-934721-02-5); PLB 29.95 Cassette & Book Package (ISBN 0-934721-07-6); Cassette Tape Vol. I, 17 min. 30 sec. 11.95, Vol. II 18 min. 22 sec. (ISBN 0-934721-00-9). Raspberry Rec.

Tommy the Timid Foal. Esta De Fossard. LC 85-15936. (Easy to Read Animal Adventures Ser.). (Illus.). 32p. (gr. 2-3). 1985. PLB 10.95 (ISBN 0-918831-37-7). Stevens Inc.

Tommy the Toothbrush. Robert D. Miller. (Illus.). 16p. (gr. 2-4). 1982. write for info. Miller OH.

Tommyknockers. Stephen King. 544p. 1987. 19.95 (ISBN 0-399-13314-3, Putnam). Putnam Pub Group.

Tommyknockers. Stephen King. 1988. pap. 5.95 (ISBN 0-451-15660-9, Sig). NAL.

Tommy's Big Problem. Lillie D. Chaffin. (Illus.). (ps-2). PLB 6.19 (ISBN 0-8313-0016-7). Lantern.

Tommy's Day. Harry Bornstein. (Signed English Ser.). 48p. 1973. pap. 5.95 (ISBN 0-913580-10-4, Clerc Bks). Gallaudet Univ Pr.

Tommy's First Speaker. facs. ed. Ed. by Thomas W. Handford. LC 71-149104. (Granger Index Reprint Ser). 1885. 15.00 (ISBN 0-8369-6229-X). Ayer Co Pubs.

Tommy's Pets. Edward W. Dolch & M. P. Dolch. (Dolch First Reading Bks.). 64p. (gr. 1-4). 1958. PLB 4.98 (ISBN 0-8116-2802-7). Garrard.

Tomochichi: Indian Friend of the Georgia Colony. Helen Todd. LC 77-75268. (Illus.). 208p. 1977. bds. 12.95 (ISBN 0-87797-040-8). Cherokee.

Tomoe Gozen. Jessica A. Salmonson. 274p. 1984. pap. 2.75 (ISBN 0-441-81653-3). Ace Bks.

Tomorrow a New World. Paul Conklin. (FDR & the Era of the New Deal Ser.). 1976. Repr. of 1959 ed. lib. bdg. 39.50 (ISBN 0-306-70805-1). Da Capo.

Tomorrow about This Time. Grace L. Hill. Repr. lib. bdg. 20.95 (ISBN 0-89190-049-7, Pub. by River City Pr). Amereon Ltd.

Tomorrow & Forever. Francesca Macklem. 256p. (Orig.). 1984. pap. 2.75 (ISBN 0-8439-2155-2, Leisure Bks). Leisure NY.

Tomorrow & Tomorrow & Tomorrow. Ed. by David G. Yellin & Marie Connors. LC 84-21908. (Illus.). 1985. 17.50x (ISBN 0-87805-247-X); pap. 8.95 (ISBN 0-87805-248-8). U Pr of Miss.

Tomorrow Began Yesterday. Sarah Holland. (Harlequin Presents Ser.). 192p. 1982. pap. 1.75 (ISBN 0-373-10536-3). Harlequin Bks.

Tomorrow Book. Doris Schwerin. LC 82-12504. (Illus.). 32p. (ps-k). 1984. 10.95 (ISBN 0-394-85459-4, Pant Bks Young); lib. bdg. 10.99 (ISBN 0-394-95459-9). Pantheon.

Tomorrow, Capitalism: The Economics of Economic Freedom. Henri Lepage. Tr. by Sheilagh C. Ogilvie from Fr. LC 82-2291. 256p. 1982. 14.95 (ISBN 0-87548-367-4); pap. 7.95 (ISBN 0-87548-424-7). Open Court.

Tomorrow Connection. T. Ernesto Bethancourt. LC 84-47836. 144p. (YA) (gr. 7 up). 1984. 10.95 (ISBN 0-8234-0543-5). Holiday.

Tomorrow File. Lawrence Sanders. 560p. 1985. pap. 4.50 (ISBN 0-425-08179-6). Berkley Pub.

Tomorrow I Die. Mickey Spillane. LC 82-60903. 260p. 1984. 14.95 (ISBN 0-89296-061-2); ltd. ed. 75.00 (ISBN 0-89296-062-0). Mysterious Pr.

Tomorrow in the Making. Ed. by John N. Andrews & Carl A. Marsden. LC 72-546. (Essay Index Reprint Ser.). Repr. of 1939 ed. 27.50 (ISBN 0-8369-2782-6). Ayer Co Pubs.

Tomorrow, Inc. SF Stories about Big Business. Ed. by Martin H. Greenberg & Joseph D. Olander. LC 76-11057. (YA) (gr. 10 up). 1976. 9.95 (ISBN 0-8008-7746-2). Taplinger.

Tomorrow Is a Better Day. Dave Atwood. 1987. 7.95 (ISBN 0-533-07122-4). Vantage.

Tomorrow Is a River. Peggy H. Dopp & Barbara F. Vroman. LC 76-52054. 390p. 1977. 14.95 (ISBN 0-931762-00-6). Phunn Pubs.

Tomorrow Is a River. Peggy H. Dopp & Barbara F. Vroman. LC 76-52054. 390p. (Orig.). 1986. pap. 9.95 (ISBN 0-931762-01-4). Phunn Pubs.

Tomorrow Is Another Day: Hope of a Better Future for Black Americans. Eliza Washington. 4.00 (ISBN 0-939354-00-4). E Washington.

Tomorrow Is for Weeping. Judith MacEachron. LC 79-63106. 1979. 8.95 (ISBN 0-914338-04-8). Regmar Pub.

Tomorrow Is Forever. Gwen Bristow. 320p. 1976. lib. bdg. 19.95x (ISBN 0-89966-027-4). Buccaneer Bks.

Tomorrow Is So Far from Now. David Kalugin. (Illus.). 1979. pap. 4.95 (ISBN 0-933586-01-9). Book Promo Pr.

Tomorrow Is Today. Shelley Bruce. LC 83-3797. (Illus.). 224p. 1983. 15.95 (ISBN 0-672-52756-1). Bobbs.

Tomorrow Knocks. Anatol Brunton. (Inner Visions Ser.: No. 1). 176p. (Orig.). 1982. pap. 9.95 (ISBN 0-917086-39-2). A C S Pubns Inc.

Tomorrow Makers: A Brave New World of Living-Brain Machines. Grant Fjermedal. 256p. 1987. 18.95 (ISBN 0-02-538560-7). Macmillan.

Tomorrow Makers: A Brave New World of Living-Brain Machines. Grant Fjermedal. 288p. 1988. pap. 8.95 (ISBN 1-55615-113-6). Microsoft.

Tomorrow Never Knows: The Beatles' Last Concert. Eric Lefcowitz. Ed. by Anita Sethi. LC 87-80730. (Illus.). 104p. (Orig.). 1987. pap. 12.95 (ISBN 0-943249-02-3). Terra Firma Bks.

Tomorrow, New Worlds of Science Fiction. Ed. by Roger Elwood. LC 75-17783. 228p. (gr. 7 up). 1975. 5.95 (ISBN 0-87131-185-2). M Evans.

Tomorrow Now Occurs Again. Robert Gover. LC 75-6142. 1975. pap. 4.95 (ISBN 0-915520-00-1). Ross-Erikson.

Tomorrow, the Stars. Ed. by Robert A. Heinlein. 1984. pap. 2.75 (ISBN 0-425-07572-9, Medallion). Berkley Pub.

Tomorrow Today. Larry Richards. 132p. 1986. pap. 5.50 (ISBN 0-89693-505-1). Victor Bks.

Tomorrow, Tomorrow. James M. Bryant. pap. 7.00 (ISBN 0-318-18289-0). Rocket Pub Co.

Tomorrow Tomorrow. James McKinley Bryant. 1976. pap. 7.00 (ISBN 0-686-15543-2). J M Bryant.

Tomorrow Triumphant: Selected Poems of Otto Rene Castillo. Tr. by Roque Dalton Cultural Brigade. Ed. by Magaly Fernandez & David Volpendesta. (Literature Ser.: No. 3). 144p. (Orig., Span. & Eng.). 1984. pap. 6.95 (ISBN 0-941842-02-9). Night Horn Books.

Tomorrow We Die. Elisaveta Fen. 245p. 1987. 40.00x (ISBN 0-7223-1575-9, Pub. by A H Stockwell England). State Mutual Bk.

Tomorrow We Live. O. Mosley. 59.95 (ISBN 0-8490-1221-X). Gordon Pr.

Tomorrow, We're Taking a Test. Donna Roppelt & Mary Mowl. 1982. Set. 3.95x (ISBN 0-932666-16-7). T J Pubs.

Tomorrow Will Always Come. Clara R. DeLima. 1965. 12.95 (ISBN 0-8392-1141-4). Astor-Honor.

Tomorrow Will Be Better. Betty Smith. 1971. pap. 2.50 (ISBN 0-06-080049-6, P49, PL). Har-Row.

Tomorrow Will Be Better: Living with a Parent Who Drinks. Ed. by Bruce Fingerhut. 64p. 1985. pap. 9.95 (ISBN 0-89651-786-1). B L Pub.

Tomorrow Will Really Be Sunday. Ron Schreiber. write for info. Calamus Bks.

Tomorrow's Bread. Beatrice Bisno. LC 74-26096. Repr. of 1938 ed. 27.00 (ISBN 0-404-58407-1). AMS Pr.

Tomorrow's Catholics - Yesterday's Church: The Two Cultures of American Catholicism. Eugene Kennedy. LC 88-45037. 208p. 1988. 17.95 (HarpT). Har-Row.

Tomorrow's Eve. Ed. by Jean M. Villiers de L'Isle-Adam. Tr. by Robert M. Adams. LC 82-13411. 256p. 1982. 22.95 (ISBN 0-252-00942-8). U of Ill Pr.

Tomorrow's Food. rev., enlarged ed. James Rorty & N. Philip Norman. LC 56-8132. pap. 77.30 (ISBN 0-317-28232-8, 2022712). Bks Demand UMI.

Tomorrow's Food. James Rorty & Philip Norman. 9.95 (ISBN 0-8159-6906-6). Devin.

Tomorrow's Global Executive. Henry Ferguson. 200p. 1987. 22.95 (ISBN 1-55623-057-5). Dow Jones-Irwin.

Tomorrow's Harvest. Hiram M. Drache. LC 78-57250. 1978. 14.95x (ISBN 0-8134-2032-6, 2032). Inter Print Pubs.

Tomorrow's Joy. Kenneth L. Hardin. (Illus.). 187p. (Orig.). 1987. pap. 4.00 (ISBN 0-9619153-1-5). K L Hardin.

Tomorrow's Love Song. Georgia Bockoven. (Temptation Ser.: No. 161). 224p. Date not set. pap. 2.25 (ISBN 0-317-63852-1). Harlequin Bks.

Tomorrow's Magic. Pamela F. Service. LC 86-32123. 208p. (gr. 4-8). 1987. 14.95 (ISBN 0-689-31320-9, Atheneum Childrens Bks). Macmillan.

Tomorrow's Magic. Pamela F. Service. (gr. 5 up). 1988. pap. 2.95 (ISBN 0-449-70305-3, Juniper). Fawcett.

Tomorrow's Marketing: A Symposium. Ed. by Earl L. Bailey. (Report Ser: No. 623). 65p. (Orig.). 1974. pap. 5.00 (ISBN 0-8237-0053-4). Conference Bd.

Tomorrow's Office Today: Managing Technological Change. D. W. Birchall & V. Hammond. 202p. 1981. 32.95x (ISBN 0-470-27236-8). Halsted Pr.

Tomorrow's Parents: A Study of Youth & Their Families. Bernice M. Moore & Wayne H. Holtzman. (Hogg Foundation Research Series). 397p. 1965. 20.00x (ISBN 0-292-73409-3). U of Tex Pr.

Tomorrow's Promise. Sandra Brown. (American Romance Ser.). 192p. 1983. pap. 2.25 (ISBN 0-373-16001-1). Harlequin Bks.

Tomorrow's Rainbow. Sara Hylton. 496p. 1988. 18.95x (ISBN 0-312-01523-2). St Martin.

Tomorrow's Sphinx. Clare Bell. LC 86-8479. 312p. (gr. 7 up). 1986. 14.95 (ISBN 0-689-50402-0, M K McElderry). Macmillan.

Tomorrow's Sphinx. Clare Bell. (gr. k-12). 1988. pap. 3.25 (ISBN 0-440-20124-1). Dell.

Tomorrow's Television. Frwd. by Frederick M. Remley. (Illus.). 256p. 1982. pap. text ed. 30.00 (ISBN 0-940690-06-3). Soc Motion Pic & TV Engrs.

Tomorrows to Come. Joseph Berry. LC 87-72433. 85p. (Orig.). 1988. pap. text ed. 3.95 (ISBN 0-87029-212-9, 20258-0). Abbey.

Tomorrow's Treason. Palma Harcourt. 224p. 1987. pap. 3.50 (ISBN 0-515-08835-8). Jove Pubns.

Tomorrow's TV. Ed. by Isaac Asimov et al. LC 81-1737. (Science Fiction Shorts Ser.). (Illus.). 48p. (gr. 5-7). 1982. PLB 15.99 (ISBN 0-8172-1735-5). Raintree Pubs.

Tomorrow's Tyrants: The Radical & the Politics of Hate. Arthur F. Ide. (Woman in History Ser.: Vol. 109). (Illus.). 340p. (Orig.). 1985. pap. 9.95 (ISBN 0-930383-05-2). Monument Pr.

Tomorrow's Universities: A World Wide Look at Educational Change. W. Werner Prange & David Jowett. (Education Ser.). 220p. 1982. lib. bdg. 36.50x (ISBN 0-86531-410-1). Westview.

Tomorrow's Wizard. Patricia MacLachlan. LC 81-47733. (Charlotte Zolotow Bks.). (Illus.). 96p. (gr. 4-6). 1982. 10.70i (ISBN 0-06-024073-3); PLB 10.89 (ISBN 0-06-024074-1). HarpJ.

Tomorrow's Workers. Michael E. Borus. LC 82-17154. 208p. 1982. 28.50x (ISBN 0-669-06090-9). Lexington Bks.

Tomorrow's World: Energy. Malcolm Brinkworth. (Illus.). 128p. 1986. 18.95 (ISBN 0-88186-402-1); pap. 9.95 (ISBN 0-563-20347-1). Parkwest Pubns.

Tomorrow's World: Food. Caroline Van Den Brul & Susan Spindler. (Illus.). 128p. 1986. 18.95 (ISBN 0-88186-401-3); pap. 9.95 (ISBN 0-563-20305-6). Parkwest Pubns.

Tomorrow's World: Medicine. Fiona Holmes. (Illus.). 128p. 1986. 18.95 (ISBN 0-88186-403-X); pap. 9.95 (ISBN 0-563-20346-3). Parkwest Pubns.

Tomorrow's World: Space Technology. Max Whitby. (Illus.). 128p. 1987. 18.95 (ISBN 0-88186-404-8, Pub. by BBC); pap. 9.95 (ISBN 0-563-20378-1, Pub. by BBC). Parkwest Pubns.

Tomorrow?...Yesterday?... Boris Zubkov. Tr. by Eleanor Yankovskaya & I. Kabakov. (Illus.). (ps-3). 1983. pap. 1.99 (ISBN 0-8285-2430-0, Pub. by Malysh Pubs USSR). Imported Pubns.

Tompkins & Other Folks: Stories of the Hudson & the Adirondacks. Philander Deming. 1972. Repr. of 1885 ed. lib. bdg. 26.50 (ISBN 0-8422-8039-1). Irvington.

Tom's Cat. Charlotte Voake. LC 85-27166. (Trophy Picture Bks.). (Illus.). 32p. (ps-2). 1986. pap. 2.50 (ISBN 0-06-443105-3, Trophy). HarpJ.

Tom's Cat. Charlotte Voake. LC 85-23904. (Illus.). 32p. (ps-2). 1986. PLB 11.89 (ISBN 0-397-32195-3, Lipp Jr Bks). HarpJ.

Toms Coons Mulattoes: Blacks in U. S. Films. Donald Bogle. 312p. 1988. pap. 14.95 (ISBN 0-8264-0416-2). Crossroad NY.

Tom's Midnight Garden. Philippa Pearce. (gr. k-6). 1986. pap. 4.95 (ISBN 0-440-48819-2, Yearling Classics). Dell.

Tom's Midnight Garden. Philippa Pearce. LC 69-12008. (Illus.). 240p. (gr. 5-7). 1984. 13.95i (ISBN 0-397-30475-7, Lipp Jr Bks). HarpJ.

Tom's Remembrance. Rebecca O'Hanlon Nunn. (Illus.). 1987. 10.95 (ISBN 0-915637-06-5). Westphalia Pr.

Tom's Tale. Judith Stinto. (Illus.). (gr. k-3). 5.95 (ISBN 0-531-04606-0, A Julia Macrae Blackbird Book). Watts.

Tom's Town: Kansas City & the Pendergast Legend. William M. Reddig. LC 85-20888. 416p. 1986. pap. 12.95 (ISBN 0-8262-0498-8). U of Mo Pr.

Tomten. Astrid Lindgren. (Illus.). (gr. 1-3). 1961. 8.95 (ISBN 0-698-20147-7, Coward). Putnam Pub Group.

Tomten. Astrid Lindgren. LC 61-10658. (Illus.). (ps-2). 1979. pap. 6.95 (ISBN 0-698-20487-5, Coward). Putnam Pub Group.

Tomten & the Fox. Astrid Lindgren. LC 65-25501. (Illus.). (ps-2). 1979. pap. 4.95 (ISBN 0-698-20488-3, Coward). Putnam Pub Group.

Ton Albert Qui T'adore: Courtship Letters of Albert Spalding to Mary V. Pyle. Ed. by Suzanne S. Winston. (Illus.). 120p. 1988. 22.50 (ISBN 0-914659-36-7). Phoenix Pub.

Ton Rire Comme un Soleil. Kerry Allyne. (Collection Harlequin Ser.). 192p. 1983. pap. 1.95 (ISBN 0-373-49346-0). Harlequin Bks.

Tonal & Rhythm Patterns. Edwin Gordon. LC 76-7947. 186p. 1976. 49.50x (ISBN 0-87395-354-1). State U NY Pr.

Tonal Coherence in Mahler's Ninth Symphony. Christopher O. Lewis. Ed. by George Buelow. LC 84-2754. (Studies in Musicology: No. 79). 148p. 1984. 37.95 (ISBN 0-8357-1585-X). UMI Res Pr.

Tonal Counterpoint in the Style of the Eighteenth Century. Ernst Krenek. LC 59-17691. 44p. 1958. pap. 11.95 (ISBN 0-913932-12-4). Boosey & Hawkes.

Tonal Grammar of Etsako. Baruch Elimelech. (UC Publications in Linguistics: Vol. 87). 1979. pap. 22.00x (ISBN 0-520-09576-6). U of Cal Pr.

Tonal Harmonic Dictation: A Workbook. Thomas L. Durham. (Illus.). 134p. 1987. 16.75 (ISBN 0-8191-6283-3). U Pr of Amer.

Tonal Harmony, with an Introduction to Twentieth Century Music. 2nd ed. Stefan Kosta & Dorothy Payne. 640p. 1989. text ed. write for info. (ISBN 0-394-36653-0); pap. text ed. wkbk. avail. (ISBN 0-394-36654-9). Knopf.

Tonal Music: Twelve Analytic Studies. Jeffrey Kresky. LC 77-74447. (Illus.). 192p. 1978. 17.50x (ISBN 0-253-37011-6). Ind U Pr.

Tonal Values: How to See Them, How to Paint Them. Angela Gair. (Illus.). 144p. 1987. 24.95 (ISBN 0-89134-220-6). North Light Bks.

Tonalamatl of the Aubin Collection. Eduard Seler. Ed. by Karl Young. (Fourth Sun Ser.). lib. bdg. cancelled (ISBN 0-932282-38-5); pap. cancelled (ISBN 0-932282-37-7). Caledonia Pr.

Tonality & Atonality in Sixteenth-Century Music. Edward E. Lowinsky. (Music Reprint Ser.). 1989. 25.00 (ISBN 0-306-76299-4). Da Capo.

Tonality, Atonality, Pantonality: A Study of Some Trends in Twentieth Century Music. Rudolph R. Reti. LC 78-6162. (Illus.). 1978. Repr. of 1958 ed. lib. bdg. 35.00x (ISBN 0-313-20478-0, RETO). Greenwood.

Tonality in Western Culture: A Critical & Historical Perspective. Richard Norton. LC 83-43030. (Illus.). 336p. 1984. 27.50x (ISBN 0-271-00359-6). Pa St U Pr.

Tonalization. Shinichi Suzuki. (Suzuki Method Ser.). (Illus.). 64p. (Orig.). 1985. pap. text ed. 9.95 (ISBN 0-87487-214-6, Suzuki Method). Birch Tree Gr.

Tondrakian Movement: Religious Movements in the Armenian Church from the Fourth to the Tenth Centuries. Vrej Nersessian. LC 88-4066. (Princeton Theological Monograph Ser.: Vol. 15). 156p. 1988. pap. 16.00 (ISBN 0-915138-99-9). Pickwick.

Tone: A Linguistic Survey. Ed. by Victoria A. Fromkin. 1978. 29.95 (ISBN 0-12-267350-6). Acad Pr.

Tone: A Study in Musical Acoustics. 2nd ed. Siegmund Levarie & Ernst Levy. LC 80-29383. (Illus.). xvii, 256p. 1981. Repr. of 1980 ed. lib. bdg. 35.00x (ISBN 0-313-22499-4, LETO). Greenwood.

Tone: A Study in Musical Acoustics. rev. ed. Siegmund Levarie & Ernst Levy. LC 80-16794. (Illus.). 280p. 1980. pap. 8.50x (ISBN 0-87338-250-1). Kent St U Pr.

Tone & Intonation on the Recorder. Edward L. Kottick. 1974. 7.00 (ISBN 0-941084-04-3). McGinnis & Marx.

Tone Deaf & All Thumbs? Frank R. Wilson. LC 87-40086. 224p. 1987. pap. 6.95 (ISBN 0-394-75354-2, Vin). Random.

Tone Deaf & All Thumbs? An Invitation to Music-Making for Late Bloomers & Non-Prodiges. Frank R. Wilson. 200p. 1986. 15.95 (ISBN 0-670-80842-3). Viking.

Tone Development Through Extented Techniques. rev. ed. Robert Dick. 60p. (Orig.). 1986. pap. 15.00 (ISBN 0-939407-00-0). Multiple Breath Music.

Tone Languages: A Technique for Determining the Number & Type of Pitch Contrasts in a Language, with Studies in Tonemic Substitution & Fusion. Kenneth L. Pike. 1948. pap. 8.50x (ISBN 0-472-08734-7). U of Mich Pr.

Tone Lexical Phonology. Douglas Pulleyblank. 1986. lib. bdg. 49.50 (ISBN 90-277-2123-8, Pub. by Reidel Holland); pap. 24.00 (ISBN 90-277-2124-6). Kluwer Academic.

Tone of Teaching. Max van Manen. 56p. 1986. pap. text ed. 6.00x (ISBN 0-435-08255-8). Heinemann Ed.

Tone Poems, Series I: Don Juan, Tod und Verklarung & Don Quixote in Full Score from the Original Editions. Richard Strauss. LC 78-67060. 1979. pap. 10.95 (ISBN 0-486-23754-0). Dover.

Tone Poems, Series II: Till Eulenspiegels Lustige Streiche, Also Sprach Zarathustra, & ein Heldenleben in Full Score from the Original Editions. Richard Strauss. LC 78-68041. 1979. pap. 10.95 (ISBN 0-486-23755-9). Dover.

Tone, Segment, & Syllable in Chinese: A Polydimensional Approach to Surface Phonetic Structure. A. Ronald Walton. LC 83-126802. (East Asia Papers Ser.: No 32). 360p. 1983. 12.00 (ISBN 0-939657-32-5). Cornell East Asia Pgm.

Tone the Bell Easy. Ed. by J. Frank Dobie. LC 33-1135. (Texas Folklore Society Publications: No. 10). (Illus.). 200p. 1965. Repr. of 1932 ed. 12.95 (ISBN 0-87074-045-8). SMU Press.

Tones & Colours. Amon Saba Saakana. 64p. 1985. pap. 5.00 (ISBN 0-907015-09-3, Pub. by Zed Pr England). Humanities.

Tones of Sechuana Nouns & a Sechuana Reader. Daniel Jones & S. T. Plaatje. 114p. Repr. text ed. 24.84x (ISBN 0-576-11455-3, Pub. by Gregg Intl Pubs England). Gregg Intl.

Tones, Tunes & Trills: Sound & Music on the Commodore 64. Timothy C. Barry et al. (Illus.). 224p. 1984. pap. cancelled (ISBN 0-88056-345-1); cancelled (ISBN 0-88056-230-7). Dilithium Pr.

Tonetti Years at Snedens Landing. 2nd ed. Isabelle K. Savelle. (Illus.). 1981. pap. 9.95 (ISBN 0-911183-05-1). Rockland County Hist.

Tonfa: An Extension of the Mind & Body. Clifford C. Crandall, Jr. 69p. 1986. 8.95 (ISBN 0-317-39352-9). Vantage.

Tonfa: Karate Weapon of Self-Defense. Fumio Demura. Ed. by Gregory Lee. LC 82-81557. (Weapons Ser.). (Illus.). 144p. (Orig.). 1982. pap. 8.95 (ISBN 0-89750-080-6, 417). Ohara Pubns.

Tonfa Police Baton Academy Manual. Sid Campbell. 85p. 1987. pap. 45.00 (ISBN 0-318-21812-7). Gong Prods.

Tonfa Police Baton Master Instructor Handbook. Sid Campbell. 225p. 1987. pap. 45.00 (ISBN 0-318-21811-9). Gong Prods.

Tonfa Tactics: A Strategy for Total Defense. Ted Gambordella. (Illus.). 144p. (Orig.). 1985. 12.00 (ISBN 0-87364-324-0). Paladin Pr.

Tonga. (Let's Visit Places & Peoples - - Nations, Dependencies, & Sovereignties of the World Ser.). (Illus.). (gr. 5 up). 1989. 12.95 (ISBN 0-7910-0138-5). Chelsea Hse.

Tonga Pictorial... a Tapestry of Pride... Kupesi 'o Tonga.. Donna Gerstle & Helen Raitt. LC 74-75535. (Illus.). 100p. (Orig.). 1974. pap. 5.95 (ISBN 0-914488-02-3). Rand-Tofua.

Tongan Music. Richard Moyle. (Illus.). 256p. 1987. 49.95 (ISBN 1-86940-007-0). Oxford U Pr.

Tongan Myths & Tales. E. W. Gifford. (BMB). Repr. of 1924 ed. 28.00 (ISBN 0-527-02111-3, BMB, NO. 8). Kraus Repr.

Tongan Place Names. E. W. Gifford. (BMB). Repr. of 1923 ed. 34.00 (ISBN 0-527-02109-1, BMB, NO. 6). Kraus Repr.

Tongan Society. E. W. Gifford. (BMB). Repr. of 1929 ed. 64.00 (ISBN 0-527-02167-9, BMB, NO. 61). Kraus Repr.

Tongan Society at the Time of Captain Cook's Visits: Discussions with Her Majesty Queen Salote Tupou. Elizabeth Bott. 187p. 1983. pap. text ed. 15.00x (ISBN 0-8248-0864-9). UH Pr.

Tongass: Alaska's Vanishing Rain Forest. Robert Ketchum & Carey D. Ketchum. (Illus.). 112p. 1987. 30.00 (ISBN 0-89381-266-8). Aperture.

Tongefaesse aus dem Brunnen Unterm Stadion-Nordwall und im Suedost-Gebiet. Werner Gauer. (Olympische Forschungen: Vol. 8). (Illus.). 254p. 1975. pap. 47.20x (ISBN 3-11-004602-4). De Gruyter.

Tongue - Our Measure. Simo Ralevic. 62p. 1987. pap. 3.95 (ISBN 0-85151-507-X). Banner of Truth.

Tongue: A Creative Force. Charles Capps. 159p. (Orig.). 1977. pap. 3.50 (ISBN 0-89274-061-2). Harrison Hse.

Tongue & Thunder. David Cloutier. (Illus.). 64p. (Orig.). 1980. pap. 4.50 (ISBN 0-914278-32-0). Copper Beech.

Tongue-Cut Sparrow. Momoko Ishii. Tr. by Katherine Paterson. LC 86-29314. (Illus.). 40p. (ps-3). 1987. 13.95 (ISBN 0-525-67199-4, 01354-410). Lodestar Bks.

Tongue Dancing. Brian Swann. (Illus.). 56p. (gr. 7-12). 1984. 12.95g (ISBN 0-937672-12-2). Rowan Tree.

Tongue Diagnosis in Chinese Medicine. Giovanni Maciocia. LC 86-83024. (Illus.). 164p. 1987. text ed. 34.50 (ISBN 0-939616-04-1). Eastland.

Tongue in Check. Joseph Stowell. 132p. pap. 5.50 (ISBN 0-88207-293-5). Victor Bks.

Tongue in Cheek. Alexander A. Lawrence. LC 79-54272. 104p. 1979. bds. 8.50 (ISBN 0-87797-047-5). Cherokee.

Tongue of Angels: The Mary Marcy Reader. Ed. by Frederick C. Giffin. LC 87-42930. 192p. 1988. 26.50x (ISBN 0-941664-91-0). Susquehanna U Pr.

Tongue of the Prophets. Robert St. John. pap. 7.00 (ISBN 0-87980-166-2). Wilshire.

Tongue of the Prophets: The Life Story of Eliezer Ben Yehuda. Robert St. John. LC 77-97303. 377p. 1972. Repr. of 1952 ed. lib. bdg. 35.00x (ISBN 0-8371-2631-2, STTP). Greenwood.

Tongue Set Free: Remembrance of a European Childhood. Elias Canetti & Joachim Neugroschel. 268p. 1983. pap. 9.95 (ISBN 0-374-51802-5). FS&G.

Tongue Speaking: The History & Meaning of the Charismatic Experience. Morton Kelsey. 256p. 1981. pap. 8.95 (ISBN 0-8245-0073-3). Crossroad NY.

Tongue Thrust Correction. 4th ed. Jeanne M. Goldberger. LC 77-90374. 100p. 1978. pap. 5.95x (ISBN 0-8134-2006-7, 2006). Inter Print Pubs.

Tongue-Tied American: Confronting the Foreign Language Crisis. Paul Simon. 224p. 1980. 12.95 (ISBN 0-8264-0022-1). Continuum.

Tongue-Tied American: Confronting the U. S. Foreign Language Crisis. Paul Simon. 1988. pap. 10.95 (ISBN 0-317-66970-2). Crossroad NY.

Tongue-Tip Taste of Tao. Bhagwan Shree Rajneesh. Ed. by Ma Prem Maneesha. (Initiation Talks Ser.). (Illus.). 350p. 1981. 8.95 (ISBN 0-88050-158-8). Chidvilas Inc.

Tongue Twister Tales for "L", "R", & "S". Esther T. Barker. LC 74-75416. vi, 74p. 1974. pap. text ed. 3.95x (ISBN 0-8134-1640-X, 1640). Inter Print Pubs.

Tongues. J. D. Whitney. 1976. 10.00 (ISBN 0-685-79200-5); pap. 5.00 (ISBN 0-685-79201-3). Elizabeth Pr.

Tongues!? Spiros Zodhiates. (I Corinthians Ser.). (Illus.). 1974. pap. 6.95 (ISBN 0-89957-512-9). AMG Pubs.

Tongues & the Holy Spirit. Frank Pack. (Way of Life Ser: No. 127). (Orig.). 1972. pap. text ed. 3.95 (ISBN 0-89112-127-7). Abilene Christ U.

Tongues & Total Surrender. Fred Smolchuck. 32p. 1974. pap. 0.50 (ISBN 0-88243-823-9, 02-0823). Gospel Pub.

Tongues in Biblical Perspective. Charles R. Smith. pap. 4.95 (ISBN 0-88469-005-9). BMH Bks.

Tongues Like As of Fire. Robert C. Dalton. 128p. 1945. pap. 1.25 (ISBN 0-88243-619-8, 02-0619). Gospel Pub.

Tongues Movement. Lewis Bauman. 1979. pap. 1.00 (ISBN 0-88469-047-4). BMH Bks.

Tongues of Conscience. facsimile ed. Robert S. Hichens. LC 75-178440. (Short Story Index Reprint Ser.). Repr. of 1900 ed. 19.00 (ISBN 0-8369-4041-5). Ayer Co Pubs.

Tongues of Fallen Angels. Selden Rodman. LC 73-89485. (Illus.). 288p. 1974. 12.00 (ISBN 0-8112-0528-2); pap. 3.75 (ISBN 0-8112-0529-0, NDP373). New Directions.

Tongues of Fire. Peter Abrahams. 1985. pap. 3.95 (ISBN 0-671-46419-1). PB.

Tongues of Fire: A Bible of Sacred Scripyures of the Pagan World. Grace H. Turnbull. 32.50 (ISBN 0-405-10634-3). Ayer Co Pubs.

Tongues of Fire: An Anthology of Religious & Poetic Experience. Ed. by Karen Armstrong. 444p. 1986. 19.95 (ISBN 0-670-80878-4). Viking.

Tongues of Fire: An Anthology of Religious & Poetic Experience. Intro. by Karen Armstrong. 352p. 1987. pap. 7.95 (ISBN 0-14-058566-4). Penguin.

Tongues of Flame. Mary W. Brown. 1986. 15.95 (ISBN 0-525-24431-X, Pub. by Seymour Lawrence). Dutton.

Tongues of Flame. Mary W. Brown. 1987. pap. 5.95 (ISBN 0-671-64157-3). WSP.

Tongues of Flame. Tim Parks. 144p. 1987. Repr. of 1985 ed. 14.95 (ISBN 0-394-55299-7). Grove.

Tongues of Flame. Tim Parks. 1988. pap. 5.95 (ISBN 0-14-010612-X). Penguin.

Tongues of Italy, Prehistory & History. Ernst Pulgram. Repr. of 1958 ed. lib. bdg. 35.00x (ISBN 0-8371-2438-7, PUTI). Greenwood.

Tongues of Man. J. R. Firth. 1937. 27.50 (ISBN 0-8274-3639-4). R West.

Tongues of Men & Speech. J. R. Firth. LC 86-22837. (Languages & Language Learning Ser.). 223p. 1986. Repr. of 1964 ed. lib. bdg. 39.75x (ISBN 0-313-25275-0, FITO). Greenwood.

Tongues of Men: Hegel & Hamann on Religious Language & History. Stephen N. Dunning. LC 79-10729. (American Academy of Religion, Dissertation Ser.: No. 27). 1979. 14.00 (ISBN 0-89130-283-2, 010127); pap. 9.95 (ISBN 0-89130-302-2). Scholars Pr GA.

Tongues of Satan. Ed. by Richard P. Salbato. The Publican Staff. LC 86-83119. 224p. (Orig.). 1986. pap. text ed. 6.00 (ISBN 0-941427-01-3). JMJ Pub.

Tongues of the Monte. J. Frank Dobie. 319p. 1980. pap. 9.95 (ISBN 0-292-78035-4). U of Tex Pr.

Tongues on Fire. Joe Towne. 352p. 1987. 19.95 (ISBN 0-89962-572-X). Todd & Honeywell.

Tongues: The Answer to the Debate. Donald L. Barnett & Jeffrey P. McGregor. 299p. (Orig.). 1988. pap. 9.95 (ISBN 0-934287-24-4). Comm Chapel Pubns.

Tongues Then & Now. George W. Marston. 1983. pap. 3.95 (ISBN 0-87552-288-2). Presby & Reformed.

Tongues Untied. Dirg Aab-Richards et al. 95p. (Orig.). 1987. pap. 7.95 (ISBN 0-85449-053-1, Pub. by GMP England). Alyson Pubns.

Toni. Grace E. Donahue. 1986. 12.95 (ISBN 0-533-06732-4). Vantage.

Toni, Roi du Cirque. Guy Des Cars. (Illus.). 24p. 1977. 12.95 (ISBN 0-686-55661-5). French & Eur.

Tonia the Tree. Sandy Stryker. (Illus.). 32p. (gr. k-8). 1988. 13.95 (ISBN 0-911655-16-6). Advocacy Pr.

Tonibah & the Rainbow. Jack L. Crowder & Faith Hill. Tr. by Clara Tohtsonie & Joe Wilson. (Illus.). 32p. (Orig., Eng. & Navajo.). (gr. 7 up). 1986. pap. 6.95 (ISBN 0-9616589-1-6). Upper Strata.

Tonic Functions of Sensory Systems. Ed. by Bernice M. Wenzel & H. Philip Zeigler. (Annals of the New York Academy of Sciences: Vol. 290). 435p. 1977. 52.00x (ISBN 0-89072-036-3). NY Acad Sci.

Tonight Josephine: And Other Undiscovered Letters. Michael Green. 1982. 5.95 (ISBN 0-395-32510-2). HM.

Tonight on This Late Road. Christine Swanberg. (Illus.). 44p. 1984. pap. 3.00 (ISBN 0-942582-06-3). Erie St Pr.

Tonight the Ballet & Russian Ballets. Adrian Stokes. LC 82-1477. (Dance Ser.). 213p. 1982. Repr. of 1935 ed. lib. bdg. 39.50 (ISBN 0-306-76152-1). Da Capo.

Toning: The Creative Power of the Voice. rev. ed. Laurel E. Keyes. LC 73-86021. 128p. 1973. pap. 4.95 (ISBN 0-87516-176-6). DeVorss.

Tonio Kroger. Thomas Mann. Ed. by Elizabeth M. Wilkinson. (Blackwell's German Texts Ser.). 228p. 1968. pap. 9.95x (ISBN 0-631-01810-7). Basil Blackwell.

Tonio Kroger. Thomas Mann. Ed. by John A. Kelly. (Illus., Orig., Ger.). (gr. 10-12). 1931. pap. text ed. 13.50 (ISBN 0-13-925065-4). P-H.

Tonkawa, an Indian Language of Texas. Harry Hoijer. pap. 5.00 (ISBN 0-685-71708-9). J J Augustin.

Tonkawa People: A Tribal History From Earliest Times to 1893. Deborah L. Newlin. Ed. by Gale Richardson. (Museum Journal Ser.). (Illus.). 119p. pap. 5.00 (ISBN 0-911618-07-4). West Tex Mus.

Tonkin Gulf Yacht Club: U. S. Carrier Operations off Vietnam. Rene Francillon. (Illus.). 265p. 1988. 24.95 (ISBN 0-87021-696-1). Naval Inst Pr.

Tonmeister Technology: Recording Environments, Sound Sources, & Microphone Techniques. Date not set. price not set (ISBN 0-9617200-0-X). Temmer Enterps.

Tono-Bungay. H. G. Wells. LC 77-28027. 317p. 1978. 24.95x (ISBN 0-8032-4702-8); pap. 5.95x (ISBN 0-8032-9701-7, BB 669, Bison). U of Nebr Pr.

Tono Bungay. H. G. Wells. 19.95 (ISBN 0-89190-698-3, Pub. by Am Repr). Amereon Ltd.

Tonopah Nevada Silver Camp. Stanley W. Paher. (Illus.). 1978. pap. 2.95 (ISBN 0-913814-18-0). Nevada Pubns.

Tonos a Lo Divino Y a Lo Humano. Ed. by Rita Goldberg. (Serie B: Textos, XXIV). 202p. (Span.). 1981. 27.00 (ISBN 0-7293-0075-7, Pub. by Tamesis Bks Ltd). Longwood Pub Group.

Tonsils: Structure, Immunology & Biochemistry. Ed. by F. Antoni & M. Staub. 1978. cancelled 17.00 (ISBN 963-05-1562-8, Pub. by Akademiai Kaido Hungary). IPS.

Tontine: From the Reign of Louis XIV to the French Revolutionary Era. Robert M. Jennings & Andrew P. Trout. LC 82-81028. (S. S. Huebner Foundation Monographs: No. 12). 91p. (Orig.). 1982. pap. 14.95 (ISBN 0-918930-12-X). Huebner Foun Insur.

Tonton-le-Vonltigeur. Beatrix Potter. Tr. by Patrice Charvet & Veronique Canal. (Original Peter Rabbit Books in French). Orig. Title: Tale of Timmy Tiptoes. (Illus., Fr.). (gr. 3-7). 1978. 5.00 (ISBN 0-7232-2048-4). Warne.

Tony & Me. Alfred Slote. (gr. 3-5). 1983. pap. 1.75 (ISBN 0-380-00438-0, 52472-4, Camelot). Avon.

Tony & Me. Alfred Slote. LC 74-5182. 160p. (gr. 4-6). 1974. 11.25i (ISBN 0-397-31507-4, Lipp Jr Bks). HarpJ.

Tony Award. Ed. by Isabelle Stevenson. LC 74-28337. 1975. 10.00 (ISBN 0-405-06485-3). Ayer Co Pubs.

Tony Award: A Complete Listing of Winners & Nominees with a History of the American Theatre Wing. 3rd ed. Isabelle Stevenson. 192p. 1987. 14.95 (ISBN 0-517-56664-8). Crown.

Tony Award: A Complete Listing of Winners & Nominees with a History of the American Theatre Wing, 1947 to Present. Ed. by Isabelle Stevenson. 188p. 1985. 12.95 (ISBN 0-517-54238-2). Crown.

Tony Award Book: Four Decades of Great American Theater. Lee A. Morrow. (Illus.). 280p. 1987. 45.00 (ISBN 0-89659-771-7). Abbeville Pr.

Tony Benn: A Political Biography. Robert Jenkins. (Illus.). 300p. 1981. 12.95 (ISBN 0-906495-35-0). Writers & Readers.

Tony Berlant: Recent Work, 1982-1987. Josine I. Starrels & Peter Clothier. LC 87-80067. (Illus.). 32p. (Orig.). 1987. pap. 12.00 (ISBN 0-936429-08-9). LA Municipal Art.

Tony Dorsett: From Heisman to Super Bowl in One Year. Dick Conrad. LC 78-11378. (Sports Stars Ser.). (Illus.). 48p. (gr. 2-8). 1979. PLB 11.27 (ISBN 0-516-04305-6); pap. 2.95 (ISBN 0-516-44305-4). Childrens.

Tony Garnier: The Cite Industrielle. Dora Wiebenson. LC 79-78051. (Planning & Cities Ser). (Illus.). 1969. 7.95 (ISBN 0-8076-0515-8). Braziller.

Tony, Grammy, Emmy, Country: A Broadway, Television & Records Awards Reference. Compiled by Don Franks. LC 85-43577. 208p. 1986. lib. bdg. 25.95x (ISBN 0-89950-204-0). McFarland & Co.

Tony Lucadello's Diamonds in the Rough. David V. Hanneman. 1989. price not set (ISBN 0-89015-666-2). Eakin Pr.

Tony: Our Journey Together. Carolyn Koons. LC 83-48432. 224p. 1985. pap. 6.95 (ISBN 0-06-064764-7, RD 546, HarpR). Har-Row.

Tony Savala. Dorothy Hamilton. LC 75-171537. (Illus.). 104p. (gr. 4-9). 1972. pap. 3.95 (ISBN 0-8361-1674-7). Herald Pr.

Tony the Night Custodian. Steven Otfinoski. (People Working Today Ser.). (Illus.). 40p. (YA) (gr. 7-12). 1977. pap. text ed. 2.65 (ISBN 0-915510-21-9). Janus Bks.

Tony the Tuna. S. Kip Farrington. (gr. 4-5). 1976. 6.95 (ISBN 0-911660-25-9). Yankee Peddler.

Tony Valenti Story. Tony Valenti & Grazia P. Yonan. LC 80-83781. 160p. (Orig.). 1981. 2.50 (ISBN 0-88243-752-6, 02-0752). Gospel Pub.

Tonya. Pappy Boyington. 16.00 (ISBN 0-933458-01-0). J B Wilson.

Tony's: A Cookbook. George Fuermann. (Illus.). 276p. 1986. 21.95 (ISBN 0-940672-38-3). Shearer Pub.

Tony's Guide to Better Painting. Anthony Quartuccio. (Illus.). 48p. (Orig.). 1982. pap. text ed. 7.95 (ISBN 0-9606934-0-8). A Quartuccio.

Tony's Hard Work Day. Reissue. ed. Alan Arkin. LC 76-183161. (Illus.). 32p. (gr. k-3). 1988. 11.70i (ISBN 0-06-020137-5); PLB 11.89 (ISBN 0-06-020138-X). HarpJ.

Tony's Shapes Come Back. Anita Trabucco. 1988. 5.95 (ISBN 0-533-07889-X). Vantage.

Tony's Tummy. Lucile Jones. Ed. by Bobbie J. Van Dolson. 32p. (gr. k up). 1981. pap. 3.95 (ISBN 0-8280-0039-5). Review & Herald.

Too. Vinnie Robinson. 64p. 1985. 5.95 (ISBN 0-9610404-1-6). Mogul Bk.

Too Big. Holly Keller. LC 82-15653. (Illus.). 32p. (gr. k-3). 1983. 10.25 (ISBN 0-688-01998-6); PLB 10.88 (ISBN 0-688-01999-4). Greenwillow.

Too Big for the Bag. Beverly Amstutz. (Illus.). (gr. k-7). 1981. pap. 2.50x (ISBN 0-937836-05-2). Precious Res.

Too Big to Spank. Jay Kesler. LC 77-90580. 160p. 1978. pap. 5.95 (ISBN 0-8307-0623-2, 5409306). Regal.

Too Bizarro. Dan Piraro. (Illus.). 1988. pap. 5.95 (ISBN 0-87701-536-8). Chronicle Bks.

Too Bright to See. Linda Gregg. LC 80-67983. 67p. 1982. pap. 9.00. Graywolf.

Too Busy for God? Think Again! Louise D'Angelo. LC 81-52423. 120p. 1981. pap. 2.50 (ISBN 0-89555-166-7). TAN Bks Pubs.

Too Busy Not to Pray. Bill Hybels. 152p. (Orig.). 1988. pap. 6.95 (ISBN 0-8308-1256-3). Inter-Varsity.

Too Busy to Cook, Vol. 2. Ed. by Bon Appetit Magazine Editors. (Illus.). 224p. 1988. 19.95 (ISBN 0-89535-214-1). Knapp Pr.

Too Clever by Half or The Diary of a Scoundrel. Alexander Ostrovsky. Tr. by Rodney Ackland from Rus. (Old Vic Theatre Collection). 120p. (Orig.). 1988. pap. 7.95 (ISBN 1-55783-023-1). Applause Theatre Bk Pubs.

Too Close Apart. Jean G. Howard. LC 77-92190. (Illus., Ltd. ed. 550 trade, 35 deluxe). 1977. 7.50 (ISBN 0-930954-01-7); deluxe ed. 75.00 (ISBN 0-930954-02-5). Tidal Pr.

Too Close for Comfort. Brooke Hastings. 1987. pap. price not set (ISBN 0-373-08528-1). Harlequin Bks.

Too Close to the Edge. Susan Dunlap. 240p. 1987. 14.95 (ISBN 0-312-00198-3). St Martin.

Too Close, Too Soon. Jim Talley & Bobbie Reed. LC 82-2132. 160p. 1982. pap. 6.95 (ISBN 0-8407-5801-4). Nelson.

Too Cool to Get Married. David Seeley. LC 88-45057. 192p. 1988. 15.95 (ISBN 0-06-015944-8, HarpT). Har-Row.

Too Dark! Susanna Gretz. LC 85-12999. (Illus.). 10p. (ps). 1986. bds. 2.95 (ISBN 0-02-737410-6, Four Winds). Macmillan.

Too Deep for Words: Rediscovering Lectio Divina. Thelma Hall. 1988. pap. 4.95 (ISBN 0-8091-2959-0). Paulist Pr.

Too Deep Then. David Stone. 160p. 1987. 15.95 (ISBN 0-7453-0140-1, Pub. by Allison & Busby England). Schocken.

Too Early Frost: A Father's Account of Losing a Son. Gerald Oosterveen. 160p. 1988. pap. 8.95 (ISBN 0-310-37771-4, 12419P). Zondervan.

Too Far from Home. T. N. Rogers. LC 87-25514. 128p. (Orig.). 1988. pap. 6.95 (ISBN 0-8262-0671-9). U of Mo Pr.

Too Far to Go. John Updike. 1982. pap. 2.75 (ISBN 0-449-20016-7, Crest). Fawcett.

Too Fat to Fly. Adelaide Holl. LC 72-12849. (Garrard Venture Ser.). (Illus.). 40p. (gr. k-3). 1973. PLB 6.69 (ISBN 0-8116-6731-6); pap. 1.19 (9028). Garrard.

Too Fat? Too Thin? Do You Have a Choice? Caroline Arnold. LC 83-23841. 112p. (gr. 5 up). 1984. PLB 10.88 (ISBN 0-688-02780-6); pap. 5.25 (ISBN 0-688-02779-2). Morrow.

Too Few Happy Endings: The Dilemma of the Humane Societies. Margaret Poynter. LC 81-2239. (Illus.). 144p. (gr. 4 up). 1981. 9.95 (ISBN 0-689-30864-7, Atheneum Childrens Bks). Macmillan.

Too Few Tomorrows: Urban Appalachians in the 1980's. Ed. by William W. Philliber & Phillip J. Obermiller. LC 86-28816. 170p. (Orig.). 1987. pap. 8.95. Appalach Consortium.

Too Funny for Words! Disney's Greatest Sight Gags. Frank Thomas & Ollie Johnston. (Illus.). 224p. 1987. 39.95 (ISBN 0-89659-747-4). Abbeville Pr.

Too Funny to Be President: Notes from the Life of a Politician. Morris Udall. 224p. 1988. 17.95 (ISBN 0-8050-0593-5). H Holt & Co.

Too Good to Be Entirely True. Donna Wyszomierski. 16p. (Orig.). 1979. pap. 3.00 (ISBN 0-917061-01-2). Top Stories.

Too Good to Be True. Francine Pascal. (Sweet Valley High Ser.: No. 11). 592p. (Orig.). (gr. 7 up). 1984. pap. 2.75 (ISBN 0-553-26824-4). Bantam.

Too Good to Eat! The Art of Dough Sculpture. Karen Mergeler. LC 72-95386. (Illus.). 84p. 1972. pap. 6.95 (ISBN 0-685-55498-8). Folk Art.

Too Great Expectations: The Academic Outlook of Young Children. Doris R. Entwisle & Leslie A. Hayduk. LC 77-23344. (Illus.). 240p. 1978. text ed. 30.00x (ISBN 0-8018-1986-5). Johns Hopkins.

Too Hot, & Other Maine Stories. Fred Bonnie. 208p. (Orig.). 1987. 16.95 (ISBN 0-937966-21-5); pap. 9.95 (ISBN 0-937966-22-3). Dog Ear.

Too Hot in Potzburg. Seymour Fleishman. LC 81-11498. (Illus.). 32p. (ps-3). 1981. PLB 10.75 (ISBN 0-8075-8024-4). A Whitman.

Too Hot to Handle. Linda Davidson. (Endless Summer Ser.: No. 2). 1988. pap. 2.95 (ISBN 0-8041-0242-2, Pub. by Ivy). Ballantine.

Too Hot to Handle. Eileen Goudge. (Senior Ser.: No. 6). 192p. (gr. 7 up). pap. 2.25 (ISBN 0-440-98812-8, YB). Dell.

Too Hot to Handle. Anne Hampson. (Harlequin Presents Ser.). 192p. 1982. pap. 1.75 (ISBN 0-373-10516-9). Harlequin Bks.

Too Hot to Handle? Social & Policy Issues in the Management of Radioactive Wastes. Ed. by Charles A. Walker et al. LC 82-20000. (Fastback Ser.: No. 26). 240p. 1983. text ed. 25.00t (ISBN 0-300-02899-7); pap. 8.95x (ISBN 0-300-02993-4). Yale U Pr.

Too Hot to Hoot: Funny Palindrome Riddles. Marvin Terban. LC 84-14942. (Illus.). 64p. (gr. 2-5). 1985. 11.95 (ISBN 0-89919-319-6, Pub. by Clarion); pap. 4.95 (ISBN 0-89919-320-X). Ticknor & Fields.

Too Late. Leon Stewart. pap. 5.95 (ISBN 0-911866-66-3). Advocate.

Too Late American Boyhood Blues. Frederick Busch. LC 83-48895. 288p. 1984. 15.95 (ISBN 0-87923-511-X). Godine.

Too Late American Boyhood Blues. Frederick Busch. 1986. pap. 6.95 (ISBN 0-452-25757-3, Plume). NAL.

Too Late for Love. (Orig.). 1986. pap. 2.50 (ISBN 0-449-13005-3, Pub. by Girls Only). Ballantine.

Too Late the Phalarope. Alan Paton. 1985. pap. 4.50 rack size (ISBN 0-684-18500-8, ScribT). Scribner.

Too Late the Phalarope. Alan Paton. 18.95 (ISBN 0-89190-392-5, Pub. by Am Repr). Amereon Ltd.

Too Late to Be Good. Craig Jones. 304p. (Orig.). 1986. pap. 3.95 (ISBN 0-345-32130-8). Ballantine.

Too Late to Die. Bill Crider. 192p. 1986. 14.95 (ISBN 0-8027-5650-6). Walker & Co.

Too Late to Say Good-Bye: My Experience with Aging Parents. Ethel McIndoo. 64p. (Orig.). 1988. pap. 3.95 (ISBN 0-936625-28-7, New Hope AL). Womans Mission Union.

Too Late to Wait. Franklin Greenwald. (Aphorisms Trilogy Ser.: Vol. 3). (Illus.). 28p. 1985. pap. 4.95 (ISBN 0-936779-02-0). No Secrets Pr.

Too Little, Too Late: Dealing with the Health Needs of Women in Poverty. Ed. by Cesar A. Perales & Lauren S. Young. LC 88-908. (Women & Health Ser.: Vol. 12, Nos. 3-4). 260p. 1988. text ed. 14.95 (ISBN 0-918393-50-7). Harrington Pk.

Too Long a Sacrifice. Mildred D. Broxon. LC 84-424. (Illus.). 226p. 1984. ltd., signed collector's ed. 35.00 (ISBN 0-312-94433-0). Bluejay Bks.

Too Long a Sacrifice: Life & Death in Northern Ireland Since 1969. Jack Holland. LC 80-27267. (Illus.). 240p. 1981. 10.95 (ISBN 0-396-07934-2). Dodd.

Too Long a Sacrifice: Life & Death in Northern Ireland since 1969. Jack Holland. 1982. pap. 7.95 (ISBN 0-14-006134-7). Penguin.

Too Long in the West. Balachandra Rajan. 1961. pap. 2.00 (ISBN 0-88253-175-1). Ind-US Inc.

Too Long Silent: Japanese Americans Speak Out. Roger W. Axford. 128p. (Orig.). 1986. pap. 9.95 (ISBN 0-939644-19-3, TLS). Media Prods & Mktg.

Too-Long Trunk. Regina Sauro. (Illus.). (ps-2). 4.25 (ISBN 0-8313-0085-X). Lantern.

Too Many Are Hungry What Can I Do? Bonnie Jorgenson & Arthur Simon. (Illus.). 32p. (Orig.). 1985. pap. 2.00 (ISBN 0-934134-17-0). Sheed & Ward MO.

Too Many Babas. Carolyn Croll. LC 78-22474. (Harper I Can Read Bks.). (Illus.). 64p. (gr. k-3). 1979. PLB 10.89 (ISBN 0-06-021384-1). HarpJ.

Too Many Balloons. Catherine Matthias. LC 81-15520. (Rookie Readers Ser.). (Illus.). 32p. (ps-2). 1982. PLB 9.93 (ISBN 0-516-03633-5); pap. text ed. 2.50 (ISBN 0-516-43633-3). Childrens.

Too Many Books. Caroline F. Bauer. (Picture Puffins Ser.). (Illus.). 32p. (ps-3). 1986. pap. 3.95 (ISBN 0-14-050632-2, Puffin). Penguin.

Too Many Books! Caroline F. Bauer. 1986. 11.95 (ISBN 0-670-81130-0). Viking.

Too Many Boys. Celia Dickenson. (Loveswept Ser.: No. 71). 160p. (Orig.) (gr. 5-6). 1984. pap. 2.50 (ISBN 0-553-26615-2). Bantam.

Too Many Brothers: The Story of Joseph. Pat Floyd. (Little Lamb Christian Storybooks Ser.). (Illus.). 24p. (gr. k-2). 1987. pap. 6.95 (ISBN 0-939697-41-6). Graded Pr.

Too Many Bunnies. Elspeth C. Murphy. LC 87-70609. (Brenda Learns about God Ser.). 1988. pap. 3.95 (ISBN 1-55513-247-2, Chariot Bks). Cook.

Too Many Clients. Rex Stout. 192p. 1986. pap. 2.95 (ISBN 0-553-25423-5). Bantam.

Too Many Cooks. Rex Stout. LC 75-46002. (Crime Fiction Ser.). 1976. Repr. of 1938 ed. lib. bdg. 21.00 (ISBN 0-8240-2394-3). Garland Pub.

Too Many Cousins. Douglas G. Browne. (Detective Stories Ser.). 192p. 1985. pap. 3.95 (ISBN 0-486-24774-0). Dover.

Too Many Eggs. M. Christina Butler. (Illus.). (gr. k-12). 1988. 13.95 (ISBN 0-87923-741-4). Godine.

Too Many Enemies. William Haggard. 15.95 (ISBN 0-88411-668-9, Pub. by Aeonian Pr). Amereon Ltd.

Too Many Ghosts. Paul Gallico. 288p. 1988. pap. 5.95 (ISBN 0-930330-80-3). Intl Polygonics.

Too Many Husbands. Charlotte Hughes. (Loveswept Ser.: No. 159). 192p. (Orig.). 1986. pap. 2.50 (ISBN 0-553-21792-5). Bantam.

Too Many Magicians. Randall Garrett. 352p. 1983. pap. 2.95 (ISBN 0-441-81698-3). Ace Bks.

Too Many Midnights. Rod McKuen. 1981. pap. 2.95 (ISBN 0-671-43111-0). PB.

Too Many Monsters. Susan Meddaugh. (Illus.). (gr. k-3). 1982. PLB 8.95 (ISBN 0-395-31862-9). HM.

Too Many Murphys. Colleen O'Shaughnessy McKenna. 144p. (gr. 3-7). Date not set. 10.95 (ISBN 0-590-41731-2, Pub. by Scholastic Hardcover). Scholastic Inc.

Too Many Pastors? The State of the Clergy Job Market. Jackson Carroll & Robert Wilson. LC 80-16037. 1980. pap. 6.95 (ISBN 0-8298-0405-6). Pilgrim NY.

Too Many Patients? A Study of the Economy of Time & Standards of Care in General Practice. John Butler & Michael Calnan. 197p. 1988. text ed. 37.00 (ISBN 0-566-05556-2, Pub. by Gower Pub England). Gower Pub Co.

Too Many Pebbles. Ted Sharpe. 1982. 15.00x (ISBN 0-906660-29-7, Pub. by New Playwrights Network). State Mutual Bk.

Too Many People? A Problem in Values. Christopher Derrick. LC 85-60469. 116p. (Orig.). 1986. pap. 6.95 (ISBN 0-89870-071-X, 85-60469). Ignatius Pr.

Too Many People & Other Reflections. facs. ed. J. B. Priestley. LC 71-128289. (Essay Index Reprint Ser). 1928. 19.00 (ISBN 0-8369-2016-3). Ayer Co Pubs.

Too Many People? Answers & Hope for the Human Family. Laurie Tychsen. 46p. (Orig.). 1986. pap. 3.25 (ISBN 0-937779-03-2). Greenlawn Pr.

Too Many Promises: The Uncertain Future of Social Security. Michael J. Boskin. 175p. 1986. 22.50 (ISBN 0-87094-779-6). Dow Jones-Irwin.

Too Many Sargeants. Mort Walker. (Beetle Bailey Ser.). (Illus.). 48p. pap. 4.95 (ISBN 0-917201-01-9). Dargaud Pub.

Too Many Schools of Education? Too Little Scholarship? Richard Wisniewski. (SPE Monograph Ser.). 1983. 4.50 (ISBN 0-933669-19-4). Soc Profs Ed.

Too Many Songs by Tom Lehrer with Not Enough Pictures by Ronald Searle. Tom Lehrer. (Illus.). 1981. pap. 10.95 (ISBN 0-394-74930-8). Pantheon.

Too Many Tomatoes, Squash, Beans, & Other Good Things: A Cookbook for When Your Garden Explodes. Lois M. Burrows & Laura G. Myers. LC 75-34581. 288p. 1976. 16.45i (ISBN 0-06-013132-2, HarpT). Har-Row.

Too Many Tomatoes...Squash, Beans, & Other Good Things: A Cookbook for When Your Garden Explodes. Lois M. Burrows & Laura G. Myers. LC 75-34581. 1980. pap. 10.95 (ISBN 0-06-090765-7, CN 765, PL). Har-Row.

Too Many, Too Long: Sudan's Twenty-Year Refugee Dilemma. John R. Rogge. LC 85-2058. (Illus.). 214p. 1985. 34.95x (ISBN 0-8476-7412-6, Rowman & Allanheld). Rowman.

Too Many Traitors. Franklin W. Dixon. (Hardy Boys Casefiles Ser.: No. 14). 160p. (Orig.). (gr. 7 up). 1988. pap. 2.75 (ISBN 0-671-64460-2). Archway.

Too Many Women? The Sex Ratio Question. Marcia Guttentag & Paul F. Secord. 336p. 1983. 32.50 (ISBN 0-8039-1918-2); pap. 16.95 (ISBN 0-8039-1919-0). Sage.

Too Much Alone. 2nd ed. Richard Gillman. LC 75-179831. (New Poetry Series). Repr. of 1965 ed. 16.00 (ISBN 0-404-56031-8). AMS Pr.

Too Much & Too Little: Waste & the World Economy. Douglas Dowd. (Institute for Policy Studies). 128p. 1989. 29.95 (ISBN 0-8133-0809-7); pap. 12.95 (ISBN 0-8133-0810-0). Westview.

Too Much: Art & Society in the Sixties, 1960-75. Robert Hewison. (Illus.). 368p. 1987. 27.95 (ISBN 0-19-520538-3). Oxford U Pr.

Too Much Flesh & Jabez. Coleman Dowell. LC 86-73236. 160p. 1987. pap. 8.00 (ISBN 0-916583-21-X). Dalkey Arch.

Too Much Garbage. Patricia Lauber. LC 74-8455. (Good Earth Ser.). (Illus.). 64p. (gr. 2-6). 1974. PLB 7.22 (ISBN 0-8116-6102-4). Garrard.

Too Much Government. Charles E. Wood. 59.95 (ISBN 0-8490-1222-8). Gordon Pr.

Too Much Holly, Not Enough Holy? Searching for Christmas. Patricia Wilson. 144p. (Orig.). 1987. pap. 6.95 (ISBN 0-8358-0566-2). Upper Room.

Too Much in Love. Brisco. (gr. 7 up). 1980. pap. 1.95 (ISBN 0-590-32199-4, Wishing Star Bks). Scholastic Inc.

Too Much in Love. Francine Pascal. (Sweet Valley High Ser.: No. 22). 160p. (Orig.). 1985. pap. 2.75 (ISBN 0-553-26745-0). Bantam.

Too Much Invested to Quit. Allan I. Teger et al. (Illus.). 1980. 29.50 (ISBN 0-08-022995-6). Pergamon.

Too Much Is Never Enough. William Evans. Ed. by James Jenkins. (Illus.). 153p. (Orig.). 1987. pap. 22.50 (ISBN 0-9619258-0-9). Clearwtr Pools Pub Co.

Too Much Is Not Enough. Orson Bean. 192p. 1988. 14.95 (ISBN 0-8184-0465-5). Lyle Stuart.

Too Much Is Not Enough. 1985. 40.00 (ISBN 0-932455-04-2). Henderikse.

Too Much Magic. Betsy Sterman & Samuel Sterman. LC 85-45861. (Illus.). 160p. (gr. 3-7). 1987. 11.70i (ISBN 0-397-32186-4, Lipp Jr Bks); PLB 11.89 (ISBN 0-397-32187-2). HarpJ.

Too Much Magic. Betsy Sterman & Samuel Sterman. (gr. 8-12). 1987. 11.95 (ISBN 0-317-57066-8). Lippincott.

Too Much Money...? Gordon Pepper & Geoffrey Wood. (Hobart Paper: No. 68). 1977. pap. 4.25 technical (ISBN 0-255-36083-5). Transatl Arts.

Too Much Noise. Ann McGovern. (gr. k-3). 1967. PLB 13.95 (ISBN 0-395-18110-0). HM.

Too Much Noise. Ann McGovern. (Illus.). 48p. (gr. k-3). pap. 2.25 (ISBN 0-317-69684-X). Scholastic Inc.

Too Much of a Good Thing. Don Carroll. 1982. 15.00x (ISBN 0-906660-24-6, Pub. by New Playwrights Network). State Mutual Bk.

Too Much of a Good Thing. John Sparrow. LC 77-6389. 1977. 9.50x (ISBN 0-226-76848-1); pap. 2.95x (ISBN 0-226-76850-3, Phoen). U of Chicago Pr.

Too Much of Everything: A Plan for Living Better Without Wealth or Excessive Material Possessions. Charles L. Mauch. LC 83-62202. 214p. (Orig.). 1984. pap. 5.95 (ISBN 0-318-00450-X). Moderation Pr.

Tools for the Electrical Trade. Richard Hunter. LC 85-702734. (Orig.). 1985. wkbk. 6.00 (ISBN 0-8064-0327-6, 819); audio visual pkg. 279.00 (ISBN 0-8064-0328-4). Bergwall.

Tools for the Simulation Profession (ESC '87) 1987. 16.00 (ISBN 0-911801-17-0). Soc Computer Sim.

Tools for the Simulation Protession (ESC 1988, Orlando) Date not set. 28.00 (ISBN 0-911801-36-7). Soc Computer Sim.

Tools for the Soft Path. International Project for Soft Energy Paths Staff & Jim Harding. 1982. pap. 11.95 (ISBN 0-913890-53-7); 25.00 (ISBN 0-913890-52-9). Friends of Earth.

Tools for the Soft Path. The International Project for Soft Energy Paths Network. (Illus.). 288p. (Orig.). 1982. pap. 11.95. Brick Hse Pub.

Tools for the Trade: Translating & the Computer 5, 1983 Conference Proceedings, 5th International, November 10-11, 1983. Ed. by Veronica Lawson. 272p. 1985. 31.50 (ISBN 0-85142-180-6). Learned Info.

Tools for the Trades & Crafts. Kenneth D. Roberts. 1976. 25.00 (ISBN 0-913602-18-3). K Roberts.

Tools for Theological Research. 8th, rev. ed. Ed. by John L. Sayre & Roberta Hamburger. 122p. 1988. pap. write for info. (ISBN 0-912832-24-X). Seminary Pr.

Tools for Thinking & Problem Solving. Moshe F. Rubinstein. (Illus.). 416p. 1986. text ed. 40.00 (ISBN 0-13-925140-5). P-H.

Tools for Thought: The History & Future of Mind-Extending Technology. Howard Rheingold. (Illus.). 320p. 1986. pap. 9.95 (ISBN 0-13-925108-1). P-H.

Tools for Thought: The People & Ideas Behind the Next Computer Revolution. Howard Rheingold. LC 85-1986. (Illus.). 335p. 1985. 17.95 (ISBN 0-671-49292-6). S&S.

Tools for Time Management: Time-Saving Tools for Managing Your Life. rev. ed. Edward R. Dayton. 224p. 1983. pap. 8.95 (ISBN 0-310-23221-X, 10675P). Zondervan.

Tools in the Learning Trade. Barbara C. Bell. LC 83-15105. 192p. 1984. pap. 8.95 (ISBN 0-8108-1743-8). Scarecrow.

Tools in the Learning Trade: A Guide to Eight Indispensable Tools for College Students. Barbara C. Bell. LC 83-15105. 192p. 1984. text ed. 15.00 (ISBN 0-8108-1655-5). Scarecrow.

Tools, Methods & Languages for Scientific & Engineering Computation. Ford et al. 1984. 89.50 (ISBN 0-444-87570-0). Elsevier.

Tools of Biochemistry. 2nd ed. Cooper. 1988. write for info. (ISBN 0-471-82358-9). Wiley.

Tools of Biochemistry. Terrance C. Cooper. LC 76-30910. 423p. 1977. 36.95 (ISBN 0-471-17116-6, Pub. by Wiley-Interscience). Wiley.

Tools of Empire: Technology & European Imperialism in the Nineteenth Century. Daniel R. Headrick. 1981. pap. text ed. 9.95x (ISBN 0-19-502832-5). Oxford U Pr.

Tools of Government. Christopher C. Hood. 192p. (Orig.). 1986. pap. text ed. 12.95x (ISBN 0-934540-52-7). Chatham Hse Pubs.

Tools of Jazz. Steven M. Schenkel. (Illus.). 144p. 1983. pap. 18.95 (ISBN 0-13-925172-3). P-H.

Tools of Learning: A Storybook Dictionary. K. R. Jones. LC 84-91385. 593p. 1986. 17.95 (ISBN 0-533-06468-6). Vantage.

Tools of My Trade: Annotated Books in Jack London's Library. David M. Hamilton. LC 84-40323. (Illus.). 350p. 1986. 25.00x (ISBN 0-295-96157-0). U of Wash Pr.

Tools of Our Trade. American Machinist Magazine Staff. LC 82-7773. 1982. text ed. 39.50 (ISBN 0-07-001547-3). McGraw.

Tools of Radio Astronomy. K. Rohlfs. (Astronomy & Astrophysics Library). (Illus.). xii, 319p. 1986. 62.00 (ISBN 0-387-16188-0). Springer-Verlag.

Tools of Science. Jean Stangl. (Illus.). 1987. 14.95 (ISBN 0-396-08965-8); pap. 9.95 (ISBN 0-396-08966-6). Dodd.

Tools of Social Science. John Madge. Ed. by Robin W. Winks. LC 83-49160. (History & Historiography Ser.). 339p. 1985. lib. bdg. 30.00 (ISBN 0-8240-6369-4). Garland Pub.

Tools of the Mind. V. Stibic. 300p. 1982. 39.25 (ISBN 0-444-86444-X, I-258-82, North-Holland). Elsevier.

Tools of the Trade. new ed. R. Bruce McQuigg. (gr. 7-12). 1979. pap. 6.00 (ISBN 0-88210-096-3). Natl Assn Principals.

Tools of the Trade. 8p. pap. 4.95 (ISBN 0-911703-04-7). CDS Assocs.

Tools of Their Trade: The Book of Professional Fiascos. Hilary MacLeod & Robin Boden. (Illus.). 144p. 1986. pap. 9.95 (ISBN 0-920792-66-9). Eden Pr.

Tools of Thought: The Practical Foundations of Formal Reasoning. Peter Barnett. 310p. 1981. 18.95x (ISBN 0-87073-655-8); pap. text ed. 11.95 (ISBN 0-87073-656-6). Schenkman Bks Inc.

Tools of War. Edgar Doleman. Ed. by Paul Dreyfus. LC 84-72888. (Vietnam Experience Ser.: Vol. XIII). (Illus.). 176p. 1984. 16.95 (ISBN 0-939526-13-1). Boston Pub Co.

Tools of War: Technology in Vietnam, 1965-1973. Ed. by Boston Publishing Company Staff & E. Doleman. (Illus.). 192p. 1985. write for info. (ISBN 0-201-11269-8). Addison-Wesley.

Tools, Skills & Business of Radio. John Hitchcock. (Illus.). 70p. 1987. pap. text ed. 9.95 (ISBN 0-943987-01-6). Origin Co.

Tools, Targets, & Troopers: The History of the Frankford Arsenal. James Zupan. 23.95 (ISBN 0-8488-0036-2, Pub. by J M C & Co). Amereon Ltd.

Tools That Started the Twentieth Century. Jene Lyon. LC 74-77922. (Illus.). 1976. 10.95 (ISBN 0-89016-008-2); pap. 6.95 (ISBN 0-89016-009-0). Lightning Tree.

Toone, Tune & Toon of America: A Family History. Lavern Toone. (Illus.). 450p. (Orig.). 1987. pap. 19.95 (ISBN 1-55618-017-9). Brunswick Pub.

Toons for Our Times: A Bloom County Book. Berke Breathed. (Orig.). 1984. pap. 7.95 (ISBN 0-316-10709-3). Little.

Toony & the Midnight Monster. Ruth Brook. LC 86-30739. (Illus.). 32p. (gr. k-3). 1987. lib. bdg. 10.89 (ISBN 0-8167-0910-6); pap. text ed. 2.95 (ISBN 0-8167-0911-4). Troll Assocs.

Toot! Taro Gomi. LC 85-32092. (Illus.). 32p. (ps-k). 1986. 11.75 (ISBN 0-688-06420-5, Morrow Junior Books); lib. bdg. 11.88 (ISBN 0-688-06421-3). Morrow.

Toot-Toot. Illus. by Carol Braken & Nina Barbaresi. (Busy Bubble Bks.). (Illus.). (ps). 2.95 (ISBN 0-671-47667-X, Little Simon). S&S.

Toot! Toot! Steven Kroll. LC 82-9356. (Illus.). 32p. (ps-3). 1983. reinforced binding 12.95 (ISBN 0-8234-0471-4). Holiday.

Toot Toot Tootsie Goodbye. Tootsie Ray. (Illus.). 128p. 1985. Cancelled (ISBN 0-89962-430-8). Todd & Honeywell.

Tooth & Claw. Gabrielle Lord. 160p. 1983. 12.95 (ISBN 0-8149-0874-8). Vanguard.

Tooth & Claw. (Phoenix Force Ser.: No. 20). Date not set. pap. 2.25 (Pub. by Worldwide). Harlequin Bks.

Tooth Book. Theo. LeSieg. LC 80-28320. (Bright & Early Ser.: No. 25). (Illus.). 48p. (ps-1). 1981. 5.95 (ISBN 0-394-84825-X, XBYR); lib. bdg. 6.99 (ISBN 0-394-94825-4). Random.

Tooth Book. Alan Nourse. (gr. 6up). 1977. 6.95 (ISBN 0-679-20376-1). McKay.

Tooth Chicken. 4 copies 5.00 (ISBN 0-934510-24-5, W013). Am Dental.

Tooth-Coloured Filling Materials in Clinical Practice. 2nd ed. L. W. Deubert & C. B. Jenkins. (Dental Practitioner Handbook Ser.: No. 16). (Illus.). 156p. 1982. pap. text ed. 22.00 (ISBN 0-7236-0628-5). PSG Pub Co.

Tooth Development & Caries, 2 vols, Vols. I & II. F. C. Driessens & J. H. Woltgens. 1986. Vol. I, 192 pgs. 2 vol. set 175.00 (ISBN 0-8493-6500-7). Vol. II, 224 pgs. CRC Pr.

Tooth Fairy. Sharon Peters. LC 81-5100. (Illus.). 32p. (gr. k-2). 1981. PLB 9.89 (ISBN 0-89375-519-2); pap. 2.95 (ISBN 0-89375-520-6). Troll Assocs.

Tooth Fairy Legend. Frank McAllister & Fran McAllister. LC 76-9595. (gr. k-4). 1976. 9.95 (ISBN 0-916864-01-4). Block.

Tooth for a Tooth: Selected Poems of Juan Larrea (1925-1932) Intro. by & tr. by David Bary. LC 86-28093. 142p. 1987. lib. bdg. 17.75 (ISBN 0-8191-5753-8). U Pr of Amer.

Tooth for the Tooth Fairy. Louise Gunther. LC 77-16422. (For Real Ser.). (Illus.). 32p. (gr. k-6). 1978. PLB 6.69 (ISBN 0-8116-4308-5). Garrard.

Tooth Mutilations & Dentistry in Pre-Columbian Mexico. S. Fastlicht. LC 74-25143. 1976. text ed. cancelled (ISBN 0-88474-020-X). U of S Cal Pr.

Tooth Mutilations & Dentistry in Pre-Columbian Mexico. Samuel Fastlicht. (Illus.). 152p. 1976. 68.00 (ISBN 0-931386-79-9). Quint Pub Co.

Tooth Survival Book. (Illus.). 1977. 5.00 (ISBN 0-685-57765-1). Am Dental.

Tooth Trip. Eva Eriksson. LC 84-28477. (Victor & Rosalie Bks.). (Illus.). 32p. (ps-3). 1985. PLB 8.95 (ISBN 0-87614-236-6). Carolrhoda Bks.

Tooth Trip. Thomas McGuire. (Illus.). 1972. pap. 6.95 (ISBN 0-394-70793-1). Random.

Tooth Witch. Nurit Karlin. LC 84-48495. (Illus.). 32p. (ps-2). 1985. 11.70i (ISBN 0-397-32119-8, Lipp Jr Bks); PLB 11.89g (ISBN 0-397-32120-1). HarpJ.

Tooth Witch. Nurit Karlin. LC 84-62553. (Trophy Picture Bks.). (Illus.). 32p. (gr. k-2). 1985. pap. 3.95 (ISBN 0-06-443079-0, Trophy). HarpJ.

Toothed World: Poems by Cori Adler. Cori Adler. Ed. & intro. by Eliza M. Young. 30p. (Orig.). Date not set. pap. 6.00 (ISBN 0-933865-15-5, 70968). Doris Pubns.

Toothing Stones: Rethinking the Political. Ed. by Robert Meagher. LC 75-189197. 289p. 1972. 12.95x (ISBN 0-8040-0566-4, Pub by Swallow). Ohio U Pr.

Toothpaste & Peanut Butter. Terry Moore. Ed. by Herb Bryce. (Illus.). 140p. (Orig.). 1987. pap. 9.95 (ISBN 0-88839-207-9). Hancock House.

Toothpaste Millionaire. Jean Merrill. LC 73-22055. (Illus.). 96p. (gr. 2-5). 1974. PLB 9.95 (ISBN 0-395-18511-4). HM.

Toothpick. Kenneth Ethridge. (YA) (gr. 7 up). Date not set. pap. 2.50. Troll Assocs.

Toothpick. Kenneth E. Ethridge. LC 85-42883. 128p. (YA) (gr. 7 up). 1985. 11.95 (ISBN 0-8234-0585-0). Holiday.

Toothpick Building Illustrated. Katrina Davis. (Illus.). 48p. (Orig.). 1980. pap. 3.95 (ISBN 0-937242-04-7). Scandia Pubs.

Toothpick House. Lee Lynch. LC 83-4093. 240p. (Orig.). 1983. pap. 8.95 (ISBN 0-930044-45-2). Naiad Pr.

Toots in Solitude. John Yount. LC 83-13802. 224p. 1983. 13.95 (ISBN 0-312-80904-2, Pub. by Marek). St Martin.

Toots in Solitude. John Yount. 192p. 1985. pap. 5.95 (ISBN 0-312-80905-0, Pub. by Marek). St Martin.

Tootsie Tanner, Why Don't You Talk? An Abby Jones, Junior Detective, Mystery. Patricia R. Giff. LC 86-32910. (Illus.). 144p. (gr. 4-7). 1987. pap. 13.95 (ISBN 0-385-29579-0). Delacorte.

Tootsietoys: World's First Diecast Models. James Wieland & Edward Force. LC 79-22376. (Illus.). 101p. 1980. pap. 15.00 (ISBN 0-87938-065-9). Motorbooks Intl.

Top & Bottom see Opposites.

Top & the Ball. Jon Erickson. LC 87-42584. (Andersen Fairy Tales Ser.). (Illus.). 32p. (gr. 2-4). 1987. PLB 9.95 (ISBN 1-55532-318-9). Stevens Inc.

Top Country & Western Records, Nineteen Seventy-Two to Nineteen Seventy-Three. new ed. Joel Whitburn. (Record Research Ser.). (Orig.). 1974. pap. text ed. 10.00 (ISBN 0-89820-016-4). Record Research.

Top Country & Western Records, 1974. Joel Whitburn. 40p. (Orig.). 1975. pap. text ed. 10.00 (ISBN 0-89820-017-2). Record Research.

Top Country & Western Records, 1975. Joel Whitburn. 40p. (Orig.). 1976. pap. text ed. 10.00 (ISBN 0-89820-018-0). Record Research.

Top Country & Western Records, 1977. Joel Whitburn. 40p. (Orig.). 1978. pap. text ed. 10.00 (ISBN 0-89820-020-2). Record Research.

Top Country & Western, 1978. new ed. Joel Whitburn. (Record Research Ser.). (Orig.). 1979. pap. text ed. 10.00 (ISBN 0-89820-033-4). Record Research.

Top Country & Western, 1979. Joel Whitburn. (Record Research Ser.). 46p. (Orig.). 1980. pap. text ed. 10.00 (ISBN 0-89820-040-7). Record Research.

Top Country & Western, 1980. Joel Whitburn. (Record Research Ser.). (Illus.). 49p. (Orig.). (YA) (gr. 8 up). 1981. pap. 10.00 (ISBN 0-89820-045-8). Record Research.

Top Cover for America: The Air Force in Alaska, 1920-1983. John H. Cloe & Michael Monaghan. LC 84-60821. (Illus.). 272p. 1984. pap. 13.95 (ISBN 0-933126-47-6). Pictorial Hist.

Top Decisions: Strategic Decision Making in Organizations. David J. Hickson et al. LC 85-10071. (Management Ser.). 1986. text ed. 32.95x (ISBN 0-87589-653-7). Jossey-Bass.

Top Dog - Bottom Dog: The Hidden Dynamics of Power, Intimacy, & Self-Respect. Robert Karen. 448p. 1988. pap. 3.95 (ISBN 1-55817-127-4). Windsor NY.

Top Dog, Bottom Dog: Coming to Grips with Power at Home, at Work, & in the Sexual Arena. Robert Karen. LC 86-46399. 288p. 1987. 18.95 (ISBN 1-556-11035-9). D I Fine.

Top Dogs. Illus. by Edward DuRose. Incl. Run, Rainey, Run. Mel Ellis. Repr. of 1967 ed; Algonquin. Dion Henderson. Repr. of 1953 ed. LC 85-28385. (Illus.). 240p. (Orig.). 1985. pap. 12.95 (ISBN 0-942802-11-X). Northword.

Top Dollar for Your Property. James E. Lumley. LC 87-36863. 1988. pap. 12.95 (ISBN 0-471-63610-X); 22.95 (ISBN 0-471-63611-8). Wiley.

Top Dollars for Technical Scholars: A Guide to Engineering, Math, Computer Science & Science Scholarships. Clark Z. Robinson. 88p. (Orig.). 1986. pap. 4.25 (ISBN 0-917760-78-6). Octameron Assocs.

Top-Down Assembly Language for Your VIC-20 & Commmodore 64. Kenneth Skier. 1984. pap. text ed. 18.95 (ISBN 0-07-057864-8). McGraw.

Top-Down Assembly Language Programming for Your VIC-20 & Commodore-64. Kenneth Skier. 434p. 1983. pap. text ed. 21.95 (ISBN 0-07-057863-X, BYTE Bks). McGraw.

Top-Down BASIC for the TRS-80 Color Computer. Kenneth Skier. LC 82-22880. (Illus.). 256p. 1983. pap. text ed. 15.95 (ISBN 0-07-057861-3, BYTE Bks). McGraw.

Top-Down Calculus. S. Gill Williamson. Ed. by Marvin Marcus. (Computers & Math Ser.). (Illus.). 429p. 1987. text ed. 27.95x (ISBN 0-88175-072-7, Computer Sci Pr). W H Freeman.

Top Down Programming with ELAN. C. H. Koster. LC 87-4065. (Computer Science Ser.). 323p. 1987. 44.95 (ISBN 0-470-20820-1, Pub. by Halsted Press). Wiley.

Top Down Structured Design Techniques. Gloria H. Swann. LC 77-27092. (PBI Series for Computer & Data Processing Professionals). 1978. text ed. 17.50 (ISBN 0-89433-094-2); pap. 12.50 (ISBN 0-89433-019-5). Petrocelli.

Top Drawer: American High Society from the Gilded Age to the Roaring Twenties. Mary Cable. LC 83-45513. (Illus.). 256p. 1984. 19.95 (ISBN 0-689-11431-1). Atheneum.

Top Easy Listening Records, Nineteen Sixty-One to Nineteen Seventy-Four. new ed. Joel Whitburn. LC 75-10541. (Record Research Ser.). (Illus., Orig.). 1975. softcover 30.00 (ISBN 0-89820-021-0). Record Research.

Top Easy Listening Records, 1975. Joel Whitburn. 28p. (Orig.). 1976. pap. text ed. 10.00 (ISBN 0-89820-022-9). Record Research.

Top Easy Listening Records, 1976. Joel Whitburn. 28p. (Orig.). 1977. pap. text ed. 10.00 (ISBN 0-89820-023-7). Record Research.

Top Easy Listening Records, 1977. Joel Whitburn. 24p. (Orig.). 1978. pap. text ed. 10.00 (ISBN 0-89820-024-5). Record Research.

Top Easy Listening Records, 1978. Joel Whitburn. 24p. (Orig.). 1979. pap. text ed. 10.00 (ISBN 0-89820-034-2). Record Research.

Top Executive Compensation, 1987. Charles A. Peck. (Report Ser.: No. 889). (Illus.). ix, 69p. (Orig.). 1986. pap. text ed. 100.00 (ISBN 0-8237-0331-2). Conference Bd.

Top Executive Pay Package. Leonard R. Burgess. LC 63-8414. 1963. 9.95 (ISBN 0-02-904990-3). Free Pr.

Top Farmer Guide to Using Options for Profitable Marketing of Farm Commodities. Top Farmers of America Staff. 76p. 1986. pap. 24.95 (ISBN 0-910939-11-X). AgriData.

Top Fifty Thousand Companies see Million Dollar Directory, 1986.

Top-Floor Killer. Walter A. Roberts. LC 73-18604. Repr. of 1935 ed. 24.50 (ISBN 0-404-11414-8). AMS Pr.

Top Forty: Making a Hit Record. Sondra Maie. (Illus.). 96p. (gr. 4-7). 1985. 9.29 (ISBN 0-671-44275-9). Messner.

Top Fueler: Inside the World of Drag Racing. B. Jackson. (Illus.). 128p. 1987. 24.95 (ISBN 0-87938-250-3). Motorbooks Intl.

Top Girls. Date not set. pap. price not set (ISBN 0-413-51510-9). Heinemann Ed.

Top Grain Cowhide History of Texas. Lee R. McCullough. 200p. 1986. pap. 9.95 (ISBN 0-89015-546-1). Eakin Pr.

Top Gun. Mike Cogan. pap. 3.50 (ISBN 0-671-61824-5). PB.

Top Gun. Gordon D. Shirreffs. 1977. pap. 1.25 (ISBN 0-505-51176-2, Pub. by Tower Bks). Leisure NY.

Top Gun From the Dakotas. Merle Constiner. 1987. pap. 2.50 (ISBN 0-317-63389-9, Charter Pub). Berkley Pub.

Top Gun: The Navy's Fighter Weapons School. George Hall. (Illus.). 136p. 1987. pap. 12.95 (ISBN 0-89141-261-1). Presidio Pr.

Top Guns: A Common Cause Guide to Defense Contractor Lobbying. Philip Simon et al. 112p. (Orig.). 1987. pap. write for info. (ISBN 0-914389-38-6). Common Cause.

Top Hand with a Gun. Harry S. Drago. 11.95 (ISBN 0-89190-162-0, Pub. by Am Repr). Amereon Ltd.

Top Management Control in Europe. Jacques H. Horovitz. 210p. 1980. 13.95x (ISBN 0-312-80908-5). St Martin.

Top Management of the Personnel Function: Current Issues & Practices. Ed. by William B. Wolf. LC 79-27383. (Frank W. Pierce Memorial Lectureship & Conference Ser.: No. 6). 88p. 1980. pap. 5.95 (ISBN 0-87546-077-1). ILR Pr.

Top Management Planning. George A. Steiner. LC 66-20539. (Studies of the Modern Corporation Ser.). (Illus.). 1969. 35.00 (ISBN 0-02-931120-9). Macmillan.

Top Management Strategy. Benjamin B. Tregoe & John W. Zimmerman. LC 80-15819. 1980. 12.95 (ISBN 0-671-25401-4); pap. 5.95. S&S.

Top Management Strategy. Benjamin B. Tregoe & John W. Zimmerman. 1983. pap. 7.95 (ISBN 0-671-25402-2, Touchstone Bks). S&S.

Top Marks: A Nautical Quiz Book. Illus. by Bill Beavis. (Illus.). 96p. 1986. 9.95 (ISBN 0-85177-418-0, Pub. by Nautical Bks England). Sheridan.

Top of the Charts. Nelson George. LC 83-8108. (Illus.). 448p. (Orig.). 1983. pap. 15.95 (ISBN 0-8329-0260-8). New Century.

Top of the City: New York's Hidden Rooftop World. Laura Rosen. (Illus.). 1982. 27.50 (ISBN 0-500-01288-1). Thames Hudson.

Top of the City: New York's Hidden Rooftop World. Photos by Laura Rosen. LC 82-80589. (Illus.). 168p. 1983. pap. 14.95f (ISBN 0-500-27269-7). Thames Hudson.

Top of the News Cumulative Index, October 1942-May 1963. 61p. 1.00x. ALA.

Top of the World. rev ed. Hans Reusch. 1973. pap. 2.50 (ISBN 0-671-78991-0). PB.

Top of the World. Hans Ruesch. 1977. pap. 2.95 (ISBN 0-671-63754-1). PB.

Top of the World. John R. Townsend. LC 76-48219. (Illus.). (gr. 1-4). 1977. 12.25 (ISBN 0-397-31728-X, Lipp Jr Bks). HarpJ.

Top One Hundred DP Almanac, 1984. Gartner Group, Inc. Staff. Ed. by William S. Cappelli & Thomas A. Ryan. (Illus.). 497p. 1984. 295.00 (ISBN 0-317-15127-4); special library price 85.00 (ISBN 0-317-15128-2). Gartner Group.

Top One Hundred Rock 'n' Roll Albums of All Time. Paul Gambaccini. (Illus.). 96p. (Orig.). 1987. pap. 12.95 (ISBN 0-517-56561-7, Harmony). Crown.

Top One Hundred, 1986. Lillian S. Clancy. (California Public Schools Ser.: How Are They Doing?). 80p. (Orig.). 1985. pap. 12.95 (ISBN 0-939580-36-5). Sindowilf Ltd.

Topics in Blood Banking. Neva M. Abelson. LC 74-8253. pap. 42.80 (ISBN 0-317-26672-1, 2055994). Bks Demand UMI.

Topics in C Programming. Steven Kochan & Patrick Wood. 400p. 1987. pap. 24.95 (ISBN 0-672-46290-7). Sams.

Topics in Calculus. 2nd ed. Morton Lowengrub & Joseph G. Stampfli. LC 7-78064. 400p. 1975. write for info. (ISBN 0-471-01088-X). Wiley.

Topics in Carbocyclic Chemistry, Vol. 1. Ed. by Douglas Lloyd. LC 74-80937. pap. 95.80 (2026310). Bks Demand UMI.

Topics in Carbon-13NMR Spectroscopy, Vol. 4. Ed. by George C. Levy. (Topics in Carbon-13 NMR Spectroscopy: 1-683). 282p. 1984. 64.50 (ISBN 0-471-09857-4, Pub. by Wiley-Interscience). Wiley.

Topics in Carciovascular Medicine. Ed. by R. W. Elsdon-Dew et al. (International Congress & Symposium ser.: No. 34). 46p. 1980. pap. 12.00 (ISBN 1-85315-066-5, Pub. by Royal Society of Medicine Services Ltd). Longwood Pub Group.

Topics in Child Neurology, Vol. 2. Ed. by G. Wise et al. (Illus.). 280p. 1983. text ed. 42.50 (ISBN 0-88331-207-7). Luce.

Topics in Classical Number Theory, 2 vols. Ed. by G. Halasz. (Colloquia Mathematica Ser.: Vol. 34). 1984. Set. 237.00 (ISBN 0-444-86509-8, North-Holland). Vol. 1 (ISBN 0-444-86781-3). Vol. 2 (ISBN 0-444-86782-1). Elsevier.

Topics in Clinical Pharmacology & Therapeutics. Ed. by R. F. Maronde. (Illus.). 530p. 1986. 85.00 (ISBN 0-387-96196-8). Springer-Verlag.

Topics in Cognitive Linguistics. Ed. by Brygida Rudzka-Ostyn. x, 704p. 1988. 114.00x (ISBN 90-272-3544-9). Benjamins North Am.

Topics in Communications Theory. David Middleton. 126p. 1987. Repr. of 1965 ed. 13.95 (ISBN 0-932146-14-7). Peninsula CA.

Topics in Complex Analysis. Ed. by D. Shaffer. LC 84-24550. (Contemporary Mathematics Ser.: Vol. 38). 142p. 1985. pap. text ed. 20.00 (ISBN 0-8218-5037-7). Am Math.

Topics in Complex Function Theory, 3 vols. C. L. Siegel. Incl. Vol. 1. Elliptical Functions & Uniformization Theory. 186p. 1969. 40.50x (ISBN 0-471-79070-2); Vol. 2. Automorphic Functions & Abelian Integrals. 193p. 1971. 48.50x (ISBN 0-471-79080-X); Vol. 3. Abelian Functions & Modular Functions of Several Variables. C. L. Siegel. (Pure & Applied Mathematics Ser.). 244p. 1973. 50.00x (ISBN 0-471-79090-7). LC 69-19931. (Pure & Applied Mathematics Ser., Pub. by Wiley-Interscience). Wiley.

Topics in Complex Functions: Automorphic Functions & Abelian Integrals, Vol. 2. C. L. Siegel. (Classics Library). 193p. 1988. pap. 29.95 (ISBN 0-471-60843-2). Wiley.

Topics in Complex Functions: Elliptic Functions & Uniformization Theory, Vol. 1. C. L. Siegel. (Classics Library). 186p. 1988. pap. 29.95 (ISBN 0-471-60844-0). Wiley.

Topics in Conditional Logic. Donald Nute. (Philosophical Studies Series in Philosophy: No. 20). 168p. 1980. lib. bdg. 31.50 (ISBN 90-277-1049-X, Pub. by Reidel Holland). Kluwer Academic.

Topics in Contemporary Mathematics. 3rd ed. Jack R. Britton & Ignacio Bello. 720p. 1984. text ed. 37.50 scp (ISBN 0-06-040992-4, HarpC). Har-Row.

Topics in Control Theory. F. Albrecht. (Lecture Notes in Mathematics: Vol. 63). 1968. pap. 10.70 (ISBN 0-387-04233-4). Springer-Verlag.

Topics in Diachronic English Syntax. Cynthia L. Allen. LC 79-6613. (Outstanding Dissertations in Linguistics Ser.). 425p. 1985. 57.00 (ISBN 0-8240-4550-5). Garland Pub.

Topics in Dietary Fiber Research. Ed. by Gene A. Spiller. LC 77-26883. 234p. 1978. 39.50x (ISBN 0-306-31126-7, Plenum Pr). Plenum Pub.

Topics in Differential & Integral Equations & Operator Theory. M. G. Krein. (Operator Theory, Advances & Applications Ser.: Vol. 7). 312p. 1983. text ed. 53.95 (ISBN 0-8176-1517-2). Birkhauser.

Topics in Differential Games. Ed. by Austin Blaquiere. LC 73-75528. 460p. 1973. 52.75 (ISBN 0-444-10467-4, North-Holland). Elsevier.

Topics in Differential Geometry, 2 vols. J. SZenthe & L. Tamassy. (Colloquia Mathematica Societatis Janos Bolyai: No. 46). 1378p. 1988. 315.75 set (ISBN 0-444-70090-0, North Holland). Elsevier.

Topics in Dynamic Bifurcation Theory. Jack K. Hale. LC 81-3445. (Conference Board of the Mathematical Sciences Ser.: No. 47). 84p. 1983. pap. 10.00 (ISBN 0-8218-1698-5). Am Math.

Topics in Employee Benefits for Association Executives - 1985. Ed. by Mary E. Brennan. 74p. (Orig.). 1985. pap. 25.00 (ISBN 0-89154-284-1). Intl Found Employ.

Topics in English Morphology. Dorothy Siegel. Ed. by Jorge Hankamer. LC 78-66592. (Outstanding Dissertations in Linguistics Ser.). 205p. 1979. lib. bdg. 31.00 (ISBN 0-8240-9675-4). Garland Pub.

Topics in Enzyme & Fermentation Bio-Technology, Vol. 8. Ed. by Alan Wiseman. LC 78-643391. 179p. 1984. text ed. 58.95x (ISBN 0-470-20058-8). Halsted Pr.

Topics in Enzyme & Fermentation Biotechnology, Vol. 2. Ed. by Alan Wiseman. LC 76-25441. 1978. 59.95x (ISBN 0-470-99318-9). Vol. 2. Halsted Pr.

Topics in Enzyme & Fermentation Biotechnology, Vol. 3. Alan Wiseman. LC 78-41290. 294p. 1979. 89.95 (ISBN 0-470-26635-X). Halsted Pr.

Topics in Enzyme & Fermentation Biotechnology, Vol. 4. Ed. by Alan Wiseman. LC 79-41466. (Topics in Enzyme & Fermentation Biotechnology Ser.). 242p. 1980. 107.00 (ISBN 0-470-26922-7). Halsted Pr.

Topics in Enzyme & Fermentation Biotechnology, Vol. 5. Alan Wiseman. LC 80-41326. (Topics in Enzyme & Fermentation Biotechnology Ser.). 300p. 1981. 125.00 (ISBN 0-470-27089-6). Halsted Pr.

Topics in Enzyme & Fermentation Biotechnology, Vol. 6. Alan Wiseman. 232p. 1982. 79.95x (ISBN 0-470-27304-6). Halsted Pr.

Topics in Enzyme & Fermentation Biotechnology, Vol. 7. Alan Wiseman. LC 77-511. 345p. 1983. 89.95x (ISBN 0-470-27366-6). Halsted Pr.

Topics in Enzyme & Fermentation Biotechnology, Vol. 10. Ed. by Alan Wiseman. LC 78-643391. 218p. 1985. 64.95 (ISBN 0-470-20215-7). Halsted Pr.

Topics in Enzyme & Fermentation Biotechnology, Vol. 19. Ed. by A. Wiseman. 192p. 1984. 52.95 (ISBN 0-470-20031-6). Halsted Pr.

Topics in Ergodic Theory. William Parry. LC 79-7815. (Cambridge Tracts in Mathematics Ser.: No. 75). 1981. 29.95 (ISBN 0-521-22986-3). Cambridge U Pr.

Topics in Fields & Solids. Ed. by C. A. Coulter & R. A. Shatas. 228p. 1968. 83.00 (ISBN 0-677-12740-5). Gordon & Breach.

Topics in Finite Elasticity. M. E. Gurtin. LC 80-53711. (CBMS-NSF Regional Conference Ser.: No. 35). v, 58p. 1981. pap. text ed. 12.50 (ISBN 0-89871-168-1). Soc Indus-Appl Math.

Topics in Fluid Film Bearing & Rotor Bearing Systems Design & Optimization: Presented at the Design Engineering Conference, Chicago, Ill., April 17-20, 1978. Fluid Film Bearing Committee of the Lubrication Division. Ed. by S. M. Rohde et al. LC 78-52526. pap. 70.00 (ISBN 0-317-11248-1, 2017648). Bks Demand UMI.

Topics in Forensic & Analytical Toxicology: Proceedings of the Annual European Meet. of the Internat. Assoc. of FornsicToxicologists, Munich, Aug. 21-25, 1983. Ed. by R. A. Maes. (Analytical Chemistry Symposia Ser.: No. 20). 214p. 1984. 84.25 (ISBN 0-444-42313-3, I-139-84). Elsevier.

Topics in Fourier Analysis & Function Spaces. Ed. by Collet's Holdings, Ltd. Staff. 1986. 189.00x (ISBN 0-317-46751-4, Pub. by Collets (UK)). State Mutual Bk.

Topics in Fourier & Geometric Analysis. Victor L. Shapiro. LC 52-42839. (Memoirs: No. 39). 100p. 1968. pap. 12.00 (ISBN 0-8218-1239-4, MEMO-39). Am Math.

Topics in Functional Analysis. A. Wilansky. (Lecture Notes in Mathematics: Vol. 45). 1967. pap. 10.70 (ISBN 0-387-03916-3). Springer-Verlag.

Topics in Functional Analysis: Essays Dedicated to M. G. Krein on the Occasion of His 70th. Birthday. Ed. by I. Gohberg & M. Kal. (Adv. in Mathematics Supplementary Studies: Vol. 3). 1978. 99.00 (ISBN 0-12-287150-2). Acad Pr.

Topics in Functional Analysis over Valued Decision Rings. J. B. Prolla. (Mathematical Studies Ser.: Vol. 77). 302p. 1983. 73.75 (ISBN 0-444-86535-7, I-466-82, North Holland). Elsevier.

Topics in General Relativity. Robert Hermann. (Interdisciplinary Mathematics Ser.: No. 5). 161p. 1973. 15.00 (ISBN 0-915692-04-X, 991600223). Math Sci Pr.

Topics in Geometry. Howard Levi. LC 75-19477. 112p. 1975. Repr. of 1968 ed. 10.50 (ISBN 0-88275-280-4). Krieger.

Topics in Geophysical Fluid Dynamics: Atmospheric Dynamics, Dynamo Theory & Climate Dynamics. M. Ghil & S. Childress. (Applied Mathematical Sciences Ser.: Vol. 60). (Illus.). 500p. 1987. pap. 39.00 (ISBN 0-387-96475-4). Springer-Verlag.

Topics in Graph Theory. Ed. by Frank Harary et al. (Annals of the New York Academy of Sciences: Vol. 328). 206p. (Orig.). 1979. write for info. (ISBN 0-89766-028-5); pap. 42.00x (ISBN 0-89766-029-3). NY Acad Sci.

Topics in Group Rings, Vol. 50. Sudarshan K. Sehgal. (Pure & Applied Mathematics Ser.). (Illus.). 264p. 1978. 55.00 (ISBN 0-8247-6755-1). Dekker.

Topics in Harmonic Analysis. Charles F. Dunkl & Donald E. Ramirez. LC 73-153387. (Century Mathematics Ser.). 1971. 34.50x (ISBN 0-89197-454-7). Irvington.

Topics in Harmonic Analysis on Homgeneous Spaces. Sigurdur Helgason. (Progress in Math. Ser.: No. 13). 160p. 1981. text ed. 19.95x (ISBN 0-8176-3051-1). Birkhauser.

Topics in Harmonic Analysis Related to the Littlewood-Paley Theory. Elias M. Stein. LC 72-83688. (Annals of Mathematics Studies: No. 63). 1969. 27.50 (ISBN 0-691-08067-4). Princeton U Pr.

Topics in Health Psychology. Maes et al. LC 88-5646. 400p. 1988. price not set (ISBN 0-471-91975-6). Wiley.

Topics in Heterocyclic Chemistry. Ed. by Raymond N. Castle. LC 71-78478. pap. 69.00 (ISBN 0-317-08776-2, 2011959). Bks Demand UMI.

Topics in Human Factors Research. John Schmid et al. 418p. 1972. pap. text ed. 12.95x (ISBN 0-8422-0186-6). Irvington.

Topics in Identification & Distributed Parameter Systems. E. Buhler & D. Franke. 1980. 35.00 (ISBN 3-528-08469-3, Pub. by Vieweg & Sohn Germany). IPS.

Topics in Information Theory. I. Csiszar & P. Elias. (Colloquia Mathematica Societatis Janos Bolyai Ser.: Vol. 16). 592p. 1977. 142.00 (ISBN 0-7204-0699-4, North Holland). Elsevier.

Topics in Inorganic & Physical Chemistry. Ed. by M. J. Clarke et al. (Structure & Bonding Ser.: Vol. 50). (Illus.). 178p. 1982. 49.00 (ISBN 0-387-11454-8). Springer-Verlag.

Topics in Intermediate Statistical Methods, Vol. 1. T. A. Bancroft. 1968. 9.95x (ISBN 0-8138-0842-1). Iowa St U Pr.

Topics in Interstellar Matter. Ed. by H. Van Woerden. (Astrophysics & Space Science Library: No. 70). 1977. lib. bdg. 39.50 (ISBN 90-277-0835-5, Pub. by Reidel Holland). Kluwer Academic.

Topics in K-Theory: Two Independent Contributions. L. H. Hodgkin. LC 75-41435. (Lecture Notes in Mathematics: Vol. 496). 1975. pap. 19.00 (ISBN 0-387-07536-4). Springer-Verlag.

Topics in Light Water Reactor Physics: Final Report of the NORA Project. (Technical Reports Ser.: No. 113). (Illus., Orig.). 1970. pap. 14.00 (ISBN 92-0-135170-4, IDC113, IAEA). UNIPUB.

Topics in Lipid Research: From Structural Elucidation to Biological Function. Ed. by R. A. Klein & B. Schmitz. (Illus.). 350p. 1987. text ed. 65.00x (ISBN 0-85186-353-1, Pub. by Royal Soc Chem). Scholium Intl.

Topics in Locally Convex Spaces. Manual Valdivia. (Mathematics Studies: Vol. 67). 510p. 1982. 94.75 (ISBN 0-444-86418-0, I-199-82, North-Holland). Elsevier.

Topics in Management Accounting. Ed. by J. Arnold et al. 300p. 1981. text ed. 38.50x (ISBN 0-86003-508-5, Pub. by Philip Allan Uk); pap. text ed. 19.95x (ISBN 0-86003-609-X). Humanities.

Topics in Management Science. 2nd ed. Robert E. Markland. LC 82-20273. 1000p. 1983. 41.95 (ISBN 0-471-09830-2). Wiley.

Topics in Mathematical Analysis for Economists. Knut Sydsaeter. LC 81-66692. 1981. 46.50 (ISBN 0-12-679980-6). Acad Pr.

Topics in Mathematical Elasticity. P. G. Ciarlet. (Studies in Mechanical Engineering). 1984. write for info. (North-Holland). Elsevier.

Topics in Mathematical Physics. Halis Odabasi & O. Akyuz. LC 77-84853. (Illus.). 1977. text ed. 29.95 (ISBN 0-87081-072-3). Colo Assoc.

Topics in Matrix Analysis. Roger A. Horn & Charles R. Johnson. (Illus.). 250p. Date not set. price not set (ISBN 0-521-30587-X). Cambridge U Pr.

Topics in Medicinal Chemistry: 4th SCI-RSC Medicinal Chemistry Symposium Special Publication. Ed. by P. R. Leeming. (Cambridge Biennial Ser.: No. 65). (Illus.). 360p. 1988. pap. text ed. 99.00x (ISBN 0-85186-706-5, Pub. by Royal Soc Chem). Scholium Intl.

Topics in Metallurgical Thermodynamics. Owen F. Devereux. LC 83-1115. 494p. 1983. 49.95x (ISBN 0-471-86963-5). Krieger.

Topics in Metallurgical Thermodynamics. Owen F. Devereux. 508p. 1989. Repr. of 1983 ed. lib. bdg. price not set (ISBN 0-89464-329-0). Krieger.

Topics in Micrometeorology: A Festschrift for Arch Dyer. Ed. by B. B. Hicks. 1988. lib. bdg. 69.00 (ISBN 90-277-2694-9, Pub. by Reidel Holland). Kluwer Academic.

Topics in Millimeter Wave Guided Propagation, Vol. 1. Ed. by Kenneth J. Button. 375p. 1988. 99.50 (ISBN 0-12-147699-5). Acad Pr.

Topics in Millimeter Wave Guided Propagation, Vol. 2. Ed. by Kenneth J. Button. 375p. 1988. 99.50. Acad Pr.

Topics in Modern Logic. D. C. Makinson. (University Paperback Ser.). 107p. 1973. pap. 5.95x (ISBN 0-416-78100-4, NO. 2309). Routledge Chapman & Hall.

Topics in Modern Mathematics: Petrovskii Seminar, No. 5. Ed. by O. A. Oleinik. (Contemporary Soviet Mathematics Ser.). 348p. 1985. 75.00x (ISBN 0-306-10980-8, Consultants). Plenum Pub.

Topics in Modern Operator Theory. Ed. by Apostol. (Operator Theory, Advances & Applications Ser.: 2). 335p. 1981. text ed. 35.95x (ISBN 0-8176-1244-0). Birkhauser.

Topics in Modern Physics: Tribute to E. U. Condon. Ed. by Wesley E. Brittin & Halis Odabasi. LC 70-135286. 1971. 22.50x (ISBN 0-87081-010-3). Colo Assoc.

Topics in Mojave Syntax. Pamela E. Munro. LC 75-25120. (American Indian Linguistics Ser.). 1976. lib. bdg. 51.00 (ISBN 0-8240-1970-9). Garland Pub.

Topics in Molecular Interactions. Ed. by W. J. Orville-Thomas & H. Ratajczak. (Studies in Physical & Theoretical Chemistry: No. 37). 472p. 1985. 155.25 (ISBN 0-444-99556-0). Elsevier.

Topics in Molecular Pharmacology, Vol. 1. Ed. by A. S. Burgen & G. C. Roberts. 250p. 1982. 107.00 (ISBN 0-444-80354-8, Biomedical Pr). Elsevier.

Topics in Molecular Pharmacology, Vol. 2. A. S. Burgen & G. C. Roberts. 1984. 109.00 (ISBN 0-444-80495-1, I-018-84). Elsevier.

Topics in Molecular Pharmacology, Vol. 4. Burgen. 1987. 97.75 (ISBN 0-444-80880-9). Elsevier.

Topics in Multivariate Approximation. Ed. by C. K. Chu & L. L. Schumaker. 352p. 1987. 39.95 (ISBN 0-12-174585-6). Acad Pr.

Topics in Neonatal Neurology. Ed. by Harvey B. Sarnat. 320p. 1984. 54.50 (ISBN 0-8089-1653-X, 793785). Grune.

Topics in Neuro-Opthalmology. Stanley H. Thompson et al. LC 78-25658. 392p. 1979. 43.50 (ISBN 0-683-08178-0, WW). Krieger.

Topics in Nevome Syntax. David L. Shaul. (UC Publications in Linguistics: Vol. 109). 1987. pap. 14.80x (ISBN 0-520-09964-8). U of Cal Pr.

Topics in Nonsmooth Mechanics. Moreau et al. 320p. 1987. 119.00 (ISBN 0-8176-1907-0). Birkhauser.

Topics in Nuclear Physics - I: A Comprehensive Review of Recent Developments Lecture Notes from Peking. Ed. by T. T. Kuo & S. S. Wong. (Lectures Notes in Physics Ser.: Vol. 144). 567p. 1981. pap. 29.50 (ISBN 0-387-10851-3). Springer Verlag.

Topics in Nuclear Physics - II: A Comprehensive Review of Recent Developments Lecture Notes from Peking. Ed. by T. T. Kuo & S. S. Wong. (Lecture Notes in Physics Ser.: Vol. 145). 511p. 1981. pap. 29.50 (ISBN 0-387-10853-X). Springer Verlag.

Topics in Number Theory. J. S. Chahal. (University Series in Mathematics). (Illus.). 183p. 1988. 35.00x (ISBN 0-306-42866-0, Plenum Pr). Plenum Pub.

Topics in Number Theory. P. Turan. (Colloquia Mathematica Societatis Janos Bolyai: Vol. 13). 456p. 1976. 92.00 (ISBN 0-7204-0454-1, North-Holland). Elsevier.

Topics in Numerical Analysis II. Ed. by J. J. Miller. 1976. 68.00 (ISBN 0-12-496952-6). Acad Pr.

Topics in Numerical Analysis III. Ed. by J. H. Miller. 1978. 99.00 (ISBN 0-12-496953-4). Acad Pr.

Topics in Numerical Analysis: Proceedings, S.E.R.C. Summer School, Lancaster, 1981. Ed. by P. R. Turner. (Lecture Notes in Mathematics Ser.: Vol. 965). 202p. 1982. pap. 14.00 (ISBN 0-387-11967-1). Springer-Verlag.

Topics in Ocean Engineering, 3 vols. Charles L. Bretschneider. Incl. Vol. 1. 428p. 1969 (ISBN 0-87201-598-X); Vol. 2. (Illus.). 229p. 1970 (ISBN 0-87201-599-8); Vol. 3. LC 78-87230. 328p. 1976. 32.00x ea. (ISBN 0-87201-600-5). LC 78-87230. 32.00x ea. Gulf Pub.

Topics in Ocean Physics: Proceedings of the International School of Physics, Enrico Fermi Course LXXX, Varenna, Italy, July 7-19, 1980. Ed. by A. R. Osborne & P. M. Rizzoli. (Enrico Fermi International Summer School of Physics Ser.: Vol. 80). 554p. 1982. 166.00 (ISBN 0-444-86160-2, I-323-82, North Holland). Elsevier.

Topics in One-Parameter Bifurcation Problems. P. Rabier. (Tata Institute Lectures on Mathematics). vi, 290p. 1985. pap. 10.00 (ISBN 0-387-13907-9). Springer-Verlag.

Topics in Operator Theory. Richard Beals. LC 70-147095. (Chicago Lectures in Mathematics Ser). (Orig.). 1971. pap. 6.00x (ISBN 0-226-03985-4). U of Chicago Pr.

Topics in Operator Theory. Ed. by C. Pearcy. LC 74-8254. (Mathematical Surveys Ser.: No. 13). 235p. 1979. pap. 35.00 (ISBN 0-8218-1513-X, SURV-13). Am Math.

Topics in Operator Theory & Interpolation. Ed. by I. Gohberg. (Operator Theory Ser.: No. 29). 243p. 1988. 55.50 (ISBN 0-8176-1960-7). Birkhauser.

Topics in Operator Theory Systems & Networks, Vol. 12. Ed. by Harry Dym et al. (Operator Theory Ser.). 300p. 1984. 68.95 (ISBN 3-7643-1550-4). Birkhauser.

Topics in Ophthalmolgy. Kanski. Date not set. write for info. (ISBN 0-7020-1103-7). Saunders.

Topics in Ordinary Differential Equations. William D. Laken & David A. Sanchez. 160p. 1982. pap. 4.50 (ISBN 0-486-61606-1). Dover.

Topics in Organic Electrochemistry. Ed. by Albert J. Fry & Wayne E. Britton. 310p. 1986. 49.50x (ISBN 0-306-42058-9, Plenum Pr). Plenum Pub.

Topics in Pali Historical Phonology. Indira Y. Junghare. 200p. 1979. text ed. 12.50 (ISBN 0-89684-095-6, Pub. by Motilal Banarsidass India). Orient Bk Dist.

Topics in Pathophysiology of Hypertension. Ed. by Herman Villarreal & Mohinder P. Sambhi. 1983. text ed. 89.50 (ISBN 0-89838-595-4, Pub. by Martinus Nijhoff Netherlands). Kluwer Academic.

Topics in Pediatric Gastroenterology. Ed. by J. A. Dodge. (Illus.). 1976. pap. text ed. 34.95 (ISBN 0-8464-0931-3). Beekman Pubs.

Topics in Pediatric Genetic Pathology: The Enid Gilbert-Barness Festschrift. Ed. by John M. Opitz et al. LC 87-16946. 492p. 1987. 90.00 (ISBN 0-8451-4242-9, 4242). A R Liss.

Topics in Peptic Ulcer Disease. Ed. by G. Bianchi Porro & K. D. Bardhan. (Perspectives in Digestive Disease Ser.: Vol. 1). 198p. 1987. text ed. 63.00 (ISBN 8-87749-021-7). Raven.

Topics in Pharamaceutical Sciences, 1985. Ed. by D. D. Breimer & P. Speiser. 480p. 1986. 169.50 (ISBN 0-444-80749-7). Elsevier.

Topics in Pharmaceutical Sciences 1987. Ed. by D. D Breimer & P. Speiser. 530p. 1988, 158.00 (ISBN 0-444-80960-0). Elsevier.

Topics in Philosophical Logic. N. Rescher. (Synthese Library: No. 17). 347p. 1968. lib. bdg. 42.00 (ISBN 90-277-0084-2, Pub. by Reidel Holland). Kluwer Academic.

Topics in Phosphorus Chemistry, Vol. 8. Ed. by Edward J. Griffith & Martin Grayson. LC 64-17051. 664p. 1976. 48.50 (ISBN 0-471-32789-1, JW). Krieger.

Topics in Phosphorus Chemistry, Vol. 9. Ed. by Edward J. Griffith & Martin Grayson. LC 64-17051. 516p. 1977. 49.00 (ISBN 0-471-32782-4, JW). Krieger.

Topics in Phosphorus Chemistry, Vol. 10. Ed. by Martin Grayson & Edward J. Griffith. LC 64-17051. (Topics in Phosphorus Chemistry Ser.). 528p. 1980. 49.50 (ISBN 0-471-05890-4, Pub. by Wiley-Interscience). Krieger.

Topics in Phosphorus Chemistry, Vol. 11. Ed. by Martin Grayson & Edward J. Griffith. LC 64-17051. (Topics in Phosphorous Chemistry Ser.). 462p. 1983. 92.00 (ISBN 0-471-89628-4, Pub. by Wiley-Interscience). Krieger.

Topics in Photomedicine. Ed. by Kendric C. Smith. LC 83-24509. 412p. 1984. 75.00x (ISBN 0-306-41510-0, Plenum Pr). Plenum Pub.

Topics in Photosynthesis Vol. 6: Photosyntheic Mechanisms & the Environment. Ed. by J. Barber & N. R. Baker. 584p. 1985. 216.50 (ISBN 0-444-80674-1). Elsevier.

Topics in Plant Population Biology. Ed. by Otto T. Solbrig et al. LC 78-27630. (Illus.). 1979. 60.00x (ISBN 0-231-04336-8). Columbia U Pr.

Topics in Plasmapheresis: A Bibliography of Therapeutic Applications & New Techniques. Ed. by Takashi Horiuchi & Helen Kambic. 1984. 25.00 (ISBN 0-936022-13-2). Intl Soc Artifical Organs.

Topics in Plasmaphersis: A Bibliography of Therapeutic Applications & New Techniques. Ed. by H. Kambie & L. Hyslop. 25.00 (ISBN 0-936022-24-8). Intl Soc Artifical Organs.

Topics in Population Genetics. Bruce Wallace. 1968. 24.95x (ISBN 0-393-09813-3). Norton.

Topics in Production Theory. Ed. by Finn R. Forsund. LC 83-40610. 220p. 1984. 27.50 (ISBN 0-312-80914-X). St Martin.

Topics in Quantum Field Theory & Gauge Theories: Proceedings of the VIII International Seminar on Theoretical Physics, Held by GIFT in Salamanca, June 13-19, 1977. Ed. by J. A. Azcarraga. (Lecture Notes in Physics Ser.: Vol. 77). 1978. pap. 20.00 (ISBN 0-387-08841-5). Springer-Verlag.

Topics in Radiation Dosimetry see Radiation Dosimetry.

Topics in Relaxation & Ellipsoidal Methods. M. Akgul. 336p. 1984. pap. 31.95 (ISBN 0-470-20401-X, Co-Pub. with Longman). Wiley.

Topics in Respiratory & Comparative Physiology. Michael Meyer & Heisler. 1986. pap. text ed. 43.00 (ISBN 0-89574-236-5, Pub. by Gustav Fischer Verlag). VCH Pubs.

Topics in Rolling Bearing Technology. Ed. by Tedric A. Harris. LC 87-4987. 624p. 1988. 69.95 (ISBN 0-471-83039-9). Wiley.

Topics in Romance Syntax. Osvaldo Jaeggli. 196p. 1981. 27.50x (ISBN 90-70176-34-3). Foris Pubns.

Topics in Scandinavian Syntax. Ed. by Lars Hellan & Kirsti K. Christiansen. 1986. lib. bdg. 59.50 (ISBN 90-277-2166-1, Pub. by Reidel Holland); pap. 24.00 (ISBN 90-277-2167-X, Pub. by Reidel Holland). Kluwer Academic.

Topics in Semiconductor Physics: Selected Papers from the First Regional Workshop, Bangkok, Thailand. Ed. by W. Sritrakool & V. Sa-yakanit. 224p. 1988. 38.00 (ISBN 9971-50-670-X). World Scientific Pub.

Topics in Several Complex Variables. E. R. Arellano. 200p. 1985. pap. 22.95 (ISBN 0-470-20404-4, Co-Pub. with Longman). Wiley.

Topics in Several Particle Dynamics. K. M. Watson & J. Nuttall. LC 67-13836. 1967. 22.95x (ISBN 0-8162-9362-7). Holden-Day.

Topics in Slavic Phonology. Ed. by Demetrius J. Koubourlis. viii, 270p. 1974. 18.95 (ISBN 0-89357-017-6). Slavica.

Topics in Small Business Management. Richard M. Hodgetts & Pamela Keel. 320p. (Orig.). 1982. shrink wrapped 27.95 (ISBN 0-8403-2680-7). Kendall-Hunt.

Topics in Soliton Theory & Exactly Solvable Nonlinear Equations: Proceedings of the Conference, Oberwolfach, F R Germany, July 27-August 2, 1986. Ed. by M. Kruskal et al. 352p. 1987. 48.00 (ISBN 9971-50-253-4). World Scientific Pub.

Topics in Statistical Information Theory. S. Kullback & J. C. Keegel. (Lecture Notes in Statistics Ser.: Vol. 42). ix, 158p. 1987. pap. 18.90 (ISBN 0-387-96512-2). Springer-Verlag.

Topics in Statistical Mechanics & Biophysics-A Memorial to Julius L. Jackson: AIP Conference Proceedings, No. 27. American Institute of Physics. Ed. by R. A. Piccirelli. LC 75-36309. 209p. 1976. 17.00 (ISBN 0-88318-126-6). Am Inst Physics.

Topics in Statistical Methodology. Suddhendu Biswas. 400p. 1988. 29.95 (ISBN 0-470-21153-9). Wiley.

Topics in Stereochemistry. Ed. by Norman L. Allinger & Ernest L. Eliel. LC 67-13943. 1979. Vol. 9, 1976, 399p. 75.00 (ISBN 0-471-02472-4, Pub. by Wiley-Interscience). Wiley.

Topics in Stereochemistry. Ed. by Ernest L. Eliel & Norman L. Allinger. LC 67-13943. 1969. Vol. 4, 280p. 38.50 (ISBN 0-471-23748-5, Pub. by Wiley); Vol. 8, 448pp. 1974. 35.00 (ISBN 0-471-23755-8, Pub. by Wiley). Krieger.

Topics in Stereochemistry, Vol. 5. Ed. by E. L. Eliel & N. L. Allinger. LC 67-13943. 338p. 1970. 30.00 (ISBN 0-471-23750-7, Pub. by Wiley). Krieger.

Topics in Stereochemistry, Vol. 10. Ed. by Ernest L. Eliel & Norman L. Allinger. LC 67-13943. pap. 91.30 (ISBN 0-317-30020-2, 2025020). Bks Demand UMI.

Topics in Stereochemistry, Vol. 13. Norman Allinger et al. LC 61-13943. 489p. 1982. 100.00 (ISBN 0-471-05680-4, Pub. by Wiley-Interscience). Wiley.

Topics in Stereochemistry, Vol. 14. Ed. by Norman L. Allinger et al. 328p. 1983. 113.00 (ISBN 0-471-89858-9, Pub. by Wiley-Interscience). Krieger.

Topics in Stereochemistry, Vol. 15. Ed. by Ernest L. Eliel et al. (Topics in Stereochemistry Ser.: No. 2-297). 337p. 1984. 110.00 (ISBN 0-471-88564-9). Wiley.

Topics in Stereochemistry, Vol. 16. Ed. by Ernest L. Eliel et al. (Topics in Stereochemistry Ser.). 341p. 1986. 110.00 (ISBN 0-471-83810-1). Wiley.

Topics in Stereochemistry, Vol. 18. Ed. by Ernest L. Eliel & Samuel H. Wilen. 346p. 1988. 99.95 (ISBN 0-471-60026-1). Wiley.

Topics in Stereochemistry, Vol. 11: 1979. Ernest L. Eliel. LC 67-13943. 344p. pap. 89.50 (2056446). Bks Demand UMI.

Topics in Stereochemistry, Vol. 17. Ed. by Ernest L. Eliel & Samuel H. Wilen. (Topics in Stereochemistry Ser.). 305p. 1987. 105.00 (ISBN 0-471-85282-1). Wiley.

Topics in Sterochemistry, Vol. 3. Ed. by Norman L. Eliel. LC 67-13943. pap. 97.30 (ISBN 0-317-08878-5, 2055275). Bks Demand UMI.

Topics in Stochastic Differential Equations. D. W. Stroock. (Tata Institute Lectures on Mathematics). 91p. 1982. pap. 9.00 (ISBN 0-387-11549-8). Springer-Verlag.

Topics in the Analysis of Causatives with an Account of Hindi Paradigms. Anuradha Saksena. LC 82-40098. (UC Publications in Linguistics: Vol. 98). 192p. 1982. pap. 16.50x (ISBN 0-520-09659-2). U of Cal Pr.

Topics in the Formal Methodology of Empirical Sciences. Ryszard Wojcicki. Tr. by Ewa Jansen from Pol. (Synthese Library: No. 135). 1980. lib. bdg. 50.00 (ISBN 90-277-1004-X, Publ by Reidel Holland). Kluwer Academic.

Topics in the General Theory of Structures. Ed. by E. R. Caianiello & M. A. Aizerman. 1987. lib. bdg. 59.00 (ISBN 90-277-2451-2, Pub. by Reidel Holland). Kluwer Academic.

Topics in the Geometric Theory of Integrable Systems. R. Hermann. (Interdisciplinary Mathematics Ser.: Vol. XXIII). 347p. 1984. 65.00 (ISBN 0-915692-36-8, 991600169). Math Sci Pr.

Topics in the Geometric Theory of Linear Systems. R Hermann. (Interdisciplinary Mathematics Ser.: Vol. XXII). 281p. 1984. 50.00 (ISBN 0-915692-35-X, 991600177). Math Sci Pr.

Topics in the Geometry of Projective Space: Recent Work of F. L. Zak. Ed. by Lazarsfeld & Van de Ven. (DMV Seminars Ser.: Band 4). 52p. 1984. pap. 12.95 (ISBN 0-317-18426-1). Birkhauser.

Topics in the History of Psychology, Vol. II. Gregory A. Kimble & Kurt Schlesinger. 448p. 1983. 39.95 (ISBN 0-89859-312-3). L Erlbaum Assocs.

Topics in the History of Psychology, Vol. I. Ed. by Gregory A. Kimble & Kurt Schlesinger. 424p. 1985. text ed. 39.95 (ISBN 0-89859-311-5). L Erlbaum Assocs.

Topics in the Homological Theory of Modules over Commutative Rings. Melvin Hochster. LC 75-1325. (CBMS Regional Conference Series in Mathematics: No. 24). 75p. 1985. pap. 12.00 (ISBN 0-8218-1674-8, CBMS-24). Am Math.

Topics in the Logic of Relevance. M. Richard Diaz. (Analytica). 144p. 1981. lib. bdg. 46.00 (ISBN 3-88405-003-6). Philosophia Pr.

Topics in the Mathematics of Quantum Mechanics. Robert Hermann. (Interdisciplinary Mathematics Ser: No. 6). 250p. 1973. 21.00 (ISBN 0-915692-05-8, 991600231). Math Sci Pr.

Topics in the Theory of Algebraic Groups. James B. Carrell et al. LC 82-17329. (Notre Dame Mathematical Lectures Ser.: No. 10a). 192p. (Orig.). 1983. pap. text ed. 9.95x (ISBN 0-268-01843-X). U of Notre Dame Pr.

Topics in the Theory of Computation: Selected Papers of the International Conference on Foundations of Computation Theory Held in Borgholm, Sweden, 21-27 August, 1983. Ed. by M. Karpinski & J. Van Leeuwen. (Mathematics Studies, Vol. 102. Annals of Discrete Mathematics, Vol. 24). 212p. 1985. 63.25 (ISBN 0-444-87647-2, North-Holland). Elsevier.

Topics in the Theory of Generative Grammar. Noam Chomsky. (Janua Linguarum, Ser. Minor: No. 56). (Orig.). 1978. pap. text ed. 10.50x (ISBN 90-279-3122-4). Mouton.

Topics in the Theory of Lifting. A. Ionescu Tulcea & C. Ionescu Tulcea. (Ergebnisse der Mathematik: Vol. 48). 1969. 26.00 (ISBN 0-387-04471-X). Springer-Verlag.

Topics in the Theory of Random Noise, 2 vols. R. L. Stratonovich. (Mathematics & Its Applications Ser.). 1963-67. Set. 182.00 (ISBN 0-677-00800-7); Vol. 1, 306p. 104.00 (ISBN 0-677-00780-9); Vol. 2, 344p. 107.00x (ISBN 0-677-00790-6). Gordon & Breach.

Topics in the Theory of Surfaces in Elliptic Space. Ed. by A. V. Pogorelov. (Russian Tracts on the Physical Sciences Ser.). (Illus.). 146p. 1962. 59.00 (ISBN 0-677-20400-0). Gordon & Breach.

Topics in the Theory of Voting. Phillip D. Straffin. (UMAP Ser.: No. 5). 76p. 1980. pap. 8.75x (ISBN 0-8176-3017-1). Birkhauser.

Topics in Theoretical Physics. Ed. by P. O. Riska. (Liperi Summer School of Theoretical Physics: Vol. 2). 416p. 1969. 136.00 (ISBN 0-677-13240-9). Gordon & Breach.

Topics in Theoretical Physics, Vol. 1. Ed. by C. Cronstrom. (Liperi Summer School of Theoretical Physics Ser.). 318p. 1969. 115.00 (ISBN 0-677-13180-1). Gordon & Breach.

Topics in Therapeutics. The Royal College of Physicians. Ed. by A. M. Breckenridge. 1974. pap. text ed. 45.00x (ISBN 0-685-83077-2). State Mutual Bk.

Topics in Therapeutics. Ed. by D. W. Vere. 224p. 1978. 27.00 (ISBN 0-8464-1144-X). Beekman Pubs.

Topics in Therapeutics, 1976. Royal College of Physicians. Ed. by R. G. Shanks. 1976. pap. text ed. 40.00x (ISBN 0-685-83078-0). State Mutual Bk.

Topics in Topicals. Ed. by R. Marks. 1985. lib. bdg. 34.25 (ISBN 0-85200-891-0, Pub. by MTP Pr England). Kluwer-Academic.

Topics in Topology. A. W. Schurle. 266p. 1979. 40.50 (ISBN 0-444-00285-5, North Holland). Elsevier.

Topics in Trade Coordination of Planned Economies. Alfred Zauberman. 108p. 1980. 32.75 (ISBN 0-8419-5085-7). Holmes & Meier.

Topics in Transcendental Algebraic Geometry. Ed. by Phillip A. Griffiths. LC 82-42593. (Annals of Mathematics Studies: No. 106). 390p. 1984. 52.50x (ISBN 0-691-08335-5); pap. text ed. 15.50x (ISBN 0-691-08339-8). Princeton U Pr.

Topics in Two-Phase Heat Transfer & Flow: Presented at the Winter Annual Meeting of ASME, San Francisco, CA, Dec. 10-15, 1978. Ed. by S. G. Bankoff. LC 78-68087. pap. 59.80 (ISBN 0-317-08175-6, 2013876). Bks Demand UMI.

Topics in Vibrational Spectroscopy: Dedicated to the Memory of Sir Harold W. Thompson. Ed. by F. A. Miller. 300p. 1985. 84.00 (ISBN 0-08-032602-1). Pergamon.

Topics in Warlpiri Grammar. David Nash. Ed. by Jorge Hankamer. (Outstanding Dissertations in Linguistics Ser.). 280p. 1985. 35.00 (ISBN 0-8240-5435-0). Garland Pub.

Topics in Wastewater Management. Sidwick. (Critical Reports on Analytical Chemistry). 1987. 59.95 (ISBN 0-471-91323-5). Wiley.

Topics of Our Times Series, 19 vols. Set. lib. bdg. 64.03 incl. catalog cards (ISBN 0-87157-800-X); Set. pap. 37.81 vinyl laminated covers (ISBN 0-87157-300-8). SamHar Pr.

Topics of Psychosomatic Research: Proceedings of the European Conference on Psychomatic Research, 9th, Vienna, April 1972. European Conference on Psychosomatic Research Staff. Ed. by H. Freyberger. (Journal: Psychotherapy & Psychosomatic Ser.: Vol. 22, Nos. 2-6). 305p. 1973. Repr. 60.00 (ISBN 3-8055-1616-9). S Karger.

Topics of West African History. Adu Boahen et al. 200p. 1986. pap. text ed. 14.95 (ISBN 0-582-58504-X). Longman.

Topics on M-Adic Topologies. S. Greco & P. Salmon. LC 76-139730. (Ergebnisse der Mathematik und Ihrer Grenzgebiete: Vol. 58). 1971. 23.00 (ISBN 0-387-05091-4). Springer-Verlag.

Topics on Nonlinear Wave Plasma Interaction. K. Baumgartel & K. Sauer. 224p. 1987. 35.00 (ISBN 0-8176-1864-3). Birkhauser.

Topics on Perfect Graphics: Annals of Discreet Mathematics, Vol. 21. Ed. by C. Berge & V. Chvatal. (Mathematics Studies: No. 88). 350p. 1984. 139.50 (ISBN 0-444-86587-X, North-Holland). Elsevier.

Topics on Real Analytic Spaces. F. Guaraldo et al. (Advanced Lectures in Mathematics Ser.). 164p. 1986. pap. 20.00 (ISBN 3-528-08963-6, Pub. by Vieweg & Sohn). IPS.

Topics on Steiner Systems. C. C. Lindner & A. Rosa. (Annals of Discrete Mathematics Ser.: Vol. 7). 350p. 1980. 100.00 (ISBN 0-444-85484-3, North-Holland). Elsevier.

Topics on Tropical Neurology. R. W. Hornabrook. LC 74-11300. (Contemporary Neurology Ser.: No. 12). (Illus.). 303p. 1975. 40.00x (ISBN 0-8036-4680-1). Davis Co.

Topics, Terms, & Research Techniques: Self-Instruction in Using Library Catalogs. Richard R. Strawn. LC 80-12569. 98p. 1980. 16.50 (ISBN 0-8108-1308-4). Scarecrow.

Topkapi Saray Museum, 3 vols. J. M. Rogers. (Illus.). 224p. 1987. 150.00 ea. Treasury (ISBN 0-8212-1672-4). Carpets (ISBN 0-8212-1679-1). Architecture (ISBN 0-8212-1680-5). NYGS.

Topkapi Saray Museum: Manuscripts. Ed. by J. M. Rogers. (Illus.). 280p. 150.00 (ISBN 0-8212-1633-3). NYGS.

Topkapi Saray Museum: Textiles. Ed. by J. M. Rogers. (Illus.). 216p. 150.00 (ISBN 0-8212-1634-1). NYGS.

Topless Tulip Caper. Lawrence Block. 192p. 1984. 13.95 (ISBN 0-8052-8202-5, Pub. by Allison & Busby, England). Schocken.

Topley & Wilson's Principles of Bacteriology, Virology & Immunity, Vol. 1. 7th ed. Graham S. Wilson. (Illus.). 552p. 1983. lib. bdg. 95.00 (ISBN 0-683-09064-X). Williams & Wilkins.

Topley & Wilson's Principles of Bacteriology, Virology & Immunity, Vol. 2. 7th ed. M. T. Parker. 576p. 1983. lib. bdg. 95.00 (ISBN 0-683-09065-8). Williams & Wilkins.

Topley & Wilson's Principles of Bacteriology, Virology & Immunity, Vol. 3. 7th ed. G. R. Smith. 576p. 1984. 91.00 (ISBN 0-683-09066-6). Williams & Wilkins.

Topley & Wilson's Principles of Bacteriology, Virology & Immunity, Vol. 4. 7th ed. F. B. Brown. 704p. 1984. 91.00 (ISBN 0-683-09067-4). Williams & Wilkins.

Topliff's Travels: Letters from Abroad in the Years 1828 & 1829. Samuel Topliff. Ed. by Ethel S. Bolton. LC 78-173189. Repr. of 1906 ed. 22.00 (ISBN 0-405-09030-7). Ayer Co Pubs.

Toplin. Michael McDowell. (Illus.). 186p. 1985. lib. bdg. 22.50 (ISBN 0-910489-11-4). Scream Pr.

Topobiology: An Introduction to Molecular Embryology. Gerald M. Edelman. LC 88-47678. (Illus.). 240p. 1988. text ed. 21.95 (ISBN 0-465-08634-9). Basic.

Topographic Histochemistry of the Cerebellum. Enrico Marani. LC 86-12132. (Progress in Histochemistry & Cytochemistry). (Illus.). 169p. 1986. pap. 70.00 (ISBN 0-89574-221-7, Pub. by Gustav Fischer Verlag). VCH Pubs.

Topographic, Hydrographic & Sedimentologic Setting of Little Lake, San Salvador Island, Bahamas. J. W. Teeter. (Occasional Papers - 1983: No. 1). 10p. 1983. pap. text ed. 1.00 (ISBN 0-935909-09-5). CCFL Bahamian.

Topographic Map--Golden Grizzly Project: Gold Exploration in Montana. (Illus.). 1981. ltd. ed. 75.00 (ISBN 0-943435-02-1). Cartographer Ink.

Topographic Mapping of Brain Electrical Activity. Frank H. Duffy. LC 85-15156. (Illus.). 320p. 1986. text ed. 55.00 (ISBN 0-409-90008-7). Butterworth.

Topographic Mapping of the Americas, Australia, & New Zealand. Mary L. Larsgaard. LC 84-3874. 192p. 1984. text ed. 45.00 (ISBN 0-87287-276-9). Libs Unl.

Topographic Terms: English & Spanish. John V. Dobbin. 1971. write for info. (G426). Am Congrs Survey.

Topographic Terms in the Ohio Valley 1748-1800. W. Bruce Finnie. (Publications of the American Dialect Society: No. 53). 144p. 1970. pap. 8.80 (ISBN 0-8173-0653-6). U of Ala Pr.

Topographic Waves in Channels & Lakes on the f-Plane. T. Stocker & K. Hutter. (Lecture Notes on Coastal & Estuarine Studies: Vol. 21). x, 176p. 1987. pap. 21.70 (ISBN 0-387-17623-3). Springer-Verlag.

Topographical Account of the District of Cunningham, Ayrshire. Timothy Pont. LC 74-174280. (Maitland Club, Glasgow. Publications: No. 74). Repr. of 1858 ed. 27.50 (ISBN 0-404-53112-1). AMS Pr.

Topographical Description of the Dominions of the United States of America. Thomas Pownall. Ed. by Lois Mulkearn. LC 75-22835. (America in Two Centuries Ser). 1975. Repr. of 1949 ed. 20.00x (ISBN 0-405-07706-8). Ayer Co Pubs.

Topographical Description of the State of Ohio, Indiana Territory, & Louisiana. Jervis Cutler. LC 78-146388. (First American Frontier Ser). (Illus.). 1971. Repr. of 1812 ed. 17.00 (ISBN 0-405-02839-3). Ayer Co Pubs.

Topographical Description of the Western Territory of North America. 3rd ed. Gilbert Imlay. 1797. 22.00 (ISBN 0-384-25685-6). Johnson Repr.

Topographical Description of the Western Territory of North America. 3rd ed. Gilbert Imlay. LC 68-55739. (Illus.). 1969. Repr. of 1797 ed. 57.50x (ISBN 0-678-00541-9). Kelley.

Topographical Dictionary of Ireland, 2 vols. Samuel Lewis. LC 83-82827. (Illus.). 1480p. 1984. Repr. of 1837 ed. Set. 75.00 (ISBN 0-8063-1063-4). Genealog Pub.

Topographical Dictionary of 2885 English Emigrants to New England, 1620-1650. Charles E. Banks. LC 63-4154. (Illus.). 295p. 1981. Repr. of 1937 ed. 17.50 (ISBN 0-8063-0019-1). Genealog Pub.

Topographical Dictionary to the Works of Shakespeare & His Fellow Dramatists. Edward H. Sugden. 1969. Repr. of 1925 ed. cancelled (ISBN 3-4870-2702-X). Adlers Foreign Bks.

Topographical Memoir. Thomas J. Cram. 126p. 1978. 12.00 (ISBN 0-87770-193-8). Ye Galleon.

Topographical Poetry in Eighteenth Century England. Robert A. Aubin. (MLA Rev. Fund Ser.). 1936. 52.00 (ISBN 0-527-03800-8). Kraus Repr.

Topographie audiovisueller Materialen (AVM) An wissenschaftlichen Einrichtungen Bundesrepublik Deutschland. Gerd Wilbert. 234p. (Ger.). 1987. lib. bdg. 27.00 (ISBN 3-598-10722-6). K G Saur.

Topographische Anatomie des Plexus Brachialis und Thoracic-Outlet-Syndrom. J. Lang. (Illus.). 74p. (Ger.). 1985. pap. 19.20x (ISBN 3-11-010160-2). De Gruyter.

Topography & Architecture. Oscar Broneer. LC 75-27618. (Isthmia Ser: Vol. 2). (Illus.). 1973. 30.00x (ISBN 0-87661-932-4). Am Sch Athens.

Topography & History of Beth-shan: With Details of the Egyptian & Other Inscriptions Found on the Site. Alan Rowe. LC 31-13812. (Publications of the Palestine Section of the Museum of the University of Pennsylvania: Vol. 1). pap. 36.00 (ISBN 0-317-28548-3, 2052030). Bks Demand UMI.

Topography & Systems in Psychoanalytic Theory. Merton M. Gill. LC 59-9821. (Psychological Issues Monograph: No. 10, Vol. 3, No. 2). 179p. (Orig.). 1963. text ed. 22.50x (ISBN 0-8236-6560-7); pap. text ed. 18.50x (ISBN 0-8236-6580-1). Intl Univs Pr.

Topography of Thebes from the Bronze Age to Modern Times. Sarantis Symeonoglou. LC 84-24890. (Illus.). 328p. 1985. text ed. 66.50x (ISBN 0-691-03576-8). Princeton U Pr.

Topoi: The Categorial Analysis of Logic. R. Goldblatt. (Studies in Logic & the Foundations of Mathematics Ser.: Vol. 98). 1980. 69.25 (ISBN 0-444-85207-7, North Holland). Elsevier.

Topoi: The Categorical Analysis of Logic. 2nd, rev. ed. (Studies in Logic & the Foundation of Mathematics: Vol. 98). 1984. 100.00 (ISBN 0-444-86711-2, I-499-83, North-Holland). Elsevier.

Topological Algebras: Selected Topics. A. Mallios. (North Holland Mathematics Studies: Vol. 124). 536p. 1986. 92.00 (ISBN 0-444-87966-8, North-Holland). Elsevier.

Topological Analysis. Gordon T. Whyburn. LC 64-12193. (Princeton Mathematical Ser.: Vol. 23). Repr. of 1964 ed. 34.30 (ISBN 0-8357-9515-2, 2015485). Bks Demand UMI.

Topological Analysis & Synthesis of Communication Networks. Wan-hui Kim & Robert T. Chien. LC 62-14636. (Illus.). pap. 80.50 (ISBN 0-317-08767-3, 2010965). Bks Demand UMI.

Topological & Geometrical Methods in Field Theory: Proceedings of the Symposium, Espoo, Finland, June 8-14, 1986. Ed. by J. Hietarinta. 460p. 1987. 71.00 (ISBN 9971-50-229-1); pap. 32.00 (ISBN 9971-50-230-5). World Scientific Pub.

Topological & Uniform Spaces. I. M. James. (Undergraduate Texts in Mathematics Ser.). (Illus.). 175p. 1987. 36.00 (ISBN 0-387-96466-5). Springer-Verlag.

Topological Approach to the Chemistry of Conjugated Molecules. A. Graovac et al. (Lecture Notes in Chemistry: Vol. 4). 1977. pap. 14.00 (ISBN 0-387-08431-2). Springer-Verlag.

Topological Degree Methods in Non-Linear Boundary Value Problems. Jean Mahwin. LC 78-31906. (CBMS Regional Conference Ser. in Mathematics: No. 40). 122p. 1981. pap. 13.00 (ISBN 0-8218-1690-X, CBMS-40). Am Math.

Topological Disorder in Condensed Matter. Ed. by F. Yonezawa & T. Ninomiya. (Springer Series in Solid State Sciences: Vol. 46). (Illus.). 270p. 1983. 39.50 (ISBN 0-387-12663-5). Springer-Verlag.

Topological Dynamics. W. H. Gottschalk & G. A. Hedlund. LC 55-12710. (Colloquium Pbns. Ser.: Vol. 36). 167p. 1982. pap. 32.00 (ISBN 0-8218-1036-7, COLL-36). Am Math.

Topological Embeddings. T. Benny Rushing. (Pure & Applied Mathematics Ser., Vol. 52). 1973. 89.00 (ISBN 0-12-603550-4). Acad Pr.

Topological Entropy & Equivalence of Dynamical Systems. R. L. Adler & B. Marcus. LC 79-15040. (Memoirs Ser.: No. 219). 84p. 1981. pap. 15.00 (ISBN 0-8218-2219-5). Am Math.

Topological Fields. Wieslaw. (Pure & Applied Mathematics Ser.). 328p. 1988. 99.75 (ISBN 0-8247-7731-X). Dekker.

Topological Geometry. 2nd ed. I. R. Porteous. LC 79-41611. 1981. 80.00 (ISBN 0-521-23160-4); pap. 34.50 (ISBN 0-521-29839-3). Cambridge U Pr.

Topological Graph Theory. Jonathan L. Gross & Thomas W. Tucker. LC 87-6221. (Discrete Mathematics Ser.). 351p. 1987. 59.95 (ISBN 0-471-04926-3, Pub. by Wiley-Interscience). Wiley.

Topological Groups. 2nd ed. Lev S. Pontryagin. (Russian Monographs). 560p. 1966. 137.00 (ISBN 0-677-20390-X). Gordon & Breach.

Topological Imbeddings in Euclidean Space: Proceedings. Steklov Institute of Mathematics, Academy of Sciences, U S S R. Ed. by L. V. Keldys. (Proceedings of the Steklov Institute of Mathematics: No. 81). 1968. 64.00 (ISBN 0-8218-1881-3, STEKLO-81). Am Math.

Topological Invariants of Quasi-Ordinary Singularities & Embedded Topological Classification of Quasi- Ordinary Singularities. Lipman & Gau. (MEMO Ser.: No. 388). 130p. 1988. 16.00 (ISBN 0-8218-2451-1). Am Math.

Topological Methods in Algebraic Geometry. F. Hirzebruch. Tr. by R. L. Schwarzberger from Ger. (Gruhdlehren der Mathematischen Wissenschaften: Vol. 131). (2nd corrected printing of the 3rd enlarged ed.). 1978. 44.00 (ISBN 0-387-03525-7). Springer-Verlag.

Topological Methods in Chemistry. Howard Simmons & Richard E. Merrifield. LC 87-30530. 1988. write for info. (ISBN 0-471-83817-9). Wiley.

Topological Methods in Nonlinear Functional Analysis. Ed. by S. P. Singh et al. LC 83-11824. (Contemporary Mathematics Ser.: Vol. 21). 218p. 1983. pap. text ed. 23.00 (ISBN 0-8218-5023-7). Am Math.

Topological Methods in the Theory of Functions of a Complex Variable. Marston Morse. (Annals of Math Ser.). 1947. 12.00 (ISBN 0-527-02731-6). Kraus Repr.

Topological Model Theory. J. Flum & M. Ziegler. (Lecture Notes in Mathematics: Vol. 769). 151p. 1980. pap. 15.00 (ISBN 3-540-09732-5). Springer-Verlag.

Topological Picturebook. G. K. Francis. (Illus.). 210p. 1987. 33.00 (ISBN 0-387-96426-6). Springer-Verlag.

Topological Properties & Global Structure of Space Time. Ed. by Peter Bergmann & Venzo De Sabbata. (NATO ASI Series B, Physics: Vol. 138). 280p. 1986. 49.50x (ISBN 0-306-42367-7, Plenum Pr). Plenum Pub.

Topological Properties of Spaces of Continuous Functions. R. A. McCoy & I. Ntantu. (Lecture Notes in Mathematics Ser.: Vol. 1315). 124p. 1988. pap. 13.90 (ISBN 0-387-19302-2). Springer-Verlag.

Topological Semifields & Their Applications to General Topology. M. Ja Antonovskii et al. LC 77-11046. (Translation Ser. No 2: Vol. 106). 142p. 1979. pap. 26.00 (ISBN 0-8218-3056-2, TRAN 2/106). Am Math.

Topological Topics: Articles on Algebra & Topology. Ed. by I. M. James. LC 83-7745. (London Mathematical Society Lecture Note Ser.: No. 86). 192p. 1983. pap. 22.95 (ISBN 0-521-27581-4). Cambridge U Pr.

Topological Transformation Groups. Deane Montgomery & Leo Zippin. LC 74-265. 302p. 1974. Repr. of 1955 ed. 22.00 (ISBN 0-88275-169-7). Krieger.

Topological Tribute. Ed. by I. M. James et al. (London Mathematical Society Lecture Note Ser.: No. 94). 250p. 1985. pap. 29.95 (ISBN 0-521-27815-5). Cambridge U Pr.

Topological Vector Space Two. G. Koethe. LC 78-84831. (Grundlehren der Mathematischen Wissenschaften: Vol. 237). 1979. 67.00 (ISBN 0-387-90400-X). Springer-Verlag.

Topological Vector Spaces. A. Grothendieck. (Notes on Mathematics & Its Applications Ser.). 256p. 1973. 68.00 (ISBN 0-677-30020-4). Gordon & Breach.

Topological Vector Spaces. Narici & Beckenstein. (Monographs & Textbooks in Pure & Applied Mathematics). 400p. 1985. 69.75 (ISBN 0-8247-7315-2). Dekker.

Topological Vector Spaces. 2nd ed. A. P. Robertson & Wendy Robertson. LC 72-89805. (Cambridge Tracts in Mathematics Ser: No. 53). 1980. pap. 13.95 (ISBN 0-521-29882-2). Cambridge U Pr.

Topological Vector Spaces. H. H. Schaefer. LC 65-24692. (Graduate Texts in Mathematics: Vol. 3). 1971. text ed. 39.00 (ISBN 0-387-90026-8). Springer-Verlag.

Topological Vector Spaces, Distributions & Kernels. Francois Treves. 1967. 69.50 (ISBN 0-12-699450-1). Acad Pr.

Topological Vector Spaces One. G. Koethe. Tr. by D. J. H. Garling. (Grundlehren der Mathematischen Wissenshaften: Vol. 159). 456p. (Second Revised Printing). 1969. 64.00 (ISBN 0-387-04509-0). Springer-Verlag.

Topologie. Paul S. Alexandroff & H. Hopf. LC 65-21833. (Ger.). 17.50 (ISBN 0-8284-0197-7). Chelsea Pub.

Topologie d'une Cite Fantome. Alain Robbe-Grillet. 204p. 1976. 20.95 (ISBN 0-686-54745-4). French & Eur.

Topology. Gustav Choquet. (Pure & Applied Mathematics Ser.: Vol. 19). 1966. 77.00 (ISBN 0-12-173450-1). Acad Pr.

Topology, 2 vols. A. Csaszar. (Colloquia Mathematica Societatis Janos Bolyai: Vol. 23). 1260p. 1980. Set. 197.50 (ISBN 0-444-85406-1, North-Holland). Elsevier.

Topology. James Dugundji. 447p. 1966. text ed. write for info. (ISBN 0-205-00271-4). Wm C Brown.

Topology. John G. Hocking & Gail S. Young. (Illus.). 384p. 1988. pap. 7.95 (ISBN 0-486-65676-4). Dover.

Topology. K. Janich. Tr. by S. Levy. (Undergraduate Texts Mathematics). (Illus.). x, 198p. 1984. 31.50 (ISBN 0-387-90892-7). Springer-Verlag.

Topology, 2 vols. Kazimierz Kuratowski. Incl. Vol. 1. 1966. 65.00 (ISBN 0-12-429201-1); Vol. 2. 1969. 76.50 (ISBN 0-12-429202-X). Acad Pr.

Topology. 2nd ed. Solomon Lefschetz. LC 56-11513. 16.95 (ISBN 0-8284-0116-0). Chelsea Pub.

Topology: A Collection of Papers. Ed. by P. Aleksandrov. LC 85-7326. (Proceedings of the Steklov Institute of Mathematics Ser.: Vol. 154). 333p. 1985. text ed. 91.00 (ISBN 0-8218-3086-4). Am Math.

Topology: A First Course. James Munkres. (Illus.). 448p. 1975. ref. ed. 44.67 (ISBN 0-13-925495-1). P-H.

Topology: An Introduction with Application to Topological Groups. George McCarty. (Illus.). 288p. 1988. pap. text ed. 6.95 (ISBN 0-486-65633-0). Dover.

Topology: An Outline for a First Course. Lewis E. Ward. LC 72-76065. (Pure & Applied Mathematics Ser.: Vol. 10). pap. 30.80 (2027126). Bks Demand UMI.

Topology & Borel Structure. J. P. Christensen. (Mathematical Studies: Vol. 10). 133p. 1974. pap. 42.75 (ISBN 0-444-10608-1, North-Holland). Elsevier.

Topology & Geometry for Physicists. Charles Nash & Siddartha Sen. 1983. 50.50 (ISBN 0-12-514080-0). Acad Pr.

Topology & Geometry for Physicists. Charles Nash & Siddharta Sen. 311p. 1988. pap. 29.00 (ISBN 0-12-514081-9). Acad Pr.

Topology & Its Applications. Ed. by S. Thomeier. (Lecture Notes in Pure & Applied Mathematics Ser.: Vol. 12). 504p. 1975. 49.75 (ISBN 0-8247-6212-6). Dekker.

Topology & Maps. Ed. by T. Husain. LC 77-10110. (Mathematical Concepts & Methods in Science & Engineering Ser.: Vol. 5). 358p. 1977. 55.00x (ISBN 0-306-31005-8, Plenum Pr). Plenum Pub.

Topology & Normed Spaces. G. J. Jameson. (Mathematics Ser.). 1974. 21.95x (ISBN 0-412-12340-1, NO. 6165, Pub. by Chapman & Hall). Routledge Chapman & Hall.

Topology & Order. Leopoldo Nachbin. LC 76-59. 128p. 1976. Repr. of 1965 ed. 14.00 (ISBN 0-88275-387-8). Krieger.

Topology & Topological Algebra. V. G. Boltyanskii et al. (Translations Ser.: No. 1, Vol. 8). 1962. 27.00 (ISBN 0-8218-1608-X, TRANS 1-8). Am Math.

Topology Conference: Proceedings. Virginia Polytechnic Institute & State University, March 22-24, 1973. Ed. by R. F. Dickman & P. Fletcher. (Lecture Notes in Mathematics: Vol. 375). x, 283p. 1974. pap. 22.00 (ISBN 0-387-06684-5). Springer-Verlag.

Topology for Analysis. Albert Wilansky. LC 81-1616. 400p. 1983. Repr. of 1970 ed. 31.00 (ISBN 0-89874-343-5). Krieger.

Topology from the Differentiable Viewpoint. John W. Milnor. LC 65-26874. (Illus.). 64p. 1965. pap. 5.95x (ISBN 0-8139-0181-2). U Pr of Va.

Topology: General & Algebraic Topology & Applications, Proceedings of the International Topological Conference Held in Leningrad, August 23-27, 1982. Ed. by L. D. Faddeev & A. A. Mal'Cev. (Lecture Notes in Mathematics Ser.: Vol. 1060). vi, 389p. 1984. 26.00 (ISBN 0-387-13337-2). Springer-Verlag.

Topology in Spaces of Holomorphic Mappings. L. Nachbin. LC 68-29710. (Ergebnisse der Mathematik, und Ihrer Grenzgebiete: Vol. 47). 1969. 19.00 (ISBN 0-387-04470-1). Springer-Verlag.

Topology of a Phantom City. Alain Robbe-Grillet. Tr. by J. A. Underwood from Fr. LC 77-77854. 1977. 8.95 (ISBN 0-394-42196-5, GP801). Grove.

Topology of a Phantom City. Alain Robbe-Grillet. Tr. by J. A. Underwood from Fr. LC 77-77854. 1977. pap. 3.95 (ISBN 0-394-17012-1, E698, Ever). Grove.

Topology of Classical Groups & Related Topics. S. Y. Husseini. (Notes on Mathematics & Its Applications Ser.). 136p. 1968. 44.00 (ISBN 0-677-02160-7). Gordon & Breach.

Topology of CW Complexes. A. T. Lundell & S. Weingram. LC 68-26689. (Illus.). vii, 216p. 1969. 25.50 (ISBN 0-387-90128-0). Springer-Verlag.

Topology of Fibre Bundles. N. E. Steenrod. (Mathematical Ser.: Vol. 14). 1951. 30.50x (ISBN 0-691-08055-0). Princeton U Pr.

Topology of Function Spaces & the Calculus of variations in the Large. L. A. Ljusternik. LC 66-25298. (Translations of Mathematical Monographs: Vol. 16). 96p. 1982. pap. 24.00 (ISBN 0-8218-1566-0, MMONO-16). Am Math.

Topology of Low-Dimensional Manifolds: Proceedings. Ed. by R. Fenn. (Lecture Notes in Mathematics: Vol. 722). 1979. pap. 14.00 (ISBN 0-387-09506-3). Springer-Verlag.

Topology of Manifolds. rev. ed. Raymond L. Wilder. LC 49-6722. (Colloquium Pbns. Ser.: Vol. 32). 403p. 1979. pap. 49.00 (ISBN 0-8218-1032-4, COLL-32). Am Math.

Topology of Surfaces. Andre Gramain. Tr. by Leo F. Boron & Charles O. Christenson. LC 84-70461. (Illus.). 160p. 1984. pap. text ed. 18.00 (ISBN 0-914351-01-X). BCS Assocs.

Topology of the Automorphism: Group of a Free Group. S. M. Gersten. (London Mathematical Society Lecture Note Ser.: No. 102). 200p. Date not set. pap. price not set. (ISBN 0-521-31523-9). Cambridge U Pr.

Topology of Uniform Convergence on Order-Bounded Sets. Y. C. Wong. (Lecture Notes in Mathematics: Vol. 531). 1976. pap. 13.00 (ISBN 0-387-07800-2). Springer-Verlag.

Topology, Ordinary Differential Equations, Dynamical Systems: A Collection of Survey Articles, Pt. II. Ed. by Mishchenko. (Proceedings of the Steklov Institute of Mathematics Ser.: Vol. 169). 260p. 1987. pap. text ed. 105.00 (ISBN 0-8218-3100-3). Am Math.

Topology: Proceedings of the Memphis State University Conference. Stanley Franklin & Barbara S. Thomas. (Lecture Notes in Pure and Applied Math Ser.: Vol. 24). 1976. 59.75 (ISBN 0-8247-6460-9). Dekker.

Topology: Theory & Applications. Ed. by A. Csaszar. (Colloquia Mathematica Societatis Janos Bolyai Ser.: Vol. 41). 728p. 1986. 152.75 (ISBN 0-444-87757-6). Elsevier.

Topology via Logic. Steven Vickers. (Cambridge Tracts in Theoretical Computer Science Ser.). (Illus.). 120p. Date not set. price not set (ISBN 0-521-36062-5). Cambridge U Pr.

Topos Theory. P. T. Johnstone. 1978. 96.00 (ISBN 0-12-387850-0). Acad Pr.

Toposes & Local Set Theories: An Introduction. J. L. Bell. (Logic Guides: No. 14). (Illus.). 350p. 1988. 75.00 (ISBN 0-19-853274-1). Oxford U Pr.

Toposes, Triples & Theories. M. Barr & C. Wells. (Grundlehren der Mathematischen Wissenschaften Ser.: Vol. 278). (Illus.). xiii, 345p. 1985. 44.00 (ISBN 0-387-96115-1). Springer-Verlag.

Topper. Thorne Smith. Repr. lib. bdg. 18.95x (ISBN 0-89190-448-4, Pub. by River City Pr). Amereon Ltd.

Topper. Thorne Smith. 208p. 1980. pap. 2.25 (ISBN 0-345-28722-3, Del Rey). Ballantine.

Topper Takes a Trip. Thorne Smith. Repr. lib. bdg. 20.95 (ISBN 0-89190-437-9, Pub. by River City Pr). Amereon Ltd.

Topper Takes a Trip. Thorne Smith et al. 240p. 1980. pap. 2.25 (ISBN 0-345-28723-1, Del Rey). Ballantine.

Topps Baseball Card Update 1986. Frank Slocum. 1986. 17.95 (ISBN 0-446-51352-0). Warner Bks.

Topps Baseball Cards: The Complete Collection, a 35 Year History 1951-1985. Frank Slocum. 736p. 1985. text ed. 79.95 (ISBN 0-446-51347-4). Warner Bks.

Topps Baseball Cards Update. Red Foley. LC 87-19012. 128p. 1988. 17.95 (ISBN 0-446-51487-X). Warner Bks.

Topps Baseball Cards Update 1987. Red Foley. LC 87-19012. 1988. 17.95 (ISBN 0-446-51421-7). Warner Bks.

Topps Football Cards: The Complete Picture Collection, A History 1956-1986. Jack Clary. 400p. 1986. 59.95 (ISBN 0-446-51336-9). Warner Bks.

TOPS. 3rd ed. Journal of Chemical Education. LC 67-25495. (Tested Overhead Projection Ser.). pap. 34.50 (ISBN 0-317-41843-2, 2025632). Bks Demand UMI.

Tops & Bottoms: The Experts Forecast the Stock Market. Donald Ribaudo. 1985. cancelled (ISBN 0-87094-592-0). Dow Jones-Irwin.

Topsail & Battleaxe: A Voyage in the Wake of the Vikings. Tom Cunliffe. (Illus.). 220p. 1988. 24.95 (ISBN 0-7153-9123-2, Pub. by David & Charles Pub England). Sterling.

Topsell's Histories of Beasts. Ed. by Malcolm South. LC 80-28838. (Illus.). 200p. 1981. text ed. 20.95x (ISBN 0-88229-642-6). Nelson-Hall.

Topsoil & Civilization. rev. ed. Vernon G. Carter & Tom Dale. (Illus.). 240p. 1981. pap. 10.95x (ISBN 0-8061-1107-0). U of Okla Pr.

Topsy & Evil. George Baxt. LC 87-82445. 232p. 1987. pap. 4.95 (ISBN 0-930330-66-8). Intl Polygonics.

Topsy-Turvies: Pictures to Stretch the Imagination. Mitsumasa Anno. LC 71-96054. (Illus.). 28p. (gr. k-5). 1970. 6.50 (ISBN 0-8348-2004-8). Weatherhill.

Topsy-Turvy. facsimile ed. Vernon Bartlett. LC 77-110179. (Short Story Index Reprint Ser.). 1927. 18.00 (ISBN 0-8369-3330-3). Ayer Co Pubs.

Topsy-Turvy. Monika Beisner. (Illus.). 32p. (ps up). 1987. 12.95 (ISBN 0-374-37679-4). FS&G.

Topsy Turvy. Monika Beisner. (Illus.). 32p. (ps up). 1988. 12.95 (ISBN 0-317-67597-4). FS&G.

Topsy Turvy Spring. V. Tendryakov. 413p. 1978. pap. 5.45 (ISBN 0-8285-1052-0, Pub. by Progress Pubs USSR). Imported Pubns.

Topsys & Turvys. Peter S. Newell. (Illus.). 76p. (gr. 3-7). pap. 3.00 (ISBN 0-486-21231-9). Dover.

Topsys & Turvys. Peter S. Newell. LC 87-51208. (gr. k-4). 1988. 12.95 (ISBN 0-8048-1551-8). C E Tuttle.

Topsys & Turvys, No. 2. Peter S. Newell. LC 87-51208. (gr. k-4). 1988. 12.95 (ISBN 0-8048-1552-6). C E Tuttle.

Topy. J. Rannap. 47p. 1985. pap. 1.99 (ISBN 0-8285-3134-X, Pub. by Perioodika Tallinn). Imported Pubns.

Toque de Diana. Rafael H. Moreno-Duran. 269p. (Span.). 1981. pap. 8.50 (ISBN 84-85859-06-5, 2009). Ediciones Norte.

Tor und der Tod. Hugo Von Hofmannsthal. Ed. by M. E. Gilbert. (German Text Ser.). 58p. 1942. pap. 9.95x (ISBN 0-631-01300-8). Basil Blackwell.

Torah: A Modern Commentary. W. Gunther Plaut & Bernard J. Bamberger. (Illus.). 1824p. 1981. 30.00 (ISBN 0-8074-0055-6). UAHC.

Torah: A Modern Commentary: Leviticus. Bernard J. Bamberger. Ed. by W. Gunther Plaut. 1979. 20.00 (ISBN 0-8074-0011-4, 3816). UAHC.

Torah: A Modern Commentary: Numbers. W. Gunther Plaut. (Torah Commentary Ser.). 476p. 1980. 20.00 (ISBN 0-8074-0039-4, 381602). UAHC.

Torah & Canon. James A. Sanders. LC 72-171504. 144p. (Orig.). 1972. pap. 5.95 (ISBN 0-8006-0105-X, 1-105). Fortress.

Torquemada. Benito P. Galdos. Tr. by Frances M. Lopez-Morillas from Span. LC 85-19560. 569p. 1986. 27.50x (ISBN 0-231-06228-1). Columbia U Pr.

Torquemada en la Hoguera, de Benito Perez Galdos. Angel Del Rio. xlviii, 131p. (Span.). bulk 0.80 (ISBN 0-318-14310-0). Hispanic Inst.

Torre. General de la Universidad de Puerto Rico Staff. 3.00 (ISBN 0-317-41477-1). U of PR pr.

Torre see Aguilas.

Torre Siniestra. new ed. Errol Lecale. Tr. by John A. Reed from Eng. (Compadre Collection, el Artifice: No. 1). Orig. Title: Castledoom. 160p. (Span.). 1974. pap. 0.85 (ISBN 0-88473-621-0). Fiesta Pub.

Torreites Sanchezi (Douville) from Jamaica see Palaeontographica Americana.

Torrent Control Terminology. (Conservation Guides: No. 6). 165p. (Eng., Span., Ital. & Ger.). 1982. pap. 12.50 (ISBN 92-5-001091-5, F2224, FAO). UNIPUB.

Torrent: Novellas & Short Stories. Anne Hebert. LC 73-83340. (French Writers of Canada Ser.). pap. 35.30 (ISBN 0-317-28416-9, 2022300). Bks Demand UMI.

Torrent of Portyngale. Ed. by E. Adam. (EETS E.S.: No.51). Repr. of 1887 ed. 25.00 (ISBN 0-527-00257-7). Kraus Repr.

Torrents of Spring. Ernest Hemingway. (Hudson River Editions Ser.). 96p. 1987. 30.00 (ISBN 0-02-550750-8). Macmillan.

Torrents of Spring, etc. facsimile ed. Ivan S. Turgenev. Tr. by Constance Garnett from Rus. LC 76-150489. (Short Story Index Reprint Ser). Repr. of 1916 ed. 19.00 (ISBN 0-8369-3830-5). Ayer Co Pubs.

Torres Strait Islanders: Custom & Colonialism. Jeremy Beckett. (Illus.). 230p. 1988. 49.50 (ISBN 0-521-33361-X). Cambridge U Pr.

Torres Strait: People & History. John Singe. (Illus.). 1980. 25.00x (ISBN 0-7022-1417-5). U of Queensland Pr.

Torres Straits Sculpture: A Study in Oceanic Primitive Art. Douglas F. Fraser. LC 77-94696. (Outstanding Dissertations in the Fine Arts Ser.). 1978. lib. bdg. 58.00 (ISBN 0-8240-3228-4). Garland Pub.

Torsion Design of Prestressed Concrete. (PCI Journal Reprints Ser.). 22p. pap. 5.00 (ISBN 0-686-40064-X, JR142). Prestressed Concrete.

Torsion Free Groups of Rank Two. Ross A. Beaumont & Richard S. Pierce. LC 52-42839. (Memoirs: No. 38). 44p. 1985. pap. 11.00 (ISBN 0-8218-1238-6, MEMO-38). Am Math.

Torsion-Free Modules. Eben Matlis. (Chicago Lectures in Mathematics Ser). 1973. 9.00x (ISBN 0-226-51073-5); pap. text ed. 7.00x (ISBN 0-226-51074-3). U of Chicago Pr.

Torsion in Concrete. 148p. 1978. 45.75 (ISBN 0-317-32095-5, B-12). ACI.

Torsion in Structures: An Engineering Approach. C. F. Kollbrunner & K. Basler. Tr. by E. C. Glauser. 1969. 35.00 (ISBN 0-387-04582-1). Springer-Verlag.

Torsion in SU-Bordism. Pierre E. Connor & E. E. Floyd. LC 52-42839. (Memoirs: No. 60). 74p. 1969. pap. 12.00 (ISBN 0-8218-1260-2, MEMO-60). Am Math.

Torsion of Reinforced Concrete. T. Hsu. 1983. 54.95 (ISBN 0-442-26401-1). VAn Nos Reinhold.

Torsion Theories. Jonathan S. Golan. LC 86-13350. (Pure & Applied Mathematics Ser.). 651p. 1987. 183.00 (ISBN 0-470-20367-6, Pub. by Halsted Press). Wiley.

Torsion Theories, Additive Semantics & Rings of Quotients. J. Lambeck. LC 70-148538. (Lecture Notes in Mathematics: Vol. 177). 1971. pap. 11.00 (ISBN 0-387-05340-9). Springer-Verlag.

Torsional Analysis of Steel Members. 1983. 16.00 (ISBN 0-318-22854-8, T114). Am Inst Steel Construct.

Torsional Strength of Reinforced & Prestressed Concrete Beams: CEB Approach. Bruno Thurlimann. (IBA Ser.: No. 92). 27p. 1979. pap. text ed. 13.95x (ISBN 0-8176-1125-8). Birkhauser.

Tort. G. H. Fridman. (Civil Law Library). 608p. 1989. 90.01 (ISBN 0-08-033080-0, Pub. by Waterlow). Pergamon.

Tort & Accident Law. Robert E. Keeton et al. LC 83-6645. (American Casebook Ser.). 1360p. 1983. text ed. 35.95 (ISBN 0-314-73467-8). West Pub.

Tort, Crime & Police in Mediaeval Britain: A Review of Some Early Law & Custom. J. W. Jeudwine. xix, 292p. 1983. Repr. of 1917 ed. lib. bdg. 25.00x (ISBN 0-8377-0742-0). Rothman.

Tort Law. R. W. Dias & B. S. Markesinis. (Illus.). 1984. 45.00x (ISBN 0-19-876150-3); pap. 29.95x (ISBN 0-19-876151-1). Oxford U Pr.

Tort Law & Alternatives, Cases & Materials On. 3rd ed. Marc A. Franklin & Robert L. Rabin. LC 83-5583. (University Casebook Ser.). 1006p. 1983. text ed. 28.00 (ISBN 0-88277-118-3). Foundation Pr.

Tort Law & Alternatives, Cases & Materials on. 4th ed. Marc A. Franklin & Robert L. Rabin. (University Casebook Ser.). 1143p. 1987. text ed. 35.40 (ISBN 0-88277-553-7). Foundation Pr.

Tort Law: Cases & Economic Analysis. Richard A. Posner. LC 81-82981. 792p. 1982. text ed. 33.00 (ISBN 0-316-71436-4). Little.

Tort Law in America: An Intellectual History. G. Edward White. 1980. text ed. 29.95x (ISBN 0-19-502586-5); pap. 9.95x (ISBN 0-19-503599-2). Oxford U Pr.

Tort Law in American History. Ed. by Kermit L. Hall. (United States Constitutional & Legal History Ser.). 600p. 1987. lib. bdg. 75.00 (ISBN 0-8240-0148-6). Garland Pub.

Tort Liability & the Music Educator. William R. Hazard. 32p. 1979. 2.50 (ISBN 0-686-37919-5, 1053). Music Ed Natl.

Tort Liability for Injuries to Pupils. Howard C. Leibee. (Illus.). 104p. 1965. pap. 5.45 (ISBN 0-87506-009-9). Campus.

Tort Liability Today. 66p. 1986. 25.00. Natl League Cities.

Tort Reform & Related Proposals: Annotated Bibliographies on Product Liability & Medical Malpractice. Ed. by Bruce A. Levin & Robert Coyne. xiii, 262p. 1979. 30.00 (ISBN 0-910058-94-6). Amer Bar Assn.

Tort Reform Packet. 1.50 (ISBN 0-317-62726-0). DC Bar Assn.

Tort UCC Warranties. Squillante. (Trial Practice Library). 1988. write for info. (ISBN 0-471-84803-4). Wiley.

Tortilla Flat. John Steinbeck. (Fiction Ser.). 224p. 1977. pap. 3.95 (ISBN 0-14-004240-7). Penguin.

Tortilla Flat. John Steinbeck. 1935. 16.95 (ISBN 0-670-72109-3). Viking.

Tortilla Flat see Short Novels of John Steinbeck.

Tortillas. Alvin J. Gordon. (Illus.). 20p. (Orig.). (gr. 1-3). 1971. pap. 6.95 (ISBN 0-916955-06-0). ARCUS Pub.

Tortillas for the Gods: A Symbolic Analysis of Zinacanteco Rituals. Evon Z. Vogt. 256p. 1976. 20.00x (ISBN 0-674-89554-1). Harvard U Pr.

Tortillitas Para Mama: And Other Nursery Rhymes, Spanish & English. Cooney et al. LC 81-4823. (Illus.). 32p. (gr. k-3). 1981. 11.95 (ISBN 0-8050-0285-5); pap. 3.95 (ISBN 0-8050-0317-7). H Holt & Co.

Tortious Liability for Unintentional Harm in the Common Law & the Civil Law, 2 vols. F. H. Lawson & B. S. Markesinis. LC 81-102302. (Cambridge Studies in International & Comparative Law). (280p ea.). 1982. Vol. 1: Texts. text ed. 55.00 (ISBN 0-521-23585-5); pap. 32.50 (ISBN 0-521-27209-2); Vol. 2: Materials. text ed. 42.50 (ISBN 0-521-23586-3); pap. 32.50 (ISBN 0-521-27210-6). Cambridge U Pr.

Tortoise & the Hare. Aesop. (Tell Me a Story Ser.). (Illus.). 26p. 1988. incl. cassette 9.95 (ISBN 1-55578-902-1). Worlds Wonder.

Tortoise & the Hare. Ken Forsse & Margaret Hughes. Ed. by Mary Becker. (Talking Mother Goose Ser.). (Illus.). 26p. (ps). 1986. 9.95 (ISBN 0-934323-21-6). Alchemy Comms.

Tortoise & the Hare. Janet Stevens. 32p. (gr. k-3). pap. 2.25 (ISBN 0-590-33677-0). Scholastic Inc.

Tortoise & the Hare. Dorothy Sword Bishop. 72p. (Fr. & Eng.). (gr. 4 up). Date not set. pap. 4.95 (ISBN 0-8442-1085-4, Passport Bks). Natl Textbk.

Tortoise & the Hare: An Aesop Fable. Janet Stevens. LC 83-18668. (Illus.). 32p. (ps-3). 1984. reinforced bdg. 12.95 (ISBN 0-8234-0510-9); Mar. 1985. pap. 5.95 (ISBN 0-8234-0564-8). Holiday.

Tortoise & the Hare, the Lion & the Mouse. (Preschool Puppet Board Bks.). (Illus.). 7p. (ps-1). 1976. 2.50 (ISBN 0-448-09742-7, G&D). Putnam Pub Group.

Tortoise & the Tree. Janina Domanska. LC 77-14572. (Illus.). 32p. (gr. k-3). 1978. 12.50 (ISBN 0-688-80132-3); PLB 12.88 (ISBN 0-688-84132-5). Greenwillow.

Tortoise by Candlelight. Nina Bawden. 16.95 (ISBN 0-88411-123-7, Pub. by Aeonian Pr). Amereon Ltd.

Tortoise Fair. (Tales from Fern Hollow Ser.). (Illus.). 22p. (ps-1). 1985. 1.98 (ISBN 0-517-45797-0). Outlet Bk Co.

Tortoise the Trickster: And Other Folktales from Cameroon. Loreto Todd. (Illus.). 121p. 1985. pap. 4.95 (ISBN 0-7102-0740-9). Routledge Chapman & Hall.

Tortoises & Terrapines. (South Group Colorguide Ser.). 1982. pap. 3.50 (ISBN 0-940842-06-8). South Group.

Tortoise's Dream: An African Folk Tale. Retold by Joanna Troughton. LC 85-15065. (Folk-Tales of the World Ser.). (Illus.). 28p. (ps-2). 1986. 12.95 (ISBN 0-87226-039-9, Bedrick Blackie). P Bedrick Bks.

Tortricidae: Olethreutinae see British Tortricoid Moths.

Torts. Edward J. Kionka. (Black Letter Ser.). 300p. 1988. pap. text ed. price not set (ISBN 0-314-43920-X). West Pub.

Torts. 1982 ed. Theodore Schussler. 171p. 5.50 (ISBN 0-87526-166-3). Gould.

Torts, 3 vols. 2nd ed. (Restatement of the Law-Library Edition: No. 1). 81.00 (ISBN 0-686-90492-3). Am Law Inst.

Torts. (Sum & Substance Ser.). 1980. write for info. (ISBN 0-940366-13-4). Herbert Legal Ser.

Torts. (Essential Principles Ser.). 1983. write for info. (ISBN 0-940366-38-X). Herbert Legal Ser.

Torts: Adaptable to Courses Utilizing Dobbs' Casebook on Torts & Compensation. Casenotes Publishing Co., Inc. Staff. Ed. by Norman S. Goldenberg et al. (Casenote Legal Briefs). (Orig.). 1987. pap. text ed. write for info. (ISBN 0-87457-148-0, 1006). Casenotes Pub.

Torts: Adaptable to Courses Utilizing Epstein, Gregory & Kalven's Casebook on Torts. Casenotes Publishing Co., Inc. Staff. Ed. by Peter Tenen et al. (Legal Briefs Ser.). 1984. pap. write for info. (ISBN 0-87457-134-0, 1003). Casenotes Pub.

Torts: Adaptable to Courses Utilizing Franklin & Rabin's Casebook on Tort Law & Alternatives. Casenotes Publishing Co., Inc. Staff. Ed. by Peter Tenen et al. (Legal Briefs Ser.). 1984. pap. write for info. (ISBN 0-87457-135-9, 1004). Casenotes Pub.

Torts: Adaptable to Courses Utilizing Henderson & Pearson's Casebook on the Torts Process. Casenotes Publishing Co., Inc. Staff. Ed. by Peter Tenen et al. (Legal Briefs Ser.). 1981. pap. write for info. (ISBN 0-87457-136-7, 1001). Casenotes Pub.

Torts: Adaptable to Courses Utilizing Keeton, Keeton, Sargentich & Steiner's Casebook on Torts. Casenotes Publishing Co., Inc. Staff. Ed. by Peter Tenen et al. (Legal Briefs Ser.). 1983. pap. write for info. (ISBN 0-87457-137-5, 1002). Casenotes Pub.

Torts: Adaptable to Courses Utilizing Materials by Franlin. Marc A. Franklin. LC 87-128751. (Legalines Ser.). 150p. Date not set. 9.95. HarBraceJ.

Torts: Adaptable to Courses Utilizing Materials by Keeton. 2nd ed. Page Keeton. LC 87-114987. (Legalines Ser.). 298p. Date not set. 12.95. HarBraceJ.

Torts: Adaptable to Courses Utilizing Materials by Prosser. 3rd ed. William L. Prosser. LC 87-116625. (Legalines Ser.). 362p. Date not set. 13.95. HarBraceJ.

Torts: Adaptable to Courses Utilizing Prosser, Wade & Schwartz's Casebook on Torts. Casenotes Publishing Co., Inc. Staff. Ed. by Peter Tenen et al. (Legal Briefs Ser.). 1985. pap. write for info. (ISBN 0-87457-138-3, 1000). Casenotes Pub.

Torts: Adaptable to Courses Utilizing Shulman, James & Grey's Casebook on Torts. Casenotes Publishing Co., Inc. Staff. Ed. by Peter Tenen et al. (Legal Briefs Ser.). 1979. pap. write for info. (ISBN 0-87457-139-1, 1005). Casenotes Pub.

Torts & Compensation: Personal Accountability & Social Responsibility for Injury. Dan B. Dobbs. LC 84-26919. (American Casebook Ser.). 955p. 1985. text ed. 31.95 (ISBN 0-314-87033-4). West Pub.

Torts & Sports: Legal Liability in Professional & Amateur Athletics. Raymond L. Yasser. LC 84-24948. xiii, 163p. 1985. lib. bdg. 36.95 (ISBN 0-89930-092-8, YLL/, Quorum). Greenwood.

Torts, Cases & Materials On. 7th ed. William L. Prosser et al. LC 82-7279. (University Casebook Ser.). 1350p. 1982. text ed. 29.50 (ISBN 0-88277-066-7). Foundation Pr.

Torts, Cases & Materials On. 8th ed. William L. Prosser et al. (University Casebook Ser.). 1247p. 1988. text ed. write for info. (ISBN 0-88277-641-X). Foundation Pr.

Torts for Wrongful Life: Individual & Eugenic Implications. Robert H. Blank. 23p. 1982. pap. text ed. 3.95x (ISBN 0-88738-638-5). Transaction Bks.

Torts in a Nutshell. Edward J. Kionka. LC 77-78248. (Nutshell Ser.). 434p. pap. text ed. 10.95 (ISBN 0-314-32999-4). West Pub.

Torts in a Nutshell: Injuries to Family, Social & Trade Relations. Wex S. Malone. LC 79-12748. (Nutshell Ser.). 358p. 1979. pap. text ed. 9.95 (ISBN 0-8299-2044-7). West Pub.

Torts in New Zealand: Cases & Materials. William C. Hodge & Joan E. Allin. (Illus.). 456p. 1988. pap. 35.00 (ISBN 0-19-558181-4). Oxford U Pr.

Torts in Private International Law. C. G. Morse. LC 78-5881. (Problems in Private International Law Ser.: Vol. 2). 412p. 1979. 92.00 (ISBN 0-444-85168-2, North Holland). Elsevier.

Torts in the Conflict of Laws. Moffatt Hancock. LC 42-36734. (Michigan Legal Publications). lviii, 288p. 1982. Repr. of 1942 ed. lib. bdg. 38.00 (ISBN 0-89941-166-5). W S Hein.

Torts: Intentional Harms, Vol. 1. 2nd ed. (Restatement of the Law-Library Edition: No. 1). 54.00 (ISBN 0-686-90474-5). Am Law Inst.

Torts: Interference, Invasion, etc, Vol. 4. 2nd ed. (Restatement of the Law-Library Edition: No. 1). 33.00 (ISBN 0-686-90484-2). Am Law Inst.

Torts: Negligence, Vol. 2. 2nd ed. (Restatement of the Law-Library Edition: No. 1). 54.00 (ISBN 0-686-90478-8). Am Law Inst.

Torts, Nineteen Eighty-One. Ed. by Win Calkins & Art Johnson. 1988. write for info. OR Bar CLE.

Torts: Personal Injury Litigation. 2nd ed. William P. Statsky. LC 81-16328. (American Casebook Ser.). 701p. 1981. text ed. 44.50 (ISBN 0-314-62125-3); instr's. manual avail. West Pub.

Torts Process. 3rd ed. James A. Henderson, Jr. & Richard N. Pearson. 1400p. 1988. text ed. 37.95 (ISBN 0-316-35615-8). Little.

Torts: Strict Liability, Vol. 3. 2nd ed. (Restatement of the Law-Library Edition: No. 1). 32.00 (ISBN 0-686-90480-X). Am Law Inst.

Torts: The Civil Law of Reparation for Harm Done by Wrongful Act. Joseph W. Little. LC 85-70058. (Anaylsis & Skills Ser.). 1985. 33.50. Bender.

Tortuga. Rudolfo A. Anaya. LC 79-89689. 1979. pap. 7.00 (ISBN 0-915808-34-X). Editorial Justa.

Tortuga. Rudolfo A. Anaya. LC 87-35665. 204p. 1988. pap. 10.95 (ISBN 0-8263-1074-5). U of NM Pr.

Tortula Hedw. Sect. Rurales de Not. Pottiaceae, Musci in der Oestlichen Holarktis. Wolfgang Kramer. (Bryophytorum Bibliotheca: 21). 250p. (Ger.). 1980. lib. bdg. 36.00x (ISBN 3-7682-1266-1). Lubrecht & Cramer.

Torture. Levaster Davis. 1987. 10.95 (ISBN 0-533-07293-X). Vantage.

Torture. Edward Peters. LC 84-21736. 160p. 1985. 29.95x (ISBN 0-631-13164-7); pap. 9.95 (ISBN 0-631-13723-8). Basil Blackwell.

Torture & English Law: An Administrative & Legal History from the Plantagenets to the Stuarts. James Heath. LC 80-24552. (Contributions in Legal Studies Ser.: No. 18). xviii, 324p. 1982. lib. bdg. 36.95 (ISBN 0-313-22598-2, HTE/). Greenwood.

Torture & the Law of Proof: Europe & England in the Accient Regime. John H. Langbein. LC 76-58314. 1977. lib. bdg. 20.00x (ISBN 0-226-46806-2). U of Chicago P.

Torture: How to Make the International Convention Effective. 60p. 1980. pap. 2.25 (ISBN 0-89192-330-6, Pub. by Intl Commission of Jurists). Interbk Inc.

Torture in Brazil: A Report. Catholic Church Staff. 1986. pap. 10.95 (ISBN 0-394-74456-X, Pub. by Vin). Random.

Torture in the Eighties. Amnesty International U. S. A. Staff. (Illus.). 224p. 1984. pap. 5.95 (ISBN 0-939994-06-2). Amnesty Intl USA.

Torture Tomb. C. Dean Anderson. 288p. (Orig.). 1987. pap. 3.50 (ISBN 0-445-20370-6, Pub. by Popular Lib). Warner Bks.

Torture Trail. Max Brand. Ed. by Tom Colgan. 208p. 1988. pap. 2.75 (ISBN 0-425-10869-4). Berkley Pub.

Tortured & the Damned. Robert Payne. LC 76-54409. (Illus.). 1978. 9.95 (ISBN 0-8180-0624-2). Horizon.

Tortured for Christ. Richard Wurmbrand. 1973. pap. 2.95 (ISBN 0-88264-001-1). Living Sacrifice Bks.

Tortured for Christ. Richard Wurmbrand. LC 86-72054. 128p. 1987. pap. 4.95 (ISBN 0-89107-408-2, Crossway Bks). Good News.

Tortured for His Faith. Haralan Popov. pap. 4.50 (ISBN 0-310-31262-0, 18070P). Zondervan.

Tortured Orchid. Stephen Cosgrove. (Snuffin Chronicles Ser.). (Illus.). (gr. k-6). 1988. pap. 3.95. Ideals.

Tortured Synthesis: The Meaning of Melville's Clarel. Joseph G. Knapp. LC 70-150099. 136p. 1971. 7.95 (ISBN 0-8022-2051-7). Philos Lib.

Toru Dutt. A. N. Dwivedi. (Indian Writers Ser.: Vol. 15). 168p. 1977. 8.50 (ISBN 0-86578-002-1). Ind-US Inc.

Toruigheacht Dhiarmuda Agus Grainne. Ed. by Standish H. O'Grady. 324p. Repr. of 1857 ed. 21.00 (ISBN 0-384-42985-8). Johnson Repr.

Torus Occipitus & Related Structures: Their Transformations in the Course of Human Evolution. Franz Weidenreich. LC 77-86451. (China. Geological Survey. Bulletin of the Geological Survey of China). 1977. Repr. of 1940 ed. 18.00 (ISBN 0-404-16694-6). AMS Pr.

Torvill & Dean. John Hennessy. LC 83-51026. (Illus.). 208p. 1984. 14.95 (ISBN 0-312-80936-0). St Martin.

Torvill & Dean. John Hennessy. (Illus.). 208p. 1985. pap. 6.95 (ISBN 0-312-80937-9). St Martin.

Tory Case. Chris Patten. LC 82-17085. pap. 52.00 (ISBN 0-317-08605-7, 2022524). Bks Demand UMI.

Tory Criticism in the Quarterly Review, 1809 - 1853. Walter Graham. LC 77-110570. 1970. Repr. of 1921 ed. 11.50 (ISBN 0-404-02889-6). AMS Pr.

Tory Democracy. William J. Wilkinson. 1980. lib. bdg. 23.00x (ISBN 0-374-98577-4, Octagon). Hippocrene Bks.

Tory Hole. Louise H. Tharp. (Illus.). (gr. 4up). 1976. pap. 7.50 (ISBN 0-686-16261-7). DCA.

Tory Lives: From Falkland to Disraeli. John Biggs-Davison. 1973. Repr. of 1952 ed. 27.50 (ISBN 0-8274-1480-3). R West.

Tory Lover. Sarah O. Jewett. (Collected Works of Sarah O. Jewett). 1988. Repr. of 1901 ed. lib. bdg. 59.00x. Am Biog Serv.

Tory Lover. Sarah O. Jewitt. 1978. Repr. of 1901 ed. lib. bdg. 30.00 (ISBN 0-8495-2730-9). Arden Lib.

Tory Lover see Collected Works.

Tory Lover see Yankee Ranger.

Tory Radical - The Life of Richard Oastler. Cecil H. Driver. LC 75-120249. 1970. Repr. of 1946 ed. lib. bdg. 40.00x (ISBN 0-374-92348-5, Octagon). Hippocrene Bks.

Tory Syndrome: Leadership Politics in the Progressive Conservative Party. George Perlin. 262p. 20.00x (ISBN 0-7735-0350-1). McGill-Queens U Pr.

Total Quality Performance: Highlights of a Conference. Ed. by Lawrence Schein & Melissa A. Berman. (Report Ser.: No. 909). (Illus.). ix, 94p. (Orig.). 1988. pap. text ed. 60.00. Conference Bd.

Total Real Estate Tax Planner. Shenkman. 1988. price not set (ISBN 0-471-61537-4); pap. 12.95 (ISBN 0-471-61536-6). Wiley.

Total Recall. Peg Case & John Migliore. Ed. by Jim Connor. 272p. (Orig.). 1987. pap. 3.95 (ISBN 0-7701-0739-7). Paperjacks US.

Total Recall. Joan Minninger. Ed. by Charles Gerras. (Illus.). 288p. 1984. 17.95 (ISBN 0-87857-515-4, 202810). Rodale Pr Inc.

Total Recall. Joan Minninger. Date not set. pap. 3.95 (ISBN 0-671-60452-X). PB.

Total Reconstruction of W. D. Gann's Stock Market Wisdom in Simple Schematical Formulations with Instances & Applications. Spencer Fleming. 149p. 1987. 177.75 (ISBN 0-86654-222-1). Inst Econ Finan.

Total Recovery. rev. ed. 1988. pap. 1.50 (ISBN 0-89230-207-0). Do It Now.

Total Rehabilitation. George N. Wright. LC 80-81957. 830p. 1980. text ed. 39.50 (ISBN 0-316-95628-7). Little.

Total Resistance. H. Von Dach. LC 66-978. (Illus.). 173p. 1965. 17.95 (ISBN 0-87364-021-7). Paladin Pr.

Total Runner: A Complete Mind-Body Guide to Optimal Performance. Jerry Lynch. (Illus.). 224p. 1986. 18.95 (ISBN 0-13-925678-4); pap. 9.95 (ISBN 0-13-925660-1). P-H.

Total Serum Cholesterol Levels of Children 4-17 Years United States, 1971-1974. Sidney Abraham et al. Ed. by Audrey Shipp. (Series 11: No. 207). 1978. pap. text ed. 1.75 (ISBN 0-8406-0125-5). Natl Ctr Health Stats.

Total Serum Cholesterol Values of Youths Twelve to Seventeen Years, United States. Paul S. Levy et al. Ed. by Taloria Stevenson. (Ser. 11, No. 156). 65p. 1976. pap. 1.50 (ISBN 0-8406-0051-8). Natl Ctr Health Stats.

Total Serum Cholestrol Levels of Adults Twenty to Seventy-Four Years of Age: United States, 1976-1980. Robinson Fulwood et al. Ed. by Klaudia Cox. 128p. 1986. pap. text ed. 2.00 (ISBN 0-8406-0337-1). Natl Ctr Health Stats.

Total Sex. Dan Abelow. 192p. 1981. pap. 3.95 (ISBN 0-441-81798-X). Ace Bks.

Total Sex. Dan Abelow. LC 76-27127. (Illus.). 96p. 1977. pap. 6.95 (ISBN 0-448-12851-9, G&D). Putnam Pub Group.

Total Sex. Herbert Otto & Roberta Otto. pap. 3.95 (ISBN 0-451-12709-9, AE2709, Sig). NAL.

Total Strangers. Terence Winch. LC 82-19278. (Illus.). 20p. (Orig.). 1982. pap. 7.50 (ISBN 0-915124-77-7, Pub. by Toothpaste). Coffee Hse.

Total Stretching. Philip J. Tyne & Matt Mitchell. (Illus.). 192p. (Orig.). 1983. pap. 7.95 (ISBN 0-8092-5567-7). Contemp Bks.

Total Surrender to God. Arthur F. Hallam. 236p. (Orig.). 1985. pap. 19.95 (ISBN 0-938770-05-5). Capitalist Pr OH.

Total Survey Error: Applications to Improve Health Surveys. Ronald Andersen et al. LC 79-88104. (Social & Behavioral Science Ser.). 1979. text ed. 35.95x (ISBN 0-87589-409-7). Jossey-Bass.

Total Syntax. Barrett Watten. 256p. 1984. pap. 13.95 (ISBN 0-8093-1179-8). S Ill U Pr.

Total Synthesis of Natural Products, 7 vols. Apsimon. 1988. Set. 445.00 (ISBN 0-471-61336-3). Wiley.

Total Synthesis of Natural Products. Ed. by John W. Apsimon. LC 72-4075. 1984. Vol. 1, 603p. 04/1973. 65.50 (ISBN 0-471-03251-4); Vol. 2, 754p. 10/1973. 78.00 (ISBN 0-471-03252-2); Vol. 3, 566p. 10/1973. 78.00x (ISBN 0-471-02392-2); Set, 6 Vols. 362.00 (ISBN 0-471-81183-1, Pub. by Wiley-Interscience). Wiley.

Total Synthesis of Natural Products, Vol. 4. Ed. by John W. Apsimon. LC 72-4075. (Total Synthesis of Natural Products Ser.). 610p. 1981. 78.00 (ISBN 0-471-05460-7, Pub. by Wiley-Interscience). Wiley.

Total Synthesis of Natural Products, Vol. 5. Ed. by John W. Apsimon. (Total Synthesis of Natural Products Ser.). 550p. 1983. 72.95 (ISBN 0-471-09808-6). Wiley.

Total Synthesis of Natural Products, Vol. 6. Ed. by John W. Apsimon. LC 72-4075. (Total Synthesis of Natural Products Ser.). 291p. 1984. 49.95 (ISBN 0-471-09900-7, Pub. by Wiley-Interscience); text ed. (ISBN 0-471-80605-6). Wiley.

Total Synthesis of Natural Products, Vol. 7. Ed. by John W. Simon. 468p. 1988. 95.00 (ISBN 0-471-88076-0). Wiley.

Total Synthesis of Natural Products: The 'Chiron' Approach. S. Hanessian. LC 83-19307. (Organic Chemistry Ser.: Vol. 3). 310p. 1983. text ed. 53.00 (ISBN 0-08-029247-X); pap. text ed. 26.00 (ISBN 0-08-030715-9). Pergamon.

Total Synthesis of Steroids. Robert T. Blickenstaff et al. 1974. 89.00 (ISBN 0-12-105950-2). Acad Pr.

Total Systems. Automated Education Center Staff. LC 62-14778. 19.00 (ISBN 0-403-04483-9). Scholarly.

TOTAL: Teacher Organized Training for the Acquisition of Language. Beth Witt & Jeanne Boose. 325p. 1983. pap. 399.00 (ISBN 0-88450-854-4, 4659-D). Communication Skill.

Total Teaching for Today's Church. rev. ed. Mary Wallace et al. Orig. Title: Centers of Interest. (Illus.). 200p. (Orig.). 1985. pap. 6.95 (ISBN 0-912315-85-7). Word Aflame.

Total Telemarketing. Robert J. McHatton. 1988. pap. 12.95 (ISBN 0-471-62755-0). Wiley.

Total Telemarketing. Robert J. McHatton. LC 87-21547. 246p. 1988. 24.95 (ISBN 0-471-62754-2). Wiley.

Total Telemarking. Brad English. LC 83-83417. (Illus., Orig.). 1984. pap. 15.95 (ISBN 0-915789-00-0). East River Pub CO.

Total Television: A Comprehensive Guide to Programming from 1948 Through 1979. rev. ed. Alex McNeil. (Illus.). 1985. pap. 14.95 (ISBN 0-14-007377-9). Penguin.

Total Tennis Training: Realizing Your Physical, Mental, & Emotional Potential. Chuck Kriese. (Illus.). 224p. (Orig.). 1988. pap. 14.95 (ISBN 0-940279-24-X). Masters Pr MI.

Total Tote Bag Book: Designer Totes to Craft & Carry. Joyce Aiken & Jean Ray Laury. LC 76-11058. (Illus.). 128p. 1977. 12.50 (ISBN 0-8008-7793-4); pap. 5.95 (ISBN 0-8008-7794-2). Taplinger.

Total Training for Motocross. Jeff Spencer. (Illus.). 124p. (Orig.). 1984. pap. 14.95 (ISBN 0-9613123-1-9). Total Train.

Total Training for Motocross. Jeffrey E. Spencer. Ed. by Rex W. Reese. (Illus.). 250p. (Orig.). 1983. lib. bdg. 19.95 (ISBN 0-317-05978-5). Total Pub.

Total Traveler by Ship. 11th ed. Ethel Blum. (Illus.). 400p. 1988. pap. 13.95t (ISBN 0-87052-024-5). Hippocrene Bks.

Total Traveler by Ship: The Cruise Traveler's Handbook. 3rd ed. Ethel Blum. (Compleat Traveler's Guides Ser.). (Illus.). 1981. pap. 8.95 (ISBN 0-89102-165-5). B Franklin.

Total Tree Chips. 56p. 1981. 9.00 (ISBN 0-935018-05-0). Forest Prod.

Total Victory at the Track: The Promise & the Performance. William L. Scott. 300p. 1988. 24.00 (ISBN 0-914861-02-6). Amicus Pr.

Total War & the Constitution. facs. ed. Edward S. Corwin. LC 70-127590. (Essay Index Reprint Ser). 1947. 18.00 (ISBN 0-8369-1796-0). Ayer Co Pubs.

Total War: Causes & Courses. rev. ed. Calvocoressi & Wint. Date not set. price not set (ISBN 0-670-80311-1). Viking.

Total War: Causes & Courses. Calvocoressi & Guy Wint. 1980. pap. 10.95 (ISBN 0-14-021422-4, Pelican). Penguin.

Total War: What It Is, How It Got That Way. Thomas Powers & Ruthven Tremain. LC 87-29951. 224p. 1988. 16.95 (ISBN 0-688-06919-3). Morrow.

Total White Blood Cell Counts for Persons 1-74 Years with Differential Leukocyte Counts for Adults Ages 25-74 Years, United States, 1971-75. (Series 11: No. 220). 44p. 3.00. Natl Ctr Health Stats.

Total Woman. Marabel Morgan. 192p. 1973. spire bks. 3.95 (ISBN 0-8007-8218-6). Revell.

Total Woman. Marabel Morgan. 1983. pap. 3.95 (ISBN 0-671-61165-8). PB.

Total Woman's Fitness Guide. Gail Shierman & Christine Haycock. LC 78-65026. (Illus.). 145p. 1979. pap. 4.95 (ISBN 0-89037-163-6). Anderson World.

Total 1-2-3. Peter G. Randall & Steven J. Bennett. (Illus.). 700p. 1989. pap. 24.95 (ISBN 0-13-925728-4). Brady Comp Bks.

Totalaction: Ideas & Activities for Teaching Children Ages 5 to 8. Pat Short & Billee Davidson. 1979. pap. 11.95 (ISBN 0-673-16452-7). Scott F.

Totalee Awesome. Lee Haney. LC 87-80978. (Illus.). 149p. 1987. pap. 12.95 (ISBN 0-934601-34-8). Peachtree Pubs.

Totalitarian Claim of the Gospels. Dora Wilson. 1935. pap. 2.50x (ISBN 0-87574-004-9, 004A). Pendle Hill.

Totalitarian Democracy & After: International Colloquium in Memory of Jacob L. Talmon, Jerusalem, 21-24 June 1982. Israel Academy of Sciences & Humanities & Hebrew University. 420p. 1986. 35.00 (ISBN 0-312-80969-7). St Martin.

Totalitarian Enemy. Franz Borkenau. LC 78-63654. (Studies in Fascism: Ideology & Practice). 256p. Repr. of 1940 ed. 29.50 (ISBN 0-404-16914-7). AMS Pr.

Totalitarian Nightmare. Enrico Arrigoni. 280p. pap. 4.00 (ISBN 0-686-35963-1). West World Pr.

Totalitarian Party: Party & People in Nazi Germany & Soviet Russia. Aryeh L. Unger. LC 73-92786. (International Studies). pap. 74.00 (2027252). Bks Demand UMI.

Totalitarian Rule: Its Nature & Characteristics. Hans Buchheim. Tr. by Ruth Hein. 112p. 1987. pap. 12.95 (ISBN 0-8195-6021-9). Wesleyan U Pr.

Totalitarian Temptation. Jean-Francois Revel. Tr. by David Hapgood. 1978. pap. 5.95 (ISBN 0-14-004841-3). Penguin.

Totalitarianism. Hannah Arendt. LC 66-22273. Orig. Title: Origins of Totalitarianism Pt. 3. 196p. (3). 1968. pap. 5.95 (ISBN 0-15-690650-3, Harv). HarBraceJ.

Totalitarianism. Michael Curtis. LC 78-66238. pap. 33.50 (ISBN 0-317-27282-9, 2024162). Bks Demand UMI.

Totalitarianism. Ed. by Michael Curtis. LC 78-66238. (Issues in Contemporary Civilization). 128p. 1979. 17.95 (ISBN 0-87855-288-X). Transaction Bks.

Totalitarianism: A Conceptual Approach. Steven P. Soper. LC 85-3240. 156p. (Orig.). 1985. lib. bdg. 26.75 (ISBN 0-8191-4598-X); pap. text ed. 12.50 (ISBN 0-8191-4599-8). U Pr of Amer.

Totalitarianism Reconsidered. Ed. by Ernest A. Menze. (National University Publications, Political Science Ser.). 1981. 27.50x (ISBN 0-8046-9268-8, Pub by Kennikat). Assoc Faculty Pr.

Totalitarianism vs. Democracy. Rodney Allen. 1986. pap. 6.95 (ISBN 0-934750-60-2). Jalamap.

Totalite et Infini. E. Levinas. (Phaenomenologica Ser: No. 8). 1971. lib. bdg. 26.35 (ISBN 90-247-5105-5, Pub. by Martinus Nijhoff Netherlands). Kluwer Academic.

Totality. Edward Sapir. (LM). 1930. pap. 16.00 (ISBN 0-527-00810-9). Kraus Repr.

Totality & Infinity. Emmanuel Levinas. Ed. by Henry J. Koren. Tr. by Alphonso Lingis. LC 69-14431. (Philosophical Ser.). 1969. text ed. 12.50x (ISBN 0-391-01004-2). Duquesne.

Totality & Infinity. Emmanuel Levinas. Tr. by Alphonso Lingis. (Martinus Nijhoff Philosophy Texts: Vol. 1). 307p. 1980. lib. bdg. 30.50 (ISBN 90-247-2288-8, Pub. by Martinus Nijhoff Netherlands). Kluwer Academic.

Totality in Essence. Vimala Thakar. 132p. 1986. pap. 7.00 (ISBN 81-208-0048-6, Pub. by Motilal Banarsidass India). Orient Bk Dist.

Totally BASIC. John Kallas. 256p. 1984. pap. 9.95 (ISBN 0-671-50638-2, Pub. by Computer Bks). S&S.

Totally Free Man: An Unauthorized Autobiography of Fidel Castro. John Krich. 192p. 1981. 15.00 (ISBN 0-916870-38-3). Creative Arts Bk.

Totally Free Man: An "Unauthorized Autobiography" of Fidel Castro. John Krich. 1988. pap. 5.95 (ISBN 0-671-64869-1, Fireside). S&S.

Totally Gross Jokes. Julius Alvin. pap. 2.50 (ISBN 0-8217-1333-7). Zebra.

Totally Hot! The Ultimate Hot Pepper Cookbook. Michael Goodwin et al. LC 86-6204. (Illus.). 312p. 1986. pap. 12.95 (ISBN 0-385-19198-7, Dolp). Doubleday.

Totally Oregon, 1988. Ed. by Robert D. Hagen. (Illus.). 432p. (Orig.). Date not set. pap. 8.95 (ISBN 0-9619833-0-2). Oregon Pride Prodns.

Totally Organized the Bonnie McCullough Way. Bonnie R. McCullough. (Illus.). 400p. 1986. pap. 10.95 (ISBN 0-312-80747-3). St Martin.

Totally Outrageous Bumper-Snickers. Mark Not-Twain & Kent Clark. Date not set. price not set. CCC Pubns.

Totally Tasteless Bumper-Stickers. Harvey Harbach & Mark Not-Twain. (Illus.). 96p. (Orig.). 1986. pap. 2.95 (ISBN 0-918259-03-7). CCC Pubns.

Totally Tasteless Jokes. Blanche Knott. pap. 8.95 (ISBN 0-345-34339-5). Ballantine.

Totally Tasteless Trivia. Ira Wasp. (Orig.). 1984. pap. 2.50 (ISBN 0-671-54219-2). PB.

Totally Topiary. Barbara Gallup & Deborah Reich. (Illus.). 256p. (Orig.). 1987. pap. 10.95 (ISBN 0-89480-318-2). Workman Pub.

Totally U. S. Simon Bond. 96p. 1988. pap. 5.95 (ISBN 0-88162-368-7). Salem Hse Pubs.

Totem. David Morrell. 256p. 1985. pap. 2.95 (ISBN 0-449-20856-7, Crest). Fawcett.

Totem & Taboo. Sigmund Freud. Tr. by James Strachey. 1962. pap. 3.95 (ISBN 0-393-00143-1, Norton Lib.). Norton.

Totem & Taboo. Sigmund Freud. Tr. by Abraham A. Brill. 1960. pap. 3.95 (ISBN 0-394-70124-0, Vin, V124). Random.

Totem Carvers: Charlie James, Ellen Neel, Mungo Martin. Phil Nuytten. LC 83-670008. (Illus.). 132p. 1983. 32.00 (ISBN 0-295-96025-6, Pub. by Panorama Pubns). U of Wash Pr.

Totem Poles & Monuments of Gitwangak Village. Canadian Government Publishing Centre Staff. 160p. 1985. pap. 17.25 (ISBN 0-660-11560-3, SSC188, SSC). UNIPUB.

Totem Poles & Tribes. Nancy Lyon. LC 77-23748. (Myth, Magic & Superstition Ser.). (Illus.). 48p. (gr. 4-5). 1977. PLB 14.65 (ISBN 0-8172-1044-X). Raintree Pubs.

Totem Poles of the Northwest. D. Allen. (Illus.). 32p. pap. 3.50 (ISBN 0-919654-83-5). Hancock House.

Totem Poles of the Pacific Northwest Coast. Ed Malin. (Illus.). 250p. 1987. 29.95 (ISBN 0-88192-068-1). Timber.

Totem Voices: Eight Plays from the Black World Repertory. Ed. by Paul C. Harrison. 608p. 1989. 24.95 (ISBN 0-8021-1053-3); pap. 14.95 (ISBN 0-8021-3126-3). Grove.

Totemic. Deirdra Baldwin. (Burning Deck Poetry Ser.). 32p. 1983. pap. 3.00 (ISBN 0-930901-13-4). Burning Deck.

Totemism. Alexander Goldenweiser. 59.95 (ISBN 0-8490-1223-6). Gordon Pr.

Totemism. Claude Levi-Strauss. (Orig.). 1963. pap. 8.95x (ISBN 0-8070-4671-X, BP157). Beacon Pr.

Totemism, the T'AO-T'iEH & the Chinese Ritual Bronzes. enl. ed. Helen F. Snow. 100p. 1986. 35.00 (ISBN 0-686-64038-1). H F Snow.

Totempole. Sanford Friedman. LC 83-63130. 416p. 1984. pap. 13.50 (ISBN 0-86547-140-1). N Point Pr.

Totems. Stanley Diamond. 96p. 1981. pap. 6.50 (ISBN 0-940170-02-7). Open Bk Pubns.

Totems. Stanley Diamond. 96p. (Orig.). 1983. pap. 6.50 (ISBN 0-317-17093-7). Station Hill Pr.

Totems & Teachers: Perspectives on the History of Anthropology. Ed. by Sydel Silverman. 328p. 1981. pap. 15.00x (ISBN 0-231-05087-9). Columbia U Pr.

Totenkult der Skythen. Renate Rolle. (Vorgeschichtliche Forschungen). (Illus.). 1979. 116.40x (ISBN 3-11-006620-3). De Gruyter.

Totentanz. Al Sarrantonio. 288p. (Orig.). 1985. pap. 3.50 (ISBN 0-8125-2558-2, Dist. by Warner Pub Services & St. Martin's Press). Tor Bks.

Totila. Giovanni Legrenzi. Ed. by Howard M. Brown. LC 76-20984. (Italian Opera 1640-1770 Ser.). 1978. lib. bdg. 77.00 (ISBN 0-8240-2608-X). Garland Pub.

Toting the Lead Row: Ruby Pickens Tartt, Alabama Folklorist. Virginia P. Brown & Laurella Owens. 208p. 1981. 19.95 (ISBN 0-8173-0074-0). U of Ala Pr.

Totline Teaching Tips. Compiled by Jean Warren & Elizabeth McKinnon. (Illus.). 64p. (Orig.). 1985. pap. 3.95 (ISBN 0-911019-08-1). Warren Pub Hse.

Totline Teaching Toys. Jean Warren. Ed. by Elizabeth S. McKinnon. LC 87-50757. (Illus.). 64p. (Orig.). 1987. pap. 3.95 (ISBN 0-911019-16-2). Warren Pub Hse.

Toto le Minet: Tom Kitten. Beatrix Potter. (Fr.). (gr. 3-7). bds. 5.00 (ISBN 0-7232-0657-0). Warne.

Toto the Timid Turtle. Howard Goldsmith. LC 80-15096. 32p. (ps-3). 1980. 13.95 (ISBN 0-87705-525-4). Human Sci Pr.

Totonac: From Clause to Discourse. Ruth Bishop. (Publications in Linguistics & Related Fields Ser.: No. 17). 185p. 1968. microfiche (2) 4.00 (ISBN 0-88312-599-4). Summer Inst Ling.

Totontepec Mixe Phonotagmemics. John C. Crawford. (Publications in Linguistics & Related Fields Ser.: No. 8). 197p. 1963. pap. 3.50 (ISBN 0-88312-008-9); microfiche(3) 6.00 (ISBN 0-88312-313-4). Summer Inst Ling.

Tot's 'n Tension. Rita T. Liberman. 100p. (Orig.). 1985. pap. 5.95 (ISBN 0-9614923-0-9). Tranquil Pr.

Tottel's Miscellany, 1557-1587, 2 vols. rev. ed. R. Tottel. Ed. by Hyder E. Rollins. LC 64-22722. 1965. Set. boxed 50.00x (ISBN 0-674-89610-6). Harvard U Pr.

Tottering State: Selected & New Poems 1963-1983. Tom Raworth. 240p. 1984. 11.50 (ISBN 0-935724-19-2). Figures.

Totters Teapot. Gordon Savage. 1985. 14.95 (ISBN 0-903852-62-4, Pub. by Milestone Pubns UK). Seven Hills Bks.

Tottie: The Tale of the Sixties. Sarah Aldridge. 181p. 1980. 5.95 (ISBN 0-930044-01-0). Naiad Pr.

Totto-Chan: The Little Girl at the Window. Tetsuko Kuroyanagi. Tr. by Dorothy Britton et al from Japanese. LC 81-80735. (Illus.). 195p. 1982. 14.95 (ISBN 0-87011-537-5). Kodansha.

Totto-Chan: The Little Girl at the Window. Tetsuko Kuroyanagi. Tr. by Dorothy Briton et al from Japanese. LC 82-80735. 208p. 1984. pap. 5.25 (ISBN 0-87011-695-9). Kodansha.

Totty. Verna Harshfield. Ed. by Margaret Burk & Marylin Hudson. (Illus.). 192p. (gr. 4-8). 1984. write for info. (ISBN 0-9612730-0-3). December Rose.

Totus Tuus: Pope John Paul II in the Philippines. Pope John Paul II. (Illus.). 1988. 12.00 (ISBN 0-317-67500-1, EP1066). Dghtrs St Paul.

T'Ou Hu: The Ancient Chinese Pitch Pot Game. G. Montell. pap. 70.00x (ISBN 0-317-68516-3, Pub. by Han-Shan Tang Ltd). State Mutual Bk.

Touareg de l'ouest. Henri Bissuel. LC 77-87620. (Illus.). Repr. of 1888 ed. 21.00 (ISBN 0-404-16447-1). AMS Pr.

Touch. Ed Catherall. LC 82-50139. (Fun with Science Ser.). 12.68 (ISBN 0-382-06648-0). Silver.

Touch. Elmore Leonard. 1987. 17.95 (ISBN 0-87795-905-6, Arbor Hse). Morrow.

Touch. Elmore Leonard. 240p. 1988. pap. 4.50 (ISBN 0-380-70386-6). Avon.

Touch. J. M. Parramon & J. J. Puig. (Child's Guide to the Five Senses Ser.). (Illus.). 32p. (Orig.). (ps). 1985. pap. 3.95 (ISBN 0-8120-3567-4); Span. ed. pap. 3.95 (ISBN 0-8120-3609-3). Barron.

Touch. Patricia Rae. 448p. 1985. pap. 3.75 (ISBN 0-8439-2187-0, Leisure Bks). Leisure NY.

Touch. F. Paul Wilson. 336p. 1986. pap. 3.95 (ISBN 0-515-08733-5). Jove Pubns.

Touch & Die. Jess Cloud. 240p. 1981. pap. 2.25 (ISBN 0-8439-0987-0, Leisure Bks). Leisure NY.

Touch & Expression in Piano Playing. Clarence G. Hamilton. LC 74-27348. Repr. of 1927 ed. 14.50 (ISBN 0-404-12950-1). AMS Pr.

Touch & Feeling. Robert Toyston. LC 85-27834. (Let's Look Up Ser.). (Illus.). 32p. (gr. 3-6). 1986. PLB 9.96 (ISBN 0-382-09176-0). Silver Burdett Pr.

Touch & Go. Elizabeth Oldfield. (Harlequin Presents Ser.: No. 1030). 192p. Date not set. pap. 1.95 (ISBN 0-317-63792-4). Harlequin Bks.

Touch Book. Jane B. Moncure. LC 82-4154. (Five Senses Ser.). (Illus.). (ps-3). 1982. PLB 11.93 (ISBN 0-516-03254-2); pap. 2.95 (ISBN 0-516-43254-0). Childrens.

Touchstone for Greatness: Essays, Addresses & Occasional Pieces about Abraham Lincoln. Roy P. Basler. LC 72-781. (Contributions in American Studies: No. 4). 1973. lib. bdg. 29.95 (ISBN 0-8371-6135-5, BTG/). Greenwood.
Touchstone for Public Leadership: A Focus on City Government. Garland S. Novosad. (Illus.). 150p. 1988. 15.00 (ISBN 0-918464-77-3). D Armstrong.
Touchstone for This Time Present. Edward Hake. LC 74-80182. (English Experience Ser.: No. 663). 96p. 1974. Repr. of 1574 ed. 7.00 (ISBN 90-221-0663-2). Walter J Johnson.
Touchstone: Historical Essays on the Reigning Diversions of the Town. James Ralph. LC 78-170491. (English Stage Ser.: Vol. 47). 1973. lib. bdg. 61.00 (ISBN 0-8240-0630-5). Garland Pub.
Touchstone: Letters Between Two Women 1953-1964. Patricia F. Lamb & Kathryn J. Hohlwein. (Hall Non-Fiction Ser.). 352p. 1986. pap. 8.95 (ISBN 0-8398-2912-4). G K Hall.
Touchstone of Dickens. Walter W. Crotch. 1973. Repr. of 1952 ed. 25.00 (ISBN 0-8274-0058-6). R West.
Touchstone of Sincerity. J. D. Albert. 256p. 1986. pap. 7.50 (ISBN 0-85398-223-6, Pub. by G Ronald England). G Ronald Pub.
Touchstone Study: Bringing the Arts to the Schools. Lillian Goldberg. 232p. (Orig.). 1984. pap. text ed. 15.00 (ISBN 0-89062-201-9). Touchstone Ctr Child.
Touchstones. Hazelden Foundation Staff. 1987. pap. 6.95 (ISBN 0-06-255445-X, HarpR). Har-Row.
Touchstones. Sallie Phillips-McClenahan. LC 82-11454. (Illus.). 300p. (Orig.). 1982. pap. 8.95 (ISBN 0-87233-066-4). Bauhan.
Touchstones. Illus. by David Spohn. (Meditation Ser.). 400p. (Orig.). 1986. pap. 5.95 (ISBN 0-89486-394-0). Hazelden.
Touchstones. Cherise Wyneken. LC 85-51973. 86p. 1986. pap. 5.95 (ISBN 1-55523-009-1). Winston-Derek.
Touchstones for Prayer. William P. Roberts. 98p. 1983. pap. text ed. 2.95 (ISBN 0-86716-023-3). St Anthony Mess Pr.
Touchstones of Matthew Arnold. John S. Eells. LC 76-136388. Repr. of 1955 ed. 22.50 (ISBN 0-404-02263-4). AMS Pr.
Touchstones of Matthew Arnold. John S. Eells, Jr. 1955. pap. 10.95x (ISBN 0-8084-0302-8). New Coll U Pr.
Touchstones: Reflections on the Best in Children's Literature, 3 vols. Children's Literature Association Publications Staff. Ed. by Perry Nodelman. 445p. 1986. Set. 60.00 (ISBN 0-937263-00-1); Vol. 1. 25.00 ea. (ISBN 0-937263-01-X). CHLA Pubns.
Touchwood: A Collection of Ojibway Prose. Ed. by Gerald Vizenor. 1987. 9.95 (ISBN 0-89823-091-8). New Rivers Pr.
Tough Act to Follow. Max Wilk. Ed. by Jim Connor. 352p. 1988. pap. 4.50 (ISBN 0-7701-0736-2). Paperjacks US.
Tough Act to Follow: A Novel. Max Wilk. 1986. 14.95 (ISBN 0-393-02219-6). Norton.
Tough Acts to Follow. George Harper. LC 87-81415. 264p. (Orig.). 1987. pap. 6.95 (ISBN 0-937959-24-3). Falcon Pr MT.
Tough & Tender: The Story of Mr. T. Veronica Michael. 64p. 1984. pap. 2.95 (ISBN 0-451-82106-8, Sig). NAL.
Tough Beans. Betty Bates. LC 88-45274. (Illus.). 96p. (gr. 3-7). 1988. 11.95 (ISBN 0-8234-0722-5). Holiday.
Tough Call. Linda Stafford. (YA) (gr. 7 up). 1982. pap. 1.95 (ISBN 0-88207-447-4). SP Pubns.
Tough Challenges for R&D Management. Ed. by James K. Brown & Lillian W. Kay. (Report Ser.: No. 895). (Illus.). viii, 48p. 1987. pap. text ed. 75.00 (ISBN 0-8237-0337-1). Conference Bd.
Tough Changes: Growing up on Your Own in America. Bernard Lefkowitz. 1987. 19.95 (ISBN 0-02-918490-8). Free Pr.
Tough Chauncey. Doris B. Smith. (Puffin Novels Ser.). 224p. (gr. 3-7). 1986. pap. 3.95 (ISBN 0-14-031928-X, Puffin). Penguin.
Tough Choices. Susan Mendonca. 128p. (gr. 7 up). 1983. pap. 1.95 (ISBN 0-590-32341-5, Vagabond). Scholastic Inc.
Tough Choices. Graydon F. Snyder. xx, 144p. (Orig.). 1988. pap. 6.95 (ISBN 0-87178-558-7). Brethren.
Tough Choices: Managers Talk Ethics. Barbara L. Toffler. LC 86-13195. (Management Series on Problem Solving, Decision Making & Strategic Thinking). 372p. 1986. 24.95 (ISBN 0-471-83022-4); cassette 15.95 (ISBN 0-471-62906-5). Wiley.
Tough Composite Materials: Recent Developments. Ed. by NASA Langley Research Center Staff. LC 85-16840. (Illus.). 466p. 1986. 54.00 (ISBN 0-8155-1039-X). Noyes.
Tough Coughs As He Ploughs the Dough: Early Cartoons & Articles by Dr. Seuss. Dr. Seuss. Ed. by Richard Marschall. LC 86-61169. (Illus.). 160p. 1987. 14.95 (ISBN 0-688-06548-1). Morrow.
Tough Country. Frank Bonham. 176p. 1983. pap. 2.25 (ISBN 0-441-81850-1). Ace Bks.
Tough Decisions: A Casebook in Medical Ethics. John M. Freeman & Kevin McDonnell. (Illus.). 202p. 1987. 24.95 (ISBN 0-19-504255-7); pap. 12.95 (ISBN 0-19-504256-5). Oxford U Pr.
Tough Eddie. Elizabeth Winthrop. LC 84-13664. (Illus.). 32p. (ps-2). 1985. 10.95 (ISBN 0-525-44164-6). Dutton.
Tough Game. H. W. Kelsey. LC 79-670266. 192p. 1979. 13.50 (ISBN 0-571-11360-5). Faber & Faber.
Tough Gazoobies on That! Sherry S. Cohen. Ed. by Billie Young. LC 73-83476. 1974. 12.95 (ISBN 0-87949-016-0). Ashley Bks.
Tough Guy Writers of the Thirties. Ed. by David Madden. LC 78-24304. (Arcturus Bks Paperbacks). 287p. 1979. pap. 9.95x (ISBN 0-8093-0912-2). S Ill U Pr.
Tough Guy Writers of the Thirties. Ed. by David Madden. LC 68-10115. (Crosscurrents-Modern Critiques Ser.). 287p. 1968. 16.95x (ISBN 0-8093-0287-X). S Ill U Pr.
Tough Guys. Mickey Spillane. 1970. pap. 2.95 (ISBN 0-451-14280-2, E9225, Sig). NAL.
Tough Guys Die Hard. JOhn Mackie. (Rat Bastards Ser.: No. 13). 208p. 1985. pap. 2.75 (ISBN 0-515-08231-7). Jove Pubns.
Tough Guys Don't Dance. Norman Mailer. LC 84-42514. 240p. 1984. slipcased ed. 75.00 (ISBN 0-394-54129-4). Random.
Tough Guys Don't Dance. Norman Mailer. 384p. 1985. pap. 3.95 (ISBN 0-345-32321-1). Ballantine.
Tough Is Not Enough. Ruth Hallman. LC 81-11490. (Hiway Bk: A High Interest-Low Reading Level Book). (Illus.). 112p. (gr. 7-10). 1981. 9.95 (ISBN 0-664-32686-2). Westminster John Knox.
Tough Little Town on the Truckee: Reno to 1900. John M. Townley. (History of Reno Ser.: Vol. 1). (Illus.). 295p. 1983. pap. 19.95 (ISBN 0-913381-00-4). Jamison Stn.
Tough Love: How Parents Can Deal with Drug Abuse. Pauline Neff. 160p. 1984. pap. 7.95 (ISBN 0-687-42407-0). Abingdon.
Tough-Luck Karen. Johanna Hurwitz. LC 82-6443. (Illus.). 160p. (gr. 4-6). 1982. 11.75 (ISBN 0-688-01485-2). Morrow.
Tough-Luck Karen. Johanna Hurwitz. (Illus.). 160p. (gr. 4-6). 1984. pap. 2.50 (ISBN 0-590-41118-7, Apple Paperbacks). Scholastic Inc.
Tough-Luck Karen see Best-Selling Apples.
Tough Luck L. A. Murray Sinclair. LC 87-71822. 224p. 1988. pap. 4.95 (ISBN 0-88739-083-8, Pub. by BlackLizard). Creative Arts Bk.
Tough Marriage. Paul A. Mickey & William Proctor. Ed. by Pat Golbitz. 256p. 1986. 14.95 (ISBN 0-688-05038-7). Morrow.
Tough Marriage: How to Make a Difficult Relationship Work. Paul A. Mickey & William Proctor. 224p. 1987. pap. 3.95 (ISBN 0-553-26861-9). Bantam.
Tough Minced Trading. Gehm. 1988. write for info. (ISBN 0-471-81233-1). Wiley.
Tough-Minded Faith for Tender Hearted People. Robert H. Schuller. 384p. 1985. pap. 3.95 (ISBN 0-553-24704-2). Bantam.
Tough Minded Faith for Tender Hearted People. Robert H. Schuller. 1985. 16.95 (ISBN 0-8161-3806-0, Large Print Bks); pap. 9.95 (ISBN 0-8161-3815-X). G K Hall.
Tough-Minded Management. Joe D. Batten. 14.95 (ISBN 0-8144-5477-1). AMACOM.
Tough-Minded Management. 3rd ed. Joe D. Batten. LC 78-15465. 240p. 1984. pap. 10.95 (ISBN 0-8144-7620-1). AMACOM.
Tough New Regulatory Environment. Law & Business Inc. Staff & Harcourt Brace Jovanovich Staff. LC 85-207366. Date not set. price not set (Pub. by Law & Business). HarBraceJ.
Tough-Nice: A Manager's Guide to Sustained High Performance. Shale Paul & Candace Paul. Ed. by Mary Hey. LC 88-70842. 200p. 1988. 16.95 (ISBN 0-913787-03-5). Delta G Pr.
Tough Princess. Martin Waddell. LC 86-8178. (Illus.). 32p. (gr. 1-5). 1987. text ed. 11.95 (ISBN 0-399-21380-5, Philomel). Putnam Pub Group.
Tough Questions: Biblical Answers Part One. Jack Cottrell. 122p. (Orig.). 1986. pap. 3.95 (ISBN 0-89900-208-0). College Pr Pub.
Tough Questions: Biblical Answers Part Two. Jack Cottvell. Orig. Title: Bible Says. 128p. 1986. pap. 3.95 (ISBN 0-89900-213-7). College Pr Pub.
Tough Row to Hoe. Ray V. Pryor, Jr. LC 88-70099. 184p. (Orig.). 1988. pap. 5.95 (ISBN 0-916383-49-0). Aegina Pr.
Tough Row to Hoe: The Nineteen Eighty-Five Farm Bill & Beyond. William A. Galston. (Illus.). 172p. (Orig.). 1985. 21.00 (ISBN 0-8191-4804-0, Pub. by Hamilton Pr); pap. 10.50 (ISBN 0-8191-4805-9). U Pr of Amer.
Tough Stuff: Hall-of-Famer Sam Huff. Leonard Shapiro. (Illus.). 256p. 1988. 18.95 (ISBN 0-312-02302-2). St Martin.
Tough, Sweet & Stuffy: An Essay on Modern American Prose Styles. Walker Gibson. LC 84-6520. xii, 179p. 1984. Repr. of 1966 ed. lib. bdg. 35.00x (ISBN 0-313-24449-9, GITS). Greenwood.
Tough Teddies & Other Bears. Simon Bond. (Illus.). 64p. 1985. pap. 3.95 (ISBN 0-517-55832-7, C N Potter Bks.). Crown.
Tough Texan. Paul E. Lehman. 1979. pap. 1.25 (ISBN 0-8439-0635-9, Leisure Bks). Leisure NY.
Tough Times. Robert Schuller. 1988. 8.95 (ISBN 1-55525-229-X). Nightingale-Conant.
Tough Times Never Last, but Tough People Do! Robert H. Schuller. LC 83-4160. (Illus.). 240p. 1983. pap. text ed. 5.95 (ISBN 0-8407-5936-3). Nelson.
Tough Times: Tender Heart. Bert Larsen. (Dest Two Ser.). 1985. pap. 6.50 (ISBN 0-8163-0594-3). Pacific Pr Pub Assn.
Tough to Tackle. Matt Christopher. (Illus.). 152p. (YA) (gr. 4-6). 1987. pap. 3.95 (ISBN 0-316-14058-9). Little.
Tough Trip Through Paradise. Andrew Garcia. LC 66-14758. (Illus.). 1976. pap. 4.50 (ISBN 0-89174-008-2). Comstock Edns.
Tough Trucks. Illus. by Nina Barbaresi. (Fast Rolling Bks.). (Illus.). 12p. (ps up). 1986. pap. 5.95 (ISBN 0-448-09884-9, G&D). Putnam Pub Group.
Tough Truths for Today's Living. Stuart Briscoe. 178p. 1984. pap. text ed. 5.95 (ISBN 0-8499-2999-7, 2999-7). Word Bks.
Tough Turf. John J. Hatch. 96p. 1988. 8.75. Carlton.
Tough Turf. Bill Sanders. 168p. (Orig.). 1985. pap. 5.95 (ISBN 0-8007-5212-0). Revell.
Tough up, Children, Away We Sing. Donna D. De la Torriente. 144p. 1983. 12.95 (ISBN 0-87881-105-2). Mojave Bks.
Tough Winter. Robert Lawson. (Story Bks Ser.). (Illus.). (gr. 3-7). 1979. pap. 3.95 (ISBN 0-14-031215-3, Puffin). Penguin.
Tough Words for American Industry. Hajime Karatsu & Karen Jones. LC 87-43206. (Japanese Management Ser.). (Illus.). 208p. 1988. 24.95 (ISBN 0-915299-25-9). Prod Press.
Toughened Composites. Ed. by Norman J. Johnson. LC 87-1387. (Special Technical Publications: No. 937). (Illus.). 478p. 1987. text ed. 69.00 (ISBN 0-8031-0934-2, 04-937000-33). ASTM.
Tougher Than Leather. B. Adler. (Illus.). 192p. (Orig.). 1987. pap. 2.95 (ISBN 0-451-15121-6, Sig). NAL.
Toughest in the Legion: Exciting French Foreign Legion Adventures. Theodore Roscoe. (Starmont Facsimile Fiction Ser.: No. 3). 128p. Date not set. lib. bdg. 17.95x (ISBN 0-8095-5452-6). Borgo Pr.
Toughing It Out. Joan L. Oppenheimer. (YA) (gr. 7 up). Date not set. pap. 2.25 (ISBN 0-317-62887-9). S&S.
Toughing It Out at Harvard: The Making of a Woman MBA. Fran W. Henrey. LC 82-24093. 256p. 1983. 14.95 (ISBN 0-399-12799-2, Putnam). Putnam Pub Group.
Toughing It Out at Harvard: The Making of a Woman MBA. Fran W. Henry. 1984. pap. text ed. 6.95 (ISBN 0-07-029324-4). McGraw.
Toughlove. Yorks & Ted Wachtel. 1985. pap. 4.50 (ISBN 0-553-26783-3). Bantam.
Toughlove Solutions. Phyllis York et al. 208p. 1985. pap. 3.95 (ISBN 0-553-25256-9). Bantam.
Toughness & Brittleness of Plastics. Ed. by Rudolph D. Deanin & Aldo M. Crugnola. LC 76-41267. (Advances in Chemistry Ser.: No. 154). 1976. 49.95 (ISBN 0-8412-0221-4). Am Chemical.
Toughness & Fracture Behavior of Titanium - STP 651. Ed. by R. G. Broadwell & C. F. Hickey. 294p. 1978. 28.50 (ISBN 0-8031-0591-6, 04-651000-30). ASTM.
Toughness Characterization & Specifications for HSLA & Structural Steels: Proceedings of a Symposium. The Metallurgical Society. Ed. by P. L. Mangonon. LC 79-52169. pap. 98.50 (ISBN 0-317-42102-6, 2026227). Bks Demand UMI.
Toughness of Ferritic Stainless Steels-STP 706. Ed. by R. A. Lula. 348p. 1978. 32.50x (ISBN 0-8031-0592-4, 04-706000-02). ASTM.
Toujours L'Amour: Poems. Ron Padgett. LC 76-7710. 1976. 12.00 (ISBN 0-915342-11-1); pap. 8.00 (ISBN 0-915342-10-3). SUN.
Toulouse in the Renaissance: The Floral Games, University & Student Life: Etienne Dolet. John C. Dawson. (Columbia University. Studies in Romance Philology & Literature: No. 33). Repr. of 1923 ed. 18.50 (ISBN 0-404-50633-X). AMS Pr.
Toulouse-Lautrec. Gotz Adriani. LC 87-50249. (Illus.). 340p. 1987. 60.00 (ISBN 0-500-09180-3). Thames Hudson.
Toulouse-Lautrec. Douglas Cooper. (Library of Great Painters Ser). (Illus.). 1956. 45.00 (ISBN 0-8109-0512-4). Abrams.
Toulouse-Lautrec. Douglas Cooper. (Masters of Art Ser.). 1984. 19.95 (ISBN 0-8109-1678-9). Abrams.
Toulouse-Lautrec. Julian Howard. (Evergreen Lives Ser.). (Illus.). 128p. cancelled (ISBN 0-312-80988-3). St Martin.
Toulouse-Lautrec. Edouard Julien. (Q L P Art Ser.). (Illus.). 1959. 12.95 (ISBN 0-517-03718-1). Crown.
Toulouse-Lautrec. Edward Lucie-Smith. (Phaidon Color Library Ser.). (Illus.). 128p. 1983. 27.50 (ISBN 0-7148-2266-3); pap. 18.95 (ISBN 0-7148-2267-1). Salem Hse Pubs.
Toulouse-Lautrec see Jewel Series.
Toulouse-Lautrec & His Contemporaries: Posters of the Belle Epoque. Ebria Feinblatt & Bruce Davis. (Illus.). 264p. (Orig.). 1985. 49.95 (ISBN 0-8109-1688-6, Co-Pub. & Dist. by Abrams); pap. 24.95 (ISBN 0-87587-125-9, Dist. by Abrams). LA Co Art Mus.
Toulouse-Lautrec & His Contemporaries: Posters of the Belle Epoque. Ebria Feinblatt & Bruce Davis. (Illus.). 264p. 1986. 35.00. Abrams.
Toulouse-Lautrec: Complete Graphic Works. Gotz Adriani. (Illus.). 1988. 60.00 (ISBN 0-500-09188-9). Thames Hudson.
Toulouse-Lautrec: Paintings. Charles F. Stuckey & Naomi E. Maurer. LC 79-90233. (Illus.). 328p. (Orig.). 1980. pap. 6.95 (ISBN 0-86559-035-4). Art Inst Chi.
Toulouse-Lautrec: The Complete Prints, 2 vols. Wolfgang Wittrock. LC 85-50981. (Illus.). 850p. 1985. Set. 295.00 (ISBN 0-85667-192-4). Sotheby Pubns.
Toulouse the Goose & Other Ridiculous Stories. Bob Karolevitz. LC 85-62753. (Illus.). 140p. (Orig.). 1985. pap. 7.95 (ISBN 0-940161-00-1). Dakota Homestead Pub.
Toulouse the Mouse. Gale Brennan. (Illus.). 16p. (Orig.). (gr. k-6). 1981. pap. 1.25. Brennan Bks.
Tour de Babel, Vol. 11. Fernando Arrabal. 120p. 1976. 19.95 (ISBN 0-686-54476-5). French & Eur.
Tour De Babil see Power of Babel: A Study of Logophilia.
Tour De Force. Christianna Brand. 272p. 1988. pap. 3.95 (ISBN 0-88184-439-X). Carroll & Graf.
Tour de France. R. Goscinny & M. Uderzo. (Illus., Ger.). 15.95 (ISBN 0-686-56254-2). French & Eur.
Tour de France '86: The American Invasion. Don Alexander & Jim Ochowicz. (Illus.). 192p. (Orig.). 1986. pap. 19.95 (ISBN 0-939353-01-6). Alexander & Alexander.
Tour de Gaulle. R. Goscinny & M. Uderzo. (Illus., Fr.). 15.95 (ISBN 0-686-56241-0). French & Eur.
Tour de Gaulle. Rene Goscinny. (Fr., Also avail. in Span.). (gr. 3-8). 15.95 (ISBN 0-685-23428-2). French & Eur.
Tour de Grammaire. 2nd. ed. Karen W. Sandler & Susan Whitebook. 318p. 1985. pap. text ed. 14.50 (ISBN 0-669-07637-6). Heath.
Tour de Role. Ed. by Renaud S. Albert. (Neuf Pieces en un Acte Ser.). 204p. (Fr.). (gr. 7-12). 1980. pap. 4.00 (ISBN 0-911409-11-4). Natl Mat Dev.
Tour du Mond du Rire. Pierre Daninos. 286p. 1963. 8.95 (ISBN 0-686-55577-5). French & Eur.
Tour du Monde en 80 Jours. Jules Verne. pap. 8.95 (ISBN 0-685-37136-0). French & Eur.
Tour du Monde en 80 Jours. Jules Verne. (Illus.). 192p. 1976. 11.95 (ISBN 0-686-55955-X). French & Eur.
Tour Eighty-Five-A. Marcia Muth. LC 86-30149. 200p. (Orig.). 1988. pap. 12.95 (ISBN 0-86534-104-4). Sunstone Pr.
Tour from the City of New York to Detroit in the Michigan Territory, Made Between the Second of May & the 22nd of September, 1818, etc. William Darby. 1977. Repr. 49.00x (ISBN 0-403-07894-6). Scholarly.
Tour from the City of New York to Detroit in the Michigan Territory. William Darby. 1988. Repr. of 1819 ed. lib. bdg. 49.00x. Am Biog Serv.
Tour Guide to North Texas. Catherine T. Gonzalez. 1982. 8.95 (ISBN 0-89015-356-6). Eakin Pr.
Tour Guide to Old Forts of Montana, Wyoming North & South Dakota, Vol. 1. Herbert M. Hart. (Illus.). 150p. 1980. pap. 4.95 (ISBN 0-87108-570-4). Pruett.
Tour Guide to Old Forts of New Mexico, Arizona, Nevada, Utah, Colorado, Vol. 2. Herbert M. Hart. (Illus.). 65p. (Orig.). 1981. pap. 4.95 (ISBN 0-87108-581-X). Pruett.
Tour Guide to Old Western Forts. Herbert M. Hart. (Illus.). 208p. 1980. 24.95 (ISBN 0-87108-568-2). Pruett.
Tour in Ireland: With General Observations on the Present State of That Kingdom Made in the Years 1776, 1777 & 1778. Arthur Young. Ed. by Constantia Maxwell. 272p. 1983. 14.95 (ISBN 0-85640-303-2, Pub. by Blackstaff Pr). Longwood Pub Group.
Tour in the Game. Irene Murrell. 1986. 32.00x (ISBN 0-86332-074-0, Pub. by Book Guild Ltd). State Mutual Bk.
Tour: New & Selected Poems. Peter Sears. LC 87-5196. 125p. 1987. 14.95 (ISBN 0-932576-48-6); pap. 8.95 (ISBN 0-932576-49-4). Breitenbush Bks.
Tour of a German Artist in England. M. J. Passavant. 60.00x (ISBN 0-7158-1355-2, Pub. by EP Pub England). State Mutual Bk.
Tour of British Bird Reserves. Valerie Russell. LC 86-1810. (Illus.). 208p. 1986. 24.95 (ISBN 0-88072-075-1, Pub. by Tanager). Longwood Pub Group.
Tour of Italian Gardens. Photos by Liberto Perugi. LC 87-43271. 224p. 1988. 27.50 (ISBN 0-8478-0908-0). Rizzoli Intl.
Tour of Mont Blanc. Andrew Harper. (Illus.). 100p. (Orig.). 1988. pap. 9.95 (ISBN 1-55650-080-7). Hunter Pub NY.
Tour of Old Ste. Genevieve. Lucille Basler. Ed. by Wehmeyer Printing Staff. (Illus.). 30p. pap. 1.00 (ISBN 0-686-32910-4). Wehmeyer Print.
Tour of Old Sturbridge Village. rev. ed. Samuel Chamberlain. 72p. 1972. pap. 1.50 (ISBN 0-8038-7128-7). Hastings.
Tour of the Summa. Paul J. Glenn. LC 78-66307. 1978. pap. 12.50 (ISBN 0-89555-081-4). TAN Bks Pubs.

Tous Feux Eteints: Carnets 1965, 1966, 1697, Carnets sans Dates et Carnets 1972. Henry de Montherlant. 192p. 1975. 19.95 (ISBN 0-686-55534-1). French & Eur.

Tous les Hommes Sont Mortels. Simone de Beauvoir. (Folio Ser.: No. 533). 544p. 1974. 9.95 (ISBN 0-686-54094-8). Schoenhof.

Toussaint L'Ouverture: A Biography & Autobiography. facs. ed. Toussaint L'Ouverture. LC 77-152924. (Black Heritage Library Collection Ser). 1863. 21.00 (ISBN 0-8369-8768-3). Ayer Co Pubs.

Toussaint Louverture: A Life with Letters. Joseph Borome. (Anvil Ser.) 1988. pap. write for info. (ISBN 0-89874-572-1). Krieger.

Toussaint L'Ouverture: Haitian Liberator. Ed. by Arthur M. Schlesinger, Jr. (World Leaders - Past & Present Ser.). (Illus.). (gr. 5-12). 1989. 16.95 (ISBN 1-55546-818-7). Chelsea Hse.

Tout a Fait Francais. Ed. by Veronique Morrison et al. (Illus.). 1979. pap. text ed. 9.95x (ISBN 0-393-09005-1). Norton.

Tout Compte Fait. Simone de Beauvoir. (Folio Ser.: No. 1022). 633p. 1978. pap. 10.95 (ISBN 0-686-54095-6). Schoenhof.

Tout de Suite: A la Microwave, 2 vols. Jean K. Durkee. Incl. Vol. I. French, Acadian & Creole Recipes, Delicious, Nutrious & Colorful. (Illus.). 224p. 1977. write for info; Vol. II. Mexican, Italian & French Recipes Tested & Tasted by the Author. (Illus.) 236p. 1980. write for info.. (Illus.). 224p. 1977. Tout de Suite.

Tout de Suite a la Microwave I: French, Acadian & Creole Recipes, Delicious, Nutrious & Colourful. Jean K. Durkee. LC 77-93096. (Illus.). 224p. 1977. plastic comb bdg. 9.95 (ISBN 0-9605362-0-5). Tout de Suite.

Tout de Suite a la Microwave II: Mexican, Italian & French Recipes Tested & Tasted by the Author. Jean K. Durkee. LC 80-53827. (Illus.). 236p. 1980. plastic comb bdg. 9.95 (ISBN 0-9605362-1-3). Tout de Suite.

Tout l'Humour du Monde. Pierre Daninos. 224p. 1958. 8.95 (ISBN 0-686-55580-5). French & Eur.

Tout Sonia: Avec: Sonia les Autres et Moi, Comment Vivre avec ou sans Sonia. Pierre Daninos. (Illus.). 435p. 1976. 12.95 (ISBN 0-686-55581-3). French & Eur.

Tout Ubu. Alfred Jarry. Incl. Ubu Roi; Ubu Cocu; Ubu Enchaine; Almanachs du Pere Ubu; Ubu sur la Butte. (Coll. Diamant). 16.50 (ISBN 0-685-34260-3). French & Eur.

Tout Ubu. Alfred Jarry. 512p. 1962. 4.95 (ISBN 0-686-54213-4). French & Eur.

Toute Epreuve. Paul Eluard. (Illus.). 104p. 1984. Additional 32 page booklet included. 75.00 (ISBN 0-8076-1102-6). Braziller.

Toute la Tendresse du Monde. Christine H. Cott. (Harlequin Seduction Ser.). 332p. 1983. pap. 3.25 (ISBN 0-373-45015-X). Harlequin Bks.

Toutes les Lumieres de Hong Kong. Margaret Mayo. (Collection Harlequin Ser.). 192p. 1983. pap. 1.95 (ISBN 0-373-49353-3). Harlequin Bks.

Toutes les Raisons du Monde. Erica Hollis. (Harlequin Seduction Ser.). 332p. 1983. pap. 3.25 (ISBN 0-373-45030-3). Harlequin Bks.

Toutonia. Pierre Daninos. 1956. pap. 8.95 (ISBN 0-685-11567-4, 154). French & Eur.

Toutounier see Duo.

Tova & Esty. 1982. pap. 2.95 (ISBN 0-87306-247-7). Feldheim.

Tova & Esty's Purim Surprise. 1982. pap. 2.95 (ISBN 0-87306-248-5). Feldheim.

Tova Difference: Tova Borgnine's Beauty Book. Tova Borgnine & Elaine C. Trebek. (Illus.). 160p. (Orig.). 1984. pap. 9.95 (ISBN 0-671-50032-5, Fireside). S&S.

Tovangar. Anne Galloway. 1978. 3.00 (ISBN 0-939046-25-3). Malki Mus Pr.

Tovareg. Leopold L. Aymard. LC 77-87625. Repr. of 1911 ed. AMS Pr.

Tovar's Classic Beauty. Tovar & Lydia P. Encinas. (Illus.). 256p. 1988. pap. 12.95 (ISBN 0-8092-4866-2). Contemp Bks.

Tovar's Classic Beauty Book. Tovar & Lydia P. Encinas. (Illus.). 256p. 1986. 18.95 (ISBN 0-8092-4867-0). Contemp Bks.

Tova's Happy Purim: In Yerusholayim. Leah Dornblatt. (Illus.). (ps-4). cancelled (ISBN 0-87306-989-7). Feldheim.

Tove Jansson. W. Glyn Jones. (World Authors Ser.: No. 716). 1984. lib. bdg. 20.95 (ISBN 0-8057-6563-8, Twayne). G K Hall.

Tovismadarak. Colleen McCullough. Tr. by Arpad Goncz & Margit Borbas. 568p. (Hungarian.). 1984. 20.00x (ISBN 0-935484-11-6). Universe Pub Co.

Toward a Balanced Curriculum. Ed. by Bonnie Spanier et al. 364p. 1984. 22.50 (ISBN 0-87073-704-X); pap. 13.95 (ISBN 0-87073-705-8). Schenkman Bks Inc.

Toward a Better Understanding: United States-Japan Relations, Report of a Conference on United States-Japan Relations, September 28-29, 1983. Ed. by Diane B. Bendahmane & Leo Moser. LC 85-600608. (Illus.). 150p. (Orig.). 1986. pap. 4.25 (S/N 044-000-02122-6). USGPO.

Toward a Better World. Mikhail S. Gorbachev. LC 87-60254. 384p. 1987. 17.95 (ISBN 0-931933-43-9). Richardson & Steirman.

Toward a Black Feminist Criticism. Barbara Smith. (Out & Out Pamphlet Ser.). 20p. pap. 2.50 (ISBN 0-918314-14-3). Crossing Pr.

Toward a Career in Business. 2nd ed. Kathryn W. Hegar. 1988. 7.16 (ISBN 0-395-45293-7). HM.

Toward a Caring Society. Robert Morris. 1974. 2.50 (ISBN 0-686-09284-8). Univ Bk Serv.

Toward a Chicano Social Science. Irene I. Blea. LC 88-6593. 192p. 1988. lib. bdg. 37.95 (ISBN 0-275-92408-4, C2408); pap. 14.95 (ISBN 0-275-92531-5, B2531). Praeger.

Toward a Christian Economic Ethic: Stewardship & Social Power. Daniel R. Finn & Prentiss L. Pemberton. LC 83-25409. 266p. 1985. pap. 10.95 (ISBN 0-86683-876-7, 7919, HarpR). Har-Row.

Toward a Christian Moral Theology. Bernard Haring. 1966. 15.95x (ISBN 0-268-00281-9). U of Notre Dame Pr.

Toward a Christian Political Ethics. Jose M. Bonino. LC 82-48541. 144p. 1983. pap. 6.95 (ISBN 0-8006-1697-9, 1-1697). Fortress.

Toward a Clearer Definition of the Role of Science & Technology in Transformation. 31p. 1981. pap. 5.00 (ISBN 92-808-0181-3, TUNU136, UNU). UNIPUB.

Toward a Code of Ethics for Management Accountants. C. Mike Merz & David E. Groebner. 160p. pap. 16.95 (ISBN 0-86641-009-0, 81129). Natl Assn Accts.

Toward a Common Body of Knowledge. Manual A. Tipgos et al. 106p. Date not set. 10.95 (ISBN 0-86641-120-8, 84172). Natl Assn Accts.

Toward a Comparative Study of Revolutions. Elbaki Hermassi. (Working Papers on Development Ser.: No. 2). 1975. pap. 1.50x (ISBN 0-87725-402-8). U of Cal Intl St.

Toward a Comprehensive Quality Assurance Program: QRB Special Edition. 84p. 1979. 20.00 (ISBN 0-86688-040-2). Joint Comm Hlthcare.

Toward a Comprehensive Test Ban. Steve Fetter. 280p. 1988. 29.95x (ISBN 0-88730-281-5). Ballinger Pub.

Toward a Consensus on Military Service. Andrew J. Goodpaster & Lloyd H. Elliott. 70p. 1983. pap. 17.95x. Transaction Bks.

Toward a Consensus on Military Service: Report of the Atlantic Council's Working Group on Military Service. Andrew J. Goodpaster. Ed. by Lloyd H. Elliott. (Illus.). 300p. 1982. text ed. 49.00 (ISBN 0-08-029399-9, K125); pap. text ed. 19.50 (ISBN 0-08-029398-0). Pergamon.

Toward a Contact Curriculum. Mario Fantini & Gerald Weinstein. 55p. 0.95 (ISBN 0-686-74916-2). ADL.

Toward a Critical Sociology. Norman Birnbaum. 1971. pap. 5.95 (ISBN 0-19-501664-5). Oxford U Pr.

Toward a Critical Sociology. Norman Birnbaum. 1983. 13.25 (ISBN 0-8446-6019-1). Peter Smith.

Toward a Cultural Theory of Education & Schooling. Ed. by Frederick Gearing & Lucinda Sangree. (World Anthropology Ser.). xiv, 260p. 1979. text ed. 37.50 (ISBN 90-279-7760-7). Mouton.

Toward a Definition of American Film Noir (1941-1949) A. M. Karimi. Ed. by Garth S. Lowett. LC 75-21431. (Dissertations of Film Ser.). 1976. lib. bdg. 22.00x (ISBN 0-405-07534-0). Ayer Co Pubs.

Toward a Definition of Clinical Social Work. Ed. by Patricia L. Ewalt. LC 80-81821. 104p. 1980. pap. 9.95x (ISBN 0-87101-086-0). Natl Assn Soc Wkrs.

Toward a Democratic Work Process. Fred H. Blum. LC 73-11840. 229p. 1974. Repr. of 1953 ed. lib. bdg. 15.00x (ISBN 0-8371-7063-X, BLDW). Greenwood.

Toward a Dependable Peace: A Proposal for an Appropriate Security System. Robert Johansen. 30p. 1978. pap. 4.95x (ISBN 0-87855-758-X). Transaction Bks.

Toward a Dependable Peace: A Proposal for an Appropriate Security System. Robert C. Johansen. (Working Papers: No. 8). (Illus.). 58p. (Orig.). 1978. pap. text ed. 3.00 (ISBN 0-911646-10-8). World Policy.

Toward a Dimensional Reality. Charles M. Perry. LC 39-11737. pap. 47.00 (ISBN 0-317-09342-8, 2016249). Bks Demand UMI.

Toward a Faculty Self-Appraisal System. John Beall et al. LC 70-630596. (Research Monograph: No. 49). 1969. spiral bdg. 10.00 (ISBN 0-88406-062-4). Ga St U Busn Pub.

Toward a Feminist Approach to Child Welfare. 1985. pap. 11.95 (ISBN 0-87868-242-2, 2422). Child Welfare.

Toward a Freudian Theory of Literature: With an Analysis of Racine's Phedre. Francesco Orlando. Tr. by Charmaine Lee from Ital. LC 78-7577. 224p. 1979. text ed. 24.00x (ISBN 0-8018-2102-9). Johns Hopkins.

Toward a Fuller Life: A Workbook for Nonprofit Homes. 14p. 1978. 1.00 (ISBN 0-943774-04-7). Am Assn Homes.

Toward a Fuller Vision: Orthodoxy & the Anglican Experience. E. C. Miller, Jr. LC 84-61015. 188p. (Orig.). 1984. pap. 8.95 (ISBN 0-8192-1351-9). Morehouse.

Toward a Functioning Federalism. David B. Walker. 1981. text ed. 18.75; pap. text ed. 13.00 (ISBN 0-673-39487-5). Scott F.

Toward a Further Definition. Ed. & intro. by Michael Tarachow. LC 76-21409. (Illus.). Date not set. 24.00 (ISBN 0-915316-42-0); pap. 12.50 (ISBN 0-915316-41-2). Pentagram.

Toward a General Theory of Action. Ed. by Talcott Parsons & Edward A. Shils. LC 51-14629. pap. 98.50 (ISBN 0-317-09500-5, 2017682). Bks Demand UMI.

Toward a General Theory of Social Control, Vol. 1: Fundamentals. Donald J. Black. LC 83-11886. (Studies on Law & Social Control). 363p. 1984. 39.95 (ISBN 0-12-102801-1). Acad Pr.

Toward a General Theory of Social Control, Vol. 2: Selected Problems. Donald Black. LC 83-11886. (Studies on Law & Social Control). 310p. 1984. 39.95 (ISBN 0-12-102802-X). Acad Pr.

Toward a General Theory of Systems: One Man's Window on our Universe. Win Wenger. (Library of the Republic of the Sciences). 35p. (Orig.). 1987. 9.95 (ISBN 0-931865-10-7). Psychegenics.

Toward a General Theory of the Paranormal. 3rd ed. Lawrence LeShan. LC 73-80027. (Parapsychological Monograph No. 9). 1969. pap. 7.00 (ISBN 0-912328-13-4). Parapsych Foun.

Toward a Generative Grammar of Blackfoot. Donald G. Frantz. (Publications in Linguistics & Related Fields Ser.: No. 34). 151p. 1971. microfiche (2) 4.00 (ISBN 0-88312-436-X). Summer Inst Ling.

Toward a Glorious Indonesia: Reminiscences & Observations of Dr. Soetomo. Tr. by Suharni Soemarmo & Paul W. Van der Veur. (CIS Southeast Asia Ser.: No. 81). 265p. 1986. pap. text ed. 13.50x (ISBN 0-89680-142-X, Ohio U Ctr Intl). Ohio U Pr.

Toward a Grammar of Passages. Richard M. Coe. (Studies in the Writing & Rhetoric). 128p. (Orig.). 1987. pap. text ed. 10.95x (ISBN 0-8093-1420-7). S Ill U Pr.

Toward a Growing Marriage. Gary Chapman. LC 79-21376. 1979. pap. 6.95 (ISBN 0-8024-8787-4). Moody.

Toward a Healing Ministry: Exploring & Implementing a Congregational Ministry. Richard J. Backmen & Steven J. Nerheim. 72p. (Orig.). 1985. pap. 7.50 (ISBN 0-8066-2176-1, 12-2022). Augsburg.

Toward a Historiography of Linguistics: Selected Essays. E. Konrad Koerner. (Studies in the History of Linguistics Ser.: No. 19). xx, 222p. 1978. 34.00x (ISBN 90-272-0960-X). Benjamins North Am.

Toward a History of Needs. Ivan Illich. 160p. 1987. pap. 8.95 (ISBN 0-930588-26-6). Heyday Bks.

Toward a History of Ukrainian Literature. George G. Grabowicz. (Harvard Ukrainian Research Institute Monograph). 112p. 1981. pap. text ed. 5.00x (ISBN 0-674-89676-9). Harvard U Pr.

Toward a Holistic Developmental Psychology. Ed. by Seymour Wapner & Bernard Kaplan. 272p. 1983. text ed. 29.95 (ISBN 0-89859-262-3). L Erlbaum Assocs.

Toward a Homeodynamic Society. R. J. Blakely. 1965. 2.50 (ISBN 0-8156-7028-1, NES 49). Syracuse U Cont Ed.

Toward a Human Rights Framework. Ed. by Peter Schwab & Adamantia Pollis. LC 82-13194. 270p. 1982. 35.00 (ISBN 0-275-90899-2, C0899). Praeger.

Toward a Human World Order: Beyond the National Security Straitjacket. Gerald Mische & Patricia Mische. LC 76-41440. 412p. 1977. pap. 4.95 (ISBN 0-8091-1977-3). Paulist Pr.

Toward a Humanistic Science of Politics: Essays in Honor of Francis Dunham Wormuth. Ed. by Dalmas H. Nelson & Richard Sklar. LC 83-1346. (Illus.). 630p. (Orig.). 1983. lib. bdg. 48.25 (ISBN 0-8191-3105-9); pap. text ed. 27.00 (ISBN 0-8191-3106-7). U Pr of Amer.

Toward a Humanitarian Diplomacy: A Primer for Policy. Tom J. Farer. LC 79-3514. 1981. 27.50x (ISBN 0-8147-2565-1). NYU Pr.

Toward a Jewish America. Eugene Kaellis. Ed. by Rhoda Kaellis. LC 87-12354. (Symposium Ser.: Vol. 20). 216p. 1987. lib. bdg. 49.95 (ISBN 0-88946-712-9). E Mellen.

Toward a Jewish Theology of Liberation. Marc H. Ellis. LC 86-23553. 160p. (Orig.). 1987. pap. 9.95 (ISBN 0-88344-358-9). Orbis Bks.

Toward a Just Social Order. Derek L. Phillips. LC 85-43303. 450p. 1986. text ed. 55.50x (ISBN 0-691-09422-5); pap. 12.95x (ISBN 0-691-02834-6). Princeton U Pr.

Toward a Just World Order, Vol. I. Richard A. Falk et al. LC 81-23744. (Studies on a Just World Order). 652p. (Orig.). 1982. lib. bdg. 54.50x (ISBN 0-86531-242-7); pap. text ed. 23.95x (ISBN 0-86531-251-6). Westview.

Toward a Larger Theatre: Seven Plays by Mordecai Gorelik. Mordecai Gorelik. LC 87-35224. 384p. (Orig.). 1988. lib. bdg. 33.50 (ISBN 0-8191-6845-9); pap. text ed. 18.50 (ISBN 0-8191-6846-7). U Pr of Amer.

Toward a Law of Global Communications Networks. Ed. by Anne W. Branscomb. (Illus.). 370p. 1986. professional ed. 49.95 (ISBN 0-582-28530-5). Longman.

Toward a Literate Society: A Report from the National Academy of Education. Ed. by John B. Carroll & Jeanne S. Chall. 352p. 1975. text ed. 26.95 (ISBN 0-07-010130-2). McGraw.

Toward a Livable World: Leo Szilard & the Crusade for Nuclear Arms Control. Leo Szilard. Ed. by Helen Hawkins et al. 484p. 1987. text ed. 50.00x (ISBN 0-262-19260-8). MIT Pr.

Toward a Marxist Anthropology: Problems & Perspectives. Ed. by Stanley Diamond. (World Anthropology Ser.). 492p. 1979. text ed. 58.25 (ISBN 90-279-7780-1). Mouton.

Toward a Marxist Theory of Nationalism. Horace B. Davis. LC 77-91740. 294p. 1980. 17.50 (ISBN 0-85345-441-8); pap. 7.50 (ISBN 0-85345-516-3). Monthly Rev.

Toward a Mature Faith. Erwin R. Goodenough. (Brown Classics in Judaica Ser.). 200p. 1988. pap. text ed. 11.75 (ISBN 0-8191-6791-6). U Pr of Amer.

Toward a Metaphysics of the Sacred: Development of the Concept of the Holy. Stephen Beasley-Murray. LC 82-8288. viii, 110p. 1982. 7.95x (MUP-M008). Mercer Univ Pr.

Toward a Model of Women's Status. Frances E. Mascia-Lees. LC 83-48762. (American University Studies XI (Anthropology & Sociology): Vol. 1). 146p. (Orig.). 1984. pap. text ed. 14.60 (ISBN 0-8204-0054-8). P Lang Pubs.

Toward a More Effective Defense. Philip A. Odeen. 66p. 1985. 14.95 (ISBN 0-317-20376-2). CSI Studies.

Toward a More Effective Defense: Report of the Defense Organization Project. Ed. by Barry M. Blechman & William J. Lynn. LC 85-11214. 264p. 1985. ref. ed. 32.00x (ISBN 0-88730-026-X). Ballinger Pub.

Toward a More Effective Defense: The Final Report of the CSIS Defense Organization Project. Philip A. Odeen. (CSIS Panel Report). 72p. (Orig.). 1985. pap. text ed. 14.95 (ISBN 0-8191-5944-1, Pub. by CSIS). U Pr of Amer.

Toward a More Natural Science: Biology & Human Affairs. Leon R. Kass. (Illus.). 359p. 1985. 23.50 (ISBN 0-02-918340-5). Free Pr.

Toward a More Perfect Union: Six Essays on the Constitution. Neil L. York. 1988. text ed. 39.50 (ISBN 0-88706-925-8); pap. text ed. 12.95 (ISBN 0-88706-926-6). State U NY Pr.

Toward a More Science: Biology & Human Affairs. Leon R. Kass. 370p. 1988. pap. 14.95x (ISBN 0-02-917071-0). Free Pr.

Toward a More Sustainable Agriculture. Raymond P. Poincelot. (Illus.). 1986. 30.95 (ISBN 0-87055-518-9). AVI.

Toward a National Antitrust Policy: Information Problems & Antitrust. Betty Bock. (Report Ser. No. 696: 696). 108p. 1976. 15.00 (ISBN 0-8237-0130-1). Conference Bd.

Toward a National Center for Higher Continuing Education. Robert B. Hudson. 1968. 2.50 (ISBN 0-87060-014-1, OCP 17). Syracuse U Cont Ed.

Toward a National Power Policy: The New Deal & the Electric Utility Industry, 1933-1941. Philip J. Funigiello. LC 72-92695. pap. 78.50 (ISBN 0-317-28770-2, 2020622). Bks Demand UMI.

Toward a National Taste: America's Quest for Aesthetic Independence. J. Meredith Neil. 415p. 1975. text ed. 15.00x (ISBN 0-8248-0340-X). UH Pr.

Toward a New Africa. Ed. by H. Noviki. (African American Conferences Ser.). 36p. (Orig.). 1985. pap. 5.00x (ISBN 0-89192-388-8). Interbk Inc.

Toward a New Africa Policy. Jane W. Jacqz. 71p. 1977. pap. text ed. 6.95 (ISBN 0-87855-754-7). Transaction Bks.

Toward a New Age. William R. Walters. LC 85-51412. 104p. 1985. 6.95 (ISBN 0-938232-87-8, Dist. by Baker & Taylor Co.). Winston-Derek.

Toward a New Age in Christian Theology. Richard H. Drummond. LC 85-5155. 272p. 1985. pap. 12.95 (ISBN 0-88344-514-X). Orbis Bks.

Toward a New Brain: Evolution & the Human Mind. Stuart Litvak & A. Wayne Senzee. 250p. 1985. 17.95 (ISBN 0-13-926056-0); pap. 8.95 (ISBN 0-13-926049-8). P-H.

Toward a New Brain: Evolution & the Human Mind. Stuart Litvak & A. Wayne Senzee. Date not set. price not set. S&S.

Toward a New Central Europe: A Symposium. Francis Wagner. (Illus.). 394p. 1970. 8.50 (ISBN 0-87934-002-9). Danubian.

Toward a New Christendom. M. Therese Lawrence. LC 81-84244. (Illus.). 80p. 1982. pap. 5.95 write for info. (ISBN 0-938034-05-7). PAL Pr.

Toward a New Deal in Baltimore: People & Government in the Great Depression. Jo Ann E. Argersinger. LC 87-21767. (Illus.). xix, 284p. 1988. 29.95x (ISBN 0-8078-1769-4). U of NC Pr.

Toward a New Definition of Health: Psychosocial Dimensions. Ed. by P. I. Ahmed & G. V. Coelho. LC 79-9066. (Current Topics In Mental Health Ser.). (Illus.). 504p. 1979. 59.50x (ISBN 0-306-40248-3, Plenum Pr). Plenum Pub.

Toward a New Dominion--Choices for Virginians: The Report of the Governor's Commission on Virginia's Future. 1984. write for info. U Va Ctr Pub Serv.

Toward a New Earth: Apocalypse in the American Novel. John R. May. LC 72-3510. 288p. 1973. pap. 8.95x (ISBN 0-268-00513-3). U of Notre Dame Pr.

Toward a Theory of War Prevention see Strategy of World Order.

Toward a Thomist Theology. Joyce A. Little. (Toronto Studies in Theology: Vol. 34). 576p. 1988. lib. bdg. 79.95x (ISBN 0-88946-779-X). E Mellen.

Toward a Typology of Juvenile Offenders: Implications for Therapy & Prevention. Sheldon Glueck & Eleanor Glueck. LC 71-115014. 200p. 1970. 49.50 (ISBN 0-8089-0648-8, 791600). Grune.

Toward a Typology of Opiate Users. William Bates & Betty Crowther. 160p. 1974. pap. text ed. 9.95 (ISBN 0-87073-960-3). Schenkman Bks Inc.

Toward a U. S. Grand Strategy. Ed. by Gregory D. Foster. 400p. 1987. 35.00 (ISBN 0-312-00831-7); pap. 14.95 (ISBN 0-312-00832-5). St Martin.

Toward a United States of Russia: Plans & Projects of Federal Reconstruction of Russia in the Nineteenth Century. Dimitri Von Mohrenschildt. LC 79-56853. (Illus.). 312p. 1981. 28.50 (ISBN 0-8386-3013-8). Fairleigh Dickinson.

Toward a Unity of Knowledge. Ed. by Marjorie Grene. LC 69-17280. (Psychological Issues Monograph: No. 22, Vol. 6, No. 2). 302p. 1969. text ed. 27.50x (ISBN 0-8236-6610-7). Intl Univs Pr.

Toward a Universal Theology of Religion. Leonard Swidler. (Faith Meets Faith Ser.). 264p. 1987. 19.95 (ISBN 0-88344-580-8); pap. 9.95 (ISBN 0-88344-555-7). Orbis Bks.

Toward a Warless World: The Travail of the American Peace Movement, 1887-1914. David S. Patterson. LC 75-28916. pap. 87.50 (ISBN 0-317-27843-6, 2056050). Bks Demand UMI.

Toward a Well-Fed World. Don Paarlberg. (Henry A. Wallace Series of Agricultural History & Rural Studies: Vol. 6). 296p. 1988. text ed. 24.95x (ISBN 0-8138-1729-3). Iowa St U Pr.

Toward a Whiteheadian Ethics. Lynne Belaief. LC 84-15248. 208p. (Orig.). 1985. lib. bdg. 27.50 (ISBN 0-8191-4229-8); pap. text ed. 13.50 (ISBN 0-8191-4230-1). U Pr of Amer.

Toward a Working Philosophy of Adult Education. Jerold W. Apps. LC 73-7425. (Occassional Papers Ser.). 65p. 1973. pap. 5.00 (ISBN 0-87060-059-1, OCP 36). Syracuse U Cont Ed.

Toward a World of Economic Stability: Optimal Monetary Framework & Policy. Ed. by Yoshio Suzuki & Mitsuaki Okabe. 350p. 1988. 44.50x (ISBN 0-86008-422-1, Pub. by U of Tokyo Japan). Columbia U Pr.

Toward Academic Quality Off-Campus. E. Kuhns & S. V. Martorana. 256p. 1984. 10.45 (ISBN 0-318-17315-8). Coun Postsecondary Accredit.

Toward Achieving Equity for Women in Social Work Education. Date not set. 6.60. Coun Soc Wk Ed.

Toward Adolescence: The Middle School Years: 79th Yearbook, Pt. 1. Ed. by Mauritz Johnson. LC 79-91183. (National Society for the Study of Education Ser.). xviii, 338p. 1980. pap. 10.00x (ISBN 0-226-60089-0). U of Chicago Pr.

Toward American English: Moving Ahead. Alan Meyers & Ethel Tiersky. 1984. pap. text ed. write for info. (ISBN 0-673-15463-7). Scott F.

Toward American English: Starting Line. Alan Meyers & Ethel Tiersky. 1984. pap. text ed. write for info. (ISBN 0-673-15462-9). Scott F.

Toward an Africanized U. S. Policy for Southern Africa: A Strategy for Increasing Political Leverage. Ronald T. Libby. LC 79-93355. (Policy Papers in International Affairs Ser.: No. 11). 120p. 1980. pap. 7.50x (ISBN 0-87725-511-3). U of Cal Intl St.

Toward an Alternative Security System: Moving Beyond the Balance of Power in the Search for World Security. Robert C. Johansen. (World Policy Paper ser.: No.24). 52p. 1983. pap. 3.00. World Policy.

Toward an American Catholic Moral Theology. Charles E. Curran. LC 86-40583. 256p. 1987. text ed. 18.95x (ISBN 0-268-01862-6). U of Notre Dame Pr.

Toward an American Revolution: The Constitution & Other Illusions. Jerry Fresia. 150p. 1988. lib. bdg. 25.00 (ISBN 0-89608-298-9); pap. 8.00 (ISBN 0-89608-297-0). South End Pr.

Toward an American Theology. Herbert W. Richardson. 1967. lib. bdg. 29.95 (ISBN 0-88946-028-0). E Mellen.

Toward an Anthropology of Women. Ed. by Rayna R. Reiter. LC 73-21476. 416p. 1975. 16.50 (ISBN 0-85345-372-1); pap. 8.00 (ISBN 0-85345-399-3). Monthly Rev.

Toward an Authentic Interpretation of the Organ Works of Cesar Franck. Rollin Smith. LC 83-8273. (Juilliard Performance Guides: No. 1). (Illus.). 191p. 1983. lib. bdg. 36.00x (ISBN 0-918728-25-8). Pendragon NY.

Toward an Ecological Society. Murray Bookchin. 315p. 1980. 34.95 (ISBN 0-919618-99-5, Dist. by U of Toronto Pr); pap. 14.95 (ISBN 0-919618-98-7, Dist. by U of Toronto Pr). Black Rose Bks.

Toward an Ecology of the Brain. R. Walsh. (Illus.). 285p. 1981. text ed. 29.95 (ISBN 0-88331-208-5). Luce.

Toward an Ecumenical Fundamental Theology. Randy L. Maddox. LC 84-13838. (American Academy of Religion Studies in Religion). 1984. 13.50 (ISBN 0-89130-771-0, 01 01 47). Scholars Pr GA.

Toward an Educational Model of Nursing Effectiveness. Joanne C. McCloskey. LC 83-9288. (Studies in Nursing Management: No. 11). pap. 48.70 (2070025). Bks Demand UMI.

Toward an Effective Pulpit Ministry. George Holmes. LC 72-152056. 176p. 1971. 4.00 (ISBN 0-88243-610-4, 02-0610). Gospel Pub.

Toward an Efficient Energy Future: Proceedings of the III International Energy Symposium III-May 23-27, 1982. Energy, Environment, & Resources Center, the University of Tennessee et al. Ed. by Robert A. Bohm & Lillian A. Clinard. (International Energy Symposia Ser.). 352p. 1983. prof. ref. 39.95x (ISBN 0-88410-878-3). Ballinger Pub.

Toward an Environmental Policy. Ed. by Paul M. Tilden. 1971. pap. cancelled (ISBN 0-940091-03-8). Natl Parks & Cons.

Toward an Equitable Representation of Minorities in School Administration. 11p. (Orig.). 1982. pap. 5.00 (ISBN 0-87652-070-0). Am Assn Sch Admin.

Toward an Exegetical Theology. Walter C. Kaiser, Jr. LC 80-68986. 224p. 1981. 14.95 (ISBN 0-8010-5425-7). Baker Bk.

Toward an Expansive Christian Theology. Vergilius Ferm. LC 64-16359. 201p. 1964. 5.95 (ISBN 0-8022-0496-1). Philos Lib.

Toward an Explanation of National Price Levels. Irving B. Kravis & Robert E. Lipsey. LC 83-18546. (Princeton Studies in International Finance Ser.: No. 52). 1983. pap. text ed. 6.50x (ISBN 0-88165-224-5). Princeton U Int Finan Econ.

Toward an Improved Fips Cost-Benefit Methodology: Descriptive Models, Data Processing, Software Development & Maintenance, 2 Vols. 1986. lib. bdg. 179.75 (ISBN 0-8490-3744-1). Gordon Pr.

Toward an Index of Preventable Mortality, Ser. 2, No. 85. Theodore D. Woolsey. Ed. by Klaudia Cox. 50p. 1980. pap. text ed. 3.25 (ISBN 0-8406-0189-1). Natl Ctr Healt.

Toward an Integrated Theory of Development: Economic & Noneconomic Variables in Rural Development. William F. Whyte & Lawrence K. Williams. LC 68-20192. (Paperback Ser.: No. 5). 96p. 1968. pap. 3.00 (ISBN 0-87546-030-5). ILR Pr.

Toward an Old Testament Theology. Walter C. Kaiser, Jr. 1978. 17.95 (ISBN 0-310-37100-7, 12320). Zondervan.

Toward an Ontology of Number Mind & Sign. Charles B. Daniels et al. (Scots Philosophical Monographs: No. 10). 176p. 1986. text ed. 22.00 (ISBN 0-08-032462-2, R132, K150, AUP); pap. 15.00. Pergamon.

Toward an Orderly Market: An Intensive Study of Japan's Voluntary Quota in Cotton Textile Exports. John Lynch. LC 68-57053. (Illus.). 1969. 6.75 (ISBN 0-8048-0652-7). C E Tuttle.

Toward an Understanding of Human Performance. 2nd ed. Ed. by Edmund J. Burke. 1980. text ed. cancelled (ISBN 0-932392-01-6); pap. 14.95 (ISBN 0-686-91525-9). Mouvement Pubns.

Toward an Understanding of Language: Charles Carpenter Fries in Perspective. Ed. by Peter H. Fries. LC 85-9168. (Current Issues in Linguistic Theory Ser.: 40). xvi, 384p. 1985. 48.00x (ISBN 90-272-3534-1). Benjamins North Am.

Toward an Understanding of the A. M. E. Zion Church, Vol. 1: A Manual for Lay Persons, Students, & Others Who Are Interested in Learning about Zion. Robert L. Clayton. 60p. 1988. lab manual 11.50 (ISBN 0-910363-04-8). Ebonics.

Toward an Understanding of the Metropolis, Pts. 1 & 2. Robert M. Haig. LC 75-38130. (Demography Ser.). 1976. Repr. of 1926 ed. 14.00x (ISBN 0-405-07984-2). Ayer Co Pubs.

Toward an Understanding of the New Testament. Lewis M. Rogers et al. 350p. 1988. 19.95 (ISBN 0-941214-76-1). Signature Bks.

Toward an Urban Ohio. John Wunder. (Illus.). 44p. 1977. pap. 2.00 (ISBN 0-318-00840-8). Ohio Hist Soc.

Toward an Urban Vision: Ideas & Institutions in Nineteenth-Century America. Thomas Bender. LC 82-47980. 296p. (Orig.). 1982. pap. text ed. 9.95x (ISBN 0-8018-2925-9). Johns Hopkins.

Toward Arab-Israeli Peace: Guidelines for American Policy. Report of a Study Group. LC 88-70490. 49p. 1988. pap. 5.95x (ISBN 0-8157-7291-2). Brookings.

Toward Awakening: An Approach to the Teaching of Gurdjieff. Jean Vaysse. LC 79-1779. 1979. pap. 5.95i (ISBN 0-06-068860-2, RD 304, HarpR). Harrow.

Toward Balance: Psycho-Physical Integration & Vibrational Therapy. Rita McNamara. (Illus.). 1988. pap. 8.95 (ISBN 0-87728-693-0). Weiser.

Toward Benevolent Neutrality: Church, State, & the Supreme Court. 3rd ed. Ed. by Robert T. Miller & Ronald B. Flowers. LC 86-72072. 612p. 1987. 36.00x (ISBN 0-918954-44-4). Baylor Univ Pr.

Toward Better Human Relations. facsimile ed. Ed. by Lloyd A. Cook. LC 70-90626. (Essay Index Reprint Ser). 1952. 17.00 (ISBN 0-8369-1284-5). Ayer Co Pubs.

Toward Better Things. Ivy Wagner. 128p. 1989. 7.95 (ISBN 0-89962-766-8). Todd & Honeywell.

Toward Better Urban Transport Planning in Developing Countries. J. Michael Thomson. (Working Paper: No. 600). 124p. 1983. 5.00 (ISBN 0-8213-0208-6, WP 0600). World Bank.

Toward Black Undergraduate Student Equality in American Higher Education. Ed. by Michael T. Nettles. LC 87-24956. (Contributions to the Study of Education Ser.: No. 25). 240p. 1988. lib. bdg. 35.95 (ISBN 0-313-25616-0, NBK/). Greenwood.

Toward Cartelization of World Steel Trade? William R. Cline. (Policy Analyses in International Economics Ser.). (Orig.). Date not set. pap. price not set (ISBN 0-88132-023-4). Inst Intl Eco.

Toward Chronopharmacology: Proceedings of Satellite Symposium to the 8th International Congress of Pharmacology, Nagasaki, Japan, 27-28 July 1981. International Congress of Pharmacology. Ed. by R. Takahashi & F. Halberg. (Illus.). 456p. 1982. 79.00 (ISBN 0-08-027977-5). Pergamon.

Toward Clean Water: A Guide to Citizen Action. Conservation Foundation Staff. 1976. pap. 8.00 (ISBN 0-89164-034-7). Conservation Foun.

Toward Collective Bargaining in Non-Profit Hospitals: Impact of New York State Law. Sara Gamm. (ILR Bulletins Ser.: No. 60). 120p. 1968. pap. 2.00 (ISBN 0-87546-220-0). ILR Pr.

Toward Communication Competency. 2nd ed. Susan R. Glaser & Anna Ablen. 256p. 1986. pap. text ed. 13.95 (ISBN 0-03-002864-7, HoltC). HR&W.

Toward Comparative Social Welfare. Ed. by Brij Mohan. (Illus.). 192p. (Orig.). 1986. 18.95 (ISBN 0-87047-025-6); pap. 11.95 (ISBN 0-87047-026-4). Schenkman Bks Inc.

Toward Comprehensive Child Care. Bank Street Consultation Service. 44p. pap. 4.00 (ISBN 0-936746-50-5, L57). Day Care Coun.

Toward Conceptual Codification: In Race & Ethnic Relations. Jonathan Udell. LC 79-84196. 1980. 7.95 (ISBN 0-87212-119-4). Libra.

Toward Continuous Misson: Strategizing for the Evangelization of Bolivia. W. Douglas Smith. LC 77-21490. 1978. pap. 4.95 (ISBN 0-87808-321-9). William Carey Lib.

Toward Creative Systems Design. Henry C. Lucas. LC 74-4129. 147p. 1974. 24.00x (ISBN 0-231-03791-0). Columbia U Pr.

Toward Defining the African Aesthetic. Ed. by Lemuel Johnson. Bernadette Cailler et al. LC 82-40408. (Annual Selected Papers of the ALA). 140p. 1983. 22.00X (ISBN 0-89410-356-3); pap. 14.00X (ISBN 0-89410-357-1). Three Continents.

Toward Economic Cooperation in Asia. David Wightman. 1963. 75.00x (ISBN 0-685-69884-X). Elliots Bks.

Toward Eden. Arthur E. Palmer. 417p. 1981. 22.50 (ISBN 0-318-17837-0). Landscape Architecture.

Toward Education for Effective Social Welfare Administrative Practice. James R. Dumpson et al. Date not set. 3.85 (78-650-09). Coun Soc WK Ed.

Toward Education with a Global Perspective. 15p. (Orig.). 1980. pap. text ed. 2.00 (ISBN 0-911696-10-5). Assn Am Coll.

Toward Educational Engineering. John Durnin. LC 81-40101. (Illus.). 134p. (Orig.). 1982. PLB 23.00 (ISBN 0-8191-2435-4); pap. text ed. 10.00 (ISBN 0-8191-2436-2). U Pr of Amer.

Toward Effective Instruction in Secondary Social Studies. Lee Ehman & Howard Mehlinger. LC 82-21894. (Illus.). 476p. 1983. pap. text ed. 22.00 (ISBN 0-8191-2916-X). U Pr of Amer.

Toward Effective Parish Religious Education for Children & Young People. 108p. 1986. 14.00 (ISBN 0-317-54823-9). Natl Cath Educ.

Toward Effective Schooling: The IGE Experience. Thomas A. Romberg. LC 85-3156. (Illus.). 246p. (Orig.). 1985. lib. bdg. 26.75 (ISBN 0-8191-4580-7); pap. text ed. 12.50 (ISBN 0-8191-4581-5). U Pr of Amer.

Toward Effective Social Work Practice. Ed. by Morley D. Glicken. LC 74-6248. 300p. 1974. text ed. 39.50x (ISBN 0-8422-5171-5). Irvington.

Toward Effective Strategic Analysis: New Applications of Information Technology. Albert Clarkson. LC 81-69202. (Special Studies in National Security & Defense Policy). 179p. 1981. lib. bdg. 33.00x (ISBN 0-86531-243-5). Westview.

Toward Equal Educational Opportunity: The Report of the Select Committee on Equal Educational Opportunity, U. S. Senate. Intro. by Francesco M. Cordasco. LC 74-8765. (Studies in Education: No. 2). 37.50 (ISBN 0-404-11622-1). AMS Pr.

Toward Equal Justice: A Comparative Study of Legal Aid in Modern Societies. Mauro Cappelletti et al. LC 75-18519. (Studies in Comparative Law: No. 13). 756p. 1975. text ed. 35.00 (ISBN 0-379-00213-2). Oceana.

Toward Equal Opportunity in Employment, the Role of State & Local Government: Proceedings. J. D. Hyman et al. LC 74-15228. (Symposia on Law and Society Ser). 1971. Repr. of 1964 ed. lib. bdg. 22.50 (ISBN 0-306-70120-0). Da Capo.

Toward Equality & Freedom: An International & Comparative Approach, Vols. 1-3. Gary L. Dorsey. LC 77-76800. 1977. Set. 105.00 (ISBN 0-379-00657-X). Oceana.

Toward Equity: An Action Manual for Women in Academe. Karen Bogart. 259p. (Orig.). 1984. pap. 17.00 (ISBN 0-911696-36-9). Assn Am Coll.

Toward European Economic Recovery in the 1980s: Report for the European Parliament. Michel Albert & James Ball. LC 84-13362. (Washington Papers: Vol. XII, No. 109). 176p. 1984. pap. 9.95 (ISBN 0-275-91597-2, B1597). Praeger.

Toward Excellence in Curriculum Inquiry. Edmund C. Short et al. 68p. (Orig.). 1985. 4.00 (ISBN 0-9613823-1-7). Nittany Pubs.

Toward Excellence in Gifted Education. Ed. by John Feldhusen. 189p. 1985. pap. text ed. 14.95 (ISBN 0-317-26976-3). Love Pub Co.

Toward Excellence in Nursing Education. 4th ed. National League for Nursing. 62p. 1983. 12.95 (ISBN 0-88737-348-8, 16-1945). Natl League Nurse.

Toward Excellence in Secondary Vocational Education: Developing Pretechnical Curricula. M. Harry Daniels et al. 48p. 1985. 5.50 (ISBN 0-318-22216-7, IN295). Natl Ctr Res Voc Ed.

Toward Excellence in Secondary Vocational Education: Elements of Program Quality. Paul B. Campbell & Phyllis Panzano. 35p. 1985. 4.75 (ISBN 0-318-22217-5, IN291). Natl Ctr Res Voc Ed.

Toward Excellence in Secondary Vocational Education: Implementing Standards. Tim L. Wentling. 29p. 1985. 4.25 (ISBN 0-318-22218-3, IN292). Natl Ctr Res Voc Ed.

Toward Excellence in Secondary Vocational Education: Improving Teaching. Gwen C. Cooke. 43p. 1985. 4.75 (ISBN 0-318-22219-1, IN293). Natl Ctr Res Voc Ed.

Toward Excellence in Secondary Vocational Education: Providing Job Training. David W. Stevens. 40p. 1985. 4.75 (ISBN 0-318-22220-5, IN296). Natl Ctr Res Voc Ed.

Toward Excellence in Secondary Vocational Education: Using Cognitive Psychology in Curriculum Planning. Janet F. Laster. 65p. 1985. 7.25 (ISBN 0-318-22221-3, IN297). Natl Ctr Res Voc Ed.

Toward Excellence in Secondary Vocational Education: Using Evaluation Results. Donald R. Brannon. 38p. 1985. 4.75 (ISBN 0-318-22222-1, IN294). Natl Ctr Res Voc Ed.

Toward Explaining Human Culture: A Critical Review of the Findings of Worldwide Cross-Cultural Research. David Levinson & Martin J. Malone. LC 80-83324. (Comparative Studies Ser.). 412p. 1980. 25.00 (ISBN 0-87536-339-3); pap. 15.00 (ISBN 0-87536-340-7). HRAFP.

Toward Fair Employment. Paul H. Norgren & Samuel E. Hill. LC 64-17756. 296p. 1964. 37.50x (ISBN 0-231-02716-8). Columbia U Pr.

Toward Fitness: Guided Exercise for Those with Health Problems. Robert Cantu. LC 79-27686. 258p. 1980. 26.95 (ISBN 0-87705-496-7). Human Sci Pr.

Toward Foundations of Information Science. Ed. by Lawrence B. Heilprin. 232p. 1985. lib. bdg. 34.95 (ISBN 0-317-67372-6). Greenwood.

Toward Freedom: A Cleveland Romance. Ilio Grossi. 1988. 12.95 (ISBN 0-533-07782-6). Vantage.

Toward Freedom & Dignity: The Humanities & the Idea of Humanity. O. B. Haradison. LC 72-4010. pap. 47.30 (ISBN 0-317-30464-X, 2024832). Bks Demand UMI.

Toward Freedom for All: North Carolina Quakers & Slavery. Hiram Hilty. 120p. 1984. pap. 9.95 (ISBN 0-913408-83-2). Friends United.

Toward Freedom in Singing. Dina S. Winter & Theodora Richards. 1986. pap. 4.50 (ISBN 0-916786-84-6). St George Bk Serv.

Toward Global Equilibrium: Collected Papers. Ed. by Dennis L. Meadows & Donella Meadows. LC 72-81804. (Illus.). 400p. 1973. 40.00x (ISBN 0-262-13143-9). MIT Pr.

Toward Gog & Magog Or? A Critical Review of the Literature of Adult Group Discussion. Ed. by F. W. Osinski et al. LC 72-6475. (Occasional Papers Ser., No. 30). 80p. (Orig.). 1972. pap. 2.00 (ISBN 0-87060-053-2, OCP 30). Syracuse U Cont Ed.

Toward Healthy Aging: Human Needs & Nursing Response. 3rd ed. Ebersole. (Illus.). 800p. 1989. 35.95 (ISBN 0-8016-2867-9). Mosby.

Toward Healthy Aging: Human Needs & Nursing Response. 2nd ed. Ebersole & Hess. 1985. 37.95 (ISBN 0-8016-1580-1). Mosby.

Toward Human Dignity: Social Work in Practice. National Association of Social Workers, Fifth Symposium, Nov. 19-22, 1977. Ed. by John W. Hanks. LC 78-65076. 269p. 1978. pap. 14.95x (ISBN 0-87101-079-8). Natl Assn Soc Wkrs.

Toward Improving Research in Social Studies Education. Jack Fraenkel. (SSEC Monographs). (Orig.). 1988. pap. 14.95 (ISBN 0-89994-325-X). Soc Sci Ed.

Toward Income Adequacy for the Elderly: Implications of the SSI Programs for New York City Recipients. Mary Zander et al. LC 84-231136. 243p. 1982. pap. 7.00 (ISBN 0-88156-004-9). Comm Serv Soc NY.

Toward Increased Judicial Activism: The Political Role of the Supreme Court. Arthur S. Miller. LC 81-20201. (Contributions in American Studies Ser.: No. 59). xii, 355p. 1982. lib. bdg. 35.00 (ISBN 0-313-23305-5, MIO/). Greenwood.

Toward Transfigured Life: The Theoria of Eastern Orthodox Ethics. Stanley Harakas. 1983. lib. bdg. 39.95x (ISBN 0-88946-027-2). E Mellen.

Toward Transformation in Social Knowledge. K. J. Gergen. (Springer Series in Social Psychology). (Illus.). 260p. 1982. 33.00 (ISBN 0-387-90673-8). Springer-Verlag.

Toward Understanding Islam: Contemporary Apologetic of Islam & Missionary Policy. Harry G. Dorman. LC 79-176727. (Columbia University. Teachers College. Contributions to Education: No. 940). Repr. of 1948 ed. 22.50 (ISBN 0-404-55940-9). AMS Pr.

Toward Understanding Power & Its Use - Machiavelli, Jesus, I-Thou. Norman W. Beck. 1988. 20.00 (ISBN 0-533-07292-1). Vantage.

Toward Understanding Sex in Marriage. Sawak Sarju. 1986. 11.95 (ISBN 0-533-06896-7). Vantage.

Toward Understanding the Social Impact of Computers. Roy Amara. 136p. 1974. 10.50 (ISBN 0-318-14427-1, R29). Inst Future.

Toward Undiscovered Ends. Anna Brinton. 1951. pap. 5.00x (ISBN 0-87574-062-6, 062). Pendle Hill.

Toward Unification in Psychology: The Banff Conference on Theoretical Psychology, 1st, 1965. Banff Conference on Theoretical Psychology Staff. Ed. by Joseph R. Royce. LC 72-505050. 1970. pap. 78.50 (ISBN 0-317-08093-8, 2014393). Bks Demand UMI.

Toward Unity Against World Imperialism. Gus Hall. 1969. pap. 0.35 (ISBN 0-87898-040-7). New Outlook.

Toward Wholeness: Rudolf Steiner Education in America. Mary C. Richards. LC 80-14905. 210p. 1980. 19.50 (ISBN 0-8195-5049-3); pap. 9.95 (ISBN 0-8195-6062-6). Wesleyan U Pr.

Toward Wider Acceptance of U N Treaties. Oscar Schachter et al. LC 79-140127. (UNITAR Studies). 1971. 10.00 (ISBN 0-405-02236-0). Ayer Co Pubs.

Toward Women: A Study of the Origins of Western Attitudes Through Greco-Roman Philosophy. Joseph P. Ghougassian. LC 77-92325. 1977. pap. 3.95x (ISBN 0-930994-01-9). Lukas & Sons.

Toward World Order & Human Dignity: Essays in Honor of Myres S. McDougal. Ed. by W. Michael Reisman & Burns H. Weston. LC 75-36109. (Illus.). 1976. 30.00 (ISBN 0-02-926290-9). Free Pr.

Toward World Peace. Henry A. Wallace. 1970. Repr. of 1948 ed. lib. bdg. 25.00x (ISBN 0-8371-3434-X, WAWP). Greenwood.

Toward World Peace. Henry A. Wallace. 1948. 10.00x (ISBN 0-686-17404-6). R S Barnes.

Toward World-Wide Christianity. Ed. by O. Frederick Nolde. LC 70-86049. (Essay & General Literature Index Reprint Ser). 1969. Repr. of 1946 ed. 23.50x (ISBN 0-8046-0581-5, Pub by Kennikat). Assoc Faculty Pr.

Towards a Better International Economic Order. pap. 1.50 (ISBN 92-1-157008-5, E.75.XV.LS/2). UN.

Towards a Better Life: Being a Series of Epistles, or Declamations. Kenneth Burke. 1966. 30.00x (ISBN 0-520-00193-1); pap. 9.95x (ISBN 0-520-04638-2). U of Cal Pr.

Towards a Better Understanding of History. Bernard Norling. 157p. 1960. pap. 5.95x (ISBN 0-268-00284-3). U of Notre Dame Pr.

Towards a Biological Awareness. George H. Kieffer. 623p. (Orig.). 1985. pap. text ed. 25.80x (ISBN 0-87563-274-2). Stipes.

Towards a Career in Europe. 5th ed. Richard Owens. LC 84-120169. 90p. 1983. 15.00 (ISBN 0-915357-00-3). AIMS.

Towards a Chaucerian Poetic. D. Brewer. (Sir Israel Gollancz Memorial Lectures in Old English Ser.). 1974. pap. 5.50 (ISBN 0-85672-104-2, Pub. by British Acad). Longwood Pub Group.

Towards a Christian Republic: Antimasonry & the Great Transition in New England, 1826-1836. Paul Goodman. (Illus.). 344p. 1988. 34.50 (ISBN 0-19-504864-4). Oxford U Pr.

Towards a Citizens Militia: Anarchist Alternatives to NATO & the Warsaw Pact. Ed. by First of May Group. 1984. lib. bdg. 79.95 (ISBN 0-87700-631-8). Revisionist Pr.

Towards a Civilization of Love. Tr. by Cardinal Ratzinger & Cardinal Suenens. LC 85-61026. 276p. (Orig., Fr., Ger. & Span.). 1985. pap. 10.95 (ISBN 0-89870-072-8). Ignatius Pr.

Towards a Comprehensive Model for Schizophrenic Disorders. Ed. by David B. Feinsilver. (Psychoanalytic Inquiry Bk.: Vol. 5). 416p. 1986. text ed. 39.95 (ISBN 0-88163-029-2). Analytic Pr.

Towards a Constitutional Charter for Canada. Albert S. Abel. 1980. pap. 8.95 (ISBN 0-8020-6399-3). U of Toronto Pr.

Towards a Contextual Grammar of English. Eugene Winter. 224p. 1983. text ed. 34.95x (ISBN 0-04-425027-4); pap. text ed. 11.95x (ISBN 0-04-425028-2). Unwin Hyman.

Towards a Critical Sociology: An Essay on Commonsense & Emancipation. Zygmunt Bauman. (Direct Edition Ser.). 1976. pap. 10.95x (ISBN 0-7100-8306-8). Routledge Chapman & Hall.

Towards a Critique of Foucault. Ed. by Mike Gane. 1987. pap. write for info. (ISBN 0-7102-0764-6, Pub. by Routledge UK). Routledge Chapman & Hall.

Towards a Cross-Linguistic Assessment of Speech Production. Ed. by Hans W. Dechert & Manfred Raupach. (Kassler Arbeiten zur Sprache und Literatur: Vol. 7). 129p. 1980. pap. 15.30 (ISBN 3-8204-6003-9). P Lang Pubs.

Towards a Cross-National Model for Cooperation in Vocational Education: Implications for Research & Development. Gert Loose. 31p. 1982. 3.25 (ISBN 0-318-22223-X, OC87). Natl Ctr Res Voc Ed.

Towards a Cultural Policy. Ed. by Satish Saberwal. 1974. 15.00 (ISBN 0-686-20320-8). Intl Bk Dist.

Towards a Cultural Policy for Honduras. Alba Alonso de Quesada. (Studies & Documents on Cultural Policies). (Illus.). 73p. 1978. pap. 5.00 (ISBN 92-3-101520-6, U875, UNESCO). UNIPUB.

Towards a Democratic Rationality: Making the Case for Swedish Labour. John Fry. 290p. 1986. text ed. 47.50 (ISBN 0-566-00761-4, Pub. by Gower Pub England). Gower Pub Co.

Towards a European Foreign Policy: Legal, Economic, & Political Dimensions. Johan K. De Vree et al. LC 87-5612. 1987. 95.00 (ISBN 9-0247-3506-8). Kluwer Academic.

Towards a Feminist Tradition: An Annotated Bibliography of Novels in English by Women, 1891-1920. Diva Daims & Janet Grimes. Ed. by Doris Robinson. 1982. lib. bdg. 91.00 (ISBN 0-8240-9523-5). Garland Pub.

Towards a Formal Description of Ada. Ed. by B. Bjorner & O. N. Oest. (Lecture Notes in Computer Science: Vol. 98). 630p. 1980. pap. 31.00 (ISBN 0-387-10283-3). Springer-Verlag.

Towards a General Comparative Linguistics. Jeffrey Ellis. (Janua Linguarum, Ser. Minor: No. 52). (Orig.). 1966. pap. text ed. 16.80x (ISBN 90-2790-584-3). Mouton.

Towards a Global Congress of the World's Religions. Ed. by Warren Lewis. LC 78-73771. 1978. write for info. (ISBN 0-932894-01-1). Rose Sharon Pr.

Towards a Global Congress of the World's Religions. Ed. by Warren Lewis. LC 79-56121. 63p. 1979. pap. 2.95 (ISBN 0-932894-03-8). Rose Sharon Pr.

Towards a Global Congress of World's Religions. Ed. by Warren Lewis. LC 80-53764. 79p. 1980. pap. 3.25 (ISBN 0-932894-07-0). Rose Sharon Pr.

Towards a Good Beginning: Teaching Early Childhood Mathematics. G. M. Burton et al. 257p. 1984. write for info. Addison-Wesley.

Towards a Hebrew University see Letters & Papers of Chaim Weizmann.

Towards a History of Adult Education in America: The Search for a Unifying Principle. Harold W. Stubblefield. 208p. 1988. text ed. 35.00 (ISBN 0-415-00563-9). Routledge Chapman & Hall.

Towards a History of Archaeology. Ed. by Glyn Daniel. 192p. 1981. 27.50 (ISBN 0-500-05039-2). Thames Hudson.

Towards a History of Phonetics. Ed. by R. E. Asher & Eugenie Henderson. 330p. 50.00x (ISBN 0-85224-374-X, Pub. by Edinburgh Univ England). State Mutual Bk.

Towards a Jurisprudence of Injury: A Summary of the Report of the A. B. A.'s Special Committee on the Tort Liability System. Roscoe Pound-American Trial Lawyers Foundation Staff. Date not set. pap. 2.50 (ISBN 0-317-57759-X). Roscoe Pound Found.

Towards a Jurisprudence of Injury: The Continuing Creation of a System of Substantive Justice in American Tort Law: Report to the American Bar Association. American Bar Association, Special Committee on the Tort Liability System & Marshall S. Shapo. LC 85-112535. 996p. 1984. 55.00. Amer Bar Assn.

Towards a Just Immigration Policy. Ed. by Ann Dummett. 1986. 20.00x (ISBN 0-900137-26-6, Pub. by NCCL UK). State Mutual Bk.

Towards a Justice with a Human Face. M. Storme. 1978. lib. bdg. 79.00 (ISBN 90-268-0974-3, Pub. by Kluwer Law Netherlands). Kluwer Academic.

Towards a Lasting Settlement. Ed. by Charles R. Buxton. LC 78-147578. (Library of War & Peace; Int'l. Organization, Arbitration & Law). 1972. lib. bdg. 46.00 (ISBN 0-8240-0343-8). Garland Pub.

Towards a Living Church: Family & Community Catechesis. Wim Saris. Tr. by Eileen Hurley. (Illus.). 176p. (Orig.). 1986. pap. 9.95 (ISBN 0-00-599644-9, Collins Liturgical). HarpR.

Towards a Metaphysics of the Sacred. Stephen Beasley-Murray. LC 82-8288. (Special Studies: No. 8). viii, 110p. 1982. pap. 7.95 (ISBN 0-86554-038-1). NABPR.

Towards a Model of Human Growth. 41p. 1979. pap. 6.75 (ISBN 92-808-0059-0, TUNU008, UNU). UNIPUB.

Towards a Modern Iran: Studies in Thought, Politics & Society. Ed. by Elie Kedourie & Sylvia G. Haim. 262p. 1980. 29.50x (ISBN 0-7146-3145-0, F Cass Co). Biblio Dist.

Towards a More General Theory of Value. Edward H. Chamberlin. LC 82-6259. xii, 318p. 1982. Repr. of 1957 ed. lib. bdg. 38.50x (ISBN 0-313-23590-2, CHTO). Greenwood.

Towards a Mythology: Studies in the Poetry of W. B. Yeats. Peter Ure. LC 85-24696. 125p. 1986. Repr. of 1946 ed. lib. bdg. 38.50x (ISBN 0-313-25055-3, URTM). Greenwood.

Towards a National Spirit. Whitfield J. Bell, Jr. 1979. pap. 3.00 (ISBN 0-89073-057-1). Boston Public Lib.

Towards a New American Poetics: Essays & Interviews: Olson, Duncan, Snyder, Creeley, Bly, Ginsberg. Ekbert Faas. LC 78-1559. 300p. 1979. 17.50 (ISBN 0-87685-389-0). Black Sparrow.

Towards a New Architecture. Le Corbusier. 320p. 1986. pap. 8.95 (ISBN 0-486-25023-7). Dover.

Towards a New Cold War: Essays on the Current Crisis & How We Got There. Noam Chomsky. LC 81-47190. 537p. 1982. pap. 11.95 (ISBN 0-394-74944-8). Pantheon.

Towards a New Consciousness. R. P. Kaushik. LC 78-59118. 1979. 8.95 (ISBN 0-918038-10-3); pap. 5.95 (ISBN 0-918038-09-X). Journey Pubns.

Towards a New Epoch. Nicolas Berdyaev. LC 73-6799. Repr. of 1949 ed. lib. bdg. 15.00 (ISBN 0-8414-3115-9). Folcroft.

Towards a New India. Karan Singh. 1974. 7.50 (ISBN 0-686-20321-6). Intl Bk Dist.

Towards a New International Economic Order. Mohammed Bedjaoui. LC 79-22943. Orig. Title: Pour un Nouvel Ordre Economique International. 287p. 1979. 38.50 (ISBN 0-8419-0585-1); pap. 27.50 (ISBN 0-8419-0588-6). Holmes & Meier.

Towards a New International Economic Order. (New Challenges to International Law Ser.). 287p. 1979. pap. 9.50 (ISBN 92-3-101670-9, U1343, UNESCO). UNIPUB.

Towards a New Iron Age. Marion Campbell. (Illus.). 100p. (Orig.). 1984. pap. 5.95 (ISBN 0-905209-23-0, Pub. by Victoria & Albert Mus UK). Faber & Faber.

Towards a New Marxism: Proceedings. International Telos Conference, 1st, Waterloo, Ont., Oct. 8-11, 1970. Ed. by Paul Piccone & Bart Grahl. LC 73-87129. 240p. 1973. 16.00 (ISBN 0-914386-03-4); pap. 5.50 (ISBN 0-914386-04-2). Telos Pr.

Towards a New Mysticism: Teilhard de Chardin & Eastern Religions. Ursula King. 320p. 1980. (HarpR); pap. 8.95 (ISBN 0-8164-2327-X). Har-Row.

Towards a New Poetry. Diane Wakoski. (Poets on Poetry Ser.). 1979. pap. 8.95 (ISBN 0-472-06307-3). U of Mich Pr.

Towards a New Price Revolution. B. Csikos-Nagy. 1981. 40.00x (ISBN 0-569-08548-9, Pub. by Collets (UK)). State Mutual Bk.

Towards a New Price Revolution. B. Csikos-Nagy. 190p. 1979. 51.25x (Pub. by Collets (UK)). State Mutual Bk.

Towards a New Theatre: Edward Gordon Craig & Hamlet. Brian Arnott. (Illus.). 1975. pap. 7.50X (ISBN 0-88884-305-4, 56521-1, Pub. by Natl Gallery Canada). U of Chicago Pr.

Towards a New Theory of Distributive Justice. Norman E. Bowie. LC 72-150315. 160p. 1971. 14.00x (ISBN 0-87023-085-9). U of Mass Pr.

Towards a New World. S. Radhakrishnan. 149p. 1983. 9.00 (ISBN 0-86578-202-4); pap. 4.25 (ISBN 0-86578-138-9). Ind-US Inc.

Towards a New World Religion. Lola A. Davis. 256p. 1983. pap. 16.00 (ISBN 0-942494-77-6). Coleman Pub.

Towards a Non-Oppressive Environment. Alexander Tzonis. LC 79-189033. 1978. 16.50x (ISBN 0-262-20038-4); pap. 6.95x (ISBN 0-262-70018-2). MIT Pr.

Towards a Nonviolent Revolution. Narayan Desai. 176p. 9.75 (ISBN 0-686-96939-1). Greenlf Bks.

Towards a Pax Africana: A Study of Ideology & Ambition. Ali A. Mazrui. LC 67-12232. (Nature of Human Society Ser). 1967. 22.00x (ISBN 0-226-51427-7). U of Chicago Pr.

Towards a People's Literature: Essays in Dialectics of Praxis & Contradiction in Philippine Writing. E San Juan. 208p. 1985. text ed. 15.00x (ISBN 0-8248-0903-3, Pub. by U of Phillippines Pr); pap. text ed. 10.00x (ISBN 0-8248-0904-1). UH Pr.

Towards a Philosophy of Administration. Christopher Hodgkinson. LC 78-676. 1978. 25.00 (ISBN 0-312-81036-9). St Martin.

Towards a Philosophy of Black Studies. Charles A. Frye. LC 77-90350. 1978. pap. 10.95 perfect bdg. (ISBN 0-88247-513-4). R & E Pubs.

Towards a Plan of Actions for Mankind, 5 vols. Ed. by Maurice Marois. Incl. Vol. 1. Long Range Mineral Resources & Growth. 1977. 150.00 (ISBN 0-08-021445-2); Vol. 2. Long Range Energetic Resources & Growth. 1977. 105.00 (ISBN 0-08-021446-0); Vol. 3. Biological Balance & Thermal Modification. 1977. 150.00 (ISBN 0-08-021447-9); Vol. 4. Design of Global System Models & Their Limitations. 1977. 145.00 (ISBN 0-08-021448-7); Vol. 5. Conclusions & Perspectives. 1977. 250.00 (ISBN 0-08-021449-5). 1977. Set. 695.00 (ISBN 0-08-021850-4). Pergamon.

Towards a Poetics of Fiction: Essays from Novel, a Forum on Fiction, 1967-1976. Mark Spilka. LC 76-48550. pap. 95.80 (2056242). Bks Demand UMI.

Towards a Political Economy for Africa: The Dialectics of Independence. Timothy M. Shaw. LC 84-8218. 150p. 1985. 22.50 (ISBN 0-312-81043-1). St Martin.

Towards a Political Economy of Nigeria: Petroleum & Politics at the Semi-Periphery. Julius O. Ihonvbere & Tim Shaw. 224p. 1988. text ed. 37.00 (ISBN 0-566-05422-1, Pub. by Gower Pub England). Gower Pub Co.

Towards a Political Economy of Urbanization in Third World Countries. Helen I. Safa. (Illus.). 1982. 10.95x (ISBN 0-19-561307-4). Oxford U Pr.

Towards a Radical Democracy: The Political Economy of the Budapest School. Douglas M. Brown. 260p. 1988. 39.95 (ISBN 0-04-330408-7). Unwin Hyman.

Towards a Rational Philosophical Anthropology. Agassi. (Van Leer Jerusalem Foundation Ser). 1977. lib. bdg. 30.00 (ISBN 90-247-2003-6, Pub. by Martinus Nijhoff Netherlands). Kluwer Academic.

Towards a Re-Definition of Development: Essays & Discussion on the Nature of Development in an International Perspective. Ed. by John P. Schlegal et al. Birou. LC 76-28753. 1977. 26.00 (ISBN 0-08-020580-1). Pergamon.

Towards a Reading-Writing Classroom. Andrea Butler & Jan Turbill. 96p. (Orig.). 1984. pap. text ed. 11.50x (ISBN 0-435-08461-5, 00584). Heinemann Ed.

Towards a Reconstructed Past: Historical Texts from Busoga, Uganda. Ed. by David W. Cohen. (Fontes Historiae Africanae Ser.). 250p. 1986. 27.95x (ISBN 0-19-726039-X). Oxford U Pr.

Towards a Reconstruction of Macroeconomics. William Fellner. LC 76-21162. 1976. pap. 19.00 (ISBN 0-8447-1318-X). Am Enterprise.

Towards a Rediscovery of the Cultural Heritage of the United States. Allan R. Crite. 23p. (Orig.). 1968. pap. 1.00 (ISBN 0-934552-24-X). Boston Athenaeum.

Towards a Regional Strategy for Eradicating Illiteracy in the Asia & Pacific Region. 59p. 1985. pap. 9.95 (UB160, UB). UNIPUB.

Towards a Renovated International System. Richard N. Cooper et al. 1977. 15.00 (ISBN 0-318-02792-5); pap. 4.95 (ISBN 0-318-02793-3). Trilateral Comm.

Towards a Revolutionary Theatre. Utpal Dutt. 1983. 5.50x (ISBN 0-8364-1022-X, Pub. by MC Sarkar Calcutta). South Asia Bks.

Towards a Romantic Conception of Nature: Coleridge's Poetry up to 1803. H. R. Rookmaaker, Jr. LC 84-24633. (Utrecht Publications in Literature (UPAL): 20). ix, 214p. 1984. 44.00x (ISBN 90-272-2205-3); pap. 28.00x (ISBN 90-272-2215-0). Benjamins North Am.

Towards a Science of Peace. Theo F. Lentz. 1955. 4.00 (ISBN 0-318-03980-X). Lentz Peace Res.

Towards a Science of Science Teaching. Michael Shayer & Philip Adey. (Orig.). 1981. pap. text ed. 16.50x (ISBN 0-435-57825-1). Heinemann Ed.

Towards a Science of Translating. Eugene A. Nida. (Illus.). 1964. 120.00x (ISBN 90-04-02605-3). Adlers Foreign Bks.

Towards a Second Green Revolution: From Chemical to New Biological Tehcnologies in Agriculture in the Tropics. Ed. by G. B. Marini-Bettolo. (Developments in Agricultural & Managed-Forest Ecology Ser.: Vol. 19). 532p. 1988. 171.00 (ISBN 0-444-98927-7). Elsevier.

Towards a Social Ecology: Contextual Appreciation of the Future in the Present. F. E. Emery & E. L. Trist. LC 70-178778. 256p. 1973. 34.50x (ISBN 0-306-30563-1, Plenum Pr). Plenum Pub.

Towards a Social Ecology: Contextual Appreciation of the Future in the Present. F. E. Emery & E. L. Trist. LC 74-26842. 256p. 1975. pap. 12.95x (ISBN 0-306-20015-5, Plenum Pr.). Plenum Pub.

Towards a Social Grammar of Language. M. Grayshon. 1977. 11.80x (ISBN 90-279-7633-3). Mouton.

Towards a Sociology of Mass Communications. D. McQuail. 1969 (97480). pap. text ed. write for info. (ISBN 0-686-66487-6). Macmillan.

Towards a Strategy for Conservation in a World of Technological Change. Colin A. Gannon. (Discussion Paper Ser.: No. 24). 1968. pap. 6.50 (ISBN 0-686-32193-6). Regional Sci Res Inst.

Towards a System of Lifelong Education: Some Practical Considerations. A. J. Cropley. LC 80-40417. (Advances in Lifelong Education Ser.: Vol. 7). (Illus.). 234p. 1980. pap. text ed. 16.25 (ISBN 0-08-026067-5). Pergamon.

Towards a Technology of Peace. Theo F. Lentz. 1972. pap. 3.00 (ISBN 0-933061-11-0). Lentz Peace Res.

Towards a Theology for Inter-Faith Dialogue. Interfaith Consultative Group, Board for Mission & Unity, Church of England. (Lambeth Study Bks.). 56p. 1986. pap. 2.25 (ISBN 0-88028-058-1). Forward Movement.

Towards a Theoretical Understanding of High Temperature Superconductivity: ICTP, Trieste, Italy, June 20-July 29, 1988. Ed. by S. Lundqvist et al. (Progress in High Temperature Superconductivity Ser.: Vol. XIV). 600p. 1988. 78.00 (ISBN 9971-50-639-4, ZB0638PP). World Scientific Pub.

Towards a Theory of Drama in Education. Gavin Bolton. (Illus.). 176p. 1980. pap. text ed. 9.95x (ISBN 0-582-36138-9). Longman.

Towards the End of Isolationism: China's Foreign Policy after Mao. Michael Yahuda. LC 83-42610. 280p. 1983. pap. 11.95x (ISBN 0-312-81141-1); 25.00x (ISBN 0-312-81142-X). St Martin.

Towards the Factory of the Future. Ed. by L. Kops. (PED: Vol. 1). 115p. 1980. 18.00 (ISBN 0-317-06809-1, G00189). ASME.

Towards the Factory of the Future: Emergence of the Computerized Factory & Its Impact on Society: Presented at the Winter Annual Meeting of the ASME, Chicago, Illinois, November 16-21, 1980. American Society of Mechanical Engineers Staff. Ed. by L. Kops. LC 80-69197. (PED Ser.: Vol. 1). pap. 31.20 (ISBN 0-317-58243-7, 2056389). Bks Demand UMI.

Towards the Gulf: A Romance of Louisiana. LC 72-3107. (Black Heritage Library Collection Ser.). Repr. of 1886 ed. 17.25 (ISBN 0-8369-9084-6). Ayer Co Pubs.

Towards the Healing of Schism: The Sees of Rome & Constantinople (Ecumenical Documents III) Ed. & tr. by E. J. Stormon. 576p. 1987. pap. 12.95 (ISBN 0-8091-2910-8). Paulist Pr.

Towards the Holocaust: The Social & Economic Collapse of the Weimar Republic. Ed. by Michael N. Dobkowski & Isidor Wallimann. LC 82-18388. (Illus.). 440p. 1983. lib. bdg. 35.00 (ISBN 0-313-22795-0, DHO/). Greenwood.

Towards the Immunological Control of Human Protozoal Diseases: Proceedings of a Royal Society Discussion Meeting Held February 22-23, 1984. Ed. by S. Cohen & G. A. Cross. (Illus.). 206p. 1985. lib. bdg. 65.00x (ISBN 0-85403-235-5, Pub. by Royal Soc London). Scholium Intl.

Towards the Information Society: Selected Papers from the Hong-Kong Computer Conference, 1983. Ed. by R. C. Barquin & G. P. Mead. 164p. 1984. 58.00 (ISBN 0-444-87564-6, North Holland). Elsevier.

Towards the Life Divine: Sri Aurobindo's Vision. Thomas O'Neil. 1979. 10.50x (ISBN 0-8364-0546-3). South Asia Bks.

Towards the Lost Domain: Letters from London, 1905. Alain-Fournier. Tr. by W. J. Strachan from Fr. (Illus.). 222p. 1986. 20.00 (ISBN 0-85635-674-3). Carcanet.

Towards the Managed Economy: Keynes, the Treasury & the Fiscal Policy Debate of the 1930's. Roger Middleton. 288p. 1985. 49.95 (ISBN 0-416-35830-6, 9523). Routledge Chapman & Hall.

Towards the Mountain. Alan Paton. 1988. 18.50 (ISBN 0-8446-6322-0). Peter Smith.

Towards the Mountain: An Autobiography. Alan Paton. 336p. 1987. pap. 9.95 (ISBN 0-684-18892-9). Scribner.

Towards the New Pattern of Education in India. 2nd ed. P. D. Shukla. 288p. 1987. text ed. 35.00x (ISBN 81-207-0666-8, Pub. by Sterling Pubs India). Apt Bks.

Towards the Planned City. Anthony Sutcliffe. 1981. 27.50 (ISBN 0-312-81039-3). St Martin.

Towards the Prevention of Alcohol Problems: Government, Business, & Community Action. Ed. by Dean R. Gerstein. 192p. 1984. pap. text ed. 14.95x (ISBN 0-309-03485-X). Natl Acad Pr.

Towards the Real Flaubert: A Study of Madame Bovary. Margaret Lowe. Ed. by A. W. Raitt. 1984. 27.00x (ISBN 0-19-815800-9). Oxford U Pr.

Towards the Renaissance of Puerto Rican Studies: Ethnic & Area Studies in University Education. Antonio M. Stevens. (Atlantic Studies on Society in Change: No. 53). Date not set. price not set. Brooklyn Coll Pr.

Towards the Sensitive Bureaucracy: Consumers, Welfare & the New Pluralism. Drew Clode et al. 160p. 1987. text ed. 38.95 (ISBN 0-566-05009-9). Gower Pub Co.

Towards the Seventies. Dick Higgins. LC 79-129807. 1969. pap. 0.75 (ISBN 0-911856-00-5). Abyss.

Towards the Sun. Margaret Chatterjee. (Writers Workshop Redbird Ser.). 1975. 8.00 (ISBN 0-88253-664-8); pap. text ed. 3.00 (ISBN 0-88253-663-X). Ind-US Inc.

Towards the Twentieth Century. facs. ed. Harold V. Routh. LC 69-17587. (Essay Index Reprint Ser). 1937. 19.00 (ISBN 0-8369-0091-X). Ayer Co Pubs.

Towards the Twenty First Century: Doing the Good. Bernhard J. Lievegoed. Ed. by Rufus Goodwin. 82p. 1979. pap. 4.95 (ISBN 0-919924-04-2, Pub. by Steiner Book Centre Canada). Anthroposophic.

Towards the Unknown: The Journey into New-Dimensional Consciousness. Dada. LC 81-65123. (Illus.). 128p. (Orig.). 1981. pap. 8.00 (ISBN 0-930608-02-X). Dada Ctr.

Towards the Year Two Thousand: The Altered Strategic Environment. Peter DeLeon. 128p. 1987. 21.00x (ISBN 0-669-14576-9). Lexington Bks.

Towards the Year 2000: International Perspectives on Museums of Science & Technology. Ed. by Victor Danilov. LC 20-84648. 94p. 1981. pap. 11.75 (ISBN 0-944040-08-X). AST Ctrs.

Towards Theory of Alternative Society. Narendra K. Singh. 1986. 26.00 (ISBN 81-7033-021-1, Pub. by Rawat). South Asia Bks.

Towards Theory of Positive Secularism. S. L. Verma. 167p. 1986. 27.00 (ISBN 81-7033-018-1, Pub. by Rawat). South Asia Bks.

Towards Third Generation Robotics. Ed. by B. Espiau. (Illus.). 650p. 1987. 120.00 (ISBN 0-387-18404-X). Springer-Verlag.

Towards Tomorrow: The Story of the African Teachers Association of South Africa. R. L. Peteni. Ed. by Cole Kitchen. LC 78-59714. 1979. pap. 7.50 (ISBN 0-917256-08-5). Ref Pubns.

Towards Total Revolution, 4 vols. Jayaprakash Narayan. Ed. by Brahmanand. LC 79-4919. 1980. Set. 50.00x (ISBN 0-295-95671-2, Pub. by Popular Prakashan India). U of Wash Pr.

Towards Understanding Climate Change: The J. O. Fletcher Lectures on Problems & Prospects of Climate Analysis & Forecasting. Ed. by Uwe Radok. (Special Studies). 200p. 1987. pap. 27.00 (ISBN 0-8133-7405-7). Westview.

Towards Understanding Galaxies at Large Redshift. Ed. by Richard G. Kron & Alvio Renzini. 1988. lib. bdg. 96.00 (ISBN 90-277-2681-7, Pub. by Reidel Holland). Kluwer Academic.

Towards Understanding India. 3rd ed. 1967. pap. 2.00 (ISBN 0-88253-398-3). Ind-US Inc.

Towards Understanding Islam. A. A. Maududi. pap. 5.50 (ISBN 0-686-18479-3). Kazi Pubns.

Towards Understanding Islam. Abul A. Maududi. Tr. by Khurshid Ahmad from Urdu. 116p. (Orig.). pap. 5.95x (ISBN 0-86037-053-4, Pub. by Islamic Found UK). New Era Pubns MI.

Towards Understanding Islam. S. A. Maududi. 5.50x (ISBN 0-87902-065-2). Orientalia.

Towards Understanding Islam. Sayyid A. Mawdudi. Tr. by Khurshid Ahmad from Urdu. 179p. (Orig.). 1980. pap. 5.95 (ISBN 0-939830-22-1, Pub. by HFSO Kuwait). New Era Pubns MI.

Towards Understanding Receptors. Ed. by J. W. Lamble. (Current Reviews in Biomedicine: Vol. 1). 234p. 1981. pap. 25.00 (ISBN 0-444-80339-4, Biomedical Pr). Elsevier.

Towards Understanding Relationships. Robert A. Hinde. LC 79-40921. (European Monographs in Social Psychology: No. 18). 1980. 58.50 (ISBN 0-12-349250-5); pap. 29.00 (ISBN 0-12-349252-1). Acad Pr.

Towards Understanding the Basics of Islam: Texts from Qur'an & Hadith. 2nd ed. Kaukab Siddique. 52p. 1986. pap. 2.50 (ISBN 0-942978-09-9). Am Soc Ed & Rel.

Towards Understanding the Bible. Perry Yoder & Elizabeth Yoder. LC 78-53649. 1978. pap. 3.95 (ISBN 0-87303-006-0). Faith & Life.

Towards Understanding the Intrinsic in Body Movement. new ed. Martha Davis. LC 74-7857. (Body Movement Perspectives in Research Ser). (Illus.). 192p. 1975. 31.00x (ISBN 0-405-06200-1). Ayer Co Pubs.

Towards Union in Palestine: Essays on Zionism & Jewish-Arab Cooperation. Ed. by Martin Buber & J. L. Magnes. LC 76-97272. (Judaica Ser.). 124p. 1972. Repr. of 1947 ed. lib. bdg. 35.00x (ISBN 0-8371-2564-2, BUUP). Greenwood.

Towards Universalization of Primary Education in Asia & the Pacific: Country Studies. (APEID Ser.). 60p. 1985. pap. 52.50 (UB172, UNESCO). UNIPUB.

Towards Universalization of Primary Education: Review of National Plans & Innovative Efforts: Report of a Regional Meeting, Bangkok, 15-23 November 1983. (Asian Programme of Educational Innovation for Development). 78p. 1985. pap. 5.00 (UB167 5071, UNESCO). UNIPUB.

Towards Utopia: A Study of Brecht. Keith A. Dickson. 1978. 49.95x (ISBN 0-19-815750-9). Oxford U Pr.

Towards Vatican III: The Work That Has to Be Done. Ed. by David Tracy et al. 1978. 14.95x (ISBN 0-8245-0397-X); pap. 5.95 (ISBN 0-8245-0398-8). Crossroad NY.

Towards Village Industry: A Strategy for Development. Liv Berg et al. (Illus.). 88p. (Orig.). 1978. pap. 9.75x (ISBN 0-903031-52-3, Pub. by Intermediate Tech England). Intermediate Tech.

Towards World Prosperity: Reshaping the Global Money System. Irving S. Friedman. 336p. 1986. 24.95 (ISBN 0-669-11564-9). Lexington Bks.

Towards Zero. Agatha Christie. 1982. pap. 3.50 (ISBN 0-671-60256-X). PB.

Towards Zero. Agatha Christie. (Popular Author Ser.). 313p. 1988. lib. bdg. 16.95x (ISBN 0-8161-4611-X, Large Print Bks). G K Hall.

Towel & the Cross. John B. Nielson. 118p. (Orig.). 1983. pap. 3.95 (ISBN 0-8341-0847-X). Beacon Hill.

Tower Abbey. Isabelle Holland. 1979. pap. 1.95 (ISBN 0-449-24044-4, Crest). Fawcett.

Tower & the Bridge: The New Art of Structural Engineering. David P. Billington. LC 85-42667. (Illus.). 328p. 1985. pap. 13.95x (ISBN 0-691-02393-X). Princeton U Pr.

Tower & the Well: A Psychological Interpretation of the Fairy Tales of Madame D'Aulnoy. Amy DeGraff. 136p. (Eng. & Fr.). 1984. pap. 12.00 (ISBN 0-917786-03-3). Summa Pubns.

Tower Anthology of the San Jose Movement in Fiction, Vol. II. Jon Ilgen et al. Ed. by Merritt Clifton. (Illus.). 1976. pap. 2.50 (ISBN 0-686-20758-0). Samisdat.

Tower at the Edge of Time. Lin Carter. (Inflation Fighter Ser.). 144p. 1982. pap. 1.50 (ISBN 0-8439-1097-6, Leisure Bks). Leisure NY.

Tower by the Sea. Meindert Dejong. (Illus.). 16.50 (ISBN 0-8446-6246-1). Peter Smith.

Tower Commission Report. 1987. pap. 5.50 (ISBN 0-317-57616-X, Co-Published with Times Books). Bantam.

Tower for Louisville: The Human Corporation-Skyscraper Competition. Ed. by Peter Arnell & Ted Bickford. (Illus.). 128p. 1982. pap. 17.50 (ISBN 0-8478-0468-2). Rizzoli Intl.

Tower in Babel: To 1933 see History of Broadcasting in the United States.

Tower of Babel. Illus. by Marilyn Hirsh. LC 80-21196. (Illus.). 32p. (gr. k-3). 1981. reinforced by 6.95 (ISBN 0-8234-0380-7). Holiday.

Tower of Babel. (Illus.). 144p. 4.00 (ISBN 0-318-14480-8). Inst Southern Studies.

Tower of Cirith Ungol & Shelob's Lair. Carl Willner. (Illus.). 32p. (YA) (gr. 10-12). 1984. pap. 7.00 (ISBN 0-915795-21-3). Iron Crown Ent Inc.

Tower of Darkness. Regina Fultz. LC 85-90157. (Endless Quest Ser.). (Illus.). 160p. (gr. 4-6). 1985. pap. 2.25 (ISBN 0-394-74180-3). Random.

Tower of David, 1964. Victor E. Reichert. 1964. 4.00 (ISBN 0-911570-12-8). Vermont Bks.

Tower of Death. Andrew J. Offutt & Keith Taylor. 256p. 1982. pap. 2.50 (ISBN 0-441-81925-7). Ace Bks.

Tower of Five Glories: A Study of the Min Chia of Ta Li. Charles P. Fitzgerald. LC 73-872. (China Studies: from Confucius to Mao Ser.). (Illus.). 280p. 1973. Repr. of 1941 ed. 23.50 (ISBN 0-88355-067-9). Hyperion Conn.

Tower of Flames. Dayle Courtney. LC 82-3270. (Thorne Twins Adventure Bks.). (Illus.). 192p. (Orig.). (gr. 5 up). 1982. pap. 2.98 (ISBN 0-87239-556-1, 2897). Standard Pub.

Tower of Geburah. White John. LC 78-2078. (Illus.). (gr. 3 up). 1978. pap. 9.95 (ISBN 0-87784-560-3). Inter-Varsity.

Tower of Glass. Ivan Angelo. Tr. by Ellen Watson. 1986. pap. 3.95 (ISBN 0-380-89607-9, Bard). Avon.

Tower of Glass. Robert Silverberg. 192p. 1987. 3.95 (ISBN 0-446-34509-1). Warner Bks.

Tower of London. Leonard E. Fisher. LC 87-1629. (Illus.). 32p. (gr. 1-5). 1987. PLB 13.95 (ISBN 0-02-735370-2). Macmillan.

Tower of London. Kenneth J. Mears. 60p. 1988. 40.00 (ISBN 0-7148-2527-1, Pub. by Salem House-Phaidon). Salem Hse Pubs.

Tower of London. Susan Saunders. (Skylark Choose Your Own Adventure Ser.: No. 19). (gr. 2-4). 1984. pap. 2.25 (ISBN 0-553-15490-7, Skylark). Bantam.

Tower of London. Derek Wilson. (Dorset Press Reprints Ser.). 268p. 1988. 17.95 (ISBN 0-88029-252-0). Hippocrene Bks.

Tower of Midnight Dreams. Margaret Weis. LC 84-91271. (Dungeons & Dragons Cartoon Show Books Ser.). (Illus.). 80p. (gr. 2-5). 1985. pap. 2.25 (ISBN 0-394-72956-0). Random.

Tower of Myriad Mirrors. Tung-Yueh. LC 88-70535. 200p. 1988. pap. 12.00 (ISBN 0-89581-501-X). Asian Human Pr.

Tower of Terror. Don Pendleton & Dick Stivers. (Able Team Ser.). 192p. 1982. pap. 1.95 (ISBN 0-373-61201-X, Pub. by Worldwide). Harlequin Bks.

Tower Site & Ohio Monongahela. Jeffrey D. Brown. LC 81-17171. (Research Papers in Archaeology Ser.: No. 3). (Illus.). 96p. 1982. pap. 7.00x (ISBN 0-87338-263-3). Kent St U Pr.

Tower Struck by Lightning. Fernando Arrabal. Tr. by Anthony Kerrigan. 1988. 16.95 (ISBN 0-670-81346-X). Viking.

Tower to the Sky. Phillip Jennings. (Orig.). 1988. pap. 3.50 (ISBN 0-671-65393-8). Baen Bks.

Tower Treasure. Franklin W. Dixon. (Hardy Boys Ser: Vol. 1). (gr. 5-9). 1927. 4.50 (ISBN 0-448-08901-7, G&D). Putnam Pub Group.

Tower Typing: Using Sears, Roebuck & Co. Business Forms. Theodore W. Ivarie. 1978. pap. 17.20 (ISBN 0-07-032066-7). McGraw.

Tower Works: Devotional Writings. St. Thomas More. Ed. by Garry E. Haupt. Tr. by Clarence Miller from Lat. LC 78-16995. (Selected Works of St. Thomas More). (Illus.). 368p. 1980. text ed. 45.00t (ISBN 0-300-02265-4). Yale U Pr.

Towering Babble: God's People Without God's Word. Vernard Eller. LC 83-4621. (Illus.). 192p. (Orig.). 1983. pap. 7.95 (ISBN 0-87178-855-1). Brethren.

Towerman. Jack Rudman. (Career Examination Ser.: C-811). (Cloth bdg. avail. on request). pap. 14.00 (ISBN 0-8373-0811-9). Natl Learning.

Towers. Norman Stahl. LC 86-82376. 1987. 17.95 (ISBN 1-55611-002-2). D I Fine.

Towers. Norman Stahl. 1988. pap. 4.95 (ISBN 1-55817-102-9). Windsor NY.

Towers: A Bibliography. Mary E. Huls. (Architecture Ser.: A 1). 5p. 1986. 3.00 (ISBN 0-89028-775-9). Vance Biblios.

Towers & Bridges. Julie Fitzpatrick. (Science Spirals Ser.). (Illus.). 32p. (gr. 3-5). 1987. PLB 8.96 (ISBN 0-382-09536-7). Silver.

Towers, Crosses. E. C. Curtsinger. 1988. pap. 15.00 (ISBN 0-941179-07-9). Latitudes Pr.

Towers in the Midst. Elizabeth Goudge. 386p. 1979. Repr. lib. bdg. 16.95x (ISBN 0-89966-109-2). Buccaneer Bks.

Towers' International Microprocessor Selector. T. D. Towers. (Illus.). 160p. 1982. vinyl 19.95x (ISBN 0-8306-1716-7, 1516). TAB Bks.

Towers' International Transistor Selector. 3rd ed. T. D. Towers. (Illus.). 280p. 1982. vinyl 19.95x (ISBN 0-8306-1416-8, 1416). TAB Bks.

Towers of Trebizond. Rose Macaulay. 277p. 1956. 20.00 (ISBN 0-374-27854-7); pap. 5.95 (ISBN 0-374-51590-5). FS&G.

Towers of Trebizond. Rose Macaulay. 277p. 1989. pap. 8.95 (ISBN 0-88184-454-3). Carroll & Graf.

Towers to the Sky. James R. Poyner. 128p. 1987. text ed. 12.50 (ISBN 0-682-40335-0). Exposition-Phoenix.

Towers with Three Bells or Less: Basingstoke. D. A. Holmes. 1986. 35.00x (ISBN 0-317-54325-3, Pub. by J Richardson UK); pap. 25.00x. State Mutual Bk.

Towhead. Fred St. Laurent. Ed. by Jean Soule et al. (Illus.). 452p. (Orig.). (gr. 1 up). Date not set. pap. 5.00 perfect bdg (ISBN 0-938447-03-3). Rendezvous Pubns.

Towkays of Sabah: Chinese Leadership & Indigenous Challenge in the Last Phase of British Rule. Edwin Lee. 256p. 1976. 14.00x (ISBN 0-8214-0475-X, Pub. by Singapore U Pr). Ohio U Pr.

Towle Family. G. T. Ridlon. LC 72-142776. (Saco Valley Settlements Ser). 1970. pap. 2.75 (ISBN 0-8048-0846-5). C E Tuttle.

Town. William Faulkner. 1957. 13.95 (ISBN 0-394-42452-2). Random.

Town. William Faulkner. 1961. pap. 4.95 (ISBN 0-394-70184-4, V184, Vin). Random.

Town. Conrad Richter. 1950. 15.45 (ISBN 0-394-44301-2). Knopf.

Town. Conrad Richter. 1981. lib. bdg. 17.95x (ISBN 0-89967-048-2). Harmony Raine.

Town. Watson. (Picture Word Bks.). (gr. k-2). 1980. 6.95 (ISBN 0-86020-391-3, Usborne-Hayes); PLB 11.96 (ISBN 0-88110-070-6); pap. 2.95 (ISBN 0-86020-392-1). EDC.

Town & City Government of New Haven. Charles H. Levermore. LC 78-63766. (Johns Hopkins University. Studies in the Social Sciences. Fourth Ser. 1886: 10). Repr. of 1886 ed. 11.50 (ISBN 0-404-61033-1). AMS Pr.

Town & City Government of New Haven. Charles H. Levermore. 1973. Repr. of 1886 ed. 12.00 (ISBN 0-384-32415-0). Johnson Repr.

Town & Country. Alice Provensen & Martin Provensen. LC 84-12693. (Illus.). 32p. (gr. k-12). 1985. Paper over board with jacket 9.95 (ISBN 0-517-55594-8, 84-12693). Crown.

Town & Country Casuals: An Accounting Clerk Practice Set. A. C. Peele. 1985. 11.55 (ISBN 0-07-049197-6). McGraw.

Town & Country Cat. Lynn Hollyn. LC 82-40389. (Illus.). 144p. 1982. 16.95 (ISBN 0-89480-214-3, 329). Workman Pub.

Town & Country Government in the English Colonies of North America. Edward Channing. LC 78-63749. (Johns Hopkins University. Studies in the Social Sciences. Second Ser. 1884: 10). Repr. of 1884 ed. 11.50 (ISBN 0-404-61018-8). AMS Pr.

Town & Country Homes. Hiawatha T. Estes. (Illus.). 1988. 2.95x. Hiawatha Homes.

Town & Country in Brazil. Marvin Harris. LC 78-82364. (Columbia Univ. Contribution to Anthropology Ser.: Vol. 37). 1969. Repr. of 1956 ed. 32.50 (ISBN 0-404-50587-2). AMS Pr.

Town & Country in Central & Eastern Africa: International African Seminar, 12th, Lusaka, Sept. 1972. Ed. by David Parkin. (Illus.). 1975. 36.00x (ISBN 0-19-724199-9). Oxford U Pr.

Town & Country Matters. John Hollander. LC 72-82864. 60p. 1972. 12.95 (ISBN 0-87923-058-4). Godine.

Town & Country under Fascism: The Transformation of Brescia 1915-1926. Alice A. Kelikian. (Illus.). 300p. 1986. text ed. 42.00x (ISBN 0-19-821970-9). Oxford U Pr.

Town & Countryside in the Transvaal: Capitalist Penetration & Popular Response. Ed. by Belinda Bozzoli. (Illus.). 466p. 1983. pap. text ed. 19.95x (ISBN 0-86975-139-5, Pub. by Ravan Pr). Ohio U Pr.

Town & County: Essays on the Structure of Local Government in the American Colonies. Ed. by Bruce C. Daniels. LC 77-14834. 1978. 22.00x (ISBN 0-8195-5020-5). Wesleyan U Pr.

Town & County Government in the English Colonies of North America. E. Channing. 1973. pap. 9.00 (ISBN 0-384-08463-X). Johnson Repr.

Town & Environs: Recreation in Town Planning. Imre Perenyi. 152p. 1978. 87.50x (ISBN 0-317-53851-9, Pub. by Collets (UK)). State Mutual Bk.

Town & Gown. facs. ed. Lynn Montross & Lois S. Montross. LC 70-132122. (Short Story Index Reprint Ser). 1923. 17.00 (ISBN 0-8369-3679-5). Ayer Co Pubs.

Town & the City. Jack Kerouac. LC 83-8466. 501p. 1970. pap. 8.95 (ISBN 0-15-690790-9, Harv). HarBraceJ.

Town At the End of the Road: A History of Waterville Valley (N.H.) Grace H. Bean. LC 83-16063. (Illus.). 256p. 1983. 15.00 (ISBN 0-914016-99-7). Phoenix Pub.

Town Beyond the Wall. Elie Wiesel. 1978. pap. 1.75 (ISBN 0-380-01590-0, 22301, Bard). Avon.

Town Beyond the Wall. Elie Wiesel. LC 81-16546. 192p. 1982. pap. 7.95 (ISBN 0-8052-0697-3). Schocken.

Town Beyond the Wall. Elie Wiesel. (Elie Wiesel Collection Ser.: Vol. 6). (Illus.). 245p. Repr. deluxe ed. 39.95 (ISBN 0-317-64929-9). Gerecor.

Town Building on the Colorado Frontier. Kathleen Underwood. LC 86-30868. (Illus.). 203p. 1987. 24.95 (ISBN 0-8263-0951-8). U of NM Pr.

Town Burning. Thomas Williams. LC 87-17123. 336p. 1988. pap. 8.95 (ISBN 0-385-24250-6, Anchor Pr). Doubleday.

Town Cats & Other Tales. Lloyd Alexander. 144p. (gr. 5 up). 1981. pap. 2.50 (ISBN 0-440-48989-X, YB). Dell.

Town Cats & Other Tales. Lloyd Alexander. (Illus.). (gr. 4-7). 1977. 11.95 (ISBN 0-525-41430-4). Dutton.

Town, City, & Nation: England. Waller. 1983. 24.95x (ISBN 0-19-219176-4); pap. 9.95x (ISBN 0-19-289163-4). Oxford U Pr.

Town Clerk. Jack Rudman. (Career Examination Ser.: C-1854). (Cloth bdg. avail. on request). pap. 14.00 (ISBN 0-8373-1854-8). Natl Learning.

Town Clock Burning. Charles Fort. 53p. (Orig.). 1985. pap. 7.95 (ISBN 0-932662-54-4). St Andrews NC.

Town Engineer. Jack Rudman. (Career Examination Ser.: C-2001). (Cloth bdg. avail. on request). pap. 14.00. Natl Learning.

Town Government in Rhode Island. W. E. Foster. 1973. pap. 9.00 (ISBN 0-384-16455-2). Johnson Repr.

Town Government in Rhode Island. William E. Foster. LC 78-6359. (John Hopkins University. Studies in the Social Sciences. Fourth Ser. 1886: 2). Repr. of 1886 ed. 11.50 (ISBN 0-404-61027-7). AMS Pr.

Town Government in the Sixteenth Century. James H. Thomas. LC 70-81148. (Illus.). 1969. Repr. of 1933 ed. 27.50x (ISBN 0-678-00508-7). Kelley.

Town Hall Power or Whitehall Pawn? Arthur Seldon. (Institute of Economic Affairs, Readings Ser.: No. 25). pap. 10.95 technical (ISBN 0-255-36135-1). Transatl Arts.

Town House. Norah Lofts. Repr. lib. bdg. 22.95 (ISBN 0-89190-230-9, Pub. by River City Pr). Amereon Ltd.

Town House, No. 3. The Miller Press Staff. LC 88-47521. (Regional Decorating Ser.). 256p. 1988. 34.95 (ISBN 0-553-05309-4). Bantam.

Town Houses of Europe. Horst Buttner & Gunter Meissner. (Illus.). 348p. sewn bdg. 45.00 (ISBN 0-317-54970-7). Apollo.

Town in Terror. E. T. Randall. LC 84-5617. (Alien Adventures Ser.). (Illus.). 128p. (gr. 3-7). 1985. PLB 9.49 (ISBN 0-8167-0332-9); pap. 2.95 (ISBN 0-8167-0333-7). Troll Assocs.

Town in the Empire: Government, Politics, & Society in Seventeenth-Century Popayan. Peter Marzahl. LC 77-620062. (Latin American Monographs: No. 45). 242p. 1978. text ed. 14.95x (ISBN 0-292-78028-1); pap. text ed. 6.95x (ISBN 0-292-78029-X). U of Tex Pr.

Town in the Library. Edith Nesbit. LC 87-8971. (Illus.). 32p. (gr. 1 up). 1988. 10.95 (ISBN 0-8037-0477-1, 01063-320). Dial Bks Young.

Town in the Ruhr: A Social History of Bochum, 1860-1914. David F. Crew. LC 78-31526. 352p. 1979. 33.00x (ISBN 0-231-04300-7). Columbia U Pr.

Town in the Ruhr: A Social History of Bochum, 1860-1914. David F. Crew. LC 78-31526. 289p. 1986. pap. 13.00x (ISBN 0-231-04301-5). Columbia U Pr.

Town in Transition: 1914-1977 see History of Hudson, New Hampshire: 1673-1913.

Town into City: Springfield, Massachusetts & the Meaning of Community, 1840-1880. Michael H. Frisch. LC 72-178075. (Studies in Urban History). (Illus.). 464p. 1972. pap. 7.95x (ISBN 0-674-89826-5). Harvard U Pr.

Town Investigator. Jack Rudman. (Career Examination Ser.: C-3067). 1988. pap. 14.00 (ISBN 0-8373-3067-X). Natl Learning.

Town Is on Fire. Larry Healey. (gr. 6 up). 1979. PLB 12.90 s&l (ISBN 0-531-02898-4). Watts.

Town Labourer, Seventeen Sixty to Eighteen Thirty-Two: The New Civilisation. J. L. Hammond & Barbara Hammond. 1979. Repr. of 1917 ed. lib. bdg. 25.00 (ISBN 0-8495-2258-7). Arden Lib.

Town Labourer, Seventeen Sixty to Eighteen Thirty-Two: The New Civilization. J. L. Hammond & Barbara Hammond. 11.25 (ISBN 0-8446-2197-8). Peter Smith.

Town Labourer, Seventeen Sixty to Eighteen Thirty-Two: The New Civilization. John L. Hammond. LC 66-22627. 1967. Repr. of 1917 ed. 37.50x (ISBN 0-678-00265-7). Kelley.

Town Life in the Fifteenth Century, 2 Vols. Alice S. Green. LC 70-171443. 920p. Repr. of 1894 ed. Set. 40.00 (ISBN 0-405-08575-3, Blom Pubns); 20.00 ea. Vol. 1 (ISBN 0-405-08576-1). Vol. 2 (ISBN 0-405-08577-X). Ayer Co Pubs.

Town Life: Poems. Jay Parini. 96p. 1988. pap. 10.95 (ISBN 0-8050-0577-3). H Holt & Co.

Town Like Alice. Nevil Shute. 1985. pap. 3.50 (ISBN 0-345-35374-9). Ballantine.

Town Maintenance Supervisor. Jack Rudman. (Career Examination Ser.: C-2764). (Cloth bdg. avail. on request). 1988. pap. 14.00 (ISBN 0-8373-2764-4). Natl Learning.

Town, Market, Mint & Port in the Mughal Empire, 1556-1707. M. P. Singh. 1985. 30.00x (ISBN 0-8364-1393-8, Pub. by Adam Pubs). South Asia Bks.

Town Meeting Forestry: Issues for the 1980's. Society of American Foresters. Ed. by H. H. Evans. (SAF Convention Proceedings Ser. -1979). (Illus.). 320p. (Orig.). 1980. pap. 17.00 (ISBN 0-939970-06-6). Soc Am Foresters.

Town Meeting Time: A Handbook of Parliamentary Law. 2nd ed. Massachusetts Moderators Association. LC 84-4354. 208p. 1984. lib. bdg. 14.50 (ISBN 0-89874-754-6). Krieger.

Town Mouse & the Country Mouse. new ed. Aesop. LC 78-18062. (Illus.). 32p. (gr. k-3). 1979. PLB 9.79 (ISBN 0-89375-131-6); pap. 1.95 (ISBN 0-89375-109-X). Troll Assocs.

Town Mouse & the Country Mouse. Lorinda B. Cauley. LC 84-11532. (Illus.). 32p. (ps-3). 1984. 11.95 (ISBN 0-399-21123-3, Putnam); pap. 5.95 (ISBN 0-399-21126-8). Putnam Pub Group.

Town Mouse, & the Country Mouse. Vicky Ireland. 38p. (Orig.). (gr. k-3). 1987. pap. 3.00 playscript (ISBN 0-87602-266-2). Anchorage.

Town Mouse & the Country Mouse. Adapted by & illus. by Janet Stevens. LC 86-14276. (Illus.). 32p. (ps-3). 1987. reinforced bdg. 13.95 (ISBN 0-8234-0633-4). Holiday.

Town of Ballymuck. Victor Power. LC 84-52121. (Illus.). 176p. (Orig.). 1984. pap. 9.50 (ISBN 0-930501-00-4). Swallows Tale Pr.

Town of Ballymuck. Victor Power. LC 84-52121. (Illus.). 162p. 1985. lib. bdg. 15.95 (ISBN 0-930501-04-7). Swallows Tale Pr.

Town of Blood. W. L. Fieldhouse. (Klaw Ser.: No. 2). (Orig.). 1981. pap. 1.75 (ISBN 0-505-51671-3, Pub. by Tower Bks). Leisure NY.

Town of Islip: A History of Its Communities & Schools. Patrick J. Curran. (Orig.). Date not set. pap. text ed. price not set (ISBN 0-9615532-0-0). Town Islip.

Town of Milan. J. A. Ryan. (Illus.). 96p. 1974. pap. 3.50 (ISBN 0-318-00869-6). Ohio Hist Soc.

Town of Tombarel. facsimile ed. William J. Locke. LC 71-150548. (Short Story Index Reprint Ser.). Repr. of 1930 ed. 18.00 (ISBN 0-8369-3845-3). Ayer Co Pubs.

Town of York, Eighteen Fifteen to Eighteen Thirty-Four: A Further Collection of Documents of Early Toronto. Ed. by Edith G. Firth. (Champlain Society, Toronto, Publications, Ontario Ser.: No. 8). pap. 119.80 (2023615). Bks Demand UMI.

Town of York, Seventeen Ninety-Three to Eighteen Fifteen: A Collection of Documents of Early Toronto. Ed. by Edith G. Firth. LC 62-4422. (Champlain Society, Toronto, Publications, Ontario Ser.: No. 5). pap. 115.50 (ISBN 0-317-26912-7, 2023614). Bks Demand UMI.

Town on Sandy Bay: A History of Rockport Massachusetts. Marshall W. Swan. LC 80-15578. (Illus.). 456p. 1980. 15.00x (ISBN 0-914016-72-5). Phoenix Pub.

Town Organizations in Prewar Tokyo. 51p. 1980. pap. 5.00 (ISBN 92-808-0086-8, TUNU060, UNU). UNIPUB.

Town, Palace & House Cult in Minoan Crete. G Gesell. (Studies in Mediterranean Archaeology: Vol. LXVII). (Illus.). 350p. 1985. pap. 80.00x (ISBN 91-86098-18-7, Pub. by P Astrom Pubs Sweden). Humanities.

Town, Palace, & House Cult in Minoan Crete. G. C. Gesell. (Illus.). 214p. (Orig.). 1985. pap. text ed. 137.50x (ISBN 91-86098-18-7, Pub. by Almqvist & Wiksell). Coronet Bks.

Town Park. Hermann Grab. Tr. by Quintin Hoare. 256p. 1988. 18.95 (ISBN 0-86091-189-6). Routledge Chapman & Hall.

Town Planning in Early South India. C. P. Ayyar. 197p. 1987. 17.50x (ISBN 0-8364-2083-7, Pub. by Mittal). South Asia Bks.

Town Planning in Frontier America. John W. Reps. LC 68-20877. (Illus.). 1969. 52.50x (ISBN 0-691-04589-5). Princeton U Pr.

Town Planning in Frontier America. John W. Reps. LC 68-20877. 336p. 1981. pap. 10.95 (ISBN 0-8262-0316-7). U of Mo Pr.

Town Planning in London: The Eighteenth & Nineteenth Centuries. Donald J. Olsen. LC 82-50440. (Illus.). 320p. 1982. text ed. 50.00t (ISBN 0-300-02914-4); pap. 16.95x (ISBN 0-300-02915-2, Y-443). Yale U Pr.

Town Planning in Practice. 2nd ed. Raymond Unwin. LC 68-56507. (Illus.). 1969. Repr. of 1934 ed. 33.00 (ISBN 0-405-09036-6). Ayer Co Pubs.

Town: Preliminary Materials, Vol. 1. William Faulkner. Ed. by Michael Millgate. (William Faulkner Manuscripts). 1986. lib. bdg. 100.00 (ISBN 0-8240-6831-9). Garland Pub.

Town Proprietors in Vermont. Florence M. Woodard. LC 68-58646. (Columbia University. Studies in the Social Sciences: No. 418). Repr. of 1936 ed. 16.50 (ISBN 0-404-51418-9). AMS Pr.

Town Proprietors of the New England Colonies. R. H. Akagi. 1963. 12.75 (ISBN 0-8446-1012-7). Peter Smith.

Town Scold. Judith Sherwin. 1977. limited ed 15.00 (ISBN 0-914378-29-5): pap. 4.95 (ISBN 0-914378-26-0). Countryman.

Town Smokes. Pinckney Benedict. LC 87-5684. 168p. (Orig.). 1987. pap. 9.95 (ISBN 0-86538-058-9). Ontario Rev NJ.

Town Tamer. Ray Hogan. 1981. pap. 1.95 (ISBN 0-451-11083-8, AJ1083, Sig). NAL.

Town Tamer see Quantrell's Raiders.

Town That Died Laughing: The Story of Austin, Nevada, Rambunctious Early-Day Mining Camp, & of its Renowned Newspaper, the Reese River Reveille. Oscar Lewis. (Vintage West Ser.). 243p. 1986. pap. 8.95 (ISBN 0-87417-109-1). U of Nev Pr.

Town That Moved. Mary J. Finsand. LC 82-9703. (Carolrhoda on my Own Bks). (Illus.). 48p. (gr. 1-4). 1983. PLB 8.95 (ISBN 0-87614-200-5). Carolrhoda Bks.

Town That Was: Ravenswood. Don Roderick. 58p. 1985. 18.50 (ISBN 0-908175-10-8, Pub. by Boolarong Pubn Australia). Intl Spec Bk.

Town That Wouldn't Die. Robert E. Haltiner. (Illus.). 144p. 1986. 16.95 (ISBN 0-9617779-0-7). J Besser Mus.

Town They Called the World - Charters Towers. Don Roderick. 64p. 1985. 19.50 (ISBN 0-317-44257-0, Pub. by Boolarong Pubns Australia). Intl Spec Bk.

Town to Tame. Joseph Chadwick. 1979. pap. 1.50 (ISBN 0-449-14234-5, GM). Fawcett.

Town Traveller. George Gissing. LC 68-54268. Repr. of 1898 ed. 18.00 (ISBN 0-404-02813-6). AMS Pr.

Town Traveller. George Gissing. 247p. 1980. Repr. of 1927 ed. lib. bdg. 25.00. Century Bookbindery.

Town Traveller. George Gissing. 1979. Repr. of 1898 ed. lib. bdg. 30.00 (ISBN 0-8492-4931-7). R West.

Town: Typescript, Vol. 2. William Faulkner. Ed. by Michael Millgate. (William Faulkner Manuscripts). 1986. lib. bdg. 100.00 (ISBN 0-8240-6830-0). Garland Pub.

Town Walks in Britain. British Automobile Association Staff. 136p. (Orig.). 1984. 19.95 (ISBN 0-86145-195-3, Pub. by Automobile Assn Brit). Salem Hse Pubs.

Town Within a City: A History of Five Points South Neighborhood. Ann M. Burkhardt. Ed. by Alice M. Bowsher. (Illus.). 92p. pap. 9.95 (ISBN 0-943994-13-6). Birmingham Hist Soc.

Town You Live In. Richard H. Turner. (Follet Success Skills Ser.). 48p. pap. 3.75 (ISBN 0-8428-2266-6). Cambridge Bk.

Towneley Cycle. Fasc. ed. A. C. Cawley & Martin Stevens. LC 75-42854. 332p. 1976. pap. 19.95 (ISBN 0-87328-113-6). Huntington Lib.

Townhouses & Condominiums: Residents' Likes & Dislikes. Carl Norcross. LC 73-82886. (Special Report Ser.). (Illus.). 105p. 1973. pap. 16.00 (ISBN 0-87420-558-1, T02). Urban Land.

Towns & Buildings. Steen E. Rasmussen. 1969. pap. 12.95s (ISBN 0-262-68011-4). MIT Pr.

Towns & Cities. Emrys Jones. LC 80-24687. (Illus.). viii, 152p. 1981. Repr. of 1966 ed. lib. bdg. 35.00x (ISBN 0-313-22724-1, JOTC). Greenwood.

Towns & Cities. Emrys Jones. (Illus., Orig.). (YA) (gr. 12). 1966. pap. 4.95x (ISBN 0-19-500337-3). Oxford U Pr.

Towns & Towns of Ottoman Anatolia: Trade, Crafts & Food Production in an Urban Setting 1520-1650. Suraiya Faroqhi. LC 83-7198. (Cambridge Studies in Islamic Civilization). (Illus.). 424p. 1984. 62.50 (ISBN 0-521-25447-7). Cambridge U Pr.

Towns in Societies. Ed. by P. Abrams & E. A. Wrigley. LC 77-82481. (Past & Present Publications). 1978. 39.50 (ISBN 0-521-21826-8); pap. 15.95 (ISBN 0-521-29594-7). Cambridge U Pr.

Towns of Destiny. Hilaire Belloc. LC 72-101273. (BCL Ser. I). (Illus.). Repr. of 1927 ed. 20.00 (ISBN 0-404-00745-7). AMS Pr.

Towns of Roman Britain. John Wacher. LC 73-91663. (Illus.). 1974. 60.00x (ISBN 0-520-02669-1). U of Cal Pr.

Townsend Family. G. T. Ridlon. LC 75-142774. (Saco Valley Settlements Ser). 1970. pap. 3.00 (ISBN 0-8048-0844-9). C E Tuttle.

Townsend Harris: First American Envoy in Japan. facsimile ed. William E. Griffis. LC 74-175698. (Select Bibliographies Reprint Ser). Repr. of 1895 ed. 21.00 (ISBN 0-8369-6613-9). Ayer Co Pubs.

Townsend Hoopes on Arms Control. Ed. by Kenneth W. Thompson. LC 87-21582. (W. Alton Jones Foundation Series on Arm Control). 138p. (Orig.). 1988. lib. bdg. 21.50 (ISBN 0-8191-6621-9, Co-pub. White Miller Center); pap. text ed. 8.75 (ISBN 0-8191-6622-7). U Pr of Amer.

Townsend Movement. Abraham Holtzman. 1973. lib. bdg. 19.00x (ISBN 0-374-93934-9, Octagon). Hippocrene Bks.

Townshend Duties Crisis: The Second Phase of the American Revolution 1767-1773. Peter D. Thomas. 290p. 1987. 52.00 (ISBN 0-19-822967-4). Oxford U Pr.

Township Thirty-Four, 7 vols. Harold K. Hochschild. (Illus.). Set. pap. 31.95 boxed (ISBN 0-8156-8026-0, Pub. by Adirondack Museum). Syracuse U Pr.

Township Thirty-Four Series, 7 vols. rev. ed. Harold K. Hochschild. (Illus.). 1952. Set. slipcased 31.95 (ISBN 0-686-74821-2). Adirondack Mus.

Townsmen. Keith Wheeler. LC 74-2180. (Old West Ser.). (Illus.). 240p. (gr. 7 up). 1975. 19.94 (ISBN 0-8094-1490-2, Pub. by Time-Life). Silver.

Townsmen. Keith Wheeler. (Old West Ser). (Illus.). 240p. 1975. 14.95 (ISBN 0-8094-1488-0). Time-Life.

Towpath. Arch Merrill. (Arch Merrill's New York Ser.: No. 4). (Illus.). 208p. 1988. pap. 7.95 (ISBN 1-55787-001-2, Empire State Bks). Heart of the Lakes.

Towpath Book. Christopher Howkins. 96p. 1987. 30.00x (ISBN 0-9509105-0-3, Countryside Bks). State Mutual Bk.

Towpath Guide to the C & O Canal: Georgetown to Cumberland. combined ed. T. F. Hahn. 226p. 1982. 12.00 (ISBN 0-933788-62-2). Am Canal & Transport.

Towpaths of England. Brian Bearshaw. 208p. 1985. 24.95x (ISBN 0-7090-2160-7, Pub. by R Hale Ltd UK). State Mutual Bk.

Towpaths to Tugboats, 1982: A History of American Canal Engineering. W. H. Shank & Mayo. 1982. 6.00 (ISBN 0-933788-40-1). Am Canal & Transport.

Towser & Sadie's Birthday. Tony Ross. LC 83-15126. (Illus.). 32p. (ps-1). 1984. (Pant Bks Young). Pantheon.

Towser & the Funny Face. Tony Ross. (Illus.). 32p. (ps-1). 1987. 5.95 (ISBN 0-86264-077-6, Pub. by Century Hutchinson). David & Charles.

Towser & the Haunted House. Tony Ross. (Illus.). 32p. (ps-1). 1987. 5.95 (ISBN 0-86264-079-2, Pub. by Century Hutchinson). David & Charles.

Towser & the Magic Apple. Tony Ross. (Illus.). 32p. (ps-1). 1987. 5.95 (ISBN 0-86264-078-4, Pub. by Century Hutchinson). David & Charles.

Towser & the Terrible Thing. Tony Ross. (Illus.). 32p. (ps-1). 1984. (Pant Bks Young). Pantheon.

Towser & the Water Rats. Tony Ross. LC 83-17392. (Illus.). 32p. (ps-1). 1984. 4.95 (ISBN 0-394-86540-5, Pant Bks Young). Pantheon.

Towson under God. Kingsley Smith. (Illus.). 1976. 2.98 (ISBN 0-317-02512-0). Friends Towson Lib.

Toxemia: The Basic Cause of Disease. John A. Tilden. 116p. pap. 3.95 (ISBN 0-317-61610-2). Natural Hygiene.

Toxemia: The Basic Cause of Disease. John H. Tilden. LC 74-82367. (Illus.). 124p. 1974. pap. 3.95 (ISBN 0-914532-07-3). Natural Hygiene.

Toxic Air Pollution. Paul J. Loiy & Joan M. Daisey. LC 86-20136. (Illus.). 300p. 1987. 49.95 (ISBN 0-87371-057-6). Lewis Pubs Inc.

Toxic & Biomedical Effects of Fibers: Asbestos, Talc, Inorganic Fibers, Man-Made Vitreous Fibers & Organic Fibers. Paul Gross & Daniel C. Braun. LC 83-23612. (Illus.). 257p. 1984. 36.00 (ISBN 0-8155-0971-5). Noyes.

Toxic & Hazardous Industrial Chemicals Safety Manual. International Technical Information Institute. 450p. 1986. 88.00 (ISBN 0-318-04390-4). Media Intl Promo.

Toxic & Hazardous Materials: A Sourcebook & Guide to Information Sources. Ed. by James K. Webster. LC 86-25710. 444p. 1987. lib. bdg. 49.95 (ISBN 0-313-24575-4, WTH/). Greenwood.

Toxic & Hazardous Wastes: Proceedings of the Eighteenth Mid-Atlantic Industrial Waste Conference. Ed. by Gregory D. Boardman. LC 86-50607. 656p. 1986. pap. 55.00 (ISBN 0-87762-479-8). Technomic.

Toxic & Hazardous Wastes: Proceedings of the Seventeenth Mid-Atlantic Industrial Waste Conference. Ed. by Irwin J. Kugelman. LC 85-51235. 602p. 1985. pap. 49.00 (ISBN 0-87762-434-8). Technomic.

Toxic & Hazardous Wastes: Proceedings of the Sixteenth Mid-Atlantic Industrial Waste Conference. Ed. by Michael D. LaGrega & David A. Long. LC 84-51326. 587p. 1984. pap. 45.00 (ISBN 0-87762-363-5). Technomic.

Toxic & Hazardous Wastes: Proceedings of the 19th Mid-Atlantic Industrial Waste Conference. Ed. by Jeffrey C. Evans. 729p. 1987. pap. 65.00 (ISBN 0-317-65574-4). Technomic.

Toxic Chemical & Explosives Facilities: Safety & Engineering Design. LC 79-9760. (Symposium Ser.: No. 96). 1979. 39.95 (ISBN 0-8412-0481-0). Am Chemical.

Toxic Chemical Emissions: A Compliance Guide for the Community Right-to-Know Act. W. Randy Kubetin. 1988. 85.00 (ISBN 0-87179-995-2). BNA.

Toxic Chemicals, Health & the Environment. Ed. by Lester B. Lave & Arthur C. Upton. LC 86-46276. (Johns Hopkins Series in Environmental Toxicology). 336p. 1987. text ed. 39.50x (ISBN 0-8018-3473-2); pap. text ed. 16.50x (ISBN 0-8018-3474-0). Johns Hopkins.

Toxic Chemicals: The Interface Between Law & Science. Earon S. Davis & Valerie A. Wilk. 153p. (Orig.). 1982. pap. 18.50x (ISBN 0-86733-073-2, 4073). Assoc Faculty Pr.

Toxic Cloud: A Cross-Country Report on the Poisoning of America's Air. Michael H. Brown. LC 87-45027. 320p. 1987. 18.95i (ISBN 0-06-015801-8, HarpT). Har-Row.

Toxic Cloud: The Poisoning of America's Air. Michael H. Brown. LC 87-45027. 320p. 1988. pap. 9.95 (PL 1509, PL). Har-Row.

Toxic Constituents in Plant Foodstuffs. I. Liener. (Food Science & Technology Ser.). 1969. 101.00 (ISBN 0-12-449950-3). Acad Pr.

Toxic Constituents of Animal Foodstuffs. Ed. by Irvin E. Liener. (Food Science & Technology Ser.). 1974. 59.00 (ISBN 0-12-449940-6). Acad Pr.

Toxic Constituents of Plant Foodstuffs. 2nd ed. Irvin E. Liener. LC 79-51681. (Food Science & Technology Ser.). 1980. 52.00 (ISBN 0-12-449960-0). Acad Pr.

Toxic Contaminants & Ecosystem Health: A Great Lakes Focus. Ed. by Marlene S. Evans. LC 87-22996. (Advances in Environmental Science & Technology Ser.). 602p. 1988. 99.95 (ISBN 0-471-85556-1). Wiley.

Toxic Contaminants in the Great Lakes. Ed. by Jerome O. Nriagu & Milagros S. Simmons. LC 83-16689. (Advances in Environmental Science & Technology Ser.: 2-010). 527p. 1984. 115.00 (ISBN 0-471-89087-1, Pub. by Wiley-Interscience). Wiley.

Toxic Contamination in Large Lakes, 4 vols. Norbert W. Schmidtke. (Illus.). 1800p. 1988. Set. 199.80 (ISBN 0-87371-088-6). Lewis Pubs Inc.

Toxic Dinoflagellate Blooms: Proceedings of the 2nd International Conference at Florida, November, 1978. Ed. by Y. Taylor & H. Seliger. LC 78-20732. (Developments in Marine Biology Ser.: Vol. 1). 206p. 1979. 107.25 (ISBN 0-444-00318-5, Biomedical Pr). Elsevier.

Toxic Dinoflagellates: Proceedings of the Third International Conference on Toxic Dinoflagellates Held in St. Andrews, New Brunswick, Canada June 8-12, 1985. D. Anderson & A. W. White. 500p. 1985. 106.00 (ISBN 0-444-01030-0). Elsevier.

Toxic Emergencies. Ed. by C. William Hanson, Jr. (Clinics in Emergency Medicine Ser.: Vol. 5). (Illus.). 336p. 1984. text ed. 37.50 (ISBN 0-443-08196-4). Churchill.

Toxic Hazard Assessment of Chemicals. Ed. & intro. by M. L. Richardson. (Illus.). 370p. 1986. text ed. 85.00x (ISBN 0-85186-897-5, Pub. by Royal Soc Chem). Scholium Intl.

Toxic Hazards of Rubber Chemicals. A. R. Nutt. 200p. 1984. 57.25 (ISBN 0-85334-242-3, Pub. by Elsevier Applied Sci England). Elsevier.

Toxic Injury of the Liver, Pt. A. Farber & Fisher. (Liver: Normal Function & Disease Ser.: Vol. 2). 1979. 89.75 (ISBN 0-8247-6838-8). Dekker.

Toxic Injury of the Liver, Pt. B. Farber & Fisher. (Liver: Normal Function & Disease: Vol. 2). 1979. 79.75 (ISBN 0-8247-6839-6). Dekker.

Toxic Interfaces of Nuerons, Smoke & Genes. Ed. by P. L. Chambers et al. (Archives of Toxicology Ser.: Supplement 9). (Illus.). 500p. 1986. pap. 108.90 (ISBN 0-387-16589-4). Springer-Verlag.

Toxic Law Reporter: BNA's Environment & Safety Service Staff. looseleaf 888.00. BNA.

Toxic Materials. Ed. by Law & Business Inc. Staff & Legal Times Seminars Staff. (Seminar Course Handbooks). 1983. pap. 30.00 (C01481, Law & Business). HarBraceJ.

Toxic Metals & Their Analysis. Eleanor Berman. LC 79-41781. (Heyden International Topics in Science Ser.). (Illus.). pap. 78.80 (ISBN 0-317-58705-6, 2029641). Bks Demand UMI.

Toxic Metals in the Atmosphere. Ed. by Jerome O. Nriagu & Cliff I. Davidson. LC 85-17783. (Environmental Science & Technology Ser.). 635p. 1986. 115.00 (ISBN 0-471-82654-5, Pub. by Wiley-Interscience). Wiley.

Toxic Nephropathies: Proceedings. Congress on Toxic Nephropathies, 6th, Parma, June 1977. Ed. by G. M. Berlyne et al. (Contributions to Nephrology Ser.: Vol. 10). (Illus.). 1978. 32.75 (ISBN 3-8055-2832-9). S Karger.

Toxic Plants. Ed. by A. Douglas Kinghorn. LC 79-16180. 1979. 32.00x (ISBN 0-231-04686-3). Columbia U Pr.

Toxic Shock Syndrome. National Research Council Staff. 1982. pap. text ed. 10.50x (ISBN 0-309-03286-5). Natl Acad Pr.

Toxic Substance Storage Tank Containment. Ecology & Environment, Inc. LC 84-22697. (Pollution Technology Review Ser.: No. 116). (Illus.). 274p. 1985. 36.00 (ISBN 0-8155-1018-7). Noyes.

Toxic Substances & Hazardous Wastes: Tenth Annual Airlie House Conference on the Environment. 25p. 1982. pap. 8.00 (ISBN 0-317-30672-3). Amer Bar Assn.

Toxic Substances & Health Biology, No. 1: Index of Modern Information. Edgar C. Tomlinson. LC 88-47850. 150p. 1988. 34.50 (ISBN 0-88164-956-2); pap. 26.50 (ISBN 0-88164-957-0). ABBE Pubs Assn.

Toxic Substances & Human Risk: Principles of Data Interpretation. Ed. by R. G. Tardiff & J. V. Rodricks. LC 87-18660. (Life Science Monographs). (Illus.). 460p. 1987. 65.00x (ISBN 0-306-42529-7, Plenum Pr). Plenum Pub.

Toxic Substances & Mental Retardation: Neurobehavioral Toxicology & Teratology. Ed. by S. Schroeder. LC 87-1776. (Monographs of the American Association on Mental Retardation: No. 8). 188p. 1987. pap. 20.00 (ISBN 0-940898-15-2). Am Assn Mental.

Toxic Substances Control Act - Law & Explanation. 160p. pap. 4.00 (ISBN 0-317-04297-1). Commerce.

Toxic Substances Control Act Compliance Guide & Service. John R. Wheeler. LC 88-80678. 900p. 1988. 125.00 (ISBN 0-945940-88-2). Environment Bks.

Toxic Substances Control Act Inspection Manual, Pt. 1, Vols. I & II. Environmental Protection Agency Staff. 341p. 1982. pap. 59.00 (ISBN 0-86587-056-X). Gov Insts.

Toxic Substances Control Act (TSCA) Chemical Substance Inventory, 5 vols. 3968p. 1986. 161.00 (ISBN 0-318-20382-0, S/N 055-000-00254-1). USGPO.

Toxic Substances Control Guide: Manufacturing, Processing & Distribution. Ed. by J. J. Keller & Associates, Inc. LC 79-54215. (21G). 600p. 1987. 95.00 (ISBN 0-934674-11-6). J J Keller.

Toxic Substances Controls Primer. 2nd ed. Mary D. Worobec. LC 86-8258. 232p. 1986. pap. text ed. 25.00 (ISBN 0-87179-517-5, 0517). BNA.

Toxic Substances: Decisions & Values. Incl. Vol. 1. Decision Making. 4.00 (ISBN 0-686-27531-4); Vol. 2. Information Flow. 5.00 (ISBN 0-686-27532-2); Vol. 3. Compensation. 6.00 (ISBN 0-686-27533-0); Vol. 4. Worldwide Problems. 8.00 (ISBN 0-686-27534-9). (Toxnet Ser.). 1979. Set. 15.00 (ISBN 0-686-77521-X). Tech Info Proj.

Toxic Substances in Agricultural Water Supply & Drainage - Searching for Solutions: Proceedings of the USCID National Meeting, 1987. 1988. 36.00 (ISBN 0-9618257-2-3). US Comm Irrigation.

Toxic Substances in Agricultural Water Supply & Drainage: Defining the Problems, Proceedings of the USCID Regional Meetings, 1986. 372p. 1986. 40.00 (ISBN 0-9618257-0-7). US Comm Irrigation.

Toxic Substances in the Aquatic Environment: An International Aspect. Ed. by P. M. Mehrle, Jr. et al. LC 85-50828. 98p. 1985. pap. 10.00 (ISBN 0-913235-35-0). Am Fisheries Soc.

Toxic Substances in the Environment. 2nd ed. Ronald J. Kendall. 112p. 1983. pap. text ed. 7.95 (ISBN 0-8403-2985-7). Kendall-Hunt.

Toxic Susceptibility: Male-Female Differences. Edward J. Calabrese. LC 85-3220. (Environmental Science & Technology Ser.). 336p. 1985. 65.00 (ISBN 0-471-80903-9). Wiley.

Toxic Terror. Elizabeth Whelan. LC 85-9807. 300p. 1985. 18.95 (ISBN 0-915463-09-1, Pub. by Jameson Bks, Dist. by Kampmann). Green Hill.

Toxic Threat: How Hazardous Substances Poison Our Lives. Stephen J. Zipko. LC 85-21563. (Illus.). 192p. (YA) (gr. 7 up). 1986. PLB 10.79 (ISBN 0-671-50963-2). Messner.

Toxic Tort Litigation. (Litigation & Administrative Practice Course Handbook: Vol. 244). 329p. 1984. 15.00 (ISBN 0-317-11463-8, H4-4925). PLI.

Toxic Tort Litigation Reference Materials. Association of Trial Lawyers of America Education Fund Staff. 104p. 1985. pap. 65.00 loose leaf (ISBN 0-941916-23-5). Assn Trial Ed.

Toxic Torts Advocacy. David Gross. LC 83-187216. (Illus.). v, 175p. Date not set. price not set (Law & Business). HarBraceJ.

Toxic Torts Advocacy (1983) 35.00 (ISBN 0-317-29549-7, #CO1864, Law & Business). HarBraceJ.

Toxic Torts Advocacy (1984) 35.00 (ISBN 0-317-29552-7, #CO2798, Law & Business). HarBraceJ.

Toxic Torts: Litigation of Hazardous Substance Cases. Gary Z. Nothstein. LC 83-27128. (Trial Practice Ser.). 906p. 1984. text ed. 90.00 (ISBN 0-07-047454-0). Shepards-McGraw.

Toxic Torts: Proposals for Compensating Victims of Hazardous Substances: 1984, 98th Congress, 2nd Session. American Enterprise Institute for Public Policy Research Staff. LC 84-243006. 32p. 1984. 6.00 (ISBN 0-8447-0260-9). Am Enterprise.

Toxic Waste: A Bibliography. Ed. by Joan Nordquist. (Contemporary Social Issues: A Bibliographic Ser.: No. 11). 60p. (Orig.). 1988. pap. 15.00 (ISBN 0-937855-21-9). Ref Rsch Serv.

Toxic Waste & Recycling. Nigel Hawkes. Ed. by Franklin Watts Ltd. (Issues Ser.). (Illus.). 32p. (YA) (gr. 7-9). 1988. 10.70 (ISBN 0-531-17080-2, Gloucester Pr). Watts.

Toxic Waste: Cleanup or Coverup? Malcolm E. Weiss. (Impact Ser.). (Illus.). (gr. 7 up). 1984. lib. bdg. 12.90 (ISBN 0-531-04755-5). Watts.

Toxic Waste: New Strategies for Controlling Toxic Contamination. Ed. by Bruce Piasecki. LC 83-24510. (Quorum Ser.). (Illus.). xix, 239p. 1984. lib. bdg. 45.00 (ISBN 0-89930-056-1, PIT/, Quorum). Greenwood.

Toxic Wastes: The Fouling of America. Knowledge Unlimited Staff. (Illus.). 24p. (gr. 4-12). 1984. tchrs' guide incl. color filmstrip 13.00. Know Unltd.

Toxicants & Drugs: Kinetics & Dynamics. Ellen O'Flaherty. LC 80-2445. 398p. 1981. 60.95 (ISBN 0-471-06047-X, Pub. by Wiley-Interscience). Wiley.

Toxicity Assessment: An International Journal. 1987. write for info. Wiley.

Toxicity of Chemicals & Pulping Wastes to Fish. Louise Louden. LC 79-64742. (Bibliographic Ser.: No. 265, Suppl. I). 1979. pap. 60.00 (ISBN 0-87010-058-0). Inst Paper Chem.

Toxicity of Chemotherapy. Ed. by Michael C. Perry & John W. Yarbro. (Clinical Oncology Monograph Ser.). 576p. 1984. 56.50 (ISBN 0-8089-1631-9, 793273). Grune.

Toxicity of Heavy Metals, Pt. 1. Oehme. (Hazardous & Toxic Substances Ser.: Vol. 2). 1978. 85.00 (ISBN 0-8247-6718-7). Dekker.

Toxicity of Heavy Metals in the Environment, Pt. 2. Oehme. (Hazardous & Toxic Substances Ser.: Vol. 2). 1979. 85.00 (ISBN 0-8247-6719-5). Dekker.

Toxicity of Hormones in Perinatal Life. Ed. by Takao Mori & Hiroshi Nagasawa. 208p. 1988. 115.00 (ISBN 0-8493-6862-6, 6862). CRC Pr.

Toxicity of Methyl Mercury. Ed. by Christine U. Eccles & Zoltan Annau. LC 86-46278. (Johns Hopkins Series in Environmental Toxicology). 256p. 1987. text ed. 39.50x (ISBN 0-8018-3449-X). Johns Hopkins.

Toxicity of Nickel & Its Inorganic Compounds. 204p. (Orig.). 1987. pap. text ed. 32.00 (ISBN 0-11-883961-6, HM1470, Pub. by Her Maj Station Ofc). UNIPUB.

Toxicity of Nitroaromatic Compounds. Ed. by Douglas E. Rickert. LC 84-8937. (Chemical Industry Institute of Toxicology Ser.). (Illus.). 295p. 1985. 62.95 (ISBN 0-89116-304-2). Hemisphere Pub.

Toxicity of Pesticides to Fish, Vol. II. Ed. by A. S. Murty. 192p. 1986. 85.00 (ISBN 0-8493-6059-5). CRC Pr.

Toxicity of Plutonium, Americium & Curium. J. C. Nenot & J. W. Stather. (Commission of the European Communities Ser.: EUR 6157). (Illus.). 1979. pap. 65.00 (ISBN 0-08-023440-2). Pergamon.

Toxicity of Pulping Wastes to Fish. (Bibliographic Ser.: No. 265). 67p. 1975. 10.00 (ISBN 0-317-34463-3). Inst Paper Chem.

Toxicity Screening Procedures Using Bacterial Systems. Liu & Dutka. (Toxicity Ser.). 448p. 1984. 85.00 (ISBN 0-8247-7171-0). Dekker.

Toxicity Testing: New Approaches & Applications in Human Risk Assessment. Ed. by A. P. Li et al. 300p. 1985. text ed. 59.50 (ISBN 0-88167-083-9). Raven.

Toxicity Testing of Dental Materials. Ed. by Harold R. Stanley. 176p. 1985. 79.00 (ISBN 0-8493-5916-3). CRC Pr.

Toxicity Testing: Strategies to Determine Needs & Priorities. National Research Council. 382p. 1984. pap. 22.50x (ISBN 0-309-03433-7). Natl Acad Pr.

Toxicity Testing Using Microorganisms, Vol. II. Bernard J. Dutka & Gabriel Bitton. 240p. 1986. 85.00 (ISBN 0-8493-5257-6). CRC Pr.

Toxicless Diet & Body Purification: The Stay-Ageless Program. 23rd,rev. ed. Paul C. Bragg & Patricia Bragg. LC 84-822373. (Illus.). pap. 3.95 (ISBN 0-87790-033-7). Health Sci.

Toxicologic & Pharmacologic Principles in Pediatrics. Sam Kacew & Simon Lock. 220p. 1987. 59.95 (ISBN 0-89116-631-9). Hemisphere Pub.

Toxicologic Emergencies. Marc J. Bayer. LC 83-15758. (Illus.). 352p. 1983. pap. text ed. 27.65 (ISBN 0-89303-188-7). P-H.

Toxicological Analysis. Muller. 768p. 1989. price not set (ISBN 0-471-91846-6). Wiley.

Toxicological & Pathological Studies on Psychoactive Drug-Involved Deaths. L. A. Gottschalk & R. H. Cravey. LC 79-56928. 470p. 1980. text ed. 31.00 (ISBN 0-931890-05-5, Biomed Pubns). PSG Pub Co.

Toxicological Aspects of Energy Production. Charles L. Sanders. 256p. 1985. 34.95x (ISBN 0-02-948960-1). Macmillan.

Toxicological Aspects of Food. Ed. by K. Miller. 458p. 1987. 117.00 (ISBN 1-85166-080-1, Pub. by Elsevier Applied Sci England). Elsevier.

Toxicological Chemistry: A Guide to Toxic Substances in Chemistry. Stanley E. Manahan. (Illus.). 375p. 1988. write for info. Lewis Pubs Inc.

Toxicological Evaluation of Certain Food Additives & Contaminants. FAO-WHO Expert Committee on Food Additives. (Vol. 20). (Illus.). 298p. 1988. pap. 24.95 (ISBN 0-521-34347-X); pap. 29.95, Vol. 22 (ISBN 0-521-36928-2). Cambridge U Pr.

Toxicological Evaluation of Certain Food Additives with a Review of General Principles & of Specifications: Report of the FAO-WHO Expert Committee on Food Additives, 17th, Rome, 1973. FAO-WHO Expert Committee on Food Additives. (Technical Report Ser.: No. 539). (Also avail. in French & Spanish). 1974. pap. 2.00 (ISBN 92-4-120539-3). World Health.

Toxicological Evaluation of Certain Food Additives with a Review of General Principles & of Specifications. (Nutrition Meetings Reports: No. 53). 40p. (Orig.). 1974. pap. 5.75 (ISBN 92-5-101837-5, F466, FAO). UNIPUB.

Toxicological Evaluation of Some Enzymes, Modified Starches & Certain Other Substances. FAO-WHO Expert Committee on Food Additives. (WHO Food Additives Ser.: Vol. 1). 109p. 1972. pap. 2.40 (ISBN 92-4-166001-5). World Health.

Toxicological Evaluation of Some Enzymes, Modified Starches & Certain Other Substances. (Nutrition Meetings Reports: No. 50A). pap. 7.50 (F1134, FAO). UNIPUB.

Toxicological Evaluation of Some Food Additives Including Anticaking Agents, Antimicrobials, Antioxidants, Emulsifiers & Thickening Agents. (Food Additive Ser.: No. 5). (Also avail. in French). 1974. pap. 9.20 (ISBN 92-4-166005-8). World Health.

Toxicological Evaluation of Some Food Additives; Including Food Colors, Thickening Agents & Others. (Nutrition Meetings Reports: No. 55a). (Illus.). 89p. 1977. pap. 9.50 (ISBN 92-5-100060-3, F1217, FAO). UNIPUB.

Toxicological Evaluation of Some Food Additives, Including Food Colors, Enzymes, Flavour Enhancers, Thickening Agents & Others. (Nutrition Meetings Reports: No. 54a). (Illus.): 204p. 1976. pap. 12.50 (ISBN 92-4-166006-6, F1243, FAO). UNIPUB.

Toxicological Evaluation of Some Food Colours, Enzymes, Flavour Enhancers, Thickening Agents & Certain Other Food Additives. (Food Additive Ser.: No. 6). (Also avail. in French). 1975. pap. 5.20 (ISBN 92-4-166006-5). World Health.

Toxicological Evaluation of Some Food Colors, Emulsifiers, Stabilizers, Anti-Caking Agents & Certain Other Substances. (Nutrition Meetings Reports: No. 46). pap. 12.50 (F1216, FAO). UNIPUB.

Toxicological Evaluation of Some Food Colours, Thickening Agents & Certain Other Substances. (Food Additive Ser.: No. 8). (Also avail. in French). 1975. pap. 4.80 (ISBN 92-4-166008-2). World Health.

Toxicological Risk Assessment: Biological & Statistical Criteria, 2 vols, Vols. I & II. Ed. by D. Krewski et al. 1985. Vol. I, 244 p. 95.00 (ISBN 0-8493-5976-7); Vol. II, 276 p. 99.00 (ISBN 0-8493-5977-5). CRC Pr.

Toxicology: A Primer on Toxicology Principles & Applications. Michael A. Kamrin. LC 87-32492. (Illus.). 145p. 1988. 27.50 (ISBN 0-87371-133-5). Lewis Pubs Inc.

Toxicology & Biological Monitoring of Metals in Humans--Including Feasability & Need. B. L. Carson et al. LC 85-23167. (Illus.). 360p. 1986. 49.95 (ISBN 0-87371-072-X). Lewis Pubs Inc.

Toxicology & Occupational Medicine. Ed. by W. B. Deichmann. (Developments in Toxicology & Environmental Science Ser.: Vol. 4). 480p. 1979. 108.50 (ISBN 0-444-00288-X, Biomedical Pr). Elsevier.

Toxicology Effects of Emissions from Diesel Engines. Lewtas. (Developments in Toxicology & Environmental Science: Vol. 10). 380p. 1982. 103.50 (ISBN 0-444-00687-7, Biomedical Pr). Elsevier.

Toxicology Handbook. Environmental Protection Agency Staff. 216p. 1986. pap. 45.00 (ISBN 0-86587-142-6). Gov Insts.

Toxicology I in Health, Science & Medicine: Research Reference Analysis with Bibliography. Jennie M. Kahndike. LC 84-45989. 150p. 1987. 34.50 (ISBN 0-88164-300-9); pap. 26.50 (ISBN 0-88164-301-7). ABBE Pubs Assn.

Toxicology in the Tropics. Ed. by R. L. Smith & E. A. Babaunumi. 280p. 1980. 42.00x (ISBN 0-85066-194-3). Taylor & Francis.

Toxicology in the Use, Misuse, & Abuse of Food, Drugs & Chemicals. Ed. by P. L. Chambers et al. (Archives of Toxicology: Suppl. 6). (Illus.). 380p. 1983. pap. 63.50 (ISBN 0-387-12392-X). Springer-Verlag.

Toxicology Laboratory Design & Management for the 80's & Beyond. Ed. by A. S. Tegeris. (Concepts in Toxicology Ser.: Vol. 1). (Illus.). xii, 320p. 1984. 99.50 (ISBN 3-8055-3797-2). S Karger.

Toxicology: Mechanisms & Analytical Methods, 2 vols. Ed. by C. P. Stewart & A. Stolman. 1960-61. Vol. 1. 106.50 (ISBN 0-12-669701-9); Vol. 2. 112.00 (ISBN 0-12-669702-7). Acad Pr.

Toxicology of Coal Conversion Processing. Robert H. Gray et al. LC 87-21546. 603p. 1988. 80.00 (ISBN 0-471-80264-6). Wiley.

Toxicology of Halogenated Hydrocarbons: Health & Ecological Effects. Ed. by M. A. Khan & R. H. Stanton. (Illus.). 350p. 1981. 92.00 (ISBN 0-08-027530-3). Pergamon.

Toxicology of Inhaled Materials. Ed. by H. Witschi & J. D. Brain. (Handbook of Experimental Pharmacology, Continuation of Handbuch der Experimentellen Pharmakologie: Vol. 75). (Illus.). 600p. 1985. 245.00 (ISBN 0-387-13109-4). Springer-Verlag.

Toxicology of Insecticides. 2nd ed. Fumio Matusmura. LC 85-12371. 618p. 1985. 45.00x (ISBN 0-306-41979-3, Plenum Pr). Plenum Pub.

Toxicology of Molluscicides. Ed. by G. Webbe. (International Encyclopedia of Pharmacology & Therapeutics Ser.: No. 125). (Illus.). 174p. 1987. 99.00 (ISBN 0-08-034209-4). Pergamon.

Toxicology of Pesticides: Exprerimental, Ckinical & Regulatory Perspectives. Ed. by L. G. Costa & C. L. Galli. (NATO ASI Ser.: Vol H 13). 335p. 1987. 79.00 (ISBN 0-387-16093-0). Springer Verlag.

Toxicology of Radioactive Substances, 2 vols. Ed. by A. A. Letavet & E. B. Kurlyandskaya. Incl. Vol. 4. Thorium-232 & Uranium-238. 1970. 50.00 (ISBN 0-08-013413-0); Vol. 5. Zinc-65. 1970. 57.00 (ISBN 0-08-013414-9). write for info. Pergamon.

Toxicology of Skin Irritation & Skin Sensitization: Standard Methods. T. Maurer. (Lectures in Toxicology: No. 19). (Illus.). 12p. 1982. 73.00 (ISBN 0-08-029790-0). Pergamon.

Toxicology of the Blood & Bone Marrow. Ed. by Richard D. Irons. (Target Organ Toxicology Ser.). 192p. 1985. text ed. 50.00 (ISBN 0-89004-837-1). Raven.

Tozer Pulpit, 8 vols. A. W. Tozer. Ed. by Gerald B. Smith. Incl. Vol. 1. Selected Quotations from the Sermons of A. W. Tozer. 158p. 1967. pap. 3.95 (ISBN 0-87509-199-7); Vol. 2. Ten Sermons on the Ministry of the Holy Spirit. 146p. 1968. pap. 3.95 (ISBN 0-87509-178-4); cloth 5.95 (ISBN 0-87509-177-6); Vol. 3. Ten Sermons from the Gospel of John. 167p. 1970; Vol. 4. Twelve Sermons on Spiritual Perfection. 144p. 1972; Vol. 5. Twelve Sermons in Peter's First Epistle. 159p. 1974; Vol. 6. Twelve Messages on Well-Known & Favorite Bible Texts. 174p. 1975. 5.95 (ISBN 0-87509-210-1); Vol. 7. Twelve Sermons Relating to the Life & Ministry of the Christian Church. 1978. 5.95 (ISBN 0-87509-213-6); Vol. 8. Ten Sermons on the Voices of God Calling Man. 5.95 (ISBN 0-87509-225-X). pap. Chr Pubns.

Tozer Pulpit, Vol. 2: Ten Sermons on the Ministry of the Holy Spirit see When He Is Come.

Tozer Pulpit, Vol. 4. Twelve Sermons on Spiritual Perfection see I Talk Back to the Devil.

Tozzetti. (Phytopathological Classics). 139p. 1952. 7.00 (ISBN 0-89054-010-1). Am Phytopathol Soc.

TpeHyiiih TpajaHa Ilecme ("Moments & Eternity") Poems. Sava Jakovic. (Illus.). xvi, 125p. (Serbian.). 1985. 6.00 (ISBN 0-915887-06-1). Kosovo Pub Co.

TPS Model Form of Conditions of Contract: For the Supply & Installation (Purchase) of Computers. Ed. by Institute of Purchasing & Supply. 40.00x (ISBN 0-317-43772-0, Pub. by Inst Purchasing Supp). State Mutual Bk.

TQ Twenty: Twenty Years of Triquarterly. Ed. by Reginald Gibbons. LC 85-60910. (Illus.). 28.00 (ISBN 0-916366-31-6). Pushcart Pr.

TQC Wisdom of Japan: Managing Total Quality Control. Hajime Karatsu. LC 87-62302. (Japanese Management Ser.). (Illus.). 176p. 1988. 34.95 (ISBN 0-915299-18-6). Prod Press.

TR for Triumph. Chris Harvey. (Illus.). 229p. 29.95 (ISBN 0-902280-94-5, P994, Pub. by Oxford Ill Pr). Haynes Pubns.

Trabajadores Frente a la Crisis. Emilio Maspero. (Coleccion Clat). 124p. (Orig., Span.). 1986. pap. 6.00 (ISBN 0-917049-04-7). Saeta.

Trabajadores Puertoriquenos y el Partido Socialista, 1932 a 1940. Blanca Silvestrini De Pacheco. Orig. Title: Puerto Rican Workers & the Socialist Party, 1932-1940. (Illus., Span.). 1979. pap. 7.50 (ISBN 0-8477-0858-6). U of PR Pr.

Trabajo Asalariado y Capital. Karl Marx. 42p. (Span.). 1979. pap. 0.95 (ISBN 0-8285-1357-0, Pub. by Progress Pubs USSR). Imported Pubns.

Trabajo, Ingreso y Bienestar en una Metropolis en Desarrollo: Consecuencias del Crecimiento en Bogota. Rakesh Mohan. Orig. Title: Work, Wages, & Welfare in a Developing Metropolis: Consequences of Growth in Bogota, Columbia. 418p. (Span.). 1988. 18.95 (IB1084). World Bank.

Trabajos Ineditos. Julio Saavedra Molina. 358p. 2.20 (ISBN 0-318-14311-9). Hispanic Inst.

Trabajos Realizados Por el Comite Juridico Interamericano Durante el Periodo Ordinario De Sesiones. OAS General Secretariat. (International Law Ser.). 147p. (CJI-42). 1980. text ed. 10.00 (ISBN 0-8270-1156-3). OAS.

Trabajos Realizados Por el Comite Juridico Interamericano Durante el Periodo Ordinario De Sesiones: Celebrado Del 4 Al 29 De Agosto De 1980. OAS General Secretariat. (Comite Juridico Interamericano). 155p. (Span., CJI-43). 1980. pap. text ed. 10.00 (ISBN 0-8270-1267-5). OAS.

Trabajos Realizados Por el Comite Juridico Interamericano Durante el Periodo Ordinario De Sesiones. Incl. Celebrado Del 21 De Julio Al 15 De Agosto De 1975. 1975. pap. 5.00 (ISBN 0-8270-2305-7); Celebrado Del 14 De Enero Al 20 De Febrero De 1974. (Span. & Eng.). pap. 1.00 (ISBN 0-8270-2250-6); Celebrado Del 16 De Agosto Al 13 De Septiembre De 1971. 1971. pap. 1.00 (ISBN 0-8270-2165-8); Celebrado Del 17 De Enero Al 11 De Febrero De 1972. 1972. pap. 1.00 (ISBN 0-8270-2190-9); Celebrado Del 25 De Julio Al 23 De Agosto De 1972. 1972. pap. 1.00 (ISBN 0-8270-2195-X); Celebrado Del 15 De Enero Al 16 De Febrero De 1973. 1973. pap. 1.00 (ISBN 0-8270-2220-4); Celebrado Del 30 De Septiembre Al 28 De Octubre De 1974. 1974. pap. 3.00 (ISBN 0-686-96809-3); Celebrado Del 26 De Julio Al 27 De Agosto De 1973. 1973. pap. 1.00 (ISBN 0-8270-2240-9). (Eng., Span. & Port.). pap. OAS.

Trabalhos Realizados Pela Comissao Juridica Interamericana Durante Seu Periodo Ordinario De Sessoes: 30 de Julho a 16 de Agosto de 1979. OAS General Secretariat. 165p. (Port.). 1980. pap. text ed. 7.00 (ISBN 0-8270-1146-6). OAS.

Trabantenstadt. Rene De Goscinny. (Asterix Ser.). (Illus., Ger.). 1976. 7.95x (ISBN 0-686-19994-4). Intl Learn Syst.

Trabantenstadt. R. Goscinny & M. Uderzo. (Illus., Ger.). 15.95 (ISBN 0-686-56265-8). French & Eur.

Trabert on Tennis: The View from Center Court. Tony Trabert & Gerald Couzens. 192p. 1988. 17.95 (ISBN 0-8092-4664-3). Contemp Bks.

Trac-Trends in Analytical Chemistry: Reference Edition, 1981-1982. P. T. Shepherd. (Trac Compendium Ser.: Vol. 1). 1984. 89.50 (ISBN 0-317-11476-X). Elsevier.

Trace, No. 1. Warren Murphy. 1983. pap. 2.95 (ISBN 0-451-12502-9, Sig). NAL.

Trace Amines: Comparative & Clinical Neurobiology. Ed. by Alan A. Boulton et al. LC 88-6847. (Experimental & Clinical Neuroscience Ser.). (Illus.). 496p. 1988. 75.00 (ISBN 0-89603-144-6). Humana.

Trace Analysis, Vol. 1. James F. Lawrence. 1981. 56.50 (ISBN 0-12-682101-1). Acad Pr.

Trace Analysis, Vol. 2. James Lawrence. (Serial Publication Ser.). 1982. 46.00 (ISBN 0-12-682102-X). Acad Pr.

Trace Analysis, Vol. 3. Ed. by James F. Lawrence. (Serial Publications). 1984. 59.00 (ISBN 0-12-682103-8). Acad Pr.

Trace Analysis, Vol. 4. James F. Lawrence. 1985. 77.00 (ISBN 0-12-682104-6). Acad Pr.

Trace Analysis & Technological Development. Ed. by M. S. Das. LC 83-12788. 407p. 1983. 45.95x (ISBN 0-470-27462-X). Halsted Pr.

Trace Analysis by Mass Spectrometry. Ed. by Arthur J. Ahearn. 1972. 102.00 (ISBN 0-12-044650-2). Acad Pr.

Trace Analysis of Atmospheric Samples. Kikuo Oikawa. LC 77-3458. 158p. 1977. 42.95 (ISBN 0-470-99013-9). Halsted Pr.

Trace Analysis: Spectroscopic Methods for Molecules. Ed. by Gary Christian & James B. Callis. LC 85-26603. (Chemical Analysis Ser.). 406p. 1986. 55.00 (ISBN 0-471-87583-X). Wiley.

Trace & Forty-Seven Miles of Rope. Warren Murphy. (Trace Ser.: No. 2). 1984. pap. 2.95 (ISBN 0-451-12858-3, Sig). NAL.

Trace Atmospheric Constituents: Properties, Transformations & Fates. Stephen E. Schwartz. LC 82-16095. (Advances in Environmental Science & Technology Ser.). 547p. 1983. 78.00 (ISBN 0-471-87640-2, Pub. by Wiley-Interscience). Wiley.

Trace Chemistry of Aqueous Solutions: General Chemistry & Radiochemistry. P. Benes & V. Majer. (Topics in Inorganic & General Chemistry Ser.: Vol. 18). 252p. 1980. 79.00 (ISBN 0-444-99798-9). Elsevier.

Trace Components of Plasma: Proceedings of the American Red Cross Scientific Symposium, 7th Annual, Washington, D.C., May, 1975. American Red Cross Scientific Symposium Staff. Ed. by G. A. Jamieson & Tibor J. Greenwalt. LC 75-38563. (Progress in Clinical & Biological Research: Vol. 5). 440p. 1976. 63.00 (ISBN 0-8451-0005-X). A R Liss.

Trace Contaminants from Coal. Ed. by S. Torrey. LC 78-61890. (Pollution Technology Review: No. 50). 249p. 1979. 39.00 (ISBN 0-8155-0724-0). Noyes.

Trace Contaminants in the Environment. 70p. 1975. pap. 22.00 (ISBN 0-8169-0089-2, S-149). Am Inst Chem Eng.

Trace Contaminants of Agriculture, Fisheries & Food in Developing Countries. LC 76-8895. (Panel Proceedings Ser.). (Illus.). 108p. 1977. pap. 12.00 (ISBN 92-0-111576-8, ISP454, IAEA). UNIPUB.

Trace Element Analytical Chemistry in Medicine & Biology. Ed. by P. Schramel. 1000p. 1980. 95.00 (ISBN 3-11-008357-4). De Gruyter.

Trace Element Analytical Chemistry in Medicine & Biology, Vol. 2. Ed. by Peter Braetter & Peter Schramel. 1189p. 1983. 181.00 (ISBN 3-11-008681-6). De Gruyter.

Trace Element Analytical Chemistry in Medicine & Biology, Vol. 3: Proceedings of the 3rd International Workshop. Ed. by P. Braetter & P. Schramel. LC 80-26803. (Illus.). xvi, 763p. 1984. 155.00 (ISBN 3-11-009821-0). De Gruyter.

Trace Element Analytical Chemistry in Medicine & Biology, Vol. 4: Proceedings of the 4th International Workshop, Neuherberg, Federal Republic of Germany, 1986. Ed. by P. Braetter & P. Schramel. xiii, 630p. 1987. lib. bdg. 191.00 (ISBN 0-89925-296-6). De Gruyter.

Trace-Element Contamination of the Environment: Fundamental Aspects of Pollution Control & Environmental Science, 7. rev. ed. D. Purves. 244p. 1985. 79.00 (ISBN 0-444-42503-9). Elsevier.

Trace Element Deficiency: Metabolic & Physiological Consequences. Ed. by L. Fowden et al. (Royal Society of London Ser.). (Illus.). 213p. 1982. lib. bdg. 65.50x (ISBN 0-85403-171-5, Pub. by Royal Soc London). Scholium Intl.

Trace Element Geochemistry in Health & Disease. Ed. by Jacob Freedman. LC 75-3801. (Geological Society of America, Special Paper: No. 155). pap. 31.50 (2027368). Bks Demand UMI.

Trace Element Measurements at the Coal-Fired Steam Plant. W. S. Lyon. LC 77-435. 146p. 1977. text ed. 44.50 (ISBN 0-8493-5118-9, CR). Krieger.

Trace Element Metabolism in Animals--2: Proceedings. International Symposium on Trace Element Metabolism in Animals (2nd: 1973: University of Wisconsin, Madison) Ed. by W. G. Hoekstra & J. W. Suttie. LC 74-11167. pap. 160.00 (ISBN 0-317-41887-4, 2025746). Bks Demand UMI.

Trace Element Metabolism in Man & Animals: Proceedings. Ed. by J. Gawthorne et al. 715p. 1982. 90.00 (ISBN 0-387-11058-5). Springer-Verlag.

Trace Element Speciation in Surface & Waters: Its Ecological Implications. Ed. by Gary C. Leppard. LC 83-2177. (NATO Conference Series I, Ecology: Vol. 6). 332p. 1983. 59.50x (ISBN 0-306-41269-1, Plenum Press). Plenum Pub.

Trace Elements. Kathryn L. Knight. 1986. 15.95 (ISBN 0-393-02333-8). Norton.

Trace Elements & Dental Disease. Martin E. Curzon. (Illus.). 430p. 1983. case bound 41.00 (ISBN 0-7236-7035-8). PSG Pub Co.

Trace Elements & Iron in Human Metabolism. Ananda S. Prasad. LC 78-13446. (Topics In Hematology Ser.). (Illus.). 408p. 1978. 65.00x (ISBN 0-306-31142-9, Plenum Med Bk). Plenum Pub.

Trace Elements & Iron in Human Metabolism. Ananda S. Prasad. LC 78-13446. (Topics in Hematology Ser.). pap. 102.00 (ISBN 0-317-26186-X, 2052077). Bks Demand UMI.

Trace Elements & Man. Henry A. Schroeder. LC 72-85731. (Illus.). 192p. 1973. pap. 6.95 (ISBN 0-8159-6907-4). Devin.

Trace Elements, Hair Analysis & Nutrition: Fact & Myth. Richard A. Passwater & Elmer M. Cranton. LC 81-83892. 1983. 18.95 (ISBN 0-87983-348-3); pap. 14.95 (ISBN 0-87983-265-7). Keats.

Trace Elements in Environmental History. Ed. by G. Grupe & B. Herrmann. (Proceedings in Life Sciences Ser.). (Illus.). 174p. 1988. 41.00 (ISBN 0-387-18718-9). Springer-Verlag.

Trace Elements in Health: A Review of Current Issues. Ed. by J. Rose. 332p. 1983. text ed. 90.00 (ISBN 0-407-00255-3). Butterworth.

Trace Elements in Health & Disease. Ed. by H. Bostrom & N. Ljungstedt. (Illus.). 285p. 1985. text ed. 45.00x (ISBN 91-22-00733-4). Coronet Bks.

Trace Elements in Human & Animal Nutrition. 4th ed. E. J. Underwood. 1977. 85.00 (ISBN 0-12-709065-7). Acad Pr.

Trace Elements in Human & Animal Nutrition, Vol. 1. 5th ed. Walter Mertz. 480p. 1987. 69.00 (ISBN 0-12-491251-6). Acad Pr.

Trace Elements in Human & Animal Nutrition, Vol. 2. 5th ed. Walter Mertz. 1986. 65.00 (ISBN 0-12-491252-4). Acad Pr.

Trace Elements in Human Nutrition: Report. WHO Expert Committee. Geneva, 1973. (Technical Report Ser.: No. 532). (Also avail. in French & Spanish). 1973. pap. 2.80 (ISBN 92-4-120532-6). World Health.

Trace Elements in Igneous Petrology. Ed. by C. J. Allegre & S. R. Hart. (Developments in Petrology: Vol. 5). 1978. Repr. 100.00 (ISBN 0-444-41658-7). Elsevier.

Trace Elements in Man & Animals. Ed. by B. Lonnerdal. (Illus.). 676p. 1988. 115.00x (ISBN 0-306-43004-5, Plenum Pr). Plenum Pub.

Trace Elements in Nutrition of Children. Ed. by Ranjit K. Chandra. (Nestle Nutrition Workshop Ser.: Vol. 8). 320p. 1985. text ed. 36.50 (ISBN 0-88167-117-7). Raven.

Trace Elements in Pathogenesis & Treatment of Inflammation. Ed. by K. D. Rainsford et al. K. Brune & Whitehouse. (AAS Ser.: No. 8). 350p. 1980. softcover 91.95x (ISBN 0-8176-1201-7). Birkhauser.

Trace Elements in Plants. M. Y. Shkolnik. (Developments in Crop Science Ser.: Vol. 6). 464p. 1984. 118.50 (ISBN 0-444-42320-6, I-136-84). Elsevier.

Trace Elements in Relation to Cardiovascular Diseases: Status of the Joint WHO-IAEA Research Programme. Ed. by R. Masironi. (Offset Pub.: No. 5). (Also avail. in French). 1974. pap. 2.80 (ISBN 92-4-170005-X). World Health.

Trace Elements in Renal Insufficiency. Ed. by E. Quellhorst et al. (Contributions to Nephrology: Vol. 38). (Illus.). x, 206p. 1984. 76.00 (ISBN 3-8055-3676-3). S Karger.

Trace Elements in Soils. H. Aubert & M. Pinta. (Developments in Soil Science: Vol. 7). 396p. 1977. 123.75 (ISBN 0-444-41511-4). Elsevier.

Trace Elements in Soils & Agriculture. (Soils Bulletins: No. 17). 70p. (Eng., Fr. & Span.). 1972. pap. 7.50 (ISBN 0-686-92718-4, F1159, FAO). UNIPUB.

Trace Elements in Soils & Plants. Ed. by Alina K. Pendias & Henry K. Pendias. 336p. 1984. 99.00 (ISBN 0-8493-6639-9). CRC Pr.

Trace Elements in Soils of the South Texas Uranium District: Concentrations, Origin, & Environmental Significance. C. D. Henry & R. R. Kapadia. (Report of Investigations Ser.: RI 101). (Illus.). 52p. 1980. 2.00 (ISBN 0-318-03243-0). Bur Econ Geology.

Trace Elements in the Environment. Ed. by Evaldo L. Kothny. LC 73-87347. (Advances in Chemistry Ser: No. 123). 1973. 29.95 (ISBN 0-8412-0185-4). Am Chemical.

Trace Elements in the Terrestrial Environment. D. C. Adriano. (Illus.). xix, 533p. 1985. 75.00 (ISBN 0-387-96158-5). Springer-Verlag.

Trace Elements: Miracle Micro Nutrients. Andrew Stanway. (Illus.). 64p. (Orig.). 1988. pap. 3.99 (Pub. by Thorsons (England)). Sterling.

Trace Formula & Base Change for GL(3) Y. Z. Flicker. (Lecture Notes in Mathematics: Vol. 927). 204p. 1982. pap. 15.00 (ISBN 0-387-11500-5). Springer-Verlag.

Trace Fossil Concepts. Ed. by Paul B. Basan. (Society of Economic Paleontologists & Mineralogists Ser.: No. 5). (Illus.). pap. 48.10 (ISBN 0-317-58122-8, 2029675). Bks Demand UMI.

Trace Fossil Zoophycos As an Indicator of Water Depth see Bulletins of American Paleontology.

Trace Fossils Two: Geological Journal Special Issue, Vol. 9. T. P. Crimes & J. C. Harper. (Liverpool Geological Society & the Manchester Geological Association Ser.). 360p. 1980. 116.00 (ISBN 0-471-27756-8, Pub. by Wiley-Interscience). Wiley.

Trace Metal Concentrations in Marine Organisms. Ed. by Eisler. 3500p. 1981. 180.00 (ISBN 0-08-025975-8). Pergamon.

Trace Metals & Inherited Metabolic Disease. Ed. by G. M. Addison et al. 144p. 1983. lib. bdg. 35.00 (ISBN 0-85200-750-7, Pub. by MTP Pr England). Kluwer Academic.

Trace Metals: Exposure & Health Effects. R. K. Di Ferrante. 1979. pap. 64.00 (ISBN 0-08-022446-6). Pergamon.

Trace Metals in Health & Disease. Ed. by Norman Kharasch. 330p. 1979. 58.00 (ISBN 0-89004-389-2). Raven.

Trace Metals in Sea Water. Ed. by C. S. Wong & Edward Boyle. (NATO Conference Series IV, Marine Sciences: Vol. 9). 934p. 1983. 125.00x (ISBN 0-306-41165-2, Plenum Press). Plenum Pub.

Trace Mineral Studies with Isotopes in Domestic Animals. (Panel Proceedings Ser.). (Illus.). 151p. 1969. pap. 10.75 (ISBN 92-0-011069-X, ISP218, IAEA). UNIPUB.

Trace of Desert Waters: The Great Basin Story. Samuel Houghton. (Illus.). 288p. 1986. pap. 11.95 (ISBN 0-935704-35-3). Howe Brothers.

Trace of Memory. Keith Laumer. 256p. (Orig.). 1984. pap. 2.95 (ISBN 0-8125-4373-4, Dist. by Warner Pub Services & Saitn Martin's Press). Tor Bks.

Trace of Perfume. Esther Vogt. 1982. pap. 3.95 (ISBN 0-87162-256-4, WP#D8235). Warner Pr.

Trace Residue Analysis: Chemometric Estimations of Sampling, Amount, & Error. Ed. by Davie A. Kurtz. (ACS Symposium Ser.: No. 284). 286p. 1985. lib. bdg. 59.95x (ISBN 0-8412-0925-1). Am Chemical.

Trace Substances & Health, Pt. II. Newberne. 224p. 1982. 45.00 (ISBN 0-8247-1850-X). Dekker.

Trace Substances & Health: A Handbook, Part 1. Ed. by P. M. Newberne. 1976. 85.00 (ISBN 0-8247-6341-6). Dekker.

Trace System: How to Get Organized, How to Stay Organized. James P. King. 1986. pap. 9.95 (ISBN 0-936895-01-2). Brown House.

Trace Theory & VLSI Design. J. L. Van de Snepscheut. (Lecture Notes in Computer Science: Vol. 200). vi, 140p. 1985. pap. 12.50 (ISBN 0-387-15988-6). Springer-Verlag.

Traceable Temperatures. J. V. Nicholas & D. R. White. (Illus.). 226p. 1982. 32.00x (ISBN 0-477-06708-5, Pub. by A Hilger UK). Taylor & Francis.

Tracer. Frederick Barthelme. 104p. 1985. 13.95 (ISBN 0-671-54253-2). S&S.

Tracer. Frederick Barthelme. 126p. 1986. pap. 4.95 (ISBN 0-14-008969-1). Penguin.

Tracer Kinetics & Physiologic Modeling - Theory & Practice: Proceedings, St. Louix, Missouri, 1983. Ed. by R. M. Lambrecht & A. Rescigno. (Lecture Notes in Biomathematics: Vol. 48). 509p. 1983. pap. 33.80 (ISBN 0-387-12300-8). Springer-Verlag.

Tracer Manual on Crops & Soils. (Technical Reports Ser.: No. 171). (Illus.). 227p. 1976. pap. 39.00 (ISBN 92-0-115076-8, IDC171, IAEA). UNIPUB.

Tracer Methods for in Vitro Kinetics: Theory & Applications. Reginald A. Shipley & Richard E. Clark. 1972. 53.50 (ISBN 0-12-640250-7). Acad Pr.

Tracer Studies on Non-Protein Nitrogen for Ruminants, 1. (Panel Proceedings Ser.). (Illus.). 179p. 1972. pap. 16.25 (ISBN 92-0-111072-3, ISP302-1, IAEA). UNIPUB.

Tracer Studies on Non-Protein Nitrogen for Ruminants, 2: Proceedings. Research Co-Ordination Meeting & Panel. (Illus.). 208p. 1975. pap. 21.50 (ISBN 92-0-111175-4, ISP389-2, IAEA). UNIPUB.

Tracer Studies on Non-Protein Nitrogen for Ruminants, 3: Proceedings (Egypt) (Panel Proceedings Ser.). (Illus.). 160p. pap. 20.00 (ISBN 92-0-111376-5, ISP455-3, IAEA). UNIPUB.

Tracer Techniques in Sediment Transport. (Technical Reports Ser.: No. 145). (Illus.). 234p. (Orig.). 1973. pap. 25.00 (ISBN 92-0-145073-7, IDC145, IAEA). UNIPUB.

Tracer Techniques in Tropical Animal Production. (Panel Proceedings Ser.). (Illus.). 209p. (Orig.). 1974. pap. 17.75 (ISBN 92-0-111074-X, ISP360, IAEA). UNIPUB.

Tracers. Vincent Caristi et al. 71p. 1987. pap. 3.75 (ISBN 0-317-62320-6). Dramatists Play.

Tracers: A Play. John Difusco et al. (Illus.). 128p. 1986. 12.95 (ISBN 0-8090-9412-6); pap. 7.95. Hill & Wang.

Tracers in Metabolic Research: Radioisotope & Stable Isotope-Mass Spectrometry Methods. Robert R. Wolfe. LC 83-19601. (Laboratory & Research Methods in Biology & Medicine Ser.: Vol. 9). 300p. 1984. 62.00 (ISBN 0-8451-1658-4). A R Liss.

Tracers in the Ocean. Compiled by H. Charnock et al. (Illus.). 236p. 1988. Repr. of 1988 ed. text ed. 90.00x (ISBN 0-85403-350-5, Pub. by Royal Soc London). Scholium Intl.

Tracers in the Sea. Wallace S. Broecker. (Illus.). 700p. 1982. text ed. 35.00 (ISBN 0-9617511-0-X). Eldigio Pr.

Tracking Toxic Wastes in New Jersey. Catherine G. Miller & Laurence M. Naviasky. 88p. 1986. pap. 15.00x (ISBN 0-918780-35-7). INFORM.

Tracking Toxic Wastes in Ohio. Catherine G. Miller & Laurence M. Naviasky. 118p. 1986. pap. 15.00x (ISBN 0-918780-37-3). INFORM.

Tracking Treasure: Romance & Fortune Beneath the Sea & How to Find It! Philip Z. Trupp. (Illus.). 208p. 1986. pap. 12.95 (ISBN 0-87491-805-7). Acropolis.

Tracking Wild Chimpanzees. Joyce Powzyk. LC 87-16099. (Illus.). 32p. (gr. 1-4). 1988. 13.95 (ISBN 0-688-06733-6); PLB 13.88 (ISBN 0-688-06734-4). Lothrop.

Trackless Seas. James L. Johnson. LC 86-72063. 306p. (Orig.). 1987. pap. 7.95 (ISBN 0-89107-400-7, Crossway Bks). Good News.

Trackman. Jack Rudman. (Career Examination Ser.: C-1066). (Cloth bdg. avail. on request). pap. 12.00 (ISBN 0-8373-1066-0). Natl Learning.

Tracks. Robyn Davidson. 1983. pap. 4.95 (ISBN 0-394-72167-5). Pantheon.

Tracks. Louise Erdrich. LC 88-93221. 1988. 18.95 (ISBN 0-8050-0895-0). H Holt & Co.

Tracks. Robert Locke. (gr. 5 up). 1986. 12.95 (ISBN 0-395-40571-8). HM.

Tracks. Malaki. LC 78-11120. (Illus.). 1979. cloth 20.00 (ISBN 0-916906-17-5); signed ed. 50.00 (ISBN 0-916906-18-3); pap. 12.00 (ISBN 0-916906-16-7). Konglomerati.

Tracks. J. D. Whitney. 1969. 4.00 (ISBN 0-685-01016-3). Elizabeth Pr.

Tracks & Landfalls of Bering & Chirikof on the Northwest Coast of America. George Davidson. 44p. 1973. (ISBN 0-87770-112-1). Ye Galleon.

Track's Greatest Champions. Cordner Nelson. (Illus.). 385p. (Orig.). 1986. pap. 15.00 (ISBN 0-911521-19-4). Tafnews.

Tracks in the Sky: Wildlife & Wetlands of the Pacific Flyway. Peter Steinhart. LC 87-9379. (Illus.). 166p. 1987. 35.00 (ISBN 0-87701-351-9). Chronicle Bks.

Tracks in the Snow. Ruthven Todd. LC 76-51349. (English Literature Ser, No. 33). 1977. lib. bdg. 42.95x (ISBN 0-8383-2159-3). Haskell.

Tracks in the Snow: Studies in English Science & Art. Ruthven Todd. 133p. 1980. Repr. of 1946 ed. lib. bdg. 29.50 (ISBN 0-8495-5152-8). Arden Lib.

Tracks in the Snow: Studies in English Science & Art (Blake) Ruthven Todd. LC 75-40220. 1975. Repr. of 1946 ed. lib. bdg. 30.50 (ISBN 0-8414-8546-1). Folcroft.

Tracks in the Snowy Forests. 3rd ed. Po Chu. Tr. by Sidney Shapiro et al from Chinese. (Illus.). 559p. 1978. pap. 7.95 (ISBN 0-917056-72-8, Pub. by Foreign Lang Pr China). Cheng & Tsui.

Tracks in the Straw: Tales Spun from the Manger. Ed Kern. (Illus.). 130p. (Orig.). 1985. pap. 9.95 (ISBN 0-931055-06-7). LuraMedia.

Tracks in the Widest Orbit: Collected Poems of J. H. Montrose. J. H. Montrose. 96p. (Orig.). 1985. pap. 4.95 (ISBN 0-930489-00-4). Russian River.

Track's Magnificent Milers. Nathan Aaseng. LC 80-27404. (Sports Heroes Library). (Illus.). (gr. 4 up). 1981. PLB 7.95 (ISBN 0-8225-1066-9). Lerner Pubns.

Tracks of a Fellow Struggler. John R. Claypool. LC 73-91553. 1976. pap. 8.95 Gift Edition (ISBN 0-8499-0324-6). Word Bks.

Tracks of Babylon & Other Poems. Edith Tiempo. 1966. pap. 0.75 (ISBN 0-8040-0293-2, Pub by Swallow). Ohio U Pr.

Tracks of Gypsy Angels. L. Bradley Law. LC 86-70545. 50p. (Orig.). 1986. pap. 5.00 (ISBN 0-933865-03-1). Doris Pubns.

Tracks on the Florida Trails. Ned Potter. 128p. 1987. 7.95 (ISBN 0-8062-2771-0). Carlton.

Tracks on the Land: Stories of Immigrants, Outlaws, Artists, & Other Texans Who Left Their Mark on the Lone State. Ed. by David C. DeBoe & Kenneth B. Ragsdale. LC 84-50969. (Illus.). 297p. 1984. pap. 9.95 (ISBN 0-87611-069-3); 18.95. Tex St Hist Assn.

Tracks, Trails & Tales in Clallam County State of Washington. Harriet U. Fish. (Illus.). 200p. (Orig.). 1983. 15.95 (ISBN 0-9612344-0-7). H U Fish.

Tract Against Usurie. Thomas Culpeper. LC 74-80170. (English Experience Ser.: No. 649). 22p. 1974. Repr. of 1621 ed. 15.00 (ISBN 90-221-0649-7). Walter J Johnson.

Tract of Time. Smith Hempstone. 224p. 1985. pap. 2.95 (ISBN 0-380-69873-0). Avon.

Tract on Monetary Reform see Collected Writings.

Tract on the Succession to the Crown, A.D. 1602. John Harington. Ed. by Clements R. Markham. 1969. Repr. of 1880 ed. lib. bdg. 29.50 (ISBN 0-8337-1577-1). B Franklin.

Tract: Questions on Divorce & Remarriage. Thomas B. Warren. 1984. each 0.60 (ISBN 0-934916-04-7); dozen 6.00; hundred 40.00. Natl Christian Pr.

Tractate Abodah. Zarah Horayoth & Edoyoth Avoth. 1988. 22.95 (ISBN 0-900689-89-7). Soncino Pr.

Tractate Baba Kamma. Ed. by I. Epstein. 1977. 22.95 (ISBN 0-900689-59-5). Soncino Pr.

Tractate Baba Kamma. Ed. by I. Epstein. 1964. student's ed. 15.00 (ISBN 0-900689-67-6). Soncino Pr.

Tractate Baba Kamma see Soncino Hebrew-English Talmud.

Tractate Baba Mezia see Soncino Hebrew-English Talmud.

Tractate Berakoth. Ed. by I. Epstein. 1960. 22.95 (ISBN 0-900689-56-0). Soncino Pr.

Tractate Berakoth see Soncino Hebrew-English Talmud.

Tractate Erubin. Ed. by I. Epstein. 1983. 22.95 (ISBN 0-900689-80-3). Soncino Pr.

Tractate Gitten. Ed. by I. Epstein. 1973. 22.95 (ISBN 0-900689-58-7). Soncino Pr.

Tractate Gittin see Soncino Hebrew-English Talmud.

Tractate Hullin. Ed. by I. Epstein. 1980. 22.95 (ISBN 0-900689-17-X). Soncino Pr.

Tractate Kethuboth. Ed. by I. Epstein. 1971. 22.95 (ISBN 0-900689-06-4). Soncino Pr.

Tractate Kethuboth see Soncino Hebrew-English Talmud.

Tractate Kiddushin see Soncino Hebrew-English Talmud.

Tractate Mourning: Regulations Relating to Death, Burial, & Mourning. Tr. by Dov Zlotnick. (Judaica Ser.: No. 17). 1966. 30.00t (ISBN 0-300-01069-9). Yale U Pr.

Tractate Nedarim. I. Epstein. 1985. 22.95 (ISBN 0-900689-90-0). Soncino Pr.

Tractate on the Jews: The Significance of Judaism for the Christian Faith. Franz Mussner. Tr. by Leonard Swidler from Ger. LC 83-5699. 352p. 1983. 9.95 (ISBN 0-8006-0707-4, 1-707). Fortress.

Tractate Pesachim. Ed. by I. Epstein. 1983. 22.95 (ISBN 0-900689-81-1). Soncino Pr.

Tractate Pesahim see Soncino Hebrew-English Talmud.

Tractate Rosh Hashana, Bezah, Shekalim. 1983. 22.95 (ISBN 0-900689-82-X). Soncino Pr.

Tractate Sanhadrin. Ed. by I. Epstein. 1969. 22.95 (ISBN 0-900689-04-8). Soncino Pr.

Tractate Sanhedrin see Soncino Hebrew-English Talmud.

Tractate Shabbath, 1 vol. Ed. by I. Epstein. 1972. Set. 35.00 (ISBN 0-900689-62-5). Soncino Pr.

Tractate Shabbath see Soncino Hebrew-English Talmud.

Tractate Shebuoth- Makkoth. 1987. 22.95. Soncino Pr.

Tractate Sukkah-Moedkattan. 1984. 22.95 (ISBN 0-900689-83-8). Soncino Pr.

Tractate Taanit, Megilla, Chagiga. 1984. write for info. (ISBN 0-900689-84-6). Soncino Pr.

Tractate Yevamoth. I. Epstein. 1984. 22.95 (ISBN 0-900689-92-7). Soncino Pr.

Tractate Yoma. Ed. by I. Epstein. 1974. 22.95 (ISBN 0-900689-63-3). Soncino Pr.

Tractate Yoma see Soncino Hebrew-English Talmud.

Tractate Zevachim. 1988. 22.95 (ISBN 0-900689-93-5). Soncino Pr.

Tractates Baba Bathra. Ed. by I. Epstein. 1976. Set. 35.00 (ISBN 0-900689-64-1). Soncino Pr.

Tractates on the Gospel of John, 1-10. St. Augustine. Tr. by John W. Rettig. (Fathers of the Church Ser.: Vol. 78). 250p. 1988. 39.95 (ISBN 0-8132-0078-4). Cath U Pr.

Tractates on the Gospel of John, 11-27. St. Augustine. Tr. by John W. Rettig. (Fathers of the Church Ser.: Vol. 79). 300p. 1988. 29.95 (ISBN 0-8132-0079-2). Cath U Pr.

Tractato di Musica. Giovanni Spataro. (Monuments of Music & Music Literature in Facsimile, Ser. II: Vol. 88). 1980. Repr. of 1531 ed. 30.00x (ISBN 0-8450-2288-1). Broude.

Tractatus Brevior see Walter Burleigh De Puritate Artis Logicae Tractus Langios.

Tractatus De Globis & Eorum Usu. Robert Hues. Ed. by C. R. Markham. Incl. Sailing Directions for the Circumnavigation of England & for a Voyage to the Straits of Gibralter. Ed. by James Gairdner. LC 1-18671. 1889. Set. lib. bdg. 34.50 (ISBN 0-8337-1759-6). B Franklin.

Tractatus De Intellectus Emendatione. facs. ed. Benedict De Spinoza. LC 78-94284. (Select Bibliographies Reprint Ser). 1899. 17.00 (ISBN 0-8369-5057-7). Ayer Co Pubs.

Tractatus de Mystica Theologia, Vol. 2. Nicolas Kempf. Ed. by James Hogg. (Analecta Cartusiana Ser.: No. 9). 574p. (Orig., Lat. & Fr.). 1973. pap. 50.00 (ISBN 3-7052-0010-0, Pub by Salzburg Studies). Longwood Pub Group.

Tractatus de Signis: The Semiotic of John Poinsot. John Deely. LC 82-17658. 1985. 75.00x (ISBN 0-520-04252-2). U of Cal Pr.

Tractatus De Successivis Attributed to William Ockham. Ed. by Philotheus Boehner. (Philosophy Ser). 1944. 8.00 (ISBN 0-686-11531-7). Franciscan Inst.

Tractatus Logico-Philosophicus. Ludwig Wittgenstein. Tr. by D. F. Pears & B. F. McGuinness. (Inter. Library Philosphy & Scientific Method). 114p. (Ger. & Eng.). 1972. text ed. 27.50x (ISBN 0-391-00359-3); pap. text ed. 7.95x (ISBN 0-7100-7923-0). Humanities.

Tractatus Logico-Philosophicus: German Text with English Translation. Ludwig Wittgenstein. Tr. by C. K. Ogden. 208p. 1981. pap. 7.95 (ISBN 0-7100-0962-3). Routledge Chapman & Hall.

Traction & Orthopaedic Appliances. 2nd ed. J. D. Stewart & J. P. Hallett. LC 74-80738. (Illus.). 316p. 1983. pap. text ed. 36.00 (ISBN 0-443-02004-3). Churchill.

Traction Classics: Interurban Freight, Vol. 3. William D. Middleton. LC 83-18482. (Illus.). 186p. Set. 38.95 (ISBN 0-317-40899-2). Gldn West Bks.

Traction Classics: The Great Wood & Steel Interurban Cars, Vol. 1. William D. Middleton. LC 83-18482. 248p. 40.95 (ISBN 0-87095-085-1). Gldn West Bks.

Traction Classics: The High Speed & Deluxe Interurban Cars, Vol. 2. William D. Middleton. LC 83-18482. (Illus.). 230p. 1985. 35.95 (ISBN 0-87095-089-4). Gldn West Bks.

Traction Engines & Steam Vehicles in Pictures. Anthony Beaumont. LC 79-93192. (Illus.). 1969. lib. bdg. 19.95x (ISBN 0-678-05549-1). Kelley.

Traction Guidebook for Model Railroaders. Ed. by Mike Schafer. LC 74-76225. (Illus.). 120p. (Orig.). 1974. pap. 4.00 (ISBN 0-89024-522-3). Kalmbach.

Traction Planbook. 2nd ed. Harold H. Carstens. (Carstens Hobby Bks.: C-16). (Illus.). 1969. pap. 6.00 (ISBN 0-911868-16-X). Carstens Pubns.

Traction Yearbook, 1983. Joseph P. Saitta. (Illus.). 128p. 1983. pap. 18.95x (ISBN 0-9610414-1-2). Traction Slides.

Tractions Drives. Shube Heilich. (Mechanical Engineering Ser.). 448p. 1983. 55.00 (ISBN 0-8247-7018-8). Dekker.

Tractor & Farm Implement & Lubrication Guide, 1986. (Illus.). 192p. Date not set. wkbk. 39.40 (ISBN 0-88098-082-6). H M Gousha.

Tractor & Self Propelled Farm Implement Guide, 1987. rev. ed. Ed. by Dan Doornbos. (Illus.). 192p. 1986. wkbk. 41.35 (ISBN 0-88098-092-3). H M Gousha.

Tractor & Small Engine Maintenance. 5th ed. Arlen D. Brown & R. Mack Strickland. 350p. 1983. 22.60 (ISBN 0-8134-2258-2); text ed. 16.95x. Inter Print Pubs.

Tractor-Implement Systems. Ralph Alcock. (Illus.). 1986. 31.95 (ISBN 0-87055-522-7). AVI.

Tractor Operator. Jack Rudman. (Career Examination Ser.: C-827). (Cloth bdg. avail. on request). pap. 14.00 (ISBN 0-8373-0827-5). Natl Learning.

Tractor-Trailer Operator. Jack Rudman. (Career Examination Ser.: C-1519). (Cloth bdg. avail. on request). pap. 14.00 (ISBN 0-8373-1519-0). Natl Learning.

Tractorization in the United States & Its Relevance for the Developing Countries. Nicholas P. Sargen. LC 78-75050. (Outstanding Dissertations in Economics Ser.). 1979. lib. bdg. 36.00 (ISBN 0-8240-4128-3). Garland Pub.

Tractors. Paul Stickland. (Working Wheels Ser.). (Illus.). 16p. (ps-1). 1988. 3.95 (ISBN 0-8249-8258-4). Ideals.

Tractors. Graham Thompson. LC 86-5689. (Wheels Ser.). (Illus.). 24p. (ps-3). 1986. PLB 9.95 (ISBN 1-55532-102-X). Stevens Inc.

Tractors & Their Power Units. 4th ed. J. B. Liljedahl et al. (Illus.). 400p. 1988. text ed. 44.95 (ISBN 0-442-25897-6). Van Nos Reinhold.

Tractors & Their Power Units. 3rd ed. John B. Liljedahl et al. 1979. 41.95 (ISBN 0-87055-472-7). AVI.

Tractors: From Yesterday's Steam Wagons to Today's Turbo-charged Giants. Jim Murphy. LC 82-48777. (Illus.). 64p. (gr. 3-6). 1984. 11.70i (ISBN 0-397-32050-7, Lipp Jr Bks); PLB 11.89 (ISBN 0-397-32051-5). HarpJ.

Tracts. David Ferguson. Ed. by David Laing. LC 70-168016. (Bannatyne Club, Edinburgh. Publications: No. 110). Repr. of 1860 ed. 20.00 (ISBN 0-404-52864-3). AMS Pr.

Tracts. Gilbert Skeyne. (Bannatyne Club, Edinburgh. Publications: No. 108). Repr. of 1860 ed. 17.50 (ISBN 0-404-52862-7). AMS Pr.

Tracts & Other Papers Relating Principally to the Origin, Settlement & Progress of the Colonies in North America, 4 vols. Ed. by Peter Force. Set. 60.00 (ISBN 0-8446-1188-3). Peter Smith.

Tracts & Other Publications on Metallic & Paper Currency. Samuel J. Overstone. LC 67-20089. 1972. Repr. of 1857 ed. 49.50x (ISBN 0-678-00902-3). Kelley.

Tracts & Pamphlets of Richard Steele. Richard Steele. Ed. by Rae Blanchard. 1966. lib. bdg. 46.00x (ISBN 0-374-90646-7, Octagon). Hippocrene Bks.

Tracts for the New Times: No. 1 Letter to a Swedenborgian. Henry James, Sr. LC 72-916. (Selected Works of Henry James, Sr.: Vol. 9). 1983. Repr. of 1850 ed. 24.50 (ISBN 0-404-10089-9). AMS Pr.

Tracts for the Times, 6 Vols. Ed. by John H. Newman et al. 1833-1841. Set. lib. bdg. 295.00 (ISBN 0-404-19560-1). Vol. 1 (ISBN 0-404-04711-4). Vol. 2 (ISBN 0-404-04712-2). Vol. 3 (ISBN 0-404-04713-0). Vol. 4 (ISBN 0-404-04714-9). Vol. 5 (ISBN 0-404-04715-7). Vol. 6 (ISBN 0-404-04716-5). AMS Pr.

Tracts on Liberty in the Puritan Revolution, 1638-1647, 3 Vols. William Haller. LC 83-1153. 1965. lib. bdg. 75.00x (ISBN 0-374-93401-0, Octagon). Hippocrene Bks.

Tracts on Liberty of Conscience & Persecution. Ed. by Edwin B. Underhill. (Philosophy Monographs: No. 11). 1968. Repr. of 1846 ed. 29.50 (ISBN 0-8337-3594-2). B Franklin.

Tracts on Our Present Money System & National Bankruptcy. Peter R. Hoare. LC 67-27467. 1969. Repr. of 1814 ed. 45.00x (ISBN 0-678-00574-5). Kelley.

Tracts on Sundry Topics of Political Economy. Oliver Putnam. LC 68-56567. 1970. Repr. of 1834 ed. 27.50x (ISBN 0-678-00600-8). Kelley.

Tracts Relating to Military Proceedings in Lancashire During the Great Civil War. Ed. by George Ormerod. 1844. 35.00 (ISBN 0-384-43700-1). Johnson Repr.

Tracy & Hepburn. Garson Kanin. 1988. pap. 8.95 (Pub. by Primus Lib Contemp). D I Fine.

Tracy Sterling, M.D. Colleen Lewis. (YA) (gr. 7 up). 1981. 9.95 (ISBN 0-686-84673-7, Avalon). Bouregy.

Tradd Street Follies. Julian Wiles. LC 76-45729. 1978. 6.50 (ISBN 0-937684-08-2). Tradd St Pr.

Trade Adjustment Assistance: New Ideas for on Old Program. LC 87-619836. (OTA-ITA Ser.: No. 346). 75p. 1987. pap. 3.25 (ISBN 0-317-62908-5, S-N 052-003-01073-9). USGPO.

Trade Adjustment Policies & Income Distribution in Three Archetype Developing Economies. Jaime de Melo & Sherman Robinson. (Working Paper: No. 442). 91p. 1980. 5.00 (ISBN 0-686-36209-8, WP-0442). World Bank.

Trade Among Capitalist Countries. P. Khvoinik. 285p. 1983. 5.95 (ISBN 0-8285-2509-9, Pub. by Progress Pubs USSR). Imported Pubns.

Trade Among Developing Countries: Theory, Policy Issues, & Principal Trends. Oil Havrylyshyn & Martin Wolf. (Working Paper: No. 479). iv, 112p. 1981. 5.00 (ISBN 0-686-36202-0, WP-0479). World Bank.

Trade among Multinationals: Intra-Industry Trade & National Competitiveness. D. C. MacCharles. 224p. 1987. lib. bdg. 62.00x (ISBN 0-7099-4618-X, Pub. by Croom Helm UK). Routledge Chapman & Hall.

Trade Amongst Growing Economies. Ian Steedman. LC 78-73818. 1980. 32.50 (ISBN 0-521-22671-6). Cambridge U Pr.

Trade & Aid: Eisenhower's Foreign Economic Policy, 1953 - 1961. Burton I. Kaufman. LC 81-15594. 325p. 1982. text ed. 34.50x (ISBN 0-8018-2623-3). Johns Hopkins.

Trade & Banking in Early Modern England. Eric Kerridge. LC 87-31369. 191p. 1988. 39.95 (ISBN 0-7190-2652-0, Pub. by Manchester Univ Pr). St Martin.

Trade & Civilisation in the Indian Ocean: An Economic History from the Rise of Islam to 1750. K. N. Chaudhuri. (Illus.). 256p. 1985. 44.50 (ISBN 0-521-24226-6); pap. 17.95 (ISBN 0-521-28542-9). Cambridge U Pr.

Trade & Co-Operation Between the Socialist Countries of Eastern Europe & the Developing Countries in the Field of Food & Agriculture. 23p. 1986. 5.00 (ISBN 92-1-112201-5, E.85.11.D.14). UN.

Trade & Commercial Activities of Southern India in the Malayo-Indonesian World, Vol. 1: Up to 1511 A. D. H. B. Sarkar. 420p. 1986. 32.50X (ISBN 0-317-53507-2, Pub. by Firma KLM). South Asia Bks.

Trade & Currency in Early Oregon. James H. Gilbert. LC 77-168145. (Columbia University. Studies in the Social Sciences: No. 68). Repr. of 1907 ed. 16.50 (ISBN 0-404-51068-X). AMS Pr.

Trade & Dependency: Studies in the Expansion of Europe. Sven H. Carlson. 188p. (Orig.). 1984. pap. text ed. 24.00x (ISBN 91-554-1628-4, Pub. by Almqvist & Wiksell). Coronet Bks.

Trade & Development: An UNCTAD Review, No. 6, 1985. 266p. 1986. 19.00 (ISBN 92-1-112211-2, E.85.II.D.20). UN.

Trade & Development: An UNTAD Review 1984, No. 5. 365p. 25.00 (ISBN 92-1-012012-4, E/F84.II.D.8). UN.

Trade & Development: Autumn: 1980. (No. 2). pap. 10.00 (UN802D8). UN.

Trade & Development Board - 14th Special Session, 10-15 & 27 June 1985: Supplement No. 1-A Report, Official Records, Vol. II. 19p. 1987. 5.00 (ISBN 0-317-58064-7, TD/B/1062). UN.

Trade & Development Board - 29th Session, 10-27 September 1984: Supplement No. 1-A Report, Official Records, Vol. II. 122p. 1987. 13.50 (ISBN 0-317-58065-5, TD/B/1026). UN.

Trade & Development Board: Proceedings of the 27th Annexes, 3-20 October & 2 November 1983. (Official Records). 38p. 1986. 7.00. UN.

Trade & Development Board: Thirty-First Session. Supplement No. 1: Resolutions & Decision, 16-27 September 1985. (TDB Official Records). 11p. 1986. pap. 4.00 (ISBN 0-317-52838-6). UN.

Trade & Development Board: Thirty-First Session. Supplement No. 4: Report of the Committee on Commodities on Its Third Special Session, 3-13 June 1985. (TDBOfficial Records). 20p. 1986. pap. 4.00 (ISBN 0-317-52839-4). UN.

Trade & Development Board, Twenty-Eighth Session, March 26- April 6, 1984: Annexes. (TDBOfficial Records). 1986. pap. 9.50 (ISBN 0-317-52479-8). UN.

Trade & Development Board, Twenty-Eight Session, Supplement No.3: Report of the Committee on Transfer of Technology on Its First Special Session. 26p. 1986. 5.00. UN.

Trade Friction & Economic Policy: Problems & Prospects for Japan & the United States. Ed. by Ryuzo Sato & Paul Wachtel. (Illus.). 304p. 1987. 34.50 (ISBN 0-521-34446-8). Cambridge U Pr.

Trade, Government & Society in Caribbean History 1700-1920: Essays Presented to Douglas Hall. Ed. by B. W. Higman. xii, 172p. (Orig.). 1983. pap. text ed. 12.50x (ISBN 0-435-08009-1). Heinemann Ed.

Trade, Growth & Anxiety: New Zealand Beyond the Welfare State. S. Harvey Franklin. (Illus.). 1978. 36.00x (ISBN 0-456-02320-8, NO. 2830). Routledge Chapman & Hall.

Trade, Growth, & Income Distribution: The Experience of the Republic of Korea. Wontack Hong. (Working Paper Ser.: No. 3). 84p. 1981. 5.00 (ISBN 0-318-16160-5). Overseas Dev Council.

Trade in Agriculture Products: Committee II, 2nd & 3rd Reports. (Fr. & Span.). 1962. pap. 5.00 (ISBN 0-686-93105-X, G21, GATT). UNIPUB.

Trade in Bodies. CIIR Staff. 160p. 1986. 30.00x (ISBN 0-317-58000-0, Pub. by CIIR). State Mutual Bk.

Trade in Manufactures. A. C. Hotson & K. L. Gardiner. (Bank of England. Discussion Papers. Technical Ser.: No. 5). pap. 20.00 (2031457). Bks Demand UMI.

Trade in Non-Factor Services: Past Trends & Current Issues. Andre Sapir & Ernst Lutz. (Workign Paper: No. 410). iii, 137p. 1980. 8.00 (ISBN 0-686-36210-1, WP-0410). World Bank.

Trade in Services: A Case for Open Markets. Jonathan D. Aaronson & Peter F. Cowhey. 1984. 7.00 (ISBN 0-8447-3570-1). Am Enterprise.

Trade in Services & the European Community. Nicholas Oulton. 170p. 1988. text ed. price not set (ISBN 0-566-05785-9, Pub. by Gower Pub England). Gower Pub Co.

Trade in Services: Economic Determinants & Development-Related Issues. Andre Sapir & Ernst Lutz. (Working Paper: No. 480). 38p. 1981. pap. 3.50 (ISBN 0-686-39776-2, WP-0480). World Bank.

Trade in the Ancient Economy. Ed. by Peter Garnsey & Keith Hopkins. LC 81-13652. 250p. 1983. text ed. 35.00x (ISBN 0-520-04803-2). U of Cal Pr.

Trade in the Eastern Seas, 1793-1813. new ed. C. Northcote Parkinson. (Illus.). 437p. 1966. 35.00x (ISBN 0-7146-1348-7, F Cass Co). Biblio Dist.

Trade in Transition: Exports from the Third World, Eighteen Forty to Nineteen Hundred. John R. Hanson. LC 79-6776. (Studies in Social Discontinuity Ser.). 1980. 22.00 (ISBN 0-12-323450-6). Acad Pr.

Trade, Income Levels & Dependence. M. Michaely. (Studies in International Economics: Vol. 8). 188p. 1984. 60.75 (ISBN 0-444-86771-6, I-191-84, North-Holland). Elsevier.

Trade, Industrial Policy & International Competition, Vol. 13. Richard G. Harris. (Collected Research Studies: No. 13). 192p. 1985. 15.95c (ISBN 0-8020-7255-0). U of Toronto Pr.

Trade, Inflation, & the Dollar. Thibaut De Saint Phalle. (Illus.). 1981. 35.00x (ISBN 0-19-502970-4). Oxford U Pr.

Trade, Inflation & the Dollar. Rev., 2nd ed. Thibaut de Saint Phalle. LC 84-6991. 464p. 1984. 42.95 (ISBN 0-275-91144-6, C1144); pap. 14.95 (ISBN 0-275-91784-3, B1784). Praeger.

Trade is a Two-Way Street. 99p. 1981. pap. 5.00 (ISBN 0-686-48033-3). Amer Bar Assn.

Trade Liberalization among Major World Trading Areas. John Whalley. (Illus.). 328p. 1985. text ed. 35.00x (ISBN 0-262-23120-4). MIT Pr.

Trade Liberalization & the National Interest. Leonard Weiss. LC 80-80932. (Significant Issues Ser.: Vol. II, No. 2). 72p. 1980. 5.95 (ISBN 0-89206-016-6). CSI Studies.

Trade Liberalization & the National Interest. Leonard Weiss. (Significant Issues Ser.: Vol. II, No. 2). 74p. (Orig.). 1980. pap. text ed. 6.95 (ISBN 0-8191-5909-3, Pub. by CSIS). U Pr of Amer.

Trade Liberalization in ASEAN: An Empirical Study of the Preferential Trading Arrangements. Gerald Tan. 104p. (Orig.). 1982. pap. text ed. 9.50x (ISBN 9971-902-46-X, Pub. by Inst Southeast Asian Stud). Gower Pub Co.

Trade Liberalization in Sri Lanka. Deepak Lal & Sarath Rajapatiraha. (Thames Essays Ser.: No. 51). 60p. 1987. pap. text ed. 16.00x (ISBN 0-566-05340-3). Gower Pub Co.

Trade Liberalization, Protectionism & Interdependence. (Studies in International Trade: No. 5). 1978. pap. 7.50 (ISBN 0-685-42363-8, G108, GATT). UNIPUB.

Trade Literature: A Review & Survey. M. J. Thompson. 52p. 1977. pap. 6.50 (ISBN 0-902914-27-8, Pub. by British Lib). Longwood Pub Group.

Trade Mark Management & Exploitation. 1987. 290.00x (ISBN 0-948641-11-8, Pub. by ESC Ltd UK). State Mutual Bk.

Trade Marks: A Guide to the Literature & Directory of Lists of Trade Names. B. M. Rimmer. 63p. (Orig.). 1976. pap. 4.50 (ISBN 0-902914-26-X, Pub. by British Lib). Longwood Pub Group.

Trade Marks & Names. W. R. Cornish. 1987. pap. 60.00x (ISBN 0-906214-35-1, Pub. by ESC Ltd UK). State Mutual Bk.

Trade Marks & Symbols, 2 vols. Yasaburo Kuwayama. Incl. Vol. 1. Alphabets. 228p. 1973. 22.95 (ISBN 0-442-24563-7); Vol. 2. Symbolized Design. 228p. 1973. 22.95 (ISBN 0-442-24564-5). 1973. Van Nos Reinhold.

Trade Marks of Saudi Arabia. Tr. by N. H. Karam. 36p. 1985. pap. 64.50 (ISBN 0-86010-629-2). Graham & Trotman.

Trade Name Creation: Processes & Patterns. Jean Praninskas. (Janua Linguarum, Ser. Practica: No. 58). 1968. pap. text ed. 12.00x (ISBN 0-686-22472-8). Mouton.

Trade Names Dictionary, 2 vols. 6th ed. Ed. by Donna Wood. 1600p. 1987. 300.00x (ISBN 0-8103-1596-3). Gale.

Trade Names Dictionary: Company Index, 2 vols. 6th ed. Ed. by Donna Wood. 1500p. 1987. 310.00x (ISBN 0-8103-1598-X). Gale.

Trade Negotiations in the Tokyo Round: A Quantitative Assessment. William R. Cline et al. LC 77-91799. 314p. 1978. 21.95 (ISBN 0-8157-1472-6). Brookings.

Trade of Elizabethan Chester. D. M. Woodward. (Occasional Papers in Economic & Social History: No. 4). 150p. 1970. pap. text ed. 7.95x (ISBN 0-900480-71-8). Humanities.

Trade Patterns in Developing Countries, 1970-1981. Lance Taylor et al. (Working Paper: No. 642). 68p. 1984. 5.00 (ISBN 0-8213-0362-7, WP 0642). World Bank.

Trade, Plunder & Settlement: Maritime Enterprise & the Genesis of the British Empire, 1480-1630. Kenneth R. Andrews. 404p. 1985. 54.50 (ISBN 0-521-25760-3); pap. 11.95 (ISBN 0-521-27698-5). Cambridge U Pr.

Trade Policies & Industralization in a Small Country: The Case of Israel. Richard W. Pomfret. 220p. 1976. lib. bdg. 53.50x (Pub. by J C B Mohr BRD). Coronet Bks.

Trade Policies for a Better Future. Gatt. 1988. lib. bdg. 52.50 (ISBN 0-89838-925-9, Pub. by Martinus Nijhoff Netherlands). Kluwer Academic.

Trade Policy & Economic Welfare. W. M. Corden. (Illus.). 1974. text ed. 44.50x o. p. (ISBN 0-19-828199-4); pap. text ed. 18.95x (ISBN 0-19-828401-2). Oxford U Pr.

Trade Policy & the New Protectionism. David Greenaway. LC 82-10621. 232p. 1983. 25.00x (ISBN 0-312-81213-2). St Martin.

Trade Policy & U. S. Competitiveness. Claude E. Barfield & John H. Makin. LC 87-18831. 160p. (Orig.). 1988. lib. bdg. 22.50 (ISBN 0-8447-3633-3); pap. text ed. 9.75 (ISBN 0-8447-3634-1). Am Enterprise.

Trade Policy Developments in Industrial Countries. S. J. Anjaria et al. (Occasional Papers: No. 5). 56p. 1981. pap. 5.00 (ISBN 0-317-04006-5). Intl Monetary.

Trade Policy for Developing Countries. Donald B. Keesing. (Working Paper: No. 353). vii, 264p. 1979. 15.00 (ISBN 0-686-36211-X, WP-0353). World Bank.

Trade Policy for Troubled Industries. Gary C. Hufbauer & Howard F. Rosen. LC 85-18105. (Policy Analyses in International Economics Ser.). 111p. (Orig.). 1986. pap. 10.00 (ISBN 0-88132-020-X). Inst Intl Eco.

Trade Policy Formation in Selected Developing Countries. Jimmy W. Wheeler & Perry Wood. 230p. 1966. pap. text ed. 50.00 (ISBN 1-55813-019-5, HI-3833-P). Hudson Inst.

Trade Policy Formation in Selected Developing Countries: Key Judgements. Jimmy W. Wheeler & Perry Wood. 46p. 1986. pap. text ed. 16.00 (ISBN 1-55813-020-9, HI-3833-S). Hudson Inst.

Trade Policy Formulation in Malaysia. Catherine Albrecht. 115p. 1986. pap. text ed. 40.00 (ISBN 1-55813-023-3, HI-3760-P). Hudson Inst.

Trade Policy Formulation in Taiwan. John Tedstrom. 64p. 1986. pap. text ed. 22.00 (ISBN 1-55813-018-7, HI-3748-P-2). Hudson Inst.

Trade Policy in the Nineteen Eighties. Ed. by William R. Cline. LC 83-4310. 810p. (Orig.). 1984. 35.00; pap. 20.00. Inst Intl Eco.

Trade Policy Issues & Developments. Shailendra J. Anjaria et al. LC 85-14544. (Occasional Papers: No. 38). 161p. 1985. pap. 7.50 (ISBN 0-939934-46-9). Intl Monetary.

Trade Policy Issues & Empirical Analysis. Ed. by Robert E. Baldwin. (National Bureau of Economic Research Conference Report Ser.). (Illus.). 352p. 1988. 42.00x (ISBN 0-226-03607-3). U of Chicago Pr.

Trade Policy Issues for the Developing Countries in the 1980's. Isaiah Frank. (Working Paper Ser.: No. 478). 52p. 1981. 5.00 (ISBN 0-686-36203-9, WP-0478). World Bank.

Trade Policy Making in Canada: Are We Doing it Right? W. R. Hines. 111p. 1985. pap. text ed. 10.00x (ISBN 0-88645-019-5, Pub. by Inst Res Pub Canada). Brookfield Pub Co.

Trade Policy of the Nineteen Eighties. C. Fred Bergsten & William R. Cline. (Policy Analyses in International Economics: No. 3). pap. 21.00 (ISBN 0-317-20818-7, 2024793). Bks Demand UMI.

Trade Policy, Protectionism & the Third World. Michael Davenport. 176p. 1986. 31.00 (ISBN 0-7099-4516-7, Pub. by Croom Helm Ltd). Routledge Chapman & Hall.

Trade Practices & Traditions: Origin & Development in India. Vipin K. Garg. 1985. 17.50x (ISBN 0-8364-1434-9, Pub. by Allied India). South Asia Bks.

Trade Problems Between Japan & Western Europe. Masamichi Hanabusa. LC 79-88567. (Illus.). 138p. 1979. 36.95 (ISBN 0-275-90360-5, C0360). Praeger.

Trade Protection in the United States: Thirty-One Case Studies. Gary C. Hufbauer et al. LC 85-18067. 371p. (Orig.). 1986. pap. 25.00 (ISBN 0-88132-040-4). Inst Intl Eco.

Trade Regulation by Negotiation: Federal Trade Commission Consent Decrees. Talbot Lindstrom & Kevin P. Tighe. LC 73-93919. pap. 160.00 (ISBN 0-317-26772-8, 2024341). Bks Demand UMI.

Trade Regulation, Cases & Materials on. 2nd ed. Milton Handler et al. LC 83-1625. (University Casebook Ser.). 1387p. 1983. text ed. 29.50 (ISBN 0-88277-112-4). Foundation Pr.

Trade Regulation: Cases & Materials on, 1985 Supplement. 2nd ed. Handler et al. (University Casebook Ser.). 172p. 1985. pap. text ed. 6.95 (ISBN 0-88277-311-9). Foundation Pr.

Trade Regulation, Cases & Materials: Teacher's Manual. 2nd ed. Milton Handler et al. (University Casebook Ser.). 172p. 1983. pap. text ed. write for info. (ISBN 0-88277-163-9). Foundation Pr.

Trade Regulation Overseas: The National Laws. Corwin D. Edwards. LC 64-23357. 768p. 1965. 32.50 (ISBN 0-379-00224-8). Oceana.

Trade Routes & Commerce of the Roman Empire. M. P. Charlesworth. LC 74-77865. 320p. 1975. Repr. 15.00 (ISBN 0-89005-063-5). Ares.

Trade Routes & Commerce of the Roman Empire. M. P. Charlesworth. 320p. (Orig.). 1986. pap. 15.00 (ISBN 0-89005-444-4). Ares.

Trade Routes: The Manager's Network of Relationships. Robert E. Kaplan & Mignon Mazique. (Technical Report Ser.: No. 22). 26p. 1983. pap. 10.00 (ISBN 0-912879-20-3). Ctr Creat Leader.

Trade Routes to Riches. F. Andrew Wolf, Jr. 200p. 1986. 14.95 (ISBN 0-933703-11-2); pap. 9.95 (ISBN 0-933703-10-4). Loiry Pubs Hse.

Trade Routes to Sustained Economic Growth. Ed. by Amnuay Viravan. LC 87-3494. 178p. 1988. 45.00 (ISBN 0-312-01263-2). St Martin.

Trade Secret Litigation: A Course Handbook. Steven J. Stein. 209p. 1985. pap. 15.00 (G4-3773). PLI.

Trade Secrets. Gabrielle Hughes. 288p. 1987. pap. 3.95 (ISBN 0-8125-8398-1, Dist. by St Martin's Pr & Warner Pub Servs). Tor Bks.

Trade Secrets. Carla Neggers. (Temptation Ser.: No. 162). 224p. Date not set. pap. 2.25 (ISBN 0-317-63854-8). Harlequin Bks.

Trade Secrets. 1988. 19.95 (ISBN 0-87857-767-X); pap. 14.95 (ISBN 0-87857-768-8). Rodale Pr Inc.

Trade Secrets: Course Manual. Kenneth B. Weckstein & Brian B. Bannon. LC 86-219059. 199p. Date not set. price not set. Fed Pubns Inc.

Trade Secrets Handbook: Strategies & Techniques for Safeguarding Corporate Information. Dennis Unkovic. 229p. 1985. 39.95 (ISBN 0-13-925926-0, Busn). P-H.

Trade Secrets Law. Melvin F. Jager. LC 85-16654. 1985. looseleaf 115.00 (ISBN 0-87632-480-4). Clark Boardman.

Trade Secrets of Washington Journalists: How to Get the Facts about What's Going on in Washington. Steve Weinberg. LC 81-66854. (Illus.). 253p. 1981. pap. 7.95 (ISBN 0-87491-085-4). Acropolis.

Trade Secrets: Protection & Remedies. Roy E. Hofer. (Corporate Practice Ser.: No. 43). 1985. 92.00 (ISBN 0-317-55350-X). BNA.

Trade Secrets: Twenty-Five Proven Success Tools for Working, Dealing & Winning with People. Martha Langdon-Dahm. LC 85-82343. 211p. (Orig.). 1986. pap. 14.95 (ISBN 0-936585-00-5). Learn Deve.

Trade Shop Assistant. (Career Examination Ser.: C-3296). Date not set. pap. 14.00 (ISBN 0-8373-3296-6). Natl Learning.

Trade Shop Manager. Jack Rudman. (Career Examination Ser.: C-3043). (Cloth bdg. avail. on request). 1988. pap. 16.00 (ISBN 0-8373-3043-2). Natl Learning.

Trade Show & Exhibition Calendars: Where to Find or Locate. Data Notes Publishing Staff. LC 83-90725. 25p. 1985. pap. 2.00 (ISBN 0-911569-65-0, Pub by Data Notes). Prosperity & Profits.

Trade Show Basics. Norman Abelson. 140p. 1987. 22.95 (ISBN 0-913247-07-3); pap. 15.95. Commerce Comns.

Trade Shows & Professional Exhibits Directory: Supplement. 2nd ed. Ed. by Robert J. Elster. 300p. 1987. 80.00x (ISBN 0-8103-2124-6). Gale.

Trade Shows & Professional Exhibits Directory. 3rd ed. Martin Connors & Charity A. Dorgan. 1988. 159.95 (ISBN 0-8103-2748-1). Gale.

Trade Shows & Professional Exhibits Directory. 2nd ed. Ed. by Robert J. Elster. LC 84-6101. 915p. 1986. 150.00x (ISBN 0-8103-2113-0). Gale.

Trade Shows in the Marketing Mix: Where They Fit & How to Make Them Pay Off. Hanlon. 26.95 (ISBN 0-317-64302-9). Van Nos Reinhold.

Trade, Society & Politics in Bristol: 1500-1640, 2 vols. David H. Sacks. Ed. by Peter Mathias & Stuart Bruchey. LC 84-46011. (British Economic History Ser.). 987p. 1985. lib. bdg. 110.00 (ISBN 0-8240-6691-X). Garland Pub.

Trade, Stability, & Macroeconomics: Essays in Honor of Lloyd A. Metzler. Ed. by George Horwich & Paul A. Samuelson. (Economic Theory & Mathematical Economics Ser.). 1974. 34.50 (ISBN 0-12-356750-5). Acad Pr.

Trade, Stability, Technology & Equity in Latin America. Ed. by Moshe Syrquin. LC 82-13890. 1982. 29.95 (ISBN 0-12-680050-2). Acad Pr.

Trade, Tactics & Territory: Britain in the Pacific 1783-1823. Margaret Steven. (Illus.). 155p. (Orig.). 1983. pap. 15.00x (ISBN 0-522-84251-8, Pub. by Melbourne U Pr). Intl Spec Bk.

Trade Talks: America Better Listen! C. Michael Aho & Jonathan D. Aronson. 192p. 1985. pap. 9.95 (ISBN 0-87609-010-2). Coun Foreign.

Trade, Technology & Soviet-American Relations. Ed. by Bruce Parrott. LC 84-48549. (CSIS Publication Series on the Soviet Union in the 1980's: Midland Bks: No. 351). (Illus.). 414p. 1985. 35.00X (ISBN 0-253-36025-0, MB 351); pap. 17.50X (ISBN 0-253-20351-1). Ind U Pr.

Trade Tests in Education. Herbert A. Toops. LC 77-177702. (Columbia University. Teachers College. Contributions to Education: No. 115). Repr. of 1921 ed. 22.50 (ISBN 0-404-55115-7). AMS Pr.

Trade Through the Himalayas. Schuyler Camman. LC 74-90477. Repr. of 1951 ed. lib. bdg. 35.00x (ISBN 0-8371-3260-6, CAHI). Greenwood.

Trade Tokens Issued in the Seventeenth Century in England, Wales, Ireland, by Corporations, Merchants, Etc, 2 vols. William Boyne. Ed. by George C. Williamson. LC 77-80246. 1970. Repr. of 1889 ed. Set. 57.50 (ISBN 0-8337-0348-X). B Franklin.

Trade Tokens of Illinois. 2nd, rev. ed. Ore Vacketta. (Illus.). 576p. 1983. 29.95 (ISBN 0-912317-05-1). World Exo.

Trade, Traders & Trading in Rural Java. Jennifer Alexander. (Illus.). 240p. 1987. pap. 29.95 (ISBN 0-19-588865-0). Oxford U Pr.

Trade, Tribute, & Transportation: The Sixteenth-Century Political Economy of the Valley of Mexico. Ross Hassig. LC 84-40687. (Civilization of the American Indian Ser.: Vol. 171). (Illus.). 364p. 1985. 24.95x (ISBN 0-8061-1911-X). U of Okla Pr.

Trade Union & Social History. H. E. Musson. 224p. 1974. 29.50x (ISBN 0-7146-3031-4, F Cass Co). Biblio Dist.

Trade Union & the Common Weal. H. Phelps Brown. (Thank-Offering to Britain Fund Lectures). 1967. pap. 5.50 (ISBN 0-85672-340-1, Pub. by British Acad). Longwood Pub Group.

Trade Union Attitudes to Producer Co-Operatives: Papers 11-15 of the Plunkett Foundation Sixth Co-Operative Seminar, Somerville College, Oxford 1981. Ed. by The Plunkett Foundation for Co-Operative Studies Staff. 28p. 20.00x (ISBN 0-85042-043-1, Pub. by Plunkett Fondation). State Mutual Bk.

Trade Union Democracy in Western Europe. Walter Galenson. LC 75-45493. 96p. 1976. Repr. of 1961 ed. lib. bdg. 35.00x (ISBN 0-8371-8752-4, GATU). Greenwood.

Trade Union Handbook. 4th ed. Arthur Marsh. 450p. 1987. text ed. 70.00x (ISBN 0-566-02749-6, Pub. by Gower Pub England). Gower Pub Co.

Trade Union Handbook. 3rd ed. Ed. by Arthur Marsh. 430p. 1984. text ed. 59.50 (ISBN 0-566-02426-8). Gower Pub Co.

Trade Union Label. Ernest R. Spedden. LC 78-63935. (Johns Hopkins University. Studies in the Social Sciences. Twenty-Eighth Ser. 1910: 2). Repr. of 1910 ed. 24.50 (ISBN 0-404-61184-2). AMS Pr.

Trade Union Leadership in India: A Sociological Perspective. Edwin Masihi. 1986. 19.00x (ISBN 0-8364-1530-2, Pub. by Ajanta). South Asia Bks.

Trade Union Mergers & Labor Conglomerates. Gideon Chitayat. LC 79-2966. (Praeger Special Studies Ser.). 240p. 1979. 42.95 (ISBN 0-275-90340-0, C0340). Praeger.

Trade Union Movement in Africa: Promise & Performance. Wogu Ananaba. 1979. 27.50x (ISBN 0-312-81221-3). St Martin.

Trade Union Movement in Nigeria. Wogu Ananaba. LC 72-106044. 1970. 29.50 (ISBN 0-8419-0039-6, Africana). Holmes & Meier.

Trade Union Officers: A Study of Full-Time Officers, Branch Secretaries & Shop Stewards in British Trade Unions. Hugh A. Clegg et al. LC 61-65475. 1961. 18.50x (ISBN 0-674-89970-9). Harvard U Pr.

Trade Union Policies in the Massachusetts Shoe Industry. Thomas L. Norton. LC 78-76630. (Columbia University. Studies in the Social Sciences: No. 372). Repr. of 1932 ed. 27.50 (ISBN 0-404-51372-7). AMS Pr.

Trade Union Rank & File: Trades Councils in Britain, 1900-1940. Alan Clinton. 262p. 1977. 23.50x (ISBN 0-87471-982-8). Rowman.

Trade Union Situation & Industrial Relations in Austria: Report of an ILO Mission. xiii, 107p. (Orig.). 1986. pap. 14.00 (ISBN 92-2-105659-7). Intl Labour Office.

Trade Union Situation & Industrial Relations in Hungary. (Reports on the Trade Union Situation & Industrial Relations in Europe). 100p. 1985. pap. 11.40 (ISBN 92-2-103894-7, ILO345, ILO). UNIPUB.

Trading for Growth: The Next Round of Trade Negotiations. Gary C. Hufbauer & Jeffrey J. Schott. LC 85-18104. (Policy Analyses in International Economics Ser.: No. 11). 109p. (Orig.). 1985. pap. 10.00 (ISBN 0-88132-033-1). Inst Intl Eco.

Trading in Banking: The Impact of Technology & Deregulation on Competition. (Illus.). 137p. (Orig.). 1987. pap. 1000.00 (ISBN 0-939853-00-0). Wilke Org.

Trading in Commodities: An Investors Chronicle Guide. 4th ed. Ed. by C. W. Granger. 158p. 1983. 20.75 (ISBN 0-85941-179-6, Pub. by Woodhead-Faulkner); pap. 14.95 (ISBN 0-85941-178-8). Longwood Pub Group.

Trading in Commodity Futures. 2nd ed. Frederick F. Horn & Victor W. Farah. LC 78-27235. (Illus.). 373p. 1979. 29.95 (ISBN 0-13-925941-4). NY Inst Finance.

Trading in Currency Options. W. H. Sutton. 1988. 39.50 (ISBN 0-13-925983-X). Prentice Hall Pr.

Trading in Financial Futures. Paul Sarnoff. LC 84-40349. 144p. 1985. 25.00x (ISBN 0-87663-362-9). Universe.

Trading in Gold Futures. Robert Beale. 180p. 1985. 28.50 (ISBN 0-89397-219-3). Nichols Pub.

Trading in Oil Futures. Sally Clubley. 180p. 1986. 28.50 (ISBN 0-89397-220-7). Nichols Pub.

Trading in Options. 3rd ed. Geoffery Chamberlain. 160p. 1985. 41.25 (ISBN 0-85941-287-3, Pub. by Woodhead-Faulkner). Longwood Pub Group.

Trading in Options: An Investor's Guide to Making High Profits in the Traded Options Market. 2nd ed. Geoffrey Chamberlain. 153p. 1982. 24.75 (ISBN 0-85941-218-0, Pub. by Woodhead-Faulkner). Longwood Pub Group.

Trading in Soft Commodity Futures. Bernard C. Savaiko. 116p. 1986. 34.95 (ISBN 0-471-81778-3, Pub. by Wiley-Interscience). Wiley.

Trading: Inside the World's Leading Stock Exchanges. Susan Goldenberg. LC 85-17570. (Illus.). 352p. 1986. 22.95 (ISBN 0-15-191005-7). HarBraceJ.

Trading Life in Western & Central Africa. 2nd ed. John Whitford. 355p. 1967. Repr. of 1877 ed. 32.50x (ISBN 0-7146-1140-9, BHA-01140, F Cass Co). Biblio Dist.

Trading on Inside Information: Problems of Defining, Detecting, Prosecuting, & Defending Insider Trading Cases, Vol. 270. Practising Law Institute. 712p. 1984. pap. 15.00 (ISBN 0-317-27560-7, #H4-4956). PLI.

Trading Options on Futures: Markets, Methods, Strategies, & Tactics. John W. Labuszewski & John E. Nyhoff. LC 87-29656. 1988. 29.95 (ISBN 0-471-60676-6). Wiley.

Trading Peasants & Urbanization in Eighteenth-Century Russia: The Central Industrial Region. Daniel Morrison. Ed. by William H. McNeill & Barbara Jelavich. (Modern European History Ser.). 415p. 1987. lib. bdg. 60.00 (ISBN 0-8240-8059-9). Garland Pub.

Trading Places. Janet Quin-Harkin. (Sugar & Spice Ser.). 192p. (Orig.). 1987. pap. 2.50 (ISBN 0-8041-0027-6, Pub. by Ivy). Ballantine.

Trading Places. Janet Quin-Harkin. (Sugar & Spice Ser.). (gr. 6 up). 1987. pap. 2.50 (ISBN 0-317-57108-7, Ivy). Fawcett.

Trading Places: How We Allowed Japan to Take the Lead. Clyde V. Prestowitz, Jr. LC 87-47775. (Illus.). 304p. 1988. 19.95 (ISBN 0-465-08680-2). Basic.

Trading Rule That Can Make You Rich: Precision Bid Commodity Trading. Edward D. Dobson. LC 79-64620. (Illus.). 1979. 25.00 (ISBN 0-934380-03-1). Traders Pr.

Trading Secrets: An Insider's Account of the Scandal at the Wall Street Journal. R. Foster Winans. 320p. 1986. 17.95 (ISBN 0-312-81227-2). St Martin.

Trading Secrets: Seduction & Scandal at the Wall Street Journal. R. Foster Winans. 1987. pap. 4.95 (ISBN 0-312-90728-1). St Martin.

Trading Stocks on the Over-the-Counter Market. The New York Institute of Finance Staff. 250p. 1988. 21.50 (ISBN 0-13-926007-2, Busn). P-H.

Trading Technology: Europe & Japan in the Middle East. Thomas L. Ilgen & T. J. Pempel. LC 86-21197. 215p. 1986. lib. bdg. 38.95 (ISBN 0-275-92483-1, C2483). Praeger.

Trading the Future: The Concentration of Economic Power in Our Food System. James Wessel & Mort Hantman. (Illus.). 260p. 1983. pap. 8.95 (ISBN 0-935028-13-7). Inst Food & Develop.

Trading under Sail off Japan, 1860 to 1899. John B. Will & G. A. Lensen. 190p. 1968. 105.00x (Pub. by Han-Shan Tang Ltd). State Mutual Bk.

Trading Up: Surviving Success As a Woman Trader on Wall Street. Nancy B. Goldstone. LC 87-19975. 1988. 17.95 (ISBN 0-525-24621-5). Dutton.

Trading Water. Linda Davidson. (Endless Summer Ser.). (YA) (gr. 10 up). 1988. pap. 2.95 (ISBN 0-317-69526-6). Ivy Books.

Trading with China: A Practical Guide. C. MacDougall. 1979. text ed. 49.95 (ISBN 0-07-084531-X). McGraw.

Trading with Saudi Arabia: A Guide to the Shipping, Trade, Investment & Tax Laws of Saudi Arabia. Leslie A. Glick. LC 79-55002. 620p. 1980. text ed. 57.50x (ISBN 0-916672-43-3, Pub. by Allanheld). Rowman.

Trading with the Future & Futures Trading. Leonardo Auernheimer. Ed. by Steve Pejovich & Henry Dethloff. (Series on Public Issues: No. 14). 23p. 1985. pap. 2.00 (ISBN 0-86599-050-6). Ctr Educ Res.

Traditio: An Introduction to the Latin Language & Its Influence. Patricia A. Johnston. 663p. 1988. text ed. write for info. (ISBN 0-02-360560-X). Macmillan.

Tradition. A. F. Moritz. LC 85-43203. (Princeton Series of Contemporary Poets). 128p. 1986. text ed. 23.50x (ISBN 0-691-06667-1); pap. 9.95 (ISBN 0-691-01427-2). Princeton U Pr.

Tradition. Edward Shils. LC 80-21643. 320p. 1981. lib. bdg. 25.00x (ISBN 0-226-75325-5). U of Chicago Pr.

Tradition. Edward Shils. LC 80-21643. viii, 334p. 1981. pap. 10.95x (ISBN 0-226-75326-3). U of Chicago Pr.

Tradition: A History of the Presidency of Clemson University. Ed. by Donald M. McKale. LC 87-31382. 252p. 1988. 35.00 (ISBN 0-86554-296-1, MUP/H262). Mercer Univ Pr.

Tradition & Adaptation: Life in a Modern Yucatan Maya Village. Irwin Press. LC 75-71. (Illus.). 288p. 1975. lib. bdg. 46.95 (ISBN 0-8371-7954-8, PYM/). Greenwood.

Tradition & Argument in Classical Indian Linguistics. Johannes Bronkhorst. 1986. lib. bdg. 39.50 (ISBN 90-277-2040-1, Pub. by Reidel Holland). Kluwer-Academic.

Tradition & Authority in Science & Theology. Alexander Thomson. (Theology & Science at the Frontiers of Knowledge Ser.: Vol. 4). 160p. 1986. 17.00 (ISBN 0-7073-0452-0, Pub. by Scot Acad Pr). Longwood Pub Group.

Tradition & Avant Garde. J. Milojkovic-Djuric. 1984. 20.00 (ISBN 0-317-18775-9). East Eur Quarterly.

Tradition & Avant Garde: Literature & Arts in Serbian Culture, 1900-1918. Jelena Milojkovic-Djuric. (East European Monographs: No. 234). 224p. 1988. 25.00 (ISBN 0-88033-131-3). East Eur Quarterly.

Tradition & Avante-Garde: The Arts in Serbian Culture Between the Two World Wars. Jelena Milojkovic-Djuric. 175p. 1984. 21.00x (ISBN 0-88033-052-X). East Eur Quarterly.

Tradition & Change. Arthur Waugh. LC 79-93385. (Essay Index Reprint Ser). 1919. 19.00 (ISBN 0-8369-1316-7). Ayer Co Pubs.

Tradition & Change: Essays in Honour of Marjorie Chibnall. Ed. by Diana Greenway & Christopher Holdsworth. 412p. 1985. 52.50 (ISBN 0-521-25793-X). Cambridge U Pr.

Tradition & Change in a Turkish Town. 2nd ed. Paul J. Magnarella. (Illus.). 210p. 1982. 18.95x (ISBN 0-87073-153-X); pap. 11.95 (ISBN 0-87073-152-1). Schenkman Bks Inc.

Tradition & Change in Jewish Experience: B.G. Rudolph Lectures in Judaic Studies. Ed. by A. Leland Jamison. 1978. pap. 5.95x (ISBN 0-8156-8097-X). Syracuse U Pr.

Tradition & Change in Swedish Education. L. Boucher. LC 81-19948. (International Studies in Education & Social Change). (Illus.). 280p. 1982. text ed. 34.00 (ISBN 0-08-025240-0, PBL). Pergamon.

Tradition & Change in Three Generations of Japanese Americans. John W. Connor. LC 76-28995. 382p. 1977. 25.95x (ISBN 0-88229-288-9). Nelson-Hall.

Tradition & Change on the Northwest Coast: The Makah, Nuu-chah-nulth, Southern Kwakiutl, & Nuxalk. Ruth Kirk. (Illus.). 256p. 1988. pap. 19.95 (ISBN 0-295-96628-9). U of Wash Pr.

Tradition & Composition in the Epistula Apostolorum. Julian Hills. LC 88-45436. (Harvard Dissertations in Religion Ser.). 1988. pap. text ed. 12.95 (ISBN 0-8006-7078-7). Fortress.

Tradition & Composition in the Parables of Enoch. David W. Suter. LC 79-17441. (Society of Biblical Literature. Dissertation Ser.: No. 47). 1979. pap. 9.95 (ISBN 0-89130-336-7, 060147). Scholars Pr GA.

Tradition & Contract: The Problem of Order. Elizabeth Colson. LC 74-82603. 152p. 1974. 19.95x (ISBN 0-202-01131-3). Aldine de Gruyter.

Tradition & Creativity: Contributions to East Asian Civilization. Ed. by Ching-I Tu. 192p. (Orig.). 1988. pap. 19.95 (ISBN 0-88738-738-1). Transaction Bks.

Tradition & Creativity in Tribal Art. Daniel Biebuyck. LC 69-12457. 1969. 47.50x (ISBN 0-520-01509-6); pap. 7.95x (ISBN 0-520-02487-7). U of Cal Pr.

Tradition & Creativity: The Engelhard of Konrad von Wurzburg - Its Strucutre & its Sources. Peter H. Oettli. (Australian & New Zealand Studies in German Language & Literature: Vol. 14). 1986. text ed. 20.55 (ISBN 0-8204-0302-4). P Lang Pubs.

Tradition & Design in the Iliad. Sir Cecil M. Bowra. LC 77-3065. 1977. Repr. of 1930 ed. lib. bdg. 35.00x (ISBN 0-8371-9561-6, BOTD). Greenwood.

Tradition & Desire: From David to Delacroix. Norman Bryson. (Studies in French). (Illus.). 220p. 1984. 44.50 (ISBN 0-521-24193-6). Cambridge U Pr.

Tradition & Desire: From David to Delacroix. Norman Bryson. (Cambridge Studies in French). (Illus.). 228p. 1987. pap. 17.95 (ISBN 0-521-33562-0). Cambridge U Pr.

Tradition & Dissent: A Rhetoric Reader. 2nd ed. Florence Greenberg & Anne P. Heffley. LC 76-145858. 602p. 1971. pap. write for info. (ISBN 0-02-346620-0). Macmillan.

Tradition & Dynamics in Small-Farm Agriculture: Economic Studies in Asia, Africa & Latin America. Ed. by Robert D. Stevens. (Illus.). 275p. 1977. 13.95x (ISBN 0-8138-0055-2). Iowa St U Pr.

Tradition & Dynamism Among Afghan Refugees: A Report on Income-Generating Activities for Afghan Refugees in Pakistan. 174p. (Orig.). 1984. pap. 11.40 (ISBN 92-2-103517-4, ILO296, ILO). UNIPUB.

Tradition & Enlightenment in the Tuscan Academies: 1690-1800. Eric W. Cochrane. LC 60-14232. pap. 73.00 (ISBN 0-317-09759-8, 2020045). Bks Demand UMI.

Tradition & Experiment in Modern Sculpture. Charles Seymour. LC 70-91378. (Contemporary Art Ser). Repr. of 1949 ed. 14.00 (ISBN 0-405-00737-X). Ayer Co Pubs.

Tradition & Experiment in Present-Day Literature. facs. ed. City Literary Institute of London Staff. LC 68-20290. (Essay Index Reprint Ser). 1968. Repr. of 1929 ed. 15.00 (ISBN 0-8369-0307-2). Ayer Co Pubs.

Tradition & Experiment in Present Day Literature. T. S. Eliot. lib. bdg. 69.95 (ISBN 0-87968-044-X). Gordon Pr.

Tradition & Experiment in Present-Day Literature. London City Literary Institute. LC 68-761. (Studies in Comparative Literature, No. 35). 1972. Repr. of 1929 ed. lib. bdg. 49.95x (ISBN 0-8383-0544-X). Haskell.

Tradition & Experiment in the Poetry of James Thomson, 1700-1748. R. R. Agrawal. Ed. by James Hogg. (Romantic Reassessment ser.). 273p. (Orig.). 1981. pap. 15.00 (ISBN 3-7052-0560-9, Pub. by Salzburg Studies). Longwood Pub Group.

Tradition & Gigli. Edgar F. Herbert-Caesari. 6.95 (ISBN 0-8008-7827-2, Crescendo). Taplinger.

Tradition & History of the Early Churches of Christ in Central Europe. Hans Grimm. pap. 1.00 (ISBN 0-88027-095-0). Firm Foun Pub.

Tradition & Hugh Walpole. Clemence Dane. LC 71-113332. 256p. 1973. Repr. of 1930 ed. 26.00x (ISBN 0-8046-1733-3, Pub by Kennikat). Assoc Faculty Pr.

Tradition & Innovation: General Education & the Reintegration of the University, a Columbia Report. Robert L. Belknap & Richard Kuhns. LC 77-3315. 130p. 1977. 23.00x (ISBN 0-231-04322-8); pap. 12.00x (ISBN 0-231-04323-6). Columbia U Pr.

Tradition & Innovation in Contemporary Austria. Ed. by Kurt Steiner. 1982. write for info. Sposs.

Tradition & Innovation in Contemporary Austria. Ed. by Kurt Steiner et al. LC 82-60869. 222p. 1982. pap. 15.00x (ISBN 0-930664-05-1). SPOSS.

Tradition & Innovation in Folk Literature. Wolfgang Mieder. LC 86-21206. (Illus.). 314p. 1987. 25.00x (ISBN 0-87451-387-1). U Pr of New Eng.

Tradition & Innovation in New Deal Art. Belisario R. Contreras. LC 81-65861. (Illus.). 256p. 1983. 35.00 (ISBN 0-8387-5032-X). Bucknell U Pr.

Tradition & Innovation: Progressivism in Primary Education since 1945' see Curriculum Change in the Primary School since 1945: Dissemination of the Progressive Ideal.

Tradition & Innovation: The Idea of Civilization As Culture & Its Significance. H. T. Wilson. (International Library of Phenomenology & Moral Sciences). 256p. 1984. 35.00x (ISBN 0-7102-0009-9). Routledge Chapman & Hall.

Tradition & Interpretation. G. W. Anderson. 1979. 38.00x (ISBN 0-19-826315-5). Oxford U Pr.

Tradition & Interpretation: A Study of the Use & Application of Formulaic Language in the So-Called Ebed YHWH-Psalms. Inger Ljung. (Coniectanea Biblica. Old Testament Ser.: No. 12). (Orig.). 1987. pap. 25.00x (ISBN 0-317-65796-8). Coronet Bks.

Tradition & Interpretation in the New Testament: Essays in Honor of E. Earle Ellis. Gerald F. Hawthorne & Otto Betz. 416p. (Orig.). 1988. pap. 35.00 (ISBN 0-8028-3644-5). Eerdmans.

Tradition & Jazz. facs. ed. Fred L. Pattee. LC 68-22937. (Essay Index Reprint Ser). 1968. Repr. of 1925 ed. 20.00 (ISBN 0-8369-0776-0). Ayer Co Pubs.

Tradition & Modern Japan. P. G. O'Neal. 320p. 1985. 75.00x (ISBN 0-904404-36-6, Pub. by Norbury Pubns Ltd). State Mutual Bk.

Tradition & Modernity: The Role of Traditionalism in the Modernization Process. Jesse G. Lutz & Salah S. El-Shakhs. LC 81-43464. 234p. 1982. lib. bdg. 30.50 (ISBN 0-8191-2326-9). U Pr of Amer.

Tradition & Modernization. Francis M. Deng. LC 78-140526. 448p. 1986. pap. 14.95x (ISBN 0-300-03756-2). Yale U Pr.

Tradition & Modernization in Japanese Culture. Ed. by Donald H. Shively. LC 69-18071. (Studies in the Modernization of Japan, No. 5). (Illus.). 1971. pap. 17.50x (ISBN 0-691-00020-4). Princeton U Pr.

Tradition & Originality in Roman Poetry. Gordon Williams. 820p. 1986. 85.00x (ISBN 0-19-814347-8). Oxford U Pr.

Tradition & Politics: The Religious Parties of Israel. Gary S. Schiff. LC 77-5723. 267p. 1977. 25.00x (ISBN 0-8143-1580-1). Wayne St U Pr.

Tradition & Progress. facs. ed. Gilbert Murray. LC 68-20323. (Essay Index Reprint Ser). 1922. 17.00 (ISBN 0-8369-0728-0). Ayer Co Pubs.

Tradition & Progress. Gilbert Murray. LC 68-20323. (Essay Index Reprint Ser.). 221p. Repr. of 1922 ed. lib. bdg. 16.00 (ISBN 0-8290-0490-4). Irvington.

Tradition & Progress, & Other Historical Essays in Culture, Religion & Politics. Ross Hoffman. LC 68-26213. 1968. Repr. of 1938 ed. 23.50x (ISBN 0-8046-0211-5, Pub by Kennikat). Assoc Faculty Pr.

Tradition & Progress in Modern Legal Culture: Proceedings of the 11th World Congress on Philosophy of Law & Social Philosophy, Helsinki. Ed. by Stig Jorgensen et al. 256p. (Orig.). 1985. pap. 48.50x (ISBN 3-515-04458-2, Pub. by Franz Steiner). Coronet Bks.

Tradition & Progress in the African Village: Non-Capitalist Reform of Rural Communities in Mali - The Sociological Problems. Klaus Ernst. LC 74-22292. 350p. 1977. 32.50x (ISBN 0-312-81235-3). St Martin.

Tradition & Re-Interpretation in Jewish & Early Christian Literature: Essays in Honour of Jurgen C. H. Lebram. J. W. Van Henten et al. (Studia Post-Biblica Ser.: Vol. 36). viii, 313p. 1986. 76.25 (ISBN 90-04-07752-9, Pub. by E J Brill). Heinman.

Tradition & Reaction in Modern Poetry. Laurence Binyon. LC 74-5434. 1926. lib. bdg. 8.50 (ISBN 0-8414-3159-0). Folcroft.

Tradition & Reform in Education. Stephen Tonsor. LC 73-82779. 262p. 1974. 9.95 (ISBN 0-87548-124-8). Open Court.

Tradition & Reform in the Teaching of English: A History. Arthur N. Applebee. LC 74-82650. 298p. (Orig.). 1974. pap. 10.75 (ISBN 0-8141-5501-4). NCTE.

Tradition & Renewal: Contemporary Art in the German Democratic Republic. David Elliott. (Illus.). 64p. 1985. pap. 12.50 (ISBN 0-87663-867-1). Universe.

Tradition & Renewal: Essays on Twentieth-Century Latin American Literature & Culture. Ed. by Merlin H. Forster. LC 74-31179. (Office of International Programs & Studies Ser: Vol. 2). 248p. 1975. 22.95 (ISBN 0-252-00440-X). U of Ill Pr.

Tradition & Renewal in "La Gloria de Don Ramiro". Gabriella Ibieta. 27.50 (ISBN 0-916379-29-9). Scripta.

Tradition & Revolt. Joyce Milton & Wendy B. Murphy. 174p. 1980. 100.00x (Pub. by Han-Shan Tang Ltd). State Mutual Bk.

Tradition & Revolution. J. Krishnamurti. 357p. 1972. 9.95. Asia Bk Corp.

Tradition & Technique in el Libro del Cavallero Zifar. Roger M. Walker. (Serie A: Monagrafias, XXXVI). 252p. (Orig.). 1974. pap. 18.00 (ISBN 0-900411-86-4, Pub. by Tamesis Bks Ltd). Longwood Pub Group.

Tradition & the Founding Fathers. Louis B. Wright. LC 74-23551. 1975. 14.95x (ISBN 0-8139-0621-0). U Pr of Va.

Tradition & the Modern World: Reformed Theology in the Nineteenth Century. B. A. Gerrish. LC 78-4982. 1978. lib. bdg. 20.00x (ISBN 0-226-28866-8). U of Chicago Pr.

Tradition & Theme in the "Annals" of Tacitus. rev. ed. Judith Ginsberg. Ed. by W. R. Connor. LC 80-2651. (Monographs in Classical Studies). 1981. lib. bdg. 20.00 (ISBN 0-405-14038-X). Ayer Co Pubs.

Tradition & Transformation in Religious Education. Ed. by Padraic O'Hare. LC 78-27506. 114p. (Orig.). 1979. pap. 6.95 (ISBN 0-89135-016-0). Religious Educ.

Tradition As Openness to the Future: Essays in Honor of Willis W. Fisher. Ed. by Fred O. Francis & Raymond P. Wallace. (Illus.). 236p. (Orig.). 1984. lib. bdg. 26.25 (ISBN 0-8191-3722-7); pap. text ed. 13.00 (ISBN 0-8191-3723-5). U Pr of Amer.

Tradition Becomes Innovation: Modern Religious Architecture in America. Bartlett Hayes. LC 82-18581. (Illus.). 176p. 1982. 27.50 (ISBN 0-8298-0635-0); pap. 12.95 (ISBN 0-8298-0624-5). Pilgrim NY.

Tradition, Change, & Modernity. S. N. Eisenstadt. LC 83-11273. 384p. 1983. Repr. of 1973 ed. text ed. 33.50 (ISBN 0-89874-642-6). Krieger.

Tradition Chevaleresque des Arabes. Boutros G. Wacyf. LC 79-8374. Repr. of 1919 ed. 29.50 (ISBN 0-404-18356-5). AMS Pr.

Tradition, Conflict & Change: Perspectives on the American Revolution. Ed. by Richard E. Brown & Don E. Fehrenbacher. (Studies in Social Discontinuity Ser.). 1977. 19.95 (ISBN 0-12-137650-8). Acad Pr.

Traditional Healer. Hakim Chisht. 416p. (Orig.). pap. 16.95 (ISBN 0-89281-225-7, Healing Arts Pr). Inner Tradit.

Traditional Healer: A Comprehensive Guide to the Principles & Practice of Unani Herbal Medicine. Hakim G. Chishti. 416p. 1988. pap. 16.95 (ISBN 0-317-66766-1, Healing Arts Pr). Inner Tradit.

Traditional Healing: New Science or New Colonialism?, Essays in Critique of Medical Anthropology. Ed. by Phillip Singer. LC 75-18490. (Trado-Medic). 250p. 1977. 17.50. Conch Mag.

Traditional Healing: New Science or New Colonialism? Essays in Critique of Medical Anthropology. Ed. by Phillip Singer. LC 75-18490. (Traditional Healing Ser.: Vol. 1). 1977. 17.50; pap. text ed. 10.00x (ISBN 0-914970-35-6). Trado-Medic.

Traditional Herbal Medicine in Northern Thailand. Viggo Brun & Trond Schumaker. (Comparative Studies of Health Systems & Medical Care: No. 19). 1986. 48.00x (ISBN 0-520-05271-4). U of Cal Pr.

Traditional History of the Jie of Uganda. John Lamphear. (Oxford Studies in African Affairs). (Illus.). 1976. 49.00x (ISBN 0-19-821692-0). Oxford U Pr.

Traditional Home & Herbal Remedies. Jan De Vries. 160p. 1987. 40.00x (ISBN 1-85158-011-5, Pub. by Mainstream Scotland); pap. 24.75x (ISBN 1-85158-012-3). State Mutual Bk.

Traditional Home & Herbal Remedies. Jan De Vries. (By Appointment Only Ser.). 158p. 1988. pap. 9.95 (ISBN 0-317-68285-7, Pub. by Mainstream Edinburgh). David & Charles.

Traditional Home Plans. 2nd ed. Ed. by Garlinghouse Co. Staff. LC 85-70893. (Illus.). 112p. 1985. pap. 2.95 (ISBN 0-938708-14-7). L F Garlinghouse Co.

Traditional Home Plans, Vol. III. Jeff Spring. 1986. pap. 4.95 (ISBN 0-9614407-0-8). Drafting Design.

Traditional Home Weaving & Decorated Textiles in Bulgaria. Gina Krusteva-Nozarova. 132p. 1981. 49.00x (ISBN 0-317-61411-8, Pub. by Collets (UK)). State Mutual Bk.

Traditional Houses in Baghdad. J. Warren & J. Fethi. 22p. (Eng. & Arabic.). 1982. 95.00x (ISBN 0-317-39174-7, Pub. by Luzac & Co Ltd). State Mutual Bk.

Traditional Hungarian Songs. Tr. by W. D. Snodgrass from Hungarian. (Fine Press Poetry Ser.). (Illus.). 1978. zaan paper covers, ltd. signed ed. 60.00 (ISBN 0-931356-01-6). Seluzicki Fine Bks.

Traditional Ideology & Ethics among the Southern Luo. A. B. Ocholla-Ayayo. 248p. 1976. pap. 24.50 (ISBN 0-8419-9719-5, Africana). Holmes & Meier.

Traditional India: Structure & Change. Ed. by Milton Singer. (American Folklore Society Bibliographical & Special Ser.: No. 10). 356p. 1959. pap. 9.95x (ISBN 0-292-73504-9). U of Tex Pr.

Traditional Indian Bags, Pouches & Containers. Monte Smith & Michele Van Sickle. (Traditional Indian Crafts Ser.). (Illus.). 96p. (Orig.). pap. cancelled (ISBN 0-943604-15-X). Eagles View.

Traditional Indian Bead & Leather Crafts. Monte Smith & Michele Van Sickle. (Traditional Indian Crafts Ser.). (Illus.). 100p. (Orig.). 1987. pap. 7.95 (ISBN 0-943604-14-1). Eagles View.

Traditional Indian Crafts. Monte Smith. (Illus.). 96p. (Orig.). 1987. pap. 7.95 (ISBN 0-943604-13-3). Eagles View.

Traditional Indian Melodies for the Sitar. Harold Schram. 1969. pap. 5.00 (ISBN 0-686-09077-2, 61478-930). Peer-Southern.

Traditional Indian Stories About Bhaskarananda see India & Her Miracle Feast-Come & Enjoy Yourself.

Traditional Indian Stories About Devadas Maharaj see India & Her Miracle Feast-Come & Enjoy Yourself.

Traditional Indian Stories About Shayama Charan Lahiri see India & Her Miracle Feast-Come & Enjoy Yourself.

Traditional Indian Stories About Troilanga Swami see India & Her Miracle Feast-Come & Enjoy Yourself.

Traditional Interpretation of the Apocalypse of St. John in the Ethiopian Orthodox Church. Roger W. Cowley. LC 80-19834. (University of Cambridge Oriental Publications Ser.: No. 33). 480p. 1983. 80.00 (ISBN 0-521-24561-3). Cambridge U Pr.

Traditional Irish Literature & Its Backgrounds: A Brief Introduction. rev. ed. George B. Saul. LC 71-120997. 115p. 1970. 14.50 (ISBN 0-8387-7686-8). Bucknell U Pr.

Traditional Irish Music for the Bagpipe. David Rickard. 60p. (Orig.). 1987. pap. 7.95 (ISBN 0-85342-802-6, Pub. by Mercier Pr Ireland). Irish Bks Media.

Traditional Irish Recipes. George L. Thomson. (Illus.). 88p. 1982. pap. 9.95 (ISBN 0-88289-339-4, Pub. by Canongate Pub Scotland). Pelican.

Traditional Islam in the Modern World. Seyyed H. Nasr. 320p. 1987. text ed. 39.95 (ISBN 0-7103-0177-4). Routledge Chapman & Hall.

Traditional Japanese Annual Brothel Festival. Jitsupenshva. (Asian Folklore & Social Life Monographs: Vol. 99). (Japanese.). 1977. 14.00x (ISBN 0-89986-329-9). Oriental Bk Store.

Traditional Japanese Design Motifs. Illus. by Joseph D'Addetta. (Pictorial Archive Ser.). (Illus.). 96p. pap. 4.00 (ISBN 0-486-24629-9). Dover.

Traditional Japanese Furniture. Kazuko Koizumi. LC 85-40067. (Illus.). 224p. 1986. 70.00 (ISBN 0-87011-722-X). Kodansha.

Traditional Japanese Furniture. Kazuko Koizumi. 128p. 1986. 240.00x (ISBN 0-317-69172-4, Pub. by Han-Shan Tang Ltd). State Mutual Bk.

Traditional Japanese Stencil Designs. Ed. by Clarence Hornung. (Pictorial Archive Ser.). 128p. 1985. pap. 5.95 (ISBN 0-486-24791-0). Dover.

Traditional Jewellery & Ornament of the Sudan. Clara Semple. (Illus.). 200p. 1987. lib. bdg. 69.95x (ISBN 0-7103-0242-8, Pub. by Routledge UK). Routledge Chapman & Hall.

Traditional Jewish Family in Historical Perspective. Jacob Katz. 1983. pap. 1.00 (ISBN 0-87495-048-1). Am Jewish Comm.

Traditional Jewish Law of Sale. Stephen Passamaneck. 1983. 20.00x (ISBN 0-686-87788-8). Ktav.

Traditional Jewish Law of Sale: Shulhan Arukh Hoshen Mishpat, Chapters 189-240. Joseph Ben Ephraim Karo. Tr. by Stephen M. Passamaneck. LC 83-4287. (Hebrew Union College Monographs No. 9). 1983. 20.00x (ISBN 0-87820-408-3). Hebrew Union Coll Pr.

Traditional Karate-Do-Okinawa Goju Ryu: Performances of the Kata, Vol. 2. Morio Higaonna. (Illus.). 200p. (Orig.). 1986. pap. 16.95 (ISBN 0-87040-596-9). Japan Pubns USA.

Traditional Karatedo: Okinawa Goju-Ryu, Vol. 1. Morio Higaonna. (Fundamental Techniques Ser.). (Illus.). 200p. (Orig.). 1985. pap. 15.95 (ISBN 0-87040-595-0). Japan Pubns USA.

Traditional Knitting. Sheila McGregor. (Illus.). 64p. 1983. pap. 9.95 (ISBN 0-7134-4336-7, Pub. by Batsford England). David & Charles.

Traditional Knitting Patterns from Scandinavia, the British Isles, France, Italy & Other European Countries. James Norbury. LC 73-79490. (Illus.). 240p. 1973. pap. 5.95 (ISBN 0-486-21013-8). Dover.

Traditional Knitting Patterns from Scandinavia, the British Isles, France, Italy & Other European Countries. James Norbury. (Illus.). 15.75 (ISBN 0-8446-5071-4). Peter Smith.

Traditional Knitting Patterns of Ireland, Scotland, & England. Gwyn Morgan. (Illus.). 128p. 1981. pap. 9.95 (ISBN 0-312-81314-7). St Martin.

Traditional Korean Art. Kim Won-yong et al. Ed. by The Korean National Commission for UNESCO. (Korean Art, Folklore, Language, & Thought Ser.: No. 1). (Illus.). viii, 153p. 1983. 20.00 (ISBN 0-89209-014-6). Pace Intl Res.

Traditional Korean Cooking: Snacks & Basic Side Dishes. Chin-hwa Noh. (Illus.). 64p. 1985. 12.50x (ISBN 0-930878-48-5). Hollym Intl.

Traditional Korean Legal Attitudes. Bong D. Chun et al. LC 80-620036. (Korean Research Monographs: No. 2). 101p. 1980. pap. 4.00x (ISBN 0-912966-30-0). IEAS.

Traditional Korean Music. Yi Hye-gu et al. Ed. by Korean National Commission for UNESCO. (Korean Art, Folklore, Language, & Thought Ser.: No. 3). (Illus.). viii, 228p. 1983. 20.00 (ISBN 0-89209-016-2). Pace Intl Res.

Traditional Korean Painting. Ch'oe Sun-u et al. Ed. by The Korean National Commission for UNESCO. (Korean Art, Folklore, Language, & Thought Ser.: No. 2). (Illus.). viii, 177p. 1983. 20.00 (ISBN 0-89209-015-4). Pace Intl Res.

Traditional Korean Theatre. Oh-Kon Cho. Tr. by Oh-Kon Cho from Korean. LC 87-71272. (Studies in Korean Religions & Culture). (Illus.). 350p. 1988. 40.00 (ISBN 0-89581-876-0). Asian Human Pr.

Traditional Land Tenure & Land Use Systems in the Design of Agricultural Projects. Raymond Noronha & Francis J. Lethem. (Working Paper: No. 561). 54p. 1983. 5.00 (ISBN 0-8213-0168-3, WP 0561). World Bank.

Traditional Life, Culture and Literature in Ghana. Ed. by J. M. Assimeng. (Africa in Transition Ser.). 200p. 1976. 17.50 (ISBN 0-914970-26-7). Conch Mag.

Traditional Literatures of the American Indian: Texts & Interpretations. Ed. by Karl Kroeber. LC 80-183338. x, 162p. 1981. 16.50x (ISBN 0-8032-2704-3); pap. 5.95x (ISBN 0-8032-7753-9, BB 765, Bison). U of Nebr Pr.

Traditional Logic. A. C. Bethel. 332p. (Orig.). 1982. pap. text ed. 14.00 (ISBN 0-8191-2616-0). U Pr of Amer.

Traditional Management of Seaweeds in the District of Leon. P. Arzel. (Fisheries Technical Papers: No. 249). 49p. 1985. pap. 7.50 (ISBN 92-5-102144-9, F2738, FAO). UNIPUB.

Traditional Marbling. rev. ed. Iris Nevins. 1988. pap. 15.00 (ISBN 0-9620400-0-2). Iris Nevins.

Traditional Math: Restored, Simplified, Condensed, Brought up to Date, Made Relevant, Programmed & All Those Good Things. John A. Hornof. (Illus.). 1977. pap. 19.95 (ISBN 0-918094-01-1); answer bk 1.00 (ISBN 0-918094-02-X). Bedous.

Traditional Medical Systems in East Asia. Seung-pyo Hong. (Bibliographies in Technology & Social Change Ser.: No. 3). 44p. (Orig.). 1988. pap. text ed. 6.00 (ISBN 0-945271-06-9). ISU-TSCP.

Traditional Medicine. Sheila Cosminsky & Ira Harrison. LC 82-49196. (Reference Library of Social Science). 275p. 1983. lib. bdg. 43.00 (ISBN 0-8240-9181-7). Garland Pub.

Traditional Medicine: Implications of Mental Health, Public Health, Maternal & Child Health & Family Planning. Ira E. Harrison & Sheila Cosminsky. LC 75-24105. (Reference Library of Social Science: Vol. 19). 150p. 1976. lib. bdg. 36.00 (ISBN 0-8240-9970-2). Garland Pub.

Traditional Medicine in Contemporary China. Ed. by Nathan Sivin. (Science, Medicine, & Technology in East Asia Ser.: No. 2). 491p. 1987. write for info. (ISBN 0-89264-073-1); pap. write for info. (ISBN 0-89264-074-X). U of Mich Ctr Chinese.

Traditional Model of Educational Excellence: Dunbar High School of Little Rock Arkansas. Faustine C. Jones. LC 81-6507. 222p. 1981. pap. 6.95 (ISBN 0-88258-098-1). Howard U Pr.

Traditional Moral Values in the Age of Technology. Hans Mark et al. (Andrew R. Cecil Lectures on Moral Values in a Free Society: Vol. VIII). 210p. 1987. text ed. 16.50x (ISBN 0-292-78098-2). U of Tex Pr.

Traditional Music in Ireland. Tomas O'Canainn. (Illus.). 1978. pap. 10.00 (ISBN 0-7100-0021-9). Routledge Chapman & Hall.

Traditional Music in Modern Java. Judith Becker. LC 80-19180. (Illus.). 1980. text ed. 30.00x (ISBN 0-8248-0563-1). UH Pr.

Traditional Music of America. Ira W. Ford. LC 78-2026. (Music Reprint Ser., 1978). 1978. Repr. of 1940 ed. lib. bdg. 49.50 (ISBN 0-306-77588-3). Da Capo.

Traditional Music of Thailand. David Morton. LC 70-142048. 1976. 43.00x (ISBN 0-520-01876-1). U of Cal Pr.

Traditional Music of the Lao: Kaen Playing & Mawlum Singing in Northeast Thailand. Terry E. Miller. LC 84-22538. (Contributions in Intercultural & Comparative Studies: No. 13). xv, 333p. 1985. lib. bdg. 48.95 (ISBN 0-313-24765-X, MKP/). Greenwood.

Traditional Ninja Weapons & Ninjutsu Techniques. Charles Daniel. LC 85-52270. 147p. (Orig.). 1986. pap. 7.95 (ISBN 0-86568-075-2, 108). Unique Pubns.

Traditional Norfolk Recipes. Geoffrey M. Dixon. 1984. 15.00x (ISBN 0-906791-24-3, Pub. by Minimax Bks UK). State Mutual Bk.

Traditional Ojibwa Religion & Its Historical Changes. Christopher Vecsey. LC 83-72209. (Memoirs Ser.: Vol. 152). 1983. 12.00 (ISBN 0-87169-152-3). Am Philos.

Traditional Papermaking & Paper Cult Figures of Mexico. Alan R. Sandstrom & Pamela E. Sandstrom. LC 85-40947. (Illus.). 336p. 1986. 24.95 (ISBN 0-8061-1972-1). U of Okla Pr.

Traditional Patchwork Patterns. Carol B. Grafton. (Illus.). 14.75 (ISBN 0-8446-5038-2). Peter Smith.

Traditional Patchwork Patterns: Full-Size Cut-Outs & Instructions for 12 Quilts. Carol B. Grafton. (Illus.). 64p. (Orig.). 1974. pap. 4.50 (ISBN 0-486-23015-5). Dover.

Traditional Pottery of Alabama: (Distributed for the Montgomery Museum of Fine Arts) Henry Willett & Joey Brackner. (Illus.). 70p. 1984. pap. 7.95 (ISBN 0-89280-020-8). U of Tenn Pr.

Traditional Pottery of Guatemala. Ruben E. Reina & Robert M. Hill, II. LC 77-17455. (Texas Pan American Ser.). (Illus.). 323p. 1978. 35.00 (ISBN 0-292-78024-9). U of Tex Pr.

Traditional Pottery Techniques of Pakistan: Field & Laboratory Studies. Owen S. Rye & Clifford Evans. LC 75-619168. (Smithsonian Contributions to Anthropology Ser.: no. 21). pap. 75.30 (ISBN 0-317-28428-2, 2020314). Bks Demand UMI.

Traditional Prayer Book for Sabbath & Festivals. 10.00 (ISBN 0-317-70172-X). Behrman.

Traditional Prayerbook for Shabbath & Festivals. rev. ed. 879p. 1960. 10.00x (ISBN 0-87441-118-1). Behrman.

Traditional Recipes of Laos. Phia Sing. (Illus.). 318p. 1981. 20.00x (ISBN 0-907325-02-5, Pub. by Prospect England); pap. 15.95x. U Pr of Va.

Traditional Rural Institutions & Their Implications for Development Planning: Studies from Hamadan Province of Iran. 15p. 1980. pap. 5.00 (ISBN 92-808-0148-1, TUNU115, UNU). UNIPUB.

Traditional Samplers. Sarah Don. LC 85-41068. (Illus.). 128p. 1986. 16.95 (ISBN 0-670-80732-X). Viking.

Traditional Sculpture from Upper Volta. (Illus.). 48p. (Orig.). 1978. pap. text ed. 5.00 (ISBN 0-89192-279-2, Pub. by African Am Inst). Interbk Inc.

Traditional Sculpture from Upper Volta. (Illus.). 1979. 3.00 (ISBN 0-686-27122-X). Mus African Art.

Traditional Sculpture from Upper Volta. (Illus.). 1979. pap. 3.00 catalog supplement (ISBN 0-89192-276-8, Pub. by Museum of African Art). Interbk Inc.

Traditional Songs of the Maori. Mervyn McLean & Margaret Orbell. 1975. text ed. 32.00x (ISBN 0-19-647976-2). Oxford U Pr.

Traditional Stepdancing from Lakeland. J. Flett & T. Flett. 104p. (Orig.). 1979. pap. text ed. 14.95 (ISBN 0-85418-123-7). Princeton Bk Co.

Traditional Symbols & the Contemporary World. Frederick Dillistone. LC 73-164751. (Bampton Lectures: 1968). 1973. text ed. 15.00x (ISBN 0-8401-0546-0). A R Allenson.

Traditional Tatting Patterns. Rita Weiss. 48p. (Orig.). 1986. pap. 2.95 (ISBN 0-486-25066-0). Dover.

Traditional Technology - Obstacle or Resource? Bamboo-Cement Rain-Water Collectors & Cooking Stoves. 18p. 1981. pap. 5.00 (ISBN 92-808-0261-5, TUNU156, UNU). UNIPUB.

Traditional Technology, a Neglected Component of Appropriate Technology. 27p. 1981. pap. 5.00 (ISBN 92-808-0250-X, TUNU112, UNU). UNIPUB.

Traditional Textiles of Tunisia & Related North African Weaving. Irmtraud Reswick. (Illus.). 272p. 1985. pap. 24.95 (ISBN 0-295-96281-X). U of Wash Pr.

Traditional Theater of Japan. Yoshinobu Inoura & Toshio Kawatake. LC 80-29635. (Illus.). 320p. 1981. 20.00 (ISBN 0-8348-0161-2). Weatherhill.

Traditional Themes & the Homeric Hymns. Cora A. Sowa. 250p. 1983. 20.00x (ISBN 0-86516-037-6). Bolchazy-Carducci.

Traditional Theory of Literature. Ray F. Livingston. LC 62-10830. pap. 49.50 (ISBN 0-317-41714-2, 2055889). Bks Demand UMI.

Traditional Tibet: A Selected & Annotated Bibliography of European Language Materials on the Pre-Communist Period. Gay D. Henderson. LC 76-24763. (Reference Library of Social Science Ser.: Vol. 28). 1976. lib. bdg. 28.00. Garland Pub.

Traditional Tole Painting: With Authentic Antique Designs & Working Diagrams for Stenciling & Brush-Stroke Painting. Roberta R. Blanchard. LC 77-78208. (Illus.). 1977. pap. 4.50 (ISBN 0-486-23531-9). Dover.

Traditional Tole Painting, with Authentic Antique Designs & Working Diagrams for Stenciling & Brush-Stroke Painting. Roberta R. Blanchard. 15.50 (ISBN 0-8446-5559-7). Peter Smith.

Traditional Tunes of the Child Ballads, 4 vols. Bertrand H. Bronson. Incl. Vol. 1. 1959; Vol. 2. 1962 (ISBN 0-691-09105-6). 87.00x (ISBN 0-686-66603-8); Vol. 3. 1966 (ISBN 0-691-09106-4); Vol. 4. 1972 (ISBN 0-691-09115-3). 87.00x (ISBN 0-686-66605-4). o.p. 210.00 set (ISBN 0-685-23096-1); 96.50x; 96.50x. Princeton U Pr.

Traditional Use of Malay Plants & Herbs. J. Kloppenburg-Versteegh. Tr. by Aileen Kaufman from Dutch. LC 79-89939. Orig. Title: Het Gebruik Van Indische Planten. (Illus.). 1985. cancelled (ISBN 0-86164-152-3, Pub by Momenta Publishing Ltd U. K.). Hunter Hse.

Traditional Values & Contemporary Federation Practices. Bernard Reisman. 1986. write for info. Coun Jewish Feds.

Traditional Victorian Cookbook. Katrina Lees & Richard Lees. LC 86-7011. (Illus.). 160p. (Orig.). Date not set. plastic comb bd. 8.95 (ISBN 0-89708-148-X, 86-070111). And Bks.

Traditional Victorian White Work to Knit & Crochet for the Home. Shelagh Hollingsworth. (Illus.). 128p. 1988. pap. 12.95x (ISBN 0-312-01253-5). St Martin.

Traditional Warwickshire Recipes. Jo Price & Merlin Price. 1984. 15.00x (ISBN 0-906791-31-6, Pub. by Minimax Bks UK). State Mutual Bk.

Traditional Woodblock Prints of Japan. Seiichiro Takahashi. LC 74-162683. (Heibonsha Survey of Japanese Art Ser.: Vol. 22). (Illus.). 176p. 1972. 20.00 (ISBN 0-8348-1002-6). Weatherhill.

Traditionalism, Nationalism, & Feminism: Women Writers of Quebec. Ed. by Paula G. Lewis. LC 84-10854. (Contributions in Women's Studies: No. 53). (Illus.). xli, 280p. 1985. lib. bdg. 36.95 (ISBN 0-313-24510-X, LTF/). Greenwood.

Traditionalism vs Modernism at Death: Allegorical Tales of Africa. John E. Njoku. (African Studies: Vol. 11). 175p. 1988. lib. bdg. 39.95 (ISBN 0-88946-188-0). E Mellen.

Traditionality & Genre in Middle English Romance. Carol Fewster. 196p. 1987. 54.00 (ISBN 0-85991-229-9, Pub. by Boydell & Brewer). Longwood Pub Group.

Traditionally Black Institutions of Higher Education: 1860 to 1982. Susan T. Hill. (Illus.). 132p. (Orig.). 1985. pap. 4.75 (ISBN 0-318-19910-6, S/N 065-000-00242-6). USGPO.

Traditionally Yours. Gail Kelley. LC 86-43230. 168p. 1987. pap. text ed. 8.95 (ISBN 0-89390-103-2). Resource Pubns.

Traditionary Anecdotes of Shakespeare. John Dowdall. Ed. by J. Payne Collier. LC 70-164782. Repr. of 1838 ed. 19.00 (ISBN 0-404-02165-4). AMS Pr.

Traditions. Alan Ebert & Janice Rotchstein. 1983. pap. 3.95 (ISBN 0-553-22838-2). Bantam.

Traditions & Change on the Northwest Coast: The Makah, Nuu-chah-nulth, Southern Kwakiutl & Nuxalk. Ruth Kirk. (Illus.). 256p. 1986. 19.95 (ISBN 0-295-96396-4). U of Wash Pr.

Traditions & Memories of American Yachting. William P. Stephens. LC 80-83038. pap. 98.00 (2026241). Bks Demand UMI.

Traditions & Superstitions of the New Zealanders. 2nd ed. Edward Shortland. LC 75-35270. Repr. of 1856 ed. 32.50 (ISBN 0-404-14439-X). AMS Pr.

Traditions & Trends in Indian Music. V. Agarwal. 82p. 1975. 7.95. Asia Bk Corp.

Traffic-Safety Education of Young Children. T. Rothengatter. 1981. pap. text ed. 28.00 (ISBN 90-265-0363-6, Pub. by Swets & Zeitlinger Netherlands). Hogrefe Intl.
Traffic Safety of Children. OECD Staff. (Road Transport Research Ser.). 110p. 1983. pap. 13.00x (ISBN 92-64-12468-3). OECD.
Traffic Safety of Elderly Road Users. OECD. (Road Transport Research Ser.). 184p. 1985. pap. 15.00x (ISBN 0-318-18489-3). OECD.
Traffic Supervisor. Jack Rudman. (Career Examination Ser.: C-2627). (Cloth bdg. avail. on request). pap. 14.00 (ISBN 0-8373-2627-3). Natl Learning.
Traffic Technician. Jack Rudman. (Career Examination Ser.: C-1522). (Cloth bdg. avail. on request). pap. 14.00 (ISBN 0-8373-1522-0). Natl Learning.
Traffic Technician I. Jack Rudman. (Career Examination Ser.: C-2335). (Cloth bdg. avail. on request). pap. 14.00 (ISBN 0-8373-2335-5). Natl Learning.
Traffic Technician II. Jack Rudman. (Career Examination Ser.: C-2336). (Cloth bdg. avail. on request). pap. 14.00 (ISBN 0-8373-2336-3). Natl Learning.
Traffic Technician III. Jack Rudman. (Career Examination Ser.: C-1887). (Cloth bdg. avail. on request). pap. 16.00 (ISBN 0-8373-1887-4). Natl Learning.
Traffic Technician Trainee. (Career Examination Ser.: C-3269). Date not set. pap. 12.00 (ISBN 0-8373-3269-9). Natl Learning.
Traffic Tickets, Fines & Other Annoying Things. Tim Matheson. 72p. 1984. pap. 4.95 (ISBN 0-8065-0883-3, Pub. by Citadel Pr). Lyle Stuart.
Traffic Transit. 8.00 (ISBN 0-317-65070-X). Am Consul Eng.
Traffic Violations. Pedro Pietri. 120p. 1983. pap. 7.95 (ISBN 0-943862-06-X). Waterfront NJ.
Traffic, with Ghosts. Rosanne Coggeshall. 13.95 (ISBN 0-395-36508-2); pap. 7.95 (ISBN 0-395-36509-0). HM.
Traffic World's Questions & Answers, Vol. 28. Ed. by Traffic World Editors. 576p. 1982. text ed. 24.50 (ISBN 0-87408-024-X). Intl Thom Trans Pr.
Traffic World's Questions & Answers, Vol. 29. Colin Barrett. 1985. 35.00 (ISBN 0-87408-035-5). Intl Thom Trans Pr.
Trafficking in Drug Users: Professional Exchange Networks in the Control of Deviance. James R. Beniger. LC 83-5251. (ASA Rose Monograph). 224p. 1984. 34.50 (ISBN 0-521-25753-0); pap. 12.95 (ISBN 0-521-27680-2). Cambridge U Pr.
Trafficking in Women & Children in India: Sexual Exploitation & Sale. M. Rita Rozario. 1988. 22.00x (Pub. by Uppal Pub Hse New Delhi). South Asia Bks.
Traffics & Discoveries. Rudyard Kipling. Ed. by Sarah Wintle. 336p. 1987. pap. 5.95 (ISBN 0-14-043286-8). Penguin.
Trafiquants Italiens Dans L'orient Hellenique. Jean Hatzfeld. LC 75-7322. (Roman History Ser.). (Fr.). 1975. Repr. 31.00x (ISBN 0-405-07086-1). Ayer Co Pubs.
Tragaluz: Experimento en dos Partes. Patricia W. O'Conner et al. 224p. (Span.). 1977. pap. text ed. write for info. (ISBN 0-02-388890-3, Pub. by Scribner). Macmillan.
Tragedi vom Grossen Abentmal see Saemtliche Schriften.
Tragedia Josephina. M. De Carvajal. Ed. by S. E. Gillet. (Elliott Monographs in the Romance Languages & Literature Ser). Repr. of 1932 ed. 28.00 (ISBN 0-527-02631-X). Kraus Repr.
Tragedian: An Essay On-Junius Brutus Booth. T. R. Gould. LC 70-87122. 190p. 1868. 15.00 (ISBN 0-405-08567-2, Pub. by Blom). Ayer Co Pubs.
Tragedian in Spite of Himself see Sea Gull.
Tragedias. Esquilo. pap. 1.95 (ISBN 0-685-11603-4). French & Eur.
Tragedie du Roi Christophe. Aime Cesaire. pap. 8.95 (ISBN 0-685-35628-0). French & Eur.
Tragedie of Cleopatra 1611. Samuel Daniel & M. Lederer. (Material for the Study of the Old English Drama Series 1: Vol. 31). pap. 11.00 (ISBN 0-8115-0280-5). Kraus Repr.
Tragedie of Cymbeline: Reprint from 1st Folio, 1623, with Collations of the 2nd, 3rd, & 4th Folios. William Shakespeare. Ed. by W. J. Craig. (New Shakespeare Society London Ser. 2: No. 11). pap. 23.00 (ISBN 0-8115-0236-8). Kraus Repr.
Tragedie of Darius. William Alexander. LC 72-6936. (English Experience Ser.: No. 293). 80p. Repr. of 1603 ed. 25.00 (ISBN 90-221-0293-9). Walter J Johnson.
Tragedie of Lodovisk Sforza, Duke of Millan: From Quarto of 1628. Robert Gomersall. Ed. by B. R. Pearn. (Material for the Study of the Old English Drama Ser.: No. 2, Vol. 8). pap. 16.00 (ISBN 0-8115-0301-1). Kraus Repr.
Tragedie Sans Masque: Notes de Theatre. Henry De Montherlant. 16.50 (ISBN 0-685-36990-0). French & Eur.
Tragedies, 2 vols. Aeschylus. Incl. Vol. 1. Suppliant Maidens, Persians, Prometheus, Seven Against Thebes (ISBN 0-674-99160-5); Vol. 2. Agamemnon, Libation Bearers, Eumenides' Fragments (ISBN 0-674-99161-3). (Loeb Classical Library: No. 145-146). 13.95x ea. Harvard U Pr.
Tragedies, 2 vols. Lucius Annaeus Seneca. (Loeb Classical Library: No. 62, 78). 13.95x. Vol. 1 (ISBN 0-674-99069-2). Vol. 2 (ISBN 0-674-99087-0). Harvard U Pr.
Tragedies. Lucius Annaeus Seneca. Ed. by Otto Zwierlein. (Classical Texts Ser.). 448p. 1986. 18.95x (ISBN 0-19-814657-4). Oxford U Pr.
Tragedies, 2 Vols. Sophocles. (Loeb Classical Library: No. 20-21). 13.95x ea. Vol. 1 (ISBN 0-674-99023-4). Vol. 2 (ISBN 0-674-99024-2). Harvard U Pr.
Tragedies de la Foi. Romain Rolland. 296p. 1970. 7.95 (ISBN 0-686-55277-6). French & Eur.
Tragedies from Drug Therapy: For Health Professionals. Ronald B. Stewart. (Illus.). 130p. 1985. 20.50 (ISBN 0-398-05105-4). C C Thomas.
Tragedies of Ennius: The Fragments. Quintus Ennius. Ed. by H. D. Jocelyn. LC 67-11525. (Cambridge Classical Texts & Commentaries Ser.: No. 10). pap. 120.30 (ISBN 0-317-29380-X, 2024481). Bks Demand UMI.
Tragedies of Euripides in English Verse, 3 vols. Euripides. Ed. by Arthur S. Way. 54.00 (ISBN 0-8369-6973-1, 7854). Ayer Co Pubs.
Tragedies of George Chapman. Ennis Rees. 1979. Repr. of 1954 ed. lib. bdg. 18.00x (ISBN 0-374-96767-9, Octagon). Hippocrene Bks.
Tragedies of Herod & Mariamne. Maurice J. Valency. LC 70-8450. Repr. of 1940 ed. 19.50 (ISBN 0-404-06750-6). AMS Pr.
Tragedies of L. Annaeus Seneca, the Philospher. Lucius Annaeus Seneca. LC 70-158326. 1976. Repr. of 1702 ed. 43.00 (ISBN 0-404-54136-4). AMS Pr.
Tragedies of Sophocles. Sophocles. Tr. by Richard C. Jebb. LC 71-39209. (Select Bibliographies Reprint Ser). Repr. of 1904 ed. 19.00 (ISBN 0-8369-6811-5). Ayer Co Pubs.
Tragedies of Vittorio Alfieri, 2 vols. Vittorio Alfieri. LC 75-98802. 1970. Repr. of 1876 ed. Vol. 2. lib. bdg. 22.50 (ISBN 0-8371-2884-6, ALTC). Greenwood.
Tragediia Grenada. V. F. Zharov. 48p. 1984. 29.00x (ISBN 0-317-40816-X, Pub. by Collets (UK)). State Mutual Bk.
Tragedy. William M. Dixon. LC 74-194357. 1974. Repr. of 1924 ed. lib. bdg. 25.00 (ISBN 0-8414-3798-X). Folcroft.
Tragedy. Clifford Leech. (Critical Idiom Ser.: Vol. 1). 1969. pap. 5.50x (ISBN 0-416-15720-3, NO. 2291). Routledge Chapman & Hall.
Tragedy & after: Euripides, Shakespeare, & Goethe. Ekbert Faas. 233p. 1984. 29.95x (ISBN 0-7735-0416-8). McGill-Queens U Pr.
Tragedy & After: Euripides, Shakespeare, Goethe. Ekbert Faas. 233p. 1986. pap. 14.95x (ISBN 0-7735-0605-5). McGill-Queens U Pr.
Tragedy & Civilization: An Interpretation of Sophocles. Charles Segal. LC 80-19765. (Modern Classical Lectures: No. 26). 544p. 1981. text ed. 32.50x (ISBN 0-674-90206-8). Harvard U Pr.
Tragedy & Comedy. Walter Kerr. (Quality Paperbacks Ser.). 350p. 1985. pap. 9.95 (ISBN 0-306-80249-X). Da Capo.
Tragedy & Comedy in the Bible. Ed. by J. Cheryl Exum. (Semeia Ser.: No. 32). 1985. pap. 9.95 (06 20 32). Scholars Pr GA.
Tragedy & Hope. Carroll Quigley. 1975. Repr. of 1966 ed. 25.00 (ISBN 0-913022-14-4). Angriff Pr.
Tragedy & Hope: A History of the World in Our Time. Caroll Quigley. 1348p. Date not set. 23.00 (ISBN 0-317-53209-X). Noontide.
Tragedy & Innocence. Harvey Birenbaum. LC 82-23828. (Illus.). 176p. (Orig.). 1983. lib. bdg. 27.50 (ISBN 0-8191-2991-7); pap. text ed. 12.00 (ISBN 0-8191-2992-5). U Pr of Amer.
Tragedy & Social Evolution. Eva Figes. 1976. 10.95 (ISBN 0-7145-3516-8). pap. 6.95 (ISBN 0-7145-3639-3). Riverrun NY.
Tragedy & the Event Continuum. J. R. Kantor. 1983. 15.00 (ISBN 0-911188-35-5). Principia Pr.
Tragedy & the Jacobean Temper: The Major Plays of John Webster. Richard Bodtke. Ed. by James Hogg. 264p. (Orig.). 1972. pap. 15.00 (ISBN 3-7052-0301-0, Pub. by Salzburg Studies). Longwood Pub Group.
Tragedy & Theory: The Problem of Conflict since Aristotle. Michelle Gellrich. 240p. 1988. text ed. 29.50 (ISBN 0-691-06738-4). Princeton U Pr.
Tragedy & Tragi-Comedy in the Plays of John Webster. Jacqueline Pearson. 151p. 1980. 27.50x (ISBN 0-389-20030-1, 06803). B&N Imports.
Tragedy & Truth: Studies in the Development of a Neoclassical Discourse. Timothy J. Reiss. LC 80-10413. 320p. 1980. 39.00x (ISBN 0-300-02461-4). Yale U Pr.
Tragedy as a Critique of Virtue: The Novel & Ethical Reflection. John D. Barbour. LC 83-20028. (Scholars Press Studies in the Humanities). 214p. 1984. text ed. 20.95 (ISBN 0-89130-661-7, 00 01 02); pap. text ed. 13.95 (ISBN 0-89130-662-5). Scholars Pr GA.
Tragedy at Tiverton. Raymond Paul. 320p. 1985. pap. 3.50 (ISBN 0-345-32262-2). Ballantine.
Tragedy in Eden: Original Sin in the Theology of Jonathan Edwards. C. Samuel Storms. LC 85-17866. 328p. 1986. lib. bdg. 28.75 (ISBN 0-8191-4936-5); pap. text ed. 13.50 (ISBN 0-8191-4937-3). U Pr of Amer.
Tragedy in the Church. W. Tozer. Ed. by Gerald Smith. 1978. pap. 3.45 (ISBN 0-87509-215-2). Chr Pubns.
Tragedy: Irony & Faith. John Tinsley. 75p. (Orig.). 1985. pap. 9.95x (ISBN 0-317-26992-5). Wyndham Hall.
Tragedy: Modern Essays in Criticism. Ed. by Laurence A. Michel & Richard B. Sewall. LC 77-13779. 1978. Repr. of 1963 ed. lib. bdg. 45.50x (ISBN 0-8371-9876-3, MITR). Greenwood.
Tragedy of a State: A Study of Jacobean Drama. J. W. Lever. (Methuen Library Reprints Ser.). 1980. 45.00x (ISBN 0-416-30550-4, NO. 2220). Routledge Chapman & Hall.
Tragedy of a Troubador (on Browning) E. H. Thomson. LC 77-24846. 1974. Repr. of 1914 ed. lib. bdg. 20.50 (ISBN 0-8414-8640-9). Folcroft.
Tragedy of Afghanistan: A First-Hand Account. Raja Anwar. Tr. by Khalid Hasan. 384p. 1988. 29.95 (ISBN 0-86091-208-6, Pub. by Verso). Routledge Chapman & Hall.
Tragedy of American Diplomacy. rev. 2nd ed. William A. Williams. 312p. 1972. pap. 9.95 (ISBN 0-385-29070-5, Delta). Dell.
Tragedy of American Diplomacy. William A. Williams. 1988. pap. 9.95 (ISBN 0-393-30493-0). Norton.
Tragedy of Antony & Cleopatra see also Antony & Cleopatra.
Tragedy of Black Lung: Federal Compensation for Occupational Disease. Peter S. Barth. LC 87-8332. 1987. 20.95 (ISBN 0-317-59126-6); pap. 13.95 (ISBN 0-88099-044-9). W E Upjohn.
Tragedy of Bolivia: A People Crucified. Alberto Ostria Gutierrez. Tr. by Eithne Golden from Span. LC 81-2424. Orig. Title: Pueblo en la Cruz. 224p. 1981. Repr. of 1958 ed. lib. bdg. 35.00 (ISBN 0-313-22935-X, GUTB). Greenwood.
Tragedy of Caesar's Revenge: Caesar & Pompey. Ed. by F. S. Boas. LC 82-45760. (Malone Society Reprint Ser.: No. 27). 1911. 40.00 (ISBN 0-404-63027-8). AMS Pr.
Tragedy of Capital Tax. Faik Okte. Tr. by Geoffrey Cox from Turkish. 144p. 1987. 39.95 (ISBN 0-7099-1964-6, Pub. by Croom Helm UK). Routledge Chapman & Hall.
Tragedy of Central Europe. rev. ed. Stephen Borsody. LC 80-51032. (Yale Russian & East European Publications Ser.: No. 2). (Illus.). xviii, 274p. 1981. 18.50 (ISBN 0-936586-01-X). Slavica.
Tragedy of Central Europe: Nazi & Soviet Conquest & Aftermath. Stephen Borsody. LC 80-51032. (Russian & East European Publications Ser.: No. 2). 274p. 1980. 18.50. Yale Russian.
Tragedy of Children under Nazi Rule. Kiryl Sosnowski. LC 81-19506. 1983. Repr. of 1962 ed. 40.00x (ISBN 0-86527-342-1). Fertig.
Tragedy of Chile. Robert J. Alexander. LC 77-91101. (Contributions in Political Science: No. 8). 1978. lib. bdg. 36.95 (ISBN 0-313-20034-3, ATC/). Greenwood.
Tragedy of Claudius Tiberius Nero. Ed. by W. W. Greg. LC 82-45778. (Malone Society Reprint Ser.: No. 47). Repr. of 1914 ed. 40.00 (ISBN 0-404-63047-2). AMS Pr.
Tragedy of Coriolanus see also Coriolanus.
Tragedy of Cymbeline see also Cymbeline.
Tragedy of Dido Queen of Carthage see Life of Marlowe.
Tragedy of Enlightenment. P. Connerton. LC 79-16102. (Cambridge Studies in the History & Theory of Politics). 1980. 37.50 (ISBN 0-521-22842-5). Cambridge U Pr.
Tragedy of Europe. Francis Neilson. 100.00 (ISBN 0-87700-003-4). Revisionist Pr.
Tragedy of Europe, Vols. I-V. Francis Neilson. 3503p. 1986. Set. 150.00 (ISBN 0-317-53294-4). Noontide.
Tragedy of German-America. John A. Hawgood. 1940. 15.00x (ISBN 0-686-17392-9). R S Barnes.
Tragedy of German-America: The Germans in the United States of America During the Nineteenth Century & after. John A. Hawgood. LC 71-129401. (American Immigration Collection, Ser. 2). 1970. Repr. of 1940 ed. 18.50 (ISBN 0-405-00554-7). Ayer Co Pubs.
Tragedy of Hamlet: A Critical Edition of the Second Quarto. Ed. by Thomas M. Parrott & Hardin Craig. LC 75-42328. 256p. 1976. Repr. of 1938 ed. 30.00x (ISBN 0-87752-172-7). Gordian.
Tragedy of Hamlet, Prince of Denmark see also Hamlet.
Tragedy of Hoffman. Henry Chettle. Ed. by Harold Jenkins & Charles Sisson. LC 82-45696. (Malone Society Reprint Ser.: No. 93). 80p. Date not set. Repr. of 1631 ed. price not set (ISBN 0-404-63093-6). AMS Pr.
Tragedy of Jane Shore. Nicholas Rowe. Ed. by Harry W. Pedicord. LC 73-85439. (Regents Restoration Drama Ser.). xxviii, 97p. 1974. 11.95x (ISBN 0-8032-0381-0); pap. 2.95x (ISBN 0-8032-5381-8, BB 277, Bison). U of Nebr Pr.
Tragedy of John Ruskin. Amabel Williams-Ellis. 1973. Repr. of 1929 ed. 30.00 (ISBN 0-8274-0560-X). R West.
Tragedy of Julia Agrippina, Empresse of Rome, with an Essay on Thomas May & the Tradegy of Nero. Thomas May. Ed. by F. E. Schmid. (Material for the Study of the Old English Drama Ser.: No. 1, Vol. 43). pap. 30.00 (ISBN 0-8115-0292-9). Kraus Repr.
Tragedy of Julius Caesar see also Julius Caesar.
Tragedy of Julius Caesar see Bibliographies to Supplement the New Variorum Editions of Shakespeare.
Tragedy of Julius Caesar: A Bibliography to Supplement the New Variorum Edition of 1913. Ed. by John W. Velz. x, 58p. 1977. 15.00 (ISBN 0-317-34925-2, Z122). Modern Lang.
Tragedy of King Lear see also King Lear.
Tragedy of King Lear. James S. Bransom. LC 71-153306. Repr. of 1934 ed. 10.50 (ISBN 0-404-01063-6). AMS Pr.
Tragedy of Libby & Andersonville Prison Camps. Daniel P. Brown. LC 79-54263. (U. S. History Civil War Ser. Ii: No. 1102). (Illus.). 1980. pap. 3.25x (ISBN 0-930860-01-2). Golden West Hist.
Tragedy of Little Hintock: New Light on Thomas Hardy's Novel, 'The Woodlanders' in Booker Memorial Studies Edited by Hill Shine. Carl Weber. 1950. Repr. 25.00 (ISBN 0-8274-3642-4). R West.
Tragedy of Locrine. Ronald B. McKerrow. LC 82-45743. (Malone Society Reprint Ser.: No. 8). Repr. of 1908 ed. 40.00 (ISBN 0-404-63008-1). AMS Pr.
Tragedy of Lynching. Arthur F. Raper. LC 72-90191. (Mass Violence in America Ser). Repr. of 1933 ed. 17.00 (ISBN 0-405-01334-5). Ayer Co Pubs.
Tragedy of Lynching. Arthur F. Raper. LC 69-14943. (Criminology, Law Enforcement, & Social Problems Ser.: No. 25). (With a new intro. by the author). 1969. Repr. of 1933 ed. 16.00x (ISBN 0-87585-025-1). Patterson Smith.
Tragedy of Macbeth see also Macbeth.
Tragedy of Man. Imre Madach. 59.95 (ISBN 0-8490-1225-2). Gordon Pr.
Tragedy of Mesopotamia. George Buchanan. LC 71-180324. (Mid-East Studies Ser.). Repr. of 1938 ed. 14.00 (ISBN 0-404-56218-3). AMS Pr.
Tragedy of Messalina: The Roman Emperesse. Nathanael Richard. Ed. by A. Skemp. (Material for the Study of the Old English Drama Ser.: No. 1, Vol. 30). pap. 24.00 (ISBN 0-8115-0279-1). Kraus Repr.
Tragedy of Miriam: The Faire Queene of Iewry. Elizabeth Faukland. LC 82-45773. (Malone Society Reprint Ser.: No. 42). Repr. of 1914 ed. 40.00 (ISBN 0-404-63042-1). AMS Pr.
Tragedy of Morant Bay: A Narrative of the Disturbances in the Island of Jamaica in 1865. facs. ed. Edward B. Underhill. LC 73-157378. (Black Heritage Library Collection Ser). 1895. 18.00 (ISBN 0-8369-8816-7). Ayer Co Pubs.
Tragedy of Nero. Thomas Jones. Ed. by Elliott M. Hill & Stephen Orgel. LC 78-66763. (Renaissance Drama Ser.). 1979. lib. bdg. 40.00 (ISBN 0-8240-9745-9). Garland Pub.
Tragedy of Nijinsky. Anatole Bourman. LC 70-98822. Repr. of 1936 ed. lib. bdg. 35.00x (ISBN 0-8371-2965-6, BOTN). Greenwood.
Tragedy of Othello, the Moor of Venice see also Othello.
Tragedy of Paraguay. Gilbert Phelps. LC 74-21750. 300p. 1975. 26.00 (ISBN 0-312-81340-6). St Martin.
Tragedy of Pelee: A Narrative of Personal Experience & Observation in Martinique. George Kennan. LC 69-18984. (Illus.). 1970. Repr. of 1902 ed. 35.00 (ISBN 0-8371-0932-9, KEP&). Greenwood.
Tragedy of Philotas by Samuel Daniel. Lawrence Michel. (Yale Studies in English: No. 110). xiv, 185p. 1970. Repr. of 1949 ed. 25.00 (ISBN 0-208-00923-X, Archon). Shoe String.
Tragedy of Philotas by Samuel Daniel. Lawrence Michel. 1949. 22.50x (ISBN 0-686-83831-9). Elliots Bks.
Tragedy of Political Science. David Ricci. LC 84-3510. 352p. 1987. pap. 13.95x (ISBN 0-300-03760-0, Y-631). Yale U Pr.
Tragedy of Political Science: Politics, Scholarship, & Democracy. David M. Ricci. LC 84-3510. 352p. 1984. 35.00t (ISBN 0-300-03088-6). Yale U Pr.
Tragedy of Quebec. Robert Sellar. LC 72-1429. (Select Bibliographies Reprint Ser.). 1972. Repr. of 1907 ed. 17.25 (ISBN 0-8369-6836-0). Ayer Co Pubs.
Tragedy of Quebec: The Expulsion of its Protestant Farmers. Robert Sellar. LC 73-90925. (Social History of Canada: No. 17). pap. 104.80 (2026388). Bks Demand UMI.
Tragedy of Rejecting Salvation. John MacArthur, Jr. (John MacArthur's Bible Studies). (Orig.). 1986. pap. 3.95 (ISBN 0-8024-5346-5). Moody.
Tragedy of Richard II. Robert J. Myers. LC 73-13017. 128p. 1973. pap. 4.95 (ISBN 0-87491-372-1). Acropolis.
Tragedy of Romeo & Juliet. William Shakespeare. 1978. reader's theatre packet of 23 scripts & directions 57.50x (ISBN 0-88020-084-7). Coach Hse.
Tragedy of Sir Francis Bacon. Harold Bayley. LC 70-133281. (English Biography Ser., No. 31). 1970. Repr. of 1902 ed. lib. bdg. 49.95x (ISBN 0-8383-1180-6). Haskell.

Tragedy of Sir John French. George H. Cassar. LC 82-49302. (Illus.). 320p. 1984. 35.00 (ISBN 0-87413-241-X). U Delaware Pr.

Tragedy of Sir John Van Olden Barnavelt. John Fletcher & Philip Massinger. LC 82-45736. (Malone Society Reprint Ser.: No. 140). Repr. of 1979 ed. 40.00 (ISBN 0-404-63141-X). AMS Pr.

Tragedy of Sohrab & Rostam from the Persian National Epic, the Shahname of Abol-Qasem Ferdowsi. Abol-Quasem Ferdowsi. Tr. by Jerome W. Clinton. 215p. 1988. 25.00x (ISBN 0-295-96577-0); pap. 12.50x (ISBN 0-295-96582-7). U of Wash Pr.

Tragedy of Tancred & Gismond. Robert Wilmot et al. LC 82-45777. (Malone Society Reprints Ser.: No. 46). Repr. of 1914 ed. 40.00 (ISBN 0-404-63046-4). AMS Pr.

Tragedy of Tenaya. Allan Shields. (Indian Culture Ser.). (gr. 6). 1974. 2.00 (ISBN 0-89992-043-8). Coun India Ed.

Tragedy of the Baltic States: A Report from Official Documents & Eyewitnesses' Stories. John A. Swettenham. LC 79-2924. (Illus.). 216p. 1981. Repr. of 1952 ed. 21.60 (ISBN 0-8305-0093-6). Hyperion Conn.

Tragedy of the Blackfoot. Walter McClintock. (Illus.). 53p. 1970. pap. 5.00 (ISBN 0-916561-63-1). Southwest Mus.

Tragedy of the Chinese Revolution. 2nd. rev ed. Harold R. Isaacs. LC 61-11101. 1961. 39.50x (ISBN 0-8047-0415-5); pap. 12.95x (ISBN 0-8047-0416-3). Stanford U Pr.

Tragedy of the Jews in Hungary: Essays & Documents. Ed. by Randolph L. Braham. (East European Monographs: No. 208). 288p. 1986. 30.00 (ISBN 0-88033-105-4). East Eur Quarterly.

Tragedy of the Korosko. Conan A Doyle. LC 80-67706. (Conan Doyle Centennial Ser.). (Illus.). 202p. 1983. 12.95 (ISBN 0-934468-47-8). Gaslight.

Tragedy of the Lady Jane Gray. Nicholas Rowe. Ed. by James Hogg. (Poetic Drama & Poetic Theory Ser.). 94p. (Orig.). 1980. pap. 15.00 (ISBN 3-7052-0892-6, Pub. by Salzburg Studies). Longwood Pub Group.

Tragedy of the Moisty Morning. Jessica A. Salmonson. (Illus.). 1978. saddlestitch 2.95 (ISBN 0-914580-10-8). Angst World.

Tragedy of the Moon. Isaac Asimov. 1978. pap. 1.50 (ISBN 0-440-18999-3). Dell.

Tragedy of the Negro in America. facsimile 2nd ed. P. Thomas Stanford. LC 75-178483. (Black Heritage Library Collection). Repr. of 1897 ed. 19.50 (ISBN 0-8369-8932-5). Ayer Co Pubs.

Tragedy of the Reformation: Being the Authentic Narrative of the History & Burning of the "Christianismi Restitution", 1553, with a Succinct Account of the Theological Controversy Between Michael Servetus, Its Author, & the Reformer, John Calvin. David Cuthbertson. LC 83-45608. Date not set. Repr. of 1912 ed. 20.00 (ISBN 0-404-19826-0). AMS Pr.

Tragedy of the Soviet Germans. John Philipps. LC 83-61289. (Illus.). 190p. (Orig.). 1983. pap. 6.50 (ISBN 0-9611412-0-4). John Philipps.

Tragedy of the Tragedies for the Life & Death of Tom Thumb the Great with the Annotations of H. Scribblerus Secundus. Henry Fielding. Ed. by James T. Hillhouse. LC 71-131704. 1971. Repr. of 1918 ed. 39.00x (ISBN 0-403-00591-4). Scholarly.

Tragedy of the Victorian Novel. Jeanette M. King. LC 77-77762. 1980. pap. 11.95 (ISBN 0-521-29744-3). Cambridge U Pr.

Tragedy of the Wahk-Shum. Lucullus McWhorter. 44p. 1968. Repr. 5.50 (ISBN 0-87770-064-8). Ye Galleon.

Tragedy of Tragedies. Henry Fielding. 1988. Repr. lib. bdg. 75.00x. Am Biog Serv.

Tragedy of Troilus & Cressida see also Troilus & Cressida.

Tragedy of Turkish Capital Tax. Faik Okte. LC 86-24034. Date not set. 34.50. Longwood Pub Group.

Tragedy of White Injustice. Marcus Garvey. 24p. pap. 2.00 (ISBN 0-933121-08-3). Black Classic.

Tragedy of X. Ellery Queen. 288p. 1986. pap. 4.95 (ISBN 0-930330-43-9). Intl Polygonics.

Tragedy of Y. Ellery Queen. 244p. 1987. pap. 4.95 (ISBN 0-930330-53-6). Intl Polygonics.

Tragedy of Z. Ellery Queen. (Library of Crime Classics). 200p. 1987. pap. 4.95 (ISBN 0-930330-58-7). Intl Polygonics.

Tragedy of Zionism. Bernard Avishai. LC 85-10235. 389p. 1985. 19.95 (ISBN 0-374-27863-6). FS&G.

Tragedy of Zionism. Bernard Avishai. 389p. 1986. pap. 8.95 (ISBN 0-374-52044-5). FS&G.

Tragedy: Plays Theory & Criticism. Richard Levin. 217p. (Orig.). 1960. pap. text ed. 11.00 net (ISBN 0-15-592346-3, HC). HarBraceJ.

Tragedy Queens of the Georgian Era. John Fyvie. LC 78-91503. 326p. 1909. 20.00 (ISBN 0-405-08544-3). Ayer Co Pubs.

Tragedy: Serious Drama in Relation to Aristotle's "Poetics". rev. & enl. ed. F. L. Lucas. 188p. 1981. pap. 9.95x (ISBN 0-389-20141-3, 06911). B&N Imports.

Tragedy: Shakespeare & the Greek Example. Adrian Poole. 272p. 1987. 24.95 (ISBN 0-631-15192-3). Basil Blackwell.

Tragedy Trail. Max Brand. 1982. pap. 2.25 (ISBN 0-671-41563-8). PB.

Tragedy's Child. Lavada Zeek. Tr. by Bill Harris. (Orig.). 1984. pap. 4.00 (ISBN 0-9611220-2-1). Crnrstn Cmns.

Trager Mentastics: Movement As a Way to Agelessness. Milton Trager & Cathy Guadagno. Ed. by George Quasha. LC 87-23454. (Illus.). 120p. 1987. 19.95 (ISBN 0-88268-048-X). Station Hill Pr.

Tragg's Choice. Clifton Adams. 192p. 1986. pap. 2.50 (ISBN 0-441-82095-6, Pub. by Charter Bks). Ace Bks.

Tragi-Comoedia. John Rowe. LC 70-170430. (English Stage Ser.: Vol. 16). 1973. lib. bdg. 61.00 (ISBN 0-8240-0599-6). Garland Pub.

Tragic Ambiguity: Anthropology, Philosophy & Sophocles' Antigone. T. C. Cudemans & A. P. Lardinois. (Brill's Studies in Intellectual History: No. 3). 280p. 1987. 68.25 (ISBN 90-04-08417-7, Pub. by E J Brill). Heinman.

Tragic Art of Ernest Hemingway. Wirt Williams. LC 81-4740. xii, 252p. 1981. text ed. 27.50 (ISBN 0-8071-0884-7). La State U Pr.

Tragic Cavalier: Governor Manuel Salcedo of Texas, 1808-1813. Felix D. Almaraz, Jr. 218p. 1971. pap. text ed. 6.95 (ISBN 0-292-78039-7). U of Tex Pr.

Tragic Choices. Guido Calabresi & Philip Bobbitt. 1978. pap. 7.95x (ISBN 0-393-09085-X). Norton.

Tragic Comedians: A Study in a Well-Known Story. (Revised Edition) facsimile ed. George Meredith. LC 74-29508. (Modern Jewish Experience Ser.). 1975. Repr. of 1922 ed. 14.00x (ISBN 0-405-06735-6). Ayer Co Pubs.

Tragic Comedians: Seven Modern British Novelists. James Hall. LC 77-18009. 1978. lib. bdg. 35.00x (ISBN 0-313-20106-4, HATC). Greenwood.

Tragic Deception: FDR & America's Involvement in World War II. Hamilton Fish. 1983. 12.95 (ISBN 0-8159-6917-1). Devin.

Tragic Drama & Modern Society: Studies in the Social & Literary Theory of Drama from 1870 to the Present. John Orr. LC 81-7978. 300p. 1981. 28.50x (ISBN 0-389-20226-6). B&N Imports.

Tragic Drama in European Literature. B. F. Harris. 1963. Repr. lib. bdg. 15.00 (ISBN 0-8414-4791-8). Folcroft.

Tragic Drama of Corneille & Racine: An Old Parallel Revisited. H. T. Barnwell. 1982. 45.00x (ISBN 0-19-815779-7). Oxford U Pr.

Tragic Drama of William Butler Yeats: Figures in a Dance. Leonard E. Nathan. LC 65-16513. 307p. 1965. 29.00x (ISBN 0-231-02765-6). Columbia U Pr.

Tragic Effect. Andre Green. Tr. by Alan Sheridan. LC 76-12629. 1979. 39.50 (ISBN 0-521-21377-0). Cambridge U Pr.

Tragic Era: The Revolution after Lincoln. Claude G. Bowers. LC 83-45716. Repr. of 1929 ed. 57.50 (ISBN 0-404-20039-7). AMS Pr.

Tragic Fate of Hungary: A Country Carved up Alive at Trianon. Ives De Daruvar. (Illus., Eng.). casebound 10.00 (ISBN 0-912404-03-5). Alpha Pubns.

Tragic History of the Sea, Fifteen Eighty-Nine to Sixteen Twenty-Two. Ed. by C. R. Boxer. (Hakluyt Society Works: No. 2, Vol. 112). Repr. of 1959 ed. 45.00 (ISBN 0-8115-0403-4). Kraus Repr.

Tragic Knowledge: Yeat's Autobiography & Hermeneutics. Daniel T. O'Hara. LC 80-26825. 224p. 1981. 32.50x (ISBN 0-231-05204-9). Columbia U Pr.

Tragic Life of the Empress Eugenie of France Compiled from Secret State Documents of the Period, 2 vols. Count de Fleury. 475p. 1987. 176.45 (ISBN 0-86722-161-5). Inst Econ Pol.

Tragic Mask: A Study of Faulkner's Heroes. John Lewis Longley, Jr. LC 63-22806. xii, 242p. 1967. pap. 8.95x (ISBN 0-8078-4005-X). U of NC Pr.

Tragic Muse. Henry James. (Modern Classics Ser.). 1978. pap. 6.95 (ISBN 0-14-004606-2). Penguin.

Tragic Muse, Vol. 1. Henry James. LC 77-158786. (Novels & Tales of Henry James: Vol. 7). Repr. of 1908 ed. lib. bdg. 28.75x (ISBN 0-678-02807-9). Kelley.

Tragic Muse, Vol. 2. Henry James. LC 77-158786. (Novels & Tales of Henry James: Vol. 8). Repr. of 1908 ed. lib. bdg. 28.75x (ISBN 0-678-02808-7). Kelley.

Tragic Muse of John Ford. George F. Sensabaugh. LC 64-14714. Repr. of 1944 ed. 17.00 (ISBN 0-405-08949-X, Blom Pubns). Ayer Co Pubs.

Tragic Myth: Lorca & Cante Jondo. Edward F. Stanton. LC 77-84067. (Studies in Romance Languages: No. 20). 152p. 1978. 14.00 (ISBN 0-8131-1378-4). U Pr of Ky.

Tragic Occasions: Essays on Several Forms. B. L. Reid. LC 72-154032. 1971. 22.50x (ISBN 0-8046-9016-2, Pub by Kennikat). Assoc Faculty Pr.

Tragic Paradox: Myth & Ritual in Greek Tragedy. J. P. Guepin. 397p. 1968. lib. bdg. 62.50x (Pub. by AM Hakkert). Coronet Bks.

Tragic Plane. H. A. Mason. 200p. 1986. 29.95x (ISBN 0-19-812843-6). Oxford U Pr.

Tragic Plight of a Border Area: Bassarabia & Bucovina. Ed. by Maria Manea. (A.R.A. Ser.: Vol. III). 300p. 1983. 18.00x. Am Romanian.

Tragic Psalms. Francis Sullivan. 1987. pap. 5.95 (ISBN 0-912405-35-X). Pastoral Pr.

Tragic Saga of the Indiana Indians. Harold Allison. LC 86-83040. 350p. 1987. 15.00 (ISBN 0-938021-07-9). Turner Pub KY.

Tragic Satire of John Webster. Travis Bogard. LC 65-13952. 1965. Repr. of 1955 ed. 18.00x (ISBN 0-8462-0585-8). Russell.

Tragic Sense of Life. Miguel Unamuno. Tr. by J. Crawford Flitch. 1921. pap. 6.00 (ISBN 0-486-20257-7). Dover.

Tragic Story of the Colleen Bawn. William McLysaght & Sigerson Clifford. (Illus.). 128p. 1982. pap. text ed. 4.95 (ISBN 0-900068-60-4, Pub. by Anvil Bks Ireland). Irish Bks Media.

Tragic Theory in the Critical Works of Thomas Rymer, John Dennis, & John Dryden. Joan C. Grace. LC 73-2892. 143p. 1975. 15.00 (ISBN 0-8386-1312-8). Fairleigh Dickinson.

Tragic Thought & the Grammar of Tragic Myth. Bradley Berke. LC 81-48675. (Illus.). 128p. 1982. 15.00X (ISBN 0-253-36027-7). Ind U Pr.

Tragic Victory: The Doctrine of Subjective Salvation in the Poetry of W. B. Yeats. Larry Brunner. LC 86-50163. 181p. 1986. 18.50x (ISBN 0-87875-315-X). Whitston Pub.

Tragic Vision & the Hebrew Tradition. W. Lee Humphreys. LC 85-47724. (Overtures to Biblical Theology Ser.). 176p. 1985. pap. 2.50 (ISBN 0-8006-1542-5). Fortress.

Tragic Vision of John Ford. Tucker Orbison. Ed. by James Hogg. (Jacobean Drama Studies). 193p. (Orig.). 1974. pap. 15.00 (ISBN 3-7052-0319-3, Pub. by Salzburg Studies). Longwood Pub Group.

Tragic Vision of Joyce Carol Oates. Mary K. Grant. LC 77-75617. xiv, 167p. 1978. 15.95 (ISBN 0-8223-0404-X). Duke.

Tragic Vision of Life in "Hamlet" & "King Lear". Jogodish Purkayastha. Ed. by James Hogg. (Jacobean Drama Studies). 207p. (Orig.). 1977. pap. 15.00 (ISBN 0-317-40110-6, Pub. by Salzburg Studies). Longwood Pub Group.

Tragic Vision: The Confrontation of Extremity see Visions of Extremity in Modern Literature.

Tragic Ways of Killing a Woman. Nicole Loraux. Tr. by Anthony Forster. LC 87-390. 112p. 1987. text ed. 17.95 (ISBN 0-674-90225-4). Harvard U Pr.

Tragic Week: A Study of Anticlericalism in Spain, 1875-1912. Joan C. Ullman. LC 67-27082. 1968. 29.50x (ISBN 0-674-90240-8). Harvard U Pr.

Tragic Wisdom & Beyond. Gabriel Marcel. Tr. by Stephen Jolin & Peter McCormick. LC 72-96700. (Studies in Phenomenology & Existential Philosophy). 250p. 1973. text ed. 25.95 (ISBN 0-8101-0414-8); pap. 13.95 (ISBN 0-8101-0614-0). Northwestern U Pr.

Tragical Comedy or Comical Tragedy of Punch & Judy. George Cruikshank. (Illus.). 1976. pap. 2.25 (ISBN 0-7100-8199-5). Routledge Chapman & Hall.

Tragical Comedy or Comical Tragedy of Punch & Judy. Ed. by Karl Leabo. LC 83-70096. (Illus.). 1983. pap. 2.50 (ISBN 0-87830-582-3). Theatre Arts.

Tragical History of Doctor Faustus. Christopher Marlowe. Ed. by Frederick S. Boas. (Works & Life of Christopher Marlowe Ser.: Vol. 5). 221p. 1966. 25.00x (ISBN 0-87752-190-5); pap. 9.75x. Gordian.

Tragical Reign of Selimus. Robert Greene. Ed. by Alexander Grosart. 1898. Repr. 20.00 (ISBN 0-8274-3643-2). R West.

Tragicall Historye of Romeus & Juliet. Arthur Broke. LC 78-26035. (English Experience Ser.: No. 134). 168p. 1969. Repr. of 1562 ed. 21.00 (ISBN 90-221-0134-7). Walter J Johnson.

Tragicomedy. David L. Hirst. (Critical Idiom Ser.: No. 43). 120p. 1984. pap. 5.50 (ISBN 0-416-32770-2, NO. 4152). Routledge Chapman & Hall.

Tragicomedy in the Courts. Ralph Slovenko. 1974. pap. 3.95 (ISBN 0-87511-112-2). Claitors.

Tragicomedy of Classical Thermodynamics: Proceedings of CISM, Department of Solids, 1971. CISM (International Center for Mechanical Sciences), Department of Mechanics of Solids Staff. Ed. by C. A. Truesdell. (CISM Pubns. Ser.: No. 70). (Illus.). 41p. 1973. pap. 9.50 (ISBN 0-387-81114-1). Springer-Verlag.

Tragicomic Construction of Cymbeline & the Winter's Tale. Caesarea Abartis. Ed. by James Hogg. (Jacobean Drama Studies). 128p. (Orig.). 1977. pap. 15.00 (ISBN 3-7052-0364-9, Salzburg Studies). Longwood Pub Group.

Tragicomical History of Thermodynamics, Eighteen Twenty-Two to Eighteen Fifty-Four. C. A. Truesdell, 3rd. LC 79-11925. (Studies in the History of Mathematics & Physical Sciences: Vol. 4). 1980. 71.50 (ISBN 0-387-90403-4). Springer-Verlag.

Tragiques, 4 tomes. Agrippa D'Aubigne. Ed. by Garnier & Plattard. (Soc. des Textes Francais Modernes). Set. 84.50 (ISBN 0-685-34180-1). French & Eur.

Tragiques. Agrippa D'Aubigne. Ed. by I. D. McFarlane. (Renaissance Library). 184p. (Fr.). 1970. 32.50 (ISBN 0-485-13803-4, Pub. by Athlone Pr UK); pap. 14.95 (ISBN 0-485-12803-9, Pub. by Athlone Pr UK). Humanities.

Tragiques Grecs: Eschyle-Sophocle. 1544p. 41.50 (ISBN 0-686-56590-8). French & Eur.

Tragiques Grecs: Euripide-Theatre Complet. 1502p. 45.00 (ISBN 0-686-56589-4). French & Eur.

Trago. Frank Bonham. 192p. 1981. pap. 1.95 (ISBN 0-425-05041-6). Berkley Pub.

Trago. Frank Bonham. 192p. 1984. pap. 2.25 (ISBN 0-441-82096-4). Ace Bks.

Tragoediae, Aeschylus. Ed. by Udalricus de Wilamowitz-Moellendorf. 280p. 1985. 15.00 (ISBN 0-89005-412-6). Ares.

Tragoediae, Euripides, 3 vols. 1985. Vol. I, xciv, 464p. 45.00 (ISBN 0-89005-415-0). Vol. II, xivi, 456p. Vol. III, xxvi, 332p. Ares.

Tragoediae, Sophocles. Ed. by G. Dindorf et al. cvi, 366p. 15.00 (ISBN 0-89005-425-8). Ares.

Traherne: An Essay. Gladys E. Willett. LC 72-12569. 1973. lib. bdg. 17.00 (ISBN 0-8414-0750-9). Folcroft.

Traherne in Dialogue: Heidegger, Lacan, & Derrida. A. Leigh DeNeef. 312p. 1988. lib. bdg. 42.50 (ISBN 0-8223-0832-0). Duke.

Traicion De Rita Hayworth see Betrayed by Rita Hayworth.

Traicionado! Stan Telchin. 160p. 1984. 3.25 (ISBN 0-88113-359-0). Edit Betania.

Traid of Knives. Tom Cooper. Date not set. pap. 3.50 (ISBN 0-317-63662-6). Harlequin bks.

Traiganme Su Cabellera. new ed. John Benteen. Tr. by Juan A. Rios from Eng. (Sundance Ser.: No. 3). Orig. Title: Bring Me His Scalp. 160p. (Span.). 1974. pap. 0.85 (ISBN 0-88473-533-8). Fiesta Pub.

Trail. (Executioner Ser.: No. 91). Date not set. pap. 2.25 (ISBN 0-317-63959-5, Pub. by Worldwide). Harlequin Bks.

Trail: A Bibliography of the Travelers on Overland Trail to California, Oregon, Salt Lake City and Montana during the Years, 1841-1864. Lannon W. Mintz. LC 86-25117. 292p. 1987. 24.95 (ISBN 0-8263-0939-9). U of NM Pr.

Trail Blazer: History of S.E. Idaho, Daughters of Pioneers. Rev., 1930 ed. Ed. by Newell Hart. 1976. 11.00 (ISBN 0-941462-02-1). Cache Valley.

Trail Blazers. J. Porter Wilhite. 4.95 (ISBN 0-89315-302-8). Lambert Bk.

Trail Blazers of Advertising: Stories of the Romance & Adventure of the Old-Time Advertising Game. Chalmers L. Pancoast. LC 75-39264. (Getting & Spending: the Consumer's Dilemma). (Illus.). 1976. Repr. of 1926 ed. 24.50x (ISBN 0-405-08037-9). Ayer Co Pubs.

Trail-Blazers of Science: Life Stories of Some Half-Forgotten Pioneers of Modern Research. facs. ed. Martin Gumpert. Tr. by Edwin L. Shuman. LC 68-29212. (Essay Index Reprint Ser). 1968. Repr. of 1936 ed. 18.00 (ISBN 0-8369-0501-6). Ayer Co Pubs.

Trail Boss. J. T. Edson. 192p. 1987. pap. 2.75 (ISBN 0-441-82097-2, Pub. by Charter Bks). Ace Bks.

Trail Boss from Texas. Barry Cord. 1979. pap. 1.25 (ISBN 0-505-51337-4, Pub. by Tower Bks). Leisure NY.

Trail Drive. Peter McCurtin. (Sundance Ser.: No. 36). 1981. pap. 1.95 (ISBN 0-8439-0878-5, Leisure Bks). Leisure NY.

Trail Driver. Zane Grey. 1986. pap. 2.50 (ISBN 0-671-45646-6). PB.

Trail Driver. Zane Grey. 1987. 20.00x (ISBN 0-86025-186-1, Pub. by Ian Henry Pubns England). State Mutual Bk.

Trail Driver. Zane Grey. 224p. 1987. pap. 2.95 (ISBN 0-671-50169-0). PB.

Trail Drivers of Texas. Ed. by J. Marvin Hunter. (Illus.). 1117p. 1985. Repr. of 1925 ed. 27.50 (ISBN 0-292-78076-1). U of Tex Pr.

Trail-Driving Rooster. Fred Gipson. (Illus.). 88p. (gr. 4-7). 1987. Repr. of 1955 ed. 8.95 (ISBN 0-89015-620-4). Eakin Pr.

Trail Dust. Douglas Meador. 1981. Repr. 7.95 (ISBN 0-89015-287-X). Eakin Pr.

Trail Dust. Clarence Mulford. 311p. 1974. Repr. of 1934 ed. lib. bdg. 19.95x (ISBN 0-88411-212-8, Pub. by Aeonian Pr). Amereon Ltd.

Trail Dust. large type ed. Clarence E. Mulford. Repr. lib. bdg. 19.95x (ISBN 0-88411-240-3, Pub. by Aeonian Pr). Amereon Ltd.

Trail Dust & Saddle Leather. Jo Mora. LC 86-19303. (Illus.). x, 246p. 1987. 21.95x (ISBN 0-8032-3114-8); pap. 7.95 (ISBN 0-8032-8145-5, Bison). U of Nebr Pr.

Trail form Taos. Don Coldsmith. (Double D Western Ser.). 1988. 12.95 (ISBN 0-385-24232-8). Doubleday.

Trail from Texas. Dale Homer. 1978. pap. 1.50 (ISBN 0-8439-0589-1, Leisure Bks). Leisure NY.

Trail Led North. Martha F. McKeown. (Illus.). 1960. 10.50 (ISBN 0-8323-0090-X). Binford-Metropolitan.

Trail Maker (David Livingstone) Robert O. Latham. 1973. pap. 3.50 (ISBN 0-87508-626-8). Chr Lit.

Trail Makers of the Middle Border. Hamlin Garland. (Collected Works of Hamlin Garland). 1988. Repr. of 1926 ed. lib. bdg. 59.00x. Am Biog Serv.

Trail Markers of the Middle Border see Collected Works.

Trail North. Hawk Greenway. (Illus.). 180p. (Orig.). 1981. pap. 7.95 (ISBN 0-933280-04-1). Island CA.

Trail of a Wilderness Wanderer. Andy Russell. 336p. 1988. 12.95 (ISBN 0-941130-93-2). N Lyons Bks.

Trail of an Artist-Naturalist: Autobiography of Ernest Thompson Seton. Ernest T. Seton. Ed. by Keir B. Sterling. LC 77-81134. (Biologists & Their World Ser.). (Illus.). 1978. Repr. of 1940 ed. lib. bdg. 36.50x (ISBN 0-405-10734-X). Ayer Co Pubs.

Trail of Ashes. Marian Babson. 1985. Walker & Co.

Trail of Ashes. Marian Babson. (Nightingale Ser.). 280p. (Orig.). 1985. pap. 9.95 (ISBN 0-8161-3904-0, Large Print Bks). G K Hall.
Trail of Ashes. Marian Babson. 1986. Walker & Co.
Trail of Bigfoot. Dayle Courtney. (Thorne Twins Adventure Bks.). (Illus.). 192p. (Orig.). (gr. 7-12). 1983. pap. 2.98 (ISBN 0-87239-681-9, 2901). Standard Pub.
Trail of Bohu: Imaro III. Charles R. Saunders. 222p. 1985. pap. 2.95 (ISBN 0-88677-087-4). DAW Bks.
Trail of Broken Promises. Caleb Pirtle, III. 188p. 1987. 12.95 (ISBN 0-89015-573-9). Eakin Pr.
Trail of Conflict. Emilie Loring. Repr. lib. bdg. 19.95x (ISBN 0-88411-381-7, Pub. by Aeonian Pr). Amereon Ltd.
Trail of Danger. James S. Wallerstein. (Illus.). 248p. (gr. 4-12). 1972. 5.95 (ISBN 0-912388-03-X). Aurelon.
Trail of Death. Rose Estes. LC 85-60429. (Find Your Fate Ser.). (Illus.). 128p. (gr. 4-7). 1985. pap. 2.95 (ISBN 0-394-86432-8, BYR). Random.
Trail of Death. Dean McElwain. (Preacher's Law Ser.: No. 2). 224p. (Orig.). 1987. pap. 2.75 (ISBN 0-8439-2528-0). Leisure NY.
Trail of Desire. Robert E. Mills. (Kansan Ser.: No. 7). 208p. (Orig.). 1981. pap. 2.25 (ISBN 0-8439-1017-8, Leisure Bks). Leisure NY.
Trail of Havoc: In the Steps of Lord Lucan. Patrick Marnham. 1988. 17.95 (ISBN 0-670-81391-5). Viking.
Trail of Iron: The CPR & the Birth of the West. Bill Mckee & Georgeen Klassen. (Illus.). 192p. 1984. 24.95 (ISBN 0-88894-399-7, Pub. by Douglas & McIntyre-Grounwood). Salem Hse Pubs.
Trail of Lewis & Clark: 1804-1904, 2 vols. Olin D. Wheeler. LC 75-177829. Repr. of 1904 ed. Set. 57.50 (ISBN 0-404-06926-6). AMS Pr.
Trail of Love. Tarla Hayford. 192p. 1981. pap. 2.95 (ISBN 0-671-43701-1, Wallaby). S&S.
Trail of Memories: The Quotations of Louis L'Amour. Compiled by Angelique L'Amour. LC 88-965. 224p. 1988. 12.95 (ISBN 0-553-05271-3). Bantam.
Trail of Miracles: Stories from a Pilgrimage in Northeast Brazil. Candace Slater. 1986. 35.00x (ISBN 0-520-05306-0). U of Cal Pr.
Trail of Peril. Yvonne Davy. Ed. by Gerald Wheeler. LC 83-17835. (Banner Bks.). (Illus.). 94p. (Orig.). (gr. k up). 1984. pap. 6.95 (ISBN 0-8280-0223-1). Review & Herald.
Trail of Tears. Gloria Jahoda. 356p. 1975. 12.95 (ISBN 0-03-014871-5). Brown BK.
Trail of Tears: The Rise & Fall of the Cherokee Nation. John Ehle. 1988. 19.95 (ISBN 0-385-23953-X, Anchor Pr). Doubleday.
Trail of the Butterfly. Calvin Bowden. 222p. 1984. 8.95 (ISBN 0-89697-191-0). Intl Univ Pr.
Trail of the Dragon. Susan Kelly. 282p. 1988. 17.95 (ISBN 0-8027-5696-4). Walker & Co.
Trail of the First Wagons Over the Sierra Nevada. 2nd ed. Charles D. Graydon. LC 86-21208. (Illus.). 80p. 1986. 19.95 (ISBN 0-935284-47-8); pap. 12.95 (ISBN 0-935284-59-1). Patrice Pr.
Trail of the Fox. David Irving. (YA) (gr. 7 up). 1978. pap. 5.95 (ISBN 0-380-40022-7). Avon.
Trail of the Fox: The True Story of the Perfect Crime. Lawrence Taylor. 352p. Date not set. pap. 4.50 (ISBN 0-671-64955-8). PB.
Trail of the Gold Spike. Aaron Allston. Ed. by Dennis Mallonee. (Hero System Ser.). (Illus.). 32p. (Orig.). 1984. pap. 6.00 (ISBN 0-917481-51-8). Hero Games.
Trail of the Goldseekers. Hamlin Garland. (Collected Works of Hamlin Garland). 1988. Repr. of 1899 ed. lib. bdg. 59.00x. Am Biog Serv.
Trail of the Goldseekers see Collected Works.
Trail of the Hare. Joel S. Savishinsky. (Library of Anthropology). (Illus.). 286p. 1974. 40.00 (ISBN 0-677-04140-3). Gordon & Breach.
Trail of the Invisible Light: From X-Strahlen to Radiobiology. E. R. Grigg. 1016p. 1965. 137.50 (ISBN 0-398-00739-X). C C Thomas.
Trail of the Lonesome Pine. John Fox. 1976. lib. bdg. 19.95x (ISBN 0-89968-040-2). Lightyear.
Trail of the Lonesome Pine. John Fox, Jr. LC 84-2234. 440p. 1984. 20.00 (ISBN 0-8131-1508-6); pap. 10.00 (ISBN 0-8131-0156-5). U Pr of KY.
Trail of the Pack Peddler. Sam Mims. 40p. pap. 2.00 (ISBN 0-911116-45-1). Pelican.
Trail of the Reaper. Peter Fox. 1988. pap. 3.95 (ISBN 0-425-11046-X). Berkley Pub.
Trail of the Sandhill Stag. Ernest Seton-Thompson. 1977. Repr. of 1900 ed. lib. bdg. 49.00 (ISBN 0-8414-7880-5). Folcroft.
Trail of the Seahawks. Ardath Mayhar. LC 86-51590. (Windwalker Bks.). 224p. (Orig.). 1987. pap. 2.95 (ISBN 0-88038-463-8). TSR Inc.
Trail of the Serpent. Jan De Hartog. LC 83-22018. 224p. 1984. pap. 6.95 (ISBN 0-452-25513-9, Plume). NAL.
Trail of the Snake from Big Bend to Baja. Michael A. Williamson. LC 85-26138. (Illus.). 128p. (Orig.). 1986. pap. 10.95 (ISBN 0-86534-077-3). Sunstone Pr.
Trail of the Spanish Bit. Don Coldsmith. 192p. 1987. pap. 2.95 (ISBN 0-553-26397-8). Bantam.
Trail of Tsathogghua. Keith Herber. Ed. by Sandy Petersen. (Illus.). 64p. 1984. pap. 10.00 incl. Call of Cthulhu roleplaying game supplement (ISBN 0-933635-05-2, 2308). Chaosium.
Trail of U. S. Grant: The Pacific Coast Years, 1852-1854. Charles G. Ellington. LC 86-50835. (Frontier Military Ser.: XIV). (Illus.). 248p. 1987. 27.50 (ISBN 0-87062-169-6). A H Clark.
Trail of '42: A Pictorial History of the Alaska Highway. Stan B. Cohen. LC 79-51360. (Illus.). 96p. 1979. pap. 5.95 (ISBN 0-933126-06-9). Pictorial Hist.
Trail Riding Book. 90p. 3.95 (ISBN 0-318-14509-X). Intl Arabian.
Trail Sinister. James Brumbaugh. LC 86-91530. (AD&D Adventure Gamebook Ser.: No. 14). 192p. (Orig.). 1987. pap. 2.95 (ISBN 0-88038-453-0). TSR Inc.
Trail Smoke. Ernest Haycox. 1982. pap. 1.95 (ISBN 0-451-11282-2, AJ1282, Sig). NAL.
Trail That Turns on Itself. Patricia Goedicke. LC 78-7551. 81p. 1978. 3.50 (ISBN 0-87886-094-0). Greenfld Rev Pr.
Trail Through Danger. William O. Steele. LC 65-25307. (Illus.). (gr. 4-6). 1965. 4.95 (ISBN 0-15-289661-9, HJ). HarBraceJ.
Trail to a Pot of Gold. Sam Mims. (Illus.). 23p. pap. 1.00 (ISBN 0-911116-46-X). Pelican.
Trail to Boot Hill. James Wesley. (YA) (gr. 7 up). 1981. 9.95 (ISBN 0-686-84694-X, Avalon). Bouregy.
Trail to Crazy Man. Louis L'Amour. 1986. pap. 2.95 (ISBN 0-553-26392-7). Bantam.
Trail to Heaven: Knowledge & Narrative in a Northern Native Community. Robin Ridington. LC 88-17098. (Illus.). 316p. 1988. text ed. 27.50x (ISBN 0-87745-212-1). U of Iowa Pr.
Trail to Justice. Terrell L. Bowers. 1986. 9.95 (ISBN 0-8034-8630-8, Avalon). Bouregy.
Trail to Mesilla. Roy Wayne. (YA) (gr. 7 up). 1979. 9.95 (ISBN 0-685-95880-9, Avalon). Bouregy.
Trail to North Star Gold. 2nd ed. Ella L. Martinsen. LC 70-98194. (Illus.). 1984. pap. 9.95 (ISBN 0-8323-0242-2). Binford-Metropolitan.
Trail to Ogallala. Benjamin Capps. 1980. pap. 2.50 (ISBN 0-441-82139-1, Pub by Charter Bks). Ace Bks.
Trail to Ogallala. Benjamin Capps. LC 85-4721. (Texas Tradition Ser.: No. 3). 285p. 1985. 16.95 (ISBN 0-87565-012-0); pap. 9.95 (ISBN 0-87565-013-9). Tex Christian.
Trail to San Jacinto. Archie P. McDonald. (Texas History Ser.). (Illus.). 45p. 1982. pap. text ed. 2.95x (ISBN 0-89641-074-9). American Pr.
Trail to San Triste. Max Brand. 192p. 1985. pap. 2.50 (ISBN 0-446-32416-7). Warner Bks.
Trail to Sonora. Ed Newsom. (YA) (gr. 7 up). 1979. 9.95 (ISBN 0-685-90728-7, Avalon). Bouregy.
Trail to the West. Louis L'Amour. 1986. 7.95 (ISBN 0-553-45009-3). Bantam.
Trail to Tucson. Ray Hogan. 256p. 1987. pap. 3.50 (ISBN 0-451-14892-4, Sig). NAL.
Trail-Use Standard Specification for Microprocessor Operating Systems Interfaces: Standard 855-1985. 173p. 1986. 23.00 (ISBN 0-471-01073-1). Wiley.
Trailberboats-West. (Illus.). 7.95 (ISBN 0-393-60021-1). Norton.
Trailbikes. Norman Barrett. (Picture Library). (Illus.). 32p. (gr. k-3). 1987. PLB 9.90 (ISBN 0-531-10277-7). Watts.
Trailbikes. David Jefferis. (Easy-Read Fact Bks.). (Illus.). 32p. (gr. k-3). 1984. lib. bdg. 10.90 (ISBN 0-531-04709-1). Watts.
Trailblazer for Jesus. Patricia Maxwell. (Hall of Faith Ser.). 77p. 1987. pap. 6.95 (ISBN 0-317-66104-3). Pacific Pr Pub Assn.
Trailblazer for the Sacred Heart. Pat Balksus. (Encounter Ser.). 1976. 3.00 (ISBN 0-8198-0476-2). Dghtrs St Paul.
Trailblazers. B. Gilbert. LC 73-76268. (Old West Ser). (Illus.). (gr. 7 up). 1973. 19.94 (ISBN 0-8094-1459-7, Pub. by Time-Life). Silver.
Trailblazers. Bil Gilbert. (Old West Ser.). (Illus.). 1973. 14.95 (ISBN 0-8094-1458-9). Time-Life.
Trailblazers for Pathfinders, Vol. 2: A Youth Enrichment Skill. Lou Gattis. (Illus., Orig.). 1987. pap. 5.00. Cheetah Pub.
Trailblazers for Translators: The Influence of the "Chichicastenago Twelve". Anna M. Dahlquist. Date not set. pap. price not set (ISBN 0-87808-205-0). William Carey Lib.
Trailer Life Campground & RV Services Directory. Ed. by Trailer Life Staff. 1400p. 1988. pap. 13.95 (ISBN 0-934798-16-8). TL Enterprises.
Trailer Life Campground & RV Services Directory: 1989 Edition. 1989. pap. 11.95 (ISBN 0-934798-19-2). TL Enterprises.
Trailer Life's RV Repair & Maintenance Manual: The Most Comprehensive & Authoritative Technical Guide Ever Published Specifically for Rvers. John Thompson & Trailer Life Editors. LC 79-66970. (Illus.). 1980. 12.98 (ISBN 0-934798-00-1). TL Enterprises.
Trailer Life's Secrets of Successful RVing: Detailed Tips & Hints for Successful RV Trips. John Thompson. (Illus.). 400p. (Orig.). 1981. pap. 12.95 (ISBN 0-934798-03-6). TL Enterprises.
Trailer Truck that Hit Me. J. Renee Himler. 72p. 1988. 6.95 (ISBN 0-8059-3117-1). Dorrance.
Trailerboating Illustrated. 2nd rev. ed. Patrick M. Royce. LC 81-11398. (Planing Hulls, Trailers, Seamanship Ser.: No. 1). (Illus.). 192p. 1981. pap. 8.95 (ISBN 0-930030-19-2). Western Marine Ent.
Trailerpark. Russell Banks. 288p. 1986. pap. 3.95 (ISBN 0-345-33077-3). Ballantine.
Trailers: How to Buy & Evaluate. M. M. Smith. (Illus., Orig.). 1983. pap. text ed. 12.95 (ISBN 0-914483-07-2). Techni-Visions.
Trailers: How to Design & Build. M. M. Smith. (Illus.). 1988. pap. text ed. 29.95 (ISBN 0-914483-23-4). Techni-Visions.
Trailers: How to Tow & Maintain. M. M. Smith. (Illus., Orig.). 1982. pap. text ed. 9.95 (ISBN 0-914483-15-3). Techni-Visions.
Trailing Back. Charles A. Seltzer. 320p. 1975. Repr. of 1936 ed. lib. bdg. 19.95x (ISBN 0-88411-107-5, Pub. by Aeonian Pr). Amereon Ltd.
Trailing Clouds of Glory: Spiritual Values in Children's Books. Madeleine L'Engle. LC 84-29081. 144p. (gr. 5-9). 1985. 12.95 (ISBN 0-664-32721-4). Westminster John Knox.
Trailing the Cowboy: His Life & Lore As Told by Frontier Journalists. Ed. by Clifford P. Westermeier. LC 77-13831. (Illus.). 1978. Repr. of 1955 ed. lib. bdg. 35.00x (ISBN 0-8371-9866-6, WETC). Greenwood.
Trailing the Holy Cross: Soldier Feet, Apache Ears & the Santa Cruz Trail. Bernard L. Fontana. Ed. by W. David Laird. (Illus.). 48p. 1988. 65.00x (ISBN 0-932337-01-5). Peccary Pr.
Trailing the Longhorns: A Century Later. Sue Flanagan. LC 74-77510. (Illus.). 290p. 1974. 18.50 (ISBN 0-89052-008-9). Madrona Pr.
Trails among the Columbine 1985: A Colorado High Country Anthology. Sundance Publications, Ltd. Staff. Ed. by Steven J. Meyers. (Illus.). 160p. 1985. 32.00x (ISBN 0-913582-37-9); pap. 22.00x (ISBN 0-913582-38-7). Sundance.
Trails among the Columbine, 1986: A Colorado High Country Anthology. Sundance Publications Ltd. Staff. Intro. by Steven J. Meyers. (Durango & Silverton Ser.). (Illus.). 160p. 1986. 32.00 (ISBN 0-913582-43-3). Sundance.
Trails among the Columbine, 1987: A Colorado High Country Anthology. Sundance Publications Ltd. Staff. Intro. by Steven J. Meyers. (Alamosa-Durango Ser.). (Illus.). 160p. 1987. 32.00 (ISBN 0-913582-08-5). Sundance.
Trails & Trails of the Berrys. Ione B. Jones. 32p. 1985. 5.95 (ISBN 0-943480-62-0). Friis-Pioneer Pr.
Trails & Trials of a Texas Ranger. William W. Sterling. (Illus.). 1979. pap. 19.95 (ISBN 0-8061-1574-2). U of Okla Pr.
Trails & Trials of the Pioneers of the Olympic Peninsula. Lucille H. Cleland. 312p. pap. 14.95 (ISBN 0-8466-0302-0, S-302). Shorey.
Trails Begin Where Rails End. Albert D. Manchester. Ed. by Mac Sebree & Paul Hammond. 160p. 1987. 35.95 (ISBN 0-87046-081-1). Interurban.
Trails from Steppingstones to Kerbstones. Russell A. Apole. LC 66-4453. (Bernice P. Bishop Museum Special Publication Ser.: No. 53). (Illus.). 85p. pap. 22.10 (2030322). Bks Demand UMI.
Trails in a Vacant Maze. Joe Hirsch. LC 84-3204. 80p. 1984. pap. 6.00 (ISBN 0-914278-42-8). Copper Beech.
Trails of a Wilderness Wanderer. Andy Russell. LC 75-118715. 1970. 15.45 (ISBN 0-394-44938-X). Knopf.
Trails of a Wilderness Wanderer. Andy Russell. 1988. pap. 12.95 (ISBN 0-317-67536-2). N Lyons Bks.
Trails of an Alaska Game Warden. Ray Tremblay. LC 85-111174. (Illus.). 192p. (Orig.). 1985. pap. 9.95 (ISBN 0-88240-273-0). Alaska Northwest.
Trails of an Alaska Trapper. Ray Tremblay. LC 83-8813. (Illus.). 170p. 1983. pap. 9.95 (ISBN 0-88240-250-1). Alaska Northwest.
Trails of the Angeles. 5th ed. John W. Robinson. LC 83-51479. (Illus.). 248p. (Orig.). 1984. pap. 11.95 (ISBN 0-89997-041-9). Wilderness Pr.
Trails of the Lancashire Witches. Hendon Publishing Co., Ltd. Staff. 1986. 40.25x (ISBN 0-317-54184-6, Pub. by Hendon Pub UK). State Mutual BK.
Trails of the Sawtooth & White Cloud Mountains. new ed. Margaret Fuller. LC 78-68661. (Illus., Orig.). 1979. pap. 8.95 (ISBN 0-913140-29-5). Signpost Bk Pub.
Trails of the Smoky Hill. Wayne C. Lee. LC 79-67199. (Illus.). 235p. (Orig.). 1980. pap. 12.95 (ISBN 0-87004-276-9). Caxton.
Trails of the Troubadours. Raimon De Loi. 1973. Repr. of 1926 ed. 30.00 (ISBN 0-8274-1394-7). R West.
Trails of Western Idaho. Margaret Fuller. LC 82-5621. (Illus.). 280p. pap. 10.95 (ISBN 0-913140-44-9). Signpost Bk Pub.
Trails of Yesterday. John Bratt. LC 79-26411. xx, 322p. 1980. 27.95x (ISBN 0-8032-1157-0); pap. 6.50 (ISBN 0-8032-6055-5, BB 723, Bison). U of Nebr Pr.
Trails Plowed Under. Charles M. Russell. 1927. pap. 19.95 (ISBN 0-385-04494-1). Doubleday.
Trails, Rails, & War: The Life of General G. M. Dodge. J. R. Perkins. Ed. by Stuart Bruchey. LC 80-1338. (Railroads Ser.). (Illus.). 1981. Repr. of 1929 ed. lib. bdg. 35.00x (ISBN 0-405-13810-5). Ayer Co Pubs.
Trails: Reflections of a Pilgrimage. Donald C. Jackson. (Illus.). 180p. 1984. 14.95 (ISBN 0-87397-261-9). Strode.
Trails South: The Wagon-Road Economy in the Dodge City-Panhandle Region. C. Robert Haywood. LC 85-40946. (Illus.). 336p. 1986. 19.95 (ISBN 0-8061-1987-X). U of Okla Pr.
Trails to Hoosier Heritage. Harry G. Black. LC 80-81608. (Illus.). 99p. (Orig.). 1981. pap. 5.95 (ISBN 0-937086-00-2). HMB Pubns.
Trails to Illinois Heritage. Harry G. Black. LC 81-85017. (Trails to Ser.). (Illus.). 110p. (Orig.). 1982. pap. 5.95 (ISBN 0-937086-01-0). HMB Pubns.
Trails to Poosey. Olive R. Cook. LC 86-8602. (Illus.). 200p. (Orig.). (gr. 3-6). 1986. pap. 5.95 (ISBN 0-930079-01-9). Misty Hill Pr.
Trails to Successful Trapping. V. E. Lynch. 170p. 1935. pap. 3.50 (ISBN 0-936622-23-7). A R Harding Pub.
Trails to Texas. Curtis Bishop et al. (Illus.). (gr. 7). 1965. text ed. 7.48 (ISBN 0-87443-039-9); tchrs' ed. 7.48 (ISBN 0-87443-040-2). Benson.
Trails to Texas: Southern Roots of Western Cattle Ranching. Terry G. Jordan. LC 80-14169. (Illus.). xviii, 220p. 1981. 19.95x (ISBN 0-8032-2554-7). U of Nebr Pr.
Trails West. LC 78-61264. (Special Publications: Series 14, No. 2). (Illus.). 1979. 7.95 (ISBN 0-87044-272-4); lib. bdg. 9.50 avail. only through Natl Geog (ISBN 0-87044-277-5). Natl Geog.
Trails West: The Genealogy of the Ohio Territory. American Family Records Association Staff. Ed. by Nita Neblock. (Illus.). 46p. 1985. pap. 6.00 (ISBN 0-913233-04-8). AFRA.
Trailsman: High Mountain Guns, No. 29. Jon Sharpe. 192p. 1984. pap. 2.50 (ISBN 0-451-12917-2, Sig). NAL.
Trailsman: Manitoba Murders, No. 67. Jon Sharpe. 192p. 1987. pap. 2.75 (ISBN 0-451-14890-8, Sig). NAL.
Trailsman No. 75: Colorado Robber. Jon Sharpe. 176p. 1988. pap. 2.75 (ISBN 0-451-15226-3, Sig). NAL.
Trailsman No. 76: Wildcat Wagons. Jon Sharpe. 176p. 1988. pap. 2.75 (ISBN 0-451-15294-8, Sig). NAL.
Trailtown. Ernest Haycox. 1981. pap. 1.95 (ISBN 0-451-15386-3, Sig). NAL.
Train. David McPhail. (gr. 3-6). 1977. 13.95 (ISBN 0-316-56316-1, Joy St Bks). Little.
Train. David McPhail. (Picture Puffins Ser). (Illus.). (ps-k). 1979. pap. 4.95 (ISBN 0-14-050302-1, Puffin). Penguin.
Train. (Press-Out Board Bks.). (Illus.). (gr. k). 1982. 3.95 (ISBN 0-448-12539-0, G&D). Putnam Pub Group.
Train see Adam & the Train.
Train Book. Phyllis Hoffman. (Colorforms Board Bks.). (Illus.). 14p. (ps-k). 1986. bds. 5.95 (ISBN 0-590-40107-6). Scholastic Inc.
Train Boy. Horatio Alger. 1975. Repr. of 1883 ed. lib. bdg. 18.95x (ISBN 0-88411-807-X, Pub. by Aeonian Pr). Amereon Ltd.
Train de 8h 47. Georges Courteline. 256p. 1959. 14.95 (ISBN 0-686-54639-3). French & Eur.
Train Dispatcher. Jack Rudman. (Career Examination Ser.: C-815). (Cloth bdg. avail. on request). pap. 14.00 (ISBN 0-8373-0815-1). Natl Learning.
Train for Tommy. (Easy Readers Ser.). (gr. k-3). 1986. 1.25 (ISBN 0-8431-4322-3). Wonder.
Train Like a Grandmaster. Alexander Kotov. (Clubplayer's Library). (Illus.). 112p. 1981. pap. 16.95 (ISBN 0-7134-3609-3, Pub. by Batsford England). David & Charles.
Train No. Eight. Julian McCall. 1988. 17.95 (ISBN 0-87949-279-1). Ashley Bks.
Train of Terror. Louise M. Foley. (Twistaplot Ser.: No. 2). (Illus.). 96p. (Orig.). (gr. 7 up). pap. 1.95 (ISBN 0-590-32499-3). Scholastic Inc.
Train Operator. Jack Rudman. (Career Examination Ser.: C-1068). (Cloth bdg. avail. on request). 1988. pap. 14.00 (ISBN 0-8373-1068-7). Natl Learning.
Train Operator, Tower Operator, Assistant Train Dispatcher. Ed. by Hy Hammer. 192p. 1985. pap. 8.00 (ISBN 0-668-06312-2). Arco.
Train Power. Ralph Creger & Barry Combs. 1981. pap. 4.99 (ISBN 0-8309-0325-9). Ind Pr MO.
Train Ride. Ted Berrigan. 48p. (Orig.). 1978. o. p. 25.00 (ISBN 0-931428-22-X); pap. 6.00 (ISBN 0-931428-21-1). Vehicle Edns.
Train Ride to Hell. J. S. Hardin. (Doc & Raider Ser.: No. 71). 192p. (Orig.). 1987. pap. 2.50 (ISBN 0-425-09713-7). Berkley Pub.
Train Robberies, Train Robbers, & the Holdup Men. William A. Pinkerton. LC 74-15748. (Popular Culture in America Ser.). (Illus.). 88p. 1975. Repr. of 1907 ed. 14.00 (ISBN 0-405-06383-0). Ayer Co Pubs.
Train Robbing Bunch. Rick Miller. LC 82-22204. (Early West Ser.). (Illus.). 175p. 1983. 13.75 (ISBN 0-932702-25-2); pap. 8.50 (ISBN 0-932702-27-9); leatherbound limited to 25 copies 75.00 (ISBN 0-932702-26-0). Creative Texas.
Train Station. Philippe Dupasquier. (Busy Places Ser.). (Illus.). 24p. (ps-1). 1984. 3.95 (ISBN 0-448-19051-6, G&D). Putnam Pub Group.
Train Talk: Guide to Lights, Hand Signals & Whistles. Roger Yepsen. LC 83-4062. (Illus.). 96p. (gr. 4-7). 1983. 9.95 (ISBN 0-394-85750-X, Pant Bks Young); lib. bdg. 9.99 (ISBN 0-394-95750-4). Pantheon.

Training for Cross-Country Ski Racing: A Physiological Guide for Athletes & Coaches. Brian J. Sharkey. LC 83-82292. 224p. 1984. pap. text ed. 13.00x (ISBN 0-931250-46-3, BSHA0046). Human Kinetics.

Training for Decisions. John Adair. 166p. Repr. of 1971 ed. text ed. 23.95x. Gower Pub Co.

Training for Development. Rolf P. Lynton & Udai Pareek. LC 78-57232. 409p. 1978. pap. 8.95x (ISBN 0-931816-25-4). Kumarian Pr.

Training for Drilling Machine Operators, 17 vols. Ed. by Engineering Industry Training Board Staff. (Illus.). 1978. Set. 69.95x (ISBN 0-89563-024-9). Trans-Atl Phila.

Training for Environmental Groups. J. Clarence Davies et al. LC 84-9443. 124p. (Orig.). 1984. pap. 11.95 (ISBN 0-89164-083-5). Conservation Foun.

Training for Evangelism. Richard Sisson. 1979. pap. 12.95 (ISBN 0-8024-8792-0). Moody.

Training for Fixed Headstock Single Spindle Automatic Lathe Setters & Operators, 30 vols. Ed. by Engineering Industry Training Board Staff. (Illus.). 1978. folder 89.95x (ISBN 0-85083-425-2). Trans-Atl Phila.

Training for Hospital Laundry Staff & a Proposed Staffing Structure. W. A. Farndale & G. Harding. 34p. 1973. 69.00x (ISBN 0-901812-12-9, Pub. by Ravenswood Pubns UK). State Mutual Bk.

Training for Industrial Site Radiography, 14 vols. Ed. by Engineering Industry Training Board Staff. Incl. Vol. 1. Introduction to Radiography; Vol. 2. Ionizing Radiations; Vol. 4. Image Formation; Vol. 5. Safety; Vol. 6. X-Ray Equipment; Vol. 7. Gamma-Ray Equipment; Vol. 8. Exposure; Vol. 9. Operations; Vol. 10. Pipe-Crawler Equipment. 69.95. (Illus.). 1977. Set. 42.50x (ISBN 0-89563-025-7). Trans-Atl Phila.

Training for Job Developers: A Job Developer's Guide. Denise Bissonnette-Lamendella & Richard Pimentel. 104p. 1987. wkbk. 19.95 (ISBN 0-942071-09-3). M Wright & Assocs.

Training for Job Developers: A Supervisor's Guide. Denise Bissonnette-Lamendella & Richard Pimentel. 129p. 1987. Repr. of 1986 ed. tchr's. ed. 94.50 (ISBN 0-942071-03-4). M Wright & Assocs.

Training for Leadership. John Adair. 158p. 1982. Repr. of 1968 ed. text ed. 23.95x (ISBN 0-566-02110-2). Gower Pub Co.

Training for Leadership in the Church. Elmer Kettner. 1.95 (ISBN 0-933350-09-0). Morse Pr.

Training for Life: A Practical Guide to Career & Life Planning. 3rd ed. Fred J. Hecklinger & Bernadette M. Curtin. 256p. 1987. pap. text ed. 17.95 (ISBN 0-8403-4344-2, 40330901). Kendall-Hunt.

Training for Manual Metal-Arc Welders, 14 vols. Ed. by Engineering Industry Training Board Staff. Incl. Vol. 1. Metal-Arc Welding; Vol. 2. Welding Electrodes; Vol. 3. Joints & Weld Symbols; Vol. 4. Limiting Distortion; Vol. 5. Basic Welding; Vol. 6. Plate Surfaces; Vol. 7. Fillet Joints; Vol. 8. Single Vee Butt Joints; Vol. 9. Pipe Welding; Vol. 10. Fault Diagnosis; Vol. 11. Branch Connections. 69.95. (Illus.). 1974. Set. 43.95x (ISBN 0-89563-026-5). Trans-Atl Phila.

Training for Mass Communication. (Reports & Papers on Mass Communications: No. 73). 44p. 1975. pap. 5.00 (ISBN 92-3-101234-7, U684, UNESCO). UNIPUB.

Training for Milling Machine Operators & Setters, 22 vols. Ed. by Engineering Industry Training Board Staff. (Illus.). 1977. Set. 69.95x (ISBN 0-89563-027-3). Trans-Atl Phila.

Training for Multi-Spindle Automatic Lathe Setters & Operators, 31 vols. Ed. by Engineering Industry Training Board Staff. (Illus.). 1979. Set. folder 89.95x (ISBN 0-85083-463-5). Trans-Atl Phila.

Training for Musicianship. Victoria Glaser. 17.95x (ISBN 0-8008-7829-9, Crescendo). Taplinger.

Training for New Technologies: Success Stories for the 1990s. 1988. write for info. (197). BNA.

Training for New Technology. David S. Bushnell. (Studies in Productivity: No. 27). 41p. 1983. pap. 39.00 (ISBN 0-08-029508-8). Work in Amer.

Training for Operators of Numerically Controlled Machines. Ed. by Engineering Industry Training Board Staff. Incl. Vol. 1. Introduction to NC Machine Tool; Vol. 2. Rotating Tool; Vol. 3. Rotating Work; Vol. 4. Milling Cutters; Vol. 5. Tape NC Machines; Vol. 6. Automatic Tool & Work Exchanging; Vol. 7. X, Y, & Z Axes; Vol. 8. Positioning of the Tool & Workpiece; Vol. 9. Emergency Stop & Switching Operations; Vol. 10. Operation. 79.95. 1973. Set. 62.50x (ISBN 0-89563-028-1). Trans-Atl Phila.

Training for Pipe Fitters, 23 vols. Engineering Industry Training Board Staff. 1976. 75.00x (ISBN 0-89563-031-1). Trans-Atl Phila.

Training for Power Press Setters & Operators, 17 vols. Ed. by Engineering Industry Training Board Staff. (Illus.). 1973. Set. folder 67.50x (ISBN 0-89563-048-6). Trans-Atl Phila.

Training for Professional Child Care. Beverly Gully et al. (Illus.). 256p. 1987. text ed. 24.95x (ISBN 0-8093-1331-6). S Ill U Pr.

Training for Public Administration & Management in Developing Countries: A Review. Samuel Paul. (Working Paper: No. 584). 131p. 1984. 8.00 (ISBN 0-8213-0234-5, WP 0584). World Bank.

Training for Retail Sales & Profit. Judith J. Howe. LC 81-66236. pap. 63.30 (ISBN 0-317-39666-8, 2023558). Bks Demand UMI.

Training for Riggers-Erectors, 15 vols. Ed. by Engineering Industry Training Board Staff. (Illus.). 1976. Set. 67.50x (ISBN 0-89563-030-3). Trans-Atl Phila.

Training for Service: A Survey of the Bible. Orrin Root. Rev. by Eleanor Daniel. 128p. 1983. pap. 3.95 (ISBN 0-87239-704-1, 3212); tchr's. ed. 4.95 (ISBN 0-87239-703-3, 3211). Standard Pub.

Training for Service Delivery to Minority Clients. Ed. by Emelicia Mizio & Anita J. Delaney. LC 80-234668. 224p. 1980. pap. 13.95 (ISBN 0-87304-180-1). Family Serv.

Training for Sliding Headstock Single Spindle Automatic Lathe (Swiss Auto) Setters & Operators, 26 vols. Ed. by Engineering Industry Training Board Staff. (Illus.). 1978. Set. folder 79.95x (ISBN 0-85083-426-0). Trans-Atl Phila.

Training for Sports. 3rd ed. Jack Wilmore & David L. Costill. 432p. 1988. text ed. write for info. (ISBN 0-697-06778-5). Wm C Brown.

Training for the Cross-Cultural Mind. 2nd ed. Pierre Casse. (Illus.). 190p. 1981. pap. 15.00 (ISBN 0-933934-06-8). Soc Intercult Ed Train & Res.

Training for the Hospitality Industry: Techniques to Improve Job Performance. Lewis C. Forrest, Jr. Ed. by Marjorie Harless. LC 82-21104. (Illus.). 354p. 1983. text ed. 36.95 (ISBN 0-86612-009-2). Educ Inst Am Hotel.

Training for the Hospitality Industry. 2nd ed. Lewis C. Forrest, Jr. Ed. by Ann Halm. (Illus.). 350p. 1988. text ed. 36.95 (ISBN 0-86612-044-0). Educ Inst Am Hotel.

Training for the Life of the Spirit. new ed. Gerald Heard. LC 74-29127. (Illus.). 192p. 1976. pap. 2.50 (ISBN 0-914896-11-3). East Ridge Pr.

Training for the Multicultural Manager. Pierre Casse. (Illus.). 191p. 1982. pap. 15.00 (ISBN 0-933934-09-2). Soc Intercult Ed Train & Res.

Training for the Public Profession of the Law. Alfred Z. Reed. LC 75-22837. (America in Two Centuries Ser). 1976. Repr. of 1921 ed. 38.50x (ISBN 0-405-07708-4). Ayer Co Pubs.

Training for the Public Profession of the Law. Alfred Z. Reed. Ed. by R. H. Helmholz & Bernard D. Reams, Jr. LC 86-62933. (Historical Writings in Law & Jurisprudence. Second Ser.: No. 2). xviii, 498p. 1986. Repr. of 1921 ed. lib. bdg. 37.50 (ISBN 0-89941-516-4). W S Hein.

Training for the Theatre. Michel Saint-Denis. Ed. by Suria Saint-Denis. (Illus.). 1982. pap. 12.95 (ISBN 0-87830-576-9). Theatre Arts.

Training for Tomorrow: Distributed Learning Through Computer & Communications Technology. Greg Kearsley. 128p. 1985. write for info. (ISBN 0-201-11652-9). Addison-Wesley.

Training for Tomorrow, Educational Aspects of Computerized Automation: Proceedings of the IFAC-IFIP Symposium, Leiden, The Netherlands, June, 1983. IFAC-IFIP Symposium Staff & Rijnsdorp. Ed. by L. Immink. (IFAC Proceedings Ser.). 600p. 1984. 92.00 (ISBN 0-08-031111-3). Pergamon.

Training for Trainers: The Technique. Robert Curry. (Serving the Elderly Ser.: Pt. 6). 1979. pap. text ed. 11.00 (ISBN 0-89634-008-2, 048). Systems Planning.

Training for Urban Management. OECD. (Urban Management Studies No. 2). 204p. (Orig.). 1979. pap. 12.50x (ISBN 92-64-11914-0). OECD.

Training for Western Horse & Rider. J'Wayne McArthur. (Illus.). 326p. pap. 16.00 (ISBN 0-318-23399-1, J'Wayne McArthur). Publishers Group.

Training for Work in the Computer Age: Policy Implications. Bryna S. Fraser & Harold Goldstein. 15p. 1986. 5.00 (ISBN 0-86510-056-X). Nat'l Inst Work.

Training Guard & Protection Dogs. Joseph A. Dobson. LC 83-26620. (Illus.). 208p. 1984. 16.95 (ISBN 0-668-05830-7, 5830). Arco.

Training Guide for Foodservice Personnel in Programs for Young Children. 200p. 1987. write for info. (ISBN 1-556720-28-9). US HHS.

Training Guide to Cerebral Palsy Sports. 3rd ed. Ed. by Jeffery A. Jones. LC 87-3081. (Illus.). 256p. 1987. pap. text ed. 20.00 (ISBN 0-87322-125-7, BJON0125). Human Kinetics.

Training, Human Decision Making & Control. Ed. by J. Patrick & K. D. Duncan. 408p. 1988. 118.50 (ISBN 0-444-70381-0, North Holland). Elsevier.

Training Human Intelligence: Developing Exploratory & Aesthetic Skills. Robert M. Travers. LC 83-82786. (Illus.). 1985. softcover 19.95 (ISBN 0-918452-51-1). Learning Pubns.

Training Human Service Managers: A Curriculum Design. Richard Liefer et al. LC 79-66521. (Human Service Management Ser.). 1979. pap. 3.95 (ISBN 0-89995-071-X). Social Matrix.

Training in Agricultural & Food Marketing at Middle Level: Report, Nairobi, Kenya, 1974. FAO In-Service Consultation on Middle-Level Training in Agricultural Marketing in African & Near East Countries Staff. (Development Documents: No. 12). 99p. 1974. pap. 7.50 (ISBN 0-686-92717-6, F1228, FAO). UNIPUB.

Training in Ambiguity: Learning Through Doing in a Mental Hospital. Rose L. Coser. LC 78-54109. (Illus.). 1979. 18.00 (ISBN 0-02-906580-1). Free Pr.

Training in Business, Industry & Government see Educational Technology Reviews Ser.

Training in Christianity. Soren Kierkegaard. Tr. by Walter Lowrie. (American-Scandinavian Foundation Ser.). 1944. pap. 9.50x (ISBN 0-691-01959-2). Princeton U Pr.

Training in Community Living Model: A Decade of Experience. Ed. by Leonard I. Stein & Mary A. Test. LC 84-82375. (Mental Health Services Ser.: No. 26). (Orig.). 1985. pap. text ed. 14.95x (ISBN 0-87589-760-6). Jossey-Bass.

Training in Consultation: Perspectives from Mental Health, Behavioral & Organizational Consultation. Judith L. Alpert & Joel Meyers. (Illus.). 268p. 1983. 23.75x (ISBN 0-398-04801-0). C C Thomas.

Training in European Enterprises. Frederic Meyers. (Monograph & Research Ser.: No. 14). 173p. 1969. 5.00 (ISBN 0-89215-015-7). U Cal LA Indus Rel.

Training in Family Planning for Health Personnel. (Public Health in Europe Ser.: No. 20). 105p. 1985. pap. 6.00 (ISBN 92-890-1156-4). World Health.

Training in High-School Mathematics Essential for Success in Certain College Subjects. Allan R. Congdon. (Columbia University. Teachers College. Contributions to Education: No. 403). Repr. of 1930 ed. 22.50 (ISBN 0-404-55403-2). AMS Pr.

Training in Human Services, Vol. I. Ed. by Thomas D. Morton & Ronald K. Green. 223p. (Orig.). 1978. pap. text ed. 5.00 (ISBN 0-89695-002-6). U Tenn CSW.

Training in Literary Appreciation: An Introduction to Criticism. F. H. Pritchard. 1978. Repr. of 1934 ed. lib. bdg. 17.50 (ISBN 0-8495-4342-8). Arden Lib.

Training in National Health Planning: Report. WHO Expert Committee. Geneva, 1970. (Technical Report Ser.: No. 456). (Also avail. in French & Spanish). 1970. pap. 2.00 (ISBN 92-4-120456-7). World Health.

Training in Objective Educational Measurements for Elementary School Teachers. Maxwell G. Park. LC 70-177143. (Columbia University. Teachers College. Contributions to Education: No. 520). Repr. of 1932 ed. 22.50 (ISBN 0-404-55520-9). Ams Pr.

Training in Organizations: Needs, Assessments, Development, & Evaluation. 2nd ed. Irwin L. Goldstein. LC 85-21348. 275p. 1985. pap. 11.25 pub net (ISBN 0-534-05604-0). Brooks-Cole.

Training in Radiological Protection for Nuclear Programs. (Technical Reports Ser.: No. 166). 116p. 1975. pap. 18.00 (ISBN 92-0-125075-4, IDC166, IAEA). UNIPUB.

Training in Small Groups: A Study of Five Methods. rev. ed. Ed. by B. Babington Smith. B. A. Farrell. 114p. 1979. 34.00 (ISBN 0-08-023689-8). Pergamon.

Training in the Automated Office: A Decision-Maker's Guide to Systems Planning & Implementation. Randy J. Goldfield. LC 86-30605. 256p. 1987. lib. bdg. 39.95 (ISBN 0-89930-112-6, EOF/, Quorum Bks). Greenwood.

Training Interventions in Job Skill Development. James E. Gardner. LC 80-23810. (Illus.). 224p. 1981. text ed. write for info. (ISBN 0-201-03097-7). Addison-Wesley.

Training Investment. Jeremy Harrison & Michaela Dungate. 172p. 1984. 40.00x (ISBN 0-86021-539-3, Pub. by Hobsons Ltd UK). State Mutual Bk.

Training: Issues & Answers for the Eighties. Michael Marquardt & Robert W. Stump. 1982. pap. 6.00 (ISBN 0-87771-030-9). Grad School.

Training Issues in Changing Technology. Ed. by Charles E. Kratz et al. 91p. 1986. 16.00 (ISBN 0-8389-7032-X). Library Admin.

Training Leaders for Family Life Education. Beth C. Fallon. LC 82-10200. (Workshop Models for Family Life Education Ser.). 124p. 1982. plastic comb 15.95 (ISBN 0-87304-188-7). Family Serv.

Training Local Midwives. Maureen Williams. 48p. 1986. 8.00x (ISBN 0-946848-52-1, Pub. by CIIR). State Mutual Bk.

Training Managers to Train. Herman Zacarelli. 96p. Date not set. 7.95. Human Res Dev Pr.

Training Managers to Train. Herman Zaccarelli. Ed. by Michael G. Crisp. LC 87-73183. (Fifty-Minute Ser.). (Illus.). 96p. 1988. pap. 7.95 (ISBN 0-931961-43-2). Crisp Pubns.

Training Manual for Central Service Technicians. American Society for Hospital Central Service Personnel Staff. LC 86-3332. (Illus.). 278p. 1986. pap. text ed. 65.00 (ISBN 0-87258-442-9, 031802). Am Hospital.

Training Manual for Staff Developers in Long Term Care. John A. Bavaro. 86p. 1987. pap. 17.95 (ISBN 0-942028-27-9); home study course 34.97. R D Anderson.

Training Manual for the BLL Battery. B. J. Hemphill. LC 81-51723. 150p. 1988. 19.95 (ISBN 0-913590-87-8). Slack Inc.

Training Manual in Development Anthropology. Ed. by William L. Partridge. (American Anthropological Association Special Publication Ser.: No. 17). 122p. 1984. pap. text ed. 9.00 (ISBN 0-913167-02-9); pap. text ed. 6.00 members. Am Anthro Assn.

Training Manual in Medical Anthropology. Ed. by Carole E. Hill. (Special Publication: No. 18). 164p. 1985. pap. text ed. 13.50 (ISBN 0-913167-08-8); pap. text ed. 9.00 members. Am Anthro Assn.

Training Manual in Nutritional Anthropology. Ed. by Sara A. Quandt & Cheryl Ritenbaugh. (Special Publication: No. 20). 154p. 1986. pap. text ed. 14.00 (ISBN 0-913167-13-4); pap. text ed. 10.50 members. Am Anthro Assn.

Training Manual in Policy Ethnography. John Van Willigen & Billie R. DeWalt. (Special Publication: No. 19). 1985. pap. text ed. 12.00 (ISBN 0-913167-11-8); pap. text ed. 8.00 members. Am Anthro Assn.

Training Manual on Food Irradiation Technology & Techniques. (Technical Reports Ser.: No. 114). (Illus.). 220p. 1982. pap. 30.50 (ISBN 92-0-115082-2, IDC114/2, IAEA). UNIPUB.

Training Methodology & Management. D. P. Chowdhry. 304p. 1986. text ed. 35.00x (ISBN 81-207-0112-7, Pub. by Sterling Pubs India). Apt Bks.

Training Needs Assessment. Allison Rossett. LC 87-9070. (Illus.). 281p. 1987. 37.95 (ISBN 0-87778-195-8). Educ Tech Pubns.

Training Needs: Assessment & Monitoring. L. Richter. viii, 83p. (Orig.). 1986. pap. 12.25 (ISBN 92-2-105458-6). Intl Labour Office.

Training Needs in Geothermal Energy: Report of the Workshop, Laugarvatu, Iceland, July 1978. 51p. 1980. pap. 5.00 (ISBN 92-808-0017-5, TUNU004, UNU). UNIPUB.

Training of an Orator, 4 vols. Quintilian. (Loeb Classical Library: No. 124-127). 13.95x ea. Vol. 1 (ISBN 0-674-99138-9). Vol. 2 (ISBN 0-674-99139-7). Vol. 3 (ISBN 0-674-99140-0). Vol. 4 (ISBN 0-674-99141-9). Harvard U Pr.

Training of "Barefoot" Architects. 53p. (Orig.). 1984. pap. 5.00 (UB150, UB). UNIPUB.

Training of Caged Birds. Nancy A. Brudigan. (Illus.). 96p. 1982. 9.95 (ISBN 0-87666-827-9, PS-788). TFH Pubns.

Training of Elementary & Secondary Teachers in Sweden. Axel G. Peterson. LC 70-177151. (Columbia University. Teachers College. Contributions to Education: No. 575). Repr. of 1934 ed. 22.50 (ISBN 0-404-55575-6). AMS Pr.

Training of Elementary School Teachers in Germany. Isaac Leon Kandel. LC 71-176926. (Columbia University. Teachers College. Contributions to Education: No. 31). Repr. of 1910 ed. 22.50 (ISBN 0-404-55031-2). AMS Pr.

Training of Good Physicians: Critical Factors in Career Choices. Fremont J. Lyden et al. LC 68-21977. (Commonwealth Fund Publications). 1968. 18.50x (ISBN 0-674-90285-8). Harvard U Pr.

Training of High School Teachers in Louisiana. James M. Smith. LC 74-177771. (Columbia University. Teachers College. Contributions to Education: No. 247). Repr. of 1926 ed. 22.50 (ISBN 0-404-55247-1). AMS Pr.

Training of Medical Laboratory Technicians: A Handbook for Tutors. A. McMinn & G. J. Russell. (Offset Pub.: No. 21). (Also avail. in French). 1975. pap. 6.00 (ISBN 92-4-170021-1). World Health.

Training of Modern Foreign Language Teachers for the Secondary Schools in the United States. Hugh Stuart. LC 70-177738. (Columbia University. Teachers College. Contributions to Education: No. 256). Repr. of 1927 ed. 22.50 (ISBN 0-404-55256-0). AMS Pr.

Training of Negro Teachers in Louisiana. Jane E. McAllister. LC 71-177016. (Columbia University. Teachers College. Contributions to Education: No. 364). Repr. of 1929 ed. 22.50 (ISBN 0-404-55364-8). AMS Pr.

Training of Personnel for Distance Education. 108p. (Orig.). 1984. pap. 6.50 (UB147, UB). UNIPUB.

Training of Primary Physicians. Ed. by Stephen J. Kunitz et al. LC 85-22745. (Illus.). 428p. (Orig.). 1986. lib. bdg. 36.25 (ISBN 0-8191-5030-4); pap. text ed. 19.50 (ISBN 0-8191-5031-2). U Pr of Amer.

Training of Prison Governors: Role Ambiguity & Socialization. P. A. Waddington. 177p. 1983. 27.00 (ISBN 0-7099-2786-X, Pub. by Croom Helm Ltd). Routledge Chapman & Hall.

Training of Research Workers in the Medical Sciences: Proceedings of the CIOMS Round Table conference, Geneva, 1970. CIOMS Round Table Conference Staff. 186p. 1972. pap. 9.60 (ISBN 92-4-156040-1, 566). World Health.

Training of Sanitary Engineers in Europe. Ed. by Robert B. Dean. 198p. 1985. pap. 9.60 (ISBN 92-890-1022-3). World Health.

Training of Sci-Tech Librarians & Library Users. Ed. by Ellis Mount. LC 81-6975. (Science & Technology Libraries: Vol. 1, No. 3). 72p. 1981. pap. text ed. 19.95 (ISBN 0-917724-75-5, B75). Haworth Pr.

Training of Science Teachers & Teacher Educators. 68p. 1986. pap. text ed. 7.50 (ISBN 0-317-43837-9, UB186, UB). UNIPUB.

Traite De Tournois, Joustes, Carrousels et Autres Spectacles Publics. Claude Menestrier. Ed. by Stephen Orgel. LC 78-68198. (Philosophy of Images Ser.: Vol. 16). (Illus.). 1980. Repr. of 1669 ed. lib. bdg. 80.00 (ISBN 0-8240-3690-5). Garland Pub.

Traite des Courbes Speciales Remarquables Planes et Gauches, 3 vols. 2nd ed. Francisco Gomes Teixeira. LC 73-113153. 1337p. (Fr.). 1972. text ed. 75.00 set (ISBN 0-8284-0255-8). Chelsea Pub.

Traite Des Degenerescences Physiques, Intellectuelles et Morales De L'espece Humaine, 2 vols. in 1. Benedict A. Morel. LC 75-16721. (Classics in Psychiatry Ser.). (Illus., Fr.). 1976. Repr. of 1857 ed. 56.50x (ISBN 0-405-07446-8). Ayer Co Pubs.

Traite des Maladies Du Cerveau et De Ses Membranes: Maladies Mentales. Antoine L. Bayle. LC 75-16682. (Classics in Psychiatry Ser.). (Fr.). 1976. Repr. of 1826 ed. 46.50x (ISBN 0-405-07414-X). Ayer Co Pubs.

Traite des tournois, joustes, carrousels et autres spectacles publics. Claude-Francois Menestrier. LC 76-43926. (Music & Theatre in France in the 17th & 18th Centuries). Repr. of 1669 ed. 60.00 (ISBN 0-404-60174-X). AMS Pr.

Traite d'orchestration d'Hector Berlioz. Richard Strauss. Tr. by Ernest Closson. LC 74-24236. Repr. of 1909 ed. 18.00 (ISBN 0-404-13104-2). AMS Pr.

Traite D'organogenie Comparee de la Fleur. I. B. Payer. Repr. of 1857 ed. 132.00x (ISBN 3-7682-0346-8). Lubrecht & Cramer.

Traite du recitatif dans la lecture, dans l'action publique, dans la declamation, et dans le chant. Jean L. Grimarest. LC 76-43921. (Music & Theatre in France in the 17th & 18th Centuries). 1977. Repr. of 1760 ed. 20.00 (ISBN 0-404-60164-2). AMS Pr.

Traite Elementaire de Comptabilite: Elementary Treatise on Accounting. J. G. Courcelle-Seneuil. Ed. by Richard P. Brief. (Dimensions of Accounting Theory & Practice Ser.). (Fr.). 1981. Repr. of 1869 ed. lib. bdg. 22.00x (ISBN 0-405-13513-0). Ayer Co Pubs.

Traite Elementaire de l'Imprimerie, ou le Manuel de l'Imprimeur. Antoine F. Momoro. (Illus.). 352p. Date not set. Repr. of 1793 ed. text ed. 62.00x (ISBN 0-576-72155-7, Pub by Gregg Untl Pubs England). Gregg Intl.

Traite Elementaire De Paleontologie Histoire Naturelle Des Animaux Fossiles Consideres Ans Leur S Rapports Zoologiques et Geologiques, 4 vols. Francois J. Pictet. Ed. by Stephen J. Gould. LC 79-8344. (History of Paleontology Ser.). (Illus., Fr.). 1980. Repr. of 1844 ed. Set. lib. bdg. 174.00x (ISBN 0-405-12734-0); lib. bdg. 43.50x ea. Vol. 1 (ISBN 0-405-12735-9). Vol. 2 (ISBN 0-405-12736-7). Vol. 3 (ISBN 0-405-12737-5). Vol. 4 (ISBN 0-405-12738-3). Ayer Co Pubs.

Traite Elementaire Theorique et Pretique De l'Art De La Danse see Elementary Treatise upon the Theory & Practice of the Art of Dancing.

Traite Maladies des Os et des Articulations Mise a Jour 1985. S. De Seze & A. Ryckewaert. (Collection Medico-Chirurgicale). (Illus.). 168p. (Fr.). 1985. 36.00 (ISBN 0-318-04694-6). S M P F Inc.

Traite Medico-Philosophique Sur L'alienation Mentale. 2nd ed. Philippe Pinel. LC 75-16727. (Classics in Psychiatry Ser.). (Fr.). 1976. Repr. of 1809 ed. 42.00 (ISBN 0-405-07450-6). Ayer Co Pubs.

Traite Neo-Manicheen du XIIIe siecle. Liber de Duobus Principiis. LC 78-63185. (Heresies of the Early Christian & Medieval Era: Second Ser.). 1979. Repr. of 1939 ed. 32.00 (ISBN 0-404-16224-X). AMS Pr.

Traite Sur L'art De la Guerre. B. Stuart. (International Archives of the History of Ideas Ser: No. 85). 1977. pap. 26.00 (ISBN 90-247-1871-6, Pub. by Martinus Nijhoff Netherlands). Kluwer Academic.

Traitement Graphique D'une Information Hydrometeorologique Relative a L'espace Maritime Du Nord Sovietique, 2 vols. Serge Bonin. Incl. Vol. 1. Documents Graphiques. (Illus.); Vol. 2. Analyses et Commentaires. 2200p. (Contributions Du Centre D' Etudes Antiques: No. 11). (Illus., Fr.). 1974. Set. pap. text ed. 34.80x (ISBN 0-686-22587-2). Mouton.

Traites de commerce. Dieudonne A. Boiteau. (Research & Source Works Ser., History, Economics & Social Science). 1971. Repr. of 1863 ed. 32.50 (ISBN 0-8337-0332-3). B Franklin.

Traites de Paix et de Commerce et Documents Divers Concernant les Relations des Chretiens avec les Arabes de l'Afrique Septentrionale Au Moyen Age, 2 Vols. Louis De Mas-Latrie. 1964. Repr. of 1886 ed. 73.00 (ISBN 0-8337-2278-6). B Franklin.

Traitor. Andre Gorz. Tr. by Richard Howard. 320p. 1988. text ed. 42.50 (ISBN 0-86091-228-0, Pub. by Verso); pap. text ed. 14.95 (ISBN 0-86091-941-2, Pub. by Verso). Routledge Chapman & Hall.

Traitor. Dan Sherman. 1987. 17.95 (ISBN 1-55611-000-6). D I Fine.

Traitor. Dan Sherman. Ed. by Jim Connor. 272p. 1988. pap. 3.95 (ISBN 0-7701-0797-4). Paperjacks US.

Traitor. William L. Shirer. 1971. pap. 0.95 (ISBN 0-671-77325-9). PB.

Traitor. James Shirley. Ed. by John S. Carter. LC 65-11520. (Regents Renaissance Drama Ser). xviii, 111p. 1965. 11.50x (ISBN 0-8032-0282-2); pap. 2.95x (ISBN 0-8032-5283-8, BB 212, Bison). U of Nebr Pr.

Traitor: The Case of Benedict Arnold. Jean Fritz. (Illus.). (gr. 3-7). 1981. 9.95 (ISBN 0-399-20834-8, Putnam). Putnam Pub Group.

Traitor to the Living. Philip Jose Farmer. 288p. (Orig.). 1985. pap. 2.95 (ISBN 0-8125-3766-1, Dist. by Warner Pub. Services & Saint Martin's Press). Tor Bks.

Traitor Trade. J. Bernard Hutton. (Illus.). 1963. 12.95 (ISBN 0-8392-1120-1). Astor-Honor.

Traitorous Hero: The Life & Fortunes of Benedict Arnold. facs. ed. Willard M. Wallace. LC 74-117896. (Select Bibliographies Reprint Ser). 1954. 24.00 (ISBN 0-8369-5349-5). Ayer Co Pubs.

Traitors. William S. Long. (Australians Ser.: No. III). (Orig.). 1981. pap. 4.50 (ISBN 0-440-18131-3). Dell.

Traitors. Chapman Pincher. 376p. 1988. pap. 7.95 (ISBN 0-14-011151-4). Penguin.

Traitors & Heroes: A Lawyer's Memoir. Martin Garbus. LC 86-47942. 352p. 1987. 19.95 (ISBN 0-689-11888-0). Atheneum.

Traitor's Blood. Reginald Hill. LC 86-16443. 256p. 1986. 16.95 (ISBN 0-88150-076-3, Foul Play). Countryman.

Traitor's Blood. Reginald Hill. 256p. (Orig.). 1987. pap. 3.95 (ISBN 0-446-34719-1). Warner Bks.

Traitor's Heir. Jasmine Cresswell. (Regency Romances Ser.: No. 7). Date not set. pap. 2.25 (ISBN 0-317-63824-6). Harlequin Bks.

Traitor's Purse. Margery Allingham. 176p. Repr. of 1941 ed. lib. bdg. 14.95 (ISBN 0-89190-199-X, Pub. by River City Pr). Amereon Ltd.

Traitors: The Anatomy of Treason. Chapman Pincher. (Illus.). 640p. 1987. 19.95 (ISBN 0-312-00696-9). St Martin.

Traitors to the Masculine Cause: The Men's Campaigns for Women's Rights. Sylvia Strauss. LC 81-20299. (Contributions in Women's Studies: No. 35). (Illus.). xix, 290p. 1982. lib. bdg. 36.95 (ISBN 0-313-22238-X, STM/). Greenwood.

Traits & Stories of the Irish Peasantry: With Illustrations by Phiz, Wrightson Lee & Others, 4 vols. facsimile ed. William Carleton. LC 79-163022. (Short Story Index Reprint Ser.). (Illus.). Repr. of 1853 ed. Set. 80.00 (ISBN 0-8369-3936-0). Ayer Co Pubs.

Traits Characteristic of Men Majoring in Physical Education at the Pennsylvania State College. Nelson S. Walke. LC 74-177668. (Columbia University. Teachers College. Contributions to Education: No. 735). Repr. of 1937 ed. 22.50 (ISBN 0-404-55735-X). AMS Pr.

Traits D'Union. Ralph Hester & Gail Wade. LC 87-80877. 512p. 1988. pap. text-ed. 29.96 (ISBN 0-395-35901-5); wkbk. lab. manual 13.95 (ISBN 0-395-44860-3); cassettes 18.36. HM.

Traits et Portraits. Natalie Barney. LC 75-12303. (Homosexuality: Lesbians & Gay Men in Society, History & Literature Ser.). (Fr.). 1975. Repr. of 1963 ed. 13.00x (ISBN 0-405-07395-X). Ayer Co Pubs.

Traits Eternels de la France. Maurice Barres. 1918. 29.50x (ISBN 0-685-89791-5). Elliots Bks.

Traits of a Happy Couple. Larry Halter. 1988. 8.95 (ISBN 0-317-66960-5). Word Bks.

Traits of a Healthy Family. Dolores Curran. 336p. 1984. pap. 3.95 (ISBN 0-345-31750-5). Ballantine.

Traits of a Healthy Family: Fifteen Traits Commonly Found in Healthy Families by Those Who Work With Them. Dolores Curran. LC 82-70489. 300p. 1983. 14.95 (ISBN 0-86683-643-8, HarpR); pap. 7.95. Har-Row.

Traits of a Healthy Family: Fifteen Traits Commonly Found in Healthy Families by Those Who Work with Them. Dolores Curran. 1984. pap. 7.95 (ISBN 0-86683-815-5, 8444, HarpR). Har-Row.

Traits of American Humor by Native Authors. 337p. 1982. Repr. lib. bdg. 50.00 (ISBN 0-8495-5213-3). Arden Lib.

Traits of American Indian Life. Peter S. Ogden. 19.95 (ISBN 0-87770-389-2). Ye Galleon.

Traits of American Indian Life & Character. 2nd ed. Peter S. Ogden. Repr. of 1933 ed. 17.45 (ISBN 0-404-07149-X). AMS Pr.

Trajectories in the Study of Religion: Addresses at the Seventy-Fifth Anniversary of the American Academy of Religion. Ed. by Ray L. Hart. LC 86-20272. (Studies in Religion & Theological Scholarship (American Academy of Religion)). 321p. 1988. 25.95 (ISBN 1-55540-064-7, 01 99 99). Scholars Pr GA.

Trajectories Through the Early Christianity. James M. Robinson. LC 79-141254. pap. cancelled (2029299). Bks Demand UMI.

Trajectory: Fueling the Future & Preserving the Black Literary Past-Essays in Criticism (1962-1986) Ruthe T. Sheffrey. (Illus.). 160p. 1986. 15.00 (ISBN 0-9610324-6-4). Morgan State.

Trajectory Spaces, Generalized Functions & Unbounded Operators. S. Van Eijndhoven & J. De Graaf. (Lecture Notes in Mathematics Ser.: Vol. 1162). iv, 272p. 1985. pap. 20.00 (ISBN 0-387-16065-5). Springer-Verlag.

Trakehnen Horses. Herbert Rudofsky. (Breed Ser.). 1977. pap. 2.95 (ISBN 0-88376-011-8). Dreenan Pr.

Trammeled University. George Kelly. 192p. 1974. text ed. 9.95x (ISBN 0-87073-434-2). Schenkman Bks Inc.

Trammels, Trenchers & Tartlets. Joyce W. Carlo. (Illus.). 144p. (Orig.). 1982. pap. 7.95 (ISBN 0-933614-13-6). Peregrine Pr Pubs.

Tramp. Jack London. (Illus.). 51p. 1948. pap. 1.95 (ISBN 0-932458-24-6). Star Rover.

Tramp. Will Thomas. 1986. 13.95 (ISBN 0-533-06958-0). Vantage.

Tramp Abroad. Samuel L. Clemens. (Works of Mark Twain). 1988. Repr. of 1906 ed. lib. bdg. 59.00x. Am Biog Serv.

Tramp Abroad, Pts. 1 & 2 see Writings of Mark Twain.

Tramp Across the Continent. Charles F. Lummis. LC 81-16194. xxvi, 270p. 1982. pap. 6.50 (ISBN 0-8032-7908-6, BB 791, Bison). U of Nebr Pr.

Tramp for the Lord. Corrie Ten Boom. 1976. pap. 2.95 (ISBN 0-515-08993-1). Jove Pubns.

Tramp for the Lord. Corrie Ten Boom. 1974. pap. 6.95 (ISBN 0-87508-028-6); pap. 3.50 (ISBN 0-87508-017-0). Chr Lit.

Tramp for the Lord. Corrie Ten Boom & Jamie Buckingham. (Illus.). 192p. 1974. pap. 6.95 (ISBN 0-8007-0769-9). Revell.

Tramp Steamer & the Silver Bullet. Jeff Kelly. 192p. (gr. 5-9). 1984. 11.95 (ISBN 0-395-36632-1). HM.

Tramp, Tramp, Tramp, the Girls Are Marching: A Self-Styled Report on the Women's Liberation Movement. Bernard M. Bane. 80p. 1982. pap. 5.00 (ISBN 0-930924-15-0). BMB Pub Co.

Tramp Virus. 1988. 3.00. Inkblot Pubns.

Trampa. Myrna Casas. Bd. with Impromptu De San Juan. (UPREX, Teatro y Cine: No. 36). pap. 1.85 (ISBN 0-8477-0036-4). U of PR Pr.

Tramper's Guide to New Zealand National Parks. Burton & Atkinson. 243p. (Orig.). 1988. pap. 12.95 (ISBN 1-55650-086-6). Hunter Pub NY.

Tramping in Europe. (One-of-a-Kind Travel Guides Ser.). 7.95 (ISBN 0-317-52027-X). P-H.

Tramping in New Zealand. Jim DuFresne. (Illus.). 168p. 1982. pap. 6.95 (ISBN 0-908086-33-4). Lonely Planet.

Tramping Out the Vintage: The Civil War Diaries & Letters of Eugene Kingman. Eugene C. Kingman. Ed. by Helene C. Phelan. (Illus.). 388p. 1983. pap. 9.95 (ISBN 0-9605836-4-5). Phelan.

Tramping with a Poet in the Rockies. Stephen Graham. 1973. Repr. of 1922 ed. 40.00 (ISBN 0-8274-1569-9). R West.

Tramping with Tramps: Studies & Sketches of Vagabond Life. Josiah Flynt Willard. LC 72-129317. (Criminology, Law Enforcement, & Social Problems Ser.: No. 140). (Illus.). 414p. (With index added). 1972. Repr. of 1907 ed. lib. bdg. 12.50x (ISBN 0-87585-140-1). Patterson Smith.

Trample an Empire Down. Mack Reynolds. 1978. pap. 1.50 (ISBN 0-8439-0585-9, Leisure Bks). Leisure NY.

Trampled Grass: Tributary States & Self-reliance in the Indian Ocean Zone of Peace. George W. Shepherd, Jr. LC 86-27116. (Contributions in Political Science: No. 169). 191p. 1987. lib. bdg. 39.95 (ISBN 0-313-25772-8, SFQ). Greenwood.

Trampled Grass: Tributary States & Self-reliance in the Indian Ocean Zone of Peace. George W. Shepherd, Jr. LC 86-17116. 187p. 1987. pap. 12.95 (ISBN 0-275-92608-7, B2608). Praeger.

Trampling Herd. Paul I. Wellman. LC 73-92636. (Illus.). 433p. 1975. Repr. of 1951 ed. lib. bdg. 25.00x (ISBN 0-8154-0490-5). Cooper Sq.

Trampling Herd: The Story of the Cattle Range in America. Paul I. Wellman. LC 88-5946. (Illus.). 433p. 1988. pap. 10.95 (ISBN 0-8032-9723-8, Bison). U of Nebr Pr.

Trampolining. Jeff T. Hennessy. (Physical Education Activities Ser.). 70p. 1968. pap. text ed. write for info. (ISBN 0-697-07034-4). Wm C Brown.

Trampolining: A Complete Handbook. rev. 2nd ed. Dennis Horne. (Illus.). 224p. 1978. pap. 6.95 (ISBN 0-571-04945-1). Faber & Faber.

Tramps & Ladies. James Bisset & P. R. Stephensen. LC 59-12193. (Illus.). 1959. 24.95 (ISBN 0-87599-014-2). S G Phillips.

Tramps & Reformers, 1873-1916: The Discovery of Unemployment in New York. Paul T. Ringenbach. LC 77-175610. (Contributions in American History: No. 27). (Illus.). 224p. 1973. lib. bdg. 46.95 (ISBN 0-8371-6266-1, RAT/). Greenwood.

Tramp's Chronicle. Thomas Callaghan. 220p. 1983. 15.95 (ISBN 0-85362-201-9, Oriel Press). Routledge Chapman & Hall.

Tramways & Trolleys: The Rise of Urban Mass Transport in Europe. John P. McKay. LC 76-3261. (Illus.). 280p. 1976. 38.00x (ISBN 0-691-05240-9). Princeton U Pr.

Trance & Treatment: Clinical Uses of Hypnosis. Herbert Spiegel & David Spiegel. LC 86-20627. (Illus.). 400p. 1987. pap. text ed. 18.95x (ISBN 0-88048-264-8, 48-264-8). Am Psychiatric.

Trance & Treatment: Clinical Uses of Hypnosis. Herbert Spiegel & David Spiegel. LC 77-20420. 1978. text ed. 19.95x (ISBN 0-465-08687-X). Basic.

Trance-Formations: Neuro-Linguistic Programming & the Structure of Hypnosis. John Grinder & Richard Bandler. Ed. by Connirae Andreas. 252p. (Orig.). 1981. 10.00 (ISBN 0-911226-22-2); pap. 8.50 (ISBN 0-911226-23-0). Real People.

Trance, Healing, & Hallucination: Three Field Studies in Religious Experience. F. D. Goodman et al. LC 80-20043. 414p. 1982. Repr. of 1974 ed. text ed. 26.50 (ISBN 0-89874-246-3). Krieger.

Trance, Healing & Hallucination: Three Field Studies in Religious Experience. Felicitas D. Goodman & Jeannette H. Henney. LC 74-4159. (Contemporary Religious Movements Ser.). pap. 78.10 (ISBN 0-317-08516-6, 2055086). Bks Demand UMI.

Trance State: How People Change. Steven Goldsmith. 140p. 1986. text ed. 16.95x (ISBN 0-8290-1465-9). Irvington.

Trancework: An Introduction to Clinical Hypnosis. Michael D. Yapko. LC 84-19758. 350p. 1984. text ed. 38.50x incl. audiocassette (ISBN 0-8290-1525-6). Irvington.

Tranches De Vie: Authentic Readings for Basic Skill Development. Brown & Young. 1987. 19.25 (ISBN 0-8384-1517-2). Heinle & Heinle.

Tranducers. Ewing. 1987. write for info. (ISBN 0-471-88724-2). Wiley.

Tranformation of Contemporary Conservatism. Ed. by Brian Girvin. (Modern Politics Ser.: Vol. 22). 256p. 1988. text ed. 47.50 (ISBN 0-8039-8145-7); pap. text ed. 18.95 (ISBN 0-8039-8146-5). Sage.

Tranformations of Romanticism in Yeats, Eliot & Stevens. George Bornstein. LC 75-43241. 1976. lib. bdg. 25.00x (ISBN 0-226-06643-6). U of Chicago Pr.

Tranquebar: A Guide to the Coins of Danish India Circa 1620 to 1845. new ed. John C. Gray. LC 74-84564. (Illus.). 96p. 1975. 20.00x (ISBN 0-88000-054-6). Quarterman.

Tranquil Ecstasy: Mark Twain's Pastorale Neigung und Ihre Literarische Gestaltung. Karl-Otto Strohmidel. (Bochumer Anglistische Studien: No. 20). 302p. 1986. pap. 37.00x (ISBN 90-6032-293-2, Pub. by B R Gruner Netherlands). Benjamins North Am.

Tranquil Heart: Boccacio. Catherine M. Carswell. LC 76-8895. 1976. Repr. of 1937 ed. lib. bdg. 35.00 (ISBN 0-8414-3639-8). Folcroft.

Tranquil Heart: Portrait of Giovanni Boccaccio. Catherine Carswell. 1978. Repr. of 1937 ed. 37.50 (ISBN 0-8492-3934-6). R West.

Tranquility, 3 vols. H. P. Sheldon. (Illus.). 540p. 1986. 45.00 (ISBN 0-932558-33-X). Willow Creek Pr.

Tranquilizer Use & Well-Being: A Longitudinal Study of Social & Psychological Effects. Robert D. Caplan et al. (ISR Research Report Ser.). 442p. (Orig.). 1984. pap. text ed. 25.00x (ISBN 0-87944-296-4). Inst Soc Res.

Tranquilizing Agents & Adverse Effects: Medical Subject Analysis & Bibliography. Jean S. Vega. LC 84-45665. 150p. 1985. 34.50 (ISBN 0-88164-198-7); pap. 26.50 (ISBN 0-88164-199-5). ABBE Pubs Assn.

Tranquilizing of America. Richard Hughes & Robert Brewin. 1980. pap. 2.95 (ISBN 0-446-93638-3). Warner Bks.

Tranquillisers: Social, Psychological & Clinical Perspectives. Jonathan Gabe & Paul Williams. 350p. 1986. 39.95 (ISBN 0-422-79930-0, 1025, Pub. by Tavistock England). Routledge Chapman & Hall.

Tranquillitas Ordinis: The Present Failure & Future Promise of American Catholic Thought on War & Peace. George Weigel, Jr. 416p. 1987. 29.95 (ISBN 0-19-504193-3). Oxford U Pr.

Tranquillity & Insight: An Introduction to the Oldest Form of Buddhist Meditation. Amadeo Sole-Leris. LC 86-11834. 176p. 1986. pap. 7.95 (ISBN 0-87773-385-6). Shambhala Pubns.

Tranquillity Base & Other Stories. Asa Baber. LC 79-89138. 140p. 1979. pap. 5.00 (ISBN 0-931362-01-6). Fiction Intl.

Trans-Am. Sylvia Wilkinson. LC 82-19721. (World of Racing Ser.). (Illus.). 48p. (gr. 4 up). 1983. PLB 13.27 (ISBN 0-516-04718-3); pap. 3.95 (ISBN 0-516-44718-1). Childrens.

Trans Am Racing, Nineteen Sixty-Six to Nineteen Eighty-Five. Albert Bochroch. LC 86-18232. (Illus.). 200p. 1986. 24.95 (ISBN 0-87938-229-5). Motorbooks Intl.

Trans-Appalachian Frontier. Malcolm J. Rohrbough. (Illus.). 1978. 29.95x (ISBN 0-19-502209-2). Oxford U Pr.

Trans-Atlantic Conservative Protestantism in the Evangelical Free & Mission Covenant Traditions. Frederick Hale. Ed. by Franklyn D. Scott. LC 78-15183. (Scandinavians in America Ser.). 1979. lib. bdg. 30.50x (ISBN 0-405-11638-1). Ayer Co Pubs.

Trans-Atlantica: Essays on Scandinavians Migration & Culture. original anthology ed. Ed. by Franklyn D. Scott. LC 78-15849. (Scandinavians in America Ser.). (Illus.). 1979. lib. bdg. 28.50x (ISBN 0-405-11659-4). Ayer Co Pubs.

Trans-Australian Wonderland. A. G. Bolam. 1979. 27.50 (ISBN 0-85564-139-8, Pub. by U of W Austral Pr). Intl Spec Bk.

Trans-Canada Canoe Trail. David Lavender. LC 77-4864. (American Trail Ser.). 1977. text ed. 11.50 (ISBN 0-07-036678-0). McGraw.

TITLE INDEX

TRANSACTIONS OF THE ROYAL

Trans-Continental Railroad. Marilyn Miller. LC 85-40167. (Turning Points in American History Ser.). (Illus.). 64p. (gr. 5 up). 1985. 14.96 (ISBN 0-382-06824-6). Silver.

Trans-Himalaya, Discoveries & Adventures in Tibet, 2 vols. Sven A. Hedin. LC 68-55194. 1970. Repr. of 1913 ed. Vol. 1. lib. bdg. 59.95 (ISBN 0-8371-0470-X, HETA); Vol. 2. lib. bdg. 59.95 (ISBN 0-8371-0815-2, HETA). Greenwood.

Trans-Mississippi Mails after the Fall of Vicksburg. Richard Krieger. Ed. by John F. Dunn. (Philatelic Foundation Monographs: No. 1). (Illus.). 76p. (Orig.). 1984. pap. 7.00 (ISBN 0-911989-13-7). Philatelic Found.

Trans-Pacific Echoes & Resonances: Listening Once Again. Joseph Needham & Lu Gwei-Djen. 106p. 1985. 23.00 (ISBN 9971-950-86-3). World Scientific Pub.

Trans-Parent: Sexual Politics in the Language of Emerson. Eric Cheyfitz. LC 80-25750. 224p. 1981. text ed. 22.50x (ISBN 0-8018-2450-8). Johns Hopkins.

Trans-Siberian Express. Ed. by Victor Kuranov. LC 79-3106. (Illus.). 376p. 17.95 (ISBN 0-943071-10-0). Sphinx Pr.

Trans-Siberian Rail Guide. Robert Strauss. (Illus.). 192p. (Orig.). 1987. pap. 11.95 (ISBN 0-946983-06-2). Hunter Pub NY.

Trans-Siberian Railway. Cornelia Veenendaal. LC 73-86246. (Illus.). 64p. 1973. pap. 7.95 (ISBN 0-914086-01-4). Alicejamesbooks.

Transaction & Meaning: Directions in the Anthropology of Exchange & Symbolic Behavior. Ed. by Bruce Kapferer. LC 76-12644. (ASA Essays in Social Anthropology Ser.: Vol. 1). (Illus.). 312p. 1979. pap. text ed. 7.95 (ISBN 0-89727-003-7). ISHI PA.

Transaction in Hearts. Edgar Saltus. LC 68-54294. Repr. of 1889 ed. 17.50 (ISBN 0-404-05515-X). AMS Pr.

Transaction of the Eighth International Conference on Structural Mechanics in Reactor Technology, Brussels, Belgium, August 19-23, 1985, 13 vols. Ed. by S. Finzi. 571p. 1985. 442.00 (ISBN 0-444-86969-7, North-Holland). Elsevier.

Transaction One: The Record of Papers Presented to the RIBA for the Sessional Programme 1981-1982. Royal Institute of British Architects. Ed. by Peter Murray. (Twentieth Century Ser.: Vol.1., No. 1). (Illus.). 126p. (Orig.). 1983. 14.95x (ISBN 0-89955-405-9, Pub. by RIBA). Intl Spec Bk.

Transactional Analysis & Family Therapy. James Horewitz. LC 79-51923. 1979. 30.00x (ISBN 0-87668-381-2). Aronson.

Transactional Analysis Bulletin: Selected Articles from Volumes 1 Thru 9. Eric Berne et al. Ed. by Paul McCormick. (Illus.). 1976. pap. 3.00x (ISBN 0-89489-000-X). TA Press.

Transactional Analysis Commnnity: The Denver Experience. Laurie Weiss. 97p. 1975. pap. 3.00 (ISBN 0-318-14601-0). Intl Transactional.

Transactional Analysis for Police Personnel. Anne T. Romano. (Illus.). 208p. 1981. spiral bdg. 23.00 (ISBN 0-398-04175-X). C C Thomas.

Transactional Analysis for Social Workers & Counsellors: An Introduction. Liz Pitman. (Library of Social Work). 172p. (Orig.). 1984. pap. 11.95x (ISBN 0-7100-9581-3). Routledge Chapman & Hall.

Transactional Analysis: Improving Communications. Thomas C. Clary et al. 1974. pap. 24.90 (ISBN 0-685-73198-7); pap. 21.50 for 2 or more (ISBN 0-685-73199-5); pap. 24.90 french ed.; pap. 0.50 leader guide (ISBN 0-685-73200-2). Didactic Syst.

Transactional Analysis in Health Care. Jean Elder. LC 78-57376. 1978. pap. text ed. write for info. (ISBN 0-201-01512-9, Hlth-Sci). Addison-Wesley.

Transactional Analysis in Psychobiology: From Prince to Frog to Principal. Franklin H. Ernst, Jr. 1981. pap. 9.50x (ISBN 0-916944-36-0). Addresso'set.

Transactional Analysis in Psychotherapy: A Systematic Individual & Social Psychiatry. Eric Berne. 1978. pap. 3.95 (ISBN 0-345-33836-7). Ballantine.

Transactional Analysis on the Job & Communicating with Subordinates. Charles Albano. Ed. by Thomasine Rendero. LC 75-20236. (Illus.). 184p. 1975. 9.95 (ISBN 0-8144-5401-1). AMACOM.

Transactional Analysis on the Job & Communicating with Subordinates. rev. ed. Charles Albano. Ed. by Thomasine Rendero. LC 75-20236. pap. 45.80 (ISBN 0-317-27194-6, 2023928). Bks Demand UMI.

Transactional Corporations & Developing Countries: New Policies for a Changing World Economy. Committee for Economic Development. 96p. 1981. lib. bdg. 6.50 (ISBN 0-87186-772-9); pap. 5.00 (ISBN 0-87186-072-4). Comm Econ Dev.

Transactional Guide to the Uniform Commercial Code, 2 vols. 2nd ed. Richard Alderman & Richard F. Dole. 1349p. 1983. 175.00 (ISBN 0-8318-0490-4, B400); pap. 25.00 supplement, 1985, 101p. (B490). Am Law Inst.

Transactional Manager: How to Solve People Problems with Transactional Analysis. Abe Wagner. (Illus.). 208p. 1981. 11.95 (ISBN 0-13-928192-4, Spec); pap. 7.95 (ISBN 0-13-928184-3). P-H.

Transactions, 6 vols. Ossianic Society. Repr. 125.00 set (ISBN 0-384-43840-7). Johnson Repr.

Transactions, 6 Vols. Ossianic Society Of Dublin. LC 78-144462. Repr. of 1858 ed. Set. 72.50 (ISBN 0-404-09070-2); 12.50 ea. AMS Pr.

Transactions, Vol. 92. 1984. lib. bdg. 595.00 (ISBN 0-89883-591-7, V92). Soc Auto Engineers.

Transactions, Vol. 93. 1985. lib. bdg. 595.00 (ISBN 0-89883-607-7, V93). Soc Auto Engineers.

Transactions, Vol. 94. 1986. 595.00 (ISBN 0-317-60938-6, V94-85). Soc Auto Engineers.

Transactions, Vol. 95. 1987. 650.00 (ISBN 0-89883-618-2, V95-86). Soc Auto Engineers.

Transactions - Eighth Congress on Irrigation & Drainage Varna (Bulgaria), 1972, 6 Vols. 90.00 (ISBN 0-318-17911-3); members 52.00 (ISBN 0-318-17912-1). US Comm Irrigation.

Transactions - Eleventh Congress on Irrigation & Drainage Grenoble (France), 1981, 4 Vols. 150.00 (ISBN 0-318-17915-6); members 112.00 (ISBN 0-318-17916-4). US Comm Irrigation.

Transactions - Fifth Congress on Irrigation & Drainage Tokyo (Japan), 1963. 51.00 (ISBN 0-318-17901-6); members 35.50 (ISBN 0-318-17902-4). US Comm Irrigation.

Transactions - Seventh Congress on Irrigation & Drainage Mexico City, 1969. 90.00 (ISBN 0-318-17908-3); members 52.00 (ISBN 0-318-17909-1). US Comm Irrigation.

Transactions - Sixth Congress on Irrigation & Drainage New Delhi (India), 1966. 57.00 (ISBN 0-318-17904-0); members 38.50 (ISBN 0-318-17905-9). US Comm Irrigation.

Transactions - Tenth Congress on Irrigation & Drainage Athens (Greece), 1978, 7 Vols. 135.00 (ISBN 0-318-17913-X); members 84.50 (ISBN 0-318-17914-8). US Comm Irrigation.

Transactions & Collections, 12 Vols. American Antiquarian Society Staff. Set. 460.00 (ISBN 0-384-01057-1); Set. pap. 400.00 (ISBN 0-685-02203-X). Johnson Repr.

Transactions in a Foreign Currency. Deborah Eisenberg. LC 85-45591. 212p. 1986. 15.45 (ISBN 0-394-54598-2). Knopf.

Transactions in a Foreign Currency: Stories. Deborah Eisenberg. 224p. 1987. pap. 6.95 (ISBN 0-14-009855-0). Penguin.

Transactions in Families. John Papajohn & John Spiegel. LC 74-6740. (Jossey-Bass Behavioral Science Ser.). pap. 83.80 (2027764). Bks Demand UMI.

Transactions in Kinship: Adoption & Fosterage in Oceania. Ed. by Ivan A. Brady. LC 76-10342. (Association for Social Anthropology in Oceania Monographs: No.4). 320p. 1976. text ed. 20.00x (ISBN 0-8248-0478-3). UH Pr.

Transactions: International Vacuum Congress - 3rd - Stuttgart - 1965, Vol. 1-2, Pts. 1-2. Ed. by H. Adam. 1967. 71.00 (ISBN 0-08-012127-6). Pergamon.

Transactions Nineteen Seventy-Eight. 1979. text ed. 22.50x (ISBN 0-87262-235-5). Am Soc Civil Eng.

Transactions Nineteen Seventy-Seven. 808p. 1978. text ed. 22.50x (ISBN 0-87262-234-7). Am Soc Civil Eng.

Transactions of Conference Held March 9 to 13, 1914 at Liberty Buildings Liverpool. Ed. by S. D. Adshead & Patrick Abercrombie. LC 84-48275. (Rise of Urban Britain Ser.). (Illus.). 168p. 1985. lib. bdg. 30.00. Garland Pub.

Transactions of Technical Conference on Metric Mechanical Fasteners. 122p. 1975. pap. text ed. 12.00 (ISBN 0-685-62576-1, E00092). ASME.

Transactions of the American Association of Cost Engineers. Ed. by K. K. Humphreys & B. G. McMillan. (Illus.). 334p. 1982. 48.50 (ISBN 0-930284-15-1); pap. 38.50 (ISBN 0-930284-14-3). Am Assn Cost Engineers.

Transactions of the American Association of Cost Engineers. Ed. by K. K. Humphreys & T. Novak. (Illus.). 360p. 1983. 48.50x (ISBN 0-930284-18-6); pap. 38.50x (ISBN 0-930284-17-8). Am Assn Cost Engineers.

Transactions of the American Association of Cost Engineers, 1984. Ed. by B. Humphreys. 1984. 65.00x (ISBN 0-930284-20-8); pap. 65.00x (ISBN 0-930284-19-4). Am Assn Cost Engineers.

Transactions of the American Association of Cost Engineers, 1985. Ed. by B. Humphreys. 374p. 1985. 65.00x (ISBN 0-930284-24-0); pap. 45.00x (ISBN 0-930284-22-4). Am Assn Cost Engineers.

Transactions of the American Association of Cost Engineers 1986. Ed. by B. Humphreys. 346p. 1986. pap. 45.00x (ISBN 0-930284-27-5). Am Assn Cost Engineers.

Transactions of the American Association of Cost Engineers, 1987. Ed. by B. Humphreys & S. Pritchard. 520p. 1987. pap. 49.50x (ISBN 0-930284-30-5). Am Assn Cost Engineers.

Transactions of the American Association of Cost Engineers, 1980. Ed. by K. K. Humphreys & B. G. McMillan. (Illus.). 429p. 1980. 40.00x (ISBN 0-930284-07-0); pap. 30.00x (ISBN 0-930284-08-9). Am Assn Cost Engineers.

Transactions of the American Association of Cost Engineers, 1981. Ed. by K. K. Humphreys & B. G. McMillan. 428p. 1981. 45.00x (ISBN 0-930284-13-5); pap. 35.00x (ISBN 0-930284-12-7). Am Assn Cost Engineers.

Transactions of the American Association of Cost Engineers, 1979. Ed. by Curtis M. Sides. Kenneth K. Humphreys. (Illus.). 1979. 40.00 (ISBN 0-930284-04-6); pap. text ed. 30.00 (ISBN 0-930284-03-8). Morgantown Print & Bind.

Transactions of the American Gynecological & Obstetrical Society, Vol. IV. Transactions Staff. 1986. 45.00 (ISBN 0-8016-5088-7). Mosby.

Transactions of the American Society of Civil Engineers, Vol. 141. 795p. 1977. 22.50x (ISBN 0-87262-341-6). Am Soc Civil Eng.

Transactions of the American Society of Civil Engineers, Vol. 144. Compiled by American Society of Civil Engineers Staff. 1980. 22.50x (ISBN 0-87262-236-3). Am Soc Civil Eng.

Transactions of the American Society of Civil Engineers, Vol. 145. 1068p. 1981. 45.00x (ISBN 0-87262-340-8). Am Soc Civil Eng.

Transactions of the American Society of Civil Engineers, Vol. 146, 1981. Compiled by American Society of Civil Engineers Staff. 1056p. 1982. 52.50x (ISBN 0-87262-309-2). Am Soc Civil Eng.

Transactions of the American Society of Civil Engineers, Vol. 147. 492p. 1983. 52.50x (ISBN 0-87262-355-6). Am Soc Civil Eng.

Transactions of the American Society of Civil Engineers, Vol. 148. 480p. 1984. 52.50x (ISBN 0-87262-394-7). Am Soc Civil Eng.

Transactions of the American Society of Civil Engineers, Vol. 149. 490p. 1985. 60.00x (ISBN 0-87262-440-4). Am Soc Civil Eng.

Transactions of the American Society of Civil Engineers, Vol. 150. 484p. 1986. 60.00x (ISBN 0-87262-514-1). Am Soc Civil Eng.

Transactions of the Asiatic Society of Japan, Vol. IX, Pt. 11. Asiatic Society of Japan Staff. 1881. 100.00x (ISBN 0-317-69461-8, Pub. by Han-Shan Tang Ltd). State Mutual Bk.

Transactions of the Blavatsky Lodge. Helena P. Blavatsky. LC 52-16841. 1946. 7.00 (ISBN 0-911500-10-3). Theos U Pr.

Transactions of the Chartered Accountants Students' Societies of Edinburgh & Glasgow: A Selection of Writings, 1886-1958. Ed. by Thomas A. Lee. LC 83-49441. (Accounting History & the Development of a Profession Ser.). 342p. 1984. lib. bdg. 35.00 (ISBN 0-8240-6308-2). Garland Pub.

Transactions of the International Astronomical Union. Ed. by Jean P. Swings. 1986. lib. bdg. 105.00 (ISBN 90-277-2321-4, Pub. by Reidel Holland). Kluwer Academic.

Transactions of the International Astronomical Union, Vol. 13a. Reports on Astronomy. Ed. by L. Perek. 1047p. 1968. lib. bdg. 66.00 (ISBN 90-277-0138-5, Pub. by Reidel Holland). Kluwer Academic.

Transactions of the International Astronomical Union, Vol. 17b. Ed. by Patrick A. Wayman. 536p. 1980. PLB 68.50 (ISBN 90-277-1159-3, Pub. by Reidel Holland). Kluwer Academic.

Transactions of the International Astronomical Union, Vol. 18b. Ed. by Richard M. West. 1983. lib. bdg. 69.50 (ISBN 90-277-1563-7, Pub. by Reidel Holland). Kluwer Academic.

Transactions of the International Astronomical Union: Proceedings of the General Assembly of I.A.U., 13th, Prague, 1967, Vol. 13b. International Astronomical Union Staff. Ed. by L. Perek. 309p. 1968. lib. bdg. 26.00 (ISBN 90-277-0139-3, Pub. by Reidel Holland). Kluwer Academic.

Transactions of the International Astronomical Union: Proceedings of the General Assembly of I.A.U., 14th, Brighton, 1970, Vol. 14b. International Astronomical Union Staff. Ed. by C. De Jager & A. Jappels. LC 30-10103. 378p. 1971. lib. bdg. 42.00 (ISBN 90-277-0190-3, Pub. by Reidel Holland). Kluwer Academic.

Transactions of the International Astronomical Union: Proceedings of the General Assembly of I.A.U., 15th, Sydney, 1973, Vol. 15b. International Astronomical Union Staff & Extraordinary General Assembly, Poland, 1973. Ed. by G. Contopoulos & A. Jappel. LC 73-81827. 334p. 1974. lib. bdg. 63.00 (ISBN 90-277-0451-1, Pub. by Reidel Holland). Kluwer Academic.

Transactions of the International Astronomical Union: Reports on Astronomy, Vol. 14a. Ed. by C. De Jager. LC 30-10103. 566p. 1970. lib. bdg. 50.00 (ISBN 90-277-0154-7, Pub. by Reidel Holland). Kluwer Academic.

Transactions of the International Astronomical Union: Reports on Astronomy, Vol. 15a. Ed. by C. De Jager. LC 73-81827. 762p. 1973. lib. bdg. 105.00 (ISBN 90-277-0340-X, Pub. by Reidel Holland). Kluwer Academic.

Transactions of the Iron & Steel Society, Vol. I. LC 83-122618. 130p. 1982. 52.00 (ISBN 0-911277-00-5). ISS Found.

Transactions of the Iron & Steel Society, Vol. II. LC 83-122618. 130p. 1983. 52.00 (ISBN 0-911277-01-3). ISS Found.

Transactions of the Iron & Steel Society, Vol. III. LC 83-122618. 134p. 1983. 52.00 (ISBN 0-911277-02-1). ISS Found.

Transactions of the Iron & Steel Society, Vol. IV. 112p. 1984. 52.00 (ISBN 0-911277-03-X). ISS Found.

Transactions of the Iron & Steel Society, Vol. V. LC 83-122618. 110p. 1985. 52.00 (ISBN 0-911277-04-8). ISS Found.

Transactions of the Iron & Steel Society, 1985, Vol. 6. 84p. 1985. 52.00 (ISBN 0-911277-05-6). ISS Found.

Transactions of the Iron & Steel Society, 1986, Vol 7. 54p. 1986. 52.00 (ISBN 0-911277-06-4). ISS Found.

Transactions of the Iron & Steel Society, 1987, Vol. 8. Collective Work Staff. 62p. 1987. pap. text ed. 52.00 (ISBN 0-911277-07-2). ISS Found.

Transactions of the Iron & Steel Society, Vol. 9, 1988. 1988. pap. 52.00 (ISBN 0-911277-08-0). ISS Found.

Transactions of the Moscow Mathematical Society. Incl. Vol. 12. 1963. 63.00 (ISBN 0-8218-1612-8, MOSCOW-12); Vol. 13. 1965. 53.00 (ISBN 0-8218-1613-6, MOSCOW-13); Vol. 14. 1967. 53.00 (ISBN 0-8218-1614-4, MOSCOW-14); Vol. 15. 1967. 63.00 (ISBN 0-8218-1615-2, MOSCOW-15); Vol. 16. 1968. 54.00 (ISBN 0-8218-1616-0, MOSCOW-16); Vol. 17. 1969. 56.00 (ISBN 0-8218-1617-9, MOSCOW-17); Vol. 18. 1969. 50.00 (ISBN 0-8218-1618-7, MOSCOW-18); Vol. 19. 1969. 45.00 (ISBN 0-8218-1619-5, MOSCOW-19); Vol. 20. 1971. 67.00 (ISBN 0-8218-1620-9, MOSCOW-20); Vol. 21. 1971. 60.00 (ISBN 0-8218-1621-7, MOSCOW-21); Vol. 22. 1972. 53.00 (ISBN 0-8218-1622-5). LC 65-4713. Am Math.

Transactions of the Moscow Mathematical Society, Vol. 25. A. D. Brjuno et al. LC 65-4713. 1973. text ed. 69.00 (ISBN 0-8218-1625-X, MOSCOW-25). Am Math.

Transactions of the Moscow Mathematical Society, Vol. 28 (1973) V. S. Afraimovic et al. LC 65-4713. 1975. 84.00 (ISBN 0-8218-1628-4, MOSCOW-28). Am Math.

Transactions of the Moscow Mathematical Society, Vol. 29 (1973) V. A. Andrunakievic et al. LC 65-4713. 1976. 73.00 (ISBN 0-8218-1629-2, MOSCOW-29). Am Math.

Transactions of the Moscow Mathematical Society, Vol. 24 (1971) V. I. Averbuh et al. LC 65-4713. 1974. 78.00 (ISBN 0-8218-1624-1, MOSCOW-24). Am Math.

Transactions of the Moscow Mathematical Society, Vol. 27 (1972) V. I. Averbvh et al. LC 65-4713. 1974. 69.00 (ISBN 0-8218-1627-6, MOSCOW-27). Am Math.

Transactions of the Moscow Mathematical Society, Vol. 26 (1972) A. D. Brjuno et al. LC 65-4713. 239p. 1974. 78.00 (ISBN 0-8218-1626-8, MOSCOW-26). Am Math.

Transactions of the Moscow Mathematical Society, Vol. 23 (1970) LC 65-4713. 310p. 1972. text ed. 76.00 (ISBN 0-8218-1623-3, MOSCOW-23). Am Math.

Transactions of the Moscow Mathematical Society, Vol. 31 (1974) P. S. Aleksandrov et al. LC 65-4713. 1976. 76.00 (ISBN 0-8218-1631-4, MOSCOW-31). Am Math.

Transactions of the Moscow Mathematical Society, Vol. 30 (1974) P. K. Rasevskii et al. 1976. 56.00 (ISBN 0-8218-1630-6, MOSCOW-30). Am Math.

Transactions of the Moscow Mathematical Society, 1975, Vol. 32. N. Ali et al. LC 65-4713. 1977. 69.00 (ISBN 0-8218-1632-2, MOSCOW-32). Am Math.

Transactions of the Oriental Ceramic Society 39, 1971-73. 128p. 1974. 100.00x (ISBN 0-317-45319-X, Pub. by Han-Shan Tang Ltd). State Mutual Bk.

Transactions of the Oriental Ceramic Society 47, 1982-1983. Oriental Ceramic Society Staff. 112p. 1984. 125.00x (ISBN 0-317-69174-0, Pub. by Han-Shan Tang Ltd). State Mutual Bk.

Transactions of the Oriental Ceramic Society 40, 1973-75. 208p. 1976. 125.00x (ISBN 0-317-45321-1, C2253, Pub. by Han-Shan Tang Ltd). State Mutual Bk.

Transactions of the Oriental Ceramic Society 41, 1975-77. 332p. 1977. 150.00x (ISBN 0-317-45322-X, Pub. by Han-Shan Tang Ltd). State Mutual Bk.

Transactions of the Oriental Ceramic Society 42, 1977-78. 92p. 1979. 62.50x (ISBN 0-317-45323-8, Pub. by Han-Shan Tang Ltd). State Mutual Bk.

Transactions of the Oriental Ceramic Society 43, 1978-79. 84p. 1980. 62.50x (ISBN 0-317-45324-6, Pub. by Han-Shan Tang Ltd). State Mutual Bk.

Transactions of the Oriental Ceramic Society 44, 1979-80. 96p. 1981. 75.00x (ISBN 0-317-45325-4, Pub. by Han-Shan Tang Ltd). State Mutual Bk.

Transactions of the Oriental Ceramic Society 45, 1980-81. 104p. 1982. 84.75x (ISBN 0-317-45326-2, Pub. by Han-Shan Tang Ltd). State Mutual Bk.

Transactions of the Oriental Ceramic Society 46, 1981-82. 94p. 1983. 89.75x (ISBN 0-317-45327-0, Pub. by Han-Shan Tang Ltd). State Mutual Bk.

Transactions of the Oriental Ceramic Society 50, 1985-86. Oriental Ceramic Society Staff. 96p. 1987. 133.00x (Pub. by Han-Shan Tang Ltd). State Mutual Bk.

Transactions of the Pacific Coast Obstetrical Gynecological Society, 1985. Transactions Staff. 1986. 40.00 (ISBN 0-8016-5089-5). Mosby.

Transactions of the Parisian Sanhedrim. Tr. by M. Diogene Tama. (Brown Classics in Judaica Ser.). 364p. 1985. pap. text ed. 16.25 (ISBN 0-8191-4488-6). U Pr of Amer.

Transactions of the Royal Historical Society, 1984. M. C. Barber et al. (RHS Transactions, 5th Ser.). 1985. 16.00 (ISBN 0-86193-104-1, Pub. by Boydell & Brewer). Longwood Pub Group.

Transactions of the Society of Actuaries. Society of Actuaries. 1981. Vol. XXXIII. 48.00 (ISBN 0-938959-06-9); Vol. XXXIV. 48.00 (ISBN 0-938959-07-7). Soc Actuaries.

Transactions of the Society of Actuaries, Vol. XXXV. Ed. by Society of Actuaries Staff & Editorial Board. Incl. Vol. XXXVI. 40.00 ea. (ISBN 0-938959-01-8). Soc Actuaries.

Transactions of the Society of Actuaries, Vol. XXXVII. 1985. 48.00 (ISBN 0-938959-03-4). Soc Actuaries.

Transactions of the Society of Actuaries, Vol. XXXVIII. 1986. 48.00 (ISBN 0-938959-04-2). Soc Actuaries.

Transactions of the Society of Actuaries, Vol. XXXIX. 1988. 48.00 (ISBN 0-938959-05-0). Soc Actuaries.

Transactions of the Society of Actuaries, Vol. XXXVI. 632p. 1984. text ed. 48.00 (ISBN 0-938959-02-6). Soc Actuaries.

Transactions of the Zoological Society of London: An Index to the Artists, 1835-1936. Nina J. Root & Bryan R. Johnson. LC 86-18484. (Reference Library of the Humanities Ser.). 444p. 1987. lib. bdg. 62.00 (ISBN 0-8240-8548-5). Garland Pub.

Transactions of the 52nd North American Wildlife & Natural Resources Conference. 780p. 25.00 (ISBN 0-318-23696-6). Wildlife Mgmt.

Transactions: Proceedings of the American Association for the Study & Prevention of Infant Mortality Meeting, 1st, New Haven, 1909. facsimile ed. American Association for the Study & Prevention of Infant Mortality Meeting Staff. LC 74-1663. (Children & Youth Ser.). 356p. 1974. Repr. of 1910 ed. 26.50x (ISBN 0-405-05944-2). Ayer Co Pubs.

Transactions Special Issue: Petroleum. 1980. 5.75 (ISBN 0-686-38292-7). IMM North Am.

Transactions: The Interplay Between Individual, Family, & Society. John Spiegel. LC 84-45129. 480p. 1983. 40.00x (ISBN 0-87668-699-4). Aronson.

Transactions: Twelfth Congress on Irrigation & Drainage, Fort Collins, Colorado, 1984, 2 vols. 1984. 300.00. US Comm Irrigation.

Transactions Two: The Record of Papers Presented to the RIBA for the Sessional Programme 1981-1982. Royal Institute of British Architects. Ed. by Peter Murry. (Twentieth Century Ser.: Vol. 1, No. 1). (Illus.). 126p. (Orig.). 14.95 (ISBN 0-89955-406-7, Pub. by RIBA). Intl Spec Bk.

Transamerica Delaval Engineering Handbook. 4th ed. Transamerica Delaval Inc. Staff. Ed. by Harold B. Crawford. (Illus.). 640p. 1983. text ed. 60.00 (ISBN 0-07-016250-6). McGraw.

Transaminases. Phillip Christen & D. E. Metzler. LC 84-3712. (Biochemistry Ser.). 643p. 1985. 142.00 (ISBN 0-471-08501-4, Pub. by Wiley-Interscience). Wiley.

Transatlantic Dialogue: Selected American Correspondence of Edmund Gosse. Edmund Gosse. Intros. by Paul F. Mattheisen & Michael Millgate. LC 65-16471. pap. 93.40 (2030733). Bks Demand UMI.

Transatlantic Discord & NATO's Crisis of Cohesion. P. H. Langer. (IFPA Foreign Policy Reports). 80p. 1986. pap. 9.95 (ISBN 0-08-034699-5, PDP). Pergamon.

Transatlantic Industrial Revolution: The Diffusion of Textile Technologies Between Britain & America, 1790-1830. David J. Jeremy. (Illus.). 384p. 1981. text ed. 45.00x (ISBN 0-262-10022-3). MIT Pr.

Transatlantic Liners Nineteen Forty-five to Nineteen Eighty. William H. Miller. LC 81-1526. (Illus.). 224p. 1981. 21.95 (ISBN 0-668-05267-8). Arco.

Transatlantic Revivalism: Popular Evangelicalism in Britain & America, 1790-1865. Richard Carwardine. LC 77-94740. (Contributions in American History Ser.: No. 75). 1978. lib. bdg. 36.95 (ISBN 0-313-20308-3, CTR/). Greenwood.

Transatlantic Sketches. Henry James. LC 72-310. (Essay Index Reprint Ser.). Repr. of 1875 ed. 21.00 (ISBN 0-8369-2797-4). Ayer Co Pubs.

Transatlantic Sketches. Henry James, Jr. 401p. 1984. Repr. of 1875 ed. lib. bdg. 50.00 (ISBN 0-89984-721-8). Century Bookbindery.

Transatlantic Slave Trade. David Killingray. (People on the Move Ser.). 64p. (gr. 6-8). 1987. 17.95 (ISBN 0-7134-5469-5, Pub. by Batsford England). David & Charles.

Transatlantic Slave Trade. James A. Rawley. 1981. 24.95 (ISBN 0-393-01471-1). Norton.

Transatlantic Symposium: Where Is South Africa Headed? (II) Michael Clough. (Seven Springs Reports). 48p. 1980. pap. 3.00 (ISBN 0-943006-12-0). Seven Springs.

Transatlantic Trends in Retailing: Takeovers & Flow of Know-How. Madhav B. Kacker. LC 84-15928. xv, 165p. 1985. lib. bdg. 38.95 (ISBN 0-89930-036-7, KEI/, Quorum). Greenwood.

Transatlantic Tunnel, Hurrah. Harry Harrison. 2.50 (ISBN 0-312-48505-0, Dist. by Warner Pub Services & Saint Martin's Press). Tor Bks.

Transatlantic Vistas: American Journalists in Europe, 1900-1940. Morrell Heald. LC 87-35901. 300p. 1988. 24.00x (ISBN 0-87338-365-6). Kent St U Pr.

Transatlantic Wanderings. John W. Oldmixon. LC 8-14417. (American Studies). 1970. Repr. of 1855 ed. lib. bdg. 17.00 (ISBN 0-384-43265-4). Johnson Repr.

Transax: The NCHS System for Producing Multiple Cause-of-Death Statistics, 1968-78. Ronald F. Chamblee & Marchsll C. Evans. Ed. by Eddie Madison. 55p. 1982. pap. text ed. 1.75 (ISBN 0-8406-0269-3). Natl Ctr Health Stats.

Transborder Data Flow. William G. Dearhammer. LC 83-8144. 36p. 1983. pap. text ed. 22.50 (ISBN 0-936742-09-7). Robt Morris Assocs.

Transborder Data Flows: Access to the International Online Database Market. United Nations Centre on Transnational Corporations Staff. (Transnational Corporation & Transborder Data Flows Ser.: Vol. 2). 130p. 1984. 44.75 (ISBN 0-444-87515-8, North Holland). Elsevier.

Transborder Data Flows: Access to the International On-Line Data-Base Market. 140p. 1983. pap. text ed. 15.00 (ISBN 92-1-104043-4, E.83.II.A.1). UN.

Transborder Data Flows & Brazil. United Nations Centre on Transnational Corporations. (Transnational Corporations & Transborder Data Flows Ser.: Vol. 3). 1984. 79.00 (ISBN 0-444-86856-9, I-087-84). Elsevier.

Transborder Data Flows & Poland. 75p. 1984. pap. 8.50 (ISBN 92-1-104081-7, E.84.II.A.8). UN.

Transborder Data Flows & Poland: Polish Case Study. United Nations Centre on Transnational Corporations. (Transnational Corporations & Transborder Data Flows Ser.: Vol. 5). 75p. 1985. 60.75 (ISBN 0-444-87630-8, North-Holland). Elsevier.

Transborder Data Flows: Proceedings of an OECD Conference Held December 1983. OECD. Ed. by Hans P. Gassmann. LC 85-1482. 504p. 1985. 105.25 (ISBN 0-444-87700-2, North Holland). Elsevier.

Transborder Data Flows: Transnational Corporations & Remote-Sensing. 74p. 8.50 (ISBN 92-1-104156-2, E.84.II.A11). UN.

Transborder Dataflow. 1987. 260.00x (ISBN 0-948641-80-0, Pub. by ESC Ltd UK). State Mutual Bk.

Transboundary Air Pollution: International Legal Aspects of the Co-Operation of States. Ed. by K. Flinterman et al. 1987. lib. bdg. 91.50 (ISBN 0-317-56087-5, Pub. by Martinus Nijhoff Netherlands). Kluwer Academic.

Transboundary Air Polution Effects & Control. (Air Pollution Studies: No. 3). 35p. 1987. pap. 11.00 (ISBN 92-1-116374-9, E.86.II.E.23). UN.

Transboundary Resources Law. Ed. by Albert E. Utton & Ludwik A. Teclaff. (Special Studies in Natural Resources & Energy Management). 321p. 1987. pap. 35.00 (ISBN 0-8133-7394-8). Westview.

Transcarceration: Essays in the Sociology of Social Control. Ed. by J. Lowman et al. (Cambridge Studies in Criminology). 370p. 1987. text ed. 39.00 (ISBN 0-566-05106-0, Pub. by Gower Pub England). Gower Pub Co.

Transcaucasia & Ararat Being Notes of a Vacation Tour in the Autumn of 1876. James Bryce. LC 73-115509. (Russia Observed, Series 1). 1970. Repr. of 1896 ed. 26.50 (ISBN 0-405-03007-X). Ayer Co Pubs.

Transcaucasia: Nationalism & Social Change - Essays in the History of Armenia, Azerbaijan & Georgia. Ed. by Ronald G. Suny. (East European Ser.: No. 2). 1983. 24.00 (ISBN 0-930042-57-3); pap. 15.00 (ISBN 0-930042-54-9). Mich Slavic Pubns.

Transcellular Membrane Potentials & Ionic Fluxes. Ed. by F. M. Snell & W. K. Noell. (Life Sciences Ser). 140p. 1964. 58.00 (ISBN 0-677-10520-7). Gordon & Breach.

Transcend: A Guide to the Spiritual Quest. Morton T. Kelsey. 240p. (Orig.). 1981. pap. 9.95 (ISBN 0-8245-0015-6). Crossroad NY.

Transcendance de L'ego: Esquisse d'une Description Phenomenologique. Jean-Paul Sartre. pap. 5.50 (ISBN 0-685-36566-2). French & Eur.

Transcendance de l'Ego: Esquisse d'une Description Phenomenoligique. 3rd ed. Jean-Paul Sartre. Ed. by S. Le Bon. (Illus.). 136p. 1972. 9.95 (ISBN 0-686-55005-6). French & Eur.

Transcendence & Hermeneutics. Alan M. Olson. (Studies in Philosophy & Religion: No. 2). 1979. lib. bdg. 35.00 (ISBN 90-247-2092-3, Pub. by Martinus Nijhoff Netherlands). Kluwer Academic.

Transcendence & Immanence: A Study in Catholic Modernism & Integralism. Gabriel Daly. 1980. 49.95x (ISBN 0-19-826652-9). Oxford U Pr.

Transcendence & Providence: Reflections of a Physicist & Priest. W. G. Pollard. (Theology & Science at the Frontiers of Knowledge Ser.: Vol. 6). 146p. 1986. 17.00 (ISBN 0-7073-0486-5, Pub. by Scot Acad Pr). Longwood Pub Group.

Transcendence & the Sacred. Ed. by Alan M.. Olson & Leroy S. Rouner. LC 81-50456. 256p. 1981. 21.95 (ISBN 0-268-01841-3). U of Notre Dame Pr.

Transcendence & Transformation: Writings from the California Institute of Integral Studies. Ed. by Vern Haddick & Michael Flanagin. LC 83-6960. 136p. (Orig.). 1983. lib. bdg. 25.75 (ISBN 0-8191-3178-4); pap. text ed. 10.00 (ISBN 0-8191-3179-2). U Pr of Amer.

Transcendence of History: Essays on the Evolution of Historical Consciousness. Joseph L. Esposito. LC 84-5217. viii, 200p. 1984. text ed. 24.95x (ISBN 0-8214-0779-1). Ohio U Pr.

Transcendence of Loss over the Life-Span. Patricia Weenolsen. LC 66-56391. (Death Education, Aging & Health Care Ser.). 500p. 1988. 70.00 (ISBN 0-89116-736-6); pap. text ed. 39.00 (ISBN 0-89116-582-7). Hemisphere Pub.

Transcendence of the Ego. Jean-Paul Sartre. 119p. (Orig.). 1957. pap. 4.95 (ISBN 0-374-50048-7). FS&G.

Transcendence of the Ego. Jean-Paul Sartre. 1972. lib. bdg. 12.00x (ISBN 0-374-97032-7, Octagon). Hippocrene Bks.

Transcendence Theory & Its Applications. A. Baker & D. W. Masser. 1978. 69.00 (ISBN 0-12-074350-7). Acad Pr.

Transcendency. Gerald Stutsman. LC 81-69736. 96p. 1982. pap. 4.75 (ISBN 0-87516-466-8). DeVorss.

Transcendent Adventure: Studies of Religion in Science Fiction-Fantasy. Ed. by Robert Reilly. LC 84-542. (Contributions to the Study of Science Fiction & Fantasy Ser.: No. 12). x, 266p. 1985. lib. bdg. 36.95 (ISBN 0-313-23062-5, RET/). Greenwood.

Transcendent Justice: The Religious Dimensions of Constitutionalism. Carl J. Friedrich. LC 64-20097. ix, 116p. 1964. 14.75 (ISBN 0-8223-0061-3). Duke.

Transcendent Meditations. Velma C. Redelfs. 72p. 1988. 7.95 (ISBN 0-8062-3019-3). Carlton.

Transcendent Nation. Chris Foster. 31p. (Orig.). 1987. pap. 4.50 (ISBN 0-9690341-1-3, B12). Foundation Hse.

Transcendent Reason: James Marsh & the Forms of Romantic Thought. Peter C. Carafiol. LC 82-13617. xviii, 222p. 1982. 26.00x (ISBN 0-8130-0732-1). U Presses Fla.

Transcendent Science: Kant's Conception of Biological Methodology. Clark Zumbach. 1984. lib. bdg. 32.00 (ISBN 90-247-2904-1, Pub. by Martinus Nijhoff Netherlands). Kluwer Academic.

Transcendent Selfhood: The Loss & Rediscovery of the Inner Life. Louis Dupre. 1976. 8.95 (ISBN 0-8164-0306-6, HarpR). Har-Row.

Transcendent Unity of Religions. Rev. ed. Frithjof Schuon. LC 84-239. 165p. 1984. pap. 7.95 (ISBN 0-8356-0587-6, Quest). Theos Pub Hse.

Transcendental Americana. Don Avery. Ed. by Jack Galef. LC 82-82852. (Unpublished Poets Ser.). 80p. (Orig.). 1983. pap. 6.95 (ISBN 0-910323-00-3). Elizabeth St Pr.

Transcendental Arguments & Science. Ed. by Rolf-Peter Horstmann et al. (Synthese Library: No. 133). 1979. lib. bdg. 34.00 (ISBN 90-277-0963-7, Pub. by Reidel Holland); pap. 16.00 (ISBN 90-277-0964-5). Kluwer Academic.

Transcendental Dancing. Margaret J. Phillippou. 1982. pap. 3.00 (ISBN 0-941500-29-2). Sharing Co.

Transcendental Magic. Eliphas Levi. Tr. by A. E. Waite from Fr. LC 72-16629. (Illus.). 1970. pap. 7.95 (ISBN 0-87728-079-7). Weiser.

Transcendental Meditation. new ed. David Haddon. 32p. (Orig.). 1975. pap. 0.75 (ISBN 0-87784-155-1). Inter-Varsity.

Transcendental Meditation. Marharishi Mahesh Yogi. 320p. 1973. pap. 4.95 (ISBN 0-451-14081-8, Sig). NAL.

Transcendental Meditation Program for Business People. Robert B. Kory. LC 76-3696. (AMA Management Briefing Ser.). pap. 22.80 (ISBN 0-317-27195-4, 2023929). Bks Demand UMI.

Transcendental Meditation: Science of Being & Art of Living. Maharishi Mahesh Yogi. (New Age Ser.). 320p. 1988. pap. 4.95 (ISBN 0-317-67301-7, Sig). NAL.

Transcendental Number Theory. Alan R. Baker. LC 74-82591. 148p. 1975. 39.50 (ISBN 0-521-20461-5). Cambridge U Pr.

Transcendental Physics: An Account of Experimental Investigations. Johann C. Zollner. Tr. by Charles C. Massey. LC 75-36924. (Occult Ser.). 1976. Repr. of 1888 ed. 17.00x (ISBN 0-405-07978-8). Ayer Co Pubs.

Transcendental Self: A Comparative Study of Thoreau & the Psycho-Philosophy of Hinduism & Buddhism. A. K. Pillai. LC 85-686. 130p. (Orig.). 1985. lib. bdg. 23.00 (ISBN 0-8191-4572-6); pap. text ed. 9.75 (ISBN 0-8191-4573-4); pap. 9.75. U Pr of Amer.

Transcendental Style in Film: Ozu, Bresson & Dreyer. Paul Schrader. (Quality Paperbacks Ser.). (Illus.). 194p. 1988. pap. 11.95 (ISBN 0-306-80335-6). Da Capo.

Transcendental Temptation: A Critique of Religion & the Paranormal. Paul Kurtz. LC 86-15082. 500p. 1986. 20.95 (ISBN 0-87975-362-5). Prometheus Bks.

Transcendental Turn: The/Foundation of Kant's Idealism. Moltke S. Gram. LC 84-22047. xii, 260p. 1985. 35.00x (ISBN 0-8130-0787-9). U Presses Fla.

Transcendental Wild Oats. Louisa May Alcott. LC 76-355426. (Illus.). 92p. 1981. 8.95 (ISBN 0-916782-21-2). Harvard Common Pr.

Transcendentalism & the Western Messenger: A History of the Magazine & Its Contributors, 1835-1841. Robert D. Habich. LC 83-49358. (Illus.). 208p. 1985. 27.50 (ISBN 0-8386-3204-1). Fairleigh Dickinson.

Transcendentalism As a Social Movement, Eighteen-Thirty to Eighteen-Fifty. Anne C. Rose. LC 81-3340. 272p. 1981. 30.00t (ISBN 0-300-02587-4). Yale U Pr.

Transcendentalism As a Social Movement, 1830-1850. Anne C. Rose. LC 81-3340. 288p. 1986. pap. 12.95x (ISBN 0-300-03757-0). Yale U Pr.

Transcendentalism; bd. with Equality. William B. Greene. LC 81-8972. (Repr. of 1849 eds.). 1981. 35.00x (ISBN 0-8201-1366-2). Schol Facsimiles.

Transcendentalism in New England: A History. Octavius B. Frothingham. LC 59-10346. 1972. pap. 16.95x (ISBN 0-8122-1038-7, Pa. Paperbacks). U of Pa Pr.

Transcendentalist Constant in American Literature. Roger Asselineau. (Gotham Library). 1981. pap. 15.00x (ISBN 0-8147-0573-1). NYU Pr.

Transcendentalists: A Review of Research & Criticism. Ed. by Joel Myerson. LC 83-19442. (Reviews of Research Ser.). 450p. 1984. 32.50 (ISBN 0-87352-260-5); pap. 20.00 (ISBN 0-87352-261-3). Modern Lang.

Transcendentalists: An Anthology. Ed. by Perry G. Miller. LC 50-7360. 1950. pap. 12.95x (ISBN 0-674-90333-1). Harvard U Pr.

Transcending Angels: Rainer Maria Rilke's "Duino Elegies". Kathleen L. Komar. LC 86-30863. xiv, 286p. 1988. 25.00x (ISBN 0-8032-2716-7). U of Nebr Pr.

Transcending Exile: Conrad, Nabokov, I. B. Singer. Asher Z. Milbauer. LC 84-22104. 155p. 1985. 21.00x (ISBN 0-8130-0815-8). U Presses Fla.

Transcending Gender: The Male-Female Double in Women's Fiction. Joanne Blum. LC 88-15592. (Challenging the Literary Canon Ser.). 102p. 1988. 34.95 (ISBN 0-8357-1886-7). UMI Res Pr.

Transcending the Hero: Reinventing the Heroic: An Essay on Andre Gide's Theater. E. San Juan, Jr. LC 87-21567. 90p. 1988. lib. bdg. 15.75 (ISBN 0-8191-6632-4). U Pr of Amer.

Transcontinental. Gary McCarthy. Ed. by Nancy Parent. 416p. 1987. pap. 3.95 (ISBN 0-7701-0688-9). Paperjacks US.

Transcontinental Railroad Legislation, 1835-1862. Thamar E. Dufwa. Ed. by Stuart Bruchey. LC 80-1279. (Railroads Ser.). 1981. lib. bdg. 18.00x (ISBN 0-405-13754-0). Ayer Co Pubs.

Transcontinental Rails. Thomas K. Hinckley. LC 71-43562. (Wild & Woolly West Ser., No. 12). (Illus., Orig.). 1969. 8.00 (ISBN 0-910584-92-3); pap. 2.00 (ISBN 0-910584-13-3). Filter.

Transcordian Connection: A Prelude to Restoration. Al Wells. 172p. (Orig.). 1983. pap. 2.95 (ISBN 0-9612318-0-7). Projections Ent.

Transcranial Doppler Sonography. Ed. by R. Aaslid. (Illus.). 190p. 1986. pap. 35.00 (ISBN 0-387-81935-5). Springer-Verlag.

Transcreation: Two Essays. P. Lal. 29p. 1973. 8.00 (ISBN 0-88253-269-3). Ind-US Inc.

Transcribed Index to Probate Records, Bk. I: Jefferson County, Texas. A. J. Guedry. 54p. 1987. 8.75 (ISBN 0-318-23274-X). A J Guedry.

Transcriber's Handbook: With the Dictionary of Sound-Alike Words. Gorton Carruth et al. LC 84-40307. 519p. 1984. 35.95x (ISBN 0-471-08876-5). Wiley.

Transcribing & Editing Oral History. Willa K. Baum. LC 77-3340. (Illus.). 127p. 1977. pap. 9.95 (ISBN 0-910050-26-0). AASLH Pr.

Transcribing Machine Operator. Jack Rudman. (Career Examination Ser.: C-1067). 1988. pap. 12.00 (ISBN 0-8373-1067-9). Natl Learning.

Transcribing Speed Studies. Arnold Condon & Alan C. Lloyd. 1974. text ed. 15.56 (ISBN 0-07-012398-5). McGraw.

Transcribing Typist. Jack Rudman. (Career Examination Ser.: C-818). (Cloth bdg. avail. on request). pap. 12.00 (ISBN 0-8373-0818-6). Natl Learning.

Transcript. Judith Doyle. 12p. (Orig.). 1981. pap. 3.00 (ISBN 0-917061-08-X). Top Stories.

Transcript of Ombudsman Workshop: Recent Experience in the United States. Ed. by Stanley V. Anderson & John E. Moore. LC 72-5772. 294p. (Orig., Ombudsman workshop, Honolulu, May 5-7, 1971). 1972. pap. 3.00x (ISBN 0-87772-154-8). UCB IGS.

Transcript of the Money Market Symposium Relating to Appraisal of Railroad & Utility Properties. Arlo Woolery. (Lincoln Institute Monograph: No. 79-1). 238p. 1979. pap. text ed. 10.00 (ISBN 0-686-28296-5). Lincoln Inst Land.

Transcript of the Registers of the Worshipful Company of Stationers, London: From 1640-1708 see Transcripts of the Registers of the Company of Stationers of London: 1554-1640.

Transcript Preparation in New Hampshire: Technical Assistance Report. National Center for State Courts Staff. 46p. 1980. manuscript 2.76 (NERO, T/A-507). Natl Ctr St Courts.

Transcript: Testimony of Dr. Robert Buckhout in the Case of State of Michigan V. Hall & McGill. R. Buckhout. (Monograph Ser.: No. CR-24). 1978. 10.00 (ISBN 1-55524-025-9). Ctr Respon Psych.

Transcriptic Van Spraak: Theoretische en Praktische Aspecten van de Symboolfonetick. W. H. Vieregge. viii, 192p. 1985. pap. write for info. (ISBN 90-6765-145-1); write for info. cass. (ISBN 90-6765-148-6). Foris Pubns.

Transcription & Skill Building, Bk. 11. Helen H. Green & Margaret A. Morton. (Hedman Stenotype System Ser.). 354p. 1978. text ed. 18.00x (ISBN 0-939056-01-1). Hedman Steno.

Transcription & Transliteration: An Annotated Bibliography on Conversion of Scripts. Hans Wellisch. LC 74-77274. 160p. 1975. 7.95 (ISBN 0-8325-9294-3). Natl TExtbk.

Transcription Dictation. Louis A. Leslie & Charles E. Zoubek. 1956. text ed. 31.25 (ISBN 0-07-037276-4). McGraw.

Transcription of DNA. rev. ed. A. A. Travers. Ed. by J. J. Head. LC 76-29378. (Carolina Biology Readers Ser.). (Illus.). 16p. (gr. 10 up). 1978. pap. 1.65 (ISBN 0-89278-275-7, 45-9675). Carolina Biological.

Transcription Skills for Information Processing, Unit 4. Anne E. Schatz & Beverley M. Funk. 1981. pap. 7.08 text workbook (ISBN 0-07-055203-7). McGraw.

Transcription Skills for Information Processing, Unit 5. Anne E. Schatz & Beverley M. Funk. 1981. pap. 7.08 text workbook (ISBN 0-07-055204-5). McGraw.

Transcription Skills for Information Processing, Unit 6. Anne E. Schatz & Beverley M. Funk. 1981. pap. 7.08 text workbook (ISBN 0-07-055205-3). McGraw.

Transcription Skills for Information Processing, Unit 7. Anne E. Schatz & Beverley M. Funk. 1981. pap. 7.08 text workbook (ISBN 0-07-055206-1). McGraw.

Transcription Skills for Information Processing, Unit 8. Anne E. Schatz & Beverley M. Funk. 1982. pap. 7.08 text workbook (ISBN 0-07-055207-X). McGraw.

Transcription Skills for Information Processing, Unit 1. Anne E. Schatz & Beverley M. Funk. 96p. 1981. pap. 7.08 (ISBN 0-07-055200-2). McGraw.

Transcription Skills for Information Processing, Unit 2. Anne E. Schatz & Beverley M. Funk. 112p. 1981. pap. 7.08 (ISBN 0-07-055201-0). McGraw.

Transcription Skills for Information Processing Unit 3: Incorporating a Sequence Language Arts Program. Anne E. Schatz & Beverley M. Funk. (Illus.). 112p. 1981. text ed. 7.08 (ISBN 0-07-055202-9). McGraw.

Transcription Specialist: A Text-Workbook. Edith E. Ennis et al. 315p. 1981. spiral bdg. net 18.95 (ISBN 0-15-592348-X, HC); instr's. manual avail. (ISBN 0-15-592349-8); tape program net 225.00 (ISBN 0-15-592350-1); key to tape program avail. (ISBN 0-15-592351-X); trainee materials 9.95 (ISBN 0-15-592352-8). HarBraceJ.

Transcription Thirty-Six. new ed. Arnold Condon et al. (Illus.). (gr. 11-12). 1976. pap. 11.68 (ISBN 0-07-012400-0). McGraw.

Transcriptional Control Mechanisms. Ed. by Daryl Granner et al. LC 86-27737. (UCLA Symposia on Molecular & Cellular Biology Ser.: Vol. 52). 516p. 1987. 78.00 (ISBN 0-8451-2651-2, 2651). A R Liss.

Transcripts by Connecticut Court Reporters. National Center for State Courts Staff. 158p. 1978. manuscript 9.48 (NERO-033). Natl Ctr St Courts.

Transcripts from Study Abroad Programs: A Workbook. Ed. by Eleanor Kramutschke & Thomas Roberts. 1987. wkbk 7.00 (ISBN 0-317-59610-1). NAFSA Washington.

Transcripts of the Registers of the Company of Stationers of London: 1554-1640, 5 vols. Ed. by Edward Arber. Incl. Transcript of the Registers of the Worshipful Company of Stationers, London: From 1640-1708, 3 vols. Set Of 8 Vols. 190.00 (ISBN 0-8446-1449-1); 24.00 ea. Peter Smith.

Transcripts of Will Book I: Mobile County Alabama, 1813-1837. Clinton P. King & Meriem A. Barlow. LC 87-81858. 200p. 1988. 20.00 (ISBN 0-943609-01-1). AL Ancestors.

Transcripts of Will Book II: Mobile County Alabama, 1837-1857. Clinton P. King & Meriem A. Barlow. 250p. 1988. 25.00t (ISBN 0-943609-03-8). AL Ancestors.

Transcualisticas. bilingual ed. Ernest Robson. Tr. by Lucy Lopez de Thorogood. LC 78-65323. (Illus., Eng. & Span.). 1978. signed limited ed. 25.00 (ISBN 0-934982-03-1); pap. 8.95 (ISBN 0-934982-04-X). Primary Pr.

Transcultural Aspects of Psychiatric Art: Proceedings. International Congress of Psychopathology of Expression, 7th, Boston, Mass., October, 1973. Ed. by Irene Jakab. (Psychiatry & Art Ser.: Vol. 4). 1975. 85.50 (ISBN 3-8055-2138-3). S Karger.

Transcultural Counseling: Needs, Programs & Techniques. Garry R. Walz & Libby Benjamin. LC 77-26253. (New Vistas in Counseling Ser.: Vol. VII). 243p. 1978. text ed. 34.95 (ISBN 0-87705-320-0). Human Sci Pr.

Transcultural Education Model: A Guide for Developing Transitional, ESL, LEP & Bilingual Programs. Judy P. Donaldson. LC 84-80658. 176p. (Orig.). 1988. pap. text ed. 19.95 (ISBN 0-918452-60-0). Learning Pubns.

Transcultural Health Care. George Henderson & Martha Primeaux. 1981. 24.50 (ISBN 0-201-03237-6, Hlth-Sci); pap. write for info. (ISBN 0-201-03452-2, Hlth-Sci). Addison-Wesley.

Transcultural Nursing: Concepts, Theories & Practices. 2nd ed. Madeleine Leininger. 1988. write for info. (ISBN 0-471-82466-6, Pub. by Wiley Med). Wiley.

Transcultural Perspectives in the Human Services: Organizational Issues & Trends. Roosevelt Wright, Jr. et al. 206p. 1983. 19.75 (ISBN 0-398-04737-5). C C Thomas.

Transcultural Picture Word List: For Teaching English to Children from Any of Twenty One Language Backgrounds, Vol. I. Judy P. Donaldson. LC 78-58532. 1980. pap. text ed. 24.95 (ISBN 0-918452-10-4, 384). Learning Pubns.

Transcultural Picture Word List: For Teaching English to Children from any of Twelve Language Backgrounds, Vol. II. Judy P. Donaldson. LC 78-58532. 204p. (Orig.). pap. text ed. 19.95 (ISBN 0-918452-38-4). Learning Pubns.

Transcultural Picture Word List, Vol. II: For Teaching English to Children, Languages Included Are: Croatian, Czech, Danish, Finnish, Hmong & Mong, Polish, Hungarian, Indonesian, Portuguese, Russian, Swedish, Thai. Judy P. Donaldson. (Illus.). (gr. 1 up). Date not set. pap. text ed. 15.95 (385). Richards Pub.

Transcultural Poetics: Corporative Studies of the Cantos by Ezra Pound & Bachittra Natak. Gurbachan Singh. 200p. 1987. 25.00x (ISBN 81-202-0178-7, Pub. by Ajanta). South Asia Bks.

Transcultural Psychiatry. Ed. by John L. Cox. 352p. 1986. 50.00 (ISBN 0-7099-3428-9, Pub. by Croom Helm Ltd). Routledge Chapman & Hall.

Transcultural Psychiatry. Ari Kiev. LC 73-163235. 1973. 14.95 (ISBN 0-02-917180-6); pap. 4.95 (ISBN 0-02-917170-9). Free Pr.

Transcultural Research in Mental Health. Ed. by William P. Lebra. (Mental Health Research in Asia & the Pacific Ser: Vol. 2). 451p. 1972. 20.00x (ISBN 0-8248-0105-9, Eastwest Ctr). UH Pr.

Transcultural Study Guide. 2nd ed. Volunteers in Asia. Ed. by Bradley Palmquist & Kenneth Darrow. 1975. pap. 4.95 (ISBN 0-917704-01-0). Volunteers Asia Pr.

Transculture; Universal Heritage: Sixty-Five Timeless Allegories. 11th ed. Mel Yosso. (Illus.). 160p. 1980. pap. 14.00 (ISBN 0-935862-00-5). Transculture Inc.

Transcutaneous Electrical Nerve Stimulation. Ed. by Steven L. Wolf. 1978. pap. 4.00 (ISBN 0-912452-21-8). Am Phys Therapy Assn.

Transcutaneous Monitoring of Oxygen. (Illus.). 1978. pap. 22.00 (ISBN 3-8055-2883-3). S Karger.

Transdanubia One. L. Horvath et al. Ed. by J. V. Megaw. Tr. by L. Bartosiewicz & Alice Choyke. (Corpus of Celtic Finds in Hungary Ser.: Vol. 1). (Illus.). 248p. 1987. text ed. 65.00 (ISBN 0-317-64656-7, Pub. by Akademia: Kiado Hungary). Humanities.

Transdermal & Related Drug Delivery Systems. Ed. by D. A. Jones. LC 84-4002. (Chemical Technology Review Ser.: No. 228). (Illus.). 305p. 1984. 45.00 (ISBN 0-8155-0984-7). Noyes.

Transdermal Controlled Systemic Medications. Chien. (Drugs & the Pharmaceutical Industries Ser.). 464p. 1987. 79.75 (ISBN 0-8247-7760-3). Dekker.

Transdermal Delivery of Drugs, 3 vols. Agis F. Kydonieus. Ed. by Bret Berner. 300p. 1987. Set. 365.00 (ISBN 0-8493-6483-3). CRC Pr.

Transdermal Drug Delivery: Developmental Issues & Research Initiative. Hadgraft & Guy. (Drugs & the Pharmaceutical Sciences Ser.). 336p. 1988. 99.75 (ISBN 0-8247-7991-6). Dekker.

Transdermal Estrogen Substitution. Ed. by Christian Lauritzen. 1987. text ed. 19.50 (ISBN 0-920887-19-8, Pub. by H Huber Canada). Hogrefe Intl.

Transdermal Nitrates in Ischaemic Heart Disease. Ed. by R. W. Elsdon-Dew & G. F. Birdwood. (International Congress & Symposium Ser.: No. 59). 45p. 1983. pap. 12.00 (ISBN 1-85315-092-4, Pub. by Royal Society of Medicine Services Ltd). Longwood Pub Group.

Transdermal Nitroglycerin Therapy. Ed. by Wulf-Dirk Bussmann & Alberto Zanchetti. (Illus.). 69p. 1985. pap. text ed. 11.00 (ISBN 3-456-81448-8, Pub. by Hans Huber Switzerland). Hogrefe Intl.

Transducer & Interfacing Techniques. Bannister & Whitehead. 1986. pap. 19.95 (ISBN 0-442-31742-5). Van Nos Reinhold.

Transducer Interfacing Handbook: A Guide to Analog Signal Conditioning. Ed. by Daniel H. Sheingold. LC 80-65520. (Illus.). 266p. 1980. 14.50 (ISBN 0-916550-05-2). Analog Devices.

Transducer Interfacing: Signal Conditioning for Processs Control. Robert G. Seippel. (Illus.). 272p. 1988. text ed. 40.00 (ISBN 0-13-928888-0). P-H.

Transducer Market. 240p. 1984. 1500.00 (ISBN 0-86621-320-1, A1403). Frost & Sullivan.

Transducer Project Book. Michael J. Andrews. (Illus.). 140p. (Orig.). 1985. 14.95 (ISBN 0-8306-0992-X, 1992H). Tab Bks.

Transducers for Automation. Michael Hordeski. LC 86-15674. (Illus.). 352p. 1987. 52.95 (ISBN 0-442-23700-6). Van Nos Reinhold.

Transducers for Biomedical Measurements: Principles & Applications. Richard S. Cobbold. LC 74-2480. (Biomedical Engineering & Health Systems Ser.). 486p. 1974. 55.50x (ISBN 0-471-16145-4). Wiley.

Transducers in Measurement & Control. P. H. Sydenham. (Illus.). 124p. 1984. pap. 37.00x (ISBN 0-85274-777-2, Pub. by A Hilger UK). Taylor & Francis.

Transducers in Mechanical & Electronic Design (TBC) Trietley. (Mechanical Engineering Ser.). 312p. 1986. 59.75 (ISBN 0-8247-7598-8). Dekker.

Transducers: Sensors & Detectors. Robert Seippel. 1983. text ed. 35.00 (ISBN 0-8359-7797-8, Reston). P-H.

Transducing. George-Therese Dichenson. LC 85-62145. 150p. (Orig.). 1985. pap. text ed. 7.50 (ISBN 0-937804-17-7). Segue NYC.

Transescence- The Child in the Middle see New Child in the Middle.

Transesophageal Echocardiography. Norbert P. Bruijn & Fiona M. Clements. (Developments in Critical Care Medicine & Anesthesiology Ser.). 1986. lib. bdg. 45.00 (ISBN 0-89838-821-X, Pub. by M Nijhoff Boston MA). Kluwer Academic.

Transfer. Madeline Hunter. 93p. (Orig.). 1971. pap. 6.95x (ISBN 0-935567-04-6). TIP Pubns.

Transfer. Thomas Palmer. LC 82-5518. 416p. 1983. 14.95 (ISBN 0-89919-130-4). Ticknor & Fields.

Transfer. Thomas Palmer. 448p. 1984. pap. 3.50 (ISBN 0-345-30996-0). Ballantine.

Transfer Across the Primate & Non Primate Placenta. Ed. by M. Young & H. Wallenburg. 264p. 1981. 67.95 (ISBN 0-275-91354-6, C1354). Praeger.

Transfer Activities: Thinking Skill Vocabulary Development. Patty Mayo & Nancy Gajewski. (Illus.). 202p. 1987. 3-ring binder 25.00 (ISBN 0-930599-13-6). Thinking Pubns.

Transfer & Development of Coal-Mine Technology in Hokkaido. Yutaka Kasuga. (Project on Technology Transfer, Transformation, & Development: The Japanese Experience). 1982. pap. 5.00 (ISBN 92-808-0335-2, TUNU192, UNU). UNIPUB.

Transfer & Expression of Eukaryotic Genes. Ed. by Harold S. Ginsberg & Henry J. Vogel. (P & S Biomedical Symposia Ser.). 1984. 44.00 (ISBN 0-12-284650-8). Acad Pr.

Transfer & Interference in Language: A Selected Bibliography. Hans W. Dechert et al. (Library & Information Sources in Linguistics Ser.: 14). xiv, 488p. 1984. 56.00 (ISBN 90-272-3735-2). Benjamins North Am.

Transfer & Transformation of Ideas & Material Culture. Ed. by Peter J. Hugill & D. Bruce Dickson. LC 87-7115. (Illus.). 304p. 1988. 29.50x (ISBN 0-89096-364-9). Tex A&M Univ Pr.

Transfer Function Techniques & Fault Location. J. Hywel Williams. LC 85-9443. (Mechanical Engineering Research Dynamics Ser.). 133p. 1985. 51.95 (ISBN 0-471-90805-3, Pub. by Research Studies Press). Wiley.

Transfer Function Techniques for Control Engineers. D. R. Towill. (Illus.). 1971. 22.50 (ISBN 0-8088-1911-9). Davey.

Transfer Function Techniques for Control Engineers. D. R. Towill. LC 74-21807. (Illus.). pap. 130.30 (ISBN 0-317-41718-5, 2025727). Bks Demand UMI.

Transfer in Power of Africa: Decolonization 1940-1960. Prosser Gifford & William R. Louis. 989p. 1988. Repr. of 1972 ed. 17.95 (ISBN 0-300-04348-1). Yale U Pr.

Transfer: Making It Work: A Community College Report. Ed. by Richard Donovan et al. 1987. 12.50 (1061). Am Assn Comm Jr Coll.

Transfer, Memory & Creativity: After-Learning As Perceptual Process. George M. Haslerud. LC 72-79096. pap. 47.80 (ISBN 0-317-41715-0, 2055873). Bks Demand UMI.

Transfer of Care: Psychiatric Deinstitutionalization & Its Aftermath. Phil Brown. 280p. 1984. 22.50x (ISBN 0-7100-9900-2). Routledge Chapman & Hall.

Transfer of Care: Psychiatric Deinstitutionalization & Its Aftermath. Phil Brown. 292p. 1988. pap. text ed. 11.95 (ISBN 0-415-00188-9, Pub. by Routledge UK). Routledge Chapman & Hall.

Transfer of Chattels in Private International Law: A Comparative Study. G. A. Zaphiriou. (University of London Legal Ser.: No. IV). xix, 227p. 1981. Repr. of 1956 ed. lib. bdg. 26.00x (ISBN 0-8377-1325-0). Rothman.

Transfer of Coal-Mining Technology from Japan to Manchuria & Manpower Problems-Focusing on the Development of the Fushun Coal Mines. (Project on Technology Transfer, Transformation & Development: The Japanese Experience Ser.). 92p. 1981. pap. 5.00 (ISBN 92-808-0225-9, TUNU167, UNU). UNIPUB.

Transfer of Development Rights: A Primer. Charles M. Haar et al. (Land Policy Roundtable: No. 206). 75p. 1981. pap. text ed. 6.00 (ISBN 0-686-30623-6). Lincoln Inst Land.

Transfer of Development Rights: Buckingham Township (Bucks County, PA) & Other Experiences. Robert E. Coughlin. Ed. by Benjamin H. Stevens. (Discussion Paper Ser.: No. 126). 61p. (Orig.). 1981. pap. 6.50 (ISBN 1-55869-003-4). Regional Sci Res Inst.

Transfer of Ideas: Historical Essays. Ed. by Craufurd C. Goodwin & I. B. Holley, Jr. LC 68-26691. pap. 47.80 (ISBN 0-317-26757-4, 2023390). Bks Demand UMI.

Transfer of Industrial Technologies to Early America. Darwin H. Stapleton. LC 86-72882. (Memoirs Ser.: Vol. 177). (Illus.). 1986. 18.00 (ISBN 0-87169-177-9). Am Philos.

Transfer of Industrial Technology of the Manufacturing Sector: The Case of Malaysia. Maisom bt Abdullah. (Studies in Technology & Social Change: No. 1). 86p. (Orig.). 1988. pap. text ed. 8.00 (ISBN 0-945271-01-8). ISU-TSCP.

Transfer of Learning: Contemporary Research & Applications. Ed. by Stephen M. Cormier & Joseph D. Hagman. (Educational Technology Ser.). 281p. 1987. 39.50 (ISBN 0-12-188950-5). Acad Pr.

Transfer of Management Technology to Developing Nations: The Role of Multinational Oil Firms in Saudi Arabia. Ibrahim A. Al-Moneef. Ed. by Stuart Brouchey. LC 80-564. (Multinational Corporations Ser.). 1980. lib. bdg. 51.50x (ISBN 0-405-13361-8). Ayer Co Pubs.

Transfer of Marine Technology to Developing Nations in International Law: OP32, LSI Occasional Paper, No. 32. Ed. by B. Boczek & A. Boleslaw. 79p. 1982. 3.75 (ISBN 0-911189-04-1). Law Sea Inst.

Transfer of Microwave Radiation in the Atmosphere. Ed. by K. S. Shifrin. 166p. 1970. text ed. 36.00x (ISBN 0-7065-0734-7, Pub. by Keter Pub Jerusalem). Coronet Bks.

Transfer of Molecular Energies by Collision: Recent Quantum Treatments. F. Gianturco. (Lecture Notes in Chemistry: Vol. 11). (Illus.). 327p. 1979. pap. 25.00 (ISBN 0-387-09701-5). Springer-Verlag.

Transfer of Power. Ilija Poplasen. (Illus.). 264p. 1984. 20.00 (ISBN 0-935352-15-5). MIR PA.

Transfer of Power in India: Nineteen Forty-Five to Nineteen Forty-Seven. Edmond W. Lumby. LC 79-1634. 1981. Repr. of 1954 ed. 25.75 (ISBN 0-88355-938-2). Hyperion Conn.

Transfer of Scholarly Scientific & Technical Information Between North & South America: Proceedings of a Conference. Ed. by Victor Rosenberg & Gretchen Whitney. LC 86-15625. (Illus.). 739p. 1986. 59.50 (ISBN 0-8108-1935-X). Scarecrow.

Transfer of Spectral Line Radiation. C. J. Cannon. (Illus.). 650p. 1985. 105.00 (ISBN 0-521-25995-9). Cambridge U Pr.

Transfer of Stock. 6th ed. Mark S. Rhodes. LC 85-50087. 1985. 79.50 (ISBN 0-318-04603-2); Suppl. 1987. 25.00; Suppl. 1988. 27.00. Lawyers Co-Op.

Transfer of Technology: A Bibliography of Materials in the English Language, 2 binders. Betty W. Taylor. (Collection of Bibliographic & Research Resources Ser.). 89p. (Orig.). 1985. included among other biliographies in looseleaf 300.00; pap. text ed. 35.00 (ISBN 0-379-20902-0). Oceana.

Transfer of Technology: Economics of Offshore Assembly, the Case of Semi-Conductor Industry. pap. 2.50 (ISBN 92-1-157019-0, E.75.XV.RR/11). UN.

Transfer of Technology to Developing Countries: The Pulp and Paper Industry. pap. 3.00 (ISBN 92-1-157049-2, E.75.XV.RR/19). UN.

Transfer of Technology to Socialist Countries: The Case of the Soviet Chemical Industry. Vladimir Sobeslavsky & Peter C. Beazley. 176p. 1980. text ed. 40.00 (ISBN 0-89946-040-2). Oelgeschlager.

Transfer of Technology: U. S. Multinationals & Eastern Europe. Marilyn L. Liebrenz. LC 81-17908. 384p. 1982. 44.95 (ISBN 0-275-90848-8, C0848). Praeger.

Transfer of Technology within Multinational Corporations: An Exploratory Analysis. Jean-Pierre Jeannet. Ed. by Stuart Bruchey. LC 80-577. (Multinational Corporations Ser.). 1980. lib. bdg. 23.00x (ISBN 0-405-13370-7). Ayer Co Pubs.

Transfer of Training & Retroaction see Two Studies in Mental Tests.

Transfer of Water Resources Knowledge: Proceedings. International Conference on Transfer of Water Resources Knowledge. 1st, Colorado State Univ., Sep. 14-16, 1972. Ed. by Evan Vlachos. LC 73-80678. 1973. 18.00 (ISBN 0-918334-05-5). WRP.

Transfer Operations in Process Industries: Design & Equipment. Ed. by Mahesh Phatia. LC 83-50699. (Process Equipment Ser.: Vol. 5). 373p. 1983. 29.00. Technomic.

Transfer Pricing. P. Yunker. 1982. 35.00 (ISBN 0-275-90928-X, C0928). Praeger.

Transfer Pricing & Multi-National Enterprises. 1979. 9.00x (ISBN 92-64-11947-7). OECD.

Transfer Pricing & Multinational Corporations: An Overview of Concepts, Mechanisms & Regulations. Sylvain R. Plasschaert. LC 79-84708. (Praeger Special Studies). 126p. 1979. 36.95 (ISBN 0-275-90407-5, C0407). Praeger.

Transfer Pricing & Multinational Enterprises: Three Taxation Issues. OECD Staff. 92p. (Orig.). 1984. pap. 12.00X (ISBN 92-64-12626-0). OECD.

Transfer Pricing Practices in the United States & Japan. Roger Y. Tang. LC 78-19780. (Praeger Special Studies). 144p. 1979. 35.00 (ISBN 0-275-90429-6, C0429). Praeger.

Transfer Pricing Problem: A Theory for Practice. Robert G. Eccles. LC 84-48024. 568p. 1985. 37.00x (ISBN 0-669-09029-8). Lexington Bks.

Transfer Pricing: Techniques & Uses. Ralph L. Benke, Jr. & James Don Edwards. 154p. pap. 16.95 (ISBN 0-86641-012-0, 80118). Natl Assn Accts.

Transfer Pricing: The Italian Experience. Ed. by Studio Trivoli. 102p. 1982. 29.00 (ISBN 90-654-4010-0, Pub. by Kluwer Law Netherlands). Kluwer Academic.
Transfer Processes. Edwards. 361p. 1979. 51.00 (ISBN 0-89116-485-5). Hemisphere Pub.
Transfer Processes in Cohesive Sediment Systems. Ed. by W. R. Parker & D. J. Kinsman. 230p. 1984. 49.50x (ISBN 0-306-41663-8, Plenum Pr). Plenum Pub.
Transfer Processes in Technical Change. Ed. by F. P. Bradbury & R. Jervis. 290p. 1978. 40.00x (ISBN 90-286-0347-6, Pub. by Sijthoff & Noordhoff). Kluwer Academic.
Transfer RNA. Ed. by Sidney Altman. (MIT Press Cell Monograph Ser.: No. 2). 1978. text ed. 47.50x (ISBN 0-262-01056-9). MIT Pr.
Transferability of Development Experience: Case Studies on Japan. 243p. 1986. pap. text ed. 16.75 (CRD178, Pub. by UNCRD). UNIPUB.
Transferable Antibiotic Resistance; Plasmids & Gene Manipulation: Fifth International Symposium on Antibiotic Resistance & Plasmids, Castle of Smolenice, Czechoslovakia, 1983. Ed. by S. Mitsuhashi et al. 420p. 1984. 41.50 (ISBN 0-387-13141-8). Springer-Verlag.
Transferable Concepts for Powerful Living. Robert Massie. 112p. (Orig.). 1985. pap. 4.95 (ISBN 0-86605-163-5). Campus Crusade.
Transference & Countertransference. Heinrich Racker. 216p. 1968. text ed. 30.00x (ISBN 0-8236-6640-9). Intl Univs Pr.
Transference & Its Context: Selected Papers on Psychoanalysis. Leo Stone. LC 83-25807. 470p. 1984. 45.00x (ISBN 0-87668-655-2). Aronson.
Transference-Countertransference. (Review of Jungian Analysis Ser.). 212p. 1984. pap. 14.95 (ISBN 0-317-44665-7). Chiron Pubns.
Transference-Countertransference Matrix: Emotional-Cognitive Dialogue in Psychotherapy, Psychoanalysis, & Supervision. Robert J. Marshall & Simone V. Marshall. (Personality, Psychopathology, & Psychotherapy: Theoretical & Clinical Perspectives Ser.). 388p. 1988. 40.00x (ISBN 0-231-06166-8). Columbia U Pr.
Transference in Brief Psychotherapy: An Approach to the Study of Psychoanalytic Process. Stanley Grand et al. 154p. 1985. text ed. 19.95 (ISBN 0-317-55305-4). Analytic Pr.
Transference in Psychotherapy: Clinical Management. Ed. by Evelyne A. Schwaber. LC 84-12958. 181p. 1986. text ed. 22.50x (ISBN 0-8236-6625-5, 06625). Intl Univs Pr.
Transference Methods in Analysis. Ronald Coifman & Guido Weiss. LC 77-24098. (Conference Board of the Mathematical Sciences Ser.: No. 31). 59p. 1977. pap. 15.00 (ISBN 0-8218-1681-0, CBMS 31). Am Math.
Transference Neurosis & Transference Psychosis. Margaret Little. LC 80-66925. 350p. 1980. 30.00x (ISBN 0-87668-421-5). Aronson.
Transferences. James Twiggs. LC 87-5081. 272p. 1987. 16.95 (ISBN 0-938626-89-2); pap. 9.95 (ISBN 0-938626-90-6). U of Ark Pr.
Transferpolitik im Foederalismus - Probleme der Kompetenzverteilung. Michaele Schreyer. (European University Studies: No. 5, Vol. 441). 293p. (Ger.). 1983. 34.75 (ISBN 3-8204-7750-0). P Lang Pubs.
Transferring Food Production Technology to Developing Nations: Economic & Social Dimensions. Ed. by Joseph J. Molnar & Howard A. Clonts. LC 83-50067. (Replica Edition Ser.). 175p. 1983. softcover 27.50x (ISBN 0-86531-957-X). Westview.
Transferring Obsessions. Judi Hollis. 24p. (Orig.). 1986. pap. 1.50 (ISBN 0-317-46562-7). Hazelden.
Transferring Responsibility: The Dangers of Transition: Report of the Miller Center Commission on Presidential Transitions & Foreign Policy. Miller Center Commission on Presidential Transitions & Foreign Policy Staff. LC 86-5536. Date not set. 2.75 (ISBN 0-8191-5344-3). U Pr of Amer.
Transferring Technology for Small Scale Farming. Ed. by N. R. Usherwood. (Illus.). 1981. pap. 5.50 (ISBN 0-89118-066-4). Am Soc Agron.
Transferring Technology to China: Prosper Giquel & the Self-Strengthening Movement. Steven A. Leibo. LC 85-60380. (China Research Monograph: No. 28). 175p. 1985. pap. 7.50 (ISBN 0-912966-76-9). IEAS.
Transferring Your Business When You Have Two or More Children. Irving L. Blackman. (Special Report Ser.: No. 12). 57p. 1987. pap. 23.00 (ISBN 0-916181-26-X). Blackman Kallick Bartelstein.
Transfers of Property in Eleventh-Century Norman Law. Emily Z. Tabuteau. LC 87-21736. (Studies in Legal History). x, 445p. 1988. 49.95x (ISBN 0-8078-1774-0). U of NC Pr.
Transfers of Technology. R. F. Brizec. 1985. text ed. 20.00. Coronet Bks.
Transfiguracion. Catharose De Petri. (Span.). 1987. pap. 6.00 (ISBN 0-317-56227-4). Rozekruis Pr.
Transfiguration. Catharose De Petri. (Rose Ser.: No. 1). 1986. pap. 6.00 (ISBN 90-70196-40-9). Rozekruis Pr.
Transfiguration. Ed. by Wolfgang Hageney. (Illus.). 112p. (Eng., Ital., Ger., Span. & Fr.). 1983. pap. 21.95 (ISBN 88-7070-036-4). R Silver.
Transfiguration. Sergiei N. Sergieev-Tsensky. Ed. by Maxim Gorky. Tr. by Marie Budberg from Rus. LC 72-90312. (Soviet Literature in English Translation Ser.). 300p. 1973. Repr. of 1926 ed. 21.60 (ISBN 0-88355-022-9). Hyperion Conn.
Transfiguration Diet. Littlegreen, Inc.'s Think Tank. LC 85-91090. (Illus.). 176p. (Orig.). 1986. pap. 7.95 (ISBN 0-936863-04-8, Littlegreen). Chris Pub UT.
Transfiguration of Christ. The Monks of New Skete Staff. Tr. by Laurence Mancuso. (Liturgical Music Series I: Great Feasts: Vol. 1). 40p. 1986. pap. text ed. 12.00 (ISBN 0-935129-02-2). Monks of New Skete.
Transfiguration of Christ in Scripture & Tradition. John A. McGuckin. LC 86-23892. (Studies in Bible & Early Christianity: Vol. 9). 333p. 1987. lib. bdg. 59.95x (ISBN 0-88946-609-2). E Mellen.
Transfiguration of History at the Center of Dante's Paradise. Jeffrey T. Schnapp. LC 85-43309. 264p. 1986. text ed. 35.00x (ISBN 0-691-06679-5). Princeton U Pr.
Transfiguration of the Commonplace: A Philosophy of Art. Arthur C. Danto. 222p. 1981. text ed. 21.00x (ISBN 0-674-90345-5). Harvard U Pr.
Transfiguration of the Commonplace: A Philosophy of Art. Arthur C. Danto. 288p. 1983. pap. text ed. 8.95x (ISBN 0-674-90346-3). Harvard U Pr.
Transfiguration: Poetic Metaphor & the Languages of Religious Belief. Frank B. Brown. LC 82-24714. (Studies in Religion). x, 230p. 1983. 27.50x (ISBN 0-8078-1560-8). U of NC Pr.
Transfigurations: Art Critical Essays on the Modern Period. Nicolas Calas. Ed. by Donald B. Kuspit. LC 85-16353. (Contemporary American Art Critics Ser.: No. 7). 290p. 1985. 37.95 (ISBN 0-8357-1690-2). UMI Res Pr.
Transfigurations: Studies in the Dynamics of Byzantine Iconography. Anthony Cutler. LC 75-1482. (Illus.). 226p. 1975. 32.50x (ISBN 0-271-01194-7). Pa St U Pr.
Transfigured Hart. Jane Yolen. LC 75-2377. (Illus.). (gr. 4 up). 1975. 12.70 (ISBN 0-690-00736-1, Crowell Jr Bks). HarpJ.
Transfixation: Atlas of Anatomical Sections for the External Fixation of Limbs. C. Faure & P. Merloz. Tr. by J. E. Robb from Fr. (Illus.). 1987. 82.00 (ISBN 0-387-17127-4). Springer-Verlag.
Transform Analysis & Electronic Networks with Applications. Joseph Kulathinal. 384p. 1989. case bound 32.95 (ISBN 0-675-20765-7). Merrill.
Transform Analysis of Generalized Functions. O. P. Misra & J. L. Lavoine. (Mathematicas Studies: Vol. 119). 332p. 1986. 73.75 (ISBN 0-444-87885-8, North-Holland). Elsevier.
Transform Circuit Analysis for Engineering & Technology. William D. Stanley. 1967. ref. ed. 38.00 (ISBN 0-13-928804-X). P-H.
Transform Coding of Images. R. J. Clarke. (Microelectronics & Signal Processing Ser.). 1985. 74.50 (ISBN 0-12-175730-7); pap. 37.50 (ISBN 0-12-175731-5). Acad Pr.
Transform Method in Linear System Analysis. J. A. Aseltine. (Electrical & Electronic Eng. Ser). 1958. text ed. 52.95 (ISBN 0-07-002389-1). McGraw.
Transform Techniques for Probability Modeling. Walter C. Giffin. (Operation Research Industrial Engineering Ser.). 1975. 70.50 (ISBN 0-12-282750-3). Acad Pr.
Transform Techniques in Chemistry. Ed. by P. R. Griffiths. LC 77-29271. (Modern Analytical Chemistry Ser.). (Illus.). 404p. 1978. 65.00x (ISBN 0-306-31070-8, Plenum Pr). Plenum Pub.
Transform Techniques in Chemistry. Ed. by Peter R. Griffiths. LC 77-29271. (Modern Analytical Chemistry). (Illus.). pap. 100.80 (ISBN 0-317-09433-5, 2019649). Bks Demand UMI.
Transform Theory. D. V. Widder. (Pure & Applied Mathematics Ser.: Vol. 42). 1971. 75.50 (ISBN 0-12-748550-3). Acad Pr.
Transformado! Raul Ries. Tr. by Rhode F. Ward from Eng. 160p. 1988. pap. 3.25 (ISBN 0-88113-288-8). Edit Betania.
Transformation. John G. Bennett. LC 78-60760. 6.95 (ISBN 0-900306-07-6). Claymont Comm.
Transformation. Edmund Plante. 352p. (Orig.). 1987. pap. 3.95 (ISBN 0-8439-2490-X, Leisure Bks). Leisure NY.
Transformation: A Guide to the Inevitable Changes in Humankind. George B. Leonard. LC 80-53151. 278p. 1987. pap. 8.95 (ISBN 0-87477-169-2). J P Tarcher.
Transformation & Continuity in Revolutionary Ethiopia. Christopher Clapham. (African Studies: No. 61). (Illus.). 304p. 1988. 42.50 (ISBN 0-521-33441-1). Cambridge U Pr.
Transformation & Convergence in the Frame of Knowledge: Exploration in the Interrelations of Scientific & Theological Enterprise. Thomas F. Torrance. LC 83-16463. Repr. of 1984 ed. 91.80 (2027552). Bks Demand UMI.
Transformation & Development of Technology in the Japanese Cotton Industry. 86p. 1980. pap. 5.00 (ISBN 92-808-0091-4, TUNU093, UNU). UNIPUB.
Transformation & Identity: The Face & Plastic Surgery. Francis C. Macgregor. 325p. 1980. pap. text ed. 5.95x (ISBN 0-934670-06-4). Eterna Pr.
Transformation & Resiliency in Africa. Ed. by Pearl T. Robinson & Elliott P. Skinner. LC 82-23211. 336p. 1982. 14.95 (ISBN 0-88258-054-X). Howard U Pr.
Transformation & Trend of Buddhism in the 20th Century. Satchidananda Dhar. 189p. 22.00 (ISBN 0-8364-1951-0, Pub. by KL Mukhopadhyay). South Asia Bks.
Transformation & Weighting in Regression. R. J. Carrol & D. Ruppert. (Monographs in Statistics & Applied Probability). 300p. 1987. text ed. 45.00 (ISBN 0-412-01421-1, 9962, Pub. by Chapman & Hall England). Routledge Chapman & Hall.
Transformation Assay of Established Cell Lines: Machanisms & Application. Ed. by H. Yamasaki. (International Agency for Research on Cancer Ser.). (Illus.). 230p. 1985. 40.00x (ISBN 0-19-723067-9). Oxford U Pr.
Transformation-Associated Cellular p53 Protein. Ed. by George Klein. (Advances in Viral Oncology Ser.: Vol. 2). 192p. 1982. text ed. 52.00 (ISBN 0-89004-857-6). Raven.
Transformation des klassischen Seinsverstandnisses: Studien zur Vorgeschichte des Neuzeitlichen Seinsbegriffs im Mittelalter. Rolf Schonberger. (Quellen und Studien zur Philosophie: Band 21). xii, 423p. 1985. 93.50x (ISBN 3-11-010296-X). De Gruyter.
Transformation Factor. Allerd Stikker. (Chrysalis Bk.). 176p. 1988. pap. 9.95 (ISBN 0-916349-56-X). Amity Hse Inc.
Transformation Geometry: An Introduction to Symmetry. G. E. Martin. (Undergraduate Texts in Mathematics Ser.). (Illus.). 240p. 1982. 36.00 (ISBN 0-387-90636-3). Springer-Verlag.
Transformation Groups. Ed. by Czes Kosniowski. LC 76-40837. (London Mathematical Society Lecture Notes Ser.: No. 26). 1977. limp bdg. 21.95 (ISBN 0-521-21509-9). Cambridge U Pr.
Transformation Groups Applied to Mathematical Physics. Nail H. Ibragimov. 1985. lib. bdg. 69.00 (ISBN 90-277-1847-4, Pub. by Reidel Holland). Kluwer Academic.
Transformation Groups: De Gruyter Studies in Mathematics, Vol.8. Tammo D. Tom. x, 312p. 1987. text ed. 59.00x (ISBN 0-89925-029-7). De Gruyter.
Transformation Groups in Differential Geometry. S. Kobayashi. LC 72-80361. (Ergebnisse der Mathematik und Ihrer Grenzgebiete: Vol. 70). 182p. 1972. 39.00 (ISBN 0-387-05848-6). Springer-Verlag.
Transformation Groups Poznan 1985. Ed. by S. Jackowski & K. Pawalowski. (Lecture Notes in Mathematics Ser.: Vol. 1217). xiv, 396p. 1986. pap. 35.80 (ISBN 0-387-16824-9). Springer-Verlag.
Transformation in Christ. George Devine. LC 70-39884. 125p. 1972. pap. 3.95 (ISBN 0-8189-0240-X). Alba.
Transformation in Late Eighteenth Century Art. R. Rosenblum. 1967. 47.00x (ISBN 0-691-03846-5); pap. 13.95x (ISBN 0-691-00302-5). Princeton U Pr.
Transformation in Metals. Paul G. Shewmon. 394p. 39.95 (ISBN 0-930745-11-6). Williams Bk Co.
Transformation: New York Period see Petersburg & Paris Period.
Transformation of a Chinese Lyrical Tradition: Chaing K'uei & Southern Sung Tz'u Poetry. Shuen-Fu Lin. LC 77-85549. (Illus.). 1978. 39.00x (ISBN 0-691-06351-6). Princeton U Pr.
Transformation of American Capitalism: From Competitive Market Structures to Centralized Private Sector Planning. John R. Munkirs. LC 83-27093. 224p. 1984. 35.00 (ISBN 0-87332-247-9); pap. 14.95 (ISBN 0-87332-270-3). M E Sharpe.
Transformation of American Foreign Policy. Charles E. Bohlen. 1969. 3.95x (ISBN 0-393-05385-7, NortonC). Norton.
Transformation of American Industrial Relations. Thomas A. Kochan et al. 1986. 23.95x (ISBN 0-465-08696-9). Basic.
Transformation of American Industrial Relations. Thomas A. Kochan et al. LC 86-47502. 304p. 1988. pap. text ed. 11.95 (ISBN 0-465-08697-7, TB-5151). Basic.
Transformation of American Law, Seventeen Eighty to Eighteen Sixty. Morton J. Horwitz. LC 76-26500. 1979. pap. text ed. 10.95x (ISBN 0-674-90371-4). Harvard U Pr.
Transformation of American Quakerism: Orthodox Friends, 1800-1907. Thomas D. Hamm. LC 86-46236. (Religion in North America Ser.). 288p. 1988. 25.00x (ISBN 0-253-36004-8). Ind U Pr.
Transformation of American Society, 1870-1890. Ed. by John A. Garraty. LC 68-65043. (Documentary History of the United States Ser). vi, 266p. 1969. 24.95x (ISBN 0-87249-124-2). U of SC Pr.
Transformation of an Indian Labor Market: The Case of Pune. Richard D. Lambert et al. LC 86-26900. (University of Pennsylvania Studies on South Asia: Vol. 3). ix, 249p. 1986. 40.00 (ISBN 0-915027-63-1). Benjamins North Am.
Transformation of Austrian Socialism. Kurt L. Shell. LC 61-8738. 305p. 1961. 49.50 (ISBN 0-87395-005-4). State U NY Pr.
Transformation of Bigfoot: Maleness, Power & Belief among the Chipewyan. Henry S. Sharp. LC 87-26422. (Ethonographic Inquiry Ser.). (Illus.). 192p. 1988. 22.50x (ISBN 0-87474-848-8). Smithsonian.
Transformation of Bill Maloney. Walter P. Garretson. 1987. 10.95 (ISBN 0-533-07321-9). Vantage.
Transformation of Britain 1830-1939. G. E. Mingay. (Making of Britain Ser.). (Illus.). 233p. 1986. 24.95 (ISBN 0-7100-9762-X). Routledge Chapman & Hall.
Transformation of Communist Ideology: The Yugoslav Case, 1945-1953. A. Ross Johnson. Ed. by William E. Griffith. (Studies in Communism, Revisionism & Revolution). 304p. 1973. 30.00x (ISBN 0-262-10012-6). MIT Pr.
Transformation of Culture. Charles Scriven. 256p. (Orig.). 1988. pap. 19.95X (ISBN 0-8361-3101-0). Herald Pr.
Transformation of Democracy. Vilfredo Pareto. Ed. by Charles Powers. Tr. by Renata Girola from Ital. 128p. (Orig.). 1984. pap. 14.95x (ISBN 0-87855-949-3). Transaction Bks.
Transformation of Egypt. Mark N. Cooper. LC 82-15317. 288p. 1982. text ed. 32.00x (ISBN 0-8018-2836-8). Johns Hopkins.
Transformation of England: Essays in the Economic & Social History of England in the Eighteenth Century. Peter Mathias. LC 80-10813. 302p. 1980. 29.50x (ISBN 0-231-05046-1). Columbia U Pr.
Transformation of English Provincial Towns, 1600-1800. Ed. by Peter Clark. LC 85-4253. (Illus.). 359p. 1984. 33.00 (ISBN 0-09-154610-9, Pub. by Hutchinson Educ); pap. 12.95 (ISBN 0-09-154611-7). Longwood Pub Group.
Transformation of Europe, 1558-1648. Charles Wilson. LC 75-17283. 1976. 45.00x (ISBN 0-520-03075-3). U of Cal Pr.
Transformation of Failure: A Critical Analysis of Character Presentation in the Novels of Wolfgang Koeppen. Carole Hanbidge. LC 83-48752. (American University Studies I (Germanic Languages & Literature): Vol. 25). 279p. (Orig.). 1983. pap. text ed. 25.80 (ISBN 0-8204-0047-5). P Lang Pubs.
Transformation of German Jewry, 1780-1840. David Sorkin. (Studies in Jewish History). (Illus.). 272p. 1987. 32.50 (ISBN 0-19-504992-6). Oxford U Pr.
Transformation of Higher Learning, 1860-1930: Expansion, Diversification, Social Opening & Professionalization in England, Germany, Russia & the United States. Konrad Jarausch. LC 82-17629. 376p. 1983. lib. bdg. 30.00x (ISBN 0-226-39367-4). U of Chicago Pr.
Transformation of Industrial Organization: Management, Labor, & Society in the U. S. Frank Hearn. 370p. 1988. pap. text ed. write for info. (ISBN 0-534-08160-6). Wadsworth Pub.
Transformation of Intellectual Life in Victorian England. T. W. Heyck. LC 82-840. 262p. 1982. 26.50x (ISBN 0-312-81427-5). St Martin.
Transformation of International Agricultural Research & Development. Ed. by J. Lin Compton. (Westview Special Studies in Agriculture Science & Policy). 275p. 1985. pap. 19.85x (ISBN 0-8133-0057-6). Westview.
Transformation of Israeli Society: An Essay in Interpretation. S. N. Eisenstadt. 608p. 1986. 51.00x (ISBN 0-8133-0306-0). Westview.
Transformation of Job: A Tale of the High Sierras. facs. ed. Frederick V. Fisher. LC 70-137729. (American Fiction Reprint Ser). 1900. 14.00 (ISBN 0-8369-7028-4). Ayer Co Pubs.
Transformation of John Foster Dulles: From Prophet of Realism to Priest of Nationalism. Mark G. Toulouse. LC 85-10467. (Illus.). xii, 278p. 1985. 29.95 (ISBN 0-86554-160-4, MUP-H150). Mercer Univ Pr.
Transformation of Man. rev. ed. Rosemary Haughton. 1980. pap. 7.95 (ISBN 0-87243-102-9). Templegate.
Transformation of Man: A Blueprint for Creative Living. George A. Jones. vii, 65p. (Orig.). 1975. 5.00 (ISBN 0-89142-015-0); pap. 2.00 (ISBN 0-89142-016-9). Sant Bani Ash.
Transformation of Metropolis. Charles L. Leven. 1978. pap. 2.00 (ISBN 0-318-00029-6, INS 18). Inst for Urban & Regional.
Transformation of Mexican Agriculture: International Structure & the Politics of Rural Change. Steven E. Sanderson. LC 85-42701. 304p. 1986. text ed. 47.00x (ISBN 0-691-07693-6); pap. text ed. 11.95x (ISBN 0-691-02239-9). Princeton U Pr.
Transformation of Morals, 2 vols. Frederick Nietzsche. (Illus.). 245p. 1986. Repr. of 1903 ed. Set. 179.86 (ISBN 0-89901-272-8). Found Class Reprints.
Transformation of Moravian Bethlehem: From Communal Mission to Family Economy. Beverly P. Smaby. (Illus.). 288p. 1988. text ed. 32.95x (ISBN 0-8122-8130-6). U of Pa Pr.
Transformaration of Nature in Art. Ananda K. Coomaraswamy. 1937. pap. 5.95 (ISBN 0-486-20368-9). Dover.
Transformation of Nature in Art. Ananda K. Coomaraswamy. 11.25 (ISBN 0-8446-0554-9). Peter Smith.
Transformation of Nicaragua: 1519-1548. Dan Stanislawski. LC 82-49326. (UC Publications in Ibero-Americana: Vol. 54). 1983. pap. 22.50x (ISBN 0-520-09680-0). U of Cal Pr.
Transformation of Old Age Security: Class & Politics in the American Welfare State. Jill Quadagno. (Illus.). 272p. 1988. 27.50x (ISBN 0-226-69923-4). U of Chicago Pr.

Transforming Natural Resources for Human Development: A Resources Systems Framework for Development Policy. (Resources Systems Theory & Methodology Ser.: No. 1). 87p. 1983. pap. text ed. 22.75 (ISBN 92-808-0469-3, TUNU221, UNU). UNIPUB.
Transforming Number One. 4th ed. Ron Smothermon. LC 81-14356. 200p. (Orig.). 1982. pap. 9.95 (ISBN 0-932654-04-5). Context Pubns.
Transforming Ordinary Income into Capital Gain. Pennsylvania Bar Institute. 43p. 1985. 15.00 (ISBN 0-318-19076-1, 282). PA Bar Inst.
Transforming Our World: A Call to Action. COTB Speakers Staff. Ed. by Rodney L. Morris. LC 88-5262. 1988. pap. 10.95 (ISBN 0-88070-222-2). Multnomah.
Transforming Political Discourse: Political Theory & Critical Conceptual History. Terence Ball. 256p. Date not set. text ed. 45.00 (ISBN 0-631-15821-9). Basil Blackwell.
Transforming Power for Peace. Lawrence S. Apsey. (FGC). 86p. 1964. 0.75 (ISBN 0-318-14158-2). Friends Genl Conf.
Transforming Power of the Bible. Wayne B. Robinson. LC 83-23680. 240p. (Orig.). 1984. pap. 9.95 (ISBN 0-8298-0706-3). Pilgrim NY.
Transforming Principle: Discovering That Genes Are Made of DNA. Maclyn McCarty. (Illus.). 256p. 1986. pap. 5.95 (ISBN 0-393-30450-7). Norton.
Transforming Principle: Discovering That Genes Are Made of DNA. Macyln McCarty. LC 84-20544. (Illus.). 288p. 1985. 14.95 (ISBN 0-393-01951-9). Norton.
Transforming Problems. Bert Ghezzi. 140p. (Orig.). 1986. pap. 5.95 (ISBN 0-89283-294-0). Servant.
Transforming Russia & China: Revolutionary Struggle in the Twentieth Century. William G. Rosenberg & Marilyn B. Young. 1982. 27.95x (ISBN 0-19-502965-8); pap. text ed. 9.95x (ISBN 0-19-502966-6). Oxford U Pr.
Transforming the Past: Tradition & Kinship among Japanese Americans. Sylvia J. Yanagisako. LC 83-42541. 304p. 1985. 39.50x (ISBN 0-8047-1199-2). Stanford U Pr.
Transforming the "Periphery" A Study of the Struggle of Social Forces in Ghana for Democracy & National Sovereignty. 29p. 1982. pap. 5.00 (TUNU178, UNU). UNIPUB.
Transforming the "Periphery" A Study of the Struggle of the Social Forces in Ghana for Democracy & National Sovereignty. Sub-project on the Transformation of the World (TW) 1981. pap. 5.00 (ISBN 92-808-0309-3, TUNU178, UNU). UNIPUB.
Transforming the School's Capacity for Problem Solving. Philip J. Runkel et al. LC 79-63379. 1979. 7.95 (ISBN 0-936276-08-8). Ctr Educ Policy Mgmt.
Transforming the State Role in Undergraduate Education: Time for a Different View. 26p. 1986. 12.50 (ISBN 0-318-22555-7, PS-86-3). Ed Comm States.
Transforming Traditional Agriculture. Theodore W. Schultz. LC 75-26314. (World Food Supply Ser). (Illus.). 1976. Repr. of 1964 ed. 21.00x (ISBN 0-405-07792-0). Ayer Co Pubs.
Transforming Traditional Agriculture. Theodore W. Schultz. LC 82-20271. xiv, 212p. 1964. pap. 7.95x (ISBN 0-226-74075-7). U of Chicago Pr.
Transforming Traditional Unit Teaching. William J. Stewart. 87p. 1982. pap. text ed. 4.95x (ISBN 0-89641-107-9). American Pr.
Transforming Traditionally: Land & Labor Use in Agriculture in Asia & Africa. Kusum Nair. LC 83-61217. (Perspectives on Asian & African Development Ser.: No. 1). 168p. 1983. 20.00 (ISBN 0-913215-00-7). Riverdale Co.
Transforming Vision: Shaping a Christian World View. Brian J. Walsh & J. Richard Middleton. LC 84-15646. 240p. (Orig.). 1984. pap. 9.95 (ISBN 0-87784-973-0). Inter-Varsity.
Transforming Words. Ed. by William Schulz. 1984. pap. 5.95 (ISBN 0-933840-22-5). Unitarian Univ.
Transforming Work. John D. Adams. (Orig.). 1984. pap. text ed. 19.95 (ISBN 0-917917-00-6). Miles River.
Transforming Your Life with Astrology. Tiffany Holmes. LC 85-73305. 192p. 1986. 16.95 (ISBN 0-86690-307-0, 2350-01). Am Fed Astrologers.
Transforms for Engineers: A Guide to Signal Processing. K. G. Beauchamp. (Illus.). 320p. 1987. 75.00 (ISBN 0-19-856174-1). Oxford U Pr.
Transforming China's in the 80's, 2 vols. Ed. by Stephen Feuchtwang. 1988. Vol. 1: The Rural Sector, Welfare &Employment, 256. 40.00 ea. (ISBN 0-8133-0556-X); pap. 21.50 ea. (ISBN 0-317-59722-1); Vol. 2:Management, Industry & the Urban Economy, 192 pgs. 38.50 (ISBN 0-8133-0557-8); pap. 18.00 (ISBN 0-8133-0558-6). Westview.
Transfrontier Movements of Hazardous Wastes: Legal & Institutional Aspects. OECD. 304p. (Orig.). 1985. pap. 28.00x (ISBN 92-64-12694-5). OECD.
Transfrontier Pollution & International Law. Ed. by Centre d'Etude et de Recherche de Droit International et de Relations Internationaies. 1987. pap. text ed. 21.50 (ISBN 90-247-3394-4, Pub. by Martinus Nijhoff Netherlands). Kluwer Academic.
Transfrontier Pollution & the Role of States. OECD Staff. 202p. (Orig.). 1981. pap. text ed. 12.50x (ISBN 92-64-12197-8). OECD.
Transfusion Medicine. Ed. by W. Hallowell Churchill & Sanford Kurtz. (Illus.). 384p. 1988. price not set (ISBN 0-86542-052-1). Blackwell Sci.
Transfusion Medicine: Recent Technological Advances. Kris Murawski & Fran Peetoom. LC 85-23740. (PCBR Ser.: Vol. 211). 372p. 1986. 56.00 (ISBN 0-8451-5061-8, 5061). A R Liss.
Transfusion: Or the Orphans of Unwalden. W. M. Godwin. 252p. 1987. text ed. 25.00 (ISBN 0-87556-695-2). Saifer.
Transfusion Therapy: Principles & Procedures. 2nd ed. Roanne C. Rutman & William V. Miller. 512p. 1985. 63.95 (ISBN 0-87189-116-6). Aspen Pub.
Transfusion-Transmitted Viral Diseases. Ed. by S. Breanndan Moore. 1987. text ed. 25.00 (ISBN 0-915355-51-5). Am Assn Blood.
Transfusion-Transmitted Viruses: Epidemiology & Pathology. Ed. by S. J. Insalaco & Jay E. Menitove. 1987. text ed. 26.00 (ISBN 0-915355-50-7). Am Assn Blood.
Transfusionsmedizin - Notfall - und Massivtransfusion, Autoimmunhaematologie, Infektionen, Stammzelluebertragung, 1987. Ed. by V. Kretschmer et al. (Contributions to Infusion Therapy Ser.: Vol. 21). (Illus.). viii, 420p. 1988. 66.75 (ISBN 3-8055-4840-0). S Karger.
Transfusionsmedizin Aktuell: Infektionen, Thrombozyten, Granulozyten. Ed. by V. Kretschmer & W. Stangel. (Beitraege zu Infusionstherapie: Vol. 15). (Illus.). viii, 294p. 1986. 44.75 (ISBN 3-8055-4340-9). S Karger.
Transfusionsmedizin und Schock. H. Reissigl & D. Schoenitzer. (Handbuch der Infusionstherapie und klinischen Ernaehrung: Band 3). xii, 256p. 1986. 83.50 (ISBN 3-8055-3744-1). S Karger.
Transfusionsmedizin 1986 - Infektionen, Autotransfusion, Lymphokine. Ed. by V. Kretschmer & W. Stangel. (Beitraege zu Infusionstherapie und klinische Ernaehrung Ser.: Vol. 18). (Illus.). xii, 412p. 1987. 66.75 (ISBN 3-8055-4696-3). S Karger.
Transgenerational Family Therapy. Stuart Lieberman. 234p. 1979. 25.00 (ISBN 0-85664-776-4, Pub. by Croom Helm Ltd). Routledge Chapman & Hall.
Transglutaminase. Ed. by Victor A. Najjar & Laszlo Lorand. (Developments in Molecular & Cellular Biochemistry). 1984. lib. bdg. 52.50 (ISBN 0-89838-593-8, Pub. by Martinus Nijhoff Netherlands). Kluwer Academic.
Transgressions: Australian Writing Now. Ed. by Don Anderson. 256p. 1986. pap. 5.95 (ISBN 0-14-008393-6). Penguin.
Transhei's Half Loaf: Race Separatism in South Africa. Newell M. Stultz. LC 78-65481. 1979. 29.50x (ISBN 0-300-02333-2). Yale U Pr.
Transhominal Criticism. E. R. Zietlow. LC 77-9229. 209p. 1978. 9.95 (ISBN 0-8022-2210-2). Philos Lib.
Transidioma: Instant Translator. 1985. 16.95 (ISBN 0-671-55296-1). S&S.
Transidioma: Ten Bilingual Dictionaries in One. 1985. pap. 7.95. S&S.
Transiency & Permanence: The Nature of Theology According to Saint Bonaventure. G. H. Tavard. 1974. Repr. of 1954 ed. 15.00 (ISBN 0-686-11588-0). Franciscan Inst.
Transient Analysis Aided by Network Theorems. Harry E. Stockman. 180p. 1984. 13.00. Sercolab.
Transient Criminality: A Model of Stress-Induced Crime. Anthony R. Mawson. LC 87-11741. 352p. 1987. lib. bdg. 45.00 (ISBN 0-275-92552-8, C2552). Praeger.
Transient Flow in Natural Gas Transmission Systems. J. F. Wilkinson et al. 273p. 1964. 5.00 (ISBN 0-318-12725-3, L20030). Am Gas Assn.
Transient Ground Water Hydraulics. Robert E. Glover. 1978. 21.00 (ISBN 0-918334-24-1). WRP.
Transient Guest & Other Episodes. Edgar Saltus. LC 76-116007. Repr. of 1889 ed. 17.50 (ISBN 0-404-05509-5). AMS Pr.
Transient Nativity: A Christmas Story. Frederick A. Raborg, Jr. (Amela Chapbook Ser.). 8p. 1987. pap. 3.50 (ISBN 0-936545-07-0). Amelia.
Transient Phenomena in Electrical Machines. P. K. Kovacs. (Studies in Electrical & Electronic Engineering: Vol. 9). 1984. 129.00 (ISBN 0-444-99663-X, I-345-83). Elsevier.
Transient Phenomena in Multiphase Flow: Proceedings of the International Centre for Heat & Mass Transfer. Ed. by Naim Afgan. 400p. 1988. 145.00 (ISBN 0-89116-682-3). Hemisphere Pub.
Transient Phenomena in Neural Development. Killackey. (Geoscience Texts Ser.). 1985. write for info. (ISBN 0-471-83632-X). Wiley.
Transient Protection of Electronic Circuits. Standler. 1989. price not set (ISBN 0-471-61121-2). Wiley.
Transient Psychosis: Diagnosis, Management, & Evaluation. Ed. by Joe P. Tupin et al. LC 83-23965. 320p. 1984. 30.00 (ISBN 0-87630-353-X). Brunner-Mazel.
Transient System Analysis on a Personal Computer. Eichenauer. 1988. write for info. (ISBN 0-471-61209-X). Wiley.
Transient Techniques in Electrochemistry. Ed. by Digby D. Macdonald. LC 77-24603. 330p. 1977. 55.00x (ISBN 0-306-31010-4, Plenum Pr). Plenum Pub.
Transient Techniques in NMR of Solids: An Introduction to Theory & Practice. B. C. Gerstein & C. R. Dybowski. 1985. 70.00 (ISBN 0-12-281180-1). Acad Pr.
Transient Two-Phase Flow: Proceedings. Safety of Nuclear Installations, Specialist Committee. Ed. by Milton Plesset et al. LC 82-23422. (Illus.). 736p. 1983. text ed. 86.95 (ISBN 0-89116-258-5). Hemisphere Pub.
Transient Two-Phase Flow: Proceedings, 2 vols. Specialists Meeting on Transient Two-Phase Flow, Toronto, Canada, Aug. 3-4, 1976. Ed. by S. Banerjee & K. Weaver. (Illus.). 1978. Set. pap. text ed. 139.00 (ISBN 0-89116-153-8). Hemisphere Pub.
Transient Unemployed. John N. Webb. LC 71-166337. (FDR & the Era of the New Deal Ser.). 1971. Repr. of 1935 ed. lib. bdg. 17.50 (ISBN 0-306-70335-1). Da Capo.
Transient Waves in Layered Media. M. Tygel & P. Hubral. (Methods in Geochemistry & Geophysics Ser.: No. 26). 342p. 1987. 87.00 (ISBN 0-444-42808-9). Elsevier.
Transients in Electric Circuits. Joseph B. Aidala & Leon Katz. (Illus.). 1980. text ed. 38.00 (ISBN 0-13-929943-2). P-H.
Transients in Pulsed Semiconductor Diodes. Y. A. Tkhorik. 152p. 1968. text ed. 33.00 (ISBN 0-7065-0601-4, Pub. by Keter Pub Jerusalem). Coronet Bks.
Transients, Settlers, & Refugees. Vaughan Robinson. (Illus.). 264p. 1985. 42.00x (ISBN 0-19-878009-5). Oxford U Pr.
Transistion from School to Work in Europe. Ed. by Peter Grootings & Michael Stefanov. 256p. 1988. lib. bdg. 49.95 (ISBN 0-415-00576-0). Routledge Chapman & Hall.
Transistor. 1987. 100.00. Data Inc.
Transistor & Integrated Electronics. 4th ed. Milton S. Kiver. 1972. text ed. 44.95 (ISBN 0-07-034942-8). McGraw.
Transistor Circuit Action. 2nd ed. H. C. Veatch. (Illus.). 1976. text ed. 39.95 (ISBN 0-07-067383-7). McGraw.
Transistor Circuit Approximations. 3rd ed. Albert P. Malvino. LC 79-18580. (Illus.). 1980. text ed. 42.95x (ISBN 0-07-039878-X). McGraw.
Transistor Circuit Design. Vincent F. Leonard, Jr. (Engineering Design Ser.). (Illus.). 583p. 1983. pap. text ed. 19.95 (ISBN 0-87119-016-8); tchr's. ed. 9.95 (ISBN 0-87119-018-4); wkbk. 10.95 (ISBN 0-87119-017-6); looseleaf with experimental pts. 59.95 (ISBN 0-87119-015-X, EE-1002). Heathkit-Zenith Ed.
Transistor Circuit Techniques. 2nd ed. Ritchie. 1987. pap. 24.95 (ISBN 0-278-00034-7). Van Nos Reinhold.
Transistor Circuit Techniques. G. Ritchie. 1983. pap. 19.95 (ISBN 0-442-30533-8). Van Nos Reinhold.
Transistor Circuits. 2nd ed. Kenneth W. Cattermole. 488p. 1964. 150.00 (ISBN 0-677-00990-9). Gordon & Breach.
Transistor Discontinued Devices. 1987. 70.00. Data Inc.
Transistor Electronics. H. H. Gerrish & W. E. Dugger, Jr. LC 81-6740. 368p. 1981. 17.60 (ISBN 0-87006-394-4); wkbk. 6.00 (ISBN 0-87006-318-9); Instr's. guide 1.00 (ISBN 0-87006-442-8). Goodheart.
Transistor Engineering. Alvin B. Phillips. LC 81-8432. 400p. 1981. Repr. of 1962 ed. 32.50 (ISBN 0-89874-355-9). Krieger.
Transistor Fundamentals & Servicing. Boyd Larson. (Illus.). 480p. 1974. 35.00 (ISBN 0-13-929992-0). P-H.
Transistor Replacement & Alternate Source Guide. Ed. by Jim Fitzerald. 200p. 1987. 85.00 (ISBN 0-317-57582-1). DATA Inc.
Transistor Theory & Circuits Made Simple. Harvey Pollack. LC 77-84638. 1982. pap. 3.50 (ISBN 0-912146-07-9). AMECO.
Transistors. Richard Hunter. LC 84-730278. (Orig.). 1984. wkbk. 7.00 (ISBN 0-8064-0313-6, 807); audio visual pkg. 299.00 (ISBN 0-8064-0314-4). Bergwall.
Transistors Fundamentals for the Integrated - Circuit Engineer. R. M. Warner, Jr. & B. L. Grung. LC 88-17417. 1988. Repr. of 1983 ed. lib. bdg. price not set (ISBN 0-89464-323-1). Krieger.
Transistors: Fundamentals for the Integrated-Circuit Engineer. R. M. Warner & B. L. Grung. LC 83-10392. 875p. 1983. 69.95 (ISBN 0-471-09208-8, Pub. by Wiley-Interscience). Krieger.
Transit Actions: Techniques for Improving Productivity & Performance. Public Technology Inc. 264p. 1979. free (DG 79611). Pub Tech Inc.
Transit & Transportation: Study of Port & Industrial Areas, Vol. 6. (Metropolitan America Ser.). 230p. 1974. 14.00 (ISBN 0-405-05419-X). Ayer Co Pubs.
Transit Captain. Jack Rudman. (Career Examination Ser.: C-819). (Cloth bdg. avail. on request). pap. 16.00 (ISBN 0-8373-0819-4). Natl Learning.
Transit Development. (Transportation Research Record Ser.). 63p. 1979. 3.40 (ISBN 0-309-02969-4). Transport Res Bd.
Transit Electrical Helper. Hammer. 192p. 1986. pap. 9.95 (ISBN 0-13-929209-8). Arco.
Transit Electrical Helper Series. Jack Rudman. (Career Examination Ser.: C-1963). (Cloth bdg. avail. on request). pap. 14.00 (ISBN 0-8373-1963-3). Natl Learning.
Transit, Land Use & Urban Form. Wayne O. Attoe. (Illus.). 200p. 1988. text ed. 20.00x (ISBN 0-934951-01-2). Ctr Study of Amer Archit.
Transit Lieutenant. Jack Rudman. (Career Examination Ser.: C-820). (Cloth bdg. avail. on request). pap. 16.00 (ISBN 0-8373-0820-8). Natl Learning.
Transit Management Analyst. Jack Rudman. (Career Examination Ser.: C-2028). (Cloth bdg. avail. on request). pap. 14.00 (ISBN 0-8373-2028-3). Natl Learning.
Transit Management Analyst Trainee. Jack Rudman. (Career Examination Ser.: C-3228). (Cloth bdg. avail. on request). 1988. pap. 12.00 (ISBN 0-8373-3228-1). Natl Learning.
Transit Management in the Northwest Passage: Problems & Prospects. Ed. by C. Lamson & D. Vanderzwaag. (Studies in Polar Research). (Illus.). 200p. 1988. 65.00 (ISBN 0-521-32065-8). Cambridge U Pr.
Transit of Civilization from England to America in the 17th Century. Edward Eggleston. (Illus.). 344p. 1981. Repr. of 1901 ed. lib. bdg. 50.00 (ISBN 0-89984-183-X). Century Bookbindery.
Transit of Civilization from England to America in the Seventeenth Century. Edward Eggleston. 10.75 (ISBN 0-8446-2025-4). Peter Smith.
Transit of Saturn. Marc Robertson. 74p. 1976. 8.50 (ISBN 0-86690-149-3). Am Fed Astrologers.
Transit Patrolman. Jack Rudman. (Career Examination Ser.: C-821). (Cloth bdg. avail. on request). pap. 14.00 (ISBN 0-8373-0821-6). Natl Learning.
Transit Planning & Operations. (Transportation Research Record Ser.). 63p. 1977. 3.20 (ISBN 0-309-02650-4). Transport Res Bd.
Transit Point Moscow. Gerald Amster & Bernard Asbell. 400p. 1986. pap. 3.95 (ISBN 0-8217-1846-0). Zebra.
Transit Postmark Collector Bound, Vol. 8. 33.00 (ISBN 0-318-18051-0). Mobile PO.
Transit Problems of Three Asian Land-Locked Countries: Afghanistan, Nepal & Laos. Martin I. Glassner. (Occasional Papers-Reprints Series in Contemporary Asian: No. 4-1983 (57)). 55p. (Orig.). 1983. pap. text ed. 3.00 (ISBN 0-942182-56-1). U MD Law.
Transit Sergeant. Jack Rudman. (Career Examination Ser.: C-822). (Cloth bdg. avail. on request). pap. 16.00 (ISBN 0-8373-0822-4). Natl Learning.
Transit System Manager. Jack Rudman. (Career Examination Ser.: C-539). (Cloth bdg. avail. on request). pap. 16.00 (ISBN 0-8373-0539-X). Natl Learning.
Transit Time Effects in Unipolar Solid-State Devices. D. Dascalu. 395p. 1974. 38.00 (ISBN 0-85626-007-X). Abacus Pr.
Transit to Narcissus: A Facsimile of the Original Typescript. Norman Mailer. LC 77-24755. 1978. 39.50x (ISBN 0-86527-315-4). Fertig.
Transition. C. Porter Aiken. 1978. pap. 5.00 (ISBN 0-933992-02-5). Coffee Break.
Transition: An Author Index. Charles L. P. Silet. LC 79-67477. 186p. 1979. 15.00x (ISBN 0-87875-168-8). Whitston Pub.
Transition & Development: Problems of Third World Socialism. Ed. by Richard Fagen et al. (MR-Censa Series on the Americas). 352p. (Orig.). 1986. 28.50 (ISBN 0-85345-704-2); pap. 12.00 (ISBN 0-85345-705-0). Monthly Rev.
Transition & Tradition in Moral Theology. Charles E. Curran. LC 78-20877. 272p. 1979. pap. text ed. 8.95 (ISBN 0-268-01838-3). U of Notre Dame Pr.
Transition & Tradition in Moral Theology. Charles E. Curran. LC 78-20877. 1979. text ed. 18.95x (ISBN 0-268-01837-5). U of Notre Dame Pr.
Transition & Turbulence. Ed. by Richard Meyer. LC 81-7903. (Mathematics Research Center Symposium & Advances Seminar Ser.). 1981. 31.50 (ISBN 0-12-493240-1). Acad Pr.
Transition Called Death. Charles Hampton. LC 79-11056. (Illus.). 1979. pap. 4.75 (ISBN 0-8356-0527-2, Quest). Theos Pub Hse.
Transition: Essays on Contemporary Literature. Edwin Muir. LC 76-26149. 1976. lib. bdg. 35.50 (ISBN 0-8414-6139-2). Folcroft.
Transition, Explained: Earth Questions - Spirit Answers As Presented by the Spirit World through the Automatic Writings of Frances Bird. Frances Bird. 172p. (Orig.). 1988. pap. 12.95 (ISBN 1-55768-700-5, Dist. by Strawberry Hill Pr). Lane Ctr Pub.
Transition: From Authoritarianism to Democracy in the Hispanic World. Ed. by Stephen Schwartz. 198p. 1986. pap. 6.95 (ISBN 0-917616-87-1). ICS Pr.
Transition from Capitalism to Socialism. John D. Stephens. LC 86-1329. 248p. 1986. 26.95 (ISBN 0-252-01332-8); pap. 9.95 (ISBN 0-252-01323-9). U of Ill Pr.
Transition from Deflagration to Detonation in Condensed Phases. A. F. Belyaev et al. 245p. 1975. text ed. 62.00x (ISBN 0-7065-1496-3, Pub. by Keter Pub Jerusalem). Coronet Bks.

Transitive Vampire: A Handbook of Grammar for the Innocent, the Eager & the Doomed. Karen E. Gordon. LC 83-40086. (Illus.). 144p. 1984. 10.95 (ISBN 0-8129-1101-6). Times Bks.

Transitivity & Discourse Continuity in Chamorro Narratives. Ann M. Cooreman. (Empirical Approaches to Language Typology Ser.: No. 4). 246p. 1987. lib. bdg. 58.00x (ISBN 0-89925-361-X). De Gruyter.

Transitivity: Grammatical Relations in Government-Binding Theory. 2nd ed. T. Hoekstra. (Linguistic Models Ser.). xii, 311p. 1987. write for info. (ISBN 90-6765-014-5); pap. write for info. (ISBN 90-6765-013-7). Foris Pubns.

Transits. Reinhold Ebertin. 136p. 1971. 6.00 (ISBN 0-86690-094-2, 1101-01). Am Fed Astrologers.

Transits: Forecasting Using the Forty-Five Degree Graphic Ephemeris. Reinhold Ebertin. Tr. by Linda Kratzsch. (Ger.). 1982. pap. text ed. 10.00. ASI Pubs Inc.

Transits of the Planets. Heber J. Smith. LC 81-71870. 64p. 4.00 (ISBN 0-86690-232-5, 1467-01). Am Fed Astrologers.

Transits of Venus. Harry Wool. Ed. by I. Bernard Cohen. LC 80-2150. (Development of Science Ser.). (Illus.). 1981. lib. bdg. 25.00x (ISBN 0-405-13959-4). Ayer Co Pubs.

Transits: The Time of Your Life. Betty Lundsted. 176p. 1980. pap. 7.95 (ISBN 0-87728-503-9). Weiser.

Transkei. (Let's Visit Places & Peoples - - Nations, Dependencies, & Sovereignties of the World Ser.). (Illus.). (gr. 5 up). 1989. 12.95 (ISBN 0-7910-0132-6). Chelsea Hse.

Translated World: A Postmodern Tour of Libraries in Literature. Debra A. Castillo. LC 84-17200. x, 358p. 1985. pap. 22.00x (ISBN 0-8130-0792-5). U Presses Fla.

Translating & the Computer: Proceedings of the Seminar in London, November, 1978. Ed. by B. Snell. 190p. 1979. 52.75 (ISBN 0-444-85302-2, North Holland). Elsevier.

Translating & the Computer: Proceedings, 8th International Conference, November 12-13, 1987. 1988. write for info. Learned Info.

Translating & the Computer, 6: Proceedings of the 6th Annual International Conference, November 20-21, 1985. Ed. by Catriona Picken. 190p. 1986. 32.00 (ISBN 0-85142-192-X). Learned Info.

Translating & the Computer 7: Proceedings of the 7th International Conference on Translation, November 14-15, 1985. Ed. by Catriona Picken. 199p. 1986. 32.00 (ISBN 0-85142-200-4). Learned Info.

Translating Chinese. Wayne Schlepp. (Oleander Language & Literature Ser.: Vol. 1). 3.50 (ISBN 0-900891-00-9). Oleander Pr.

Translating Commitment to Reality: Third Annual Symposium on Nursing Faculty Practice. American Academy of Nursing Staff. (Illus.). 120p. (Orig.). 1986. pap. 16.50 (ISBN 0-317-60353-1, G-169). ANA.

Translating Neruda: The Way to Macchu Picchu. John Felstiner. LC 79-67773. (Illus.). xii, 284p. 1980. 30.00x (ISBN 0-8047-1079-1); pap. 9.95 (ISBN 0-8047-1327-8, SP 178). Stanford U Pr.

Translating Poetic Discourse: Questions of Feminist Strategies in Adrienne Rich. Myriam Diaz-Diocaretz. LC 84-28245. (Critical Theory Ser.: No. 2). vii, 167p. 1985. 34.00x (ISBN 0-915027-52-6); pap. 21.95x (ISBN 0-915027-53-4). Benjamins North Am.

Translating Relational Queries into Interactive Programs. J. C. Freytag. (Lecture Notes in Computer Science Ser.: Vol. 261). xi, 131p. 1987. pap. 15.40 (ISBN 0-387-18000-1). Springer-Verlag.

Translating Translating Apollinaire. B. P. Nichol. 1979. pap. 6.00 (ISBN 0-87924-031-8). Membrane Pr.

Translating World Affairs. Ruth A. Roland. LC 82-6521. 192p. 1982. lib. bdg. 21.95x (ISBN 0-89950-047-1). McFarland & Co.

Translatio Studii: Manuscript & Library Studies Honoring Oliver L. Kapsner, OSB. Ed. by Julian G. Plante. LC 73-76553. xii, 288p. (Ger. & Span.). 1972. 20.00 (ISBN 0-940250-75-6). Hill Monastic.

Translation. Julian J. Joyce. 1979. 9.95 (ISBN 0-89962-010-8). Todd & Honeywell.

Translation & Interpretation in Principle & Practice: From English into Chinese & from Chinese into English. Joseph D. Lowe. LC 88-90988. (Illus.). xviii, 450p. 1988. 70.00 (ISBN 0-930325-00-1). Lowe Pub.

Translation & Poetization in the Quaderna via Study & Edition of the Libro de Miseria D'Omme. Jane Ellen Connolly. (Spanish Ser.: No. 33). 260p. 1987. 20.00 (ISBN 0-942260-81-3). Hispanic Seminary.

Translation Debate. Eugene H. Glassman. LC 80-29286. 128p. (Orig.). 1981. pap. 5.95 (ISBN 0-87784-467-4). Inter Varsity.

Translation Determined. Robert Kirk. 236p. 1986. 42.00x (ISBN 0-19-824921-7). Oxford U Pr.

Translation Guide to Nineteenth-Century Polish-Language Civil-Registration Documents (Birth, Marriage & Death Records) Judith R. Frazin. (Illus.). 128p. (Orig.). 1984. pap. 10.00 (ISBN 0-9613512-0-9). Jewish Genealogical.

Translation Guide to Nineteenth Century Polish-Language Civil-Registration Documents (Birth, Marriage & Death Records) 2nd ed. Judith R. Frazin. (Illus.). 160p. 1988. pap. 16.00 (ISBN 0-9613512-1-7). Jewish Genealogical.

Translation Lattices. Richard S. Pierce. LC 52-42839. (Memoirs: No. 32). 66p. 1983. pap. 16.00 (ISBN 0-8218-1232-7, MEMO-32). Am Math.

Translation: Literary, Linguistic & Philosophical Approaches. Ed. by William Frawley. LC 82-40479. (Illus.). 224p. 1984. 27.50 (ISBN 0-87413-226-6). U Delaware Pr.

Translation of Computer Languages. Frederick W. Weingarten. LC 72-83240. 330p. 1973. text ed. 24.95x (ISBN 0-8162-9423-2). Holden-Day.

Translation of Film-Video Terms into Series, 5 bks. Verne Carlson. Incl. French (ISBN 0-943288-00-2); German (ISBN 0-943288-01-0); Italian (ISBN 0-943288-02-9); Spanish (ISBN 0-943288-03-7); Japanese (ISBN 0-943288-04-5). LC 84-203565. 1984. pap. 17.95 ea.; 59.95 set (ISBN 0-943288-05-3). Double C Pub.

Translation of Glanville: (A Treatise on the Laws & Customs of the Kingdom of England) Ranulph de Glanville. Tr. by John Beames from Lat. xl, 362p. 1980. Repr. of 1812 ed. lib. bdg. 30.00x (ISBN 0-8377-0313-1). Rothman.

Translation of Lao Tzu's "Tao Te Ching" & Wang Pi's "Commentary.". Paul J. Lin. (Michigan Monographs in Chinese Studies: No. 30). 232p. (Orig.). 1977. pap. 8.50 (ISBN 0-89264-030-8). U of Mich Ctr Chinese.

Translation of the Greek Expressions in the Text of The Gospel of John, A Commentary by Rudolf Bultmann. Walter Eisenbeis. 160p. (Orig.). 1984. lib. bdg. 23.25 (ISBN 0-8191-3884-3); pap. text ed. 12.00 (ISBN 0-8191-3885-1). U Pr of Amer.

Translation of the Orpheus of Angelo Politian & the Aminta of Torquato Tasso. Angelo Poliziano. Tr. by Louis E. Lord. LC 78-59036. 1985. Repr. of 1931 ed. 16.00 (ISBN 0-88355-708-8). Hyperion Conn.

Translation of the Orpheus of Angelo Politian & the Aminta of Torquato Tasso. Angelo Poliziano. LC 86-3172. 198p. 1986. Repr. of 1931 ed. lib. bdg. 38.50X (ISBN 0-313-25211-4, LOTR). Greenwood.

Translation of Things Past: Chinese History & Historiography. Ed. by George Kao. LC 82-165579. 202p. 1982. 25.00x (ISBN 0-295-95910-X, Pub. by Chinese Univ Hong Kong). U of Wash Pr.

Translation Series, 4 vols. Viking Society for Northern Research. Repr. of 1947 ed. 120.00 set (ISBN 0-404-60010-7). AMS Pr.

Translation Services Directory. 6th, rev. ed. American Translators Association Staff. 1986. 20.00 (ISBN 0-938734-16-4). Learned Info.

Translation Spectrum: Essays in Theory & Practice. Marilyn Rose. LC 80-20302. 172p. 1980. 34.50x (ISBN 0-87395-436-X); pap. 10.95x (ISBN 0-87395-437-8). State U NY Pr.

Translation Studies. Susan Bassnett-McGuire. (New Accents Ser.). 1981. pap. 10.95x (ISBN 0-416-72880-4, NO. 2364). Routledge Chapman & Hall.

Translation Textbook. Madeleine Sergent & Kay Wilkins. LC 85-17989. 140p. 1986. lib. bdg. 23.25 (ISBN 0-8191-4959-4); pap. text ed. 9.25 (ISBN 0-8191-4960-8). U Pr of Amer.

Translational Control. Ed. by Michael B. Mathews. (Current Communications in Molecular Biology Ser.). 192p. (Orig.). 1986. pap. text ed. 27.00 (ISBN 0-87969-191-3). Cold Spring Harbor.

Translational Regulation of Gene Expression. Ed. by J. Ilan. LC 87-15322. (Illus.). 510p. 1987. 75.00 (ISBN 0-306-42640-4, Plenum Pr). Plenum Pub.

Translationes Operum Sinensium de Geseneriaceis--I. L. E. Skog & H. M. Whetzel. (Contributions from the New York Botanical Garden Ser.: Vol. 16). 1986. pap. text ed. 12.00x (ISBN 0-89327-305-8). NY Botanical.

Translations. Brian Friel. 72p. 1981. pap. 8.50 (ISBN 0-571-11742-2). Faber & Faber.

Translations. rev. ed. Ezra Pound. LC 53-11965. 1953. pap. 10.00 (ISBN 0-8112-0164-3, NDP145). New Directions.

Translations. Henry David Thoreau. Ed. by Elizabeth Witherell. LC 83-42589. (Writings of Henry D. Thoreau). (Illus.). 250p. 1986. 27.50x (ISBN 0-691-06531-4). Princeton U Pr.

Translations. Charles Tomlinson. (Contemporary Poetry Ser.). 1983. 15.95x (ISBN 0-19-211958-3). Oxford U Pr.

Translations, "A". Saul Yurkievich et al. Ed. by Don Wellman. Tr. by Cola Franzen. (Translations: Experiments in Reading Ser.). (Illus.). 72p. (Orig.). 1983. pap. 4.50 (ISBN 0-942030-04-4). O ARS.

Translations & Other Rhymes. Henry C. Lea. 59.95 (ISBN 0-8490-1226-0). Gordon Pr.

Translations & Reprints from the Original Sources of European History, 6 Vols. rev. ed. Pennsylvania University - Department Of History. LC 75-143179. Repr. of 1900 ed. Set. lib. bdg. 135.00 (ISBN 0-404-08970-4); 22.50 ea. AMS Pr.

Translations, "B". Joseph Guglielmi. Ed. by Don Wellman. Tr. by Christopher Duncan. (Translations: Experiments in Writing Ser.). (Illus.). 96p. (Orig.). 1983. pap. 4.50 (ISBN 0-942030-05-2). O ARS.

Translations, "C". Bruce Andrews et al. Ed. by Don Wellman et al. Tr. by Jerome Rothenberg et al. (Translations: Experiments in Reading Ser.). (Illus.). 104p. (Orig.). 1983. pap. 4.50 (ISBN 0-942030-06-0). O ARS.

Translations: Experiments in Reading. Henri Michaux et al. Ed. by Don Wellman et al. Tr. by Charles Simic et al from Fr., Ger., Chinese, & Japanese. (Illus.). 272p. (Orig.). casebound o.p. 15.00; pap. 12.00 (ISBN 0-942030-03-6). O ARS.

Translations from C. Baudelaire. Richard H. Shepherd. LC 77-11485. Repr. of 1869 ed. 13.50 (ISBN 0-404-16345-9). AMS Pr.

Translations from Early Japanese Literature. 2nd abr. ed. Edwin O. Reischauer & Joseph K. Yamagiwa. LC 72-79310. (Harvard-Yenching Institute Studies: No. 29). 352p. 1972. pap. 12.00x (ISBN 0-674-90422-2). Harvard U Pr.

Translations from Hispanic Poets. Henry Thomas. 1938. 5.00 (ISBN 0-87535-045-3). Hispanic Soc.

Translations from Lu Yu. David Gordon. (Juniper Bks: No. 25). 1978. pap. 5.00 (ISBN 1-55780-024-3). Juniper Pr Wi.

Translations from the Ancient Tanbara. Harold James. LC 87-60012. 190p. (Orig.). 1986. pap. 9.95 (ISBN 0-930122-00-3, SP-2-00-3). Straightline Fresno.

Translations from the Classics into English from Caxton to Chapman, 1477-1620. Henry B. Lathrop. 1967. Repr. lib. bdg. 23.00x (ISBN 0-374-94826-7, Octagon). Hippocrene Bks.

Translations from the Icelandic. Ed. & tr. by W. C. Green. 1976. lib. bdg. 59.95 (ISBN 0-8490-2757-8). Gordon Pr.

Translations from the Icelandic. Ed. by William C. Green. LC 66-30733. (Medieval Library). Repr. of 1926 ed. 17.50x (ISBN 0-8154-0089-6). Cooper Sq.

Translations from the Old English. Albert S. Cook et al. Incl. Andreas: The Legend of St. Andrew: No. 7. Robert K. Root. Repr. of 1899 ed; Elene of Cynewulf: No. 21. Lucius H. Holt. Repr. of 1904 ed; Genesis: No. 48. Lawrence A. Mason. Repr. of 1915 ed; King Alfred's Version of St. Augustine's Soliloquies: No. 22. Henry L. Hargrove. Repr. of 1904 ed; Old English Physiologus: No. 63. Albert S. Cook & James H. Pitman. Repr. of 1921 ed. (Yale Studies in English Ser.). 274p. 1970. Set. 29.50 (ISBN 0-208-00909-4, Archon). Shoe String.

Translations from the Philosophical Writings of Gottlob Frege. 3rd ed. Gottlob Frege. Ed. by Peter Geach & Max Black. 228p. 1980. pap. 15.95x (ISBN 0-8476-6287-X). Rowman.

Translations from the Poetry of Rainer Maria Rilke. Rainer M. Rilke. Tr. by M. Herter Norton. (Ger. & Eng.). 1962. pap. 7.95 (ISBN 0-393-00156-3, Norton Lib). Norton.

Translations from the Unconscious. Clyde F. Smith. 32p. 1986. pap. 4.00 (ISBN 0-929170-10-5). Paper Plant.

Translations of Ancient Arabian Poetry. Charles J. Lyall. LC 79-2872. 200p. 1987. Repr. of 1885 ed. 20.50 (ISBN 0-8305-0042-1). Hyperion Conn.

Translations of Bengali Works into English: A Bibliography. Dipali Ghosh. 280p. 1986. 64.00x (ISBN 0-7201-1809-3). Mansell.

Translations of Beowulf: A Critical Bibliography. Chauncey B. Tinker. LC 68-58234. (Bibliography & Reference Ser.: No. 90). 1969. Repr. of 1903 ed. 13.50 (ISBN 0-8337-3539-X). B Franklin.

Translations of Beowulf: A Critical Biography. Chauncey B. Tinker. LC 67-21717. 148p. 1967. Repr. of 1903 ed. 20.00x (ISBN 0-87752-114-X). Gordian.

Translations of Eastern Poetry & Prose. Reynold A. Nicholson. LC 86-21110. (Illus.). 216p. 1987. pap. 15.00 (ISBN 0-391-03463-4, Pub. by Humanities Press & Curzon Pr England). Humanities.

Translations of Eastern Poetry & Prose. Tr. by Reynold A. Nicholson. Repr. of 1922 ed. lib. bdg. 22.50 (ISBN 0-8371-2301-1, NIEP). Greenwood.

Translations of German Poetry in American Magazines. E. Z. Davis. 59.95 (ISBN 0-8490-1227-9). Gordon Pr.

Translations of German Poetry in American Magazines, 1741-1810. Edward Z. Davis. LC 66-27663. 240p. 1966. Repr. of 1905 ed. 35.00x (ISBN 0-8103-3209-4). Gale.

Translations of Hispanic Poets. 271p. 1938. 5.00 (ISBN 0-317-00548-0, Pub. by Hispanic Soc). Interbk Inc.

Translations of Lucian: Complete Works of St. Thomas More Ser, Vol. 3, Pt. 1. St. Thomas More. Ed. by Craig R. Thompson. 1974. 31.00t (ISBN 0-300-01472-4). Yale U Pr.

Translations of Seneca's Troas Thyestes & Hercules Furens: 1559, 1560 & 1561. Jasper Heywood. Ed. by H. De Vocht. (Material for the Study of the Old English Drama Ser.: No. 1, Vol. 41). pap. 36.00 (ISBN 0-8115-0290-2). Kraus Repr.

Translations of the Gospel Back into Tongues. C. D. Wright. LC 82-17047. (SUNY Poetry Ser.). 84p. 1983. 24.50x (ISBN 0-87395-652-4); pap. 7.95 (ISBN 0-87395-685-0). State U NY Pr.

Translations: Series 2, Vol. 6. American Mathematical Society Staff. pap. 126.70 (ISBN 0-317-58776-5, 2029659). Bks Demand UMI.

Translations Without Originals. Julio Marzan. 50p. 1986. pap. 3.95 (ISBN 0-918408-23-7). Reed & Cannon.

Translator. Pat Goodheart. 160p. 1983. pap. 4.95 (ISBN 0-941324-07-9). Van Vactor & Goodheart.

Translator-Warrior Speaks: A Personal History of the American Translators Association, 1959-1970. Bernard Bierman. Ed. by Evelyn Rothstein. (Illus.). 220p. (Orig.). 1987. pap. text ed. 19.95 (ISBN 0-913935-43-3). ERA-CCR.

Translator's Art: Essays in Honor of Betty Radice. Ed. by Barbara Reynolds & William Radice. 272p. 1988. pap. 8.95 (ISBN 0-14-009226-9). Penguin.

Translator's Guide to Paul's First Letter to the Corinthians. Robert G. Bratcher. LC 82-6951. (Helps for Translators Ser.). 176p. 1982. pap. 6.00x (ISBN 0-8267-0185-X, 08566). Am Bible.

Translator's Guide to Paul's Letters to Timothy & to Titus. Robert G. Bratcher. LC 83-4823. (Helps for Translators Ser.). viii, 138p. 1983. softcover 5.50x (ISBN 0-8267-0190-6, 08781, Pub. by United Bible). Am Bible.

Translator's Guide to Paul's Second Letter to the Corinthians. Robert G. Bratcher. LC 83-1383. (Helps for Translators Ser.). vii, 160p. 1983. pap. 5.50x (ISBN 0-8267-0186-8, 08571, Pub. by United Bible). Am Bible.

Translator's Guide to Selected Psalms. Heber F. Peacock. LC 81-176690. (Helps for Translators Ser.). 154p. 1981. pap. 5.50x (ISBN 0-8267-0299-6, 08737, Pub. by United Bible). Am Bible.

Translator's Guide to Selections from the First Five Books of the Old Testament. Hebert F. Peacock. LC 82-130980. (Helps for Translators Ser.). 323p. 1982. pap. 7.00x (ISBN 0-8267-0298-8, 08765, Pub. by United Bible). Am Bible.

Translator's Guide to the Gospel of Luke. Robert G. Bratcher. LC 82-213977. (Helps for Translators Ser.). 388p. 1982. pap. 7.00x (ISBN 0-8267-0181-7, 08712, Pub. by United Bible). Am Bible.

Translator's Guide to the Gospel of Mark. Robert G. Bratcher. LC 81-176668. (Helps for Translators Ser.). 236p. 1981. pap. 7.00x (ISBN 0-8267-0180-9, 08711, Pub. by United Bible). Am Bible.

Translator's Guide to the Gospel of Matthew. Robert G. Bratcher. LC 82-213977. (Helps for Translators Ser.). 388p. 1981. pap. 7.00x (ISBN 0-8267-0179-5, 08710, Pub. by United Bible). Am Bible.

Translator's Guide to the Letters from James, Peter, & Jude. Robert G. Bratcher. LC 83-18159. (Helps for Translators Ser.). viii, 200p. 1983. 6.00x (ISBN 0-8267-0192-2, 08572, Pub. by United Bible). Am Bible.

Translator's Guide to the Revelation to John. R. G. Bratcher. LC 84-8670. (Helps for Translators Ser.). viii, 204p. 1984. flexible bdg. 6.00x (ISBN 0-8267-0195-7, 08790, Pub. by United Bible). Am Bible.

Translator's Handbook. Ed. by Catriona Picken. 270p. 1983. pap. 25.00 (ISBN 0-85142-185-7). Learned Info.

Translator's Handbook on Paul's First Letter to the Corinthians. Paul Ellingworth & Howard Hatton. LC 85-1142. (Helps for Translators Ser.). viii, 352p. 1985. flexible 4.20x (ISBN 0-8267-0140-X, 08578, Dist. by American Bible Society). United Bible.

Translator's Handbook on Paul's Letters to the Colossians & to Philemon. Robert G. Bratcher & Eugene A. Nida. LC 79-110968. (Helps for Translators Ser.). 149p. 1977. soft cover 5,50x (ISBN 0-8267-0145-0, 08529, Pub. by United Bible). Am Bible.

Translator's Handbook on Paul's Letter to the Ephesians. Robert G. Bratcher & Eugene A. Nida. LC 81-19691. (Helps for Translators Ser.). viii, 199p. 1982. pap. 3.75x (ISBN 0-8267-0143-4, 08780, Pub. by United Bible). Am Bible.

Translator's Handbook on Paul's Letter to the Galatians. D. C. Arichea, Jr. & E. A. Nida. LC 79-115359. (Helps for Translators Ser.). 176p. Repr. of 1976 ed. soft cover 5.50x (ISBN 0-8267-0142-6, 08527, Pub. by United Bible). Am Bible.

Translator's Handbook on Paul's Letter to the Philippians. I. Loh & E. A. Nida. LC 82-17585. (Helps for Translators Ser.). 167p. 1977. 5.50x (ISBN 0-8267-0144-2, 08528, Pub. by United Bible). Am Bible.

Translator's Handbook on Paul's Letter to the Romans. B. M. Newman & E. A. Nida. LC 75-2229. (Helps for Translators Ser.). 325p. 1973. 6.50x (ISBN 0-8267-0139-6, 08517, Pub. by United Bible). Am Bible.

Translator's Handbook on Paul's Letter to the Thessalonians. P. Ellingworth & E. A. Nida. LC 79-318783. (Helps for Translators Ser.). 229p. 1975. 6.50x (ISBN 0-8267-0146-9, 08526, Pub. by United Bible). Am Bible.

Translator's Handbook on the Acts of the Apostles. B. M. Newman, Jr. & E. A. Nida. LC 73-162720. (Helps for Translators Ser.). 542p. 1972. 8.50x (ISBN 0-8267-0138-8, 08514, Pub. by United Bible). Am Bible.

Translator's Handbook on the Book of Amos. J. De Waard & W. A. Smalley. LC 80-490970. (Helps for Translators Ser.). 274p. 1979. 6.25x (ISBN 0-8267-0128-0, 08577, Pub. by United Bible). Am Bible.

Translator's Handbook on the Book of Jonah. Brynmor F. Price & Eugene A. Nida. LC 79-311312. (Helps for Translators Ser.). 95p. 1978. 3.75x (ISBN 0-8267-0199-X, 08552, Pub. by United Bible). Am Bible.

Transnational Economic & Monetary Law Transactions & Contracts, 10 binders. Leonard Lazar. LC 77-8398. 1977. looseleaf incl. chronology binder 850.00 (ISBN 0-379-10215-3); Chronology BDR available separately 100.00 (ISBN 0-379-10220-X). Oceana.

Transnational Enterprises in a New International System. Klaus W. Grewlich. 240p. 1981. 42.50 (ISBN 90-286-0650-5, Pub. by Sijthoff & Noordhoff). Kluwer Academic.

Transnational Industrial Relations. Hans Gunter. 1972. 36.00 (ISBN 0-312-81480-1). St Martin.

Transnational Law. Philip C. Jessup. 1956. 39.50x (ISBN 0-685-89792-3). Elliots Bks.

Transnational Law of International Commercial Transactions. Ed. by Norbert Horn & Clive M. Schmitthoff. 420p. 1983. 75.00 (ISBN 90-654-4092-5, Pub. by Kluwer Law Netherlands). Kluwer Academic.

Transnational Legal Practice: A Guide to Selected Countries, 2 vols. Ed. by D. Campbell. 410p. write for info. (ISBN 90-6544-028-3). Kluwer Academic.

Transnational Legal Practice in the EEC & the United States. Linda S. Spedding. 350p. lib. bdg. 52.00 (ISBN 0-941320-36-7). Transnatl Pubs.

Transnational Legal Problems, Materials & Text: 1982 Case & Documentary Supplement. Henry J. Steiner & Detlev F. Vagts. (University Casebook Ser.). 273p. 1982. pap. text ed. 5.75 (ISBN 0-88277-092-6). Foundation Pr.

Transnational Legal Problems, Materials & Text. 3rd ed. Henry J. Steiner & Detlev F. Vagts. LC 85-24720. (University Casebook Ser.). 1122p. 1985. text ed. 31.00 (ISBN 0-88277-302-X). Foundation Pr.

Transnational Media & Third World Development: The Structure & Impact of Imperialism. William H. Meyer. (Contributions to the Study of Mass Media & Communications Ser.: No. 11). 1988. 37.85 (ISBN 0-313-26264-0, MYN/). Greenwood.

Transnational Monopoly Capitalism. Keith Cowling & Roger Sugden. LC 87-4965. 265p. 1987. 35.00 (ISBN 0-312-00954-2). St Martin.

Transnational Oil: Issues, Policies & Perspectives. Zuhayr Mikdashi. LC 85-30364. 280p. 1986. 29.95x (ISBN 0-312-81482-8). St Martin.

Transnational Parties: Organizing the World's Precincts. Ed. by Ralph M. Goldman. LC 83-12369. (Illus.). 374p. 1983. lib. bdg. 32.50 (ISBN 0-8191-3400-7); pap. text ed. 16.25 (ISBN 0-8191-3401-5). U Pr of Amer.

Transnational Reinsurance Operations: A Technical Paper. 51p. 1980. pap. 6.00 (ISBN 92-1-104034-5, E.80.II.A.10). UN.

Transnational Relations & World Politics. Ed. by Robert O. Keohane & Joseph S. Nye, Jr. LC 76-178076. (Center for International Affairs Ser). (Illus.). 1972. pap. 10.95x (ISBN 0-674-90482-6). Harvard U Pr.

Transnational Retailing. Ed. by Erdener Kaynak. 374p. 1988. lib. bdg. 49.95x (ISBN 0-89925-150-1). De Gruyter.

Transnational Terror. J. Bowyer Bell. LC 75-27369. 1975. pap. 8.50 (ISBN 0-8447-3187-0). Am Enterprise.

Transnational Terrorism: A Chronology of Events, 1968-1979. Edward F. Mickolus. LC 79-6829. xxxviii, 967p. 1980. lib. bdg. 85.00 (ISBN 0-313-22206-1, MTT/). Greenwood.

Transnationalism in World Politics & Business. Ed. by Forest L. Grieves. LC 79-1397. (Pergamon Policy Studies). 240p. 1979. 54.00 (ISBN 0-08-023892-0). Pergamon.

Transnationals. Profulla Roychoudhury. 1983. 12.50x (ISBN 0-8364-0949-3, Pub. by Mukhopadhyay India). South Asia Bks.

Transnationals & the Third World: The Struggle for Culture. Armand Mattelart. (Illus.). 192p. 1985. 27.95 (ISBN 0-89789-030-2); pap. 14.95 (ISBN 0-89789-100-7). Bergin & Garvey.

Transonic Aerodynamics. J. D. Cole & L. P. Cook. (Applied Mathematics & Mechanics Ser.: Vol. 30). 474p. 1986. 50.25 (ISBN 0-444-87958-7, North-Holland). Elsevier.

Transonic Aerodynamics. Carlo Ferrari & Francesco Tricomi. Tr. by R. H. Cramer. LC 67-23156. 1968. 119.50 (ISBN 0-12-253950-8). Acad Pr.

Transonic Aerodynamics, PAAS81. Ed. by David Nixon. LC 82-4027. (Illus.). 669p. 1982. 79.50 (ISBN 0-915928-65-5). AIAA.

Transonic Flow Problems in Turbomachinery: Proceedings. Project Squid Workshop on Transonic Flow Problems in Turbomachinery, Feb. 1976. Ed. by T. C. Adamson & M. F. Platzer. LC 77-22185. (Illus.). 660p. 1977. text ed. 85.95 (ISBN 0-89116-069-8). Hemisphere Pub.

Transonic, Shock, & Multidimensional Flows: Advances in Scientific Computing. Ed. by Richard E. Meyer. (Mathematics Research Center Symposium Ser.). 1982. 35.50 (ISBN 0-12-493280-0). Acad Pr.

Transorganizational Development. Thomas G. Cummings. 240p. Date not set. 26.95x (ISBN 0-88730-168-1). Ballinger Pub.

Transpacific Steam: The Story of Steam Navigation from the Pacific Coast of North America to the Far East and the Antipodes, 1867-1941. E. Mowbray Tate. LC 84-45642. (Illus.). 272p. 1986. 39.95 (ISBN 0-8453-4792-6, Cornwall Bks). Assoc Univ Prs.

Transparence of the World: A Selection of Poems by Jean Follain in French & English. Tr. by W. S. Merwin. LC 76-86550. 1969. 6.95 (ISBN 0-689-10195-3). Atheneum.

Transparencies. Vesle Fenstermaker. 48p. (Orig.). 1985. pap. 5.95 (ISBN 0-935306-36-6). Barnwood Pr.

Transparencies. S. Fox. 1978. pap. 2.95 (ISBN 0-942396-23-5). Blackberry ME.

Transparencies. Judith J. Sherwin. (Illus.). 1978. pap. 3.95 (ISBN 0-914378-37-6). Countryman.

Transparencies & Projections. Halvard Johnson. (Illus.). 1969. signed ltd ed o.p. 10.00 (ISBN 0-685-02579-9); pap. 3.00 (ISBN 0-912284-04-8). New Rivers Pr.

Transparencies for Understanding Medical Terminology. 7th ed. Agnes C. Frenay & Rose M. Mahoney. (Illus.). 43p. pap. text ed. 40.00 (ISBN 0-87125-120-5, 921). Cath Health.

Transparencies to Accompany Marketing. William G. Zikmund & Michael D'Amico. 152p. 1984. 25.00 (ISBN 0-471-80314-6). Wiley.

Transparency. Colin Rowe et al. (Academy Architecture Ser.). (Illus.). 72p. Date not set. 9.95 (ISBN 0-312-81497-6). St Martin.

Transparency for Positive Adjustment: Identifying & Evaluating Government Intervention. OECD Staff. 257p. (Orig.). 1983. pap. text ed. 19.00x (ISBN 92-64-12467-5). OECD.

Transparency Making Made Easy: A Programmed Primer. (Illus.). 1977. 3.75 (ISBN 0-9601006-2-8). G T Yeamans.

Transparent Designs: Reading, Performance, & Form in the "Spectator" Papers. Michael G. Ketcham. LC 84-24046. 224p. 1985. 25.00x (ISBN 0-8203-0771-8). U of Ga Pr.

Transparent God. Claude Esteban. Tr. by David Cloutier from Fr. LC 80-84603. (Modern Poets in Translation Ser.: Vol. II). ix, 107p. (Orig.). 1983. text ed. 17.00 (ISBN 0-916426-07-6); pap. 6.95 (ISBN 0-916426-08-4). KOSMOS.

Transparent Jungle. George Snelling. 100p. (Orig.). 1986. pap. text ed. 4.95 (ISBN 0-935805-00-1). Innerlogic Cir.

Transparent Landscapes. Alane Rollings. LC 83-27036. 96p. (Orig.). 1984. pap. 6.95 (ISBN 0-918518-30-X). Ion Books.

Transparent Lyric. David Walker. LC 84-1986. 235p. 1984. text ed. 25.00x (ISBN 0-691-06606-X). Princeton U Pr.

Transparent Minds: Narrative Modes for Presenting Consciousness in Fiction. Dorritt Cohn. LC 78-51161. 1978. 28.50x (ISBN 0-691-06369-9); pap. 13.95x (ISBN 0-691-10156-6). Princeton U Pr.

Transparent Motives: Glass on a Large Scale. Karen S. Chambers. (Illus.). 36p. 1986. pap. 12.95 (ISBN 0-917562-41-0). Contemp Arts.

Transparent Self: Self-Disclosure & Well-Being. 2nd ed. Sidney M. Jourard. 1971. pap. 13.95 (ISBN 0-442-24192-5). Van Nos Reinhold.

Transparent Simulacra: Spanish Fiction, 1902-1926. Robert C. Spires. LC 88-4882. 224p. 1988. text ed. 26.00 (ISBN 0-8262-0695-6). U of Mo Pr.

Transparent Things. Vladimir Nabokov. LC 72-3989. 128p. 1972. text ed. 9.95 (ISBN 0-07-045734-4). McGraw.

Transparent Tree: Fictions. Robert Kelly. LC 85-2951. 200p. 1985. 20.00 (ISBN 0-914232-68-1); pap. 10.00 (ISBN 0-914232-70-3); deluxe ed. 50.00 (ISBN 0-914232-69-X). McPherson & Co.

Transparent Watercolor. Edward D. Walker. (Illus.). 176p. 1985. 24.95 (ISBN 0-89134-163-3). North Light Bks.

Transparent Watercolor: Ideas & Techniques. Gerald F. Brommer. LC 72-97154. 1973. 15.95 (ISBN 0-87192-052-2). Davis Mass.

Transparent Watercolor: Painting Methods & Materials. Inessa Derkatsch. (Illus.). 1980. text ed. 25.95 (ISBN 0-13-930321-9, Spec); pap. text ed. 14.95 (ISBN 0-13-930313-8, Spec). P-H.

Transparentizing of Paper. (Bibliographic Ser.: No. 201). 98p. 1963. 9.00 (ISBN 0-317-34464-1). Inst Paper Chem.

Transparentizing of Paper. Jack Weiner & Vera Pollock. LC 63-5444. (Bibliographic Ser.: No. 201, Suppl. 1). 1973. pap. 10.00 (ISBN 0-87010-015-7). Inst Paper Chem.

Transparenz der Wirklichkeit: Edzard Schaper und die innere Spannung in der christlichen Literatur des zwanzigsten Jahrhunderts. Irene Sonderegger-Kummer. (Quellen und Forschungen zur Sprach- und Kulturgeschichte der germanischen Voelker, No. 37). (Ger). 1971. 48.40x (ISBN 3-11-001845-4). De Gruyter.

Transpersonal Actor: The Whole Person in Acting. Ned Manderino. 1977. pap. 12.00 (ISBN 0-9601194-1-8). Manderino Bks.

Transpersonal Approaches to Counseling & Psychotherapy. Gay Hendricks & Barry Weinhold. 199p. 1982. pap. text ed. 12.95 (ISBN 0-89108-112-7). Love Pub Co.

Transpersonal Psychologies. Ed. by Charles T. Tart. (Illus.). 504p. 1983. pap. text ed. 12.95x (ISBN 0-912149-00-0). Psych Processes Inc.

Transpersonal Psychology for Daily Life. Paul Philips. LC 80-66662. (Illus.). 98p. (Orig.). 1984. pap. 8.95 (ISBN 0-930149-01-7). AAP Calif.

Transplacental Carcinogenesis. Jerry M. Rice. Date not set. price not set (ISBN 0-89004-565-8). Raven.

Transplacental Carcinogenesis. Ed. by L. Tomatis & U. Mohr. (Illus.). 181p. 1986. pap. 25.95 (ISBN 0-19-723003-2). Oxford U Pr.

Transplacental Carcinogenesis: Proceedings. Medizinische Hochschule Meeting. Hannover, Federal Republic of Germany. Oct. 6-7, 1971. Ed. by L. Tomatis et al. (IARC Scientific Pub.: No. 4). 1973. 16.00 (ISBN 0-686-16794-5). World Health.

Transplantation. H. Cotlier et al. Ed. by W. Masshoff. (Handbuch der Allgemeinen Pathologie: Bund 6, Teil 8). (Illus.). 1977. 275.00 (ISBN 0-387-07751-0). Springer-Verlag.

Transplantation. John S. Najarian & Richard L. Simmons. LC 73-135689. (Illus.). Repr. of 1972 ed. 120.00 (ISBN 0-8357-9424-5, 2014566). Bks Demand UMI.

Transplantation & Clinical Immunology: Immunosuppression, Vol. 15. Ed. by J. L. Touraine et al. (Symposia Foundation Merieux Ser.: Vol. 9). 294p. 1984. 93.25 (ISBN 0-444-90373-9, I-019-84, Excerpta Medica). Elsevier.

Transplantation & Clinical Immunology. Ed. by J. L. Touraine et al. (Symposia Foundation Merieux: Vol. 8). 302p. 1983. 82.00 (ISBN 0-444-90288-0, Excerpta Medica). Elsevier.

Transplantation & Clinical Immunology, Vol. 11. J. L. Touraine et al. (Symposia Foundation Merieux Ser.: Vol. 3). 338p. 1980. 94.25 (ISBN 0-444-90118-3, Excerpta Medica). Elsevier.

Transplantation & Clinical Immunology, Vol. 12. Ed. by J. L. Touraine et al. (Symposia Foundation Merieux Ser.: Vol. 4). 294p. 1981. 79.00 (ISBN 0-444-90184-1, Excerpta Medica). Elsevier.

Transplantation & Clinical Immunology: Proceedings of the 16th International Course, Lyon, France, 28-30 May; 1984 Symposia Fondation Merieux, 10, Vol. XVI. Ed. by J. L. Touraine et al. 312p. 1985. 126.50 (ISBN 0-444-80682-2, Excerpta Medica). Elsevier.

Transplantation & Clinical Immunology: Proceedings of the 9th International Course, Lyon, 1977. Ed. by J. L. Touraine et al. (International Congress Ser.: No. 447). 1979. 94.25 (ISBN 0-444-90042-X, Excerpta Medica). Elsevier.

Transplantation & Clinical Immunology, Vol. XVII--the Hyperimmunized Patient: Proceedings of the Seventeenth International Course, Lyon, France, 20-22 May 1985. Ed. by J. L. Touraine et al. (Symposia Foundation Merieux Ser.: Vol. 11). 264p. 1986. 99.50 (ISBN 0-444-80760-8). Elsevier.

Transplantation & Clinical Immunology, Vol. XVIII: Risk Factors in Organ Transplantation: Proceedings of the Eighteenth International Course, Lyon, May 12-14, 1986. Ed. by J. L. Touraine et al. (Symposia Fondation Merieux Ser.: No. 12). 424p. 1987. 123.75 (ISBN 0-444-80850-7). Elsevier.

Transplantation & Clinical Immunology, Vol. 13: Proceedings of the International Course, 13th, Lyon, June 15-17, 1981. Ed. by J. L. Touraine et al. (Symposia Foundation Merieux 1981 Ser.: Vol. 7). 284p. 1982. 86.50 (ISBN 0-444-90205-8, Excerpta Medica). Elsevier.

Transplantation & Clinical Immunology: Volume XIX - Long Term Transplant Patient. Ed. by J. L. Touraine et al. (Symposia Foundation Merieux Ser.: Vol. 13). 308p. 1988. 102.75 (ISBN 0-444-80948-1). Elsevier.

Transplantation Antigens: A Study in Serological Data Analysis. Neville Selwood & Alan Hedges. LC 78-5708. Repr. of 1978 ed. 38.30 (ISBN 0-8357-9995-6, 2016180). Bks Demand UMI.

Transplantation: Approaches to Graft Rejection. Ed. by Harold T. Meryman. (Progress in Clinical & Biological Research Ser.: Vol. 224). 368p. 1986. 58.00 (ISBN 0-8451-5074-X, 5074). A R Liss.

Transplantation Immunology. Ed. by R. Y. Calne. (Illus.). 1984. 75.00x (ISBN 0-19-261414-2). Oxford U Pr.

Transplantation in Primates. Ed. by G. P. Murphy. (Primates in Medicine: Vol. 7). 1972. 39.50 (ISBN 3-8055-1408-5). S Karger.

Transplantation in the Nineteen Eighties: Recent Advances. Ed. by Rex Jamison. LC 84-6783. 128p. 1984. 25.00 (ISBN 0-275-91436-4, C1436). Praeger.

Transplantation of Endocrine Tissue: Prospects & Constraints. Mandel. (Modern Concepts in Immunology Ser.). 1985. write for info. (ISBN 0-471-86565-6). Wiley.

Transplantation of Lyophilized Cartilage in Maxillo-Facial Surgery. H. F. Sailer. (Illus.). x, 138p. 1983. 76.75 (ISBN 3-8055-3570-8). S Karger.

Transplantation of the Pancreas. Ed. by Jules Traeger & Jean-Michel Dubernard. (Transplantation Proceedings Reprint Ser.). 248p. 1981. 56.00 (ISBN 0-8089-1396-4, 794646). Grune.

Transplantation Reviews. 2nd ed. Morris & Tilney. 240p. 1988. write for info. (ISBN 0-7216-2869-9). Saunders.

Transplantation Reviews, Vol. 1. Morris & Tilney. 1987. price not set (ISBN 0-8089-1884-2). Grune.

Transplantation Theorems & Multiplier Theorems for Jacobi Series. Muckenhoupt. LC 86-22270. (Memoirs of the American Mathematical Society Ser.: Vol. 356). 86p. 1986. pap. text ed. 13.00 (ISBN 0-8218-2418-X). Am Math.

Transplantation Therapeutics. Ed. by A. P. Monacco. (Journal: Nephron: Vol. 46, Suppl. 1, 1987). (Illus.). iv, 60p. 1987. pap. 15.50 (ISBN 3-8055-4642-4). S Karger.

Transplantation Today, Vol. VII. Ed. by Leslie Brent et al. (Transplantation Proceedings Reprint Ser.). 1983. 105.00 (ISBN 0-8089-1603-3, 790659). Grune.

Transplantation Today, Vol. V. Ed. by Rafaello Cortesini & Felix T. Rapaport. (Transplantation Proceedings Reprint Ser.). 1256p. 1979. 105.00 (ISBN 0-8089-1210-0, 790908). Grune.

Transplantation Today, Vol. IX. Ed. by Pekka Hayry et al. 3000p. 1987. 198.00 (ISBN 0-8089-1855-9, 791951). Grune.

Transplantation Today, Vol. III. Ed. by M. Schlesinger et al. (Transplanation Proceedings Reprint Ser.). (Illus.). 960p. 1975. 70.00 (ISBN 0-8089-0892-8, 793893). Grune.

Transplantation Today: Proceedings, Vol. VI. International Congress of the Transplantation Society 8th, June 29, July 5, 1980. Ed. by Felix Rapaport. 1305p. 1981. 96.50 (ISBN 0-8089-1398-0, 792973). Grune.

Transplantation Today: Proceedings of the Tenth International Congress of the Transplantation Society, Vol. VIII. Ed. by John S. Najarian et al. LC 79-3077. 1684p. 1985. 145.00 (ISBN 0-8089-1734-X, 793077). Grune.

Transplanted: A History of Immigrants in Urban America. John Bodnar. LC 84-48041. (Interdisciplinary Studies in History). (Illus.). 320p. 1987. 27.50x (ISBN 0-253-31347-3); pap. 8.95 (ISBN 0-253-20416-X). Ind U Pr.

Transplanted & Artificial Body Organs. Arnold Madison. LC 81-3805. (Illus.). 128p. (gr. 7 up). 1981. 10.95 (ISBN 0-8253-0050-9). Beaufort Bks NY.

Transplanted Christianity: Documents Illustrating Aspects of New Zealand Church History. Ed. by A. K. Davidson & P. J. Lineham. 372p. (Orig.). 1987. pap. 31.95 (ISBN 0-9597775-6-3, Pub. by Methodist Theol). ANZ Religious Pubns.

Transplanted Family: A Study of Social Adustment of the Polish Immigrant Family to the United States after the Second World War. Danuta Mostwin. Ed. by Francesco Cordasco. LC 80-881. (American Ethnic Groups Ser.). 1981. lib. bdg. 38.50x (ISBN 0-405-13442-8). Ayer Co Pubs.

Transplanted Woman: A Study of French-American Marriages in France. Gabrielle Varro. LC 87-29093. 272p. 1988. lib. bdg. 42.95 (ISBN 0-275-92856-X, C2856). Praeger.

Transplanting Success. 80p. 1983. 3.00 (ISBN 0-317-36798-6, 611-83310). Assn Supervision.

Transplants in Man. David J. Gerrick. (Illus.). 1978. 20.00 (ISBN 0-916750-68-X). Dayton Labs.

Transplants in Soil Blocks. Rev. ed. David Tresemer. (Illus.). 32p. 1986. pap. text ed. 3.00 (ISBN 0-938670-05-0). By Hand & Foot.

Transplants: Today's Medical Miracles. Gerald Leinwand. LC 84-27101. 128p. (gr. 7 up). 1985. PLB 11.90 (ISBN 0-531-04930-2). Watts.

Transplutonium Elements. B. F. Myasoedov. (Analytical Chemistry of the Elements Ser.). 380p. 1970. text ed. 75.00x (ISBN 0-7065-1375-4, Pub. by Keter Pub Jerusalem). Coronet Bks.

Transplutonium Elements--Production & Recovery. Ed. by Wallace W. Schulz & James Navratil. LC 81-7999. (ACS Symposium Ser.: No. 161). 1981. 39.95 (ISBN 0-8412-0638-4). Am Chemical.

Transplutonium Nineteen Seventy-Five: Proceedings. Ed. by W. Muller & R. Lindner. 1976. 50.00 (ISBN 0-444-11049-6, North-Holland). Elsevier.

Transporation Geography: A Bibliography. 3rd ed. William R. Siddall. LC 73-633686. (Libraries Bibliography: No. 1). 1972. Repr. 2.50 (ISBN 0-686-20817-X). KSU.

Transport. Ed. by H. Schadee & M. H. Claringbloud. 1983. Looseleaf. 114.00 (ISBN 0-686-40936-1, Pub. by Kluwer Law Netherlands). Kluwer Academic.

Transport. Illus. by Michael Twinn. (Concertina Ser.). (Illus.). 12p. (Orig.). (ps-2). 1977. 4.50 (ISBN 0-85953-006-X, Pub. by Child's Play England). Playspaces.

Transport Across Multi-Membrane Systems. Ed. by G. Giebisch. (Membrane Transport in Biology: Vol. 3). (Illus.). 1978. 99.00 (ISBN 0-387-08596-3). Springer-Verlag.

Transport Across Single Biological Membranes. Ed. by D. C. Tosteson. LC 78-17668. (Membrane Transport in Biology: Vol. 2). (Illus.). 1979. 99.00 (ISBN 0-387-08780-X). Springer-Verlag.

Transport Acts 1981 & 1982: Penalty Points-Drink & Driving-Fixed Penalties. Peter S. Wallis. 115p. 1985. 72.00x (ISBN 0-906840-92-9, Pub. by Fourmat England). State Mutual Bk.

Transport & Bioenergetics In Biomembranes. Ed. by Ryo Sato & Yasuo Kagawa. 262p. 1982. 49.50x (ISBN 0-306-41282-9, Plenum Pr). Plenum Pub.

Transport & Communication Bulletin for Asia & the Pacific, No. 58. 1986. pap. 8.50 (ISBN 0-317-66532-4, E.86.II.F.10). UN.

Transportation, Vol. 2 (incl. 1980-1984 Supplements) Ed. by Eleanor C. Goldstein. (Social Issues Resources Ser.). 1985. 75.00 (ISBN 0-89777-050-1). Soc Issues.

Transportation - Nautical Education for Offshore Extractive Industries. 2nd ed. G. H. Hoffmann et al. (Nautical Education for Offshore Extractive Industries Ser.). (Illus.). 206p. pap. 16.00 (ISBN 0-934114-71-4, BK-113). Marine Educ.

Transportation - Railroads: Companies, a Bibliography. E. Willard Miller & Ruby M. Miller. (Public Administration Ser.: P 2039). 48p. 1986. 12.50 (ISBN 1-55590-079-8). Vance Biblios.

Transportation - Railroads: Economics & Government, a Bibliography. E. Willard Miller & Ruby M. Miller. (Public Administration Ser.: P 2038). 52p. 1986. 13.50 (ISBN 1-55590-078-X). Vance Biblios.

Transportation - Railroads: Equipment & Operations, a Bibliography. E. Willard Miller & Ruby M. Miller. (Public Administration Ser.: P 2040). 70p. 1986. 16.50 (ISBN 1-55590-080-1). Vance Biblios.

Transportation - Water: Waterways, Shipping & Ports, a Bibliography. E. Willard Miller & Ruby M. Miller. (Public Administration Ser.: P 2121). 42p. 1987. 11.25 (ISBN 1-55590-241-3). Vance Biblios.

Transportation: A Pictorial Archive From 19th Century Sources with 400 Copyright-Free Illustrations for Artists & Designs. Ed. by Jim Harter. (Illus.). 160p. (Orig.). 1983. pap. 6.95 (ISBN 0-486-24499-7). Dover.

Transportation: A Survey of Current Methods of Study & Instruction & of Research & Experimentation. Victor Topping & S. J. Dempsey. 1926. pap. 49.50x (ISBN 0-686-51321-5). Elliots Bks.

Transportation Accounting & Control: Guidelines for Distribution & Financial Management. Ernst & Whinney & Cleveland Consulting Association Staff. 232p. Date not set. 50.00 (ISBN 0-318-22916-1, 83143). Natl Assn Accts.

Transportation Accounting & Control: Guidelines for Distribution Management. Ernst & Whinney Staff & Cleveland Consulting Associates Staff. 1983. non-members 50.00 (ISBN 0-86641-092-9); members 25.00. Coun Logistics Mgt.

Transportation Act 1920. Rogers Macveagh. Ed. by Stuart Bruchey. LC 80-1330. (Railroads Ser.). 1981. Repr. of 1923 ed. lib. bdg. 85.00x (ISBN 0-405-13804-0). Ayer Co Pubs.

Transportation: America's Lifeline. Ed. by Mark Siegel et al. (Information Aides Ser.). 104p. 1987. pap. 16.95 (ISBN 0-936474-72-6). Info Plus TX.

Transportation: An Annotated Bibliography. British Computer Society (BCS) Staff. 48p. 1981. pap. 31.95 (ISBN 0-471-26203-X). Wiley.

Transportation Analyst. (Career Examination Ser.: C-3380). Date not set. pap. 14.00 (ISBN 0-8373-3380-6). Natl Learning.

Transportation & Central City Unemployment: Appendices. Ed. by Edward Kalachek & John M. Goering. 100p. 1970. pap. 3.00 (INS 5A). Inst for Urban & Regional.

Transportation & Communication Policy. new ed. Ed. by Alan Altshuler. 1977. pap. 8.00 (ISBN 0-918592-22-4). Policy Studies.

Transportation & Commuting in Virginia, 1980. (Nineteen Eighty Census Analysis Ser.: Vol. 2). 1984. 7.32 (ISBN 0-317-69883-4). U Va Ctr Pub Serv.

Transportation & Economic Opportunity. (Illus.). 96p. (B). 1974. 10.00 (ISBN 0-318-16388-8, 119); members 7.00 (ISBN 0-318-16389-6). Regional Plan Assn.

Transportation & Economic Stagnation in Spain, 1750-1850. David R. Ringrose. LC 78-101131. pap. 53.30 (ISBN 0-317-20423-8, 2023441). Bks Demand UMI.

Transportation & Energy. Compiled by American Society of Civil Engineers Staff. 456p. 1978. pap. 15.00x (ISBN 0-87262-135-9). Am Soc Civil Eng.

Transportation & Industrial Development in the Middle West. William F. Gephart. 1971. lib. bdg. 18.50x (ISBN 0-374-93027-9, Octagon). Hippocrene Bks.

Transportation & Land Development. Institute of Transportation Engineers Staff et al. (Illus.). 320p. 1988. text ed. 46.00 (ISBN 0-13-930413-4). P-H.

Transportation & Land Development. (Special Report). 49p. 1978. 3.60 (ISBN 0-309-02803-5). Transport Res Bd.

Transportation & Land Use Planning Abroad. (Special Report). 77p. 1976. 3.60 (ISBN 0-309-02487-0). Transport Res Bd.

Transportation & Marketing of Natural Gas: Update 1986. William Mogel. 1985. pap. 75.00 (ISBN 0-88057-466-6). Exec Ent Pubns.

Transportation & Marketing of Natural Gas. William Mogel. 1985. pap. 125.00 (ISBN 0-88057-346-5). Exec Ent Pubns.

Transportation & Mobility in an Era of Transition. Ed. by G. R. Jansen et al. (Studies in Regional Science & Urban Economics: Vol. 13). 388p. 1985. 84.25 (ISBN 0-444-87749-5, North Holland). Elsevier.

Transportation & the Environment. G. B. Hutchins. 106p. 1977. 12.95 (ISBN 0-8464-1146-6). Beekman Pubs.

Transportation & the 1977 Clean Air Act Amendments. LC 80-66291. 440p. 1980. pap. 34.00x (ISBN 0-87262-242-8). Am Soc Civil Eng.

Transportation & Traffic Engineering Handbook. 2nd. ed. Institute of Transportation Engineers. (Illus.). 992p. 1982. 80.00 (ISBN 0-13-930362-6). P-H.

Transportation & Traffic Management, 4 vols. 16th ed. E. Albert Ovens. Ed. by Robert M. Butler & William J. Haugh. LC 74-19874. (Illus.). 1191p. 1981. Set. pap. text ed. 85.00 (ISBN 0-87408-012-6); Vol. I, 273 pgs. pap. text ed. 23.00 (ISBN 0-87408-029-0); Vol. II, 262 pgs. pap. text ed. 23.00 (ISBN 0-87408-030-4); Vol. III, 310 pgs. pap. text ed. 23.00 (ISBN 0-87408-031-2); Vol. IV, 346 pgs. pap. text ed. 23.00 (ISBN 0-87408-032-0). Intl Thom Trans Pr.

Transportation & Traffic Theory. Ed. by N. H. Gartner. N. N. Wilson. 505p. 1987. 94.25 (ISBN 0-444-01227-3). Elsevier.

Transportation & Traffic Theory Eighth International Symposium. Ed. by H. V. Hurdle & E. Hauer. 736p. 1983. 40.00x (ISBN 0-8020-2461-0). U of Toronto Pr.

Transportation & Traffic Theory: Proceedings of the 9th International Symposium, Delft, 1984. Ed. by J. Volmuller & R. Hamerslag. 608p. 1984. lib. bdg. 117.50X (ISBN 90-6764-008-5). Coronet Bks.

Transportation & Urban Land. Lowdon Wingo, Jr. LC 77-86416. (Resources for the Future Ser.). 144p. Repr. of 1961 ed. 25.00 (ISBN 0-404-60346-7). AMS Pr.

Transportation & World Development. Wilfred Owen. LC 87-4154. 176p. 1987. text ed. 22.50x (ISBN 0-8018-3495-3). Johns Hopkins.

Transportation Assistant. Jack Rudman. (Career Examination Ser.: C-2358). (Cloth bdg. avail. on request). pap. 12.00 (ISBN 0-8373-2358-4). Natl Learning.

Transportation: Basic Terms. Douglas Moore & Harris Winitz. (All about Language Ser.). (Illus.). 35p. (Orig.). 1987. pap. text ed. 4.00 (ISBN 0-939990-51-2). Intl Linguistics.

Transportation Bleves: Causes - Effects - Guidelines. Robert C. Barr. Ed. by Paul R. Lyons. LC 78-720334. 1979. pap. 49.50 incl. slides & tape (ISBN 0-87765-139-6, SL-36). Natl Fire Prot.

Transportation Buttons, Vol. I: Railroads. Donald P. Van Court. LC 87-90092. (Transportation Uniform Buttons Ser.). (Illus.). 280p. 1987. 34.50 (ISBN 0-9618301-0-7). D P Van Court.

Transportation Century. Ed. by George F. Mott. LC 67-29273. xii, 280p. 1967. 32.50 (ISBN 0-8071-0625-9). La State U Pr.

Transportation Costs & Costing, 1917-1973: A Select Annotated Chronological Bibliography. Emanuel B. Ocran, Jr. LC 75-2027. (Reference Library of Social Science: No. 10). 775p. 1975. 103.00 (ISBN 0-8240-1087-6). Garland Pub.

Transportation Decision-Making: A Guide to Social & Environmental Considerations. (National Cooperative Highway Research Program Report). 135p. 1975. 7.20 (ISBN 0-309-02331-9). Transport Res Bd.

Transportation Demand Analysis. Adib Kanafani. (Illus.). 352p. 1983. text ed. 46.95 (ISBN 0-07-033271-1). McGraw.

Transportation Deregulation: What's Deregulated & What Isn't. Daniel Sweeney et al. LC 86-60020. 309p. 1986. 50.00 (ISBN 0-9616271-0-7). NASSTRAC.

Transportation-Distribution Costs and Cost Analysis see Correspondence Course.

Transportation Economics. National Bureau Of Economic Research. (Universities-National Bureau Conference Ser.: No. 17). 482p. 1965. 29.00 (ISBN 0-87014-308-5, Dist. by Columbia U Pr). Natl Bur Econ Res.

Transportation Economics: A Guide to Information Sources. Ed. by James P. Rakowski. LC 73-17584. (Economics Information Guide Series: Vol. 5). 232p. 1976. 68.00x (ISBN 0-8103-1307-3). Gale.

Transportation Economics & Public Policy: With Urban Extensions. Alan Abouchar. LC 76-51828. 354p. 1977. 29.50 (ISBN 0-471-02101-6, Pub. by JW). Krieger.

Transportation: Educational Coloring Book. Spizzirri Publishing Co. Staff. Ed. by Linda Spizzirri. (Illus.). 32p. (gr. 1-8). 1981. pap. 1.49 (ISBN 0-86545-038-2). Spizzirri.

Transportation Eighty One. 200p. (Orig.). 1981. pap. text ed. 37.50x (ISBN 0-85825-158-2, Pub. by Inst Engineering Australia). Brookfield Pub Co.

Transportation Electronics: Proceedings of the International Congress on Transportation Electronics (Convergence '86) 1986. 55.00 (ISBN 0-89883-747-2, P 183). Soc Auto Engineers.

Transportation, Energy & Economic Development: A Dilemma in the Developing World. F. Moavenzadeh & D. Geltner. (Energy Research Ser.: Vol. 5). 530p. 1984. 152.75 (ISBN 0-444-42338-9, I-247-84). Elsevier.

Transportation Energy & the Future. Lloyd J. Money. (Illus.). 144p. 1984. text ed. 38.00 (ISBN 0-13-930230-1). P-H.

Transportation Energy Conservation & Demand, 6 Reports. (Transportation Research Record Ser.). 68p. 1976. 5.00 (ISBN 0-309-02471-4). Transport Res Bd.

Transportation Engineering: Introduction to Planning, Design & Operation. J. C. Yu. 512p. 1982. 46.50 (ISBN 0-444-00564-1). Elsevier.

Transportation Engineering: Planning & Design. 2nd ed. Radnor J. Paquette et al. LC 80-17112. 679p. 1982. write for info. (ISBN 0-471-04878-X). Wiley.

Transportation Engineering, Planning & Design. 3rd ed. Wright. 1988. write for info. (ISBN 0-471-83874-8). Wiley.

Transportation Engineering 1972: Conference Proceedings. 180p. 1973. 39.00 (ISBN 0-901948-69-1, Pub. by T Telford UK). Am Soc Civil Eng.

Transportation Environmental & Conservation Concerns: Energy, Noise & Air Quality. (Transportation Research Record Ser.). 76p. 1977. 4.80 (ISBN 0-317-36108-2). Transport Res Bd.

Transportation Facilities. 572p. 1975. pap. 25.00x (ISBN 0-87262-107-3). Am Soc Civil Eng.

Transportation Facility Negligence. National Transportation Facility Negligence Institute Staff & American Bar Association Staff. Date not set. price not set. Amer Bar Assn.

Transportation Finance & Charges, Programming & Costs. (Transportation Research Record Ser.). 53p. 1978. 3.40 (ISBN 0-317-36109-0). Transport Res Bd.

Transportation for Cities: The Role of Federal Policy. Wilfred Owen. LC 75-44508. 70p. 1976. pap. 8.95 (ISBN 0-8157-6773-0). Brookings.

Transportation for Marketing & Business Students. Paul T. McElhiney. (Quality Paperback: No. 290). 232p. (Orig.). 1975. pap. 5.95 (ISBN 0-8226-0290-3). Littlefield.

Transportation for the Elderly: Changing Lifestyles, Changing Needs. Martin Wachs. 1979. 32.50x (ISBN 0-520-03691-3). U of Cal Pr.

Transportation for the Elderly, Handicapped & Disadvantaged: An Annotated Bibliography of Technical Reports. Joseph J. Galin. (Public Administration Ser.: P 1658). 19p. 1985. 3.00 (ISBN 0-89028-368-0). Vance Biblios.

Transportation for the Elderly, Handicapped & Disadvantaged: A Bibliography of Articles. Joseph J. Galin. (Public Administration Ser.: P 1659). 9p. 1985. 2.00 (ISBN 0-89028-369-9). Vance Biblios.

Transportation for the Poor: Research in Rural Mobility. Hal S. Maggied. (Studies in Applied Regional Science). 1982. lib. bdg. 30.00 (ISBN 0-89838-081-2, Pub. by Kluwer-Nijhoff (Netherlands)). Kluwer Academic.

Transportation for the Poor, the Elderly & the Disadvantaged, 5 reports. (Transportation Research Record Ser.). 157p. 1974. 2.20 (ISBN 0-309-02360-2). Transport Res Bd.

Transportation Forecasting & Travel Behavior. (Transportation Research Record Ser.). 211p. 1978. 11.00 (ISBN 0-309-02813-2). Transport Res Bd.

Transportation Fuel Alternatives for North America into the 21st Century. 1987. 18.00 (ISBN 0-89883-452-X, P190). Soc Auto Engineers.

Transportation Fun Book. Patti Carson & Janet Dellosa. (Stick-Out-Your-Neck Ser.). (Illus.). 32p. (ps-2). 1984. pap. 1.59 (ISBN 0-88724-022-4, CD-8037). Carson-Dellos.

Transportation Futures: An Option for Tomorrow? 146p. 1988. 25.00 (ISBN 0-934292-07-8). Natl Waterways.

Transportation Geography: A Bibliography. 3rd ed. William R. Siddall. 1972. Repr. of 1969 ed. 2.50 (ISBN 0-318-22154-3). KSU.

Transportation Health & Safety Representative. (Career Examination Ser.: C-3379). Date not set. pap. 16.00 (ISBN 0-8373-3379-2). Natl Learning.

Transportation Improvements in Madison, Wisconsin: Preliminary Analysis of Pricing Programs for Roads & Parking in Conjunction with Transit Changes. Franklin Spielberg. 65p. 1978. pap. 6.00x (ISBN 0-87766-234-7, 22400). Urban Inst.

Transportation in America. Donald Altschiller. LC 82-11190. (Reference Shelf Ser.: Vol. 54, No. 3). 204p. 1982. pap. text ed. 10.00 (ISBN 0-8242-0667-3). Wilson.

Transportation in America: Users, Carriers, Government. 2nd ed. Donald V. Harper. (Illus.). 624p. 1982. text ed. write for info (ISBN 0-13-930297-2). P-H.

Transportation in Cities. E. O. Pederson. 1981. 19.00 (ISBN 0-08-024666-4). Pergamon.

Transportation in Eastern Europe. Bogdan Mieczkowski. (Eastern European Monographs: No. 38). 240p. 1978. 24.00x (ISBN 0-914710-31-1). East Eur Quarterly.

Transportation in the Future. Mark Lambert. (Tomorrow's World Ser.). (Illus.). 48p. (gr. 4-6). 1986. PLB 12.40 (ISBN 0-531-18076-X, Pub. by Bookwright). Watts.

Transportation in the Puget Sound Region: Past, Present & Future. Scott. (Occasional Papers: No. 6). 1986. pap. 4.00 (ISBN 0-318-23325-8). WWU CPNS.

Transportation in the World of the Future. rev. ed. Hal Hellman. LC 73-86220. (World of the Future Ser.). (Illus.). 188p. (gr. 7 up). 1974. 6.95 (ISBN 0-87131-155-0). M Evans.

Transportation Industries, 1889-1946: A Study of Output, Employment & Productivity. Harold Barger. LC 75-19692. (National Bureau of Economic Research Ser.). (Illus.). 1975. Repr. of 1951 ed. 23.50x (ISBN 0-405-07573-1). Ayer Co Pubs.

Transportation Information Sources. Ed. by Kenneth N. Metcalf. LC 65-24657. (Management Information Guide Ser.: No. 8). 308p. 1965. 68.00x (ISBN 0-8103-0808-8). Gale.

Transportation Issues: The Disadvantaged, the Elderly & Citizen Involvement. (Transportation Research Record Ser.). 58p. 1976. 2.60 (ISBN 0-309-02597-4). Transport Res Bd.

Transportation Law. 4th ed. John Guandolo. 1072p. 1984. 58.00 (ISBN 0-205-11566-7, H1566-2). Allyn.

Transportation Law: Institute 82 (A Practice Primer for the Eighties - 15th Annual) University of Denver College of Law Staff & Motor Carriers Lawyers Association Staff. 203p. 1983. 35.00 (ISBN 0-409-20176-6). Butterworth Legal Pubs.

Transportation-Logistics Dictionary. 2nd ed. Ed. by Joseph L. Cavinato. 323p. 1982. 14.00 (ISBN 0-87408-022-3). Intl Thom Trans Pr.

Transportation Management. 4th ed. Kenneth U. Flood & Oliver G. Callson. 736p. 1984. 43.00 (ISBN 0-205-11564-0, H1564-7). Allyn.

Transportation: Management, Economics, Policy. John L. Hazard. LC 77-22414. (Illus.). 607p. 1977. 18.00x (ISBN 0-87033-229-5). Cornell Maritime.

Transportation Markings: International Traffic Control Devices. Brian Clearman. LC 80-6184. (Study in Communication Monograph: Vol. II, Pt. E.). (Illus.). 269p. (Orig.). 1984. pap. 9.95 (ISBN 0-918941-00-8). Mt Angel Abbey.

Transportation Models for Agricultural Products. Ed. by Won W. Koo. (Special Studies in Agriculture Science & Policy). 175p. 1985. pap. text ed. 30.50x (ISBN 0-8133-0252-8). Westview.

Transportation Networks: A Quantitative Treatment. Dusan Teodorovic. (Transportation Studies: Vol. 6). 222p. 1986. text ed. 80.00 (ISBN 0-677-21380-8). Gordon & Breach.

Transportation Noise Reference Book. Ed. by Paul M. Nelson. LC 86-29944. (Illus.). 576p. 1987. text ed. 95.00 (ISBN 0-408-01446-6). Butterworth.

Transportation Not Necessary. C. B. Adderley. LC 83-49228. (Crime & Punishment in England 1850-1922 Ser.). 134p. 1984. lib. bdg. 30.00 (ISBN 0-8240-6202-7). Garland Pub.

Transportation of Hazardous Materials. LC 86-600542. (OTA-SET-304 Ser.). (Illus.). 277p. (Orig.). 1986. pap. 13.00 (ISBN 0-318-21319-2, S/N 052-003-01042-9). USGPO.

Transportation of Hazardous Materials: State & Local Activities. Office of Technology Assessment Staff. LC 87-3555. 100p. 1988. Repr. of 1985 ed. lib. bdg. 14.50 (ISBN 0-89464-218-9). Krieger.

Transportation of Radioactive Materials & Waste: A Bibliography of Politics & Law. Frederick Frankena & Joann K. Frankena. (Public Administration Ser.: P 2004). 20p. 1986. 5.00 (ISBN 1-55590-004-6). Vance Biblios.

Transportation of Soviet Energy Resources. Matthew J. Sagers & Milford B. Green. LC 86-15508. 200p. 1986. 32.50x (ISBN 0-8476-7504-1). Rowman.

Transportation of Spent Fuel, High Level Wastes, & Transuranic Wastes. 66p. 1984. 10.00 (ISBN 1-55516-471-4). Natl Conf State Legis.

Transportation Planning Aide. Jack Rudman. (Career Examination Ser.: C-2846). (Cloth bdg. avail. on request). 1988. pap. 14.00 (ISBN 0-8373-2846-2). Natl Learning.

Transportation Planning & Policy Decision Making: Behavioral Science Contributions. Richard M. Michaels. LC 79-24820. 264p. 1980. 40.95 (ISBN 0-275-90524-1, C0524). Praeger.

Transportation Planning & Policy: The Role of Analytical Methods in Government. D. N. Starkie. 1976. text ed. 38.00 (ISBN 0-08-020909-2); pap. text ed. 17.00 (ISBN 0-08-020908-4). Pergamon.

Transportation Planning & Public Policy see Progress in Planning.

Transportation Planning As Response to Controversy: Participation & Conflict in the Boston Case. Ralph Gakenheimer. LC 75-35905. 432p. 1975. 37.50x (ISBN 0-262-07065-0). MIT Pr.

Transportation Planning for Small & Medium-Sized Communities. (Special Report). 100p. 1980. 5.60 (ISBN 0-309-02982-1). Transport Res Bd.

Transportation Planning for Small Urban Areas. (National Cooperative Highway Research Program Report). 71p. 1976. 4.80 (ISBN 0-309-02506-0). Transport Res Bd.

Transportation Planning in a Changing World. P. Nijkamp & S. Reichman. 320p. 1986. text ed. 55.50 (ISBN 0-566-05250-4, Pub. by Gower Pub England). Gower Pub Co.

Transportation Planning in the Boston Metropolitan Area: A Selected Bibliography, 1930-1982. Toby Pearlstein. LC 83-20954. (Bibliography Ser.: No. 128). 1983. 10.00. CPL Biblios.

Transportation Planning in the Boston Metropolitan Area: A Selected Bibliography, 1930-1982. Toby Pearlstein. (CPL Bibliogrpahies Ser.: No. 128). 53p. 1983. 10.00. Coun Plan Librarians.

Transportation Planning Models. Florian. 1984. 100.00 (ISBN 0-444-87581-6). Elsevier.

Trash into Treasure: Recycling Ideas for Library-Media Centers Containing 100 Easy-to-Do Ideas. Eleanor Silverman. LC 87-36449. (Illus.). 176p. 1988. 22.50 (ISBN 0-8108-2101-X). Scarecrow.
Trash to Treasure. (Americana Books Ser.). (Illus.). 1979. 3.00 (ISBN 0-911410-48-1). Applied Arts.
Trash to Treasures: An Idea Book for Classroom & Media Center Materials. Ann Christensen & Lee Green. 178p. 1982. pap. text ed. 18.50 (ISBN 0-87287-338-2). Libs Unl.
Trash Trio: Three Screenplays by John Waters; Pink Flamingos, Desperate Living, Flamingos Forever. John Waters. (Orig.). 1988. 10.95 (ISBN 0-394-75986-9, Vin). Random.
Trash: True Revelations & Strange Happenings, Vol. 1. Ed. by John Dagion. (Illus.). 192p. (Orig.). 1985. pap. 10.95 (ISBN 0-917342-07-0). Gay Sunshine.
Trashing of America. Charles Pirmell. 1975. 7.00 (ISBN 0-686-11117-6); pap. 3.50 (ISBN 0-686-11118-4). Kulchur Foun.
Trask. Don Berry. LC 60-5835. 376p. 1976. pap. 3.95 (ISBN 0-89174-001-5). Comstock Edns.
Tratado De Instrumentos Negociables. 2nd, enl.,rev. ed. Basilio Santiago Romero. LC 79-22321. (Illus.). 1980. 42.00 (ISBN 0-8477-2636-3). U of PR Pr.
Tratado de Tordesillas ("Treaty of Tordesillas") Ed. by Francisco M. Padron & Juan P. De Tudela. (Christopher Columbus Collection). 16p. (Span.). 1985. lib. bdg. 300.00x (ISBN 0-8115-3740-4, Pub. by Coleccion Tabula Americae). Kraus Repr.
Tratado Interamericano De Asistencia Reciproca. Incl. Vol. 1. Aplicaciones, 1948-1959. 5.00 (ISBN 0-8270-0670-5); Vol. 2. Aplicaciones, 1960-1972. 5.00 (ISBN 0-8270-0675-6); Vol. 3. Aplicaciones, 1973-1976. (Eng. & Span.). 2.00. (Serie De Tratados Multilaterales, Convenciones y Acuerdos). (Span.). OAS.
Tratado Sobre el Titulo de Duque. Juan De Mena. Ed. by Louise V. Fainberg. (Serie B: Textos, XVI). 134p. (Span.). 1976. 22.00 (ISBN 0-7293-0009-9, Pub. by Tamesis Bks Ltd). Longwood Pub Group.
Tratado Sobre la Predicacion. J. A. Broadus. Tr. by Ernesto Barocio. Orig. Title: On the Preparation & Delivery of Sermons. 336p. 1985. pap. 6.25 (ISBN 0-311-42034-6). Casa Bautista.
Tratados E Convencoes Firmados Na Sexta Conferencia Internacional Americana. (Treaty Ser.: No. 35). (Port.). 1928. pap. 1.00 (ISBN 0-8270-0450-8). OAS.
Tratados Sobre el Canal De Panama Suscritos Entre la Republica De Panama y los Estados Unidos De America. OAS General Secretariat Bureau of Legal Affairs. (Serie Sobre Tratados: No. 57 & 57a). 157p. 1979. text ed. 9.00. OAS.
Tratados y Convenciones Interamerianos. OAS General Secretariat. (Serie Sobre Tratados: No. 9). 303p. 1980. 15.00. OAS.
Trattato...di Canto Figurato. Pietro Aaron. (Monuments of Music & Music Literature, Ser. II: Vol. 129). 1979. Repr. of 1525 ed. 30.00x (ISBN 0-8450-2329-2). Broude.
Trattato...Sopra Gli Errori Degli Architetti... Teofilo Gallaccini. 94p. 1767. Repr. text ed. 41.40x (ISBN 0-576-15403-2, Pub. by Gregg Intl Pubs England). Gregg Intl.
Traum Ein Leben. F. Grillparzer. Ed. by W. E. Yates. 1968. text ed. 9.95x (ISBN 0-521-05154-1). Cambridge U Pr.
Traum und Wirklichkeit in der Romantik und Bei Heine. Ilse Weidekampf. 18.00 (ISBN 0-384-66456-3); pap. 13.00 (ISBN 0-384-66455-5). Johnson Repr.
Trauma. Robert Craig. 224p. 1984. pap. 2.95 (ISBN 0-451-12758-7, Sig). Nal.
Trauma. J. C. Dosch. (Radiology of the Spine Ser.). (Illus.). xiii, 94p. 1985. 69.00 (ISBN 0-387-13767-X). Springer-Verlag.
Trauma. Ed. by Bernard D. Fine & Herbert F. Waldhorn. Bd. with Symbolism. LC 73-6942. (Kris Study Group Monograph: No.5). 102p. 1973. text ed. 17.50 (ISBN 0-8236-6643-3). Intl Univs Pr.
Trauma. John J. Fried & John G. West. 336p. 1987. pap. 3.95 (ISBN 0-7701-0453-3). Paperjacks US.
Trauma. Ed. by Maurice King. (Primary Surgery Ser.: No. 2). (Illus.). 400p. 1987. pap. 18.95 (ISBN 0-19-261599-8). Oxford U Pr.
Trauma. Ed. by Kenneth L. Mattox et al. 944p. 1987. 125.00 (ISBN 0-8385-9004-7). Appleton & Lange.
Trauma. P. J. Shaughnessy. 320p. 1988. pap. 3.95 (ISBN 1-55785-006-2). Bart Books.
Trauma & Its Metabolic Problems. Ed. by R. N. Barton. (British Medical Bulletin Ser.: Vol. 41, No. 3). (Illus.). 104p. 1985. pap. text ed. 51.00 (ISBN 0-443-03250-5). Churchill.
Trauma & Its Wake: The Study & Treatment of Post-Traumatic Stress Disorder, Vol. 1. Ed. by Charles R. Figley. LC 84-29344. (Psychosocial Stress Ser.: No. 4). 475p. 1985. 40.00 (ISBN 0-87630-385-8). Brunner-Mazel.
Trauma & Its Wake, Vol. 2: Traumatic Stress Theory, Research, & Intervention. Ed. by Charles R. Figley. LC 84-29344. (Psychosocial Stress Ser.: No. 8). 368p. 1986. 40.00 (ISBN 0-87630-431-5). Brunner-Mazel.
Trauma & Mastery in Life & Art. Gilbert Rose. LC 86-28089. 224p. 1987. 27.50 (ISBN 0-300-03842-9). Yale U Pr.
Trauma & Pregnancy. C. E. Haycock. (Illus.). 224p. 1985. 27.00 (ISBN 0-88416-467-5). PSG Pub Co.
Trauma & Regeneration. H. Adams. (Acta Neurochirurgica: Supplement 32). (Illus.). 150p. 1983. pap. 37.00 (ISBN 0-387-81775-1). Springer-Verlag.
Trauma & the Anaesthetist. J. C. Stoddart. (Illus.). 210p. 1984. 17.95 (ISBN 0-7216-0969-4, Bailliere-Tindall). Saunders.
Trauma Care. R. Adams Cowley. LC 65-7412. 1987. Set. text ed. 49.95 (ISBN 0-397-50578-7, Lippincott Medical); Vol. I, surgical management. text ed. 29.00; Vol. II, medical management. text ed. 29.00. Lippincott.
Trauma Care. Ed. by William Odling-Smee & Alan Crockard. 657p. 1981. 74.50 (ISBN 0-8089-1271-2, 793186). Grune.
Trauma Care: Medical Management, Vol. II. Cowley et al. LC 65-7404. 1987. text ed. 29.00 (ISBN 0-397-50577-9, Lippincott Medical). Lippincott.
Trauma Care: Surgical Management, Vol. I. Cowley et al. LC 65-7396. 1987. text ed. 29.00 (ISBN 0-397-50576-0, Lippincott Medical). Lippincott.
Trauma Care Systems: Clinical, Financial, & Political Considerations. Ed. by John G. West et al. 208p. 1983. 35.00 (ISBN 0-275-91418-6, C1418). Praeger.
Trauma Centers & Emergency Departments. 35.00 (ISBN 0-317-29654-X, #CO3700, Law & Business). HarBraceJ.
Trauma: Emergency Surgery & Critical Care, 2 vols. Ed. by John H. Siegel. (Illus.). 1206p. 1986. text ed. 150.00 (ISBN 0-443-08330-4). Churchill.
Trauma, Growth, & Personality. Phyllis Greenacre. LC 71-75188. 1969. Repr. of 1952 ed. text ed. 37.50x (ISBN 0-8236-6645-X). Intl Univs Pr.
Trauma in Children. Randall Marcus. 288p. 1986. 65.00 (ISBN 0-87189-369-X). Aspen Pub.
Trauma in the Lives of Children: Crisis & Stress Management Techniques for Teachers, Counselors, & Student Service Professionals. Kendall Johnson. 256p. 1988. 19.95 (ISBN 0-89793-055-X); pap. 12.95 (ISBN 0-89793-056-8). Hunter Hse.
Trauma Management. 2nd ed. Burke. 1988. 90.00 (ISBN 0-8151-1455-9). Year Bk Med.
Trauma Management. David J. Kreis & Geraldo Gomez. 600p. 1988. text ed. write for info. (ISBN 0-316-50371-1). Little.
Trauma Management for Civilian & Military Physicians. Stanley L. Wiener & John Barrett. (Illus.). 582p. 1986. 68.00 (ISBN 0-7216-1806-5). Saunders.
Trauma Management in the Dog & Cat. John E. Houlton & Polly Taylor. (Illus.). 172p. 1987. pap. 16.00 (ISBN 0-7236-0696-X). PSG Pub Co.
Trauma Nurse. Patricia Rae. (Orig.). 1982. pap. 2.95 (ISBN 0-8217-1036-2). Zebra.
Trauma Nursing. Ed. by Virginia D. Cardona. 275p. 1984. pap. 24.50 (ISBN 0-87489-341-0). Med Economics.
Trauma Nursing. Eleanor Howell et al. 1988. text ed. write for info. (ISBN 0-673-39728-9). Scott F.
Trauma Nursing: Principles & Practice. Barbara A. Knezevich. 640p. 1986. 39.95 (ISBN 0-8385-9006-3). Appleton & Lange.
Trauma Nursing: Resuscitation Through Rehabilitation. Cardona et al. 944p. 1988. write for info. Saunders.
Trauma of Decolonization: The Dutch & West New Guinea. Arend Lijphart. LC 66-12506. (Yale Studies in Political Science Ser.). pap. 79.00 (ISBN 0-317-11338-0, 2022014). Bks Demand UMI.
Trauma of the Central Nervous System. Ed. by Ralph G. Dacey, Jr. et al. (Seminars in Neurological Surgery Ser.). (Illus.). 360p. 1985. text ed. 87.00 (ISBN 0-88167-111-8). Raven.
Trauma of the Middle Ear. Michael Strohm. (Advances in Oto-Rhino-Laryngology Ser.: Vol. 35). (Illus.). x, 254p. 1986. 116.00 (ISBN 3-8055-4087-6). S Karger.
Trauma of Time: A Psychoanalytic Investigation. Irvine Schiffer. LC 77-92182. 279p. 1978. text ed. 32.50x (ISBN 0-8236-6646-8). Intl Univs Pr.
Trauma of Transparency: A Biblical Approach to Inter-Personal Communication. J. Grant Howard. LC 79-87716. (Critical Concern Bks). 1979. pap. 7.95 (ISBN 0-930014-73-1). Multnomah.
Trauma of War: Stress & Recovery in Viet Nam Veterans. Ed. by Stephen M. Sonnenberg et al. John A. Talbott. LC 85-6094. 464p. 1985. text ed. 28.95x (ISBN 0-88048-048-3, 48-048-3). Am Psychiatric.
Trauma Reference Manual. Ed. by Virginia Cardona. 416p. 1984. pap. text ed. 24.95 (ISBN 0-89303-900-4). Appleton & Lange.
Trauma, Sepsis, & Shock: The Physiological Basis of Therapy. Clowes. (Science & Practice of Surgery Ser.). 608p. 1988. 125.00 (ISBN 0-8247-7502-3). Dekker.
Trauma Surgery. Joseph A. Moylan. LC 65-8873. (Illus.). 579p. 1987. 79.50 (ISBN 0-397-50723-2, Lippincott Medical). Lippincott.
Trauma: The First Hour. Ed. by William G. Baxt. 336p. 1984. 45.00 (ISBN 0-8385-9005-5). Appleton & Lange.
Trauma, Trance & Transformation: A Clinical Guide to Hypnotherapy. M. Gerald Edelstien. LC 81-10175. 176p. 1981. 25.00 (ISBN 0-87630-278-9). Brunner-Mazel.
Traumatic Abuse & Neglect of Children. Gertrude Williams & John Money. LC 79-3684. 1980. pap. 16.95x (ISBN 0-8018-2926-7). Johns Hopkins.
Traumatic Aphasia: Its Syndromes, Psychology & Treatment. A. R. Luria. Tr. by Douglas Bowden. LC 68-17903. (Janua Linguarum, Ser. Major: No. 5). 1970. text ed. 69.50x (ISBN 0-686-22421-3). Mouton.
Traumatic Brain Edema. Ed. by F. Cohadon et al. (FIDIA Research Ser.). 195p. 1987. 35.00 (ISBN 0-387-96507-6). Springer-Verlag.
Traumatic Brain Injury: Pathophysiology & Neuropsychological Evaluation, Vol. 1. Ralph M. Reitan & Deborah Wolfson. LC 86-60951. (Illus.). 425p. 1986. text ed. 59.95 (ISBN 0-934515-06-9). Neuropsych Pr.
Traumatic Brain Injury: Recovery & Rehabilitation, Vol. 2. Ralph M. Reitan & Deborah Wolfson. LC 86-60952. (Illus.). 400p. 1987. text ed. 59.95 (ISBN 0-934515-07-7). Neuropsych Pr.
Traumatic Dislocation of the Hip. Herman Epstein. LC 79-9482. 336p. (Orig.). 1980. 43.00 (ISBN 0-683-02906-1, WW). Krieger.
Traumatic Disorders of the Ankle. Ed. by W. C. Hamilton. (Illus.). 300p. 1984. 82.00 (ISBN 0-387-90831-5). Springer-Verlag.
Traumatic Hip Dislocation in Childhood. A. Barquet. (Illus.). 160p. 1987. 71.00 (ISBN 0-387-17009-X). Springer-Verlag.
Traumatic Injuries of the Teeth. 2nd ed. J. O. Andreasen. (Illus.). 462p. 1981. 95.00 (ISBN 0-7216-1249-0). Saunders.
Traumatology see Reconstruction Surgery & Traumatology.
Traumatology & Orthopaedics in the U. S. S. R. Advances in Science & Technology in the U. S. S. R. M. V. Volkov & N. A. Lyuboshitz. 216p. 1983. pap. 30.00x (Pub. by Collets (UK)). State Mutual Bk.
Traumatology of the Skull Base: Anatomy, Clinical & Radiological Diagnosis, Operative Treatment. Ed. by M. Samii & J. Brihaye. (Illus.). 260p. 1983. 49.00 (ISBN 0-387-12528-0). Springer-Verlag.
Travail. Emile Zola. 666p. 1957. 7.95 (ISBN 0-686-55806-5). French & Eur.
Travail see Quatre Evangiles.
Travail & Triumph: Black Life & Culture in the South Since the Civil War. Arnold H. Taylor. LC 76-5264. (Contributions in Afro-American & African Studies: No. 26). (Orig.). 1976. lib. bdg. 35.00 (ISBN 0-8371-8912-8, TTT/). Greenwood.
Travail & Triumph: Black Life & Culture in the South Since the Civil War. Arnold H. Taylor. LC 76-5264. (Contributions in Afro-American & African Studies: No. 26). 1977. pap. text ed. 9.95 (ISBN 0-313-20162-5, TTTPB). Greenwood.
Travail de la Femme dans la Grece Ancienne. Pieter Herfst. Ed. by Moses Finley. LC 79-4982. (Ancient Economic History Ser.). (Fr.). 1980. Repr. of 1922 ed. lib. bdg. 12.00x (ISBN 0-405-12368-X). Ayer Co Pubs.
Travail et l'Usure dans l'Antiquite. Charles Lelievre. LC 72-179395. (Research & Source Works Ser.: No. 894). 36p. (Fr.). 1972. Repr. of 1866 ed. 16.00 (ISBN 0-8337-2065-1). B Franklin.
Travail et Regimes Fonciers au Niger see Cahiers de l'Institut de Science Economique Appliquee.
Travail of Nature: The Ambiguous Ecological Promise of Christian Theology. H. Paul Santmire. LC 84-47934. 288p. 1985. 16.95 (ISBN 0-8006-1806-8, 1-1806). Fortress.
Travail, Salaire, Production: Le Controle des Cadences, Tome I. Alfred Willener et al. (Societe, Mouvements Sociaux et Ideologies: Etudes 12). (Illus.). 1972. pap. 14.00x (ISBN 90-2797-054-8). Mouton.
Travail, Salaire, Production: Pouvoir et Remuneration, Tome II. Alfred Willener et al. (Societe, Mouvements Sociaux et Ideologies: Etudes 13). (Illus.). 1972. pap. 12.80x (ISBN 90-2797-064-5). Mouton.
Travailes of an Englishman. Job Hortop. LC 79-38203. (English Experience Ser.: No. 469). 32p. 1972. Repr. of 1591 ed. 20.00 (ISBN 90-221-0469-9). Walter J Johnson.
Travailleurs de la Mer. Victor Hugo. (Illus.). 60p. 1966. 18.95 (ISBN 0-686-54046-8). French & Eur.
Travailleurs Estrangers en Europe Occidentale: Actes Du Colloque Organise Par la Commission Nationale Pour les Etudes et les Recherches Inter-Ethniques, Paris-Sorbonne, Du 5 Au 7 Juin 1974. Philippe J. Bernard. (Publications de l'Institut d'Etudes et de Recherches Interethniques et Inter Culturelles: No. 6). (Fr.). 1976. pap. text ed. 26.80x (ISBN 0-686-22611-9). Mouton.
Travaux d'Approche. Michel Butor. (Coll. Poesie). 9.95 (ISBN 0-685-37261-8). French & Eur.
Travaux Geophysiques. Ed. by Collet's Holdings, Ltd. Staff. 404p. 1984. 224.00x (ISBN 0-317-46752-2, Pub. by Collets (UK)). State Mutual Bk.
Travaux preparatoires-Deliberations. Institut en seance plenieres, Session d'Oslo, 1977. Ed. by Instiut de Droit International Staff. (Institut de Droit International. Annuaire: Vol. 57, Tome II). (Illus.). 1978. 236.75 (ISBN 3-8055-2880-9). S Karger.
Travaux Publics des Etats-Unis Amerique en 1870: Souvenirs d'une Mission. J. Malezieux & E. Malezieux. (Industrial Antiquities Ser.). (Illus.). 256p. (Fr.). 1987. Repr. of 1874 ed. 65.00 (ISBN 1-85297-014-6). Archival Facsimiles.
Travel Accounts of Indiana, 1679-1961: A Collection of Observations by Wayfaring Foreigners, Itinerants & Peripatetic Hoosiers. Shirley S. McCord. (Illus.). 340p. 1970. 10.00x (ISBN 0-253-36040-4). Ind U Pr.
Travel Agency Bookkeeping Made Simple. Douglas Thompson & Mary Miller-Marshall. 200p. 1986. 45.00 (ISBN 0-936831-04-9). Dendrobium Bks.
Travel Agency Management. George C. Brownell. LC 75-15476. 1975. pap. 12.50x (ISBN 0-87651-206-6). Southern U Pr.
Travel Agency of San Diego. Margaret Ames. 1986. write for info. simulation (ISBN 0-538-25730-X, Y73). SW Pub.
Travel Agency Personnel Manual. Laurence Stevens. LC 78-60277. (Travel Management Library). 90p. 1979. 21.95 (ISBN 0-916032-04-3). Delmar.
Travel Agent: Dealer in Dreams. 2nd ed. Aryear Gregory. (Illus.). 270p. 1985. pap. 19.95x (ISBN 0-8403-3539-3). Natl Pub Black Hills.
Travel Agent Training Workbook, 6 pts. Claudine Dervaes. (Illus.). 750p. 1985. Set. 65.00. Solitaire Pub.
Travel Agent Training Workbook, 1987-88, 6 sections. Claudine Dervaes. Incl. Section 1. Geography. 3-ring binder 30.00 (ISBN 0-933143-00-1); ans. key 10.00; Section 2. Domestic Airlines. 30.00 (ISBN 0-933143-02-8); ans. key 10.00; Section 3. Supplemental Sales. 30.00 (ISBN 0-933143-03-6); ans. key 10.00 (ISBN 0-933143-09-5); Section 4. International Travel. 30.00 (ISBN 0-933143-04-4); ans. key 10.00 (ISBN 0-933143-10-9); Section 5. Cruises. 30.00 (ISBN 0-933143-05-2); ans. key 10.00 (ISBN 0-933143-11-7); Section 6. Review, Sales, Computers. 30.00 (ISBN 0-933143-06-0); ans. key 10.00 (ISBN 0-933143-12-5). 950p. 1987. Set. 150.00 (ISBN 0-933143-01-X). Solitaire Pub.
Travel Air: Wings Over the Prairie. Ed. by Edward H. Phillips. LC 82-82791. (Illus.). 128p. 1982. 21.95 (ISBN 0-911139-00-1). Flying Bks.
Travel & Adventure in South-East Africa: Being the Narrative of the Last Eleven Years Spent by This Author on the Zambesi & Its Tributaries. Fredrick C. Selous. LC 72-5527. (Black Heritage Library Collection Ser). 1972. Repr. of 1893 ed. 44.75 (ISBN 0-8369-9148-6). Ayer Co Pubs.
Travel & Adventure in Southeast Africa. Frederick Selous. (Century Classic Ser.). 503p. 1988. pap. 13.95 (ISBN 0-7126-0445-6, Pub. by Century Hutchinson). David & Charles.
Travel & Communications. (Children's Encyclopedia Ser.). (Illus.). 96p. (gr. 3-8). 1987. PLB 240.00 set (ISBN 0-317-62835-6); pap. 13.27 (ISBN 0-317-62836-4). Raintree Pubs.
Travel & Description, 1765-1865. Solon J. Buck. LC 71-147150. (Research & Source Works Ser.: No. 827). 1971. Repr. of 1914 ed. lib. bdg. 29.50 (ISBN 0-8337-0411-7). B Franklin.
Travel & Entertainment: Business or Pleasure? 56p. 1985. pap. 2.50 (ISBN 0-317-04237-8, 5471). Commerce.
Travel & Entertainment: Business or Pleasure? 56p. (Orig.). 1987. pap. 3.50 (5261). Commerce.
Travel & Entertainment Deduction Guide: With Answers to Vital Questions on How to Nail Down Big Cash Savings under the All-New T&E Setup. Executive Reports Corporation Staff. LC 85-1619. 1985. 35.00 (ISBN 0-13-930090-2). Exec Reports.
Travel & Lodging Law. John R. Goodwin & James M. Rovelstad. LC 79-12189. (Law Ser.). 456p. 1980. text ed. 30.95 (ISBN 0-88244-188-4, Pub. by Grid). Wiley.
Travel & Roads in England. Virginia A. LaMar. LC 61-1916. (Folger Guides to the Age of Shakespeare). 1961. 3.95 (ISBN 0-918016-23-1). Folger Bks.
Travel & Sports Guide. John C. Dean. Ed. by Jane C. Edmunds. (Illus.). 512p. (Orig.). 1988. pap. 9.95 (ISBN 0-942427-02-5). Travel & Sports SF.
Travel & Tourism: An Introduction to Travel Agency Operations. Armin D. Lehmann. LC 77-12589. 1978. pap. 26.56 scp (ISBN 0-672-97090-2). Bobbs.
Travel & Tourism Audiovisual Guide. 2nd ed. Ed. by Jeanne Gay. 1982. pap. write for info. (ISBN 0-935638-05-9). Travel & Tourism.
Travel & Tourism Bibliography & Resource Guide, 6 vols. 2nd ed. Ed. by Jeanne Gay. (Orig.). 1982. pap. write for info. (ISBN 0-935638-04-0). Travel & Tourism.
Travel & Tourism Industry: Strategies for the Future. Ed. by A. Hodgson. LC 86-25296. (Illus.). 168p. 1987. text ed. 36.00 (ISBN 0-08-033892-5, PBL); pap. text ed. 17.75 (ISBN 0-08-033893-3, PBL). Pergamon.
Travel & Tourism Law Bibliography, Vol. 1, No. 1. Ed. by Jeanne Gay. (Tourism Information System Bibliographies Ser.). 125p. 1988. pap. text ed. 20.00x (ISBN 0-935638-18-0). Travel & Tourism.
Travel & Tourism Law Bibliography, Vol. 1, No. 2. (Tourism Information System Bibliographies Ser.). 140p. (Orig.). 1988. pap. 20.00x (ISBN 0-935638-19-9). Travel & Tourism.
Travel & Tourism Marketing Techniques. 280p. 1988. 21.95 (ISBN 0-8273-3301-3). Delmar.
Travel & Tourism Personnel Directory. 2nd ed. Ed. by Jeanne Gay. (Orig.). 1982. pap. cancelled (ISBN 0-935638-06-7). Travel & Tourism.

Traveler's French. Institute for Language Study Staff. (Language Ser.). (Fr.). 1980. pap. 17.95 (ISBN 0-06-463610-0, EH 610, B&N Bks). Har-Row.

Travelers from an Antique Land: A Series of 6 Paperbound Chapbooks. R. Martin Helick. 504p. (Gaelic.). 1987. pap. 2.00 ea. (ISBN 0-912710-15-2). Regent Graphic Serv.

Traveler's German. Institute for Language Study Staff. (Language Ser.). (Gr.). 1980. pap. 17.95 (ISBN 0-06-463611-9, EH 611, B&N Bks). Har-Row.

Traveler's Guide to American Gardens. rev. ed. Ed. by Mary H. Ray & Robert P. Nicholls. (Illus.). xv, 375p. 1988. 22.50 (ISBN 0-8078-1787-2); pap. 9.95 (ISBN 0-8078-4214-1). U of NC Pr.

Travelers' Guide to Asian Customs & Manners. Kevin Chambers. 370p. 1988. pap. 7.95 (ISBN 0-671-65888-3). Meadowbrook.

Traveler's Guide to Chinese History. Madge Huntington. LC 86-4767. (Illus.). 224p. 1987. pap. 11.95 (ISBN 0-8050-0097-6). H Holt & Co.

Traveler's Guide to El Dorado & the Inca Empire. rev. ed. Lynn Meisch. (Penguin Handbooks Ser.). 464p. 1984. pap. 14.95 (ISBN 0-14-046639-8). Penguin.

Travelers' Guide to European Customs & Manners. Nancy Braganti & Elizabeth Devine. Ed. by Louise Delagran. LC 83-23700. (Illus.). 273p. (Orig.). 1984. pap. 6.95 (ISBN 0-671-54493-4). Meadowbrook.

Traveler's Guide to Herb Gardens. 1986. 3.75 ea. Herb Society.

Traveler's Guide to Jewish Landmarks in Europe. Bernard Postal & Samuel H. Abramson. LC 79-154636. (Illus.). 1971. pap. 14.95 (ISBN 0-8303-0163-1). Fleet.

Travelers' Guide to Latin American Customs & Manners. Nancy L. Braganti & Elizabeth Devine. (Illus.). 240p. 1988. pap. 10.95 (ISBN 0-312-02303-0). St Martin.

Traveler's Guide to Montana. Gary Turbak. LC 83-808928. (Illus.). 256p. (Orig.). 1983. pap. 7.95 (ISBN 0-934318-14-X). Falcon Pr MT.

Traveler's Guide to Ocean Going Ferries: Southern Seas, Vol. 1. Michael Murphy & Laura Murphy. 156p. (Orig.). 1986. pap. 14.95 (ISBN 0-317-40505-5). Hippocrene Bks.

Traveler's Guide to Ocean Going Ferry Liners of Europe: Northern Seas, Vol. 2. Michael Murphy & Laura Murphy. 156p. 1986. pap. 14.95 (ISBN 0-87052-240-X). Hippocrene Bks.

Traveler's Guide to the Great Art Treasures of Europe. Davis L. Morton. 575p. 1987. lib. bdg. 45.00x (ISBN 0-8161-8733-9, Hall Reference); pap. 12.95x (ISBN 0-8161-8931-5). G K Hall.

Traveler's Guide to the History of Biology & Medicine. Eric T. Pengelley & Daphne Pengelley. 238p. 1986. pap. text ed. 12.50 (ISBN 0-9616695-0-0). Trevor Hill Pr.

Traveler's Guide to the Smoky Mountains Region. Jeff Bradley. LC 84-25119. (Illus.). 288p. (Orig.). 1985. 19.95 (ISBN 0-916782-63-8); pap. 10.95 (ISBN 0-916782-64-6). Harvard Common Pr.

Traveler's Handbook. Ed. by Melissa Shales. 820p. 1988. pap. 15.95 (ISBN 0-87106-654-8). Globe Pequot.

Travelers' Health Abroad: A Guide for Physicians. LC 82-130700. 44p. 8.00 (ISBN 0-89970-122-1, OP-098). AMA.

Travelers' Health Guide: How to Stay Fit Whenever & Wherever You Go in the U. S. & Around the World. Patrick J. Doyle & James E. Banta. LC 78-6773. (Illus.). 1978. 9.95 (ISBN 0-87491-192-3); pap. 4.95. Acropolis.

Travelers in Disguise: Narratives of Eastern Travel. rev. ed. Lincoln D. Hammond & Ludovico De Varthema. Ed. by Poggio Bracciolini. Tr. by John W. Jones. LC 63-2569. (Texts from the Romance Languages Ser). 1963. pap. 3.25x (ISBN 0-674-90645-4). Harvard U Pr.

Traveler's I.Q. Test: Rate Your Globetrotting Knowledge. George Blagowidow. 256p. 1987. pap. 6.95 (ISBN 0-87052-307-4). Hippocrene Bks.

Traveler's Italian. Institute for Language Study Staff. (Language Ser.). (Ital.). 1980. pap. 17.95 (ISBN 0-06-463612-7, EH 612, B&N Bks). Har-Row.

Traveler's Journal. Running Press Editors. (Illus.). 96p. 1986. text ed. 6.98 (ISBN 0-89471-432-5, Pub. by Courage Bks). Running Pr.

Traveler's Journal. LC 82-13338. 96p. pap. 5.95 (ISBN 0-89471-185-7); 15.90 (ISBN 0-89471-186-5). Running Pr.

Traveler's Joy. Juliette De Bairacli Levy. LC 78-61327. 1979. 8.95 (ISBN 0-87983-182-0); pap. 4.95 (ISBN 0-87983-183-9). Keats.

Traveler's Key to Ancient Egypt: A Guide to the Sacred Places of Ancient Egypt. John A. West. Ed. by Toinette Lippe. LC 84-48786. (Illus.). 512p. 1985. pap. 18.45 (ISBN 0-394-51441-6). Knopf.

Traveler's Key to Ancient Greece: A Guide to the Sacred Places of Ancient Greece. Richard G. Geldard. LC 88-45268. (Illus.). 416p. 1989. pap. 19.95 (ISBN 0-394-55631-3). Knopf.

Traveler's Key to Medieval France. John James. LC 86-45394. 336p. 1986. 18.45 (ISBN 0-394-55531-7). Knopf.

Traveler's Key to Northern India: A Guide to the Sacred Places of Northern India. Alistair Shearer. LC 83-47887. (Illus.). 1989. pap. 18.95 (ISBN 0-394-51652-4). Knopf.

Traveler's Key to Sacred England. John Michell. LC 87-46041. (Illus.). 1988. pap. 18.95 (ISBN 0-394-55573-2). Knopf.

Traveler's Map Guide. Date not set. cancelled. Barron.

Traveler's Medical Manual. Angelo Scotti. 256p. 1986. pap. 4.95 (ISBN 0-425-07758-6). Berkley Pub.

Traveler's Narrative: Written to Illustrate the Episode of the Bab. rev. ed. Abdu'l-Baha. Tr. by Edward G. Browne from Persian, Modern. LC 79-19025. 1980. 13.95 (ISBN 0-87743-134-5, 106-027); pap. 8.95 (ISBN 0-686-96668-6, 106-028). Baha'i.

Travelers on the Western Frontier. Ed. by John F. McDermott. LC 77-100375. (Illus.). Repr. of 1970 ed. 69.00 (ISBN 0-8357-9700-7, 2014920). Bks Demand UMI.

Traveler's Phrasebook. Constantine et al. 1985. 6.95 (ISBN 0-8120-3558-5). Barron.

Travelers' Picture Language. Norma W. Gann. (Illus.). 108p. 1984. pap. 3.95 (ISBN 0-317-02658-5). Lawton Pub Co.

Traveler's Reading Guide: Ready-Made Reading List for the Armchair Traveler. Ed. by Maggie Simony. 848p. 1988. pap. 18.95 (ISBN 0-8160-1932-0). Facts on File.

Traveler's Reading Guide: Ready Made Reading Lists for the Armchair Traveler. Maggy Simony. 848p. 40.00 (ISBN 0-8160-1244-X). Facts on File.

Traveler's Rest. William Wise. 1979. pap. 2.00 (ISBN 0-88680-194-X); royalty 35.25. I E Clark.

Traveler's Spanish. Institute for Language Study Staff. (Language Ser.). (Span.). 1980. pap. 17.95 (ISBN 0-06-463609-7, LEH 609, B&N Bks). Har-Row.

Traveler's Tree: New & Selected Poems. William J. Smith. (Illus.). 167p. 1981. pap. 6.95 (ISBN 0-89255-051-1). Persea Bks.

Traveler's Trivia Test: One Thousand & One Questions & Answers for the Sophisticated Globetrotter. George Blagowidow. 100p. (Orig.). 1985. pap. 3.95 (ISBN 0-87052-063-6). Hippocrene Bks.

Traveler's Workbook: Based on the People's Travel Book Index. Frieda Carrol. 50p. 1983. 3.95 (ISBN 0-939476-52-5, Pub. by Biblio Pr Ga). Prosperity & Profits.

Travelin' An Odyssey in Oz. Virginia G. Koste. 44p. (Orig.). 1984. pap. 2.50 (ISBN 0-88020-112-6). Coach Hse.

Travelin Man, No. 241. Charlotte Hughes. 192p. (Orig.). 1988. pap. 2.50 (ISBN 0-553-21871-9, Loveswept). Bantam.

Travelin' On: The Slave Journey to an Afro-Baptist Faith. Mechal Sobel. (Andrew E. Murray, Journal of American History). (Illus.). 352p. 1988. pap. text ed. 12.95 (ISBN 0-691-00603-2). Princeton U Pr.

Travelin' Woman. Katherine Gibbs. (Orig.). 1980. pap. 1.95 (ISBN 0-8439-0728-2, Leisure Bks). Leisure NY.

Traveling. Nancy King. (Orig.). 1982. pap. 2.00 (ISBN 0-936563-01-X). Signpost.

Traveling a Road of Success. Jean R. Nave. (Illus.). 30p. (Orig.). 1985. pap. 12.95 (ISBN 0-930115-05-8). Windemere Pr.

Traveling Around Mt. St. Helens. Dan Youra & Pat Thompson. (Illus.). 64p. (Orig.). 1981. pap. 2.50 (ISBN 0-940828-01-4). Olympic Pub.

Traveling Around Mt. St. Helens. 3rd ed. Dan Youra & Pat Thompson. (Illus.). 64p. 1981. pap. 3.50 (ISBN 0-940828-03-0). Olympic Pub.

Traveling Around Mt. St. Helens: 400 Mile Scenic Loop. 2nd ed. Dan Youra & Pat Thompson. (Illus.). 64p. 1981. pap. 3.50 (ISBN 0-940828-02-2). Olympic Pub.

Traveling at Home. Wendell Berry. Ed. by John Wheatcroft. (Bucknell University Fine Editions: A Series in Contemporary Poetry). (Illus.). 60p. 1988. ltd. ed. 125.00 (ISBN 0-916375-09-9). Press Alley.

Traveling Bird. Robert Burch. (gr. 1-4). 1959. 9.95 (ISBN 0-8392-3038-9). Astor-Honor.

Traveling by Bike. Bike World Editors. 96p. 1977. pap. 3.95 (ISBN 0-89037-065-6). Anderson World.

Traveling Exhibitions: An Overview of Not-for-Profit Traveling Exhibition Services. Victor J. Danilov. (Illus.). 48p. 1978. pap. 7.00 (ISBN 0-944040-09-8). AST Ctrs.

Traveling in Africa. Gwen Cottman. 36p. 1982. 3.00 (ISBN 0-912444-24-X). Gaus.

Traveling in Mark Twain. Richard Bridgman. (Quantum Books: No. 30). (Illus.). 176p. 1987. 25.00 (ISBN 0-520-05952-2). U of Cal Pr.

Traveling Jewish in America: For Business & Pleasure. rev. ed. Brynna C. Bloomfield et al. 472p. 1987. pap. 9.95 (ISBN 0-9617104-1-1). Wandering You Pr.

Traveling Jewish in America: The Complete Guide for 1986 for Business & Pleasure. Brynna C. Bloomfield & Jane M. Moskowitz. 407p. (Orig.). 1986. pap. 9.95 (ISBN 0-9617104-0-3). Wandering You Pr.

Traveling Light. Daniel F. Manning. (Illus., Orig.). 1979. pap. 5.00x (ISBN 0-933192-00-2). Dancin Bee.

Traveling Light. Eugene H. Peterson. 204p. 1988. pap. 7.95 (ISBN 0-939443-08-2). Helmers Howard Pub.

Traveling Light. Steve Toth. LC 76-29720. (Illus.). 1977. pap. 4.95 (ISBN 0-912652-19-5, Dynamite Books). Blue Wind.

Traveling Light: Every Woman's Guide to Getting There in Style. Leah Feldon. (Illus.). 160p. 1986. 13.95 (ISBN 0-399-13042-X). Putnam Pub Group.

Traveling Light: Monologues by Jim Stowall. Jim Stowell. Ed. by Emilie Buchwald. LC 88-42976. (Illus.). 112p. (Orig.). 1988. pap. 8.95 (ISBN 0-915943-31-X). Milkweed Ed.

Traveling...Like Everybody Else: A Practical Guide for Disabled Travelers. Jacqueline Freedman & Susan Gersten. 224p. 1987. pap. 11.95 (ISBN 0-915361-77-9, Dist. by Watts). Adama Pubs Inc.

Traveling Like Everybody Else: A Practical Guide for Disabled Travelers. Jacqueline Freedman & Susan Gersten. 224p. (gr. 12 up). 1987. pap. 11.95 (Dist. by Watts). Adama Pubs Inc.

Traveling Man: The Life Story of Henry Watkins Allen. Vincent Cassidy & Amos Simpson. 1967. 4.50 (ISBN 0-87511-017-7). Claitors.

Traveling Men of Ballycoo. Eve Bunting. LC 82-15799. (Illus.). 32p. (ps-3). 1983. 12.95 (ISBN 0-15-289792-5, HJ). HarBraceJ.

Traveling Mind. Walt Kaufmann. 66p. 1976. 6.95 (ISBN 0-87881-044-7). Mojave Bks.

Traveling on Credit. Daniel Halpern. LC 74-75745. pap. 2.25 (ISBN 0-670-00366-2). Small Pr Dist.

Traveling on Credit: Poems. Daniel Halpern. LC 72-75745. 80p. 1972. 9.95 (ISBN 0-670-72479-3). Viking.

Traveling Photographer. Ann Purcell & Carl Purcell. (Illus.). 144p. 1988. 27.50 (ISBN 0-8174-6200-7, Amphoto); pap. 18.95 (ISBN 0-8174-6201-5, Amphoto). Watson-Guptill.

Traveling Photographer's Guide to San Francisco: How to Find & Photograph the Classic San Francisco Scenes. Mary A. Schatz. LC 85-52229. (Illus.). 34p. (Orig.). 1986. pap. 4.95 (ISBN 0-9616197-0-8). Travel Photo.

Traveling Psychoanalyst. new ed. Lawrence J. Friedman. LC 72-180305. (Illus.). 1978. pap. 5.95 (ISBN 0-8397-8375-2). Eriksson.

Traveling Salesman: How to Find Answers for Lots of Things for Lots of People Especially Salesman. Larry Moriarty. LC 81-50012. (Illus.). 170p. 1981. 14.95x (ISBN 0-939102-13-7). MLM Pubs.

Traveling Salesman Problem: A Guided Tour of Combinatorial Optimization. E. L. Lawler et al. LC 85-3158. (Discrete Mathematics Ser.). 1985. 64.95 (ISBN 0-471-90413-9). Wiley.

Traveling Shoes. Noel Streatfeild. 256p. (gr. 4-7). 1984. pap. 2.95 (ISBN 0-440-48732-3, YB). Dell.

Traveling Texas Borders. Ann Ruff & Michael Burke. LC 83-11972. (Illus.). 136p. (Orig.). 1983. pap. 9.95x (ISBN 0-88415-074-7, Lone Star Bks). Gulf Pub.

Traveling the Trans-Canada: From Newfoundland to British Columbia. William Howarth. Ed. by Donald J. Crump. (Special Publications Ser. 22: No. 3). (Illus.). 200p. 1987. 7.95 (ISBN 0-87044-626-6); lib. bdg. 9.50 (ISBN 0-87044-631-2). Natl Geog.

Traveling the Way. Drusilla McGowen. 1977. 6.35 (ISBN 0-686-20047-0). Rod & Staff.

Traveling Toward Sunrise. Charles E. Cowman. 1988. price not set (ISBN 0-310-35390-4). Zondervan.

Traveling Toward Sunrise see Streams in the Desert.

Traveling Well: The Comprehensive Health Guide for Every Traveler. W. Scott Harkonen. 304p. 1984. pap. 11.95 (ISBN 0-396-08394-3). Dodd.

Traveling West: Nineteenth Century Women on the Overland Routes. Martha M. Allen. LC 86-51207. (Southwestern Studies: No. 80). 96p. 1987. pap. 5.00 (ISBN 0-87404-161-9). Tex Western.

Traveling with Children in the U. S. A. A Guide to Pleasure, Adventure, Discovery. Leila Hadley. (Americans-Discover-America Ser.). 1977. 4.95 (ISBN 0-688-03132-3). Morrow.

Traveling with Coyotes. Jennifer Moyer. 34p. 1987. pap. 3.00 (ISBN 0-933180-92-6). Spoon Riv Poetry.

Traveling with Man's Best Friend: A Selective Guide to California's Bed & Breakfasts, Inns, Hotels, & Resorts That Welcome You & Your Dog. rev. ed. Dawn Habgood & Robert Habgood. Ed. by Ruth W. Somerville. (Traveling with Man's Best Friend Ser.). (Illus.). 225p. 1988. pap. 10.95 (ISBN 0-933603-17-7). Dawbert Pr.

Traveling with Man's Best Friend: A Selective Guide to New England's Bed & Breakfasts, Inns, Hotels, & Resorts That Welcome You & Your Dog. Dawn Habgood & Robert Habgood. Ed. by Ruth W. Somerville. (Traveling with Man's Best Friend Ser.). (Illus.). 280p. (Orig.). 1987. pap. 10.95 (ISBN 0-933603-20-7). Dawbert Pr.

Traveling with Sherlock Holmes & Dr. Watson. Herman A. Litzinger. 264p. 1988. 10.95 (ISBN 0-8059-3090-6). Dorrance.

Traveling with Your Baby. Vicki Lansky. 112p. (Orig.). 1985. pap. 2.95 (ISBN 0-553-34153-7). Bantam.

Traveling Woman. Roberta Allen. (Illus.). 128p. (Orig.). 1986. pap. 12.00 (ISBN 0-931428-14-9). Vehicle Edns.

Travelingue. Marcel Ayme. 1965. 12.95 (ISBN 0-685-23912-8). French & Eur.

Traveller. Richard Adams. LC 87-46187. 248p. 1988. 18.45 (ISBN 0-394-57055-3). Knopf.

Traveller & His Road. Gostan Zarian. Tr. by Ara Baliozian from Armenian. LC 80-22809. 160p. (Orig.). 1981. pap. 5.95 (ISBN 0-935102-04-3). Ashod Pr.

Traveller Child. Jose Patterson. (Way We Live Ser.). (Illus.). 32p. (gr. 1-3). 1986. 9.95 (ISBN 0-241-11573-6, Pub. by Hamish Hamilton England). David & Charles.

Traveller-Gypsies. Judith Okely. LC 82-9478. (Illus.). 228p. 1983. 39.50 (ISBN 0-521-24641-5); pap. 14.95 (ISBN 0-521-28870-3). Cambridge U Pr.

Traveller in China. Christina Dodwell. (Illus.). 160p. 1986. 15.95 (ISBN 0-8253-0371-0). Beaufort Bks NY.

Traveller in Little Things. William H. Hudson. Repr. of 1923 ed. 35.00 (ISBN 0-404-03412-8). AMS Pr.

Traveller in Romance: Uncollected Writings, 1901-1964. W. Somerset Maugham. Ed. by John Whitehead. 256p. 1985. 16.95 (ISBN 0-517-55618-9, C N Potter Bks). Crown.

Traveller in Southern Italy. H. V. Morton. (Illus.). 1987. pap. 14.95 (ISBN 0-396-08926-7). Dodd.

Traveller in Time. Alison Uttley. (Illus.). 331p. (gr. 3-7). 1981. 9.95 (ISBN 0-571-06182-6). Faber & Faber.

Traveller in Turkey. Daniel Fearson. 224p. 1987. pap. 12.95 (ISBN 0-7102-1213-5, Pub. by Routledge UK). Routledge Chapman & Hall.

Traveller of the East. Thomas Mofolo. Tr. by H. Ashton. 1934. 18.00 (ISBN 0-8115-3032-9). Kraus Repr.

Traveller: Stories of Two Continents. Victor Kelleher. 218p. 1988. pap. 8.95 (ISBN 0-7022-2103-1). U of Queensland Pr.

Traveller Tales of the Pan-American Countries. Hezekiah Butterworth. LC 71-130986. (Illus.). Repr. of 1902 ed. 19.00 (ISBN 0-404-01255-8). AMS Pr.

Traveller Through Time: A Photographic Journey with Freya Stark. Malise Ruthven. 144p. 1986. 19.95 (ISBN 0-670-80183-6). Viking.

Traveller to Turkey. Daniel Farson. 224p. 1985. 19.95 (ISBN 0-7102-0281-4). Routledge Chapman & Hall.

Traveller's Alphabet. Marty Cohen. Ed. by Vi Gale. LC 79-84509. (Prescott First Bk.). (Illus.). 1979. ltd. ed. 20.00 (ISBN 0-915986-15-9); pap. 5.00 (ISBN 0-915986-16-7). Prescott St Pr.

Traveller's Bed & Breakfast. rev. ed. Jean Knight. 80p. 1985. 4.95 (ISBN 0-9613481-0-0). Travellers Bed.

Traveller's Breviant, or an Historical Description of the Most Famous Kingdomes. Giovanni Botero. LC 72-175. (English Experience Ser.: No. 143). 180p. 1969. Repr. of 1601 ed. 35.00 (ISBN 90-221-0143-6). Walter J Johnson.

Travellers by Land & Sea. Mikhail Kuzmin. Tr. by John Barnstead from Rus. 140p. 1987. 17.95 (ISBN 0-88233-810-2); pap. 5.00 (ISBN 0-88233-811-0). Ardis Pubs.

Traveller's Dictionary of Quotations: Who Said What, about Where. Ed. by Peter Yapp. 1022p. 1985. pap. 19.95 (ISBN 0-7102-0672-0). Routledge Chapman & Hall.

Travellers Directory. (FGC). 112p. cancelled (ISBN 0-318-14159-0). Friends Genl Conf.

Travellers' Guide to Asian Customs & Manners. Elizabeth Devine & Nancy L. Braganti. (Illus.). 352p. 1986. pap. 9.95 (ISBN 0-312-81610-3). St Martin.

Traveller's Guide to Astral Plane. Steve Richards. pap. 7.99 (ISBN 0-85030-337-0, Pub. by Aquarian Pr England). Sterling.

Traveller's Guide to Celtic Britain. Anne Ross. (Traveller's Guides Ser.). (Illus.). 128p. 1985. 18.95 (ISBN 0-7102-0632-1). Routledge Chapman & Hall.

Traveller's Guide to Celtic Britain. Anne Ross & Michael Cyprien. (Traveller's Guide Ser.). (Illus.). 128p. 1985. 14.95 (ISBN 0-918678-06-4). Historical Times.

Traveller's Guide to Central & Southern Africa. 248p. 1985. 12.95 (ISBN 0-531-03851-3). Watts.

Traveller's Guide to Crete. Rev. ed. John Bowman. 320p. 1985. pap. 14.95 (ISBN 0-224-02285-7, Pub. by Jonathan Cape). Salem Hse Pubs.

Traveller's Guide to Early Medieval Britain. Anthony Goodman. Ed. by Michael Cyprien. (A Traveller's Guide Ser.). 1986. 14.95 (ISBN 0-918678-16-1). Historical Times.

Traveller's Guide to Health Protection Abroad. W. H. Jopling. 1986. 34.00x (ISBN 0-86332-035-X, Pub. by Book Guild Ltd). State Mutual Bk.

Traveller's Guide to Medieval Britain. Anthony Goodman. 128p. 1987. 22.50 (ISBN 0-7102-0942-8, Pub. by Routledge UK). Routledge Chapman & Hall.

Traveller's Guide to Norman Britain. Trevor Rowley & Michael Cyprien. (Traveller's Guide Ser.). (Illus.). 128p. 1986. 18.95 (ISBN 0-317-40583-7). Routledge Chapman & Hall.

Traveller's Guide to Places of Worship. Charles Kightly. 1986. 14.95 (ISBN 0-918678-18-8). Historical Times.

Traveller's Guide to Places of Worship. Charles Kightly. 128p. 1987. 22.50 (ISBN 0-7102-0941-X, Pub. by Routledge UK). Routledge Chapman & Hall.

Traveller's Guide to Pubs of the North Island. Ian Jenkins. 228p. 1984. pap. 9.95 (ISBN 0-86863-416-6, Pub. by Heinemann Pubs New Zealand). Intl Spec Bk.

Traveller's Guide to Roman Britain. Patrick Ottaway. 1986. 14.95 (ISBN 0-918678-19-6). Historical Times.

Traveller's Guide to Roman Britain. Patrick Ottaway & Michael Cyprien. 128p. 1987. 22.50 (ISBN 0-7102-0943-6, Pub. by Routledge UK). Routledge Chapman & Hall.

Traveller's Guide to Royal Roads. Charles Kightly. (Illus.). 128p. 1985. 14.95 (ISBN 0-918678-09-9). Historical Times.

Traveller's Guide to Spurgeon Country. Eric W. Hayden. 1974. pap. 1.95 (ISBN 0-686-10527-3). Pilgrim Pubns.

Traveller's Guide to the Astral Plane. Steve Richards. LC 86-18043. 110p. 1986. lib. bdg. 19.95x (ISBN 0-8095-7006-8). Borgo Pr.

Traveller's Guide to the Belgian Congo & Ruanda Urundi. 2nd ed. (Illus.). 1956. 12.50 (ISBN 0-685-02660-4). Univ Place.

Traveller's Guide to the Best Cathouses in Nevada. rev. ed. Jerry R. Schwartz. (Illus.). 172p. 1988. pap. 5.95. Straight Pubs.

Traveller's Guide to the Food of France. Glynn Christian. (Illus.). 192p. 1986. pap. 9.95 (ISBN 0-03-008529-2, Owl Bks). H Holt & Co.

Travellers Guide to the Food of Italy. Valentina Harris. LC 87-82904. (Owl Bks.). 1988. 11.95 (ISBN 0-8050-0631-1). H Holt & Co.

Traveller's Guide to the Royal Roads. Ed. by Charles Knightly. (Traveller's Guides Ser.). (Illus.). 128p. 1985. 18.95 (ISBN 0-7102-0689-5). Routledge Chapman & Hall.

Traveller's Guide to the Scotland of Robert the Bruce. Nigel Tranter. LC 85-21914. (Illus.). 127p. 1985. 14.95 (ISBN 0-918678-10-2). Historical Times.

Traveller's Guide to the Scotland of Robert the Bruce. Nigel Tranter & Michael Cyprien. (Traveller's Guide Ser.). (Illus.). 128p. 1986. 18.95 (ISBN 0-7102-0688-7). Routledge Chapman & Hall.

Traveller's Health Guide. 2nd rev. ed. A. C. Turner. 188p. 1986. 9.95 (ISBN 0-903909-51-0). Bradt Ent.

Traveller's History of Greece see Pelican History of Greece.

Travellers in a Bygone Shetland, 1550-1850. Derek Flinn. 1987. 20.00 (ISBN 0-7073-0524-1, Pub. by Scot Acad Pr). Longwood Pub Group.

Travellers in Eighteenth-Century England. Rosamond Bayne-Powell. LC 74-174875. (Illus.). Repr. of 1951 ed. 20.00 (ISBN 0-405-08245-2, Blom Pubns). Ayer Co Pubs.

Travellers' India: An Anthology. H. K. Kaul. 1979. 34.95x (ISBN 0-19-560654-X). Oxford U Pr.

Traveller's Quest: Original Contributions Towards a Philosophy of Travel. Maurice A. Michael. Ed. by M. A. Michael. LC 72-5673. (Essay Index Reprint Ser.). 1972. Repr. of 1950 ed. 22.00 (ISBN 0-8369-7297-X). Ayer Co Pubs.

Traveller's Rest. facs. ed. Philip Gosse. LC 70-84308. (Essay Index Reprint Ser.). 1937. 17.50 (ISBN 0-8369-1132-6). Ayer Co Pubs.

Travellers Rest. Peter Johnson. 1982. 15.00x (ISBN 0-903653-85-0, Pub. by New Playwrights Network). State Mutual Bk.

Travellers' Songs from England & Scotland. Ewan MacColl & Peggy Seeger. LC 76-2854. 1977. 34.95x (ISBN 0-87049-191-1). U of Tenn Pr.

Traveller's Tales. Enid M. Dinnis. LC 72-5908. (Short Story Index Reprint Ser.). Repr. of 1927 ed. 13.50 (ISBN 0-8369-4211-6). Ayer Co Pubs.

Travellers Tales. Anthony Jenkins. 128p. (Orig.). 1985. pap. 8.95 (ISBN 0-908086-84-9). Lonely Planet.

Travellers' Weather: Europe & North Africa. Bengt Ahlstrom & John Pohlman. 192p. 1986. pap. 19.00x (ISBN 0-7090-2167-4, Pub. by R Hale Ltd UK). State Mutual Bk.

Travellers's Guide to Norman Britain. Trevor Rowley. (Traveller's Guide Ser.). (Illus.). 128p. 1986. 14.95 (ISBN 0-918678-11-0). Historical Times.

Travelling Circus: Part One of Cesar Cascabel. Jules Verne. 4.95 (ISBN 0-87497-044-X). Assoc Bk.

Travelling Companions. facsimile ed. Henry James. LC 75-37552. (Short Story Index Reprint Ser.). Repr. of 1919 ed. 17.00 (ISBN 0-8369-4111-X). Ayer Co Pubs.

Travelling Games for Babies. Julie Hagstrom. Date not set. pap. 3.50 (ISBN 0-671-61920-9). PB.

Travelling in. Monica Furlong. LC 84-71182. 125p. 1984. pap. 6.00 (ISBN 0-936384-20-4). Cowley Pubns.

Travelling in Amherst: A Poet's Journal 1931-1954. Robert Francis. LC 85-62398. 120p. (Orig.). 1986. pap. 9.95 (ISBN 0-937672-19-X). Rowan Tree.

Travelling in the Family. Carlos Drummond. Ed. by Thomas Colchie. Tr. by Elizabeth Bishop et al. Date not set. pap. 19.45 (ISBN 0-394-52478-0). Random.

Travelling Jobs for Women: A Guide to Exciting Career Opportunities. rev. ed. Sylvia B. Coppersmith. LC 73-135315. 48p. 1976. pap. 2.00 (ISBN 0-87576-037-6). Pilot Bks.

Travelling Light. Bill Barich. (Penguin Nonfiction Ser.). 1985. pap. 6.95 (ISBN 0-14-007418-X). Penguin.

Travelling Light. William B. McClain. (Orig.). 1981. pap. 3.75 (ISBN 0-377-00109-0). Friendship Pr.

Travelling Light. Ken MCullough. 110p. (Orig.). 1987. pap. 8.95 (ISBN 0-938410-45-8). Thunder's Mouth.

Travelling Men. Eric Lane. (Dedalus Modern Fiction Ser.). 192p. (Orig.). 1986. pap. 4.95 (ISBN 0-946626-00-6, Pub. by Dedalus Bks England). Hippocrene Bks.

Travelling My Shadow. Sue B. Walker. LC 82-80016. (Illus.). 60p. 1982. pap. text ed. 5.00 (ISBN 0-942544-02-1). Negative Capability Pr.

Travelling Naturalists. Clare Lloyd. LC 85-11266. (Illus.). 160p. 1985. 25.00 (ISBN 0-295-96304-2). U of Wash Pr.

Travelling Sketches. Anthony Trollope. Ed. by N. John Hall. LC 80-1884. (Selected Works of Anthony Trollope Ser.). 1981. Repr. of 1866 ed. lib. bdg. 15.00 (ISBN 0-405-14147-5). Ayer Co Pubs.

Travelling the Miracle Road. Betty Palmer. Ed. by Nita Scoggan. LC 88-909635. (Illus.). 224p. (Orig.). Date not set. 10.00 (ISBN 0-910487-17-0); pap. 4.95 (ISBN 0-910487-16-2). Royalty Pub.

Travelling with a Sunbeam: A Novel. Kusum Ansal. (Vikas Library of Modern Indian Writing: No. 29). vi, 138p. 1983. text ed. 17.95x (ISBN 0-7069-2219-0, Pub. by Vikas India). Advent NY.

Travelling with Women. Harry Polkinhorn. 56p. 1983. pap. 5.00 (ISBN 0-317-63763-0). Atticus Pr.

Travelling Workshops Experiment in Library User Education. D. Clark et al. (R&D Report 5602). (Illus.). 259p. (Orig.). 1981. pap. 24.00 (ISBN 0-905984-63-3, Pub. by British Lib). Longwood Pub Group.

Travelog. Charles Harbutt. 1974. pap. 8.95 (ISBN 0-262-58026-8). MIT Pr.

Travelogues. Peter Frank. LC 82-80710. (Contemporary Literature Ser.: No. 12). 48p. (Orig.). 1982. pap. 4.00 (ISBN 0-940650-15-0). Sun & Moon CA.

Travels. Yehuda Amichai. Tr. by Ruth Nevo. LC 85-27814. 137p. (Orig., Eng. & Hebrew.). 1986. 13.95 (ISBN 0-935296-62-X, Dist. by Persea Bks.); pap. 9.95 (ISBN 0-935296-63-8). Sheep Meadow.

Travels. William Bartram. 1928. pap. 6.95 (ISBN 0-486-20013-2). Dover.

Travels. William Bartram. Ed. by Mark Van Doren. (Illus.). 15.50 (ISBN 0-8446-1600-1). Peter Smith.

Travels. William Bartram. 452p. 1988. pap. 7.95 (ISBN 0-14-017008-1). Penguin.

Travels. Michael Crichton. LC 87-46040. 1988. 17.95 (ISBN 0-394-56236-4). Knopf.

Travels. Marco Polo. Ed. by T. Wright. Tr. by Marsden. LC 68-57871. (Bohn's Antiquarian Library Ser). Repr. of 1854 ed. 41.50 (ISBN 0-404-50023-4). AMS Pr.

Travels Amongst the Great Andes of the Equator. Edward Whymper. (Illus.). 524p. 1987. Repr. of 1896 ed. 24.95 (ISBN 0-87905-281-3, Peregrine Smith). Gibbs Smith Pub.

Travels & Adventures in Canada & the Indian Territories Between 1760 & 1776. Alexander Henry. Ed. by James Bain. (Research & Source Works Ser.: No. 342). (American Classics in History & Social Science Ser., No. 74). 1969. Repr. of 1901 ed. 18.50 (ISBN 0-8337-1665-4). B Franklin.

Travels & Adventures; in Canada & the Indian Territories: Between the Years 1760 & 1776. Alexander Henry. Ed. & illus. by James Bain. LC 72-108491. (Illus.). 375p. 1972. Repr. of 1901 ed. 12.00 (ISBN 0-403-00393-8). Scholarly.

Travels & Adventures of Benjamin the Third. Mendele M. Seforim. LC 49-9256. 124p. 1985. pap. 5.50 (ISBN 0-8052-0176-9). Schocken.

Travels & Adventures of Edward Brown, Esq. John Campbell. LC 75-170599. (Foundations of the Novel Ser.: Vol. 70). 1973. lib. bdg. 61.00 (ISBN 0-8240-0582-1). Garland Pub.

Travels & Archaeology in South Chile. Junius B. Bird. LC 87-30245. (Illus.). 278p. 1988. text ed. 25.00x (ISBN 0-87745-202-4). U of Iowa Pr.

Travels & Life in Ashanti & Jaman. Richard A. Freedman. 559p. 1967. Repr. of 1898 ed. 42.50x (ISBN 0-7146-1808-X, BHA-01808, F Cass Co). Biblio Dist.

Travels & Politics in the Near East. William Miller. LC 70-135822. (Eastern Europe Collection Ser). 1970. Repr. of 1898 ed. 30.00 (ISBN 0-405-02764-8). Ayer Co Pubs.

Travels & Researches among the Lakes & Mountains of Eastern & Central Africa. new ed. J. F. Elton. Ed. by H. B. Cotterill. (Illus.). 417p. 1968. 45.00x (ISBN 0-7146-1806-3, F Cass Co). Biblio Dist.

Travels & Researches in Caffraria. Stephan Kay. 1834. 49.00x (ISBN 0-403-00374-1). Scholarly.

Travels & Researches in Chaldaea & Susiana; with an Account of Excavations in Warka, the 'Erech' of Nimrod, & Shush, 'Shushan the Palace' of Esther, in 1849-1852. William K. Loftus. 452p. Repr. of 1857 ed. text ed. 74.52x (ISBN 0-576-03106-2, Pub. by Gregg Intl Pubs England). Gregg Intl.

Travels & Researches in Crete, 2 vols. in 1. T. A. Spratt. (Illus.). 848p. 1984. Repr. of 1865 ed. lib. bdg. 137.50x (ISBN 90-256-0893-0, Pub. by AM Hakkert). Coronet Bks.

Travels & Traditions of Waterfowl. H. Albert Hochbaum. (Illus.). 1967. pap. 2.95 (ISBN 0-8166-0448-7, MP8). U of Minn Pr.

Travels & Works of Captain John Smith, President of Virginia & Admiral of New England, 2 Vols. rev. ed. John Smith. Ed. by Edward Arber & A. G. Bradley. (Illus.). 1965. 75.50 (ISBN 0-8337-0080-4). B Franklin.

Travels During the Years 1787, 1788 & 1789, 2 Vols. 2nd ed. Arthur Young. LC 79-115008. Repr. of 1794 ed. Set. 145.00 (ISBN 0-404-07068-X). AMS Pr.

Travels from St. Petersburgh in Russia. John Bell. 554p. 1788. leather, rubbed & spines cracked 1260.00x (Pub. by Han-Shan Tang Ltd). State Mutual Bk.

Travels in Alaska. John Muir. LC 77-19358. (Illus.). Repr. of 1915 ed. 19.50 (ISBN 0-404-16075-1). AMS Pr.

Travels in Alaska. John Muir. LC 77-19358. 1979. pap. 8.95 (ISBN 0-395-28522-4). HM.

Travels in Alaska. John Muir. LC 70-145196. 1915. Repr. 39.00x (ISBN 0-403-01120-5). Scholarly.

Travels in Alaska. John Muir. LC 87-26311. (John Muir Library). 352p. 1988. pap. 9.95 (ISBN 0-87156-783-0). Sierra.

Travels in Alaska. John Muir. 1988. Repr. of 1915 ed. lib. bdg. 49.00x. Am Biog Serv.

Travels in America: A Large Print Anthology. Roy Bongartz. (General Ser.). 475p. 1988. lib. bdg. 19.95 (Large Print Bks). G K Hall.

Travels in America Eighteen Fifty One to Eighteen Fifty Five. Rosalie Roos. Tr. by Carl L. Anderson. LC 81-187. 1982. 19.95 (ISBN 0-8093-1018-X). Swedish Am.

Travels in America: From the Voyages of Discovery to the Present: An Annotated Bibliography of Travel Articles in Periodicals, 1955-1980. Garold L. Cole. LC 84-40273. 344p. 1985. 48.50x (ISBN 0-8061-1791-5). U of Okla Pr.

Travels in America, 1816-1817. E. De Montule. Tr. by E. D. Seeber. Repr. of 1950 ed. 21.00 (ISBN 0-527-64550-8). Kraus Repr.

Travels in America, 1851-1855. Rosalie Roos. Ed. by Carl L. Anderson. LC 81-187. 170p. 1982. 19.95x. S Ill U Pr.

Travels in Arabia. John L. Burckhardt. 478p. 1968. Repr. of 1829 ed. 55.00x (ISBN 0-7146-1982-5, F Cass Co). Biblio Dist.

Travels in Arabia. John L. Burckhardt. (Arab Background Ser.). 25.00x (ISBN 0-86685-007-4). Intl Bk Ctr.

Travels in Arabia. B. Taylor. 336p. 1986. 200.00x (ISBN 1-85077-084-0, Pub. by Darf). State Mutual Bk.

Travels in Arabia Deserta. Charles M. Doughty. Ed. by Edward Garnett. (Illus.). 12.00 (ISBN 0-8446-1159-X). Peter Smith.

Travels in Arabia Deserta, 2 vols. Charles M. Doughty. Set. 36.00 (ISBN 0-8446-5750-6); Vol. I. (ISBN 0-8446-5751-4); Vol. II. (ISBN 0-8446-5752-2). Peter Smith.

Travels in Arabia Deserts, 2 vols. Charles M. Doughty. (Illus.). 1980. Vol. 1. pap. 14.95 (ISBN 0-486-23825-3); Vol. 2. pap. 14.95 (ISBN 0-486-23826-1). Dover.

Travels in Arabia, 1845-1848. Georg A. Wallin. (Arabia Past & Present Ser.: Vol. 8). (Illus.). 1979. 26.00 (ISBN 0-900891-53-X). Oleander Pr.

Travels in Asia & Africa, 1325-1354. Ibn Batuta. LC 73-93906. 1969. Repr. of 1929 ed. lib. bdg. 39.50x (ISBN 0-678-06523-3). Kelley.

Travels in Assyria, Media, & Persia, Including a Journey from Bagdad by Mont Zagros, to Hamadan, the Ancient Ecbatana, Researchers in Ispahan & the Ruins of Persepolis. James S. Buckingham. 562p. 1829. Repr. text ed. 74.52x (ISBN 0-576-03165-8, Pub. by Gregg Intl Pubs England). Gregg Intl.

Travels in Brazil. Henry Koster. Ed. by Harvey C. Gardiner. LC 65-16537. (Latin American Travel Ser.). 216p. 1966. 5.85x (ISBN 0-8093-0205-5). S Ill U Pr.

Travels in Central Asia. Arminius Vambery. LC 73-115592. (Russia Observed, Series I). 1970. Repr. of 1865 ed. 33.75 (ISBN 0-405-03073-8). Ayer Co Pubs.

Travels in Chili & La Plata, 2 Vols. John Miers. LC 76-128416. Repr. of 1826 ed. Set. 67.50 (ISBN 0-404-04317-8). AMS Pr.

Travels in Circassia, Krim Tartary. Edmund Spencer. 834p. Repr. of 1837 ed. text ed. 74.52x (ISBN 0-576-03319-7, Pub. by Gregg Intl Pubs England). Gregg Intl.

Travels in Eastern Africa, 2 vols. Lyons McLeod. 1971. Repr. of 1860 ed. 95.00x (ISBN 0-7146-1832-2, F Cass Co). Biblio Dist.

Travels in Egypt, Vols. 1 & 2. V. Denon. 1986. 180.00x ea. (Pub. by Darf Pubs Ltd). Vol. 1, 346p (ISBN 1-85077-098-0). Vol. 2, 332p (ISBN 1-85077-099-9). State Mutual Bk.

Travels in Egypt & Nubia, Syria & Asia Minor. C. Irby & J. Mangles. 614p. 1985. 350.00x (ISBN 1-85077-082-4, Pub. by Darf). State Mutual Bk.

Travels in Egypt, Arabia Petraea &the Holy Land, 2 vols. in one. Stephen Olin. Ed. by Moshe Davis. LC 77-70727. (America & the Holy Land Ser.). 1977. lib. bdg. 74.00x (ISBN 0-405-10273-9). Ayer Co Pubs.

Travels in England: A Ramble with the City & Town Missionaries. John Shaw. LC 84-48282. (Rise of Urban Britain Ser.). 393p. 1985. 50.00 (ISBN 0-8240-6284-1). Garland Pub.

Travels in France & Italy. Arthur Young. 1976. 14.95x (ISBN 0-460-00720-3, Evman). Biblio Dist.

Travels in France During the Years 1787, 1788, 1789. Arthur Young. Ed. by Jeffry Kaplow. 13.25 (ISBN 0-8446-3223-6). Peter Smith.

Travels in Greeneland: The Cinema of Graham Greene. Quentin Falk. (Illus.). 230p. 1985. 22.95 (ISBN 0-7043-2425-3, Pub. by Quartet Bks). Salem Hse Pubs.

Travels in Hawaii. Robert Louis Stevenson. Ed. & intro. by A. Grove Day. LC 72-91621. (Illus.). 250p. 1973. 10.50 (ISBN 0-8248-0257-8). UH Pr.

Travels in Holland, the United Provinces, England, Scotland & Ireland. William Brereton. Repr. of 1844 ed. 20.00 (ISBN 0-384-05670-9). Johnson Repr.

Travels in Hyperreality: Essays. Umberto Eco. Ed. by Helen Wolff & Kurt Wolff. Tr. by William Weaver from Ital. LC 85-24810. 236p. 1986. 15.95 (ISBN 0-15-191079-0). HarBraceJ.

Travels in India, 2 vols. 2nd ed. Jean-Baptiste Tavernier. Ed. by William Crooke. Tr. by V. Ball from Fr. Repr. of 1925 ed. Set. text ed. 67.50x. Coronet Bks.

Travels in India, Ceylon & Borneo. Basil Hall. Ed. by H. G. Rawlinson. LC 76-174846. Repr. of 1931 ed. 22.00 (ISBN 0-405-08593-1, Blom Pubns). Ayer Co Pubs.

Travels in India Including Sinde & the Punjab, 2 vols. Leopold Von Orlinch. 315p. 67.50 (ISBN 0-8364-1630-9, Pub. by Usha). South Asia Bks.

Travels in Jewry. cancelled (ISBN 0-686-76271-1). Feldheim.

Travels in Kamtchatka & Siberia: With a Narrative of a Residence in China. Peter Dobell. LC 78-115529. (Russia Observed Ser., No. 1). 1970. Repr. of 1830 ed. 33.00 (ISBN 0-405-03021-5). Ayer Co Pubs.

Travels in Kamtschatka, During the Years 1787 & 1788. Jean De Lesseps. LC 72-115557. (Russia Observed, Series I). 1970. Repr. of 1790 ed. 32.00 (ISBN 0-405-03043-6). Ayer Co Pubs.

Travels in Madeira, Sierra Leone, Teneriffe, St. Jago, Cape Coast, Fernando Po, Princes Island, Ect. Etc. 2nd ed. James Holman. LC 72-5529. (Black Heritage Library Collection Ser). 1972. Repr. of 1840 ed. 29.25 (ISBN 0-8369-9142-7). Ayer Co Pubs.

Travels in Mesopotamia, with Researches on the Ruins of Babylon. James S. Buckingham. 588p. Repr. of 1827 ed. text ed. 74.52x (ISBN 0-576-03342-1, Pub. by Gregg Intl Pubs England). Gregg Intl.

Travels in Mexico & California. A. B. Clarke. Ed. by Anne M. Perry. LC 88-1490. (Essays on the American West Ser.: No. 10). (Illus.). 1988. 17.50 (ISBN 0-89096-354-1). Tex A&M Univ Pr.

Travels in Mexico, South America, 2 vols. Godfrey T. Vigne. LC 70-177865. (Illus.). Repr. of 1863 ed. 49.50 (ISBN 0-404-06766-2). AMS Pr.

Travels in My Homeland: A Portuguese Classic. Almeida Garrett. Tr. & intro. by John M. Parker. LC 87-61378. (Unesco Collection of Representative Works - European Ser.). 256p. 1987. 22.50 (ISBN 0-7206-0663-2, Pub. by P Owen Ltd). Dufour.

Travels in New England & New York, 4 Vols. Timothy Dwight. Ed. by Barbara M. Solomon. LC 69-12735. (John Harvard Library). (Illus.). 1969. Repr. of 1821 ed. Set. boxed 50.00x (ISBN 0-674-90670-5). Harvard U Pr.

Travels in North America, During the Years 1834-36, Including a Summer with the Pawnees. 2nd ed. Charles A. Murray. LC 68-54845. (American Scene Ser.). 878p. 1974. Repr. of 1839 ed. lib. bdg. 85.00 (ISBN 0-306-71021-8). Da Capo.

Travels in North-America, in the Years 1780-1782, 2 Vols. Francois J. De Chastellux. LC 67-29046. (Eyewitness Accounts of the American Revolution Ser., No. 1). 1968. Repr. of 1787 ed. Set. 24.00 (ISBN 0-405-01109-1); Vol. 1. 14.00 (ISBN 0-405-01135-0); Vol. 2. 11.50 (ISBN 0-405-01127-X). Ayer Co Pubs.

Travels in North America, the Years, 1841-2: Geological Observations on the United States, Canada & Nova Scotia, 2 vols. in one. Charles Lyell. Ed. by Claude C. Albritton, Jr. LC 77-6525. (History of Geology Ser.). (Illus.). 1978. Repr. of 1845 ed. lib. bdg. 40.00x (ISBN 0-405-10447-2). Ayer Co Pubs.

Travels in North America, 1827-1828, 3 vols. in 1. Basil Hall. LC 73-13135. (Foreign Travelers in America, 1810-1935 Ser.). (Illus.). 1318p. 1974. Repr. 87.00x (ISBN 0-405-05457-2). Ayer Co Pubs.

Travels in Nubia. J. L. Burckhardt. 656p. 1987. 350.00x (ISBN 1-85077-172-3, Pub. by Darf Pubs Ltd). State Mutual Bk.

Travels in Nubia. John L. Burckhardt. LC 74-15014. Repr. of 1882 ed. 61.00 (ISBN 0-404-12009-1). AMS Pr.

Travels in Nubia. John L. Burckhardt. 646p. Repr. of 1822 ed. text ed. 99.36x (ISBN 0-576-79103-2, Pub. by Gregg Intl Pubs England). Gregg Intl.

Travels in Oman. Philip Ward. (Arabia Past & Present Ser.: Vol. 21). (Illus.). 584p. 1986. 55.00 (ISBN 0-906672-51-1). Oleander Pr.

Travels in Persia, Georgia & Koordistan; with Sketches of the Cossacks & the Caucasus, 3 vols. Moritz Wagner. 976p. Repr. of 1856 ed. text ed. 149.04x (ISBN 0-576-03330-8, Pub. by Gregg Intl Pubs England). Gregg Intl.

Travels in Persia, Sixteen Seventy-Three - Sixteen Seventy-Seven. John Chardin. (Illus.). 336p. 1988. pap. 7.95t (ISBN 0-486-25636-7). Dover.

Travels in Persia, 1627-1629. Thomas Herbert. Ed. by William Foster. LC 78-39468. (Select Bibliographies Reprint Series). 1972. Repr. of 1929 ed. 21.75 (ISBN 0-8369-9912-6). Ayer Co Pubs.

Travels in Poland & Russia. William Coxe. LC 73-115524. (Russia Observed, Ser.). 1970. Repr. of 1802 ed. 53.00 (ISBN 0-405-03017-7). Ayer Co Pubs.

Travels in Provence. Marion Deschamps. 176p. 1988. pap. 13.95 (ISBN 0-946576-80-7, Pub. by Phoenix Pub). David & Charles.

Travels in Russia. William R. Wilson. LC 75-115598. (Russia Observed, Series I). 1970. Repr. of 1828 ed. 37.50 (ISBN 0-405-03071-1). Ayer Co Pubs.

Travels in Russia, the Krimea, the Caucasus & Georgia. Robert Lyall. LC 74-115560. (Russia Observed, Ser., No. 1). 1970. Repr. of 1825 ed. 47.50 (ISBN 0-405-03046-0). Ayer Co Pubs.

Travels in Siberia. S. S. Hill. LC 71-115546. (Russia Observed, Series I). 1970. Repr. of 1854 ed. 42.00 (ISBN 0-405-03034-7). Ayer Co Pubs.

Travels in Siberia: Including Excursions Northwards, Down the Obi, to the Polar Circle, & Southwards, to the Chinese Frontier. Adolph Erman. LC 70-115535. (Russia Observed, Ser., No. 1). 1970. Repr. of 1848 ed. 51.00 (ISBN 0-405-03025-8). Ayer Co Pubs.

Travels in South Africa, Undertaken at the Request of the London Missionary Society, 2 Vols. in 1. John Campbell. 1968. Repr. of 1822 ed. 55.00 (ISBN 0-384-07260-7). Johnson Repr.

Travels in South America, 2 vols. Francois R. de Pons. LC 71-128420. Repr. of 1807 ed. Set. 75.00 (ISBN 0-404-02115-8). AMS Pr.

Travels in Southern Abyssinia: Through the Country of Adal to the Kingdom of Shoa, 2 vols. Charles Johnston. LC 72-3885. (Black Heritage Library Collection Ser.). Repr. of 1844 ed. Set. 53.00 (ISBN 0-8369-9099-4). Ayer Co Pubs.

Travels in Southern Abyssinia Through the Country of Adal to the Kingdom of Shoa, 2 vols. Charles Johnston. 964p. Repr. of 1844 ed. 165.60x (ISBN 0-576-17315-0, Pub. by Gregg Intl Pubs England). Gregg Intl.

Travels in Southern California. John Xantus. Tr. by Theodore Schoenman & Helen B. Schoenman. LC 76-23224. (Illus.). 216p. 1976. 19.95x (ISBN 0-8143-1570-4). Wayne St U Pr.

Travels in Syria & the Holy Land. John L. Burckhardt. LC 77-87614. (Illus.). 720p. 1983. Repr. of 1822 ed. 76.50 (ISBN 0-404-16437-4). AMS Pr.

Travels in Tartary. Evariste-Regis Huc. 1927. 40.00 (ISBN 0-686-17241-8). Scholars Ref Lib.

Travels in Tartary, Thibet & China. 2nd ed. E. R. Huc. 304p. 1855. 385.00x (Pub. by Han-Shan Tang Ltd). State Mutual Bk.

Travels in Tartary, Thibet & China, 1844-1846. Evariste-Regis Huc & Joseph Gabet. 864p. 1987. pap. 14.95 (ISBN 0-486-25438-0). Dover.

Travels in Tartary, Tibet & China During the Years 1844-5-6, 2 vols. in 1. M. Huc. (Illus.). 342p. 1981. Repr. of 1900 ed. lib. bdg. 100.00 (ISBN 0-89984-271-2). Century Bookbindery.

Travels in the Central Portions of the Mississippi Valley. Henry R. Schoolcraft. LC 1-6591. 1975. Repr. of 1825 ed. 32.00 (ISBN 0-527-03224-7). Kraus Repr.

Travels in the Confederate States: A Bibliography. E. Merton Coulter. xiv, 289p. 1981. Repr. of 1948 ed. 25.00 (ISBN 0-916107-02-7). Broadfoot.

Travels in the Confederation, 1783-1784. Johann D. Schoepf. Tr. by A. J. Morrison. LC 68-56584. (Research & Source Works Ser.: No. 206). 1968. Repr. of 1911 ed. Set. 38.00 (ISBN 0-8337-3158-0). B Franklin.

Travels in the Congo. Andre Gide. (Travel Library). 320p. 1986. pap. 7.95 (ISBN 0-14-009555-1). Penguin.

Travels in the Dordogne. Fiona Fennell. (Illus.). 158p. 1988. pap. 13.95 (ISBN 0-946576-78-5, Pub. by Phoenix Pub). David & Charles.

Travels in the Free States of Central America, 2 Vols. Karl Scherzer. LC 79-128430. 1970. Repr. of 1857 ed. Set. 45.00 (ISBN 0-404-05600-8). AMS Pr.

Travels in the Great Desert of Sahara, 1845-1846, 2 vols. James Richardson. (Illus.). 1970. Repr. of 1847 ed. 95.00x set (ISBN 0-7146-1850-0, BHA-01850, F Cass Co). Biblio Dist.

Travels in the Great Western Prairies, 2 vols. in 1. Thomas J. Farnham. LC 68-16231. (American Scene Ser.). 612p. 1973. Repr. of 1843 ed. lib. bdg. 75.00 (ISBN 0-306-71012-9). Da Capo.

Travels in the Interior Districts of Africa. Mungo Park & James Rennell. 15.00 (ISBN 0-405-18974-5, 16889). Ayer Co Pubs.

Travels in the Interior Inhabited Parts of North America in the Years 1791 & 1792. Patrick Campbell. Ed. by H. H. Langton. LC 68-28611. 1968. Repr. of 1937 ed. lib. bdg. 24.00x (ISBN 0-8371-5061-2, CATI). Greenwood.

Travels in the Interior of Africa. G. Mollien. Ed. by T. E. Bowdich. (Illus.). 408p. 1967. 45.00x (ISBN 0-7146-1077-1, F Cass Co). Biblio Dist.

Travels in the Interior of America in the Years 1809, 1810 & 1811. John Bradbury. LC 85-24615. 320p. 1986. pap. 7.95 (ISBN 0-8032-6076-8, Bison). U of Nebr Pr.

Travels in the Interior of Brazil. George Gardner. LC 75-128421. Repr. of 1846 ed. 37.50 (ISBN 0-404-02678-8). AMS Pr.

Travels in the Interior of Brazil. George Gardner. LC 77-88571. 1977. Repr. of 1846 ed. lib. bdg. 50.00 (ISBN 0-89341-278-3). Longwood Pub Group.

Travels in the Interior of Mexico in 1825, 1826, 1827 & 1828: In Baja California & Around the Sea of Cortes. R. W. Hardy. (Beautiful Rio Grande Classics Ser.). 606p. Repr. of 1828 ed. 25.00 (ISBN 0-87380-146-6). Rio Grande.

Travels in the Ionian Isles, Albania, Thessaly, Macedonia, etc. Henry Holland. 15.00 (ISBN 0-405-18970-2, 16885). Ayer Co Pubs.

Travels in the Land of the Gods: The Japan Diaries of Richard Gordon Smith. Richard G. Smith. Ed. by Victoria Manthorpe. (Illus.). 224p. 1986. 25.00. P-H.

Travels in the Mughal Empire AD 1656-1668. 2nd ed. Francois Bernier. Tr. by Archibald Constable. (Illus.). 500p. Repr. of 1914 ed. text ed. 38.50x. Coronet Bks.

Travels in the New South: A Bibliography, 2 vols. Thomas D. Clark. LC 62-10772. (American Exploration & Travel Ser.: No. 36). (Illus.). 284p. Vol. 1, The Postwar South, 1865-1900: An Era of Reconstruction & Readjustment. pap. 73.90 (2029819); Vol. 2, The Twentieth-Century South, 1900-1955: An Era of Change, Depression & Emergence. pap. 82.20 (2029819). Bks Demand UMI.

Travels in the North of Germany, 2 Vols. Thomas Hodgskin. LC 68-55735. 1969. Repr. of 1820 ed. 87.50x (ISBN 0-678-00587-7). Kelley.

Travels in the Old South: A Bibliography. 1st ed. Ed. by Thomas D. Clark. LC 56-8016. (American Exploration & Travels Ser.: No. 19). Vol. 1. pap. 85.80 (ISBN 0-317-10655-4, 2016201); Vol. 2. pap. 75.50 (ISBN 0-317-10656-2); Vol. 3. pap. 104.30 (ISBN 0-317-10657-0). Bks Demand UMI.

Travels in the Regions of the Upper & Lower Amxoor & the Russian Acquisitions on the Confines of India & China. Thomas W. Atkinson. 584p. Repr. of 1860 ed. text ed. 82.80x (ISBN 0-576-03345-6, Pub. by Gregg Intl Pubs England). Gregg Intl.

Travels in the Slavonic Provinces of Turkey-In-Europe. Georgena M. Mackenzie & A. P. Irby. LC 78-135816. (Eastern Europe Collection Ser). 1970. Repr. of 1866 ed. 40.00 (ISBN 0-405-02758-3). Ayer Co Pubs.

Travels in the South of France. Stendhal. 12.95 (ISBN 0-7145-0818-7); pap. 6.95 (ISBN 0-7145-1108-0). Riverrun NY.

Travels in the United States of America, in the Years 1806 & 1807, & 1809, 1810, & 1811. John Melish. (American Studies). 1970. Repr. of 1818 ed. 42.00 (ISBN 0-384-38095-6). Johnson Repr.

Travels in the West: Cuba with Notices of Porto Rico & the Slave Trade. David Turnbull. LC 76-177576. Repr. of 1840 ed. 19.50 (ISBN 0-404-06528-7). AMS Pr.

Travels in the West, Cuba: With Notices of Porto Rico & the Slave Trade. David Turnbull. LC 74-91667. 1970. Repr. of 1840 ed. 35.00 (ISBN 0-8371-2075-6, TCU&). Greenwood.

Travels in Three Continents, Europe, Africa, Asia. James M. Buckley. LC 72-5586. (Black Heritage Library Collection). 1972. Repr. of 1894 ed. 55.00 (ISBN 0-8369-9136-2). Ayer Co Pubs.

Travels in Turkey, Asia-Minor, Syria & Across the Desert into Egypt During the Years 1799, 1800 & 1801 in Company with the Turkish Army, & the British Military Mission. W. Wittman. 612p. Repr. of 1803 ed. text ed. 99.36x (ISBN 0-576-03344-8, Pub. by Gregg Intl Pubs England). Gregg Intl.

Travels in Upper & Lower Egypt. Charles N. De Manoncourt. 788p. Repr. of 1800 ed. text ed. 124.20x (ISBN 0-576-17110-7, Pub. by Gregg Intl Pubs England). Gregg Intl.

Travels in Upper & Lower Egypt, 3 vols. in 1. Vivant Denon. LC 73-6275. (Middle East Ser.). Repr. of 1803 ed. 86.00 (ISBN 0-405-05331-2). Ayer Co Pubs.

Travels in Various Parts of Peru, 2 Vols. Edmond Temple. LC 76-12824. Repr. of 1833 ed. Set. 52.00 (ISBN 0-404-06359-4). AMS Pr.

Travels in West Africa. 3rd rev. ed. Mary Kingsley. (Illus.). 743p. 1965. 37.50x (ISBN 0-7146-1824-1, F Cass Co). Biblio Dist.

Travels in West Africa. Mary Kingsley. 288p. 1987. pap. 7.95 (ISBN 0-460-01587-7, Evman). Biblio Dist.

Travels in West Africa. Mary Kingsley. LC 87-42856. (Virago-Beacon Traveler Ser.). (Illus.). 768p. 1988. pap. 12.95 (ISBN 0-8070-7105-6, BP 780). Beacon Pr.

Travels in Western Africa in 1845 & 1846, 2 vols. John Duncan. 1968. Repr. of 1847 ed. 85.00x set (ISBN 0-7146-1804-7, F Cass Co). Biblio Dist.

Travels into Bokhara, 3 vols. Sir Alexander Burnes. (Oxford in Asia Historical Reprints). 1973. Set. 39.95x (ISBN 0-19-636061-7). Oxford U Pr.

Travels into Dalmatia. Alberto Fortis. LC 70-135806. (Eastern Europe Collection Ser). 1970. Repr. of 1778 ed. 37.50 (ISBN 0-405-02748-6). Ayer Co Pubs.

Travels into Poland. William Coxe. LC 76-135802. (Eastern Europe Collection Ser). (Illus.). 226p. 1970. Repr. of 1785 ed. 16.00 (ISBN 0-405-02744-3). Ayer Co Pubs.

Travels into the Poor Man's Country: The Work of Henry Mayhew. Ann Humpherys. (Illus.). 250p. 1980. 19.75 (ISBN 0-904573-29-X, Pub. by Caliban Bks). Longwood Pub Group.

Travels of a Layman. Brooks Smith. (Illus.). 1986. pap. 10.00 (ISBN 0-931611-08-3). D R Benbow.

Travels of a Photographer in China, 1933-1946. Hedda Morrison. (Illus.). 276p. 1987. 29.95 (ISBN 0-19-584098-4). Oxford U Pr.

Travels of Alexine. Penelope Gladstone. (Illus.). 1971. 12.50 (ISBN 0-7195-2044-4). Transatl Arts.

Travels of Ali Bey in Morocco, Tripoli, Cyprus, Egypt, Arabia, Syria & Turkey, Between the Years 1803 & 1807, 2 vols. Domingo Badia y Leyblich. 766p. Repr. of 1816 ed. text ed. 99.36x (ISBN 0-576-03580-7, Pub. by Gregg Intl Pubs England). Gregg Intl.

Travels of an Alchemist. Li Chih-Ch'ang. LC 75-36233. Repr. of 1931 ed. 14.50 (ISBN 0-404-14481-0). AMS Pr.

Travels of Babar. Jean De Brunhoff. (Illus.). (ps). 1967. 7.95 (ISBN 0-394-80576-3, BYR); lib. bdg. 7.99 (ISBN 0-394-90576-8). Random.

Travels of Babar. Jean De Brunhoff. LC 85-2236. (Illus.). 48p. (ps up). 1985. 15.95 (ISBN 0-394-87453-6, BYR). Random.

Travels of Ben Sira. Stanley Nelson. LC 77-82687. (Illus.). 70p. (Orig.). 1978. pap. 3.00 (ISBN 0-912292-44-X). The Smith.

Travels of Certaine Englishmen into Africa, Asia & to the Blacke Sea, Finished 1608. William Biddulph & Peter Biddulph. LC 72-6344. (English Experience Ser.: No. 22). 144p. 1968. Repr. of 1609 ed. 25.00 (ISBN 90-221-0022-7). Walter J Johnson.

Travels of Charlie. Charles G. Mortimer. LC 75-29684. (Illus.). 368p. 1975. pap. 6.95 (ISBN 0-914896-29-6). East Ridge Pr.

Travels of Faith. Faith A. Sand. LC 85-17751. (Illus.). 152p. (Orig.). 1986. pap. 4.95 (ISBN 0-932727-03-4). Hope Pub Hse.

Travels of Freddie & Frannie Frog. Betsy Maestro. LC 86-81491. (Golden Storytime Bks.). (Illus.). 24p. (ps-1). 1987. pap. 2.95 (ISBN 0-307-11966-1, Pub. by Golden Bks). Western Pub.

Travels of Ibn Battuta, A.D. 1325-1354, 2 vols. in one. H. A. Gibb. Tr. by C. Defremery & B. R. Sanguimetti. (Hakluyt Society Works Series II: Vol. 110-117). (Illus.). 1962. 95.00 (ISBN 0-8115-0401-8). Kraus Repr.

Travels of Ibn Batuta. Ibn Batuta. LC 74-172523. (Oriental Translation Fund, Publications: No. 1). Repr. of 1829 ed. 18.50 (ISBN 0-8337-2051-1). B Franklin.

Travels of Ibn Batuta. S. Lee. 264p. 1985. 200.00x (ISBN 1-85077-035-2, Pub. by Darf Pubs Ltd). State Mutual Bk.

Travels of Ibn Jubayr. 2nd ed. Muhammad Ibn Ahmad. Ed. by William Wright. LC 77-173005. Repr. of 1907 ed. 24.50 (ISBN 0-404-03480-2). AMS Pr.

Travels of J. B. Rabbit. Doris S. Smith. LC 82-80876. Orig. Title: Vacances de Jeremy. (Illus.). 48p. (gr. k-2). 1982. 5.95 (ISBN 0-448-16585-6, G&D). Putnam Pub Group.

Travels of John Heckewelder in Frontier America. Ed. by Paul A. Wallace. LC 84-22085. Orig. Title: Thirty Thousand Miles with John Heckewelder. (Illus.). 496p. 1985. pap. 12.95 (ISBN 0-8229-5369-2). U of Pittsburgh Pr.

Travels of John Sanderson in the Levant, 1584-1602. Ed. by William Foster. (Hakluyt Society Works Ser. 2: Vol. 67). (Illus.). Repr. of 1930 ed. 38.00 (ISBN 0-8115-0371-2). Kraus Repr.

Travels of Lady Hester Stanhope, 3 Vols. Lady Hester Stanhope. Ed. by James Hogg. Incl. Vol. 1. 372p (ISBN 3-7052-0579-X); Vol. 2. 400p (ISBN 3-7052-0580-3); Vol. 3. 423p (ISBN 3-7052-0581-1). (Romantic Reassessment ser.). (Orig.). 1983. pap. 15.00 ea. (Pub. by Salzburg Studies). Longwood Pub Group.

Travels of Lao Can. Liu E. 176p. 1983. pap. 4.95 (ISBN 0-8351-1075-3). China Bks.

Travels of Lao Ts'an. E. Liu. Tr. & intro. by Harold Shadick. LC 86-1867. 301p. 1986. Repr. of 1952 ed. lib. bdg. 48.50x (ISBN 0-313-25164-9, LITR). Greenwood.

Travels of Leo of Rozmital. Ed. by Malcolm Letts. (Hakluyt Society Works Ser. 2: Vol. 108). (Illus.). Repr. of 1955 ed. 25.00 (ISBN 0-8115-0400-X). Kraus Repr.

Travels of Ludovico di Varthema in Egypt, Syria, Arabia Deserta & Arabia Felix, Persia, India & Ethiopia: A.D. 1503 to 1508. Lodovico De Varthema. Intro. by George P. Badger. LC 63-24804. (Hakluyt Society Ser: No. 32). 1964. Repr. of 1863 ed. 28.50 (ISBN 0-8337-1862-2). B Franklin.

Travels of Macarius: Extracts from the Diary of the Travels of Macarius, Patriarch of Antioch. Ed. by Laura Ridding. LC 77-115577. (Russia Observed Ser). 1971. Repr. of 1936 ed. 12.00 (ISBN 0-405-03089-4). Ayer Co Pubs.

Travels of Marco Polo. L. F. Bendetto. 439p. 1931. 280.00x (ISBN 0-317-69177-5, Pub. by Han-Shan Tang Ltd). State Mutual Bk.

Travels of Marco Polo. Adapted by Vincent Buranelli. LC 85-40435. (Silver Burdett Classics for Kids Ser.). (Illus.). 32p. (gr. 3 up). 1985. PLB 5.96 (ISBN 0-382-09098-5); pap. 3.60 (ISBN 0-382-09104-3). Silver.

Travels of Marco Polo. Manuel Komroff. 1982. pap. 9.95 (ISBN 0-87140-132-0). Liveright.

Travels of Marco Polo. Tr. by Ronald E. Latham. (Classics Ser.). 1958. pap. 4.95 (ISBN 0-14-044057-7). Penguin.

Travels of Marco Polo. Edward W. Marsden. 1987. 17.95 (ISBN 0-88029-135-4, Pub. by Dorset Pr). Hippocrene Bks.

Travels of Marco Polo. Intro. by John Masefield. 478p. 1983. pap. text ed. 5.95x (ISBN 0-460-11306-2, Evman). Biblio Dist.

Travels of Marco Polo. Marco Polo. (Airmont Classics Ser.). (gr. 9 up). 1968. pap. 1.50 (ISBN 0-8049-0186-4, CL-186). Airmont.

Travels of Marco Polo. Marco Polo. Ed. by Manuel Komroff. 1953. 11.95 (ISBN 0-87140-898-8). Liveright.

Travels of Marco Polo. Marco Polo. Tr. by Ronald Latham from Fr. (Illus.). 318p. 1982. 35.00x (ISBN 0-89835-058-1). Abaris Bks.

Travels of Marco Polo. Marco Polo. 1982. Repr. lib. bdg. 18.95x (ISBN 0-89967-045-8). Harmony Raine.

Travels of Marco Polo. Milton Rugoff. 1982. pap. 3.50 (ISBN 0-451-51717-2, Sig Classics). NAL.

Travels of Marco Polo. Tr. by Teresa Waugh. (Illus.). 218p. 19.95 (ISBN 0-87196-890-8). Facts on File.

Travels of Olearius in Seventeenth-Century Russia. Adam Olearius. Tr. by Samuel H. Baron. (Illus.). 1967. 35.00x (ISBN 0-8047-0219-5). Stanford U Pr.

Travels of Pedro De Cieza De Leon 1532-50. Pedro De Cieza De Leon. Tr. by Clements R. Markham. 1964. Repr. of 1864 ed. 60.50 (ISBN 0-8337-2235-2). B Franklin.

Travels of Pedro Teixeira. Pedro Teixeira. Notes by William F. Sinclair. Bd. with King of Harmuz. Pedro Teixeira; King of Persia: Extract. Pedro Teixeira. (Hakluyt Society Works Series 2: Vol. 9). Repr. of 1901 ed. 60.00 (ISBN 0-8115-0331-3). Kraus Repr.

Travels of Peter Munday in Europe & Asia, 1608-1667, 5 vols. Ed. by Richard C. Temple et al. (Hakluyt Society Works Series 2: Vols. 17, 35, 45,46, 55, & 78). 1905-1936. 300.00 (ISBN 0-8115-0338-0). Kraus Repr.

Travels of Peter Mundy. John Keast. 1985. 20.00x (ISBN 0-907566-75-8, Pub. by Dyllansow & Truran). State Mutual Bk.

Travels of Pietro Della Valle to India, 2 Vols. Pietro Della Valle. Ed. by Edward Grey. Tr. by G. Hovers. (Illus.). 58.00 (ISBN 0-8337-0822-8). B Franklin.

Travels of Sebastien Manrique, 1629-1643, 2 vols. Sebastiao Manrique. (Hakluyt Society Works Ser.: No. 2, Vols. 59 & 61). (Illus.). 1926. Set. 140.00 (ISBN 0-8115-0362-3). Kraus Repr.

Travels of Sir John Mandeville. Josef Krasa. Tr. by Peter Kussi from Czech. LC 83-12283. (Illus.). 128p. 1983. 45.00 (ISBN 0-8076-1054-2). Braziller.

Travels of Sir John Mandeville. John Mandeville. Tr. by Charles W. Moseley. (Penguin Classics Ser.). 208p. 1984. pap. 5.95 (ISBN 0-14-044435-1). Penguin.

Travels of Sir John Mandeville: The Version of the Cotton Manuscript in Modern Spelling. Intro. by A. W. Pollard. 1978. Repr. of 1900 ed. lib. bdg. 35.00 (ISBN 0-8495-3722-3). Arden Lib.

Travels of Soc. (MicroSoc Thinking Games Ser.). (gr. k-8). 1985. 12.50 (ISBN 0-88671-209-2). Am Guidance.

Travels of the Abbe Carre in India & the Near East: 1672 to 1674, 3 vols. in 1. Ed. by Charles Fawcett & Richard Burn. (Hakluyt Society Works Ser.: No. 2, Vols. 95-97). (Illus.). Repr. of 1947 ed. 150.00 (ISBN 0-8115-0391-7). Kraus Repr.

Travels of the Golden Fish & Other Bilingual Children's Stories. Rafael A. Urena. LC 85-90097. 37p. 1985. 5.95 (ISBN 0-533-06610-7). Vantage.

Travels of the Itinerant Freda Aharon. Myra Sklarew. (Orig.). 1985. special ed 25.00 (ISBN 0-931956-24-2); pap. 6.00 (ISBN 0-931956-22-6). Water Mark.

Travels of the Naturalist Charles A. Lesueur in North America, 1815-1837. Ernest T. Hamy. Ed. by H. F. Raup. LC 67-65271. pap. 29.50 (2027305). Bks Demand UMI.

Travels of the Russian Mission Through Mongolia to China. Egor F. Timkovsky. 496p. 1821. 2200.00x (Pub. by Han-Shan Tang Ltd). State Mutual Bk.

Travels, or Observations Relating to Several Parts of Barbary & the Levant. Thomas Shaw. 526p. Repr. of 1738 ed. text ed. 82.80x (ISBN 0-576-03335-9, Pub. by Gregg Intl Pubs England). Gregg Intl.

Travels: People & Places in My Life. Edward Heath. (Illus.). 1979. 12.95 (ISBN 0-8317-8810-0, Mayflower Bks). Smith Pubs.

Treasure Hunting: The Treasure Hunter's Own Book of Land Caches & Bullion Wrecks. Harold T. Wilkins. LC 73-12206. (Beautiful Rio Grande Classics Ser.). (Illus.). 400p. 1983. Repr. of 1939 ed. lib. bdg. 15.00 (ISBN 0-87380-104-0). Rio Grande.

Treasure Hunting with a Metal Detector. Pisces Books Staff & Steve Blount. LC 86-30357. (Illus.). 96p. 1987. 9.95 (ISBN 0-86636-049-2). PBC Intl Inc.

Treasure Hunts. Harriet H. Green & Sue G. Martin. 144p. (gr. 4-7). 1983. wkbk. 9.95 (ISBN 0-86653-115-7, GA 469). Good Apple.

Treasure in Clay: The Autobiography of Fulton J. Sheen. Fulton J. Sheen. LC 81-43271. (Illus.). 384p. 1982. pap. 9.95 (ISBN 0-385-17709-7, Im). Doubleday.

Treasure in Earthen Vessels. James M. Gustafson. xiv, 142p. 1985. pap. text ed. 7.95 (ISBN 0-226-31101-5). U of Chicago Pr.

Treasure in Roubles. David Williams. 224p. 1988. pap. 2.95 (ISBN 0-380-70546-X). Avon.

Treasure in Roubles: A Mark Treasure Mystery. David Williams. 208p. 1987. 14.95 (ISBN 0-312-00697-7). St Martin.

Treasure in the Dust: Enduring Gold & Silver's Century of Divorce. Becky Boudway. (Illus.). 196p. 1986. casebound 22.50 (ISBN 0-317-44748-3); pap. 10.95 (ISBN 0-317-44749-1). Panorama West.

Treasure in the Yukon. Jeri Massi. (Light Line Ser.). (Illus.). 136p. (Orig.). (gr. 4-6). 1986. pap. 5.83 (ISBN 0-89084-365-1). Bob Jones Univ Pr.

Treasure Island. Aurand Harris. (gr. 4 up). 1983. pap. 3.50 (ISBN 0-87602-253-0). Anchorage.

Treasure Island. Jean Howarth. (Fiction Ser.). 208p. 1985. pap. 5.95 (ISBN 0-14-007066-4). Penguin.

Treasure Island. Ed. by William A. Kottmeyer. 1972. text ed. 7.96 (ISBN 0-07-034020-X). McGraw.

Treasure Island. Marcia Sohl & Gerald Dackerman. (Now Age Illustrated Ser.). 16p. (gr. 4-10). 1976. pap. 1.25 student activity bk. (ISBN 0-88301-185-9). Pendulum Pr.

Treasure Island. Robert Louis Stevenson. (Airmont Classics Ser.). (gr. 7 up). pap. 1.95 (ISBN 0-8049-0002-7, CL-2). Airmont.

Treasure Island. Robert Louis Stevenson. (Literature Ser). (gr. 7-12). 1969. pap. text ed. 7.00 (ISBN 0-87720-718-6). AMSCO Sch.

Treasure Island. Robert Louis Stevenson. (Illus.). 208p. (gr. 7-12). 1981. pap. 1.75 (ISBN 0-553-21099-8, Bantam Classics). Bantam.

Treasure Island. Robert Louis Stevenson. (Illus.). (gr. 1-9). 1947. deluxe ed. 10.95 (ISBN 0-448-06025-6, G&D). Putnam Pub Group.

Treasure Island. Robert Louis Stevenson. (Hardy Boys' Favorite Classics). (Illus.). (gr. 6-9). 1978. 2.95 (ISBN 0-448-14920-6, G&D). Putnam Pub Group.

Treasure Island. Robert Louis Stevenson. (RL 6). pap. 1.50 (ISBN 0-451-51729-6, CW1729, Sig Classics). NAL.

Treasure Island. new ed. Robert Louis Stevenson. Ed. by John Norwood. LC 73-75459. (Now Age Illustrated Ser.). (Illus.). 64p. (Orig.). (gr. 5-10). 1973. 7.50 (ISBN 0-88301-221-9); pap. 2.95 (ISBN 0-88301-106-9). Pendulum Pr.

Treasure Island. Robert Louis Stevenson. (Story Bks.). 224p. (gr. 2-5). 1984. pap. 2.25 (ISBN 0-14-035016-0, Puffin). Penguin.

Treasure Island. Robert Louis Stevenson. Adapted by Jane Edwards. LC 79-24100. (Short Classics Ser.). (Illus.). (gr. 4-12). 1980. PLB 15.99 (ISBN 0-8172-1655-3). Raintree Pubs.

Treasure Island. Robert Louis Stevenson. (Regents Illustrated Classics Ser.). (gr. 7-12). 1982. pap. text ed. 3.50 (ISBN 0-13-930629-3, 20521). Prentice ESL.

Treasure Island. Robert Louis Stevenson. LC 78-74010. (Illus.). (gr. 5-12). 1979. pap. 4.95 (ISBN 0-8052-0620-5). Schocken.

Treasure Island. Robert Louis Stevenson. (gr. 7-12). 1972. pap. 2.25 (ISBN 0-590-40105-X, Schol Pap). Scholastic Inc.

Treasure Island. Robert Louis Stevenson. LC 81-8788. (Scribner's Illustrated Classics). (Illus.). 273p. (gr. 3 up). 1981. 20.95 (ISBN 0-684-17160-0, Pub. by Scribner). Macmillan.

Treasure Island. Robert Louis Stevenson. (Bambi Classics Ser.). (Illus.). 304p. (Orig.). (YA) (gr. 9-12). 1981. pap. 3.95 (ISBN 0-89531-051-1, 0221-48). Sharon Pubns.

Treasure Island. Robert Louis Stevenson. Adapted by June Edwards. LC 79-24100. (Short Classics Ser.). (Illus.). 48p. (gr. 4-12). 1983. pap. 9.27 (ISBN 0-8172-2026-7). Raintree Pubs.

Treasure Island. Robert Louis Stevenson. LC 80-54133. (Silver Burdett Classics for Kids Ser.). (Illus.). 32p. (gr. 3 up). 1984. 5.96 (ISBN 0-382-06810-6); pap. 3.60 (ISBN 0-382-06953-6). Silver.

Treasure Island. Robert Louis Stevenson. (Illus.). 336p. 1985. 11.95 (ISBN 0-396-08532-6). Dodd.

Treasure Island. Robert Louis Stevenson. Date not set. price not set. S&S.

Treasure Island. Robert Louis Stevenson. LC 80-54133. (Silver Burdett Classics for Kids Ser.). 288p. (gr. 6 up). 1985. pap. 3.67 (ISBN 0-382-09996-6). Silver.

Treasure Island. Robert Louis Stevenson. Ed. by Emma Letley. (WC-P Ser.). (YA) (gr. 7-12). 1985. pap. 2.25 (ISBN 0-19-281681-0). Oxford U Pr.

Treasure Island. Robert Louis Stevenson. (gr. 5-6). 17.95 (ISBN 0-89190-236-8, Pub. by Am Repr). Amereon Ltd.

Treasure Island. Robert Louis Stevenson. (Oxford Progressive English Readers Ser.). (Illus.). (YA) (gr. 7-12). 1982. pap. 3.75 (ISBN 0-19-581379-0). Oxford U Pr.

Treasure Island. Robert Louis Stevenson. (YA) (gr. 7 up). 1965. pap. 1.75 (ISBN 0-451-51917-5, Sig Classics). NAL.

Treasure Island. Robert Louis Stevenson. (gr. k-6). 1986. 7.98 (618168). Outlet Bk Co.

Treasure Island. Robert Louis Stevenson. 1986. Limited Edition 500.00X (ISBN 0-245-54356-2, Pub. by Harrap Ltd England). State Mutual Bk.

Treasure Island. Robert Louis Stevenson. 224p. (Orig.). (gr. 4-7). 1988. pap. 2.50 (ISBN 0-590-41617-0, Pub. by Apple Classics). Scholastic Inc.

Treasure Island. Robert Louis Stevenson. (Classics Ser.). (YA) (gr. 7 up). Date not set. pap. 3.95. Longman Trade.

Treasure Island. Robert Louis Stevenson & L. Steadman. 1986. pap. 64.75X (ISBN 0-245-54266-3, Pub. by Harrap Ltd England). State Mutual Bk.

Treasure Island. (Illustrated Junior Library). (Illus.). 352p. (gr. 3-9). 1981. pap. 7.95 (ISBN 0-448-11025-3, G&D). Putnam Pub Group.

Treasure Island. (Classics Ser.). (ps-6). 1988. pap. 3.95 (ISBN 0-582-54163-8). Longman.

Treasure Island. Wilkes. (Children's Classics Ser.). (gr. 3-6). 1982. (Usborne-Hayes); PLB 11.96 (ISBN 0-88110-063-3); pap. 2.95 (ISBN 0-86020-574-6). EDC.

Treasure Island see Good Literature for Slow Readers.

Treasure Island see Kidnapped.

Treasure Island see New Method Supplementary Readers.

Treasure Island see Serie Illustrada, "Now Age".

Treasure Island: A Stevenson Study. David Barnett. 1979. 42.50 (ISBN 0-685-65707-8). Bern Porter.

Treasure Island & Kidnapped Notes. O. L. Mishk. 73p. (Orig.). 1974. pap. text ed. 3.25 (ISBN 0-8220-1306-1). Cliffs.

Treasure Island: San Francisco's Exposition Years. Richard Reinhardt. LC 73-78446. (Illus.). 176p. 1973. pap. 6.95 (ISBN 0-916290-09-3). Squarebooks.

Treasure Island with Reader's Guide. Robert Louis Stevenson. (Amsco Literature Program Ser.). (gr. 10-12). 1972. text ed. 11.58 (ISBN 0-87720-840-9); pap. text ed. 7.83 (ISBN 0-87720-817-4); model ans. bk. 8.16 (ISBN 0-87720-917-0). AMSCO Sch.

Treasure Legends of the Civil War. C. A. Mills. Date not set. price not set (ISBN 0-945598-02-5). Apple Cheeks Pr.

Treasure Legends of Virginia. C. A. Mills. Date not set. price not set (ISBN 0-945598-00-9). Apple Cheeks Pr.

Treasure Maps & Charts in the Library of Congress: A Descriptive List by a Reference Librarian. Ed. by Richard S. Ladd. LC 64-60033. 1988. pap. 5.00 (ISBN 0-87380-161-X). Rio Grande.

Treasure Mountain. Louis L'Amour. 192p. (Orig.). 1984. pap. 2.95 (ISBN 0-553-25508-8). Bantam.

Treasure of Alpheus Winterborn. John Bellairs. 192p. (gr. 3-8). 1985. pap. 2.75 (ISBN 0-553-15527-X, Skylark). Bantam.

Treasure of Andor: A Robo Force Adventure. Regina King. LC 84-62070. (Robo Force Mini-Storybks.). (Illus.). 32p. (ps-3). 1985. pap. 1.25 (ISBN 0-394-87174-X, BYR). Random.

Treasure of Atlantis. J. Allan Dunn. (Time-Lost Ser.). (Illus.). 1971. 5.00 (ISBN 0-87818-006-0); pap. 0.75 (ISBN 0-87818-002-8). Centaur.

Treasure of El Dorado. rev. ed. Joseph Whitfield. LC 86-50360. (Illus.). 216p. 1987. Repr. of 1977 ed. 13.95 (ISBN 0-912119-02-0). Treasure Publications.

Treasure of El Lahun: Metropolitan Museum of Art (Department of Egyptian Art Publications, Vol. 4) Herbert E. Winlock. LC 73-168416. (Metropolitan Museum of Art Publications in Reprint). (Illus.). 130p. 1972. Repr. of 1934 ed. 22.00 (ISBN 0-405-02254-9). Ayer Co Pubs.

Treasure of Euonymus: Conteyninge the Hid Secretes of Nature. Conrad Gesner. Tr. by P. Morwyng. LC 63-6477. (English Experience Ser.: No. 97). 408p. 1969. Repr. of 1559 ed. 45.00 (ISBN 90-221-0097-9). Walter J Johnson.

Treasure of Green Knowe. L. M. Boston. 13.00 (ISBN 0-8446-6275-5). Peter Smith.

Treasure of Green Knowe. Lucy M. Boston. LC 77-16689. (Illus.). (gr. 4-7). 1978. pap. 1.95 (ISBN 0-15-691302-X, VoyB). HarBraceJ.

Treasure of Guatavita: El Tesoro De Guatavita. Adapted by Harriet Rohmer & Jesus G. Rea. LC 76-29081. (Fifth World Tales Ser.). (Illus.). 24p. (gr. k-6). 1976. pap. 5.95 spanish bilingual ed. (ISBN 0-89239-010-7). Childrens Book Pr.

Treasure of Homestake Gold: The Story of Homestake Gold Mine. Mildred Fielder. LC 70-113967. (Illus.). 478p. 1970. 13.95 (ISBN 0-87970-115-3). North Plains.

Treasure of Hymns. facs. ed. Amos R. Wells. LC 70-128330. (Essay Index Reprint Ser). 1945. 19.50 (ISBN 0-8369-2096-1). Ayer Co Pubs.

Treasure of My Heart Two. Carrol R. Bailey. 79p. 1988. 6.95 (ISBN 0-533-07094-5). Vantage.

Treasure of Nagyszenimiklos. Laszlo Gyula & Istvan Racz. 184p. 1984. 114.00x (ISBN 0-317-61412-6, Pub. by Collets (UK)). State Mutual Bk.

Treasure of Pawley's Island. Celia C. Halford. (Illus.). 190p. (Orig.). 1987. pap. 7.65 (ISBN 0-87844-068-2). Sandlapper Pub Co.

Treasure of Plunderell Manor. Bruce Clements. LC 87-25218. 192p. (YA) (gr. 7 up). 1987. 12.95 (ISBN 0-374-37746-4). FS&G.

Treasure of Sierra Madre. Ed. by James Naremore. LC 78-53298. (Screenplay Ser.). (Illus.). 206p. 1979. 18.95x (ISBN 0-299-07680-6); pap. 8.95 (ISBN 0-299-07684-9). U of Wis Pr.

Treasure of Sierra Madre. B. Traven. 15.95 (ISBN 0-89190-161-2, Pub. by Am Repr). Amereon Ltd.

Treasure of Stonewycke. Michael Phillips & Judith Pella. (Stonewycke Legacy Ser.). 352p. (Orig.). (YA) (gr. 11 up). 1988. pap. 6.95 (ISBN 0-87123-902-7). Bethany Hse.

Treasure of Superstition Mountains. Gary Jennings. (Illus.). 256p. 1974. 7.95 (ISBN 0-393-08678-X). Norton.

Treasure of the Atocha: A Sixteen Year Undersea Adventure. R. Duncan Mathewson, III. LC 85-30978. (Illus.). 192p. 1986. 19.95 (ISBN 0-525-24497-2). Dutton.

Treasure of the City of Ladies: Or the Book of Three Virtues. Christine De Pisan. Tr. by Sarah Lawson. (Classics Ser.). 192p. 1985. pap. 5.95 (ISBN 0-14-044453-X). Penguin.

Treasure of the Heart. Pat Louis. (Superromances Ser.). 384p. 1982. pap. 2.50 (ISBN 0-373-70014-8, Pub. by Worldwide). Harlequin Bks.

Treasure of the Humble. Maurice Maeterlinck. Tr. by Alfred Sutro. LC 77-10276. Repr. of 1897 ed. 20.00 (ISBN 0-404-16328-9). AMS Pr.

Treasure of the Land of Darkness: The Fur Trade & Its Significance for Medieval Russia. Janet L. Martin. (Illus.). 296p. 1987. 39.50 (ISBN 0-521-32019-4). Cambridge U Pr.

Treasure of the Lost City. Aaron Fletcher. 1976. pap. 1.25 (ISBN 0-685-73461-7, LB391, Leisure Bks). Leisure NY.

Treasure of the Magi: A Story of Modern Zoroastrianism. James H. Moulton. LC 73-173004. Repr. of 1917 ed. 21.75 (ISBN 0-404-04508-1). AMS Pr.

Treasure of the Magi: A Study of Modern Zoroastrianism. J. H. Moulton. lib. bdg. 59.95 (ISBN 0-8490-2759-4). Gordon Pr.

Treasure of the Sangre De Cristos: Tales & Traditions of the Spanish Southwest. Arthur L. Campa. LC 63-17162. (Illus.). 1984. pap. 6.95 (ISBN 0-8061-1176-3). U of Okla Pr.

Treasure of the Scroll. Valerie Reddix. (Pennypinchers Ser.). 128p. (gr. 5-9). 1984. pap. 2.95 (ISBN 0-89191-884-1, 58842). Cook.

Treasure of the Sierra Madre. B. Traven. LC 79-10456. 1980. Repr. of 1967 ed. lib. bdg. 14.00x (ISBN 0-8376-0436-2). Bentley.

Treasure of the Sierra Madre. B. Traven. (American Century Ser.). 308p. 1935. pap. 6.95 (ISBN 0-8090-0160-8). Hill & Wang.

Treasure of Victoria Peak. Phil A. Koury. 200p. 1986. pap. 9.95 (ISBN 0-88740-060-4). Schiffer.

Treasure of Wonderwhat: A Farstar & Son Novel. Bill Starr. 240p. 1983. pap. 2.50 (ISBN 0-345-30968-5, Del Rey). Ballantine.

Treasure on the Chesapeake Bay. Bob Trevillian & Frank Carter. (Illus.). 85p. (Orig.). 1983. pap. 9.95 (ISBN 0-913487-01-5). Spyglass Pro.

Treasure, People, Ships & Dreams. John L. Davis. (Illus.). 75p. 1977. pap. 5.95 (ISBN 0-933164-20-3). U of Tex Inst Tex Culture.

Treasure Preserved. David Williams. 224p. 1987. pap. 2.95 (ISBN 0-380-70256-8). Avon.

Treasure Ranch. Charles A. Seltzer. 273p. 1975. Repr. of 1940 ed. lib. bdg. 18.95x (ISBN 0-88411-110-5, Pub. by Aeonian Pr). Amereon Ltd.

Treasure Recovery from Sand & Sea. Charles Garrett. Ed. by Hal Dawson. LC 87-63128. (Illus.). 409p. 1988. pap. 12.95 (ISBN 0-915920-51-4). Ram Pub.

Treasure Ship. E. J. Hall. 64p. 1984. text ed. 2.60 (ISBN 0-07-025751-5). McGraw.

Treasure Ship; Rory Aforesaid; the Happy War: Three Plays. John Brandane. LC 79-50019. (One-Act Plays in Reprint Ser.). 1980. Repr. of 1928 ed. 21.50x (ISBN 0-8486-2043-7). Roth Pub Inc.

Treasure Sock. Pat Thomson. LC 87-443. (Share-a-Story Bks.). (Illus.). 32p. (gr. k-2). 1987. pap. 8.95 (ISBN 0-385-29600-2). Delacorte.

Treasure Sock. Pat Thomson & Tony Ross. (Orig.). (gr. k-6). 1987. pap. 2.50 (ISBN 0-440-48814-1, YB). Dell.

Treasure State Treasury: Banks, Bankers & Banking in Montana, 1863-1984. William C. Skidmore. (Illus.). 200p. 1985. 29.95 (ISBN 0-9612006-0-X). Montana Bankers.

Treasure Tales of the Rockies. 3rd ed. Perry Eberhart. LC 61-14373. (Illus.). 315p. 1969. 15.95 (ISBN 0-8040-0295-9, Pub by Swallow). Ohio U Pr.

Treasure Tales: Shipwrecks & Salvage. Thomas H. Sebring. (Illus.). 150p. 1986. lib. bdg. 24.95 (ISBN 0-9617735-0-2). T H Sebring.

Treasure: The World's First One-Step Guide to Success, Prosperity & Happiness. Morris D. Armstrong, III. 136p. 1984. 8.95 (ISBN 0-8059-2951-7). Dorrance.

Treasure to the Naked Eye. Glenna Luschei & Sally Wilson. (6 copies) 200.00 (ISBN 0-318-23705-9). Solo Pr.

Treasure Trail. Van W. Tilford. (Orig.). 1981. pap. 1.75 (ISBN 0-505-51673-X, Pub. by Tower Bks). Leisure NY.

Treasure Trail from Tucson. Nelson Nye. 1987. pap. 2.75 (ISBN 0-515-09267-3). Jove Pubns.

Treasure Trails. R. J. Santschi. (Doodlebug Edition Ser.). 1974. 6.00; pap. 4.00 (ISBN 0-89316-601-4). Exanimo Pr.

Treasure Transfer: A Resale & Consignment Guide for Orange County, Los Angeles County & San Diego County. Starr Phillips. (Illus.). 170p. (Orig.). 1985. pap. 6.50 (ISBN 0-933911-00-9). DC Pub Co.

Treasure Vault of Atlantis. Olof W. Anderson. Ed. by R. Reginald & Douglas Melville. LC 77-84194. (Lost Race & Adult Fantasy Ser.). 1978. Repr. of 1925 ed. lib. bdg. 26.50x (ISBN 0-405-10952-0). Ayer Co Pubs.

Treasure Wreck: The Fortunes & Fate of the Pirate Ship Whydah. Arthur T. Vanderbilt, II. (Illus.). 160p. 1986. 16.95 (ISBN 0-395-39975-0). HM.

Treasured Alabama Recipes. rev. & enl. ed. Kathryn T. Windham. LC 67-28975. (Illus.). 1967. 5.95 (ISBN 0-87397-009-8). Strode.

Treasured Catholic Prayers & Devotions. David Konstant. LC 86-50715. 1987. pap. 4.95 (ISBN 0-89622-312-4). Twenty-Third.

Treasured Georgia Recipes. Kathryn T. Windham. LC 73-87005. 1973. 4.95 (ISBN 0-87397-045-4). Strode.

Treasured Greek Proverbs. E. Bucuvalas. (Gr. & Eng.). 1980. 6.50 (ISBN 0-686-64282-1). Divry.

Treasured Polish Christmas Customs & Traditions. 8.95 (ISBN 0-685-37594-3). Polanie.

Treasured Polish Folk Rhythms, Songs & Games. 1976. 5.95 (ISBN 0-685-84287-8). Polanie.

Treasured Polish Recipes for Americans. 4.95 (ISBN 0-685-22650-6). Polanie.

Treasured Polish Songs. (Eng. & Pol.). 10.00 (ISBN 0-685-22652-2). Polanie.

Treasured Recipes of Country Inns. Ed. by Berkshire Traveller Staff. LC 73-91008. (Illus.). 134p. 1973. pap. 5.95 (ISBN 0-912944-08-0). Berkshire Traveller.

Treasured Tennessee Recipes. Kathryn T. Windham. LC 72-91391. 1972. 5.95 (ISBN 0-87397-021-7). Strode.

Treasurer's & Controller's Desk Book. Daniel L. Gotthilf. 512p. 1977. 54.95 (ISBN 0-13-930727-3). P-H.

Treasurer's & Controller's New Equipment Leasing Guide. Albert R. McMeen, III. LC 84-6994. 251p. 1984. 59.95 (ISBN 0-13-930876-8, Busn). P-H.

Treasurer's Guide. E R C Editorial Staff. 1976. 131.50 (ISBN 0-13-930503-3). P-H.

Treasurer's Guide. Executive Reports Corporation Editorial Staff. 1976. 97.50. Exec Reports.

Treasurer's Office Inventory. rev. & enl. ed. Compiled by Emily Salmon. xx, 55p. 1981. pap. 5.00 (ISBN 0-88490-103-3). VA State Lib.

Treasurer's Report; And Other Aspects of Community Singing. Robert Benchley. (Illus. by Guyas Williams). 1976. Repr. of 1938 ed. lib. bdg. 17.95x (ISBN 0-88411-304-3, Pub. by Aeonian Pr). Amereon Ltd.

Treasures. Darwin Gross. LC 88-90607. 150p. (Orig.). 1988. pap. 6.95 (ISBN 0-931689-11-2). SOS Pub OR.

Treasures see Word Studies in the Greek New Testament, for the English Reader.

Treasures & Rarities - Renaissance, Mannerist & Baroque: A Picture Book. LC 72-198355. (Illus.). 39p. 1971. pap. 4.00 (ISBN 0-911886-21-4). Walters Art.

Treasures Beneath the Sea. Robert Silverberg. (Illus.). 80p. (gr. 4-6). 1986. pap. 2.25 (ISBN 0-590-40245-5). Scholastic Inc.

Treasures Beyond the Snows. Marie A. Gouffe. LC 77-95392. Orig. Title: Jigme. (Illus.). (gr. 3-9). 1970. 3.75 (ISBN 0-8356-0026-2, Quest). Theos Pub Hse.

Treasures Found off Sinan Coast. Cultural Assets Maintenance Bureau Staff. 314p. 1983. 190.00x (ISBN 0-317-45328-9, Pub. by Han-Shan Tang Ltd). State Mutual Bk.

Treasures from Bible Times. Alan Millard. (Illus.). 192p. 14.95 (ISBN 0-85648-587-X). Lion USA.

Treasures from Chatsworth: The Devonshire Inheritance. Ed. by Anthony Blunt. LC 79-89141. (Illus.). 236p. (Orig.). 1979. soft bdg. 12.00 (ISBN 0-88397-007-4, Pub. by Intl Exhibit Foun). C E Tuttle.

Treasures from Earth's Storehouse. Juliet B. Ballard. 311p. (Orig.). 1980. pap. 8.95 (ISBN 0-87604-128-4). ARE Pr.

Treasures from Grandma. Arleta Richardson. (Grandma's Attic Ser.). (gr. 3 up). 1984. pap. 3.50 (59345). Cook.

Treasures from Holy Scripture. T. B. Maston. (Orig.). 1987. pap. 3.95 (ISBN 0-8054-5043-2). Broadman.

Treasures from India: The Clive Collection at Powis Castle. Mildred Archer et al. (Illus.). 144p. 1987. 25.00 (ISBN 0-941533-01-8). New Amsterdam Bks.

Treasures from Japan. Honolulu Academy of Arts Staff. (Illus.). 92p. 1957. 70.00x (ISBN 0-317-69284-4, Pub. by Han-Shan Tang Ltd). State Mutual Bk.

TITLE INDEX TREASURY OF AMERICAN SACRED

Treasures from Korea: Art Through 5000 Years. Roger Goepper & Roderick Whitfield. (Illus.). 224p. (Orig.). 1985. 40.00x (ISBN 0-253-36050-1); pap. 20.00x (ISBN 0-253-28860-6). Ind U Pr.
Treasures from Moscow Museums. B. Brodsky. 374p. 1980. 85.00x (ISBN 0-686-97673-8, Pub. by Collets (UK)). State Mutual Bk.
Treasures from Near Eastern Looms. Ernest H. Roberts. LC 81-68474. (Illus.). 1981. pap. 10.00 (ISBN 0-916606-02-3). Bowdoin Coll.
Treasures from Paul's Letters, Vol. I. A. M. Coniaris. 1978. pap. 7.95 (ISBN 0-937032-05-0). Light&Life Pub Co MN.
Treasures from Paul's Letters, Vol. II. A. M. Coniaris. 1979. pap. 7.95 (ISBN 0-937032-06-9). Light&Life Pub Co MN.
Treasures from Private Museums of Art in Japan. Tanaka. 1986. 580.00x (ISBN 0-317-68549-X, Pub. by Han-Shan Tang Ltd). State Mutual Bk.
Treasures from the Bodleian Library. A. G. Hassall et al. Intro. by D. R. Hunt. 180p. 1976. 210.00x (ISBN 0-900406-52-6, Pub. by Gordon Fraser). State Mutual Bk.
Treasures from the Bronze Age of China. Metropolitan Museum of Art Staff. 192p. 1980. 53.00x (ISBN 0-317-68602-X, Pub. by Han-Shan Tang Ltd). State Mutual Bk.
Treasures from the East: Chinese Export Porcelain for the Collector. rev. ed. Ed. by Elinor Gordon. LC 84-15515. (Illus.). 192p. 1984. pap. 11.95 (ISBN 0-915590-58-1). Main Street.
Treasures from the Kremlin: E. S. Sizov, Chief Curator of the State Museums of the Moscow Kremlin. E. S. Sizov. Tr. by John E. Bowlt. LC 79-1051. (Illus.). 224p. 1979. 9.95 (ISBN 0-87099-193-0); pap. 29.95 (ISBN 0-87099-192-2, MPLD2081). Metro Mus Art.
Treasures from the Language of Jesus. Rocco A. Errico. LC 87-70912. 131p. 1987. pap. 9.95 (ISBN 0-87516-594-X). DeVorss.
Treasures from the Meher Baba Journals. Meher Baba et al. Ed. by Jane B. Haynes. LC 79-92169. (Illus.). 246p. 1980. pap. 6.95 (ISBN 0-913078-37-9). Sheriar Pr.
Treasures from the Metropolitan Museum of Art. Laurance Roberts. 93p. 1979. 50.00x (ISBN 0-317-46380-2, Pub. by Han-Shan Tang Ltd). State Mutual Bk.
Treasures from the National Museum of American Art. William Kloss. LC 85-61846. (Illus.). 256p. 1986. 39.95 (ISBN 0-87474-594-2, KLTN). Smithsonian.
Treasures from The New York Public Library. Ed. by Richard Newman. (Illus.). 132p. (Orig.). 1985. pap. 12.95 (ISBN 0-87104-286-X). NY Pub Lib.
Treasures from the Rietberg Museum. Helmut Brinker & Eberhard Fischer. LC 80-12528. (Illus.). 176p. 1980. 19.95 (ISBN 0-87848-055-2). Asia Soc.
Treasures from the Shanghai Museum: 6,000 Years of Chinese Art. Rene-Yvon L. D'Argence. 191p. 1983. 98.00x (ISBN 0-317-46371-3, Pub. by Han-Shan Tang Ltd). State Mutual BK.
Treasures from the Shanghai Museum: 6,000 Years of Chinese Art. Ed. by Rene-Yvon Lefebvre d'Argence. LC 83-70559. (Illus.). 188p. 1983. pap. 14.95 (ISBN 0-295-96363-8, Pub by Museum of Fine Arts Houston). U of Wash Pr.
Treasures from the Shoso-In. Tokyo National Museum Staff. 151p. 1959. 150.00x (Pub. by Han-Shan Tang Ltd). State Mutual Bk.
Treasure's Golden Dream. Myra Rowe. 1988. pap. 3.95 (ISBN 0-446-32614-3). Warner Bks.
Treasures in Earthen Vessels: The Vows, a Wholistic Approach. Joyce Ridick. LC 84-2817. 166p. 1984. pap. 9.95 (ISBN 0-8189-0467-4). Alba.
Treasures in the Pages. Grace Slwooko. 1985. 6.95 (ISBN 0-8062-2252-2). Carlton.
Treasures in the Sea see Books for Young Explorers.
Treasures in Truck & Trash. Carl Drepperd. LC 78-86067. (Essay & General Literature Index Reprint Ser). 1969. Repr. of 1950 ed. 21.50x (ISBN 0-8046-0592-0, Pub by Kennikat). Assoc Faculty Pr.
Treasures, No. 2: Stories & Art by Students in Oregon. Ed. by Chris Weber. 256p. (Orig.). (gr. k-12). 1988. pap. 9.95 (ISBN 0-9616058-1-2). OR Students Writing.
Treasures of a Chinese Studio. T. C. Lai. 152p. 1976. 40.00x (ISBN 0-317-68696-8, Pub. by Han-Shan Tang Ltd). State Mutual Bk.
Treasures of Age. Peggy Scarborough. (International Correspondence Program Ser.). (Orig.). 1985. pap. text ed. 6.95 (ISBN 0-87148-856-6). Pathway Pr.
Treasures of American Architecture in Geneva, New York. H. Edmund Wirtz. (Illus., Orig.). 1986. pap. 6.95 (ISBN 0-9613821-2-0). Geneva Hist Soc Mus.
Treasures of American Folk Art: From the Abby Aldrich Rockefeller Folk Art Center. Beatrix T. Rumford & Carolyn J. Weekley. (Illus.). 1989. 35.00 (ISBN 0-8212-1726-7). NYGS.
Treasures of American West: Selections from the Collection of Harrison Eiteljorg. Harrison Eiteljorg. (Illus.). 176p. 1982. 45.00 (ISBN 0-9607596-0-3). Eiteljorg Pubns.
Treasures of Ancient Nigeria. Frank Willet & Ekpo Eyo. LC 79-3497. (Illus.). 1980. pap. 16.95 (ISBN 0-394-73858-6). Knopf.
Treasures of Ancient Oriental Art. 38p. 1964. pap. 105.00x (ISBN 0-317-68517-1, Pub. by Han-Shan Tang Ltd). State Mutual Bk.
Treasures of Asian Art from the Idemitsu Collection. Henry Trubner & William Rathbun. LC 81-52557. (Illus.). 204p. 1981. pap. 13.95 (ISBN 0-932216-06-4). Seattle Art.
Treasures of Britain. 3rd ed. Ed. by Automobile Association of England Staff. (Illus.). 1986. 27.95 (ISBN 0-393-08743-3). Norton.
Treasures of Chanukah. Illus. by Greg Hildebrandt. Ed. by Jean L. Scrocco. (Illus.). 48p. (ps up). 1987. 14.95 (ISBN 0-88101-071-5). Unicorn Pub.
Treasures of China. Annette Juliano. (Illus.). 192p. 1981. 35.00 (ISBN 0-399-90105-1, Marek). Putnam Pub Group.
Treasures of Christmas: The Guideposts Family Christmas Book. 80p. pap. 7.95 (ISBN 0-687-42560-3). Abingdon.
Treasures of Darkness: A History of Mesopotamian Religon. Thorkild Jacobsen. LC 75-27576. (Illus.). 1976. pap. 10.95x (ISBN 0-300-02291-3). Yale U Pr.
Treasures of Darkness: Meet the Carib! Minnie Pearman. 144p. 1984. 8.95 (ISBN 0-89962-428-6). Todd & Honeywell.
Treasures of Disney Animation Art. Robert E. Abrams & John Canemaker. LC 82-72998. (Illus.). 320p. 1982. 49.98 (ISBN 0-89659-581-1). Abbeville Pr.
Treasures of Esztergom Cathedral. Pal Csfalvay. 1984. 30.00x (ISBN 0-569-08828-3, Pub. by Collets (UK)). State Mutual Bk.
Treasures of Everyday Art. 1979. 25.00x (ISBN 0-8364-0519-6). South Asia Bks.
Treasures of Everyday Art: Raja Dinkar Kelkar Museum. Jyotindra Jain et al. LC 80-901921. (Illus.). 135p. 1979. 22.50x (ISBN 0-89684-459-5). Orient Bk Dist.
Treasures of Galveston Bay. Carroll Lewis. (Illus.). 1967. 10.00 (ISBN 0-87244-052-4). Texian.
Treasures of Half-Truths. Pat Bagley. 100p. 1986. pap. 4.95 (ISBN 0-941214-47-8). Signature Bks.
Treasures of History: Historic Buildings in Chaves County 1870-1935. Ed. by William E. Gibbs et al. LC 85-72824. (Illus.). 144p. (Orig.). 1986. pap. 6.95 (ISBN 0-9615310-2-9). Chaves Hist.
Treasures of Independence. John Milley. (Illus.). 224p. 1980. 25.00 (ISBN 0-8317-8593-4, Mayflower Bks). Smith Pubs.
Treasures of Indian Textiles. Calico Museum, Ahmedabad Staff. (Illus.). 148p. 1980. 49.95x (ISBN 0-940500-44-2). Asia Bk Corp.
Treasures of Iowa. Ed. by Charles W. Roberts & Mary Hirsch. (Illus.). 76p. (Orig.). 1987. pap. 4.95 (ISBN 0-317-61645-5). Mid Am Pub.
Treasures of Irish Art 1500 BC to 1500 AD. (Illus.). 224p. 1980. Repr. of 1977 ed. 36.95 (ISBN 0-85342-577-9, Pub. by Mercier Pr Ireland). Irish Bks Media.
Treasures of Kosan-JI Temple. Kyoto National Museum Staff. (Illus.). 250p. 1981. pap. 200.00x (Pub. by Han-Shan Tang Ltd). State Mutual Bk.
Treasures of Medieval Russia. B. Fabritsky & I Shmeliov. 336p. 1974. 40.00x (ISBN 0-317-14303-4, Pub. by Collets (UK)). State Mutual Bk.
Treasures of My Heart. Marjorie McLachlan Booker. 112p. 1978. 7.95 (ISBN 0-87881-068-4). Mojave Bks.
Treasures of Nature: Birds. Illus. by Gary Carpenter. (Illus.). 128p. (Orig.). 1988. pap. 4.95 (ISBN 0-89594-303-4). Crossing Pr.
Treasures of Nature: Ferns. Ed. by John Streams. 128p. (Orig.). 1987. pap. 4.95 (ISBN 0-89594-242-9). Crossing Pr.
Treasures of Nishihonganji Temple. Kyoto National Museum Staff. (Illus.). 142p. 1980. 250.00x (Pub. by Han-Shan Tang Ltd). State Mutual Bk.
Treasures of Simple Living: A Family's Search for a Simpler & More Meaningful Life in the Middle of a Forest. Tyra Arraj & James Arraj. LC 87-5990. (Illus.). 216p. (Orig.). 1987. pap. 11.95 (ISBN 0-914073-04-4). Inner Growth Bks.
Treasures of Taliesin: Seventy-Six Unbuilt Designs of Frank Lloyd Wright. Frank Lloyd Wright. Ed. by Bruce B. Pfeiffer. (Illus.). 168p. 1985. 60.00 (ISBN 0-8093-1235-2, Co-Pub. by Cal State Pr). S Ill U Pr.
Treasures of the American Arts & Crafts Movement 1890-1920. Tod Volpe & Beth Cathers. Text by Alastair Duncan. 1988. 49.50 (ISBN 0-8109-1695-9). Abrams.
Treasures of the Aquarians: The Sixties Rediscovered. Richard Davis & Jeff Stone. (Nonfiction Ser.). 96p. (Orig.). 1985. pap. 5.95 (ISBN 0-14-008036-8). Penguin.
Treasures of the Ashmolean Museum. Ashmolean Museum Staff. (Illus.). 112p. (Orig.). 1985. 25.00x (ISBN 0-907849-09-1, Pub. by Ashmolean Museum). State Mutual Bk.
Treasures of the Ashmolean Museum. Ashmolean Museum Staff. (Illus.). 112p. (Orig.). 1985. pap. 12.50 (ISBN 0-317-58686-6, Pub. by Ashmolean Mus). Longwood Pub Group.
Treasures of the Barrier Reef. Geoffrey T. Williams. (Illus.). 64p. (gr. 1-5). 1988. 9.95 (ISBN 0-8431-1941-1); incl. cass. 13.95 (ISBN 0-8431-1975-6). Price Stern.
Treasures of the British Museum. Marjorie Caygill. (Illus.). 240p. 1985. 29.95 (ISBN 0-8109-1687-8). Abrams.
Treasures of the Centuries. Ed. by Ivan Owechko. 112p. 1981. write for info. Ukrainian Pol.
Treasures of the Deep: Adventure Box I. Stephanos Attalides. LC 85-45420. (Illus.). 28p. (ps up). 1986. 3.95 (ISBN 0-694-00082-5). HarpJ.
Treasures of the Deep: Adventures of Undersea Exploration. Walter Oleksy. LC 83-22088. 190p. (YA) (gr. 7 up). 1984. PLB 9.79g (ISBN 0-671-42269-3). Messner.
Treasures of the Earth. Jessica Stirling. 384p. 1985. 15.95 (ISBN 0-312-81651-0). St Martin.
Treasures of the Forbidden City. Zhu Jiajin. LC 85-51256. 264p. 1986. 75.00 (ISBN 0-670-80795-8). Viking.
Treasures of the Heras Institute. Kalpana Desai. LC 76-905157. (Illus.). 1976. 20.00x (ISBN 0-88386-923-3). South Asia Bks.
Treasures of the Holy Land: A Visit to the Places of Christian Origins. Veselin Kesich & Lydia W. Kesich. LC 85-18403. (Illus., Orig.). 1985. pap. 7.95 (ISBN 0-88141-045-4). St Vladimirs.
Treasures of the Israel Museum, Jerusalem. The Israel Museum. (Illus.). 120p. 1985. 49.50 (ISBN 0-295-96444-8, Pub. by Israel Museum). U of Wash Pr.
Treasures of the Jewish Museum. Vivian B. Mann & Norman Kleeblatt. LC 85-28913. (Illus.). 216p. 1986. text ed. 35.00x (ISBN 0-87663-493-5); pap. 19.95 (ISBN 0-87663-890-6). Universe.
Treasures of the Library of Congress. Charles A. Goodrum. (Illus.). 456p. 1980. 55.00 (ISBN 0-8109-1661-4, 1661-4). Abrams.
Treasures of the New York Public Library. Marshall B. Davidson et al. 1988. 60.00 (ISBN 0-8109-1354-2). Abrams.
Treasures of the Night: Collected Poems of Jean Genet. Jean Genet. Tr. by Steven Finch from Fr. (Illus.). 120p. (Orig.). 1981. 25.00x (ISBN 0-917342-75-5); pap. 6.95 (ISBN 0-917342-76-3). Gay Sunshine.
Treasures of the Old West: Paintings & Sculpture from the Thomas Gilcrease Institute of American History & Art. Peter H. Hassrick. LC 83-13519. (Illus.). 128p. 1984. 35.00 (ISBN 0-8109-1781-5). Abrams.
Treasures of the Oregon Country: No. IV. Maynard C. Drawson. (Illus.). 1977. pap. 9.95 (ISBN 0-934476-03-9). Dee Pub Co.
Treasures of the Orthodox Church Museum in Finland. (Illus.). 124p. (Orig.). 1985. pap. text ed. 72.50x (Pub. by Almqvist & Wiksell). Coronet Bks.
Treasures of the Precious Moments. Ed. by Sal St. John Buttaci & Susan L. Gerstle. LC 85-61728. 140p. 1985. 18.98 (ISBN 0-917398-14-9). New Worlds.
Treasures of the Psychic Realm. Jack J. Studer. (Illus.). 1976. pap. 3.95 (ISBN 0-87516-226-6). DeVorss.
Treasures of the Royal Photographic Society. Intro. by Tom Hopkins. (Illus.). 24p. 1980. pap. 4.50 (ISBN 0-88397-028-7, Pub. by Intl Exhibit Foun). C E Tuttle.
Treasures of the Russian Museum. V. Pushkariov. 266p. 1975. 39.00x (ISBN 0-317-14324-7, Pub. by Collets (UK)). State Mutual Bk.
Treasures of the Sea: Marine Life of the Pacific Northwest. James A. Cribb. (Illus.). 1983. 24.95 (ISBN 0-19-540418-1). Oxford U Pr.
Treasures of the Smithsonian. Edwards Park. LC 83-40203. (Illus.). 496p. 1983. 60.00 (ISBN 0-89599-012-1, Dist. by Harry N. Abrams). Smithsonian Bks.
Treasures of the Smithsonian. Edwards Park. (Illus.). 496p. 1983. 60.00 (ISBN 0-8109-1680-0). Abrams.
Treasures of the Snow. Patricia St. John. (gr. 5-8). 1950. pap. 4.50 (ISBN 0-8024-0008-6). Moody.
Treasures of the Tropic Seas. Rene Catala. (Illus.). 336p. 1986. 50.00 (ISBN 0-8160-1590-2). Facts on File.
Treasures of the U. S. S. R. Diamond Fund. N. Ia. Baulin. 1980. 80.00x (ISBN 0-317-14304-2, Pub. by Collets (UK)). State Mutual Bk.
Treasures of the Vatican. M. Calvesi. 39.95 (ISBN 0-517-62643-8). Outlet Bk Co.
Treasures of Thrace. Gerda Von Bulow. (Illus.). 146p. 1988. 14.95x (ISBN 0-312-01524-0). St Martin.
Treasures of Wisdom: Studies in Colossians & Philemon. Homer A. Kent, Jr. pap. 5.95 (ISBN 0-88469-062-8). BMH Bks.
Treasures Old & New: Interpretations of "Spirit-Baptism" in the Charismatic Renewal Movement. Henry I. Lederle. 368p. 1987. pap. 14.95 (ISBN 0-913573-75-2). Hendrickson MA.
Treasures on Earth. James L. Brown. 1979. pap. 7.80. Academy Santa Clara.
Treasures on Earth. James L. Brown. LC 79-54075. 282p. 1979. pap. 7.50. J L Brown.
Treasures on Earth. Jessica Stirling. (Critic's Choice Paperbacks Ser.). 1989. pap. 3.95 (ISBN 1-55547-287-7, Univ Bks). Lyle Stuart.
Treasures on Earth. Carter Wilson. 256p. 1983. pap. 3.95 (ISBN 0-380-63305-1, 63305-1, Bard). Avon.
Treasures on the Tibetan Middle Way. Herbert V. Guenther. 156p. 1971. pap. 26.00x (ISBN 0-317-69464-2, Pub. by Han-Shan Tang Ltd). State Mutual Bk.
Treasures Originally from the Horyu-Ji. Tokyo National Museum Staff. 14p. 1959. 150.00x (Pub. by Han-Shan Tang Ltd). State Mutual Bk.
Treasures: Stories & Art by Students in Oregon. Ed. by Chris Weber. (Illus.). 256p. (Orig.). 1985. pap. 12.95 (ISBN 0-9616058-0-4). OR Students Writing.
Treasurie or Store-House of Similies. Robert Cawdrey. LC 75-171738. (English Experience Ser.: No. 365). 880p. 1971. Repr. of 1600 ed. 150.00 (ISBN 90-221-0365-X). Walter J Johnson.
Treasury Bills: Fourteen Point One Percent to Sixteen Percent. Financial Publishing Co. Staff. 128p. 1980. pap. 29.95 (ISBN 0-87600-566-0). Finan Pub.
Treasury Bills: Six Percent to Twelve Percent. Financial Publishing Co. Staff. 374p. 1983. pap. 35.00 (ISBN 0-87600-068-5). Finan Pub.
Treasury Bills: Sixteen Percent to Eighteen Percent. Financial Publishing Co. Staff. 128p. 1980. pap. 29.95 (ISBN 0-87600-666-7). Finan Pub.
Treasury Bills: Twelve Percent to Fourteen Percent. Financial Publishing Co. Staff. 127p. 1979. pap. write for info. (ISBN 0-87600-466-4). Finan Pub.
Treasury Bills: Two Percent To Six Percent. Financial Publishing Co. Staff. 374p. 1983. pap. 35.00 (ISBN 0-87600-066-9). Finan Pub.
Treasury Control: The Co-ordination of Financial & Economic Policy in Great Britain. Samuel H. Beer. LC 82-11843. viii, 138p. 1982. Repr. of 1957 ed. lib. bdg. 35.00x (ISBN 0-313-23626-7, BETRC). Greenwood.
Treasury Department's View of Oil Imports in 1975, 1979, & 1984: A Study in Contrasts. G. Henry Schuler. (Significant Issues Ser.: Vol. VII, No. 5). 98p. (Orig.). 1985. pap. text ed. 6.95 (ISBN 0-8191-6072-5, Pub. by CSIS). U Pr of Amer.
Treasury Department's View of Oil Imports in 1975, 1979, & 1984: A Study in Contrasts. Henry M. Schuler. (Significant Issues Ser.: Vol. VII, No. 5). 92p. 1985. 6.95 (ISBN 0-89206-082-4). CSI Studies.
Treasury Division Three of the Organization Executive Course see Organization Executive Course: An Encyclopedia of Scientology Policy (1950-1951, 1953-1974.
Treasury Enforcement Agent. 5th ed. Arco Publishing Company Staff & Eve P. Steinberg. LC 85-11235. 1985. 10.00 (ISBN 0-668-06418-8). Arco.
Treasury Enforcement Agent. Jack Rudman. (Career Examination Ser.: C-823). (Cloth bdg. avail. on request). pap. 15.00 (ISBN 0-8373-0823-2). Natl Learning.
Treasury Enforcement Agent. Eve P. Steinberg. Date not set. write for info. S&S.
Treasury for the Free World. Ed. by Ben Raeburn. LC 72-5771. (Essay Index Reprint Ser). 1972. Repr. of 1946 ed. 25.00 (ISBN 0-8369-7293-7). Ayer Co Pubs.
Treasury for Word Lovers. Morton Freeman. (Professional Writing Ser.). 333p. 1983. 19.95 (ISBN 0-89495-026-6); pap. 14.95 (ISBN 0-89495-027-4). ISI Pr.
Treasury Holiday. William Harmon. LC 78-120263. (Wesleyan Poetry Program: Vol. 53). (Orig.). 1970. 17.00x (ISBN 0-8195-2053-5); pap. 8.95 (ISBN 0-8195-1053-X). Wesleyan U Pr.
Treasury Line. Greg Whitwell. 320p. 1986. text ed. 29.95x (ISBN 0-86861-727-X). Unwin Hyman.
Treasury Management Handbook for Small Cities & Other Governmental Units. Municipal Finance Officers Association. LC 78-71725. (Illus.). 93p. 1978. 15.00 (ISBN 0-686-84374-6). Municipal.
Treasury Management: International Banking Operations. Alasdair Watson & Ron Altringham. 1985. 114.00x (ISBN 0-85297-142-7, Pub. by Inst of Bankers). State Mutual Bk.
Treasury Management Practioners' Handbook: A Practical Approach to Treasury Management in the Multinational Corporation. John B. Giannotti & Richard W. Smith. LC 8-1523. 536p. 1981. 64.50x (Pub. by Wiley Interscience). Wiley.
Treasury Note & Bond Futures Conversion Tables. Financial Publishing Co. Staff. 32p. 1982. pap. 6.50 (ISBN 0-87600-765-5). Finan Pub.
Treasury of A. W. Tozer. A. W. Tozer. 1979. 9.95 (ISBN 0-87509-281-0). Chr Pubns.
Treasury of African Art from the Harrison Eiteljorg Collection. Theodore Celenko. LC 82-47954. (Illus.). 240p. 1984. 57.50x (ISBN 0-253-11057-2). Ind U Pr.
Treasury of African Folklore. Harold Courlander. 640p. 1974. 14.95 (ISBN 0-517-51670-5). Crown.
Treasury of Afro-American Folklore. Harold Courlander. 1976. 14.95 (ISBN 0-517-52348-5); pap. 6.95 o. p. (ISBN 0-517-52584-4). Crown.
Treasury of Albert Schweitzer. facs. ed. Albert Schweitzer. Ed. by Thomas Kiernan. LC 73-136651. (Biography Index Reprint Ser). 1965. 21.00 (ISBN 0-8369-8046-8). Ayer Co Pubs.
Treasury of American Pen & Ink Illustration: 222 Drawings by 99 Artists, 1890-1930. Ed. by Fridolf Johnson. (Illus.). 176p. 1982. pap. 6.50 (ISBN 0-486-24280-3). Dover.
Treasury of American Poetry: A Collection of the Finest by America's Poets. Intro. by Nancy Sullivan. LC 77-92232. 1978. 21.50 (ISBN 0-385-12032-X). Doubleday.
Treasury of American Sacred Song. facs. ed. W. G. Horder. LC 74-76944. (Granger Index Reprint Ser). 1896. 18.00 (ISBN 0-8369-6019-X). Ayer Co Pubs.

Treasury of American Verse. Walter Learned. LC 74-86799. (Granger Index Reprint Ser). 1897. 26.50 (ISBN 0-8369-6081-5). Ayer Co Pubs.
Treasury of American Wildlife, 4 vols. Set. 39.00 (ISBN 0-87827-354-9). Ency Brit Ed.
Treasury of American Writers from Harpers Magazine. 1985. 7.98 (ISBN 0-517-48074-3). Outlet Bk Co.
Treasury of Animal Stories. Linda Yeatman. Ed. by Kate Klimo. (Illus.). 160p. (gr. k-4). 1982. 6.95 (ISBN 0-671-45632-6, Little Simon). S&S.
Treasury of Aphoristic Jewels: The Subhasitaratnanidhi of Sa Skya Pandita in Tibetan & Mongolian. James E. Bosson. (Uralic & Altaic Ser: Vol. 92). 1969. pap. text ed. 19.95x (ISBN 0-87750-080-0). Res Ctr Lang Semiotic.
Treasury of Art Nouveau Design & Ornament. Carol B. Grafton. (Pictorial Archive Ser.). (Illus.). 144p. (Orig.). 1980. pap. 5.95 (ISBN 0-486-24001-0). Dover.
Treasury of Art Nouveau Design & Ornament. Carol Belanger Grafton. 1983. 15.75 (ISBN 0-8446-5949-5). Peter Smith.
Treasury of Asian Literature. Ed. by John D. Yohannan. 1959. pap. 4.95 (ISBN 0-451-62395-9, ME1936, Ment). NAL.
Treasury of Authentic Art Nouveau: Alphabets, Decorative Initials, Monograms, Frames & Ornaments. Ed. by L. Petzendorfer. (Lettering, Caligraphy, Typography Ser.). 160p. 1984. pap. 6.95 (ISBN 0-486-24653-1). Dover.
Treasury of Ba-Suto Lore, 2 vols. in 1. E. Jacottet. LC 78-67723. (Folktale Ser.). Repr. of 1908 ed. 27.50 (ISBN 0-404-16098-0). AMS Pr.
Treasury of Baby Names. Alan Benjamin. 1983. pap. 2.95 (ISBN 0-451-13356-0, Sig). NAL.
Treasury of Bed & Breakfast. 2nd ed. American Bed & Breakfast Association. Ed. by Sarah W. Sonke. (Illus.). 201p. 1986. pap. 14.95 (ISBN 0-934473-01-3). Am Bed & Breakfast.
Treasury of Bed & Breakfast. 2nd, rev. ed. American Bed & Breakfast Association Staff. 201p. 1986. pap. 14.95 (ISBN 0-915765-23-3). Am Bed & Breakfast.
Treasury of Bed & Breakfast. 3rd, rev. ed. American Bed & Breakfast Association Staff. 189p. 1987. pap. 14.95. Am Bed & Breakfast.
Treasury of Bedtime Stories. Illus. by Hilda Offen. (Illus.). 160p. (ps-3). 1981. 8.95 (ISBN 0-671-44463-8, Little Simon). S&S.
Treasury of Best Loved Songs: 114 All-Time Family Favorites. Ed. by Reader's Digest Editors. LC 71-183858. (Illus.). 288p. 1972. Lie-flat spiral bdg. 26.95 (ISBN 0-89577-007-5, Pub. by RD Assn). Random.
Treasury of Bible Subjects. Mrs. John G. Weaver. 1986. 6.75. Rod & Staff.
Treasury of Bookplates from the Renaissance to the Present. Fridolf Johnson. (Illus.). 1978. pap. 6.50 (ISBN 0-486-23485-1). Dover.
Treasury of Bookplates from the Renaissance to the Present. Ed. by Fridolf Johnson. (Illus.). 14.75 (ISBN 0-8446-5587-2). Peter Smith.
Treasury of Books for Family Enjoyment: Books for Children from Infancy to Grade 2. Elouise Daniel. (Illus.). 122p. (Orig.). 1983. pap. text ed. 8.95 (ISBN 0-9611370-0-2). Blue Engine.
Treasury of British Eloquence. Robert Cochrane. 1902. Repr. 50.00 (ISBN 0-8274-3644-0). R West.
Treasury of British Humor. facs. ed. Ed. by Morris Bishop. (Granger Index Reprint Ser). 1942. 35.00 (ISBN 0-8369-6194-3). Ayer Co Pubs.
Treasury of British Humour. Morris Bishop. 1977. Repr. of 1942 ed. lib. bdg. 30.00 (ISBN 0-8495-0302-7). Arden Lib.
Treasury of Calligraphy: Two Hundred Nineteen Great Examples, 1522-1840. Jan Tschichold. 244p. 1984. pap. 9.95 (ISBN 0-486-24700-7). Dover.
Treasury of Canadian Verse. facs. ed. Theodore H. Rand. LC 76-75717. (Granger Index Reprint Ser). 1900. 21.00 (ISBN 0-8369-6039-4). Ayer Co Pubs.
Treasury of Catholic Digest: Favorite Stories of Fifty Years, 1936-1986. Henry Lexau. LC 86-81597. 598p. 1986. 24.95 (ISBN 0-89870-115-5). Ignatius Pr.
Treasury of Catholic Wisdom. John A. Hardon. LC 86-19648. 768p. 1987. pap. 27.50 (ISBN 0-385-23079-6). Doubleday.
Treasury of Charted Designs for Needleworkers. Georgia Gorham & Jeanne Warth. (Illus.). 1978. pap. 2.50 (ISBN 0-486-23558-0). Dover.
Treasury of Chassidic Tales on the Festivals, 2 vols. Shlomo Y. Zevin. Tr. by Uri Kaploun from Hebrew. (Art Scroll Judaica Classics Ser.). 320p. 1981. Vol. 1 Rosh Hashanah-Yom Kippur-Succos-Chanukah-Purim. 14.95 (ISBN 0-89906-912-6); pap. 11.95; Vol. 2 Pesach-Shavuos-Tisha B'av. 14.95 (ISBN 0-89906-914-2); pap. 11.95 (ISBN 0-89906-915-0); slipcased 31.95. Mesorah Pubns.
Treasury of Chassidic Tales: On the Torah, 2 vols. Shlomo Y. Zevin. Tr. by Uri Kaploun. (Art Scroll Judaica Classics Ser.). 352p. 1980. 14.95; Vol. I: Bereishis-Shemous. pap. 11.95 (ISBN 0-89906-901-0) (ISBN 0-89906-902-9). Vol. II: Vayikra-Bamidbar-Devarim. pap. 11.95 (ISBN 0-89906-903-7); Set. 31.95 (ISBN 0-89906-904-5). Mesorah Pubns.
Treasury of Children's Classics in Spanish & English. (Illus.). 176p. (gr. 4 up). Date not set. pap. 7.95 (ISBN 0-8442-7145-4, Passport Bks). Natl Textbk.
Treasury of Chinese Design Motifs. Joseph D'Addetta. (Illus.). 108p. pap. 4.95 (ISBN 0-486-24167-X). Dover.
Treasury of Christian Classics. Bd. with Greatest Thing in the World; As a Man Thinketh; Acres of Diamonds; Practice of the Presence of God. (Christian Library). 241p. 6.95 (ISBN 0-916441-47-4). Barbour & Co.
Treasury of Christian Poetry. Compiled by Lorraine Eitel. 192p. 1982. 12.95 (ISBN 0-8007-1291-9). Revell.
Treasury of Christmas Songs & Carols. 2nd ed. Henry A. Simon. 1973. 16.95 (ISBN 0-395-17786-3); pap. 9.95 (ISBN 0-395-17785-5). HM.
Treasury of Civil War Stories. Ed. by Martin Greenberg & Bill Pronzini. 7.98 (46781X). Outlet Bk Co.
Treasury of Civil War Tales. Webb Garrison. 1988. 14.95 (ISBN 0-934395-95-0). Rutledge Hill Pr.
Treasury of Classical & Islamic Coins: The Collection of Anman Museum. Adia Dr. Arif. 1986. text ed. 45.00 (ISBN 0-317-66009-8). Intl Bk Ctr.
Treasury of Clean Business Jokes. Tal D. Bonham. LC 85-4134. 1985. pap. 3.50 (ISBN 0-8054-5712-7). Broadman.
Treasury of Clean Church Jokes. Tal D. Bonham. LC 85-26837. 1986. pap. 3.50 (ISBN 0-8054-5719-4). Broadman.
Treasury of Clean Country Jokes. Tal D. Bonham. LC 85-28045. 1986. pap. 3.50 (ISBN 0-8054-5717-8). Broadman.
Treasury of Clean Jokes. Tal D. Bonham. LC 80-67639. (Orig.). 1981. pap. 3.50 (ISBN 0-8054-5703-8). Broadman.
Treasury of Clean Jokes for Children. Tal D. Bonham. (Orig.). (gr. 1-6). 1987. pap. 3.50 (ISBN 0-8054-5721-6). Broadman.
Treasury of Clean Senior Adult Jokes. Tal D. Bonham & Jack Gulledge. (Orig.). 1989. pap. 3.50 (ISBN 0-8054-5736-4). Broadman.
Treasury of Clean Sports Jokes. Tal D. Bonham. LC 85-27997. 1986. pap. 3.50 (ISBN 0-8054-5718-6). Broadman.
Treasury of Clean Teenage Jokes. Tal D. Bonham. LC 85-4134. (gr. 7 up). 1985. pap. 3.50 (ISBN 0-8054-5713-5, 4257-13). Broadman.
Treasury of Comfort. Ed. by Sidney Greenberg. 1967. 12.50 (ISBN 0-87677-022-7). Hartmore.
Treasury of Comfort. Ed. by Sidney S. Greenberg. pap. 5.00 (ISBN 0-87980-167-0). Wilshire.
Treasury of Crochet Patterns. Liz Blackwell. (Illus.). 1979. 16.95 (ISBN 0-684-16320-9, ScribT). Scribner.
Treasury of Crocheted Sweaters. LC 84-52752. (Illus.). 168p. 1985. 18.95 (ISBN 0-02-496730-0, Pub by Sedgewood Press). MacMillan.
Treasury of Cross-Stitch Samplers. Sharon Perna. LC 86-23146. (Illus.). 144p. 1988. 19.95 (ISBN 0-8069-6474-X). Sterling.
Treasury of Damon Runyon. Damon Runyon. Ed. by Clark Kinnaird. LC 58-6363. 1958. 6.95 (ISBN 0-394-60444-X). Modern Lib.
Treasury of David, 7 vols. C. H. Spurgen. 1983. Set. 75.00 (ISBN 0-686-40818-7). Pilgrim Pubns.
Treasury of David, 2 vols. Charles H. Spurgeon. 1983. Set. 45.00 (ISBN 0-8010-8256-0). Baker Bk.
Treasury of David - A Commentary on the Psalms, 3 vols. C. H. Spurgeon. 2912p. Date not set. 49.95 (ISBN 0-917006-25-9). Hendrickson MA.
Treasury of Design for Artists & Craftsmen. Gregory Mirow. LC 69-18877. (Pictoral Archive Ser). 1969. pap. 4.95 (ISBN 0-486-22002-8). Dover.
Treasury of Designs for Artists & Craftsmen. Gregory Mirow. (Illus.). 14.75 (ISBN 0-8446-0804-1). Peter Smith.
Treasury of Designs for Lace Net Embroidery. Ed. by Rita Weiss. (Embroidery, Needlepoint, Charted Designs Ser.). 48p. 1985. pap. 2.95 (ISBN 0-486-24840-2). Dover.
Treasury of Devotion. A. J. Russell. 432p. 1986. 15.95 (ISBN 0-396-08885-6). Dodd.
Treasury of Disney Little Golden Books. (ps-2). 1972. 7.95 (ISBN 0-307-17865-X, Golden Bks). Western Pub.
Treasury of Early Music. Carl Parrish. (Illus.). 1964. pap. 8.95x (ISBN 0-393-09444-8, NortonC). records avail. Norton.
Treasury of Edith Hamilton. Ed. by Doris F. Reid. LC 70-90989. 1969. 5.00 (ISBN 0-393-04313-4). Norton.
Treasury of Embroidery Samples. Ondori Publishing Company Staff. LC 80-84416. (Illus.). 96p. 1981. pap. 6.50 (ISBN 0-87040-496-2). Japan Pubns USA.
Treasury of English Church Music 1545-1650. Ed. by Peter Le Huray. 250p. 1982. pap. 19.95 (ISBN 0-521-28405-8). Cambridge U Pr.
Treasury of English Literature. Kate Warren. 1977. Repr. of 1906 ed. 27.00. Century Bookbindery.
Treasury of English Prose. Ed. by Logan P. Smith. 215p. Repr. of 1984 ed. lib. bdg. 27.50 (ISBN 0-89987-948-9). Darby Bks.
Treasury of English Verse: New & Old. facsimile ed. Ed. by A. S. Collins. LC 79-168778. (Granger Index Reprint Ser.). Repr. of 1931 ed. 22.00 (ISBN 0-8369-6298-2). Ayer Co Pubs.
Treasury of Evangelical Writings. Ed. by David O. Fuller. LC 61-9768. 472p. 1974. pap. 11.95 (ISBN 0-8254-2613-8). Kregel.
Treasury of Fairy Tales with Classic Illustrations. Ed. by Michal Foss. (Illus.). 160p. 1986. 29.00x (ISBN 0-948397-30-6, Pub. by M O'Mara UK). State Mutual Bk.
Treasury of Fantastic & Mythological Creatures: 1,087 Renderings from Historic Sources. Richard Huber. (Illus.). 160p. (Orig.). 1981. pap. 6.95 (ISBN 0-486-24174-2). Dover.
Treasury of Farm & Ranch Humor. James E. Myers. (Illus.). 325p. 1989. pap. 10.95 (ISBN 0-942936-15-9). Lincoln Herndon Pr.
Treasury of Flower Designs for Artists, Embroiderers & Craftsmen: 100 Garden Favorites. Susan Gaber. (Illus.). 80p. (Orig.). 1981. pap. 3.95 (ISBN 0-486-24096-7). Dover.
Treasury of French Dolls. Lydia Richter. LC 84-80436. (Illus.). 128p. 1984. 19.95 (ISBN 0-89586-329-4). Price Stern.
Treasury of Georgia Folklore. Ronald G. Killion & Charles T. Waller. LC 72-88901. (Illus.). 288p. 1972. bds. 14.95 (ISBN 0-87797-022-X). Cherokee.
Treasury of Georgia Tales. Webb Garrison. LC 87-23255. (Illus.). 160p. 1987. 8.95 (ISBN 0-934395-66-7). Rutledge Hill Pr.
Treasury of German Dolls. Lydia Richter. LC 84-80438. (Illus.). 160p. 1984. 19.95 (ISBN 0-89586-328-6). Price Stern.
Treasury of German Trademarks: 1850-1925, Vol. 1. Leslie Cabarga. LC 81-71799. (Illus.). 160p. 1982. 17.50 (ISBN 0-910158-89-4). Art Dir.
Treasury of German Trademarks, 1925-1950, Vol. 2. Leslie Cabarga. LC 81-71799. 156p. 17.50 (ISBN 0-88108-007-1). Art Dir.
Treasury of Great Books. Ed. by Reader's Digest Editors. LC 80-50421. (Illus.). 640p. 1980. 17.97 (ISBN 0-89577-084-9). RD Assn.
Treasury of Great Historical Novels, 2 Vols. Ed. by Reader's Digest Editors. LC 83-17664. (Illus.). 1248p. 1984. Set. 19.95 (ISBN 0-89577-176-4). RD Assn.
Treasury of Great Hymns: And Their Stories. Guye Johnson. 382p. (Orig.). 1985. pap. 11.95 (ISBN 0-89084-249-3). Bob Jones Univ Pr.
Treasury of Handicapping Methods. rev. ed. Ed. by Henry D. Bomze. 172p. pap. 9.95 (ISBN 0-89709-169-8). Liberty Pub.
Treasury of Hawaiian Words: In One Hundred & One Categories. Harold W. Kent. LC 86-788. 504p. 1986. text ed. 30.00x (ISBN 0-8248-1071-6). UH Pr.
Treasury of Helpful Verse. facsimile ed. Ed. by John W. Chadwick & Annie H. Chadwick. LC 73-76933. (Granger Index Reprint Ser). 1896. 17.00 (ISBN 0-8369-6007-6). Ayer Co Pubs.
Treasury of His Promises. Graham Miller. 386p. (Orig.). 1986. pap. 14.95 (ISBN 0-85151-472-3). Banner of Truth.
Treasury of Home Business Opportunities. Bernard H. Porter. 1986. 42.50 (ISBN 0-317-55094-2). Bern Porter.
Treasury of Home Business Opportunities. 1987. lib. bdg. 79.00 (ISBN 0-8490-3882-0). Gordon Pr.
Treasury of Home Business Opportunities. Russ Von Hoelscher. 344p. 1984. 14.95 (ISBN 0-940398-08-7). Profit Ideas.
Treasury of Home Business Opportunities. rev. ed. Russ Von Hoelscher. 382p. 1985. 14.95 (ISBN 0-940398-13-3). Profit Ideas.
Treasury of Home Remedies. Myra Cameron. 340p. 1987. 21.95 (ISBN 0-13-930637-4); pap. 9.95 (ISBN 0-13-930645-5). Prentice Hall Pr.
Treasury of Houseplants. Rob Herwig & Margot Schubert. (Illus.). 368p. 1984. write for info. (ISBN 0-02-551170-X); pap. 14.95 (ISBN 0-02-063120-0, Collier). Macmillan.
Treasury of Humor in Large Print. Ed. by Pinky Chin & Daphne Abeel. (Large Print Books-Reference). 616p. 1985. lib. bdg. 17.95 (ISBN 0-8161-3937-7). G K Hall.
Treasury of Humorous Poetry. facs. ed. Ed. by Frederic L. Knowles. LC 71-75713. (Granger Index Reprint Ser). 1902. 22.00 (ISBN 0-8369-6023-8). Ayer Co Pubs.
Treasury of Humorous Writing. Ed. by Reader's Digest Editors. LC 85-19636. (Illus.). 640p. 1988. 19.95 (ISBN 0-89577-224-8). RD Assn.
Treasury of Illuminated Borders in Full Color. Ed. by Carol B. Grafton. (Pictorial Archive Ser.). (Illus.). 48p. (Orig.). 1988. pap. 7.95t (ISBN 0-486-25699-5). Dover.
Treasury of Indian Tales: Book I. Shankar. (Illus.). (YA) (gr. 8-12). 1979. 4.95 (ISBN 0-89744-170-2). Auromere.
Treasury of Indian Tales: Book II. Shankar. (Illus.). (YA) (gr. 8-12). 1979. 4.95 (ISBN 0-89744-171-0). Auromere.
Treasury of Investment Literature. Ed. by Charles D. Ellis. 250p. 1988. 37.50 (ISBN 1-55623-098-2). Dow Jones-Irwin.
Treasury of Irish Folklore. rev. ed. Ed. by Padraic Colum. (YA) (gr. 9 up). 1969. 14.95 (ISBN 0-517-50294-1). Crown.
Treasury of Irish Poetry in the English Tongue. Ed. by Stopford A. Brooke & T. W. Rolleston. 1971. Repr. of 1932 ed. 79.00 (ISBN 0-403-00841-7). Scholarly.
Treasury of Irish Religious Verse. Ed. by Patrick Murray. 1986. 17.95 (ISBN 0-8245-0776-2). Crossroad NY.
Treasury of Irish Saints. John Irvine. (gr. 1 up). Date not set. 7.95 (ISBN 0-85105-902-3, Pub. by Colin Smythe Ltd Britain). Dufour.
Treasury of Jamaican Poetry. Ed. by John E. McFarlane. 1977. lib. bdg. 59.95 (ISBN 0-8490-2760-8). Gordon Pr.
Treasury of Japanese Designs & Motifs for Artists & Craftsmen. Ed. by Carol B. Grafton. (Illus.). 96p. (Orig.). 1982. pap. 4.50 (ISBN 0-486-24435-0). Dover.
Treasury of Jewels & Gems. M. Curran. 1960. 12.95 (ISBN 0-87523-139-X). Emerson.
Treasury of Jewish Folklore. Ed. by Nathan Ausubel. 1948. 14.95 (ISBN 0-517-50293-3). Crown.
Treasury of Jewish Folksong. Ed. by Ruth Rubin. LC 50-14685. (Illus.). 224p. 1976. 12.50 (ISBN 0-8052-0528-4). Schocken.
Treasury of Jewish Humor. Ed. by Nathan Ausubel. 768p. 1988. pap. 14.95 (ISBN 0-87131-546-7). M Evans.
Treasury of Jewish Quotations. Ed. by Joseph L. Baron. LC 85-3857. 623p. 1985. 25.00 (ISBN 0-87668-894-6). Aronson.
Treasury of Kahlil Gibran. Kahlil Gibran. 7.95 (ISBN 0-8065-0260-6, Pub. by Citadel Pr). Lyle Stuart.
Treasury of Kahlil Gibran. Kahlil Gibran. Ed. by Martin L. Wolf. Tr. by Anthony R Ferris from Arabic. 448p. 1974. pap. 7.95 (ISBN 0-8065-0410-2, Pub. by Citadel Pr). Lyle Stuart.
Treasury of Kathe Kruse Dolls. Lydia Richter. LC 84-80437. (Illus.). 128p. 1984. 19.95 (ISBN 0-89586-331-6). Price Stern.
Treasury of Knitting Patterns. Barbara G. Walker. (Illus.). 320p. 1981. pap. 16.95 (ISBN 0-684-17314-X, ScribT). Scribner.
Treasury of Little Golden Books. Ed. by Ellen L. Buell. 96p. (ps-2). 1982. 8.95 (ISBN 0-307-96540-6, Golden Bks). Western Pub.
Treasury of Mahayana Sutras: Selections from the Maharatnakuta Sutra. Ed. by Garma C. C. Chang. Tr. by Buddhist Association of the United States. LC 82-42776. (Institute for Advanced Study of World Religions (IASWR) Ser.). 512p. 1983. 26.75x (ISBN 0-271-00341-3). Pa St U Pr.
Treasury of Mandaya & Mansaka Folk Literature. Tr. by Vilma M. Fuentes & Edito T. De La Cruz. (Illus.). 130p. (Mandaya & Mansaka.). 1980. newsprint 5.00x (ISBN 0-686-28808-4, Pub by New Day Pub.). Cellar.
Treasury of Marketing of Physicians. Ed. by Eleanor M. Walker. (Treasury of Healthcare Marketing Ser.: Vol. 2). (Illus.). 88p. (Orig.). 1988. pap. 77.00 (ISBN 0-932577-03-2). Wentworth Pub.
Treasury of Middle English Verse. Margot R. Adamson. LC 73-9719. 1930. lib. bdg. 30.00 (ISBN 0-8414-2858-1). Folcroft.
Treasury of Mississippi River Folklore. B. A. Botkin. 640p. 1984. 9.98 (ISBN 0-517-24605-8). Crown.
Treasury of Mme. Alexander Dolls. Jan Foulke. (Illus.). 102p. pap. 9.95 (ISBN 0-87588-147-5, 2270). Hobby Hse.
Treasury of Modern Asian Stories. Ed. by William Clifford & Daniel Milton. pap. 2.95 (ISBN 0-452-25052-8, Z5052, Plume). NAL.
Treasury of Modern Biography: A Gallery of Literary Sketches of Eminent Men & Women of the 19th Century. Robert Cochrane. 1881. Repr. 50.00 (ISBN 0-8274-3645-9). R West.
Treasury of Modern Biography: A Gallery of Literary Sketches of Eminent Men & Women of the Nineteenth Century. Ed. by Robert Cochrane. 544p. 1984. Repr. of 1885 ed. lib. bdg. 75.00 (ISBN 0-918377-20-X). Russell Pr.
Treasury of Mother Goose. Illus. by Hilda Offen. (Illus.). (gr. 1 up). Date not set. 8.95 (ISBN 0-671-50118-6, Little Simon). S&S.
Treasury of Nebraska Pioneer Folklore. Compiled by Roger L. Welsch. LC 66-10876. (Illus.). xviii, 391p. 1984. pap. 9.95 (ISBN 0-8032-9707-6, BB 883, Bison). U of Nebr Pr.
Treasury of Needlecraft Gifts for the New Baby. Jean R. Laury. LC 76-12186. (Illus.). 192p. 1976. 12.95 (ISBN 0-8008-7858-2). Taplinger.
Treasury of New England Folklore. Benjamin A. Botkin. 640p. 1984. 9.98 (ISBN 0-517-10918-2). Crown.
Treasury of New Testament Synonyms. Stewart Custer. 161p. 1975. 8.95 (ISBN 0-89084-025-3). Bob Jones Univ Pr.
Treasury of North American Birdlore. Rev. ed. Ed. by Paul S. Eriksson & Joseph W. Krutch. Alan Pistorious. LC 62-16745. 420p. 1987. 24.95 (ISBN 0-8397-8372-8). Eriksson.
Treasury of Novenas. Lawrence G. Lovasik. 352p. 1986. pap. 4.95 (ISBN 0-89942-345-0, 345/22). Catholic Bk Pub.
Treasury of Old & Historical American & British Furniture. Charles E. Dunsworth. (Illus.). 187p. 1983. 137.45 (ISBN 0-86650-067-7). Gloucester Art.
Treasury of Orthodox Hymnology: The Triodion. Savas J. Savas. 1983. pap. 4.95 (ISBN 0-937032-32-8). Light&Life Pub Co MN.
Treasury of Our Western Heritage: The Favell Museum of Western Art & Indian Artifacts. (Illus.). 1986. 19.75 (ISBN 0-317-57138-9). Favell Mus.

Treasury of Outdoor Life: The Greatest Hunting, Fishing, and Survival Stories from America's Favorite Sportsman's Magazine. Ed. by William E. Rae. (Illus.). 520p. 1983. 24.95 (ISBN 0-943822-17-3). Stackpole.

Treasury of Parenthood & Its Folklore. Claudia De Lys. 5.00 (ISBN 0-8315-0016-6). Speller.

Treasury of Peter Rabbit & Other Stories. Beatrix Potter. (Illus.). (gr. k up). 1985. 5.98 (ISBN 0-517-23948-5). Outlet Bk Co.

Treasury of Pineapple Designs for Crocheting. Ed. by Linda Macho. (Illus.). 48p. (Orig.). 1983. pap. 2.75 (ISBN 0-486-24494-6). Dover.

Treasury of Plays for Women. Ed. by Frank Shay. LC 79-50030. (One-Act Plays in Reprint Ser.). 1980. 34.50x (ISBN 0-8486-2054-2). Roth Pub Inc.

Treasury of Prayer. E. M. Bounds. LC 53-9865. 192p. 1981. pap. 5.95 (ISBN 0-87123-543-9, 210543). Bethany Hse.

Treasury of Quotations on Religious Subjects. F. B. Proctor. LC 76-15741. 832p. 1976. 21.95 (ISBN 0-8254-3500-5). Kregel.

Treasury of Raw Foods. Edmond B. Szekely. (Illus.). 48p. 1981. pap. 2.95 (ISBN 0-89564-042-2). IBS Intl.

Treasury of Russian Life & Humor. Ed. by John Cournos. 676p. 1984. Repr. of 1943 ed. lib. bdg. 45.00. Century Bookbindery.

Treasury of Russian Life & Humor. Ed. by John Cournos. 676p. 1984. Repr. of 1943 ed. lib. bdg. 75.00 (ISBN 0-89987-199-2). Darby Bks.

Treasury of Russian Literature. Ed. by Bernard G. Guerney. LC 43-17369. (Illus.). 1050p. 25.00 (ISBN 0-8149-0113-1). Vanguard.

Treasury of Russian Verse. facs. ed. Ed. by Avrahm Yarmolinsky. LC 79-80370. (Granger Index Reprint Ser). 1949. 21.00 (ISBN 0-8369-6093-9). Ayer Co Pubs.

Treasury of San Marco, Venice. David Buckton. (Illus.). 354p. 1984. pap. 30.00 (ISBN 0-295-96327-1). U of Wash Pr.

Treasury of San Marco, Venice. (Illus.). 340p. 1987. 60.00 (ISBN 0-8109-1684-3). Abrams.

Treasury of Satsuma. Sandra Andacht. 160p. 1981. 24.95 (ISBN 0-87069-318-2); price guide 1.50 (ISBN 0-87069-319-0). Wallace-Homestead.

Treasury of Science Jokes. Morris Goran. (Illus.). 136p. (Orig.). 1987. pap. 8.95 (ISBN 0-942936-09-4); pap. 8.95. Lincoln-Herndon Pr.

Treasury of Scripture Knowledge. R. A. Torrey. 784p. 1973. 21.95 (ISBN 0-8007-0324-3). Revell.

Treasury of Scripture Knowledge. R. A. Torrey. 778p. Date not set. 17.95 (ISBN 0-917006-22-4). Hendrickson MA.

Treasury of Scripture Knowledge. 778p. 1987. bonded leather 19.95 (ISBN 0-916441-99-7). Barbour & Co.

Treasury of Sephardic Laws & Customs. Dobrinsky. Date not set. pap. 16.95. Ktav.

Treasury of Sephardic Laws & Customs. Hebert Dobrinsky. 500p. 1986. 29.50x (ISBN 0-88125-031-7); pap. text ed. 16.95. Ktav.

Treasury of Smocking Designs. Allyne S. Holland. 48p. (Orig.). 1985. pap. 3.50 (ISBN 0-486-24991-3). Dover.

Treasury of Stencil Designs for Artists & Craftsmen. Ed. by Martin Isaacson & Dorothy Rennie. LC 75-46105. (Pictorial Archive Ser.). (Illus.). 64p. (Orig.). 1976. pap. 3.50 (ISBN 0-486-23307-3). Dover.

Treasury of Stencil Designs for Artists & Craftsmen. Martin J. Isaacson & Dorothy A. Rennie. 12.50 (ISBN 0-8446-5469-8). Peter Smith.

Treasury of Success Unlimited. Og Mandino. 1984. pap. 3.95. PB.

Treasury of Successful Appeal Letters. Ed. by Joseph Dermer. 1985. pap. 49.50 (ISBN 0-914977-07-5). Public Serv Materials.

Treasury of Tennessee Churches. Mayme H. Johnson. (Illus.). 160p. 1986. 29.95 (ISBN 0-939298-60-0, 600). J M Prods.

Treasury of Tennessee Tales. James Ewing. LC 85-18256. (Illus.). 144p. 1985. 7.95 (ISBN 0-934395-04-7). Rutledge Hill Pr.

Treasury of the Art of Living. Sidney Greenberg. pap. 5.00 (ISBN 0-87980-168-9). Wilshire.

Treasury of the Art of Living. Ed. by Sidney Greenberg. 1964. 12.50 (ISBN 0-87677-019-7). Hartmore.

Treasury of the Bible, 8 vols. Charles H. Spurgeon. 295.00 (ISBN 0-8010-8210-2). Baker Bk.

Treasury of the Great Children's Book Illustrators. Susan E. Meyer. LC 83-2500. (Illus.). 272p. 1983. 45.00 (ISBN 0-8109-0782-8). Abrams.

Treasury of the Great Children's Book Illustrators. 272p. 1987. 19.95 (ISBN 0-8109-8081-9). Abrams.

Treasury of the Sierra Nevada. Robert Reid. LC 82-62811. (Illus.). 256p. (Orig.). 1983. 16.95 (ISBN 0-89997-032-X); pap. 11.95 (ISBN 0-89997-023-0). Wilderness Pr.

Treasury of the Theatre, 3 vols. Ed. by John Gassner. Incl. Vol. 1. From Aeschylus to Ostrovsky. 1968. o.p. (ISBN 0-671-20137-9); Vol. 2. From Ibsen to Sartre (ISBN 0-671-75610-9); Vol. 3. From Wilde to Eugene Ionesco. 1951. 24.95 ea.. S&S.

Treasury of the World's Great Sermons. Compiled by Warren W. Wiersbe. LC 77-72366. 1977. 24.95 (ISBN 0-8254-4011-4). Kregel.

Treasury of the World's Greatest Opera Stories. Anthony J. Rudel. 512p. 1985. pap. 9.95 (ISBN 0-671-45943-0, Fireside). S&S.

Treasury of Themes & Illustrations. R. C. Rein. (Illus.). 1983. pap. 19.95 (ISBN 0-317-17226-3, 15N0386). Northwest Pub.

Treasury of Thought. Ed. by D. Runes Dagobert. LC 66-18815. 1966. pap. 3.95 (ISBN 0-317-65278-8). Philos Lib.

Treasury of Tips for the Antiquarian Bookseller. Hoffman Research Services Staff. 24p. (Orig.). 1983. pap. 7.95 (ISBN 0-910203-00-8). Hoffman Res.

Treasury of Tradition. Ed. by Norman Lamm. Walter S. Wurzburger. 462p. 1967. 9.95 (ISBN 0-88482-434-9). Hebrew Pub.

Treasury of Traditional Stained Glass Designs. Ann V. Winterbotham. (Illus.). 80p. (Orig.). 1981. pap. 3.95 (ISBN 0-486-24084-3). Dover.

Treasury of Traditional Wisdom. Whitall N. Perry. 1986. pap. 19.95 (ISBN 0-06-250671-4, PL 4136, HarpR). Har-Row.

Treasury of Turkish Designs: Six Hundred Seventy Motifs from Iznik Pottery. Azade Akar. (Pictorial Archive Ser.). (Illus.). 128p. 1988. pap. 5.95 (ISBN 0-486-25594-8). Dover.

Treasury of Turkish Folktales for Children. Barbara K. Walker. 200p. (gr. 3-7). Date not set. lib. bdg. price not set (Linnet). Shoe String.

Treasury of Unfamiliar Lyrics. Norman Ault. 1938. 35.00 (ISBN 0-686-17670-7). Quaker City.

Treasury of Vance Havner: Twentieth-Century Prophet, Preacher, Pilgrim. Vance Havner. Compiled by Betsey D. Scanlan. 254p. (Orig.). 1988. 14.95 (ISBN 0-8010-4319-0). Baker Bk.

Treasury of Verse for Little Children. Pogany Edgar. 1986. 24.75x (ISBN 0-245-54313-9, Pub. by Harrap Ltd England). State Mutual Bk.

Treasury of Victorian Detective Stories. Ed. by Everett F. Bleiler. 416p. 1982. pap. 3.95 (ISBN 0-684-17640-8, ScribT). Scribner.

Treasury of Victorian Ghost Stories. Everett F. Bleiler. 368p. 1983. pap. 7.95 (ISBN 0-684-17823-0, ScribT). Scribner.

Treasury of Victorian Murder. Rick Geary. 64p. (Orig.). 1987. pap. 6.95x (ISBN 0-918348-41-2). NBM.

Treasury of Victorian Printers' Frames, Ornaments, & Initials. Carol B. Grafton. 128p. 1984. pap. 5.95 (ISBN 0-486-24703-1). Dover.

Treasury of Winnie-the-Pooh, 4 bks. A. A. Milne. Incl. Winnie-the-Pooh; House at Pooh Corner; Now We Are Six; When We Were Very Young. (Illus.). 1987. pap. 13.00 boxed set (ISBN 0-440-49580-6). Dell.

Treasury of Winning Basketball Tips. Bob Samaras. LC 83-22104. 247p. 19.95 (ISBN 0-13-930199-2, Parker). P-H.

Treasury of Wit & Wisdom. Ed. by F. Seymour Smith. 80p. 1966. 3.95 (ISBN 0-212-35832-4). Dufour.

Treasury of Witchcraft. Harry E. Wedeck. 271p. 1983. pap. 6.95 (ISBN 0-8065-0038-7, Pub. by Citadel Pr). Lyle Stuart.

Treasury of Women's Health Marketing. Ed. by Eleanor M. Walker. (Treasury of Healthcare Marketing: Vol. 1). (Illus.). 88p. (Orig.). 1988. pap. 77.00 (ISBN 0-932577-02-4). Wentworth Pub.

Treasury of Woodcarving Designs. Alan Bridgewater & Gill Bridgewater. LC 87-29628. (Illus.). 192p. (Orig.). 1988. pap. 12.95 (ISBN 0-8069-6766-8). Sterling.

Treasury of World Literature. Ed. by Dagobert D. Runes. 1956. 15.00 (ISBN 0-8022-1454-1). Philos Lib.

Treasury of World Science. Dagobert D. Runes. (Quality Paperback Ser.: No. 108). 978p. (Orig.). 1962. pap. 4.95 (ISBN 0-8226-0108-7). Littlefield.

Treasury of World War II. Ed. by Martin Greenberg & Bill Pronzini. 1986. 7.98 (467828). Outlet Bk Co.

Treasury of Worship. Helena Dickinson. 59.95 (ISBN 0-8490-1230-9). Gordon Pr.

Treasury of Yiddish Poetry. Ed. by Irving Howe & Eliezer Greenberg. LC 76-9422. 1976. pap. 10.95 (ISBN 0-8052-0546-2). Schocken.

Treasury of Yiddish Stories. Ed. by Irving Howe & Eliezer Greenberg. LC 54-9599. (Illus.). 630p. 1973. pap. 13.95 (ISBN 0-8052-0400-8). Schocken.

Treasury Rules: Recurrent Themes in British Economic Policy. Adrian Ham. 15.95 (ISBN 0-7043-2267-6, Pub. by Quartet England). Charles River Bks.

Treasury: The Evolution of a British Institution. Henry Roseveare. 1970. 35.00x (ISBN 0-231-03405-9). Columbia U Pr.

Treat It Gentle: An Autobiography. Sidney Bechet. LC 74-23412. (Roots of Jazz Ser.). (Illus.). vi, 245p. 1978. lib. bdg. 27.50 (ISBN 0-306-70657-1); pap. 6.95 (ISBN 0-306-80086-1). Da Capo.

Treat Me Right. Eileen Goudge. (Senior Ser.: No. 19). (Orig.). (gr. 6 up). 1986. pap. 2.25 (ISBN 0-440-98845-4, LFL). Dell.

Treat Me Right: Essays on Medical Law & Ethics. Ian Kennedy. (Illus.). 320p. 1988. 48.00 (ISBN 0-19-825559-4); pap. 24.95 (ISBN 0-19-825558-6). Oxford U Pr.

Treat Yourself: Statement One. Jack P. Prince. 1986. 13.95 (ISBN 0-533-06698-0). Vantage.

Treat Yourself to a Better Sex Life. Harvey L. Gochros & Joel Fischer. (Illus.). 1980. (Spec); pap. 8.95 (ISBN 0-13-930677-3). P-H.

Treatement of Hemifacial Microsomia. Egil P. Harvold. LC 83-18758. 258p. 1983. 53.00 (ISBN 0-8451-0229-X). A R Liss.

Treaties & Agreements & the Proceedings of the Treaties & Agreements of the Tribes & Bands of the Sioux Nation. (American Indian Treaty Ser.: No. 1). 20.00 (ISBN 0-944253-17-2). Inst Dev Indian Law.

Treaties & Agreements of the Chippewa Indians. (American Indian Treaty Ser.: No. 7). 15.00 (ISBN 0-317-57356-X). Inst Dev Indian Law.

Treaties & Agreements of the Eastern Oklahoma Indians. (American Indian Treaty Ser.: No. 4). 12.00 (ISBN 0-944253-14-8). Inst Dev Indian Law.

Treaties & Agreements of the Five Civilized Tribes. (American Indian Treaty Ser.: No. 6). 20.00 (ISBN 0-944253-16-4). Inst Dev Indian Law.

Treaties & Agreements of the Indian Tribes of the Great Lakes Region. (American Indian Treaty Ser.: No. 8). 10.00 (ISBN 0-944253-18-0). Inst Dev Indian Law.

Treaties & Agreements of the Indian Tribes of the Northern Plains. (American Indian Treaty Ser.: No. 3). 15.00 (ISBN 0-944253-13-X). Inst Dev Indian Law.

Treaties & Agreements of the Indian Tribes of the Pacific Northwest. (American Indian Treaty Ser.: No. 2). 12.00 (ISBN 0-944253-12-1). Inst Dev Indian Law.

Treaties & Agreements of the Indian Tribes of the Southwest. (American Indian Treaty Ser.: No. 5). 15.00 (ISBN 0-944253-15-6). Inst Dev Indian Law.

Treaties & Agreements with & Concerning China, 1894-1919, 2 vols. Ed. by John V. MacMurray. LC 77-114588. 1729p. 1974. Repr. of 1921 ed. Set. 125.00x (ISBN 0-86527-195-X). Fertig.

Treaties & Agreements with & Concerning China, 1919-29. Carnegie Endowment for International Peace Staff. LC 75-39021. (China Studies: Perspectives on the Revolution Ser.). xiv, 282p. 1977. Repr. of 1929 ed. 23.10 (ISBN 0-88355-378-3). Hyperion Conn.

Treaties & Alliances of the World. 4th ed. Ed. by Henry Degenhardt. 495p. 1987. 95.00x (ISBN 0-8103-2347-8, Pub. by Longman). Gale.

Treaties & Conventions Signed at the Second International Conference on American States. (Treaty Series). 82p. 1902. 1.00 (ISBN 0-8270-0430-3). OAS.

Treaties & Federal Constitutions. James M. Hendry. LC 75-1361. 186p. 1975. Repr. of 1955 ed. lib. bdg. 35.00x (ISBN 0-8371-8010-4, HETF). Greenwood.

Treaties Between the Empire of China & Foreign Powers. 5th ed. William F. Mayers. 354p. 1906. 126.00x (Pub. by Han-Shan Tang Ltd). State Mutual Bk.

Treaties Between the Empire of China & Foreign Powers. Ed. by William F. Mayers. 1976. lib. bdg. 59.95 (ISBN 0-8490-2761-6). Gordon Pr.

Treaties Concerning the Utilization of International Water Courses for Other Purposes than Navigation: Africa. (Natural Resources-Water Ser.: No. 13). 98p. (Eng. & Fr.). 1984. pap. 13.50 (EF84.11.A.7). UN.

Treaties, Conventions, International Acts, Protocols & Agreements Between the United States of America & Other Powers, 4 vols. 1969. Repr. Vol. 1. (TRCA). Vol. 2. lib. bdg. 70.00 (ISBN 0-8371-0855-1, TRCB); Vol. 3. lib. bdg. 70.00 (ISBN 0-8371-0856-X, TRCC); Vol. 4. lib. bdg. 70.00 (ISBN 0-8371-0857-8, TRCD). Greenwood.

Treaties, Conventions, International Acts, Protocols, Agreements Between the U. S. & Other Powers, 4 Vols, 1910-1938. U. S. Treaties. LC 10-35763. 1968. Repr. Set. 225.00x. Scholarly.

Treaties for the Eighteen Sixties with the Southern Cheyenne & Arapaho. Raymond J. DeMaille. 15.00 (ISBN 0-944253-58-X). Inst Dev Indian Law.

Treaties in Force: A List of Treaties & Other International Agreements of the United States inForce on January 1, 1987. (State Department Publication Ser.: 9433). 360p. 1987. pap. 16.00 (ISBN 0-318-23532-3, S/N 044-000-02183-8). USGPO.

Treaties of Puget Sound, 1854-1855. Robert B. Lane & Barbara Lane. (Treaty Manuscripts Ser.: No. 6). 60p. 12.50 (ISBN 0-944253-28-8). Inst Dev Indian Law.

Treaties of Seventeen Seventy-Eight & Allied Documents. Ed. by Gilbert Chinard. LC 73-181911. (BCL Ser.: No. I). Repr. of 1928 ed. 15.00 (ISBN 0-404-52421-4). AMS Pr.

Treaties of Seventeen Seventy-Eight: Proceedings of French Treaties, 1774-1792 (Louis XVI) & United States Treaties, Feb. 7, 1778. Gilbert Chinard. 1979. 12.00 (ISBN 0-405-10595-9). Ayer Co Pubs.

Treaties on Analytical Chemistry: Theory & Practice, Pt. 1, Vol. 7. Ed. by Izaak M. Kolthoff & Philip J. Elving. LC 78-1707. pap. 160.00 (2032002). Bks Demand UMI.

Treaties on the Panama Canal Signed Between the United States of American & the Republic of Panama. (Treaty). 254p. 1979. 9.00 set. OAS.

Treaties on Trial: The Continuing Controversy over Northwest Indian Fishing Rights. Fay G. Cohen et al. LC 85-40396. (Illus.). 280p. 1986. 20.00x (ISBN 0-295-96263-1); pap. 9.95 (ISBN 0-295-96268-2). U of Wash Pr.

Treaties on Utilization of International Water Courses for Other Purposes than Navigation: Africa. (Natural Resources-Water Ser.: No.13). 13.50 (ISBN 92-1-104225-9, EF.84.II.A.7). UN.

Treaties Series, Vol. 907. (12952-12965). 302p. pap. 22.00 (ISBN 0-686-95451-3, TS907/908). UN.

Treaties, Their Making & Enforcement. Samuel B. Crandall. LC 74-76672. (Columbia University Studies in the Social Sciences: No. 54). Repr. of 1904 ed. 19.50 (ISBN 0-404-51054-X). AMS Pr.

Treating Addictive Behaviors: Processes of Change. Ed. by William R. Miller & Nick H. Heather. (Applied Clinical Psychology Ser.). 450p. 1986. 45.00x (ISBN 0-306-42248-4, Plenum Pr). Plenum Pub.

Treating Adult Children of Alcholics: A Developmental Perspective. Stephanie Brown. (Personality Processes Ser.). 333p. 1988. 34.95 (ISBN 0-471-85300-3). Wiley.

Treating & Drying Trees on the Stump. P. S. Zakharov. LC 61-9225. (Illus.). pap. 20.00 (ISBN 0-317-08275-2, 2020664). Bks Demand UMI.

Treating & Overcoming Anorexia Nervosa. Steven Levenkron. 224p. 1983. pap. 3.95 (ISBN 0-446-32743-3). Warner Bks.

Treating & Preventing Obesity. William G. Johnson. (Advances in Eating Disorders Ser.: Vol. 1). 1987. 56.50 (ISBN 0-89232-814-2). Jai Pr.

Treating Anxiety Disorders. Ed. by Rodrigo A. Munoz. LC 85-81896. (Mental Health Services Ser.: No. 32). (Orig.). 1986. pap. text ed. 14.95x (ISBN 1-55542-989-0). Jossey-Bass.

Treating Anxiety Disorders: A Guide for Human Service Professionals. Bruce A. Thyer. (Sage Human Services Guides Ser.: Vol. 45). 160p. (Orig.). 1987. pap. 9.95 (ISBN 0-8039-2792-4). Sage.

Treating Articulation Disorders: For Clinicians by Clinicians. Ed. by Harris Winitz. LC 83-14657. (Illus.). 352p. 1984. text ed. 24.00x (ISBN 0-936104-97-X, 1333). Pro Ed.

Treating Auditory Processing Difficulties in Children. Christine Sloan. LC 85-17462. (Clinical Updates Ser.). (Illus.). 229p. (Orig.). 1985. pap. text ed. 31.00 (ISBN 0-316-79840-1, 798401). College-Hill.

Treating Bites & Stings. Jennifer Holvoet & James Lent. (Taking Care of Simple Injuries Ser.). (Illus.). 80p. (Orig.). 1979. pap. 8.95 (ISBN 0-8331-1253-8). Hubbard Sci.

Treating Bruises & Nosebleeds. Jennifer Holvoet & James Lent. (Taking Care of Simple Injuries Ser.). (Illus.). 64p. (Orig.). 1979. pap. text ed. 7.95 (ISBN 0-8331-1252-X). Hubbard Sci.

Treating Bulimia: A Psychoeducational Approach. Lillie Weiss et al. (Psychology Practitioner Guidebks.). 144p. 1985. pap. text ed. 12.95 (ISBN 0-08-032399-5). Pergamon.

Treating Burns. Jennifer Holvoet & James Lent. (Taking Care of Simple Injuries Ser.). 56p. (Orig.). 1979. pap. text ed. 7.95 (ISBN 0-8331-1251-1). Hubbard Sci.

Treating Cerebral Palsy. Ed. by Eugene T. McDonald. LC 86-22568. (For Clinicians by Clinicians Ser.). (Illus.). 312p. 1987. pap. text ed. 21.00x (ISBN 0-89079-141-4, 1412). Pro Ed.

Treating Chemically Dependent Women. Josette Mondanaro. 160p. 1988. 29.95x. Lexington Bks.

Treating Child-Abusive Families: Intervention Based on Skills Training Principles. Jeffrey A. Kelly. (Applied Clinical Psychology). 234p. 1983. 29.50x (ISBN 0-306-41417-1, Plenum Pr). Plenum Pub.

Treating Child Sex Offenders & Victims: A Practical Guide. Anna C. Salter. 320p. 1988. text ed. 35.00 (ISBN 0-8039-3181-6); pap. text ed. 16.95 (ISBN 0-8039-3182-4). Sage.

Treating Childhood & Adolescent Obesity. Ed. by Daniel S. Kirschenbaum & William G. Johnson. (Psychology Practitioner Guidebooks Ser.). 160p. 1987. 22.50 (ISBN 0-08-032414-2, PBI); pap. 12.95 (ISBN 0-08-032413-4, PBI). Pergamon.

Treating Children in Groups: A Behavioral Approach. Sheldon D. Rose. LC 78-189609. (Social & Behavioral Science Ser.). 1972. 27.95x (ISBN 0-87589-130-6). Jossey-Bass.

Treating Children's Fears & Phobias: A Behavioral Approach. Richard J. Morris & Thomas R. Kratochwill. LC 82-10186. (Pergamon General Psychology Ser.: No. 114). (Illus.). 375p. 1983. text ed. 54.00 (ISBN 0-08-025999-5, J115); pap. text ed. 17.50 (ISBN 0-08-025998-7). Pergamon.

Treating Chronically Mentally Ill Women. Leona Bachrach & Carol Nadelson. LC 87-31830. (Clinical Insights Ser.). 194p. 1988. pap. text ed. 19.95 (ISBN 0-88048-144-7). Am Psychiatric.

Treating Common Diseases of Your Horse. George H. Conn. pap. 5.00 (ISBN 0-87980-255-3). Wilshire.

Treating Couples in Crisis: The Fundamentals & Practice of Marital Therapy. Robert L. Barker. 304p. 1984. 23.95x (ISBN 0-02-901790-4). Free Pr.

Treating Couples: The Intersystem Model of the Marriage Council of Philadelphia. Ed. by Gerald R. Weeks. 350p. 1989. 37.50 (ISBN 0-87630-534-6). Brunner-Mazel.

Treating Eating Disorders. Gloria R. Leon. LC 83-17550. (Applied Clinical Psychology Ser.). 128p. 1984. text ed. 14.95 (ISBN 0-86616-026-4). Greene.

Treating Families in the Home: An Alternative to Placement. Marvin Bryce & June C. Lloyd. (Illus.). 352p. 1981. 39.25x (ISBN 0-398-04085-0). C C Thomas.

Treating Fearful Dental Patients: A Patient Management Handbook. Peter Milgrom et al. 1985. text ed. 25.95 (ISBN 0-8359-7829-X); pap. text ed. 19.95 (ISBN 0-8359-7828-1). Appleton & Lange.

Treating Hemostatic Disorders: A Problem Oriented Approach. Kathy McMillian & Jean Otter. (Illus.). 1984. pap. text ed. 8.00 (ISBN 0-915355-09-4). Am Assn Blood.

Treating Incest: A Multimodal Systems Perspective. Ed. by Terry Trepper & Mary Jo Barrett. LC 86-4719. (Journal of Psychotherapy & the Family: Vol. 2, No. 2). 140p. 1986. text ed. 22.95 (ISBN 0-86656-512-4); pap. text ed. 19.95 cancelled (ISBN 0-86656-513-2). Haworth Pr.

Treating Language Disorders: For Clinicians by Clinicians. Ed. by Harris Winitz. LC 82-23682. (Illus.). 272p. 1983. pap. text ed. 19.00x (ISBN 0-8391-1813-9, 1334). Pro Ed.

Treating Loneliness in Child Protection. Norman A. Polansky. 12.00 (ISBN 0-87868-239-2, G-21, 2392). Child Welfare.

Treating Malpractice: Report of the Twentieth Century Fund Task Force on Medical Malpractice Insurance. Andrew Tobias. 70p. (Orig.). 1986. pap. text ed. 7.50x (ISBN 0-87078-173-1). Priority Pr Pubns.

Treating Mental Illness. Robert Byck. (Encyclopedia of Psychoactive Drugs Ser.). (Illus.). (YA) (gr. 7 up). 1986. 17.95 (ISBN 0-87754-774-2). Chelsea Hse.

Treating of Alcoholism: An Alcoholics Anonymous Approach. Norman K. Denzin. (Sage Human Services Guides Ser.: Vol. 46). 160p. (Orig.). 1987. pap. 9.95 (ISBN 0-8039-2907-2). Sage.

Treating Oil Field Emulsions. 3rd ed. Ron Baker. Ed. by Lydia Taylor. (Illus.). 112p. 1974. pap. text ed. 8.00 (ISBN 0-88698-121-2, 3.50030). PETEX.

Treating Persons As Ends: An Essay on Kant's Moral Philosophy. P. C. Lo. 368p. (Orig.). 1987. lib. bdg. 30.00 (ISBN 0-8191-6100-4); pap. text ed. 16.75 (ISBN 0-8191-6101-2). U Pr of Amer.

Treating Resistant Depression. Ed. by Joseph Zohar & R. H. Belmaker. LC 85-14424. 496p. 1987. text ed. 50.00 (ISBN 0-89335-225-X). PMA Pub Corp.

Treating Schizophrenic Patients: A Critical Analytical Approach. Michael H. Stone & David Forest. Ed. by Harry D. Albert. (Illus.). 352p. 1982. text ed. 32.50 (ISBN 0-07-001917-7). McGraw.

Treating Sexual Problems in Medical Practice. David K. Kentsmith & Merrill T. Eaton. LC 78-16836. (Illus.). 1979. pap. text ed. 15.95 (ISBN 0-668-04050-5). Arco.

Treating Sexually Abused Children & Their Families. Beverly James & Maria Nasjleti. 166p. 1983. pap. 13.00 (ISBN 0-89106-023-5, 7310). Consulting Psychol.

Treating Straw for Animal Feeding: An Assessment of Its Technical & Economic Feasibility. M. G. Jackson. (Animal Production & Health Papers: No. 10). 84p. (Eng., Fr. & Span.). 1978. pap. 7.50 (ISBN 92-5-100584-2, F1480, FAO). UNIPUB.

Treating Stress in Families. Ed. by Charles R. Figley. (Psychosocial Stress Ser.: No. 13). 300p. 1989. 30.00 (ISBN 0-87630-530-3). Brunner-Mazel.

Treating the Adolescent Victim of Abuse. Darlene A. Merchant. Date not set. pap. 19.95 (ISBN 1-55691-017-7). Learning Pubns.

Treating the Alcoholic: A Developmental Model of Recovery. Stephanie Brown. LC 85-3172. (Personality Processes Ser.). 348p. 1985. 35.95 (ISBN 0-471-81736-8, Pub. by Wiley-Interscience). Wiley.

Treating the Aphasic Patient. John C. Rosenbek et al. (Orig.). 1988. pap. text ed. 27.50 (ISBN 0-316-75719-5, 757195). College-Hill.

Treating the Cocaine Abuser. 80p. (Orig.). 1985. pap. 5.95 (ISBN 0-89486-279-0). Hazelden.

Treating the Criminal Offender. A. B. Smith & L. Berlin. (Criminal Justice & Public Safety Ser.). (Illus.). 416p. 1988. 45.00x (ISBN 0-306-42885-7, Plenum Pr). Plenum Pub.

Treating the Disorder, Treating the Family. Ed. by Jim Orford. LC 87-3159. 304p. 1987. text ed. 32.50x (ISBN 0-8018-3536-4). Johns Hopkins.

Treating the Elderly with Psychotherapy. Ed. by Joel Sadavoy. Molyn Leszcz. LC 86-10487. 1987. 37.50x (ISBN 0-8236-6647-6, BN-06647). Intl Univs Pr.

Treating the Homeless: Urban Psychiatry's Challenge. Billy E. Jones. LC 85-30626. (Clinical Insights Monograph). 128p. 1986. pap. text ed. 12.00x (ISBN 0-88048-080-7, 48-080-7). Am Psychiatric.

Treating the Long-Term Mentally Ill. H. Richard Lamb. LC 82-48391. (Social & Behavioral Science Ser.). 1982. text ed. 27.95x (ISBN 0-87589-553-0). Jossey-Bass.

Treating the Marijuana-Dependent Person. Robin De Silva & Robert L. DuPont. LC 82-198647. 59p. 1981. pap. 3.00 (ISBN 0-942348-04-4). Am Council Drug Ed.

Treating the Mentally Disabled. Ed. by Gary E. McCuen. LC 87-91952. (Ideas in Conflict Ser.). (Illus.). 140p. 1988. lib. bdg. 11.95. G E McCuen Pubns.

Treating the Oedipal Patient in Brief Psychotherapy. Ed. by Althea J. Horner. LC 84-24300. 256p. 1985. 25.00x (ISBN 0-87668-759-1). Aronson.

Treating the Remarried Family. Clifford J. Sager et al. LC 82-17811. 450p. 1983. 30.00 (ISBN 0-87630-323-8). Brunner-Mazel.

Treating the School Age Stutterer: A Guide for Clinicians, No. 14. Carl W. Dell, Jr. LC 79-67284. 110p. (Orig.). pap. 1.50 (ISBN 0-933388-11-X). Speech Found Am.

Treating the Treatment Failures: The Challenge of Chronic Schizophrenia. Arnold M. Ludwig. LC 75-155998. 236p. 1971. 69.50 (ISBN 0-8089-0707-7, 792595). Grune.

Treating the Troubled Family. Nathan W. Ackerman. LC 66-27943. 1966. pap. 10.95x (ISBN 0-465-09522-4, TB5023). Basic.

Treating Troubled Adolescents: A Family Therapy Approach. H. Charles Fishman. LC 87-47838. 320p. 1988. text ed. 24.95 (ISBN 0-465-08742-6). Basic.

Treating Type A Behavior: And Your Heart. Meyer Friedman & Diane Ulmer. LC 83-47939. (Illus.). 1984. 15.45 (ISBN 0-394-52286-9). Knopf.

Treating Women's Fear of Failure. Ed. by Esther D. Rothblum & Ellen Cole. LC 87-25132. (Women & Therapy Ser.). 110p. 1987. text ed. 14.95 (ISBN 0-86656-676-7). Haworth Pr.

Treating Women's Fear of Failure: From Worry to Enlightenment. Ed. by Esther D. Rothblum & Ellen Cole. LC 87-25132. (Women & Therapy Ser.). 110p. 1987. pap. write for info. (ISBN 0-918393-41-8). Harrington Pk.

Treatise see **Treatise on Etching.**

Treatise Against Dicing, Dancing, Plays & Interludes. John Northbrooke. LC 77-149667. Repr. of 1843 ed. 19.00 (ISBN 0-404-04793-9). AMS Pr.

Treatise Against Judicial Astrology, 2 pts. John Chamber. LC 77-6872. (English Experience Ser.: No. 860). 1977. Repr. of 1601 ed. lib. bdg. 20.00 (ISBN 90-221-0860-0). Walter J Johnson.

Treatise Concerning Enthusiasme. Meric Casaubon. LC 77-119864. 1970. Repr. of 1656 ed. 45.00x (ISBN 0-8201-1077-9). Schol Facsimiles.

Treatise Concerning Eternal & Immutable Morality. Ralph Cudworth. Ed. by Rene Wellek. LC 75-11214. (British Philosophers & Theologians of the 17th & 18th Centuries Ser.: Vol. 17). 1976. Repr. of 1731 ed. lib. bdg. 51.00 (ISBN 0-8240-1768-4). Garland Pub.

Treatise Concerning Political Enquiry & the Liberty of the Press. Tunis Wortman. LC 78-122162. (Civil Liberties in American History Ser). 1970. Repr. of 1800 ed. lib. bdg. 39.50 (ISBN 0-306-71967-3). Da Capo.

Treatise Concerning the Arte of Limning. Nicholas Hilliard. LC 77-94584. 1979. Repr. of 1912 ed. lib. bdg. 15.00 (ISBN 0-89341-242-2). Longwood Pub Group.

Treatise, Concerning the Causes of the Magnificence & Greatness of Cities. Giovanni Botero. LC 79-84090. (English Experience Ser.: No. 910). 128p. 1979. Repr. of 1606 ed. lib. bdg. 25.00 (ISBN 90-221-0910-0). Walter J Johnson.

Treatise Concerning the Division Between the Spirituality & Temporality. Christopher Saint German. LC 72-6027. (English Experience Ser.: No. 453). 94p. 1972. Repr. of 1532 ed. 14.00 (ISBN 90-221-0453-2). Walter J Johnson.

Treatise Concerning the Principles of Human Knowledge. George Berkeley. Ed. by Colin M. Turbayne. LC 57-1290. 1957. pap. 4.79 scp (ISBN 0-672-60225-3, LLA53). Bobbs.

Treatise Concerning the Principles of Human Knowledge. George Berkeley. Ed. & intro. by Kenneth Winkler. LC 82-2876. (HPC Philosophical Classics Ser.). 156p. 1982. lib. bdg. 17.50 (ISBN 0-915145-40-5); pap. text ed. 3.95 (ISBN 0-915145-39-1). Hackett Pub.

Treatise Concerning the Principles of Human Knowledge: Berkeley. Ed. by Colin M. Turbayne. 1957. pap. text ed. write for info. (ISBN 0-02-421690-9). Macmillan.

Treatise Concerning the Principles of Human Knowledge: Three Dialogues Between Hylas & Philonous. George Berkeley. 288p. 1985. pap. 5.95 (ISBN 0-87548-446-8). Open Court.

Treatise How by the Worde of God, Christian Mens Almose Oght to Be Distributed. Martin Bucer. LC 76-57360. (English Experience Ser.). 1977. Repr. of 1557 ed. lib. bdg. 3.50 (ISBN 90-221-0779-5). Walter J Johnson.

Treatise of All the Degrees & Symptoms of the Venereal Disease in Both Sexes...Gonoslogium Novum...by Way of Appendix. John Marten. LC 83-48589. (Marriage, Sex & the Family in England Ser.). 716p. 1985. lib. bdg. 90.00 (ISBN 0-8240-5913-1). Garland Pub.

Treatise of Civil Government & a Letter Concerning Toleration. John Locke. Ed. by Charles L. Sherman. 1965. pap. text ed. 6.95x (ISBN 0-89197-519-5). Irvington.

Treatise of Commerce. Wheeler John. Ed. by Mira Wilkins. LC 76-29979. (European Business Ser.). 1977. Repr. of 1931 ed. lib. bdg. 37.50x (ISBN 0-405-09745-X). Ayer Co Pubs.

Treatise of Crypto-Analysis. (Illus.). 137p. (Fr.). 1988. 127.65 (ISBN 0-86722-180-1). Inst Econ Pol.

Treatise of Daunces. Bd. with Godly Exhortation by Occasion of the Late Judgement of God at Parris Garden. John Fields. (English Stage Ser.: Vol. 5). 1974. lib. bdg. 61.00 (ISBN 0-8240-0588-0). Garland Pub.

Treatise of Ecclesiastical Discipline. Matthew Sutcliffe. LC 73-7082. (English Experience Ser.: No. 626). 1973. Repr. of 1590 ed. 21.00 (ISBN 90-221-0626-8). Walter J Johnson.

Treatise of Femme Coverts: Or, the Lady's Law. Intro. by Lance E. Dickson. viii, 280p. 1974. Repr. of 1732 ed. text ed. 22.50x (ISBN 0-8377-2129-6). Rothman.

Treatise of Health & Long Life with the Future Means of Attaining It. Leonard Lessius & Luigi Cornaro. Ed. by Robert Kastenbaum. Tr. by Timothy Smith. LC 78-22206. (Aging & Old Age Ser.). 1979. Repr. of 1743 ed. lib. bdg. 14.00x (ISBN 0-405-11821-X). Ayer Co Pubs.

Treatise of Human Nature, 2 vols. David Hume. Ed. by T. H. Green & T. H. Grose. 1025p. 1981. Repr. of 1898 ed. lib. bdg. 200.00 (ISBN 0-89987-377-4). Darby Bks.

Treatise of Human Nature. David Hume. Ed. by L. A. Selby-Bigge & P. H. Nidditch. 1978. pap. text ed. 10.95x (ISBN 0-19-824588-2). Oxford U Pr.

Treatise of Human Nature. David Hume. Ed. by Ernest G. Mossner. (Classics Ser.). 680p. 1986. pap. 6.95 (ISBN 0-14-043244-2). Penguin.

Treatise of Man. Rene Descartes. Tr. & commentary by Thomas S. Hall. LC 76-173412. (Monographs in the History of Science Ser). (Illus., Fr. & Eng.). 1972. 17.50x (ISBN 0-674-90710-8). Harvard U Pr.

Treatise of Melancholie, Containing the Causes Thereof. Timothy Bright. LC 72-176. (English Experience Ser.: No. 212). 1969. Repr. of 1586 ed. 35.00 (ISBN 90-221-0212-2). Walter J Johnson.

Treatise of Morall Philosophie. rev. ed. William Baldwin. LC 67-10126. 1967. Repr. of 1620 ed. 50.00x (ISBN 0-8201-1003-5). Schol Facsimiles.

Treatise of Musick, Speculative, Practical & Historical. A. Malcolm. LC 69-16676. (Music Ser.). 1970. Repr. of 1721 ed. lib. bdg. 75.00 (ISBN 0-306-71099-4). Da Capo.

Treatise of One Hundred & Thirteen Diseases of the Eyes. Richard Banister. LC 79-37135. (English Experience Ser.: No. 297). 480p. Repr. of 1622 ed. 35.00 (ISBN 90-221-0297-1). Walter J Johnson.

Treatise of Schemes & Tropes. Richard Sherry. LC 61-5030. 1977. Repr. of 1550 ed. 40.00x (ISBN 0-8201-1258-5). Schol Facsimiles.

Treatise of Spousals or Marriage Contracts. Henry Swinburne. LC 83-48610. (Marriage, Sex & the Family in England Ser.). 256p. 1985. lib. bdg. 33.00 (ISBN 0-8240-5902-6). Garland Pub.

Treatise of the Canker of Englands Common Wealth. Gerard De Malynes. LC 77-7412. (English Experience Ser.: No. 880). 1977. Repr. of 1601 ed. lib. bdg. 10.50 (ISBN 90-221-0880-5). Walter J Johnson.

Treatise of the Donation of Gyfts & Endowment of Possessyons Gyven & Graunted Unto Sylvester Pope of Rome by Constantyne Emperour of Rome. Constantine I. Tr. by William Marshall. LC 79-84096. (English Experience Ser.: No. 916). 152p. 1979. Repr. of 1534 ed. lib. bdg. 35.00 (ISBN 90-221-0916-X). Walter J Johnson.

Treatise of the First Part of Chirurgerie. Alexander Read. LC 76-57411. (English Experience Ser.: No. 826). 1977. Repr. of 1638 ed. lib. bdg. 24.00 (ISBN 90-221-0826-0). Walter J Johnson.

Treatise of the Hypochondriack & Hysterick Diseases. Bernard Mandeville. LC 76-45623. 1976. Repr. of 1732 ed. 60.00x (ISBN 0-8201-1277-1). Schol Facsimiles.

Treatise of the Hypochondriack & Hysterick Passions. Bernard De Mandeville. LC 75-16717. (Classics in Psychiatry Ser.). 1976. Repr. of 1711 ed. 23.50x (ISBN 0-405-07445-X). Ayer Co Pubs.

Treatise of the Lawes of the Forest. John Manwood. LC 76-57398. (English Experience Ser.: No. 814). 1977. Repr. of 1615 ed. lib. bdg. 51.00 (ISBN 90-221-0814-7). Walter J Johnson.

Treatise of the Organ of Hearing. Guichard J. Duverney. LC 77-147969. Repr. of 1737 ed. 21.50 (ISBN 0-404-08221-1). AMS Pr.

Treatise of the Passions & Faculties of the Soule of Man. Edward Reynolds. LC 79-161935. (Hist. of Psych. Ser.). 1971. 75.00x (ISBN 0-8201-1095-7). Schol Facsimiles.

Treatise of the Plague: Containing the Nature, Signes & Accidents of the Same. Thomas Lodge. LC 79-84119. (English Experience Ser.: No. 938). 92p. 1979. Repr. of 1603 ed. lib. bdg. 20.00 (ISBN 90-221-0938-0). Walter J Johnson.

Treatise of the Pleas of the Crown: Or, a System of the Principal... William Hawkins. LC 70-37977. (American Law Ser.: The Formative Years). 876p. 1972. Repr. of 1726 ed. 58.50 (ISBN 0-405-04020-2). Ayer Co Pubs.

Treatise of the Pool. Obadyah Maimonides. Tr. by Paul Fenton. 1981. 22.95 (ISBN 0-900860-87-1, Pub. by Octagon Pr England). Ins Study Human.

Treatise of the Relative Rights & Duties of Belligerent & Neutral Powers in Maritime Affairs: In Which the Principles of Armed Neutralities & the Opinions of Hubner & Schlegel Are Fully Discussed. Robert Ward. viii, 180p. 1988. Repr. of 1875 ed. lib. bdg. 27.50x (ISBN 0-8377-1347-1). Rothman.

Treatise of the Structure & Preservation of the Violin. Jacob A. Otto. 1988. Repr. of 1891 ed. lib. bdg. 59.00x. Am Biog Serv.

Treatise of the Structure & Preservation of the Violin. Jacob Agustus Otto. 1976. lib. bdg. 39.00x (ISBN 0-403-03760-3). Scholarly.

Treatise of the Venereal Disease. Jean Astruc. Ed. by William Barrowby. LC 83-48590. (Marriage, Sex & the Family in England Ser.). 1015p. 1985. lib. bdg. 121.00 (ISBN 0-8240-5914-X). Garland Pub.

Treatise of Usurie. Roger Fenton. LC 74-28855. (English Experience Ser.: No. 736). 1975. Repr. of 1611 ed. 20.00 (ISBN 9-0221-0736-1). Walter J Johnson.

Treatise of Weights, Mets & Measures of Scotland. Alexander Huntar. LC 74-80191. (English Experience Ser.: No. 671). 58p. 1974. Repr. of 1624 ed. 8.00 (ISBN 90-221-0671-3). Walter J Johnson.

Treatise on Adhesion & Adhesives, Vols. 1-2. Ed. by R. L. Patrick. Incl. Vol. 1. Theory. 1967. pap. 99.75 soft cover (ISBN 0-8247-7037-4); Vol. 2. Materials. 1969. Dekker.

Treatise on Adhesion & Adhesives, Vol. 3. Robert L. Patrick. LC 66-11285. pap. 67.80 (2026808). Bks Demand UMI.

Treatise on Adhesion & Adhesives, Vol. 5. Patrick. 416p. 1981. 79.75 (ISBN 0-8247-1399-0). Dekker.

Treatise on Adhesion & Adhesives, Vol. 6. Patrick. 296p. 1988. 99.75 (ISBN 0-8247-7587-2). Dekker.

Treatise on All the Diseases Incident to Women. Jean Astruc. LC 83-48603. (Marriage, Sex & the Family in England Ser.). 480p. 1985. lib. bdg. 66.00 (ISBN 0-8240-5927-1). Garland Pub.

Treatise on American Citizenship. John S. Wise. (Studies in Constitutional Law). viii, 340p. 1981. Repr. of 1906 ed. lib. bdg. 30.00x (ISBN 0-8377-1306-4). Rothman.

Treatise on Analysis, 6 vols. J. A. Dieudonne. Incl. Vol. 1. 1960. 33.75 (ISBN 0-12-215550-5); Vol. 2. rev. ed. 1970. 67.50 (ISBN 0-12-215502-5); Vol. 3. 1972. 68.50 (ISBN 0-12-215503-3); Vol. 4. 1974. 67.50 (ISBN 0-12-215504-1); Vol. 5. 1977. 49.50 (ISBN 0-12-215505-X); Vol. 6. 1978. 47.50 (ISBN 0-12-215506-8). (Pure & Applied Mathematics Ser.). Acad Pr.

Treatise on Analysis, Vol. 7. Jean Dieudonne. Tr. by Laura Fainsilber. (Pure & Applied Mathematics Ser.: Vol. 10-VII). 329p. 1988. price not set (ISBN 0-12-215507-6). Acad Pr.

Treatise on Analytical Chemistry, Vol. 6. 2nd ed. Kolthoff. 1988. price not set (ISBN 0-471-07994-4). Wiley.

Treatise on Analytical Chemistry, Vol. 9. 2nd ed. Kolthoff. 1988. write for info. (ISBN 0-471-08669-X). Wiley.

Treatise on Analytical Chemistry, Vol. 11, Pt. 1. Kolthoff. (Chemical Analysis Ser.). 1988. price not set (ISBN 0-471-89689-6). Wiley.

Treatise on Analytical Chemistry, Vol. 13. 2nd ed. Kolthoff. 1988. write for info. (ISBN 0-471-80647-1). Wiley.

Treatise on Analytical Chemistry: Analytical Chemistry of Inorganic & Organic Compounds, Vol. 16, Pt. 2. I. M. Kolthoff & P. J. Elving. (Analytical Chemistry Ser.). 560p. 1980. 87.50 (ISBN 0-471-05857-2). Wiley.

Treatise on Analytical Chemistry, Pt. 1, Vol. 2: Theory & Practice. 2nd ed. Ed. by Izaak M. Kolthoff & Philip J. Elving. LC 78-1707. (Illus.). 815p. pap. 160.00 (2056452). Bks Demand UMI.

Treatise on Analytical Chemistry, Pt. 2, Vol. 15: Analytical Chemistry of Inorganic & Organic Compounds. Izaak M. Kolthoff & Philip J. Elving. LC 78-1707. (Illus.). 509p. pap. 132.40 (2056453). Bks Demand UMI.

Treatise on Analytical Chemistry: Theory & Practice, Vol. 3. 2nd ed. I. M. Kolthoff & Philip J. Elving. LC 78-1707. 592p. 1983. 95.00 (ISBN 0-471-49969-2, Pub. by Wiley-Interscience). Wiley.

Treatise on Analytical Chemistry: Theory & Practice, Vol. 4, Pt. 1. 2nd ed. Ed. by I. M. Kolthoff & Philip J. Elving. (Treatise on Analytical Chemisty Ser.: 1-299). 675p. 1984. 84.00 (ISBN 0-471-01836-8, Pub. by Wiley-Interscience). Wiley.

Treatise on Analytical Chemistry: Theory & Practice, Vol. 5, Pt. 1. 2nd ed. I. M. Kolthoff & Philip J. Elving. LC 78-1707. (Treatise on Analytical Chemistry Ser.). 668p. 1982. 126.00 (ISBN 0-471-01837-6, Pub. by Wiley-Interscience). Wiley.

Treatise on Analytical Chemistry: Theory & Practice, Vol. 8, Pt. 1. 2nd ed. Ed. by I. M. Kolthoff et al. (Treatise on Analytical Chemistry Ser.). 767p. 1986. 105.00 (ISBN 0-471-07995-2, Pub. by Interscience). Wiley.

Treatise on Analytical Chemistry: Theory & Practice, Vol. 14, Pt. 1. 2nd ed. Ed. by Philip J. Kolthoff et al. (Analytical Chemistry Ser.). 795p. 1986. 90.00 (ISBN 0-471-80648-X). Wiley.

Treatise on Analytical Dynamics. L. A. Pars. LC 79-87498. 1979. Repr. of 1965 ed. 75.00 (ISBN 0-918024-07-2). Ox Bow.

Treatise on Ancient Hindu Music. A. Bhattacharya. 176p. 1978. 12.95. Asia Bk Corp.

Treatise on Ancient Indian Music. Arun Bhattacharya. 1978. 12.00x (ISBN 0-8364-0051-8). South Asia Bks.

Treatise on Ancient Painting. George Turnbull. 248p. 1971. Repr. of 1940 ed. 98.00x (ISBN 3-7705-0506-9). Adlers Foreign Bks.

Treatise on Angel Magic, Being a Complete Transcription of Ms. Harley 6482 in the British Library. Rudd. Ed. by Adam Mclean. (Magnum Opus Hermetic Sourceworks Ser.: No. 15). (Illus.). 173p. (Orig.). 1987. pap. 18.00 (ISBN 0-933999-07-0). Phanes Pr.

Treatise on Aphasia & Other Speech Defects. Henry C. Bastian. LC 78-72786. (Brainedness, Handedness & Mental Ability Ser.). Repr. of 1898 ed. 37.50 (ISBN 0-404-60851-5). AMS Pr.

Treatise on Architecture: Being the Treatise by Antonio di Piero Averlino, Known As Filarete. Antonio A. Filarete. Tr. by John R. Spencer. LC 65-12547. (Yale Publications in the History of Art Ser.: No. 16). Vol. 1 (Translation) pap. 112.50 (ISBN 0-317-10501-9, 2013374); Vol. 2 (Facsimile) pap. 52.50 (ISBN 0-317-10502-7). Bks Demand UMI.

Treatise on Atonement. Hosea Ballou. Ed. by Ernest Cassara. 1986. pap. 7.95 (ISBN 0-933840-26-8, 0495000). Unitarian Univ.

Treatise on Basic Philosophy: Epistemology & Methodology I. Mario Bunge. 1983. lib. bdg. 64.00 (ISBN 90-277-1511-4, Pub. by Reidel Holland); pap. text ed. 34.00 (ISBN 90-277-1523-8, Pub. by Reidel Holland). Kluwer Academic.

Treatise on Basic Philosophy: Epistemology & Methodology II, Vol. 6. Mario Bunge. 1983. lib. bdg. 50.00 (ISBN 90-277-1634-X, Pub. by Reidel Holland); pap. text ed. 28.00 (ISBN 90-277-1635-8, Pub. by Reidel Holland). Kluwer Academic.

Treatise on Basic Philosophy: Semantics II, Interpretation & Truth, Vol. 2. Mario Bunge. LC 74-83872. 1974. lib. bdg. 39.50 (ISBN 90-277-0535-6, Pub. by Reidel Holland); pap. 24.00 (ISBN 90-277-0573-9). Kluwer Academic.

Treatise on Basic Philosophy: Semantics I, Sense & Reference, Vol. 1. Mario Bunge. LC 74-83872. 183p. 1974. lib. bdg. 37.00 (ISBN 90-277-0534-8, Pub. by Reidel Holland); pap. 21.000 (ISBN 90-277-0572-0). Kluwer Academic.

Treatise on Basic Philosophy, Vol. 3: Ontology I--the Furniture of the World. Mario Bunge. 1977. lib. bdg. 55.00 (ISBN 90-277-0780-4, Pub. by Reidel Holland); pap. 29.00 (ISBN 90-277-0785-5). Kluwer Academic.

Treatise on Basic Philosophy, Vol. 4: Ontology 11. Mario Bunge. (Treatise on Basic Philosophy Ser.: No. 4). 1979. lib. bdg. 50.00 (ISBN 90-277-0944-0, Pub. by Reidel Holland); pap. 27.50 (ISBN 90-277-0945-9). Kluwer Academic.

Treatise on Basic Philosophy, Vol. 7: Epistemology & Methodology III, Philosophy of Science & Technology Pt I: Formal & Physical Science. Mario Bunge. 1985. lib. bdg. 39.00 (ISBN 90-277-1903-9, Pub. by Reidel Holland); pap. text ed. 22.00 (ISBN 90-277-1904-7). Kluwer Academic.

Treatise on Basic Philosophy, Vol. 7: Epistemology & Methodology III, Philosophy of Science & Technology Part II: Life Science, Social Science & Technology. Mario Bunge. 1985. lib. bdg. 49.00 (ISBN 90-277-1913-6, Pub. by Reidel Holland); pap. text ed. 24.50 (ISBN 90-277-1914-4). Kluwer Academic.

Treatise on Biogenesis by Henry Drummond. Henry Drummond. (Illus.). 129p. 1982. Repr. of 1886 ed. 127.75 (ISBN 0-89901-069-5). Found Class Reprints.

Treatise on Book Selection. Ajit K. Chakabarti. 300p. 1983. text ed. 32.50x (ISBN 0-86590-129-5). Apt Bks.

Treatise on Byzantine Music. S. G. Hatherly. LC 77-75226. 1977. Repr. of 1892 ed. lib. bdg. 20.00 (ISBN 0-89341-071-3). Longwood Pub Group.

Treatise on Children's Diseases. Tirthankar Datta. 1984. 69.00x (ISBN 0-317-38808-8, Pub. by Current Dist). State Mutual Bk.

Treatise on Civil Architecture. 3rd ed. William Chambers. Ed. by John Harris. LC 68-17154. (Illus.). Repr. of 1791 ed. 38.50 (ISBN 0-405-08349-1, Blom Pubns). Ayer Co Pubs.

Treatise on Civil Government, 3 pts. Josiah Tucker. Incl. Pt. 1. Notion of Mr. Locke & His Followers, Concerning the Origin, Extent & End of Civil Government, Examined & Confuted; Pt. 2. True Basis of Civil Government Set Forth; Pt. 3. England's Former Gothic Constitution Censured & Exposed. LC 65-26384. v, 428p. 1967. Repr. of 1781 ed. 45.00x (ISBN 0-678-00217-7). Kelley.

Treatise on Clean Surface Technology, Vol. 1. Ed. by K. L. Mittal. 326p. 1987. 59.50x (ISBN 0-306-42420-7, Plenum Pr). Plenum Pub.

Treatise on Coatings, Vol. 2, Part 1. Ed. by Raymond R. Myers & J. S. Long. LC 67-21701. pap. 160.00 (2026411). Bks Demand UMI.

Treatise on Colon Classification. P. N. Kaula. 1985. text ed. 40.00x (ISBN 0-86590-696-3, Pub. by Sterling Pubs India). Apt Bks.

Treatise on Communication by Telegraph. Morris Gray. LC 12-14201. 1988. Repr. of 1885 ed. 18.45. Little.

Treatise on Constitutional Conventions Their History, Powers & Modes of Proceeding. John A. Jameson. LC 73-166332. (American Constitutional & Legal History Ser). 1972. Repr. of 1887 ed. lib. bdg. 75.00 (ISBN 0-306-70243-6). Da Capo.

Treatise on Constitutional Law, 1987: Substance & Procedure, 3 vols. John Nowak & Ronald Rotunda. 292p. 1987. Pocket Parts. write for info. (ISBN 0-314-42493-8). West Pub.

Treatise on Contempt Including Civil & Criminal Contempts of Judicial Tribunals, Justices of the Peace, Legislative Bodies, Municipal Boards, Committees, Notaries, Commissioners, Referees & Other Officers Exercising Judicial & Quasi-judicial Functions: With Practice & Forms. Stewart Rapalje. xliv, 273p. 1981. Repr. of 1890 ed. lib. bdg. 32.50x (ISBN 0-8377-1030-8). Rothman.

Treatise on Cosmic Fire. Alice A. Bailey. 1973. 49.00 (ISBN 0-85330-017-8); pap. 30.00 1982 (ISBN 0-85330-117-4). Lucis.

Treatise on Court Marshall. J. Payne Adye. 284p. Repr. of 1800 ed. 44.00 (ISBN 0-932051-70-7, Pub. by Am Repr Serv). Am Biog Serv.

Treatise on Criminal Law. K. K. Dutta. 625p. 1984. 240.00x (ISBN 0-317-54744-5, Pub. by Eastern Bk India). State Mutual Bk.

Treatise on Criminal Law & Criminal Procedure. Charles E. Chadman. LC 77-156008. (Foundations of Criminal Justice Ser). Repr. of 1906 ed. 64.00 (ISBN 0-404-09108-3). AMS Pr.

Treatise on Critical Reason. Hans Albert. Tr. by Mary V. Rorty. LC 84-15095. 270p. 1985. text ed. 33.50x (ISBN 0-691-07295-7). Princeton U Pr.

Treatise on Cryptography: An English Translation of the Original "Traite de Cryptographie". Andre Lange & E. A. Soudart. 181p. 1982. lib. bdg. 30.80 (ISBN 0-89412-121-9); pap. text ed. 22.80 (ISBN 0-89412-055-7). Aegean Park Pr.

Treatise on Currency & Banking. 2nd ed. Condy Raguet. LC 65-26375. 1967. Repr. of 1840 ed. 39.50x (ISBN 0-678-00215-0). Kelley.

Treatise on Daguerreotype, Pts. 1-4. Levi L. Hill & W. McCartey, Jr. LC 72-9210. (Literature of Photography Ser.). Repr. of 1850 ed. 16.00 (ISBN 0-405-04918-8). Ayer Co Pubs.

Treatise on Deeds. Robert F. Norton. LC 81-83533. lxxxii, 772p. 1981. Repr. of 1928 ed. lib. bdg. 80.00x (ISBN 0-912004-17-7). W W Gaunt.

Treatise on Dinitrogen Fixation: Agronomy & Ecology, Sect. 4. R. W. Hardy. LC 76-15278. 542p. 1977. 69.95x (ISBN 0-471-02343-4, Pub. by Wiley-Interscience). Krieger.

Treatise on Disputed Handwriting & the Determination of Genuine from Forged Signatures. W. E. Hagan. LC 76-38666. Repr. of 1894 ed. 23.00 (ISBN 0-404-09175-X). AMS Pr.

Treatise on Domestic Education. facs. ed. Daniel A. Payne. LC 75-157373. (Black Heritage Library Collection Ser). 1885. 16.00 (ISBN 0-8369-8811-6). Ayer Co Pubs.

Treatise on Environmental Law, 5 vols. Frank P. Grad. 1973. looseleaf 390.00 (323); Updates 1985 179.00; 1986 256.00. Bender.

Treatise on Etching. Maxime Lalanne. Tr. by S. R. Koehler from Fr. Orig. Title: Treatise. (Illus.). 120p. 1982. pap. 3.95 (ISBN 0-486-24182-3). Dover.

Treatise on Facts As Subjects of Inquiry by a Jury. 3rd ed. James Ram & John N. Townshend. 486p. 1982. Repr. of 1873 ed. lib. bdg. 35.00x (ISBN 0-8377-1033-2). Rothman.

Treatise on Files & Rasps. William T. Nicholson. (Illus.). 80p. 7.95 (ISBN 0-317-12565-6). Early Am Indus.

Treatise on Fishing with a Hook. Juliana Berners. LC 79-20603. 1979. Repr. 15.00 (ISBN 0-88427-038-6). North River.

Treatise on Fracture, 7 vols. Harold A. Liebowitz. Incl. Vol. 1. Microscopic & Macroscopic Fundamentals of Fracture. 1969. 86.00 (ISBN 0-12-449701-2); Vol. 2. Mathematical Fundamentals of Fracture. 1969. 90.00 (ISBN 0-12-449702-0); Vol. 3. Engineering Fundamentals & Environmental Effects. 1971. 90.00 (ISBN 0-12-449703-9); Vol. 4. 1969. 72.00 (ISBN 0-12-449704-7); Vol. 5. 1969. 80.50 (ISBN 0-12-449705-5); Vol. 6. 1969; Vol. 7. 1972. 134.00 (ISBN 0-12-449707-1). Acad Pr.

Treatise on Fugue. Andre Gedalge. Tr. by A. Levin. 1964. 25.00 (ISBN 0-910648-02-6). Gamut Music.

Treatise on God As First Principle. rev. ed. John D. Scotus & Allan Wolter. LC 65-28880. 393p. 1983. 15.00 (ISBN 0-8199-0860-6). Franciscan Herald.

Treatise on Good Taste in the Art of Musick. 2nd ed. Francesco Geminiani. LC 68-16233. (Music Reprint Ser). 1969. Repr. of 1749 ed. lib. bdg. 21.50 (ISBN 0-306-70985-6). Da Capo.

Treatise on Grace & Other Posthumous Published Writings Including Observations on the Trinity. Jonathan Edwards. Ed. by Paul Helm. 141p. 1971. 17.00 (ISBN 0-227-67739-0). Attic Pr.

Treatise on Happiness. St. Thomas Aquinas. Tr. by John A. Oesterle. LC 83-17091. 224p. 1983. text ed. 15.95x (ISBN 0-268-01848-0, 85-18482); pap. text ed. 7.95x (ISBN 0-268-01849-9, 85-18490). U of Notre Dame Pr.

Treatise on Harmony. Jean-Philipe Rameau. Tr. by Philip Gossett. 9.95 (ISBN 0-486-22461-9). Dover.

Treatise on Harpsichord Tuning by Jean Denis. Ed. & tr. by Vincent J. Panetta. (Cambridge Musical Texts & Monographs). 120p. 1987. 29.95 (ISBN 0-521-30628-0); pap. 12.95 (ISBN 0-521-31402-X). Cambridge U Pr.

Treatise on Heavy-Ion Science, Vol. 1: Elastic & Quasi-Elastic Phenomena. Ed. by D. Allan Bromley. LC 84-8384. 750p. 1984. 115.00x (ISBN 0-306-41571-2, Plenum Pr). Plenum Pub.

Treatise on Heavy-Ion Science, Vol. 2: Fusion & Quasi-Fusion Phenomena. Ed. by D. Allan Bromley. 752p. 1985. 115.00x (ISBN 0-306-41572-0, Plenum Pr). Plenum Pub.

Treatise on Heavy-Ion Science, Vol. 3: Compound Systems Phenomena. Ed. by D. Allan Bromley. 610p. 1985. 95.00x (ISBN 0-306-41573-9, Plenum Pr). Plenum Pub.

Treatise on Heavy-Ion Science, Vol. 4: Extreme Nuclear States. D. Allan Bromley. 722p. 1985. 92.50x (ISBN 0-306-41574-7, Plenum Pr). Plenum Pub.

Treatise on Heavy-Ion Science, Vol. 5: High-Energy Atomic Physics. Ed. by D. Allan Bromley. 518p. 1985. 79.50x (ISBN 0-306-41575-5, Plenum Pr). Plenum Pub.

Treatise on Heavy Ion Science, Vol. 6: Astrophysics, Chemistry, & Condensed Matter. Ed. by D. Allan Bromley. 452p. 1985. 69.50x (ISBN 0-306-41786-3, Plenum Pr). Plenum Pub.

Treatise on Heavy Ion Science, Vol. 7: Instrumentation & Techniques. Ed. by D. Allan Bromley. 494p. 1985. 79.50x (ISBN 0-306-41787-1, Plenum Pr). Plenum Pub.

Treatise on Heavy-Ion Science, Vol. 8: Nuclei Far from Stability. Ed. by D. A. Bromley. (Illus.). 735p. Date not set. price not set (ISBN 0-306-42949-7, Plenum Pr). Plenum Pub.

Treatise on Heliochromy. Levi Hill. LC 71-173025. 192p. 1972. Repr. text ed. 14.95 (ISBN 0-87601-005-2). Carnation.

Treatise on Hindu Law. S. Venkatarman. (Orient Longman Law Library). 550p. 1980. pap. text ed. 18.95x (ISBN 0-86131-211-2, Pub. by Orient Longman Ltd India). Apt Bks.

Treatise on Human Nature, 3 vols. David Hume. LC 78-67528. (Scottish Enlightenment Ser.). Repr. of 1740 ed. Set. 97.50 (ISBN 0-404-17653-4). Vol. 1 (ISBN 0-404-17654-2). Vol. 2 (ISBN 0-404-17655-0). V0l. 3 (ISBN 0-404-17656-9). AMS Pr.

Treatise on Hygiene & Public Health, 2 vols. Albert H. Buck. Ed. by Barbara G. Rosenkrantz. LC 76-25654. (Public Health in America Ser.). 1977. Repr. of 1879 ed. Set. lib. bdg. 106.00x (ISBN 0-405-09810-3); lib. bdg. 53.00x ea. Vol. 1 (ISBN 0-405-09811-1). Vol. 2 (ISBN 0-405-09812-X). Ayer Co Pubs.

Treatise on Inorganic Chemistry, 2 vols. H. Remy. Ed. by J. Kleinberg. Incl. Vol. 1: Introduction & Main Groups of the Periodic Tables. 866p. 116.00 (ISBN 0-444-40470-8); Vol. 2: Subgroups of the Periodic Table & General Topics. 798p. 83.00 (ISBN 0-444-40471-6). 1956. Elsevier.

Treatise on Insanity see Responsibility in Mental Disease.

Treatise on Insanity & Other Disorders Affecting the Mind. James C. Prichard. LC 73-2412. (Mental Illness & Social Policy; the American Experience Ser.). Repr. of 1837 ed. 24.50 (ISBN 0-405-05222-7). Ayer Co Pubs.

Treatise on Insanity in Its Medical Relations. William A. Hammond. LC 73-2402. (Mental Illness & Social Policy; the American Experience Ser.). Repr. of 1883 ed. 45.50 (ISBN 0-405-05208-1). Ayer Co Pubs.

Treatise on International Law Including American Diplomacy. Cushman K. Davis. xiii, 368p. 1982. Repr. of 1901 ed. lib. bdg. 30.00x (ISBN 0-8377-0441-3). Rothman.

Treatise on Invertebrate Paleontology, Pt. A: Introduction (Fossilization, Biogeography & Biostratigraphy) Ed. by Richard A. Robison & Curt Tiechert. LC 53-12913. 1979. 29.00 (ISBN 0-8137-3001-5). Geol Soc.

Treatise on Invertebrate Paleontology, Pt. C: Protista 2 (Foraminiferida, et, 2 vols. Ed. by Raymond C. Moore. LC 53-12913. 1964. 43.00 (ISBN 0-8137-3003-1). Geol Soc.

Treatise on Invertebrate Paleontology, Pt. D: Protista 3 (Radiolaria, Tintinnina) Ed. by Raymond C. Moore. LC 53-12913. (Illus.). 1954. 20.00 (ISBN 0-8137-3004-X). Geol Soc.

Treatise on Invertebrate Paleontology, Part E, Vol. 1: Archaeocyatha. rev. & enl. ed. Dorothy Hill. Ed. by Curt Teichert. LC 53-12913. (Illus.). 158p. 1972. 20.00 (ISBN 0-8137-3105-4). Geol Soc.

Treatise on Invertebrate Paleontology, Pt. F: Coelenterata. Ed. by Raymond C. Moore. LC 53-12913. (Illus.). 1956. 27.50 (ISBN 0-8137-3006-6). Geol Soc.

Treatise on Invertebrate Paleontology, Pt. F, Suppl. 1: Coelenterata (Anthozoa: Rugosa & Tabulata) Ed. by Dorothy Hill. LC 53-12913. (Illus.). 1981. 44.00 (ISBN 0-8137-3029-5). Geol Soc.

Treatise on Invertebrate Paleontology, Part G: Bryozoa. Ed. by Raymond C. Moore. LC 53-12913. 1953. 12.50 (ISBN 0-8137-3007-4). Geol Soc.

Treatise on Invertebrate Paleontology, Part G: Bryoza, Vol. 1. rev. ed. Ed. by R. A. Robison. 1983. 52.00 (ISBN 0-8137-3107-0). Geol Soc.

Treatise on Invertebrate Paleontology, Pt. H: Brachiopoda, 2 vols. Ed. by Raymond C. Moore. LC 53-12913. (Illus.). 1965. 43.50 (ISBN 0-8137-3008-2). Geol Soc.

Treatise on Invertebrate Paleontology, Pt. I: Mollusca 1. Ed. by Raymond C. Moore. LC 53-12913. (Illus.). 1960. 30.00 (ISBN 0-8137-3009-0). Geol Soc.

Treatise on Invertebrate Paleontology, Pt. K: Mollusca 3. Ed. by Raymond C. Moore. LC 53-12913. (Illus.). 1964. 27.75 (ISBN 0-8137-3011-2). Geol Soc.

Treatise on Invertebrate Paleontology, Pt. N: Mollusca 6 (Bivalvia, Vols. 1-2. Ed. by Raymond C. Moore. LC 53-12913. (Illus.). 1969. 44.25 (ISBN 0-8137-3014-7). Geol Soc.

Treatise on Invertebrate Paleontology, Pt. N: Mollusca 6 (Bivalvia, Vol. 3 (Oysters) Ed. by Raymond C. Moore. LC 53-12913. (Illus.). 1971. 23.50 (ISBN 0-8137-3026-0). Geol Soc.

Treatise on Invertebrate Paleontology, Pt. O: Arthropoda 1. Ed. by Raymond C. Moore. LC 53-12913. (Illus.). 1959. 27.50 (ISBN 0-8137-3015-5). Geol Soc.

Treatise on Invertebrate Paleontology, Pt. P: Arthropoda 2. Ed. by Raymond C. Moore. LC 53-12913. (Illus.). 1955. 18.00 (ISBN 0-8137-3016-3). Geol Soc.

Treatise on Invertebrate Paleontology, Pt. Q: Arthropoda 3. Ed. by Raymond C. Moore. LC 53-12913. (Illus.). 1961. 26.75 (ISBN 0-8137-3017-1). Geol Soc.

Treatise on Invertebrate Paleontology, Pt. R. Arthropoda 4, Vols. 1-2. Ed. by Raymond C. Moore. LC 53-12913. (Illus.). 1969. 32.00 (ISBN 0-8137-3018-X). Geol Soc.

Treatise on Invertebrate Paleontology, Pt. S: Echinodermata 1, 2 vols. Ed. by Raymond C. Moore. LC 53-12913. (Illus.). 1968. 32.00 (ISBN 0-8137-3020-1). Geol Soc.

Treatise on Invertebrate Paleontology: Part T: Echinodermata 2 (Crinoidea, 3 vols. Ed. by Raymond C. Moore & Curt Teichert. LC 53-12913. (Illus.). 1978. Set. 61.00 (ISBN 0-8137-3021-X); Vol. 1. 31.00 (ISBN 0-686-82905-0); Vol. 2. 30.00 (ISBN 0-686-82906-9); Vol. 3. 17.00 (ISBN 0-686-82907-7). Geol Soc.

Treatise on Invertebrate Paleontology, Pt. U: Echinodermata 3, 2 vols. Raymond C. Moore. LC 53-12913. (Illus.). 1966. 33.50 (ISBN 0-8137-3022-8). Geol Soc.

Treatise on Invertebrate Paleontology, Pt. V: Graptolithina. rev. ed. Ed. by Raymond C. Moore. LC 53-12913. (Illus.). 1970. 16.75 (ISBN 0-8137-3123-2). Geol Soc.

Treatise on Invertebrate Paleontology, Pt. W: Miscellanea. Ed. by Raymond C. Moore. LC 53-12913. (Illus.). 1962. 18.00 (ISBN 0-8137-3024-4). Geol Soc.

Treatise on Invertebrate Paleontology, Pt. W., Suppl. 1: Miscellanea, (Trace Fossils & Problematica) 2nd. rev. & enl. ed. Walter Hartzschel. LC 53-12913. (Illus.). 1975. 24.00 (ISBN 0-8137-3027-9). Geol Soc.

Treatise on Invertebrate Paleontology, Pt. W, Suppl. 2: Conodonta. Ed. by R. A. Robison. LC 53-12913. (Illus.). 1981. 22.00 (ISBN 0-8137-3028-7). Geol Soc.

Treatise on Irreversible & Statistical Thermophysics: An Introduction to Nonclassical Thermodynamics. Wolfgang Yourgrau et al. (Illus.). xx, 268p. 1982. pap. 7.00 (ISBN 0-486-64313-1). Dover.

Treatise on Judicial Evidence, Extracted from the Manuscripts of Jeremy Bentham. M. Dumont. xvi, 366p. 1981. Repr. of 1825 ed. lib. bdg. 35.00x (ISBN 0-8377-0318-2). Rothman.

Treatise: On Lathes & Turning. W. Henry Northcott. (Illus.). 328p. 1988. pap. 14.95 (ISBN 0-941936-10-4). Linden Pub Fresno.

Treatise on Laughter. Laurent Joubert. Tr. by Gregory D. de Rocher from Fr. LC 79-16796. 224p. 1980. 17.95 (ISBN 0-8173-0026-0). U of Ala Pr.

Treatise on Law. St. Thomas Aquinas. 1963. pap. 4.50 (ISBN 0-89526-918-X). Regnery Gateway.

Treatise on Life Insurance Accounts: Forming Pt. II on "Life Insurance in 1872", 2 vols. in one. Thomas B. Sprague. Ed. by Richard P. Brief. LC 80-1526. (Dimensions of Accounting Theory & Practice Ser.). 1981. Repr. of 1911 ed. lib. bdg. 27.50x (ISBN 0-405-13547-5). Ayer Co Pubs.

Treatise on Limnology, 3 vols. G. Evelyn Hutchinson. Incl. Vol. 1. Treatise on Limnology, 2 pts. G. Evelyn Hutchinson. 1015p. 1957. Set. 93.50 (ISBN 0-471-42570-2); Set. pap. 59.95 (ISBN 0-471-42567-2); Vol. 1, Pt. 1. Geography & Physics of Lakes. 672p. 1957. pap. 32.50 o (ISBN 0-471-42568-0); Vol. 1, Pt. 2. Chemistry of Lakes. 474p. 1975. pap. 32.50x (ISBN 0-471-42569-9); Vol. 2. Introduction to Lake Biology & the Limnoplankton. G. Evelyn Hutchinson. 1115p. 1967. 104.00 (ISBN 0-471-42572-9); Vol. 3. Limnological Botany. 660p. 1975. 54.50x (ISBN 0-471-42574-5). LC 57-8888. 1986. Set. 209.95 (ISBN 0-471-85025-X). Wiley.

Treatise on Limnology see Treatise on Limnology.

Treatise on Madness. William Battie & John Monro. (Illus.). 160p. 1962. Repr. of 1758 ed. 18.50x (ISBN 0-8464-0936-4). Beekman Pubs.

Treatise on Magnetism & Hallucinations As an Expression of Nervous Disorders. A. Brierre De Boismont. (Illus.). 137p. 1988. 167.45 (ISBN 0-89920-180-6). Am Inst Psych.

Treatise on Man & the Development of His Faculties. Lambert A. Quetelet. LC 68-56761. (Illus.). 1968. Repr. of 1842 ed. 15.00 (ISBN 0-8337-2874-1). B Franklin.

Treatise on Man & the Development of His Faculties, 1842. Lambert A. Quetelet. LC 77-81364. (History of Psychology Ser.). (Illus.). 1969. 35.00x (ISBN 0-8201-1061-2). Schol Facsimiles.

Treatise on Man: His Intellectual Faculties & His Education, 2 Vols. Claude A. Helvetius. Tr. by W. Hooper. Repr. of 1810 ed. 55.50 (ISBN 0-8337-1652-2). B Franklin.

Treatise on Marine Ecology & Paleoecology. National Research Council, Committee on a Treatise on Marine Ecology & Paleoecology Staff. Ed. by Joel W. Hedgpeth. LC 57-4669. (Geological Society of America. Memoir Ser.: No. 67, Vol. 1). pap. 160.00 (2031784). Bks Demand UMI.

Treatise on Markets: Spot, Futures, & Options. Joseph M. Burns. 1979. pap. 9.00 (ISBN 0-8447-3340-7). Am Enterprise.

Treatise on Materials Science, Vols. 1-12. Ed. by Herbert Herman. Incl. Vol. 1. 1972. 67.50 (ISBN 0-12-341801-1); Vol. 2. 1973. 82.50 (ISBN 0-12-341802-X); Vol. 3. Ultrasonic Investigation of Mechanical Properties. Robert E. Green, Jr. 1973. 39.50 (ISBN 0-12-341803-8); Vol. 4, 1974. 76.00 (ISBN 0-12-341804-6); Vol. 5. 1974. 76.00 (ISBN 0-12-341805-4); Vol. 6. Plastic Deformation of Materials. 1975. 82.00 (ISBN 0-12-341806-2); Vol. 7. Microstructure of Irradiated Materials. 1975. 52.50 (ISBN 0-12-341807-0); Vol. 8. 1975. 67.50 (ISBN 0-12-341808-9); Vol. 9. Ceramic Fabrication Processes. Ed. by F. F. Wang. 1976. 80.00 (ISBN 0-12-341809-7); Vol. 10. Properties of Solid Polymeric Materials: Part A. Ed. by J. M. Schulz. 1977. 81.00 (ISBN 0-12-341810-0); Vol. 10. Properties of Solid Polymeric Materials: Part B. Ed. by J. M. Schultz. 1977. 82.00 (ISBN 0-12-341841-0); Vol. 11. Properties & Microstructure. Ed. by R. K. MacCrone. 1977. 85.00 (ISBN 0-12-341811-9); Vol. 12. Glass I: Interaction with Electromagnetic Radiation. Ed. by Minoru Tomozawa. 1977. 80.00 (ISBN 0-12-341812-7). LC 78-27077. Acad Pr.

Treatise on Materials Science & Technology, Vol. 17: Glass 11. Ed. by Herbert Herman. 1979. 89.50 (ISBN 0-12-341817-8). Acad Pr.

Treatise on Materials Science & Technology, Vol. 24. Ed. by H. Herman & K. N. Tu. 306p. 1982. 79.50 (ISBN 0-12-341824-0). Acad Pr.

Treatise on Materials Science & Technology: Experimental Methods, Vol. 19B. Herbert Herman. LC 77-182672. 1983. 79.50 (ISBN 0-12-341842-9). Acad Pr.

Treatise on Materials Science & Technology: Embrittlement of Engineering Alloys, Vol. 25. Herbert Herman. 1983. 99.50 (ISBN 0-12-341825-9). Acad Pr.

Treatise on Materials Science & Technology, Vol. 16: Erosion. Ed. by Herbert Herman. (Treatise on Materials Science & Technology Ser.). 1979. 99.50 (ISBN 0-12-341816-X). Acad Pr.

Treatise on Materials Science & Technology, Vol. 19: Experimental Methods, Pt. A. Herbert Herman. LC 77-182672. 1980. 79.50 (ISBN 0-12-341819-4). Acad Pr.

Treatise on Materials Science & Technology, Vol. 15: Neutron Scattering in Materials Science. Ed. by Herbert Herman. (Treatise on Materials Science & Technology Ser.). 1979. 99.50 (ISBN 0-12-341815-1). Acad Pr.

Treatise on Materials Science & Technology, Vol. 27: Analytical Techniques for Thin Films. Herbert Herman. Ed. by K. N. Tu & R. Rosenberg. 493p. 1988. 89.95 (ISBN 0-12-341827-5). Acad Pr.

Treatise on Materials Science & Technology, Vol. 21: Electronic Structure & Properties. Herbert Herman & F. Frandin. LC 81-2457. 1981. 89.50 (ISBN 0-12-341821-6). Acad Pr.

Treatise on Materials Science & Technology, Vol. 26: Glass IV. Ed. by Herbert Herman. 1985. 79.50 (ISBN 0-12-341826-7). Acad Pr.

Treatise on Materials Science & Technology, Vol. 22: Glass III. Ed. by Herbert Herman & Minoru Tomozawa. LC 77-378180. 1982. 79.50 (ISBN 0-12-341822-4). Acad Pr.

Treatise on Materials Science & Technology, Vol. 28: Materials for Marine Systems & Structures. Ed. by Herbert Herman et al. (Materials Science & Technology Ser.). 430p. 1988. price not set (ISBN 0-12-341828-3). Acad Pr.

Treatise on Materials Science & Technology, Vol. 29: Structural Cerammics. Ed. by John B. Wachtsman & Herbert Herman. 484p. 1988. price not set (ISBN 0-12-341829-1). Acad Pr.

Treatise on Materials Science & Technology, Vol. 20: Ultrarapid Quenching of Liquid Alloys. Ed. by Herbert Herman. LC 81-22860. 1981. 94.50 (ISBN 0-12-341820-8). Acad Pr.

Treatise on Materials Science & Technology, Vol. 30: Auger Electron Spectroscopy. Ed. by C. L. Briant et al. 282p. 1988. price not set (ISBN 0-12-341830-5). Acad Pr.

Treatise on Media & Methods Used in Bacteriological Techniques. 2nd ed. V. Iswaran. 189p. 1980. 12.00 (ISBN 0-88065-132-6, Pub. by Messers Today & Tomorrows Printers & Publishers India). Scholarly Pubns.

Treatise on Mental Diseases. Henry J. Berkley. Ed. by Gerald N. Grob. LC 78-22549. (Historical Issues in Mental Health Ser.). (Illus.). 1979. Repr. of 1900 ed. lib. bdg. 46.00x (ISBN 0-405-11903-8). Ayer Co Pubs.

Treatise on Modern Instrumentation & Orchestration. Hector Berlioz. 1976. 69.00x (ISBN 0-403-06679-4, Regency). Scholarly.

Treatise on Modern Instrumentation & Orchestration. Hector Berlioz. 1988. Repr. of 1948 ed. lib. bdg. 79.00x. Am Biog Serv.

Treatise on Money, 2 vols. John M. Keynes. LC 75-41162. Repr. of 1930 ed. 75.00 set (ISBN 0-404-15000-4). Vol. 1 (ISBN 0-404-15001-2). Vol. 2 (ISBN 0-404-15002-0). AMS Pr.

Treatise on Money, the Applied Theory of Money see Collected Writings.

Treatise on Money, the Pure Theory of Money see Collected Writings.

Treatise on Photography. N. P. Lerebours. LC 72-9215. (Literature of Photography Ser.). Repr. of 1843 ed. 17.00 (ISBN 0-405-04923-4). Ayer Co Pubs.

Treatise on Photogravure. Herbert Denison. Ed. by Nathan Lyons. (Reprint & Research Ser.). (Illus.). 142p. 1974. 11.95 (ISBN 0-89822-001-7); pap. 6.50. Visual Studies.

Treatise on Physiological Optics. Hermann Von Helmholtz. 103p. 1987. 117.55 (ISBN 0-89920-187-3). Am Inst Psych.

Treatise on Planetary Spirits, Witchcraft & Divination. August M. Layard. (Illus.). 141p. 1982. Repr. of 1876 ed. 137.75 (ISBN 0-89901-049-0). Found Class Reprints.

Treatise on Poisons in Relation to Medical Jurisprudence, Physiology & the Practice of Physic. Robert Christison. LC 79-156011. Repr. of 1845 ed. 45.00 (ISBN 0-404-09111-3). AMS Pr.

Treatise on Political Economy. A. Destutt De Tracy. LC 67-23018. 1970. Repr. of 1817 ed. 45.00x (ISBN 0-678-00656-3). Kelley.

Treatise on Political Economy. George Opdyke. LC 68-56559. Repr. of 1851 ed. 45.00x (ISBN 0-678-00802-7). Kelley.

Treatise on Political Economy. Jean-Baptiste Say. LC 63-23524. Repr. of 1880 ed. 45.00x (ISBN 0-678-00028-X). Kelley.

Treatise on Political Economy or the Production, Distribution & Consumption of Wealth, 2 vols. Jean-Baptiste Say. Tr. by C. R. Prinsep. 467p. 1987. Repr. of 1830 ed. 457.75 (ISBN 0-86654-241-8). Inst Econ Finan.

Treatise on Practical Seamanship. William Hutchinson. Repr. of 1777 ed. 60.00 (ISBN 0-85967-566-1). Scolar.

Treatise on Prayer: An Explanation of the Services of the Orthodox Church. Symeon of Thessalonike. Intro. by N. M. Vaporis. Tr. by H. L. Simmons from Gr. (Archbishop Iakovos Library of Ecclesiastical & Historical Sources: No. 9). Orig. Title: Peri Theias Kai Hieras Proseuches. (Orig.). 1984. 12.95 (ISBN 0-917653-05-X); pap. text ed. 7.95 (ISBN 0-917653-06-8). Hellenic Coll Pr.

Treatise on Prayer & Meditation. Dominic Devas. Repr. of 1926 ed. lib. bdg. 25.00 (ISBN 0-8495-1026-0). Arden Lib.

Treatise on Presumptions of Law & Fact, with the Theory & Rules of Presumptive or Circumstantial Proof in Criminal Cases. W. M. Best. 222p. 1981. Repr. of 1845 ed. lib. bdg. 25.00x (ISBN 0-8377-0319-0). Rothman.

Treatise on Private International Law, or the Conflict of Laws with Principal Reference to Its Practice in the English & Other Cognate Systems of Jurisprudence, & Numerous References to American Authorities. John Westlake. 251p. 1986. Repr. of 1859 ed. lib. bdg. 32.50x (ISBN 0-8377-2732-4). Rothman.

Treatise on Probability. John M. Keynes. LC 75-41163. Repr. of 1921 ed. 31.50 (ISBN 0-404-14563-9). AMS Pr.

Treatise on Probability see Collected Writings.

Treatise on Response & Retribution. Lao Tze. Tr. by Paul Carus & D. T. Suzuki. LC 6-28775. (Illus.). 139p. 1973. pap. 1.95 (ISBN 0-87548-244-9). Open Court.

Treatise on Social Security & Labour Law. S. C. Srivastava. 1985. 180.00x (ISBN 0-317-57707-7, Pub. by Eastern Bk India). State Mutual Bk.

Treatise on Social Theory: The Methodology of Social Theory, 2 vols. W. G. Runciman. LC 82-4493. (Illus.). 400p. 1983. Vol. 1. 57.50 (ISBN 0-521-24906-6); Vol. 1. pap. 18.95 (ISBN 0-521-27251-3); Vol. 2, 400 p., 1988. price not set (ISBN 0-521-24959-7); Vol. 2, 400 p., 1988. pap. price not set (ISBN 0-521-36983-5). Cambridge U Pr.

Treatise on Soil Science. K. D. Glinka. 680p. 1963. text ed. 135.00x (ISBN 0-317-46451-5, Pub. by Keter Pub Jerusalem). Coronet Bks.

Treatise on Solid State Chemistry, 7 vols. Ed. by N. Bruce Hannay. Incl. Vol. 1, The Chemical Structure of Solids. LC 73-13798. 540p. 1973. 79.50x (ISBN 0-306-35051-3); Vol. 2, Defects in Solids. LC 74-22197. 528p. 1975. 79.50x (ISBN 0-306-35052-1); Vol. 3, Crystalline & Non-Crystalline Solids. LC 76-18863. 774p. 1976. 89.50x (ISBN 0-306-35053-X); Vol. 4, Reactivity of Solids. LC 76-20827. 722p. 1976. 89.50x (ISBN 0-306-35054-8); Vol. 5, Changes of State. LC 73-13799. 600p. 1975. 85.00x (ISBN 0-306-35055-6); Vol. 6A, Surfaces, I. LC 73-13799. 492p. 1976. 75.00x (ISBN 0-306-35056-4); Vol. 6B, Surfaces, II. 418p. 1976. 75.00x (ISBN 0-306-35057-2). (Plenum Pr.). Plenum Pub.

Treatise on Stair Building & Hand Railing. William Mowat & Alexander Mowat. LC 85-6916. (Illus.). 390p. 1985. pap. 19.95 (ISBN 0-941936-02-3). Linden Pub Fresno.

Treatise on State & Federal Control of Persons & Property in the United States, 2 vols. 2nd ed. Christopher G. Tiedeman. LC 72-38673. Repr. of 1900 ed. Set. 85.00 (ISBN 0-404-09185-7). AMS Pr.

Treatise on Sunday Laws: The Sabbath-the Lord's Day, Its History & Observance, Civil & Criminal. George E. Harris. xxiii, 338p. 1980. Repr. of 1892 ed. lib. bdg. 32.50x (ISBN 0-8377-2232-2). Rothman.

Treatise on the Acute Diseases of Infants. Walter Harris. LC 83-48619. (Marriage, Sex & the Family in England Ser.). 234p. 1984. lib. bdg. 30.00. Garland Pub.

Treatise on the Admissibility of Parol Evidence in Respect to Written Instruments. Irving Browne. xlviii, 510p. 1982. Repr. of 1893 ed. lib. bdg. 38.50x (ISBN 0-8377-0325-5). Rothman.

Treatise on the American Law of Landlord & Tenant. John N. Taylor. Ed. by R. H. Helmholz & Reams D. Bernard, Jr. LC 80-84857. (Historical Writings in Law & Jurisprudence Ser.: No. 14, Bk. 17). xxv, 477p. 1981. Repr. of 1844 ed. lib. bdg. 45.00 (ISBN 0-89941-069-3). W S Hein.

Treatise on the American Law Relating to Mines & Mineral Lands Within the Public Land States & Territories & Governing the Acquisition & Enjoyment of Mining Rights in Lands of the Public Domain, 2 vols. 2nd ed. Curtis H. Lindley. LC 72-2853. (Use & Abuse of America's Natural Resources Ser). 1972. Repr. of 1903 ed. 132.00 (ISBN 0-405-04517-4); 66.00 ea. Vol. 1 (ISBN 0-405-04546-8). Vol. 2 (ISBN 0-405-04547-6). Ayer Co Pubs.

Treatise on the Analytical Dynamics of Particles & Rigid Bodies. E. T. Whittaker. (Cambridge Mathematical Library). 456p. Date not set. pap. 24.95 (ISBN 0-521-35883-3). Cambridge U Pr.

Treatise on the Analytical Dynamics of Particles & Rigid Bodies: With an Introduction to the Problem of Three Bodies. 4th ed. Edmund T. Whittaker. LC 83-45485. 1937. 78.50 (ISBN 0-404-20288-8). AMS Pr.

Treatise on the Art of Pianoforte Construction. Samuel Wolfenden. 288p. 1984. soft linen-type cover 40.00x (ISBN 0-905418-09-3, Pub. by Gresham England). State Mutual Bk.

Treatise on the Astrolabe. Walter W. Skeat. 45.00 (ISBN 0-8274-3646-7). R West.

Treatise on the Blessed Body see Treatise on the Passion: Complete Works of St. Thomas More.

Treatise on the Calculus of Finite Differences. 5th ed. George Boole. LC 76-119364. text ed. 14.95 (ISBN 0-8284-1121-2). Chelsea Pub.

Treatise on the Canon of Medicine of Avicenna. Avicenna. LC 73-12409. Repr. of 1930 ed. 45.00 (ISBN 0-404-11231-5). AMS Pr.

Treatise on the Chemical Constitution of the Brain. J. L. Thudichum. xxiii, 262p. 1962. Repr. of 1884 ed. 27.50 (ISBN 0-208-00575-7, Archon). Shoe String.

Treatise on the Circle & the Sphere. Julian L. Coolidge. LC 78-128872. 1971. text ed. 29.50 (ISBN 0-8284-0236-1). Chelsea Pub.

Treatise on the Circumstances Which Determine the Rate of Wages & the Conditions of the Labouring Classes. John R. McCulloch. LC 64-56231. Repr. of 1851 ed. 22.50x (ISBN 0-678-00005-0). Kelley.

Treatise on the Coins of the Realm. Charles J. Liverpool. LC 67-29513. 1968. Repr. of 1880 ed. 39.50x (ISBN 0-678-00412-9). Kelley.

Treatise on the Commerce & Police of the River Thames. Patrick Colquhoun. LC 69-14917. (Criminology, Law Enforcement & Social Problems Ser.: No. 41). (Map). 1969. Repr. of 1800 ed. 30.00x (ISBN 0-87585-041-3). Patterson Smith.

Treatise on the Constitutional Limitations. Thomas M. Cooley. LC 78-87510. (American Constitutional & Legal History Ser). 720p. 1972. Repr. of 1868 ed. lib. bdg. 75.00 (ISBN 0-306-71403-5). Da Capo.

Treatise on the Construction of the Statutes, 13 Eliz. C.5. & 27 Eliz. C.4. Relating to Voluntary & Fraudulent Conveyances, & on the Nature & Force of Different Considerations to Support Deeds & Other Legal Instruments, in the Courts of Law & Equity. 2nd ed. William Roberts. xv, 667p. 1979. Repr. of 1825 ed. lib. bdg. 35.00x (ISBN 0-8377-1028-6). Rothman.

Treatise on the Criminal Law As Now Administered in the United States, 2 vols. Emlin McClain. Incl. Vol. 1. Criminal Law - United States (ISBN 0-404-09166-0); Vol. 2. Criminal Procedure (ISBN 0-404-09167-9). LC 74-156026. Repr. of 1897 ed. Set. 125.00 (ISBN 0-404-09127-X). AMS Pr.

Treatise on the Doctrine of Ultra Vires. Howard A. Street. LC 81-83532. lxxxviii, 591p. 1981. Repr. of 1930 ed. lib. bdg. 75.00x (ISBN 0-912004-18-5). W W Gaunt.

Treatise on the Family. Gary S. Becker. LC 81-1306. (Illus.). 320p. 1981. text ed. 25.00x (ISBN 0-674-90696-9). Harvard U Pr.

Treatise on the Family. Gary S. Becker. 304p. 1985. pap. text ed. 8.95x (ISBN 0-674-90697-7). Harvard U Pr.

Treatise on the Flute. Richard S. Rockstro. LC 76-22348. (Illus.). 1976. Repr. of 1928 ed. lib. bdg. 50.00 (ISBN 0-89341-007-1). Longwood Pub Group.

Treatise on the Fugue. Andre Gedalge. Tr. by Ferdinand Davis. LC 65-11241. Repr. of 1965 ed. 110.50 (ISBN 0-8357-9744-9, 2016219). Bks Demand UMI.

Treatise on the Fundamental Principles of Violin Playing. 2nd ed. Leopold Mozart. Tr. by Editha Knocker. (Early Music Ser.). (Illus.). 1985. pap. 18.95x (ISBN 0-19-318513-X). Oxford U Pr.

Treatise on the Heathen Superstitions that Today Live among the Indians Native to this Day in New Spain, 1629. Hernando Ruiz de Alarcon. Ed. by J. Richard Andrews & Ross Hassig. LC 83-47842. (Civilization of the American Indian Ser.: Vol. 164). (Illus.). 540p. 1984. text ed. 48.50x (ISBN 0-8061-1832-6). U of Okla Pr.

Treatise on the Heathen Superstitions: That Today Live among the Indians Native to This New Spain, 1629. Hernando Ruiz de Alarcon. Ed. by J. Richard Andrews & Ross Hassig. LC 83-47842. (Civilization of the American Indian Ser.: Vol. 164). (Illus.). 432p. 1987. pap. 16.95x (ISBN 0-8061-2031-2). U of Okla Pr.

Treatise on the History & Construction of the Violin. G. Foucher. LC 77-94578. 1978. Repr. of 1897 ed. lib. bdg. 15.00 (ISBN 0-89341-407-7). Longwood Pub Group.

Treatise on the Law & Practice of Injunctions. William W. Kerr. LC 81-81500. 743p. 1981. Repr. of 1927 ed. lib. bdg. 85.00x (ISBN 0-912004-16-9). W W Gaunt.

Treatise on the Law of Agency, 2 Vols. 2nd ed. Floyd R. Mechem. LC 14-14927. (Business Enterprises Reprint Ser.). 1982. Repr. of 1914 ed. Set. lib. bdg. 115.00 (ISBN 0-89941-165-7). W S Hein.

Treatise on the Law of Carriers of Goods & Passengers, by Land & by Water. Joseph K. Angell. LC 72-37694. (American Law Ser.: The Formative Years). 796p. 1972. Repr. of 1849 ed. 45.00 (ISBN 0-405-03991-3). Ayer Co Pubs.

Treatise on the Law of Circumstantial Evidence: Illustrated by Numerous Cases. Arthur P. Will. xvi, 555p. 1982. Repr. of 1896 ed. lib. bdg. 39.50x (ISBN 0-8377-1318-8). Rothman.

Treatise on the Law of Citizenship in the United States. Prentiss Webster. xxiii, 338p. 1980. Repr. of 1891 ed. lib. bdg. 30.00x (ISBN 0-8377-1307-2). Rothman.

Treatise on the Law of Contracts Not Under Seal. William W. Story. LC 71-37988. (American Law Ser.: The Formative Years). 522p. 1972. Repr. of 1844 ed. 30.00 (ISBN 0-405-04033-4). Ayer Co Pubs.

Treatise on the Law of Descents, in the Several United States of America. Tapping Reeve. Ed. by R. H. Helmholz & Bernard D. Reams, Jr. LC 80-84864. (Historical Writings in Law & Jurisprudence Ser.: No. 12, Bk. 15). iv, 515p. 1981. Repr. of 1825 ed. lib. bdg. 45.00 (ISBN 0-89941-067-7). W S Hein.

Treatise on the Law of Evidence, 3 vols. Simon Greenleaf. LC 73-37975. (American Law Ser.: The Formative Years). 2070p. 1972. Repr. of 1850 ed. Set. 120.00 (ISBN 0-405-04015-6); 40.00 ea. Vol. 1 (ISBN 0-405-04016-4). Vol. 2 (ISBN 0-405-04017-2). Vol. 3 (ISBN 0-405-04018-0). Ayer Co Pubs.

Treatise on the Law of Fire & Life Insurance. Joseph K. Angell. LC 76-37965. (American Law Ser.: The Formative Years). 600p. 1972. Repr. of 1854 ed. 35.50 (ISBN 0-405-03992-1). Ayer Co Pubs.

Treatise on the Law of Highways. 3rd ed. George F. Choate. Ed. by R. H. Helmholz & Bernard D. Reams, Jr. (Historical Writings in Law & Jurisprudence, Second Ser.: No. 9). xl, 625p. 1986. Repr. of 1886 ed. lib. bdg. 45.00 (ISBN 0-89941-524-5). W S Hein.

Treatise on the Law of Libel & the Liberty of the Press, Showing the Origin, Use & Abuse of the Law of Libel. Thomas Cooper. LC 78-125688. (American Journalists Ser). 1970. Repr. of 1830 ed. 20.00 (ISBN 0-405-01665-4). Ayer Co Pubs.

Treatise on the Law of Libel & the Liberty of the Press. Thomas Cooper. LC 71-107408. (Civil Liberties in American History Ser). 1970. Repr. of 1833 ed. lib. bdg. 25.00 (ISBN 0-306-71892-8). Da Capo.

Treatise on the Law of Master & Servant Covering the Relations, Duties & Liabilities of Employers & Employees. Horace G. Wood. Ed. by R. H. Helmholz & Bernard D. Reams, Jr. LC 80-84866. (Historical Writings in Law & Jurisprudence Ser.: No. 15, Bk. 18). xxxiv, 956p. 1981. Repr. of 1877 ed. lib. bdg. 48.00 (ISBN 0-89941-070-7). W S Hein.

Treatise on the Law of Negligence. Thomas G. Shearman & Amasa A. Redfield. Ed. by R. H. Helmholz & Bernard D. Reams, Jr. LC 79-56321. (Historical Writings in Law & Jurisprudence Ser.: No. 7, Bk. 10). lix, 748p. 1980. Repr. of 1870 ed. lib. bdg. 40.00 (ISBN 0-89941-046-4). W S Hein.

Treatise on the Law of Principal & Agent: And of Sales by Auction, Vol. I & II. Samuel Livermore. Ed. by R. H. Helmholz & Bernard B. Reams, Jr. LC 86-62943. (Historical Writings in Law & Jurisprudence, Second Ser.: No. 11). 1986. Repr. of 1818 ed. Set. lib. bdg. 88.00 (ISBN 0-89941-526-1). W S Hein.

Treatise on the Law of Principal & Agent, Chiefly with Reference to Mercantile Transactions. 2nd ed. William Paley. xvi, 202p. 1982. Repr. of 1840 ed. lib. bdg. 25.00x (ISBN 0-8377-1010-3). Rothman.

Treatise on the Law of Private Corporations, Aggregate. Joseph Angell & Samuel Ames. LC 70-37966. (American Law Ser.: The Formative Years). 600p. 1972. Repr. of 1832 ed. 35.50 (ISBN 0-405-03993-X). Ayer Co Pubs.

Treatise on the Law of Private Corporations, 2 vols. Henry O. Taylor. 1976. Set. lib. bdg. 200.00 (ISBN 0-8490-2762-4). Gordon Pr.

Treatise on the Law of Property in Intellectual Productions in Great Britain & the United States. Eaton S. Drone. liv, 774p. 1972. Repr. of 1879 ed. lib. bdg. 45.00x (ISBN 0-8377-2027-3). Rothman.

Treatise on the Law of Taxation: Including the Law of Local Assessments. 2nd ed. Thomas M. Cooley. Repr. of 1886 ed. 63.00 (ISBN 0-384-09775-8). Johnson Repr.

Treatise on the Law of Warranties in the Sale of Chattels. Arthur Biddle. xx, 308p. 1981. Repr. of 1884 ed. lib. bdg. 30.00x (ISBN 0-8377-0316-6). Rothman.

Treatise on the Law of Watercourses. 5th rev. ed. Joseph K. Angell. Repr. of 1854 ed. 54.00 (ISBN 0-384-01472-0). Johnson Repr.

Treatise on the Law Relating to Insurance in Three Parts: Of Marine Insurance, of Insurance on Lives & of Insurance Against Fire. David Hughes. Ed. by R. H. Helmholz & Bernard D. Reams, Jr. LC 80-84860. (Historical Writings in Law & Jurisprudence Ser.: No. 13, Bk. 16). xxxii, 472p. 1981. Repr. of 1883 ed. lib. bdg. 48.00 (ISBN 0-89941-068-5). W S Hein.

Treatise on the Law Relative to Sales of Personal Property. George Long. xvi, 288p. 1982. Repr. of 1823 ed. lib. bdg. 30.00x (ISBN 0-8377-2403-1). Rothman.

Treatise on the Laws & Customs of the Realm of England Commonly Called Glanvill. Ed. by G. D. Hall. LC 83-80258. 1983. Repr. of 1965 ed. lib. bdg. 60.00x (ISBN 0-912004-25-8). W W Gaunt.

Treatise on the Liability of Stockholders in Corporations. Seymour D. Thompson. xxxix, 528p. 1983. Repr. of 1879 ed. lib. bdg. 42.50x (ISBN 0-8377-1130-4). Rothman.

Treatise on the Limitations of Police Power in the United States. C. G. Tiedeman. LC 73-150421. (American Constitutional & Legal History Ser). 1971. Repr. of 1886 ed. lib. bdg. 65.00 (ISBN 0-306-70104-9). Da Capo.

Treatise on the Line Complex. Charles H. Jessop. LC 68-55945. 1969. Repr. of 1903 ed. 16.95 (ISBN 0-8284-0223-X). Chelsea Pub.

Treatise on the Love of God, 2 vols. St. Francis de Sales. Tr. by John K. Ryan. 1975. Set. pap. 10.00 (ISBN 0-89555-064-4); Vol. 1. pap. (ISBN 0-89555-062-8, 166-I); Vol. 2. pap. 13.50 (ISBN 0-89555-063-6). TAN Bks Pubs.

Treatise on the Mathematical Theory of Elasticity. 4th ed. Augustus E. Love. (Illus.). 1927. pap. text ed. 12.50 (ISBN 0-486-60174-9). Dover.

Treatise on the Measure of Damages, or an Inquiry into the Principles Which Govern the Amount of Compensation Recovered in Suits at Law. Theodore Sedgwick. LC 77-37984. (American Law Ser.: The Formative Years). 648p. 1972. Repr. of 1847 ed. 37.50 (ISBN 0-405-04027-X). Ayer Co Pubs.

Treatise on the Medical Jurisprudence of Insanity. 5th ed. Isaac Ray. LC 75-16732. (Classics in Psychiatry Ser.). 1976. Repr. of 1871 ed. 49.50x (ISBN 0-405-07453-0). Ayer Co Pubs.

Treatise on the Medical Jurisprudence of Insanity. Isaac Ray. (Historical Foundations of Forensic Psychiatry & Psychology Ser.). xvi, 480p. 1983. Repr. of 1838 ed. lib. bdg. 45.00 (ISBN 0-306-76181-5). Da Capo.

Treatise on the Method of Government Surveying. Shobal V. Clevenger. 1978. pap. 8.50 (ISBN 0-686-25541-0). CARBEN Survey.

Treatise on the Methods of Observation & Reasoning in Politics, 2 vols. in 1. George C. Lewis. LC 73-14166. (Perspectives in Social Inquiry Ser.). 984p. 1974. Repr. 54.00x (ISBN 0-405-05511-0). Ayer Co Pubs.

Treatise on the Military Band. H. E. Adkins. 1977. lib. bdg. 59.95 (ISBN 0-8490-2763-2). Gordon Pr.

Treatise on the Millennium. Samuel Hopkins. LC 70-38450. (Religion in America, Series 2). 162p. 1972. Repr. of 1793 ed. 14.00 (ISBN 0-405-04070-9). Ayer Co Pubs.

Treatise on the Mule. Harvey Riley. (Illus.). 112p. pap. 5.00 spiral bdg (ISBN 0-318-12511-0). Am Donkey.

Treatise on the Nature, Symptoms, Causes & Treatment of Insanity. William C. Ellis. LC 75-16700. (Classics in Psychiatry Ser.). 1976. Repr. of 1838 ed. 27.50x (ISBN 0-405-07427-1). Ayer Co Pubs.

Treatise on the Novel. Robert Liddell. LC 83-45913. Repr. of 1947 ed. 21.00 (ISBN 0-404-20160-1). AMS Pr.

Treatise on the Operation & Construction of Retroactive Laws, As Affected by Constitutional Limitations & Judicial Interpretations. William P. Wade. xlviii, 391p. 1982. Repr. of 1880 ed. lib. bdg. 35.00x (ISBN 0-8377-1319-6). Rothman.

Treatise on the Operations of Surgery. Samuel Sharpe. LC 77-91540. 1977. Repr. of 1769 ed. lib. bdg. 35.00 (ISBN 0-89341-503-0). Longwood Pub Group.

Treatise on the Organization, Jurisdiction & Practice of the Courts of the U. S., to Which Is Added an Appendix. Alfred Conkling. LC 85-80031. 1985. Repr. of 1831 ed. lib. bdg. 80.00x (ISBN 0-912004-27-4). W W Gaunt.

Treatise on the Passion see Treatise on the Passion: Complete Works of St. Thomas More.

Treatise on the Passion: Complete Works of St. Thomas More, Vol. 13. St. Thomas More. Ed. by Garry E. Haupt. Incl. Treatise on the Passion; Treatise on the Blessed Body; Instructions & Prayers. LC 63-7949. 1976. text ed. 62.00t (ISBN 0-300-01794-4). Yale U Pr.

Treatise on the Passions, So Far As They Regard the Stage. Samuel Foote. LC 72-144608. Repr. of 1747 ed. 11.50 (ISBN 0-404-02448-3). AMS Pr.

Treatise on the Patriarchal, or Co-Operative System of Society. facsimile 2nd ed. Zaphaniah Kingsley. LC 78-126240. (Select Bibliographies Ser). Repr. of 1829 ed. 10.00 (ISBN 0-8369-5467-X). Ayer Co Pubs.

Treatise on the Police & Crimes of the Metropolis. John Wade. LC 71-129306. (Criminology, Law Enforcement, & Social Problems Ser.: No. 128). 410p. (With intro. added). 1972. Repr. of 1829 ed. 18.00x (ISBN 0-87585-128-2). Patterson Smith.

Treatise on the Police of the Metropolis. 7th ed. Patrick Colquhoun. LC 69-14918. (Criminology, Law Enforcement & Social Problems Ser.: No. 42). 1969. Repr. of 1806 ed. 30.00x (ISBN 0-87585-042-1). Patterson Smith.

Treatise on the Practice of the Supreme Court of Judicature of the State of New York in Civil Actions. William Wyche. LC 70-37993. (American Law Ser.: The Formative Years). 374p. 1972. Repr. of 1794 ed. 24.50 (ISBN 0-405-04040-7). Ayer Co Pubs.

Treatise on the Principles & Practical Influence of Taxation & the Funding System. J. R. McCulloch. Ed. by D. P. O'Brien. 520p. 1975. 32.00 (ISBN 0-8419-5700-2). Holmes & Meier.

Treatise on the Principles & Practical Influence of Taxation & the Funding System. John R. McCulloch. LC 68-56739. (Research & Source Works Ser.: No. 220). 1968. Repr. of 1863 ed. 20.00 (ISBN 0-8337-2317-0). B Franklin.

Treatise on the Principles & Practical Influence of Taxation & the Funding System. 2nd ed. John R. McCulloch. LC 67-28411. 1986. Repr. of 1852 ed. 45.00x (ISBN 0-678-00331-9). Kelley.

Treatise on the Principles of American Constitutional Law & Legislation: The Constitutional Convention; Its History, Powers & Modes of Proceeding. 2nd ed. John A. Jameson. xix, 561p. 1981. Repr. of 1869 ed. lib. bdg. 42.50x (ISBN 0-8377-0734-X). Rothman.

Treatise on the Principles of Pleading, in Civil Actions. James Gould. LC 70-37974. (American Law Ser.: The Formative Years). 540p. 1972. Repr. of 1832 ed. 23.00 (ISBN 0-405-04014-8). Ayer Co Pubs.

Treatise on the Property Rights of Husband & Wife, Under the Community or Ganancial System: Adapted to the Statutes & Decisions of Louisiana, Texas, California, Nevada, Washington, Idaho, Arizona & New Mexico. Richard A. Ballinger. xiii, 543p. 1981. Repr. of 1895 ed. lib. bdg. 38.50x (ISBN 0-8377-0320-4). Rothman.

Treatise on the Right of Personal Liberty & on Writ of Habeas Corpus. Rollin Carlos Hurd. LC 77-37767. (American Constitutional & Legal History Ser). 670p. 1972. Repr. of 1876 ed. lib. bdg. 75.00 (ISBN 0-306-70431-5). Da Capo.

Treatise on the Right of Property in Tide Waters & in the Soil & Shores Thereof. Joseph K. Angell. 435p. 1983. Repr. of 1826 ed. lib. bdg. 37.50x (ISBN 0-8377-0214-3). Rothman.

Treatise on the Rules Which Govern the Interpretation & Construction of Statutory & Constitutional Law. 2nd ed. Theodore Sedgwick. Ed. by John N. Pomeroy. xlviii, 692p. 1981. Repr. of 1874 ed. lib. bdg. 49.50x (ISBN 0-8377-1115-0). Rothman.

Treatise on the Seven Rays, 5 vols. Alice A. Bailey. Incl. Vol. 1. Esoteric Psychology. 1979. 20.00 (ISBN 0-85330-018-6); pap. 9.00 1984 (ISBN 0-85330-118-2); Vol. 2. Esoteric Psychology. 1982. 28.00 (ISBN 0-85330-019-4); pap. 17.00 1982 (ISBN 0-85330-119-0); Vol. 3. Esoteric Astrology. 1975. 28.00 (ISBN 0-85330-020-8); pap. 17.00 1983 (ISBN 0-85330-120-4); Vol. 4. Esoteric Healing. 1978. 28.00 (ISBN 0-85330-021-6); pap. 17.00 1984 (ISBN 0-85330-121-2); Vol. 5. The Rays & the Initiations. 1988. 28.00 (ISBN 0-85330-022-4); pap. 17.00 (ISBN 0-85330-122-0). pap. Lucis.

Treatise on the Shift Operator. N. K. Nikol'skii. Tr. by J. Peetre from Rus. LC 84-26869. (Grundlehren der Mathematischen Wissenschaften: Vol. 273). (Illus.). 504p. 1985. 84.00 (ISBN 0-387-15021-8). Springer-Verlag.

Treatise on the Specific Performance of Contracts. 3rd ed. John N. Pomeroy & John C. Mann. Ed. by R. H. Hemholz & Bernard D. Reams, Jr. LC 86-62940. (Historical Writings in Law & Jurisprudence, Second Ser.: No. 8). xi, 1045p. 1986. Repr. of 1926 ed. lib. bdg. 52.50 (ISBN 0-89941-523-7). W S Hein.

Treatise on the Supposed Hereditary Properties of Diseases...(London, 1814) Joseph Adams. Ed. by Charles Rosenberg. LC 83-48528. (History of Hereditarian Thought Ser.). 125p. 1985. Repr. of 1814 ed. lib. bdg. 22.00 (ISBN 0-8240-5800-3). Garland Pub.

Treatise on the Teeth. John A. Skinner. (Illus.). 1967. Repr. of 1801 ed. 15.00 (ISBN 0-87266-027-3). Argosy.

Treatise on the Theory & Practice of Landscape Gardening Adapted to North America. Andrew J. Downing. (Illus.). 1976. Repr. of 1875 ed. 20.00 (ISBN 0-913728-23-3). Theophrastus.

Treatise on the Unconstitutionality of American Slavery: Together with the Powers & Duties of the Federal Government, in Relation to That Subject. facs. ed. Joel Tiffany. LC 78-83905. (Black Heritage Library Collection Ser). 1849. 11.25 (ISBN 0-8369-8666-0). Ayer Co Pubs.

Treatise on the Virtues. St. Thomas Aquinas. Tr. by John A. Oesterle. LC 84-10691. 171p. 1984. pap. text ed. 7.95 (ISBN 0-268-01855-3, 85-18557). U of Notre Dame Pr.

Treatise on the Wealth, Power & Resources of the British Empire. 2nd ed. Patrick Colquhoun. 1815. 60.00 (ISBN 0-384-09710-3). Johnson Repr.

Treatise on Theatres. George Saunders. Incl. LC 68-21227. (Illus.). 1968. 33.00 (ISBN 0-405-08917-1). Ayer Co Pubs.

Treatise on Thoroughbred Selection. new ed. Donald Lesh. 7.95 (ISBN 0-85131-296-9, BL6783, Pub. by J A Allen U K). S R Smith Sporting Bks.

Treatise on Trial by Jury: Including Questions of Law & Fact. With an Introductory Chapter on the Origin & History of Jury Trial. John Proffatt. viii, 608p. 1986. Repr. of 1877 ed. lib. bdg. 47.50x (ISBN 0-8377-2506-2). Rothman.

Treatise on Trusts & Monopolies, Containing an Exposition of the Rule of Public Policy Against Contracts & Combinations in Restraint of Trade, & a Review of Cases, Ancient & Modern. Thomas C. Spelling. xxvii, 274p. 1981. Repr. of 1893 ed. lib. bdg. 27.50x (ISBN 0-8377-1116-9). Rothman.

Treatise on White Magic. Alice A. Bailey. 1979. 28.00 (ISBN 0-85330-023-2); pap. 17.00 1987 (ISBN 0-85330-123-9). Lucis.

Treatise on Wills. 8th ed. Thomas Jarman et al. (Legal Reprint Ser.). (Illus.). 1986. Repr. of 1951 ed. Vol. 1 - p.ccclxiv, 1-628; Vol. 2 - p.629-1542; Vol. 3 - p.1543-2197. lib. bdg. 180.00x set (ISBN 0-421-35530-1). Rothman.

Treatise on Wood Engraving, Historical & Practical. William A. Chatto. LC 69-16477. (Illus.). 698p. 1969. Repr. of 1861 ed. 65.00x (ISBN 0-8103-3531-X). Gale.

Treatise Ta'anit of the Babylonian Talmud. Tr. & Henry Malter. LC 78-1171. (JPS Library of Jewish Classics). 528p. 1978. 6.50 (ISBN 0-8276-0108-5, 422). JPS Phila.

Treatise Touching the Inconveniences, That the Importation of Tobacco Out of Spaine, Hath Brought into This Land. Edward Bennett. LC 77-6856. (English Experience Ser.: No. 846). 1977. Repr. of 1620 ed. lib. bdg. 15.00 (ISBN 90-221-0846-5). Walter J Johnson.

Treatise Upon Cable or Rope Traction As Applied to the Working of Street & Other Railways. J. Bucknall Smith & George W. Hilton. LC 76-53131. (Illus.). 1978. Repr. 14.50 (ISBN 0-913896-08-X). Owlswick Pr.

Treatise Upon the Law of Eminent Domain. Henery E. Mills. lxvii, 404p. 1982. Repr. of 1879 ed. lib. bdg. 35.00x (ISBN 0-8377-0841-9). Rothman.

Treatise Upon the Law, Privileges, Proceedings & Usage of Parliament. E. May. (Parliamentary & Congressional Ser). xvi, 469p. 1971. Repr. of 1844 ed. 24.00x (ISBN 0-7165-2014-1). Rothman.

Treatise Wherein Dicing, Dauncing, Vaine Playes or Enterluds Are Reproved. John Northbrooke. LC 72-170401. (English Stage Ser.: Vol. 1). 1973. lib. bdg. 61.00 (ISBN 0-8240-0584-8). Garland Pub.

Treatise Wherein Is Declared the Sufficiencie of English Medicines, for Cure of All Diseases, Cured with Medicine. Timothy Bright. LC 77-6860. (English Experience Ser.: No. 854). 1977. Repr. of 1580 ed. lib. bdg. 6.00 (ISBN 90-221-0854-6). Walter J Johnson.

Treatises & Essays on Subjects Connected with Economical Policy. John R. McCulloch. LC 67-20088. 1968. Repr. of 1853 ed. 45.00x (ISBN 0-678-00255-X). Kelley.

Treatises & Sermons of Meister Eckhart. Meister Eckhart et al. Tr. by James M. Clark & John V. Skinner. 267p. 1983. Repr. of 1958 ed. lib. bdg. 21.00 (Octagon). Hippocrene Bks.

Treatises & the Pastoral Prayer. Aelred of Rievaulx. pap. 5.00 (ISBN 0-87907-902-9). Cistercian Pubns.

Treatises I: Apologia, Precept & Dispensation. Bernard of Clairvaux. (Cistercian Fathers Ser.: No. 1). 190p. 7.95 (ISBN 0-87907-101-X). Cistercian Pubns.

Treatises of Benvenuto Cellini on Goldsmithing & Sculpture. Benvenuto Cellini. Tr. by C. R. Ashbee. (Illus.). 1966. pap. 6.95 (ISBN 0-486-21568-7). Dover.

Treatises on Marriage & Other Subjects. St. Augustine. LC 73-75002. (Fathers of the Church Ser.: Vol. 27). 456p. 1955. 34.95x (ISBN 0-8132-0027-X). Cath U Pr.

Treatises on Various Moral Subjects. St. Augustine. LC 65-18319. (Fathers of the Church Ser.: Vol. 16). 479p. 1952. 24.95x (ISBN 0-8132-0016-4). Cath U Pr.

Treatises Upon Several Subjects. John Norris. Ed. by Rene Wellek. LC 75-11244. (British Philosophers & Theologians of the 17th & 18th Centuries Ser.). 1978. Repr. of 1698 ed. lib. bdg. 51.00 (ISBN 0-8240-1796-X). Garland Pub.

Treatment & Disposal Methods for Waste Chemicals. (IRPTC Data Profile Ser.: No. 5). 303p. 1986. 50.00 (ISBN 92-807-1106-7, E.85.III.D.2). UN.

Treatment & Disposal of Industrial Wastewaters & Residues. (Illus.). 1978. pap. 5.00x (ISBN 0-686-26017-1, 1WW8). Info Transfer.

Treatment & Disposal of Industrial Wastewaters & Residues. (Illus.). 1977. 10.00x (ISBN 0-686-26018-X, 1WW7); softcover 5.00x (ISBN 0-686-26019-8). Info Transfer.

Treatment & Disposal of Liquid & Solid Industrial Wastes: Proceedings of the Third Turkish-German Environmental Engineering Symposium, Istanbul, July 1979. K. Curi. LC 80-40993. (Illus.). 515p. 1980. 125.00 (ISBN 0-08-023999-4). Pergamon.

Treatment & Management in Adult Psychiatry. G. E. Berrios & H. Dowson. (Illus.). 432p. 1983. 52.00 (ISBN 0-7216-0808-6, Bailliere-Tindall). Saunders.

Treatment & Management of Urban Solid Waste. David G. Wilson. LC 70-182527. 210p. 1972. pap. 14.95 (ISBN 0-87762-077-6). Technomic.

Treatment & Prevention of Alcohol Problems. W. Miles Cox. (Personality, Psychopathology, & Psychotherapy Ser.). 1986. 45.00 (ISBN 0-12-194470-0). Acad Pr.

Treatment & Prevention of Dehydration in Diarrheal Diseases: A Guide for Use at the Primary Level. (Also avail. in French). 1976. 2.40 (ISBN 92-4-154052-4). World Health.

Treatment & Prevention of Reading Problems: The Neuropsychological Approach. Carl H. Delacato. (Illus.). 136p. 1971. 17.25x (ISBN 0-398-00421-8). C C Thomas.

Treatment & Reuse of Wastewater. Ed. by Asit K. Biswas & Abdullah Arar. (Illus.). 208p. 1988. text ed. 90.00 (ISBN 0-408-02335-X). Butterworth.

Treatment & the Cure. Peter Kocan. LC 85-14818. 1985. 14.95 (ISBN 0-8008-7867-1). Taplinger.

Treatment & the Cure. Peter Kocan. 246p. 1987. pap. 7.95 (ISBN 0-207-14974-7, Pub. by Angus & Robertson). Salem Hse Pubs.

Treatment & Use of Sewage Effluent for Irrigation. A. Arar & M. B. Pescod. (Illus.). 392p. 1988. text ed. write for info. (ISBN 0-408-02622-7). Butterworth.

Treatment Approaches to Language Disorders in Children: Psycholinguistic & Neurolinguistic Approaches. Merlin J. Mecham & Mary L. Willbrand. (Illus.). 246p. 1985. 32.75 (ISBN 0-398-05148-8). C C Thomas.

Treatment Aspects of Drug Dependence. Ed. by Arnold Schecter. (Uniscience Ser.). 1978. 66.00 (ISBN 0-8493-5476-5). CRC Pr.

Treatment, Conditioning & Disposal of Iodine-129. (Technical Reports Ser.: No. 276). 84p. (Orig.). 1987. pap. text ed. 25.00 (ISBN 92-0-125287-0, IDC276, IAEA). UNIPUB.

Treatment Custody Role Conflict in Community Based Correctional Workers: Causes & Effects. Ronald J. Scott. LC 76-56470. 1977. soft bdg. 12.95 (ISBN 0-88247-450-2). R & E Pubs.

Treatment, Disposal & Management of Human Wastes: Proceedings of an IAWPRC Conference Held in Tokyo, Japan, 30 September-4 October 1985. Ed. by J. Matusmoto & T. Matusuo. LC 82-645900. (Water Science & Technology Ser.: No. 18). (Illus.). 428p. 1987. pap. 105.00 (ISBN 0-08-035192-1). Pergamon.

Treatment Effectiveness in Communication Disorders: A Meta-Analysis. Chad Nye. (Orig.). 1988. pap. text ed. 24.50 (ISBN 0-316-61739-3, 617393). College-Hill.

Treatment for Psychosomatic Problems. Ed. by John M. Kuldau. LC 81-48484. (Mental Health Services Ser.: No. 15). 1982. pap. text ed. 14.95x (ISBN 0-87589-909-9). Jossey-Bass.

Treatment Formulations & Clinical Social Work. Ed. by Phyllis Caroff. LC 82-62378. 52p. (Orig.). 1982. pap. text ed. 7.95 (ISBN 0-87101-118-2). Natl Assn Soc Wkrs.

Treatment in Crisis Situations. Naomi Golan. LC 77-85350. (Treatment Approaches in the Human Services Ser., Gen. Ed. Francis J. Turner). 1978. text ed. 20.95 (ISBN 0-02-912060-8). Free Pr.

Treatment in Dermatology. Ed. by J. Verbov. (New Clinical Applications Dermatology Ser.). 1987. lib. bdg. 38.25 (ISBN 0-85200-955-0, Pub. by MTP Pr England). Kluwer Academic.

Treatment Interventions In Human Sexuality. Ed. by Carol C. Nadelson & David B. Marcotte. LC 83-4078. (Critical Issues In Psychiatry Ser.). 502p. 1983. 65.00x (ISBN 0-306-41082-6, Plenum Pr). Plenum Pub.

Treatment Issues & Innovations in Mental Retardation. Ed. by Johnny L. Matson & Frank Andrasik. (Applied Clinical Psychology Ser.). 666p. 1983. 69.50x (ISBN 0-306-40935-6, Plenum Pr). Plenum Pub.

Treatment Manual for Patients with Pulmonary Emphysema. Alvan L. Barach. LC 70-75403. (Illus.). 114p. 1969. 29.50 (ISBN 0-8089-0030-7, 790425). Grune.

Treatment Modalities in Lung Cancer. Ed. by R. Arriagada & T. Le Chevalier. (Antibiotics & Chemotherapy Ser.: Vol. 41). (Illus.). viii, 212p. 1988. 124.75 (ISBN 3-8055-4775-7). S Karger.

Treatment of Acute Psychotic Episodes. Ed. by Steven T. Levy & Philip T. Ninan. 250p. 1988. cancelled (ISBN 0-87668-988-8). Aronson.

Treatment of Adult Survivors of Childhood Abuse. Eliana Gil. LC 88-80275. 250p. (Orig.). 1988. pap. 16.95 (ISBN 0-9613205-6-7, 0007). Launch Pr.

Treatment of Affective Disorders in the Elderly. Charles A. Shamoian. LC 85-6103. (Progress in Psychiatry Ser.). 112p. 1985. text ed. 17.95x (ISBN 0-88048-086-6, 48-086-6). Am Psychiatric.

Treatment of Airborne Radioactive Wastes. (Proceedings Ser.). (Illus.). 818p. 1968. pap. 48.00 (ISBN 92-0-020068-0, ISP195, IAEA). UNIPUB.

Treatment of Alcoholism. Edgar P. Nace. LC 87-11691. 304p. 1987. 30.00 (ISBN 0-87630-468-4). Brunner-Mazel.

Treatment of Alcoholism & Other Addictions: A Self-Psychology Approach. Jerome D. Levin. LC 87-19563. 433p. 1987. 35.00x (ISBN 0-87668-947-0). Aronson.

Treatment of Ancient Legend & History in Bodmer. Anthony Scenna. LC 37-9711. (Columbia University. Germanic Studies, New Ser.: No. 5). Repr. of 1937 ed. 17.00 (ISBN 0-404-50455-8). AMS Pr.

Treatment of Antisocial Behavior in Children & Adolescents: Alternative Interventions & Their Effectiveness Treatment. Alan E. Kazdin. (Dorsey Professional Bks.). 366p. 1985. 35.00 (ISBN 0-256-03486-9). Dorsey.

Treatment of Antisocial Syndromes. Ed. by William H. Reid. 288p. 1981. 27.95 (ISBN 0-442-25630-2). Van Nos Reinhold.

Treatment of Aphasia: A Language-Oriented Approach. Cynthia M. Shewan & Donna L. Bandur. LC 86-2305. (Clinical Updates Ser.). (Illus.). 310p. (Orig.). 1986. pap. text ed. 29.50 (ISBN 0-316-78570-9, 785709). College-Hill.

Treatment of Autistic Children. Patricia Howlin & Michael Rutter. LC 86-24628. (Studies in Child Psychiatry). 299p. 1987. 59.95 (ISBN 0-471-10262-8). Wiley.

Treatment of Black Alcoholics. Ed. by Frances L. Brisbane & Maxine Womble. LC 85-13975. (Alcoholism Treatment Quarterly Ser.: Vol. 2, No. 3-4). 270p. 1985. text ed. 32.95 (ISBN 0-86656-403-9, B403). Haworth Pr.

Treatment of Bleeding Disorders with Blood Components. Ed. by E. F. Mammen et al. (Reviews of Hematology: Vol. I). 1980. 39.95 (ISBN 0-915340-01-1). PJD Pubns.

Treatment of Brain Tumors. 1983. 1.50 (ISBN 0-318-03973-7). Assn Brain Tumor.

Treatment of Burns. Ed. by Ch-Ch Yang. (Illus.). 450p. 1982. 125.00 (ISBN 0-387-10770-3). Springer-Verlag.

Treatment of Burns: Principles & Practice. William W. Monafo & Carlos Pappalardo. LC 71-138827. (Illus.). 286p. 1971. 22.50 (ISBN 0-87527-055-7). Green.

Treatment of Cancer. Ed. by Keith E. Halnan. LC 81-82118. (Illus.). 912p. 1982. monograph 75.00 (ISBN 0-89640-058-1). Igaku-Shoin.

Treatment of Cardiac Emergencies. 5th ed. Goldberger. (Illus.). 498p. 1989. 41.95 (ISBN 0-8016-2931-4). Mosby.

Treatment of Cardiac Emergencies. 4th ed. Emanuel Goldberger & Myron W. Wheat, Jr. (Illus.). 336p. 1984. pap. text ed. 39.00 (ISBN 0-8016-1904-1). Mosby.

Treatment of Cats by Homoeopathy. K. Sheppard. 62p. 1960. 4.95x (ISBN 0-8464-1055-9). Beekman Pubs.

Treatment of Cats by Homoeopathy. K. Sheppard. 1979. pap. 3.95x (ISBN 0-85032-120-4, Pub. by C. W. Daniels). Formur Intl.

Treatment of Cats by Homoeopathy. K. Sheppard. 1980. 17.50x (ISBN 0-85032-187-5, Pub. by Daniel Co England). State Mutual Bk.

Treatment of Cerebral Edema. Ed. by A. Hartmann & M. Brock. (Illus.). 176p. 1982. pap. 35.00 (ISBN 0-387-11751-2). Springer-Verlag.

Treatment of Cerebral Infarction. J. Suzuki. (Illus.). 400p. 1987. 91.50 (ISBN 0-387-81933-9). Springer-Verlag.

Treatment of Children Through Social Group Work: A Developmental Approach. James A. Garland & Ralph Kolodny. 1980. text ed. 20.00x (ISBN 0-89182-016-7); pap. text ed. 10.00 (ISBN 0-89182-017-5). Charles River Bks.

Treatment of Children's Phonetic Disorders. Paul R. Hoffman et al. 320p. (Orig.). 1988. pap. text ed. 27.50 (ISBN 0-316-36837-7, 368377). College-Hill.

Treatment of Communication Disorders in Culturally & Linguistically Diverse Populations. Ed. by Orlando Taylor. LC 85-22431. 200p. 1986. pap. 25.50 (ISBN 0-316-83377-0). College-Hill.

Treatment of Complicated Epilepsies in Adults. Ed. by P. Berner & L. W. Diehl. (Bibliotheca Psychiatrica Ser.: No. 158). (Illus.). 1978. 38.75 (ISBN 3-8055-2814-0). S Karger.

Treatment of Depression: An Interpersonal Systems Approach. Ian H. Gotlib & Catherine A. Colby. (Psychology Practioner Guidebks.: No. 5). 180p. 1987. text ed. 22.50 (ISBN 0-08-033634-5, PBI); pap. text ed. 12.95 (ISBN 0-08-033633-7). Pergamon.

Treatment of Depression: Old Controversies & New Approaches. Ed. by Paula J. Clayton & James E. Barrett. (American Psychopathological Association Ser.). 352p. 1983. text ed. 80.00 (ISBN 0-89004-745-6). Raven.

Treatment of Depressions & Related Moods: A Manual for Psychotherapists. Daniel W. Badal. LC 87-33665. 600p. 1988. 45.00x (ISBN 0-87668-981-0). Aronson.

Treatment of Disordered Function from Pain to Sexual Complaints: An Introduction to the Edagawa Method. Lawrence W. Friedmann & Naoyushi Edagawa. (Illus.). 192p. 1981. 20.00x (ISBN 0-682-49665-0, University). Exposition-Phoenix.

Treatment of Dogs by Homoeopathy. K. Sheppard. 1980. 4.95 (ISBN 0-8464-1056-7). Beekman Pubs.

Treatment of Dogs by Homoeopathy. K. Sheppard. 1981. pap. 3.95x (ISBN 0-85032-079-8, Pub. by C. W. Daniels). Formur Intl.

Treatment of Dogs by Homoeopathy. K. Sheppard. 1980. 17.50x (ISBN 0-85032-188-3, Pub. by Daniel Co England). State Mutual Bk.

Treatment of Domestic & Industrial Wastewaters in Large Plants: Proceedings of a Workshop Held in Vienna, Austria, Sept. 1979. S. H. Jenkins. (Progress in Water Technology: Vol. 12, Nos. 3 & 5). 550p. 1981. 110.00 (ISBN 0-08-026033-0). Pergamon.

Treatment of Drinking Problems. G. Edwards. 1984. text ed. 24.95 (ISBN 0-07-019036-4). McGraw.

Treatment of Drinking Water for Organic Contaminants: Proceedings of the Second National Conference on Drinking Water, Edmonton, Alberta, Canada, 7-8 April 1986. Ed. by P. M. Huck & P. Toft. (Illus.). 388p. 1987. 92.00 (ISBN 0-08-031876-2). Pergamon.

Treatment of Emotional Disorders. Seymour L. Halleck. LC 77-18374. 544p. 1978. 35.00x (ISBN 0-87668-263-8). Aronson.

Treatment of End-Stage Coronary Artery Disease. P. J. Walter. (Advances in Cardiology Ser.: Vol. 36). (Illus.). x, 306p. 1988. 126.00 (ISBN 3-8055-4717-X). S Karger.

Treatment of End Stage Renal Disease in Children. Richard N. Fine & Alan Gruskin. (Illus.). 590p. 1984. write for info. (ISBN 0-7216-1025-0). Saunders.

Treatment of Families in Conflict: The Clinical Study of Family Process. Group for the Advancement of Psychiatry Staff. LC 84-45131. 352p. 1983. 30.00x (ISBN 0-87668-724-9). Aronson.

Treatment of Families in Crisis. Donald G. Langsley & David M. Kaplan. LC 68-29400. 208p. 1968. 42.50 (ISBN 0-8089-0251-2, 792440). Grune.

Treatment of Family Violence: Sourcebook. Ammerman. (Personality Processes Ser.). 1989. price not set (ISBN 0-471-61023-2). Wiley.

Treatment of Final Vowels in Early Neo-Babylonian. James P. Hyatt. LC 78-63567. (Yale Oriental Series Researches: No. 23). Repr. of 1941 ed. 20.00 (ISBN 0-404-60323-8). AMS Pr.

Treatment of Fractures in Children & Adolescents. Ed. by B. G. Weber. LC 79-16985. (Illus.). 1980. 139.00 (ISBN 0-387-09313-3). Springer-Verlag.

Treatment of Glioma. Ed. by J. Suzuki. (Illus.). 225p. 1988. 89.70 (ISBN 0-387-70029-3). Springer-Verlag.

Treatment of Haemoglobinopathies & Allied Disorders: Report. WHO Scientific Group. Geneva, 1971. (Technical Report Ser.: No. 509). (Also avail. in French & Spanish). 1972. pap. 2.00 (ISBN 92-4-120509-1). World Health.

Treatment of Hand Injuries: Preservation & Restoration of Function. Elden C. Weckesser. LC 72-86353. pap. 73.90 (ISBN 0-317-58154-6, 2029741). Bks Demand UMI.

Treatment of Heart Disease in the Adult. 2nd ed. Ira L. Rubin & Harry Gross. LC 79-175466. pap. 130.50 (ISBN 0-317-26706-X, 2056008). Bks Demand UMI.

Treatment of Hodgkin's Disease. Enrico Anglesio. Ed. by P. Rentchnick. LC 68-56205. (Recent Results in Cancer Research Ser.: Vol. 18). 1969. 20.00 (ISBN 0-387-04681-X). Springer-Verlag.

Treatment of Homosexuals with Mental Health Disorders. Ed. by Michael Ross & John P. DeCecco. LC 87-30826. (Journal of Homosexuality: No. 15). (Illus.). 230p. 1988. pap. 12.95 (ISBN 0-918393-47-7). Harrington Pk.

Treatment of Horses by Acupuncture. Erwin Westermayer. 1980. 25.00x (ISBN 0-85032-161-1, Pub. by Daniel Co England). State Mutual Bk.

Treatment of Horses by Homeopathy. G. MacLeod. 182p. 1977. 19.95x (ISBN 0-8464-1284-5). Beekman Pubs.

Treatment of Horses by Homoeopathy. G. MacLeod. 1980. 17.50x (ISBN 0-85032-155-7, Pub. by Daniel Co England). State Mutual Bk.

Treatment of Hydrocephalus: Computer Tomography. Ed. by R. Wuellenweber et al. (Advances in Neurosurgery Ser.: Vol. 6). (Illus.). 1978. pap. 46.00 (ISBN 0-387-09031-2). Springer-Verlag.

Treatment of Hyperlipoproteinemia. Ed. by Lars A. Carlson & Anders G. Olsson. 304p. 1984. text ed. 75.50 (ISBN 0-89004-341-8). Raven.

Treatment of Hypertension with Urapidil-Preclinical & Clinical Update. Ed. by A. Amery. (International Congress & Symposium Ser.: No. 101). 186p. 1986. pap. 30.00 (ISBN 0-905958-29-2, Pub. by Royal Society of Medicine Services Ltd). Longwood Pub Group.

Treatment of Imprecise Goals: The Case of the Regional Science. Horst Zimmerman. (Discussion Paper Ser.: No. 9). 1966. pap. 6.50 (ISBN 0-686-32178-2). Regional Sci Res Inst.

Treatment of Incorporated Transuranium Elements. (Technical Reports Ser.: No. 184). (Illus.). 170p. 1978. pap. 23.00 (ISBN 92-0-125278-1, IDC184, IAEA). UNIPUB.

Treatment of Industrial Effluents. Ed. by A. Callely et al. LC 76-54909. 378p. 1977. 45.95x (ISBN 0-470-98934-3). Halsted Pr.

Treatment of Infantile Hydrocephalus, 2 vols. Concezio Di Rocco. 1987. Set. 195.00 (ISBN 0-8493-5720-9). Vol. I, 160 pgs. Vol. II, 160 pgs. CRC Pr.

Treatment of Infective Endocarditis. Ed. by Alan Bisno. LC 81-7080. 352p. 1981. 51.50 (ISBN 0-8089-1450-2, 790598). Grune.

Treatment of Injuries to Athletes. 4th ed. Don H. O'Donoghue. (Illus.). 736p. 1984. 89.00 (ISBN 0-7216-6928-X). Saunders.

Treatment of Insanity. John M. Galt. LC 73-2397. (Mental Illness & Social Policy; the American Experience Ser.). Repr. of 1846 ed. 32.00 (ISBN 0-405-05205-7). Ayer Co Pubs.

Treatment of Integral Equations by Numerical Methods. Christopher T. Baker & Geoffrey F. Miller. 1983. 54.50 (ISBN 0-12-074120-2). Acad Pr.

Treatment of Low- & Intermediate-Level Liquid Radioactive Wastes. (Technical Reports Ser.: No. 236). (Illus.). 145p. 1985. pap. 29.00 (ISBN 92-0-125184-X, IDC236, IAEA). UNIPUB.

Treatment of Low & Intermediate-Level Solid Radioactive Wastes. (Technical Reports Ser.: No. 223). (Illus.). 93p. 1983. pap. 21.00 (ISBN 92-0-125183-1, IDC223, IAEA). UNIPUB.

Treatment of Male Infertility. Ed. by J. Bain et al. (Illus.). 330p. 1982. 88.50 (ISBN 0-387-10990-0). Springer-Verlag.

Treatment of Market Power: Antitrust Regulation & Public Enterprise. William G. Shepherd. LC 75-19459. 272p. 1975. 32.00x (ISBN 0-231-03773-2). Columbia U Pr.

Treatment of Mental Disorders. Ed. by John H. Greist & James W. Jefferson. 1982. pap. text ed. 24.95x (ISBN 0-19-503107-5). Oxford U Pr.

Treatment of Mental Illness: Science, Faith & the Therapeutic Community. T. M. Caine & D. J. Smail. LC 78-88569. 192p. (Orig.). 1969. text ed. 25.00x (ISBN 0-8236-6648-4). Intl Univs Pr.

Treatment of Metastasis: Problems & Prospects. K. Hellman & S. A. Eccles. 430p. 1985. 88.00x (ISBN 0-85066-294-X). Taylor & Francis.

Treatment of Migraine: Pharmacological & Biofeedback Considerations. Ed. by R. J. Mathew. (Illus.). 170p. 1981. text ed. 27.50 (ISBN 0-88331-209-3). Luce.

Treatment of Multiple Personality Disorder. Ed. by Bennett G. Braun. LC 86-10903. 232p. 1986. pap. text ed. 17.50x (ISBN 0-88048-096-3, 48-096-3). Am Psychiatric.

Treatment of Mycosis with Imidazole Derivatives. W. Raab. (Illus.). 180p. 1980. pap. 16.60 (ISBN 0-387-09800-3). Springer-Verlag.

Treatment of Nature in Dante's Divina Comedia. L. Oscar Kuhns. LC 70-118412. 1971. Repr. of 1897 ed. 23.00x (ISBN 0-8046-1189-0, Pub by Kennikat). Assoc Faculty Pr.

Treatment of Nature in English Poetry Between Pope & Wordsworth. 2nd ed. Myra Reynolds. LC 76-170847. (Ces 3: No. 3). Repr. of 1909 ed. 36.00 (ISBN 0-404-50263-6). AMS Pr.

Treatment of Nature in English Poetry Between Pope & Wordsworth. Myra Reynolds. LC 66-29468. 388p. 1966. Repr. of 1909 ed. 40.00x (ISBN 0-87752-091-7). Gordian.

Treatment of Nature in German Literature from Guenther to Goethe's Werner. Max Batt. 1976. lib. bdg. 59.95 (ISBN 0-8490-2764-0). Gordon Pr.

Treatment of Nature in German Literature from Gunther to the Appearance of Goethe's Werther. Max Batt. LC 72-91034. 1969. Repr. of 1902 ed. 17.00x (ISBN 0-8046-0644-7, Pub by Kennikat). Assoc Faculty Pr.

Treatment of Neoplastic Lesions of the Nervous System: Proceedings of a Symposium Sponsored by the European Organization for Research & Treatment of Cancer (EORTC), Brussels, April, 1980. European Organization for Research & Treatment of Cancer Staff. Ed. by J. Hildebrand & D. Gangji. (Illus.). 178p. 1982. 67.00 (ISBN 0-08-027989-9). Pergamon.

Treatment of Oil-Containing Wastewater. V. V. Pushkarev et al. LC 83-70667. viii, 214p. 1983. 42.50 (ISBN 0-89864-004-0). Allerton Pr.

Treatment of Pain. Ed. by Harold J. Wain & Dionisios P. Devaris. LC 81-65783. 208p. 1982. 30.00x (ISBN 0-87668-607-2). Aronson.

Treatment of Palestinians in Israeli-Occupied West Bank & Gaza. National Lawyers Guild 1977 Middle East Delegation. LC 78-21553. 1978. 12.50 (ISBN 0-9602188-1-5). Natl Lawyers Guild.

Treatment of Patients in the Borderline Spectrum. William W. Meissner. LC 88-10526. 450p. 1988. 40.00x (ISBN 0-87668-917-9). Aronson.

Treatment of Primitive Mental States. Peter Giovacchini. LC 78-74990. 536p. 1978. 35.00x (ISBN 0-87668-347-2). Aronson.

Treatment of Prisoners under International Law. Nigel S. Rodley. LC 86-16433. 1987. 74.00x (ISBN 0-19-825551-9, Pub. by Clarendon Pr); pap. 28.50 (ISBN 0-19-825563-2). Oxford U Pr.

Treatment of Problem Waters in the Northeast. 25.00 (ISBN 0-317-59381-1). NE Agri Engineer.

Treatment of Psychiatric Disorders: Revised for the DSM-III-R. rev. & enl. ed. William H. Reid. 450p. 1988. 42.50 (ISBN 0-87630-536-2). Brunner-Mazel.

Treatment of Psychopathology in the Aging. Ed. by Carl Eisdorfer & William E. Fann. (Springer Psychiatry Ser.: Vol. 2). 304p. 1982. text ed. 31.95 (ISBN 0-8261-3810-1). Springer Pub.

Treatment of Religion in Elementary School Social Studies Textbooks. Judah Harris. 72p. 0.65 (ISBN 0-686-74917-0). ADL.

Treatment of Religion In Public Schools & the Impact On Private Education. 61p. 1984. 6.00 (ISBN 0-318-17960-1, LEC-84-4). Ed Comm States.

Treatment of Renal Anemia with Recombinant Human Erythropoietin. Ed. by K. M. Koch. (Contributions to Nephrology Ser.: Vol. 66). (Illus.). viii, 212p. 1988. 105.50 (ISBN 3-8055-4764-1). S Karger.

Treatment of Schizophrenia. Ed. by M. J. Goldstein et al. xii, 223p. 1986. pap. 34.50 (ISBN 0-387-16628-9). Springer-Verlag.

Treatment of Schizophrenia. Leland E. Hinsie. Ed. by Gerald N. Grob. LC 78-22565. (Historical Issues in Mental Health Ser.). 1979. Repr. of 1930 ed. lib. bdg. 16.00x (ISBN 0-405-11919-4). Ayer Co Pubs.

Treatment of Schizophrenia: Progress & Prospects. L. J. West & D. E. Flinn. LC 76-47510. (Illus.). 320p. 1976. 63.50 (ISBN 0-8089-0970-3, 794805). Grune.

Treatment of Seasonal Unemployment Under Unemployment Insurance. Merrill G. Murray. 84p. 1972. pap. 1.00 (ISBN 0-911558-29-2). W E Upjohn.

Treatment of Sex Offenders in Social Work & Mental Health Settings. Pref. by John S. Wodarski & Daniel L. Whitaker. (Journal of Social Work & Human Sexuality Ser.: Vol. 7, No. 2). (Illus.). 169p. 1988. text ed. 19.95 (ISBN 0-86656-791-7). Haworth Pr.

Treatment of Sexual Disorders: Concepts & Techniques of Couple Therapy. Ed. by Gerd Arentewicz & Gunter Schmidt. LC 83-71214. 1983. 29.95x (ISBN 0-465-08748-5). Basic.

Treatment of Sexual Dysfunction: A Bio-Psycho-Social Approach. new ed. William Hartman & Marilyn A. Fithian. LC 74-5314. 304p. 1974. Repr. 30.00x (ISBN 0-87668-725-7). Aronson.

Treatment of Sexual Dysfunction: A Bio-Psycho Social Approach. William E. Hartman & Marilyn A. Fithian. LC 72-93106. (Illus.). 282p. 1972. 14.95 (ISBN 0-9600626-1-0). Ctr Marital Sexual.

Treatment of Sexual Problems in Individual & Couples Therapy. R. A. Brown & J. R. Field. LC 88-319. 460p. 1988. 47.50 (ISBN 0-89335-301-9). PMA Pub Corp.

Treatment of Sexual Problems in Recovery: Issues in Clinical Management. Ed. by David J. Powell. LC 84-12764. (Alcoholism Treatment Quarterly: Vol. 1, No. 3). 145p. 1984. text ed. 22.95 (ISBN 0-86656-365-2). Haworth Pr.

Treatment of Shakespeare's Text by His Earlier Editors. Ronald B. McKerrow. LC 74-20679. 1933. lib. bdg. 18.50 (ISBN 0-8414-5948-7). Folcroft.

TITLE INDEX TREE BY LEAF.

Treatment of Shakespeare's Text by His Earlier Editors, 1709-1768. Ronald B. McKerrow. LC 79-109656. (Select Bibliographies Reprint Ser). 1933. 12.00 (ISBN 0-8369-5265-0). Ayer Co Pubs.
Treatment of Shame & Guilt in Alcoholism Counseling. Ed. by Patricia Potter-Efron. LC 88-853. (Alcoholism Treatment Quarterly Ser.). (Illus.). 200p. 1988. text ed. 22.95. Haworth Pr.
Treatment of Shame & Guilt in Alcoholism Counseling. Ed. by Patricia S. Potter-Efron & Ronald T. Potter-Efron. LC 87-29724. (Alcoholism Treatment Quarterly Ser.). (Illus.). 220p. 1987. text ed. 22.95 (ISBN 0-86656-718-6). Haworth Pr.
Treatment of Shock: Principles & Practice. 2nd ed. Ed. by John Barrett & Lloyd M. Nyhus. LC 85-18170. (Illus.). 242p. 1986. text ed. 27.50 (ISBN 0-8121-1008-0). Lea & Febiger.
Treatment of Small Bowel Diseases: Proceedings. Symposium on Hepato-Gastroenterology of the University Hospital Center of Nice, 1st, August 1972. Ed. by J. Delmont. (Illus.). 200p. 1973. 29.50 (ISBN 3-8055-1490-5). S Karger.
Treatment of Sounds in Language & Literature. Raymond Chapman. Ed. by David Crystal. (Language Library). 272p. 1984. 29.95x (ISBN 0-631-13657-6). Basil Blackwell.
Treatment of Special Population with Ericksonian Approaches. Ed. by Stephen R. Lankton & Jeffrey K. Zeig. LC 87-35514. (Ericksonian Monographs: No. 3). 160p. 1988. 25.00 (ISBN 0-87630-494-3). Brunner-Mazel.
Treatment of Stuttering. Charles Van Riper. (Illus.). 464p. 1973. 38.00 (ISBN 0-13-930594-7). P-H.
Treatment of Stuttering in Early Childhood: Methods & Issues. Ed. by David Prins & Roger J. Ingham. LC 82-17914. (Illus.). 156p. 1983. 20.50 (ISBN 0-316-71940-4). College-Hill.
Treatment of Substance Abuse: Psychosocial Occupational Therapy Approaches. Ed. by Diane Gibson. (Occupational Therapy in Mental Health Ser.: Vol. 8, No. 2). (Illus.). 94p. 1988. text ed. 19.95 (ISBN 0-86656-838-7). Haworth Pr.
Treatment of Substance Abusers. Leon Brill et al. Ed. by Francis J. Turner & Herbert S. Strean. LC 81-66433. (Fields of Practice Ser.). 256p. 1981. 21.95 (ISBN 0-02-905160-6). Free Pr.
Treatment of the Alcohol-Abusing Offender. Robert R. Ross & Lynn O. Lightfoot. 164p. 1985. 21.75x (ISBN 0-398-05090-2). C C Thomas.
Treatment of the Borderline Adolescent: A Developmental Approach. James F. Masterson. LC 85-4236. 308p. 1985. Repr. of 1972 ed. 30.00 (ISBN 0-87630-394-7). Brunner-Mazel.
Treatment of the Borderline Personality. Patricia M. Chatham. LC 84-20425. 585p. 1985. 40.00x (ISBN 0-87668-754-0). Aronson.
Treatment of the Capital Sins. R. J. Ianucci. LC 70-140024. (Catholic University Studies in German: No. 17). Repr. of 1942 ed. 21.00 (ISBN 0-404-50237-7). AMS Pr.
Treatment of the Chronic Schizophrenic Patient. Ed. by Diane Gibson. LC 86-18451. (Occupational Therapy in Mental Health Ser.: No. 6). 87p. 1986. text ed. 24.95 (ISBN 0-86656-578-7). Haworth Pr.
Treatment of the DSM-III Psychiatric Disorders. William H. Reid & George U. Balis. LC 83-7503. 240p. 1983. 27.50 (ISBN 0-87630-339-4). Brunner-Mazel.
Treatment of the Edentulous Patient. Victor O. Lucia. LC 85-30060. (Illus.). 1986. text ed. 120.00x (ISBN 0-86715-122-6, 1226). Quint Pub Co.
Treatment of the Holocaust in Textbooks: The Federal Republic of Germany, Israel, the United States. Walter Renn et al. (Holocaust Studies). 288p. 1987. text ed. 30.00 (ISBN 0-88033-955-1). East Eur Quarterly.
Treatment of the Insane Without Mechanical Restraints. John Conolly. LC 73-2392. (Mental Illness & Social Policy; the American Experience Ser.). Repr. of 1856 ed. 25.50 (ISBN 0-405-05200-6). Ayer Co Pubs.
Treatment of the Jews in the Christian Writers of the First Three Centuries, Vol. 81. Robert Wilde. (Patristic Studies). 255p. 1984. Repr. of 1949 ed. 38.00x (ISBN 0-939738-28-7). Zubal Inc.
Treatment of the Narcissistic Neuroses. Hyman Spotnitz & Phyllis W. Meadow. LC 76-6716. 256p. 1976. 30.00 (ISBN 0-916850-01-3). CMPS NYC.
Treatment of the Obsessive Personality. Leon Salzman. LC 84-46127. 544p. 1985. 40.00x (ISBN 0-87668-881-4). Aronson.
Treatment of the Seriously Ill Psychiatric Patient. Ed. by Alexander Gralnick. 133p. 1985. 35.00x (ISBN 0-8147-2998-3); pap. 13.50x (ISBN 0-8147-2999-1). NYU Pr.
Treatment of the Severely Disturbed Adolescent. Donald B. Rinsley. LC 80-66922. 368p. 1983. 35.00x (ISBN 0-87668-415-0). Aronson.
Treatment of the Spinal Cord Injured: An Interdisciplinary Perspective. M. G. Eisenberg & J. A. Falconer. (Illus.). 152p. 1979. photocopy ed. 21.75x (ISBN 0-398-03833-3). C C Thomas.
Treatment of the Young Stutterer in the School, No. 4. Charles Van Riper. LC 82-80348. 64p. 1964. pap. 0.50 (ISBN 0-933388-02-0). Speech Found Am.
Treatment of Traumatized Incisor in the Child Patient. Ronald Johnson. Ed. by D. Walter Cohen. (Continuing Dental Education Ser.). 116p. 1981. pap. 20.00 (ISBN 0-931386-29-2). Quint Pub Co.
Treatment of Tricyclic-Resistant Depression: Progress in Psychiatry Ser. Ed. by Irl L. Extein. 128p. 1988. text ed. price not set (ISBN 0-88048-140-4, 48-140-4). Am Psychiatric.
Treatment of Water by Granular Activated Carbon. Ed. by Michael J. McGuire & Irwin H. Suffet. LC 82-22662. (Advances in Chemistry Ser.: No. 202). 599p. 1983. lib. bdg. 64.95 (ISBN 0-8412-0665-1). Am Chemical.
Treatment or Diagnosis: A Study of Repeat Prescriptions in General Practice. Michael Balint et al. 208p. 1984. pap. text ed. 17.95 (ISBN 0-422-78770-1, 4004). Routledge Chapman & Hall.
Treatment Planning & Dose Calculation & Treatment Planning in Radiation Oncology. Gunilla C. Bentel et al. (Illus.). 265p. 1982. text ed. 49.00 (ISBN 0-08-027176-6, H230); pap. text ed. 21.50 (ISBN 0-08-027175-8). Pergamon.
Treatment Planning in Psychiatry. Ed. by Jerry M. Lewis & Gene Usdin. LC 82-3985. (Illus.). 456p. 1982. 19.95x (ISBN 0-89042-045-9, 42-045-9). Am Psychiatric.
Treatment Planning in the Radiation Therapy of Cancer. Ed. by J. M. Vaeth & J. Meyer. (Frontiers of Radiation Therapy & Oncology Ser.: Vol. 21). (Illus.). x, 342p. 1987. 216.75 (ISBN 3-8055-4377-8). S Karger.
Treatment Plant Hydraulics for Environmental Engineers. Larry D. Benefield et al. (Illus.). 240p. 1984. 59.00 (ISBN 0-13-930248-4). P-H.
Treatment Procedures in Communicative Disorders. M. N. Hegde. LC 85-14934. (Illus.). 271p. 1985. text ed. 25.50 (ISBN 0-316-35433-3, 354333). College-Hill.
Treatment, Recovery, & Disposal Processes for Radioactive Wastes: Recent Advances. Ed. by J. I. Duffy. LC 82-22260. (Pollution Technology Review No.95, Chemical Technology Review No. 216). (Illus.). 287p. 1983. 39.00 (ISBN 0-8155-0922-7). Noyes.
Treatment Services for Adolescent Substance Abusers. Alfred S. Friedman & George M. Beschner. (DHHS Publication Ser.: No. ADM 85-1342). 242p. (Orig.). 1985. pap. 8.50 (ISBN 0-318-19911-4, S/N 017-024-01243-2). USGPO.
Treatment Services for Adolescent Substance Abusers. 1986. lib. bdg. 79.95 (ISBN 0-8490-3496-5). Gordon Pr.
Treatment Techniques for Common Mental Disorders. Joan Atwood & Robert Chester. LC 87-17471. 300p. 1987. 30.00x (ISBN 0-87668-962-4). Aronson.
Treatment Techniques for Controlling Trihalomethanes in Drinking Water. (AWWA Handbooks-General Ser.). (Illus.). 312p. 1982. pap. text ed. 16.80 (ISBN 0-89867-279-1). Am Water Wks Assn.
Treatment Unit Clerk. Jack Rudman. (Career Examination Ser.: C-319). (Cloth bdg. avail. on request). pap. 14.00 (ISBN 0-8373-0319-2). Natl Learning.
Treatment with Autogenic Neutralization see Autogenic Therapy.
Treatments. Ed. by Matthew Cahill. LC 87-18073. (Nurses Reference Library). 716p. 1988. pap. 27.95 (ISBN 0-87434-124-8). Springhouse Pub.
Treatments for the Alzheimer Patient: The Long Haul. Ed. by Lissy F. Jarvik & Carol H. Winograd. 288p. 1988. 28.95 (ISBN 0-8261-6000-X). Springer Pub.
Treats. Christopher Hampton. 62p. 1976. pap. 4.95 (ISBN 0-571-10967-5). Faber & Faber.
Treats for My Sweets. Gail C. Jay. 124p. cancelled (ISBN 0-939114-00-3). Wimmer Bks.
Treats for My Sweets. Gail C. Jaye. (Illus.). 128p. 1981. pap. 6.50 (ISBN 0-686-31566-9). G C Jaye.
Treaty Between the U. S. & the Indians of the Willamette Valley. facs. ed. Isaac I. Stevens. 8p. pap. 3.00 (ISBN 0-8466-0112-5, S112). Shorey.
Treaty Between the U. S. & the Nisqually & Other Bands of Indians. facs. ed. Isaac I. Stevens. 8p. pap. 3.00 (ISBN 0-8466-0109-5, S109). Shorey.
Treaty Between the U. S. & the Yakima Nation of Indians. facs. ed. Isaac I. Stevens. 8p. pap. 3.00 (ISBN 0-8466-0110-9, S110). Shorey.
Treaty Between the United States of America & the Union of Soviet Socialist Republics on the Elimination of Their Intermediate-Range & Shorter-Range Missiles. 412p. (Orig.). 1988. pap. 12.00 (S/N 052-070-06411-1). USGPO.
Treaty Between the United States of America & the Union of Soviet Socialist Republics on the Elimination of Their Intermediate-Range & Shorter-Range Missiles, Dec. 1987. (State Department Selected Documents 25, State Department Publication Ser.: No. 9555). 60p. (Orig.). 1987. pap. 6.00 (S/N 044-000-02208-7). USGPO.
Treaty Conflict & Political Consideration: The Dialectic of Duplicity. Guyora Binder. 1988. price not set (ISBN 0-275-93046-7, C3046). Praeger.
Treaty Interpretation: Theory & Reality. Edward S. Yambrusic. 310p. (Orig.). 1987. lib. bdg. 28.50 (ISBN 0-8191-6145-4); pap. text ed. 15.75 (ISBN 0-8191-6146-2). U Pr of Amer.
Treaty Making & Treaty Rejection by the Federal Government in California 1850-1852. George E. Anderson et al. (No. 9). 1978. pap. 7.95 (ISBN 0-87919-071-X). Ballena Pr.
Treaty-Making Power of International Organizations. J. W. Schneider. 154p. (Orig.). 1963. pap. text ed. 18.00x (ISBN 0-317-56053-0, Pub. by Droz Switzerland). Coronet Bks.
Treaty of Eighteen Forty-Two Between the United States & the Chippewa Indians of the Mississippi & Lake Superior. Robert Keller. (Treaty Manuscripts Ser.: No. 32). 58p. 12.50 (ISBN 0-944253-54-7). Inst Dev Indian Law.
Treaty of Eighteen Thirty-Six Between the Ottawa & Chippewa Nations of Indians & the U. S. Government. Robert Keller. (Treaty Manuscripts Ser.: No. 31). 55p. 12.50 (ISBN 0-317-57475-2). Inst Dev Indian Law.
Treaty of Medicine Lodge: A Programmed Text. Lynn Kickingbird & Curtis Berkey. (Treaty Manuscripts Ser.: No. 20). 22p. 7.50 (ISBN 0-944253-42-3). Inst Dev Indian Law.
Treaty of Medicine Lodge, 1867, Between the United States & the Kiowa, Comanche & Apache Indians. R. J. DeMallie & Lynn Kickingbird. (Treaty Manuscripts Ser.: No. 26). 65p. 15.00 (ISBN 0-944253-48-2). Inst Dev Indian Law.
Treaty of Nineteen Eleven & the Immigration & Alien Land Law Issue Between the U. S. & Japan, 1911-1913. Teruko O. Kachi. Ed. by Roger Daniels. LC 78-54821. (Asian Experience in North American Ser.). 1979. lib. bdg. 23.00x (ISBN 0-405-11277-7). Ayer Co Pubs.
Treaty of Paris (1738) in a Changing States System: Papers from a Conference January 26-27, 1984. Ed. by Prosser Gifford. LC 85-9139. 218p. (Orig.). 1985. lib. bdg. 34.75 (ISBN 0-8191-4752-4, Pub. by Woodrow Wilson Intl. Ctr.); pap. text ed. 19.75 (ISBN 0-8191-4753-2). U Pr of Amer.
Treaty of Trianon & European Peace: Four Lectures Delivered in London in November 1933. Stephen Bethlen. LC 73-135795. (Eastern European Collection Ser). 1970. Repr. of 1934 ed. 13.00 (ISBN 0-405-02737-0). Ayer Co Pubs.
Treaty of Union of Scotland & England. Scotland. Treaties. Ed. by George S. Pryde. LC 78-24202. 1979. Repr. of 1950 ed. lib. bdg. 35.00x (ISBN 0-313-20829-8, SCTR). Greenwood.
Treaty of Versailles & After, Annotations of the Text & Treaty. U. S. Department Of State. 1968. Repr. of 1947 ed. 49.00x (ISBN 0-403-00054-8). Scholarly.
Treaty of Waitangi. T. Lindsay Buick. LC 72-1294. (Select Bibliographies Reprint Ser.). 1972. Repr. of 1936 ed. 29.00 (ISBN 0-8369-6822-0). Ayer Co Pubs.
Treaty of Washington: Its Negotiation, Execution & the Discussions Relating Thereto. facsimile ed. Caleb Cushing. LC 72-114872. (Select Bibliographies Reprint Ser.). 1873. 19.00 (ISBN 0-8369-5277-4). Ayer Co Pubs.
Treaty on the Little Arkansas River, 1865. R. J. DeMallie & Lynn Kickingbird. (Treaty Manuscripts Ser.: No. 25). 55p. 12.50 (ISBN 0-944253-47-4). Inst Dev Indian Law.
Treaty Ports & China's Modernization: What Went Wrong? Rhoads Murphey. (Michigan Monographs in Chinese Studies: No. 7). 84p. (Orig.). 1970. pap. 6.00 (ISBN 0-89264-007-3). U of Mich Ctr Chinese.
Treaty Ports in China: A Study in Diplomacy. En-Sai Tai. LC 75-32311. (Studies in Chinese History & Civilization). 202p. 1977. 17.50 (ISBN 0-89093-083-X). U Pubns Amer.
Treaty Series, Vol. 1012. 1976. 22.00. UN.
Treaty Series, Vol. 1013. 1976. 22.00. UN.
Treaty Series, Vol. 1015. 400p. 1976. 22.00. UN.
Treaty Series, Vol. 1016. 407p. 1976. 22.00. UN.
Treaty Series, Vol. 1030. 468p. 1976. 22.00 (ISBN 0-317-16457-0). UN.
Treaty Series, Vol. 1033. 365p. 1977. 22.00. UN.
Treaty Series, Vol. 1035. 380p. 1977. 22.00. UN.
Treaty Series, Vol. 1042. 456p. 1977. 22.00. UN.
Treaty Series, Vol. 1048. 416p. 1977. 22.00. UN.
Treaty Series, Vol. 1054. 378p. 1977. 22.00. UN.
Treaty Series, Vol. 1055. 390p. 1977. 22.00. UN.
Treaty Series, Vol. 1058. 417p. 1977. 22.00. UN.
Treaty Series, Vol. 1062. 414p. 1977. 22.00. UN.
Treaty Series, Vols. 903/904. (12899-12916). 328p. pap. 22.00. UN.
Treaty Series, Vol. 911-912. pap. 22.00 (TS911/912). UN.
Treaty Series, Vols. 925/926. (13184-13214 (1) 713-715 (2)). 314p. pap. 22.00. UN.
Treaty Series, Vol. 936. (13303-13326). 457p. pap. 22.00. UN.
Treaty Series, Vol. 941. (13400-3415 (I) 720-721 (II)). 358p. pap. 22.00. UN.
Treaty Series, Vol. 946. (13488-13490). 554p. pap. 22.00. UN.
Treaty Series, Vol. 947. (13488-13490). 611p. pap. 22.00. UN.
Treaty Series, Vol. 894. (12781-12793). 345p. pap. 22.00. UN.
Treaty Series, Vol. 899-900. pap. 22.00 (TS899/900). UN.
Treaty Series: Cumulative Index No. 13, Vols. 801-850. 334p. 22.00. UN.
Treaty Series: Treaties & International Agreements Registered or Filed & Recorded with the Secretariat of United Nations, Nos. 14021-14040, Vol. 969. United Nations. 1982. 22.00. UN.
Treaty Series: Treaties & International Agreements Registered or Filed & Recorded with the Secretariat of the United Nations, Nos. 14041-14053, Vol. 970. United Nations. 1982. 22.00. UN.
Treaty Series: Treaties & International Agreements Registered or Filed & Recorded with the Secretariat of the United Nations, Nos. 13630-13673, Vol. 954. United Nations. 1982. 22.00. UN.
Treaty Series 1973, Vol.886-887. pap. 22.00 (TS886/887). UN.
Treaty Series: 1975, Vol. 962. pap. 22.00 (TS962). UN.
Treaty Series: 1975, Vol. 970. pap. 22.00 (TS970). UN.
Treaty Veto of the American Senate. Denna F. Fleming. LC 76-168039. Repr. of 1930 ed. 25.00 (ISBN 0-404-02409-2). AMS Pr.
Treaty Veto of the American Senate. Denna F. Fleming. LC 72-147598. (Library of War & Peace; International Law). 1972. lib. bdg. 46.00 (ISBN 0-8240-0359-4). Garland Pub.
Treaty with the Makah. Kenneth C. Hansen. (Treaty Manuscripts Ser.: No. 8). 30p. 10.00 (ISBN 0-944253-30-X). Inst Dev Indian Law.
Treaty with the Quinaielt & Quileute Indian. Lynn Kickingbird & Curtis Berkey. (Treaty Manuscripts Ser.: No. 7). 21p. 7.50 (ISBN 0-944253-29-6). Inst Dev Indian Law.
Treatyse of Fysshinge with an Angle. J. Barnes. (English Dialect Society Publications: No. 41a). pap. 15.00 (ISBN 0-8115-0467-0). Kraus Repr.
Trebizond: The Last Greek Empire. William Miller. 140p. Repr. of 1926 ed. lib. bdg. 32.50x (Pub. by AM Hakkert). Coronet Bks.
Treble Clef & Notes. Mary Lou Walker. (Music Ser.). 24p. (gr. 1 up). 1980. wkbk. 5.00 (ISBN 0-8209-0274-8, MU-3). ESP.
Treble Exposure. Anne Morice. 192p. 1988. 13.95x (ISBN 0-312-01525-9). St Martin.
Treble V. R. Guild Gray. 1986. 18.95 (ISBN 0-533-06759-6). Vantage.
Treblinka. Jean-Francis Steiner. 320p. 1979. pap. 4.50 (ISBN 0-451-62566-8, Ment). NAL.
Treblinka. Jean-Francois Steiner. 304p. pap. 3.50 (ISBN 0-686-95096-8). ADL.
Trece Lecciones de Doctrina Biblica. Denver Sizemore. Tr. by Raul Martinez from Eng. 114p. (Span.). pap. 2.95 (ISBN 0-89900-300-1). College Pr Pub.
Trece Relatos Sombrios. Ignacio R. Galbis. LC 79-64142. (Senda Narrativa Ser.). (Orig., Span.). 1979. pap. 4.95 (ISBN 0-918454-14-X). Senda Nueva.
Trechos de "Meu Caminho Para Rotary". Paul Harris. 58p. (Port.). 1984. 3.00 (ISBN 0-915062-20-8). Rotary Intl.
Tree. Althea Braithwaite. (Life Cycle Bks.). (ps-6). 1988. PLB 7.95 (ISBN 0-88462-196-0); pap. 2.95 (ISBN 0-88462-197-9). Longman Crown.
Tree. David Burnie. LC 88-1572. (Illus.). 64p. (gr. 5 up). 1988. 12.95 (ISBN 0-394-89617-3); lib. bdg. 13.99 (ISBN 0-394-99617-8). Knopf.
Tree. John Fowles. (Illus.). 1980. 24.95 (ISBN 0-316-28957-4). Little.
Tree. John Fowles. 125p. (Orig.). 1983. 13.25 (ISBN 0-88001-033-9); pap. 7.95 (ISBN 0-88001-040-1). Ecco Pr.
Tree. 2nd ed. J. Marvin Spiegelman. LC 74-81034. 480p. 1982. pap. 12.95 (ISBN 0-941404-04-8). Falcon Pr Az.
Tree, A Blade of Grass. Shinzo Maeda. (Natural Beauty of Japan Ser.). 96p. 1986. Repr. of 1983 ed. 36.95 (ISBN 4-766-10278-9, Pub. by Graphic Sha Japan). Bks Nippan.
Tree & Leaf. J. R. R. Tolkien. 1965. 8.95 (ISBN 0-395-08253-6). HM.
Tree & the Vine. Dola De Jong. 3.00 (ISBN 0-8184-0143-5). Lyle Stuart.
Tree Army: A Pictorial History of the Civilian Conservation Corps 1933-1943. Stan Cohen. LC 80-81071. 172p. 1980. pap. 8.95 (ISBN 0-933126-10-7). Pictorial Hist.
Tree at the Center of the World: The Story of the California Missions. Bruce W. Barton. LC 79-26434. (Illus., Orig.). 1980. lib. bdg. 19.95 (ISBN 0-915520-30-3); pap. 12.95 (ISBN 0-915520-29-X). Ross-Erikson.
Tree Automata. F. Gecseq & M. Steinby. 1984. 139.00x (ISBN 0-569-08794-5, Pub. by Collets (UK)). State Mutual Bk.
Tree Automata. Geeseg & Steinby. 1984. cancelled 30.00 (ISBN 963-05-3170-4, Pub. by Akademiai Kaido Hungary). IPS.
Tree-Bird. Lalitha Venkateswaran. 8.00 (ISBN 0-89253-749-3); flexible cloth 4.80 (ISBN 0-89253-750-7). Ind-US Inc.
Tree Book: Teaching Responsible Enviromental Education, Vol. 1. Toni Christenson & Marian R. Feia. (Illus.). 78p. (Orig.). 1981. tchr's ed. 6.95 (ISBN 0-686-36286-1). Creative Curriculum.
Tree Boy. Adapted by & tr. by Mark C. Setton. (Korean Folk Tales Ser.: No. 13). (Illus.). 32p. (Eng. & Korean.). (gr. 1-8). 1986. PLB write for info. (ISBN 0-87296-012-9, Pub. by Si-sa-yong-o-sa Korea); bilingual cassette incl. Si-sa-yong-o-sa.
Tree by Leaf. Cynthia Voigt. LC 87-17512. 208p. (gr. 4-8). 1988. 13.95 (ISBN 0-689-31403-5, Atheneum Childrens Bks). Macmillan.

Tree Calendar. Hilary Llewellyn-Williams. LC 87-73284. 72p. (Orig.). 1988. pap. 11.95 (ISBN 0-907476-77-5, Pub. by Poetry Wales Pr. UK). Dufour.
Tree Care. rev. ed. John M. Haller. LC 76-50995. (Illus.). 1986. pap. 16.95 (ISBN 0-02-062870-6, Pub. by Audel). Macmillan.
Tree Climber: A Play in Two Acts. 2nd ed. Tawfiq Al-Hakim. Tr. by Denys Johnson-Davis from Arabic. LC 82-74256. (Illus.). 87p. 1985. 12.00 (ISBN 0-89410-204-4); pap. 7.00 (ISBN 0-89410-205-2). Three Continents.
Tree Climbing. Susan Mernit. 60p. (Orig.). 1981. pap. 2.00 (ISBN 0-87924-036-9). Membrane Pr.
Tree Crop Physiology. Ed. by M. R. Sethuraj & A. S. Raghavendra. (Developments in Agricultural & Managed-Forest Ecology Ser.: No. 18). 362p. 1987. 97.75 (ISBN 0-444-42841-0). Elsevier.
Tree Crops: A Permanent Agriculture. rev. ed. J. Russell Smith. (Illus.). 408p. 1987. pap. 19.95 (ISBN 0-8159-6908-2). Devin.
Tree Crops: A Permanent Agriculture. J. Russell Smith. (Conservation Classics Ser.). (Illus.). 415p. 1987. pap. 19.95 (ISBN 0-933280-44-0). Island CA.
Tree Detailing. Michael Littlewood. (Illus.). 176p. 1988. pap. 29.95 (ISBN 0-442-20571-6). Van Nos Reinhold.
Tree Disease Concepts in Relation to Forest & Urban Tree Management Practice. Paul D. Manion. (Illus.). 400p. 1981. text ed. 43.00 (ISBN 0-13-930701-X). P-H.
Tree Ecology & Preservation. A. Bernatzky. (Developments in Agricultural & Managed-Forest Ecology Ser.: Vol. 2). 358p. 1978. 100.00 (ISBN 0-444-41606-4). Elsevier.
Tree Farm Business Management. 3rd ed. Vardaman. 1990. price not set (ISBN 0-471-60919-6). Wiley.
Tree Farm Business Management. 2nd ed. James M. Vardaman. LC 78-1610. 213p. 1978. 26.50 (ISBN 0-471-07263-X, Pub. by Wiley-Interscience). Wiley.
Tree Finder: A Manual for Identifying Trees by Their Leaves East of Rockies. May T. Watts. 1963. pap. 1.50 (ISBN 0-912550-01-5). Nature Study.
Tree: Five, the Snake, the Apple. Ed. by David Meltzer. (Illus.). 200p. (Orig.). 1975. pap. 5.00 (ISBN 0-686-10822-1). Tree Bks.
Tree Flowers. Millicent E. Selsam. LC 83-17353. (Illus.). 32p. (gr. 4 up). 1984. 11.75 (ISBN 0-688-02768-7); PLB 11.88 (ISBN 0-688-02769-5). Morrow.
Tree for Me. Norma LeValley. LC 87-70974. (Illus.). 50p. (ps-2). 1987. pap. 5.95 (ISBN 0-9618740-0-7). Caring Tree.
Tree! For Me! Frankie Maynard. (Illus.). 60p. 1985. 15.00 (ISBN 0-912783-02-8). Upton Sons.
Tree for Poverty: Somali Poetry & Prose. Margaret Laurence. 146p. 1954. 15.00x (ISBN 0-7165-1415-X, BBA 02223, Pub. by Cuala Press Ireland). Biblio Dist.
Tree: Four, Raa. Ed. by David Meltzer. (Illus., Orig.). pap. 5.00 (ISBN 0-686-17262-0). Tree Bks.
Tree Frog. annual Hidetomo Oda. Ed. by Kathy Pohl. LC 85-28194. (Nature Close-Ups Ser.). (Illus.). 32p. (gr. 4). 1986. PLB 15.33 (ISBN 0-8172-2546-3); pap. text ed. 9.27 (ISBN 0-8172-2571-4). Raintree Pubs.
Tree Frogs. Sylvia A. Johnson. LC 86-2721. (Lerner Natural Science Bks.). (Illus.). 48p. (gr. 4-10). 1986. PLB 12.95 (ISBN 0-8225-1467-2). Lerner Pubns.
Tree Fruit Production. 3rd ed. Benjamin J. Teskey & James S. Shoemaker. (Illus.). 1978. 30.95 (ISBN 0-87055-265-1). AVI.
Tree Full of Angels: Seeing the Holy in the Ordinary. Macrina Wiederkehr. LC 87-45727. 160p. 1988. 13.95 (ISBN 0-06-254842-5, HarpR). Har-Row.
Tree Giants. Bill Schneider. LC 88-80225. (Interpreting the Great Outdoors Ser.). (Illus.). 32p. 1988. pap. 4.95 (ISBN 0-937959-40-5). Falcon Pr MT.
Tree Grows in Brooklyn. Betty Smith. 321p. 1981. Repr. lib. bdg. 17.95x (ISBN 0-89966-303-6). Buccaneer Bks.
Tree Grows in Brooklyn. Betty Smith. 1968. pap. 5.50 (ISBN 0-06-080126-3, P126, PL). Har-Row.
Tree Growth & Environmental Stresses. Theodore T. Kozlowski. LC 78-10815. (Geo. S. Long Publication Ser.). (Illus.). 184p. 1979. 15.00x (ISBN 0-295-95636-4). U of Wash Pr.
Tree Harvesting Techniques. Ed. by K. A. Staaf. (Forestry Sciences Ser.). 1984. lib. bdg. 53.50 (ISBN 90-247-2994-7, Pub. by Martinus Nijhoff Netherlands). Kluwer-Academic.
Tree Hound Record Book. Billy C. Littlejohn. 17p. 1988. pap. 5.95 (ISBN 0-533-07577-7). Vantage.
Tree House. Edna P. Weegmann. 1985. 7.95 (ISBN 0-317-28979-9). Vantage.
Tree House Detective Club. Elizabeth Bolton. LC 84-8762. (Illus.). 48p. (gr. 2-4). 1985. PLB 9.29 (ISBN 0-8167-0404-X); pap. text ed. 1.95 (ISBN 0-8167-0405-8). Troll Assocs.
Tree House Fun. Rose Greydanus. (Illus.). 32p. (gr. k-2). 1980. PLB 5.41 (ISBN 0-89375-391-2); pap. 1.50 (ISBN 0-89375-291-6). Troll Assocs.
Tree House Mystery. Gertrude C. Warner. LC 77-91744. (Boxcar Children Mysteries Ser.). (Illus.). 128p. (gr. 3-7). 1969. PLB 8.95 (ISBN 0-8075-8086-4). A Whitman.
Tree Identification Book. George W. Symonds. LC 58-5359. 272p. 1973. 22.95 (ISBN 0-688-00039-8); pap. 14.95 (ISBN 0-688-05039-5). Morrow.
Tree in Architecture: A Selected Bibliography. Anthony G. White. (Architecture Ser.: A 1686). 5p. 1986. 3.00 (ISBN 1-55590-036-4). Vance Biblios.
Tree in Art. Ed. by Stephen Longstreet. (Master Draughtsman Ser). (Illus., Orig.). treasure trove bdg. 10.95x (ISBN 0-87505-047-6); pap. 4.95 (ISBN 0-87505-200-2). Borden.
Tree in Bud: The Hawaiian Kingdom, 1889-1893. M. G. Bosseront d'Anglade. Tr. by Alfons L. Korn from Fr. LC 87-10841. (Illus.). 208p. 1987. text ed. 24.00X (ISBN 0-8248-1101-1). UH Pr.
Tree in the Trail. Holling C. Holling. (Illus.). (gr. 4-6). PLB 15.95 (ISBN 0-395-18228-X). HM.
Tree Is a Tree. King Vidor. Ed. by Bruce S. Kupelnick. LC 76-52132. (Classics of Film Literature Ser.). 1978. lib. bdg. 22.00 (ISBN 0-8240-2896-1). Garland Pub.
Tree Is Lighted. Ellen Davies-Rogers. LC 84-90673. (Illus.). 1984. 5.00 (ISBN 0-317-19588-3). Plantation.
Tree Is Nice. Janice M. Udry. LC 56-5153. (Illus.). (ps-1). 1956. 11.95i (ISBN 0-06-026155-2); PLB 11.89 (ISBN 0-06-026156-0). HarpJ.
Tree Is Nice. Janice M. Udry. LC 56-5153. (Trophy Picture Bks.). (Illus.). 32p. (ps-3). 1987. pap. 4.95 (ISBN 0-06-443147-9, Trophy). HarpJ.
Tree Key. Herbert L. Edlin. (Illus.). 1978. 14.95 (ISBN 0-684-15886-8, ScribT). Scribner.
Tree Life of Argyll. Picton Publishing Staff. 1987. 9.00x (Pub. by Picton UK). State Mutual Bk.
Tree-Lines. Robin Fulton. (Illus.). 1974. signed ed. o.p. 10.00 (ISBN 0-685-46815-1); pap. 2.50 (ISBN 0-912284-58-7); 5.00. New Rivers Pr.
Tree Lore in the Bible. Lonsdale Ragg. Repr. of 1935 ed. lib. bdg. 30.00 (ISBN 0-8495-4528-5). Arden Lib.
Tree Maintenance. 5th ed. P. P. Pirone. (Illus.). 1978. 49.95 (ISBN 0-19-502321-8). Oxford U Pr.
Tree Maintenance. 6th ed. P. P. Pirone et al. (Illus.). 512p. 1988. 45.00 (ISBN 0-19-504370-7). Oxford U Pr.
Tree Meditation & Others. Alan Stephens. LC 70-132580. 53p. 1971. 6.95 (ISBN 0-8040-0296-7, Pub by Swallow); pap. 4.50 (ISBN 0-8040-0622-9, Pub by Swallow). Ohio U Pr.
Tree Mycoplasmas & Mycoplasmas Diseases. Ed. by C. Hiruki. xvi, 245p. 1988. 40.00x (ISBN 0-88864-126-5, Pub. by Univ of Alta Pr Canada). U of Nebr Pr.
Tree of Appomattox: A Story of the Civil War's Close. Joseph A. Altsheler. (Joseph A. Altsheler Civil War Ser.). 1985. 21.95 (ISBN 0-317-28292-1, Pub. by American Hse.). Amereon Ltd.
Tree of Death. Marcia Muller. 1987. pap. 3.50 (ISBN 0-451-14749-9, Sig). NAL.
Tree of Evil. rev. ed. William G. Gray. LC 84-51741. 1984. pap. 7.95 (ISBN 0-87728-539-X). Weiser.
Tree of Freedom. Rebecca Caudill. (Puffin Newbery Library). (gr. 5-9). 1988. pap. 3.95 (ISBN 0-14-032908-0, Puffin Bks). Penguin.
Tree of Gernika: A Field Study of Modern War. George L. Steer. 1974. lib. bdg. 69.95 (ISBN 0-685-51640-7). Revisionist Pr.
Tree of Gold. Rosalind Laker. LC 85-31210. 360p. 1986. 17.95 (ISBN 0-385-23193-8). Doubleday.
Tree of Hands. Ruth Rendell. 273p. 1985. 13.45 (ISBN 0-394-53098-5). Pantheon.
Tree of Hands. Ruth Rendell. LC 85-8148. 320p. 1986. pap. 3.50 (ISBN 0-345-31200-7). Ballantine.
Tree of Healing: Psychological & Biblical Foundations for Counseling & Pastoral Care. Roger F. Hurding. Orig. Title: Roots & Shoots. 464p. 1987. Repr. of 1986 ed. 18.95 (ISBN 0-310-25140-0, 11022). Zondervan.
Tree of Hope. Jessica Goronwy. 1985. 20.00x (ISBN 0-7223-1827-8, Pub. by A H Stockwell England). State Mutual Bk.
Tree of Hope. 74p. 1983. pap. 2.95 (ISBN 1-55586-849-5). US Catholic.
Tree of Knowledge. Louis A. Gottschalk. LC 85-71701. (Illus.). 236p. (gr. 8 up). 1985. text ed. 12.50x (ISBN 0-939373-01-7). Eden Press.
Tree of Knowledge see Author of Beltraffio.
Tree of Knowledge of Good & Evil. Omraam M. Aivanhov. (Izvor Collection Ser.: Vol. 210). (Illus.). 160p. (Orig.). 1983. pap. 5.95 (ISBN 2-85566-237-0, Pub. by Prosveta France). Prosveta USA.
Tree of Knowledge: The Biological Roots of Human Understanding. Humberto R. Maturana & Francisco J. Varela. LC 86-29698. (New Science Library). (Illus.). 263p. 1987. 24.95 (ISBN 0-87773-373-2); pap. 17.95 (ISBN 0-87773-403-8). Shambhala Pubns.
Tree of Liberty: A Documentary History of Rebellion & Political Crime in America. Ed. by Nicholas N. Kittrie & Eldon D. Wedlock, Jr. LC 85-24068. (Illus.). 832p. 1986. text ed. 48.00x (ISBN 0-8018-2497-4). Johns Hopkins.
Tree of Life. Jim Goure. (Illus.). 62p. (Orig.). 1981. pap. 5.00 (ISBN 0-915235-04-8). United Res.
Tree of Life. Z'ev Ben Shimon Halevi. Orig. Title: Introduction to the Cabala. 1973. pap. 10.95 (ISBN 0-87728-189-0). Weiser.
Tree of Life. Hugh Nissenson. LC 84-48615. (Illus.). 224p. 1985. 15.45i (ISBN 0-06-015143-9, HarpT). Har-Row.
Tree of Life. Hugh Nissenson. LC 84-48615. 224p. 1986. pap. 6.95 (ISBN 0-06-091362-2, PL-1362, PL). Har-Row.
Tree of Life, a Study in Magic. Israel Regardie. LC 70-16403. 1972. pap. 9.95 (ISBN 0-87728-149-1). Weiser.
Tree of Life: An Anthology. De Solo Pinto et al. 1981. Repr. of 1929 ed. lib. bdg. 35.00 (ISBN 0-89984-390-5). Century Bookbindery.
Tree of Life: Diversity, Creativity, & Flexibility in Jewish Law. Louis Jacobs. (Littman Library of Jewish Civilization). 32.50x (ISBN 0-19-710039-2). Oxford U Pr.
Tree of Life: Image for the Cosmos. Roger Cook. LC 88-50248. (Art & Imagination Ser.). (Illus.). 128p. (Orig.). 1988. pap. 11.95 (ISBN 0-500-81007-9). Thames Hudson.
Tree of Man. Patrick White. 1955. 13.95 (ISBN 0-670-72875-6). Viking.
Tree of Man. Patrick White. 480p. 1984. pap. 6.95 (ISBN 0-14-001657-0). Penguin.
Tree of Memories Nature Essays. 6.00 (ISBN 0-9608926-0-5). McClain.
Tree of Mythology, Its Growth & Fruitage. Charles Mills. 1976. lib. bdg. 59.95 (ISBN 0-8490-2765-9). Gordon Pr.
Tree of Shelter. 1979. pap. 5.00. Vedanta Ctr.
Tree of Song. 2nd rev. ed. Federico Garcia Lorca. Tr. by Alan Brilliant from Span. LC 70-134743. (Keepsake Ser.: Vol. 3). (Illus.). 14p. (Eng. & Span.). 1973. 10.00 (ISBN 0-87775-046-7); pap. 4.00 (ISBN 0-87775-047-5). Unicorn Pr.
Tree of Swords & Jewels. C. J. Cherryh. 1987. pap. 2.95 (ISBN 0-87997-850-3). DAW Bks.
Tree of Yoga. B. K. Iyengar. Ed. by Kendra Crossen. 206p. (Orig.). 1989. pap. 9.95 (ISBN 0-87773-464-X). Shambhala Pubns.
Tree Pathology. William H. Smith. 1970. 34.50 (ISBN 0-12-652650-8). Acad Pr.
Tree Planting Practices in African Savannas. (Forestry Papers: No. 14). (Illus.). 185p. 1974. pap. 38.25 (ISBN 92-5-101094-3, F479, FAO). UNIPUB.
Tree Planting Practices in Asia. (Forestry Development Papers: No. 11). pap. 30.00 (F2389, FAO). UNIPUB.
Tree Planting Practices in Temperate Asia: Burma, India and Pakistan. (Forestry Development Papers: No. 14). pap. 5.75 (F482, FAO). UNIPUB.
Tree Plantings in Semi-Arid Regions: Proceedings of a Symposium on Establishment & Productivity. Ed. by P. Felker. 435p. 1987. Repr. 129.00 (ISBN 0-444-42735-X). Elsevier.
Tree Pruner Supervisor. Jack Rudman. (Career Examination Ser.: C-3049). (Cloth bdg. avail. on request). 1988. pap. 14.00 (ISBN 0-8373-3049-1). Natl Learning.
Tree-Ring Dating & Archaeology. M. G. Baillie. LC 81-16079. (Illus.). 1982. lib. bdg. 28.00x (ISBN 0-226-03630-8). U of Chicago Pr.
Tree Rings. Fritz H. Schweingruber. 1988. lib. bdg. 149.00 (ISBN 90-277-2445-8, Pub. by Reidel Holland). Kluwer Academic.
Tree Rings & Telescopes: The Scientific Career of A. E. Douglass. George E. Webb. LC 83-1152. 242p. 1983. 19.50x (ISBN 0-8165-0798-8). U of Ariz Pr.
Tree: Six, Messiah. Ed. by David Meltzer. (Illus., Orig.). pap. 5.00 (ISBN 0-686-31720-3). Tree Bks.
Tree Surgery: The Complete Guide. Peter Bridgeman. LC 75-31320. (Illus.). 160p. 1976. 19.95 (ISBN 0-7153-7050-2). David & Charles.
Tree Taking Root. David Wilk. 40p. 1977. 3.00 (ISBN 0-916562-10-7). Truck Pr.
Tree Talk: The People & Politics of Timber. Ray Raphael. (Illus.). 304p. (Orig.). 1981. pap. 14.95 (ISBN 0-933280-10-6). Island Ca.
Tree Tall & the Horse Race. Shirlee Evans. LC 86-7659. (Tree Tall Ser.: No. 2). (Illus.). 136p. (Orig.). (gr. 3-8). 1986. pap. 3.95 (ISBN 0-8361-3414-1). Herald Pr.
Tree Tall & the Whiteskins. Shirlee Evans. LC 85-13952. (Illus.). 112p. (gr. 9 up). 1985. pap. 3.95 (ISBN 0-8361-3402-8). Herald Pr.
Tree Tall to the Rescue. Shirlee Evans. LC 87-8615. (Tree Tall Ser.: No. 3). (Illus.). 144p. (Orig.). (gr. 4-9). 1987. pap. 4.50 (ISBN 0-8361-3444-3). Herald Pr.
Tree That Always Said No. Leo Price. LC 73-90617. (Illus.). 1973. plastic bdg. 2.75 (ISBN 0-8198-0330-8); pap. 1.75 (ISBN 0-8198-0331-6). Dghtrs St Paul.
Tree That Made a Million Dollars. James W. Sprague. 105p. 1985. 5.95 (ISBN 0-917802-18-7). Theoscience Found.
Tree: The Complete Book of Saxon Witchcraft. Raymond Buckland. LC 74-79397. (Illus.). 158p. 1974. pap. 6.95 (ISBN 0-87728-258-7). Weiser.
Tree: Three, Shekinah. Ed. by David Meltzer. (Illus., Orig.). pap. 7.50 (ISBN 0-686-27969-7). Tree Bks.
Tree Trimmer. Jack Rudman. (Career Examination Ser.: C-1526). (Cloth bdg. avail. on request). pap. 12.00 (ISBN 0-8373-1526-3). Natl Learning.
Tree Trimmer Foreman. Jack Rudman. (Career Examination Ser.: C-2574). (Cloth bdg. avail. on request). pap. 14.00 (ISBN 0-8373-2574-9). Natl Learning.
Tree, Turf & Ornamental Pesticide Guide. rev. ed. W. T. Thomson. 150p. 1987. pap. text ed. 14.00 (ISBN 0-913702-46-3). Thomson Pubns.
Tree: Two, Yetzirah. Ed. by David Meltzer. (Illus., Orig.). pap. 7.50 (ISBN 0-686-27968-9). Tree Bks.
Tree Vipers. Bargar & Johnson. (Snake Discovery Library Set II). (Illus.). 24p. (gr. 1-4). 1987. PLB 69.96 6 bk. set (ISBN 0-317-60589-5); PLB 11.66 (ISBN 0-86592-245-4). Rourke Corp.
Tree Where Man Was Born. Peter Mattiessen. 353p. 1983. pap. 8.95 (ISBN 0-525-48032-3, Obelisk). Dutton.
Tree Within. Octavio Paz. Tr. by Eliot Weinberger. LC 88-19666. 176p. 1988. pap. 8.95 (ISBN 0-8112-1071-5). New Directions.
Tree Worship in Ancient India. B. C. Sinha. xv, 103p. 1979. 15.00 (ISBN 1-55528-057-9, Pub. by Messers Today & Tomorrow Printers & Publishers). Scholarly Pubns.
Tree You Can Never Climb. Gloria Whiteman. 1985. 12.95 (ISBN 0-533-06532-1). Vantage.
Treeful of Pigs. Arnold Lobel. LC 78-1810. (Illus.). 32p. (gr. k-3). 1979. PLB 12.88 (ISBN 0-688-84177-5). Greenwillow.
Treeful of Pigs. Arnold Lobel. (Illus.). 32p. (gr. k-3). 1988. pap. 3.95 (ISBN 0-590-41280-9, Blue Ribbon Bks). Scholastic Inc.
Treehorn's Treasure. Florence P. Heide. LC 81-4043. (Illus.). 64p. (gr. 3-6). 1981. 10.95 (ISBN 0-8234-0425-0). Holiday.
Treehorn's Wish. Florence P. Heide. LC 83-6240. (Illus.). 64p. (gr. 3-6). 1984. reinforced bdg 8.95 (ISBN 0-8234-0493-5). Holiday.
Treehouse of the Mind. William Swarts, 3rd. 24p. (Orig.). 1981. 2.00 (ISBN 0-9603840-2-2). Andrew Mtn Pr.
Treelike: The Poetry of Kinoshita Yuji. Ed. by Thomas Fitzsimmons. Tr. by Robert Epp. LC 82-81181. (Asian Poetry in Translation Ser.: Japan, No. 4). (Illus.). 278p. (Orig., Japanese & Eng.). 1982. pap. 20.00 (ISBN 0-942668-04-9). Katydid Bks.
Trees. Ed. by Y. S. Bajaj. LC 85-17309. (Biotechnology in Agriculture & Forestry Ser.: Vol. 1). (Illus.). 550p. 1985. 110.00 (ISBN 0-387-15581-3). Springer-Verlag.
Trees. Carolyn Boulton. LC 84-50016. (Action Science Ser.). (Illus.). 32p. (gr. 2-4). 1984. PLB 11.90 (ISBN 0-531-04635-4). Watts.
Trees. Sharon Gordon. LC 82-20291. (Now I Know Ser.). (Illus.). 32p. (gr. k-2). 1982. lib. bdg. 9.89 (ISBN 0-89375-901-5); pap. text ed. 2.95 (ISBN 0-8167-0879-7). Troll Assocs.
Trees. Martyn Hamer. (Easy Read Fact Bk.). (Illus.). 32p. (gr. 2-4). 1983. PLB 10.90 (ISBN 0-531-04513-7). Watts.
Trees. Riki H. Kondo. (Instant Nature Guides Ser.). (Illus.). 1979. pap. 2.95 (ISBN 0-448-12674-5, G&D). Putnam Pub Group.
Trees. rev. ed. Andrew Langley. Ed. by Franklin Watts Ltd. (Easy-Read Fact Bks.). (Illus.). 32p. (ps-6). 1988. 10.90 (ISBN 0-531-10446-X). Watts.
Trees. Benjamin Perkins. (Illus.). 176p. 1987. 24.95 (ISBN 0-88162-225-7). Salem Hse Pubs.
Trees. Illa Podendorf. LC 81-12313. (New True Bks.). (Illus.). 48p. (gr. k-4). 1982. PLB 12.60 (ISBN 0-516-01657-1); pap. 3.95 (ISBN 0-516-41657-X). Childrens.
Trees. Conrad Richter. 1940. 18.45 (ISBN 0-394-44951-7). Knopf.
Trees. J. P. Serre. 140p. 1980. 32.00 (ISBN 0-387-10103-9). Springer-Verlag.
Trees. Olenus L. Sponsler. 1939. 3.50x (ISBN 0-685-21809-0). Wahr.
Trees. Thompson. (First Nature Bks.). (gr. 2-5). 1980. (Usborne-Hayes); PLB 11.96 (ISBN 0-88110-071-4); pap. 3.95 (ISBN 0-86020-473-1). EDC.
Trees. Time-Life Books Editors. (Illus.). 1988. 12.95 (ISBN 0-8094-6616-3); lib. bdg. write for info. (ISBN 0-8094-6617-1). Time-Life.
Trees. Herbert S. Zim & Alexander C. Martin. (Golden Guide Ser.). (Illus.). (gr. 6 up). 1952. pap. 3.95 (Golden Pr). Western Pub.
Trees Alive. Sarah R. Riedman. (Illus.). 128p. (gr. 5 up). 1974. 11.75 (ISBN 0-688-41574-1). Lothrop.
Trees: An Introduction to Trees & Forest Ecology for the Amateur Naturalist. Laurence C. Walker. (Illus.). 288p. 1984. 23.95 (ISBN 0-13-930157-7). P-H.
Trees & Buildings. Ed. by Tony Aldous. 95p. 1980. pap. 11.25 (ISBN 0-900630-73-6, Pub. by RIBA). Intl Spec Bk.
Trees & Hills: Methodology for Maximising Functions of Systems of Linear Relations. R. Greer. (Mathematical Studies, No. 96; Annals of Discrete Mathematics). 1984. 68.50 (ISBN 0-444-87578-6). Elsevier.
Trees & Leaves for Quilters. Betty Boyink. 60p. (Orig.). 1982. pap. 9.50 (ISBN 0-9612608-1-5). B Boyink.
Trees & Networks in Biological Models. N. MacDonald. 216p. 1984. 57.95x (ISBN 0-471-10508-2, Pub. by Wiley-Interscience). Wiley.
Trees & Other Poems. Joyce Kilmer. LC 82-14061. 72p. 1982. Repr. of 1914 ed. 12.95 (ISBN 0-89783-024-5). Larlin Corp.
Trees & Other Woody Plants of Maine. Fay Hyland & Ferdinand H. Steinmetz. 72p. pap. 3.50 (ISBN 0-89621-018-9). U Maine Orono.

Trends & Differentials in Births to Unmarried Women: United States, Nineteen Seventy to Nineteen Seventy-Six. Stephanie J. Ventura. Ed. by Mary Olsted. (Series 21: No. 36). 1979. pap. text ed. 1.85 (ISBN 0-8406-0172-7). Natl Ctr Health Stats.

Trends & Directions in Hydrology. Stephens J. Burges. (Special Publications). 192p. 13.50 (ISBN 0-317-66489-1). Am Geophysical.

Trends & Issues in Foreign Direct Investment & Related Flows. 96p. 1986. 11.00 (ISBN 92-1-104170-8, E.85.II.A.15). UN.

Trends & Needs in Home Management: An Analytical Study of Home Management in Higher Institutions, in Order to Ascertain Trends & to Formulate Policies. Helen J. Bond. LC 77-176922. (Columbia University. Teachers College. Contributions to Education Ser.: No. 365). Repr. of 1929 ed. 22.50 (ISBN 0-404-55365-6). AMS Pr.

Trends & Patterns see Future of the International Legal Order.

Trends & Perspectives in Musicology: Proceedings of the World Music Conference. Ed. by Royal Swedish Academy of Music. (Illus.). 166p. (Orig.). 1983. pap. text ed. 28.00x (ISBN 91-85428-42-6, Pub. by Almqvist & Wiksell). Coronet Bks.

Trends & Perspectives in Parasitology, No. 1. Ed. by D. W. Crompton & B. A. Newton. LC 80-42159. (Illus.). 150p. 1981. 29.95 (ISBN 0-521-23821-8); pap. 11.95 o. p. (ISBN 0-521-28242-X). Cambridge U Pr.

Trends & Perspectives in Parasitology, No. 2. Ed. by D. W. Crompton & B. A. Newton. LC 80-42159. (Illus.). 91p. 1982. 21.95 (ISBN 0-521-24830-2); pap. 8.95 (ISBN 0-521-28989-0). Cambridge U Pr.

Trends & Perspectives in Parasitology, Vol. 2. Ed. by D. W. Crompton & B. A. Newton. LC 81-642963. pap. 25.30 (2027281). Bks Demand UMI.

Trends & Practices. Ed. by Ron McBeath & Phillip Sleeman. (Instructional Media & Technology Ser.: Vol. 1). 210p. (Orig.). 1983. pap. text ed. 11.50x (ISBN 0-89503-041-1). Baywood Pub.

Trends & Problems in Science & Technology Education in Asia. (Illus.). 1977. pap. 6.00 (ISBN 0-685-80109-8, UB11, UB). UNIPUB.

Trends & Problems in the Distribution of Property Liability Insurance. John S. Bickley. 1956. pap. text ed. 3.00 (ISBN 0-87776-091-8, R91). Ohio St U Admin Sci.

Trends & Progress in System Identification. Ed. by P. Eykhoff. LC 80-41994. (IFAC Series for Graduate, Research Workers & Practicing Engineers: Vol. 1). (Illus.). 410p. 1981. 94.00 (ISBN 0-08-025683-X). Pergamon.

Trends & Status of Minority Aging, Vol. 8. Ed. by E. P. Stanford & Shirley Lockery. (Proceedings of the Institute on Minority Aging). 150p. (Orig.). 1982. pap. 10.00 (ISBN 0-916304-57-4). SDSU Press.

Trends & Teaching in Clinical Genetics. Ed. by Daniel Bergsma et al. LC 77-24643. (Birth Defects Original Article Ser.: Vol. XIII, No. 6). 200p. 1977. 28.00 (ISBN 0-8451-1015-2). A R Liss.

Trends & Traditions in Japanese Art. (Illus.). 36p. 1984. 3.00 (ISBN 0-912303-34-4). Michigan Mus.

Trends & Variations in Fertility in the United States. Clyde V. Kiser et al. LC 68-25613. (Vital & Health Statistics Monographs, American Public Health Association). (Illus.). 1968. 24.50x (ISBN 0-674-90780-9). Harvard U Pr.

Trends in African Contemporary Art. Kojo Fosu. LC 79-51527. (Illus.). 1980. 45.00 (ISBN 0-933184-02-6); pap. 35.00 (ISBN 0-933184-03-4). Flame Intl.

Trends in American Economic Growth, 1929-1982. Edward F. Denison. LC 85-17413. 141p. 1985. 31.95 (ISBN 0-8157-1810-1); pap. 11.95 (ISBN 0-8157-1809-8). Brookings.

Trends in American Electoral Behavior. 2nd ed. David B. Hill & Norman R. Luttbeg. LC 83-61557. 165p. 1983. pap. 9.95 (ISBN 0-87581-296-1). Peacock Pubs.

Trends in American Geological Education During the Critical Years 1954-1969. John Tomikel. LC 72-183704. 1972. 5.00 (ISBN 0-910042-08-X); pap. 2.50 (ISBN 0-910042-11-X). Allegheny.

Trends in American Higher Education. Joseph Ben-David. LC 78-177370. (Midway Reprints Ser.). xii, 138p. 1981. pap. 9.00x (ISBN 0-226-04225-1). U of Chicago Pr.

Trends in Applications of Pure Mathematics to Mechanics. Ed. by E. Kroner & K. Kirchgassner. (Lecture Notes in Physics Ser.: Vol. 249). viii, 523p. 1986. pap. 36.40 (ISBN 0-387-16467-7). Springer-Verlag.

Trends in Automatic Pharmacology, Vol. 3. Ed. by S. Kalsner. 366p. 1985. 99.00x (ISBN 0-85066-327-X). Taylor & Francis.

Trends in Banking in OECD Countries. OECD. 72p. (Orig.). 1985. pap. 12.00x (ISBN 0-318-18490-7). OECD.

Trends in Behavior Therapy. Ed. by Per-Olow Sjoden & Sandra Bates. 1979. 39.95 (ISBN 0-12-647450-8). Acad Pr.

Trends in Biotechnology & Chemical Patent Law. 230p. 1985. 15.00 (G4-3772). PLI.

Trends in Birth Rates in the United States Since 1870. Bernard Okun. LC 78-64229. (Johns Hopkins University. Studies in the Social Sciences. Seventy-Sixth Ser. 1958: No. 1). Repr. of 1958 ed. 19.50 (ISBN 0-404-61334-9). AMS Pr.

Trends in Breast Feeding Among American Mothers. Charles Hirschman & Gerry E. Hendershot. Ed. by Audrey Shipp. (Ser. 23: No. 3). 1979. pap. text ed. 1.75 (ISBN 0-8406-0159-X). Natl Ctr Health Stats.

Trends in British Politics Since 1945. Ed. by Christopher Cook & John Ramsden. LC 77-17789. 1978. 25.00x (ISBN 0-312-81754-1). St Martin.

Trends in Business Ethics: Implications for Decision Making. Cees Van Dam & Luud M. Stallaert. (Nijenrode Studies in Business: Vol. 3). 1978. lib. bdg. 19.00 (ISBN 90-207-0691-8, Pub. by Martinus Nijhoff Netherlands). Kluwer Academic.

Trends in Cancer Incidence: Causes & Practical Implications. Ed. by Knut Magnus. LC 81-13205. (Illus.). 446p. 1982. 55.00 (ISBN 0-89116-235-6). Hemisphere Pub.

Trends in Cancer Incidence in Singapore, 1968-1982. Ed. by H. P. Lee et al. (IARC Scientific Publications: No. 91). (Illus.). 160p. 1988. pap. 55.00 (ISBN 92-832-1191-X). Oxford U Pr.

Trends in Cancer Incidences: Causes & Practical Implications. K. Magnus. 1982. text ed. 79.50 (ISBN 0-07-039501-2). McGraw.

Trends in Cancer Research. 84p. (Eng., Fr. & Rus.). 1966. pap. 2.80 (ISBN 92-4-156000-2). World Health.

Trends in Change in Telecommunications Policy. OECD. (Information Computer Communications Policy Ser.: No. 13). 354p. (Orig.). 1987. pap. 25.00x (ISBN 92-64-12940-5). OECD.

Trends in Child Abuse & Neglect: A National Perspective. Alene B. Russell & Cynthia M. Trainor. (Orig.). 1984. pap. text ed. 15.00 (ISBN 0-930915-00-3). Am Humane Assn.

Trends in Cluster Headache: Proceedings of the International Workshop on Trends in Cluster Headache, Chieti-Montesilvano (PE), Italy, 7-10 September, 1986. Ed. by F. L. Sicuteri et al. (International Congress Ser.: No. 731). 396p. 1987. 116.00 (ISBN 0-444-80871-X, Excerpta Medica). Elsevier.

Trends in Collective Bargaining. Twentieth Century Fund. Labor Committee Staff. Ed. by S. T. Williamson. H. Harris. LC 46-64. 1945. 26.00 (ISBN 0-527-02809-6). Kraus Repr.

Trends in Computer Algebra. R. Janssen. (Lecture Notes in Computer Science Ser.: Vol. 296). v, 197p. 1988. pap. 21.80 (ISBN 0-387-18928-9). Springer-Verlag.

Trends in Computer-Processed Electrocardiograms: Proceedings of the IFPPtC4 Working Conference, Amsterdam, 1976. IFPtC4 Working Conference Staff. Ed. by J. H. Van Bemmel & J. L. Willems. LC 77-1801. 438p. 1977. 76.50 (ISBN 0-7204-0723-0, North-Holland). Elsevier.

Trends in Consumer Behavior Research. Robert A. Peterson. LC 76-45657. (American Marketing Association Monograph Ser.: No. 6). pap. 20.00 (ISBN 0-317-28135-6, 2022481). Bks Demand UMI.

Trends in Consumer Credit Legislation. Barbara A. Curran. LC 65-17284. (Illus.). pap. 101.50 (ISBN 0-317-09650-8, 2020192). Bks Demand UMI.

Trends in Contraceptive Practice in the United States. William D. Mosher et al. (Series 23: No. 10). 47p. 1981. pap. 3.00 (ISBN 0-8406-0241-3). Natl Ctr Health Stats.

Trends in Coronary Heart Disease Mortality: The Influence of Medical Care. Ed. by Millicent W. Higgins & Russell V. Luepker. (Illus.). 384p. 1988. 45.00 (ISBN 0-19-505297-8). Oxford U Pr.

Trends in Dyeing & Finishing: A Global View. (Symposium Papers). 67p. 1986. 46.00 (ISBN 0-318-12154-9). Am Assn Text.

Trends in Ecological Research for the Nineteen Eighties. Ed. by June H. Cooley & Frank B. Golley. LC 84-26316. (NATO Conference Series I, Ecology: Vol. 7). 352p. 1984. 65.00x (ISBN 0-306-41889-4, Plenum Pr). Plenum Pub.

Trends in Educational Occupations. Marjorie Rankin. LC 74-177179. (Columbia University. Teachers College. Contributions to Education Ser.: No. 412). Repr. of 1930 ed. 22.50 (ISBN 0-404-55412-1). AMS Pr.

Trends in Electric Utility Research: Proceedings of the Electric Utility Research Conference, Chicago, April 1984. Ed. by C. Bullard & P. Wameldorff. 500p. 1984. pap. 105.00 (ISBN 0-08-030982-8). Pergamon.

Trends in Electronics: TENCON '84. Phang. 1984. 110.75 (ISBN 0-444-87582-4). Elsevier.

Trends in Employee Counseling Programs. Brenda McGowan. (Studies in Productivity: Highlights of the Literature Ser.: Vol. 37). 55p. 1984. pap. 39.00 (PS37). Work in Amer.

Trends in Employee Counseling Programs. Brenda McGowan. (Studies in Productivity: Highlights of the Literature Ser.: No. 37). 55p. 1984. pap. 39.00 (ISBN 0-08-032361-8, PS37). Work in Amer.

Trends in Employment & Earnings for Nineteen Graduating Classes of a Teachers College: As Shown by the Record of the 1927-1936 Classes of the New Jersey State Teachers College at Newark, New Jersey. John S. French. LC 79-176786. (Columbia University. Teachers College. Contributions to Education Ser.: No. 911). Repr. of 1945 ed. 22.50 (ISBN 0-404-55911-5). AMS Pr.

Trends in Enzyme Histochemistry & Cytochemistry. Ciba Foundation Staff. (Ciba Symposium Ser.: No. 73). 1980. 58.50 (ISBN 0-444-90135-3). Elsevier.

Trends in Enzyme Histochemistry & Cytochemistry. Ciba Foundation Staff. LC 80-11757. (Ciba Foundation Symposium, New Ser.: 73). pap. 80.50 (ISBN 0-317-29754-6, 2022192). Bks Demand UMI.

Trends in Enzymology: Proceedings, 2 vols. Incl. Enzyme Regulation & Mechanism of Action. Ed. by P. Mildner & B. Bries. 1980. 180.00 (ISBN 0-08-024417-3); Industrial & Clinical Enzymology. Ed. by L. J. Vitale & V. Simeon. 1980. (FEBS Ser.: Vols. 60 & 61). (Illus.). 730p. 1980. Pergamon.

Trends in Ergonomics Human Factors II. Ed. by R. E. Eberts & C. G. Eberts. 652p. 1985. 105.25 (ISBN 0-444-87751-7, North Holland). Elsevier.

Trends in Ergonomics: Human Factors III. Ed. by W. Karwowski. 1210p. 1986. 184.25 (ISBN 0-444-70036-6, North-Holland). Elsevier.

Trends in Ergonomics-Human Factors IV: Proceedings of the Annual Internat. Industrial Ergonomics & Safety Conf., Miami, FL, 9-12 June 1987. Ed. by S. S. Asfour. 1136p. 1987. 210.75 (ISBN 0-444-70246-6, North Holland). Elsevier.

Trends in Ethnic Group Relations in Asia & Oceania. (Race & Society Ser.). (Illus.). 292p. 1979. pap. 8.00 (ISBN 92-3-101603-2, U1008, UNESCO). UNIPUB.

Trends in European Multiple Sclerosis Research: Proceedings of the European Committee for Treatment & Research in Multiple Sclerosis Congress, Lyon, France, 3-5 Sept., 1987. Ed. by C. Confavreux et al. (International Congress Ser.). 428p. 1988. 131.50 (ISBN 0-444-80978-3, Excerpta Medica). Elsevier.

Trends in Fertility in the United States. Ed. by Taloria Stevenson. (Series 21, No. 28). 1977. pap. text ed. 1.95 (ISBN 0-8406-0108-5). Natl Ctr Health Stats.

Trends in Financial Decision Making: Planning & Capital Investment Decisions. Cees Van Dam. (Nijenrode Studies in Business: Vol. 2). 1978. lib. bdg. 27.00 (ISBN 90-207-0692-6, Martinus Nijhoff Pubs). Kluwer Academic.

Trends in Fish Utilization. J. J. Connell & R. Hardy. 116p. 1982. 25.00x (Pub. by Fishing News England). State Mutual Bk.

Trends in Fish Utilization. J. J. Connell & R. Hardy. (Illus.). 116p. 1982. pap. 17.95 (ISBN 0-85238-120-4, FN96, FNB). UNIPUB.

Trends in Food & Nutrient Availability in China, 1950-1981. Alan Piazza. (Working Paper: No. 607). 148p. 1983. 8.00 (ISBN 0-8213-0217-5, WP 0607). World Bank.

Trends in Foreign Language Requirements & Placement see Foreign Languages: Reading, Literature, Requirements.

Trends in Genetic Analysis. G. Pontecorvo. LC 58-8805. (Columbia Biological Ser.: No. 18). 1958. 27.50x (ISBN 0-231-02268-9). Columbia U Pr.

Trends in Government Financing. Morris A. Copeland. LC 75-19710. (National Bureau of Economic Research Ser.). (Illus.). 1975. Repr. 18.00x (ISBN 0-405-07590-1). Ayer Co Pubs.

Trends in Hepatology. Ed. by L. Bianchi et al. 1985. lib. bdg. 48.00 (ISBN 0-85200-868-6, Pub. by MTP Pr Netherlands). Kluwer Academic.

Trends in Indian Transport System: A District-Wise Study. D. Panduranga Rao. (Illus.). 484p. 1985. text ed. 125.00x (ISBN 0-86590-701-3, Pub. by Inter Pubns N. Delhi). Apt Bks.

Trends in Indonesia, Vol. II. Ed. by Leo Suryadinata & Sharon Siddique. (Illus.). 176p. 1981. pap. 10.00x (ISBN 9971-69-039-X, Pub. by Singapore U Pr). Ohio U Pr.

Trends in Industrial Location & Their Impact on Regional Economic Development. Benjamin H. Stevens et al. (Discussion Paper Ser.: No. 31). 1969. pap. 6.50 (ISBN 0-686-32200-2). Regional Sci Res Inst.

Trends in Inflammation Research One. Ed. by G. P. Velo. (Agents & Actions Supplement Ser.: Vol. 7). 362p. 1980. text ed. 93.95x (ISBN 0-8176-1177-0). Birkhauser.

Trends in Inflammation Research Two. Ed. by H. Bekemeier. R. Hirschelmann. (Agents & Actions Supplements Ser.: Vol. 10). 315p. 1982. text ed. 39.95 (ISBN 0-8176-1344-7). Birkhauser.

Trends in Information Processing Systems: Proceedings. Ed. by A. Duijvestijn & P. C. Lockemann. (Lecture Notes in Computer Science Ser.: Vol 123). 349p. 1981. pap. 22.00 (ISBN 0-387-10885-8). Springer-Verlag.

Trends in Information Systems: TC 8 Anthology. Ed. by B. Langefors & A. A. Verrijn-Stuart. 450p. 1986. 53.00 (ISBN 0-444-87949-8, North Holland). Elsevier.

Trends in Information Technology: A Handbook for Senior Management Who Must Understand Information Technology in a Competitive Context. 3rd ed. Andersen, Arthur & Co. (Illus.). 88p. (Orig.). 1987. pap. 9.95 (ISBN 0-942319-00-1). A Andersen.

Trends in Information Technology: A Handbook for Senior Management Who Must Understand Information Technology in a Competitive Context. Andersen, Arthur, & Co. Staff. 128p. (Orig., Japanese.). pap. text ed. write for info. (ISBN 0-942319-02-8). A Andersen.

Trends in Information Transfer. Ed. by Philip J. Hills. LC 82-3021. vii, 191p. 1982. 35.00 (ISBN 0-313-23600-3, HIT/). Greenwood.

Trends in Instructional Technology. Ed. by James W. Brown. 54p. 1984. 6.95 (ISBN 0-937597-07-4, IR-66). ERIC Clear.

Trends in Interfacial Electrochemistry. Ed. by A. Fernando Silva. 1986. lib. bdg. 99.00 (ISBN 90-277-2271-4, Pub. by Reidel Holland). Kluwer Academic.

Trends in International Trade in Manufactured Goods & Structural Change in the Industrial Countries. Bela Balassa & Kenneth Meyers. (Working Paper: No. 611). 44p. 1983. 5.00 (ISBN 0-8213-0251-5, WP 0611). World Bank.

Trends in Linguistics. H. Ivic. Tr. by Muriel Heppel. (Janua Linguarum, Series Minor: No. 42). (Orig.). 1965. pap. text ed. 19.60x (ISBN 0-686-22473-6). Mouton.

Trends in Macromolecular Science. Ed. by H-G Elias. LC 73-86253. (Midland Macromolecular Monographs). 132p. 1973. 32.00 (ISBN 0-677-15860-2). Gordon & Breach.

Trends in Management Thinking, 1960-1970. Harold R. Pollard. 331p. 1978. 18.00x (ISBN 0-87201-880-6). Gulf Pub.

Trends in Managerial & Financial Accounting: Income Determining & Financial Reporting. Cees Van Dam. (Nijenrode Studies in Business: Vol. 1). 1978. lib. bdg. 22.00 (ISBN 90-207-0693-4, Pub. by Martinus Nijhoff Netherlands). Kluwer Academic.

Trends in Manpower & Educational Development: A British Perspective. Keith Hampson. 18p. 1985. 2.75 (ISBN 0-318-22225-6, OC104). Natl Ctr Res Voc Ed.

Trends in Mathematical Optimization. Hoffmann et al. (International Series of Numerical Mathematics: No. 84). 390p. 1988. 60.50 (ISBN 0-8176-1919-4). Birkhauser.

Trends in Mathematical Psychology. E. Degreef & J. Van Buggenhaut. (Advances in Psychology Ser.: Vol. 20). 1984. 97.50 (ISBN 0-444-87512-3, I-241-84). Elsevier.

Trends in Medicinal Chemistry: Proceedings of the 9th International Symposium on Medicinal Chemistry. Ed. by E. Mutschler & E. Winterfeldt. 634p. 1987. pap. text ed. 107.00 (ISBN 0-89573-616-0). VCH Pubs.

Trends in Memory Development Research. Ed. by M. T. Chi. (Contributions to Human Development Ser.: Vol. 9). (Illus.). xii, 128p. 1983. pap. 32.75 (ISBN 3-8055-3661-5). S Karger.

Trends in Modern American Society. Intro. by Clarence Morris. LC 86-22762. (Benjamin Franklin Lectures of the University of Pennsylvania, 7th Series). 191p. 1986. Repr. of 1962 ed. lib. bdg. 38.50x (ISBN 0-313-22106-5, MOTM). Greenwood.

Trends in Modern Chinese Paintings. Li Chu-tsing. 246p. 1979. 128.00x (ISBN 0-317-68698-4, Pub. by Han-Shan Tang Ltd). State Mutual Bk.

Trends in Municipal Administration: The Periodical Literature, 1980-1984. Dale E. Casper. (Public Administration Ser.: P 1769). 22p. 1985. 3.00 (ISBN 0-89028-569-1). Vance Biblios.

Trends in Natural Resource Commodities: Statistics of Prices, Output, Consumption, Foreign Trade, & Employment in the United States, 1870-1957. Neal Potter & Francis T. Christy. Ed. by Pauline Manning. LC 62-11711. pap. 145.00 (ISBN 0-317-26474-5, 2023809). Bks Demand UMI.

Trends in New Medical Schools. Ed. by Hans P. Popper. (Illus.). 184p. 1967. 49.50 (ISBN 0-8089-0366-7, 793358). Grune.

Trends in Nonprofit Organizations Law. Howard L. Oleck. 176p. 1977. pap. 5.00 (ISBN 0-317-31050-X, B227/B228); 1979 supplement incl. Am Law Inst.

Trends in Nursing & Related Care Homes & Hospitals: United States, Selected Years 1969-1980. Geneive Strahan. Ed. by Kaludia Cox. (Series 14: No. 30). 60p. 1984. pap. text ed. 2.75 (ISBN 0-8406-0290-1). Natl Ctr Health Stats.

Trends in Optical & Video Disks. (Special Interest Packages Ser.). pap. 25.00 (ISBN 0-317-06201-8, PO23). Assn Inform & Image Mgmt.

Trends in Oral Contraception. Ed. by R. F. Harrison et al. 70p. 1983. text ed. 15.00 (ISBN 0-85200-771-X, Pub. by MTP Pr England). Kluwer Academic.

Trends in Pharmacological Research on Platelet Activating Factor (PAF) in Japan. Y. Ogura & K. Kisara. (Illus.). 208p. 1988. 28.00 (ISBN 0-912791-67-5). Ishiyaku Euro.

Trends in Photobiology. Ed. by Claude Helene et al. LC 80-29512. 686p. 1982. 65.00x (ISBN 0-306-40644-6, Plenum Pr). Plenum Pub.

Trends in Protestant Social Idealism. Neal Hughley. LC 74-167359. (Essay Index Reprint Ser.). Repr. of 1948 ed. 18.00 (ISBN 0-8369-2771-0). Ayer Co Pubs.

Trends in Reactor Pressure Vessel & Circuit Development. Ed. by R. W. Nichols. (Illus.). 380p. 1980. 90.00 (ISBN 0-85334-872-3, Pub. by Elsevier Applied Sci England). Elsevier.

Trends in Relief Expenditures, 1910-1935. Ann E. Geddes. LC 74-166327. (Research Monograph Ser.: Vol. 10). 1971. Repr. of 1937 ed. lib. bdg. 19.50 (ISBN 0-306-70342-4). Da Capo.

Trends in Research & in the Application of Science & Technology for Arid Zone Development. (MAB Technical Notes Ser.: No. 10). 53p. 1979. pap. 5.00 (ISBN 92-3-101597-4, U907, UNESCO). UNIPUB.

Trends in Romance Linguistics & Philology, Vol. 2. Ed. by Rebecca Posner & John Green. (Synchronic Romance Linguistics Ser.). 422p. 1981. 64.00x (ISBN 90-279-7896-4). Mouton.

Trends in Rural Savings & Private Capital Formation in India. Raj Krishna & G. S. Raychaudhuri. (World Bank Staff Working Paper: No. 382). 43p. 1980. pap. 3.50 (ISBN 0-686-39734-7, WP-0382). World Bank.

Trends in Scandinavian Taxation. G. Lindencrona. 46p. 1979. lib. bdg. 10.00 (ISBN 90-200-0584-7, Pub. by Kluwer Law Netherlands). Kluwer Academic.

Trends in Scholarly Publishing. British Library Staff. (R&D Report 5299). 94p. (Orig.). 1976. pap. 8.25 (ISBN 0-85350-141-6, Pub. by British Lib). Longwood Pub Group.

Trends in School Library Media Research as Reflected in the ERIC Database. Barbara B. Minor. 44p. 1986. 6.00 (ISBN 0-937597-11-2, IR-70). ERIC Clear.

Trends in Scientific & Technical Primary Journal Publishing in the U. S. A. Peter W. Lea. (R&D Report 5272). 34p. (Orig.). 1976. pap. 8.25 (ISBN 0-85350-138-6, Pub. by British Lib). Longwood Pub Group.

Trends in Singapore. Chee M. Seah. 164p. 1975. pap. 5.00x (ISBN 0-8214-0510-1, 82-93433, Pub. by Singapore U Pr). Ohio U Pr.

Trends in Social Work, Eighteen Seventy-Four to Nineteen Fifty-Six: A History Based on the Proceedings of the National Conference of Social Work. 2nd ed. Frank J. Bruno. LC 80-19210. xviii, 462p. 1980. Repr. of 1957 ed. lib. bdg. 45.50x (ISBN 0-313-22665-2, BRTI). Greenwood.

Trends in Solid Mechanics. Ed. by J. F. Besseling & A. M. Van Der Heijden. 256p. 1980. 45.00x (ISBN 90-286-0699-8, Pub. by Sijthoff & Noordhoff). Kluwer Academic.

Trends in Soviet Theoretical Linguistics. Ed. by F. Kiefer. LC 72-95890. (Foundations of Language Supplementary Ser: No. 18). 1973. lib. bdg. 66.00 (ISBN 90-277-0274-8, Pub. by Reidel Holland). Kluwer Academic.

Trends in Special Librarianship. Ed. by Jack Burkett. 205p. 1969. 20.00 (ISBN 0-208-00856-X, Archon). Shoe String.

Trends in Specialization: Tomorrow's Medicine. Ed. by Donald G. Langsley & James H. Darragh. LC 85-73107. (Illus.). 128p. 1985. lib. bdg. 29.95 (ISBN 0-934277-06-0). Am Bd Med Spec.

Trends in Student Personnel Work As Represented in the Positions of Dean of Women & Dean of Girls in Colleges & Universities, Normal Schools, Teachers Colleges, & High Schools. Sarah M. Sturtevant et al. LC 79-177732. (Columbia University. Teachers College. Contributions to Education Ser.: No. 787). Repr. of 1940 ed. 22.50 (ISBN 0-404-55787-2). AMS Pr.

Trends in Teaching Genetics. Ed. by Daniel Bergsma. (Alan R. Liss Ser.: Vol. 13, No. 6). 1977. 23.00 (ISBN 0-686-23125-2). March of Dimes.

Trends in Technology in the Modern Real Estate Office. James A. Young & Joseph M. Lord. (Illus.). 120p. 1985. write for info. (ISBN 0-935351-03-5); pap. 14.95 (ISBN 0-318-18987-9). Gross Johnson.

Trends in Teenage Childbearing, United States, 1970-81. (Series 21: No. 41). 22p. 1.75. Natl Ctr Health Stats.

Trends in the Accreditation Relationships of U. S. Postsecondary Institutions: 1978-1985. H. R. Kells & Richard M. Parrish. 12p. 1986. 8.95 (ISBN 0-318-21996-4). Coun Postsecondary Accredit.

Trends in the American Economy in the Nineteenth Century. Conference on Research in Income & Wealth. LC 75-19709. (National Bureau of Economic Research Ser.). (Illus.). 1975. Repr. of 1960 ed. 58.50x (ISBN 0-405-07588-X). Ayer Co Pubs.

Trends in the Biology of Fermentations for Fuels & Chemicals. Ed. by A. Hollaender et al. LC 81-5928. (Basic Life Sciences Ser.: Vol. 18). 604p. 1981. 95.00x (ISBN 0-306-40752-3, Plenum Pr). Plenum Pub.

Trends in the Design & Building of Skyscrapers: Journal Articles, 1980-1985. Dale E. Casper. (Architecture Ser.: A 1620). 8p. 1986. 3.00 (ISBN 0-89028-910-7). Vance Biblios.

Trends in the Information Economy. OECD Staff. (Information Computer Communications Policy Ser.: No. 11). 42p. (Orig.). 1986. pap. 8.00 (ISBN 92-64-12861-1). OECD.

Trends in the Ohio Economy. Paul G. Craig & James C. Yocum. 1955. pap. text ed. 2.00 (ISBN 0-87776-079-9, R79). Ohio St U Admin Sci.

Trends in the Philippines, Vol. II. Ed. by M. Rajaretnam. 1978. pap. 6.00x (ISBN 0-8214-0511-X, Pub. by Singapore U Pr). Ohio U Pr.

Trends in the Relocation of U.S. Manufacturing. Christina M. Kelton. Ed. by Fred Bateman. LC 83-9117. (Research in Business Economics & Public Policy Ser.: No. 6). 194p. 1983. 42.95 (ISBN 0-8357-1445-4). UMI Res Pr.

Trends in the Services for Youth. Ed. by J. H. Leicester & W. A. Farndale. 1967. 71.00 (ISBN 0-08-011604-3). Pergamon.

Trends in the Size, Growth & Cost of the Literature since 1955. Christopher B. Wootton. (R&D Report 5323). (Illus.). 100p. (Orig.). 1977. pap. 8.25 (ISBN 0-85350-146-7, Pub. by British Lib). Longwood Pub Group.

Trends in the Soviet Oil & Gas Industry. Robert W. Campbell. LC 76-15940. (Resources for the Future Ser). (Illus.). 144p. 1977. 12.00x (ISBN 0-8018-1870-2). Johns Hopkins.

Trends in the Soviet Oil & Gas Industry. Robert W. Campbell. LC 76-15940. 141p. pap. 36.70 (2030193). Bks Demand UMI.

Trends in the Study of Morbidity & Mortality. D. Curiel et al. (Public Health Paper Ser: No. 27). 196p. (Eng., Fr., Rus. & Span.). 1965. pap. 3.60 (ISBN 92-4-130027-2). World Health.

Trends in the Theory & Practice of Non-Linear Analysis. Ed. by V. Lakshmikantham. (Mathematical Studies: Vol. 110). 1985. 55.00 (ISBN 0-444-87704-5, North-Holland). Elsevier.

Trends in the United States Ferrous Industry. Jonathan P. Raymond. (Illus.). 58p. 1987. pap. 3.00 (003-009-00510-8). USGPO.

Trends in the World Aluminum Industry. Sterling Brubaker. LC 67-16035. pap. 68.50 (ISBN 0-317-26024-3, 2023790). Bks Demand UMI.

Trends in Theoretical Computer Science. Egon Borger. (Principles of Computer Science Ser.). (Illus.). 400p. 1987. text ed. 39.95x (ISBN 0-88175-084-0, Computer Sci Pr). W H Freeman.

Trends in Theory & Practice of Non-Linear Differential Equations. Lakshmikantham. (Lecture Notes in Pure & Applied Mathematics). 576p. 1983. 65.00 (ISBN 0-8247-7130-3). Dekker.

Trends in Transport Investment & Expediture in 1979: Statistical Report on Road Accidents in 1980, Vol. II. Ministers of Transport, European Conference Staff. 108p. (Orig.). 1982. pap. 10.00x (ISBN 92-821-1076-1). OECD.

Trends in Transport Investment & Performance in 1981 & Statistical Report on Road Accidents in 1982: Report of the ECMT, Vol. II. OECD. 122p. (Orig.). 1985. pap. 13.00x (ISBN 92-821-1095-8). OECD.

Trends in Transport Investment & Performance in 1980 & Statistical Report on Road Accidents in 1981: ECMT's 29th Annual Report, Vol. 2. 92p. (Orig.). 1984. pap. 10.00X (ISBN 92-821-1086-9). OECD.

Trends in United States Merchandise Trade, 1953-1970. (Studies in International Trade: No. 3). (Illus.). 53p. (Orig.). 1972. pap. 7.50 (ISBN 0-685-29062-X, G96, GATT). UNIPUB.

Trends in Urban Firefighting: Periodical Literature, 1980-1984. Dale E. Casper. (Public Administration Ser.: P 1801). 11p. 1985. 2.00 (ISBN 0-89028-631-0). Vance Biblios.

Trends in Urbanisation in India. Raj Bala. 1986. 49.50X (ISBN 81-7033-012-2, Pub. by Rawat). South Asia Bks.

Trends in Veterinary Pharmacology & Toxicology: Proceedings of the 1st European Congress. Ed. by A. S. Van Miert. (Developments in Animal & Veterinary Science Ser.: Vol. 6). 364p. 1980. 97.50 (ISBN 0-444-41878-4). Elsevier.

Trends in Welding Research. Ed. by S. A. David. 1982. 82.00 (ISBN 0-87170-150-2). ASM.

Trends in White Attitudes Toward Negroes. Mildred Schwartz. (Report Ser: No. 119). 1967. 3.00x (ISBN 0-932132-11-1). NORC.

Trends in World Production & Trade. (Trade & Development Ser.). 36p. 1983. pap. text ed. 6.00 (ISBN 92-1-112141-8, E.82.11.D.13). UN.

Trends in World Social Development: The Social Progress of Nations, 1980-1986. Richard J. Estes. LC 87-36132. 240p. 1988. lib. bdg. 39.95 (ISBN 0-275-92613-3). Praeger.

Trends Influence Curriculum. 2nd ed. Ed. by Lutian R. Wootton & John C. Reynolds. 1974. 29.50x (ISBN 0-8422-5177-4). Irvington.

Trends of Mental Disease. American Psychopathological Association Staff. Ed. by Gerald N. Grob. LC 78-22547. (Historical Issues in Mental Health Ser.). (Illus.). 1979. Repr. of 1945 ed. lib. bdg. 14.00x (ISBN 0-405-11901-1). Ayer Co Pubs.

Trends of Occupational Mobility among Migrants. Sunanda Pande. 232p. 1986. 31.00x (ISBN 81-7033-023-8, Pub. by Rawat). South Asia Bks.

Trends of Professional Opportunities in the Liberal Arts College. Merle S. Kuder. LC 74-176940. (Columbia University. Teachers College. Contributions to Education Ser.: No. 717). Repr. of 1937 ed. 22.50 (ISBN 0-404-55717-1). AMS Pr.

Trends of Urbanization in Taiwan, 2 vols. in one. Lung Kwan-Hai. (Asian Folklore & Social Life Monograph: Nos. 39-40). (Chinese.). 1972. 17.00x (ISBN 0-89986-039-7). Oriental Bk Store.

Trends, Policies & Prospects in Trade among Countries Having Different Economic & Social Systems: Selected Studies. 145p. 1985. 16.50 (ISBN 92-1-112162-0, E.83.II.D.11). UN.

Trends, Techniques & Problems in Theoretical Computer Science. Ed. by A. Kelemenova & J. Kelemen. (Lecture Notes in Computer Science Ser.: Vol. 281). vi, 213p. 1988. pap. 21.80 (ISBN 0-387-18535-6). Springer-Verlag.

Trends Toward the Future in Physical Education. Ed. by John D. Massengale. LC 86-34282. (Illus.). 200p. 1987. text ed. 24.00x (ISBN 0-87322-103-6). Human Kinetics.

Trent Intervenes. E. C. Bentley. 259p. 1981. pap. 4.50 (ISBN 0-486-24098-3). Dover.

Trent Motor Traction Co., Ltd., 1913-1986: A Pictorial Record. Trent Valley Publications Staff. (Illus.). 128p. 1988. 70.00x (Pub. by Trent Valley UK); cardcover 52.00x (Pub. by Trent Valley UK). State Mutual Bk.

Trent, Museo Provinciale d'arte, Biblioteca Musicale L. Feininger N.S. Ed. by Alexander Silbiger. (Seventeenth-Century Keyboard Music). 225p. 1988. lib. bdg. 60.00 (ISBN 0-8240-8015-7). Garland Pub.

Trente Ans de Vie Sociale: Vers les Temps Meileurs, 1915-1925, Vol. 4. Anatole France et al. 216p. 1973. 12.50 (ISBN 0-686-55879-0). French & Eur.

Trente et une Chansons Musicales: Claude de Sermisy, Clement Janequin et al see Maitres Musiciens de la Renaissance Francaise.

Trente-Sept Sous de Monsieur Montaudouin. Eugene Labiche. 9.95 (ISBN 0-686-54256-8). French & Eur.

Trente-Sixieme Dessous. Pierre Daninos. 1974. 8.95 (ISBN 0-686-55582-1). French & Eur.

Trenton Pickle Ordinance & Other Bonehead Legislation. Dick Hyman. LC 75-41874. (Illus.). 132p. 1976. 7.95 (ISBN 0-8289-0278-X). Greene.

Trenton Pickle Ordinance & Other Bonehead Legislation. Dick Hyman. LC 75-41874. 115p. 1984. pap. 4.95 (ISBN 0-8289-0537-1). Greene.

Trent's Last Case. E. C. Bentley. LC 75-44955. (Crime Fiction Ser). 1976. Repr. of 1912 ed. lib. bdg. 21.00 (ISBN 0-8240-2353-6). Garland Pub.

Trent's Last Case. E. C. Bentley. 1978. pap. 3.50 (ISBN 0-06-080440-8, P 440, PL). Har-Row.

Trent's Last Case. E. C. Bentley. 1976. lib. bdg. 18.95x (ISBN 0-89968-165-4). Lightyear.

Trent's Last Case. E. C. Bentley. 265p. 24.95x (ISBN 0-7090-2201-8, Pub. by R Hale Ltd UK). State Mutual Bk.

Trent's Own Case. E. C. Bentley & H. Warner Allen. 324p. 1988. pap. 3.95 (ISBN 0-88184-349-0). Carroll & Graf.

Treponema Pallidum: A Bibliographical Review of the Morphology, Culture & Survival of T. Pallidum & Associated Organisms. (WHO Bulletin Supplement Ser.: Vol. 35). 1966. pap. 4.80 (ISBN 92-4-068351-8). World Health.

Treponematoses Research: A Report. WHO Scientific Group, Geneva, 1969. (Technical Report Ser: No. 455). 91p. 1970. pap. 2.80 (ISBN 92-4-120455-9, 1526). World Health.

Trepostomatous Ectoprocta (Bryozoa) from the Lower Chickamauga Group(Middle Ordovician), Wills Valley, Alabama see Bulletins of American Paleontology.

Tres a la Vez. new ed. Rogelio Rios. (Pimienta Collection Ser). (Illus.). 160p. (Span.). 1975. pap. 1.25 (ISBN 0-88473-231-2). Fiesta Pub.

Tres Breve Relation sur la Destruction des Indes: Suivie de les Trent Propositions Tres Juridiques. Don Fray Bartolome De Las Casas. (Archontes Ser.: No. 2). 140p. (Fr.). 1975. pap. text ed. 16.00x (ISBN 90-2797-865-4). Mouton.

Tres Caras Del Amor. Josh McDowell & Paul Lewis. 96p. 1983. 2.50 (ISBN 0-88113-289-6). Edit Betania.

Tres Cuentos. 2nd ed. Carlos Garcia-Prada & William E. Wilson. LC 59-4973. (Span). 1959. pap. text ed. 16.76 (ISBN 0-395-04482-0). HM.

Tres de la Madrugada. Bunuel. (EMC Easy Readers: Series A). 1972. pap. 3.95 (ISBN 0-88436-061-X, 70265). EMC.

Tres Dramas De Navidad. Belia Perez. 24p. 1985. pap. 0.95 (ISBN 0-311-08221-1). Casa Bautista.

Tres Dramas Romanticos. Jose Zorilla et al. LC 73-111116. (Play Anthology Reprint Ser). 1962. 20.25 (ISBN 0-8369-8209-6). Ayer Co Pubs.

Tres Farsas Contemporaneas y un Secuestro. Antonio M. Ballesteros. Ed. by Angel R. Maroto & Charles E. Whitehead. (Orig.). (gr. 10-12). 1980. pap. text ed. 4.75x (ISBN 0-88334-125-5). Ind Sch Pr.

Tres Fuentes y las Tres Partes Integrantes Del Marxismo. Lenin. 68p. (Span.). 1977. pap. 0.95 (ISBN 0-8285-1409-7, Pub. by Progress Pubs USSR). Imported Pubns.

Tres Goldaras En la Poesia Del Siglo XX. Jose L. Goldaras et al. LC 80-7043. (Coleccion Espejo de Paciencia). (Illus.). 143p. (Orig., Span.). 1981. pap. 7.95 (ISBN 0-89729-280-4). Ediciones.

Tres grandes metros - el eneasilabo, el tredecasilabo, y el decasilabo. Julio Saaredra Molina. 122p. (Span.). 1.60 (ISBN 0-318-14312-7). Hispanic Inst.

Tres Macho, He Said: Padre Gallegos, New Mexico's First Congressman. Angelico Chavez. 1985. 15.00 (ISBN 0-88307-669-1). Gannon.

Tres Mosqueteros. Alexandre Dumas. LC 84-52574. (Silver Burdett Classics for Kids Ser.). (Illus.). 32p. (Span.). (gr. 3 up). 1985. pap. 3.60 (ISBN 0-382-09022-5). Silver.

Tres Novelas. Ivan S. Turgenev. 269p. (Span.). 1980. 5.95 (ISBN 0-8285-1344-9, Pub. by Progress Pubs USSR). Imported Pubns.

Tres Obras (El Senor Presidente, el Alhajadito, Leyendas de Guatemala) Miguel A. Asturias. (Ayacucho Library Collection Ser.: Vol. 19). (Span.). 1985. 35.00 (ISBN 0-317-56297-5, Pub. by Biblioteca Ayacucho); pap. 17.50 (ISBN 0-317-56298-3, Pub. by Biblioteca Ayacucho). Humanities.

Tres Pasos Adelante. Charles Swindoll. 176p. 1983. 3.75 (ISBN 0-88113-363-9). Edit Betania.

Tres Relatos. Chinguiz Aitmatov. 280p. (Span.). 1978. 4.95 (ISBN 0-8285-1327-9, Pub. by Progress Pubs USSR). Imported Pubns.

Tres Representaciones Literarias de la Vida Politica Cubana. Ada Ortuzar-Young. LC 79-901197. (Senda de Estudios y Ensayos). (Orig., Span.). 1979. pap. 10.95 (ISBN 0-918454-17-4). Senda Nueva.

Tres Riches Heures du Duc de Berry. (Illus.). 616p. 1984. 12500.00 (ISBN 0-8109-4999-7). Abrams.

Tres Riches Heures of Jean, Duke of Berry. Millard Meiss. LC 73-90120. (Illus.). 290p. (Gold slipcased). slipcase 80.00 (ISBN 0-8076-0512-3). Braziller.

Tresor d'Arlatan. Alphonse Daudet. (Illus.). 160p. 1897. 11.95 (ISBN 0-686-55602-X). French & Eur.

Tresor de Felibridge: Dictionnaire Provencal-Francais, 2 vols. Frederic Mistral. 2375p. (Fr.). Set. 250.00 (ISBN 0-686-56736-6, M-6414). French & Eur.

Tresor de la Francaise: Dictionnaire du XIXe et du XXe Siecles (1789-1960, 4 vols. Centre de Recherche pour un Tresor de la Langue Francaise Staff. Set. 175.00 (ISBN 0-685-36650-2). French & Eur.

Tresor De Rackham le Rouge. Herge. (Illus.). 62p. (Fr.). (gr. 7-9). looseleaf bdg. 15.95 (ISBN 0-685-28413-1). French & Eur.

Tresor des Humbles. Maurice Maeterlinck. 222p. 1949. 9.95 (ISBN 0-686-56292-5). French & Eur.

Tresor des pianistes, 23 vols. Ed. by Aristide Farrenc & Louise Farrenc. LC 77-8873. (Music Reprint Ser.). (Illus.). 1978. Repr. of 1872 ed. lib. bdg. 47.50 ea.; lib. bdg. 950.00 set (ISBN 0-306-77380-5). Da Capo.

Tresors de la Mer Rouge. Romain Gary. pap. 9.50 (ISBN 0-685-34128-3). French & Eur.

Tresors des Musees de Province, 5 tomes. Set. 209.95 (ISBN 0-685-35924-7). French & Eur.

Tresors Du Tibet. Pierre Colombel & Rinnie Tang. 118p. 1987. pap. 137.00x (Pub. by Han-Shan Tang Ltd). State Mutual Bk.

Trespass. Phillip Finch. 1987. 17.95 (ISBN 0-531-15044-5). Watts.

Trespass. Fletcher Knebel. 1987. pap. 3.95 (ISBN 0-441-82336-X, Pub. by Charter Bks). Ace Bks.

Trespasser. D. H. Lawrence. Ed. by Elizabeth Mansfield. LC 80-41663. (Cambridge Edition of the Works of D. H. Lawrence Ser.). 350p. 1982. 44.50 (ISBN 0-521-22264-8); pap. 14.95 (ISBN 0-521-29424-X). Cambridge U Pr.

Trespasser. D. H. Lawrence. 1971. Repr. of 1912 ed. 39.00 (ISBN 0-403-01067-5). Scholarly.

Trespasser. D. H. Lawrence. Ed. by Elizabeth Mansfield. LC 82-42740. (Cambridge Edition Ser.). 256p. 1983. 20.00 (ISBN 0-670-72991-4). Viking.

Trespasser. D. H. Lawrence. 1988. Repr. of 1912 ed. lib. bdg. 49.00x. Am Biog Serv.

Trespasser. Gilbert Parker. 1976. lib. bdg. 13.85x (ISBN 0-89968-083-6). Lightyear.

Trespassers. Andrew Coburn. (Orig.). 1980. pap. 2.50 (ISBN 0-671-83048-1). PB.

Trespassers on the Roof of the World. Peter Hopkirk. (Illus.). 288p. 1983. 13.95 (ISBN 0-87477-257-5). J P Tarcher.

Trespassers on the Roof of the World. Peter Hopkirk. 274p. 1984. pap. 35.00x (ISBN 0-317-69432-4, Pub. by Han-Shan Tang Ltd). State Mutual Bk.

Trespassing Stoplights & Attitudes. Mary McGrath. (Illus.). 44p. (Orig.). 1980. pap. 5.00 (ISBN 0-930012-43-7). J Mudfoot.

Tretii Rim. Georgii Ivanov. Ed. by Vadim Kreid. LC 87-4114. 380p. (Rus.). 1987. pap. 14.00 (ISBN 0-938920-77-4). Hermitage.

Tretyakov Art Gallery: A Guide. V. Volodarsky. 184p. 1977. 25.00x (ISBN 0-317-14325-5, Pub. by Collets (UK)). State Mutual Bk.

Tretyakov Gallery. X. Antonova. 375p. 1983. 75.00 (ISBN 0-8285-2662-1, Pub. by Aurora Pubs USSR). Imported Pubns.

Tretyakov Gallery, Moscow: A Panorama of Russian & Soviet Art, Painting, Graphic Art, Sculpture. N. Adaskina. (Illus.). 376p. 1983. 308.00x (ISBN 0-317-57473-6, Pub. by Collets UK). State Mutual Bk.

Tretyakov Gallery: Paintings. 192p. 1981. 48.00x (ISBN 0-317-14328-X, Pub. by Collets (UK)). State Mutual Bk.

Trevayne. Jonathon Ryder. 1986. pap. 3.95 (ISBN 0-440-19069-X). Dell.

Treve. Albert P. Terhune. 19.95 (ISBN 0-89190-366-6, Pub. by Am Repr). Amereon Ltd.

Trevelyan Papers, 3 Vols. (Vol. 67, 0-384-61497-3; vol. 84, 0-384-61514-7; vol. 105, 0-384-61525-2). 1857-1872. 37.00 ea. Johnson Repr.

Trevelyan Papers, 1856-72, 3 Vols. Trevelyan. Ed. by J. Payne Collier et al. (Camden Society, London, Publications, First Ser.: Nos. 67, 84, & 105). Set. 110.00 (ISBN 0-404-50206-7); 37.00 ea. No. 67 (ISBN 0-404-50167-2). No. 84 (ISBN 0-404-50184-2). No. 105 (ISBN 0-404-50205-9). AMS Pr.

Trever's First Strike: A Former Minuteman Missile Launch Officer Zeroes in on the Arms Race. John Trever & Gene Copeland. LC 83-15352. (Illus.). 112p. (Orig.). 1983. pap. 4.95 (ISBN 0-931790-63-8). Brick Hse Pub.

Trevi Fountain. John A. Pinto. LC 85-2480. 320p. 1986. 32.00x (ISBN 0-300-03335-4). Yale U Pr.

Trevor Howard: A Gentleman & a Player. Vivienne Knight. (Illus.). 288p. 1987. 17.95 (ISBN 0-8253-0430-X). Beaufort Bks NY.

Trevor Huddleston: Essays on His Life & Work. Ed. by Deborah D. Honore. (Illus.). 224p. 1988. 29.95 (ISBN 0-19-826692-8). Oxford U Pr.

Trevor's Place: The Story of the Boy Who Brings Hope to the Homeless. Frank Ferrell et al. LC 84-48768. (Illus.). 138p. 1985. 13.45 (ISBN 0-06-062531-7, HarpR). Har-Row.

Trewe Mirrour of Glase Wherin We Maye Beholde the Wofull State of Thys Our Realme of Englande. Laurence Saunders. LC 74-28884. (English Experience Ser.: No. 761). 1975. Repr. of 1556 ed. 3.50 (ISBN 90-221-0761-2). Walter J Johnson.

TRH & Spinocerebellar Degeneration. Ed. by I. Sobue. 268p. 1986. 110.75 (ISBN 0-444-80721-7). Elsevier.

Tri & Tetra-hydric Alcohols, Their Oxidation Products & Derivatives see Rodd's Chemistry of Carbon Compounds.

Tri-Color Pottery of the T'ang Dynasty. National Museum of History Staff. 92p. 1977. 140.00x (ISBN 0-317-68519-8, Pub. by Han-Shan Tang Ltd). State Mutual Bk.

Tri-Nim: The Game for Compleat Strategysts. Bruce Hicks & Hervey Hicks. 6.00 (ISBN 0-911624-35-X). Wffn Proof.

Tri-Play Crosswords, No. 1. Len Fellows. Ed. by Henry Hook. (Illus.). 64p. 1984. 6.95 (ISBN 0-671-50320-0, Fireside). S&S.

Tri Portreta. Lev Kopelev & Raisa Orlova. 125p. (Rus.). cancelled (ISBN 0-88233-861-7). Ardis Pubs.

Tri-X Chronicles. Bil Paul. LC 73-86842. (Illus.). 1972. pap. 3.45 (ISBN 0-9600650-0-8). Alchemist-Light.

Triable Either-Way Cases: Crown Court or Magistrates' Court? D. Riley & J. Vennard. (Home Office Research Study Ser.: No. 98). (Illus.). 51p. 1988. pap. 11.00 (ISBN 0-11-340890-0, HM3288, Pub. by Her Maj Station Offc). UNIPUB.

Triad -- Modern Irish Fiction. Ronit Lentin et al. 176p. 1986. 17.95 (ISBN 0-86327-056-5, Pub. by Wolfhound Pr Ireland); pap. 7.95 (ISBN 0-86327-057-3, Pub. by Wolfhound Pr Ireland). Irish Bks Media.

Triad of Genius. Edith Sitwell & Osbert Sitwell. 1979. Repr. of 1953 ed. lib. bdg. 30.00 (ISBN 0-8492-2985-5). R West.

Triad of Knives. Tom Cooper. 384p. 1986. pap. 3.50 (ISBN 0-373-97020-X, Pub. by Worldwide). Harlequin Bks.

Triad Optical Illusions & How to Design Them. Harry Turner. LC 77-81212. (Illus.). 1977. pap. 3.50 (ISBN 0-486-23549-1). Dover.

Triad Power: The Coming Shape of Global Competition. Kenichi Ohmae. LC 84-26068. 192p. 1985. 21.95 (ISBN 0-02-923470-0). Free Pr.

Triad Reader. Ed. by Joseph S. Renzulli & Sally M. Reis. 218p. 1986. pap. 19.95 (ISBN 0-936386-35-5). Creative Learning.

Triad System. Walter G. Allan. Ed. by Silent Partners, Inc. Staff. (Illus.). 38p. (Orig.). 1987. pap. text ed. 79.95 (ISBN 0-9619483-0-2). W G Allan.

Triada. Sam Hamill. LC 78-58877. 1978. 25.00x (ISBN 0-914742-34-5); pap. 6.00 (ISBN 0-914742-35-3). Copper Canyon.

Triadic Heart of Siva: Kaula Tantricism of Abhinavagupta in the Non-Dual Shaivism of Kashmir. Paul E. Muller-Ortega. (Shaiva Traditions of Kashmir Ser.). 416p. 1988. 49.50x (ISBN 0-88706-786-7); pap. 14.95x (ISBN 0-88706-787-5). State U NY Pr.

Triadic Mysticism. Paul E. Murphy. 1986. 23.00X (ISBN 81-208-0010-9, Pub. by Motilal Banarsidass). South Asia Bks.

Triadic Mysticism: The Mystic Theology of the Shaivism of Kashmir. Paul E. Murphy. 226p. 1986. 22.00 (ISBN 81-208-0010-9, Pub. by Motilal Banarsidass India). Orient Bk Dist.

Triads of Ireland. Ed. by Kuno Meyer. LC 78-72688. (Royal Irish Academy. Todd Lecture Ser.: Vol. 13). Repr. of 1906 ed. 14.50 (ISBN 0-404-60573-7). AMS Pr.

Triads: The Wisdom of the Welsh Witches. Rhuddlwm Gawr. LC 85-73755. (Illus.). 140p. (Orig.). 1988. 14.95 (ISBN 0-931760-45-3, CP 10123); pap. 10.95 (ISBN 0-931760-23-2). Camelot GA.

Triage & Justice: The Ethics of Rationing Life-Saving Medical Resources. Gerald R. Winslow. LC 81-10434. 240p. 1982. 28.00x (ISBN 0-520-04328-6). U of Cal Pr.

Trial. Lindsey P. Dew. 237p. 1988. pap. 4.95 (ISBN 0-87579-157-3). Deseret Bk.

Trial. Philip L. Dew. LC 84-12711. 250p. 1984. 8.95 (ISBN 0-87747-874-0). Deseret Bk.

Trial. Linda DuBreuil. 1975. pap. 1.50 (ISBN 0-685-52172-9, LB245DK, Leisure Bks). Leisure NY.

Trial. rev. ed. Franz Kafka. 1937. 16.45 (ISBN 0-394-44955-X). Knopf.

Trial. Franz Kafka. LC 68-59195. (Illus., Definitive edition with Kafka's own drawings). 1968. pap. 6.95 (ISBN 0-8052-0416-4). Schocken.

Trial. Franz Kafka. 179p. 1983. Repr. lib. bdg. 19.95x (ISBN 0-89966-453-9). Buccaneer Bks.

Trial. Franz Kafka. LC 87-32345. 288p. 1988. pap. 6.95 (ISBN 0-8052-0848-8). Schocken.

Trial Advocacy: A Systematic Approach. Leonard Packel & Dolores B. Spina. LC 84-70166. 206p. 1984. 60.00 (ISBN 0-8318-0453-X, B453). Am Law Inst.

Trial Advocacy: Cases, Exercises & Problems. Richard B. Parnell & Glen W. Shellhaas. LC 82-2668. 171p. 1982. pap. text ed. 9.95 (ISBN 0-314-66859-4). West Pub.

Trial Advocacy in a Nutshell. Paul B. Bergman. LC 78-27734. (Nutshell Ser.). 402p. 1979. pap. text ed. 9.95 (ISBN 0-8299-2030-7). West Pub.

Trial Advocacy Materials. 2nd ed. Kent Sinclair, Jr. 823p. 1985. incl. administrator's manual 50.00 (H10850). PLI.

Trial Advocate Quarterly: 1981-1986, 5 vols. Bound Set. 137.50x (ISBN 0-686-90058-8). Rothman.

Trial & Condemnation of Mervyn Lord Audley, Earl of Castlehaven. LC 83-48599. (Marriage, Sex & the Family in England Ser.). 154p. 1984. lib. bdg. 30.00. Garland Pub.

Trial & Death of Jesus. H. Cohn. 14.95x (ISBN 0-87068-432-9). Ktav.

Trial & Death of Jesus Christ. James A. Stalker. (Stalker Trilogy Ser.). 176p. 1984. pap. 7.95 (ISBN 0-310-44171-4, 12616P). Zondervan.

Trial & Death of Socrates. Plato. Tr. by John Warrington. 1969. Repr. of 1963 ed. 14.95x (ISBN 0-460-00457-3, Evman). Biblio Dist.

Trial & Death of Socrates. Plato. Tr. by G. M. Grube from Gr. LC 75-33058. (HPC Philosophical Classics Ser.). 64p. (Orig.). 1975. pap. 2.95 (ISBN 0-915144-15-8). Hackett Pub.

Trial & Error. Robert Kee. (Illus.). 224p. 1987. pap. 14.95 (ISBN 0-241-12324-0, Pub. by Hamish Hamilton). David & Charles.

Trial & Error. Jack Woodford. LC 80-54882. 1980. pap. 10.95 (ISBN 0-9601574-2-5). Woodford Mem.

Trial & Error: The American Controversy over Creation & Evolution. Edward J. Larson. LC 85-7144. 232p. 1985. 21.95 (ISBN 0-19-503666-2). Oxford U Pr.

Trial & Error: The Autobiography of Chaim Weizmann. Chaim Weizmann. LC 70-156215. 498p. 1972. Repr. of 1949 ed. lib. bdg. 38.50x (ISBN 0-8371-6166-5, WETE). Greenwood.

Trial & Error: The Detroit School Segregation Case. Eleanor P. Wolf. LC 80-25025. 372p. 1981. 27.00x (ISBN 0-8143-1673-5). Wayne St U Pr.

Trial & Flagellation & Other Studies in the Chester Cycle. LC 82-45684. (Malone Society Reprints Ser.: No. 81). Repr. of 1935 ed. 40.00 (ISBN 0-404-63081-2). AMS Pr.

Trial & Imprisonment of Jonathan Walker at Pensacola, Florida, for Aiding Slaves to Escape from Bondage, with an Appendix Containing a Sketch of His Life. Jonathan Walker. Intro. by Joe M. Richardson. LC 74-19173. (Floridiana Facsimile & Reprint Ser.). 1974. Repr. of 1845 ed. 11.00 (ISBN 0-8130-0371-7). U Presses Fla.

Trial & Practice Skills in a Nutshell. Kenney F. Hegland. LC 78-2731. (Nutshell Ser.). 346p. 1978. pap. text ed. 9.95 (ISBN 0-8299-2001-3). West Pub.

Trial & Triumph Genesis B: Leader's Guide. (New Horizons Bible Study Ser.). 1981. pap. 1.95 (ISBN 0-89367-054-5). Light & Life.

Trial & Triumph Genesis B: Study Guide. (New Horizons Bible Study Ser.). 68p. 1981. pap. 2.50 (ISBN 0-89367-055-3). Light & Life.

Trial Attorney's Evidence Code Notebook. California Continuing Education of the Bar Staff. LC 82-73213. 481p. 1982. looseleaf 55.00 (ISBN 0-88124-107-5). Cal Cont Ed Bar.

Trial Attorney's Evidence Code Notebook Annotated. 3rd. ed. 483p. 1987. 55.00 (CP-30290); May '86 supp. 40.00; May '87 supp. 42.00. Cal Cont Ed Bar.

Trial Balance: The Collected Short Stories of William March. William March. LC 87-5900. (Library of Alabama Classics). 528p. 1987. pap. 15.95t (ISBN 0-8173-0372-3). U of Ala Pr.

Trial Begins. Abram Tertz & Sinyavsky Andrei. Tr. by Max Hayward & George Denis. Bd. with On Socialist Realism. 220p. 1982. pap. 9.95x (ISBN 0-520-04677-3). U of Cal Pr.

Trial Bibliography of American Trade-Union Publications. Ed. by George E. Barnett. LC 78-63900. (Johns Hopkins Univesity. Studies in the Social Sciences. Twenty-Second Ser. 1904: 1-2). Repr. of 1904 ed. 16.00 (ISBN 0-404-61153-2). AMS Pr.

Trial by Death & Fire. D. Carl Anderson. LC 80-14446. (Orion Ser.). 160p. 1980. pap. 3.95 (ISBN 0-8127-0292-1). Review & Herald.

Trial by Fire. Richard Austin. (Guardians Ser.: No. 2). 240p. 1987. pap. 2.75 (ISBN 0-515-08681-9). Jove Pubns.

Trial by Fire. Carolyn Keene. (Nancy Drew Files Ser.: No. 15). 160p. (Orig.). (YA) (gr. 7 up). 1987. pap. 2.75 (ISBN 0-671-64138-7). Archway.

Trial by Fire. Anne S. White. 108p. (Orig.). 1975. pap. 3.50 (ISBN 0-89228-045-X). Impact Bks MO.

Trial by Fire: A People's History of the Civil War & Reconstruction. Page Smith. LC 81-18573. 1024p. 1982. text ed. 29.95 (ISBN 0-07-058571-7). McGraw.

Trial by Fire & Water: The Medieval Judicial Ordeal. Robert Bartlett. 1986. 39.95x (ISBN 0-19-821973-3). Oxford U Pr.

Trial by Fire & Water: The Medieval Judicial Ordeal. Robert Bartlett. (Illus.). 192p. 1988. pap. 17.95 (ISBN 0-19-822735-3). Oxford U Pr.

Trial by Fury. J. A. Jance. 224p. 1986. pap. 2.95 (ISBN 0-380-75138-0). Avon.

Trial by Fury. Craig Rice. 224p. 1988. pap. 3.50 (ISBN 0-553-26858-9). Bantam.

Trial by Jury. Patrick Devlin. (Legal Reprint Ser.). viii, 216p. 1988. Repr. of 1966 ed. lib. bdg. 24.00x (ISBN 0-8377-2035-4). Rothman.

Trial by Jury. Kevin King. 1984. pap. text ed. 8.95 (ISBN 0-88377-370-8). Newbury Hse.

Trial by Jury. Jo Kolanda & Patricia Curley. Ed. by Maury Solomon. (First Book Ser.). (Illus.). 96p. (gr. 5 up). 1988. 10.40 (ISBN 0-531-10610-1). Watts.

Trial by Medicine: The Insanity Defense in Victorian England. Roger Smith. 238p. 1981. 33.00x (ISBN 0-85224-407-X, Pub. by Edinburgh U Pr Scotland). Columbia U Pr.

Trial by Prejudice. Arthur G. Hays. LC 79-109550. (Civil Liberties in American History Ser). 1970. Repr. of 1933 ed. lib. bdg. 45.00 (ISBN 0-306-71904-5). Da Capo.

Trial by Television & Other Encounters. Michael Straight. LC 79-17889. (In Great Decades Ser.: Vol. III). (Illus.). 1979. pap. 6.95 (ISBN 0-934160-03-1); Boxed Set Of In Great Decades. 30.00. Devon Pr.

Trial by Terror--The Child-Hostage Crisis in Cokeville, Wyoming. Hartt Wixom & Judene Wixom. LC 87-80151. 256p. 1987. 17.95 (ISBN 0-88290-289-X). Horizon Utah.

Trial by Trial: Destiny of a Believer. Don Stephens. LC 85-80485. 176p. (Orig.). 1985. pap. 6.95 (ISBN 0-89081-498-8). Harvest Hse.

Trial by Virgins. David Larg. 1973. Repr. of 1933 ed. 30.00 (ISBN 0-8274-0316-X). R West.

Trial by Wilderness. David Mathieson. LC 84-27766. 176p. (gr. 7 up). 1985. 11.95 (ISBN 0-395-37697-1). HM.

Trial Court Review of Verdicts: A National Survey, Vol. 3. National Center for State Courts Staff. (Post-Adjudication Ser.). 165p. 1982. manuscript 9.90 (NERO-118). Natl Ctr St Courts.

Trial Ethics. Richard H. Underwood & William H. Fortune. 800p. 1988. 85.00 (ISBN 0-316-88810-9). Little.

Trial Evidence. 157p. 1984. 10.00 (ISBN 0-318-02448-9). ICLE Georgia.

Trial Evidence Foundations. John A. Tarantino & James R. Nanko. LC 86-216436. Date not set. price not set (ISBN 0-938065-15-7). James Pub Santa Ana.

Trial Handbook. Kent Sinclair. 337p. looseleaf 75.00 (ISBN 0-317-18594-2, H1-2972). PLI.

Trial Handbook for Arkansas Lawyers. John W. Hall, Jr. LC 85-82390. 1986. 79.50 (ISBN 0-318-19875-4); Suppl. 1988. 32.50. Lawyers Co-Op.

Trial Handbook for Connecticut Lawyers. John T. Asselin. LC 86-83060. 1987. 72.50; Suppl. 1988. 32.00. Lawyers Co-Op.

Trial Handbook for Florida Lawyers. 2nd ed. William M. Hicks. LC 74-121653. 479p. 69.50; Suppl. 1986. 25.00. Lawyers Co-Op.

Trial Handbook for Georgia Lawyers. Jack Kleiner. LC 73-92581. 433p.. 72.50; Suppl. 1987. 27.50. Lawyers Co-Op.

Trial Handbook for Illinois Lawyers. 5th ed. Robert S. Hunter. LC 83-80621. (Illinois Practice Library). xlix, 1374p. 1984. 79.50; Suppl. 1987. 25.00. Lawyers Co-Op.

Trial Handbook for Indiana Lawyers. 72.50 (ISBN 0-318-11933-1); Suppl. 1986. 28.50 (ISBN 0-318-11934-X); Suppl. 1987. 31.00 (ISBN 0-318-11935-8). Lawyers Co-Op.

Trial Handbook for Kentucky Lawyers. Thomas L. Osborne & Earl T. Osborne. LC 84-81064. 1984. 72.50 (ISBN 0-318-03857-9); Suppl. 1986. 27.00; Suppl. 1987. 28.50. Lawyers Co-Op.

Trial Handbook for Louisiana Lawyers. Eldon E. Fallon. LC 81-81708. 72.50; Suppl. 1987. 24.50; Suppl. 1986. 22.50; Suppl. 1988. 26.50. Lawyers Co-Op.

Trial Handbook for Maryland Lawyers. 2nd ed. Jacob A. Stein. LC 85-82441. (Maryland Practice Library). 1986. 72.50; Suppl. 1988. 30.00. Lawyers Co-Op.

Trial Handbook for Massachusetts Lawyers. Edward M. Swartz. LC 72-76293. 416p. 69.50; Suppl. 1987. 27.50; Suppl. 1986. 22.50. Lawyers Co-Op.

Trial Handbook for Michigan Lawyers. 2nd ed. Harry M. Philo. LC 72-97629. 369p. 69.50. Lawyers Co-Op.

Trial Handbook for Michigan Lawyers. 2nd ed. Harry M. Philo. LC 87-82165. 1987. 69.50. Lawyers Co-Op.

Trial Handbook for Mississippi Lawyers. Stanford Young. LC 86-80878. 1986. 79.50 (ISBN 0-318-21803-8). Lawyers Co-Op.

Trial Handbook for Missouri Lawyers. J. William Turley. LC 84-82477. 1985. 72.50 (ISBN 0-318-04387-4); Suppl. 1987. 25.00. Lawyers Co-Op.

Trial Handbook for New Jersey Lawyers. Janet W. Freeman & Fred Freeman. LC 72-76294. 520p. 1972. 69.50; Suppl. 1985. 23.00; Suppl. 1988. 28.00. Lawyers Co-Op.

Trial Handbook for New York Lawyers. 2nd ed. Aaron J. Broder. LC 85-82119. 1986. 69.50 (ISBN 0-318-19876-2); Suppl. 1987. 24.00; Suppl. 1988. 26.00. Lawyers Co-Op.

Trial Handbook for Ohio Lawyers. Richard M. Markus. LC 72-97628. 354p. 72.50; Suppl. 1987. 26.00; Suppl. 1986. 24.00; Suppl. 1988. 28.00. Lawyers Co-Op.

Trial Handbook for Pennsylvania Lawyers. Jack Kleiner & Edwin P. Rome. LC 80-82243. 72.50; Suppl. 1986. 28.00; Suppl. 1987. 30.00. Lawyers Co-Op.

Trial Handbook for Tennessee Lawyers. Robert E. Burch. LC 79-83775. 450p. 72.50; Suppl. 1987. 31.50. Lawyers Co-Op.

Trial Handbook for Virginia Lawyers. Craig D. Johnston. LC 85-82118. 1986. 72.50 (ISBN 0-318-19877-0); Suppl. 1987. 24.00; Suppl. 1988. 27.50. Lawyers Co-Op.

Trial Handbook for Wisconsin Lawyers. Ted M. Warshafsky. LC 81-82645. 72.50; Suppl. 1986. 26.50; Suppl. 1987. 57.00. Lawyers Co-Op.

Trial Judge: The Candid, Behind the Bench Story of Justice Bernard Botein. Bernard Botein. (American Constitutional & Legal History Ser.). 337p. 1974. Repr. of 1952 ed. lib. bdg. 39.50 (ISBN 0-306-70630-X). Da Capo.

Trial Lawyer. Stanley M. Rosenblatt. LC 84-73. 416p. 1984. 19.95 (ISBN 0-8184-0360-8); pap. 9.95 (ISBN 0-8184-0361-6). Lyle Stuart.

Trial Lawyer & the Federal Rules of Evidence. Ed. by Jeffrey R. White. 630p. 1980. 25.00 (ISBN 0-941916-03-0). Assn Trial Ed.

Trial Lawyer's Guide, 27 vols. Ed. by John J. Kennelly. 750.00. Callaghan.

Trial Lawyers: The Nation's Top Litigators Tell How They Win. Emily Couric. 384p. 1988. 19.95 (ISBN 0-312-02305-7). St Martin.

Trial Manual Four for the Defense of Criminal Cases, 2 vols. 4th ed. Anthony G. Amsterdam. 950p. 1984. looseleaf 175.00 (ISBN 0-8318-0440-8, B440). Am Law Inst.

Trial Masters: A Handbook of Strategies & Techniques That Win Cases. Bertram G. Warshaw. LC 84-11575. 1984. 49.95 (ISBN 0-13-930892-X). P-H.

Trial Mechanics & Discovery in Medical Malpractice, Products Liability & Personal Injury Cases. Practising Law Institute Staff et al. LC 86-60312. (Litigation & Administrative Practice Ser.). 272p. 1986. 15.00 (ISBN 0-317-52274-4, H44990). PLI.

Trial Notebook. LC 81-68305. 215p. 1981. pap. 19.50 (ISBN 0-317-63786-X, 531-0034-01). Amer Bar Assn.

Trial Notebook. Thomas Vesper. 1985. lectern-binder 60.00. NJ Inst CLE.

Trial Notes. Herberth Czermak. (Orig.). 1976. pap. text ed. 3.50 (ISBN 0-8220-1304-5). Cliffs.

Trial Objections. 127p. 1984. 20.00 (ISBN 0-318-03912-5, 257). PA Bar Inst.

Trial of a Toxic Tort Case. Massachusetts Continuing Legal Education Staff. LC 84-61754. 486p. write for info. Mass CLE.

Trial of Accident Cases, 8 vols. 3rd ed. Louis E. Schwartz. 1958. looseleaf set 585.00 (610); Updates avail. 1985 412.50; 1984 395.00. Bender.

Trial of an Administration Case. William J. Kolasky. LC 86-102592. 112p. Date not set. price not set. HarBraceJ.

Trial of an Antitrust Price-Fixing Case. American Bar Association National Institutes Staff. 271p. 1981. looseleaf 75.00 (ISBN 0-317-30576-X). Amer Bar Assn.

Trial of Andrew Johnson--Impeachment, 3 vols. 1970. Repr. of 1868 ed. lib. bdg. 95.00 (ISBN 0-89941-606-3). W S Hein.

Trial of Andrew Johnson, President of the U. S, 3 vols. in 2. Andrew Johnson. LC 69-11326. (Law, Politics, & History Ser). 1970. Repr. of 1868 ed. Set. lib. bdg. 145.00 (ISBN 0-306-71184-2). Da Capo.

Trial of Annie Besant & Charles Bradlough. Roger Manvell. LC 75-37491. 192p. 1976. 8.95 (ISBN 0-8180-0819-9). Horizon.

Trial of Beyers Naude: Christian Witness & the Rule of Law. International Commission of Jurists, Geneva. 1975. pap. 5.95 (ISBN 0-377-00057-4, Pub. by Search Pr England). Friendship Pr.

Trial of C. B. Reynolds. Robert G. Ingersoll. 44p. (Orig.). 1986. pap. 3.00 (ISBN 0-910309-25-6, 5532). Am Atheist.

Trial of Champions. Ian Livingstone & Steve Jackson. (Fighting Fantasy Gamebooks: No. 21). (Orig.). (gr. k-12). 1987. pap. 2.50 (ISBN 0-440-98689-3, LFL). Dell.

Trial of Chivalry. LC 77-133748. (Tudor Facsimile Texts. Old English Plays Ser.: No. 104). Repr. of 1912 ed. 49.50 (ISBN 0-404-53404-X). AMS Pr.

Trial of Christopher Okigbo. Ali Mazrui. (African Writers Ser.). 1971. pap. text ed. 7.00 (ISBN 0-435-90097-8). Heinemann Ed.

Trial of D. M. Bennett: Upon the Charge of Depositing Prohibited Matter in the Mail. Bennett M. De Robigne. LC 72-8110. (Civil Liberties in American History Ser.). 202p. 1973. Repr. of 1879 ed. lib. bdg. 27.50 (ISBN 0-306-70525-7). Da Capo.

Trial of Dedan Kimathi. Ngugi. (African Writers Ser.). 1977. pap. text ed. 6.50 (ISBN 0-435-90191-5). Heinemann Ed.

Trial of Dr. Mesmer: A Play. Norman Cousins. Date not set. 15.00 (ISBN 0-393-01845-8). Norton.

Trial of Duncan Terig. Duncan Terig. LC 79-176140. (Bannatyne Club, Edinburgh. Publications: No. 40). Repr. of 1831 ed. 17.50 (ISBN 0-404-52746-9). AMS Pr.

Trial of Education in Two Cities Omaha & Manila. Natividad T. Nacianceno & Floyd T. Waterman. 100p. (Orig.). 1985. pap. 6.00 (ISBN 1-55719-057-7). U Ne Ctr Applied Urban Rsch.

Trial of Elizabeth Gurley Flynn by the American Civil Liberties Union. Ed. by Corliss Lamont. (Documents of Civil Liberties Ser.: Vol. 1). 1969. 5.95 (ISBN 0-8180-0804-0). Horizon.

Trial of Faith: Discussions Concerning Mormonism & Neo-Mormonism. William Call. 215p. (Orig.). Date not set. pap. write for info. (ISBN 0-916095-11-8). Pubs Pr UT.

Trial of Faith: Religion & Politics in Tocqueville's. Doris S. Goldstein. LC 75-4753. pap. 39.00 (2026263). Bks Demand UMI.

Trial of Faith: Religion & Politics in Tocqueville's Thought. Doris Goldstein. 144p. 1975. 21.00 (ISBN 0-444-99001-1). Elsevier.

Trial of Father Dillingham. John Broderick. 224p. 1981. 14.95 (ISBN 0-7145-2747-5, Dist by Scribner). M Boyars Pubs.

Trial of Feargus O'Connor & Fifty-Eight Other Chartists. Feargus O'Connor. LC 71-109591. 1970. Repr. of 1843 ed. 45.00x (ISBN 0-678-00608-3). Kelley.

Trial of Generals: Homma, Yamashita, MacArthur. Lawrence Taylor. (Illus.). 256p. 1981. 13.95 (ISBN 0-89651-775-6). B L Pub.

Trial of God. Elie Wiesel. (Elie Wiesel Collection Ser.: Vol. 16). (Illus.). Repr. deluxe ed. 39.95 (ISBN 0-935613-16-1). Gerecor.

Trial of God: A Play in Three Acts. Elie Wiesel. Tr. by Marion Wiesel. LC 85-27625. 176p. 1986. pap. 7.95 (ISBN 0-8052-0809-7). Schocken.

Trial of Inez Garcia. Kenneth Salter. LC 75-42992. 368p. 1976. pap. 10.00 (ISBN 0-685-65556-3). Editorial Justa.

Trial of Jesus. Giovanni Rosadi. 1977. lib. bdg. 59.95 (ISBN 0-8490-2767-5). Gordon Pr.

Trial of Jesus Christ. Aristarchus Vassilakos. Ed. by Orthodox Christian Educational Society. 64p. (Orig.). 1950. pap. 2.75x (ISBN 0-938366-47-5). Orthodox Chr.

Trial of Jesus from a Lawyer's Standpoint, 2 vols. Walter M. Chandler. LC 83-82312. 1983. Repr. of 1925 ed. 115.00 set (ISBN 0-89941-294-7). W S Hein.

Trial of John Frost for High Treason under a Special Commission Held at Monmouth in December 1839 & January 1840. John Frost. Ed. by Dorothy Thompson. (Chartism, Working-Class Politics in the Industrial Revolution Ser.). 778p. 1987. lib. bdg. 100.00 (ISBN 0-8240-5587-X). Garland Pub.

Trial of John W. Hinckley, Jr. A Case Study in the Insanity Defense. Peter Low et al. (University Casebook Ser.). 137p. 1986. pap. text ed. 6.95 (ISBN 0-88277-333-X). Foundation Pr.

Trial of Judaism in Contemporary Jewish Writing. Josephine Z. Knopp. LC 74-18319. 180p. 1975. 15.95 (ISBN 0-252-00386-1). U of Ill Pr.

Trial of Klaus Barbie. Le Monde. Tr. by Ann Krooth. (Illus.). 1988. pap. price not set. Harvest Pubns.

Trial of Leonard Peltier. Jim Messerschmidt. LC 82-61152. 250p. 1983. 20.00 (ISBN 0-89608-164-8); pap. 9.00 (ISBN 0-89608-163-X). South End Pr.

Trial of Levi Weeks. Estelle Kleiger. (Illus.). 176p. 1988. 14.95 (ISBN 0-89733-297-0). Academy Chi Pubs.

Trial of Louis Riel. Frederick G. Walsh. LC 65-63477. 142p. 1965. pap. 3.00 (ISBN 0-911042-11-3). N Dak Inst.

Trial of Luther. Daniel Olivier. 1979. pap. 9.50 (ISBN 0-570-03785-9, 12-2743). Concordia.

Trial of Pakistani Prisoners of War: Pleadings. pap. 10.00 (ICJ426). UN.

Trial of Patrolman Thomas Shea. Thomas Hauser. 288p. 1983. pap. 3.50 (ISBN 0-380-62778-7, 62778-7, Discus). Avon.

Trial of Samuel Chase, an Associate Justice of the Supreme Court Impeached by the House of Representatives, 2 vols. Samuel Chase. LC 69-11324. (Law, Politics, & History Ser). 1970. Repr. of 1805 ed. Set. lib. bdg. 79.50 (ISBN 0-306-71181-8). Da Capo.

Trial of Scott Nearing & the American Socialist Party. Rand School of Social Science. LC 73-147523. (Library of War & Peace; Labor, Socialism & War). 1973. lib. bdg. 46.00 (ISBN 0-8240-0311-X). Garland Pub.

Trial of Scott Nearing & the American Socialist Society. LC 76-122159. (Civil Liberties in American History Ser). 1970. Repr. of 1919 ed. lib. bdg. 29.50 (ISBN 0-306-71966-5). Da Capo.

Trial of Socrates. I. F. Stone. 320p. 1988. 18.95 (ISBN 0-316-81758-9). Little.

Trial of Socrates. I. F. Stone. 1989. pap. 9.95 (ISBN 0-385-26032-6, Anchor Pr). Doubleday.

Trial of Soren Qvist. Janet Lewis. LC 72-94405. 256p. 1959. pap. 9.95 (ISBN 0-8040-0297-5, Pub by Swallow). Ohio U Pr.

Trial of Stephen Ward. Ludovic Kennedy. 256p. 1988. pap. 9.95 (ISBN 0-575-04194-3, Pub. by Gollancz England). David & Charles.

Trial of Strength. Jean Earle. 64p. (Orig.). 1980. pap. 7.50 (ISBN 0-85635-298-5). Carcanet.

Trial of the Assassin Guiteau: Psychiatry & the Law in the Gilded Age. Charles E. Rosenberg. LC 68-16713. 1976. pap. 10.00x (ISBN 0-226-72717-3, P682, Phoen). U of Chicago Pr.

Trial of the Assassin Guiteau: Psychiatry & the Law in the Gilded Age. Charles E. Rosenberg. LC 68-16712. (Illus.). 1968. 15.00x (ISBN 0-226-72716-5). U of Chicago Pr.

Trial of the Assassins & Conspirators for the Murder of Abraham Lincoln, & the Attempted Assassination of Vice-President Johnson & the Whole Cabinet. LC 81-90340. (Illus.). 1981. pap. 15.00 (ISBN 0-939128-04-7). J L Barbour.

Trial of the British Soldiers. facs. ed. LC 75-79023. (Black Heritage Library Collection Ser). 1807. 12.25 (ISBN 0-8369-8670-9). Ayer Co Pubs.

Trial of the Christmas Bells. Nancy Forquer. 1984. pap. 4.95 (ISBN 0-912963-05-0). Eldridge Pub.

Trial of the Constitution. Sidney G. Fisher. LC 70-164511. (American Constitutional & Legal History Ser.). 1972. Repr. of 1864 ed. lib. bdg. 45.00 (ISBN 0-306-70281-9). Da Capo.

Trial of the Constitution. Sidney G. Fisher. LC 69-18977. 1969. Repr. of 1862 ed. 35.00 (ISBN 0-8371-0896-9, FIC&). Greenwood.

Trial of the Expert: A Study of Expert Evidence & Forensic Experts. Ian Freckelton. 324p. 1987. 72.00 (ISBN 0-19-554566-4). Oxford U Pr.

Trial of the Major War Criminals Before the International Military Tribunal, 44 vols. Nuremberg War Trials. LC 70-145536. Repr. of 1949 ed. Set. write for info. (ISBN 0-404-53650-6). AMS Pr.

Trial of the Poet: An Interpretation of the First Edition of "Leaves of Grass". Ivan Marki. LC 76-18792. 1976. 32.50x (ISBN 0-231-03984-0). Columbia U Pr.

Trial of the Templars. M. C. Barber. LC 77-85716. 320p. 1978. 54.50 (ISBN 0-521-21896-9); pap. 16.95 (ISBN 0-521-28018-4). Cambridge U Pr.

Trial of the Templars. Edward J. Martin. LC 76-29845. Repr. of 1928 ed. 24.50 (ISBN 0-404-15424-7). AMS Pr.

Trial of Theodore Parker: For the Misdemeanor of a Speech in Fanenil Hall Against Kidnapping. facs. ed. Theodore Parker. LC 70-154087. (Black Heritage Library Collection Ser). 1855. 15.75 (ISBN 0-8369-8798-5). Ayer Co Pubs.

Trial of Tom Sawyer. Virginia G. Koste. (gr. 4 up). 1978. 3.00 (ISBN 0-87602-213-1). Anchorage.

Trial of Treasure. LC 70-133749. (Tudor Facsimile Texts. Old English Plays Ser.: No. 38). Repr. of 1908 ed. 49.50 (ISBN 0-404-53338-8). AMS Pr.

Trial of Warren Hastings in House of Lords Sessional Papers: 1794-95, 9 vols, Vols. 1-9. LC 70-141328. 1974. 750.00 set (ISBN 0-379-20014-7). Oceana.

Trial on Trial. Lawrence Dennis. 1978. lib. bdg. 75.00 (ISBN 0-87700-292-4). Revisionist Pr.

Trial on Trial. Lawrence Dennis & Maximillian St. George. 502p. 1984. pap. 11.00 (ISBN 0-939484-20-X). Inst Hist Rev.

Trial Practice Cases & Materials. Joseph R. Nolan. LC 80-29182. (American Casebook Ser.). 518p. 1981. text ed. 27.95 (ISBN 0-8299-2129-X). West Pub.

Trial Practice for the General Practitioner. Ed. by Leonard Packel et al. 114p. 1980. pap. 5.00 (ISBN 0-686-32427-7, B190). Am Law Inst.

Trial Practice-Negligence. 78p. 1975. pap. 3.00 (ISBN 0-686-48306-5). Amer Bar Assn.

Trial Preparation for Prosecutors. Marcus. (Trial Practice Library). 1988. write for info. (ISBN 0-471-84895-6). Wiley.

Trial Process. Ed. by Bruce D. Sales. LC 80-20487. (Perspectives In Law & Psychology Ser.: Vol. 2). 522p. 1981. 52.50x (ISBN 0-306-40491-5, Plenum Pr). Plenum Pub.

Trial Process: Law, Tactics, & Ethics. J. Alexander Tanford. (Contemporary Legal Education Ser.). (Illus.). 1983. 25.00x (ISBN 0-87215-668-0). Michie Co.

Trial Psychology: Communication & Persuasion in the Courtroom. Margaret Covington. 508p. 1988. 95.00 (ISBN 0-409-25105-4). Butterworth TX.

Trial Run. Dick Francis. 1985. pap. 3.50 (ISBN 0-671-50732-X). PB.

Trial Tactics. Mark A. Dombroff. Date not set. reference manual 25.00 (ISBN 0-318-23985-X, 999); audiotapes 50.00 (ISBN 0-318-23986-8); videotape 325.00 (ISBN 0-318-23987-6). Natl Prac Inst.

Trial Tactics. West Virginia Trial Lawyers Association Staff. 466p. 1966. 25.00 (ISBN 0-913338-21-4). Condyne-Oceana.

Trial Tactics. Irving Younger. write for info. (ISBN 0-316-97720-9). Little.

Trial Tactics & Methods. 2nd ed. Robert E. Keeton. 480p. 1973. 31.00 (ISBN 0-316-48572-1). Little.

Trial Techniques. Irving Younger. Ed. by Robert Oliphant. LC 78-71017. 98p. 1978. 15.00 (ISBN 0-686-31598-7, 670); audiotapes 115.00; videotape 750.00. Natl Prac Inst.

Trial Techniques: A Compendium of Course Materials. 6th ed. 1987. 12.50 (ISBN 0-318-18679-9). Natl Coll DA.

Trial Techniques: A Young Lawyer's Guide to Civil Trial Advocacy. Pennsylvania Bar Institute staff. 212p. 1985. 50.00 (ISBN 0-318-19077-X, 321). PA Bar Inst.

Trial Techniques, 1984. Ed. by Anne R. Grant. (Trial Annuals Ser.). (Illus.). 144p. (Orig.). 1985. pap. 22.00 (ISBN 0-941916-21-9). Assn Trial Ed.

Trial Valley. Reissue. ed. Vera Cleaver & Bill Cleaver. LC 76-54303. 160p. (YA) (gr. 7 up). 1987. 12.25i (ISBN 0-397-31722-0, Lipp Jr Bks); PLB 12.89 (ISBN 0-397-32246-1). HarpJ.

Trialbook. John Sonsteng et al. LC 85-3273. 300p. 1985. 40.00 (ISBN 0-314-85989-6). West Pub.

Trialbook: A Total System for Preparation & Presentation of a Case. John O. Sonsteng et al. LC 84-15292. (Hornbook Series Student Edition). 404p. 1984. pap. text ed. 18.95 (ISBN 0-314-85865-2). West Pub.

Trialbook: Forms. West's Editorial Department Staff. 99p. 1985. pap. text ed. write for info. (ISBN 0-314-95553-4). West Pub.

Trialogue Between Jew, Christian & Muslim. Ignay Maybaum. (Littman Library of Jewish Civilization). 192p. 1973. 18.50x (ISBN 0-19-710032-5). Oxford U Pr.

Trialogue of Abrahamic Faiths. I. R. Al Farugi. 88p. (Orig.). 1986. pap. 7.50 (ISBN 0-317-52454-2). New Era Pubns MI.

Trials. Vicente Segrelles. Tr. by T. Nantier from Span. (Mercenary Ser.). 48p. 1986. 7.95x (ISBN 0-918348-16-1). NBM.

Trials & Punishments. R. A. Duff. LC 85-15128. (Cambridge Studies in Philosophy). 220p. 1986. 34.50 (ISBN 0-521-30818-6). Cambridge U Pr.

Trials & the Sacrifice. Vicente Segrelles. (Mercenary Ser.). 96p. 1988. pap. 12.95x (ISBN 0-918348-49-8). NBM.

Trials & Tribulations. William Kunstler. LC 84-73209. 201p. 1985. 22.50 (ISBN 0-394-54611-3, E-991, Ever); pap. 7.95 (ISBN 0-394-62060-7). Grove.

Trials & Tribulations of Little Red Riding Hood: Versions of the Tale in Sociopolitical Context. Jack Zipes. (Illus.). 320p. 1983. 34.95 (ISBN 0-89789-023-X); pap. 16.95 (ISBN 0-89789-057-4). Bergin & Garvey.

Trials & Tribulations of Staggerlee Booker T. Brown: A Play in Two Acts. Don Evans. 1985. pap. 3.50x (ISBN 0-317-18648-5). Dramatists Play.

Trials & Triumphs: George Washington's Foreign Policy. Frank T. Reuter. LC 83-675. (A.M. Pate, Jr., Series on the American Presidency: No. 2). 249p. 1983. 19.50x (ISBN 0-912646-70-5). Tex Christian.

Trials & Triumphs of Eva Grant. Effie M. Williams. 94p. pap. 1.00 (ISBN 0-686-29173-5). Faith Pub Hse.

Trials & Triumphs of Marcus Garvey. Len S. Nembhard. LC 76-51869. 1978. lib. bdg. 45.00 (ISBN 0-527-66570-3). Kraus Repr.

Trials for Adultery or the History of Divorces, Being Select Trials...from the Year 1760 to the Present Time.., 7 vols. Ed. by Randolph Trumbach. LC 83-48611. (Marriage, Sex & the Family in England 1660-1800 Ser.). 2797p. 1985. lib. bdg. 385.00 (ISBN 0-8240-5908-5). Garland Pub.

Trials in Burma. Maurice Collis. LC 74-179181. Repr. of 1945 ed. 22.50 (ISBN 0-404-54812-1). AMS Pr.

Trials in Collections: An Index to Famous Trials Throughout the World. John M. Ross. LC 82-21635. 218p. 1983. 17.50 (ISBN 0-8108-1603-2). Scarecrow.

Trials of Ada Adams. Philippa Ruth. write for info. World Pr Ltd.

Trials of British Freedom: Being Some Studies in the History of the Fight for Democratic Freedom in Britain. Thomas A. Jackson. LC 68-56759. (Research & Source Works Ser.: No. 244). 1968. Repr. of 1940 ed. 17.00 (ISBN 0-8337-1816-9). B Franklin.

Trials of Character: The Eloquence of Ciceronian Ethos. James M. May. LC 87-13884. viii, 216p. 1988. 27.50x (ISBN 0-8078-1759-7). U of NC Pr.

Trials of Counsel: Francis Bacon in 1621. Jonathan Marwil. LC 75-33650. 254p. 1976. text ed. 24.50x (ISBN 0-8143-1549-6). Wayne St U Pr.

Trials of Daniel. As told by Catherine Storr. (People of the Bible Ser.). (Illus.). 32p. (gr. k-4). 1985. PLB 11.33 (ISBN 0-8172-2040-2). Raintree Pubs.

Trials of Desire: Renaissance Defenses of Poetry. Margaret W. Ferguson. LC 82-8525. (Illus.). 280p. 1983. pap. text ed. 29.00x (ISBN 0-300-02787-7). Yale U Pr.

Trials of Discipleship: The Story of William Clayton, a Mormon. James B. Allen. LC 86-11328. 402p. 1987. 22.95 (ISBN 0-252-01369-7). U of Ill Pr.

Trials of Israel Lipski: A True Story of a Victorian Murder in the East End of London. Martin L. Friedland. (Illus.). 224p. 1985. 14.95 (ISBN 0-8253-0278-1). Beaufort Bks NY.

Trials of Jawaharlal Nehru. Ram Gopal. 133p. 1964. 24.00x (ISBN 0-7146-1557-9, F Cass Co). Biblio Dist.

Trials of Mrs. Lincoln. Samuel A. Schreiner, Jr. LC 86-82181. (Illus.). 336p. 1987. 18.95 (ISBN 1-55611-009-X). D I Fine.

Trials of Oscar Wilde. H. Montgomery Hyde. (Illus.). 327p. 1973. pap. 6.50 (ISBN 0-486-20216-X). Dover.

Trials of Prophylactic Agents for the Control of Communicable Diseases: A Guide to Their Organization & Evaluation. T. M. Pollock. (Monograph Ser: No. 52). 92p. (Eng., Fr., Rus. & Span.). 1966. 4.80 (ISBN 0-686-09188-4, 92-4-140052). World Health.

Trial(s) of Psychoanalysis. Francoise Meltzer. 296p. 1988. 28.00x (ISBN 0-226-51969-4); pap. 13.95 (ISBN 0-226-51970-8). U of Chicago Pr.

Trials of Rumpole. John Mortimer. 206p. 1981. pap. 3.95 (ISBN 0-14-005162-7). Penguin.

Trials of Rumpole. John Mortimer. 15.95 (ISBN 0-89190-276-7, Pub. by Am Repr). Amereon Ltd.

Trials of the Human Heart, 4 vols. in 2. Susanna Rowson. LC 78-64091. Repr. of 1795 ed. 75.00 set (ISBN 0-404-17360-8). AMS Pr.

Trials of the Self: Heroic Ordeals in the Epic Tradition. George D. Lord. LC 83-11727. x, 249p. 1983. 27.50 (ISBN 0-208-02013-6, Archon Bks). Shoe String.

Trials of Thinking, Feeling & Willing. Carl Unger. 1980. pap. 3.00 (ISBN 0-916786-47-1). St George Bk Serv.

Trials on Trial: The Pure Theory of Legal Procedure. Gordon Tullock. LC 80-13113. 264p. 1980. 30.00x (ISBN 0-231-04952-8). Columbia U Pr.

Triangle. Fantasimulations Associates Staff. (Star Trek Ser.). 92p. (Orig.). 1985. pap. 12.00 (ISBN 0-931787-25-4). FASA Corp.

Triangle. Sondra Marshak & Myrna Culbreath. (Gregg Press Science Fiction - Star Trek Ser.). 192p. 1986. lib. bdg. 11.95x (ISBN 0-8398-2934-5, Gregg). G K Hall.

Triangle, No. 9. Sondra Marshak & Myrna Culbreath. pap. 3.50 (ISBN 0-671-60548-8). PB.

Triangle Broadcasting Company: A Word Information Processing Simulation. Betty S. Johnson & Gayle A. Nagai. 192p. (Orig.). 1985. pap. text ed. 16.00 scp (ISBN 0-672-98562-4); scp instr's. guide 7.33 (ISBN 0-672-98565-9); scp wkbk. 4.00 (ISBN 0-672-98563-2); scp 3 tapes 66.00 (ISBN 0-672-98564-0). Bobbs.

Triangle Fire. Mary Fell. (Shadow Press U. S. A. Poetry Chapbook Ser.: No. 2). 12p. (Orig.). 1983. pap. 2.50 numbered copies (ISBN 0-937724-02-5); pap. 5.00 lettered & signed copies. Shadow Pr.

Triangle Fire. Leon Stein. 224p. 1985. pap. 7.95 (ISBN 0-88184-126-9). Carroll & Graf.

Triangle Has Four Sides: True-to-Life Stories Show How Teens Deal with Feelings & Problems. Phyllis R. Naylor. LC 83-72123. 128p. (Orig.). (YA) (gr. 7-10). 1984. pap. 4.50 (ISBN 0-8066-2067-6, 10-6700). Augsburg.

Triangle Noir: Laclos, Goysa, Saint-Just. Andre Malraux. 13.15 (ISBN 0-685-34272-7). French & Eur.

Triangle of Love. Colman. 1985. pap. 2.25 (ISBN 0-671-49631-X). Archway.

Triangle of Love: Intimacy, Passion, & Commitment. Robert J. Sternberg. LC 88-47692. 288p. 1988. 18.95 (ISBN 0-465-08746-9). Basic.

Triangle of the Lost. Warren Smith. 222p. 1975. pap. 1.75 (ISBN 0-89083-125-4). Zebra.

Triangle Shirtwaist Fire: Mini-Play. (Women's Studies). (gr. 5 up). 1975. 6.50 (ISBN 0-89550-369-7). Stevens & Shea.

Triangle: The Betrayed Wife. Evelyn M. Berger. LC 70-170883. 224p. 1971. 18.95 (ISBN 0-911012-13-3). Nelson-Hall.

Triangles. Graham Percy. (Shape Ser.). 16p. (ps). 1986. bds. 3.95 (ISBN 0-915391-17-1, Pub by Mad Hatter Bks). Slawson Comm.

Triangles. Paul Vigyikan. 186p. 1978. 8.95 (ISBN 0-8059-2502-3). Dorrance.

Triangles: A Novel. Ruth Geller. LC 84-15632. (Feminist Ser.). 192p. (Orig.). 1984. 20.95 (ISBN 0-89594-152-X); pap. 7.95 (ISBN 0-89594-151-1). Crossing Pr.

Triangles & Quadrangles: Level Four Texts. rev. ed. (Math Components Ser.). 56p. 1983. 3.25 (ISBN 0-88336-841-2). New Readers.

Triangles in the Afternoon. Ron Padgett. LC 70-25069. 46p. (Orig.). pap. 5.00 (ISBN 0-915342-31-6). SUN.

Triangles of Fire. Torkom Saraydarian. LC 77-82155. 1977. pap. 3.00 (ISBN 0-911794-35-2). Aqua Educ.

Triangles, Parallel Lines, Similar Polygons see Key to Geometry Series.

Triangular & Jordan Representations of Linear Operators. M. S. Brodskii. LC 74-162998. (Translations of Mathematical Monographs: Vol. 32). 1972. 38.00 (ISBN 0-8218-1582-2, MMONO-32). Am Math.
Triangular Clause Relationship in Aelfric's Lives of Saints & in Other Works. Ed. by Ruth Waterhouse. LC 83-5399. (American Universtiy Studies IV: English Language & Literature: Vol. 1). 119p. (Orig.). 1983. pap. text ed. 12.10 (ISBN 0-8204-0007-6). P Lang Pubs.
Triangular Connection: America, Israel & American Jews. Edward B. Glick. 160p. 1982. text ed. 14.95x (ISBN 0-04-353008-7). Unwin Hyman.
Triangular Pattern of Life. Donna Hitz. LC 79-84851. 94p. 1980. 7.95 (ISBN 0-8022-2249-8). Philos Lib.
Triangular Plates & Slabs. K. Breitschuh. (Illus.). 199p. (Eng. & Ger.). 1974. cancelled (ISBN 3-4330-0647-4). Adlers Foreign Bks.
Triangular Products of Group Representations & Their Applications. S. M. Vovsi. (Progress in Mathematics Ser.: No. 17). 150p. 1982. text ed. 19.95x (ISBN 0-8176-3062-7). Birkhauser.
Triangulated Categories in the Representation Theory of Finite-Dimensional Algebras. D. Happel. (London Mathematical Society Lecture Note: Series 119). 200p. 1988. pap. 24.95 (ISBN 0-521-33922-7). Cambridge U Pr.
Triangulation Short-Cut Layouts. 4th ed. Joseph J. Kaberlein. (gr. 9 up). 1985. 21.00 (ISBN 0-02-819410-1). Glencoe.
Triarchic Mind: A New Theory of Human Intelligence. Robert J. Sternberg. LC 87-40431. 461p. 1988. 19.95 (ISBN 0-670-80364-2). Viking.
Triassic-Jurassic Rift Basin Sedimentology. John C. Lorenz. 272p. 1987. 42.95 (ISBN 0-442-26041-5). Van Nos Reinhold.
Triathalon Training Book. Mark Sisson. 1984. pap. 6.95 (ISBN 0-02-029610-X, Collier). Macmillan.
Triathlon: A Triple Fitness Sport. Sally Edwards. 10.95 (ISBN 0-8092-5555-3). Contemp Bks.
Triathlon: Going the Distance. Mike Plant. (Sportsperformance Ser.: The Cutting Edge in Today's Sports). (Illus.). 128p. (Orig.). 1987. pap. 6.95 (ISBN 0-8092-4774-7). Contemp Bks.
Triathlon: Lifestyle of Fitness. Dave Horning & Gerald Couzens. Date not set. pap. 9.95 (ISBN 0-671-54081-5). PB.
Triathlon Training. Date not set. 6.95. Anderson World.
Triathlon Training & Racing Book. Sally Edwards. (Illus.). 128p. (Orig.). 1985. pap. 8.95 (ISBN 0-8092-5430-1). Contemp Bks.
Triathloning for Ordinary Mortals. Steven Jonas. (Illus.). 1986. 19.95 (ISBN 0-393-02251-X); pap. 12.95 (ISBN 0-393-30279-2). Norton.
Triazoles. K. T. Finley. LC 80-13323. (Chemistry of Heterocyclic Compounds, Series of Monographs: Vol. 39). 349p. 1980. 188.50x (ISBN 0-471-07827-1). Wiley.
Triazoles One, Two, Four, Vol. 37. Caroll Temple & John A. Montgomery. LC 80-15637. (Chemistry of Heterocyclic Compounds, a Series of Monographs). 791p. 1981. 333.50 (ISBN 0-471-04656-6, Pub. by Wiley-Interscience). Wiley.
Tribal Administration in India. Amir Hasan. 242p. 1988. text ed. 37.50x (ISBN 81-7018-475-4, Pub. by B R Corp Delhi). Apt Bks.
Tribal & Peasant Life in Nineteenth Century India. V. Ball. 1986. Repr. of 1880 ed. 60.00x (ISBN 0-8364-1583-3, Pub. by Usha). South Asia Bks.
Tribal Crafts of Uganda, by M. T. & K. P. Wachsmann. Margaret Trowell. LC 74-15098. (Illus.). Repr. of 1953 ed. 57.50 (ISBN 0-404-12147-0). AMS Pr.
Tribal Culture & Economy: The Mal Paharias of Santal Parganas. Alok Kumar. xviii, 328p. 1986. text ed. 45.00x (ISBN 81-210-0044-0, Pub. by Inter India Pubns N Delhi). Apt Bks.
Tribal Custom in Anglo-Saxon Law Being an Essay Supplemental to 'The English Village Community' & 'The Tribal System in Wales' Frederic Seebohm. xvi, 538p. 1972. Repr. of 1911 ed. lib. bdg. 25.00x (ISBN 0-8377-2605-0). Rothman.
Tribal Design. Deborah Christine & Stevie Mack. (Programs Ser.). 50p. (gr. 4-12). 1988. pap. 235.00 (ISBN 0-318-23702-4); audio visual incl. Crizmac.
Tribal Development in Madhya Pradesh: A Planning Perspective. Ajit Raizada. (Tribal Studies of India: T112). (Illus.). xvi, 214p. 1984. text ed. 50.00x (ISBN 0-86590-361-1, Pub. by Inter Pubns N Delhi). Apt Bks.
Tribal Development Programmes & Administration in India. Ashok R. Basu. 1985. 34.00x (ISBN 0-8364-1506-X, Pub. by Natl Bk Organ). South Asia Bks.
Tribal Dispossession & the Ottawa Indian University Fraud. William E. Unrau & H. Craig Miner. LC 84-19534. (Illus.). 224p. 1985. 17.95 (ISBN 0-8061-1896-2). U of Okla Pr.
Tribal Distribution in Oregon. J. V. Berreman. LC 37-20181. (American Anthropological Association Memoirs). pap. 15.00 (ISBN 0-527-00546-0). Kraus Repr.
Tribal Economy in Transition: A Study of Meghalaya. M. K. Nair. (Illus.). 159p. Date not set. price not set (ISBN 81-210-0180-3, Pub. by Inter India Pubns N-Delhi). Apt Bks.
Tribal Economy: Problems & Prospects. V. S. Ramamani. 1988. 34.00x (Pub. by Chugh Pubns India). South Asia Bks.
Tribal Government of the Oglala Sioux of Pine Ridge, South Dakota. Ira H. Grinnell. 1967. 5.00 (ISBN 1-55614-012-6). U of SD Gov Res Bur.
Tribal Guerillas: The Santals of West Bengal & the Naxalite Movement. Edward Duyker. (Illus.). 228p. 1987. 19.95 (ISBN 0-19-561938-2). Oxford U Pr.
Tribal Health: Socio-Cultural Dimensions. Ed. by Buddhadeb Chaudhari. (Illus.). xxxvi, 350p. 1986. text ed. 50.00x (ISBN 81-210-0049-1, Pub by Inter India Pubns N Delhi). Apt Bks.
Tribal Heritage of Madhya Pradesh: An Annotated Bibliography. H. L. Shukla. (Illus.). xiv, 208p. 1987. text ed. 30.00x (ISBN 81-7018-341-3, Pub. by B R Pub Corp Delhi). Apt Bks.
Tribal History of Eastern India. E. T. Dalton. (Illus.). 327p. 1978. Repr. of 1872 ed. 30.00 (ISBN 0-89684-123-5, Pub. by Cosmo Pubns India). Orient Bk Dist.
Tribal Innovators: Tswana Chiefs & Social Change, 1795-1940. I. Schapera. (London School of Economies Monographs on Social Anthropology: No. 43). 280p. 1970. 46.50 (ISBN 0-485-19543-7, Pub. by Athlone Pr UK). Humanities.
Tribal Movements & Political History in India: A Case Study from Orissa, 1803-1949. D. M. Praharaj. (Tribal Studies of India: No. T 127). 228p. 1988. text ed. 45.00x (ISBN 81-210-0208-7, Pub. by Inter India Pubns N. Delhi). Apt Bks.
Tribal Movements in India, Vol. 1. Ed. by K. S. Singh. 1982. 25.00X (ISBN 0-8364-0901-9, Pub. by Manohar India). South Asia Bks.
Tribal Movements in India, Vol. 2. K. S. Singh. 1983. 27.00x (ISBN 0-8364-1027-0, Pub. by Manohar India). South Asia Bks.
Tribal Myths of Orissa. Verrier Elwin. Ed. by Richard M. Dorson. LC 80-746. (Folklore of the World Ser.). 1980. Repr. of 1954 ed. lib. bdg. 74.50x (ISBN 0-405-13312-X). Ayer Co Pubs.
Tribal Occupational Mobility. D. N. Majumdar & D. Datta Ray. 1985. 18.50x (ISBN 0-8364-1396-2, Pub. by Research India). South Asia Bks.
Tribal Peasantry: Dynamics of Development. Jaganath Pathy. 233p. 1984. text ed. 30.00x (ISBN 0-86590-240-2, Pub. by Inter India Pubns India). Apt Bks.
Tribal Peoples & Economic Development: Human Ecologic Considerations. Robert Goodland. 111p. (Eng. & Span.). 1982. Eng. Ed. 5.00 (ISBN 0-8213-0010-5, BK0010); Span. Ed. avail. World Bank.
Tribal Politics & State Systems in Pre-Colonial & Eastern & Northeastern India. Surajit Sinha. 366p. 1987. 22.50x (ISBN 81-7074-014-2, Pub. by KP Bagchi India). South Asia Bks.
Tribal Religion: Religious Beliefs & Practices Among the Santals. J. Troisi. 1979. 18.00x (ISBN 0-8364-0197-2). South Asia Bks.
Tribal Revolt of Chotanagpur, Nineteen Thirty-One to Nineteen Thirty-Two. Jagdish C. Jha. 356p. 1987. 14.00x (ISBN 0-8364-2045-4, Pub. by Usha). South Asia Bks.
Tribal Rugs of Southern Persia. James Opie. LC 81-90582. 223p. text ed. 70.00 (ISBN 0-9611144-0-1). J Opie Oriental.
Tribal Scars. Sembene Ousmane. LC 87-25035. (African Writers Ser.). 128p. 1987. pap. text ed. 7.00 (ISBN 0-435-90142-7). Heinemann Ed.
Tribal Situation in India. Ed. by K. Surah Singh. 639p. 1986. Repr. of 1969 ed. lib. bdg. 45.00 (ISBN 81-208-0074-5, Pub. by Motilal Banarsidass India). Orient Bk Dist.
Tribal Situation in India. Ed. by K. Suresh Singh. 1986. 47.50X (ISBN 81-208-0074-5, Pub. by Motilal Banarsidass). South Asia Bks.
Tribal Society in India. K. S. Singh. 1986. 32.00x (ISBN 0-8364-1541-8, Pub. by Manohar India). South Asia Bks.
Tribal Songs of Northeast India Choudhury, Amalendu B Kar. 1985. 10.00x (ISBN 0-8364-1259-1, Pub. by Muklopadhyaya India). South Asia Bks.
Tribal Studies in Northern Nigeria, 2 vols. Charles K. Meek. LC 74-15066. Repr. of 1931 ed. Set. 92.00 (ISBN 0-404-12107-1). AMS Pr.
Tribal Studies in Northern Nigeria, 2 vols. Charles K. Meek. LC 32-2870. Repr. of 1931 ed. Set. 92.00 (ISBN 0-527-62650-3). Kraus Repr.
Tribal Style: Selections from the African Collection at the Peabody Museum of Salem. John R. Grimes. (Illus.). 1984. pap. 12.50 (ISBN 0-87577-150-5). Peabody Mus Salem.
Tribal Visions. Ed. by Peter E. Saunders & Michael David. (Illus.). 1981. pap. 35.00 (ISBN 0-87544-002-9). Museum Bks.
Tribal Warfare in Organizations. Peg Neuhauser. 240p. 1988. 19.95 (ISBN 0-88730-355-2). Ballinger Pub.
Tribal Woman Labourers: Aspects of Economic & Physical Exploitation. Sushama S. Prasad. 1988. 32.00x (ISBN 0-8364-2295-3, Pub. by Gian Pub Hse India). South Asia Bks.
Tribal Women in Changing Society. K. Mann. 178p. 1987. 21.00x (ISBN 0-8364-2034-9, Pub. by Mittal). South Asia Bks.
Tribal Women of India. S. S. Shashi. 163p. 1978. 16.95. Asia Bk Corp.
Tribaliks: Contemporary Congolese Stories. Henri Lopes. Tr. by Andres Leskes from Fr. (African Writers Ser.). Orig. Title: Tribaliques. 112p. (Orig.). 1987. pap. 7.00 (ISBN 0-435-90762-X). Heinemann Ed.
Tribaliques see Tribaliks: Contemporary Congolese Stories.
Tribalism & Society in Islamic Iran 1500-1629. Ed. by James J. Reid. (Studies in Near Eastern Culture & Society Ser.: Vol. 4). 215p. 1983. 24.50x (ISBN 0-89003-125-8, 82-50984); pap. 18.50x (ISBN 0-89003-124-X). Undena Pubns.
Tribalism in Crisis: Federal Indian Policy, 1953-1961. Larry W. Burt. LC 82-4864. 190p. 1982. 17.50 (ISBN 0-8263-0633-0). U of NM Pr.
Tribalism in India. Kamaladevi Chattopadhyaya. 302p. 1978. 19.95. Asia Bk Corp.
Tribe. Bari Wood. 1981. pap. 3.95 (ISBN 0-451-14004-4, Sig). NAL.
Tribe Alasmidontini: Unionidae Anodontinae. Arthur Clarke. LC 80-23747. (Smithsonian Contributions to Zoology Ser.: No. 326). pap. 20.00 (ISBN 0-317-26683-7, 2025112). Bks Demand UMI.
Tribe & Intertribal Relations in Australia. Gerald C. Wheeler. Repr. of 1910 ed. 17.00 (ISBN 0-384-67850-5). Johnson Repr.
Tribe & Polity in Late Prehistoric Europe: Demography, Production, & Exchange in the Evolution of Complex Social Systems. Ed. by D. B. Gibson & M. N. Geselowitz. LC 88-9940. (Illus.). 248p. 1988. 42.50x (ISBN 0-306-42913-6, Plenum Pr). Plenum Pub.
Tribe & State in Bahrain: The Transformation of Social & Political Authority in an Arab State. Fuad I. Khuri. LC 80-13528. (Publications of the Center for Middle Eastern Studies: No. 14). (Illus.). 1981. lib. bdg. 22.00x (ISBN 0-226-43473-7). U of Chicago Pr.
Tribe in Transition. H. L. Deb Roy. 222p. 1981. text ed. 18.50x (ISBN 0-391-02911-8). Humanities.
Tribe of Ben: Pre-Augustan Classical Verse in English. Ed. by A. C. Partridge. LC 75-116473. (English Library). 192p. (Orig.). 1970. pap. text ed. 5.95x (ISBN 0-87249-159-5). U of SC Pr.
Tribe of Dina: A Jewish Women's Anthology. Ed. by Irena Klepfisz & Melanie Kaye-Kantrowitz. (Illus.). 336p. (Orig.). 1986. pap. 9.95 (ISBN 0-931103-02-9). Sinister Wisdom Bks.
Tribes: A Process for Social Development & Cooperative Learning. rev. ed. Jeanne Gibbs. LC 86-72796. (Illus.). 220p. 1987. pap. 19.95 (ISBN 0-932762-08-5). Ctr Source Pubns.
Tribes & Castes of Bengal, 2 vols. H. H. Risley. 1981. Repr. of 1891 ed. Set. 75.00 (ISBN 0-8364-0693-1, Pub. by Mukhopadhyay India). South Asia Bks.
Tribes & Tribunes. Philip Sauvain. 1984. pap. 9.95 (ISBN 0-7175-1237-1). Dufour.
Tribes in Oman. J. R. Carter. 176p. 1982. 125.00x (ISBN 0-907151-02-7, Pub. by Immel UK). State Mutual Bk.
Tribes of California. Stephen Powers. LC 74-7994. Repr. of 1877 ed. 45.50 (ISBN 0-404-11881-X). AMS Pr.
Tribes of California. Stephen Powers. LC 75-13150. 1977. 40.00x (ISBN 0-520-03023-0); pap. 11.95x (ISBN 0-520-03172-5). U of Cal Pr.
Tribes of India: The Struggle for Survival. Christoph Von Furer-Haimendorf. LC 80-28647. (Illus.). 360p. 1982. 38.00x (ISBN 0-520-04315-4). U of Cal Pr.
Tribes of Israel: An Investigation into Some of the Presuppositions of Martin Noth's Amphictyony Hypothesis. C. H. De Geus. (Studia Semitica Neerlandica: No. 18). 270p. 1976. text ed. 33.00 (ISBN 90-232-1337-8, Pub. by Van Gorcum Holland). Longwood Pub Group.
Tribes of Nagaland. Sipra Sen. 1987. 44.00x (ISBN 0-8364-2220-1, Pub. by Mittal). South Asia Bks.
Tribes of North East India. Sudhangshu B. Saha. 1987. 27.50x (ISBN 0-8364-2127-2, Pub. by KL Mukhopadhyay). South Asia Bks.
Tribes of Northeast India. Ed. by S. Karotempral. 1984. 32.50x (ISBN 0-8364-1135-8, Pub. by Mukhopadhyaya). South Asia Bks.
Tribes of Northern & Central Kordofan. H. A. Macmichael. 260p. 1967. Repr. of 1912 ed. 47.50x (ISBN 0-7146-1113-1, F Cass Co). Biblio Dist.
Tribes of Southern Region: A Select Bibliography. Ed. by P. K. Misra et al. vii, 171p. 1986. text ed. 37.50x (ISBN 81-210-0042-4, Pub. by Inter India Pubns N Delhi). Apt Bks.
Tribes of the Columbia Valley & the Coast of Washington & Oregon. Albert B. Lewis. LC 6-44808. (American Anthrop. Assoc. Ser.). 1906. pap. 15.00 (ISBN 0-527-00501-0). Kraus Repr.
Tribes of the Extreme Northwest, Alaska, the Aleutians & Adjacent Territories. George Gibbs et al. (Illus.). 156p. pap. 9.95 (ISBN 0-8466-4018-X, I18). Shorey.
Tribes of the Liberian Hinterland. George Schwab. Ed. by G. W. Harley. (HU PMP). (Illus.). 1947. 93.00 (ISBN 0-527-01278-5). Kraus Repr.
Tribes of the Niger Delta: Their Religion & Customs. M. F. Perham. 1976. lib. bdg. 59.95 (ISBN 0-8490-2768-3). Gordon Pr.
Tribes of the Niger Delta: Their Religions & Customs. Percy A. Talbot. (Illus.). 350p. 1967. Repr. of 1932 ed. 37.50x (ISBN 0-7146-1013-5, F Cass Co). Biblio Dist.
Tribes of the Rif. Carleton S. Coon. (Harvard African Studies: Vol. 9). 1931. 79.00 (ISBN 0-527-01032-4). Kraus Repr.
Tribes of the Sahara. Lloyd C. Briggs. LC 60-7988. pap. 82.00 (ISBN 0-317-10935-9, 2006009). Bks Demand UMI.
Tribes of Yahweh: A Sociology of the Religion of Liberated Israel, 1250-1050 B.C. Norman K. Gottwald. LC 78-24333. 944p. (Orig.). 1979. pap. 19.95 (ISBN 0-88344-499-2). Orbis Bks.
Tribes on the Hill: The United States Congress - Rituals & Realities. rev. ed. J. McIver Weatherford. 320p. 1985. 29.95 (ISBN 0-89789-071-X); pap. 14.95 (ISBN 0-89789-072-8). Bergin & Garvey.
Tribes That Slumber: Indians of the Tennessee Region. Thomas M. Lewis & Madeline Kneberg. LC 58-12085. (Illus.). 1958. 17.95x (ISBN 0-87049-020-6); pap. 8.95 (ISBN 0-87049-021-4). U of Tenn Pr.
Tribes: Their Environments & Culture. Ed. by Maheshwari Prasad. 344p. 1987. text ed. 50.00x (ISBN 81-85061-51-3, Pub. by Amar Prakashan). Advent NY.
Tribes with Flags: A Dangerous Passage Through the Chaos of the Middle East. Charles Glass. 1989. 18.95 (ISBN 0-87113-267-2). Atlantic Monthly.
Tribesmen. Marshall D. Sahlins. (Illus., Orig.). 1968. pap. 14.00 ref. ed. (ISBN 0-13-930925-X). P-H.
Tribesmen & Patriots: Political Culture in a Poly-Ethnic African State. Ndiva Kofele-Kale. LC 80-5734. 375p. 1981. lib. bdg. 31.25 (ISBN 0-8191-1395-6); pap. text ed. 16.25 (ISBN 0-8191-1396-4). U Pr of Amer.
Tribesmen of Gor, No. 10. John Norman. (Science Fiction Ser.). 1986. pap. 3.50 (ISBN 0-88677-026-2). DAW Bks.
Tribhuvan University Charter: An Act Promulgated for the Establishment & Organization of a Teaching & Affiliating University. 39p. 1959. 7.50 (ISBN 0-318-23190-5). Am-Nepal Ed.
Tribochemistry. Gerqard Heinicke. (Hanser Publications). (Illus.). 496p. 1985. 69.00 (ISBN 0-19-520731-9). Oxford U Pr.
Tribology. Szeri. 548p. 1980. 52.00 (ISBN 0-89116-509-6). Hemisphere Pub.
Tribology: A Systems Approach to the Science & Technology of Friction, Lubrication & Wear. Czichos. (Tribology Ser.: Vol. 1). 400p. 1978. 118.50 (ISBN 0-444-41676-5). Elsevier.
Tribology & Mechanics of Magnetic Storage Systems, 25 papers. 191p. 1984. 80.00 (ISBN 0-318-17681-5, SP-16). Soc Tribologists.
Tribology Handbook. Ed. by M. J. Neale. (Illus.). 540p. 1973. text ed. 125.00 (ISBN 0-408-00082-1). Butterworth.
Tribology in Metalworking. John A. Schey. 1983. 115.00 (ISBN 0-87170-155-3). ASM.
Tribology in Particulate Technology. Ed. by B. J. Briscoe & M. J. Adams. 464p. 1987. 149.00x (ISBN 0-85274-425-0, Pub by A Hilger UK). Taylor & Francis.
Tribology of Natural & Artificial Joints. J. H. Dumbleton. (Tribology Ser.: Vol. 3). 460p. 1981. 108.00 (ISBN 0-444-41898-9). Elsevier.
Tribology of Thin Layers. I. Iliuc. (Tribology Ser.: Vol. 4). 226p. 1980. 71.00 (ISBN 0-444-99768-7). Elsevier.
Tribonian. Tony Honore. LC 77-79701. 292p. 1978. 49.50x (ISBN 0-8014-1148-3). Cornell U Pr.
Tribophysics. Nam P. Suh. 528p. 1986. text ed. 80.00 (ISBN 0-13-930983-7). P-H.
Triborough Plan. Jose Ramon. 1986. 6.95 (ISBN 0-533-06589-5). Vantage.
Tribu de Wagap (Nouvelle-Caledonie) A. Colomb. LC 75-32812. Repr. of 1890 ed. 26.50 (ISBN 0-404-14116-1). AMS Pr.
Tribulaciones de Jonas. Edgardo Rodriguez. LC 81-66836. (Nave y el Puerto Ser.). (Illus.). 108p. 1981. pap. 5.50 (ISBN 0-940238-38-1). Ediciones Huracan.
Tribulat Bonhomet. Auguste de Villiers De L'Isle-Adam. 192p. 19.95 (ISBN 0-686-55725-5). French & Eur.
Tribulation & the Church. Chuck Smith. 64p. (Orig.). 1980. pap. 1.50 (ISBN 0-936728-01-9). Word for Today.
Tribulation Period Will Last Longer Than 7 Years. Walter E. Adams. (Orig.). 1988. pap. 3.95 (ISBN 0-937408-99-9). GMI Pubns Inc.
Tribulation Temple. Dale A. Howard. (Illus.). 80p. 1987. pap. 5.00 (ISBN 0-940517-03-5). JCMC Louisiana.
Tribulation Temple. Gordon Lindsay. (Revelation Ser.). 1.25 (ISBN 0-89985-038-3). Christ Nations.
Tribulations d'un Chinois en Chine. 4th ed. Jules Verne. 192p. 1976. 10.95 (ISBN 0-686-55956-8). French & Eur.
Tribulations d'un Chinois en Chine. Jules Verne. (Illus.). 8.95 (ISBN 0-686-55957-6). French & Eur.
Tribulations of a Chinese Gentleman. Jules Verne. 4.95 (ISBN 0-87497-045-8). Assoc Bk.
Tribulations of Veneguay. Jim Stickter. LC 78-53364. (Illus., Orig.). 1978. pap. 7.50 (ISBN 0-930770-08-0). Hemisphere Hse.
Tribunal. Vladimir Voinovich. 94p. 1984. cancelled (ISBN 0-88233-530-8). Ardis Pubs.

Triggers. Donald Guravich. 32p. 1984. pap. 3.50 (ISBN 0-939180-25-1). Tombouctou.

Triggers: A New Approach to Self-Motivation. Stanley Mann. 216p. 1986. 19.95 (ISBN 0-13-930793-1); pap. 8.95 (ISBN 0-13-930785-0). P-H.

Triggers for Six. Nelson Nye. 256p. pap. 2.50 (ISBN 0-8439-2011-4, Leisure Bks). Leisure NY.

Trigmaster. Bela Kainez. 1974. pap. 3.95 (ISBN 0-686-17776-2). Vertex.

Trigoniaceae. Eduardo Lleras. LC 77-91706. (Flora Neotropica Monograph: No. 19). 1978. pap. 7.25x (ISBN 0-89327-198-5). NY Botanical.

Trigoniaceae & Vochysiaceae. R. Spichiger & P. A. Loizeau. (Flora del Paraquay Ser.). (Illus.). 36p. (Orig., Span.). 1985. pap. 5.00 (ISBN 0-915279-04-5). Miss Botan.

Trigonometric Series, Vols. I & II. 2nd ed. A. Zygmund. (Cambridge Mathematical Library). 776p. 1988. pap. 44.50 (ISBN 0-521-35885-X). Cambridge U Pr.

Trigonometric Series: A Survey. Ralph L. Jeffery. LC 56-59071. (Canadian Mathematical Congress Lecture Ser.: No. 2). pap. 20.00 (ISBN 0-317-08877-7, 2014260). Bks Demand UMI.

Trigonometrie, or the Doctrine of Triangles, 2 pts. Richard Norwood. LC 78-171779. (English Experience Ser.: No. 404). 362p. 1971. Repr. of 1631 ed. 75.00 (ISBN 90-221-0404-4). Walter J Johnson.

Trigonometry. Frank Ayres, Jr. (Schaum's Outline Ser). (Orig.). 1954. pap. text ed. 8.95 (ISBN 0-07-002651-3). McGraw.

Trigonometry. John Baley & Martin Holstege. 385p. 1988. text ed. 28.75 (ISBN 0-394-35461-3, RanC). Random.

Trigonometry. Marvin L. Bittinger & Judith A. Beecher. (Illus.). 1988. pap. text ed. price not set (ISBN 0-201-09184-4). Addison-Wesley.

Trigonometry. C. B. Douthitt & J. A. McMillan. 1977. text ed. 28.95 (ISBN 0-07-017670-1). McGraw.

Trigonometry. Isidore Dressler & Barnett Rich. (gr. 10-12). 1975. pap. text ed. 10.33 (ISBN 0-87720-219-2). AMSCO Sch.

Trigonometry. Roy Dubisch. LC 55-6084. pap. 102.50 (ISBN 0-317-08418-6, 2012451). Bks Demand UMI.

Trigonometry. John R. Durbin. LC 86-28193. 416p. 1987. write for info. (ISBN 0-471-03366-9). Wiley.

Trigonometry. 2nd ed. Harley Flanders & Justin J. Price. 1982. text ed. 38.75 (ISBN 0-03-057802-7, CBS C). SCP.

Trigonometry. Gehrmann & Lester. (College Outline Ser.). 278p. 1988. pap. 10.95 (ISBN 0-15-601693-1, BFP). HarBraceJ.

Trigonometry. Vivian S. Groza. 1980. text ed. 34.75 (ISBN 0-7216-4325-6, CBS C). SCP.

Trigonometry. 2nd ed. Marshall D. Hestenes & Richard O. Hill. (Illus.). 320p. 1986. text ed. write for info. (ISBN 0-13-930744-3). P-H.

Trigonometry. Leonard I. Holder. 271p. 1982. text ed. write for info. (ISBN 0-534-01014-8). Wadsworth Pub.

Trigonometry. Jerome E. Kaufmann. 384p. 1988. text ed. 27.00 (ISBN 0-534-92106-X). PWS Kent Pub.

Trigonometry. 2nd ed. Larson. 400p. 1988. text ed. 27.00 (ISBN 0-669-16266-3); solutions guide 6.50 (ISBN 0-669-16268-X); study & solutions guide 7.00 (ISBN 0-669-19540-5); instr's. guide 2.00 (ISBN 0-669-16267-1). Heath.

Trigonometry. Roland E. Larson & Robert P. Hostetler. LC 84-80506. 322p. 1985. text ed. 27.00 (ISBN 0-669-08611-8); instr's guide 2.00 (ISBN 0-669-08612-6); compl. sols. guide 6.50 (ISBN 0-669-12001-4); Archive trig. pkg. Apple 150.00 (ISBN 0-669-13039-7). Heath.

Trigonometry. 3rd ed. Margaret L. Lial & Charles D. Miller. 1985. text ed. write for info. (ISBN 0-673-18016-6). Scott F.

Trigonometry. 4th ed. Margaret L. Lial & Charles D. Miller. 1988. text ed. write for info. (ISBN 0-673-38248-6). Scott F.

Trigonometry. Charles P. McKeague. 1984. 22.00 (ISBN 0-12-484785-4); 10.00 (ISBN 0-12-484786-2). Acad Pr.

Trigonometry. 2nd ed. Charles P. McKeague. 339p. 1988. text ed. 26.00 (ISBN 0-15-592362-5, HC). HarBraceJ.

Trigonometry. Jack Rudman. (College Level Examination Ser.: CLEP-28). 25.95 (ISBN 0-8373-5378-5); pap. 13.95 (ISBN 0-8373-5328-9). Natl Learning.

Trigonometry. Howard A. Silver. (Illus.). 320p. 1986. text ed. write for info. (ISBN 0-13-930801-6). P-H.

Trigonometry. Ralph C. Steinlage. 408p. 1985. text ed. 37.75 (ISBN 0-314-86662-0). West Pub.

Trigonometry. Dennis Zill & Jacqueline Dewar. 450p. 1989. text ed. price not set (ISBN 0-394-35675-6). Random.

Trigonometry: A Calculus Approach. Herman R. Hyatt & Laurence Small. LC 81-13120. 430p. 1982. 32.50 (ISBN 0-471-07985-5); student supp. o.p. 13.95 (ISBN 0-471-08069-1); tchr's manual avail. (ISBN 0-471-86938-4). Wiley.

Trigonometry: A Complete & Concrete Approach. Harold S. Engelsohn. (Illus.). 1981. text ed. 35.95 (ISBN 0-07-019419-X). McGraw.

Trigonometry: A Modern Approach. 2nd ed. Joseph Elich et al. LC 84-9287. 1985. text ed. write for info. (ISBN 0-201-10523-3); write for info. solutions manual (ISBN 0-201-10526-8); write for info. instr's. manual (ISBN 0-201-10524-1). Addison-Wesley.

Trigonometry: A New Approach. Richard T. Kuechle. 410p. 1984. text ed. write for info. (ISBN 0-534-01137-3). Wadsworth Pub.

Trigonometry: A Skills Approach. J. Louis Nanney & John L. Cable. 384p. 1979. pap. text ed. write for info. (ISBN 0-205-06603-8). Wm C Brown.

Trigonometry: A Straightforward Approach. Zuckerman. 352p. 1988. write for info. (ISBN 0-471-09602-4). Wiley.

Trigonometry: A Unitized Approach. Reuben W. Farley et al. (Illus.). 1975. pap. text ed. write for info (ISBN 0-13-930909-8). P-H.

Trigonometry: An Analytic Approach. 5th ed. Irving Drooyan & Walter Hadel. (Illus.). 1987. text ed. write for info. (ISBN 0-02-330650-5). Macmillan.

Trigonometry & Its Applications. C. R. Hirsch & H. Schoen. LC 84-23391. 544p. 1985. text ed. 38.95 (ISBN 0-07-029059-8). McGraw.

Trigonometry for College Students. 4th ed. Karl J. Smith. (Mathematics Ser.). 416p. 1986. text ed. 25.00 pub. net (ISBN 0-534-06552-X). Brooks-Cole.

Trigonometry for the Practical Worker. 4th ed. J. E. Thompson. 208p. 1982. pap. 10.95 (ISBN 0-442-28271-0). Van Nos Reinhold.

Trigonometry Self-Taught. Peter H. Selby. (Orig.). 1964. pap. text ed. 6.95 (ISBN 0-07-056069-2). McGraw.

Trigonometry: Student Solutions Guide. 2nd ed. Judith M. Barclay. 166p. 1988. pap. text ed. 6.00 net (ISBN 0-15-592364-1). HarBraceJ.

Trigonometry the Easy Way. Downing. (Easy Way Ser.). 225p. 1984. pap. 8.95 (ISBN 0-8120-2717-5). Barron.

Trigonometry: Triangles & Functions. 3rd ed. Mervin L. Keedy & Marvin L. Bittinger. LC 81-14974. 1982. Stu Sol. o.p. 2.00 (ISBN 0-201-13409-8); write for info. (ISBN 0-201-13411-X). Addison-Wesley.

Trigonometry: Triangles & Functions. 4th ed. Mervin L. Keedy & Marvin L. Bittinger. 400p. 1986. pap. text ed. write for info. (ISBN 0-201-13332-6); instr's. manual avail. (ISBN 0-201-13333-4); student's guide avail. (ISBN 0-201-13334-2); test bank avail. (ISBN 0-201-13335-0); placement test avail. Addison-Wesley.

Trigonometry Using Calculators. Carlotta J. Elich & Joseph Elich. LC 79-18934. (Illus.). 1980. text ed. write for info. (ISBN 0-201-03186-8); instr's. manual o.p. 4.00 (ISBN 0-201-03187-6). Addison-Wesley.

Trigonometry with Analytic Geometry. Arnold R. Steffensen & L. M. Johnson. 1983. pap. text ed. write for info. (ISBN 0-673-15633-8). Scott F.

Trigonometry with Applications. Dale Ewen & Lynn R. Akers. (Illus.). 384p. 1984. write for info. (ISBN 0-201-11312-0); write for info. instr's. manual (ISBN 0-201-11314-7). Addison-Wesley.

Trigonometry with Applications. L. Murphy Johnson & Arnold R. Steffensen. 1988. text ed. write for info. (ISBN 0-673-18799-3). Scott F.

Trigonometry with Applications. Terry H. Wesner et al. 480p. 1986. text ed. write for info. (ISBN 0-697-00236-5); instr's. manual avail. (ISBN 0-697-00366-3); workbook-solutions manual avail. (ISBN 0-697-00365-5). Wm C Brown.

Trihalomethane Reduction in Drinking Water: Technologies, Costs, Effectiveness, Monitoring, Compliance. Ed. by Gordon Culp. LC 84-14906. (Pollution Technology Review Ser.: No. 114). (Illus.). 251p. 1985. 42.00 (ISBN 0-8155-1002-0). Noyes.

Triiodothyronines in Health & Disease. I. J. Chopra. (Monographs in Endocrinology: Vol. 18). (Illus.). 160p. 1981. 48.00 (ISBN 0-387-10400-3). Springer-Verlag.

Trilateral Commission Task Force Reports, Nos. 9-14. Incl. Collaboration with Communist Countries in Managing Global Problems: Am Examination of the Options. Chihiro Hosoya & Henry D. Owen. 1976; Problem of International Confrontations. Egidio Ortona & J. Robert Schaetzel. 1976; Reform of International Institutions. C. Fred Bergsten & Georges Berthoin. 1978; New Regime for the Oceans. Michael Hardy & Ann L. Hollick. 1976; Seeking a New Accommodation in World Commodity Markets. Carl E. Beigie & Wolfgang Hager. 1976; Toward a Renovated International System. Richard N. Cooper & Karl Kaiser. 1977. 30.00 (ISBN 0-318-03634-7). Trilateral Comm.

Trilateral Commission Task Force Reports, Nos. 15-19. Incl. Collective Bargaining & Employee Participation in Western Europe, North America & Japan. Benjamin C. Roberts & George C. Lodge. 1979; Energy: Managing the Transition. John Sawhill & Keichi Oshima. 1978; Industrial Policy & the International Economy. William Diebold & Takashi Hosomi. 1979; Overview of East-West Relations. Jeremy R. Azrael & Richard Lowenthal. 1978; Reducing Malnutrition in Developing Countries: Increasing Rice Production in South & Southeast Asia. Toshio Shishido & D. Gale Johnson. 1978. 30.00 (ISBN 0-318-03635-5). Trilateral Comm.

Trilateral Countries & the Middle East. Joseph J. Sisco & Shlomo Avineri. write for info. Trilateral Comm.

Trilateral Countries in the International Economy of the 1980's. Miriam Camps & Ryokichi Hirono. 1982. write for info. Trilateral Comm.

Trilateral Relations at the Threshold of the New Decade. Robert R. Bowie et al. write for info. Trilateral Comm.

Trilateral Security: Defense & Arms Control Policies in the 1980s - Report of the Trilateral Task Force on Security & Arms Limitation to the Trilateral Commission. Trilateral Task Force on Security & Arms Limitation et al. LC 83-5100. (Triangle Papers: No. 26). 1983. write for info. Trilateral Comm.

Trilateral-Soviet Relations in Transition. Seweryn Bialer et al. write for info. Trilateral Comm.

Trilateral Template. Bernard M. Bane. 6p. 1982. pap. 0.25 (ISBN 0-930924-13-4). BMB Pub Co.

Trilateralism in Asia: Problems & Prospects in U. S.-Japan-ASEAN Relations. Ed. by K. S. Nathan & M. Pathmanathan. 224p. 1986. text ed. 18.00x (ISBN 967-80-0005-9, Pub. by Antara Bk Co); pap. text ed. 12.00x (ISBN 967-80-0004-0). UH Pr.

Trilateralism: The Trilateral Commission & Elite Planning for World Management. Ed. by Holly Sklar. LC 80-51040. 1980. 30.00 (ISBN 0-89608-104-4); pap. 15.00 (ISBN 0-89608-103-6). South End Pr.

Trilaterals Over Washington, 2 vols. Anthony C. Sutton & Patrick M. Wood. 390p. 1981. Set. pap. 11.90 (ISBN 0-933482-03-5); pap. 5.95 ea. Vol. 1 (ISBN 0-933482-01-9). Vol. 2 (ISBN 0-933482-02-7). August Corp.

Trilby, a Novel. George Du Maurier. 1977. Repr. of 1895 ed. lib. bdg. 35.00 (ISBN 0-8414-1857-8). Folcroft.

Trilby's Trumpet. Sarah A. Stapler. LC 87-397. (Illus.). 16p. (ps-1). 1988. 12.95i (ISBN 0-06-025827-6). HarpJ.

Trilemma of World Oil Politics. Sheikh R. Ali & Jeffrey M. Elliot. LC 84-275. (Great Issues of the Day Ser.: No. 2). 160p. (Orig.). 1988. lib. bdg. 19.95x (ISBN 0-89370-168-8); pap. text ed. 9.95x (ISBN 0-89370-268-4). Borgo Pr.

Trilingual Compendium of the United Nations Terminology, 4 vols. rev. ed. 1987. Vol. I, 561p. 75.00 (ISBN 92-1-002048-0, E/F/G.86.I.20). Vol. II. 571p (E/F/G.86.I.20). UN.

Trilingual Compendium of United Nations Terminology, 4 vols. (Eng., Fr. & Ger.). 1986. 75.00 (ISBN 0-317-66530-8, EFG.86.I.20). UN.

Trilingual Dictionary of Fisheries Technological Terms: Curing. 85p. 1960. pap. 12.00 (ISBN 92-5-000856-2, F483, FAO). UNIPUB.

Trilingual Education: Sign Language, Spanish, English. Kathee M. Christensen & C. Ben Christensen. (Illus., Span. & Eng.). Date not set. 9.00 (ISBN 0-916304-70-1). SDSU Press.

Trillion Dollar Budget: How to Stop the Bankrupting of America. Glenn Pascall. LC 84-40665. (Illus.). 328p. 1985. 25.00 (ISBN 0-295-96217-8); pap. 12.95 (ISBN 0-295-96237-2). U of Wash Pr.

Trillion Dollar Trick. Bennett A. Williams. 1989. pap. 3.95 (ISBN 0-8125-1231-6). Tor Bks.

Trillion Year Spree. Brian Aldiss & David Wingrove. LC 86-47682. (Illus.). 512p. 1986. 24.95 (ISBN 0-689-11839-2). Atheneum.

Trillion Year Spree: The History of Science Fiction. Brian W. Aldiss. 528p. 1988. pap. 9.95 (ISBN 0-380-70461-7). Avon.

Trillions. Nicholas Fisk. (gr. 5 up). 1973. Pantheon.

Trillium Basal Math-Ware: Apple Diskette. Helen Oliver & Bob Oliver. (gr. 1-6). incl. tchr's manual 29.95 (ISBN 0-89824-080-8). Trillium Pr.

Trilobites in British Stratigraphy. A. T. Thomas et al. (Illus.). 80p. 1984. pap. text ed. 24.50x (ISBN 0-632-01201-3). Blackwell Pubns.

Trilogiia. Aleksandr V. Sukhovo-Kobylin. Intro. by Leonid Grossman. 560p. 1985. Repr. cancelled (ISBN 0-88233-957-5). Ardis Pubs.

Trilogy. Harriette S. Arnow. 1986. 70.00 (ISBN 0-8131-1607-4). U Pr of Ky.

Trilogy. Hilda Doolittle, pseud. Incl. The Walls Do Not Fall; Tribute to the Angels; The Flowering of the Rod. LC 73-78848. 128p. 1973. pap. 7.95 (ISBN 0-8112-0491-X, NDP362). New Directions.

Trilogy. Spiros Zodhiates. Vol. 1 The Patience of Hope. 7.95 ea.; Vol. 2 The Work of Faith. 6.95; Vol. 3 The Labor of Love. 8.95; Set. 21.95 (ISBN 0-89957-558-7). AMG Pubs.

Trilogy: More than Many Sparrows, Wisdom Shall Enter & Many Are One, 3 bks. in 1 vol. Leo J. Trese. 271p. 1984. pap. 6.95 (ISBN 971-117-023-X, Pub. by Sinag-Tala Pubs Philippines). Scepter Pubs.

Trilogy of Armageddon. David. LC 85-90253. 138p. 1986. 10.95 (ISBN 0-533-06739-1). Vantage.

Trilogy of Prizewinning Plays. Norman Holland. 1982. 15.00x (ISBN 0-903653-17-6, Pub. by New Playwrights Network). State Mutual Bk.

Trilogy of Treason: An Intertextual Study of Juan Goytisolo. Michael Ugarte. LC 81-10288. 192p. 1982. text ed. 21.00x (ISBN 0-8262-0353-1). U of Mo Pr.

Trilogy on Wisdom & Celibacy. J. Massingberd Ford. 1967. 21.95x (ISBN 0-268-00285-1). U of Notre Dame Pr.

Trilogy: Or Dante's Three Visions, 3 vols. Dante Alighieri. Tr. by John Thomas. 1978. Repr. of 1859 ed. lib. bdg. 100.00 set (ISBN 0-8492-0669-3). R West.

Trilogy: The Nazarene, the Apostle, Mary. Sholem Asch. Boxed set. pap. cancelled (ISBN 0-88184-142-0). Carroll & Graf.

Trim-a-Tree Books, 6 bks. Kathleen N. Daly. (Illus., Orig.). (gr. k-3). 1986. Set. pap. 4.95 (ISBN 0-590-33411-5). Scholastic Inc.

Trim & Finish Models see D.A.E Project: Instructional Materials for Dental Health Professions.

Trim & Thin 4-Ingredient Cookbook. Shirley Atwater McClay & Marilyn Miech. 320p. (Orig.). 1988. pap. 6.95 (ISBN 0-89586-724-9, HP Bks). Price Stern.

Trim-the-Tree Counting Book. Illus. by Pat Sustendal. LC 83-63314. (Illus.). 12p. (ps). 1984. bds. 1.95 (ISBN 0-394-86748-3, BYR). Random.

Trimblerigg: A Book of Revelation. Laurence Housman. LC 75-145094. 1971. Repr. of 1924 ed. 29.00x (ISBN 0-403-01032-2). Scholarly.

Trimethoprim-Sulfamethoxazole. Ed. by Maxwell Finland & Edward H. Kass. LC 73-92601. viii, 392p. 1974. 17.95x (ISBN 0-226-24916-6). U of Chicago Pr.

Trimetre Iambique Des Iambographes a la Comedie Nouvelle. J. Descroix. Ed. by Leonardo Taran. (Ancient Greek Literature Ser.). 383p. 1987. lib. bdg. 60.00 (ISBN 0-8240-7755-5). Garland Pub.

Trimetric Secret. Marvin Pietruszka & Paulette Lambert. LC 85-61325. (Illus.). 300p. 1986. 9.95 (ISBN 0-934249-01-6). Quail Valley.

Trimmers, Trucklers & Temporizers: Notes of Murat Halstead from the Political Conventions of 1856. Ed. by William B. Hesseltine & Rex Fisher. LC 61-62506. 114p. 1961. 3.50 (ISBN 0-87020-044-5). State Hist Soc Wis.

Trimming & Clipping. Valerie Watson. (Illus.). 24p. (Orig.). 1987. pap. 6.95 (ISBN 0-901366-42-0, Pub. by Threshold Bks). Half Halt Pr.

Trimming Float to Build Earnings. 104p. 1986. 99.95 (ISBN 0-929097-29-7, 18291). US League Savi Inst.

Trimotor & Trail. Earl Cooley. LC 84-9757. (Illus.). 288p. 1984. 14.95 (ISBN 0-87842-173-4). Mountain Pr.

Trimtab Factor: How Business Executives Can Help Solve the Nuclear Weapons Crisis. Harold Willens. LC 83-17202. 180p. 1984. 10.95 (ISBN 0-688-02661-3). Morrow.

Trinet Directory of Leading U. S. Companies. Date not set. Set. 395.00 (ISBN 0-317-57793-X); 175.00 ea. The Top 1500, 86-637903. The Second 1500, 85-643077. The Tops 1500 Private, 85-640131. Trinet.

Trinet Directory of Leading U. S. Companies: The Second Fifteen Hundred. LC 82-73381. 1984. 175.00 (ISBN 0-86692-001-3). Trinet.

Trinet Directory of Leading US Companies: The Second 1500. LC 85-643077. 175.00 (ISBN 0-317-63821-1). Trinet.

Trinet Directory of Leading US Companies: The Top 1500. LC 86-647903. 175.00 (ISBN 0-317-63826-2). Trinet.

Trinet Directory of Leading US Companies: The Top 1500 Private. LC 85-640131. write for info. Trinet.

Trini. Estela Portillo Trambley. LC 85-73394. (United States Hispanic Creative Literature Ser.). 248p. 1986. lib. bdg. 19.00x (ISBN 0-916950-61-1); pap. text ed. 12.00x (ISBN 0-916950-62-X). Biling Rev-Pr.

Trinidad & Tobago. Frances Chambers. (World Bibliographical Ser: No. 74). 213p. 1986. 35.00 (ISBN 1-85109-020-7). ABC-Clio.

Trinidad & Tobago. Patricia R. Urosevich. (Places & People of the World Ser.). (Illus.). 96p. 1988. lib. bdg. 12.95x (ISBN 1-55546-778-4). Chelsea Hse.

Trinidad & Tobago see American Nations Past & Present.

Trinidad & Tobago: Consolidated Index of Statutes & Subsidiary Legislation. Ed. by C. J. Hammett. (West Indian Legislation Indexing Project Ser.). v, 116p. (Orig.). 1986. pap. text ed. 20.00 (ISBN 0-317-60548-8, Pub. by UWI Fac Law). W W Gaunt.

Trinidad & Tobago: Democracy & Development in the Caribbean. Scott B. MacDonald. LC 86-539. 240p. 1986. 35.00 (ISBN 0-275-92004-6, C2004). Praeger.

Trinidad Awakening: West Indian Literature of the Nineteen-Thirties. Reinhard W. Sander. LC 87-31777. (Contributions in Afro-American & African Studies: No. 114). 180p. 1988. lib. bdg. 37.95 (ISBN 0-313-24562-2, SNT/). Greenwood.

Trinidad Del Hombre. Dennis Bennett & Rita Bennett. Ed. by Andy Carrodeguas. Tr. by Francisco Lievano from Span. Orig. Title: Trinity of Man. 224p. 1982. pap. 3.50 (ISBN 0-8297-1298-4). Life Pubs Intl.

Trinidad in Transition: The Years after Slavery. Donald Wood. 328p. 1986. pap. text ed. 17.95x (ISBN 0-19-827269-3). Oxford U Pr.

Trinidad Village. Melville J. Herskovits & Frances S. Herskovits. 1964. lib. bdg. 26.00x (ISBN 0-374-93876-8, Octagon). Hippocrene Bks.

Trinitarian & Mystical Theology of St. Symeon the New Theologian. Constine N. Tsirpanlis. 42p. 1981. pap. 5.00 (ISBN 0-686-36331-0). EO Pr.
Trinitarian Concept of God. Wade H. Horton. 1964. pap. 1.95 (ISBN 0-87148-833-7). Pathway Pr.
Trinitarian Controversy. Ed. by William G. Rusch. LC 79-8889. (Sources of Early Christian Thought Ser.). 192p. 1980. pap. 7.95 (ISBN 0-8006-1410-0, 1-1410). Fortress.
Trinitarian Faith. T. F. Torrance. 376p. 1988. 43.95 (ISBN 0-567-09483-9, Pub. by T & T Clark Ltd UK). Fortress.
Trinitarian Theology East & West: St. Thomas Aquinas - St. Gregory Palamas. Micheal J. Fahey & John Meyendorff. 43p. 1986. pap. 2.45. Holy Cross Orthodox.
Trinitas. Michael O'Carroll. LC 86-45326. (Orig.). 1986. 35.00 (ISBN 0-89453-595-1). M Glazier.
Trinity. St. Augustine. LC 63-72482. (Fathers of the Church Ser.: Vol. 45). 539p. 1963. 27.95x (ISBN 0-8132-0045-8). Cath U Pr.
Trinity. Edward H. Bickersteth. LC 59-13770. 182p. 1976. pap. 5.95 (ISBN 0-8254-2226-4). Kregel.
Trinity. Gordon H. Clark. (Trinity Papers: No. 8). 139p. (Orig.). 1985. pap. 8.95 (ISBN 0-940931-08-7). Trinity Found.
Trinity. rev. ed. Robert Crossley. 32p. 1987. pap. 0.75 (ISBN 0-87784-077-6). Inter-Varsity.
Trinity. St. Hilary Of Poitiers. LC 67-28585. (Fathers of the Church Ser: Vol. 25). 555p. 1954. 34.95 (ISBN 0-8132-0025-3). Cath U Pr.
Trinity. Nancy Kress. 1988. pap. 3.50 (ISBN 0-441-82415-3). Ace Bks.
Trinity. Harry Smith. 72p. 1975. 6.95 (ISBN 0-8180-1575-6). Horizon.
Trinity. Leon Uris. 1983. pap. 4.95 (ISBN 0-553-25846-X). Bantam.
Trinity. Leon Uris. LC 75-14844. 384p. 1976. 19.95 (ISBN 0-385-03458-X). Doubleday.
Trinity Alps. 2nd ed. Luther Linkhart. LC 85-41029. (Illus.). 192p. 1986. pap. 14.95 (ISBN 0-89997-064-8). Wilderness Pr.
Trinity & Culture. Charles S. MacKenzie. (American University Studies Series VIII Theology & Religion: Vol. 34). 150p. 1987. text ed. 25.95 (ISBN 0-317-62568-3). P Lang Pubs.
Trinity & Duke, 1892-1924: Foundations of Duke University. Earl W. Porter. LC 64-15199. (Illus.). xii, 274p. 1964. pap. 10.95 (ISBN 0-8223-0350-7). Duke.
Trinity & Other Stories. Nancy Kress. 288p. 1985. 15.95 (ISBN 0-312-94438-1, Dist. by St. Martin). Bluejay Bks.
Trinity & Society: Theology & Liberation. Leonardo Boff. Tr. by Paul Burns from Port. 236p. (Orig.). 1988. 26.95 (ISBN 0-88344-623-5); pap. 13.95 (ISBN 0-88344-622-7). Orbis Bks.
Trinity & Temporality. John J. O'Donnell. (Oxford Theological Monographs). 1983. 32.50x (ISBN 0-19-826722-3). Oxford U Pr.
Trinity & the Kingdom. Jurgen Moltmann. LC 80-8352. 320p. 1981. 21.95 (ISBN 0-06-065906-8, HarpR). Har-Row.
Trinity & the Religious Experience of Man: Icon, Person, Mystery. Raimundo Panikkar. LC 73-77329. pap. 24.50 (ISBN 0-317-26668-3, 2025122). Bks Demand UMI.
Trinity-by-the-Stove. Ed. by Bee Harper. (Illus.). 320p. 1987. 12.95 (ISBN 0-9618615-0-9). TBTC ECW.
Trinity College Dublin, 1592-1952: An Academic History. R. B. McDowell & D. A. Webb. LC 81-12262. (Illus.). 678p. 1982. 89.00 (ISBN 0-521-23931-1). Cambridge U Pr.
Trinity College Historical Society Historical Papers, Series 1-32. Duke University Staff. LC 74-115989. Repr. of 1956 ed. Set. 735.00 (ISBN 0-404-51750-1); 24.50 ea. AMS Pr.
Trinity College Historical Society Papers, Series 1: Reconstruction & State Biography. Duke University Staff. Repr. of 1897 ed. 24.50 (ISBN 0-404-51751-X). AMS Pr.
Trinity College Historical Society Papers, Series 11: 1915. Duke University Staff. Repr. 24.50 (ISBN 0-404-51761-7). AMS Pr.
Trinity College Historical Society Papers, Series 15: 1925. Duke University Staff. Repr. 24.50 (ISBN 0-404-51765-X). AMS Pr.
Trinity College Historical Society Papers, Series 14: 1922. Duke University Staff. Repr. 24.50 (ISBN 0-404-51764-1). AMS Pr.
Trinity College Historical Society Papers, Series 10: 1914. Duke University Staff. Repr. 24.50 (ISBN 0-404-51760-9). AMS Pr.
Trinity College Historical Society Papers, Series 13: 1919. Duke University Staff. Repr. 24.50 (ISBN 0-404-51763-3). AMS Pr.
Trinity College Historical Society Papers, Series 12: 1916. Duke University Staff. Repr. 24.50 (ISBN 0-404-51762-5). AMS Pr.
Trinity College Historical Society Papers, Series 2: Legal & Biographical Studies. Duke University Staff. Repr. of 1898 ed. 24.50 (ISBN 0-404-51752-8). AMS Pr.
Trinity College Historical Society Papers, Series 3: Gov. W. W. Holden & Revolutionary Documents. Duke University Staff. Repr. of 1899 ed. 24.50 (ISBN 0-404-51753-6). AMS Pr.
Trinity College Historical Society Papers, Series 4: 1900. Duke University Staff. Repr. 24.50 (ISBN 0-404-51754-4). AMS Pr.
Trinity College Historical Society Papers, Series 5: 1905. Duke University Staff. Repr. 24.50 (ISBN 0-404-51755-2). AMS Pr.
Trinity College Historical Society Papers, Series 6: 1906. Duke University Staff. Repr. 24.50 (ISBN 0-404-51756-0). AMS Pr.
Trinity College Historical Society Papers, Series 7: 1907. Duke University Staff. Repr. 24.50 (ISBN 0-404-51757-9). AMS Pr.
Trinity College Historical Society Papers, Series 8: 1908-1909. Duke University Staff. Repr. 24.50 (ISBN 0-404-51758-7). AMS Pr.
Trinity College Historical Society Papers, Series 9: 1912. Duke University Staff. Repr. 24.50 (ISBN 0-404-51759-5). AMS Pr.
Trinity College, Washington, DC: The First Eighty Years, 1897-1977. Columba Mullaly. 500p. 1987. 40.00 (ISBN 0-87061-140-2); pap. 35.00 (ISBN 0-87061-139-9). Chr Classics.
Trinity County Beginnings, Texas. Trinity County Book Committee. (Illus.). 866p. 1986. 62.50 (ISBN 0-88107-072-6). Curtis Media.
Trinity Factor. Sean Flannery. 418p. (Orig.). 1982. pap. 2.95 (ISBN 0-441-82402-1, Pub. by Charter Bks). Ace Bks.
Trinity in the Gospel of John. Royce G. Gruenler. 1986. pap. 9.95 (ISBN 0-8010-3806-5). Baker Bk.
Trinity in the Universe. 2nd ed. Nathan R. Wood & G. Campbell Morgan. LC 78-5483. 220p. 1984. pap. 6.95 (ISBN 0-8254-4018-1). Kregel.
Trinity: Is the Doctrine Biblical-Is It Important? F. Donald Harris & Ronald A. Harris. LC 77-123613. 1971. pap. 1.50 (ISBN 0-87213-310-9). Loizeaux.
Trinity of Man. Dennis Bennett & Rita Bennett. LC 87-82616. 196p. 1987. pap. 6.95 (ISBN 0-89221-149-0). New Leaf.
Trinity of Man see Trinidad Del Hombre.
Trinity of Terror. William Doran. 48p. (Orig.). 1980. pap. 2.95 (ISBN 0-89288-045-7). Maverick.
Trinity, or the Tri-Personal Being of God. J. A. Synan. pap. 2.95 (ISBN 0-911866-00-0). Advocate.
Trinity Story. Calvin B. Hanson. LC 83-81575. 1983. 8.95 (ISBN 0-911802-58-4). Free Church Pubns.
Trinity Teacher Training Workshop Booklet. Larry Christenson. (Trinity Bible Ser.). 80p. (gr. 4-6). 1975. pap. 2.95 (ISBN 0-87123-552-8, 240552). Bethany Hse.
Trinity University: A Record of One Hundred Years. Donald E. Everett. LC 68-24632. (Illus.). 1968. 5.00 (ISBN 0-911536-21-3). Trinity U Pr.
Trinity's Child. William Prochnau. LC 83-4595. 400p. 1983. 16.95 (ISBN 0-399-12777-1, Putnam). Putnam Pub Group.
Trinity's Child. William Prochnau. 416p. 1985. pap. 3.95 (ISBN 0-425-07787-X). Berkley Pub.
Trinkum-Trinkums of Fifty Years. F. B. Kettlewell. LC 76-24119. 1976. Repr. of 1927 ed. lib. bdg. 27.50 (ISBN 0-8414-5505-8). Folcroft.
Trio. Dorothy D. Baker. LC 77-5686. 1977. lib. bdg. 35.00x (ISBN 0-8371-9647-7, BATR). Greenwood.
Trio. Osbert Sitwell. LC 78-107738. (Essay Index Reprint Ser). 1938. 18.00 (ISBN 0-8369-1535-6). Ayer Co Pubs.
Trio: A Book of Stories, Plays & Poems. 6th ed. Harold P. Simonson. 784p. pap. text ed. 20.50t scp (ISBN 0-06-046187-X, HarpC). Har-Row.
Trio Five. Dennis Greig et al. (Trio Poetry Ser.). 72p. 1987. pap. 6.95 (ISBN 0-85640-376-8, Pub. by Blackstaff Pr). Longwood Pub Group.
Trio for Piano, Violin & Cello. Rebecca Clarke. LC 80-20960. (Women Composer Ser.: No. 5). (Illus.). 64p. 1980. Repr. of 1928 ed. 26.50 (ISBN 0-306-76053-3). Da Capo.
Trio for Piano, Violin & Cello in D Minor, Opus 11. Fanny Hensel. LC 80-20958. (Women Composer Ser.: No. 6). (Illus.). 58p. 1980. Repr. of 1850 ed. lib. bdg. 26.50 (ISBN 0-306-76052-5). Da Capo.
Trio in E Minor for Piano, Flute & Cello: Opus 45. Louise Farrenc. LC 78-31122. (Women Composers Ser.: No. 3). 86p. 1979. Repr. of 1862 ed. 27.50 (ISBN 0-306-79553-1). Da Capo.
Trio in G. Al Glover. (Illus.). 92p. (Orig.). 1971. pap. 3.00 (ISBN 0-686-05063-0). Frontier Press Calif.
Trio: New Poets from Edinburgh. Roderick Watson et al. (Illus.). 1971. 4.50 (ISBN 0-912284-14-5); pap. 2.50 (ISBN 0-912284-13-7). New Rivers Pr.
Trio of Talks. Gerard Smith. 44p. pap. 4.95 (ISBN 0-87462-440-1). Marquette.
Trio Poetry. Will Colhoun et al. (Trio Peotry Ser.: 1). 72p. 1980. pap. 1.50 (ISBN 0-85640-164-1, Pub. by Blackstaff Pr). Longwood Pub Group.
Trio Poetry. Damian Gorman et al. (Trio Poetry Ser.: 2). 72p. (Orig.). 1981. pap. 1.50 (ISBN 0-85640-216-8, Pub. by Blackstaff Pr). Longwood Pub Group.
Trio Poetry. Johnston Kirkpatrick et al. (Trio Poetry Ser.: 3). 72p. (Orig.). 1982. pap. 5.95 (ISBN 0-85640-276-1, Pub. by Blackstaff Pr). Longwood Pub Group.
Trio: Portrait Intimate. Aram Saroyan. 272p. 1986. pap. 4.95 (ISBN 0-14-008884-9). Penguin.
Trio: Portrait of an Intimate Friendship. Aram Saroyan. 1985. 15.95 (ISBN 0-671-50919-5, Pub. by Linden Pr). S&S.
Trio Waltz. (Ballroom Dance Ser.). 1985. lib. bdg. 64.50 (ISBN 0-87700-816-7). Revisionist Pr.
Trio Waltz. (Ballroom Dance Ser.). 1986. lib. bdg. 79.95 (ISBN 0-8490-3417-5). Gordon Pr.
Trio 4. Andrew Elliott et al. (Trio Poetry Ser.). 69p. (Orig.). 1985. pap. 5.95 (ISBN 0-85640-333-4, Pub. by Blackstaff Pr). Longwood Pub Group.
Triod' Postnaja see Tserkovno-Pjevcheskiji Sbornik.
Triod' Tsvjetnaja see Tserkovno-Pjevcheskiji Sbornik.
Triometon. (Specifications for Plant Protection Products Ser.: No. 44). 1977. pap. 7.50 (ISBN 92-5-100553-2, F2021, FAO). UNIPUB.
Triomphe de la Raison. Romain Rolland. 88p. 1971. 4.95 (ISBN 0-686-55278-4). French & Eur.
Trionfo Di Camilla, Regina De 'Volsci. Giovanni Bononcini. Ed. by Howard M. Brown. LC 76-21029. (Italian Opera 1640-1770 Ser.: Vol. 17). 1978. lib. bdg. 77.00 (ISBN 0-8240-2616-0). Garland Pub.
Trionfo di Clelia. Johann A. Hasse & Howard M. Brown. (Italian Opera Ser., 1640-1770: No. 2). 83.00 (ISBN 0-8240-4822-9). Garland Pub.
Trip. Ezra Keats. LC 77-24907. (Illus.). 32p. (gr. k-3). 1978. PLB 12.88 (ISBN 0-688-84123-6). Greenwillow.
Trip. Ezra J. Keats. (ps-3). 1987. pap. 3.95 (ISBN 0-688-07328-X, Mulberry). Morrow.
Trip. Mercer Mayer. LC 87-83013. (Golden Easy Readers Ser.). (Illus.). 40p. (gr. k-2). 1988. 3.95 (ISBN 0-307-11661-1). Western Pub.
Trip a Go-Go. Harry Barba. (Mini-Book Ser). (Orig.). 1970. pap. 1.50 (ISBN 0-911906-03-7). Harian Creative.
Trip Across the Plains in Eighteen Forty-Nine. Martha M. Morgan. 32p. 1983. pap. 4.95 (ISBN 0-87770-295-0). Ye Galleon.
Trip Around Buzzards Bay Shores. E. G. Perry. LC 76-3145. (Illus.). 1976. Repr. 25.00 (ISBN 0-88492-013-5). W S Sullwold.
Trip Around the World Quilt. Date not set. pap. 4.98 (ISBN 0-317-03203-8). Gick.
Trip Around the World Quilts. Blanche Young & Helen Young. (Illus.). 96p. pap. text ed. 13.95 (ISBN 0-914881-16-7). C & T Pub.
Trip Day. Harriet Ziefert. (Illus.). (gr. 2-5). 1987. 7.95 (ISBN 0-316-98765-4). Little.
Trip Day (Mr. Rose's Class) Harriet Ziefert. (Illus.). 64p. 1988. pap. 2.50 (ISBN 0-553-15618-7, Skylark). Bantam.
Trip from California to Carolina. Robert Pope. LC 85-90241. 57p. 1987. 7.95 (ISBN 0-533-06743-X). Vantage.
Trip from the Dalles, Oregon, to Fort Owen, Montana & Overland Diary. Charles A. Frush & William H. Frush. 15p. 1986. pap. write for info. (ISBN 0-87770-302-7). Ye Galleon.
Trip into Your Unconscious. W. A. Mambert & Frank Foster. LC 72-12393. 200p. 1973. 12.50 (ISBN 0-87491-147-8); pap. 4.95 (ISBN 0-87491-148-6). Acropolis.
Trip of a Drip. Vicki Cobb. (How the World Works Science Ser.). (Illus.). 64p. (gr. 3-5). 1986. 11.95 (ISBN 0-316-14900-4). Little.
Trip on a Jet Plane: Photos & Fun for Boys & Girls. Peggy Space. (Sarah Ser.). (Illus.). 32p. (gr. 3-7). 1981. pap. 2.50 (ISBN 0-942772-00-8). Image Pubns.
Trip Out, Fall Back. Joanne Kyger. (Illus.). 1974. wrappers 5.00 (ISBN 0-913537-12-8). Arif.
Trip Relationships in Urban Areas. H. Holzapfel. 190p. 1986. text ed. 38.00 (ISBN 0-566-05235-0, Pub. by Gower Pub England). Gower Pub Co.
Trip Through Cambodia. Bridgette Diep. LC 73-159478. (Illus.). 32p. (ps-3). 8.95 (ISBN 0-87592-054-3). Scroll Pr.
Trip Through the Magic Valley. Florence Barton. (Illus.). pap. 5.95 (ISBN 0-89015-421-X). Eakin Pr.
Trip Through the Seasons. Allen Miles. 66p. 1984. 4.45 (ISBN 0-89697-156-2). Intl Univ Pr.
Trip Through Time. Donald Salvucci. (Literacy Volunteers of America Readers Ser.). 48p. (Orig.). 1983. pap. 1.95 (ISBN 0-8428-9615-5). Cambridge Bk.
Trip Through Time: Principles of Historical Geology. John D. Cooper et al. 608p. 1986. text ed. 39.95 (ISBN 0-675-20140-3). Merrill.
Trip to a Pow Wow. Richard Red Hawk. (Illus.). 45p. (Orig.). (gr. k-3). 1988. pap. 5.95 (ISBN 0-940113-14-7). Sierra Oaks Pub.
Trip to Bodie Bluff & the Dead Sea of the Westin 1863. J. Ross Browne. Pref. by William R. Jones. (Illus.). 1978. pap. 3.95 (ISBN 0-89646-076-2). Outbooks.
Trip to Heaven. Tom Kohls. (Sunshine Ser.). 31p. 1987. pap. 2.95 (ISBN 0-8163-0708-3). Pacific Pr Pub Assn.
Trip to Italy & France. Lawrence Ferlinghetti. LC 80-36778. 64p. 1981. signed limited ed. 50.00 (ISBN 0-8112-0782-X). New Directions.
Trip to Mars. Fenton Ash. LC 74-15948. (Science Fiction Ser). (Illus.). 326p. 1975. Repr. of 1909 ed. 24.50x (ISBN 0-405-06274-5). Ayer Co Pubs.
Trip to New England: With a Character of the Country & People. Edward Ward. LC 68-57126. (Research & Source Works Ser.: No. 312). Orig. Title: Club for Colonial Reprints, Vol. (2). 1969. Repr. of 1905 ed. 19.00 (ISBN 0-8337-3686-8). B Franklin.
Trip to the Dentist. Margot Linn. LC 87-14884. (Illus.). 20p. (ps-k). 1988. 9.95i (ISBN 0-06-025829-2); PLB 10.89 (ISBN 0-06-025834-9). HarpJ.
Trip to the Doctor. Margot Linn. LC 87-15004. (Illus.). 20p. (ps-k). 1988. 9.95i (ISBN 0-06-025839-X); PLB 10.89 (ISBN 0-06-025843-8). HarpJ.
Trip to the Jungle. Susan Butler. (Illus.). 40p. (Orig.). (ps-2). 1978. pap. 3.95 (ISBN 0-931416-00-0). Open Books.
Trip to the Moon see Gulliveriana, No. 1.
Trip to the Moon: Containing an Account of the Island of Noibla, 2 vols. in 1. Francis Gentleman. Ed. by Michael F. Shugrue. (Flowering of the Novel, 1740-1775 Ser.: Vol. 68). 1975. lib. bdg. 61.00 (ISBN 0-8240-1167-8). Garland Pub.
Trip to the People's Republic of China: The Great Adventure. Harold L. Enarson. 63p. (Orig.). 1975. pap. 2.50x (ISBN 0-8142-0261-6). Ohio St U Pr.
Trip to the Prairies & in the Interior of North America 1837-1838 Travel Notes. Francesco Arese. LC 74-12556. (Illus.). 216p. 1974. Repr. of 1934 ed. lib. bdg. 20.00x (ISBN 0-8154-0496-4). Cooper Sq.
Trip to the Rockies. B. R. Corwin. LC 78-39693. (Select Bibliographies Reprint Ser). 1972. Repr. of 1890 ed. 9.50 (ISBN 0-8369-9934-7). Ayer Co Pubs.
Trip to the West & Texas: Far Western Frontier. Amos Andrew Parker. LC 72-9463. (Illus.). 1972. Repr. of 1835 ed. 22.00 (ISBN 0-405-04991-9). Ayer Co Pubs.
Trip to the West Indies. E. W. Howe. (Collected Works of E. W. Howe). 1988. Repr. of 1910 ed. lib. bdg. 59.00x. Am Biog Serv.
Trip to the West Indies see Collected Works.
Trip to Venus: A Novel. John Munro. LC 75-10655. (Classics of Science Fiction Ser.). 254p. 1976. 15.00 (ISBN 0-88355-360-0); pap. 10.00 (ISBN 0-88355-460-7). Hyperion Conn.
Trip to Wonderful Alaska. facs. ed. L. D. MacDowell. 33p. pap. 2.95 (ISBN 0-8466-2063-4, S63). Shorey.
Trip with Father. Hotchkis. 1979. 7.00 (ISBN 0-910312-52-4). Calif Hist.
Tripartism in Labour Policy. K. Mathur & N. R. Sheth. 1969. 11.25 (ISBN 0-89684-520-6). Orient Bk Dist.
Tripartite Declaration of Principles Concerning Multinational Enterprises & Social Policy: History, Contents, Follow-up & Relationship with Relevant Instruments of Other Organisations. Hans Gunter. (Working Paper Ser.: No. 18). iii, 29p. (Orig.). 1982. pap. 10.50 (ISBN 92-2-102909-3). Intl Labour Office.
Tripartite Life of St. Patrick. pap. text ed. 3.95 (ISBN 0-686-25557-7). Eastern Orthodox.
Tripartite Life of St. Patrick, with Other Documents Related to the Saint with Translation & Indexes, 2 vols. Ed. by Whitley Stokes. (Rolls Ser.: No. 89). Repr. of 1888 ed. Set. 88.00 (ISBN 0-8115-1165-0). Kraus Repr.
Tripartite Relationship: Government, Foreign Investors & Local Investors During Egypt's Economic Opening. Kate Gillespie. LC 83-21221. 236p. 1984. 35.00 (ISBN 0-275-91171-3, C1171). Praeger.
Tripartite Structure of Christopher Marlowe's Tamburlaine Plays & Edward II. Lawrece M. Benaquist. Ed. by James Hogg. (Elizabethan & Renaissance Studies). 200p. (Orig.). 1975. pap. 15.00 (ISBN 3-7052-0689-3, Pub. by Salzburg Studies). Longwood Pub Group.
Tripartite Technical Meeting for the Food Products & Drink Industries, Second: General Report. 1978. pap. 10.00 (ISBN 92-2-101878-4, ILO107, ILO). UNIPUB.
Triplanetary. E. E. Smith. (Lensman Ser.: No. 1). 1982. pap. 2.95 (ISBN 0-425-09055-8). Berkley Pub.
Triple. Ken Follett. LC 78-73869. 1980. 18.95 (ISBN 0-87795-223-X, Arbor Hse). Morrow.
Triple. Ken Follett. 352p. 1980. pap. 4.50 (ISBN 0-451-13988-7, Sig). NAL.
Triple Bond: Audience, Actors & Renaissance Playwrights. Ed. by Joseph G. Price. LC 74-15140. 256p. 1975. 24.95x (ISBN 0-271-01177-7). Pa St U Pr.
Triple Collision of Modernization. Harlan Cleveland. 17p. 1979. pap. 1.50 (ISBN 0-89940-000-0). LBJ Sch Pub Aff.
Triple Crown. Jon L. Breen. 192p. 1986. 13.95 (ISBN 0-8027-5627-1). Walker & Co.
Triple Crown: Chicano, Puerto Rican & Cuban American Poetry. Roberto Duran & Judith Ortiz Cofer. LC 87-70081. 168p. 1987. pap. 10.00 (ISBN 0-916950-71-9). Biling Rev-Pr.
Triple Demism of Sun Yat-Sen (San Min Chu I) Sun Yat-Sen. LC 78-38069. Repr. of 1931 ed. 50.00 (ISBN 0-404-56929-3). AMS Pr.
Triple Detente. Piers Anthony. 256p. 1988. pap. 3.95 (ISBN 0-8125-3129-9). Tor Bks.
Triple Divide: High Sierra Hiking Guide. 2nd ed. Andy Selters. (Illus.). 120p. 1987. pap. 7.95 (ISBN 0-89997-088-5). Wilderness Pr.
Triple-Entry Bookkeeping & Income Momentum, Vol. 18. Yuji Ijiri. LC 82-71118. (Studies in Accounting Research). 53p. 1982. 9.00 (ISBN 0-86539-041-X). Am Accounting.
Triple Espera: Novelas Cortas de Hispanoamerica. Ed. by Djelal Kadir. 235p. (Span.). 1976. pap. text ed. 10.00 net (ISBN 0-15-592353-6, HC). HarBraceJ.

Triple Fugue. facs. ed. Osbert Sitwell. LC 74-134980. (Short Story Index Reprint Ser). 1925. 18.00 (ISBN 0-8369-3710-4). Ayer Co Pubs.
Triple Goddess: An Exploration of the Archetypal Feminine. Adam Mclean. 1987. pap. 15.00 (ISBN 0-317-57172-9). Phanes Pr.
Triple Hoax. Carolyn Keene. (Nancy Drew Ser.: No. 57). (Illus.). 192p. (gr. 3-7). 1987. pap. 3.50 (ISBN 0-671-64278-2). Wanderer Bks.
Triple Hoax. Carolyn Keene. (Nancy Drew Boxed Gift Set Ser.: No. 57). (gr. 2-7). 1984. 8.85. Wanderer Bks.
Triple Jeopardy. Richard Speight. LC 87-40405. 272p. 1988. 16.95 (ISBN 0-446-51394-6). Warner Bks.
Triple Jump Encyclopedia. Ernie Bullard & Larry Knuth. LC 77-4265. 1977. pap. 9.95 (ISBN 0-87095-057-6, Athletic). Gldn West Bks.
Triple Murder. Daniel D. Mancini. 1986. 7.95 (ISBN 0-533-06295-0). Vantage.
Triple Nickles: America's First All-Black Paratroop Unit. Bradley Biggs. LC 85-28732. (Illus.). x, 92p. 1986. 17.50 (ISBN 0-208-02037-3, Archon Bks). Shoe String.
Triple Secreto Del Espiritu Santo. James H. McConkey. Tr. by Beatrice Agostini from Eng. Orig. Title: Three Fold Secret of the Holy Spirit. 112p. (Span.). 1980. pap. 2.50 (ISBN 0-311-09090-7). Casa Bautista.
Triple Soul: Browning's Theory of Knowledge. Norton B. Crowell. 235p. 1963. text ed. 29.50x (ISBN 0-8290-0228-6). Irvington.
Triple Stream. Antony Brett-James. 1978. Repr. of 1954 ed. lib. bdg. 36.50 (ISBN 0-8495-0351-5). Arden Lib.
Triple Stream: Four Centuries of English, French & German Literature 1531-1930. Anthony Brett-James. LC 74-13161. 1973. lib. bdg. 27.00 (ISBN 0-8414-5306-3). Folcroft.
Triple Struggle: Latin American Peasant Women. Audrey Bronstein. 268p. 1983. 20.00 (ISBN 0-89608-180-X); pap. 8.50 (ISBN 0-89608-179-6). South End Pr.
Triple Thinkers. Edmund Wilson. 1976. Repr. of 1976 ed. lib. bdg. 19.00x (ISBN 0-374-98651-7, Octagon). Hippocrene Bks.
Triple Thinkers & the Wound & the Bow: A Combined Volume. Edmund Wilson. 259p. 1984. pap. 11.95x (ISBN 0-930350-67-7). NE U Pr.
Triple Threat. Helen MacInnes. 22.95 (ISBN 0-89190-104-3, Pub. by Am Repr). Amereon Ltd.
Triple Trouble at Fairwood High, No. 3. Nancy Norton. (Homeroom Ser.). (gr. 7-12). 1988. pap. 2.50 (ISBN 0-590-41975-7). Scholastic Inc.
Triple Way. George Peck. LC 77-79824. 321p. (Orig.). 1977. pap. 2.50x (ISBN 0-87574-213-0). Pendle Hill.
Triple Western. Incl. Gun Brat. Wes Yancey; Breed Blood. Ben Jefferson; Renegade Rides. Brett Austin. 288p. pap. 2.75 (ISBN 0-505-51788-4, Pub. by Tower Bks). Leisure NY.
Triple Your Reading Speed. rev. ed. Wade Cutler. 193p. 1987. pap. 7.95 (ISBN 0-13-930975-6). P-H.
Triple Your Reading Speed. Wade E. Cutler. LC 70-93505. (Prog. Bk.). 1970. lib. bdg. 7.50 o. p. (ISBN 0-668-02084-9); pap. 5.00 (ISBN 0-668-02083-0). Arco.
Triplet. Timothy Zahn. 1987. pap. 3.95 (ISBN 0-671-65341-5). Baen Bks.
Triplet State ODMR Spectroscopy: Techniques & Applications to Biophysical Systems. Ed. by Richard H. Clarke. LC 81-10486. 566p. 1982. 78.00 (ISBN 0-471-07988-X, Pub. by Wiley-Interscience). Wiley.
Triplet States One. A. Devaquet et al. (Topics in Current Chemistry Ser.: Vol. 54). (Illus.). iv, 164p. 1975. 42.00 (ISBN 0-387-07107-5). Springer-Verlag.
Triplets. Mollie Gregory. 1988. 18.95 (ISBN 0-531-15067-4). Watts.
Tripods Trilogy, 3 bks. John Christopher. Incl. White Mountains; the City of Gold & Lead; Pool of Fire. (gr. 5-9). 1980. Boxed Set. pap. 11.95 (ISBN 0-02-042570-8, Collier). Macmillan.
Tripods Trilogy. 2nd ed. John Christopher. 224p. (YA) (gr. 7 up). 1970. Boxed Set. pap. 11.95 (ISBN 0-02-042571-6, Collier). Macmillan.
Tripoli: A Modern Arab City. John Gulick. LC 67-14340. (Middle Eastern Studies: No. 12). (Illus.). 1967. 19.50x (ISBN 0-674-90915-1). Harvard U Pr.
Tripoli: Portrait of a City. Philip Ward. (Libya Past & Present Ser.: Vol. 1). (Illus.). 12.50 (ISBN 0-902675-06-0). Oleander Pr.
Trippensee Transparent Simplified Celestial Globe. T. R. Stoeckley. 17p. 1968. pap. text ed. 5.65 (ISBN 0-943956-03-X). Trippensee Pub.
Tripping Devices for Radical & Heavy Vertical Drilling Machines. (Guidance Note PM Ser.: No. 10). 3p. (Orig.). 1987. pap. text ed. 5.00 (ISBN 0-11-883974-8, HM1471, Pub. by Her Maj Station Ofc). UNIPUB.
Tripping in America. John Bennett. 160p. 1984. pap. 5.95 (ISBN 0-912824-33-6). Vagabond Pr.
Trippings of Tom Pepper; or the Results of Romancing: An Autobiography, 2 vols. Charles F. Briggs. LC 78-64066. (Harry Franco, pseud.). Repr. of 1847 ed. o.p. 75.00 set (ISBN 0-404-17170-2). AMS Pr.
Trips & Tails: Family Camps, Short Hikes, & View Roads Around the North Cascades, Vol. 1. 3rd ed. E. M. Sterling. (Illus.). 220p. 1985. pap. 9.95 (ISBN 0-89886-115-2). Mountaineers.
Trips & Tours Manual. Kenneth Ostrand. 147p. Date not set. 29.95 (ISBN 0-914951-04-1). LERN.
Trips & Trails. 3 ed. E. M. Sterling. Incl. One: Family Camps, Short Hikes & View Roads Around the North Cascades. (Trips & Trails Ser.). (Illus.). 220p. 1985. 9.95; Two: Olympics, South Cascades, & Mt. Rainier. (Trips & Trails Ser.). 228p. 1983. 9.95 (ISBN 0-89886-069-5). Mountaineers.
Trips & Treks see New Jersey Day Trips: A Guide to Outings in New Jersey, New York, Pennsylvania & Delaware.
Trips & Trivia: A Guide to Western Massachusetts. 2nd ed. Linda K. Fuller. Ed. by Robert S. Friedman. LC 87-22297. (Illus.). 1988. pap. 14.95 (ISBN 0-89865-552-8). Donning Co.
Trips for Those over Fifty. Harriet Webster. Ed. by Mark Corsey. (Magazine Guidebook Ser.). (Illus.). 176p. (Orig.). 1988. pap. 9.95 (ISBN 0-89909-158-X). Yankee Bks.
Trips: New York City & Out-of-Town. rev. ed. Elizabeth M. Murray. (Illus.). 112p. 1980. pap. 3.95 (ISBN 0-936426-10-1). Play Schs.
Trips on Twos. rev. ed. Leslie Bergstrom & Kim Bergstrom. (Illus.). 72p. pap. 4.50 (ISBN 0-9612668-2-1). Talk Town.
Trips on Wheels. Leslie Bergstrom. (Illus.). 128p. pap. 7.95 (ISBN 0-9612668-1-3). Talk Town.
Trips with Children in New England. 3rd ed. Harriet Webster. LC 85-50067. (Yankee Magazine Guidebook Ser.). (Illus.). 256p. 1985. pap. 9.95 (ISBN 0-89909-075-3). Yankee Bks.
Tripticks. Ann Quin. 160p. 1979. 9.95 (ISBN 0-7145-0816-0, Dist by Scribner). M Boyars Pubs.
Triptych. Max Frisch. Tr. by Geoffrey Skelton. LC 80-8747. (Helen & Kurt Wolff Bk.). 128p. 1981. 7.95 (ISBN 0-15-191157-6). HarBraceJ.
Triptych. Sy Kahn et al. 1964. 2.00 (ISBN 0-686-20736-X). Sydon.
Triptych. rev. ed. Claude Simon. Tr. by Helen R. Lane from Fr. 180p. (Orig.). 1986. pap. 8.95 (ISBN 0-7145-3787-X). Riverrun NY.
Triptych for the Atomic Age. John W. Andrews. 12.00 (ISBN 0-8283-1281-8). Branden Pub Co.
Triptych: Gifts of the Spirit Through the Illumined Road. Dane Rudhyar. LC 87-31476. 318p. 1987. lib. bdg. 11.95x (ISBN 0-8095-6306-1). Borgo Pr.
Tripura: A Profile. Surendra N. Chatterjee. (Illus.). xii, 67p. 1984. text ed. 22.50x (ISBN 0-86590-327-1, Pub. by Inter-India Pubns N Delhi). Apt Bks.
Tripwire. Jay Brandon. 250p. (Orig.). 1987. pap. 3.50 (ISBN 0-553-26279-3). Bantam.
Tripwire. Brian Garfield. 185p. 1985. pap. 3.95 (ISBN 0-317-19148-9). Mysterious Pr.
Trisagion. Hellenic College-Holy Cross Faculty. 16p. 1986. pap. 0.50 (ISBN 0-917651-25-1). Holy Cross Orthodox.
Triscomy, Twenty-One: An International Symposium. Ed. by G. R. Burgio et al. (Human Genetics Supplementa Ser.: Vol. 2). (Illus.). 265p. 1981. pap. 27.00 (ISBN 0-387-10653-7). Springer-Verlag.
Trisection Problem. Robert C. Yates. LC 77-176232. (Classics in Mathematics Education Ser.: Vol. 3). (Illus.). 68p. 1971. 8.00 (ISBN 0-87353-038-1). NCTM.
Trish for President. Lael Littke. LC 84-4587. 160p. (gr. 7 up). 1984. 13.95 (ISBN 0-15-290512-X, HJ). HarBraceJ.
Trish for President. Lael Littke. (gr. k up). 1986. pap. 2.50 (ISBN 0-671-55175-2). Archway.
Trish for President. Lael Littke. (gr. 4-9). 1988. pap. 2.50. Scholastic Inc.
Tristan. Ed. by C. E. Pickford. 676p. Facsimile. 45.00 (ISBN 0-85991-157-8, Pub. by Boydell & Brewer). Longwood Pub Group.
Tristan. Suzanne Schuurman. 248p. 1987. 19.95 (ISBN 0-85398-248-1); pap. 9.50 (ISBN 0-85398-249-X). G Ronald Pub.
Tristan. Gottfried Von Strassburg. (Classics Ser). 1960. pap. 4.95 (ISBN 0-14-044098-4). Penguin.
Tristan. Gottfried Von Strassburg. Ed. by Francis G. Gentry. (German Library). 320p. 1988. 27.50x (ISBN 0-8264-0314-X); pap. 12.95x (ISBN 0-8264-0315-8). Continuum.
Tristan & Iseult, Pts. 1 & 2. Tr. by Jessie L. Weston from Ger. LC 71-141784. Repr. of 1899 ed. 22.50 ea. Pt. 1 (ISBN 0-404-00472-5). Pt. 2 (ISBN 0-404-00473-3). Set. 45.00 (ISBN 0-404-10038-4). AMS Pr.
Tristan & Isolde. Richard Wagner. Ed. by Nicholas John. Tr. by Andrew Porter from Ger. (English National Opera Guide Ser.: No. 6 Libretto, Articles). (Illus., Orig.). 1981. pap. 4.95 (ISBN 0-7145-3849-3). Riverrun NY.
Tristan & Isolde: Complete Orchestral Score. Richard Wagner. Ed. by Felix Mottl. 672p. 1973. pap. 18.95 (ISBN 0-486-22915-7). Dover.
Tristan & Isolt: A Study of the Sources of the Romance, 2 vols. in 1. 2nd ed. Gertrude Loomis. LC 71-131396. (Research & Source Work Ser.: No. 541). 1970. Set. 32.50 (ISBN 0-8337-3161-0). B Franklin.
Tristan & the Round Table: a Translation of La Tavola Ritonda. Tr. by Anne Shaver from Ital. LC 82-14140. (Medieval & Renaissance Texts & Studies: Vol. 28). (Illus.). 368p. 1983. 15.00 (ISBN 0-86698-053-9). Medieval & Renaissance NY.
Tristan De Luna, Conquistador of the Old South: A Study of Spanish Imperial Strategy. Herbert I. Priestley. LC 80-21168. (Perspectives in American History Ser.: No. 49). (Illus.). 215p. 1981. Repr. lib. bdg. 25.00x (ISBN 0-87991-375-4). Porcupine Pr.
Tristan Legend: A Study in Sources. Sigmund Eisner. LC 69-18373. Repr. of 1969 ed. 51.80 (ISBN 0-8357-9474-1, 2015293). Bks Demand UMI.
Tristan Studies. Renee L. Curtis. 96p. 1985. 27.00 (ISBN 0-85991-188-8, Pub. by Boydell & Brewer). Longwood Pub Group.
Tristan und Isolde in Auswahl. 4th ed. Strassburg Gottfried. Ed. by Friedrich Maurer. (Sammlung Goeschen, No.2204). 1977. 3.90x (ISBN 3-11-006841-9). De Gruyter.
Tristana. Benito P. Galdos. (Easy Readers, Series B). 96p. (Span.). 1976. pap. text ed. 4.95 (ISBN 0-88436-279-5, 70269). EMC.
Triste Deleytacion: An Anonymous Fifteenth Century Castilian Romance. Ed. by E. Michael Gerli. LC 82-15742. 160p. (Orig., Span. & Eng.). 1983. lib. bdg. 14.95 (ISBN 0-87840-086-9). Georgetown U Pr.
Triste Historia De Mi Vida Oscura: A Peticion Popular. Armando Couto. LC 78-70332. 1978. pap. 5.95 (ISBN 0-89729-196-4). Ediciones.
Tristes Tropiques. rev. ed. Claude Levi-Strauss. (Illus., Fr.). 1984. 9.00x (ISBN 2-266-01394-7). Adlers Foreign Bks.
Tristes-Tropiques. Claude Levi-Strauss. Tr. by John Weightman & Doreen Weightman. LC 79-162975. (Illus.). 1974. pap. 10.95 (ISBN 0-689-70122-5, 48). Atheneum.
Tristes Tropiques. Claude Levi-Strauss. 1982. pap. 4.95 (ISBN 0-671-45850-7). WSP.
Tristessa. Jack Kerouac. (McGraw-Hill Paperbacks Ser.). 1978. pap. text ed. 5.95 (ISBN 0-07-034205-9). McGraw.
Tristesse de Saint Louis: Jazz under the Nazis. Mike Zwerin. 224p. 1987. 16.95 (ISBN 0-688-06537-6, Pub. by Beech Tree Bks). Morrow.
Tristia. Ovid. Tr. by L. R. Lind. LC 73-88363. 180p. 1975. 10.00x (ISBN 0-8203-0330-5). U of Ga Pr.
Tristia, & Ex Ponto. Ovid. (Loeb Classical Library: No. 151). 13.95x (ISBN 0-674-99167-2). Harvard U Pr.
Tristia, Ibis, Ex Ponto, Halieutica, Fragmenta. Ovid. Ed. by S. G. Owen. (Oxford Classical Texts Ser). 1915. 18.95x (ISBN 0-19-814626-4). Oxford U Pr.
Tristia of Ovid. Tr. by David R. Slavitt from Lat. (Illus.). 143p. 1986. 14.95 (ISBN 0-934958-04-1). Bellflower.
Tristia: Poems by Osip Mandelstam. Tr. by Bruce McClelland. LC 86-32305. (Illus.). 120p. 1987. 13.95 (ISBN 0-88268-041-2). Station Hill Pr.
Tristitia Christi: Complete Works of St. Thomas More, Vol. 14, Pts. 1 & 2. St. Thomas More. Ed. by Clarence H. Miller. LC 63-7949. 1976. 92.00t (ISBN 0-300-01793-6). Yale U Pr.
Tristram Shandy see also Life & Opinions of Tristram Shandy, Gentleman.
Tristram Shandy. Max Byrd. Ed. by Claude Rawson. (Unwin Critical Library). 192p. 1985. text ed. 27.95x (ISBN 0-04-800033-7). Unwin Hyman.
Tristram Shandy. Laurence Sterne. (Airmont Classics Ser.). (gr. 11 up). 1967. pap. 1.95 (ISBN 0-8049-0152-X, CL-152). Airmont.
Tristram Shandy. Laurence Sterne. 1978. pap. 4.95x (ISBN 0-460-01617-2, Evman). Biblio Dist.
Tristram Shandy. Laurence Sterne. pap. 4.95 (ISBN 0-451-51868-3, CE1868, Sig Classics). NAL.
Tristram Shandy. Laurence Sterne. Ed. by Howard Anderson. LC 79-277. (Norton Critical Editions Ser.). 1980. 24.95 (ISBN 0-393-01244-1); pap. 10.95x (ISBN 0-393-95034-4). Norton.
Tristram Shandy Notes. Charles Parish. (Orig.). 1968. pap. 3.95 (ISBN 0-8220-1311-8). Cliffs.
Tristram Shandy: The Life & Opinions of a Gentleman. Ed. by James A. Work. 722p. 1940. pap. text ed. write for info. (ISBN 0-02-430030-6). Macmillan.
Tristram Shandy: The Life & Opinions of Tristram Shandy, Gentleman. Laurence J. Sterne. Ed. by James A. Work. 1940. pap. 11.49scp (ISBN 0-672-63128-8). Odyssey Pr.
Trisulti: Art & Architecture. James Hogg. (Analecta Cartusiana Ser.: No. 74-2). (Orig.). 1984. pap. 25.00 (ISBN 3-7052-0110-7, Pub. by Salzburg Studies). Longwood Pub Group.
Triticale. Ed. by R. A. Forsberg. 82p. 1985. 12.00 (ISBN 0-89118-519-4). Crop Sci Soc Am.
Triticale: Results & Problems. Arne Muntzing. (Advances in Plant Breeding Ser.: Vol. 10). (Illus.). 103p. (Orig.). 1979. pap. text ed. 35.00 (ISBN 3-489-76210-X). Parey Sci Pubs.
Tritium & Its Compounds. 2nd ed. Eustace A. Evans. LC 75-313264. (Illus.). pap. 160.00 (ISBN 0-317-41698-7, 2025716). Bks Demand UMI.
Tritium & Other Environmental Isotopes in the Hydrological Cycle. (Technical Reports Ser.: No. 73). (Illus.). 83p. 1967. pap. 10.50 (ISBN 92-0-145067-2, IDC73, IAEA). UNIPUB.
Tritium & Other Radionuclide Labeled Organic Compounds Incorporated in Genetic Material. LC 79-84486. (NCRP Reports Ser.: No. 63). 1979. 15.00 (ISBN 0-913392-47-2). NCRP Pubns.
Tritium in Organic Chemistry. E. Buncel. (Isotopes in Organic Chemistry Ser.: Vol. 4). 300p. 1978. 108.00 (ISBN 0-444-41741-9). Elsevier.
Tritium in Some Typical Ecosystems. (Technical Reports Ser.: No. 207). (Illus.). 118p. 1981. pap. 20.00 (ISBN 92-0-125181-5, IDC207, IAEA). UNIPUB.
Tritium in the Environment. LC 79-63514. (NCRP Reports Ser.: No. 62). 1979. 14.00 (ISBN 0-913392-46-4). NCRP Pubns.
Tritium Measurement Techniques. LC 76-16301. (NCRP Reports Ser.: No. 47). 1976. 13.00 (ISBN 0-913392-29-4). NCRP Pubns.
Triton. Daniel Torres. (Rocco Vargas Adventures Ser.). (Illus.). 50p. (Orig.). 1986. pap. 10.95 (ISBN 0-87416-025-1). Catalan Communs.
Triton in Exile: WW II Poems. Starling. 1984. 15.00 (ISBN 0-317-02727-1). Byzantine Pr.
Tritonian Ring. L. Sprague De Camp. LC 76-56969. (Illus.). 1977. Repr. of 1953 ed. 12.50 (ISBN 0-913896-09-8). Owlswick Pr.
Tritton's Guide to Better Wine & Beer Making for Beginners. S. M. Tritton. (Illus.). 160p. (Orig.). 1969. pap. 4.50 (ISBN 0-571-09171-7). Faber & Faber.
Triumph. Juanita M. Boeckel. 1986. 11.95 (ISBN 0-533-06665-4). Vantage.
Triumph. Ernest K. Gann. 408p. 1986. 17.45 (ISBN 0-671-52829-7). S&S.
Triumph. Ernest K. Gann. 1987. pap. 4.50 (ISBN 0-671-64549-8). PB.
Triumph. Arthur Moore. (Orig.). 1979. pap. 2.50 (ISBN 0-89083-522-5). Zebra.
Triumph. Steve Swanson. (Pennypinchers Ser.). 128p. (gr. 5-9). 1984. pap. 2.95 (ISBN 0-89191-793-4, 57935). Cook.
Triumph see First Transatlantic Flight, Nineteen-Nineteen.
Triumph & the Cycles. Adrian C. Van Dyk, Jr. (Illus.). 96p. (Orig.). 1978. pap. 5.95 (ISBN 0-686-02012-X). Van Dyk.
Triumph & the Fall of the Moghul Empire with Important Chronological Lists of the Mohammedan Dynasties, 2 vols. Stanley Lane-Poole. 265p. 1987. Repr. of 1906 ed. Set. 189.75 (ISBN 0-89901-326-0). Found Class Reprints.
Triumph & Tragedy, 6 vols. Winston S. Churchill. 1986. pap. 9.95 (ISBN 0-395-41060-6). HM.
Triumph & Tragedy see Second World War.
Triumph at Perth: The America's Cup Story. Bruce Stannard et al. (Illus.). 212p. 1987. 39.95 (ISBN 0-911378-74-X). Sheridan.
Triumph GT6 Mk III Driver's Handbook. British Leyland Motors Staff. 66p. Date not set. 8.95 (ISBN 0-946489-84-X). Bentley.
Triumph GT6 Mk III Parts Catalogue. British Leyland Motors Staff. 140p. Date not set. 19.95 (ISBN 0-948207-93-0). Bentley.
Triumph in Adversity: Studies in Hungarian Civilization in Honor of Professor Ferenc Somogyi. Ed. by Steven B. Vardy & Agnes H. Vardy. (East European Monographs: No. 253). 480p. 1988. 55.00 (ISBN 0-88033-150-X). East Eur Quarterly.
Triumph in Defeat: Infallibility, Vatican I, & the French Minority Bishops. Margaret O'Gara. 352p. 1988. 48.95x (ISBN 0-8132-0641-3). Cath U Pr.
Triumph in the West. Arthur Bryant. LC 73-22634. (Illus.). 438p. 1974. Repr. of 1959 ed. lib. bdg. 69.50x (ISBN 0-8371-7344-2, BRTR). Greenwood.
Triumph of Achilles. Louise Gluck. 60p. 1987. pap. 7.50 (ISBN 0-88001-082-7). Ecco Pr.
Triumph of Achilles, No. 32. Louise Gluck. (American Poetry Ser.). 64p. 1985. 13.50 (ISBN 0-88001-081-9). Ecco Pr.
Triumph of American Painting: A History of Abstract Expressionism. Irving Sandler. (Icon Editions Ser.). (Illus.). 302p. 1976. pap. 14.95 (ISBN 0-06-430075-7, IN-75, HarpT). Har-Row.
Triumph of Art for the Public, 1785-1848, Vol. I. Elizabeth G. Holt. LC 83-60461. (Illus.). 560p. 1984. pap. 16.95x (ISBN 0-691-00349-1). Princeton U Pr.
Triumph of Barabbas. Giovanni Giglio. Tr. by E. Mosbacher. LC 74-180401. Repr. of 1937 ed. 29.00 (ISBN 0-404-56125-X). AMS Pr.
Triumph of Bolshevism: Revolution or Reaction? Stuart R. Tompkins. LC 66-22714. (Illus.). 331p. (Orig.). 1967. 19.50x (ISBN 0-8061-0727-8). U of Okla Pr.
Triumph of Conservatism: A Reinterpretation of American History, 1900-1916. Gabriel Kolko. LC 63-16588. 1977. pap. 11.95x (ISBN 0-02-916650-0). Free Pr.
Triumph of Culture: Eighteenth Century Perspectives. Paul Fritz & David Williams. LC 80-80055. (McMaster 18th Century Studies). 398p. 1979. lib. bdg. 48.00 (ISBN 0-8240-4001-5). Garland Pub.
Triumph of Death. David Rudkin. 60p. 1982. pap. 6.95 (ISBN 0-413-49110-2, NO. 3645). Heinemann Ed.
Triumph of Death & Other Unpublished & Uncollected Poems by Mary Sidney, Countess of Pembroke, 1561-1621. G. F. Waller. Ed. by James Hogg. (Elizabethan & Renaissance Studies). 227p. (Orig.). 1977. pap. 15.00 (ISBN 3-7052-0708-3, Pub. by Salzburg Studies). Longwood Pub Group.
Triumph of Death: Resurrection of Life. Stephen Sweigart. (Parpaglion Poetry Ser.: No. 8). (Orig.). 1987. Computer program. 10.00x (ISBN 0-9604252-3-3). Parpaglion.

Troia Bretanica, or Great Britaines Troy. Thomas Heywood. LC 74-80187. (English Experience Ser.: No. 667). 466p. 1974. Repr. of 1609 ed. 75.00 (ISBN 90-221-0667-5). Walter J Johnson.

Troika: Introduction to Russian Letters & Sounds. Reason A. Goodwin. LC 80-81788. (Orig.). (gr. 11-12). 1980. text ed. 14.50 (ISBN 0-936368-00-4); pap. text ed. 6.95 (ISBN 0-936368-01-2). Lexik Hse.

Troiley Lives. Steven Sher. 48p. 1985. 7.95 (ISBN 0-931694-28-0). Wampeter Pr.

Troilus & Cressida see also Tragedy of Troilus & Cressida.

Troilus & Cressida. Jane Adamson. 130p. 1988. 17.95 (ISBN 0-8057-8701-1, Twayne); pap. 8.95 (ISBN 0-8057-8704-6). G K Hall.

Troilus & Cressida. Bay Area Community College. 48p. 1981. 4.50 (ISBN 0-8403-2636-X). Kendall-Hunt.

Troilus & Cressida. William Shakespeare. Ed. by Arthur Quiller-Couch et al. (New Shakespeare Ser). 1969. pap. 5.95x (ISBN 0-521-09503-4). Cambridge U Pr.

Troilus & Cressida. William Shakespeare. Ed. by Willard E. Farnham. LC 66-12978. (Crofts Classics Ser.). 1966. pap. text ed. 0.85x (ISBN 0-88295-084-3). Harlan Davidson.

Troilus & Cressida. William Shakespeare. Ed. by David Seltzer. 1974. pap. 2.75 (ISBN 0-451-51946-9, Sig Classics). NAL.

Troilus & Cressida. William Shakespeare. Ed. by Virgil K. Whitaker. (Shakespeare Ser.). 1958. pap. 2.95 (ISBN 0-14-071413-8, Pelican). Penguin.

Troilus & Cressida. William Shakespeare. Ed. by Louis B. Wright & Virginia A. La Mar. (Folger Library). 336p. (gr. 11 up). pap. 1.95 (ISBN 0-671-49116-4). WSP.

Troilus & Cressida. William Shakespeare. Ed. by Kenneth Muir. (Oxford Shakespeare Ser.). (Illus.). 1984. 26.00x (ISBN 0-19-812903-3); pap. 6.95x (ISBN 0-19-281439-7). Oxford U Pr.

Troilus & Cressida. William Shakespeare. Ed. by Kenneth Palmer. LC 83-7987. (Arden Shakespeare Ser.). 300p. 1982. 37.00x (ISBN 0-416-47680-5, NO. 2298); pap. 7.95 (ISBN 0-416-17790-5, NO. 2305). Routledge Chapman & Hall.

Troilus & Cressida. William Shakespeare. Intro. by R. A. Foakes. 240p. 1987. pap. 3.75 (ISBN 0-14-070741-7). Penguin.

Troilus & Cressida: An Opera in Three Parts (Musical Score by Sir William Walton) 2nd ed. Christopher Hassall. (Orig.). 1976. pap. 3.75 (ISBN 0-19-338603-8). Oxford U Pr.

Troilus & Cressida in Modern English Verse. Geoffrey Chaucer. Tr. by George P. Krapp. 1957. pap. 3.16 (ISBN 0-394-70142-9, Vin, V142). Random.

Troilus & Cressida: Modern Text with Introduction. Ed. by A. L. Rowse. LC 86-11032. (Contemporary Shakespeare Ser.). 146p. (Orig.). 1986. pap. text ed. 3.45 (ISBN 0-8191-3932-7). U Pr of Amer.

Troilus & Cressida Notes. James K. Lowers. (Orig.). 1964. pap. 3.50 (ISBN 0-8220-0091-1). Cliffs.

Troilus & Criseyde see also Book of Troilus & Criseyde.

Troilus & Criseyde. Geoffrey Chaucer. 1974. 13.95x (ISBN 0-460-10992-8, Evman). Biblio Dist.

Troilus & Criseyde. Geoffrey Chaucer. Tr. by Nevill Coghill. (Classics Ser). 1971. pap. 4.95 (ISBN 0-14-044239-1). Penguin.

Troilus & Criseyde. Geoffrey Chaucer. Ed. by Barry A. Windeatt. 1983. pap. text ed. 90.00x (ISBN 0-582-49072-3). Longman.

Troilus & Criseyde. Geoffrey Chaucer. Tr. by Stanley-Wrech. 1983. 40.00x (ISBN 0-900000-55-4, Pub. by Centaur Bks). State Mutual Bk.

Troilus & Criseyde (Abridged) Geoffrey Chaucer. Ed. by D. S. Brewer & L. E. Brewer. 1977. pap. 5.95x (ISBN 0-7100-6642-2). Routledge Chapman & Hall.

Troilus & Criseyde: Studies in Interpretation. Robert A. Jelliffe. LC 73-12946. 1956. Repr. lib. bdg. 47.00 (ISBN 0-8414-5256-3). Folcroft.

Troilus-Cressida Story. Hyder E. Rollins. 1917. lib. bdg. 20.00 (ISBN 0-8414-7472-9). Folcroft.

Troilus-Cressida Story from Chaucer to Shakespeare. Hyder Rollins. LC 76-100782. (English Literature Ser., No. 33). 1970. Repr. of 1917 ed. lib. bdg. 24.95x (ISBN 0-8383-0338-2). Haskell.

Trois Ages de la Nuit. Francoise Mallet-Joris. 1968. 12.95 (ISBN 0-686-56317-4); pap. 3.95 (ISBN 0-686-56318-2). French & Eur.

Trois Albums. Victor Hugo. 1963. 22.50 (ISBN 0-686-54047-6). French & Eur.

Trois Chansonniers Francais Du XV Siecle. Ed. by Eugenie Droz et al. LC 77-26063. (Music Reprint Ser.). 1978. Repr. of 1927 ed. lib. bdg. 35.00 (ISBN 0-306-77561-1). Da Capo.

Trois Contes. Gustave Flaubert. (Coll. GF). 1963. pap. 8.95 (ISBN 0-685-11604-2, 1958). French & Eur.

Trois Contes. Gustave Flaubert. Ed. by Maynial. (Class. Garnier). pap. 29.95 (ISBN 0-685-34904-7). French & Eur.

Trois Contes. Gustave Flaubert. Ed. by Maynial. (Coll. Prestige). 49.95 (ISBN 0-685-34905-5). French & Eur.

Trois Dialogues de L'Exercice de Sauter et Voltiger en L'Air. Arcangelo Tucarro. (Books of the Monarchs of England). (Illus.). 416p. (Fr.). 1987. Repr. of 1599 ed. 115.00 (ISBN 1-85297-009-X). Archival Facsimiles.

Trois Dumas. Andre Maurois. 25.95 (ISBN 0-685-36969-2). French & Eur.

Trois Essais de Montaigne. 4th ed. Michel de Montaigne et al. 150p. 1967. 15.00 (ISBN 0-686-54778-0). French & Eur.

Trois Figures Saintes. Paul Claudel. 148p. 1953. 8.95 (ISBN 0-686-54441-2). French & Eur.

Trois Fils De Rois. Ed. by F. J. Furnivall. (EETS, ES Ser.: No. 67). Repr. of 1895 ed. 35.00 (ISBN 0-527-00271-2). Kraus Repr.

Trois Maitres. Alexandre Dumas. 288p. 1977. 19.95 (ISBN 0-686-55212-1). French & Eur.

Trois Mots Magiques. Charlotte Lamb. (Collection Harlequin Ser.). 192p. 1983. pap. 1.95 (ISBN 0-373-49367-3). Harlequin Bks.

Trois Mousquetaires. Alexandre Dumas. Ed. by Samaran. (Coll. Prestige). 35.00 (ISBN 0-685-34892-X). French & Eur.

Trois Mousquetaires, 2 vols. Alexandre Dumas. 1973. pap. 9.95 ea. French & Eur.

Trois Mousquetaires, 3 vols. Alexandre Dumas. (Illus.). 950p. 1974. Set. 160.00 (ISBN 0-686-55214-8). French & Eur.

Trois Mousquetaires. Alexandre Dumas, Sr. Ed. by Samaran. 1961. pap. 9.95 (ISBN 0-685-11605-0). French & Eur.

Trois Mousquetaires see Oeuvres Illustrees.

Trois Mousquetaires & Vingt Ans Apres. Alexandre Dumas. 1800p. 45.00 (ISBN 0-686-56508-8). French & Eur.

Trois Mousquetaires: Avec Vingt Ans Apres. Alexandre Dumas. 1800p. 1962. 35.00 (ISBN 0-686-55213-X). French & Eur.

Trois Nouvelles. Georges Duhamel. (Illus.). 25.00 (ISBN 0-686-55198-2). French & Eur.

Trois Petits Amis et la Decouverte du Gumbo. David Theriot. (Illus.). 41p. (Fr.). (gr. 3). 1979. pap. 1.25 (ISBN 0-911409-04-1). Natl Mat Dev.

Trois Pieces Medievales: Le Jeu d'Adam, le Miracle de Theophile, la Farce du Cuvier. Ed. by Arthur R. Harden. LC 67-20813. (Medieval French Literature Ser). (Orig., Fr.). 1967. pap. text ed. 9.95x (ISBN 0-89197-455-5). Irvington.

Trois Pieces Surrealistes: Les Maries de la Tour Eiffel; L'Armoire a Glace un Beau Soir; Victor ou les Enfants au Pouvoir. Ed. by Robert G. Marshall & Frederic St Aubyn. LC 75-89864. (Illus., Fr.). 1969. pap. text ed. 14.95x (ISBN 0-89197-456-3). Irvington.

Trois Portraits de Femme: La Duchesse de Devonshire, la Comtesse D'Albany, Henriette de France. Andre Maurois. (Coll. les Soirees Du Luxembourg). 21.50 (ISBN 0-685-36965-X). French & Eur.

Trois Primitifs. Joris-Karl Huysmans. (Illus.). 188p. 1966. 9.95 (ISBN 0-686-54184-7). French & Eur.

Trois Recits. Francois Mauriac. pap. 9.50 (ISBN 0-685-34306-5). French & Eur.

Trois Versions Rimees de l'Evangile De Nicodeme Par Chretien, Andre De Coutances, et un Anonyme. Chretien De Troyes et al. 1885. pap. 28.00 (ISBN 0-384-04210-4). Johnson Repr.

Trois Villes, 3 pts. Emile Zola. Incl. Lourdes; Rome; Paris. 7.95 ea. French & Eur.

Troisieme Fascicule des 150 Psaumes see Maitres Musiciens de la Renaissance Francaise.

Troisieme livre de chansons see Monuments de la musique francaise au temps de la Renaissance.

Troisieme Sibylle. Valentin Nikiprowetzky. (Etudes Juives: No. 9). 1970. pap. 34.40x (ISBN 0-686-21819-1). Mouton.

Troja. Heinrich Schliemann. LC 66-29425. (Illus.). Repr. of 1884 ed. 25.00 (ISBN 0-405-08933-3, Pub. by Blom). Ayer Co Pubs.

Trojan Ending. Laura Riding. 443p. 1985. Repr. of 1937 ed. 18.50 (ISBN 0-85635-524-0). Carcanet.

Trojan Generals Talk: Memoirs of the Greek War. Phillip Parotti. LC 87-34282. (Illinois Short Fiction Ser.). 192p. 1988. 11.95 (ISBN 0-252-01510-X). U of Ill Pr.

Trojan Gold. Elizabeth Peters. LC 86-26486. 288p. 1987. 15.95 (ISBN 0-689-11621-7). Atheneum.

Trojan Gold. Elizabeth Peters. 416p. 1988. pap. 3.95 (ISBN 0-8125-0758-4). Tor Bks.

Trojan Heritage: A Pictorial History of USC Football. Mal Florence. LC 80-84556. (Illus.). 184p. 1980. 16.95 (ISBN 0-938694-01-4). JCP Corp VA.

Trojan Horse. Paul Nizan. 1975. Repr. 25.00x (ISBN 0-86527-317-0). Fertig.

Trojan Horse. Catherine Storr. LC 84-18292. (Stories Clippers Ser.). (Illus.). 32p. (gr. 2-5). 1985. PLB 15.33 (ISBN 0-8172-2114-X); pap. 9.27 (ISBN 0-8172-2257-X). Raintree Pubs.

Trojan Horse: A Radical Look at Foreign Aid. rev ed. Steve Weissman. LC 74-32606. (Reader Ser). (Illus.). 250p. 1975. 10.00 (ISBN 0-87867-060-2). Ramparts.

Trojan Horse: How the Greeks Won the War. Emily Little. LC 87-43118. (Step into Reading Bks.). (Illus.). 48p. (Orig.). (gr. 2-4). 1988. PLB 6.99 (ISBN 0-394-99674-7, BYR); pap. 2.95 (ISBN 0-394-89674-2, BYR). Random.

Trojan Horse: Imagery in Psychology, Literature, Art & Politics. Akhter Ahsen. LC 84-72150. 287p. 1984. 35.00 (ISBN 0-913412-20-1). Brandon Hse.

Trojan Horse in America. Martin Dies. Ed. by Gerald Grob. LC 76-46072. (Anti-Movements in America Ser.). 1977. Repr. of 1940 ed. lib. bdg. 29.00x (ISBN 0-405-09945-2). Ayer Co Pubs.

Trojan Orbit. Mack Reynolds & Dean Ing. 384p. 1988. pap. 2.95 (ISBN 0-671-55942-7). Baen Bks.

Trojan Trilogy of Euripides. Ruth Scodel. (Classical Antiquity Ser.). 1980. pap. cancelled (ISBN 3-525-25156-4). Adlers Foreign Bks.

Trojan War. Olivia Coolidge. (Illus.). (gr. 7-12). 1952. 14.95 (ISBN 0-395-06731-6). HM.

Trojan War. Bernard Evslin. 160p. (gr. 5 up). 1988. pap. 2.95 (ISBN 0-590-41626-X). Scholastic Inc.

Trojan War. Ed. by William A. Kottmeyer. 1962. pap. 7.96 (ISBN 0-07-033733-0). McGraw.

Trojan Women. Euripides. Adapted by Jean-Paul Sartre. pap. 1.65 (ISBN 0-394-71074-6, V-74, Vin). Random.

Trojan Women. Euripides. Ed. by S. Barlow. 49.00x (ISBN 0-86516-094-5); pap. 16.50x (ISBN 0-86516-069-4). Bolchazy Carducci.

Trojan Women. Lucius Annaeus Seneca. Tr. & intro. by Frederick Ahl. LC 86-47636. (Masters of Latin Literature Ser.). 128p. 1986. pap. 5.95x (ISBN 0-8014-9431-1). Cornell U Pr.

Trojans: A Story of Southern California Football. Ken Rappoport. LC 74-81346. (College Sports Ser.). Orig. Title: Southern Cal Football. 1981. 12.95 (ISBN 0-87397-033-0). Strode.

Troll, a Truck, & a Cookie. Phylliss Adams et al. (BTR Series). (Illus.). 32p. (gr. k-3). 1982. lib. bdg. 4.95 (ISBN 0-8136-5396-7, Dist. by Caroline Hse); pap. 2.25 (ISBN 0-8136-5896-9). Modern Curr.

Troll & the Elephant Prince. Max Bush. (gr. 4 up). 1985. pap. 3.00 (ISBN 0-87602-254-9). Anchorage.

Troll Book. Michael Berenstain. LC 79-5268. (Illus.). 72p. (gr. 1-7). 1980. bds. o.p. 5.95 (ISBN 0-394-84295-2). Random.

Troll Country. Edward Marshall. LC 79-19324. (Easy-to-Read Bks.). (Illus.). 56p. (ps-3). 1980. PLB 9.89 (ISBN 0-8037-6211-9); pap. 4.95 (ISBN 0-8037-6210-0, 0481-140). Dial Bks Young.

Troll Garden. Willa Cather. 160p. 1984. pap. 3.95 (ISBN 0-452-00714-3, Mer). NAL.

Troll Garden see Early Novels & Stories.

Troll Garden: A Definitive Edition. Willa Cather. Ed. by James L. Woodress. LC 82-20138. xxx, 176p. 1983. 15.95 (ISBN 0-8032-1417-0). U of Nebr Pr.

Troll Music. Anita Lobel. LC 66-7117. (Illus.). (ps-3). PLB 11.89 (ISBN 0-06-023930-1). HarpJ.

Troll Tales. new ed. Corinne Denan. LC 79-66327. (Illus.). 48p. (gr. 3-6). 1980. lib. bdg. 9.59 (ISBN 0-89375-322-X); pap. 1.95 (ISBN 0-89375-321-1); cassette avail. Troll Assocs.

Trolley Car Family. Eleanor Clymer. (Illus.). 224p. (gr. 4-6). 1987. pap. 2.50 (ISBN 0-590-40732-5, Apple Paperback). Scholastic Inc.

Trolley Cars Across America. Ed. by James A. Ekken. 96p. 1984. 12.95 (ISBN 0-912113-01-4). Railhead Pubns.

Trolley Days in Pasadena. Charles Sems. LC 82-21146. (Illus.). 196p. 1982. 17.50 (ISBN 0-87095-086-X). Gldn West Bks.

Trolley Song. Sheila Raescild. (Orig.). 1981. pap. 3.50 (ISBN 0-89083-889-5). Zebra.

Trolley Talk, Vols. 1-8, Nos. 1-160. Incl. Vol. 1, Nos. 1-20. 1954-1958. 1975. Repr. of 1963 ed. pap. 6.60 (ISBN 0-914196-01-4); Vol. 2, Nos. 21-40. 1959-1962. 1971. Repr. of 1966 ed; Vol. 3, Nos. 41-60. 1962-1966. 1978. pap. 10.00 (ISBN 0-914196-07-3); Vol. 4, Nos. 61-80. 1966-1970. 1972. pap. 10.00 (ISBN 0-914196-13-8); Vol. 5, Nos. 81-100. 1970-1973. 1978. pap. 10.00 (ISBN 0-914196-19-7); Vol. VI, 1974-1977, Nos. 101-120. 1980. pap. 10.00 (ISBN 0-914196-21-9); Vol. 7, nos. 121-140, 1977-1980. 1985. pap. 11.75 (ISBN 0-914196-23-5); Vol. 8, Nos. 141-160. 1980-1983. 1986. pap. 14.00 (ISBN 0-914196-24-3). pap. Trolley Talk.

Trolley to the Past: A Companion to & History of the Operating Trolley Museums of North America. A. D. Young. Ed. by Jim Walker. (Special Ser.: No. 85). (Illus.). 160p. 1983. pap. 19.95 (ISBN 0-916374-56-4). Interurban.

Trolley Trails Through the West, Vols. 1-6. Robert S. Wilson. Incl. Vol. 1. Yakima Valley. (Illus.). 1978 (ISBN 0-934944-01-6); Vol. 2. Seattle. (Illus.). 1978 (ISBN 0-934944-02-4); Vol. 3. Portland. (Illus.). 1978 (ISBN 0-934944-03-2); Vol. 4. Tacoma, Spokane, Bellingham, Miscellaneous Washington & Oregon Communities. (Illus.). 1978 (ISBN 0-934944-04-0); Vol. 5. Montana & Utah. (Illus.). 1978 (ISBN 0-934944-05-9); Vol. 6. Western Canada. (Illus.). 1979 (ISBN 0-934944-06-7). (Illus.). 1978. pap. 5.00 ea. Wilson Bros.

Trolley Trails Through the West: Council Bluffs, Miscellany & Summing Up, Vol. 10. Robert S. Wilson. (Illus.). 32p. (Orig.). 1982. pap. 7.00 (ISBN 0-934944-10-5). Wilson Bros.

Trolley Trails Through the West: Northern California. Robert S. Wilson. (Trolley Trails Through the West Ser.: Vol. 7). (Illus.). 1979. pap. 5.00 (ISBN 0-934944-07-5). Wilson Bros.

Trolley Trails Through the West: San Diego, Colorado, Minnesota; Plus System Maps, Vol. 9. Robert S. Wilson. (Illus.). 40p. (Orig.). 1981. pap. 9.00 (ISBN 0-934944-09-1). Wilson Bros.

Trolley Trails Through the West: Southern California, Vol. 8. Robert S. Wilson. (Illus., Orig.). 1980. pap. 5.00 (ISBN 0-934944-08-3). Wilson Bros.

Trolley Visit to Make-Believe. Fred Rogers. (Illus.). 14p. (ps-k). 1987. 6.95 (ISBN 0-394-88617-8, BYR). Random.

Trolleys & Streetcars on American Picture Postcards. Ed. by Ray D. Appelgate. LC 78-64854. (Illus.). 1979. pap. 5.95 (ISBN 0-486-23749-4). Dover.

Trolleys from the Mines: Street Railways of Centre, Clearfield, Indiana & Jefferson Counties, Pennsylvania. Richard C. Albert. (Illus.). 100p. (Orig.). 1980. pap. 10.00 (ISBN 0-911940-32-4). Cox.

Trolleys of Bucks County, Pennsylvania. Harry Foesig et al. (Illus.). 72p. (Orig.). 1985. pap. 10.00 (ISBN 0-911940-41-3). Cox.

Trolleys of Lower Delaware Valley, Pennsylvania. Paul Schieck & Harold Cox. (Illus., Orig.). 1970. pap. 10.00 (ISBN 0-911940-10-3). Cox.

Trolleys of the Triple Cities. Shelden S. King. (Illus.). 48p. pap. 8.00 (ISBN 0-932334-98-9). Heart of the Lakes.

Trolleys to Augusta, Maine. O. R. Cummings. (Transportation Bulletin Ser.: No. 76). (Illus.). 1969. 7.50 (ISBN 0-910506-03-5). De Vito.

Trollope: A Commentary. Michael Sadleir. 435p. 1975. Repr. of 1947 ed. lib. bdg. 29.00x (ISBN 0-374-97013-0, Octagon). Hippocrene Bks.

Trollope: A Commentary. Michael Sadleir. Repr. of 1945 ed. 29.50 (ISBN 0-8492-9972-1). R West.

Trollope: A Commentary. Ed. by Michael Sadleir. (Illus.). 435p. 1980. Repr. lib. bdg. 52.50 (ISBN 0-89987-760-5). Darby Bks.

Trollope & Comic Pleasure. Christopher Herbert. LC 86-11367. xii, 246p. 1987. lib. bdg. 24.00x (ISBN 0-226-32741-8). U of Chicago Pr.

Trollope & the Law. R. D. McMaster. LC 86-1279. 144p. 1986. 27.50 (ISBN 0-312-81891-2). St Martin.

Trollope Centenary Essays. Ed. by John Halperin. LC 81-21326. 192p. 1982. 25.00x (ISBN 0-312-81894-7). St Martin.

Trollope Critics. Ed. by N. John Hall. 278p. 1981. 29.50x (ISBN 0-389-20044-1). B&N Imports.

Trollope in the Post Office. Robert H. Super. 1981. text ed. 12.95x (ISBN 0-472-10013-0). U of Mich Pr.

Trollope: Interviews & Recollections. R. C. Terry. (Illus.). 288p. 1987. 29.95 (ISBN 0-312-00368-4). St Martin.

Trollope-to-Reader: A Topical Guide to Digressions in the Novels of Anthony Trollope. Compiled by Mary L. Daniels. LC 83-10873. xxi, 393p. 1983. lib. bdg. 46.95 (ISBN 0-313-23877-4, DTR/). Greenwood.

Trollopes: Chronicle of a Writing Family. Lucy Stebbins & Richard P. Stebbins. LC 71-182720. Repr. of 1945 ed. 26.50 (ISBN 0-404-06228-8). AMS Pr.

Trollope's Palliser Novels: Theme & Pattern. Juliet McMaster. LC 77-17333. (Illus.). 1978. 34.00x (ISBN 0-19-520036-5). Oxford U Pr.

Troll's Christmas. Jill Wolf. (Illus.). 24p. (gr. 3-7). 1981. pap. 1.95 (ISBN 0-89954-460-6). Antioch Pub Co.

Troll's Grindstone. Elizabeth H. Boyer. 352p. (Orig.). 1986. pap. 3.50 (ISBN 0-345-32182-0, Del Rey). Ballantine.

Trolls of Omberg. Paul Karlsson. (Illus.). 40p. 1985. pap. 4.95 (ISBN 0-916871-08-8). Welcome Pr.

Trolls of the Misty Mountains. Mike Creswell & John Creswell. Ed. by Peter Fenlon. (Middle-Earth Ready-to-Run Adventure Ser.: No. 3). 32p. (Orig.). (YA) (gr. 10-12). 1986. pap. 6.00 (ISBN 0-915795-49-3). Iron Crown Ent Inc.

Trombone Chamber Music. 2nd ed. Harry J. Arling. Ed. by Stephen L. Glover. LC 83-19669. (Brass Research Ser.: No. 8). 1983. pap. text ed. 10.00x (ISBN 0-914282-29-8). Brass Pr.

Trombone: Its History & Music, 1697-1811. David M. Guion. (Musicology Ser.: Vol. 6). 352p. 1988. text ed. 65.00 (ISBN 2-88124-211-1). Gordon & Breach.

Trombone Teaching Techniques. 2nd ed. Donald Knaub. 1977. pap. 5.95 (ISBN 0-918194-09-1). Accura.

Trombone Technique. 2nd ed. Denis Wick. 1984. pap. 13.95x (ISBN 0-19-322378-3). Oxford U Pr.

Trombonist's Handbook: A Complete Guide to Playing & Teaching. Reginald H. Fink. LC 76-55601. (Illus.). 1977. 24.95 (ISBN 0-918194-01-6). Accura.

Trompe-L'Oeil Architecture. Miriam Milman. LC 85-43549. (Illus.). 128p. 1986. 37.50 (ISBN 0-8478-0713-4). Rizzoli Intl.

Trompe L'Oeil Painting: The Illusion of Reality. Miriam Milman. Ed. by Skira-Rizzoli Staff. LC 82-42851. (Illus.). 130p. pap. 25.00 (ISBN 0-8478-0817-3). Rizzoli Intl.

Trompette Dans L'Egypte Ancienne. Hans Hickmann. (Brass Research Ser: No. 4). (Illus.). 1976. pap. text ed. 10.00x (ISBN 0-914282-17-4). Brass Pr.

Trompowski Opening & Torre Attack. Robert Bellin. (Illus.). 96p. 1983. 17.95 (ISBN 0-7134-2399-4, Pub. by Batsford England). David & Charles.

Tron. Brian Daley. 1982. pap. 2.75 (ISBN 0-345-30352-0, Del Rey). Ballantine.

Tropical Oyster Culture: A Selected Bibliography. D. B. Quayle. 40p. 1975. pap. 5.00 (ISBN 0-88936-066-9, IDRC52, IDRC). UNIPUB.
Tropical Paradise, Gulf Coast Florida. D. C. Kip. (Illus.). 26p. (Orig.). 1985. pap. 5.00 (ISBN 0-9614549-1-1). Maedon.
Tropical Pasture & Fodder Plants. A. V. Bogdan. LC 76-14977. (Tropical Agriculture Ser.). (Illus.). 1977. text ed. 48.00x (ISBN 0-582-46676-8). Wiley.
Tropical Pasture & Fodder Plants: Grasses & Legumes. A. V. Bogden. LC 76-14977. (Tropical Agriculture Ser.). pap. 122.30 (ISBN 0-317-29850-X, 2019606). Bks Demand UMI.
Tropical Pasture Science. Peter C. Whiteman. (Illus.). 1980. 58.00x (ISBN 0-19-859470-4); pap. 24.50x (ISBN 0-19-859471-2). Oxford U Pr.
Tropical Pasture Seed Production. L. R. Humphreys. (Plant Production & Protection Papers: No. 8). 203p. 1987. pap. 16.25 (ISBN 92-5-100670-9, F2980, FAO). UNIPUB.
Tropical Pastures & Fodder Crops. 2nd ed. Leonard R. Humphreys. (Intermediate Tropical Agriculture Ser.). 168p. 1988. pap. 14.95 (ISBN 0-470-20938-0). Wiley.
Tropical Pathology. H. Spencer et al. (Spezielle Pathologische Anatomie Ser. Special Ed.: Vol. 8). (Illus.). 765p. 1973. 150.00 (ISBN 0-387-06208-4). Springer Verlag.
Tropical Plains Frontier: The Llanos of Colombia, 1531-1831. Jane M. Rausch. LC 84-13072. (Illus.). 333p. 1984. 29.95x (ISBN 0-8263-0761-2). U of NM Pr.
Tropical Plant Diseases. H. D. Thurston. LC 84-81534. 208p. 1984. 16.00 (ISBN 0-89054-063-2). Am Phytopathol Soc.
Tropical Plant Types. B. G. Jamieson & J. F. Reynolds. 1967. pap. text ed. 23.00 (ISBN 0-08-012120-9). Pergamon.
Tropical Poems from Ghana. Mark D. Hayford. 1983. 20.00x (ISBN 0-946270-00-7, Pub. by Pentland Pr UK). State Mutual Bk.
Tropical Polytpores. W. A. Murrill. 1973. Repr. of 1915 ed. 30.00x (ISBN 3-7682-0914-8). Lubrecht & Cramer.
Tropical Provenance & Progeny Research & International Cooperation. J. Burley & G. Nikles. 1973. 100.00x (ISBN 0-85074-022-3, Pub. by For Lib Comm England). State Mutual Bk.
Tropical Pulses. J. Smartt. (Tropical Agriculture Ser.). (Illus.). 1976. text ed. 36.00x (ISBN 0-582-46679-2). Wiley.
Tropical Pulses. J. Smartt. LC 76-361820. (Tropical Agriculture Ser.). pap. 89.50 (ISBN 0-317-27857-6, 2025258). Bks Demand UMI.
Tropical Rain Forest. M. Jacobs. (Illus.). 300p. 1988. pap. text ed. 39.95 (ISBN 0-387-17996-8). Springer-Verlag.
Tropical Rain Forest. Paul W. Richards. LC 79-50507. (Illus.). 1952. 90.00 (ISBN 0-521-06079-6); pap. 34.50 (ISBN 0-521-29658-7). Cambridge U Pr.
Tropical Rain Forest: A Study of Irradiation & Ecology at El Verde, Puerto Rico, 3 Vols. AEC Technical Information Center Staff. Ed. by Howard T. Odum & Robert F. Pigeon. LC 70-606844. 1652p. 1970. Set. pap. 49.25 (ISBN 0-87079-230-X, TID-24270); microfiche 6.50 (ISBN 0-87079-340-3, TID-24270). DOE.
Tropical Rain Forest Ecology. D. J. Maberlev. (Tertiary Level Biology Ser.). 170p. 1983. 39.95 (ISBN 0-412-00431-3, NO. 5058); pap. 18.95 (ISBN 0-412-00441-0, NO. 5059). Routledge Chapman & Hall.
Tropical Rain Forest Ecosystems, Part A: Structure & Function. Ed. by F. B. Gollery & M. J. Werger. (Ecosystems of the World Ser.: Vol. 14A). 382p. 1983. 147.50 (ISBN 0-444-41986-1, I-488-82). Elsevier.
Tropical Rain Forest Engagement Calendar 1989. Peter Carmichael. 1988. 8.95 (ISBN 0-318-23875-6). Basic Found.
Tropical Rain Forest Silviculture: A Research Project Report. T. J. Synnott. 1980. 30.00x (ISBN 0-85074-050-9, Pub. by For Lib Comm England). State Mutual Bk.
Tropical Rain-Forest: The Leed Symposium. Ed. by A. C. Chadwick & S. L. Sutton. (Illus.). 335p. 1984. 50.00 (ISBN 0-9501921-3-9, Pub. by Leeds Philoso & Lit Soc). Longwood Pub Group.
Tropical Rain Forests & the World Atmosphere. Ed. by Ghillean T. Prance. (AAAS Selected Symposium Ser.). 105p. 1986. pap. 20.00 (ISBN 0-8133-7176-7). Westview.
Tropical Rain Forests of the Far East. 2nd ed. T. C. Whitmore. (Illus.). 352p. 1984. 95.00x (ISBN 0-19-854136-8). Oxford U Pr.
Tropical Rain Forests of the Far East. 2nd ed. T. C. Whitmore. (Illus.). 368p. 1988. pap. 55.00 (ISBN 0-19-854241-0). Oxford U Pr.
Tropical Rainfall Measurements: An International Symposium Proceedings. Ed. by John S. Theon & Nobuyoshi Fugone. 1988. write for info. (ISBN 0-937194-14-X). A Deepak Pub.
Tropical Rainforests. James D. Nations. Ed. by Henry Rasof. (Illus.). 144p. (YA) (gr. 7-12). 1988. 12.90 (ISBN 0-531-10604-7). Watts.
Tropical Root Crops: Postharvest Physiology & Processing. Ed. by Ikuzo Uritani & Edilberto D. Reyes. (Illus.). 328p. (Orig.). 1984. pap. 26.00x (ISBN 4-7622-6358-3, Pub. by Japan Sci Soc Japan). Intl Spec Bk.
Tropical Root Crops: Root Crops & the African Food Crisis. E. R. Terry et al. 197p. (Orig.). 1987. pap. text ed. 18.00 (ISBN 0-88936-498-2, IRDC258, Intl Soc Tropical Foresters). UNIPUB.
Tropical Savannas. F. Bourliere. (Ecosystems of the World Ser.: Vol. 13). 730p. 1983. 258.00 (ISBN 0-444-42035-5). Elsevier.
Tropical Shrubs. Horace F. Clay & James C. Hubbard. LC 77-7363. (Hawai'i Garden Ser.: No. 2). (Illus.). 312p. 1987. pap. 24.95 (ISBN 0-8248-1128-3). UH Pr.
Tropical Snappers & Groupers: Biology & Fisheries Management. Ed. by Jeffrey J. Polovina & Stephen Ralston. (Special Studies in Ocean Science & Policy). 659p. 1986. pap. 47.00 (ISBN 0-8133-7179-1). Westview.
Tropical Soils & Soil Survey. A. Young. LC 75-19573. (Cambridge Geographical Studies: No. 9). 1976. Cambridge U Pr.
Tropical Soils & Soil Survey. A. Young. LC 75-19573. (Cambridge Geographical Studies: No. 9). 468p. 1980. pap. 19.95 (ISBN 0-521-29768-0). Cambridge U Pr.
Tropical Soils: Classification, Fertility & Management. F. S. Kalpage. LC 75-20866. 300p. 1976. 26.00 (ISBN 0-312-81935-8). St Martin.
Tropical Soils of Nigeria in Engineering Practice. S. Ola. 336p. 1983. text ed. 43.50 (ISBN 90-6191-264-4, Pub. by A A Balkema). Brookfield Pub Co.
Tropical Splendor: An Architectural History of Florida. Hap Hatton. LC 87-45238. (Illus.). 240p. 1987. 40.00 (ISBN 0-394-55594-5). Knopf.
Tropical Tempest. Flora Kidd. (Harlequin Presents Ser.). 192p. 1983. pap. 1.95 (ISBN 0-373-10643-2). Harlequin Bks.
Tropical Timber for Building Materials in the Andean Group Countries of South America. F. J. Keenan & Marcelo Tejada. (Illus.). 151p. 1985. pap. 10.00 (ISBN 0-88936-423-0, IDRCTS49, IDRC). UNIPUB.
Tropical Timbers of the World. (Agriculture Handbook: No. 607). (Illus.). 469p. 1984. pap. 16.00 (ISBN 0-318-22465-8, S/N 001-001-00609-2). USGPO.
Tropical Traveller. John Hatt. (Illus.). 253p. 1984. pap. 6.95 (ISBN 0-330-26577-6). Hippocrene Bks.
Tropical Trees & Forests: An Architectural Analysis. F. Halle et al. 1978. 84.00 (ISBN 0-387-08494-0). Springer-Verlag.
Tropical Trees: Found in the Carribbean, South American, Central America, Mexico. Dorothy Hargreaves & Bob Hargreaves. LC 65-19767. (Illus.). 1965. pap. 3.85 (ISBN 0-910690-05-7). Ross Hargreaves.
Tropical Trees of Hawaii. Dorothy Hargreaves & Bob Hargreaves. LC 64-23259. (Illus.). 1964. pap. 3.85 (ISBN 0-910690-02-2). Ross Hargreaves.
Tropical Trees of the Pacific. Dorothy Hargreaves & Bob Hargreaves. LC 72-113702. (Illus.). 1970. pap. 3.85 (ISBN 0-910690-09-X). Ross Hargreaves.
Tropical Tuber Crops: Yam, Cassava, Sweet Potato, Cocoyams. I. C. Onwueme. LC 77-20932. Repr. of 1978 ed. 47.20 (ISBN 0-8357-9996-4, 2051823). Bks Demand UMI.
Tropical Visions. John Millington. (Illus.). 144p. 1988. text ed. 39.95x (ISBN 0-7022-2079-5). U of Queensland Pr.
Tropical Zooplankton. H. J. Dumont & J. G. Tundisi. (Developments in Hydrobiology Ser.: No. 23). 344p. 1984. 84.00 (ISBN 90-6193-774-4, Pub. by Junk Pubs Netherlands). Kluwer Academic.
Tropicalism. Kenward Elmslie. LC 75-26459. 80p. (Orig.). 1976. pap. 5.00 (ISBN 0-915990-00-8). Z Pr.
Tropicals. Gordon Courtright. (Illus.). 126p. 1988. 35.95 (ISBN 0-88192-098-3). Timber.
Tropics: A General Bibliography of Books with Subject Index. Leslie E. Sponsel. (Public Administration Ser.: P 1908). 27p. 1986. 7.50 (ISBN 0-89028-828-3). Vance Biblios.
Tropics & Economic Development: A Provocative Inquiry into the Poverty of Nations. Andrew M. Kamarck. LC 76-17242. (World Bank Ser). 128p. 1977. 17.00x (ISBN 0-8018-1891-5); pap. 6.95x (ISBN 0-8018-1903-2). Johns Hopkins.
Tropics of Discourse: Essays in Cultural Criticism. Hayden White. LC 78-58297. 304p. 1985. pap. 10.95x (ISBN 0-8018-2741-8). Johns Hopkins.
Tropics: Their Resources, People & Future. C. R. Enock. 1976. lib. bdg. 59.95 (ISBN 0-8490-2770-5). Gordon Pr.
Tropism. Photos by Ralph Gibson. (Illus.). 160p. 1987. 39.50 (ISBN 0-89381-255-2). Aperture.
Tropismes. Nathalie Sarraute. 1957. pap. 7.25 (ISBN 0-685-11606-9). French & Eur.
Tropisms. Nathalie Sarrante. Tr. by Maria Jolas from Fr. 1986. 9.95 (ISBN 0-7145-0045-3). Riverrun NY.
Tropisms. Nathalie Sarraute. Tr. by Maria Jolas. LC 67-18211. (Orig.). pap. 4.95 (ISBN 0-8076-0412-7). Braziller.
Tropologue. Dawn Kolokithas. 72p. 1986. 30.00 (ISBN 0-918395-07-0); pap. 9.00 (ISBN 0-918395-04-6). Poltroon Pr.
Troposcatter Radio Links. Giovanni Roda. (Telecommunications Applications Library). 250p. 1988. text ed. 66.00 (ISBN 0-89006-293-5). Artech Hse.
Tropospheric Chemistry with Emphasis on Sulphur & Nitrogen Cycles & the Chemistry of Clouds & Precipitation: A Selection of Papers from the Fifth International Conference of the Commission on Atmospheric Chemistry & Global Pollution. Ed. by P. Goldsmith. (Illus.). 467p. 1985. 110.00 (ISBN 0-08-031448-1, Pub. by P P L). Pergamon.
Tropospheric Ozone. Ed. by Ivar S. Isaksen. 1988. lib. bdg. 99.00 (ISBN 90-277-2676-0, Pub. by Reidel Holland). Kluwer Academic.
Trorenija Svatago Efrema Sirina, Vol. 1. Saint John Moschus. 475p. 21.00 (ISBN 0-317-28899-7); pap. 16.00 (ISBN 0-317-28900-4). Holy Trinity.
Trot, Trot to Boston. Carol F. Ra. LC 86-7354. (Illus.). 32p. (ps). 1987. 11.75 (ISBN 0-688-06190-7); PLB 11.88 (ISBN 0-688-06191-5). Lothrop.
Trotsky. David King et al. (Illus.). 336p. 1986. 29.95 (ISBN 0-631-14689-X). Basil Blackwell.
Trotsky: A Documentary. Francis Wyndham & David King. (Illus.). 1973. pap. 7.95 (ISBN 0-14-003522-2). Penguin.
Trotsky & the Jews Behind the Russian Revolution. 1982. lib. bdg. 59.95 (ISBN 0-87700-423-4). Revisionist Pr.
Trotsky Bibliography. Wolfgang Lubitz. 458p. 1982. lib. bdg. 50.00 (ISBN 3-598-10469-3). K G Saur.
Trotsky Bibliography. 2nd. rev. ed. Wolfgang Lutz. xxxi, 581p. 1988. lib. bdg. 120.00 (ISBN 3-598-10754-4). K G Saur.
Trotsky for Beginners. Tariq Ali. (Illus.). 1980. pap. 6.95 (ISBN 0-394-73885-3). Pantheon.
Trotsky, Trotskyism & the Transition to Socialism. Peter Beilharz. 208p. 1987. 28.50 (ISBN 0-389-20698-9, N 8256). B&N Imports.
Trotskyism & Maoism: Theory & Practice in France & the U. S. Belden Fields. (Illus.). 288p. 1984. 26.95 (ISBN 0-275-91813-0, C1813). Praeger.
Trotskyism & Maoism: Theory & Practice in France & the United States. Belden Fields. 1988. 29.95 (ISBN 0-275-92035-6, C2035). Praeger.
Trotskyism & the Dilemma of Socialism. Christopher Z. Hobson & Ronald D. Tabor. LC 88-3093. (Contributions in Political Science Ser.: No. 215). 584p. 1988. lib. bdg. 49.95 (ISBN 0-313-26237-3, HTY/). Greenwood.
Trotsky's Anaylysis of Soviet Bureaucratization: A Critical Essay. David W. Lovell. LC 85-14968. (Flinders Politcal Monographs). 82p. (Orig.). 1985. pap. 11.50 (ISBN 0-7099-4112-9, Pub. by Croom Helm Ltd). Routledge Chapman & Hall.
Trotsky's Diary in Exile, 1935. Leon Trotsky. 236p. 1976. 17.50x (ISBN 0-674-91006-0). Harvard U Pr.
Trotsky's Notebooks, 1933-1935: Writings on Lenin, Dialectics, & Evolutionism. Tr. & annotations by Philip Pomper. LC 85-29955. 160p. 1986. 27.50 (ISBN 0-231-06302-4). Columbia U Pr.
Trotsky's Run. Richard Hoyt. 320p. 1983. pap. 3.50 (ISBN 0-523-48079-2, Dist. by Warner Pub. Services & Saint Martin's Press). Tor Bks.
Trotsky's Run. Richard Hoyt. 320p. 1988. pap. 3.95 (ISBN 0-8125-0485-2). Tor Bks.
Trotter-Nama. I. Allan Sealy. LC 87-45262. 640p. 1987. 19.95 (ISBN 0-394-56364-6). Knopf.
Trotter Ross. James Hogard. 1981. 12.00 (ISBN 0-914476-89-0). Thorp Springs.
Trou de l'Enfer. Alexandre Dumas. 1975. 9.95 (ISBN 0-686-55215-6). French & Eur.
Troubadors. Henry J. Chaytor. LC 74-102836. 1970. Repr. of 1912 ed. 21.00x (ISBN 0-8046-0751-6, Pub by Kennikat). Assoc Faculty Pr.
Troubadour. Giuseppe Verdi. Ed. by Nicholas John. Tr. by T. Hammond from Ital. (English National Opera - Royal Opera House Guide Ser.: Libretto, Articles: No. 20). (Illus.). 128p. (Orig.). 1983. pap. 4.95 (ISBN 0-7145-3877-9). Riverrun NY.
Troubadour Bertram D'Alamanon. Bertran D'Alamanon. Repr. of 1902 ed. 25.00 (ISBN 0-384-04080-2). Johnson Repr.
Troubadour Elias De Barjols. Elias De Barjols. liv, 159p. Repr. of 1906 ed. 21.00 (ISBN 0-384-14110-2). Johnson Repr.
Troubadour for the Lord: The Story of John Michael Talbot. Dan O'Neill. 160p. 1987. pap. 3.50 (ISBN 0-553-26900-3). Bantam.
Troubadour for the Lord: The Story of John Michael Talbot. Daniel O'Neill. 192p. 1983. 9.95 (ISBN 0-8245-0567-0). Crossroad NY.
Troubadour Guilhem Montanhagol. Jules Coulet. Repr. of 1898 ed. 20.00 (ISBN 0-384-39860-X). Johnson Repr.
Troubadour Raimon Jordan, Vicomte De Saint-Antonin. Raimon Jordan. LC 80-2189. Repr. of 1922 ed. 25.00 (ISBN 0-404-19016-2). AMS Pr.
Troubadours. Francis Hueffer. LC 74-24121. Repr. of 1878 ed. 28.00 (ISBN 0-404-12979-X). AMS Pr.
Troubadours. B. Sargent. LC 73-93396. (Resources of Music Ser.: No. 7). (Illus.). 400p. 1974. record 7.95 (ISBN 0-521-20476-3). Cambridge U Pr.
Troubadours & Love. L. T. Topsfield. LC 74-14440. (Illus.). 304p. 1975. pap. 15.95 (ISBN 0-521-09897-1). Cambridge U Pr.
Troubadours at Home: Their Lives, Personalities & Songs, 2 vols. Justin Smith. Set. PLB 200.00 (ISBN 0-8490-1232-5). Gordon Pr.
Troubadours, Leur Vies, Leurs Oeuvre, Leur Influence. Joseph Anglade. LC 78-38487. Repr. of 1908 ed. 22.00 (ISBN 0-404-08344-7). AMS Pr.
Troubadours of Dante: Being Selections from the Works of the Provencal Poets Quoted by Dante, with Introduction, Notes, Concise Grammar & Glossary. Henry J. Chaytor. LC 79-178520. Repr. of 1902 ed. 27.50 (ISBN 0-404-56533-6). AMS Pr.
Troubadours of Provence. John A. Fleming. LC 77-806. 1977. Repr. of 1952 ed. lib. bdg. 40.00 (ISBN 0-685-76861-9). Folcroft.
Troubadour's Romance. Robyn Carr. 288p. 1985. 16.95 (ISBN 0-316-12976-3). Little.
Troubadour's Romance. Robyn Carr. 320p. 1987. pap. 3.95 (ISBN 0-671-61708-7). PB.
Troubadours: Their Loves & Their Lyrics with Remarks on Their Influence, Social & Literary. John Rutherford. 1977. lib. bdg. 59.95 (ISBN 0-8490-2771-3). Gordon Pr.
Trouble. Helen Cresswell. (Illus.). 32p. (ps-2). 1988. 10.95 (ISBN 0-525-44396-7, 01063-320). Dutton.
Trouble. Michael Gilbert. LC 86-46067. (Harper Novel of Suspense Ser.). 256p. 1987. 15.45i (ISBN 0-06-015741-0, HarpT). Har-Row.
Trouble & Strife: Women & the Labour Party. Sarah Perrigo. 128p. (Orig.). 1986. pap. 5.95 (ISBN 0-86104-648-X, Pub. by Pluto Pr). Longwood Pub Group.
Trouble at Aquitaine. Nancy Livingston. 192p. 1985. 12.95 (ISBN 0-312-81975-7). St Martin.
Trouble at Crossed Forks. B. A. Collier. (YA) (gr. 7 up). 1979. 9.95 (ISBN 0-685-93880-8, Avalon). Bouregy.
Trouble at Goodewoode Manor. Linda Heller. LC 80-27417. (Illus.). 32p. (gr. k-3). 1981. 8.95 (ISBN 0-02-743570-9). Macmillan.
Trouble at Moon Pass. Burt Arthur. 1978. pap. 1.25 (ISBN 0-505-51257-2, Pub. by Tower Bks.). Leisure NY.
Trouble at Mrs. Portwine's. John Wood. (Illus.). 128p. (gr. 4-8). 1987. 14.95 (ISBN 0-86327-147-2, Pub. by Wolfhound Pr Ireland). Irish Bks Media.
Trouble at Pena Blanca. Nelson Nye. 1987. pap. 2.75 (ISBN 0-515-09139-1). Jove Pubns.
Trouble at Quinn's Crossing. Nelson Nye. 1987. pap. 2.50 (ISBN 0-441-82432-3, Pub. by Charter Bks). Ace Bks.
Trouble at the Gabourys' Joan L. Oppenheimer. 1987. 16.95 (ISBN 0-8027-0981-8). Walker & Co.
Trouble at the Glory Barn. Tom C. McKenney. LC 85-51173. (Illus.). 128p. (Orig.). 1985. pap. 4.95 (ISBN 0-934527-05-9). Words Living Minis.
Trouble at the Mines. Doreen Rappaport. LC 84-45339. (Illus.). 96p. (gr. 3-7). 1987. 11.25i (ISBN 0-690-04445-3, Crowell Jr Bks); PLB 10.89 (ISBN 0-690-04446-1). HarpJ.
Trouble at Windy Acres. Mary M. Landis. (gr. 5-10). 1976. 6.95 (ISBN 0-686-15486-X). Rod & Staff.
Trouble Begins at Eight: Mark Twain's Lecture Tours. Frederick W. Lorch. LC 68-17493. (Illus.). 391p. pap. 101.70 (2030318). Bks Demand UMI.
Trouble Borrower. Giles Lutz. 192p. 1986. pap. 2.50 (ISBN 0-441-82459-5, Pub. by Charter Bks). Ace Bks.
Trouble Brand. Russ Kidd. (Lythway Ser.). 184p. 1988. lib. bdg. 17.50x (ISBN 0-7451-0685-4, Pub. by Chivers Pr UK). G K Hall.
Trouble Brewing: A Social Psychological Analysis of the Ansells Brewery Dispute. D. P. Waddington. 1987. text ed. 39.95 (ISBN 0-566-05374-8, Pub. by Gower Pub England). Gower Pub Co.
Trouble Crossing the Pyrenees. Gaylord Larsen. 1986. pap. 3.95 (ISBN 0-345-33641-0, Pub. by Ballantine Epiphany). Ballantine.
Trouble Downtown: The Local Context of Twentieth Century America. Henry F. Bedford. (Harbrace History of the United States Ser.). (Illus.). 213p. 1978. pap. text ed. 11.00 net (ISBN 0-15-592369-2, HC). HarBraceJ.
Trouble Enough: Joseph Smith & the Book of Mormon. Ernest H. Taves. LC 84-42790. (Illus.). 280p. 1984. 22.95 (ISBN 0-87975-261-0). Prometheus Bks.
Trouble for Lucia, Pt. VI. E. F. Benson. LC 83-48945. (Make Way for Lucia Ser.). 288p. 1986. pap. 5.95 (ISBN 0-06-091376-2, PL 1376, PL). Har-Row.
Trouble for Lucy. Carla Stevens. LC 79-10445. (Illus.). (gr. 2-6). 1979. 8.95 (ISBN 0-395-28971-8, Clarion). HM.
Trouble for Lucy. Carla Stevens. LC 79-10445. 80p. (gr. 3-6). 1987. pap. 3.95 (ISBN 0-89919-523-7, Pub. by Clarion). Ticknor & Fields.
Trouble for Trumpets. Peter Cross. LC 83-43115. (Illus.). (gr. 3 up). 1984. 9.95 (ISBN 0-394-86513-8, BYR). Random.
Trouble-Free Swimming Pools. Dan Ramsey. (Illus.). 176p. (Orig.). 1985. pap. 11.95 (ISBN 0-8306-1808-2, 1808P). TAB Bks.
Trouble Halfway. Jan Mark. LC 85-20028. (Illus.). 129p. (gr. 4-6). 1986. 11.95 (ISBN 0-689-31210-5, Atheneum Childrens Bks). Macmillan.
Trouble in Bugland. William Kotzwinkle. LC 82-49338. (Illus.). 160p. 1986. pap. 9.95 (ISBN 0-87923-555-1). Godine.
Trouble in Eden: A Comparison of the British & Swedish Economies. Eli Schwartz. LC 80-17073. 160p. 1980. 35.00 (ISBN 0-275-90547-0, C0547). Praeger.
Trouble in Form Six. Cyprian O. Ekwensi. 1966. text ed. 3.95x (ISBN 0-521-04884-2). Cambridge U Pr.

Troubled Waters: New Policies for Managing Water in the American West. Mohamed T. El-Ashry & Diana C. Gibbons. LC 86-62910. 104p. (Orig.). 1986. pap. text ed. 10.00 (ISBN 0-915825-15-5). World Resources Inst.

Troubled Youth, Troubled Families. James Garbarino et al. Ed. by James K. Whittaker. LC 85-20154. (Modern Applications of Social Work Ser.). (Illus.). 369p. (Orig.). 1986. pap. 32.95 (ISBN 0-202-36039-3). Aldine de Gruyter.

Troublemaker. Emily Chase. (Girls of Canby Hall Ser.: No. 22). 176p. (Orig.). (YA) (gr. 7 up). 1987. pap. 2.50 (ISBN 0-590-40711-2). Scholastic Inc.

Troublemaker. Lynn Hall. (Illus.). 94p. (gr. 3-5). 1975. pap. 1.75 (ISBN 0-380-00434-8, 52373-6, Camelot). Avon.

Troublemaker. Joseph Hansen. LC 81-4820. (Dave Brandsetter Mystery Ser.). 160p. 1981. pap. 3.95 (ISBN 0-03-057487-0, Owl Bks). H Holt & Co.

Troublemaker. Robert McKay. 192p. (gr. 7 up). 1972. pap. 1.50 (ISBN 0-440-99122-6, LFL). Dell.

Troublemaker. Francine Pascal. (Sweet Valley High Ser.: No. 47). 1988. pap. 2.95. Bantam.

Troubles. J. G. Farrell. 448p. 1986. 4.95 (ISBN 0-88184-269-9). Carroll & Graf.

Troubles. Naomi May. (Orig.). 1979. pap. 5.95 (ISBN 0-7145-3606-7). Riverrun NY.

Troubles at the Metabolic Mill-Ketosis. David J. Gerrick. (Illus.). 1978. 20.00 (ISBN 0-916750-70-1). Dayton Labs.

Trouble's Child. Mildred P. Walter. LC 84-16387. 128p. (gr. 4 up). 1985. 10.25 (ISBN 0-688-04214-7). Lothrop.

Troubles Dans les Andains. Boris Vian. 144p. 1976. 7.95 (ISBN 0-686-55708-5). French & Eur.

Troubles de L'invention: Etude sur le doute poetique de Joe Bousquet. Joseph Brami. LC 87-62927. 168p. (Fr.). 1988. lib. bdg. 21.95 (ISBN 0-917786-58-0). Summa Pubns.

Troubles in the External Field Problem for Invariant Wave Equations see Fundamental Interactions at High Energy Three: Tracts in Mathematics & Natural Sciences.

Troubles of a Bibliophile or Outpourings from the Heart of a Bookloving Worldling. Martin Breslauer. 1970. 5.00 (ISBN 0-910330-16-6). Grant Dahlstrom.

Troubles on the East Bank: Challenges to the Domestic Stability of the Middle East. Robert B. Satloff. LC 86-18675. (Washington Papers: No. 124). 151p. 1986. lib. bdg. 29.95 (ISBN 0-275-92617-6, C2617); pap. 9.95 (ISBN 0-275-92618-4, B2618). Praeger.

Troubles on the East Bank: Challenges to the Domestic Stability of Jordan. Robert B. Satloff. (Washington Papers: No. 123). 138p. 1986. pap. 9.95 (ISBN 0-317-63124-1, B2618); lib. bdg. 29.95 (C2617). Praeger.

Troubleshooter. Ronald Weber. 208p. 1988. 14.95 (ISBN 0-312-01839-8, Pub. by J Kahn). St Martin.

Troubleshooting. 3rd ed. William Herman & Jeffrey M. Young. 352p. 1986. pap. text ed. 16.95 (ISBN 0-03-002133-2, HoltC). HR&W.

Troubleshooting & Repairing Audio Equipment. Homer L. Davidson. (Illus.). 336p. 1987. 24.95 (ISBN 0-8306-7167-6, 2867); pap. 16.95 (ISBN 0-8306-2867-3). TAB Bks.

Troubleshooting & Repairing Compact Disc Players. Homer L. Davidson. (Illus.). 368p. 1988. 26.95 (ISBN 0-8306-9107-3, 3107); pap. 17.95 (ISBN 0-8306-3107-0, 3107). TAB Bks.

Troubleshooting & Repairing Electronic Test Equipment. 2nd, rev. & enl. ed. Mannie Horowitz. 1986. pap. 17.95 (ISBN 0-8306-1663-2, 1663P). TAB Bks.

Troubleshooting & Repairing Satellite TV Systems. Richard Maddox. (Illus.). 400p. 1985. 26.95 (ISBN 0-8306-0977-6, 1977). TAB Bks.

Troubleshooting & Repairing Small Home Appliances. Bob Wood. (Illus.). 256p. 1988. 23.95 (ISBN 0-8306-9912-0); pap. 14.95 (ISBN 0-8306-2912-2). TAB Bks.

Troubleshooting & Repairing Solid-State TVs. Homer L. Davidson. (Illus.). 480p. 1986. 26.95 (ISBN 0-8306-0307-7, 2707H); pap. 17.95 (ISBN 0-8306-2707-3, 2707P). TAB Bks.

Troubleshooting & Repairing the New Personal Computer. Art Margolis. (Illus.). 416p. (Orig.). 1987. 26.95 (ISBN 0-8306-0209-7); pap. 17.95 (ISBN 0-8306-2809-6). TAB Bks.

Troubleshooting & Repairing TVRO Systems. Stan Prentiss. (Illus.). 224p. 1988. 24.95 (ISBN 0-8306-0592-4); pap. 16.95 (ISBN 0-8306-2992-0). TAB Bks.

Troubleshooting & Repairing Your Commodore 64. Art Margolis. (Illus.). 288p. (Orig.). 1985. 22.95 (ISBN 0-8306-0889-3, 1889); pap. 16.95 (ISBN 0-8306-1889-9). TAB Bks.

Troubleshooting & Repairing Your Commodore 128. Art Margolis. (Illus.). 400p. 1988. 27.95 (ISBN 0-8306-9099-9, 3099); pap. 18.95 (ISBN 0-8306-9399-8, 3099). TAB Bks.

Troubleshooting & Servicing Air Conditioning Equipment. S. Don Swenson. 250p. 1985. text ed. 29.95 (ISBN 0-8273-2710-2). Delmar.

Troubleshooting: Basic Writing Skills. 2nd ed. William Herman & Jeffrey M. Young. 1982. pap. text ed. 14.95 (ISBN 0-03-059118-X). HR&W.

Troubleshooting Classroom Problems: A Practical Guide. Murray Tillman. 1982. pap. 10.95 (ISBN 0-673-16032-7). Scott F.

Troubleshooting Electrical Components. Peter Novellino. (Orig.). 1983. wkbk. 5.00 (ISBN 0-8064-0173-7, 461); audio visual pkg. 179.00 (ISBN 0-8064-0174-5). Bergwall.

Troubleshooting Electronic Equipment Without Service Data. Robert G. Middleton. LC 83-13772. (Illus.). 303p. 1984. 24.95 (ISBN 0-13-931097-5, Busn). P-H.

Troubleshooting Electronic Equipment Without Service Data. 2nd ed. Robert G. Middleton. (Illus.). 400p. 1987. pap. 14.95 (ISBN 0-13-931155-6, Busn). P-H.

Troubleshooting Guide to Christian Education. John Cionca. LC 85-73069. 176p. 1986. pap. 7.95 (ISBN 0-89636-191-8). Accent Bks.

Troubleshooting Home Video Microprocessing. Bob Goodman. (Illus.). 384p. 1986. 24.95 (ISBN 0-8306-0158-9); pap. 16.95 (ISBN 0-8306-2758-8, NO. 2758). TAB Bks.

Troubleshooting Microprocessor Based Systems. Allan H. Robbins & Brian Lundeen. (Illus.). 320p. 1987. text ed. 32.00 (ISBN 0-13-931296-X). P-H.

Troubleshooting Microprocessor Based Systems. G. B. Williams. 1984. pap. text ed. 20.00 (ISBN 0-08-029988-1). Pergamon.

Troubleshooting Natural Gas Processing: From Wellhead to Transmission. Norman P. Lieberman. 208p. 1987. 63.95 (ISBN 0-87814-308-4). PennWell Bks.

Troubleshooting Old Cars. Ron Bishop. (Illus.). 182p. 1982. pap. 9.25 (ISBN 0-8306-2075-3, 2075). TAB Bks.

Troubleshooting Process Operations. 2nd ed. Norman P. Lieberman. 440p. 1984. 69.95 (ISBN 0-87814-263-0, P-4359). PennWell Bks.

Troubleshooting, Servicing, & Theory of AM, FM, & FM Stereo Receivers. 2nd ed. Clarence Green & Robert Bourque. (Illus.). 608p. 1987. text ed. 40.00 (ISBN 0-13-931114-9). P-H.

Troubleshooting Solid State Circuits. George C. Loveday & Arthur H. Seidman. LC 80-21954. 110p. 1981. pap. text ed. 14.95 (ISBN 0-471-08371-2). Wiley.

Troubleshooting the Data Comm Network. Gabriel Kasperek. 292p. 1984. looseleaf 59.95 (ISBN 0-935506-27-6). Carnegie Pr.

Troubleshooting the High School Band: How to Detect & Correct Common & Uncommon Performance Problems. Carrol M. Butts. LC 80-24776. 224p. 1981. 22.95x (ISBN 0-13-931105-X, Parker). P-H.

Troubleshooting: The Troubleshooting Course or Debug d'Bugs. Robert F. Mager. LC 82-81980. 1983. pap. 11.95 (ISBN 0-8224-9370-5). D S Lake Pubs.

Troubleshooting with the Oscilloscope. 5th ed. Robert G. Middleton. 224p. 1987. pap. 16.95 (ISBN 0-672-22473-9). Sams.

Troubleshooting with the Vat Forty. John Primi. LC 80-730756. (Orig.). 1980. wkbk. 5.00 (ISBN 0-8064-0147-8, 441); audio visual pkg. 339.00 (ISBN 0-8064-0148-6). Bergwall.

Troublesome Border. Oscar J. Martinez. LC 87-34294. (PROFMEX Ser.). 177p. 1988. 22.95x (ISBN 0-8165-1033-4). U of Ariz Pr.

Troublesome Business: The Labour Party & the Irish Question. Geoffrey Bell. 168p. 1982. pap. 8.95 (ISBN 0-86104-373-1, Pub by Pluto Pr). Longwood Pub Group.

Troublesome Engines. Reverend W. Awdry. (Railway Ser.). (Illus.). 64p. (gr. k-2). 1985. Repr. of 1950 ed. 6.95 (ISBN 0-7182-0004-7, Pub. by Kaye & Ward). David & Charles.

Troublesome People. Caroline Moorehead. LC 86-28699. 344p. 1987. 19.95 (ISBN 0-917561-35-X). Adler & Adler.

Troublesome Pig. Priscilla Lamont. As told by & illus. by Priscilla Lamont. LC 84-7717. (Illus.). 32p. (ps-1). 1985. 7.95 (ISBN 0-517-55546-8). Crown.

Troublesome Raigne of John King of England. Ed. by J. W. Sider & Stephen Orgel. LC 78-66778. (Renaissance Drama Ser.). 1979. lib. bdg. 37.00 (ISBN 0-8240-9733-5). Garland Pub.

Troublesome Reign of King John. LC 75-133750. (Tudor Facsimile Texts. Old English Plays: No. 59). Repr. of 1911 ed. 49.50 (ISBN 0-404-53359-0). AMS Pr.

Troublesome Reign of King John: Being the Original of Shakespeare's "Life & Death of King John". J. F. Furnivall & John Munro. LC 72-195924. 1973. Repr. of 1913 ed. lib. bdg. 25.00 (ISBN 0-8414-4291-6). Folcroft.

Troubling Problems in Medical Ethics: Proceedings of Ethics, Humanisms & Medicine Conference, University of Michigan, Ann Arbor, MI 1981. Ethics, Humanisms & Medicine Conference Staff & Marc D. Basson. LC 81-20723. (Progress in Clinical & Biological Research: Vol. 76). 306p. 1981. 31.00 (ISBN 0-8451-0076-9). A R Liss.

Troublous Times in Canada: A History of the Fenian Raids of 1866 & 1870. John A. MacDonald. 255p. 1987. 91.00x (Pub. by Picton UK). State Mutual Bk.

Troublous Times in New Mexico, 1659-1670. France V. Scholes. LC 75-41242. (New Mexico Hist. Society. Publications in History: Vol. 11). Repr. of 1942 ed. 21.50 (ISBN 0-404-14701-1). AMS Pr.

Troupe. Gordon Linzner. 1988. pap. 3.50 (ISBN 0-671-66354-2). PB.

Trouping Through Texas: Harley Sadler & His Tent Show. Clifford Ashby & Suzanne D. May. LC 81-82503. 194p. 1982. 14.95 (ISBN 0-87972-184-7); pap. 8.95 (ISBN 0-87972-185-5). Bowling Green Univ.

Trouser Press Guide to New Wave Records. Ed. by Ira A. Robbins. (Illus.). 288p. 1983. (ScribT); pap. 12.95 (ISBN 0-684-17944-X). Scribner.

Trout. Ray Bergman & Edward C. Janes. 1976. 24.50 (ISBN 0-394-49957-3); pap. 15.95 (ISBN 0-394-73144-1). Knopf.

Trout, 2 Vols. Ernest Schwiebert. (Illus.). 1800p. 1984. Set. 125.00 (ISBN 0-525-24269-4). Dutton.

Trout. Dick Sternberg & Parker Bauer. (Hunting & Fishing Library). (Illus.). 160p. 1988. 17.95 (ISBN 0-86573-027-X); pap. 12.95 (ISBN 0-86573-028-8). Cy De Cosse.

Trout Almanac: Rocky Mountain Region. Kim Long. (Illus.). 160p. (Orig.). 1987. pap. 8.95 (ISBN 1-55566-014-2). Johnson Bks.

Trout & Salmon Culture (Hatchery Methods) Earl Leitritz & Robert C. Lewis. (Illus.). 1980. pap. 5.00x (ISBN 0-931876-36-2, 4100). ANR Pubns CA.

Trout & Salmon Fishing. Roy Eaton. LC 80-68897. (Illus.). 192p. 1981. 29.95 (ISBN 0-7153-8117-2). David & Charles.

Trout & Salmon Fly Index. Dick Surette. LC 78-24196. (Illus.). 144p. 1979. pap. 16.95 (ISBN 0-8117-2093-4). Stackpole.

Trout & Salmon of Pacific Coast. facs. ed. David S. Jordan. 16p. pap. 1.95 (ISBN 0-8466-0071-4, S71). Shorey.

Trout Biology: An Angler's Guide. William B. Willers. LC 81-50829. 224p. 1981. 22.50 (ISBN 0-299-08720-4). U of Wis Pr.

Trout Bum. John Gierach. LC 84-4805. 227p. 1986. 19.95 (ISBN 0-87108-715-4). Pruett.

Trout Bum: Essays on Fly-Fishing As a Way of Life. John Gierach. (Illus.). 224p. 1988. pap. 7.95 (ISBN 0-671-64413-0, Fireside). S&S.

Trout Chaser's Journal: A Diary for the Trout & Salmon Fisherman. Tully Stroud. (Illus.). 144p. 1986. 14.95 (ISBN 0-87701-404-3). Chronicle Bks.

Trout Farming Handbook. 4th ed. Stephen D. Sedgwick. (Illus.). 164p. (Orig.). 1985. pap. 22.50 (ISBN 0-85238-135-2, Pub. by Fishing News Ltd). Scholium Intl.

Trout Farming Manual. 2nd ed. J. P. Stevenson. (Illus.). 271p. 1987. flexbound 32.50 (ISBN 0-85238-149-2, Pub. by Fishing News Ltd). Scholium Intl.

Trout Farming Manual. John P. Stevenson. 1980. 60.75x (ISBN 0-686-64739-4, Pub. by Fishing News England). State Mutual Bk.

Trout Fisherman's Bible. rev. ed. Dan Holland. LC 78-55853. (Illus.). 1979. pap. 7.95 (ISBN 0-385-14406-7, Outdoor Bible). Doubleday.

Trout Fishing in America. Richard Brautigan. Bd. with Pill Versus the Springhill Mine Disaster; In Watermelon Sugar. (Illus.). 156p. 1979. pap. 10.00 (ISBN 0-385-28860-3, Sey Lawr). Delacorte.

Trout Fishing in America. Richard Brautigan. 182p. 1979. pap. 3.50 (ISBN 0-440-39125-3). Dell.

Trout Fishing in America, the Pill Versus the Spring Hill Mine Disaster & in Watermelon Sugar. Richard Brautigan. 1989. pap. 9.95 (ISBN 0-395-50076-1). HM.

Trout Fishing in California. Ron Kovach. (Illus.). 240p. (Orig.). 1987. pap. 13.95 (ISBN 0-934061-04-1). Marketscope Bks.

Trout Fishing the Southern Appalachians. Wayne J. Fears. 192p. pap. 7.95 (ISBN 0-317-65075-0). Globe Pequot.

Trout Hunting. F. Woolner. (Illus.). 10.00 (ISBN 0-87691-196-3). Brown Bk.

Trout in the Milk: An Arnold Landon Novel. Roy Lewis. 208p. 1986. 13.95 (ISBN 0-312-82009-7). St Martin.

Trout on a Fly. Lee Wulff. (Illus.). 160p. 1986. 15.95 (ISBN 0-941130-17-7). N Lyons Bks.

Trout River. Text by Nick Lyons. 1988. 49.50 (ISBN 0-8109-1697-5). Abrams.

Trout Strategies: Observations on Modern Fly Fishing, Including Tested Methods of Matching the Hatch, Fishing the Nymph, Bucktails & Streamers, Wet & Dry Flies; & Techniques for Eastern & Western Lakes, Ponds, Rivers & Streams--Drawn from the Author's Masterwork "Trout". Ernest Schwiebert. (Illus.). 288p. 1983. pap. 10.95 (ISBN 0-525-48052-8). Dutton.

Trout Streams of Michigan. 1978. pap. 7.95 (ISBN 0-933112-03-3). Mich United Conserv.

Trout the Magnificent. Sheila Turnage. LC 82-15865. (Illus.). 48p. (ps-3). 1984. 12.95 (ISBN 0-15-290962-1, HJ). HarBraceJ.

Trout Waters in the Adirondack Mountains. pap. 2.00 (ISBN 0-686-31387-9). Outdoor Pubns.

Trout's Best Friend. Bud Lilly & Paul Schullery. (Illus.). 200p. (Orig.). 1988. pap. 13.95 (ISBN 0-87108-745-6); 18.95 (ISBN 0-87108-744-8). Pruett.

Trova. 2nd ed. Andrew Kagan. (Illus.). 366p. 1988. 75.00 (ISBN 0-8109-1696-7). Abrams.

Trova: The Profile Cantos. Udo Kulterman. Ed. by Pace Gallery. (Illus.). 20p. (Orig.). 1973. pap. text ed. 4.00 (ISBN 0-938608-38-X). Pace Pubns.

Troy: a Study in Homeric Geography. facsimile ed. Walter Leaf. LC 70-150191. (Select Bibliographies Reprint Ser). Repr. of 1912 ed. 36.00 (ISBN 0-8369-5704-0). Ayer Co Pubs.

Troy & Her Legend. Arthur M. Young. LC 76-141272. (Illus.). 1971. Repr. of 1948 ed. lib. bdg. 35.00 (ISBN 0-8371-5862-1, YOTR). Greenwood.

Troy & Its Remains. Heinrich Schliemann. LC 68-21228. (Illus.). Repr. of 1875 ed. 28.00 (ISBN 0-405-08934-1, Pub. by Blom). Ayer Co Pubs.

Troy & the Early Greeks. Cambridge School Classics Project Foundation Course Staff. Ed. by M. Forrest. (Illus.). 1973. text ed. 12.50x (ISBN 0-521-08467-9). Cambridge U Pr.

Troy Chimneys. Margaret Kennedy. (Virago Modern Classics Ser.). 256p. 1985. pap. 6.95 (ISBN 0-14-016112-0). Penguin.

Troy Dossier. Manny Meyers. (Crime Court Ser.). 240p. 1986. pap. 2.95 (ISBN 0-8439-5006-4, Leisure Bks). Leisure NY.

Troy: Excavations Conducted by the University of Cincinnati, 1932-1938, 3 vols. University of Cincinnati, Excavations in the Troad. Ed. by Carl W. Blegen et al. Vol. 2, Pt. 1. pap. 86.80 (ISBN 0-317-10368-7, 2001131); Vol. 2, Pt. 2. pap. 52.30 (ISBN 0-317-10369-5); Vol. 3, Pt. 1. pap. 112.00 (ISBN 0-317-10370-9); Vol. 3, Pt. 2. pap. 75.00 (ISBN 0-317-10371-7); Vol. 4, Pt. 1. pap. 89.50 (ISBN 0-317-10372-5); Vol. 4, Pt. 2. pap. 58.80 (ISBN 0-317-10373-3). Bks Demand UMI.

Troy H. Middleton: A Biography. Frank J. Price. LC 73-90869. (Illus.). xvii, 416p. 1974. 37.50. La State U Pr.

Troy State University: Nineteen Thirty-Seven to Nineteen Seventy, Troy Alabama. Charles B. Smith. (Illus.). 1972. pap. 3.50x (ISBN 0-916624-34-X). Troy State Univ.

Troy State University Writings & Research, Vol. III. Daniel S. Gray. 32p. 1974. pap. 1.95 (ISBN 0-686-97227-9). Troy State Univ.

Troy State University Writings & Research, Vol. I. 60p. 1969. pap. 1.95 (ISBN 0-686-97224-4). Troy State Univ.

Troy State University Writings & Research, Vol. II, No. 1. Joseph B. Roberts, Jr. & John Ciardi. 64p. 1971. pap. 1.95 (ISBN 0-686-97225-2). Troy State Univ.

Troy State University Writings & Research, Vol. II, No. 2. Carl E. Purinton. 52p. 1971. pap. 1.95 (ISBN 0-686-97226-0). Troy State Univ.

Troy: Terracotta Figurines of the Hellenistic Period. D. Thompson. (U. of Cincinnati Supplementary Monograph: No. 3). 1963. 52.50x (ISBN 0-691-03527-X). Princeton U Pr.

Troy: The Archaeological Geology. Ed. by George Rapp & John A. Gifford. LC 50-9752. (Illus.). 232p. 1982. 73.00x (ISBN 0-691-03559-8). Princeton U Pr.

Troy the Coins. Alfred R. Bellinger. LC 81-50603. (Illus.). 1979. Repr. of 1961 ed. lib. bdg. 30.00 (ISBN 0-915262-32-0). S J Durst.

Troy Town. Arthur T. Quiller-Couch. 224p. 1982. pap. 7.50 (ISBN 0-907746-09-8, Pub. by A Mott Ltd). Longwood Pub Group.

TRS-DOS 2.3 Decoded & Other Mysteries. James L. Farvour. (TRS-80 Information Ser.: Vol. 6). (Illus.). 298p. (Orig.). 1982. pap. 29.95 (ISBN 0-936200-07-3). Blue Cat.

TRS-80, Vol. 1. Henry A. Taitt & Kathy Taitt. (Thinking-Learning-Creating: TLC for Growing Minds Ser.). 53p. (gr. 4-12). 1983. pap. text ed. 11.95 (ISBN 0-88193-011-3). Create Learn.

TRS-80, Vol. 2. Henry A. Taitt & Kathy Taitt. (Thinking-Learning-Creating: TLC for Growing Minds Ser.). 56p. (gr. 4-12). 1983. pap. text ed. 11.95 (ISBN 0-88193-012-1). Create Learn.

TRS-80, Vol. 3. Henry A. Taitt & Jennifer Taitt. (Thinking-Learning-Creating: TLC for Growing Minds Ser.). 53p. (gr. 5-12). 1983. pap. text ed. 11.95 (ISBN 0-88193-013-X). Create Learn.

TRS-80, Vol. 4. Henry A. Taitt & Jennifer Taitt. (Thinking-Learning-Creating: TLC for Growing Minds Ser.). 56p. (gr. 5-12). 1983. pap. text ed. 11.95 (ISBN 0-88193-014-8). Create Learn.

TRS-80, Vol. 5. Henry A. Taitt & Jennifer Taitt. (Thinking-Learning-Creating: TLC for Growing Minds Ser.). 57p. (gr. 6-12). 1983. pap. text ed. 11.95 (ISBN 0-88193-015-6). Create Learn.

TRS-80, Vol. 6. Henry A. Taitt & Jennifer Taitt. (Thinking-Learning-Creating: TLC for Growing Minds Ser.). 54p. (gr. 6-12). 1984. pap. text ed. 11.95 (ISBN 0-88193-016-4). Create Learn.

TRS-80 BASIC: A Self Teaching Guide. Bob Albrecht et al. LC 80-10268. (Self Teaching Guides Ser.: No. 1581). 351p. 1980. pap. 12.95 (ISBN 0-471-06466-1). Wiley.

TRS-80 Beginner's Guide to Games & Graphics. Tom Dempsey. 1984. 16.95 (ISBN 0-317-06048-1); pap. 16.95 (ISBN 0-936200-10-3). Blue Cat.

TRS-80 COBOL. Robert T. Grauer. (Illus.). 352p. 1983. text ed. 38.00 (ISBN 0-13-931212-9); pap. text ed. 30.00 (ISBN 0-13-931204-8). P-H.

TRS-80 Color Computer Program Writing Workbook. Ron Clark. 96p. pap. 4.95 (ISBN 0-86668-816-1). ARCsoft.

TRS-80 Color Programs. Ted Lewis. 350p. 1983. pap. 39.95 incl. disk (ISBN 0-88056-154-8). Dilithium Pr.

TRS-80 Color Programs. Tom Rugg & Phil Feldman. 323p. 1982. pap. 14.95 (ISBN 0-918398-61-4); incl. cassette 19.95. Weber Systems.

TRS-80 Disk & Other Mysteries. Harvard C. Pennington. (TRS-80 Information Ser.: Vol. I). (Illus.). 128p. (Orig.). 1979. pap. 22.50 (ISBN 0-936200-00-6). Blue Cat.

TRS-80 Disk BASIC for Business for the Model II & Model III. Alan J. Parker. 1982. pap. 14.95 (ISBN 0-8359-7872-9, Reston). P-H.

TRS-80 Educational Software Sourcebook. 1983. pap. 6.95 (ISBN 0-318-01175-1). Radio Shack.

TRS-80 for Kids from Eight to Eighty, 2 vols. Michael P. Zabinski. LC 82-61990. 136p. 1982. pap. 10.95 ea. (22046-6). Vol. 1 (ISBN 0-672-22046-6). Vol. 2 (ISBN 0-672-22070-9). Sams.

TRS-80 Graphics. David A. Kater & Susan Thomas. (Illus.). 256p. 1982. pap. text ed. 15.95 (ISBN 0-07-033303-3, BYTE Bks). McGraw.

TRS-80 Microcomputer Information Handbook for Educators. 1981. pap. 2.50 (ISBN 0-318-01174-3). Radio Shack.

TRS-80 Model I-III Computer Writing Workbook. Mark Lewis. 96p. 1983. 4.95 (ISBN 0-86668-815-3). ARCsoft.

TRS-80 Model 100 User's Guide. Oymax et al. 160p. 1984. pap. 16.95 (ISBN 0-471-80536-X, Pub. by Wiley Pr). Wiley.

TRS-80 Programming for Learning & Teaching: Forty Plus Application Programs. Frederick Bell. 1984. text ed. 30.00 (ISBN 0-8359-7863-X, Reston); pap. text ed. 24.00 (ISBN 0-8359-7862-1). P-H.

TRS-80 ROM Routines Documented. Jack Decker. 126p. 1983. pap. text ed. 19.95 (ISBN 0-915363-01-1). Alter Source.

TRS-80 Teaching Aid: Ready-to-Run Programs for the Classroom & Home. Edward Burns. (Illus.). 1984. 24.00 (ISBN 0-8359-7877-X, Reston); pap. 16.95 (ISBN 0-8359-7875-3). P-H.

TRS-80 User's Encyclopedia: Color Computer & MC-10. Gary Phillips & Guier S. Wright. Ed. by Michael F. Mellin & Andrew Klein. 246p. (Orig.). 1983. pap. 14.95 (ISBN 0-912003-11-1). Bk Co.

TRS-80 User's Encyclopedia: Model 100. Gary Phillips & Jacquelyn Smith. Ed. by Michael F. Mellin & Robert Sandberg. 350p. (Orig.). 1983. pap. 14.95 (ISBN 0-912003-13-8). Bk Co.

TRS-80 User's Encyclopedia: Models I, III & 4. Gary Phillips & James E. Potter. pap. 19.95 (ISBN 0-912003-12-X). Bk Co.

TRS-80 Word Processing Applications Using SuperScripsit. Carol Lehman et al. 1984. pap. text ed. write for info. (ISBN 0-8359-7878-8, Reston); instr's. manual avail. (ISBN 0-8359-7880-X). P-H.

TRS-80 Word Processing Applications Using Super SCRIPSIT. Carol Lehman et al. 1986. pap. text ed. 20.00 (ISBN 0-89787-420-X); tchr's. material 7.00 (ISBN 0-89787-422-6); Training disk for DOS 6.2 or DOS 1.3. 20.00x. Gorsuch Scarisbrick.

TRS-80 Word Processing with Scripsit. David A. Kater. 176p. 1985. pap. text ed. 21.95 (ISBN 0-07-033360-2, BYTE Bks). McGraw.

Truancy & Non-Attendance in the Chicago Schools: A Study of the Social Aspects of the Compulsory Education & Child Labor Legislation of Illinois. Edith Abbott & Sophonisba P. Breckinridge. LC 74-12526. (Rise of Urban America Ser.). 1970. Repr. of 1917 ed. 26.50 (ISBN 0-405-02432-0). Ayer Co Pubs.

Truant Bather. Mark Taksa. 48p. 1986. pap. write for info. (ISBN 0-917658-24-8). BPW & P.

Truant State. Nicholas Hasluck. 320p. 1988. pap. 6.95 (ISBN 0-14-010466-6). Penguin.

Truants. Ron Carlson. 1987. pap. 7.95 (ISBN 0-393-30508-2). Norton.

Truants from Life: The Rehabilitation of Emotionally Disturbed Children. Bruno Bettelheim. LC 55-7331. 516p. 1955. 18.95 (ISBN 0-02-903440-X); pap. 10.95 (ISBN 0-02-903450-7). Free Pr.

Trubloff: The Mouse Who Wanted to Play the Balalaika. John Burningham. (ps). 1965. lib. bdg. write for info. (ISBN 0-394-97316-X, BYR). Random.

Trubner's Bibliographical Guide. Nikolaus Trubner. 35.00 (ISBN 0-8490-1233-3). Gordon Pr.

Truce of God. Rowan Williams. 128p. (Orig.). 1983. pap. 3.95 (ISBN 0-8298-0660-1). Pilgrim NY.

Truce with Time. Parke Godwin. LC 86-47891. 288p. 1988. pap. 16.95 (ISBN 0-553-05201-2, Spectra). Bantam.

Trucial States. Donald Hawley. (Illus.). 379p. 1971. 39.50 (ISBN 0-686-66022-6); pap. text ed. 14.95x (ISBN 0-8290-0454-8). Irvington.

Truck. Donald Crews. LC 79-19031. (Illus.). 32p. (ps-2). 1980. 11.95 (ISBN 0-688-80244-3); PLB 11.88 (ISBN 0-688-84244-5). Greenwillow.

Truck. Donald Crews. LC 84-18137. (Illus.). 32p. (ps). 1985. pap. 3.95 (ISBN 0-14-050506-7, Puffin). Penguin.

Truck Ability Prediction Procedure. 98p. 1975. 12.00 (ISBN 0-89883-360-4, HS-82). Soc Auto Engineers.

Truck Ability Work Sheet Pad. 150p. 8.00 (HS-83). Soc Auto Engineers.

Truck & Bus Industry Glossary. 1988. 25.00 (ISBN 0-89883-659-X, SP732). Soc Auto Engineers.

Truck & Loader. Helen R. Haddad. LC 81-6823. (Greenwillow Read-Alone Bks.). (Illus.). 56p. (gr. 1-3). 1982. lib. bdg. 8.88 (ISBN 0-688-00827-5). Greenwillow.

Truck & Tractor Pullers. Rosemary Grimm. Ed. by Carnival Enterprises Staff. LC 87-30592. (Super-Charged! Ser.). (Illus.). 48p. (gr. 5-6). 1988. PLB 10.95 (ISBN 0-89686-358-1). Crestwood Hse.

Truck & Tractor Pulling: Motorsports' Heavyweight Powerhouses. Michael Bargo. (Illus.). 128p. 1988. 24.95 (ISBN 0-87938-283-X). Motorbooks Intl.

Truck & Van Prices Buyer's Guide, 1979. Ed. by Michael L. Green. (Buyer's Guide Reports Ser.). 1978. pap. 1.95 (ISBN 0-89552-052-4). DMR Pubns.

Truck & Vertebral Column see Physiology of the Joints.

Truck Book. Lawrence DiFiori. LC 83-83106. (Golden Sturdy Shape Bks.). (Illus.). (ps). 1984. 2.95 (ISBN 0-307-12299-9, Golden Bks). Western Pub.

Truck Book. Bill Gere. (Golden Super Shape Bks.). (Illus.). 24p. (ps-k). 1987. pap. write for info. (ISBN 0-307-10051-0, Pub. by Golden Bks). Western Pub.

Truck Book. Bill Gere. (Illus.). (gr. k-9). 1988. pap. 1.29. Scholastic Inc.

Truck Book. Harry McNaught. LC 77-79851. (Picturebacks Ser.). (ps-2). 1978. (BYR); pap. 1.95 (ISBN 0-394-83703-7). Random.

Truck Book. Robert L. Wolfe. LC 80-15683. (Carolrhoda Photo Bks.). (Illus.). 32p. (ps-3). 1981. PLB 8.95 (ISBN 0-87614-125-4). Carolrhoda Bks.

Truck Company Fire Ground Operations. Hal Richman. LC 76-57667. 1977. pap. 13.95 (ISBN 0-87618-059-4). Brady Comp Bks.

Truck Company Fireground Operations. 2nd ed. Harold Richman. (Illus.). 224p. 1987. 27.00 (ISBN 0-317-63591-3, FSP-76H). Natl Fire Prot.

Truck Dance: A Novel. LC 87-46146. 288p. 1988. 16.95 (ISBN 0-06-015937-5, HarpT). Har-Row.

Truck Driver. Jack Rudman. (Career Examination Ser.: C-1161). (Cloth bdg. avail. on request). 1988. pap. 14.00 (ISBN 0-8373-1161-6). Natl Learning.

Truck Driver. Judith B. Stamper. LC 88-10039. (What's It Like to Be a... Ser.). (Illus.). 32p. (gr. k-2). 1988. PLB 9.89 (ISBN 0-8167-1424-X); pap. text ed. 1.95 (ISBN 0-8167-1425-8). Troll Assocs.

Truck Driver Training Manual. Neil Darmstadter. 91p. 1981. pap. text ed. 4.50 (ISBN 0-88711-008-8). Am Trucking Assns.

Truck Driving Techniques. (Training Aids Ser.: No. 1). 28p. 4.00 (ISBN 0-317-58433-2). Natl Asphalt Pavement.

Truck Electronic Control Systems. 1985. 18.00 (ISBN 0-89883-916-5, SP645). Soc Auto Engineers.

Truck Facts Buyer's Guide, 1981. rev. ed. Ed. by Michael Green. 96p. (Orig.). write for info. DMR Pubns.

Truck Facts, 1979. Ed. by Michael L. Green. (Buyer's Guide Reports Ser.). 1978. pap. 1.95 (ISBN 0-89552-053-2). DMR Pubns.

Truck Facts, 1980. Michael L. Green. (Truck Facts, 1980). 1979. pap. 2.25 (ISBN 0-89552-062-1). DMR Pubns.

Truck Fire Protection. National Fire Protection Association Staff. 1984. 10.50 (ISBN 0-317-63483-6, 513-84). Natl Fire Prot.

Truck Guide, Vols. 1-2. James E. Brumbaugh. Incl. Vol. 1. Engines & Auxiliary Systems. (Audel). 370p. 16.95 (ISBN 0-672-23356-8); Vol. 2. Transmissions, Steering & Brakes. 304p. 16.95 (ISBN 0-672-23357-6); Vol. 3. 16.95 (ISBN 0-672-23406-8). 1984. 45.95 set (ISBN 0-672-23392-4, Pub. by Audel). Macmillan.

Truck Leasing Markets. (Reports Ser.: No. 192). 212p. 1982. 1285.00x (ISBN 0-88694-192-X). Intl Res Dev.

Truck Lubrication Guide, 1985. rev. ed. (Illus.). 100p. 1985. pap. 33.40x (ISBN 0-88098-061-3). H M Gousha.

Truck Lubrication Guide, 1986. (Illus.). 96p. Date not set. wkbk. 34.75 (ISBN 0-88098-083-4). H M Gousha.

Truck Lubrication Guide, 1987. rev. ed. Chek-Chart Staff. Ed. by Roger Fennema. (Illus.). 96p. 1987. wkbk. 35.80 (ISBN 0-88098-091-5). H M Gousha.

Truck Parts Edition. Hollander Publishing Company Inc. (Truck Interchange Ser.). 510p. 1972. 43.75 (ISBN 0-943032-02-4). Hollander Co.

Truck Safety: An Agenda for the Future. 1986. 45.00 (ISBN 0-89883-745-6, P 181). Soc Auto Engineers.

Truck Song. Diane Siebert. LC 83-46173. (Illus.). 32p. (ps-3). 1984. 12.70i (ISBN 0-690-04410-0, Crowell Jr Bks); PLB 12.89 (ISBN 0-690-04411-9). HarpJ.

Truck Song. Diane Siebert. LC 83-46173. (Trophy Picture Bks.). (Illus.). 32p. (ps-3). 1987. pap. 3.95 (ISBN 0-06-443134-7, Trophy). HarpJ.

Truck Steering System from Hand Wheel to Road Wheel. J. W. Durstine. 78p. 1973. pap. 18.00 (ISBN 0-89883-152-0, SP-374). Soc Auto Engineers.

Truck System. George Hilton. LC 75-11877. 166p. 1975. Repr. of 1960 ed. lib. bdg. 35.00x (ISBN 0-8371-8130-5, HITS). Greenwood.

Truck Tech Talk. Ruth Radlauer & Ed Radlauer. LC 86-9684. (Tech Talk Ser.). (Illus.). 64p. (gr. 4 up). 1986. PLB 14.60 (ISBN 0-516-08257-4); pap. 3.95 (ISBN 0-516-48257-2). Childrens.

Truck-Tractor Identification. Lee S. Cole. 69p. (Orig.). 1988. pap. 12.00 (ISBN 0-939818-15-9). Lee Bks.

Truck Transportation. (Illus.). 32p. (gr. 6-12). 1973. pap. 1.25x (ISBN 0-8395-3371-3, 3371). BSA.

Trucker Favorites. Thomas L. Hakes. (Illus.). Date not set. pap. 4.50x ltd. ed. (ISBN 0-915020-53-X). Bardic.

Truckers Atlas. American Trucking Associations & Creative Sales Corporation. 336p. 1988. pap. text ed. 8.95 spiral bdg. (ISBN 0-88711-087-8). Am Trucking Assns.

Trucker's Atlas. 1982. 9.95 (ISBN 0-933162-04-9). Creative Sales.

Trucker's Atlas. Date not set. price not set. Am Map.

Truckin' Eight Hundred: The Special Commodities Directory. 3rd ed. Dale Wilson. (Truckin' 800 Ser.: Vol. 1, No. 3). (Illus.). 400p. 1986. pap. text ed. write for info. (ISBN 0-9610616-2-6). Cargo Serv Inc.

Trucking: A Truck Driver's Enhanced Workbook. Ken Gilliland. Ed. by S. Michele McFadden. LC 79-90760. 1986. pap. text ed. 24.50x (ISBN 0-89262-029-3); Guide. 50.00 (ISBN 0-89262-122-2). Career Pub.

Trucking: A Truck Driver's Training Handbook. Ed. by S. Michele McFadden et al. LC 79-90760. (Illus.). 434p. (Orig.). 1986. pap. text ed. 24.50x (ISBN 0-89262-025-0). Career Pub.

Trucking & Intermodal Freight Issues. LC 84-1956. (Transportation Research Record Ser.: No. 920). 1983. 10.80 (ISBN 0-309-03608-9). Transport Res Bd.

Trucking & the Public Interest: The Emergence of Federal Regulation 1914-1940. William R. Childs. LC 85-5315. 260p. 1985. text ed. 19.95x (ISBN 0-87049-473-2). U of Tenn Pr.

Trucking: Instructor's Guide. Ken Gilliland. Ed. by S. Michele McFadden. 1982. pap. text ed. 50.00 (ISBN 0-89262-030-7). Career Pub.

Trucking Permit Guide: Private, Contract, Common, Exempt. rev. ed. J. J. Keller & Associates, Inc. Staff. LC 75-16944. (1G). 1987. loose-leaf 119.00 (ISBN 0-934674-00-0). J J Keller.

Trucking Safety Guide: Driver, Vehicles, Cargo, Highway. rev. ed. J. J. Keller & Associates, Inc. LC 74-31865. (8G). 1987. loose-leaf 119.00 (ISBN 0-934674-03-5). J J Keller.

Trucking Terminal Impact & Community Response: Case Studies in the Philadelphia Region. Thomas A. Reiner. (Discussion Paper Ser.: No. 86). 1975. pap. 5.50 (ISBN 0-686-32252-5). Regional Sci Res Inst.

Trucking Trends. Spence Murray. LC 77-84296. (Pickups & Vans Ser.). (Illus., Orig.). (gr. 9-12). 1977. pap. 3.95 (ISBN 0-8227-5017-1). Petersen Pub.

Truckline Cafe. Maxwell Anderson. (Lost Play Ser.). 1986. pap. 3.95 (ISBN 0-912262-86-9). Proscenium.

Trucks. N. S. Barrett. LC 84-50700. (Picture Library). (Illus.). 32p. (gr. k-3). 1984. PLB 10.90 (ISBN 0-531-03723-1). Watts.

Trucks. Byron Barton. LC 85-47901. (Illus.). 32p. (ps-k). 1986. 4.95 (ISBN 0-694-00062-0, Crowell Jr Bks); PLB 9.89 (ISBN 0-690-04530-1). HarpJ.

Trucks. Ray Broekel. LC 82-17907. (New True Bks.). (Illus.). 48p. (gr. k-4). 1983. PLB 12.60 (ISBN 0-516-01688-1); pap. 3.95 (ISBN 0-516-41688-X). Childrens.

Trucks. J. Ronald Cave. (What About Ser.). (Illus.). 32p. (ps-3). 1982. PLB 10.90 (ISBN 0-531-04421-1). Watts.

Trucks. Gail Gibbons. LC 81-43039. (Illus.). 32p. (ps-2). 1981. 12.70i (ISBN 0-690-04118-7, Crowell Jr Bks); PLB 12.89 (ISBN 0-690-04119-5). HarpJ.

Trucks. Gail Gibbons. LC 81-43039. (Trophy Picture Bks.). (Illus.). 32p. (ps-1). 1985. pap. 2.95 (ISBN 0-06-443069-3, Trophy). HarpJ.

Trucks. Harry McNaught. LC 79-63901. (Shape Bks.). (Illus.). (ps-1). 1979. 3.95 (ISBN 0-394-84268-5). Random.

Trucks. Harry McNaught. LC 75-36463. (Illus.). 14p. (ps-1). 1976. 3.95 (ISBN 0-394-83240-X). Random.

Trucks. Kate Petty. (First Library). (Illus.). 32p. (gr. 4-6). 1987. lib. bdg. 10.90 (ISBN 0-531-10285-8). Watts.

Trucks. Anne Rockwell. LC 84-1556. (Illus.). 24p. (ps-1). 1984. 8.95 (ISBN 0-525-44147-6). Dutton.

Trucks. Anne Rockwell. LC 84-1556. (Unicorn Paperbacks Ser.). (Illus.). 24p. (ps-1). 1988. pap. 3.95 (ISBN 0-525-44432-7, 0383-120). Dutton.

Trucks. Illus. by Art Seiden. (Teddy Board Bks.). (Illus.). (ps). 1983. 3.95 (ISBN 0-448-40873-2, G&D). Putnam Pub Group.

Trucks. Paul Stickland. (Working Wheels Ser.). (Illus.). 16p. (ps-1). 1988. 3.95 (ISBN 0-8249-8259-2). Ideals.

Trucks. (Illus.). 8p. 1981. 1.95 (ISBN 0-8431-0710-3). Price Stern.

Trucks: An Educational Coloring Book. Spizzirri Publishing Co. Staff. Ed. by Linda Spizzirri. (Illus.). 32p. 1979. pap. 1.49 (ISBN 0-86545-051-X). Spizzirri.

Trucks & Associated OEM Product Market. Frost & Sullivan, Inc. Staff. write for info. (ISBN 0-86621-781-9, A1600). Frost & Sullivan.

Trucks & Cars. Illus. by Tony Tallarico. (Baby's First Bks.). (Illus.). 14p. (ps). 1980. 2.50 (ISBN 0-448-16275-X, G&D). Putnam Pub Group.

Trucks & Trailers. Marc Arceneaux. (E-Z Color & Fold Bks.). (gr. 1-4). 1983. pap. 2.50 (ISBN 0-448-11053-9, G&D). Putnam Pub Group.

Trucks & Trucking. Ruth Wolverton & Mike Wolverton. LC 82-6967. (First Bks.). (Illus.). 72p. (gr. 4-8). 1982. PLB 10.40 (ISBN 0-531-04468-8). Watts.

Trucks in Your Neighborhood. Illus. by Joe Mathieu. (Wheel Bks.). (Illus.). 14p. (ps-k). 1988. bds. 2.95 (ISBN 0-394-89951-2, BYR). Random.

Trucks of Every Sort. Ken Robbins. (Illus.). 48p. (gr. 2-4). 1981. lib. bdg. 9.95 (ISBN 0-517-54164-5). Crown.

Trucks of Every Sort. Ken Robbins. (Illus.). 48p. (gr. 2-4). 1988. pap. 4.95 (ISBN 0-517-56640-0). Crown.

Trucks, Trouble & Triumph: The Norwalk Truck Line Company. Wayne G. Broehl, Jr. LC 75-41749. (Companies & Men: Business Enterprises in America). (Illus.). 1976. Repr. of 1954 ed. 29.00x (ISBN 0-405-08066-2). Ayer Co Pubs.

Trucksource: Sources of Trucking Industry Information. American Trucking Associations. Ed. by Linda S. Rothbart. 154p. 1987. pap. text ed. 15.00 (ISBN 0-88711-098-3). Am Trucking Assns.

Trucos de Clifford (Clifford's Tricks) Norman Bridwell. Tr. by Argentina Palacios. 32p. (Span.). (gr. k-3). pap. 2.95 (ISBN 0-590-40123-8). Scholastic Inc.

Trucos De Eva: La Ninta De G.O.C.E. new ed. Rod Gray. Tr. by Jairo Ibero. (Pimienta Collection Ser.). (Illus.). 160p. (Span.). 1975. pap. 1.25 (ISBN 0-88473-232-0). Fiesta Pub.

Truculentus see Stichus.

Trudeau. George Radwanski. LC 78-67827. 1978. 14.95 (ISBN 0-8008-7897-3). Taplinger.

Trudnaia Missiia. N. M. Kharlamov. 224p. (Rus.). 1983. 29.00x (ISBN 0-317-40875-5, Pub. by Collets (UK)). State Mutual Bk.

Trudy I Dni Lavinii Monakhini Iz Ordena Obrezaniia Serdtsa (Ot Rozhdestva do Paskhi) Elena Shvarts. 1216p. (Rus.). 1987. cancelled (ISBN 0-87501-040-7); pap. 7.50 (ISBN 0-87501-041-5). Ardis Pubs.

True Adventures. Dan Geeenburg. 256p. (Orig.). 1985. pap. 8.95 (ISBN 0-88191-023-6). Freundlich.

True Adventures of Grizzly Adams. Robert M. McClung. LC 85-8886. (Illus.). 208p. (gr. 5 up). 1985. 10.25 (ISBN 0-688-05794-2, Morrow Junior Books). Morrow.

True Adventures of Huckleberry Finn. 2nd ed. As told by John Seelye. LC 87-8581. 368p. 1988. 27.50 (ISBN 0-252-01446-4); pap. 8.95 (ISBN 0-252-01432-4). U of Ill Pr.

True Adventures of John Steinbeck, Writer: A Biography. Jackson J. Benson. (Illus.). 1038p. 1984. 35.00 (ISBN 0-670-16685-5). Viking.

True Adventures of the Rolling Stones. Stanley Booth. 600p. 1985. 4.95 (ISBN 0-394-74110-2, Vin). Random.

True Alchemy or the Quest for Perfection, Vol. 221. Omraam M. Aivanhov. (IZVOR Collection ser.). 191p. (Orig.). 1986. pap. 5.95 (ISBN 2-85566-384-9, 221). Prosveta USA.

True Americanism: Green Berets & War Resisters: A Study of Commitment. David M. Mantell. LC 74-2230. 1974. pap. 10.95x (ISBN 0-8077-2452-1). Tchrs Coll.

True & Almost Incredible Report of an Englishman That Travelled by Land Through Many Kingdoms. Robert Coverte. LC 72-186. (English Experience Ser.: No. 302). 1971. Repr. of 1612 ed. 11.50 (ISBN 90-221-0302-1). Walter J Johnson.

True & Authentic Register of Persons...Who in the Year 1709...Journeyed from Germany to America. Ulrich Simmendinger. LC 70-23539. 20p. 1984. pap. 3.00 (ISBN 0-8063-0313-1). Genealog Pub.

True & Fair View in Company Accounts. D. Flint. 1982. pap. 16.95 (ISBN 0-85258-223-4). Van Nos Reinhold.

True & False Democracy. facsimile ed. Nicholas M. Butler. LC 78-93323. (Essay Index Reprint Ser). 1907. 14.00 (ISBN 0-8369-1278-0). Ayer Co Pubs.

True & False Monkey. Ed. by Gao Maingyou. (Monkey Ser.: No. 17). (Illus.). 73p. (gr. 1-4). 1986. pap. 7.95 (ISBN 0-8351-1731-6). China Bks.

True & False Paths in Spiritual Investigation. Rudolf Steiner. Tr. by A. H. Parker from Ger. 222p. 1986. pap. 10.95. Anthroposophic.

True & False Repentance. Charles G. Finney. LC 66-10576. (Charles G. Finney Memorial Library). 122p. 1975. pap. 4.50 (ISBN 0-8254-2617-0). Kregel.

True & False Universality of Christianity. Ed. by Claude Geffre & Jean-pierre Jossua. (Concilium Ser.: Vol. 135). 128p. (Orig.). 1980. pap. 5.95 (ISBN 0-8164-2277-X, HarpR). Har-Row.

True & Historical Narrative of the Colony of Georgia in America. facsimile ed. Patrick Tailfer et al. LC 74-168522. (Black Heritage Library Collection). Repr. of 1741 ed. 12.75 (ISBN 0-8369-8874-4). Ayer Co Pubs.

True & Incredible Adventures of Doktor Thrill. Linderman. LC 84-6001739. (Illus.). 155p. 1984. 40.00 (ISBN 0-87358-366-3). Paradise Hse.

True & Invisible Rosicrucian Order. Paul F. Case. LC 85-3185. (Illus.). 352p. 1985. 22.50 (ISBN 0-87728-608-6). Weiser.

True & Perfect Description of Three Voyages by the Ships of Holland & Zeland. Gerrit de Veer. Tr. by W. Phillip. LC 75-25746. (English Experience Ser.: No. 274). 164p. 1970. Repr. of 1609 ed. 21.00 (ISBN 90-221-0274-2). Walter J Johnson.
True & the False: The Domain of the Pragmatic. Charles Travis. (Pragmatics & Beyond Ser.: II: 2). vi, 165p. (Orig.). 1981. pap. 20.00x (ISBN 90-272-2512-5). Benjamins North Am.
True Arte of Defence see Three Elizabethan Fencing Manuals.
True Authorship of the New Testament. Abelard Reuchlin. 1979. pap. 4.00 (ISBN 0-930808-02-9). Vector Assocs.
True BASIC: A Complete Manual. Henry Simpson. (Illus.). 208p. 1985. pap. 14.95 (ISBN 0-8306-1970-4, 1970P). TAB Bks.
True BASIC: A Tutorial. Larry J. Goldstein et al. Date not set. write for info. S&S.
True BASIC: Programs & Subroutines. John C. Craig. (Illus.). 256p. (Orig.). 1985. 24.95 (ISBN 0-8306-0990-3, 1990); pap. 16.95 (ISBN 0-8306-1990-9, 1990P). Tab Bks.
True Basis of Civil Government Set Forth see Treatise on Civil Government.
True Bear Stories. Joaquin Miller. Ed. by James Robertson. (Illus.). 216p. 1987. pap. 7.95 (ISBN 0-88496-259-8). Capra Pr.
True Bear Stories. Joaquin Miller. 96p. 1988. Repr. lib. bdg. 19.95x (ISBN 0-8095-4051-7). Borgo Pr.
True Bear Tales. David E. Young. (True Bear Tales Ser.). (Illus.). 50p. 1987. pap. 3.50 (ISBN 0-318-23859-4). Gold Oak Bks.
True Believer. Eric Hoffer. 1966. pap. 4.95 (ISBN 0-06-080071-2, P71, PL). Har-Row.
True Believers. Alyce Rohrer. LC 85-18521. 1987. 18.95 (ISBN 0-87949-253-8). Ashley Bks.
True Black Man's History. Douglas Taylor. LC 76-47244. 94p. 1977. 9.95 (ISBN 0-8022-2192-0). Philos Lib.
True Blood Professors Seminar Accounting & Auditing Case Studies 1983, 2 vols. Touche Ross. Student Case Bk, 91 pgs. 6.00 (ISBN 0-86539-046-0); Discussion Leaders Guide, 192 pgs. 6.00 (ISBN 0-86539-045-2). Am Accounting.
True-Blue Laws of Connecticut & New Haven & the False Blue-Laws Invented by the Rev. Samuel Peters to Which Are Added Specimens of the Laws & Judicial Proceedings of Other Colonies & Some Blue-Laws of England in the Reign of James I. Ed. by J. Hammond Trumbull. 360p. 1987. Repr. of 1876 ed. 35.00x (ISBN 0-8377-2632-8). Rothman.
True Blue: The Davie Cooper Story. Ed. by Davie Cooper & Graham Clark. 192p. 1987. 50.00x (ISBN 1-85158-069-7, Pub. by Mainstream Scotland). State Mutual Bk.
True-Born Englishman: Being the Life of Henry Fielding. M. P. Willcocks. LC 74-8472. 1947. lib. bdg. 40.00 (ISBN 0-8414-9529-7). Folcroft.
True Boundaries of the Holy Land: Described in Numbers XXIV: 1-12: Solving the Many Diversified Theories As to Their Location. Samuel H. Isaacs. Ed. by Moshe Davis. LC 77-70706. (America & the Holy Land Ser.). (Illus.). 1977. Repr. of 1917 ed. lib. bdg. 17.00x (ISBN 0-405-10256-9). Ayer Co Pubs.
True Bounds of Christian Freedom. 1978. pap. 6.45 (ISBN 0-85151-083-3). Banner of Truth.
True Bride. Amy Gerstler. LC 85-81091. 71p. (Orig.). 1986. 18.00 (ISBN 0-932499-03-1); pap. 9.50 (ISBN 0-932499-04-X). Lapis Pr.
True Bridge Humor. Mike Lawrence. 60p. 1980. pap. 3.95 (ISBN 0-939460-11-4). M Hardy.
True Cat Stories. Marguerite P. Dolch. LC 75-2146. (Dolch Basic Vocabulary Ser.). (Illus.). 176p. (gr. 1-6). 1975. PLB 6.57 (ISBN 0-8116-2516-8). Garrard.
True Christian Science. Hani R. Abdu. 64p. 1981. 5.00 (ISBN 0-682-49632-4). Exposition-Phoenix.
True Christianity. H. A Williams. 1975. 5.95 (ISBN 0-87243-059-6). Templegate.
True Christianity: Twelve Lives of True Christians. Hugo G. Walter. LC 86-91688. 209p. 1988. 12.95 (ISBN 0-533-07352-9). Vantage.
True Church & the Poor. Jon Sobrino. Tr. by Mathew J. O'Connell from Span. LC 84-5661. Orig. Title: Resureccion de la Verdadera Iglesia, Los Pobres Lugar Teologica de la Eclesiologia. 384p. (Orig.). 1984. pap. 13.95 (ISBN 0-88344-513-1). Orbis Bks.
True Church of Christ. Sebastian Dabovich. pap. 0.25 (ISBN 0-686-11506-6). Eastern Orthodox.
True Civilization, an Immediate Necessity, & the Last Ground of Hope for Mankind. Josiah Warren. 1965. Repr. of 1863 ed. 22.50 (ISBN 0-8337-3689-2). B Franklin.
True Colors: 1004 Days as a Prisoner of War. James Thompson. Ed. by Judy Hilvosky. 1988. 18.95 (ISBN 0-87949-282-1). Ashley Bks.
True Confession of the Faith, Which Wee Falsley Called Brownists, Doo Hold. Henry Ainsworth. LC 78-26338. (English Experience Ser.: No. 158). 24p. 1969. Repr. of 1956 ed. 25.00 (ISBN 90-221-0158-4). Walter J Johnson.
True Confessions. John G. Dunne. 1983. pap. 4.50 (ISBN 0-671-65874-3). PB.
True Confessions & False Romances. William Hathaway. LC 72-182981. 64p. 1972. 2.95 (ISBN 0-87886-013-4). Greenfld Rev Pr.
True Confessions of a Sunday School Teacher. Hawley. 1983. 3.95 (ISBN 0-88207-285-4). Victor Bks.
True Confessions of an Albino Terrorist. Breyten Breytenbach. LC 84-25966. 396p. 1985. 18.95 (ISBN 0-374-27935-7). FS&G.
True Confessions of an Albino Terrorist. Breyten Breytenbach. 480p. 1986. pap. text ed. 5.95 (ISBN 0-07-007674-X). McGraw.
True Confessions: Owning up to the Secret Everybody Knows. Philip Yancey. (Christian Essentials Ser.). 48p. (Orig.). 1987. pap. 1.95 (ISBN 0-89283-324-6, Pub. by Vine Books). Servant.
True Copie of a Discourse Written by a Gentleman, Employed in the Late Voyage of Spaine & Portingale. Robert Devereux & Anthony Wingfield. LC 78-38172. (English Experience Ser.: No. 449). 1972. Repr. of 1589 ed. 9.50 (ISBN 90-221-0449-4). Walter J Johnson.
True Copie of a Letter from the Queens Maiesty to the Lord Mayor of London. Queen Elizabeth. LC 70-25636. (English Experience Ser.: No. 167). 8p. 1969. Repr. of 1586 ed. 25.00 (ISBN 90-221-0167-3). Walter J Johnson.
True Copy of the Record of the Official Proceedings at the Council in the Walla Walla Valley, 1855. Darrell Scott & Isaac I. Stevens. LC 85-17781. 124p. 1985. 12.95 (ISBN 0-87770-355-8). Ye Galleon.
True Correspondence: A Phenomenology of Thomas Hardy's Novels. Bruce Johnson. LC 83-3456. 176p. 1983. 22.00x (ISBN 0-8130-0764-X). U Presses Fla.
True Country: Themes in the Fiction of Flannery O'Connor. Carter W. Martin. LC 68-29047. pap. 65.80 (ISBN 0-317-27620-4, 2025065). Bks Demand UMI.
True Crime. Max A. Collins. 1984. 15.95 (ISBN 0-312-82045-3). St Martin.
True Crime. Max A. Collins. 384p. 1986. pap. 3.95 (ISBN 0-8125-0152-7, Dist. by Warner Pub Services & St. Martin's Press). Tor Bks.
True Declaration of the Troublesome Voyage of M. John Hawkins to the Parties of Guynea & the West Indies. John Hawkins. LC 73-6137. (English Experience Ser.: No. 602). 36p. 1973. Repr. of 1569 ed. 3.50 (ISBN 90-221-0602-0). Walter J Johnson.
True Description of the Lake Superior Country. John R. St. John. LC 76-27042. (Illus.). 1976. 15.00 (ISBN 0-912382-20-1). Black Letter.
True Detective. Max Collins. 384p. 1986. pap. 3.95 (ISBN 0-8125-0150-0, Dist. by Warner Pub Service & St. Martin's Press). Tor Bks.
True Detective. Max A. Collins. (Illus.). 368p. 1983. 14.95 (ISBN 0-312-82051-8). St Martin.
True Detective. Theodore Weesner. 464p. 1987. 17.95 (ISBN 0-671-40024-X). Summit Bks.
True Detective. Theodore Weesner. 400p. 1988. pap. 4.50 (ISBN 0-380-70499-4). Avon.
True Detectives. William Parkhurst. 1989. 19.95 (ISBN 0-517-56554-4). Crown.
True Devotion. Louis De Montfort. LC 63-12679. 1973. 3.50 (ISBN 0-8198-0517-3); pap. 2.50. Dghtrs St Paul.
True Devotion to Mary. Eddie Doherty. pap. 3.95 (ISBN 0-910984-02-6). Montfort Pubns.
True Devotion to Mary. De Montfort Louis. Ed. by The Fathers of the Company of Mary. LC 85-50571. 215p. 1985. pap. 5.00 (ISBN 0-89555-279-5). Tan Bks Pubs.
True Devotion to the Blessed Virgin. St. Louis Marie De Montfort. 4.95 (ISBN 0-910984-49-2); pap. 3.95 (ISBN 0-910984-50-6). Montfort Pubns.
True Difference Between Christian Subjection & Unchristian Rebellion. Thomas Bilson. LC 70-38154. (English Experience Ser.: No. 434). 854p. 1972. Repr. of 1585 ed. 143.00 (ISBN 90-221-0434-6). Walter J Johnson.
True Discipleship. expanded ed. William MacDonald. pap. 3.25 (ISBN 0-937396-50-8). Walterick Pubs.
True Discipleship. William MacDonald. pap. 2.50 (ISBN 0-937396-49-4). Walterick Pubs.
True Discourse Historical, of the Succeeding Governors in the Netherlands. Emanuel van Meteren. Tr. by T. Churchyard & R. Robinson. LC 68-54653. (English Experience Ser.: No. 57). 154p. 1968. Repr. of 1602 ed. 16.00 (ISBN 90-221-0057-X). Walter J Johnson.
True Discourse of the Present Estate of Virginia. Ralphe Hamor. LC 72-25512. (English Experience Ser.: No. 320). 70p. 1971. Repr. of 1615 ed. 30.00 (ISBN 90-221-0320-X). Walter J Johnson.
True Discourse of the Present State of Virginia. Ralph Hamor. LC 57-9000. (Publications Ser: No. 3). 1957. pap. 3.00 (ISBN 0-88490-044-4). VA State Lib.
True Doctrine of Ultra Vires in the Law of Corporations, Being a Concise Presentation of the Doctrine in Its Application to the Powers & Liabilities of Private & Municipal Corporations. Reuben A. Reese. lxxi, 338p. 1981. Repr. of 1897 ed. lib. bdg. 30.00x (ISBN 0-8377-1031-6). Rothman.
True Exemplary & Remarkable History of the Earle of Tirone. Thomas Gainsford. LC 68-54644. (English Experience Ser.: No. 25). 1968. Repr. of 1619 ed. 8.00 (ISBN 90-221-0025-1). Walter J Johnson.
True Face of Japan. Nohara Komankichi. 288p. 1936. 140.00x (ISBN 0-317-69180-5, Pub. by Han-Shan Tang Ltd). State Mutual Bk.
True Family. G. T. Ridlon. LC 76-142777. (Saco Valley Settlements Ser). 1970. pap. 1.50 (ISBN 0-8048-0847-3). C E Tuttle.
True FBI Story. pap. cancelled (ISBN 0-915598-18-3). Church of Scient Info.
True Founder of Christianity & the Hellenistic Philosophy. Max Rieser. 89p. (Orig.). 1979. pap. 19.00x (ISBN 90-6296-081-2, Pub. by Gieben Amsterdam). Benjamins North Am.
True Francine. Marc Brown. (Snuggle & Read Story Bks.). (Illus.). 32p. (ps-3). 1982. pap. 1.95 (ISBN 0-380-57083-1, 57083-1, Camelot). Avon.
True Francine. Marc Brown. (Illus.). 32p. (ps-3). 1981. 13.95 (ISBN 0-316-11212-7, Joy St Bks). Little.
True Francine. Marc Brown. (Illus.). (ps-3). 1987. pap. 4.95 (ISBN 0-316-11243-7, Joy St Bks). Little.
True Gen: An Intimate Portrait of Hemingway by Those Who Knew Him. Denis Brian. (Illus.). 288p. 1987. 19.95 (ISBN 0-8021-0006-6). Grove.
True Genius of Oliver Goldsmith. Robert H. Hopkins. LC 69-15760. (Illus.). pap. 64.00 (ISBN 0-317-41738-X, 2025856). Bks Demand UMI.
True George Washington. Paul L. Ford. 1981. Repr. of 1896 ed. lib. bdg. 30.00 (ISBN 0-8495-1622-6). Arden Lib.
True George Washington. facsimile ed. Paul L. Ford. LC 70-160973. (Select Bibliographies Reprint Ser). Repr. of 1896 ed. 26.50 (ISBN 0-8369-5841-1). Ayer Co Pubs.
True Ghost Stories. Brad Steiger. 1982. pap. 7.95 (ISBN 0-914918-35-4). Para Res.
True Glory: The Story of the Royal Navy. Warren Tute. 192p. 1982. 45.00x (ISBN 0-356-07915-5, Pub. by MacDonald & Co Pubs England). State Mutual Bk.
True God. Enoch Zadock. (Illus.). 45p. 1987. pap. text ed. 3.00 (ISBN 0-940517-06-X). JCMC Louisiana.
True Gospel of Salvation Revealed Anew by Jesus, 3 Vols. James E. Padgett. Vol. I, III. pap. 7.50 ea. (ISBN 0-686-37147-X); Vols. II, III. pap. 9.00 ea. New Age Min Spiritualist.
True Grasses. Eduard Hackel. Tr. by F. Lamson-Scribner & E. A. Southworth. (Illus.). 228p. 1982. Repr. of 1896 ed. text ed. 12.00 (ISBN 0-934454-98-1). Lubrecht & Cramer.
True Grit. Charles Portis. (RL 8). pap. 2.95 (ISBN 0-451-13734-5, AE2707, Sig). NAL.
True Hauntings in Montana. David F. Curran. Ed. & illus. by Patricia A. Curran. (Illus.). 40p. (Orig.). 1986. pap. 1.50 (ISBN 0-318-21289-7). D F Curran Prods.
True History of Joshua Davidson, 1872. Eliza L. Linton. Ed. by Robert L. Wolff. LC 75-1524. (Victorian Fiction Ser.). 1975. lib. bdg. 73.00 (ISBN 0-8240-1596-7). Garland Pub.
True History of Mexico. C. Morris. 1976. lib. bdg. 59.95 (ISBN 0-8490-2772-1). Gordon Pr.
True History of the Church of Scotland: From the Beginnings of the Reform to the End of the Reign of King James VI, 8 vols. David Calderwood. Ed. by Thomas Thomson. LC 83-45577. Date not set. Repr. of 1842 ed. Set. 525.00 (ISBN 0-404-19894-5). AMS Pr.
True History of the Elephant Man. Michael Howell & Peter Ford. 1980. pap. 4.95 (ISBN 0-14-005622-X). Penguin.
True History on the Walls. Roderick Watson. 1983. 20.00x (ISBN 0-904265-15-3, Pub. by Macdonald Pub UK). State Mutual Bk.
True Horoscope of the U. S. Helen M. Boyd. LC 75-7188. 1975. 7.25 (ISBN 0-88231-007-0). ASI Pubs Inc.
True Horror Stories of Science: Research & Medicine in American College Education. Jack Formacarr. LC 83-48722. 171p. 1984. 24.95 (ISBN 0-88164-077-8); pap. 19.95 (ISBN 0-88164-074-3). ABBE Pubs Assn.
True Humanism. Jacques Maritain. Tr. by M. R. Adamson. LC 71-114888. (Select Bibliographies Reprint Ser). 1938. 22.00 (ISBN 0-8369-5292-8). Ayer Co Pubs.
True Humanism. 3rd ed. Jacques Maritain. Tr. by Margot Adamson. Repr. of 1941 ed. lib. bdg. 38.50x (ISBN 0-8371-2902-8, MAHU). Greenwood.
True Identification. Lillian De Waters. pap. 4.00 (ISBN 0-686-05707-4). L De Waters.
True Image: Christ as the Origin & Destiny of Man. Philip E. Hughes. 1988. pap. 19.95 (ISBN 0-8028-0314-8). Eerdmans.
True India. C. F. Andrews. 251p. 1986. Repr. text ed. 37.50x (ISBN 81-210-0036-X, Pub. by Inter India Pubns N Delhi). Apt Bks.
True India. C. F. Andrews. 251p. 1985. 34.95. Asia Bk Corp.
True Intellectual System of the Universe. Ralph Cudworth. Repr. of 1678 ed. cancelled (ISBN 3-7728-0103-X). Adlers Foreign Bks.
True Intellectual System of the Universe, 2 vols. Ralph Cudworth. Ed. by Rene Wellek. LC 75-11213. (British Philosophers & Theologians of the 17th & 18th Centuries Ser.: Vol. 16). 1978. Repr. of 1678 ed. Set. lib. bdg. 101.00 (ISBN 0-8240-1767-6). Garland Pub.
True Interest & Political Maxims of the Republic of Holland. Pieter De La Court. LC 78-38278. (Evolution of Capitalism Ser.). 520p. 1972. Repr. of 1746 ed. 34.50 (ISBN 0-405-04117-9). Ayer Co Pubs.
True Interest of Britain Set Forth in Regard to the Colonies & the Only Means of Living in Peace & Harmony with Them, Including Five Different Plans for Effecting This Desirable Event. Josiah Tucker. LC 76-141126. (Research Library of Colonial Americana). 1971. Repr. of 1776 ed. 18.00 (ISBN 0-405-03337-0). Ayer Co Pubs.
True Jaguar. Warren Norwood. 336p. 1988. pap. 3.95 (ISBN 0-553-27127-X, Spectra). Bantam.
True Journal of the Sally Fleet, with the Proceedings of the Voyage. John Dunton. LC 71-25745. (English Experience Ser.: No. 242). 26p. 1970. Repr. of 1637 ed. 20.00 (ISBN 90-221-0242-4). Walter J Johnson.
True Joy from Assisi. Raphael Brown. 276p. 1978. 8.95 (ISBN 0-8199-0688-3). Franciscan Herald.
True Joy of Positive Living. Norman V. Peale. 288p. 1985. pap. 3.95 (ISBN 0-449-20833-8, Pub. by Crest). Fawcett.
True Law of Population: Shown to Be Connected with the Food of the People. 2nd ed. Thomas Doubleday. LC 67-17492. 1967. Repr. of 1847 ed. 39.50x (ISBN 0-678-00244-4). Kelley.
True Lies. Philip Ross. 288p. 1988. 16.95x (ISBN 0-312-93057-7). Tor Bks.
True Life. Lewis Foster. LC 77-83656. 96p. (Orig.). 1978. pap. 2.25 (ISBN 0-87239-192-2, 40047). Standard Pub.
True-Life Adventure. Julie Smith. 1985. 15.95 (ISBN 0-89296-120-1). Mysterious Pr.
True-Life Adventure. Julie Smith. 256p. 1986. pap. 3.95 (ISBN 0-445-40505-8). Mysterious Pr.
True Life of Billy the Kid. Edmund Fable, Jr. LC 80-18408. 78p. (Orig.). 1980. Repr. of 1881 ed. collector's edition 95.00 (ISBN 0-932702-11-2). Creative Texas.
True Life of Jesus of Nazareth - the Confessions of St. Paul. Alexander Smyth. (Illus.). 1968. 8.95 (ISBN 0-932642-15-2); pap. write for info. (ISBN 0-932642-56-X). Unarius Pubns.
True Life of Sir Richard F. Burton. G. M. Stisted. 436p. 1984. 250.00x (ISBN 1-85077-049-2, Pub. by Darf Pubs Ltd). State Mutual Bk.
True Life of Sweeney Todd: A Novel in Collage. Cozette De Charmoy. (Paperback Ser.). (Illus.). 1977. pap. 5.95 (ISBN 0-306-80060-8). Da Capo.
True Life Reader for Children & Parents. Philip Thody. 1977. 10.00 (ISBN 0-7045-0311-5). State Mutual Bk.
True-Life Treasure Hunts. Judy Donnelly. LC 84-4777. (Step-up Bks.). (Illus.). 72p. (gr. 2-5). 1984. 4.95 (ISBN 0-394-86801-3, Pub. by BYR); lib. bdg. 8.99 (ISBN 0-394-96801-8). Random.
True Likeness: The Black South of Richard Samuel Roberts, 1920-1936. Ed. by Philip Dunn. Thomas L. Johnson. (Illus.). 188p. (Orig.). 1986. 34.50 (ISBN 0-912697-48-2, Co-pub. by Bruccoli-Clark); ltd. ed. slipcased 100.00 (ISBN 0-912697-47-4); pap. 19.95 (ISBN 0-912697-50-4). Algonquin Bks.
True Love. Created by Francine Pascal. (Caitlin Ser.: No. 3). 208p. 1986. pap. 2.95 (ISBN 0-553-25295-X, Skylark). Bantam.
True Love: A Novel. Herbert Gold. LC 85-45939. 224p. 1986. pap. 3.95 (ISBN 0-394-62220-0, BC). Grove.
True Love Story. G. A. Holland. 1987. 14.95 (ISBN 0-533-06799-5). Vantage.
True Love Works. Stephen Stanley. 200p. (Orig.). 1989. pap. 12.95 (ISBN 1-55618-038-1). Brunswick Pub.
True Meaning of Christ's Teaching, Vol. 215. Omraam M. Aivanhov. (Izvor Collection Ser.). (Illus.). 203p. (Orig.). 1985. pap. 5.95 (ISBN 2-85566-322-9). Prosveta USA.
True Meaning of the Lord of Heaven. Matteo Ricci. Tr. by Douglas Lancashire & Peter Hu Kuo-chen. Ed. by Edward J. Malatesta. LC 84-80944. (Jesuit Primary Sources in English Translations Series I: No. 6). (Illus.). 300p. (Eng. & Chinese.). 1985. 39.00 (ISBN 0-912422-78-5); smyth sewn 34.00 (ISBN 0-912422-77-7). Inst Jesuit.
True Men. Mary Q. Steele. LC 76-5482. 144p. (gr. 5-9). 1976. PLB 11.88 (ISBN 0-688-84052-3). Greenwillow.
True Mexico: Tenochtitlan. A. Deverdun. 1976. lib. bdg. 59.95 (ISBN 0-8490-2773-X). Gordon Pr.
True Names. Vernor Vinge. (Illus.). 160p. 1984. pap. 7.95 (ISBN 0-312-94444-6); cancelled signed ltd. ed. (ISBN 0-312-94445-4). Bluejay Bks.
True Names & Other Dangers. Vernor Vinge. 1987. pap. 2.95 (ISBN 0-671-65363-6). Baen Bks.
True Nature of Discounts & Interest Charges. Charles H. Hoffman. Ed. by James J. Andover. 1980. pap. 6.95 (ISBN 0-934914-31-1). NACM.
True Newes from One of Sir F. Veres Companie. Francis Vere. LC 78-38227. (English Experience Ser.: No. 491). 24p. 1972. Repr. of 1591 ed. 5.00 (ISBN 90-221-0491-5). Walter J Johnson.
True Ocean Found: Paludanus's Letters on Dutch Voyages to the Kara Sea, 1595-1596. Ed. by James D. Tracy. LC 80-13962. (Publication from the James Ford Bell Library at the University of Minnesota). (Illus.). 1980. 10.00x (ISBN 0-8166-0961-6). U of Minn Pr.

Truly Tasteless Jokes V. Blanche Knott. 1988. pap. 2.95 (ISBN 0-317-65543-4). St Martin.
Truly Tasteless Jokes 2. Blanche Knott. 1985. pap. 3.50 (ISBN 0-345-32921-X). Ballantine.
Truly Tasteless Jokes 3. Blanche Knott. 1983. pap. 3.50 (ISBN 0-345-32922-8). Ballantine.
Truly Unusual Soups. 2nd ed. Lu Lockwood. LC 77-88839. 144p. 1977. 6.95 (ISBN 0-87106-931-8). Globe Pequot.
Trumai Indians of Central Brazil. Robert F. Murphy. LC 84-45523. (American Ethnological Society Monographs: No. 24). 1988. Repr. of 1955 ed. 22.00 (ISBN 0-404-62923-7). AMS Pr.
Truman. Roy Jenkins. (Illus.). 232p. 1986. 17.45i (ISBN 0-06-015580-9, HarpT). Har-Row.
Truman. Roy Jenkins. LC 85-45643. (Illus.). 256p. 1987. pap. 7.95 (ISBN 0-06-091422-X, PL 1422, PL). Har-Row.
Truman: A Centenary Remembrance of Robert H. Ferrell. Robert H. Ferrell. (Illus.). 272p. 1984. 25.00 (ISBN 0-670-36196-8). Viking.
Truman Administration & the Problems of Postwar Labor 1945-1948. Arthur F. McClure. LC 68-57718. 267p. 1969. 25.00 (ISBN 0-8386-6999-9). Fairleigh Dickinson.
Truman Administration's Legacy for Black America. Philip Vaughan. LC 76-5294. 1976. 9.00 (ISBN 0-87881-047-1). Mojave Bks.
Truman, American Jewry, & Israel, 1945-1948. Zvi Ganin. 238p. 1979. 34.50 (ISBN 0-8419-0401-4); pap. 22.50 (ISBN 0-8419-0497-9). Holmes & Meier.
Truman & Taft-Hartley: A Question of Mandate. R. Alton Lee. LC 80-17251. viii, 254p. 1980. Repr. of 1966 ed. lib. bdg. 35.00x (ISBN 0-313-22618-0, LETT). Greenwood.
Truman & the Eightieth Congress. Susan Hartmann. LC 78-149008. 254p. 1971. 28.00x (ISBN 0-8262-0105-9). U of Mo Pr.
Truman & the Russians. Herbert Druks. 1981. pap. 12.50 (ISBN 0-8315-0183-9). Speller.
Truman & the Steel Seizure Case: The Limits of Presidential Power. Maeva Marcus. LC 77-4095. (Contemporary American History Ser.). 390p. 1977. 37.50x (ISBN 0-231-04126-8); pap. 17.50 (ISBN 0-231-04127-6). Columbia U Pr.
Truman Capote. Helen S. Garson. LC 80-5336. (Literature & Life Ser.). (Illus.). 216p. 1980. 16.95x (ISBN 0-8044-2229-X). Ungar.
Truman Capote. Kenneth T. Reed. (United States Authors Ser.). 1981. lib. bdg. 16.95 (ISBN 0-8057-7321-5, Twayne). G K Hall.
Truman Capote: A Bibliography. Ed. by Kenneth Starosciak. 1973. ltd ed 7.50 (ISBN 0-686-05289-7). K Starosciak.
Truman Capote: A Reference Guide. Robert J. Stanton. 1980. lib. bdg. 24.50 (ISBN 0-8161-8108-X, Hall Reference). G K Hall.
Truman Capote: Conversations. M. T. Inge. LC 86-19116. (Literary Conversations Ser.). 390p. 1987. 25.95x (ISBN 0-87805-274-7); pap. 14.95 (ISBN 0-87805-275-5). U Pr of Miss.
Truman Capote: Dear Heart, Old Buddy. John M. Brinnin. (Illus.). 176p. 1986. pap. 16.95 (ISBN 0-385-29509-X, Sey Lawr). Delacorte.
Truman Capote: Dear Heart, Old Buddy. John M. Brinnin. (Illus.). 176p. 1988. pap. 9.95 (ISBN 0-385-29621-5, Delta). Delacorte.
Truman Capote: Dear Heart, Old Buddy. John M. Brinnin. 1988. pap. 9.95 (ISBN 0-317-66972-9, Delta). Dell.
Truman Committee: A Study in Congressional Responsibility. Donald H. Riddle. LC 63-16306. pap. 54.30 (ISBN 0-317-08280-9, 2050638). Bks Demand UMI.
Truman Doctrine. Charles M. Dobbs. 1988. price not set (ISBN 0-89874-988-3). Krieger.
Truman Doctrine & the Origins of McCarthyism: Foreign Policy, Domestic Policy, & Internal Security, 1946-48. Richard M. Freeland. 448p. 1985. 50.00x (ISBN 0-8147-2575-9); pap. 18.50x (ISBN 0-8147-2576-7). NYU Pr.
Truman Era, Nineteen Forty-Five to Nineteen Fifty-Two. I. F. Stone. (Nonconformist History of Our Times Ser.). 264p. 1988. 17.95 (ISBN 0-316-81761-9); pap. 8.95 (ISBN 0-316-81772-4). Little.
Truman G. Blocker, Jr. History of Medicine Collections Books & Manuscripts. Ed. by Larry J. Wygant. (Illus.). 432p. 1986. text ed. 50.00X (ISBN 0-292-78093-1, Pub. by Univ of Tx Medical Branch at Galvestar). U of Tex Pr.
Truman in Cartoon & Caricature. James N. Giglio & Greg G. Thielen. LC 84-9088. (Illus.). 165p. 1984. 14.95 (ISBN 0-8138-1806-0). Iowa St U Pr.
Truman-MacArthur Controversy & the Korean War. John W. Spanier. 1965. pap. 7.95 (ISBN 0-393-00279-9, Norton Lib). Norton.
Truman Nelson Reader. Ed. by William Schafer. 336p. (Orig.). 1989. lib. bdg. 40.00x (ISBN 0-87023-647-4); pap. text ed. 14.95 (ISBN 0-87023-648-2). U of Mass Pr.
Truman Period As a Research Field: A Reappraisal, 1972. Richard S. Kirkendall. LC 73-80585. 256p. 1974. 28.00x (ISBN 0-8262-0152-0). U of Mo Pr.
Truman Persuasions. William R. Underhill. (Illus.). 372p. 1981. 24.95x (ISBN 0-8138-1640-8). Iowa St U Pr.
Truman Presidency: Intimate Perspectives. Ed. by Kenneth W. Thompson. (Portraits of American Presidents Ser.). 200p. 1984. lib. bdg. 24.50; pap. text ed. 9.00 (ISBN 0-8191-3699-9). U Pr of Amer.
Truman Presidency: The Origins of the Imperial Presidency & the National Security State. Ed. by Athan Theoharis. 1979. text ed. 39.50x (ISBN 0-930576-12-8). E M Coleman Ent.
Truman Scandals & the Politics of Morality. Andrew J. Dunar. LC 84-2205. 224p. 1984. 24.00 (ISBN 0-8262-0443-0). U of Mo Pr.
Truman Speaks. Harry S. Truman. Ed. by Cyril Clemens. 1946. 15.00 (ISBN 0-527-90950-5). Kraus Repr.
Truman Speaks: On the Presidency, the Constitution, & Statecraft. Harry S. Truman. LC 60-8389. 160p. 1975. 30.00x (ISBN 0-231-02384-7); pap. 15.00x (ISBN 0-231-08339-4). Columbia U Pr.
Truman White House: The Administration of the Presidency, 1945-1953. Ed. by Francis H. Heller. LC 79-15713. (Illus.). xxiv, 248p. 1980. 25.00x (ISBN 0-7006-0193-7). U Pr of KS.
Truman Years. (Political Profiles Ser.). 748p. 1982. 65.00x (ISBN 0-87196-453-8). Facts on File.
Truman's Court: A Study in Judicial Restraint. Frances H. Rudko. LC 88-5664. (Contributions in Legal Studies: No. 45). 184p. 1988. lib. bdg. 37.95 (ISBN 0-313-26316-7, RTC/). Greenwood.
Truman's Crises: A Political Biography of Harry S. Truman. Harold F. Gosnell. LC 79-7360. (Contributions in Political Science Ser.: No. 33). 1980. lib. bdg. 36.95 (ISBN 0-313-21273-2, GTC/). Greenwood.
Truman's Two-China Policy. June Grasso. 216p. 1987. text ed. 27.50 (ISBN 0-87332-411-0). M E Sharpe.
Trumbull Stickney. Amberys R. Whittle. LC 72-425. 164p. 1973. 15.00 (ISBN 0-8387-1154-5). Bucknell U Pr.
Trumbull: The Declaration of Independence. Irma B. Jaffe. (Art in Context Ser.). (Illus.). 124p. 1979. 17.95x (ISBN 0-8464-1199-7). Beekman Pubs.
Trump Card. Margaret Hobbs. 224p. (Orig.). 1986. pap. 2.95 (ISBN 0-345-32637-7). Ballantine.
Trump: The Art of the Deal. Donald Trump & Tony Schwartz. LC 87-42663. (Illus.). 256p. 1987. 19.95 (ISBN 0-394-55528-7). Random.
Trump: The Art of the Deal. Donald Trump & Tony Schwartz. 1988. pap. 5.95. Warner Bks.
Trump: The Building of an Empire. Jhon Dooley. 192p. 1988. pap. 3.50 (ISBN 1-55547-262-1). Critics Choice Paper.
Trump: The Remarkable, Unfinished Saga of an Extraordinary American. Jerome Tuccille. 1988. pap. 7.95 (ISBN 1-55611-089-8, Pub. by Primus Lib Contemp). D I Fine.
Trump: The Saga of America's Masterbuilder. rev. & updated ed. Jerome Tuccille. LC 86-80053. (Illus.). 262p. 1986. pap. 9.95 (ISBN 0-917657-69-1, Pub. by Primus). D I Fine.
Trump: The Saga of America's Most Powerful Real Estate Baron. Jerome Tuccille. LC 85-70277. 243p. 1985. 17.95 (ISBN 0-917657-25-X). D I Fine.
Trump Tower. Jonathan Mandell & Sy Rubin. 200p. 1984. 30.00 (ISBN 0-8184-0354-3, Pub. by Citadel Pr). Lyle Stuart.
Trumpet & Trombone in Graphic Arts, Fifteen Hundred to Eighteen Hundred. Tom L. Naylor. Ed. by Stephen L. Glover. LC 79-10044. (Brass Research Ser.: No. 9). (Illus.). 1979. lib. bdg. 30.00x (ISBN 0-914282-20-4). Brass Pr.
Trumpet at a Distant Gate. Tim Mowl & Brian Earnshaw. LC 84-73358. (Illus.). 288p. 1985. 35.00 (ISBN 0-87923-602-7). Godine.
Trumpet Book. Melvin Berger. LC 78-836. (Illus.). (gr. 3-7). 1978. o. p. 11.25 (ISBN 0-688-41832-5); PLB 11.88 (ISBN 0-688-51832-X). Lothrop.
Trumpet in Darkness: Preaching to Mourners. Robert Hughes. LC 85-47719. (Fortress Resources for Preaching Ser.). 112p. 1985. pap. 5.95 (ISBN 0-8006-1141-1). Fortress.
Trumpet in the Twilight of Time. Raymond McCarty. LC 80-53734. (Illus.). 144p. (Orig.). 1981. 10.95 (ISBN 0-938310-00-3); pap. 6.95 (ISBN 0-938310-01-1). Volunteer Pubns.
Trumpet Judgments. Date not set. pap. 0.95 (ISBN 0-937408-10-7). GMI Pubns Inc.
Trumpet-Major. Thomas Hardy. LC 77-70257. (Hardy New Wessex Editions Ser.). 1977. pap. 3.95 (ISBN 0-312-82146-8). St Martin.
Trumpet-Major. Thomas Hardy. (Nonfiction Ser.). 320p. 1985. pap. 4.95 (ISBN 0-14-043142-X). Penguin.
Trumpet of Terror. Deborah L. Goodman. (Choose Your Own Adventure Ser.: No. 55). 128p. (Orig.). (gr. 4). 1986. pap. 2.25 (ISBN 0-553-25491-X). Bantam.
Trumpet of the Last Judgement Against the Athiest & Antichrist: An Ultimatum. Bruno Bauer. Tr. by Lawrence Stepelevich from Ger. (Studies in German Thought & History: Vol. 5). 224p. 1988. lib. bdg. 49.95x (ISBN 0-88946-356-5). E Mellen.
Trumpet of the Swan. E. B. White. LC 72-112484. (Illus.). (gr. 4-6). 10.95i (ISBN 0-06-026397-0); PLB 11.89 (ISBN 0-06-026398-9). HarpJ.
Trumpet of the Swan. E. B. White. LC 72-112484. (Trophy I Can Read Bks.). (Illus.). 222p. (gr. 3 up). 1973. pap. 2.95 (ISBN 0-06-440048-4, Trophy). HarpJ.
Trumpet of the Swan. E. B. White. (gr. k-9). 1988. pap. 1.95. Scholastic Inc.
Trumpet of the Swan see E. B. White Boxed Set.
Trumpet Shall Sound: A Study of Cargo Cults in Melanesia. Peter Worsley. LC 67-26995. (Illus.). 1968. pap. 8.95 (ISBN 0-8052-0156-4). Schocken.
Trumpet Soundeth: William Jennings Bryan & His Democracy, 1896-1912. Paul W. Glad. LC 85-24695. (Illus.). x, 256p. 1986. Repr. of 1960 ed. lib. bdg. 48.50x (ISBN 0-313-25049-9, GLTS). Greenwood.
Trumpet Sounds. Eunice Y. Smith. LC 85-17596. (Illus.). 272p. 1985. 14.95 (ISBN 0-88208-198-5). Chicago Review.
Trumpet to Arms. Bruce Lancaster. 1976. Repr. of 1944 ed. lib. bdg. 21.95x (ISBN 0-88411-681-6, Pub. by Aeonian Pr). Amereon Ltd.
Trumpet to Arms: Alternative Media in America. David Armstrong. 350p. 1984. pap. 9.00 (ISBN 0-89608-193-1). South End Pr.
Trumpeter of Krakow. Eric P. Kelly. LC 66-16712. (Illus.). 224p. (gr. 7 up). 1966. 13.95 (ISBN 0-02-750140-X); pap. 3.95 (ISBN 0-02-044150-9). Macmillan.
Trumpeter Swan Bibliography. Ed. by James A. Cooper & David K. Weaver. 55p. (Orig.). 1986. pap. text ed. 10.00 (ISBN 0-9619936-3-4); software disk 25.00 (ISBN 0-9619936-5-0). Trumpeter Swan Soc.
Trumpeter Swan: Its History, Habits, & Population in the United States. Winston E. Banko. LC 80-12533. (Illus.). x, 214p. 1980. pap. 5.95 (ISBN 0-8032-6057-1, BB 731, Bison). U of Nebr Pr.
Trumpeters' & Kettledrummers' Art (1795) J. Ernst Altenburg. Tr. by Edward H. Tarr from Ger. LC 74-4026. (Illus.). 168p. 1974. 15.00x (ISBN 0-914282-01-8). Brass Pr.
Trumpeter's Guide to Orchestral Excerpts. 2nd ed. Ed. by Anne Hardin. LC 86-70740. 70p. 1986. 18.00x (ISBN 0-938100-44-0); pap. 12.00x (ISBN 0-938100-46-7). Camden Hse.
Trumpeter's Handbook: A Comprehensive Guide to Playing & Teaching the Trumpet. Roger C. Sherman. LC 78-73020. (Illus.). 1979. 24.95 (ISBN 0-918194-02-4). Accura.
Trumpets & Raspberries. Dario Fo. 75p. 1987. pap. write for info. (ISBN 0-86104-676-5). Routledge Chapman & Hall.
Trumpets from the Islands of Their Eviction. Martin Espada. LC 87-71581. 96p. 1987. pap. 7.00 (ISBN 0-916950-72-7). Biling Rev-Pr.
Trumpets, Horns & Music. J. Murray Barbour. 1964. 10.00 (ISBN 0-87013-079-X). Mich St U Pr.
Trumpets in Grumpetland. Peter Dallas-Smith. LC 84-11491. (Illus.). 32p. (gr. 3 up). 1985. 8.95 (ISBN 0-394-87028-X). Random.
Trumpets of Company K. William Chamberlain. 1982. pap. 1.95 (ISBN 0-345-30551-5). Ballantine.
Trumpets of War. Robert Adams. (Horseclans Ser.: No. 16). 224p. 1987. pap. 3.50 (ISBN 0-451-14715-4, Sig). NAL.
Trumpets Sounding: Propanda Plays of the American Revolution. Ed. by Norman Philbrick. LC 77-184007. 1977. Repr. of 1972 ed. lib. bdg. 20.00x (ISBN 0-405-11192-4, Pub. by Blom Pubns). Ayer Co Pubs.
Trumps of Doom. Roger Zelazny. (Amber Ser.). 157p. 1985. 14.95 (ISBN 0-87795-718-5). Morrow.
Trumps of Doom. Roger Zelazny. 1986. pap. 3.50 (ISBN 0-380-89635-4). Avon.
Truncated & Censored Samples from Normal Applications. Schneider. 328p. 1986. 49.75 (ISBN 0-8247-7591-0). Dekker.
Trundlewheel. Katrina Van Tassel. (Lamont Hall Chapbook Series for Poetry). 16p. (Orig.). 1981. 1.25 (ISBN 0-9603840-1-4). Andrew Mtn Pr.
Trunkful of Observations. Myldred Hutchins. LC 86-72120. 1986. pap. 5.00 (ISBN 0-931611-07-5). D R Benbow.
Truro, Cape Cod, Mass: Or Land Marks & Sea Marks. Shebnah Rich. 1988. 32.50 (ISBN 0-8048-7025-X). C E Tuttle.
Truro City Trail. Christine Oates. 1985. 12.00x (ISBN 0-907566-16-2, Pub. by Dyllansow & Truran). State Mutual Bk.
Trusses: A Revision of A 713. Mary Vance. (Architecture Ser.: A 1580). 14p. 1986. 3.75 (ISBN 0-89028-810-0). Vance Biblios.
Trust. Mary Flanagan. LC 87-24402. 292p. 1988. 17.95 (ISBN 0-689-11986-0). Atheneum.
Trust. Robert Merchant. (Literacy Volunteers of America Readers Ser.). 32p. (Orig.). 1983. pap. 1.95 (ISBN 0-8428-9618-X). Cambridge Bk.
Trust. Cynthia Ozick. 640p. 1983. pap. 11.95 (ISBN 0-525-48066-8, Obelisk). Dutton.
Trust: A New View of Personal & Organizational Development. Jack R. Gibb. 1978. 15.00 (ISBN 0-89615-006-2); pap. 8.95. Omicron Pr.
Trust Administration & Taxation, 4 vols. rev. ed. Walter L. Nossaman & Joseph L. Wyatt, Jr. 1966. looseleaf set 260.00 (470); Updates. 1985 159.00; 1986 171.00. Bender.
Trust & Corporation Problems. Henry R. Seager & Charles A. Gulick, Jr. LC 73-2534. (Big Business; Economic Power in a Free Society Ser.). Repr. of 1929 ed. 44.00 (ISBN 0-405-05112-3). Ayer Co Pubs.
Trust & Power: Two Works. Niklas Luhmann. Ed. by Tom Burns & Gianfranco Poggi. Tr. by Howard Davis et al. LC 79-40579. 228p. pap. 59.30 (2030528). Bks Demand UMI.
Trust Audit Manual. Bank Administration Institute Staff. 133p. 1976. 36.00 (ISBN 0-317-33834-X, 322). Bank Admin Inst.
Trust Business. 2nd ed. John M. Clarke et al. (Illus.). 260p. 1988. text ed. 37.50 (ISBN 0-89982-350-5). Am Bankers.
Trust Companies in the United States. George Cator. LC 78-63889. (Johns Hopkins University. Studies in the Social Sciences. Twentieth Ser. 1902: 5-6). Repr. of 1902 ed. 24.50 (ISBN 0-404-61143-5). AMS Pr.
Trust Department Accounting. Bank Administration Institute Staff. 244p. 1976. 36.00 (ISBN 0-317-33836-6, 108). Bank Admin Inst.
Trust Department Administration & Operations, 2 vols. Victor P. Whitney. 1981. looseleaf 130.00 (754); Updates 1985 38.50; 1986 39.50. Bender.
Trust Doctrines in Church Controversies. Dallin H. Oaks. LC 83-25058. xiv, 125p. 1984. 13.95x (ISBN 0-86554-104-3, MUP/H96). Mercer Univ Pr.
Trust Functions & Services. 1978. 24.00 (ISBN 0-89982-158-8, 050500). Am Bankers.
Trust in Love. Cloverdale Press Staff. (Sweet Dreams Ser.: No. 147). 176p. (Orig.). 1988. pap. 2.50 (ISBN 0-553-27229-2, Sweet Dreams). Bantam.
Trust in Summer Madness. Carole Mortimer. (Harlequin Presents Ser.). 192p. 1984. pap. 1.95 (ISBN 0-373-10669-6). Harlequin Bks.
Trust in the Unexpected. Gunnel Linde. LC 83-73165. (Illus.). 144p. (gr. 3-7). 1984. 10.95 (ISBN 0-689-50300-8, M K McElderry). Macmillan.
Trust Industry in Transition. 1983. 60.00 (ISBN 0-318-04487-0, TRIN). Bank MKTG Assn.
Trust Is the Key. Roxanne Sumners. (Illus.). 52p. (Orig.). 1983. pap. 4.95 (ISBN 0-913627-00-3). Agadir Pr.
Trust: Its Book. Ed. by James H. Bridge. LC 73-1995. (Big Business; Economic Power in a Free Society Ser.). Repr. of 1902 ed. 18.00 (ISBN 0-405-05077-1). Ayer Co Pubs.
Trust: Learn the Value Of... Ser. Elaine Goley. (Illus.). 32p. (gr. 1-4). 1987. PLB 106.00 10 bk. set (ISBN 0-317-60395-7); PLB 10.60 (ISBN 0-86592-378-7). Rourke Corp.
Trust Magic: The Ultimate Tax Shelter. Eagle Legal Services Staff. 1985. 19.95. Lifecraft.
Trust: Making & Breaking Cooperative Relations. Ed. by Diego Gambetta. 280p. 1988. text ed. 49.95 (ISBN 0-631-15506-6). Basil Blackwell.
Trust Marketing Handbook. Victor P. Whitney. LC 76-46444. 288p. pap. 74.90 (2052226). Bks Demand UMI.
Trust Me. John Updike. 1987. 17.95 (ISBN 0-394-55833-2). Knopf.
Trust Me. John Updike. 1988. pap. 4.95 (ISBN 0-449-21498-2, Crest). Fawcett.
Trust Me, Jennifer. Val Call. LC 82-72081. (Comic Tale Easy Reader Ser.). (Illus.). 176p. (Orig.). (gr. 5-12). 1985. pap. 4.50x (ISBN 0-943864-01-1). Davenport.
Trust Me on This. Donald E. Westlake. LC 87-22098. 272p. 1988. 16.95 (ISBN 0-89296-176-7). Mysterious Pr.
Trust Problem. Jeremiah W. Jenks & Walter E. Clark. Ed. by John J. Quigley. LC 73-2513. (Big Business; Economic Power in a Free Society Ser.). Repr. of 1929 ed. 34.00 (ISBN 0-405-05094-1). Ayer Co Pubs.
Trust Software Directory. 1982. 50.000 (ISBN 0-89982-058-1, 366900); members 7.50. Am Bankers.
Trust Territory Reports, 8 vols. 1987. Vol. 1, 1951-1958. 33.00; Vol. 2, 1959-1964. 33.00; Vol. 3, 1965-1968. 33.00; Vol. 4, 1968-1969. 33.00; Vol. 5, 1970-1972. 33.00; Vol. 6, 1972-1974. 33.00; Vol. 7, 1974-1978. 33.00; Vol. 8, 1979-1987. write for info. Equity Pub NH.
Trust the Liar. Susan Zannos. 1987. 16.95 (ISBN 0-8027-5697-2). Walker & Co.
Trust the Spirit, Share the Struggle. William A. Dudde. 1986. pap. 4.50 (ISBN 0-377-00158-9). Friendship Pr.
Trust Thy Fellow Man. Thomas L. Hakes. 5p. 1983. pap. 1.75x (ISBN 0-915020-14-9). Bardic.
Trust to Good Verses: Herrick Tercentenary Essays. Ed. by Roger B. Rollin & J. Max Patrick. LC 77-74547. (Illus.). 1977. 29.95x (ISBN 0-8229-3353-5). U of Pittsburgh Pr.
Trust Your Children: Voices Against Censorship in Children's Literature. Mark I. West. 150p. 1987. pap. text ed. 19.95 (ISBN 1-55570-021-7). Neal-Schuman.
Trust Your Heart: An Autobiography. Judy Collins. (Illus.). 320p. 1987. 18.95 (ISBN 0-395-41285-4). HM.
Trust Yourself to Life. Clara M. Codd. LC 75-4245. 116p. 1975. pap. 1.75 (ISBN 0-8356-0464-0, Quest). Theos Pub Hse.
Trust Yourself! You Have the Power. Tony Larsen. LC 79-12837. 248p. 1979. pap. 8.95 (ISBN 0-915166-18-6). Impact Pubs Cal.
Trusted Network Interpretation of the Trusted Computer System Evaluation Criteria. (NCSC TG). 298p. (Orig.). 1987. pap. 13.00 (ISBN 0-318-23850-0, S/N 008-000-00486-2). USGPO.

Trustee from the Toolroom. Nevil Shute. 311p. 1976. Repr. of 1960 ed. lib. bdg. 21.95x (ISBN 0-89244-016-3). Queens Hse-Focus Serv.

Trustee Game: The Foundation of MacTitle-MacTrust; How to Be an Unlicensed, Undercapitalized, Inexperienced Success. United Entrepreneurs Association of America Staff & Al Rotola. LC 86-104624. (Megatactics Ser.). (Illus.). xiii, 197p. Date not set. price not set. Am Entrepreneurs.

Trustee Handbook. 5th ed. Francis Parkman et al. 1984. pap. 7.75 (ISBN 0-934338-54-X). NAIS.

Trustee of a Small Public Library. Virginia Young. (Small Public Library). 12p. 1978. pap. 2.50x (ISBN 0-8389-5514-2). ALA.

Trustee Tool Kit for Library Leadership. Caltac Tool Kit Committee 1985. 425p. 1987. pap. 25.00 (ISBN 0-318-23784-9). Cal State Lib.

Trustees & Officers of Indiana University 1950-1982. Eleanor L. Roehr. LC 83-47510. (Illus.). 320p. 1983. 15.00x (ISBN 0-253-36095-1). Ind U Pr.

Trustees & the Future of Foundations. John W. Nason. LC 77-76677. 112p. 1977. pap. 12.00 (ISBN 0-913892-00-9). Coun Found.

Trustee's Guide to Hospital Law. Arthur H. Bernstein. LC 81-53758. 300p. 1981. 24.95 (ISBN 0-931028-14-0); pap. 19.95 (ISBN 0-931028-13-2). Teach'em.

Trustees Handbook: A Basic Text on Labor-Management Employee Benefit Plans. 3rd ed. Ed. by Claude L. Kordus. 545p. 1979. pap. text ed. 35.00 (ISBN 0-89154-113-6). Intl Found Employ.

Trustees, Trusteeship, & the Public Good: Issues of Accountability for Hospitals, Museums, Universities, & Libraries. James C. Baughman. LC 86-25574. 205p. 1987. lib. bdg. 35.00 (ISBN 0-89930-195-9, BLT/, Quorum Bks). Greenwood.

Trusteeship & the Future of Community Hospitals. Basil J. F. Mott. LC 83-25683. 72p. 1984. pap. 13.75 (ISBN 0-939450-04-6, 196121). AHPI.

Trusteeship & the Management of Foundations. Donald R. Young & Wilbert E. Moore. LC 75-87819. 158p. 1969. 14.95x (ISBN 0-87154-970-0). Russell Sage.

Trusteeship Council: Official Records, Resolutions: 51st Session, Supplement No. 3. 3.00. UN.

Trusteeship Council, Sixteenth Special Session, 4-6 February 1986: 53rd Session, 12 May-30 June 1986, Resolution & Decisions, Official Records, Supplement No. 3. 1987. 4.00 (ISBN 0-317-63242-6). UN.

Trusteeship Council, Thirty-Forth Session: Report of the United Nations Visiting Mission to Observe the Plebiscite in Palau, Trust Territory of the Pacific Islands, December 1986, Official Records, Supplement No. 1. 43p. 1987. 6.00 (ISBN 0-317-63239-6). UN.

Trusteeship Council: 51st Session, 14 May-July 1984, Sessional Fascicle. (Official Records). 30p. 1986. 4.00. UN.

Trusteeship Council: 52nd Session, 13 May-11 July 1985, Sessional Fascicle. 23p. 1986. 4.00. UN.

Trusteeship Council 53rd Session-Supplement No. 1 (May-June 1986) Report of the United Nations Visiting Mission to the Trust Territory of the Pacific Islands, 1985. (Official Records). 50p. 1986. 7.00. UN.

Trusteeship Council 53rd Session, Supplement No. 2 (May-June 1986) Report of the United Nations Visiting Mission to Observe the Plebiscite in Palau, Trust Territory of the Pacific Islands, February 1986. 48p. 1986. 7.00. UN.

Trusteeship in the Private College. Miriam M. Wood. LC 85-8051. 208p. 1986. text ed. 22.50x (ISBN 0-8018-3270-5). Johns Hopkins.

Trusteeship Presidency: Jimmy Carter & the United States Congress. Charles O. Jones. LC 87-24379. (Illus.). 264p. 1988. 24.95 (ISBN 0-8071-1426-X). La State U Pr.

Trusteeships: What Are They? 1980. 0.75. Natl Lawyers Guild.

Trustful Surrender to Divine Providence: The Secret of Peace & Happiness. Jean B. Saint-Jure & Claude De La Colombiere. LC 83-50252. 139p. 1983. pap. 3.00 (ISBN 0-89555-216-7). TAN Bks Pubs.

Trusting & the Maimed. James Plunkett. 12.50 (ISBN 0-8159-6909-0). Devin.

Trusting God. David R. Reagan. (Orig.). 1987. pap. 6.95 (ISBN 0-910311-15-3). Huntington Hse Inc.

Trusting Heart: Great News about Type A Behavior. Redford Williams. (Illus.). 288p. 1989. 17.95 (ISBN 0-8129-1675-1). Times Bks.

Trusting the Stones. Linda Levitz. LC 87-81207. 80p. 1987. 8.00x (ISBN 0-8233-0431-0). Golden Quill.

Trusting Together in God. Myron Chartier & Jan Chartier. LC 83-73132. (Illus.). 172p. (Orig.). 1984. pap. 6.95 (ISBN 0-87029-193-9, 20285-3). Abbey.

Trusting Your Life to Water & Eternity. Olav H. Hauge. Tr. by Robert Bly. LC 87-42897. 56p. 1987. 12.95 (ISBN 0-915943-23-9); pap. 6.95 (ISBN 0-915943-28-X). Milkweed Ed.

Trusts. 6th ed. George T. Bogert. (Hornbook Ser.). 637p. 1987. Student edition. text ed. 25.95 (ISBN 0-314-35139-6). West Pub.

Trusts. 6th ed. George T. Bogert. (Hornbook Ser.). 950p. 1987. Practitioner's Edition. text ed. 46.95 (ISBN 0-314-35140-X). West Pub.

Trusts. 1977 ed. 1979. 5.00 (ISBN 0-87526-212-0). Gould.

Trusts: Adaptable to Courses Utilizing Bogert & Oak's Casebook on Law of Trusts. Casenotes Publishing Co., Inc. Staff. Ed. by Peter Tenen et al. (Legal Briefs Ser.). 1982. pap. write for info. (ISBN 0-87457-140-5, 1230). Casenotes Pub.

Trusts: Adaptable to Courses Utilizing Wellmans, Waggoners & Browder's Casebook on Trusts. Ed. by Norman Goldenberg et al. (Legal Brief Ser.). 1985. pap. write for info. (ISBN 0-87457-141-3, 1231). Casenotes Pub.

Trusts & Estates: A Basic Course. Lewis D. Solomon. (Contemporary Legal Education Ser.). 600p. 1981. text ed. 25.00x (ISBN 0-672-84345-5); Paperback Documentary & Statutory Appendix. 5.00x (ISBN 0-672-84344-7); Supplement 1985. 8.00x (ISBN 0-87215-798-9). Michie Co.

Trusts & Trust Companies in Canada: What You Need to Know to Avoid Getting Taken. 1st ed. Alix Granger. 92p. 1978. 3.95 (ISBN 0-88908-046-1). ISC Pr.

Trusts, Estates & Minors under 1986 Tax Reform. 88p. (Orig.). 1986. pap. 6.00 (5368). Commerce.

Trusts for the Continent & for the Protection of Wealth. 1987. 310.00x (ISBN 0-948641-06-1, Pub. by ESC Ltd UK). State Mutual Bk.

Trusts in Midcentury: Transition, Taxation & Trends. LC 76-54603. 701p. 1977. 20.00 (ISBN 0-686-47967-X). Amer Bar Assn.

Trusts or Industrial Combinations & Coalitions in the United States. Ernst Von Halle. xvi, 350p. 1983. Repr. of 1900 ed. lib. bdg. 30.00x (ISBN 0-8377-1234-3). Rothman.

Trustworthiness of Religious Experience. D. E. Trueblood. LC 78-24656. 1979. pap. 4.95 (ISBN 0-944350-00-3). Friends United.

Truth. George Sterling. LC 70-119656. Repr. of 1923 ed. 11.50 (ISBN 0-404-06260-1). AMS Pr.

Truth: A Psychological Cure. Robert Firestone & Joyce Catlett. 234p. 1982. pap. 6.95 (ISBN 0-89696-167-2, An Everest House Book). Dodd.

Truth about AIDS: Evolution of an Epidemic. Ann G. Fettner & William A. Check. LC 83-22799. 320p. 1985. pap. 8.95 (ISBN 0-03-005622-5, Owl Bks). H Holt & Co.

Truth about an Author. Arnold Bennett. LC 74-17055. (Collected Works of Arnold Bennett Ser.: Vol. 84). 1976. Repr. of 1911 ed. 20.25 (ISBN 0-518-19165-6). Ayer Co Pubs.

Truth about Armageddon. William S. LaSor. 240p. 1987. pap. 6.95 (ISBN 0-8010-5637-3). Baker Bk.

Truth about Astral Projection. Llewellyn Staff. Ed. by Carl L. Weschcke. (Educational Guide Ser.). 32p. (Orig.). 1983. pap. 2.00 (ISBN 0-87542-350-7, L-350). Llewellyn Pubns.

Truth about Black Biblical Hebrew Israelites (Jews) Ella J. Hughley. (Orig.). 1982. pap. 5.00 (ISBN 0-9605150-1-1). Hughley Pubns.

Truth about Boulwarism: Trying to do Right Voluntarily. Lemuel R. Boulware. LC 77-91413. pap. 48.00 (ISBN 0-317-29423-7, 2024305). Bks Demand UMI.

Truth about... Can Astrology Predict the Future. Llewellyn Publications Staff. Ed. by Phyllis Galde. (Truth about Ser.). 32p. 1987. pap. 2.00 (ISBN 0-87542-376-0). Llewellyn Pubns.

Truth about Carlyle. David A. Wilson. 1978. Repr. of 1913 ed. lib. bdg. 25.00 (ISBN 0-8495-5803-4). Arden Lib.

Truth about Carlyle. David A. Wilson. LC 73-462. 1973. lib. bdg. 17.00 (ISBN 0-8414-1528-5). Folcroft.

Truth about CB Antennas. 2nd ed. William I. Orr & Stuart D. Cowan. LC 70-164932. (Illus.). 240p. 1971. 11.95 (ISBN 0-933616-08-2). Radio Pubns.

Truth about Christmas. Ralph Becker. pap. 0.50 (ISBN 0-685-41826-X). Reiner.

Truth about Corporate Planning: International Research into the Practice of Planning. Ed. by David E. Hussey. (Illus.). 388p. 1983. 47.00 (ISBN 0-08-025833-6). Pergamon.

Truth about Cottages. John Woodforde. LC 76-115402. (Illus.). 1970. lib. bdg. 19.95x (ISBN 0-678-06528-4). Kelley.

Truth about Cottages. John Woodforde. (Illus.). 1979. pap. 8.95 (ISBN 0-7100-0165-7). Routledge Chapman & Hall.

Truth about Creative Visualization. Llewellyn Publications Staff. Ed. by Carl L. Weschcke. (Educational Guide Ser.). 32p. (Orig.). 1984. pap. 2.00 (ISBN 0-87542-353-1, L-353). Llewellyn Pubns.

Truth about Crystals in Healing. The Llewellyn Publications Staff. Ed. by Phyllis Galde. 32p. (Orig.). 1987. pap. 2.00 (ISBN 0-87542-360-4). Llewellyn Pubns.

Truth about Geronimo. Britton Davis. Ed. by M. M. Quaife. LC 75-37958. (Illus.). xxx, 265p. 1976. pap. 7.95 (ISBN 0-8032-5840-2, BB 622, Bison). U of Nebr Pr.

Truth about Gorillas. Susan Meyers. LC 79-19393. (Smart Cat Bks.). (Illus.). 40p. (gr. 1-4). 1980. 7.95 (ISBN 0-525-41564-5). Dutton.

Truth about Herbs. Mrs. C. F. Leyel. 106p. 1985. pap. 6.50 (ISBN 0-89540-145-2, SB-145). Sun Pub.

Truth about Hitler & the Roman Catholic Church. A. Ratcliffe. 1982. lib. bdg. 59.95 (ISBN 0-87700-362-9). Revisionist Pr.

Truth about Hungary. Herbert Aptheker. LC 57-2931. 1976. Repr. of 1957 ed. 28.00 (ISBN 0-527-03001-5). Kraus Repr.

Truth about Japan. Ed. by Andrew Watt. 1988. pap. 5.95 (ISBN 0-8048-1562-3). C E Tuttle.

Truth about Kent State. Peter Davies. (Illus.). 241p. 1973. 10.00 (ISBN 0-374-27938-1). FS&G.

Truth about Kent State. Peter Davies. 1973. pap. 3.50 (ISBN 0-374-51041-5, Noonday). FS&G.

Truth about Lorin Jones. Alison Lurie. 336p. 1988. 18.95 (ISBN 0-316-53720-9). Little.

Truth about Mars. Ernest L. Norman. (Illus.). 116p. 1956. pap. 4.95 (ISBN 0-932642-12-8). Unarius Pubns.

Truth about Mary Rose. Marilyn Sachs. (Illus.). 160p. (gr. 4-6). 1987. pap. 2.50 (ISBN 0-590-40402-4, Apple Paperbacks). Scholastic Inc.

Truth about Mesopotamia, Palestine & Syria. John D. Wakehurst. LC 79-2887. 221p. 1982. Repr. of 1923 ed. 21.25 (ISBN 0-8305-0054-5). Hyperion Conn.

Truth about Nelson Rockefeller. Emanuel Josephson. (Blacked-Out History Ser.). 1979. 50.00 (ISBN 0-685-91971-4). Chedney.

Truth about Past Life Regression. The Llewellyn Publications Staff. Ed. by Phyllis Galde. (Educational Guide Ser.). 32p. (Orig.). 1986. pap. 2.00 (ISBN 0-87542-359-0). Llewellyn Pubns.

Truth about Pearl Harbor. John T. Flynn. 1984. lib. bdg. 79.95 (ISBN 0-87700-613-X). Revisionist Pr.

Truth about Peter Harley. James Mills. 272p. 1983. pap. 2.95 (ISBN 0-345-29005-4). Ballantine.

Truth about Psychic Powers. The Llewellyn Publications Staff. (Educational Guide Ser.). 32p. (Orig.). Date not set. pap. 2.00 (ISBN 0-87542-355-8). Llewellyn Pubns.

Truth about Publishing. 8th ed. Stanley Unwin. 1976. 24.95 (ISBN 0-04-655014-3). Unwin Hyman.

Truth about Publishing. 8th ed. Stanley Unwin & Philip Unwin. 256p. 1982. pap. 6.95 (ISBN 0-89733-064-1). Academy Chi Pubs.

Truth about Rainbows. Steve Lail. (Orig.). 1987. pap. 5.95 (ISBN 0-9618697-2-0). Lail Press.

Truth about Reparations & War Debts. David Lloyd George. LC 68-9609. 1970. Repr. 22.50x (ISBN 0-86527-197-6). Fertig.

Truth about Rockefeller. Emanuel Josephson. 280p. Date not set. 3.75 (ISBN 0-317-53212-X). Noontide.

Truth about Rockefeller. Emanuel M. Josephson. 1979. write for info. (ISBN 0-685-96471-X). Revisionist Pr.

Truth about Rockefeller "Public Enemy No. 1". Emanuel Josephson. LC 64-20630. (Blacked-Out History Ser.). 277p. 1964. 5.00 (ISBN 0-686-32439-0); pap. 2.00 (ISBN 0-686-32440-4). A-albionic Res.

Truth about Santa Claus. James C. Giblin. LC 85-47541. (Illus.). 96p. (gr. 3-7). 1985. 12.89 (ISBN 0-690-04483-6, Crowell Jr Bks); PLB 12.89 (ISBN 0-690-04484-4). HarpJ.

Truth about Self Protection. Massad F. Ayoob. (Illus.). 417p. 1983. 4.95 (ISBN 0-317-64452-1). Police Bkshelf.

Truth about Self-Protection: Streetfighting Techniques, Mace, Improvised Weapons & Firearms, Locks, Alarms, & Dogs. M. Ayoob. 1986. lib. bdg. 79.95 (ISBN 0-8490-3667-4). Gordon Pr.

Truth about Selling. Samuel S. Susser. LC 73-83178. 176p. 1973. 5.95 (ISBN 0-8397-8395-7). Eriksson.

Truth about Soviet Lies. R. H. Shackford. 1962. 12.50 (ISBN 0-8183-0215-1). Pub Aff Pr.

Truth about Stacey. Ann M. Martin. (Baby-Sitter's Club Ser.: No. 3). 144p. (Orig.). (gr. 3-7). 1986. pap. 2.75 (ISBN 0-590-42124-7, Apple Paperbacks). Scholastic Inc.

Truth about Stacey. Ann M. Martin. (Babysitter's Club Ser.: No. 3). 167p. (gr. 4-7). Date not set. Repr. of 1986 ed. 8.95 (ISBN 0-942545-64-8); lib. bdg. 9.95 (ISBN 0-942545-74-5). Grey Castle.

Truth About Stone Hollow. Zilpha K. Snyder. (gr. k-6). 1986. pap. 3.25 (ISBN 0-440-48846-X, YB). Dell.

Truth about Subliminals. Llewellyn Publications Staff. Ed. by David Dix. (Educational Guide Ser.). 32p. (Orig.). 1985. pap. 2.00 (ISBN 0-87542-356-6, L-356). Llewellyn Pubns.

Truth about Sugar in Cuba. Antonio Barro Y Segura. 1976. lib. bdg. 59.95 (ISBN 0-8490-2775-6). Gordon Pr.

Truth about Taffy Sinclair. Betsy Haynes. 128p. (Orig.). 1988. pap. 2.75 (ISBN 0-553-15607-1, Skylark). Bantam.

Truth about the American Flag. Robert Morris. LC 76-12730. (Illus.). 1976. 10.80 (ISBN 0-9601476-1-6); pap. 7.65 (ISBN 0-9601476-2-4). Wynnehaven.

Truth about the Betsy Ross Story. Robert Morris. LC 82-70798. (Illus.). 1982. 15.95 (ISBN 0-9601476-3-2); pap. 12.95 (ISBN 0-9601476-4-0). Wynnehaven.

Truth about the Heavens. Micheal Cyrek. 1987. 14.95 (ISBN 0-533-07236-0). Vantage.

Truth about the Indian Press. J. N. Sahni. 154p. 1974. 13.95. Asia Bk Corp.

Truth about the Jews. A. Ratcliffe. 1982. lib. bdg. 59.95 (ISBN 0-87700-421-8). Revisionist Pr.

Truth about the Ku Klux Klan. Milson Meltzer. (Illus.). 129p. (gr. 7 up). 1982. PLB 11.90 (ISBN 0-531-04498-X). Watts.

Truth about the Lie. David R. Mains. 128p. 1987. pap. 6.95 (ISBN 0-310-34831-5, 12750P). Zondervan.

Truth about the Moon. Clayton Bess. (Illus.). 48p. (gr. k-3). 1983. PLB 8.95 (ISBN 0-395-34551-0). HM.

Truth about the Movies. L. Hughes. 1976. lib. bdg. 59.95 (ISBN 0-8490-2776-4). Gordon Pr.

Truth about the Russian Church Abroad. M. Rodzianko. Tr. by Michael P. Hilko from Rus. LC 74-29321. (Illus.). 48p. (Orig.). 1975. pap. 1.50 (ISBN 0-88465-004-9). Holy Trinity.

Truth about the Territory. Rich Ives. 530p. (Orig.). 1987. text ed. 21.00 (ISBN 0-937669-27-X); pap. text ed. 14.00 (ISBN 0-937669-26-1). Owl Creek Pr.

Truth about the Trinity. Roy D. Mixon. 43p. (Orig.). 1986. pap. 2.25 (ISBN 0-934942-64-1, 3874). White Wing Pub.

Truth about the West African Land Question. J. E. Hayford. 208p. 1971. Repr. of 1913 ed. 28.50x (ISBN 0-7146-1755-5, F Cass Co). Biblio Dist.

Truth about Tristrem Varick. Edgar Saltus. LC 74-95394. Repr. of 1888 ed. 17.50 (ISBN 0-404-05505-2). AMS Pr.

Truth about Uri Geller. rev. ed. James Randi. LC 82-60951. (Illus.). 234p. 1982. pap. 12.95 (ISBN 0-87975-199-1). Prometheus Bks.

Truth about Witchcraft Today. Scott Cunningham. Ed. by Tom Lawless. LC 88-45197. (New Age Ser.). 200p. (Orig.). 1988. 3.95 (ISBN 0-87542-127-X). Llewellyn Pubns.

Truth about Witchcraft Today. The Llewellyn Publications Staff. Ed. by Tom Lawless. (Educational Guide Ser.). 32p. 1987. pap. 2.00 (ISBN 0-87542-357-4). Llewellyn Pubns.

Truth about Woman: Biological, Historical, Anthropological, Sociological. C. G. Hartley. 1974. lib. bdg. 69.95 (ISBN 0-685-51360-2). Revisionist Pr.

Truth about Women: How Women Can Advance the World. Carolyn H. Bray. 144p. (Orig.). 1986. pap. write for info. (ISBN 0-935834-51-6). Rainbow Books.

Truth about You. Arthur F. Miller & Ralph T. Mattson. 1987. pap. 8.95 (ISBN 0-89815-194-5). Ten Speed Pr.

Truth about Your Diet. Mary Morris. 1988. pap. 9.95 (ISBN 0-934791-15-5). W Mulvey Inc.

Truth Against the World: Frank Lloyd Wright Speaks for an Organic Architecture. Ed. by Patrick J. Meehan. LC 86-19114. 448p. 1987. 39.95 (ISBN 0-471-84509-4). Wiley.

Truth & Actuality: Conversations on Science & Consciousness. J. Krishnamurti. LC 77-20450. 176p. 1980. pap. 8.95 (ISBN 0-06-064875-9, RD 334, HarpR). Har-Row.

Truth & Beauty: Aesthetics & Motivations in Science. S. Chandrasekhar. (Illus.). 208p. 1987. 23.95x (ISBN 0-226-10086-3). U of Chicago Pr.

Truth (& Beauty) in Radiation Measurement. John H. Harley. LC 85-15292. (Lauriston S. Taylor Lecture Ser.: No. 9). 37p. (Orig.). 1985. pap. text ed. 11.00 (ISBN 0-913392-78-2). NCRP Pubns.

Truth & Beauty in the Total Extension of Man & of His Universe, 2 vols. John Ruskin. (Illus.). 460p. 1988. Set. 228.85 (ISBN 0-89266-623-4). Am Classical Coll Pr.

Truth & Compassion: Essays on Judaism & Religion in Memory of Rabbi Dr. Solomon Frank, Vol. 12. Ed. by Howard Joseph et al. 217p. 1983. pap. text ed. 13.95x (ISBN 0-919812-17-1, Pub. by Wilfrid Laurier Canada). Humanities.

Truth & Consequence in Medieval Logic. Ernest A. Moody. LC 76-44307. (Studies in Logic & the Foundations of Mathematics). 1976. Repr. of 1953 ed. lib. bdg. 35.00 (ISBN 0-8371-9053-3, MOTC). Greenwood.

Truth & Consequences of Sexually Transmitted Diseases. Carole Marsh. (Sex Stuff for Kids Ser.). 48p. (Orig.). 1987. pap. 7.95elled (ISBN 1-55609-212-1). Gallopade Pub Group.

Truth & Error: Or, the Science of Intellection. John W. Powell. LC 75-3322. Repr. of 1898 ed. 31.50 (ISBN 0-404-59318-6). AMS Pr.

Truth & Falsehood in Visual Images. Mark Roskill & David Carrier. LC 83-5123. (Illus.). 160p. 1983. lib. bdg. 18.00x (ISBN 0-87023-404-8); pap. text ed. 9.95x (ISBN 0-87023-405-6). U of Mass Pr.

Truth & Fiction: Relating to My Life, 6 vols. Johann Wolfgang Von Goethe. Ed. by Nathan H. Dole. Tr. by John Oxenford. 2400p. 1986. Repr. of 1902 ed. lib. bdg. 400.00 (ISBN 0-8495-2106-8). Arden Lib.

Truth & Health. Fannie B. James. 1970. 8.95 (ISBN 0-686-24356-0). Divine Sci Fed.

Truth & Ideology. Hans Barth. Tr. by Frederic Lilge from Ger. LC 74-81430. Orig. Title: Wahrheit und Ideologie. 1977. 35.00x (ISBN 0-520-02820-1). U of Cal Pr.

Truth & Interpretation: Perspectives on the Philosophy of Donald Davidson. Ed. by Ernest LePore. 528p. 1986. text ed. 60.00x (ISBN 0-631-14811-6). Basil Blackwell.

Truth & Knowledge. 2nd ed. Rudolph Steiner. Ed. by Paul M. Allen. Tr. by Rita Stebbing from Ger. LC 81-51762. 112p. 1987. pap. 6.50 (ISBN 0-89345-212-2, Steinerbks). Garber Comm.

Truth & Knowledge: Introduction to "Philosophy of Spiritual Activity", Vol. 14. 2nd ed. Rudolf Steiner. Ed. by Paul M. Allen. Tr. by Rita Stebbing from Ger. LC 81-51762. (Spiritual Science Library). 112p. 1981. lib. bdg. 13.00 (ISBN 0-89345-008-1, Spiritual Sci Lib); pap. 7.50. Garber Comm.
Truth & Lies in Literature: Essays & Reviews. Stephen Vizinczey. x, 340p. 1988. pap. 12.95 (ISBN 0-226-85884-7). U of Chicago Pr.
Truth & Lies in Literature: Reviews & Essays. Stephen Vizinczey. Ed. by Bryan Brady. LC 86-70253. 340p. 1986. 16.95 (ISBN 0-87113-078-5). Atlantic Monthly.
Truth & Light: Brief Explanations. M. R. Bawa Muhaiyaddeen. LC 74-76219. (Illus.). 144p. 1974. pap. 3.95 (ISBN 0-914390-04-X). Fellowship Pr PA.
Truth & Maud: A Modern Allegory. John B. Gerald. Date not set. 7.00 (ISBN 0-941917-11-8). Gerald & Maas.
Truth & Meaning: Essays in Semantics. Ed. by Garth Evans & John McDowell. 1976. 54.00x (ISBN 0-19-824517-3). Oxford U Pr.
Truth & Meaning in Political Science: An Introduction to Political Inquiry. 2nd ed. Maria J. Falco. LC 82-25095. 160p. 1983. pap. text ed. 12.00 (ISBN 0-8191-3048-6). U Pr of Amer.
Truth & Method. Hans-Georg Gadamer. 516p. 1982. pap. 16.95x (ISBN 0-8264-0431-6). Continuum.
Truth & Method. Hans-Georg Gadamer. (Crossroad Paperback Ser.). 516p. 1982. pap. 16.95 (ISBN 0-8245-0431-3). Crossroad NY.
Truth & Method. Rev. ed. Hans-Georg Gadamer. Ed. by Donald G. Marshall & Joel C. Weinsheimer. 600p. 1988. 34.50x (ISBN 0-8264-0401-4). Continuum.
Truth & Nonviolence: A UNESCO Symposium on Gandhi. Ed. by T. K. Mahadevan. 1970. 21.50x (ISBN 0-8046-8816-8, Pub by Kennikat). Assoc Faculty Pr.
Truth & Other Enigmas. Michael Dummett. LC 77-12777. 528p. 1978. 42.00x (ISBN 0-674-91075-3); pap. 14.95x (ISBN 0-674-91076-1). Harvard U Pr.
Truth & Peace in the Middle East: A Critical Analysis of the Quaker Report. Arnold Soloway et al. 112p. pap. 1.25 (ISBN 0-686-74978-2). ADL.
Truth & Reality. Otto Rank. 1978. pap. 5.95 (ISBN 0-393-00899-1, Norton Lib). Norton.
Truth & Reality in Marx & Hegel: A Reassessment. Czeslaw Prokopczyk. LC 80-7976. 144p. 1980. lib. bdg. 13.50x (ISBN 0-87023-307-6). U of Mass Pr.
Truth & Science: A Bibliography. Norman Ansley et al. 1982. 13.95. Am Polygraph.
Truth & Scientific Knowledge in the Thought of Henry of Ghent. Steven P. Marrone. LC 84-62885. (Speculum Anniversary Monographs: No. 11). 164p. 1985. 12.50x (ISBN 0-910956-91-X); pap. 6.50x (ISBN 0-910956-92-8). Medieval Acad.
Truth & Symbol. Karl Jaspers. (Orig.). 1959. pap. 5.95x (ISBN 0-8084-0303-6). New Coll U Pr.
Truth & the Disputed Questions on Truth. St. Thomas Aquinas. (Illus.). 107p. 1987. 117.50 (ISBN 0-89266-582-3). Am Classical Coll Pr.
Truth & the Historicity of Man. Ed. by George F. McLean. (Proceedings of the American Catholic Philosophical Association: Vol. 43). 1969. pap. 15.00 (ISBN 0-918090-03-2). Am Cath Philo.
Truth & the War. Edmund D. Morel. LC 70-147478. (Library of War & Peace; the Character & Causes of War). 1972. lib. bdg. 46.00 (ISBN 0-8240-0270-9). Garland Pub.
Truth & Tradition in Chinese Buddhism. Karl Reichelt. 59.95 (ISBN 0-8490-1234-1). Gordon Pr.
Truth & Tragedy: A Tribute to Hans J. Morgenthau. Ed. by Kenneth Thompson & Robert J. Myers. 386p. (Orig.). 1983. pap. 18.95 (ISBN 0-87855-866-7). Transaction Bks.
Truth & Value In Nietzsche: A Study of His Metaethics & Epistemology. John T. Wilcox. LC 82-45066. 250p. 1982. pap. text ed. 13.50 (ISBN 0-8191-2354-4). U Pr of Amer.
Truth & Vision in Katherine Anne Porter's Fiction. Darlene H. Unrue. LC 84-23925. 280p. 1985. 24.00x (ISBN 0-8203-0768-8). U of Ga Pr.
Truth-Antidote for Error. Anthony D. Palma. LC 76-52177. (Radiant Life Ser.). 128p. 1977. pap. 2.50 (ISBN 0-88243-904-9, 02-0904); teacher's guide 3.95 (ISBN 0-88243-174-9, 32-0174). Gospel Pub.
Truth Apparent: Essays on Biblical Preaching. Jay E. Adams. 1982. pap. 4.95 (ISBN 0-87552-077-4). Presby & Reformed.
Truth As a Way of Life. Robert E. Birdsong. (Aquarian Academy Monograph: Ser. F, Lecture No. 3). 1977. pap. 1.50 (ISBN 0-917108-17-5). Sirius Bks.
Truth Barriers: Poems by Tomas Transtromer. Tomas Transtromer. Tr. by Robert Bly from Swedish. LC 80-13310. (Illus.). 64p. 1980. 9.95 (ISBN 0-87156-235-9); pap. 5.95 (ISBN 0-87156-239-1). Sierra.
Truth, Beauty & Goodness. Rudolf Steiner. 1986. pap. 1.50 (ISBN 0-916786-86-2). St George Bk Serv.
Truth Beyond Relativism: Karl Mannheim's Sociology of Knowledge. Gregory Baum. LC 77-76605. (Pere Marquette Ser.). 1977. 7.95 (ISBN 0-87462-509-2). Marquette.
Truth Beyond Words: Problems & Prospects for Anglican-Roman Catholic Unity. Paul Avis. LC 85-22399. 142p. (Orig.). 1985. pap. 7.95 (ISBN 0-936384-26-3). Cowley Pubns.
Truth Concerning the Invention of Photography: Nicephore Niepce-His Life, Letters, & Works (1867) Victor Fouque. LC 72-9198. (Literature of Photography Ser.). Repr. of 1935 ed. 17.00 (ISBN 0-405-04907-2). Ayer Co Pubs.
Truth Disguised: Allegorical Structure & Technique in Gracian's "Criticon". Theodore L. Kassier. (Serie A: Monagrafias, LIII). 150p. 1976. 22.00 (ISBN 0-7293-0006-4, Pub. by Tamesis Bks Ltd). Longwood Pub Group.
Truth Fairy: Weird Tales of an Eleemosynarian. Date not set. price not set. Mainespring.
Truth for Germany. Udo Walendy. 1984. lib. bdg. 79.95 (ISBN 0-87700-607-5). Revisionist Pr.
Truth for Life. John Blanchard. 1986. pap. 14.95 (ISBN 0-87552-756-6, Evangel Pr UK). Presby & Reformed.
Truth for Life Bible Studies. Lela Birky. (gr. 7-9). pap. write for info (ISBN 0-686-15481-9). Rod & Staff.
Truth for Today. George Merritt. 5.50 (ISBN 0-89225-202-2). Gospel Advocate.
Truth Has No Alternative. Benny C. Watson. 96p. 1988. write for info. Entrtnmnt Galore.
Truth, Images & Distortions: A View of the Indian Press. Sunny Thomas. 1985. 17.50x (ISBN 0-8364-1372-5, Pub. by Heritage India). South Asia Bks.
Truth Imagined. Eric Hoffer. LC 83-47914. 112p. 1983. 11.45i (ISBN 0-06-015215-X, HarpT). Har-Row.
Truth in Accounting. Kenneth MacNeal. LC 74-75709. 1970. Repr. of 1939 ed. text ed. 15.00 (ISBN 0-914348-04-3). Scholars Bk.
Truth in Advertising. Arthur Gibson et al. LC 72-7241. 45p. 1984. Repr. of 1972 ed. 19.95x (ISBN 0-88946-912-1). E Mellen.
Truth in Advertising: An AMA Research Report. John T. Lucas & Richard Gurman. LC 72-79980. (AMA Research Report Ser.). pap. 20.00 (ISBN 0-317-28460-6, 2051309). Bks Demand UMI.
Truth in Crisis: The Controversy in the Southern Baptist Convention. James C. Hefley. LC 86-70962. 208p. 1986. pap. 7.95 (ISBN 0-937969-00-1). Criterion Pubns.
Truth in Crisis, Vol. 2: The Controversy in the Southern Baptist Convention. James C. Hefley. 218p. Date not set. pap. 7.95 (ISBN 0-929292-00-6). Hannibal Bks.
Truth in Crisis, Vol. 3: The Controversy in the Southern Baptist Convention. James C. Hefley. 260p. 1988. pap. 7.95 (ISBN 0-929292-01-4). Hannibal Bks.
Truth in History. Oscar Handlin. LC 78-24157. 1979. 29.50x (ISBN 0-674-91025-7, Belknap Pr); pap. 10.95 (ISBN 0-674-91026-5). Harvard U Pr.
Truth in Lending: A Comprehensive Guide. Roland E. Brandel et al. LC 84-22423. 850p. 1985. Supplements avail. 85.00 (ISBN 0-15-004372-4, #H43724, Law & Business). HarBraceJ.
Truth in Lending & Consumer Credit Agreements. J. Karpinski & S. Fielding. 288p. 1985. pap. 32.00 (ISBN 0-08-039200-8). Pergamon.
Truth in Lending & Real Estate, 1981. Kent J. Levine. Date not set. write for info. Prof Pubns & Educ.
Truth-in-Lending & Regulation Z. Dennis Replansky. 297p. 1984. 75.00 (ISBN 0-317-55927-3, B242). Am Law Inst.
Truth in Lending Case Summaries. 3rd ed. National Consumer Law Center Staff. 350p. (Orig.). 1983. pap. 15.00 (ISBN 0-941077-04-7, 22,250). NCLS Inc.
Truth-in-Lending Compliance Manual. Morrison & Foerster Law Offices Staff. 178p. (Orig.). 1981. 65.00 (ISBN 0-318-16992-4). Credit Union Natl Assn.
Truth-in-Lending Manual: Cumulative Supplementation, 2 vols. 5th ed. Ralph C. Clontz, Jr. 1982. Set. 115.00 (ISBN 0-88262-757-0). Warren Gorham & Lamont.
Truth in Lending Simplification: A Compliance Manual for Creditors & Attorneys on Regulation E. Dennis H. Replansky et al. 329p. 1986. pap. 45.00 (ISBN 0-941161-08-0). PES Inc WI.
Truth in Lending Simplification: Countdown to Final Compliance. ABA National Institutes Staff. 300p. 1982. 75.00. Amer Bar Assn.
Truth in Lending Simplification: Understanding & Applying Procedures to Regulation Z. 15.00 (ISBN 0-686-95628-1, 626500, 626501). Am Bankers.
Truth in Lending: 1986 & 1987 Supplement. National Consumer Law Center Staff. (Consumer Credit & Sales Legal Practice Ser.). (Orig.). 1986. pap. 57.00 (ISBN 0-943116-44-9). Nat Consumer Law.
Truth in Money Book. Rev. 2nd. ed. Theodore R. Thoren & Richard F. Warner. LC 83-51421. (Illus.). 263p. 1984. pap. 8.50 (ISBN 0-9606938-1-5). Truth in Money.
Truth in Painting. Jacques Derrida. Tr. by Geoffrey Bennington & Ian McLeod. (Illus.). xvi, 386p. 1987. 49.95x (ISBN 0-226-14323-6); pap. 19.95x (ISBN 0-226-14324-4). U of Chicago Pr.
Truth in the World Doctrine. Dennis L. Maxberry. 32p. 1988. 7.00 (ISBN 0-8062-3346-X). Carlton.
Truth, Interpretation & Information: Selected Papers of the 3rd Amsterdam Colloquium. Ed. by J. Groenendyk et al. (Grass Ser.). viii, 182p. 1984. pap. write for info. (ISBN 90-6765-001-3). Foris Pubns.
Truth, Invention & the Meaning of Life. D. Wiggins. (Philosophical Lectures (Henriette Hertz Trust)). 1976. pap. 5.50 (ISBN 0-85672-309-6, Pub. by British Acad). Longwood Pub Group.
Truth Is a Neighborhood with Nothing in-Between. Francis Schwanauer. 127p. 1977. pap. text ed. 9.75 (ISBN 0-8191-0240-7). U Pr of Amer.
Truth Is Immortal: The Story of Baptists in Europe. Irwin Barnes. 127p. 1950. 4.50 (ISBN 0-87921-015-X); pap. 2.50 (ISBN 0-87921-019-2). Attic Pr.
Truth Is My Sword. Bo Hi Pak. LC 78-74661. 110p. (Orig.). 1978. pap. 2.00 (ISBN 0-318-03063-2). HSA Pubns.
Truth Is Not Sober. Winifred Holtby. LC 77-121564. (Short Story Index Reprint Ser). 1934. 18.00 (ISBN 0-8369-3521-7). Ayer Co Pubs.
Truth Is Stranger Than Dogma. John O. Fisher. 1988. 14.95 (ISBN 0-533-07747-8). Vantage.
Truth is Stranger than Publicity. Alton Delmore. Ed. by Charles K. Wolfe. 188p. 1977. pap. 5.95 (ISBN 0-915608-05-7). Country Music Found.
Truth Is Symphonic: Aspects of Christian Pluralism. Hans U. Von Balthasar. Tr. by Graham Harrison from Ger. LC 86-83131. 192p. 1987. pap. 9.95 (ISBN 0-89870-141-4). Ignatius Pr.
Truth, Knowledge & Modality: Philosophical Papers, Vol. III. G. H. Von Wright. 248p. 1985. 34.95x (ISBN 0-631-13367-4). Basil Blackwell.
Truth, Knowledge, & Reality: Inquiries into the Foundations of 17th Century Rationalism. Ed. by George H. Parkinson. (Studia Leibnitiana Ser.: No. 9). 167p. (Orig.). 1981. pap. 48.50x (ISBN 3-515-03350-5, Pub. by Franz Steiner). Coronet Bks.
Truth, Lie Detectors, & Other Problems in Labor Arbitration: Thirty-First Annual Meeting, 1978. (Library of Labor Arbitration). 490p. 1978. 35.00 (ISBN 0-87179-288-5, 0288). BNA.
Truth, Love, & Immortality: An Introduction to McTaggart's Philosophy. P. T. Geach. LC 78-62842. 1979. 30.00x (ISBN 0-520-03755-3). U of Cal Pr.
Truth Machine see Heinemann Guided Readers.
Truth Maintenance Systems. David McAllester & Drew McDermott. (Illus.). 75p. 1988. pap. text ed. 5.00x (ISBN 0-929280-11-3). Amer Artificial.
Truth of a Hopi. 2nd ed. Edmund Nequatewa. LC 73-78419. (Illus.). 137p. 1985. pap. 8.95 (ISBN 0-87358-386-8). Northland.
Truth of Authority: Ideology & Communication in the Soviet Union. Thomas F. Remington. LC 88-4745. (Pitt Series in Russian & East European Studies). (Illus.). 256p. (Orig.). 1989. 26.95x (ISBN 0-8229-3590-2); pap. 13.95 (ISBN 0-8229-5408-7). U of Pittsburgh Pr.
Truth of Christmas Beyond the Myths: The Gospel of the Infancy of Christ. Rene Laurentin. (Studies in Scripture: Vol. III). 1986. pap. 29.95 (ISBN 0-932506-34-8). St Bedes Pubns.
Truth of Freedom. John M. Anderson. LC 78-26932. 1978. pap. 2.95 (ISBN 0-932540-01-5). Dialogue Pr Man World.
Truth of Imagination: Essays & Reviews by Edwin Muir. P. H. Butter. 274p. 1988. text ed. 23.51 (ISBN 0-08-036392-X, AUP). Pergamon.
Truth of Poetry: Tensions in Modern Poetry from Baudelaire to the 1960s. Michael Hamburger. 356p. 1982. Repr. of 1969 ed. 11.95x (ISBN 0-416-34240-X, NO. 3764). Routledge Chapman & Hall.
Truth of Poetry: Tensions in Modern Poetry from Baudelaire to the 1960s. Michael Hamburger. 347p. 1984. 21.00 (ISBN 0-85635-438-4). Carcanet.
Truth of the Gospel: An Exposition of Galatians. Gerhard Ebeling. LC 84-47918. 288p. 1985. 3.95 (ISBN 0-8006-0728-7, 1-728). Fortress.
Truth of the Matter. John Lutz. LC 87-72700. 176p. 1988. pap. 4.95 (ISBN 0-88739-090-0, Pub. by Black Lizard Bks). Creative Arts Bk.
Truth of the Matter. Barbara Stretton. LC 83-4305. 256p. (gr. 7-12). 1983. lib. bdg. 10.99 (ISBN 0-394-96144-7); PLB 10.95 (ISBN 0-394-86144-2). Knopf.
Truth of the Matter. Barbara Stretton. 256p. 1984. pap. 2.25 (ISBN 0-399-21147-0). Putnam Pub Group.
Truth of the Stock Tape. W. D. Gann. (Illus.). 1923. 25.00 (ISBN 0-939093-04-9). Lambert Gann Pub.
Truth of Time & Space. Richard R. Thorgrimson. 1988. 13.95 (ISBN 0-533-07759-1). Vantage.
Truth of War: Owen, Rosenburg & Blunden. Desmond Graham. 168p. 20.00 (ISBN 0-85635-496-1). Carcanet.
Truth Option. Will Schutz. LC 83-40025. 128p. (Orig.). 1984. 12.95 (ISBN 0-89815-108-2); pap. 7.95 (ISBN 0-89815-107-4). Ten Speed Pr.
Truth or Dare. Susan B. Pfeffer. LC 83-20635. 128p. (gr. 4-6). 1984. 9.95 (ISBN 0-02-774680-1, Four Winds). Macmillan.
Truth or Dare. Susan B. Pfeffer. 176p. (gr. 5-8). 1986. pap. 2.50 (ISBN 0-590-41104-7, Apple Paperbacks). Scholastic Inc.
Truth or Dare: Encounters with Power, Authority, & Mystery. Starhawk. 370p. Date not set. 19.95 (ISBN 0-317-70114-2). Har-Row.
Truth or Dare Trap. Nancy J. Hopper. LC 85-7014. (Illus.). 128p. (gr. 5-9). 1985. 10.95 (ISBN 0-525-44218-9). Dutton.
Truth or Dare Trap. Nancy J. Hopper. (gr. 7 up). 1988. pap. 2.50 (ISBN 0-380-70269-X, Flare). Avon.
Truth or Tradition: What Is the Gospel? Maralene Wesner & Miles Wesner. LC 86-71139. 100p. 1986. pap. 4.95 (ISBN 0-936715-03-0). Diversity Okla.
Truth Out of Africa. Ivor Benson. 1984. pap. 5.75 (ISBN 0-949667-34-X). Concord Bks.
Truth Out of Africa. Ivor Benson. 111p. 1986. pap. 4.00 (ISBN 0-317-53269-3). Noontide.
Truth Out of Africa: How the African Crisis Is Manipulated. I. Benson. 1986. Gordon Pr.
Truth Seekers. Myrtle A. Pohle. (Daybreak Ser.). 144p. 1983. pap. 1.49 (ISBN 0-8163-0529-3). Pacific Pr Pub Assn.
Truth Shall Make You Free. David T. Demola. 24p. 1987. pap. 1.50 (ISBN 0-88144-092-2). Christian Pub.
Truth Shall Make You Free: An Inquiry into the Legend of God. Robert A. Steiner. LC 80-80646. (Illus.). 56p. (Orig.). (gr. 6 up). 1980. pap. 3.95 (ISBN 0-9604044-0-6). Penseur Pr.
Truth Shall Spring out of the Earth, Vol. I. David T. Harris. 240p. 1988. 12.95 (ISBN 0-8062-3333-8). Carlton.
Truth Shall Triumph. 9th ed. Ralph V. Reynolds. 111p. 1983. pap. 2.95 (ISBN 0-912315-07-5). Word Aflame.
Truth-Speaking & Power among Friends (Quakers) Ethical Alternatives & Consequences. Paul Barton-Kriese & Kenneth Ives. (Studies in Quakerism: No. 15). 52p. 1987. pap. 5.00 (ISBN 0-89670-018-6). Progresiv Pub.
Truth Speaks. Richard E. Tottress. 1975. 5.00 (ISBN 0-682-48160-2). Exposition-Phoenix.
Truth Syntax & Modality: Proceedings of the Temple University Conference on Alter Semantics. H. Liblanc. (Proceedings). 1973. 73.75 (ISBN 0-444-10487-9). Elsevier.
Truth Tales: Contemporary Writings by Indian Women. Kali for Women Staff. 1987. 10.00x (ISBN 0-8364-2197-3, Pub. by Manohar India). South Asia Bks.
Truth, Tall Tales, & Blatant Lies. William E. Gratwick. LC 81-65246. (Illus.). 192p. 1981. 20.00 (ISBN 0-89822-016-5); pap. 10.95 (ISBN 0-89822-017-3). Visual Studies.
Truth That Frees. Gerard Smith. (Aquinas Lecture). 1956. 7.95 (ISBN 0-87462-121-6). Marquette.
Truth That Goes Unclaimed. Jean K. Foster. Ed. by Jim Gross. (Trilogy of Truth Ser.: Bk. 2). 176p. (Orig.). 1987. pap. 8.95 (ISBN 0-912949-08-2). Uni-Sun.
Truth That Killed. Georgi Markov. Tr. by Liliana Brisby. LC 84-20. 304p. 1984. 15.95 (ISBN 0-89919-296-3). Ticknor & Fields.
Truth, the Millennium, & the Battle of Armageddon. Leslie G. Thomas. 1979. pap. 2.50 (ISBN 0-89225-188-3). Gospel Advocate.
Truth the Poet Sings. Illus. by Alan W. Peterson. (Illus.). 220p. 1984. 5.95 (ISBN 0-87159-160-X). Unity School.
Truth Twisters: How Disinformation Ruins Lives. Richard Deacon. 288p. 1987. 24.95x (ISBN 0-356-12216-6, Pub. by MacD & CO). Trans-Atl Phila.
Truth vs. Traditon. Howard M. Hart. LC 87-81508. (Illus.). 176p. (Orig.). 1987. pap. 7.95 (ISBN 0-9618908-0-0). Herald Pub.
Truth Will Prevail. Marian Slingova. 126p. 1968. 2.75 (ISBN 0-85036-212-1, Pub. by Merlin Pr UK). Longwood Pub Group.
Truth Within. Dadaji. Ed. by Ann Mills. (Illus.). 400p. (Orig.). 1987. pap. 14.95 (ISBN 0-942687-00-0). Amida Pr.
Truth Within Us All. David Howlett. 384p. 1989. 25.00 (ISBN 0-89962-771-4). Todd & Honeywell.
Truth-Wrought-Words. Rudolf Steiner. 209p. 12.95 (ISBN 0-910142-82-3). Anthroposophic.
Truthful Lens. Lucien Goldschmidt & Weston J. Naef. LC 80-66237. (Illus.). 241p. 1980. 125.00x (ISBN 0-8139-1036-6, Grolier Club). U Pr of Va.
Truthfulness & Tragedy: Further Investigations in Christian Ethics. Stanley Hauerwas & Richard Bondi. LC 76-30425. 1977. 21.95x (ISBN 0-268-01831-6); pap. text ed. 9.95 (ISBN 0-268-01832-4). U of Notre Dame Pr.
Truths from the West Indies. Studholme Hodgson. (Illus.). text ed. 19.25 (ISBN 0-8369-9224-5, 9078). Ayer Co Pubs.
Truths of Love. Javad Nurbakhsh. Tr. by Leonard Lewisohn. 1982. pap. 6.00x (ISBN 0-933546-08-4). KhaniQahi Nimatullahi-Sufi.
Truths of Others: An Essay on Nativistic Intellectuals in Mexico. Alicja Iwanska. LC 76-40139. (Illus.). 124p. 1978. 18.95x (ISBN 0-87073-558-6); pap. text ed. 9.95x (ISBN 0-87073-559-4). Schenkman Bks Inc.
Truths That Transform. D. James Kennedy. 160p. 1974. power bks. 6.95 (ISBN 0-8007-5148-5). Revell.
Truths the Hand Can Touch: The Theatre of Athol Fugard. Russell Vandenbroucke. LC 85-2760. 268p. 1985. lib. bdg. 22.50 (ISBN 0-930452-42-9); pap. 12.50 (ISBN 0-930452-45-3). Theatre Comm.

Truths to Live by. facsimile ed. John E. Ross. LC 72-37834. (Essay Index Reprint Ser). Repr. of 1929 ed. 19.00 (ISBN 0-8369-2622-6). Ayer Co Pubs.

Try Again, Sally Jane. Mary Diestel-Feddersen. LC 86-42810. (Illus.). 30p. (gr. 2-3). 1987. PLB 11.25 (ISBN 1-55532-150-X). Stevens Inc.

Try Another Way Training Manual. Marc Gold. LC 80-52142. 114p. (Orig.). 1980. pap. 10.95 (ISBN 0-87822-222-7, 2227). Res Press.

Try Being a Teenager: A Challenge to Parents to Stay In Touch. Earl Wilson. LC 82-8314. 250p. 1982. pap. 6.95 (ISBN 0-930014-97-9). Multnomah.

Try Being Healthy. Alec Forbes. 184p. 1976. pap. 5.50x (ISBN 0-8464-1057-5). Beekman Pubs.

Try Being Healthy. Alec Forbes. 1980. 15.00x (ISBN 0-85032-140-9, Pub. by Daniel Co England). State Mutual Bk.

Try God, You'll Like Him. Katie Tonn. (Uplook Ser.). 1975. pap. 0.99 (ISBN 0-8163-0178-6, 20340-6). Pacific Pr Pub Assn.

Try It. Phillip Auerbach. 121p. 1976. pap. 20.00. NJ Inst CLE.

Try It On: Buying Clothing. Marilyn Thypin & Lynne Glasner. LC 78-12440. (Consumer Education Ser.). 1979. pap. text ed. 3.95 (ISBN 0-88436-508-5, 30254). EMC.

Try It! Simple Vegetarian Recipes for the Non-Vegetarian. Sandra Bartiromo & Debbie Weir. (Illus., Orig.). 1984. spiral bd. 4.95 (ISBN 0-916005-02-X). Silver Sea.

Try Marriage Before Divorce. James Kilgore. 1984. Repr. 5.95 (ISBN 0-8499-2995-4). Word Bks.

Try Thai. Sharon Wong Hoy. 100p. 1987. pap. 6.95 (ISBN 0-9607508-3-5). Benshaw Pub.

Try the Rabbit: A Handbook on Rabbit Raising for Beginners. S. O. Adajre. (Illus.). 40p. (Orig.). 1984. pap. 7.50x (ISBN 0-946688-61-3, Pub. by Intermediate Tech England). Intermediate Tech.

Try to Live to See This! Kabir. Tr. by Robert Bly. 1976. pap. 2.50 (ISBN 0-915408-12-0). Ally Pr.

Try to Remember. Vanessa James. (Nightingale Paperbacks Ser.). 328p. 1987. pap. 10.95 (ISBN 0-8161-4318-8, Large Print Bks). G K Hall.

Try Us: Washington Artillery in World War 2. P. A. Casey. 1971. 15.00 (ISBN 0-87511-588-8). Claitors.

Tryal of the Witnesses of the Resurrection of Jesus. 2nd ed. Thomas Sherlock. Ed. by Rene Wellek. Bd. with Use & Extent of Prophecy. LC 75-25131. (British Philosophers & Theologians of the 17th & 18th Centuries Ser.). 348p. 1979. lib. bdg. 51.00 (ISBN 0-8240-1761-7). Garland Pub.

Tryall of Private Devotions. Henry Burton. LC 77-6863. (English Experience Ser.: No. 856). 1977. Repr. of 1628 ed. lib. bdg. 20.00 (ISBN 90-221-0856-2). Walter J Johnson.

Trying Cases to Win. Herbert Stern. 180p. 1985. 3-ring Binder 47.70 (ISBN 0-317-42512-9). Hamline Law.

Trying Freedom: The Case for Liberating Education. Richard Meisler. LC 83-22543. 320p. 1984. 16.95 (ISBN 0-15-191358-7). HarBraceJ.

Trying Hard to Hear You. Sandra Scoppettone. LC 74-2611. 272p. (YA) (gr. 7up). 1974. PLB 13.89 (ISBN 0-06-025247-2). HarpJ.

Trying Not to Love You. (YA) (gr. 7-9). pap. 2.25 (ISBN 0-671-54394-6). Archway.

Trying Out. Caroline B. Cooney. (Cheerleaders Ser.: No. 1). 192p. (Orig.). (gr. 7 up). 1985. pap. 2.50 (ISBN 0-590-41034-2). Scholastic Inc.

Trying Out see Cheerleaders Boxed Set.

Trying-Out of Moby Dick. Howard P. Vincent. LC 80-16962. (Illus.). 400p. 1980. pap. 8.50x (ISBN 0-87338-247-1). Kent St U Pr.

Trying Sociology. Kurt H. Wolff. LC 74-13165. (Illus.). pap. 120.00 (ISBN 0-317-08702-9, 2017412). Bks Demand UMI.

Trying Times: Alabama Photographs, Nineteen-Seventeen to Nineteen Forty-Five. Michael V. Thomason. LC 84-16329. (Illus.). xiii, 302p. 1985. 39.50 (ISBN 0-8173-0254-9). U of Ala Pr.

Trying To Be a Christian. 4.95. Pilgrim NY.

Trying to Be an Honest Woman. Judith Barrington. LC 85-80278. 80p. 1985. pap. 6.95 (ISBN 0-933377-00-2). Eighth Mount Pr.

Trying to Explain. Donald Davie. (Poets on Poetry Ser.). 1979. pap. 8.95 (ISBN 0-472-06310-3). U of Mich Pr.

Trying to Make Sense. Peter Winch. 224p. Date not set. text ed. 34.95 (ISBN 0-631-15336-5). Basil Blackwell.

Trying to Surprise God. Peter Meinke. LC 80-54062. (Pitt Poetry Ser). 88p. 1981. 16.95x (ISBN 0-8229-3434-5); pap. 8.95 (ISBN 0-8229-5326-9). U of Pittsburgh Pr.

Trying to Understand What It Means to Be a Feminist: Essays on Women Writers. Rochelle Ratner. (Contact II Criticism Ser.). 100p. (Orig.). 1983. pap. 5.00 (ISBN 0-936556-10-2, Pub by Inland Book Co.). Contact Two.

Tryon Palace Mystery. Carole Marsh. (History Mystery Ser.). 104p. (Orig.). (gr. 3-12). 1986. pap. 7.95 (ISBN 0-935326-58-8). Gallopade Pub Group.

Trypanosomiasis: A Veterinary Perspective. L. E. Stephen. LC 86-2446. (Illus.). 572p. 1986. 125.00 (ISBN 0-08-032017-1). Pergamon.

Trypanosomiasis Control & African Rural Development. Anthony M. Jordan. 357p. 1986. 79.95 (ISBN 0-470-20665-9, Co-Pub. with Longman). Wiley.

Trypanotolerant Cattle & Livestock Development in West & Central Africa, Vol. II. A. P. Shaw & C. H. Hoste. 320p. (Orig.). 1987. pap. text ed. 31.50 (ISBN 92-5-102618-1, F3158, FAO). UNIPUB.

Trypanotolerant Cattle & Livestock Development in West & Central Africa, Vol. 1: The International Supply & Demand for Breeding Stock. A. P. Shaw & C. H. Hoste. (FAO Animal Production & Health Paper: No. 67-1). (Illus.). 183p. (Orig.). 1987. pap. 18.00 (ISBN 92-5-102617-3, F3141, FAO). UNIPUB.

Trypanotolerant Livestock in West & Central Africa. (Animal Production & Health Papers: No. 20-1 & 20-2). (Eng. & Fr.). 1980. Set. pap. 31.00 (ISBN 92-5-100978-3, F2152, FAO). Vol. 1, General Study, 155p. Vol. 2, Country Studies, 308p. UNIPUB.

Tryst. Grace L. Hill. Repr. lib. bdg. 20.95x (ISBN 0-89190-050-0, Pub. by River City Pr). Amereon Ltd.

Tryst. Elswyth Thane. 1974. Repr. of 1939 ed. lib. bdg. 19.95x (ISBN 0-88411-956-4, Pub. by Aeonian Pr). Amereon Ltd.

Tryst. Linda Trint. 1987. pap. 3.95 (ISBN 0-451-40010-0, Onyx). NAL.

Tryst with Education in the Technetronic Society. V. R. Taneja. 98p. 1984. text ed. 10.95x (ISBN 0-86590-180-5, Pub. by Sterling India). Apt Bks.

Tryst with Freedom: A Pictorial Saga. Subhash Kashyap. LC 73-906266. (Illus.). 89p. 1974. 17.50x (ISBN 0-89684-460-9). Orient Bk Dist.

T.S. Eliot & the Myth of Adequation. Alan Weinblatt. Ed. by A. Walton Litz. LC 83-17863. (Studies in Modern Literature: No. 29). 194p. 1984. 37.95 (ISBN 0-8357-1465-9). UMI Res Pr.

T.S. Eliot & the Politics of Voice: The Argument of "The Waste Land". John X. Cooper. Ed. by A. Walton Litz. LC 87-10896. (Studies in Modern Literature: No. 79). 134p. 1987. 39.95 (ISBN 0-8357-1824-7). UMI Res Pr.

T.S. Eliot As Editor. Shahid Ali Agha. Ed. by A. Walton Litz. LC 86-1263. (Studies in Modern Literture: No. 60). 183p. 1986. 39.95 (ISBN 0-8357-1751-8). UMI Res Pr.

T.S. Eliot on Shakespeare. Charles Warren. Ed. by A. Walton Litz. LC 86-14658. (Studies in Modern Literature: No. 66). 149p. 1986. 39.95 (ISBN 0-8357-1784-4). UMI Res Pr.

T.S. Eliot's Poems in French Translation: Pierre Leyris & Others. Joan F. Hooker. Ed. by A. Walton Litz. LC 83-9246. (Studies in Modern Literature: No. 26). 344p. 1983. 44.95 (ISBN 0-8357-1456-X). UMI Res Pr.

TSA Manual Release 1. J. D. Henstridge. 165p. (Orig.). 1982. pap. 13.72 (ISBN 0-317-52235-3, Pub. by Numer Algo UK). Numer Algorithms.

Tsa'ar Ba'ale Hayim. 1976. 6.95 (ISBN 0-87306-127-6). Feldheim.

Ts'ai Yuan-P'ei: Educator of Modern China. William J. Duiker. LC 76-43212. (Penn State Studies: No. 41). 1977. pap. 5.95x (ISBN 0-271-00504-1). Pa St U Pr.

Tsalagi. Carroll Arnett. 1976. pap. 5.00 (ISBN 0-685-79197-1). Elizabeth Pr.

Tsali. Denton R. Bedford. LC 72-91136. (Illus.). 256p. 1972. pap. 15.00 (ISBN 0-913436-24-0). Indian Hist Pr.

Tsaniia T. Razmyshleniia. Fyodor Dostoyevsky. 464p. 1983. 39.00x (Pub. by Collets UK). State Mutual Bk.

Ts'ao Yin & the K'Ang-Hsi Emperor: Bondservant & Master. Jonathan D. Spence. LC 87-51374. 352p. 1988. 13.95 (ISBN 0-300-04278-7); text ed. 35.00 (ISBN 0-300-04277-9). Yale U Pr.

TSAR. Christopher Egerton-Thomas. 350p. 1988. cancelled (ISBN 0-938311-01-8). Atlantic Intl Pubns.

Tsar Alexander First: Paternalistic Reformer. Allen McConnell. LC 70-101949. (Europe Since 1500 Ser.). 1970. pap. 9.95x (ISBN 0-88295-745-7). Harlan Davidson.

Tsar Alexis, His Reign & His Russia. Joseph T. Fuhrman. (Russian Ser.: No. 34). 1981. 25.00 (ISBN 0-87569-040-8). Academic Intl.

Tsar & Cossack, Eighteen Fifty-Five to Nineteen Fourteen. Robert H. McNeal. LC 85-1942. 288p. 1987. 27.50 (ISBN 0-312-82188-3). St Martin.

Tsar & the Amazing Cow. Patrick J. Lewis. LC 86-29255. (Illus.). 32p. (ps-3). 1988. 10.95 (ISBN 0-8037-0410-0, 01063-320); PLB 10.89 (ISBN 0-8037-0411-9). Dial Bks Young.

Tsar Ivan Fourth's Reply to Jan Roktya. Valerie A. Tumins. LC 79-114575. (Slavistic Printings & Reprintings Ser.: No. 84). (Illus.). 1971. text ed. 72.00x (ISBN 90-2791-764-7). Mouton.

Tsar Maksimilian. Aleksei M. Remizov. 128p. (Rus.). 1988. pap. 8.00 (ISBN 0-933884-55-9). Berkeley Slavic.

Tsar Nicholas I & the Jews: The Transformation of Jewish Society in Russia, 1825-1855. Michael Stanislawski. (Illus.). 272p. 1983. 18.95 (ISBN 0-8276-0216-2, 497). JPS Phila.

Tsardom & Imperialism in the Far East & Middle East, 1880-1914. B. H. Sumner. 43p. 1968. Repr. of 1940 ed. 12.50 (ISBN 0-208-00057-7, Archon). Shoe String.

Tsardom of Moscow, Fifteen Forty-Seven to Sixteen Eighty-Two. George Vernadsky. LC 43-1903. (History of Russia Ser.: Vol. 5). Pt. 1. pap. 125.00 (ISBN 0-317-10883-2, 2022048); Pt. 2. pap. 102.50 (ISBN 0-317-10884-0). Bks Demand UMI.

Tsarist Economy, Eighteen Fifty to Nineteen Seventeen. Peter Gatrell. LC 85-25014. 304p. 1986. 29.95 (ISBN 0-312-82191-3). St Martin.

Tsarist Russia & Balkan Nationalism: Russian Influence in International Affairs of Bulgaria & Serbia, 1879-1886. Charles Jelavich. LC 77-26080. (Russian & East European Studies). (Illus.). 1978. Repr. of 1958 ed. lib. bdg. 35.00x (ISBN 0-313-20085-8, JETR). Greenwood.

Tsar's Loyal German: The Riga German Community, Social Change & the Nationality Question, 1855-1905. Anders Henriksson. 218p. 1983. 24.00x (ISBN 0-88033-020-1). East Eur Quarterly.

Tsar's Viceroys: Russian Provincial Governors in the Last Years of the Empire. Richard G. Robbins, Jr. LC 87-47700. 328p. 1987. 32.95x (ISBN 0-8014-2046-6). Cornell U Pr.

Tsar's Window. facsimile ed. Lucy H. Hooper. LC 74-164566. (American Fiction Reprint Ser). Repr. of 1881 ed. 23.50 (ISBN 0-8369-7043-8). Ayer Co Pubs.

Tsar's Woman. Hill. 1988. pap. 3.50 (ISBN 0-312-90668-4). St Martin.

Tsar's Woman. Pamela Hill. 1987. pap. 3.50 (ISBN 0-317-54103-X). St Martin.

TSCA Compliance-Enforcement Guidance Manual. Ed. by U. S. Environmental Protection Agency Staff. 500p. 1984. pap. 68.00 (ISBN 0-86587-072-1). Gov Insts.

TSCA Handbook. McKenna, Conner & Cuneo Law Firm. 414p. 1987. pap. 79.00 (ISBN 0-86587-711-4). Gov Insts.

TSCA Inspection Manual, Pt. II. Environmental Protection Agency Staff. 216p. 1986. pap. 53.00 (ISBN 0-86587-143-4). Gov Insts.

TSCA Policy Compendium. U. S. Environmental Protection Agency Staff. 656p. 1985. pap. text ed. 99.00 (ISBN 0-86587-036-5). Gov Insts.

TSCA's Impact on Society & Chemical Industry. Ed. by George W. Ingle. LC 83-2733. (Symposium Ser.: No. 213). 244p. 1983. lib. bdg. 34.95 (ISBN 0-8412-0766-6). Am Chemical.

Tschiffely's Ride. A. Tschiffely. 1976. lib. bdg. 34.95 (ISBN 0-8490-2777-2). Gordon Pr.

Tschudi: The Harpsichord Maker. William Dale. LC 77-75208. 1977. Repr. of 1913 ed. lib. bdg. 12.50 (ISBN 0-89341-069-1). Longwood Pub Group.

Tsekh Poetov: I. (Rus.). 1978. 12.50 (ISBN 0-88233-370-4); pap. 3.50 (ISBN 0-88233-375-5). Ardis Pubs.

Tseng Kuo-Fan's Private Bureaucracy. Jonathan Porter. LC 72-619560. (China Research Monographs: No. 9). 148p. 1972. pap. 2.50x (ISBN 0-912966-10-6). IEAS.

Tsereteli: A Democrat in the Russian Revolution. Roobol. (Studies in Social History: No. 1). 1976. lib. bdg. 45.00 (ISBN 90-247-1915-1, Pub. by Martinus Nijhoff Netherlands). Kluwer Academic.

Tserkov' Boga Ahivago, Stolp i Utverzhdjenije Istini. Archpriest Kyrill Zaits. 92p. 1956. pap. 2.00 (ISBN 0-317-29113-0). Holy Trinity.

Tserkov', Rus' i Rim. N. N. Voieivkov. 512p. 1983. text ed. 25.00 (ISBN 0-88465-016-2); pap. text ed. 20.00 (ISBN 0-88465-015-4). Holy Trinity.

Tserkovni Bratsva v Ukraini. Wasyl Luciw. 1976. pap. 3.50 (ISBN 0-317-12225-8). Slavia Lib.

Tserkovnij Ustav. Alexander Svirelin. 143p. 1981. pap. text ed. 6.00 (ISBN 0-317-30282-5). Holy Trinity.

Tserkovno-Obshchestvennye Voprosky v Epokhu: Tasaria-Osvoboditelia 1855-1870. A. A. Papkov. 192p. Repr. of 1902 ed. text ed. 49.68x (ISBN 0-576-99281-X, Pub. by Gregg Intl Pubs England). Gregg Intl.

Tserkovno-Pjevcheskiji Sbornik, 5 Vols. Incl. Vol. 1. Vsjenoshchnoje Bdjenije. 394p. 27.00 (ISBN 0-317-30454-2); Vol. 2. Bozhestvjennaja Liturgija (Nachjalo) 381p. Pt. 1. 26.00 (ISBN 0-317-30455-0); Vol. 2. Bozhestvjennaja Liturgija (Konjets) 621p. Pt. 2. 33.00 (ISBN 0-317-30456-9); Vol. 3. Triod' Postnaja. 532p. Pt. 1. 31.00 (ISBN 0-317-30457-7); Vol. 3. Strastnaja Sedmitsa. 1059p. Pt. 2. 40.00 (ISBN 0-317-30458-5); Vol. 4. Triod' Tsvjetnaja. 680p. 33.00 (ISBN 0-317-30459-3); Vol. 5. Oktojikh. 421p. 26.00 (ISBN 0-317-30460-7). 216.00 set (ISBN 0-317-30453-4). Holy Trinity.

Tsese-Ma'Heone-Nemeototse: Cheyenne Spiritual Songs. Ed. by David Graber. LC 82-83401. 227p. (Eng. & Cheyenne.). 1982. 29.95 (ISBN 0-87303-078-8). Faith & Life.

Tsewa'a Gift: Magic & Meaning in an Amazonian Society. Michael F. Brown. LC 85-40401. (Ethnographic Inquiry Ser.). (Illus.). 220p. 1986. 19.95x (ISBN 0-87474-294-3, BRTG). Smithsonian.

TSFR: The Taoist Way to Total Sexual Fitness for Men. Bruce M. Wong. 80p. 1982. pap. 9.95 (ISBN 0-910295-00-X). Golden Dragon Pub.

Tshi-Speaking Peoples of the Gold Coast of West Africa. Alfred B. Ellis. 1964. 18.50x (ISBN 0-910216-02-9). Benin.

Tshombe. Anthony Bouscaren. 1967. pap. 0.95 (ISBN 0-912080-05-1). Guild Bks.

Tsimshian & Their Neighbors of the North Pacific Coast. Ed. by Jay Miller & Carol Eastman. LC 83-28364. (Illus.). 366p. 1985. 35.00x (ISBN 0-295-96126-0). U of Wash Pr.

Tsimshian Indians & Their Arts. Viola E. Garfield & Paul S. Wingert. LC 68-87177. (American Ethnological Society Numbered Publications: No. 18). (Illus.). 108p. 1966. pap. 4.95 (ISBN 0-295-74042-6). U of Wash Pr.

Tsimshian Mythology Based on Texts Recorded by Henry W. Tate. Franz Boas. (Landmarks in Anthropology Ser.). (Illus.). Repr. of 1916 ed. 60.00 (ISBN 0-384-04880-3). Johnson Repr.

Tsimshian Narratives, No. 1: Tricksters, Shamans & Heroes. Marius Barbeau & William Beynon. Ed. by John J. Cove & George F. MacDonald. (Mercury Ser.). (Illus.). 354p. 1988. pap. 19.95 (ISBN 0-660-10761-9, Pub. by CN Mus of Civilization Canada). U of Chicago Pr.

Tsimshian Narratives, No. 2: Trade & Warfare. Marius Barbeau & William Beynon. Ed. by John J. Cove & George F. MacDonald. (Mercury Ser.). (Illus.). 268p. 1988. pap. 17.95 (ISBN 0-660-10770-8, Pub. by CN Mus of Civilization Canada). U of Chicago Pr.

Tsimshian Texts. Franz Boas. Repr. of 1902 ed. 39.00x (ISBN 0-403-03716-6). Scholarly.

Tsimshian: Their Arts & Music. Viola E. Garfield et al. LC 84-4549. (American Ethnological Society Publications: No. 18). Date not set. Repr. of 1951 ed. 45.00 (ISBN 0-404-58168-4). AMS Pr.

TSM in Nineteen Eighty: State of the Art & Future Directions. (Special Report). 70p. 1980. 5.60 (ISBN 0-309-02996-1). Transport Res Bd.

Tso Tsung T'ang: Soldier & Statesman of Old China. W. I. Bales. lib. bdg. 79.95 (ISBN 0-87968-475-5). Krishna Pr.

TSOHAR. Rabbi Nachman of Breslov. Tr. by Avraham Greenbaum from Hebrew. 64p. (Orig.). 1986. pap. text ed. 1.50 (ISBN 0-930213-26-2). Breslov Res Inst.

Tsonakwa & Yolaikia: Legends in Stone, Bone, & Wood. Intro. by Linda Crawford & Jo West. (Illus.). 64p. (Orig.). 1986. pap. write for info. (ISBN 0-938541-03-X). Origins Program.

Tsong Khapa's Speech of Gold in the Essence of True Eloquence: Robert Thurman. LC 83-43096. (Library of Asian Translations). (Illus.). 475p. 1984. 55.50x (ISBN 0-691-07285-X). Princeton U Pr.

Tsotsi. Athol Fugard. 1983. pap. 4.95 (ISBN 0-14-006272-6). Penguin.

Tstoriia Russkoi Tserkvi. N. M. Nikol'skii. 320p. (Rus.). 1983. 59.00x (ISBN 0-317-40812-7, Pub. by Collets (UK)). State Mutual bk.

Tsuba & Japanese Sword Fittings in the Collection of the Cooper-Hewitt: The Smithsonian Institution's National Museum of Design. Henry Rosin. LC 80-67169. (Cooper-Hewitt Museum Collection Handbook Ser.). (Illus.). 36p. (Orig.). 1980. pap. 3.95x (ISBN 0-910503-10-9). Cooper-Hewitt Museum.

Tsubas in Southern California. W. M. Hawley. 302p. 1973. 175.00x (ISBN 0-317-69183-X, Pub. by Han-Shan Tang Ltd). State Mutual Bk.

Tsubas in Southern California. 1986. Repr. of 1973 ed. 30.00 (ISBN 0-910704-62-7). Hawley.

Tsubo: Vital Points for Oriental Therapy. Katsusuke Serizawa. (Illus.). 256p. 1976. 22.95 (ISBN 0-87040-350-8). Japan Pubns USA.

Tsuen-Wan Township: Study Group Report on Its Development. Gerald Moore. pap. 20.00 (ISBN 0-317-11282-1, 2017719). Bks Demand UMI.

Tsuga Canadensis & Related Species. John C. Swartley. (Illus.). 1977. 15.00 (ISBN 0-913728-28-4). Theophrastus.

Tsujigahana: The Flower of Japanese Textile Art. Toshiko Ito. Tr. by Monica Bethe. LC 84-48967. (Illus.). 202p. 1985. 55.00 (ISBN 0-87011-397-6). Kodansha.

Tsunami! Walter C. Dudley & Min Lee. LC 87-19070. (Illus.). 152p. 1988. pap. 10.95 (ISBN 0-8248-1125-9). UH Pr.

Tsunami. Richard M. Stern. 1988. 17.95 (ISBN 0-393-02529-2). Norton.

Tsunami Research Symposium, 1974: Proceedings of an International Symposium of Tsunami Research. (Illus.). 258p. 1976. pap. 12.75 (ISBN 92-3-101330-0, U771, UNESCO). UNIPUB.

Tsunamis in the Pacific Ocean. Ed. by William M. Adams. 1970. 30.00x (ISBN 0-8248-0095-8, Eastwest Ctr). UH Pr.

Tsunamis: Their Science & Engineering. Ed. by T. Iwasaki & K. Iida. 1983. lib. bdg. 113.00 (ISBN 0-686-39790-8, Pub. by Reidel Holland). Kluwer Academic.

Tsungli Yamen: Its Organization & Functions. S. M. Meng. LC 62-53393. (East Asian Monographs: No. 13). 1962. pap. 11.00x (ISBN 0-674-91095-8). Harvard U Pr.

Tsuni-Ilgoam. facsimile ed. Theophilus Hahn. LC 70-164388. (Black Heritage Library Collection). Repr. of 1880 ed. 18.00 (ISBN 0-8369-8847-7). Ayer Co Pubs.

Tsurezure Gusa see Miscellany of a Japanese Priest.

Tsushima. Aleksei S. Novikov-Priboi. Tr. by E. Paul & C. Paul. LC 75-39005. (Soviet Literature in English Translation Ser.). (Illus.). 407p. 1978. Repr. of 1936 ed. 27.50 (ISBN 0-88355-408-9). Hyperion-Conn.

Tsutsugaki Textiles of Japan. Ed. by S. Yoshioka. 178p. 1988. 49.95 (ISBN 4-879-40501-9). Bks Nippan.
Tsvetaeva i Parnok. S. Poliakova. (Illus.). 128p. (Rus.). 1982. 19.50 (ISBN 0-88233-830-7). Ardis Pubs.
Tswana. I. Schapera. 112p. 1985. pap. 14.95x (ISBN 0-7103-0096-4). Routledge Chapman & Hall.
TTL & CMOS Circuits. Heath Company Staff. (Circuit Files Ser.). (Illus.). 124p. looseleaf with experimental pts. 59.95 (ISBN 0-87119-001-X, EH-702). Heathkit-Zenith Ed.
TTL Cookbook. Donald E. Lancaster. LC 73-90295. (Illus.). 336p. (Orig.). 1974. pap. 14.95 (ISBN 0-672-21035-5). Sams.
TTL Data Book, Vol. IV. Texas Instruments Engineering Staff. LC 83-51810. 350p. (Orig.). 1986. pap. text ed. 9.95 (ISBN 0-89512-154-9, SDZD001B). Tex Instr Inc.
TTL Data Book, Vol. III. Texas Instruments Engineering Staff. LC 83-51810. 800p. (Orig.). 1986. pap. text ed. 12.95 (ISBN 0-89512-153-0, SDAD001B). Tex Instr Inc.
TTL Data Book, Vol. II. Texas Instruments Engineering Staff. LC 83-51810. 1100p. (Orig.). 1984. pap. text ed. 17.85 (ISBN 0-89512-096-8, SDLD001). Tex Instr Inc.
TTL Data Book, Vol. I. Texas Instruments Engineering Staff. LC 83-51810. 320p. (Orig.). 1984. pap. text ed. 7.95 (ISBN 0-89512-090-9, SDYD001). Tex Instr Inc.
Tu. Cid Corman. 48p. 1983. pap. 12.50 (ISBN 0-915124-79-3, Pub. by Toothpaste). Coffee Hse.
Tu' A Moving Collection of Romantic Poetry. Armando De Peralta et al. Ed. by Marilyn A. Ward. LC 85-73610. (Illus.). 90p. 1986. 14.95 (ISBN 0-938727-00-1). Scorpio Pr.
Tu Bishvat. Norma Simon. (Festival Series of Picture Storybooks). (Illus.). (ps-k). 1961. plastic cover 4.50 (ISBN 0-8381-0709-5). United Syn Bk.
Tu Cours apres l'Ete, et l'Hiver te Rattrape. Charles M. Schulz. (Fr.). pap. 5.95 (ISBN 0-03-061651-4). H Holt & Co.
Tu Es Dans le Vent, Charlie Brown. Charles M. Schulz. (Fr). 1971. 1.50 (ISBN 0-03-086657-X). H Holt & Co.
Tu es le Plus Beau, Charlie Brown. Charles M. Schulz. (Fr.). pap. 1.50 (ISBN 0-03-089255-4). H Holt & Co.
Tu estais Si Gentil Quand Tu Etais Petit see Pieces Secretes.
Tu Etais Si Gentil Quand Tu etais Petit. Jean Anouilh. 1973. pap. 9.95 (ISBN 0-686-50126-8). French & Eur.
Tu Fe. Ed. by John McPhee. Tr. by Olimpia Diaz. (Span.). (YA) (gr. 9-12). 1980. pap. 1.95 (ISBN 0-89243-124-5, 48290). Liguori Pubns.
Tu Fu's Gedichte, 2 Vols. Tu Fu. Ed. by James R. Hightower. Tr. by Erwin Von Zach. LC 52-10980. (Harvard-Yenching Institute Studies: No. 8). 1952. Set. pap. 20.00x (ISBN 0-674-34125-2). Harvard U Pr.
Tu Ne Tueras Point see Thou Shalt Not Kill.
Tu N'En Reviendras Pas, Charlie Brown. Charles M. Schulz. (Fr.). pap. 1.50 (ISBN 0-03-086658-8). H Holt & Co.
Tu Puedes! James D. Freeman. LC 82-70490. 256p. 1982. 5.95 (ISBN 0-87159-158-8). Unity School.
Tu y Tu Dinero. Malcolm MacGregor & Stanley G. Baldwin. 160p. (Span.). 1984. 3.95 (ISBN 0-88113-369-8). Edit Betania.
Tuala Speaks. Tuala. Ed. by Jeanne Tamalelagi. LC 80-67870. 220p. (Orig.). 1980. pap. 8.95 (ISBN 0-87516-425-0). DeVorss.
Tuamatuan Stone Structures. K. P. Emory. (BMB Ser.). Repr. of 1934 ed. 16.00 (ISBN 0-527-02224-1). Kraus Repr.
Tuamotuan Legends (Island of Anaa), Pt. 1: The Demigods. J. F. Stimson. (BMB). Repr. of 1937 ed. 23.00 (ISBN 0-527-02256-X). Kraus Repr.
Tuamotuan Religion. J. F. Stimson. (BMB Ser.). Repr. of 1933 ed. 23.00 (ISBN 0-527-02209-8). Kraus Repr.
Tuamotuan Religious Structures & Ceremonies. K. P. Emory. (BMB Ser.). Repr. of 1947 ed. 15.00 (ISBN 0-527-02299-3). Kraus Repr.
Tuan. Eva Boholm-Olsson. Tr. by Dianne Jonasson. (Illus.). 32p. (YA) (ps up). 1988. 11.95 (ISBN 91-29-58766-2, Pub. by R & S Bks). FS&G.
Tuaregs: Their Islamic Legacy & Its Diffusion in the Sahel. H. T. Norris. 252p. 1975. text ed. 45.00x (ISBN 0-85668-031-1, Pub. by Aris & Phillips UK). Humanities.
Tuba Music Guide. Ed. by R. Winston Morris. pap. 7.00 (ISBN 0-686-15895-4). Instrumental Co.
Tubbo: The Great Peter's Run. Paul DeServille. 1982. 45.00x (ISBN 0-19-554304-1). Oxford U Pr.
Tubby the Little Green Frog. Erma Lively. (Illus.). 32p. (gr. 1-2). 1987. 10.95 (ISBN 0-89962-580-0). Todd & Honeywell.
Tube Bundle Thermal-Hydraulics. Ed. by P. A. Pfund & S. C. Yao. 73p. 1982. 20.00 (G00212). ASME.
Tube Leaks: A Consumer's & Worker's Guide to Steam Generator Problems at Nuclear Power Plants. Critical Mass Energy Project. Ed. by Richard Udell. (Illus.). 64p. 1982. saddle-stitched 3.50 (ISBN 0-937188-21-2). Pub Citizen Inc.
Tube of Plenty: The Evolution of American Television. Erik Barnouw. (Illus.). 1982. rev. ed. 22.50x (ISBN 0-19-501949-0). Oxford U Pr.
Tube of Plenty: The Evolution of American Television. rev. ed. Erik Barnouw. (Illus.). 1982. pap. 11.95 (ISBN 0-19-503092-3). Oxford U Pr.
Tube Strips. Bill Plympton. 1976. pap. 5.00 (ISBN 0-918266-04-1). Smyrna.
Tube Substitution Handbook. 21st ed. Howard W. Sams Engineering Staff. LC 80-13842. 128p. 1980. pap. 5.95 (ISBN 0-672-21746-5). Sams.
Tube Type Dilatometers: Applications from Cyrogenic to Elevated Temperatures. Joseph H. Valentich. LC 80-82116. 240p. 1981. text ed. 28.75x (ISBN 0-87664-468-X). Instru Soc.
Tuberculin Skin Test Reaction among Adults 25-74 Years: United States, 1971-1972. Ed. by Audrey Shipp. (Series 11 No. 204). 1977. pap. 1.75 (ISBN 0-8406-0086-0). Natl Ctr Health Stats.
Tuberculin Test in Clinical Practice. Maxwell Caplin. (Illus.). 1982. pap. text ed. 20.95 (ISBN 0-7216-0710-1, Bailliere-Tindall). Saunders.
Tuberculosis, 2 pts. Anthony Lowell. Incl. Pt. 1. Tuberculosis Morbidity & Mortality & Its Control. Anthony M. Lowell; Pt. 2. Tuberculosis Infection. Lydia B. Edwards & Carroll E. Palmer. LC 79-82296. (Vital & Health Statistics Monographs, American Public Health Association). 256p. 1969. text ed. 17.50x set (ISBN 0-674-91135-0). Harvard U Pr.
Tuberculosis. Ed. by D. Schlossberg. (Clinical Topics in Infectious Disease Ser.). (Illus.). 225p. 1988. 79.00 (ISBN 0-387-96552-1). Springer-Verlag.
Tuberculosis. Incl. Vol. 21, No. 1. 144p. 1959. pap. o. p. (ISBN 0-686-09225-2); Vol. 31, No. 2. 146p. 1964. pap. 3.60 (ISBN 0-686-09226-0); Vol. 33, No. 3. 146p. 1965. pap. 3.60 (ISBN 0-686-09227-9); Vol. 34, No. 4. 172p. 1966. pap. o. p. (ISBN 0-686-09228-7); Vol. 35, No. 4. 192p. 1966. pap. 3.60 (ISBN 0-686-09229-5); Vol. 36, No. 5. 168p. 1967. pap. 3.60 (ISBN 0-686-09230-9); Vol. 37, No. 6. 164p. 1967. pap. 3.60 (ISBN 0-686-09231-7); Vol. 39, No. 5. 198p. 1968. pap. 3.60 (ISBN 0-686-09232-5); Vol. 41, No. 1. 178p. 1969. pap. 4.80 (ISBN 0-686-09233-3); Vol. 43, No. 1. 206p. 1970. (Bulletin of WHO Ser.). (Eng. & Fr.). pap. World Health.
Tuberculosis. Gerald B. Webb. LC 75-23667. (Clio Medica Ser.: No. 16). (Illus.). Repr. of 1936 ed. 18.50 (ISBN 0-404-58916-2). AMS Pr.
Tuberculosis: A Half-Century of Study & Conquest. Jay A. Myers. LC 75-96989. (Illus.). 378p. 1970. 17.50 (ISBN 0-87527-059-X). Green.
Tuberculosis among Certain Indian Tribes of the United States. Ales Hrdlicka. 96p. 1980. Repr. of 1909 ed. deluxe ed. 29.00 (ISBN 0-403-02467-6). Scholarly.
Tuberculosis among Certain Indian Tribes of the United States. Ales Hrdlicka. 1988. Repr. of 1909 ed. lib. bdg. 49.00x. Am Biog Serv.
Tuberculosis & Its Prevention. Stefan Grzybowski. (Illus.). 114p. 1983. 19.75. Green.
Tuberculosis As a Disease of the Masses & How to Combat It. S. Adolphus Knopf. Ed. by Barbara G. Rosenkrantz. LC 76-40633. (Public Health in America Ser.). 1977. Repr. of 1908 ed. lib. bdg. 17.00x (ISBN 0-405-09824-3). Ayer Co Pubs.
Tuberculosis Movement: A Public Health Campaign in the Progressive Era. LC 87-29432. (Contributions in Medical Studies: No. 22). 192p. 1988. lib. bdg. 37.95 (ISBN 0-313-25748-5, TCD/). Greenwood.
Tuberculosis Nurse. Ellen N. LaMotte. Ed. by Susan Reverby. (History of American Nursing Ser.). 35.00 (ISBN 0-8240-6517-4). Garland Pub.
Tuberculosis of the Bones & Joints. Ed. by M. Martini. (Illus.). 230p. 1988. 84.50 (ISBN 0-387-18166-0). Springer-Verlag.
Tuberculous Meningitis; Tuberculomas & Spinal Tuberculosis: A Handbook for Clinicians. 2nd ed. Malcolm Parsons. (Illus.). 92p. 1988. 29.95 (ISBN 0-19-261721-4). Oxford U Pr.
Tuberoses & Nine-Patch. Ruth Dyer. Ed. by Sherri York. LC 87-42905. 65p. 1988. pap. 5.95 (ISBN 1-55523-112-8). Winston-Derek.
Tuberous Begonias: Origin & Development. J. Haegeman. 1979. lib. bdg. 48.00x (ISBN 3-7682-1219-X). Lubrecht & Cramer.
Tuberous Sclerosis. 2nd ed. Ed. by Manuel R. Gomez. (Illus.). 288p. 1988. text ed. 69.00 (ISBN 0-88167-397-8). Raven.
Tubes. Alfred Gray. 250p. 1988. 40.95 (ISBN 0-201-15676-8). Addison-Wesley.
Tubex: The Ultimate Body Exercise. Dand Kulund & Booton Herndon. LC 85-40867. (Illus.). 136p. 1986. pap. 9.95 incl. exercise tube & instruction card (ISBN 0-394-74411-X, Vin). Random.
Tubicolous Annelids see Enchytroids.
Tubingen Studies in Language & Literature, 1980. 1980. 7.00 (ISBN 0-936072-15-6). Soc New Lang Study.
Tubinger Predigten. Johann Von Staupitz. (Ger.). 34.00 (ISBN 0-384-57712-1); pap. 28.00 (ISBN 0-384-57711-3). Johnson Repr.
Tubtime for Thaddeus. Joan W. Anglund. (Bath & Beach Play Sets Ser.). (Illus.). 10p. (ps). 1986. 3.95 (ISBN 0-394-88134-6). Random.
Tubtime for Thaddeus. Joan W. Anglund. (Bathtime Bks.). (Illus.). 10p. (ps). 1986. 2.95 (ISBN 0-394-87542-7). Random.
Tubular Members in Offshore Structures. W. F. Chen. 296p. 1985. 59.95 (ISBN 0-470-20441-9, Co-Pub. with Longman). Wiley.
Tubulo-Interstitial Nephropathies. Ed. by Ramzi Cotran. (Contemporary Issues in Nephrology Ser.: Vol. 10). (Illus.). 381p. 1982. text ed. 49.50 (ISBN 0-443-08258-8). Churchill.
Tuc Overseas: The Roots of Policy. Marjorie Nicholson. 220p. 1986. text ed. 45.00X (ISBN 0-04-331103-2). Unwin Hyman.
Tuc: The Growth of a Pressure Group Eighteen Sixty-Eight to Nineteen Seventy-Six. Ross M. Martin. 1980. text ed. 59.00x (ISBN 0-19-822475-3). Oxford U Pr.
Tuck. Mamie Swallow. 264p. 1987. pap. 10.95 (ISBN 0-918292-14-X). Griggs Print.
Tuck Everlasting. Natalie Babbitt. LC 75-33306. 160p. (gr. 3 up). 1975. 11.95 (ISBN 0-374-37848-7, Sunburst); pap. 3.50 (ISBN 0-374-48009-5). FS&G.
Tuck in Chaps! Traditional British Grub. Jane Pettigrew. (Illus.). 128p. 1988. 19.95 (ISBN 0-7063-6595-X, Pub. by Ward Lock). David & Charles.
Tucker. Louis L'Amour. 192p. 1984. pap. 2.95 (ISBN 0-553-25022-1). Bantam.
Tucker Boone. Joan E. Pickart. (Loveswept Ser.: No. 285). 192p. 1988. pap. 2.50. Bantam.
Tucker Trails Through Southside Virginia. B. DeRoy Beale. LC 85-71124. 321p. (Orig.). 1986. pap. 22.00 (ISBN 0-9602132-2-8). B D Beale.
Tucker's Countryside. George Selden. LC 69-14975. (Illus.). 176p. (gr. 3 up). 1969. 12.95 (ISBN 0-374-37854-1). FS&G.
Tucking Mommy In. Morag Loh. LC 87-16740. (Illus.). 40p. (ps-2). 1988. 12.95 (ISBN 0-531-05740-2); PLB 12.99 (ISBN 0-531-08340-3). Orchard Bks Watts.
Tucson. Bernice Cosulich. (Illus., Orig.). 1987. pap. 12.00 (ISBN 0-918080-36-3). Treasure Chest.
Tucson. A. R. Riefe. (Fortune West Ser.: No. 1). 336p. 1988. pap. 4.50 (ISBN 0-451-15470-3, Sig). NAL.
Tucson: A Short History. Charles W. Polzer et al. LC 85-63503. (Illus.). 160p. (Orig.). 1986. pap. 8.95 (ISBN 0-915076-11-X). SW Mission.
Tucson Adventures for Toys Through Teens. Nan Rosenthal. 76p. 1985. pap. 4.00 (ISBN 0-918080-27-4). Treasure Chest.
Tucson Meteorites: Their History from Frontier Arizona to the Smithsonian. Richard R. Willey. LC 86-42742. (Illus.). 48p. (Orig.). 1987. pap. 8.95 (ISBN 0-87474-983-2, WITMP). Smithsonian.
Tucson: The Life & Times of an American City. C. L. Sonnichsen. LC 82-40329. (Illus.). 400p. 1982. 29.95 (ISBN 0-8061-1823-7). U of Okla Pr.
Tucson: The Life & Times of an American City. C. L. Sonnichsen. (Illus.). 384p. 1987. pap. 15.95 (ISBN 0-8061-2042-8). U of Okla Pr.
Tucson Twosome. Jory Sherman. (Gunn Ser.: Vol. 17). 1983. pap. 2.25 (ISBN 0-8217-1236-5). Zebra.
Tucsoneses: The Mexican Community in Tucson, 1854-1941. Thomas E. Sheridan. LC 86-11404. 327p. 1986. 29.95 (ISBN 0-8165-0876-3). U of Ariz Pr.
Tude Ever Lasting. Rabbitt Natalie. 160p. (gr. 2 up). 1975. 10.95 (ISBN 0-317-65291-5); pap. 3.45 (ISBN 0-317-65292-3). FS&G.
Tudor Age. James A. Williamson. (History of England Ser.). (Illus.). 496p. 1979. pap. text ed. 16.95 (ISBN 0-582-49074-X). Longman.
Tudor Age & Beyond: England from the Black Death to the End of the Age of Elizabeth. Arthur J. Slavin. LC 86-2723. 252p. (Orig.). 1987. pap. text ed. 9.50 (ISBN 0-89874-945-X). Krieger.
Tudor & Early Stuart Voyaging. B. Penrose. LC 79-65985. (Folger Guides to the Age of Shakespeare). 1979. pap. 3.95 (ISBN 0-918016-12-6). Folger Bks.
Tudor & Jacobean Portraits, 2 vol. Roy Strong. (Illus.). 700p. 1980. Set. 160.00x (ISBN 0-312-82220-0). St Martin.
Tudor & Jacobean Tournaments. Alan Young. (Illus.). 230p. 1987. 34.95 (ISBN 0-911378-75-8). Sheridan.
Tudor & Stuart Britain. 2nd ed. Roger Lockyer. (Illus.). Date not set. price not set (ISBN 0-312-82254-5). St Martin.
Tudor & Stuart Drama. 2nd ed. Irving Ribner & Clifford C. Huffman. LC 76-5215. (Goldentree Bibliographies in Language & Literature). 1978. text ed. 24.95x (ISBN 0-88295-572-1); pap. text ed. 14.95x (ISBN 0-88295-554-3). Harlan Davidson.
Tudor Books of Private Devotion. Helen C. White. LC 78-21661. (Illus.). 1979. Repr. of 1951 ed. lib. bdg. 35.00x (ISBN 0-313-21063-2, WHTB). Greenwood.
Tudor Books of Saints & Martyrs. Helen C. White. LC 63-13741. pap. 73.00 (ISBN 0-317-07866-6, 2004164). Bks Demand UMI.
Tudor Church Music. Ed. by P. C. Buck & E. H. Fellowes. Incl. Vol. 1. John Taverner - Part One; Vol. 2. William Byrd - English Church Music, Part One (ISBN 0-8450-1852-3); Vol. 3. John Tavernen - Part Two; Vol. 4. Orlando Gibbons; Vol. 5. Robert White; Vol. 6. Thomas Tallis; Vol. 7. William Byrd; Vol. 8. Thomas Tomkins; Vol. 9; Vol. 10. Hugh Aston & John Marbeck (ISBN 0-8450-1860-4). 1963. Repr. of 1922 ed. 750.00x set (ISBN 0-8450-1850-7); 85.00x ea.; appendix 50.00x. Broude.
Tudor Church Music. Denis Stevens. LC 73-4335. (Music Reprint Ser.). 144p. 1973. Repr. of 1955 ed. lib. bdg. 25.00 (ISBN 0-306-70579-6). Da Capo.
Tudor Constitution: Documents & Commentary. 2nd ed. Geoffrey R. Elton. LC 81-15216. 522p. 1982. 77.50 (ISBN 0-521-24506-0); pap. 23.95 (ISBN 0-521-28757-X). Cambridge U Pr.
Tudor Court. David Loades. LC 86-20612. (Illus.). 272p. 1986. 30.00x (ISBN 0-389-20676-8). B&N Imports.
Tudor Drama. Charles F. Brooke. LC 75-144902. 1911. Repr. 69.00 (ISBN 0-403-00840-9). Scholarly.
Tudor Drama: A History of English National Drama to the Retirement of Shakespeare. C. F. Brooke. xiii, 461p. 1970. Repr. of 1939 ed. 35.00 (ISBN 0-208-00578-1, Archon). Shoe String.
Tudor Drama & Politics: A Critical Approach to Topical Meaning. David M. Bevington. LC 68-17637. 1968. 27.00x (ISBN 0-674-91230-6). Harvard U Pr.
Tudor Drama & Religious Controversy. James C. Bryant, Jr. LC 84-10850. (Mercer Sesquicentennial Ser.). x, 168p. 1984. 14.50x (ISBN 0-86554-129-9, MUP-H120). Mercer Univ Pr.
Tudor England. John Guy. (Illus.). 600p. 1988. 35.00 (ISBN 0-19-873088-8). Oxford U Pr.
Tudor England, Vol. 5. S. T. Bindoff. 1950. pap. 5.95 (ISBN 0-14-020212-9, Pelican). Penguin.
Tudor England Through Venetian Eyes. Emma Gurney-Salter. 1977. lib. bdg. 59.95 (ISBN 0-8490-2778-0). Gordon Pr.
Tudor England, 1485-1603. Mortimer Levine. LC 68-12060. (Conference on British Studies. Bibliographical Handbooks). pap. 31.80 (2027230). Bks Demand UMI.
Tudor Facsimile Texts, 149 titles in 146 vols. Ed. by John S. Farmer. Repr. of 1914 ed. Set. 7227.00 (ISBN 0-404-53300-0); 49.50 ea. AMS Pr.
Tudor Figures of Rhetoric. Warren Taylor. LC 75-186416. 1972. text ed. 10.00 (ISBN 0-912386-03-7). Language Pr.
Tudor Foreign Policy. P. S. Crowson. LC 73-81733. 288p. 1973. 25.00 (ISBN 0-312-82285-5). St Martin.
Tudor Geography, 1485-1583. Eva G. Taylor. 1968. lib. bdg. 23.50x (ISBN 0-374-97847-6, Octagon). Hippocrene Bks.
Tudor Homes & Other Popular Designs. Ed. by National Plan Service, Inc. Staff. (Illus.). 32p. (Orig.). 1987. pap. 3.95 (ISBN 0-934039-02-X). Natl Plan Serv.
Tudor Household. Jean Ellenby. (Cambridge Information Books for Children). (Illus.). 32p. (gr. 2-8). pap. 2.95 (ISBN 0-521-27899-6). Cambridge U Pr.
Tudor Interludes "Nice Wanton" & "Impatient Poverty". Leonard Tennenhouse. Ed. by Stephen Orgel. (Renaissance Imagination Ser.). 227p. 1984. lib. bdg. 39.00 (ISBN 0-8240-5462-8). Garland Pub.
Tudor Ireland: Crown Community & the Conflict of Cultures 1470-1603. Steven G. Ellis. 432p. 1985. pap. text ed. 17.95 (ISBN 0-582-49341-2). Longman.
Tudor Law of Treason: An Introduction. John G. Bellamy. LC 79-303364. (Studies in Social History). pap. 76.30 (2056137). Bks Demand UMI.
Tudor Men & Institutions: Studies in English Law & Government. Ed. by Arthur J. Slavin. LC 72-79337. x, 294p. 1972. 32.50 (ISBN 0-8071-0227-X). La State U Pr.
Tudor Mercenaries & Auxiliaries, 1485-1547. Gilbert J. Millar. LC 79-22164. (Illus.). 223p. 1980. 14.95x (ISBN 0-8139-0818-3). U Pr of Va.
Tudor Music. David Wulstan. LC 85-51090. (Illus.). 384p. 1986. 27.50s (ISBN 0-87745-135-4). U of Iowa Pr.
Tudor Parliaments: Crown, Lords, & Commons 1485-1603. Michael A. Graves. 176p. 1985. pap. text ed. 13.95 (ISBN 0-582-49190-8). Longman.
Tudor Play of Mind: Rhetorical Inquiry & the Development of Elizabethan Drama. Joel B. Altman. LC 76-52022. 1978. 42.00x (ISBN 0-520-03427-9). U of Cal Pr.
Tudor Problems. Parker Woodward. 1978. Repr. of 1912 ed. lib. bdg. 65.00 (ISBN 0-8495-5635-X). Arden Lib.
Tudor Puritanism: A Chapter in the History of Idealism. Marshall M. Knappen. LC 39-10082. 1965. pap. 3.45x (ISBN 0-226-44627-1, P194, Phoen). U of Chicago Pr.
Tudor Rebellions. 2nd rev. ed. Anthony Fletcher. (Seminar Studies in History). (Illus.). 176p. 1973. pap. text ed. 7.25x (ISBN 0-582-35255-X). Longman.
Tudor Regime. Penry Williams. 1979. 13.95x (ISBN 0-19-822678-0). Oxford U Pr.
Tudor Royal Proclamations, Vols. 2 - 3, The Later Tudors, 1553-1603. Ed. by Paul L. Hughes & James F. Larkin. LC 63-13965. 1969. Set. 100.00x (ISBN 0-300-00103-7). Yale U Pr.
Tudor Rule & Revolution. DeLloyd J. Guth & John W. McKenna. LC 82-4266. 400p. 1983. 59.50 (ISBN 0-521-24841-8). Cambridge U Pr.
Tudor School Boy Life. new ed. Juan L. Vives. 247p. 1970. 25.00x (ISBN 0-7146-2279-6, F Cass Co). Biblio Dist.
Tudor Songs & Ballads from MS Cotton Vespasian A-25. Peter J. Seng. (Illus.). 1978. 16.00x (ISBN 0-674-91285-3). Harvard U Pr.

Tudor Story: The Return of Anne Boleyn. W. S. Pakenham-Walsh. 200p. 1963. 8.95 (ISBN 0-227-67678-5). Attic Pr.

Tudor Studies Presented to Albert Frederick Pollard. facs. ed. London University, Board of Studies in History. Ed. by R. W. Seton-Watson. LC 69-17582. (Essay Index Reprint Ser.). 1924. 18.00 (ISBN 0-8369-0083-9). Ayer Co Pubs.

Tudor Translations. Arthur F. Clements. 1978. Repr. of 1940 ed. lib. bdg. 35.50 (ISBN 0-8495-0831-2). Arden Lib.

Tudor Translations, 56 vols. Incl. Vols. 1-44. First Series. Ed. by William E. Henley. Repr. of 1909 ed. Set. 1980.00 (ISBN 0-685-24312-5); 45.00 ea.; Vols. 1-12. Second Series. Ed. by Charles Whibley. Repr. of 1927 ed. 540.00 set (ISBN 0-685-24313-3); 45.00 ea.. Set. 2520.00 (ISBN 0-404-51850-8). AMS Pr.

Tudor Translations: An Anthology. Judge Clements. LC 74-7478. 1940. lib. bdg. 25.00 (ISBN 0-8414-3577-4). Folcroft.

Tudor Translations of the Colloquies of Erasmus, 1536-1568, 7 vols. in one. Desiderius Erasmus. LC 74-161931. 384p. 1972. 55.00x (ISBN 0-8201-1097-3). Schol Facsimiles.

Tudor Verse Satire. Ed. by K. W. Grandsen. (Renaissance Library). 182p. 1970. pap. 16.95 (ISBN 0-485-12601-X, Pub. by Athlone Pr UK). Humanities.

Tudor Wales. Trevor Herbert & Gareth E. Jones. (Welsh History & Its Sources Ser.). 160p. 1988. pap. text ed. 15.00 (ISBN 0-7083-0971-2, Pub. by U of Wales Pr). Humanities.

Tudor Wales. W. S. Thomas. 211p. 1983. 35.50x (ISBN 0-85088-718-6, Pub. by Gomer Pr). State Mutual Bk.

Tudor Wench. Elswyth Thane. Repr. lib. bdg. 22.95x (ISBN 0-88411-972-6, Pub. by Aeonian Pr). Amereon Ltd.

Tudor Women: Commoners & Queens. Pearl Hogrefe. LC 75-20248. pap. 48.00 (2029470). Bks Demand UMI.

Tudor York. D. M. Palliser. (Historical Monographs). (Illus.). 1979. text ed. 38.50x (ISBN 0-19-821878-8). Oxford U Pr.

Tudors & Stuarts. M. B. Synge et al. Repr. of 1934 ed. 22.00 (ISBN 0-686-19864-6). Ridgeway Bks.

Tudors Briefings Unit. David Birt & Ian Carstairs. (History Units Ser.). (Illus., Incl. 10 briefing, tchr's guide & ans. key). 1975. pap. text ed. 18.95 (ISBN 0-582-39616-6). Longman.

Tudors in French Drama. L. A. Hill. 1973. Repr. of 1932 ed. 16.00 (ISBN 0-384-23257-4). Johnson Repr.

Tudors: Personalities & Practical Politics in Sixteenth Century England. facs. ed. Conyers Read. LC 68-24854. (Essay Index Reprint Ser). 1936. 18.00 (ISBN 0-8369-0812-0). Ayer Co Pubs.

Tudors: Personalities & Practical Politics in Sixteenth-Century England. Conyers Read. (Illus.). 1969. pap. 7.95 (ISBN 0-393-00129-6, Norton Lib). Norton.

Tuers sans Gages see Theatre.

Tuesday Club Murders. 192p. 1971. pap. 2.50 (ISBN 0-440-19136-X). Dell.

Tuesday Timely Teasers. Thomas J. Palumbo. (Illus.). 64p. (gr. 3-8). 1985. wkbk. 6.95 (ISBN 0-86653-309-5). Good Apple.

Tuesdays & Thursday. Abby Mann. 1979. pap. 2.50 (ISBN 0-671-82506-2). PB.

Tuesdays at Ten: A Garnering from the Talks of Thirty Years on Poets, Dramatists & Essayists. facs. ed. Cornelius Weygandt. LC 67-30235. (Essay Index Reprint Ser). 1928. 17.75 (ISBN 0-8369-0985-2). Ayer Co Pubs.

Tuesday's Child. Nancy Baron. LC 84-2944. 120p. (gr. 4-6). 1984. 10.95 (ISBN 0-689-31042-0, Atheneum Childrens Bks). Macmillan.

Tueur Sans Gages. Eugene Ionesco. (Folio Ser.: No. 576). 6.95 (ISBN 0-686-54202-9). Schoenhof.

Tuf Voyaging. George R. Martin. 1987. pap. 3.50 (ISBN 0-671-65624-4). Baen Bks.

Tuffa & Her Friends. Binette Schroeder. LC 82-46088. (Very First Bks.). (Illus.). 12p. (ps-2). 1983. bds. 3.95 (ISBN 0-8037-9894-6, 0383-120). Dial Bks Young.

Tuffa & the Bone. Binette Schroeder. LC 82-46089. (Very First Bks.). (Illus.). 12p. (ps-k). 1983. bds. 3.95 (ISBN 0-8037-9893-8, 0383-120). Dial Bks Young.

Tuffa & the Ducks. Binette Schhroeder. LC 82-46090. (Very First Bks.). (Illus.). 12p. (ps-k). 1983. bds. 3.95 (ISBN 0-8037-9892-X, 0383-120). Dial Bks Young.

Tuffa & the Picnic. Binette Schroeder. LC 82-46087. (Very First Bks.). (Illus.). 12p. (ps-k). 1983. bds. 3.95 (ISBN 0-8037-9896-2, 0383-120). Dial Bks Young.

Tufflavas & Ignimbrites. Ed. by Earl F. Cook. 1966. 23.95 (ISBN 0-444-00008-9, North Holland). Elsevier.

Tuffy the Tiger. Tom LaFleur & Gale Brennan. (Illus.). 16p. (gr. k-6). 1982. pap. 1.25. Brennan Bks.

Tuffy's Bike Race. Linda P. Silbert & Alvin J. Silbert. (Little Twirps Understanding People Bks.). (Illus.). (gr. k-4). 1978. pap. 2.98 (ISBN 0-89544-058-X). Silbert Bress.

Tuft of Primroses, with Other Late Poems for "the Recluse". William Wordsworth. Ed. by Joseph F. Kishel. LC 84-27403. (Wordsworth Ser.). (Illus.). 408p. 1986. 45.00x (ISBN 0-8014-1819-4). Cornell U Pr.

TuFu - Kenneth Rexroth - Brice Marden. TuFu. Tr. by Kenneth Rexroth from Chinese. (Illus.). 114p. 1987. letterpress 47.50 (ISBN 0-935875-04-2). Blumarts Inc.

Tug Hill Country. 6th ed. Harold E. Samson. 1982. 11.95 (ISBN 0-932052-13-4). North Country.

Tug Hill Program: A Regional Planning Option for Rural Areas. Cynthia D. Dyballa et al. LC 81-8999. (Illus.). 208p. 1981. pap. text ed. 11.95x (ISBN 0-8156-2241-4). Syracuse U Pr.

Tug of Love. Pam Lyons. (Heartlines Ser.: No. 7). (Orig.). (gr. 6 up). 1986. pap. 2.50 (ISBN 0-440-98818-7, LFL). Dell.

Tug of Loyalties. Ed. by Esmond Wright. 92p. 1975. pap. 14.95 (ISBN 0-485-12902-7, Pub. by Athlone Pr UK). Humanities.

Tug of War. Created by Francine Pascal. (Sweet Valley Twins Ser.: No. 14). 112p. (Orig.). (YA) (gr. 7-12). 1987. pap. 2.75 (ISBN 0-553-15663-2, Skylark). Bantam.

Tug of War. Janet Quin-Harkin. (Sugar & Spice Ser.). 192p. (Orig.). 1987. pap. 2.50 (ISBN 0-8041-0058-6, Pub. by Ivy). Ballantine.

Tug of War. Cheryl Zach. (Smyth vs Smith Ser.: No. 3). 144p. (Orig.). (YA) 1988. pap. 2.95 (ISBN 1-55802-073-X). Lynx Bks.

Tug of War, No. 16. Francine Pascal. (Sweet Valley Twins Ser.). 112p. (Orig.). 1988. pap. 2.75 (Skylark). Bantam.

Tug of War: The Battle for Italy, 1943-1945. Dominick Graham & Shelford Bidwell. (Illus.). 432p. 1986. 24.95 (ISBN 0-312-82323-1). St Martin.

Tugboat Book. Al Plant. 56p. 1983. pap. text ed. 5.95 (ISBN 0-8403-2886-9). Kendall-Hunt.

Tugboats I Have Known. Fred G. Godfrey. (Illus.). 128p. 1987. 10.95 (ISBN 0-89962-609-2). Todd & Honeywell.

Tugent Spyl: Nach der Ausgabe des Magister Johann Winckel von Strassburg. Sebastian Brant. Ed. by Hans G. Roloff. (Ausgaben Deutscher Literatur des 15 bis 18 Jahrh). (Ger). 1968. 23.60x (ISBN 3-11-000350-3). De Gruyter.

Tugford Wanted to Be Bad. Audrey Wood. LC 83-318. (Let-Me-Read Ser.). (Illus.). 32p. (ps-3). 1983. pap. 4.95 (ISBN 0-15-291084-0, VoyB). HarBraceJ.

Tugford Wanted to Be Bad. Audrey Wood & Audrey Wood. LC 83-318. (Let Me Read Ser.). (Illus.). 32p. (ps-3). 1983. PLB 9.95 (ISBN 0-15-291083-2, HJ). HarBraceJ.

Tughlug Dynasty. Agha M. Husain. 718p. 150.00X (ISBN 0-317-52161-6, Pub. by S Chand India). State Mutual Bk.

Tughluq Dynasty. A. M. Husain. (Illus.). 1976. Repr. of 1935 ed. 75.00x (ISBN 0-89684-461-7). Orient Bk Dist.

Tugman's Passage. Edward Hoagland. 1982. 12.00 (ISBN 0-394-52268-0). Random.

Tugman's Passage. Edward Hoagland. 224p. 1983. pap. 6.95 (ISBN 0-14-006685-3). Penguin.

Tugs, Towboats & Towing. Edward M. Brady. LC 67-17537. (Illus.). 242p. 1967. 15.00x (ISBN 0-87033-127-2). Cornell Maritime.

Tugwell's Thoughts on Planning. Rexford G. Tugwell. Ed. by Salvador M. Padilla. 1975. pap. 6.25 (ISBN 0-8477-2429-8). U of PR Pr.

Tuhami: Portrait of a Moroccan. Vincent Crapanzano. LC 79-24550. xvi, 188p. 1980. lib. bdg. 17.50x (ISBN 0-226-11870-3). U of Chicago Pr.

Tuhami: Portrait of a Moroccan. Vincent Crapanzano. LC 79-24550. xvi, 1888p. 1986. pap. 8.95 (ISBN 0-226-11871-1). U of Chicago Pr.

Tuhft al-Nafis see Precious Gift.

Tuimarishe Kiswahili Chetu: Kitabu Cha Wanafunzi Wa Mwaka Wa Pili-Tatu: Building Proficiency in Kiswahili: A Manual for Second-Third Year Swahili Students. Lioba J. Moshi. LC 87-27466. (Illus.). 180p. (Orig.). 1988. lib. bdg. 22.50 (ISBN 0-8191-6739-8); pap. text ed. 11.75 (ISBN 0-8191-6740-1). U Pr of Amer.

Tuition Aid Case Study Series, 4 vols. 1979. Set. pap. text ed. 22.50 (ISBN 0-86510-021-7). Natl Inst Work.

Tuition Aid Revisited: Tapping the Untapped Resource. Willard Wirtz. (Tuition Aid Case Study Ser.). 31p. (Orig.). 1979. pap. text ed. 5.00 (ISBN 0-86510-025-X). Natl Inst Work.

Tuition & Student Aid Policy in Minnesota: A Case Study. 42p. 1985. 7.50 (ISBN 0-318-22550-6, PS-85-1A). Ed Comm States.

Tuition-Fees, Financial Aid Statistics: Private Colleges Awarding the Bachelor's As the Highest Degree. Intro. by John Minter. (Institutional Research Reports). 50p. 1986. lib. bdg. write for info. (ISBN 0-937767-09-3). Nat Data Service.

Tuition-Fees, Financial Aid Statistics: Public Colleges Awarding the Bachelor's As the Highest Degree. Ed. & intro. by John Minter. (Institutional Research Reports). 50p. 1987. lib. bdg. write for info. (ISBN 0-937767-42-5). Nat Data Service.

Tuition-Fees, Financial Aid Statistics: Private Colleges & Universities Awarding the Master's As the Highest Degree. Intro. by John Minter. (Institutional Research Reports). 50p. 1986. lib. bdg. write for info. (ISBN 0-937767-15-8). Nat Data Service.

Tuition-Fees, Financial Aid Statistics: Public Colleges & Universities Awarding the Comprehensive As the Highest Degree. Ed. & intro. by John Minter. (Institutional Research Reports). 50p. 1987. lib. bdg. write for info. (ISBN 0-937767-47-6). Nat Data Service.

Tuition-Fees, Financial Aid Statistics: Private Universities Awarding the Doctoral's As the Highest Degree. Intro. by John Minter. (Institutional Research Reports). 50p. 1987. lib. bdg. write for info. (ISBN 0-937767-21-2). Nat Data Service.

Tuition Tax Credits & Alternatives. (Legislative Analysis Ser.). 1978. pap. 6.00 (ISBN 0-8447-0209-9). Am Enterprise.

Tuition Tax Credits: Fact & Fiction. James S. Catterall. LC 82-63057. (Fastback Ser.: No. 188). 50p. 1983. pap. 0.90 (ISBN 0-87367-188-0). Phi Delta Kappa.

Tuition Tax Credits for Private Education: An Economic Analysis. Donald E. Frey. (Illus.). 120p. 1983. pap. text ed. 10.50x (ISBN 0-8138-1826-5). Iowa St U Pr.

Tuition Tax Deductions & Parent School Choice: A Case Study of Minnesota. Linda Darling-Hammond et al. LC 85-16965. 1985. 10.00 (ISBN 0-8330-0670-3, R-3294-NIE). Rand Corp.

Tuk, the Timid: The Story of a Sea Otter. Jean G. Howard. LC 84-50217. (Illus.). 80p. (Orig.). (gr. 3 up). 1984. pap. 10.95 stitched pages (ISBN 0-930954-20-3). Tidal Pr.

Tukarama, His Person & His Religion: A Relio-Historical, Phenomenological & Typological Enquiry. Ajit Lokhande. (European University Studies: Series 20, Philosophy: Vol. 22). 210p. 1976. 23.50 (ISBN 3-261-02009-1). P Lang Pubs.

Tukumba Pounding Songs: A Device for Resolving Familial Conifict. Enoch T. Mvula. (Graduate Student Term Paper Ser.). 19p. 1984. pap. text ed. 2.00 (ISBN 0-941934-45-4). Indiana Africa.

Tula Art Museum. S. F. Nechaeva. 224p. 1983. 116.00x (ISBN 0-317-57476-0, Pub. by Collets UK). State Mutual Bk.

Tula of the Toltecs: Excavations & Survey. Ed. by Dan M. Healan. LC 88-18996. (Illus.). 280p. 1988. text ed. 45.00x (ISBN 0-87745-209-1); computer disk incl. U of Iowa Pr.

Tula: The Toltec Capital of Ancient Mexico. Richard A. Diehl. LC 82-51256. (New Aspects of Antiquity Ser.). (Illus.). 1983. 29.95 (ISBN 0-500-39018-5). Thames Hudson.

Tulane, Vols. 1-22. 1974. 25.00x. Claitors.

Tulane Law Review: 1916-1986, 60 vols. Bound set. 2112.00x (ISBN 0-686-90060-X). Rothman.

Tulane Tax Institute, Vols. 1-32. Date not set. Set. price not set; Vols. 1-22. price not set; Vols. 23, 24. price not set; Vols. 25-30. 30.00 ea.; Vols. 31, 32. 35.00 ea.; Vol. 33. 40.00 ea. Claitors.

Tulane University Medical Center: One Hundred & Fifty Years of Medical Education. John Duffy. (Illus.). 253p. 1985. text ed. 25.00 (ISBN 0-8071-1195-3). La State U Pr.

Tulapai to Tokay: A Bibliography of Alcohol Use & Abuse Among Native Americans of North America. Patricia D. Mail & David R. McDonald. LC 80-81243. (Bibliographies Ser.). 372p. 1981. 25.00 (ISBN 0-87536-253-2). HRAFP.

Tularemia Gambit. Steve Perry. 224p. (Orig.). 1981. pap. 2.25 (ISBN 0-449-14411-9, GM). Fawcett.

Tularosa: Last of the Frontier West. rev. ed. C. L. Sonnichsen. LC 80-52286. 344p. 1980. pap. 9.95 (ISBN 0-8263-0561-X). U of NM Pr.

Tule. Frederick A. Raborg, Jr. (Amelia Chapbooks). (Illus.). 24p. (Orig.). 1986. pap. 5.95 (ISBN 0-936545-01-1). Amelia.

Tule Elk. Caroline Arnold. (Nature Watch Bks.). (Illus.). 48p. (gr. 2-5). 1988. 12.95 (ISBN 0-87614-343-5). Carolrhoda Bks.

Tule Lake. Edward T. Miyakawa. Ed. by Carol S. Van Strum. (Orig.). 1979. 12.95 (ISBN 0-686-25250-0); pap. 7.95 (ISBN 0-686-25251-9). Hse by the Sea.

Tule Springs, Nevada: With Other Evidences of Pleistocene Man in North America. M. R. Harrington & R. D. Simpson. 146p. 1961. pap. 5.00 (ISBN 0-916561-65-8). Southwest Mus.

Tulip Evermore: Emma Butler & William Paisley, Their Lives in Letters: 1857-1887. Ed. by Elizabeth P. Huckaby & Ethel C. Simpson. LC 84-27873. (Illus.). 490p. 1985. 35.00 (ISBN 0-938626-34-5); pap. 12.00 (ISBN 0-938626-35-3). U of Ark Pr.

Tulip: Five Points of Calvinism. Duane E. Spencer. LC 78-73445. (Direction Bks). pap. 3.50 (ISBN 0-8010-8161-0). Baker Bk.

Tulip: The Universal List of Indian Periodicals. Murari L. Nagar & Sarla D. Nagar. 186p. (Orig.). 1986. pap. 45.00 (ISBN 0-943913-00-4). Intl Lib Ctr.

Tulip: The Universal List of Indian Periodicals. Murari L. Nagar & Sarla D. Nagar. 208p. (Orig.). 1988. pap. 45.00 (ISBN 0-943913-04-7). Intl Lib Ctr.

Tulip: The Universal List of Indian Periodicals, Vol. 2. Murari L. Nagar & Sarla D. Nagar. 207p. (Orig.). 1986. pap. 45.00 (ISBN 0-943913-02-0). Intl Lib Ctr.

Tulip: The Universal List of Indian Periodicals, Vol. 3. Murari L. Nagar & Sarla D. Nagar. 221p. (Orig.). 1987. pap. 45.00 (ISBN 0-943913-03-9). Intl Lib Ctr.

Tulip Tree. Mary A. Gibbs. 1979. pap. 1.75 (ISBN 0-449-50000-4, Coventry). Fawcett.

Tulipanes en Diciembre. Eddie Valencia. 96p. (Orig.). 1988. pap. 3.25 (ISBN 0-311-37026-8, Edit Mundo). Casa Bautista.

Tulipe. Romain Gary. pap. 9.50 (ISBN 0-685-34129-1). French & Eur.

Tulipe Noire. Alexandre Dumas. (Illus.). 1973. 10.95 (ISBN 0-686-55216-4). French & Eur.

Tulips. Kathleen Pohl. (Nature Close-Ups Ser.). (Illus.). 32p. (gr. 3-4). 1986. PLB 15.33 (ISBN 0-8172-2709-1); pap. 9.27 (ISBN 0-8172-2727-X). Raintree Pubs.

Tulips & Chimneys. e. e. Cummings. Ed. by George J. Firmage. 1976. 10.00 (ISBN 0-87140-622-5). Liveright.

Tulips, Arabesques & Turbans: Decorative Arts from the Ottoman Empire. Ed. by Yanni Petsopoulos. LC 81-20534. (Illus.). 208p. 1982. 60.00 (ISBN 0-89659-279-0). Abbeville Pr.

Tulips: Taxonomy, Morphology, Cytology, Phytogeography & Physiology. Z. Botschantzeva. Ed. by H. Varekamp. 282p. 1982. text ed. 107.50 (ISBN 90-6191-029-3, Pub. by A A Balkema). Brookfield Pub Co.

Tulku. Peter Dickinson. (MagicQuest Ser.: No. 5). 224p. 1984. pap. 2.25 (ISBN 0-441-82630-X, Pub. by Tempo). Ace Bks.

Tully the Tree Kangaroo. Georgeanne Irvine. (Zoo Babies Ser.). (Illus.). 16p. (Orig.). (gr. k-6). 1983. pap. 1.25 (ISBN 0-8249-8058-1). Ideals.

Tulpa. J. N. Williamson. 240p. 1985. pap. 2.95 (ISBN 0-8439-2228-1, Leisure Bks). Leisure NY.

Tulpa. J. N. Williamson. 240p. 1988. pap. 3.50 Mass Market (ISBN 0-8439-2586-8). Leisure NY.

Tulpehocken Church Records, 1730 to 1800: Christ (Little Tulpehocken) Church & the Altalaha Church at Rehrersburg. (Sources & Documents Ser.: No. 7). 1982. 15.00 (ISBN 0-911122-45-1). Penn German Soc.

Tulsa. Hank Mitchum. (Stagecoach Station Ser.: No. 26). 192p. (Orig.). 1986. pap. 2.75 (ISBN 0-553-26229-7). Bantam.

Tulsa Kid. Ron Padgett. Ed. by Kenward Elmslie. (Illus., Orig.). 1980. 10.00 (ISBN 0-915990-16-4); pap. 5.00 (ISBN 0-915990-17-2). Z Pr.

Tulsa Law Journal: 1964-1986, Vols. 1-21. Bound set. 720.00x (ISBN 0-686-90064-2). Rothman.

Tulsa Race War of 1921. R. Halliburton. LC 74-31767. 1975. soft bdg. 12.95 (ISBN 0-88247-333-6). R & E Pubs.

Tulsa: Tale of Two Cities. Dorothy M. DeWitty. 144p. 1989. 12.95 (ISBN 0-89962-803-6). Todd & Honeywell.

Tulsa-Tbilisi. Ed. by Fran Ringold. 168p. 1985. pap. 5.50 (ISBN 0-317-60730-8). Art & Human Council Tulsa.

Tulsi: The Union Lists of Serials: History; Literature; Philosophy. Murari L. Nagar. Ed. by Sarla D. Nagar. 230p. (Orig.). 1986. pap. 23.00 (ISBN 0-943913-12-8). Intl Lib Ctr.

Tulsidas. Devendra Singh. (National Biography Ser.). (Orig.). 1979. pap. 3.25 (ISBN 0-89744-207-5, Pub. by Natl Bk Trust India). Auromere.

Tulso Parton. Cecile Tormay. 1977. Repr. of 1936 ed. 11.00 (ISBN 0-918570-04-2). Karpat.

Tuluak & Amaulik. Stacey Day. LC 73-93517. (Illus.). 176p. 1973. 6.50 (ISBN 0-912922-07-9). U of Minn Bell Mus.

Tulum: An Archaeological Study of the East Coast of Yucaton. Samuel K. Lothrop. 1976. lib. bdg. 69.95 (ISBN 0-8490-2779-9). Gordon Pr.

Tumacacori. Peter Wild. (Illus.). 1974. wrappers, limited to 100 copies 12.50x (ISBN 0-685-46856-9). Twowindows Pr.

Tumble, Tumble, Tumbleweed. Pat L. Collins. Ed. by Ann Fay. LC 81-23968. (Illus.). 32p. (gr. 1-3). 1982. PLB 10.75 (ISBN 0-8075-8122-4). A Whitman.

Tumbledown. Paul Rogers. LC 87-11558. (Illus.). 32p. (gr. k-3). 1988. 12.95 (ISBN 0-689-31392-6, Atheneum Childrens Bks). Macmillan.

Tumbler of Our Lady & Other Miracles. Gautier De Coinci. Tr. by A. Kemp-Welch. (Medieval Library). (Illus.). Repr. of 1926 ed. 17.50x (ISBN 0-8154-0076-4). Cooper Sq.

Tumbleweed. Janwillen Van de Wetering. 1987. pap. 3.50 (ISBN 0-345-33127-3). Ballantine.

Tumbleweed Gourmet: Cooking with Wild Southwestern Plants. Carolyn Niethammer. LC 87-5948. 229p. 1987. 20.00 (ISBN 0-8165-1021-0). U of Ariz Pr.

Tumbleweeds. Marta Roberts. LC 74-22805. Repr. of 1940 ed. 22.50 (ISBN 0-404-58461-6). AMS Pr.

Tumbleweeds. Tom K. Ryan. (Tumbleweed Ser.). (Illus.). 144p. 1981. pap. 1.75 (ISBN 0-449-13756-2, GM). Fawcett.

Tumbleweeds. Tom K. Ryan. (Tumbleweed Ser.: No. 5). (Illus.). 1980. pap. 1.50 (ISBN 0-449-13789-9, GM). Fawcett.

Tumbleweeds: A Therapist's Guide to Treatment of ACOAs. Paul J. Curtin. 90p. (Orig.). 1985. pap. 6.95 (ISBN 0-934391-03-3). Quotidian.

Tumbleweeds Corral. Tom K. Ryan. (Orig.). 1987. pap. 2.25 (ISBN 0-449-13245-5, GM). Fawcett.

Tumbleweeds Express. Tom K. Ryan. 128p. (Orig.). 1981. pap. 1.75 (ISBN 0-449-14407-0, GM). Fawcett.

Tumbleweeds Rodeo! Tom K. Ryan. (Orig.). 1987. pap. 2.25 (ISBN 0-449-13244-7, GM). Fawcett.

Tumbling Book. Jack Wiley. (Illus.). (gr. 7 up). 1978. 8.95 (ISBN 0-679-20418-0). McKay.

Tumbling Book. 2nd ed. Jack Wiley. LC 85-62755. (Illus.). 152p. (YA) (gr. 7 up). 1985. pap. 17.95 (ISBN 0-913999-07-5). Solipaz Pub Co.

Tumbling Down. Billy Roche. 160p. 1986. 17.95 (ISBN 0-86327-052-2, Pub. by Wolfhound Pr Ireland); pap. 7.95 (ISBN 0-86327-053-0, Pub. by Wolfhound Pr Ireland). Irish Bks Media.

Tumbling Run, No. 3. Elizabeth Levy. (Gymnasts Ser.). 128p. (gr. 3-7). 1988. pap. 2.50 (ISBN 0-590-41564-6). Scholastic Inc.

Tumbling: Stories. Kermit Moyer. LC 87-34284. (Illinois Short Fiction Ser.). 136p. 1988. 11.95 (ISBN 0-252-01525-8). U of Ill Pr.

Tummy: An Owner's Manual. Judson P. Cone. 63p. (Orig.). 1974. pap. 1.95 (ISBN 0-89074-008-9). Charing Cross.

Tummy Tickler Desserts. Vinnie Prochilo & Jeff Myers. 48p. (Orig.). 1987. pap. 4.00 (ISBN 0-930791-02-9). Designed Impacts.

Tumor Aneuploidy. Ed. by T. Buchner et al. LC 85-9897. (Illus.). 140p. 1985. pap. 19.50 (ISBN 0-387-15376-4). Springer-Verlag.

Tumor Antigenicity & Approaches to Tumor Immunotherapy: An Outline. D. Weiss. (Current Topics in Microbiology & Immunology Ser.: Vol. 89). 70p. 1980. 20.00 (ISBN 0-387-09789-9). Springer-Verlag.

Tumor Associated Antigens & Their Specific Immune Responses. Ed. by F. Spreafico & R. Arnon. (Serono Symposium Ser.). 1979. 76.00 (ISBN 0-12-658350-1). Acad Pr.

Tumor Blood Circulation: Angiogenesis, Vascular Morphology & Blood Flow of Experimental & Human Tumors. Hans-Inge Peterson. 240p. 1979. 89.00 (ISBN 0-8493-5695-4). CRC Pr.

Tumor Cell Differentiation: Biology & Pharmacology. Ed. by Jarle Aarbakke et al. LC 87-17012. (Experimental Biology & Medicine Ser.). (Illus.). 383p. 1987. 64.50 (ISBN 0-89603-134-9). Humana.

Tumor Cell Heterogeneity: Origins & Implications. Ed. by Albert H. Owens. (Bristol-Myers Cancer Symposium Ser.). 1982. 70.50 (ISBN 0-12-531520-1). Acad Pr.

Tumor Cell Surfaces & Malignancy: Proceedings. Ed. by R. Hynes & C. Fred Fox. LC 80-7798. (Progress in Clinical & Biological Research Ser.: Vol. 41). 970p. 1980. 172.00 (ISBN 0-8451-0041-6). A R Liss.

Tumor Diagnosis by Electron Microscopy, Vol. 2. Jose Russo & Sheldon Sommers. 250p. 1988. text ed. 65.00 (ISBN 0-02-404910-7). Macmillan.

Tumor Immunity in Prognosis. Haskill. (Immunology Ser.). 464p. 1982. 79.75 (ISBN 0-8247-1837-2). Dekker.

Tumor Immunology: Mechanisms Diagnosis Therapy. Otter Den. (Research Monographs in Immunology: Vol. 11). 1987. 134.25 (ISBN 0-444-80866-3). Elsevier.

Tumor Invasion & Metastasis. L. A. Liotta & I. R. Hurt. 1982. 99.00 (ISBN 90-247-2611-5, Pub. by Martinus Nijhoff Netherlands). Kluwer Academic.

Tumor Lipids: Biochemistry & Metabolism. Ed. by Randall Wood. 324p. 1974. 12.00 (ISBN 0-935315-00-4). Am Oil Chemists.

Tumor Markers & Their Significance in the Management of Breast Cancer. Thomas Dao & Angela Brodie. LC 85-23902. (PCBR Ser.: Vol. 204). 160p. 1986. 36.00 (ISBN 0-8451-5054-5, 5054). A R Liss.

Tumor Markers & Tumor Associated Antigens. Ed. by B. C. Ghosh & L. Ghosh. 336p. 1987. text ed. 59.50 (ISBN 0-07-023167-2). McGraw.

Tumor Markers: Biology & Clinical Applications. Ed. by Nasser Javadpour. LC 85-30014. (Cancer Research Monographs: Vol. 4). 304p. 1986. lib. bdg. 65.00 (ISBN 0-275-92145-X, C2145). Praeger.

Tumor Markers: Clinical & Laboratory Studies. J. V. Klavins. LC 85-6799. 214p. 1985. 48.00 (ISBN 0-8451-0248-6). A R Liss.

Tumor Markers in Cancer Control. Herbert E. Nieburgs et al. LC 85-15850. 362p. 1985. 68.00 (ISBN 0-8451-4201-1). A R Liss.

Tumor Necrosis Factor & Related Cytotoxins. CIBA Staff. (CIBA Foundation Symposia Ser.: No. 131). 241p. 1987. 49.95 (ISBN 0-471-91097-X, Pub. by Wiley-Interscience). Wiley.

Tumor Necrosis Factor-Cachectin & Related Cytokines. Ed. by B. Bonavida et al. (Illus.). viii, 212p. 1988. 132.00 (ISBN 3-8055-4755-2). S Karger.

Tumor Promoters: Biological Approaches for Mechanistic Studies & Assay Systems. Ed. by Robert Langenbach et al. (Progress in Cancer Research & Therapy Ser.: Vol. 34). 480p. 1988. text ed. 75.00 (ISBN 0-88167-451-6). Raven.

Tumor Specific Transplantation Antigen. P. Koldovsky. LC 78-82896. (Recent Results in Cancer Research Ser.: Vol. 22). (Illus.). 1969. 20.00 (ISBN 0-387-04684-4). Springer-Verlag.

Tumor Surgery of the Head & Neck. R. S. Pollack. (Illus.). x, 206p. 1975. 48.75 (ISBN 3-8055-2092-1). S Karger.

Tumor Therapy with Tumor Cells & Neuraminidase: Cell Physiological, Immunological, & Oncological Aspects. H. H. Sedlacek. (Beitraege zur Onkologie, Contributions to Oncology Ser.: Vol. 27). (Illus.). viii, 96p. 1987. 23.50 (ISBN 3-8055-4549-5). S Karger.

Tumor Viruses & Differentiation. Edward M. Scolnick & Arnold J. Levine. LC 83-9808. (UCLA Symposia on Molecular & Cellular Biology Ser.: Vol. 5). 478p. 1983. 88.00 (ISBN 0-8451-2604-0). A R Liss.

Tumorbiologie. J. G. Birkmayer. (Illus.). viii, 230p. 1984. 38.00 (ISBN 3-8055-3892-8). S Karger.

Tumorimmunologie & Tumortherapie. H. H. Sedlacek. (Beitraege zur Onkologie, Contributions to Oncology Ser.: Vol. 25). (Illus.). x, 186p. 1986. 42.00 (ISBN 3-8055-4447-2). S Karger.

Tumors & Tumor-Like Lesions of Bone & Joints. F. Schajowicz. (Illus.). 650p. 1981. 210.00 (ISBN 0-387-90492-1). Springer-Verlag.

Tumors & Tumorlike Conditions of the Ovary. Ed. by Lawrence M. Roth & Bernard Czernobilsky. (Contemporary Issues in Surgical Pathology Ser.: Vol. 6). (Illus.). 296p. 1985. text ed. 65.00 (ISBN 0-443-08289-8). Churchill.

Tumors Arising from the Blood Vessels of the Brain: Angiomatous Malformations & Hemangioblastomas. Harvey Cushing & Percival Bailey. (Illus.). 232p. 1928. photocopy ed. 28.25x (ISBN 0-398-04238-1). C C Thomas.

Tumors in Aquatic Animals. Ed. by F. Homburger. (Progress in Experimental Tumor Research Ser.: Vol. 20). 400p. 1976. 102.75 (ISBN 3-8055-2254-1). S Karger.

Tumors in Domestic Animals. 2nd ed. Ed. by Jack Moulton. 1978. 60.00x (ISBN 0-520-02386-2). U of Cal Pr.

Tumors of Skin Appendages. Ken Hashimoto et al. (Practical Dermatopathology Ser.). (Illus.). 225p. 1987. text ed. 49.95 (ISBN 0-409-95159-5). Butterworth.

Tumors of Soft Tissue: Proceedings of the Fifty-Second Annual Anatomic Pathology Slide Seminar of the American Society of Clinical Pathologists. Sharon W. Weiss et al. LC 87-1041. 120p. 1987. pap. text ed. 28.00 (ISBN 0-89189-253-2). Am Soc Clinical.

Tumors of the Brain. Ed. by N. M. Bleehen. (Illus.). 230p. 1986. 69.00 (ISBN 0-387-15412-4). Springer-Verlag.

Tumors of the Breast: Proceedings of the Fifty Third Annual Anatomic Pathology Slide Seminar of the American Society of Clinical Pathologists. Ed. by Paul P. Rosen & Harold A. Oberman. LC 87-35131. 1988. 28.00 (ISBN 0-89189-271-0, 50-1-054-00). Am Soc Clinical.

Tumors of the Cranial Base: Diagnosis & Treatment. Ed. by Laligam N. Sekhar & Victor L. Schramm, Jr. (Illus.). 728p. 1987. Monograph. 140.00 (ISBN 0-87993-302-X). Futura Pub.

Tumors of the Head & Neck in Children. Robert O. Greer et al. LC 82-19114. 430p. 1983. 56.95 (ISBN 0-275-91391-0, C1391). Praeger.

Tumors of the Kidney. Jean B. DeKernion. (Surgery Ser.). 340p. 1986. 86.75 (ISBN 0-683-02426-4). Williams & Wilkins.

Tumors of the Kidney & Urinary Tract. Steen Olsen. (Illus.). 291p. 1985. 83.00 (ISBN 0-7216-1588-0). Saunders.

Tumors of the Larynx & Hypoharynx. Kleinsasser. (Illus.). 373p. 1988. 145.00 (ISBN 0-86577-290-8). Thieme Med Pubs.

Tumors of the Liver. Ed. by G. T. Pack & A. H. Islami. LC 71-99868. (Recent Results in Cancer Research Ser.: Vol. 26). (Illus.). 1970. 42.00 (ISBN 0-387-04991-6). Springer-Verlag.

Tumors of the Male Genital System. International Symposium of the "Gesellschaft Zur Bekampfung De Krebskran Kheiten Nordrhein-West-Falen E. V.", 7th, Dusseldorf, Oct. 1975. Ed. by E. Grundmann & W. Vahlensuck. (Recent Results in Cancer Research Ser.: Vol. 60). 1977. 43.00 (ISBN 0-387-08029-5). Springer-Verlag.

Tumors of the Nervous System. T. H. Moss. (Illus.). 170p. 1986. 116.50 (ISBN 0-387-16858-3). Springer-Verlag.

Tumors of the Spine. Ed. by L. Jeanmart. (Radiology of the Spine Ser.). (Illus.). 130p. 1985. 49.50 (ISBN 0-387-15326-8). Springer-Verlag.

Tumorviruses, Neoplastic Transformation & Differentiation. Ed. by T. Graf & R. Jaenisch. (Current Topics in Microbiology & Immunology Ser.: Vol. 101). (Illus.). 198p. 1982. 62.00 (ISBN 0-387-11665-6). Springer-Verlag.

Tumour Localization with Radioactive Agents. LC 76-7616. (Panel Proceedings Ser.). (Illus.). 142p. 1977. pap. 16.00 (ISBN 92-0-111276-9, ISP451, IAEA). UNIPUB.

Tumours in a Tropical Country: A Survey of Uganda (1964-1968) Ed. by A. C. Templeton. LC 72-96042. (Recent Results in Cancer Research Ser.: Vol. 41). (Illus.). 346p. 1973. 60.00 (ISBN 0-387-06114-2). Springer-Verlag.

Tumours in Children. 2nd, rev. & enl. ed. Ed. by H. B. Marsden. J. K. Stewart. LC 76-6091. (Recent Results in Cancer Research Ser.: Vol. 13). (Illus.). 1976. 56.00 (ISBN 0-387-07632-8). Springer-Verlag.

Tumours, Lymphomas & Selected Paraproteinaemias. Ed. by Julian L. Verbov. (New Clinical Applications Dermatology Ser.). 1988. lib. bdg. 51.00 (ISBN 0-7462-0082-X, Pub. by MTP Pr England). Kluwer Academic.

Tumours of the Brain & Skull see Handbook of Clinical Neurology.

Tumours of the Hand. J. Glicenstein & J. Ohana. (Illus.). 250p. 1988. 113.00 (ISBN 0-387-17439-7). Springer-Verlag.

Tumours of the Larynx. E Meyer-Breiting & A. Burkhardt. (Illus.). 240p. 1988. 160.00 (ISBN 0-387-16342-5). Springer-Verlag.

Tumours of the Spine & Spinal Cord see Handbook of Clinical Neurology.

Tumours That Secrete Catecholamines: A Study of Their Natural History & Their Diagnosis. Ronald Robinson. LC 79-41731. 132p. 1980. 75.95 (ISBN 0-471-27748-7). Wiley.

Tumours That Secrete Catecholamines: Their Detection & Clinical Chemistry. Ronald Robinson. LC 79-41731. pap. 36.00 (ISBN 0-317-29342-7, 2024034). Bks Demand UMI.

Tumpline Economy: Production & Distribution Systems in Sixteenth-Century Eastern Guatemala. Lawrence H. Feldman. LC 85-50097. (Illus.). 160p. (Orig.). 1985. pap. 20.00x (ISBN 0-911437-16-9). Labyrinthos.

Tumult. Botho Strauss. Tr. by Michael Hulse from Ger. 136p. 1984. 14.95 (ISBN 0-85635-472-4). Carcanet.

Tumult. Botho Strauss. Tr. by Michael Hulse. 136p. (Ger.). 1987. pap. 7.50 (ISBN 0-85635-588-7). Carcanet.

Tumult & the Shouting: Beerbohm, Sinclair Lewis, James Joyce, Etc. George Slocombe. 1936. Repr. 20.00 (ISBN 0-8274-3653-X). R West.

Tumult for John Berryman: A Homage to John Berryman. Ed. by Marguerite Harris. LC 76-8553. 1976. pap. 5.95 (ISBN 0-931848-15-6). Dryad Pr.

Tumult in the Clouds. James A. Goodson. 1986. pap. 4.95. St Martin.

Tumult in the Clouds: A Story of the Eagle Squadron. James A. Goodson. (Illus.). 256p. 1984. 13.95 (ISBN 0-312-82327-4). St Martin.

Tumult of Inner Voices. Douglas R. Hofstadter. (Grace A. Tanner Lecture in Human Values Ser.). 24p. 1982. text ed. 9.50 (ISBN 0-910153-01-9). E T Woolf.

Tumultuous Years - Schwenkfelder Chronicles Fifteen Eighty to Seventeen Fifty: The Reports of Martin John, Jr. & Balthazar Hoffmann. L. Allen Viehmeyer. 157p. (Orig.). 1980. pap. write for info. (ISBN 0-935980-00-8). Schwenkfelder Lib.

Tumultuous Years: The Presidency of Harry S. Truman, 1949-1953. Robert J. Donovan. (Illus.). 1982. 19.95 (ISBN 0-393-01619-6). Norton.

Tumultuous Years: The Presidency of Harry S. Truman, 1949-1953. Robert J. Donovan. (Illus.). 448p. 1984. pap. 9.95 (ISBN 0-393-30164-8). Norton.

Tun Huang. Yasushi Inoue. Tr. by Jean Oda Moy from Japanese. LC 77-75969. 1978. 12.95x (ISBN 0-87011-314-3); pap. 4.95 (ISBN 0-87011-576-6). Kodansha.

Tun Razak: His Life & Times. W. S. Shaw. (Illus.). 1976. text ed. 14.50x (ISBN 0-582-72414-7). Longman.

Tun-Ta-Ca-Tun: More Stories & Poems in English & Spanish for Children. Ed. by Sylvia C. Pena. LC 84-72297. 80p. (Orig., Eng. & Span.). (ps up). 1985. pap. 8.50 (ISBN 0-934770-43-3). Arte Publico.

Tuna & Billfish: Fish Without a Country. 2nd ed. James Joseph et al. LC 80-81889. (Illus.). 53p. (Orig.). (gr. 7-12). 1980. pap. 7.95 (ISBN 0-9603078-1-8). Inter-Am Tropical.

Tuna Chopper. Robert P. Goshen. LC 80-50122. 14.95 (ISBN 0-9602964-0-9). Zoom.

Tuna: Distribution & Migration. Hiroshi Nakamura. 1978. 40.00x (ISBN 0-685-63462-0). State Mutual Bk.

Tuna Fishing with Pole & Line. M. Ben-Yami. 1980. 21.50x (ISBN 0-686-64740-8, Pub. by Fishing News England); pap. 19.50x (ISBN 0-686-77604-6). State Mutual Bk.

Tuna Fishing with Pole & Line: An FAO Fishing Manual. Ed. by M. Ben-Yami. (Illus.). 168p. 1981. pap. 21.50 (ISBN 0-85238-111-5, FN88, FNB). UNIPUB.

Tuna: Status, Trends, & Alternative Management Arrangements. Saul B. Saila & Virgil J. Norton. LC 73-20846. (Resources for the Future, Program of International Studies of Fishery Arrangements, Paper: No. 6). pap. 20.00 (ISBN 0-317-26479-6, 2023814). Bks Demand UMI.

Tunable Lasers. Ed. by L. F. Mollenauer & J. C. White. (Topics in Applied Physics Ser.: Vol 59). (Illus.). 425p. 1987. 65.50 (ISBN 0-387-16921-0). Springer-Verlag.

Tunable Lasers & Applications. Ed. by A. Mooradian et al. (Optical Sciences Ser: Vol. 3). 1976. 39.00 (ISBN 0-387-07968-8). Springer-Verlag.

Tunable Solid State Lasers. Ed. by P. Hammerling et al. (Springer Series in Optical Sciences: Vol. 47). (Illus.). 210p. 1985. 41.50 (ISBN 0-387-15135-4). Springer-Verlag.

Tunable Solid State Lasers. LC 87-60706. (Technical Digest Series 1987: Vol. 20). 270p. (Orig.). 1987. lib. bdg. 62.00 postconference ed. (ISBN 0-936659-68-8); pap. 35.00 conference ed. (ISBN 0-936659-48-3). Optical Soc.

Tunable Solid State Lasers for Remote Sensing. Ed. by R. L. Byer et al. (Springer Series in Optical Sciences: Vol. 51). (Illus.). 160p. 1985. 34.00 (ISBN 0-387-16168-6). Springer-Verlag.

Tunable Solid-State Lasers II. Ed. by A. B. Budgor et al. (Springer Series in Optical Sciences: Vol. 52). (Illus.). 380p. 1987. 50.00 (ISBN 0-387-17320-X). Springer-Verlag.

Tunafish Sandwiches. Patty Wolcott. LC 84-40795. 1975. 6.70i (ISBN 0-201-14249-X, Lipp Jr Bks). HarpJ.

Tunbridge Wells As It Was: Fourth Impression. Hendon Publishing Co., Ltd. Staff. 1986. 21.00x (ISBN 0-317-54186-2, Pub. by Hendon Pub UK). State Mutual BK.

Tunc: A Novel. Lawrence Durrell. 1979. pap. 5.95 (ISBN 0-14-005184-8). Penguin.

Tundra. William F. Hallstead. LC 84-7053. 128p. (gr. 6 up). 1984. 8.95 (ISBN 0-517-55266-3). Crown.

Tundra & People. Ian Barrett. LC 82-50395. (Nature's Landscape Ser.). PLB 15.96 (ISBN 0-382-06670-7). Silver.

Tundra Ecosystems. Ed. by L. C. Bliss et al. LC 79-50913. (International Biological Programme Ser.: No. 25). (Illus.). 1000p. 1981. 147.50 (ISBN 0-521-22776-3). Cambridge U Pr.

Tundra Tales. Nola M. Zobarskas. 1967. 5.00 (ISBN 0-87141-021-4). Manyland.

Tundra: The Arctic Land. Bruce Hiscock. LC 85-28769. (Illus.). 144p. (gr. 5 up). 1986. 13.95 (ISBN 0-689-31219-9, Atheneum Childrens Bks). Macmillan.

Tune & Repair Your Own Piano. Michael Johnson & Robin Mackworth-Young. LC 78-51046. (Illus.). 82p. 1978. 3.95 (ISBN 0-15-191383-8). HarBraceJ.

Tune In. Ed. by Herman C. Ahrens, Jr. LC 68-54031. (Illus.). 1968. pap. 3.95 (ISBN 0-8298-0138-3). Pilgrim NY.

Tune in, America. Daniel G. Mason. LC 72-90664. (Essay Index Reprint Ser). 1931. 17.00 (ISBN 0-8369-1228-4). Ayer Co Pubs.

Tune in America! A Study of Our Coming Musical Independence. Daniel G. Mason. LC 72-1720. Repr. of 1931 ed. 16.45 (ISBN 0-404-08328-5). AMS Pr.

Tune in on Telephone Calls. Tom Kneitel. (Illus.). 160p. 1988. pap. 12.95 (ISBN 0-939780-08-9). CRB Res.

Tune in the World. LC 76-13248. (Illus.). 12.00 (ISBN 0-87259-006-2). Am Radio.

Tune in the World: The Listener's Guide to International Shortwave Radio. Kenneth D. MacHarg. LC 83-62842. (Illus.). 110p. 1983. pap. 9.99 (ISBN 0-914021-01-X). L Miller Pub.

Tune in the World with Ham Radio. LC 76-13248. (Illus.). with cassette & tapes 15.00 (ISBN 0-87259-455-6). Am Radio.

Tune in to a Television Career. T. R. Hollingsworth. LC 82-42787. 160p. (YA) (gr. 7 up). 1983. PLB 9.29 (ISBN 0-671-45581-8). Messner.

Tune in to English. Uwe Kind. (Illus.). 108p. (gr. 7-12). 1980. pap. text ed. 6.50 (ISBN 0-13-932807-6, 18845); cassettes 25.00 (ISBN 0-13-932815-7, 58846). Prentice ESL.

Tune in Tomorrow. Mary Anderson. LC 83-15656. 192p. (gr. 5 up). 1984. 11.95 (ISBN 0-689-31009-9, Atheneum Childrens Bks). Macmillan.

Tune in Tomorrow. Mary Anderson. 192p. (gr. 7 up). 1985. pap. 2.50 (ISBN 0-380-69870-6, Flare). Avon.

Tune in Tonight. Alexis Finger. 1985. pap. text ed. 11.50 (ISBN 0-88377-286-8); cassettes 25.75 (ISBN 0-88377-979-X). Newbury Hse.

Tune In, Tune Out: Broadcasting Regulation in the United States. Ann E. Weiss. (Illus.). (gr. 5-8). 1981. 8.95 (ISBN 0-395-31610-3). HM.

Tune in Workbook. Nancy L. Tubesing & Donald A. Tubesing. 132p. 1973. wkbk. 10.00 (ISBN 0-938586-14-9). Whole Person.

Tune into Limericks. Elizabeth Nichols. 1979. 7.50 (ISBN 0-913650-05-6). Columbia Pictures.

Tune on the Stairs. Ellen Garwood. 131p. 1988. 14.95 (ISBN 0-89526-562-1). Regnery Gateway.

Tune: The Structure of Melody. Imogen Holst. 1969. 9.50 (ISBN 0-8079-0126-1); pap. 5.95 (ISBN 0-8079-0127-X). October.

Tune Time, 2 pts. rev. ed. Sarah L. Dittenhaver et al. Ed. by Louise Goss. (Frances Clark Library for Piano Students). 48p. (gr. k-6). 1973. pap. text ed. 7.95 Pt. A (ISBN 0-87487-194-8); pap. text ed. 7.95 Pt. B (ISBN 0-87487-195-6). Birch Tree Gr.

Tune-Up Ignition & Fuel Induction Systems. rev. ed. Bob Leigh et al. Ed. by Roger L. Fennema & Leslie A. Wiseman. (Automobile Mechanics Refresher Course Ser.: Book 1). (Illus.). 104p. 1981. pap. 9.95x wkbk. (ISBN 0-88098-062-1); cassette tape 13.90 (ISBN 0-88098-068-0). H M Gousha.

Turbine-Generators. (Principles of Steam Generation Ser.: Module 12). (Illus.). 135p. 1982. spiral bdg. 26.50x (ISBN 0-87683-262-1). GP Pub.

Turbine Lube-Oil System. Center for Occupational Research & Development Staff. (EUTEC Power Plant Operator Curriculum Ser.). (Illus.). 20p. 1985. pap. text ed. write for info. (ISBN 1-55502-240-5). Ctr Res & Dev.

Turbine Lube Oil System Flushing & Cleaning. (Fossil Power Plant Startup Training Ser.: Module 8). (Illus.). 108p. 1982. spiral bdg. 21.50x (ISBN 0-87683-365-2). GP Pub.

Turbine Lubrication. 92p. 1984. 15.00 (ISBN 0-318-17675-0, SP-12). Soc Tribologists.

Turbine Operation. Center for Occupational Research & Development Staff. (EUTEC Power Plant Operator Curriculum Ser.). (Illus.). 40p. 1985. pap. text ed. write for info. (ISBN 1-55502-251-0). Ctr Res & Dev.

Turbine Protective System. Center for Occupational Research & Development Staff. (EUTEC Power Plant Operator Curriculum Ser.). (Illus.). 34p. 1985. pap. text ed. write for info. (ISBN 1-55502-241-3). Ctr Res & Dev.

Turbine Steam Path Components. William P. Sanders. (Turbomachinery International Publications Monograph: No. S-2). 1987. 19.95 (ISBN 0-937506-18-4). Turbo Intl Pubn.

Turbine Steam Path Maintenance & Repair Methods. William P. Sanders. (Turbomachinery International Publications Monograph: No. S-5). 1985. 19.95 (ISBN 0-937506-21-4). Turbo Intl Pubn.

Turbine Steam Path: Manufacturing Errors & Their Potential to Influence Blade System Performance. William P. Sanders. (Turbomachinery International Publications Monograph: No. S-3). 1987. 19.95 (ISBN 0-937506-19-2). Turbo Intl Pubn.

Turbine Steam Path Performance. William P. Sanders. (Turbomachinery International Publications Monograph: No. S-1). 1987. 19.95 (ISBN 0-937506-17-6). Turbo Intl Pubn.

Turbine Turning-Gear Operation. Center for Occupational Research & Development Staff. (EUTEC Power Plant Operator Curriculum Ser.). (Illus.). 24p. 1985. pap. text ed. write for info. (ISBN 1-55502-242-1). Ctr Res & Dev.

Turbines. Center for Occupational Research & Development Staff. (EUTEC Power Plant Operator Curriculum Ser.). (Illus.). 28p. 1985. pap. text ed. write for info. (ISBN 1-55502-239-1). Ctr Res & Dev.

Turbines & Jet Nozzles with Two-Phase Flows. V. C. Venediktov. LC 70-130509. 253p. 1969. 22.00 (ISBN 0-403-04543-6). Scholarly.

Turbines Westward. Thomas R. Lee. 1975. 16.95 (ISBN 0-686-00363-2). AG Pr.

Turbio-Medium Theory for Reflectance Spec. Billmeyer. 1987. write for info. (ISBN 0-471-07297-4). Wiley.

Turbo BASIC. Stern. (Higher Education Ser.). 1988. price not set (ISBN 0-471-63794-7). Wiley.

Turbo BASIC Instant Reference. Douglas Hergert. (Prompter Ser.). 393p. (Orig.). 1987. pap. 12.95 (ISBN 0-89588-485-2). Sybex.

Turbo BASIC Programs for Scientists & Engineers. Alan R. Miller. 276p. (Orig.). 1987. pap. 19.95 (ISBN 0-89588-429-1). Sybex.

Turbo Building Blocks. David D. McLeod. 1987. 16.95 (ISBN 0-87455-126-9). Compute Pubns.

Turbo "C". M. Tim Grady. Ed. by Raleigh Wilson. 408p. 1988. pap. text ed. price not set (ISBN 0-394-39497-6). Knopf.

Turbo C. Al Kelley & Ira Pohl. (Illus.). 450p. 1988. text ed. 20.95 (ISBN 0-8053-7880-4). Benjamin-Cummings.

Turbo C & Quick C Functions: Building Blocks for Efficient Code. Barden. 1988. pap. price not set (ISBN 0-471-61132-8). Wiley.

Turbo C at Any Speed. Richard S. Wiener. LC 87-30531. (Borland-Wiley Higher Education Ser.). 310p. 1988. pap. 27.95 (ISBN 0-471-63478-6). Wiley.

Turbo C Bible. The Waite Group Staff. (Illus.). 950p. (Orig.). 1988. pap. 24.95 (ISBN 0-672-22631-6). Sams.

Turbo C Developer's Library. Edward Rought & Thomas Hoops. 450p. (Orig.). 1988. pap. 24.95 (ISBN 0-672-22642-1). Sams.

Turbo C DOS Utilities. Robert Alonso. LC 87-33248. 1988. pap. 19.95 (ISBN 0-471-60910-2). Wiley.

Turbo C for Turbo Pascal Programmer's. Tom Swan. 375p. 1988. pap. 19.95 (ISBN 0-672-48422-6). Sams.

Turbo C: Memory Resident Utilities, Screen I-O & Programming Techniques. Al Stevens. 315p. (Orig.). 1987. pap. 24.95 (ISBN 0-943518-35-0); with disk 44.95 (ISBN 0-317-58971-7). MIS Press.

Turbo C Programmer's Guide. Nathan Goldenthal. 440p. (Orig.). 1988. pap. 24.95. Weber Systems.

Turbo C Programmer's Library. Kris Jamsa. (Borland Osborne-McGraw-Hill Business Ser.). 650p. 1988. 22.95 (ISBN 0-07-881394-8). Osborne-McGraw.

Turbo C Programmer's Resource Book. Frederick Holtz. (Illus.). 260p. 1987. pap. 17.95 (ISBN 0-8306-3030-9, 3030). TAB Bks.

Turbo C Programming. Miller. (Higher Education Ser.). 1988. pap. write for info. (ISBN 0-471-60861-0). Wiley.

Turbo C Programming. rev. ed. The Waite Group Staff. (Illus.). 700p. 1988. pap. 22.95 (ISBN 0-672-22660-X). Sams.

Turbo C Programming for the IBM. Robert Lafore. 600p. 1987. 22.95 (ISBN 0-672-22614-6). Sams.

Turbo C Survival Guide. Larry Miller & Alec Quilici. (Illus.). 1988. pap. 22.95 (ISBN 0-471-61708-3). Wiley.

Turbo C: The Art of Advanced Program Design, Optimization, & Debugging. Stephen R. Davis. 448p. 1987. pap. 24.95 (ISBN 0-934375-38-0); book & disk 39.95 (ISBN 0-934375-45-3). M & T Pub Inc.

Turbo C: The Complete Reference. Herbert Schildt. 850p. 1988. cancelled (ISBN 0-07-881373-5); pap. text ed. 24.95 (ISBN 0-07-881346-8). Osborne-McGraw.

Turbo C: The Pocket Reference. Herbert Schildt. 128p. 1988. pap. text ed. 5.95 (ISBN 0-07-881381-6). Osborne-McGraw.

Turbo C Trilogy: A Complete Library for Turbo C Programmers. Eric P. Bloom. (Illus.). 510p. 1988. pap. 22.95 (ISBN 0-8306-9370-X, 3070). TAB Bks.

Turbo Cowboys: Jump Start, No. 1. Tony Phillips. (gr. 3 up). 1988. pap. 2.95 (ISBN 0-345-35121-5). Ballantine.

Turbo Genealogy: The Computer-Enhanced "How-to-Find-Your-Roots" Handbook. John C. Cosgriff & Carolyn H. Cosgriff. 128p. (Orig.). 1987. 27.95 (ISBN 0-917255-05-4); pap. text ed. 17.95 (ISBN 0-917255-04-6). Progenesys Pr.

Turbo Hydra-matic 350 Handbook. Ron Sessions. LC 85-80861. 256p. pap. 17.95 (ISBN 0-89586-051-1). Price Stern.

Turbo Pascal. H. Paul Haiduk. 672p. 1989. pap. text ed. price not set (ISBN 0-394-39504-2). Knopf.

Turbo PASCAL. Paul L. Schlieve. (Applied Skills Ser.). 1987. pap. text ed. write for info. (ISBN 0-673-18787-X). Scott F.

Turbo Pascal: A Problem Solving Approach. E. B. Koffman. 600p. 1986. pap. text ed. 29.25 (ISBN 0-201-11743-6). Addison-Wesley.

Turbo Pascal-Advanced Applications. Ed. by Judith E. Overbeek. LC 86-26207. (Illus.). 108p. 1987. pap. text ed. 19.95 (ISBN 0-939621-00-2, 005.133). Rockland Publishing.

Turbo Pascal DOS Utilities. Robert Alonso. 163p. 1987. pap. 19.95 (ISBN 0-471-85995-8). Wiley.

Turbo Pascal Express: Two Hundred Fifty Plus Routines to Make Your Programs Faster, More Powerful, & Easier to Use. rev. ed. Robert Jourdain. 1988. incl. 2 disks 39.95 (ISBN 0-13-933193-X). Brady Comp Bks.

Turbo Pascal for BASIC Programmers. Paul Garrison. LC 85-62363. 410p. 1985. pap. 18.95 (ISBN 0-88022-167-4, 184); disk IBM-PC format 29.95 (ISBN 0-88022-233-6, 232); CP-M format 29.95. Que Corp.

Turbo Pascal for Electronics. Edward J. Pasahow. 208p. 1988. pap. text ed. 14.85 (ISBN 0-07-048732-4). McGraw.

Turbo Pascal for the IBM PC. Radford & Haigh. 1986. pap. text ed. 24.00 (ISBN 0-534-06426-4, 27R8000, Pub. by PWS Engineering). PWS Kent Pub.

Turbo Pascal for the Mac: A Quick Path to Programming Power. Paul Goodman & Alan Zeldin. 400p. (Orig.). 1988. pap. 19.95 (ISBN 0-13-933011-9). Brady Comp Bks.

Turbo Pascal for the MAC: Programming with Business Applications. Leon A. Wortman. 288p. 1987. pap. 17.95 (ISBN 0-8306-2927-0). TAB Bks.

Turbo Pascal Handbook. Ed Faulk. (Orig.). 1986. pap. 16.95 (ISBN 0-87455-037-8). Compute Pubns.

Turbo Pascal: Power Programmer's Guide. Stephen O'Brien. (Borland Osborne-McGraw-Hill Business Ser.: No. 5). 650p. 1988. 22.95 (ISBN 0-07-881420-0). Osborne-McGraw.

Turbo Pascal: Procedures & Functions for IBM PCs & Compatibles. Patrick Philippot. 188p. 1988. pap. 27.95 (ISBN 0-471-91632-3). Wiley.

Turbo Pascal Program Library. Tom Rugg & Phil Feldman. LC 86-60590. 617p. (Orig.). 1986. pap. 19.95 (ISBN 0-88022-244-1, 35); 29.95 (ISBN 0-88022-300-6, 264). Que Corp.

Turbo Pascal Program Reference Guide. Bomanns. 140p. 1987. text ed. 9.95 (ISBN 0-317-59244-0). Abacus Soft.

Turbo Pascal: Programmer's Guide. Paul M. Chirlian. 250p. 1986. pap. 17.95 (ISBN 0-938862-66-9). Weber Systems.

Turbo Pascal: Programmer's Library. Kris Jamsa & Steven Nameroff. (Borland-Osborne-McGraw-Hill Programming Ser.). 625p. 1987. pap. text ed. 21.95 (ISBN 0-07-881286-0). Osborne-McGraw.

Turbo Pascal Programmer's Library Version 4. Kris Jamsa & Steven Nameroff. 600p. 1988. pap. text ed. 22.95 (ISBN 0-07-881368-9). Osborne-McGraw.

Turbo Pascal: Programming & Problem Solving. Mickey Settle & Michel Boillot. 536p. 1988. pap. text ed. 32.75 (ISBN 0-314-62308-6). West Pub.

Turbo Pascal: Programming & Problem Solving (HC) Mickey Settle & Michel Boillot. 535p. 1988. pap. text ed. 33.75 (ISBN 0-314-62309-4). West Pub.

Turbo Pascal: Programming Examples & Subroutines. Paul Chirlian. 150p. 1986. pap. 15.95 (ISBN 0-938862-68-5). Weber Systems.

Turbo Pascal Programming Today. Steven L. Mandell. (Illus.). 561p. (Orig.). 1987. pap. text ed. 34.25 (ISBN 0-314-34628-7); write for info. instr's. manual (ISBN 0-314-35260-0). West Pub.

Turbo Pascal Programming Visual Masters. Donald D. Spencer. (Illus.). 96p. 1987. pap. 13.95 (ISBN 0-89218-108-7, NO. 3003). Camelot Pub.

Turbo Pascal Programming with Applications. Leon A. Wortman. 240p. 1986. pap. 17.95 (ISBN 0-8306-0127-9). TAB Bks.

Turbo Pascal Programs for Scientists & Engineers. Alan R. Miller. 332p. (Orig.). 1987. pap. 19.95 (ISBN 0-89588-424-0). Sybex.

Turbo Pascal Solutions. Jeff Duntemann. 1987. pap. 21.95 (ISBN 0-673-18584-2). Scott F.

Turbo Pascal: The Complete Reference. Stephen O'Brien. (Borland-Osborne McGraw-Hill Programming Ser.). 640p. 1987. pap. text ed. 24.95 (ISBN 0-07-881290-9). Osborne-McGraw.

Turbo Pascal: The Complete Reference. Stephen O'Brien. 640p. 1987. 27.95. Osborne-McGraw.

Turbo Pascal Tips, Tricks and Traps. Tom Rugg & Phil Feldman. LC 86-61149. 490p. 1986. pap. 19.95 (ISBN 0-88022-266-2, 65). Que Corp.

Turbo Pascal Toolbook. Ed. by Namir Clement Shammas. 1986. pap. 25.95 (ISBN 0-934375-25-9); bk. & Disk 45.95 (ISBN 0-934375-61-5). M & T Pub Inc.

Turbo Pascal Toolbox. Frank Dutton. 405p. (Orig.). 1988. pap. 18.95. Sybex.

Turbo Pascal Toolbox-A Programmer's Guide. Paul Garrison. 288p. 1987. pap. 17.95 (ISBN 0-8306-2852-5). TAB Bks.

Turbo Pascal Tricks & Tips. 2nd ed. J. Sgonina & A. Warner. 230p. 1986. pap. 19.95 (ISBN 0-916439-30-5). Abacus Soft.

Turbo Pascal Trilogy: A Complete Library for Turbo Pascal Programmers. Eric P. Bloom & Jeremy G. Soybel. (Illus.). 510p. 1988. 34.95 (ISBN 0-8306-9080-8, 3080); pap. 24.95 (ISBN 0-8306-9380-7, 3080). TAB Bks.

Turbo Pascal Version 4: The Pocket Reference. Kris Jamsa. 128p. 1988. pap. text ed. 5.95 (ISBN 0-07-881379-4). Osborne-McGraw.

Turbo Pascal 4.0: An Introduction to the Art & Science of Programming. 2nd ed. Walter J. Savitch. 880p. 1989. pap. text ed. 28.95 (ISBN 0-8053-0410-X); instr's. guide avail. (ISBN 0-8053-0411-8); programming software package avail. (ISBN 0-8053-0413-4); algorithms in action tutorial software avail. (ISBN 0-8053-8406-5). Benjamin-Cummings.

Turbo Pascaz. Jean Gonzalez & Gonzalo Chiriboga. (Computer-Programming Languages Ser.). (Illus.). 476p. pap. 18.95 (ISBN 0-938661-02-7). Franklin Beedle.

Turbo Power: Building with Superkey, Sidekick, & Turbo Lightning. Frank Iritz & Maxine Iritz. (Business Productivity Library). 1987. pap. 19.95 (ISBN 0-553-34437-4). Bantam.

Turbo Prolog. Dan Kauffman & Ralph Cafolla. 224p. 1989. case bound 24.95 (ISBN 0-675-20816-5). Merrill.

Turbo Prolog Advanced Programming Techniques. Philip Seyer & Safaa Hashim. (Illus.). 300p. 1988. pap. 18.95 (ISBN 0-8306-9308-4, 3008). TAB Bks.

Turbo Prolog: An Introduction. Paul Chirlian. 240p. 1988. pap. 28.95 (ISBN 0-675-20846-7); supplements avail. Merrill.

Turbo PROLOG: An Introduction to Artificial Intelligence. Patrice Bihan. LC 87-16074. 146p. 1987. 24.95 (ISBN 0-471-91633-1). Wiley.

Turbo Prolog: Features for Programmers. Sanjiva Nath. 272p. (Orig.). 1986. pap. 22.95 (ISBN 0-943518-68-7). MIS Press.

TURBO Prolog Primer. Andrew J. Bradbury et al. 376p. 1988. 32.95 (ISBN 0-07-707090-9). McGraw.

Turbo Prolog Primer. Jean B. Rogers. LC 86-28707. (Illus.). 240p. 1987. pap. text ed. 23.75x (ISBN 0-201-12198-0). Addison-Wesley.

Turbo Prolog Primer. rev. ed. Dan Shafer. 320p. (Orig.). 1987. pap. 19.95 (ISBN 0-672-22615-4). Sams.

Turbo Prolog Programmer's Guide. Nathan Goldenthal. 300p. 1987. pap. 19.95 (ISBN 0-938862-83-9). Weber Systems.

Turbocharged High Performance Engines. 1984. 14.00 (ISBN 0-89883-339-6, SP568). Soc Auto Engineers.

Turbochargers. Hugh MacInnes. LC 81-83821. (Illus.). 1976. pap. 12.95 (ISBN 0-89586-135-6). Price Stern.

Turbochargers & Turbocharged Engines. LC 79-50459. 158p. 1979. Twelve papers. 36.00 (ISBN 0-89883-214-4, SP442). Soc Auto Engineers.

Turbochargers: Theory, Installation, Maintenance & Repair. Todd Curless. LC 84-16425. (Illus.). 176p. (Orig.). 1984. TAB Bks.

Turbocharging Diesel & Gasoline Engines. 1981. 60.00 (ISBN 0-89883-111-3, PT23). Soc Auto Engineers.

Turbomachinery. Logan. 160p. 1981. 37.50 (ISBN 0-8247-1509-8). Dekker.

Turbomachinery Developments in Steam & Gas Turbines: Presented at the Winter Annual Meeting of the American Society of Mechanical Engineers, Atlanta, Georgia, November 27-December 2, 1977. American Society of Mechanical Engineers Staff. Ed. by W. G. Steltz. LC 77-88002. (Illus.). pap. 26.00 (ISBN 0-317-11146-9, 2013321). Bks Demand UMI.

Turbomachinery Diffuser Design Technology. David Japikse. LC 85-90311. (Design Technology Ser.: DTS 1). (Illus.). 400p. 1984. text ed. 1450.00 (ISBN 0-933283-00-8). Concepts ETI.

Turbomachinery International Handbook. 50.00 (ISBN 0-686-31377-1). Busn Journals.

Turbomachinery Maintenance Handbooks, 3 vols. Ea. 60.00 (ISBN 0-686-31375-5). Busn Journals.

Turbomechanics: A Guide to Design, Selection & Theory. Ed. by O. E. Balje. LC 80-21524. 513p. 1981. 64.95 (ISBN 0-471-06036-4, Pub. by Wiley-Interscience). Wiley.

Turbotrains. Wolfgang Stoffels. 124p. 1983. 25.95 (ISBN 0-8176-1172-X). Birkhauser.

Turbott Wolfe. William Plomer. (Twentieth-Century Classics Ser.). 224p. 1985. pap. 5.95 (ISBN 0-19-281890-2). Oxford U Pr.

Turbott Wolfe. William Plomer. 1987. pap. 7.95 (ISBN 0-15-691490-5, Harv). HarBraceJ.

Turbulence. 2nd ed. J. O. Hinze. 1975. text ed. 61.95 (ISBN 0-07-029037-7). McGraw.

Turbulence & Diffusion in Stable Environments. Ed. by J. C. Hunt. (Institute of Mathematics & It's Applications Conference Ser.). (Illus.). 336p. 1985. 55.00x (ISBN 0-19-853604-6). Oxford U Pr.

Turbulence & Predictability in Geophysical Fluid Dynamics & Climate Dynamics: Proceedings of the International School of Physics, Enrico Fermi Course LXXXVIII, Varenna, Italy, 14 June-24 June, 1983. Ed. by M. Ghil et al. (Enrico Fermi Ser.: Vol. 88). 464p. 1985. 113.25 (ISBN 0-444-86936-0, North-Holland). Elsevier.

Turbulence & Random Processes in Fluid Mechanics. M. T. Landahl & E. Mollo-Christensen. (Illus.). 160p. 1987. pap. 17.95 (ISBN 0-521-34687-8). Cambridge U Pr.

Turbulence in Fluids: Stochastic & Numerical Modelling. Marcel Lesieur. 1987. lib. bdg. 68.50 (ISBN 90-247-3470-3, Pub. by Martinus Nijhoff Netherlands). Kluwer Academic.

Turbulence in Internal Flows: Turbomachinery & Other Engineering Applications, Proceedings. Project Squid Workshop on Turbulence in Internal Flows: Turbomachinery & Other Applications, Airlie House, Warrenton, Va., June 14-15, 1976. Ed. by S. N. Murthy. LC 77-15615. (Illus.). 573p. 1977. 91.25 (ISBN 0-89116-073-6). Hemisphere Pub.

Turbulence in Lakes & Rivers. J. R. Smith. 1975. 11.00x (ISBN 0-900386-21-5, Pub. by Freshwater Bio). State Mutual Bk.

Turbulence in Mixing Operations: Theory & Application to Mixing & Reaction. Symposium at Pittsburgh, Penn., June, 1974. Ed. by Robert S. Brodkey. 1975. 68.50 (ISBN 0-12-134450-9). Acad Pr.

Turbulence in the Ocean. A. S. Monin & R. V. Ozmidov. 1984. lib. bdg. 44.50 (ISBN 90-277-1735-4, Pub. by Reidel Holland). Kluwer Academic.

Turbulence Management & Relaminarisation. Ed. by H. W. Liepmann & R. Narashima. (Illus.). xxiii, 550p. 1987. 89.70 (ISBN 0-387-18574-7). Springer-Verlag.

Turbulence Measurement & Flow Modeling. Ed. by Ching Jen Chen & Forrest M. Holly, Jr. 869p. 1986. 125.00 (ISBN 0-89116-558-4). Hemisphere Pub.

Turbulence Models & Their Application in Hydraulics: A State of the Art Review. Wolfgang Rodi. 116p. 1984. text ed. 23.00 (ISBN 90-2127-002-1, Pub. by A A Balkema). Brookfield Pub Co.

Turbulence over the Middle East: Israel & the Nations in Confrontation & the Coming Kingdom of Peace on Earth. Louis Goldberg. (Illus.). 320p. 1982. pap. 7.95 (ISBN 0-87213-240-4). Loizeaux.

Turbulent Buoyant Jets & Plumes, Vol. 6. Ed. by W. Rodi. (HMT Ser.). 192p. 1982. text ed. 50.00 (ISBN 0-08-026492-1). Pergamon.

Turbulent City: Paris 1783 to 1871. facs. ed. Andre Castelot. Tr. by Denise Folliot. LC 76-117867. (Select Bibliographies Reprint Ser). 1962. 25.50 (ISBN 0-8369-5320-7). Ayer Co Pubs.

Turbulent Combustion, PAAS58. Ed. by Lawrence A. Kennedy. LC 78-479. (Illus.). 485p. 1978. 59.50 (ISBN 0-915928-22-1). AIAA.

Turbulent Diffusion in the Environment. G. T. Csanady. LC 72-92527. (Geophysics & Astrophysics Monographs: No. 3). (Illus.). 248p. 1973. lib. bdg. 37.00 (ISBN 90-277-0260-3); pap. text ed. 21.00 (ISBN 90-277-0261-6). Kluwer Academic.

Turbulent Dream: Passion & Politics in the Poetry of W. B. Yeats. Geoffrey Thurley. LC 83-5728. 235p. 1984. 29.95 (ISBN 0-7022-1962-2). U of Queensland Pr.

Turbulent Era: A Diplomatic Record of Forty Years, 1904-1945, 2 Vols. Joseph C. Grew. Ed. by Walter Johnson. LC 72-114880. (Select Bibliographies Reprint Ser). 1952. Set. 88.00 (ISBN 0-8369-5284-7). Ayer Co Pubs.

Turkish Embroideries, Sixteenth to Nineteenth Centuries. M. Gonul. (Illus.). 1975. pap. 7.50. Heinman.

Turkish Embroidery. Pauline Johnstone. (Illus.). 112p. (Orig.). 1985. pap. 11.95 (ISBN 0-948107-02-2, Pub. by Victoria & Albert Mus UK). Faber & Faber.

Turkish-English - English-Turkish. 254p. (Orig.). 1986. pap. 5.95 (ISBN 0-87052-241-8). Hippocrene Bks.

Turkish-English Contrastive Analysis: Turkish Morphology & Corresponding English Structures. H. I. Sebuktekin. LC 75-120352. (Janua Linguarum, Series Practica: No. 84). (Orig.). 1970. pap. text ed. 12.00x (ISBN 0-686-22402-7). Mouton.

Turkish-English Dictionary. 2nd ed. H. C. Hony. (Turkish & Eng.). 1957. 39.95x (ISBN 0-19-864108-7). Oxford U Pr.

Turkish-English Dictionary, 3 pts. James W. Redhouse. (Turkish & Eng.). 1976. Repr. of 1958 ed. Set. 270.00 (ISBN 0-518-19005-6). Ayer Co Pubs.

Turkish-English, English-Turkish Dictionary: New Red House, 2 Vols. (Turkish & Eng.). Set. 90.00; Turkish-English, 7th ed. 45.00; English-Turkish, 12th ed. 45.00. Heinman.

Turkish-English, English-Turkish Dictionary (The Redhouse Portable Dictionary) Ed. by Robert Avery et al. (Turkish & Eng.). 17.50. Heinman.

Turkish Folk Music from Asia Minor. Bela Bartok. Ed. by Benjamin Suchoff. LC 75-23186. (Studies in Musicology). 1976. 34.00x (ISBN 0-691-09120-X). Princeton U Pr.

Turkish for Travellers. Berlitz Editors. 1975. pap. 4.95 (ISBN 0-02-964230-2, Berlitz). Macmillan.

Turkish Foreign Policy During the Second World War: An Active Neutrality. Selim Deringil. (LSE Monographs in International Studies). (Illus.). 248p. Date not set. price not set (ISBN 0-521-34466-2). Cambridge U Pr.

Turkish Grammar. G. L. Lewis. 328p. 1986. pap. 14.95x (ISBN 0-19-815838-6). Oxford U Pr.

Turkish Grammar. J. Nemeth. (Publications in the Near & Middle East Studies, Series B: No. 1). 1962. 13.20x (ISBN 90-2790-100-7). Mouton.

Turkish Grammar. Robert Underhill. LC 75-46535. 1976. text ed. 35.00x (ISBN 0-262-21006-1). MIT Pr.

Turkish History, 3 Vols. 6th ed. Richard Knolles. LC 72-153621. Repr. of 1687 ed. Set. lib. bdg. 200.00 (ISBN 0-404-09510-0); lib. bdg. 70.00 ea. Vol. 1 (ISBN 0-404-09511-9). Vol. 2 (ISBN 0-404-09512-7). Vol. 3 (ISBN 0-404-09513-5). AMS Pr.

Turkish Instruments of Music in the Seventeenth Century. Ewliya Chelebi. Ed. by Henry G. Farmer. LC 76-42034. 1977. Repr. of 1937 ed. lib. bdg. 12.50 (ISBN 0-89341-068-3). Longwood Pub Group.

Turkish Intonation: An Instrumental Study. Rose Nash. LC 71-120351. (Janua Linguarum, Series Practica: No. 114). (Illus.). 190p. (Orig.). 1973. pap. text ed. 28.80x (ISBN 90-2792-369-8). Mouton.

Turkish Life in Town & Country. Lucy M. Garnett. LC 77-87629. Repr. of 1904 ed. 28.00 (ISBN 0-404-16454-4). AMS Pr.

Turkish Literature. facsimile ed. LC 77-111117. (Play Anthology Reprint Ser). 1901. 23.50 (ISBN 0-8369-8210-X). Ayer Co Pubs.

Turkish Literature. Epiphanius Wilson. 1973. Repr. of 1901 ed. 40.00 (ISBN 0-8274-1603-2). R West.

Turkish Literature. Epiphanus Wilson. 69.95 (ISBN 0-8490-1235-X). Gordon Pr.

Turkish Miniatures. G. M. Meredith-Owens. (Illus.). 32p. (Orig.). 1970. pap. 2.95 (ISBN 0-7141-0641-0, Pub. by British Lib). Longwood Pub Group.

Turkish Nationalism & Western Civilization: Selected Essays of Ziya Gokalp. Ziya Gokalp. Ed. & tr. by Niyazi Berkes. LC 81-13235. 336p. 1982. Repr. of 1959 ed. lib. bdg. 35.00x (ISBN 0-313-23196-6, GOTN). Greenwood.

Turkish Newspaper Reader. John D. Murphy & Metin Somay. LC 88-70934. 330p. 1988. text ed. 31.50 (ISBN 0-931745-35-7). Dunwoody Pr.

Turkish Ordeal. Halide E. Adivar. LC 79-3081. (Illus.). 407p. 1981. Repr. of 1928 ed. 35.50 (ISBN 0-8305-0057-X). Hyperion Conn.

Turkish People: Their Social Life, Religious Beliefs & Institutions & Domestic Life. Lucy M. Garnett. LC 77-87630. (Illus.). 352p. Repr. of 1909 ed. 36.00 (ISBN 0-404-16455-2). AMS Pr.

Turkish Revolution & the Indian Freedom Movement. Mohammad Sadiq. 1984. 17.50x (ISBN 0-8364-1155-2, Pub. by Macmillan India). South Asia Bks.

Turkish Rugs: The Rachel B. Stevens Memorial Collection. Intro. by Joseph V. McMullan. (Illus.). 63p. 1968. pap. 6.50 (ISBN 0-87405-000-6). Textile Mus.

Turkish Straits. Christos L. Rozakis & Petros N. Stagos. LC 86-28581. (International Straits of the World Ser.: Vol. 9). 1987. write for info. (ISBN 9-02-473464-9, Pub. by Kluwer-Nijhoff (Netherlands)). Kluwer-Academic.

Turkish Theatre. Nicholas N. Martinovitch. LC 68-20241. (Illus.). 1968. Repr. of 1933 ed. 12.50 (ISBN 0-405-08761-6, Pub. by Blom). Ayer Co Pubs.

Turkish Treasures from the Collection of Edwin Binney, 3rd. Edwin Binney, 3rd. (Illus.). 250p. (Orig.). 1979. pap. 15.00 (ISBN 0-295-96136-8, Pub. by Portland Art Museum). U of Wash Pr.

Turkish Waters Pilot. Rod Heikell. 256p. 1984. 120.00x (ISBN 0-85288-094-4, Pub. by Imray Laurie Norie & Wilson England). State Mutual Bk.

Turkish Workers in Europe: An Interdisciplinary Study. Ed. by Ilhan Basgoz & Norman Furniss. LC 85-71750. (Turkish Studies: Indiana University). (Illus.). 198p. 1986. pap. 10.95x (ISBN 0-253-39809-6). Ind U Pr.

Turkistan Tumult. Aitchen Wu. (Illus.). 1985. pap. 12.95x (ISBN 0-19-583839-4). Oxford U Pr.

Turkmen: Tribal Carpets & Traditions. Ed. by Louise W. Mackie & Jon Thompson. LC 80-53159. (Illus.). 240p. 75.00 (ISBN 0-87405-014-6). Textile Mus.

Turkmenistan. (Let's Visit Places & Peoples - - Nations, Dependencies, & Sovereignties of the World Ser.). (Illus.). (gr. 5 up). 1989. 12.95 (ISBN 0-7910-0176-8). Chelsea Hse.

Turkoman Carpet. George W. O'Bannon. (Illus.). 168p. 1974. 95.00 (ISBN 0-7156-0740-5, Pub. by Duckworth London). Longwood Pub Group.

Turks & Caicos: Consolidated Index of Statutes & Subsidiary Legislation. Ed. by C. J. Hammett. (West Indian Legislation Indexing Project Ser.). vi, 54p. (Orig.). 1986. pap. text ed. 20.00 (ISBN 0-317-60549-6, Pub. by UWI Fac Law). W W Gaunt.

Turmoil. 2nd ed. Arthur Moore. 1979. pap. 2.25 (ISBN 0-89083-490-3). Zebra.

Turmoil in Hungary: An Anthology of Twentieth Century Hungarian Poetry. Ed. by Nicholas Kolumban. LC 82-81365. (Illus.). 186p. 1982. pap. 6.00 (ISBN 0-89823-039-X). New Rivers Pr.

Turmoil in New Mexico, 1846-1868. William A. Keleher. LC 82-11113. (Illus.). 560p. 1982. pap. 12.95 (ISBN 0-8263-0632-2). U of NM Pr.

Turmoil of the World. Francis Neilson. 1979. lib. bdg. 39.95 (ISBN 0-685-96645-3). Revisionist Pr.

Turmoil to Triumph: The Odyssey of Captain Harris O. Machus Through Six War Devastated Countries in Search of Survival. Angus D. McKellar. LC 86-72281. (Illus.). 257p. 1987. 18.95 (ISBN 0-939528-00-2). Brookside Pub.

Turn About, Think About, Look About Book. Beau Gardner. LC 80-12885. (Illus.). 32p. (gr. k-6). 1980. 11.75 (ISBN 0-688-41969-0); PLB 11.75 (ISBN 0-688-51969-5). Lothrop.

Turn Again Tiger. Samuel Selvon. (Caribbean Writers Ser.). (Orig.). 1980. pap. text ed. 6.00 (ISBN 0-435-98780-1). Heinemann Ed.

Turn Again to Life. Abraham Schmitt. LC 86-33581. 136p. (Orig.). 1987. pap. 8.95 (ISBN 0-8361-3436-2). Herald Pr.

Turn Again to Me. Helen Adam. 1977. 7.00x (ISBN 0-686-22908-8); pap. 3.50x (ISBN 0-686-22909-6). Kulchur Foun.

Turn Around One Hundred Times. Ian Hickingbotham. 1988. pap. 30.00x (ISBN 0-7223-1917-7, Pub. by A H Stockwell England). State Mutual Bk.

Turn Around Twice. Elizabeth Ogilvie. Repr. lib. bdg. 13.95x (ISBN 0-88411-339-6, Pub. by Aeonian Pr). Amereon Ltd.

Turn Back the Night: A Christian Response to Popular Culture. Stephen R. Lawhead. LC 84-72005. 192p. (Orig.). 1985. pap. 6.95 (ISBN 0-89107-340-X, Crossway Bks). Good News.

Turn-from Poverty to Prosperity. Samarjit Ghosh. 140p. 1986. 21.95. Asia Bk Corp.

Turn Here for the Big Hole. Mary P. Berthold. 1970. 3.95 (ISBN 0-8187-0025-4). Harlo Pr.

Turn Home Again. Herbert Harker. 245p. 1984. 6.95 (ISBN 0-934126-57-7). Randall Bk Co.

Turn Homeward, Hannalee. Patricia Beatty. LC 84-8960. 208p. (gr. 5-9). 1984. 11.75 (ISBN 0-688-03871-9, Morrow Junior Books). Morrow.

Turn in the South. V. S. Naipaul. LC 88-45346. 320p. 1989. 18.45 (ISBN 0-394-56477-4). Knopf.

Turn in the Trail. Walt Sandberg. 215p. 1980. 15.95 (ISBN 0-932558-14-3). Willow Creek Pr.

Turn It Up! Todd Strasser. (gr. 6-12). 1985. pap. 2.50 (ISBN 0-440-99059-9, LFL). Dell.

Turn Me Over - I'm Reversible: Quick & Easy Reversible Quilts. Kaye Wood. (Illus.). 60p. (Orig.). 1988. pap. 9.95 (ISBN 0-944588-03-4). K Wood Pub.

Turn Not Pale, Beloved Snail: A Book About Writing & Other Things. Jacqueline Jackson. 192p. (YA) (gr. 7 up). 1974. 14.95 (ISBN 0-316-45481-8). Little.

Turn of the Cards. Georgina Grey. (Regency Romance Ser.). 1979. pap. 1.75 (ISBN 0-449-23969-1, Crest). Fawcett.

Turn of the Century American Journalist, Ray Stannard Baker. Vivian G. Rosenberg. (Illus., LC A-935092). 1977. 10.00 (ISBN 0-686-15375-8); pap. 8.00 (ISBN 0-686-15376-6). V G Rosenberg.

Turn-of-the-Century Cabaret: Paris, Barcelona, Berlin, Munich, Vienna, Cracow, Moscow, St. Petersburg, Zurich. Harold B. Segel. LC 86-31699. (Illus.). 325p. 1987. 30.00 (ISBN 0-231-05128-X). Columbia U Pr.

Turn of the Century Glass: The Murray Collection of Glass. Ed. by Philip D. Zimmerman. LC 83-40054. (Illus.). 96p. 1983. pap. 20.00 (ISBN 0-87451-280-8). U Pr of New Eng.

Turn-of-the-Century Houses, Cottages & Villas. R. W. Shoppell. 1984. 16.25 (ISBN 0-8446-6110-4). Peter Smith.

Turn of the Century Houses, Cottages & Villas: Floor Plans & Illustrations of 120 Homes from Shoppell's Catalogs. R. W. Shoppell. (Architecture Ser.). 128p. (Orig.). 1984. pap. 6.95 (ISBN 0-486-24567-5). Dover.

Turn-of-the-Century Posters. (Shorewood Art Programs for Education Ser.). 12p. 1983. tchr's ed 86.00 (ISBN 0-88185-073-X); mounted prints 119.00. Shorewood Fine Art.

Turn of the Clock: A Book of Modern Parables. Peter Kreeft. LC 87-81571. 91p. (Orig.). 1987. pap. 5.95 (ISBN 0-89870-168-6). Ignatius Pr.

Turn of the Screw. Henry James. (Airmont Classics Ser.). (gr. 9 up). 1967. pap. 1.75 (ISBN 0-8049-0155-4, CL-155). Airmont.

Turn of the Screw. Henry James. Repr. lib. bdg. 16.95 (ISBN 0-89190-315-1, Pub. by River City Pr). Amereon Ltd.

Turn of the Screw. Henry James. 1975. (Evman); pap. 1.95x (ISBN 0-460-01912-0, Evman). Biblio Dist.

Turn of the Screw. Henry James. Bd. with Daisy Miller. 192p. 1978. pap. 2.95 (ISBN 0-440-39154-7, LE). Dell.

Turn of the Screw. Henry James. Ed. by Robert Kimbrough. (Norton Critical Edition Ser.). 1966. pap. 5.95x (ISBN 0-393-09669-6). Norton.

Turn of the Screw. Henry James. (Now Age Illustrated V Ser.). (Illus.). 64p. (gr. 4-12). 1979. text ed. 7.50 (ISBN 0-88301-408-4); pap. text ed. 2.95 (ISBN 0-88301-396-7); student activity bk. 1.25 (ISBN 0-88301-420-3). Pendulum Pr.

Turn of the Screw. Henry James. 1977. Repr. of 1898 ed. lib. bdg. 21.95x (ISBN 0-89244-046-5). Queens Hse-Focus Serv.

Turn of the Screw. Henry James. Adapted by Diana Stewart. LC 81-5217. (Short Classics Ser.). (Illus.). 48p. (gr. 4 up). 1981. PLB 15.99 (ISBN 0-8172-1672-3). Raintree Pubs.

Turn of the Screw. Henry James. Adapted by Diana Stewart. LC 81-5217. (Short Classics Ser.). (Illus.). 48p. (gr. 4-12). 1983. pap. 9.27 (ISBN 0-8172-2027-5). Raintree Pubs.

Turn of the Screw see Aspern Papers.

Turn of the Screw & Other Short Fiction. Henry James. 416p. (Orig.). (gr. 9-12). 1981. pap. 1.95 (ISBN 0-553-21059-9, Bantam Classics). Bantam.

Turn of the Screw & Other Short Novels. Henry James. 456p. (Orig.). pap. 1.95 (ISBN 0-451-51669-9, Sig Classics). NAL.

Turn of the Screw & Other Stories. Henry James. 1970. pap. 1.95 (ISBN 0-14-003026-3). Penguin.

Turn of the Screw & Washington Square. Henry James. LC 80-54134. (Silver Burdett Classics for Kids Ser.). 288p. (gr. 6 up). 1985. pap. 3.67 (ISBN 0-382-09997-4). Silver.

Turn of the Screw Notes see Daisy Miller Notes.

Turn of the Wheel. Oliver Friggieri. Tr. by Grazio Falzon from Maltese. LC 87-70813. (Unesco Collection of Representative Works - European Ser.). 77p. 1987. pap. 13.95 (ISBN 0-905075-25-0, Pub. by Wilfion Bks Scotland). Dufour.

Turn of the Wheel. Roger Vailland. Tr. by Peter Wiles from Fr. LC 77-20080. 1978. Repr. of 1962 ed. lib. bdg. 35.00 (ISBN 0-313-20014-9, VATW). Greenwood.

Turn of the Years. V. S. Pritchett. 1982. ltd. ed. 17.00 (ISBN 0-394-52501-9). Random.

Turn of Traitors. Palma Harcourt. 1986. pap. 3.50 (ISBN 0-515-08504-9). Jove Pubns.

Turn of Zero. Won Ko. (Poetry Ser.). (Illus.). 1974. signed ltd. ed. 15.00x (ISBN 0-89304-048-7); pap. 4.50x (ISBN 0-89304-003-7). Cross Cult.

Turn Off Your Age see Think Young-Be Young!.

Turn on the Dark. Phyllis Martin. (Happy Day Bks.). (Illus.). 24p. (ps-2). 1985. 1.59 (ISBN 0-87239-881-1, 3681). Standard Pub.

Turn on the Light at Christmas. Earl Paulk. 32p. 1987. pap. 1.50 (ISBN 0-917595-23-8). K-Dimension.

Turn on to Reading (All Night Long) Sylvia Blake & Sy Kaufman. 1984. wkbk. 1.00 (ISBN 0-910307-04-0). Comp Pr.

Turn on, Tune in & Drop the Lot. Bhagwan Shree Rajneesh. Ed. by Ma Prem Maneesha. (Initiation Talks Ser.). (Illus.). 312p. (Orig.). 1980. pap. 8.95 (ISBN 0-88050-660-1). Chidvilas Inc.

Turn-Ons! One Hundred Eighty-Five Strategies for the Secondary Classroom. Stephen K. Smuin. LC 77-92903. (gr. 7-12). 1978. pap. 10.95 (ISBN 0-8224-7051-9). D S Lake Pubs.

Turn Right at Death Valley. John Merrill. 1986. 30.00x (ISBN 0-907496-26-1, Pub. by JNM Pubns UK). State Mutual Bk.

Turn South at the Second Bridge. Leon Hale. LC 80-5517. 224p. 1980. Repr. of 1965 ed. 15.95 (ISBN 0-89096-100-X). Tex A&M Univ Pr.

Turn the Battle to the Gate. Betsey Frye. 48p. 1988. pap. 2.95 (ISBN 0-88144-099-X). Christian Pub.

Turn the Dial. Harriet Ziefert. (Magic Touch Bks.). (Illus.). 24p. (ps). 1984. 4.95 (ISBN 0-448-19103-2, G&D). Putnam Pub Group.

Turn: The Journal of an Artist. Anne Truitt. 256p. 1986. 16.95 (ISBN 0-670-81175-0). Viking.

Turn: The Journal of an Artist. Anne Truitt. 224p. 1987. pap. 6.95 (ISBN 0-14-009249-8). Penguin.

Turn the Key. Harriet Ziefert. (Magic Touch Bks.). (Illus.). 24p. (ps). 1984. 4.95 (ISBN 0-448-19104-0, G&D). Putnam Pub Group.

Turn the Page, Wendy. Margaret Hill. LC 80-26784. (Illus.). 144p. (gr. 5 up). 1981. 9.50g (ISBN 0-687-42700-2). Abingdon.

Turn to the Lord: A Call to Repentance. Michael Scanlan. 32p. (Orig.). 1984. pap. text ed. 1.25 (ISBN 0-89283-258-4). Servant.

Turn to the Right: The Ideological Origins & the Development of Ukrainina Nationalism, 1919-1929. Alexander J. Motyl. (East European Monographs: No. 65). 212p. 1980. 20.00x (ISBN 0-914710-58-3). East Eur Quarterly.

Turn to the South: Essays on Southern Jewry. Ed. by Nathan M. Kaganoff & Melvin I. Urofsky. LC 78-9306. 205p. 1979. 10.95x (ISBN 0-8139-0742-X). U Pr of Va.

Turn Toward Life: The Bible & Peacemaking. Jorg Zink. Tr. by Victoria Rhodin from Ger. LC 84-48709. 128p. 1985. pap. 1.00 (ISBN 0-8006-1829-7, 1-1829). Fortress.

Turn Toward Violence, Nineteen Twenty to Nineteen Twenty-Nine. Ed. by Aaron Klieman & Howard M. Sachar. (Rise of Israel Ser.). 440p. 1987. lib. bdg. 90.00 (ISBN 0-8240-4938-1). Garland Pub.

Turn Us, Lord. Robert Campbell & Michael Sherer. 1985. 2.95 (ISBN 0-89536-728-9, 5812). CSS of Ohio.

Turn West on Twenty-Third. Robert Baral. LC 65-24028. (Illus.). 1966. 10.95 (ISBN 0-8303-0055-4). Fleet.

Turn West, Turn East: Mark Twain & Henry James. Henry S. Canby. LC 65-23485. 1951. 12.00 (ISBN 0-8196-0154-3). Biblo.

Turn Your Craft Hobbies into Cash. 2nd ed. Mary Woods. 132p. 1981. pap. 13.95 (ISBN 0-939640-01-5). MWS Pubns.

Turn Your Good Idea into a Profitable Home Video. Matthew White. (Illus.). 288p. 1987. pap. 12.95 (ISBN 0-312-01043-5). St Martin.

Turn Your Hurts into Healing. V. Gilbert Beers. 192p. 1988. text ed. 9.95 (ISBN 0-8007-1598-5). Revell.

Turn Your Pressure Valve Down. Richard Flint. 100p. 1982. pap. 10.00 (ISBN 0-937851-15-9). Pendelton Lane.

Turn Your World Upside Down. Kathy Berry & Esther Burroughs. 88p. (Orig.). 1985. pap. 2.95 (ISBN 0-937170-29-1). Home Mission.

Turnabout. Dilys Gater. 1982. 15.00x (ISBN 0-86319-002-2, Pub. by New Playwrights Network). State Mutual Bk.

Turnabout Children. Mary MacCracken. 256p. 1987. pap. 3.95 (ISBN 0-451-14877-0, Sig). NAL.

Turnabout Children: Overcoming Dyslexia & Other Learning Disabilities. Mary MacCracken. 1986. 16.95 (ISBN 0-316-55540-1). Little.

Turnabout: Help for a New Life. Jean Kirkpatrick. 1978. 7.95 (ISBN 0-686-30132-3). WFS.

Turnabout: New Help for the Woman Alcholic. Jean Kirkpatrick. LC 77-79558. 184p. 1986. pap. 8.95. Madrona Pubs.

Turnaround: A Book of Rhymes, Riddles, & Sounds. Katherine T. McAvoy. 94p. 1980. text ed. 7.50x spiral (ISBN 0-8134-2111-X). Inter Print Pubs.

Turnaround Manager's Handbook. Richard S. Sloma. 192p. 1985. 16.95 (ISBN 0-02-929290-5). Free Pr.

Turnaround Selling: How to Cash in on Hidden Big-Money Opportunities in Everyday Sales Situation. Richard F. Gabriel. 1977. 49.50 (ISBN 0-13-933176-X). Exec Reports.

Turnaround: The No-Nonsense Guide to Corporate Renewal. Marvin A. Davis. 1987. 17.95 (ISBN 0-8092-4780-1). Contemp Bks.

Turnaround: The No-Nonsense Guide to Corporate Renewal. Marvin A. Davis. 208p. 1988. pap. 9.95 (ISBN 0-8092-4578-7). Contemp Bks.

Turnaround Time: The Best of Computerworld's Q & A's. Larry Long. 192p. 1988. pap. 14.95 (ISBN 0-13-933029-1). P-H.

Turnaround Wind. Arnold Lobel. LC 87-45293. (Illus.). 32p. (ps-3). 1988. 12.70i (ISBN 0-06-023987-5); PLB 12.89 (ISBN 0-06-023988-3). HarpJ.

Turnbulls. Taylor Caldwell. 1974. Repr. of 1943 ed. lib. bdg. 26.95x (ISBN 0-88411-155-5, Pub. by Aeonian Pr). Amereon Ltd.

Turnbulls. Taylor Caldwell. 512p. (Orig.). 1985. pap. 4.50 (ISBN 0-515-08044-6). Jove Pubns.

Turncoat. Jack Lynn. 1976. pap. 8.95 (ISBN 0-440-09133-0). Delacorte.

Turncoat: The Strange Case of British Traitor Sergeant Harold Cole, "The Worst Traitor of the War". Brendan Murphy. (Illus.). 1987. 19.95 (ISBN 0-15-191410-9). HarBraceJ.

Turned-Around Taxi: Book & Cassette. Craig McKee & Margaret Holland. (Predictable Reading Bks.). (Illus.). (gr. k-4). 1985. 4.95 (ISBN 0-87406-025-7). Willowisp Pr.

Turned-Bowl Design. Richard Raffan. LC 87-72008. (Illus.). 176p. 1987. pap. 17.95 (ISBN 0-918804-82-5). Taunton.

Turned Funny: A Memoir. Celestine Sibley. 1988. 16.95 (ISBN 0-317-67531-1). Har-Row.

Turning Wheels: The Great Boer Trek. Stuart Cloete. 435p. 1987. Repr. of 1937 ed. lib. bdg. 45.00 (ISBN 0-89987-246-8). Darby Bks.
Turning Wishes into Reality. Neva Coyle. 192p. (Orig.). 1988. pap. 5.95 (ISBN 0-87123-997-3). Bethany Hse.
Turning Wood with Richard Raffan. Richard Raffan. LC 84-52130. (Illus.). 176p. 1985. pap. 17.95 (ISBN 0-918804-24-8, Dist. by W W Norton). Taunton.
Turning Wool into a Cottage Industry. Paula Simmons. LC 84-27231. 200p. (Orig.). 1985. pap. 9.95 (ISBN 0-88089-004-5). Madrona Pubs.
Turning World. Selected by D. J. Brindley. 1987. 30.00x (ISBN 0-7217-0219-8, Pub. by Schofield & Sims). State Mutual Bk.
Turning Your Inside Out: Avonda. Avonda Robinson. 64p. 1988. 7.95 (ISBN 0-89962-713-7). Todd & Honeywell.
Turning Your Vision to Success. David A. Fitch. Ed. by Grace Lessner. 80p. 1986. pap. 7.98 (ISBN 0-9616406-0-X). Visions Success.
Turnings of Darkness & Light: Essays in Philosophical & Systematic Theology. Kenneth Surin. 352p. Date not set. price not set (ISBN 0-521-34159-0). Cambridge U Pr.
Turnip. Tr. by Fainna Solasko. 12p. 1984. pap. 1.99 (ISBN 0-8285-2850-0, Pub. by Malysh Pubs USSR). Imported Pubns.
Turnip. A. Tolstoy. 16p. 1978. pap. 1.49 (ISBN 0-8285-1251-5, Pub. by Progress Pubs USSR). Imported Pubns.
Turnip Pie. Rebecca Cummings. (Orig.). 1986. pap. 8.95 (ISBN 0-913006-36-X). Puckerbrush.
Turnip's Blood. Cassin Maxine. Ed. by Everette Maddox et al. (Illus.). 112p. (Orig.). 1985. pap. 5.00 (ISBN 0-9614371-0-3). Sisters Grim Pr.
Turnover. Myles Spicer. 1988. 10.95 (ISBN 0-533-07715-X). Vantage.
Turnpike Optimality in Input-Output Systems: Theory & Application for Planning. J. Tsukui & Y. Murakami. (Contributions to Economic Analysis Ser.: Vol. 122). 260p. 1979. 84.25 (ISBN 0-444-85221-2, North Holland). Elsevier.
Turns. John Matthias. LC 75-535. 111p. 1975. 8.95 (ISBN 0-8040-0689-X, Pub by Swallow). Ohio U Pr.
Turns. John Matthias. 112p. (Orig.). 1975. pap. 7.95 (ISBN 0-85646-023-0, Pub. by Anvil Pr Poetry). Longwood Pub Group.
Turns & Movies & Other Tales in Verse. Conrad Aiken. 1978. Repr. of 1916 ed. lib. bdg. 35.00 (ISBN 0-8495-0054-0). Arden Lib.
Turns & Movies & Other Tales in Verse. Conrad Aiken. LC 73-18103. Repr. of 1916 ed. lib. bdg. 35.00 (ISBN 0-8414-2947-2). Folcroft.
Turnstile Maintainer. Jack Rudman. (Career Examination Ser.: C-825). (Cloth bdg. avail. on request). pap. 12.00 (ISBN 0-8373-0825-9). Natl Learning.
Turolian Fauna from the Island of Samos, Greece. N. Solounias. (Contributions to Vertebrate Evolution Ser.: Vol. 6). (Illus.). xvi, 232p. 1981. pap. 32.75 (ISBN 3-8055-2692-X). S Karger.
Turpentine. Jack Weiner & Vera Pollock. LC 74-77350. (Bibliographic Ser.: No. 260). 1974. pap. 15.00 (ISBN 0-87010-020-3). Inst Paper Chem.
Turpin Francais, dit le Turpin I: Edition Critique. Ed. by Ronald N. Walpole. (Toronto Medieval Texts & Translations Ser.: No. 3). 276p. (Fr.). 1985. 40.00x (ISBN 0-8020-2536-6). U of Toronto Pr.
Turquie en 1962 see Cahiers de l'Institut de Science Economique Appliquee.
Turquois: A Study in the History, Minerology, Geology, Ethnology, Archaeology, Mythology, Folklore & Technology. Joseph E. Pogue. LC 70-175059. (Beautiful Rio Grande Classics Ser.). 300p. 1983. Repr. of 1914 ed. lib. bdg. 25.00 (ISBN 0-686-89218-6). Rio Grande.
Turquoise. Naomi Cocanower. (Illus.). 64p. 24.00 (ISBN 0-88014-010-0). Mosaic Pr OH.
Turquoise. S. A. Northrop et al. (Illus.). 1973. pap. 2.25 (ISBN 0-89013-060-4). Museum NM Pr.
Turquoise. Richard M. Pearl. 1976. pap. 1.35 (ISBN 0-940566-08-7). R M Pearl Bks.
Turquoise & Six-Guns: The Story of Cerrillos, New Mexico. 3rd ed. Marc Simmons. LC 85-30350. (Illus.). 64p. 1988. pap. 6.95 (ISBN 0-86534-082-X). Sunstone Pr.
Turquoise Dragon. David R. Wallace. LC 84-5471. 256p. 1985. 12.95 (ISBN 0-87156-819-5). Sierra.
Turquoise Dragon. David R. Wallace. LC 84-5471. 230p. 1987. pap. 6.95 (ISBN 0-87156-710-5). Sierra.
Turquoise Jewelry of the Indians of the Southwest. Edna M. Bennett & John F. Bennett. (Illus.). 1973. 15.00 (ISBN 0-917834-01-1). Turquoise Bks.
Turquoise Lament. John D. Macdonald. LC 73-14806. 1973. 14.50i (ISBN 0-397-00987-9). Har-Row.
Turquoise Mask. Phyllis A. Whitney. 1981. pap. 3.50 (ISBN 0-449-23470-3, Crest). Fawcett.
Turquoise: The Gem of the Centuries. O. T. Branson. (Illus.). 1975. pap. 9.95 (ISBN 0-918080-01-0). Treasure Chest.
Turquoise Toad Mystery. Georgess McHargue. LC 81-69664. 160p. (gr. 4-6). 1982. 9.95 (ISBN 0-385-29057-8). Delacorte.
Turquoise Trail. Shirley Seifert. 1976. Repr. of 1950 ed. lib. bdg. 22.95 (ISBN 0-89190-140-X, Pub. by River City Pr). Amereon Ltd.
Turret. Margery Sharp. 144p. (gr. 3 up). 1974. pap. 2.75 (ISBN 0-440-48630-0, YB). Dell.
Turret Room. Charlotte Armstrong. Repr. lib. bdg. 13.95x (ISBN 0-88411-566-6, Pub. by Aeonian Pr). Amereon Ltd.
Turritella Zonation Across the Cretaceous-Tertiary Boundary, California. Lou E. Saul. LC 83-1317. (UC Publications in Geological Sciences: Vol. 125). 176p. 1983. pap. text ed. 15.95x (ISBN 0-520-09679-7). U of Cal Pr.
Turtle. Hidetomo Oda. Ed. by Kathy Pohl. LC 85-28234. (Nature Close-Ups Ser.). (Illus.). 32p. (gr. 4). 1986. PLB 15.33 (ISBN 0-8172-2547-1); pap. text ed. 9.27 (ISBN 0-8172-2572-2). Raintree Pubs.
Turtle see Ten Top Stories.
Turtle & Rabbit. Valjean McLenighan. (Beginning-to-Read Ser.). (Illus.). 32p. (gr. 2). 1980. PLB 4.39 (ISBN 0-8136-5086-0, Dist. by Caroline Hse); pap. 1.95 (ISBN 0-8136-5586-2). Modern Curr.
Turtle & Snail. Zibby Oneal. LC 78-14826. (Lippincott I-Like-to-Read Bks.). (Illus.). (gr. k-2). 1979. 11.25i (ISBN 0-397-31829-4, Lipp Jr Bks). HarpJ.
Turtle & the Monkey. Paul Galdone. (Illus.). 32p. (ps-3). 1982. 13.95 (ISBN 0-89919-145-2, Clarion). HM.
Turtle & Tortoise. Vincent Serventy. LC 84-15881. (Animals in the Wild Ser.). (Illus.). 24p. (gr. k-3). 1985. PLB 10.65 (ISBN 0-8172-2403-3). Raintree Pubs.
Turtle & Tortoise. Vincent Serventy. (Animals in the Wild Ser.). (Illus.). 24p. (gr. 1-4). 1987. pap. 1.95 (ISBN 0-590-40228-5). Scholastic Inc.
Turtle Beach. Blanche D'Alpuget. 288p. 1983. 14.50 (ISBN 0-671-49241-1). S&S.
Turtle Dance: Poems of Hawaii. Aelbert C. Aehegma. Ed. by Ray Freed. (Illus.). 72p. 1984. pap. 7.95 (ISBN 0-916467-00-7, 101A). Oceanic Pub Co.
Turtle Diary. Russell Hoban. 1982. pap. 1.95 (ISBN 0-380-39081-7, 39081, Bard). Avon.
Turtle Diary. Russell Hoban. 1986. pap. 3.95 (ISBN 0-671-61833-4). PB.
Turtle Diary. Russell Hoban. pap. 3.95 (ISBN 0-317-56821-3). WSP.
Turtle Geometry: The Computer As a Medium for Exploring Mathematics. Harold Abelson & Andrea DiSessa. (Artificial Intelligence Ser.). (Illus.). 477p. 1981. text ed. 30.00x (ISBN 0-262-01063-1). MIT Pr.
Turtle Geometry: The Computer As a Medium for Exploring Mathematics. Harold Abelson & Andrea DiSessa. 504p. 1986. pap. text ed. 14.95x (ISBN 0-262-51037-5). MIT Pr.
Turtle Island. Gary Snyder. LC 74-8542. (Illus.). 128p. 1974. pap. 4.95 (ISBN 0-8112-0546-0, NDP381). New Directions.
Turtle Lady. Patsy R. McCleery. Ed. by Meg Tynan & John Forsyth. 32p. (Orig.). (gr. 1 up). 1988. pap. 6.95 (ISBN 0-915101-03-3). Texas Geograph.
Turtle Lore. (Illus.). pap. 1.50 (ISBN 0-685-57147-5). E A Seemann.
Turtle Mazes: Educational Activity-Coloring Book. Peter M. Spizzirri. Ed. by Linda Spizzirri. (Illus.). 32p. (gr. k-5). 1984. pap. 0.99 (ISBN 0-86545-059-5). Spizzirri.
Turtle on Her Toe. Edna L. Glines. LC 83-17870. (Illus.). 66p. (ps up). 1984. 9.95 (ISBN 0-9612160-0-X). Tumbleweed Pub Co.
Turtle Street Trading Co. Jill R. Klevin. LC 82-70312. (Illus.). 144p. (gr. 4-6). 1982. 11.95 (ISBN 0-385-29043-8); PLB 11.95. Delacorte.
Turtle, Swan. Mark Doty. LC 87-371. 80p. 1987. 14.95 (ISBN 0-87923-697-3); pap. 9.95 (ISBN 0-87923-698-1). Godine.
Turtle Tail & Other Tender Mercies: Traditional Chinese Pediatrics. Robert S. Flaws. (Illus.). 172p. (Orig.). 1985. pap. 14.95 (ISBN 0-936185-00-7). Blue Poppy.
Turtle Talk: A Beginner's Book of Logo. Seymour Simon. LC 85-47890. (Let's-Read-&-Find-Out Science Bks.). (Illus.). 32p. (gr. 1-4). 1986. 12.70 (ISBN 0-690-04521-2, Crowell Jr Bks); PLB 12.89 (ISBN 0-690-04522-0). HarpJ.
Turtle Talk: A Beginner's Book of Logo. Seymour Simon. LC 85-47890. (Trophy Let's-Read-&-Find-Out Bks.). (Illus.). 32p. (gr. 1-4). 1986. pap. 4.95 (ISBN 0-06-445051-1, Trophy). HarpJ.
Turtle Time. Jeanne Betancourt. 112p. 1985. pap. 2.50 (ISBN 0-380-89675-3, Camelot). Avon.
Turtle Watch. George Ancona. LC 87-9316. (Illus.). 48p. (gr. 1-5). 1987. PLB 13.95 (ISBN 0-02-700910-6). Macmillan.
Turtle Who Wanted to Run. J. Grey. LC 68-56813. (Illus.). 32p. (gr. 1-3). 1968. PLB 9.95 (ISBN 0-87783-045-2). Oddo.
Turtles. Janet Craig. LC 81-11448. (Now I Know Ser.). (Illus.). 32p. (gr. k-2). 1982. PLB 9.89 (ISBN 0-89375-664-4). Troll Assocs.
Turtles. John M. Mehrtens. (Illus.). 80p. 1984. pap. text ed. 5.95 (ISBN 0-86622-235-9, PB-129). TFH Pubns.
Turtles. Mervin F. Roberts. (Illus.). 96p. 1980. 9.95 (ISBN 0-87666-928-3, KW-051). TFH Pubns.
Turtles. H. Wilkie. (Pet Care Ser.). 1983. pap. 3.95 (ISBN 0-8120-2631-4). Barron.
Turtles. Ed. by Wildlife Education, Ltd. Staff. (Illus.). 20p. (Orig.). 1985. pap. 1.95 (ISBN 0-937934-41-0). Wildlife Educ.
Turtles All the Way Down. John Grinder & Judith DeLozier. LC 87-80282. 392p. 1987. 24.95x (ISBN 0-929514-01-7). Grinder DeLozier.
Turtles & Tortoises of the World. David Alderton. (Of the World Ser.). (Illus.). 192p. 1988. 22.95x (ISBN 0-8160-1733-6). Facts on File.
Turtle's Darshan for All the Animals. Bob Brown. (Illus.). 32p. (gr. 2 up). 1973. pap. 2.00 (ISBN 0-913078-17-4). Sheriar Pr.
Turtles for Home & Garden. Willy Jocher. (Illus.). 1973. 6.95 (ISBN 0-87666-777-9, PS-307). TFH Pubns.
Turtles in Kansas. Janalee P. Caldwell & Joseph T. Collins. LC 81-66138. Date not set. pap. text ed. 5.25. AMS Kansas.
Turtles of the United States. Carl H. Ernst & Roger W. Barbour. LC 72-81315. (Illus.). 384p. 1972. 45.00x (ISBN 0-8131-1272-9). U Pr of KY.
Turtles: Perspective & Research. Ed. by Marion Harless & Henry Morlock. 1979. Repr. of 1979 ed. lib. bdg. write for info. Krieger.
Turtles: Perspectives & Research. Marion Harless & Henry Morlock. LC 78-16177. 712p. 1988. Repr. of 1979 ed. 80.50x (ISBN 0-89464-319-3, Pub. by Wiley-Interscience). Krieger.
Turtle's Sourcebook. Jim Muller et al. 1983. 23.95 (ISBN 0-8359-7890-7, Reston). P-H.
Turtles Together Forever! Jill R. Klevin. LC 82-70313. (Illus.). 160p. (gr. 4-6). 1982. pap. 9.95 (ISBN 0-385-29045-4); pap. 9.89 (ISBN 0-385-29046-2). Delacorte.
Turtles, Tortoises & Terrapins. Fritz J. Obst. (Illus.). 208p. 1986. 19.95 (ISBN 0-312-82362-2). St Martin.
Turturado por Cristo. Richard Wurmbrand. 1986. pap. 2.95 (ISBN 0-88264-134-4). Living Sacrifice Bks.
Tus Cinco Sentidos. Ray Broekel. LC 84-7603. (Spanish - New True Bks. Ser.). 48p. (Span.). (gr. k-4). 1987. PLB 13.00 (ISBN 0-516-31932-9); pap. 3.95 (ISBN 0-516-51932-8). Childrens.
Tus Ojos y Yo. Uva A. Clavijo. (Coleccion Espejo de Paciencia Ser.). 14p. (Orig., Span.). 1985. pap. 4.50 (ISBN 0-89729-373-8). Ediciones.
Tuscaloosa: Portrait of An Alabama County, An Illustrated History. G. Ward Hubbs. LC 87-8307. 128p. 1987. 22.95 (ISBN 0-89781-202-6). Windsor Pubns Inc.
Tuscan Cookbook. Wilma Pezzini. LC 77-15809. 288p. 1982. pap. 6.95 (ISBN 0-689-70598-0, 279). Atheneum.
Tuscan in the Kitchen: Recipes & Tales from My Home. Pino Luongo et al. (Illus.). 1988. 22.95 (ISBN 0-517-56916-7, C N Potter Bks). Crown.
Tuscan Year. Elizabeth Romer. LC 84-45670. (Illus.). 192p. 1985. 12.95 (ISBN 0-689-11568-7). Atheneum.
Tuscans & Their Families: A Study of the Florentine Catasto to 1427. David Herlihy & Christiane Klapisch-Zuber. LC 84-40195. (Economic History Ser.). 416p. 1984. text ed. 37.50t (ISBN 0-300-03056-8). Yale U Pr.
Tuscany. Franco Cardini. LC 87-60282. (Illus.). 128p. (Orig.). 1988. pap. 13.95 (ISBN 0-935748-86-5). Scala Books.
Tuscany & the Low Countries: An Introduction to the Series & an Inventory of Four Florentine Libraries. Henk T. Van Veen & Andrew P. McCormick. 182p. (Orig.). 1985. pap. 28.00x (ISBN 88-7038-097-1, Pub. by Centro Di Italia). Benjamins North Am.
Tuscany Terror. (Executioner Ser.: No. 52). 192p. 1983. pap. 1.95 (ISBN 0-373-61052-1, Pub. by Worldwide). Harlequin Bks.
Tuscarora Language. Elton Green. 1969. 5.00 (ISBN 0-930230-27-2). Johnson NC.
Tuscarora Legacy of J. N. B. Hewitt: Materials for the Study of the Tuscarora Language & Culture. Blair A. Rudes & Dorothy Crouse. (Mercury Ser.). 670p. 1988. Set. pap. 39.95x (ISBN 0-660-10773-2, Pub. by CN Mus of Civilization Canada). U of Chicago Pr.
Tuscaroras, Vol. 1: Mythology, Medicine & Culture. F. Roy Johnson. (Illus.). 1968. 7.50 (ISBN 0-930230-28-0). Johnson NC.
Tuscaroras, Vol. 2: History, Tradition & Cultural Modificatications. F. Roy Johnson. (Illus.). 1968. 9.50 (ISBN 0-930230-29-9). Johnson NC.
Tusculan Disputations. Cicero. (Loeb Classical Library: No. 141). 1927. 13.95x (ISBN 0-674-99156-7). Harvard U Pr.
Tusculanarum Disputationum I-V. Cicero. 190p. (Lat.). 1985. 15.00 (ISBN 0-89005-462-2). Ares.
Tuskegee Airmen: The Story of the Negro in the U. S. Air Force. Charles E. Francis. (Illus.). 1988. 16.95 (ISBN 0-8283-1386-5). Branden Pub Co.
Tuskegee & Its People: Their Ideals & Achievements. facsimile ed. Ed. by Booker T. Washington. LC 74-161276. (Black Heritage Library Collection). Repr. of 1905 ed. 20.75 (ISBN 0-8369-8835-3). Ayer Co Pubs.
Tuskegee & the Black Belt. Anne K. Walker. 1945. 3.00 (ISBN 0-685-09016-7). Dietz.
Tuskegee: Its Story & Its Work. facsimile ed. Max B. Thrasher. LC 77-161274. (Black Heritage Library Collection). Repr. of 1900 ed. 19.25 (ISBN 0-8369-8833-7). Ayer Co Pubs.
Tussie-Mussies & More. Paulette S. Jarvey. (Illus.). 28p. 1985. pap. 4.50 (ISBN 0-9605904-9-8). Hot Off Pr.
Tut-Ankh-Amun-& His Friends. Cyril Aldred. (gr. 8). pap. 2.95 (ISBN 0-88388-043-1). Bellerophon Bk.
Tutankhamen. Christiane Desroches-Noblecourt. LC 63-15145. (Illus.). 312p. 1976. pap. 16.45 (ISBN 0-8212-0695-8, 857017). NYGS.
Tutankhamen: Amenism, Atenism & Egyptain Monotheism. E. Wallis Budge. LC 79-160615. (Illus.). Repr. of 1923 ed. 12.75 (ISBN 0-405-08323-8, Blom Pubns). Ayer Co Pubs.
Tutankhamen & Other Essays. Arthur Weigall. LC 73-115210. 1971. Repr. of 1924 ed. 24.50x (ISBN 0-8046-1103-3, Pub by Kennikat). Assoc Faculty Pr.
Tutankhamen: The Untold Story. Thomas Hoving. 384p. 1984. pap. 12.95 (ISBN 0-671-24370-5, Touchstone Bks). S&S.
Tutankhamon. Edward L. Jones. 1978. pap. 14.00 (ISBN 0-9602458-2-0). Ed Lynne Jones.
Tutankhamon: A Novel of Ancient Egypt. Paul Startzman. 1979. 9.00 (ISBN 0-682-49218-3, Banner). Exposition-Phoenix.
Tutankhamun's Painted Box. Nina M. Davies. 22p. 1962. pap. 48.00x (ISBN 0-900416-22-X, Pub. by Aris & Phillips UK). Humanities.
Tutelary Pluralism: A Critical Approach to Venezuelan Democracy. Luis J. Oropeza. (Harvard Studies in International Affairs: No. 46). 144p. 1984. lib. bdg. 18.75 (ISBN 0-8191-4052-X); pap. text ed. 10.00 (ISBN 0-8191-4120-8). U Pr of Amer.
Tutelary Tales. Villy Sorensen. Tr. by Paula Hostrup-Jessen. 1988. 21.00 (ISBN 0-8032-4185-2). U of Nebr Pr.
Tutelle: Etudes De Droit Prive Normand, Vol. 3. Robert Genestal. LC 80-2027. Repr. of 1930 ed. 29.00 (ISBN 0-404-18564-9). AMS Pr.
Tutelo Rituals on Six Nations Reserve, Ontario. Gertrude Kurath. 184p. 10.00 (ISBN 0-318-16571-6). Soc Ethnomusicology.
Tutor. Bertolt Brecht. Tr. by Pip Broughton from Ger. (Old Vic Theatre Collection). 86p. (Orig.). 1988. pap. 7.95 (ISBN 1-55783-022-3). Applause Theatre Bk Pubs.
TUTOR. 6th ed. Ruth J. Colvin & Jane Root. Ed. by V. K. Lawson. 103p. 1987. pap. 9.50. Lit Vol Am.
Tutor! A Handbook for Tutorial Programs. Lillie Pope. 144p. 1976. pap. text ed. 6.95 (ISBN 0-87594-139-7). Book-Lab.
Tutor & the Soldiers. J. M. Lenz. Ed. by Kenneth Northcott. Tr. by William E. Yuill from Ger. LC 72-80812. (German Literary Classics in Translation Ser). 1973. pap. 1.95x (ISBN 0-226-47211-6, P469, Phoen). U of Chicago Pr.
Tutor Book. Marian Arkin & Barbara Shollar. LC 81-13697. (Illus.). 352p. (Orig.). 1982. pap. text ed. 17.95 (ISBN 0-582-28233-0); tutor supplements o.p. 4.95x (ISBN 0-686-32740-3). Longman.
Tutor Laughter: The Joy & Adventure in Remedial Tutoring. Treb Sona. 1980. pap. 4.50 (ISBN 0-930480-02-3). R H Barnes.
Tutor-Notetaker. Russel T. Osguthorpe. 98p. (Orig.). 1980. pap. text ed. 8.50 (ISBN 0-88200-131-0, N6680). Alexander Graham.
Tutor to Astronomy & Geography. 3rd rev., enl. ed. Joseph Moxon. LC 68-56778. (Research & Source Works Ser.: No. 264). (Illus.). 1968. Repr. of 1674 ed. 24.50 (ISBN 0-8337-2478-9). B Franklin.
Tutoraids. Sivasailam Thiagarajan. Ed. by Danny G. Langdon. LC 77-25137. (Instructional Design Library). (Illus.). 88p. 1978. 23.95 (ISBN 0-87778-124-9). Educ Tech Pubns.
Tutorial. C. E. Mandel, Sr. & Billy Livesay. LC 62-38584. 160p. (Orig.). 1987. pap. 40.00 (ISBN 0-915414-96-1). Inst Environ Sci.
Tutorial: Analysis of Particulate Contaminants: Microscopical Methods. 43p. pap. text ed. 25.00. Inst Environ Sci.
Tutorial & Study Guide to Accomany General Chemistry Prepared by Philip C. Keller & Jill L. Keller. Raymond Chang. write for info (ISBN 0-394-35536-9, RanC). Random.
Tutorial & User Experience. Ed. by Network Staff. 1982. 49.00x (ISBN 0-904999-17-3, Pub. by Network Events Ltd). State Mutual Bk.
Tutorial Automatic Testing. Ed. by Network Staff. 1985. 100.00x (ISBN 0-907634-28-1, Pub. by Network Events Ltd). State Mutual Bk.
Tutorial: De: Development of a Test-Verified Finite-Element Model. Richard C. Stroud & Robert Coppolino. LC 62-38584. 126p. (Orig.). 1987. pap. 35.00 (ISBN 0-915414-95-3). Inst Environ Sci.
Tutorial: Environmental Stress Screening & Defect Induced Failure Mechanisms Accelerated by Environmental Stress Screening. C. E. Mandel & Billy R. Livesay. LC 62-38584. 161p. (Orig.). 1988. pap. text ed. 50.00 (ISBN 0-915414-99-6). Inst Environ Sci.
Tutorial Essays in Psychology, Vol. 1. Ed. by Norman S. Sutherland. 182p. 1977. 29.95x (ISBN 0-89859-148-1). L Erlbaum Assocs.
Tutorial Essays in Psychology: A Guide to Recent Advances, Vol. 2. Ed. by N. S. Sutherland. 160p. 1979. 29.95x (ISBN 0-89859-199-6). L Erlbaum Assocs.
Tutorial for Using the TERAK-RT-11. Robert L. Smith. 136p. 1982. pap. text ed. 10.95 (ISBN 0-8403-2697-1). Kendall-Hunt.

TV Trivia Book. Michael Uslan & Bruce Solomon. 160p. 1979. o. p. 10.00 (ISBN 0-517-53780-X, Harmony Bks); pap. 4.95 (ISBN 0-517-53776-1). Crown.

TV Trivia II. Fred Miranda & Bill Ginch. 256p. (Orig.). 1985. pap. 3.50 (ISBN 0-345-32974-0). Ballantine.

TV Trivia Teasers. W. Wilson Casey. (Illus.). 260p. 1984. pap. 12.50 (ISBN 0-87650-164-1). Pierian.

TV Use & Social Interaction in Adolescence: A Longitudinal Study. Ulla Johnsson-Smaragdi. 239p. 1983. text ed. 29.95x (ISBN 91-22-00623-0, Pub. by Almqvist & Wiksell). Humanities.

T.V. Vet Book for Pig Farmers. 4th ed. Ed Straiton. (T.V. Vet Ser.). (Illus.). 160p. 1976. Repr. of 1967 ed. 21.95 (ISBN 0-85236-073-8, Pub. by Farming Pr UK). Diamond Farm Bk.

T.V. Vet Book for Stock Farmers: Calving the Cow & Care of the Calf, No. 2. Ed. Straiton. (T.V. Vet Ser.). (Illus.). 164p. 21.95 (ISBN 0-85236-011-8, Pub. by Farming Pr UK). Diamond Farm Bk.

T.V. Vet Book for Stock Farmers: Recognition & Treatment of Common Cattle Ailments. 4th ed. Eddie Straiton. (T. V. Ser.). (Illus.). 176p. 1976. 21.95 (ISBN 0-85236-072-X, Pub. by Farming Pr UK). Diamond Farm Bk.

T.V. Vet Dog: Recognition & Treatment of Common Dog Ailments & Treatment. 3rd ed. Ed Straiton. (T.V. Vet Ser.). (Illus.). 208p. 1980. 21.95 (ISBN 0-85236-105-X, Pub. by Farming Pr UK). Diamond Farm Bk.

T.V. Vet Horse Book: Recognition & Treatment of Common Horse & Pony Ailments. 6th ed. (T.V. Vet Ser.). 1979. 21.95 (ISBN 0-85236-095-9, Pub. by Farming Pr UK). Diamond Farm Bk.

T.V. Vet Sheep: Recognition & Treatment of Common Sheep Ailments. 3rd ed. (T.V. Vet Ser.). (Illus.). 178p. 1976. 21.95 (ISBN 0-85236-065-7, Pub. by Farming Pr UK). Diamond Farm Bk.

TV Violence & the Child: The Evolution & Fate of the Surgeon General's Report. Douglass Cater & Stephen P. Strickland. LC 74-83207. 168p. 1975. 15.00x (ISBN 0-87154-203-X). Russell Sage.

TVA & the Dispossessed: The Resettlement of Population in the Norris Dam Area. Michael J. McDonald & John Muldowny. LC 81-16333. (Illus.). 352p. 1982. 33.95x (ISBN 0-87049-345-0). U of Tenn Pr.

TVA & the Tellico Dam, 1936 - 1979: A Bureaucratic Crisis in Post-Industrial America. William B. Wheeler & Michael J. McDonald. LC 85-22224. (Illus.). 304p. 1986. text ed. 34.50x (ISBN 0-87049-492-9). U of Tenn Pr.

TVA: Bridge Over Troubled Waters. North Callahan. LC 79-21586. (Illus.). 420p. 1980. 17.95 (ISBN 0-8453-2490-X, Cornwall Bks). Assoc Univ Prs.

TVA: Fifty Years of Grass-Roots Bureaucracy. Ed. by Erwin C. Hargrove & Paul K. Conkin. LC 83-6475. 368p. 1983. 24.95 (ISBN 0-252-01086-8). U of Ill Pr.

TVEI & Secondary Education: A Critical Appraisal. Ed. by Denis Gleeson. 224p. 1987. 65.00 (ISBN 0-335-15539-1, Open Univ Pr); pap. 24.00 (ISBN 0-335-15538-3). Taylor & Francis.

Tverskoi Bul'Var. B. Kraevskii. 60p. 1982. 25.00 (ISBN 0-317-40704-X, Pub. by Collets UK). State Mutual Bk.

Tvorcheskie Raboty Uchenikov Tolstogo v Yasnoi Polyane. Intro. by Thomas G. Winner. LC 72-2453. (Brown University Slavic Reprint Ser.: No. 10). 148p. 1974. pap. 8.00x (ISBN 0-87057-135-4). U Pr of New Eng.

Tvorcheskii Put'F. V. Karzhavina. S. R. Dolgova. 152p. 1984. 39.00x (Pub. by Collets UK). State Mutual Bk.

Tvorchestvo I. S. Sokolova-Mikitova. V. G. Bazanov. 296p. 1986. 39.00x (ISBN 0-317-40824-0, Pub. by Collets (UK)). State Mutual Bk.

Tvortsi Netlinnoi Krasy. Wasyl Luciw. (Ukrainian.). 1972. pap. text ed. 10.00 (ISBN 0-918884-05-5). Slavia Lib.

TVR: Nineteen Sixty to Nineteen Eighty. R. M. Clarke. (Brooklands Bks). (Illus.). 100p. 1982. 13.95 (ISBN 0-907073-20-4, Pub. by Brooklands Bks England). Motorbooks Intl.

TVR's: Collectors Guide. 2nd ed. Graham Robson. (Collector's Guide Ser.). (Illus.). 128p. 1987. 29.95 (ISBN 0-947981-17-9, Pub. by Motor Racing England). Motorbooks Intl.

Twachtman in Gloucester: His Last Years, 1900-1902. Richard Boyle et al. Ed. by Lisa Peters. (Illus.). 64p. (Orig.). 1987. pap. 12.95 (ISBN 0-87663-526-5). Universe.

Twain Shall Meet: The Current Study of English in China. Donald J. Ford. LC 88-42521. 208p. 1988. lib. bdg. 24.95 (ISBN 0-89950-348-9). McFarland & Co.

Twain: Wit & Wisecracks. Mark Twain. 1961. 5.95 (ISBN 0-88088-546-7). Peter Pauper.

Twain's Heroes, Twain's Worlds. Andrew J. Hoffman. 192p. 1988. 23.95 (ISBN 0-8122-8139-X). U of Pa Pr.

Twana Twined Basketry. D. L. Nordquist & G. E. Nordquist. (Illus.). 100p. (Orig.). 1983. pap. 19.95 (ISBN 0-916552-27-6). Acoma Bks.

Twas Seeding Time. John L. Ruth. LC 76-41475. 220p. 1976. pap. 7.95 (ISBN 0-8361-1800-6). Herald Pr.

Twas the Night Before Christmas. Clement C. Moore. LC 85-61305. (Illus.). 24p. (ps up). 1985. 5.95 (ISBN 0-88088-548-3, 885483). Peter Pauper.

Twas the Night Before Christmas: A Visit from St. Nicholas. Clement C. Moore. (Illus.). (ps-2). 1912. 12.95 (ISBN 0-395-06952-1). HM.

Tweed Ring. Alexander B. Callow. LC 81-6528. (Illus.). xi, 351p. 1981. Repr. of 1966 ed. lib. bdg. 35.00x (ISBN 0-313-22761-6, CATR). Greenwood.

Tweedle-De-Dee Tumbleweed. Bob Reese. LC 81-6155. (Critterland Desert Adventures Ser.). (Illus.). 24p. (ps-2). 1981. PLB 9.27 (ISBN 0-516-02307-1); pap. 1.95 (ISBN 0-516-42307-X). Childrens.

Tweedles & Foodles for Young Noodles. Malvina Reynolds. LC 73-80670. (Illus.). 42p. (gr. k-4). 1961. pap. 3.00 (ISBN 0-915620-00-6). Schroder Music.

Tweedlioop. Steven Barnes. 240p. 1988. pap. 3.95 (ISBN 0-8125-3155-8, Dist. by St Martin's Pr & Warner Pub Servs). Tor Bks.

Tweedlioop. Stanley Schmidt. 1986. pap. 8.95. Tor Bks.

Tweeds. Clayton R. Graham. LC 86-27645. 257p. (Orig.). 1987. pap. 8.95 (ISBN 0-915175-20-7). Knights Pr.

Tweeg & the Bounders. Ken Forsse. (Teddy Ruxpin Adventure Ser.). (Illus.). 26p. (ps). 1985. incl. audio-cassette 9.95 (ISBN 0-934323-10-0). Alchemy Comms.

Tweeg Gets the Tweezles. Ken Forsse & Michelle Baron. (Teddy Ruxpin Adventure Ser.). (Illus.). 34p. (ps). 1987. incl. cassettes 9.95 (ISBN 0-934323-41-0). Alchemy Comms.

Tweens at Deep Lake: An Original American Fantasy. Douglas A. Ploss. LC 79-90996. (Illus.). 88p. (gr. 3 up). 1979. PLB 13.50 (ISBN 0-9603632-0-3); pap. 8.50 (ISBN 0-9603632-1-1). OPC.

Twelfth Annual Exhibition: National Academy of Western Art, 1984. Ed. by Sara Dobberteen. (Illus.). 100p. (Orig.). 1984. pap. 15.00 (ISBN 0-932154-14-X). Natl Cowboy Hall of Fame.

Twelfth Annual Review of Project Performance Results. Operations Evaluation Department Staff. 1987. 12.00 (ISBN 0-8213-0936-6, BK0936). World Bank.

Twelfth Armored Division Association History. Twelfth Armored Division Association Staff. LC 86-51588. 264p. 1987. 45.00 (ISBN 0-938021-09-5). Turner Pub KY.

Twelfth Assembling Annual. Ed. by Charles Dorta et al. (Illus.). 100p. (Orig.). 1986. pap. 10.00; pap. 25.00 art supplement. Assembling Pr.

Twelfth Census, 1900: Manufactures, Special Reports on Selected Industries see American Industry & Manufactures in the Nineteenth Century.

Twelfth Census, 1900: Manufactures, States & Territories see American Industry & Manufactures in the Nineteenth Century.

Twelfth Census, 1900: Manufactures, U. S. by Industries see American Industry & Manufactures in the Nineteenth Century.

Twelfth-Century Decretal Collections & Their Importance in English History. Charles Duggan. 220p. 1963. 75.00 (ISBN 0-485-13112-9, Pub. by Athlone Pr UK). Humanities.

Twelfth-Century Homilies in Ms. Bodley 343, Pt. I: Text. Ed. by A. O. Belfour. (EETS OS Ser.: Vol. 137). pap. 28.00 (ISBN 0-8115-3369-7). Kraus Repr.

Twelfth Century Renaissance. Christopher Brooke. (History of European Civilization Library). (Illus.). 216p. 1969. pap. text ed. 11.00 net (ISBN 0-15-592385-4, HC). HarBraceJ.

Twelfth-Century Renaissance. Charles L. Young. 12.00 (ISBN 0-8446-0973-0). Peter Smith.

Twelfth Century Renaissance. Ed. by Charles R. Young. LC 77-23066. (European Problems Studies Ser.). 122p. 1977. pap. text ed. 6.50 (ISBN 0-88275-590-0). Krieger.

Twelfth Century Studies. Josiah C. Russell. LC 77-83792. (Studies in the Middle Ages: No. 1). 34.50 (ISBN 0-404-16022-0). AMS Pr.

Twelfth Conference on Local Computer Networks: Proceedings. 208p. 1987. 56.00 (ISBN 0-8186-0803-X, EZ803). IEEE Comp Soc.

Twelfth Gun. Ronald Watson. 1979. pap. 1.50 (ISBN 0-8439-0643-X, Leisure Bks). Leisure NY.

Twelfth I. S. C. E. R. G. Symposium. (Documenta Ophthalmologica Proceedings Ser.: Vol. 10). 1974. lib. bdg. 74.00 (ISBN 90-6193-150-9, Pub. by Junk Pubs Netherlands). Kluwer Academic.

Twelfth Juror. B. M. Gill. 192p. 1985. pap. 2.95 (ISBN 0-345-32516-8). Ballantine.

Twelfth Man: A Story of Texas A & M Football. Wilbur Evans & H. B. McElroy. LC 74-81347. (College Sports Ser.). 1982. 10.95 (ISBN 0-87397-217-1). Strode.

Twelfth Mid-Atlantic Industrial Wastewater Conference. (Illus.). 1980. pap. 12.00 (ISBN 0-318-01366-5). Hazardous Mat Control.

Twelfth Night. Ed. by Elizabeth S. Donno. (New Cambridge Shakespeare Ser.). 200p. 1985. 29.95 (ISBN 0-521-22752-6); pap. 6.95 (ISBN 0-521-29633-1). Cambridge U Pr.

Twelfth Night. Ed. by Alan Durband. (Shakespeare Made Easy Ser.). 288p. 1985. pap. 4.95 (ISBN 0-8120-3604-2). Barron.

Twelfth Night. Ed. by Lois Potter. (Text & Performance Ser.). 80p. 1985. pap. text ed. 8.50x (ISBN 0-333-33995-9, Pub. by Macmillan UK). Humanities.

Twelfth Night. Ed. by A. L. Rowse. LC 84-15387. (Contemporary Shakespeare Ser.: Vol. II). 112p. (Orig.). 1985. pap. text ed. 3.45 (ISBN 0-8191-3912-2). U Pr of Amer.

Twelfth Night. William Shakespeare. (Airmont Shakespeare Ser.). (gr. 10 up). pap. 1.75 (ISBN 0-8049-1008-1, S8). Airmont.

Twelfth Night. William Shakespeare. Ed. by J. M. Lothian & T. W. Craik. (Arden Shakespeare Ser.). 1975. 37.00x (ISBN 0-416-17950-9, NO. 2496); pap. 7.95 (ISBN 0-416-17960-6, NO. 2497). Routledge Chapman & Hall.

Twelfth Night. William Shakespeare. pap. 2.75 (ISBN 0-451-52129-3, Sig Classics). NAL.

Twelfth Night. William Shakespeare. Ed. by Louis B. Wright & Virginia A. LaMar. (Folger Library). (Illus.). (gr. 12 up). 1960. pap. text ed. 2.95. PB.

Twelfth Night. William Shakespeare. Ed. by M. M. Mahood. 1981. pap. 3.75 (ISBN 0-14-070711-5). Penguin.

Twelfth Night. William Shakespeare. Ed. by Charles T. Prouty. (Shakespeare Ser.). 1958. pap. 2.95 (ISBN 0-14-071411-1, Pelican). Penguin.

Twelfth Night. William Shakespeare. Ed. by J. H. Walter. (Players' Shakespeare Ser). (YA) (gr. 9 up). 1959. 3.50 (ISBN 0-8238-0118-7). Plays.

Twelfth Night. William Shakespeare. (BBC TV Shakespeare Ser.). (Illus.). 96p. 1980. pap. 2.95 (ISBN 0-8317-8913-1, Mayflower Bks). Smith Pubs.

Twelfth Night. William Shakespeare. Ed. by Louis B. Wright & Virginia A. La Mar. (Folger Library Ser.). 256p. pap. 2.95 (ISBN 0-671-49947-5). WSP.

Twelfth Night. abr. ed. William Shakespeare. Adapted by Cecil Pickett. (Illus.). 36p. (YA) (gr. 7 up). 1984. pap. 1.50 (ISBN 0-88680-213-X). I E Clark.

Twelfth Night. William Shakespeare. (Book Notes Ser.). 1985. pap. 2.50 (ISBN 0-8120-3548-8). Barron.

Twelfth Night. William Shakespeare. (Classics Ser.). 160p. 1988. pap. 2.75 (ISBN 0-553-21308-3, Bantam Classics). Bantam.

Twelfth Night. William Shakespeare. 1988. text ed. 16.67 (ISBN 0-87720-823-9); pap. text ed. 11.67 (ISBN 0-87720-822-0). Amsco Sch.

Twelfth Night. William Shakespeare. Ed. by Roma Gill. (School Shakespeare Ser.). (Illus.). 136p. (ps-5). 1987. pap. 6.95 (ISBN 0-19-831947-9). Oxford U Pr.

Twelfth Night: An Annotated Bibliography. Ed. by William L. Godshalk. 1984. lib. bdg. 20.00 (ISBN 0-8240-9324-0). Garland Pub.

Twelfth Night: Complete Study Edition. William Shakespeare. Ed. by Sidney Lamb. (Illus., Orig.). pap. 3.95 (ISBN 0-8220-1444-0). Cliffs.

Twelfth Night: Critical Essays. Stanley Wells. LC 82-48288. 150p. 1985. 54.00 (ISBN 0-8240-9239-2). Garland Pub.

Twelfth Night Notes. Marilynn Harper. (Orig.). 1982. pap. 3.50 (ISBN 0-8220-0094-6). Cliffs.

Twelfth Night of Ramadan. Kendal J. Peel. 229p. 1984. 12.95 (ISBN 0-8149-0881-0). Vanguard.

Twelfth Night of Shakespeare's Audience. John W. Draper. 1972. lib. bdg. 21.50x (ISBN 0-374-92277-2, Octagon). Hippocrene Bks.

Twelfth Night, or What You Will: A Bibliography to Supplement the New Variorum Edition of 1901. Compiled by William C. McAvoy. LC 84-6546. (New Variorum Edition of Shakespeare Ser.). 57p. 1984. pap. 10.00x (ISBN 0-87352-285-0). Modern Lang.

Twelfth of April. Roy Doliner. 320p. 1985. 16.95 (ISBN 0-517-55735-5). Crown.

Twelfth of April. Roy Doliner. 1986. pap. 3.95 (ISBN 0-671-60456-2). PB.

Twelfth of June. Marilyn Gould. LC 85-45173. 192p. (gr. 4-7). 1986. 11.70i (ISBN 0-397-32130-9, Lipp Jr Bks); PLB 11.89 (ISBN 0-397-32131-7). HarpJ.

Twelfth Planet. Zecharia Sitchin. 448p. 1978. pap. 4.50 (ISBN 0-380-39362-X, 67751-1). Avon.

Twelfth Texas Symposium on Relativistic Astrophysics, Vol. 470. Ed. by Mario Livio & Giora Shaviv. 100.00 (ISBN 0-89766-335-7); 100.00 (ISBN 0-89766-336-5). NY Acad Sci.

Twelfth Transforming. Pauline Gedge. LC 84-47570. 544p. 1984. 16.45i (ISBN 0-06-015338-5, HarpT). Har-Row.

Twelfth Virginia Cavalry. Dennis E. Frye. (Illus.). 188p. 1988. 16.45 (ISBN 0-930919-52-1). H E Howard.

Twelfth Virginia Infantry. William D. Henderson. (Virginia Regimental Histories Ser.). (Illus.). 174p. 1985. 16.45 (ISBN 0-930919-12-2). H E Howard.

Twelve. Leslie Flynn. 156p. 1982. pap. 5.95 (ISBN 0-88207-310-9). Victor Bks.

Twelve. Carlos Franqui. Tr. by Albert Teicher. LC 68-10011. 1968. 4.50 (ISBN 0-8184-0089-7). Lyle Stuart.

Twelve. Elaine Kittredge. (Illus.). 84p. (Orig.). (gr. 4 up). 1983. pap. 6.95 (ISBN 0-9611266-1-2). Optext.

Twelve Against Empire: The Anti-Imperialist, 1898-1900. Robert L. Beisner. LC 84-24116. 310p. 1985. pap. 9.95x (ISBN 0-226-04171-9). U of Chicago Pr.

Twelve Against the Gods. William Bolitho. 356p. 1985. Repr. of 1929 ed. lib. bdg. 35.00 (ISBN 0-89987-999-3). Darby Bks.

Twelve American Plays. Ed. by Richard Corbin & Miriam Belf. LC 69-11437. 480p. 1969. pap. text ed. write for info. (ISBN 0-02-325180-8, Pub. by Scribner). Macmillan.

Twelve American Poets Before Nineteen Hundred. facs. ed. Rica Brenner. LC 68-22092. (Essay Index Reprint Ser). 1933. 18.00 (ISBN 0-8369-0250-5). Ayer Co Pubs.

Twelve American Women. Elizabeth Anticaglia. LC 74-23229. (Illus.). 272p. 1975. 23.95x (ISBN 0-88229-102-5); pap. 11.95x (ISBN 0-88229-758-9). Nelson-Hall.

Twelve Americans: Their Lives & Times. facsimile ed. Howard Carroll. LC 70-37154. (Essay Index Reprint Ser.). Repr. of 1883 ed. 30.00 (ISBN 0-8369-2489-4). Ayer Co Pubs.

Twelve & One-Half Keys. Edward Hays. Ed. by Thomas Turkle. LC 81-50505. (Illus.). 152p. (Orig.). 1981. pap. 6.95 (ISBN 0-939516-00-4). Forest Peace.

Twelve & Other Poems. Aleksandr Blok. Tr. by Anselm Hollo. 1971. pap. 4.00 (ISBN 0-917788-04-4). Gnomon Pr.

Twelve & the Scythians. Alexander Blok. Tr. by Jack Lindsay from Russ. (Illus., Orig.). 1985. pap. 4.50 (ISBN 0-904526-49-6, Journeyman Pr England). Riverrun NY.

Twelve Angry Men: A Screen Adaptation, Directed by Sidney Lumet. Reginald Rose. Ed. by George P. Garrett et al. LC 71-135273. (Film Scripts Ser.). 1988. pap. text ed. 18.95x (ISBN 0-89197-970-0). Irvington.

Twelve Apostles. William J. Coughlin. 1988. pap. 3.95 (ISBN 0-451-13604-7, Sig). NAL.

Twelve Bad Men. facs. ed. Sidney Dark. LC 68-54343. (Essay Index Reprint Ser). 1929. 20.00 (ISBN 0-8369-0361-7). Ayer Co Pubs.

Twelve Becoming, Biographies of Mennonite Disciples from the Sixteenth to the Twentieth Century. Cornelius J. Dyck. LC 73-75174. 1973. pap. 4.50 (ISBN 0-87303-865-7). Faith & Life.

Twelve Becoming: Leader's Guide for Juniors. new ed. Bertha F. Harder. (Illus.). 61p. 1973. pap. 2.00x (ISBN 0-87303-866-5). Faith & Life.

Twelve Bells for Santa. Crosby Bonsall. LC 76-58714. (Trophy I Can Read Bks.). (Illus.). 64p. (ps-3). 1985. pap. 3.50 (ISBN 0-06-444086-9, Trophy). HarpJ.

Twelve Bells for Santa. Crosby N. Bonsall. LC 76-58714. (Harper I Can Read Bks.). (Illus.). 64p. (ps-3). 1977. PLB 10.89 (ISBN 0-06-020582-2). HarpJ.

Twelve Below Zero. Anthony Bukoski. 1986. 7.00 (ISBN 0-89823-072-1). New Rivers Pr.

Twelve Best Short Stories in the English Language. Adam L. Gowans. 1920. 30.00 (ISBN 0-932062-68-7). Sharon Hill.

Twelve Blessings. Ed. by George King. 63p. 1958. 9.25 (ISBN 0-937249-02-5). Aetherius Soc.

Twelve Caesars. Suetonius. Tr. by Robert Graves. (Classics Ser.). (Orig.). 1957. pap. 4.95 (ISBN 0-14-044072-0). Penguin.

Twelve Caesars: An Illustrated Edition. Suetonius. Tr. by Robert Graves. (Illus.). 320p. 1979. pap. 18.95 (ISBN 0-14-005416-2). Penguin.

Twelve Cats for Christmas. Martin Leman & Jill Leman. 1988. 9.95 (ISBN 0-7207-1403-6). Viking.

Twelve Centuries of Bookbindings: Four Hundred to Sixteen Hundred. Paul Needham. LC 79-52345. (Illus.). 368p. 1979. 75.00 (Co-pub by Oxford U Pr); pap. 39.95 (ISBN 0-686-68488-5). Pierpont Morgan.

Twelve Clever Brothers & Other Fools. Mirra Ginsburg. LC 79-2409. (Illus.). (gr. 3-6). 1979. (Lipp Jr Bks); PLB 11.89 (ISBN 0-397-31862-6). HarpJ.

Twelve Contemporary Russian Stories. Ed. & tr. by Vytas Dukas. LC 74-4969. 130p. 1977. 16.50 (ISBN 0-8386-1491-4). Fairleigh Dickinson.

Twelve Crimes of Christmas. Ed. by Carol-Lynn R. Waugh et al. 256p. (Orig.). 1981. pap. 2.95 (ISBN 0-380-78931-0). Avon.

Twelve Dancing Princesses. I. E. Clark. 40p. 1969. pap. 2.25 (ISBN 0-88680-197-4); royalty 35.25 (ISBN 0-317-03614-9). I E Clark.

Twelve Dancing Princesses. I. E. Clark. (Illus.). 53p. (Director's Production Script Ser.). 1969. pap. 10.00 (ISBN 0-88680-198-2). I E Clark.

Twelve Dancing Princesses. Jacob Grimm & Wilhelm K. Grimm. LC 78-18077. (Illus.). 32p. (gr. k-4). 1979. PLB 9.79 (ISBN 0-89375-139-1); pap. 1.95 (ISBN 0-89375-117-0). Troll Assocs.

Twelve Dancing Princesses. Errol LeCain. 32p. (ps-k). 1981. pap. 3.95 (ISBN 0-14-050322-6, Puffin). Penguin.

Twelve Dancing Princesses. Retold by Freya Littledale. (Illus.). 32p. (gr. 1-4). 1988. pap. 2.50 (ISBN 0-590-41185-3). Scholastic Inc.

Twelve Dancing Princesses. Marianna Mayer. (Illus.). (ps-5). 1988. 12.95 (ISBN 0-688-02024-0); PLB 12.88 (ISBN 0-688-02026-7). Morrow.

Twelve Dancing Princesses & Other Fairy Tales. Alfred David & Mary E. Meek. LC 73-16517. (Midland Bks.: No. 173). (Illus.). 320p. (gr. 1-6). 1974. 20.00x (ISBN 0-253-36100-1); pap. 8.95x (ISBN 0-253-20173-X). Ind U Pr.

Twelve Dancing Princesses & Other Tales from Grimm. Ed. by Naomi Lewis. LC 85-6964. (Illus.). 100p. (ps up). 1986. 14.95 (ISBN 0-8037-0237-X, 01451-440). Dial Bks Young.

Twelve Daughters of Democracy. facs. ed. Eleanor M. Sickels. LC 68-55858. (Essay Index Reprint Ser). 1941. 16.00 (ISBN 0-8369-0879-1). Ayer Co Pubs.

Twelve Daughters of Zion. Raymond Ridgell. 1988. 14.95 (ISBN 0-533-07401-0). Vantage.

Twelve Days of Christmas. Illus. by Louise Brierley. LC 86-45290. (Illus.). 32p. (gr. 1-5). 1986. 12.95 (ISBN 0-8050-0035-6). H Holt & Co.

Twelve Days of Christmas. Parachute Press Staff. (Sing-A-Story Ser.). 24p. 1988. pap. 2.50 (ISBN 0-553-15638-1, Bantam Aud Pub). Bantam.

Twelve Days of Christmas. Illus. by Erika Schneider. LC 84-9489. (Illus.). 12p. (gr. 1 up). 1984. 4.95 (ISBN 0-907234-62-3). Picture Bk Studio.

Twelve Days of Christmas. Illus. by Christina L. Sterchele. (Cut & Paste Ser.). (Illus.). (ps-6). 1981. 3.50 (ISBN 0-913545-07-4). Moonlight FL.

Twelve Days of Christmas. Illus. by Susan E. Swan. LC 80-28097. (Illus.). 32p. (gr. k-4). 1981. PLB 9.79 (ISBN 0-89375-474-9); pap. text ed. 1.95 (ISBN 0-89375-475-7). Troll Assocs.

Twelve Days of Christmas. 12p. 1985. paper wrapped limited ed. 10.00 (ISBN 0-317-38833-9). Walrus Pr.

Twelve Days of Christmas. Illus. by Sophie Windham. (Illus.). 32p. (ps-1). 1986. pap. 13.95 (ISBN 0-399-21327-9, Putnam). Putnam Pub Group.

Twelve Days of Christmas Cookbook. Ruth Moorman & Lalla Williams. (Cookbook Ser.: No. 1). (Illus.). 80p. 1978. pap. 5.95 (ISBN 0-937552-00-3). Quail Ridge.

Twelve Days of Christmas: The Twelve Stages of a Soul (The Creation of a Universe) John D. Rea & Alayna Rea. 40p. (Orig.). 1987. pap. 4.95 (ISBN 0-938183-04-4). Two Trees Pub.

Twelve Days of Christmas: 14 Delightful Ornament Designs. Annette Bradshaw & Gwyn Franson. 48p. (Orig.). 1981. pap. 5.00 (ISBN 0-88290-151-6, 2803). Horizon Utah.

Twelve Days of Turkey. Christine Allen. (Illus.). 48p. 1983. pap. 2.95 (ISBN 0-89286-224-6). One Hund One Prods.

Twelve Deaths of Christmas. Marian Babson. 192p. 1987. pap. 3.25 (ISBN 0-440-19183-1). Dell.

Twelve Decisive Battles of the Mind: The Story of Propaganda During the Christian Era, with Abridged Versions of Texts That Have Shaped History. Gorham B. Munson. LC 72-167388. (Essay Index Reprint Ser.). Repr. of 1942 ed. 18.00 (ISBN 0-8369-2705-2). Ayer Co Pubs.

Twelve Descants. Ellen Sibrava. 36p. (Orig.). 1985. pap. 4.95 (ISBN 0-934553-00-9). Wainwright.

Twelve Doors to the Soul. Jane Evans. LC 78-64907. (Illus., Orig.). 1979. pap. 5.75 (ISBN 0-8356-0521-3, Quest). Theos Pub Hse.

Twelve Dreams. James Lapine. LC 82-81974. 55p. 1982. pap. 3.95 (ISBN 0-933826-33-8). PAJ Pubns.

Twelve Dynamic Bible Study Methods. Richard Warren. 252p. 1981. pap. 8.95 (ISBN 0-88207-815-1). Victor Bks.

Twelve English Authoresses. Ed. by Lucy B. Walford. LC 72-1314. (Essay Index Reprint Ser.). Repr. of 1893 ed. 16.00 (ISBN 0-8369-2871-7). Ayer Co Pubs.

Twelve Englishmen of Mystery. Earl Bargainnier. LC 83-72499. 1984. 22.95 (ISBN 0-87972-249-5); pap. 11.95 (ISBN 0-87972-250-9). Bowling Green Univ.

Twelve Entry Points to Legal Research: A User Friendly System. Berton E. Ballard. LC 86-26611. (Illus.). 375p. (Orig.). 1986. pap. 19.95 (ISBN 0-940199-00-9). B E Ballard.

Twelve Facsimiles of Old English Manuscripts. Walter W. Skeat. LC 77-94620. 1979. Repr. of 1892 ed. lib. bdg. 15.00 (ISBN 0-89341-191-4). Longwood Pub Group.

Twelve Famous Plays of the Restoration & Eighteenth Century, 3 vols. Repr. of 1933 ed. 150.00x (ISBN 0-403-03071-4). Somerset Pub.

Twelve for Twelve. Edward F. Cox. 64p. 1982. pap. 3.50 (ISBN 0-8341-0787-2). Beacon Hill.

Twelve Frights of Christmas. Ed. by Isaac Asimov et al. 272p. 1986. pap. 3.50 (ISBN 0-380-75098-8). Avon.

Twelve from the Sixties. Ed. by Richard Kostelanetz. 1978. pap. 10.00 (ISBN 0-932360-03-3). RK Edns.

Twelve Geometric Essays. H. S. Coxeter. 288p. 1968. text ed. 7.00x (ISBN 0-8093-0303-5). S Ill U Pr.

Twelve German Novellas. Ed. by Harry Steinhauer. Tr. by Harry Steinhauser from Ger. 648p. 1977. 32.00x (ISBN 0-520-03504-6); pap. 11.95x (ISBN 0-520-03002-8). U of Cal Pr.

Twelve Gifts for Santa Claus. Mauri Kunnas. (ps-2). 1988. PLB 10.95 (ISBN 0-517-56631-1). Crown.

Twelve Good Men & True: The Criminal Trial Jury in England, 1200-1800. Ed. by J. S. Cockburn & Thomas A. Green. (Illus.). 375p. 1988. text ed. 44.00 (ISBN 0-691-05511-4). Princeton U Pr.

Twelve Good Musicians: From John Bull to Henry Purcell. Frederick Bridge. LC 77-75210. 1977. Repr. of 1920 ed. lib. bdg. 17.50 (ISBN 0-89341-110-8). Longwood Pub Group.

Twelve Good Musicians: From John Bull to Henry Purcell. Frederick Bridge. 152p. 1984. pap. cancelled (ISBN 0-89341-527-8). Longwood Pub Group.

Twelve Great Modernists. facs. ed. Lawrence F. Abbott. LC 76-84292. (Essay Index Reprint Ser). 1927. 20.25 (ISBN 0-8369-1118-0). Ayer Co Pubs.

Twelve Great Western Philosophers. H. Ozmon. LC 68-16403. (Illus.). 48p. (gr. 4 up). 1967. PLB 9.95 (ISBN 0-87783-046-0); pap. 3.94 deluxe ed (ISBN 0-87783-115-7). Oddo.

Twelve Groups of Animals. Eugen Kolisko. pap. cancelled (ISBN 0-906492-06-8, Pub by Kolisko Archives). St George Bk Serv.

Twelve Harmonies. Rudolf Steiner. Tr. by Daisy Aldan. 1986. pap. 3.95 (ISBN 0-317-55959-1). Folder Edns.

Twelve Healers of the Zodiac. Peter Damian. (Illus.). 96p. 1986. pap. 5.95 (ISBN 0-87728-653-1). Weiser.

Twelve Houses. Howard Sasportas. pap. 14.95 (ISBN 0-85030-385-0, Pub. by Aquarian Pr England). Sterling.

Twelve Houses: An Introduction to the Houses in Astrological Interpretation. Howard Sasportas. 400p. 1988. Repr. lib. bdg. 29.95x (ISBN 0-8095-7059-9). Borgo Pr.

Twelve Hundred & Four-the Unholy Crusade. John Godfrey. (Illus.). 1980. 39.95x (ISBN 0-19-215834-1). Oxford U Pr.

Twelve-Hundred Bottles Priced: A Price Guide & Classification System (with Index, Vol. 1. rev. ed. John C. Tibbitts. LC 70-121084. (Illus.). 1970. spiral bdg. 5.00 (ISBN 0-911508-08-2). Little Glass.

Twelve Hundred Bottles Priced: A Price Guide & Classification System (with Index, Vol. 2. John C. Tibbitts & Don Smith. LC 70-121084. (Illus.). 184p. (Orig.). 1973. spiral bdg. 5.00 (ISBN 0-911508-09-0). Little Glass.

Twelve Hundred Fifty Health-Care Questions Women Ask. Joe S. McIlhaney, Jr. & Susan Nethery. 700p. 1985. text ed. 24.95 (ISBN 0-8010-6193-8). Baker Bk.

Twelve Hundred Notes, Quotes, & Anecdotes. Ed. by A. Naismith. 237p. 1987. pap. 12.95 (ISBN 0-310-55311-3, 190210P). Zondervan.

Twelve in Arcady. Agnes Reilly. 200p. 1986. 13.50 (ISBN 0-85640-351-2, Pub. by Blackstaff Pr); pap. 5.95 (ISBN 0-85640-338-5). Longwood Pub Group.

Twelve Iron Sandals: And other Czechoslovak Tales. Vit Horejs. LC 84-22272. (Illus.). 128p. (gr. 4-6). 1985. 11.95 (ISBN 0-13-934159-5). P-H.

Twelve Is Too Old. updated ed. Peggy Mann. 140p. (YA) (gr. 6-9). 1987. pap. 6.95 (ISBN 0-942493-00-1). Woodmere Press.

Twelve Jews. Hector Bolitho. 1934. Repr. 35.00 (ISBN 0-8274-3655-6). R West.

Twelve Jews. facs. ed. Ed. by Hector Bolitho. LC 67-23179. (Essay Index Reprint Ser). 1934. 20.00 (ISBN 0-8369-0223-8). Ayer Co Pubs.

Twelve Key Strategies to Improve Cash Flow in Medical Groups. David H. Zimmerman. 127p. 1985. 25.00 (ISBN 0-933948-91-3). Ctr Res Ambulatory.

Twelve Keys to an Effective Church. Kennon L. Callahan. LC 83-47718. 1983. pap. 14.45 (ISBN 0-06-061297-5, HarpR). Har-Row.

Twelve Keys to an Effective Church: Leader's Guide. Kennon Callahan. 1987. 11.45 (ISBN 0-06-061295-9, HarpR). Har-Row.

Twelve Keys to an Effective Church: The Planning Workbook. Kennon Callahan. 1988. pap. 4.95 (ISBN 0-06-061294-0, HarpR). Har-Row.

Twelve Labors of Hercules. Corinne Heline. (In the Zodiacal School of Life Ser.). pap. 2.50 (ISBN 0-87613-029-5). New Age.

Twelve Lays of the Gypsy. Kostis Palamas. 146p. 1971. deluxe ed. 22.00 (ISBN 0-8464-0939-9). Beekman Pubs.

Twelve Lead EKG. rev. ed. Carolyn G. Smith-Marker. 53p. 1984. pap. text ed. 7.00 (ISBN 0-932491-01-4); video 297.00 (ISBN 0-932491-14-6); audiocassette & workbk. set 17.50 (ISBN 0-932491-00-6); slide set cancelled 215.00 (ISBN 0-932491-27-8). Res Appl Inc.

Twelve Little Housemates. Karl Von Frisch. Tr. by A. T. Sugar. LC 78-40341. 1979. 21.00 (ISBN 0-08-021959-4); pap. 9.25 (ISBN 0-08-021958-6). Pergamon.

Twelve Mayors of Boston: 1900-1970. Ed. by Philip J. McNiff. (Illus.). 1970. 2.00 (ISBN 0-89073-033-4). Boston Public Lib.

Twelve Melodious Studies for Piano, Op. 63. L. Streabbog. Ed. by Hans T. Seifert. (Carl Fischer Music Library: No. 363). 1982. pap. 4.50 (ISBN 0-8258-0113-3, L363). Fischer Inc NY.

Twelve Men. Theodore Dreiser. LC 74-144985. 1971. Repr. of 1919 ed. 49.00x (ISBN 0-403-00914-6). Scholarly.

Twelve Men. Theodore Dreiser. 1988. Repr. of 1919 ed. lib. bdg. 49.00x. Am Biog Serv.

Twelve Men of Action in Graeco-Roman History. facs. ed. Arnold J. Toynbee. LC 69-17592. (Essay Index Reprint Ser). 1952. 14.00 (ISBN 0-8369-0095-2). Ayer Co Pubs.

Twelve Men Who Shook the World. Philip Knoche & Keith Knoche. 1983. pap. 1.99 (ISBN 0-317-28277-8). Pacific Pr Pub Assn.

Twelve Messages on Well-Known & Favorite Bible Texts see Tozer Pulpit.

Twelve-Metre Yacht: Its Evolution & Design 1906-1987. Chris Freer. (Illus.). 160p. 1986. 24.95 (ISBN 0-85177-398-2, Pub. by Nautical Bks England). Sheridan.

Twelve Miles from a Lemon. facsimile ed. Mary A. Dodge. LC 76-37512. (Essay Index Reprint Ser). Repr. of 1873 ed. 20.00 (ISBN 0-8369-2544-0). Ayer Co Pubs.

Twelve Million Black Voices. Text by Richard Wright. (Classic Reprint Ser.). 150p. 1988. pap. 15.95 (ISBN 0-938410-44-X); 27.00. Thunder's Mouth.

Twelve Million Black Voices: A Folk History of the Negro in the U. S. Richard Wright. LC 69-18562. (American Negro: His History & Literature Ser., No. 2). 1969. Repr. of 1941 ed. 17.00 (ISBN 0-405-01909-2). Ayer Co Pubs.

Twelve Minor Prophets. George L. Robinson. pap. 5.95 (ISBN 0-8010-7669-2). Baker Bk.

Twelve Minor Prophets. George L. Robinson. 203p. 1981. Repr. of 1926 ed. lib. bdg. 35.00 (ISBN 0-89984-434-0). Century Bookbindery.

Twelve Minutes over Fatima. John McMillin & Jim Glenn. 1986. 10.95 (ISBN 0-533-06492-9). Vantage.

Twelve Modern Apostles & Their Creeds. facs. ed. G. K. Chesterton et al. LC 68-16982. (Essay Index Reprint Ser). 1926. 17.00 (ISBN 0-8369-0955-0). Ayer Co Pubs.

Twelve Moons. Mary Oliver. LC 79-10428. 1979. pap. 8.95 (ISBN 0-316-65000-5). Little.

Twelve More Ladies. facs. ed. Sidney Dark. LC 70-86744. (Essay Index Reprint Ser). 1932. 18.00 (ISBN 0-8369-1177-6). Ayer Co Pubs.

Twelve Mormon Homes Visited in Succession on a Journey Through Utah to Arizona. Elizabeth W. Kane. 149p. 1974. 12.00 (ISBN 0-941214-40-0). Signature Bks.

Twelve Muscle Tones. L. C. Phillips. 104p. 1980. 16.95 (ISBN 0-912282-08-8). Pulse-Finger.

Twelve Nigerian Languages. Elizabeth Dunstan. LC 70-95611. 185p. (Orig.). 1969. pap. 14.50 (ISBN 0-8419-0031-0, Africana). Holmes & Meier.

Twelve O'Clock High! Beirne Lay, Jr. & Sy Bartlett. Ed. by James Gilbert. LC 79-7278. (Flight: Its First Seventy-Five Years Ser.). (Illus.). 1979. Repr. of 1948 ed. lib. bdg. 23.00x (ISBN 0-405-12187-3). Ayer Co Pubs.

Twelve on the River St. John. Charles Bennett. Date not set. text ed. price not set (ISBN 0-8130-0913-8). U Presses Fla.

Twelve One-Act Plays for Study & Production. S. Marion Tucker. 1975. Repr. of 1929 ed. 40.00 (ISBN 0-8274-4038-3). R West.

Twelve Original Essays on Great American Novels. Ed. by Charles Shapiro. LC 57-13316. (Waynebooks: No. 13). 304p. (Orig.). 1958. pap. text ed. 8.95x (ISBN 0-8143-1086-9). Wayne St U Pr.

Twelve Panegyrici Latini. Ed. by Roger A. Mynors. (Oxford Classical Texts Ser.). 1964. 29.50x (ISBN 0-19-814647-7). Oxford U Pr.

Twelve Papers in Algebra. Ed. by Lev J. Leifman. LC 82-24434. (Translations Series II: Vol. 119). 36.00 (ISBN 0-8218-3074-0). Am Math.

Twelve Papers in Logic & Algebra. M. I. Semenenko et al. Ed. by Ben Silver. LC 79-9994. (American Mathematical Society Translations Series 2: Vol. 113). 1979. 39.00 (ISBN 0-8218-3063-5, TRANS 2-113). Am Math.

Twelve Papers on Algebra, Algebraic Geometry & Topology. S. N. Cernikov et al. LC 51-5559. (Translations Ser.: No. 2, Vol. 84). 1969. 40.00 (ISBN 0-8218-1784-1, TRANS 2-84). Am Math.

Twelve Papers on Algebra & Real Functions. S. N. Cernikov et al. LC 51-5559. (Translations Ser.: No. 2, Vol. 17). 1961. 33.00 (ISBN 0-8218-1717-5, TRANS 2-17). Am Math.

Twelve Papers on Algebra, Number Theory & Topology. M. S. Calenko et al. LC 51-5559. (Translations Ser.: No. 2, Vol. 58). 1966. 38.00 (ISBN 0-8218-1758-2, TRANS 2-58). Am Math.

Twelve Papers on Analysis. (Translations Series Two: Vol. 115). 1980. 45.00 (ISBN 0-8218-3065-1). Am Math.

Twelve Papers on Analysis & Applied Mathematics. Ju. M. Berezanskii et al. LC 51-5559. (Translations Ser.: No. 2, Vol. 35). 1964. 33.00 (ISBN 0-8218-1735-3, TRANS 2-35). Am Math.

Twelve Papers on Analysis, Applied Mathematics & Algebraic Topology. E. A. Barbasin et al. LC 51-5559. (Translations Ser.: No. 2, Vol. 25). 1963. 30.00 (ISBN 0-8218-1725-6, TRANS 2-25). Am Math.

Twelve Papers on Approximations & Integrals. K. I. Babenko et al. LC 51-5559. (Translations Ser.: No. 2, Vol. 44). 1966. Repr. of 1965 ed. 27.00 (ISBN 0-8218-1744-2, TRANS 2-44). Am Math.

Twelve Papers on Function Theory, Probability, & Differential Equations. A. E. Andreev et al. LC 51-5559. (Translations Ser.: No. 2, Vol. 8). 1957. 47.00 (ISBN 0-8218-1708-6, TRANS 2-8). Am Math.

Twelve Papers on Functional Analysis & Geometry. V. T. Fomenko et al. LC 51-5559. (Translations Ser.: No. 2, Vol. 85). 1969. 38.00 (ISBN 0-8218-1785-X, TRANS 2-85). Am Math.

Twelve Papers on Logic & Algebra. N. I. Feldman et al. LC 51-5559. (Translations Ser.: No. 2, Vol. 59). 1966. 40.00 (ISBN 0-8218-1759-0, TRANS 2-59). Am Math.

Twelve Papers on Logic & Differential Equations. M. S. Gel'fand et al. LC 51-5559. (Translations Ser.: No. 2, Vol. 29). 1963. 33.00 (ISBN 0-8218-1729-9, TRANS 2-29). Am Math.

Twelve Papers on Number Theory & Function Theory. A. O. Gel'fond et al. LC 51-5559. (Translations Ser.: No. 2, Vol. 19). 1962. 30.00 (ISBN 0-8218-1719-1, TRANS 2-19). Am Math.

Twelve Papers on Real & Complex Function Theory. I. I. Eremin et al. LC 51-5559. (Translations Ser.: No. 2, Vol. 88). 1970. 41.00 (ISBN 0-8218-1788-4, TRANS 2-88). Am Math.

Twelve Papers on Topology, Algebra & Number Theory. V. A. Andrunakievic et al. LC 51-5559. (Translations Ser.: No. 2, Vol. 52). 1966. 40.00 (ISBN 0-8218-1752-3, TRANS 2-52). Am Math.

Twelve Pathways to Feeling Better about Yourself. Dov P. Elkins. LC 79-88299. 1980. pap. 7.50 (ISBN 0-918834-08-2). Growth Assoc.

Twelve Photographers of the American Social Landscape. Ed. by Thomas H. Garver. (Illus.). 1968. 15.00 (ISBN 0-8079-0128-8). October.

Twelve Photographic Portraits. John H. Griffin. LC 74-134755. (Keepsake Ser.: Vol. 4). (Illus.). 1973. 8.00 (ISBN 0-87775-036-X); pap. 3.00 (ISBN 0-87775-077-7). Unicorn Pr.

Twelve Photographs of Yellowstone. Ronald Koertge. 1976. pap. 2.50 (ISBN 0-88031-030-8). Invisible-Red Hill.

Twelve Pioneers of Science. Harry Sootin. LC 60-15074. (Illus.). 254p. (gr. 7-11). 1960. 13.95 (ISBN 0-8149-0410-6). Vanguard.

Twelve Poems: With Preludes & Postludes. Joseph Langland. 40p. (Orig.). 1988. pap. 5.00 (ISBN 0-938566-37-7); limited ed. 8.00. Adastra Pr.

Twelve Portraits of the French Revolution. facs. ed. Henri Beraud. Tr. by M. Boyd. LC 68-16909. (Essay Index Reprint Ser). 1928. 18.00 (ISBN 0-8369-0197-5). Ayer Co Pubs.

Twelve Powers of Man. rev. ed. Charles Fillmore. 1985. 5.95 (ISBN 0-87159-157-X). Unity School.

Twelve Principles of Efficiency. 5th ed. Harrington Emerson. LC 76-5897. (Management History Ser.: No. 32). 441p. Repr. of 1919 ed. 23.75 (ISBN 0-87960-042-X). Hive Pub.

Twelve Problems in Health Care Ethics. Thomas A. Shannon. LC 84-22654. (Studies in Health & Human Services: Vol. 2). 320p. 1985. lib. bdg. 49.95x (ISBN 0-88946-127-9). E Mellen.

Twelve: Profiles of the Twelve Apostles. Sue Wallace. (Illus.). 88p. 1988. pap. 2.50 (ISBN 0-8198-7338-1). Dghtrs St Paul.

Twelve Prophetic Voices. Mariano Di Gangi. 168p. 1985. pap. 6.50 (ISBN 0-89693-536-1). Victor Bks.

Twelve Prophets. A. Cohen. 368p. 1948. 12.95 (ISBN 0-900689-31-5). Soncino Pr.

Twelve Prophets. Ed. by K. Elliger. (Biblia Hebraica Stuttgartensia Ser.). x, 96p. 1970. pap. 3.00x (ISBN 3-438-05210-5, 61261, Pub. by German Bible Society). Am Bible.

Twelve Prophets, Vol. 1. Peter C. Craigie. LC 84-2372. (Daily Study Bible-Old Testament Ser.). 1984. 14.95 (ISBN 0-664-21810-5); pap. 7.95 (ISBN 0-664-24577-3). Westminster John Knox.

Twelve Prophets, Vol. 2. Peter C. Craigie. LC 84-2372. (Daily Study Bible-Old Testament). 260p. 1985. 15.95 (ISBN 0-664-21813-X); pap. 8.95 (ISBN 0-664-24582-X). Westminster John Knox.

Twelve Religions of the Bible. Rolland E. Wolfe. LC 82-20401. (Studies in the Bible & Early Christianity: Vol. 2). (Illus.). 440p. 1983. lib. bdg. 69.95x (ISBN 0-88946-600-9). E Mellen.

Twelve Romantic Scottish Ballads, with the Original Airs. Robert Chambers. LC 77-17101. 1977. Repr. of 1844 ed. lib. bdg. 27.00 (ISBN 0-8414-1824-1). Folcroft.

Twelve Royal Ladies. facsimile ed. Sidney Dark. LC 73-99689. (Essay Index Reprint Ser.). 1929. 24.50 (ISBN 0-8369-1459-7). Ayer Co Pubs.

Twelve Seasons. Joseph Krutch. LC 72-134106. (Essay Index Reprint Ser). 1949. 16.00 (ISBN 0-8369-1970-X). Ayer Co Pubs.

Twelve Seconds to the Moon. rev. ed. Rosamond Young & Catharine Fitzgerald. LC 78-71073. (Illus.). 208p. 1983. 13.95 (ISBN 0-9611634-0-2). US Air Force Mus.

Twelve Sermons in Peter's First Epistle see Tozer Pulpit.

Twelve Sermons on Holiness. C. H. Spurgeon. pap. 3.95 (ISBN 0-685-88395-7). Reiner.

Twelve Sermons on Spiritual Perfection see Tozer Pulpit.

Twelve Sermons Relating to the Life & Ministry of the Christian Church see Tozer Pulpit.

Twelve Ships a'Sailing: Thirty-Five Years of British Home-Water Cruising. Jim Andrews. (Illus.). 224p. 1986. 25.95 (ISBN 0-7153-8787-1). David & Charles.

Twelve Sons of Israel. Compiled by Norman L. Heap. 196p. 1988. 12.50 (ISBN 0-945905-04-1). Family Hstory Pubns.

Twelve-Spoked Wheel Flashing. Marge Piercy. LC 77-15020. 1978. pap. 6.95 (ISBN 0-394-73488-2). Knopf.

Twelve Steps. Hazelden Foundation Staff & Karen Elliot. 1987. pap. 6.95 (ISBN 0-06-255444-1, HarpR). Har-Row.
Twelve Steps - a Spiritual Journey: A Working Guide Based on Biblical Teachings. Friends in Recovery Staff. Ed. by Ronald S. Halvorson & Valerie B. Deilgat. 224p. (Orig.). 1988. wkbk. 14.95 (ISBN 0-941405-02-8). Recovery SD.
Twelve Steps - a Way Out: A Working Guide for Adult Children of Alcoholic & Other Dysfunctional Families. Friends in Recovery Staff. Ed. by Ronald S. Halvorson & Valerie B. Deilgat. 194p. (Orig.). wkbk. 14.95 (ISBN 0-941405-04-4). Recovery SD.
Twelve Steps & Twelve Traditions. LC 53-5454. 192p. 1953. 2.70 (ISBN 0-916856-01-1). AAWS.
Twelve Steps & Twelve Traditions. 192p. 1965. 2.90 (ISBN 0-916856-06-2). AAWS.
Twelve Steps for Adult Children: Of Alcoholic & Other Dysfunctional Families. Friends in Recovery Staff. Ed. by Ronald S. Halvorson & Valerie B. Deilgat. 93p. (Orig.). pap. 6.95 (ISBN 0-317-68951-7). Recovery SD.
Twelve Steps for Christian Living: Growth in a New Way of Living. Vernon J. Bittner. 140p. 1988. 11.95 (ISBN 0-933173-14-8). Prince Peace Pub.
Twelve Steps for Everyone. rev. ed. LC 77-78480. 148p. 1979. pap. 5.95 (ISBN 0-89638-136-6). CompCare.
Twelve Steps for Overeaters: An Interpretation of the Twelve Steps of Overeaters Anonymous. Elisabeth L. LC 87-46206. 144p. 1988. pap. 7.95 (ISBN 0-06-255478-6, PL-4274, HarpR). Har-Row.
Twelve Steps for Smokers. Jeanne E. 24p. (Orig.). 1984. pap. 1.15 (ISBN 0-89486-229-4). Hazelden.
Twelve Steps ot Holiness & Salvation. St. Alphonsus Liquori. LC 86-50419. Orig. Title: School of Christian Rejections. 246p. 1986. pap. 6.00 (ISBN 0-89555-298-1). TAN Bks Pubs.
Twelve Steps Revisited. Ronald L. Rogers et al. LC 88-9119. 96p. 1988. pap. 5.95 (ISBN 0-88089-028-2). Madrona Pubs.
Twelve Steps to a Pain-Free Back. Ray C. Mulry et al. (Illus.). 1983. pap. 2.95 (ISBN 0-451-82080-0, Sig). NAL.
Twelve Steps to Finding a Job under 30,000 Dollars in Four Weeks. Mike Marcon & Margot Worthington. (Illus.). 160p. 1984. pap. 9.95 (ISBN 0-13-933433-5, Busn). P-H.
Twelve Steps to Happiness. Joe Klaas. 78p. 4.95 (ISBN 0-89486-156-5). Hazelden.
Twelve Steps to Self-Parenting. Philip Oliver-Diaz & Patricia A O'Gorman. 1988. pap. 7.95 (ISBN 0-932194-96-6). Health Comm.
Twelve Stories. S. S. Blicher. Repr. of 1945 ed. 26.00 (ISBN 0-527-08950-8). Kraus Repr.
Twelve Stories & a Dream. facsimile ed. H. G. Wells. LC 72-152963. (Short Story Index Reprint Ser.). Repr. of 1905 ed. 18.00 (ISBN 0-8369-3878-X). Ayer Co Pubs.
Twelve String Quartets: Opus 55, 64 & 71 Complete. Joseph Haydn. 288p. 1980. pap. 8.95 (ISBN 0-486-23933-0). Dover.
Twelve Systems of Higher Education: Six Decisive Issues. Clark Kerr et al. 214p. (Orig.). 1978. pap. text ed. 8.00 (ISBN 0-89192-211-3, Pub. by ICED). Interbk Inc.
Twelve Tarot Games. Michael Dummett. (Illus.). 242p. 1980. 14.95 (ISBN 0-7156-1485-1); pap. 9.95 (ISBN 0-7156-1488-6). US Games Syst.
Twelve Ten from San Antone: Only the Swift. Kirk Hamilton. (Orig.). 1980. pap. 2.25 (ISBN 0-8439-0741-X, Leisure Bks). Leisure NY.
Twelve Tens. Victoria S. Morris. 1978. pap. 1.00 (ISBN 0-914318-08-X). V S Morris.
Twelve: The Lives of the Apostles After Calvary. C. Bernard Ruffin. LC 83-63168. 194p. (Orig.). 1984. pap. 7.95 (ISBN 0-87973-609-7, 609). Our Sunday Visitor.
Twelve Therapists: How They Live & Actualize Themselves. Arthur Burton. LC 72-83966. (Jossey-Bass Behavioral Science Ser.). pap. 85.50 (2027747). Bks Demand UMI.
Twelve Thousand Minibiografias. 2nd ed. Ed. by Maria E. Alvarez del Real. LC 81-72104. (Illus.). 800p. (Span.). pap. 6.00x (ISBN 0-944499-12-0). Editorial Amer.
Twelve Thousand Students & Their English Teachers: Tested Units in Teaching Literature, Language, Composition. Ed. by Commission on English Staff. LC 67-30437. 389p. 1968. pap. 8.50 spiral bdg. (ISBN 0-87447-097-8, 295725). College Bd.
Twelve Thousand Words: A Supplement to Webster's Third New International Dictionary. Ed. by Merriam Webster Editorial Staff. 240p. 1986. 10.95 (ISBN 0-87779-207-0). Merriam-Webster Inc.
Twelve Thrones. Jim Lewis. LC 83-91008. 85p. (Orig.). 1983. pap. 5.95 (ISBN 0-942482-06-9). Unity Church Denver.
Twelve Times Twelve: One Forty Four Sun-Ascendant Combinations. Joan McEvers. 304p. 1984. pap. 9.95 (ISBN 0-917086-61-9). A C S Pubns Inc.
Twelve Tissue Remedies of Schuessler. William Boericke & Willis Dewey. 9.95 (ISBN 0-89378-065-0, Pub. by Harjeet). Formur Intl.
Twelve to Sixteen: Early Adolescence. Ed. by Jerome Kagan et al. (Illus.). 1972. pap. text ed. 9.95x 1972 (ISBN 0-393-09621-1). Norton.
Twelve Traditions for All of Us. Joe Klaas. 61p. (Orig.). 1986. pap. 3.95 (ISBN 0-89486-357-6). Hazelden.
Twelve Traps in Today's Marriage. Brent A. Barlow. LC 86-13429. 1986. 9.95 (ISBN 0-87579-039-9). Deseret Bk.
Twelve Tribes: From Jacob Until Joseph see Torah Anthology: Mem Lo'ez.
Twelve, Twenty & Five: A Doctor's Year in Vietnam. John A. Parrish. 288p. (Orig.). 1986. pap. 3.50 (ISBN 0-553-26029-4). Bantam.
Twelve Types. Gilbert K. Chesterton. LC 75-30017. Repr. of 1906 ed. 18.00 (ISBN 0-404-14022-X). AMS Pr.
Twelve Virginia Counties Where the Western Migration Began. John H. Gwathmey. LC 79-66025. (Illus.). 469p. 1981. Repr. of 1937 ed. 20.00 (ISBN 0-8063-0861-3). Genealog Pub.
Twelve-Volt Bible. Miner Brotherton. (Illus.). 174p. 1985. 12.95 (ISBN 0-915160-81-1). Seven Seas.
Twelve-Volt Bible for Boats. Miner Brotherton. Date not set. pap. write for info. S&S.
Twelve Volt Doctor's Alternator Book. Edgar J. Beyn. (Illus.). 1983. 18.75 (ISBN 0-911551-10-7). SPA Creek.
Twelve Volt Doctor's Practical Handbook: For the Boat's Electric System. rev. ed. Edgar J. Beyn. (Illus.). 1983. 24.95 (ISBN 0-911551-07-7). SPA Creek.
Twelve Ways to Build a Vocabulary. Archibald Hart. (Orig.). 1964. pap. 3.50 (ISBN 0-06-463293-8, EH 293, B&N Bks). Har-Row.
Twelve Ways to Develop a Positive Attitude. Galloway. 1975. pap. 1.95 (ISBN 0-8423-7550-3). Tyndale.
Twelve Ways to Sell Your Old, Used & Rare Books. Ernest L. Sackett. 32p. (Orig.). 1980. pap. 2.95 (ISBN 0-89288-036-8). Maverick.
Twelve Who Followed: The Story of Jesus & His First Disciples. Harry N. Huxold. LC 86-30218. 128p. (Orig.). 1987. pap. 7.95 (ISBN 0-8066-2242-3, 10-6722). Augsburg.
Twelve Who Made It Big. Jason Marks. LC 81-68767. (Illus.). 112p. (Orig.). 1981. pap. write for info. (ISBN 0-9606858-0-4). Alumni Assn.
Twelve Who Ruled. Robert R. Palmer. 1941. 38.00x (ISBN 0-691-05119-4); pap. 8.95x (ISBN 0-691-00761-6). Princeton U Pr.
Twelve Wings of the Eagle: Spiritual Evolution Through the Ages of the Zodiac. Maria K. Simms. (Illus.). 304p. (Orig.). 1988. pap. 12.95 (ISBN 0-917086-95-3). A C S Pubns Inc.
Twelve Words of the Gypsy. Kostes Palamas. Tr. & intro. by Frederic Will. LC 64-17223. xxiv, 205p. 1964. 19.95x (ISBN 0-8032-0141-9). U of Nebr Pr.
Twelve World Teachers. Manly P. Hall. pap. 6.50 (ISBN 0-89314-816-4). Philos Res.
Twelve Year Sentence: Radical Views of Compulsory Schooling. Ed. by William F. Rickenbacker. LC 73-23107. 236p. 1974. 6.95 (ISBN 0-8126-9075-3). Open Court.
Twelve Years - First & Last. Jack Petersen. LC 87-81107. (Illus.). 100p. 1987. lib. bdg. 50.00 (ISBN 0-87208-203-2). Island Pr Pubs.
Twelve Years a Slave. Solomon Northup. Ed. by Sue Eakin & Joseph Logsdon. LC 68-13454. (Library of Southern Civilization: No. 1). (Illus.). xxxviii, 274p. 1968. pap. text ed. 9.95 (ISBN 0-8071-0150-8). La State U Pr.
Twelve Years: An American Boyhood in East Germany. Joel Agee. 324p. 1981. 14.95 (ISBN 0-374-27958-6); pap. 6.95 (ISBN 0-374-51715-0). FS&G.
Twelve Years in America Being Observations on the Country, the People, Institutions, & Religion. James Shaw. text ed. 25.50 (ISBN 0-8369-9234-2, 9088). Ayer Co Pubs.
Twelve Years in China: The People, the Rebels, & the Mandarins. John Scarth. LC 72-79838. (China Library). (Illus.). 1972. Repr. of 1860 ed. lib. bdg. 35.00 (ISBN 0-8420-1365-2). Scholarly Res Inc.
Twelve Years in the Saddle. John L. Sullivan. LC 67-6749. (Concordance Ser., No. 37). 1970. lib. bdg. 51.95x (ISBN 0-8383-1106-7). Haskell.
Twelve Years with Sri Aurobindo. Nirodbaran. 306p. 1973. pap. 5.00 (ISBN 0-89071-244-1). Aurobindo Assn.
Twelve Years with the Sufi Herb Doctors. Najib Siddiqui. 1983. 4.95 (ISBN 0-86304-014-4, Pub. by Octagon Pr England). Ins Study Human.
Twelvemonth & a Day. Christopher Rush. 196p. 1985. text ed. 20.00 (ISBN 0-08-032428-2, Pub. by Aberdeen Scotland). Pergamon.
Twelvemonth & a Day. Christopher Rush. 296p. 1986. pap. text ed. 8.25 (ISBN 0-08-032469-X, R145, R150, K150, P110, AUP). Pergamon.
Twende! A Practical Swahili Course. Joan E. Maw. (Illus.). 352p. 1986. 24.95x (ISBN 0-19-713605-2). Oxford U Pr.
Twenties America & the Meaning of Jazz. Kathy J. Ogren. (Illus.). 256p. 1989. 19.95 (ISBN 0-19-505153-X). Oxford U Pr.
Twenties: American Writing in the Postwar Decade. Frederick J. Hoffman. 1965. pap. text ed. 9.95 (ISBN 0-02-914780-8). Free Pr.
Twenties: An Anthology. Ed. by Carl Proffer & Ellendea Proffer. 480p. 1987. 37.50 (ISBN 0-88233-820-X); pap. 18.00 (ISBN 0-88233-821-8). Ardis Pubs.
Twenties: Fords, Flappers, & Fanatics. Ed. by George E. Mowry. (Orig.). 1962. pap. 5.95 (ISBN 0-13-934968-5, Spec). P-H.
Twenties: Fords, Flappers & Fanatics. Ed. by George E. Mowry. 19.25 (ISBN 0-8446-2624-4). Peter Smith.
Twenties: From Notebooks & Diaries of the Period. Edmund Wilson. Ed. & intro. by Leon Edel. LC 74-34339. 608p. 1975. 10.00 (ISBN 0-374-27963-2). FS&G.
Twenties in America. 2nd ed. Paul A. Carter. LC 74-26538. (American History Ser.). 1975. pap. 7.95x (ISBN 0-88295-717-1). Harlan Davidson.
Twenties in the Sixties. Richard Kostelanetz. LC 77-90708. 1978. pap. 10.00 (ISBN 0-685-81506-4, Wild & Woolley). Assembling Pr.
Twenties in the Sixties: Previously Uncollected Critical Essays. Ed. by Richard Kostelanetz. LC 78-20012. 1979. lib. bdg. 36.95 (ISBN 0-313-21205-8, KTW/). Greenwood.
Twenties: The Lawless Decade. Paul Sann. (Quality Paperbacks Ser.). (Illus.). 240p. 1984. pap. 12.95 (ISBN 0-306-80216-3). Da Capo.
Twentieth AAMI Annual Meeting - Proceedings: Transitions in Health Care Delivery. (Illus.). 110p. 1985. pap. text ed. 6.00 (ISBN 0-910275-48-3); pap. text ed. 5.00. Assn Adv Med Instrn.
Twentieth Anniversary Catalogue. Idemitsu Museum of Arts. 1986. 140.00x (ISBN 0-317-68520-1, Pub. by Han-Shan Tang Ltd). State Mutual Bk.
Twentieth Anniversary Exhibition of the Vogel Collection. Georgia Coopersmith. (Illus.). 94p. 1982. pap. 12.50 (ISBN 0-942746-03-1). SUNYP R Gibson.
Twentieth Anniversary Symposium -- PCMR: Maximizing the Quality of Life for Individuals with Mental Retardation & Other Developmental Disabilities. 194p. write for info. (ISBN 1-556720-08-4). US HHS.
Twentieth Annual Immigration & Naturalization Institute. (Litigation & Administrative Practice Ser.). 465p. 1987. 45.00 (H4-5029). PLI.
Twentieth Annual in Anaheim, 1986: Convention Program. 271p. 1986. 6.00 (ISBN 0-317-52208-6). Tchrs Eng Spkrs.
Twentieth Annual Plating & Metal Finishing Forum: Proceedings. 1984. 20.00 (ISBN 0-89883-701-4, P145). Soc Auto Engineers.
Twentieth Annual Workshop on Microprogramming (MICRO-20) Proceedings. 171p. 1987. 40.00 (ISBN 0-89791-250-0, EZ831). IEEE Comp Soc.
Twentieth Century. Trevor Cairns. LC 82-4251. (Cambridge Introduction to World History Course: Bk. 10). (Illus.). 144p. (YA) (gr. 7 up). 1984. pap. 7.95 (ISBN 0-521-28270-5). Cambridge U Pr.
Twentieth Century. Trevor Cairns. (Cambridge Introduction to History Ser.). (Illus.). 168p. (gr. 5 up). 1984. PLB 14.95 (ISBN 0-8225-0810-9). Lerner Pubns.
Twentieth Century. Rosemary Lambert. LC 80-40456. (Cambridge Introduction to the History of Art: No. 7). (Illus.). 90p. 1981. pap. 9.95 (ISBN 0-521-29622-6). Cambridge U Pr.
Twentieth Century see American Painting.
Twentieth Century: A Brief Global History. rev., 2nd ed. Richard Goff et al. 425p. 1986. pap. text ed. 12.00 net (ISBN 0-394-35464-8, KnopfC). Knopf.
Twentieth Century: A People's History. Howard Zinn. LC 83-48397. 336p. 1984. pap. 7.95 (ISBN 0-06-091103-4, CN 1103, PL). Har-Row.
Twentieth-Century Africa. Ed. by P. J. McEwan. (Readings in African History Ser). 1968. 32.50x (ISBN 0-19-215663-2). Oxford U Pr.
Twentieth Century Almanac. E. H. Ferrell. 1986. 64.75X (ISBN 0-245-54393-7, Pub. by Harrap Ltd England). State Mutual Bk.
Twentieth-Century America: Recent Interpretations. 2nd ed. Ed. by Barton J. Bernstein & Allen J. Matusow. 582p. (Orig.). 1972. pap. text ed. 13.00 (ISBN 0-15-592391-9, HC). HarBraceJ.
Twentieth-Century American City. Jon C. Teaford. LC 85-24214. (American Moment Ser.). 192p. 1986. text ed. 20.00x (ISBN 0-8018-3094-X); pap. text ed. 8.95x (ISBN 0-8018-3096-6). Johns Hopkins.
Twentieth-Century American Dramatists, 2 vols. Ed. by John MacNicholas. (Dictionary of Literary Biography Ser.: Vol. 7). (Illus.). 848p. 1981. 190.00x set (ISBN 0-8103-0928-9). Gale.
Twentieth Century American Drawings from the Whitney Museum of American Art. Paul Cummings. 1987. 29.95 (ISBN 0-393-02483-0). Norton.
Twentieth-Century American Historians. Ed. by Clyde N. Wilson. (Dictionary of Literary Biography Ser.: Vol. 17). 536p. 1983. 95.00x (ISBN 0-8103-1144-5). Gale.
Twentieth-Century American-Jewish Fiction Writers. Ed. by Daniel Walden. LC 84-4014. (Dictionary ofLiterary Biography Ser.: Vol. 28). 384p. 1984. 95.00x (ISBN 0-8103-1706-0, Pub by Bruccoli). Gale.
Twentieth-Century American Literary Naturalism: An Interpretation. Donald Pizer. LC 81-5606. (Crosscurrents-Modern Critiques-New Ser.). 187p. 1982. 17.95x (ISBN 0-8093-1027-9). S Ill U Pr.
Twentieth-Century American Literature, 8 vols. Ed. by Harold Bloom. 1985. Set. 495.00 (ISBN 0-87754-800-5); 65.00 ea. Vol. 1 650 pgs., 1985 (ISBN 0-87754-801-3). Vol. 2 650 pgs., 1986 (ISBN 0-87754-802-1). Vol. 3 650 pgs., 1986 (ISBN 0-87754-803-X). Vol. 4 650 pgs., 1986 (ISBN 0-87754-804-8). Vol. 5 650 pgs., 1987 (ISBN 0-87754-805-6). Vol. 6 650 pgs., 1987 (ISBN 0-87754-806-4). Vol. 7 650 pgs., 1988 (ISBN 0-87754-807-2). Chelsea Hse.
Twentieth-Century American Literature. Marjorie N. Bond. 1977. Repr. of 1933 ed. lib. bdg. 10.00 (ISBN 0-8495-0325-6). Arden Lib.
Twentieth Century American Literature, 1 of 7 vols. Intro. by Warren French. (Great Writers Library). 668p. pap. 14.95 (ISBN 0-312-34712-X). Academy Chi Pubs.
Twentieth-Century American Literature, Vol. 8: Bibliographical Supplement & Index. Ed. by Harold Bloom & S. T. Joshi. (Chelsea House Library of Literary Criticism). 200p. 1988. text ed. 40.00x (ISBN 1-55546-773-3). Chelsea Hse.
Twentieth-Century American Masters: Barber, Berstein, Cage, Carter, Copland, Cowell, Gershwin, Ives, Sessions, & Thomson. William Austin et al. Ed. by Stanley Sadie. (New Grove Composer Biography Ser.). (Orig.). 1988. 19.95x (ISBN 0-393-01698-6); pap. 12.95 (ISBN 0-393-30353-5). Norton.
Twentieth-Century American Nicknames. Ed. by Laurence Urdang. LC 79-23390. 398p. 1979. 32.00 (ISBN 0-8242-0642-8). Wilson.
Twentieth-Century American Painting: The Thyssen-Bornemisza Collection. Gail Levin. LC 87-61728. (Illus.). 320p. 1988. 95.00 (ISBN 0-85667-332-3, Pub. by P Wilson Pubs). Sotheby Pubns.
Twentieth Century American Quilts, 1900-1950. Thomas K. Woodard & Blanche Greenstein. (Illus.). 144p. 1988. 35.00 (ISBN 0-525-24244-9); pap. 22.50 (ISBN 0-525-48115-X). Dutton.
Twentieth-Century American Science Fiction Writers, 2 vols. Ed. by David Cowart. (Dictionary of Literary Biography Ser.: Vol. 8). 688p. 1981. 190.00x set (ISBN 0-8103-0918-1, Bruccoli Clark). Gale.
Twentieth Century American West: Contributions to an Understanding. Gerald D. Nash et al. Ed. by Thomas G. Alexander & Thomas F. Bluth. (Charles Redd Monographs in Western History: No. 12). 119p. (Orig.). 1983. pap. 5.50 (ISBN 0-941214-09-5, Dist. by Signature Bks). C Redd Ctr.
Twentieth Century: An Almanac. Ed. by Robert H. Ferrell & John S. Bowman. 512p. 1984. 24.95. Ballantine.
Twentieth Century: An Almanac. Ed. by Robert H. Ferrell & John S. Bowman. (Illus.). 512p. 1985. 24.95 (ISBN 0-345-31708-4); pap. 12.95 (ISBN 0-345-32630-X). Pharos Bks NY.
Twentieth Century: An American History. Arthur S. Link & William A. Link. LC 82-22080. (Illus.). 384p. 1983. text ed. 27.95x (ISBN 0-88295-815-1); pap. text ed. 18.95 (ISBN 0-88295-816-X). Harlan Davidson.
Twentieth Century Art, No. 51. 30.00 (ISBN 0-8148-0758-5). L Amiel Pub.
Twentieth Century Art, No. 52. 30.00 (ISBN 0-8148-0752-6). L Amiel Pub.
Twentieth Century Art, No. 55. 30.00 (ISBN 0-8148-0759-3). L Amiel Pub.
Twentieth Century Art - No. 39. Ed. by G. Di San Lazzaro. (Illus., Eng. & Fr.). 19.95 (ISBN 0-8148-0566-3). L Amiel Pub.
Twentieth Century Art-No. 35: Panorama '70. Ed. by G. Di San Lazzaro. (Illus., Fr. & Eng.). 19.95 (ISBN 0-8148-0493-4). L Amiel Pub.
Twentieth Century Art-No. 38: Panorama '72. Ed. by G. Di San Lazzaro. (Illus., Fr., Abridged English trans). 1972. 19.95 (ISBN 0-8148-0539-6). L Amiel Pub.
Twentieth Century Art, No. 42: Surrealism, Pt. 1. Ed. by G. Di San Lazzaro. (Illus.). 1975. 30.00 (ISBN 0-8148-0683-X). L Amiel Pub.
Twentieth Century Art, No. 43: Surrealism, Pt.2. Ed. by G. Di San Lazzaro. (Illus., French, abridged Eng. trans.). 1975. 30.00 (ISBN 0-8148-0684-8). L Amiel Pub.
Twentieth Century Art, No. 44: The Imaginary Reality, Pt. 1. Ed. by Alain Jouffroy. (Illus., Fr.). 1975. 30.00 (ISBN 0-8148-0685-6). L Amiel Pub.
Twentieth Century Art, No. 45: The Imaginary Reality, Pt. 2. Ed. by Alain Jouffroy. (Illus., Fr.). 1975. 30.00 (ISBN 0-8148-0686-4). L Amiel Pub.
Twentieth Century Art: Painting & Sculpture in the Ludwig Museum. Karl Ruhrberg. LC 86-42724. (Illus.). 356p. 1986. 45.00 (ISBN 0-8478-0755-X). Rizzoli Intl.
Twentieth Century Art: Panorama '76 Total Art Pt. 1, No.47. Ed. by Alain Jouffroy. 1976. 30.00 (ISBN 0-8148-0688-0). L Amiel Pub.
Twentieth-Century Artists on Art. Ed. by Dore Ashton. (Illus.). 1986. 24.45 (ISBN 0-394-52276-1); pap. 14.95 (ISBN 0-394-73489-0). Pantheon.
Twentieth-Century Artists on Art: An Index to Artists Writings, Statements, & Interviews. Jack S. Robertson. (Visual Arts Ser.). 350p. 1985. lib. bdg. 35.00 (ISBN 0-8161-8714-2). G K Hall.
Twentieth-Century Author Biographies Master Index. Ed. by Barbara McNeil. 539p. 1984. 64.00x (ISBN 0-8103-2095-9); pap. 30.00x (ISBN 0-8103-2096-7). Gale.

Twentieth-Century Literary Theory: An Introductory Anthology. Vassilis Lambropoulos & David N. Miller. LC 86-5837. 521p. (Orig.). 1987. 56.50 (ISBN 0-88706-265-2); pap. 18.95x (ISBN 0-88706-266-0). State U NY Pr.

Twentieth Century Literature Criticism, Vol. 30: Archives. Ed. by Paula Kepos & Dennis Poupard. 1988. 95.00 (ISBN 0-8103-2412-1). Gale.

Twentieth Century Literature in Retrospect. Ed. by Reuben Brower. LC 76-168430. (English Studies: No. 2). viii, 363p. 1971. pap. 8.95x (ISBN 0-674-91424-4). Harvard U Pr.

Twentieth Century: Major Composers of Our Time. Denes Agay. (Anthology of Piano Music Ser.: Vol. 4). 238p. 1971. pap. 12.95 (ISBN 0-8256-8044-1, Yorktown). Music Sales.

Twentieth Century Man. Gloria North. 16p. 1979. pap. 1.00 (ISBN 0-686-27736-8). Samisdat.

Twentieth Century Masters of Erotic Art. Bradley Smith. LC 80-36666. (Illus.). 1985. 30.00 (ISBN 0-517-54236-6). Gemini Smith.

Twentieth-Century Mexico. Ed. by W. Dirk Raat & William H. Beezley. LC 85-14109. (Illus.). xviii, 318p. 1986. 25.95x (ISBN 0-8032-3868-1); pap. 9.95x (ISBN 0-8032-8914-6). U of Nebr Pr.

Twentieth Century Mind: Essays on Contemporary Thought. Donald A. Zoll. LC 67-13892. Repr. of 1967 ed. 30.40 (ISBN 0-8357-9393-1, 2051674). Bks Demand UMI.

Twentieth Century Moliere: Bernard Shaw. Augustin Hamon. LC 72-10092. 1972. Repr. of 1916 ed. lib. bdg. 35.00 (ISBN 0-8414-0470-4). Folcroft.

Twentieth-Century Montana: A State of Extremes. K. Ross Toole. LC 75-177348. (Illus.). 278p. (Orig.). 1983. 24.95 (ISBN 0-8061-0992-0); pap. 12.95 (ISBN 0-8061-1826-1). U of Okla Pr.

Twentieth Century Music. Richard Burbank. LC 80-25040. (Illus.). 500p. 1984. 50.00 (ISBN 0-87196-464-3). Facts on File.

Twentieth-Century Music. Robert P. Morgan. (Introduction to Music History Ser.). 1988. price not set (ISBN 0-393-95272-X). Norton.

Twentieth-Century Music. Ellen Rosand. (Garland Library of the History of Western Music). 350p. 1985. lib. bdg. 50.00 (ISBN 0-8240-7459-9). Garland Pub.

Twentieth Century Music: An Introduction. 3rd ed. Eric Salzman. (Illus.). 352p. 1988. pap. text ed. 24.00 (ISBN 0-13-935057-8). P-H.

Twentieth Century Music: An Introduction. 2nd ed. E. Solzman. 1974. pap. 23.00 (ISBN 0-13-935007-1). P-H.

Twentieth-Century Music for Trumpet & Organ: An Annotated Bibliography. Philip T. Cansler. LC 84-20422. (Research Ser.: No. 11). 1984. pap. 10.00x (ISBN 0-914282-30-1). Brass Pr.

Twentieth Century Music: How It Developed, How to Listen to It. Marion Bauer. (Music Ser.). 354p. 1978. Repr. of 1933 ed. lib. bdg. 37.50 (ISBN 0-306-79503-5). Da Capo.

Twentieth-Century Music Idioms. G. Welton Marquis. LC 81-4197. xvi, 269p. 1981. Repr. of 1964 ed. lib. bdg. 35.00x (ISBN 0-313-22624-5, MATC). Greenwood.

Twentieth-Century Music in Western Europe: The Compositions & Recordings. Arthur Cohn. LC 70-39297. 510p. 1972. Repr. of 1965 ed. lib. bdg. 59.50 (ISBN 0-306-70460-9). Da Capo.

Twentieth Century Music: Its Evolution from the End of the Harmonic Era into the Present Era of Sound. Peter Yates. LC 80-23310. xv, 367p. 1981. Repr. of 1967 ed. lib. bdg. 35.00 (ISBN 0-313-22516-8, YATC). Greenwood.

Twentieth-Century Music: The Sense Behind the Sound. Joan Peyser. LC 79-57286. (Illus.). 1980. pap. 5.95 (ISBN 0-02-871880-1). Schirmer Bks.

Twentieth Century Negro Literature. Ed. by D. W. Culp. LC 69-18586. (American Negro: His History & Literature Ser., No. 2). 1969. Repr. of 1902 ed. 23.00 (ISBN 0-405-01856-8). Ayer Co Pubs.

Twentieth Century Negro Literature. facs. ed. Ed. by Daniel W. Culp. LC 73-89416. (Black Heritage Library Collection Ser). 1902. 24.00 (ISBN 0-8369-8551-6). Ayer Co Pubs.

Twentieth-Century Novel in English: A Checklist. 2nd ed. E. C. Bufkin. LC 83-6598. 192p. 1983. 20.00x (ISBN 0-8203-0685-1). U of Ga Pr.

Twentieth Century Odyssey: A Study of Heimito Von Doderer's "Die Damonen". Elizabeth C. Hesson. LC 81-69885. (Studies in German Literature, Linguistics & Culture: Vol. 9). (Illus.). 220p. 1982. 26.00x (ISBN 0-938100-07-6). Camden Hse.

Twentieth-Century Pentecostal Explosion. Vinson Synan. (Orig.). 1987. pap. 8.95 (ISBN 0-88419-203-2, Creation Hse). Strang Comms Co.

Twentieth-Century Pentecostal Explosion. Vinson Synan. LC 87-71623. 238p. 1987. 13.95 (ISBN 0-88419-206-7, Creation Hse). Strang Comms Co.

Twentieth-Century Pessimism & the American Dream. Ed. by Raymond C. Miller. LC 79-26081. (Franklin Memorial Lectures Ser.: Vol. VIII). (Illus.). ix, 104p. 1980. Repr. of 1961 ed. lib. bdg. 35.00x (ISBN 0-313-22122-7, MITW). Greenwood.

Twentieth-Century Philosophy: The Analytic Tradition. Morris Weitz. LC 66-10366. 1966. pap. text ed. 14.95 (ISBN 0-02-934990-7). Free Pr.

Twentieth Century Physics. Claude Garrod. 385p. Date not set. pap. text ed. 11.20x (ISBN 0-915141-00-0). Faculty Pub C A.

Twentieth Century Physics. Claude Garrod. (Illus.). 390p. 1988. Repr. of 1984 ed. text ed. 29.95 (ISBN 0-86542-331-8). Blackwell Pubns.

Twentieth Century Pilgrimage: Walter Lippmann & the Public Philosophy. Charles Wellborn. LC 69-17624. viii, 200p. 1969. 25.00 (ISBN 0-8071-0303-9). La State U Pr.

Twentieth Century Pioneer. Edna W. Shannon. 1987. pap. write for info. (ISBN 0-9602284-5-4). Long Haul.

Twentieth Century Pittsburgh: Government, Business & Environmental Change. Roy Lubove. 189p. 1969. pap. text ed. write for info (ISBN 0-394-34196-1, RanC). Random.

Twentieth Century Pleasures: Prose on Poetry. Robert Hass. LC 83-16394. 296p. 1984. 17.95 (ISBN 0-88001-045-2). Ecco Pr.

Twentieth Century Pleasures: Prose on Poetry. Robert Hass. LC 83-16394. 308p. 1985. pap. 9.50 (ISBN 0-88001-046-0). Ecco Pr.

Twentieth Century Poetry. Ed. by Martin Grahman & P. N. Furbank. 464p. 1975. pap. 21.00x (ISBN 0-335-05117-0, Pub. by Open Univ Pr). Taylor & Francis.

Twentieth Century Poetry. Harold Monro. Repr. of 1929 ed. lib. bdg. 19.50 (ISBN 0-8414-6633-5). Folcroft.

Twentieth Century Poetry see Houghton Books in Literature.

Twentieth Century Poetry see St. James Reference Guide to English Literature.

Twentieth Century Poetry, an Anthology. Ed. by Harold Monro. Repr. of 1946 ed. 29.00x (ISBN 0-403-03062-5). Somerset Pub.

Twentieth-Century Poetry, Fiction, Theory. Ed. by Harry R. Garvin & John D. Kirkland, Jr. (Bucknell Review Ser.: Vol. 22, No. 2). 231p. 16.50 (ISBN 0-8387-1934-1). Bucknell U Pr.

Twentieth Century Poetry: Landscapes of the Mind. Weimer. (American Literature Ser.). (gr. 10-12). 1973. pap. text ed. 7.62 (ISBN 0-88343-138-6); tchrs'. manual o.p. 2.70 (ISBN 0-88343-139-4). McDougal-Littell.

Twentieth Century Polish Theatre. Ed. by Bohdan Drozdowsky. 256p. 1983. 12.95 (ISBN 0-7145-3738-1). Riverrun NY.

Twentieth-Century Popular Culture in Museums & Libraries. Fred Schroeder. LC 80-85197. 1981. 30.00 (ISBN 0-87972-162-6). Bowling Green Univ.

Twentieth-Century Poster. Dawn Ades et al. LC 83-73420. (Illus.). 208p. 1984. 55.00 (ISBN 0-89659-433-5); pap. 27.50 (ISBN 0-89659-434-3). Abbeville Pr.

Twentieth-Century Protestant Church Music in America. Talmage W. Dean. LC 87-35522. 1988. text ed. 12.95 (ISBN 0-8054-6813-7). Broadman.

Twentieth Century Psalms: Reflections on This Life. Justin F. Stone. 100p. (Orig.). 1988. pap. 9.95. Good Karma Bks.

Twentieth Century Psychiatry: Its Contribution to Man's Knowledge of Himself. William A. White. LC 73-2428. (Mental Illness & Social Policy; the American Experience Ser.). Repr. of 1936 ed. 17.00 (ISBN 0-405-05236-7). Ayer Co Pubs.

Twentieth Century Psychology: Recent Developments. Ed. by Philip Harriman et al. LC 75-128255. (Essay Index Reprint Ser). 1946. 37.50 (ISBN 0-8369-1948-3). Ayer Co Pubs.

Twentieth Century Publications in Scottish Gaelic. Donald J. MacLeod. 232p. 1981. 27.00x (ISBN 0-7073-0266-8, Pub. by Scot Acad Pr). Longwood Pub Group.

Twentieth Century Pulpit, Vol. II. Ed. by James W. Cox & Patricia P. Cox. LC 77-21997. 1981. pap. 9.95 (ISBN 0-687-42716-9). Abingdon.

Twentieth Century Religion Thought: The Frontiers of Philosophy & Theology, 1900-1980. rev. ed. John Maquarrie. 429p. 1981. pap. text ed. write for info. (ISBN 0-02-374500-2, Pub. by Scribner). Macmillan.

Twentieth Century Religious Thought. John Macquarrie. LC 81-9349. 1981. pap. text ed. 18.95x (ISBN 0-684-17334-4). Scribner.

Twentieth-Century Richmond: Planning, Politics, & Race. Christopher Silver. LC 83-16848. (Twentieth-Century America Ser.). (Illus.). 352p. 1984. 34.95x (ISBN 0-87049-421-X); pap. 16.95x (ISBN 0-87049-422-8). U of Tenn Pr.

Twentieth-Century Romance & Gothic Writers. Ed. by James Vinson & D. L. Kirkpatrick. 898p. 1982. 95.00x (ISBN 0-8103-0226-8, Pub. by Macmillan England). Gale.

Twentieth Century Rumania. Stephen Fischer-Galati. LC 77-108838. (Illus.). 1970. 35.00x (ISBN 0-231-02848-2). Columbia U Pr.

Twentieth Century Russia. 6th ed. Donald W. Treadgold. 580p. 1988. 48.50 (ISBN 0-8133-0506-3); pap. 24.95 (ISBN 0-8133-0507-1). Westview.

Twentieth-Century Russian Drama: From Gorky to the Present. Harold B. Segel. LC 79-11673. (Illus.). 520p. pap. 135.20 (2029830). Bks Demand UMI.

Twentieth-Century Russian Literature. Harry T. Moore & Albert Parry. LC 74-13812. (Crosscurrents-Modern Critiques Ser.). 208p. 1974. 7.95x (ISBN 0-8093-0703-0). S Ill U Pr.

Twentieth-Century Schwenkfelders: A Narrative History. W. Kyrel Meschter. 1984. pap. write for info (ISBN 0-935980-03-2). Schwenkfelder Lib.

Twentieth-Century Science-Fiction Writers. 2nd ed. Ed. by Curtis C. Smith. 1986. 75.00 (ISBN 0-912289-27-9); Standing Order. 67.50. St James Pr.

Twentieth Century Science Fiction Writers. Ed. by Curtis S. Smith. LC 81-8944. (Twentieth Century Writers Ser.). 649p. 1981. 65.00x (ISBN 0-312-82420-3). St Martin.

Twentieth Century Sculptors. facs. ed. Stanley Casson. LC 67-23189. (Essay Index Reprint Ser). 1930. 19.00 (ISBN 0-8369-0283-1). Ayer Co Pubs.

Twentieth-Century Shapers of American Popular Religion. Ed. by Charles H. Lippy. 1989. 55.85 (ISBN 0-313-25356-0, LTW/). Greenwood.

Twentieth Century Short Stories Explication, Supplement III to Third Edition. Warren S. Walker. 486p. 1987. lib. bdg. 45.00 (ISBN 0-208-02122-1). Shoe String.

Twentieth-Century Short Story Explication: Interpretations, 1900-1975, of Short Fiction since 1800. 3rd ed. Warren S. Walker. LC 76-30666. vii, 880p. 1977. 50.00 (ISBN 0-208-01570-1, SSP). Shoe String.

Twentieth-Century Short Story Explication: Supplement One to Third Edition. Warren S. Walker. LC 80-16175. (Short Story Explication Ser.). v, 257p. 1980. 35.00 (ISBN 0-208-01813-1, SSP). Shoe String.

Twentieth Century Short Story Explication: Supplement Two to the Third Edition. Warren S. Walker. LC 80-16175. 348p. 1984. 39.00 (ISBN 0-208-02005-5, SSP). Shoe String.

Twentieth Century Sociology. facs. ed. Ed. by Georgy D. Gurvich & Wilbert E. Moore. LC 78-134090. (Essay Index Reprint Ser). 1945. 38.50 (ISBN 0-8369-2110-0). Ayer Co Pubs.

Twentieth Century Spanish-American Novel: A Bibliographic Guide. David W. Foster. LC 75-25787. 234p. 1975. 17.50 (ISBN 0-8108-0871-4). Scarecrow.

Twentieth Century Stage Decoration, 2 vols. in 1. Ed. by Rene Fuerst & Samuel J. Hume. LC 67-28846. (Illus.). 428p. 1968. 33.00 (ISBN 0-405-08540-0, Blom Pubns). Ayer Co Pubs.

Twentieth Century Style & Design: Nineteen Hundred to the Present. Philippe Garner. LC 84-3706. 320p. 1986. 48.95 (ISBN 0-442-23008-7). Van Nos Reinhold.

Twentieth Century Table of Houses. A. LeRoi Simmons. 202p. 1972. text ed. 6.00 (ISBN 0-9605126-2-4). Aquarian Bk Pubs.

Twentieth Century Theater, 2 vols. Glenn Loney. LC 81-19587. (Illus.). 540p. 1983. Set. 75.00x (ISBN 0-87196-463-5). Facts on File.

Twentieth Century Theatre. William L. Phelps. LC 68-16302. 1968. Repr. of 1920 ed. 20.50x (ISBN 0-8046-0368-5, Pub by Kennikat). Assoc Faculty Pr.

Twentieth Century Theatre: Observations on the Contemporary English & American Stage. facs. ed. William L. Phelps. LC 67-28764. (Essay Index Reprint Ser). 1918. 15.00 (ISBN 0-8369-0787-6). Ayer Co Pubs.

Twentieth Century Thinkers in Adult Education. Ed. by Peter Jarvis. (International Perspectives on Adult Education Ser.). 256p. 1987. 34.50 (ISBN 0-7099-1482-2, Pub. by Croom Helm UK). Routledge Chapman & Hall.

Twentieth-Century Type Designers. Sebastian Carter. (Illus.). 168p. 1987. 24.95 (ISBN 0-8008-7916-3). Taplinger.

Twentieth Century Views of Musical History. William Hays. 1972. lib. rep. ed. 30.00x (ISBN 0-684-15149-9, ScribT). Scribner.

Twentieth-Century Warriors: The Development of the Armed Forces of the Major Military Nations in the Twentieth Century. Lord Carver. Ed. by William Strachan. LC 87-33976. 448p. 1988. 25.00 (ISBN 1-55584-187-2). Weidenfeld.

Twentieth Century Watercolors. Christopher Finch. (Illus.). 312p. 1988. 85.00 (ISBN 0-89659-811-X). Abbeville Pr.

Twentieth Century Welsh Poems. Joseph P. Clancy. 253p. 1982. 29.95 (ISBN 0-85088-406-3). Dufour.

Twentieth-Century Western Writers. Ed. by James Vinson & D. L. Kirkpatrick. 941p. 1983. 95.00x (ISBN 0-8103-0227-6, Pub. by Macmillan England). Gale.

Twentieth Century Wildlife Artists. Ed. by Nicholas Hammond. LC 86-5341. (Illus.). 224p. 1986. 60.00 (ISBN 0-87951-221-0). Overlook Pr.

Twentieth Century Women. Arthur Vogelsang. LC 87-19200. (Contemporary Poetry Ser.). 80p. 1988. 13.95x (ISBN 0-8203-0995-8); pap. 6.95 (ISBN 0-8203-0996-6). U of Ga Pr.

Twentieth Century Women Novelists. Ed. by Thomas F. Staley. LC 82-1740. 240p. 1982. text ed. 28.50x (ISBN 0-389-20272-X). B&N Imports.

Twentieth Century Women Poets. Ed. by Roth Publishing, Inc Staff. LC 82-84763. (World's Best Poetry Ser.). 375p. 1987. 49.95x (ISBN 0-89609-270-4). Roth Pub Inc.

Twentieth-Century World. Carter V. Findley et al. LC 87-71109. 526p. pap. text ed. 21.96 (ISBN 0-395-35037-9); instr's manual & test items 2.36 (ISBN 0-395-42426-7). HM.

Twentieth-Century World: An International History. William R. Keylor. (Illus.). 1984. pap. 12.95x (ISBN 0-19-503370-1). Oxford U Pr.

Twentieth Century World History: A Select Bibliography. Freda Harcourt & Francis Robinson. LC 79-10154. 154p. 1979. text ed. 27.50x (ISBN 0-06-492680-X). B&N Imports.

Twentieth IECEC Proceedings. 1985. 190.00 (ISBN 0-89883-725-1, P 164). Soc Auto Engineers.

Twentieth Maine. John Pullen. 1980. 17.50 (ISBN 0-89029-055-5); pap. 9.95. Pr of Morningside.

Twentieth March, a Day Like Any Other. K. A. Abbas. 134p. 1978. 11.95. Asia Bk Corp.

Twentieth Oil Shale Symposium Proceedings. Frwd. by James H. Gary. (Illus.). 238p. 1987. pap. text ed. 25.00 (ISBN 0-918062-76-4). Colo Sch Mines.

Twentieth Publication Design Annual. Society of Publication Designers Staff. (Illus.). 224p. 1968. 39.95 (ISBN 0-942604-10-5). Madison Square.

Twentieth Reunion & Other Poems. ltd. ed. Gladys Merrifield. LC 84-70671. (Living Poets Ser.: No. 31). 1984. 5.00 (ISBN 0-934218-31-5). Dragons Teeth.

Twentieth Son of Ornon. Mike Sirota. (Orig.). 1980. pap. 1.95 (ISBN 0-89083-685-X). Zebra.

Twenty Activities for Developing Managerial Effectiveness: A Management Skills Training Manual. Mike Lewis & Graham Kelly. 288p. 1986. text ed. 134.50x (ISBN 0-566-02515-9, Pub. by Gower Pub England). Gower Pub Co.

Twenty Activities for Improving Sales Effectiveness. Ed. by Marketing Improvements Ltd. Staff. 300p. 1987. text ed. 130.00 (ISBN 0-566-02707-0, Pub. by Gower Pub England). Gower Pub Co.

Twenty Alabama Books. Rucker Agee. LC 75-44472. (Illus.). 1976. 8.95 (ISBN 0-912458-48-8). E A Seemann.

Twenty & Ten. Claire H. Bishop. (Illus.). (ps-3). 1978. pap. 3.95 (ISBN 0-14-031076-2, Puffin). Penguin.

Twenty & Ten. Claire H. Bishop. (Illus.). (gr. 5-9). 1984. 13.75 (ISBN 0-8446-6168-6). Peter Smith.

Twenty Artists: Yale School of Art, 1950-1970. Irving Sandler. LC 80-54616. (Illus.). 64p. 1981. pap. 7.50x (ISBN 0-89467-016-6). Yale Art Gallery.

Twenty Best European Plays on the American Stage. Ed. by John Gassner. (Best Plays Ser.). (gr. 9 up). 1957. 22.50 (ISBN 0-517-50963-6). Crown.

Twenty Best Film Plays, 2 vols. John Gassner & Dudley Nichols. LC 76-52104. (Classics of Film Literature Ser.: Vol. 13). 1977. Repr. of 1943 ed. Set. lib. bdg. 69.00 ea. (ISBN 0-8240-2877-5). Garland Pub.

Twenty Best Plays of the Modern American Theatre. Ed. by John Gassner. (Best Plays Ser). (gr. 9 up). 1939. 22.50 (ISBN 0-517-50964-4). Crown.

Twenty Best Short Stories in Ray Long's Twenty Years As an Editor. 603p. 1983. lib. bdg. 40.00 (ISBN 0-8495-3411-9). Arden Lib.

Twenty Bicycle Tours in & Around New York City. rev. ed. Dan Carlinsky & David Heim. (Bicycle Tours Ser.). (Illus.). 136p. 1988. pap. 7.95 (ISBN 0-88150-123-9). Backcountry Pubns.

Twenty Bicycle Tours in the Finger Lakes. 1983. 6.95 (ISBN 0-317-03672-6). Countryman.

Twenty Bicycle Tours in the Finger Lakes: Scenic Routes to Central New York's Best Waterfalls, Wineries, Beaches & Parks. rev. ed. Mark Roth & Sally Walters. LC 87-1004. (Illus.). 160p. 1987. pap. 7.95 (ISBN 0-942440-39-0). Backcountry Pubns.

Twenty Candles. Ed Gilmorgan. 1982. 15.00x (ISBN 0-906660-73-4, Pub. by New Playwrights Network). State Mutual Bk.

Twenty Cases Suggestive of Reincarnation. 2nd, rev. & enl. ed. Ian Stevenson. LC 79-93627. 396p. 1980. pap. 11.95 (ISBN 0-8139-0872-8). U Pr of Va.

Twenty Centuries in Sedlescombe. Beryl Lucey. 523p. 1984. 40.00x (ISBN 0-7212-0548-8, Pub. by Regency Pr). State Mutual Bk.

Twenty Centuries of Catholic Church Music. Erwin E. Nemmers. LC 78-17248. 1978. Repr. of 1949 ed. lib. bdg. 25.00x (ISBN 0-313-20542-6, NETW). Greenwood.

Twenty Centuries of Ecumenism. Jacques Desseaux. 1984. pap. 4.95 (ISBN 0-8091-2617-6). Paulist Pr.

Twenty Centuries of Education. Edgar W. Knight. LC 83-45904. Repr. of 1940 ed. 47.50 (ISBN 0-404-20147-4). AMS Pr.

Twenty Centuries of Mexican Art: Viento Siglos de Arte Mexicano. New York City Museum of Modern Art Staff. LC 79-169322. (Museum of Modern Art in Reprint Ser.). (Illus.). 200p. 1972. Repr. of 1940 ed. 23.00 (ISBN 0-405-01580-1). Ayer Co Pubs.

Twenty Colorado Artists. Denver Art Museum Staff. LC 78-89063. 1977. pap. 5.00 (ISBN 0-914738-12-7). Denver Art Mus.

Twenty Contemporary Norwegian Poets: A Bilingual Anthology. Ed. by Terje Johanssen. LC 83-16002. 232p. 1984. 20.00 (ISBN 0-312-82422-X). St Martin.

Twenty Days. Dorothy Kunhardt & Philip Kunhardt. 320p. 1985. pap. 14.95 (ISBN 0-87877-079-8). Newcastle Pub.

Twenty Days: A Narrative in Text & Pictures of the Assassination of Abraham Lincoln. Dorothy M. Kunhardt & Philip Kunhardt. LC 85-9919. 312p. 1985. Repr. lib. bdg. 29.95x (ISBN 0-89370-679-5). Borgo Pr.

Twenty Decoding Games. Marla Love. (gr. 2-6). 1982. pap. 10.95 (ISBN 0-8224-5801-2). D S Lake Pubs.

Twenty-Four Art Nouveau Postcards in Full Colors: From Classic Posters. Ed. by Hayward Cirker & Blanche Cirker. (Illus.). 12p. (Orig.). 1983. pap. 3.50 (ISBN 0-486-24389-3). Dover.
Twenty-Four Blacksmithing Projects. Percy W. Blandford. (Illus.). 130p. 1988. pap. 8.95 (ISBN 0-8306-2974-2). TAB Bks.
Twenty-Four British Potters: Exhibition Catalogue. William Hull. (Illus.). 48p. 1976. pap. 3.00 (ISBN 0-911209-08-5). Penn St Art.
Twenty-Four Caprices in the Form of Etudes for Violin. Pierre Rode. Ed. by Gustave Saenger. (Carl Fischer Music Library: No.583). 52p. 1910. pap. 6.50 (ISBN 0-8258-0076-5, L583). Fischer Inc NY.
Twenty-Four Conversations with Borges: Interviews by Roberto Alifano 1981-1983. Ed. by Roberto Alifano. Tr. by Nicomedes S. Arauz et al. LC 83-49422. (Illus.). 157p. 1984. 17.95 (ISBN 0-394-53879-X, GP 921). Grove.
Twenty-Four Conversations with Borges: Interviews by Roberto Alifano 1981-1983. Ed. by Roberto Alifano. Tr. by Nicomedes S. Arauz et al. LC 83-49422. (Illus.). 157p. 1984. pap. 8.95 (ISBN 0-394-62192-1, E940, Ever). Grove.
Twenty-Four Days Before Christmas. Madeleine L'Engle. (gr. k-6). 1988. pap. 2.95 (ISBN 0-440-40105-4, YB). Dell.
Twenty-Four Days Before Christmas: An Austin Family Story. Madeleine L'Engle. LC 84-5540. (Illus.). 48p. 1984. 8.95 (ISBN 0-87788-843-4). Shaw Pubs.
Twenty-Four Doors: Advent Calendar Poems. Nance Van Winckel. (Illus., Orig.). 1985. pap. 40.00x (ISBN 0-931460-24-7). Bieler.
Twenty Four Early American Country Dances Cotillions & Reels for the Year 1976. James E. Morrison. LC 76-3969. (Illus.). 1976. spiral bdg. 8.00 (ISBN 0-917024-04-4). Country Dance & Song.
Twenty-Four Exercises for Violin, Op. 33. A. Blumenstengel. (Carl Fischer Music Library: No. 621). 1911. pap. 6.50 (ISBN 0-8258-0082-X, L621). Fischer Inc NY.
Twenty-Four Eyes. Sakae Tsuboi. Tr. by Akira Miura from Japanese. LC 82-51098. 256p. 1983. pap. 8.50 (ISBN 0-8048-1462-7). C E Tuttle.
Twenty-Four Favorite One-Act Plays. Ed. by Van H. Cartmell & Bennett Cerf. LC 58-13274. 1963. pap. 6.95 (ISBN 0-385-06617-1, C423, Dolp). Doubleday.
Twenty Four Favorite One Act Plays. Ed. by Bennett Cerf & Van H. Cartmell. 24.95 (ISBN 0-88411-264-0, Pub. by Aeonian Pr). Amereon Ltd.
Twenty Four Haiku After the Japanese. Tom Weigel. Ed. by Maureen Owen. (Summer Ser.). 1982. pap. 3.00 (ISBN 0-686-43221-5). Telephone Bks.
Twenty-four Hour Christian. Earl Palmer. LC 87-14306. (Orig.). 1987. pap. 5.95 (ISBN 0-87784-993-5). Inter-Varsity.
Twenty-Four Hour Drink Book. Ralph Maloney. (Illus.). 1962. 10.95 (ISBN 0-8392-1121-X). Astor-Honor.
Twenty-Four Hour Trading: The Global Network of Financial & Currency Markets. Diamond. 1988. 29.95 (ISBN 0-471-60072-5). Wiley.
Twenty-Four Hours a Day. Faith Baldwin. 1976. Repr. of 1937 ed. 19.95x (ISBN 0-88411-605-0, Pub. by Aeonian Pr). Amereon Ltd.
Twenty-Four Hours a Day. large print ed. Alan L. Roeck. 195p. 1980. pap. 7.95 (ISBN 0-89486-108-5). Hazelden.
Twenty-Four Hours a Day. rev. ed. 365p. 1975. 4.95 (ISBN 0-89486-012-7). Hazelden.
Twenty-Four Hours a Day. 384p. (Orig.). 1985. pap. 5.95 (ISBN 0-86683-500-8, HarpR). Har-Row.
Twenty-Four Hours a Day. (Hazelden Bks.). scp 5.50 (ISBN 0-317-46478-7). Har-Row.
Twenty-Four Hours a Day for Everyone. Alan L. Roeck. LC 78-52007. 383p. (Orig.). 1977. pap. 5.95 (ISBN 0-89486-040-2). Hazelden.
Twenty-Four Hundred Jokes to Brighten Your Speeches. Robert Orben. LC 83-25392. 240p. 1984. 14.95 (ISBN 0-385-17230-3). Doubleday.
Twenty-Four Hundred Tennessee Pensioners: Revolution & War of 1812. Zella Armstrong. LC 75-971. 121p. 1981. pap. 7.50 (ISBN 0-8063-0665-3). Genealog Pub.
Twenty-Four Love Songs. Edward Dorn. 1969. pap. 2.00 (ISBN 0-686-18964-7). Frontier Press Calif.
Twenty-Four Metalworking Projects. Percy W. Blandford. pap. 9.95 (ISBN 0-8306-2784-7, 2784). Tab Bks.
Twenty-Four Negro Melodies. S. Coleridge-Taylor. LC 80-10532. (Music Reprint Ser.: 1980). 1980. Repr. of 1905 ed. lib. bdg. 35.00 (ISBN 0-306-76023-1). Da Capo.
Twenty-Four Papers on Statistics & Probability. A. Aleskjavicene et al. LC 61-9803. (Selected Translations in Mathematical Statistics & Probability Ser.: Vol. 7). 1968. 41.00 (ISBN 0-8218-1457-5, STAPRO-7). Am Math.
Twenty-Four Papers on Statistics & Probability. D. V. Anosov et al. LC 61-9803. (Selected Translations in Mathematical Statistics & Probability: Vol. 14). 296p. 1978. 65.00 (ISBN 0-8218-1464-8, STAPRO-14). Am Math.
Twenty-Four Practice Hairstyles. rev. ed. Anthony B. Colletti. 1981. pap. text ed. 7.07 (ISBN 0-912126-47-7, 1265-00). Keystone Pubns.
Twenty-Four Robbers. Audrey Woods. (Illus.). 32p. (ps-2). 1981. 5.50 (ISBN 0-85953-100-7, Pub. by Child's Play England). Playspaces.
Twenty-Four Router Projects. Percy W. Blandford. (Illus.). 120p. 1988. pap. 6.95 (ISBN 0-8306-9062-X, 9062P). TAB Bks.
Twenty Four Silicon-Controlled Rectifier Projects. Robert J. Traister. (Illus.). 160p. 1986. 17.95 (ISBN 0-8306-0386-7, 1586); pap. 9.95 (ISBN 0-8306-0486-3, 1586P). Tab Bks.
Twenty-Four Table Saw Projects. Percy W. Blandford. (Illus.). 128p. 1988. pap. 6.95 (ISBN 0-8306-2964-5). TAB Bks.
Twenty-Four Tested Ready-to-Run Game Programs in BASIC. Ken Tracton. (Illus.). 1978. pap. 10.25 (ISBN 0-8306-1085-5, 1085). TAB Bks.
Twenty-Four Ways to Improve Your Teaching. Kenneth O. Gangel. LC 74-77453. 131p. 1974. pap. 5.50 (ISBN 0-89693-235-4). Victor Bks.
Twenty-Four Women's Programs: Please Pass the Fruit. Jeanette Lockerbie. 96p. (Orig.). 1986. pap. 4.95 (ISBN 0-87403-226-1, 2979). Standard Pub.
Twenty-Four Years in the Argentine Republic. J. Anthony King. LC 71-161042. Repr. of 1846 ed. 28.50 (ISBN 0-404-03691-0). AMS Pr.
Twenty Fourth Infantry: Past & Present. William G. Muller. (Illus.). 1972. pap. 6.95 (ISBN 0-88342-219-0). Old Army.
Twenty Grand. Taggard. (gr. 7 up). 1975. pap. 2.50 (ISBN 0-590-08909-9). Scholastic Inc.
Twenty Grand Short Stories. Ed. by Ernestine Taggard. (gr. 6-12,RL 5). 1984. pap. 3.95 (ISBN 0-553-26266-1). Bantam.
Twenty Great American Guns. Merrill Lindsay. (Illus.). 34p. 1976. pap. 1.75 (ISBN 0-686-15689-7). Arma Pr.
Twenty Greatest Hits: The Beatles. Ed. by Milton Okun. 72p. 1982. pap. 7.95 (ISBN 0-89524-173-0, 1338). Cherry Lane.
Twenty-Gun Ship Blandford. Peter Goodwin. (Anatomy of the Ship Ser.). (Illus.). 120p. 1988. 21.95 (ISBN 0-87021-058-0). Naval Inst Pr.
Twenty Holy Hours. Mateo C. Boevey. 1978. pap. 5.00 (ISBN 0-8198-0563-7). Dghtrs St Paul.
Twenty Hours Forty Minutes: Our Flight in the Friendship. Amelia Earhart. Ed. by James Gilbert. LC 79-7249. (Flight: Its First Seventy-Five Years Ser.). (Illus.). 1979. Repr. of 1928 ed. lib. bdg. 21.00x (ISBN 0-405-12161-X). Ayer Co Pubs.
Twenty Infallible Systems to Beat the Roulette & Gain at Faro in Any Gambling Spot in the World. Frederick M. Lake. (Illus.). 112p. 1983. Repr. of 1901 ed. 131.45 (ISBN 0-89901-116-0). Found Class Reprints.
Twenty Innovative Electronics Projects for Your Home. Joseph O'Connell. (Illus.). 256p. 1988. 21.95 (ISBN 0-8306-0947-4); pap. 13.95 (ISBN 0-8306-2947-5). TAB Bks.
Twenty Jataka Tales. Noor I. Khan. (Illus.). 136p. (Orig.). (YA) (gr. 10 up). 1985. pap. 6.95 (ISBN 0-89281-103-X). Inner Tradit.
Twenty Lectures Delivered at the International Congress of Mathematicians in Vancouver, 1974. Ed. by D. V. Anosov. LC 77-9042. (Translation Ser. No. 2: Vol. 109). 129p. 1982. pap. 30.00 (ISBN 0-8218-3059-7, TRANS 2/109). Am Math.
Twenty Lectures on Chinese Culture: An Intermediary Chinese Textbook. Parker P. Huang et al. 1967. pap. text ed. 15.95 (ISBN 0-300-00127-4). Yale U Pr.
Twenty Lectures on Chinese Culture: Exercise Book. Parker Po-fei Huang. LC 66-21520. 1967. pap. text ed. 15.95x (ISBN 0-300-00128-2). Yale U Pr.
Twenty Lectures: Sociological Theory since World War II. Jeffrey C. Alexander. LC 86-17106. 432p. 1987. 35.00x (ISBN 0-231-06210-9). Columbia U Pr.
Twenty Lectures: Sociological Theory since World War II. Jeffrey C. Alexander. 393p. 1988. pap. 13.00x (ISBN 0-231-06211-7). Columbia U Pr.
Twenty Lines a Day. Harry Mathews. 120p. (YA) 1988. 20.00 (ISBN 0-916583-27-9). Dalkey Arch.
Twenty Love Poems & a Song of Despair. Pablo Neruda. LC 70-481699. (Cape Editions Ser.). 1976. pap. 4.95 (ISBN 0-14-042205-6). Penguin.
Twenty Major Wall Street Classics with Pertinent Commentaries which, Properly Applied, Will Guide You to the Accumulation of the Fortune You Are After. C. M. Flumiani. (Illus.). 117p. 1986. 57.75 (ISBN 0-86654-187-X). Inst Econ Finan.
Twenty Million Yankees. LC 84-28030. (Civil War Ser.). 1985. lib. bdg. 19.94 (ISBN 0-8094-3951-4, Pub. by Time-Life). Silver.
Twenty Modern Men. National Observer. 1973. Repr. of 1891 ed. 25.00 (ISBN 0-8274-0806-4). R West.
Twenty Months a Prisoner of War. Bernhard Domschke. LC 85-46015. 1987. 19.50 (ISBN 0-8386-3286-6). Fairleigh Dickinson.
Twenty Months in Auschwitz. Pelagia Lewinska. Tr. by Albert Teichner. 1968. 4.95 (ISBN 0-8184-0090-0). Lyle Stuart.
Twenty Months in Captivity: Memoirs of a Union Officer in Confederate Prisons. Bernhard Domschcke. Ed. by Frederic Trautmann. LC 85-46015. 176p. 1987. 26.50x (ISBN 0-317-64558-7). Fairleigh Dickinson.
Twenty Most Asked Questions about the Amish & Mennonites. Merle Good & Phyllis Good. LC 79-54804. (People's Place Booklet Ser.: No.1). (Illus.). 96p. 1979. pap. 4.50 (ISBN 0-934672-00-8). Good Bks PA.
Twenty Most Valuable Books for Speculative Success in the Stock Market with Elucidations Sufficient to Master the Content of Each Single Book. Spencer Fleming. (Illus.). 97p. 1984. pap. 54.75 (ISBN 0-86654-133-0). Inst Econ Finan.
Twenty-Mule Team & a Sketch of Its Famous Driver - Borax Bill. (Illus.). 1981. wrappers 1.50 (ISBN 0-930704-05-3). Sagebrush Pr.
Twenty Mule Team Days in Death Valley. 7th ed. Harold O. Weight. 1985. pap. 1.95 (ISBN 0-912714-00-X). Calico Pr.
Twenty New Ways of Teaching the Bible. Donald L. Griggs. (Griggs Educational Resources Ser.). 1979. pap. 7.25 (ISBN 0-687-42740-1). Abingdon.
Twenty New Ways to Get the Minister Out of Moneyraising. E. F. Brose. 1976. 2.50 (ISBN 0-941500-18-7). Sharing Co.
Twenty Nine Fifty Nine Deluxe Prayer Plan. Date not set. price not set (ISBN 0-918403-01-4). Agape Ministries.
Twenty Nine Fifty Nine Regular Prayer Plan. Date not set. price not set (ISBN 0-918403-00-6). Agape Ministries.
Twenty-Nine Most Common Writing Mistakes & How to Avoid Them. Judy Delton. LC 84-27117. (Writer's Basic Bookshelf Ser.). 73p. 1985. 9.95 (ISBN 0-89879-172-3). Writers Digest.
Twenty-Nine Papers on Statistics & Probability. A. Aksomaitis et al. LC 61-9803. (Selected Translations in Mathematical Statistics & Probability Ser.: Vol. 9). 1971. 41.00 (ISBN 0-8218-1459-1, STAPRO-9). Am Math.
Twenty-Nine Puppet Plays for the Lollipop Dragon & Friends. Betty Foster. 64p. 1986. wkbk 4.95 (ISBN 0-87239-999-0, 3359). Standard Pub.
Twenty-Nine Reasons Not to Go to Law School. 3rd, rev. ed. Ralph Warner & Toni Ihara. LC 82-99889. 142p. 1987. pap. 8.95 (ISBN 0-87337-053-8). Nolo Pr.
Twenty-Nine Tales from the French. facsimile ed. Ed. by Alys E. Macklin. Tr. & intro. by Robert Herrick. LC 72-157785. (Short Story Index Reprint Ser.). Repr. of 1922 ed. 19.00 (ISBN 0-8369-3897-6). Ayer Co Pubs.
Twenty-Nine Years in the West Indies & Central Africa. 2nd rev ed. H. M. Waddell. 1970. Repr. of 1863 ed. 35.00x (ISBN 0-7146-1881-0, BHA 01881, F Cass Co). Biblio Dist.
Twenty-Ninth Annual Antitrust Law Institute. (Corporate Law & Practice Course Handbook Ser.). Date not set. 45.00 (B46829). PLI.
Twenty-Ninth Day. Lester Brown. 1978. 11.95 (ISBN 0-393-05664-3); pap. 7.95 (ISBN 0-393-05673-2). Norton.
Twenty-Ninth Estate Planning Institute. 228p. 1984. 12.00 (ISBN 0-318-02396-2). ICLE Georgia.
Twenty-Ninth Midwest Symposium on Circuits & Systems. Ed. by M. Ismail. 1001p. 1987. 159.00 (ISBN 0-444-01201-X, North Holland). Elsevier.
Twenty Notches. Max Brand. 224p. 1987. pap. 2.75 (ISBN 0-515-08897-8). Jove Pubns.
Twenty of the Plays, 4 Vols. William Shakespeare. Ed. by George Steevens. LC 68-55094. Repr. of 1766 ed. Set. lib. bdg. 195.00 (ISBN 0-404-05820-5). AMS Pr.
Twenty One Afternoons of Biology. Stephan O. Schiff & Mimi Bres. 198p. 1987. pap. text ed. 22.95 (ISBN 0-8403-4137-7). Kendall Hunt.
Twenty-One Americans. facsimile ed. Niven Busch. LC 72-99686. (Essay Index Reprint Ser.). 1930. 24.50 (ISBN 0-8369-1552-6). Ayer Co Pubs.
Twenty-One, & Over. William L. Fox. Ed. by Kirk Robertson. (Illus.). 36p. 1982. pap. 3.00 (ISBN 0-916918-18-1); pap. 10.00 (ISBN 0-916918-19-X). Duck Down.
Twenty-One Balloons. William P. Du Bois. (Newbery Library). (Illus.). 184p. (gr. 5-9). 1986. pap. 3.95 (ISBN 0-14-032097-0, Puffin). Penguin.
Twenty One Balloons. William Pene Du Bois. (Illus.). 192p. (gr. 4-8). 1982. pap. 2.75 (ISBN 0-440-49183-5, YB). Dell.
Twenty-One Balloons. William Pene Du Bois. (Illus.). (gr. 5-9). 1947. 12.95 (ISBN 0-670-73441-1). Viking.
Twenty-One Balloons see Newberry Library Award.
Twenty-One Days to a Trained Dog. Dick Maller & Jeffrey Feinman. 1979. pap. 6.95 (ISBN 0-671-25193-7, Fireside). S&S.
Twenty-One Fifty A.D. Thea Alexander. 281p. (Orig.). 1971. pap. 6.50 (ISBN 0-913080-03-9). Macro Bks.
Twenty-One Great Stories. Ed. by Abraham Lass & Norma Tasman. (Orig.). 1969. pap. 3.95 (ISBN 0-451-62521-8, Ment). NAL.
Twenty One Lessons in Acting: A Workbook for Young Actors. Donald Wait Keyes & Dorothy Sands. 112p. 1980. 19.95 (ISBN 0-318-16876-6). World Modeling.
Twenty-One Letters of Ambrose Bierce. limited ed. Samuel Loveman. LC 73-12618. 1922. Repr. lib. bdg. 30.00 (ISBN 0-8414-5652-6). Folcroft.
Twenty-One Letters: Robert Bridges & R. C. Trevelyan. Robert Bridges. 1955. lib. bdg. 25.00 (ISBN 0-8414-2897-2). Folcroft.
Twenty-One Medieval Latin Poems. Ed. by Edwardj. Martin. 1931. Repr. 20.00 (ISBN 0-8274-3656-4). R West.
Twenty-One Mile Swim. Matt Christopher. LC 79-15197. (gr. 3-7). 1979. 11.95 (ISBN 0-316-13979-3). Little.
Twenty-One Poems. Lionel Johnson. Ed. by W. B. Yeats. 40p. 1971. Repr. of 1904 ed. 15.00x (ISBN 0-7165-1331-5, Pub. by Cuala Press Ireland). Biblio Dist.
Twenty-One Poems. Jack Lindeman. 1963. pap. 6.00 (ISBN 0-685-62609-1). Atlantis Edns.
Twenty-One Poems. Marco A. Montes de Oca. Ed. by Yvette E. Miller. Tr. by Laura Villasenor. LC 82-20833. 73p. 1982. pap. 9.00 (ISBN 0-935480-09-9). Lat Am Lit Rev Pr.
Twenty-One Poems. Katherine Tynan. Ed. by William B. Yeats. 48p. 1971. Repr. of 1907 ed. 15.00x (ISBN 0-7165-1336-6, BBA 02083, Pub. by Cuala Press Ireland). Biblio Dist.
Twenty-One Poems: Old & New. Naomi Replansky. (Orig.). 1988. pap. 5.95 (ISBN 0-9619869-0-5). Gingko Pr.
Twenty-One Stories. Y. Agnon. Ed. by Nahum N. Glatzer. LC 71-108902. 1971. pap. 8.95 (ISBN 0-8052-0313-3). Schocken.
Twenty-One Stories. Graham Greene. 200p. 1981. pap. 4.95 (ISBN 0-14-003093-X). Penguin.
Twenty-One Texas Short Stories. Ed. by William Peery. 272p. 1954. pap. 8.95 (ISBN 0-292-73452-2). U of Tex Pr.
Twenty-One Things Shortly to Come to Pass in Israel. Gordon Lindsay. 1.25 (ISBN 0-89985-192-4). Christ Nations.
Twenty One-Twenty One: Funny Stories & How to Tell Them. Winston K. Pendleton. LC 64-22702. 1977. pap. 9.95 (ISBN 0-8272-3622-0). CBP.
Twenty-One Waking Dreams. Roger Weaver. 60p. (Orig.). 1985. pap. 4.95 (ISBN 0-916155-01-3). Trout Creek.
Twenty-One Wins: The Gambler's Edge. Jere Russell. LC 81-70297. (Illus.). 240p. (Orig.). 1981. pap. text ed. 12.50 (ISBN 0-941922-00-6). Bon Chance Ent.
Twenty-One Years of World Cup Ski Racing. Serge Lang. (Illus.). 200p. 1987. 19.95 (ISBN 1-55566-009-6). Johnson Bks.
Twenty Painters St. Ives. Marion Whybrow. 1985. 9.00x (ISBN 0-907566-93-6, Pub. by Dyllansow & Truran). State Mutual Bk.
Twenty Papers on Analytic Functions & Ordinary Differential Equations. V. G. Boltyanskii et al. LC 51-5559. (Translations Ser.: No. 2, Vol. 18). 1961. 33.00 (ISBN 0-8218-1718-3, TRANS 2-18). Am Math.
Twenty Papers on Statistics & Probability. M. Arato et al. (Selected Translations in Mathematics Statistics & Probability Ser.: Vol. 13). 1973. 61.00 (ISBN 0-8218-1463-X, STAPRO 13). Am Math.
Twenty Papers on Statistics & Probability. Ch'En Hsi-Ju et al. LC 61-9803. (Selected Translations in Mathematical Statistics & Probability Ser.: Vol. 12). 1973. 50.00 (ISBN 0-8218-1462-1, STAPRO-12). Am Math.
Twenty Plays for Young People. Frwd. by William B. Birner. (YA) (gr. 12 up). 1967. 20.00 (ISBN 0-87602-015-5). Anchorage.
Twenty Plays of the No Theatre. Ed. by Donald Keene. Tr. by Tyler et al from Japanese. LC 74-121556. (Records of Civilization Sources & Studies & Translations of the Oriental Classics Ser.). 336p. 1970. pap. 17.50x (ISBN 0-231-03455-5). Columbia U Pr.
Twenty Poems. 3rd ed. John Haines. LC 78-134756. 1982. pap. 4.00 (ISBN 0-87775-045-9). Unicorn Pr.
Twenty Poems of Anna Akhmatova. Anna Akhmatova. Tr. by Jane Kenyon & Vera S. Dunham. 54p. 1985. pap. 6.95 (ISBN 0-915408-30-9). Ally Pr.
Twenty Poems of Rolf Jacobsen. Rolf Jacosen. Ed. by Robert Bly. 1977. pap. 3.50 (ISBN 0-685-88845-2). Eighties Pr.
Twenty Problems--Twenty Solutions: The Basic Design Workbook. Raymond Dorn. (Illus.). 88p. 1980. pap. 12.95 (ISBN 0-931368-03-0). Ragan Comm.
Twenty Progressive Exercises for Violin, Op. 38a. J. Dont. (Carl Fischer Music Library: No. 357). 1964. pap. 6.00 (ISBN 0-8258-0044-7, L357). Fischer Inc NY.
Twenty Prose Poems. rev. ed. Charles Baudelaire. Tr. & intro. by Michael Hamburger. 64p. 1988. pap. 4.95 (ISBN 0-87286-216-X). City Lights.
Twenty Proven Ways to Profit from Real Estate. R. J. Turner. 192p. 1988. 16.95 (ISBN 0-8092-4502-7). Contemp Bks.
Twenty Questions: An Introduction to Philosophy. G. Lee Bowie et al. 782p. 1988. pap. text ed. 17.00 (ISBN 0-15-592388-9, HC). HarBraceJ.
Twenty Questions for the Writer: A Rhetoric with Readings. 4th ed. Jacqueline Berke. 630p. 1985. pap. text ed. 13.00 net (ISBN 0-15-592403-6, HC); instr's. manual avail. (ISBN 0-15-592404-4). HarBraceJ.
Twenty Reading Comprehension Games. Marla Love. (Makemaster Bk.). (gr. 4-6). 1977. pap. 8.95 (ISBN 0-8224-5800-4). D S Lake Pubs.

Twister of Twists, a Tangler of Tongues. Alvin Schwartz. LC 72-1434. (Illus.). 126p. (gr. 6 up). 1972. 11.70i (ISBN 0-397-31387-X, Lipp Jr Bks); pap. 1.95 o. p. (ISBN 0-397-31412-4, LSC-22). HarpJ.

Twister Talk. Debbie Harrison. 10p. (gr. 5). 1983. pap 21.95 (ISBN 0-88450-846-3, 4617-B). Communication Skill.

Twisting Shadows. Emma Darcy. (Harlequin Presents Ser.). 192p. 1983. pap. 1.95 (ISBN 0-373-10648-3). Harlequin Bks.

Twisting the Rope. R. A. MacAvoy. 256p. (Orig.). 1986. pap. 3.50 (ISBN 0-553-26026-X, Spectra). Bantam.

Twisting the Truth. Bruce Tucker. 192p. (Orig.). 1987. pap. 5.95 (ISBN 0-87123-931-0). Bethany Hse.

Twistor Geometry & Field Theory. R. S. Ward & R. O. Wells, Jr. (Cambridge Monographs on Mathematical Physics). 350p. Date not set. price not set (ISBN 0-521-26890-7). Cambridge U Pr.

Twistor Geometry & Non-Linear Systems: Proceedings, Primorsko, Bulgaria, 1980. Ed. by H. D. Doebner & T. D. Palev. (Lecture Notes in Mathematics Ser.: Vol. 970). 216p. 1982. pap. 14.00 (ISBN 0-387-11972-8). Springer-Verlag.

Twitchell the Wishful. Marjorie W. Sharmat. LC 80-16845. (Illus.). 40p. (gr. k-3). 1981. reinforced bdg. 9.95 (ISBN 0-8234-0379-3). Holiday.

Twits. Roald Dahl. 96p. 1982. pap. 2.75 (ISBN 0-553-15343-9). Bantam.

Twits. Roald Dahl & Mary Tannen. LC 80-18410. (Illus.). 96p. (ps-5). 1981. lib. bdg. 7.99 (ISBN 0-394-94599-9). Knopf.

Twixt Land & Sea: Three Tales. Joseph Conrad. Intro. by Boris Ford. 240p. 1988. pap. 4.95 (ISBN 0-14-043294-9). Penguin.

Twixt North & South. H. M. Calhoun. 1974. 10.00 (ISBN 0-87012-166-9). McClain.

Twixt Sand & Sea. C. F. Grant & L. Grant. 622p. 1986. 350.00x (ISBN 1-85077-094-8, Pub. by Darf Pubs Ltd). State Mutual Bk.

Twixt: Teens Yesterday & Today. Ernie Anastos & Jack Levin. (Illus.). 244p. 1983. pap. 9.95 (ISBN 0-531-09953-9). Watts.

Twixt Wind & Water. Leona R. Phillips. LC 80-12218. 183p. 1984. 11.95 (ISBN 0-87949-179-5). Ashley Bks.

Two. Harry Crews. 40p. 1984. deluxe ed. 50.00 Signed Ed. (ISBN 0-935716-32-7). Lord John.

Two. Ron Elisha. 56p. (Orig.). 1987. pap. 7.95 (ISBN 0-936839-70-8). Applause Theatre Bk Pubs.

Two. John D. MacDonald. 104p. 1983. pap. 2.50 (ISBN 0-88184-011-4). Carroll & Graf.

Two. Brian Pomeroy. LC 88-90559. 87p. (Orig.). 1988. pap. 4.95 (ISBN 0-9620101-0-3). Phase One Pr.

Two Abnormal Busycon Shells see Palaeontographica Americana.

Two Addresses. James W. Nesmith. 56p. 1978. 7.95 (ISBN 0-87770-200-4); pap. 5.95 (ISBN 0-87770-202-0). Ye Galleon.

Two Admirals: A Tale. James Fenimore Cooper. (Writings of James Fenimore Cooper). (Orig.). (YA) (gr. 9-12). 1989. text ed. 44.50x (ISBN 0-88706-905-3); pap. 14.95X (ISBN 0-88706-907-X). State U NY Pr.

Two Aesthetic Realism Papers: Opposites in the Drama; Opposites in Myself. Martha Baird. LC 79-268159. 1971. pap. 2.95 (ISBN 0-910492-15-8). Definition.

Two Against Cape Horn. Hal Roth. 272p. 1981. 35.00x (ISBN 0-540-07144-7). State Mutual Bk.

Two Against Cape Horn. Hal Roth. (Illus.). 288p. 1985. pap. 8.95 (ISBN 0-393-30259-8). Norton.

Two Against One. Frederick Barthelme. 1988. 17.95 (ISBN 1-55584-214-3). Weidenfeld.

Two Against the Tide. Bruce Clements. 224p. (gr. 4 up). 1987. pap. 3.50 (ISBN 0-374-48016-8, Sunburst). FS&G.

Two Against Time. Joy N. Humes. LC 78-3474. (Studies in the Romance Languages & Literatures: No. 200). 172p. 1978. pap. 15.00x (ISBN 0-8078-9200-9). U of NC Pr.

Two Alone. Erin St. Claire. (Intimate Moments Ser.). pap. 2.74 (ISBN 0-373-07213-9). Harlequin Bks.

Two American Political Systems: Society, Economics, & Politics. Creel Froman. (Illus.). 288p. 1984. pap. text ed. 22.00 (ISBN 0-13-934902-2). P-H.

Two Ancient Christologies: A Study in the Christological Thought of the Schools of Alexandria & Antioch in the Early History of Christian Doctrine. (Church Historical Society. Publications, New Series, 38.) Robert V. Sellers. LC 82-45824. (Orthodoxies & Heresies in the Early Church Ser.). Date not set. Repr. of 1940 ed. 32.50 (ISBN 0-404-62394-8). AMS Pr.

Two & the One. Mircea Eliade. Tr. by J. M. Cohen. LC 79-2268. 1979. pap. 10.00 (ISBN 0-226-20389-1, P811). U of Chicago Pr.

Two & Three Part Inventions (Fifteen Inventions & Fifteen Symphonies) Johann S. Bach. Ed. by Eric Simon. LC 68-11918. (Facsimile Series of Musical Manuscripts). (Orig.). 1969. pap. 5.95 (ISBN 0-486-21982-8). Dover.

Two & Three-Part Inventions for Piano. J. S. Bach. Ed. by Carl Czerny. (Carl Fischer Music Library: No. 304). 63p. (Eng. & Ger.). 1903. pap. 6.50 (ISBN 0-8258-0102-8, L 304). Fischer Inc NY.

Two & Two Are Four. Carolyn Haywood. LC 86-4619. (Illus.). 180p. (gr. k-3). 1986. pap. 4.95 (ISBN 0-15-291771-3, VoyB). HarBraceJ.

Two Angry Women of Abingdon. Henry Porter. LC 70-133722. (Tudor Facsimile Texts. Old English Plays: No. 87). Repr. of 1911 ed. 49.50 (ISBN 0-404-53387-6). AMS Pr.

Two Angry Women of Abingdon. Henry Porter. LC 82-45763. (Malone Society Reprint Ser.: No. 31). Repr. of 1912 ed. 40.00 (ISBN 0-404-63031-6). AMS Pr.

Two Angry Women of Abingdon: A Critical Edition. Henry Porter. Ed. by Marianne B. Evett. LC 79-54336. (Renaissance Drama Ser.). 304p. 1980. lib. bdg. 40.00 (ISBN 0-8240-4454-1). Garland Pub.

Two Applications of Logic to Mathematics. Gaisi Takeuti. (Publications of the Mathematical Society of Japan Ser.: No. 13). 1978. 28.00x (ISBN 0-691-08212-X). Princeton U Pr.

Two Are Twins. June Albertsen. LC 86-70195. (Illus.). 31p. (ps-3). 1987. pap. 5.95 (ISBN 0-9615839-0-8). Double Talk.

Two at One Piano. Jon George. Ed. by Frances Clark & Louise Goss. Incl. Bk 1. 1969. pap. text ed. 5.95 (ISBN 0-87487-141-7); Bk 2. 1972. pap. text ed. 5.95 (ISBN 0-87487-142-5); Bk 3. 1976. pap. text ed. 5.95 (ISBN 0-87487-143-3). (Frances Clark Library for Piano Students Ser.). pap. Birch Tree Gr.

Two at the Net. H. R. Sheffer. Ed. by Howard Schroeder. LC 80-28429. (Teamates Ser.). (Illus.). 48p. (gr. 3 up). 1981. PLB 7.95 (ISBN 0-89686-108-2). Crestwood Hse.

Two Augustans: John Locke, Jonathan Swift. Ricardo Quintana. LC 77-91059. 156p. 1978. 26.50x (ISBN 0-299-07420-X). U of Wis Pr.

Two Aztec Wood Idols: Iconographic & Chronologic Analysis. H. B. Nicholson & Rainer Berger. LC 68-58701. (Studies in Pre-Columbian Art & Archaeology: No.5). (Illus.). 28p. 1968. pap. 3.00x (ISBN 0-88402-026-6). Dumbarton Oaks.

Two-B & the Rock & Roll Band. Sherry Paul. (See How I Read Ser.). (Illus.). 32p. (gr. 1). 1981. pap. write for info. Modern Curr.

Two-B & the Rock 'n' Roll Band. Sherry Paul. (See How I Read Ser.). (Illus.). 32p. (Orig.). (ps-2). pap. 14.10 set (ISBN 0-675-01082-9); Bks & Skillmasters set 16.20. CPI Pub.

Two-B & the Space Visitor. Sherry Paul. (See How I Read Ser.). (Illus.). 32p. (Orig.). (ps-2). pap. 14.10 bks. only; pap. 16.20 Bks. & Skill Masters. CPI Pub.

Two-B & the Space Visitor. Sherry Paul. (See How I Read Ser.). (Illus.). 32p. (gr. 1). 1981. pap. write for info. Modern Curr.

Two Babylons. Alexander Hislop. 9.95 (ISBN 0-87213-330-3). Loizeaux.

Two Babylons. Gordon Lindsay. (Revelation Ser.). 1.25 (ISBN 0-89985-046-4). Christ Nations.

Two Bacchises see Amphitryon.

Two Bad Ants. Chris Van Allsburg. (Illus.). 32p. (ps up). 1988. 15.95 (ISBN 0-395-48668-8). HM.

Two Bad Mice Pop-Up Book. Beatrix Potter. (Illus.). (ps-3). 1986. 11.95 (ISBN 0-7232-3360-8). Warne.

Two Battles of the Little Horn. Ed. by John M. Carroll. (Illus.). 1985. pap. 18.95 (ISBN 0-8488-0029-X, Pub. by J M C & Co). Amereon Ltd.

Two Bear Cubs. Ann Jonas. LC 82-2860. (Illus.). 24p. (gr. k-3). 1982. PLB 11.88 (ISBN 0-688-01408-9). Greenwillow.

Two Become One. J. Allan Petersen et al. 1973. pap. 3.95 (ISBN 0-8423-7620-8). Tyndale.

Two Birds Flying. Phyllis S. Prokop. Ed. by Frances B. Goodman. (Illus.). 1984. 8.95 (ISBN 0-89896-150-5). Larksdale.

Two Bishops. Agnes S. Turnbull. 1980. 10.95 (ISBN 0-395-29201-8). HM.

Two-Bit Culture: The Paperbacking of America. Kenneth C. Davis. LC 83-22767. 430p. 1984. 18.95 (ISBN 0-395-34398-4); pap. 9.95 (ISBN 0-395-35535-4). HM.

Two Bites at a Cherry, with Other Tales. facsimile ed. Thomas B. Aldrich. 1972. Repr. of 1894 ed. lib. bdg. 27.00 (ISBN 0-8422-8002-2). Irvington.

Two Bites at a Cherry, with Other Tales. Thomas B. Aldrich. 1986. pap. text ed. 6.95x (ISBN 0-8290-2044-6). Irvington.

Two Black Folk Artists: Clementine Hunter & Nellie Mae Rowe. Sterling Cook. LC 86-62956. 16p. 1986. pap. 5.00 (ISBN 0-940784-09-2). Miami Univ Art.

Two Black Teachers During the Civil War: Mary S. Peake: The Colored Teacher at Fortress Monroe. Lewis C. Lockwood & Charlotte L. Forten. 1970. 10.00 (ISBN 0-405-01931-9, 16381). Ayer Co Pubs.

Two Black Views of Liberia: Four Months in Liberia, or African Colonization Exposed Four Years in Liberia, a Sketch of the Life of Rev. Samuel Williams. William Nesbit & Samuel Williams. LC 70-92234. (American Negro: His History & Literature, Ser. No. 3). 1970. Repr. of 1855 ed. 13.00 (ISBN 0-405-01936-X). Ayer Co Pubs.

Two Blades of Grass: A History of Scientific Development in the U. S. Department of Agriculture. T. Swann Harding. Ed. by I. Bernard Cohen. LC 79-7966. (Three Centuries of Science in America Ser.). (Illus.). 1980. Repr. of 1947 ed. lib. bdg. 32.50x (ISBN 0-405-12547-X). Ayer Co Pubs.

Two Blocks Down. Jina Delton. 128p. 1982. pap. 1.50 (ISBN 0-451-11477-9, AW1477, Sig Vista). NAL.

Two Blocks from Happiness. Lois Morse. 176p. 1985. pap. 6.95 (ISBN 0-87239-860-9, 3005). Standard Pub.

Two Books on Stanzas of Dzyan. Blavatsky. 6.75 (ISBN 0-8356-7223-9). Theos Pub Hse.

Two Books...of the Proficience & Advancement of Learning. Francis Bacon. LC 70-25525. (English Experience Ser.: No. 218). 236p. Repr. of 1605 ed. 39.00 (ISBN 90-221-0218-1). Walter J Johnson.

Two-Boy Cruise. Bonnie Towne. 128p. (gr. 6-8). 1986. 1.95 (ISBN 0-87406-149-0). Willowisp Pr.

Two Boys, A Girl, & Enough: Reproductive & Economic Decisionmaking on the Mexican Periphery. Jeanne M. Simonelli. (Women in Cross-Cultural Perspective Ser.). xx, 232p. 1986. pap. 21.50 (ISBN 0-8133-7190-2). Westview.

Two Brahman Sources of Emerson & Thoreau, 1822-1832. Ed. by William B. Stein. LC 67-10340. 1967. 50.00x (ISBN 0-8201-1043-4). Schol Facsimiles.

Two Brahmanical Institutions-Gotra & Charana. G. S. Ghurye. 312p. 1972. 15.95. Asia Bk Corp.

Two Branches of the Same Stream. E. N. Griswold. (Maccabaean Lectures in Jurisprudence Ser.). 1962. pap. 2.25 (ISBN 0-902732-47-1, Pub. by British Acad). Longwood Pub Group.

Two Brazilian Capitals: Architecture & Urbanism in Rio de Janeiro & Brasilia. Norma Evenson. LC 72-91293. (Illus.). 416p. 1973. 50.00x (ISBN 0-300-01540-2). Yale U Pr.

Two-Bridge Knotts Have Property P. Moto-O Takahashi. LC 80-26113. (MEMO: No. 239). 104p. 1981. pap. 11.00 (ISBN 0-8218-2239-X). Am Math.

Two Brothers. James M. Bryant. LC 69-17331. 1974. pap. 6.50 (ISBN 0-686-09047-0). J M Bryant.

Two Brothers. James M. Bryant. pap. 6.50 (ISBN 0-318-18286-6). Rocket Pub Co.

Two Brothers. 1982. pap. 2.95 (ISBN 0-87306-242-6). Feldheim.

Two Brothers & Their Magic Gourds. Ed. by Edward B. Adams. (Korean Folk Stories for Children Ser.). (Illus.). 32p. (gr. 3). 1981. 6.50 (ISBN 0-8048-1474-0, Pub. by Seoul Intl Tourist Korea). C E Tuttle.

Two Bunnykins Out to Tea. Warrener. LC 83-23531. (Illus.). 24p. (ps-3). 1985. 4.95 (ISBN 0-670-80053-8, Viking Kestrel). Viking.

Two Burlettas of Kane O'Hara, Midas & the Golden Pippin: An Edition with Commentary. Ed. by Stephen Orgel. (Satire & sense Ser.). 634p. 1987. lib. bdg. 95.00 (ISBN 0-8240-6023-7). Garland Pub.

Two Busy Bears. Charles E. Reasoner. (Mother & Baby Bks.). (Illus.). 12p. (ps). 1987. bds. 4.95 (ISBN 0-8431-1770-2). Price Stern.

Two by Astley: A Kindness Cup - The Acolyte. Thea Astley. 288p. 1988. 18.95 (ISBN 0-399-13363-1). Putnam Pub Group.

Two by Ralph Waldo Trine. Ralph W. Trine. LC 86-10294. (Pivot Family Reader Ser.). 306p. (Orig.). pap. 4.50 (ISBN 0-87983-382-3). Keats.

Two by Terry Plus One. 1st limited ed. Megan Terry & Rochelle L. Holt. 3.95 (ISBN 0-317-14940-7). Merging Media.

Two by Terry Plus One: An Anthology of Plays by Women. Bd. with Pro Game. Megan Terry; Pioneer. Megan Terry; Walking into the Dawn: A Celebration. Rochelle L. Holt. (Illus.). 64p. (Orig.). 1984. pap. 3.50 (ISBN 0-88680-218-0); royalty 60.45 (ISBN 0-317-11922-2). I E Clark.

Two by Thomas Hardy. Thomas Hardy. LC 87-50438. 97p. 1987. pap. 3.95 (ISBN 0-940561-08-5). White Rose Pr.

Two by Two. Bo Beskow. 128p. 1981. pap. 2.95 (ISBN 0-380-55210-8, 55210-8, Bard). Avon.

Two by Two. Henrietta Gambill. (Little Happy Day Bks.). (Illus.). 24p. (ps-2). 1985. pap. 0.49 (ISBN 0-87239-936-2, 2192). Standard Pub.

Two by Two Romance, No. 1: Cassie & Chris. Sara Casey. 192p. (Orig.). 1983. pap. 1.95 (ISBN 0-446-30801-3). Warner Bks.

Two by Two Romance, No. 10: Just the Way you Are. Lisa Norby. 192p. 1984. pap. 1.95 (ISBN 0-446-32032-3). Warner Bks.

Two by Two Romance, No. 11: Kiss for Good Luck. Carol Ellis. 176p. (Orig.). 1984. pap. 1.95 (ISBN 0-446-32014-5). Warner Bks.

Two by Two Romance, No. 12: Here To Stay. M. L. Kennedy. 192p. (Orig.). 1984. pap. 2.25 (ISBN 0-446-32016-1). Warner Bks.

Two by Two Romance, No. 13: Secret Hearts. Janice Harrell. 192p. (Orig.). 1984. pap. 2.25 (ISBN 0-446-32168-0). Warner Bks.

Two by Two Romance, No. 14: Looking at You. Mark Emerson. (Romance Ser.). (Illus.). 160p. 1984. pap. 2.25 (ISBN 0-446-32170-2). Warner Bks.

Two by Two Romance, No. 2: Jed & Jessie. Abby Connell. 192p. (Orig.). 1983. pap. 1.95 (ISBN 0-446-30802-1). Warner Bks.

Two by Two Romance, No. 3: Change of Heart. Patricia Aks. 192p. (Orig.). 1983. pap. 1.95 (ISBN 0-446-30803-X). Warner Bks.

Two by Two Romance, No. 4: Only a Dream Away. Kathryn Makris. 192p. 1983. pap. 1.95 (ISBN 0-446-30804-8). Warner Bks.

Two by Two Romance, No. 5: One Special Summer. Janice Harrell. 192p. (Orig.). 1984. pap. 1.95 (ISBN 0-446-30805-6). Warner Bks.

Two by Two Romance, No. 6: Handle with Care. Lucy Malone. 192p. (Orig.). 1984. pap. 1.95 (ISBN 0-446-30806-4). Warner Bks.

Two by Two Romance, No. 7: In-Between Love. Kim Kennedy. 192p. (Orig.). 1984. pap. 1.95 (ISBN 0-446-32006-4). Warner Bks.

Two by Two Romance, No. 8: Falling in Love Again, No. 8. Peter Filichia. 192p. (Orig.). 1984. pap. 1.95 (ISBN 0-446-32028-5). Warner Bks.

Two by Two Romances, No. 9: Weekends for Us. Kathryn Makris. 192p. (Orig.). 1984. pap. 1.95 (ISBN 0-446-32030-7). Warner Bks.

Two by Two: The Untold Story. Kathryn Hewitt. LC 84-4579. (Illus.). 32p. (ps-3). 1984. PLB 12.95 (ISBN 0-15-291801-9, HJ). HarBraceJ.

Two Californias: The Truth about the Split-State Movement. Michael DiLeo & Eleanor Smith. (Illus.). 250p. (Orig.). 1983. pap. 12.95 (ISBN 0-933280-16-5). Island CA.

Two Called Together. George Gerl & George Lane. 1978. pap. text ed. 4.00 (ISBN 0-8294-0274-8); tchr's ed. 4.00 (ISBN 0-8294-0277-2). Loyola.

Two Can Play. Trevor Rhone. Ed. by Terry Tucker. 84p. 1984. wkbk. 3.50 (ISBN 0-910475-27-X). KET.

Two Can Toucan. David McKee. (Illus.). 32p. (gr. k-3). 1987. 12.95 (ISBN 0-86264-094-6, Pub. by Century Hutchinson). David & Charles.

Two-Career Marriage. G. Wade Rowatt, Jr. & Mary Jo Rowatt. LC 79-28408. (Christian Care Bks.: Vol. 5). 120p. 1980. pap. 7.95 (ISBN 0-664-24298-7). Westminster John Knox.

Two Careers: One Marriage. William M. Jones & Ruth A. Jones. 1980. 12.95 (ISBN 0-8144-5589-1). AMACOM.

Two Carlyles. O. Burdett. LC 71-130269. (English Biography Ser., No. 31). 1970. Repr. of 1931 ed. lib. bdg. 52.95x (ISBN 0-8383-1176-8). Haskell.

Two Carlyles. Osbert Burdett. 1977. Repr. of 1931 ed. lib. bdg. 20.00 (ISBN 0-8495-0319-1). Arden Lib.

Two Carlyles. facsimile ed. Osbert Burdett. LC 78-164591. (Select Bibliographies Reprint Ser.). Repr. of 1930 ed. 21.00 (ISBN 0-8369-5875-6). Ayer Co Pubs.

Two Carlyles. Osbert Burdett. 319p. 1980. Repr. lib. bdg. 25.00. Darby Bks.

Two Carlyles. Osbert Burdett. 1973. lib. bdg. 15.75 (ISBN 0-8414-2545-0). Folcroft.

Two Carolines. Gloria Martinis. (Orig.). 1976. pap. 1.50 (ISBN 0-685-64018-3, LB339DK, Leisure Bks). Leisure NY.

Two Cartographers: Gudbrandur Thorlaksson & Thordur Thorlaksson. Haandor Hermannsson. LC 27-13445. (Islandica Ser.: Vol. 17). 1926. 23.00 (ISBN 0-527-00347-6). Kraus Repr.

Two Cents Pieces. 2nd ed. M. Kliman. LC 82-70831. (Illus.). 1983. pap. 10.00 (ISBN 0-915262-84-3). S J Durst.

Two Centuries of African English. Lalage Bown. (African Writers Ser.). 1973. pap. text ed. 7.50 (ISBN 0-435-90132-X). Heinemann Ed.

Two Centuries of American Agriculture. Ed. by V. Wiser. 1976. cancelled. McNally & Loftin.

Two Centuries of American Banking: A Pictorial Essay. Vladimir Clain-Stefanelli & Elvira Clain-Stefanelli. LC 75-24641. 143p. 1975. 14.95; pap. 7.95 (ISBN 0-87491-031-5). Acropolis.

Two Centuries of American Medicine: 1776-1976. James Bordley, III & A. McGehee Harvey. LC 75-19841. (Illus.). 750p. 1976. text ed. 58.00 (ISBN 0-7216-1873-1). Saunders.

Two Centuries of American Planning. Ed. by Daniel Schaffer. LC 86-31293. 336p. 1988. text ed. 48.50x (ISBN 0-8018-3647-6); pap. text ed. 14.95x (ISBN 0-8018-3719-7). Johns Hopkins.

Two Centuries of Bach. Friedrich Blume. Tr. by Stanley Godman. LC 77-27291. (Music Reprint Ser.). 1978. Repr. of 1950 ed. lib. bdg. 21.50 (ISBN 0-306-77567-0). Da Capo.

Two Centuries of Ceramics in the Richelieu Valley. pap. write for info. (Pub. by Natl Mus Canada). U of Chicago Pr.

Two Centuries of Costume in America, 2 vols. Alice Earle. 824p. 1974. Repr. of 1903 ed. Set. 60.00 (ISBN 0-87928-054-9). Corner Hse.

Two Centuries of Costume in America, 2 Vols. Alice M. Earle. LC 68-56468. (Illus.). 1968. Repr. of 1903 ed. Set. 40.00 (ISBN 0-405-08477-3, Blom Pubns); 20.00 ea. Vol. 1 (ISBN 0-405-08478-1). Vol. 2 (ISBN 0-405-08479-X). Ayer Co Pubs.

Two Centuries of Ecumenism. Georges H. Tavard. LC 78-6449. 1978. Repr. of 1960 ed. lib. bdg. 35.00x (ISBN 0-313-20490-X, TATC). Greenwood.

Two Centuries of Hispanic Theatre in the Southwest. Nicolas Kanellos. 1985. 2.00 (ISBN 0-317-06977-2). Arte Publico.

Two Centuries of Life & Art in America. Howard E. Wooden. LC 87-51156. (Illus.). 80p. 1987. pap. 5.00 (ISBN 0-939324-31-8). Wichita Art Mus.

Two Centuries of Prints in America, 1680-1880: A Selective Catalogue of the Winterthur Collection. E. McSherry Fowble. LC 87-611. (Illus.). 512p. 1988. 60.00 (ISBN 0-8139-1124-9). U Pr of VA.

Two Centuries of Spanish & English Bilingual Lexicography, 1590-1800. Roger J. Steiner. LC 74-110958. (Janua Linguarum, Ser. Practica: No. 108). (Orig.). 1970. pap. text ed. 13.60x (ISBN 90-2790-743-9). Mouton.

Two Ears of Corn: A Guide to People-Centered Agricultural Improvement. 2nd ed. Roland Bunder. (Illus.). 250p. (Orig.). 1985. pap. 7.95 (ISBN 0-317-62186-6). World Neigh.
Two-Edged Sword: Armed Force in the Modern World, The Reith Lectures 1981. Laurence Martin. 1982. 13.95 (ISBN 0-393-01655-2). Norton.
Two Elizabethan Puritan Diaries. Richard Rogers & Samuel Ward. Ed. by Marshall M. Knappen. 1933. 11.75 (ISBN 0-8446-1387-8). Peter Smith.
Two Elizabethan Stage Abridgements: The Battle of Alcazar & Orlando Furioso, 2 vols. Ed. by W. W. Greg. LC 82-45784. (Malone Society Reprints Ser.: No. 53). Date not set. Repr. of 1922 ed. Set. 80.00 (ISBN 0-404-63053-7). AMS Pr.
Two Elizabethan Writers of Fiction: Thomas Nashe & Thomas Deloney. R. G. Howarth. LC 77-3511. 1956. lib. bdg. 16.50 (ISBN 0-8414-4711-X). Folcroft.
Two Energy Futures: A National Choice for the Eighty's. rev. ed. American Petroleum Institute Staff. LC 81-7926. (Illus.). 187p. 1986. pap. text ed. write for info. (ISBN 0-89364-041-7, 877-71850). Am Petroleum.
Two Equals One. Peter Dagmar. 1986. 35.00x (ISBN 0-86332-000-7, Pub. by Book Guild Ltd). State Mutual Bk.
Two Essays: A Forgotten Aspect of the University Question & The Day of the Rabblement. F. J. Skeffington. LC 74-18057. 1974. Repr. of 1957 ed. lib. bdg. 29.50 (ISBN 0-8414-7724-8). Folcroft.
Two Essays by Wilhelm Roepke: The Problem of Economic Order, Welfare, Freedom & Inflation. Intro. by Johannes Overbeek. LC 86-33982. 114p. (Orig.). 1987. lib. bdg. 19.25 (ISBN 0-8191-6125-X); pap. text ed. 8.50 (ISBN 0-8191-6126-8). U Pr of Amer.
Two Essays on Entropy. Rudolf Carnap. Ed. by Abner Shimony. LC 73-94444. (Studies in the Logic of Science). 1978. 30.00x (ISBN 0-520-02715-9). U of Cal Pr.
Two Essays: On the Foundation of Civil Government & On the Constitution of the United States. Thomas Cooper. LC 72-99477. (American Constitutional & Legal History Ser). 1970. Repr. of 1826 ed. lib. bdg. 19.50 (ISBN 0-306-71852-9). Da Capo.
Two Essays on the Liberty of the Press. George Hay. LC 75-112703. (Civil Liberties in American History Ser). 1970. Repr. of 1803 ed. lib. bdg. 19.50 (ISBN 0-306-71918-5). Da Capo.
Two Essays on the Scientific Study of History. Lars Bo Rasmussen. 119p. 1975. 18.25 (ISBN 3-261-01650-7). P Lang Pubs.
Two Essays on Vegetarianism. Percy Bysshe Shelley. LC 75-12545. 1975. lib. bdg. 27.50 (ISBN 0-8414-7844-9). Folcroft.
Two Essays: Relation of the State to Industrial Action & Economics & Jurisprudence. Henry C. Adams. Ed. by Joseph Dorfman. LC 75-76510. (Reprints of Economic Classics). 1969. Repr. of 1954 ed. 25.00x (ISBN 0-678-00494-3). Kelley.
Two Essays Upon Matthew Arnold with Some of His Letters to the Author. Arthur Galton. LC 74-16286. 1897. lib. bdg. 15.00 (ISBN 0-8414-4550-8). Folcroft.
Two Exiles: Lord Byron & D. H. Lawrence. Graham Hough. LC 76-23314. 1956. lib. bdg. 16.00 (ISBN 0-8414-4741-1). Folcroft.
Two Fables. Roald Dahl. (Illus.). 63p. 1987. 12.95 (ISBN 0-374-28018-5). FS&G.
Two-Faced Press? Tom Goldstein. (Twentieth Century Fund Paper). 54p. (Orig.). 1986. pap. text ed. 7.50x (ISBN 0-87078-204-5). Priority Pr Pubns.
Two Faces see Aspern Papers.
Two Faces of Chemistry: The Benefits & the Risks of Chemical Technology. Luciano Caglioti & Mirella Giacconi. LC 82-12706. 240p. 1985. 22.50x (ISBN 0-262-03088-8); pap. 9.95 (ISBN 0-262-53064-3). MIT Pr.
Two Faces of Co-Existence. Alfreds Berzins. 1967. 10.95 (ISBN 0-8315-0018-2). Speller.
Two Faces of Dr. Collier. Elizabeth Seifert. 18.95 (ISBN 0-89190-937-0, Pub. by Am Repr). Amereon Ltd.
Two Faces of Ionesco. Ed. by Rosette C. Lamont & Melvin J. Friedman. LC 76-51038. 285p. 1978. 15.00x (ISBN 0-87875-110-6). Whitston Pub.
Two Faces of January. Patricia Highsmith. 288p. 1988. pap. 7.95 (ISBN 0-87113-209-5). Atlantic Monthly.
Two Faces of Malnutrition. Erik P. Eckholm & Francis Record. LC 76-47787. (Worldwatch Papers). 1976. pap. 4.00 (ISBN 0-916468-08-9). Worldwatch Inst.
Two Faces of Man: Two Studies on the Sense of Time & on Ambivalence. Joost A. Meerloo. LC 54-12141. (Illus.). pap. 62.80 (ISBN 0-317-10297-4, 2010703). Bks Demand UMI.
Two Faces of Management: An American Approach to Leadership in Business & Management. Joseph L. Bower. LC 83-141. 288p. 1983. 19.95 (ISBN 0-395-33119-6). HM.
Two Faces of Reality. Robert Jastrow. Date not set. 14.95 (ISBN 0-393-02400-8). Norton.
Two Faces of Time. Lawrence W. Fagg. LC 85-40412. (Illus.). 210p. (Orig.). 1985. pap. 7.75 (ISBN 0-8356-0599-X, Quest). Theos Pub Hse.
Two Faces of Tomorrow. James P. Hogan. 1984. pap. 2.95 (ISBN 0-345-32387-4, Del Rey Bks). Ballantine.
Two Faiths or One? David Cox. 1985. 10.00x (ISBN 0-317-62226-9, Guild of Pastoral Psych). State Mutual Bk.
Two Farms. Mary E. Pearce. 192p. 1985. 12.95 (ISBN 0-312-82684-2). St Martin.
Two Feet Between the Rails: The Early Years, Vol. 1. Robert C. Jones. (Illus.). 416p. 1979. 45.00x (ISBN 0-913582-17-4). Sundance.
Two Feet Between the Rails: The Mature Years, Vol. II. Robert C. Jones. (Illus.). 416p. 1980. 45.00x (ISBN 0-913582-18-2). Sundance.
Two Feet to Tidewater: The Wiscasset Waterville & Farmington Railway. Robert C. Jones & David L. Register. (Illus.). 275p. 1987. 34.95 (ISBN 0-87108-729-4). Pruett.
Two Fevers - Gold & Typhoid: A Social History of Western Australia 1891-1900. Vera Whittington. 692p. 1988. 55.00 (ISBN 0-85564-274-2); pap. 44.00 (ISBN 0-85564-275-0, Pub. by U of W Austral Pr). Intl Spec Bk.
Two Fifteenth-Century Cookery-Books. Ed. by T. Austin. (EETS OS Ser.: Vol. 91). Repr. of 1888 ed. 38.00 (ISBN 0-8115-0148-5). Kraus Repr.
Two Figures in Circular Dance. Katherine Privett. 12p. 1985. pap. 1.00 (ISBN 0-317-39892-X). Samisdat.
Two First Centuries of Florentine History. Pasquale Villari. LC 77-153609. Repr. of 1908 ed. 37.50 (ISBN 0-404-09294-2). AMS Pr.
Two Fish to You. Ken Schauer. 76p. 1985. pap. 4.95 (ISBN 0-933350-46-5). Morse Pr.
Two-Fisted Banana: Electric & Gothic. Mary Beach. LC 79-14957. 1980. pap. 4.00x (ISBN 0-916156-35-4). Cherry Valley.
Two-Five A System: Molecular & Clinical Aspects of the Interferon-Regulated Pathway. Bryan R. Williams & Robert H. Silverman. LC 85-19858. (PCBR, Ser.: Vol. 202). 502p. 1985. 68.00 (ISBN 0-8451-5052-9). A R Liss.
Two Flamboyant Fathers. Nicolette Devas. (Illus.). 288p. 1985. pap. 11.95 (ISBN 0-241-11404-7, Pub. by Hamish Hamilton England). David & Charles.
Two Flappers in Paris. LC 86-80058. (Classics of the Victorian Imagination Ser.). 1986. pap. 7.95 (ISBN 0-394-62209-X, Ever). Grove.
Two Flappers in Paris. pap. 13.95 (ISBN 0-394-55386-1). Grove.
Two Foolish Cats. Yoshiko Uchida. LC 86-12660. (Illus.). 32p. (gr. 4-8). 1987. 13.95 (ISBN 0-689-50397-0, M K McElderry). Macmillan.
Two for America: The True Story of a Swiss Immigrant. Gloria Jacobson. (Illus.). 36p. (gr. 4). 1986. 12.95x (ISBN 0-9618399-0-2); pap. 8.50 (ISBN 0-9618399-1-0). G Jacobson.
Two for Jack Spicer. Stephen Jonas. 1974. pap. 1.00 (ISBN 0-686-18859-4). Man-Root.
Two for One. Jana Ellis. LC 88-12384. (Merivale Mall Ser.). 160p. (YA) (gr. 7 up). 1988. pap. text ed. 2.50 (ISBN 0-8167-1354-5). Troll Assocs.
Two for Survival. Arnold Roth. (gr. 7 up). 1985. pap. 1.75 (ISBN 0-380-44651-0, 56408-4, Flare). Avon.
Two for Tanner. Lawrence Block. 192p. 1985. pap. 2.95 (ISBN 0-515-08688-6). Jove Pubns.
Two for Texas. James L. Burke. 167p. (Orig.). 1982. pap. 2.25 (ISBN 0-671-44112-4). PB.
Two for the Road. J. Nichels. 39.00x (ISBN 0-317-43671-6, Pub. by Regency Pr). State Mutual Bk.
Two for the Road. (Leisure Reading Ser.). 32p. 1979. 1.85 (ISBN 0-88336-319-4). New Readers.
Two for the Road. Kit Windham. (Second Chance at Love Ser.: No. 447). 1988. pap. 2.50 (ISBN 0-425-10946-1). Berkley Pub.
Two Foraminieral Assemblages from the Duplin Marl in Georgia & South Carolina see Bulletins of American Paleontology.
Two Forces of Creation. Christopher A. Anderson. LC 88-71660. (Illus.). 90p. (Orig.). 1988. pap. text ed. 9.00 (ISBN 0-931353-14-9). Andersons Pubns.
Two, Four, Six, Eight, When You Gonna Integrate? Frank A. Petroni & Ernest A. Hirsch. 1971. pap. 2.75 (ISBN 0-87140-241-6). Liveright.
Two Franklins. Bernard Fay. LC 70-93277. Repr. of 1933 ed. 18.50 (ISBN 0-404-02372-X). AMS Pr.
Two Fremont Sites & Their Position in Southwestern Perehistory. Dee C. Taylor. (Utah Anthropological Papers: No. 29). Repr. of 1957 ed. 37.50 (ISBN 0-404-60629-6). AMS Pr.
Two French Moralists. Odette De Mourgues. LC 77-82506. (Major European Authors Ser.). 1978. 39.50 (ISBN 0-521-21823-3). Cambridge U Pr.
Two Frenchmen. David Thomson. LC 75-8806. 255p. 1975. Repr. of 1951 ed. lib. bdg. 25.00x (ISBN 0-8371-8115-1, THTWF). Greenwood.
Two Friendly Elephants. Charles E. Reasoner. (Mother & Baby Bks.). (Illus.). 12p. (ps). 1987. bds. 4.95 (ISBN 0-8431-1768-0). Price Stern.
Two Friends. Guy De Maupassant. Ed. by Ann Redpath. (Creative's Classic Short Stories Ser.). (Illus.). 32p. (gr. 4 up). 1985. PLB 8.95 (ISBN 0-88682-003-0). Creative Ed.
Two Friends II. Menke Katz & Harry Smith. (Illus.). 112p. 1988. 20.00 (ISBN 0-913559-09-1); pap. 11.95 (ISBN 0-913559-10-5). Birch Brook Pr.
Two Friends in Love: Growing Together in Marriage. Ed Neuenschwander & Candee Neuenschwander. LC 85-28402. 1986. pap. 6.95 (ISBN 0-88070-121-8). Multnomah.
Two Frisky Cats. Charles E. Reasoner. (Mother & Baby Bks.). (Illus.). (ps). 1987. bds. 4.95 (ISBN 0-8431-1769-9). Price Stern.
Two from Armageddon. Merritt Clifton. (Illus.). 20p. 1976. pap. 1.00 (ISBN 0-686-20756-4). Samisdat.
Two from Egypt: Bits of Wisdom. Jeanne Fournier-Merrill. 128p. (Orig.). 1987. pap. 4.95 (ISBN 0-9619622-0-8). Sun Flower Ent Prize.
Two from Galilee. Marjorie Holmes. 224p. 1982. 2.95 (ISBN 0-553-22623-1, 13077-3); pap. 3.50 (ISBN 0-553-25343-3). Bantam.
Two from Galilee. Marjorie Holmes. 224p. 1972. pap. 5.95 (ISBN 0-8007-5089-6, Power Bks); pap. 3.50 (ISBN 0-8007-8155-4, Spire Bks). Revell.
Two from the Dead. Hilary Milton. LC 83-10848. 224p. (gr. 5up). 1983. 6.95 (ISBN 0-395-34557-X). HM.
Two Fronts, a Small Town at War. Paul Fridlund. 200p. 1985. 19.95 (ISBN 0-87770-326-4). Ye Galleon.
Two Galilees. Khalil Nakhleh. (Occasional Paper: No. 7). 27p. (Orig.). 1982. pap. text ed. 1.50 (ISBN 0-937694-57-6). Assn Arab-Amer U Grads.
Two Geese. Theodore Enslin. 1980. pap. 5.00 (ISBN 0-915316-86-2). Pentagram.
Two Generations of Soviet Man. John Kosa. 1962. pap. 9.95 (ISBN 0-8084-0304-4). New Coll U Pr.
Two Generations of Soviet Man: A Study in the Psychology of Communism. John Kosa. 17.50 (ISBN 0-8078-0860-1, U of North Carolina Pr). Lib Soc Sci.
Two Generations of Zionism. Bernard A. Rosenblatt. LC 67-18134. 1967. 8.95 (ISBN 0-88400-017-6). Shengold.
Two Gentlemen & a Lady. facs. ed. Alexander Woollcott. LC 79-134984. (Short Story Index Reprint Ser). (Illus.). 1928. 12.00 (ISBN 0-8369-3714-7). Ayer Co Pubs.
Two Gentlemen of China: An Intimate Description of the Private Life of Two Patrician Chinese Families. Dorothea Hosie. LC 79-2941. (Illus.). 316p. 1983. Repr. of 1924 ed. 29.00 (ISBN 0-8305-0106-1). Hyperion Conn.
Two Gentlemen of Rome: Keats & Shelley. Ernest Raymond. 69.95 (ISBN 0-8490-1238-4). Gordon Pr.
Two Gentlemen of Verona. 2nd ed. William Shakespeare. Ed. by Clifford Leech. (Arden Shakespeare Ser.). 1969. 37.00x (ISBN 0-416-47490-X, NO. 2498); pap. 8.95 (ISBN 0-416-70080-2, NO. 2499). Routledge Chapman & Hall.
Two Gentlemen of Verona. William Shakespeare. Date not set. pap. 2.50 (ISBN 0-451-51649-4, CE1649, Sig Classics). NAL.
Two Gentlemen of Verona. William Shakespeare. Ed. by Norman Sanders. 1981. pap. 3.75 (ISBN 0-14-070717-4). Penguin.
Two Gentlemen of Verona. William Shakespeare. Ed. by Berners Jackson. (Shakespeare Ser.). 1965. pap. 3.50 (ISBN 0-14-071431-6, Pelican). Penguin.
Two Gentlemen of Verona. William Shakespeare. Ed. by Louis B. Wright & Virginia A. La Mar. (Folger Library). 224p. (gr. 10 up). 1983. pap. 3.95 (ISBN 0-671-46754-9). WSP.
Two Gentlemen of Verona: Modern Text with Introduction. Ed. by A. L. Rowse. LC 86-11026. (Contemporary Shakespeare Ser.). 106p. (Orig.). 1986. pap. text ed. 3.45 (ISBN 0-8191-3933-5). U Pr of Amer.
Two Gentlemen to See You, Sir: The Autobiography of a Villain. Victor Carasov. LC 76-155091. 1971. 5.50 (ISBN 0-8008-7920-1). Taplinger.
Two German Crowns: Monarchy & Empire in Medieval German. Otis C. Mitchell. LC 85-51753. 97p. (Orig.). 1985. pap. text ed. 9.95 (ISBN 0-932269-66-4). Wyndham Hall.
Two German Economies. Herbert Wilkens. 194p. 1981. text ed. 44.50x (ISBN 0-566-00304-X). Gower Pub Co.
Two Germanies since 1945: East & West. Henry A. Turner, Jr. LC 87-6205. 230p. 1987. 17.95 (ISBN 0-300-03865-8). Yale U Pr.
Two Germans of Genius. Oswald Mosley. Afterword by Diana Mosley. 44p. 1987. 30.00x (ISBN 0-930126-22-X). Typographeum.
Two: Gertrude Stein & Her Brother & Other Early Portraits, Vol. One Of Unpublished Works Of Gertrude Stein In 8 Vols. Gertrude Stein. LC 74-103667. (Select Bibliographies Reprint Ser). 1951. 27.50 (ISBN 0-8369-5167-0). Ayer Co Pubs.
Two Gether. Palmer L. Gedder. 1983. pap. 5.95 (12N1725). Northwest Pub.
Two Ghosts on a Bench. Marjorie W. Sharmat. LC 81-47734. (Illus.). 64p. (gr. k-3). 1982. 10.70i (ISBN 0-06-025518-8); PLB 10.89 (ISBN 0-06-025519-6). HarpJ.
Two Girls & a Kite. Edith Parker-Hinckley. Ed. by Larry Burgess. LC 84-61445. (Illus.). 64p. 1984. 12.50 (ISBN 0-914167-01-4). Moore Hist.
Two Girls, One Boy. Janet Quin-Harkin. (Sugar & Spice Ser.). 192p. (Orig.). 1987. pap. 2.50 (ISBN 0-8041-0021-7). Ivy Books.
Two Good Friends. Judy Delton. (Illus.). 32p. (ps-3). 1986. pap. 2.95 (ISBN 0-517-55949-8). Crown.
Two Grains of Sand. Sandra Trump. 48p. 1987. 6.95 (ISBN 0-8062-2982-9). Carlton.
Two Grateful Magpies see Golden Axe.
Two Great Indian Artists. Ed. by Prasanta Daw. 1978. 8.00x (ISBN 0-8364-0277-4). South Asia Bks.
Two Great Scientists of the Nineteenth Century: Correspondence of Emil Du Bois-Reymond & Carl Ludwig. Ed. by Paul F. Cranefield. Tr. by Sabine L. Ayed from Ger. LC 79-24140. 204p. 1982. text ed. 22.50x (ISBN 0-8018-2351-X). Johns Hopkins.
Two Great Scouts & Their Pawnee Battalion: The Experiences of Frank J. North & Luther H. North, Pioneers in the Great West, 1856-1882, & Their Defence of the Building of the Union Pacific Railroad. George B. Grinnell. LC 29-2718. pap. 76.50 (ISBN 0-317-20462-9, 2023005). Bks Demand UMI.
Two Greedy Bears: Adapted from a Hungarian Folk Tale. Mirra Ginsburg. LC 76-8819. (Illus.). 32p. (ps-2). 1976. 12.95 (ISBN 0-02-736450-X). Macmillan.
Two Group Reactor Theory. J. L. Meem. 430p. 1967. 108.00 (ISBN 0-677-00520-2). Gordon & Breach.
Two Groups of Thessalian Gold. Stella Miller. LC 77-80473. (UC Publications in Classical Studies: Vol. 18). 1979. pap. 23.00x (ISBN 0-520-09580-4). U of Cal Pr.
Two Guadalupes: Hispanic Legends & Magic Tales from Northern New Mexico. Intro. by Marta Weigle. LC 86-71416. (Illus.). 176p. (Orig.). 1987. 19.95 (ISBN 0-941270-33-5); pap. 9.95 (ISBN 0-941270-32-7). Ancient City Pr.
Two Gulls, One Hawk: Two Long Poems. James Hoggard. 1983. lib. bdg. 11.95 (ISBN 0-933384-10-6); pap. 7.95 (ISBN 0-933384-08-4). Prickly Pear.
Two Guys Fooling Around With the Moon & Other Drawings. B. Kliban. LC 81-43780. (Illus.). 144p. 1982. pap. 3.95 (ISBN 0-89480-198-8, 474). Workman Pub.
Two Guys Notice Me...& Other Miracles. Marjorie Sharmat. (gr. 5-8). 1986. pap. 2.50 (ISBN 0-440-98846-2, LFL). Dell.
Two Hague Conferences. Joseph H. Choate. (Reprints in Government & Political Science Ser). 1970. Repr. of 1913 ed. 13.00 (ISBN 0-384-08915-1). Johnson Repr.
Two Hague Conferences. Joseph H. Choate. LC 13-4133. 1969. Repr. of 1913 ed. 35.00 (ISBN 0-527-16850-5). Kraus Repr.
Two Hague Conferences & Their Contributions to International Law. W. I. Hull. LC 8-28855. Repr. of 1908 ed. 39.00 (ISBN 0-527-43200-8). Kraus Repr.
Two Hague Conferences & Their Contributions to International Law. William I. Hull. 1978. Repr. of 1908 ed. lib. bdg. 30.00 (ISBN 0-8495-2253-6). Arden Lib.
Two Hague Conferences & Their Contributions to International Law. William I. Hull. LC 73-147582. (Library of War & Peace; Int'l. Organization, Arbitration & Law). 1972. lib. bdg. 46.00 (ISBN 0-8240-0346-2). Garland Pub.
Two Halves of the Same Silence. Susan A. Katz. LC 84-71176. 76p. 1985. pap. 6.95 (ISBN 0-917652-46-0). Confluence Pr.
Two Handed Tennis: How to Play a Winner's Game. Jeffrey F. McCullogh. LC 83-20759. (Illus.). 192p. 1984. 14.95 (ISBN 0-87131-425-8); pap. 7.95 (ISBN 0-87131-491-6). M Evans.
Two Harmonies: Poetry & Prose in the Seventeenth Century. Kenneth G. Hamilton. LC 77-18929. 1978. Repr. of 1963 ed. lib. bdg. 35.00x (ISBN 0-313-20180-3, HATH). Greenwood.
Two Harness Textiles, the Loom Controlled Weaves, the Open Work Weaves, Brocade. Harriet Tidball. LC 87-80655. (Shuttle Craft Guild Monographs: No. 20, 21, 22). (Illus.). 118p. 1987. pap. 13.95 (ISBN 0-317-63457-7). Shuttle Craft.
Two-Headed Monster. C. B. Cox. 62p. 1985. pap. 8.50 (ISBN 0-85635-618-2). Carcanet.
Two-Headed Poems. Margaret Atwood. 1981. (Touchstone Bks); pap. 6.95 (ISBN 0-671-25373-5). S&S.
Two-Headed Woman. Lucille Clifton. LC 80-5379. 72p. 1980. lib. bdg. 10.00x (ISBN 0-87023-309-2); pap. 5.95 (ISBN 0-87023-310-6). U of Mass Pr.
Two Heads Are Better Than One. Peter Warnock. (Illus.). 72p. (Orig.). 1985. pap. 4.95 (ISBN 0-943456-09-6). Bearly Ltd.
Two Hearts Are Better Than One. Bob Mandel. LC 85-29922. 220p. (Orig.). 1986. pap. 8.95 (ISBN 0-89087-454-9). Celestial Arts.
Two Hearts Bid. Carol Gaye. (Lythway). 256p. 1988. lib. bdg. 19.50x (ISBN 0-7451-0634-X, Pub. by Chivers Pr UK). G K HAll.
Two Hearts in a Melting Pot. Paul Kolesar. 104p. 1983. 8.95x (ISBN 0-87141-074-5). Manyland.
Two Hearts Too Wild. Lindsay Randall. 1988. pap. 3.95 (Pageant). Crown.
Two Hemispheres--One Brain: Functions of the Corpus Callosum. Ed. by Franco Lepore et al. LC 85-23968. (Neurology & Nuerbiology Ser.: Vol. 17). 582p. 1986. 124.00 (ISBN 0-8451-2719-5, 2719). A R Liss.
Two Heroines of Plumplington. Anthony Trollope. Ed. by John K. Shannon. (Harting Grange Library). (Illus.). 116p. 1980. pap. 6.95 (ISBN 0-932282-49-0). Caledonia Pr.
Two Histories of Ireland. James Ware. LC 71-171796. (English Experience Ser.: No. 421). 500p. 1971. Repr. of 1633 ed. 80.00 (ISBN 90-221-0421-4). Walter J Johnson.

Two Jamaicas: The Role of Ideas in a Tropical Colony, 1830-1865. Philip D. Curtin. LC 69-10082. (Illus.). 1968. Repr. of 1955 ed. lib. bdg. 35.00x (ISBN 0-8371-0055-0, CUTJ). Greenwood.

Two Japanese Novelists: Soseki & Toson. Edwin McClellan. LC 76-81223. pap. 45.00 (ISBN 0-317-10055-6, 2007276). Bks Demand UMI.

Two Jerusalems in Prophecy. David Clifford. LC 78-14922. (Illus.). 1978. pap. 3.50 (ISBN 0-87213-081-9). Loizeaux.

Two Jewish Justices: Outcasts in the Promised Land. Robert A. Burt. 200p. 1987. 19.95 (ISBN 0-520-06110-1). U of Cal Pr.

Two Journeys. Cambridge School Classics Project Foundation Course Staff. (Roman World Ser.). (Illus.). 1978. 2.95x (ISBN 0-521-21603-6). Cambridge U Pr.

Two Jungle Books, 2 vols. in one. facsimile ed. Rudyard Kipling. LC 71-150477. (Short Story Index Reprint Ser.). Repr. of 1895 ed. 27.50 (ISBN 0-8369-3818-6). Ayer Co Pubs.

Two Kafka Plays: Kafka's Dick. Alan Bennett. Bd. with Insurance Man. 128p. (Orig.). 1987. pap. 7.95 (ISBN 0-571-14727-5). Faber & Faber.

Two Kinds of Power: An Essay on Bibliographic Control. Patrick Wilson. 1978. 40.00x (ISBN 0-520-03515-1). U of Cal Pr.

Two Kinds of Time. Graham Peck. LC 83-45833. (Illus.). Repr. of 1950 ed. 67.50 (ISBN 0-404-20198-9). AMS Pr.

Two Kings of Uganda: Or, Life by the Shores of Victoria Nyanza. Robert P. Ashe. (Illus.). 354p. 1970. Repr. of 1889 ed. 30.00x (ISBN 0-7146-1862-4, BHA 01862, F Cass Co). Biblio Dist.

Two Kin's Pumpkins. Adapted by & tr. by John Holstein. (Korean Folk Tales Ser.: No. 1). (Illus.). 35p. (Eng. & Korean.). (gr. 1-8). 1986. PLB write for info. (ISBN 0-87296-000-5, Pub. by Si-Sa-Yong-O-Sa Korea); incls. cassette. Si-Sa-Yong-O-Sa.

Two Kittens Are Born. Betty Schilling. (Illus.). 40p. (gr. k-3). pap. 2.25 (ISBN 0-590-33722-X). Scholastic Inc.

Two Korean Brothers: The Story of Hungbu & Nolbu. Grace S. Yoo. LC 73-18023. (Oriental Stories: No. 7). (gr. k-3). 1970. 6.95 (ISBN 0-912580-01-1). Far Eastern Res.

Two Koreas. Bruce Cumings. LC 84-81643. (Headline Ser.: 269). (Illus.). 80p. 1984. 4.00 (ISBN 0-87124-092-0). Foreign Policy.

Two Koreas in East Asian Affairs. Ed. by William J. Barnds. LC 75-27379. 216p. 1976. 30.00x (ISBN 0-8147-0988-5). NYU Pr.

Two Koreas-One Future? A Report Prepared for the American Friends Service Committee. Ed. by John Sullivan & Roberta Foss. LC 86-30762. (Illus.). 176p. (Orig.). 1987. lib. bdg. 22.50 (ISBN 0-8191-6049-0, Pub. by Am Friends Serv); pap. text ed. 10.75 (ISBN 0-8191-6050-4, Pub. by Am Friends Serv). U Pr of Amer.

Two Ladies of Colonial Algeria: The Lives & Times of Aurelie Picard & Isabelle Eberhardt. Ursula K. Hart. (CIS Africa Ser.: No. 49A). 140p. 1986. pap. text ed. 9.00x (ISBN 0-89680-143-8, Ohio U Ctr Intl). Ohio U Pr.

Two Lamentable Tragedies. Robert Yarington. (Tudor Facsimile Texts. Old English Plays: No. 96). Repr. of 1913 ed. 49.50 (ISBN 0-404-53396-5). AMS Pr.

Two Languages & Two Cultures in Education, 3 vols. 1988. Vol. 1. 42.00x (ISBN 1-85359-014-2, Pub. by Multilingual Matters); Vol. 2. 42.00x (ISBN 1-85359-015-0, Pub. by Multilingual Matters); Vol. 3. 42.00x (ISBN 1-85359-016-9, Pub. by Multilingual Matters). Taylor & Francis.

Two Lectures on Machinery. T. Twiss. (The Development of Industrial Society Ser.). 76p. 1971. Repr. of 1844 ed. 17.50x (ISBN 0-7165-1778-7, BBA 02145, Pub. by Irish Academic Pr Ireland). Biblio Dist.

Two Lectures on Population: Delivered Before the University of Oxford. Nassau W. Senior. LC 75-38143. (Demography Ser.). 1976. Repr. of 1828 ed. 14.00x (ISBN 0-405-07996-6). Ayer Co Pubs.

Two Lectures on Shakespeare. Leo Kirschbaum. 1961. 15.00 (ISBN 0-686-00064-1). Ridgeway Bks.

Two Lectures on the Subjects of Slavery & Abolition. facsimile ed. Compiled by Charles Olcott. LC 71-164391. (Black Heritage Library Collection). Repr. of 1838 ed. 15.50 (ISBN 0-8369-8850-7). Ayer Co Pubs.

Two Lefist Parties of India, 1982. Shiv Lal. 200p. 1986. 120.00x (ISBN 0-317-61987-X, Pub. by Archives Pubs). State Mutual Bk.

Two Legends: Oedipus & Theseus. Andre Gide. Tr. by John Russell. 1958. pap. 2.95 (ISBN 0-394-70066-X, V66, Vin). Random.

Two Leggings: The Making of a Crow Warrior. Peter Nabokov. LC 82-6979. (Illus.). xxx, 242p. 1982. pap. 6.95 (ISBN 0-8032-8351-2, BB 807, Bison). U of Nebr Pr.

Two Letters & Short Rules of a Good Life. Robert Southwell. Ed. by Nancy P. Brown. (Documents Ser). 1978. 19.00x (ISBN 0-918016-53-3). Folger Bks.

Two Literary Riddles in the Exeter Book: Riddle 1 & the Easter Riddle. James E. Anderson. LC 85-40471. (Illus.). 288p. 1986. 27.50x (ISBN 0-8061-1947-0). U of Okla Pr.

Two Little Bears. Hanna Muschg. LC 85-24352. (Illus.). 80p. (gr. 1-4). 1986. 8.95 (ISBN 0-02-767660-9). Bradbury Pr.

Two Little Devils. Robert E. Holt. 1979. 8.95 (ISBN 0-682-49362-7). Exposition-Phoenix.

Two Little Farm Girls of the 1920's. Elizabeth H. Martin. 1987. 4.95 (ISBN 0-533-07208-5). Vantage.

Two Little Kittens. Fang Yiqun. (Illus.). 22p. (Orig.). (gr. 2-4). 1982. pap. 2.50 (ISBN 0-8351-1142-3). China Bks.

Two Little Rich Girls. Mignon G. Eberhart. 223p. Repr. of 1971 ed. lib. bdg. 15.95x (ISBN 0-88411-768-5, Pub. by Aeonian Pr). Amereon Ltd.

Two Little Savages. Ernest T. Seton. (Illus.). 286p. (gr. 4-8). 1903. pap. 5.95 (ISBN 0-486-20985-7). Dover.

Two Little Savages. Ernest T. Seton. (Illus.). 13.50 (ISBN 0-8446-2909-X). Peter Smith.

Two Little Savages. Ernest T. Seton. 552p. 1982. Repr. of 1903 ed. lib. bdg. 49.50 (ISBN 0-89984-443-X). Century Bookbindery.

Two Little Savages. Ernest T. Seton. 18.95 (ISBN 0-89190-919-2, Pub. by Am Repr). Amereon LTd.

Two Little Savages: Being the Adventures of Two Boys Who Lived as Indians & What They Learned. Ernest T. Seton. 552p. 1983. Repr. of 1903 ed. lib. bdg. 49.50 (ISBN 0-89987-794-X). Darby Bks.

Two Liturgies, A. D. Fifteen Forty-Nine, & A. D. Fifteen Fifty-Seven. 1844. 51.00 (ISBN 0-384-62140-6). Johnson Repr.

Two Lives & a Dream. Marguerite Yourcenar. Tr. by Walter Kaiser from Fr. 250p. 1987. 16.95 (ISBN 0-374-28019-3). FS&G.

Two Lives & a Dream. Marguerite Yourcenar. Tr. by Walter Kaiser. 245p. 1988. pap. 8.95 (ISBN 0-374-52091-7). FS&G.

Two Lives: My Spirit & I. Jane T. Creider. 178p. 1988. pap. 5.95 (ISBN 0-7043-4006-2, Pub. by Women's Press). Salem Hse Pubs.

Two Lives of Charlemagne. Einhard & Notker. Tr. & intro. by Lewis Thorpe. (Classics Ser.). 240p. 1969. pap. 4.95 (ISBN 0-14-044213-8). Penguin.

Two Lives of Saint Cuthbert. Ed. by Bertram Colgrave. 388p. 1985. 49.50 (ISBN 0-521-30925-5); pap. 17.95 (ISBN 0-521-31385-6). Cambridge U Pr.

Two Lives, One Russia. Nicholas Daniloff. (Illus.). 320p. 1988. 19.95 (ISBN 0-395-44601-5). HM.

Two Lives to Lead: Bisexuality in Men & Women. Ed. by Fritz Klein & Timothy J. Wolf. LC 85-5868. 255p. 1985. pap. 14.95 (ISBN 0-918393-22-1). Harrington Pk.

Two Living & One Dead. Sigurd Christiansen. Tr. by Edwin Bjorkman from Norwegian. LC 73-22751. 288p. 1975. Repr. of 1932 ed. lib. bdg. 35.00x (ISBN 0-8371-7348-5, CHTL). Greenwood.

Two "Loaf-Givers" Or a Tour Through the Gastronomic Libraries of Katherine Golden Bitting & Elizabeth Pennell. Leonard N. Beck. LC 82-13107. (Illus.). 224p. 1984. 20.00 (ISBN 0-317-59994-1). Lib Congress.

Two Lost Plays of Euripides. Dana F. Sutton. (American University Studies: Classical Languages & Literature: Vol. 4). 170p. 1987. text ed. 28.00 (ISBN 0-8204-0366-0). P Lang Pubs.

Two Loves. Vincent A. McCrossen. LC 78-61110. 383p. 1979. 13.95 (ISBN 0-8022-2237-4). Philos Lib.

Two Loves" & "A Worthier Pen" The Enigmas of Shakespeare's Sonnets. K. D. Sethna. 304p. 1984. text ed. 22.50x (ISBN 0-391-02934-7). Humanities.

Two Loves for Tina. Maurine Miller. (Caprice Ser.: No. 22). 144p. 1985. pap. 1.95 (ISBN 0-441-83380-2, Pub by Tempo). Ace Bks.

Two Loves: Nursing Disarry in American Hospitals. Alice C. Ream. 1988. 10.95 (ISBN 0-533-07840-7). Vantage.

Two Maids of Moreclacke. Robert Armin. LC 77-133634. (Tudor Facsimile Texts. Old English Plays: No. 127). Repr. of 1913 ed. 49.50 (ISBN 0-404-53427-9). AMS Pr.

Two Marine Quaternary Localities see Palaeontographica Americana.

Two Marxisms: Contradictions & Anomalies in the Development of Theory. Alvin W. Gouldner. 1982. pap. 10.95 (ISBN 0-19-503066-4). Oxford U Pr.

Two Masters, Browning-Turgenief. Philip S. Moxom. LC 76-28217. 1912. lib. bdg. 16.00 (ISBN 0-8414-6137-6). Folcroft.

Two Masters of Irony: Oscar Wilde & Lytton Strachey. Margaret M. Yu. LC 79-8090. Repr. of 1957 ed. 13.50 (ISBN 0-404-18398-0). AMS Pr.

Two Masters of Irony: Wilde & Strachey. Margaret M. Yu. 1980. Repr. of 1957 ed. lib. bdg. 22.00 (ISBN 0-8492-3118-3). R West.

Two Masters-Prior Engagements. Frank Manley. (Illus.). 176p. (Orig.). 1987. pap. 6.95 (ISBN 0-932419-14-3). Susan Hunter.

Two Maya Monuments in Yucatan: The Palace of the Stuccoes at Acanceh & the Temple of the Owls at Chicken Itza. Hasso Von Winning. (Frederick Webb Hodge Publications: No. XII). (Illus.). 104p. (Orig.). 1985. pap. write for info. (ISBN 0-916561-68-2). Southwest Mus.

Two Measures of Rice. T. S. Pillai. Tr. by M. A. Shakoor from Malayalam. 118p. 1975. pap. 2.50 (ISBN 0-88253-169-7). Ind-US Inc.

Two Memoirs of Renaissance Florence: The Diaries of Buonaccorso Pitti & Gregorio Dati. Buonaccorso Pitti & Gregorio Dati. pap. 6.95x (ISBN 0-06-131333-5, TB1333, Torch). Har-Row.

Two Men: A Novel. Elizabeth D. Stoddard. LC 1-22016. Repr. 15.00 (ISBN 0-384-58316-4). Johnson Repr.

Two Men for Modern Music. Vivian Perlis. (I. S. A. M. Monographs: No. 9). (Illus.). 35p. 1978. pap. 5.00 (ISBN 0-914678-09-4). Inst Am Music.

Two Men in Me. facsimile ed. Henry Daniel-Rops. Tr. by Gil Meynier from Fr. LC 76-163024. (Short Story Index Reprint Ser.). Repr. of 1931 ed. 17.00 (ISBN 0-8369-3938-7). Ayer Co Pubs.

Two Menaechmuses see Casina.

Two Merry Milkmaids. LC 79-133751. (Tudor Facsimile Texts. Old English Plays: No. 137). Repr. of 1914 ed. 49.50 (ISBN 0-404-53437-6). AMS Pr.

Two Mexico City Choirbooks of 1717: An Anthology of Sacred Polyphony from the Cathedral of Mexico. Tr. by Steven Barwick. LC 82-3047. 213p. 1982. 16.95x (ISBN 0-8093-1065-1). S Ill U Pr.

Two Millenia of International Relations in Higher Education. William W. Brickman. 263p. 1980. Repr. of 1976 ed. lib. bdg. 40.00 (ISBN 0-8414-1660-5). Folcroft.

Two Millennia of Poetry in Latin: An Anthology of Works of Cultural & Historic Interest, Vol. 1: The Late Classical Period & the Early Middle Ages. Ed. by Jan Oberg. (Illus.). 284p. (Orig., Eng. & Lat.). 1987. pap. 68.50x. Coronet Bks.

Two Million Dollar Hit. James A. Cran. (Illus.). 232p. (Orig.). 1983. 19.95x (ISBN 0-913495-00-X); pap. 9.95x (ISBN 0-913495-01-8). Taurus Pub Co.

Two Million Unnecessary Arrests: Removing a Social Service Concern from the Criminal Justice System. American Bar Foundation Staff. 211p. 1971. 10.00 (ISBN 0-910058-41-5, 765-0049-01); pap. 5.00 (ISBN 0-910058-42-3, 765-0038-01). Amer Bar Assn.

Two-Minute Bedtime Stories. Mary Packard. LC 87-83202. (Golden Book Two-Minute Stories Ser.). (Illus.). 36p. (ps-1). 1988. 3.95 (ISBN 0-307-12183-6). Western Pub.

Two-Minute Mysteries. Donald J. Sobol. 160p. (Orig.). (gr. 5-8). 1986. pap. 2.50 (ISBN 0-590-41292-2, Apple Paperbacks). Scholastic Inc.

Two Minute Philosopher. Lindy H. Lumbert. Date not set. 19.00 (ISBN 0-943280-01-X); pap. 8.50 (ISBN 0-943280-02-8). Blossom Bks.

Two Minutes of Silence. H. C. Branner. Tr. by Vera L. Vance. 244p. 1966. 17.50x (ISBN 0-299-04161-1). U of Wis Pr.

Two Minutes with God: One Minute to Listen, One Minute to Pray. Leslie F. Brandt. LC 88-6326. 128p. 1988. pap. 6.95 (ISBN 0-8066-2350-0, 10-6724). Augsburg.

Two Models of an Open Economy. Ed. by Bengt-Christer Ysander. (Illus.). 161p. 1986. text ed. 47.50x (Pub. by Almqvist & Wiksell). Coronet Bks.

Two Monographs on Japanese Canadians. Ed. by Roger Daniels. LC 78-3222. (Asian Experience in North America Ser.). 1979. lib. bdg. 14.00x (ISBN 0-405-11304-8). Ayer Co Pubs.

Two Monsters. David McKee. LC 85-22344. (Illus.). 32p. (ps-2). 1986. 12.95 (ISBN 0-02-765760-4). Bradbury Pr.

Two Monsters: A Fable. Lucretia Fisher. LC 76-21684. (Illus.). 48p. (ps up). 1976. pap. 3.95 (ISBN 0-916144-08-9). Stemmer Hse.

Two Months with Mary: Short Reflections for Every Day of May & October. Ed. by Joseph A. Viano. (Illus.). 94p. (Orig.). 1984. pap. 4.95 (ISBN 0-8189-0466-6). Alba.

Two Moral Essays: Human Personality & on Human Obligations. Simone Weil. 1981. Repr. 2.50x (ISBN 0-686-79299-8). Pendle Hill.

Two Morrow's Legacy. Arthur E. Morrow & Edith M. Morrow. As told to & intro. by O. Ray Dodson. (Illus.). 1988. 17.95 (ISBN 0-9620550-0-X). Dodson Assocs.

Two Mothers see Three Exemplary Novels.

Two Mountains & a River. Harold W. Tilman. LC 50-196. pap. 69.30 (ISBN 0-317-11324-0, 2050720). Bks Demand UMI.

Two-Move Chess Problems: Being 257 Orthodox Twoers by 108 U. S. Problemists. Robert C. Moore. LC 84-43199. (Illus.). 170p. 1986. lib. bdg. 18.95x (ISBN 0-89950-177-X). McFarland & Co.

Two Moves to Better Golf. Dudley Wolford. LC 88-70792. (Orig.). 1988. pap. 12.95 (ISBN 0-929091-00-0). Brentwood Productions.

Two Mrs. Greenvilles Scrap Book see Don't Cry for Me, Locust Valley! Ann Woodward Scrap Book.

Two Mrs. Grenvilles. Dominick Dunne. LC 85-445. 384p. 1985. 14.95 (ISBN 0-517-55713-4). Crown.

Two Mrs. Grenvilles. Dominick Dunne. 384p. 1986. pap. 4.50 (ISBN 0-553-25891-5). Bantam.

Two Mrs. Grenvilles. Dominick Dunne. (General Ser.). 552p. 1986. lib. bdg. 18.95 (ISBN 0-8161-4059-6, Large Print Bks). G K Hall.

Two Mrs. Grenville's Scrap Book: Photo Reportage of Ann & Billy Woodward's Lives & Ultimately Deaths. Compiled by Dick Frost. (Illus.). 200p. 1986. pap. 30.00 (ISBN 0-933883-02-1). Aquarius Rising Pr.

Two Mystic Communities in America. John E. Jacoby. LC 75-326. (Radical Tradition in America Ser). 104p. 1975. Repr. of 1931 ed. 15.00 (ISBN 0-88355-230-2). Hyperion Conn.

Two Mystic Poets & Other Essays. K. M. Loudon. LC 72-194763. 1922. lib. bdg. 20.50 (ISBN 0-8414-5888-X). Folcroft.

Two Nations. Christopher Hollis. 69.95 (ISBN 0-87968-230-2). Gordon Pr.

Two Nations Over Time: Spain & the United States, 1776-1977. James W. Cortada. LC 77-94752. (Contributions in American History: No. 74). 1978. lib. bdg. 35.00 (ISBN 0-313-20319-9, CTN/). Greenwood.

Two Nativity Dramas. Edward S. Long. 1984. 4.75 (ISBN 0-89536-697-5, 4874). CSS of Ohio.

Two NATO Allies at the Threshhold of War: Cyprus: A Firsthand Account of Crisis Management, 1965-1968. Parker T. Hart. (Illus.). 1989. lib. bdg. price not set (ISBN 0-934742-53-7); pap. text ed. price not set (ISBN 0-934742-54-5). Geo U Sch For Serv.

Two Natures in Christ. Martin Chemnitz. Tr. by J. A. Preus. LC 74-115465. Orig. Title: De Duabus Naturis in Christo. 1970. 24.95 (ISBN 0-570-03210-5, 15-2109). Concordia.

Two Naval Journals: 1864-Battle of Mobile Bay. Ed. by C. Carter Smith. (Illus.). 1964. pap. 6.95 (ISBN 0-87651-210-4). Southern U Pr.

Two New Houses. Mandeville. (Ladybird Ser.). (gr. 2-7). 1977. 2.50 (ISBN 0-87508-871-6). Chr Lit.

Two New Sciences, Including Centers of Gravity & Force of Percussion. Galileo Galilei & Stillman Drake. LC 73-2043. pap. 91.30 (ISBN 0-317-55783-1, 2029307). Bks Demand UMI.

Two New Sneakers. Nancy Tafuri. LC 87-8418. (Illus.). 12p. (ps). 1988. 3.95 (ISBN 0-688-07462-6). Greenwillow.

Two Nichols: Spent for Missions. Jester Summers. LC 81-70910. (Meet the Missionary Ser.). (gr. 4-6). 1982. 5.95 (ISBN 0-8054-4279-0, 4242-79). Broadman.

Two Nixon Shocks & Japan-U. S. Relations. Atsushi Kusano. (Research Monograph: No. 50). 46p. 1987. 8.00 (ISBN 0-318-22897-1). Princeton CIS.

Two Noble Kinsmen. John Fletcher & William Shakespeare. LC 72-133736. (Tudor Facsimile Texts. Old English Plays: No. 141). Repr. of 1910 ed. 49.50 (ISBN 0-404-53441-4). AMS Pr.

Two Noble Kinsmen. John Fletcher & William Shakespeare. Ed. by G. R. Proudfoot. LC 74-80902. (Regents Renaissance Drama Ser). xxvi, 141p. 1970. 15.50x (ISBN 0-8032-0286-5); pap. 3.95x (ISBN 0-8032-5287-0, BB 234, Bison). U of Nebr Pr.

Two Noble Kinsmen. William Shakespeare. Ed. by N. W. Bawcutt. 1981. pap. 3.75 (ISBN 0-14-070730-1). Penguin.

Two Noble Kinsmen. William Shakespeare & John Fletcher. Ed. by Eugene M. Waith. (Shakespeare Ser.). (Illus.). 256p. 1989. 39.95 (ISBN 0-19-812939-4). Oxford U Pr.

Two Noble Kinsmen: A Tragic Romance. William Shakespeare & John Fletcher. (Swan Theatre Plays). 64p. pap. 6.95 (ISBN 0-413-40530-3, 1034). Heinemann Ed.

Two Noble Kinsmen, Titus Andonicus, Pericles. William Shakespeare. 1977. pap. 3.95 (ISBN 0-451-51639-7, Sig). NAL.

Two Noble Kinsmen. 71. John Fletcher. Bd. with Quarto of 1634, Pt. 1. rev. ed. (New Shakespeare Soc., London, Ser. 2: Nos. 7,8 & 15). pap. 59.00 (ISBN 0-8115-0235-X). Kraus Repr.

Two Noble Ladies. Rebecca G. Rhoads. LC 82-45798. (Malone Society Reprints Ser.: No. 68). Repr. of 1930 ed. 40.00 (ISBN 0-404-63068-5). AMS Pr.

Two Notebooks of Thomas Carlyle: From 23rd March 1822 to 16th May 1832. Ed. by Charles E. Norton. 1972. Repr. of 1898 ed. 10.00x (ISBN 0-911858-21-0). Appel.

Two Novels by Peter Handke. Peter Handke. 1985. pap. 2.75 (ISBN 0-380-48033-6, Bard). Avon.

Two Novels of Mexico: The Flies & The Bosses. Mariano Azuela. Tr. by Lesley B. Simpson. 1956. pap. 7.95X (ISBN 0-520-00053-6). U of Cal Pr.

Two Novels: You Didn't Even Try & Imaginary Speeches for a Brazen Head. Philip Whalen. LC 85-51335. 272p. 1985. 16.95 (ISBN 0-939010-07-0); pap. 9.95 (ISBN 0-939010-06-2); signed ed. 25.00. Zephyr Pr.

Two-Ocean War: A Short History of United States Navy in the Second World War. Samuel E. Morison. (Illus.). 1963. 35.00 (ISBN 0-316-58366-9, Pub. by Atlantic Monthly Pr). Little.

Two of a Kind. Darcy O'Brien. 1987. pap. 4.50 (ISBN 0-451-14643-3, Sig). NAL.

Two of a Kind. Susan Shaw. (Caprice Romance Ser.: No. 59). 176p. 1985. pap. 2.25 (ISBN 0-441-83432-9, Pub by Tempo). Ace Bks.

Two of a Kind: An English Rifle. Rosemary Edghill. 272p. 1988. 16.95 (ISBN 0-312-01840-1). St Martin.

Two of a Kind: The Hillside Stranglers. Darcy O'Brien. 448p. 1985. 17.95 (ISBN 0-453-00499-7). NAL.

Two of the Saxon Chronicles Parallel with Supplementary Extracts from the Others, 2 Vols. Ed. by Charles Plummer. 463p. 1983. Repr. of 1899 ed. lib. bdg. 150.00 set (ISBN 0-89984-833-8). Century Bookbindery.

Two Revolutions: Antonio Gramsci & the Dilemmas of Marxism. Carl Boggs. LC 84-50943. 250p. (Orig.). 1984. 20.00 (ISBN 0-89608-226-1); pap. 9.50 (ISBN 0-89608-225-3). South End Pr.
Two Revolutions in Economic Policy: The First Economic Reports of Presidents Kennedy & Reagan. Ed. by James Tobin & Murray Weidenbaum. 460p. (Orig.). 1988. text ed. 30.00x (ISBN 0-262-20070-8); pap. text ed. 13.95x (ISBN 0-262-70034-4). MIT PR.
Two Rivers to Freedom. Stella Wuerffel. LC 80-66578. 385p. 1980. 11.95 (ISBN 0-915644-20-7). Clayton Pub Hse.
Two Rivulets. Walt Whitman. 120p. 1980. Repr. of 1876 ed. lib. bdg. 42.00 (ISBN 0-8414-9461-4). Folcroft.
Two Roads. Patt Bucheister. (Loveswept Ser.: No. 227). 192p. 1987. pap. 2.50 (ISBN 0-553-21864-6, Loveswept). Bantam.
Two Roads to Dodge City. Nigel Nicolson & Adam Nicolson. LC 86-45675. (Cornelia & Michael Bessie Book). 352p. 1987. 17.00i (ISBN 0-06-039064-6, C&M Bessie Bks). Har-Row.
Two Roads to Ignorance: A Quasi Biography. Eliseo Vivas. LC 79-757. 318p. 1979. 18.95x (ISBN 0-8093-0916-5). S Ill U Pr.
Two Roads to Sumter. William Catton & Bruce Catton. 1971. pap. text ed. 6.95 (ISBN 0-07-010255-4). McGraw.
Two Rosetos. Carla Bianco. LC 73-16523. (Illus.). Repr. of 1974 ed. 62.30 (ISBN 0-8357-9249-8, 2055234). Bks Demand UMI.
Two Royall Entertainments, Lately Given to Charles, Prince of Great Britaine, by Philip the Fourth of Spaine. Andres De Almansa & Andres De Mendoza. LC 77-6847. (English Experience Ser.: No. 842). 1977. Repr. of 1623 ed. lib. bdg. 8.00 (ISBN 90-221-0842-2). Walter J Johnson.
Two R's: Paragraph to Essay. Shirley Fencl & Susan G. Jager. LC 78-16026. 1979. pap. text ed. write for info. (ISBN 0-673-15723-7). Scott F.
Two Runaways. Jerry Jenkins. (Bradford Family Adventures Ser.). 128p. (Orig.). (gr. 3-7). 1984. pap. 2.95 (ISBN 0-87239-792-0, 2942). Standard Pub.
Two Runaways & Other Stories. facsimile ed. Harry S. Edwards. 1972. Repr. of 1889 ed. lib. bdg. 24.00 (ISBN 0-8422-8042-1). Irvington.
Two Russian Thinkers: An Essay in Berdyaev & Shestov. James C. Wernham. LC 68-85112. pap. 33.00 (ISBN 0-317-08859-9, 2014455). Bks Demand UMI.
Two Saints: St. Bernard & St. Francis. G. G. Coulton. 1923. lib. bdg. 25.00 (ISBN 0-8414-3513-8). Folcroft.
Two Saunters: Summer & Winter 1978. 1986. 20.00 (ISBN 0-9615665-0-7). Pencil Pr.
Two Score & Growing Up. Christine Callahan. 144p. 1985. 8.95 (ISBN 0-89962-456-1). Todd & Honeywell.
Two Screenplays. Jean Cocteau. Tr. by Carol Martin-Sperry from Fr. Incl. Blood of the Poet; Testament of Orpheus. (Illus.). 152p. 1985. pap. 7.95 (ISBN 0-7145-0580-3, Dist. by Kampmann & Co). M Boyars Pubs.
Two Screenplays: The Blood of a Poet, The Testament of Orpheus. Jean Cocteau. Tr. by Carol Martin-Sperry from Fr. LC 63-30778. (Illus.). 144p. 1968. 16.95 (ISBN 0-910278-07-5). Boulevard.
Two-Sector General Equilibrium Model: A New Approach. C. L. Dinwiddy & F. J. Teal. LC 87-36935. 160p. 1988. 45.00 (ISBN 0-312-01877-0). St Martin.
Two-Sector Model of Economic Growth with Technological Progress. Frederick O. Goddard. LC 75-625421. (University of Florida Social Sciences Monographs: No. 36). 1969. pap. 6.00x (ISBN 0-8130-0270-2). U Presses Fla.
Two Select Bibliographies of Medieval Historical Study. Margaret F. Moore. 1912. 21.00 (ISBN 0-8337-2452-5). B Franklin.
Two Selves of Jessica Throckmorton: An Aesthetic Realism Lesson. Eli Siegel. 1971. pap. 2.00x (ISBN 0-911492-10-0). Aesthetic Realism.
Two Serious Ladies. Jane Bowles. 208p. 1984. pap. 8.95 (ISBN 0-525-48324-1, Obelisk). Dutton.
Two Sermons. John Cotton. LC 79-141108. (Research Library of Colonial Americana). 1971. Repr. of 1642 ed. 22.00 (ISBN 0-405-03322-2). Ayer Co Pubs.
Two Shall Be One. C. M. Ward. (Orig.). 1986. pap. text ed. 3.95 (ISBN 0-88368-184-6). Whitaker Hse.
Two Sheffield Poets: James Montegomery & Ebenezer Elliott. W. Odom. 1973. 25.00 (ISBN 0-8274-1148-0). R West.
Two Shoes, New Shoes. Shirley Hughes. LC 86-2733. (Illus.). 24p. (ps). 1986. 4.95 (ISBN 0-688-04207-4). Lothrop.
Two Short Paris Summertime Plays of Nineteen Seventy-Four. William Saroyan. (Santa Susana Press Ser.). 1979. numbered 60.00 (ISBN 0-937048-17-8); lettered o.p. 85.00 (ISBN 0-937048-26-7); with laid-in block print 110.00 (ISBN 0-937048-27-5). CSUN.
Two Sides of a Coin. Charles Hunter & Frances Hunter. 1973. pap. 4.95 (ISBN 0-917726-36-7). Hunter Bks.
Two Sides of a Coin. Rev. ed. 167p. (Span.). 1986. pap. 3.00 (ISBN 0-917726-77-4). Hunter Bks.
Two Sides of a Poem. Katherine J. Bellamann. LC 70-179811. (New Poetry Ser.). Repr. of 1955 ed. 16.00 (ISBN 0-404-56011-3). AMS Pr.
Two Sides, the Best of Personal Opinion, 1964-1984. John H. Redekop. 306p. (Orig.). 1984. pap. 9.95 (ISBN 0-919797-13-X). Kindred Pr.
Two Sieges of Rhodes. Eric Brockman. LC 71-436060. 1969. text ed. 10.00x (ISBN 0-8401-0241-0). A R Allenson.
Two Sisters. Gore Vidal. 1987. pap. 4.95 (ISBN 0-345-33117-6). Ballantine.
Two Sisters for Social Justice: A Biography of Grace & Edith Abbott. Lela B. Costin. LC 82-21790. (Illus.). 336p. 1983. 22.50 (ISBN 0-252-01013-2). U of Ill Pr.
Two Sites on Martha's Vineyard, Vol. 1 No. 1. D. Byers & F. Johnson. LC 40-3078. 1940. 4.00 (ISBN 0-939312-00-X). Peabody Found.
Two-Six Compounds. B. Ray. LC 72-93126. 1969. 57.00 (ISBN 0-08-006624-0). Pergamon.
Two Small Bodies. Neal Bell. pap. 3.50x (ISBN 0-686-63171-4). Dramatists Play.
Two Social Psychologies. Cookie W. Stephan & Walter C. Stephan. 448p. 1985. 34.00x (ISBN 0-256-03108-8); study guide 12.00 (ISBN 0-256-03251-3). Dorsey.
Two Society Comedies: A Woman of No Importance & Ideal Husband. Oscar Wilde. Ed. by Ian Small & Russell Jackson. (New Mermaids Ser.). 1984. pap. text ed. 7.95x (ISBN 0-393-90055-X). Norton.
Two Songs This Archangel Sings. George C. Chesbro. LC 86-47668. 320p. 1987. 14.95 (ISBN 0-689-11659-4). Atheneum.
Two Songs This Archangel Sings. George C. Chesbro. 1988. pap. 3.95 (ISBN 0-440-20105-5). Dell.
Two Sons of Heaven: Studies in Sung-Liao Relations. Jing-shen Tao. LC 88-1330. 180p. 1988. 26.95x (ISBN 0-8165-1051-2). U of Ariz Pr.
Two-Source Hypothesis: A Critical Appraisal. Ed. by Arthur J. Bellinzoni. LC 84-29447. x, 486p. 1985. 39.95 (ISBN 0-86554-096-9, MUP/H88). Mercer Univ Pr.
Two Sources of Morality & Religion. Henri Bergson. LC 74-10373. 308p. 1975. Repr. of 1935 ed. lib. bdg. 27.50x (ISBN 0-8371-7679-4, BETS). Greenwood.
Two Sources of Morality & Religion. Henri Bergson. Tr. by R. Ashley Audra from Fr. LC 77-89762. 1977. pap. text ed. 9.95 (ISBN 0-268-01835-9). U of Notre Dame Pr.
Two Soviet Studies on Frege. B. V. Birjukov. Tr. by Ignacio Angelelli from Rus. (Sovietica Ser.: No. 15). 101p. 1964. lib. bdg. 18.50 (ISBN 90-277-0072-9, Pub by Reidel Holland). Kluwer Academic.
Two Space Six. Peter Ganick. 36p. (Orig.). 1982. pap. 3.00 (ISBN 0-318-20083-X). Potes Poets.
Two Spanish Picaresque Novels. Tr. by Michael Alpert. Incl. Lazarillo De Tormes; Swindler. Francisco Quevedo. (Classics Ser). (Orig.). 1969. pap. 5.95 (ISBN 0-14-044211-1). Penguin.
Two Spanish-Quiche Dance Dramas of Rabinal, Vol. 3. Carroll E. Mace. 221p. 1970. pap. 7.00 (ISBN 0-912788-02-X). Tulane Romance Lang.
Two Speeches by Malcolm X. Malcolm X. (Orig.). pap. 0.75 (ISBN 0-87348-087-2). Path Pr NY.
Two Speeches on Conciliation With American & Two Letters on Irish Questions. Edmund Burke. (Illus.). 284p. 1983. 35.00 (ISBN 0-317-00584-7). Century Bookbindery.
Two Spine Rows in a Florida Busycon Contrarium see Palaeontographica Americana.
Two Standards. William F. Barry. Ed. by Robert L. Wolff. LC 75-466. (Victorian Fiction Ser). 1976. Repr. of 1898 ed. lib. bdg. 73.00 (ISBN 0-8240-1544-4). Garland Pub.
Two State Universe. Angelo A. Molinaro. 1988. pap. 14.95 (ISBN 0-8283-1997-9). Branden Pub Co.
Two Statesmen of Medieval Islam: Vizir Ibn Hubayra (499-560 A. H., 1105-1165 A. D.) & Calif*h* an-Nasir Li Din Allah (553-622 A. H., 1158-1225 A. D.) Herbert Mason. 146p. 1972. text ed. 15.20x (ISBN 90-2796-979-5). Mouton.
Two-Step: Dancing Toward Intimacy. Eileen McCann. LC 85-14764. (Illus.). 180p. 1985. 17.50 (ISBN 0-394-55016-1). Grove.
Two-Step: Dancing Toward Intimacy. Eileen McCann. LC 85-14764. (Illus.). 160p. 1985. pap. 9.95 (ISBN 0-394-62050-X, Ever). Grove.
Two Step Formal Advertising. (Monographs: No. 12). 75p. 1979. 7.00 (ISBN 0-935165-14-2). GWU Gov Contracts.
Two Steps at a Time. Marce H. Stein. 96p. 1982. 7.95 (ISBN 0-89962-211-9). Todd & Honeywell.
Two Stochastic Processes. John A. Beekman. 192p. (Orig.). 1974. text ed. 28.00x (Pub. by Almqvist & Wiksell). Coronet Bks.
Two Stories. Giambattista Basile. Tr. & intro. by Felix Stefanile. (Poverty Pamphlets Ser.: No. 50). 28p. (Orig.). 1986. pap. text ed. 2.50x (ISBN 0-935552-21-9). Sparrow Pr.
Two Stories. 2nd ed. Thomas Mann. Ed. by William Witte. Incl. Unordnung und Fruhes Leid; Mario und der Zauberer. (German Text Ser.). 128p. 1971. pap. 15.00 (ISBN 0-631-01870-0). Basil Blackwell.
Two Stories. Brian Moore. (Santa Susana Press Ser.). 1979. numbered 35.00 (ISBN 0-937048-22-4); lettered 60.00 (ISBN 0-937048-29-1). CSUN.
Two Stories Jesus Told. Lucy Diamond. (Ladybird Ser). (Illus.). 1959. bds. 2.50 (ISBN 0-87508-870-8). Chr Lit.
Two Story Homes. 288p. 1986. pap. 6.95 (ISBN 0-918894-50-6). Home Planners.
Two-Story Outhouse. Norman D. Weis. (Illus., Orig.). 1988. pap. 12.95 (ISBN 0-87004-326-9). Caxton.
Two Strange Tales. Mircea Eliade. Tr. by William A. Coates from Romanian. LC 86-13026. 130p. 1986. pap. 6.95 (ISBN 0-87773-386-4). Shambhala Pubns.
Two Strikes, Four Eyes. Ned Delaney. (Illus.). (gr. k-3). 1976. PLB 11.95 reinforced bdg. (ISBN 0-395-24744-6). HM.
Two-Stroke Tuner's Handbook. Gordon Jennings. (Illus.). 156p. 1974. pap. 5.95 (ISBN 0-912656-41-7). Price Stern.
Two Studies. David Daiches. LC 77-1314. 1977. Repr. of 1958 ed. lib. bdg. 15.00 (ISBN 0-8414-3817-X). Folcroft.
Two Studies. David Daiches. 32p. 1980. Repr. of 1958 ed. lib. bdg. 15.00 (ISBN 0-8492-4225-8). R West.
Two Studies in Automobile Franchising. H. O. Helmers et al. (Vol. 1, No. 1: No. 1). 265p. 1974. 9.50 (ISBN 0-87712-160-5). UMI Div Res GSBA.
Two Studies in Chinese Literature. Li Chi & Dale Johnson. (Michigan Monographs in Chinese Studies: No. 3). (Illus.). 98p. 1968. pap. 1.50 (ISBN 0-89264-003-0). U of Mich Ctr Chinese.
Two Studies in Early Mughal History. Yusuf Husain. 1976. 7.50x (ISBN 0-89684-462-5). Orient Bk Dist.
Two Studies in Later Roman & Byzantine Administration. Arthur E. Boak. Repr. of 1924 ed. 37.00 (ISBN 0-384-38814-0). Johnson Repr.
Two Studies in Latin Phonology. Andrew M. Devine & Laurence D. Stephens. (Studia Linguistica et Philologica: No. 3). 1978. pap. 29.50 (ISBN 0-915838-42-7). Anma Libri.
Two Studies in Mental Tests. Carl Brigham. Bd. with Radiometric Apparatus for Use in Psychological Optics. C. E. Ferree. Repr. of 1917 ed; Transfer of Training & Retroaction. L. E. Webb. Repr. of 1917 ed; Reliability of Mental Tests in the Division of an Academic Group. B. Ruml. Repr. of 1917 ed; Analysis of Mental Functions. C. Rosenow. Repr. of 1917 ed. (Psychology Monographs General & Applied: Vol. 24). pap. 36.00 (ISBN 0-8115-1423-4). Kraus Repr.
Two Studies in Middle American Comparative Linguistics. David Oltrogge & Calvin Rensch. (SIL Publications in Linguistics: No. 55). 108p. 1977. 5.00x (ISBN 0-88312-068-2); microfiche (2) 4.00x (ISBN 0-88312-474-2). Summer Inst Ling.
Two Studies in Roman Nomenclature. D. R. Bailey. (American Philological Association, American Classical Studies). 1974. pap. 9.00 (ISBN 0-89130-716-8, 400403). Scholars Pr GA.
Two Studies in Romantic Reviewing: Edinburgh Reviewers & the English Tradition, the Reviewing of Walter Scott's Poetry 1805-1817, 2 vols. J. H. Alexander. Ed. by James Hogg. 437p. (Orig.). 1976. pap. 30.00 (ISBN 3-7052-0504-8, Pub. by Salzburg Studies). Longwood Pub Group.
Two Studies in Soviet Terms of Trade, (1918-1970) Michael Dohan & Edward Hewett. (Studies in East European & Soviet Planning, Development, & Trade: No. 21). 1973. pap. text ed. 3.00 (ISBN 0-89249-001-2). Intl Development.
Two Studies on Ethnic Group Relations in Africa: Senegal, United Republic of Tanzania. (Race & Society Ser.). 156p. 1974. pap. 5.00 (ISBN 92-3-101101-4, U688, UNESCO). UNIPUB.
Two Studies on Israel. Ayad Al-Qazzaz & Ibrahim Oweiss. (Information Papers: No. 13). 29p. (Orig.). 1974. pap. text ed. 2.75 (ISBN 0-937694-29-0). Assn Arab-Amer U Grads.
Two Studies on Ming History. Charles O. Hucker. (Michigan Monographs in Chinese Studies: No. 12). (Illus.). 83p. 1971. pap. 6.00 (ISBN 0-89264-012-X). U of Mich Ctr Chinese.
Two Studies on Roman Expansion: An Original Anthology. A. Afzelius. LC 75-7301. (Roman History Ser.). (Ger.). 1975. Repr. of 1975 ed. 30.00x (ISBN 0-405-07178-7). Ayer Co Pubs.
Two Studies on the Lacandones of Mexico. Phil Baer & William R. Merrifield. (Publications in Linguistics & Related Fields Ser.: No. 33). 272p. 1971. microfiche (3) 6.00 (ISBN 0-88312-435-1). Summer Inst Ling.
Two Studies on the Palestinians Today & American Policy. Ibrahim Abu-Lughod & Edward Said. (Information Paper: No. 17). 22p. (Orig.). 1976. pap. 2.75 (ISBN 0-937694-33-9). Assn Arab-Amer U Grads.
Two Studies on the Roman Lower Classes: An Original Anthology. M. E. Park & M. Maxey. LC 75-7347. (Roman History Ser.). 1975. Repr. 16.00x (ISBN 0-405-07069-1). Ayer Co Pubs.
Two Studies on the Roman Pontifices. P. Preibisch. LC 75-10647. (Ancient Religion & Mythology Ser.). 1976. 12.00x (ISBN 0-405-07271-6). Ayer Co Pubs.
Two Studies on Unemployment Among Educated Young People, 2 Pts. Simone Morio & Yarrise Zoctizum. (Illus.). 1980. Pt. 1: Unemployment in the Developed Market Economy Countries. pap. 5.00, set (ISBN 92-3-101618-0, U996, UNESCO). Pt. 2: Unemployment in the French-Speaking Developing Countries. UNIPUB.
Two Studies on Venetian Government. D. Quellen. (Estudes de Philologie d'Histoire: No. 33). 180p. 1977. lib. bdg. 44.50 (ISBN 0-317-65826-3). Coronet Bks.
Two Suffolk Friends. Francis H. Groome. 133p. 1980. Repr. lib. bdg. 17.50 (ISBN 0-89984-227-5). Century Bookbindery.
Two Suites for Harpsichord. Thomas Chilcot. Ed. by Gwilym Beechey. LC 72-626211. (Penn State Music Series, No. 22). pap. 4.00 (ISBN 0-271-09122-3). Pa St U Pr.
Two Summer Sequences. Gerald Locklin. 1979. 2.50 (ISBN 0-917554-10-8). Maelstrom.
Two Sung Texts on Chinese Painting & the Landscape Styles of the 11th & 12th Centuries. Robert J. Maeda. LC 77-94706. (Outstanding Dissertations in the Fine Arts Ser.). 1978. lib. bdg. 33.00 (ISBN 0-8240-3238-1). Garland Pub.
Two Surprises. Lucy Conley. (Jewel Bk.). 1986. pap. 1.95. Rod & Staff.
Two Symphonies. Andre Gide. 1977. pap. 5.95 (ISBN 0-394-72454-2, Vin). Random.
Two Tactics of Social Democracy in the Democratic Revolution. Vladimir I. Lenin. 132p. 1970. pap. 0.95 (ISBN 0-8285-0177-7, Pub. by Progress Pubs USSR). Imported Pubns.
Two Tahitian Villages: A Study in Comparison. Douglas L. Oliver. 1983. text ed. 24.95x (ISBN 0-939154-22-6). Inst Polynesian.
Two Tales: Betrothed & Edo & Enam. S. Y. Agnon. Tr. by Walter Lever from Hebrew. 256p. 1986. pap. 6.95 (ISBN 0-8052-0814-3). Schocken.
Two Tales for Autumn. Berry Fleming. LC 79-88065. 332p. 1979. 9.95 (ISBN 0-9604810-0-1); pap. 4.95 (ISBN 0-9604810-1-X). Cotton Lane.
Two Tales in Afro-American History: The Denmark Vesey Revolt & a Story of Reconstruction. Illus. by Jon F. Rice. (Illus.). 51p. 1980. 2.50 (ISBN 0-937352-00-4). Committee IL.
Two Tales: Man Who Would Be King & Without Benefit of Clergy. Rudyard Kipling. pap. 3.00 (ISBN 0-8283-1460-8, 2, IPL). Branden Pub Co.
Two Tales of the East Indies: The Last House in the World & The Counselor. Beb Vuyk & H. J. Friedericy. Intro. by E. M. Beekman. Tr. by Andre Lefevere & Hans Koning. LC 83-4812. (Library of the Indies). 216p. 1983. lib. bdg. 20.00x (ISBN 0-87023-403-X). U of Mass Pr.
Two Tales: Rip Van Winkle & the Legend of Sleepy Hollow. Washington Irving. (Illus.). 112p. (gr. 1 up). 1986. 17.95 (ISBN 0-15-192280-2). HarBraceJ.
Two-Ten Conspiracy. Leon LeGrand. 320p. 1988. pap. 3.95 (ISBN 1-55547-242-7). Critics Choice Paper.
Two Terrible Frights. Jim Aylesworth. LC 86-25859. (Illus.). 32p. (ps-2). 1987. PLB 13.95 (ISBN 0-689-31327-6, Atheneum Childrens Bks). Macmillan.
Two Thackerays: Anne Thackeray Richie's Centenary Biographical Introductions to the Works of William Makepeace Thackeray, 2 vols. Carol H. MacKay et al. LC 85-48065. (Studies in the Nineteenth Century: No. 5). 1988. Set. 165.00 (ISBN 0-404-61483-3). AMS Pr.
Two That Were Tough. Robert Burch. (Illus.). (gr. 6-8). 1976. 9.95 (ISBN 0-670-73684-8). Viking.
Two Theban Monuments from the Reign of Amenhotep II. Charles C. Van Siclen, III. (Illus.). 46p. 1982. pap. text ed. 9.00x (ISBN 0-933175-01-9). Van Siclen Bks.
Two Theories of Morality. S. Hampshire. (Thank-Offering to Britain Fund Lectures). 1976. 8.00 (ISBN 0-85672-344-4, Pub. by British Acad). Longwood Pub Group.
Two Thieves. facsimile ed. Theodore F. Powys. LC 79-167466. (Short Story Index Reprint Ser.). Repr. of 1933 ed. 18.00 (ISBN 0-8369-3992-1). Ayer Co Pubs.
Two Thousand. Gilles Aussant. 1986. 10.00 (ISBN 0-533-06957-2). Vantage.
Two Thousand & Eighty-one: A Hopeful View of the Human Future. Gerard K. O'Neill. 1982. pap. 6.25 (ISBN 0-671-44751-3). S&S.
Two Thousand & One: A Space Odyssey. Arthur C. Clarke. 1972. pap. 3.50 (ISBN 0-451-13469-9, Sig). NAL.
Two Thousand & One Free Things for the Garden. Marilyn Hendrickson & Robert Hendrickson. 256p. 1983. cancelled (ISBN 0-312-82746-6). St Martin.
Two Thousand & One French & English Idioms: Idiotismes Francais et Anglais 2001. Francois Denoeu & David Sices. 1982. pap. text ed. 9.95 (ISBN 0-8120-0435-3). Barron.
Two Thousand & One Italian & English Idioms: 2001 Locuzione Italiane e Inglese. Robert R. Hall, Jr. & Frances A. Hall. LC 81-66403. (Ital. & Eng.). 1981. pap. text ed. 9.95 (ISBN 0-8120-0467-1). Barron.
Two Thousand & One Modismos Espanoles e Ingleses. Eugene Savaiano & Lynn W. Winget. LC 81-3628. (Barron's Educational Ser.). 336p. 1981. pap. 4.95 (ISBN 0-8120-2314-5). Barron.
Two Thousand & One Spanish & English Idioms: 2001 Modismos Espanoles y Ingleses. rev. ed. Eugene Saviano & Lynn W. Winget. LC 75-11955. (Span. & Eng.). 1977. pap. 4.95 (ISBN 0-8120-0711-5); pap. text ed. 9.95 (ISBN 0-8120-0438-8). Barron.
Two Thousand & One the Church in Crisis. Leonidas C. Contos. 60p. 1981. pap. 2.95 (ISBN 0-916586-46-4). Holy Cross Orthodox.

Two Thousand Dollars an Hour. David Bendah. 1985. pap. 10.00 (ISBN 0-933301-11-1). Lion Pub.
Two Thousand Fifty. Peter Bosto. 48p. 1987. 6.95 (ISBN 0-89962-606-8). Todd & Honeywell.
Two Thousand Five Hundred Fiber Optics Patent Abstracts: 1881-1979. LC 79-93149. (Illus.). 382p. 1980. 167.50x (ISBN 0-935714-00-6). Patent Data.
Two Thousand Five Hundred Ninety-Seven Keeney Relatives. Roscoe C. Keeney, Jr. 1978. 10.00 (ISBN 0-87012-324-6). McClain.
Two Thousand Five Hundred Tips & Tricks for the Apple Macintosh. Anthony R. Curtis. (Illus.). 320p. (Orig.). 1988. pap. 24.95 (ISBN 0-86668-066-7). ARCsoft.
Two Thousand Insults for All Occasions. Louis A. Safian. 1965. pap. 5.95 (ISBN 0-8065-0039-5, C276, Pub. by Citadel Pr). Lyle Stuart.
Two Thousand Insults for All Occasions. Louis A. Safian. 256p. 1983. pap. 2.95 (ISBN 0-671-47430-8). PB.
Two Thousand Maniacs. 2nd, rev. ed. Herschell G. Lewis. (Illus.). 144p. 1988. pap. 9.95 (ISBN 0-938782-08-8). Fantaco.
Two Thousand Mile Turtle & Other Episodes from Editor Harold Smith's Private Journal. H. B. Fox. LC 75-1600. (Illus.). 128p. 1975. 7.95 (ISBN 0-89052-014-3). Madrona Pr.
Two Thousand Miles on the Appalachian Trail. Donald J. Fortunato. (Illus.). 153p. (Orig.). 1984. pap. 6.95 (ISBN 0-9613494-0-9). Fortunato Bks.
Two Thousand Miles' Ride Through the Argentine Provinces, 2 Vols. William MacCann. LC 70-128433. Repr. of 1853 ed. Set. 52.00 (ISBN 0-404-04102-7). AMS Pr.
Two Thousand More Insults. Louis A. Safian. 192p. 1984. pap. 2.95 (ISBN 0-671-50326-X). PB.
Two Thousand More Insults. Louis H. Safian. 224p. 1976. pap. 4.95 (ISBN 0-8065-0521-4, Pub. by Citadel Pr). Lyle Stuart.
Two Thousand New Laughs for Speakers. Bob Orben. pap. 5.00 (ISBN 0-87980-382-7). Wilshire.
Two Thousand Nine Hundred & Fifty-Nine Plan. Peter Lord. pap. 7.95 (ISBN -08010-5600-4). Baker Bk.
Two Thousand Notable American Women. Ed. by J. M. Evans. 500p. 1987. 135.00 (ISBN 0-934544-45-X). Am Biog Inst.
Two Thousand Notable Americans. 2nd ed. Ed. by J. M. Evans. LC 83-73395. (Illus.). 500p. 1985. 125.00 (ISBN 0-934544-35-2). Am Biog Inst.
Two Thousand Notable Americans. 3rd ed. Ed. by J. M. Evans. LC 83-73395. (Illus.). 500p. 1987. 135.00 (ISBN 0-934544-39-5). Am Biog Inst.
Two Thousand One: A Sports Odyssey Hypnosis Cybernetics Conditioning Biofeedback. Judd Biasiotto. 160p. (Orig.). 1984. pap. 8.00 (ISBN 0-933079-04-4). World Class Enterprises.
Two Thousand One Great Radio Promotions. Jeffrey Green. 300p. 1988. pap. 19.95 (ISBN 0-939735-02-4). Prof Desk Ref.
Two Thousand One Hundred & Fifty A. D. Thea Alexander. 288p. (Orig.). 1976. pap. 4.50 (ISBN 0-446-32214-8). Warner Bks.
Two Thousand One Hundred Laughs for All Occasions. Robert Orben. LC 82-45448. 240p. 1986. pap. 7.95 (ISBN 0-385-23488-0). Doubleday.
Two Thousand One Hundred Ninety-Four Days of War. Ed. by Cesare Salmaggi & Fredo Pallavisini. LC 79-738. (Illus.). 1979. 24.95 (ISBN 0-8317-8941-7, Mayflower Bks). Smith Pubs.
Two Thousand One Southern Superstitions. 1.95 (ISBN 0-936672-34-X). Aerial Photo.
Two-Thousand-Pound Goldfish. Betsy Byars. LC 81-48652. 160p. (gr. 5 up). 1982. 12.70i (ISBN 0-06-020889-9); PLB 12.89g (ISBN 0-06-020890-2). HarpJ.
Two-Thousand-Pound Goldfish. Betsy Byars. (gr. 4-6). 1983. pap. 2.50 (ISBN 0-590-40224-2, Apple Paperbacks). Scholastic Inc.
Two-Thousand-Pound Goldfish. Betsy Byars. 160p. (gr. 4-6). 1988. pap. 2.50 (ISBN 0-590-40562-4). Scholastic Inc.
Two-Thousand-Pound Goldfish see Betsy Byars Boxed Set.
Two Thousand Seasons. Ayi Kwei Armah. LC 74-980017. 1980. pap. 12.95 (ISBN 0-88378-051-8); pap. 6.95. Third World.
Two Thousand Six Hundred Definitions of Technical Terms According to Din: English-German, German-English. H. G. Freeman. write for info. (ISBN 0-686-39804-1, 10804-1, Pub. by DIN Germany). IPS.
Two Thousand Sixty-One: Odyssey Three. Arthur C. Clarke. 1988. 17.95 (ISBN 0-345-35173-8, Del Rey). Ballantine.
Two Thousand Sons: The Story of Cal Farley's Boys Ranch. Cal Farley & E. L. Howe. LC 87-14040. (Illus.). 300p. 1987. 20.00 (ISBN 0-914659-23-5). Phoenix Pub.
Two Thousand Sure Fire Jokes for Speakers & Writers. Robert Orben. LC 86-24240. 240p. 1986. pap. 6.95 (ISBN 0-385-23465-1). Doubleday.
Two Thousand Ten: Odyssey Two. Arthur C. Clark. 1984. pap. 4.95 (ISBN 0-345-30306-7, Del Rey). Ballantine.
Two Thousand Ten: Odyssey Two. Arthur C. Clarke. 1988. pap. 3.95 (ISBN 0-345-00661-5). Ballantine.
Two Thousand Twenty-Two Modismos Esenciales en Ingles. Ed. by Maria E. Alvarez del Real. (Illus.). 288p. (Orig., Eng., Span.). 1987. pap. 4.00x (ISBN 0-944499-19-8). Editorial Amer.
Two Thousand Ways To Save On Probate, Inflation, Taxes. Art Linkletter & Ferd A. Nuaheim. 1977. pap. 4.95 (ISBN 0-87491-199-0). Acropolis.
Two Thousand Years of Calligraphy. Dorothy E. Miner et al. LC 78-20698. (Illus.). 1980. pap. 13.95 (ISBN 0-8008-7919-8, Pentalic). Taplinger.
Two Thousand Years of Calligraphy: A Three-Part Exhibition Organized by the Baltimore Museum of Art, Peabody Institute Library & Walters Art Gallery June 6-July 18, 1965: A Comprehensive Catalog. Ed. by Dorothy E. Miner et al. (Illus.). 201p. 1980. Repr. of 1972 ed. 24.50x (ISBN 0-87471-091-X). Rowman.
Two Thousand Years of Chinese Ceramics. V. Reynolds. 72p. 1978. 20.00x (ISBN 0-317-45299-1, Pub. by Han-Shan Tang Ltd). State Mutual Bk.
Two Thousand Years of Tapestry Weaving: A Loan Exhibition. (Illus.). 86p. 1952. pap. 2.50 (ISBN 0-317-13607-0). Wadsworth Atheneum.
Two Thyrdes. Bertie Denham. 304p. 1986. 15.95 (ISBN 0-312-82752-0). St Martin.
Two Thyrdes. Bertie Denham. 1988. pap. 3.95 (ISBN 0-312-90649-8). St Martin.
Two Tickets for Tangier. F. Van Wyck Mason. 1976. Repr. of 1955 ed. lib. bdg. 18.95 (ISBN 0-89190-354-2, Pub. by River City Pr). Amereon Ltd.
Two-Tier Partnerships & Other Alternatives: Five Approaches. American Bar Association, Economics of Law Practice Staff. LC 86-72163. 75p. 1986. pap. 34.95 (ISBN 0-89707-267-7). Amer Bar Assn.
Two Times Two Equals Four. Anatolii Shteiger. LC 80-54026. (Russica Poetry Ser.: No. 1). 104p. (Orig., Rus.). 1982. pap. 6.95 (ISBN 0-89830-029-0). Russica Pubs.
Two to Conquer. Marion Zimmer Bradley. 1987. pap. 3.50 (ISBN 0-88677-174-9). DAW Bks.
Two to Three Years: Playing & Learning with a Two Year Old Including Pictures, Anecdotes & Suggestions for Activities. Marilyn M. Segal & Don Adcock. Ed. by Monica M. Segal. (Family Center Child Development Ser.: Vol. 3). (Illus.). 300p. cancelled (ISBN 0-914799-06-1); pap. cancelled (ISBN 0-914799-05-3). Mailman Family.
Two Tocquevilles, Father & Son: Herve & Alexis de Tocqueville on the Coming of the French Revolution. Ed. by R. R. Palmer. (Illus.). 264p. 1987. text ed. 28.50 (ISBN 0-691-05495-9). Princeton U Pr.
Two Too Thin: Two Women Who Triumphed over Anorexia Nervosa. Camie Ford & Sunny Hale. LC 83-61378. 370p. 1983. pap. 6.95 (ISBN 0-941478-15-7). Paraclete Pr.
Two Toreadors from Vasukovka Village. V. Nestaiko. 311p. 1983. 9.95 (ISBN 0-8285-2670-2, Pub. by Raduga Pubs USSR). Imported Pubns.
Two Towers. J. R. R. Tolkien. 1967. 11.95 (ISBN 0-395-08255-2). HM.
Two Towers. J. R. R. Tolkien. pap. 3.95 (ISBN 0-345-33971-1, Del Rey). Ballantine.
Two Towers: Being the Second Part of the Lord of the Rings. J. R. Tolkien. (Illus.). 356p. 1988. 16.95 (ISBN 0-395-48933-4); pap. 7.95 (ISBN 0-395-27222-X). HM.
Two Towns in Provence: Map of Another Town & a Considerable Town. M. K. Fisher. LC 83-6901. (Illus.). 512p. 1983. pap. 9.95 (ISBN 0-394-71631-0, Vin). Random.
Two Tracts on Civil Liberties. Richard Price. LC 74-169641. (Era of the American Revolution Ser.). 1972. Repr. lib. bdg. 42.50 (ISBN 0-306-70233-9). Da Capo.
Two Traditions of Meditation in Ancient India. Johannes Bronkhorst. 157p. (Orig.). 1986. pap. 34.00x (ISBN 3-515-04238-5, Pub. by Franz Steiner). Coronet Bks.
Two Tragedies: Hector & La Reine d'Escosse. Antoine De Montchrestien. Ed. by C. N. Smith. (Renaissance Library). 152p. (Fr.). 1972. 36.50 (ISBN 0-485-13805-0, Pub. by Athlone Pr UK); pap. 16.95 (ISBN 0-485-12805-5, Pub. by Athlone Pr UK). Humanities.
Two Tragedies: Hippolyte & Marc Antoine. Robert Garnier. Ed. by Christine M. Hill & Mary G. Morrison. (Renaissance Library). 181p. (Fr.). 1975. 36.50 (ISBN 0-485-13809-3, Pub. by Athlone Pr UK); pap. 16.95 (ISBN 0-485-12809-8, Pub. by Athlone Pr UK). Humanities.
Two Trails to Rosas. Dusty Richards. 126p. 1984. 6.95 (ISBN 0-89697-181-3). Intl Univ Pr.
Two Travellers & Other Korean Short Stories. So Ki-won et al. Ed. by The Korean National Commission for UNESCO. Tr. by Mun Sang-duk et al from Korean. (Modern Korean Short Stories Ser.: No. 7). viii, 144p. 1983. 20.00 (ISBN 0-89209-208-4). Pace Intl Res.
Two Treatises Concerning the Perservation of Eye-Sight. Walter Bailey. LC 74-28827. (English Experience Ser.: No. 709). 1975. Repr. of 1616 ed. 20.00 (ISBN 90-221-0709-4). Walter J Johnson.
Two Treatises: In the One of Which the Nature of Bodies; In the Other the Nature of Man's Soule is Look'd into the Way of Discovery of the Immortality of Reasonable Souls. Sir Kenelme Digby. Ed. by Rene Wellek. LC 75-11217. (British Philosophers & Theologians of the 17th & 18th Centuries Ser.). 514p. 1978. lib. bdg. 51.00 (ISBN 0-8240-1771-4). Garland Pub.
Two Treatises of Government. John Locke. 1975. 12.95x (ISBN 0-460-00751-3, Evman); pap. 4.95x (ISBN 0-460-01751-9, Evman). Biblio Dist.
Two Treatises of Government. John Locke. Ed. & intro. by Thomas I. Cook. Bd. with Patriarcha. Robert Filmer. (Library of Classics Ser: No. 2). text ed. 9.95x (ISBN 0-02-848500-9). Hafner.
Two Treatises of Government. John Locke. pap. 4.95 (ISBN 0-451-62586-2, Ment). NAL.
Two Treatises of Government. 3rd, rev. ed. John Locke. Ed. by Peter Laslett. (Cambridge Texts in the History of Political Thought Ser.). 200p. Date not set. price not set (ISBN 0-521-35448-X); pap. price not set (ISBN 0-521-35730-6). Cambridge U Pr.
Two Treatises of Government with a Supplement Containing Sir Robert Filmer's Patriarcha. John Locker. 1974. pap. 10.95 (ISBN 0-317-60442-2). Free Pr.
Two Treatises of Philo of Alexandria: A Commentary on De Gigantibus & Quod Deus Sit Immutabilis. David Winston & John Dillon. LC 82-786. (Brown Judaic Studies). 416p. 1983. pap. 15.00 (ISBN 0-89130-563-7, 14 00 25). Scholars Pr GA.
Two Treatises of Proclus. Proclus. 175p. 1980. 15.00 (ISBN 0-89005-329-4). Ares.
Two Treatises of Servetus on the Trinity. Michael Servetus. Tr. by Earl M. Wilbur. (Harvard Theological Studies). 1932. 26.00 (ISBN 0-527-01016-2). Kraus Repr.
Two Treatises on the Accentuation of the Old Testament. rev. ed. William Wickes. 1970. 35.00x (ISBN 0-87068-004-8). Ktav.
Two Treatises on the Christian Priesthood, 3 Vols. George Hickes. (Library of Anglo-Catholic Theology: No. 9). Repr. of 1848 ed. Set. 87.50 (ISBN 0-404-52100-2). AMS Pr.
Two Trends in Modern Quaker Thought. Albert Fowler. 1961. pap. 2.50x (ISBN 0-87574-112-6, 112). Pendle Hill.
Two Trips to Gorilla Land & the Cataracts of the Congo, 2 Vols. in 1. Richard F. Burton. (Illus.). 1876. 45.00 (ISBN 0-384-06651-8). Johnson Repr.
Two Truths in My Pocket. Lois Ruby. LC 81-70401. 156p. (gr. 7 up). 1982. 9.95 (ISBN 0-670-73724-0). Viking.
Two Truths in My Pocket. Lois Ruby. 128p. 1983. pap. 1.95 (ISBN 0-449-70070-4, Juniper). Fawcett.
Two Tudor Interludes. Ed. by Ann Lancashire. LC 79-3123. (Revels Plays Ser.). 1980. 20.00x (ISBN 0-8018-2338-2). Johns Hopkins.
Two Turtles of Paradise: A Love Story for Children & Adults. Joan S. Logan. (Illus.). 20p. 1988. pap. 1.95 (ISBN 0-944208-01-0). Seventh-Wing Pubns.
Two Twelfth Century Texts on Chinese Painting. Robert J. Maeda. (Michigan Monographs in Chinese Studies: No.8). 74p. 1970. pap. 1.50 (ISBN 0-89264-008-1). U of Mich Ctr Chinese.
Two Tycoons: Charles Clore & Jack Cotton. Charles Gordon. (Illus.). 288p. 1984. 22.95 (ISBN 0-241-11256-7, Pub. by Hamish Hamilton England). David & Charles.
Two Tycoons: Jack Cotton & Charles Clore. Charles Gordon. (Illus.). 256p. 1986. pap. 14.95 (ISBN 0-241-11785-2, Pub. by Hamish Hamilton England). David & Charles.
Two Types of Faith. Martin Buber. 256p. 1986. pap. 7.95 (ISBN 0-02-084180-9, Collier). Macmillan.
Two Types of Rural Schools, with Some Facts Showing Economic & Social Conditions. Ernest Burnham. LC 79-176613. (Columbia University. Teachers College. Contributions to Education: No. 51). Repr. of 1912 ed. 22.50 (ISBN 0-404-55051-7). AMS Pr.
Two under Par. reinforced ed. Kevin Henkes. LC 86-7556. (Illus.). 128p. (gr. 2-6). 1987. 10.25 (ISBN 0-688-06708-5). Greenwillow.
Two under the Covers. Jean MacCready & Vicki Quade. (Illus., Orig.). 1981. pap. 2.95 (ISBN 0-9602604-1-2). V Quade.
Two under the Indian Sun. Jon Godden & Rumer Godden. (Illus.). 208p. 1987. pap. 8.95 (ISBN 0-688-07422-7, Quill). Morrow.
Two University Latin Plays: Philip Parsons' Atlanta & Thomas Atkinson's Homo. William E. Mahaney. Ed. by James Hogg. (Elizabethan & Renaissance). 191p. (Orig.). 1973. pap. 15.00 (ISBN 3-7052-0665-6, Pub. by Salzburg Studies). Longwood Pub Group.
Two-Valued Iterative Systems of Mathematical Logic. Emil L. Post. (Annals of Math Studies). 1941. pap. 16.00 (ISBN 0-527-02721-9). Kraus Repr.
Two Vanrevels. Booth Tarkington. 1975. lib. bdg. 15.80x (ISBN 0-89966-175-0). Buccaneer Bks.
Two Vectors & Mechanics (Draft Edition) P. G. Lewis. LC 70-134616. (School Mathematics Project Ser). 1971. text ed. 9.95 (ISBN 0-521-08045-2). Cambridge U Pr.
Two Versions of Mariano Azuela's "Los De Abajo" A Comparative Study. Thomas W. Renaldi. 1978. lib. bdg. 69.95 (ISBN 0-8490-1396-8). Gordon Pr.
Two Versions of Waerferth's Translation of Gregory's Dialogues: An Old English Thesaurus. David Yerkes. LC 79-10546. (Toronto Old English Ser.). 1979. 22.50x (ISBN 0-8020-5464-1). U of Toronto Pr.
Two Very Notable Commentaries, of the Originall of Turcks, Etc. Andrea Cambini. Tr. by J. Shute. LC 75-25772. (English Experience Ser.: No. 235). 1970. Repr. of 1562 ed. 45.00 (ISBN 90-221-0235-1). Walter J Johnson.
Two Vietnams: A Political & Military Analysis. Bernard B. Fall. (Encore Ser.). 498p. 1985. pap. 60.50x (ISBN 0-8133-0092-4). Westview.
Two Views of Freedom in Process & Thought. George R. Lucas. LC 79-12287. (American Academy of Religion, Dissertation Ser.: No. 28). 1979. 14.00 (ISBN 0-89130-285-9, 010128); pap. 9.95 (ISBN 0-89130-304-9). Scholars Pr GA.
Two Views of Life: Secular Humanism & Radical Fundamentalism. Brian Bolton. (Orig.). 1988. pap. 7.95 (ISBN 0-943099-01-3). M&M Pr.
Two Village Sites in Southwestern Missouri: A Lithic Analysis. F. A. Calabrese et al. Ed. by W. Raymond Wood. LC 72-628906. (Research Ser.: No. 7). (Illus.). 50p. (Orig.). 1969. pap. 2.00 (ISBN 0-943414-09-1). MO Arch Soc.
Two Villages: Story of Chelsea & Kensington. Mary C. Borer. (Illus.). 288p. 1974. 12.50 (ISBN 0-491-01061-3). Transatl Arts.
Two Virgins. Kamala Markandaya. LC 73-4293. (John Day Bk.). 256p. 1973. o.s.i 10.45i (ISBN 0-381-98244-0). T Y Crowell.
Two Voyages to Russian America, 1802-1807. Gavriil Davydov. Ed. by Richard A. Pierce. Tr. by Colin Bearne. (Alaska History Ser.: No. 10). (Illus.). 1977. 16.50x (ISBN 0-919642-75-6). Limestone Pr.
Two Way Bilingual Songs for Elementary School. Ursula O. Ronnholm. 41p. (gr. k-12). 1987. pap. text ed. 8.00 (ISBN 0-941911-06-3); cassettes incl. Two Way Bilingual.
Two-Way Cable Television: Experiences with Pilot Projects in North America, Japan, & Europe. Proceedings of a Symposium Held in Munich, Germany, April 27-29, 1977. Ed. by W. Kaiser et al. LC 77-13725. (Illus.). 1977. pap. 26.00 (ISBN 0-387-08498-3). Springer-Verlag.
Two Way Cut. Peter Turnbull. 192p. 1988. 14.95 (ISBN 0-312-02306-5). St Martin.
Two Way Land Mobile Radio. 261p. 1984. 1550.00 (ISBN 0-86621-429-1, A1399). Frost & Sullivan.
Two-Way Mirror. David Meltzer. 1977. 6.95 (ISBN 0-685-80005-9); sewn in wrappers 2.95 (ISBN 0-685-80006-7). Oyez.
Two-Way Pitcher. Bonner. (YA) (gr. 7 up). PLB 6.19 (ISBN 0-8313-0008-6). Lantern.
Two-Way Prayer. Clifton King. 91p. (Orig.). 1987. pap. 4.95 (ISBN 0-87516-590-7). DeVorss.
Two-Way Radio Troubleshooting & Repair. Joseph Carr. (Orig.). 1987. pap. cancelled (ISBN 0-672-22557-3). Sams.
Two-Way Street: The Klepsch Report on U. S. A. - Europe Arms Procurement. E Klepsch & T. Normantoe. 95p. 1979. pap. 13.50 (ISBN 0-08-027011-5). Pergamon.
Two Ways About It. Judy F. Mearian. LC 79-10029. (gr. 5 up). 1979. 7.95 (ISBN 0-8037-8797-9). Dial Bks Young.
Two Ways to Count to Ten. Ruby Dee. LC 86-33513. 32p. (gr. k-3). 1988. 12.95 (ISBN 0-8050-0407-6). H Holt & co.
Two Weeks in the Midday Sun: A Cannes Notebook. Roger Ebert. LC 87-25183. (Illus.). 192p. (Orig.). 1987. pap. 8.95 (ISBN 0-8362-7942-5). Andrews & McMeel.
Two Weeks in the Yosemite & Vicinity. facs. ed. J. M. Buckley. (Illus.). 36p. pap. 3.95 (ISBN 0-8466-0153-2, S153). Shorey.
Two Weeks Off. Kirk Robertson. (Illus.). 48p. (Orig.). 1984. pap. 5.00 (ISBN 0-912449-11-X). Floating Island.
Two Weeks with the Psychic Surgeons. Marti Sladek. LC 76-45732. (Illus.). 1977. 8.95 (ISBN 0-917816-01-3). Doma.
Two Welsh Revivalists. Eifion Evans. pap. 3.25 (ISBN 0-317-65606-6). ChR Lit.
Two Were Prisoners. G. J. Parle. 493p. 1986. 20.00X (ISBN 0-7223-1941-X, Pub. by A H Stockwell England). State Mutual Bk.
Two Wesleys. C. H. Spurgeon. 1975. pap. 1.95 (ISBN 0-686-16834-8). Pilgrim Pubns.
Two-Wheeled Athlete. Ed Burke. LC 85-52407. (Illus.). 144p. (Orig.). 1986. pap. 10.95 (ISBN 0-941950-09-3). Velo-News.
Two-Wheeled Terror. Jake Mackenzie. (Secret Files of Dakota King: No. 2). 96p. (Orig.). (gr. 4-6). 1988. pap. 2.50 (ISBN 0-590-40751-1). Scholastic Inc.
Two Wheels & a Taxi: A Slightly Daft Adventure in the Andes. Virginia Urrutia. (Illus.). 276p. 1987. 14.95 (ISBN 0-89886-141-1). Mountaineers.
Two Wheels for Grover. Dan Elliott. LC 84-4732. (Sesame STreet Start-to-Read Bks.). (Illus.). 40p. (ps-3). 1984. 4.95 (ISBN 0-394-86586-3, Pub. by BYR); lib. bdg. 6.99 (ISBN 0-394-96586-8). Random.
Two Who Were There: A Biography of Stanley Nowak, Polish UAW Pioneer & Michigan's First Labor Legislator. Margaret C. Nowak. (Illus.). 320p. 1988. 32.50x (ISBN 0-8143-1883-5). Wayne St U Pr.

Two Willow Chairs. Jess Wells. 192p. (Orig.). 1987. pap. 8.95 (ISBN 0-940721-01-5). Libr B Bks.
Two Wills - His & Mine. Mother M. Angelica. 27p. (Orig.). 1977. pap. text ed. 2.00 (ISBN 1-55794-019-3, B52). Eternal Wrd TV.
Two Winchester Bibles. Walter Oakshott. (Illus.). 1981. 375.00x (ISBN 0-19-818235-X). Oxford U Pr.
Two Wings to Veil My Face. Leon Forrest. 320p. 1988. pap. 8.95 (ISBN 0-9614644-4-5). Another Chicago Pr.
Two Winters & Three Summers. Fyodor Abramov. 1984. 17.95 (ISBN 0-15-192300-0). HarBraceJ.
Two Winters & Three Summers. Fyodor Abramov. Tr. by D. B. Powers & Doris C. Powers. Orig. Title: Dve Zimy i Tri Leta. 1984. 19.50 (ISBN 0-88233-983-4); pap. 7.50 (ISBN 0-88233-984-2). Ardis Pubs.
Two Wise Men & All the Rest Fools. LC 72-133752. (Tudor Facsimile Texts. Old English Plays: No. 135). Repr. of 1913 ed. 49.50 (ISBN 0-404-53435-X). AMS Pr.
Two Witnesses. Gordon Lindsay. (Revelation Ser.). 1.25 (ISBN 0-89985-039-1). Christ Nations.
Two Witnesses. Date not set. pap. 0.95 (ISBN 0-937408-12-3). GMI Pubns Inc.
Two Women. Harry Mulisch. Tr. by Els Early from Dutch. 1981. 11.95 (ISBN 0-7145-3810-8). Riverrun NY.
Two Women in One. Nawal El-Saadawi. Tr. by Osman Nusairi & Jana Gough. LC 86-3675. 124p. 1986. 14.95 (ISBN 0-931188-41-5); pap. 7.95 (ISBN 0-931188-40-7). Seal Pr Feminist.
Two Women, Two Shores. M. McGuekian & Nuala Archer. (New Poets Ser.: Vol. 16). 64p. (016783633). 1988. pap. 5.95 (ISBN 0-932616-19-4). New Poets.
Two Wonder of Women, or the Tragedy of Sophonisba. William Kemp. Ed. by Stephen Orgel. LC 78-66805. (Renaissance Drama Ser.). 215p. 1979. lib. bdg. 28.00 (ISBN 0-8240-9744-0). Garland Pub.
Two-Word Sentence in Child Language Developement: A Study Based on Evidence Provided by Dutch-Speaking Triplets. A. M. Schaerlaekens. 1973. text ed. 27.20x (ISBN 90-2792-541-0). Mouton.
Two-Word Verbs in English. J. N. Hook. 198p. (Orig.). 1981. pap. text ed. 12.00 net (ISBN 0-15-592506-7, HC). HarBraceJ.
Two Words into One Word Puzzle. Edison C. Generoso. 32p. 1986. 5.95 (ISBN 0-8062-2909-8). Carlton.
Two Works of Grace. H. M. Riggle. 56p. pap. 0.40 (ISBN 0-686-29168-9); pap. 1.00 3 copies (ISBN 0-686-29169-7). Faith Pub Hse.
Two Works on Free Will see Teacher, The Free Choice of the Will, Grace & Free Will.
Two World Wars. David Killingray. Ed. by Malcolm Yapp & Margaret Killlingray. (World History Ser.). (Illus.). 32p. (gr. 6-11). 1980. lib. bdg. 6.95; pap. text ed. 2.45 (ISBN 0-89908-209-2). Greenhaven.
Two World Wars & Economic Development. Ed. by Barbara Ingham & Colin Simmons. (Journal of World Development Ser.: No. 9). 100p. 1984. 48.00 (ISBN 0-08-028944-4). Pergamon.
Two Worlds. David Daiches. 1971. 8.50x (ISBN 0-85621-001-3, Pub. by Scot Acad Pr). Longwood Pub Group.
Two Worlds - Two Monetary Systems. A. Atchkassov & O. Preksin. 252p. 1986. 6.95 (ISBN 0-8285-3243-5, Pub. by Progress Pubs USSR). Imported Pubns.
Two Worlds & Their Ways. Ivy Compton-Burnett. 1949. 20.95 (ISBN 0-575-02610-3, Pub by Gollancz England). David & Charles.
Two Worlds: Christianity & Communism. James Bales. pap. 2.25 (ISBN 0-686-80419-8). Lambert Bk.
Two Worlds for Our Children. 2nd ed. Myron E. Gruenwald. (Illus.). 36p. 1985. pap. 3.50 (ISBN 0-9601536-3-2). M E Gruenwald.
Two Worlds of Andrew Wyeth. Thomas Hoving. (Illus.). 1978. 25.00 (ISBN 0-395-27089-8); pap. 10.95 (ISBN 0-395-27080-4). HM.
Two Worlds of Childhood: U. S. & U. S. S. R. Urie Brofenbrenner. (Illus.). (gr. 10 up). 1979. pap. 9.95 (ISBN 0-671-21238-9). PB.
Two Worlds of Coral Harper. Leigh G. Tarlton. LC 82-48758. 160p. (gr. 5 up). 1983. 12.95 (ISBN 0-15-292371-3, HJ). HarBraceJ.
Two Worlds of Jill. Patricia Aks. 192p. (Orig.). (gr. 7 up). 1981. pap. 1.95 (ISBN 0-590-31801-2, Wishing Star Bks). Scholastic Inc.
Two Worlds of Liberalism: Religion & Politics in Hobbes, Locke, & Mill. Eldon J. Eisenach. LC 80-27255. (Chicago Original Paperback Ser.). 272p. 1981. lib. bdg. 20.00x (ISBN 0-226-19533-3). U of Chicago Pr.
Two Worlds of Music. Berta Geissmar. LC 74-28326. Orig. Title: Baton & the Jackboot. (Illus.). 327p. 1975. Repr. of 1946 ed. lib. bdg. 39.50 (ISBN 0-306-70664-4). Da Capo.
Two Worlds of Paul Miliukov see Outlines of Russian Culture: The Origins of Ideology.
Two Worlds of William March. Roy S. Simmonds. LC 83-1100. xix, 367p. 1984. text ed. 30.00x (ISBN 0-8173-0167-4). U of Ala Pr.
Two Worlds, One Love. Meg Hudson. (Superromances Ser.). 384p. 1983. pap. 2.95 (ISBN 0-373-70079-2, Pub. by Worldwide). Harlequin Bks.
Two Worlds: Studies in the Protestant Culture of Ontario, 1820-1870. William Westfall. (Studies in the History of Religion). (Illus.). 320p. 1989. text ed. 29.95x (ISBN 0-7735-0669-1). McGill-Queens U Pr.
Two Worlds: The Indian Encounter with the European, 1492-1509. S. Lyman Tyler. 272p. 1988. 25.00x (ISBN 0-87480-297-0). U of Utah Pr.
Two Writers & the Cultural Revolution: Lao She & Chen Jo-hsi. Ed. by George Kao. (Renditions Ser.). 170p. 1980. 25.00x (ISBN 0-295-95747-6, Pub by Chinese Univ Hong Kong). U of Wash Pr.
Two X Two Game. Anatol Rapoport et al. LC 74-25947. (Illus.). 1976. text ed. 14.50x (ISBN 0-472-08742-8). U of Mich Pr.
Two Yachts, Two Voyages. Eric Hiscock. 1985. 15.95 (ISBN 0-393-03307-4). Norton.
Two-Year College Mathematics Readings. Ed. by Warren Page. LC 80-81044. 312p. 1980. pap. 24.50 (ISBN 0-88385-435-X). Math Assn.
Two-Year Mountain. Phil Deutschle. LC 86-4026. 256p. 1986. 15.95 (ISBN 0-87663-471-4). Universe.
Two Years After. John Kiang. LC 86-63770. 96p. (Orig.). 1987. pap. 4.95 (ISBN 0-916301-02-8). One World Pub.
Two Years Ago. Charles Kingsley. 540p. 1983. Repr. of 1887 ed. lib. bdg. 30.00 (ISBN 0-8495-3100-4). Arden Lib.
Two Years Before the Mast. Charles H. Dana. (Regents Illustrated Classics Ser.). (gr. 7-12). 1982. pap. text ed. 3.50 (ISBN 0-13-935123-X, 20571). Prentice ESL.
Two Years Before the Mast. Richard Dana. 1981. Repr. lib. bdg. 19.95x (ISBN 0-89966-426-1). Buccaneer Bks.
Two Years Before the Mast. Richard H. Dana. (Airmont Classics Ser.). (gr. 8 up). pap. 2.25 (ISBN 0-8049-0085-X, CL-85). Airmont.
Two Years Before the Mast. Richard H. Dana. 1972. 12.95x (ISBN 0-460-00588-X, Evman); pap. 3.50x (ISBN 0-460-01588-5, Evman). Biblio Dist.
Two Years Before the Mast. new & abr. ed. Richard H. Dana. Ed. by John N. Fago. (Now Age Illustrated III Ser.). (Illus.). (gr. 4-12). 1977. text ed. 7.50 (ISBN 0-88301-282-0); pap. text ed. 2.95 (ISBN 0-88301-270-7). Pendulum Pr.
Two Years Before the Mast. Richard H. Dana, Jr. 383p. Date not set. pap. 3.50 (ISBN 0-451-51764-4, CE1764, Sig Classics). NAL.
Two Years Before the Mast. Richard H. Dana, Jr. Ed. by Thomas Philbrick. (Pengiun American Library). 1981. pap. 4.95 (ISBN 0-14-039008-1). Penguin.
Two Years Before the Mast: Student Activity Book. Marcia Sohl & Gerald Dackerman. (Now Age Illustrated Ser.). (Illus.). (gr. 4-12). wkbk. 1.25 (ISBN 0-88301-294-4). Pendulum Pr.
Two Years Experience Among the Shakers. David R. Lamson. LC 71-134418. Repr. of 1848 ed. 30.00 (ISBN 0-404-08477-X). AMS Pr.
Two Years in Limbo. Robert H. Stone. (Illus.). 85p. 1981. text ed. 7.50 (ISBN 0-9609192-1-X). R H Stone.
Two Years in Revolutionary China, 1925-27. Vera V. Vishnyakova-Akimova. Tr. by Stephen I. Levine from Rus. LC 78-148942. (East Asian Monographs Ser: No. 40). xviii, 352p. 1971. pap. 11.00x (ISBN 0-674-91601-8). Harvard U Pr.
Two Years in the French West Indies. gacsimile ed. Lafcadio Hearn. LC 73-104479. (Illus.). 431p. Repr. of 1890 ed. lib. bdg. 39.50 (ISBN 0-8398-0775-9). Irvington.
Two Years in the Jungle. William T. Hornaday. Repr. of 1926 ed. 20.00 (ISBN 0-686-19882-4). Ridgeway Bks.
Two Years in the Melting Pot. rev. ed. Liu Zongren. Date not set. 16.95 (ISBN 0-8351-2048-1); pap. 9.95 (ISBN 0-8351-2035-X). China Bks.
Two Years in the Melting Pot: China Books & Periodicals. Liu Zongren. LC 84-2090. 208p. 1984. 14.95 (ISBN 0-8351-1371-X); pap. 8.95 (ISBN 0-8351-1370-1). China Bks.
Two Years in the Pacific & Arctic Oceans & China, Being a Journal of Events Peculiar to a Whaling Voyage. James Munger. 80p. 1967. Repr. 14.95 (ISBN 0-87770-019-2). Ye Galleon.
Two Year's Journal in New York & Part of Its Territories in America. Charles Wolley. LC 73-5949. (Illus.). 96p. 1973. Repr. of 1902 ed. 7.50 (ISBN 0-916346-01-3). Harbor Hill Bks.
Two Years of French Foreign Policy: Vichy, 1940-1942. Adrienne D. Hytier. LC 74-7448. (Etudes D'histoire Economique Politique et Sociale: No. 25). 402p. 1974. Repr. of 1958 ed. lib. bdg. 35.00x (ISBN 0-8371-7551-8, HYFP). Greenwood.
Two Years on the Muckamuck Line. Helen Potrebenko. (Illus.). 11p. (Orig.). 1981. pap. 3.00 (ISBN 0-317-67952-X). Left Bank.
Two Years' Service on the Reorganized State Board of Insanity in Massachusetts, August, 1914 to August, 1916. Lloyd V. Briggs. Ed. by Gerald N. Grob. LC 78-22551. (Historical Issues in Mental Health Ser.). (Illus.). 1979. Repr. of 1930 ed. lib. bdg. 46.00x (ISBN 0-405-11905-4). Ayer Co Pubs.
Two Years Under the Crescent. H. C. Seppings Wright. 360p. 1985. 250.00x (ISBN 1-85077-056-5, Pub. by Darf). State Mutual Bk.
Two Years with the Chinese Communists. Claire Band & William Band. LC 75-36219. (Illus.). Repr. of 1948 ed. 30.00 (ISBN 0-404-14470-5). AMS Pr.
Two Yemens. Robin Bidwell. LC 82-15352. 350p. 1983. lib. bdg. 36.00X (ISBN 0-86531-295-8). Westview.
Two Young Dancers: Their World of Ballet. Alexandra Collard. LC 83-26435. (Illus.). 192p. (gr. 7 up). 1984. 10.29 (ISBN 0-671-47074-4). Messner.
Two Zen Classics: Mumonkan & Hekiganroku. Ed. by A. V. Grimstone. Tr. by Katsuki Sekida from Chinese. LC 77-2398. 1977. 13.50 (ISBN 0-8348-0131-0); pap. 8.95 (ISBN 0-8348-0130-2). Weatherhill.
Two Zions: Reminiscences of Jerusalem & Ethiopia. Edward Ullendorff. 264p. 1988. 36.00 (ISBN 0-19-212275-4). Oxford U Pr.
Twofold Vibration. Raymond Federman. LC 81-47831. 192p. 1982. 10.95 (ISBN 0-253-18989-6). Ind U Pr.
Twofold Voice: Essays in Honour of Ramesh Mohan. S. N. Rizvi. Ed. by James Hogg. (Poetic Drama & Poetic Theory Ser.). 232p. (Orig.). 1982. pap. 15.00 (ISBN 3-7052-0886-1, Pub by Salzburg Studies). Longwood Pub Group.
Two's a Crowd. Diana Gregory. (Sweet Dreams Ser.: No. 90). 144p. (Orig.). (gr. 6 up). 1985. pap. 2.25 (ISBN 0-553-24992-4). Bantam.
Two's Company. Bev Bennett. (Illus.). 224p. 1985. 16.95 (ISBN 0-8120-5596-9). Barron.
Two's Company. Betty Cavanna. (Illus.). 190p. (gr. 5-9). 1951. 6.95 (ISBN 0-664-32080-5). Westminster John Knox.
Twyborn Affair. Patrick White. 432p. 1981. pap. 6.95 (ISBN 0-14-005544-4). Penguin.
Twyllyp. Peter Farrow & Diane Lampert. (Illus.). (gr. 3-7). 1963. 10.95 (ISBN 0-8392-3040-0). Astor-Honor.
TY Algebra. P. Abbot. (Teach Yourself Ser.). 1980. pap. 8.95 (ISBN 0-679-10386-4). McKay.
TY Calculus. P. Abbott. (Teach Yourself Ser.). 1976. pap. 9.95 (ISBN 0-679-10391-0). McKay.
Ty Cobb. Charles C. Alexander. (Illus.). 1984. pap. 8.95 (ISBN 0-19-503598-4). Oxford U Pr.
Ty Cobb: Baseball's Fierce Immortal. Charles C. Alexander. LC 83-17409. (Illus.). 272p. 1984. 21.95x (ISBN 0-19-503414-7). Oxford U Pr.
TY Dutch Dictionary. P. King & M. King. (Teach Yourself Ser.). 1974. pap. 9.95 (ISBN 0-679-10251-5). McKay.
TY French Dictionary. (Teach Yourself Ser.). (Fr.). 1977. pap. 8.95 (ISBN 0-679-10245-0). McKay.
Tybee Trimble's Hard Times. Lila Perl. LC 84-4310. 160p. (gr. 4-7). 1984. PLB 10.95 (ISBN 0-89919-288-2, Clarion). HM.
Tycho Brahe: A Picture of Scientific Life & Work in the Sixteenth Century. John L. Dreyer. (Illus.). 13.25 (ISBN 0-8446-1996-5). Peter Smith.
Tychonic & Semi-Tychonic World Systems. Christine J. Schofield. Ed. by I. Bernard Cohen. LC 80-2094. (Development of Science Ser.). (Illus.). 1981. lib. bdg. 35.00x (ISBN 0-405-13859-8). Ayer Co Pubs.
Tycoon. George Alexanders. LC 86-46400. 352p. 1987. 18.95 (ISBN 1-55611-030-8). D I Fine.
Tycoon. George Alexanders. Ed. by Jim Connor. 1988. pap. 4.50 (ISBN 0-7701-0888-1). PaperJacks US.
Tycoon Boy. Richard Grossman. LC 83-50108. 72p. 1983. pap. 5.00 (ISBN 0-939358-02-6). Zygote Pr.
Tycoon: The Life of James Goldsmith. Geoffrey Wansell. LC 87-11473. 388p. 1987. 19.95 (ISBN 0-689-11817-1). Atheneum.
Tycoon's Daughter. Lynn Scott-Drennan. (Starlight Romance Ser.). 1988. 12.95 (ISBN 0-385-24497-5). Doubleday.
Tyee Cookbook of the University of Washington. Carol James et al. 185p. (Orig.). 1981. pap. 8.95 (ISBN 0-89716-102-5). Peanut Butter.
Tyendinaga Tales. Compiled by & intro. by Rona Rustige. (Illus.). 96p. 1988. 15.95 (ISBN 0-7735-0650-0). McGill-Queens U Pr.
Tygers of Wrath: Poems of Hate, Anger, & Invective. Ed. by X. J. Kennedy. LC 80-23212. 272p. 1981. 20.00 (ISBN 0-8203-0535-9). U of Ga Pr.
Tying & Fishing the Wests' Best Dry Flies. Bob Wilson & Richard Parks. (Illus.). 111p. (Orig.). 1978. pap. 12.95 (ISBN 0-936608-22-6). F Amato Pubns.
Tying Arrangements. William A. Montgomery. (Corporate Practice Ser.: No. 39). 1984. 92.00 (ISBN 0-317-55352-6). BNA.
Tying the Swisher-Richards Flies. Doug Swisher & Carl Richards. (Illus.). 48p. 1980. pap. 9.95 (ISBN 0-8117-2099-3). Stackpole.
Tying up Strings. John P. Schumake & Caroline L. Schumake. 125p. (Orig.). 1987. pap. text ed. 7.95 (ISBN 0-9616789-1-7, A2); tchr's ed. 7.95 (ISBN 0-9616789-2-5, A3). Earnest Pubns.
Tyl Eulenspiegel & the Talking Donkey. Robert Masters et al. (Children's Theatre Musical Playscript Ser.). (gr. k-12). 1961. pap. 2.00x (ISBN 0-88020-062-6); piano score 5.00x (ISBN 0-88020-060-X). Coach Hse.
Tyler County, West Virginia, Marriage Records: 1815-1852. Mary D. Atkinson. LC 80-67521. 73p. 1980. pap. text ed. 10.00 (ISBN 0-937436-01-1). Atkinson.
Tyler Family. G. T. Ridlon. LC 73-142779. (Saco Valley Settlements Ser). 1970. pap. 2.00 (ISBN 0-8048-0848-1). C E Tuttle.
Tyler Graphics: Catlogue Raisonne, 1974-1985. Kenneth Tyler et al. (Illus.). 430p. 1987. 195.00 (ISBN 0-89659-757-1). Abbeville Pr.
Tyler Graphics: The Extended Image. Elizabeth Armstrong et al. (Illus.). 256p. 1987. 45.00 (ISBN 0-89659-750-4). Abbeville Pr.
Tyler Hick's Encyclopedia of Wealth-Building Secrets. Tyler G. Hicks. 454p. 1982. pap. 6.95 (ISBN 0-13-935247-3, Reward). P-H.
Tyler Toad & the Thunder. Robert L. Crowe. LC 80-347. (Illus.). 32p. (ps-1). 1980. 9.95 (ISBN 0-525-41795-8). Dutton.
Tyler Toad & the Thunder. Robert L. Crowe. LC 80-347. (Unicorn Paperback Ser.). (Illus.). 32p. (ps-1). 1986. pap. 4.95 (ISBN 0-525-44243-X). Dutton.
Tyler Twins: Latchkey Kids. Hilda Stahl. 128p. (Orig.). (gr. 6-8). 1988. 3.50 (ISBN 0-8423-7628-3). Tyndale.
Tyler Twins: Pet Show Panic. Hilda Stahl. (Windrider Ser.). 112p. (Orig.). (gr. 6-8). 1986. 3.50 (ISBN 0-8423-7627-5). Tyndale.
Tyler Twins: The Mystery of the Missing Grandfather, No. 6. Hilda Stahl. 128p. 1988. pap. 3.50 (ISBN 0-8423-7630-5). Tyndale.
Tyler Twins: Tree House Hideaway, No. 5. Hilda Stahl. (WindRider Book Ser.). 128p. (gr. 3-5). 1988. pap. 3.50 (ISBN 0-8423-7629-1). Tyndale.
Tyler's Quarterly Historical & Genealogical Magazine: Genealogies of Virginia Families from Tyler's Quarterly Historical & Genealogical Magazine, 4 vols. LC 81-82083. (Illus.). 3621p. 1981. 125.00 (ISBN 0-8063-0947-4). Genealog Pub.
Tyll Ulenspiegel's Merry Pranks. Moritz A. Jagendorf. (Illus.). (gr. 5-6). 1938. 10.95 (ISBN 0-8149-0337-1). Vanguard.
Tylman's Theory & Practice of Fixed Prosthodontics. 8th ed. William F. Malone & David L. Koth. 550p. 1988. 49.50 (ISBN 0-912791-48-9). Ishiyaku Euro.
Tyme, Inc. Player Manual. Gates. 1987. 19.95 (ISBN 0-256-05564-5). Irwin.
Tympanoplasty & Stapedectomy: A Manual of Techniques. Ugo Fisch. (Illus.). 82p. 1980. pap. 31.95 (ISBN 0-913258-78-4). Thieme Med Pubs.
Tyndale Library of Great Biblical Novels, 6 vols. 27.35 (ISBN 0-8423-7643-7). Tyndale.
Tyne Bytes: A Computerised Sociolinguistic Study of Tyneside, Vol. 11. Val Jones-Sargent. (Bamberger Beitroge zur Engleschen Sprach wissenschaft). 374p. 1983. 40.00 (ISBN 3-8204-7655-5). P Lang Pubs.
Tyneside Songs & Drolleries: Readings & Temperance Songs. Joe Wilson. 472p. 1980. Repr. of 1890 ed. lib. bdg. 65.00 (ISBN 0-8414-9700-1). Folcroft.
Type. David Gates. 208p. 1973. 24.95 (ISBN 0-8230-5522-1). Watson-Guptill.
Type A Behavior - Your Heart. Meyer Friedman & Diane Ulmer. 1985. pap. 3.95 (ISBN 0-449-20826-5, Crest). Fawcett.
Type A Behavior & Your Heart. Meyer Friedman & Ray H. Rosenman. 320p. 1981. pap. 6.95 (ISBN 0-449-90059-2, Columbine). Fawcett.
Type A Behavior & Your Heart. Meyer Friedman & Ray H. Rosenman. 1974. 16.45 (ISBN 0-394-48011-2). Knopf.
Type A Behavior Pattern: A Model for Research & Practice. Virginia A. Price. 1983. 24.95 (ISBN 0-12-564680-1). Acad Pr.
Type a Behavior Pattern: Research, Theory, & Intervention. Ed. by B. Kent Houston & C. R. Snyder. LC 87-31705. (Health Psychology-Behavioral Medicine Ser.). 362p. 1988. 39.95 (ISBN 0-471-84591-4). Wiley.
Type & Events of Disasters: Organization in Various Disaster Situations. Ed. by R. Frey & P. Safar. (Disaster Medicine Ser.: Vol. 1). (Illus.). 1980. pap. 52.00 (ISBN 0-387-09043-6). Springer-Verlag.
Type & Figured Specimens of Fossil Vertebrates in the Collection of the University of Kansas Museum of Natural History: Part I. Fossil Fishes. Hans-Peter Schultze et al. (Miscellaneous Papers: No. 73). 53p. 1982. 8.25 (ISBN 0-317-04815-5). U of KS Mus Nat Hist.
Type & Image. Phillip B. Meggs. (Illus.). 228p. 1988. 32.95 (ISBN 0-442-25846-1). Van Nos Reinhold.
Type & Motif-Index of the Folktales of England & North America. Ernest W. Baughman. 1966. pap. text ed. 44.80x (ISBN 90-2790-046-9). Mouton.
Type & Typefaces. 2nd ed. J. Ben Lieberman. LC 77-24401. (Illus.). 1978. 19.95 (ISBN 0-918142-01-6); pap. 14.95 (ISBN 0-918142-02-4). Myriade.
Type & Typography. rev. ed. Ben Rosen. 461p. 1976. pap. 19.95 (ISBN 0-442-27020-8). Van Nos Reinhold.
Type-Caster: Universal Copyfitting. Stanley Rice. 96p. 1980. 19.95 (ISBN 0-442-22565-2). Van Nos Reinhold.
Type Certification of New Aircraft Technology. 1987. 30.00 (ISBN 0-89883-998-X, SP727). Soc Auto Engineers.
Type Composition in the Private Press. H. W. Larken. 128p. 1983. 35.00x (ISBN 0-946095-11-6, Pub. by Gresham England). State Mutual Bk.
Type Crossings: Sentential Meaninglessness in the Border Area of Linguistics & Philosophy. Theodore Drange. (Janua Linguarum, Ser. Minor: No. 44). (Orig.). 1966. pap. text ed. 19.20x (ISBN 90-2790-578-9). Mouton.

Type: Design, Color, Character & Use. Michael Beaumont. (Illus.). 176p. 1986. 24.95 (ISBN 0-89134-191-9). North Light Bks.

Type Designations, Areas of Use, Maintenance & Operation of Powered Industrial Trucks. (Five Hundred Ser.). 1973. pap. 2.00 (ISBN 0-685-58223-X, 505). Natl Fire Prot.

Type du Valet chez Moliere et Ses Successeurs: Regnard, Dufresny, Dancourt, et Lesage. Caracteres et Evolution. Gerard R. Gouvernet. LC 84-47806. (American University Studies II (Romance Languages & Literature): Vol. 15). 358p. (Fr.). 1985. text ed. 29.00 (ISBN 0-8204-0141-2). P Lang Pubs.

Type E Woman. Harriet B. Braiker. 304p. 1987. pap. 4.50 (ISBN 0-451-14999-8, Sig). NAL.

Type E Women: How to Overcome the Stress of Being Everything to Everybody. Harriet B. Braiker. 304p. 1986. 16.95 (ISBN 0-396-08677-2). Dodd.

Type, Graphics, & Macintosh: A Hands-on Intructional Manual Designed to Teach the Finer Points of Macintosh-Based Type & Graphics. John R. Balint. (Illus.). 92p. (Orig.). (YA) (gr. 10 up). 1987. spiral bd. 17.95 (ISBN 0-941929-00-0). Computer Based Pubns.

Type One Super Robot. Alison Prince. LC 87-14835. (Illus.). 128p. (gr. 3-6). 1988. PLB 12.95 (ISBN 0-02-775201-1, Pub. by Four Winds Pr). Macmillan.

Type One Supernovae: Proceedings. Texas Workshop on Type I Supernovae, Austin, March 17-19, 1980. Ed. by J. C. Wheeler. LC 80-52944. (Illus.). 1980. pap. 10.00 (ISBN 0-9603796-1-4). U of Tex Dept Astron.

Type One-Type Two Allergy Relief Program. Alan S. Levin & Merla Zellerbach. LC 83-4744. 228p. 1984. pap. 6.95 (ISBN 0-87477-328-8). J P Tarcher.

Type One-Type Two Allergy Relief Program. Alan S. Levin & Merla Zellerbach. 240p. 1985. pap. 3.50 (ISBN 0-425-09044-2). Berkley Pub.

Type Processing: The Word Processing-Typesetting Connection. Dean P. Lem. Ed. by James O. Cremeans. LC 85-82365. 152p. (Orig.). 1986. pap. text ed. 39.50 (ISBN 0-914218-08-5). D Lem Assocs.

Type Processing: The Word Processing-Typesetting Connection. 4th ed. Dean P. Lem. LC 85-82365. 156p. 1988. 69.50 (ISBN 0-914218-06-9). D Lem Assocs.

Type Rating (Airplane) Flight Test Guide (AC 61-57A) Federal Aviation Administration. 1975. pap. text ed. 4.25 (ISBN 0-86677-010-0, Pub. by Cooper Aviation). Aviation.

Type Right! A Complete Program for Business Typewriting. Altholz et al. LC 78-73160. 1980. text ed. 17.20 (ISBN 0-8224-2128-3); tchrs' manual o.p. 7.96 (ISBN 0-8224-2129-1); stationary supplies 7.80 (ISBN 0-8224-2131-3); classroom mgmt manual (3 ring binder) 1981 30.00 (ISBN 0-8224-2132-1). Glencoe.

Type Specimen Book. 648p. 1974. pap. 22.95 (ISBN 0-442-27915-9). Van Nos Reinhold.

Type Specimens in the Insect Collections of the Milwaukee Public Museum. Gerald R. Noonan. (Contributions in Biology & Geology Ser.: No. 58). 14p. 1984. 2.75 (ISBN 0-89326-105-X). Milwaukee Pub Mus.

Type-Specimens of Birds in the British Museum (Natural History) Vol. 1, Non-Passerines. Rachel L. Warren. ix, 320p. 1966. pap. 32.50x (ISBN 0-565-00651-7, Pub. by Brit Mus Nat Hist). Sabbot-Natural Hist Bks.

Type-Specimens of Birds in the British Museum (Natural History) Vol. 3, Systematic Index. Rachel L. Warren & C. J. Harrison. xi, 76p. 1973. pap. 13.50x (ISBN 0-565-00716-5, Pub. by Brit Mus Nat Hist). Sabbot-Natural Hist Bks.

Type Specimens of Birds in the British Museum (Natural History) Vol. 2, Passerines. Rachel M. Warren & C. J. Harrison. vi, 628p. 1971. pap. 62.00x (ISBN 0-565-00691-6, Pub. by Brit Mus Nat Hist). Sabbot-Natural Hist Bks.

Type Specimens of Recent Mammals in the Museum of Vertebrate Zoology, University of California, Berkeley. Blair Csuti. (UC Publications in Zoology: Vol. 114). 80p. 1981. pap. 22.00x (ISBN 0-520-09622-3). U of Cal Pr.

Type Studies of North American & Other Related Taxa of Stipitate Hydnums: Genera Hydnellum, Phellodon, Sarcodon. Richard E. Baird. (Bibliotheca Micologica Ser.: No. 13). 90p. 1986. 34.50X (ISBN 3-443-59004-7). Lubrecht & Cramer.

Type Studies: The Norstedt Collection of Matrices in the Typefoundry of the Royal Printing Office; A History & Catalogue. Christian Axel-Nilsson. (Illus.). 199p. 1985. 87.50 (ISBN 0-8390-0350-1). Abner Schram Ltd.

Type Study of American Banking. Ed. by Russell A. Stevenson. Stuart Bruchey. LC 80-1169. (Rise of Commercial Banking Ser.). (Illus.). 1981. Repr. of 1953 ed. lib. bdg. 22.00x (ISBN 0-405-13679-X). Ayer Co Pubs.

Type Talk: The Sixteen Personality Types That Determine How We Live, Love & Work. Otto Kroeger & Janet M. Thuesen. 288p. 1988. pap. 16.95 (ISBN 0-385-29648-7). Delacorte.

Type Three Company. Georges Archier & Herve Serieyx. 200p. 1987. 32.50 (ISBN 0-89397-282-7). Nichols Pub.

Type VII U-Boat. David Westwood. (Anatomy of the Ship Ser.: No. 3). (Illus.). 95p. 1985. 21.95 (ISBN 0-87021-886-7). Naval Inst Pr.

Typecast, No. 5. Kristi Andrews. 176p. (Orig.). (YA) 1988. pap. 2.50 (ISBN 0-553-26569-5). Bantam.

Typee. Herman Melville. (Airmont Classics Ser.). (gr. 10 up). pap. 1.50 (ISBN 0-8049-0053-1, CL-53). Airmont.

Typee. Herman Melville. pap. 3.50 (ISBN 0-451-51854-3, CE1854, Sig Classics). NAL.

Typee. Herman Melville. LC 67-11990. (Writings of Herman Melville Ser.). (Illus.). 1968. 36.95x (ISBN 0-8101-0161-0); pap. 12.95 (ISBN 0-8101-0159-9). Northwestern U Pr.

Typee. Herman Melville. Ed. by George Woodcock. (English Library Ser.). 1972. pap. 3.95 (ISBN 0-14-043070-9). Penguin.

Typee: Four Months Residence in the Marquesas Islands. Herman Melville. (Pacific Basin Bks.). 300p. (Orig.). 1985. pap. 12.95 (ISBN 0-7103-0132-4, Kegan Paul). Routledge Chapman & Hall.

Typee Notes see Billy Budd Notes.

Typee, Omoo, Mardi. Herman Melville. Ed. by G. Thomas Tanselle. Incl. Omoo: A Narrative of Adventures in the South Seas; Mardi; And a Voyage Thither. LC 81-18600. 1333p. 1982. 27.50 (ISBN 0-940450-00-3). Library of America.

Typefounding in America, 1787-1825. Rollo G. Silver. LC 65-19396. pap. 50.00 (ISBN 0-317-10827-1, 2007195). Bks Demand UMI.

Typencyclopedia: A User's Guide to Better Typography. Frank Romano. 186p. 1984. pap. 34.95 (ISBN 0-8352-1925-9). Bowker.

Types & Emblems. C. H. Spurgeon. 288p. Date not set. pap. write for info. Pilgrim Pubns.

Types & Problems of Philosophy. 3rd ed. Hunter Mead. LC 59-6277. 1959. text ed. 37.95x (ISBN 0-03-006240-3). Irvington.

Types Approach to Literature. Irvin Ehrenpreis. LC 73-19263. 1945. lib. bdg. 27.50 (ISBN 0-685-44515-1). Folcroft.

Types in Hebrews. Robert Anderson. LC 78-9545. (Sir Robert Anderson Library). 192p. 1978. pap. 4.95 (ISBN 0-8254-2129-2). Kregel.

Types in the Old Testament. Ada R. Habershon. LC 88-12126. 304p. 1988. pap. 9.95 (ISBN 0-8254-2856-4). Kregel.

Types, Levels-Irregularities of Response to a Nursery School Situation of 40 Children Observed with Special Reference to the Home Environment. E. C. Slater. (SRCD M). 1939. 15.00 (ISBN 0-527-01509-1). Kraus Repr.

Types Litteraires et Fantaises Esthetiques. Emile Montegut. Repr. of 1882 ed. 26.00 (ISBN 0-384-39870-7). Johnson Repr.

Types of Building Construction. 1974. pap. 2.00 (ISBN 0-685-58207-8, 220-T). Natl Fire Prot.

Types of Children's Literature. Walter Barnes. 59.95 (ISBN 0-8490-1239-2). Gordon Pr.

Types of Drama. 5th ed. Sylvan Barnet et al. 1988. pap. text ed. price not set (ISBN 0-673-39876-5). Scott F.

Types of Drama: Plays & Essays. 4th ed. Sylvan Barnet et al. 1984. pap. text ed. write for info. (ISBN 0-673-39192-2). Scott F.

Types of Economic Theory: From Mercantilism to Institutionalism, 2 vols. Wesley C. Mitchell. Ed. by J. Dorfman. LC 67-16418. 1967-1969. Set. 75.00x (ISBN 0-678-00234-7). Kelley.

Types of Elementary Teaching & Learning. Samuel C. Parker. 585p. 1980. Repr. of 1923 ed. lib. bdg. 25.00 (ISBN 0-89984-399-9). Century Bookbindery.

Types of English Drama. Ed. by John W. Ashton. Repr. of 1940 ed. 79.00x (ISBN 0-403-07209-3). Somerset Pub.

Types of Ethical Theory, 2 vols. James Martineau. 1616p. 1980. Repr. of 1885 ed. Set. lib. bdg. 100.00 (ISBN 0-8495-3794-0). Arden Lib.

Types of Formalization in Small-Group Research. Joseph Berger et al. LC 79-27703. (Illus.). x, 159p. 1980. Repr. of 1962 ed. lib. bdg. 35.00x (ISBN 0-313-22328-9, BETF). Greenwood.

Types of Injuries & Impairment Due to Injuries, United States: PHS 86-1587. John G. Collins. Ed. by Mary Olmsted. (Series 10: No. 159). 171p. pap. text ed. 4.00 (ISBN 0-8406-0352-5). Natl Ctr Health Stats.

Types of International Society. Evan Luard. LC 75-43173. 1976. 22.50 (ISBN 0-02-919450-4). Free Pr.

Types of Jewish-Palestinian Piety from 70 BCE to 70 CE. Adolf Buchler. 264p. Repr. of 1922 ed. text ed. 62.10x (ISBN 0-576-80135-6, Pub. by Gregg Intl Pubs England). Gregg Intl.

Types of Mankind: Or, Ethnological Researches. facs. ed. J. C. Nott & George R. Gliddon. LC 76-89386. (Black Heritage Library Collection Ser). (Illus.). 1854. 41.50 (ISBN 0-8369-8639-3). Ayer Co Pubs.

Types of Modern & Ancient Chinese Love-Songs. Liang Ch'i-Ch'ao. (Asian Folklore & Social Life Monograph: No. 8). (Chinese.). 1970. 14.00x (ISBN 0-89986-011-7). Oriental Bk Store.

Types of Modern Theology. Young O. Kim. LC 83-80105. 296p. 1983. pap. 11.95 (ISBN 0-910621-32-2). Rose Sharon Pr.

Types of Musical Form & Composition: Fifty Ready-to-Use Activities. Audrey J. Adair. (Music Curriculum Activities Library). 112p. 1987. text ed. 12.95 (ISBN 0-13-934985-5). P-H.

Types of Naval Officers, Drawn from the History of the British Navy. facs. ed. Alfred T. Mahan. LC 77-84323. (Essay Index Reprint Ser). 1901. 22.75 (ISBN 0-8369-1093-1). Ayer Co Pubs.

Types of Naval Officers: Drawn from the History of the British Navy. Alfred T. Mahan. LC 77-84323. (Essay Index Reprint Ser.). 500p. Repr. of 1901 ed. lib. bdg. 21.75 (ISBN 0-8290-0473-4). Irvington.

Types of Norwegian Folktales. Ornulf Hodne. 1984. 38.00x (ISBN 82-00-06849-8). Oxford U Pr.

Types of Poetry. H. J. Hall. 1927. 30.00 (ISBN 0-686-17682-0). Quaker City.

Types of Qualified Plans. David C. Rothman. (Kinds of Qualified Plans Ser.). 55p. 1979. pap. 2.50 (ISBN 0-317-32264-8, B330). Am Law Inst.

Types of Religious Culture see Sociology of Religion: A Study of Christendom.

Types of Religious Experience: Christian & Non-Christian. Joachim Wach. LC 51-9885. 275p. 1972. pap. 2.45x (ISBN 0-226-86710-2, P482, Phoen). U of Chicago Pr.

Types of Religious Man see Sociology of Religion: A Study of Christendom.

Types of Scenery & Their Influence on Literature. Archibald Geikie. LC 72-113335. 1970. Repr. of 1898 ed. 16.50x (ISBN 0-8046-0954-3, Pub by Kennikat). Assoc Faculty Pr.

Types of Schedules Training Aid. Spencer B. Smith. LC 82-73447. 30p. 1982. 25.00 (ISBN 0-935406-22-0). Am Prod & Inventory.

Types of Shape. John Hollander. LC 68-9726. (Orig.). 1969. pap. 5.95 (ISBN 0-689-10127-9). Atheneum.

Types of Society in Medieval Literature. Frederick Tupper. LC 67-29555. 1968. Repr. of 1926 ed. 15.00 (ISBN 0-8196-0212-4). Biblo.

Types of Society in Medieval Literature. Frederick Tupper. (English Literary Reference Ser). Repr. of 1926 ed. 14.00 (ISBN 0-384-61990-8). Johnson Repr.

Types of Thematic Structure. Eugene H. Falk. LC 67-16775. 1967. 15.00x (ISBN 0-226-23609-9). U of Chicago Pr.

Types of Thinking: Including a Survey of Greek Philosophy. John Dewey. Ed. by Samuel Meyer. LC 83-13245. 251p. 1984. 15.95 (ISBN 0-8022-2404-0). Philos Lib.

Types of Weltschmerz in German Poetry. Wilhelm A. Braun. LC 5-33195. (Columbia University. Germanic Studies, Old Ser.: No. 6). Repr. of 1905 ed. 14.50 (ISBN 0-404-50406-X). AMS Pr.

Typescript: Crime Club Ser. Anthony Trench. LC 87-36481. 192p. 1988. 12.95 (ISBN 0-385-24623-4). Doubleday.

Typesetting by Microcomputer. Michael L. Kleper. (Illus.). 1982. pap. 10.00 (ISBN 0-930904-04-4). Graphic Dimensions.

Typewriter Guerillas: Closeups of Twenty Top Investigative Reporters. John C. Behrens. LC 77-3439. 282p. 1977. 21.95x (ISBN 0-88229-266-8). Nelson-Hall.

Typewriter Poems. Peter Finch. 1971. pap. 7.50 (ISBN 0-87110-078-9). Ultramarine Pub.

Typewriter Profits. 1987. lib. bdg. 39.95 (ISBN 0-8490-3869-3). Gordon Pr.

Typewriter Repair Manual. Howard Hutchison. pap. 11.95 (ISBN 0-8306-1336-6, 1336). TAB Bks.

Typewriter Repairman (Electric) Jack Rudman. (Career Examination Ser.: C-1646). (Cloth bdg. avail. on request). pap. 12.00 (ISBN 0-8373-1646-4). Natl Learning.

Typewriter Repairman (Manual) Jack Rudman. (Career Examination Ser.: C-1645). (Cloth bdg. avail. on request). 1988. pap. 12.00 (ISBN 0-8373-1645-6). Natl Learning.

Typewriter Revolution & Other Poems. D. J. Enright. LC 73-158612. 143p. 1973. 7.95 (ISBN 0-912050-07-1, Library Pr). Open Court.

Typewriting: A Comprehensive Program. Robert E. Gades & Birdie H. Holder. 248p. 1979. pap. text ed. 21.95 (ISBN 0-8403-3023-5, 40302301). Kendall-Hunt.

Typewriting: A Comprehensive Program, Working Papers. Robert Gades & Birdie H. Holder. 1979. pap. text ed. 14.95 (ISBN 0-8403-2047-7). Kendall-Hunt.

Typewriting Dictionary. Edith Mackay. (Illus.). 1977. text ed. 17.95 (ISBN 0-8464-0940-2). Beekman Pubs.

Typewriting Drills for Speed & Accuracy. 4th ed. John L. Rowe & Faborn Etier. LC 76-50096. 1977. pap. 12.76 (ISBN 0-07-054151-5). McGraw.

Typewriting for the Modern Office: A Self-Paced Learning Activity Program. 2nd ed. Ellen Pate & Barbara Spengler. 224p. 1985. pap. 16.95 (ISBN 0-8403-3693-4). Kendall-Hunt.

Typewriting Identification (I.S.Q.T.) Identification System for Questioned Typewriting. Billy P. Bates. (Illus.). 112p. 1971. photocopy ed. 16.25 (ISBN 0-398-00110-3). C C Thomas.

Typewriting-Jr. H. S. Jack Rudman. (Teachers License Examination Ser.: T-63). (Cloth bdg. avail. on request). pap. 13.95 (ISBN 0-8373-8063-4). Natl Learning.

Typewriting Office Practice for Colleges: OfficePower, Inc. 3rd ed. Robert P. Bell & Joanna D. Hanks. 1982. write for info. (ISBN 0-538-11770-2, K77). SW Pub.

Typhoid & Paratyphoid Fevers: A Report. (World Health Statistics Ser: Vol. 22, No. 12). (Eng. & Fr.). 1969. pap. 2.00 (ISBN 0-686-09179-5). World Health.

Typhoid & the Politics of Public Health in Nineteenth Century Philadelphia. Michael P. McCarthy. LC 86-72881. (Memoirs Ser.: Vol. 179). (Illus.). 150p. (Orig.). 1988. pap. 12.00 (ISBN 0-87169-179-5). Am Philos.

Typhoid Fever: Its Nature, Mode of Spreading & Prevention. William Budd. Ed. by Barbara G. Rosenkrantz. LC 76-25656. (Public Health in America Ser.). (Illus.). 1977. Repr. of 1931 ed. lib. bdg. 19.00x (ISBN 0-405-09809-X). Ayer Co Pubs.

Typhoon - The Other Enemy: The Third Fleet & the Pacific Storm of December 1944. C. R. Calhoun. LC 81-38384. 261p. 1981. 18.95 (ISBN 0-87021-510-8). Naval Inst Pr.

Typhoon & Other Stories. Joseph Conrad. Ed. & intro. by Cedric Watts. (World's Classics Ser.). 336p. 1987. pap. 2.95 (ISBN 0-19-281711-6). Oxford U Pr.

Typhoon & Other Tales. Joseph Conrad. pap. 3.95 (ISBN 0-451-51779-2, CE1779, Sig Classics). NAL.

Typhoon & Tempest Story. Chris Thomas & Christopher Shores. (Illus.). 176p. 1988. 49.95 (ISBN 0-85368-878-8, Pub. by Arms & Armour). Sterling.

Typhoon in Tokyo: The Occupation & Its Aftermath. Henry Wildes. 1978. Repr. of 1954 ed. lib. bdg. 23.00x (ISBN 0-374-98572-3, Octagon). Hippocrene Bks.

Typhoon Shipments. Kevin Klose & Philip A. McCombs. 280p. 1974. 6.95 (ISBN 0-393-08693-3). Norton.

Typhoon, Typhoon: An Illustrated Haiku Sequence. Lucille M. Bogue. LC 75-94026. (Illus.). 1969. pap. 1.25 (ISBN 0-8048-0605-5). C E Tuttle.

Typhus & Doughboys: The American Polish Typhus Relief Expedition, Nineteen Nineteen to Nineteen Twenty-One. Alfred E. Cornebise. LC 81-70530. (Illus.). 240p. 1982. 24.50 (ISBN 0-87413-216-9). U Delaware Pr.

Typical & Atypical Antidepressants: Clinical Practice. Ed. by E. Costa & G. Racagni. (Advances in Biochemical Psychopharmacology Ser.: Vol. 32). 422p. 1982. text ed. 73.00 (ISBN 0-89004-830-4). Raven.

Typical & Atypical Antidepressants: Molecular Mechanisms. Ed. by E. Costa & G. Racagni. (Advances in Biochemical Psychopharmacology Ser.: Vol. 31). 416p. 1982. text ed. 81.00 (ISBN 0-89004-686-7). Raven.

Typical Architectural Styles of Greek, Etruscan & Roman Architecture, 2 vols. Henry M. Ferguson. (Illus.). 247p. 1988. Set. 187.75 (ISBN 0-86650-240-8). Gloucester Art.

Typical Battle Scenes in the Illiad: Studies in the Narrative Techniques of Homeric Battle Description. Bernard Fenik. 268p. (Orig.). 1968. pap. 52.50x (ISBN 3-515-00242-1, Pub. by Franz Steiner). Coronet Bks.

Typical Elizabethan Plays. facs. ed. Ed. by Felix E. Schelling & Matthew W. Black. LC 78-132140. (Play Anthology Reprint Ser). 1949. 37.00 (ISBN 0-8369-8219-3). Ayer Co Pubs.

Typical Forms of English Literature. Alfred H. Upham. 281p. 1982. Repr. of 1917 ed. lib. bdg. 30.00 (ISBN 0-89987-825-3). Darby Bks.

Typical Forms of English Literature: An Introduction to the Historical & Critical Study of English Literature for College Classes. Alfred H. Upham. 1979. Repr. of 1917 ed. lib. bdg. 22.50 (ISBN 0-8492-2753-4). R West.

Typical Girls: Young Women from School to the Full-Time Job Market. Christine Griffin. 1985. 22.95x; pap. 12.95. Routledge Chapman & Hall.

Typical Photovoltaic Systems Applications. (SERI-SP 273-2428 Ser.). 32p. 1986. pap. 1.75 (S/N 061-000-00680-0). USGPO.

Typical Residential, Commercial & Industry Bills: Investor-Owned Utilities. 75p. Winter Issue. semi-annual 12.50 ea. (04048004). Summer Issue (04048011). Edison Electric.

Typically Australian: Porcelain Art in Australia Today, Bk. 2. Tricia Bradford. 112p. (Orig.). 1985. 29.95 (ISBN 0-86417-041-6, Pub. by Kangaroo Pr). Intl Spec Bk.

Typing. college ed. Verleigh Ernest. LC 72-142516. 1971. pap. 15.12 scp (ISBN 0-672-96002-8); tchrs' manual o.p. 7.95 (ISBN 0-672-96003-6); wkbk. o.p. 11.50 (ISBN 0-672-96004-4). Bobbs.

Typing by Design. Herbert L. Becker. 1982. pap. 6.56 (ISBN 0-8224-7191-4). Glencoe.

Typing for Beginners. Betty Owen. 1976. pap. 3.95 (ISBN 0-399-50820-1, G&D). Putnam Pub Group.

Typing for Beginners. rev. ed. Betty Owen. (Practical Handbook Ser.). 80p. (Orig.). 1985. pap. 5.95 (ISBN 0-399-51147-4, Perigee). Putnam Pub Group.

Typing for Beginners. Speedwriting Institute. 1976. pap. 4.95 (ISBN 0-671-18138-6). Monarch Pr.

Typing for Everyone. rev. ed. Nathan Levine. LC 80-80741. (Illus.). 160p. 1980. easel-back 7.95 (ISBN 0-668-04975-8). Arco.

Typing for Everyone. Nathan Levine. 160p. 1985. spiral bdg. 9.95 (ISBN 0-668-06081-6). Arco.

Typing for Individual Achievement. Jack Heller. Ed. by Audrey S. Rubin. LC 80-26244. (Illus.). 192p. 1981. text ed. 26.36 (ISBN 0-07-027921-7). McGraw.

Typing for the Physically Handicapped: Methods & Keyboard Presentation Charts. Jack Heller. (gr. 10-12). 1978. text ed. 250.00 (ISBN 0-07-028079-7). McGraw.

Typing for Tots. Christina Dinklocker. (Illus.). 24p. (gr. 1-9). 1983. pap. 3.95 Tchr Enrichment Bk (ISBN 0-88047-019-4, 8305). DOK Pubs.

Typing for Your Needs. Marion J. Russell & Donald A. Boyer. (gr. 7-12). 1957. pap. text ed. 3.50x (ISBN 0-910286-11-6). Boxwood.

Typing from Rough Drafts. Harry R. Moon. 1984. 14.05 (ISBN 0-87350-335-X); tchr's manual 11.35 (ISBN 0-87350-343-0); work papers packet 5.40 (ISBN 0-87350-306-6). Milady Pub.

Typing Fun. Mary E. Switzer. (Gifted & Talented Ser.). 48p. (gr. 3-6). 1977. 4.95 (ISBN 0-88160-027-X, LW 212). Learning Wks.

Typing Improvement Practice for Manual Typists. Robert L. Grubbs & David H. Weaver. 1984. write for info. (ISBN 0-07-025065-0). McGraw.

Typing in Ten Minutes: On Any Keyboard - At Any Age. Carole Marsh. (Tomorrow's Books for Today's Children). (Illus.). 56p. (gr. k-12). 1983. 7.95 (ISBN 0-935326-12-X). Gallopade Pub Group.

Typing Made Easy. 5th ed. Diane Bellauance. (Illus.). 20p. (Orig.). 1987. pap. 2.50 (ISBN 0-317-66761-0). DBA BKS.

Typing Made Easy. 5th ed. Diane Bellavance. (Illus.). 24p. (Orig.). 1987. pap. 2.50x. DBA Bks.

Typing Mailable Letters. 3rd ed. Parker Liles et al. Ed. by Audrey S. Rubin. (Illus.). (gr. 9-12). 1978. pap. 10.68 (ISBN 0-07-037855-X). McGraw.

Typing One: General Course. Alan C. Lloyd et al. (Illus.). (gr. 9-12). 1976. text ed. 21.44 (ISBN 0-07-038241-7). McGraw.

Typing One: General Course Gregg Typing. Alan C. Lloyd et al. LC 81-15629. (Gregg Typing, Ser. 7). (Illus.). 288p. 1982. text ed. 21.24 (ISBN 0-07-038281-6). McGraw.

Typing Power -- Spelling Power, Vol. I. Norman W. Elliott et al. LC 75-8458. 1975. pap. 9.63 scp (ISBN 0-672-96415-5); scp tchr's manual 3.67 (ISBN 0-672-96791-X). Bobbs.

Typing Power Drills. 3rd ed. Alan C. Lloyd & Fred E. Winger. LC 83-8592. (Illus.). 96p. 1984. pap. 12.80 (ISBN 0-07-038176-3). McGraw.

Typing Seventy-Five. Alan C. Lloyd et al. Incl. Basic; Advanced. text ed. 11.20 (ISBN 0-07-038166-6); Expert. text ed. 11.20 (ISBN 0-07-038167-4); Professional. 1971. text ed. 25.25 (ISBN 0-07-038168-2). 1970-71. McGraw.

Typing Seventy Five: Advanced. Ed. by Alan C. Lloyd et al. (Gregg College Typing Ser.: 4). 1979. pap. 24.10 (ISBN 0-07-038257-3). McGraw.

Typing Seventy Five: Expert. 4th ed. Ed. by Alan C. Lloyd et al. (Gregg College Typing Ser.: 4). 1978. pap. 24.10 (ISBN 0-07-038258-1). McGraw.

Typing Seventy-Five: Intermediate. Alan C. Lloyd et al. (Gregg College Typing Ser.: No. 5). 1984. text ed. 26.15 (ISBN 0-07-038323-5). McGraw.

Typing Skill Drills. E. C. Archer & LeRoy A. Pemberton. 1973. pap. text ed. 4.35 (ISBN 0-89420-103-4, 143000). Natl Book.

Typing Skill Drives. 2nd ed. Alan C. Lloyd et al. 1974. text ed. 13.40 (ISBN 0-07-038161-5). McGraw.

Typing Sourcebook. Jordan Hale. LC 77-25064. 1978. pap. 10.83 scp (ISBN 0-672-97324-3); scp tchr's kit 7.33 (ISBN 0-672-97184-4). Bobbs.

Typing Techniques for Speed & Accuracy. Boyd. 1988. pap. cancelled (Perigee Bks). Putnam Pub Group.

Typing the Easy Way. Lieberman & Schimmel. (Easy Way Ser.). 1982. pap. 8.95 (ISBN 0-8120-2284-X). Barron.

Typing the Easy Way. 2nd ed. Warrent T. Schimmel & Stanley A. Lieberman. (Easy Way Ser.). 128p. 1988. pap. 9.95 spiral bdg. (ISBN 0-8120-4080-5). Barron.

Typing Three Hundred, 2 vols. John L, Rowe et al. (Illus.). 288p. (gr. 9-12). 1972. 22.64 ea.; Vol. 1 General Course. text ed. 23.96 (ISBN 0-07-054090-X). McGraw.

Typing Two, Advanced Course. Alan C. Lloyd et al. (Illus.). (gr. 9-12). 1977. pap. text ed. 21.44 (ISBN 0-07-038244-1). McGraw.

Typing Two: Advanced Course Gregg Typing. Alan C. Lloyd et al. LC 81-15629. (Gregg Typing, Ser. 7). (Illus.). 288p. 1982. text ed. 21.24 (ISBN 0-07-038282-4). McGraw.

Typings. Christopher Knowles. 112p. 1979. 12.50 (ISBN 0-931428-36-X); pap. 7.50 (ISBN 0-931428-09-2). Vehicle Edns.

Typist. Jack Rudman. (Career Examination Ser.: C-826). (Cloth bdg. avail. on request). pap. 12.00 (ISBN 0-8373-0826-7). Natl Learning.

Typographia: Or the Printers Instructor. Thomas F. Adams. LC 78-7449. (Nineteenth Century Bookarts & Printing Ser.). 295p. 1980. lib. bdg. 33.00 (ISBN 0-8240-3893-2). Garland Pub.

Typographia Scoto-Gadelica. D. Maclean. 384p. 1972. Repr. of 1915 ed. 35.00x (ISBN 0-7165-2058-3, BBA 02173, Pub. by Irish Academic Pr Ireland). Biblio Dist.

Typographic Aesthetics. Date not set. text ed. write for info. (ISBN 0-88362-080-4, 0203). Graphic Arts Tech Found.

Typographic Design: Form & Communication. Rob Carter et al. LC 85-667. (Illus.). 256p. 1985. pap. 38.95 (ISBN 0-442-26166-7). Van Nos Reinhold.

Typographic Samples, Pictures & Polemics. Michael Corris. 1986. 35.00 (ISBN 0-932526-11-X). Nexus Pr.

Typographic Scene: A Review of Typographic Design. Walter Tracy. 128p. 1988. 99.00x (ISBN 0-86092-112-3, Pub. by Gordon Fraser). State Mutual Bk.

Typographic Spec's. Date not set. text ed. write for info. (ISBN 0-88362-083-9, 0205). Graphic Arts Tech Found.

Typographic Years: A Printer's Journey Through a Half Century. Joseph Blumenthal. LC 82-71904. (Illus.). 153p. 26.50 (ISBN 0-913720-38-0). Beil.

Typographical Antiquities or the History of Printing in England, Scotland & Ireland, 4 vols. Joseph Ames. 2337p. Repr. of 1819 ed. Set. lib. bdg. 500.00x (Pub. by G Olms BRD). Coronet Bks.

Typographical Gazetteer. Henry Cotton. LC 76-159922. 222p. 1975. Repr. of 1825 ed. 40.00x (ISBN 0-8103-4121-2). Gale.

Typographical Journey Through the Inland Printer 1883-1900. Intro. by Maurice Annenberg. LC 77-89269. casebound 45.00 (ISBN 0-916526-04-6). Maran Pub.

Typographical Miscellany, Historical & Practical. Joel Munsell. LC 72-83618. (Illus.). 268p. 1972. Repr. of 1850 ed. 21.00 (ISBN 0-8337-2482-7). B Franklin.

Typographical Printing-Surfaces: The Technology & Mechanism of Their Production. Lucien Legros & John C. Grant. Ed. by John Bidwell. LC 78-74403. (Nineteenth-Century Book Arts & Printing History Ser.: Vol. 16). (Illus.). 1980. lib. bdg. 94.00 (ISBN 0-8240-3890-8). Garland Pub.

Typography. 40p. 1981. 16.00 (ISBN 0-88362-042-1, 0201). Graphic Arts Tech Found.

Typography, No. 2. Date not set. text ed. write for info. (0202). Graphic Arts Tech Found.

Typography, Vol. 9. Type Directors Club Staff. (Illus.). 208p. 1988. 37.50 (ISBN 0-8230-5543-4). Watson-Guptill.

Typography & Design. Boston Public Library Staff. 10.00 (ISBN 0-685-60072-6). Boston Public Lib.

Typography & Typesetting. Ronald LaBuz. (Illus.). 375p. 1987. 35.95 (ISBN 0-442-25966-2). Van Nos Reinhold.

Typography Instructor Guide. Date not set. write for info. (ISBN 0-88362-082-0, 0200). Graphic Arts Tech Found.

Typography: Its History & Use. Day. 3.00 (ISBN 0-318-19216-0). Quill & Scroll.

Typography 2: (Identifying Typefaces) Clare Nadorlik. Ed. by Robert J. Schneider, Jr. (Illus.). 28p. (Orig.). 1986. pap. text ed. 16.00 (ISBN 0-88362-079-0). Graphic Arts Tech Found.

Typologia: Studies in Type Design & Type Making with Comments on the Invention of Typography, the First Types, Legibility & Fine Printing. Frederic W. Goudy. 1978. pap. 7.95 (ISBN 0-520-03278-0). U of Cal Pr.

Typologies in England, 1650-1820. Paul J. Korshin. LC 81-47139. (Illus.). 448p. 1982. 44.00x (ISBN 0-691-06485-7). Princeton U Pr.

Typology, 2 vols. in 1. Patrick Fairbairn. 918p. 1989. lib. bdg. price not set (ISBN 0-8254-2631-6); pap. price not set (ISBN 0-8254-2628-6). Kregel.

Typology & English Medieval Literature. Ed. by Hugh T. Keenan. (Georgia State Literary Studies: No. 7). 1988. 45.00 (ISBN 0-404-63207-6). AMS Pr.

Typology & Seventeenth-Century Literature. Joseph A. Galdon. (De Proprietatibus Litterarum Series: Major 28). 164p. 1975. text ed. 22.40x (ISBN 90-2793-366-9). Mouton.

Typology & Structure of Roman Historical Reliefs. Mario Torelli. (Jerome Lectures Fourteenth Ser.). 1982. text ed. 25.00x (ISBN 0-472-10014-9). U of Mich Pr.

Typology & the Gospel. George W. Buchanan. LC 87-8276. 152p. (Orig.). 1987. lib. bdg. 23.75 (ISBN 0-8191-6377-5); pap. text ed. 11.50 (ISBN 0-8191-6378-3). U Pr of Amer.

Typology in Scripture: A Study of Hermeneutical Tupos Structures. Richard M. Davidson. (Andrews University Seminary Doctoral Dissertation Ser.: Vol. 2). 496p. (Orig.). 1981. pap. 10.95 (ISBN 0-943872-34-0). Andrews Univ Pr.

Typology of Community Residential Services: Task Force Report Twenty-One. LC 82-24467. (Illus.). 96p. 1982. pap. 5.00x (ISBN 0-89042-221-4, 42-221-4). Am Psychiatric.

Typology of Reflexives. Emma Geniusiene. (Empirical Approaches to Language Typology Ser.: No. 2). 435p. 1987. lib. bdg. 109.00 (ISBN 3-11-010677-9). De Gruyter.

Typology of Resultative Constructions. Ed. by Vladimir P. Nedjalkov & Bernard Comrie. LC 88-2598. (Typological Studies in Language: Vol. 12). xvi, 573p. 1988. 98.00x (ISBN 0-915027-78-X); pap. 39.00x (ISBN 0-915027-79-8). Benjamins North Am.

Typology of Subordination in Georgian & Abkhaz. Brian G. Hewitt. (Empirical Approaches to Language Typology: No. 5). 292p. 1987. lib. bdg. 82.75 (ISBN 0-89925-113-7). De Gruyter.

Typology of the Early Codex. Eric G. Turner. LC 75-10125. (Haney Foundation Ser). pap. 40.30 (ISBN 0-8357-9750-3, 2055282). Bks Demand UMI.

Typology of the Racehorse. Franco Varola. (Illus.). Repr. write for info. (ISBN 0-85131-196-2, BL2491, Pub. by J A Allen U K). S R Smith Sporting Bks.

Typology of the Racehorse. Franco Varola. (Illus.). 35.00 (ISBN 0-87556-270-1). Saifer.

Typology of the Ting in the Shang Dynasty: A Tentative Chronology of the Yin-Hsu Period. Ursula Lienert. 410p. (Orig.). 1979. pap. 52.50x (ISBN 3-515-02808-0, Pub. by Franz Steiner). Coronet Bks.

Typology Relationship & Time. Ed. by Vitalij V. Shevoroshkin & T. L. Markey. xxxii, 129p. 1986. pap. 14.50 (ISBN 0-89720-072-1). Karoma.

Typophily. H. Jackson. 59.95 (ISBN 0-8490-1240-6). Gordon Pr.

Tyrannobot: Punch-out Robot Dinosaur. Jim Razzi. 32p. (gr. 1-3). pap. 4.95 (ISBN 0-590-40790-2). Scholastic Inc.

Tyrannosaurus. Janet Riehecky. LC 88-1692. (Dinosaurs Ser.). (Illus.). 32p. (gr. k-4). 1988. PLB 8.95 (ISBN 0-89565-424-5). Childs World.

Tyrannosaurus Game. Steven Kroll. LC 75-37078. (Illus.). 40p. (ps-3). 1976. reinforced bdg. 12.95 (ISBN 0-8234-0275-4); pap. 5.95 (ISBN 0-8234-0620-2). Holiday.

Tyrannosaurus Rex. Millicent Selsam. LC 77-25677. (Illus.). (gr. 3-5). 1978. PLB 12.89 (ISBN 0-06-025424-6). HarpJ.

Tyrannosaurus Was a Beast. Jack Prelutsky. LC 87-25131. (Illus.). 32p. (ps-6). 1988. 11.95 (ISBN 0-688-06442-6); lib. bdg. 11.88 (ISBN 0-688-06443-4). Greenwillow.

Tyrannosaurus Wrecks. Noelle Sterne. LC 78-22499. (Trophy Picture Bks.). (Illus.). 32p. (gr. 1-4). 1983. pap. 3.50 (ISBN 0-06-443043-X, Trophy). HarpJ.

Tyrannosaurus Wrecks: A Book of Dinosaur Riddles. Noelle Sterne. LC 78-22499. (Illus.). (gr. 1-4). 1979. (Crowell Jr Bks); PLB 12.89 (ISBN 0-690-03960-3). HarpJ.

Tyrannous Reign of Mary Stewart. George Buchanan. Tr. by W. A. Gatherer from Lat. LC 78-3556. (Edinburgh University Publication: History, Philosophy, & Economics: No. 10). 1978. Repr. of 1958 ed. lib. bdg. 35.00x (ISBN 0-313-20343-1, BUTR). Greenwood.

Tyrannsasaurus Rex: The Fierce Dinosaur. Elizabeth Sandell. Ed. by Marjorie Oelerich & Howard Schroeder. LC 88-958. (Dinosaur Discovery Era Ser.). (Illus.). 32p. (gr. k-5). 1988. PLB 9.95 (ISBN 0-944280-00-5); pap. 4.95 (ISBN 0-944280-06-4). BSP Pub Inc.

Tyrannus Nix? Lawrence Ferlinghetti. LC 71-94522. 1969. pap. 1.25 (ISBN 0-8112-0047-7, NDP288). New Directions.

Tyranny & Fall of Edward II: 1321-1326. Natalie Fryde. LC 78-56179. 1979. 42.50 (ISBN 0-521-22201-X). Cambridge U Pr.

Tyranny & Freedom: Series One, Volume III. Ed. by Lynchburg College Faculty Staff. LC 82-45156. (Classical Selections on Great Issues, Symposium Readings Ser.). 538p. (Orig.). 1982. lib. bdg. 24.00 (ISBN 0-8191-2466-4); pap. text ed. 9.25 (ISBN 0-8191-2467-2). U Pr of Amer.

Tyranny & Legitimacy: A Critique of Political Theories. James S. Fishkin. LC 79-11177. 176p. 1979. text ed. 19.50x (ISBN 0-8018-2206-8); pap. text ed. 8.95x (ISBN 0-8018-2256-4). Johns Hopkins.

Tyranny of Change: America in the Progressive Era, 1900-1917. John W. Chambers. (Twentieth Century United States History Ser.). 280p. 1980. write for info. (ISBN 0-312-82758-X). St Martin.

Tyranny of Colour: A Study of the Indian Problem in South Africa. P. S. Joshi. LC 72-89266. 344p. 1973. Repr. of 1942 ed. 34.50x (ISBN 0-8046-1754-6, Pub by Kennikat). Assoc Faculty Pr.

Tyranny of Malice: Exploring the Dark Side of Character & Culture. Joseph Berke. 576p. 1988. 22.95 (ISBN 0-671-49753-7). Summit Bks.

Tyranny of Malice: Exploring the Dark Side of Character & Culture. Joseph Berke. 1988. 22.95. Summit Bks.

Tyranny of Survival: And Other Pathologies of Civilized Life. Daniel Callahan. LC 85-5316. (Illus.). 300p. 1985. pap. text ed. 11.50 (ISBN 0-8191-4636-6). U Pr of Amer.

Tyranny of the Dark. Hamlin Garland. (Collected Works of Hamlin Garland). 1988. Repr. of 1905 ed. lib. bdg. 59.00x. Am Biog Serv.

Tyranny of the Dark see **Collected Works.**

Tyranny of the Group. Andrew Malcolm. (Quality Paperback: No. 294). 190p. (Orig.). 1975. pap. 2.95 (ISBN 0-8226-0294-6). Littlefield.

Tyranny of the Household: Investigative Essays on Women's Work. Ed. by Nirmala Banerjee & Devaki Jain. 272p. 1985. text ed. 35.00x (ISBN 0-7069-2785-0, Pub. by Vikas India). Advent NY.

Tyranny of the Status Quo. Milton Friedman & Rose Friedman. LC 83-22637. 192p. 1984. 10.95 (ISBN 0-15-192379-5). HarBraceJ.

Tyranny of the Urgent. Charles Hummel. pap. 0.75 (ISBN 0-87784-128-4). Inter-Varsity.

Tyranny of Tide: An Oral History of the East Sutherland Fisherfolk. Nancy C. Dorian. (Illus.). 145p. 1984. pap. 10.50 (ISBN 0-89720-062-4). Karoma.

Tyranny of Time. Robert Banks. LC 84-28855. 265p. 1985. pap. 8.95 (ISBN 0-87784-338-4). Inter-Varsity.

Tyranny of Words. Stuart Chase. LC 38-27108. 396p. 1959. pap. 7.95 (ISBN 0-15-692394-7, Harv). HarBraceJ.

Tyranny on Trial: The Evidence at Nuremberg. Whitney R. Harris. LC 54-11298. (Illus.). 648p. 1970. Repr. of 1954 ed. 21.95x (ISBN 0-87074-073-3). SMU Press.

Tyranny-Two Thousand: The Justice Conflict. William Hester. LC 87-90616. 372p. (Orig.). 1988. pap. 12.00 (ISBN 0-945665-01-6); condensed ref. 9.00 (ISBN 0-945665-02-4). Cole & Sherwood.

Tyranny Unmasked. John Taylor. x, 185p. 1988. Repr. of 1822 ed. 18.95 (ISBN 0-940973-05-7). James River Pr.

Tyrant. Patricia Veryan. (Golden Chronicles Ser.: No. 3). 400p. 1987. 17.95 (ISBN 0-312-00199-1). St Martin.

Tyrant & Victim in Dostoevsky. Gary Cox. 119p. 1984. pap. 10.95 (ISBN 0-89357-125-3). Slavica.

Tyrant from Illinois. Blair Bolles. LC 73-16641. 248p. 1974. Repr. of 1951 ed. lib. bdg. 35.00x (ISBN 0-8371-7205-5, BOTI). Greenwood.

Tyrant in Cap & Gown. Carl W. Salser, Jr. LC 73-91074. 1974. 12.95 (ISBN 0-89420-100-X, 110055, Halcyon). Natl Book.

Tyrant or Father? A Study of Calvin's Doctrine of God. Garret Wilterdink. 185p. (Orig.). 1985. pap. 9.95 (ISBN 0-932269-19-2). Wyndham Hall.

Tyrant Slayers. rev. ed. Michael Taylor. Ed. by W. R. Connnor. LC 80-2671. (Monographs in Classical Studies). (Illus.). 1981. lib. bdg. 25.00 (ISBN 0-405-14054-1). Ayer Co Pubs.

Tyrants. Charles E. Jarvis. LC 77-78167. (Illus.). 1977. pap. text ed. 2.95 (ISBN 0-915940-02-7). Ithaca Pr Ma.

Tyrants of the Twentieth Century. Philip Clark. LC 81-86279. (In Profile Ser.). PLB 13.96 (ISBN 0-382-06633-2). Silver.

Tyrian Influence in the Upper Galilee. Richard S. Hanson. LC 79-11775. (Meiron Excavation Project Ser.: Vol. 2). (Illus.). 89p. 1980. text ed. 12.00x (ISBN 0-89757-504-0, Am Sch Orient Res); pap. text ed. 8.00x (ISBN 0-89757-505-9). Eisenbrauns.

Tyro: A Review of the Arts of Painting, Sculpture & Design, Nos. 1 & 2, 1921-22. new ed. Ed. by Wyndham Lewis. (Illus.). 120p. 1970. 65.00x (ISBN 0-7146-2116-1, F Cass Co). Biblio Dist.

Tyrol. Alan Proctor. (Visitor's Guide Ser.). (Illus.). 144p. (Orig.). 1986. pap. 8.95 (ISBN 0-935161-42-2). Hunter Pub NY.

Tyrol Travel Guide. Berlitz Editors. 128p. 1984. 4.95 (ISBN 0-02-969920-7, Berlitz). Macmillan.

Tyrone Folk Quest. Michael J. Murphy. 95p. 1983. pap. 7.50 (ISBN 0-85640-038-6, Pub. by Blackstaff Pr). Longwood Pub Group.

Tyrone Goes Camping. Linda P. Silbert & Alvin J. Silbert. (Little Twirps Understanding People Bks.). (Illus.). (gr. k-4). 1978. pap. 2.98 (ISBN 0-89544-055-5). Silbert Bress.

Tyrone Power: The Last Idol. Fred L. Guiles. 1980. pap. 2.75 (ISBN 0-425-04619-2). Berkley Pub.

Tyrone the Horrible. Hans Wilhelm. (Illus.). 32p. (gr. 1-3). Date not set. 10.95 (ISBN 0-590-41471-2, Pub. by Scholastic Hardcover). Scholastic Inc.

Tyronne the Horrible. Hans Wilhelm. (Illus.). 32p. (gr. k-3). 1988. 10.95. Scholastic Inc.

Tyrrell County North Carolina Minutes Court of Pleas & Quarter Sessions, 1735-1754, Bk. 1. Produced by Betty Fagan Burr. 137p. (Orig.). 1981. pap. 14.50 (ISBN 0-911619-01-1). B F Burr.

Tyrrell County North Carolina Minutes Court of Pleas & Quarter Sessions: 1755-1761, Bk. 2. LC 81-120466. (Illus.). 154p. 1983. pap. 15.50 (ISBN 0-911619-03-8). B F Burr.

Ty's One-Man Band. Mildred P. Walter. 48p. (gr. k-3). 1985. pap. 3.95 (ISBN 0-590-40178-5). Scholastic Inc.

Ty's One-man Band. Mildred P. Walter. LC 80-11224. (Illus.). 40p. (gr. k-3). 1987. Repr. of 1980 ed. PLB 12.95 (ISBN 0-02-792300-2, Pub. by Four Winds Pr). Macmillan.

Tysiacha I Odin Izbrannyi Sovetskii Politicheshii Anekdot. Yulius Telesin. LC 85-30588. 220p. (Rus.). 1986. pap. 10.00 (ISBN 0-938920-65-0). Hermitage.

Tysiachiletie Dreveishidh Monet. M. P. Sotnikova & J. G. Spasskii. 238p. 1983. 39.00x (ISBN 0-317-40819-4, Pub. by Collets (UK)). State Mutual Bk.

Tysk-Dansk: Dansk-Tysk Ordbog. F. Albertus. 532p. (Danish & Ger.). 1982. 39.95 (ISBN 0-686-92489-4, M-1293). French & Eur.

Tysk-Dansk Dansk-Tysk Special Ordbog. E. Fryd. 175p. (Ger. & Danish.). 1974. 49.95 (ISBN 0-686-92491-6, M-1274). French & Eur.

Tysk-Dansk Ordbog. E. Bork & E. Kaper. 550p. (Ger. & Danish.). 1981. 45.00 (ISBN 0-686-92483-5, M-1282). French & Eur.

Tysk-Dansk Teknisk Ordbog. A. Warrern. 275p. (Ger. & Danish.). 1974. 75.00 (ISBN 0-686-92486-X, M-1291). French & Eur.

Tysk-Norsk Ordbog. Ed. by J. Haukoy & W. Zickfedt. 360p. (Ger. & Norwegian.). 1978. 39.95 (ISBN 0-686-92285-9, M-9465). French & Eur.

Tzacones. Stam C. Caratzas. (Supplementa Byzantina: Vol. 4). 1976. 148.00x (ISBN 3-11-004799-3). De Gruyter.

Tzaddik. Rabbi Nathan. Tr. by Avraham Greenbaum from Hebrew. Orig. Title: Chayey Moharan. 1988. 18.00 (ISBN 0-930213-17-3). Breslov Res Inst.

Tzaddik in Our Time. Simcha Raz. Tr. by Charles Wengrow from Hebrew. (Illus.). 1976. 15.95 (ISBN 0-87306-130-6). Feldheim.

Tzaddik in Our Time: Life & Times of Rav Aryeh Levin of Jerusalem, Celebrated Tzaddik of Jerusalem. Simcha Raz. Tr. by Charles Wengrov from Hebrew. (Illus.). 1978. pap. 11.95 (ISBN 0-87306-986-2). Feldheim.

Tzadik Yesod Olam. Luria. 124p. 1960. 12.00 (ISBN 0-943688-21-3). Res Ctr Kabbalah.

Tzbrannaya Proza v Dvuch Tomach T L Beey Koriolor: The White Corridor - Selected Prose, Vol. I. 2nd ed. Vladislav Khodasevich. Ed. by Gregory Poliak & Joceph Prodsky. 320p. (Orig., Rus.). pap. 17.50 (ISBN 0-940294-10-9). Silver Age Pub.

Tzbrannye Stat'i. T. V. Kireevskii. 384p. 1984. 49.00 (ISBN 0-317-40701-5, Pub. by Collets UK). State Mutual Bk.

Tzedakah. Amye Rosenberg. (Jewish Awareness Ser.). (Illus.). (gr. k-1). 1979. pap. text ed. 3.50x (ISBN 0-87441-279-X). Behrman.

Tzedakah see Mitzvah of the Month.

Tzedakah: Can Jewish Philanthropy Buy Jewish Survival? Jacob Neusner. Ed. by David Altshuler. (Basic Jewish Ideas Ser.). 160p. 1982. pap. 7.95 (ISBN 0-940646-07-2). Rossel Bks.

Tzedakah Workbook. Jan Rabinowitz. (Illus.). 32p. (Orig.). (gr. 4-5). 1986. pap. text ed. 3.95 (ISBN 0-933873-07-7). Torah Aura.

Tzelta Folk Zoology: The Classification of Discontinuities in Nature. Eugene S. Hunn. LC 76-56205. (Language, Thought & Culture Ser.). 1977. 49.50 (ISBN 0-12-361750-2). Acad Pr.

Tzeltal Numerical Classifiers: A Study in Ethnographic Semantics. Brent Berlin. (Janua Linguarum, Ser. Practica: No. 70). (Orig.). 1968. pap. text ed. 50.50x (ISBN 0-686-22422-1). Mouton.

Tzeltal Tales of Demons & Monsters: Modern Folk Tales from the Tzeltal Maya Town of Tenejapa, Chiapas, Pt. 2. Ed. by Richard Diehl et al. Tr. by Brian Stross. LC 78-622530. (Museum Briefs Ser.: No. 24). iv, 40p. 1978. pap. 2.00 (ISBN 0-913134-24-4). Mus Anthro Mo.

Tz'ena Ur'enah: Bereishis with Haftoros, Vol. I. Tr. by Miriam S. Zakon from Yiddish. (ArtScroll Judaica Classics). (Illus.). 316p. 1983. 15.95 (ISBN 0-89906-925-8); pap. 12.95 (ISBN 0-89906-926-6). Mesorah Pubns.

Tz'enah Ur'enah: Bamidbar Devarim with Haftoros, Vol. III. Tr. by Miriam S. Zakon from Yiddish. (ArtScroll Judaica Classics). 1110p. 1984. 15.95 (ISBN 0-89906-929-0); pap. 12.95 (ISBN 0-89906-930-4). Mesorah Pubns.

Tz'enah Ur'enah: Sh'mos-Vayikra with Haftoros, Vol. II. Tr. by Miriam S. Zakon from Yiddish. (ArtScroll Judaica Classics). (Illus.). 688p. 1983. 15.95 (ISBN 0-89906-927-4); pap. 12.95 (ISBN 0-89906-928-2). Mesorah Pubns.

Tzenah Ur'enah: The Complete Set. Tr. by Miriam S. Zakon from Yiddish. (Artscroll Judaica Classics Ser.). (Illus.). 1110p. 1985. slipcase 49.95 (ISBN 0-89906-931-2); lib. bdg. 69.95 leatherbound (ISBN 0-89906-932-0). Mesorah Pubns.

Tzili: The Story of a Life. Aharon Appelfeld. 192p. 1984. pap. 5.95 (ISBN 0-14-007058-3). Penguin.

Tzintzuntzan. rev. ed. G. M. Foster. 416p. 1979. pap. 15.50 (ISBN 0-444-99070-4). Elsevier.

Tzintzuntzan: Mexican Peasants in a Changing World. George M. Foster. 404p. 1988. pap. 10.95 (ISBN 0-88133-315-8). Waveland Pr.

Tzorchei Tzibbur: Community & Responsibility in the Jewish Tradition. 6.00 (ISBN 0-686-96047-5); tchr's ed. 8.50 (ISBN 0-686-99687-9). United Syn Bk.

Tzotzil Grammar. Marian M. Cowan. (Publications in Linguistics & Related Fields Ser.: No. 18). 119p. 1969. microfiche (2) 4.00 (ISBN 0-88312-420-3). Summer Inst Ling.

Tzutujil Grammar. Jon P. Dayley. LC 84-28118. (UC Publications in Linguisitics: Vol. 107). 1985. pap. 34.00x (ISBN 0-520-09962-1). U of Cal Pr.

Tzutujil Mayas: Continuity & Change, 1250-1630. Sandra L. Orellana. LC 83-47837. (Civilization of the American Indian Ser.: Vol. 162). (Illus.). 320p. 1984. 32.50x (ISBN 0-8061-1739-7). U of Okla Pr.

Tzvika's Class: The Big Suprise, Vol. 3. 1982. pap. 1.50 (ISBN 0-87306-227-2). Feldheim.

Tzvika's Class: The Outing, Vol. 5. pap. 1.50 (ISBN 0-686-76272-X). Feldheim.

Tzvika's Class: The Rosh Chodesh Party, Vol. 4. 1982. pap. 1.50 (ISBN 0-87306-228-0). Feldheim.

Tzvika's Class: The Snow, Vol. 1. 1982. pap. 1.50 (ISBN 0-87306-188-8). Feldheim.

Tzvika's Class: The Traffic Accident, Vol. 2. 1982. pap. 1.50 (ISBN 0-87306-226-4). Feldheim.

U

U. Sal J. Martingnetti. 1988. 8.95 (ISBN 0-533-07466-5). Vantage.

U. A. R. in Africa: Egypt's Policy Under Nasser. Tareq Y. Ismael. LC 73-126902. Repr. of 1971 ed. 51.70 (ISBN 0-8357-9475-X, 2015299). Bks Demand UMI.

U. B. Phillips: A Southern Mind. John H. Roper. LC 84-682. vi, 204p. 1984. 16.95 (ISBN 0-86554-112-4, MUP/H103). Mercer Univ Pr.

U-Boat Commander. Peter Cremer. 272p. 1986. pap. 3.50 (ISBN 0-515-08459-X). Jove Pubns.

U-Boat Commander: A Periscope View of the Battle of the Atlantic. Peter Cremer. 288p. 1984. 18.95 (ISBN 0-87021-969-3). Naval Inst Pr.

U-Boat: Evolution & Technical History of German Submarines. Eberhard Rossler. LC 81-81198. (Illus.). 464p. 1981. 48.95 (ISBN 0-87021-966-9). Naval Inst Pr.

U-Boat Intelligence, 1914-1918. Robert M. Grant. (Illus.). 192p. 1969. 25.00 (ISBN 0-208-00898-5, Archon). Shoe String.

U-Boat Peril: An Anti-Submarine Commander's Story. Bob Whinney. (Illus.). 160p. 1987. 24.95 (ISBN 0-7137-1821-8, Pub. by Blandford Pr England). Sterling.

U-Boat Wars: 1916-1945. John Terraine. 512p. 1989. 22.95 (ISBN 0-399-13291-0, Putnam). Putnam Pub Group.

U-Boats: A Pictoral History. Edwin P. Hoyt. (Illus.). 256p. 1987. text ed. 19.95 (ISBN 0-07-030620-6). McGraw.

U-Boats Against Canada: German Submarines in Canadian Waters. Michael L. Hadley. 416p. 1985. 29.95 (ISBN 0-7735-0584-9). McGill-Queens U Pr.

U-Boats at War. Harold Busch. 1982. pap. 2.50 (ISBN 0-345-30755-0). Ballantine.

U-Boats in Action. (Warships in Action Ser.). (Illus.). 1984. pap. 5.95 (ISBN 0-89747-054-0, 4001). Squad Sig Pubns.

U-Boats of World War Two, Vol. 1. Robert C. Stern. (Warships Illustrated Ser.: No. 13). (Illus.). 64p. (Orig.). 1988. pap. 9.95 (ISBN 0-85368-813-3, Pub. by Arms & Armour). Sterling.

U-Boats Offshore. Edwin P. Hoyt. 304p. 1985. pap. 3.95 (ISBN 0-515-07427-6). Jove Pubns.

U-Boats under the Swastika. rev. ed. Jak P. Showell. (Illus.). 144p. 1987. 19.95 (ISBN 0-87021-970-7). Naval Inst Pr.

U. D. A. G. A Public - Private Partnership. Gloria Fitzgibbons. 168p. (Orig.). 1982. pap. text ed. 14.95x (ISBN 0-940438-01-1). Innovations Pr.

U. D. I. The International Politics of the Rhodesian Rebellion. Robert C. Good. 1973. 43.50x (ISBN 0-691-05647-1). Princeton U Pr.

U. F. O. Abduction at Mirassol: A Biogenetic Experiment. Walter K. Buhler et al. Tr. by Wendelle C. Stevens from Portuguese. (Factbooks Ser.). (Illus.). 416p. 1986. lib. bdg. 16.95 (ISBN 0-9608558-8-2). UFO Photo.

U. H. F. O. Harrison Fisher. 60p. (Orig.). 1982. pap. 4.50 (ISBN 0-933442-05-X). Dianas Bimonthly.

U. K. Adhesion Fundamentals & Practice U. K. Ministry of Technology Staff. 322p. 1971. 108.00 (ISBN 0-677-61430-6). Gordon & Breach.

U. K. Banking after Deregulation. Andy Mullineux. 192p. 1987. lib. bdg. 55.00x (ISBN 0-7099-4689-9, Pub. by Croom Helm UK). Routledge Chapman & Hall.

U. K. Banking Supervision: Evolution, Practice & Issues. Edward P. Gardner. (Studies in Financial Institutions & Markets Ser.: No. 2). 380p. 1986. text ed. 44.95x (ISBN 0-04-332102-X). Unwin Hyman.

U. K. Blood Lead Monitoring Programme, 1984-1987: Results for 1985. 130p. (Orig.). 1987. pap. 16.00 (ISBN 0-11-752036-5, HM1406, Pub. by Her Maj Station Ofc). UNIPUB.

U. K. Cinema Today: 1986. 190.00x (ISBN 0-686-71958-1, Pub. by Euromonitor). State Mutual Bk.

U. K. Commodities Yearbook. Ed. by A. Buckley. 1977. 14.00 (ISBN 0-85941-050-1). State Mutual Bk.

U. K. Consumer Electronics Markets. International Resource Development Staff. 185p. 1986. 1650.00x (ISBN 0-88694-699-9). Intl Res Dev.

U. K. Economy: An Intergrated Approach. N. Proctor. 150p. 1986. 39.00 (ISBN 1-85313-004-4, Checkmate Pubs). State Mutual Bk.

U. K. Economy: Manual of Applied Economics. 6th ed. Ed. by A. R. Prest & D. J. Coppock. 1977. 19.95x (ISBN 0-8464-0942-9). Beekman Pubs.

U. K. Energy: Structure, Prospects & Policies. Richard Bending & Richard Eden. (Illus.). 320p. 1985. 49.50 (ISBN 0-521-26708-0). Cambridge U Pr.

U. K. Finance Directory: A Directory of Sources of U. K. Corporate Finance. Ed. by M. Morgano. 600p. 1987. 490.00x (ISBN 0-86010-342-0, Pub. by Graham & Trotman England); pap. 60.00x (ISBN 0-86010-341-2). State Mutual Bk.

U. K. Financial Accounting Standards: A Descriptive & Analytical Approach. Raymond K. Ashton. 234p. 1983. 32.95 (ISBN 0-85941-201-6, Pub. by Woodhead-Faulkner); pap. 16.50 (ISBN 0-85941-202-4). Longwood Pub Group.

U. K. Health Markets. 100p. 1987. 170.00x (ISBN 0-686-71959-X, Pub. by Euromonitor). State Mutual Bk.

U. K. Holiday & Tourism: 1986. 150p. 190.00x (ISBN 0-686-71960-3, Pub. by Euromonitor). State Mutual Bk.

U. K. Household Chemical Markets. 1986. 190.00x (ISBN 0-686-71961-1, Pub. by Euromonitor). State Mutual Bk.

U. K. in Nineteen Eighty: The Hudson Report. Hudson Institute. LC 74-25234. 127p. 1975. 24.95x (ISBN 0-470-41855-9). Halsted Pr.

U. K. Labor Market Guide. Kenneth Walsh & Richard Pearson. LC 84-13814. (Institute of Manpower Studies: No. 5). 288p. 1984. 32.95x (ISBN 0-566-00718-5). Gower Pub Co.

U. K. Life Assurance Industry: A Study in Applied Economics. Peter J. Franklin & Caroline Woodhead. (Illus.). 390p. 1980. 80.00 (ISBN 0-85664-654-7, Pub. by Croom Helm Ltd). Routledge Chapman & Hall.

U. K. Marine Pollution Law. J. H. Bates. 1984. 85.00 (ISBN 1-850-44028-X). Lloyds London Pr.

U. K. Market for Toys & Games. 1986. 190.00x (ISBN 0-686-71962-X, Pub. by Euromonitor). State Mutual Bk.

U. K. Menswear Markets. 1986. 256.00x (ISBN 0-686-71963-8, Pub. by Euromonitor). State Mutual Bk.

U. K. Monetary & Financial System: An Introduction. J. H. Gilbody. 256p. 1988. lib. bdg. 55.00 (ISBN 0-415-00435-7). Routledge Chapman & Hall.

U. K. Occupation & Employment Trends to 1990. Ed. by Richard Pearson. 224p. 1986. text ed. 49.95 (ISBN 0-408-02980-3). Butterworth.

U. K. Oil & Gas Tax Legislation. Ed. by J. Gordon McClure & Anne G. Lavies. 216p. 1981. 37.00 (ISBN 0-86010-367-6). Graham & Trotman.

U. K. Publishing Industry. Peter J. Curwen. (Illus.). 176p. 1981. text ed. 24.00 (ISBN 0-08-024081-X). Pergamon.

U. K. Smoking Statistics. Nicholas Wald et al. (Illus.). 208p. 1988. pap. 62.00 (ISBN 0-19-261572-6). Oxford U Pr.

U. K. Tax Policy & Applied General Equilibrium Analysis. J. Piggott & J. Whalley. 345p. 1985. 47.50 (ISBN 0-521-30148-3). Cambridge U Pr.

U. K. Telecommunication Market Opportunities. Int'l Resource Development Inc. 201p. 1987. 1650.00x (ISBN 0-88694-734-0). Intl Res Dev.

U. L. & Wire-Cable Industry. 15.00 (ISBN 0-318-03189-2, 7518). Wire Assn Intl.

U. N. see United Nations.

U. N., UNESCO & the Politics of Knowledge. Clare Wells. LC 86-6567. 300p. 1987. 32.50 (ISBN 0-312-83277-X). St Martin.

U Nas Byla Velikaia Epokha. Eduard Limonov. 150p. (Orig., Rus.). 1988. pap. price not set (ISBN 0-89830-124-6). Russica Pubs.

U Neba Na Vidu. Lev Druskin. LC 85-29265. 204p. (Rus.). 1986. pap. 9.50 (ISBN 0-938920-61-8). Hermitage.

U Nikh V Michigane. Pavel Leonidov. LC 85-61782. 120p. (Orig.). 1987. pap. 12.05 (ISBN 0-89830-100-9). Russica Pubs.

U Nu of Burma. rev. ed. Richard Butwell. (Illus.). 1969. 35.00x (ISBN 0-8047-0155-5). Stanford U Pr.

U Nu: Saturday's Son. U Nu. Ed. by U Kyaw Win. Tr. by U Law Yone. LC 74-79835. (Illus.). 372p. 1975. 37.00x (ISBN 0-300-01776-6). Yale U Pr.

U-One Hundred Sixty-Eight Incident. Steve Reynolds & H. E. Carver. LC 84-51393. (Mercenary Adventure Ser.). 260p. (Orig.). 1985. 14.95 (ISBN 0-918379-01-6); pap. 6.95 (ISBN 0-317-14780-3). Wild Geese.

U. P. Agricultural Credit Act, 1973. 4th ed. B. C. Shukla. 1985. Repr. 90.00x (ISBN 0-317-54766-6, Pub. by Eastern Bk India). State Mutual Bk.

U. P. Consolidation of Holdings Act. Surendra Malik. 250p. 1980. 82.50x (ISBN 0-317-54837-9, Pub. by Eastern Bk India). State Mutual Bk.

U. P. Land Records Manual. Vijay Malik. 138p. 1975. 37.50x (ISBN 0-317-54592-2, Pub. by Eastern Bk India). State Mutual Bk.

U. P. Police Regulations. P. L. Malik. 1985. 65.00x (ISBN 0-317-56723-3, Pub. by Eastern Bk India). State Mutual Bk.

U. P. Sales Tax Act, Nineteen Forty-Eight: Together with Rules & Notifications. P. L. Malik. 220p. 1985. 108.00x (ISBN 0-317-54852-2, Pub. by Eastern Bk India). State Mutual Bk.

U. P. Trail. Zane Grey. 1983. pap. 2.95 (ISBN 0-671-49844-4). PB.

U. P. Urban Buildings (Regulation of Letting, Rent & Eviction) Act, 1972. V. K. Sircar. 833p. 1983. 315.00x (ISBN 0-317-57704-2, Pub. by Eastern Bk India). State Mutual Bk.

U R What You Drive. Tom Couch. 1987. pap. 8.95 (ISBN 0-671-63874-2, Fireside). S&S.

U. S. see United States.

U. S.--Japan Foreign Trade: An Annotated Bibliography of Socioeconomic Perspectives. Ed. by Rita Neri. (Garland Reference Library of Social Science). 332p. 1988. lib. bdg. 40.00 (ISBN 0-8240-8471-3). Garland Pub.

U. S.- Japan Relations: Technology, Economics, & Security. Harold Brown. 48p. 1987. 4.00 (ISBN 0-87641-228-2). Carnegie Ethics & Intl Affairs.

U. S. A. - Anglo-Saxon Rhythms in Screed. Jack Saunders & Jack Remick. (White Paper Ser.: No. 4). 50p. (Orig.). 1983. pap. 3.00 (ISBN 0-912824-30-1). Vagabond Pr.

U. S. A. A. F. at War in the Pacific. David Mondey. (Illus.). 160p. 1980. 7.95 (ISBN 0-684-16702-6, ScribT). Scribner.

U. S. A. A History in Art. Bradley Smith. 1977. pap. 17.95 (ISBN 0-385-11409-5). Doubleday.

U. S. A.: Anatomy of the Arms Race. Ed. by I. Usachev. 198p. 1986. 6.95 (ISBN 0-8285-3244-3, Pub. by Progress Pubs USSR). Imported Pubns.

U. S. A. & China see Through Russian Eyes: American-Chinese Relations.

U. S. A. & Russia. P. J. Larkin. (World History in 20th Century Ser.). (Illus.). 158p. pap. 9.95 (ISBN 0-7175-0063-2). Dufour.

U. S. A. & the Soviet Myth. Lev E. Dobriansky. 9.50 (ISBN 0-8159-7005-6). Devin.

U. S. A. Aspects of Political & Social Life. D. Siegmund-Schultze. 164p. 1980. 17.50x (ISBN 0-317-53849-7, Pub. by Collets (UK)). State Mutual Bk.

U. S. A. by Bus & Train. Gary Hawkins. 1985. pap. 9.95. Pantheon.

U. S. A., Canada, Mexico - Delicious Recipes: Collected from the Finest Award-Winning Restaurants & Inns. Marilyn S. Howard. 104p. (Orig.). 1985. pap. text ed. 8.95 (ISBN 0-9616125-0-9). M Serrett Howard.

U. S. A. Country Guide. Berlitz Editors. 256p. 1984. 7.95 (ISBN 0-02-969900-2, Berlitz). Macmillan.

U. S. A. Customs & Institutions, Vol. 4. Tiersky. (gr. 7 up). 1976. pap. 5.50 (ISBN 0-13-939828-7, 18438). Prentice ESL.

U. S. A. F. E. A Primer for Modern Air Combat in Europe. Michael Skinner. (Airpower Bk.). (Illus.). 144p. (Orig.). 1983. pap. 12.95 (ISBN 0-89141-151-8). Presidio Pr.

U. S. A. F. Europe Eighteen Forty-Eight to Nineteen Sixty-Five in Color. (Fighting Colors Ser.). (Illus.). 36p. 1984. pap. 5.95 (ISBN 0-89747-132-6, 6504). Squad Sig Pubns.

U. S. A. F. in Color Today. Dana Bell. (Warbirds Illustrated Ser.: No.29). (Illus.). 1984. pap. 12.95 (ISBN 0-85368-679-3, Arms & Armour Pr). Sterling.

U. S. A. for Africa, Rock Aid in the Eighties. Gilda Berger. LC 86-24718. (Illus.). 96p. (gr. 7-12). 1987. lib. bdg. 11.90 (ISBN 0-531-10299-8). Watts.

U. S. A. for Business Travelers, 1987. Steve Birnbaum. (Illus.). 592p. 1986. pap. 7.95 (ISBN 0-395-42576-X). HM.

U. S. A. for Business Travelers, 1989. Stephen Birnbaum. (Birnbaum's Travel Guides Ser.). (Illus.). 624p. Date not set. pap. 8.95 (ISBN 0-395-48161-9). HM.

U. S. A. Guide. 8.95 (ISBN 0-685-37584-6). Pan Am Pubns.

U. S. A., Imperialists & Anti-Imperialists. I. Dementyev. 351p. 1979. 7.45 (Pub. by Progress Pubs USSR). Imported Pubns.

U. S. A. in the Twentieth Century. Peter Lane. (gr. 5up). 1978. 14.95 (ISBN 0-7134-0975-4, Pub. by Batsford England). David & Charles.

U. S. A. in the World Economy. Arnold Heertje. LC 84-81000. 1984. text ed. 12.50 (ISBN 0-87735-801-X); pap. text ed. 6.90 (ISBN 0-87735-802-8). Freeman Cooper.

U. S. A. Men & Machines, Vol. 3. Rachael L. Chapman. (gr. 7 up). 1968. pap. 5.50 (ISBN 0-13-939810-4, 18437). Prentice ESL.

U. S. A. Militarism & the Economy - A Soviet View. R. A. Faramazyan. 271p. 1975. 15.95 (ISBN 0-8464-0941-0). Beekman Pubs.

U. S. A. Products Liability Litigation Institute. Mark A. Dombroff. LC 85-139119. (Illus.). write for info. Lawyers Co-op.

U. S. A. Tennis Course. Victor Tantalo. Ed. by Jacqueline Hartt. LC 86-50302. (Illus.). 208p. (Orig.). 1986. 24.95x (ISBN 0-936577-01-0); pap. 14.95x (ISBN 0-936577-00-2). USA Pubs.

U. S. A. The Forty-Second Parallel, Nineteen Nineteen, The Big Money. John Dos Passos. (Illus.). 1963. 20.00 (ISBN 0-395-07627-7). HM.

U. S. A. The Message of Justice, Peace & Love. Pope John Paul II. 1979. 5.95 (ISBN 0-8198-0630-7); pap. 4.95 (ISBN 0-8198-0631-5). Dghtrs St Paul.

U. S. A., the Permanent Revolution. Fortune Magazine Editors & Russell W. Davenport. LC 80-15776. 267p. 1980. Repr. of 1951 ed. lib. bdg. 35.00x (ISBN 0-313-22500-1, FMUS). Greenwood.

U. S. A. The Unfolding Story of America. Ed. by Groisser. Levine. (YA) (gr. 11-12). 1987. text ed. 23.75 (ISBN 0-87720-643-0). AMSCO Sch.

U. S. A., Tierra Condenada. Alberto Muller. LC 80-70473. (Coleccion Espejo de paciencia). 49p. (Span.). 1981. pap. 5.00 (ISBN 0-89729-281-2). Ediciones.

U. S. A. Today Cartoon Book. Illus. by Dean Vietor et al. 1986. pap. 6.95 (ISBN 0-8362-2077-3). Andrews & McMeel.

U. S. A. Today Crossword Puzzle Book. Ed. by Charles Preston. 80p. 1986. pap. 5.95 (ISBN 0-399-52053-8, Perigee); 10-copy counterpack 59.50. Putnam Pub Group.

U. S. A. Today Crossword Puzzle Book, No. 2. Ed. by Charles Preston. 80p. 1987. pap. 5.95 (ISBN 0-399-52055-4, Perigee Bks). Putnam Pub Group.

U. S. A. Today Crossword Puzzle Book, No. 4. Ed. by Charles Preston. (U. S. A. Today Crossword Puzzle Ser.). 80p. 1988. pap. 5.95 (ISBN 0-399-52069-4, Perigee Bks). Putnam Pub Group.

U. S. A. Today Crossword Puzzle Book, No. 5. Charles Preston. 80p. (Orig.). 1988. pap. 5.95 (ISBN 0-399-52075-9, Perigee Bks). Putnam Pub Group.

U. S. A. Today: Tracking Tomorrow's Trends. What We Think about Our Lives & Our Future. Anthony M. Casale. 1986. pap. 8.95 (ISBN 0-8362-7934-4). Andrews & McMeel.

U. S. A. Today Travel Tips. U. S. A. Today Editors. 160p. (Orig.). 1987. pap. 6.95 (ISBN 0-8362-9101-8). Andrews & McMeel.

U. S. A. Vol. 1, the Land & the People. rev. ed. Robert J. Dixson. (Illus.). 169p. (gr. 7 up). 1975. pap. 5.50 (ISBN 0-13-939373-0, 18435). Prentice ESL.

U. S. A. Vol. 2, Men & History. rev. ed. Robert J. Dixson & Herbert Fox. (Illus.). 179p. 1975. pap. 5.50 (ISBN 0-13-939422-2, 18436). Prentice ESL.

U. S. A., Western Europe, Japan: Triangle of Rivalry. A. Bogdanov. 253p. 1985. pap. 3.95 (ISBN 0-8285-3366-0, Pub. by Progress pubns USSR). Imported Pubns.

U. S. A. Within a World View. Margaretta M. Styles. (Credentialing in Nursing: Contemporary Developments & Trends Ser.). (Illus.). 29p. (Orig.). 1986. pap. 100.00 set of 10 monographs (ISBN 0-317-60356-6, G-172). ANA.

U. S.-Canadian Range Management, Nineteen Thirty to Nineteen Seventy-Seven: Selected Bibliography on Ranges, Pastures, Wildlife, Livestock & Ranching. Ed. by John F. Vallentine. 356p. 1978. Vol. 1: 1935-1977. lib. bdg. 93.50x (ISBN 0-912700-11-4). Oryx Pr.

U. S.-Caribbean-Grenada Relations: Before & After Bishop. Linus A. Hoskins. (International Affairs Ser.). 130p. (Orig.). 1984. pap. text ed. 6.00 (ISBN 0-9613067-0-X). L A Hoskins.

U. S.-China Business Services Directory, 1983. 46.00 (ISBN 0-318-04701-2). Natl Coun US China.

U. S.-China Nuclear Agreement: Blueprint for Proliferation. Ken Bossong. 13p. 1985. pap. 1.50 (ISBN 0-937188-34-4). Critical Mass.

U. S.-Chinese Trade Negotiations. John W. DePauw. LC 80-27254. 252p. 1981. 44.95 (ISBN 0-275-90603-5, C0603). Praeger.

U. S.-Chippewa Treaty at La Pointe, 1854. 12.50 (ISBN 0-317-66462-X). Inst Dev Indian Law.

U. S.-Japan Mutual Security: The Next Twenty Years. Edwin J. Feulner & Hideaki Kase. 161p. 1981. pap. 5.00 (ISBN 0-89195-030-3). Heritage Found.

U. S.-Japan Mutual Security: The Next Twenty Years. Ed. by Edwin J. Feulner, Jr. & Hideaki Kase. LC 81-818367. 161p. 1981. 5.00 (ISBN 0-317-07526-8). Heritage Found.

U. S.-Japan Relations: A Partnership in Search of Definition. Alan D. Romberg. (Critical Issues 1988 Ser.: No. 1). 32p. 1988. pap. 3.95 (ISBN 0-87609-031-5). Coun Foreign.

U. S.-Japan Relations: New Attitudes for a New Era. Ed. by Richard B. Finn. 221p. 1984. pap. 14.95x (ISBN 0-88738-666-0). Transaction Bks.

U. S.-Japan Relations: Toward a New Equilibrium. Ed. by Richard B. Finn. 185p. 1983. pap. 14.95x (ISBN 0-88738-667-9). Transaction Bks.

U. S.-Japan Relations: Towards Burden Sharing. Ed. by Richard B. Finn. 182p. 1982. pap. 14.95x (ISBN 0-88738-668-7). Transaction Bks.

U. S.-Japan Science & Technology Exchange Patterns of Interdependence. Ed. by Cecil H. Uyehara. (WVSS in International Economics & Issues). 312p. 1988. 28.50 (ISBN 0-8133-7415-4). Westview.

U. S.-Japanese Agricultural Trade Relations. Emery N. Castle et al. 463p. 1982. 35.00 (ISBN 0-8018-2815-5); pap. 14.95 (ISBN 0-8018-2814-7). Resources Future.

U. S.-Japanese Competition in International Markets: A Study of the Trade - Investment Cycle in Modern Capitalism. John E. Roemer. LC 75-620086. (Research Ser.: No. 22). (Illus.). 225p. 1975. pap. 3.95x (ISBN 0-87725-122-3). U of Cal Intl St.

U. S.-Japanese Competition in the Semiconductor Industry: A Study in International Trade & Technological Development. Michael Borrus et al. LC 82-81106. (Policy Papers in International Affairs Ser.: No. 17). (Illus.). x, 155p. 1982. pap. 8.50x (ISBN 0-87725-517-2). U of Cal Intl St.

U. S.-Japanese Energy Relations: Cooperation & Competition. Ed. by Charles K. Ebinger & Ronald A. Morse. (Replica Edition Ser.). 275p. 1984. softcover 31.00x (ISBN 0-86531-833-6). Westview.

U. S.-Japanese Security Relations: A Historical Perspective. Richard L. Sneider. (Occassional Papers of East Asian Institute Ser.). 116p. (Orig.). 1982. pap. 5.00 (ISBN 0-913418-01-3). Columbia U E Asian Inst.

U. S.-Korean Relations, 1882-1982. Ed. by Tai-Hwan Kwak & John Chay. 433p. 1983. lib. bdg. 36.00x (ISBN 0-86531-608-2). Westview.

U. S.-Latin American Policy in the Nineteen Nineties: Toward Realism & Maturity. Georges A. Fauriol. (CSIS Significant Issues Ser.). 1988. write for info. CSI Studies.

U. S.-Latin American Trade Relations: Issues & Concerns. Ed. by Michael R Czinkota. Juan Luis Colaiacovo et al. LC 83-2311. 316p. 1983. 42.95 (ISBN 0-275-90966-2, C0966). Praeger.

U. S.-Mexican Economic Relations: Prospects & Problems. Ed. by Khosrow Fatemi. LC 88-311. (Illus.). 216p. 1988. lib. bdg. 39.95 (ISBN 0-275-92955-8, C2955). Praeger.

U. S.-Mexican Relations, Nineteen Ten to Nineteen Forty: An Interpretation. Alan Knight. (Monograph Ser.: No. 28). 146p. (Orig.). 1987. pap. text ed. 15.00 (ISBN 0-935391-76-2, MN28). Ctr Mex Studies.

U. S.-Mexico Border Region. Cesar Sepuivada & Albert E. Utton. LC 64-63319. 452p. 1984. pap. 15.00 (ISBN 0-87404-091-4). Tex Western.

U S Navy in Pensacola: From Sailing Ships to Naval Aviation, 1825-1930. George F. Pearce. LC 80-12167. (Illus.). vii, 207p. 1980. 20.00 (ISBN 0-8130-0665-1). U Presses Fla.

U. S.-Pakistan Relations. Ed. by Leo E. Rose & Noor A. Husain. LC 85-80563. (Research Papers & Policy Studies: No. 13). 245p. 1985. pap. 8.50 (ISBN 0-912966-78-5). IEAS.

U. S.-Republic of China Economic Issues: Problems & Prospects. Ed. by Martin L. Lasater. 68p. 1988. pap. 6.00. Heritage Found.

U S S R in World War II, 1941-1945. Leonid Yeremeyev. 112p. 1985. 20.00x (ISBN 0-317-42844-6, Pub by Collets (UK)). State Mutual Bk.

U. S. S. R. Memoranda see U. S. S. R. & Far East Memoranda.

U. S.-Seneca Treaty, 1842. 5.00 (ISBN 0-317-66465-4). Inst Dev Indian Law.

U. S.-South Korean Alliance. Ed. by Gerald L. Curtis & Sung-Joo Han. LC 82-49205. (Illus.). 256p. 1983. 33.00x (ISBN 0-669-06438-6). Lexington Bks.

U. S.-Soviet Cultural Exchanges, 1958-1986: Who Wins? Yale Richmond. (WVSS on the Soviet Union & Eastern Europe Ser.). 170p. 1986. pap. 29.00 (ISBN 0-8133-7275-5). Westview.

U. S.-Soviet Relations: A Strategy for the Eighties. UNA-USA National Policy Panel to Study US-Soviet Relations. 102p. (Orig.). 1981. pap. 4.00 (ISBN 0-934654-32-8). UNA-USA.

U. S.-Soviet Relations: The Next Phase. Ed. by Arnold L. Horelick. LC 85-48274. 304p. 1986. 36.50x (ISBN 0-8014-1912-3); pap. 9.95x (ISBN 0-8014-9383-8). Cornell U Pr.

U. S., the Gulf, & Israel: Emerging Regional Security Policies & the United States Middle East Central Command. Dore Gold. 130p. 1988. pap. 18.00 (ISBN 0-8133-0719-8). Westview.

U. S., the U. N., & the Management of Global Change. Ed. by Toby T. Gati. (Una-Usa Book). 392p. 1983. 45.00x (ISBN 0-8147-2986-X); pap. 20.00x (ISBN 0-8147-2987-8). NYU Pr.

U. S.-Third World Conflict: A Glossary. John M. Starrels. 70p. 1983. pap. 3.00 (ISBN 0-89195-207-1). Heritage Found.

U. S.-UAR Diplomatic Relations. Andrew Carvely. LC 73-86351. 1969. pap. 2.00 (ISBN 0-686-05635-3). Bks Intl DH-TE.

U. S.-U. S. S. R.: Agenda for Communication: Proceedings. LC 74-80143. (Annals Ser.: No. 414). 300p. (Orig.). 1974. pap. 7.95 (ISBN 0-87761-179-3). Am Acad Pol Soc Sci.

U. S.-U. S. S. R. Nuclear Weapons Balance. Edward Luttwak. (Washington Papers: Vol. II, No. 13). 72p. (Orig.). 1974. pap. text ed. 7.95 (ISBN 0-8191-5972-7, Pub. by CSIS). U Pr of Amer.

U-Shaped Behavioral Growth. Ed. by Sidney Strauss. LC 81-17662. (Developmental Psychology Ser.). 1981. 47.00 (ISBN 0-12-673020-2). Acad Pr.

U Thant: Divinity's Smile and Humanity's Cry. pap. 4.95 (ISBN 0-88497-341-7). Aum Pubns.

U Thant in New York. Ramses Nassit. 180p. 1988. 24.95. St Martin.

U-2 4 the People. Tony Scott. (Illus.). 64p. 1986. pap. 7.95 (ISBN 0-89524-307-5). Cherry Lane.

UA. Helynn Hoffa. (Illus.). 48p. 1981. 20.00 (ISBN 0-88014-029-1). Mosaic Pr OH.

UAE. Middle East Economic Digest Staff. Ed. by Trevor Mostyn. (MEED Practical Guides Ser.). (Illus.). 324p. (Orig.). 1986. pap. 16.95x (ISBN 0-946510-03-2). Lynne Rienner.

Uanga--Fetico: Romance Folclorico Angolano. 2nd ed. Oscar B. Ribas. (Port.). 1969. 22.00 (ISBN 0-8115-3019-1). Kraus Repr.

UAW & Walter Reuther. I. Howe & B. J. Widick. LC 72-2375. (FDR & the Era of the New Deal Ser.). 324p. 1973. Repr. of 1949 ed. lib. bdg. 39.50 (ISBN 0-306-70485-4). Da Capo.

UAW Politics in the Cold War Era. Martin Halpern. (American Labor History Ser.). 320p. 1988. 44.50x (ISBN 0-88706-671-2); pap. 16.95x (ISBN 0-88706-672-0). State U NY Pr.

Uaxactun, Guatemala: Excavations of 1931-1937. Augustus L. Smith. LC 77-11523. (Carnegie Institution of Washington. Publication: No. 588). Repr. of 1950 ed. 30.50 (ISBN 0-404-16288-6). AMS Pr.

Ubena of the Rivers. Arthur T. Culwick & G. M. Culwick. LC 76-44707. Repr. of 1935 ed. 57.50 (ISBN 0-404-15883-8). AMS Pr.

Uber Die Altgermanischen Relativsatze. Gustav Neckel. (Ger). 18.00; pap. 13.00 (ISBN 0-685-02114-9). Johnson Repr.

Uber die Aussagekraft statisticher Methoden fur die linguistische Stilanalyse. Ursula Pieper. (Ars Linguistica: 5). 157p. (Orig., Ger.). 1980. pap. 24.00x (ISBN 3-87808-355-6). Benjamins North Am.

Uber Die Epochen der Neueren Geschichte & das Politische Gesprach und Andere Schdriften Zur Wissenschaftslehre, 2 vols. in one. Leopold Von Ranke. LC 78-67376. (European Political Thought Ser.). 1979. Repr. of 1925 ed. lib. bdg. 17.00x (ISBN 0-405-11726-4). Ayer Co Pubs.

Uber die Hoffnung see On Hope.

Uber die Leibnizsche Logik Mit Besonderer Berucksictigung des Problems der Intension und der Extension. Raili Kauppi. Ed. by R. C. Sleigh, Jr. LC 84-48421. (Philosophy of Leibniz Ser.). 279p. 1985. lib. bdg. 35.00 (ISBN 0-8240-6534-4). Garland Pub.

Uber die Musik der Nordamerikanischen Wilden. Theodore Baker. LC 71-38496. Repr. of 1882 ed. 15.00 (ISBN 0-404-08337-4). AMS Pr.

Uber Finanzen und Monopole Im Alten Griechenland: Zur Theorie und Geschichte der antiken Stadtwirtschaft. Kurt Riezler. Ed. by Moses Finley. LC 79-5002. (Ancient Economic History Ser.). (Ger.). 1980. Repr. of 1907 ed. lib. bdg. 12.00x (ISBN 0-405-12391-4). Ayer Co Pubs.

Uber Ideenflucht. Ludwig Binswanger. LC 78-66767. (Phenomenology Ser.). 200p. 1980. lib. bdg. 26.00 (ISBN 0-8240-9568-5). Garland Pub.

Uber Politisch-Satirische Gedichte Aus der Schottischen Reformationszeit. Franz Wollmann. 12.00 (ISBN 0-384-69075-0). Johnson Repr.

Uber Zacharias Werners Sohne Des Tals. R. Palgen. pap. 9.00 (ISBN 0-384-44600-0). Johnson Repr.

Ubergang Vom Feudalen Zum Burgerlichen Weltbild. Franz Borkenau. LC 74-25740. (European Sociology Ser.). 574p. 1974. Repr. 43.00x (ISBN 0-405-06496-9). Ayer Co Pubs.

Ubersetzer Nicolaus Von Wyle. Bruno Strauss. (Ger). 27.00 (ISBN 0-685-02167-X); pap. 22.00 (ISBN 0-685-02168-8). Johnson Repr.

UBIK: The Screenplay. Philip K. Dick. Ed. by Ira M. Thornhill. (Illus.). 160p. 1985. 23.00 (ISBN 0-911169-06-7); text ed. write for info. (ISBN 0-911169-07-5). Corroboree Pr.

Ubiquitin. Ed. by M. Rechsteiner. LC 88-9809. (Illus.). 364p. 1988. 59.50x (ISBN 0-306-42850-4, Plenum Pr). Plenum Pub.

Ubiquity of Metaphor: Metaphor in Language & Thought. Wolf Paprotte & Rene Dirven. LC 85-10143. (Current Issues in Linguistic Theory: No. 29). xiii, 628p. 1986. 72.00x (ISBN 90-272-3521-X). Benjamins North Am.

Ubiquity of the Finite: Hegel, Hiedegger, & the Entitlements of Philosophy. Dennis J. Schmidt. (Studies in Contemporary German Social Thought). 200p. 1988. text ed. 22.50x (ISBN 0-262-19270-5). MIT Pr.

Ubiystvo Emigranta. Mark Girshin. LC 83-159. 145p. (Rus.). 1983. pap. 6.00 (ISBN 0-938920-29-4). Hermitage.

Ubu Cocu see Tout Ubu.

Ubu Cuckolded see Ubu Plays.

Ubu Enchaine see Tout Ubu.

Ubu Enchained see Ubu Plays.

Ubu Guide to New French-Language Plays in English Translations. Ubu Repertory Theater Staff. 54p. (Orig.). 1986. pap. 5.00 (ISBN 0-913745-22-7). Ubu Repertory.

Ubu Plays. Alfred Jarry. Tr. by Cyril Connolly & Simon W. Taylor. Incl. Ubu Rex; Ubu Cuckolded; Ubu Enchained. 1969. pap. 9.95 (ISBN 0-394-17485-2, E496, Ever). Grove.

UBU Repertory Theater Publications, Vols. 1-5. Ubu Repertory Theater Publications Staff. Set. pap. 28.00 (ISBN 0-913745-13-8). UBU Repertory.

UBU Repertory Theater Publications, Vol. 6-10. Ubu Repertory Theater Publications Staff. Set. pap. 28.00 (ISBN 0-913745-14-6). UBU Repertory.

Ubu Rex see Ubu Plays.

Ubu Roi. Alfred Jarry. Tr. by Barbara Wright. LC 61-10124. (Illus.). 1961. pap. 6.95 (ISBN 0-8112-0072-8, NDP105). New Directions.

Ubu Roi see Tout Ubu.

Ubu Roi: An Analytical Study, Vol. 6. Judith Cooper. 120p. 1974. pap. 7.00 (ISBN 0-912788-05-4). Tulane Romance Lang.

Ubu sur la Butte see Tout Ubu.

Ubu: Ubu Roi, Ubu Cocu, Ubu Enchaine, Ubu sur la Butte. Alfred Jarry. Ed. by Noel Arnaud & Henri Bordillon. 533p. 1978. 5.50 (ISBN 0-686-54214-2). French & Eur.

Ubungen zur Projektiven Geometrie. H. Herrmann. (Mathematische Reihe Ser.: No. 18). (Illus.). 168p. (Ger.). 1952. 19.95x (ISBN 0-8176-0170-8). Birkhauser.

UC Irvine. Melinda Wortz. LC 75-37097. (Illus.). 96p. 1975. 7.00X (ISBN 0-686-99815-4). La Jolla Mus Contemp Art.

U.C.C. Adaptable to Courses Utilizing Epstein & Martin's Casebook on Basic Uniform Commercial Code. Casenotes Publishing Co., Inc. Staff. Ed. by Norman S. Goldenberg et al. (Legal Briefs Ser.). 1982. pap. write for info. (ISBN 0-87457-142-1, 1410). Casenotes Pub.

U.C.C. Amendments to Article Eight, 1977: Official Text with Comments. 1978. pap. 3.95 (ISBN 0-685-91310-4). West Pub.

U.C.C. Amendments to Article Nine, 1972: Official Text with Comments. 1978. pap. 3.95 (ISBN 0-685-91309-0). West Pub.

UCC-Pertinent Commercial Statutes, 2 vols. Gould Editorial Staff. Set. text ed. 10.95 looseleaf (ISBN 0-686-47976-9). Gould.

UCC Skills - Articles 3, 4, 5 & 9: Commercial Paper. William C. Hillman. 390p. 1985. 15.00 (A4-4122). PLI.

Uch Tepe I, Tell Razuk, Tell Ahmed al-Mughir, Tell Ajamat. Ed. by McGuire Gibson et al. Ingolf Thuesen & John C. Sanders. (Chicago-Copenhagen Expedition to the Hamrin Ser.). (Illus.). xi, 198p. 1981. pap. 25.00x (ISBN 0-918986-34-6). Oriental Inst.

Uchenije o Pravoslavnom Bogosluzhenii. V. Mikhailovsky. 146p. pap. text ed. 6.00 (ISBN 0-317-30287-6). Holy Trinity.

Uchinanchu: A History of Okinawans in Hawaii. Ed. by University of Hawaii Ethnic Studies Oral History Project. 696p. 1982. 25.00 (ISBN 0-8248-0749-9, Ethnic Stud Oral Hist). UH Pr.

Uchjebnik Tserkovnago Penija. A. Ryazhsky. 105p. 1966. pap. 5.00 (ISBN 0-317-30382-1). Holy Trinity.

UCLA-Alaska Law Review: 1971-1983, Vols. 1-12. Bound set. 330.00x (ISBN 0-686-90065-0). Rothman.

UCLA Architecture Journal, Vol. 2. 1988. 24.00. Knapp Pr.

UCLA Business Forecast for the Nation & California in 1981. 1981. 40.00 (ISBN 0-913404-05-5). UCLA Busn Forecasting.

UCLA Business Forecast for the Nation & California in 1979. Ed. by Robert M. Williams. 1979. pap. 25.00 (ISBN 0-913404-03-9). UCLA Busn Forecasting.

UCLA Business Forecast for the Nation & California in 1976. Ed. by Robert M. Williams. (Orig.). 1976. pap. 20.00 (ISBN 0-913404-00-4). UCLA Busn Forecasting.

UCLA Business Forecast for the Nation & California in 1980. Ed. by Robert M. Williams. 1980. 35.00 (ISBN 0-913404-04-7). UCLA Busn Forecasting.

UCLA Business Forecast for the Nation & California in 1978. Ed. by Robert M. Williams. 1978. pap. 25.00 (ISBN 0-913404-02-0). UCLA Busn Forecasting.

UCLA Business Forecast for the Nation & California in 1982: Proceedings of the 30th Annual Business Forecasting Conference, Graduate School of Management at UCLA, Dec. 10, 1981. Ed. by Robert M. Williams. (Illus.). 110p. 1982. 50.00 (ISBN 0-686-87238-X). UCLA Busn Forecasting.

UCLA Business Forecast for the Nation & California in 1983: Proceedings of an Annual Conference, December 15, 1982. Ed. by Robert M. Williams. 1983. 60.00x. UCLA Busn Forecasting.

UCLA Football: Touchdown UCLA. Hendrick Van Leuven. LC 81-85248. (College Sports Ser.). 1982. 12.95 (ISBN 0-87397-227-9). Strode.

UCLA Handbook of Psychiatry. Guze. 1988. 16.00 (ISBN 0-8151-3644-7). Year Bk Med.

UCLA-Intramural Law Review: 1952-1953, 1 Vol. Bound set. 30.00x (ISBN 0-686-90068-5). Rothman.

UCLA Law Review: 1953-1986, 33 vols. Bound set. 1380.00x (ISBN 0-686-90071-5). Rothman.

UCLA Rock Art Archive Unpublished Documents: A Catalog. Helen Michaelis & Catherine Weinerth. (Occasional Paper: 12). 55p. 1984. pap. 5.00x (ISBN 0-917956-45-1). UCLA Arch.

UCSD Pascal: A Beginner's Guide to Programming Microcomputers. R. C. Holt & J. N. Hume. 368p. 1982. 30.00 (ISBN 0-8359-7915-6, Reston); pap. 25.00 (ISBN 0-8359-7913-X). P-H.

UCSD Pascal Examples & Exercises. David V. Moffat. (Illus.). 224p. 1986. pap. text ed. 16.00 (ISBN 0-13-935396-8). P-H.

UCSD Pascal: Featuring the Apple IIe & II Plus. Roger Haigh & Loren Radford. 461p. 1984. text ed. 21.00 (ISBN 0-87150-457-X, 8090). PWS Kent Pub.

UCSD Pascal for the IBM PC. Iain MacCallum. Date not set. write for info. S&S.

UCSD Pascal for the IBM PC. Iain MacCallum. (Illus.). 608p. 1986. pap. text ed. 30.00 (ISBN 0-13-935982-6). P-H.

UCSD Pascal Handbook. Randy Clark & Stephen Koehler. (Software Ser.). (Illus.). 384p. 1982. text ed. 30.00 (ISBN 0-13-935544-8); pap. text ed. 23.95 (ISBN 0-13-935536-7). P-H.

UCSD Pascal Programming. Seymour V. Pollack. 1985. pap. text ed. 21.95x (ISBN 0-03-069393-4). HR&W.

Uda: Japan's First County. John R. Terry. (Illus.). 200p. 1988. pap. 9.95 (ISBN 0-933704-67-4). Dawn Pr.

Udana, or the Solemn Utterances of the Buddha. Tr. by D. M. Strong from Pali. LC 78-70131. Repr. of 1902 ed. 20.50 (ISBN 0-404-17399-3). AMS Pr.

Udderly Inviting. Ruth Seeley-Scheel. (Illus.). 1987. pap. 6.95 (ISBN 0-9619815-1-2). Laugh Goose.

Uddhava Gita or Last Message of Sri Krishna. Tr. by Madhavananda from Sanskrit. 425p. pap. 4.95 (ISBN 0-87481-211-9). Vedanta Pr.

Udo Fahrt Nach Koln. Peter Lunt. LC 73-20464. (Ger). 1971. pap. text ed. 8.16 (ISBN 0-395-11058-0). HM.

Udvalgte digte see Selected Poems.

Ugo Betti: An Introduction. Emanuele Licastro. LC 84-43202. 188p. 1985. lib. bdg. 21.95x (ISBN 0-89950-141-9). McFarland & Co.

Ugo Foscolo: Poet of Exile. Glauco Cambon. LC 79-3193. 360p. 1980. 34.00x (ISBN 0-691-06424-5). Princeton U Pr.

UH-1 Huey in Action. (Illus.). 1986. pap. 5.95 (ISBN 0-89747-179-2, 1075). Squad Sig Pubns.

UH-1 Iroquois & Hueycobra: Modern Combat Aircraft No. 19. Jerry Scutts. (Illus.). 112p. 1984. 23.95 (ISBN 0-7110-1416-7, Pub. By Ian Allen England). Motorbooks Intl.

UH-1C Huey. Peter W. Harlem. LC 85-70918. (Crewchief Ser.: No. 1). (Illus.). 56p. (Orig.). 1985. pap. 6.50 (ISBN 0-933907-00-1, CE-1). Cobra Co.

Uhlands Gedichte und das Deutsche Mittelalter. Hermann Schneider. 18.00 (ISBN 0-384-54186-0); pap. 13.00 (ISBN 0-384-54185-2). Johnson Repr.

Uhr Schlaegt Eins: Ein historisches Drama aus der Gegenwart. Helen Swediuk-Cheyne. 110p. 1977. pap. 18.25 (ISBN 3-261-02125-X). P Lang Pubs.

Uhura's Song, No. 21. Janet Kagan. pap. 3.50 (ISBN 0-671-54730-5). PB.

UIA International Exhibition of Architecture, Cairo 1985. Ed. by Jorge Glusberg. (Academy Architecture Ser.). (Illus.). 88p. 1985. pap. 14.95 (ISBN 0-312-82780-6). St Martin.

UIA Journal of Architectural Theory & Criticism, Vol. I: Vision of the Modern. Ed. by The International Union of Architects Staff. Catherine Cooke. (Illus.). 96p. 1988. pap. 25.00 (ISBN 0-8478-5489-2). Rizzoli Intl.

Uibhist A Deas. Domhnall L. MacDhomhnaill. 1985. 27.00x (ISBN 0-86152-021-1, Pub. by Acair Ltd Scotland). State Mutual Bk.

Uj Egtajak. Ed. by Gyorgy Gomori & Vilmos Juhasz. LC 71-94112. (Hung). 1969. pap. 6.00 (ISBN 0-911050-35-3). Occidental.

Ujamaa: Essays on Socialism. Julius K. Nyerere. 1968. pap. 6.95 (ISBN 0-19-501474-X). Oxford U Pr.

UJAMAA Villages in Tanzania: A Bibliography. Dean E. McHenry, Jr. 69p. 1982. pap. 12.50 (ISBN 0-8419-9738-1, Africana). Holmes & Meier.

Ujamaa Villages in Tanzania: Analysis of a Social Experiment. Michaela Von Freyhold. LC 79-13401. 201p. 1981. 14.50 (ISBN 0-85345-512-0); pap. 5.95 (ISBN 0-85345-513-9). Monthly Rev.

UK Import Market Reports, No. 1: Knitwear. Date not set. 105.00x (Pub. by Trade Rsch Pubns UK). State Mutual Bk.

UK Import Market Reports, No. 2: Furniture. Trade Research Publications Staff. Date not set. 70.00x (ISBN 0-904783-17-0, Pub. by Trade Rsch Pubns UK). State Mutual Bk.

UK Military R & D. Council for Science & Society Staff. (Illus.). 90p. 1986. pap. 8.95 (ISBN 0-19-859930-7). Oxford U Pr.

Ukazanije Puti v Tsarstvije Nebsnoje. Metropolitan Innocent of Moscow Staff. 59p. pap. 2.00 (ISBN 0-317-28978-0). Holy Trinity.

Ukifune: Love in the Tale of Genji. Ed. by Andrew J. Pekarik. LC 82-1157. 264p. 1982. 29.50x (ISBN 0-231-04598-0). Columbia U Pr.

Ukiyo-E. Marco Fagioli. 31p. 1983. 24.00x (ISBN 0-317-69465-0, Pub. by Han-Shan Tang Ltd). State Mutual Bk.

Ukiyo-E. Tadashi Kobayashi. Tr. by Mark A. Harbison. LC 81-84909. (Great Japanese Art Ser.). (Illus.). 48p. 1982. 24.95 (ISBN 0-87011-518-9). Kodansha.

Ukiyo-E A - a Journal of the Floating World. 1400.00x (ISBN 0-317-68604-6, Pub. by Han-Shan Tang Ltd). State Mutual Bk.

Ukiyo-e Collection, 3 Vols. Phillip Franz Von Siebold. (Illus.). Set. limited edition 1250.00 (ISBN 0-384-64941-6). Johnson Repr.

Ukiyo-E Masterpieces in Europe Collections, Vol. 2. Muneshige Narazaki. LC 87-81680. (Illus.). 278p. 1988. 250.00 (ISBN 0-87011-869-2). Kodansha.

Ukiyo-E Masterpieces in European Collections: Museum fur Ostasiatische Kunst, Berlin, Vol. 12. Contrib. by Muneshige Narazaki. 260p. 1988. 300.00 (ISBN 0-87011-882-X); Until 12/31/88. 250.00. Kodansha.

Ukiyo-E Masterpieces in European Collections: Vol. 1: British Museum I. LC 87-81680. (Ukiyo-E Masterpieces Ser.). (Illus.). 268p. 1988. 250.00 (ISBN 0-87011-855-2). Kodansha.

Ukiyo-E Masterpieces in European Collections, Vol. 10: Museo d'Arte Orientale, Genoa I, Vol. 10. Muneshige Narazaki. LC 87-81680. (Ukiyo-E Masterpieces Ser.). (Illus.). 232p. 1988. 250.00 (ISBN 0-87011-856-0). Kodansha.

Ukiyo-E Masterpieces in European Collections, Vol. 3: British Museum III. Ed. by Muneshige Narazaki. 278p. 1988. 250.00 (ISBN 0-87011-874-9). Kodansha.

Ukiyo-E: Two Hundred & Fifty Years of Japanese Art. Susugu Yoshida & Roni Neuer. LC 79-13327. (Illus.). 384p. 1980. 19.98 (ISBN 0-8317-9041-5, Mayflower Bks). Smith Pubs.

Ukiyoe. Galerie Zacke. 1986. 100.00x (Pub. by Han-Shan Tang Ltd). State Mutual Bk.

Ukomno'm: The Yuki Indians of Northern California. Virginia P. Miller. (Ballena Press Anthropological Papers: No. 14). (Illus.). 1979. pap. 8.95 (ISBN 0-87919-083-3). Ballena Pr.

Ukraine. (Let's Visit Places & Peoples - - Nations, Dependencies, & Sovereignties of the World Ser.). (Illus.). (gr. 5 up). 1988. 12.95. Chelsea Hse.

Ukraine - Questions & Answers. S. Lazebnik & P. Orlenko. 92p. 1983. 25.00x (ISBN 0-317-39537-8, Pub. by Collets UK). State Mutual Bk.

Ukraine: A Brief History. 2nd ed. Roman Shporluk. 162p. 1982. write for info. Ukrainian Pol.

Ukraine: A Historical Atlas. Paul R. Magocsi. 64p. 1985. 35.00x (ISBN 0-8020-3428-4); pap. 16.95 (ISBN 0-8020-3429-2). U of Toronto Pr.

Ukraine in the United Nations: A Study in Soviet Foreign Policy, 1944-1950. Konstantin Sawczuk. LC 74-83055. (East European Monographs: No. 9). 158p. 1975. 20.00x (ISBN 0-914710-02-8). East Eur Quarterly.

Ukraine: Nineteen Seventeen to Nineteen Twenty-One: A Study in Revolution. Ed. by Taras Hunczak. (Ser. in Ukrainian Studies). 1978. 18.50x (ISBN 0-674-92009-0). Harvard U Pr.

Ukrainer Pogromen in Yor 1919. Elias Tcherikower. (Bibliotek Fun Yivo). 372p. (Yiddish.). 1965. 10.00 (ISBN 0-914512-09-9, HE66-1617). Yivo Inst.

Ukrainian Americans: Roots & Aspirations. Myron B. Kuropas. LC 85-80955. (Harvard Ukrainian Research Institute Monograph). 1988. 24.95x (ISBN 0-916458-13-X, Dist. by Harvard University Press). Harvard Ukrainian.

Ukrainian Catholic Church: 1945-1975. Ed. by Miroslav Labunka & Leonid Rudnytzky. LC 76-26753. 1976. 7.50 (ISBN 0-686-28475-5). St Sophia Religious.

Ukrainian Catholics in America: A History. Bohdan Procka. 170p. 1982. write for info. Ukrainian Pol.

Ukrainian Catholics in America: A History. Bohdan P. Procko. LC 81-43718. 184p. (Orig.). 1982. lib. bdg. 29.25 (ISBN 0-8191-2409-5); pap. text ed. 12.25 (ISBN 0-8191-2410-9). U Pr of Amer.

Ukrainian Culinary Glossary. Natalia Chaplenko. LC 80-54687. 113p. 1980. pap. 6.00 (ISBN 0-317-36114-7). UNWLA.

Ukrainian Culture at Pennsylvania State University: Papers, Articles & Synopses of Lectures. Ed. by W. O. Luciw. (Illus.). 256p. 1980. 30.00 (ISBN 0-686-63321-0). Slavia Lib.

Ukrainian Egg Mystery. George E. Stanley. 112p. 1986. pap. 2.50 (ISBN 0-380-89962-0, Camelot). Avon.

Ukrainian Embroidery Techniques. Tania D. O'Neill. LC 84-52257. (Illus.). 158p. (Eng. & Ukrainian.). 1985. text ed. 35.00 (ISBN 0-9614540-0-8). STO Pub.

Ukrainian-English Dictionary. Ed. by C. H. Andrusyshen. 1200p. (Ukrainian & Eng.). 1981. pap. 27.50 (ISBN 0-8020-6421-3). U of Toronto Pr.

Ukrainian-English Dictionary. 2nd ed. Ed. by M. L. Podvesko. 37.50 (ISBN 0-87557-088-7, 088-7). Saphrograph.

Ukrainian-English, English-Ukrainian Pocket Dictionary. (Ukrainian & Eng.). 12.50. Heinman.

Ukrainian Experience in the United States: A Symposium. Ed. by Paul R. Magocsi. LC 78-59968. (Sources & Documents Ser.). (Orig.). 1979. pap. 7.50x (ISBN 0-916458-04-0). Harvard Ukrainian.

Ukrainian Folklore in Canada: An Immigrant Complex in Transition. Robert B. Klymasz. Ed. by Richard M. Dorson. LC 80-731. (Folklore of the World Ser.). 1980. lib. bdg. 32.50x (ISBN 0-405-13318-9). Ayer Co Pubs.

Ukrainian Helsinki Group: Five Years of Struggle in Defense of Rights. LC 81-85108. 45p. 1981. pap. 1.50 (ISBN 0-914834-46-0). Smoloskyp.

Ukrainian Helsinki Group, 1978-1982: A Collection of Documents & Materials. Ed. by O. Zinkewych. LC 83-60960. 998p. (Ukrainian.). 1983. 29.75 (ISBN 0-914834-50-9). Smoloskyp.

Ukrainian Herald, Issue 6: Dissent in Ukraine. Ed. by Lesya Jones & Bohdan Yasen. Tr. by Lesya Jones. LC 75-39367. 1977. 6.95 (ISBN 0-914834-05-3); pap. 3.95 (ISBN 0-914834-06-1). Smoloskyp.

Ukrainian Herald, Issue 7-8: Ethnocide of Ukrainians in the U. S. S. R. 2nd ed. Compiled by Maksym Sahaydak. Tr. by Bohdan Yasem & Olena Saciuk. Intro. by Robert Conquest. LC 75-38397. 209p. 1981. 8.95 (ISBN 0-914834-45-2). Smoloskyp.

Ukrainian Language in the First Half of the Twentieth Century (1900-1941) Its State & Status. George Y. Shevelov. LC 88-81195. (Monograph Ser.). 240p. 1988. text ed. 20.00X (ISBN 0-916458-30-X). Harvard Ukrainian.

Ukrainian Literature: Studies of the Leading Authors. facsimile ed. Clarence A. Manning. LC 70-86771. (Essay Index Reprint Ser). Repr. of 1944 ed. 18.00 (ISBN 0-8369-2244-1). Ayer Co Pubs.

Ukrainian Nationalism. 2nd ed. John A. Armstrong. LC 79-25529. 361p. 1980. Repr. of 1963 ed. 30.00 (ISBN 0-87287-193-2). Libs Unl.

Ukrainian Nationalism in the Post-Stalin Era: Myth, Symbols & Ideology in Soviet Nationalities Policy. Kenneth C. Farmer. (Studies in Contemporary History: Vol. 4). 253p. 1980. lib. bdg. 36.50 (ISBN 90-247-2401-5, Pub. by Martinus Nijhoff). Kluwer Academic.

Ukrainian Revolution, Nineteen Seventeen to Nineteen Twenty: A Study in Nationalism. John S. Reshetar, Jr. LC 72-4292. (World Affairs Ser.: National & International Viewpoints). 376p. 1972. Repr. of 1952 ed. 29.00 (ISBN 0-405-04584-0). Ayer Co Pubs.

Ukrainian Revolution: The Nineteen Nineteen to Nineteen Twenty-One Documents: Editor's Text in English, Documents in French, Polish, Russian & Ukrainian. Taras Hunczak. (Sources of modern History of the Ukrain Ser.). (Illus.). 464p. 1984. 25.00 (ISBN 0-916381-00-5). Ukrainian Arts Sci.

Ukrainian Struggle for National Liberation. Yaroslav Stetsko. Ed. by John Kolasky. LC 87-6948. (Illus.). 700p. 1988. 59.95 (ISBN 0-8022-2537-3). Philos Lib.

Ukrainian Women in the Soviet Union: Documented Persecution. Nina Strokata. (Illus.). 64p. 1980. 3.25 (ISBN 0-914834-43-6). Smoloskyp.

Ukrainian Women's Bibliography Beyond the Borders of Ukraine. Natalia Chaplenko. 54p. 1974. pap. 2.00 (ISBN 0-317-36115-5). UNWLA.

Ukrainians & the Polish Revolt of Eighteen Sixty-Three. rev. ed. Wasyl O. Luciw. 100p. (Orig.). 1980. pap. text ed. 8.00 (ISBN 0-686-63322-9). Slavia Lib.

Ukrainians in America. Myron Kuropas. LC 72-3588. (In America Bks.). (Illus.). 88p. (gr. 5-11). 1972. PLB 8.95 (ISBN 0-8225-0221-6); pap. 3.95 (ISBN 0-8225-1024-3). Lerner Pubns.

Ukrainians in America 1608-1975: A Chronology & Fact Book. Vladimir Wertsman. LC 76-6679. (Ethnic Chronology Ser.: No. 25). 140p. 1976. lib. bdg. 8.50 (ISBN 0-379-00523-9). Oceana.

Ukrainians in Canada & the United States: A Guide to Information Sources. Ed. by Aleksander Sokolyszyn & Vladimir Wertsman. (Ethnic Studies Information Guide Ser.: Vol. 7). 256p. 1981. 68.00x (ISBN 0-8103-1494-0). Gale.

Ukrainians in Canada & the United States, Vol. 7. 236p. 1981. write for info. Ukrainian Pol.

Ukrainians in the Making: Their Kingston Story. Lubomyr Y. Luciuk. (Builders of Canada Ser.: No. 1). (Illus.). 1980. 16.50x (ISBN 0-919642-91-8). Limestone Pr.

Ukrainians in the United States. Wasyl Halich. LC 78-129399. (American Immigration Collection, Ser. 2). (Illus.). 1970. Repr. of 1937 ed. 13.00 (ISBN 0-405-00552-0). Ayer Co Pubs.

Ukrainians of Maryland. Stephen Basarab et al. LC 77-85157. (Illus.). 519p. (Orig.). 1977. pap. 8.95 (ISBN 0-9606178-0-9). Ukrainian Ed Assn.

Ukranian see **Spohady Memoirs.**

Ukranian Olympic Champions. Osyp Zinkewych. LC 84-51196. 158p. 1984. 9.75 (ISBN 0-914834-54-1); pap. 7.50 (ISBN 0-914834-56-8). Smoloskyp.

Ukrayinsky Pravozakhysny Rukh: Ukrainian Movement in Defense of Rights: Documents of Kiev Ukrainian Helsinki Group. (Ukrainian.). 12.75 (ISBN 0-914834-17-7); soft cover 9.75. Smoloskyp.

UKSC Conference on Computer Simulation: (UKSC 1987, United Kingdom) Date not set. 50.00 (ISBN 0-911801-23-5). Soc Computer Sim.

Ukulele: A Portuguese Gift to Hawaii. John H. Felix et al. LC 80-66299. (Illus.). 75p. (Orig.). (gr. 4-12). 1980. pap. 5.95x (ISBN 0-9604190-0-4). Nunes.

Ukulele by "Ear", Hawaiian Style. Hideo M. Kimura. 57p. 1977. pap. 8.95 (ISBN 0-917822-02-1). Heedays.

Ukulele Music. Peter Reading. 128p. 1986. pap. 9.95 (ISBN 0-436-40986-0, Pub. by Secker & Warburg UK). David & Charles.

Ula Li'i & the Magic Shark. Donivee M. Laird. LC 86-3390. (Illus.). 42p. (gr. k-3). 1985. 6.95x (ISBN 0-940350-09-2). Barnaby Bks.

Ulam Problem of Optimal Motion of Line Segments. V. A. Dubovitskij. Tr. by J. T. Ellis from Rus. LC 84-19035. xiii, 113p. 1985. 27.00 (ISBN 0-387-90946-X). Springer-Verlag.

Ulam Problem of Optimal Motion of Line Segments. V. A. Dubovitskij. Ed. by A. V. Balakrishnan. LC 84-19035. (Translations Series in Mathematics & Engineering). 128p. 1985. text ed. 24.00 (ISBN 0-911575-04-9). Optimization Soft.

Ulay & Marina Abramovic. Sarah Rogers-Lafferty. (Illus.). cancelled. Contemp Arts.

Ulcer & Non-Ulcer Dyspepsias. Ed. by M. J. Smith. (Practical Clinical Medicine Ser.). 1987. lib. bdg. 44.50 (ISBN 0-85200-970-4, Pub. by MTP Pr England). Kluwer Academic.

Ulcer Diet Cookbook. Harold Rubin. LC 63-9769. 224p. 1963. 6.95 (ISBN 0-87131-100-3); pap. 3.95 (ISBN 0-87131-248-4). M Evans.

ULF Pulsations in the Magnetosphere. D. J. Southwood. 1981. 29.50 (ISBN 90-277-1232-8, Pub. by Reidel Holland). Kluwer Academic.

ULI Development Trends: 1987. ULI the Urban Land Institute. Ed. by Libby Howland. Orig. Title: Development Review & Outlook. 48p. 1987. pap. 8.00 (ISBN 0-87420-669-3, D47). Urban Land.

ULI Market Profiles: 1987. ULI the Urban Land Institute. Ed. by Julie Stern. Orig. Title: Development Review & Outlook. 205p. 1987. pap. 110.00 (ISBN 0-87420-668-5). Urban Land.

ULI-UMTA Policy Forum on Joint Development of Rail Transit Facilities. ULI Urban Land. 105p. 1987. pap. 20.00 (ISBN 0-87420-671-5, I01). Urban Land.

Ulithi: A Micronesian Design for Living. William A. Lessa. (Illus.). 118p. 1986. pap. text ed. 7.50x (ISBN 0-88133-212-7). Waveland Pr.

Uller Uprising. H. Beam Piper. 1983. pap. 2.75 (ISBN 0-441-84292-5, Pub. by Ace Science Fiction). Ace Bks.

Ullmann's Encyclopedia of Industrial Chemistry: Abrasives to Aluminium Oxide, Vol. A1. 5th ed. LC 84-25829. 594p. 1985. 180.00 (ISBN 0-89573-151-7). VCH Pubs.

Ullmann's Encyclopedia of Industrial Chemistry: Benzyl Alcohol to Calcium Sulfate, Vol. A4. 5th ed. Ed. by W. Gerhartz. 584p. 1986. lib. bdg. 180.00 (ISBN 0-89573-154-1); Avail. through subscription. 155.00. VCH Pubs.

Ullmann's Encyclopedia of Industrial Chemistry: Cancer Chemotherapy to Ceramics Colorants, Vol. A5. 5th ed. Ed. by W. Gerhartz. 556p. 1985. lib. bdg. 180.00 (ISBN 0-89573-155-X); lib. bdg. 155.00; through subscription avail. VCH Pubs.

Ullmann's Encyclopedia of Industrial Chemistry: Ceramics to Chlorohydrins, Vol. A6. 5th ed. Ed. by W. Gerhartz. 576p. 1987. lib. bdg. 180.00 (ISBN 0-89573-156-8); lib. bdg. 155.00; through subscription avail. VCH Pubs.

Ullmann's Encyclopedia of Industrial Chemistry: Chlorophenols to Copper Compunds, Vol. A7. 5th ed. Ed. by W. Gerhartz. 576p. 1987. lib. bdg. 180.00 (ISBN 0-89573-157-6); lib. bdg. 155.00; through Subscription avail. VCH Pubs.

Ullmann's Encyclopedia of Industrial Chemistry: Coronary Therapeutics to Display Technology, Vol. A8. 5th ed. Ed. by W. Gerhartz. 624p. 1987. lib. bdg. 180.00 (ISBN 0-89573-158-4); Avail. through subscription. 145.00. VCH Pubs.

Ullmann's Encyclopedia of Industrial Chemistry: Dithiocarbamic Acid to Ethanol, Vol. A9. 5th ed. Ed. by W. Gerhartz. (Illus.). 653p. 1988. lib. bdg. 180.00 (ISBN 0-89573-159-2). VCH Pubs.

Ullmann's Encyclopedia of Industrial Chemistry: Ethanolamines to Fibers, 4, Synthetic Organic, Vol. A10. Ed. by W. Gerhartz. 1988. lib. bdg. 180.00 (ISBN 0-89573-160-6). VCH Pubs.

Ullmann's Encyclopedia of Industrial Chemistry, Index to Volumes A1 to A7. Ed. by W. Gerhartz. 1987. lib. bdg. 24.95 (ISBN 0-89573-181-9). VCH Pubs.

Ullmann's Encyclopedia of Industrial Chemistry, Vol. 2: Amines, Aliphatics to Antibiotics. 5th ed. 557p. 1985. lib. bdg. 180.00 (ISBN 0-89573-152-5). VCH Pubs.

Ullmann's Encyclopedia of Industrial Chemistry, Vol. 3: Antidiabetic Drugs to Benzoquinone & Naphthoquinone Dyes. 5th ed. W. Gerhartz. (Illus.). 578p. 1985. lib. bdg. 180.00. VCH Pubs.

Ullstein Lexikon der Medizin. (Ger.). 1970. 49.95 (ISBN 3-550-06017-3, M-7674, Pub. by Ullstein Verlag/VVA). French & Eur.

Ullstein Lexikon der Pflanzenwelt. Hartmut Bastian. (Ger.). 1973. 49.95 (ISBN 0-686-56471-5, M-7675, Pub. by Ullstein Verlag VA). French & Eur.

Ullstein Lexikon der Tierwelt. Hartmut Bastian. (Ger.). 1967. 49.95 (ISBN 3-550-06014-9, M-7676, Pub. by Ullstein Verlag/VVA). French & Eur.

Ullstein Lexikon des Rechts. Otto Gritschneder. (Ger.). 1971. 75.00 (ISBN 3-550-06018-1, M-7677, Pub. by Ullstein Verlag/VVA). French & Eur.

Ulpian. Tony Honore. 1982. 79.00x (ISBN 0-19-825358-3). Oxford U Pr.

Ulpian Fullwell's 'The Art of Flattery'; 1576. Roberta Buchanan. Ed. by James Hogg. (Elizabethan & Renaissance Studies). (Orig.). 1984. pap. 15.00 (ISBN 3-7052-0777-6, Pub. by Salzburg Studies). Longwood Pub Group.

Ulrea Rich: How Much Is Too Much? Vance Packard. 1989. 22.95 (ISBN 0-316-68752-9). Little.

Ulrich Becker: A Computer-Assisted Case Study of the Reception of an Exile. Nancy A. Zeller. LC 82-84614. (American University Studies, Ser. I: Germanic Languages & Literature: Vol. 7). 426p. 1983. pap. text ed. 46.85 (ISBN 0-8204-0006-8). P Lang Pubs.

Ulrich Bonnell Phillips: Historian of the Old South. Merton L. Dillon. LC 85-10229. (Southern Biography Ser.). 190p. 1985. text ed. 22.50 (ISBN 0-8071-1206-2). La State U Pr.

Ulrich Fuetrer's Parzival: Material & Sources. James Boyd. 1977. lib. bdg. 59.95 (ISBN 0-8490-2782-9). Gordon Pr.

Ulrich Von Hutten. David F. Strauss. Tr. by Mrs. G. Sturge from Ger. LC 77-130624. Repr. of 1874 ed. 27.50 (ISBN 0-404-06296-2). AMS Pr.

Ulrich Von Hutten & the German Reformation. Hajo Holborn. Tr. by Roland H. Bainton. LC 77-25067. (Yale Historical Publications Studies: No. XI). (Illus.). 1978. Repr. of 1937 ed. lib. bdg. 35.00x (ISBN 0-313-20125-0, HOUV). Greenwood.

Ulrich Von Hutten und Die Reformation: Eine Kritische Geschichte Seiner Wichtigsten Lebenszeit und der Entscheidungsjahre der Reformation, 1517-1523. Paul Kalkoff. (Ger). pap. 55.00 (ISBN 0-384-28511-2). Johnson Repr.

Ulrich Von Turheim. Eberhard K. Busse. pap. 13.00 (ISBN 0-685-02229-3). Johnson Repr.

Ulrich's International Periodicals Directory, 1988-1989, 3 vols. Ed. by Bowker, R. R., Staff. 1988. Set. 279.95 (ISBN 0-8352-2563-1). Vol. 1 (ISBN 0-8352-2565-8). Vol. 2 (ISBN 0-8352-2566-6). Vol. 3 (ISBN 0-8352-2623-9). Bowker.

TITLE INDEX ULTIMATE TRANSFORMATION.

Ulrichs: The Life & Works of Karl Heinrich Ulrichs, Pioneer of the Modern Gay Movement. Hubert Kennedy. 200p. 1988. 17.95 (ISBN 1-55583-124-9); pap. 8.95 (ISBN 1-55583-109-5). Alyson Pubns.
Ulrichs Von Lichtenstein Frauendienst: Untersuchungen Uber Den Hofischen Sprachstil. Hans Arens. (Ger). 18.00 (ISBN 0-384-01898-X); pap. 13.00 (ISBN 0-685-02208-0). Johnson Repr.
Ulster. Stephen Gwynn. 59.95 (ISBN 0-8490-1241-4). Gordon Pr.
Ulster. Lord Longford & Anne McHardy. 272p. 1981. 22.00x (ISBN 0-297-77971-0, GWN 01008, Pub. by Weidenfeld & Nicolson England). Biblio Dist.
Ulster: A Case Study in Conflict Theory. R. S. Elliot & John Ickie. LC 78-182186. 180p. 1971. 29.50 (ISBN 0-8290-0213-8); pap. text ed. 14.95x (ISBN 0-8290-0683-4). Irvington.
Ulster Childhood. Lynn Doyle. 164p. (Orig.). 1985. pap. 5.95 (ISBN 0-85640-349-0, Pub. by Blackstaff Pr). Longwood Pub Group.
Ulster County in the Revolution. Ed. by Ruth P. Heidgerd. 297p. 1976. 9.50. Huguenot Hist.
Ulster County, New York Atlas. Orange County Genealogical Society & F. W. Beers. 130p. 1984. Repr. of 1875 ed. lib. bdg. 30.00 (ISBN 0-9604116-8-2). Orange County Genealog.
Ulster Folk Ways. Alan Gailey. 2.95 (ISBN 0-913714-20-8). Legacy Bks.
Ulster Folklore. Elizabeth Andrews. 1978. Repr. of 1913 ed. lib. bdg. 39.50 (ISBN 0-8495-0113-X). Arden Lib.
Ulster Joke Book. Compiled by Geoff Hill. (Illus.). 80p. 1987. pap. 6.95 (ISBN 0-85640-392-X, Pub. by Blackstaff Ireland). Irish Bks Media.
Ulster Museum, Pt. 1. 20.00 (ISBN 0-317-70068-5, Pub. by British Acad). Longwood Pub Group.
Ulster Presbyterianism: The Historical Perpective. Peter Brooke. LC 87-16705. 256p. 1987. 35.00 (ISBN 0-312-01271-3). St Martin.
Ulster Question, 1603-1973. 4th ed. T. W. Moody. (Illus.). 136p. 1980. pap. 5.75 (ISBN 0-85342-399-7, Pub. by Mercier Pr Ireland). Irish Bks Media.
Ulster Reciter. Joe McPartland. 90p. (Orig.). 1984. pap. 4.50 (ISBN 0-85640-321-0, Pub. by Blackstaff Pr). Longwood Pub Group.
Ulster Sails West. William F. Marshall. LC 76-56641. 79p. 1984. pap. 5.00 (ISBN 0-8063-0754-4). Genealog Pub.
Ulster under Home Rule: A Study of the Political & Economic Problems of Northern Ireland. Ed. by Thomas Wilson. LC 86-2291. 253p. 1986. Repr. of 1955 ed. lib. bdg. 48.50 (ISBN 0-313-25169-X, WIUL). Greenwood.
Ulster's Uncertain Defenders: Protestant Political, Paramilitary & Community Groups & the Northern Ireland Conflict. Sarah Nelson. (Irish Studies). 206p. 1984. text ed. 32.00x (ISBN 0-8156-2316-X). Syracuse U Pr.
Ulster's Uncertain Defenders: Protestant Political, Paramilitary, & Community Groups & the Northern Ireland Conflict. Sarah Nelson. (Irish Studies). 206p. 1987. pap. text ed. 12.95 (ISBN 0-8156-2418-2). Syracuse U Pr.
Ulterior Motives: The Killing & Dark Legacy of Tycoon Henry Kyle. Suzanne Finstad. LC 87-10981. 384p. 1987. 18.95 (ISBN 0-688-06902-9). Morrow.
Ultima Llamada. Jack T. Chick. (Illus.). 64p. (Orig., Span.). 1972. pap. 1.95 (ISBN 0-937958-02-6). Chick Pubns.
Ultima Noche Que Pase Contigo (40 anos de farandula cubana) 1910-1959. Bobby Collazo. (Illus.). 466p. (Span.). pap. 18.00 (ISBN 0-89729-451-3). Ediciones.
Ultima Thule. Henry H. Richardson. 314p. 1984. Repr. of 1929 ed. lib. bdg. 20.00 (ISBN 0-89984-877-X). Century Bookbindery.
Ultimate Album Cover Album. Roger Dean & David Howells. (Illus.). 224p. (Orig.). 1987. pap. 19.95 (ISBN 0-13-935750-5). P-H.
Ultimate Alchemy, 2 vols. Bhagwan Shree Rajneesh. Ed. by Ma Ananda Prem. LC 75-905370. (Upanishad Ser.). (Illus.). 1976. Vol. I, 442 pgs. 9.95 ea. (ISBN 0-88050-161-8). Vol. II, 424 pgs (ISBN 0-88050-162-6). Chidvilas Inc.
Ultimate Alphabet. Mike Wilks. (Illus.). 64p. 1986. 21.95 (ISBN 0-8050-0076-3); wkbk. 2.50 (ISBN 0-8050-0159-X); Set, shrink-wrapped. 22.45 (ISBN 0-8050-0160-3). H Holt & Co.
Ultimate Asteroid Book. Lee Lehman. Ed. by Julie Lockhart. (Illus.). 250p. (Orig.). 1988. pap. 18.95 (ISBN 0-914918-78-8, Pub. by Whitford Pr). Schiffer.
Ultimate Automobiles. Alberto Martinez & Jose Rosinski. (Illus.). 189p. 1985. Repr. 14.98 (ISBN 0-87938-200-7, Pub. by Edns Presse AudioVisual France). Motorbooks Intl.
Ultimate Baby Catalog. Michelle I. Haber & Barbara Kantrowitz. LC 82-60064. (Illus.). 192p. 1982. pap. 7.95 (ISBN 0-89480-174-0, 494). Workman Pub.
Ultimate Baseball Book. Daniel Okrent & Harris Lewine. (Illus.). 352p. 1984. pap. 15.95 (ISBN 0-395-36145-1). HM.
Ultimate Baseball Quiz Book. Dom Forker. (Orig.). 1988. pap. 4.95 (ISBN 0-451-15236-0, Sig). NAL.
Ultimate Baseball Trivia Book. Richard L. Vicknoy & Herbert A. Ruth. 250p. (Orig.). 1986. pap. 8.95 (ISBN 0-8246-0311-7). Jonathan David.
Ultimate Benefit Book: How to Raise 50,000-Plus for Your Organization. Marilyn E. Brentlinger & Judith M. Weiss. LC 87-12171. 232p. 1987. 22.95 (ISBN 0-940601-01-X). Octavia Ohio.
Ultimate Black Book. Date not set. pap. price not set (ISBN 0-935047-05-0). Americas Group.
Ultimate Book of Baccarat. Lyle Stuart. (Illus.). 224p. postponed 15.00 (ISBN 0-8184-0339-X). Lyle Stuart.
Ultimate Breakfast. Phillip Scully & Annie Gilbar. LC 87-8229. (Illus.). 288p. 1988. 19.95 (ISBN 1-55584-074-4). Weidenfeld.
Ultimate Cat Catalog. L. Sussman & S. Bordwell. 208p. 1985. pap. text ed. 9.95 (ISBN 0-07-062333-3). McGraw.
Ultimate Christmas Fake Book. (Fake Bks.). 84p. (gr. 4-12). 1985. 9.95 (ISBN 0-88188-381-6, HL00240063). H Leonard Pub Corp.
Ultimate Cigar. Stuart Kaufman. 41p. 1985. pap. 7.95 (ISBN 0-910829-05-5). First East.
Ultimate Coercive Sanction: A Cross-Cultural Study of Capital Punishment. Keith F. Otterbein. LC 86-80163. 164p. 1987. pap. 14.00 (ISBN 0-87536-346-6). HRAFP.
Ultimate Computing: Biomolecular Consciouness & Nano Technology. S. R. Hameroff. 358p. 1987. 78.00 (ISBN 0-444-70283-0). Elsevier.
Ultimate Con Man. Steve Wexler. 300p. (Orig.). 1987. pap. write for info. (ISBN 0-89894-038-9). Advocate Pub Group.
Ultimate Conspiracy. Jacqueline Lapidus. 84p. (Orig.). 1987. pap. 7.95 (ISBN 0-9619598-0-0). Lynx Pubns.
Ultimate Consumer: A Study in Economic Illiteracy. Ed. by J. Grist Brainerd. LC 75-39236. (Getting & Spending: the Consumer's Dilemma). 1976. Repr. of 1934 ed. 20.00x (ISBN 0-405-08012-3). Ayer Co Pubs.
Ultimate Country Fake Book Update. (Fake Bks.). 95p. 1985. plastic comb 8.95 (ISBN 0-88188-389-1, HL00240047). H Leonard Pub Corp.
Ultimate Crossword Puzzle Index. Douglas M. Hershey. LC 81-3591. (Illus.). 192p. 1981. pap. 7.95 (ISBN 0-498-02557-8). A S Barnes.
Ultimate Defense: A Practical Plan to Prevent Man's Self-Destruction. Frederic F. Clair. LC 59-6490. 157p. 1959. 5.95 (ISBN 0-8048-7019-5). C E Tuttle.
Ultimate Dessert Book. Linda Lewis. (Illus.). Date not set. 12.95 (ISBN 0-394-41276-1). Random.
Ultimate Destination. W. Norman Cooper. 95p. 1980. 7.50 (ISBN 0-87516-413-7); pap. 4.50 (ISBN 0-87516-381-5). DeVorss.
Ultimate Deterrent: Foundations of U. S.-U. S. S. R. Security under Stable Competition. William G. Shepherd. LC 86-20486. 147p. 1986. lib. bdg. 35.00 (ISBN 0-275-92368-1, C2368). Praeger.
Ultimate Dilemma: Obligation Conflicts in Wartime. C. Ashford Baker. LC 87-10736. 156p. 1988. lib. bdg. 21.50 (ISBN 0-8191-6500-X). U Pr of Amer.
Ultimate Enemy. Fred Saberhagen. (Berserkers! Ser.). 240p. (Orig.). 1988. pap. 2.95 (ISBN 0-671-65414-4). Baen Bks.
Ultimate Enemy: British Intelligence & Nazi Germany, 1933-1939. Wesley K. Wark. LC 85-4685. (Cornell Studies in Security Affairs). 336p. 1985. 32.50x (ISBN 0-8014-1821-6). Cornell U Pr.
Ultimate Entrepreneur: The Story of Ken Olsen & Digital Equipment Corporation. Glen Rifkin & George Harrar. 320p. 1988. 19.95 (ISBN 0-8092-4559-0). Contemp Bks.
Ultimate Evil. Maury Terry. 608p. 1988. pap. 4.95 (ISBN 0-553-27601-8). Bantam.
Ultimate Evil: An Investigation into America's Most Dangerous Satanic Cult. Maury Terry. LC 86-29203. (Illus.). 528p. 1987. pap. 17.95 (ISBN 0-385-23452-X, Dolp). Doubleday.
Ultimate Fake Book, Vol. 2. (Fake Bk.). 823p. 1985. plastic comb 29.95 (ISBN 0-88188-344-1). H Leonard Pub Corp.
Ultimate Fate of the Universe. Jumal N. Islam. LC 82-14558. 150p. 1983. 15.95 (ISBN 0-521-24814-0). Cambridge U Pr.
Ultimate Fitness Book: Physical Fitness Forever. Charles Corbin & Ruth Lindsey. LC 84-47519. (Illus.). 272p. 1984. pap. 12.95 (ISBN 0-88011-232-8, PCOR0232). Leisure Pr.
Ultimate Football Quiz Book. R. Etheredge & W. Etheredge. 1988. pap. 2.95 (ISBN 0-451-15774-5, Sig). NAL.
Ultimate Frontier. rev. & expanded ed. Eklal Kueshana. (Illus.). 1984. pap. 6.95 (ISBN 0-9600308-1-6). Stelle.
Ultimate: Fundamentals of the Sport. Irv Kalb & Tom Kennedy. LC 81-90610. (Illus.). 104p. (Orig.). 1982. pap. 7.95. Rev Pubns.
Ultimate Game. Ralph Glendinning. 1981. 13.95 (ISBN 0-671-42016-X, Wyndham Bks). S&S.
Ultimate Game. Tom Zito. Date not set. price not set (ISBN 0-393-01916-0). Norton.
Ultimate Game: The Rise & Fall of Bhagwan Shree. Kate Strelley. 1987. 17.95i (ISBN 0-06-250821-0). Har-Row.
Ultimate Goals of Israel's World Policies, 2 vols. Isaac Waterman. (Illus.). 117p. 1983. 175.45 (ISBN 0-86722-017-1). Inst Econ Pol.
Ultimate Good Luck. Richard Ford. (Vintage Contemporaries Ser.). 1987. pap. 5.95 (ISBN 0-394-75089-6, Vin). Random.
Ultimate Guide to Residential Real Estate Loans. Andrew J. McLean. 1989. pap. 12.95 (ISBN 0-471-61713-X). Wiley.
Ultimate Guide to Winning Scrabble. Michael Lawrence & John Ozag. 192p. (Orig.). 1987. pap. 8.95 (ISBN 0-553-34306-8). Bantam.
Ultimate Healing System. Don Lepore. 1987. 29.95 (ISBN 0-913923-57-5); pap. 19.95 (ISBN 0-913923-63-X). Woodland UT.
Ultimate Heat Sink & Directly Associated Heat Transport Systems for Nuclear Power Plants: A Safety Guide. (Safety Ser.: No. 50-SG-D6). (Illus.). 62p. 1981. pap. 12.25 (ISBN 92-0-123581-X, ISP581, IAEA). UNIPUB.
Ultimate Hollywood Trivia Quiz. Karen Warner & Michael Iapoce. LC 86-2428. (Illus.). 240p. (Orig.). 1986. pap. 7.95 (ISBN 0-89286-263-7). One Hund One Prods.
Ultimate in Sports. Edgar Phillips. 32p. 1982. pap. write for info. (ISBN 0-9608576-1-3). Busn Pro Bks.
Ultimate Insiders: U. S. Senators in the National Media. Stephen Hess. LC 85-48177. 151p. 1986. 22.95 (ISBN 0-8157-3598-7); pap. 8.95 (ISBN 0-8157-3597-9). Brookings.
Ultimate Issue. George Markstein. 336p. (Orig.). 1982. pap. 2.75 (ISBN 0-345-29031-3). Ballantine.
Ultimate Kick. Bill Wallace. LC 86-51504. 230p. (Orig.). 1987. pap. 11.50 (ISBN 0-86568-088-4, 406). Unique Pubns.
Ultimate Kid. Jeff Goelitz. 145p. 1986. 8.95 (ISBN 0-916438-61-9). Univ of Trees.
Ultimate Kingdom. 2nd ed. Earl Paulk. 264p. (Orig.). 1987. pap. 7.95 (ISBN 0-917595-13-0). K-Dimension.
Ultimate Kingdom see Ultimo Reino.
Ultimate L. A. Food Guide: Shopping for Quality Ingredients & Prepared Foods. LC 83-9262. 220p. 1983. pap. 7.95 (ISBN 0-87477-269-9). J P Tarcher.
Ultimate Lawyers Joke Book. Larry Wilde. 192p. 1987. pap. 2.95 (ISBN 0-553-26736-1). Bantam.
Ultimate Load Design of Concrete Structures. 104p. 1964. 16.00 (ISBN 0-901948-64-0, Pub. by T Telford UK). Am Soc Civil Eng.
Ultimate Load Design of Continuous Concrete Beams. Derrick Beckett. LC 67-31269. pap. 31.50 (ISBN 0-317-08608-1, 2020707). Bks Demand UMI.
Ultimate Load Test of a Segmentally Constructed Prestressed Concrete I-Beam. (PCI Journal Reprints Ser.). 16p. pap. 5.00 (ISBN 0-686-40065-8, JR146). Prestressed Concrete.
Ultimate Loss: Coping with the Death of a Child. Joan W. Bordow. LC 81-18182. 192p. 1982. 12.95 (ISBN 0-8253-0091-6). Beaufort Bks NY.
Ultimate Martial Art: Renbukai, Vol. II. Ronald L. Marchini. 144p. 1982. pap. 7.95 (ISBN 0-940522-01-2). ROMARC Inc.
Ultimate Martial Art: Renbukai, Vol. III. Ronald L. Marchini. 152p. 1982. pap. 7.95 (ISBN 0-940522-02-0). ROMARC Inc.
Ultimate Martial Art: Renbukai, Vol. 1. Ronald L. Marchini. 128p. (Orig.). 1981. pap. 6.95 (ISBN 0-940522-00-4). ROMARC Inc.
Ultimate MASH Quiz Book. Kevin John. lib. bdg. 20.95 (ISBN 0-89190-814-5, Pub. by Am Repr); pap. 10.95 (ISBN 0-89190-747-5). Amereon Ltd.
Ultimate Meaning of Jules De Gaultier. Gerald M. Spring. LC 74-30744. 80p. 1975. 5.95 (ISBN 0-8022-2161-0). Philos Lib.
Ultimate Monkees Trivia Book. Ellen L. Puerzer. 142p. (Orig.). 1987. pap. 9.95 (ISBN 0-9618809-0-2). Puerzer Pub.
Ultimate New York Yankee Record Book. Walter LeConte. (Illus.). 240p. 1984. pap. 12.95 (ISBN 0-88011-231-X). Scribner.
Ultimate Officers Cookbook. C. I. Nightingdale. (Illus.). 160p. (Orig.). 1988. lib. bdg. 14.95 (ISBN 0-9620210-0-8). C I Nightingdale.
Ultimate Official Jewish Joke Book. Larry Wilde. 192p. (Orig.). 1986. pap. 2.95 (ISBN 0-553-26227-0). Bantam.
Ultimate Opera Quiz Book. Kenn Harris. (Illus.). 256p. 1982. pap. 7.95 (ISBN 0-14-005884-2). Penguin.
Ultimate Paper Airplane. Richard Kline & Floyd Fogelman. 1985. pap. 8.95 (ISBN 0-671-55551-0). S&S.
Ultimate Peanut Butter Cookbook. Arthur Boze. 128p. 1987. 6.95 (ISBN 0-940481-01-4); lib. bdg. 6.95 (ISBN 0-940481-02-2); pap. 4.95 (ISBN 0-940481-00-6). Hillcrest Pub.
Ultimate Penalties: Capital Punishment, Life Imprisonment, Physical Torture. Leon S. Sheleff. LC 87-5553. 492p. 1987. 27.50 (ISBN 0-8142-0436-8). Ohio St U Pr.
Ultimate Personal Success Programme. Victor Dunstan. 1986. 39.00x (ISBN 0-317-54485-3, Pub. by Megiddo Pr Cardiff). State Mutual Bk.
Ultimate Pipe Book. Richard C. Hacker. LC 84-72427. (Illus.). 305p. 1984. 18.95 (ISBN 0-931253-00-4). Autumngold Pub.
Ultimate Pleasure. Marc Meshorer & Judith Meshorer. 256p. 1987. pap. 4.50 (ISBN 0-451-15095-3, Sig). NAL.
Ultimate Pleasure: The Secrets of Easily Orgasmic Women. Marc Meshorer & Judith Meshorer. 272p. 1986. 15.95 (ISBN 0-312-82826-8). St Martin.
Ultimate Porno. PierNico Solinas. LC 80-69871. 1981. 15.95 (ISBN 0-938112-00-7). Eyecontact.
Ultimate Priority. John MacArthur, Jr. 1983. pap. 6.95 (ISBN 0-8024-0186-4). Moody.
Ultimate Purpose & Fundamental Principles of Life. Josef G. Lowder. LC 85-701. (What in the World Are You Doing with Your Life Ser.: No. 1). 72p. 9.95 (ISBN 0-935597-00-X); pap. 3.95 (ISBN 0-935597-01-8); software diskette 9.95 (ISBN 0-935597-04-2). Comm Architects.
Ultimate Questions. John Blanchard. pap. 1.50 (ISBN 0-87552-764-7, Pub. by Evangel Pr UK); pap. 12.50 set of 10 (ISBN 0-317-65339-3). Presby & Reformed.
Ultimate Questions: A Theological Primer. Clyde R. Crews. 176p. 1986. pap. 6.95 (ISBN 0-8091-2774-1). Paulist Pr.
Ultimate Questions: An Anthology of Modern Russian Religious Thought. Ed. by Alexander Schmemann. 310p. 1977. pap. 9.95 (ISBN 0-913836-46-X). St Vladimirs.
Ultimate Reality. Hugh M. Woodman. LC 84-90244. 145p. 1985. 10.95 (ISBN 0-533-06292-6). Vantage.
Ultimate Reality & Spiritual Discipline. Ed. by James P. Duerlinger. (God Ser.). 237p. (Orig.). 1984. text ed. 22.95 (ISBN 0-913757-09-8, Pub. by New Era Bks); pap. text ed. 12.95 (ISBN 0-913757-08-X, Pub. by New Era Bks). Paragon Hse.
Ultimate Relationship. Dora Panorelli. 1987. 8.95 (ISBN 0-8062-2454-1). Carlton.
Ultimate Resource. Julian L. Simon. LC 80-8575. 336p. 1982. pap. 9.95 (ISBN 0-691-00369-6). Princeton U Pr.
Ultimate Rip-Off: A Taxing Tale. Iris W. Collett. LC 87-83032. 1988. pap. 9.95 (ISBN 0-913878-39-1). T Horton & Dghts.
Ultimate Ripoff. Bill Stringfellow. LC 81-49329. 176p. 1981. pap. 3.95 (ISBN 0-939286-00-9). Concerned Pubns.
Ultimate Roots: Readings in Physical Anthropology. J. Mavalwala. 240p. 1984. pap. text ed. 16.50 (ISBN 0-8403-3474-5). Kendall-Hunt.
Ultimate Salad Dressing Book. Claire Stancer. (Illus.). 1989. pap. 12.95 (ISBN 0-07-549598-8). McGraw.
Ultimate Sandwich Book: With Over 700 Delicious Sandwich Creations. Louis P. De Gouy et al. LC 82-537. (Illus.). 160p. 1982. lib. bdg. 15.90 (ISBN 0-89471-163-6); pap. 6.95 (ISBN 0-89471-164-4). Running Pr.
Ultimate Secret. John Taylor. 1987. text ed. 25.00x (ISBN 0-566-05193-1, Pub. by Gower Pub England). Gower Pub Co.
Ultimate Secret to Getting Absolutely Everything You Want. Mike Hernacki. Ed. by Sallye Levanthal. 112p. (Orig.). 1988. pap. 3.50 (ISBN 0-425-10686-1). Berkley Pub.
Ultimate Secrets of Total Self-Confidence. Robert Anthony. 240p. 1987. pap. 3.50 (ISBN 0-425-09143-0). Berkley Pub.
Ultimate Seduction. Madeline Harper. (Temptation Ser.: No. 165). 224p. Date not set. pap. 2.25 (ISBN 0-317-63859-9). Harlequin Bks.
Ultimate Series Love & Wedding. (Piano-Vocal-Guitar Ser.). 295p. 1985. perfect bound 14.95 (ISBN 0-88188-365-4); plastic comb 17.95 (ISBN 0-88188-366-2). H Leonard Pub Corp.
Ultimate Sex. Linda Du Breuil. 1976. pap. 1.50 (ISBN 0-8439-0347-3, Leisure Bks). Leisure NY.
Ultimate Shopper's Catalogue. Elena dela Iglesia. LC 86-45089. 288p. (Orig.). 1987. 18.45i (ISBN 0-06-055017-1, HarpT). Har-Row.
Ultimate Skateboard Book. Albert Cassorla. (Illus.). 128p. (Orig.). (YA) (gr. 6 up). 1988. PLB 19.80 (ISBN 0-89471-565-8); pap. 8.95 (ISBN 0-89471-564-X). Running Pr.
Ultimate Solution. Eric Norden. (Gryphon Special Edition Ser.). (Illus.). 144p. Date not set. pap. 9.95 (ISBN 0-936071-03-6). Gryphon Pubns.
Ultimate Solution of the American Negro Problem. Edward Eggleston. LC 78-144604. Repr. of 1913 ed. 22.50 (ISBN 0-404-00155-6). AMS Pr.
Ultimate Soyfoods Cookbook. Richard Leviton. LC 83-47675. 250p. Date not set. pap. 15.95 (ISBN 0-87983-340-8). Keats.
Ultimate Sports Nutrition: A Scientific Approach to Peak Athletic Performance. Fred Hatfield. (Illus.). 192p. (Orig.). 1987. pap. 11.95 (ISBN 0-8092-4887-5). Contemp Bks.
Ultimate Stranger: The Autistic Child. rev. ed. Carl H. Delacato. 240p. 1984. pap. 9.00 (ISBN 0-87879-446-8, 446-8, Arena Press). Acad Therapy.
Ultimate Strength Design of Reinforced Concrete Columns. 50p. 1969. pap. 4.00 (ISBN 0-89312-124-X, EB009D). Portland Cement.
Ultimate Student Handbook. Steve Lawhead & Alice Lawhead. LC 83-71749. 248p. 1984. pap. 7.95 (ISBN 0-89107-297-7, Crossway Bks). Good News.
Ultimate Tax Book. David Ingram. 192p. (Orig.). 1988. pap. text ed. 12.95 (ISBN 0-88839-208-7). Hancock House.
Ultimate Tennis: The Pleasure Game. Al Secunda. LC 84-15107. 320p. 1984. 21.95 (ISBN 0-13-935438-7); pap. 14.95 (ISBN 0-13-935420-4). P-H.
Ultimate Terror. Gar Wilson. (Phoenix Force Ser.: No. 9). 192p. 1984. pap. 2.25 (ISBN 0-373-61309-1, Pub. by Worldwide). Harlequin Bks.
Ultimate Transformation. 2nd ed. R. P. Kaushik. LC 77-85215. 1977. 8.95 (ISBN 0-918038-05-7); pap. 5.95 (ISBN 0-918038-04-9). Journey Pubns.

Ultimate Travel Journal. F. Michael & Irene Sisavic. LC 87-81868. 128p. (Orig.). 1987. 19.95 (ISBN 0-9619093-1-5); deluxe ed. 44.95 (ISBN 0-9619093-2-3); pap. 9.95 (ISBN 0-9619093-0-7). Florian Group.

Ultimate Tyranny: The Majority Over the Majority. Eugene McCarthy. LC 79-3530. 256p. 1980. 12.95 (ISBN 0-15-192581-X). HarBraceJ.

Ultimate View: The Himalayan Journeys of Samuel Bourne (1863-1866) Clark Worswick. (Illus.). 152p. (Orig.). 1983. 55.00 (ISBN 0-940492-05-9). Asian Conserv Lab.

Ultimate Weapon. Marco Lalla. (Illus.). 95p. (Orig.). 1987. pap. 12.95 (ISBN 0-939427-82-6, 05052). Alpha Pubns OH.

Ultimate Weapon. Anne Walters. 1966. pap. 1.00x (ISBN 0-88020-076-6). Coach Hse.

Ultimate Wood Block Book: Castles, Bridges & Other Engineering Marvels. Sam Bingham. (Illus.). 176p. (Orig.). 1988. pap. 12.95 (ISBN 0-8069-6662-9). Sterling.

Ultimate Workout Journal (for Nautilus Enthusiasts) A Personal Workout Guide. 2nd ed. Joseph Mullen. 150p. 1986. 12.95 (ISBN 0-935783-03-2). Fitness Ctr Info.

Ultimate World Series Quiz Book. Dom Forker. 1982. pap. 2.50 (ISBN 0-451-11788-3, AJ1788, Sig). NAL.

Ultimately Fiction: Design in Modern American Literary Biography. Dennis W. Petrie. LC 80-84578. 250p. 1981. 10.95 (ISBN 0-911198-62-8). Purdue U Pr.

Ultimatum: PU 94. Uri Dan & Peter Mann. 1977. pap. 1.95 (ISBN 0-8439-0523-9, Leisure Bks). Leisure NY.

Ultimax Man. Keith Laumer. 1987. pap. 2.95 (ISBN 0-671-65652-X). Baen Bks.

Ultimo Giorno di Pomoei & Excerpts from Niobe, Vol. 32. Giovanni Pacini. (Italian Opera II Ser.). 315p. 1985. lib. bdg. 85.00 (ISBN 0-8240-6581-6). Garland Pub.

Ultimo Reino. Earl Paulk. Orig. Title: Ultimate Kingdom. 268p. (Orig., Span.). 1987. pap. 3.50 (ISBN 0-917595-19-X). K-Dimension.

Ultra & Mediterranean Strategy. Ralph Bennett. (Illus.). 352p. Date not set. 19.95 (ISBN 0-688-08175-4). Morrow.

Ultra & the History of the United States. LC 80-52057. 224p. 1981. 27.00 (ISBN 0-89093-245-X). U Pubns Amer.

Ultra Deadly. Neil Randall. LC 87-51355. (Sniper! Gamebook Ser.). (Illus.). 192p. (Orig.). (YA) (gr. 7-12). 1988. pap. 2.95 (ISBN 0-88038-549-9). TSR Inc.

Ultra-Fashionable Peerage of America. facsimile ed. Charle W. De Lyon Nichols. LC 75-1864. (Leisure Class in America Ser.). 1975. Repr. of 1904 ed. 13.00x (ISBN 0-405-06930-8). Ayer Co Pubs.

Ultra Fiche. write for info. West Pub.

Ultra Function Plot. John Losse. 50p. 1982. pap. text ed. 15.95 (ISBN 0-930182-31-6). Avant Garde Pub.

Ultra Guitar Method: Arpeggios, Vol. 4. Michael E. Fletcher. (Illus.). 65p. (Orig.). 1988. pap. text ed. 19.95 (ISBN 0-943355-03-6). Ultra Guitar Pubns.

Ultra Guitar Method: Minor Key Signatures, Vol. 5. Michael E. Fletcher. (Illus.). 65p. (Orig.). 1988. pap. text ed. 19.95 (ISBN 0-943355-04-4). Ultra Guitar Pubns.

Ultra Guitar Method: Progressions, Vol. 2. Michael E. Fletcher. (Illus.). 65p. (Orig.). 1988. pap. text ed. 19.95 (ISBN 0-943355-01-X). Ultra Guitar Pubns.

Ultra Guitar Method: The Power of Pentatonics & Substitution Principles, Vol. 3. Ed. by Michael E. Fletcher. (Illus.). 65p. (Orig.). 1988. pap. text ed. 19.95 (ISBN 0-943355-02-8). Ultra Guitar Pubns.

Ultra Guitar Method: Unlocking the Fingerboard, Vol. 1. Michael E. Fletcher. (Illus.). 63p. (Orig.). 1986. pap. text ed. 19.95 (ISBN 0-943355-00-1). Ultra Guitar Pubns.

Ultra-High Modulus Polymers. Ed. by A. Ciferri & I. M. Ward. (Illus.). 362p. 1979. 83.00 (ISBN 0-85334-800-6, Pub. by Elsevier Applied Sci England). Elsevier.

Ultra-High Pressure Equipment & Techniques Mainly for Synthesizing Diamond & Cubic Boron Nitride. W. Johnson & A. G. Mamalis. 1979. 28.00 (ISBN 3-18-143702-6, Pub. by VDI W Germany). IPS.

Ultra-High-Sensitivity Mass Spectrometry with Accelerators. Ed. by A. E. Litherland et al. (Illus.). 200p. 1987. text ed. 82.00x (ISBN 0-85403-323-8, Pub. by Royal Soc London). Scholium Intl.

Ultra High Strength Materials. K. Friedrich et al. Ed. by E. Hornbogen. (Progress Report of the VDI-Z Ser.: No. 82). 125p. 1984. pap. 38.00 cancelled (ISBN 3-18-148205-6, Pub. by VDI Verlag Gmbh Dusseldorf). IPS.

Ultra-high Vacuum Practice. G. F. Weston. (Illus.). 304p. 1985. text ed. 95.00 (ISBN 0-408-01485-7). Butterworth.

Ultra Large Scale Integrated Microelectronics. David K. Ferry et al. (Illus.). 256p. 1988. text ed. 50.00 (ISBN 0-13-935735-1). P-H.

Ultra-lite Stealhead Fishing. Ralph F. Quinn. LC 85-30586. (Illus.). 180p. (Orig.). 1986. pap. 12.95 (ISBN 0-934802-26-2). ICS Bks.

Ultra, Magic & the Allies. Ed. by John Mendelsohn. (Covert Warfare Ser.). 320p. 1987. lib. bdg. 60.00 (ISBN 0-8240-7950-7). Garland Pub.

Ultra Plot: Complete Mailing. Don Jones. (Label & Filing System Interface Ser.). (Illus.). 50p. 1981. 19.95 (ISBN 0-930182-23-5). Avant-Garde Pub.

Ultra Ripped Abs. Robert Kennedy. LC 87-10124. (Musclebuilder's Body Part Ser.). (Illus.). 128p. (Orig.). 1987. pap. 7.95 (ISBN 0-8069-6416-2). Sterling.

Ultra-Royalism & the French Restoration. Nora E. Hudson. LC 73-670. 209p. 1973. Repr. of 1936 ed. lib. bdg. 17.00x (ISBN 0-374-94027-4, Octagon). Hippocrene Bks.

Ultra Secret. F. W. Winterbotham. 288p. 1975. pap. 3.25 (ISBN 0-440-19061-4). Dell.

Ultra-Short Laser Pulses. D. J. Bradley et al. (Phil. Strans. Ser. A: Vol. 298). (Illus.). 204p. 1981. text ed. 60.00x (ISBN 0-85403-147-2, Pub. by Royal Soc London). Scholium Intl.

Ultra-Solutions: How to Fail Most Successfully. Paul Watzlawick. 1988. 12.95 (ISBN 0-393-02514-4). Norton.

Ultracytochemistry of Intracellular Membrane Glycoconjugates. W. F. Neiss. (Advances in Anatomy, Embryology & Cell Biology Ser.: Vol. 99). 100p. 1986. pap. 35.80 (ISBN 0-387-16726-9). Springer-Verlag.

Ultradian Rhythms in Physiology & Behavior. Ed. by H. Schulz & P. Lavie. LC 85-17241. (Experimental Brain Research Series: Suppl. 12). (Illus.). 350p. 1985. 34.50 (ISBN 0-387-15439-6). Springer-Verlag.

Ultrafast Laser Probe Phenomena in Bulk & Microstructure Semiconductors. Ed. by Alfano. 200p. 1987. 43.00 (ISBN 0-89252-828-1, 793). SPIE.

Ultrafast Laser Probe Phenomena in Bulk & Microstructure Semiconductors, No. II. Ed. by Alfano. 1988. 50.00 (ISBN 0-89252-977-6, 942). SPIE.

Ultrafast Phenomena IV. Ed. by D. H. Auston & K. B. Eisenthal. (Chemical Physics Ser.: Vol. 38). (Illus.). xvi, 509p. 1984. 45.00 (ISBN 0-387-13834-X). Springer-Verlag.

Ultrafast Phenomena V, Vol. 46. Ed. by G. R. Fleming & A. E. Siegman. (Chemical Physics Ser.). (Illus.). 575p. 1986. 49.00 (ISBN 0-387-17077-4). Springer-Verlag.

Ultrafiltration & Reverse Osmosis Food Processing Applications. N. W. Hurst & J. Mann. 250p. 1986. lib. bdg. write for info. (ISBN 0-89573-402-8). VCH Pubs.

Ultrafiltration Handbook. Munir Cheryan. LC 86-50330. 369p. 1986. 65.00 (ISBN 0-87762-456-9). Technomic.

Ultrafiltration Membranes & Applications. Ed. by Anthony R. Cooper. LC 80-18685. (Polymer Science & Technology Ser.: Vol. 13). 724p. 1981. 105.00x (ISBN 0-306-40548-2, Plenum Pr). Plenum Pub.

Ultrafine Grinding & Separation of Industrial Minerals. Subhas G. Malaghan. LC 83-82078. 177p. 1983. pap. 15.00x (ISBN 0-89520-419-3, 419-3). Soc Mining Eng.

Ultrafine Particles. Symposium on Ultrafine Particles Indianapolis, 1961. Ed. by W. E. Kuhn. LC 63-20239. (Electrochemical Society Ser.). pap. 143.50 (ISBN 0-317-11065-9, 2007076). Bks Demand UMI.

Ultrahigh Resolution Chromatography. Ed. by Satinder Ahuja. LC 84-2792. (ACS Symposium Ser.: No. 250). 231p. 1984. lib. bdg. 44.95x (ISBN 0-8412-0835-2). Am Chemical.

Ultralight Accessory Book. Hal Adkins. (Illus.). 224p. 1986. pap. 13.95 (ISBN 0-8306-2388-4, 2388). TAB Bks.

Ultralight Aircraft Log. 1981. leatherette 3.95 (ISBN 0-317-01150-2, A-1). Ultralight Pubns.

Ultralight Aircraft: The Basic Handbook Aviation Ser. Michael A. Markowski. LC 82-60021. (No. 1). (Illus.). 288p. (Orig.). 1981. 21.95 (ISBN 0-938716-01-8); pap. 14.95 (ISBN 0-938716-00-X). Ultralight Pubns.

Ultralight Aircraft: The Basic Handbook of Ultralight Aviation. 3rd, rev. ed. Michael A. Markowski. LC 83-50244. (Ultralight Aviation Ser.: No. 1). (Illus., Orig.). 1983. pap. 15.95 (ISBN 0-938716-16-6). Ultralight Pubns.

Ultralight Airman's Manual. Ben Millspaugh. (Illus.). 160p. 1987. pap. 14.95 (ISBN 0-8306-2391-4, NO. 2391). TAB Bks.

Ultralight Airmanship: How to Master the Air in an Ultralight. Jack Lambie. Ed. by Michael A. Markowski. LC 81-71888. (Ultralight Aviation Ser.: No. 2). (Illus., Orig.). 1984. 17.95 (ISBN 0-938716-03-4); pap. 10.95 (ISBN 0-938716-02-6). Ultralight Pubns.

Ultralight Boatbuilding. Tom Hill. (Illus.). 160p. 1987. pap. 19.95 (ISBN 0-87742-244-3). Intl Marine.

Ultralight Engine Log. 1981. leatherette 3.95 (ISBN 0-317-01151-0, E-1). Ultralight Pubns.

Ultralight Flight: The Pilot's Handbook of Ultralight Knowledge. Michael A. Markowski. LC 81-71889. (Ultralight Aviation Ser.: No. 3). (Illus.). 206p. (Orig.). 1984. 20.95 (ISBN 0-938716-07-7); pap. 13.95 (ISBN 0-938716-06-9). Ultralight Pubns.

Ultralight Flying for the Private Pilot. Joe Christy. (Illus.). 192p. 1985. pap. 12.95 (ISBN 0-8306-2382-5, 2382P). TAB Bks.

Ultralight Pilot Flight Log. 1981. leatherette 3.95 (ISBN 0-317-01149-9, P-1). Ultralight Pubns.

Ultralight Technique: How to Fly & Navigate Ultralight Air Vehicles. Michael A. Markowski. LC 83-50057. (Ultralight Aviation Ser.: No. 5). (Illus., Orig.). 1983. pap. 14.95 (ISBN 0-938716-12-3). Ultralight Pubns.

Ultralights. James E. Mrazek & James E. Mrazek, Jr. (Illus.). 215p. 1982. cancelled (ISBN 0-312-82852-7). St Martin.

Ultralights: The Flying Featherweights. Charles I. Coombs. LC 83-17411. (Illus.). 160p. (gr. 5 up). 1984. 11.75 (ISBN 0-688-02775-X). Morrow.

Ultramafic & Related Rocks. Ed. by Peter J. Wyllie. LC 78-12080. 484p. (Orig.). 1979. Repr. of 1967 ed. 37.50 (ISBN 0-88275-755-5). Krieger.

Ultraman - All Monsters. (Champion Graphic Ser.). (Illus.). 1984. 6.95 (ISBN 0-318-02756-9). Bks Nippan.

Ultramarathoning: The Next Challenge. Tom Osler & Ed Dodd. LC 78-68612. (Illus.). 240p. 1980. 14.95 (ISBN 0-89037-169-5). Anderson World.

Ultramarathons: The World's Most Punishing Races. Nathan Aaseng. (Sports Talk Ser.). (Illus.). 72p. (gr. 4 up). 1987. PLB 8.95 (ISBN 0-8225-1534-2). Lerner Pubns.

Ultramarine. Raymond Carver. LC 86-10221. 128p. 1986. 14.95 (ISBN 0-394-55379-9). Random.

Ultramarine. Raymond Carver. LC 87-40081. 160p. 1987. pap. 6.95 (ISBN 0-394-75535-9, Vin). Random.

Ultramarine. Malcolm Lowry. 203p. 1986. pap. 7.95 (ISBN 0-88184-258-3). Carroll & Graf.

Ultramicroelectrodes. Martin Fleischmann et al. (Illus.). 363p. 1987. 44.95 (ISBN 0-9618927-0-6). Datatech Systems.

Ultramicroelectrodes. Martin Fleischmann et al. (Illus.). 363p. 1988. lib. bdg. 44.95 (ISBN 0-9618927-1-4). Datatech Systems.

Ultramicrotomy. Ed. by Norma Reid. (Practical Methods in Electron Microscopy Ser.: Vol. 3, Pt. 2). 353p. 1975. pap. text ed. 17.75 (ISBN 0-444-10667-7, North-Holland). Elsevier.

Ultraprecision in Manufacturing Engineering. Ed. by M. Weck & R. Hartel. (Illus.). 364p. 1988. 83.50 (ISBN 0-387-19241-7). Springer-Verlag.

Ultraprecision Machining & Automated Fabrication of Optics. Ed. by Decker. 172p. 1986. 43.00 (ISBN 0-89252-711-0, 676). SPIE.

Ultrapurity: Methods & Techniques. Ed. by Morris Zief et al. LC 72-179387. (Illus.). pap. 160.00 (ISBN 0-317-07978-6, 2055009). Bks Demand UMI.

Ultrarelativistic Heavy Ion Collisions. Baym & McLerran. 352p. 1988. 43.25 (ISBN 0-201-15670-9). Addison-Wesley.

Ultras in the U. S. A. V. Nikitin. 349p. 1981. 7.00 (ISBN 0-8285-2142-5, Pub. by Progress Pubs USSR). Imported Pubns.

Ultrasensitive Laser Spectroscopy. Ed. by David S. Kliger. LC 82-18417. (Quantum Electronics Ser.). 1983. 65.50 (ISBN 0-12-414980-4). Acad Pr.

Ultrashort Laser Pulses & Applications. Ed. by W. Kaiser. (Topics in Applied Physics Ser.: Vol. 60). (Illus.). 440p. 1988. 87.50 (ISBN 0-387-18605-0). Springer-Verlag.

Ultrashort Pulse Spectroscopy & Applications. Ed. by M. J. Soileau. 164p. 1985. 43.00 (ISBN 0-89252-568-1, 533). SPIE.

Ultrasoft X-Ray Microscopy: Its Application to Biological & Physical Sciences. Ed. by Donald F. Parsons. (Annals of the New York Academy of Sciences: Vol. 342). 402p. 1980. 72.00x (ISBN 0-89766-066-8); pap. 72.00x (ISBN 0-89766-067-6). NY Acad Sci.

Ultrasonic Absorption: An Introduction to the Theory of Sound Absorption & Dispersion in Gases, Liquids & Solids. A. B. Bhatia. 440p. 1985. pap. 9.95 (ISBN 0-486-64917-2). Dover.

Ultrasonic Bioinstrumentation. Douglas Christenson. 240p. 1988. write for info. (ISBN 0-471-60496-8); solutions manual avail. Wiley.

Ultrasonic Diagnosis: Index of Modern Information. Carl L. Rossi. LC 88-47847. 150p. 1988. 34.50 (ISBN 0-88164-964-3); pap. 26.50 (ISBN 0-88164-965-1). ABBE Pubs Assn.

Ultrasonic Diagnosis: Medical Subject Analysis with Bibliography. Marvin N. Seymour. LC 87-47616. 160p. 1987. 34.50 (ISBN 0-88164-526-5); pap. 26.50 (ISBN 0-88164-527-3). ABBE Pubs Assn.

Ultrasonic Diagnosis of Cerebrovascular Disease. Ed. by Merrill P. Spencer. (Developments in Cardiovascular Medicine Ser.). 1987. lib. bdg. 79.50 (ISBN 0-89838-836-8, Pub. by Martinus Nijhoff Netherlands). Kluwer Academic.

Ultrasonic Diagnosis of Ectopic Pregnancy. Nabil F. Maklad. 260p. (Orig.). 1988. 27.50 (ISBN 0-87527-222-3). Green.

Ultrasonic Differential Diagnosis of Tumors. Ed. by George Kossoff & Morimuchi Fukuda. LC 83-174. (Illus.). 315p. 1984. 65.00 (ISBN 0-89640-093-X). Igaku-Shoin.

Ultrasonic Energy: Biological Investigations & Medical Applications. Ed. by Elizabeth Kelly. LC 65-10078. (Illus.). Repr. of 1965 ed. 99.00 (ISBN 0-8357-9701-5, 2019048). Bks Demand UMI.

Ultrasonic Fatigue. Ed. by Joseph M. Wells et al. LC 82-61407. (Illus.). 660p. 1982. 10.00 (ISBN 0-89520-397-9). Metal Soc.

Ultrasonic Inspection of Heavy Section Steel Components: The PISC II Final Report. Ed. by R. W. Nichols & S. Crutzen. 698p. 1988. 174.50 (ISBN 1-85166-155-7). Elsevier.

Ultrasonic Investigation of Mechanical Properties see Treatise on Materials Science.

Ultrasonic Measurements for Process Control: Theory, Techniques, Applications. Lawrence C. Lynnworth. 628p. 1988. price not set (ISBN 0-12-460585-0). Acad Pr.

Ultrasonic Methods in Evaluation of Inhomogeneous Materials. Ed. by Adriano Alippi & Walter G. Mayer. 1987. lib. bdg. 112.00 (ISBN 90-247-3490-8, Pub. by Martinus Nijhoff Netherlands). Kluwer Academic.

Ultrasonic Question & Answer Book C. 1980. member 19.50 (ISBN 0-318-21521-7, 2028); non-member 24.35. Am Soc Nondestructive.

Ultrasonic Scanning of the Kidneys. J. K. Kristensen. (Illus.). 256p. (Orig.). 1979. pap. text ed. 29.50x (ISBN 91-22-00282-0, Pub. by Almqvist & Wiksell). Coronet Bks.

Ultrasonic Sectional Anatomy. Ed. by Patricia Morley et al. LC 81-71720. (Illus.). 238p. 1983. text ed. 100.00 (ISBN 0-443-01690-9). Churchill.

Ultrasonic Spectral Analysis for Nondestructive Evaluation. Dale Fitting & Laszlo Adler. LC 80-14991. 364p. 1981. 69.50x (ISBN 0-306-40484-2, Plenum Pr). Plenum Pub.

Ultrasonic Testing, 3 Vols. (Programmed Instruction Handbooks). 903p. Set. member 40.00 (ISBN 0-318-17229-1, 1504); non-member 50.00 (ISBN 0-318-17230-5); of programmed instruction handbooks 155.00 set. Am Soc Nondestructive.

Ultrasonic Testing. 207p. member 11.00 (ISBN 0-318-17237-2, 1610); non-member 15.00. Am Soc Nondestructive.

Ultrasonic Testing of Materials. 3rd ed. Josef Krautkramer & Herbert Krautkramer. 600p. 1983. member 88.50 (ISBN 0-318-21482-2, 324); non-member 102.00. Am Soc Nondestructive.

Ultrasonic Testing of Steel Castings. 1976. 10.00 (ISBN 0-686-44985-1). Steel Founders.

Ultrasonic Tissue Characterization. Ed. by J. M. Thijsen & D. Nicholas. 1983. 34.50 (ISBN 90-247-2757-X, Pub. by Martinus Nijhoff Netherlands). Kluwer Academic.

Ultrasonic Tomography in Obstetrics & Gynaecology. E. G. Loch. (Advances in Obstetrics & Gynaecology Ser.: Vol. 51). (Illus.). 1973. 26.75 (ISBN 3-8055-1585-5). S Karger.

Ultrasonic Transducer Materials. Ed. by Oskar E. Mattiat. LC 71-131885. 186p. 1971. 45.00x (ISBN 0-306-30501-1, Plenum Pr). Plenum Pub.

Ultrasonic Transducers for Nondestructive Testing. Silk. 1984. 68.00x (ISBN 0-85274-436-6, Pub. by A Hilger UK). Taylor & Francis.

Ultrasonics. A. P. Cracknell. 200p. 1980. pap. 18.00x (ISBN 0-85109-770-7). Taylor & Francis.

Ultrasonics. A. P. Cracknell & J. L. Clark. LC 79-26250. (Wykeham Science Ser.: No. 55). 200p. 1980. pap. 18.00x (ISBN 0-8448-1330-3, Pub. by Crane Russak & Co). Taylor & Francis.

Ultrasonics. Woodcock. (Medical Physics Handbook: Vol. 1). 1979. 40.00x (ISBN 0-85274-506-0, Pub. by A Hilger UK). Taylor & Francis.

Ultrasonics as a Medical Diagnostic Tool. Ed. by J. I. DiStasio. LC 79-26029. (Radiology Review Ser.: No. 1). (Illus.). 330p. 1980. 32.00 (ISBN 0-8155-0785-2). Noyes.

Ultrasonics: Fundamentals, Technology, Application. 2nd, rev. & expanded ed. Ensminger. (Mechanical Engineering Ser.). 600p. 1988. 99.75 (ISBN 0-8247-7659-3). Dekker.

Ultrasonics in Early Pregnancy: Diagnostic Scanning & Fetal Motor Activity. E. Reinold. Ed. by P. J. Keller. (Contributions to Gynecology & Obstetrics Ser.: Vol. 1). 1976. 39.50 (ISBN 3-8055-2332-7). S Karger.

Ultrasonics in Medicine: Proceedings at Dubrovnik, May, 1981. Ed. by V. Latin. (International Congress Ser.: Vol. 547). 146p. 1981. pap. 34.25 (ISBN 0-444-90200-7, Excerpta Medica). Elsevier.

Ultrasonics in the Chemical Industry. Vladimir A. Nosov. LC 64-23248. (Soviet Progress in Applied Ultrasonics Ser.: Vol. 2). pap. 42.80 (ISBN 0-317-10629-5, 2020692). Bks Demand UMI.

Ultrasonics International, 1983. 680p. (Orig.). 1983. pap. text ed. 110.00 (ISBN 0-408-22163-1). Butterworth.

Ultrasonics International 87: Conference Proceeding. (Ultrasonics International Ser.). (Illus.). 968p. 1987. 195.00 (ISBN 0-408-02348-1). Butterworth.

Ultrasonics of Snow. Isobel Thrilling. 72p. 1985. 21.00x (ISBN 0-947612-09-2, Pub. by Rivelin Grapheme Pr). State Mutual Bk.

Ultrasonics: The Low & High-Intensity Applications. Dale Ensminger. LC 72-90963. (Illus.). pap. 146.80 (ISBN 0-317-07982-4, 2055005). Bks Demand UMI.

Ultrasonographic Diagnosis in Obstetrics & Gynecology. H. Schams & J. Bretscher. (Illus.). 230p. 1975. text ed. 48.00 (ISBN 0-387-07254-3). Springer-Verlag.

Ultrasonography: Basic Principles & Clinical Applications. Ross E. Brown. LC 72-13842. (Illus.). 320p. 1975. 28.50 (ISBN 0-87527-095-6). Green.

Ulysses & the Sirens: Studies in Rationality & Irrationality. Jon Elster. 330p. 1985. pap. 12.95 (ISBN 0-521-26984-9). Cambridge U Pr.
Ulysses Annotated. Don Gifford. 1988. 65.00x (ISBN 0-520-05639-6). U of Cal Pr.
Ulysses: "Circe": A Facsimile of Page Proofs for Episode 15. James Joyce. Ed. by Michael Groden. LC 77-14656. (James Joyce Archive Ser.). 1978. lib. bdg. 125.00 (ISBN 0-8240-2820-1). Garland Pub.
Ulysses: "Circe" & "Eumaeus": A Facsimile of Manuscripts & Typescripts for Episodes 15 (Part II) & 16. James Joyce. Ed. by Michael Groden. LC 77-11971. (James Joyce Archive Ser.). 1978. lib. bdg. 125.00 (ISBN 0-8240-2825-2). Garland Pub.
Ulysses: "Circe" & "Eumaeus". A Facsimile of Placards for Episodes 15-16. James Joyce. Ed. by Michael Groden. (James Joyce Archive Ser.). 125.00 (ISBN 0-8240-2814-7). Garland Pub.
Ulysses: "Cyclops" & "Nausicaa", & "Oxen of the Sun": a Facsimile of Page Proofs of Episode 12-14. James Joyce. Ed. by Michael Groden. LC 77-14655. (James Joyce Archive Ser.). 1978. lib. bdg. 125.00 (ISBN 0-8240-2819-8). Garland Pub.
Ulysses: "Eumaeus," "Ithaca," & "Penelope": A Facsimile of Page Proofs for Chapters 16-18. James Joyce. Ed. by Michael Groden. LC 77-14657. (James Joyce Archive Ser.). 1978. lib. bdg. 125.00 (ISBN 0-8240-2821-X). Garland Pub.
Ulysses Found. Ernie Bradford. (Century Classic Ser.). 238p. 1988. pap. 11.95 (ISBN 0-7126-0844-3, Pub. by Century Hutchinson). David & Charles.
Ulysses in Progress. Michael Groden. 256p. 1987. pap. text ed. 14.50x (ISBN 0-691-10215-5). Princeton U Pr.
Ulysses in Traction. Albert Innaurato. 1978. pap. 3.50x (ISBN 0-685-91028-8). Dramatists Play.
Ulysses: "Ithaca" & "Penelope." A Facsimile of Manuscripts & Typescripts for Episodes 17 & 18. Ed. by Michael Groden. LC 77-10882. (James Joyce Archive Ser.: Vol. 16). 1978. lib. bdg. 125.00 (ISBN 0-8240-2826-0). Garland Pub.
Ulysses Notes. Edward A. Kopper. (Orig.). 1981. pap. text ed. 3.95 (ISBN 0-8220-1315-0). Cliffs.
Ulysses: Notes & "Telemachus" - "Scylla" & "Charybdis": A Facsimile of Notes for the Book & Mauscripts for Episodes 1-9. James Joyce. Ed. by Michael Groden. LC 78-16032. (James Joyce Archive Ser.). 1978. lib. bdg. 125.00 (ISBN 0-8240-2822-8). Garland Pub.
Ulysses on the Liffey. Richard Ellmann. 1972. 21.95x (ISBN 0-19-519665-1); pap. 7.95 (ISBN 0-19-501663-7). Oxford U Pr.
Ulysses: "Oxen of the Sun," & "Circe": A Facsimile of Drafts, Manuscripts, & Typescripts 14 & 15 (Part 1) James Joyce. Ed. by Michael Groden. LC 77-22764. (James Joyce Archive Ser.). 1978. lib. bdg. 125.00 (ISBN 0-8240-2824-4). Garland Pub.
Ulysses S. Grant. Louis A. Coolidge. Ed. by John T. Morse, Jr. LC 75-128953. (American Statesmen: No. 32). Repr. of 1917 ed. 43.00 (ISBN 0-404-50894-4). AMS Pr.
Ulysses S. Grant. Ed. by Carol B. Fitzgerald. (Meckler's Bibliographies of the Presidents of the United States, 1789-1989 Ser.: No. 18). (Illus.). 1989. lib. bdg. 45.00x (ISBN 0-88736-132-3). Meckler Corp.
Ulysses S. Grant. Hamlin Garland. (Collected Works of Hamlin Garland). 1988. Repr. of 1898 ed. lib. bdg. 59.00x. Am Biog Serv.
Ulysses S. Grant. Herman J. Viola. (World Leaders--Past & Present Ser.). (Illus.). 112p. (gr. 5 up). Date not set. 16.95x (ISBN 0-317-62981-6). Chelsea Hse.
Ulysses S. Grant see Collected Works.
Ulysses S. Grant & the Period of National Preservation & Reconstruction. William C. Church. LC 73-14437. (Heroes of the Nation Ser.). Repr. of 1897 ed. 49.50 (ISBN 0-404-58255-9). AMS Pr.
Ulysses S. Grant, Eighteen Twenty-Two to Eighteen Eighty-Five: Chronology, Documents, Bibliographical Aids. P. Moran. LC 68-23568. (Presidential Chronology Ser: No. 6). 114p. 1968. 8.00 (ISBN 0-379-12056-9). Oceana.
Ulysses S. Grant: Essays & Documents. Ed. by David L. Wilson & John Y. Simon. LC 81-18246. (Illus.). 137p. 1981. 14.95x (ISBN 0-8093-1019-8). S Ill U Pr.
Ulysses S. Grant: 18th President of the United States. Lucille Falkof. Ed. by Richard G. Young. LC 87-32817. (Presidents of the United States Ser.). (Illus.). 128p. (gr. 5-9). PLB 12.95 (ISBN 0-944483-02-X). Garrett Ed Corp.
Ulysses' Sail: An Ethnographic Odyssey of Power, Knowledge, & Geographical Distance. Mary W. Helms. (Illus.). 312p. 1988. text ed. 45.00 (ISBN 0-691-09435-7); pap. text ed. 14.95 (ISBN 0-691-02840-0). Princeton U Pr.
Ulysses: "Sirens," "Cyclops," "Nausicaa," & "Oxen of the Sun." A Facsimile of Placards for Episodes 11-14. Ed. by Michael Groden. LC 78-11931. (James Joyce Archive Ser.: Vol. 19). 1979. lib. bdg. 125.00 (ISBN 0-8240-2813-9). Garland Pub.
Ulysses Smiled. Charles E. Ziavras. (Illus.). 1986. pap. 15.95 (ISBN 0-915940-08-6); pap. 4.95 (ISBN 0-915940-09-4). Ithaca Pr MA.
Ulysses: "Telemachus," "Nestor," "Proteus" Calypso" "Lotus Eaters," & "Hades": a Facsimile of Placards for Episodes 1-6. James Joyce. Ed. by Michael Groden. LC 78-16032. (James Joyce Archive Ser.: Vol. 17). 1978. lib. bdg. 125.00 (ISBN 0-8240-2811-2). Garland Pub.
Ulysses: The Corrected Text. James Joyce. LC 85-28279. 608p. 1986. 24.95 (ISBN 0-394-55373-X); pap. 15.95 (ISBN 0-394-74312-1). Random.
Ulysses: The Mechanics of Meaning. 2nd ed. David Hayman. LC 81-70007. 174p. 1982. 18.50 (ISBN 0-299-09020-5); pap. 9.95 (ISBN 0-299-09024-8). U of Wis Pr.
Ulysses, The Waste Land, & Modernism. Stanley Sultan. (Literary Criticism Ser). 1977. 16.50x (ISBN 0-8046-9144-4, Pub by Kennikat). Assoc Faculty Pr.
Ulysses Voyage. Tim Severin. (Illus.). 256p. 1987. 21.95 (ISBN 0-525-24614-2). Dutton.
Ulysses: "Wandering Rocks" & "Sirens" A Facsimile of Page Proofs for Episodes 10-11. James Joyce. Ed. by Michael Groden. LC 77-14654. (James Joyce Archive Ser.). 1978. lib. bdg. 125.00 (ISBN 0-8240-2818-X). Garland Pub.
Ulysses: "Wandering Rocks," "Sirens," "Cyclops," "Nausicaa": Facsimile of Drafts & Typescripts for Episodes 10-13. Ed. by Michael Groden. LC 77-10196. (James Joyce Archive Ser.). 1978. lib. bdg. 125.00 (ISBN 0-8240-2823-6). Garland Pub.
UMAP Modules Nineteen Eighty-One: Tools for Teaching. 746p. 1982. text ed. 47.95 (ISBN 0-8176-3085-6). Birkhauser.
UMAP Modules Nineteen Eighty-Six: Tools for Teaching 1986. COMAP, Inc. Staff. Ed. by Paul J. Campbell. (Illus.). 350p. 1987. pap. text ed. 35.00 (ISBN 0-912843-11-X). COMAP Inc.
UMAP Modules Nineteen Eighty-Two: Tools for Teaching. Ed. by COMAP, Inc. Staff. 544p. (Orig.). 1983. pap. 25.00 (ISBN 0-912843-03-9). COMAP Inc.
UMAP Modules, Ninteen Seventy-Seven to Nineteen Seventy-Nine: Tools for Teaching. Compiled by UMAP Central Staff. 727p. 1982. text ed. 47.95x (ISBN 0-8176-3049-X). Birkhauser.
UMAP Modules 1984: Tools for Teaching. Ed. by Philip D. Straffin, Jr. & Paul J. Campbell. 360p. (Orig.). 1985. pap. 25.00 (ISBN 0-912843-07-1). COMAP Inc.
UMAP Modules 1985: Tools for Teaching. Ed. by Philip D. Straffin, Jr. & Paul J. Campbell. 336p. (Orig.). 1986. pap. 25.00 (ISBN 0-912843-08-X). COMAP Inc.
Umar the Great, 2. Shibli Naumani. 12.50 ea. Kazi Pubns.
Umar the Great (Al-Farqu, 2 vols. M. Z. Khan & M. Saleem. 1970. Vol. 1. 12.50x (ISBN 0-87902-196-9); Vol. 2. 12.50x (ISBN 0-685-33011-7). Orientalia.
Umayyad, Abbasid & Tulunid Glass Weights & Vessel Stamps. Paul Balog. (Numismatic Studies: No. 13). (Illus.). 377p. 1976. 60.00 (ISBN 0-89722-066-8). Am Numismatic.
Umayyad Caliphate: A Political Study. Abd'al-Ameer'Abd Dixon. 222p. 1971. 95.00x (ISBN 0-317-39182-8, Pub. by Luzac & Co Ltd). State Mutual Bk.
Umayyads & Abbasids. Jirji Zaydan. Tr. by D. S. Margoliuth from Arabic. LC 79-2889. 325p. 1982. Repr. of 1907 ed. 29.00 (ISBN 0-8305-0056-1). Hyperion Conn.
Umayyads & Abbasids: Islamic Civilisation. G. Zaydan. 332p. 1987. 250.00x (ISBN 1-85077-171-5, Pub. by Darf Pubs Ltd). State Mutual Bk.
Umbanda: Religion & Politics in Urban Brazil. Diana D. Brown. Ed. by Conrad Kottak. LC 85-20962. (Studies in Cultural Anthropology: No. 7). 270p. 1985. 44.95 (ISBN 0-8357-1556-6). UMI Res Pr.
Umberto Menghi Seafood Cookbook. Umberto Menghi. (Illus.). 192p. 1987. spiral bdg. 14.95 (ISBN 1-55013-039-0, Pub. by Key Porter Canada). U of Toronto Pr.
Umberto Saba: Thirty-One Poems. Tr. by Felix Stephanile from Ital. 1978. 20.00 (ISBN 0-686-59679-X); pap. 8.00 (ISBN 0-686-59680-3). Elizabeth Pr.
Umbral Calculus. Steven Roman. LC 83-11940. (Pure & Applied Mathemnatics Ser.). 1983. 49.50 (ISBN 0-12-594380-6). Acad Pr.
Umbral Calculus & Hopf Algebras. Ed. by Robert Morris. LC 81-22756. (Contemporary Mathematics Ser.: Vol. 6). 84p. 1982. pap. 12.00 (ISBN 0-8218-5003-2, 6). Am Math.
Umbrella. Taro Yashima. (Illus.). (ps-1). 1977. pap. 3.95 (ISBN 0-14-050240-8, Puffin). Penguin.
Umbrella. Taro Yashima. (Illus.). (ps-1). 1958. lib. bdg. 13.95 (ISBN 0-670-73858-1). Viking.
Umbrella Book, 3 vols. Rev. ed. LC 81-216095. (Illus.). 1500p. 1979. Set looseleaf. write for info. (ISBN 0-941360-00-8). Griffin Comns.
Umbrella Garden: A Picture of Student Life in Red China. Ed. by Maria Yen & Richard M. McCarthy. LC 78-12991. 1979. Repr. of 1954 ed. lib. bdg. 35.00 (ISBN 0-313-21214-7, YEUG). Greenwood.
Umbrella Named Umbrella. Tobi Tobias. LC 76-8659. (gr. 2-4). 1976. Knopf.
Umbrella of Glass. Henry Alley. LC 88-11729. 170p. 1988. 14.95 (ISBN 0-932576-61-3). Breitenbush Bks.
Umbrella Parade. Kathy Feczko. LC 84-8650. (Giant First Start Reader Ser.). (Illus.). 32p. (gr. k-2). 1985. PLB 9.89 (ISBN 0-8167-0356-6); pap. text ed. 2.95 (ISBN 0-8167-0436-8). Troll Assocs.
Umbrella Thief. Sybil Wettasinghe. (Illus.). 32p. (ps-3). 1987. 11.95 (ISBN 0-916291-12-X). Kane-Miller Bk.
Umbrellas & Parasols. Jerry Farrell. (Costume Accessories Ser.). (Illus.). 96p. 1986. text ed. 15.95x (ISBN 0-7134-4874-1, Pub. by Batsford England). Drama Bk.
Umbstandliche und Eigentliche Beschreibung Von Africa. Olfert Dapper. (Illus.). 1967. Repr. of 1670 ed. 78.00 (ISBN 0-384-10825-3). Johnson Repr.
Umfang des Fassungsvermogens: Anselm Stalder. Anselm Stalder. 64p. 1984. 45.00 (ISBN 0-935875-01-8). Blumarts Inc.
Umgang mit schwierigen Kindern und Jugendlichen. H. J. Von Schumann. (Psychologische Praxis Ser.: No. 48). 80p. 1973. 13.00 (ISBN 3-8055-1561-8). S Karger.
Umi to Dokuyaku see Sea & Poison: A Novel.
Umpire Strikes Back. Ron Luciano & David Fisher. 1984. pap. 3.95 (ISBN 0-553-24846-4). Bantam.
Umpire's Handbook. J. Brinkman & C. Euchner. 1987. 9.95 (ISBN 0-8289-0550-9). Greene.
Umpire's Handbook. rev. ed. Joe Brinkman & Charlie Euchner. 192p. 1987. pap. 9.95 (ISBN 0-8289-0628-9). Greene.
Umpiring Baseball. Jay Baum. (Orig.). 1979. pap. 4.95 (ISBN 0-8092-7476-0). Contemp Bks.
Umpiring Made Easy: How to Command Respect! Glen D. Eley. (Illus.). 24p. (Orig.). 1983. pap. 4.95 (ISBN 0-940934-03-5). GDE Pubns OH.
Umpoled Synthons: A Survey of Sources & Uses in Synthesis. Ed. by Tapio A. Hase. LC 86-26702. 387p. 1987. 59.95 (ISBN 0-471-80667-6). Wiley.
Umpqua Valley, Oregon, & Its Pioneers. Harold A. Minter. LC 67-1952. (Illus.). 1967. 10.50 (ISBN 0-8323-0036-5). Binford-Metropolitan.
Umstrittene Ruhm Alexander Popes. Rudolf Stamm. 1973. Repr. of 1940 ed. 20.00 (ISBN 0-8274-0623-1). R West.
Umstrittenes Taufertum 1525-1975. Ed. by Hans-Jurgen Goertz. 1975. 22.50x (ISBN 0-8361-1128-1). Herald Pr.
Umweltbelastung der Nahrung; Gefahr fuer den Menschen? Environmental Contamination of Foods: Danger to Man? Ed. by J. C. Somogyi & D. Hotzel. (Bibliotheca Nutritio et Dieta: No. 41). (Illus.). vi, 114p. 1987. 73.50 (ISBN 3-8055-4661-0). S Karger.
Umweltvorsorge im Rahmen der Landesplanung Nordrhein - Westfalen: Eine Integrationsorientierte Untersuchung, Vol. 3. Robert Weimar & Guido Leidig. (Forschungen der Europaischen Fakultat fur Bodenordnung). 313p. (Ger.). 1983. 37.35 (ISBN 3-8204-7669-5). P Lang Pubs.
UN see United Nations.
Un-American Activities in the State of Washington. Vern Countryman. 1951. 27.00 (ISBN 0-384-09920-3). Johnson Repr.
Un Dans L'autre. Andre Breton. (Coll. Desordee). 8.50 (ISBN 0-685-37240-5). French & Eur.
Un de Beaumugnes see Oeuvres Romanesques.
Un-Diet Book. Robert J. DuPuis. 222p. 1980. pap. 1.95 (ISBN 0-8439-8033-8, Leisure Bks). Leisure NY.
Un-Divine Comedy. Zygmunt Krasinski. Tr. by Harriette Kennedy & Zofia Uminska. LC 74-5774. 1976. Repr. of 1924 ed. lib. bdg. 35.00x (ISBN 0-8371-7513-5, KRUD). Greenwood.
Un-Dudding of Roger Judd. Harriett Luger. LC 82-50362. 144p. (gr. 7 up). 1983. 11.95 (ISBN 0-670-73886-7, Viking Kestrel). Viking.
UN-ECE Standard for Poultry Meat & Explanatory Brochure: ECE-AGRI-86. 30p. 1986. pap. 9.00 (ISBN 92-1-116355-2, E.85.II.E.41). UN.
Un-Expressionism: Art Beyond the Post-Modern Era. Germano Celant. LC 88-42711. (Illus.). 416p. 1988. 50.00 (ISBN 0-8478-0984-6); pap. 35.00 (ISBN 0-8478-0985-4). Rizzoli Intl.
Un Jardin a Hammamet see Garden at Hammamet.
Un-Marxian Socialist: A Study of Proudhon. Henry De Lubac. 1978. Repr. of 1948 ed. lib. bdg. 20.50x (ISBN 0-374-95138-1, Octagon). Hippocrene Bks.
Un-Terrible Tiger. Miroslav Zahradka. LC 78-155815. (Illus.). 32p. (ps-3). 7.95 (ISBN 0-87592-056-X). Scroll Pr.
Una Agenda para la Excelencia Academica. Rafael Cartagena. LC 84-681. (Illus.). 128p. (Orig.). 1984. pap. 9.95 (ISBN 0-913480-60-6). Inter Am U Pr.
Una Interpretacion Del Apocalipsis. Domingo S. Fernandez. 234p. (Span.). 1985. pap. 5.50 (ISBN 0-311-04312-7). Casa Bautista.
Una Isla, la Mas Bella. Nieves Del Rosario Marquez. LC 81-65414. (Coleccion Espejo De Paciencia Ser.). 62p. (Orig.). 1981. pap. 4.50 (ISBN 0-89729-288-X). Ediciones.
Una Nueva Ilusion. Dale E. Galloway. Tr. by Rhode F. Ward. 169p. (Span.). 1982. pap. 5.75 (ISBN 0-89922-158-0). Edit Caribe.
Una Stubbs - Fairy Tales. 96p. 1987. 29.00x (ISBN 0-7063-6561-5, Pub. by Ward Lock Educ Co Ltd). State Mutual Bk.
Una Troubridge: Friend of Radcliff Hall. Richard Ormrod. 340p. (Orig.). 1985. 18.95 (ISBN 0-88184-193-5). Carroll & Graf.
Una Vez Mas. James H. Couch et al. (gr. 10-12). 1982. pap. 8.95x (ISBN 0-88334-164-6); tests 3.50 (ISBN 0-317-02593-7). Ind Sch Pr.
Una Vita: A Grandfather's Story. Nicholas Romanelli. Ed. by Dorothy H. Romanelli. (Illus.). 185p. (Orig.). 1981. pap. 6.50 (ISBN 0-9606104-0-5). Port Pr.
Unabashed Self-Promoter's Guide: Getting Ahead by Exploiting the Media. 1986. lib. bdg. 79.95 (ISBN 0-8490-3911-8). Gordon Pr.
Unabashed Self-Promoter's Guide: What Every Man, Woman, Child & Organization in America Needs to Know About Getting Ahead by Exploiting the Media. Jeffrey L. Lant. (Enterprise Ser.: Vol. II). 366p. (Orig.). 1983. pap. text ed. 30.00 (ISBN 0-940374-06-4). JLA Pubns.
Unaborted Socrates. Peter J. Kreeft. LC 83-8430. 180p. 1983. pap. 7.95 (ISBN 0-87784-810-6). Inter-Varsity.
Unabridged Bible Commentary, 3 vols. Jamieson et al. 1974. 79.95 (ISBN 0-8028-8033-9). Eerdmans.
Unabridged Crossword Puzzle Dictionary. A. F. Sisson. 1964. pap. 14.95 thumb-indexed edition (ISBN 0-385-01350-7). Doubleday.
Unabridged Dictionary of F-rts. Donald Wetzel. 80p. 1986. 3.95 (ISBN 0-8092-4884-0). Contemp Bks.
Unabridged Edgar Allan Poe. Edgar Allan Poe. LC 83-16023. (Illus.). 1280p. (Orig.). 1983. lib. bdg. 24.80 (ISBN 0-89471-234-9); pap. 12.95 (ISBN 0-89471-233-0). Running Pr.
Unabridged Edgar Allan Poe. Edgar Allan Poe. (Illus.). 1280p. 1985. 12.98 (ISBN 0-89471-245-4, Pub. by Courage Bks). Running Pr.
Unabridged Jack London. Jack London. Ed. by Lawrence Teacher & Richard Nicholls. LC 81-4383. (Illus.). 1143p. (Orig.). 1981. 12.95 (ISBN 0-89471-124-5, Pub. by Courage Bks); lib. bdg. 24.80. Running Pr.
Unabridged Marilyn: Her Life from A to Z. Randall Riese & Neal Hitchens. (Illus.). 608p. 1987. 25.00 (ISBN 0-86553-176-5). Congdon & Weed.
Unabridged Marilyn: Her Life from A to Z. Randall Riese & Neal Hitchens. (Illus.). 592p. 1988. pap. 14.95 (ISBN 0-86553-167-6). Congdon & Weed.
Unabridged Mark Twain. Mark Twain. Ed. by Lawrence Teacher. LC 76-43094. (Illus.). 1250p. (Orig.). 1976. lib. bdg. 24.80 (ISBN 0-914294-53-9); pap. 12.95 (ISBN 0-914294-54-7). Running Pr.
Unabridged Mark Twain. Mark Twain. LC 76-43094. 1312p. 1985. 12.98 (ISBN 0-89471-072-9, Pub. by Courage Books). Running Pr.
Unabridged Mark Twain, No. 2. Mark Twain. Ed. by Lawrence Teacher. LC 79-9576. (Illus.). 1118p. 1979. lib. bdg. 24.80 (Pub. by Courage Bks); pap. 12.95. Running Pr.
Unabridged, Uncensored, Unbelievable Garfield. Jim Davis. (Orig.). 1986. pap. 5.95 (ISBN 0-345-33772-7, Pub. by Ballantine Trade). Ballantine.
Unabridged Vegetable Cookbook. Nika Hazelton. LC 76-23451. (Illus.). 384p. 1976. 14.95 (ISBN 0-87131-213-1). M Evans.
Unabridged Woman. Bobbie McKay. LC 79-14297. (Orig.). 1979. pap. 5.95 (ISBN 0-8298-0369-6). Pilgrim NY.
Unacceptable Essays. M. F. Roe. 112p. 1987. 35.00x (ISBN 0-946095-19-1, Pub. by Gresham England). State Mutual Bk.
Unacceptable Offer. Mary Balogh. 1988. pap. 2.95 (ISBN 0-451-15314-6, Sig). NAL.
Unaccompanied Children: Care & Protection in Wars, Natural Disasters & Refugee Movements. Everett M. Ressler et al. 432p. 1987. 49.95 (ISBN 0-19-504091-0); pap. 18.95 (ISBN 0-19-504937-3). Oxford U Pr.
Unaccustomed As I Am. 2nd ed. Lorin J. Badskey. 1974. pap. 7.95 (ISBN 0-686-81687-0). Loru Co.
Unaccustomed to Fear: Biography of Gen. Roy S. Geiger. 2nd ed. Roger Willock. 333p. Repr. of 1968 ed. 9.95 (ISBN 0-940328-05-4). Marine Corps.
Unacknowledged Harmony: Philo-Semitism & the Survival of European Jewry. Alan Edelstein. LC 81-1563. (Contributions in Ethnic Studies: No. 4). xii, 235p. 1982. lib. bdg. 35.00 (ISBN 0-313-22754-3, EDP/). Greenwood.
Unacknowledged Legislator. Bonamy Dobree. LC 73-13656. 1973. lib. bdg. 15.00 (ISBN 0-8414-3656-8). Folcroft.
Unacknowledged Legislator: Shelley & Politics. P. M. Dawson. 1980. 65.00x (ISBN 0-19-812095-8). Oxford U Pr.
Unadjusted Girl, with Cases & Standpoint for Behavior Analysis. William I. Thomas. LC 69-14951. (Criminology, Law Enforcement, & Social Problems Ser.: No. 26). 1969. Repr. of 1923 ed. 12.00x (ISBN 0-87585-026-X). Patterson Smith.
Unadjusted Man: A New Hero for Americans. Peter R. Viereck. LC 74-178795. 339p. 1973. Repr. of 1956 ed. lib. bdg. 35.00x (ISBN 0-8371-6285-8, VUMA). Greenwood.
Unafraid. facsimile ed. Winnifred K. Rugg. LC 73-114891. (Select Bibliographies Reprint Ser). 1930. 17.00 (ISBN 0-8369-5295-2). Ayer Co Pubs.
Unamerican Activities: The Campaign Against the Underground Press. Geoffrey Rips. 160p. 1981. pap. 7.95 (ISBN 0-87286-127-9). City Lights.
Unamericans in Paris: A Novel. Jack Grant. 184p. (Orig.). 1988. pap. 7.95 (ISBN 0-89087-525-1). Celestial Arts.

Uncertain Magic. Laura Kinsale. 384p. 1987. pap. 3.95 (ISBN 0-380-75140-2). Avon.
Uncertain Mandate: Politics of the U. N. Congo Operation. Ernest W. Lefever. LC 67-22890. pap. 67.50 (ISBN 0-317-28789-3, 2020540). Bks Demand UMI.
Uncertain Passage: China's Transition to the Post-Mao Era. A. Doak Barnett. LC 73-22482. pap. 101.30 (ISBN 0-317-30179-9, 2025361). Bks Demand UMI.
Uncertain Phoenix: Adventures Toward a Post-Cultural Sensibility. David L. Hall. LC 80-67033. xviii, 426p. 1982. 40.00 (ISBN 0-8232-1053-7); pap. 20.00 (ISBN 0-8232-1054-5). Fordham.
Uncertain Physician: Dilemmas & Decisions in Medical Practice. Kurt Link. LC 86-43081. 160p. 1987. pap. 14.95x (ISBN 0-89950-266-0). McFarland & Co.
Uncertain Power: The Struggle for a National Energy Policy. Ed. by Dorothy Zinberg. (Illus.). 250p. 1983. text ed. 49.00 (ISBN 0-08-029388-3); pap. text ed. 16.50 (ISBN 0-08-029387-5). Pergamon.
Uncertain Princess: A Children's Book with a Science Hook. rev. ed. Faith Flagg. (Illus.). 182p. (gr. 5-10). 1986. pap. 7.00 (ISBN 0-940023-01-6). MacCactus Pr.
Uncertain Profession: Harvard & the Search for Educational Authority. Arthur G. Powell. LC 79-260960. (Illus.). 1980. 24.50x (ISBN 0-674-92045-7). Harvard U Pr.
Uncertain Saints. Alan Graebner. LC 75-1573. (Contributions in American History: No. 42). 320p. 1975. lib. bdg. 46.95 (ISBN 0-8371-7963-7, GUS/). Greenwood.
Uncertain Search for Environmental Quality. Bruce A. Ackerman et al. LC 73-21305. (Illus.). 1974. 16.95 (ISBN 0-02-900200-1). Free Pr.
Uncertain Self: Whitman's Drama of Identity. Fred E. Carlisle. 1973. 8.50 (ISBN 0-87013-172-9). Mich St U Pr.
Uncertain the Final Run to Winter. William Kloefkorn. 1977. pap. 4.95 (ISBN 0-931534-01-1). Windflower Pr.
Uncertain Tradition: American Secretaries of State in the Twentieth Century. Ed. by Norman A. Graebner. LC 79-26791. (McGraw-Hill Ser. in American History). 341p. 1980. Repr. of 1961 ed. lib. bdg. 35.00x (ISBN 0-313-22317-3, GRUT). Greenwood.
Uncertain Tradition: Constitutionalism & the History of the South. Ed. by Kermit L. Hall & James W. Ely, Jr. LC 88-5579. 416p. 1989. 40.00x (ISBN 0-8203-1055-7); pap. 17.95x (ISBN 0-8203-1075-1). U of Ga Pr.
Uncertain Triumph: Federal Education Policy in the Kennedy & Johnson Years. Hugh D. Graham. LC 83-23424. xxi, 280p. 1984. 25.00x (ISBN 0-8078-1599-3). U of NC Pr.
Uncertain Victory: Social Democracy & Progressivism in European & American Thought, 1870-1920. James T. Kloppenberg. 528p. 1986. text ed. 39.95x (ISBN 0-19-503749-9). Oxford U Pr.
Uncertain Victory: Social Democracy & Progressivism in European & American Thought, 1870-1920. James T. Kloppenberg. 556p. 1988. pap. text ed. 12.95 (ISBN 0-19-505304-4). Oxford U Pr.
Uncertain Years: Chinese-American Relations, 1947-1950. Ed. by Dorothy Borg & Waldo Heinrichs. LC 79-28297. (Studies of the East Asian Institute). 1980. 32.00x (ISBN 0-231-04738-X). Columbia U Pr.
Uncertainity Analysis. Yigal Ronen. 272p. 1988. 165.00 (ISBN 0-8493-6714-X, 6714). CRC Pr.
Uncertainties. H. L. Van Brunt. LC 68-22413. (Illus.). 94p. 6.00 (ISBN 0-912292-00-8); pap. 3.00 (ISBN 0-912292-01-6). The Smith.
Uncertainties & Rest, Poems. Timothy Steele. LC 78-15063. 64p. 1979. o. p. 13.95x (ISBN 0-8071-0480-9); pap. 6.95 (ISBN 0-8071-0481-7). La State U Pr.
Uncertainties in French Grammar. Lewis Harmer. Ed. by P. Rickard & G. S. Combe. LC 78-58793. 1980. 85.00 (ISBN 0-521-22233-8). Cambridge U Pr.
Uncertainties in Peasant Farming: A Colombian Case. Sutti R. De Ortiz. (London School of Economics Monographs on Social Anthropology: No. 46). (Illus.). 294p. 1973. 38.50 (ISBN 0-485-19546-1, Pub. by Athlone Pr UK). Humanities.
Uncertainty Analysis for Engineers. Ed. by Vincent W. Uhl & Walter E. Lowthian. LC 82-24443. (AIChE Symposium: Vol. 78). 1982. pap. 20.00 (ISBN 0-8169-0244-5, S-220). Am Inst Chem Eng.
Uncertainty Analysis for Performance Assessments of Radioactive Waste Disposal Systems. OECD. 258p. (Fr.). 1987. pap. 25.00x (ISBN 92-64-03011-5). OECD.
Uncertainty Analysis Loads & Safety in Structural Engineering. Gary C. Hart. (Illus.). 240p. 1982. 51.00 (ISBN 0-13-935619-3). P-H.
Uncertainty & Conservatism in the Seismic Analysis & Design of Nuclear Facilities: Working Group on Quantification of Uncertainties. 302p. 1986. 23.00x (ISBN 0-87262-547-8). Am Soc Civil Eng.
Uncertainty & Control. Ed. by J. Ackermann. (Lecture Notes in Control & Information Sciences Ser.: Vol. 70). iv, 236p. 1985. pap. 21.50 (ISBN 0-387-15533-3). Springer-Verlag.
Uncertainty & Expectations in Economics: Essays in Honour of G.L.S. Schakle. Ed. by C. F. Carter & J. L. Ford. LC 72-184239. 299p. 1972. lib. bdg. 37.50x (ISBN 0-678-06277-3). Kelley.
Uncertainty & Forecasting of Water Quality. Ed. by M. B. Beck & G. Van Straten. (Illus.). 386p. 1983. 39.00 (ISBN 0-387-12419-5). Springer-Verlag.
Uncertainty & the Labor Market: Recent Developments in Job-Search Theory. C. J. McKenna. LC 85-1988. 165p. 1985. 22.50 (ISBN 0-312-82861-6). St Martin.
Uncertainty & the Theory of International Trade. Earl L. Grinols. (Fundamentals of Pure & Applied Economics Ser.: Vol. 15). 100p. 1987. pap. text ed. 25.00 (ISBN 3-7186-0356-X). Harwood Academic.
Uncertainty: Behavioral & Social Dimensions. Ed. by Seymour Fiddle. LC 80-82073. 410p. 1980. 46.95 (ISBN 0-275-90480-6, C0480). Praeger.
Uncertainty Business. W. J. Maunder. 1987. 49.95 (ISBN 0-416-36100-5). Routledge Chapman & Hall.
Uncertainty in Artificial Intelligence. Ed. by L. N. Kanal & J. F. Lemmer. 524p. 1986. 73.25 (ISBN 0-444-70058-7, North-Holland). Elsevier.
Uncertainty in Artificial Intelligence, Vol. 2. Ed. by J. F. Lemmer & L. N. Kaanal. (Machine Intelligence & Pattern Recognition: No. 2). 484p. 1988. 105.25 (ISBN 0-444-70396-9, North Holland). Elsevier.
Uncertainty in Economics: Readings & Exercises. Ed. by Peter Diamond & Michael Rothschild. (Economic Theory Econometrics & Mathematical Economic Ser.). 1978. 34.95 (ISBN 0-12-214850-9). Acad Pr.
Uncertainty in Knowledge-Based Systems. B. Bouchon & R. R. Yager. (Lecture Notes in Computer Science Ser.: Vol. 286). vii, 405p. 1987. pap. 33.30 (ISBN 0-387-18579-8). Springer-Verlag.
Uncertainty in Microeconomics. John D. Hey. LC 79-63434. 1979. cobee o.p. 35.00x (ISBN 0-8147-3398-0); pap. 15.00x cobee (ISBN 0-8147-3399-9). NYU Pr.
Uncertainty in Risk Assessment, Risk Management & Decision Making. Ed. by Lester B. Lave & Vincent T. Covello. (Advances in Risk Analysis Ser.: Vol. 4). 538p. 1987. 85.00x (ISBN 0-306-42557-2, Plenum Pr). Plenum Pub.
Uncertainty, Information & Communication: Essays in Honor of Kenneth J. Arrow, Vol. III. Ed. by Walter P. Heller et al. (Illus.). 309p. 1986. 34.50 (ISBN 0-521-32704-0). Cambridge U Pr.
Uncertainty Management in AI Systems. Judea Pearl & Glenn Shafer. (Illus.). 105p. 1988. pap. text ed. 5.00x (ISBN 0-929280-16-4). Amer Artificial.
Uncertainty Modeling: With Applications to Multidimensional Civil Engineering. Ove Ditlevsen. (Illus.). 448p. 1981. text ed. 83.95 (ISBN 0-07-017046-0). McGraw.
Uncertainty Models for Knowledge-Based Systems: A Unified Approach to the Measurement of Uncertainty. Ed. by I. R. Goodman & H. T. Nguyen. LC 85-10275. 644p. 1985. 105.25 (ISBN 0-444-87796-7, North-Holland). Elsevier.
Uncertainty of Analysis: Problems in Truth, Meaning, & Culture. Timothy J. Reiss. LC 88-47741. 312p. 1988. 29.95x (ISBN 0-8014-2162-4). Cornell U Pr.
Uncertainty of Strangers & Other Stories. Patrick Franklin. LC 85-7653. 152p. 1985. pap. 7.95 (ISBN 0-912516-91-7). Grey Fox.
Uncertainty Principle & Foundations of Quantum Mechanics: A Fifty Years' Survey. Ed. by William C. Price & Seymour S. Chissick. LC 76-18213. 572p. 1977. 184.95 (ISBN 0-471-99414-6). Wiley.
Uncertainty Principle & Foundations of Quantum Mechanics: A Fifty Years' Survey. Ed. by William C. Price & Seymour S. Chissick. LC 76-18213. 590p. pap. 153.40 (2030478). Bks Demand UMI.
Uncertainty: Studies in Philosophy, Economics & Socio-Political Theory. Luigi Bonatti. (Bochumer Studien zur Philosophie Ser.: Vol. 2). xii, 132p. 1984. 32.00x (ISBN 90-6032-230-4, Pub. by B R Gruener Netherlands). Benjamins North Am.
Unchallenged Violence: An American Ordeal. Robert B. Toplin. LC 75-72. 1975. lib. bdg. 35.00 (ISBN 0-8371-7748-0, TLV/); pap. 9.95 (ISBN 0-313-20163-3, TLVPB). Greenwood.
Uncharged Battery. Edra D. Blixseth. Ed. by Cheryl Hodgson. 256p. 1988. text ed. 16.95 (ISBN 0-945033-00-1). Portland Ent.
Uncharged Misconduct Evidence. Edward J. Imwinkelried. LC 84-7619. 706p. 1984. 75.00 (ISBN 0-317-06219-0). Callaghan.
Uncharted Journey. Reynolds. 5.00 (ISBN 0-8065-0337-8, Pub. by Citadel Pr). Lyle Stuart.
Uncharted Places. Nora Johnson. 320p. 1988. 17.95 (ISBN 0-671-66136-1). S&S.
Uncharted Seas. Emilie Loring. Repr. lib. bdg. 19.95x (ISBN 0-88411-373-6, Pub. by Aeonian Pr). Amereon Ltd.
Unchartered Stars. Andre Norton. 256p. 1983. pap. 2.50 (ISBN 0-441-84466-9). Ace Bks.
Unchaste. Thakazhi S. Pillai. Tr. by M. K. Bhaskaran. 112p. 1971. pap. 2.10 (ISBN 0-88253-067-4). Ind-US Inc.
Unchosen. Nan Gilbert. (YA) (gr. 7 up). 1963. PLB 12.89 (ISBN 0-06-021971-8). HarpJ.
Unchosen. Charles Judah & George W. Smith. cancelled (ISBN 0-698-10381-5, Coward). Putnam Pub Group.
Unchosen Presidents: The Vice-President & Other Frustrations of Presidential Succession. Allan P. Sindler. LC 75-46041. (Quantum Book: No. 7). 1976. 22.50x (ISBN 0-520-03185-7); pap. 5.95 (ISBN 0-520-03493-7). U of Cal Pr.
Unchurched: Who They Are & Why They Stay Away. J. Russell Hale. LC 79-2993. 192p. 1980. 12.00 (ISBN 0-06-063560-6, HarpR). Har-Row.
UNCITRAL Legal Guide on Electronic Funds Transfers. 150p. 1987. 17.00 (ISBN 92-1-133299-0, E.87.V.9). UN.
UNCITRAL Model Law of International Commercial Arbitration: A Documentary History. Igor I. Kavaas & Arnold Liivak. LC 85-81187. 1985. 95.00 (ISBN 0-317-59127-4). W S Hein.
UNCITRAL: The United Nations Commission on International Trade Law. 199p. 1987. 15.00 (ISBN 92-1-133284-2, E.86.V.8). UN.
Uncitral's Model Law on International Commercial Arbitration. Ed. by P. Sanders. 1984. pap. text ed. 30.00 (ISBN 90-6544-183-2, Pub. by Kluwer Law Netherlands). Kluwer Academic.
Uncivil Liberties. Calvin Trillin. 224p. 1987. pap. 7.95 (ISBN 0-14-010255-8). Penguin.
Uncivil Liberty: An Essay to Show the Injustice & Impolicy of Ruling Woman Without Her Consent. Ezra H. Heywood. (Libertarian Broadsides: No. 8). (Illus.). 1978. pap. 1.00 (ISBN 0-87926-023-8). R Myles.
Uncivil Religion: Interreligious Hostility in America. Robert Bellah & Frederick Greenspahn. 256p. 1986. 16.95. Crossroad NY.
Uncivil Religions: Interreligious Hostility. Ed. by Robert N. Bellah & Frederick E. Greenspahn. 1987. 17.95 (ISBN 0-8245-0796-7). Crossroad NY.
Uncivil Seasons. Michael Malone. 336p. Date not set. pap. 3.95 (ISBN 0-671-65838-7). PB.
Uncivil War: The Southern Backcountry During the American Revolution. Ed. by Ronald Hoffman et al. LC 84-19632. (U. S. Capitol Historical Society, Perspectives on the American Revolution Ser.). 346p. 1985. text ed. 25.00x (ISBN 0-8139-1051-X). U Pr of Va.
Uncivil Wars. Padraig O'Malley. 1984. pap. 9.95 (ISBN 0-395-36570-8). HM.
Unclaimed Children: The Failure of Public Responsibility to Children & Adolescents in Need of Mental Health Services. Jane Knitzer et al. LC 82-72900. 160p. (Orig.). 1982. pap. 10.50 (ISBN 0-938008-06-4). Children's Defense.
Unclaimed Property Law & Reporting Forms, 4 vols. David J. Epstein & Andrew W. McThenia, Jr. 1984. Set, updates avail. looseleaf 425.00 (136); Updates 1985. 135.00; 1986 197.50. Bender.
Unclaimed Treasures. Patricia MacLachlan. LC 83-47714. (Charlotte Zolotow Bks.). 160p. (gr. 5-7). 1984. 11.70i (ISBN 0-06-024093-8); PLB 11.89g (ISBN 0-06-024094-6). HarpJ.
Unclaimed Treasures. Patricia MacLachlan. LC 83-47714. (Trophy I Can Read Bks.). 128p. (gr. 5-7). 1987. 2.95 (ISBN 0-06-440189-8, Trophy). HarpJ.
Unclaimed Treasures. Baruch Silverstein. 1983. 15.00x (ISBN 0-88125-029-5). Ktav.
Unclassed. George Gissing. LC 68-54269. Repr. of 1896 ed. 15.00 (ISBN 0-404-02811-X). AMS Pr.
Unclassed. George Gissing. 1983. pap. 8.95 (ISBN 0-686-47743-X, NO. 3879). Routledge Chapman & Hall.
Unclassed. George Gissing. Ed. by Jacob Korg. 327p. 24.50. Fairleigh Dickinson.
Unclassed see Works of George Gissing.
Unclassifiable Leukemias. Ed. by M. Bessis. (Illus.). 270p. 1975. pap. 29.00 (ISBN 0-387-07242-X). Springer-Verlag.
Unclassified Buildings & Substructures, Nos. 3-12. Linton Satterthwaite, Jr. (Piedras Negras Archaeology,Architecture: Pt. 6). (Illus.). 92p. 1954. pap. 10.00 (ISBN 0-318-01016-X). Univ Mus of U PA.
Unclay. Theodore F. Powys. LC 76-145247. (Literature Ser). 328p. 1972. Repr. of 1932 ed. 39.00x (ISBN 0-403-01162-0). Scholarly.
Uncle. Julia Markus. 1987. pap. 3.95 (ISBN 0-440-39187-3, LE). Dell.
Uncle Abner & the Devil's Tools. Melville D. Post. 12.95 (ISBN 0-89190-987-7, Pub. by Am Repr). Amereon Ltd.
Uncle Abner & the Doomsdorf Mystery. Melville D. Post. 12.95 (ISBN 0-89190-988-5, Pub. by Am Repr). Amereon Ltd.
Uncle & Nephew in the Old French Chansons De Geste. William O. Farnsworth. LC 70-168008. (Columbia University. Studies in Romance Philology & Literature: No. 14). Repr. of 1913 ed. 22.00 (ISBN 0-404-50614-3). AMS Pr.
Uncle & Other Stories. Joan Shaw. Ed. by Angela Jaffray. LC 82-70936. 101p. 1983. pap. 6.00 (ISBN 0-932274-31-5); o. p. signed 15.00 (ISBN 0-932274-32-3). Cadmus Eds.
Uncle Aron: Alabama Desparado. Nora L. Hicks. (Illus.). 80p. (Orig.). 1981. pap. 5.95 (ISBN 0-89962-217-8). Todd & Honeywell.
Uncle Ben's Instant Clip Quotes. Benjamin R. De Jong. 128p. 1985. pap. 5.95 (ISBN 0-8010-2954-6). Baker Bk.
Uncle Ben's Quotebook. Benjamin R. De Jong. 1976. 14.95 (ISBN 0-8010-2851-5). Baker Bk.
Uncle Ben's Quotebook. Benjamin R. DeJong. 320p. 1976. pap. 10.95 (ISBN 0-89081-023-0). Harvest Hse.
Uncle Bernac: A Memory of the Empire. Arthur Conan Doyle. 9.95 (ISBN 0-7195-0392-2). Transatl Arts.
Uncle Billy: The Ancestors & Descendants of William B. Shoemaker of Jasper County. Mattie S. Holliday. 257p. 1987. pap. 30.00 (ISBN 0-9619875-0-2). M S Holliday.
Uncle Bob's Animal Stories. Bob Devine. (Illus., Orig.). 1986. pap. 5.95 (ISBN 0-8024-9058-1). Moody.
Uncle Bob's Bible Stories. Bob Wolf. (Illus.). 108p. (Orig.). (gr. 4-8). 1982. pap. 1.75 (ISBN 0-89323-028-6). Bible Memory.
Uncle Cam. James Hefley & Marti Hefley. Tr. by James C. Yu from Eng. 288p. (Orig., Chinese.). 1987. pap. text ed. 5.50. Evangel Lit.
Uncle Charles Has Locked Himself In. Georges Simenon. Tr. by Howard Curtis. 1987. 19.95 (ISBN 0-15-192685-9). HarBraceJ.
Uncle Charlie's Poems. Charles N. Douglas. 1977. Repr. 25.00 (ISBN 0-403-08367-2). Scholarly.
Uncle Dan Drumheller Tells Thrills of Western Trails in 1854. Dan Drumheller. (Illus.). 131p. pap. 4.95 (ISBN 0-8466-0234-2, S234). Shorey.
Uncle Dan Drumheller Tells Thrills of Western Trails in 1854. Dan Drumheller. 123p. 1985. 12.95 (ISBN 0-87770-366-3). Ye Galleon.
Uncle Dick Wootton: The Pioneer Frontiersman of the Rocky Mountain Region. Howard L. Conard. Ed. by Milo M. Quaife. LC 79-19038. (Illus.). xxiv, 462p. 1980. 35.00x (ISBN 0-8032-1408-1); pap. 7.50 (ISBN 0-8032-6306-6, BB 730, Bison). U of Nebr Pr.
Uncle Don's Adventure down East Cookbook. Donald B. Drew. (Illus.). 217p. 1987. pap. 8.95 (ISBN 0-9617940-0-3). D B Drew.
Uncle Dudley's Odd Hours; Western Sketches, Indian Trail Echoes. facsimile ed. Morris C. Russell. LC 73-104558. (Illus.). 255p. Repr. of 1904 ed. lib. bdg. 22.00 (ISBN 0-8398-1768-1). Irvington.
Uncle Elephant. Arnold Lobel. LC 80-8944. (Harper I Can Read Bks.). (Illus.). 64p. (gr. k-3). 1981. 8.70i (ISBN 0-06-023979-4); PLB 10.89g (ISBN 0-06-023980-8). HarpJ.
Uncle Elephant. Arnold Lobel. LC 80-8944. (Trophy I Can Read Bks.). (Illus.). 64p. (gr. k-3). 1986. pap. 3.50 (ISBN 0-06-444104-0, Trophy). HarpJ.
Uncle Ezra's Short Stories for Children. Ezra Meeker. 100p. pap. 4.95 (ISBN 0-8466-0242-3, S242). Shorey.
Uncle Foster's Hat Tree. Doug Cushman. LC 88-3573. (Easy Readers Ser.). (Illus.). 48p. (ps-3). 1988. 9.95 (ISBN 0-525-44410-6, 0966-290). Dutton.
Uncle Fred in the Springtime. P. G. Wodehouse. 1976. pap. 3.95 (ISBN 0-14-000971-X). Penguin.
Uncle Gene's Breadbook for Kids! Eugene Bove. (Illus.). 64p. (gr. 5-12). 1986. pap. 11.95 (ISBN 0-937395-00-5). Happibook Pr.
Uncle George Washington & Harriot's Guitar. Miriam A. Bourne. (Illus.). 64p. (gr. 3-6). 1983. pap. 8.95 (ISBN 0-698-20573-1, Coward). Putnam Pub Group.
Uncle Grubby. Will Ryan. Ed. by Ken Forsse. (Teddy Ruxpin Adventure Ser.). (Illus.). 26p. (ps). 1985. 9.95 (ISBN 0-934323-20-8); audio cassette incl. Alchemy Comms.
Uncle Happy's Cat. C. Mongo. (Illus., Orig.). (gr. 2-3). plastic bdg. 2.00 (ISBN 0-8198-0166-6); pap. 1.25 (ISBN 0-8198-0167-4). Dghtrs St Paul.
Uncle Harry: An Autobiography. H. E. Wierwille. LC 78-73348. 55p. 1978. 5.95 (ISBN 0-910068-15-1). Am Christian.
Uncle Henry & Aunt Henrietta's Honeymoon. Nicole Rubel. LC 85-15944. (Illus.). 32p. (ps-2). 1986. 10.95 (ISBN 0-8037-0246-9, 01063-320); PLB 10.89 (ISBN 0-8037-0247-7). Dial Bks Young.
Uncle Henry & Aunt Henrietta's Honeymoon. Nicole Rubel. LC 85-15944. (Pied Piper Bk.). 32p. (ps-2). 1988. pap. 3.95 (ISBN 0-8037-0498-4, 0383-120). Dial Bks Young.
Uncle Ike. Linda S. Chandler. LC 80-70520. (gr. 1-6). 1981. 5.95 (ISBN 0-8054-4264-2, 4242-64). Broadman.
Uncle Isaac. facsimile ed. William D. Powers. LC 74-170703. (Black Heritage Library Collection). Repr. of 1899 ed. 18.00 (ISBN 0-8369-8893-0). Ayer Co Pubs.
Uncle Ivan's Magic Box. Helen Z. Jensen. LC 86-32903. (Illus.). 32p. (ps-4). 1988. 11.95 (ISBN 0-8037-0095-4, 01160-350). Dial Bks Young.
Uncle Jack among the English. John W. Loughary. (Illus.). 60p. (Orig.). 1984. pap. 3.95 (ISBN 0-915671-00-X). United Learn.
Uncle Jacob's Ghost Story. Donn Kushner. LC 85-14124. 144p. (gr. 4-9). 1986. 12.95 (ISBN 0-03-006502-X). H Holt & Co.
Uncle Jim's Book of Pancakes. 2ed ed. James E. Banks. (Wild & Woolly West Ser., No. 3). (Illus., Orig.). 1979. 8.00 (ISBN 0-910584-58-3); pap. 1.50 (ISBN 0-910584-44-3). Filter.
Uncle Joe Cannon: The Story of a Pioneer American. Joe Cannon. Ed. by L. White Busbey. LC 77-144924. (Illus.). 1971. Repr. of 1927 ed. 29.00 (ISBN 0-403-00887-5). Scholarly.
Uncle Joe's Record Guide: Eric Clapton, Jimi Hendrix, The Who. Joe Benson. 288p. 1988. pap. 9.95 (ISBN 0-943031-03-6). J Benson Unlimit.

Uncommon Guide to Carmel, Monterey & Big Sur. Laclan P. MacDonald. (Illus.). 1982. pap. 6.95 (ISBN 0-914598-21-X). Padre Prods.
Uncommon Guide to San Luis Obispo County California. rev. 2nd ed. Lachlan P. MacDonald. LC 75-2794. (Illus.). 1982. pap. 5.95 (ISBN 0-686-69421-X). Padre Prods.
Uncommon Hero: One Mother Who Went to Jail to Protect Her Child from Sexual Abuse. Stephen T. Curwood. LC 88-40094. 320p. 1988. 18.95 (ISBN 0-446-51448-9). Warner Bks.
Uncommon Infections & Special Topics. Ed. by Louis Keith. 1985. lib. bdg. 72.00 (ISBN 0-85200-861-9, Pub. by MTP Pr England). Kluwer-Academic.
Uncommon Man. Coman Leavenworth. 96p. 1987. 9.95 (ISBN 0-89962-615-7). Todd & Honeywell.
Uncommon Man in American Business. Wallace J. Johnson. 1966. 6.95 (ISBN 0-8159-7001-3). Devin.
Uncommon Man: The Triumph of Herbert Hoover. Richard N. Smith. (Illus.). 448p. 1984. 22.95 (ISBN 0-671-46034-X). S&S.
Uncommon Market: Capital, Class & Power in the European Community. Stuart Holland. 1980. 12.95x (ISBN 0-312-82867-5). St Martin.
Uncommon Market: Capital, Class & Power in the European Community. Stuart Holland. 183p. 73.00x (ISBN 0-85124-378-9, Pub. by Bertrand Russell Hse); pap. 15.00x (ISBN 0-85124-373-8). State Mutual Bk.
Uncommon Obdurate: The Several Public Careers of J. F. W. Des Barres. Geraint N. Evans. LC 72-84547. (Illus.). 1969. 12.50 (ISBN 0-87577-000-2). Peabody Mus Salem.
Uncommon Places. Stephen Shore. (Illus.). 64p. 1982. 30.00. ltd. ed. 250.00 (ISBN 0-89381-104-1). Aperture.
Uncommon Poet for the Common Man: A Study of the Poetry of Philip Larkin. Lolette Kuby. (De Proprietatibus Litterarum, Ser. Practica: No. 60). 190p. 1974. pap. text ed. 16.80x (ISBN 90-2792-720-0). Mouton.
Uncommon Prayer: Approaching Intimacy with God. Kenneth Swanson. 1987. 10.95 (ISBN 0-345-33783-2, Pub. by Ballantine Epiphany). Ballantine.
Uncommon Prayers: For Young Adults at Work. Daniel R. Seagren. 3.50 (ISBN 0-8010-8129-7). Baker Bk.
Uncommon Psychiatric Syndromes. 2nd ed. M. Enoch & W. Trethowan. 208p. Repr. of 1981 ed. 31.00 (ISBN 0-7236-0517-3). PSG Pub Co.
Uncommon Sailor: A Portrait of Sir William Penn. Lucie Street. 176p. 1988. 12.95x (ISBN 0-312-01526-7, Pub. by Thomas Dunne Bks). St Martin.
Uncommon Sense. J. Robert Oppenheimer. Ed. by N. Metropolis et al. LC 84-439. 195p. 1984. 16.95 (ISBN 0-8176-3165-8). Birkhauser.
Uncommon Sense: Manuscript Two of the Humanist Papers. pap. 5.00 (ISBN 0-938722-02-6). Word Ent.
Uncommon Sense: The Life & Thought of Ludwig von Bertalanffy (1901-1972), Father of General Systems Theory. Mark Davidson. LC 82-16900. 256p. 1983. 15.95 (ISBN 0-87477-165-X). HM.
Uncommon Sense: The Life & Thought of Ludwig von Bertalanffy, Father of the General Systems Theory. Mark Davidson. 240p. 1984. pap. 8.95 (ISBN 0-87477-334-2). J P Tarcher.
Uncommon Sense: The World's Fullest Compendium of Wisdom. Joseph Telushkin. 238p. 1987. 14.95 (ISBN 0-933503-48-2). Shapolsky Pubs.
Uncommon Subject: Drawings & Prints by Sharon Ellis. Georgia Coopersmith & Sharon Ellis. 1986. pap. 0.75 (ISBN 0-942746-11-2). SUNYP R Gibson.
Uncommon Therapy. Jay Haley. 1987. pap. 5.95 (ISBN 0-393-30424-8). Norton.
Uncommon Therapy: The Psychiatric Techniques of Milton H. Erickson, M.D. Jay Haley. 1986. 19.95 (ISBN 0-393-02304-4). Norton.
Uncommon Tongue: The Poetry & Criticism of Geoffrey Hill. Vicent Sherry. 272p. 1987. 29.50x (ISBN 0-472-10084-X). U of Mich Pr.
Uncommon Valor: A Game-by-Game History of the Army-Navy Football Rivalry. Wesley F. Gill. (Illus.). 304p. pap. cancelled (ISBN 0-88011-245-X). Leisure Pr.
Uncommon Valor: Marine Divisions in Action. George McMillan et al. (Elite Unit Ser.: 5th). (Illus.). 272p. 1986. Repr. of 1946 ed. 19.95 (ISBN 0-89839-094-X). Battery Pr.
Uncommon Wisdom. Fritjof Capra. (New Age Ser.). 224p. 1989. pap. 9.95 (ISBN 0-553-34610-5). Bantam.
Uncommon Wisdom: Conversations with Remarkable People. Fritjof Capra. 336p. 1988. 19.95 (ISBN 0-671-47322-0). S&S.
Uncommon Women & Others. Wendy Wasserstein. 1979. pap. 2.95 (ISBN 0-380-45997-3, 80580-4, Bard). Avon.
Uncompahgre. Muriel Marshall. LC 80-11666. (Illus.). 210p. (Orig.). 1980. pap. 6.95 (ISBN 0-87004-282-3). Caxton.
Uncompensated Hospital Care: Rights & Responsibilities. Ed. by Frank A. Sloan et al. LC 85-45045. (Contemporary Medicine & Public Health Ser.). 224p. 1986. text ed. 25.00x (ISBN 0-8018-2867-8). Johns Hopkins.
Uncompleted Past. Martin Duberman. Ed. by Robin W. Winks. LC 83-49169. (History & Historiography Ser.). 356p. 1985. lib. bdg. 35.00 (ISBN 0-8240-6359-7). Garland Pub.
Uncompleted Past. Martin Duberman. 1971. pap. 2.45 (ISBN 0-525-47290-8). Dutton.
Uncompleted Past: Postwar German Novels & the Third Reich. Judith Ryan. LC 83-6744. 184p. 1983. 24.50x (ISBN 0-8143-1728-6). Wayne St U Pr.
Uncomplicated Christian. LeRoy Dugan. LC 78-66886. 128p. 1978. pap. 2.50 (ISBN 0-87123-572-2, 200572). Bethany Hse.
Uncompromising Chess: The Games of Viktor Kupreichik. Gene McCormick. 66p. (Orig.). 1986. pap. 5.00 (ISBN 0-931462-58-4). Chess Ent Inc.
Uncompromising Fictions of Cynthia Ozick. Sanford Pinkster. LC 86-30788. 128p. 1987. pap. 8.95 (ISBN 0-8262-0635-2). U of Mo Pr.
Uncompromising Life: Daniel One, Three, & Six. John MacArthur. (John MacArthur's Bible Studies). 1988. pap. 3.95 (ISBN 0-8024-5364-3). Moody.
Unconcious Contracts: A Psychoanalytic Theory of Society. Michael Allingham. 176p. 1988. text ed. 42.00 (ISBN 0-7102-0996-7, Pub. by Routledge UK). Routledge Chapman & Hall.
Unconditional Democracy: Education & Politics in Occupied Japan, 1945 to 1952. Toshio Nishi. (Publication Ser.: No. 244). 408p. 1982. 19.95x (ISBN 0-8179-7441-5). Hoover Inst Pr.
Unconditional Good News: Toward an Understanding of Biblical Universalism. Neal Punt. LC 80-10458. pap. 44.80 (ISBN 0-317-39671-4, 2023222). Bks Demand UMI.
Unconditional Hatred: German War Guilt Post W.W.II. Russell Grenfell. 1953. 9.95 (ISBN 0-8159-7002-1). Devin.
Unconditional in Human Knowledge: Four Early Essays (1794-1796) by F. W. J. Schelling. Fritz Marti. Tr. by F. W. Schelling. LC 77-74407. 272p. 1980. 25.00 (ISBN 0-8387-2020-X). Bucknell U Pr.
Unconditional Love. John Powell. LC 78-74154. 1978. pap. 3.50 (ISBN 0-89505-029-3). Tabor Pub.
Unconditional Love & Forgiveness. Edith R. Staufer. (Illus.). 224p. (Orig.). 1987. pap. 9.95 (ISBN 0-940111-03-9). Triangle Burbank.
Unconditional Surrender: God's Program for Victory. 2nd ed. Gary North. LC 82-84385. 280p. 1983. pap. text ed. 9.95 (ISBN 0-939404-06-0). Geneva Ministr.
Unconditional Surrender: God's Program for Victory. Gary North. 417p. 1988. pap. 5.95 (ISBN 0-930464-12-5). Inst Christian.
Unconfined Vapor Cloud Explosions. Keith Gugan. LC 78-74101. 168p. 1979. 45.00x (ISBN 0-87201-887-3). Gulf Pub.
Unconfirmed Kill. (Vietnam Ground Zero Ser.: No. 3). Date not set. pap. 2.75 (Pub. by Worldwide). Harlequin Bks.
Unconformities in Shakespeare's Early Comedies. Kristian Smidt. LC 86-6666. 240p. 1986. 29.95 (ISBN 0-312-82868-3). St Martin.
Unconjugated Pterins & Related Biogenic Amines. Ed. by H. Curtius et al. 398p. 1987. lib. bdg. 135.50x (ISBN 0-89925-368-7). De Gruyter.
Unconjugated Pterins in Neurobiology: Basic & Clinical Aspects. Ed. by W. Lovenberg & R. A. Levine. LC 86-23177. (Topics in Neurochemistry & Neuropharmacology Ser.: Vol. 1). 250p. 1987. 66.00x (ISBN 0-85066-370-9). Taylor & Francis.
Unconquerable Spirit. Simon Zuker. Ed. by Gertrude Hirschler. (Illus.). 160p. 1980. pap. 9.95 (ISBN 0-89906-203-2). Mesorah Pubns.
Unconquerable Spirit: Vignettes of the Jewish Religious Spirit the Nazis Could Not Destroy. Simon Zuker. Ed. by Gertrude Hirschler. (ArtScroll History Ser.). (Illus.). 160p. 1980. 12.95 (ISBN 0-89906-202-4). Mesorah Pubns.
Unconquered. Bertrice Small. 1982. pap. 3.95 (ISBN 0-345-31401-8). Ballantine.
Unconquered. Jeffrey Wallman. 1977. pap. 1.75 (ISBN 0-8439-0442-9, Leisure Bks). Leisure NY.
Unconquered Country. Ryman. 1987. pap. 2.95 (ISBN 0-553-26654-3, Spectra). Bantam.
Unconquered: Journal of a Year's Adventure Among the Fighting Peasants of North China. James M. Bertram. (China in the 20th Century Ser.). (Illus.). ix, 340p. 1975. Repr. of 1939 ed. lib. bdg. 39.50 (ISBN 0-306-70688-1). Da Capo.
Unconquered Knight: A Chronicle of the Deeds of Don Pero Nino. Diaz De Gamez. Tr. by Joan Evans. LC 78-63494. Repr. of 1928 ed. 27.50 (ISBN 0-404-17143-5). AMS Pr.
Unconquered Souls: The Resistentialists. C. L. Sulzberger. LC 72-81087. 224p. 1973. 7.95 (ISBN 0-87951-004-8); 14.95. Overlook Pr.
Unconscious: A Conceptual Analysis. Alasdair C. MacIntyre. (Studies in Philosophical Psychology). 1976. pap. text ed. 7.95x (ISBN 0-391-00336-4). Humanities.
Unconscious: A Guide to the Sources. Natalino Caputi. LC 85-1979. (ATCA Bibliography Ser.: No. 16). 161p. 1985. 17.50 (ISBN 0-8108-1798-5). Scarecrow.
Unconscious, a Symposium. facs. ed. Charles M. Child et al. LC 67-22125. (Essay Index Reprint Ser). 1928. 17.00 (ISBN 0-8369-0957-7). Ayer Co Pubs.
Unconscious & the Theory of Psychoneuroses. Zvi Giora. Ed. by Leo Goldberger. (Psychoanalytic Crosscurrents Ser.). 256p. 1988. 35.00x (ISBN 0-8147-3021-3). NYU Pr.
Unconscious Before Freud. L. L. Whyte. (Classics in Psychology & Psychiatry Ser.). 256p. 1978. 19.50 (ISBN 0-86187-349-1, Pub. by Frances Pinter); pap. 7.75 (ISBN 0-86187-309-2). Longwood Pub Group.
Unconscious Communication in Everyday Life. Robert Langs. LC 82-1669. 224p. 1983. 20.00x (ISBN 0-87668-492-4). Aronson.
Unconscious Conspiracy: Why Leaders Can't Lead. Bennis G. Warren. LC 75-37851. pap. 46.30 (ISBN 0-317-42056-9, 2056091). Bks Demand UMI.
Unconscious God. Victor Frankl. 1976. pap. 5.95 (ISBN 0-671-22426-3, Touchstone Bks). S&S.
Unconscious God. Viktor Frankl. 1985. pap. 3.50 (ISBN 0-671-54728-3). WSP.
Unconscious Humourist: And Other Essays. E. Lacon Watson. LC 72-13313. (Essay Index Reprint Ser.). Repr. of 1896 ed. 16.75 (ISBN 0-8369-8177-4). Ayer Co Pubs.
Unconscious Reconsidered. Ed. by Kenneth S. Bowers & Donald Meichenbaum. LC 84-5201. (Personality Processes Ser. (1-341)). 311p. 1984. 33.95x (ISBN 0-471-87558-9, Pub. by Wiley-Interscience). Wiley.
Unconscious Structure in Dostoevsky's "The Idiot" A Study in Literature & Psychoanalysis. Elizabeth Dalton. LC 78-70287. 1979. 30.50x (ISBN 0-691-06364-8). Princeton U Pr.
Unconscious: The Fundamentals of Human Personality Normal & Abnormal. 2nd ed. Morton Prince. LC 73-2411. (Mental Illness & Social Policy; the American Experience Ser.). Repr. of 1921 ed. 40.00 (ISBN 0-405-05221-9). Ayer Co Pubs.
Unconscious Today: Essays in Honor of Max Schur. Ed. by Mark Kanzer. LC 74-14337. 544p. 1971. text ed. 50.00x (ISBN 0-8236-6680-8). Intl Univs Pr.
Unconscious Victorious & Other Stories. Stanley Berne. LC 69-20442. (Archives of Post-Modern Literature). (Illus.). 1969. pap. 9.95 (ISBN 0-913844-04-7). Am Canadian.
Unconscious Victorious & Other Stories. Stanley Berne. 304p. 1973. pap. 9.95 (ISBN 0-8180-0616-1). Horizon.
Unconstitutionality of Slavery. 2nd ed. Lysander Spooner. 1965. 20.50 (ISBN 0-8337-3353-2). B Franklin.
Uncontested Divorces & Annulments in New York. 2nd ed. James P. Gitlitz. 175p. (Supplemented annually). text ed. 25.00. Gould.
Uncontrollable Spending for Social Services Grants. Martha Derthick. LC 75-5155. 139p. 1975. pap. 9.95 (ISBN 0-8157-1813-6). Brookings.
Uncontrolled Chancellor: Charles Townshend & His American Policy. Cornelius P. Forster. LC 78-63017. 155p. 1978. 9.95 (ISBN 0-917012-16-X). RI Pubns Soc.
Unconventional Aircraft. Peter M. Bowers. (Illus.). 288p. (Orig.). 1984. pap. 17.95 (ISBN 0-8306-2384-1, 2384). TAB Bks.
Unconventional Approaches to Fusion. Ed. by B. Brunelli & G. G. Leotta. LC 82-3836. (Ettore Majorana International Science Series, Physical Sciences: Vol. 13). 544p. 1982. 95.00x (ISBN 0-306-41002-8, Plenum Pr). Plenum Pub.
Unconventional Courtship. Dorothy Mack. 224p. 1987. pap. 2.75 (ISBN 0-451-14925-4, Sig). NAL.
Unconventional Electron Microscopy for Molecular StructureDetermination. Ed. by W. Hoppe & R. Mason. 1979. 55.50 (ISBN 3-528-08117-1, Pub. by Vieweg & Sohn Germany). IPS.
Unconventional Imaging, Science & Technology: Advanced Printing of Paper Summaries, the 22nd Fall Symposium, November 15-18, 1982, Key Bridge Marriott Hotel, Arlington, Virginia. Society of Photographic Scientists & Engineers. pap. 21.50 (ISBN 0-317-29897-6, 2019357). Bks Demand UMI.
Unconventional Invention Book. Bob Stanish. (gr. 3-12). 1981. 8.95 (ISBN 0-86653-035-5, GA 263). Good Apple.
Unconventional Natural Gas: Resources, Potential & Technology. M. Satriana. LC 80-15215. (Energy Technology Review: No. 56). 358p. (Orig.). 1980. 42.00 (ISBN 0-8155-0808-5). Noyes.
Unconventional Perceptions of Yugoslavia. Ed. by Steven K. Pavlowitch. 256p. 1985. 25.00x (ISBN 0-88033-081-3, Dist. by Columbia U Pr). East Eur Quarterly.
Unconventional Sources of Dietary Fiber. Ed. by Ivan Furda. LC 83-2691. (Symposium Ser.: No. 214). 315p. 1983. lib. bdg. 58.95x (ISBN 0-8412-0768-2). Am Chemical.
Unconventional Warfare Devices & Techniques: Incendiaries. 1982. lib. bdg. 75.00 (ISBN 0-87700-325-4). Revisionist Pr.
Unconventional Wisdom. Pat Quigley. 160p. (Orig.). 1988. pap. 7.95 (ISBN 0-917895-21-5). Cordillera Co.
Unconventional Women. Margaret Hess. 1981. pap. 5.95 (ISBN 0-88207-340-0). Victor Bks.
Uncook Book: Raw Food Adventures to a New Health High. Elizabeth Baker & Elton Baker. 210p. 1981. pap. 5.95. Comm Creat.
Uncook Book: Raw Food Adventures to a New Health High. Elizabeth Baker & Elton Baker. (Illus.). 198p. 1981. pap. 5.95 (ISBN 0-937766-05-4). Drelwood Pubns.
Uncorrected World. Kenneth Hanson. LC 73-6012. (Wesleyan Poetry Program: Vol. 67). 1973. pap. 8.95 (ISBN 0-8195-1067-X). Wesleyan U Pr.
Uncorrupted Heart: Journal & Letters of Frederick Julius Gustorf 1800-1845. Frederick Gustorf & Gisela Gustorf. LC 70-93049. 192p. 1969. 21.00x (ISBN 0-8262-0079-6). U of Mo Pr.
Uncoupling: How & Why Relationship Come Apart. Diane Vaughan. LC 87-40065. 324p. 1987. pap. 4.95 (ISBN 0-394-75539-1, Vin). Random.
Uncoupling: Turning Points in Intimate Relationships. Diane Vaughan. LC 86-5401. 272p. 1986. 15.95 (ISBN 0-19-503910-6). Oxford U Pr.
Uncovered Wagon. Hart Stilwell. (Classic Ser.). 315p. 1985. pap. 9.95 (ISBN 0-87719-018-6). Texas Month Pr.
Uncovered Wagon. Mae Urbanek. 207p. 3.50x (ISBN 0-940514-08-7). Urbanek.
Uncovering Soviet Disasters. James E. Oberg. LC 87-42658. (Illus.). 336p. 1988. 19.95 (ISBN 0-394-56095-7). Random.
Uncovering the Ancient World. H. V. Winstone. (Illus.). 394p. 24.95 (ISBN 0-8160-1578-3). Facts on File.
Uncovering the Dome. Amy Klobuchar. (Illus.). 174p. 1986. pap. text ed. 8.50x (ISBN 0-88133-218-6). Waveland Pr.
Uncovering the Forces for War. Conrad Grieb. 115p. pap. 4.00 (ISBN 0-89562-096-0). Sons Lib.
Uncovering the Forces for War. Conrad Grieb. 115p. 1986. pap. 3.75 (ISBN 0-317-53286-3). Noontide.
Uncovering the News: A Journalist's Search for Information. Lauren Kessler & Duncan McDonald. 243p. 1987. pap. text ed. write for info. (ISBN 0-534-06954-1). Wadsworth Pub.
Uncovering the Sixties: The Life & Times of the Underground Press. Abe Peck. LC 84-42970. 1985. 22.45 (ISBN 0-394-52793-3). Pantheon.
Uncovering Up: A Guide to Excellence in School Public Relations. William L. Jones & Charles S. Stough. LC 75-43576. 1977. pap. 9.95 (ISBN 0-88280-038-8). ETC Pubns.
Uncoverings, 1980. Ed. by Sally Garoutte. LC 81-649486. (Research Papers of American Quilt Study Group Ser.: Vol. 1). (Illus.). 76p. (Orig.). 1981. pap. 15.00x (ISBN 0-9606590-0-5). Am Quilt.
Uncoverings, 1981. Ed. by Sally Garoutte. LC 81-649486. (Research Papers of American Quilt Study Group Ser.: Vol. 2). (Illus.). 112p. (Orig.). 1982. pap. 15.00x (ISBN 0-9606590-1-3). Am Quilt.
Uncoverings, 1982. Ed. by Sally Garoutte. LC 81-649486. (Research Papers of American Quilt Study Group: Vol. 3). (Illus.). 140p. (Orig.). 1983. pap. 15.00x (ISBN 0-9606590-2-1). Am Quilt.
Uncoverings, 1983. Ed. by Sally Garoutte. LC 81-649486. (Research Papers of American Quilt Study Group Ser.: Vol. 4). (Illus.). 150p. (Orig.). 1984. pap. 15.00x (ISBN 0-9606590-3-X). Am Quilt.
Uncoverings, 1984. Ed. by Sally Garoutte. LC 81-649486. (Research Papers of American Quilt Study Group: Vol. 5). (Illus.). 176p. (Orig.). 1985. pap. 15.00x (ISBN 0-9606590-4-8). Am Quilt.
Uncoverings, 1985. Intro. by Sally Garoutte. LC 81-649486. (Research Papers: Vol. 6). (Illus.). 170p. (Orig.). 1987. pap. 15.00x (ISBN 0-9606590-5-6). Am Quilt.
Uncoverings, 1986. Ed. by Sally Garoutte. LC 81-649486. (Research Papers of American Quilt Study Group: Vol. 7). (Illus., Orig.). 1987. pap. 15.00x (ISBN 0-9606590-6-4). Am Quilt.
Uncreated Energy. George Maloney. (Wellspring Bk.). 128p. 1988. pap. 7.95 (ISBN 0-916349-20-9). Amity Hse Inc.
Uncreating Word: Romanticism & the Object. Irving J. Massey. LC 77-126213. Repr. of 1970 ed. 27.40 (ISBN 0-8357-9250-1, 2013020). Bks Demand UMI.
Uncrowned King. H. B. Wright. 1982. Repr. lib. bdg. 17.95x (ISBN 0-89966-439-3). Buccaneer Bks.
Uncrowned Prime Ministers. D. R. Thorpe. 272p. 1980. 35.00x (Pub. by Darkhorse England). State Mutual Bk.
UNCTAD Commodity Yearbook 1986. 584p. 1987. 60.00 (ISBN 92-1-112228-7, E.86.II.D.8). UN.
UNCTAD Liner Code: United States Maritime Policy at the Crossroads. Lawrence Juda. (Replica Edition Ser.). 350p. 1983. softcover 28.50x (ISBN 0-86531-996-0). Westview.
UNCTAD Rules of Procedures. rev. 2nd ed. 37p. 1987. 6.00 (ISBN 92-1-112230-9, E.87.II.D.4). UN.
UNCTC Bibliography 1974-1987. 83p. 1988. pap. 12.00 (ISBN 92-1-104218-6, E.87.II.A.23). UN.
Und Transzedentale Logik: Herausgegeben Von Paul Janssen, No. 1. Husserl. (Studienausgaben Husserl Ser). 1977. pap. 10.00 (ISBN 90-247-1976-3, Martinus Nijhoff Netherlands). Kluwer Academic.
Undaunted Heroes: A Soviet Vietnam Diary. Sergei Vysotsky & Ilya Glazunov. (Illus.). 177p. 1975. 15.00 (ISBN 0-8464-0944-5). Beekman Pubs.
Undaunted River. Richard Cox. 1966. pap. 1.00x (ISBN 0-88020-080-4). Coach Hse.
Undecidability of the Domino Problem. Robert Berger. LC 52-42839. (Memoirs: No. 66). 72p. 1966. pap. 11.00 (ISBN 0-8218-1266-1, MEMO-66). Am Math.

Under the Greenwood Tree. Thomas Hardy. Ed. & intro. by Simon Gatrell. (World's Classics Ser.). (Illus.). 224p. 1986. pap. 3.95 (ISBN 0-19-281706-X). Oxford U Pr.
Under the Greenwood Tree. William Shakespeare. Ed. by Barbara Holdridge. (Stemmer House Poetry for Young People Ser.). (Illus.). 80p. (gr. 4 up). 1986. 17.95 (ISBN 0-88045-028-2); pap. 9.95 (ISBN 0-88045-029-0); cassette & Bk. 21.90 (ISBN 0-88045-103-3); cassette only 8.95 (ISBN 0-88045-100-9). Stemmer Hse.
Under the Grey Gull's Wing. Alta Ashley. (Illus.). 135p. (Orig.). 1984. 6.95 (ISBN 0-9614592-0-4). Grey Gull Pubns.
Under the Ground. Eugene Booth. LC 77-8037. (Spotlight Bks.). (Illus.). (gr. k-3). 1977. PLB 13.32 (ISBN 0-8393-0110-3). Raintree Pubs.
Under the Ground. Eugene Booth. LC 77-8037. (Spotlight Ser.). (Illus.). 24p. (gr. k-3). 1985. pap. 9.27 (ISBN 0-8393-0171-5). Raintree Pubs.
Under the Ground. Andrew Langley. LC 85-71730. (Topics Ser.). (Illus.). 32p. (gr. k-6). 1986. PLB 11.90 (ISBN 0-531-18049-2, Pub. by Bookwright Pr). Watts.
Under the Gun. Gerald Eaton. 48p. (Orig.). 1985. pap. 6.95 (ISBN 0-934553-01-7). Wainwright.
Under the Gun: Weapons, Crime, & Violence in America. James Wright et al. 360p. 1986. pap. text ed. 17.95 (ISBN 0-202-30306-3). Aldine de Gruyter.
Under the Gun: Weapons, Crime, & Violence in America. James D. Wright et al. LC 83-2615. 362p. 1983. text ed. 34.95x (ISBN 0-202-30305-5). Aldine de Gruyter.
Under the Guns in Beirut. Terry Raburn. LC 80-65308. 160p. 1980. pap. 2.50 (ISBN 0-88243-634-1, 02-0634). Gospel Pub.
Under the Hawthorne. Ellen Frye. LC 87-60530. 240p. (Orig.). 1987. pap. 7.95 (ISBN 0-934678-12-X). New Victoria Pubs.
Under the Hermes, & Other Stories. Clotilde I. Graves. LC 70-121554. (Short Story Index Reprint Ser). 1917. 20.00 (ISBN 0-8369-3510-1). Ayer Co Pubs.
Under the High Seas: New Frontiers in Oceanography. Margaret Poynter & Donald Collins. LC 82-16338. (Illus.). 160p. (gr. 5 up). 1983. 11.95 (ISBN 0-689-30977-5, Atheneum Childrens Bks). Macmillan.
Under the House. Leslie H. Pinder. LC 87-43217. 184p. 1988. 15.95 (ISBN 0-394-56932-6). Random.
Under the Indian Turquois Sky. Rosemary Davey & Grace Nutley. (Illus.). 93p. 1985. 9.00 (ISBN 0-87770-339-6). Ye Galleon.
Under the Influence. W. E. Butterworth. LC 78-22127. 256p. (gr. 7 up). 1979. 9.95 (ISBN 0-02-716240-0, Four Winds). Macmillan.
Under the Influence. Reginald Ikin. 1986. 8.95 (ISBN 0-533-06820-7). Vantage.
Under the Influence - Myths-Realities-Alcoholism. Milam & Ketcham. 1987. pap. 4.95 (ISBN 0-553-26758-2). Bantam.
Under the Influence - Myths-Realities-Alcoholism. Milan & Ketcham. 1984. pap. 4.95 (ISBN 0-553-27487-2). Bantam.
Under the Influence: A Charles Bukowski Checklist. Charles Bukowski. Ed. by Jeffrey Weinberg. (Illus.). 50p. (Orig.). 1987. pap. 10.00 (ISBN 0-934953-13-9). Water Row Pr.
Under the Influence: A Guide to the Myths & Realities of Alcoholism. James Milam & Katherine Ketcham. LC 81-12360. 224p. 1981. 14.95 (ISBN 0-914842-69-2). Madrona Pubs.
Under the Jaguar Sun. Italo Calvino. Tr. by William Weaver. 96p. 1988. 12.95 (ISBN 0-15-192820-7). HarBraceJ.
Under the Lake. Stuart Woods. 1987. 17.95 (ISBN 0-671-63332-5). S&S.
Under the Lake. Stuart Woods. (Illus.). 473p. 1987. Repr. lib. bdg. 18.95 (ISBN 0-89621-846-5). Thorndike Pr.
Under the Lake. Stuart Woods. 288p. 1988. pap. 4.50 (ISBN 0-380-70519-2). Avon.
Under the Lights: A Young Model at Work. Barbara Beirne. (Illus.). 56p. (gr. 2-5). 1988. PLB 12.95 (ISBN 0-87614-316-8). Carolrhoda Bks.
Under the Lilacs. Louisa May Alcott. (Illus.). (gr. 7 up). 1877. 16.45i (ISBN 0-316-03099-6). Little.
Under the Lineage's Shadow. Jack Goody. (Radcliffe-Brown Lectures in Social Anthropology Ser.). 1986. pap. 5.50 (ISBN 0-85672-529-3, Pub. by British Acad). Longwood Pub Group.
Under the Looking Glass: The Color Photographs of Olivia Parker. Olivia Parker. LC 83-61445. (Illus.). 80p. 1983. 34.00i (ISBN 0-8212-1556-6, 887323). NYGS.
Under the Mercy: A Sequel to a Severe Mercy. Sheldon Vanauken. 263p. 1988. pap. 9.95 (ISBN 0-89870-213-5). Ignatius Pr.
Under the Mexican Flag: The Mexican Struggle Outlined. C. J. Velarde. 1976. lib. bdg. 59.95 (ISBN 0-8490-2783-7). Gordon Pr.
Under the Mountain. Molly F. Knudtsen. LC 82-8552. (Illus.). 130p. 1982. 11.95 (ISBN 0-87417-072-9). U of Nev Pr.
Under the Mountain Wall. Peter Matthiessen. 1987. pap. 8.95 (ISBN 0-14-009548-9). Penguin.
Under the Mountain Wall. Peter Matthiessen. 1988. 16.75 (ISBN 0-8446-6304-2). Peter Smith.
Under the Net. Iris Murdoch. 1977. pap. 6.95 (ISBN 0-14-001445-4). Penguin.
Under the North Star. Ted Hughes. LC 80-17894. (Illus.). 48p. 1981. 16.95 (ISBN 0-670-73942-1, Studio). Viking.
Under the Nuptial Canopy. Rosenblatt. 1975. 6.00 (ISBN 0-87306-109-8). Feldheim.
Under the Ocean. Eugene Booth. LC 77-7983. (Raintree Spotlight Book). (Illus.). (gr. k-3). 1977. PLB 13.32 (ISBN 0-8393-0108-1). Raintree Pubs.
Under the Ocean. Eugene Booth. LC 77-7983. (Spotlight Ser.). (Illus.). 24p. (gr. k-3). 1985. pap. 9.27 (ISBN 0-8393-0172-3). Raintree Pubs.
Under the Old Flag, 2 vols. James H. Wilson. 1971. Repr. of 1912 ed. Vol. 2. lib. bdg. 18.00 (ISBN 0-8371-5810-9, WIUH). Greenwood.
Under the Redwoods. Bret Harte. LC 72-113674. (Short Story Index Reprint Ser.). 1901. 19.00 (ISBN 0-8369-3403-2). Ayer Co Pubs.
Under the Roofs of Paris. Henry Miller. 240p. 1984. pap. cancelled (ISBN 0-440-09173-X, Pub. by Grove). Dell.
Under the Roofs of Paris. Henry Miller. LC 84-73204. Orig. Title: Opus Pistorum. 288p. 1985. pap. 3.95 (ISBN 0-394-62030-5, BC). Grove.
Under the Same Roof: A Guide for Parents in Recovery. Kay M. Porterfield. 32p. 1985. pap. 1.25 (ISBN 0-89486-285-5). Hazelden.
Under the Same Stars. Dean Hughes. 143p. (gr. 4-8). 1988. pap. 4.95 (ISBN 0-87579-159-X). Deseret Bk.
Under the Same Stars. Dean T. Hughes. LC 79-10472. (gr. 7-12). 1979. 6.95 (ISBN 0-87747-750-7). Deseret Bk.
Under the Sangre de Cristo. Paul Horgan. (Charlotte Ser.). 90p. 1985. 150.00x (ISBN 0-911292-00-4). Rydal.
Under the Sangre de Cristo. Paul Horgan. LC 86-46374. 86p. 1987. 14.95 (ISBN 0-87358-440-6); pap. 9.95 (ISBN 0-87358-441-4). Northland.
Under the Sea. Brenda Thompson & Cynthia Overbeck. LC 76-22470. (Lerner First Fact Bks.). (Illus.). (gr. k-3). 1977. PLB 4.95 (ISBN 0-8225-1363-3). Lerner Pubns.
Under the Shade of a Coolibah Tree: Australian Studies in Consciousness. Richard A. Hutch & Peter G. Fenner. LC 84-20854. 352p. (Orig.). 1985. lib. bdg. 31.25 (ISBN 0-8191-4348-0); pap. text ed. 15.50 (ISBN 0-8191-4349-9). U Pr of Amer.
Under the Shadow of War: Fascism, Anti-Fascism, & Marxists, 1918-1939. Larry Ceplair. LC 86-32652. 272p. 1987. 30.00 (ISBN 0-231-06532-9). Columbia U Pr.
Under the Shadow of Your Wings. Craig D. Erickson. Ed. by Michael L. Sherer. LC 86-28348. (Orig.). 1987. pap. 6.75 (ISBN 0-89536-844-7, 7803). CSS of Ohio.
Under the Shelter of His Wings. Glenn Clark. pap. 0.20 (ISBN 0-910924-50-3). Macalester.
Under the Sidewalks of New York: The Story of the World's Greatest Subway System. rev. ed. Brian J. Cudahy. LC 88-1255. (Illus.). 176p. Date not set. 17.95 (ISBN 0-8289-0685-8). Greene.
Under the Sign of Ambiguity: Saint John Perse - Alexis Leger. Erika Ostrovsky. LC 85-8946. 280p. 1987. pap. 15.00x (ISBN 0-8147-6166-6). NYU Pr.
Under the Sign of Ambiguity: Saint John Perse-Alexis Leger. Erika Ostrovsky. LC 85-9846. (Studies in French Culture & Civilization). (Illus.). 219p. 1985. 35.00x. NYU Pr.
Under the Sign of Saturn. Susan Sontag. 300p. 1980. 10.95 (ISBN 0-374-28076-2). FS&G.
Under the Sign of Saturn. Susan Sontag. LC 81-40073. 224p. 1981. pap. 3.95 (ISBN 0-394-74742-9, Vin). Random.
Under the Sign of Saturn. 1989. pap. 7.95 (ISBN 0-374-52115-8, Noonday). FS&G.
Under the Sign of the Waterbearer: A Life of Thomas Merton. James T. Baker. 1976. pap. 2.95 (ISBN 0-915216-15-9). Marathon Intl Pub Co.
Under the Skin. Nina Bawden. 17.95 (ISBN 0-88411-124-5, Pub. by Aeonian Pr). Amereon Ltd.
Under the Skin. Ken Norris. 24p. 1976. pap. 1.00 (ISBN 0-916696-00-6). Cross Country.
Under the Skin: The Death of White Rhodesia. David Caute. 447p. 1983. 32.95x (ISBN 0-8101-0658-2). Northwestern U Pr.
Under the Skylights. Henry B. Fuller. 1972. Repr. of 1901 ed. lib. bdg. 34.00 (ISBN 0-8422-8056-1). Irvington.
Under the Skylights. Henry B. Fuller. 1984. Repr. of 1901 ed. deluxe ed. 59.00x (ISBN 0-403-04590-8). Scholarly.
Under the Skylights. Henry B. Fuller. (Collected Works of Henry B. Fuller). 1988. Repr. of 1901 ed. lib. bdg. 59.00x. Am Biog Serv.
Under the Snowball Tree. Ellie Kirby. (Illus.). 32p. 1986. text ed. 14.95. Fox Creek Pr.
Under the Southern Cross: South America, Australia, Africa. G. B. Redmore. (Life & Livelihood Geographies Ser.: Bk. 2). (Illus.). pap. 8.95 (ISBN 0-685-20646-7). Transatl Arts.
Under the Starry Plough: Recollections of the Irish Citizen Army. Frank Robbins. (Illus.). 256p. 1977. (Pub. by Univ Pr of Ireland); pap. 7.95 (ISBN 0-906187-07-9). Longwood Pub Group.
Under the Stars & Bars: Memories of Four Years Service with the Oglethorpes of Augusta, Georgia. Walter A. Clark. LC 87-82696. (Georgia Military History Ser.). 250p. 1987. Repr. of 1900 ed. 14.50 (ISBN 0-944259-02-2). Freedom Hill.
Under the Stars & the Bars. J. T. Edson. 192p. (Orig.). 1987. pap. 2.50 (ISBN 0-425-09782-X). Berkley Pub.
Under the Streets of Nice. Ken Follett. 1989. pap. 3.95. PaperJacks US.
Under the Streets of Nice: The Bank Heist of the Century. Rene L. Maurice & Ken Follett. Ed. by Wendy Slossburg. (Zenith Edition Ser.). Orig. Title: Gentlemen of 16 July. 175p. 1986. pap. 5.95 (ISBN 0-915765-25-X). Natl Pr Inc.
Under the Sun. Erik Jay. LC 87-61377. 152p. 1987. 18.95 (ISBN 0-7206-0654-3, Pub. by P Owen Ltd). Dufour.
Under the Sun. George Junghanns. 1969. 4.50 (ISBN 0-686-05524-1); pap. 2.45 (ISBN 0-686-05525-X). Gauntlet Bks.
Under the Sun: Myth & Realism in Western American Literature. Ed. by Barbara H. Meldrum. LC 85-50609. (Illus.). vi, 231p. 1986. 22.50x (ISBN 0-87875-303-6). Whitston Pub.
Under the Sunday Tree. Eloise Greenfield. LC 87-29373. (Illus.). 48p. (ps up). 1988. 19.95i (ISBN 0-06-022254-9); PLB 12.89 (ISBN 0-06-022257-3). HarpJ.
Under the Sunset. Bram Stoker. Ed. by R. Reginald & Douglas Menville. LC 80-19564. (Newcastle Forgotten Library Ser.: Vol. 17). 190p. 1980. Repr. of 1978 ed. lib. bdg. 22.95x (ISBN 0-89370-516-0). Borgo Pr.
Under the Sweetwater Rim. Louis L'Amour. 1984. pap. 2.95 (ISBN 0-553-24760-3). Bantam.
Under the Ten Sleep Rim. rev., 2nd ed. Paul Frison. LC 85-8109. (Illus.). 175p. pap. cancelled (ISBN 0-914565-11-7). Capstan Pubns.
Under the Texas Sun: Adventures of a Young Cowpuncher. Anna M. Dana. LC 86-14401. (Wardlaw Bk.). 112p. 1987. 12.50 (ISBN 0-89096-284-7). Tex A&M Univ Pr.
Under the Third Roof. Terence G. Abreu. 1987. 7.95 (ISBN 0-533-07229-8). Vantage.
Under the Tonto Rim. Zane Grey. 1986. pap. 2.95 (ISBN 0-671-60499-6). PB.
Under the Tumtum Tree: From Nonsense to Sense. Marlene Dolitsky. LC 84-28471. (Pragmatics & Beyond Ser.: Series V: 1). vii, 118p. (Orig.). 1984. pap. 28.00x (ISBN 0-915027-39-9). Benjamins North Am.
Under the Volcano. Malcolm Lowry. LC 65-11640. 1984. 15.45i (ISBN 0-06-015367-9). Har-Row.
Under the Volcano. Malcolm Lowry. 1984. pap. 9.95 (ISBN 0-452-25595-3, Plume). NAL.
Under the Volcano. Malcolm Lowry. 1984. pap. 3.95 (ISBN 0-451-13213-0, Sig). NAL.
Under the Vulture Tree. David Bottoms. Ed. by Maria D. Guarnaschelli. LC 86-33178. 88p. (Orig.). 1987. 17.95 (ISBN 0-688-06834-0); pap. 5.95 (ISBN 0-688-07148-1). Morrow.
Under the Weight of the Sky. Kirk Robertson. LC 77-23446. 1978. pap. 2.50x (ISBN 0-916156-22-2). Cherry Valley.
Under the Wheat. Rick DeMarinis. LC 86-7007. (Drue Heinz Literature Prize Ser.). 160p. 1986. 16.95 (ISBN 0-8229-3544-9). U of Pittsburgh Pr.
Under the Wheat. Rick DeMarinis. 157p. (Orig.). 1987. pap. 7.50 (ISBN 0-88001-149-1). Ecco Pr.
Under the Wheel. Gregory Benford et al. 1987. 3.50 (ISBN 0-671-65611-2). Baen Bks.
Under the Wheel. Hamlin Garland. (Collected Works of Hamlin Garland). 1988. Repr. of 1890 ed. lib. bdg. 59.00x. Am Biog Serv.
Under the Wheel see Collected Works.
Under the White Boar. Mary D. Few. LC 70-161090. (Illus.). 219p. 1973. 9.95 (ISBN 0-87667-069-9). Carolina Edns.
Under Their Vine & Fig Tree: Travels Through America in 1797-1799, 1805 with Some Further Account of Life in New Jersey, Vol. 14. Ed. by Julian U. Niemcewicz. (Illus.). 398p. 20.00 (ISBN 0-686-81808-3). NJ Hist Soc.
Under Thirty-Five: The New Generation of American Poets. Ed. by Nicholas Christopher. 1989. pap. 9.95 (ISBN 0-385-26035-0, Anchor Pr). Doubleday.
Under This Roof. Nancy King. 24p. (Orig.). 1983. pap. text ed. write for info (ISBN 0-932460-03-8). Summer Stream.
Under Three: A Comprehensive Guide to Caring for Your Baby & Toddler. Ed. by John S. O'Shea. LC 84-27023. 240p. 1987. 24.95 (ISBN 0-442-27247-2). Van Nos Reinhold.
Under Tropic Skies. facsimile ed. Louis Becke. LC 73-113650. (Short Story Index Reprint Ser.). 1905. 17.00 (ISBN 0-8369-3379-6). Ayer Co Pubs.
Under Twenty-Five: Duke Narrative & Verse, 1945-1962. William M. Blackburn. LC 63-9005. pap. 62.50 (ISBN 0-317-42244-8, 2026187). Bks Demand UMI.
Under Twenty-Five: Duke Narrative & Verse, 1945-1962: A Collection of Short Stories & Verse by Sixteen Duke Authors. Ed. by William M. Blackburn. LC 63-9005. xi, 240p. 1963. 12.95 (ISBN 0-8223-0349-3). Duke.
Under Two Flags, 3 vols. in 2. Ouida, pseud. LC 79-8187. Repr. of 1867 ed. Set. 84.50 (ISBN 0-404-62088-4); Vol. 1 o.p. (ISBN 0-404-62089-2); Vol. 2 o.p. (ISBN 0-404-62090-6). AMS Pr.
Under Venus. Peter Straub. 304p. 1985. pap. 3.95 (ISBN 0-425-07033-6). Berkley Pub.
Under Water: The Northern Lakes. Douglas R. Stamm. (Illus.). 128p. 1977. pap. 9.95 (ISBN 0-299-07264-9). U of Wis Pr.
Under Western Eyes. Joseph Conrad. Ed. by Boris Ford. (Classics Ser.). 352p. 1986. pap. 4.95 (ISBN 0-14-043243-4). Penguin.
Under Western Eyes. Joseph Conrad. 1987. pap. 3.50 (ISBN 0-451-52114-5, Sig Classics). NAL.
Under-Wood. Jeffrey Kindley. LC 66-20629. 1966. 3.50 (ISBN 0-916228-11-8). Phoenix Bk Shop.
Under Words. Robert Kelly. LC 83-12325. 164p. 1983. 25.00 (ISBN 0-87685-595-8); pap. 10.00 (ISBN 0-87685-594-X). Black Sparrow.
Under World. Subhas C. Saha. (Redbird Ser.). 1975. 8.00 (ISBN 0-88253-666-4); pap. text ed. 4.00 (ISBN 0-88253-665-6). Ind-US Inc.
Under Your Feet: The Story of the American Mound Builders. facsimile ed. Blanche B. King. LC 73-152990. (Select Bibliographies Reprint Ser). Repr. of 1939 ed. 22.00 (ISBN 0-8369-5742-3). Ayer Co Pubs.
Underachievement Syndrome: Causes & Cures. Sylvia B. Rimm. (Illus.). 313p. (Orig.). 1986. pap. 15.00 (ISBN 0-937891-00-2). Apple Pub Wisc.
Underachievers in School: Issues & Interventions. Nava Butler-Por. LC 87-8295. 187p. 1987. 39.95 (ISBN 0-471-91109-7). Wiley.
Underachievers: New York City Elementary Education Through the Eyes of a Teacher. Paul Friedman. LC 79-84194. 1980. 7.95 (ISBN 0-87212-110-0). Libra.
Underachieving Gifted see Reaching for the Stars: A Minicourse for Education of Gifted Students.
Underbelly Poems. James A. Costello. 1981. pap. 2.95 (ISBN 0-9605098-0-1). En Passant Poet.
Underbrush. Francis Fike. 20p. 1986. pap. 4.00 (ISBN 0-941150-50-X). Barth.
Underburner's Diet. Barbara Edelstein. 1988. pap. 4.50 (ISBN 0-440-20057-1). Dell.
Underburner's Diet: How to Rid Your Body of Excess Fat Forever. Barbara Edelstein. 224p. 1987. 14.95 (ISBN 0-02-534940-6). Macmillan.
Underclass. Ken Auletta. LC 82-40433. 368p. 1983. pap. 6.95 (ISBN 0-394-71388-5, Vin). Random.
Underconsumption Theories: A History & Critical Analysis. M. Bleaney. pap. text ed. 17.95 (ISBN 0-8464-0945-3). Beekman Pubs.
Undercooled Alloy Phases. Ed. by E. W. Collings & C. C. Koch. LC 86-33243. (Illus.). 520p. 1987. text ed. 98.00 (ISBN 0-87339-059-8). Metal Soc.
Undercover. Richard Girard & Cynthia Copeland. (Amazon Mutual Live-Action Ser.). (Illus.). cancelled (ISBN 0-940918-23-4). Dragon Tree.
Undercover. Soledad Santiago. 272p. 1988. pap. 3.95 (ISBN 0-553-26995-X). Bantam.
Undercover. Raymond C. Williams. 80p. 1986. 6.50 (ISBN 0-8233-0419-1). Golden Quill.
Undercover Agents in the Russian Revolutionary Movement: The SR Party, 1902-14. Nurit Scheifman. LC 86-21888. 250p. 1987. 29.95 (ISBN 0-312-00077-4). St Martin.
Undercover Cop. Jose L. Guzman & Carl Fick. (Orig.). 1979. pap. 2.25 (ISBN 0-89083-488-1). Zebra.
Undercover Exercise: Turn Everyday Activities into Fitness & Fun. Mardi Erdman & Barbara K. Koplan. (Illus.). 224p. 1984. 15.95 (ISBN 0-13-935453-0); pap. 8.95 (ISBN 0-13-935446-8). P-H.
Undercover Fighters: The British 22nd SAS Regiment. LC 85-40983. (Villard Military Ser.: The Elite Forces). (Illus.). 96p. 1986. 4.95 (ISBN 0-394-74405-5, Pub. by Villard Bks). Random.
Undercover Investigation. 2nd ed. J. Kirk Barefoot. 130p. 1983. text ed. 21.95 (ISBN 0-409-95076-9). Butterworth.
Undercover Lover. David Grote. (Illus.). 39p. (Director's Production Script). 1978. pap. 10.00 (ISBN 0-88680-200-8). I E Clark.
Undercover Operations & Persuasion. R. D. Hicks. (Illus.). 104p. 1973. 15.25x (ISBN 0-398-02807-9). C C Thomas.
Undercover: Police Surveillance in America. Gary Marx. (Twentieth Century Fund Book: No. 1). (Illus.). 280p. 1988. 25.00 (ISBN 0-520-06286-8). U of Cal Pr.
Undercover Run. Lew Dykes. Ed. by Damaris Rowland. 352p. (Orig.). 1988. pap. text ed. 3.95 (ISBN 0-425-10751-5). Berkley Pub.
Undercover: The Secret Lives of a Federal Agent. Donald Goddard. (Illus.). 320p. 1988. 18.95. Times Bks.
Undercover Work: A Complete Handbook. Burt Rapp. LC 85-82011. 152p. (Orig.). 1985. pap. 9.95 (ISBN 0-915179-32-6). Loompanics.
Undercurrent. Andrew J. Lane. 14.95 (ISBN 0-533-06051-6). Vantage.
Undercurrent. Bill Pronzini. 213p. 1984. pap. 4.95 (ISBN 0-88150-033-X, Foul Play). Countryman.
Undercurrents. Ridley Pearson. 416p. 1988. 18.95 (ISBN 0-312-01841-X). St Martin.
Undercurrents in American Politics. Arthur T. Hadley. Repr. of 1915 ed. 22.00 (ISBN 0-384-20688-3, P516). Johnson Repr.

TITLE INDEX UNDERGROUND STORAGE TANK: MODEL

Undercurrents of Influence in English Romantic Poetry. Margaret P. Sherwood. LC 70-155612. Repr. of 1934 ed. 9.50 (ISBN 0-404-05959-7). AMS Pr.

Undercurrents of Influence in English Romantic Poetry. facs. ed. Margaret P. Sherwood. LC 68-26474. (Essay Index Reprint Ser). 1934. 20.00 (ISBN 0-8369-0875-9). Ayer Co Pubs.

Underdeveloping the Amazon: Extraction, Unequal Exchange, & the Failure of the Modern State. Stephen G. Bunker. LC 83-18197. 296p. 1985. 24.50 (ISBN 0-252-01121-X). U of Ill Pr.

Underdeveloping the Amazon: Extraction, Unequal Exchange, & the Failure of the Modern State. Stephen G. Bunker. (Illus.). xvi, 280p. 1988. pap. 14.95 (ISBN 0-226-08032-3). U of Chicago Pr.

Underdevelopment & Agrarian Structure in Pakistan. Mahmood H. Khan. (Replica Edition Ser.). 275p. 1981. lib. bdg. 37.00 (ISBN 0-86531-134-X). Westview.

Underdevelopment & Economic Growth. Ivan T. Berend & Gyorgy Ranki. (Studies in Hungarian Economic & Social History). 299p. 1979. 68.75x (Pub. by Collets (UK)). State Mutual Bk.

Underdevelopment & Industrialization in Tanzania: A Study of Perverse Capitalist Industrial Development. Justinian Rweyemamu. (Illus.). 1973. 14.95x (ISBN 0-19-572268-X). Oxford U Pr.

Underdevelopment & Rural Structures in Southeastern Turkey. Zulkuf Aysin. (Durham Middle East Monographs). 301p. 1986. 29.00 (ISBN 0-86372-034-X, Pub. by Ithaca England). Evergreen Dist.

Underdevelopment & Spatial Inequality: Approaches to the Problems of Regional Planning in the Third World see Progress in Planning.

Underdevelopment & the Development of Law: Corporations & Corporation Law in Nineteenth-Century Colombia. Robert C. Means. LC 79-23936. (Studies in Legal History). xx, 327p. 1980. 32.50x (ISBN 0-8078-1423-7). U of NC Pr.

Underdevelopment & the Transition to Socialism: Mozambique & Tanzania. James H. Mittelman. LC 81-2728. (Studies in Social Discontinuity Ser.). 1981. 24.95 (ISBN 0-12-500660-8). Acad Pr.

Underdevelopment in Kenya: The Political Economy of Neo-Colonialism, 1964-1971. Colin Leys. LC 74-76387. 1975. 35.00x (ISBN 0-520-02731-0); pap. 11.95x (ISBN 0-520-02770-1). U of Cal Pr.

Underdevelopment Is a State of Mind: The Latin American Case. Lawrence E. Harrison. 210p. (Orig.). 1988. pap. 9.95 (ISBN 0-8191-6490-9, Pub. by Madison Bks). U Pr of Amer.

Underdevelopment of African Education: A Black Zimbabwean Perspective. Dickson A. Mungazi. LC 82-13696. (Illus.). 274p. (Orig.). 1982. pap. text ed. 14.00 (ISBN 0-8191-2670-5). U Pr of Amer.

Underdevelopment State & Mode of Production in Bangladesh: A Sociological Outline. Hasanuzzaman Chowdhury. 120p. 1986. 12.50x (ISBN 0-8364-1561-2, Pub. by Minerva India). South Asia Bks.

Underdog. Marilyn Sachs. LC 84-24676. 128p. (gr. 4-6). 1985. pap. 11.95 (ISBN 0-385-17609-0). Doubleday.

Underdog. Marilyn Sachs. 128p. (gr. 3-6). 1987. pap. 2.50 (ISBN 0-590-40406-7, Apple Paperbacks). Scholastic Inc.

Underdog-A Play. J. P. Das. (Library of Modern Indian Writing). 48p. 1984. pap. text ed. 8.95x (ISBN 0-7069-2582-3, Pub. by Vikas India). Advent NY.

Underdog & Other Stories. Agatha Christie. 192p. 1969. pap. 2.25 (ISBN 0-440-19228-5). Dell.

Underdog & Other Stories. Agatha Christie. 224p. 1986. pap. 3.50 (ISBN 0-425-06808-0). Berkley Pub.

Underdog & Other Stories. 02/1988 ed. Agatha Christie. (HC Collections). pap. 9.95 (ISBN 0-553-35070-6). Bantam.

Underdog Appeal. Vladimir Volkoff. 229p. 1984. 14.95 (ISBN 0-914707-02-7). Ren Pr GA.

Underdogs. Mariano Azuela. 160p. 1986. Repr. lib. bdg. 15.95x (ISBN 0-89966-515-2). Buccaneer Bks.

Underdogs. Mariano Azuelo. Tr. by E. Munguia, Jr. (Orig.). pap. 3.50 (ISBN 0-451-52102-1, CE1741, Sig Classics). NAL.

Underdogs & Tricksters. Susan Niditch. LC 86-46209. 224p. 1987. 18.95 (ISBN 0-06-254605-8, HarpR). Har-Row.

Underemployment from a Human Perspective. David P. Meyer. 63p. 1985. 6.25 (IN303). Natl Ctr Res Voc Ed.

Underglaze Blue & Red. Shanghai Museum Staff. 248p. 1987. 280.00x (Pub. by Han-Shan Tang Ltd). State Mutual Bk.

Underglaze Decoration. Marc Bellaire. 3.95 (ISBN 0-934706-01-8). Prof Pubns Ohio.

Underglaze Soft Sculpture. Jean Kriefer. LC 86-63579. 52p. 1986. pap. text ed. 8.95 (ISBN 0-916809-15-3). Scott Pubns MI.

Undergraduate Admissions: The Realities of Institutional Policies, Practices, & Procedures. LC 80-70480. (Illus.). 72p. (Orig.). 1980. pap. 8.50 (ISBN 0-87447-136-2, 001362). College Bd.

Undergraduate Algebra. S. Lang. (Undergraduate Texts in Mathematics Ser.). (Illus.). 250p. 1986. 36.00 (ISBN 0-387-96404-5). Springer-Verlag.

Undergraduate Algebra: A First Course. C. W. Norman. 400p. 1986. 39.95 (ISBN 0-19-853249-0). Oxford U Pr.

Undergraduate Algebraic Geometry. M. Reid. (London Mathematical Society Students Texts Ser.: No. 11). (Illus.). 120p. Date not set. price not set; pap. price not set (ISBN 0-521-35662-8). Cambridge U Pr.

Undergraduate Analysis. S. Lang. (Undergraduate Texts in Mathematics Ser.). (Illus.). 545p. 1983. Repr. of 1968 ed. 36.00 (ISBN 0-387-90800-5). Springer-Verlag.

Undergraduate Career Decisions: Correlates of Occupational Choice. James A. Davis. LC 64-15604. (NORC Monographs in Social Research Ser.: No. 2). (Illus.). 1965. 9.95x (ISBN 0-202-09007-8). NORC.

Undergraduate Engineering Laboratory. Ed. by Edward W. Ernst. LC 83-82477. 226p. (Orig.). 1983. pap. 15.00 (ISBN 0-939204-21-5, 83-14). Eng Found.

Undergraduate Field Instruction Programs: Current Issues & Predictions. Ed. by Kristen Wenzel. Date not set. 3.00 (72-400-03). Coun Soc WK Ed.

Undergraduate Field Instructions Program. Date not set. 3.30. Coun Soc Wk Ed.

Undergraduate Guides Set, 1989, 2 vols. Date not set. Set. 56.00 (ISBN 0-87866-809-8); Set. pap. 27.50 (ISBN 0-87866-808-X). Petersons Guides.

Undergraduate Instrumental Analysis. 4th, rev. & enl. ed. Robinson. 664p. 1986. 34.75 (ISBN 0-8247-7406-X). Dekker.

Undergraduate Mathematics Education in the People's Republic of China: Report of a 1983 North American Delegation. Ed. by Lynn Steen. (MAA Notes Ser.: Vol. 3). 100p. 1984. pap. 6.75 (ISBN 0-88385-053-2). Math Assn.

Undergraduate Medical Education & the Elective System: Experience with the Duke Curriculum, 1966-75. Ed. by James F. Gifford. LC 77-84615. pap. 64.30 (ISBN 0-317-26746-9, 2023383). Bks Demand UMI.

Undergraduate Obstetrics & Gynaecology. 2nd ed. M. G. Hull et al. (Illus.). 320p. 1986. 16.00 (ISBN 0-7236-0832-6). PSG Pub Co.

Undergraduate Papers (1857-1858) An Oxford Journal Conducted by A. C. Swinburne. LC 74-12387. 220p. 1974. lib. bdg. 35.00x (ISBN 0-8201-1134-1). Schol Facsimiles.

Undergraduate Physical Education Programs: Issues & Approaches. Ed. by Hal A. Lawson. pap. 28.00 (2026622). Bks Demand UMI.

Undergraduate Program Field Test Series. Jack Rudman. (Cloth bdg. avail. on request). pap. write for info. (ISBN 0-8373-6000-5). Natl Learning.

Undergraduate Social Work Education: Today & Tomorrow. Date not set. 3.10. Coun Soc Wk Ed.

Undergraduate Topology. Robert H. Kasriel. LC 76-18783. 302p. 1977. Repr. of 1971 ed. 21.50 (ISBN 0-88275-444-0). Krieger.

Undergraduate Tuition & Fees: Trends 1977 to 1986. Ed. & intro. by John Minter. 250p. 1987. lib. bdg. 95.00 (ISBN 0-937767-31-X). Nat Data Service.

Underground. Richard Corben. (Richard Corben Complete Works: No. 1). (Illus.). 80p. (Orig.). 1985. pap. 10.95 (ISBN 0-87416-018-9). Catalan Communs.

Underground. Corrinne Hales. Ed. by Dale K. Boyer. LC 85-72151. (Ahsahta Press Modern & Contemporary Poetry of the West). 60p. (Orig.). 1986. pap. 4.50 (ISBN 0-916272-30-3). Ahsahta Pr.

Underground. David Macaulay. (Illus.). (gr. 1 up). 1976. 14.95 (ISBN 0-395-24739-X). HM.

Underground. David Macaulay. (Illus.). 112p. (gr. 5 up). 1983. 5.95 (ISBN 0-395-34065-9). HM.

Underground. Brian Read. LC 86-6531. (Let's Look Up Ser.). (Illus.). 32p. (gr. 3-6). 1986. PLB 9.96 (ISBN 0-382-09278-3). Silver Burdett Pr.

Underground Armoured Cable Protected Against Solvent Penetration & Corrosive Attack. EEMUA Staff. 1974. 75.00x (ISBN 0-85931-142-2, Pub. by EEMUA). State Mutual Bk.

Underground Army. Chaika Grossman. 1988. pap. 17.95 (ISBN 0-89604-078-X). Holocaust Pubns.

Underground Atlanta. Norman Shavin. (Illus.). 40p. 1979. pap. 3.50 (ISBN 0-910719-02-0). Capricorn Corp.

Underground Atlas: A Gazetteer of the World's Cave Regions. John Middleton & Tony Waltham. (Illus.). 240p. 1987. 16.95 (ISBN 0-312-01101-6). St Martin.

Underground Banquet & Other Stories. Joyce Warren. 166p. (Orig.). 1988. pap. 13.95 (ISBN 0-937672-23-8). Rowan Tree.

Underground Blue Book: A Guide to Buying & Selling New & Used Cars, Trucks & R. V.'s. Lee. 136p. (Orig.). 1987. pap. 9.95 (ISBN 0-9617946-0-7). Diamond S Pub.

Underground Cable Thermal Backfill: Proceedings. Symposium on Underground Cable Thermal Backfill, Toronto, Ont., Canada, Sept. 1981. Ed. by S. A. Boggs et al. (Illus.). 248p. 1982. 61.00 (ISBN 0-08-025387-3). Pergamon.

Underground Canals: Wonders of the Industrial Revolution. Ronald Howarth. 1986. 32.00x (ISBN 0-317-54397-0, Pub. by Hesketh UK). State Mutual Bk.

Underground Coal Gasification. G. H. Lamb. LC 77-77022. (Energy Technology Review Ser.: No. 14). (Illus.). 255p. 1977. 36.00 (ISBN 0-8155-0670-8). Noyes.

Underground Coal Gasification: The State of the Art. Ed. by William B. Krantz & Robert D. Gunn. LC 83-11741. (AIChE Symposium: Vol. 79, No. 226). 195p. 1983. pap. 50.00 (ISBN 0-8169-0251-8). Am Inst Chem Eng.

Underground Construction: A Bibliography. Mary Vance. (Architecture Ser.: Bibliography A 1353). 1985. pap. 2.25 (ISBN 0-89028-323-0). Vance Biblios.

Underground Corrosion - STP 741. Ed. by E. Escalante. 210p. 1981. 26.00 (ISBN 0-8031-0703-X, 04-741000-27). ASTM.

Underground Disposal of Radioactive Wastes: Basic Guidance. (Safety Ser.: No. 54). 56p. 1981. pap. 12.00 (ISBN 92-0-123381-7, ISP579, IAEA). UNIPUB.

Underground Disposal of Radioactive Wastes: Proceedings, 2 Vols. (Proceedings Ser.). 1980. pap. 72.75 (ISBN 92-0-020180-6, ISP528 1, IAEA); pap. 85.00 (ISBN 92-0-020280-2, ISP528 2). UNIPUB.

Underground Economies. Ed. by Edgar L. Feige. (Illus.). 400p. Date not set. price not set (ISBN 0-521-26230-5). Cambridge U Pr.

Underground Economy: An Annotated Bibliography. Nancy K. Humphreys. (CompuBibs Ser.: No. 9). 75p. 1985. pap. 15.00x (ISBN 0-914791-08-7). Vantage Info.

Underground Economy in the United States & Abroad. Ed. by Vito Tanzi. LC 80-8887. 352p. 1982. 35.00x (ISBN 0-669-04400-8). Lexington Bks.

Underground Empire: Where Crime & Governments Embrace. James Mills. LC 86-2111. 1176p. 1986. 22.95 (ISBN 0-385-17535-3). Doubleday.

Underground Empire: Where Crime & Governments Embrace. James Mills. 1987. pap. 5.95 (ISBN 0-440-19206-4). Dell.

Underground Excavations in Rock. E. Hoek & E. T. Brown. 532p. 1980. text ed. 69.00x (ISBN 0-900488-54-9); pap. text ed. 43.25x (ISBN 0-900488-55-7). IMM North Am.

Underground Fate: The Idiom of Romance in the Later Novels of Graham Greene. Brian Thomas. LC 87-12538. 256p. 1988. 28.00x (ISBN 0-317-67985-6). U of GA Pr.

Underground Government: The Off-Budget Public Sector. James T. Bennett & Thomas J. DiLorenzo. 184p. 1983. pap. 8.95 (ISBN 0-932790-37-2). Cato Inst.

Underground Guide to Kauai, Hawaii. 1980-1986 rev. & exp. ed. Lenore W. Horowitz. (Illus.). 1986. pap. 5.95 (ISBN 0-9615498-0-7). Papaloa Pr.

Underground Homes. rev. ed. Louis Wampler. LC 80-18701. (Illus.). 121p. 1980. pap. 5.95 (ISBN 0-88289-273-8). Pelican.

Underground Kingdom. Edward Packard. (Choose Your Own Adventure Ser.: No. 18). (ps-7). 1983. pap. 2.25 (ISBN 0-553-25989-X). Bantam.

Underground Leakage of Flammable & Combustible Liquids. National Fire Protection Association Staff. 25p. 1987. 12.00 (ISBN 0-317-63415-1, 329-87). Natl Fire Prot.

Underground Leakage of Flammable & Combustible Liquids. (Thirty Ser.). 56p. 1972. pap. 2.00 (ISBN 0-685-46064-9, 329). Natl Fire Prot.

Underground Life. Allan Roberts. LC 82-23582. (New True Bks.). (Illus.). 48p. (gr. k-4). 1983. PLB 12.60 (ISBN 0-516-01689-X). Childrens.

Underground Literature, 2 vols. in 1. 80p. 1.95 (ISBN 0-686-74969-3). ADL.

Underground Literature During the Emergency, India. Sajal Bose. 1978. 10.00x (ISBN 0-8364-0034-8). South Asia Bks.

Underground Man. Edward F. Abood. LC 72-97331. 189p. 1973. pap. 9.95 (ISBN 0-88316-048-X). Chandler & Sharp.

Underground Man. Gabriel Tarde. Tr. by C. Bereton from Fr. LC 73-13268. (Classics of Science Fiction Ser.). 206p. 1974. 15.00 (ISBN 0-88355-122-5); pap. 10.00 (ISBN 0-88355-151-9). Hyperion Conn.

Underground Man & Raskolnikov: A Comparative Study. Preben Villadsen. (Odense Slavic Studies: No. 3). 159p. (Orig.). 1981. pap. 22.00x (ISBN 87-7492-326-9, Pub. by Odense Universitets Forlag (Odense Denmark)). Coronet Bks.

Underground Manual for Spiritual Survival. Larry Neagle. (Orig.). 1986. pap. 4.95 (ISBN 0-8024-9052-2). Moody.

Underground Marketplace: A Guide to New England & the Middle Atlantic States. Jonathan Webster & Harriet Webster. LC 80-54401. 176p. 1981. 12.50x (ISBN 0-87663-348-3); pap. 6.95 o. p. (ISBN 0-87663-555-9). Universe.

Underground Mining Methods & Technology: Proceedings of the International Symposium, Nottingham, September 8-13, 1986. Ed. by A. B. Szwilski & M. J. Richards. (Advances in Mining Science & Technology Ser.: No. 1). 472p. 1987. 112.25 (ISBN 0-444-42845-3). Elsevier.

Underground Mining Methods Handbook. Ed. by William H. Hustrulid. LC 80-70416. (Illus.). 1754p. 1982. 120.00x (ISBN 0-89520-049-X). Soc Mining Eng.

Underground Notes. 2nd ed. Mihajlo Mihajlov et al. Tr. by Maria M. Ivusic & Christopher Ivusic. LC 80-65723. 208p. 1982. lib. bdg. 20.00 (ISBN 0-89241-132-5); pap. 6.95 (ISBN 0-89241-131-7). Caratzas.

Underground Operation's Conference: 1985. 260p. 1985. pap. text ed. 39.00x (ISBN 0-909520-92-5, Pub. by Australian inst M & M). Brookfield Pub Co.

Underground Picnic. Carol B. Kaplan. Ed. by Janet L. Bolinske. (Animal Tales Ser.). (Illus.). 24p. (Orig.). 19.95 (ISBN 0-317-64810-1). Milliken Pub Co.

Underground Piping Handbook. L. A. Peggs. LC 83-19906. 296p. 1985. lib. bdg. 25.50 (ISBN 0-89874-616-7). Krieger.

Underground Plastic Pipe. ASCE Pipeline Division, New Orleans, March, 1981. Ed. by B. J. Schrock. LC 81-65630. 553p. 1981. pap. 38.00x (ISBN 0-87262-265-7). Am Soc Civil Eng.

Underground Press: Die Untergrundpresse der U. S. A. als Bestandteil des "New Journalism" Phaenomens. Hanns-Peter Bushoff. (European University Studies: No. 3, Vol. 203). 388p. (Ger.). 1983. 40.00 (ISBN 3-8204-7848-5). P Lang Pubs.

Underground Press in America. Robert J. Glessing. LC 84-6521. (Illus.). xvi, 207p. 1984. Repr. of 1970 ed. lib. bdg. 35.00x (ISBN 0-313-24450-2, GLUP). Greenwood.

Underground Processing of Fuels. 168p. 1963. text ed. 34.00x (ISBN 0-7065-0217-5, Pub. by Keter Pub Jerusalem). Coronet Bks.

Underground Railroad. William M. Mitchell. LC 78-106887. Repr. of 1860 ed. 35.00x (ISBN 0-8371-3283-5, MIU&). Greenwood.

Underground Railroad. William Still. LC 68-29019. (American Negro: His History & Literature Ser., No. 1). (Illus.). 1968. Repr. of 1872 ed. 29.00 (ISBN 0-405-01838-X). Ayer Co Pubs.

Underground Railroad. William Still. LC 74-102982. (Ebony Classics Ser). (Illus.). 1970. 10.50 (ISBN 0-87485-033-9). Johnson Chi.

Underground Railroad: First-Person Narratives of Escapes to Freedom in the North. Charles L. Blockson. (Illus.). 320p. 1987. 18.95 (ISBN 0-13-935743-2). P-H.

Underground Railroad from Slavery to Freedom. Wilbur H. Siebert. LC 68-29016. (American Negro: His History & Literature Ser., No. 1). 1968. Repr. of 1898 ed. 19.00 (ISBN 0-405-01835-5). Ayer Co Pubs.

Underground Railroad in Connecticut. Horatio T. Strother. LC 62-15122. 356p. 1962. pap. 8.95 (ISBN 0-8195-6012-X). Wesleyan U Pr.

Underground Railroad in Pennsylvania. Charles L. Blockson. LC 80-69847. (Illus.). 225p. 1981. 13.95 (ISBN 0-933184-21-2); pap. 6.95 (ISBN 0-933184-22-0). Flame Intl.

Underground Reservation: Osage Oil. Terry P. Wilson. LC 84-26974. (Illus.). xvi, 263p. 1985. 22.95x (ISBN 0-8032-4733-8). U of Nebr Pr.

Underground Rock Chambers: Symposium held during the ASCE National Meeting on Water Resources Engineering, Phoenix, Arizona, Jan. 13-14, 1971. Symposium on Underground Rock Chambers. LC 78-322140. pap. 151.50 (ISBN 0-317-08299-X, 2019554). Bks Demand UMI.

Underground Russia. Sergiei M. Kravchinsky. LC 73-846. (Russian Studies: Perspectives on the Revolution Ser.). 272p. 1973. Repr. of 1883 ed. 24.75 (ISBN 0-88355-041-5). Hyperion Conn.

Underground Shadows. Valery Oistenau. 1977. pap. 1.50 (ISBN 0-9601870-0-6). Pass.

Underground Shopper's Guide to Health & Fitness. Sue Goldstein. 1987. pap. 10.95 (ISBN 0-449-90228-5, Columbine). Fawcett.

Underground Shoppers Guide to Off-Price Shopping. Sue Goldstein. 528p. (Orig.). 1984. pap. 3.95 (ISBN 0-446-32531-7). Warner Bks.

Underground Shopper's Guide to Off-Price Shopping. Sue Goldstein. Date not set. pap. 4.50 (ISBN 0-446-32890-1). Warner Bks.

Underground Siting of Nuclear Power Plants: Internationales Symposium, 1981. F. Bender. (Illus.). 409p. (Ger. & Eng.). 1982. 90.00x (ISBN 3-510-65108-1). Lubrecht & Cramer.

Underground Siting of Nuclear Power Plants. Ed. by F. Bender. (Illus.). 416p. (Orig.). 1982. pap. text ed. 115.00x (ISBN 0-317-63454-2, Pub. by E Schweizerbartsche). Coronet Bks.

Underground Sound: Application of Seismic Waves. J. E. White. (Methods in Geochemistry & Geophysics Ser.: Vol. 18). 254p. 1983. 76.50 (ISBN 0-444-42139-4). Elsevier.

Underground Storage of Oil & Gas in Salt Deposits & Other Non-Hard Rocks. Wolfgang Dreyer. (Geology of Petroleum Ser.). 207p. 1982. pap. 26.95 (ISBN 0-470-27138-8). Halsted Pr.

Underground Storage Systems - Leak Detection & Monitoring. Todd G. Schwendeman et al. LC 87-3661. (Illus.). 250p. 1987. 44.95 (ISBN 0-87371-045-2). Lewis Pubs Inc.

Underground Storage Tank Management: A Practical Guide. 2nd ed. Raymond W. Kane & Albert D. Young, Jr. 312p. 1987. pap. 49.00 (ISBN 0-86587-726-2). Gov Insts.

Underground Storage Tank: Model Legislation. Paul Doyle. 24p. (Orig.). 1986. pap. 10.00 (ISBN 1-55516-479-X). Natl Conf State Legis.

Underground Systems Reference Book. 592p. 1955. 14.50 (ISBN 0-317-34113-8, 045516). Edison Electric.
Underground Tank Leak Detection Methods: A State-of-the-Art Review. Shahzad Niaki & John A. Broscious. 136p. 1988. 40.00 (ISBN 0-89116-098-1). Hemisphere Pub.
Underground Tank Leak Detection Methods. Shahzad Niaki & John A. Broscious. LC 86-31159. (Pollution Technology Review Ser.: No. 139). (Illus.). 123p. 1987. 36.00 (ISBN 0-8155-1117-5). Noyes.
Underground Tank Leak Insurance: Maximizing Your Coverage. Richard Levy & Leslie Foster. Ed. by Lindsay Hutter. 710p. 1988. 49.95 (ISBN 0-9620337-0-7). Petro Mkts Assn.
Underground Tea Party. Carol B. Kaplan. Ed. by Janet L. Bolinske. (Animal Tales Ser.). (Illus.). 24p. (Orig.). (ps-k). spiral-bound Big Book 17.95 (ISBN 0-88335-758-5). Milliken Pub Co.
Underground Terminal Stations: A Selected Bibliography. Anthony G. White. (Architecture Ser.: A 1697). 8p. 1986. 3.00 (ISBN 1-55590-067-4). Vance Biblios.
Underground: The London Alternative Press, 1966-74. Nigel Fountain. (Comedia Bks.). 350p. 1988. pap. text ed. 13.95 (ISBN 0-415-00728-3). Routledge Chapman & Hall.
Underground Transmission of Electric Power. B. M. Weedy. 294p. 1979. text ed. 64.95x (ISBN 0-471-27700-2, Pub. by Wiley-Interscience). Wiley.
Underground Waters & Subsurface Temperatures of the Woodbine Sand in Northeast Texas. F. B. Plummer & E. C. Sargent. (Bull Ser.: No. 3138). (Illus.). 178p. 1931. 1.00 (ISBN 0-686-29351-7). Bur Econ Geology.
Underground Worlds. Donald Jackson. (Planet Earth Ser.). 1982. lib. bdg. 19.94 (ISBN 0-8094-4321-X, Pub. by Time-Life). Silver.
Underground Worlds. (Planet Earth Ser.). 14.95x (ISBN 0-8094-4320-1). Time Life.
Underhill Edge Tool Co., Eighteen Fifty-Nine Price List Axes & Mechanics' Tools. 1980. pap. 2.50 (ISBN 0-913602-37-X). K Roberts.
Underlay. Barry N. Malzberg. 256p. 1986. pap. 4.95 (ISBN 0-930330-41-2). Intl Polygonics.
Underlying Word Order: German as a VSO Language. Barbara J. Beckman. (German Language & Literature-European University Studies: No. 1, Vol. 322). 155p. 1979. pap. 21.95 (ISBN 3-8204-6633-9). P Lang Pubs.
Undermining Capitalism. Joel Krieger. LC 83-42563. 328p. 1983. 32.00x (ISBN 0-691-07662-6). Princeton U Pr.
Undermining Rural Development with Cheap Credit. Dale W. Adams et al. (Special Studies in Social, Political, & Economic Development Ser.). 350p. 1984. lib. bdg. 39.50x (ISBN 0-86531-768-2). Westview.
Underneath English Towns. Martin Carver. (Illus.). 176p. 1987. 45.00 (ISBN 0-7134-3637-9, Pub. by Batsford England); pap. 29.95 (ISBN 0-7134-3638-7, Pub. by Batsford England). David & Charles.
Underneath I'm Different. Ellen Rabinowich. LC 82-14919. 192p. (gr. 7 up). 1983. 12.95. Delacorte.
Undersanding Cancer. John Laszlo. LC 86-46079. (Illus.). 320p. 1988. pap. 8.95 (ISBN 0-06-091491-2, PL-1491, PL). Har-Row.
Underscore. Frank Skinner. 1960. 9.95 (ISBN 0-910468-09-5). Criterion Mus.
Undersea. Paul Hazel. 1987. pap. 3.50 (ISBN 0-553-26697-7, Spectra). Bantam.
Undersea Archaeology. Christopher F. Lampton. Ed. by Maury Solomon. (First Bk.). (Illus.). 96p. (gr. 5 up). 1988. 9.90 (ISBN 0-531-10492-3). Watts.
Undersea City. Frederik Pohl & Jack Williamson. pap. 1.95 (ISBN 0-345-30814-X, Del Rey). Ballantine.
Undersea Dinosaur Action Set. Malcolm Whyte. (Illus.). 24p. (gr. 1 up). 1988. 4.95 (ISBN 0-8431-1954-3). Price Stern.
Undersea Giants. Patrick Geistdoefer. LC 87-34531. (Illus.). 38p. (gr. k-5). 1988. 4.95 (ISBN 0-944589-02-2, 022). Young Discovery Lib.
Undersea Homes. Althea. (Cambridge Natural History Ser.). 24p. (gr. 2 up). 1985. 5.95 (ISBN 0-521-30297-8); pap. 2.95. Cambridge U Pr.
Undersea Life. Joseph S. Levine. LC 85-2833. (Illus.). 224p. 1987. 29.95 (ISBN 0-941434-70-2); pap. 18.95 (ISBN 0-941434-94-X). Stewart Tabori & Chang.
Undersea Lightwave Communications. Ed. by P. R. Trischitta. LC 86-10670. 644p. 1986. 64.45 (ISBN 0-87942-201-7). Inst Electrical.
Undersea Machines. R. J. Stephen. LC 85-52093. (Picture Library). (Illus.). 32p. (gr. k-6). 1987. lib. bdg. 10.90 (ISBN 0-531-10187-8). Watts.
Undersea Mountain. Harold Norse. LC 79-179808. (New Poetry Ser.). Repr. of 1953 ed. 16.00 (ISBN 0-404-56008-3). AMS Pr.
Undersea Quest. Frederik Pohl & Jack Williamson. 160p. 1982. pap. 1.95 (ISBN 0-345-30701-1, Del Rey). Ballantine.
Undersea Terror: U-Boat Wolf Packs in World War II. Ernest McKay. LC 82-12529. (Illus.). 192p. (YA) (gr. 9 up). 1982. PLB 9.79 (ISBN 0-671-44196-5). Messner.
Undersea Treasures. Ed. by National Geographic Society. LC 74-1563. (Special Publications Series 9: No. 2). (Illus.). 200p. 1974. avail. only from Natl. Geog. 7.95 (ISBN 0-87044-147-7). Natl Geog.
Undersea World. Thomas Wright. LC 81-51497. (Exploration & Discovery Ser.). (gr. 5 up). PLB 14.96 (ISBN 0-382-06616-2). Silver.
Underseas Possessions: Selected Poems. Hans-Juergen Heise. (Oleander Modern Poets Ser.: Vol. 1). 1974. 4.95 (ISBN 0-902675-33-8). Oleander Pr.
Underseas Victory I, 1941-1943: Against the Odds. W. J. Holmes. (World at War Ser.: No. 10). 352p. 1980. pap. 2.50 (ISBN 0-89083-613-2). Zebra.
Underseas Victory II, 1943-1945: The Tide Turns. W. J. Holmes. (World at War Ser.: No. 11). 1979. pap. 2.50 (ISBN 0-89083-448-2). Zebra.
Underserved: Our Young Gifted Children. Ed. by Merle B. Karnes. 240p. 1983. pap. 17.80 (ISBN 0-86586-147-1). Coun Exc Child.
Undershirts & Other Stories. Cathy Cockrell. 1982. pap. 6.00 (ISBN 0-914610-30-9). Hanging Loose.
Underside of American History: Since 1865, Vol. 2. 5th ed. Thomas R. Frazier. 436p. 1987. pap. text ed. 11.50 net (ISBN 0-15-592853-8, HC). HarBraceJ.
Underside of American History: To 1877, Vol. 1. 5th ed. Thomas R. Frazier. 482p. 1987. pap. text ed. 11.50 net (ISBN 0-15-592852-X, HC). HarBraceJ.
Underside of High-Tech: Technology & the Deformation of Human Sensibilities. Ed. by John W. Murphy et al. LC 85-27265. (Contributions in Sociology Ser.: No. 59). 226p. 1986. 36.95 (ISBN 0-313-24612-2). Greenwood.
Underside of History: A View of Women Through Time. Elise Boulding. LC 75-30558. 750p. 1976. pap. 27.95x (ISBN 0-89158-056-5). Westview.
Underside of the Leaf. M. B. Goffstein. LC 75-188252. 144p. (gr. 7 up). 1972. 11.95 (ISBN 0-374-38031-7). FS&G.
Undersides of Leaves. Joseph Hutchison. LC 85-50797. (Illus.). 64p. 1985. ltd. ed 15.00 (ISBN 0-933573-03-0); pap. 7.00 (ISBN 0-933573-02-2). Wayland Pr.
Understains: The Sense & Seduction of Advertising. Kathy Myers. (Comedia Bks.). 160p. 1988. pap. text ed. 13.95 (ISBN 0-906890-98-5). Routledge Chapman & Hall.
Understand Employee Regulations. 85p. 1984. 20.00 (30). Am Consul Eng.
Understand Employee Regulations. 130p. 1984. 25.00 (ISBN 0-317-65516-7, 55-1562). Natl Ret Merch.
Understand Employee Regulations: An Employer's Guide to Federal Law. Sheldon I. London. 96p. (Orig.). 1984. pap. 9.95 (ISBN 0-9613262-0-4). London Pub.
Understand-It-All with Professor Know-It-All. Wilmac. 1962. pap. text ed. 3.25 (ISBN 0-940630-21-4, T-7153 (PROF-F-123)). Playette Corp.
Understand It! Developing Comprehension. (Golden Activity Book 'n' Tapes). (Illus.). (ps-3). pap. write for info. incl. cassette (ISBN 0-307-13802-X, Golden Bks). Western Pub.
Understand Those Financial Reports: Question & Answer Guide for Investors & Nonfinancial Business Persons. Raymond J. Lipay. LC 83-16652. 266p. 1984. 19.95 (ISBN 0-471-86571-0). Wiley.
Understand Your Backache: A Guide to Prevention, Treatment, & Relief. Rene Cailliet. LC 83-24071. (Illus.). 194p. 1984. pap. text ed. 11.95x (ISBN 0-8036-1647-3). Davis Co.
Understandable Approach to Basic Mathematics. Gilbert M. Peter & Daniel R. Peterson. 1982. text ed. write for info. (ISBN 0-673-16045-9). Scott F.
Understandable Guide to Music Theory. 2nd, rev. ed. Charles Q. Bufe. (Illus.). 75p. 1987. pap. 7.95 (ISBN 0-9613289-2-4). See Sharp Pr.
Understandable Statistics: Concepts & Methods. 3rd ed. Charles H. Brase & Corrinne P. Brace. LC 86-81382. 544p. 1987. text ed. 26.00 (ISBN 0-669-12181-9); instr's guide 2.00 (ISBN 0-669-12182-7); compstat manual & Apple disk 8.00 (ISBN 0-669-15122-X); compstat manual & IBM disk 8.00 (ISBN 0-669-15124-6). Heath.
Understanding. Churches Alive, Inc. Staff. LC 79-52129. (Love One Another Bible Study Ser.). (Illus.). 1979. wkbk. 3.00 (ISBN 0-934396-02-7). Churches Alive.
Understanding, Bk. 1. C. Anson Smith. LC 84-90151. 123p. 1985. 10.95 (ISBN 0-533-06218-7). Vantage.
Understanding a Company. Jeffrey Little. (Basic Investors Library). (Illus.). 48p. 1987. lib. bdg. 9.95x (ISBN 1-55546-622-2). Chelsea Hse.
Understanding a Company's Finances. W. R. Purcell, Jr. (Illus.). 148p. 1983. pap. 4.95 (ISBN 0-06-463583-X, EH 583, B&N Bks). Har-Row.
Understanding: A Guide to Impaired Fertility for Family & Friends. Patricia I. Johnston. 28p. 1983. pap. 3.50 (ISBN 0-9609504-1-9). Perspect Indiana.
Understanding: A Phenomenological-Pragmatic Analysis. LC 81-4233. (Contributions in Philosophy Ser.: No. 19). 344p. 1982. lib. bdg. 36.95 (ISBN 0-313-22483-8, MUN/). Greenwood.
Understanding a Woman's Depression. Brenda Poinsett. LC 83-51595. 256p. 1984. pap. 6.95 (ISBN 0-8423-7764-6). Tyndale.
Understanding Abnormal Behavior. 2nd ed. Stanley Sue et al. LC 85-60475. 672p. 1986. text ed. 44.36 (ISBN 0-395-36947-9); instr's manual 3.96 (ISBN 0-395-37807-9); study guide 14.36 (ISBN 0-395-37808-7). HM.
Understanding Abnormal Behavior: Description, Explanation, Management. Leonard D. Goodstein & James F. Calhoun. LC 81-17669. (Illus.). 1982. text ed. write for info (ISBN 0-394-34768-4, RanC); study guide 5.75 (ISBN 0-394-34769-2). Random.
Understanding Abortion. Mary Pipes. 182p. 1987. 5.95 (ISBN 0-7043-3982-X, Pub. by Quartet Bks). Salem Hse Pubs.
Understanding Abstract Art. Frank Whitford. (Illus.). 160p. 1987. 29.95 (ISBN 0-525-24575-8); pap. 22.50 (ISBN 0-525-48343-8). Dutton.
Understanding Abusive Families. James Garbarino & Gwen Gilliam. LC 79-47983. 288p. 1980. pap. 14.00x (ISBN 0-669-09782-9). Lexington Bks.
Understanding Academic Lectures. Abelle Mason. (Illus.). 208p. 1983. pap. text ed. write for info (ISBN 0-13-936419-6). P-H.
Understanding Accounting. Stanley Stern. LC 82-18434. 128p. 1983. pap. 5.95 (ISBN 0-668-05673-8). Arco.
Understanding Accounts. Couldery. 1979. pap. 20.95 (ISBN 0-85258-183-1). Van Nos Reinhold.
Understanding Accreditation: Contemporary Perspectives on Issues & Practices in Evaluating Educational Quality. Kenneth E. Young et al. LC 83-11260. (Higher Education Ser.). 1983. text ed. 39.95x (ISBN 0-87589-570-0). Jossey-Bass.
Understanding ADA: A Software Engineering Approach. David Pokrass & Gary Bray. LC 84-26998. 352p. 1985. pap. text ed. 24.95 (ISBN 0-471-87833-2). Wiley.
Understanding Adolescence. Ronald L. Koteskey. 168p. 1987. pap. 6.50 (ISBN 0-89693-249-4). Victor Bks.
Understanding Adolescents & Safety at Home & on the Job. Betty L. Brace & Tonita Croghan. LC 79-21803. (Lifeworks Ser.). (Illus.). 1980. pap. 12.96 (ISBN 0-07-060912-8). McGraw.
Understanding Adolescents & Young Adults with Learning Disabilities--A Focus on Employability & Career Placement: A Guide for Rehabilitation Counselors. Ernest F. Biller. (Illus.). 114p. 1988. pap. text ed. 19.50x (ISBN 0-398-05455-X). C C Thomas.
Understanding Adoption: Resources & Activities for Teaching Adults About Adoption. (Adoption Builds Families Ser.). (Orig.). 1980. pap. 14.95 (ISBN 0-89994-258-X). Soc Sci Ed.
Understanding Advanced Solid State Electronics. Don L. Cannon. Ed. by Charles W. Battle & Gerald Luecke. LC 85-52068. (Understanding Ser.). (Illus.). 280p. 1985. pap. 17.95 (ISBN 0-672-27058-7, LCB8453). Sams.
Understanding African Poetry: A Study of Ten Poets. Ken Goodwin. 256p. 1982. text ed. 25.00x (ISBN 0-435-91325-5); pap. text ed. 15.00x (ISBN 0-435-91326-3). Heinemann Ed.
Understanding Africa's Rural Households & Farming Systems. Ed. by Joyce Lewinger Moock. 275p. 1986. pap. 18.85 (ISBN 0-8133-7175-9). Westview.
Understanding Aging & Human Needs. Didactic Systems. 72p. 1978. pap. 19.95. Van Nos Reinhold.
Understanding Aging & Human Needs. Didactic Systems staff. pap. 19.95 (ISBN 0-686-60069-X). Van Nos Reinhold.
Understanding Aging Parents. Andrew D. Lester & Judith L. Lester. LC 80-17832. (Christian Care Bks.: Vol. 8). 120p. 1980. pap. 7.95 (ISBN 0-664-24329-0). Westminster John Knox.
Understanding Agriculture: New Directions for Education. 80p. 1988. pap. 6.95 (ISBN 0-309-03936-3). Natl Acad Pr.
Understanding AIDS. Arun & Anadi K. Dasa. 1987. 11.95. Asia Bk Corp.
Understanding AIDS. Seymour Bakerman. 187p. 1988. text ed. 19.50 (ISBN 0-945577-01-X). Interpret Lab Data.
Understanding AIDS. Ethan A. Lerner. (Coping with Modern Problems Ser.). (Illus.). 70p. (gr. 3-6). 1987. PLB 9.95 (ISBN 0-8225-0024-8). Lerner Pubns.
Understanding Aircraft Structures. John Cutler. (Illus.). 170p. 1986. pap. text ed. 26.50x (ISBN 0-00-383246-5, Pub. by Collins England). Sheridan.
Understanding Alcohol. Jean Kinney & Gwen Leaton. LC 81-22557. (Mosby Medical Library). (Illus.). 270p. 1982. pap. 8.95 (ISBN 0-452-25338-1, 2706-0, Plume). NAL.
Understanding Alcohol. Jean Kinney & Gwen Leaton. 268p. 1982. pap. 8.95 (ISBN 0-8016-2706-0). Mosby.
Understanding Algebra & Trigonometry. Gene Sellers. 1979. text ed. 33.95 (ISBN 0-675-08306-0). Additional supplements may be obtained from publisher. Merrill.
Understanding Alzheimer's Disease: What It Is, How to Treat It, How to Cope with It. Alzheimer's Disease & Related Disorders Association Staff. Ed. by Miriam K. Aronson. (Illus.). 256p. 1988. 15.95 (ISBN 0-684-18475-3, ScribT). Scribner.
Understanding Amateur Radio. American Radio Relay League Staff. LC 63-10833. 5.00 (ISBN 0-87259-603-6). Am Radio.
Understanding American Government. 2nd ed. Robert Weissberg. 650p. 1986. text ed. 21.00 (ISBN 0-394-35299-8, RanC). Random.
Understanding American Government Workbook. 2nd ed. Robert Weisberg. 1986. write for info (ISBN 0-394-35574-1, RanC). Random.
Understanding American Jewish Philanthropy. Marc L. Raphael. 20.00x (ISBN 0-87068-689-5). Ktav.
Understanding American Jewry. Ed. by Marshall Sklare. LC 81-14795. 300p. 1982. text ed. 27.95x (ISBN 0-87855-454-8). Transaction Bks.
Understanding American Judaism: Toward the Description of a Modern Religion, 2 vols. Jacob Neusner. Incl. Vol. 1. The Synagogue & the Rabbi (ISBN 0-87068-280-6); Vol. 2. Reform, Orthodoxy, Conservatism, & Reconstructionism (ISBN 0-87068-279-2). pap. 14.95 ea. Ktav.
Understanding American Judaism: Toward the Description of Modern Religion, 2 vols. Ed. by Jacob Neusner. Incl. Vol.1. Synagogue & the Rabbi; Vol.II. Reform, Orthodoxy, Conservatism, & Reconstruction. pap. 9.95 (ISBN 0-686-95149-2). ADL.
Understanding American Sentences. Kapili & Kapili. 457p. 1986. pap. text ed. 10.00 net (ISBN 0-15-592857-0, Pub. by HC). HarBraceJ.
Understanding America's Drinking Problem: How to Combat the Hazards of Alcohol. Don Cahalan. LC 87-45418. (Social & Behavioral Science Ser.). 1987. text ed. 24.95x (ISBN 1-55542-057-5). Jossey-Bass.
Understanding America's Government. Fred R. Harris et al. 1988. pap. text ed. write for info. (ISBN 0-673-18731-4). Scott F.
Understanding Ancient Coins: An Introduction for Archaeologists & Historians. P. J. Casey. LC 86-4028. (Illus.). 168p. 1986. 22.50x (ISBN 0-8061-2003-7). U of Okla Pr.
Understanding & Accepting Human Needs. Vincent W. Kafka. 12p. 1987. pap. 3.95 (ISBN 0-913261-17-3). Effect Learn Sys.
Understanding & Applying the Bible. Robertson McQuilkin. (Orig.). 1983. pap. 9.95 (ISBN 0-8024-0457-X). Moody.
Understanding & Being: An Introduction & Companion to Insight. Bernard J. F. Lonergan. Ed. by Elizabeth A. Morelli & Mark D. Morelli. (Toronto Studies in Theology: Vol. 5). xii, 368p. 1980. lib. bdg. 59.95x (ISBN 0-88946-909-1). E Mellen.
Understanding & Being Understood. Sanford Berman. LC 72-75526. 77p. 1972. pap. text ed. 4.00x (ISBN 0-918970-13-X). Intl Gen Semantics.
Understanding & Believing: Essays. Joachim Wach. Ed. by Joseph M. Kitagawa. LC 75-31987. 204p. 1976. Repr. of 1968 ed. lib. bdg. 35.00x (ISBN 0-8371-8488-6, WAUB). Greenwood.
Understanding & Changing Criminal Behavior. Michael J. Lillyquist. (Ser. in Criminal Justice). 1980. text ed. 36.00 (ISBN 0-13-935528-6). P-H.
Understanding & Conceiving Chemical Processes. 31p. 1974. pap. 22.00 (ISBN 0-8169-0039-6, M-8). Am Inst Chem Eng.
Understanding & Conducting Qualitative Research. Susan Stainback & William Stainback. Date not set. price not set. Coun Exc Child.
Understanding & Conducting Research: Applications in Education & the Behavioral Sciences. Emanuel J. Mason & William J. Bramble. (Illus.). 1977. text ed. 42.95 (ISBN 0-07-040697-9). McGraw.
Understanding & Controlling Crime: Toward a New Research Strategy. D. P. Farrington et al. LC 86-11823. (Research in Criminology Ser.). 215p. 1986. 25.00 (ISBN 0-387-96298-0). Springer-Verlag.
Understanding & Counseling Ethnic Minorities. George Henderson. (Illus.). 552p. 1979. 39.25x (ISBN 0-398-03916-X). C C Thomas.
Understanding & Counseling the Alcoholic. rev. ed. Howard J. Clinebell, Jr. LC 56-10143. 1968. 13.95 (ISBN 0-687-42803-3). Abingdon.
Understanding & Developing the Skills of Oral Communication: Speaking & Listening. Richard Hunsaker. 232p. (gr. 12). 1983. pap. text ed. 10.95x (ISBN 0-89582-096-X). Morton Pub.
Understanding & Developing Your Child's Natural Psychic Ability. Alex Tanous & Katherine F. Donnely. (Illus.). 224p. 1987. 5.95 (ISBN 0-671-65904-9, Fireside). S&S.
Understanding & Educating the Deaf-Blind - Severely & Profoundly Handicapped: An International Perspective. photocopy ed. Sara R. Walsh & Robert Holzberg. (Illus.). 328p. 1981. 34.00 (ISBN 0-398-04514-3). C C Thomas.
Understanding & Experiencing Prayer. E. J. Thomas. (Lets Discuss It Ser.). pap. 3.25 (ISBN 0-88172-130-1). Believers Bkshelf.
Understanding & Explanation. Karl-Otto Apel. 320p. 1988. Repr. of 1984 ed. text ed. 11.95x (ISBN 0-262-51041-3, Pub. by Bradford). MIT Pr.
Understanding & Explanation. Stephan Strasser. LC 84-21176. (Duquesne Studies-Philosophical Ser.: Vol. 39). 220p. 1985. text ed. 18.50x (ISBN 0-8207-0173-4). Duquesne.
Understanding & Explanation: A Transcendental Pragmatic Perspective. Karl O. Apel. Tr. by Georgia Warnke from Ger. (Studies in Contemporary German Social Thought). 320p. 1984. text ed. 30.00x (ISBN 0-262-01079-8). MIT Pr.

Understanding Austria: The Political Reports & Analyses of Martin F. Herz, Political Officer of the U. S. Legation in Vienna, 1945-1948. Ed. by Reinhold Wagnleitner. 653p. (Orig.). 1984. pap. 55.00x (ISBN 3-85376-043-0, Pub. by Wolfgang Neugebauer Verlag). Geo U Sch For Serv.

Understanding Authority for Effective Leadership. rev. ed. Doyle Harrison. 122p. (Orig.). 1985. pap. 3.50 (ISBN 0-89274-379-4). Harrison Hse.

Understanding Automation Systems. 2nd ed. Neil M. Schmitt & Robert F. Farwell. LC 84-51472. (Understanding Ser.). 280p. 1984. pap. 17.95 (ISBN 0-672-27014-5, LCB8472). Sams.

Understanding Automotive Electronics. 2nd. ed. William B. Ribbens & Norman Mansour. LC 84-51470. (Understanding Ser.). (Illus.). 256p. (Orig.). 1984. pap. 17.95 (ISBN 0-672-27017-X, LCB5771). Sams.

Understanding Automotive Electronics. 2nd ed. Wm. B. Ribbens. (Understanding Series Library). (Illus.). 320p. 1988. pap. 17.95. Sams.

Understanding Automotive Specifications & Data. James Flammang. (Illus.). 208p. 1986. pap. 12.95 (ISBN 0-8306-0316-6). TAB Bks.

Understanding Avalanches: A Handbook for Snow Travelers in the Sierra & Cascades. Barbara Diltz-Siler. (Illus.). 32p. 1977. pap. 2.95 (ISBN 0-913140-24-4). Signpost Bk Pub.

Understanding Baking. Joseph Amendola. 216p. 1983. pap. 19.95 (ISBN 0-8436-0521-9). Van Nos Reinhold.

Understanding BASIC. rev. ed. Richard G. Peddicord. (Alfred Handy Guide Ser.). 1982. 3.50 (ISBN 0-88284-146-7). Manusoft.

Understanding Basic Energy Terms. Robert V. Nelson. LC 81-2888. 1981. lib. bdg. 10.00 (ISBN 0-86663-806-7); pap. text ed. 2.95 (ISBN 0-86663-807-5). Ide Hse.

Understanding BASIC in Business. Michel Boillot. 276p. 1978. pap. text ed. 33.25 (ISBN 0-8299-0206-6). West Pub.

Understanding Basic Statistics. Harvey W. Kushner & Gerald De Maio. LC 78-54195. 1980. text ed. 29.95x (ISBN 0-8162-4874-5); sol. manual 6.00x (ISBN 0-686-76791-8, 0-8162-8475). Holden-Day.

Understanding Beckett: A Study of Monologue & Gesture in the Works of Samuel Beckett. Peter Gidal. LC 85-8304. 246p. 1986. 27.50 (ISBN 0-312-83080-7). St Martin.

Understanding Behavior: Foundations & Applications. Ray Denny & Robert Davis. 1981. 21.50 (ISBN 0-88252-113-6). Paladin Hse.

Understanding Behavioral Science: Research Methods for Research Consumers. R. L. Rosnow & R. Rosenthal. 1984. text ed. 16.95 (ISBN 0-07-053809-3). McGraw.

Understanding Bernard Malamud. Jeffrey Helterman. LC 85-16413. (Understanding Contemporary American Literature Ser.). 168p. 1985. 19.95x (ISBN 0-87249-469-1); pap. 9.95 (ISBN 0-87249-470-5). U of SC Pr.

Understanding Bible Doctrine: Leader's Guide. (Electives Ser.). 1983. pap. 2.50 (ISBN 0-8024-0308-5). Moody.

Understanding Biblical Symbols. Charles L. Edwards. 96p. 1981. 6.00 (ISBN 0-682-49704-5). Exposition-Phoenix.

Understanding Big Government: The Programme Approach. Richard Rose. LC 83-51198. iii, 261p. 1984. 39.95 (ISBN 0-8039-9778-7); pap. 16.50 (ISBN 0-8039-9779-5). Sage.

Understanding Bilingualism. Ed. by Werner Hullen. (Forum Linguisticum: Vol. 27). 163p. 1979. pap. 18.95 (ISBN 3-8204-6417-4). P Lang Pubs.

Understanding Biology. Burton S. Guttman & Johns W. Hopkins, III. 978p. 1983. text ed. 29.00 net (ISBN 0-15-592701-9, HC); pap. text ed. test file avail. (ISBN 0-15-592704-3); study guide net 12.00 (ISBN 0-15-592702-7); instr's. manual avail. (ISBN 0-15-592703-5). HarBraceJ.

Understanding Biology. Raven & Johnson. (Illus.). 1418p. 1987. text ed. 41.95 (ISBN 0-8016-2518-1); International ed. pap. text ed. 25.00 (ISBN 0-8016-3402-4). Mosby.

Understanding Black Africa: Data & Analysis of Social Change & Nation Building. Donald G. Morrison et al. (Illus.). 220p. 1988. text ed. 49.50x (ISBN 0-8290-2228-7). Irvington.

Understanding Black Africa: Data & Analysis of Social Change & Nation-Building. Donald G. Morrison et al. (Illus.). 220p. 1988. pap. text ed. 19.95x (ISBN 0-8290-1371-7). Irvington.

Understanding Black Africa: Data & Analysis of Social Change & Nation Building. Donald G. Morrison et al. 255p. 1988. pap. 19.95 (ISBN 0-88702-043-7). Paragon Hse.

Understanding Boat Design: A Basic Introduction for the Boat Buyer, Amateur Builder & Beginning Yacht Designer. 3rd ed. Edward S. Brewer & Jim Betts. LC 72-147872. pap. 20.00 (2026803). Bks Demand UMI.

Understanding Body Movement: An Annotated Bibliography. Martha Davis. LC 73-37652. 1676p. 1971. 21.00 (ISBN 0-405-00286-6). Ayer Co Pubs.

Understanding Body Movement: An Annotated Bibliography. Martha Davis. LC 82-1096. (Advances in Semiotics Ser.). 200p. 1982. 20.00x (ISBN 0-253-36163-X). Ind U Pr.

Understanding Book. John Pavao. Ed. by Ruth L. Perle. (Illus.). (gr. 1). 1977. pap. text ed. 1.75 (ISBN 0-89796-863-8). Arista Corp NY.

Understanding Book-Collecting. Grant Uden. (Understanding Ser.). (Illus.). 280p. 1986. 29.50 (ISBN 0-907462-13-8). Antique Collect.

Understanding Boy Scouts with Handicaps. (Illus.). 1975. pap. 1.50x (ISBN 0-8395-6557-7, 6557A). BSA.

Understanding Brain Damage: A Primer of Neuropsychological Evaluation. Kevin W. Walsh. LC 84-21438. (Illus.). 264p. 1985. text ed. 52.00 (ISBN 0-443-02224-0). Churchill.

Understanding Breast Cancer. Rich & Hager. 448p. 1983. 59.75 (ISBN 0-8247-7137-0). Dekker.

Understanding Britain: A History of the British People & Their Culture. John Randle. (Illus.). 232p. 1981. 24.95x (ISBN 0-631-12471-3); pap. 9.95 (ISBN 0-631-12883-2). Basil Blackwell.

Understanding Broadcasting. 2nd ed. Eugene S. Foster. (Illus.). 544p. 1982. pap. text ed. write for info (ISBN 0-394-35000-6, RanC). Random.

Understanding Buddhism. Nolan P. Jacobson. 224p. (Orig.). 1985. text ed. 19.95x (ISBN 0-8093-1224-7); pap. text ed. 12.95x (ISBN 0-8093-1225-5). S Ill U Pr.

Understanding Building Codes & Standards in the United States. National Association of Home Builders. 35p. 1986. pap. 7.00 (ISBN 0-86718-279-2). Nat Assn H Build.

Understanding Buildings: A Multidisciplinary Approach. Esmond Reid. (Illus.). 256p. 1984. text ed. 27.50x (ISBN 0-262-18116-9). MIT Pr.

Understanding Buildings: A Multidisciplinary Approach. Esmond Reid. (Illus.). 232p. 1988. pap. 12.50 (ISBN 0-262-68054-8). MIT Pr.

Understanding Business. Nickels. 800p. 1986. text ed. 37.95 (ISBN 0-8016-3627-2); International student ed. text ed. 15.95. Mosby.

Understanding Business & Consumer Law. 6th ed. R. Robert Rosenberg & John E. Whitcraft. (Illus.). (YA) (gr. 11-12). 1978. text ed. 24.52 (ISBN 0-07-053631-7). McGraw.

Understanding Business & Personal Law. 7th ed. G. W. Brown. 576p. 1983. text ed. 23.84 (ISBN 0-07-053635-X). McGraw.

Understanding Business & Personal Law. 8th ed. G. W. Brown. 608p. 1987. pap. text ed. 23.12 (ISBN 0-07-008433-5). McGraw.

Understanding Business & Personal Law. 8th ed. Gordon W. Brown & P. Sukys. 1987. pap. text ed. 26.50 (ISBN 0-07-008438-6). Gregg-McGraw.

Understanding Business & Personal Law: Performance Guide. 7th ed. Gordon W. Brown & R. Robert Rosenberg. (Illus.). 144p. 1983. pap. text ed. 9.12 (ISBN 0-07-053636-8). McGraw.

Understanding Business Communication. Richard L. Weaver, II. (Illus.). 352p. 1985. text ed. write for info. (ISBN 0-13-936998-8). P-H.

Understanding Business Contracts in China, Nineteen Forty-Nine to Nineteen Sixty-Three. Richard M. Pfeffer. 1973. text ed. 11.00x (ISBN 0-674-92095-3). Harvard U Pr.

Understanding Business Forecasting. 2nd ed. C. L. Jain. LC 87-82280. 261p. 1988. pap. text ed. 27.95 (ISBN 0-932126-15-4). Graceway.

Understanding Business Forecasting: A Manager's Guide. Ed. by Al Migliaro & Jain L. Chaman. 234p. (Orig.). 1985. pap. 25.95 (ISBN 0-932126-12-X). Graceway.

Understanding C. Bruce H. Hunter. LC 83-51569. (Illus.). 320p. 1984. pap. 19.95 (ISBN 0-89588-123-3). SYBEX.

Understanding C. Carlton Shrum. 1984. pap. 3.50 (ISBN 0-88284-300-1). Manusoft.

Understanding C. Carl Townsend. (Illus.). 275p. (Orig.). 1988. pap. 17.95 (ISBN 0-672-27278-4). Sams.

Understanding CAD-CAM. Daniel J. Bowman & Annette C. Bowman. 304p. 1986. pap. 17.95 (ISBN 0-672-27068-4). Sams.

Understanding Calcium & Osteoporosis. American Allergy Association Staff. Ed. by Irene T. McPherrin. (Illus.). 16p. 1987. pap. 4.00 (ISBN 0-9616708-4-3). Allergy Pubns.

Understanding Canada. Ed. by William Metcalfe et al. 624p. 1982. 40.00x (ISBN 0-8147-5382-5); pap. 20.00x (ISBN 0-8147-5383-3). NYU Pr.

Understanding Cancer. 3rd, rev. ed. Mark Renneker. 472p. (Orig.). 1988. pap. 19.95 (ISBN 0-915950-86-3). Bull Pub.

Understanding Cancer. Mark Renneker & Steven Leib. LC 78-31769. 1979. 19.95 (ISBN 0-915950-29-4); pap. text ed. 12.95 (ISBN 0-915950-26-X). Bull Pub.

Understanding Cancer: A Leading Expert Tells You What He Wishes Everyone Knew. John Laszlo. LC 86-46079. (Illus.). 288p. 1987. 17.95i (ISBN 0-06-015754-2, HarpT). Har-Row.

Understanding Capital. Duncan K. Foley. (Illus.). 208p. 1986. text ed. 21.00x (ISBN 0-674-92087-2); pap. text ed. 9.95x (ISBN 0-674-92088-0). Harvard U Pr.

Understanding Capitalism: Competition, Command & Change in the U. S. Economy. Samuel Bowles & Richard Edwards. 419p. 1985. pap. 21.95 scp (ISBN 0-06-040897-9, HarpC). Har-Row.

Understanding Cardiac Pacing: A Guide for Nurses. Kevan Metcalfe. 192p. 1986. pap. 27.95 (ISBN 0-8385-9258-9). Appleton & Lange.

Understanding Catholic Christianity. Thomas Zanzig. (Illus.). 304p. 1988. pap. text ed. 9.50x (ISBN 0-88489-182-8). St Mary's.

Understanding Catholicism. Monika K. Hellwig. LC 81-80047. 200p. (Orig.). 1981. pap. 6.95 (ISBN 0-8091-2384-3). Paulist Pr.

Understanding Cats. Gibbs. (Animal World Ser.). (gr. 3-6). 1981. (Usborne-Hayes); PLB 12.96 (ISBN 0-88110-088-9); pap. 4.95 (ISBN 0-86020-185-6). EDC.

Understanding Celine. Ed. by James Flynn. LC 84-10281. 270p. (Orig.). 1984. pap. 12.50x (ISBN 0-915781-00-X). Genitron Press.

Understanding Cell Structure. M. W. Steer. (Illus.). 120p. 1981. 34.50 (ISBN 0-521-23745-9); pap. text ed. 13.95 (ISBN 0-521-28198-9). Cambridge U Pr.

Understanding Central America. John A. Booth & Thomas W. Walker. 130p. 1986. lib. bdg. 26.50x (ISBN 0-8133-0002-9); pap. text ed. 12.95x (ISBN 0-8133-0003-7). Westview.

Understanding Cereal Crops, No. 2: Maize, Sorghum, Rice, & Millet. Roy M. Stephen & Betsey Eisendrath. (Technical Paper: No. 55). 19p. 1987. write for info. (ISBN 0-86619-272-7). Vols Tech Asst.

Understanding Cereal Crops: Wheat, Oats, Barley, & Rye, No. 1. Roy M. Stephen & Betsey Eisendrath. Ed. by Margaret Crouch. (Technical Paper: No. 50). 19p. 1987. write for info. (ISBN 0-86619-267-0). Vols Tech Asst.

Understanding Change in Education: An Introduction. A. M. Huberman. (Experiments & Innovations in Education Ser.: No. 4). (Illus.). 99p. (Orig., 3rd Printing 1979). 1973. pap. 5.00 (ISBN 92-3-101116-2, U689, UNESCO, IBE). UNIPUB.

Understanding Characters: Advanced Level. James A. Giroux & Glenn R. Williston. Ed. by Edward Spargo. (Comprehension Skills Ser). (Illus.). 64p. (gr. 9 up). 1974. pap. text ed. 4.00x (ISBN 0-89061-014-2, CB-3A). Jamestown Pubs.

Understanding Characters: Middle Level. Glenn R. Williston. (Comprehension Skills Ser.). (Illus.). 64p. (gr. 6-12). 1976. pap. text ed. 4.00x (ISBN 0-89061-066-5, CB-3M). Jamestown Pubs.

Understanding Chemical Patents: A Guide for the Inventor. John T. Maynard. LC 77-28097. 1978. 19.95 (ISBN 0-8412-0347-4). Am Chemical.

Understanding Chemical Thermodynamics. George C. Pimentel & Richard D. Spratley. LC 69-13419. (Illus.). 1969. pap. text ed. 22.00x (ISBN 0-8162-6791-X). Holden-Day.

Understanding Chemistry. H. J. Bruckman & A. Cruickshanks. 560p. 1988. 37.45 (ISBN 0-471-79684-0). Wiley.

Understanding Chemistry. J. Dudley Herron. 515p. 1981. text ed. write for info (ISBN 0-394-32087-5, RanC); wkbk, by Elizabeth Kean o.p 9.00 (ISBN 0-394-32423-4); write for info (ISBN 0-394-32437-4). Random.

Understanding Chemistry. 2nd ed. J. Dudley Herron. 515p. 1986. text ed. write for info (ISBN 0-394-34043-4, RanC). Random.

Understanding Chemistry. Lawrence P. Lessing. LC 59-14418. pap. 48.00 (ISBN 0-317-08764-9, 2007397). Bks Demand UMI.

Understanding Chemistry. Robert J. Ouellette & Jason H. Manchester. 194p. 1987. write for info. lab manual (ISBN 0-02-389720-1); write for info. study guide (ISBN 0-02-389740-6). Macmillan.

Understanding Chemistry. George C. Pimentel & Richard D. Spratley. LC 70-142944. 1971. 36.00x (ISBN 0-8162-6761-8). Holden-Day.

Understanding Chest Radiographers. Rau. 1985. 22.95 (ISBN 0-8016-4026-1). Mosby.

Understanding Chest Radiographs. Joseph L. Rau & Douglas J. Pearce. LC 83-62443. (Illus.). 150p. (Orig.). 1984. text ed. 22.95x (ISBN 0-940122-11-1). Mosby Multi-Media.

Understanding Chicano Literature. Carl R. Shirley & Paula W. Shirley. Ed. by Matthew J. Bruccoli. (Understanding Contemporary American Literature Ser.). 180p. 1988. text ed. 19.95x (ISBN 0-87249-575-2); pap. 9.95xt (ISBN 0-87249-576-0). U of SC Pr.

Understanding Child Behavior Disorders. 2nd ed. Donna M. Gelfand et al. LC 87-19753. (Illus.). 512p. 1988. text ed. 31.95 (ISBN 0-03-016618-7). HR&W.

Understanding Child Development. Rosalind Charlesworth. LC 81-66763. (Child Care Ser.). (Illus.). 246p. (Orig.). 1983. instr's. guide 6.00 (ISBN 0-8273-1856-1). Delmar.

Understanding Child Development. Sara Meadows. (Illus.). 256p. 1986. pap. 13.50 (ISBN 0-09-164121-7, Pub. by Hutchinson Educ). Longwood Pub Group.

Understanding Child Development. Spencer A. Rathus. (Illus.). 688p. 1988. text ed. price not set (ISBN 0-03-001837-4). HR&W.

Understanding Child Development. Peter K. Smith & Helen Cowie. (Illus.). 430p. (Orig.). Date not set. text ed. 55.00 (ISBN 0-631-15722-0); pap. text ed. 19.95 (ISBN 0-631-15723-9). Basil Blackwell.

Understanding Child Development: For Adults Who Work with Young Children. 2nd ed. Rosalind Charlesworth. LC 86-31910. 512p. 1987. text ed. 25.95 (ISBN 0-8273-2786-2); instr's. guide 8.00 (ISBN 0-8273-2787-0). Delmar.

Understanding Child Variance. William C. Morse & Judith M. Smith. LC 79-57303. 117p. (Orig.). 1980. pap. 10.95 (ISBN 0-86586-099-8). Coun Exc Child.

Understanding Children. Richard A. Gardner. LC 84-45133. 258p. 1983. Repr. of 1973 ed. 25.00x (ISBN 0-87668-726-5). Aronson.

Understanding Children: A Parents Guide to Child Rearing. Richard A. Gardner. LC 79-20004. 258p. 1979. Repr. of 1973 ed. 12.50 (ISBN 0-933812-01-9). Creative Therapeutics.

Understanding Children & Youth with Emotional & Behavioral Problems: A Handbook for Parents & Professionals. Paul Zionts & Richard Simpson. LC 87-29798. 192p. (Orig.). 1988. pap. 17.00x (ISBN 0-89079-170-8, 1429). Pro Ed.

Understanding Children Spelling. Jennifer E. Barr. (SCRE Publication Ser.: No. 90). (Illus.). 60p. 1986. pap. 6.95x (ISBN 0-947833-12-9, Pub. by Scot Council Research). Humanities.

Understanding Children Through Observation. Sherrill Richarz. 222p. 1980. pap. text ed. 19.00 (ISBN 0-8299-0337-2). West Pub.

Understanding Children's Behavior Disorders. Donna M. Gelfand & William R. Jensen. 1982. text ed. 36.95 (ISBN 0-03-044211-7). HR&W.

Understanding Children's Play. Ruth E. Hartley et al. LC 52-1138. (Illus.). 1952. 24.00x (ISBN 0-231-01899-1). Columbia U Pr.

Understanding Chinese Painting. T. C. Lai. LC 84-23467. (Illus.). 239p. 1985. 13.95 (ISBN 0-8052-3960-X). Schocken.

Understanding Christian Ethics. Ed. by William M. Tillman, Jr. LC 87-36752. (Orig.). 1988. pap. 10.95 (ISBN 0-8054-6129-9). Broadman.

Understanding Christian Missions. J. Herbert Kane. 16.95 (ISBN 0-8010-5344-7). Baker Bk.

Understanding Chronic Illness: The Medical & Psychosocial Dimensions of Nine Diseases. Toba S. Kerson & Lawrence A. Kerson. LC 84-28622. 368p. 1985. 28.95 (ISBN 0-02-918200-X). Free Pr.

Understanding Chronicles One & Two. John Heading. pap. 7.95 (ISBN 0-937396-10-9). Walterick Pubs.

Understanding Church Finances: The Economics of the Local Church. Loyde H. Hartley. LC 83-23769. 192p. (Orig.). 1984. pap. 10.95 (ISBN 0-8298-0708-X). Pilgrim NY.

Understanding Church Growth. rev. ed. Donald McGavran. 488p. (Orig.). 1980. pap. 12.95 (ISBN 0-8028-1849-8). Eerdmans.

Understanding Church Growth & Decline, 1950-78. Ed. by Dean R. Hoge & David A. Roozen. LC 79-4166. (Illus.). 1979. pap. 9.95 (ISBN 0-8298-0358-0). Pilgrim NY.

Understanding Cities. David Clow. LC 82-84486. (Development Component Ser.). (Illus.). 63p. (Orig.). 1982. pap. 11.00 (ISBN 0-87420-617-0, D25). Urban Land.

Understanding Civil Procedure. Joseph W. Glannon. LC 86-82424. 350p. (Orig.). 1987. pap. 15.95 (ISBN 0-316-31595-8). Little.

Understanding Civilizations: The Shape of History. James K. Feibleman. 1975. 8.95 (ISBN 0-8180-0816-4). Horizon.

Understanding Classroom Management: An Observation Guide. Julie P. Sanford & Edmund T. Emmer. (Illus.). 96p. 1988. pap. text ed. 12.00 (ISBN 0-13-935693-2). P-H.

Understanding Climatic Change: A Program for Action. LC 79-22423. (Illus.). 264p. 1980. Repr. of 1975 ed. 55.00x (ISBN 0-8103-1019-8). Gale.

Understanding COBOL. Richard G. Peddicord. 47p. 1981. pap. 3.50 (ISBN 0-88284-147-5). Manusoft.

Understanding Colonial Handwriting. 2nd ed. Harriet Stryker-Rodda. 26p. 1987. 3.50 (3647). Genealog Pub.

Understanding Color Infrared Photography. William H. Klein. (Illus.). 16p. 1982. pap. text ed. 3.00 (ISBN 0-938361-02-3). Austin Univ Forestry.

Understanding Commodore 64 BASIC. Richard G. Peddicord. (Handy Guide Ser.). 64p. (Orig.). 1984. pap. 3.50. Manusoft.

Understanding Commodore 64 Graphics. Richard G. Peddicord. (Handy Guide Ser.). 64p. (Orig.). 1984. pap. 3.50 (ISBN 0-88284-282-X). Manusoft.

Understanding Communication: A Workbook Approach. Douglas B. Hoehn. 368p. 1986. pap. text ed. 23.95 (ISBN 0-8403-3641-1). Kendall-Hunt.

Understanding Communication & Control. Lionel Bender. LC 85-40218. (Understanding Science Ser.). 64p. (gr. 5 up). 1985. PLB 13.96 (ISBN 0-382-09082-9). Silver.

Understanding Communication: Hidden Insight into Human Communication. Dana Britton. 35p. (Orig.). 1987. pap. 5.00 (ISBN 0-944478-00-X). Dock Pub Co.

Understanding Communication: The Signifying Web. D. J. Crowley. (Communication & the Human Condition Ser.). 211p. 1983. 46.00 (ISBN 0-677-05920-5). Gordon & Breach.

Understanding Communications Systems. 2nd. ed. Don L. Cannon & Gerald Luecke. LC 84-51469. (Understanding Ser.). (Illus.). 288p. (Orig.). 1984. pap. 17.95 (ISBN 0-672-27016-1, LCB8474). Sams.

Understanding Elementary Algebra. Arthur Goodman & Lewis Hirsch. LC 85-20243. (Illus.). 452p. 1986. text ed. 37.00 (ISBN 0-314-93532-0). West Pub.

Understanding Elementary Algebra. Richard G. Moon. (Mathematics Ser.). 1979. text ed. 32.95 (ISBN 0-675-08406-7). Merrill.

Understanding Elementary Algebra. 2nd ed. Robert Moon & Gus Klentos. 572p. 1987. Additional supplements may be obtained from publisher. text ed. 32.95 (ISBN 0-675-20418-6); study guide 13.95 (ISBN 0-675-20781-9); solutions manual 12.95 (ISBN 0-675-20858-0). Merrill.

Understanding Elementary Algebra: A Text-Workbook. Arthur Goodman & Lewis Hirsch. (Illus.). 616p. (Orig.). 1987. pap. text ed. 37.00 (ISBN 0-314-28493-1). West Pub.

Understanding: Eliminating Stress & Dissatisfaction in Life & Relationships. Jane Nelsen. LC 85-63353. 141p. 1986. pap. 7.95 (ISBN 0-9606896-2-1). Sunrise Pr.

Understanding: Eliminating Stress & Finding Serenity in Life & Relationships. rev. ed. Jane Nelson. Ed. by Bookman Productions Staff. 160p. 1988. pap. 8.95 (ISBN 0-914629-72-7, Dist. by St. Martin's). Prima Pub Comm.

Understanding Energy. Neil Ardley. LC 85-27784. (Understanding Science Ser.). (Illus.). 64p. (gr. 5 up). 1986. PLB 15.96 (ISBN 0-382-09184-1). Silver Burdett Pr.

Understanding English. rev. ed. Mary Jane Carrell. 1982. pap. 3.50 (ISBN 0-88323-182-4, 197). Richards Pub.

Understanding English Grammar. 2nd ed. Martha Kolin. 407p. 1986. text ed. write for info. (ISBN 0-02-366060-0). Macmillan.

Understanding Enzymes. Trevor Palmer. 405p. 1981. 84.95x (ISBN 0-470-27186-8). Halsted Pr.

Understanding Enzymes. 2nd ed. Trevor Palmer. LC 85-14040. (Biochemistry & Biotechnology Ser.). 411p. 1985. 47.95 (ISBN 0-470-20173-8). Halsted Pr.

Understanding Events. David R. Heise. LC 78-2417. (American Sociological Association Rose Monograph Ser.). (Illus.). 1979. o. p. 29.95 (ISBN 0-521-22539-6); pap. 11.95 (ISBN 0-521-29544-0). Cambridge U Pr.

Understanding Evolution. Earl D. Hanson. (Illus.). 1981. text ed. 29.95x (ISBN 0-19-502784-1). Oxford U Pr.

Understanding Evolution. 5th. ed. Peter E. Volpe. 288p. 1985. pap. text ed. write for info. (ISBN 0-697-04944-2). Wm C Brown.

Understanding Excel for the IBM. Bill O'Brien. 1988. pap. 19.95 (ISBN 0-673-38151-X). Scott F.

Understanding Exceptional Children. Peter Knoblock. 1987. text ed. write for info. (ISBN 0-673-39086-1). Scott F.

Understanding Exceptional People. Colleen J. Mandell & Edward D. Fiscus. (Illus.). 517p. 1981. text ed. 37.25 (ISBN 0-8299-0394-1). West Pub.

Understanding Executive Stress. Cary L. Cooper & Judi Marshall. LC 77-16077. 1978. text ed. 17.50 (ISBN 0-89433-059-4). Petrocelli.

Understanding Exodus. Moshe Greenberg. 214p. 1969. pap. 9.95x (ISBN 0-87441-265-X). Behrman.

Understanding Expert Systems. Louis E. Frenzel. (Understanding Ser.). (Orig.). 1987. pap. 17.95 (ISBN 0-672-27065-X). Sams.

Understanding Expert Systems. The Waite Group & Mike Van Horn. 320p. (Orig.). 1986. pap. 14.95 (ISBN 0-553-34168-5). Bantam.

Understanding Expository Text: A Theoretical & Practical Handbook for Analizing Explanatory Text. Ed. by Bruce K. Britton & John B. Black. (Psychology of Reading & Reading Instruction Ser.). 424p. 1984. text ed. 39.95 (ISBN 0-89859-412-X). L Erlbaum Assocs.

Understanding Fabrics: From Fiber to Finished Cloth. Debbie A. Gioello. (Language of Fashion Ser.). (Illus.). 350p. 1982. text ed. 30.00 (ISBN 0-87005-377-9). Fairchild.

Understanding Factoring & Trade Credit. Ed. by S. Crichton & C. W. Ferrier. (Business Library). (Illus.). 256p. 1986. pap. 22.00 (ISBN 0-08-039204-0, Pub. by Waterlow). Pergamon.

Understanding Family Policy: Theoretical Approaches. Shirley L. Zimmerman. 200p. 1988. text ed. 26.00 (ISBN 0-8039-2798-3); pap. text ed. 12.95 (ISBN 0-8039-3226-X). Sage.

Understanding Family Violence within U. S. Refugee Communities: A Training Manual. Refugee Women in Development Staff. Ed. by Beth Richie. 1988. 8.00 (ISBN 0-9620653-0-7). Ref Women Dev.

Understanding Far Eastern Art. Julia Hutt. (Illus.). 208p. 1987. 29.95 (ISBN 0-525-24521-9, 02908-870); pap. 19.95 (ISBN 0-525-48295-4, 01937-580). Dutton.

Understanding Far Eastern Art. Julia Hutt. 208p. 1987. 137.00x (ISBN 0-317-68524-4, Pub. by Han-Shan Tang Ltd). State Mutual Bk.

Understanding Farm Animals. Thompson. (Animal World Ser.). (gr. 3-6). 1978. (Usborne-Hayes); PLB 12.96 (ISBN 0-88110-090-0); pap. 4.95 (ISBN 0-86020-186-4). EDC.

Understanding Fashion. Elizabeth Rouse. 224p. 1988. write for info (ISBN 0-00-383063-2, Pub. by Collins England). Sheridan.

Understanding Fiber Optics. Jeff Hecht. 456p. 1987. pap. 17.95 (ISBN 0-672-27066-8). Sams.

Understanding Fibonacci Numbers. Edward D. Dobson. 16p. 1984. pap. 5.00 (ISBN 0-934380-08-2). Traders Pr.

Understanding Fiction. 3rd ed. Robert Penn Warren & Cleanth Brooks. 1979. pap. text ed. write for info (ISBN 0-13-936690-3). P-H.

Understanding Figurative Language: What Effect Did the Author Intend? Walter Pauk. (Skill at a Time Ser.). 64p. (gr. 9 up). 1975. pap. text ed. 4.00x (ISBN 0-89061-023-1, ST-3). Jamestown Pubs.

Understanding Filipino Values: A Management Approach. Tomas D. Andres. 180p. 1981. pap. 7.50x (ISBN 0-686-32452-8, Pub. by New Day Philippines). Cellar.

Understanding Finance with the Financial Times. Terry Byland. 1988. 49.00x (ISBN 0-245-54509-3, Pub. by Harrap Ltd England). State Mutual Bk.

Understanding Financial Statements. 2nd ed. Lyn Fraser. (Illus.). 192p. 1988. text ed. write for info. (ISBN 0-13-936246-0). P-H.

Understanding Financial Statements: Through the Maze of a Corporate Annual Report. Adlyn Fraser. 1984. 24.95 (ISBN 0-8359-8042-1, Reston); pap. 19.33 (ISBN 0-8359-8041-3). P-H.

Understanding Financial Statements: What the Executive Should Know About the Accountant's Statements. John N. Myer. 1968. pap. 3.50 (ISBN 0-451-62354-1, ME2051, Ment). NAL.

Understanding Finite Math. James Radlow. 640p. 1981. text ed. write for info. (ISBN 0-87150-328-X, 33L 2621, Prindle). PWS Kent Pub.

Understanding Finnegans Wake: A Guide to the Narrative of James Joyce's Masterpiece. Danis Rose & John O'Hanlon. LC 82-9237. 341p. 1982. lib. bdg. 31.00 (ISBN 0-8240-2899-6). Garland Pub.

Understanding Fish Preservation & Processing. Richard T. Carruthers. Ed. by Margaret Crouch. (Technical Paper: No. 44). 10p. (Orig.). 1987. write for info. (ISBN 0-86619-258-1). Vols Tech Asst.

Understanding Flying. Robert Taylor. (Eleanor Friede Book Ser.). 342p. 1987. 22.50 (ISBN 0-02-616660-7). Macmillan.

Understanding Foreign Policy Decisions: The Chinese Case. David B. Bobrow et al. LC 78-24667. (Illus.). 1979. 22.95 (ISBN 0-02-904410-3). Free Pr.

Understanding FORTH. Joseph Reymann. (Alfred Handy Guide). 47p. 1983. 3.50 (ISBN 0-88284-237-4). Alfred Pub.

Understanding FORTRAN. 3rd ed. Michel Boillot. (Illus.). 592p. 1985. pap. text ed. 34.25 (ISBN 0-314-85219-0). West Pub.

Understanding FORTRAN. Herbert R. Ludwig. (Alfred Handy Guide Ser.). 62p. 1981. 3.50 (ISBN 0-88284-148-3). Manusoft.

Understanding FORTRAN-77 with Structured Problem Solving. Michel Boillot. (Illus.). 592p. 1984. pap. text ed. 30.75 (ISBN 0-314-77845-4); write for info. instr's guide (ISBN 0-314-77846-2). West Pub.

Understanding Fortran 77 with Structured Problem Solving. 2nd ed. Michel Boillot. LC 86-26662. (Illus.). 527p. 1987. pap. text ed. 35.50 (ISBN 0-314-27031-0); instr's. manual avail. (ISBN 0-314-34720-8). West Pub.

Understanding Franchise Contracts. David C. Hjelmfelt. LC 84-1848. 45p. 1984. pap. 3.95 (ISBN 0-87576-110-0). Pilot Bks.

Understanding Futures Markets. Robert W. Kolb. 1985. pap. text ed. write for info. (ISBN 0-673-15976-0). Scott F.

Understanding Futures Markets. 2nd ed. Robert W. Kolb. 1988. pap. text ed. write for info. (ISBN 0-673-18901-5). Scott F.

Understanding Gabriel Garcia Marquez. Kathleen McNerney. Ed. by James N. Hardin. (Understanding Contemporary European & Latin Literature Ser.). 176p. 1988. text ed. 19.95x (ISBN 0-87249-563-9); pap. 9.95 (ISBN 0-87249-564-7). U of SC Pr.

Understanding Gap: A Guide to Fine-Tuning Your Dataq. 1987. 35.00 (ISBN 0-929097-30-0, 19166). US League Savi Inst.

Understanding Genesis. Jack P. Lewis. 63p. (Orig.). 1987. pap. 3.95 (ISBN 0-89225-300-2). Gospel Advocate.

Understanding Genesis: The Heritage of Biblical Israel. Nahum M. Sarna. LC 66-23626. 1970. pap. 8.95 (ISBN 0-8052-0253-6). Schocken.

Understanding Genetics. E. B. Ford. LC 79-63132. (Illus.). 1979. text ed. 15.00x (ISBN 0-87663-728-4, Pica Pr). Universe.

Understanding Genetics. 4th ed. Norman Rothwell. (Illus.). 728p. 1988. text ed. 39.95 (ISBN 0-19-505108-4). Oxford U Pr.

Understanding Genetics. 3rd ed. Norman V. Rothwell. (Illus.). 1983. text ed. 37.95x (ISBN 0-19-503123-7). Oxford U Pr.

Understanding George Garrett. R. H. Dillard. Ed. by Matthew J. Bruccoli. (Understanding Contemporary American Literature Ser.). 176p. 1988. text ed. 19.95x (ISBN 0-87249-550-7); pap. 9.95 (ISBN 0-87249-551-5). U of SC Pr.

Understanding Glass Recycling. W. Richard Ott. Ed. by Margaret Crouch. (Technical Paper: No. 43). 14p. 1987. write for info. (ISBN 0-86619-257-3). Vols Tech Asst.

Understanding Gliding: The Principles of Soaring Flight. Derek Piggott. LC 77-371531. (Illus.). 259p. 1977. 26.95x (ISBN 0-06-495568-0). B&N Imports.

Understanding God's Word see How to Understand Your Bible.

Understanding Graciliano Ramos. Celso L. De Oliveira. (Understanding Contemporary European & Latin Literature Ser.). 176p. 1988. text ed. 19.95x (ISBN 0-87249-560-4); pap. 9.95 (ISBN 0-87249-561-2). U of SC Pr.

Understanding Grammar. Paul M. Roberts. 1954. text ed. 25.95 scp (ISBN 0-06-045480-6, HarpC). Har-Row.

Understanding Group Behavior: A Discussion Guide. rev. ed. Harry L. Miller. pap. 24.80 (ISBN 0-317-10607-4, 2000637). Bks Demand UMI.

Understanding Gunter Grass. Alan F. Keele. Ed. by James N. Hardin. (Understanding Contemporary European & Latin Literature Ser.). 127p. 1988. text ed. 19.95x (ISBN 0-87249-546-9); pap. 9.95 (ISBN 0-87249-547-7). U of SC Pr.

Understanding Harmony. Robert L. Jacobs. LC 85-31691. Orig. Title: Harmony for the Listener. 192p. 1986. Repr. of 1969 ed. lib. bdg. 35.00x (ISBN 0-313-25092-8, JAHA). Greenwood.

Understanding Health Care Budgeting: An Introduction. Allen G. Herkimer, Jr. 208p. 1988. 29.95 (ISBN 0-87189-772-5). Aspen Pub.

Understanding Health Economics. John Rapoport et al. LC 81-14987. 554p. 1982. text ed. 49.95 (ISBN 0-89443-380-6). Aspen Pub.

Understanding Hearing Loss & What Can Be Done To Help. Susan Sundstrom. 64p. 1983. pap. text ed. 3.95x (ISBN 0-8134-2266-3). Inter Print Pubs.

Understanding Heart. 1966. 5.95 (ISBN 0-88088-554-8). Peter Pauper.

Understanding Heart Sounds & Murmurs: With an Introduction to Lung Sounds. 2nd ed. Ara G. Tilkian & Mary B. Conover. (Illus.). 288p. 1984. pap. 31.95 (ISBN 0-7216-8847-0). Saunders.

Understanding Heartbreak. L. K. Mickelson. 1979. 9.95 (ISBN 0-686-26186-0). Risk Ent.

Understanding Heat Pumps, Ground Water, & Wells. 1983. 10.00 (ISBN 0-318-23030-5). Natl Water Well.

Understanding Hebrew Literature: A Guide to a Better Understanding of the Bible As a Source Book for the Humanities. John C. Kersten. 2.25 (ISBN 0-89942-145-8, 145/04). Catholic Bk Pub.

Understanding Herbert Hoover: Ten Perspectives. Lee Nash. 1988. 21.95 (ISBN 0-8179-8541-7). Hoover Inst Pr.

Understanding High Blood Pressure & Its Treatment. Richard A. Schacht. (Illus.). 203p. (Orig.). 1987. pap. 10.95 (ISBN 0-941827-00-3). Ricca Bks.

Understanding High Technology. David L. Goetsch. Ed. by Barbara Rock. 223p. 1987. 34.95 (ISBN 0-87814-313-0). PennWell Bks.

Understanding Histochemistry: Selection, Evaluation & Design of Biological Stains. Richard V. Horobin. (Biochemistry & Biotechnology Ser.). 172p. 1988. 59.95 (ISBN 0-470-21060-5). Wiley.

Understanding Historical Research: A Search for Truth. Jack Block. (Illus.). 156p. 1971. pap. text ed. 7.00x (ISBN 0-9600478-0-8). Research Pubns.

Understanding History: A Primer of Historical Method. Louis M. Gottschalk. 1969. pap. 10.00 (ISBN 0-394-30215-X, KnopfC). Knopf.

Understanding History: Marxist Essays. Rev. ed. George Novack. LC 75-186684. 1980. lib. bdg. 20.00 (ISBN 0-87348-606-4); pap. 6.95 (ISBN 0-87348-605-6). Path Pr NY.

Understanding History of Education. 2nd ed. Ed. by Robert R. Sherman. 345p. 1984. text ed. 18.95 (ISBN 0-87073-338-9); pap. text ed. 11.95 (ISBN 0-87073-339-7). Schenkman Bks Inc.

Understanding History Through the American Experience. Bernard Norling & Charles Poinsatte. LC 76-637. 208p. 1976. text ed. 16.95x (ISBN 0-268-01910-X); pap. 6.95x (ISBN 0-268-01911-8). U of Notre Dame Pr.

Understanding Holography. Michael Wenyon. LC 78-965. (Illus.). 176p. 1984. 14.95 (ISBN 0-668-06414-5); pap. 8.95 (ISBN 0-668-06203-7). Arco.

Understanding Horse Psychology see Farnam Horse Library Series.

Understanding Hospital Financial Management. 2nd ed. Allen G. Herkimer, Jr. 416p. 1986. 39.95 (ISBN 0-87189-392-4). Aspen Pub.

Understanding Hospitality Accounting I. Raymond Cote. Ed. by Kent Premo. LC 87-15724. (Illus.). 329p. 1987. text ed. 36.95 (ISBN 0-86612-035-1). Educ Inst Am Hotel.

Understanding Hospitality Accounting II. Raymond Cote. Ed. by Kent Premo et al. LC 87-15724. (Illus.). 384p. 1988. text ed. 36.95 (ISBN 0-86612-038-6). Educ Inst Am Hotel.

Understanding Hotel-Motel Law. Jack P. Jefferies. Ed. by Susan J. Berman. LC 83-16351. (Illus.). 310p. 1983. 36.95 (ISBN 0-86612-015-7). Educ Inst Am Hotel.

Understanding How Components Fail. 256p. 1985. 52.00 (ISBN 0-87170-189-8). ASM.

Understanding How to Fight the Good Fight of Faith. Kenneth E. Hagin. 1987. pap. 3.50 (ISBN 0-89276-510-0). Hagin Ministries.

Understanding Human Action: Social Explanation of the Vision of Social Science. Michael A. Simon. LC 88-5280. (Systematic Philosophy Ser.). 226p. 1981. 49.50 (ISBN 0-87395-498-X); pap. 16.95x (ISBN 0-87395-499-8). State U NY Pr.

Understanding Human Anatomy & Physiology. Eldra P. Solomon & Gloria A. Phillips. (Illus.). 400p. 1987. pap. 21.95 (ISBN 0-7216-1994-0). Saunders.

Understanding Human Behavior: A Guide for Health Care Providers. 4th ed. Mary E. Milliken. LC 86-16758. 304p. 1987. text ed. 20.96 (ISBN 0-8273-2798-6); pap. text ed. 15.95 (ISBN 0-8273-2797-8); instr's. guide 8.00 (ISBN 0-8273-2799-4). Delmar.

Understanding Human Behavior: An Introduction to Psychology. 5th ed. James V. McConnell. 768p. 1986. text ed. 29.95 (ISBN 0-03-071096-0); instr's manual 19.95 (ISBN 0-03-006617-4); student manual 12.95 (ISBN 0-03-062337-5); PSI mastery wkbk. 12.95 (ISBN 0-03-062336-7). HR&W.

Understanding Human Behavior & the Social Environment. Charles Zastrow & Karen Kirst-Ashman. (Illus.). 629p. 1987. 28.95x (ISBN 0-8304-1122-4). Nelson-Hall.

Understanding Human Behavior for Effective Police Work. 2nd ed. Harold E. Russell & Allan Beigel. LC 75-7261. (Illus.). 1982. 20.95x (ISBN 0-465-08862-7). Basic.

Understanding Human Behavior in Health & Illness. 3rd ed. Richard C. Simons & Herbert Pardes. 800p. 1985. text ed. 28.95 (ISBN 0-683-07741-4); study guide & self examination review, 250p 34.95 (ISBN 0-683-04571-7). Williams & Wilkins.

Understanding Human Communication. Ronald B. Adler & George Rodman. 1985. pap. text ed. 17.95 (ISBN 0-03-059468-5). HR&W.

Understanding Human Communication. 3rd ed. Ronald B. Adler & George Rodman. LC 87-17719. 464p. 1988. pap. text ed. price not set (ISBN 0-03-013363-7). HR&W.

Understanding Human Disease. 2nd ed. Abner Golden & Deborah E. Powell. 700p. 1985. 29.95 (ISBN 0-683-03724-2). Williams & Wilkins.

Understanding Human Emotions. Ed. by Fred D. Miller, Jr. & Thomas W. Attig. (Bowling Green Studies in Applied Philosophy: Vol. 1). 101p. 1979. 10.00 (ISBN 0-935756-01-9). BGSU Dept Phil.

Understanding Human Evolution. Frank E. Poirier. (Illus.). 336p. 1987. pap. text ed. 22.00 (ISBN 0-13-935875-7). P-H.

Understanding Human Nature. Alfred Adler. 1981. pap. 2.25 (ISBN 0-449-30833-2, Prem). Fawcett.

Understanding Human Nature: A Popular Guide to the Effects of Technology on Man & His Behavior. James K. Feibleman. LC 77-77126. 1978. 8.95 (ISBN 0-8180-1322-2). Horizon.

Understanding Human Relations: A Practical Guide to People at Work. Baron. 1985. 30.00 (ISBN 0-205-08287-4, 798287). Allyn.

Understanding Human Relations: The Individual, Organization & Management. Gerald H. Graham. 416p. 1982. text ed. write for info. (ISBN 0-574-19520-3, 13-2520); instr's. guide avail. (ISBN 0-574-19521-1, 13-2521). SRA.

Understanding Human Resources. Eli Ginzberg. 1984. 34.25 (ISBN 0-89011-602-4). Abt Bks.

Understanding Human Resources. Eli Ginzberg. 762p. 1986. lib. bdg. 36.00 (ISBN 0-8191-4869-5, ABT Bks). U Pr of Amer.

Understanding Human Sexuality. 2nd ed. Janet S. Hyde. 640p. 1982. text ed. 30.95 (ISBN 0-07-031567-1). McGraw.

Understanding Human Sexuality. 3rd ed. Janet S. Hyde. 768p. 1986. text ed. 33.95 (ISBN 0-07-031581-7). McGraw.

Understanding Human Values: Individual & Societal. Milton Rokeach. LC 78-24753. (Illus.). 1979. 17.95 (ISBN 0-02-926760-9). Free Pr.

Understanding Hydropower. Walter C. Eshenaur. 60p. 1984. 9.95 (ISBN 0-86619-205-0). Vols Tech Asst.

Understanding HyperCard. Greg Harvey. 581p. (Orig.). 1988. pap. 24.95 (ISBN 0-89588-506-9). Sybex.

Understanding HyperTalk 1.2. Dan Shafer. (Illus.). 300p. (Orig.). 1988. pap. 17.95 (ISBN 0-672-27283-0). Sams.

Understanding Hypertension: Causes & Treatments. Timothy N. Caris. Date not set. pap. 3.95. Warner Bks.

Understanding Hypnosis: A Brief Guide. Wladyslaw Michaluk. 4.95 (ISBN 0-939628-00-7, Pub. by Hypnos Pr). Borden.

Understanding IC Operational Amplifiers. 3rd ed. Roger Melen & Harry Garland. 256p. 1986. pap. 12.95 (ISBN 0-672-22484-4). Sams.

Understanding Imperial Russia: State & Society in the Old Regime. Marc Raeff. Tr. by Arthur Goldhammer. LC 83-26241. 240p. 1984. 25.00 (ISBN 0-231-05842-X); pap. 13.00x (ISBN 0-231-05843-8). Columbia U Pr.

Understanding Indian Classical Music. G. N. Joshi. (Illus.). xii, 46p. 1981. text ed. 25.00x (ISBN 0-86590-046-9, Pub. by Taraporevala India). Apt Bks.

Understanding Indian Classical Music. G. N. Joshi. (Illus.). 110p. 1957. 26.96. Asia Bk Corp.

Understanding Indian Music. Baburao Joshi. LC 73-15055. 102p. 1974. Repr. of 1963 ed. lib. bdg. 35.00x (ISBN 0-8371-7156-3, JOIM). Greenwood.

Understanding Military Specifications & Purchase Descriptions. Larry G. Best & Ronald R. Shook. 326p. 1987. wkbk. 100.00 (ISBN 0-933427-18-2). Shipley.

Understanding Miniature British Pottery & Porcelain. M. Milboun & E. Milboun. (Illus.). 184p. 1985. 29.50 (ISBN 0-907462-30-8). Apollo.

Understanding Miniature British Pottery & Porcelain, 1730-the Present Day. Maurice Milbourn & Evelyn Milbourn. (Understanding Ser.). (Illus.). 184p. 1983. 29.50. Antique Collect.

Understanding Minority Dominant Relations: Sociological Contributions. F. James Davis. LC 77-90671. 1979. pap. text ed. 19.95x (ISBN 0-88295-210-2). Harlan Davidson.

Understanding Modern Architecture. George Barford. LC 86-70903. (Illus.). 192p. 1986. 19.95 (ISBN 0-87192-179-0). Davis Mass.

Understanding Modern Art. Frances Mordecai & Helen S. Stone. (Illus.). 1970. pap. 7.00 (ISBN 0-8283-1038-6). Branden Pub Co.

Understanding Modern Business Data Processing see Introduction to Data Processing.

Understanding Modern Business Maths. Morison. pap. 20.95 (ISBN 0-85258-142-4). Van Nos Reinhold.

Understanding Modern Ethical Standards, 2 vols. Deanne C. Siemer & National Institute for Trial Advocacy, U. S. A. LC 86-145601. 1986. Set. 59.95 (ISBN 0-317-63740-1); Vol. 1. 35.00 (ISBN 0-317-63741-X); Vol. 2. 35.00 (ISBN 0-317-63742-8). Natl Inst Trial Ad.

Understanding Modern Telecommunications. H. S. Dordick. 336p. 1986. text ed. 42.95 (ISBN 0-07-017662-0). McGraw.

Understanding Modern Theology I: Cultural Revolutions & New World. Jeffery Hopper. LC 86-45210. 192p. 1986. 14.95 (ISBN 0-8006-1929-3). Fortress.

Understanding Modern Theology II: Reinterpreting Christian Faith for Changing Worlds. Jeffrey Hopper. LC 86-45210. 176p. 1988. pap. 12.95 (ISBN 0-8006-2050-X, 1-2050). Fortress.

Understanding Modernity: Towards a New Perspective Going Beyond Durkheim & Webber. Richard Munch. (International Library of Sociology). 356p. 1988. text ed. 65.00 (ISBN 0-7102-1217-8, Pub. by Kegan Paul). Routledge Chapman & Hall.

Understanding Molecular Properties. Ed. by John Avery et al. 1987. lib. bdg. 98.00 (ISBN 90-277-2419-9, Pub. by Reidel Holland); pap. text ed. 34.00 (ISBN 90-277-2439-3, Pub. by Reidel Holland). Kluwer Academic.

Understanding Motor Development: Infants, Children, Adolescents. 2nd ed. David L. Gallahue. LC 87-70628. (Illus.). 400p. 1988. text ed. 21.95 (ISBN 0-936157-22-4). Benchmark Pr.

Understanding Mourning: A Guide for Those Who Grieve. Glen W. Davidson. LC 84-14527. 112p. (Orig.). 1984. pap. 6.95 (ISBN 0-8066-2080-3, 10-6805). Augsburg.

Understanding Movement. Ralph Hancock. LC 85-40216. (Understanding Science Ser.). (Illus.). (gr. 5 up). 1985. PLB 13.96 (ISBN 0-382-09084-5). Silver.

Understanding Movies. 4th ed. Louis D. Giannetti. (Illus.). 512p. 1987. pap. text ed. 23.00 (ISBN 0-13-936329-7). P-H.

Understanding MS-DOS. Waite Group. (Understanding Ser.). 236p. (Orig.). 1986. pap. 17.95 (ISBN 0-672-27067-6). Sams.

Understanding Multiple Sclerosis. Robert Shuman & Janice Schwartz. 240p. 1988. 17.95 (ISBN 0-684-18989-5). Scribner.

Understanding Music. Antony Hopkins. (Illus.). 255p. 1980. Repr. of 1979 ed. 17.50x (ISBN 0-460-04376-5, Pub. by J. M. Dent England). Biblio Dist.

Understanding Music Fundamentals. Phyllis Gelineau. (Illus.). 256p. 1986. pap. text ed. write for info. (ISBN 0-13-937004-8). P H.

Understanding Music Through Sound Exploration & Experiments. Janet Moore. LC 85-29462. 134p. (Orig.). 1986. pap. text ed. 9.00 (ISBN 0-8191-5231-5). U Pr of Amer.

Understanding My Church. rev. ed. Samuel J. Stoesz. LC 82-73214. 216p. 1983. pap. 5.95 (ISBN 0-87509-325-6); leader's guide 2.95 (ISBN 0-87509-331-0). Chr Pubns.

Understanding Natural Fibre Concrete: Its Application As a Building Material. Barrie Evans. (Illus.). 44p. (Orig.). 1986. pap. 9.75x (ISBN 0-946688-77-X, Pub. by Intermediate Tech England). Intermediate Tech.

Understanding Natural Gas Accounting. Joe Caggiano. 1988. pap. 75.00 (ISBN 0-88057-858-0). Exec Ent Pubns.

Understanding Natural Language. Terry Winograd. 1972. 19.95 (ISBN 0-12-759750-6). Acad Pr.

Understanding Negro History. Ed. & commentary by Dwight W. Hoover. LC 68-26441. 1968. pap. 3.95 (ISBN 0-317-39766-4). Brown Bk.

Understanding Negro History. Ed. by Dwight W. Hoover. LC 68-26441. (Quadrangle Original Paperback Ser.). 432p. (Orig.). 1968. pap. text ed. 5.95x. Wiener Pub Inc.

Understanding Neural Networks: A Primer. 75p. 1988. 95.00 (ISBN 0-937587-04-4). Graeme Pub.

Understanding Neuropsychology. Graham J. Beaumont. (Illus.). 160p. (Orig.). Date not set. text ed. 34.95 (ISBN 0-631-15719-0); pap. text ed. 15.95 (ISBN 0-631-15721-2). Basil Blackwell.

Understanding New Zealand. facs. ed. Frederick L. Wood. LC 75-134163. (Essay Index Reprint Ser). 1944. 21.50 (ISBN 0-8369-2097-X). Ayer Co Pubs.

Understanding News. John Hartley. (Studies in Communication). 160p. 1982. pap. 9.95 (ISBN 0-416-74550-4, NO. 3622). Routledge Chapman & Hall.

Understanding Non-Christian Religions. Josh McDowell & Don Stewart. LC 81-86543. (Handbook of Today's Religion Ser.). 208p. 1982. pap. 6.95 (ISBN 0-86605-092-2, 402834). Heres Life.

Understanding Non-Fuel Uses of Woodwastes. Jon Vogler. Ed. by Margaret Crouch. (Technical Paper: No. 47). 1987. write for info. (ISBN 0-86619-261-1). Vols Tech Asst.

Understanding Normal & Clinical Nutrition. 2nd ed. Eleanor N. Whitney & Connie B. Cataldo. 787p. 1987. text ed. 48.75 (ISBN 0-314-24245-7). West Pub.

Understanding Normal & Clinical Nutrition. Eleanor N. Whitney & Corrine Cataldo. (Illus.). 1065p. 1983. text ed. 42.75 (ISBN 0-314-69685-7); tchrs.' manual avail. (ISBN 0-314-71137-6). West Pub.

Understanding Nuclear Power. H. A. Cole. 300p. 1987. text ed. 35.00x (ISBN 0-291-39704-2, Pub. by Gower England). Gower Pub Co.

Understanding Nuclear Weapons & Arms Control: A Guide to the Issues. 3rd, rev. ed. T. K. Mayers. (Illus.). 128p. 1986. text ed. 16.95 (ISBN 0-08-034483-6, PDP); pap. text ed. 9.95 (ISBN 0-08-034482-8). Pergamon.

Understanding Nurses: The Social Psychology of Nursing. Ed. by Suzanne Skevington. LC 83-14509. 190p. 1984. 32.00x (ISBN 0-471-90277-2, Pub. by Wiley Med). Wiley.

Understanding Nursing Care. 3rd ed. Ed. by Anne M. Chilman & Margaret Thomas. LC 85-24653. (Illus.). 681p. (Orig.). 1987. pap. text ed. 25.75 (ISBN 0-443-03040-5). Churchill.

Understanding Nutrition. 4th ed. Eleanor N. Whitney & Eva M. Hamilton. (Illus.). 573p. 1987. text ed. 41.00 (ISBN 0-314-24247-3); instr's. manual avail. (ISBN 0-314-35438-7); study guide 15.00 (ISBN 0-314-35443-3). West Pub.

Understanding of Animals. Ed. by Georgina Ferry. (New Scientist Guides Ser.). (Illus.). 336p. 1984. 29.95x (ISBN 0-85520-729-9); pap. 11.95 (ISBN 0-85520-728-0). Basil Blackwell.

Understanding of Jane Austen's Novels: Character, Value & Ironic Perspective. John Odmark. 240p. 1981. 27.50x (ISBN 0-389-20216-9, 06998). B&N Imports.

Understanding of Love According to the Anchoress Julian of Norwich. Patricia M. Vinje. Ed. by James Hogg. (Elizabethan & Renaissance Studies). 238p. (Orig.). 1983. pap. 15.00 (ISBN 3-7052-0749-0, Pub. by Salzburg Studies). Longwood Pub group.

Understanding of Music. 5th ed. Charles R. Hoffer. 544p. 1985. text ed. write for info. (ISBN 0-534-03939-1). Wadsworth Pub.

Understanding of Music. 6th ed. Charles R. Hoffer. Date not set. text ed. write for info. (ISBN 0-534-09810-X). Wadsworth Pub.

Understanding Organic Chemistry. Margot K. Schumm. 544p. 1985. text ed. write for info. (ISBN 0-02-408200-7). Macmillan.

Understanding Organizational Behavior: A Managerial Viewpoint. Robert Callahan et al. 576p. (Additional supplements may be obtained from publisher). 1986. text ed. 35.95 (ISBN 0-675-20198-5). Merrill.

Understanding Organizational Behavior. 2nd ed. Stuart M. Klein & R. Richard Ritti. LC 83-18715. 692p. 1984. text ed. 33.00 (ISBN 0-534-03119-6). PWS Kent Pub.

Understanding Organizational Behavior. Denis D. Umstot. (Management Ser.). (Illus.). 455p. 1984. text ed. 40.00 (ISBN 0-314-77850-0); instrs.' manual avail. (ISBN 0-314-79073-X). West Pub.

Understanding Organizational Behavior: A Casebook. Bud Knudson et al. 320p. 1986. pap. text ed. 19.50 (ISBN 0-675-20481-X). Merrill.

Understanding Organizations. Charles Handy. 1986. pap. 6.95 (ISBN 0-14-009110-6). Penguin.

Understanding Organizations. Charles B. Handy. 496p. 1986. 24.95x (ISBN 0-8160-1390-X). Facts On File.

Understanding Oriental Philosophy. James K. Feibleman. 1984. pap. 9.95 (ISBN 0-452-00710-0, Mer). NAL.

Understanding Orthopedics. Jerzy M. Sikorski. (Illus.). 248p. 1986. pap. text ed. 29.95 (ISBN 0-409-49098-9). Butterworth.

Understanding Oscillators. 2nd ed. Irving M. Gottlieb. (Illus.). 224p. 1987. 16.95 (ISBN 0-8306-0715-3); pap. 12.95 (ISBN 0-8306-2715-4). TAB Bks.

Understanding Other Cultures. C. Sandbacka. (Acta Philosophica Fennica Ser.: Vol. No. 42). 193p. (Orig.). 1987. pap. 39.50x (ISBN 951-95055-8-X). Coronet Bks.

Understanding Other People. Stuart Palmer. 208p. 1977. pap. 1.75 (ISBN 0-449-30815-4, Prem). Fawcett.

Understanding Others. Elaine Goley. (Learn the Value Of... Ser.). (Illus.). 32p. (gr. 1-4). 1987. PLB 106.00 10 bk. set (ISBN 0-317-60461-9); PLB 10.60 (ISBN 0-86592-382-5). Rourke Corp.

Understanding Our Atmospheric Environment. 2nd ed. Morris Neiburger et al. LC 81-15160. (Illus.). 453p. 1982. text ed. 26.95 (ISBN 0-7167-1348-9). W H Freeman.

Understanding Our Environment. Ed. & intro. by R. E. Hester. (Illus.). 348p. 1986. text ed. 77.00x (ISBN 0-85186-907-6, Pub. by Royal Soc Chem). Scholium Intl.

Understanding Our Sexuality. 2nd ed. Bryan Strong & Christine DeVault. 566p. 1988. text ed. 35.50 (ISBN 0-314-62316-7). West Pub.

Understanding Our Sexuality. Bryan Strong & Rebecca Reynolds. (Illus.). 530p. 1982. pap. text ed. 29.00 (ISBN 0-314-63294-8). West Pub.

Understanding Our World: An Integral Ontology. Hendrik Hart. LC 84-17238. 498p. (Orig.). 1985. 34.75 (ISBN 0-8191-4257-3, Pub. by Inst Christ Stud); pap. 20.75 (ISBN 0-8191-4258-1). U Pr of Amer.

Understanding Ourselves As Adults. Paul B. Maves. LC 59-4795. pap. 54.30 (ISBN 0-317-10345-8, 2001254). Bks Demand UMI.

Understanding Overvue. Steven S. Cobb. 325p. (Orig.). 1985. pap. 22.95 (ISBN 0-936767-01-4). Cobb Group.

Understanding OverVUE. Steven S. Cobb. Ed. by Marjorie Phifer. LC 85-73825. (Illus.). 342p. (Orig.). 1985. pap. 22.95 (ISBN 0-317-61513-0). Cobb Group.

Understanding Pacemakers. Emil A. Naclerio et al. LC 80-22912. (Illus.). 176p. 1982. 24.95 (ISBN 0-935576-04-5); pap. 12.95 (ISBN 0-935576-05-3). Kesend Pub Ltd.

Understanding Pacemakers. David Sonnenburg et al. 1986. pap. 4.50 (ISBN 0-671-55674-6). PB.

Understanding Pain: Interpretation & Philosophy. Mitchell T. Smolkin. 1989. price not set (ISBN 0-89464-308-8). Krieger.

Understanding Paint & Painting Processes. 3rd ed. Gerald L. Schneberger. (Illus.). 176p. (Orig.). Date not set. pap. 25.00 (ISBN 0-933931-05-0). Hitchcock Pub.

Understanding Paintings. Fred Malins. 1981. pap. 9.95 (ISBN 0-13-936724-1). P-H.

Understanding Paper Recycling. Jon Vogler & Peter Sarjeant. Ed. by Margaret Crouch. (Technical Paper: No. 53). 16p. Date not set. price not set (ISBN 0-86619-270-0). Vols Tech Asst.

Understanding Pascal. George Ledin. (Alfred Handy Guide Ser.). 63p. 1981. 3.50 (ISBN 0-88284-149-1). Manusoft.

Understanding Pascal. F. R. Skilton. 400p. 1984. pap. text ed. write for info. (ISBN 0-697-08256-3); instr's. manual avail. (ISBN 0-697-08279-2). Wm C Brown.

Understanding Passive Cooling Systems. Daniel Halacy. Ed. by Margaret Crouch. (Technical Paper: No. 48). 21p. (Orig.). 1987. write for info. (ISBN 0-86619-265-4). Vols Tech Asst.

Understanding Paul. Richard L. Anderson. LC 83-72103. 448p. 1983. 10.95 (ISBN 0-87747-984-4). Deseret Bk.

Understanding Pedal Power. David G. Wilson. Ed. by Margaret Crouch. (Technical Paper: No. 51). 13p. (Orig.). 1987. write for info. (ISBN 0-86619-268-9). Vols Tech Asst.

Understanding Pennsylvania Civics. William Cornell. (gr. 7-12). 1985. pap. 6.95 (ISBN 0-931992-45-1). Penns Valley.

Understanding Pennsylvania Civics. William A. Cornell. (YA) (gr. 7-12). 1987. 10.45 (ISBN 0-931992-57-5). Penns Valley.

Understanding People. Lawrence J. Crabb. pap. 12.95 (ISBN 0-88469-200-0). BMH Bks.

Understanding People. Howard Wilson. (Orig.). 1969. pap. 1.50 (ISBN 0-910022-00-3). ARA.

Understanding People at Work: A Manager's Guide to the Behavioral Sciences. Thomas Quick. (Illus.). 1976. pap. 15.95 (ISBN 0-917386-17-5). Exec Ent Pubns.

Understanding People: Children, Youth, Adults. J. Omar Brubaker & Robert E. Clark. LC 75-172116. 96p. 1981. pap. text ed. 5.95 (ISBN 0-910566-15-1); looseleaf instr's guide with binder 9.95 (ISBN 0-910566-25-9). Evang Tchr.

Understanding People: Deep Longings for Relationship. Lawrence J. Crabb, Jr. 224p. 1987. 12.95 (ISBN 0-310-22600-7, 10171). Zondervan.

Understanding People in Organizations. Robert C. Dailey. 525p. 1988. text ed. 26.00 (ISBN 0-314-24254-6). West Pub.

Understanding People in Social Life: Introduction to Sociology. H. Paul Chalfant & Emily E. LaBeff. 326p. 1988. pap. text ed. 26.00 (ISBN 0-314-28603-9). West Pub.

Understanding People or, How to Be Your Very Own Shrink. Julie Rogers. LC 78-31175. 232p. 1979. 19.95x (ISBN 0-88229-273-0). Nelson-Hall.

Understanding Personal & Business Finance. 2nd ed. W. Reay Tolfree. 208p. (Orig.). 1986. pap. 10.50 (ISBN 0-85941-362-4, Pub. by Woodhead-Faulkner). Longwood Pub Group.

Understanding Personal Computers: Home Study Course. Harry M. Brobst. (Home Study Ser.). 36p. 1987. 28.00 (ISBN 0-939926-38-5); cassette tape incl. Fruition Pubns.

Understanding Personal Relationships. Steve Duck & Daniel Perlman. 1985. 29.95 (ISBN 0-8039-9701-9). Sage.

Understanding Personnel Management. Thomas H. Stone. 600p. 1982. text ed. 33.95x (ISBN 0-03-045671-1); instr's manual 20.95 (ISBN 0-03-045676-2). Dryden Pr.

Understanding Persons: Personal & Impersonal Relations. F. M. Berenson. LC 80-19004. 25.00 (ISBN 0-312-83154-4). St Martin.

Understanding Persuasion. Raymond S. Ross & Mark Ross. (P-H Speech Communication Ser.). (Illus.). 224p. 1981. P-H.

Understanding Persuasion: Foundations & Practice. 2nd ed. Raymond S. Ross & Mark Ross. (Illus.). 240p. 1985. pap. text ed. write for info (ISBN 0-13-937053-6). P-H.

Understanding Photography. Carl Shipman. LC 74-82518. (Illus.). 224p. 1974. pap. 12.95 (ISBN 0-912656-24-7). Price Stern.

Understanding Physical Anthropology & Archaeology. 3rd ed. Robert Jurmain et al. LC 86-26789. (Illus.). 597p. 1986. pap. text ed. 39.00 (ISBN 0-314-30395-2); instr's. manual avail. (ISBN 0-314-35254-6). West Pub.

Understanding Physical Chemistry. 3rd ed. Arthur W. Adamson. 1980. 27.95 (ISBN 0-8053-0128-3). Benjamin Cummings.

Understanding Physician: Writings of Charles D. Aring, M.D. rev., enl. ed. Charles D. Aring. LC 73-143496. pap. 55.00 (2027650). Bks Demand UMI.

Understanding Physics. Isaac Asimov. (Dorset Press Reprints Ser.). 768p. 1988. 24.95 (ISBN 0-88029-251-2). Hippocrene Bks.

Understanding Physics: Light, Magnetism & Electricity. Isaac Asimov. (Signet Science Ser). 1969. pap. 3.95 (ISBN 0-451-62304-5, ME2304, Ment). NAL.

Understanding Physics: Motion, Sound & Heat. Isaac Asimov. (Signet Science Ser.). 1969. pap. 4.50 (ISBN 0-451-62365-7, ME2202, Ment). NAL.

Understanding Physics: The Electron, Proton & Neutron. Isaac Asimov. (Signet Science Ser.). 1969. pap. 4.50 (ISBN 0-451-62402-5, ME2190, Ment). NAL.

Understanding Piaget. R. Droz & M. Rahmy. Tr. by Joyce Diamanti from Fr. LC 75-18509. Orig. Title: Lire Piaget. 212p. 1976. text ed. 27.50x (ISBN 0-8236-6690-5). Intl Univs Pr.

Understanding Piaget. rev. ed. Mary Ann Pulaski. LC 80-7595. 256p. 1980. 15.45i (ISBN 0-06-013454-2, HarpT). Har-Row.

Understanding Pictures: A Study in the Design of Appropriate Visuals for Education in Developing Countries. David A. Walker. (Illus.). 406p. 1980. pap. 6.50 (ISBN 0-932288-55-3). Ctr Intl Ed U of MA.

Understanding PILOT. Victor Ledin. (Handy Guide Ser.). 64p. (Orig.). 1983. pap. 3.50 (ISBN 0-88284-251-X). Manusoft.

Understanding Plato. D. J. Melling. (Illus.). 190p. 1987. 32.00 (ISBN 0-19-219129-2); pap. text ed. 9.95 (ISBN 0-19-289116-2). Oxford U Pr.

Understanding Police Human Relations. Dilip K. Das. LC 87-4734. 273p. 1987. 25.00 (ISBN 0-8108-1994-5). Scarecrow.

Understanding Political Develpment. Ed. by Myron Weiner & Samuel P. Huntington. 1987. pap. text ed. 15.25 (ISBN 0-673-39489-1). Scott F.

Understanding Political Theory: An Introduction. Thomas S. Spragens, Jr. LC 75-33578. 150p. 1976. pap. text ed. write for info. (ISBN 0-312-83195-1). St Martin.

Understanding Political Variables. 4th ed. William Buchanan. 395p. 1988. pap. text ed. write for info. (ISBN 0-02-316360-7). Macmillan.

Understanding Politics: Ideas, Institutions, & Issues. 2nd ed. Thomas M. Magstadt & Peter M. Schotten. LC 87-60556. 500p. 1988. text ed. write for info. (ISBN 0-312-00320-X); write for info. instr's. manual (ISBN 0-312-00321-8). St Martin.

Understanding Popular Culture: Europe from the Middle Ages to the Nineteenth Century. Ed. by Steven L. Kaplan. LC 84-1001. (New Babylon, Studies in the Social Sciences: No. 40). viii, 31?p. 1984. 71.25 (ISBN 3-11-009600-5). Mouton.

Understanding PostScript Programming. David A. Holzgang. 457p. (Orig.). 1987. pap. 22.95 (ISBN 0-89588-396-1). Sybex.

Understanding PostScript Programming. David A. Holzgang. 500p. (Orig.). 1988. pap. 24.95 (ISBN 0-89588-566-2). Sybex.

Understanding Prader-Willi Syndrome: A Literature Review for Educators & Families. E. Raab. 58p. 1986. 3.75 (ISBN 0-318-21993-X). Prader-Willi.

Understanding Pregnancy & Childbirth. rev. ed. Sheldon Cherry. 192p. 1984. pap. 3.95 (ISBN 0-553-23934-1). Bantam.

Understanding Pregnancy & Childbirth. rev. ed. Sheldon H. Cherry. LC 82-17800. 272p. 1983. 11.95 (ISBN 0-672-52758-8). Bobbs.

Understanding Pregnancy & Childbirth. Sheldon H. Cherry. 1985. 16.95 (ISBN 0-02-524720-4). Bobbs.

Understanding Prescription Drugs. Dorothy L. Smith. 496p. 1987. pap. 4.50 (ISBN 0-671-63782-7). PB.

Understanding Spoken Language. D. E. Walker & R. E. Fikes. (Artificial Intelligence Ser.: Vol. 5). 252p. 1978. 44.00 (ISBN 0-444-00272-3, North-Holland); pap. 26.50 (ISBN 0-444-00287-1). Elsevier.

Understanding Station Carrier, Vol. VI. Kenneth C. Wilson. 1975. 9.95 (ISBN 0-686-98062-X). Telecom Lib.

Understanding Statistical Process Control. Donald J. Wheeler & David S. Chambers. 340p. 1986. pap. 35.00 (ISBN 0-945320-01-9). Stat Process Controls.

Understanding Statistics. Chalmer. (Statistics: Textbook & Monographs). 448p. 1986. 39.95 (ISBN 0-8247-7322-5). Dekker.

Understanding Statistics. 3rd ed. Arnold Naiman & Robert Rosenfeld. (Illus.). 368p. 1983. text ed. 40.95 (ISBN 0-07-045863-4). McGraw.

Understanding Statistics. 2nd ed. Arnold Naiman et al. (Illus.). 1976. text ed. 35.95 (ISBN 0-07-045860-X). McGraw.

Understanding Statistics: An Informal Introduction for the Behavioral Sciences. R. L. Wright. (Illus.). 500p. 1976. text ed. 26.00 net (ISBN 0-15-592877-5, HC); net 9.00 (ISBN 0-15-592879-1); instr's manual (ISBN 0-15-592878-3). HarBraceJ.

Understanding Statistics in the Behavioral Sciences. 2nd ed. Robert R. Pagano. (Illus.). 486p. 1986. text ed. 42.50 (ISBN 0-314-93403-0). West Pub.

Understanding Street Gangs. Robert K. Jackson & Wesley D. McBride. LC 84-71415. (Illus.). 140p. (Orig.). 1985. pap. 12.95 (ISBN 0-942728-17-3). Custom Pub Co.

Understanding Stress. (Orig.). 1987. Vol. 1: Introduction, 116 pgs. pap. 23.00 (ISBN 0-11-430019-4, HM1727, Pub. by Her Maj Station Ofc); Vol. 2: Line Manager's Guide, 52 pgs. pap. 11.50 (ISBN 0-11-430020-8, HM1728); Vol. 3: Trainer's Guide, 76 pgs. pap. 13.50 (ISBN 0-11-430021-6, HM1729); Vol. 4: Welfare Officer's Guide, 32 pgs. pap. 8.50 (ISBN 0-11-430022-4, HM1730). UNIPUB.

Understanding Structural Analysis. David Brohn. (Illus.). 224p. 1984. pap. text ed. 26.50x (ISBN 0-246-12238-2, Pub. by Granada England). Sheridan.

Understanding Structured COBOL. 2nd ed. Michel Boillot. LC 85-22719. (Illus.). 622p. 1986. pap. text ed. 35.25 (ISBN 0-314-93155-4). West Pub.

Understanding Structures & Materials. Robin Kerrod. LC 86-27782. (Understanding Science Ser.). (Illus.). 64p. (gr. 5 up). 1986. PLB 15.96 (ISBN 0-382-09182-5). Silver Burdett Pr.

Understanding Stupidity. 2nd ed. James F. Welles. 266p. 1987. pap. 7.95 (ISBN 0-9617729-0-5). Mt Pleasant Pr.

Understanding Success & Failure. Lois S. Roets. 36p. (gr. 5 up). 1985. 8.00 (ISBN 0-911943-07-2). Leadership Pubs.

Understanding Sunday School. LC 81-67935. 96p. 1980. pap. text ed. 5.95 (ISBN 0-910566-31-3); looseleaf instr's guide with binder by Robert E. Clark 9.95 (ISBN 0-910566-32-1). Evang Tchr.

Understanding Swine Production. Vernon M. Meyer & Douglas Henderson. Ed. by Margaret Crouch. (Technical Paper: No. 39). 22p. (Orig.). 1987. write for info. (ISBN 0-86619-251-4). Vols Tech Asst.

Understanding Systems Failures. Victor Bignell & Joyce Fortune. LC 83-12016. 272p. 1984. pap. 10.00 (ISBN 0-7190-0973-1, Pub. by Manchester Univ Pr). St Martin.

Understanding Teaching. Kenneth O. Gangel. LC 68-24579. 96p. 1979. pap. text ed. 5.95 (ISBN 0-910566-14-3); looseleaf instr's guide with binder 9.95 (ISBN 0-910566-26-7). Evang Tchr.

Understanding Technical Change: An Evolutionary Process. R. R. Nelson. (Lectures in Economics: Theory, Institutions, Policy: No. 8). 80p. 1987. 37.50 (ISBN 0-444-70207-5, North Holland). Elsevier.

Understanding Technical English, 3 bks. K. Methold et al. (English As a Second Language Bk.). (Illus.). 60p. 1975. pap. text ed. 4.95 ea. Bk. 1, 1973 (ISBN 0-582-69032-3). Bk. 2, 1974 (ISBN 0-582-69035-8). Bk. 3, 1980 (ISBN 0-582-69036-6). Longman.

Understanding Technological Change. Chris De Bresson. 400p. 1987. 38.95 (ISBN 0-920057-26-8, Dist by U of Toronto Pr); pap. 18.95 (ISBN 0-920057-27-6, Dist. by U of Toronto). Black Rose Bks.

Understanding Technology. Charles Susskind. LC 72-12344. pap. 43.80 (ISBN 0-317-20640-0, 2024131). Bks Demand UMI.

Understanding Technology. Charles Susskind. (Illus.). 1985. pap. 7.50 (ISBN 0-911302-53-0). San Francisco Pr.

Understanding Technology New to the Blood Bank. Ed. by Virginia Vengelen-Tyler & Michael L. Baldwin. 1988. text ed. price not set (ISBN 0-915355-59-0). Am Assn Blood.

Understanding Teenagers: A Guide for Parents. James J. Digiacomo & Edward Wakin. LC 83-70289. 148p. (Orig.). 1983. pap. 6.95 (ISBN 0-89505-129-X). Tabor Pub.

Understanding Teenagers' Reading: Reading Processes & the Teaching of Literature. Jack Thomson. 264p. (Orig.). 1987. pap. 24.95 (ISBN 0-89397-289-4). Nichols Pub.

Understanding Telephone Electronics. 2nd ed. J. L. Fike & G. E. Friend. LC 84-50902. (Understanding Ser.). 277p. 1984. pap. text ed. 17.95 (ISBN 0-672-27018-8, LCB8482). Sams.

Understanding Television: Essays on Television As a Social & Cultural Force. Ed. by Richard Adler. 456p. 1981. 44.95 (ISBN 0-275-90575-6, C0575); pap. 18.95 (ISBN 0-275-91507-7, B1507). Praeger.

Understanding Television Production. Frank Iezzi. (Illus.). 158p. 1984. 18.95 (ISBN 0-13-937078-1); pap. 9.95 (ISBN 0-13-937060-9). P-H.

Understanding Terence. Sander M. Goldberg. LC 85-43285. 232p. 1986. text ed. 28.50x (ISBN 0-691-03586-5). Princeton U Pr.

Understanding Terrorism: Groups, Strategies, & Responses. James M. Poland. (Illus.). 288p. 1988. pap. text ed. 19.00 (ISBN 0-13-936113-8). P-H.

Understanding Testing in Occupational Licensing: Establishing Links Between Principles of Measurement & Practices of Licensing. Jim C. Fortune et al. LC 84-43026. (Social & Behavioral Science Ser.). 1985. text ed. 26.95x (ISBN 0-87589-644-8). Jossey-Bass.

Understanding Texas Insurance. Douglas Caddy. LC 83-40499. 180p. 1984. 14.95 (ISBN 0-89096-179-4). Tex A&M Univ Pr.

Understanding Textiles. 3rd ed. Phyllis G. Tortora. (Illus.). 415p. 1987. text ed. write for info. (ISBN 0-02-421140-0). Macmillan.

Understanding the Academic Role: A Handbook for New Faculty. 64p. 1986. pap. 16.95 (ISBN 0-88737-268-6, 15-2163). Natl League Nurse.

Understanding the Alcoholic's Mind: The Nature of Craving & How to Control It. Arnold M. Ludwig. 208p. 1987. 16.95 (ISBN 0-19-504878-4). Oxford U Pr.

Understanding the Alpha Child at Home & School: Left & Right Hemispheric Function in Relation to Personality & Learning. Jack L. Fadely & Virginia N. Hosler. (Illus.). 256p. 1979. photocopy ed. 28.50x (ISBN 0-398-03862-7). C C Thomas.

Understanding the American Past: A Survey of American History since 1865, Vol. II. 2nd ed. Joseph L. Conlin. 253p. 1987. pap. text ed. 18.00 (ISBN 0-15-502372-1); study guide 9.00 (ISBN 0-15-502375-6). HarBraceJ.

Understanding the Anointing. Kenneth Hagin. 1983. pap. 3.50 (ISBN 0-89276-507-0). Hagin Ministries.

Understanding the Antitrust Laws. 9th ed. Jerold G. Van Cise et al. 391p. 1986. text ed. 60.00 (ISBN 0-317-52203-5, B1-1304). PLI.

Understanding the Apple II. Jim Sather. LC 84-111632. 1983. 22.95 (ISBN 0-912985-01-1, 5011). Quality Soft.

Understanding the Apple IIe. James F. Sather. (Illus.). 368p. (Orig.). 1985. pap. 24.95 (ISBN 0-8359-8019-7, 0197). Quality Soft.

Understanding the Arts. John Hospers. (Illus.). 416p. 1982. pap. write for info. ref. ed. (ISBN 0-13-935965-6). P-H.

Understanding the Atonement for the Mission of the Church. John Driver. LC 86-3133. 288p. (Orig.). 1986. pap. 19.95 (ISBN 0-8361-3403-6). Herald Pr.

Understanding the Automobile. John H. Beck. 88p. pap. 7.40 (ISBN 0-8428-2288-7). Cambridge Bk.

Understanding the Bible. 2nd ed. Stephen L. Harris. 1985. pap. 19.95 (ISBN 0-87484-696-X). Mayfield Pub.

Understanding the Bible. 2nd ed. John R. Stott. 192p. 1985. pap. 7.95 (ISBN 0-310-41431-8, 12610P). Zondervan.

Understanding the Bible & Science. Paul L Walker. LC 75-25343. (Illus.). 1976. pap. 1.99 (ISBN 0-87148-878-7). Pathway Pr.

Understanding the Bible Through History & Archaeology. Harry M. Orlinsky. 1969. 15.00x (ISBN 0-87068-096-X). Ktav.

Understanding the Black Family: A Guide for Scholarship & Research. Wade W. Nobles & Lawford L. Goddard. 137p. 1984. 10.00 (ISBN 0-939205-00-9). Blk Fam Inst Pub.

Understanding the Child with a Chronic Illness in the Classroom. Ed. by Janet Fithian. LC 83-43250. (Illus.). 264p. 1984. lib. bdg. 38.50 (ISBN 0-89774-083-1). Oryx Pr.

Understanding the Christian Faith. Charles D. Barrett. (Illus.). 1980. text ed. write for info. (ISBN 0-13-935882-X). P-H.

Understanding the Christian Faith. Georgia Harkness. (Festival Ser.). 192p. 1981. pap. 1.95 (ISBN 0-687-42955-2). Abingdon.

Understanding the Cold War. Howard Roffman. LC 75-5251. 198p. 1976. 18.50 (ISBN 0-8386-1740-9). Fairleigh Dickinson.

Understanding the Common Cold. Charles J. Cheslock. 142p. 1987. 10.95 (ISBN 0-533-07066-X). Vantage.

Understanding the Constitution. 10th ed. J. W. Peltason. LC 84-28982. 368p. 1985. pap. text ed. 17.95 (ISBN 0-03-071176-2, HoltC). HR&W.

Understanding the Cosmos. Matthew Irvine. LC 85-27757. (Understanding Science Ser). (Illus.). 64p. (gr. 5 up). 1986. PLB 15.96 (ISBN 0-382-09186-8). Silver Burdett Pr.

Understanding the Cults. Josh McDowell & Don Stewart. LC 81-81850. (Handbook of Today's Religion Ser.). 199p. 1982. pap. 6.95 (ISBN 0-86605-090-6, 402826). Heres Life.

Understanding the Difficult Words of Jesus. David Bivin & Roy B. Blizzard, Jr. LC 83-61850. (Illus.). 172p. (Orig.). 1983. pap. 8.95 (ISBN 0-918873-00-2). Ctr Judaic-Christ Studies.

Understanding the Dollar Crisis. Enlarged Ed. ed. Percy L. Greaves, Jr. LC 84-148895. 332p. (gr. 11-12). 1984. 14.00 (ISBN 0-930902-02-5); pap. 7.00 (ISBN 0-930902-03-3). Free Market.

Understanding the Earth. Tom Williamson. LC 85-40215. (Understanding Science Ser.). (Illus.). 64p. (gr. 5 up). 1985. PLB 13.96 (ISBN 0-382-09083-7). Silver.

Understanding the Economy: For People Who Can't Stand Economics. Alfred Malabre, Jr. 1977. pap. 3.50 (ISBN 0-451-62140-9, ME2140, Ment). NAL.

Understanding the Elements of Literature. Richard Taylor. LC 81-9295. 256p. 1982. 19.95x (ISBN 0-312-83216-8). St Martin.

Understanding the Environment. Kenneth E. Watt. 1982. pap. text ed. 34.33 (ISBN 0-205-07265-8, 677265-X); tchr's. ed. avail. (ISBN 0-205-07266-6). Allyn.

Understanding the Essay. Edward O. Shakespeare et al. 1978. pap. text ed. 5.50x (ISBN 0-88334-109-3). Ind Sch Pr.

Understanding the Faith of the Church. Richard A. Norris. (Church's Teaching Ser.: Vol. 4). 288p. 1979. 5.95 (ISBN 0-8164-0421-6, HarpR); pap. 3.95 (ISBN 0-8164-2217-6, Crossroad Bks). Har-Row.

Understanding the Fear of the Lord. Dennis Burke. 1982. pap. 2.75 (ISBN 0-89274-265-8, HH-265). Harrison Hse.

Understanding the Feasts of the Lord, God's Time Clock for the Ages. Roger V. Houtsma. 195p. (Orig.). 1986. pap. 6.95 (ISBN 0-9617623-0-6). World Outreach.

Understanding the Filipino. Tomas D. Andres & Pilar B. Ilada-Andres. xii, 184p. (Orig.). 1987. pap. 9.50x (ISBN 971-10-0337-6, Pub. by New Day Pub Philippines). Cellar.

Understanding the French Revolution. Albert Soboul. Ed. by Betty Smith. Tr. by April A. Knutson from Fr. LC 88-1215. 346p. (Orig.). 1988. pap. 10.95 (ISBN 0-7178-0658-8). Intl Pubs Co.

Understanding the Gold Market. Daniel Rosenthal & Ellen Young. 132p. 1987. pap. text ed. 92.00 (ISBN 0-938689-04-5). Inst Preserv Wealth.

Understanding the Heart. rev. ed. Francis Larkin. LC 80-81066. 127p. 1980. pap. 5.95 (ISBN 0-89870-007-8). Ignatius Pr.

Understanding the High Holyday Service. Jeffrey M. Cohen. 218p. 1983. 12.50 (ISBN 0-7100-9566-X). Hebrew Pub.

Understanding the History & Records of Non-Conformity. 1987. 30.00x (Pub. by Birmingham Midland Soc UK). State Mutual Bk.

Understanding the Human Jesus: A Journey in Scripture & Imagination. Andrew Canale. LC 84-61027. 208p. 1985. pap. 7.95 (ISBN 0-8091-2654-0). Paulist Pr.

Understanding the Immune System: The Immune System in the Human Body & How It Works. 1984. lib. bdg. 79.95 (ISBN 0-87700-620-2). Revisionist Pr.

Understanding the Japanese Mind. James C. Moloney. LC 68-23316. 1968. Repr. of 1954 ed. lib. bdg. 27.50x (ISBN 0-8371-0172-7, MOJM). Greenwood.

Understanding the Japanese Spirit, 2 vols. Masaharu Nesaki. (Illus.). 215p. 1985. Set. 167.75 (ISBN 0-86722-105-4). Inst Econ Pol.

Understanding the Jewish Experience. 54p. 2.00 (ISBN 0-686-74981-2). ADL.

Understanding the Language of Banking. American Bankers Association Staff. (Illus.). 258p. (Orig.). 1986. pap. text ed. 43.50 (ISBN 0-89982-302-5). Am Bankers.

Understanding the Language of Medicine: A Programmed Learning Text. Patricia J. Bernthal & James D. Spiller. (Illus.). 1981. pap. text ed. 19.95x (ISBN 0-19-502879-1). Oxford U Pr.

Understanding the Law: A Handbook on Educating the Public. Robert Peck & Charles J. White. LC 84-164846. (Illus.). 232p. 1983. 10.95 (ISBN 0-89707-111-5). Amer Bar Assn.

Understanding the Law: An Advocates Guide to the Law & Developmental Disabilities. Steven J. Taylor & Douglas Biklen. 67p. 1980. pap. 4.25 (ISBN 0-937540-10-2, HPP-13). Human Policy Pr.

Understanding the Laws of Hospitality. Jack P. Jefferies. Ed. by Marj Harless. (Illus.). 360p. 1989. text ed. 36.95 (ISBN 0-86612-050-5). Educ Inst Am Hotel.

Understanding the Learning Disabled Athlete: A Guide for Parents, Coaches, & Professionals. Andrew G. Yellen & Heidi L. Yellen. 126p. 1987. 24.75x (ISBN 0-398-05316-2). C C Thomas.

Understanding the Liver: A History. Thomas S. Chen & Peter S. Chen. LC 83-22631. (Contributions in Medical History Ser.: No. 14). (Illus.). xiii, 293p. 1984. lib. bdg. 46.95 (ISBN 0-313-23472-8, CLV/). Greenwood.

Understanding the Living Word. G. Hansel. 1980. pap. 8.95 (ISBN 0-8163-0372-X). Pacific Pr Pub Assn.

Understanding the Main Idea: Advanced Level. James A. Giroux & Glenn R. Williston. Ed. by Edward Spargo. (Comprehension Skills Ser). (Illus.). 64p. (gr. 9 up). 1974. pap. text ed. 4.00x (ISBN 0-89061-012-6, CB-1). Jamestown Pubs.

Understanding the Main Idea: Middle Level. Glenn R. Williston. (Comprehension Skills Ser.). (Illus.). 64p. (gr. 6-12). 1976. pap. text ed. 4.00x (ISBN 0-89061-064-9, CB-1M). Jamestown Pubs.

Understanding the Male Temperament: What Every Man Would Like to Tell His Wife About Himself...but Won't. Tim LaHaye. 192p. 1977. pap. 6.95 (ISBN 0-8007-5009-8, Power Bks). Revell.

Understanding the Mass. rev. ed. Maynard Kolodziej. 80p. 1987. pap. 1.50 (ISBN 1-55805-000-0). Franc Pubs WI.

Understanding the Mathematics Teacher: A Study of Practice in First Schools. Charles Desforges & Anne D. Cockburn. 180p. 1987. 36.00x (ISBN 1-85000-212-6, Falmer Pr); pap. 17.00x (ISBN 1-85000-213-4, Falmer Pr). Taylor & Francis.

Understanding the Metric System. Mary J. Carrell. 68p. 1978. pap. text ed. 3.75 (ISBN 0-88323-140-9, 229); tchr's. key 1.00 (274). Richards Pub.

Understanding the Micro. Bill Bennett & Judy Tatchell. (Usborne Electronics Ser.). (Illus.). 48p. (gr. 7-9). 1982. (Usborne-Hayes); PLB 9.96 (ISBN 0-88110-008-0); pap. 2.95 (ISBN 0-86020-637-8). EDC.

Understanding the Microscope. Paul Geisert. (EMI Programmed Biology Ser.). 1967. pap. text ed. 3.00 (ISBN 0-88462-018-2, 3304-18, Ed Methods). Longman Finan.

Understanding the Mid-Life Crisis. Peter O'Connor. 1988. pap. 6.95 (ISBN 0-8091-2976-0). Paulist Pr.

Understanding the Middle East. Joe E. Pierce. LC 70-172002. 1971. 6.25 (ISBN 0-8048-0670-5). C E Tuttle.

Understanding the Modern Predicament. Dwight D. Murphey. LC 81-40345. (Orig.). 1982. lib. bdg. 33.75 (ISBN 0-8191-2135-5); pap. text ed. 16.75 (ISBN 0-8191-2136-3). U Pr of Amer.

Understanding the Multicultural Experience in Early Childhood Education. Ed. by Olivia N. Saracho & Bernard Spodek. 168p. 1983. pap. text ed. 5.50 (ISBN 0-912674-84-9, NAEYC #125). Natl Assn Child Ed.

Understanding the New ALTA Title Insurance Policy Forms. 169p. 1987. pap. 22.00 (RE-49110). Cal Cont Ed Bar.

Understanding the New Economy. Alfred L. Malabre, Jr. 1988. 19.95 (ISBN 1-55623-117-2). Dow Jones-Irwin.

Understanding the New Religions. Ed. by Jacob Needleman & George Baker. 1978. (HarpR); pap. 8.95 (ISBN 0-8164-2188-9). Har-Row.

Understanding the New Right & Its Impact on Education. Joe L. Kincheloe. LC 83-61782. (Fastback Ser.: No. 195). 50p. 1983. pap. 0.90 (ISBN 0-87367-195-3). Phi Delta Kappa.

Understanding the New Technologies of the Mass Media. George E. Whitehouse. (Illus.). 256p. 1986. pap. text ed. write for info. (ISBN 0-13-937020-X). P H.

Understanding the New Telephone Service. Quincy Harris. LC 86-91167. (Illus.). 72p. (Orig.). 1986. pap. text ed. 10.00 (ISBN 0-682-40299-0). Exposition-Phoenix.

Understanding the New Testament. 4th ed. Howard C. Kee. (Illus.). 464p. 1983. text ed. 33.00 (ISBN 0-13-936591-5). P-H.

Understanding the New Testament. O. Jessie Lace. (Cambridge Bible Commentary on the New English Bible, New Testament Ser.). pap. 10.95 (ISBN 0-521-09281-7). Cambridge U Pr.

Understanding the New Testament. Francis B. Rhein. LC 65-23532. 1974. pap. text ed. 6.95 (ISBN 0-8120-0027-7). Barron.

Understanding the New Testament, 10 vols. 1982. Set. pap. 37.50 (ISBN 0-8054-1346-4). Broadman.

Understanding the New Testament: Acts. Ralph P. Martin. LC 78-9086. 1982. pap. 3.95 (ISBN 0-8054-1331-6). Broadman.

Understanding the New Testament: Ephesians-2 Thessalonians. W. L. Lane. LC 78-9675. 1982. pap. 3.95 (ISBN 0-8054-1336-7). Broadman.

Understanding the New Testament: John. R. E. Nixon. LC 78-9114. 1982. pap. 3.95 (ISBN 0-8054-1330-8). Broadman.

Understanding the New Testament: Luke. E. M. Blaiklock. LC 78-9119. 1982. pap. 3.95 (ISBN 0-8054-1329-4). Broadman.

Understanding the New Testament: Mark. I. Howard Marshall. LC 78-9118. 1982. pap. 3.95 (ISBN 0-8054-1328-6). Broadman.

Understanding the New Testament: Matthew. F. F. Bruce. LC 78-9115. 1982. pap. 3.95 (ISBN 0-8054-1327-8). Broadman.

Understanding the New Testament: Romans. E. M. Blaiklock. LC 78-9794. 1982. pap. 3.95 (ISBN 0-8054-1332-4). Broadman.

Understanding the New Testament: 1 Corinthians-Galatians. Ralph P. Martin. LC 78-9793. 1982. pap. 3.95 (ISBN 0-8054-1334-0). Broadman.

Understanding the New Testament: 1 Peter-Revelation. H. L. Ellison. LC 78-9116. 1982. pap. 3.95 (ISBN 0-8054-1341-3). Broadman.

Understanding Your Pension Scheme: A Guide to Occupational Pensions. D. Hancox & J. P. McMahon. 136p. 1987. 60.00x (ISBN 0-946679-04-5, Pub. by Mgmt Update UK); pap. 40.00x (ISBN 0-946679-03-7). State Mutual Bk.
Understanding Your Pet: The Eckstein Method of Pet Therapy & Behavior Training. Warren Eckstein & Fay Eckstein. LC 85-4754. (Illus.). 246p. 1986. 15.95 (ISBN 0-03-000699-6). H Holt & Co.
Understanding Your School-Age Child. (Successful Parenting Ser.). Orig. Title: Looking Ahead. (Illus.). 1988. price not set. Time-Life.
Understanding Your Sikh Neighbour. P. S. Sambhi. 55p. 9.50 (ISBN 0-7188-2422-9, Pub. by Lutterwrth). Attic Pr.
Understanding Your Social Agency. 2nd ed. Armand Lauffer. LC 84-18014. 168p. 1984. pap. 9.95 (ISBN 0-8039-2349-X). Sage.
Understanding Your Temperament: A Self-Analysis with a Christian Viewpoint. Peter Blitchington & Robert J. Cruise. 38p. (Orig.). 1979. pap. 2.95 (ISBN 0-943872-67-7). Andrews Univ Pr.
Understanding Yourself. Intro. by Christopher Evans. 1980. pap. 4.95 (ISBN 0-451-13453-2, Sig). NAL.
Understanding Yourself. Mark L. Prophet. LC 76-28089. 144p. 1982. pap. 3.95 (ISBN 0-916766-46-2). Summit Univ.
Understanding Yourself & Others. Bill Kvols-Riedler & Kathy Kvols-Riedler. (Illus.). 260p. (Orig.). 1980. pap. 10.95 (ISBN 0-933450-01-X). RDIC Pubns.
Understanding Yourself Through Birth Order. Clifford E. Isaacson. (Illus.). 120p. (Orig.). 1988. pap. 7.95 (ISBN 0-945156-00-6). Upper Des Moines Counsel.
Understanding Z: A Specification Language & Its Formal Semantics. J. M. Spivey. (Cambridge Tracts in Theoretical Computer Science Ser.: No. 3). 160p. 1988. 27.95 (ISBN 0-521-33429-2). Cambridge U Pr.
Understanding Zoo Animals. Cox. (Animal World Ser.). (gr. 3-6). 1980. (Usborne-Hayes); PLB 12.96 (ISBN 0-88110-092-7); pap. 4.95 (ISBN 0-86020-251-8). EDC.
Understandings of Man. Perry LeFevre. LC 66-10432. 186p. 1966. pap. 6.95 (ISBN 0-664-24678-8). Westminster John Knox.
Understandings of Prayer. Perry LeFevre. LC 81-11622. 212p. 1981. pap. 10.95 (ISBN 0-664-24382-7). Westminster John Knox.
Understandings of the Church. Ed. by E. Glenn Hinson. LC 86-45227. (Sources of Early Christian Thought Ser.). 128p. 1986. pap. 7.95 (ISBN 0-8006-1415-1, 1-1415). Fortress.
Understandings: Photographs of Decatur County, Georgia. Paul Kwilecki. LC 81-2958. (Duke University Center for Documentary Photography Ser.). (Illus.). x, 118p. 1981. 19.95 (ISBN 0-8078-1486-5). U of NC Pr.
Understatements & Hedges in English. Alex Huebler. LC 84-10981. (Pragmatics & Beyond (P & B) Ser.: Vol. IV, No. 6). ix, 192p. (Orig.). 1984. pap. 40.00x (ISBN 0-915027-29-1). Benjamins North Am.
Understood Betsy. Dorothy Canfield. 219p. 1981. Repr. PLB 14.95 (ISBN 0-89966-342-7). Buccaneer Bks.
Understood Betsy. Dorothy Canfield. 213p. 1980. Repr. PLB 14.95x (ISBN 0-89967-016-4). Harmony Raine.
Understood Betsy. Dorothy C. Fisher. (Illus.). 220p. (gr. 5-9). 1973. pap. 1.75 (ISBN 0-380-01595-1, 49692-5, Camelot). Avon.
Understood Betsy. Dorothy C. Fisher. (gr. k-6). 1987. pap. 4.95 (ISBN 0-440-49179-7, Pub. by Yearling Classics). Dell.
Understructure of Writing for Film & Television. Ben Brady & Lance Lee. 282p. (Orig.). 1988. text ed. 28.95x (ISBN 0-292-78514-3); pap. 12.95 (ISBN 0-292-78515-1). U of Tex Pr.
Understudies. facs. ed. Mary E. Wilkins Freeman. LC 70-86141. (Short Story Index Reprint Ser.). 1901. 19.00 (ISBN 0-8369-3045-2). Ayer Co Pubs.
Understudies: Theatre & Sexual Politics. Michelene Wandor. 80p. 1981. pap. 8.95 (ISBN 0-413-40060-3, NO. 3503). Heinemann Ed.
Understudy. Jack Weyland. LC 85-1468. 126p. 1985. 7.95 (ISBN 0-87747-673-X). Deseret Bk.
Undertaker's Garland. John Bishop & Edmund Wilson. LC 74-14616. 1922. lib. bdg. 27.00 (ISBN 0-8414-0504-2). Folcroft.
Undertaker's Garland. John P. Bishop & Edmund Wilson. LC 74-4263. (American Literature Ser., No. 49). 1974. lib. bdg. 42.95x (ISBN 0-8383-2041-4). Haskell.
Undertaker's Gone Bananas. Paul Zindel. (gr. 6-12). 1979. pap. 2.95 (ISBN 0-553-26424-9). Bantam.
Undertaker's Gone Bananas. Paul Zindel. LC 78-54606. 256p. (YA) (gr. 7 up). 1978. PLB 10.89 (ISBN 0-06-026846-8). HarpJ.
Undertow. Drake Douglas. 400p. 1987. pap. 3.95 (ISBN 0-8439-2495-0, Leisure Bks). Leisure NY.
Underutilized Resources as Animal Feedstuffs. 296p. 1983. 21.95x (ISBN 0-309-03382-9). Natl Acad Pr.
Underwater Acoustic Positioning Systems. P. H. Milne. LC 83-80348. 288p. 1983. 55.00x (ISBN 0-87201-012-0). Gulf Pub.
Underwater Acoustic System Analysis. William S. Burdic. (Illus.). 480p. 1984. 60.00 (ISBN 0-13-936716-0). P-H.
Underwater Acoustics: A Linear Theory Approch. Lawerence J. Ziomek. 1985. 53.50 (ISBN 0-12-781720-4). Acad Pr.
Underwater Acoustics & Signal Processing. Ed. by L. Bjorno. 1981. 87.00 (ISBN 90-277-1255-7, Pub. by Reidel Holland). Kluwer Academic.
Underwater Acoustics Handbook. 2nd ed. Vernon M. Albers. LC 64-15069. (Illus.). 1965. 32.00x (ISBN 0-271-73106-0). Pa St U Pr.
Underwater Acoustics Instrumentation. Vernon M. Albers. LC 76-84217. pap. 24.80 (ISBN 0-317-08626-X, 2051122). Bks Demand UMI.
Underwater Adventure Book Featuring "20,000 Leagues Under the Sea". Walt Disney Productions. LC 77-90198. (Disney's World of Adventure Ser). (gr. 3-7). 1978. 3.95 (ISBN 0-394-83602-2, BYR); lib. bdg. 4.99 (ISBN 0-394-93602-7). Random.
Underwater Archaelogy: The Proceedings of the Thirteenth Conference on Underwater Archaeology. Ed. by Donald H. Keith. (Illus.). 116p. 1984. pap. text ed. 18.00x (ISBN 0-910651-04-3). Fathom Eight.
Underwater Archaeology: A Nascent Discipline. LC 72-76249. (Museums & Monuments Ser.: No. 13). (Illus.). 306p. 1972. 12.75 (ISBN 92-3-101011-5, U690, UNESCO). UNIPUB.
Underwater Archaeology: The Challenge Before Us. Ed. by Gordon P. Watts, Jr. (Illus.). 368p. (Orig.). 1981. pap. text ed. 16.00x (ISBN 0-910651-01-9). Fathom Eight.
Underwater Archaeology: The Proceedings of the Eleventh Conference on Underwater Archaeology. Ed. by Calvin R. Cummings. (Illus.). 200p. (Orig.). 1982. pap. text ed. 14.00x (ISBN 0-910651-03-5). Fathom Eight.
Underwater Archaeology: The Proceedings of the Fourteenth Conference on Underwater Archaeology. Ed. by Calvin R. Cummings. 100p. (Orig.). 1986. pap. text ed. 18.00x (ISBN 0-910651-14-0). Fathom Eight.
Underwater California. Wheeler North. LC 75-13153. (Natural History Guide: No.39). (Illus.). 1976. pap. 8.95 (ISBN 0-520-03039-7). U of Cal Pr.
Underwater Communication: Hand Signals for Scuba Diving. Norris W. Eastman & Gerald Landrum. (Illus.). 48p. 1984. pap. 6.95 (ISBN 0-916622-30-4). Princeton Bk Co.
Underwater Construction: Development & Potential. Ed. by Society for Underwater Technology (SUT) Staff. 1987. lib. bdg. 66.00 (ISBN 0-86010-861-9, Pub. by Graham & Trotman). Kluwer Academic.
Underwater Crime Scene Investigation: Organizing, Training & Equipping - The Dive Team on a Budget. Eric Tackett. Ed. by PADI Staff. (Emergency Service - Public Safety Dive Teams). (Illus.). 144p. (Orig.). 1987. pap. 15.95 (ISBN 0-318-22519-0); instr's. guide 12.95 (ISBN 0-943155-05-3, 1011). Lasertech.
Underwater Dive. Antony Jensen & Stephen Bolt. LC 88-42907. (Young Explorers Ser.). (Illus.). 32p. (gr. 2). 1989. PLB 9.95 (ISBN 1-55532-918-7). Stevens Inc.
Underwater Engineering Surveys. P. H. Milne. LC 80-65129. (Illus.). 370p. 1980. 55.00x (ISBN 0-87201-884-9). Gulf Pub.
Underwater Farming. George S. Fichter. (Illus.). 140p. 1988. 16.95 (ISBN 0-910923-48-5). Pineapple Pr.
Underwater Fun with the Snorks. (Bathtime Bks.). (Illus.). 10p. (ps). 1985. pap. 2.95 vinyl (ISBN 0-394-86953-2, BYR). Random.
Underwater Guide to Hawai'i. Ann Fielding. LC 86-30841. (Illus.). 144p. 1987. 14.95 (ISBN 0-8248-1104-6). UH Pr.
Underwater Guide to Hawaiian Reef Fishes. John E. Randall. LC 79-27625. (Illus.). 1980. plastic bdg. 11.95 (ISBN 0-915180-02-2). Harrowood Bks.
Underwater Handbook: A Guide to Physiology & Performance for the Engineer. Ed. by Charles W. Shilling et al. LC 76-7433. (Illus.). 912p. 1977. 135.00x (ISBN 0-306-30843-6, Plenum Pr). Plenum Pub.
Underwater Life. rev. ed. Dean Morris. LC 87-16693. (Read About Animals Ser.). (Illus.). 48p. (gr. 3). 1987. PLB 15.33 (ISBN 0-8172-3214-1). Raintree Pubs.
Underwater Logging. John E. Cayford & Ronald E. Scott. LC 64-18585. (Illus.). 92p. 1964. pap. 3.00 (ISBN 0-87033-128-0). Cornell Maritime.
Underwater Minerals. David S. Cronan. (Ocean Science Resources & Technology Ser.). 1980. 82.50 (ISBN 0-12-197480-4). Acad Pr.
Underwater Photography. Charles R. Seaborn. (Illus.). 144p. 1988. 27.50 (ISBN 0-8174-6335-6, Amphoto); pap. 18.95 (ISBN 0-8174-6336-4, Amphoto). Watson-Guptill.
Underwater Photography & Television for Scientists. Ed. by J. D. George et al. (Illus.). 1985. 57.50x. Oxford U Pr.
Underwater Photography Now. Peter J. Diamondis. LC 83-136151. (Illus.). 154p. 1983. 14.95 (ISBN 0-9612110-0-8). P J Diamondis.
Underwater Physiology. Ed. by Christian J. Lambertsen. 1971. 39.95 (ISBN 0-12-434750-9). Acad Pr.
Underwater Prospecting Techniques: The Gold Divers Handbook. 10th, rev. ed. LC 60-4754. (Illus.). 1983. pap. 3.00 (ISBN 0-686-38066-5). Merlin Engine Wks.
Underwater Recreation. 2.50 (ISBN 0-87505-261-4). Borden.
Underwater Soil Sampling, Testing, & Construction Control: A Symposium Presented at the Seventy-Fourth Annual Meeting, American Society for Testing & Materials, 1971. Symposium on Underwater Soil Sampling, Testing & Construction Control, Atlantic City (1971: Atlantic City) LC 77-185536. (ASTM Special Technical Publication: 501). pap. 61.80 (ISBN 0-317-26537-7, 2023988). Bks Demand UMI.
Underwater Tools. Donald J. Hackman & Don W. Caudy. LC 81-4399. (Illus.). 152p. 1981. 32.95 (ISBN 0-935470-08-5). Battelle.
Underwater Tour. Margaret Webb. (Illus.). 16p. (gr. 3-5). 1984. 4.95 (ISBN 0-533-05927-5). Vantage.
Underwater Warriors. Wyatt Blassingame. LC 81-787. (Landmark Paperback: No. 11). (Illus.). 160p. (gr. 3-8). 1982. pap. 2.95 (ISBN 0-394-84884-5). Random.
Underwater Welding of Offshore Platforms & Pipelines, OPP: Proceedings of the AWS Conference, 1980. AWS Conference Staff. 189p. 1981. 25.00 (ISBN 0-87171-215-6). Am Welding.
Underwater Wilderness. C. Roessler. 320p. 1987. text ed. 29.95 (ISBN 0-07-053503-5). McGraw.
Underwater Wilderness: Life Around the Great Reefs. Carl Roessler. LC 77-77800. (Illus.). 319p. 1977. 35.00 (ISBN 0-918810-00-0). Chanticleer.
Underwater Work: A Manual of Scuba Commercial Salvage & Construction Operations. 2nd ed. John E. Cayford. LC 66-28081. (Illus.). 271p. 1966. 13.50x (ISBN 0-87033-129-9). Cornell Maritime.
Underwear! Mary Monsell. Ed. by Abby Levine. (Illus.). 24p. (ps-2). 1988. PLB 9.95 (ISBN 0-8075-8308-1). A Whitman.
Underwear & Footwear see Independence Training.
Underweight Infant, Child & Adolescent. Stanley Cohen. 352p. 1985. 55.00 (ISBN 0-8385-9280-5). Appleton & Lange.
Underwood & Holt's Professional Negligence. Hilton Harrop-Griffiths & Jane Bennington. 136p. 1985. 88.00x (ISBN 0-906840-90-2, Pub. by Fourmat England). State Mutual Bk.
Underworld. J. Goodman & L. Will. 1986. 49.75X (ISBN 0-245-54267-1, Pub. by Harrap Ltd England). State Mutual Bk.
Underworld: A New Daiziel-Pascoe Murder Mystery. Reginald Hill. 288p. 1988. 14.95 (ISBN 0-684-18931-3). Scribner.
Underwriter. Jack Rudman. (Career Examination Ser.: C-2011). (Cloth bdg. avail. on request). pap. 14.00 (ISBN 0-8373-2011-9). Natl Learning.
Underwriters Laboratories, Inc. Fact-Finding Report: A Study of Existing Flammability Tests & Requirements for Upholstered Furniture, Project 76 NK 5338. 100p. 1977. 4.25 (ISBN 0-318-13666-X). Busn Inst Furn.
Underwriting Decisions under Uncertainity: A Catastrophe Market. David E. Ayling. 240p. 1984. text ed. 36.95x (ISBN 0-566-00692-8). Gower Pub Co.
Underwriting in Life & Health Insurance Companies. Ed. by Richard Bailey. LC 85-50140. (FLMI Insurance Education Program Ser.). 1985. 29.00 (ISBN 0-915322-74-9). LOMA.
Underwriting Principles & Practices. Robert B. Holtom. LC 80-81848. 1981. text ed. 25.00 (ISBN 0-87218-308-4). Natl Underwriter.
Underwriting the Physical Risk. Paul S. Entmacher & Edward A. Lew. (FLMI Insurance Education Program Ser.). 1971. pap. 5.00 (ISBN 0-915322-22-6). LOMA.
Undesirable Journalist. Gunter Wallraff. LC 78-70935. 192p. 1983. 22.50 (ISBN 0-87951-095-1); pap. 10.95 (ISBN 0-87951-169-9). Overlook Pr.
Undesirable Versus Desirable Societies. Mihai C. Botez & Mariana Celac. (Project on Goals, Processes & Indicators of Development). 74p. 1983. pap. text ed. 7.50 (ISBN 92-808-0450-2, TUNU215, UNU). UNIPUB.
Undesirables. Y. Fries & T. Bibib. 1985. 24.95. Asia Bk Corp.
Undesirables, Early Immigrants & the Anti-Japanese Movement in San Francisco: 1892-1893. Donald T. Hata, Jr. Ed. by Roger Daniels. LC 78-54817. (Asian Experience in North American Ser.). 1979. lib. bdg. 16.00x (ISBN 0-405-11273-4). Ayer Co Pubs.
Undesirables: The Expatriation of the Tamil People of Recent Indian Origin from the Plantations in Sri Lanka. Yvonne Fries & T. Bibin. 1985. 18.50x (ISBN 0-8364-1344-X, Pub. by KP Bagchi India). South Asia Bks.
Undeveloped West; or, Five Years in the Territories. John H. Beadle. LC 72-9427. (Far Western Frontier Ser.). (Illus.). 828p. 1973. Repr. of 1873 ed. 51.00 (ISBN 0-405-04958-7). Ayer Co Pubs.
UNDEX Series "C" Cumulative Edition, 1974-1978, Vols. 1-4. M. Mittleman & M. Pease. LC 78-27483. 1800p. 1980. Set. 215.00x (ISBN 0-89111-009-7). UNIFO Pubs.
Undici Mesi In Viaggio. Augusto Torlonia. 151p. 1892. 600.00x (ISBN 0-317-68457-4, Pub. by Han-Shan Tang Ltd). State Mutual Bk.
Undimensional Scaling. John P. McIver & Edward G. Carmines. (Sage University Papers: Quantitative Applications in the Social Sciences: Vol. 24). (Illus.). 1981. pap. 6.50 (ISBN 0-8039-1736-8). Sage.
Undiminished Man: A Political Biography of Robert Walker Kenny. Janet Stevenson. LC 80-10889. (Illus.). 218p. 1980. 10.95 (ISBN 0-88316-538-4); pap. 6.95. Chandler & Sharp.
Undine. Friedrich H. La Motte-Foque. Tr. by Edmund Gosse from Ger. LC 76-48431. (Library of World Literature Ser.). 1985. Repr. of 1912 ed. 22.50 (ISBN 0-88355-558-1). Hyperion Conn.
Undine. Olive Schreiner. Repr. of 1928 ed. 26.00 (ISBN 0-384-54279-4). Johnson Repr.
Undine. Olive Schreiner. 1978. Repr. of 1928 ed. lib. bdg. 29.50 (ISBN 0-8492-2592-2). R West.
Undine & Other Stories. Fouque La Motte. 25.00. Darby Bks.
Undiplomatic Diary. Harry H. Bandholtz. LC 77-160009. Repr. of 1933 ed. 27.50 (ISBN 0-404-00494-6). AMS Pr.
Undiplomatic Incidents. Apa B. Pant. 1987. text ed. 12.50x (ISBN 0-86131-690-8, Pub. by Orient Longman Ltd India). Apt Bks.
Undiscovered Europe. Ed. by Marian V. Cooper. 610p. 1988. 14.95 (ISBN 0-945332-07-6). Agora Inc MD.
Undiscovered Continent: Emily Dickinson & the Space of the Mind. Suzanne Juhasz. LC 82-49014. 200p. 1983. 17.50x (ISBN 0-253-36164-8). Ind U Pr.
Undiscovered Country. John Hay. (Illus.). 157p. 1982. 12.95 (ISBN 0-393-01571-8). Norton.
Undiscovered Country. John Hay. (Illus.). 192p. 1984. pap. 4.95 (ISBN 0-393-30015-3). Norton.
Undiscovered Country. William D. Howells. 1973. lib. bdg. 30.00 (ISBN 0-8414-5178-8). Folcroft.
Undiscovered Country. William D. Howells. LC 71-129976. 1971. Repr. of 1880 ed. 24.00x (ISBN 0-403-00133-1). Scholarly.
Undiscovered Country. Arthur Schnitzler. Tr. by Tom Stoppard. 94p. 1981. pap. 5.95 (ISBN 0-571-11575-6). Faber & Faber.
Undiscovered Denver Dining. 2nd ed. David Engelken et al. (Illus.). 84p. 1983. pap. 3.95 (ISBN 0-9610064-0-4). Undiscovered.
Undiscovered Dostoyevsky. Ronald Hingley. LC 74-5549. (Illus.). 241p. 1975. Repr. of 1962 ed. lib. bdg. 35.00x (ISBN 0-8371-7506-2, HIUD). Greenwood.
Undiscovered Genre: A Search for the German Gothic Novel. Michael Hadley. (Canadian Studies in German Language & Literature: Vol. 20). 155p. 1978. pap. 19.60 (ISBN 3-261-03106-9). P Lang Pubs.
Undiscovered Islands of the Caribbean. Burl Willes. Ed. by Richard Harris. (Illus.). 256p. (Orig.). 1988. pap. 12.95 (ISBN 0-912528-80-X). John Muir.
Undiscovered Self. C. G. Jung. 1974. pap. 3.95 (ISBN 0-451-62539-0, ME1946, Ment). NAL.
Undiscovered Self. Carl G. Jung. 1958. 12.95 (ISBN 0-316-47693-5, Pub. by Atlantic Monthly Pr); pap. 6.95 (ISBN 0-316-47694-3, Pub. by Atlantic Monthly Pr). Little.
Undiscovered: The Fascinating World of Undiscovered Places, Graves, Wrecks & Treasure. Ian Wilson. (Illus.). 192p. 1987. 16.95 (ISBN 0-688-07278-X, Pub. by Beech Tree Bks). Morrow.
Undiscovered Zane Grey Fishing Stories. Zane Grey. Ed. by George Reiger. LC 83-17082. (Illus.). 200p. 1983. deluxe slipcased ed. 29.95 (ISBN 0-8329-0342-6, Pub. by Winchester Pr). New Century.
Undiscovered Zane Grey Fishing Stories. Zane Grey. Ed. by George Reiger. LC 83-17082. (Illus.). 200p. 1983. 17.95 (ISBN 0-8329-0316-7). New Century.
Undisturbed Soldier. Ed Irsch. 1983. 4.25 (ISBN 0-89536-602-9, 2105). CSS of Ohio.
Undocumented Aliens & Crime: The Case of San Diego County. Daniel Wolf. (Monograph Ser.: No. 29). (Illus., Orig.). Date not set. pap. text ed. 12.00 (ISBN 0-935391-77-0, MN29). Ctr Mex Studies.
Undocumented Aliens in the New York Metropolitan Area: An Exploration into Their Social & Labor Market Incorporation. Demetrios G. Papademetriou & Nicholas DiMarzio. (Migration & Ethnicity Ser.). 1986. pap. 14.95 (ISBN 0-913256-99-4). Ctr Migration.
Undoing Yourself Too. Christopher S. Hyatt. LC 88-80928. (Orig.). 1988. pap. 9.95 (ISBN 0-941404-52-8). Falcon Pr AZ.
Undoing Yourself with Energized Meditation & Other Devices. Christopher S. Hyatt. LC 82-83293. 180p. 1982. pap. 9.95 (ISBN 0-941404-06-4). Falcon Pr Az.
Undream'd of Shores. Frank Harris. 1978. Repr. of 1924 ed. lib. bdg. 25.00 (ISBN 0-8492-5261-X). R West.
Undulating Weft Effects. Harriet Tidball. LC 76-24001. (Shuttle Craft Guild Monographs: No. 9). (Illus.). 25p. 1963. pap. 6.95 (ISBN 0-916658-09-0). Shuttle Craft.
Undying Dedication. R. Vernon Boyd. 1985. pap. 5.95 (ISBN 0-89225-281-2). Gospel Advocate.
Undying Flame. Ed. by Ellen Garwood. 226p. 1985. 14.95 (ISBN 0-931727-01-4). Am Studies Ctr.
Undying Love. Carole Mortimer. (Harlequin Presents Ser.). 192p. 1983. pap. 1.95 (ISBN 0-373-10645-9). Harlequin Bks.

Unemployment Under Capitalism: The Sociology of British & American Labour Markets. David N. Ashton. LC 85-21874. (Contributions in Economics & Economic History Ser.: No. 65). (Illus.). 1985. lib. bdg. 27.50 (ISBN 0-313-25201-7, AUT/). Greenwood.

Unemployment Upon the Status of the Man in Fifty-Nine Families. LC 79-137174. (Poverty, U. S. A.: The Historical Record Ser.). 1971. Repr. of 1940 ed. 8.00 (ISBN 0-685-47396-1). Ayer Co Pubs.

Unemployment, Vacancy Durations, & Wage Increases: Applications of Markov Processes to Labour Market Dynamics. Nils H. Schager. (Industrial Institute for Economic & Social Research Report Ser.: No. 29). 217p. (Orig.). 1987. pap. text ed. 42.50x (ISBN 91-7204-280-X, Pub. by Almqvist & Wiksell). Coronet Bks.

Unemployment Versus Inflation. Milton Friedman. Ed. by David Laidler. (IEA Occaisional Paper: No. 44). 1975. pap. 4.25 technical (ISBN 0-255-36069-X). Transatl Arts.

Unended Quest: An Intellectual Autobiography. rev. ed. Karl Popper. LC 76-2155. 264p. 1985. 12.95 (ISBN 0-87548-366-6); pap. 9.95 (ISBN 0-87548-343-7). Open Court.

Unending Blues: Poems. Charles Simic. 64p. 1986. pap. 5.95 (ISBN 0-15-692831-0, Harv); 14.95 (ISBN 0-15-192830-4). HarBraceJ.

Unending Vigil: History of the Commonwealth War Graves Commission. Philip Longworth. (Illus.). 256p. 1986. 39.95 (ISBN 0-436-25689-4, Pub. by Secker & Warburg UK). David & Charles.

Unending Work & Care: Managing Chronic Illness at Home. Juliet M. Corbin & Anselm Strauss. LC 87-46343. (Health Ser.). 1988. text ed. 34.95x (ISBN 1-55542-082-6). Jossey-Bass.

Unenlightened & Other Korean Short Stories. Yi Kwang-su et al. Tr. by Chang Wang-rok et al from Korean. (Modern Korean Short Stories Ser.: No. 3). viii, 234p. 1983. 20.00 (ISBN 0-89209-204-1). Pace Intl Res.

Unequal Access to Information: Problems & Needs of the World's Information Poor. Ed. by Jovian P. Lang. 250p. 1988. pap. 35.00 (ISBN 0-87650-239-7). Pierian.

Unequal Access: Women Lawyers in a Changing America. Ronald Chester. 160p. 1984. 29.95 (ISBN 0-89789-052-3). Bergin & Garvey.

Unequal Alliance. Robin Broad. 1988. 35.00 (ISBN 0-520-05905-0). U of Cal Pr.

Unequal Allies. R. Bell. 1977. 20.00x (ISBN 0-522-84115-5, Pub. by Melbourne U Pr). Intl Spec Bk.

Unequal Americans: Practices & Politics of Intergroup Relations. John Slawson. LC 78-67909. (Contributions in Political Science: No. 24). 1979. lib. bdg. 46.95x (ISBN 0-313-21118-3, SUA/). Greenwood.

Unequal Beginnings: Agriculture & Economic Development in Quebec & Ontario Until 1870. John McCallum. (State & Economic Life Ser.). 1980. 15.00x (ISBN 0-8020-5455-2); pap. 11.95c (ISBN 0-8020-6362-4). U of Toronto Pr.

Unequal Breadwinner. Ruth Lister & Leo Wilson. 1976. 20.00x (ISBN 0-901108-57-X, Pub. by NCCL UK). State Mutual Bk.

Unequal Care: A Case Study of Interorganizational Relations. Murray Milner, Jr. LC 80-15612. (Illus.). 224p. 1980. 35.00x (ISBN 0-231-05006-2). Columbia U Pr.

Unequal Colleagues: The Entrance of Women into the Professions, 1890-1940. Penina Glazer & Miriam Slater. (Douglass Series on Womens Lives & the Meaning of Gender). (Illus.). 220p. 1987. text ed. 28.00 (ISBN 0-8135-1186-0); pap. text ed. 9.95 (ISBN 0-8135-1187-9). Rutgers U Pr.

Unequal Development: An Essay on the Social Formations of Peripheral Capitalism. Samir Amin. Tr. by Brian Pearce from Fr. LC 75-15364. 1977. pap. 8.50 (ISBN 0-85345-433-7). Monthly Rev.

Unequal Education: A Study of Sex Differences in Secondary-School Curricula. Beatrice Dupont. (Illus.). 88p. 1981. pap. 5.00 (ISBN 92-3-101823-X, U1175, UNESCO). UNIPUB.

Unequal Educational Provision in England & Wales: The Nineteenth-Century Roots. W. E. Marsden. 224p. 1986. 29.50x (ISBN 0-7130-0178-X, Pub. by Woburn Pr England). Biblio Dist.

Unequal Exchange. Ranjit Sau. (Illus.). 1985. pap. 10.95x (ISBN 0-19-561620-0). Oxford U Pr.

Unequal Exchange & the Evolution of the World System: Reconsidering the Impact of Trade on North-South Relations. Kunibert Raffer. LC 86-31306. 336p. 1987. 40.00 (ISBN 0-312-00440-0). St Martin.

Unequal Growth: Urban & Regional Employment Change in the U. K. Stephen Fothergill & Graham Gudgin. 210p. 1982. text ed. 25.50x (ISBN 0-435-84370-2). Gower Pub Co.

Unequal Justice. Jerold S. Auerbach. 1976. 29.95x (ISBN 0-19-501939-3). Oxford U Pr.

Unequal Justice: Lawyers & Social Change in Modern America. Jerold S. Auerbach. LC 75-7364. 1976. pap. 10.95 (ISBN 0-19-502170-3). Oxford U Pr.

Unequal Knowledge Distribution: The Schooling Experience in a Togolese Secondary School. Karen Biraimah. (Special Studies in Comparative Education: No. 9). 56p. (Orig.). 1983. pap. text ed. 5.00 (ISBN 0-937033-00-6). SUNY Compar Educ Ctr.

Unequal Laws unto a Savage Race: European Legal Traditions in Arkansas, 1686-1836. Morris S. Arnold. LC 84-168. (Illus.). 240p. 1985. 23.00x (ISBN 0-938626-33-7); pap. 12.00x (ISBN 0-938626-76-0). U of Ark Pr.

Unequal Lovers. Alison Stewart. (Illus.). 208p. Date not set. 49.50 (ISBN 0-913870-44-7). Abaris Bks.

Unequal Opportunities: The Case of Women & the Media. Margaret Gallagher. 221p. 1981. pap. 11.50 (ISBN 92-3-101897-3, U1201, UNESCO). UNIPUB.

Unequal Opportunities: Women's Employment in England 1800-1918. Ed. by Angela V. John. 256p. 1986. text ed. 49.95x (ISBN 0-631-13955-9); pap. text ed. 14.95x (ISBN 0-631-13956-7). Basil Blackwell.

Unequal Partnership: U. S. Economic Relations with the Developing Countries. Rudolf Zimenkov. 110p. 1986. text ed. 15.00x (ISBN 81-207-0120-8, Pub. by Sterling Pubs India). Apt Bks.

Unequal Taxation: Its Unconstitutionality. 100p. 1981. 65.00 (ISBN 0-318-16627-5). T Jefferson Equal Tax.

Unequal Trade: The Economics of Discriminatory International Trade Policies. Richard Pomfret. 288p. Date not set. text ed. 39.95 (ISBN 0-631-15341-1). Basil Blackwell.

Unequal Treaties: China & the Foreigner. Rodney V. Gilbert. LC 75-32314. (Studies in Chinese History & Civilzation). 248p. 1977. Repr. of 1929 ed. 19.50 (ISBN 0-89093-075-9). U Pubns Amer.

Unequal Treatment: A Study in the Neoclassical Theory of Discrimination. Mats Lundahl & Eskil Wadensjo. 336p. 1985. 45.00x (ISBN 0-8147-5012-5). NYU PR.

Unequal Treaty, Eighteen Ninety-Eight to Nineteen Ninety-Seven: China, Great Britain, & Hong Kong's New Territories. Peter Wesley-Smith. LC 84-135396. (Illus.). write for info. Amer Bar Assn.

Unequal Treaty, Eighteen Ninety-Eight to Nineteen Ninety-Seven: China, Great Britain & Hong Kong's New Territories. Peter Wesley-Smith. LC 81-204259. (East Asian Historical Monographs). (Illus.). 1983. pap. 15.95x (ISBN 0-19-583727-4). Oxford U Pr.

Unequal Victims: Poles & Jews During World War II. Israel Gutman & Shmuel Krakowski. LC 86-81417. 1987. 20.95 (ISBN 0-89604-055-0); pap. 13.95 (ISBN 0-89604-056-9). Holocaust Pubns.

Unequal Yoke. Edmund W. Gosse. LC 75-31652. 52p. 1975. lib. bdg. 30.00x (ISBN 0-8201-1163-5). Schol Facsimiles.

Unequally Yoked. 2nd ed. William S. Deal. LC 80-67387. 112p. 1987. pap. 4.95 (Crossway Bks). Good News.

Unequally Yoked Wives. C. S. Lovett. 1968. pap. 5.45 (ISBN 0-938148-22-2). Personal Christianity.

Unequivocal Americanism: Right-Wing Novels in the Cold War Era. Macel D Ezell. LC 77-3725. 160p. 1977. 17.50 (ISBN 0-8108-1033-6). Scarecrow.

UNESCO Activites in the field of Science & Technology in the Arab Region. (Science Documents & Policy Studies: No. 65). 62p. (Orig.). 1986. pap. text ed. 5.00 (ISBN 0-317-66422-0, UI603, UNESCO). UNIPUB.

UNESCO & Library Development Planning. Stephen Parker. 512p. 1985. 60.00 (ISBN 0-85365-863-3, Pub. by Library Assn Pub London). ALA.

UNESCO Bulletin for Libraries: Cumulative Index 1962-1976 (Volumes 1-15) 1983. 30.00 (ISBN 0-317-01053-0). Learned Info.

UNESCO Courier. pap. 16.00 year (UNESCO). UNIPUB.

UNESCO Dictionary of the Social Sciences. Julius Gould & W. J. Kolb. LC 64-20307. 1964. 40.00 (ISBN 0-02-917490-2). Free Pr.

UNESCO General History of Africa, Vol. III. Ed. by M. El Fasi. 1988. 35.00x (ISBN 0-520-03914-9). U of Cal Pr.

UNESCO General History of Africa, 8 vols. Incl. Vol. I. Methodology & African Prehistory. Ed. by J. Ki-Zerbo. 1980. 35.00x (ISBN 0-520-03912-2); Vol. II. Ancient Africa. Ed. by G. Mokhtar. 35.00x (ISBN 0-520-03913-0); Vol. IV. Africa from the XII to the XVI the Century. Ed. by D. T. Niane. 1984p. 35.00x (ISBN 0-520-03915-7); Vol VII. Africa under Colonial Domination, 1880-1935. Ed. by A. Adu Boahen. 35.00x (ISBN 0-520-03918-1). 1980. U of Cal Pr.

UNESCO Handbook for Biology Teachers in Africa. (Illus.). 329p. (Orig.). 1987. pap. text ed. 12.75 (ISBN 92-3-102210-5, UI547, UNESCO). UNIPUB.

UNESCO Handbook for Science Teachers. 208p. (Co-published with Heinemann Educational Books, London; and Unipub, New York). 1980. pap. 19.50 (ISBN 92-3-101666-0, U1029, UNESCO). UNIPUB.

UNESCO: IBE Education Thesaurus. 4th, rev. ed. (IBEdata). 345p. 1986. pap. text ed. 22.50 (ISBN 92-3-102061-7, U1363, UNESCO). UNIPUB.

Unesco in Asia & the Pacific: Forty Years on Bibliographical Supplement. (Belletin of the UNESCO Regional Office for Education in Asia & the Pacific Ser.: No. 27). 186p. (Orig.). 1987. pap. text ed. 7.50 (ISBN 0-317-58381-6, UB229, UB). UNIPUB.

UNESCO in Asis & the Pacific: Forty Years On. Intro. by Makaminar Makagiansar. (Belletin of the UNESCO Regional Office for Education in Asia & the Pacific: No. 27). (Illus.). 265p. (Orig.). 1987. pap. text ed. 22.50 (ISBN 0-317-58384-0, UB228, UB). UNIPUB.

Unesco: In Retrospect & Prospect. Ed. by U. S. Pajpai & S. Viswam. 197p. 1986. 25.00x (ISBN 81-7062-000-7, Pub. by Lancer India). South Asia Bks.

UNESCO: Its Purpose & Its Philosophy. Julian Huxley. 1979. pap. 4.50 (ISBN 0-8183-0216-X). Pub Aff Pr.

UNESCO List of Documents & Publications: 1972-76, 2 Vols. (Vol. 1 - Annoted List of Documents and Publications; Personal Name Index; Conference Index. Vol. 2 Subject Index). 1979. Set. pap. 11.50 (ISBN 92-3-101607-5, U1063, UNESCO). UNIPUB.

UNESCO List of Documents & Publications 1977: Part I: Cumulative Masterfile Listing (20531-35818). Part II: Cumulative Indexes for 1977, 2 Pts. 180p. 1981. pap. 11.50 set (ISBN 92-3-101607-5, U1063, UNESCO). UNIPUB.

UNESCO List of Documents & Publications, 1977-1980, Vols. 1 & 2. 1643p. (Eng. , Fr. & Span.). 1984. pap. 42.00 (ISBN 92-3-002179-2, U1369, UNESCO). UNIPUB.

UNESCO: Purpose, Progress, Prospects. W. H. Laves & C. A. Thomson. LC 57-10728. 1968. Repr. of 1957 ed. 39.00 (ISBN 0-527-55300-X). Kraus Repr.

UNESCO Regional Seminar on the Educational Role of Museums. Ed. by G. H. Riviere. (Educational Studies & Documents: No. 38). pap. 13.00 (ISBN 0-8115-1362-9). Kraus Repr.

UNESCO Report: Marine Science Report 1-9. 435p. pap. 42.50 (U1154, UNESCO). UNIPUB.

UNESCO Report of the Director General on the Activities of the Organizations: 1977-1978. 256p. 1980. pap. 10.50 (ISBN 92-3-101738-1, U967, UNESCO). UNIPUB.

UNESCO Science & Technology Activities in Asia & the Pacific. (Science Policy Studies & Documents: No. 51). 37p. 1983. pap. 5.00 et (ISBN 92-3-102066-8, U1325, UNESCO). UNIPUB.

UNESCO Sourcebook for Out-of-School Science & Technology Education. (Illus.). 145p. (Orig.). 1987. pap. text ed. 12.75 (ISBN 92-3-102386-1, U1580, UNESCO). UNIPUB.

UNESCO Statistical Digest. 335p. (Orig., Eng., Fr. & Span.). 1987. pap. 10.00 (ISBN 92-3-002481-3, U1639, UNESCO). UNIPUB.

UNESCO Statistical Digest 1984. 335p. (Eng., Fr. & Span.). 1985. pap. 7.50 (ISBN 92-3-002260-8, U1448, UNESCO). UNIPUB.

UNESCO Statistical Digest 1986. 336p. (Orig., Eng., Span. & Fr.). 1987. pap. text ed. 7.50 (ISBN 92-3-002446-5, U1590, UNESCO). UNIPUB.

UNESCO Statistical Yearbook. (Orig.). 1987. pap. text ed. 81.00 (ISBN 92-3-002480-5, U1622, UNESCO). UNIPUB.

UNESCO Statistical Yearbook: 1977. 1979. pap. 42.00 (ISBN 92-3-001598-9, U883, UNESCO). UNIPUB.

UNESCO Statistical Yearbook, 1981. 1982. 59.00 (ISBN 92-3-001965-8, U1169, UNESCO). UNIPUB.

UNESCO Statistical Yearbook: 1983. (Illus.). 1064p. (Eng., Fr. & Span.). 1983. pap. 25.25 (ISBN 92-3-002285-3, U1316, UNESCO). UNIPUB.

UNESCO Statistical Yearbook, 1986. (Illus.). 1000p. (Eng., Fr. & Span.). 1987. pap. 67.25 (ISBN 92-3-002445-7, U1552, UNESCO). UNIPUB.

UNESCO Symposium. 408p. 1981. pap. 17.00 (ISBN 92-3-101664-4, U1099, UNESCO). UNIPUB.

UNESCO Thesaurus: A Structured List of Descriptors for Indexing & Retrieving Literature in the fields of Education, Science, Social Science, Culture & Communication, 2 Vols. Compiled by Jean Aitchison. 1977. Set. 52.50 (ISBN 92-3-101469-2, U816, UNESCO). Vol. 1: Introduction, Classified Thesaurus, Permuted Index, Hierarchical Display, 485 p. Vol. 2: Alphabetical Thesaurus, 530 p. UNIPUB.

UNESCO: Universality & International Intellectual Cooperation. Amadou-Mahtar M'Bow. 149p. (Orig.). 1987. pap. text ed. 7.50 (ISBN 92-3-102450-7, U1562, UNESCO). UNIPUB.

UNESCO Yearbook of Peace Corps, 1981. cancelled (ISBN 0-8002-3324-7). Intl Pubns Serv.

UNESCO Yearbook on Peace & Conflict Studies Nineteen Eighty-Three. United Nations Educational, Scientific, & Cultural Organization. (United Nations Educational, Scientific, & Cultural Organization Annuals Ser.). (Illus.). xiv, 406p. 1985. lib. bdg. 40.00 (ISBN 0-313-24833-8, UN83). Greenwood.

UNESCO Yearbook on Peace & Conflict Studies: 1982. Yuri K. Babansky & Liviu Bota. 269p. (Orig.). 1984. pap. 52.50 (ISBN 92-3-102119-2, U1339, UNESCO). UNIPUB.

UNESCO Yearbook on Peace & Conflict Studies, 1987. UNESCO Staff. 1989. 55.85 (ISBN 0-313-26485-6, UN87). Greenwood.

UNESCO Yearbook on Peace & Conflict Studies 1980. 311p. 1982. 36.75 (ISBN 92-3-101254-1, U1165, UNESCO). UNIPUB.

UNESCO Yearbook on Peace & Conflict Studies, 1981. 396p. (Co-published with Greenwood Press Inc.). 1982. text ed. 50.00 (ISBN 92-3-102032-3, U1285, UNESCO). UNIPUB.

UNESCO Yearbook on Peace & Conflict Studies, 1980. The United Nations Educational, Scientific & Cultural Organization. 384p. 1981. lib. bdg. 30.00 (ISBN 0-313-22922-8, UN80). Greenwood.

UNESCO Yearbook on Peace & Conflict Studies 1981. United Nations Educational, Scientific, & Cultural Organzation. (United Nations Educational, Scientific & Cultural Organization Annuals Ser.). (Illus.). 576p. 1982. lib. bdg. 35.00 (ISBN 0-313-22923-6, UN81). Greenwood.

UNESCO Yearbook on Peace & Conflict Studies, 1982. United Nations Educational, Scientific & Cultural Organization. (United Nations Educational, Scientific & Cultural Organization Annuals Ser.). (Illus.). xiv, 269p. 1983. lib. bdg. 35.00 (ISBN 0-313-22924-4, UN82). Greenwood.

UNESCO Yearbook on Peace & Conflict Studies 1984. United Nations Educational, Scientific, & Cultural Organization Staff. (United Nations Educational, Scientific & Cultural Organization Annuals Ser.). 240p. 1986. 40.00 (ISBN 0-313-25442-7, UN84/). Greenwood.

UNESCO Yearbook on Peace & Conflict Studies 1985. United Nations Educational, Scientific, & Cultural Organization. 250p. 1987. lib. bdg. 49.95 (ISBN 0-313-26122-9, UN85). Greenwood.

UNESCO 1979-1980: Report of the Director-General on the Activities of the Organization in 1979-1980. (Illus.). 276p. 1981. pap. 13.00 (ISBN 92-3-101959-7, U1173, UNESCO). UNIPUB.

UNESCO, 1984-1985: Introduction to the Draft Programme & Budget. Amandou-Mahtar MBow. 120p. 1983. pap. text ed. 5.00 (ISBN 92-3-102149-4, U1306, UNESCO). UNIPUB.

UNESCO 1984-1985, Report of the Director General. (Annual Ser.). (Illus.). 314p. (Orig.). 1987. pap. text ed. 15.00 (ISBN 92-3-102441-8, U1578, UNESCO). UNIPUB.

Unescorted Women. Ed. by Bibliotheca Press Staff. 1986. pap. 3.00 (ISBN 0-939476-26-6, Pub. by Biblio Pr GA). Prosperity & Profits.

UNESCO's Activities in Science & Technology in the European & North American Region. (Science Policy Studies & Documents: No. 45). 49p. 1979. pap. 5.00 (ISBN 92-3-101727-6, U930, UNESCO). UNIPUB.

UNESCO's Standard-Setting Instruments. 667p. 1982. binder 59.00 (U1193, UNESCO). UNIPUB.

UNESCO's Standard-Setting Instruments. (X Incl. Basic volume, 960p., & Suppl. 1, 168 p. loose-leaf binder). 1983. pap. 59.00 (ISBN 92-3-102155-9, U1193, UNESCO). UNIPUB.

UNESCO's Standard-Setting Instruments. 20p. (Orig.). 1986. pap. text ed. 12.60 (ISBN 92-3-102462-0, U1619, UNESCO). UNIPUB.

Uneven Development & Regionalism: State, Territory & Class in Southern Europe. Cotis Hadjimichalis. Ed. by Alan Wilson et al. (Geography & Environment Ser.). 352p. 1986. 50.00 (ISBN 0-7099-3700-8, Pub. by Croom Helm UK). Routledge Chapman & Hall.

Uneven Development in Southern Europe. Ed. by J. Lewis & R. Hudson. 328p. 1985. 65.00 (ISBN 0-416-32840-7, 9527). Routledge Chapman & Hall.

Uneven Development: Nature, Capital & the Production of Space. Neil Smith. 256p. 1984. 34.95x (ISBN 0-631-13564-2); pap. 14.95 (ISBN 0-631-13685-1). Basil Blackwell.

Uneven Developments: The Ideological Work of Gender in Mid-Victorian England. Mary Poovey. (Women in Culture & Society Ser.). 224p. 1988. 37.50x (ISBN 0-226-67529-7); pap. 14.95x (ISBN 0-226-67530-0). U of Chicago Pr.

Unevenness of the Abilities of Dull & of Bright Children. Andrew W. Brown. LC 70-176596. (Columbia University. Teachers College. Contributions to Education: No. 220). Repr. of 1926 ed. 22.50 (ISBN 0-404-55220-X). AMS Pr.

Unexamined Wife. Sherril Jaffe. LC 83-11915. 188p. 1983. 14.00 (ISBN 0-87685-570-2); pap. 8.50 (ISBN 0-87685-569-9); signed ed. 25.00 (ISBN 0-87685-571-0). Black Sparrow.

Unexpected Community: Portrait of an Old Age Subculture. Arlie R. Hochschild. LC 77-91733. 1978. pap. 8.95x (ISBN 0-520-03624-7). U of Cal Pr.

Unexpected Developments. R. B. Dominic. 225p. 1983. 11.95 (ISBN 0-312-83278-8, J Kahn). St Martin.

Unexpected Hanging & Other Mathematical Diversions. Martin Gardner. 1972. pap. 6.75 (ISBN 0-671-21425-X, Fireside). S&S.

Unexpected Hanging: And Other Mathematical Diversions. Martin Gardner. 256p. 1986. pap. 7.95 (ISBN 0-671-62819-4, Touchstone Bks). S&S.

Unexpected Japan: Why American Business Should Return to Its Own Traditional Values--& Not Imitate the Japanese. Donald R. Riccomini & Philip M. Rosenzweig. 144p. 1985. 12.95 (ISBN 0-8027-0858-7). Walker & Co.

Unexpected Journeys: The Art & Life of Remedios Varo. Janet Kaplan. (Illus.). 288p. 1988. 35.00 (ISBN 0-89659-797-0). Abbeville Pr.

Unexpected Meditations Late in the Twentieth Century. James V. Schall. 142p. 1986. 9.95 (ISBN 0-8199-0885-1). Franciscan Herald.

Unexpected Miracle. Demos Shakarian. 224p. 1987. cancelled (ISBN 0-8407-7618-7). Nelson.

Unexpected Mrs. Pollifax. Dorothy Gilman. 1985. pap. 2.95 (ISBN 0-449-20828-1, Crest). Fawcett.

Unexpected News: Reading the Bible with Third World Eyes. Robert M. Brown. LC 84-2380. 166p. 1984. pap. 7.95 (ISBN 0-664-24552-8). Westminster John Knox.

Unexpected Peace. Jack Kelly. 240p. 1983. pap. 2.50 (ISBN 0-8439-2003-3, Leisure Bks). Leisure NY.

Unexpected Real Consequences of Floating Exchange Rates. Rachel McCulloch. LC 83-10857. (Essays in International Finance Ser.: No. 153). 1983. pap. text ed. 4.50x (ISBN 0-88165-060-9). Princeton U Int Finan Econ.

Unexpected Rebellion: Ethnic Activism in Contemporary France. William R. Beer. LC 79-3515. 1980. 30.00x (ISBN 0-8147-1029-8). NYU Pr.

Unexpected Revolution: Social Forces in the Hungarian Uprising. Paul Kecskemeti. 1961. 17.50x (ISBN 0-8047-0085-0). Stanford U Pr.

Unexpected Twist Series. Paul J. Payack. (Illus.). 1976. pap. 1.00 (ISBN 0-686-16728-7). Chthon Pr.

Unexpected Universe. Loren Eiseley. LC 67-20308. 239p. 1972. pap. 4.95 (ISBN 0-15-692850-7, Harv). HarBraceJ.

Unexpected Universe of Doris Lessing: A Study of in Narrative Technique. Katherine Fishburn. LC 85-9913. (Contributions to the Study of Science Fiction & Fantasy Ser.: No. 17). 184p. 1985. lib. bdg. 35.00 (ISBN 0-313-23424-8, FTW/). Greenwood.

Unexpected Vista: A Physicist's View of Nature. James Trefil. Ed. by B. Lippman. 224p. 1985. pap. 7.95 (ISBN 0-02-096780-2, Collier). Macmillan.

Unexplained at Sea: A Collection of the Sea's Greatest Mysteries. Robert Stanton. 1984. 25.00x (ISBN 0-906549-31-0, Pub. by J Clare Bks); pap. 12.00x (ISBN 0-906549-32-9, Pub. by J Clare Bks). State Mutual Bk.

Unexplained Laughter. Alice T. Ellis. LC 86-46063. 160p. 1987. 14.45i (ISBN 0-06-015722-4, HarpT). Har-Row.

Unexplained: Mysteries of Mind, Space & Time. Ed. by Peter Brookesmith. (Illus.). 1152p. 1983. lib. bdg. 169.95x (ISBN 0-86307-098-1). Marshall Cavendish.

Unexplained Sniglits of the Universe. Rich Hall. 1986. pap. 5.95 (ISBN 0-02-040400-X, Collier). Macmillan.

Unexplored New Guinea. Wilfred N. Beaver. LC 75-32799. (Illus.). Repr. of 1920 ed. 36.50 (ISBN 0-404-14102-1). AMS Pr.

Unexplored Relationships Between Early Seventeenth Century Venetian Opera & Contemporary Music in France & England. R. Leppard. (Italian Lectures). 1969. pap. 5.50 (ISBN 0-85672-284-7, Pub. by British Acad). Longwood Pub Group.

Unexpurgated Code: A Complete Manual of Survival & Manners. J. P. Donleavy. LC 75-8956. 283p. 1975. 20.00 (ISBN 0-317-58041-8). Ultramarine Pub.

Unextinguished Hearth. Newman I. White. 397p. 1966. Repr. of 1938 ed. 25.00x (ISBN 0-7146-2097-1, BHA-02097, F Cass Co). Biblio Dist.

Unextinguished Hearth. Newman I. White. 1966. lib. bdg. 27.50x (ISBN 0-374-98474-3, Octagon). Hippocrene Bks.

Unfair Advantage. Summers. 1987. pap. 4.50 (ISBN 0-312-90847-4). St Martin.

Unfair Advantage (PG) Tom Miller. 170p. (Orig.). 1986. pap. 13.95 (ISBN 0-9613034-2-5). Horsesense Inc.

Unfair Advantage, "R". Tom Miller. 170p. (Orig.). 1986. pap. 13.95 (ISBN 0-9613034-1-7). Horsesense Inc.

Unfair Advantage: The Mental Part of Sports & Business. James A. Davis. LC 84-50120. (Illus.). 215p. (Orig.). 1984. 19.95 (ISBN 0-915377-00-4); pap. 13.95 (ISBN 0-915377-01-2). Trad Pub.

Unfair & Deceptive Acts & Practices. 2nd ed. (Consumer Credit & Sales Legal Practice Ser.). 350p. 1988. pap. 60.00x (ISBN 0-943116-61-9). Nat Consumer Law.

Unfair & Deceptive Acts & Practices: 1982 & 1987 Supplement. LC 82-81234. 108p. 1982. pap. 48.00 (ISBN 0-943116-01-5). Nat Consumer Law.

Unfair Arguments with Existence. Lawrence Ferlinghetti. LC 63-21384. 1963. pap. 1.00 (ISBN 0-8112-0048-5, NDP143). New Directions.

Unfair at Any Gridiron. C. W. Staley. LC 80-66404. 250p. 1981. 14.95 (ISBN 0-9604324-0-X, 8012 800326). CWS Group Pr.

Unfair, but Not Too Unfair. Dave Jackson. (Caring Parents Storybooks Ser.). 32p. (ps-2). 1986. pap. 3.95 (ISBN 0-89191-278-9). Cook.

Unfair Competition & Unfair Trade Practices. Beverly W. Pattishall & David C. Hilliard. LC 85-73650. (Case & Materials Ser.). 1986. tchrs. guide 27.50. Bender.

Unfair Exchange. Marian Babson. 192p. 1986. 15.95 (ISBN 0-8027-5660-3). Walker & Co.

Unfair Trade Practices & Consumer Protection Cases & Comments on, 1986 Supplement. Chesterfield Oppenheim et al. (American Casebook Ser.). 148p. 1986. pap. 9.95 (ISBN 0-314-21435-6). West Pub.

Unfair Trade Practices & Consumer Protection. 4th ed. S. Chesterfield Oppenheim & Glen E. Weston. LC 83-6884. (American Casebook Ser.). 1038p. 1983. text ed. 34.95 (ISBN 0-314-70365-9); pap. text ed. write for info. teachrs' manual avail. (ISBN 0-314-86143-2). West Pub.

Unfair Trade Practices & Intellectual Property. Roger E. Schechter. (Black Letter Ser.). 272p. 1986. pap. text ed. 15.95 (ISBN 0-314-98619-7). West Pub.

Unfair Trade Practices in a Nutshell. Charles R. McManis. LC 82-13597. (Nutshell Ser.). 444p. 1982. text ed. 10.95 (ISBN 0-314-68094-2). West Pub.

Unfair Trade Practices in a Nutshell. 2nd ed. Charles R. McManis. (Nutshell Ser.). 420p. 1988. pap. text ed. write for info. (ISBN 0-314-38860-5). West Pub.

Unfair Trial Tactics: Recognizing & Avoiding Them in Litigation. Mark A. Dombroff. Date not set. 25.00 (ISBN 0-318-23988-4, 5315); audiotapes 115.00 (ISBN 0-318-23989-2); videotape 750.00 (ISBN 0-318-23990-6). Natl Prac Inst.

Unfairly Structured Cities. Blair Badcock. 448p. 1984. 39.95x (ISBN 0-631-13395-X); pap. 14.95x (ISBN 0-631-13396-8). Basil Blackwell.

Unfamiliar Masterpieces of Painting. Walter Scheidig. (Illus.). 1965. 43.50 (ISBN 0-8079-0163-6). October.

Unfathered Child & Other Poems. Lela G. Sitzman. 32p. 1988. 6.95 (ISBN 0-8062-3218-8). Carlton.

Unfathomed Mind: A Handbook of Unusual Mental Phenomena. William R. Corliss. LC 81-85081. (Illus.). 760p. 1982. 19.95 (ISBN 0-915554-08-9). Sourcebook.

Unfavorable Result in Plastic Surgery. 2nd ed. Robert M. Goldwyn. 1134p. 1984. text ed. 165.00 2 vols. in slipcase (ISBN 0-316-31975-9). Little.

Unfettered. Sutton E. Griggs. LC 79-144623. Repr. of 1902 ed. 14.00 (ISBN 0-404-00168-8). AMS Pr.

Unfettered Has Nothing to Do with a Nude Bird. Evelyn G. Fisher. (Illus.). 192p. (Orig.). 1984. pap. 5.95 (ISBN 0-9614144-0-5). See-Saw Pr.

Unfettered Mind: Writings of the Zen Master to the Sword Master. Takuan Soho. LC 86-45072. 92p. 1986. 13.95 (ISBN 0-87011-776-9). Kodansha.

Unfettered Mind: Writings of the Zen Master to the Sword Master. Takuan Soho. 104p. 1988. pap. 4.95 (ISBN 0-87011-851-X, 300). Kodansha.

Unfinished Agenda. Ralph Harris et al. 152p. (Orig.). 1986. pap. text ed. 15.95x (ISBN 0-255-36191-2, Pub. by Inst Econ Affairs UK). Transatl Arts.

Unfinished Agenda. Manning Nash. LC 84-51416. 160p. 1984. 35.00x (ISBN 0-86531-759-3). Westview.

Unfinished Agenda. The National Commission on Secondary Vocational Education. 35p. 1985. 4.75 (ISBN 0-318-22226-4, IN289). Natl Ctr Res Voc Ed.

Unfinished Agenda: An Autobiography. Lesslie Newbigin. (Illus.). 280p. (Orig.). 1985. pap. 12.95 (ISBN 0-8028-0091-2). Eerdmans.

Unfinished Agenda for Civil Servivce Reform: Implications of the Grace Commission Report. Ed. by Charles H. Levine. LC 85-71183. (Dialogue on Public Policy Ser.). 142p. 1985. pap. 10.95 (ISBN 0-8157-5251-2). Brookings.

Unfinished Autobiography. Alice A. Bailey. 1986. 19.00 (ISBN 0-85330-024-0); pap. 10.00 1986 (ISBN 0-85330-124-7). Lucis.

Unfinished Building. Henry J. Ambers. LC 74-19535. 400p. 1974. 10.95 (ISBN 0-9600874-2-7). Edelweiss Pr.

Unfinished Business. John Houseman. (Illus.). 508p. (Orig.). 1988. pap. 12.95 (ISBN 1-55783-024-X). Applause Theatre Bk Pubs.

Unfinished Business. Maggie Scarf. 1988. pap. 4.95 (ISBN 0-345-00650-X). Ballantine.

Unfinished Business. Nicola West. (Harlequin Presents Ser.: No. 998). 192p. Date not set. pap. 1.95 (ISBN 0-317-63739-8). Harlequin Bks.

Unfinished Business of Civil Service Reform. William Carpenter. LC 72-86539. 136p. 1973. Repr. of 1952 ed. 21.50x (ISBN 0-8046-1748-1, Pub by Kennikat). Assoc Faculty Pr.

Unfinished Business of Civil Service Reform. William S. Carpenter. LC 79-16863. 1980. Repr. of 1952 ed. lib. bdg. 35.00x (ISBN 0-313-22051-4, CACS). Greenwood.

Unfinished Business of Doctor Hermes. Richard Grossinger. 1976. pap. 4.00 (ISBN 0-913028-43-6). North Atlantic.

Unfinished Business of Living. Elwood N. Chapman. Ed. by Michael G. Crisp. LC 86-71572. (Illus.). 256p. (Orig.). 1987. pap. 10.95 (ISBN 0-931961-19-X). Crisp Pubns.

Unfinished Business: Pressure Points in the Lives of Women. Maggie Scarf. LC 78-22352. 1980. 14.95 (ISBN 0-385-12248-9). Doubleday.

Unfinished Business: The Theory & Practice of Personal Process Work in Training. Neil Clark et al. LC 84-8134. 200p. 1984. text ed. 35.50x (ISBN 0-566-02514-0). Gower Pub Co.

Unfinished Cathedral. T. S. Stribling. LC 85-20857. 400p. 1986. 27.50 (ISBN 0-8173-0252-2); pap. 12.95 (ISBN 0-8173-0253-0). U of Ala Pr.

Unfinished Church: A Brief History of the Union of the Evangelical United Brethern Church & the Methodist Church. Paul Washburn. 176p. 14.95 (ISBN 0-687-01378-X). Abingdon.

Unfinished Clue. Georgette Heyer. Repr. lib. bdg. 19.95 (ISBN 0-89190-648-7, Pub. by River City Pr). Amereon Ltd.

Unfinished Clue. Georgette Heyer. 1985. pap. 3.95 (ISBN 0-03-003297-0, Owl Bks). H Holt & Co.

Unfinished Constitution: Philosophy & Constitutional Practice. John Arthur. Date not set. pap. text ed. write for info. (ISBN 0-534-10014-7). Wadsworth Pub.

Unfinished Democracy: The American Political System. 2nd ed. Harrell R. Rodgers, Jr. & Michael Harrington. 1985. pap. text ed. write for info. (ISBN 0-673-15873-X). Scott F.

Unfinished Democracy: Women in Nordic Politics. Ed. by E. Haavio-Mannila. (Illus.). 228p. 1985. text ed. 28.00 (ISBN 0-08-031811-8, Pub. by P P L). Pergamon.

Unfinished Design: The Humanities & Social Sciences in Undergraduate Engineering Education. 1988. pap. price not set (ISBN 0-911696-42-3). Assn Am Coll.

Unfinished Dialogue: Martin Buber & the Christian Way. John M. Oesterreicher. LC 85-12410. 128p. 1986. 14.95 (ISBN 0-8022-2495-4). Philos Lib.

Unfinished Dialogue: Martin Buber & the Christian Way. John M. Osterreicher. 136p. 1987. pap. 5.95 (ISBN 0-8065-1050-1, Pub. by Citadel Pr). Lyle Stuart.

Unfinished Dream: The Musical World of Red Callender. Red Callender & Elaine Cohen. 1986. 11.95 (ISBN 0-318-19366-3, Pub. by Quartet). Salem Hse Pubs.

Unfinished... Essays in Honor of Ray L. Hart. Ed. by Mark C. Taylor. (JAAR Thematic Studies). 1981. pap. 13.50 (ISBN 0-89130-680-3, 01-24-81). Scholars Pr GA.

Unfinished Heartbeats: Poems. David L. Thompson. 1987. text ed. 8.95 (ISBN 0-682-40346-6). Exposition-Phoenix.

Unfinished Image. George McCauley. 462p. (Orig.). 1983. pap. 10.95 (ISBN 0-8215-9903-8). Sadlier.

Unfinished Journey. Shiva Naipaul. 144p. 1987. 15.95 (ISBN 0-670-81368-0). Viking.

Unfinished Journey. Shiva Naipaul. 144p. 1988. pap. 6.95 (ISBN 0-14-010925-0). Penguin.

Unfinished Journey: America since World War II. William H. Chafe. (Illus.). 516p. 1986. 35.00 (ISBN 0-19-503639-5); pap. 14.95 (ISBN 0-19-503640-9). Oxford U Pr.

Unfinished Liberation of Chinese Women, 1949-1980. Phyllis Andors. LC 81-48323. 224p. 1983. 22.50x (ISBN 0-253-36022-6). Ind U Pr.

Unfinished Man. Nissim Ezekiel. 6.75 (ISBN 0-89253-686-1); cancelled (ISBN 0-89253-687-X). Ind-US Inc.

Unfinished Man & the Imagination: Toward an Ontology & a Rhetoric of Revelation. Ray Hart. (Reprints & Translations Ser.). 1985. pap. text ed. 12.95 (ISBN 0-89130-937-3, 00-07-15). Scholars Pr GA.

Unfinished Mystery. John Walchars. (Orig.). 1978. pap. 5.95 (ISBN 0-8164-2184-6, HarpR). Har-Row.

Unfinished Plays. Eugene O'Neill. LC 87-30926. 256p. 1988. 24.95 (ISBN 0-8044-2674-0). Ungar.

Unfinished Portrait. Mary Westmacott, pseud. 1969. pap. 1.50 (ISBN 0-440-19217-X). Dell.

Unfinished Portrait. Mary Westmacott, pseud. 1987. pap. 3.95 (ISBN 0-515-09171-5). Jove Pubns.

Unfinished Reformation. facs. ed. Charles C. Morrison. LC 68-20322. (Essay Index Reprint Ser). 1953. 17.50 (ISBN 0-8369-0723-X). Ayer Co Pubs.

Unfinished Revolution: Marxism & Communism in the Modern World. rev. ed. Adam B. Ulam. 1979. lib. bdg. 42.00x (ISBN 0-89158-485-4); pap. 15.95x (ISBN 0-89158-496-X). Westview.

Unfinished Revolution: Russia, 1917-1967. Isaac Deutscher. LC 67-23012. 1967. pap. 7.95 (ISBN 0-19-500786-7). Oxford U Pr.

Unfinished Sequence. Edward Butscher. Ed. by Stanley H. Barkan. (Cross-Cultural Review Chapbook 6: American Poetry 3). 20p. 1980. pap. 2.25 (ISBN 0-89304-805-4). Cross Cult.

Unfinished Sequence & Other Poems. Sean Lucy. 64p. 1979. 9.95 (ISBN 0-905473-37-X, Pub. by Wolfhound Pr Ireland); pap. 5.95 (ISBN 0-905473-38-8). Irish Bks Media.

Unfinished Song: The Life of Victor Jara. Joan Jara. LC 83-24265. (Illus.). 288p. 1984. 15.95 (ISBN 0-89919-279-3). Ticknor & Fields.

Unfinished Stories for Facilitating Decision Making in the Elementary Classroom. Ed. by Elizabeth H. Weiner. 78p. 1980. pap. 7.95 (ISBN 0-8106-1678-5). NEA.

Unfinished Syntheses: Biological Hierarchies & Modern Evolutionary Thought. Niles Eldredge. (Illus.). 256p. 1988. pap. 14.95 (ISBN 0-19-505574-8). Oxford U Pr.

Unfinished Synthesis: Biological Hierarchies & Modern Evolutionary Thought. Niles Eldredge. LC 85-5008. (Illus.). 1985. 24.95x (ISBN 0-19-503633-6). Oxford U Pr.

Unfinished Tales. J. R. R. Tolkien. Ed. by Christopher Tolkien. (Illus.). 368p. 1980. 15.00 (ISBN 0-395-29917-9). HM.

Unfinished Tales. J. R. R. Tolkien. 1982. pap. 8.95 (ISBN 0-395-32441-6). HM.

Unfinished Task. Compiled by John E. Kyle. LC 84-11727. 1984. pap. 6.95 (ISBN 0-8307-0983-5, 5418342). Regal.

Unfinished Universe. Louise B. Young. 1986. 17.95 (ISBN 0-671-52376-7). S&S.

Unfinished Universe. Louise B. Young. 240p. 1987. pap. 8.95 (ISBN 0-671-63316-3, Touchstone Bks). S&S.

Unfinished Voyages. Graeme Henderson. 288p. 1980. 31.95 (ISBN 0-85564-176-2, Pub. by U of West Australia). Intl Spec Bk.

Unfinished War: Vietnam & the American Conscience. Walter H. Capps. LC 81-66193. 192p. 1983. pap. 9.95x (ISBN 0-8070-0401-4, BP 657). Beacon Pr.

Unfinished Woman. Lillian Hellman. LC 76-75019. (Illus.). 1970. 13.95 (ISBN 0-316-35518-6). Little.

Unfinished Women Cry in No Man's Land while a Bird Cries in a Gilded Cage. Aishah Rahman. 84p. (Orig.). 1984. pap. 8.95 (ISBN 0-915833-21-2). Drama Jazz Hse Inc.

Unfit for Glory. Art Fettig. LC 86-81726. 1987. pap. 5.95 (ISBN 0-916927-02-4). Growth Unltd.

Unfit Mothers. Sue Mahan. Ed. by R. Reed. LC 81-83616. (Illus.). 125p. 1982. pap. 11.95 (ISBN 0-88247-622-X). R & E Pubs.

Unfit to Manage: How Mis-Management Endangers America & What Working People Can Do about It. Ernest Liberman. 336p. 1988. text ed. 17.95 (ISBN 0-07-037815-0). McGraw.

Unfogettable Days in Southern Football. Clyde Bolton. (Sports Ser.). (Illus.). 255p. 1974. 10.95 (ISBN 0-87397-057-8). Strode.

Unfolding & Determinacy Theorems for Subgroups of A & K. James Damon. LC 84-9333. (Memoirs of the American Mathematical Society Ser.: Vol. 306). 90p. 1984. pap. 12.00 (ISBN 0-8218-2306-X). Am Math.

Unfolding Beauty: The Art of The Fan. Anna Bennett. Ed. by Janet Silver. LC 86-63853. (Illus.). 264p. 1987. 29.95 (ISBN 0-87846-279-1); pap. 45.00. Mus Fine Arts Boston.

Unfolding Beauty: The Art of the Fan. Anna G. Bennett. Ed. by Janet G. Silver. (Illus.). 270p. 1988. 45.00 (ISBN 0-500-23520-1). Thames Hudson.

Unfolding Daniel. R. A. Anderson. LC 75-16526. (Dimension Ser.). 192p. 1975. pap. 6.95 (ISBN 0-8163-0180-8, 21390-0). Pacific Pr Pub Assn.

Unfolding Drama of the Bible: Eight Studies Introducing the Bible as a Whole. 3rd ed. Bernhard W. Anderson. LC 87-4588. 96p. 1988. pap. 4.95 (ISBN 0-8006-2098-4). Fortress.

Unfolding Drama: Studies in U. S. History by Herbert Aptheker. Herbert Aptheker. Ed. by Bettina Aptheker. LC 78-21025. 188p. 1979. 11.00 (ISBN 0-7178-0560-3); pap. 3.50 (ISBN 0-7178-0501-8). Intl Pubs Co.

Unfolding Meaning: A Weekend of Dialogue with David Bohm. Ed. by Donald Factor. 192p. 1987. pap. 6.95 (ISBN 0-7448-0064-1, Ark Paperbacks). Routledge Chapman & Hall.

Unfolding Misconceptions: A Study of the Arkansas State Prison System. Clyde Crosley. LC 86-21426. (Illus.). vi, 155p. (Orig.). 1986. pap. 12.95 (ISBN 0-935175-05-9). Lib Arts Pr.

Unfolding of Anarchism: Its Origins & Historical Development to the Year 1864. Max Nettlau. (Men & Movements in the History & Philosophy of Anarchism Ser.). 1978. lib. bdg. 49.95 (ISBN 0-685-06650-9). Revisionist Pr.

Unfolding of Artistic Activity: Its Basis, Processes, & Implications. Henry Schaefer-Simmern. (Illus.). 1948. 35.00x (ISBN 0-520-01141-4). U of Cal Pr.

Unfolding of the Seasons. Ralph Cohen. LC 70-82867. pap. 87.50 (ISBN 0-317-19884-X, 2023088). Bks Demand UMI.

Unfolding Plan of Redemption. Leland M. Haines. 1982. 3.50 (ISBN 0-87813-517-0). Christian Light.

Unfolding Self: Psyhosynthesis & Counseling. Molly Y. Brown. LC 83-61449. (Illus.). 170p. (Orig.). 1983. pap. 12.95 (ISBN 0-9611444-0-8). Psychosynth Pr.

Unfolding the Mind: The Unconscious in American Romanticism & Literary Theory. Jeffrey Steele. Ed. by Stephen Orgel. (Harvard Dissertations in American & English Literature Ser.). 285p. 1987. lib. bdg. 45.00 (ISBN 0-8240-0076-5). Garland Pub.

Unfolding the Petals: A New Sanskrit Grammar. David Teplitz. 1982. cancelled 44.00 (ISBN 0-8364-0908-6, Pub. by Tulsi Pub Hse). South Asia Bks.

Unfolding the Revelation. Roy A. Anderson. LC 61-10884. (Dimension Ser.). 223p. 1961. pap. 6.95 (ISBN 0-8163-0027-5, 21400-7). Pacific Pr Pub Assn.

Unfolding the Third Eye. Robert G. Chaney. (Adventures in Esoteric Learning Ser.). 48p. 1970. pap. 4.25 (ISBN 0-918936-18-7). Astara.

Unfolding Universe. Patrick Moore. (Illus.). 256p. 1982. 17.95 (ISBN 0-517-54836-4). Crown.

Unfolding Westward in Treaty & Law: Land Documents in United States History from the Appalachians to the Pacific, 1783-1934. Frederick E. Hosen. LC 87-29879. 440p. 1988. 45.00x (ISBN 0-89950-308-X). McFarland & Co.

Unforeseen. Dorothy Macardle. Repr. lib. bdg. 18.95x (ISBN 0-89190-113-2, Pub. by River City Pr). Amereon Ltd.

Unforeseen Joy: Serving a Friends Meeting As Recording Clerk. Damon D. Hickery. (Illus.). 40p. 1987. pap. text ed. 2.00x (ISBN 0-942727-16-9). NC Yrly Pubns Bd.
Unforeseen Tendencies of Democracy. E. L. Godkin. 1976. lib. bdg. 59.95 (ISBN 0-8490-2784-5). Gordon Pr.
Unforeseen Tendencies of Democracy. facsimile ed. Edwin L. Godkin. LC 76-37153. (Essay Index Reprint Ser). Repr. of 1898 ed. 20.00 (ISBN 0-8369-2500-9). Ayer Co Pubs.
Unforgettable British Weekends. Angela Lansbury. (Illus.). 148p. 1988. pap. 11.95 (ISBN 0-87052-438-0). Hippocrene Bks.
Unforgettable Fire - Awkward Instant. Michael Action, Jr. 32p. 1986. 6.95 (ISBN 0-8062-2933-0). Carlton.
Unforgettable Fire: Past, Present, & Future--the Definitive Biography of U2. Eamon Dunphy. LC 87-40607. 1988. 16.95 (ISBN 0-446-51459-4). Warner Bks.
Unforgettable Fire: Pictures Drawn by Atomic Bomb Survivors. Ed. by Japan Broadcasting Corporation. (Illus.). 1981. pap. 11.95 (ISBN 0-394-74823-9). Pantheon.
Unforgettable Fire: The Definitive Biography of U2. Eamon Dunphy. (Illus.). 336p. Date not set. pap. 9.95 (ISBN 0-446-38974-9). Warner Bks.
Unforgettable Hollywood. Nat Dallinger. LC 82-3479. (Illus.). 1982. 20.00 (ISBN 0-688-01323-6). Morrow.
Unforgettable Hollywood. Nat Dallinger. LC 83-60483. (Illus.). 256p. 1983. pap. 12.95 (ISBN 0-688-02475-0, Quill NY). Morrow.
Unforgettable Months & Years. Vo-Nguyen-Giap. (Cornell University, Southeast Asia Program, Data Paper: No. 99). pap. 31.00 (ISBN 0-317-29631-0, 2021847). Bks Demand UMI.
Unforgettable Musical Memories. Ed. by Reader's Digest Editors. (Illus.). 252p. 1984. Lie-flat spiral bdg. 26.95 (ISBN 0-89577-178-0, Pub. by RD Assn). Random.
Unforgettable Season. G. H. Fleming. LC 80-18299. (Illus.). 336p. 1981. 16.95 (ISBN 0-03-056221-X). H Holt & Co.
Unforgettable Sounds. Elbert D. Godfrey. (Mental Therapy Ser.). 128p. 1981. 6.50 (ISBN 0-89962-030-2). Todd & Honeywell.
Unforgettable Strategies for Success. George R. Allen. 96p. (Orig.). 1987. pap. 6.95 (ISBN 0-933554-50-8). Tech Ed Pub.
Unforgettable Ulendo. Xana Hampson. 1986. 37.00x (ISBN 0-86332-082-1, Pub. by Book Guild Ltd). State Mutual Bk.
Unforgiven. Alan LeMay. 1987. pap. 3.50 (ISBN 0-515-09061-1). Jove Pubns.
Unforgiven. Patricia J. MacDonald. (Orig.). 1981. pap. 3.95 (ISBN 0-440-19123-8). Dell.
Unforgiveness. Kenneth Hagin, Jr. 1983. pap. 0.50mini bk (ISBN 0-89276-716-2). Hagin Ministries.
Unforgiving Minutes. Mary M. Pulver. 336p. 1988. 17.95x (ISBN 0-312-01528-3). St Martin.
Unforgotten Things. (Illus.). 6.95 (ISBN 0-686-46782-5). Inspiration Conn.
Unforgotten Years (Whitman) Logan P. Smith. 296p. Repr. of 1939 ed. lib. bdg. 25.00 (ISBN 0-89987-947-0). Darby Bks.
Unforsaken Hero. Sterling E. Lanier. pap. 2.95 (ISBN 0-345-30228-1). Ballantine.
Unfortunate Colonel Despard & Other Studies. Charles W. Oman. 1922. 22.50 (ISBN 0-8337-2626-9). B Franklin.
Unfortunate Duke: Henry Pelham, Fifth Duke of Newcastle, 1811-1864. F. Darrell Munsell. LC 84-20882. 352p. 1985. text ed. 30.00x (ISBN 0-8262-0456-2). U of Mo Pr.
Unfortunate Fall: Theodicy & the Moral Imagination of Andrew Marvell. John Klause. LC 83-13521. xi, 208p. 1984. 25.00 (ISBN 0-208-02026-8, Archon Bks). Shoe String.
Unfortunate Mother's Advice...(with) Additional Letter on the Management...of Infant Children. Sarah Pennington. (Marriage, Sex & the Family in England Ser.). 136p. 1985. lib. bdg. 25.00 (ISBN 0-8240-5932-8). Garland Pub.
Unfortunate Traveller & Other Stories. Thomas Nashe. Ed. by J. B. Steane. (English Library). 512p. 1972. pap. 6.95 (ISBN 0-14-043067-9). Penguin.
Unfortunate Traveller or the Life of Jack Wilton: With an Essay on the Life & Writings of Thomas Nash by Edmund Gosse. Thomas Nash. 216p. 1986. Repr. of 1892 ed. lib. bdg. 75.00 (ISBN 0-89984-780-3). Century Bookbindery.
Unfortunate Woman. Barry Gifford. LC 83-82560. 192p. (Orig.). 1984. 14.95 (ISBN 0-916870-73-1, Donald S. Ellis); pap. 7.95 (ISBN 0-916870-74-X). Creative Arts Bk.
Unfortunately Harriet. Rosemary Wells. LC 76-181786. (Illus.). 32p. (ps-3). 1972. PLB 4.58 (ISBN 0-8037-9169-0). Dial Bks Young.
Unfortunately, She Was Also Wired for Sound. G. B. Trudeau. (Illus.). 1982. pap. 5.25 (ISBN 0-03-061731-6). H Holt & Co.
Unfought War of Nineteen Sixty-Two. J. R. Saigal. 180p. 1979. 11.95. Asia Bk Corp.
Unfractioned Idiom: Hart Crane & Modernism. Maria F. Bennett. LC 86-21084. (American University Studies XIX-General Literature: Vol. 3). 244p. 1987. text ed. 35.40 (ISBN 0-8204-0355-5). P Lang Pubs.
Unframed Originals: Recollections. W S Merwin. LC 81-70063. 256p. 1983. 14.95 (ISBN 0-689-11284-X); pap. 8.95 (ISBN 0-689-11424-9). Atheneum.
Unfree Associations. Michael Covino. 64p. (Orig.). 1982. pap. 3.95. BPW & P.
Unfree Labor: American Slavery & Russian Serfdom. Peter Kolchin. LC 86-14909. (Illus.). 528p. 1987. text ed. 27.00x (ISBN 0-674-92097-X, Belknap Pr). Harvard U Pr.
Unfriendly Book. Charlotte Zolotow. LC 74-19581. (Ursula Nordstrom Bks.). (Illus.). (ps-3). 1975. PLB 10.89 (ISBN 0-06-026931-6). HarpJ.
Unfriendly Governor. Anthony A. Lee. (Stories About 'Abdu'l-Baha Ser.). (Illus.). 24p. (gr. k-5). 1980. pap. 2.50 (ISBN 0-933770-02-2). Kalimat.
Unfriendly Natives of the Pacific. Glen Wright. Ed. by Carol Murphy. (Illus.). (gr. 3-6). 1981. PLB 6.95 (ISBN 0-89868-116-2, Read Res); pap. text ed. 4.95 (ISBN 0-89868-123-5, Read Res). ARO Pub.
Unfriendly Skies: An Aviation Watergate. 2nd, rev. ed. Ed. by Rodney Stich. LC 79-52680. 1980. pap. 15.95 (ISBN 0-932438-02-4). Diablo West Pr.
Unfulfilled Promise: Collective Bargaining in California Agriculture. Philip L. Martin et al. (Special Study on Agriculture Science & Policy Ser.: No. 2). 217p. 1988. 21.50 (ISBN 0-8133-7628-9). Westview.
Unfulfilled Promise of Synthetic Fuels: Technological Failure, Policy Immobilism, or Commercial Illusion. Ed. by Ernest J. Yanarella & William C. Green. LC 87-247. (Contributions in Political Science Ser.: No. 179). 243p. 1987. lib. bdg. 39.95 (ISBN 0-313-25666-7, YUN/). Greenwood.
Unfurling of Entity: Metaphor in Poetic Theory. Aileen Ward. Ed. by Stephen Orgel. (Harvard Dissertations in American & English Literature Ser.). 540p. 1987. lib. bdg. 80.00 (ISBN 0-8240-0081-1). Garland Pub.
Ungainsayable Presence. Ed. by Centaur Books Staff. 1985. 25.00x (ISBN 0-900000-89-9, Pub. by Centaur Bks). State Mutual Bk.
Ungame Cards-Complete. 6.00 set (ISBN 0-317-15788-4). Chr Marriage.
Ungaretti. F. J. Jones. 229p. 1977. 18.00x (ISBN 0-85224-299-9, Pub. by Edinburgh U Pr Scotland). Columbia U Pr.
Ungarische Grammatik. Jozsef Tompa. (Janua Linguarum, Series Practica: No. 96). 1968. 49.60x (ISBN 90-2790-674-2). Mouton.
Unger's Bible Dictionary. Merrill F. Unger. 1961. 23.95 (ISBN 0-8024-9035-2). Moody.
Unger's Bible Handbook. Merrill F. Unger. LC 66-16224. 1966. 10.95 (ISBN 0-8024-9039-5). Moody.
Unger's Bible Handbook see Manual Biblico de Unger.
Unger's Concise Bible Dictionary: With Complete Pronunciation Guide to Bible Names by W. Murray Severance. Merrill F. Unger. 296p. 1985. pap. 9.95 (ISBN 0-8010-9208-6). Baker Bk.
Unger's Survey of the Bible. Merrill F. Unger. LC 81-82675. 432p. 1981. pap. 12.95 (ISBN 0-89081-298-5). Harvest Hse.
Unglueckselige Atalanta. J. L. Rost. 560p. Repr. of 1717 ed. 60.00 (ISBN 0-384-52101-0). Johnson Repr.
Ungovernable City: The Politics of Urban Problems & Policy Making. Douglas Yates. 1977. pap. 8.95x (ISBN 0-262-74013-3). MIT Pr.
Ungovernable People: The English & Their Law in the Seventeenth & Eighteenth Centuries. Ed. by John Brewer & John Styles. 1980. 35.00x (ISBN 0-8135-0891-6); pap. 14.00 (ISBN 0-8135-0976-9). Rutgers U Pr.
Ungovernable Rock: A History of the Anglo-Corsian Kingdom & Its Role in Britain's Mediterranean Strategy During the Revolutionary War. Desmond Gregory. LC 83-49345. (Illus.). 216p. 1985. 28.50 (ISBN 0-8386-3225-4). Fairleigh Dickinson.
Ungrateful Governess. Mary Balogh. 1988. pap. 2.95 (ISBN 0-451-15727-3, Sig). NAL.
Ungrund und Mitwissenschaft: Das Problem der Freiheit in der Spaetphilosophie Schellings. Hideki Mine. (European University Studies: No. 20, Vol. 119). 152p. (Ger.). 1983. 19.45 (ISBN 3-8204-7801-9). P Lang Pubs.
Unguarded Frontier: A History of American-Canadian Relations. Edgar W. McInnis. LC 72-102518. 1970. Repr. of 1942 ed. 13.50x (ISBN 0-8462-1286-2). Russell.
Unguarded Moment. Sara Craven. (Harlequin Presents Ser.). 1982. pap. 1.75 (ISBN 0-373-10551-7). Harlequin Bks.
Unguarded Moment. L. F. James. 1977. pap. 1.50 (ISBN 0-8439-0438-0, Leisure Bks). Leisure NY.
Unhallowed Ground: A Young Boy's Search for His Father & Brother. Paul Guernsey. Ed. by Maria D. Guarnaschelli. LC 86-8430. 356p. 1986. 16.95 (ISBN 0-688-06366-7). Morrow.
Unhappy Consciousness: The Poetic Plight of Samuel Beckett. Eugene F. Kaelin. 348p. 1982. 48.00 (ISBN 90-277-1313-8, Pub. by Reidel Holland). Kluwer Academic.
Unhappy Families: Clinical & Research Perspectives on Family Violence. E. Newberger & R. Bourne. 192p. 1985. pap. 18.50 (ISBN 0-88416-504-3). PSG Pub Co.
Unhappy Hippopotamus. Nancy Moore & Edward Leight. (Illus.). (ps-3). 12.95 (ISBN 0-8149-0368-1). Vanguard.
Unhappy India. rev. 2nd enl. ed. Lala Lajpat Rai. LC 72-171642. Repr. of 1928 ed. 36.45 (ISBN 0-404-03803-4). AMS Pr.
Unhappy King. Hannah Gruenbaum. (Illus.). (ps-3). 1.50 (ISBN 0-685-86208-9). Feldheim.
Unhappy Loves of Men of Genius: Gibbon, Johnson, Goethe, Mozart & Irving. Thomas Hitchcock. 1979. Repr. of 1892 ed. lib. bdg. 25.00 (ISBN 0-8492-5322-5). R West.
Unhappy Medium: Spirtualism & the Life of Margaret Fox. Earl W. Fornell. LC 64-10317. pap. 55.00 (ISBN 0-317-10609-0, 2000824). Bks Demand UMI.
Unhealed Wounds: France & the Klaus Barbie Affair. Erna Paris. LC 86-218. 256p. 1986. Repr. of 1985 ed. 27.50 (ISBN 0-394-55390-X). Grove.
Unhealthful Air. Elliott Baker. 1988. 16.95 (ISBN 0-670-81750-3). Viking.
Unhealthiness of London & the Necessity of Remedial Measures. Hector Gavin. Ed. by Lynn H. Lees & Andrew Lees. LC 84-48271. (Rise of Urban Britain Ser.). 164p. 1985. 33.00 (ISBN 0-8240-6273-6). Garland Pub.
Unheard Cry for Meaning. Victor E. Frankl. 1979. pap. 8.95 (ISBN 0-671-24736-0, Touchstone Bks). S&S.
Unheard Cry for Meaning. Viktor Frankl. 1985. pap. 3.95 (ISBN 0-671-54163-3). WSP.
Unheard Melodies: Narrative Film Music. Claudia Gorbman. LC 86-45941. (Illus.). 200p. 1987. 25.00x (ISBN 0-253-33987-1); pap. 9.95x (ISBN 0-253-20436-4). Ind U Pr.
Unheard Voices: Labor & Economic Policy in a Competitive World. Ray Marshall. LC 83-46084. 288p. 1987. 19.95 (ISBN 0-465-08869-4). Basic.
Unheard Voices: Labor & Economic Policy in a Competitive World. Ray Marshall. LC 83-46084. 353p. 1988. pap. 9.95 (ISBN 0-465-08870-8, PL 5227). Basic.
Unheard Words: Women & Literature in Africa, Asia & Latin America. Ed. by Mineke Schipper. Tr. by Barbara P. Fasting from DUTCH. (Illus.). 288p. 1985. pap. 8.95 (ISBN 0-8052-8243-2, Pub. by Allison & Busby England). Schocken.
Unheavenly City Revisited: A Revision of the Unheavenly City. Edward C. Banfield. 1974. pap. text ed. write for info. (ISBN 0-673-39419-0). Scott F.
Unheeded Cry. Abraham Fuchs. (ArtScroll History Ser.). (Illus.). 288p. 1984. 14.95 (ISBN 0-89906-468-X); pap. 11.95 (ISBN 0-89906-469-8). Mesorah Pubns.
Unheeded Teachings of Christ or Christ Rejected. Emanuel M. Josephson. 1979. write for info. (ISBN 0-685-96472-8). Revisionist Pr.
Unheeded Teachings of Jesus Christ or Christ Rejected: The Strangest Story Never Told. Emanuel Josephson. LC 59-15870. (Blacked-Out History Ser.). (Illus.). 96p. 1959. 3.50 (ISBN 0-686-32441-2); pap. 3.00 (ISBN 0-686-32442-0). A-albionic Res.
Unheeded Teachings of Jesus: Christ Rejected. Emanuel M. Josephson. (Illus.). 50.00 (ISBN 0-685-07976-7). Chedney.
Unheeded Warning. Manes Sperber. (All Our Yesterday's Trilogy Ser.: Vol. 2). 1988. 32.50 (ISBN 0-8419-1032-4); pap. 17.50 (ISBN 0-8419-1086-3). Holmes & Meier.
Unheralded Majority: Contemporary Women As Mothers. Lydia N. O'Donnell. LC 83-49530. 192p. 1984. 27.00x (ISBN 0-669-08274-0). Lexington Bks.
Unheralded Triumph: City Government in America, 1870-1900. Jon C. Teaford. LC 83-12082. 416p. 1984. pap. text ed. 14.95x (ISBN 0-8018-3063-X). Johns Hopkins.
Unheroic Hero in the Novels of Stendahl, Balzac & Flaubert. Raymond Giraud. 1969. lib. bdg. 19.00x (ISBN 0-374-93154-2, Octagon). Hippocrene Bks.
Unheroic Muse. Barriss Mills. 1978. 20.00 (ISBN 0-686-59681-1); pap. 8.00 (ISBN 0-686-59682-X). Elizabeth Pr.
Unholy. Anderson. 1988. pap. 3.50 (ISBN 0-312-90976-4). St Martin.
Unholy. Michael F. Anderson. 224p. 1987. 15.95 (ISBN 0-312-00699-3). St Martin.
Unholy Alliance. Serita D. Stevens. (gr. 5 up). 1988. pap. 2.50 (ISBN 0-449-70232-4, Juniper). Fawcett.
Unholy Alliances: New Fiction by Women. Ed. by Louise Rafkin. 160p. (Orig.). 1988. 21.95 (ISBN 0-939416-14-X); pap. 9.95 (ISBN 0-939416-15-8). Cleis Pr.
Unholy Bible: Blake, Jung & the Collective Unconscious. June Singer. LC 85-22139. (Illus.). 272p. (Orig.). 1986. 24.95 (ISBN 0-938434-24-1); pap. 12.95 (ISBN 0-938434-25-X). Sigo Pr.
Unholy Child. Catherine Breslin. 1985. pap. 4.50 (ISBN 0-451-13844-9, AE2378, Sig). NAL.
Unholy Communion. Adrian Savage. 256p. (Orig.). Date not set. pap. 3.50 (ISBN 0-671-64743-1). PB.
Unholy Devotion: Why Cults Lure Christians. Harold L. Bussell. 160p. 1983. pap. 6.95 (ISBN 0-310-37251-8, 12388P). Zondervan.
Unholy Dying. R. T. Campbell. 128p. 1985. pap. 4.95 (ISBN 0-486-24977-8). Dover.
Unholy Goddess. Baker Stein. (Orig.). 1981. pap. 2.95 (ISBN 0-89083-846-1). Zebra.
Unholy Loves. Joyce Carol Oates. 320p. 1981. pap. 2.95 (ISBN 0-449-24457-1, Crest). Fawcett.
Unholy Loves. Joyce Carol Oates. LC 79-64396. 1979. 17.95 (ISBN 0-8149-0813-6). Vanguard.
Unholy Matrimony. John Dillman. 288p. 1988. pap. 3.95 (ISBN 0-317-67136-7). Berkley Pub.
Unholy Matrimony. Liz Hodgkinson. 1988. 49.00x (Pub. by Harrap Ltd England). State Mutual Bk.
Unholy Matrimony: A True Story of Murder & Obsession. John Dillmann. (Illus.). 240p. 1986. 17.95 (ISBN 0-02-531680-X). Macmillan.
Unholy Moses. William DeAndrea. Ed. by Jim Connor. 192p. 1988. pap. 3.50 (ISBN 0-7701-0840-7). PaperJacks US.
Unholy Pleasure: The Idea of Social Class. P. N. Furbank. 1987. pap. 7.95 (ISBN 0-19-285147-0). Oxford U Pr.
Unholy Smile. Gregory A. Douglas. 1981. pap. 2.50 (ISBN 0-89083-796-1). Zebra.
Unholy Spirits: Occultism & New Age Humanism. Gary North. write for info. Am Bur Eco Res.
Unholy Terror: The Sikhs & International Terrorism. Ian Mulgrew. 256p. 1988. 24.95 (ISBN 1-55013-052-8, Pub. by Key Porter Canada). U of Toronto Pr.
Unholy Toledo. Harry R. Illman. (Illus.). 1986. 14.95 (ISBN 0-317-56484-6). Polemic Pr Pubns.
Unholy Trade. Richard Findlater. 1978. Repr. of 1952 ed. lib. bdg. 25.00 (ISBN 0-8495-1623-4). Arden Lib.
Unholy Tricks. rev. ed. Terence Reese & David Bird. 160p. 1988. pap. 13.95 (ISBN 0-575-04263-X, Pub. by Gollancz England). David & Charles.
Unholy Warfare. Ed. by David Martin & Peter Mullen. 224p. 1983. pap. 9.95 (ISBN 0-631-13454-9). Basil Blackwell.
Unholy Writ. David Williams. LC 83-63284. 1984. pap. 3.95 (ISBN 0-89296-089-2). Mysterious Pr.
Unhurried Chase That Ended at L'Abri. Betty Carlson. LC 83-62688. 158p. 1984. pap. 5.95 (ISBN 0-89107-304-3). Good News.
Unhurried View of Copyright. Benjamin Kaplan. LC 67-13539. (James S. Carpentier Lectures, 1966). pap. 39.50 (2055780). Bks Demand UMI.
Uni- the New International Language. Elisabeth Wainscott. (Illus.). 346p. 1974. 10.95 (ISBN 0-912904-00-3); pap. 5.95 (ISBN 0-912904-01-1). Uniline Div.
Unichtozhenie Prioroda Obostrenie Ekologicheskogo Krizisa V SSSR see Destruction of Nature in the Soviet Union.
Unicode, ein Verfahren Zur Optimierung der Begrifflichen Gehirnleistung. David Szekely. (Interdisciplinary Systems Research Ser.: No. 66). 400p. (Ger.). 1980. pap. 51.95x (ISBN 0-8176-1069-3). Birkhauser.
Unicon II. David J. Schlink. 1983. Repr. of 1974 ed. 3.50 (ISBN 0-912327-00-6). Unicon Ent.
Unicorn. Sri Donato. Ed. by Morningland Publications, Inc. Staff. (Illus.). 207p. (Orig.). 1981. pap. 10.00 (ISBN 0-935146-16-4). Morningland.
Unicorn. N. Hathaway. 192p. 1984. 12.98 (ISBN 0-517-44902-1, Avenel). Outlet Bk Co.
Unicorn. Dorothea Manusch. 160p. 1984. 8.50 (ISBN 0-682-40153-6). Exposition-Phoenix.
Unicorn. Iris Murdoch. 312p. 1987. pap. 6.95 (ISBN 0-14-002476-X). Penguin.
Unicorn. Martin Walser. Tr. by B. Ellis-Jones from Ger. 283p. 1983. pap. 7.95 (ISBN 0-7145-0886-1, Dist. by Kampmann & Co). M Boyars Pubs.
Unicorn & Dragon. Lynn Abbey. LC 86-90768. (Byron Preiss Bk.). (Illus.). 240p. 1987. pap. 5.95 (ISBN 0-380-75061-9). Avon.
Unicorn & Dragon, Vol. 1. Lynn Abbey. 240p. 1988. pap. 3.50 (ISBN 0-380-75567-X). Avon.
Unicorn & Other Poems. Anne M. Lindbergh. LC 72-4548. 1972. pap. 3.95 (ISBN 0-394-71822-4, Vin). Random.
Unicorn & the Garden. Ed. by Betty Parry. LC 78-64531. (Illus.). 1978. perfect bdg. 10.00 (ISBN 0-915380-04-8). Word Works.
Unicorn & the Lake. Marianna Mayer. LC 82-71356. (Illus.). 32p. (gr. k up). 1982. 12.95 (ISBN 0-8037-9337-5, 01258-370); PLB 12.89 (ISBN 0-8037-9338-3). Dial Bks Young.
Unicorn & the Lake. Marianna Mayer. LC 81-5469. (Pied Piper Bk.). (Illus.). 32p. (gr. k up). 1987. pap. 3.95 (ISBN 0-8037-0436-4, 0383-120). Dial Bks Young.
Unicorn & the Plow. Louise Moeri. (Illus.). 32p. (gr. 2 up). 1982. 10.95 (ISBN 0-525-45116-1). Dutton.
Unicorn Caper. James W. Lampp. 1980. pap. 1.95 (ISBN 0-8439-0817-3, Leisure Bks). Leisure NY.
Unicorn Crossing. Nancy Luenn. LC 87-995. (Illus.). 64p. (gr. 2-5). 1987. 11.95 (ISBN 0-689-31384-5, Atheneum Childrens Bks). Macmillan.
Unicorn Crossing. Nancy Luenn. (gr. 2-9). Date not set. pap. 2.95. Troll Assocs.
Unicorn Dancer. R. A. Salsitz. 1986. pap. 2.95 (ISBN 0-451-14393-0, Sig). NAL.
Unicorn Dilemma. John Lee. 384p. 1988. pap. 3.95 (ISBN 0-8125-4402-1, Dist. by St Martin's Pr & Warner Pub Servs). Tor Bks.
Unicorn Expedition: And Other Fantastic Tales of India. Satyajit Ray. (Illus.). 208p. 1987. 16.95 (ISBN 0-525-24544-8). Dutton.

Unicorn from the Stars see Where There Is Nothing.

Unicorn Journal, Nos. 2-4. Ed. by Teo Savory. (Illus.). 125p. 1972. pap. 3.00 ea. (ISBN 0-87775-019-X). Unicorn Pr.

Unicorn Magic. Ida M. McIntyre. LC 72-1922. (Garrard Venture Ser.). (Illus.). (gr. 1-3). 1972. PLB 6.89 (ISBN 0-8116-6965-3). Garrard.

Unicorn Moon. Gale Copper. LC 84-1634. (Illus.). 32p. (ps up). 1984. 11.95 (ISBN 0-525-44148-4). Dutton.

Unicorn Mountain. Michael Bishop. 352p. 1988. 18.45 (ISBN 0-87795-953-6, Arbor Hse). Morrow.

Unicorn Notebook. Green. LC 81-10670. 96p. pap. 5.95 (ISBN 0-89471-146-6); 15.90 (ISBN 0-89471-147-4). Running Pr.

Unicorn Notebook: An Illustrated Book with Space for Notes. Illus. by Michael Green. (Illus.). 96p. (gr. 5 up). 1985. 6.98 (ISBN 0-89471-395-7, Pub. by Courage Bks). Running Pr.

Unicorn Postcard Book. 64p. 1986. pap. 6.95 (ISBN 0-89471-423-6). Running Pr.

Unicorn Quest. John Lee. 384p. (Orig.). 1986. pap. 2.95 (ISBN 0-8125-4400-5, Dist. by Warner Pub Services & St. Martin's Press). Tor Bks.

Unicorn Rampant. Nigel Tranter. 1984. 14.95 (ISBN 0-340-33720-6). Beaufort Bks NY.

Unicorn Riders of the Orb. Michael G. Moore. (Illus.). 227p. 1986. pap. 2.95 (ISBN 0-9613282-1-5). MGM Bks.

Unicorn Treasury: Stories, Poems & Unicorn Lore. Compiled by Bruce Coville. (Illus.). 176p. (gr. 3 up). 1988. pap. 14.95 (ISBN 0-385-24000-7). Doubleday.

Unicorn Variations. Roger Zelazny. 256p. 1987. pap. 3.50 (ISBN 0-380-70287-8). Avon.

Unicorn Was There. Elizabeth Pool. LC 81-4747. (Illus.). 64p. 1981. pap. 5.95 (ISBN 0-87233-061-3). Bauhan.

Unicornis: On the History & Truth of the Unicorn. 2nd ed. Michael Green. (Illus.). 112p. (YA) (gr. 9 up). 1988. 19.95 (ISBN 0-89471-570-4); pap. 12.95 (ISBN 0-89471-550-X). Running Pr.

Unicornis: On the History & Truth of the Unicorn. Annotations by Michael Green. Tr. by James O'Donnell from Latin. LC 83-3168. (Illus.). 64p. (Orig.). 1983. 19.95; pap. 12.95. Running Pr.

Unicorns! Jack Dann. (Magic Tales Ser.). 320p. 1985. pap. 2.95 (ISBN 0-441-85444-3) (ISBN 0-317-31898-5). Ace Bks.

Unicorns. James G. Huneker. LC 72-6581. Repr. of 1917 ed. 22.50 (ISBN 0-404-10529-7). AMS Pr.

Unicorns & Dreams. Wanda W. Waller. Ed. by Ron Lopez. (Illus.). 39p. (Orig.). (gr. k-6). 1985. pap. 4.95 (ISBN 0-930825-00-4). Lola Library.

Unicorns Are Real: A Right-Brained Approach to Learning. Barbara M. Vitale. LC 82-83064. (Right Brain-Whole Brain Learning Ser.). (Illus.). 120p. (Orig.). (gr. k-8). 1982. pap. 10.95 (ISBN 0-915190-35-4). Jalmar Pr.

Unicorns Are Real: A Right-Brained Approach to Learning. Barbara M. Vitale. 240p. 1986. pap. 3.95 (ISBN 0-446-32340-3). Warner Bks.

Unicorns for Everyone: Large Type. Marilyn R. Riddle. (Illus.). 24p. (Orig.). 1980. pap. 3.00 (ISBN 0-9603748-1-7). Sandpiper OR.

Unicorns I Have Known. Robert Vavra. LC 83-61566. (Illus.). 200p. 1983. 39.95 (ISBN 0-688-02203-0). Morrow.

Unicorns in Soft Sculpture, Bk. 1. Bonnie Arthur. (Illus., Orig.). 1982. pap. 3.50 (ISBN 0-941284-14-X). Deco Design Studio.

Unicorns in the Rain. Barbara Cohen. 176p. (gr. 7 up). 1988. pap. 2.95 (ISBN 0-02-042210-5, Collier). Macmillan.

Unicorns of Kilimanjaro. Robert Vavra. Ed. by Andrew Ambraziejus. 200p. 1988. text ed. 39.95 (ISBN 0-688-06850-2). Morrow.

Unicorn's Secret: A Murder in the Age of Aquarius. Steven Levy. (Illus.). 384p. 1988. 18.95 (ISBN 0-13-937830-8). Prentice Hall Pr.

Unicornucopia: The Capture, Care & Feeding of Your Own Pet Unicorn. O. Keith Hallam, Jr. LC 83-61860. (Illus.). 85p. (Orig.). 1983. pap. 7.95 (ISBN 0-913679-00-3). Promotions Ltd.

Unicycles & Artistic Bicycles Illustrated. Jack Wiley. LC 86-61015. (Illus.). 168p. (YA) (gr. 7 up). 1986. pap. 26.95 (ISBN 0-913999-15-6). Solipaz Pub Co.

Unideal Principles of Editing Old English Verse. E. G. Stanley. (Sir Israel Gollancz Memorial Lectures in Old English). 1986. pap. 5.50 (ISBN 0-85672-515-3, Pub. by British Acad). Longwood Pub Group.

Unidentified Flying Objects. Isaac Asimov. LC 87-42604. (Isaac Asimov's Library of the Universe). (Illus.). (gr. 2-3). 1988. PLB 10.95 (ISBN 1-55532-355-3). Stevens Inc.

Unidentified Flying Objects. Jim Collins. LC 77-13040. (Great Unsolved Mysteries Ser.). (Illus.). 48p. (gr. 4-5). 1977. PLB 15.33 (ISBN 0-8172-1065-2). Raintree Pubs.

Unidentified Flying Objects. Jim Collins. LC 77-13040. (Great Unsolved Mysteries Ser.). (Illus.). 48p. (gr. 4up). 1983. pap. 9.27 (ISBN 0-8172-2169-7). Raintree Pubs.

Unidentified Flying Reject. R. Eugene Jackson. 56p. 1982. pap. 2.50 (ISBN 0-88680-201-6); royalty 25.00 (ISBN 0-317-03576-2). I E Clark.

Unidentified Flying Riddles. Joanne Bernstein & Paul Cohen. Ed. by Ann Fay. LC 83-17097. (Illus.). 32p. (gr. 1-5). 1983. PLB 7.95 (ISBN 0-8075-8329-4). A Whitman.

Unidentified Sign. Henry F. Lutz. LC 72-995. (University of California Publications in Semitic Philology: Vol. 10, No. 2). pap. 20.00 (ISBN 0-317-10202-8, 2021473). Bks Demand UMI.

Unidentified Woman. Mignon G. Eberhart. 176p. 1988. pap. 3.50 (ISBN 0-446-31461-7). Warner Bks.

Unidimensional Scaling of Social Variables: Concepts & Procedures. Raymond L. Gorden. LC 76-26443. 1977. 18.00 (ISBN 0-02-912580-4). Free Pr.

Unidirectional Wave Motion. H. Levine. (Applied Mathematics & Mechanics Ser.: Vol. 23). 502p. 1978. 89.50 (ISBN 0-444-85043-0, North-Holland). Elsevier.

Unification & Comparative Law in Theory & Practice. Ed. by C. S. Hondius. 1984. lib. bdg. 50.00 (ISBN 90-654-4173-5, Pub. by Kluwer Law Netherlands). Kluwer Academic.

Unification & Differentiation in Socialist Criminal Justice. T. Szabo. 260p. 1978. 69.00x (ISBN 0-569-08472-5, Pub. by Collets (UK)). State Mutual Bk.

Unification & Supersymmetry. R. N. Mohapatra. (Contemporary Physics Ser.). (Illus.). xiv, 328p. 1986. 34.00 (ISBN 0-387-96285-9). Springer-Verlag.

Unification Church in America: Sects & Cults in America. Michael J. Mickler. LC 83-48225. (Bibliographical Guides Ser.). 130p. 1986. lib. bdg. 19.00 (ISBN 0-8240-9040-3). Garland Pub.

Unification Church in the United States: A Bibliography. Michael J. Mickler. Ed. by J. Gordon Melton. LC 83-48225. (Sects & Cults in America, Biographica, Guides Ser.: Vol. 9 Ref. Library of Social Science). 1987. lib. bdg. 30.00 (ISBN 0-317-58486-3). Garland Pub.

Unification Church Policy on South Africa. Dibinga wa Said. (Christian Churches Policies on South Africa Ser.). 14p. (Orig.). 1986. pap. write for info. (ISBN 0-943324-26-2). Omenana.

Unification of Elementary Forces & Gauge Theories: Proceedings. Ed. by D. B. Cline & F. E. Mills. 792p. 1980. lib. bdg. 83.00 (ISBN 0-906346-00-2). Harwood Academic.

Unification of Finite Element Methods. Ed. by H. Kardestuncer. (Mathematics Studies: Vol. 94). 344p. 1984. 48.25 (ISBN 0-444-87519-0, I-265-84, North Holland). Elsevier.

Unification of Finite Element Software Systems. Ed. by H. Kardestuncer. 240p. 1986. pap. 60.00 (ISBN 0-444-87998-6, North-Holland). Elsevier.

Unification of Fundamental Particle Interactions II. Ed. by John Ellis & Sergio Ferrara. 530p. 1983. 89.50x (ISBN 0-306-41166-0, Plenum Pr). Plenum Pub.

Unification of Germany, 1848-1871. Ed. by Otto Pflanze. LC 78-23470. (European Problem Studies). 128p. 1979. pap. 6.50 (ISBN 0-88275-803-9). Krieger.

Unification of Italy, 1859-1861, Cavour, Mazzini, or Garibaldi? Ed. by Charles F. Delzell. LC 76-15352. (European Problem Studies Ser.). 126p. 1976. pap. text ed. 6.50 (ISBN 0-88275-658-3). Krieger.

Unification of the Armed Forces. Ed. by Frank Feidel & Ernest May. (Harvard Dissertations in American History & Political Science Ser.). 442p. 1988. lib. bdg. 75.00 (ISBN 0-8240-5134-3). Garland Pub.

Unification of the Fundamental Particle Interactions. Ed. by Sergio Ferrara et al. LC 80-24447. (Ettore Majorana International Science Series, Physical Sciences: Vol. 7). 740p. 1981. 125.00x (ISBN 0-306-40575-X, Plenum Pr). Plenum Pub.

Unification Policy of South & North Korea: A Comparative Study. Hak-Joon Kim. 341p. 1984. text ed. 18.00x (ISBN 0-8248-0964-5, Pub. by Seul U Pr). UH Pr.

Unification Theology. Young O. Kim. LC 80-52872. 294p. 1980. pap. 8.95 (ISBN 0-318-11689-8). Rose Sharon Pr.

Unification Theology & Christian Thought. Young O. Kim. LC 74-32590. 302p. 1976. pap. 6.95 (ISBN 0-318-11688-X). Rose Sharon Pr.

Unification Theology & Christian Thought. Dr. Young Oon Kim. pap. 4.00 (ISBN 0-686-13407-9). Unification Church.

Unification Theology Seminar, Virgin Islands: Proceedings. Ed. by Darrol Bryant. LC 80-52594. 323p. 1980. pap. 9.95. Rose Sharon Pr.

Unification Thought. 1975. pap. 5.00 (ISBN 0-686-13405-2); Study Guide. pap. text ed. 1.50 (ISBN 0-686-13406-0). Unification Church.

Unificationism: A New Philosophy & Worldview. Sebastian A. Matczak. LC 81-86036. (Philosophical Questions Ser.: No. 11). 500p. 1982. 45.00x (ISBN 0-912116-14-5). Learned Pubns.

UNIFIED--A Course on Truth & Practical Guidance from Babaji. Roger G. Lanphear. LC 86-72570. 160p. (Orig.). 1987. pap. 7.95 (ISBN 0-87516-585-0). DeVorss.

Unified Analysis & Solutions of Heat & Mass Diffusion. M. D. Mikhailov & M. N. Ozisik. LC 83-14562. 524p. 1984. 72.00 (ISBN 0-471-89830-9, Pub. by Wiley-Interscience). Wiley.

Unified Applied Technical Physics. Roy S. Jones. 720p. 1987. pap. text ed. 49.95 (ISBN 0-8403-4273-X). Kendall-Hunt.

Unified Applied Technical Physics Lab Manual. Roy S. Jones. 280p. 1986. pap. text ed. 24.95 (ISBN 0-8403-4051-6). Kendall-Hunt.

Unified Approach to Dosage Calculation. Billie A. Wilson & Margaret T. Shannon. 192p. 1986. pap. 18.95 (ISBN 0-8385-9295-3). Appleton & Lange.

Unified Approach to the Computerization of Museum Catalogues. M. F. Porter et al. LC 78-304072. (R & D Report: No. 5338). (Illus.). 82p. (Orig.). 1976. pap. 8.25 (ISBN 0-905984-01-3, Pub. by British Lib). Longwood Pub Group.

Unified Approach to Zero-Crossings & Nonuniform Sampling for Single & Multidimensional Signals & Systems. F. A. Marvasti. (Illus.). 213p. 1987. pap. text ed. write for info. (ISBN 0-9618167-0-8). Farok Marvasti.

Unified Concepts in Applied Physics. E. Dierauf, Jr. & J. Court. 1979. write for info (ISBN 0-13-938753-6). P-H.

Unified Court System for Vermont: Full Report. National Center for State Courts Staff. 278p. 1974. manuscript 5.00 (ISBN 0-89656-015-5, R-017). Natl Ctr St Courts.

Unified Design of Reinforced Concrete Members. 2nd. ed. Benjamin Forsyth. LC 80-16123. 520p. 1982. 48.50 (ISBN 0-89874-189-0). Krieger.

Unified Development Ordinance. Michael Brough. LC 85-70182. (Illus.). 215p. (Orig.). 1985. pap. 34.95 (ISBN 0-918286-39-5). Planners Pr.

Unified Directory of Area Codes & Zip Codes, Including Canadian Area Codes, with Population Figures for All Major U. S. & Canadian Cities. LC 83-108785. 192p. (Orig.). 1982. pap. 29.95x (ISBN 0-8486-9999-8, Pub. by Unified Directories). Roth Pub Inc.

Unified English Composition. 4th ed. Gerald D. Sanders et al. LC 66-13967. 1966. text ed. 9.95x (ISBN 0-89197-458-X); wkbk (instructor's key to wkbk avail. free) 5.95x (ISBN 0-89197-459-8). Irvington.

Unified Field. Joseph A. Uphoff, Jr. LC 88-2440. 32p. Date not set. pap. text ed. 2.00 (ISBN 0-943123-06-2). Arjuna Lib Pr.

Unified Field Theories of More Than Four Dimensions Including Exact Solutions: Proceedings of the 8th Course of the International School Cosmology & Gravitation Erice, Trapani, Sicily, May 20-June 1, 1982. Ed. by V. De Sabbata & E. Schmutzer. viii, 458p. 1983. 59.00 (ISBN 9971-950-50-2). World Scientific Pub.

Unified Gas Supply System of the U. S. S. R. Ed. by L. A. Melentiev. (Soviet Technology Reviews: Section A Energy Reviews Ser.). 400p. 1985. text ed. 170.00 (ISBN 3-7186-0152-4). Harwood Academic.

Unified in Hope: Arabs & Jews Talk About Peace. Carol J. Birkland. 160p. 1987. pap. 8.95 (ISBN 0-377-00177-5). Friendship Pr.

Unified Integration. E. J. McShane. LC 82-16266. (Pure & Applied Mathematics Ser.). 1983. 71.00 (ISBN 0-12-486260-8). Acad Pr.

Unified Introduction to Linear Algebra: Models, Methods & Theory. Alan Tucker. 1988. write for info. (ISBN 0-02-421580-5). Macmillan.

Unified Methodology for Developing Systems. R. N. Charette et al. 288p. 1986. text ed. 39.95 (ISBN 0-07-010646-0). McGraw.

Unified Model of the Universe: The Geometrically Unified Field Solution. Sean Sheeter. LC 80-27648. (Unified Theory of Process: Vol. 1, No. 1). (Illus.). 170p. 1981. pap. 9.50 (ISBN 0-9605378-1-3). Process Pr.

Unified Numbering System for Metals & Alloys: And Cross Index of Chemically-Similar Specification - A Joint Activity of the Society of Automotive Engineers, American Society for Testing & Materials. American Society for Testing & Materials Staff. LC 77-89064. (American Society for Testing & Materials Ser.: No. DS-56A). pap. 72.00 (ISBN 0-317-29433-4, 2024296). Bks Demand UMI.

Unified Numbering System for Metals & Alloys: Metals & Alloys Currently Covered by UNS Numbers, July, 1974. American Society for Testing & Materials Staff. LC 75-309848. pap. 46.50 (ISBN 0-317-11264-3, 2021525). Bks Demand UMI.

Unified Numbering System for Metals & Alloys. 4th ed. 1986. casebound 90.00 (ISBN 0-89883-419-8, HS-J1086H); pap. 78.00 (HS-J1086P). Soc Auto Engineers.

Unified Planning & Budgeting in a Free Society. Herman I. Shaller. LC 76-49389. 1977. 15.00 (ISBN 0-9601104-1-0). Oakview.

Unified Reading. Fred Justus. (Early Education Ser.). 24p. (gr. 2). 1981. wkbk. 5.00 (ISBN 0-8209-0212-8, K-14). ESP.

Unified Ring: Narrative Art & the Science Fiction Novel. Frank Sadler. Ed. by Robert Scholes. LC 84-16232. (Studies in Speculative Fiction: No. 11). 134p. 1984. 37.95 (ISBN 0-8357-1598-1). UMI Res Pr.

Unified Science. Ed. by Brian F. McGuinness. 1987. lib. bdg. 84.00 (ISBN 90-277-2484-9, Pub. by Reidel Holland). Kluwer Academic.

Unified String Theories: Proceedings of the Workshop on Unifed String Theories, Santa Barbara, July 29-August 16, 1985. Ed. by M. B. Green & D. J. Gross. LC 86-1699. 620p. 1986. 86.00 (ISBN 9971-50-031-0); pap. 41.00 (ISBN 9971-50-032-9, Pub. by World Sci Singapore). World Scientific Pub.

Unified Technical Concepts. 2nd, with supplement ed. Center for Occupational Research & Development Staff. (Unified Technical Concepts Ser.). (Illus.). 520p. 1984. pap. text ed. 24.00 (ISBN 1-55502-161-1). Ctr Res & Dev.

Unified Theory & Strategies of Survey Sampling. A. Chaudhuri & J. W. Vos. (North-Holland Series in Statistics & Probability: No. 4). 414p. 1988. 100.00 (ISBN 0-444-70357-8, North-Holland). Elsevier.

Unified Theory of Estimation & Inference for Nonlinear Dynamic Models. A. Ronald Gallant & Halbert White. 176p. text ed. 49.95 (ISBN 0-631-15765-4). Basil Blackwell.

Unified Theory of Ether, Field & Matter. 3rd ed. R. B. Driscoll. 310p. 1966. pap. 10.00x (ISBN 0-9601374-1-6). R B Driscoll.

Unified Theory of Fracture. K. Jagannadham & M. J. Marcinkowski. (Materials Science Surveys Ser.: Vol. 1). 800p. 1983. text ed. 90.00x (ISBN 0-87849-523-1). Trans Tech.

Unified Theory of Nonlinear Operator & Evolution Equation with Applications. Altman. 456p. 1986. 69.75 (ISBN 0-8247-7613-5). Dekker.

Unified Theory of Syntactic Categories. Joseph E. Emonds. (Studies Generative Grammar Ser.: No. 19). 360p. 1985. 54.00 (ISBN 9-067-65091-9); pap. 26.90 (ISBN 9-067-65092-7). Foris Pubns.

Unified Theory of the Mechanical Behavior of Matter. M. J. Marcinkowski. LC 78-27799. pap. 68.80 (ISBN 0-317-28028-7, 2055722). Bks Demand UMI.

Unified Theory of the Nucleus. K. Wildermuth & Y. C. Tang. (Clustering Phenomena in Nuclei Ser.: Vol. 1). (Illus.). 390p. 1977. 49.00 (ISBN 3-528-08373-5, Pub. by Vieweg & Sohn). IPS.

Unified Thermodynamic Treatment of Heat, Mass & Momentum Exchange. Henri Soumerai. LC 86-34028. 1987. 59.50 (ISBN 0-471-81854-2). Wiley.

Unified Valence Bond Theory of Electronic Structure-Applications. N. D. Epiotis. (Lecture Notes in Chemistry: Vol. 34). 585p. 1983. pap. 48.00 (ISBN 0-387-12000-9). Springer-Verlag.

Unified View of the Macro & Micro Cosmos. Ed. by A. de Rujula. 680p. 1987. 83.00 (ISBN 9971-50-393-X); pap. 44.00 (ISBN 9971-50-394-8). World Scientific Pub.

UNIFIL: International Peacekeeping in Lebanon, 1978-1988. Bjorn Skogmo. 265p. 1989. lib. bdg. 28.50 (ISBN 1-55587-135-6). Lynne Rienner.

Uniform Administrative Code. 1985. pap. 8.65. Intl Conf Bldg Off.

Uniform Administrative Code. 1988. 8.65. Intl Conf Bldg Off.

Uniform Algebras. 2nd ed. Theodore W. Gamelin. LC 83-72339. 270p. text ed. 17.95 (ISBN 0-8284-0311-2). Chelsea Pub.

Uniform Algebras & Jensen Measures. Theodore W. Gamelin. LC 78-16213. (London Mathematical Society Lecture Note Ser.: 32). pap. 42.50 (ISBN 0-317-20600-1, 2024488). Bks Demand UMI.

Uniform Building Code. 1985. pap. 50.75; loose-leaf 58.30. Intl Conf Bldg Off.

Uniform Building Code. 1988. loose leaf 58.30; pap. 50.75. Intl Conf Bldg Off.

Uniform Building Code & Related Publications Supplement 1986. pap. 6.95. Intl Conf Bldg Off.

Uniform Building Code Application Interpretation Manual. 22.50 (ISBN 0-318-00051-2). Intl Conf Bldg Off.

Uniform Building Code Standards. 1985. pap. 70.70. Intl Conf Bldg Off.

Uniform Building Code Standards. 1988. 70.70. Intl Conf Bldg Off.

Uniform Building Security Code. LC 81-86613. (Illus.). 1985. 8.65. Intl Conf Bldg Off.

Uniform Building Security Code. 1988. 8.65. Intl Conf Bldg Off.

Uniform Burner Rating Method for Aggregate Dryers. (Information Ser.: No. 76). 1981. 6.00 (ISBN 0-317-58434-0). Natl Asphalt Pavement.

Uniform Civil Jury Instruction: 1985 Supplement. Date not set. price not set. Oregon St Bar.

Uniform Code for Building Conservation. 23.95 (ISBN 0-318-22266-3). Intl Conf Bldg Off.

Uniform Code for Solar Energy Installations. 1986 ed. 8.65 (ISBN 0-318-22265-5). Intl Conf Bldg Off.

Uniform Code for the Abatement of Dangerous Buildings. 1985. pap. 8.65. Intl Conf Bldg Off.

Uniform Code for the Abatement of Dangerous Buildings. 1988. 8.65. Intl Conf Bldg Off.

Uniform Coding for Fire Protection. National Fire Protection Association Staff. 103p. 1986. 15.50 (ISBN 0-317-63509-3, 901-86). Natl Fire Prot.

Uniform Coding for Fire Protection. (Eight Hundred & Nine Hundred Ser.). 170p. 1973. pap. 3.50 (ISBN 0-685-44144-X, 901). Natl Fire Prot.

Uniform Commercial Code, 11 vols. 3rd ed. Ronald A. Anderson. LC 81-837763. 1981. 654.50 (ISBN 0-686-14491-0); legal forms vol. 99.00 (ISBN 0-686-14492-9); pleading & practice forms 2 vols. 99.00 (ISBN 0-686-14493-7); Suppl. 1987. 57.00. Lawyers Co-Op.

Uniform Commercial Code. 700p. 1979. 11.95 (ISBN 0-87526-251-1). Gould.
Uniform Commercial Code. 2nd ed. James J. White & Robert S. Summers. (Hornbook Ser.). 1250p. 1980. 28.95. West Pub.
Uniform Commercial Code: An Operational Translation. Robert LeVine. LC 80-68569. 1980. 16.50 (ISBN 0-933718-00-4). Browning Pubns.
Uniform Commercial Code, Article 9 Reprint, 1962 Official Text with Comments: Secured Transactions; Sale of Accounts Contract Rights & Chattel Paper. 1976. pap. 1.95 (ISBN 0-685-71471-3). West Pub.
Uniform Commercial Code Bibliography. J. Mitchel Ezer & Alphonse M. Squinante. 539p. 1972. Incl. 1978 suppl. 42.00 (ISBN 0-317-30896-3, B396); Suppl. 1978 only. pap. 18.00 (ISBN 0-317-30897-1, B398); Study outline. pap. 2.48 (ISBN 0-317-30898-X, B390). Am Law Inst.
Uniform Commercial Code Case Digest & Code Volume, 21 vols. Ed. by Pike & Fischer. LC 70-126080. 1976. 700.00 (ISBN 0-317-11804-8); Suppl., 1982. 414.00; Supp., 1983. 389.00. Callaghan.
Uniform Commercial Code: Code Service, 2 vols. Ed. by Pike & Fischer & John Willis. LC 82-9735. 1982. 87.50 (ISBN 0-317-12222-3); Suppl., 1982. 65.00; Suppl., 1983. 65.00. Callaghan.
Uniform Commercial Code Commentary & Law Digest. Thomas M. Quinn. (Commercial Law Ser.). 1978. Cumulative Suppls. avail. 98.00 (ISBN 0-88262-174-2, 78-50306). Warren Gorham & Lamont.
Uniform Commercial Code Drafts: Issued by the American Law Institute & the National Conference of Commissioners on Uniform State Laws Through the 1962 Official Text with Comments, 23 vols. Elizabeth S. Kelly. 1984. Set. text ed. 1150.00x (ISBN 0-8377-1235-1). Rothman.
Uniform Commercial Code in a Nutshell. 2nd ed. Bradford Stone. LC 84-17356. (Nutshell Ser.). 516p. 1984. pap. text ed. 11.95 (ISBN 0-314-84695-6). West Pub.
Uniform Commercial Code Law Journal: 1968-1987, 19 vols. Bound set. 855.00x (ISBN 0-686-90073-1). Rothman.
Uniform Commercial Code of Kentucky. David J. Leibson & Richard H. Nowka. 1023p. 1983. 75.00x (ISBN 0-87215-622-2). Michie Co.
Uniform Commercial Code of the State of California: Annotated. Bancroft-Whitney Staff. LC 87-400267. 7p. Date not set. price not set. Bancroft Whitney Co.
Uniform Commercial Code: Official Text with Comments. 994p. 1978. write for info. West Pub.
Uniform Commercial Code Reporting: 1965-1983, 42 vols. Ed. by Pike & Fischer. 850.00 (ISBN 0-317-11803-X); Suppl., 1982. 485.00; Suppl., 1983. 545.00. Callaghan.
Uniform Commercial Code Series, 6 vols. William Hawkland. LC 82-9735. 1982. 450.00 (ISBN 0-317-12224-X). Callaghan.
Uniform Commercial Code Simplified. Jesse S. Raphael. LC 67-15469. pap. 79.10 (ISBN 0-317-09564-1, 2012370). Bks Demand UMI.
Uniform Commercial Code State Service, 3 vols. Gould Editorial Staff. 1985. Set. 45.00 (ISBN 0-87526-296-1). Gould.
Uniform Commercial Code Study Outline. 1965. pap. 2.48 (B390). Am Law Inst.
Uniform Commercial Code: 1972 Amendments to Article 9. American Law Institute Staff & National Conference of Commissioners on Uniform State Laws Staff. 304p. 1978. 3.95 (ISBN 0-686-90969-0). Am Law Inst.
Uniform Commercial Code: 1977 Amendments to Article 8. American Law Institute Staff & National Conference of Commissioners on Uniforms State Laws Staff. 249p. 1978. 3.95 (ISBN 0-686-90957-7). Am Law Inst.
Uniform Consumer Credit Code & Real Estate (1981) Kent J. Levine. Date not set. price not set. Prof Pubns & Educ.
Uniform Contract Compliance: A Working Labor Compliance Program. Lynn Goad. 148p. (Orig.). 1988. pap. 18.95 wkbk. (ISBN 0-9620455-1-9). Paige Pubs.
Uniform Credit Analysis. 244p. 1982. 78.00 (ISBN 0-318-18146-0); members 55.00 (ISBN 0-318-18147-9). Robt Morris Assocs.
Uniform Criminal Jury Instructions: 1985 Supplement. Date not set. write for info. Oregon St Bar.
Uniform Disaster Mitigation Plan. 7.80 (ISBN 0-318-00048-2). Intl Conf Bldg Off.
Uniform Distribution of Sequences. Lauwerens Kuipers & H. Niederreiter. LC 73-20497. (Pure & Applied Mathematics (Wiley) Ser.). pap. 101.00 (ISBN 0-317-08710-X, 2055524). Bks Demand UMI.
Uniform Distribution of Sequences of Integers in Residue Classes. W. Narkiewicz. (Lecture Notes in Mathematics Ser.: Vol. 1087). vii, 125p. 1984. pap. 11.00 (ISBN 0-387-13872-2). Springer-Verlag.
Uniform Fire Code. 1985. pap. 31.10; loose-leaf 35.85. Intl Conf Bldg Off.
Uniform Fire Code. 1988. loose leaf 35.85; pap. 31.10. Intl Conf Bldg Off.
Uniform Fire Code Standards. 1985. pap. 52.15. Intl Conf Bldg Off.
Uniform Fire Code Standards. 1988. 52.15. Intl Conf Bldg Off.
Uniform Housing Code. 1985. pap. 8.65. Intl Conf Bldg Off.
Uniform Housing Code. 1988. 8.65. Intl Conf Bldg Off.
Uniform Insignia of the United States Military Forces. Jack L. Britton. LC 80-83871. (Illus.). 1980. 14.95 (ISBN 0-912958-14-6); pap. 8.95 (ISBN 0-912958-06-5). MCN Pr.
Uniform Land Transactions Act, Uniform Simplification of Land Transfers Act, Uniform Condominium Act: 1877 Official Text with Comments. 462p. 1978. pap. write for info. West Pub.
Uniform Law Cases, 1959-1970. International Institute for the Unification of Private Law. Oceana.
Uniform Law for International Sales under the Nineteen Eighty United Nations Convention. John Honnold. 580p. 1982. 52.00 (ISBN 90-654-4045-3, Pub. by Kluwer Law Netherlands); pap. 32.00 (ISBN 90-654-4056-9). Kluwer Academic.
Uniform Law Review: Combining Coverage of Uniform Law Cases & Yearbook, 1973 & Following. International Institute for the Unification of Private Law (UNIDROIT) 30.00 (ISBN 0-317-30328-7). Oceana.
Uniform Laws Annotated: Uniform Commercial Code. Master ed. write for info. West Pub.
Uniform Limit Theorems for Sums of Independent Randon Variables. Arak & Zaitsev. (STEKLO Ser.: Vol. 174). 230p. 1988. pap. text ed. 101.00. Am Math.
Uniform Marking of Fire Hydrants. (Twenty Ser.). 1974. pap. 2.00 (ISBN 0-685-58114-4, 291). Natl Fire Prot.
Uniform Mechanical Code. 1985. pap. 31.90; loose-leaf 36.75. Intl Conf Bldg Off.
Uniform Mechanical Code. 1988. loose leaf 36.75; pap. 31.90. Intl Conf Bldg Off.
Uniform Plumbing Code. 1985. pap. 35.70; loose-leaf 39.90. Intl Conf Bldg Off.
Uniform Plumbing Code. 1988. loose leaf 39.90; pap. 35.70. Intl Conf Bldg Off.
Uniform Probate Code in a Nutshell. 2nd ed. Lawrence H. Averill, Jr. (Nutshell Ser.). 455p. 1987. pap. text ed. 11.95 (ISBN 0-314-35852-8). West Pub.
Uniform Probate Code Practice Manual, 2 vols. 2nd ed. Ed. by Richard V. Wellman. LC 76-46049. (Illus.). xvi, 859p. 1977. Set. 72.00 (B194). Am Law Inst.
Uniform Product Disclosure for Roll Film Readers: AIIM MS27-1982. Association for Information & Image Management Staff. (Standards & Recommended Practices Ser.). 4p. 1982. pap. 30.00 (ISBN 0-89258-078-X, MS27). Assn Inform & Image Mgmt.
Uniform Rules for Collections. Bernard Wheble & Hon Fib. 1985. 20.00x (ISBN 0-85297-088-9, Pub. by Inst of Bankers). State Mutual Bk.
Uniform Rules for Collections. V. Wheble. 1980. 25.00x (ISBN 0-317-20366-5, Pub. by Inst of Bankers). State Mutual Bk.
Uniform Rules of Criminal Procedure: Comparison & Analysis. 2nd ed. 223p. 1977. pap. 5.00 (ISBN 0-686-47921-1). Amer Bar Assn.
Uniform Rules of Criminal Procedure for All Courts. Russell Chapin. 66p. 1983. pap. 7.00 (ISBN 0-8447-3530-2). Am Enterprise.
Uniform Securities Agent State Law: Blue Sky. (NASD Ser.: No. 63). 1984. 35.00 (ISBN 0-88171-044-X). Insurance Achiev.
Uniform Sign Code. 1985. pap. 8.65. Intl Conf Bldg Off.
Uniform Sign Code. 1988. 8.65. Intl Conf Bldg Off.
Uniform Simplification in a Full Neighborhood of a Transition Point. Yasataka Sibuya. LC 74-11246. (Memoirs: No. 149). 106p. 1974. pap. 12.00 (ISBN 0-8218-1849-X, MEMO-149). Am Math.
Uniform Spaces. John R. Isbell. LC 64-16541. (Mathematical Surveys Ser.: No. 12). 175p. 1964. 27.00 (ISBN 0-8218-1512-1, SURV-12). Am Math.
Uniform Structures on Topological Groups & Their Quotients. W. Roelcke & S. Dierolf. (Illus.). 352p. 1982. text ed. 62.95x (ISBN 0-07-053412-8). McGraw.
Uniform System for Accounts for Wastewater Utilities ('70) (Manual of Practice Ser.: No. 10). 73p. 1970. pap. 11.00 (ISBN 0-943244-10-2, M0011). Water Pollution.
Uniform System of Accounts & Expense Dictionary for Small Hotels, Motels, & Motor Hotels. Fourth ed. Ed. by George Glazer. (Illus.). 1987. text ed. 29.95 (ISBN 0-86612-030-0). Educ Inst Am Hotel.
Uniform System of Accounts for Restaurants. Laventhol & Horwath Staff. 160p. 1983. pap. 14.95 (ISBN 0-317-57883-9, MG936). Natl Restaurant Assn.
Uniform System of Accounts for Restaurants. 21.95x (ISBN 0-911202-17-X). Radio City.
Uniformed Court Officer. Jack Rudman. (Career Examination Ser.: C-852). (Cloth bdg. avail. on request). pap. 12.00 (ISBN 0-8373-0852-6). Natl Learning.
Uniformitarianism in Linguistics. Craig Christy. (Studies in the History of Linguistics: 31). xiv, 139p. 1983. 22.00x (ISBN 90-272-4513-4). Benjamins North Am.
Uniformity & Diversity: Development of Classification Concepts in Double Entry Accounting. Hans P. Hain. Ed. by Richard P. Brief. LC 80-1498. (Dimensions of Accounting Theory & Practice Ser.). 1981. lib. bdg. 57.00x (ISBN 0-405-13492-4). Ayer Co Pubs.
Uniformity of Cement Strength. Ed. by Emery Farkas & Paul Klieger. LC 87-17469. (Special Technical Publications: No. 961). (Illus.). 105p. 1987. text ed. 18.00 (ISBN 0-8031-0961-X, 04-961000-07). ASTM.
Uniformity with God's Will. St. Alphonsus de Liguori. 1977. pap. 1.00 (ISBN 0-89555-019-9). TAN Bks Pubs.
Uniforms & Insignia of the German Foreign Office & Government Ministries, 1938-1945. Jill Halcomb. (Illus.). 200p. 23.95 (ISBN 0-934870-09-8). Johnson Ref Bks.
Uniforms & Nonuniforms: Communication Through Clothing. Nathan Joseph. LC 86-7677. (Contributions in Sociology Ser.: No. 61). 257p. 1986. 36.95 (ISBN 0-313-25195-9, JUN/). Greenwood.
Uniforms & Traditions of the German Army, Vol. 3. John R. Angolia & Adolf Schlicht. (Illus.). 480p. 1987. 34.95 (ISBN 0-912138-37-8). Bender Pub CA.
Uniforms, Badges & Intelligence Data, etc. of the German Force. Ed. by Factus Staff. (War Documents Ser.: No. 24). (Illus.). 64p. 1983. pap. 5.95 (ISBN 0-86663-993-4). Ide Hse.
Uniforms Commercial Code. American Law Institute Staff & National Conference of Commissioners on Uniform State Laws Staff. 994p. 1978. 9.50 (ISBN 0-686-90955-0). Am Law Inst.
Uniforms of the British Yeomanry Forces 1794-1914: Duke of Lancaster's Own Yeomanry. L. Barlow & R. J. Smith. 1986. 30.00x (ISBN 0-85936-287-6, Pub. by Spellmount Ltd Pubs). State Mutual Bk.
Uniforms of the British Yeomanry Forces 1794-1914: Royal Engineers (Volunteers) 1859-1908. L. Barlow & R. J. Smith. 1986. 30.00x (ISBN 0-9508530-0-3, Pub. by Spellmount Ltd Pubs). State Mutual Bk.
Uniforms of the British Yeomanry Forces 1794-1914: The Lovat Scouts. L. Barlow & R. J. Smith. 1986. 30.00x (ISBN 0-946771-87-1, Pub. by Spellmount Ltd Pubs). State Mutual Bk.
Uniforms of the British Yeomanry Forces 1794-1914: The North Somerset Yeomanry. L. Barlow & R. J. Smith. 1986. 25.00x (ISBN 0-85936-249-3, Pub. by Spellmount Ltd Pubs). State Mutual Bk.
Uniforms of the British Yeomanry Forces 1794-1914: The Sussex Yeomanry. L. Barlow & R. J. Smith. 1986. 25.00x (ISBN 0-85936-183-7, Pub. by Spellmount Ltd Pubs). State Mutual Bk.
Uniforms of the British Yeomanry Forces 1794-1914: The Yorkshire Hussars. L. Barlow & R. J. Smith. 1986. 25.00x (ISBN 0-85936-250-7, Pub. by Spellmount Ltd Pubs). State Mutual Bk.
Uniforms of the British Yeomanry Forces, 1794-1914: Westmoreland & Cumberland Yeomanry. L. Barlow & R. J. Smith. 1986. 25.00x (ISBN 0-85936-285-X, Pub. by Spellmount Ltd Pubs). State Mutual Bk.
Uniforms of the British Yeomanry Forces 1794-1914: Worcestershire & Warwickshire Yeomanry. L. Barlow & R. J. Smith. 1986. 30.00x (ISBN 0-317-58028-0, Pub. by Spellmount Ltd Pubs). State Mutual Bk.
Uniforms of the British Yeomanry Forces 1794-1914: Yorkshire Dragoons. L. Barlow & R. J. Smith. 1986. 29.00x (ISBN 0-946771-82-0, Pub. by Spellmount Ltd Pubs). State Mutual Bk.
Uniforms of the British Yeomanry Forces, 1794-1914: 3rd County of London. L. Barlow & R. J. Smith. 1986. 29.00x (ISBN 0-85936-286-8, Pub. by Spellmount Ltd Pubs). State Mutual Bk.
Uniforms of the Continental Army. Philip Katcher. LC 80-54450. (Illus.). 230p. 1981. 35.00 (ISBN 0-87387-036-0). Shumway.
Uniforms of the Imperial Russian Army. Boris Mollo. (Illus.). 160p. 1987. pap. 12.95 (ISBN 0-7137-1939-7, Pub. by Blandford Pr England). Sterling.
Uniforms of the Indo-China & Vietnam Wars. Leroy Thompson. (Illus.). 160p. 1984. 29.95 (ISBN 0-7137-1264-3, Pub. by Blandford Pr England). Sterling.
Uniforms of the Serbian Army Eighteen Hundred Eight to Nineteen Eighteen. Pavie Vasich. 206p. 1980. 150.00x (ISBN 0-317-61413-4, Pub. by Collets (UK)). State Mutual Bk.
Uniforms of the Soldiers of Fortune. Leroy Thompson. (Illus.). 175p. 1985. 14.95 (ISBN 0-7137-1328-3, Pub. by Blandford Pr England). Sterling.
Uniforms of the World's Great Armies. I. T. Schick. (Illus.). 256p. 9.98 (ISBN 0-8317-9073-3). Smith Pubs.
Uniforms of the World's Police: With Brief Data on Organizations, Systems, & Weapons. James Cramer. (Illus.). 216p. 1968. photocopy ed. 28.50x (ISBN 0-398-00355-6). C C Thomas.
Uniforms, Organization & History of the Panzertruppe. Roger J. Bender & Warren W. Odegard. (Illus.). 336p. 1980. 24.95 (ISBN 0-912138-18-1). Bender Pub CA.
Uniforms, Organization & History of the Waffen-SS. R. J. Bender & Hugh P. Taylor. Incl. Vol. 1. 160p. 19.95 (ISBN 0-912138-02-5); Vol. 2. 176p. 19.95 (ISBN 0-912138-03-3); Vol. 3. 176p. 19.95 (ISBN 0-912138-08-4); Vol. 4. 208p. 19.95 (ISBN 0-912138-13-0); Vol. 5. 256p. 19.95 (ISBN 0-912138-25-4). (Illus.). 1986. Bender Pub CA.
Uniforms, Organization of the Afrikakorps. 2nd ed. Roger J. Bender & Richard D. Law. (Illus.). 256p. 1986. 24.95 (ISBN 0-912138-09-2). Bender Pub CA.
Uniforms, Weapons & Equipment of the World War II G. I. Stephen W. Sylvia & Micheal J. O'Donnell. (Illus.). 224p. 1982. 25.00 (ISBN 0-943522-06-4). Moss Pubns VA.
Unifying Concept: Approaches to the Structure of Cervantes' Comedias. Edward H. Friedman. LC 81-50484. 186p. 1981. 18.00x (ISBN 0-938972-00-6). Spanish Lit Pubns.
Unifying Concepts of Leukemia: Proceedings. International Symposium on Comparative Leukemia Research, 5th, Padova-Venice, 1971. Ed. by R. M. Dutcher. (Bibliotheca Haematologica Ser.: No. 39). 1973. 150.75 (ISBN 3-8055-1383-6). S Karger.
Unifying Individual & Family Therapies. David M. Allen. LC 87-46328. (Social & Behavioral Science Ser.). 1988. text ed. 27.95x (ISBN 1-55542-078-8). Jossey-Bass.
Unifying Influence: Essays of Raynard Coe Swank. Ed. by David W. Heron. LC 80-28595. 237p. 1981. 16.50 (ISBN 0-8108-1407-2). Scarecrow.
Unifying Moment: The Psychological Philosophy of William James & Alfred North Whitehead. Craig R. Eisendrath. LC 70-135550. 1971. 24.50x (ISBN 0-674-92100-3). Harvard U Pr.
Unifying Principles of the Mind. Edward J. Bartek. 178p. (Orig.). 1969. pap. 8.95 (ISBN 0-9609866-5-0). Selene Bks.
Unifying Strategies in Virginia Woolf's Experimental Literature. A. Velicu. 120p. (Orig.). 1985. pap. text ed. 20.00x (ISBN 91-554-1655-1, Pub. by Almqvist & Wiksell). Coronet Bks.
Unilateral Measurements to Prevent Double Taxation, LXVIb. 550p. 1982. write for info. (ISBN 90-6544-007-0). Kluwer Academic.
Unilateral Nuclear Disarmament Measures. (Disarmament Study Ser.: No. 13). 5.00 (ISBN 92-1-142078-4, E.85.IX.2). UN.
Unilateral Problems in Structural Analysis. Ed. by G. Del Piero & F. Maceri. (CISM International Centre for Mechanical Sciences Ser.: Vol. 288). (Illus.). vii, 387p. pap. 34.00 (ISBN 0-387-81859-6). Springer-Verlag.
Unilateral Problems in Structural Analysis 2. Ed. by G. Del Piero & F. Maceri. (CISM Ser.: Vol. 304). (Illus.). vi, 314p. Date not set. pap. 39.39 (ISBN 0-387-82036-1). Springer-Verlag.
Unilateral Renal Function Studies: Proceedings. International Symposium on Unilateral Renal Function Studies, 1st, Montecatini Terme, May 1977 et al. Ed. by S. Giovannetti & S. Thomas. (Contributions to Nephrology Ser.: Vol. 11). (Illus.). 1978. 52.00 (ISBN 3-8055-2858-2). S Karger.
Unilateralism, Idealogy, & U. S. Foreign Policy: The United States in & out of UNESCO. Roger A. Coate. LC 87-32225. 150p. 1988. lib. bdg. 24.50x (ISBN 1-55587-088-0). Lynne Rienner.
Unilever Overseas: The Anatomy of a Multinational. David K. Fieldhouse. LC 78-20358. (Publications Ser.: No. 205). 1979. 25.00x (ISBN 0-8179-7051-7). Hoover Inst Pr.
Unimodality, Convexity & Applications. Ed. by Sudhakar Dharmadhikari & Kumar Joag-dev. (Probability & Mathematical Statistics Ser.: Vol. 27). 236p. 1988. 64.50 (ISBN 0-12-214690-5). Acad Pr.
Unimpressible Race: A Century of Educational Struggle by the Chinese in San Francisco. Victor Low. 236p. 1982. 15.50 (ISBN 0-934788-04-9); pap. 9.95 (ISBN 0-934788-03-0). E-W Pub Co.
Uninformed Choice: The Failure of the New Presidential Nominating System. Scott Keeter & Cliff Zukin. (American Political Parties & Elections Ser.). 272p. 1983. 35.00 (ISBN 0-275-91022-9, C1022). Praeger.
Uninhabited & Deserted Islands. Jon Fisher. (Illus.). 1983. pap. 7.95 (ISBN 0-317-03309-3). Loompanics.
Uninhabited House see Five Victorian Ghost Novels.
Uninsured & Underinsured Motorist Coverage, 2 vols. 2nd ed. Alan I. Widiss. 1985. Set. 200.00; Suppls. avail. pap. 90.00. Anderson Pub Co.
Uninsured Families: Problems & Solutions. Ed. by Carol Huber. 70p. (Orig.). 1988. pap. 8.00 (ISBN 0-932622-13-5). Ctr Public Rep.
Unintended Consequences of Social Action. Raymond Boudon. LC 81-21372. 240p. 1982. 27.50x (ISBN 0-312-83303-2). St Martin.
Unintended Reader: Feminism & Manon Lescaut. Naomi Segal. (Studies in French). 275p. 1986. 47.50 (ISBN 0-521-30723-6). Cambridge U Pr.

Uninterrupted Poetry: Selected Writings of Paul Eluard. Paul Eluard. Tr. by Lloyd Alexander from Fr. LC 77-22122. 1977. Repr. of 1975 ed. lib. bdg. 35.00x (ISBN 0-8371-9779-1, ELSW). Greenwood.

Uninterruptible Power Supplies. Frost & Sullivan, Inc. Staff. 270p. 1986. 2150.00 (ISBN 0-86621-754-1, E825). Frost & Sullivan.

Uninterruptible Power Supply Market. Frost & Sullivan, Inc Staff. 201p. 1986. 1725.00 (ISBN 0-86621-793-2, A1613). Frost & Sullivan.

Uninterruptible Power Systems. 1983. 15.00 (ISBN 0-318-18030-8, PE 1-1983). Natl Elec Mfrs.

Uninterruptible Power Systems & Power Line Conditioning Equipment. 131p. 1985. 1285.00x (ISBN 0-88694-635-2). Intl Res Dev.

Uninvited. John Farris. 288p. 1987. pap. 3.95 (ISBN 0-8125-1776-8, Dist. by St Martin's Pr & Warner Pub Servs). Tor Bks.

Uninvited. William W. Johnstone. (Orig.). 1982. pap. 2.95 (ISBN 0-89083-933-6). Zebra.

Uninvited. William W. Johnstone. 448p. 1988. pap. 3.95 (ISBN 0-8217-2258-1). Zebra.

Uninvited. Dorothy Macardle. 342p. 1976. Repr. of 1942 ed. lib. bdg. 20.95x (ISBN 0-89244-068-6, Pub. by Queens Hse). Amereon Ltd.

Uninvited Corpse. Michael Underwood. 224p. 1987. 15.95 (ISBN 0-312-00023-5). St Martin.

Uninvited Dilemma. Kim E. Stuart. (Human Condition Ser.). (Illus.). 173p. (Orig.). 1985. 17.95 (ISBN 0-943920-19-1); pap. 9.95 (ISBN 0-943920-17-5); Research Supplement. 9.95 (ISBN 0-943920-25-6). Metamorphous Pr.

Uninvited Ghosts. Penelope Lively. LC 84-26035. (Illus.). 128p. (gr. 4-7). 1985. 11.95 (ISBN 0-525-44165-4). Dutton.

Uninvited Guest. Frank Egan. (Illus.). 44p. (gr. 1-3). 1986. 9.95 (ISBN 0-86327-082-4, Pub. by Wolfhound Pr Ireland). Irish Bks Media.

Uninvited Guest. Barbara Kennedy. 256p. 1981. pap. 2.50 (ISBN 0-449-14421-6, GM). Fawcett.

Uninvited Guests: A Documented History of U. F. O. Sightings, Alien Encounters & Coverups. Richard Hall. 384p. 1988. pap. 14.00 (ISBN 0-943358-32-9). Aurora Press.

Union: A Guide to Federal Archives Relating to the Civil War. Kenneth W. Munden & Henry P. Beers. LC 86-8363. 721p. 1986. Repr. of 1962 ed. text ed. 25.00 (ISBN 0-911333-46-0, 100050). Natl Archives & Records.

Union & Anti-Slavery Speeches. facs. ed. Charles D. Drake. LC 77-83961. (Black Heritage Library Collection Ser). 1864. 18.00 (ISBN 0-8369-8552-4). Ayer Co Pubs.

Union & Communion. Hudson Taylor. 96p. 1971. pap. 2.95 (ISBN 0-87123-571-4, 200571). Bethany Hse.

Union & Its Retired Workers: A Case Study of the UAW. Richard Korn. (Key Issues Ser.: No. 21). 60p. 1976. pap. 3.00 (ISBN 0-87546-230-8). ILR Pr.

Union & Oneness. Sri Chinmoy. 50p. (Orig.). 1976. pap. 2.00 (ISBN 0-88497-266-6). Aum Pubns.

Union & the Black Musician: The Narrative of William Everett Samuels & Chicago Local 208. Donald Spivey. (Illus.). 158p. (Orig.). 1984. lib. bdg. 26.75 (ISBN 0-8191-3741-3); pap. text ed. 12.50 (ISBN 0-8191-3742-1). U Pr of Amer.

Union & the Coal Industry. Morton S. Baratz. LC 82-25141. (Yale Studies in Economics: Vol. 4). xvii, 170p. 1983. Repr. of 1955 ed. lib. bdg. 35.00x (ISBN 0-313-23698-4, BAUC). Greenwood.

Union & the States. Jain et al. 1972. 25.00 (ISBN 0-89684-488-9). Orient Bk Dist.

Union Army Operations in the Southwest. LC 61-18715. 140p. 1982. lib. bdg. 29.95x (ISBN 0-89370-739-2). Borgo Pr.

Union at Risk: Jacksonian Democracy, States' Rights & the Nullification Crisis. Richard E. Ellis. 256p. 1987. 32.50x (ISBN 0-19-503785-5). Oxford U Pr.

Union Bay: The Life of a City Marsh. Harry W. Higman & Earl J. Larrison. LC 51-13089. (Illus.). 325p. 1951. 15.00x (ISBN 0-295-73976-2). U of Wash Pr.

Union Bibliography of Ohio Printed State Documents, 1803-1970. The Ohio Historical Society Staff. 750p. 1973. 20.00 (ISBN 0-318-03190-6). Ohio Hist Soc.

Union Bookshelf: A Selected Civil War Bibliography. Michael Mullins & Rowena Reed. LC 82-71852. (Illus.). 100p. 1982. pap. text ed. 17.00x (ISBN 0-916107-12-4). Broadfoot.

Union Brotherhood, Union Town: The History of the Carpenters' Union of Chicago, 1863-1987. Richard Schneirov & Thomas J. Suhrbur. (Illus.). 224p. 1988. text ed. 24.95x (ISBN 0-8093-1352-9); 14.95x (ISBN 0-8093-1353-7). S Ill U Pr.

Union Busting in the Tri State: The Oklahoma, Kansas, & Missouri Metal Workers Strike of 1935. George G. Suggs. LC 86-6910. (Illus.). 296p. 1986. 22.50x (ISBN 0-8061-2012-6). U of Okla Pr.

Union Camp Papers. D. R. Wagner. 1968. pap. 2.00 (ISBN 0-912136-02-2); pap. 7.50x ea. signed ed. twenty copies. Twowindows Pr.

Union Cases: A Collector's Guide to the Art of America's First Plastics. Clifford Krainik & Carl Walvoord. (Illus.). 240p. 1988. 85.00 (Amphoto). Watson-Guptill.

Union Catalog of Audiovisual Materials: Microfiche Catalog of AV Materials in OCLC Libraries on Long Island. 1988. 5.00 (ISBN 0-938435-03-5). LI Lib Resources.

Union Catalog of Clemens Letters. Ed. by Paul Machlis. (UC Publications in Catalogs & Bibliographies: Vol. I). 1986. 55.00x (ISBN 0-520-09688-6). U of Cal Pr.

Union Catalog of Government Documents: Microfiche Catalog of Federal Documents in Libraries on Long Island. 1988. 5.00 (ISBN 0-938435-02-7). LI Lib Resources.

Union Catalogue of Arabic Books in French Libraries 1952-1983. Ed. by Georges Haddad et al. 2670p. 1984. lib. bdg. 330.00 (ISBN 3-598-10510-X). K G Saur.

Union Catalogue of the Documentary Materials on Middle East, 1965. Ed. by Institute of Asian Economic Affairs. 188p. 1965. 20.00 (ISBN 0-379-00281-7). Oceana.

Union Catalogues of Serials: Guidelines for Creation & Maintenance, with Recommended Standards for Bibliographic & Holdings Control. Jean Whiffin. LC 83-8586. (Serials Librarian Ser.: Vol. 8, No. 1). 138p. 1983. text ed. 24.95 (ISBN 0-86656-238-9, B238). Haworth Pr.

Union Cavalry in the Civil War: From Fort Sumter to Gettysburg, Vol. 1. Stephen Z. Starr. LC 78-26751. (Illus.). xiv, 522p. 1979. 35.00 (ISBN 0-8071-0484-1). La State U Pr.

Union Cavalry in the Civil War: The War in the East, from Gettysburg to Appomattox, 1863-1865, Vol. II. Stephen Z. Starr. LC 78-26751. (Illus.). xvi, 568p. 1981. 35.00 (ISBN 0-8071-0859-6). La State U Pr.

Union Cavalry in the Civil War: The War in the West, 1861-1865, Vol. III. Stephen Z. Starr. LC 78-26751. (Illus.). xx, 616p. 1985. 35.00 (ISBN 0-8071-1209-7). La State U Pr.

Union Challenge to Management Control. Neil W. Chamberlain. LC 67-19507. xx, 338p. 1967. Repr. of 1948 ed. 30.00 (ISBN 0-208-00586-2, Archon). Shoe String.

Union Contract Application & Interpretation. Charles E. Hooper. 53p. 1978. 4.50 (ISBN 0-318-13503-5). Assn U Busn & Econ Res.

Union Control of Pension Funds: Will the North Rise Again? George J. Borjas. LC 79-66581. 41p. 1979. pap. 2.00 (ISBN 0-917616-36-7). ICS Pr.

Union Cook Book. 1987. 3.00 (ISBN 0-317-55310-0). United Elec R&M.

Union Corporate Campaigns. Charles R. Perry. LC 86-82727. (Employee Relations & Collective Bargaining Ser.). (Orig.). 1987. pap. 30.00 (ISBN 0-89546-065-3). Indus Res Unit-Wharton.

Union County (New Jersey) District Court Pro Se Assistance Program. National Center for State Courts Staff. (Paul Reardon Ser.). 85p. 1981. manuscript 5.10 (PRS-018). Natl Ctr St Courts.

Union County, South Carolina, Will Abstracts 1787-1849. Brent H. Holocomb. 175p. 1987. 25.00 (ISBN 0-913363-09-X). SCMAR.

Union Dale Cemeteries, Vol. 2. Ed. by Ken McFarland. 112p. pap. text ed. 11.95 perfect bound (ISBN 0-933227-25-6). Closson Pr.

Union Dale Cemetery, Vol. I. Ed. by Ken McFarland. 109p. pap. text ed. 11.95 (ISBN 0-933227-24-8). Closson Pr.

Union Democracy & Landrum Griffin. Clyde W. Summer et al. 52p. 1986. pap. 3.00 (ISBN 0-9602244-3-2). Assn Union Demo.

Union Democracy in the Construction Trades. Ed. by Herman Benson et al. 33p. 1985. pap. 2.00 (ISBN 0-9602244-2-4). Assn Union Demo.

Union Democracy Review. 200p. ann. subscr. 7.00, 6 per year (ISBN 0-318-13505-1); institut. subscr. 10.00 (ISBN 0-318-13506-X); bound volume with index 1972-81 35.00 (ISBN 0-318-13507-8); index alone 10.00 (ISBN 0-318-13508-6). Assn Union Demo.

Union Democracy Review: 27-49; 1982-1985. 1987. 35.00 (ISBN 0-9602244-5-9). Assn Union Demo.

Union Democracy Review: 27-49; 1982-1985--Index. 1987. 10.00 (ISBN 0-9602244-6-7). Assn Union Demo.

Union Democracy: The Internal Politics of the International Typographical Union. Seymour M. Lipset et al. LC 56-6202. (Illus.). 1977. pap. text ed. 14.95 (ISBN 0-02-919210-2). Free Pr.

Union Des Provinces De L'amerique Britannique Du Nord. Joseph E. Cauchon. 1865. 14.00 (ISBN 0-384-07945-8). Johnson Repr.

Union Des Provinces De L'amerique Britannique Du Nord, (Quebec, 1865) Joseph Cauchon. (Canadiana Avant 1867: No. 6). 1968. 11.20x (ISBN 90-2796-334-7). Mouton.

Union Dues. John Sayles. 1977. pap. 7.95 (ISBN 0-316-77234-8, Atlantic-Little, Brown). Little.

Union Epidemic: A Prescription for Supervisors. Warren H. Chaney & Thomas R. Beech. LC 76-24132. 180p. 1977. 43.50 (ISBN 0-912862-28-9). Aspen Pub.

Union-Free Labor Relations: A Step-by-Step Guide to Staying Union Free. James L. Dougherty. LC 80-11777. 227p. 1980. 3 ring binder 69.00x (ISBN 0-87201-302-2). Gulf Pub.

Union-Free Supervisor. James L. Dougherty. LC 74-11836. 230p. 1974. 19.00x (ISBN 0-87201-882-2). Gulf Pub.

Union Government & Organization. James Wallihan. 270p. 1985. 23.00 (ISBN 0-87179-480-2); pap. 18.00 (ISBN 0-87179-481-0). BNA.

Union Government & the Law: British & American Experiences. Joseph R. Grodin. (Monograph & Research Ser.: No. 8). 209p. 1961. 5.00 (ISBN 0-89215-010-6). U Cal LA Indus Rel.

Union Haggadah. 1977. Repr. of 1923 ed. 4.75 (ISBN 0-916694-08-9). Central Conf.

Union Home Prayerbook. 1951. 7.95 ea. (ISBN 0-916694-19-4); leatherbound 7.00 ea. (ISBN 0-916694-60-7). Central Conf.

Union Jack - the New York City Ballet. Ed. by Lincoln Kirstein. LC 77-94845. 1977. pap. 6.95x (ISBN 0-87130-047-8). Eakins.

Union Labor Report. BNA's Labor Services Staff. looseleaf 440.00. BNA.

Union List of African Censuses Development Plans & Statistical Abstracts. Compiled by Victoria K. Evalds. xiv, 232p. 1985. lib. bdg. 36.00 (ISBN 3-598-10576-2). K G Saur.

Union List of Arabic Serials in the United States: The Arabic Serials Holdings of Seventeen Libraries. Mohamed M. El-Hadi. LC 67-157. (University of Illinois Graduate School of Library Science Occasional Papers Ser.: No. 75). pap. 20.00 (ISBN 0-317-29753-8, 2017405). Bks Demand UMI.

Union List of Commonwealth Periodicals in London, Oxford & Cambridge. A. R. Hewitt. (Commonwealth Studies). 101p. 1960. 75.00 (ISBN 0-485-15005-0, Pub. by Athlone Pr UK). Humanities.

Union List of Film Periodicals: Holdings of Selected American Collections. Ed. by Anna Brady et al. LC 83-22585. xxvi, 316p. 1984. 40.95 (ISBN 0-313-23702-6, BRL/). Greenwood.

Union List of Geologic Field Trip Guidebooks of North America. 4th ed. Ed. by Geoscience Information Society Guidebooks Committee. LC 86-71946. 200p. 1986. pap. 47.50 (ISBN 0-913312-88-6). Am Geol.

Union List of Legal Serials in Selected Libraries of the Federal Republic of Germany Including West Berlin, 2 Vols. 2nd ed. Ed. by Staatsbibliothek Preussischer Kulturbesitz Staff. 1896p. 1984. lib. bdg. 250.00 (ISBN 3-598-10525-8). K G Saur.

Union List of Legislative Histories: 47th Congress, 1881-97th Congress, 1982. 5th ed. Compiled by Law Librarian's Society of the District of Columbia Staff. LC 85-10736. xxvi, 481p. 1985. loose-leaf 85.00x (ISBN 0-8377-2701-4). Rothman.

Union List of Population-Family Planning Periodicals. Ed. by Susan K. Pasquariella. 135p. 1978. 25.00 (ISBN 0-318-03477-8, LC-78-60528); members 10.00 (ISBN 0-318-03478-6). Assn Pop Lib.

Union List of Printed Indic Texts & Translations in American Libraries. Compiled by Murray B. Emeneau. (Amer Oriental Ser.). 1935. 40.00 (ISBN 0-527-02681-6). Kraus Repr.

Union List of Sanborn Fire Insurance Maps Held by Institutions in the United States & Canada: Volume 2 (Montana to Wyoming, Canada & Mexico, with a Supplement & Corrigenda to Volume 1. rev. ed. William S. Peterson-Hunt & Evelyn L. Woodruff. LC 76-6129. (Western Association of Map Libraries: Occasional Paper; No. 3). (Illus.). 216p. (Orig.). 1977. pap. 6.00x (ISBN 0-939112-03-5); pap. 10.00x Vols. 1 & 2 (ISBN 0-939112-04-3). Western Assn Map.

Union List of Sanborn Fire Insurance Maps Held by Institutions in the United States & Canada: Alabama to Missouri, Vol.1. R. Philip Hoehn. LC 76-6129. (Western Association of Map Libraries: Occasional Paper: No.2). (Illus.). 195p. 1976. pap. 5.00x (ISBN 0-939112-02-7). Western Assn Map.

Union List of Selected Western Books on China in American Libraries. 2nd ed. Charles S. Gardner. LC 70-126771. (Bibliography & Reference Ser.: No. 345). 1970. Repr. of 1938 ed. 20.50 (ISBN 0-8337-1281-0). B Franklin.

Union List of Serials in Libraries of United States & Canada. 3rd ed. Ed. by Edna B. Titus. 4649p. (5 Vols). 1965. Set. 175.00. Vol. 1 (ISBN 0-8242-0055-1). Vol. 2 (ISBN 0-8242-0056-X). Vol. 3 (ISBN 0-8242-0057-8). Vol. 4 (ISBN 0-8242-0058-6). Vol. 5 (ISBN 0-8242-0059-4). Wilson.

Union List of Victorian Serials: A Union List of Selected Nineteenth Century British Serials Available in the U. S. & Canadian Libraries. Richard D. Fulton. (Reference Library of the Humanities). 758p. 1984. lib. bdg. 103.00 (ISBN 0-8240-8846-8). Garland Pub.

Union Lists: Issues & Answers. Ed. by Dianne Ellsworth. LC 82-81471. (Current Issues in Serials Management Ser.: No. 2). 1982. 24.50 (ISBN 0-87650-141-2). Pierian.

Union Maids Not Wanted: Organizing Domestic Workers Eighteen Seventy to Nineteen Forty. Donna Van Raaphorst. 328p. 1988. lib. bdg. 39.95 (ISBN 0-275-92288-X, C2288). Praeger.

Union-Management Cooperation in the "Stretch-Out". R. Carter Nyman & E. D. Smith. 1934. 59.50x (ISBN 0-685-69848-3). Elliots Bks.

Union-Management Cooperation on the Railroads. Louis A. Wood. LC 74-22765. (Labor Movement in Fiction & Non-Fiction). Repr. of 1931 ed. 32.00 (ISBN 0-404-58518-3). AMS Pr.

Union-Management Cooperation: Structure, Process & Impact. Michael H. Schuster. LC 84-17373. 235p. 1984. text ed. 19.95 (ISBN 0-88099-023-6); pap. text ed. 12.95 (ISBN 0-88099-024-4). W E Upjohn.

Union-Management in a Changing Economy. Alan Balfour. (Illus.). 464p. 1987. text ed. write for info. (ISBN 0-13-938804-4). P-H.

Union Member's Guide to Free Speech. 1980. 0.75. Natl Lawyers Guild.

Union Member's Right to Vote. 0.75. Natl Lawyers Guild.

Union Miners Cemetary & the Mother Jones Monument. John Keiser. 40p. 1980. 14.95 (ISBN 0-916884-09-0, Pub. by Illinois Labor History Society). C H Kerr.

Union Nationale: Quebec Nationalism from Duplessis to Levesque. rev ed. Herbert F. Quinn. 1980. pap. 10.95 (ISBN 0-8020-6347-0). U of Toronto Pr.

Union of Eagles El Paso-Juarez. 1988. 49.95 (ISBN 0-944551-00-9). Rainbow Tree Pubns.

Union of England & Scotland 1603-1608. Bruce Galloway. 208p. 1986. text ed. 39.95x (ISBN 0-85976-143-6, Pub. by John Donald Pub UK). Humanities.

Union of Honour. James Yorke. LC 72-240. (English Experience Ser.: No. 148). 76p. 1969. Repr. of 1640 ed. 58.00 (ISBN 90-221-0148-7). Walter J Johnson.

Union of Individuals: The Formation of the American Newspaper Guild, 1933-36. Daniel J. Leab. LC 75-110603. 362p. 1970. 37.50x (ISBN 0-231-03367-2). Columbia U Pr.

Union of Lublin: Polish Federalism in the Golden Age. Harry E. Dembrowski. (East European Monographs: No. 116). 380p. 1982. 35.00x (ISBN 0-88033-009-0). East Eur Quarterly.

Union of Opposites: A General Theory of Physical & Human Processes Towards an American Humanism. Hector C. Sabelli. LC 87-70324. 360p. (Orig.). 1988. pap. 24.95 (ISBN 1-55618-019-5). Brunswick Pub.

Union of Soviet Socialist Republics see U.S.S.R.

Union of Soviet Socialist Republics. Abraham Resnick. LC 84-7602. (Illus.). 128p. (gr. 5-9). 1984. lib. bdg. 22.60 (ISBN 0-516-02789-1). Childrens.

Union of Soviet Socialist Republics. (Let's Visit Places & Peoples - - Nations, Dependencies, & Sovereignties of the World Ser.). (Illus.). (gr. 5 up). 1988. 12.95 (ISBN 0-222-00921-7). Chelsea Hse.

Union of Soviet Socialist Republics & Eastern Europe: Their Economies Today & the Outlook for East-West Trade. Hudson Research, Europe, Ltd. (Research Memorandum: No. 24). 73p. 1976. 25.00 (ISBN 0-318-14357-7, HI-2416-P). Hudson Inst.

Union of Tanganyika & Zanzibar: A Study in Political Integration. Martin Bailey. (Foreign & Comparative Studies Program, Eastern African Ser.: No.9). 114p. 1973. pap. 5.50x (ISBN 0-915984-06-7). Syracuse U Foreign Comp.

Union Officer in the Reconstruction. John W. De Forest. Ed. by David M. Potter & James H. Croushore. LC 68-12523. xxx, 211p. 1968. Repr. of 1948 ed. 20.00 (ISBN 0-208-00097-6, Archon). Shoe String.

Union Organization & Militancy Conclusions from a Study of the United Mine Workers of America, 1940-1974. Makoto Takamiya. 262p. 1978. pap. text ed. 30.00 (ISBN 3-445-01834-0). Oelgeschlager.

Union Organizing & Public Policy: Failure to Secure First Contracts. William N. Cooke. LC 85-3239. 1985. text ed. 18.95 (ISBN 0-88099-026-0); pap. text ed. 11.95 (ISBN 0-88099-027-9). W E Upjohn.

Union Organizing & Staying Organized. Kenneth Gagala. 1983. text ed. 24.33 (ISBN 0-8359-8064-2, Reston); pap. text ed. write for info. (ISBN 0-8359-8063-4). P-H.

Union Organizing: Management & Labor Conflict. William E. Fulmer. LC 82-16172. 240p. 1982. 35.00 (ISBN 0-275-90797-X, C0797). Praeger.

Union Pacific. Donald C. Porter. (Winning the West Ser.). 320p. (Orig.). 1988. pap. 3.95 (ISBN 0-553-26708-6). Bantam.

Union Pacific Country. Robert G. Athearn. LC 75-11707. (Illus.). 480p. 1976. 27.50x (ISBN 0-8032-0858-8); pap. 11.95 (ISBN 0-8032-5829-1, BB 610, Bison). U of Nebr Pr.

Union Pacific Forties...on the Move. George R. Cockle. LC 81-65096. (Overland Railbook Ser.). (Illus.). 208p. 1985. pap. 23.50 (ISBN 0-916160-10-6). G R Cockle.

Union Pacific: Mainline West. William E. Botkin et al. (Illus.). 80p. 1986. pap. 11.95 (ISBN 0-918654-38-6). CO RR Mus.

Union Pacific Railroad: A Case in Premature Enterprise. Robert W. Fogel. LC 78-64234. (Johns Hopkins University. Studies in the Social Sciences. Seventy-Eighth Ser. 1960: 2). Repr. of 1960 ed. 24.50 (ISBN 0-404-61339-X). AMS Pr.

Union Pacific Railway. John P. Davis. LC 73-2501. (Big Business; Economic Power in a Free Society Ser.). Repr. of 1894 ed. 20.00 (ISBN 0-405-05082-8). Ayer Co Pubs.

Union Pacific Three-Nine-Eight-Five. William E. Botkin et al. LC 85-9929. (Illus.). 64p. 1985. pap. 9.95 (ISBN 0-918654-36-X). CO RR Mus.

Union Pacific, Vol. 1: Birth of a Railroad, 1862-1893. Maurice Klein. LC 86-16732. (Illus.). 704p. 1987. pap. 27.50 (ISBN 0-385-17728-3). Doubleday.

Union Pacific...Nineteen Seventy-Seven to Nineteen Eighty. George R. Cockle. LC 77-81546. (Illus.). 208p. 1980. pap. 18.95 (ISBN 0-916160-03-3). G R Cockle.

Union Pacific's Snow Fighters. G. R. Cockle. LC 81-65095. (Overland Railbook Ser.). (Illus.). 208p. 1984. pap. 23.50 (ISBN 0-916160-09-2). G R Cockle.

Union Pacific's Stromsburg Branch: Pictorial Review of a Rural Neb. Rail Line. James J. Reisdorff & Forrest H. Bahm. (Illus.). 52p. 1987. pap. 12.95 (ISBN 0-942035-02-X). South Platte.

Union Pamphlets of the Civil War, 1861-1865, 2 Vols. Ed. by Frank B. Freidel. LC 67-17309. (John Harvard Library). 1967. Set. 70.00x (ISBN 0-674-92130-5). Harvard U Pr.

Union Policies & Industrial Management. Sumner H. Slichter. LC 73-89763. (American Labor, from Conspiracy to Collective Bargaining Ser., No.1). 611p. 1969. Repr. of 1941 ed. 32.00 (ISBN 0-405-02148-8). Ayer Co Pubs.

Union Policy & Incentive Wage Methods. Van Dusen Kennedy. LC 68-58598. (Columbia University Studies in the Social Sciences: No. 513). Repr. of 1945 ed. 21.00 (ISBN 0-404-51513-4). AMS Pr.

Union Policy & the Older Worker. Melvin K. Bers. LC 76-14986. 1976. Repr. of 1957 ed. lib. bdg. 38.50x (ISBN 0-8371-8655-2, BEUP). Greenwood.

Union Politic: The CIO Political Action Committee. James C. Foster. LC 74-22240. 257p. 1975. 28.00x (ISBN 0-8262-0171-7). U of Mo Pr.

Union Portraits. facs. ed. Gamaliel Bradford. LC 68-29194. (Essay Index Reprint Ser.). 1916. 18.00 (ISBN 0-8369-0243-2). Ayer Co Pubs.

Union Portraits. Gamaliel Bradford. 1978. Repr. of 1916 ed. lib. bdg. 25.00 (ISBN 0-8492-3524-3). R West.

Union Power & American Democracy: The UAW & the Democratic Party, 1972-83. Dudley W. Buffa. 296p. 1984. 29.50 (ISBN 0-472-10053-X). U of Mich Pr.

Union Power & New York: Victor Gotbaum & District Council 37. Jewel Bellush & Bernard Bellush. LC 84-15926. 496p. 1984. 38.95 (ISBN 0-275-91126-8, C1126). Praeger.

Union Powers & Union Functions: Toward a Better Balance. 52p. 1964. 1.00 (ISBN 0-317-33998-2, 012P). Comm Econ Dev.

Union Prayerbook, 2 vols. 1977. Vol. 1. . 16.00 (ISBN 0-916694-09-7). Central Conf.

Union Professional: The Staff Rep in Action. Duane Beeler. 109p. 1977. pap. 3.95 (ISBN 0-317-12247-9). Union Rep.

Union Regulations see NEA Series.

Union Relative Wage Effects: A Survey. H. Gregg Lewis. LC 85-8663. 1986. lib. bdg. 37.50x (ISBN 0-226-47721-5). U of Chicago Pr.

Union Representation Elections: Law & Reality. Julius G. Getman et al. LC 78-13271. 218p. 1976. 18.50x (ISBN 0-87154-302-8). Russell Sage.

Union Representative's Guide to Federal Labor Relations. Dennis K. Reischl. (Illus.). 100p. (Orig.). 1988. pap. text ed. 8.95 (ISBN 0-317-67340-8). Fed Person Mgmt.

Union Representative's Guide to NLRB RC & CA Cases. Gloria Busman. (Policy & Practice Publication). 112p. 1984. 9.00 (ISBN 0-89215-127-7). U Cal LA Indus Rel.

Union Republics in Soviet Diplomacy: A Study of Soviet Federalism in the Service of Soviet Foreign Policy. Vernon V. Aspaturian. LC 83-22696. 228p. 1984. Repr. of 1960 ed. lib. bdg. 35.00x (ISBN 0-313-24368-9, ASUP). Greenwood.

Union Sourcebook: Membership, Structure, Finance, Directory. Leo Troy & Niel Sheflin. 200p. 1985. 25.00 (ISBN 0-9613923-0-4). IRDIS.

Union Square. Meredith Tax. 448p. 1988. 18.95 (ISBN 0-688-05069-7). Morrow.

Union Station Massacre. Merle Clayton. 1977. pap. 1.50 (ISBN 0-8439-0430-5, Leisure Bks). Leisure NY.

Union Station Remembered. 2nd ed. Joseph Pallotta. (Illus.). 173p. 1985. pap. 19.95 (ISBN 0-9616091-0-9). J & C Bks.

Union Street. Pat Barker. 256p. 1984. pap. 3.50 (ISBN 0-345-31501-4). Ballantine.

Union Tactics & Economic Change: A Case Study of Three Philadelphia Textile Unions. Gladys L. Palmer. LC 71-156438. (American Labor Ser., No. 2). 1971. Repr. of 1932 ed. 17.00 (ISBN 0-405-02936-5). Ayer Co Pubs.

Union, the Civil War & John W. Tuttle: A Kentucky Captains Account. Ed. by Hambleton Tapp & James C. Klotter. LC 79-89244. 1980. 20.00 (ISBN 0-916968-08-1). Kentucky Hist.

Union Violence: The Record & the Response by Courts, Legislatures & the NLRB. Armand J. Thieblot, Jr. & Thomas Haggard. Frwd. by Herbert R. Northrup. LC 83-81085. (Labor Relations & Public Policy Ser.: No. 25). (Illus.). 540p. (Orig.). 1984. Repr. of 1983 ed. clth. bd. 38.00 (ISBN 0-89546-040-8). Indus Res Unit-Wharton.

Union Vision. Sri Chinmoy. (Talks Delivered at the United Nations). 102p. (Orig.). 1977. pap. 3.00. Aum Pubns.

Union with Christ. Date not set. price not set (ISBN 0-918403-15-4). Agape Ministries.

Union with God. Jeanne Guyon. Ed. by Gene Edwards. 117p. 1981. pap. 5.95 (ISBN 0-940232-05-7). Christian Bks.

Union with the Lord in Prayer: Beyond Meditation to Affective Prayer, Aspiration & Contemplation. Venard Poslusney. (Illus., Orig.). 1973. pap. 2.95 (ISBN 0-914544-03-9). Living Flame Pr.

Union World Catalog of Manuscript Books Vol. 3: A List of Printed Catalogs of Manuscript Books. Ernest C. Richardson. Ed. by American Library Association Committee on Bibliography. LC 70-132686. v, 386p. 1972. Repr. of 1935 ed. 23.50 (ISBN 0-8337-2991-8). B Franklin.

Unionism & Relative Wages in the United States. H. Gregg Lewis. LC 63-20915. (Midway Reprint Ser.). 1973. pap. 13.00x (ISBN 0-226-47720-7). U of Chicago Pr.

Unionism, Economic Stabilization & Incomes Policies: European Experience. Robert J. Flanagan & David W. Soskice. LC 83-71459. 705p. 1983. 39.95 (ISBN 0-8157-2856-5); pap. 18.95 (ISBN 0-8157-2855-7). Brookings.

Unionists Divided: Arthur Balfour, Joseph Chamberlain & the Unionist Free Traders. Richard A. Rempel. (Library of Politics & Society Ser.). 236p. 1972. 26.00 (ISBN 0-208-01308-3, Archon). Shoe String.

Unionization of Professional Societies. Eileen B. Hoffman. LC 76-17475. (Report Ser.: No. 690). (Illus.). 58p. 1976. pap. 30.00 (ISBN 0-8237-0124-7). Conference Bd.

Unionization of Teachers: A Case Study of the UFT. Stephen Cole. Ed. by Harriet Zuckerman & Robert K. Merton. LC 79-8986. (Dissertations on Sociology Ser.). 1980. Repr. of 1969 ed. lib. bdg. 20.00x (ISBN 0-405-12959-9). Ayer Co Pubs.

Unions. Alvin Schwartz. (Illus.). (gr. 7 up). 1972. PLB 10.00 (ISBN 0-670-74098-5). Viking.

Unions Against Revolution. G. Munis & J. Zerzan. 1975. pap. 1.25x (ISBN 0-934868-12-3). Black & Red.

Unions & Economic Crisis: Britain, West Germany & Sweden. George Ross et al. 250p. 1984. text ed. 44.95x (ISBN 0-04-331094-X). Unwin Hyman.

Unions & Leaders in Ghana: A Model of Labor & Development. Paul S. Gray. LC 80-18482. 1981. 35.00 (ISBN 0-914970-57-7); pap. text ed. 17.50 (ISBN 0-914970-58-5). Conch Mag.

Unions & Politics in Mexico: The Case of the Automobile Industry. Ian Roxborough. (Cambridge Latin American Studies: No. 49). (Illus.). 224p. 1984. 44.50 (ISBN 0-521-25987-8). Cambridge U Pr.

Unions & Politics in Washington State, 1885-1935. Jonathan Dembo. Ed. by Robert E. Burke & Frank Freidel. (Modern American History Ser.). 83.00 (ISBN 0-8240-5654-X). Garland Pub.

Unions & Public Schools: The Effects of Collective Bargaining on American Education. Randall W. Eberts et al. LC 82-148862. (Politics of Education Ser.). 224p. 1984. 30.00x (ISBN 0-669-06372-X). Lexington Bks.

Unions & Racism. Shelby Shapiro. 1980. pap. 1.00 (ISBN 0-686-46447-8). Indus Workers World.

Unions & the Cities. Harry H. Wellington & Ralph K. Winter, Jr. LC 79-179327. (Brookings Institution Studies of Unionism in Government). pap. 60.00 (2025417). Bks Demand UMI.

Unions, Change & Crisis: French & Italian Union Strategy & the Political Economy, 1945-1980. Peter Lange & George Ross. 280p. 1983. text ed. 39.95x (ISBN 0-04-331088-5). Unwin Hyman.

Unions for Academic Library Support Staff: Impact on Workers & the Workplace. James M. Kusack. LC 86-7709. (New Directions in Information Management Ser.: No. 10). 121p. 1986. lib. bdg. 35.00 (ISBN 0-313-24991-1, KUA/). Greenwood.

Unions in America: A British View. Benjamin C. Roberts. LC 82-6257. x, 136p. 1982. Repr. of 1959 ed. lib. bdg. 35.00x (ISBN 0-313-23623-2, ROUA). Greenwood.

Unions in American National Politics. Graham K. Wilson. LC 79-15559. 1979. 25.00x (ISBN 0-312-83305-9). St Martin.

Unions in Conflict: A Comparative Study Four South Indian Textile Centres, 1918-1939. Eamon Murphy. 1982. 18.00x (ISBN 0-8364-0874-8, Pub. by Australia Nat Univ). South Asia Bks.

Unions in Crisis & Beyond. Richard C. Edwards et al. 400p. 1986. 35.00x (ISBN 0-86569-127-4). Auburn Hse.

Unions in Emerging Societies: Frustration & Politics. Sidney C. Sufrin. LC 64-14084. pap. 32.50 (ISBN 0-317-52020-2, 2027414). Bks Demand UMI.

Unions in Post-Industrial Society. John Schmidman. LC 78-112229. 1979. text ed. 17.95x (ISBN 0-271-00209-3). Pa St U Pr.

Unions in Transition. Jerry Bornstein. LC 81-13996. 192p. (gr. 7 up). 1981. PLB 10.79 (ISBN 0-671-41913-7). Messner.

Unions in Transition: Entering the Second Century. Ed. by Seymour M. Lipset. 506p. 1986. 29.95 (ISBN 0-917616-74-X); pap. 12.95 (ISBN 0-917616-73-1). ICS Pr.

Unions of States: Theory & Practice of Confederation. Murray G. Forsyth. LC 80-29044. 360p. 1981. 42.50 (ISBN 0-8419-0691-2); pap. 19.50 (ISBN 0-8419-0729-3). Holmes & Meier.

Unions on Campus. Frank R. Kemerer & J. Victor Baldridge. LC 75-24009. (Jossey-Bass Series in Higher Education). pap. 65.80 (2027758). Bks Demand UMI.

Unions, Parties, & Political Development: A Study of Mineworkers in Zambia. Robert H. Bates. LC 78-158135. pap. 75.80 (ISBN 0-317-29593-4, 2021980). Bks Demand UMI.

Unions' Rights to Company Information. rev. ed. James T. O'Reilly & Jodi C. Aronson. LC 85-82257. (Labor Relations & Public Policy Ser.). 300p. 1987. pap. 30.00. Indus Res Unit-Wharton.

Unions' Rights to Company Information. James T. O'Reilly & Gale P. Simon. LC 80-53300. (Labor Relations & Public Policy Ser.: No. 21). pap. 73.00 (ISBN 0-317-41895-5, 2025913). Bks Demand UMI.

Unions: Structure, Development, & Management. 3rd ed. Marten Estey. 153p. 1981. pap. text ed. 9.00 net (ISBN 0-15-592952-6, HC). HarBraceJ.

Unions, Unemployment, & Innovation. Eric Batstone & Stephen Gourlay. 304p. 1986. 50.00 (ISBN 0-631-14961-9). Basil Blackwell.

Unions, Wages & Inflation. Daniel J. Mitchell. LC 79-3776. 304p. 1980. 29.95 (ISBN 0-8157-5752-2); pap. 10.95 (ISBN 0-8157-5751-4). Brookings.

Unions, Workers, & the Law. Betty W. Justice. (George Meany Center for Labor Studies Ser.: No. 2). 312p. 1983. pap. 17.00 (ISBN 0-87179-400-4). BNA.

Uniontown, Maryland: A Walking Tour. Joseph M. Getty. LC 83-61818. 54p. (Orig.). 1983. pap. 10.00 (ISBN 0-913281-00-X). Noodle-Doosey.

Unipix: Universal Language of Pictures. Cindy Drolet. Ed. by Ken Drolet. LC 82-90721. (Illus.). 58p. (Orig.). 1982. pap. 8.95 (ISBN 0-9609464-0-3). Imaginart Pr.

Unipotent Algebraic Groups. T. Kambayashi et al. (Lecture Notes in Mathematics: Vol. 414). vi, 165p. 1974. pap. 14.00 (ISBN 0-387-06960-7). Springer-Verlag.

Unique Animal. Don D. Davis. (Illus.). 336p. 1981. 25.00 (ISBN 0-907152-02-3); pap. 12.95 (ISBN 0-907152-01-5). Prytaneum Pr.

Unique Experience. Carolyn T. Anderson. 173p. (Orig.). 1987. pap. 6.00 (ISBN 0-935132-08-2). C H Fairfax.

Unique Ghost Towns & Mountain Spots. Caroline Bancroft. 96p. 1961. pap. 4.50 (ISBN 0-933472-24-2). Johnson Bks.

Unique Golf Resorts of the World. Gwen Williams. 204p. 1983. 34.95 (ISBN 0-9612294-0-3). Unique Golf Res.

Unique Golf Resorts of the World. 2nd ed. Gwen Williams. 300p. 1987. 34.95. Unique Golf Res.

Unique Hopewellian Mask-Headdress. R. Baby. (Illus.). 2p. 1956. pap. 0.50 (ISBN 0-318-00853-X). Ohio Hist Soc.

Unique Meeting Places in Greater Washington: Distinctive Conference & Party Facilities Found Only in the Capital Area. Elise Ford. (Illus.). 250p. (Orig.). 1988. pap. 11.95 (ISBN 0-939009-08-0). EPM Pubns.

Unique New York & Long Branch. Don Wood et al. LC 85-71330. (Illus.). 240p. 1985. 25.95 (ISBN 0-917451-10-4). Audio-Visual.

Unique New Zealand. Glen Pownall. 156p. 1980. 7.95 (ISBN 0-85467-003-3, Pub. by Viking Sevenseas). Intl Spec Bk.

Unique Position: A Biography of Edith Dircksey Cowan, 1861-1932. Peter Cowan. 1979. 35.00 (ISBN 0-85564-135-5, Pub. by U of W Austral Pr). Intl Spec Bk.

Unique Potato Salad Cookbook. Vera Klein. LC 86-82992. 152p. (Orig.). 1987. pap. 7.95 (ISBN 0-940995-00-X). Entrepen Wrkshps Pubns.

Unique Power Systems Solved. O. C. Seevers. 1982. text ed. 39.00 (ISBN 0-915586-60-6). Fairmont Pr.

Unique Program for Staying Healthy, Young, & Trim. Riette Ormond & George Ormond. 44p. (Orig.). 1982. pap. 6.95 (ISBN 0-9620518-0-2). Ormond Assocs.

Unique Properties of Melanocytes: Proceedings. International Pigment Cell Conference, Houston, Tex., Pt. 2, Jan, 1975. Ed. by V. Riley. (Pigment Cell Ser.: Vol. 3). (Illus.). 1977. 102.00 (ISBN 3-8055-2371-8). S Karger.

Unique Status of Man. Herbert W. Carr. 1977. Repr. of 1928 ed. lib. bdg. 20.00 (ISBN 0-8492-0496-8). R West.

Unique Three-in-One Research & Development Directory: Annual. 640p. 1987. pap. 15.00 (ISBN 0-318-00176-4). Gov Data Pubns.

Unique World of Mitsumasa Anno: Selected Works 1968-1977. Mitsumasa Anno. Tr. by Samuel Morse. LC 80-12827. (Illus.). 64p. (gr. 7 up). 1980. 19.95 (ISBN 0-399-20743-0, Philomel). Putnam Pub Group.

Uniquely You. Betty Nethery & Beverly B. Smith. LC 83-51176. (Illus.). 224p. 1984. pap. 9.95 (ISBN 0-8423-7792-1). Tyndale.

Uniquely Yours: A Collection of Over 700 Suggestions to Individualize Your Wedding. Michelle M. Pattarozzi. 104p. 1983. 9.95. M M Pattarozzi.

Uniqueness & Diversity in Human Evolution: Morphometric Studies of Australopithecines. Charles Oxnard. LC 74-16689. viii, 134p. 1975. text ed. 17.50x (ISBN 0-226-64253-4). U of Chicago Pr.

Uniqueness & Non-Uniqueness in the Cauchy Problem. Claude Zuily. (Progress in Mathematics Ser.). 250p. 1983. text ed. 16.95 (ISBN 0-8176-3121-6). Birkhauser.

Uniqueness of Man. John Lewis. 1974. pap. 7.95x (ISBN 0-8464-0948-8). Beekman Pubs.

Uniqueness of Pastoral Psycholtherapy. William Kyle. 1985. 10.00x (ISBN 0-317-62229-3, Guild of Pastoral Psych). State Mutual Bk.

Uniqueness of the Good & the Psychology of Activity. John Dewey. 147p. 1987. 137.75 (ISBN 0-89920-165-2). Am Inst Psych.

Uniqueness of the Individual. 2nd rev. ed. P. B. Medawar. 13.50 (ISBN 0-8446-5903-7). Peter Smith.

Uniqueness of the Individual. Peter B. Medawar. 192p. 1981. pap. 5.95 (ISBN 0-486-24042-8). Dover.

Uniqueness: The Human Pursuit of Difference. C. R. Snyder & Howard L. Fromkin. LC 79-18764. (Perspectives In Social Psychology Ser.). (Illus.). 250p. 1980. 27.50x (ISBN 0-306-40376-5, Plenum Pr). Plenum Pub.

Uniqueness Theorems in Linear Elasticity. R. J. Knops & L. E. Payne. LC 70-138813. (Springer Tracts in Natural Philosophy: Vol. 19). 1971. 28.00 (ISBN 0-387-05253-4). Springer-Verlag.

Unisex Tennis. Bill Lenz. LC 76-7981. (Illus., Orig.). 1977. pap. 9.95x (ISBN 0-8046-9147-9, Pub by Kennikat). Assoc Faculty Pr.

Unit & Bulk Materials Handling. Ed. by F. J. Loeffler & C. R. Proctor. 289p. 1980. 60.00 (ISBN 0-686-69864-9, H00163). ASME.

Unit Conversions & Formulas Manual. Ed. by Nicholas P. Cheremisinoff & Paul N. Cheremisinoff. LC 79-55140. (Illus.). 1980. pap. 9.95 (ISBN 0-250-40331-5). Butterworth.

Unit Costs of Salaries in Teachers College & Normal Schools. Herman J. MaGee. LC 73-177046. (Columbia University. Teachers College. Contributions to Education: No. 489). Repr. of 1931 ed. 22.50 (ISBN 0-404-55489-X). AMS Pr.

Unit Costs of School Building. Henry H. Bormann. LC 78-176582. (Columbia University. Teachers College. Contributions to Education: No. 842). Repr. of 1941 ed. 22.50 (ISBN 0-404-55842-9). AMS Pr.

Unit Groups of Classical Rings. Gregory Karpilovsky. 320p. 1989. 75.00 (ISBN 0-19-853557-0). Oxford U Pr.

Unit Histories of the United States Air Forces: Including Privately Printed Personal Narratives & United States Air Force History: a Guide to Documentary Sources. Charles E. Dornbusch & Lawrence J. Paszek. Ed. by James Gilbert. LC 79-7247. (Flight: Its First Seventy-Five Years Ser.). (Illus.). 1979. Repr. of 1958 ed. lib. bdg. 28.50x (ISBN 0-405-12159-8). Ayer Co Pubs.

Unit-Load & Package Conveyors: Application & Design. Henry C. Keller. LC 66-21856. (Illus.). pap. 62.30 (ISBN 0-317-11121-3, 2012434). Bks Demand UMI.

Unit Method of Clothing Construction: Women's & Men's Wear. 6th ed. Iowa Home Economics Association. Ed. by Phyllis Brackelsberg & Bertha Shaw. (Illus.). 172p. 1977. text ed. 10.95x (ISBN 0-8138-1710-2). Iowa St U Pr.

Unit of Measure. Marilyn R. Rosenberg. 18p. 1977. pap. 7.00 (ISBN 0-913615-04-8). M Rosenberg.

Unit Operations & Chemical Engineering. 4th ed. Warren L. McCabe & J. C. Smith. 3040p. 1985. text ed. 57.95 (ISBN 0-07-044828-0). McGraw.

Unit Operations in Cane Sugar Production. J. H. Payne. (Sugar Technology Ser.: Vol. 4). 204p. 1982. 76.50 (ISBN 0-444-42104-1). Elsevier.

Unit Operations in Chemical Engineering. 3rd ed. Warren L. McCabe & Julian C. Smith. (Engineering Ser.). 1975. text ed. 44.95 (ISBN 0-07-044825-6). McGraw.

Unit Operations in Food Processing. 2nd ed. R. L. Earle. (Illus.). 220p. 1983. text ed. 53.00 (ISBN 0-08-025537-X); pap. text ed. 24.00 (ISBN 0-08-025536-1). Pergamon.

Unit Operations in Resource Recovery Engineering. P. Vesiland et al. (Illus.). 1980. text ed. 56.00 (ISBN 0-13-937953-3). P-H.

Unit Operations Models for Solid Waste Processing. G. M. Savage. LC 86-5154. (Pollution Technology Review Ser.: No. 133). (Illus.). 214p. 1986. 36.00 (ISBN 0-8155-1086-1). Noyes.

Unit Operations of Sanitary Engineering. Linvil G. Rich. LC 61-15410. soft bdg. 15.00 (ISBN 0-686-11818-9). Rich SC.

Unit Plan: A Plan for Curriculum Organizing & Teaching. Earl J. Ogletree et al. LC 79-48018. 499p. 1980. pap. text ed. 18.50 (ISBN 0-8191-0996-7). U Pr of Amer.

Unit Processes in Hydrometallurgy: Papers, Dallas, Texas, February 24-28, 1963. Ed. by Milton E. Wadsworth & Franklin T. Davis. LC 65-7413. (Metallurgical Society Conferences Ser.: Vol. 24). pap. 160.00 (ISBN 0-317-10396-2, 2001512). Bks Demand UMI.

Unit Processes of Extractive Metallurgy. R. M. Pehlke. 400p. 1973. 34.50 (ISBN 0-444-00130-1). Elsevier.

Unit Processes of Sanitary Engineering. Linvil G. Rich. LC 63-14067. soft bdg. 15.00 (ISBN 0-686-15000-7). Rich SC.

United Nations Commission of International Trade Law Yearbook, Vol. XV. 1984. 38.00 (ISBN 92-1-133275-3, E.86.V.2). UN.

U. N. Commission on Human Rights. Howard Tolley. LC 86-32580. (Special Study). 320p. 1987. pap. 39.95 (ISBN 0-8133-7288-7). Westview.

United Nations Commission on International Trade Law Yearbook, Vol. XII. 1981. 23.00 (ISBN 92-1-133181-1, E.82.V.6). UN.

United Nations Commission on International Trade Law Yearbook: 1982, Vol. XIII. 432p. 38.00 (ISBN 92-1-133261-3, E.84.V.5). UN.

United Nations Commission on International Trade Law Yearbook: 1983, Vol. XIV. 1986. 41.00 (ISBN 92-1-133265-6, E.85.V.3). UN.

United Nations Commodity Conference. Incl. Tin, 1970. pap. 1.50 (ISBN 0-686-93618-3, UN70/2D/10); Wheat, 1971. pap. 1.50 (ISBN 0-686-93620-5, UN71/2D10); Cocoa, 1972. pap. 2.00 (ISBN 0-686-93621-3, UN73/2D/9); Olive Oil, 1973. pap. 1.50 (ISBN 0-686-93623-X, UN73/2D/15); Cocoa, 1975. pap. 3.50 (ISBN 0-686-93622-1, UN76/2D9); Tin, 1975. pap. 3.00 (ISBN 0-686-93619-1, UN76/2D4); Sugar, 1977. pap. 3.50 (ISBN 0-686-93625-6, UN78/2D/17); Olive Oil, 1978. pap. 1.50 (ISBN 0-686-93624-8, UN76/2D/16). UN.

United Nations Conference on Contracts for the International Sale of Goods: Vienna, 10 March-11 April, 1980; Official Records. 33.00 (ISBN 92-1-133249-4, E.82.V.5). UN.

United Nations Conference on Human Settlements, Vancouver, B. C., 1976: Human Settlements, National Reports: Summaries & Reference Guides. International Institute for Environment & Development (I.I.E.D.) Compiled by Mary Anglemeyer & Signe R. Ottersen. LC 76-14569. 1976. pap. 57.00 (ISBN 0-08-021243-3). Pergamon.

United Nations Conference on Succession of States in Respect of Treaties: Official Records, Vol. II. 12.00 (ISBN 92-1-133253-2, E.79.V.9). UN.

United Nations Conference on Succession of States in Respect of Treaties: Official Records, Vol. III. 14.00 (ISBN 92-1-133252-4, E.79.V.10). UN.

United Nations Conference on the Law of the Sea, 3rd: Summary Records of Meetings, Documents Resumed Eighth Session, Vol.12. 115p. 1980. pap. 9.00 (E.80.V.12). UN.

United Nations Conference on Trade & Development: An Organization Betraying its Mission. Stanley J. Michalak. 78p. 1983. pap. 3.00 (ISBN 0-89195-206-3). Heritage Found.

United Nations Conference on Trade & Development: Fourth Session, Nairobi. Incl. Vol. 1. Report & Annexes (UN76/2D10); Vol. 2. Summaries of Statements by Heads of Delegations & Summary Records of Plenary Meetings (UN76/2D11); Vol. 3. Basic Documents (UN76/2D12). pap. 13.00 ea. UN.

United Nations Conference on Trade & Development, Sixth Conference - Report & Annexes: Proceedings. 167p. 1985. 17.50 (E.83.II.D.6). Vol. 1 (E.83.II.D.7). Vol. 2. 35.00 (ISBN 92-1-112209-0, E.83.II.D.8); Vol. 3. 33.00 (ISBN 92-1-112210-4). UN.

United Nations Conference on Trade & Development: Third Session, Santiago, Chile, 4 Vols. Incl. Vol. 1. Report of the United Nations Conference on Trade & Development. pap. 15.50 (ISBN 0-686-93660-4, UN73/2D4); Vol. 2. Merchandise Trade. pap. 8.50 (ISBN 0-686-93661-2, UN73/2D/5); Vol. 3. Financing & Invisibles. pap. 5.50 (ISBN 0-686-93662-0, UN73/2D/6); Vol. 4. General Review & Special Issues. pap. 12.00 (ISBN 0-686-93663-9, UN73/2D7). UN.

United Nations Conspiracy. Robert W. Lee. 296p. 1981. 10.00 (ISBN 0-88279-236-9). Western Islands.

United Nations: Constitutional Developments, Growth & Possibilities. Benjamin V. Cohen. LC 61-16691. (Oliver Wendell Holmes Lectures Ser: 1961). 1961. 11.00x (ISBN 0-674-92265-4). Harvard U Pr.

U. N. Convention & the Law of the Sea, 1983. Kenneth R. Simmonds. LC 83-7206. 312p. 1983. pap. 20.00 (ISBN 0-379-01068-2). Oceana.

United Nations Convention on Contracts for the International Sale of Goods. Columbia University, Parker School of Foreign & Comparative Law Staff. Ed. by Nina M. Galston et al. 1984. 75.00 (768). Bender.

U. N. Convention on the Elimination of All Forms of Racial Discrimination. Natan Lerner. LC 80-51738. 278p. 1980. 37.50x (ISBN 90-286-0160-0, Pub. by Sijthoff & Noordhoff). Kluwer Academic.

U. N. Convention on the Law of the Sea: Impact & Implementation P19, 19th Annual Conference Proceedings. Ed. by E. D. Brown & Robin Churchill. 700p. 1988. 38.50 (ISBN 0-911189-16-5). Law Sea Inst.

U. N. Convention on the Law of the Sea: Impacts on Tuna Regulation. W. T. Burke. (Legislative Studies: No. 26). 19p. (An FAO-EEZ Programme Activity, Norway Funds-in-Trust). 1982. pap. text ed. 7.50 (ISBN 92-5-101292-X, F2398, FAO). UNIPUB.

United Nations Convention on the Law of the Sea 1982. Ed. by Myron H. Nordquist. 1985. lib. bdg. 100.00 (ISBN 90-247-3145-3, Pub. by Martinus Nijhoff Netherlands). Kluwer Academic.

United Nations Correspondece Manual: A Compendium of Rules Relating to the Drafting, Typing & Dispatch of Official United Nations Communications. LC 84-46787. 108p. 9.00 (ISBN 92-1-100253-2, E.84.I.11). UN.

United Nations Crime Conference: Fifth U. N. Conference of Crime & the Treatment of Prisoners--Geneva 1975, 2 vols. United Nations. LC 76-10067. 700p. 1976. Set, Keynote Documents Ed. 65.00x (ISBN 0-89111-007-0); silver halide fiche & 30p. index 85.00x (ISBN 0-686-33120-6). UNIFO Pubs.

U. N. Decade for Women: Documents & Dialogue. Arvonne S. Fraser. 200p. 1986. pap. 18.85 (ISBN 0-8133-7249-6). Westview.

United Nations Decade for Women World Conference. Ed. by Naomi B. Lynn. LC 84-4559. (Women & Politics Ser.: Vol. 4, No. 1). 93p. 1984. text ed. 24.95 (ISBN 0-86656-150-1, B150). Haworth Pr.

United Nations Decision Making. J. Kaufmann. 300p. 1980. 40.00x (ISBN 90-286-0410-3, Pub. by Sijthoff & Noordhoff). Kluwer Academic.

U. N. Declaration on Friendly Relations & the System of Sources of International Law. G. Arangio-Ruiz. 354p. 1979. 27.50x (ISBN 90-286-0149-X, Pub. by Sijthoff & Noordhoff). Kluwer Academic.

U. N. Declaration on the Elimination of Religious Intolerance & Discrimination. Sidney Liskofsky. 20p. 1982. pap. 2.00 (ISBN 0-87495-041-4). Am Jewish Comm.

United Nations Development Fund for Women: Development Co-operation with Women: The Experience & Future Directions of the Fund. 195p. 1986. pap. 19.50 (ISBN 92-1-130101-7, E.85.IV.6). UN.

United Nations Development Program: Failing the World's Poor. Richard E. Bissell. 46p. 1985. pap. 5.00 (ISBN 0-89195-215-2). Heritage Found.

U. N. Developmet Aid: Criteria & Methods of Evaluation. William R. Leonard et al. LC 75-140126. (UNITAR Studies). 1971. 20.00 (ISBN 0-405-02235-2). Ayer Co Pubs.

United Nations Directory of Agencies & Institutions in Public Administration & Finance. United Nations Department of Technical Cooperation for Development. LC 81-151890. 289p. 20.00 (ISBN 92-1-023001-9, E.81.II.H.1). UN.

United Nations Disarmament Yearbook, 6 Vols. & 1 Suppl. Incl. Vol. 1. 18.00 (UN77/9/2); Vol. 2. 1977. pap. 18.00 (ISBN 0-686-93589-6, UN78/9/4); Vol. 7. 1982. 632p. 22.00 (UN83/9/7CL). UN.

United Nations Disarmament Yearbook, Vol. 5. United Nations. 481p. 1980. 35.00x (ISBN 0-8002-2969-X). Intl Pubns Serv.

United Nations Disarmament Yearbook, Vol. 9. 623p. 1984. 35.00 (ISBN 92-1-142081-4, E.85.IX.4). UN.

United Nations Disarmament Yearbook, Vol. 10. 577p. 1985. pap. 35.00 (ISBN 92-1-142121-7, E.86.IX.7). UN.

United Nations Disarmament Yearbook, Vol. 11, 1986. 492p. 1987. 37.50 (ISBN 92-1-142129-2, E.87.IX.1). UN.

United Nations Disarmament Yearbook, 1982, Vol. VII. LC 78-641027. 648p. 1984. 35.00 (ISBN 0-8002-3153-8). Intl Pubns Serv.

United Nations Disarmament Yearbook: 1983, Vol. 8. UN Department for Disarmament Affairs. 553p. 1985. 25.00 (ISBN 92-1-142080-6, E.84.IX.3). UN.

United Nations Discussions on Palestine, 1947. Ed. by Michael J. Cohen & Howard M. Sachar. (Rise of Israel Ser.). 220p. 1987. lib. bdg. 60.00 (ISBN 0-8240-4935-7). Garland Pub.

United Nations, Divided World: The U. N.'s Roles in International Relations. Ed. by Adam Roberts & Benedict Kingsbury. (Illus.). 290p. 1988. 48.00 (ISBN 0-19-827544-7). Oxford U Pr.

United Nations Document Series Symbols, 1978-1984. 160p. 18.50 (ISBN 92-1-100281-8, E.85.I.21). UN.

United Nations Documents Index. Cumulated Index to Vols. 1-13 of the United Nation Document Index (UNDI, 4 vols. 1974. Set. 250.00 (ISBN 0-527-91530-0). UNIPUB-Kraus Intl.

U. N. Draft Model Taxation Convention. Ed. by International Fiscal Association. (Congress Seminar Ser. of the International Fiscal Association: No. 4). 76p. 1980. pap. 14.00 (ISBN 9-0200-0601-0, Pub. by Kluwer Law Netherlands). Kluwer Academic.

U. N. Draft Model Taxation Convention. (IFA Congress Seminar Ser.: Vol. 4). 76p. 1980. pap. 12.00 (ISBN 0-686-41008-4). Kluwer Academic.

U. N. Draft Model Taxation Convention: Trends in Income Tax Treaties Involving Developing Countries (with Special Reference to the U. N. Group of Experts on Tax Treaties Between Developed & Developing Countries) U. N. Group of Experts on Tax Treaties Between Developed & Developing Countries Staff & International Fiscal Association Staff. LC 82-106896. (IFA Congress Seminar Ser.: No. 4). (Illus.). 76p. 1979. write for info. (ISBN 9-02-000600-2). Kluwer Academic.

United Nations Economic & Social Council - Official Records, 1985, Supplement No. 9: Committee for Development Planning, Report on the Twenty-First Session & Resumed Twenty-First Session. 46p. 1985. 7.00. UN.

United Nations Economic & Social Council: Official Records, 1981, Plenary Meetings: Summary Records of the Meetings Held During the Year 1981. 260p. 1985. 27.00. UN.

United Nations Economic & Social Council: Official Records, 1981, Plenary Meetings: Report on the Ninth Session, April 8-17, 1985. 55p. 1985. 7.00. UN.

United Nations Economic & Social Council: Official Records, 1985, Supplement No. 8: Commission on Transnational Corporations, Report on the Eleventh Session. 53p. 1985. 7.00. UN.

United Nations Economic & Social Council Official Records, 1985, Supplement No. 1A: Resolutions & Decisions of Economic & Social Council. 39p. 1985. 7.00. UN.

United Nations Economic & Social Council Official Records, 1985, Supplement No. 12: Economic & Social Commission for Asia & the Pacific, Annual Report. 192p. 1985. 19.00. UN.

United Nations Economic & Social Council, 1984, Supplement No. 12: Economic Commission for Latin America & the Caribbean Report. 298p. 1985. 27.00. UN.

United Nations Economic & Social Council, 1985, Supplement No. 13: Economic Commission for Europe, Annual Report. 1985. 16.50. UN.

U. N. Economic Commission for Europe, 1947-1987. 140p. 1987. 15.00 (ISBN 92-1-116390-0, E.87.II.E.17). UN.

United Nations Economic Commission Manual on Licensing Procedures, in Member Countries, 2 vols. LC 80-19578. 1980. 150.00 (ISBN 0-87632-339-5). Clark Boardman.

United Nations Editorial Manual. 1983. 50.00x (ISBN 0-8002-3462-6). Intl Pubns Serv.

United Nations Editorial Manual. 524p. 1983. pap. text ed. 50.00 (ISBN 92-1-100185-4, E.83.1.16). UN.

United Nations Efforts to Control Arms in Outer Space: A Brief History with Key Documents. P. K. Menon. LC 87-24727. (Studies in World Peace: Vol. 1). 275p. 1987. lib. bdg. 49.95 (ISBN 0-88946-587-8). E Mellen.

United Nations Emergency Force: Basic Documents. Compiled by E. Lauterpacht. (International & Comparative Law Quarterly Special Supplement Ser.: No. 3). pap. 11.00 (ISBN 0-8115-3194-5). Kraus Repr.

United Nations Environment Programme: Environmental Data Report. (Illus.). 304p. (Orig.). Date not set. text ed. 49.95 (ISBN 0-631-15684-4). Basil Blackwell.

United Nations Environment Programme, Report of the Governing Council on the Work of Its Thirteenth Session: 40th Session, Supplement No. 25. 80p. 8.50. UN.

United Nations General Assembly & Disarmament, 1984. 263p. 1986. 25.00 (ISBN 92-1-142113-6, E.85.IX.7). UN.

United Nations General Assembly & Disarmament 1985. 309p. 1987. 30.00 (ISBN 92-1-142126-8, E.86.IX.11). UN.

United Nations General Assembly & Disarmament, 1986. 229p. 1987. 23.50 (ISBN 92-1-142132-2, E.87.IX.6). UN.

United Nations General Assembly: Official Records, 39th Session, Supplement No. 3: Report of the Economic & Social Council for the Year 1984. 89p. 1985. 11.00. UN.

United Nations General Assembly: Official Records, 40th Session Supplement No. 8: Report of the Commission on Human Settlements on the Work of its Eighth Session, April 29 - May 10, 1985. 50p. 1985. 7.00. UN.

U. N. General Assembly Resolutions: A Selection of the Most Important Resolutions During the Period 1949 Through 1974, Sessions I-XXVII. Knud Krakau et al. xiii, 442p. 1975. text ed. 33.00x. Rothman.

United Nations: General Assembly: 13th Special Session Supplement: Resolutions & Decisions Adopted by the General Assembly During Its Thirteen Special Session, 27 May-1 June 1986, No. 2. 15p. 1987. pap. 4.00 (ISBN 0-317-59487-7). UN.

United Nations: General Assembly: 14th Special Session Supplement: Resolutions & Decisions Adopted by the General Assembly During Its Fourteen Special, 17-20 September 1986, No. 1. 7p. 1987. pap. 3.00 (ISBN 0-317-59488-5). UN.

United Nations: General Assembly: 29th Session: Plenary Meetings, Verbatim Records of the 2233rd to 2265th Meeting: 17 Sep.-10 Oct. 1974, Official Records, Vol. 1. 649p. 1987. 60.00 (ISBN 0-317-59486-9). UN.

United Nations General Assembly 30th Session, Plenary Meetings: Verbatim Records of the 2351st to 2382nd Meetings 16 Sept.-9 Oct 1975, Official Records, Vol. I. 1987. 60.00 (ISBN 0-317-64758-X). UN.

United Nations General Assembly 30th Session, Plenary Meetings: Verbatim Records of the 2383rd to 2413th Meetings 10 Oct.-20 Nov. 1975, Official Records, Vol. II. 1987. 42.00 (ISBN 0-317-64760-1). UN.

United Nations General Assembly 30th Session, Plenary Meetings: Verbatim Records of the 2414th to 2444th Meetings 21 Nov.-17 Dec. 1975, Official Records, Vol. III. 1987. 45.00 (ISBN 0-317-64761-X). UN.

United Nations, General Assembly: 34th Session, Plenary Meetings, Official Records, Vol. III. 2098p. 1987. 41.00 (ISBN 0-317-63349-X). UN.

United Nations General Assembly, 34th Session Plenary Meetings: Verbatim Records of the 33rd to 76th Meetings, 3 vols, Vol. II. 1985. 39.00. UN.

United Nations General Assembly, 35th Session Plenary Meetings: Verbatim Records of the 80th to 114th Meetings, 3 vols, Vol. III. 1985. 45.00. UN.

United Nations General Assembly, 37th Session, Annexes: Agenda Items 72-142, September 21-December 21, 1982 & May 10-13 & September 1983, 2 vols, Vol. II. 1985. 33.00. UN.

United Nations General Assembly, 37th Session Annexes: Agenda Items 3-71, 2 vols, Vol. I. 1985. 38.00. UN.

United Nations: General Assembly: 37th Session, Plenary Meetings: Verbatim Records of the 78th to 122nd Meetings, 24 November - 21 December 1982, 10-13 May & 19 September 1983, Official Records, Vol. II. 2062p. 1987. 55.00 (ISBN 0-317-58061-2, A/37/PV.78-122). UN.

United Nations General Assembly, 39th Session, Suppelment No. 15: Report for the Trade & Development Board, 29th Session, Vol. II. 43p. 1985. 7.00. UN.

United Nations General Assembly 39th Session, Supplement No. 29: Report of the Ad Hoc Committee on the Indiam Ocean. LC 85-45781. 8p. 1985. 3.00. UN.

United Nations General Assembly, 39th Session, Supplement No. 51: Resolutions & Decisions Adopted by the General Assembly During Its 39th Session, September 18 - December 18, 1984 & April 9-12, 1985. 351p. 1985. 33.00. UN.

United Nations General Assembly, 39th Session, Supplement No. 7: First to Seventeenth Reports on the Programme Budget for the Biennium, 1984-1985. United Nations Advisory Committee on Administrative & Budgetary Questions. 117p. 1985. 12.50. UN.

United Nations General Assembly, 40th Session, Supplement No. 15: Report of the Trade & Development Board, Vol. I. United Nations Conference on Trade & Development. 40p. 1985. 6.00. UN.

United Nations General Assembly, 40th Session, Supplement No. 11: Report of the Committee on Contributions. 38p. 1985. 5.00. UN.

United Nations General Assembly, 40th Session, Supplement No. 17: Report of the United Nations Commission on International Trade Law on the Work of its Eighteenth Session. 95p. 1985. 11.00. UN.

United Nations General Assembly, 40th Session, Supplement No. 19: Report of the World Food Council on the Work of Its Eleventh Session, June 10-13, 1985. 36p. 1985. 6.00. UN.

United Nations General Assembly 40th Session, Supplement No. 15: Report of the Trade & Development Board, Vol. II. 44p. 1986. 7.00. UN.

United Nations General Assembly, 40th Session, Supplement No. 16: Report of the Industrial Development Board. United Nations Industrial Development Organization. 57p. 1985. 7.00. UN.

United Nations General Assembly, 40th Session, Supplement No. 20: Report of the Committee on the Peaceful Uses of Outer Space. 32p. 1985. 5.00. UN.

United Nations General Assembly, 40th Session, Supplement No. 28: Report of the Ad Hoc Committee on the World Disarmament Conference. 1985. 3.00. UN.

United Nation's General Assembly 40th Session, Supplement No. 29: Report of the Ad Hoc Committee on the Indian Ocean. 8p. 1986. 3.00. UN.

United Nations General Assembly, 40th Session, Supplement No. 33: Report of the Special Committee on the Charter of the United Nations & on the Strenghtening of the Role of the Organization. 59p. 1985. 7.00. UN.

United Nations General Assembly, 40th Session, Supplement No. 34: Report of the Joint Inspection Unit. 25p. 1985. 4.00. UN.

United Nations General Assembly, 40th Session, Supplement No. 37: Report of the Intergovernmental Committee on Science & Technology for Development. 56p. 1985. 7.00. UN.

United Nations General Assembly, 40th Session, Supplement No. 38: Report of the Committee for Programme & Co-Ordination on the Work of Its Twenty-Fifth Session. 157p. 1985. 16.50. UN.

United Nations General Assembly, 40th Session, Supplement No. 41: Report of the Special Committee on Enhancing the Effectiveness of the Principle of Non-Use of Force in International Relations. 39p. 1985. 6.00. UN.

United Nations General Assembly, 40th Session, Supplement No. 42: Report of the Disarmament Commission. 47p. 1985. 6.00. UN.

United Nations General Assembly, 40th Session, Supplement No. 43: Report of the Ad Hoc Committee on the Drafting of an International Convention Against the Recruitement, Use, Financing & Training of Mercenaries. 39p. 1985. 6.00. UN.

United Nations General Assembly, 40th Session, Supplement No. 40: Report of the Human Rights Committee. 244p. 1985. 23.00. UN.

United Nations General Assembly, 40th Session, Supplement No. 5B: Financial Report & Audited Financial Statements for the Year Ended December 31, 1984 & Report of the Board of Auditors. United Nations Children's Fund. 75p. 1985. 9.50. UN.

United Nations General Assembly, 40th Session, Supplement No. 5A: Financial Report & Audited Financial Statements for the Year Ended December 31, 1984 & Report of the Board of Auditors. United Nations Development Programme. 112p. 1985. 15.00. UN.

United Nations General Assembly, 40th Session, Supplement No. 5G: Financial Report & Audited Financial Statements for the Year Ended December 31, 1984 & Report of the Board of Auditors. United Nations Fund for Population Activities. 34p. 1985. 5.00. UN.

United Nations General Assembly, 40th Session, Supplement No. 5E: Voluntary Funds Administered by the United Nations High Commissioner for Refugees - Audited Financial Statements for the Year Ended December 31, 1984 & Report of the Board of Auditors. 69p. 1985. 8.50. UN.

United Nations General Assembly, 40th Session, Supplement No. 52: Report of the Ad Hoc Committee to Review the Implementation of the Charter of Economic Rights & Duties of States. 12p. 1985. 3.00. UN.

United Nations General Assembly, 40th Session, Supplement No. 5I: Financial Report & Audited Financial Statements for the Year Ended December 31, 1984 & Report of the Board of Auditors. United Nations Industrial Development Fund. 19p. 1985. 4.00. UN.

United Nations General Assembly, 40th Session, Supplement No. 5D: Financial Report & Audited Financial Statements for the Year Ended December 31, 1984 & Report of the Board of Auditors. United Nations Institute for Training & Research. 27p. 1985. 5.00. UN.

United Nations General Assembly, 40th Session, Supplement No. 5C: Financial Report & Audited Financial Statements for the Year Ended December 31, 1984 & Report of the Board of Auditors. United Nations Relief & Works Agency for Palestine Refugees in the Near East. 84p. 1985. 9.00. UN.

United Nations General Assembly, 40th Session, Supplement No. 7: First Report on the Proposed Programme Budget for the Biennium, 1986-1987. United Nations Advisory Committee on Administrative & Budgetary Questions. 216p. 1985. 21.00. UN.

United Nations General Assembly 41st Session, Supplement No. 53: Resolutions & Decisions Adopted by the General Assembly During Its 41st Session , 16 Sep.-19 Dec. 1986, Official Records. 321p. 1987. 36.00. UN.

United Nations General Assembly 41st Session. Supplement No. 7: Advisory Committee on Administrative & Budgetary Questions, 1st to 12th Reports on the Programme Budget for the Biennium 1986-1987, Official Records. 60p. 1987. 7.50 (ISBN 0-317-64762-8). UN.

United Nations: General Assembly: 41st Session Supplement: Report of the Preparatory Committee for UN Conference for the Promotion of International Co-operation in the Peaceful Uses of Nuclear Energy, Official Records, No. 47. 16p. 1987. pap. 3.00 (ISBN 0-317-59489-3). UN.

United Nations General Assembly 41st Session, Supplement 5-C: United Nations Relief & Works Agency for Palestine Refugees in the Near East, Financial Report & Audited Financial Statements for the Year Ended Dec. 31 1986 & Rpt. of the Board of Auditors, Official Records. 53p. 1987. 7.50 (ISBN 0-317-64825-X). UN.

United Nations General Assembly 42nd Session, Supplement No. 11: Report of the Committee on Contributions, Official Records. 14p. 1987. pap. 3.00 (ISBN 0-317-64767-9). UN.

United Nations General Assembly 42nd Session, Supplement No. 12: Report of the United Nations High Commissioner for Refugees, Official Records. 42p. 1987. 6.00 (ISBN 0-317-64829-2). UN.

United Nations General Assembly 42nd Session, Supplement No. 19: Report of the World Food Council on the Work of Its 13th Session, 8-11 Jun. 1987, Official Records. 30p. 1987. 5.00 (ISBN 0-317-64830-6). UN.

United Nations: General Assembly 42nd Session. Supplement No. 10: Report of the International Law Commission on the Work of its 39th Session, 4 May-27 July 1987, Official Records. 136p. 1987. 17.00 (ISBN 0-317-68000-5). UN.

United Nations: General Assembly 42nd Session, Supplement No. 18: Report of the Committee on the Elimination of Racial Discrimination, Official Records. 186p. 1987. 21.00 (ISBN 0-317-68003-X). UN.

United Nations General Assembly 42nd Session, Supplement No. 29: Report of the Ad Hoc Committee on the Indian Ocean, Official Records. 7p. 1987. pap. 3.00 (ISBN 0-317-64833-0). UN.

United Nations: General Assembly 42nd Session, Supplement No. 27: Report of the Conference on Disarmament, Official Records. 204p. 1987. 21.00 (ISBN 0-317-68004-8). UN.

United Nations General Assembly 42nd Session, Supplement No. 38: Report of the Committee on the Elimination of Discrimination Against Women, Official Records, 6th Sess. 94p. 1987. 12.00 (ISBN 0-317-64770-9). UN.

United Nations General Assembly 42nd Session, Supplement No. 39: Report of the High-Level Committee on the Review of Technical Co-operation among Developing Countries, Official Records. 43p. 1987. 6.00 (ISBN 0-317-64777-6). UN.

United Nations General Assembly 42nd Session, Supplement No. 34: Report of the Joint Inspection Unit, Official Records. 26p. 1987. 5.00 (ISBN 0-317-64834-9). UN.

United Nations: General Assembly 42nd Session, Supplement No. 30: Report of the International Civil Service Commission for the Year 1987, Official Records. 143p. 1987. 19.00 (ISBN 0-317-68005-6). UN.

United Nations: General Assembly 42nd Session, Supplement No. 32: Report of the Committee on Conferences, Official Records. 90p. 1987. 12.00 (ISBN 0-317-68006-4). UN.

United Nations: General Assembly 42nd Session, Supplement No. 37: Report of the Intergovernmental Committee on Science & Technology for Development, Official Records. 55p. 1987. 7.50 (ISBN 0-317-68007-2). UN.

United Nations General Assembly 42nd Session, Supplement No. 41: Report of the Special Committee on Enhancing the Effectiveness of the Principle of Non-use of Force in International Relations, Official Records. 25p. 1987. pap. 4.00 (ISBN 0-317-64781-4). UN.

United Nations General Assembly 42nd Session, Supplement No. 42: Report of the Disarmament Commission, Official Records. 46p. 1987. 6.00 (ISBN 0-317-64783-0). UN.

United Nations General Assembly 42nd Session, Supplement No. 46: Report of the Preparatory Committee for the Third Special Session of the General Assembly Devoted to Disarmament, Official Records. 8p. 1987. pap. 3.00 (ISBN 0-317-64786-5). UN.

United Nations General Assembly: 42nd Session, Supplement No. 4: Report of the International Court of Justice, 1 August 1986-31 July 1987, Official Records. 16p. 1987. 4.00 (ISBN 0-317-67999-6). UN.

United Nations: General Assembly 42nd Session, Supplement No. 40: Report of the Human Rights Committee, Official Records. 187p. 1987. 20.00 (ISBN 0-317-68009-9). UN.

United Nations General Assembly 42nd Session, Supplement No. 5-A: UNDP Financial Report & Audited Financial Statement for the Year Ended 31 Dec. 1986 & Report of the Board of Auditors, Offical Records. 186p. 1987. 20.00 (ISBN 0-317-64823-3). UN.

United Nations General Assembly 42nd Session, Supplement No. 5-B: United Nations Children's Fund, Financial Report & Audited Financial Statements for the Year Ended 31 Dec. 1986 & Report of the Board of Auditors, Official Records. 113p. 1987. 13.50 (ISBN 0-317-64824-1). UN.

United Nations General Assembly 42nd Session, Supplement No. 5-E: Voluntary Funds Administered by the United Nations High Commissioner for Refugees, Audited Financial Statements for the Year Ended 31 Dec. 1986 & Report of the Board of Auditors, Official Records. 76p. 1987. 10.00 (ISBN 0-317-64827-6). UN.

United Nations General Assembly 42nd Session, Supplement No. 5-G: UNFPA Financial Report & Audited Financial Statements for the Year Ended 31 Dec. 1986 & Rpt. of the Board of Auditors, Official Records. 41p. 1987. 6.00 (ISBN 0-317-64828-4). UN.

United Nations General Assembly 42nd Session, Supplement No. 8: Reports of the Commission on Human Settlements on the Work of Its 10th Session, 6-16 Apr. 1987, Official Records. 66p. 1987. 7.50 (ISBN 0-317-64764-4). UN.

United Nations: General Assembly: 9th Emergency Special Session: Plenary Meetings Verbatim Records of Meetings; Annexes - 29 January - 5 February 1982, Official Records. 159p. 1987. 16.50 (ISBN 0-317-58058-2). UN.

United Nations Giving Countenance to Soviet Strategic Penetrations of Africa. 16p. 1977. stitched 2.50 (ISBN 90-27-11333-5). Kluwer Academic.

United Nations: How It Works & What It Does. Evan Luard. LC 78-21471. 187p. 1985. pap. 11.95 (ISBN 0-312-83311-3). St Martin.

United Nations in a Changing World. Leland M. Goodrich. LC 74-893. (Columbia University Studies in International Organization). 280p. 1976. 35.00x (ISBN 0-231-03824-0). Columbia U Pr.

United Nations in Bangladesh. Thomas W. Oliver. LC 77-85554. 1978. 34.00x (ISBN 0-691-07593-X). Princeton U Pr.

United Nations in Economic Development: Need for a New Strategy. Sudhir Sen. LC 70-83745. 351p. 1969. lib. bdg. 14.00 (ISBN 0-379-00385-6). Oceana.

U. N. in International Politics. Ed. by Leon Gordenker. LC 71-132239. (Center of International Studies Ser.). 224p. 1971. 30.50x (ISBN 0-691-05615-3). Princeton U Pr.

United Nations in the 1970's: A Strategy for a Unique Era in the Affairs of Nations. UNA-USA National Policy Panel. LC 79-177235. (Illus.). 88p. 1971. pap. text ed. 1.00x (ISBN 0-934654-08-5). UNA-USA.

United Nations, International Law & the Rhodesian Independence Crisis. Jericho C. Nkala. 1985. 69.00x (ISBN 0-19-825394-X). Oxford U Pr.

United Nations: International Organization & World Politics. Robert Riggs & Jack Plano. 432p. 1987. text ed. 35.00 (ISBN 0-256-05525-4); pap. text ed. 26.00 (ISBN 0-256-06061-4). Dorsey.

United Nations: Its Problems & What to Do About Them. U. N. Assessment Project Staff. 36p. 1986. 4.00. Heritage Found.

United Nations Juridical Yearbook. 1980. 25.00 (ISBN 92-1-133162-5, E.83.V.1). UN.

United Nations Juridical Yearbook: 1973. cloth 13.00 (ISBN 0-686-89645-9, E.75.V.1). UN.

United Nations Juridical Yearbook, 1981. United Nations. 25.00 (ISBN 92-1-133332-6, E.84.V.1). UN.

United Nations Juridical Yearbook 1981. 235p. 1985. pap. 25.00 (UN84/5/1, UN). UNIPUB.

U. N. Law-Fundamental Rights: Two Topics in International Law. Ed. by A. Cassese. 268p. 1979. 38.00x (ISBN 90-286-0828-1, Pub. by Sijthoff & Noordhoff). Kluwer Academic.

United Nations Law Making: Cultural & Ideological Relativism & International Law for an Era of Transition. Edward McWhinney. 310p. 1984. 34.50 (ISBN 0-8419-0948-2); pap. 24.50 (ISBN 0-8419-1008-1). Holmes & Meier.

U. N. Law Reports: Sept. 1984 to Aug. 1985, Vol. 19. 1982. 75.00. Walker & Co.

United Nations Law Reports: September 1984-August 1985, Vol. 22. Ed. by John Carey. limited ed. with index o.p 35.00 (ISBN 0-686-66952-5) (ISBN 0-8027-2992-4) (ISBN 0-8027-2993-2). 90.00 (ISBN 0-8027-2978-9). Walker & Co.

United Nations Library Catalogue: Part I. 22.00 (ISBN 92-1-000024-2, G.V.E.79.0.2). UN.

United Nations of Time Square. Bruce Benderson. LC 87-42542. 24p. 1987. pap. 3.00 (ISBN 0-87376-056-5). Red Dust.

United Nations Operation in the Congo, 1960-1964. Georges Abi-Saab. (International Crises & the Role of Law Ser.). 1979. pap. 11.95x (ISBN 0-19-825323-0). Oxford U Pr.

United Nations: Pacific Settlement of the Dispute with the Republic of South Africa. 23p. 1978. stitched 5.00 (ISBN 90-27-11511-7). Kluwer Academic.

U. N. Peacekeeping Activities in Korea: A Study of India's Role, 1947-1953. Alka Gupta. 1977. 11.00x (ISBN 0-88386-850-4). South Asia Bks.

United Nations Peacekeeping, Documents & Commentary: Europe 1946-1979, Vol. 4. Rosalyn Higgins. (Illus.). 1981. 98.00x (ISBN 0-19-218322-2). Oxford U Pr.

United Nations Peacekeeping, 1946-1967: Documents & Commentary, Africa, Vol. 3 Africa. Rosalyn Higgins. 1980. 89.00x (ISBN 0-19-218321-4). Oxford U Pr.

United Nations Peacemaking: The Conciliation Commission for Palestine. David P. Forsythe. LC 71-181557. pap. 55.50 (ISBN 0-317-42329-0, 2025814). Bks Demand UMI.

United Nations Philately, 2 vols. Ed. by Arleigh Gaines. (Illus.). 978p. 1983. Set. 38.00x (ISBN 0-938152-03-3). R & D Pubns.

United Nations Philately, 2 vols. Ed. by Arleigh Gaines. (Illus.). 1000p. 1985. Set. 42.00x (ISBN 0-938152-04-1). R & D Pubns.

U. N. Protection of Civil & Political Rights, Vol. 8. John Carey. (Procedural Aspects of International Law Ser.). 205p. 1970. 20.00x (ISBN 0-8156-2146-9). U Pr of Va.

United Nations: Reality & Ideal. Peter R. Baehr & Leon Gordenker. LC 84-3155. 192p. 1984. 35.00 (ISBN 0-275-91122-5, C1122). Praeger.

United Nations Resolutions. Dusan Djonovich. (Second Series - Security Council: Vol. 1). 1988. lib. bdg. write for info. (ISBN 0-379-14401-8). Oceana.

United Nations Resolutions on Palestine & the Arab-Israeli Conflict, 1947-74, Vol. 1. George J. Torreh. 294p. 1988. 29.95. Inst Palestine.

United Nations Resolutions on Palestine & the Arab-Israeli Conflict, 1975-81, Vol. 2. Ed. by Regina Sharif. 333p. 1988. 29.95. Inst Palestine.

United Nations Resolutions on Palestine & the Arab-Israeli Conflict, 1982-1986, Vol. 3. Ed. by Michael Simpson. 340p. 1988. text ed. 29.95. Inst Palestine.

United Nations Resolutions: Series I, General Assembly, 24 vols. Dusan J. Djonovich. LC 72-13009. 1973. Vols. 1-14. 42.50 ea. (ISBN 0-379-14260-0); Vols. 15-24. 50.00 ea. Oceana.

United Nations Resolutions: Series II, Security Council, Vol. 1. Dusan Djonovich. 1988. lib. bdg. 50.00 (ISBN 0-379-14400-X). Oceana.

United Nations Secretariat. Syracuse University. Maxwell Graduate School of Citizenship & Public Affairs. Ed. by W. S. Sayre. LC 78-2884. (Carnegie Endowment for International Peace, United Nations Studies: No. 4). 1978. Repr. of 1950 ed. lib. bdg. 18.50x (ISBN 0-313-20331-8, UNNS). Greenwood.

United Nations Security Council - Official Records. Incl. 31st Year: 1975th Meeting. 12p. 3.00; 31st Year: 1976th Meeting. 1p. 1.50; 31st Year: 1977th Meeting. 10p. 3.00; 31st Year: 1978th Meeting. 1p. 1.50; 31st Year: 1979th Meeting. 23p. 4.00; 31st Year: 1980th Meeting. 17p. 4.00; 31st Year: 1981st Meeting. 10p. 3.00; 31st Year: 1982nd Meeting. 16p. 4.00. 1985. UN.

United Nations Security Council - Official Records. Incl. 35th Year: 2199th Meeting. 21p. pap. 4.00 (ISBN 0-317-57538-4); 35th Year: 2200th Meeting. 27p. pap. 4.00 (ISBN 0-317-57539-2); 35th Year: 2201st Meeting. 23p. pap. 4.00 (ISBN 0-317-57540-6); 35th Year: 2202nd Meeting. 21p. pap. 4.00 (ISBN 0-317-57541-4); 35th Meeting: 2203rd Meeting. 7p. pap. 3.00 (ISBN 0-317-57542-2); 35th Year: 2204th Meeting. 20p. pap. 4.00 (ISBN 0-317-57543-0); 35th Year: 2205th Meeting. 12p. pap. 3.00 (ISBN 0-317-57544-9); 35th Year: 2206th Meeting. 12p. pap. 3.00 (ISBN 0-317-57545-7); 35th Year: 2207th Meeting. 13p. pap. 3.00 (ISBN 0-317-57546-5); 35th Year: 2208th Meeting. 13p. pap. 3.00 (ISBN 0-317-57547-3); 35th Year: 2209th Meeting. 9p. pap. 3.00 (ISBN 0-317-57548-1); 35th Year: 2210th Meeting. 9p. pap. 4.00 (ISBN 0-317-57549-X); 35th Year: 2211th Meeting. 16p. pap. 4.00 (ISBN 0-317-57550-3); 35th Year: 2213th Meeting. 9p. pap. 3.00 (ISBN 0-317-57551-1); 35th Year: 2214th Meeting. 9p. pap. 3.00 (ISBN 0-317-57552-X); 35th Year: 2215th Meeting. 9p. pap. 3.00 (ISBN 0-317-57553-8); 35th Year: 2217th Meeting. 9p. pap. 3.00 (ISBN 0-317-57554-6); 35th Year: 2218th Meeting. 17p. pap. 4.00 (ISBN 0-317-57555-4); 35th Year: 2219th Meeting. 9p. pap. 3.00 (ISBN 0-317-57556-2). 1987. pap. UN.

United Nations Security Council: Official Records. Incl. 38th Year - Supplement for October, November, December 1983. 162p. 17.50; 31st Year: 1924th Meeting. 10p. 3.00; 31st Year: 1928th Meeting. 14p. 3.00; 31st Year: 1933rd Meeting. 9p. 3.00; 31st Year: 1935th Meeting. 13p. 3.00; 31st Year: 1937th Meeting. 11p. 3.00; 31st Year: 1939th Meeting. 28p. 4.00; 31st Year: 1940th Meeting. 14p. 3.00; 31st Year: 1944th Meeting. 11p. 3.00; 31st Year: 1945th Meeting. 22p. 4.00; 31st Year: 1946th Meeting. 19p. 4.00; 31st Year: 1947th Meeting. 12p. 3.00; 31st Year: 1948th Meeting. 17p. 4.00; 31st Year: 1953rd Meeting. 13p. 3.00; 31st Year: 1959th Meeting. 18p. 4.00; 31st Year: 1960th Meeting. 9p. 3.00; 31st Year: 1961st Meeting. 13p. 3.00; 31st Year: 1962nd Meeting. 4p. 1.50; 31st Year: 1963rd Meeting. 22p. 4.00; 31st Year: 1964th Meeting. 12p. 3.00; 31st Year: 1965th Meeting. 1p. 1.50; 31st Year: 1966th Meeting. 21p. 4.00; 31st Year: 1967th Meeting. 27p. 4.00; 31st Year: 1968th Meeting. 8p. 3.00; 31st Year: 1969th Meeting. 11p. 3.00; 31st Year: 1970th Meeting. 22p. 4.00; 31st Year: 1971st Meeting. 13p. 3.00; 31st Year: 1972nd Meeting. 22p. 4.00; 31st Year: 1973rd Meeting. 1p. 1.50. 1985. UN.

United Nations Security Council Official Records, 31st Year. Incl. Meeting Number 1941 - July 12, 1976. 21p. 4.00; Meeting Number 1942 - July 13, 1976. 24p. 4.00; Meeting Number 1949 - August 12, 1976. 4p. 1.50; Meeting Number 1950 - August 13, 1976. 7p. 3.00; Meeting Number 1951 - August 16, 1976. 1p. 1.50; Meeting Number 1954 - August 31, 1976. 10p. 3.00 (ISBN 0-317-41002-4); Meeting Number 1951 - August 16, 1976. 5p. 1.50 (ISBN 0-317-41003-2); Meeting Number 1955 - September 10, 1976. 7p. 3.00 (ISBN 0-317-41004-0); Meeting Number 1957 - September 30, 1976. 13p. 3.00 (ISBN 0-317-41005-9). 1985. UN.

U. N. Security Council Resolution 242: A Case Study in Diplomatic Ambiguity. Caradon & Arthur J. Goldberg. LC 81-1671. 64p. 1981. 5.50 (ISBN 0-934742-11-1, Inst Study Diplomacy). Geo U Sch For Serv.
U. N. Security Council Resolution 242: A Case Study in Diplomatic Ambiguity. Lord Caradon et al. 64p. 1985. pap. text ed. 5.25 (ISBN 0-8191-5061-4, Inst for Study Diplomacy). U Pr of Amer.
United Nations Security Council: Towards Greater Effectiveness. Davidson Nicol et al. LC 82-240243. (Illus.). xvi, 334p. 1982. write for info. UNITAR.
United Nations Statistical Yearbook: 1981. 1070p. (Eng. & Fr.). 1983. text ed. 65.00 (E.83.XVII.1); pap. 55.00 (E.83.XVII.1). UN.
United Nations: The Next Twenty-Five Years. Organization of Peace Commission. Ed. by Louis B. Sohn. LC 42-18205. 1971. 15.00 (ISBN 0-379-13353-9). Oceana.
United Nations Trade & Development Board - Official Records: 13th Special Session, Supplement No. 1A Report, April 2-6, 1984. 12p. 4.00. UN.
United Nations Trade & Development Board Official Records: 28th Session, March 26 - April 6, 1984. 11.00. UN.
United Nations Trade & Development Board Official Records, 29th Session, Supplement No. 2: Report of the Special Committee on Preferences on Its Twelfth Session. 42p. 1985. 7.00. UN.
United Nations Treaties on Outer Space. LC 84-46787. 37p. 2.00 (ISBN 92-1-100238-9, E.84.I.10). UN.
United Nations Treaty Ser. write for info. Oceana.
United Nations Treaty Series. Incl. Vol. 1004. 606p. 1976 (ISBN 0-317-41432-1); Vol. 1005. 589p. 1976 (ISBN 0-317-41433-X); Vol. 1039. 473p. 1976; Vol. 1046. 421p. 1977; Vol. 1047. 445p. 1976; Vol. 1053. 524p. 1977; Vol. 1056. 404p. 1977; Vol. 1057. 427p. 1977; Vol. 1063. 352p. 1977; Vol. 1064. 516p. 1978; Vol. 1065. 580p. 1978; Vol. 1068. 463p. 1978; Vol. 1069. 469p. 1978; Vol. 1070. 414p. 1978; Vol. 1071. 392p. 1978; Vol. 1073. 450p. 1978; Vol. 1074. 376p. 1978; Vol. 1076. 352p. 1978; Vol. 1080. 424p. 1978; Vol. 1085. 418p. 1978; Vol. 1093. 377p. 1978; Vol. 1050. 441p; Vol. 1077. 374p. 1978; Vol. 1087. 384p. 1978; Vol. 1088. 441p. 1978; Vol. 1090. 388p. 1978; Vol. 1092. 433p. 1978; Vol. 1075. 374p. 1986; Vol. 1082. 379p. 1986. 22.00 ea. UN.
United Nations Treaty Series. Incl. Vol. 1024. 435p; Vol. 1027. 419p; Vol. 1032. 379p; Vol. 1040. 394p; Vol. 1052. 435p; Vol. 1059. 477p; Vol. 1067. 382p; Vol. 1072. 413p; Vol. 1083. 375p; Vol. 1090. 381p; Vol. 1106. 413p; Vol. 1110. 388p; Vol. 1111. 475p; Vol. 1115. 371p; Vol. 1130. 361p; Vol. 1132. 446p. 1985. 22.00 ea. UN.
United Nations Treaty Series. Incl. Vol. 1089. 408p. 1986; Vol. 1098. 399p. 1986; Vol. 1105. 438p. 1986; Vol. 1108. 457p. 1986; Vol. 1139. 427p. 1986. 22.00 ea. UN.
United Nations Treaty Series. 1987. 22.00 ea. Vol. 1079, 366 pgs. Vol. 1086, 351 pgs. Vol. 1088, 441 pgs. Vol. 1091, 379 pgs. Vol. 1095, 345 pgs. Vol. 1189, 728 pgs. UN.
United Nations Treaty Series. Incl. Volume 1113. 370p; Volume 1119. 389p; Volume 1125. 699p; Volume 1126. 458p; Volume 1129. 412p; Volume 1137. 949p; Volume 1143. 373p; Volume 1144. 410p; Volume 1163. 386p; Volume 1187. 412p; Volume 1191. 441p. 1987. 22.00 (ISBN 0-317-64632-X). UN.
United Nations Treaty Series. (Eng. & Fr.). 1987. 22.00 ea. Vol. 1103, 398 pp. Vol. 1117, 352 pp. Vol. 1133, 429 pp. Vol. 1140, 400 pp. Vol. 1147, 385 pp. Vol. 1155, 533 pp. UN.
United Nations Treaty Series. (Eng. & Fr.). 1988. pap. 22.00 ea. Vol. 1156, 500 pgs. Vol. 1166, 437 pgs. Vol. 1167, 466 pgs. Vol. 1175, 477 pgs. Vol. 1182, 424 pgs. Vol. 1186, 419 pgs. UN.
United Nations Treaty Series. (Eng. & Fr.). 1988. 22.00 ea. Vol. 1066, 371 pgs.; Vol. 1114, 379 pgs. Vol. 1123, 437 pgs; Vol. 1136, 462 pgs. Vol. 1148, 454 pgs.; Vol. 1162, 465 pgs. Vol. 1164, 423 pgs.; Vol. 1169, 395 pgs. Vol. 1185, 714 pgs.; Vol. 1197, 439 pgs. Vol. 1206, 439 pgs.; Vol. 1235, 622 pgs. UN.
United Nations Trusteeship Council - Official Records: 15th Special Session, December 16-20, 1982; 50th Session, May 16 - November 28, 1983. 48p. 1985. 6.00. UN.
United Nations Trusteeship Council: Official Records: Fifteenth Special Session, December 16-20, 1982; Fiftieth Session, May 16 - November 28, 1983: Supplement No. 1: Resolutions. 17p. 1985. 3.00. UN.
U. N. under Attack. Jeffrey Harrod & Nico Schrijver. 160p. 1988. text ed. 44.40 (ISBN 0-566-05695-X, Pub. by Gower Pub England). Gower Pub Co.
United Nations Water Conference: Summary & Main Documents. new ed. Ed. by Asit K. Biswas. LC 77-30461. 1978. 65.00 (ISBN 0-08-022392-3); 15.40 (ISBN 0-08-023410-0). Pergamon.
U. N. World Assembly on the Elderly: The Aging as a Resource; The Aging as a Concern & the Situation of the Elderly in Austria. Ed. by Charlotte Nusberg. 52p. (Orig.). 1981. pap. text ed. 3.50 (ISBN 0-910473-08-0). Intl Fed Ageing.
United Nations Yearbook of the International Law Commission: 1984, Vol. 1. 35.00 (ISBN 92-1-133336-9, E.85.V.6). UN.
United Nations Yearbook of the Internaitonal Law Commission: 1984, Vol. II, Pt. 2. 13.50 (ISBN 92-1-133337-7, E.85.V.7). UN.
United Negro College Fund Archives: A Guide & Index to the Microfiche. (Illus.). 422p. 1985. 95.00 (ISBN 0-8357-0678-8, Pub. by Collections & Curr). Univ Microfilms.
United Order Among the Mormons (Missouri Phase) An Unfinished Experiment in Economic Organization. Joseph A. Geddes. LC 72-8247. Repr. of 1924 ed. 32.00 (ISBN 0-404-11001-0). AMS Pr.
United Roumania. Charles U. Clark. LC 79-135799. (Eastern Europe Collection Ser). 1970. Repr. of 1932 ed. 25.50 (ISBN 0-405-02741-9). Ayer Co Pubs.
United State Supreme Court Manual. Joseph M. Kadans. 160p. 1984. (incl. s upp. to date of purchase) 45.00 (ISBN 0-931907-00-4). Legal Pr Serv.
United States. Laurie Anderson. LC 82-48315. (Illus.). 224p. 1984. 29.45i (ISBN 0-06-015243-5, HarpT); pap. 21.95 (ISBN 0-06-091110-7). Har-Row.
United States. rev. ed. Ed. by Jerry E. Jennings et al. LC 83-82539. (Illus.). (gr. 5 up). 1985. text ed. 12.95 (ISBN 0-88296-479-8); tchr's. guide 9.95 (ISBN 0-88296-349-X). Gateway Pr MI.
United States. Louis A. Knafla. (Bibliographies on the History of Crime & Criminal Justice Ser.: vol. 2). 1988. lib. bdg. 45.00x (ISBN 0-88736-158-7). Meckler Corp.
United States. Len Martelli & Alma Graham. (Our Nation, Our World Ser.). 128p. (gr. 5). 1983. text ed. 23.56 (ISBN 0-07-039945-X). McGraw.
United States. (International Blank Bks.). 128p. 1982. 3.95 (ISBN 0-941434-12-5). Stewart Tabori & Chang.
United States. LC 84-52692. (Library of Nations Ser.). 1985. lib. bdg. 18.60 (ISBN 0-8094-5303-7, Pub. by Time-Life). Silver.
United States. (Library of Nations Ser.). 1986. 14.95 (ISBN 0-8094-5112-3). Time-Life.
United States. (Economist Business Traveller's Guides Ser.). (Illus., Orig.). 1987. 17.95 (ISBN 0-13-234881-0). P-H.
United States. (Let's Visit Places & Peoples - - Nations, Dependencies, & Sovereignties of the World Ser.). (Illus.). (gr. 5 up). 1988. 12.95 (ISBN 0-222-01014-2). Chelsea Hse.
United States see Commercial Business & Trade Laws.
U. S. - Arab Economic Relations: A Time of Transition. Ed. by Michael Czinkota & Scot Marciel. LC 85-3614. 368p. 1985. 48.95 (ISBN 0-275-90081-9, C0081). Praeger.
U. S. - Arab Relations: Security in the Arabian Peninsula & Gulf States, 1974-84, No. 7. J. E. Peterson. 180p. (Orig.). 1984. pap. 10.00 (ISBN 0-916729-12-5). Natl Coun Arab.
U. S. - Arab Relations: The Evangelical Dimension, No. 3. Ruth Mouly. (Orig.). 1985. pap. 5.00 (ISBN 0-317-20009-7). Natl Coun Arab.
U. S. - Arab Relations: The Economic Dimension, No. 6. Joseph Story. 40p. (Orig.). 1985. pap. 5.00 (ISBN 0-916729-07-9). Natl Coun Arab.
U. S. - Arab Relations: The European Dimension, No. 10. John P. Richardson. 40p. (Orig.). pap. 5.00. Natl Coun Arab.
U. S. - Arab Relations: The Iranian Dimension, No. 9. James A. Bill. (Orig.). 1984. pap. 5.00 (ISBN 0-916729-06-0). Natl Coun Arab.
U. S. - Arab Relations: The Iran-Iraq War & the Gulf Cooperation Council, No. 12. John D. Anthony. (Orig.). 1984. pap. 2.00 (ISBN 0-916729-10-9). Natl Coun Arab.
U. S. - Arab Relations: The Iran-Iraq War & U. S.-Iraq Relations: An Iraqi Perspective, No. 11. Anthony H. Cordesman. 40p. (Orig.). pap. 5.00. Natl Coun Arab.
U. S. - Arab Relations: The Iraq Dimension, No. 5. Fred Axelgard. 45p. (Orig.). 1985. pap. 4.00 (ISBN 0-916729-05-2). Natl Coun Arab.
U. S. - Arab Relations: The Literary Dimension, No. 2. Gregory Orfalea. 44p. (Orig.). 1985. pap. 4.00 (ISBN 0-916729-01-X). Natl Coun Arab.
U. S. - Arab Relations: The Syrian Dimension, No. 4. Talcott Seelye. 40p. (Orig.). 1985. pap. 4.00 (ISBN 0-916729-02-8). Natl Coun Arab.
U. S. - Arab Relations: The Strategic Dimension, No. 8. Anthony H. Cordesman. 80p. (Orig.). 1984. pap. 8.00 (ISBN 0-916729-08-7). Natl Coun Arab.
U. S. - Bangladesh Relations: A Study of the Political & Economic Developments During 1971-1981. Jayasee Biswas. 1985. 12.50x (ISBN 0-8364-1309-1). South Asia Bks.
U. S. - Canada Free Trade Agreement: The Complete Resource Guide, 3 vols. 1988. Set. looseleaf 350.00 (ISBN 1-55871-000-0, 365); Legal Guide. 75.00. BNA.
U. S. - Canadian Economic Relations: Next Steps? Ed. by Edward R. Fried & Philip H. Trezise. LC 84-72025. (Dialogue on Public Policy Ser.). 141p. 1984. pap. 10.95 (ISBN 0-8157-2925-1). Brookings.
U. S. - Canadian Softwood Lumber: Trade Dispute Negotiations. Charles F. Doran & Timothy J. Naftali. 62p. (Orig.). 1987. pap. text ed. 7.00 (ISBN 0-941700-11-9). JH FPI SAIS.
U. S. - Canadian Tables of Feed Composition. 148p. 1982. 11.50x (ISBN 0-309-03245-8). Natl Acad Pr.
U. S. - China Normalization: An Evaluation of Foreign Policy. Joanne Chang. (World Affairs Ser.: Vol. 22, Bk 4). (Orig.). 1986. pap. 9.95 (ISBN 0-87940-083-8). Monograph Series.
U. S. - China Relations. Laurence W. Levine. 7.95 (ISBN 0-8315-0136-7). Speller.
U. S. - China Trade Negotiations. Rosalie L. Tung. (Pergamon Policy Studies on Business & Economics Ser.). 245p. 1982. 49.00 (ISBN 0-08-027187-1). Pergamon.
U. S. - China Trade: Problems & Prospects. Ed. by Eugene K. Lawson. LC 88-3214. 352p. 1988. lib. bdg. 49.95 (ISBN 0-275-92494-7, C2494). Praeger.
U. S. - Iana. 2nd ed. Ed. by Wright Howes. 1978. Repr. 49.95 (ISBN 0-8352-0103-1). Bowker.
U. S. - Japan Relations. Ed. by Richard B. Finn. 343p. 1986. pap. 14.95x (ISBN 0-88738-661-X). Transaction Bks.
U. S. - Japan Seminar of Piezoelectric Polymers, Proceedings: Honolulu, Hawaii, July 1983. Ed. by K. D. Pae. (Ferroelectric & Related Materials Ser.). 354p. 1984. text ed. 149.00 (ISBN 0-677-16555-2). Gordon & Breach.
U. S. - Japan Strategic Reciprocity: A Neo-Internationalist View. Edward A. Olsen. (Publication Ser.: No. 307). xiii, 194p. 1985. pap. 10.95x (ISBN 0-8179-8072-5). Hoover Inst Pr.
U. S. - Japan Trade Law Conference 1979. Federal Bar Association Staff. 198p. 35.00 (ISBN 0-318-14102-7). Federal Bar.
United States - Japanese Political Relations: The Critical Issues Affecting Asia's Future. Center for Strategic Studies Staff. LC 80-12143. (Center for Strategic Studies, Georgetown University Special Report: No. 7). ix, 104p. 1980. Repr. of 1968 ed. lib. bdg. 35.00x (ISBN 0-313-22376-9, CSUS). Greenwood.
U. S. - Latin American Relations. Michael J. Kryzanek. LC 85-6510. 272p. 1985. 40.95 (ISBN 0-275-90131-9, C0131). Praeger.
U. S. - Mexican Trade Relations: From the Generalized System of Preferences to a Formal Bilateral Trade Treaty. Gustavo Del Castillo V. (Research Report Ser.: No. 14). 27p. (Orig.). 1985. pap. 5.50 (ISBN 0-935391-13-4). Ctr Mex Studies.
U. S. - Mexico Relations: Agriculture & Rural Development. Ed. by Bruce F. Johnston et al. LC 86-23103. 416p. 1987. 42.50x (ISBN 0-8047-1319-7). Stanford U Pr.
U. S. - Mexico Relations: Economic & Social Aspects. Ed. by Clark W. Reynolds & Carlos Tello. LC 81-86450. xvi, 373p. 1983. 35.00x (ISBN 0-8047-1163-1); pap. 12.95x (ISBN 0-8047-1286-7). Stanford U Pr.
U. S. - Mexico Trade Law. Federal Bar Association Staff. 183p. 35.00 (ISBN 0-318-14103-5). Federal Bar.
U. S. - Pakistan & India Strategic Relations. Rajvir Singh. 1986. 28.50x (ISBN 0-8364-1631-7, Pub. by Chugh Pubns India). South Asia Bks.
U. S. - Panama Relations, 1903-1978: A Study in Linkage Politics. David Farnsworth & James McKenney. (Replica Edition Ser.). 314p. 1983. 35.50x (ISBN 0-86531-969-3). Westview.
U. S. - South Africa Relations: The Technological Factor. Aaron Segal. 30p. 1984. pap. text ed. 3.50 (ISBN 0-941934-42-X). Indiana Africa.
U. S. - Soviet Cooperation in Space: A Technical Memorandum. Intro. by John H. Gibbons. LC 85-600561. (OTA-TM-STI-27). (Illus.). 123p. (Orig.). 1985. pap. 4.50 (ISBN 0-318-18860-0, S/N 052-003-01004-6). USGPO.
U. S. - Soviet Relations. Simon Serfaty. 84p. (Orig.). Date not set. pap. text ed. 11.00 (ISBN 0-941700-30-5). JH FPI SAIS.
U. S. - Soviet Security Cooperation: Achievements, Failures, Lessons. Ed. by Alexander George et al. 768p. 1988. 42.00 (ISBN 0-19-505397-4); pap. text ed. 18.95 (ISBN 0-19-505398-2). Oxford U Pr.
United States - Soviet Summit Meetings, 1967-1985: A Checklist. Alva W. Stewart. (Public Administration Ser.: P 1987). 10p. 1986. 3.00 (ISBN 0-89028-967-0). Vance Biblios.
U. S. - Soviet Summits: An Account of East-West Diplomacy at the Top, 1955-1985. Gordon R. Weihmiller. 230p. (Orig.). 1986. lib. bdg. 24.75 (ISBN 0-8191-5442-3, Pub. by Inst Study Diplomacy); pap. text ed. 10.25 (ISBN 0-8191-5443-1). U Pr of Amer.
U. S. - Soviet Summits: An Account of East-West Diplomacy at the Top, 1955-1985. Gordon R. Weihmiller & Dusko Doder. LC 86-11023. 230p. (Orig.). 1986. lib. bdg. 24.75 (ISBN 0-934742-35-9, Inst Study Diplomacy); pap. text ed. 10.25 (ISBN 0-934742-36-7, Inst Study Diplomacy). Geo U Sch For Serv.
U. S. - U. S. S. R. Grain Agreement. Roger B. Porter. 144p. 1984. 32.50 (ISBN 0-521-23676-2). Cambridge U Pr.
United States- Korea Relations. Ed. by Robert A. Scalapino & Han Sung-joo. LC 86-2388. (Research Papers & Policy Studies: No. 19). xii, 226p. (Orig.). 1986. pap. 20.00x (ISBN 0-912966-93-9). IEAS.
United States: A Contemporary Human Geography. Paul L. Knox. LC 87-3166. 287p. 1988. pap. 31.95 (ISBN 0-470-20845-7). Wiley.
U. S. A Cultural Mosaic. 380p. (gr. 6-8). 12.50 (ISBN 0-686-74871-9). ADL.
United States: A Guide to Library Holdings in the United Kingdom. Compiled by Peter Snow. 750p. 1982. 85.00x (ISBN 0-930466-45-4). Meckler Corp.
U. S. A Statistical Portrait of the American People. Ed. by Andrew Hacker & Lorrie Millman. 1983. pap. 8.95 (ISBN 0-14-006579-2). Penguin.
United States Abridged Life Tables: 1919-1920. U. S. Department of Commerce, Bureau of the Census Staff & Elbertie Foudray. LC 75-37268. (Demography Ser.). (Illus.). 1976. Repr. of 1923 ed. 14.00x (ISBN 0-405-08000-X). Ayer Co Pubs.
U. S. Academic Community & the Training of Foreign Medical Graduates for Careers in Asia. 112p. 1.50 (ISBN 0-318-17483-9, 2). A B M A C.
U. S. Acquires the Philippines: Consensus vs. Reality. Louis J. Halle. LC 85-9233. (Credibility of Institutions, Policies & Leadership Ser.: Vol. 15). 72p. (Orig.). 1985. lib. bdg. 14.75 (ISBN 0-8191-4759-1, Co-Pub. by White Burket Miller Center of Public Affairs, University of Virginia, Charlottesville); pap. 5.00 (ISBN 0-8191-4760-5). U Pr of Amer.
U. S. Acres Counts Its Chickens. Jim Davis. (Illus.). 128p. (ps up). 1987. pap. 5.95 (ISBN 0-345-34881-8). Pharos Bks NY.
U. S. Acres Goes Half Hog. Jim Davis. 128p. 1987. pap. 5.95 (ISBN 0-345-34392-1). Pharos Bks NY.
U. S. Acres Rules the Roost. Jim Davis. 128p. 1988. pap. 5.95 (ISBN 0-345-35514-8). Pharos Bks NY.
United States Administrative Citations, 13 vols. Shepard's Editorial Staff. (Specialized Citations Ser.). 315.00. Shepards-McGraw.
United States After the World War. facsimile ed. James C. Malin. LC 77-37897. (Select Bibliographies Reprint Ser). Repr. of 1930 ed. 29.00 (ISBN 0-8369-6735-6). Ayer Co Pubs.
United States After War. facs. ed. A. H. Hansen et al. LC 69-18571. (Essay Index Reprint Ser). 1945. 16.50 (ISBN 0-8369-1069-9). Ayer Co Pubs.
United States Agricultural Export Policy. Ed. by Sheila M. Geoghegan. (Wisconsin International Law Journal Ser.: Vol. 1 (1982)). 150p. (Orig.). 1983. pap. text ed. 8.00 (ISBN 0-933431-00-7). U Wisc Law Madison.
U. S. Agricultural Policies: A Market Process Approach. E. C. Pasour. 184p. 1986. pap. 7.95 (ISBN 0-910614-73-3). Foun Econ Ed.
U. S. Agricultural Policy: The Nineteen Eighty-Five Farm Legislation. Ed. by Bruce L. Gardner. 26.50 (ISBN 0-8447-2256-1); pap. 14.00 (ISBN 0-8447-2255-3). Am Enterprise.
U. S. Agriculture & Third World Development: The Critical Linkage. Ed. by Randall B. Purcell & Elizabeth Morrison. LC 86-29860. 240p. 1987. lib. bdg. 28.50x (ISBN 1-55587-011-2). Lynne Rienner.
United States Agriculture in a Global Economy: Agriculture Yearbook, Nineteen Eighty-Five. Ed. by Larry B. Marton. LC 85-600627. (Illus.). 420p. 1985. 10.00 (ISBN 0-318-19913-0, S/N 001-000-04452-4). USGPO.
U. S. Aid to the Developing World: A Free Market Agenda. Ed. by Doug Bandow. LC 85-80362. 152p. 1985. pap. 8.00. Heritage Found.
U. S. Air Force. Bernard Fitzsimons. LC 84-6502. (Illus.). 144p. 1984. 16.95 (ISBN 0-668-06201-0, 6201). Arco.
United States Air Force in Korea: 1950-1953. rev. ed. Robert E. Futrell. LC 81-60776. 843p. 1983. 18.00 (ISBN 0-318-11837-8, S/N 008-070-00488-7). USGPO.
U. S. Airborne. Ian Padden. (Fighting Elite Ser.: No. 7). 160p. (Orig.). 1986. pap. 2.95 (ISBN 0-553-26146-0). Bantam.
U. S. Airborne Forces of World War Two. Cameron P. Laughlin. (Uniforms Illustrated Ser.: No.18). (Illus.). 72p. 1987. pap. 9.95 (ISBN 0-85368-737-4, Pub. by Arms & Armour). Sterling.
United States Airborne Forces, 1940-1986. Leroy Thompson. (Illus.). 128p. (Orig.). 1987. pap. 12.95 (ISBN 0-7137-1921-4, Pub. by Blandford Pr England). Sterling.
U. S. Aircraft Carriers: A Bibliography. A. Lani Low & James F. Muche. (Orig.). 1986. pap. text ed. 15.00x (ISBN 0-910651-12-4). Fathom Eight.
U. S. Aircraft Carriers: An Illustrated Design History. Norman Friedman. (Illus.). 488p. 1983. 46.95 (ISBN 0-87021-739-9). Naval Inst Pr.
U. S. Airfreight Industry. Nawal K. Taneja. LC 78-24840. 272p. 1979. 30.00x (ISBN 0-669-02853-3). Lexington Bks.
U. S. Airline Industry: End of an Era. Paul Biederman. LC 81-17845. 222p. 1982. 35.00 (ISBN 0-275-90763-5, C0763). Praeger.
United States Airlines: Trunk & Regional Carriers, Their Operations & Management. Leo G. Fradenburg. 480p. (Orig.). 1979. pap. text ed. 27.95 (ISBN 0-8403-2128-7). Kendall-Hunt.

United States & the Developing Economies. rev. ed. Gustav Ranis. (Problems of Modern Economy Ser.). 1973. 8.95x (ISBN 0-393-05461-6, NortonC); pap. 5.95x (ISBN 0-393-09999-7). Norton.

U. S. & the Developing World: Agenda for Action, 1974. James W. Howe & Overseas Development Council Staff. LC 74-4234. (Agenda Ser.). 228p. 1974. pap. 3.95 (ISBN 0-686-28670-7). Overseas Dev Council.

United States & the Developing World: Agenda for Action, 1973. Overseas Development Council Staff & Robert E. Hunter. LC 73-76292. (Agenda Ser.). 172p. 1973. pap. 2.50 (ISBN 0-686-28671-5). Overseas Dev Council.

United States & the Development of the Puerto Rican Status Question, 1936-1968. Surendra Bhana. LC 74-7077. x, 294p. 1975. 29.95x (ISBN 0-7006-0126-0). U Pr of KS.

United States & the Direct Broadcast Satellite: The Politics of International Broadcasting in Space. Sara F. Luther. 240p. 1988. 39.95. Oxford U Pr.

United States & the Disruption of the Spanish Empire, 1810-1822. Charles C. Griffin. 1968. lib. bdg. 21.50x (ISBN 0-374-93287-5, Octagon). Hippocrene Bks.

United States & the European Community: Policies for a Changing World Economy. 75p. 1971. 2.50 (ISBN 0-317-33999-0, 744); pap. 1.50 (ISBN 0-317-34000-X, 044P). Comm Econ Dev.

United States & the Far East. 2nd ed. American Assembly Staff. Ed. by Willard L. Thorp. LC 62-12831. pap. 48.00 (ISBN 0-317-08145-4, 2050840). Bks Demand UMI.

United States & the Global Environment: A Guide to American Organizations Concerned with International Environment Issues. Pref. by Thaddeus C. Trzyna. LC 79-53313. (Who's Doing What Ser.: No. 9). 72p. (Orig.). 1983. pap. 25.00x (ISBN 0-912102-45-4). Cal Inst Public.

United States & the Global Struggle for Minerals. Alfred E. Eckes, Jr. LC 78-11082. 365p. 1979. text ed. 20.00x (ISBN 0-292-78506-2); pap. 9.95x (ISBN 0-292-78511-9). U of Tex Pr.

United States & the Hawaiian Kingdom: A Political History. Merze Tate. LC 80-14045. (Illus.). ix, 374p. 1980. Repr. of 1965 ed. lib. bdg. 35.00x (ISBN 0-313-22441-2, TAUS). Greenwood.

United States & the Inter-American System: Are There Functions for the Forms, No. 17. Tom J. Farer. (Studies in Transnational Legal Policy). 77p. 3.50 (ISBN 0-318-13190-0). Am Soc Intl Law.

United States & the International Labor Organization. LC 81-151047. 132p. cancelled. Comm Peace.

United States & the Italo-Ethiopian Crisis. Brice Harris, Jr. 1964. 17.50x (ISBN 0-8047-0243-8). Stanford U Pr.

United States & the Korean Problem, Documents, 1943-1953. U. S. Congress. Senate, Committee on Foreign Relations. LC 72-38089. Repr. of 1953 ed. 20.00 (ISBN 0-404-56962-5). AMS Pr.

United States & the Latin American Sphere of Influence, 2 vols. Ed. by Robert F. Smith. Incl. Vol. 1. Era of Caribbean Intervention, 1890-1930. 104p. 1983. pap. 6.50 (ISBN 0-89874-153-X); Vol. 2. Era of Good Neighbors, Cold Warriors & Hairshirts, 1930-1982. 1983. pap. 6.50 (ISBN 0-89874-154-8). LC 80-13478. Krieger.

United States & the Materials Advance in Russia, 1881-1906. George S. Queen. Ed. by Stuart Bruchey & Eleanor Bruchey. LC 76-5030. (American Business Abroad Ser.). (Illus.). 1976. lib. bdg. 22.00x (ISBN 0-405-09297-0). Ayer Co Pubs.

United States & the Middle East. American Assembly Staff. LC 64-14027. 192p. pap. 50.00 (2029870). Bks Demand UMI.

United States & the Middle East. American Assembly Staff & G. G. Stevens. (New Reprints in Essay & General Literature Index Ser.). 1975. Repr. of 1964 ed. 20.25 (ISBN 0-518-10195-9, 10195). Ayer Co Pubs.

United States & the Middle East. Ed. by Georgiana G. Stevens. LC 64-14027. 1964. 4.95 (ISBN 0-936904-05-4); pap. 1.95 (ISBN 0-936904-30-5). Am Assembly.

United States & the Near East. rev. ed. Ephraim A. Speiser. LC 73-100244. (Illus.). 1971. Repr. of 1950 ed. lib. bdg. 35.00x (ISBN 0-8371-4031-5, SPUS). Greenwood.

United States & the New Law of the Sea: Territorial Claims & Sea Bed Exploitation in the 1980's. Tim J. Watts. (Public Administration Ser.: P 2251). 30p. 1987. 7.50 (ISBN 1-55590-491-2). Vance Biblios.

United States & the Origins of the Cold War, 1941-1947. John L. Gaddis. LC 75-186388. (Contemporary American History Ser.). 396p. 1972. 37.50x (ISBN 0-231-03289-7); pap. 14.00x (ISBN 0-231-08302-5). Columbia U Pr.

United States & the Pacific Economy in the 1980's. Ed. by Kermit Hanson & Thomas Roehl. LC 80-16599. (ITT Key Issue Lecture Ser.). 160p. 1980. pap. text ed. 10.28 scp. Bobbs.

United States & the Palestinian People. Michael E. Jansen. 215p. 1970. 5.95 (ISBN 0-88728-107-9). Inst Palestine.

United States & the Palestinians. Mohammed K. Shadid. 240p. 1981. 26.00x (ISBN 0-312-83315-6). St Martin.

United States & the Persian Gulf: An ANVIL Original. Joseph S. Roucek & Michael V. Belok. LC 84-19366. (Anvil Ser.). 208p. 1985. pap. text ed. 8.25 (ISBN 0-89874-574-8). Krieger.

United States & the Philippine Bases. Evelyn Colbert. 28p. (Orig.). 1987. pap. text ed. 8.00 (ISBN 0-941700-26-7). JH FPI SAIS.

United States & the Philippines. American Assembly Staff. Ed. by Frank H. Golay. LC 66-22802. 192p. pap. 50.00 (2029871). Bks Demand UMI.

United States & the Philippines. Ed. by Frank H. Golay. LC 66-22802. 1966. pap. 1.95 (ISBN 0-936904-06-2). Am Assembly.

United States & the Philippines: A Study of Neocolonialism. Stephen R. Shalom. LC 80-29357. (Studies in Political Economy). (Illus.). 320p. 1981. 22.00 (ISBN 0-89727-014-2). ISHI PA.

United States & the Philippines: Background for Policy. Claude A. Buss. LC 77-22589. 1977. pap. 9.00 (ISBN 0-8447-3258-3). Am Enterprise.

United States & the Problem of Recovery After 1893. Gerald T. White. LC 80-39558. 176p. 1982. 13.75 (ISBN 0-8173-0069-4). U of Ala Pr.

United States & the Regional Organization of Asia & the Pacific. W. W. Rostow. (Ideas & Action Ser.: No. 6). 281p. 1986. text ed. 30.00x (ISBN 0-292-78512-7). U of Tex Pr.

United States & the Republic of Panama. William D. McCain. LC 72-111724. (American Imperialism: Viewpoints of United States Foreign Policy). Repr. of 1937 ed. 19.00 (ISBN 0-405-02036-8). Ayer Co Pubs.

United States & the Second Hague Peace Conference: American Diplomacy & International Organization, 1899-1914. Calvin D. Davis. LC 75-17353. x, 380p. 1976. 35.00 (ISBN 0-8223-0346-9). Duke.

U. S. & the Southern Cone: Argentina, Chile, Uruguay. Ed. by Arthur P. Whitaker. (American Foreign Policy Library). 1977. 29.50x (ISBN 0-674-92841-5). Harvard U Pr.

United States & the Spanish Civil War. F. Jay Taylor. LC 76-159232. 1971. Repr. of 1956 ed. lib. bdg. 20.50x (ISBN 0-374-97849-2, Octagon). Hippocrene Bks.

United States & the United Nations. Ed. by Franz B. Gross. 1965. 24.50x (ISBN 0-8061-0631-X). U of Okla Pr.

United States & the United Nations. William A. Scott & Stephen B. Withey. (National Studies on International Organization - the Carnegie Endowment for International Peace). (Illus.). 314p. 1974. Repr. of 1958 ed. lib. bdg. 35.00x (ISBN 0-8371-7537-2, SCUS). Greenwood.

United States & the United Nations Treaty on Racial Discrimination, No. 9. (Studies in Transnational Legal Policy). 94p. 3.00 (ISBN 0-318-13191-9). Am Soc Intl Law.

United States & the Washington Conference, 1921-1922. Thomas H. Buckley. LC 79-100409. pap. 59.00 (ISBN 0-317-20137-9, 2023166). Bks Demand UMI.

United States & The World see Colonies in America.

United States & the World Court. Philip C. Jessup. Incl. What's Wrong with International Law? Wolfgang Friedman; Foreign Policy of a Free Democracy. Philip C. Jessup; Fallacy of a "Preventive" War. Philip C. Jessup; Legal Process & International Order. Hans Kelsen. LC 70-147750. (Library of War & Peace; International Law). 1973. lib. bdg. 46.00 (ISBN 0-8240-0490-6). Garland Pub.

United States & the World Court. Philip C. Jessup. LC 30-269. 1971. Repr. of 1929 ed. 14.00 (ISBN 0-384-27190-1). Johnson Repr.

United States & the World Economy. Ed. by John N. Yochelson. 123p. 1985. 15.00. CSI Studies.

United States & the World Economy: The Postwar Years. Leonard S. Silk. 35.00 (ISBN 0-405-06671-6). Ayer Co Pubs.

United States & Turkey & Iran. Lewis V. Thomas & Richard N. Frye. LC 75-147379. (Illus.). xii, 291p. 1971. Repr. of 1951 ed. 29.50 (ISBN 0-208-00998-1, Archon). Shoe String.

United States & UNESCO. L. H. Evans. LC 75-37631. 224p. 1971. 12.00 (ISBN 0-379-00130-6). Oceana.

United States & Vatican Policies, 1914-1918. Dragan Zivojinovic. LC 78-52438. 1978. 22.50x (ISBN 0-87081-112-6). Colo Assoc.

U. S. & West German Housing Markets. Konrad Stahl & Raymond J. Struyk. 175p. 1985. text ed. 20.00x (ISBN 0-87766-388-2). Urban Inst.

United States & World Development: Agenda 1979. Martin M. McLaughlin & Overseas Development Council. LC 78-71589. 1979. 38.95 (ISBN 0-275-90392-3, C0392). Praeger.

United States & World Development: Agenda 1980. John W. Sewell. LC 80-82415. 256p. 1980. 38.95 (ISBN 0-275-90549-7, C0549); pap. 15.95 (ISBN 0-03-058992-4). Praeger.

U. S. & World Energy Resources: Prospects & Priorities. Ed. by Dorthea El Mallakh & Ragaei El Mallakh. LC 77-88785. (Illus.). 1977. 12.50x (ISBN 0-918714-03-6). Intl Res Ctr Energy.

United States & World Energy Sources. Ed. by Larry L. Berg et al. LC 81-21171. 320p. 1982. 44.95 (ISBN 0-275-90760-0, C0760). Praeger.

U. S. & World Order. R. Cox. write for info. (ISBN 0-275-90000-2, C0000). Praeger.

United States & World Organization, 1920-1933. Denna F. Fleming. LC 70-168040. Repr. of 1938 ed. 41.50 (ISBN 0-404-02435-1). AMS Pr.

U. S. & World Trade. William Hart. LC 85-10486. (Economics Impact Books Ser.). (Illus.). 103p. (gr. 7 up). 1985. PLB 12.90 (ISBN 0-531-10067-7). Watts.

U. S. & Worldwide Travel Accommodations Guide: For 6 to 18 Dollars per Day. 8th ed. Ed. by Mary J. Jensen. 72p. (Orig.). 1988. pap. 11.95 (ISBN 0-945499-00-0). Campus Travel.

United States Anti-Apartheid Movement: Local Activism in Global Politics. Janice Love. LC 85-3564. 316p. 1985. 42.95 (ISBN 0-275-90139-4, C0139). Praeger.

U. S. Antitrust Law in International Patent & Know-How Licensing. LC 81-65600. 78p. 1981. pap. 10.00 (ISBN 0-89707-035-6). Amer Bar Assn.

United States Antitrust Laws & Multinational Business. Barry E. Hawk. (Seven Springs Studies). 28p. 1981. pap. 3.00 (ISBN 0-943006-06-6). Seven Springs.

U. S. Apparel Industry: International Challenge - Domestic Response. Jeffrey S. Arpan et al. LC 88-6647. (Research Monograph: No. 88). 1982. pap. 24.95 (ISBN 0-88406-141-8). Ga St U Busn Pub.

U. S. Approach to the Latin American Debt Crisis. Michael T. Clark et al. 92p. (Orig.). 1988. pap. text ed. 11.00 (ISBN 0-941700-32-1). JH FPI SAIS.

United States Arctic Interests: The 1980's & 1990's. Ed. by W. E. Westermeyer & K. M. Shusterich. (Illus.). 304p. 1984. 42.50 (ISBN 0-387-96009-0). Springer-Verlag.

U. S. Armored Cruisers: A Design & Operational History. Ivan Musicant. (Illus.). 176p. 1985. 28.95 (ISBN 0-87021-714-3). Naval Inst Pr.

U. S. Arms Exports: Policies & Contractors. Paul L. Ferrari et al. LC 87-80032. 368p. (Orig.). 1987. pap. 60.00 (ISBN 0-931035-12-0). IRRC Inc DC.

U. S. Arms Exports: Policies & Contractors, 1988. Ed. by Paul L. Ferrari. Ballinger 376p. 1988. 45.00x (ISBN 0-88730-282-3). Ballinger Pub.

U. S. Arms Sales Policy: Background & Issues. Roger Labrie et al. 87p. 1982. pap. 7.00 (ISBN 0-8447-3491-8). Am Enterprise.

United States Army Air Arm: April 1861 to April 1917. Juliette A. Hennessy. (USAF Historical Studies: No. 98). 271p. pap. text ed. 27.00x (ISBN 0-89126-014-5). MA-AH Pub.

U. S. Army Air Arm, April 1861 to April 1917. Juliette A. Hennessy. (USAF General Histories Ser.). (Illus.). 258p. 1986. pap. 13.00 (ISBN 0-912799-34-X). Off Air Force.

U. S. Army Air Forces in World War II, Vol. 1. Jeffrey Ethell. (Warbirds Illustrated Ser.: No. 38). (Illus.). 72p. (Orig.). 1986. pap. 9.95 (ISBN 0-85368-722-6, Pub. by Arms & Armour). Sterling.

United States Army & Reconstruction, 1865-1877. James E. Sefton. LC 80-15136. (Illus.). xx, 284p. 1980. Repr. of 1967 ed. lib. bdg. 35.00x (ISBN 0-313-22602-4, SEUS). Greenwood.

U. S. Army Cloth Insignia - 1941 to the Present: An Illustrated Reference Guide for Collectors. Brian L. Davis. (Illus.). 68p. 1988. 14.95 (ISBN 0-85368-850-8, Pub. by Arms & Armour). Sterling.

U. S. Army Command & General Staff Colllege: A Centennial History. Boyd L. Dastrup. (Illus.). 154p. 1982. 40.00x (ISBN 0-89745-033-7). Sunflower U Pr.

U. S. Army Corps of Engineers: Albuquerque District, 1935-1985. Michael Welsh. LC 87-5912. (Illus.). 275p. 1987. 22.50x (ISBN 0-8263-0966-6). U of NM Pr.

U. S. Army Counterterrorism Handbook. 1986. lib. bdg. 79.95 (ISBN 0-8490-3493-0). Gordon Pr.

U. S. Army Counterterrorism Manual. 130p. Date not set. pap. 11.95. Lancer.

U. S. Army Enlisted Men's Clothing: Quartermaster Supply Catalog QM 3-1. Repr. of 1946 ed. 8.95 (ISBN 0-938242-03-2). Portrayal.

U. S. Army Guard & Reserves: Rhetoric, Realities, Risks. Martin Binkin & William W. Kaufmann. 160p. 1988. pap. 8.95t (ISBN 0-8157-0979-X). Brookings.

United States Army in Peacetime. Ed. by Robin Higham & Carol Brandt. 1975. 9.95 (ISBN 0-686-00372-1). AG Pr.

United States Army in Peacetime: Essays in Honor of the Bicentennial 1775-1975. Ed. by Robin Higham & Carol Brandt. (Illus.). 234p. (Orig.). 1975. 10.00x (ISBN 0-89126-018-8); pap. 5.00x (ISBN 0-89126-019-6). MA-AH Pub.

United States Army in the Korean War: Medic's War. Albert E. Cowdrey. (CMH Pub. Ser.: 20-5). (Illus.). 409p. 1987. text ed. 21.00 (ISBN 0-318-23533-1, 008-029-00147-1). USGPO.

United States Army in the Korean War, South to the Naktong, North to the Yalu (June-November 1950) Ed. by Roy E. Appleman. LC 60-60043. (Center of Military History Publication: No. 20-2). (Illus.). 841p. 1986. Repr. of 1961 ed. 25.50 (ISBN 0-317-59467-2, S/N 008-029-00079-2). USGPO.

United States Army in Transition. Zeb B. Bradford, Jr. & Frederic J. Brown. (Armed Forces & Society Ser.). 256p. 1973. 25.00 (ISBN 0-8039-0211-5). Seven Locks Pr.

United States Army in World War 2: European Theater of Operations, Cross-Channel Attack. Gordon A. Harrison. LC 51-61669. (Illus.). 519p. 1985. Repr. of 1951 ed. 29.00 (ISBN 0-318-22740-1, S/N 008-029-00020-2). USGPO.

United States Army in World War 2, European Theater of Operations: The Last Offensive. Charles B. MacDonald. LC 71-183070. (Illus.). 532p. 1973. 25.50 (ISBN 0-318-22956-0, S/N 008-029-00087-3). USGPO.

United States Army in World War 2, Pictorial Record, War Against Germany: Europe & Adjacent Areas. Ed. by Kenneth E. Hunter et al. 460p. 1985. Repr. of 1951 ed. 15.00 (ISBN 0-318-22957-9, S/N 008-029-00042-3). USGPO.

United States Army in World War 2, Pictorial Record: War Against Japan. Compiled by Kenneth E. Hunter et al. (Center of Military History Pulication: No. 12-1). (Illus.). 483p. 1986. Repr. of 1952 ed. 15.00 (ISBN 0-318-22959-5, S/N 008-029-00043-1). USGPO.

United States Army in World War 2. Special Studies, Manhattan: The Army & the Atomic Bomb. Vincent C. Jones. LC 84-12407. (Center for Military History Publication: No. 10-11). (Illus.). 682p. 1985. 21.00 (ISBN 0-318-18863-5, S/N 008-029-00132-2). USGPO.

U. S. Army in World War 2, Technical Services, The Corps of Engineers: The War Against Germany. Alfred M. Beck. LC 84-11376. (Center for Military History Publication: No. 10-22). (Illus.). 626p. 1985. 31.00 (ISBN 0-318-18859-7, S/N 008-029-00131-4). USGPO.

United States Army in World War 2, War in the Pacific: Campaign in the Marianas. Philip A. Crowl. LC 60-60000. (Center of Military History Pulication: No. 5-7). (Illus.). 505p. 1985. Repr. of 1960 ed. 19.00 (ISBN 0-318-22960-9, S/N 008-029-00040-7). USGPO.

United States Army in World War 2: War in the Pacific, Leyte, the Return to the Philippines. M. Hamlin Cannon. LC 53-61979. (CMH Publications: Nos. 5-9). (Illus.). 420p. 1954. 15.00 (ISBN 0-318-22739-8, S/N 008-029-00036-9). USGPO.

United States Army in World War 2: War in the Pacific, Okinawa, the Last Battle. Roy E. Appleman et al. LC 49-45742. (Illus.). 529p. 1948. 22.00 (ISBN 0-318-22738-X, S/N 008-029-00066-1). USGPO.

United States Army in World War 2: War in the Pacific, Triumph in the Philippines. Robert R. Smith. LC 62-60000. (Illus.). 756p. 1963. 25.00 (ISBN 0-318-22737-1, S/N 008-029-00033-4). USGPO.

United States Army Invades the New River Valley May 1964. Patricia G. Johnson. 137p. (Orig.). 1981. 18.00 (ISBN 0-9614765-7-5); pap. 10.00 (ISBN 0-317-61019-8). Pat G Johnson.

U. S. Army Military Academy. Robert Krist. (Illus.). 112p. 1987. 35.00 (ISBN 0-916509-16-8); deluxe ed. 125.00. Harmony Hse Pub LO.

United States Army Mobilization & Logistics in the Korean War: A Reseaarch Approach. Terrence J. Gough. LC 87-1781. (CMH Pub Ser.: No. 70-19). (Illus.). 134p. (Orig.). 1987. pap. 4.25 (S/N 008-029-00154-3). USGPO.

U. S. Army Order of Battle: European Theater of Operations, 1943-1945. LC 83-81812. 200p. 1983. Supp. 13.95 (ISBN 0-941052-71-0, 71); Supp. pap. 9.95 (ISBN 0-941052-15-X, 21). Valor Pub.

U. S. Army Order of Battle: Mediterranean & Europe 1942-1945. Ed. by W. Victor Madej. 190p. 1984. 13.95 (ISBN 0-941052-70-2, 70); pap. 9.95 (ISBN 0-941052-26-5, 20). Valor Pub.

U. S. Army Order of Battle: Pacific Theater, 1941-1945. W. Victor Madej. 1984. 13.95 (ISBN 0-941052-72-9, 72); pap. 9.95 (ISBN 0-941052-19-2, 22). Valor Pub.

U. S. Army: Pacific Theater Command & Marine Corps, Suppl. 1. LC 83-81812. 176p. 1984. 13.95 (ISBN 0-941052-73-7, 73); pap. 9.95 (ISBN 0-941052-16-8, 23). Valor Pub.

U. S. Army Ships & Watercraft of World War II. David H. Grover. (Illus.). 352p. 1987. 48.95 (ISBN 0-87021-766-6). Naval Inst Pr.

U. S. Army Sniper Training Manual. (Illus.). 196p. 1969. pap. 14.95 (ISBN 0-87364-120-5). Paladin Pr.

U. S. Army Sniper Training Manual. 1986. lib. bdg. 79.95 (ISBN 0-8490-3666-6). Gordon Pr.

U. S. Army Special Forces. Ian Padden. (Fighting Elite Ser.). 144p. 1986. pap. 2.95 (ISBN 0-553-25358-1). Bantam.

U. S. Army Special Forces Medical Handbook. G. K. Craig. 1986. lib. bdg. 79.95 (ISBN 0-8490-3487-6). Gordon Pr.

U. S. Army Special Forces Medical Handbook. rev. ed. (Illus.). 608p. 1988. pap. 19.95. Paladin Pr.

U. S. Army Special Forces Medical Handbook. U. S. Military Institute for Military Assistance Staff. (Illus.). 424p. 1987. pap. 9.95 (ISBN 0-8065-1045-5, Pub. by Citadel Pr). Lyle Stuart.

United States Army Special Warfare Counter-Insurgency Planning Guide. 1982. lib. bdg. 75.00 (ISBN 0-87700-374-2). Revisionist Pr.

United States Army Special Warfare, Its Origins, Psychological & Unconventional Warfare 1941-1952. Alfred H. Paddock, Jr. LC 82-600513. 230p. (Orig.). 1982. pap. 6.00 (ISBN 0-318-20158-5, S/N 008-020-00905-9). USGPO.

U. S. Army Standard Military Motor Vehicles, 1943. 560p. 1980. 45.00x (ISBN 0-905418-46-8, Pub. by Gresham England). State Mutual Bk.

U. S. Army Total Fitness Program. Dianne Hales & Robert E. Hales. LC 84-16992. (Illus.). 1985. 14.95 (ISBN 0-517-55550-6). Crown.

U. S. Army Tradoc Evaluation Methodology. Paul R. Lees-Haley. 257p. 1983. 395.00 (ISBN 0-938124-03-X). Rubicon.

U. S. Army Uniforms & Equipment, 1889: Specifications for Clothing, Camp & Garrison Equipage & Clothing & Equipage Materials. Quartermaster General of the Army Staff. LC 86-6972. (Illus.). x, 375p. 1986. 26.50x (ISBN 0-8032-4552-1); pap. 9.95 (ISBN 0-8032-9552-9, Bison). U of Nebr Pr.

U. S. Army Uniforms: Europe, Nineteen Forty-Four to Nineteen Forty-Five. C. P. Laughlin & J. P. Langellier. (Uniforms Illustrated Ser.: No. 14). (Illus.). 68p. (Orig.). 1986. pap. 9.95 (ISBN 0-85368-727-7, Pub. by Arms & Armour). Sterling.

United States Army Unit Histories: A Reference & Bibliography. Compiled by James T Controvich. 591p. 1983. 60.00x (ISBN 0-89126-121-4). MA-AH Pub.

U. S. Army Vehicle Guide. Frank Chadwick & Loren Wiseman. (Twilight: 2000 Ser.). (Illus.). 49p. (Orig.). 1986. pap. 7.00 (ISBN 0-943580-54-4). Game Designers.

U. S. Army War College Guide to the Battle of Gettysburg. Jay Luvaas & Harold W. Nelson. LC 86-46083. (Illus.). 256p. 1987. pap. 8.95 (ISBN 0-06-097096-0, PL 7096, PL). Har-Row.

U. S. Army War College Guide to the Battle of Antietam: The Maryland Campaign of 1862. Jay Luvaas & Harold W. Nelson. LC 87-46233. (Illus.). 320p. 1988. pap. 8.95 (ISBN 0-06-097160-6, PL-7160, PL). Har-Row.

U. S. Army War College Guide to the Battle of Gettysburg. Ed. by Jay Luvaas & Harold W. Nelson. (Illus.). 256p. 1986. 19.95 (ISBN 0-937339-00-8, 008). South Mtn Pr.

U. S. Army War College Guide to the Battle of Antietam: The Maryland Campaign of 1862. Ed. by Jay Luvaas & Harold W. Nelson. (Illus.). 336p. 1987. 21.95 (ISBN 0-937339-01-6). South Mtn Pr.

United States Army Weapon Systems, 1987. 169p. 1987. pap. 9.50 (ISBN 0-318-22588-3, S/N 008-020-01107-0). USGPO.

United States Army Weapon Systems, 1988. (Illus.). 153p. 1988. pap. 9.00 (S/N 008-020-01131-2). USGPO.

United States Art Directory & Year-Book. S. R. Koehler. Ed. by H. Barbara Weinberg. Incl. Vol. 1. Guide for Artists, Art Students, Travellers, Etc; Vol. 2. Chronicle of Events in the Art World, & a Guide for All Interested in the Progress of Art in America. LC 75-28874. (Art Experience in Late 19th Century America Ser.: Vol. 10). (Illus.). 1976. Repr. of 1884 ed. lib. bdg. 88.00 (ISBN 0-8240-2234-3). Garland Pub.

U. S. As a World Power. Archibald Coolidge. 1988. Repr. of 1927 ed. lib. bdg. 59.00x. Am Biog Serv.

U. S. As a World Power. Archibald C. Coolidge. 1981. Repr. lib. bdg. 59.00 (ISBN 0-403-00907-3). Scholarly.

United States as Seen by Spanish American Writers: 1776-1890. Jone De Onis. 226p. 4.00 (ISBN 0-318-14313-5). Hispanic Inst.

United States As Seen by Spanish American Writers (1776-1890) Jose De Onis. LC 74-26684. (Cultural Relations Between the U. S. & the Hispanic World Ser.: Vol. 1). 236p. 1975. Repr. of 1952 ed. 25.00x (ISBN 0-87752-184-0). Gordian.

U. S. Asian Relations: The National Security Paradox. Ed. by James C. Hsiung. 220p. 1983. 35.00 (ISBN 0-275-91013-X, C1013). Praeger.

United States at War. United States, Bureau of the Budget, Committee on Records of War Administration. LC 79-169909. (FDR & the Era of the New Deal Ser.). 553p. 1972. Repr. of 1946 ed. lib. bdg. 65.00 (ISBN 0-306-70330-0). Da Capo.

U. S. at War, Nineteen Forty-One to Nineteen Forty-Five. Gary R. Hess. Ed. by John H. Franklin & Abraham Eisenstadt. LC 85-20728. (American History Ser.). 184p. 1986. pap. text ed. 7.95 (ISBN 0-88295-834-8). Harlan Davidson.

United States Atlases. Ed. by Clara E. Le Gear. LC 71-154058. (Library of Congress Publications in Reprint Ser). 1971. Repr. of 1950 ed. 20.00 (ISBN 0-405-03424-5). Ayer Co Pubs.

U. S. Attorney General's Asbestos Liability Report to the Congress. U. S. Department of Justice Research Staff. 275p. (Orig.). 1986. pap. 19.95 (ISBN 0-917097-06-8). SourceFinders.

United States Aviation Reports. Ed. by Christopher R. Knauth & J. P. Leuzzi. LC 29-3034. 1974. Vols. 1-50, 1928-1967. lib. bdg. 50.00 ea.; Vols. 51-82, 1968-1982. lib. bdg. 45.00 ea. (ISBN 0-379-14100-0); Cumulative Digest, 1969-1980, 4th, 4 vols. lib. bdg. 100.00 ea.. Oceana.

U. S. Battery Industry. Business Communications Staff. 153p. 1987. 1950.00 (GB-086). BCC.

U. S. Battery Industry. Business Communications Staff. 153p. 1987. pap. 1950.00 (ISBN 0-89336-528-9, GB-086). BCC.

U. S. Battleships: A Bibliography. A. Lani Low & James F. Muche. (Orig.). 1985. pap. text ed. 15.00x (ISBN 0-910651-10-8). Fathom Eight.

U. S. Battleships: An Illustrated Design History. Norman Friedman. LC 85-13769. (Illus.). 512p. 1985. 46.95 (ISBN 0-87021-715-1). Naval Inst Pr.

U. S. Battleships in Action. Robert Stern. 50p. 1985. pap. 5.95 (ISBN 0-89747-157-1, 4004). Squad Sig Pubns.

U. S. Battleships in Action. 1980. pap. 5.95 (ISBN 0-89747-107-5). Squad Sig Pubns.

United States Battleships: The History of America's Greatest Fighting Fleet. Ed. by Alan F. Pater. LC 68-17423. 1968. 19.95 (ISBN 0-917734-07-6). Monitor.

United States: Becoming a World Power, Vol. II. 6th ed. Leon F. Litwack et al. (Illus.). 512p. 1987. pap. text ed. write for info. (ISBN 0-13-938432-4). P-H.

United States Beet Sugar Industry & the Tariff. Roy G. Blakey. LC 77-76717. (Columbia University. Studies in the Social Sciences: No. 119). Repr. of 1912 ed. 22.50 (ISBN 0-404-51119-8). AMS Pr.

U. S. Bicentennial Music I. Richard Jackson. LC 77-66. (I.S.A.M. Special Publications: No. 1). 20p. (Orig.). 1977. pap. 1.50 (ISBN 0-914678-06-X). Inst Am Music.

U. S. Bilateral Assistance in Africa: The Case of Cameroon. Peter Agbor-Tabi. (Illus.). 192p. (Orig.). 1984. lib. bdg. 24.25 (ISBN 0-8191-3909-2); pap. text ed. 12.25 (ISBN 0-8191-3910-6). U Pr of Amer.

U. S. Blowers & Fans Industry: A Product-by-Product Marketing Analysis & Competitor Profile. 275p. 1986. 650.00 (ISBN 0-317-55212-0). Busn Trend.

U. S. Bomber Force Modernization. Mike Syner et al. LC 86-21401. (National Security Paper: No. 7). 1986. 5.00 (ISBN 0-89549-078-1). Inst Foreign Policy Anal.

U. S. Books Abroad: Neglected Ambassadors. 1985. write for info. Lib Congress.

U. S. Bottled Water Market. 3rd ed. Ed. by Peter Allen. 300p. 1986. pap. 1250.00 (ISBN 0-931634-31-8). FIND-SVP.

United States Branch Mint at Dahlonega, Georgia: Its History and Coinage. Clair M. Birdsall. (Illus.). 122p. 27.50 (ISBN 0-89308-520-0). Southern Hist Pr.

United States: Brief Edition. Richard Hofdstadter et al. (Illus.). 1979. P-H.

United States, Brief Edition, Vol. II. 6th ed. Winthrop D. Jordan et al. (Illus.). 320p. 1987. pap. text ed. write for info. (ISBN 0-13-939117-7); write for info. study guide (ISBN 0-13-938457-X). P-H.

United States: Brief Edition, Vol. 1. Winthrop D. Jordan et al. (Illus.). 272p. 1987. pap. text ed. write for info. (ISBN 0-13-939109-6). P-H.

United States, Britain & Appeasement 1936-1939. C. A. MacDonald. LC 79-27121. 224p. 1980. 27.50 (ISBN 0-312-83313-X). St Martin.

U. S. Broadcasting to the Soviet Union. Ludmilla Alexeyeva. 136p. 1986. 10.00 (ISBN 0-938579-87-8). Fund Free Expression.

United States Budget in Brief, Fiscal Year 1988. (Illus.). 114p. (Orig.). 1987. pap. 2.75 (ISBN 0-318-22442-9, 041-001-00317-7). USGPO.

United States Budget in Brief, Fiscal Year 1987. (Illus.). 120p. (Orig.). 1988. pap. 3.25 (S/N 041-001-00329-1). USGPO.

U. S. Business Corporation: An Institution in Transition. Ed. by John R. Meyer & James M. Gustafson. 400p. 1988. 34.95x (ISBN 0-88730-354-4). Ballinger Pub.

United States Business Directory & Industry Register. 1979. pap. 194.40 (ISBN 0-686-24297-1). World Mktg Systems.

U. S. Business Investments in Foreign Countries: A Supplement to the Survey of Current Business. U. S. Department of Commerce. Ed. by Stuart Bruchey & Eleanor Bruchey. LC 76-5038. (American Business Abroad Ser.). (Illus.). 1976. Repr. of 1960 ed. 17.00x (ISBN 0-405-09304-7). Ayer Co Pubs.

United States, Canada & the New International Economic Order. Ed. by Ervin Laszlo & Joel Kurtzman. (Policy Studies). 1979. 33.00 (ISBN 0-08-025113-7). Pergamon.

United States-Canada Free Trade: An Evaluation of the Agreement. Jeffrey J. Schott. LC 88-9106. (Policy Analyses in International Economics Ser.: No. 24). 48p. (Orig.). 1988. pap. 3.95 (ISBN 0-88132-072-2). Inst Intl Eco.

U. S. Canadian Automotive Products Agreement of 1965: An Evaluation for Its Twentieth Year. Sidney Weintraub. LC 85-50653. (Policy Research Project Ser.: No. 68). 169p. 1985. 8.50 (ISBN 0-89940-670-X). LBJ Sch Pub Aff.

U. S. Capitalism in Crisis. Union of Radical Political Economists. 346p. 1978. pap. 4.00 (ISBN 0-85345-449-3). Monthly Rev.

United States Capitol: An Annotated Bibliography. Ed. by John R. Kerwood. LC 72-870. 465p. 1973. 29.50x (ISBN 0-8061-1030-9); pap. 15.00x (ISBN 0-8061-1253-0). U of Okla Pr.

United States Cartridge Co.-Lowell, Mass: Catalog 1891. (Illus.). pap. 3.50 (ISBN 0-686-20762-9). Sand Pond.

U. S. Catholic Elementary & Secondary & Secondary Schools, 1986-1987. Frank H. Bredeweg. 1987. 7.30 (ISBN 0-317-60173-3). Natl Cath Educ.

United States Catholic Elementary & Secondary Schools. Incl. 1981-1982. (Statistical Report on Schools, Enrollment, Staffing, & Finances). 64p. 1982. 9.55 (ISBN 0-318-12105-0); 1982-1983. 3.55 (ISBN 0-318-12106-9); 1983-1984. 6.00 (ISBN 0-318-12107-7); United States Catholic Elementary & Secondary Schools: 1981-1982. 64p. 1982. 9.55. Natl Cath Educ.

United States Catholic Elementary & Secondary Schools, 1984-85. Frank H. Bredeweg. 1985. 6.60. Natl Cath Educ.

U. S. Catholic Elementary & Secondary Schools, 1987-88. Frank H. Bredeweg. 21p. (Orig.). 1988. pap. 7.30 (ISBN 1-55833-002-X). Natl Cath Educ.

United States Catholic Elementary & Secondary Schools, 1985-86. Frank H. Bredweg. 21p. 1986. 7.30 (ISBN 0-318-20578-5). Natl Cath Educ.

United States Catholic Elementary & Secondary Schools: 1981-1982 see United States Catholic Elementary & Secondary Schools.

U. S. Catholic Elementary Schools & Their Finances, 1987. Frank H. Bredeweg. 1987. 6.75 (ISBN 0-317-60174-1). Natl Cath Educ.

United States Catholic Elementary Schools & Their Finances 1988. Frank H. Bredeweg. (Data Bank Ser.). 14p. 1988. pap. 6.60 (ISBN 1-55833-006-2). Natl Cath Educ.

United States Catholic Elementary Schools & their Finances, 1986. Frank H. Bredweg. 1986. 6.00 (ISBN 0-318-20577-7). Natl Cath Educ.

United States Catholic Elementary Schools & Their Finances 1984. 6.00 (ISBN 0-318-03695-9). Natl Cath Educ.

U. S. Catholic Institutions & Labor Unions, 1960-1980. Patrick J. Sullivan. LC 85-20171. 550p. (Orig.). 1986. lib. bdg. 42.75 (ISBN 0-8191-4970-5); pap. text ed. 24.00 (ISBN 0-8191-4971-3). U Pr of Amer.

U. S. Catholic Schools: 1973 to 1974. 92p. 1974. 2.40. Natl Cath Educ.

U. S. Catholic Seminaries & Their Future. Intro. by Francis J. Butler. 148p. 1988. pap. 5.95 (ISBN 1-55586-202-0). US Catholic.

United States Cavalry: An Illustrated History. Gregory J. Urwin. (Illus.). 192p. 1986. 24.95 (ISBN 0-7137-1219-8, Pub. by Blandford Pr England); pap. 12.95 (ISBN 0-7137-1817-X). Sterling.

U. S. Census of Eighteen Fifty, Barbour County, Ala. Helen S. Foley. 178p. 1976. 15.00 (ISBN 0-89308-178-7). Southern Hist Pr.

U. S. Census of Eighteen Sixty, Barbour County, Ala. Helen S. Foley. 228p. 1976. pap. 15.00 (ISBN 0-89308-179-5). Southern Hist Pr.

U. S. Centers for Disease Control: Index of Modern Activities. Ellis W. Watkins. LC 88-47795. 150p. (Orig.). 1988. 34.50 (ISBN 0-88164-886-8); pap. 26.50 (ISBN 0-88164-887-6). ABBE Pubs Assn.

U. S. Championship, 1983. Larry Christiansen. (U. S. Tournament Ser.). (Illus.). 135p. (Orig.). 1984. pap. 6.50 (ISBN 0-931462-28-2). Chess Ent Inc.

U. S. Cheese Market: A Product-by-Product Marketing Analysis & Competitor Profile. 260p. 1986. 595.00 (ISBN 0-317-55184-1). Busn Trend.

U. S. Chemotherapy Market. The Leading Edge Group. 325p. 1987. 1950.00 (ISBN 0-317-63102-0). Busn Trend.

U. S. Chess Championship, 1845-1985. Gene H. McCormick & Andy Soltis. LC 83-42900. (Illus.). 304p. 1986. lib. bdg. 19.95x (ISBN 0-89950-056-0). McFarland & Co.

U. S. Chess Federation's (U. S. C. F.) Official Rules of Chess. 1987. pap. 7.95 (ISBN 0-679-14154-5). McKay.

U. S. Chief of Counsel for the Prosecution of Axis Criminality, 11 vols. LC 70-180435. Repr. of 1948 ed. 57.00 ea.; Set. 620.00 (ISBN 0-404-56180-2). AMS Pr.

United States Children's Bureau, 1912-1972: An Original Anthology. LC 74-1712. (Children & Youth Ser.: Vol. 16). (Illus.). 1974. 16.00x (ISBN 0-685-50597-9). Ayer Co Pubs.

United States, Chile & Peru in the Tacna & Arica Plebiscite. Joe F. Wilson. LC 78-66124. (Orig.). 1979. pap. text ed. 15.00 (ISBN 0-8191-0685-2). U Pr of Amer.

United States, China & Arms Control. Ralph N. Clough et al. LC 75-15650. pap. 41.30 (ISBN 0-317-20793-8, 2025370). Bks Demand UMI.

U. S. China Policy & the Problem of Taiwan. William M. Bueler. LC 79-25371. 143p. 1980. Repr. of 1971 ed. lib. bdg. 35.00x (ISBN 0-313-22153-7, BUUS). Greenwood.

U. S. China Relations since World War II. Dorothy Hoobler & Thomas Hoobler. LC 80-25343. (Impact Bks). 1981. 11.90 (ISBN 0-531-04264-2). Watts.

United States-China Trade Law Conference Summary: Proceedings of the Federal Bar Association, Conference, April 1979. Federal Bar Association Staff. 73p. 35.00 (ISBN 0-318-14104-3). Federal Bar.

United States Circuit Judge Nominating Commission: Its Members, Procedures & Candidates. Larry C. Berkson & Susan B. Carbon. 260p. 1980. 7.50 (ISBN 0-938870-09-2, 8561). Am Judicature.

United States Citizenship Examination. (Career Examination Ser.: C-3487). Date not set. pap. 15.00 (ISBN 0-8373-3487-X). Natl Learning.

United States Civil Service Commission: Its History, Activities & Organization. Darrell H. Smith. LC 72-3065. (Brookings Institution. Institute for Government Research. Service Monographs of the U. S. Government: No. 49). Repr. of 1928 ed. 30.00 (ISBN 0-404-57149-2). AMS Pr.

U. S. Civil War Store Cards. rev. ed. George Fuld & Melvin Fuld. LC 75-1785. (Illus.). 704p. 1975. 50.00x (ISBN 0-88000-135-6). Quarterman.

United States Claims Court Post-Traumatic Stress Disorder: V. A. Disability Claims Review & Military Review. rev. ed. Randall F. Lepore. Ed. by Anna Kirwin-Vogel. 400p. Date not set. pap. 34.95x (ISBN 0-9617076-1-5). Dominus Vobiscum Pub.

U. S. Coal & the Electric Power Induustry. Richard L. Gordon. LC 74-24403. (Resources for the Future Ser.). 232p. 1975. 17.50x. Johns Hopkins.

U. S. Coal & the Electric Power Industry. Richard L. Gordon. 228p. 1975. 17.50 (ISBN 0-8018-1697-1). Resources Future.

U. S. Coal Goes Abroad: A Social Action Perspective in Interorganizational Networks. Kathryn S. Rogers. LC 85-12467. 272p. 1985. 42.95 (ISBN 0-275-90036-3, C0036). Praeger.

U. S. Coal Industry: The Economics of Policy Choice. Martin B. Zimmerman. 256p. 1981. text ed. 37.50x (ISBN 0-262-24023-8). MIT Pr.

U. S. Coast Guard Cutters & Craft of World War II. Robert L. Scheina. (Illus.). 384p. 1982. 35.95 (ISBN 0-87021-717-8). Naval Inst Pr.

U. S. Coast Guard in World War II. Malcolm F. Willoughby. LC 79-6163. (Navies & Men Ser.). (Illus.). 1980. Repr. of 1957 ed. lib. bdg. 40.00x (ISBN 0-405-13081-3). Ayer Co Pubs.

U. S. Coast Guard Licenses & Certificate. Gregory Szczurek. 222p. 1988. 14.95 (ISBN 0-317-67976-7). Azure Comns.

United States Coastal Charts, 1783-1860. Peter Guthorn. LC 84-51187. (Illus.). 272p. 1984. 59.00 (ISBN 0-88740-019-1). Schiffer.

United States Code Annotated: Crimes and Criminal Procedure, 15 vols. write for info. West Pub.

United States Code Service: Lawyers Edition, 131 vols. LC 72-76254. write for info. Lawyers Co-Op.

United States Code: Supplement 3, Vol. 3. 1337p. 1986. Repr. of 1982 ed. 45.00 (ISBN 0-318-21360-5, S/N 052-001-00260-1). USGPO.

United States Coin Collector's Check List & Record Book. (Illus.). Date not set. pap. 1.95 (ISBN 0-307-19091-9, Whitman). Western Pub.

U. S. Coins of Value. Norman Stack. 1987. pap. 3.50 (ISBN 0-440-19227-7). Dell.

U. S. Coins of Value, 1989. Norman Stack. (Orig.). (YA) (gr. 7 up). 1989. pap. price not set (ISBN 0-440-20229-9). Dell.

United States: Combined Edition. 6th ed. Winthrop D. Jordan et al. (Illus.). 896p. 1987. text ed. write for info. (ISBN 0-13-938473-1). P-H.

United States, Common Market & International Antitrust: A Comparative Guide. Barry E. Hawk. 110p. 1979. 85.00 (ISBN 0-317-06013-9, H39735, Law & Business). HarBraceJ.

United States, Common Market, & International Antitrust: A Comparative Guide, 3 vols. 2nd ed. Barry E. Hawk. LC 84-27790. 1984-85. Supplements avail. 225.00 (ISBN 0-15-004385-6, #H43856, Law & Business). HarBraceJ.

United States, Communism & the Emergent World. Bernard P. Kiernan. LC 72-75636. Repr. of 1972 ed. 64.00 (ISBN 0-8357-9251-X, 2015826). Bks Demand UMI.

U. S. Commuter Airline Industry. James F. Molloy, Jr. LC 83-48826. 224p. 1984. 32.00x (ISBN 0-669-07605-8). Lexington Bks.

U. S. Companies & Fair Employment Practices in Northern Ireland. Helen E. Booth. 92p. (Orig.). 1988. pap. 50.00 (ISBN 0-931035-22-8). IRRC Inc DC.

U. S. Companies & Support for the South African Government: The Legal Requirements. 41p. 1985. 25.00 (ISBN 0-317-52535-2). IRRC Inc DC.

U. S. Competitiveness in the World Economy. Ed. by Bruce R. Scott & George C. Lodge. LC 84-15714. (Illus.). 552p. 1985. 32.50 (ISBN 0-87584-160-0, Dist. by Harper & Row Pubs., Inc.); pap. 16.95 (ISBN 0-87584-173-2). Harvard Busn.

U. S. Concerns Regarding Mexico's Oil & Gas: Evolution of the Debate, 1977-1980. Olga P. De Brody. (Research Report Ser.: No. 10). 21p. (Orig.). 1981. pap. 5.00 (ISBN 0-935391-09-6, RR-10). Ctr Mex Studies.

U. S. Conference of Mayors: Rebuilding America's Cities. LC 85-30780. 320p. 1986. prof. ref. 29.95x (ISBN 0-88730-051-0). Ballinger Pub.

United States Congress. Robert Goehlert & John Sayre. 320p. 1981. text ed. 50.00 (ISBN 0-02-911900-6). Free Pr.

United States Congress. Dennis Hale. LC 83-7992. 360p. 1984. pap. 19.95 (ISBN 0-87855-939-6). Transaction Bks.

U. S. Congress - Proceedings of Thomas P. O'Neal Jr. Symposium. Ed. by Dennis Hale. 300p. 1981. pap. 10.95 (ISBN 0-317-69296-8). BU Poli Sci.

United States Congress & the Making of U. S. Policy Toward Mexico. Don L. Wyman. (Research Report Ser.: No. 13). 74p. (Orig.). 1981. pap. 6.50 (ISBN 0-935391-12-6, RR-13). Ctr Mex Studies.

U. S. Congress & the West German Bundestag: Comparisons of Democratic Processes. Ed. by Uwe Thaysen et al. (Special Study). 500p. 1988. pap. 42.50 (ISBN 0-8133-7346-8). Westview.

United States Congress, Immigration Hearings. Ed. by Carlos E. Cortez. LC 80-7793. (Hispanics in the United States Ser.). 1981. Repr. of 1970 ed. lib. bdg. 23.00x (ISBN 0-405-13186-0). Ayer Co Pubs.

United States Congress, Immigration 1976. Ed. by Carlos E. Cortez. LC 80-7794. (Hispanics in the United States Ser.). lib. bdg. 25.00x (ISBN 0-405-13187-9). Ayer Co Pubs.

United States Congress: People, Place, & Policy. Charles O. Jones. 1982. 31.00x (ISBN 0-256-02663-7). Dorsey.

United States Congress: Proceedings of the Thomas P. O'Neill, Jr., Symposium on the U. S. Congress, Boston College, 1981. Ed. by Dennis Hale. LC 82-71847. 360p. (Orig.). 1982. pap. text ed. 10.00 (ISBN 0-943360-00-5). Boston Coll.

U. S. Congress. Senate. Select Committee on Small Business. Annual Report, 1950-1974, Vols. 1-25. Bound set. 295.00x (ISBN 0-686-90074-X). Rothman.

United States Congressional Directories, 1789-1840. Ed. by James S. Young et al. 400p. 1973. 60.00x (ISBN 0-231-03365-6). Columbia U Pr.

U. S. Congressional Districts & Data, 1843-1883. Stanley B. Parsons et al. LC 85-67582. (Illus.). 254p. 1986. lib. bdg. 67.95 (ISBN 0-313-22045-X, PUN/). Greenwood.

United States Congressional Districts, 1788-1841. Stanley Parsons et al. LC 77-83897. (Illus.). 1978. lib. bdg. 56.95 (ISBN 0-8371-9828-3, PUS/). Greenwood.

U. S. Connector Market. 213p. 1984. 1550.00 (ISBN 0-86621-324-4, A1407). Frost & Sullivan.

United States: Conquering a Continent, Vol. I. 6th ed. Winthrop D. Jordan et al. (Illus.). 448p. 1987. pap. text ed. write for info. (ISBN 0-13-938374-3); write for info. study guide (ISBN 0-13-938382-4). P-H.

United States Conquest of California: An Original Anthology. Lewis & Emory. Ed. by Carlos E. Cortes. LC 76-7303. (Chicano Heritage Ser.). (Illus.). 1976. 52.00x (ISBN 0-405-09542-2). Ayer Co Pubs.

U. S. Constitution. Joseph T. Keenan. 1985. pap. 10.00x (ISBN 0-256-01615-1). Dorsey.

U. S. Constitution. Donald A. Richie. (Know Your Government Ser.). (Illus.). 112p. (YA) (gr. 7-12). 1989. 12.95. Chelsea Hse.

United States Constitution: A National Historic Landmark Theme Study. Harry A. Butowsky. (Illus.). 113p. 1987. pap. 5.50 (ISBN 0-318-22587-5, S/N 024-005-01017-3). USGPO.

U. S. Constitution & Amendments: Constitucion de Estados Unidos Y Enmiendas. 3rd ed. Tr. by Carlos B. Vega. LC 82-90658. 40p. (Orig., Span.). 1981. pap. 7.95 (ISBN 0-88174-000-4). C B Vega.

U. S. Constitution for Beginners. Steven Bachmann. (Documentary Comic Bks.). (Illus.). 192p. (Orig.). 1987. pap. 7.95 (ISBN 0-86316-126-X). Writers & Readers.

U. S. Constitution for Everyone: A Guide to the Most Important Document Written by & for the People of the United States. Mort Gerberg. (Illus.). 64p. 1987. pap. 4.95 (ISBN 0-399-51305-1, Perigee); 10-copy counterpack 49.50 (ISBN 0-399-52054-6). Putnam Pub Group.

United States Constitution: Personalities, Principles, & Issues. Walter B. Mead. LC 87-16162. 220p. 1987. text ed. 24.95x (ISBN 0-87249-520-5); pap. text ed. 14.95 (ISBN 0-87249-523-X). U of SC Pr.

United States Constitution: Supreme Court Cases. Denis Killeen. 374p. (Orig.). 1987. pap. 19.95 (ISBN 0-944830-00-5). Hartfordshire.

United States Constitution: 1787-1987. Pref. by Warren Burger. (Illus.). 70p. 1987. ltd. ed. 500.00 (ISBN 0-910457-11-5). Arion Pr.

U. S. Constitutional History & Law. Albert H. Putney. 599p. 1985. Repr. of 1908 ed. lib. bdg. 45.00x (ISBN 0-8377-1021-9). Rothman.

United States Constitutions Subject Index, Release 1. B. F. Sachs. 1982. 35.00 (ISBN 0-379-20413-4); Release 6. 35.00 (ISBN 0-379-20412-6). Oceana.

U. S. Consumer Market 1987. Stanley J. Marks & Ethel M. Marks. 1987. pap. 14.95 (ISBN 0-317-55313-5). Bur Intl Aff.

United States Control of Petroleum Imports: A Study of the Federal Government's Role in the Management of Domestic Oil Supplies. Torleif Meloe. Ed. by Stuart Bruchey. LC 78-22701. (Energy in the American Economy Ser.). (Illus.). 1979. lib. bdg. 25.50x (ISBN 0-405-12003-6). Ayer Co Pubs.

U. S. Conventional Force Structure at a Crossroads. Harlan K. Ullman. 74p. 1985. 14.95 (ISBN 0-89206-088-3). CSI Studies.

U. S. Conventional Force Structure at a Crossroads. Ed. by Harlan K. Ullman. (CSIS Panel Report). 78p. (Orig.). 1985. pap. text ed. 14.95 (ISBN 0-8191-5947-6, Pub. by CSIS). U Pr of Amer.

U. S. Conventional Oil & Gas Production to the Year 2000. Joseph P. Riva, Jr. et al. (WVSS in Natural Resources & Energy Management Ser.). 150p. 1985. pap. text ed. 31.00x (ISBN 0-8133-7066-3). Westview.

United States Copper Cents Eighteen Sixteen to Eighteen Fifty-Seven. Howard R. Newcomb. LC 81-50923. (Illus.). 288p. 1981. Repr. of 1944 ed. lib. bdg. 50.00x (ISBN 0-88000-127-5). Quarterman.

U. S. Corporate Personnel Reduction Policies. Michael Cross. 144p. 1981. text ed. 35.50x (ISBN 0-566-00501-8). Gower Pub Co.

U. S. Corporate Profitability & Capital Formation: Are Rates of Return Sufficient? Herman I. Liebling. (Pergamon Policy Studies). 1980. 36.00 (ISBN 0-08-024622-2). Pergamon.

U. S. Corporate Withdrawal from South Africa: The Likely Impact on Social & Political Change. 30p. 1986. 35.00 (ISBN 0-317-52537-9). IRRC Inc DC.

United States Corporation Histories, 1965-1985: A Bibliography. Wahib Nasrallah. LC 86-33560. (Reference Library of Social Sciences: Vol. 391). 1987. lib. bdg. 30.00 (ISBN 0-8240-9847-1). Garland Pub.

U. S. Counterintelligence Today. Francis J. McNamara. Ed. by Nathan Hale Institute Staff. 88p. (Orig.). 1985. 9.95 (ISBN 0-935067-06-X). Nathan Hale Inst.

U. S. Cruise Missile Programs: Development, Deployment & Implications for Military Balance. C. A. Sorrels. (Brasseys Ser.). 300p. 1983. 38.50 (ISBN 0-08-030527-X). Pergamon.

U. S. Cruisers: An Illustrated Design History. Norman Friedman. (Illus.). 480p. 1984. 46.95 (ISBN 0-87021-718-6). Naval Inst Pr.

U. S. Crusade in China, Nineteen Thirty-Eight to Nineteen Forty-Five. Michael Schaller. LC 78-15032. 1979. 32.50x (ISBN 0-231-04454-2). Columbia U Pr.

U. S. Cubans, Puerto Ricans, & Mexicans: Do They Speak the Same Language? Carlos B. Vega. 300p. pap. write for info. C B Vega.

United States Cultural History: A Guide to Information Sources. Ed. by Philip I. Mitterling. LC 79-24061. (American Government & History Information Guide Ser.: Vol. 5). 592p. 1980. 68.00x (ISBN 0-8103-1369-3). Gale.

United States Customs & International Trade Guide, 4 vols. Peter Buck Feller. 1979. Set. looseleaf 300.00 (757); Updates 1985. 255.00; Supplement 1986. 200.00. Bender.

U. S. Customs & the Madero Revolution. Michael D. Carman. (Southwestern Studies Ser.: No. 48). 1976. pap. 5.00 (ISBN 0-87404-105-8). Tex Western.

U. S. Customs Unconventional Weapons "Lookout" Manual. rev. ed. (Illus.). 24p. pap. text ed. 6.00 (ISBN 0-87364-357-7). Paladin Pr.

United States Cutting Tool Handbook. 7th ed. U. S. Cutting Tool Institute Staff. 900p. 1988. 38.95x (ISBN 0-8311-1177-1). Indus Pr.

U. S. D. Drug Information for the Health Care Provider. 1982. 24.95 (ISBN 0-8016-5191-3). Mosby.

U. S. Debate on Industrial Policy: A Bibliography, 1980-1985. Michael Stevenson. (Public Administration Ser.: P 1728). 9p. 1985. 2.00 (ISBN 0-89028-498-9). Vance Biblios.

U. S. Declaration of Independence: Declaracion de Independencia de Estados Unidos. 3rd ed. Tr. by Carlos B. Vega. 16p. (Orig., Span.). 1982. pap. 4.95 (ISBN 0-88174-001-2). C B Vega.

United States Decorated Stoneware. Carmen A. Guappone. (Orig.). 1988. pap. 24.95 (ISBN 0-9615230-9-3). Guappones Pubs.

U. S. Defense Acquisition: A Process in Trouble. Intro. by Amos A. Jordan. (Panel Report Ser.). 85p. (Orig.). 1987. pap. 14.95 (ISBN 0-89206-101-4). CSI Studies.

U. S. Defense Bases in the United Kingdom: A Matter for Joint Decision? Simon Duke. LC 87-4318. 260p. 1987. 45.00 (ISBN 0-312-00769-8). St Martin.

U. S. Defense Economy: A Selected Checklist. Alva W. Stewart. (Public Administration Ser.: P 1843). 11p. 1986. 3.75 (ISBN 0-89028-713-9). Vance Biblios.

U. S. Defense Mobilization Infrastructure: Problems & Priorities. Ed. by Robert Pfaltzgraff, Jr. & Uri Ra'anan. LC 82-16381. 292p. 1982. lib. bdg. 32.50 (ISBN 0-208-01984-7, Archon). Shoe String.

U. S. Defense Planning: A Critique. John M. Collins. LC 82-51148. 338p. 1982. lib. bdg. 31.50x (ISBN 0-86531-549-3); pap. text ed. 19.95x (ISBN 0-86531-554-X). Westview.

U. S. Defense Planning for a More Proliferated World. Lewis Dunn. 248p. 1979. 20.00 (ISBN 0-318-14358-5, HI29562RR). Hudson Inst.

U. S. Defense Policy. 3rd ed. Congressional Quarterly, Inc. Staff. LC 83-7555. 248p. 1983. pap. 11.95 (ISBN 0-87187-258-7). Congr Quarterly.

U. S. Defense Policy. Ed. by Christopher A. Kojm. (Reference Shelf: Vol. 54, No. 2). 224p. 1982. pap. text ed. 10.00 (ISBN 0-8242-0666-5). Wilson.

U. S. Defense Posture. Walter Laqueur. (Task Force on the Eighties Ser.). 24p. 1981. pap. 2.50 (ISBN 0-87495-036-8). Am Jewish Comm.

U. S. Defense Spending: How Much is Enough. Ed. by Carol C. Collins. 256p. 24.95x (ISBN 0-87196-816-9). Facts on File.

United States Democratic Review, 42 vols., lacks vol. 39, Vol. 1-43. Repr. of 1859 ed. Set. lib. bdg. 3200.00 (ISBN 0-404-19561-X). AMS Pr.

United States Department of Agriculture: A Study in Administration. William L. Wanlass. LC 78-63970. (Johns Hopkins University. Studies in the Social Sciences. Eighth Ser. 1920: 1). 136p. 1982. Repr. of 1920 ed. 24.50 (ISBN 0-404-61216-4). AMS Pr.

United States Department of Justice-Antitrust Division, Grand Jury Manual. 1976. pap. 15.00 (ISBN 0-87945-036-3). Fed Legal Pubn.

United States Department of Justice & Individual Rights, 1937-1962. John T. Elliff. Ed. by Harold Hyman & Stuart Bruchey. (American Legal & Constitutional History Ser.). 814p. 1987. lib. bdg. 85.00 (ISBN 0-8240-8261-3). Garland Pub.

United States Department of Labor: The First Seventy-Five Years. (Illus.). 56p. (Orig.). 1988. pap. 2.00 (S/N 029-000-00423-4). USGPO.

U. S. Department of Labor's Occupational Outlook Handbook. Ed. by United States Department of Labor. 528p. pap. 17.95 (ISBN 0-8442-6689-2, NTC Busn Bks). NAtl Textbk.

U. S. Department of Transportation Inconsistency Rulings. Barbara Foster. (State Legislative Reports: Vol. 13, No. 6). 44p. 1988. pap. 5.00 (ISBN 1-55516-191-X). Natl Conf State Legis.

U. S. Dept. of the Interior. Paul Metcalf. LC 80-66485. (Illus.). 88p. (Orig.). 1980. pap. 5.00 (ISBN 0-917788-23-0). Gnomon Pr.

United States Destroyer Operations in World War II. Theodore Roscoe. LC 53-4273. (Illus.). 581p. 1953. 34.95x (ISBN 0-87021-726-7). Naval Inst Pr.

United States Destroyer Operations in World War Two see United States Submarine Operations in World War Two.

U. S. Destroyers: An Illustrated Design History. Norman Friedman. (Illus.). 544p. 1982. 46.95 (ISBN 0-87021-733-X). Naval Inst Pr.

United States Dimes. A. Kosoff. 1964. soft cover 8.00 (ISBN 0-317-27389-2). S J Durst.

United States Diplomatic Codes & Ciphers, 1775-1938. Ralph E. Weber. (Illus.). 656p. 1979. 34.95. Precedent Pub.

United States Diplomatic Codes & Ciphers, 1775-1938. Ralph E. Weber. 490p. 1973. 34.95. Transaction Bks.

U. S. Diplomats in Europe, Nineteen Nineteen to Nineteen Forty-One. Ed. by Kenneth P. Jones. LC 82-24402. (Topics in Diplomatic History Ser.). 240p. 1983. 16.95x (ISBN 0-317-56346-7); pap. 10.95x (ISBN 0-317-56347-5); pap. text ed. 8.75x (ISBN 0-317-56348-3). Regina Bks.

U. S. Direct Investment in the Latin American-Caribbean Region: Trends & Issues. Ramesh F. Ramsaran. LC 84-18364. 224p. 1985. 35.00 (ISBN 0-312-83317-2). St Martin.

U. S. Directory of Systems & Vendors. rev. ed. Charles M. Foundyller. Ed. by Bruce L. Jenkins. (CAD-CAM Computer Graphics Ser.). (Illus.). 450p. 1983. cancelled (ISBN 0-938484-14-1). Daratech.

U. S. Directory of Systems & Vendors, 1982: CAD-CAM Computer Graphics: Survey & Buyers Guide. rev. ed. Charles M. Foundyller. Ed. by Jane A. Murphy. (Illus.). 374p. 1982. cancelled (ISBN 0-938484-08-7). Daratech.

U. S. Directory of Vendors see CAD-CAM, CAE: Survey, Review & Buyers' Guide.

U. S. Directory of Vendors, 1983. (CAD-CAM Computer Graphics: Pt. 3). (Illus.). 458p. 1983. cancelled (ISBN 0-938484-10-9). Daratech.

United States District Judge Nominating Commissions: Their Members, Procedures & Candidates. Alan Neff. LC 80-70512. (Federal Judicial Selection During the Carter Administration Ser.). 204p. (Orig.). 1981. pap. 7.50 (ISBN 0-938870-03-3, 8568). Am Judicature.

United States Doctoral Dissertations in Third World Studies, 1869-1978. Michael Sims. 436p. 1980. 60.00 (ISBN 0-918456-37-1, Crossroads). African Studies Assn.

U. S. Documents in the Prop. Fide Archives: A Calendar, Vol. 11. Ed. by Mathias C. Kiemen & James Mc. Manamon. 339p. 1988. 55.00 (ISBN 0-88382-237-7). AAFH.

United States Documents in the Propaganda Fide Archiives, Vol. 8. Ed. by Debevec et al. 1980. 40.00 (ISBN 0-88382-208-3). AAFH.

United States Documents in the Propaganda Fide Archives, Vol. 9. Ed. by Debevec et al. 1982. 40.00 (ISBN 0-88382-210-5). AAFH.

United States Documents in the Propaganda Fide Archives, Vol. 10. Ed. by Mathias Kiemen et al. 1984. 40.00 (ISBN 0-88382-211-3). AAFH.

United States Documents in the Propaganda Fide Archives: Index to Calendar, 7 Vols. Finbar Kenneally. (Propaganda Fide Ser.). (Illus.). 1981. 40.00 ea. (ISBN 0-88382-209-1). AAFH.

United States Dressage Federation Bulletin. 80p. (B). write for info. US Dressage Fed.

United States Dressage Federation Calender of Competitions. 96p. write for info. US Dressage Fed.

U. S. Driver's Manual. (Gr.). 7.00 (ISBN 0-685-25478-X). Divry.

United States During the Civil War. Auguste Laugel. Ed. by A. Nevins. LC 61-13716. (Indiana University Civil War Centennial Ser). 1968. Repr. of 1961 ed. 29.00 (ISBN 0-527-55050-7). Kraus Repr.

U. S. Economic History. 2nd ed. Albert W. Niemi, Jr. LC 87-10730. (Illus.). 492p. 1987. pap. text ed. 19.75 (ISBN 0-8191-6335-X). U Pr of Amer.

United States Economic Penetration of Venezuela & Its Effects on Diplomacy, 1895-1906. Charles Carreras. Ed. by Stuart Bruchey. (Foreign Economic Policy of the United States Ser.). 250p. 1987. lib. bdg. 40.00 (ISBN 0-8240-8077-7). Garland Pub.

U. S. Economic Policies Affecting Industrial Trade: A Quantative Assessment. Peter Morici & Laura L. Megna. LC 83-60013. (Committee on Changing International Realities Ser.). 140p. (Orig.). 1983. pap. 12.00 (ISBN 0-89068-068-X, CIR-13). Natl Planning.

U. S. Economic Policy in an Era of Detente. Marina N. Whitman & William K. McInally Memorial Lecture, 7th. 24p. 1973. pap. 1.00 (ISBN 0-87712-163-X). UMI Div Res GSBA.

U. S. Economic Policy toward the Association of Southeast Asian Nations: Meeting the Japanese Challenge. Lawrence B. Krause. LC 82-9656. 98p. 1982. 26.95 (ISBN 0-8157-5026-9); pap. 9.95 (ISBN 0-8157-5025-0). Brookings.

U. S. Economy. John Davenport. LC 64-25754. 1965. pap. 1.25 (ISBN 0-911956-09-3). Constructive Action.

U. S. Economy Demystified: What Major Economic Statistics Mean & Their Significance for Business. rev. ed. Albert T. Sommers & Lucie R. Blau. LC 84-48451. 192p. 1988. pap. 19.95x (ISBN 0-669-17383-5); pap. text ed. 13.95x (ISBN 0-669-17385-1). Lexington Bks.

U. S. Economy in Crisis: Adjusting to the New Realities. Pearl M. Kamer. 1988. price not set (ISBN 0-275-93072-6, C3072). Praeger.

U. S. Economy in the Nineteen Fifties: An Economic History. Harold G. Vatter. LC 84-16269. xii, 308p. 1985. Repr. of 1963 ed. 12.00x (ISBN 0-226-85153-2). U of Chicago Pr.

U. S. Economy in the 1950's: An Economic History. Harold G. Vatter. LC 84-6727. xii, 308p. 1984. Repr. of 1963 ed. lib. bdg. 41.50x (ISBN 0-313-24531-2, VAUS). Greenwood.

U. S. Economy in World War II. Harold G. Vatter. LC 85-7789. (Columbia Studies in Business, Government, & Society). 224p. 1985. 26.50x (ISBN 0-231-05768-7). Columbia U Pr.

U. S. Economy in World War Two. Harold G. Vatter. (Columbia Studies in Business, Government & Society). (Illus.). 198p. 1988. pap. 12.50x (ISBN 0-231-05769-5). Columbia U Pr.

United States Educational System: Marxist Approaches. Ed. by Marvin J. Berlowitz & Frank E. Chapman, Jr. LC 80-12394. (Studies in Marxism: Vol. 6). 240p. 1980. 18.95x (ISBN 0-930656-12-1); pap. 7.50 (ISBN 0-930656-11-3). MEP Pubns.

U. S. Elite Forces - Vietnam. (In Action Ser.). (Illus.). 50p. 1986. pap. 5.95 (ISBN 0-89747-170-9, 3007). Squad Sig Pubns.

United States' Emergence As a Southeast Asian Power, 1940-1950. Gary R. Hess. LC 86-18861. 528p. 1987. 45.00x (ISBN 0-231-06190-0). Columbia U Pr.

United States Emerges, 1783-1800. Naunerle Farr. Ed. by D'Ann Calhoun & Lawrence W. Bloch. (Basic Illustrated History of America). (Illus.). (gr. 4-12). 1977. text ed. 7.50 (ISBN 0-88301-250-2). Pendulum Pr.

United States Emerges: 1783-1800. Naunerle Farr & Dennis Dostert. Ed. by Lawrence W. Bloch. (Basic Illustrated History of America Ser.). (Illus., Orig.). (gr. 4-12). 1976. pap. text ed. 2.95 (ISBN 0-88301-233-2). Pendulum Pr.

United States Employment & Training Programs: A Selected Annotated Bibliography. Compiled by Frederick A. Raffa et al. Clyde A. Haulman & Djehane A. Hosni. LC 82-25108. xvi, 152p. 1983. lib. bdg. 36.95 (ISBN 0-313-23872-3, RUE/). Greenwood.

U. S. Employment Opportunities. Joseph Ryan. (III Ser.). 300p. (YA) (gr. 12). looseleaf (includes quarterly updates) 184.00 (ISBN 0-937801-01-1). Wash Res Assocs.

U. S. Employment Opportunities. 5th ed. Joseph Ryan. 260p. 1987. looseleaf binder 184.00. Wash Res Assocs.

United States Employment Service: Its History, Activities & Organization. Darrell H. Smith. LC 72-3042. (Brookings Institution. Institute for Government Research. Service Monographs of the U. S. Government: No. 28). Repr. of 1923 ed. 24.00 (ISBN 0-404-57128-X). AMS Pr.

U. S. Ends & Means in Central America: A Debate. Ernest Van den Haag & Tom J. Farer. 275p. 1988. 19.95 (ISBN 0-306-42857-1, Plenum Pr). Plenum Pub.

U. S. Forty Today: Thirty Years of Landscape Change in America. Thomas R. Vale & Geraldine R. Vale. LC 83-50081. (Illus.). 208p. 1983. 27.50 (ISBN 0-299-09480-4); pap. 14.95 (ISBN 0-299-09484-7). U of Wis Pr.

U. S. Frogmen of World War II. Wyatt Blassingame. (Landmark Ser.: No. 106). (gr. 5-9). 1964. Random.

U. S. Geological Survey: Its History, Activities & Organization. Brookings Institution, Washington, D. C. Institute for Government Research Staff. LC 72-3014. (Service Monographs of the U. S. Government: No. 1). Repr. of 1918 ed. 21.50 (ISBN 0-404-57101-8). AMS Pr.

United States Geological Survey Yearbook, Fiscal Year 1985. (Illus.). 160p. 1986. pap. 11.00 (ISBN 0-318-22466-6, S/N 024-001-03551-1). USGPO.

United States-German Economic Survey 1986. Heinz J. Dielman. 212p. (Ger.). 1986. write for info. (ISBN 0-86640-024-9). German Am Chamber.

United States-German Economic Yearbook, 1987: Deutsch-Amerikanisches Wirtschaftsjahrbuch, 1987. 13th ed. Ed. by Richard C. Jacob. 225p. (Ger.). 1988. write for info. (ISBN 0-86640-026-5). German Am Chamber.

U. S. Government: A Resource Book for Secondary Schools. Marie J. Turner & Sara Lake. (Social Studies Resources for Secondary School Librarians, Teachers, & Students). 200p. 1989. 28.50 (ISBN 0-87436-535-X). ABC-Clio.

U. S. Government & the Vietnam War: Executive & Legislative Roles & Relationships. William C. Gibbons. (U. S. Government & the Vietnam War Ser.). 1986. Part I: 1945-1960, 384 pgs. PLB 31.50x (ISBN 0-691-07714-2); Part II: 1961-1964, 448 pgs. PLB 36.00x (ISBN 0-691-07715-0); Part I. pap. 8.95x (ISBN 0-691-02254-2); Part II. pap. 9.95x (ISBN 0-691-02255-0). Princeton U Pr.

U. S. Government & the Vietnam War: Executive & Legislative Roles & Relationships, 1965-66, Part III. William C. Gibbons. 475p. 1988. 47.50 (ISBN 0-691-07733-9); pap. 12.50 (ISBN 0-691-02263-1). Princeton U Pr.

U. S. Government Directories, 1970-1981: A Selected, Annotated Bibliography. Ed. by Constance S. Gray. 1984. lib. bdg. 35.00 (ISBN 0-87287-414-1). Libs Unl.

U. S. Government Documents: A Practical Guide for Library Assistants in Academic & Public Libraries. Elizabeth J. Pokorny. 175p. 1989. lib. bdg. 23.50 (ISBN 0-87287-507-5). Libs Unl.

U. S. Government: Executive Branch: Syllabus. Robert E. Adam. (U. S. Government Ser.). (gr. 7-12). 1979. pap. text ed. 7.35 student syllabus (ISBN 0-89420-089-5, 194030); cassette recordings 150.05 (ISBN 0-89420-189-1, 194000). Natl Book.

United States Government: How & Why It Works. Jane W. Smith & Carol Sullivan. (Illus.). 312p. 1987. text ed. 12.95 (ISBN 0-86601-615-5); tchr's ed. 9.95 (ISBN 0-86601-616-3); wkbk. 3.95 (ISBN 0-86601-617-1); software disk. & bk. pkg. 99.95 (ISBN 0-86601-620-1); IBM PC software 99.95 (ISBN 0-86601-622-8). Media Materials.

U. S. Government: How It Functions: Syllabus. Carl W. Salser. (U. S. Government Ser.). 1976. pap. text ed. 4.55 (ISBN 0-89420-090-9, 196051); cassette recordings 36.05 (ISBN 0-89420-190-5, 196040). Natl Book.

U. S. Government: How Our Laws Are Made: Syllabus. Carl W. Salser. 1976. pap. text ed. 4.55 (ISBN 0-89420-091-7, 196033); cassette recordings 36.05 (ISBN 0-89420-191-3, 196000). Natl Book.

United States Government Manual. annual 890p. 20.00 (ISBN 0-318-17587-8). Office Fed Register.

United States Government Market for Wind Energy Systems. U. S. Department of Energy. 110p. 1981. pap. 55.00 (ISBN 0-88016-015-2). Windbks.

U. S. Government Offices in California: A Directory. 3rd ed. (California Information Guides Ser.). 42p. (Orig.). 1987. pap. 16.50 (ISBN 0-912102-81-0). Cal Inst Public.

United States Government Policy on Refugees, 1933-1940. Barbara M. Stewart. Ed. by Frank Freidel. LC 80-8475. (Modern American History Ser.). 620p. 1981. lib. bdg. 85.00 (ISBN 0-8240-4870-9). Garland Pub.

United States Government Printing Office Style Manual, (Illus.). 448p. 1984. 15.00 (ISBN 0-318-04559-1, S/N 021-000-00121-0). USGPO.

United States Government Printing Office: Style Manual. paper ed. LC 84-600037. 488p. 1984. pap. 11.00 (ISBN 0-318-21699-X, S/N 021-000-00120-1). USGPO.

U. S. Government Publications for Small & Medium-Sized Public Libraries: Public Library Reporter, No. 20. Gladys Sachse. LC 81-14998. 206p. 1981. pap. 10.00x (ISBN 0-8389-3268-1). ALA.

United States Government Publications Catalogs. Steven D. Zink. LC 81-18352. (SLA Bibliography Ser.: No. 8). pap. 29.80 (ISBN 0-317-27926-2, 2025125). Bks Demand UMI.

United States Government Publications Catalogs. 2nd ed. Ed. by Steven D. Zink. 312p. 1987. pap. 20.00 (ISBN 0-87111-335-X). SLA.

United States Government Purchasing & Sales Directory. 199p. 1984. pap. 5.50 (ISBN 0-318-21321-4, S/N 045-000-00226-8). USGPO.

U. S. Government Response to Terrorism: In Search of an Effective Strategy. William R. Farrell. LC 82-50665. (National & International Terrorism Ser.). 142p. 1982. lib. bdg. 31.00x (ISBN 0-86531-402-0). Westview.

U. S. Government Scientific & Technical Periodicals. Philip A. Yannarella & Rao Aluri. LC 75-38740. 271p. 1976. 19.00 (ISBN 0-8108-0888-9). Scarecrow.

U. S. Government Surplus: A Complete Buyer's Manual. 6th ed. James J. Senay. LC 80-18466. 120p. (Orig.). 1981. pap. 7.95 (ISBN 0-936218-01-0). Rainbow Pub Co.

U. S. Grant & the American Military Tradition. Bruce Catton. (Library of American Biography Ser.). (Orig.). 1972. pap. text ed. write for info. (ISBN 0-673-39327-5). Scott F.

U. S. Grant & the American Military Tradition. Bruce Catton. 1985. 15.95 (ISBN 0-8488-0279-9, Pub. by J M C & Co). Amereon Ltd.

United States, Great Britain, & the Cold War: 1944-1947. Terry H. Anderson. LC 80-25838. 272p. 1981. text ed. 29.00x (ISBN 0-8262-0328-0). U of Mo Pr.

United States, Greece & Turkey: The Troubled Triangle. Theodore A. Couloumbis. Ed. by Alvin Z. Rubinstein. (Studies of Influence in International Relations). 256p. 1983. pap. 16.95 (ISBN 0-275-91566-2, B1566). Praeger.

U. S. Ground Forces & the Defense of Central Europe. William P. Mako. LC 83-2817. (Studies in Defense Policy). 137p. 1983. 26.95 (ISBN 0-8157-5444-2); pap. 9.95 (ISBN 0-8157-5443-4). Brookings.

U. S. Guerilla Warfare. 1987. lib. bdg. 75.00 (ISBN 0-8490-3932-0). Gordon Pr.

U. S. Guide to Literary Landmarks. Geri Bass & Eben Bass. (Illus.). 144p. (Orig.). 1984. pap. 8.95 (ISBN 0-939332-09-4). J Pohl Assocs.

U. S. Gunboat Carondolet, 1861-1865. Myron J. Smith, Jr. 195p. 1982. 25.00x (ISBN 0-89126-104-4). MA-AH Pub.

United States Half Cents. Illus. by D. Bowers & J. Ruddy. LC 83-51003. (Illus.). 1984. soft cover 10.00 (ISBN 0-317-27384-1). S J Durst.

United States Half Dimes. D. W. Valentine et al. LC 84-70699. 1984. Repr. of 1931 ed. lib. bdg. 35.00 (ISBN 0-942666-39-9). S J Durst.

United States Half Dimes. Daniel W. Valentine. LC 74-80917. (Illus.). 384p. 1975. Repr. 40.00x (ISBN 0-88000-049-X). Quarterman.

U. S. Halftracks of World War Two. Steven J. Zaloga. (Tanks Illustrated Ser.: Vol. 15). (Illus.). 64p. (Orig.). 1985. pap. 9.95 (ISBN 0-85368-697-1, Pub by Arms & Armour). Sterling.

U. S. Health Care System: A Look to the 1990's. Ed. by Eli Ginzberg. (Conservation of Human Resources Ser.: Vol. 26). 160p. 1985. 22.00x (ISBN 0-8476-7468-1, Rowman & Allanheld). Rowman.

U. S. Health System: Origins & Functions. 2nd ed. Marshall W. Raffel. LC 84-11826. 447p. 1984. text ed. 25.95x (ISBN 0-471-88673-4). Wiley.

United States Higher Civil Service Study: Careers of High-Level Employees, 1963. David T. Stanley. 1973. write for info., codebk (ISBN 0-89138-064-7). ICPSR.

U. S. Higher Education: A Guide to Information Sources. Ed. by Franklin Parker & Betty J. Parker. (Education Information Guide Ser.: Vol. 9). 688p. 1980. 68.00x (ISBN 0-8103-1476-2). Gale.

U. S. Highway Atlas. 4.95. Am Map.

U. S. Hispanic Market. Ed. by Peter Allen. 260p. 1984. pap. 295.00 (ISBN 0-931634-48-2). FIND SVP.

U. S. Historic Flag Project Book, 2 vols. Norman H. Ludlow, Jr. (Illus.). 1974. pap. 4.85x (ISBN 0-916706-07-9); Vol. 1. narration (ISBN 0-916706-20-6); Vol. 2. workbook (ISBN 0-916706-21-4). N H Ludlow.

United States History, 2 vols. Nelson Klose. Incl. Vol. I. To 1877. pap. 8.95 (ISBN 0-8120-2250-5); Vol. II. Since 1865. 1983. pap. 8.95 (ISBN 0-8120-2251-3). LC 64-8317. pap. Barron.

U. S. History - One, 4 vols. Richard G. Allen et al. Incl. Vol. 1: America - Its Discovery, Independence & Early Problems. 290p. 7.95 (ISBN 0-86624-001-2, UT1); Vol. 2: Strengthening the New Nation. 270p. 7.95 (ISBN 0-86624-002-0, UT2); Vol. 3: The Republic Expands. 192p. 7.95 (ISBN 0-86624-003-9, UT3); Vol. 4: Expansion, Destruction & Reconstruction. 156p. 7.95 (ISBN 0-86624-004-7, UT4); Teacher's Guide. available 3.95 (UT5); End of Unit Test (UT6). (Illus.). 1981. pap. text ed. 5.95 ea. Bilingual Ed Serv.

U. S. History - Two, 5 vols. Richard G. Allan et al. Incl. Vol. 1: Modern America Takes Shape. 242p. 7.95 (ISBN 0-86624-005-5, UU4); Vol. 2: Imperialism to Progressivism. 192p. 7.95 (ISBN 0-86624-006-3, UU5); Vol. 3: War, Prosperity & Depression. 180p. 7.95 (ISBN 0-86624-007-1, UU6); Vol. 4: The Roosevelt Years of Depression & War. 184p. 7.95 (ISBN 0-86624-008-X, UU7); Vol. 5: The Cold War Years. 244p. 7.95 (ISBN 0-86624-009-8, UU8); Teacher's Guide. available 3.95 (UV9); End of Unit Test. available 3.95 (UV0). (Illus.). 1981. pap. text ed. 5.95 ea. Bilingual Ed Serv.

United States History: A Resource Book for Secondary Schools. James R. Giese & Laurel R. Singleton. (Social Studies Resources for Secondary School Librarians, Teachers & Students). 1989. Set. 45.50 (ISBN 0-87436-525-2); Vol. 1, 200p. 28.50 (ISBN 0-87436-505-8); Vol. 2, 200p. 28.50 (ISBN 0-87436-506-6). ABC-Clio.

United States History Atlas. Hammond Incorporated Editors. LC 78-78283. 64p. (gr. 7-12). 1984. text ed. 5.99x (ISBN 0-8437-7465-7). Hammond Inc.

United States History, Bk. I: To 1877. John L. Napp. (Illus.). 344p. (YA) (gr. 7-12). 1988. text ed. 12.95 (ISBN 0-86601-692-9); tchr's. ed. 9.95 (ISBN 0-86601-693-7); wkbk. 3.95 (ISBN 0-86601-694-5); Apple software 99.95 (ISBN 0-86601-697-X); IBM-pc software 99.95 (ISBN 0-86601-698-8). Media Materials.

U. S. History Cartoons: For Young People 8-14. Cobblestone Publishing, Inc. Staff. (Illus.). 36p. (gr. 4-8). 1987. pap. text ed. 4.95 (ISBN 0-942389-02-6). Cobblestone Pub.

U. S. History Crosswords: For Young People 8-14. Cobblestone Publishing Inc. Staff. (Illus.). 36p. (gr. 4-8). 1987. pap. text ed. 4.95 (ISBN 0-942389-01-8). Cobblestone Pub.

U. S. History: Focus on the Individual. Robert G. Hanvey & Ellen Harrington. (Intercom: Nos. 94-95). (Illus.). 72p. 5.00 (ISBN 0-318-14214-7). Amer Forum.

U. S. History Word Finds: For Young People 8-14. Cobblestone Publishing, Inc. Staff. (Illus.). 36p. (gr. 4-8). 1987. pap. 4.95 (ISBN 0-9607638-9-9). Cobblestone Pub.

U. S. Hot Beverage Market. 1988. 750.00 (ISBN 0-686-38412-1, 126). Busn Trend.

United States House of Representatives. James T. Currie. LC 87-16898. (Anvil Ser.). 248p. 1988. pap. 11.50 (ISBN 0-89874-882-8). Krieger.

United States House of Representatives Telephone Directory, Spring, 1988. 317p. (Orig.). 1988. pap. 13.00 (S/N 052-001-00289-0). USGPO.

U. S. Household Consumption, Income & Demographic Changes, 1975-2025. Philip Musgrove & Adele Shapanka. 250p. 1982. 15.00 (ISBN 0-8018-2868-6). Resources Future.

U. S. I. Q. Game. W. Cleon Skousen et al. 29.95 (ISBN 0-88080-026-7). Natl Ctr Constitutional.

U. S. Identification Manual 1986. Drivers License Guide Co. Staff. (Illus.). 700p. 1986. text ed. 103.50 (ISBN 0-938964-10-0). Drivers License.

U. S. Immigration & Refugee Policy. Ed. by Mary Kritz. LC 82-47513. (Illus.). 448p. 1982. 33.00x (ISBN 0-669-05543-3). Lexington Bks.

United States Immigration for Businesses, Investors & Workers. Arthur M. Gellman et al. LC 81-80685. viii, 108p. lib. bdg. 30.00 (ISBN 0-89941-098-7); pap. text ed. 15.00 (ISBN 0-89941-099-5). W S Hein.

U. S. Immigration in the 1980s: Reappraisal & Reform. Ed. by David E. Simcox. 230p. 1988. 30.00 (ISBN 0-8133-7542-8). Westview.

U. S. Immigration Law & the Control of Labor, 1820-1924. Kitty Calavita. LC 84-45222. (Law, State, & Society Ser.). 1984. 47.50 (ISBN 0-12-155052-4). Acad Pr.

U. S. Immigration Policy. Ed. by Richard R. Hofstetter. LC 83-20815. (Duke Press Policy Studies). vii, 310p. 1984. 31.75 (ISBN 0-8223-0476-7). Duke.

U. S. Imperialism: The Spanish American War to the Iranian Revolution. Mansour Farhang. LC 81-50136. 250p. 1981. 20.00 (ISBN 0-89608-095-1); pap. 7.00 (ISBN 0-89608-094-3). South End Pr.

United States Import Relief Laws: Current Developments in Law & Policy: A Course Handbook. Harvey M. Applebaum & A. Paul Victor. 365p. 1985. pap. 15.00 (A4-4137). PLI.

U. S. Import Statistics for Agricultural Commodities (1981-1986) Kevin M. Yokoyana et al. 620p. 1988. 89.95. Transaction Bks.

U. S. Import Trade Regulation. Eugene T. Rossides. 725p. 1985. 85.00 (ISBN 0-87179-454-3, 0454). BNA.

United States in a Chaotic World see No Break Here.

United States in a Disarmed World: A Study of the U. S. Outline for General & Complete Disarmament. Washington Center of Foreign Policy Research & Arnold Wolfers. LC 66-16036. pap. 62.50 (ISBN 0-317-19862-9, 2023114). Bks Demand UMI.

United States in Central America: An Analysis of the Kissinger Commission Report. Larry G. Hufford. LC 87-25704. (Edwin Mellen Press Text Ser.). 260p. 1987. lib. bdg. 49.95 (ISBN 0-88946-006-X). E Mellen.

United States in Crisis. Ed. by Lajos Biro & Marc J. Cohen. LC 78-61686. (Studies in Marxism: Vol. 4). 256p. 1979. x 8.95 (ISBN 0-930656-08-3); pap. 3.00 (ISBN 0-930656-07-5). MEP Pubns.

United States in Crisis - the Communist Solution. 1969. pap. 0.75 (ISBN 0-87898-042-3). New Outlook.

United States in Crisis, Vol. I. Eli Raitport. (Nineteen Eighty-Six to Nineteen Eighty-Seven Ser.). (Illus.). 192p. (Orig.). 1988. pap. 19.50x (ISBN 0-944182-00-3). Raitport Co.

United States in East Asia: A Historical Bibliography. (ABC-Clio Research Guides: No. 4). 298p. 1985. 34.00 (ISBN 0-87436-452-3). ABC-Clio.

United States in Eighteen Hundred: Henry Adams Revisited. Noble E. Cunningham, Jr. LC 88-5514. 75p. 1988. text ed. 14.95x (ISBN 0-8139-1182-6). U Pr of VA.

United States in International Banking. Siegfried Stern. Ed. by Stuart Bruchey & Eleanor Bruchey. LC 76-5036. (American Business Abroad Ser.). 1976. Repr. of 1952 ed. 37.50x (ISBN 0-405-09302-0). Ayer Co Pubs.

U. S. in Norwegian History. Sigmund Skard. LC 76-5263. (Contributions in American Studies: No. 26). (Orig.). 1976. lib. bdg. 29.95 (ISBN 0-8371-8909-8, SKU/). Greenwood.

United States in Panamanian Politics. G. A. Mellander. LC 76-141903. 218p. 1971. text ed. 7.95x (ISBN 0-8134-1219-6, 1219). Inter Print Pubs.

United States in Prague, 1945-1948. Walter Ullmann. (East European Monographs: No. 36). 205p. 1978. 20.00x (ISBN 0-914710-29-X). East Eur Quarterly.

U. S. in Space: Issues & Policy Choices for a New Era. Ed. by Edmund S. Muskie. 100p. 1988. 16.75 (ISBN 0-944237-24-X); pap. 7.75 (ISBN 0-944237-23-1). Ctr National Policy.

United States in the Civil War. Don Lawson. LC 76-54932. (Young People's History of America's Wars Ser.). (Illus.). (gr. 7 up). 1977. PLB 12.89 (ISBN 0-200-00176-0, Crowell Jr Books). HarpJ.

United States in the Indian Wars. Don Lawson. LC 75-6684. (Young People's History of America's Wars Ser.). (Illus.). (gr. 7 up). 1975. 12.70 (ISBN 0-200-00158-2, Crowell Jr Books). HarpJ.

United States in the Indian Wars. Reissue. ed. Don Lawson. LC 75-6684. (Young People's History of America's Wars Ser.). (Illus.). 145p. (YA) (gr. 7 up). 1988. PLB 12.89 (ISBN 0-690-04713-4, Crowell Jr Bks). HarpJ.

United States in the International Telecommunication Union & in Pre-ITU Conferences. Mildred L. B. Feldman. LC 76-2971. 1976. 10.00 (ISBN 0-9606700-0-9). Feldman.

United States in the Mexican War. Don Lawson. LC 76-11022. (Young People's History of America's Wars Ser.). (Illus.). (gr. 7 up). 1976. 12.70i (ISBN 0-200-00169-8, Crowell Jr Books); PLB 12.89 (ISBN 0-690-04723-1). HarpJ.

United States in the Middle East: A Historical Dictionary. David Shavit. LC 87-24965. 480p. 1988. lib. bdg. 65.00 (ISBN 0-313-25341-2, SHV/). Greenwood.

United States in the Middle East: Interests & Obstacles. Seth P. Tillman. LC 81-47777. (Midland Bks: No. 335). 352p. 1982. 35.00x (ISBN 0-253-36172-9); pap. 12.95x (ISBN 0-253-20335-X). Ind U Pr.

United States in the Orient. Charles A. Conant. LC 72-137936. (Economic Thought, History & Challenge Ser.). 1971. Repr. of 1900 ed. 26.50x (ISBN 0-8046-1441-5, Pub by Kennikat). Assoc Faculty Pr.

United States in the Spanish-American War. Don Lawson. LC 75-34165. (Illus.). (gr. 7-9). 1976. PLB 12.89 (ISBN 0-200-00163-9, Crowell Jr Books). HarpJ.

United States in the Supreme War Council: American War Aims & Inter-Allied Strategy 1917-1918. David F. Trask. LC 77-16237. 1978. Repr. of 1961 ed. lib. bdg. 35.00x (ISBN 0-313-20006-8, TRUS). Greenwood.

United States in the Twentieth Century. Melvyn Dubofsky et al. LC 77-13246. (Illus.). 1978. pap. write for info. ref. ed. (ISBN 0-13-938712-9). P-H.

United States in the Vietnam War. Don Lawson. LC 80-2460. (Illus.). 160p. (YA) (gr. 7 up). 1981. 12.89 (ISBN 0-690-04104-7, Crowell Jr Bks); PLB 12.70 (ISBN 0-690-04105-5). HarpJ.

U. S. in the Vietnam War, 1954-1975: A Selected, Annotated Bibliography. Louis A. Peake. LC 84-45409. (WUS-SS Ser.). 600p. 1986. lib. bdg. 70.00 (ISBN 0-8240-8946-4). Garland Pub.

United States in the World Economy. Martin Feldstein. (NBER Conference Report Ser.). 712p. 1988. 74.95x (ISBN 0-226-24077-0); pap. 24.95x (ISBN 0-226-24078-9). U of Chicago Pr.

United States in the World Economy. Hal B. Lary et al. LC 75-26859. (Economic Series: No. 23). 216p. 1975. Repr. of 1943 ed. lib. bdg. 35.00x (ISBN 0-8371-8257-3, LAUS). Greenwood.

United States in the World-Economy: A Regional Geography. John Agnew. (Geography of the World-Economy Ser.). (Illus.). 272p. 1987. 34.50 (ISBN 0-521-30410-5); pap. 9.95 (ISBN 0-521-31684-7). Cambridge U Pr.

United States in the World Economy: Selected Papers of C. Fred Bergsten, 1981 to 1982. C. Fred Bergsten. LC 82-49336. 256p. 1983. 26.00x (ISBN 0-669-06617-6). Lexington Bks.

United States in the 1980's. Ed. by Peter Duignan & Alvin Rabushka. LC 79-5475. (Publication Ser.: No. 228). 1980. 20.00 (ISBN 0-8179-7281-1). Hoover Inst Pr.

United States in World Affairs: Leadership, Partnership, or Disengagement. Ed. by Robert A. Bauer. LC 74-14990. (Essays on Alternatives of U. S. Foreign Policy Ser.). pap. 36.00 (2027724). Bks Demand UMI.

TITLE INDEX U. S. MARITIME POLICY

United States in World War One: Story of General John J. Pershing & the American Expeditionary Forces. Don Lawson. (Young People's History of America's Wars Ser.). (Illus.). (gr. 7 up). 1963. 12.70i (ISBN 0-200-71939-4, B86940, Crowell Jr Books). HarpJ.

United States in 1800. Henry Adams. 142p. 1955. pap. 5.95x (ISBN 0-8014-9014-6). Cornell U Pr.

U. S. Income Tax Guide, 1978. rev. ed. Ed. by Internal Revenue Service. (Illus.). 1977. pap. 1.95 (ISBN 0-89552-010-9). DMR Pubns.

U. S. Income Tax Guide, 1979. Ed. by Michael L. Green. (Buyer's Guide Reports Ser.). 1978. pap. 1.95 (ISBN 0-89552-054-0). DMR Pubns.

U. S. Income Tax Guide, 1980. Ed. by Michael L. Green. (Buyer's Guide Ser.). 1979. pap. 2.25 (ISBN 0-89552-064-8). DMR Pubns.

U. S. Income Tax Guide, 1981. rev. ed. Ed. by Michael L. Green. (Buyer's Guide Ser.). 80p. (Orig.). pap. 2.50 (ISBN 0-89552-074-5). DMR Pubns.

United States, India, & the Bomb. Shelton L. Williams. LC 74-79299. (Washington Center of Foriegn Policy Research Studies in International Affairs: No. 12). pap. 17.70 (ISBN 0-317-08622-7, 2016058). Bks Demand UMI.

U. S. Industrial Competitiveness: The Case of the Textile & Apparel Industry. Fariborz Ghadar et al. LC 86-46341. (Illus.). 128p. 1987. 24.00x (ISBN 0-669-15689-2). Lexington Bks.

U. S. Industrial Fastener Industry: Past Performance, Current Trends & Opportunities for Growth. 210p. 1986. 650.00 (ISBN 0-317-55203-1). Busn Trend.

United States Industrial Outlook, 1988, with Expanding Coverage of the Services Sector, Construction, High- Tech, & Emerging Industries. 29th ed. (Illus.). 643p. 1988. pap. 24.00 (S/N 003-009-00522-1). USGPO.

United States Infantry: An Illustrated History, 1775-1918. Gregory J. Urwin & Darby Erd. (Illus.). 176p. 1988. 24.95 (ISBN 0-7137-1757-2, Pub. by Blandford Pr England). Sterling.

U. S. Infantry Combat Vehicles Today. Steven J. Zaloga & Michael Green. (Tanks Illustrated Ser.: Vol.13). 1984. pap. 9.95 (ISBN 0-85368-663-7, Arms & Armour Pr). Sterling.

United States Infantry Regiments. C. Gallagher & R. Pigeon. 1986. 14.98 (614944). Outlet Bk Co.

U. S. Infantry: Vietnam. Jim Mesko. (Weapons in Action Ser.: No. 3006). (Illus.). 50p. 1983. pap. 5.95 (ISBN 0-89747-151-2). Squad Sig Pubns.

U. S. Information Agency. Fitzhugh Green. (WV Library of Federal Department Agencies & Systems Ser.). 285p. 1983. lib. bdg. 25.00 cancelled (ISBN 0-86531-228-1). Westview.

U. S. Information Agency: Public Diplomacy in the Computer Age. Allen C. Hansen. LC 83-24515. 250p. 1984. 35.00 (ISBN 0-275-91186-1, C1186). Praeger.

U. S. Intelligence & the Soviet Strategic Threat. Lawrence Freedman. LC 85-43345. 236p. 1986. text ed. 37.00x (ISBN 0-691-07696-0); pap. 9.95x (ISBN 0-691-02242-9). Princeton U Pr.

U. S. Intelligence Community. Jeffrey Richelson. LC 84-24385. 392p. 1985. prof. ref. 39.95x (ISBN 0-88730-024-3); pap. text ed. 16.95 (ISBN 0-88730-025-1). Ballinger Pub.

U. S. Intelligence Community. 2nd ed. Jeffrey Richelson. 392p. 1988. 39.95 (ISBN 0-88730-245-9); pap. text ed. 16.95 (ISBN 0-88730-226-2). Ballinger Pub.

U. S. Intelligence Community. Stafford T. Thomas. LC 83-1246. 134p. (Orig.). 1983. PLB 25.25 (ISBN 0-8191-3098-2); pap. text ed. 8.75 (ISBN 0-8191-3099-0). U Pr of Amer.

U. S. Intelligence Community: Foreign Policy & Domestic Activities. Lyman B. Kirkpatrick, Jr. 224p. 1985. pap. 31.00x (ISBN 0-8133-7093-0). Westview.

U. S. Intelligence: Evolution & Anatomy. Mark M. Lowenthal. LC 83-27039. 1984. pap. 9.95 (ISBN 0-275-91617-0, B1617). Praeger.

U. S. Intelligence Requirements for the Late 1980s. Leo Cherne. 1986. write for info. (ISBN 0-935067-10-8). Nathan Hale Inst.

U. S. Interest Rates & the Interest Rate Dilemma for the Developing World. J. Pierre Benoit. LC 85-12348. (Illus.). 248p. 1986. lib. bdg. 40.95 (ISBN 0-89930-120-3, BIR/, Quorum Bks). Greenwood.

U. S. Interests & Global Natural Resources: Energy, Minerals, Food. Ed. by Emery N. Castle & Kent A. Price. 147p. 1983. 18.00 (ISBN 0-8018-3099-0); pap. 9.95 (ISBN 0-8018-3106-7). Resources Future.

U. S. Interests & Policies in the Caribbean & Central America. Jorge I. Dominguez. 1982. pap. 6.00 (ISBN 0-8447-1097-0). Am Enterprise.

U. S. Interests in Africa: Diversity of Decision Making. Helen Kitchen. LC 83-2408. 119p. 1983. pap. 9.95 (ISBN 0-275-91575-1, B1575). Praeger.

United States Internal Revenue Tax-Paid Stamps Printed on Tin-Foil & Paper Tobacco Wrappers, Vol. 1. John A. Hicks. LC 87-82283. (Illus.). 200p. 1988. price not set (ISBN 0-9619611-0-4). Hicks Philatelic.

United States Internal Revenue Tax System. Ed. by Charles W. Eldridge et al. LC 86-62932. (Historical Writings in Law & Jurisprudence. Second Ser.: No. 1). vii, 722p. 1986. Repr. of 1895 ed. lib. bdg. 46.00 (ISBN 0-89941-515-6). W S Hein.

U. S. International Broadcasting & National Security. James L. Tyson. 151p. (Orig.). 1983. pap. text ed. 7.95 (ISBN 0-915071-00-2). Ramapo Pr.

U. S. International Competitiveness: Evolution or Revolution? John C. Hilke & Philip B. Nelson. LC 88-1137. (Illus.). 256p. 1988. lib. bdg. 37.95 (ISBN 0-275-92964-7, C2964). Praeger.

U. S. International Economic Policy in Action. Stephen D. Cohen & Ronald L. Meltzer. LC 82-15059. 224p. 1982. 36.95 (ISBN 0-275-90773-2, C0773). Praeger.

U. S. International Economic Policy in an Interdependent World, 4 vols. Commission of International Trade & Investment Policy Staff. (Final Reports & Compendium of Papers: Nos. 1 & 2). 1985. Repr. of 1971 ed. Set. lib. bdg. 180.00 (ISBN 0-89941-420-6). W S Hein.

United States International Electricity Trade: Projections Through 1995. Christopher J. Freitas & Thomas Petersik. (DOE-EIA Ser.: No. 0496). 61p. 1986. pap. 3.25 (ISBN 0-318-21642-6, S/N 061-003-00494-6). USGPO.

U. S. International Monetary Policy: Markets, Power & Ideas as Sources of Change. J. S. Odell. 1982. pap. 11.95x (ISBN 0-691-02212-7). Princeton U Pr.

U. S. International Trade Laws: Program Materials, March 14-15, 1985, Washington, D.C., May 8-9, 1985, San Francisco, CA. Georgetown University, Law Center Staff. LC 86-102194. Date not set. price not set. Grgtwn U Law Ctr.

U. S. International Trade Laws. Ed. by Alan M. Stowell. 536p. 1986. pap. text ed. 30.00 (ISBN 0-87179-518-3, 0518). BNA.

U. S. International Trade Reports, 7 binders. Edwin S. Newman & Eugene M. Wypyski. LC 81-11181. (First Ser.). 1981. Set. looseleaf 525.00 (ISBN 0-379-20722-2); New Series. 2 bdrs. looseleaf 200.00. Oceana.

United States International Visitor Program: Strengthening the Community Organization. John S. Gibson. 108p. 1979. 1.00 (ISBN 0-318-15385-8). Natl Coun Intl Visitors.

U. S. Intervention in the Exchange Market for DM, 1977-80. Paul Wonnacott. LC 82-21263. (Princeton Studies in International Finance Ser.: No. 51). 1982. pap. text ed. 6.50x (ISBN 0-88165-222-9). Princeton U Int Finan Econ.

U. S. Interventionism in South America: The OAS & the Dominican Crisis. Shiv Kumar. LC 86-73078. 250p. 1987. text ed. 22.50x (ISBN 0-89891-012-9). Advent NY.

United States Investment in the Forest-Based Sector in Latin America: Problems & Potentials. Hans M. Gregersen & Arnoldo Contreras. LC 74-21754. pap. 32.00 (ISBN 0-317-26461-3, 2023797). Bks Demand UMI.

U. S. Investments in the Latin American Economy. U. S. Department of Commerce. Ed. by Stuart Bruchey & Eleanor Bruchey. LC 76-5039. (American Business Abroad Ser.). (Illus.). 1976. Repr. of 1957 ed. 21.00 (ISBN 0-405-09305-5). Ayer Co Pubs.

U. S. Investor's Guide to Gold & Silver Penny Stocks. James E. Ryan. 288p. (Orig.). 1984. pap. 14.95 (ISBN 0-9610202-1-0). NW Silver Pr.

United States-Iranian Relations. Benson L. Grayson. LC 81-40305. 194p. (Orig.). 1981. pap. text ed. 12.25 (ISBN 0-8191-1797-8). U Pr of Amer.

United States: It's Past, Purpose & Promise. Diane Hart. (Illus.). 256p. (gr. 6-12). 1988. text ed. 13.95 (ISBN 0-88102-059-1); Part 1, 128 pp. pap. text ed. 5.95 ea. (ISBN 0-88102-057-5). Part 2, 128 p (ISBN 0-88102-058-3). tchr's ed. 14.95 (ISBN 0-88102-060-5). Janus Bks.

United States-Japan Economic Problem. 2nd ed. C. Fred Bergsten & William R. Cline. LC 86-83417. (Policy Analyses in International Economics: No. 13). 180p. 1987. pap. 10.00 (ISBN 0-88132-060-9). Inst Intl Eco.

United States-Japan Relations: A Surprising Partnership--Annual Review, 1986. Ed. by Richard B. Finn. (U. S.-Japan Relations Ser.). 288p. 1987. pap. 14.95 (ISBN 0-88738-685-7). Transaction Bks.

U. S. Japan Seminar on Polymer Liquid Crystals: Journal of Applied Polymer Science Symposium, No. 41. J. L. White & S. Onogi. 1985. pap. write for info. (ISBN 0-471-88171-6). Wiley.

United States-Japan Technological Exchange Symposium: Sponsored by the Japan-American Society of Washington, 1981. Ed. by Cecil H. Uyehara. LC 82-40064. 142p. (Orig.). 1982. PLB 25.50 (ISBN 0-8191-2423-0); pap. text ed. 10.00. U Pr of Amer.

United States-Japan Trade Relations: A Critical Juncture. (CED Program Statement Ser.). 29p. 1987. pap. 4.00 (ISBN 0-87186-113-5). Comm Econ Dev.

United States-Japanese Economic Relations: Cooperation, Competition & Confrontation. Ed. by Diane Tasca et al. (Policy Studies). 1980. 29.00 (ISBN 0-08-025129-3). Pergamon.

United States-Japanese Relations: The 1970's. Ed. by Priscilla Clapp & Morton H. Halperin. LC 74-80441. 256p. 1974. text ed. 18.50x (ISBN 0-674-92571-8). Harvard U Pr.

U. S. Jet Fighters Since Nineteen Forty-Five. Robert F. Dorr. (Illus.). 128p. (Orig.). 1988. pap. 14.95 (ISBN 0-7137-1948-6, Pub. by Blandford Pr England). Sterling.

U. S. Joint Ventures in China: A Progress Report. 1987. 95.00. Natl Coun US China.

U. S. Labor & Employment Laws, 1987 Edition. Ed. by Ruth C. Trussell. 432p. 1987. pap. text ed. 30.00 (ISBN 0-87179-560-4, 0560). BNA.

U. S. Labor & the Vietnam War. Phillip S. Foner & Betty Smith. 264p. (Orig.). 1988. pap. 8.95 (ISBN 0-7178-0672-3). Intl Pubs Co.

U. S. Labor Movement & Latin America: A History of Workers' Response to Intervention, Vol. I, 1846-1919. Philip S. Foner. 240p. 1988. text ed. 39.95 (ISBN 0-89789-131-7). Bergin & Garvey.

U. S. Labour Unions Today: Basic Problems & Trends - A Soviet View. A. Mkrtchian. 203p. 1975. 15.95 (ISBN 0-8464-0949-6). Beekman Pubs.

United States Land Grant Records, Pickens County, Alabama. Ed. by Rose G. Lovett. 195p. (Orig.). 1988. text ed. 13.00x (ISBN 0-942301-14-5). Birm Pub Lib.

United States Large Cents 1793-1857. Ed. by Warren A. Lapp & Herbert A. Silberman. LC 74-27611. (Gleanings from the Numismatist Ser.). (Illus.). 640p. 1975. 50.00 (ISBN 0-88000-058-9). Quarterman.

United States-Latin America: A Special Relationship? Edmund Gaspar. 1978. pap. 7.00 (ISBN 0-8447-3287-7). Am Enterprise.

United States-Latin American Relations. Michael J. Kryzanek. LC 85-6510. 256p. 1987. pap. 14.95 (ISBN 0-275-92715-6, B2715). Praeger.

United States-Latin American Trade & Financial Relations: Some Policy Recommendations. S. Weintraub. (CEPAL Manuals). pap. 3.00 (ISBN 92-1-121048-8, E.81.11.G.63). UN.

U. S. Law of Sovereign Immunity. 1984. 150.00 (ISBN 0-8002-3170-8). Intl Pubns Serv.

U. S. Law Schools: A Directory of Courses & Other Special Programs Available at the American Law Schools. Abayomi Moses. LC 81-52882. 180p. 1981. 14.00 (ISBN 0-9606958-0-X); pap. 11.00 (ISBN 0-9606958-1-8). Sekoni Pubs.

United States Law Week. BNA's Legal Services Staff. looseleaf 544.00. BNA.

U. S. Law Week's Supreme Court Review: 1986-1987 Term. Law Week's Editors. 178p. 1987. write for info. BNA.

U. S. Leadership in Asia & the Middle East: The Credibility of Institutions, Policies & Leadership, Vol. 18. Ed. by Kenneth W. Thompson. LC 85-670. 156p. (Orig.). 1985. lib. bdg. 25.25 (ISBN 0-8191-4426-6); pap. text ed. 9.25 (ISBN 0-8191-4427-4). U Pr of Amer.

U. S. Leadership in the International Economy. John N. Yochelson. (CSIS Significant Issues Ser.). 1988. write for info. CSI Studies.

U. S. Legal System: A Practice Handbook. Dennis Campbell. 1983. lib. bdg. 56.50 (ISBN 90-247-2782-0, Pub. by Martinus Nijhoff Netherlands). Kluwer Academic.

United States Legislation on Foreign Relations & International Commerce: 1789-1979, 5 vols. Ed. by Igor I. Kavass & Michael J. Blake. LC 76-51898. 1977. Set. lib. bdg. 625.00 (ISBN 0-930342-00-3); Vol. 5 1970-1979. 125.00; looseleaf service binder,1980 75.00. W S Hein.

United States Letter Rates to Foreign Destinations, 1847 to GPU-UPU. Charles J. Starnes. Ed. by Leonard H. Hartmann. LC 82-80070. (Illus.). 160p. 1982. 27.50 (ISBN 0-917528-04-2). L H Hartmann.

U. S. Liberty Album. Ed. by David S. Macdonald. (Illus.). 416p. (gr. 6 up). 1984. text ed. 18.95 (ISBN 0-937458-29-5). Harris & Co.

U. S. Library of Congress Directory to Quilt Collections in the United States & Canada. Lisa T. Oshins. (Illus.). 300p. 1987. 24.95; pap. 18.95. Acropolis.

United States Licensed: Indian Trader. J. B. Moore. (Illus.). 136p. 1988. pap. 16.50 (Pub. by Avanyu Pub). U of NM Pr.

United States Life-Saving Service: Eighteen Eighty. J. H. Merryman. Ed. by William R. Jones. (Illus.). 1981. pap. 4.95 (ISBN 0-89646-071-1). Outbooks.

United States Life Tables by Dentulous or Edentulous Condition, 1971 & 1957-58. T. N. Greville. LC 74-7204. (Data Evaluation & Methods Research Ser. 2: No. 64). 60p. 1974. pap. text ed. 1.50 (ISBN 0-8406-0018-6). Natl Ctr Health Stats.

United States Life Tables: 1890, 1901, 1910, & 1901-1910. U. S. Department of Commerce, Bureau of the Census Staff & James W. Glover. LC 75-37267. (Demography Ser.). (Illus.). 1976. Repr. of 1921 ed. 46.50x (ISBN 0-405-07997-4). Ayer Co Pubs.

U. S. Lighting Fixtures Industry: A Product-by-Product Marketing Analysis & Competitor Profile. 275p. 1986. 675.00 (ISBN 0-317-55198-1). Busn Trend.

U. S. Loans, 1776-1892: An Illustrated History. Gene Hessler. (Illus.). 320p. 1986. 75.00. BNR Pr.

U. S. Local Histories in the Library of Congress - A Bibliography, 4 vols. Ed. by Marion J. Kaminkow. LC 74-25444. 4500p. 1975. 225.00 (ISBN 0-910946-17-5). Magna Carta Bk.

U. S. Local Histories in the Library of Congress: Supplement & Index. LC 74-25444. 569p. 1976. 25.00 (ISBN 0-910946-18-3). Magna Carta Bk.

U. S. Machine Postmarks, 1871-1925. R. F. Hanmer. LC 84-82081. (Illus.). xiv, 121p. 1984. pap. 15.00 (ISBN 0-318-03728-9). R F Hanmer.

United States: MacKaey Blue Book, 1988, 3 vols. 1988. Set. 125.00. Manufacturers.

U. S. McMaster Glossary of FORTRAN-77. W. H. Fleming & K. A. Redish. 64p. 1983. pap. text ed. 5.50 (ISBN 0-8403-3052-9). Kendall-Hunt.

U. S. Man-Made Fibers Industry: Global Challenges & Strategies for the Future. David A. Ricks et al. LC 84-10376. (Industrial Policy & Strategy Ser.). 272p. 1984. text ed. 75.00x (ISBN 0-87249-452-7). U of SC Pr.

United States Manufactured Exports & Export-Related Employment: Profiles of the 50 States & 33 Selected Metropolitan Areas for 1983. Georg Mehl. (Illus.). 117p. (Orig.). 1987. pap. 5.50 (ISBN 0-318-22736-3, S/N 003-009-00501-9). USGPO.

U. S. Manufacturers Directory: Eastern Region, Vol. 2. American Business Directories, Inc. Staff. Ed. by Andrew D. Bock. 1200p. Date not set. pap. 349.00 (ISBN 0-945041-01-2). Am Busn Direct.

U. S. Manufacturers Directory: Western Region, Vol. 1. American Business Directories, Inc. Staff. Ed. by Andrew D. Bock. 800p. Date not set. pap. 295.00 (ISBN 0-945041-02-0). Am Busn Direct.

U. S. Manufacturers Directory, Vol. 3. American Business Directores, Inc. Staff. Ed. by Andrew D. Bock. 2000p. Date not set. pap. 495.00 (ISBN 0-945041-00-4). Am Busn Direct.

U. S. Marine Corps. Ed. by Arthur M. Schlesinger, Jr. (Know Your Government Ser.). (Illus.). (gr. 5 up). 1989. 14.95 (ISBN 1-55546-110-7). Chelsea Hse.

U. S. Marine Corps Aviation 1912-Present. Peter B. Mersky. LC 83-13290. (Illus.). 320p. 1983. 22.95 (ISBN 0-933852-39-8). Nautical & Aviation.

U. S. Marine Corps Story. Abr. ed. J. Robert Moskin. 800p. 1983. pap. text ed. 14.95 (ISBN 0-07-043454-9). McGraw.

U. S. Marine Corps Story. 2nd, rev. ed. J. Robert Moskin. 864p. 1988. pap. text ed. 14.95 (ISBN 0-07-043457-3). McGraw.

U. S. Marine Operations in Korea 1950-53, 4 Vols. Lynn Montross & Nicholas A. Canzona. 1971. Repr. of 1962 ed. Set. 195.00 (ISBN 0-403-00030-0); 50.00 ea. Scholarly.

U. S. Marine Operations in Korea, 1950-53, 4 vols. Lynn Montross & Ca Montross. 1988. Repr. of 1962 ed. Set. lib. bdg. 295.00x. Am Biog Serv.

U. S. Marine Operations in Korea, 4 Vols. U. S. Marine Corps. 1968. Repr. Set. 250.00 (ISBN 0-403-03719-0); 25.00 ea. Scholarly.

U. S. Marines & Amphibious War. Isely & Crowl. (Illus.). 636p. Date not set. Repr. of 1951 ed. 11.95 (ISBN 0-686-31000-4). Marine Corps.

U. S. Marines in Action. LC 85-40981. (Villard Military Ser.: The Elite Forces). (Illus.). 96p. 1986. 4.95 (ISBN 0-394-74402-0, Pub. by Villard Bks). Random.

United States Marines in Grenada, 1983. Ronald H. Spector. LC 87-691831. (Illus.). 43p. 1987. pap. 2.25 (ISBN 0-317-62819-4, S/N 008-055-00170-6). USGPO.

U. S. Marines in Lebanon 1982-1984. Benis M. Frank. (Illus.). 206p. 1987. pap. 10.00 (ISBN 0-318-23857-8, S/N 008-055-00171-4). USGPO.

United States Marines in Lebanon, 1982-1984. Benis M. Frank. (Illus.). 206p. 1987. pap. 10.00 (S/N 008-055-00171-4). USGPO.

United States Marines in North China. John A. White. LC 74-80832. (New Ser). (Illus.). 228p. 1974. 10.00 (ISBN 0-9603242-0-8). J A White.

United States Marines in Vietnam, 1967: Fighting the North Vietnamese. Gary L. Telfer et al. LC 77-604776. (United States Marines in Vietnam Ser.). (Illus.). 354p. 1984. pap. 10.00 (S/N 008-055-00165-0). USGPO.

United States Marines in Vietnam, 1970-1971: Vietnamization & Redeployment. Cosmas et al. LC 77-604776. (Illus.). 499p. 1986. 29.00 (ISBN 0-318-22584-0, S/N 008-055-00169-2). USGPO.

U. S. Marines in World War II. Robert C. Stern. (Uniforms Illustrated Ser.: No. 11). (Illus.). 68p. (Orig.). 1986. pap. 9.95 (ISBN 0-85368-755-2, Pub. by Arms & Armour). Sterling.

U. S. Marines on Iwo Jima. 6th ed. Raymond Henri et al. (Elite Unit Ser.). 294p. 1987. Repr. of 1945 ed. 19.95 (ISBN 0-89839-095-8). Battery Pr.

United States Marines Seventeen Seventy-Five to Nineteen Seventy-Five. E. H. Simmons. 342p. 1976. lib. bdg. 2.95 (ISBN 0-670-74101-9). Marine Corps.

U. S. Maritime Industry In the National Interest. Irwin M. Heine. pap. 11.95 (ISBN 0-317-55862-5). Acropolis.

U. S. Maritime Industry in the National Interest: A Comprehensive Historical & Statistical Reference. Irwin M. Heine. 1981. pap. 11.95 (ISBN 0-87491-518-X). Acropolis.

U. S. Maritime Policy: History & Prospects. H. David Bess & Martin T. Farris. LC 81-1503. 238p. 1981. 44.95 (ISBN 0-275-90584-5, C0584). Praeger.

U. S. Maritime Strategy. Norman Friedman. (Illus.). 288p. 1988. 30.00 (ISBN 0-7106-0500-5). Janes Info Group.

U. S. Market for Animal Health Products: A Strategic Marketing Analysis & Biennial Review. 200p. 1986. 595.00 (ISBN 0-317-55211-2). Busn Trend.

U. S. Market for Food Additives, 1984. write for info. (ISBN 0-86621-125-X, A1181). Frost & Sullivan.

U. S. Market for Foreign Machine Tools, Parts & Accessories. 229p. 1984. 1450.00 (ISBN 0-86621-177-2, A1239). Frost & Sullivan.

U. S. Market for Household Paper Products: A Strategic Marketing Analysis & Biennial Review. 235p. 1986. 650.00 (ISBN 0-317-55202-3). Busn Trend.

U. S. Market for Petroleum Refinery Process Units. 237p. 1984. 1275.00 (ISBN 0-86621-185-3, A1247). Frost & Sullivan.

U. S. Markets for Infant Products: Past Performance, Current Trends & Opportunities for Growth. 215p. 1986. 595.00 (ISBN 0-317-55181-7). Busn Trend.

United States Marshal. Jack Rudman. (Career Examination Ser.: C-853). (Cloth bdg. avail. on request). pap. 15.00 (ISBN 0-8373-0853-4). Natl Learning.

United States Marshals of New Mexico & Arizona Territories, 1846 - 1912. Larry D. Ball. LC 76-57543. (Illus.). 325p. 1982. pap. 10.95 (ISBN 0-8263-0617-9). U of NM Pr.

U. S. Master Producers & British Music Scene Book: Stories, Text, Forms, Contracts. Walter E. Hurst & Walter S. Hale. LC 68-4500. (Entertainment Industry Ser., No. 4). (Illus.). 1968. 25.00 (ISBN 0-911370-04-8). Seven Arts.

U. S. Master Tax Guide, 1984: Permanent Edition. 564p. 18.00 (ISBN 0-317-04239-4); pap. 12.00 (ISBN 0-317-04240-8). Commerce.

U. S. Master Tax Guide 1985. 564p. 1984. 19.50 (5885); pap. 13.00 (5955). Commerce.

U. S. Master Tax Guide, 1987. Commerce Clearing House Staff. 576p. 1987. 22.50 (ISBN 0-317-30559-X, 5887); pap. 15.50 (ISBN 0-317-30558-1, 5957). Commerce.

U. S. Master Tax Guide 1987. 1576p. 1986. 22.50 (5887); pap. 15.50 (5957). Commerce.

U. S. Master Tax Guide, 1988. 636p. (Orig.). 1987. pap. 17.50 (5958). Commerce.

U. S. Master Tax Guide, 1988: Permanent Edition. 636p. 1987. 25.00 (5888). Commerce.

U. S. Master Tax Guide, 1989. 636p. Date not set. pap. 19.50 (5959). Commerce.

U. S. Master Tax Guide, 1989. Date not set. 27.50 (5889). Commerce.

United States Match & Medicine Stamps. Christopher West. LC 80-80786. (C. & S. Revenue Ser.). (Illus.). 144p. 24.95x (ISBN 0-9603498-1-2). Castenholz Sons.

U. S. Mechanized Firepower Today. Steven Zaloga & Arnold Meisner. (Tanks Illustrated Ser.: No. 26). (Illus.). 72p. (Orig.). 1988. pap. 9.95 (ISBN 0-85368-732-3, Pub. by Arms & Armour). Sterling.

U. S. Medical Care Industry: The Economist's Point of View. Ed. by Joseph C. Morreale. (Michigan Business Papers: No. 60). 131p. 1974. pap. 5.50 (ISBN 0-87712-166-4). UMI Div Res GSBA.

U. S. Medical Directory. 7th ed. LC 72-92344. 1986. 125.00 (ISBN 0-916524-24-8, 604-7). US Direct Serv.

U. S. Medical Licensure Statistics Nineteen Eighty-Five & Licensure Requirements Nineteen Eighty-Six. American Medical Association Staff. 53p. (Orig.). 1987. pap. 32.50 (ISBN 0-89970-309-7, OP-190/7). AMA.

U. S. Medical Licensure Statistics 1986, Licensure Requirements 1987. American Medical Association Staff. 53p. (Orig.). 1988. pap. 35.00 (OP-190/8). AMA.

United States Memoranda, 2 vols. Incl. U. S. Research Memoranda. (Nos. 1-8). (Nos. 1-236). 1945. 165.00 (ISBN 3-601-00023-7). Kraus Intl.

U. S. Merchant Marine Academy. Photos by Mike Yamashita. (First Edition Ser.). (Illus.). 112p. 1988. 35.00 (ISBN 0-916509-45-1); deluxe ed. 125.00 slipcased. Harmony Hse Pub LO.

U. S. Merchant Marine: In Search of an Enduring Maritime Policy. Ed. by Clinton W. Whitehurst, Jr. LC 83-13467. (Illus.). 320p. 1983. 28.95 (ISBN 0-87021-737-2). Naval Inst Pr.

U. S. Merchant Tokens: 1845-1860. 2nd ed. Russ Rulau. (Illus.). 150p. pap. 9.95 (ISBN 0-87341-083-1). Krause Pubns.

United States Metallurgical Coal Industry. James E. Spearman. 209p. 1980. 12.50 (ISBN 0-937058-00-9). West Va U Pr.

U. S. Microelectronics Industry: Technical Change, Industry Growth, & Social Impact. Nico Hazewindus & N. V. Phillips. LC 82-12191. (Technology & Economic Growth Ser.). (Illus.). 165p. 1982. 39.00 (ISBN 0-08-029376-X). Pergamon.

United States-Middle East Diplomatic Relations 1784-1978: An Annotated Bibliography. Thomas A. Bryson. LC 78-26754. 219p. 1979. lib. bdg. 20.00 (ISBN 0-8108-1197-9). Scarecrow.

U. S. Middle East Policy: The Domestic Setting. Ed. by Shai Feldman. (Publications of JCSS: No. 142). 100p. 1988. 18.00 (ISBN 0-8133-0721-X). Westview.

United States Military Buttons of the Land Services, 1787-1902: A Guide & Classificatory System. Martin A. Wyckoff. (Illus.). 121p. 1984. pap. text ed. 12.00 (ISBN 0-943788-01-3). McLean County.

U. S. Military Communications: The Force Multiplier. Fred J. Ricci & Danile Schutzer. LC 84-23783. 263p. 1986. text ed. 45.95 (ISBN 0-88175-016-6, Computer Sci Pr). W H Freeman.

U. S. Military Doctrine. G. Trofimenko. 222p. 1986. 9.95 (ISBN 0-8285-3278-8, Pub. by Progress Pubs USSR). Imported Pubns.

U. S. Military Firearms. James E. Hicks. 18.95 (ISBN 0-87505-109-X). Borden.

U. S. Military-Industrial Complex is a Threat to Peace. Ye Burgrow. 56p. 1984. 5.00x (Pub. by Collets (UK)). State Mutual Bk.

U. S. Military Intervention: Law & Morality. William V. O'Brien. (Washington Papers: Vol. VII, No. 68). 88p. (Orig.). 1979. pap. text ed. 7.95 (ISBN 0-8191-6015-6, Pub. by CSIS). U Pr of Amer.

U. S. Military Involvement in Southern Africa. Western Massachusetts ACAS. LC 78-64519. 262p. 1978. 20.00 (ISBN 0-89608-042-0); pap. 8.00 (ISBN 0-89608-041-2). South End Pr.

U. S. Military Management Thought, 1979-1984: A Selected Bibliography. Anthony G. White. (Public Administration Ser.: P 1965). 10p. 1986. 3.00 (ISBN 0-89028-925-5). Vance Biblios.

United States Military Posture for FY 1987. (Illus.). 108p. (Orig.). 1986. pap. 4.00 (ISBN 0-318-20159-3, S/N 008-004-00023-4). USGPO.

United States Military Posture for FY 1988. (Illus.). 108p. (Orig.). 1987. pap. 5.00 (ISBN 0-318-22467-4, S/N 008-004-00025-1). USGPO.

United States Military Posture for Fiscal Year 1989. (Illus.). 118p. (Orig.). 1988. pap. 7.50 (S/N 008-004-00027-7). USGPO.

U. S. Military Power & Rapid Deployment Requirements in the 1980s. Sherwood S. Cordier. 156p. 1983. pap. 24.50x (ISBN 0-86531-968-5). Westview.

U. S. Military Presence in the Middle East: Problems & Prospects. Robert J. Hanks. LC 82-84308. (Foreign Policy Reports Ser.). 77p. 1982. 7.50 (ISBN 0-89549-047-1). Inst Foreign Policy Anal.

United States Military Saddles, 1812-1943. Randy Steffen. LC 72-9268. (Illus.). 1980. 22.95 (ISBN 0-8061-1074-0). U of Okla Pr.

United States Military Saddles, 1812-1943. Randy Steffen. LC 72-9268. (Illus.). 176p. 1988. pap. 14.95 (ISBN 0-8061-2102-5). U of Okla Pr.

United States Military Small Arms, 1816-1865. Robert M. Reilly. 1983. 35.00 (ISBN 0-88227-019-2). Gun Room.

U. S. Military Vehicles, Nineteen Forty-One to Nineteen Forty-Five. Arthur Bryson. 100p. 1987. pap. 9.95. Portrayal.

U. S. Military Wheeled Vehicles. Major F. Crismon. Ed. by George H. Dammann. LC 82-73699. (Automotive Ser.). 472p. 1983. 34.95 (ISBN 0-912612-21-5). Crestline.

U. S. Millwork Industry: A Product-by-Product Marketing Analysis & Biennial Review. 205p. 1986. 650.00 (ISBN 0-317-55196-5). Busn Trend.

United States Mineral Lands. Henry N. Copp. Ed. by Stuart Bruchey. LC 78-53539. (Development of Public Land Law in the U. S. Ser.). 1979. Repr. of 1882 ed. lib. bdg. 45.00x (ISBN 0-405-11373-0). Ayer Co Pubs.

U. S. Mint. Paul Wolman. (Know Your Government Ser.). (Illus.). 96p. 1987. lib. bdg. 12.95 (ISBN 0-87754-829-3). Chelsea Hse.

U. S. Mint & Coinage. Don Taxay. LC 66-18413. 1983. Repr. of 1966 ed. lib. bdg. 35.00 (ISBN 0-915262-68-1); supplement incl. S J Durst.

U. S. Mississippi Census 1890 Union Veterans. Ronald V. Jackson. (Illus.). lib. bdg. 15.00 (ISBN 0-317-17039-2). Accelerated Index.

U. S. Monetary Policy. facsimile & rev. ed. American Assembly Staff. Ed. by Neil H. Jacoby. LC 79-164586. (Select Bibliographies Reprint Ser). Repr. of 1964 ed. 18.00 (ISBN 0-8369-5702-4). Ayer Co Pubs.

United States Monetary Policy. rev. ed. American Assembly Staff. Ed. by Neil H. Jacoby. LC 64-7956. (Illus.). 255p. pap. 66.30 (2029872). Bks Demand UMI.

U. S. Monetary Policy & European Responses in the 1980's. Kenneth King. (Chatham House Papers in Foreign Policy). 128p. (Orig.). 1982. pap. 10.95x (ISBN 0-7100-9337-3). Routledge Chapman & Hall.

United States Monetary Policy: Discussion & Research, 1981-1985. Dale E. Casper. (Public Administration Ser.: P 2048). 15p. 1986. 3.75 (ISBN 1-55590-088-7). Vance Biblios.

U. S. Monopolies & Developing Countries. V. D. Shchetinin. 178p. 1985. pap. 3.95 (ISBN 0-8285-3400-4, Pub. by Progress pubs USSR). Imported Pubns.

U. S. Motion Picture Theatre Industry: A Strategic Marketing Analysis & Biennial Review. 220p. 1986. 595.00 (ISBN 0-317-55186-8). Busn Trend.

United States Multinational Companies. 1986. lib. bdg. 79.95 (ISBN 0-8490-3783-2). Gordon Pr.

U. S. Multinationals & Worker Participation in Management: The American Experience in the European Community. Ton Devos. LC 80-23597. xv, 229p. 1981. lib. bdg. 36.95 (ISBN 0-89930-004-9, DUM/, Quorum). Greenwood.

United States Music: Sources of Bibliography. Richard Jackson. LC 73-80637. (I.S.A.M. Monographs: No. 1). 80p. (Orig.). 1973. pap. 5.00 (ISBN 0-914678-00-0). Inst Am Music.

U. S. N. Seal Combat Manual. 240p. Date not set. pap. 14.95. Lancer.

United States National Bank Notes & Their Seals. Dewitt G. Prather. Ed. by J. S. Prather & Angela Prather. (Illus.). 200p. 1986. 40.00x (ISBN 0-9616836-0-0); deluxe ed. 60.00 (ISBN 0-317-58449-9). D G Prather.

U. S. National Bibliography & the Copyright Law: An Historical Study. Joseph W. Rogers. LC 60-15545. pap. 29.80 (ISBN 0-317-10597-3, 2050963). Bks Demand UMI.

U. S. National Congress of Applied Mechanics, 9th: Proceedings. 480p. 1982. 75.00 (H00228). ASME.

U. S. National Economic Policy, 1917-1985. Anthony S. Campagna. LC 86-30316. 640p. 1987. lib. bdg. 55.00 (ISBN 0-275-92426-2, C2426). Praeger.

U. S. National Economic Policy, 1917-1985. Anthony S. Campagna. LC 86-30316. (Illus.). 672p. 1988. lib. bdg. 19.95 (ISBN 0-275-92907-8, B2907). Praeger.

U. S. National Health Policy: An Analysis of the Federal Role. Jennie J. Kronenfeld & Marcia L. Whicker. LC 84-2169. 304p. 1984. 36.95 (ISBN 0-275-91207-8, C1207). Praeger.

U. S. National Income & Product Accounts: Selected Topics. Murray F. Foss. LC 82-11081. (National Bureau of Economic Research-Studies in Income & Wealth: No. 47). (Illus.). 1983. lib. bdg. 50.00x (ISBN 0-226-25728-2). U of Chicago Pr.

United States National Interests in a Changing World. Donald E. Nuechterlein. LC 73-77255. (Illus.). 216p. 1973. 19.00 (ISBN 0-8131-1287-7). U Pr of Ky.

U. S. National Labor Relations Board: Annual Report, 1936-1965, Vols. 1-30. Bound set. 405.00x (ISBN 0-686-90070-6). Rothman.

U. S. National Report to ICA, 1984. Ed. by Judy M. Olson. LC 83-83405. 100p. 1984. pap. 6.00 (ISBN 0-9613459-0-X, C164). Am Congrs Survey.

United States National Report to International Union of Geodesy & Geophysics: 1971-1974, 2 Vols. (Special Publications Reprints: Antarctic Research Series). 504p. Vol. 1, 504p. pap. 10.00 (ISBN 0-317-32678-3, SP0005); Vol. 2, 1108p. 20.00 (ISBN 0-317-32679-1, SP006). Am Geophysical.

U. S. National Report to the International Union of Geodesy & Geophysics 1967-1970. 504p. pap. 5.00 (ISBN 0-317-66486-7). Am Geophysical.

U. S. National Report to the International Union of Geodesy & Geophysics 1971-1974. 1108p. 1975. pap. 10.00 (ISBN 0-317-66487-5). Am Geophysical.

U. S. National Security: A Framework for Analysis. Ed. by Daniel J. Kaufman et al. LC 84-48809. 608p. 1985. 39.00x (ISBN 0-669-09812-4); pap. text ed. 19.95x (ISBN 0-669-09851-5). Lexington Bks.

U. S. National Security & the Third World: Toward an Integrated Approach. William Perry. 1983. 6.00 (ISBN 0-89206-049-2). CSI Studies.

U. S. National Security & the Third World: Toward an Integrated Approach. Ed. by William Perry. (CSIS Panel Report). 22p. 1983. pap. text ed. 6.95 (ISBN 0-8191-5942-5, Pub. by CSIS). U Pr of Amer.

United States National Security Policy & Aid to the Thailand Police. Thomas Lobe. (Monograph Series in World Affairs: Vol. 14, 1976-77 Ser., Bk. 2). 161p. (Orig.). 1977. pap. 5.95 (ISBN 0-87940-051-X). Monograph Series.

U. S. National Security Policy & Strategy: Documents & Policy Proposals. Sam C. Sarkesian & Robert A. Vitas. (Documentary Reference Collections). 1988. price not set (ISBN 0-313-25482-6, SML/). Greenwood.

U. S. National Security: Policymakers, Processes, & Politics. Sam C. Sarkesian. 300p. Date not set. lib. bdg. 35.00 (ISBN 1-55587-022-8); pap. 16.95 (ISBN 1-55587-023-6). Lynne Rienner.

U. S. National Wage Stabilization Board, Jan. 1, 1946-Feb. 24, 1947: A Documentary History with Brief Explanations of Its Formation, Organization & Activities. viii, 594p. 1973. Repr. of 1947 ed. text ed. 25.00x (ISBN 0-8377-0901-6). Rothman.

United States, NATO & Israeli-Arab Peace. Peter Grose. (Seven Springs Reports). 54p. 1980. pap. 3.00 (ISBN 0-943006-11-2). Seven Springs.

U. S. Naval Academy. Dan Dry. (Illus.). 112p. 1987. 35.00 (ISBN 0-916509-15-X); deluxe ed. 125.00. Harmony Hse Pub LO.

U. S. Naval Academy: An Illustrated History. Jack Sweetmen. LC 78-70778. (Illus.). 208p. 1979. 24.95 (ISBN 0-87021-730-5). Naval Inst Pr.

U. S. Naval Airpower: Supercarrier in Action. Neil Leifer & Bill Sweetman. LC 87-12294. (Illus.). 128p. 1987. 12.98 (ISBN 0-87938-246-5). Motorbooks Intl.

U. S. Naval & Marine Aircraft Today. Don Linn. (Warbirds Illustrated Ser.: No. 34). (Illus.). 72p. (Orig.). 1985. pap. 9.95 (ISBN 0-85368-730-7, Pub. by Arms & Armour). Sterling.

U. S. Naval Armament: Aircraft-a Bibliography. A. Lani Low & James F. Muche. (Orig.). 1986. pap. text ed. 25.00x (ISBN 0-910651-16-7). Fathom Eight.

U. S. Naval Armament: Ships-A Bibliography. A. Lani Low & James F. Muche. (Orig.). 1986. pap. text ed. 25.00x (ISBN 0-910651-15-9). Fathom Eight.

United States Naval Aviation, 1910-1980. Clarke Van Fleet & William Armstrong. (NAVAIR 00-80p-1). (Illus.). 562p. (Orig.). 1981. text ed. 17.00 (ISBN 0-318-22470-4, S/N 008-046-00107-3). USGPO.

U. S. Naval Developments. Jan S. Breemer. LC 83-13289. 1987. 24.95 (ISBN 0-933852-36-3). Nautical & Aviation.

United States Naval Institute, Intellectual Forum of the New Navy: 1873-1889. new ed. Lawrence C. Allin. 381p. (Orig.). 1978. pap. 38.00x (ISBN 0-89126-066-8). MA-AH Pub.

U. S. Naval Institute Proceedings Cumulative Index Eighteen Seventy-Four to Nineteen Seventy-Seven. U. S. Naval Institute Staff. 384p. 1982. 18.95x (ISBN 0-87021-025-4). Naval Inst Pr.

United States Naval Power in a Changing World. Edwin B. Hooper. 288p. 1988. write for info. (ISBN 0-275-92738-5, C2738). Praeger.

U. S. Naval Vessels, 1943. U. S. Navy Department Staff. (Illus.). 288p. 1986. 12.95 (ISBN 0-87021-724-0). Naval Inst Pr.

U. S. Naval Weapons. Norman Friedman. LC 82-61473. (Illus.). 256p. 1982. 26.95 (ISBN 0-87021-735-6). Naval Inst Pr.

U. S. Navy. Richard Humble. LC 84-6497. (Illus.). 144p. 1984. 16.95 (ISBN 0-668-06163-4, 6163). Arco.

United States Navy. 1986. 24.95 (ISBN 0-317-62762-7, Pub. by Naval Inst Pr). H Holt & Co.

United States Navy: A Two Hundred-Year History. Edward L. Beach. (Illus.). 592p. 1987. pap. 12.95 (ISBN 0-395-43289-8). HM.

United States Navy Aircraft Since 1911. 2nd ed. Gordon Swanborough & Peter M. Bowers. LC 76-12910. 518p. 1977. 24.95 (ISBN 0-87021-968-5). Naval Inst Pr.

U. S. Navy Aircraft 1921-1941 & U. S. Marine Corps Aircraft 1941-1959. William T. Larkins. 1988. 27.50 (ISBN 0-517-56920-5, Orion Bks). Crown.

U. S. Navy Airships: A Bibliography. A. Lani Low & James F. Muche. (Orig.). 1986. pap. text ed. 15.00x (ISBN 0-910651-13-2). Fathom Eight.

U. S. Navy: An Illustrated History. Nathan Miller. (Illus.). 416p. 1977. 39.95 (Co-pub. by American Heritage); deluxe ed. 39.95 slipcased; bulk rates avail. Naval Inst Pr.

United States Navy & Coast Guard, 1946-1983: A Bibliography of English-Language Works & 16mm Films. Myron J. Smith, Jr. LC 84-42605. 559p. 1984. lib. bdg. 65.00x (ISBN 0-89950-122-2). McFarland & Co.

United States Navy & Defense Unification, 1947-1953. Paolo E. Coletta. LC 77-74410. (Illus.). 550p. 1981. 37.50 (ISBN 0-87413-126-X). U Delaware Pr.

United States Navy & Marine Corps Bases, Domestic. Ed. by Paolo E. Coletta & K. Jack Bauer. LC 84-4468. xv, 740p. 1985. lib. bdg. 95.00 (ISBN 0-313-23133-8, CUN/). Greenwood.

United States Navy & Marine Corps Bases, Overseas. Ed. by Paolo E. Coletta & K. Jack Bauer. LC 84-4470. 480p. 1985. lib. bdg. 76.95 (ISBN 0-313-24504-5, COU/). Greenwood.

United States Navy & the Vietnam Conflict, Vol. 1: The Setting of the Stage. Edwin B. Hooper et al. LC 76-600006. (Illus.). 419p. 1987. pap. 12.00 (ISBN 0-318-22961-7, S/N 008-046-00070-1). USGPO.

United States Navy & the Vietnam Conflict, V. 2: From Military Assistance to Combat 1959-1963. Edward J. Marolda & Oscar P. Fitzgerald. LC 76-600006. (Illus.). 607p. 1986. 22.00 (ISBN 0-318-22469-0, S/N 008-046-00114-6). USGPO.

U. S. Navy Carrier Bombers of WWII. (Illus.). 1987. pap. 9.95 (ISBN 0-89747-195-4, 6205). Squad Sig Pubns.

U. S. Navy Carrier Fighters of WWII. (Illus.). 1987. pap. 9.95 (ISBN 0-89747-194-6, 6204). Squad Sig Pubns.

U. S. Navy Cruisers: A Bibliography. A. Lani Low & James F. Muche. (Orig.). 1986. pap. text ed. 20.00x (ISBN 0-910651-17-5). Fathom Eight.

U. S. Navy Divers: A Bibliography. A. Lani Low & James F. Muche. (Orig.). 1987. pap. 25.00x (ISBN 0-910651-19-1). Fathom Eight.

United States Navy, Diving Manual, Vol. 1: Air Diving. rev. ed. Intro. by C. S. Maclin. (NAVSEA 0994-LP-001-9010 Ser.). (Illus.). 357p. 1985. wkbk. 21.00 (ISBN 0-318-19917-3, S/N 008-046-00110-3). USGPO.

U. S. Navy Fights. facs. ed. Walter A. Roberts. (Essay Index Reprint Ser). 1942. 21.00 (ISBN 0-8369-2068-6). Ayer Co Pubs.

U. S. Navy Helicopters: A Bibliography. A. Lani Low & James F. Muche. 1987. pap. text ed. 25.00x (ISBN 0-910651-18-3). Fathom Eight.

U. S. Programs That Impede U. S. Export Competitiveness: The Regulatory Environment. Robert A. Flammang. (Significant Issues Ser.: Vol. II, No. 3). 54p. (Orig.). 1980. pap. text ed. 6.95 (ISBN 0-8191-5910-7, Pub. by CSIS). U Pr of Amer.

U. S. Public Attitudes Towards Arms Control. 23p. 1986. write for info. Comm Present Danger.

U. S. Public Attitudes Toward Arms Control. 55p. 1987. write for info. Comm Present Danger.

U. S. Public Attitudes Toward the Defense Effort: Program, Priorities & Budget. 1984. write for info. Comm Present Danger.

U. S. Public Attitudes Toward the Geneva Summit & Arms Control. 49p. 1985. write for info. Comm Present Danger.

U. S. Public Attitudes Toward the Nuclear Freeze & Other Nuclear Arms Issues. 65p. 1984. write for info. Comm Present Danger.

U. S. Public Attitudes Toward the Strategic Defense Initiative & the U. S. Defense Effort. 67p. 1985. write for info. Comm Present Danger.

United States Public Opinion, the Fatalism of the Multitudes & the Tyranny of the Majority. James Bryce. (Illus.). 141p. 1986. 137.45 (ISBN 0-89901-284-1). Found Class Reprints.

United States Public Policy: A Geographical View. Ed. by John W. House. (Illus.). 1983. 39.95x (ISBN 0-19-874116-2); pap. 19.95x (ISBN 0-19-874117-0). Oxford U Pr.

United States-Puerto Rico Relations. Ed. by Raoul Gordon. 1976. lib. bdg. 59.95 (ISBN 0-8490-1245-7). Gordon Pr.

United States Pulp & Paper Industry: Global Challenges & Strategies. Jeffrey S. Arpan et al. LC 86-19296. 483p. 1987. text ed. 75.00 (ISBN 0-87249-501-9). U of SC Pr.

U. S. Pump & Compressor Industry: An Analysis of Current Markets & Prospects for Future Growth. 360p. 1986. 750.00. Busn Trend.

U. S. Pursuit Aircraft: A Pictorial Survey. 96p. 1981. 25.00x (ISBN 0-85153-185-7, Pub. by D B Barton England). State Mutual Bk.

United States Puzzlers. Candy Colborn. 1987. lib. bdg. 18.50 (ISBN 0-87287-573-3). Libs Unl.

U. S. Radio Broadcasting to Cuba: Policy Implications. 1982. write for info. Cuban Amer Natl Fndtn.

U. S. Rapid Deployment Forces. D. Eshel. 1986. lib. bdg. 79.95 (ISBN 0-8490-3665-8). Gordon Pr.

U. S. Rapid Deployment Forces. David Eshel. (Illus.). 208p. 1984. 19.95 (ISBN 0-668-06211-8, 6211-8). Arco.

U. S. Rapid Deployment Forces. David Eshel. 1987. pap. 14.95 (ISBN 0-668-06278-9). Arco.

U. S. Ratification of the Human Rights Treaties: With or Without Reservations? Ed. by Richard B. Lillich. LC 80-28995. (Human Rights Law Group Ser). 203p. 1981. 15.00x (ISBN 0-8139-0881-7). U Pr of Va.

U. S. Reclamation Service: Its History, Activities & Organization. Brookings Institution, Washington, D. C., Institute for Government Research Staff. LC 72-3015. (Service Monographs of the U. S. Government: No. 2). Repr. of 1919 ed. 24.50 (ISBN 0-404-57102-6). AMS Pr.

U. S. Refinery Policy in the 1980's: Security, Economics & Equity. Ed. by Bettina Silber & Clarice R. Feldman. LC 80-68123. (Orig.). 1980. 7.00 (ISBN 0-934458-02-2). Americans Energy Ind.

U. S. Refugee Policy. 1985. write for info. US Comm Refugees.

U. S. Regional Publications Directory. William T. Harrison. 288p. 1986. pap. 43.95 (ISBN 0-936045-00-0). Bradley Comm.

U. S. Register of American Writers: Professional Communicators in Science, Technology, & Business. Ed. by Robert S. Kellner. 176p. 1986. 24.95x (ISBN 0-938039-01-6). Am Archives Pubs.

United States Regulations for Fruits & Vegetables. Hui. 1988. write for info. (ISBN 0-471-85437-9). Wiley.

U. S. Relation with China, 2 vols. U. S. Department of State Staff. 1988. Repr. of 1949 ed. Set. lib. bdg. 52.00x. Am Biog Serv.

U. S. Relations with China, 2 vols. U. S. Department of State. LC 76-145342. xli, 1054p. 1972. Repr. of 1949 ed. 49.00x (ISBN 0-403-01293-7). Scholarly.

United States Relations with Mexico. Ed. by Richard D. Erb & Stanely R. Ross. 291p. 1981. pap. 12.00 (ISBN 0-8447-1343-0). Am Enterprise.

U. S. Relations with South Africa: An Analytic Survey & Bibliographic Research Guide. Y. G-M. Lulat. 450p. 1988. pap. 35.00 (ISBN 0-8133-7138-4). Westview.

United States Reports: Cases Adjudged in the Supreme Court at Oct. Term, 1983, Jan. 23 Through Mar. 23, 1984, Together with Opinions of Individual Justices in Chambers, V. 465. Ed. by Henry C. Lind. 1206p. 1986. 36.00 (ISBN 0-318-22472-0, S/N 028-001-00435-1). USGPO.

United States Reports of Tax Court, Vol. 86, Jan. 1, 1986 to June 30, 1986. Ed. by Mary T. Pittman. 1407p. 1986. 37.00 (ISBN 0-318-22594-8, S/N 028-005-00156-0). USGPO.

United States Reports, Vol. 461: April 20 Through June 3, 1983. Intro. by Henry C. Lind. (Supreme Court Reports). 1212p. 1985. 36.00 (ISBN 0-318-20160-7, S/N 028-001-00430-0). USGPO.

United States Reports, Vol. 463: June 24 Through September 27, 1983. Ed. by Henry C. Lind. (Supreme Court Reports). 1413p. 1986. 37.00 (ISBN 0-318-21633-7, S/N 028-001-00433-4). USGPO.

United States Reports, Vol. 464: October3, 1983 Through January 18, 1984. Ed. by Henry C. Lind. (Supreme Court Reports). 1430p. 1968. 38.00 (ISBN 0-318-21695-7, S/N 028-001-00434-2). USGPO.

United States Reports, Vol. 466, Cases Adjudged in the Supreme Court at Oct. Term, 1983, Mar. 26 through May 15, 1984, Together. Henry C. Lind. 1986. 35.00 (ISBN 0-318-22583-2, S/N 028-001-00436-9). USGPO.

United States Reports, Vol. 467, Cases Adjudged in the Supreme Court at Oct. Term, 1983, May 21 through June 26, 1984. Ed. by Henry C. Lind. 1349p. text ed. 37.00 (ISBN 0-318-22582-4, S/N 028-001-00437-7). USGPO.

United States Reports, Vol. 468, Cases Adjudged in the Supreme Court at Oct. Term, 1963, June 27, through Sept. 19, 1984, Together with Opinions of Individual Justices in Chambers, End of Term. Ed. by Henry C. Lind. 1106p. 1987. 36.00 (ISBN 0-318-22581-6, S/N 028-001-00438-5). USGPO.

United States, Republic of Korea Combined Operations: A Korean Perspective. Taek-Hyung Rhee. (National Security Affairs Monograph). 61p. (Orig.). 1986. pap. 2.00 (ISBN 0-318-20161-5, S/N 008-020-01074-0). USGPO.

U. S. Research Memoranda see United States Memoranda.

U. S. Research Reactors. AEC Technical Information Center Staff. Ed. by Joel W. Chastain. 78p. 1957. pap. 13.95 (ISBN 0-87079-380-2, TID-7013); microfiche 6.50 (ISBN 0-87079-483-3, TID-7013). DOE.

U. S. Reserve Forces: The Problem of the Weekend Warrior. Martin Binkin. LC 73-23109. (Studies in Defense Policy). 63p. 1974. pap. 7.95 (ISBN 0-8157-0959-5). Brookings.

United States Response to Turkish Nationalism & Reform, 1914-1939. Roger R. Trask. LC 74-153505. pap. 72.50 (ISBN 0-317-29475-X, 2055923). Bks Demand UMI.

U. S. Rifle Caliber .30 Model 1903. 2.00 (ISBN 0-913150-16-9). Pioneer Pr.

U. S. Rifle Model 1866 Springfield. 1.75 (ISBN 0-913150-14-2). Pioneer Pr.

U. S. Rifle Model 1870 Remington. 1.75 (ISBN 0-913150-15-0). Pioneer Pr.

United States Road Atlas. Rev. ed. 80p. 1984. 2.95 (ISBN 0-88098-074-5). H M Gousha.

U. S. Roads Atlas. Date not set. price not set. Am Map.

U. S. Rockets Hypersonic Mach Busters Guide. Jerry Irvine & Charles E. Rogers. 60p. 1985. 25.00 (ISBN 0-912468-26-2). CA Rocketry.

U. S. Rockets Multi-Stage Flight Sheet Guide. Jerry Irvine & Charles E. Rogers. 26p. 1985. 9.95 (ISBN 0-912468-25-4). CA Rocketry.

U. S. Rockets Single Stage Flight Sheet Guide, No. 1. Jerry Irvine & Charles E. Rogers. 26p. 1984. 8.95 (ISBN 0-912468-10-6). CA Rocketry.

U. S. S. A. James N. Frey. 496p. 1987. pap. 3.95 (ISBN 0-8217-2068-6). Zebra.

U. S. S. A. S. N. Lewitt. (Young Adult Ser.: Bk. 4). 176p. 1987. pap. 2.95 (ISBN 0-380-75183-6). Avon.

U. S. S. A. S. C. Sykes. (Young Adult Ser.: Bk. 3). 195p. 1987. pap. 2.95 (ISBN 0-380-75182-8). Avon.

U. S. S. A. Book 1. Tom DeHaven. LC 86-91605. (Young Adult Ser.: Bk. 1). 185p. 1987. pap. 2.95 (ISBN 0-380-75180-1, Flare). Avon.

U. S. S. A. Book 1. S. N. Lewitt. LC 86-91605. (Young Adult Ser.: Bk. 2). 176p. 1987. pap. 2.95 (ISBN 0-380-75181-X, Flare). Avon.

U. S. S. Cassin Young (DD-793) A Fletcher Class Destroyer. J. Scott Harmon. LC 84-63014. (Illus.). 1985. pap. 5.95 (ISBN 0-933126-58-1). Pictorial Hist.

U. S. S. Enterprise (CV-Six), the Most Decorated Ship of World War II: A Pictorial History. Steve Ewing. LC 82-61737. (Illus.). 168p. 1982. 9.95 (ISBN 0-933126-24-7). Pictorial Hist.

U. S. S. New Jersey (BB-62) Refit to Recommissioning. A. Lani Low & James F. Muche. (Illus., Orig.). 1985. pap. 5.95x (ISBN 0-910651-08-6). Fathom Eight.

U. S. S. R. Harry Robinson. 1981. 20.00x (ISBN 0-7231-0696-7, Pub. by Univ Tutorial Pr Ltd). State Mutual Bk.

U. S. S. R. Marion Sichel. (National Costume Reference Ser.). (Illus.). 80p. (YA) (gr. 7-12). 1986. 12.95 (ISBN 1-55546-157-3). Chelsea Hse.

U. S. S. R. Marilyn Tolhurst. (People & Places Ser.). (Illus.). 48p. (gr. 4-8). 1988. PLB 12.96 (ISBN 0-382-09507-3). Silver.

U. S. S. R. A Concise History. 4th ed. Basil Dmytryshyn. (Illus.). 697p. 1984. pap. text ed. write for info. (ISBN 0-02-330430-8, Pub. by Scribner). Macmillan.

U. S. S. R. Academy of Arts. V. Kemenov. 413p. 1983. 65.00 (ISBN 0-8285-2412-2, Pub. by Aurora Pubs USSR). Imported Pubns.

U. S. S. R. after Brezhnev. Seweryn Bialer. LC 83-83061. (Headline Ser.: No. 265). (Illus.). 64p. (Orig.) (gr. 11-12). 1983. pap. 4.00 (ISBN 0-87124-086-6). Foreign Policy.

U. S. S. R. & Africa: Foreign Policy under Khrushchev. Dan C. Heldman. LC 81-4975. 204p. 1981. 35.00 (ISBN 0-275-90642-6, C0642). Praeger.

U. S. S. R. & Countries of Africa. E. A. Tarabrin et al. 1980. 8.95 (ISBN 0-8285-1919-6, Pub. by Progress Pubs USSR). Imported Pubns.

U. S. S. R. & Developing Countries Economic Cooperation. 142p. 1984. 5.00x (Pub. by Collets (U. K.)). State Mutual Bk.

U. S. S. R. & Far East Memoranda, 1 vol. Bd. with U. S. S. R. Memoranda. (Nos. 1-26); Far East Memoranda. (Nos. 1-26). (Nos. 1-5). 1945. 83.00 (ISBN 3-601-00022-9). Kraus Intl.

U. S. S. R. & the Middle East. Ed. by M. Confino & Shimon Shamir. 441p. 1973. casebound 21.95x (ISBN 0-87855-160-3). Transaction Bks.

U. S. S. R. & the Muslim World. Yaacov Ro'i. (Illus.). 352p. 1984. text ed. 44.95x (ISBN 0-04-301171-3). Unwin Hyman.

U. S. S. R. & the U. N.'s Economic & Social Activities. Harold K. Jacobson. LC 63-19327. (Notre Dame University, Committee on International Relations, International Studies). pap. 81.80 (ISBN 0-317-42107-7, 2025947). Bks Demand UMI.

U. S. S. R. & World Peace. facs. ed. Andrei Vyshinsky. Ed. by Jessica Smith. LC 70-76919. (Essay Index Reprint Ser). 1949. 14.00 (ISBN 0-8369-1071-0). Ayer Co Pubs.

U. S. S. R. Aujourd'hui et Demain. (Collection Marxisme-Leninisme). 270p. (Fr.). 1982. pap. 11.25 (ISBN 0-08-027060-3). Pergamon.

U. S. S. R. Eastern Europe & the Development of the Law of the Sea. William E. Butler. 1983. Set. 2 bdrs. looseleaf including bibliography bdr. 200.00; Bibliography. binder sold separately 100.00 (ISBN 0-379-20851-2). Oceana.

U. S. S. R. Economic Handbook. (Economic Handbook Ser.). 250p. 1986. 80.00x (ISBN 0-86338-156-1, Pub. by Euromonitor Pubns). Gale.

U. S. S. R. Economy in 1976-1980. F. Kotov & Y. Ivanov. 144p. 1977. 3.00x (Pub. by Collets (U. K.)). State Mutual Bk.

U. S. S. R. Energy Atlas. United States Central Intelligence Agency. (Illus.). 80p. (Orig.). 1985. pap. 35.00x (ISBN 0-87201-904-7). Gulf Pub.

U. S. S. R. Energy Atlas. (Illus.). 79p. (Orig.). 1985. pap. 13.00 (ISBN 0-318-18858-9, S/N 041-015-00160-4). USGPO.

U. S. S. R. Facts & Figures Annual, 1977-1985, Vols. 1-11. Ed. by John L. Scherer. (UFFA Ser.). 1979. 69.50 ea. Academic Intl.

U. S. S. R. Foreign Policies after Detente. rev. ed. Richard Staar. 1987. 13.95 (ISBN 0-8179-8592-1). Hoover Inst Pr.

U. S. S. R. From an Idea by Karl Marx. Marc Polonsky & Russell Taylor. (Orig.). 1986. pap. 8.95 (ISBN 0-571-13842-X). Faber & Faber.

U. S. S. R.-German Aggression Against Lithuania: 1918-1945. Bronis Kaslas. 17.95 (ISBN 0-8315-0135-9). Speller.

U. S. S. R. in Crisis: The Failure of an Economic System. Marshall I. Goldman. 1983. 15.00 (ISBN 0-393-01715-X); pap. 6.95x (ISBN 0-393-95336-X). Norton.

U. S. S. R. in Figures for 1985. Central Statistical Board of USSR. 253p. 1986. pap. 5.95 (ISBN 0-8285-3285-0, Pub. by Progress Pubs USSR). Imported Pubns.

U. S. S. R. in Maps. Ed. by J. C. Dewdney. LC 52-1242. 128p. 1982. 45.00 (ISBN 0-8419-0760-9). Holmes & Meier.

U. S. S. R. in Third World Conflicts: Soviet Arms & Diplomacy in Local Wars, 1945-1980. Bruce D. Porter. LC 83-26265. (Illus.). 256p. 1984. 37.50 (ISBN 0-521-26308-5). Cambridge U Pr.

U. S. S. R. in Third World Conflicts: Soviet Arms & Diplomacy in Local Wars, 1945-1980. Bruce D. Porter. (Illus.). 256p. 1986. pap. 10.95 (ISBN 0-521-31064-4). Cambridge U Pr.

U. S. S. R. in World Politics. Nikolai Lebedev. 320p. 1982. 19.75x (ISBN 0-317-53826-8, Pub. by Collets (UK)). State Mutual Bk.

U. S. S. R.-India: The Path to the Stars. Vladimir Shatalov. (Illus.). 188p. 1986. text ed. 35.00x (ISBN 0-7069-2733-8, Pub. by Vikas India). Advent NY.

U. S. S. R. It's People, Its Society, Its Culture. Thomas Fitzsimmons et al. LC 74-12074. (Illus.). 590p. 1974. Repr. of 1960 ed. lib. bdg. 48.50x (ISBN 0-8371-7667-0, FIUS). Greenwood.

U. S. S. R.-Land of the Russian Bear. Ed. by Natalie Rifkin. LC 78-730222. (National Wildlife Challenge Kit Ser.). (gr. 3-6). 1978. 35.00 (ISBN 0-912186-26-7). Natl Wildlife.

U. S. S. R: Languages & Realities: Nations, Leaders, & Scholars. Michael Bruchis. (East European Monographs: No. 250). 280p. 1988. 35.00 (ISBN 0-88033-147-X). East Eur Quarterly.

U. S. S. R. Proposes Disarmament: 1920s-1980s. Ed. by Y. Potyarkin & S. Kortunov. 344p. 1986. pap. 4.95 (ISBN 0-8285-3206-0, Pub. by Progress Pubs USSR). Imported Pubns.

U. S. S. R. Sub-Saharan Africa in the 1980s. David E. Albright. (Washington Papers: No. 101). 144p. 1983. pap. 9.95 (ISBN 0-275-91558-1, B1558). Praeger.

U. S. S. R. The Politics of Oligarchy. rev. ed. Darrell P. Hammer. 250p. 1986. 35.00x (ISBN 0-8133-0051-7); pap. text ed. 15.95x (ISBN 0-8133-0052-5). Westview.

U. S. S. R., the U. S. A., & the People's Revolution in China. A. Ledovsky. 251p. 1982. 4.95 (ISBN 0-8285-2457-2, Pub. by Progress Pubs U. S. s. r.). Imported Pubns.

U. S. S. R. Today. 7th ed. Fred Schulze. Tr. by Current Digest of the Soviet Press Staff. 200p. (Orig.). 1988. pap. 20.00x (ISBN 0-913601-77-2). Current Digest.

U. S. S. R. Today & Tomorrow: Problems & Challenges. Uri Ra'anan & Charles M. Perry. LC 86-45960. 160p. 1986. 25.00x (ISBN 0-669-14813-X); pap. text ed. 12.95 (ISBN 0-669-16465-8). Lexington Bks.

U. S. S. R. Today: Facts & Interpretations. 3rd ed. Leo Hecht. LC 87-13041. (Illus.). 1987. pap. 12.95 (ISBN 0-9606754-3-4). Scholasticus.

U. S. S. R. Today: Perspectives from the Soviet Press. 5th ed. Ed. by Fred Schulze & Gordon Livermore. 242p. 1981. pap. 5.00 (ISBN 0-913601-75-6). Current Digest.

U. S. S. R. Today: Perspectives from the Soviet Press. 6th. ed. Ed. by Fred Schulze & Gordon Livermore. 313p. 1985. pap. 15.00 (ISBN 0-913601-76-4). Current Digest.

U. S. S. Texas (BB-35) A Remembrance. James F. Muche. (Illus., Orig.). 1984. pap. 3.50x (ISBN 0-910651-06-X). Fathom Eight.

U. S. Secret Service. Gregory Matvsky & John P. Hayes. (Know Your Government Ser.). (Illus.). 96p. (gr. 5 up). 1988. lib. bdg. 12.95 (ISBN 1-55546-130-1). Chelsea Hse.

U. S. Securities & Exchange Commission: Annual Report, 1935-1967, Vols. 1-33. Bound set. 346.00x (ISBN 0-686-90077-4). Rothman.

United States Security Assistance: The Political Process. Ed. by Ernest Graves & Steven A. Hildreth. LC 84-47688. 208p. 1984. 35.00x (ISBN 0-669-08355-0). Lexington Bks.

U. S. Security in the Twenty First Century. Barry M. Blechman. (Westview Special Studies in National Security & Defense Policy). 128p. 1986. pap. 18.95 (ISBN 0-8133-7315-8). Westview.

U. S. Security Interests in Asia. J. Hsiung. write for info. (ISBN 0-275-90013-4, C0013). Praeger.

United States Senate: A Bicameral Perspective. Richard F. Fenno, Jr. 47p. 1982. pap. 7.00 (ISBN 0-8447-3499-3). Am Enterprise.

U. S. Senate: Paralysis or a Search for Consensus? George E. Reedy. LC 86-8906. 1986. 16.95 (ISBN 0-517-56239-1). Crown.

U. S. Senate: Paralysis or a Search for Consensus? George E. Reedy. 224p. 1988. pap. 4.95 (ISBN 0-451-62608-7, Ment). NAL.

U. S. Senators & Their World. Donald R. Matthews. LC 80-17163. (Illus.). xvi, 303p. 1980. Repr. of 1960 ed. lib. bdg. 35.00x (ISBN 0-313-22664-4, MASE). Greenwood.

United States Sentencing Commission Unpublished Public Hearings, 1986. U. S. Sentencing Commission Staff. LC 88-80878. iii, 601p. Date not set. lib. bdg. 52.00 (ISBN 0-89941-639-X). W S Hein.

United States Service Industries Handbook. Ed. by Wray O. Candilis. LC 87-7292. 254p. 1988. lib. bdg. 45.00 (ISBN 0-275-92367-3, C2367). Praeger.

U. S. Servicewoman - Ground Combat Debate: A Selected Bibliography. Anthony G. White. (Public Administration Ser.: P 2013). 9p. 1986. 3.00 (ISBN 1-55590-013-5). Vance Biblios.

U. S. Servicewomen - Academy Cadets: A Selected Bibliography. Anthony G. White. (Public Administration Ser.: P 2011). 5p. 1986. 3.00 (ISBN 1-55590-011-9). Vance Biblios.

U. S. Servicewomen - Air Combat Debate: A Selected Sourcelist. Anthony G. White. (Public Administration Ser.: P 2014). 6p. 1986. 3.00 (ISBN 1-55590-014-3). Vance Biblios.

U. S. Servicewomen - Sea Duty Debate: A Selected Bibliography. Anthony G. White. (Public Administration Ser.: P 2012). 4p. 1986. 3.00 (ISBN 1-55590-012-7). Vance Biblios.

U. S. Shipbuilding Industry: Past, Present & Future. Clinton H. Whitehurst, Jr. (Illus.). 393p. 1986. 27.95 (ISBN 0-87021-723-2). Naval Inst Pr.

U. S. Shipping Act of 1984: A Scrutiny of Controversial Provisions. N. Sashikumar. LC 87-62805. (Illus.). 104p. (Orig.). 1987. pap. 14.95 (ISBN 0-9619447-0-6). Maine Maritime Pr.

U. S. Shipping Act 1984. John W. McConnell. 328p. 80.00 (ISBN 1-85044-036-0). Lloyds London Pr.

United States Shipping Board: Its History, Activities & Organization. Darrell H. Smith & Paul V. Betters. LC 72-3080. (Brookings Institution. Institute for Government Research. Service Monographs of the Government: No. 63). Repr. of 1931 ed. 42.50 (ISBN 0-404-57163-8). AMS Pr.

United States Shipping Policy. Wytze Gorter. LC 77-6767. 1977. Repr. of 1956 ed. lib. bdg. 35.00x (ISBN 0-8371-9657-4, GOUS). Greenwood.

TITLE INDEX

UNITED STATES VS CHARLES

United States Since Eighteen Sixty-Five. John A. Krout & Arnold S. Rice. LC 76-18396. (Illus.). 310p. (Orig.). 1977. pap. 7.95 (ISBN 0-06-460168-4, COS CO 168, B&N Bks). Har-Row.

United States Since Nineteen Forty-Five: The Ordeal of Power. Dewey W. Grantham. (Modern America Ser.). 1975. text ed. 21.95 (ISBN 0-07-024116-3). McGraw.

United States Ski Team. Ed. by John Dankin & Kristi Scott. LC 83-82974. (Illus.). 160p. 1983. 24.95 (ISBN 0-913927-01-5). Intl Sport Pubns.

U. S. Sky Spies since World War I. Michael O'Leary. (Illus.). 128p. (Orig.). 1986. 24.95 (ISBN 0-7137-1555-3, Pub. by Blandford Pr England); pap. 12.95 (ISBN 0-7137-1692-4, Pub. by Blandford Pr England). Sterling.

U. S. Small Combatants: An Illustrated Design History Including PT-Boats, Subchasers, & the Brown-Water Navy. Norman Friedman. (Illus.). 500p. 1987. 46.95 (ISBN 0-87021-713-5). Naval Inst Pr.

U. S. Soft Drink Market: Past Performance, Current Trends & Opportunities for Growth. 260p. 1986. 750.00 (ISBN 0-317-55175-2). Busn Trend.

U. S. Soviet Conventional Arms Transfer Negotiations. Barry M. Blechman & Janne E. Nolan. 48p. (Orig.). 1987. pap. text ed. 6.00 (ISBN 0-941700-06-2). JH FPI SAIS.

U. S. Soviet Military Balance Nineteen Eighty to Nineteen Eighty-Five. John M. Collins. (Illus.). 400p. 1985. 50.00 (ISBN 0-08-033131-9, Pub. by P-B); pap. 29.95 (ISBN 0-08-033130-0). Pergamon.

United States-Soviet Relations: Building a Consensus Policy. Dick Clark. 62p. (Orig.). 1985. pap. text ed. 7.00 (ISBN 0-8191-5852-6, Pub. by Aspen Inst for Humanistic Studies). U Pr of Amer.

U. S. Soviet Relations in the Era of Detente: A Tragedy of Errors. Richard Pipes. LC 80-27121. 228p. (Orig.). 1981. pap. text ed. 15.95x (ISBN 0-86531-155-2). Westview.

United States, Soviet Russia, Europe, the Middle East, Israel & the Rigid Pressure of the Kondratieff Cycle. Clancey G. Taranfeld. (Illus.). 139p. 1983. 97.75x (ISBN 0-86722-035-X). Inst Econ Pol.

United States-Soviet Summitry: Roosevelt Through Carter. Ed. by John W. McDonald, Jr. & Diane B. Bendahmane. LC 87-619871. (Study of Foreign Affairs Ser.). 170p. (Orig.). 1987. pap. 9.00 (ISBN 0-318-23851-9, S/N 044-000-02206-1). USGPO.

United States Space Law: National & International Regulation, 3 bdrs. looseleaf. Ed. by Stephen Gorove. LC 81-22465. 1982. o.p. 100.00 ea. (ISBN 0-379-20695-1). Oceana.

U. S. Space Program after Challenger. Alan Stern. (Impact Ser.). (Illus.). 128p. 1987. lib. bdg. 11.90 (ISBN 0-531-10412-5). Watts.

United States Spanish-American War Fortifications at the Sabine Pass, Texas. Mildred S. Wright & William D. Quick. LC 82-99801. (Illus.). x, 50p. (Orig.). 1982. pap. 15.00x (ISBN 0-917016-23-8). M S Wright.

United States-Spanish Relations: Wolfram & World War II. John W. Cortrada. 134p. 1971. 10.00 (ISBN 0-939738-11-2). Zubal Inc.

U. S. Special Forces Nineteen Forty-Five to Present. Leroy Thompson. (Uniforms Illustrated Ser.: No. 3). (Illus.). 72p. 1984. pap. 9.95 (ISBN 0-85368-625-4, Pub. by Arms & Armour Pr). Sterling.

U. S. Special Forces Nineteen Forty-One to Nineteen Eighty-Seven. Leroy Thompson. (Illus.). 128p. (Orig.). 1987. pap. 12.95 (ISBN 0-7137-1543-X, Pub. by Blandford Pr England). Sterling.

U. S. Special Forces of World War II, No. 1. Leroy Thompson. (Uniforms Illustrated Ser.: No. 1). (Illus.). 68p. 1984. pap. 7.95 (ISBN 0-85368-624-6, Pub. by Arms & Armour Pr). Sterling.

U. S. Special Forces Recon Manual. 1986. lib. bdg. 79.95 (ISBN 0-8490-3578-3). Gordon Pr.

U. S. Special Forces Recon Manual. 120p. Date not set. pap. 11.95. Lancer.

U. S. Spyplanes. Michael O'Leary. (Warbirds Illustrated Ser.: No. 24). (Illus.). 72p. 1984. pap. 9.95 (ISBN 0-85368-626-2, Pub. by Arms & Armour Pr). Sterling.

United States-State Agricultural Data, 1986. Letricia M. Womack & Larry G. Traub. (Agriculture Information Bulletin Ser.: No. 512). 105p. 1987. pap. 4.75 (ISBN 0-318-22962-5, S/N 001-019-00513-1). USGPO.

U. S. Statistical Rankings, 1983. Joe B. Williams & Joann Williams. 138p. 1983. 12.50 (ISBN 0-939644-13-4). Media Prods & Mktg.

U. S. Statistical Rankings, 1987. 4th ed. 150p. 1987. 29.00 (ISBN 0-939644-34-7). Media Prods & Mktg.

United States Steel Corporation: A Study of the Growth & Influence of Combination in the Iron & Steel Industry. Abraham Berglund. LC 72-76677. (Columbia University Studies in the Social Sciences Ser.: No. 73). 1968. Repr. of 1907 ed. 16.50 (ISBN 0-404-51073-6). AMS Pr.

U. S. Steel Industry in Recurrent Crisis: Policy Options in a Competitive World. Robert W. Crandall. LC 81-4642. 184p. 1981. 26.95 (ISBN 0-8157-1602-8); pap. 9.95 (ISBN 0-8157-1601-X). Brookings.

United States Store Cards. Edgar Adams. LC 80-70824. 1981. Repr. of 1920 ed. softcover 12.00 (ISBN 0-915262-60-6). S J Durst.

U. S. Strategic Airlift Choices. William S. Cohen et al. LC 86-21425. (National Security Paper: No. 8). 1986. 5.00 (ISBN 0-89549-079-X). Inst Foreign Policy Anal.

U. S. Strategic Airlift: Requirements & Capabilities. Jeffrey Record. LC 85-23927. (National Security Papers: No. 2). 43p. 1986. 6.00 (ISBN 0-89549-068-4). Inst Foreign Policy Anal.

U. S. Strategic Interests in Southwest Asia. Shirin Tahir-Keli. Ed. by Mack Lipkin. LC 82-5305. 236p. 1982. 35.00 (ISBN 0-275-90915-8, C0915). Praeger.

U. S. Strategic Interests in the Gulf Region. William J. Olson. (Studies in Regional Security). 1985. pap. 29.50x (ISBN 0-8133-7119-8). Westview.

U. S. Strategic Security in the Nineteen Eighties. Herman Kahn. (Hudson Perspective Ser.: No. 3). 52p. 1980. 40.00 (ISBN 0-318-14360-7, HI3212P). Hudson Inst.

U. S. Strategy at the Crossroads: Two Views. Jeffrey Record & Robert J. Hanks. LC 82-82774. (Foreign Policy Reports Ser.). 69p. 1982. 7.50 (ISBN 0-89549-044-7). Inst Foreign Policy Anal.

U. S. Strategy in the Gulf. Leila Meo. (Monograph: No. 14). 130p. (Orig.). 1981. pap. 6.00 (ISBN 0-937694-50-9). Assn Arab-Amer U Grads.

United States Studies Program. R. Dryer & J. Downey. Ed. by Stan Harper & Elizabeth Yockstick. (Work-A-Text Ser.). (Illus.). 1982. of 105 435.00 set (ISBN 0-943068-99-1). Graphic Learning.

United States Studies Program: Activity Manual. 2nd ed. J. Fisher & R. Dryer. Ed. by Elizabeth Yockstick. (Illus.). 126p. (gr. 5). 1981. Duplication Masters 49.00 (ISBN 0-943068-16-9); Teacher's Guide 5.00 (ISBN 0-943068-69-X). Graphic Learning.

United States Submarine Operations in World War II. Theodore Roscoe. LC 50-5198. (Illus.). 577p. 1949. 34.95x (ISBN 0-87021-731-3). Naval Inst Pr.

United States Submarine Operations in World War Two. Theodore Roscoe. Incl. United States Destroyer Operations in World War Two. Set. 62.95x (ISBN 0-87021-732-1). Naval Inst Pr.

U. S. Submarines: A Bibliography. A. Lani Low & James F. Muche. (Orig.). 1986. pap. text ed. 25.00x (ISBN 0-910651-11-6). Fathom Eight.

U. S. Subs in Action. (Warships in Action Ser.). (Illus.). 50p. 1984. pap. 5.95 (ISBN 0-89747-085-0, 4002). Squad Sig Pubns.

United States Supermarkets: Characteristics & Services. Charlene C. Price & Doris J. Newton. (Agriculture Information Bulletin Ser.: No. 502). 30p. 1986. pap. 1.75 (ISBN 0-318-21906-9, S/N 001-019-00489-4). USGPO.

U. S. Supreme Court & the Uses of Social Science Data. Ed. by Abraham L. Davis. LC 73-8983. 150p. 1975. pap. text ed. 7.95x (ISBN 0-8422-0338-9). Irvington.

U. S. Supreme Court Appointments: 1961-1986: A Brief Bibliography. Alva W. Stewart. (Public Administration Ser.: P 2129). 11p. 1987. 3.75 (ISBN 1-55590-249-9). Vance Biblios.

United States Supreme Court Cases & Comments: Criminal Law & Procedure. William H. Erickson et al. 1985. looseleaf 85.00 (765); updates 45.00. Bender.

United States Supreme Court Decisions: An Index to Excerpts, Reprints & Discussions. 2nd ed. Nancy A. Guenther. LC 82-10518. (Illus.). 864p. 1983. 55.00 (ISBN 0-8108-1578-8). Scarecrow.

U. S. Supreme Court Digest: Annotated, 20 vols. in 31 bks. write for info. Lawyers Co-Op.

United States Supreme Court Justices Biographical Data, 1789-1958. John R. Schmidhauser. 1972. codebk. write for info. (ISBN 0-89138-052-3). ICPSR.

U. S. Supreme Court Reports: Lawyers Edition, 65 vols. LC 17-25985. (Second Ser.). write for info. Lawyers Co-Op.

U. S. Supreme Court Restricts Imposition of Death Penalty on Non-Triggerman Accomplices in Felony Murder Cases. Benjamin B. Sendor. LC 83-620653. (Administration of Justice Memoranda: No. 82-06). 1982. pap. 2.00 (ISBN 0-318-00252-3). U of NC Inst Gov.

United States Synchronized Swimming 1987 Directory. U. S. Synchronized Swimming, Inc. Staff. 50p. (Orig.). 1987. pap. 5.00 (ISBN 0-911543-06-6). US Synch Swim.

United States Synchronized Swimming 1987-1988 Official Rules. U. S. Synchronized Swimming Inc. Staff. 139p. (Orig.). 1987. pap. 10.00 (ISBN 0-911543-02-3). Us Synch Swim.

U. S. Tactical Air Power: Missions, Forces, & Costs. William D. White. LC 74-20695. (Studies in Defense Policy). 121p. 1974. pap. 7.95 (ISBN 0-8157-9371-5). Brookings.

U. S. Tank Destroyers of World War II. Steven J. Zaloga. (Tanks Illustrated Ser.: No. 19). (Illus.). 64p. (Orig.). 1986. pap. 9.95 (ISBN 0-85368-770-6, Pub. by Arms & Armour). Sterling.

U. S. Tanks of World War II in Action. George Forty. (In Action Ser.). (Illus.). 160p. 1986. pap. 14.95 (ISBN 0-7137-1818-8, Pub. by Blandford Pr England). Sterling.

U. S. Tax Cases. write for info. (17). Commerce.

U. S. Tax Conventions, 16 vols. Sidney I. Roberts. (Roberts & Holland Collection). 1986. looseleaf 1395.00 (ISBN 0-89941-379-X). W S Hein.

U. S. Tax Conventions, 4 vols. U. S. Congress. Joint Committee on Internal Revenue Taxation. LC 62-60650. 1979. Repr. of 1962 ed. Set. lib. bdg. 140.00 (ISBN 0-930342-99-2). W S Hein.

United States Tax Court, An Historical Analysis. Dubroff. 504p. 1985. 17.50 (ISBN 0-317-44576-6, 5223). Commerce.

United States Taxation & Developing Countries. Ed. by Robert Hellawell. LC 79-25138. (Columbia U Center for Law & Economic Studies). 1980. 58.00x (ISBN 0-231-04820-3). Columbia U Pr.

United States Taxation of Foreign Investment Income: Issues & Arguments. Peggy B. Musgrave. LC 68-58098. (Illus.). 186p. (Orig.). 1969. pap. 6.00x (ISBN 0-915506-10-6). Harvard Law Intl Tax.

U. S. Taxation of International Operations. (Information Services Ser.). Date not set. price not set ring bound l'leaf. P-H.

U. S. Taxes & Tax Policy. David G. Davies. LC 85-31414. 1986. 37.50 (ISBN 0-521-30169-6); pap. 11.95 (ISBN 0-521-31769-X). Cambridge U Pr.

U. S. Technology & Export Controls. 1978. 10.00 (ISBN 0-686-27829-1). M & A Products.

U. S. Telecommunications Law & Policy. Ed. by Robert Bruce et al. 1986. 40.00. Butterworth Legal Pubs.

U. S. Television Network News: A Guide to Sources in English. Myron J. Smith, Jr. LC 82-42885. 255p. 1984. lib. bdg. 39.95x (ISBN 0-89950-080-3). McFarland & Co.

U. S. Ten Cent Stamps of 1855-59. Mortimer L. Neinken. (Illus.). 252p. 1960. 30.00x (ISBN 0-912574-07-0). Collectors.

United States Territories. (Let's Visit Places & Peoples - - Nations, Dependencies, & Sovereignties of the World Ser.). (Illus.). (gr. 5 up). 1989. 12.95 (ISBN 0-7910-0136-9). Chelsea Hse.

U. S. Territories & Possessions (Guam, Puerto Rico, U. S. Virgin Islands, American Samoa, North Mariana Islands) Thomas G. Aylesworth & Virginia L. Aylesworth. (Let's Discover the States Ser.). (Illus.). 66p. 1988. lib. bdg. 14.95x (ISBN 1-55546-567-6). Chelsea Hse.

U. S. Territories Freely Associated States. Terry Dunnahoo. Ed. by Jennie Rakos. (Venture Ser.). (Illus.). 96p. 1988. 10.90 (ISBN 0-531-10605-5). Watts.

U. S. Textile Mills Products Industry: Challenges & Strategies for the Future for the 1980's & Beyond. University of South Carolina, Center for Industry Policy & Strategy Staff & David A. Ricks. LC 83-10432. 322p. 1984. 75.00x (ISBN 0-87249-430-6). U of SC Pr.

United States-Thailand Relations. Ed. by Karl D. Jackson & Wiwat Mungkandi. LC 86-82801. (Research Papers & Policy Studies: No. 20). xii, 332p. (Orig.). 1986. pap. 20.00x (ISBN 0-912966-95-5). IEAS.

United States, the United Nations, & Human Rights: The Eleanor Roosevelt & Jimmy Carter Eras. A. Glenn Mower, Jr. LC 78-22134. (Studies in Human Rights Ser.: No. 4). xii, 215p. 1979. lib. bdg. 35.00 (ISBN 0-313-21090-X, MUH/). Greenwood.

United States Three-Cent & Five-Cent Pieces: An Action Guide for the Collector & Investor. Q. David Bowers. (Illus.). 168p. 1988. pap. text ed. 9.95 (ISBN 0-943161-06-1, BBM-303). Bowers & Merena.

U. S. Timber Resources in a World Economy. John A. Zivnuska. LC 67-21585. (Resources for the Future Ser.). Repr. of 1967 ed. 34.30 (ISBN 0-8357-9290-0, 2016069). Bks Demand UMI.

United States to Eighteen Seventy-Seven. 7th rev. ed. John A. Krout. (Orig.). 1971. pap. 6.95 (ISBN 0-06-460029-7, CO 29, B&N Bks). Har-Row.

U. S. Today: An Overview of Reproducible Pages. Ed. by World Eagle Staff. (World Eagle's Today Ser.). (Illus.). lib. bdg. cancelled (ISBN 0-930141-02-4); pap. text ed. cancelled (ISBN 0-930141-00-8); cancelled looseleaf (ISBN 0-930141-01-6). World Eagle.

United States Trade Deficit of the 1980's: Origins, Meanings, & Policy Responses. Chris C. Carvounis. LC 87-2561. 197p. 1987. lib. bdg. 35.00 (ISBN 0-89930-219-X, CTD/, Quorum Bks). Greenwood.

U. S. Trade Dollar. J. Willem. (Illus.). 1983. Repr. of 1961 ed. lib. bdg. 20.00 supplement included (ISBN 0-915262-98-3). S J Durst.

United States Trade Performance in 1985 & Outlook. 3rd annual ed. Frwd. by Bruce Smart. (Illus.). 166p. 1986. pap. 8.50 (ISBN 0-318-21563-2, S/N 003-009-00481-1). USGPO.

U. S. Trade Policies in a Changing World Economy. Ed. by Robert Stern. (Illus.). 408p. 1987. text ed. 25.00x (ISBN 0-262-19253-5). MIT Pr.

U. S. Trade Policy & Developing Counties. Ed. by Ernest H. Preeg. (U. S. Third World Policy Perspectives Ser.). 192p. 1985. pap. 12.95 (ISBN 0-87855-987-6); cloth 19.95 (ISBN 0-88738-043-3). Transaction Bks.

United States Trade Policy Legislation: A Canadian View. Rodney Grey. 130p. (Orig.). 1982. pap. text ed. 7.95x (ISBN 0-920380-86-7, Pub. by Inst Res Pub Canada). Brookfield Pub Co.

U. S. Trade Policy Toward Mexico: Are There Reasons to Expect Special Treatment? Olga P. De Brody. (Research Report Ser.: No. 9). 24p. (Orig.). 1981. pap. 5.00 (ISBN 0-935391-08-8). Ctr Mex Studies.

U. S. Trade Problems in Steel: Japan, West Germany & Italy. Albert W. Harris. (Illus.). 288p. 1983. 36.95 (ISBN 0-275-90998-0, C0998). Praeger.

U. S. Trademark Law: Rules of Practice, Forms & Federal Statutes. LC 84-50807. 1984. looseleaf 49.95 (ISBN 0-939190-02-8). US Trademark.

United States, Transnational Business, & the Law. Columbia Law School Alumni Association Staff & Columbia Law School Association of the United Kingdom Staff. Ed. by Beverly A. Allen & Christian S. Ward. LC 85-61594. 132p. 1985. lib. bdg. 25.00 (ISBN 0-379-20783-4). Oceana.

United States Treasure Atlas, Vols. 1-10. rev. ed. Thomas P. Terry. Incl. (Ala; Ark; Ariz; Alaska Ser.: Vol. 1). 103p. (Orig.). pap. 9.95x (ISBN 0-939850-16-8); rev. ed. (Cal; Colo Ser.: Vol. 2). 111p. (Orig.). pap. 9.95x (ISBN 0-939850-17-6); rev. ed. (Conn; Dela; Fla; Ga; Hawaii; Ida; Ill Ser.: Vol. 3). 119p. (Orig.). pap. 9.95x (ISBN 0-939850-18-4); rev. ed. (Ind; Iowa; Kansas; Ky; La Ser.: Vol. 4). 119p. (Orig.). pap. 9.95x (ISBN 0-939850-19-2); rev. ed. (Maine; Md; Mass; Mich; Minn; Ms Ser.: Vol. 5). 103p. (Orig.). pap. 9.95x (ISBN 0-939850-20-6); rev. ed. (Mo; Mont; Neb; Nev; NHamp; NJ Ser.: Vol. 6). 111p. (Orig.). pap. 9.95x (ISBN 0-939850-21-4); rev. ed. (NM; NY; NC; ND; Ohio Ser.: Vol. 7). 119p. (Orig.). pap. 9.95x (ISBN 0-939850-22-2); rev. ed. (Okla; Ore; Penn; RI; SC; SD Ser.: Vol. 8). 111p. (Orig.). pap. 9.95x (ISBN 0-939850-23-0); rev. ed. (Tenn; Tex; Utah Ser.: Vol. 9). 119p. (Orig.). pap. 9.95x (ISBN 0-939850-24-9); rev. ed. (Vt; Va; Wash; WV; Wis; Wyo Ser.: Vol. 10). 103p. (Orig.). pap. 9.95x (ISBN 0-939850-25-7). 1127p. (Orig.). 1985. Set. pap. 99.50x (ISBN 0-939850-26-5). Spec Pub.

United States Treasury System: Debt Bondage or a Debtless Economy. Silas W. Adams. 1979. lib. bdg. 59.95 (ISBN 0-8490-3012-9). Gordon Pr.

U. S. Treaty with the Sioux-Brule, Oglala, Miniconjou, Yanktoni, Hunkpapa, Blackfeet, Cuthead, Two Kettle, Sans Arcs, & Santee & Arapaho, 1868. Lynn Kickingbird. (Treaty Manuscripts Ser.: No. 28). 30p. 10.00 (ISBN 0-944253-50-4). Inst Dev Indian Law.

U. S. Treaty with the Walla Walla, Cayuse, Wascoes, etc., 1855. 5.00 (ISBN 0-944253-27-X). Inst Dev Indian Law.

U. S. Troops in Europe. Phil Williams. (Chatham House Papers). 128p. 1985. pap. 10.95x (ISBN 0-7102-0422-1). Routledge Chapman & Hall.

U. S. Truck Driver Anthropometric & Truck Work Space: Survey & Recommended Practices. 1987. 60.00 (ISBN 0-89883-983-1, SP712). Soc Auto Engineers.

U. S. U. S.-U. S. S. R. James Gardner. 1987. 24.95 (ISBN 0-941831-05-1); pap. 14.95 (ISBN 0-941831-02-7). Beyond Words Pub.

U. S. University Activity Abroad: Implications of the Mexican Case. Charles N. Myers. 1968. pap. 1.50 (ISBN 0-89192-245-8, Pub. by ICED). Interbk Inc.

U. S. Utilization of ISO Aerospace Standards. 1984. 7.00 (ISBN 0-89883-826-6, SP605). Soc Auto Engineers.

United States v. Crime in the Streets. Thomas E. Cronin et al. LC 80-8842. pap. 55.50 (2056221). Bks Demand UMI.

U. S. Veterans on U. S. Vessels Union Veterans. Ronald V. Jackson. (Illus.). lib. bdg. 15.00 (ISBN 0-317-17040-6). Accelerated Index.

U. S. Videodisc Market: Forecasts & Analysis to 1990. Rockley Miller. (Monitor Report Ser.). (Illus.). 300p. (Orig.). 1985. 795.00 (ISBN 0-938907-01-8). Future Syst.

U. S. Virgin Islands Alive. 2nd ed. Arnold Greenberg & Harriet Greenberg. (Alive Travel Ser.). (Illus.). 250p. pap. 9.95 (ISBN 0-935572-14-7). Alive Pubns.

U. S. Virgin Islands Alive. Harriet Greenberg. 1983. pap. 5.95 (ISBN 0-935572-11-2). Alive Pubns.

United States Virgin Islands: History to 1916. LC 86-60194. (Illus.). 192p. 1986. 10.95. Mainespring.

U. S. Virgin Islands: Jewels of the Caribbean--St. Croix, St. Thomas, St. John. Katharine R. Bailey & Gloria Bourne. LC 86-82891. (Illus.). 48p. (Orig.). (YA) (gr. 7-12). 1987. pap. 4.95 (ISBN 0-88714-012-2). KC Pubns.

U. S. Virgin Islands, Part 1: History to 1916. L. K. Zabriskie & George F. Bush. Ed. by Helen Nash. (Illus.). 192p. (Orig.). 1985. pap. 8.95. Mainespring.

U. S. Voluntary Aid to the Third World: What is Its Future? John G. Sommer. LC 75-43481. (Development Papers: No. 20). 68p. 1975. pap. 1.50 (ISBN 0-686-28677-4). Overseas Dev Council.

U. S. Voluntary Resettlement Agencies' Programs for Refugee Women. 1985. write for info. US Comm Refugees.

United States vs Charles J. Guiteau; Supreme Court Holding a Criminal Term No.14056. District of Columbia Supreme Court Staff et al. 141.00. Ayer Co Pubs.

U. S. vs. Downing: Opinion of U. S. Court of Appeals, Third Circuit, Reversing Due to Exclusion of Expert Opinion on Eyewitness Identification, 753 Fed. 2nd, 1224. (Monograph Ser.: No. CR-51). 1985. 4.00 (ISBN 1-55524-052-6). Ctr Respon Psych.

United States vs. Nixon: The President Before the Supreme Court. Ed. by Leon Friedman. LC 74-16403. 644p. 1980. pap. 11.95 (ISBN 0-87754-144-2). Chelsea Hse.

U. S. vs. Schubert. (Monograph Ser.: No. CR-49). 1985. 8.00 (ISBN 1-55524-050-X). Ctr Respon Psych.

U. S. vs. Steven F. Soliah. S. Otis. (Monograph Ser.: No. CR-6). 1975. 4.00 (ISBN 1-55524-006-2). Ctr Respon Psych.

United States vs. United Shoe Machinery Corporation: An Economic Analysis of an Anti-Trust Case. Carl Kaysen. LC 56-7215. (Economic Studies: No. 99). 1956. 27.50x (ISBN 0-674-92895-4). Harvard U Pr.

United States vs. William Laite. W. E. Laite. LC 75-184718. 1972. 9.95 (ISBN 0-87491-324-1). Acropolis.

U. S. War Aims. Walter Lippman. LC 76-16079. 235p. 1976. Repr. of 1944 ed. lib. bdg. 29.50 (ISBN 0-306-70773-X). Da Capo.

U. S. War Machine: An Illustrated Encyclopedia of American Military Equipment & Strategy. rev. ed. James E. Dornan, Jr. 1983. pap. 10.95 (ISBN 0-517-54984-0). Crown.

U. S. War Machine & Politics. R. Bogdanov. 284p. 1985. pap. 3.95 (ISBN 0-8285-3399-7, Pub. by Progress Pubs USSR). Imported Pubns.

U. S. War Relocation Authority, 11 vols. U. S. War Relocation Authority. Incl. Administrative Highlights of the WRA Program. LC 73-5422. 1946. Vol. 1. 16.00 (ISBN 0-404-58001-7); Community Government in War Relocation Centers. LC 73-5423. 1946. Vol. 2. 16.00 (ISBN 0-404-58002-5); Evacuated People, a Quantitative Description. LC 73-5424. Vol. 3. 65.00 (ISBN 0-404-58003-3); Legal & Constitutional Phases of the WRA Program. LC 73-5425. 1946. Vol. 4. 16.00 (ISBN 0-404-58004-1); People in Motion: The Postwar Adjustment of the Evacuated Japanese Americans. LC 73-5426. 1947. Vol. 5. 39.00 (ISBN 0-404-58005-X); Relocation Program: A Guidebook for the Residents of Relocation Centers. LC 73-5427. 1943. Vol. 6. 16.00 (ISBN 0-404-58006-8); Relocation Program. LC 73-5428. 1946. Vol. 7. 16.00 (ISBN 0-404-58007-6); Token Shipment: The Story of America's War Refugee Shelter. LC 73-5430. 1946. Vol. 8. 16.00 (ISBN 0-404-58008-4); WRA, a Story of Human Conservation. LC 73-5431. Vol. 9. 40.00 (ISBN 0-404-58009-2); Wartime Exile, the Exclusion of the Japanese Americans from the West Coast. LC 73-5432. 1946. Vol. 10. 24.00 (ISBN 0-404-58010-6); Wartime Handling of Evacuee Property. LC 73-5433. 1946. Vol. 11. 16.00 (ISBN 0-404-58011-4). 1946. Set. 280.00 (ISBN 0-404-58000-9). AMS Pr.

U. S. Warships since Nineteen Forty-Five. Paul H. Silverstone. 240p. 1987. 18.95 (ISBN 0-87021-769-0). Naval Inst Pr.

U. S. Wartime Aid to Britain, 1940-1946. Alan P. Dobson. LC 85-27920. 240p. 1986. 27.50x (ISBN 0-312-83319-9). St Martin.

United States Water Well Industry. 180p. 100.00 (ISBN 0-318-17407-3). Natl Water Well.

United States Water Well Marketplace. 1986. 125.00 (ISBN 0-318-22990-0). Natl Water Well.

U. S. West Audit Report. 1986. 10.00 (ISBN 0-318-21756-2). NARUC.

United States, Western Europe & Military Intervention Overseas. Ed. by Christopher Coker. LC 87-26111. 200p. 1988. 39.95 (ISBN 0-312-01620-4). St Martin.

United States, Western Europe, & the Third World: Allies & Adversaries. Simon Serfaty. LC 80-50588. (Significant Issues Ser.: Vol. II, No. 4). 64p. 1980. 5.95 (ISBN 0-89206-018-2). CSI Studies.

United States, Western Europe, & the Third World: Allies & Adversaries. Simon Serfaty. (Significant Issues Ser.: Vol. II, No. 4). 60p. (Orig.). 1980. pap. text ed. 6.95 (ISBN 0-8191-5911-5, Pub. by CSIS). U Pr of Amer.

United States Wheel of Destiny. Diana Stone. LC 76-23512. 132p. 1976. 4.50 (ISBN 0-86690-162-0, 1469-01). Am Fed Astrologers.

United States Will Planning Guide. Jens C. Appel & F. Bruce Gentry. 40p. (Orig.). 1987. wkbk 9.25 (ISBN 0-936499-01-X). Spectrum Bus Syst.

U. S. Wine Market. 305p. 1987. 795.00 (ISBN 0-686-38415-6, 131). Busn Trend.

United States with an Excursion into Mexico see Baedeker's United States.

United States Women in Aviation, 1930-1939. Claudia M. Oakes. LC 85-600019. (Smithsonian Studies in Air & Science: No. 6). pap. 20.00 (ISBN 0-317-41864-5, 2026175). Bks Demand UMI.

U. S. Wood-Based Industry: Industrial Organization & Performance. Paul V. Ellefson & Robert N. Stone. LC 84-8278. 508p. 1984. 48.95 (ISBN 0-275-91150-0, C1150). Praeger.

U. S. World Development. Incl. Agenda 1976. Roger D. Hansen & Overseas Development Council Staff. LC 76-4936. 240p. 1976. 4.95 (ISBN 0-275-85670-4); Agenda 1975. James W. Howe & Overseas Development Council Staff. LC 75-11641. 288p. 1975. 4.95 (ISBN 0-275-89310-3); Agenda 1979. Martin M. McLaughlin & Overseas Development Council Staff. LC 78-71589. 280p. 1979. 5.95 (ISBN 0-318-12104-2); Agenda 1977. John Sewell & Overseas Development Council Staff. LC 76-30725. 273p. 1977. 4.95 (ISBN 0-275-65000-6); Agenda 1980. John W. Sewell & Overseas Development Council Staff. LC 80-82415. 242p. 1980. 28.95. (Agenda Ser.). Overseas Dev Council.

U. S. Z. Kush. (Voices in the Wind Ser.: No. 1). (Illus.). 108p. 1983. pap. 5.00 (ISBN 0-938392-03-4). Homeward Pr.

United States 1789-1890. W. R. Brock. (Sources of History Ser.). 352p. 1975. 29.95x (ISBN 0-8014-0723-0). Cornell U Pr.

United States: 1830-1850. Frederick J. Turner. (Illus.). 13.25 (ISBN 0-8446-1454-8). Peter Smith.

United States 1984. Steve Birnbaum. 1982. 11.95 (ISBN 0-395-34631-2). HM.

United States, 1985. Steve Birnbaum. (Stephen Birnbaum Travel Guides Ser.). pap. 11.95. HM.

United States, 1989. Stephen Birnbaum. (Birnbaum's Travel Guides Ser.). 1008p. 1988. pap. 12.95. HM.

U. S. 40: A Roadscape of the American Experience. Thomas J. Schlereth. (Indiana Historical Society Ser.). (Illus.). 150p. 1985. 27.50X (ISBN 0-253-36201-6); pap. 13.95x (ISBN 0-253-28861-4). Ind U Pr.

United Synod: The Southern New School Presbyterian Church. Harold M. Parker, Jr. LC 87-37564. (Contributions to the Study of Religion: No. 20). 368p. 1988. lib. bdg. 42.95 (ISBN 0-313-26289-6, PSY/). Greenwood.

United to Christ. Tony Floyd. (Illus.). 80p. (Orig.). 1983. pap. 6.95 (ISBN 0-85819-420-1, Pub. by JBCE). ANZ Religious Pubns.

United Way: The Next Hundred Years. William Aramony. LC 86-46401. 127p. 1987. 13.95 (ISBN 1-55611-039-1). D I Fine.

United We Fall. Ed. by Pat Works & Jan Works. LC 77-84030. 17.95 (ISBN 0-930438-03-5); pap. 11.95 (ISBN 0-930438-02-7). RWU Parachuting.

United We Stand. Arthur L. Clanton. (Illus.). 207p. 1970. pap. 5.95 (ISBN 0-912315-42-3). Word Aflame.

United We Stood. Carl Lundquist. 128p. 1985. 12.50 (ISBN 0-89962-442-1). Todd & Honeywell.

Unites d'Habitation: Meaux, Briey, Berlin-Charlotteburg. Brooks. (Corbusier Ser.). 1984. lib. bdg. 200.00 (ISBN 0-8240-5078-9). Garland Pub.

Unites States Congress, Western Hemisphere Immigration. Ed. by Carlos E. Cortez. LC 80-7795. (Hispanics in the United States Ser.). 1981. Repr. of 1976 ed. lib. bdg. 37.00x (ISBN 0-405-13188-7). Ayer Co Pubs.

Unities & Diversities in Chinese Religion. Robert P. Weller. LC 86-9085. 250p. 1986. 22.50x (ISBN 0-295-96397-2). U of Wash Pr.

Unities: Studies in the English Novel. H. M. Daleski. LC 84-8842. 304p. 1985. 35.00x (ISBN 0-8203-0743-2). U of Ga Pr.

Uniting a Nation: The Postal & Telecommunications Services of Papua New Guinea. James Sinclair. (Illus.). 287p. 1984. 39.95x (ISBN 0-19-554437-4). Oxford U Pr.

Uniting of Europe: Political, Social & Economic Forces, 1950-1957. rev. ed. Ernst B. Haas. 1968. 45.00x (ISBN 0-8047-0515-1). Stanford U Pr.

Unitive Thinking. Tom McArthur. 192p. (Orig.). 1988. pap. 9.99 (ISBN 0-85030-621-3, Pub. by Aquarian Pr England). Sterling.

Unitization of Oil & Gas Fields in Texas: A Study of Legislative, Administrative, & Judicial Policies. Jacqueline L. Weaver. 555p. 1986. lib. bdg. 37.50 (ISBN 0-915707-20-9). Resources Future.

Unitized Experiments in Organic Chemistry. 4th ed. Ray Q. Brewster et al. 577p. 1977. pap. text ed. write for info. (ISBN 0-534-21051-1). Wadsworth Pub.

Unitl the Mashiach: The Life of Rabbi Nachman. Aryeh Kaplan. Ed. by Dovid Shapiro. 379p. 1986. text ed. 15.00 (ISBN 0-930213-08-4). Breslov Res Inst.

Units & Standards of Electromagnetism. Vigoreaux. (Wykeham Science Ser.: No. 15). 82p. 1971. pap. 18.00x (ISBN 0-85109-190-3). Taylor & Francis.

Units & Standards of Electromagnetism. P. Vigoureux & R. A. Tricker. LC 77-153869. (Wykeham Science Ser.: No. 15). 82p. 1971. 18.00x (ISBN 0-8448-1117-3, Pub. by Crane Russak & Co). Taylor & Francis.

Units Based on a Theme. 1984. Eleven Topics. 3.50 ea. (ISBN 0-939418-54-1). Ferguson-Florissant.

Units in Woodworking. 2nd ed. J. H. Douglass et al. LC 79-8737. (Industrial Arts Ser.). 320p. 1981. pap. text ed. 19.95 (ISBN 0-8273-1333-0); instr's. guide 6.00 (ISBN 0-8273-1334-9); comprehensive tests 5.00 (ISBN 0-8273-1335-7). Delmar.

Units of Expression for Wastewater Management. rev. ed. (Manual of Practice: No. 6). 47p. 1982. pap. text ed. 11.00 (ISBN 0-943244-06-4, M0006). Water Pollution.

Units of Language Acquisition. Ann M. Peters. LC 82-22161. (Cambridge Monographs & Texts in Applied Psycholinguistics I). 131p. 1983. pap. 12.95 (ISBN 0-521-27071-5). Cambridge U Pr.

Units of Measure. Fred Justus. (Math Ser.). 24p. (gr. 3-5). 1979. wkbk. 5.00 (ISBN 0-8209-0120-2, A-30). ESP.

Units of Measurement: An Encyclopaedic Dictionary of Units, Both Scientific & Popular, & the Quantities They Measure. Stephen Dresner. LC 72-187346. pap. 75.80 (ISBN 0-317-26195-9, 2052071). Bks Demand UMI.

Units of Weight & Measure: International (Metric) & U. S. Customary. L. J. Chisholm. LC 74-20726. (Illus.). 256p. 1975. Repr. of 1967 ed. 40.00x (ISBN 0-8103-4163-8). Gale.

Units of Work & Centers of Interest in the Organization of the Elementary School Curriculum. Sadie Goggans. LC 70-176809. (Columbia University. Teachers College. Contributions to Education: No. 803). Repr. of 1940 ed. 22.50 (ISBN 0-404-55803-8). AMS Pr.

Unity. David Miller. 32p. (Orig.). 1981. pap. 3.00x (ISBN 0-935162-03-8). Singing Horse.

Unity: A Quest for Truth. Eric Butterworth. (Orig.). 1965. pap. 3.00 (ISBN 0-8315-0020-4). Speller.

Unity: A Quest for Truth. Eric Butterworth. 160p. 1985. 5.95 (ISBN 0-87159-165-0, X1965, ROBERT SPELLER & SONS PUB.). Unity School.

Unity & Design in Horace's Odes. Matthew S. Santirocco. LC 85-20964. x, 251p. 1986. 25.00x (ISBN 0-8078-1691-4). U of NC Pr.

Unity & Development in Plato's Metaphysics. William J. Prior. LC 85-5073. 202p. 1985. 23.95 (ISBN 0-8126-9000-1). Open Court.

Unity & Disintegration in International Alliances. O. R. Holsti et al. LC 72-10150. 293p. 1973. 21.00 (ISBN 0-471-40835-2, Pub. by Wiley). Krieger.

Unity & Disintegration in International Alliances. Ole R. Holsti et al. (Illus.). 306p. 1985. pap. text ed. 13.50 (ISBN 0-8191-4387-1). U Pr of Amer.

Unity & Diversity: Essays in the History, Literature, & Religion of the Ancient Near East. Ed. by Hans Goedicke & J. J. Roberts. LC 74-24376. (Johns Hopkins University Near Eastern Studies). pap. 60.00 (ISBN 0-317-11301-1, 2016572). Bks Demand UMI.

Unity & Diversity in the New Testament: An Inquiry into the Character of Earliest Christianity. James D. Dunn. LC 77-22598. 488p. 1984. Westminster John Knox.

Unity & Diversity: Thirteen Original Essays on America's Ethnics & Minorities. 2nd ed. Ed. by Joseph M. Collier. 1985. pap. text ed. 10.95 (ISBN 0-942738-10-1). Amer Studies.

Unity & Jesus Forsaken. Chiara Lubich. LC 85-72397. 105p. 1985. pap. 4.95 (ISBN 0-911782-53-2). New City.

Unity & Language: A Study in the Philosophy of Johann Georg Hamann. James C. O'Flaherty. LC 52-4007. (North Carolina. University. Studies in the Germanic Languages & Literatures: No. 6). Repr. of 1952 ed. 27.00 (ISBN 0-404-50906-1). AMS Pr.

Unity & Multiplicity: Multilevel Consciousness of Self in Hypnosis, Psychiatric Disorder & Mental Health. John O. Beahrs. LC 81-38538. 256p. 1981. 32.50 (ISBN 0-87630-273-8). Brunner-Mazel.

Unity & Reform: Selected Writings of Nicholas De Cusa. Nicolas De Cusa. Ed. by John P. Dolan. 1962. 22.95x (ISBN 0-268-00287-8). U of Notre Dame Pr.

Unity & Struggle: Speeches & Writings. Amilcar Cabral. LC 79-2337. 298p. 1979. 16.50 (ISBN 0-85345-510-4); pap. 10.00 (ISBN 0-85345-625-9). Monthly Rev.

Unity & Synthesis in the Work of Heinrich Heine. Frederick E. Hueppe. (European University Studies: Series 1, German Language & Literature: Vol. 289). 68p. 1979. pap. 8.85 (ISBN 3-261-04638-4). P Lang Pubs.

Unity & Variety in Muslim Civilization. Armand Abel et al. Ed. by Gustave E. Von Grunebaum. LC 55-11191. (Comparative Studies of Cultures & Civilizations: No. 7). pap. 99.30 (ISBN 0-317-11328-3, 2013614). Bks Demand UMI.

Unity & Variety in the Philosophy of Samuel Alexander. Michael A. Weinstein. LC 83-21294. 136p. 1984. 14.50 (ISBN 0-911198-70-9). Purdue U Pr.

Unity from Diversity: Extracts from Selected Pennsylvania Colonial Documents, 1681 to 1780, in Commemoration of the Tercentenary of the Commonwealth. Louis M. Waddell. (Illus.). 89p. 1980. pap. 4.00 (ISBN 0-89271-009-8). Pa Hist & Mus.

Unity, Heresy, & Reform, 1378-1460. Christopher Crowder. 1987. pap. 15.50x (ISBN 0-919642-10-1). Limestone Pr.

Unity in Action. John MacArthur, Jr. (John MacArthur Bible Studies Ser.). 1987. pap. 3.95 (ISBN 0-8024-5307-4). Moody.

Unity in Christ. Leonard Mullens. 1958. 3.00 (ISBN 0-88027-053-5). Firm Foun Pub.

Unity in Creation. Russell Maatman. 143p. (Orig.). 1978. pap. 4.95 (ISBN 0-932914-00-4). Dordt Coll Pr.

Unity in Diversity. Ed. by O. P. Ghai. 132p. 1986. text ed. 15.95x (ISBN 0-86590-762-5, Pub. by Sterling Pubs India). Apt Bks.

Unity in Diversity. Ed. by Henry O. Thompson. LC 83-51715. 436p. (Orig.). 1984. pap. 12.95 (ISBN 0-932894-20-8). Rose Sharon Pr.

Unity in Diversity: An Index to the Publications of Conservative & Libertarian Institutions. The New American Foundation. Ed. by Carol L. Birch. LC 82-20552. 284p. 1983. 20.00 (ISBN 0-8108-1599-0). Scarecrow.

Unity in Diversity: Italian Communism & the Communist World. Donald L. Blackmer. (Studies in Communism, Revisionism & Revolution). 1968. 37.50x (ISBN 0-262-02030-0). MIT Pr.

Unity in Hardy's Novels: Repetitive Symmetries. Peter J. Casagrande. xii, 252p. 1982. 29.95x (ISBN 0-7006-0209-7). U Pr of KS.

Unity in Shakespearian Tragedy. Brents Stirling. LC 66-19086. 212p. 1966. Repr. of 1956 ed. 27.50x (ISBN 0-87752-105-0). Gordian.

Unity in the Ghazals of Hafez. Michael C. Hillmann. LC 74-27614. (Studies in Middle Eastern Literatures: No. 6). 1976. 25.00x (ISBN 0-88297-010-0). Bibliotheca.

Unity in the Work of Service - John Paul II: On the Occasion of His Second Pastoral Visit to the United States. Pope John Paul, II. 208p. (Orig.). 1987. pap. 8.95 (ISBN 1-55586-177-6). US Catholic.

Unity of Anglicanism: Catholic & Reformed. Henry R. McAdoo. 48p. 1983. pap. 4.95 (ISBN 0-8192-1324-1). Morehouse.

Unity of English-German Contrasts: A Case Study in Language Variation. John A. Hawkins. 200p. cancelled (ISBN 0-85664-931-7, Pub. by Croom Helm Ltd). Routledge Chapman & Hall.

Unity of European History: A Political & Cultural Survey. rev. & expanded ed. John Bowle. 1970. pap. 6.95 (ISBN 0-19-501249-6). Oxford U Pr.

Unity of Forces in the Universe, 2 vols. A. Zee. 1104p. 1982. Set. 107.00 (ISBN 9971-950-38-3); Set. pap. 47.00 (ISBN 9971-950-39-1, Pub. by World Sci Singapore). World Scientific Pub.

Unity of Good. Mary Baker Eddy. Indonesian ed. 12.50 (ISBN 0-87952-177-5); French Ed. 7.50 (ISBN 0-87952-123-6). First Church.

Unity of Good. Mary Baker Eddy. 63p. Braille ed. 68.00 (ISBN 0-87952-052-3). First Church.

Unity of Good. Mary Baker Eddy. 64p. pap. 7.50 (ISBN 0-87952-233-X). First Church.

Unity of Good, Rudimental Divine Science. Mary Baker Eddy. pap. 4.50 (ISBN 0-87952-043-4). First Church.

Unity of Good, Two Sermons. Mary Baker Eddy. Danish 12.50 (ISBN 0-87952-106-6); Norwegian 12.50 (ISBN 0-87952-197-X); German o.p. 6.00 (ISBN 0-87952-159-7). First Church.

Unity of Homer. John A. Scott. LC 65-15246. 1921. 15.00 (ISBN 0-8196-0152-7). Biblo.

Unity of Isaiah. Oswald T. Allis. 1952. pap. 7.95 (ISBN 0-87552-105-3). Presby & Reformed.

Unity of Isaiah: A Study in Prophecy. Oswald T. Allis. 1974. pap. 7.95 (ISBN 0-8010-0111-0). Baker Bk.

Unity of Kant's Critique of Pure Reason: Experience, Language, & Knowledge. Terence C. Williams. (Studies in the History of Philosophy: No. 4). 1986. lib. bdg. 39.95x (ISBN 0-88946-301-8). E Mellen.

Unity of Knowledge & Action: A Study in Wang Yang-Ming's Moral Psychology. A. S. Cua. LC 81-23060. 147p. 1982. text ed. 12.95x (ISBN 0-8248-0786-3). UH Pr.

Unity of Law & Morality: A Refutation of Legal Positivism. M. J. Detmold. (International Library of Philosophy). 288p. 1984. 25.00x (ISBN 0-7102-0030-7). Routledge Chapman & Hall.

Unity of Law: As Exhibited in the Relation of Physical, Social, Mental & Moral Science. Henry C. Carey. LC 67-18575. (Illus.). 1967. Repr. of 1872 ed. 45.00x (ISBN 0-678-00247-9). Kelley.

Unity of Luke's Theology: An Analysis of Luke-Acts. Robert F. O'Toole. LC 84-81246. (Good News Studies Ser.: Vol. 9). 1984. pap. 8.95 (ISBN 0-89453-438-6). M Glazier.

Unity of Mistakes: A Phenomenological Interpretation of Medical Work. Marianne A. Paget. LC 87-26716. 224p. 1988. 27.95 (ISBN 0-87722-533-8). Temple U Pr.

Unity of Nature. Carl F. Von Weizsacker. Ed. by Francine J. Zucker. 406p. 1980. 20.00 (ISBN 0-374-28100-9); pap. 12.95 (ISBN 0-374-51602-2). FS&G.

Unity of One. George L. Pink. 160p. 1982. 8.00 (ISBN 0-682-49838-6). Exposition-Phoenix.

Unity of Plato's Thought. Paul Shorey. LC 78-66598. (Ancient Philosophy Ser.). 88p. 1980. lib. bdg. 15.00 (ISBN 0-8240-9585-5). Garland Pub.

Unity of Religious Ideals. Hazrat I. Khan. (Collected Works of Hazrat Inayat Khan Ser.). 264p. 1979. 9.95 (ISBN 0-930872-09-6); pap. 6.95 (ISBN 0-930872-10-X). Omega Pr NY.

Unity of Science. Robert L. Causey. (Synthese Library: No. 109). 1977. lib. bdg. 34.00 (ISBN 90-277-0779-0, Pub. by Reidel Holland). Kluwer Academic.

Unity of the Bible. Harold H. Rowley. LC 78-2684. 1978. Repr. of 1953 ed. lib. bdg. 35.00x (ISBN 0-313-20346-6, ROUB). Greenwood.

Universal Sikhism. A. S. Sethi. 1972. 5.95 (ISBN 0-88253-767-9). Ind-US Inc.
Universal Soil Loss Equation: Past, Present & Future. Ed. by A. G. Peterson & J. B. Swan. 53p. 1979. pap. 3.75 (ISBN 0-89118-766-9). Soil Sci Soc Am.
Universal Stitches for Weaving, Embroidery, & Other Fiber Arts. Nancy A. Hoskins. LC 82-80789. (Illus.). 128p. 1982. pap. 19.95 (ISBN 0-295-96274-7). U of Wash Pr.
Universal Story. Clive Hirschhorn. LC 83-7840. 19.95 (ISBN 0-517-55001-6). Crown.
Universal Subgoaling & Chunking: The Automatic Generation & Learning of Goal Hierarchies. Dr. John Laird et al. 1986. lib. bdg. 39.95 (ISBN 0-89838-243-0). Kluwer Academic.
Universal Supplementary Exercisebook. Kathleen Ruhl. 1981. pap. text ed. write for info. (ISBN 0-673-15453-X). Scott F.
Universal Supplementary Exercisebook (U. S. E.) Form B. Kathleen Ruhl. 1983. pap. text ed. write for info. (ISBN 0-673-15619-2). Scott F.
Universal Television: The Studio & Its Programs, 1950-1980. Jeb H. Perry. LC 83-4269. 499p. 1983. 35.00 (ISBN 0-8108-1628-8). Scarecrow.
Universal Theory of Automata. H. Ehrig. (Illus.). 1976. pap. 20.95x (ISBN 3-519-02054-8). Adlers Foreign Bks.
Universal Theosophy. Robert Crosbie. 171p. 1963. pap. 5.00 (ISBN 0-938998-31-5). Theosophy.
Universal Transcription. James L. Clark & Lyn R. Clark. LC 84-23328. 224p. 1985. pap. 21.50 (ISBN 0-534-04530-8). PWS Kent Pub.
Universal Traveler: A Soft-Systems Guide to Creativity, Problem-Solving & the Process of Reaching Goals. rev. ed. Don Koberg & Jim Bagnall. LC 81-17123. (Illus.). 130p. (Orig.). 1981. pap. 9.95 (ISBN 0-86576-017-9). W Kaufmann.
Universal Treatise of Nicholas of Autrecourt. Leonard Kennedy. (Medieval Philosophical Texts in Translation: No. 20). 172p. 1971. pap. 7.95 (ISBN 0-87462-220-4). Marquette.
Universal Turing Machine: A Half-Century Survey. Rolf Herken. 640p. 1988. 145.00 (ISBN 0-19-853741-7). Oxford U Pr.
Universal Typing. 3rd ed. Edith Mackay. 192p. 1988. 23.50x (ISBN 0-273-02706-9, Pub. by Pitman Pub Ltd London). Trans-Atl Phila.
Universal Variable Life Insurance Pocket Guide. Rich White. Date not set. write for info. S&S.
Universal White Brotherhood Is Not a Sect. Omraam M. Aivanhov. (Izvor Collection Ser.: Vol. 206). (Illus.). 197p. (Orig.). 1982. pap. 5.95 (ISBN 2-85566-194-3, Pub. by Prosveta France). Prosveta USA.
Universal Yarn Finder. Maggie Righetti. 1987. pap. 10.95 (ISBN 0-13-940065-6). P-H.
Universalism in America. Ed. by Ernest Cassara. 1984. pap. 5.95 (ISBN 0-933840-21-7). Unitarian Univ.
Universalism Versus Relativism in Language & Thought: Proceedings of a Colloquium on the Sapir-Whorf Hypothesis. Ed. by Rik Pinxten. (Contributions to the Sociology of Language Ser.: No. 11). 1977. text ed. 32.80x (ISBN 90-2797-791-7). Mouton.
Universality in Chaos. Cvitanovic. 1984. 81.00x (ISBN 0-85274-766-7, Pub. by A Hilger UK); pap. 35.00x (ISBN 0-85274-765-9, Pub. by A Hilger UK). Taylor & Francis.
Universality, Selectivity & Effectiveness in Social Policy. Bleddyn Davies. LC 80-457434. (Studies in Social Policy & Welfare). 1978. text ed. 31.00 (ISBN 0-435-82266-7). Gower Pub Co.
Universalizability. Wlodzimierz Rabinowics. (Synthese Library: No. 141). 1979. lib. bdg. 24.00 (ISBN 90-277-1020-1, Pub. by Reidel Holland). Kluwer Academic.
Universals & Scientific Realism, Vol. 1: Nominalism & Realism. D. M. Armstrong. LC 77-80824. 1978. 37.50 (ISBN 0-521-21741-5); pap. 12.95 (ISBN 0-521-28033-8). Cambridge U Pr.
Universals & Scientific Realism, Vol. 2: A Theory of Universals. D. M. Armstrong. LC 77-80824. 1978. 32.50 (ISBN 0-521-21950-7); pap. 10.95 (ISBN 0-521-28032-X). Cambridge U Pr.
Universals of Human Language, 4 vols. Ed. by Joseph H. Greenberg et al. Incl. Vol. I. Method & Theory. 22.50x (ISBN 0-8047-0965-3); Vol. II. Phonology. 40.00x (ISBN 0-8047-0966-1); Vol. III. Word Structure. 35.00x (ISBN 0-8047-0968-8); Vol. IV. Syntax. 45.00x (ISBN 0-8047-0969-6). LC 77-89179. 1978. Set. 142.50x (ISBN 0-8047-1012-0). Stanford U Pr.
Universals of Human Thought: Some African Evidence. Ed. by Barbara Lloyd & John Gay. LC 79-41471. (Illus.). 300p. 1981. 57.50 (ISBN 0-521-22953-7). Cambridge U Pr.
Universals: Studies in Indian Logic & Linguistics. Frits Staal. (Illus.). x, 268p. 1988. 47.50x (ISBN 0-226-76999-2); pap. 18.95x (ISBN 0-226-77000-1). U of Chicago Pr.
Universe. Isaac Asimov. 1980. 15.95 (ISBN 0-8027-0655-X). Walker & Co.
Universe. Eric Chaisson. (Illus.). 544p. 1988. text ed. 42.67 (ISBN 0-13-938391-3). P-H.
Universe. rev. ed. Larry Ciupik. LC 87-20805. (Read About Science Ser.). (Illus.). 48p. (gr. 3). 1987. PLB 15.33 (ISBN 0-8172-3264-8). Raintree Pubs.
Universe. Heather Couper. (Illus.). 1985. 19.45 (ISBN 0-394-54691-1). Random.
Universe. William J Kaufmann, III. LC 84-13830. (Illus.). 640p. 1984. 34.95 (ISBN 0-7167-1673-9); slides 45.00 (ISBN 0-7167-1744-1). W H Freeman.
Universe. 2nd ed. William J. Kaufmann, III. LC 87-15050. 688p. 1987. 36.95 (ISBN 0-7167-1927-4). W H Freeman.
Universe. Josip Kleczek. (Geophysics & Astrophysics Ser.: Monograph 11). 1976. lib. bdg. 37.00 (ISBN 90-277-0684-0, Pub. by Reidel Holland); pap. 21.000 (ISBN 90-277-0685-9). Kluwer Academic.
Universe. Scudder Klyce. LC 75-3217. Repr. of 1921 ed. 54.00 (ISBN 0-404-59213-9). AMS Pr.
Universe. Ed. by Patrick Moore & Laian Nicolson. (Illus.). 256p. 1985. text ed. 50.00 (ISBN 0-02-922110-2). Macmillan.
Universe. James Muirden. (Illustrated Encyclopedia Ser.). (Illus.). 128p. (gr. 5-9). 1988. PLB 14.95 (ISBN 0-671-64493-9, Little Simon). S&S.
Universe. Ed. by Byron Preiss. LC 87-47572. 336p. 1987. 27.95 (ISBN 0-553-05227-6). Bantam.
Universe, No. 10. Ed. by Terry Carr. 1982. pap. 2.50 (ISBN 0-8217-1114-8). Zebra.
Universe, No. 11. Ed. by Terry Carr. 1983. pap. 2.50 (ISBN 0-8217-1143-1). Zebra.
Universe Against Her. James H. Schmitz. 192p. 1984. pap. 2.75 (ISBN 0-441-84577-0, Pub. by Ace Science Fiction). Ace Bks.
Universe & Civilization. V. Sevastyanov. 240p. 1981. pap. 4.00 (ISBN 0-8285-2009-7, Pub. by Progress Pubs USSR). Imported Pubns.
Universe & Dr. Einstein. Lincoln Barnett. 16.95 (ISBN 0-8488-0146-6, Pub. by Amereon Hse). Amereon Ltd.
Universe & Life. facsimile ed. Herbert S. Jennings. (Select Bibliographies Reprint Ser). Repr. of 1933 ed. 14.00 (ISBN 0-8369-6695-3). Ayer Co Pubs.
Universe & Life: Origins & Evolution. G. Siegfried Kutter. 1987. text ed. 40.00 (ISBN 0-86720-033-2). Jones & Bartlett.
Universe & Other Fictions. Paul West. 1988. 17.95 (ISBN 0-87951-303-9). Overlook Pr.
Universe & Other Poems. Dennis Keene. 104p. 1984. pap. 8.50 x (ISBN 0-85635-506-2). Carcanet.
Universe Around Us. J. H. Jeans. 1929. 37.00 (ISBN 0-686-17428-3). Ridgeway Bks.
Universe as Journey: Conversations with W. Norris Clarke, S.J. Ed. by Gerald A. McCool. LC 88-80357. 200p. 1988. text ed. 40.00 (ISBN 0-8232-1208-4). Fordham.
Universe As Pictured in Milton's Paradise Lost. William F. Warren. LC 73-12894. 1915. lib. bdg. 20.00 (ISBN 0-8414-9418-5). Folcroft.
Universe As Pictured in Milton's Paradise Lost: An Illustrated Study for Personal & Class Use. William F. Warren. LC 68-59037. (Illus.). 80p. 1968. Repr. of 1915 ed. 15.00x (ISBN 0-87752-117-4). Gordian.
Universe At Your Fingertips. R. Robert Robbins & Andrew Fraknoi. 96p. 1985. 9.95 (ISBN 0-937707-07-4, BO 99). Astron Soc Pacific.
Universe Between. Alan E. Nourse. 176p. Date not set. pap. 2.95 (ISBN 0-441-85456-7, Pub. by Ace Science Fiction). Ace Bks.
Universe City. Randy Russell. 48p. (Orig.). 1987. pap. 3.00 (ISBN 0-944388-00-0). TBS Pubns.
Universe Earth & Man. Rudolf Steiner. (Russian Language Ser.). 136p. 1985. pap. 8.00 (ISBN 0-89345-903-8, Steiner). Garber Comm.
Universe Fifteen. Terry Carr. 1987. pap. 3.50 (ISBN 0-8125-3265-1, Dist. by St Martin's Pr & Warner Pub Servs). Tor Bks.
Universe Fourteen. Ed. by Terry Carr. 224p. 1986. pap. 2.95 (ISBN 0-8125-3271-6, Dist. by Warner Pub. Services & St. Martin's Press). Tor Bks.
Universe: From Flat Earth to Quasar. Isaac Asimov. 1976. pap. 3.95 (ISBN 0-380-01596-X, 62208-4, Discus). Avon.
Universe from Your Backyard: A Guide to Deep Sky Objects from Astronomy Magazine. David J. Eicher. LC 88-8920. (Illus.). 188p. 1988. 24.95 (ISBN 0-913135-05-4). AstroMedia.
Universe from Your Backyard: An Atlas of Deep Sky Objects. Astronomy Editors & David J. Eicher. (Illus.). 200p. Date not set. 24.95 (ISBN 0-521-36299-7). Cambridge U Pr.
Universe, God, & God-Realization: From the Viewpoint of Vedanta. Swami Satprakashananda. LC 77-79829. 310p. 1977. 12.50 (ISBN 0-916356-57-4). Vedanta Soc St Louis.
Universe: God, Science & the Human Person. Adam Ford. LC 87-50830. 228p. 1987. pap. 9.95 (ISBN 0-89622-336-1). Twenty-Third.
Universe Guide to Stars & Planets. Ian Ridpath & Wil Tirion. LC 84-24133. (Illus.). 384p. 1985. 19.95 (ISBN 0-87663-366-1); pap. 11.95 (ISBN 0-87663-859-0). Universe.
Universe in the Classroom: A Resource Guide for Teaching Astronomy. Andrew Fraknoi. 269p. (Orig.). 1985. pap. text ed. 9.95 (ISBN 0-7167-1692-5). W H Freeman.
Universe Is a Green Dragon: A Cosmic Creation Story. Brian Swimme. LC 84-72255. (Illus.). 176p. (Orig.). 1984. pap. 8.95 (ISBN 0-939680-14-9). Bear & Co.
Universe, Life & Mind. 5th ed. Shklovskii. 1988. write for info. (ISBN 0-471-87536-8). Wiley.
Universe Next Door. rev. ed. James W. Sire. LC 88-8852. 240p. (YA) (gr. 7-12). 1988. pap. 8.95 (ISBN 0-8308-1220-2). Inter-Varsity.
Universe Next Door: A Basic World View Catalog. James W. Sire. LC 75-32129. 240p. (Orig.). 1976. pap. 7.95 (ISBN 0-87784-772-X). Inter-Varsity.
Universe of Babies: In the Beginning There Were No Words. Caleb Gattegno. 133p. 1973. pap. 4.95 (ISBN 0-87825-023-9). Ed Solutions.
Universe of Cartoons. Jack Nemec. LC 87-91984. (Illus.). 120p. (Orig.). 1987. pap. 5.95 (ISBN 0-9618998-3-2). Nemec Pub.
Universe of Galaxies. Ed. by Paul W. Hodge. (Readings from Scientific American Ser.). (Illus.). 113p. 1984. 20.95 (ISBN 0-7167-1675-5); pap. 11.95 (ISBN 0-7167-1676-3). W H Freeman.
Universe of Knowledge. Ed. by Derek Langridge & Esther Herman. LC 68-66990. (Student Contribution Ser.: No. 2). 1969. pap. 3.50 (ISBN 0-911808-04-3). U of Md Lib Serv.
Universe of Language. George Watson. 1979. Repr. of 1878 ed. lib. bdg. 50.00 (ISBN 0-8492-2963-4). R West.
Universe of Maurice Barres. Gordon Shenton. (Studies in the Romance Languages & Literatures: No. 214). 160p. 1980. pap. 12.50x (ISBN 0-8078-9214-9). U of NC Pr.
Universe of Motion. Dewey B. Larson. LC 84-60388. (Illus.). 460p. 1984. 19.00 (ISBN 0-913138-11-8). North Pacific.
Universe of Numbers. Ed. by Ralph M. Lewis. LC 83-51126. 209p. (Orig.). 1984. pap. 7.95 (ISBN 0-912057-11-4, G-649). AMORC.
Universe of Robert Herrick. S. Musgrove. LC 75-20062. 1950. lib. bdg. 17.50 (ISBN 0-8414-6049-3). Folcroft.
Universe of Science. H. Levy. LC 74-26272. (History, Philosophy & Sociology of Science Ser). 1975. Repr. 21.00x (ISBN 0-405-06600-7). Ayer Co Pubs.
Universe of Shabbetai Donnolo. A. Sharf. 20.00x (ISBN 0-87068-485-X). Ktav.
Universe of the Mind. George E. Owen. LC 76-125674. (Seminar in the History of Ideas Ser: No. 4). (Illus.). 368p. 1971. 37.50x (ISBN 0-8018-1131-7); pap. 12.95x (ISBN 0-8018-1179-1). Johns Hopkins.
Universe: Past, Present & Future. David J. Darling. LC 84-23068. (Discovering Our Universe Ser.). (Illus.). 64p. (gr. 4 up). 1985. PLB 10.95 (ISBN 0-87518-286-0). Dillon.
Universe That Isn't. J. H. Hacsi. 236p. (Orig.). 1985. pap. 9.95 (ISBN 0-9612146-1-9). Champagne Pr.
Universe Thirteen. Ed. by Terry Carr. 256p. 1985. pap. 2.95 (ISBN 0-8125-3269-4, Dist. by Warner Pub. Services & Saint Martin's Press). Tor Bks.
Universe Twelve. Ed. by Terry Carr. 1983. pap. 2.95 (ISBN 0-8217-1303-5). Zebra.
Universe Unified. Douglas Walsh. 48p. 1987. 6.95 (ISBN 0-89962-595-9). Todd & Honeywell.
Universele Taalkunde: Een Inleiding in de Algemene Taal Wetenschep. 3rd, rev. ed. V. Fromkiin & R. Rodman. Ed. & tr. by A. Neyt. xii, 320p. 1986. pap. write for info. (ISBN 90-6765-260-1). Foris Pubns.
Universes of E. E. Smith. Ron Ellik & Bill Evans. LC 66-9092. (Illus.). 1966. pap. 6.00 (ISBN 0-911682-03-1). Advent.
Universidad de la Palabra. Dick Eastman. Tr. by Jose D. Silva from Eng. 239p. (Span.). 1986. pap. text ed. 3.50 (ISBN 0-8297-0443-4). Life Pubs Intl.
Universidade da Palavra. Dick Eastman. Orig. Title: University of the World. (Port.). 1986. write for info. (ISBN 0-8297-0442-6). Life Pubs Intl.
Universitaets-Klinik und Poliklinik fuer Hals -, Nasen- und Ohren-Krankheiten Basel 1876-1976. 1976. 12.75 (ISBN 3-8055-2405-6). S Karger.
Universitas 15: Enciclopedia Cultural, 15 vols. 4500p. (Span.). 1971. Set. 695.00 (ISBN 84-345-3054-6, S-50485). French & Eur.
Universitat Gottingen unter dem Nationalsozialismus: Das Verdrangte Kapitel Ihrer 250 Jahrigen Gestichte. Ed. by Heinrich Becker et al. 616p. (Ger.). 1987. lib. bdg. 40.00 (ISBN 3-598-10676-9). K G Saur.
Universitats-Selbstverwaltung: Ihre Geschichte und Gegenwartige Rechtsform. Alexander Kluge. Ed. by Walter P. Metzger. LC 76-55205. (Academic Profession Ser.). 1977. Repr. of 1958 ed. lib. bdg. 20.00x (ISBN 0-405-10033-7). Ayer Co Pubs.
Universitatsbibliothek Freiburg im Dritten Reich. Ingo Toussaint. 272p. (Ger.). 1984. lib. bdg. 16.00 (ISBN 3-598-10547-9). K G Saur.
Universite de la Parole. Dick Eastman. Ed. by Annie Cosson. Tr. by Vera Sayous from Eng. Orig. Title: Universoty of the WORD. 240p. (Fr.). 1985. pap. 2.00 (ISBN 0-8297-0441-8). Life Pubs Intl.
Universites Americaines: Dynamismes et Traditions. J. Bodelle & G. Nicolaon. 416p. (Orig., Fr.). 1985. pap. 30.00 (ISBN 0-318-18948-8, Pub. by Technique et Documentation). S M P F Inc.
Universities, Academics & the Great Schism. R. N. Swanson. LC 78-56764. (Cambridge Studies in Medieval Life & Thought: 3rd Ser., No. 12). 1979. Cambridge U Pr.
Universities, Adult Education & Social Criticism. S. Raybould. (Tolley Medal Ser). 1970. 1.50 (ISBN 0-686-52207-9, WPT 3). Syracuse U Cont Ed.
Universities: American, English, German. Abraham Flexner. 381p. 1980. Repr. of 1930 ed. lib. bdg. 40.00 (ISBN 0-89984-200-3). Century Bookbindery.
Universities & Colleges: A Simple Critique for Making Money & Excellence. Brad B. Mortel. LC 88-47608. 150p. 1988. 34.50 (ISBN 0-88164-798-5); pap. 26.50 (ISBN 0-88164-799-3). ABBE Pubs Assn.
Universities & Environmental Education. (Development of Higher Education Ser.). (Illus.). 127p. (Orig.). 1986. pap. text ed. 10.50 (ISBN 92-3-102364-0, U1504, Unesco). UNIPUB.
Universities & National Development: A Report of the Nordic Association for the Study of Education in Developing Countries. Ed. by Atle Hetland. 174p. (Orig.). 1984. pap. text ed. 30.00x (ISBN 91-22-00726-1, Pub. by Almqvist & Wiksell). Coronet Bks.
Universities & Scientific Life in the United States. Maurice Caullery. LC 74-26257. (History, Philosophy & Sociology of Science Ser). 1975. Repr. of 1922 ed. 24.50x (ISBN 0-405-06585-X). Ayer Co Pubs.
Universities & Scientific Life in the United States. Maurice J. Caullery. LC 72-94312. (American Scientific Community, 1790-1920 Ser.). 1973. Repr. of 1922 ed. lib. bdg. 30.00 (ISBN 0-8420-1677-5). Scholarly Res Inc.
Universities & State Governments: Study in Policy Analysis. Irwin Feller. LC 86-520. 188p. 1986. lib. bdg. 35.00 (ISBN 0-275-92094-1, C2094). Praeger.
Universities & the International Distribution of Knowledge. Ed. by Irving J. Spitzberg, Jr. LC 80-16569. 222p. 1980. 38.95 (ISBN 0-275-90556-X, C0556). Praeger.
Universities & the Myth of Cultural Decline. Jerry S. Herron. LC 88-10081. 128p. 1988. 16.00x (ISBN 0-8143-2068-6); pap. 9.95x (ISBN 0-8143-2069-4). Wayne St U Pr.
Universities & the Public: A History of Adult Higher Education in the United States. David N. Portman. LC 78-9333. 228p. 1979. text ed. 21.95x (ISBN 0-88229-116-5). Nelson-Hall.
Universities & the Social Problem: An Account of the University Settlements in East London. John M. Knapp. Ed. by Lynn H. Lees & Andrew Lees. LC 84-48281. (Rise of Urban Britain Ser.). 235p. 1985. 35.00 (ISBN 0-8240-6283-3). Garland Pub.
Universities & Women Faculty: Why Some Organizations Discriminate More Than Others. Robert F. Szafran. LC 83-23104. 1984. 35.00 (ISBN 0-275-91282-5, C1282). Praeger.
Universities: Commonwealth & American; a Comparative Study. Oliver C. Carmichael. LC 70-167323. (Essay Index Reprint Ser.). Repr. of 1959 ed. 20.25 (ISBN 0-8369-2760-5). Ayer Co Pubs.
Universities for All. George Z. Bereday. LC 72-11624. (Jossey-Bass Series in Higher Education). pap. 43.80 (2027746). Bks Demand UMI.
Universities in Politics: Case Studies from the Late Middle Ages & Early Modern Period. Ed. by John W. Baldwin & Richard A. Goldthwaite. LC 73-183041. (Johns Hopkins Symposia in Comparative History Ser.). pap. 36.00 (ISBN 0-317-41614-6, 2025829). Bks Demand UMI.
Universities in the Caribbean Region - Struggles to Democratize: An Annotated Bibliography. Barbara A. Waggoner & George R. Waggoner. (Reference Publications in Areas Studies). 450p. 1986. lib. bdg. 55.00 (ISBN 0-8161-8159-4). G K Hall.
Universities in the Modern World. B. Fletcher. 1968. pap. 10.25 (ISBN 0-08-012762-2). Pergamon.
Universities in Transition, the U. S. Presence in Latin American Higher Education. Ed. by Richard R. Renner. LC 73-8234. 147p. 1973. pap. 10.00 (ISBN 0-8130-0422-5). U Presses Fla.
Universities in Tudor England. Craig R. Thompson. LC 79-65982. (Folger Guides to the Age of Shakespeare). 1979. pap. 3.95 (ISBN 0-918016-09-6). Folger Bks.
Universities, Information Technology, & Academic Libraries. Robert M. Hayes. LC 85-22879. (Libraries & Information Science Ser.). 192p. 1986. text ed. 35.00 (ISBN 0-89391-266-2). Ablex Pub.
Universities of Ancient Greece. facsimile ed. John W. Walden. LC 70-109635. (Select Bibliographies Reprint Ser). 1909. 24.50 (ISBN 0-8369-5244-8). Ayer Co Pubs.
Universities of Europe. Willis Rudy. LC 82-49281. 176p. 1984. 22.50. Fairleigh Dickinson.
Universities of Europe in the Middle Ages, Vol. III: English Universities-Student Life. Hastings Rashdall. Ed. by F. M. Powicke & A. B. Emden. 588p. 1987. 94.00 (ISBN 0-19-822983-6). Oxford U Pr.
Universities of Europe in the Middle Ages, Vol. II: Italy-Spain-France-Germany-Scotland, etc. Hastings Rashdall. Ed. by F. M. Powicke & A. B. Emden. 352p. 1987. 69.00 (ISBN 0-19-822982-8). Oxford U Pr.
Universities of Europe in the Middle Ages, Vol. I: Salerno-Bologna-Paris. Hastings Rashdall. Ed. by F. M. Powicke & A. B. Emden. 638p. 1987. 98.00 (ISBN 0-19-822981-X). Oxford U Pr.
Universities of Puerto Rico: A Historical, Sociological & Cultural Study Including a Directory of Puerto Rico Scholars. Winifred Melendez. 1979. lib. bdg. 75.00 (ISBN 0-8490-1247-3). Gordon Pr.
Universities under Scrutiny. OECD. 114p. (Orig.). 1987. pap. 18.00x (ISBN 92-64-12922-7). OECD.
University Administration in India & U. S. A. Pradeep Mehendiratta. 1985. 28.50 (ISBN 0-8364-1308-3, Pub. by Oxford IBH). South Asia Bks.

University Adult Education in England & the U. S. A. A Reappraisal of the Liberal Tradition. Richard Taylor et al. LC 85-8743. (Radical Forum on Adult Education Ser.). 272p. 1985. 29.50 (ISBN 0-7099-2431-3, Pub. by Croom Helm Ltd). Routledge Chapman & Hall.

University Adult Education: The Career for Experiment in Education. A. A. Liveright. 1961. 2.50 (ISBN 0-87060-080-X, PUC 21). Syracuse U Cont Ed.

University Algebra. 1986. 4.00 (ISBN 0-471-63873-0). Wiley.

University & Community Education. Kenneth Haygood. 1962. 2.50 (ISBN 0-8156-7017-6, NES 36). Syracuse U Cont Ed.

University & Community Service: Perspectives for the Seventies. J. Whipple & D. Chertow. LC 74-118676. (Notes & Essays Series, No. 64). pap. text ed. 2.50 (ISBN 0-87060-028-1, NES 64). Syracuse U Cont Ed.

University & Community: The New Partnership. Fein & Gatner. LC 75-165286. 1971. 15.00 (ISBN 0-913252-03-4); pap. 8.50 (ISBN 0-913252-04-2). LIU Univ.

University & Government in Mexico: Autonomy in a Authoritarian System. Daniel C. Levy. LC 79-21134. 190p. 1980. 35.00 (ISBN 0-275-90512-8, C0512). Praeger.

University & Historical Addresses. facs. ed. James B. Bryce. LC 68-55842. (Essay Index Reprint Ser). 1913. 20.00 (ISBN 0-8369-0262-9). Ayer Co Pubs.

University & the City: From Medieval Origins to the Present. Ed. by Thomas Bender. 304p. 1988. 34.50 (ISBN 0-19-505273-0). Oxford U Pr.

University & the Community: The Problems of Changing Relationships. OECD Staff. 162p. 1982. pap. 14.50 (ISBN 92-64-12370-9). OECD.

University & the Man of Tomorrow. 1967. 11.95x (ISBN 0-8156-6008-1, Am U Beirut). Syracuse U Pr.

University & the State. Ed. by Sidney Hook et al. LC 77-26375. 296p. 1978. 18.95 (ISBN 0-87975-098-7). Prometheus Bks.

University Archives: Kit & Flyer 107. Office of Management Studies Staff. 108p. 1984. 20.00 (ISBN 0-318-18198-7). Assn Res Lib.

University As Usual-in an Unusual World. Herbert G. Heneman, Jr. (Edward Shann Memorial Lectures: No. 13). 1974. pap. 3.00x (ISBN 0-85564-081-2, Pub. by U of W Austral Pr). Intl Spec Bk.

University at Prayer. Alfred C. Payne. LC 86-14613. (Illus.). 1987. 13.95x (ISBN 0-9617635-0-7). VA Tech Educ Found.

University at the Crossroads: Addresses & Essays. Henry E. Sigerist. LC 73-167419. (Essay Index Reprint Ser.). Repr. of 1946 ed. 15.00 (ISBN 0-8369-2861-X). Ayer Co Pubs.

University Budgeting for Critical Mass & Competition. L. R. Jones. LC 84-26416. 304p. 1985. 36.95 (ISBN 0-275-90124-6, C0124). Praeger.

University Capacity in Eastern & Southern African Countries. Eastern & Southern African Universities Research Programme. xx, 260p. 1987. text ed. 45.00x (ISBN 0-435-08024-5). Heinemann Ed.

University Chemical Dependency Project. Steven Ungerleider & Steven A. Bloch. 113p. (Orig.). 1987. write for info. (ISBN 0-943277-00-0). Integrated Res Servs.

University Chemical Education: Proceedings of an International Symposium, Frascati, Rome, 1969. International Union of Pure & Applied Chemistry. 222p. 1976. 53.00 (ISBN 0-08-020821-5). Pergamon.

University Chemistry. 3rd ed. Bruce H. Mahan. LC 74-19696. 1975. text ed. write for info. (ISBN 0-201-04405-6). Addison-Wesley.

University Chemistry. 4th ed. Bruce M. Mahan & Rollie J. Myers. LC 86-14063. (Chemistry Ser.). (Illus.). 1076p. 1987. text ed. 44.95 (ISBN 0-201-05833-2); study guide 14.95 (ISBN 0-201-05835-9); solutions manual 13.95 (ISBN 0-201-05838-3). Benjamin-Cummings.

University Collection, Reading. write for info. (Pub. by British Acad). Longwood Pub Group.

University College of Wales. Ed. by The Plunkett Foundation for Co-Operative Studies. 67p. 25.00x (ISBN 0-85042-027-X, Pub. by Plunkett Foundation). State Mutual Bk.

University Control. J. McKeen Cattell. Ed. by Walter P. Metzger. LC 76-55179. (Academic Profession Ser.). 1977. Repr. of 1913 ed. lib. bdg. 36.50x (ISBN 0-405-10007-8). Ayer Co Pubs.

University Council on Education for Public Responsibility, 1961-1975. Granville D. Davis. LC 75-2281. 130p. 1975. pap. 2.75 (ISBN 0-87060-068-0, OCP 43). Syracuse U Cont Ed.

University Course in Digital Seismic Methods Used in Petroleum Exploration. 294p. 1980. 25.00 (ISBN 0-910835-04-7). Goose Pond Pr.

University Drama in the Tudor Age. Frederick S. Boas. LC 65-20049. (Illus.). 1914. 27.50 (ISBN 0-405-08277-0, Blom Pubns). Ayer Co Pubs.

University Education. Henry P. Tappan. LC 78-89243. (American Education: Its Men, Institutions & Ideas, Ser. 1). 1969. Repr. of 1851 ed. 14.00 (ISBN 0-405-01480-5). Ayer Co Pubs.

University Education & the Labour Market in the Arab Republic of Egypt. B. C. Sanyal. (Illus.). 277p. 1982. 57.00 (ISBN 0-08-028123-0); pap. 26.00 (ISBN 0-08-028122-2). Pergamon.

University Education for Business. James H. Bossard & J. Frederic Dewhurst. LC 73-1993. (Big Business; Economic Power in a Free Society Ser.). Repr. of 1931 ed. 36.50 (ISBN 0-405-05076-3). Ayer Co Pubs.

University Education in Botswana. N. O. Setidisho. 1985. 13.95 (ISBN 0-533-05939-9). Vantage.

University Expansion & Finance. M. Pickford. 1975. 15.00x (ISBN 0-85621-041-2, Pub. by Scot Acad Pr). Longwood Pub Group.

University Fitness Program: Aerobics Lifting Diet & Nutrition. Sharon Stoll. 121p. (Orig.). 1986. pap. 8.95 (ISBN 0-89301-106-1). U of Idaho Pr.

University Gradebook-Class Recordkeeping Software. Herrick. (Free to Adopter of any Benjamin-Cummings Textbook). 1987. 49.95 (ISBN 0-8053-2268-X). Benjamin Cummings.

University in a Changing World. facs. ed. Ed. by Walter M. Kotschnig & Elined Prys. LC 71-86766. (Essay Index Reprint Ser). 1932. 17.00 (ISBN 0-8369-1183-0). Ayer Co Pubs.

University in Process. John O. Riedl. (Aquinas Lecture Ser.). 1965. 7.95 (ISBN 0-87462-130-5). Marquette.

University in Society. N. T. Phillipson. 200p. 1983. 20.00x (ISBN 0-85224-461-4, Pub. by Edinburgh U Pr Scotland). Columbia U Pr.

University in Transition. James A. Perkins. 1966. pap. 7.50x (ISBN 0-691-02806-0). Princeton U Pr.

University-Industry Research Partnerships: The Major Legal Issues in Research & Development Agreements. Bernard D. Reams, Jr. LC 85-9589. (Illus.). 365p. 1986. lib. bdg. 46.95 (ISBN 0-89930-121-5, RUI/, Quorum). Greenwood.

University Jokes Told with Class. S. C. Lee. (Illus.). 202p. (Orig.). 1983. pap. 4.95 (ISBN 0-87397-223-6). Strode.

University Liberaries in Transition: Responding to Technological Change. Ed. by Lonora Welzenvach. 112p. 1987. pap. 15.00 (ISBN 0-915164-29-9). Nacubo.

University Librarianship. J. F. Stirling. 246p. 1981. 30.00 (ISBN 0-85365-621-5, Pub. by Library Assn Pub London). ALA.

University Libraries & the Antiquarian Book Trade: Fragments of Library History. Lawrence S. Thompson. (University of Kentucky Libraries Occasional Papers: No. 4). 26p. 1983. pap. 5.00 (ISBN 0-317-27435-X). U of KY Libs.

University Libraries in Developing Countries: Structure & Function in Regard to Information Transfer for Science & Technology. Ed. by Anthony J. Loveday & Gunter Gattermann. (IFLA Publication Ser.: 33). 183p. 1985. lib. bdg. 20.00 (ISBN 3-598-20397-7). K G Saur.

University Library Administration. Rutherford D. Rogers & David C. Weber. LC 75-116997. (Illus.). 454p. 1971. 23.00 (ISBN 0-8242-0417-4). Wilson.

University Library History: An International Review. Ed. by James Thompson. 336p. 1980. 35.00 (ISBN 0-85157-304-5, Pub. by Bingley England). ALA.

University Library in the United States: Its Origins & Development. Arthur Hamlin. 1981. 36.95x (ISBN 0-8122-7795-3). U of Pa Pr.

University Library Practices in Developing Countries. Nazir Ahmad. (Illus.). 220p. 1985. 45.00x (ISBN 0-7103-0058-1). Routledge Chapman & Hall.

University Library Problems. Uppsala University Library Staff. 124p. 1977. text ed. 26.50x (Pub. by Almqvist & Wiksell). Coronet Bks.

University Library System in India. K. S. Deshpande. 1985. text ed. 25.00x (ISBN 0-86590-697-1, Pub. by Sterling Pubs India). Apt Bks.

University Life in Ancient Athens. William W. Capes. LC 77-445. 1977. Repr. of 1922 ed. lib. bdg. 20.00 (ISBN 0-8414-3561-8). Folcroft.

University Life in Ancient Athens. William W. Capes. 134p. 1980. Repr. of 1922 ed. lib. bdg. 25.00 (ISBN 0-8492-3864-1). R West.

University of Alabama: A Guide to the Campus. Robert Mellown. LC 87-26205. (Illus.). 115p. 1988. pap. 7.95 (ISBN 0-8173-0395-2). U of Ala Pr.

University of Alabama: A Pictorial History. Suzanne R. Wolfe. LC 82-2626. (Illus.). 264p. 1983. 30.00 (ISBN 0-8173-0119-4). U of Ala Pr.

University of Alaska Anthropological Papers: An Index. David A. Hales et al. LC 79-624596. (Elmer E. Rasmuson Library Occasional Papers: No. 6). 198p. 1979. pap. text ed. 7.50x (ISBN 0-937592-02-1). U Alaska Rasmuson Lib.

University of British Columbia Hispanic Studies. Ed. by Harold Livermore. (Serie A: Monagrafias, XL). 86p. (Orig., Span. & Eng.). 1974. pap. 9.00 (ISBN 0-900411-82-1, Pub. by Tamesis Bks Ltd). Longwood Pub Group.

University of California: A Pictorial History. Albert G. Pickerell & May Dornin. (Illus.). 1968. 30.00 (ISBN 0-520-01010-8). U of Cal Pr.

University of California-Berkeley. Jim Sugar. (Illus.). 112p. 1987. 35.00 (ISBN 0-916509-10-9); deluxe ed. 125.00. Harmony Hse Pub LO.

University of California Prototype On-Line Catalog: Preliminary Specifications for the Patron Interface. Katharina Klemperer & Michael Berger. (Working Paper: No. 7). 1980. 5.00 (ISBN 0-686-87248-7). UCDLA.

University of California Sotheby Book of California Wine. Ed. by Doris Muscatine et al. LC 83-47666. (Illus.). 640p. 1984. 75.00 (ISBN 0-520-05085-1). U of Cal Pr.

University of California Union Catalog-Conversion of Catalog Cards to Machine-Readable Form: Phase I-Bibliographic Characteristics of University of California Cataloging. Katharina Klemperer & Bruce D'Ambrosio. (UCULAP PAper: No. 78-1). 1978. pap. 5.00 (ISBN 0-914602-91-8). UCDLA.

University of California Union Catalog: Conversion of Catalog Cards to Machine-Readable Form, Phase III-Comparison Study of Existing Data Bases for the Use of Retrospective Conversion. Katharina Klemperer & Kitty M. Shih. (Working Paper: No. 6). 1979. 5.00 (ISBN 0-686-87247-9). UCDLA.

University of California Union Catalog System Design Overview. Michael Berger et al. (Working Paper: No. 5). 1979. 5.00 (ISBN 0-686-87245-2). UCDLA.

University of Cambridge from the Earliest Times to the Royal Injunctions of 1535, 3 Vols. James B. Mullinger. 1969. Repr. of 1873 ed. Set. 195.00 (ISBN 0-384-40500-2). Johnson Repr.

University of Chicago Graduate Problems in Physics with Solutions. Jeremiah A. Cronin et al. 1979. pap. 12.00x (ISBN 0-226-12109-7, P809, Phoen). U of Chicago Pr.

University of Chicago Law Review: 1933-1986, 53 vols. Bound set. 1860.00x (ISBN 0-686-90082-0). Rothman.

University of Chicago Reading in Western Civilization, Vol. 9: Twentieth Century Europe. Ed. by John W. Boyer & Jan Goldstein. LC 85-16328. (RWC Ser.). 656p. text ed. 40.00x (ISBN 0-226-06953-2); pap. text ed. 14.95x (ISBN 0-226-06954-0). U of Chicago Pr.

University of Chicago Readings in Western Civilization: Medieval Europe, Vol. 4. Ed. by John W. Boyer & Julius Kirshner. LC 85-16328. x, 462p. 1986. lib. bdg. 30.00x (ISBN 0-226-06942-7); pap. 11.95x (ISBN 0-226-06943-5). U of Chicago Pr.

University of Chicago Readings in Western Civilization: The Church in the Roman Empire, Vol. 3. Ed. by John W. Boyer & Julius Kirshner. LC 85-16328. 1986. lib. bdg. 20.00x (ISBN 0-226-06938-9); pap. text ed. 7.95x (ISBN 0-226-06939-7). U of Chicago Pr.

University of Chicago Readings in Western Civilization: The Greek Polis, Vol. 1. Ed. by John W. Boyer & Julius Kirshner. LC 85-16328. (Readings in Western Civilization Ser.). viii, 368p. 1986. lib. bdg. 25.00x (ISBN 0-226-06934-6); pap. text ed. 8.95x (ISBN 0-226-06935-4). U of Chicago Pr.

University of Chicago Readings in Western Civilization: The Renaissance, Vol. 5. Ed. by John W. Boyer & Julius Kirshner. LC 85-16328. (Readings in Western Civilization Ser.). x, 448p. 1986. lib. bdg. 30.00x (ISBN 0-226-06944-3); pap. text ed. 11.95x (ISBN 0-226-06945-1). U of Chicago Pr.

University of Chicago Readings in Western Civilization, Vol. 2: Rome: Late Republic & Principate. Ed. by John W. Boyer & Julius Kirshner. LC 85-16328. (Readings in Western Civilization Ser.). vii, 316p. 1986. lib. bdg. 25.00x (ISBN 0-226-06936-2); pap. text ed. 8.95x (ISBN 0-226-06937-0). U of Chicago Pr.

University of Chicago Readings in Western Civilization, Vol. 6, Early Modern Europe: Crisis of Authority. Ed. by John W. Boyer & Julius Kirshner. LC 85-16328. (RWC Ser.). x, 608p. 1988. text ed. 37.50x (ISBN 0-226-06947-8); pap. text ed. 14.95x (ISBN 0-226-06948-6). U of Chicago Pr.

University of Chicago Readings in Western Civilization, Vol. 7: The Old Regime & the French Revolution. Ed. by John W. Boyer & Julius Kirshner. LC 85-16328. (Readings in Western Civilization Ser.). x, 466p. 1987. text ed. 37.50x (ISBN 0-226-06949-4); pap. text ed. 11.95x (ISBN 0-226-06950-8). U of Chicago Pr.

University of Chicago Readings in Western Civilization, Vol. 8, Nineteenth-Century Europe: Liberalism & Its Critics. Ed. by Jan Boyer & John W. Boyer. LC 86-16328. (RWC Ser.). x, 576p. 1988. text ed. 37.50x (ISBN 0-226-06951-6); pap. text ed. 13.95x (ISBN 0-226-06952-4). U of Chicago Pr.

University of Chicago Spanish Dictionary. 4th ed. Ed. by Lincoln Canfield. (Illus.). viii, 476p. 1987. lib. bdg. 19.95 (ISBN 0-226-10400-1); pap. 6.95 (ISBN 0-226-10402-8). U of Chicago Pr.

University of Chicago Spanish Dictionary. 3rd rev. enl. ed. Carlos Castillo & Otto F. Bond. (Span.). 1977. 16.95 (ISBN 0-226-09673-4, Phoen); pap. 6.95 (ISBN 0-226-09674-2). U of Chicago Pr.

University of Chicago Spanish-English, English-Spanish Dictionary. 3rd ed. Carlos Castillo & Otto F. Bond. pap. 3.95 (ISBN 0-317-56745-4). PB.

University of Cincinnati Law Review: 1927-1986, Vols. 1-54. Bound set. 1910.00x (ISBN 0-686-90083-9). Rothman.

University of Colorado Investigations of Paleolithic & Epipaleolithic Sites in the Sudan, Africa. Lee F. Irwin. (Nubian Ser.: No. 3). Repr. of 1968 ed. 20.00 (ISBN 0-404-60699-7). AMS Pr.

University of Delaware. Photos by Kevin Fleming. (First Edition Ser.). (Illus.). 112p. 1988. 35.00 (ISBN 0-916509-43-5); deluxe ed. 125.00 slipcased. Harmony Hse Pub LO.

University of Georgia. Photos by Sam Abell. (Illus.). 112p. 1987. 35.00 (ISBN 0-317-57499-X); deluxe ed. 125.00 deluxe slipcased (ISBN 0-317-57500-7). Harmony Hse Pub LO.

University of Georgia: A Bicentennial History, 1785-1985. Thomas G. Dyer. LC 84-232. 448p. 1985. 35.00 (ISBN 0-8203-0725-4). U of Ga Pr.

University of Georgia Under Sixteen Administrations, 1785-1955. Robert P. Brooks. LC 56-7979. 260p. 1956. 15.00 (ISBN 0-8203-0195-7). U of Ga Pr.

University of Hard Knocks. Ralph Parlette. 1966. standard ed. 6.95 (ISBN 0-915720-05-1); graduation ed. 6.95 (ISBN 0-915720-03-5). Brownlow Pub Co.

University of Illinois. Barth Falkenberg. (Illus.). 112p. 1988. 35.00 (ISBN 0-916509-19-2); deluxe ed. 125.00. Harmony Hse Pub LO.

University of Illinois Administrator Evaluation Project Report: 1975-1977. Peter E. Yankwich. 776p. 1979. pap. 22.50 (ISBN 0-252-00839-1). U of Ill Pr.

University of Illinois Football: The Fighting Illini. Lon Eubanks. LC 76-7853. (College Sports Ser.). 1976. 12.95 (ISBN 0-87397-065-9). Strode.

University of Iowa. Photos by Jim Richardson. (First Edition Ser.). (Illus.). 112p. 1988. 35.00 (ISBN 0-916509-32-X); deluxe ed. 125.00 slipcased. Harmony Hse Pub LO.

University of Iowa Football: The Hawkeyes. Chuck Bright. LC 82-50031. (College Sports Ser.). 1982. 10.95 (ISBN 0-87397-233-3). Strode.

University of Kansas: A History. Clifford S. Griffin. LC 73-12349. (Illus.). xiv, 810p. 1974. 25.00x (ISBN 0-7006-0106-6). U Pr of KS.

University of Kentucky: The Maturing Years. Charles G. Talbert. LC 65-11827. (Illus.). 224p. 1965. 18.00 (ISBN 0-8131-1095-5). U Pr of Ky.

University of Life. Mehdi N. Bahadori. (Illus.). 83p. (Orig.). (YA) (gr. 12). 1988. pap. 6.95 (ISBN 0-9620384-0-7). M N Bahadori.

University of Maine at Farmington. Richard Mallett. LC 74-20199. (Illus.). 304p. 1975. 10.95 (ISBN 0-87027-157-1); pap. 6.95 (ISBN 0-87027-158-X). Cumberland Pr.

University of Melborune - Nucleus Multi-Electrode Cochlear Implant. G. M. Clark et al. (Advances in Oto-Rhino-Laryngology Ser.: Vol. 38). (Illus.). x, 190p. 1987. 89.50 (ISBN 3-8055-4575-4). S Karger.

University of Melbourne: An Illustrated Perspective. John Bechervaise. (Illus.). 86p. 1985. 12.50 (ISBN 0-522-84295-X, Pub. by Melbourne U Pr). Intl Spec Bk.

University of Miami. Photos by Brian Smith. (First Edition Ser.). (Illus.). 112p. 1988. 35.00 (ISBN 0-916509-34-6); deluxe ed. 125.00 slipcased. Harmony Hse Pub LO.

University of Miami Dictionary, English-Spanish - Spanish-English. 2nd ed. Ed. by Maria E. Alvarez del Real. LC 81-71536. 512p. 1986. pap. text ed. 3.75x (ISBN 8-459910-45-8). Editorial Amer.

University of Miami Hispanic-American Studies. facs. ed. Miami University - Hispanic American Institute. Ed. by R. E. McNicoll & J. R. Owre. LC 70-117825. (Essay Index Reprint Ser). 1941. 20.00 (ISBN 0-8369-1997-1). Ayer Co Pubs.

University of Miami Law Center's Philip E. Heckerling Institute on Estate Planning: Twentieth Annual Institute. Ed. by John T. Gaubatz. 1986. looseleaf 80.00 (755); Updates. 1985 69.00; 1986 74.50. Bender.

University of Michigan: A Pictorial History. Ruth B. Bordin. LC 66-17029. (Illus.). 1967. 6.50 (ISBN 0-472-16400-7). U of Mich Pr.

University of Michigan Trivia. Susan K. McCann. LC 86-60715. (Illus.). 194p. (Orig.). 1986. pap. 7.95 (ISBN 0-933341-48-2). Quinlan Pr.

University of Missouri: An Illustrated History. James C. Olson & Vera B. Olson. LC 88-1158. (Illus.). 320p. 1988. 29.95 (ISBN 0-8262-0678-6). U of Mo Pr.

University of Missouri Studies: A Quarterly of Research. Ed. by Robert J. Kerner. 77p. 1980. Repr. of 1927 ed. lib. bdg. 22.50 (ISBN 0-8495-5409-8). Arden Lib.

University of Montana: A Pictorial History. Stan B. Cohen & Don C. Miller. LC 80-53616. (Illus.). 96p. 1980. pap. 5.95 (ISBN 0-933126-12-3). Pictorial Hist.

University of Newark Law Review: 1936-1942, Vols. 1-7. Bound set. 85.00x (ISBN 0-686-90084-7). Rothman.

University of North Carolina at Chapel Hill: The First 200 Years. Ed. by Hugh Norton, Jr. & Jane Collins. LC 87-71526. (Illus.). 160p. 1987. write for info. (ISBN 0-917631-04-8). Capitol Broadcasting.

University of North Carolina Studies in the Germanic Language & Literatures, 52 vols. North Carolina University. Repr. of 1949 ed. Set. 1452.00 (ISBN 0-404-50900-2). AMS Pr.

University of Northern Iowa Department of Art Annual Faculty Exhibition. Daniel E. Stetson. Ed. by Kevin Boatright. LC 82-50565. 16p. (Orig.). 1982. pap. text ed. 2.00. U of NI Dept Art.

University of Notre Dame. Ed. by William Strode. (First Edition Ser.). (Illus.). 112p. 1988. 35.00 (ISBN 0-916509-35-4); deluxe ed. 125.00 slipcased. Harmony Hse Pub LO.

University of Notre Dame: A Contemporary Portrait. Robert Schmuhl. LC 86-40246. 160p. 1986. text ed. 16.95x (ISBN 0-268-01916-9). U of Notre Dame Pr.

University of Notre Dame: A Contemporary Portrait. rev. ed. Robert Schmuhl. (Illus.). 1988. pap. text ed. 9.95x (ISBN 0-268-01918-5). U of Notre Dame Pr.

University of Notre Dame: A Portrait of Its History & Campus. Thomas J. Schlereth. LC 74-27890. 1976. pap. text ed. 9.95x (ISBN 0-268-01905-3). U of Notre Dame Pr.

University of Oklahoma & World War II: A Personal Account, 1941-1946. George L. Cross. LC 80-16934. (Illus.). 320p. 1980. 19.95 (ISBN 0-8061-1662-5). U of Okla Pr.

University of Oregon Centennial Lectures, 3 vols. B. Jessup et al. 1959. pap. 2.50 boxed (ISBN 0-87114-008-X). U of Oreg Bks.

University of Oregon Charter. George N. Belknap. 1976. pap. 1.25 (ISBN 0-87114-081-0). U of Oreg Bks.

University of Papua New Guinea: A Case Study in the Sociology of Higher Education. V. Lynn Meek. LC 81-14727. (Scholars' Library). (Illus.). 263p. 1982. text ed. 37.50x (ISBN 0-7022-1638-0). U of Queensland Pr.

University of Pennsylvania Law Review: 1852-1986, 134 vols. Bound set. 5408.00x (ISBN 0-686-90085-5). Rothman.

University of Reading. Percy N. Ure & Annie D. Ure. (Corpus Vasorum Antiquorum, Great Britain: Fasc. 12, Reading, Fasc. 1). (Illus.). 61p. 1954. portfolio bdg. 40.00 (ISBN 0-85672-600-1, Pub. by British Acad). Longwood Pub Group.

University of Rhode Island 1975 Accident Report. John McAniff. 1977. 2.00 (ISBN 0-916974-14-6). NAUI.

University of Rochester. Photos by Ira Block. (First Edition Ser.). (Illus.). 112p. 1988. 35.00 (ISBN 0-916509-36-2); deluxe ed. 125.00 slipcased. Harmony Hse Pub LO.

University of San Francisco. Photos by Phil Schermeister. (Illus.). 112p. 1987. 35.00 (ISBN 0-916509-24-9); deluxe ed. 125.00 deluxe slipcased. Harmony Hse Pub LO.

University of San Francisco Law Review: 1966-1986, 20 vols. Bound set. 690.00x (ISBN 0-686-90086-3). Rothman.

University of Santa Clara: A History, 1851-1977. Gerald McKevitt. LC 78-65396. (Illus.). 1979. 32.50x (ISBN 0-8047-1024-4). Stanford U Pr.

University of South Carolina: Volume 1, South Carolina College, Vol. 1. Daniel W. Hollis. LC 52-195. xiv, 346p. 1951. 22.95 (ISBN 0-87249-032-7). U of SC Pr.

University of Southern California. Photos by Bob Holmes. (Illus.). 112p. 1987. 35.00 (ISBN 0-916509-26-5); deluxe ed. 125.00 deluxe slipcased (ISBN 0-317-57501-5). Harmony Hse Pub LO.

University of Spiritualism. Harry Boddington. 59.95 (ISBN 0-8490-1248-1). Gordon Pr.

University of Tennessee, Memphis 75th Anniversary: Medical Accomplishments. James E. Hammer, III. LC 86-16170. (Illus.). 320p. 1986. 25.00 (ISBN 0-9616311-3-9). Univ TN Alumni.

University of Texas Medical Branch at Galveston: A Seventy-five Year History. Medical Branch of The University of Texas. (Illus.). 457p. 1967. 22.50x (ISBN 0-292-73697-5). U of Tex Pr.

University of the Word. Dick Eastman. LC 83-17763. 1983. pap. 3.95 (ISBN 0-8307-0903-7, 5018301). Regal.

University of the World see Universidade da Palavra.

University of Toronto Doctoral Theses, 1897-1967: A Bibliography. Judy Mills & Irene Dombre. LC 75-354611. pap. 49.30 (ISBN 0-317-41719-3, 2055822). Bks Demand UMI.

University of Toulouse in the Middle Ages. Cyril E. Smith. 1959. 19.00 (ISBN 0-87462-402-9). Marquette.

University of Tulsa: A History, Eighteen Eighty-Two to Nineteen Seventy-Two. Guy Logsdon. LC 76-54950. (Oklahoma Horizons Ser.: Vol. 1). (Illus.). 358p. 1977. 16.95x (ISBN 0-8061-1397-9). U of Okla Pr.

University of Utah Anthropological Papers, 81 vols. Utah. University. Department of Anthropology. Incl. Glen Canyon Series, 32 vols. Repr. of 1966 ed. Set. 1089.00 (ISBN 0-404-60630-X); Upper Colorado Series, 9 vols. Repr. of 1963 ed. Set. 252.00 (ISBN 0-404-60670-9); Nubian Series, 4 vols. Repr. of 1969 ed. Set. 116.50 (ISBN 0-404-60690-3); Miscellaneous Collected Papers, 4 vols. Repr. of 1967 ed. Set. 93.50 (ISBN 0-404-60700-4). LC 78-123. Repr. of 1973 ed. Set. 2425.00 (ISBN 0-404-60600-8). AMS Pr.

University of Vermont Baily-Howe Library Folklore & Oral History Catalogue. Intro. by Connell B. Gallagher. 58p. (Orig.). 1981. pap. text ed. 5.00x (ISBN 0-944277-07-1). U VT Ctr Rsch VT.

University of Vermont Graduate College Theses on Vermont Topics in Arts & Sciences. Compiled by Kristin Peterson-Ishaq. (Occasional Papers, Supplement to No. 1). 30p. (Orig.). 1982. pap. text ed. 2.50x (ISBN 0-944277-08-X). U VT Ctr Rsch VT.

University of Vermont Student Research on Vermont Topics. Ed. by Carolyn Perry. (Occasional Papers: No. 1). 66p. (Orig.). 1979. pap. text ed. 2.50x (ISBN 0-944277-02-0). U VT Ctr Rsch VT.

University of Washington Multidisciplinary Pain Center: Theory & Practice in the Management of Current Pain. Ed. by John D. Loeser & Kelly J. Egan. 1988. text ed. price not set (ISBN 0-88167-464-8). Raven.

University of Washington Nursing Simulations: The Family Nurse Practitioner: Women's Health Care. Delecki et al. 1987. Ten Apple disks & resource manuals. price not set (ISBN 0-7216-1795-6); Five IBM PC disks, resource manual, 128 K, & disk drive. price not set (ISBN 0-7216-1793-X). Saunders.

University of Western Ontario. John De Visser. (First Edition Ser.). (Illus.). 112p. 1988. 35.00 (ISBN 0-916509-38-9); deluxe ed. 125.00 slipcased. Harmony Hse Pub LO.

University of Wisconsin-Madison & the Local & State Economies: A Second Look. William A. Strang et al. 1985. pap. 10.00 (ISBN 0-86603-019-0). Bur Busn Wis.

University of Wisconsin Medical School: A Chronicle, 1848-1948. Paul F. Clark. (Illus.). 286p. 1967. 19.95 (ISBN 0-299-04350-9). U of Wis Pr.

University of Wisconsin: One Hundred & Twenty-Five Years. Ed. by Allan G. Bogue & Robert Taylor. LC 74-27306. (Illus.). 302p. 1975. 17.50x (ISBN 0-299-06840-4). U of Wis Pr.

University on Trial. Robert Dentler. 1983. text ed. 31.00 (ISBN 0-89011-588-5). Abt Bks.

University on Trial: The Case of the University of North Carolina. Robert A. Dentler et al. 212p. 1984. Repr. of 1983 ed. lib. bdg. 32.75 (ISBN 0-8191-4083-X). U Pr of Amer.

University Optics, 2 vols. D. W. Tenquist et al. 1970. Set. 175.00 (ISBN 0-677-62090-X); Vol. 1, 350p. 99.00 (ISBN 0-677-62070-5); Vol. 2, 390p. 99.00x (ISBN 0-677-62080-2). Gordon & Breach.

University Organization: A Matrix Analysis of the Academic Professions. James L. Bess. LC 81-8127. 334p. 1982. 34.95 (ISBN 0-89885-036-3). Human Sci Pr.

University Outside Europe. facsimile ed. Ed. by Edward Bradby. LC 71-107684. (Essay Index Reprint Ser.). 1939. 20.00 (ISBN 0-8369-1548-8). Ayer Co Pubs.

University Physics. George Arfken. 1984. text ed. 34.00 (ISBN 0-12-059860-4); student's solution manual 8.00 (ISBN 0-12-059867-1); study guide 10.00 (ISBN 0-12-059868-X); instr's. manual 2.00 (ISBN 0-12-059865-5); transparency masters 50.00 (ISBN 0-12-059870-1). Acad Pr.

University Physics. Alvin Hudson & Rex Nelson. 975p. 1982. text ed. 37.00 net (ISBN 0-15-592960-7, HC); instr's. manual avail. (ISBN 0-15-592961-5); net study guide 12.00 (ISBN 0-15-592962-3). HarBraceJ.

University Physics. 6th ed. Francis W. Sears et al. LC 81-17551. (Physics Ser.). (Illus.). 900p. 1982. write for info. study guide (ISBN 0-201-07224-6); solutions guide o.p. 9.95 (ISBN 0-201-07225-4); answer book o.p. 1.00 (ISBN 0-201-07226-2). Addison-Wesley.

University Physics. 7th ed. Francis W. Sears et al. LC 85-28801. (Illus.). 976p. 1987. write for info. (ISBN 0-201-06681-5); Vol. I. write for info. (ISBN 0-201-06682-3); Vol. II. write for info. (ISBN 0-201-06683-1); write for info. study guide (ISBN 0-201-06684-X); write for info. solutions manual (ISBN 0-201-06686-6); write for info. answer book (ISBN 0-201-06685-8). Addison-Wesley.

University Physics I. Kenneth Jesse. 306p. 1988. pap. 10.95 (ISBN 0-15-601668-0, BFP). HarBraceJ.

University Physics: International Edition. George Arfken. 1984. 20.00 (ISBN 0-12-059858-2). Acad Pr.

University Physics Two. Kenneth E. Jesse. (College Outline Ser.). 350p. 1988. pap. 10.95 (ISBN 0-15-601685-0). HarBraceJ.

University Piano Series, 4 bks. Hershal Pyle. 1964. Bk. 1. pap. 6.25 (ISBN 0-87506-019-6); Bk. 2. pap. 6.25 (ISBN 0-87506-020-X); Bk. 3. pap. 4.75 (ISBN 0-87506-021-8); Bk, 4. pap. 4.75 (ISBN 0-87506-022-6). Campus.

University (Pictorial) Phil Davis. LC 67-30753. 1967. 14.95 (ISBN 0-472-27900-9). U of Mich Pr.

University Portrait: Nine Paintings. Carolyn G. Plochmann. 1959. 6.95x (ISBN 0-8093-0022-2). S Ill U Pr.

University Problems in the United States. Daniel C. Gilman. LC 75-89182. (American Education: Its Men, Institutions & Ideas, Ser. 1). 1969. Repr. of 1898 ed. 15.00 (ISBN 0-405-01419-8). Ayer Co Pubs.

University Problems in the United States. Daniel C. Gilman. 1972. Repr. of 1898 ed. lib. bdg. 29.00 (ISBN 0-8422-8058-8). Irvington.

University Problems in the United States. Daniel C. Gilman. 1971. Repr. 32.00 (ISBN 0-384-18562-2). Johnson Repr.

University Professor John M. Dorsey. John M. Dorsey. LC 79-25046. (Illus.). 280p. 1980. 25.00x (ISBN 0-8143-1645-X). Wayne St U Pr.

University Programs in Ground Water Science. 1987. 5.00 (ISBN 0-318-23035-6). Natl Water Well.

University Reform of Tsar Alexander I, 1802-1835. James T. Flynn. xiv, 283p. 1988. 39.95x (ISBN 0-8132-0653-7). Cath U Pr.

University Research Park: The First Twenty Years. Dean W. Colvard et al. 128p. 1988. 19.95 (ISBN 0-945344-00-7). UNC Charlotte Urban Inst.

University Research: Social & Political Implications: A Bibliography. Ed. by Joan Nordquist. (Contemporary Social Issues: A Bibliographic Ser.: No. 3). 1986. pap. text ed. 15.00 (ISBN 0-937855-05-7). Ref Rsch Serv.

University Research System: The Public Policies of the Home of Scientists. Ed. by Bjorn Wittrock & Aant Elzinga. 220p. (Orig.). 1985. pap. text ed. 33.00x (ISBN 91-22-00743-1, Pub. by Almqvist & Wiksell). Coronet Bks.

University Roles in Inservice Education: Planning for Change. Lou M. Carey & David D. Marsh. 102p. (Orig.). 1980. pap. text ed. write for info. (ISBN 0-89333-018-3). AACTE.

University Science & Engineering Libraries. 2nd ed. Ellis Mount. LC 84-6530. (Contributions in Librarianship & Information Science Ser.: No. 49). (Illus.). x, 303p. 1985. lib. bdg. 36.95 (ISBN 0-313-23949-5, MOU/). Greenwood.

University Student: A Study of Behavior & Values. Charles D. Bolton & Kenneth C. Kammeyer. 1967. 15.95x (ISBN 0-8084-0307-9); pap. 11.95x (ISBN 0-8084-0308-7). New Coll U Pr.

University Student: Background Profile & Stance. Krishna Chakrabortty. 1985. 10.00x (ISBN 0-8364-1480-2, Pub. by KP Bagchi India). South Asia Bks.

University Students & African Politics. Ed. by William J. Hanna. LC 73-89778. 400p. 1975. 35.00 (ISBN 0-8419-0145-7, Africana). Holmes & Meier.

University Students & Revolution in Cuba, 1920-1968. Jaime Suchlicki. LC 69-19866. 1969. 10.95 (ISBN 0-87024-108-7). U of Miami Pr.

University Teacher & His World. Richard Startup. 192p. 1979. text ed. 33.25x (ISBN 0-566-00295-7). Gower Pub Co.

University Teacher As Artist. 1st ed. Joseph Axelrod. LC 73-3773. (Jossey-Bass Series in Higher Education). pap. 65.50 (ISBN 0-317-42098-4, 2052159). Bks Demand UMI.

University Without Walls: Correspondence Education in India. Satyapal Anand. 69p. 1979. text ed. 15.00x (ISBN 0-7069-0826-0, Pub. by Vikas India). Advent NY.

University Work of the United Lutheran Church in America: A Study of the Work Among Lutheran Students at Non-Lutheran Institutions. Howard M. Le Sourd. LC 70-176990. (Columbia University. Teachers College. Contributions to Education: No. 377). Repr. of 1929 ed. 22.50 (ISBN 0-404-55377-X). AMS Pr.

Universo, Vida, Intelecto. I. S. Shklovski. 383p. (Span.). 1977. 5.95 (ISBN 0-8285-1700-2, Pub. by Mir Pubs USSR). Imported Pubns.

Universoty of the WORD see Universite de la Parole.

UNIX, 2 vols. Bell Labs Staff. 1983. Vol. 1, 208 p. pap. 37.45 (ISBN 0-03-061742-1); Vol. II, 320 p. pap. 37.45 (ISBN 0-03-061743-X). HR&W.

UNIX: A Minimal Manual. Jim Moore. 200p. 1988. pap. 16.95t (ISBN 0-7167-8195-6). W H Freeman.

UNIX: A Practical Introduction for Users. R. J. Whiddett et al. LC 85-16401. (Computers & Their Applications Ser.). 195p. 1985. pap. 22.95 (ISBN 0-470-20233-5). Halsted Pr.

UNIX Ada. Narain Gehani. (Illus.). 368p. 1987. pap. text ed. 28.00 (ISBN 0-13-938325-5). P-H.

UNIX Administration Guide for System V. Rebecca Thomas & Rik Farrow. (Illus.). 500p. 1988. pap. 34.95 (ISBN 0-13-942889-5). P-H.

UNIX: An Introduction for Computer Users. Silvester. 200p. 1984. write for info. (ISBN 0-471-90205-5). Wiley.

UNIX & XENIX: A Step by Step Approach for Micros. D. W. Topham & H. Trong. (Illus.). 528p. 1985. pap. 21.95 (ISBN 0-89303-918-7). Brady Comp Bks.

Unix & Xenix Demystified. Lee P. Clukey. LC 85-2658. (Illus.). 250p. 1985. 21.95 (ISBN 0-8306-0874-5, 1874); pap. 16.95 (ISBN 0-8306-1874-0, 1874P). TAB Bks.

Unix Applications Software Directory. 3rd ed ed. Ray A. Jones. 380p. pap. 60.00 (ISBN 0-936491-00-0). Onager Pub.

UNIX C Language Programming. Arthur. 1988. write for info. (ISBN 0-471-83963-9). Wiley.

UNIX C Shell Field Guide. Gail Anderson & Paul Anderson. (Illus.). 374p. 1986. pap. text ed. 28.95 (ISBN 0-13-937468-X). P-H.

UNIX Command Reference Guide: The Top 50 UNIX Commands-What They Are, How They Work, How To Use Them. Kaare Christian. LC 87-20969. 1987. pap. 23.95 (ISBN 0-471-85580-4). Wiley.

UNIX Command Summary System III. Rev. ed. Specialized Systems Consultants. 32p. 1983. pap. 6.00 (ISBN 0-916151-01-8). Specialized Sys.

UNIX Command Summary (System V) Specialized Systems Consultants. 48p. (Orig.). 1984. pap. 6.00 (ISBN 0-916151-09-3). Specialized Sys.

UNIX Communications. The Waite Group. 350p. 1987. pap. 26.95 (ISBN 0-672-22511-5). Sams.

UNIX Dictionary. Christian. LC 88-14208. 1988. 24.95 (ISBN 0-471-60929-3); pap. 16.95 (ISBN 0-471-60931-5). Wiley.

UNIX Environment. Andy Walker. LC 84-13046. 151p. 1984. pap. 21.95 (ISBN 0-471-90564-X). Wiley.

UNIX for Beginners: A Step-by-Step Introduction. Byran Strong & Josy Hosler. LC 84-29138. 385p. 1987. pap. 29.95 (ISBN 0-471-80666-8, Pub. by Wiley-Interscience). Wiley.

UNIX for Beginners: Basic Word Processing Skills with ED. Bryan Strong & Jay Hosler. 450p. 1988. pap. 22.95 (ISBN 0-471-80664-1, Pub. by Wiley-Interscience); Primer. pap. write for info. (ISBN 0-471-80665-X). Wiley.

UNIX for People. Patrick Brown & John Muster. 1984. pap. text ed. 35.00 (ISBN 0-13-937442-6). P-H.

Unix for Programmers. Daniel Farkas. 350p. 1987. pap. 22.95 (ISBN 0-471-83812-8). Wiley.

UNIX for Programmers: An Introduction. Daniel Farkas. LC 87-29824. 381p. 1988. 29.95 (ISBN 0-471-83799-7). Wiley.

Unix for Super-Users. Eric Foxley. 213p. 1985. pap. text ed. write for info. (ISBN 0-201-14228-7). Addison-Wesley.

UNIX for the IBM-PC. Paul M. Chirlian. 192p. 1987. pap. text ed. 19.95 (ISBN 0-675-20785-1). Merrill.

UNIX in a Nutshell: Berkeley Edition. 2nd ed. (Nutshell Handbooks (For Beginning & Advanced Users)). 290p. 1987. pap. 19.50 (ISBN 0-937175-20-X). O'Reilly & Assocs.

UNIX in a Nutshell: System V Edition. 2nd ed. (Nutshell Handbooks (For Beginning & Advanced Users)). 275p. 1987. pap. 19.50 (ISBN 0-937175-19-6). O'Reilly & Assocs.

Unix Internals: A Systems Operations Handbook. Myril C. Shaw & Susan S. Shaw. (Illus.). 320p. 1987. pap. 17.95 (ISBN 0-8306-2951-3). TAB Bks.

Unix-Like Utility Package for MS-DOS. Allen Holub. 60p. 1986. pap. 29.95 (ISBN 0-934375-12-7). M & T Pub Inc.

Unix Markets. 183p. 1984. 1285.00x (ISBN 0-88694-626-3). Intl Res Dev.

UNIX nroff-troff: A User's Guide. Kevin P. Roddy. LC 85-27223. 362p. 1987. pap. text ed. write for info. HR&W.

UNIX Operating System. 2nd ed. Kaare Christian. (Illus.). 450p. 1988. pap. 22.95 (ISBN 0-471-84781-X). Wiley.

UNIX Operating System. 2nd. ed. Kaare Christian. LC 87-34560. 455p. 1988. 29.95 (ISBN 0-471-84782-8). Wiley.

UNIX Papers. The Waite Group. 576p. 1987. 26.95 (ISBN 0-672-22578-6). Sams.

UNIX: Power User's Guide. Stephen Mikes. 500p. 1988. pap. text ed. 22.95 (ISBN 0-07-881423-5). Osborne-McGraw.

UNIX Primer. Ann N. Lomuto & Nico Lomuto. (P-H Software Ser.). (Illus.). 256p. 1983. pap. text ed. 28.95 (ISBN 0-13-937731-X). P-H.

UNIX Primer Plus. Waite Group. LC 83-60162. 416p. 1983. pap. 22.95 (ISBN 0-672-22028-8, 22028). Sams.

UNIX Products Directory: Summer 1986 Edition. 6th ed. 1000p. 1987. cancelled. USR Group.

UNIX Products Directory: Winter 1986 Edition. 5th ed. 984p. 1986. pap. 10.00 (ISBN 0-936593-00-8). USR Group.

UNIX Products Directory: 1987 Edition. 6th ed. 576p. 1987. 50.00 (ISBN 0-936593-02-4). USR Group.

UNIX Products for Europe, 1985. 200p. 1985. pap. 45.00 (ISBN 0-387-15906-1). Springer-Verlag.

UNIX Programmer's Manual, Vol. 1. AT&T Staff. 560p. 1986. pap. text ed. 28.95 (ISBN 0-03-009317-1, HoltC). HR&W.

UNIX Programmer's Manual, Vol. 2. AT&T Staff. 512p. pap. text ed. 28.95 (ISBN 0-03-009314-7, HoltC). HR&W.

UNIX Programmer's Manual, Vol. 3. AT&T Staff. 160p. 1986. pap. text ed. 19.95 (ISBN 0-03-009313-9, HoltC). HR&W.

UNIX Programmer's Manual, Vol. 4. AT&T Staff. 1986. pap. text ed. 28.95 (ISBN 0-317-47172-4, HoltC). HR&W.

UNIX Programmer's Manual, Vol. 5. AT&T Staff. 1986. pap. text ed. 37.95 (ISBN 0-317-47175-9, HoltC). HR&W.

UNIX Programming Environment. Brian W. Kernighan & Robert Pike. LC 83-62851. (P-H Software Ser.). 368p. 1984. text ed. 33.33 (ISBN 0-13-937699-2); pap. text ed. 24.95 (ISBN 0-13-937681-X). P-H.

UNIX Programming: Methods & Tools. James F. Peters, III. 447p. 1988. pap. text ed. 20.00 (ISBN 0-15-593021-4, HC); instr's. manual 6.00 (ISBN 0-15-593022-2). HarBraceJ.

UNIX Programming on the 80286-80386. Alan Deikman. (Illus.). 352p. (Orig.). 1988. pap. 24.95 (ISBN 0-934375-83-6); pap. 39.95 incl. disk (ISBN 0-934375-91-7). M & T Pub Inc.

UNIX-R System Readings & Applications, Vol. II. AT&T Bell Laboratories Staff. (Illus.). 352p. 1987. pap. text ed. 19.00 (ISBN 0-13-939845-7). P-H.

Unkonventionelle Rheumatherapie. Ed. by A Weintraub et al. (Fortbildungskurse fuer Rheumatologie: Vol. 7). (Illus.). viii, 192p. (Ger.). 1985. pap. 50.00 (ISBN 3-8055-4005-1). S Karger.

Unlacing: Ten Irish-American Women Poets. Tess Gallagher et al. Ed. by Patricia Monaghan. 128p. 1987. pap. 7.95 (ISBN 0-914221-09-4). Fireweed Pr AK.

Unladylike & Unprofessional: Academic Women & Academic Unions (MLA Commission on the Status of Women in the Profession) Ed. by Elaine Reuben & Leonore Hoffmann. vi, 54p. (Orig.). 1975. pap. 9.00 (ISBN 0-87352-327-X, B86). Modern Lang.

Unlawful Gain & Legitimate Profit in Islamic Law: Riba, Gharar, & Islamic Banking. Nabil A. Saleh. LC 85-25547. (Studies in Islamic Civilization). 1986. 37.50 (ISBN 0-521-32298-7). Cambridge U Pr.

Unlawful Sex: Offences, Victims & Offenders in the Criminal Justice System of England & Wales. Howard League for Penal Reform, London, UK. (Waterlow's Legal & Social Policy Library). 264p. 1985. pap. 15.25 (ISBN 0-08-039220-2, Pub. by Waterlow). Pergamon.

Unlearned Language: New Studies in Xenoglossy. Ian Stevenson. LC 83-12525. 223p. 1984. 17.50x (ISBN 0-8139-0994-5). U Pr of Va.

Unlearned Lessons: Current & Past Reforms for School Improvement. Barbara Z. Presseisen. LC 85-29659. 258p. 1986. 31.00x (ISBN 1-85000-079-4, Falmer Pr); pap. 14.00x (ISBN 1-85000-080-8). Taylor & Francis.

Unlearning "Indian" Stereotypes. Council on Interracial Books for Children, Inc. Staff. LC 77-88826. 56p. 1977. pap. 4.95 (ISBN 0-930040-36-8). CIBC.

Unlearning the Lie: Sexism in School. Barbara G. Harrison. 1973. 6.95 (ISBN 0-87140-559-8). Liveright.

Unleash the Tremendous Potential Within You & Achieve the Success You've Always Dreamed Of! Bill W. Wayman. 190p. 1987. pap. 10.95 (ISBN 0-941155-01-3). Positive Liv Pubns.

Unleashing Multiplan. Daniel Sueltz & Bruce Kinder. 1984. pap. 14.95 (ISBN 0-13-937210-5). P-H.

Unleashing SuperCalc. Daniel Sueltz & Bruce Kinder. 1984. 22.95 (ISBN 0-13-937269-5); pap. 14.95. P-H.

Unleashing the Church. Frank R. Tillapaugh. LC 82-9783. 1985. pap. 7.95 (ISBN 0-8307-1024-8, 5418433). Regal.

Unleashing the Church: Leader's Guide. Bob Massie. (Regal Study & Grow Electives Ser.). 64p. 1985. 3.95 (ISBN 0-8307-1020-5, 6102049). Regal.

Unleashing the Power of Lotus. Roger J. Seymour. 1988. pap. 21.95 (ISBN 0-13-510181-6). Brady Comp Bks.

Unleashing the Right Side of the Brain: The LARC Creativity Program. Robert Williams & John Stockmyer. 128p. 1987. pap. 9.95 (ISBN 0-8289-0620-3). Penguin.

Unleashing the Right Side of the Brain: The LARC Creativity Program. Robert Williams & John Stockmyer. 1987. pap. 9.95 (ISBN 0-317-61853-9). Greene.

Unleashing the Wild Physique: Ultimate Bodybuilding for Men & Women. Vince Gironda & Robert Kennedy. LC 84-8451. (Illus.). 192p. 1984. pap. 9.95 (ISBN 0-8069-7888-0). Sterling.

Unleashing VisiCalc. Daniel Sueltz & Bruce Kinder. 1984. pap. 14.95 (ISBN 0-13-937277-6). P-H.

Unleashing Your Potential: Discovering Your God-Given Opportunities for Ministry. Frank R. Tillapaugh. Ed. by Earl Roe. 244p. (Orig.). 1988. pap. 7.95 (ISBN 0-8307-1186-4, 5418972). Regal.

Unleavened Bread. Robert Grant. LC 68-20014. (Americans in Fiction Ser.). 431p. Repr. of 1900 ed. lib. bdg. 29.00 (ISBN 0-8398-0665-5). Irvington.

Unleavened Bread. Robert Grant. 431p. 1986. pap. text ed. 6.95x (ISBN 0-8290-2046-2). Irvington.

Unleaving. Jill Paton Walsh. LC 76-8857. 160p. (gr. 7 up). 1976. 9.95 (ISBN 0-374-38042-2). FS&G.

Unleaving. Jill P. Walsh. (YA) (gr. 7 up). 1986. pap. 1.95 (ISBN 0-380-01785-7, 59360-2, Flare). Avon.

Unless Haste Is Made: A French Skeptic's Account of the Sandwich Islands in 1836. Theodore-Adolphe Barrot. Ed. by Penny Pagliaro. Tr. by Daniel Dole from Fr. LC 77-27597. Orig. Title: Visit of the French Frigate Sloop of War to the Sandwich Islands, 1836. (Illus.). 1978. 10.00 (ISBN 0-916630-05-6); pap. 4.95 (ISBN 0-916630-04-8). Pr Pacifica.

Unless I See. John W. Bowman. LC 76-42859. (Illus.). 1977. pap. 8.00 (ISBN 0-89430-002-4). Palos Verdes.

Unless One Is Born Anew. Dorothy Hutchinson. LC 65-26994. (Orig.). 1965. pap. 2.50x (ISBN 0-87574-143-6, 143). Pendle Hill.

Unless Soul Clap Its Hands: Portraits & Passages. Erika Duncan. 160p. 1984. 17.95 (ISBN 0-8052-3916-2). Schocken.

Unless You Become Like a Little Child. Jean Gill. 88p. (Orig.). 1985. pap. 4.95 (ISBN 0-8091-2717-2). Paulist Pr.

Unless You Believe, You Shall Not Understand: Logic, University, & Society in Late Medieval Vienna. Michael H. Shank. 355p. 1988. text ed. 35.00 (ISBN 0-691-05523-8). Princeton U Pr.

Unlikely Beginnings. Gerald H. Bidlack. LC 82-90984. 1984. 10.95 (ISBN 0-87212-164-X). Libra.

Unlikely Cast: Dramatic Monologues for Advent. Alan E. Siewert. 1976. pap. 3.50 (ISBN 0-89536-245-7, 2107). CSS of Ohio.

Unlikely Catechism: Some Challenges for the Creedless Catholic. William Reiser. 184p. (Orig.). 1985. pap. 6.95 (ISBN 0-8091-2706-7). Paulist Pr.

Unlikely Firemaster. 170p. 1968. pap. 5.25 (ISBN 0-685-46046-0, FSP-31). Natl Fire Prot.

Unlikely Heroines: Nineteenth-Century Women Writers & the Woman Question. Ann R. Shapiro. LC 86-22750. (Contributions in Women's Studies: No. 81). 163p. 1987. lib. bdg. 29.95 (ISBN 0-313-25422-2, SUH/). Greenwood.

Unlikely Liberators: The Men of the 100th & the 442nd. Masayo U. Duus. Tr. by Peter Duus from Japanese. LC 87-6013. (Illus.). 288p. 1987. 19.95 (ISBN 0-8248-1081-3). UH Pr.

Unlikely Meeting see Sentimental Talks.

Unlikely Ones. Mary Brown. 432p. 1986. text ed. 15.95 (ISBN 0-07-008296-0). McGraw.

Unlikely Ones. Mary Brown. 1987. 3.95 (ISBN 0-671-65361-X). Baen Bks.

Unlikely Partners. Jacqueline Diamond. (American Romance Ser.: No. 218). 245p. Date not set. pap. 2.50 (ISBN 0-317-63713-4). Harlequin Bks.

Unlikely Stories, Mostly. Alisdair Gray. (Illus.). 280p. 1984. pap. 6.95 (ISBN 0-14-006925-9). Penguin.

Unlikely Warriors: General Benjamin H. Grierson & His Family. William H. Leckie & Shirley A. Leckie. LC 84-40275. (Illus.). 384p. 1984. 19.95 (ISBN 0-8061-1912-8). U of Okla Pr.

Unlimited Community: A Study of the Possibility of Social Science. Julius W. Friend & James K. Feibleman. LC 75-3144. Repr. of 1936 ed. 40.00 (ISBN 0-404-59152-3). AMS Pr.

Unlimited Dream Company. J. G. Ballard. 1985. pap. 4.50 (ISBN 0-671-60537-2). WSP.

Unlimited Power. Anthony Robbins. 1987. pap. 9.95 (ISBN 0-449-90280-3). Fawcett.

Unlimited Power: The New Science of Personal Achievement. Anthony Robbins. 327p. 1986. 17.95 (ISBN 0-671-61088-0). S&S.

Unlimited Purpose. Joshua K. Ogawa. 1986. pap. 3.50 (ISBN 9971-972-46-8). OMF Bks.

Unlimited You. Don Clowers. 146p. (Orig.). 1985. pap. text ed. 8.50 (ISBN 0-914307-31-2). Word Faith.

Unlisted Legion. Jock Purves. 1978. pap. 4.95 (ISBN 0-85151-245-3). Banner of Truth.

Unlisted Securities Market. J. Cucksey & D. Medland. (Waterlow Executive Bulletins Ser.). 72p. 1984. pap. 12.25 (ISBN 0-08-039197-4). Pergamon.

Unlit Lamp. Radclyffe Hall. LC 74-145067. 343p. 1972. Repr. of 1924 ed. 29.00 (ISBN 0-403-01010-1). Scholarly.

Unlit Lamp. Radclyffe Hall. 1988. Repr. of 1924 ed. lib. bdg. 80.00x. Am Biog Serv.

Unlock Your Bible. W. Brian Gee. (Illus.). 111p. 1988. pap. 9.95 (ISBN 0-89390-134-2). Resource Pubns.

Unlock Your Child's Potential: Through Ten Minutes a Day of Games & Activities. Dean L. Hummel & Carl McDaniels. 1982. pap. 8.95 (ISBN 0-87491-493-0). Acropolis.

Unlock Your Mind. Judy Hevenly. Ed. by Karnie Starrett. (Illus.). 1988. pap. 10.00 (ISBN 0-915157-00-4). Star Moon Pub.

Unlock Your Mind & Be Free! A Practical Approach to Hypnotherapy. Edgar Barnett. 153p. 1984. pap. 8.95 (ISBN 0-930298-49-7). Westwood Pub Co.

Unlock Your Potential: Know Your Brain & How to Use It. Margaret A. Golton. LC 82-2490. 80p. (Orig.). 1982. pap. 5.95 (ISBN 0-942952-00-6). Frank Pubns.

Unlocked Book: A Memoir of John Wilkes Booth by His Sister. Asia Clarke. LC 74-88533. (Illus.). 1938. 22.00 (ISBN 0-405-08363-7, Blom Pubns). Ayer Co Pubs.

Unlocking: A Guide to Creative Living. Daniel Sankowsky. 206p. (Orig.). 1987. lib. bdg. 24.50 (ISBN 0-8191-6519-0); pap. text ed. 12.75 (ISBN 0-8191-6520-4). U Pr of Amer.

Unlocking Doors to Friendship. C. Lynn Fox & Francine L. Weaver. LC 83-60148. (Creative Teaching Ser.). 150p. (Orig.). 1983. pap. 14.95 (ISBN 0-935266-14-3, MS-09). Jalmar Pr.

Unlocking Nature's Secrets: Recent Discoveries from the Natural World. Michael Bright. 206p. 1987. pap. 5.95 (ISBN 0-563-20322-6, Pub. by BBC). Parkwest Pubns.

Unlocking Nontraditional Careers. 1981. Set. 44.00 (ISBN 0-318-22281-7, RD215); Communication Skills, by Judith A. Sechler. 14.00 (ISBN 0-318-22282-5, RD215A); Enhancing Placement, by Judith A. Sechler. 20.00 (ISBN 0-318-22283-3, RD215B); Parent Awareness, by Vivien Canora. 5.10 (ISBN 0-318-22284-1, RD215C); Recruitment Skills, by Rodney K. Spain. 5.50 (ISBN 0-318-22285-X, RD215D). Natl Ctr Res Voc Ed.

Unlocking Omnis Three Plus-Express. David Swain. 1988. 24.95 (ISBN 0-13-936080-8). Brady Comp Bks.

Unlocking Personal Creativity: A Course in Idea Mapping. David D. Thornburg. (Illus.). 124p. (Orig.). 1986. pap. 8.95 (ISBN 0-942207-00-9). Innovision.

Unlocking Potential: College & Other Choices for Learning Disabled People--A Step-by-Step Guide. Barbara Scheiber & Jeanne Talpers. LC 86-14205. 195p. 1987. 27.95 (ISBN 0-917561-29-5); pap. 12.95 (ISBN 0-917561-30-9). Adler & Adler.

Unlocking Potential: College & Other Choices for Learning-Disabled People: A Step-By-Step Guide. Barbara Scheiber & Jeanne Talpers. 1987. 27.95 (4025); pap. 12.95 (4031). Am Assn Comm Jr Coll.

Unlocking Secrets of the Feminine: The Path Beyond Sexism. Kathleen Wagner. LC 86-61355. 148p. (Orig.). 1986. pap. 7.95 (ISBN 0-934134-79-0). Sheed & Ward MO.

Unlocking Shakespeare's Language: Help for the Teacher & Student. Randal Robinson. (Theory & Research into Practice Ser.). 1988. pap. 9.95 (ISBN 0-8141-5568-5). NCTE.

Unlocking the Cabinet: Cabinet Structures in Comparative Perspective. Thomas T. Mackie & Brian Hogwood. (Modern Politics Ser.: No. 10). 192p. (Orig.). 1986. pap. text ed. 17.95 (ISBN 0-8039-9725-6). Sage.

Unlocking the Doors of Your Heart: A New Look at Love. Russell M. Abata. LC 83-83442. 1984. pap. 4.95 (ISBN 0-89243-204-7). Liguori Pubns.

Unlocking the Family Door: A Systematic Approach to the Understanding & Treatment of Anorexia Nervosa. Helm Stierlin & Gunthard Weber. 240p. 1989. 25.00 (ISBN 0-87630-541-9). Brunner-Mazel.

Unlocking... the Illinois Lottery. Robert Serotic. 180p. 1988. pap. 4.95 (ISBN 0-941271-18-8). Lottery Systs Intl.

Unlocking the Mysteries of Creation. Dennis Petersen. (Illus.). 207p. 1988. 18.95 (ISBN 0-89051-137-3). Master Bks.

Unlocking the Mystery of How the Mind Creates Time: An Engineer's Analysis. Ernest Defoggi. (Illus.). 1979. 8.95 (ISBN 0-9602372-1-6). E Defoggi.

Unlocking the Mystery of Revelation. James H. Knotek. (Illus.). 145p. (Orig.). 1987. Set. deluxe tchrs.' ed. & 9 students guide 49.00 (ISBN 0-939925-07-9); pap. 5.95 (ISBN 0-939925-02-8); tchr's ed. 7.95 (ISBN 0-939925-03-6). R C Law & Co.

Unlocking the Mystery of the Force. Rev. ed. Frank Allnutt. LC 83-72138. 208p. 1983. pap. 2.95 (ISBN 0-934374-02-3). Allnutt Pub.

Unlocking... the New York Lottery. Robert Serotic. 160p. 1988. pap. 4.95 (ISBN 0-941271-24-2). Lottery Systs Intl.

Unlocking the Old Testament. Victor L. Ludlow. LC 81-68266. (Illus.). 239p. 1981. 8.95 (ISBN 0-87747-873-2). Deseret Bk.

Unlocking... the Pennsylvania Lottery. Robert Serotic. 160p. 1988. pap. 4.95 (ISBN 0-941271-26-9). Lottery Systs Intl.

Unlocking the People Puzzle. Vincent W. Kafka. 50p. 1988. pap. 11.95 (ISBN 0-913261-21-1). Effect Learn Sys.

Unlocking the Scriptures. Hans Finzel. 144p. 1986. 7.95 (ISBN 0-89693-276-1). Victor Bks.

Unlocking the Secrets of Research. Anita M. Meinbach & Liz C. Rothlein. 1986. pap. 9.95 (ISBN 0-673-18171-5). Scott F.

Unlocking the Stories Within You. Jewell R. Coburn. LC 86-70472. (Illus.). 141p. (Orig.). 1986. pap. text ed. 8.95 (ISBN 0-918060-05-2). Burn-Hart.

Unlocking Your Bowels for Better Health. Salem Kirban. 1981. pap. 5.00 (ISBN 0-912582-41-3). Kirban.

Unlocking Your Creative Gifts. Dan Zadra. (Value of Self-Esteem Ser.). 32p. Date not set. lib. bdg. 11.65 (ISBN 0-88682-157-6). Creative Ed.

Unlocking Your Potential. Dan Zadra. (Self-Esteem Ser.). 1987. lib. bdg. 11.65 (ISBN 0-88682-155-X). Creative Ed.

Unloosing Monsters: Plunging to the Depths of Human Wisdom. Fred Leavitt. LC 84-90338. 1984. 10.00 (ISBN 0-87212-179-8). Libra.

Unloved. John Saul. 368p. 1988. pap. 4.50. Bantam.

Unlovelinesse of Love-Lockes. William Prynne. LC 76-57410. (English Experience Ser.: No. 825). 1977. Repr. of 1628 ed. lib. bdg. 25.00 (ISBN 90-221-0825-2). Walter J Johnson.

Unlovely Child. Norman Williams. LC 84-47908. 64p. (Orig.). 1985. 13.45 (ISBN 0-394-53770-X); pap. 6.95 (ISBN 0-394-72763-0). Knopf.

Unloving Care: The Nursing Home Tragedy. Bruce C. Vladeck. LC 79-3076. 305p. 1980. pap. 9.95 (ISBN 0-465-08881-3, CN-5072). Basic.

Unmaking of a Dancer. Joan Brady. Date not set. pap. 4.95. PB.

Unmaking of a Dancer: An Unconventional Life. John Brady. 1983. pap. 4.95. WSP.

Unmaking of Palestine. W. Abboushi. 250p. (Orig.). 1987. 17.95 (ISBN 0-915597-66-7); pap. 9.95 (ISBN 0-915597-61-6). Amana Bks.

Unmaking of Palestine. Wasif Abboushi. 230p. 1985. lib. bdg. 27.50x (ISBN 0-906559-20-0). Lynne Rienner.

Unmaking of Rabbit. Constance C. Greene. 128p. (gr. 4-6). 1972. lib. bdg. 11.95 (ISBN 0-670-74136-1). Viking.

Unmanageable Revolutionaries: Women & Irish Nationalism. Margaret Ward. 296p. 1983. pap. 11.25 (ISBN 0-86104-700-1, Pub. by Pluto Pr). Longwood Pub Group.

Unmanly Man: Concept of Sexual Defamation in Early Northern Society. Preben M. Sorensen. 115p. (Orig.). 1983. pap. 22.50x (ISBN 87-7492-436-2, Pub. by Odense Universitets Forlag (Odense Denmark)). Coronet Bks.

Unmanned Aircraft. Michael Armitage. (Aircraft Weapons & Technology Ser.: No. 3). (Illus.). 150p. 1988. 28.91 (ISBN 0-08-034744-4); pap. 15.91 (ISBN 0-08-034743-6). Pergamon.

Unmanned Aircraft. A. Reed. 110p. 1979. 30.95 (ISBN 0-08-027026-3). Pergamon.

Unmanned Exploration of the Solar System. Ed. by G. W. Morgenthaler & R. G. Morra. (Advances in the Astronautical Sciences Ser.: Vol. 19). 1965. 45.00x (ISBN 0-87703-021-9, Pub. by Am Astronaut). Univelt Inc.

Unmarried Educated Women in India: Working Women's Attitude Towards Marriage & Career. Majula Rathaur. 165p. 1988. text ed. 22.50x (Pub. by Radiant Pubs India). Advent NY.

Unmarried Heterosexual Cohabitation. Carl Danziger. LC 78-62233. 1978. soft cover 11.95 (ISBN 0-88247-535-5). R & E Pubs.

Unmarried Mother: A Study of 500 Cases. Percy G. Kammerer. LC 69-14935. (Criminology, Law Enforcement, & Social Problems Ser.: No. 58). 1969. Repr. of 1918 ed. 15.00x (ISBN 0-87585-058-8). Patterson Smith.

Unmarried Mother in German Literature. O. H. Werner. 59.95 (ISBN 0-8490-1250-3). Gordon Pr.

Unmarried Mother in German Literature. Oscar H. Werner. LC 17-18727. (Columbia University. Germanic Studies, Old Ser.: No. 22). Repr. of 1917 ed. 15.00 (ISBN 0-404-50422-1). AMS Pr.

Unmarried Mothers. Clark E. Vincent. LC 80-16580. x, 308p. 1980. Repr. of 1961 ed. lib. bdg. 35.00x (ISBN 0-313-22474-9, VIMO). Greenwood.

Unmasking. Jan Van Rijckenborgh. 70p. 1987. pap. 3.00 (ISBN 0-317-56231-2). Rozekruis Pr.

Unmasking Culture: Cross-Cultural Perspectives in the Social & Behavioral Sciences. Ed. & pref. by Liucija Baskauskas. LC 86-4225. (Publications in Anthropology & Related Fields). (Illus.). 160p. (Orig.). 1986. pap. text ed. 9.95x (ISBN 0-88316-554-6). Chandler & Sharp.

Unmasking of Medicine. Ian Kennedy. 256p. 1985. pap. 6.95 (ISBN 0-586-08433-9). Academy Chi Pubs.

Unmasking: Ten Women in Metamorphosis. Ed. by Valerie H. Sheehan. LC 72-96163. 286p. 1973. 6.95 (ISBN 0-8040-0626-1, 82-73393, Pub by Swallow). Ohio U Pr.

Unmasking the Face. 2nd ed. Paul Ekman & Wallace v. Friesen. (Illus.). xii, 212p. 1984. pap. 10.00 (ISBN 0-89106-024-3, 7281). Consulting Psychol.

Unmasking the Forger: The Dossena Deception. David Sox. (Illus.). 212p. 1988. 17.95 (ISBN 0-87663-690-3). Universe.

Unmasking the New Age. Douglas R. Groothuis. LC 85-23832. 200p. (Orig.). 1986. pap. 6.95 (ISBN 0-87784-568-9). Inter-Varsity.

Unmasking the Powers: The Invisible Forces That Determine Human Existence. Walter Wink. LC 85-45480. 224p. 1986. pap. 12.95 (ISBN 0-8006-1902-1, 1-1902). Fortress.

Unmasking the Psychopath: Antisocial Personality & Related Syndromes. Ed. by William H. Reid et al. (Professional Bks.). 1986. text ed. 34.95 (ISBN 0-393-70025-9). Norton.

Unmasterable Past: History, Holocaust, & German National Identity. Charles S. Maier. 240p. 1988. text ed. 22.50 (ISBN 0-674-92975-6). Harvard U Pr.

Unmastered Past: The Autobiographical Reflections of Leo Lowenthal. Leo Lowenthal. Intro. by Martin Jay. LC 86-24942. (Illus.). 240p. 1987. 25.00 (ISBN 0-520-05638-8). U of Cal Pr.

Unmatched Pair: The Story of E. W. & Ellen Browning Scripps. Charles O. Preece. 90p. (Orig.). 1989. pap. text ed. 12.95 (ISBN 0-9619349-4-8). C O Preece.

Unmedical Book: How to Conquer Disease, Lose Weight, Avoid Suffering & Save Money. Elizabeth Baker & Elton Baker. 280p. 1987. pap. 8.95 (ISBN 0-918880-14-9). Comm Creat.

Unmentionable Cuisine. Calvin W. Schwabe. LC 79-15977. (Illus.). 476p. 1980. pap. 24.95x (ISBN 0-8139-0811-6). U Pr of Va.

Unmentionable Cuisine. Calvin W. Schwabe. LC 79-15957. (Illus.). 476p. (Orig.). 1988. pap. 14.95 (ISBN 0-8139-1162-1); 24.95. U Pr of Va.

Unmentionable Vice: Homosexuality in the Later Medieval Period. Michael Goodich. LC 78-13276. 179p. 1980. pap. 7.95. Ross-Erikson.

Unmet Needs: The Growing Crisis in America. League of Women Voters Education Fund Staff. 72p. 1988. pap. 5.00 (ISBN 0-89959-409-3, 853). LWV US.

Unmet Promise of Alternatives to Incarceration. Barry Krisberg & Jim Austin. 1982. 4.50 (ISBN 0-318-02054-8). Natl Coun Crime.

Unmusical New York: A Brief Criticism of Triumphs, Failures, & Abuses. Herman Klein. LC 79-1278. (Music Reprint Ser.). 1979. Repr. of 1910 ed. lib. bdg. 25.00 (ISBN 0-306-79517-5). Da Capo.

Unmuzzled Ox. Ed. by Michael Andre. (Illus.). 78p. 1974. pap. 4.95 (ISBN 0-317-60998-X). Unmuzzled OX.

Unpublished Personal Names Indexes in Record Offices & Libraries. 1987. 30.00x (Pub. by Birmingham Midland Soc UK). State Mutual Bk.

Unpublished Plays of Thomas Holley Chivers. Thomas H. Chivers. LC 79-29747. 75.00x (ISBN 0-8201-1350-6). Schol Facsimiles.

Unpublished Stories. William Faulkner. Ed. by Thomas McHaney. (William Faulkner Manuscripts). 1987. lib. bdg. 100.00 (ISBN 0-8240-6837-8). Garland Pub.

Unpublished Velins of Lamarck, 1802 to 1809: Illustrations of Fossils of the Paris Basin Eocene. Katherine V. Palmer. (Illus.). 67p. 1977. 15.00 (ISBN 0-87710-373-9). Paleo Res.

Unpuzzling Your Past: A Basic Guide to Genealogy. Emily A. Croom. LC 82-24514. (Illus.). 128p. 1983. pap. 7.95 (ISBN 0-932620-21-3). Betterway Pubns.

Unquestionable Right to Be Free: Essays in Black Theology from South Africa. Ed. by Itumeleng J. Mosala & Buti Tlhagale. 224p. (Orig.). 1986. pap. 11.95 (ISBN 0-88344-251-5). Orbis Bks.

Unquestionably the Family Circus. Bil Keane. 1985. pap. 5.95 (ISBN 0-449-90147-5, Columbine). Fawcett.

Unquestioning Obedience to the President: The ACLU Case Against the Legality of the War in Vietnam. Leon Friedman & Burt Neuborne. LC 76-169044. 1972. pap. 3.95x (ISBN 0-393-05470-5). Norton.

Unquiet Dead: A Psychologist Treats Spiritual Possession. Edith Fiore. 1988. pap. 3.95. Ballantine.

Unquiet Dead: A Psychologist Works with Spirit Possession. Edith Fiore. LC 86-29096. 192p. 1987. 15.95 (ISBN 0-385-23904-1, Dolp). Doubleday.

Unquiet Grave. Cyril Connolly. 156p. 1982. cancelled 12.95 (ISBN 0-89255-074-0); pap. 9.95 (ISBN 0-89255-058-9). Persea Bks.

Unquiet Grave. Janet LaPierre. 240p. 1987. 15.95 (ISBN 0-312-01102-4). St Martin.

Unquiet Landscape. Ed. by Denys Brunsden & John C. Doornkamp. LC 77-15583. 168p. 1978. Repr. of 1972 ed. 31.95x (ISBN 0-470-99345-6). Halsted Pr.

Unquiet Soul: A Biography of Charlotte Bronte. Margot Peters. LC 85-48115. 480p. 1986. pap. 12.95 (ISBN 0-689-70707-X, 341). Atheneum.

Unquiet Souls: Fourteenth-Century Saints & Their Religious Milieu. Richard Kieckhefer. LC 84-210. 248p. 1984. lib. bdg. 24.95x (ISBN 0-226-43509-1). U of Chicago Pr.

Unquiet Souls: Fourteenth Century Saints & Their Religious Milieu. Richard Kieckhefer. LC 84-210. (Illus.). viii, 238p. 1987. pap. 10.95x (ISBN 0-226-43510-5). U of Chicago Pr.

Unratified Treaty Between the Kiowas, Comanches & Apaches & the United States of 1863. R. J. DeMallie. (Treaty Manuscripts Ser.: No. 24). 8p. 5.00 (ISBN 0-944253-46-6). Inst Dev Indian Law.

Unraveling Fatherhood. Ed. by T. Knyu & A. C. Mulder. (Women's Studies). viii, 180p. 1986. pap. write for info. (ISBN 90-6765-278-4). Foris Pubns.

Unraveling Mathematical Concepts. Edith Silver & Betty Cornelius. 1978. wire coil bdg. 21.50 (ISBN 0-88252-084-9). Paladin Hse.

Unraveling of America: A History of Liberalism in the 1960s. Allen J. Matusow. LC 83-48019. (New American Nations Ser.). 560p. 1984. 22.45i (ISBN 0-06-015224-9, HarpT). Har-Row.

Unraveling of America: A History of Liberalism in the 1960s. Allen J. Matusow. LC 83-48019. (New American Nations Ser.). 560p. 1985. pap. 10.95x (ISBN 0-06-132058-7, TB2058, Torch). Har-Row.

Unraveling the Big Questions about God. Kenneth Boa. 192p. 1988. pap. 8.95 (ISBN 0-310-33651-1, 12771P). Zondervan.

Unraveling the Integral Knot Concordance Group. N. Stoltzfus. LC 77-10133. (Memoirs Ser.: No. 192). 91p. 1977. pap. 15.00 (ISBN 0-8218-2192-X, MEMO 192). Am Math.

Unraveling the Mystery of Health: How People Manage Stress & Stay Well. Aaron Antonovsky. LC 86-27386. (Social & Behavioral Science Ser.). 1987. text ed. 23.95x (ISBN 1-55542-028-1). Jossey-Bass.

Unravelling Animal Behaviour. M. S. Dawkins. LC 85-10230. 159p. 1986. pap. 17.95 (ISBN 0-470-20657-8, Pub. by Halsted Press). Wiley.

Unravelling Japan's Mystique. John R. Terry. (Illus.). 200p. 1988. pap. 9.95 (ISBN 0-933704-33-X). Dawn Pr.

Unravelling Social Policy. David Gil. 180p. 1982. 18.95x (ISBN 0-87073-458-X); pap. 9.95 (ISBN 0-87073-459-8). Schenkman Bks Inc.

Unreachable Child: An Introduction to Early Childhood Autism. Sam B. Morgan. 208p. 1981. pap. text ed. 7.95 (ISBN 0-87870-201-6). Memphis St Univ.

Unreached Peoples The Future of World Evangelization: The Lausanne Movement. World Vision International. 383p. 7.95 (ISBN 0-317-36187-2, 138). World Vision Intl.

Unreached Peoples '79: The Challenge of the Church's Unfinished Business. Lausanne Committee for World Evangelization. LC 78-57642. 349p. 1979. pap. 7.95 (ISBN 0-912552-49-2). Missions Adv Res Com Ctr.

Unreached Peoples '80. LC 79-57522. 383p. 1980. pap. 7.95 (ISBN 0-912552-50-6). Missions Adv Res Com Ctr.

Unreached Peoples '81. LC 80-69556. 465p. pap. 7.95 (ISBN 0-912552-51-4). Missions Adv Res Com Ctr.

Unreached Peoples '82. LC 81-69100. 435p. pap. 7.95 (ISBN 0-912552-52-2). Missions Adv Res Com Ctr.

Unreached People's '83: The Refugees Among Us. LC 82-61991. 523p. 1983. pap. 7.95 (ISBN 0-912552-38-7). Missions Adv Res Com Ctr.

Unreached Peoples '86: Clarifying the Task. Ed. by Harley Schreck & David Barrett. 302p. pap. 7.95 (ISBN 0-912552-58-1). Missions Adv Res Com Ctr.

Unreal City: Urban Experience in Modern European Literature & Art. Ed. by Edward Timms & David Kelley. LC 85-2209. 256p. 1985. 25.00 (ISBN 0-312-83348-2). St Martin.

Unreal Estate. Brian Swann. LC 82-2799. (Illus.). 48p. 1982. signed 35.00 (ISBN 0-915124-39-4, Pub. by Toothpaste); pap. 8.50 (ISBN 0-915124-40-8). Coffee Hse.

Unreal Past & Other Poems. K. R. Narayanaswamy. 6.75 (ISBN 0-89253-710-8); flexible cloth 3.00 (ISBN 0-89253-711-6). Ind-US Inc.

Unrealists. Harvey Wickham. LC 78-105051. (Essay Index Reprint Ser). 1930. 19.00 (ISBN 0-8369-1736-7). Ayer Co Pubs.

Unrealists. Harvey Wickham. LC 73-105851. (Essay & General Literature Index Reprint Ser). 1971. Repr. of 1931 ed. 24.00x (ISBN 0-8046-1338-9, Pub by Kennikat). Assoc Faculty Pr.

Unreality & Time. Robert S. Brumbaugh. LC 83-5084. (Philosophy Ser.). 164p. 1984. 56.50 (ISBN 0-87395-799-7); pap. 19.95x (ISBN 0-87395-798-9). State U NY Pr.

Unreasonable American. Houston Branch & Wendell Smith. Date not set. 9.95 (ISBN 0-317-63446-1). Acropolis.

Unrecognized Patriots: The Jews in the American Revolution. Samuel Rezneck. LC 74-15160. (Illus.). 1975. lib. bdg. 35.00 (ISBN 0-8371-7803-7, RRJ/). Greenwood.

Unredeemed Rhetoric: Thomas Nashe & the Scandal of Authorship. Jonathan Crewe. LC 82-6554. 144p. 1982. text ed. 17.50x (ISBN 0-8018-2848-1). Johns Hopkins.

Unreformed Cambridge: A Study of Certain Aspects of the University in the Eighteenth Century. D. A. Winstanley. Ed. by Walter P. Metzger. LC 76-55194. (Academic Profession Ser.). 1977. Repr. of 1935 ed. lib. bdg. 32.00x (ISBN 0-405-10023-X). Ayer Co Pubs.

Unreformed House of Commons, 2 Vols. Edward Porritt. LC 63-21104. 1963. Repr. of 1903 ed. 95.00x (ISBN 0-678-00012-3). Kelley.

Unreformed Local Government System. Bryan Keith-Lucas. 173p. 1980. 27.00 (ISBN 0-85664-877-9, Pub. by Croom Helm Ltd). Routledge Chapman & Hall.

Unregierbarkeit der Staedte. Gottlieb Duttweiler Institut Staff. 250p. (Ger.). 1982. pap. 13.00 (ISBN 0-89192-368-3). Interbk Inc.

Unrelated Business Income Tax. Joseph M. Galloway. LC 81-23166. (Professional Accounting & Business Ser.). 186p. 1982. 52.95x (ISBN 0-471-09916-3). Wiley.

Unrelenting Struggle: War Speeches. facsimile ed. Winston S. Churchill. Compiled by Charles Eade. LC 78-167325. (Essay Index Reprint Ser). Repr. of 1942 ed. 20.00 (ISBN 0-8369-2450-9). Ayer Co Pubs.

Unreliable History. Maurice Baring. 1934. 25.00 (ISBN 0-8274-3662-9). R West.

Unremarkable Wordsworth. Geoffrey Hartman. LC 86-24887. (Theory & History of Literature Ser.: Vol. 34). 276p. (Orig.). 1987. 29.50x (ISBN 0-8166-1175-0); pap. 13.95 (ISBN 0-8166-1176-9). U of Minn Pr.

Unremembered Country. Susan Griffin. LC 86-73197. 144p. (Orig.). 1987. 15.00 (ISBN 1-55659-000-8); pap. 9.00 (ISBN 1-55659-001-6). Copper Canyon.

Unrequired Reading: An Annotated Bibliography for Teachers & School Administrators. 2nd ed. Compiled by Iris M. Tiedt & Sidney W. Tiedt. LC 63-63839. (Bibliographic Ser.: No. 7). 128p. (Orig.). 1967. pap. 6.95x (ISBN 0-87071-127-X). Oreg St U Pr.

Unrequited. Adina Joy. 136p. (Orig.). (YA) (gr. 7 up). 1985. pap. 2.25 (ISBN 0-590-33255-4, Point). Scholastic Inc.

Unresolvable Plot: Reading Contemporary Fiction. Elizabeth Dipple. 288p. 1988. text ed. 45.00 (ISBN 0-415-00661-9, Pub. by Routledge UK); pap. text ed. 14.95 (ISBN 0-415-00662-7, Pub. by Routledge UK). Routledge Chapman & Hall.

Unresolved Conflict: India & China. Bhim Sandhu. 300p. 1988. text ed. 37.50x (ISBN 81-7027-116-9, Pub. by Radiant Pubs India). Advent NY.

Unresolved Problems in Haemophilia. C. D. Forbes. (Illus.). 245p. 1981. text ed. 29.95 (ISBN 0-85200-388-9, Pub. by MTP Pr England). Kluwer Academic.

Unresolved Problems in Marine Microbiology see Marine Biology.

Unresponsive Bystander: Why Doesn't He Help? Bibb Latane & John M. Darley. LC 79-123548. (Psychology Ser). (Orig.). 1970. 18.00 (ISBN 0-13-938613-0). P-H.

Unresponsive: Resistant or Neglected? Homogeneous Unit Principal Illustrated by the Hakka Chinese in Taiwan. David Liao. LC 73-175494. 160p. 1979. pap. 5.95 (ISBN 0-87808-735-4). William Carey Lib.

Unrest in Brazil: Political Military Crises, 1955-1964. John W. Dulles. (Illus.). 465p. 1970. 27.50x (ISBN 0-292-70006-7). U of Tex Pr.

Unrest in the Middle East. Francis Neilson. 1979. lib. bdg. 39.95 (ISBN 0-685-96646-1). Revisionist Pr.

Unretouched Woman. Eve Arnold. 1976. Knopf.

Unriddling. Alvin Schwartz. LC 82-48778. (Illus.). 128p. (gr. 3-7). 1983. 11.70i (ISBN 0-397-32029-9, Lipp Jr Bks); PLB 10.89 (ISBN 0-397-32030-2). HarpJ.

Unriddling: All Sorts of Riddles to Puzzle Your Guessary. Alvin Schwartz. LC 82-48778. (Trophy Nonfiction Bks.). (Illus.). 128p. (gr. 4 up). 1987. pap. 4.95 (ISBN 0-06-446057-6, Trophy). HarpJ.

Unrolling Time: Huygens & the Mathematization of Nature. Joella G. Yoder. (Illus.). 264p. Date not set. price not set (ISBN 0-521-34140-X). Cambridge U Pr.

Unromantic Agony: An Exhibition. Intro. by Dominique De Menil. (Illus.). 1965. pap. 2.50 (ISBN 0-914412-26-4). Inst for the Arts.

Unsafe at Any Margin: Interpreting Congressional Elections. Thomas E. Mann. LC 78-10892. 1978. pap. 9.00 (ISBN 0-8447-3322-9). Am Enterprise.

Unsafe at Any Meal. Earl Mindell. 208p. 1987. 16.95 (ISBN 0-446-34670-5). Warner Bks.

Unsafe at Any Meal. Earl Mindell. 288p. Date not set. pap. 4.95. Warner Bks.

Unsafe on Any Sea-L.H.A. Ships of the U. S. Navy. Earl Kent. 1976. pap. text ed. 25.00 (ISBN 0-918782-00-7). E Kent.

Unsafe Sky. William Norris. 224p. 1982. 14.95 (ISBN 0-393-01596-3). Norton.

Unsaid Anna Karenina. Judith M. Armstrong. LC 87-30765. 192p. 1988. 35.00 (ISBN 0-312-01676-X). St Martin.

Unsatisfactory Results in Hand Surgery: Vol. 3, HUL. McFarlane. 1987. 60.00 (ISBN 0-443-03387-0). Churchill.

Unsaturated & Polyunsaturated Fatty Acid in Health & Disease. James F. Mead & Armand J. Fulco. (Illus.). 208p. 1976. 30.25x (ISBN 0-398-03413-3). C C Thomas.

Unsaturated Fatty Acids in Atherosclerosis. 2nd ed. J. Enselme. 1969. 57.00 (ISBN 0-08-013060-7). Pergamon.

Unsaturated Nitro Compounds. V. V. Perekalin. 344p. 1964. text ed. 77.00x (ISBN 0-7065-0526-3, Pub. by Keter Pub Jerusalem). Coronet Bks.

Unsaturated Polyester Technology. Paul F. Bruins. LC 74-12774. 448p. 1976. 88.00 (ISBN 0-677-21160-0). Gordon & Breach.

Unscheduled Love. Beverly Sommers. (Harlequin American Romance Ser.). 256p. 1983. pap. 2.25 (ISBN 0-373-16026-7). Harlequin Bks.

Unscientific Americans. Roz Chast. (Illus.). 128p. 1986. pap. 9.95 (ISBN 0-385-27622-2, Dolp). Doubleday.

Unscientific Essays. facs. ed. Frederic W. Jones. LC 67-23236. (Essay Index Reprint Ser). 1967. Repr. of 1924 ed. 15.00 (ISBN 0-8369-0578-4). Ayer Co Pubs.

Unsealed Book: An Amillennial View of Revelation. Wade Jernigan. 1975. pap. 4.95 (ISBN 0-89265-028-1). Randall Hse.

Unsearchable Riches. David N. Power. 160p. (Orig.). 1984. pap. 12.95 (ISBN 0-916134-62-8). Pueblo Pub Co.

Unsearchable Riches of Christ. D. Martyn Lloyd-Jones. 1980. 14.95 (ISBN 0-8010-5597-0). Baker Bk.

Unsearchable Wisdom of God: A Study of Providence in Richardson's Pamela. James L. Fortuna, Jr. LC 80-14919. (University of Florida Humanities Monographs: No. 49). vii, 130p. 1980. pap. 12.00x (ISBN 0-8130-0676-7). U Presses Fla.

Unseasonal Migrations: The Effects of Rural Labor Scarcity in Peru. Jane L. Collins. (Illus.). 200p. 1988. text ed. 27.50 (ISBN 0-691-07744-4). Princeton U Pr.

Unsecular America. Paul Johnson et al. Ed. by Richard J. Neuhaus. (Encounter Ser.). 176p. (Orig.). 1986. pap. 8.95 (ISBN 0-8028-0202-8). Eerdmans.

Unsecular Man: The Persistence of Religion. Andrew M. Greeley. LC 85-2459. 297p. 1985. pap. 8.95 (ISBN 0-8052-0794-5). Schocken.

Unseen Bird. S. C. Saha. 6.75 (ISBN 0-89253-727-2); flexible cloth 4.00 (ISBN 0-89253-728-0). Ind-US Inc.

Unseen Danger: A Tragedy of People, Government, & the Centralia Mine Fire. David DeKok. LC 85-31454. (Illus.). 384p. 1986. pap. text ed. 18.95 (ISBN 0-8122-1226-6). U of Pa Pr.

Unseen Dimensions of Wealth Towards a Generalized Economic Theory. Henry K. Woo. 1984. 35.00 (ISBN 0-9613204-0-0). Victoria Pr.

Unseen Elderly. J. Kevin Eckert. (Illus.). 243p. (Orig.). 1981. 16.00 (ISBN 0-916304-47-7); pap. 6.00 (ISBN 0-916304-45-0). SDSU Press.

Unseen Forces. Manly P. Hall. pap. 3.95 (ISBN 0-89314-385-5). Philos Res.

Unseen Hand. Assembly of Elementary Schools. 87p. 6.50 (ISBN 0-318-14824-2, AES 4); members 3.50 (ISBN 0-318-14825-0). Mid St Coll & Schl.

Unseen Hand: An Introduction to the Conspiratorial View of History. A. Ralph Epperson. (Illus.). 474p. (Orig.). 1985. pap. 12.95 (ISBN 0-9614135-0-6). Publius Pr.

Unseen Hand & Other Plays. Sam Shepard. 304p. (Orig.). 1986. pap. 7.95 (ISBN 0-553-34263-0). Bantam.

Unseen Hand & Other Plays. Sam Shepard. 233p. 1988. 21.95 (ISBN 0-317-65861-1); pap. 9.95 (ISBN 0-317-65862-X). Applause Theatre Bk Pubs.

Unseen Hands: The Story of Revival in Ethiopia. Nona Freeman. Ed. by David Bernard. LC 87-23263. (Illus.). 224p. (Orig.). 1987. pap. 6.95 (ISBN 0-932581-22-6). Word Aflame.

Unseen Holocaust: A Sad Record of Nuclear Accidents, Leakages, Mismanagement & Cover-Ups. Teddy Milne. 24p. 1987. pap. 2.20 (ISBN 0-938875-09-4). Pittenbruach Pr.

Unseen Influences. Dick Sutphen. (Orig.). 1983. pap. 3.50 (ISBN 0-671-55221-X). PB.

Unseen King. Tyson Blue. (Starmont Studies in Literary Criticism: No. 26). 203p. 1988. Repr. lib. bdg. 19.95x (ISBN 0-8095-5106-3). Borgo Pr.

Unseen Kingdoms. Bill Cox. (Illus.). 68p. (Orig.). 1983. pap. 8.95 saddle stitch. Life Understanding.

Unseen Kingdoms: UFOs & Invisible Elemental Forces. Bill Cox. (Illus.). 72p. 1983. pap. 9.95 saddle-stitch. Global Comm.

Unseen New York. Mark Feldstein. (Illus.). 11.25 (ISBN 0-8446-5184-2). Peter Smith.

Unseen Rain: Quatrains of Rumi. Mevlana J. Rumi. Tr. by John Moyne & Coleman Barks. LC 86-50782. 96p. (Orig.). 1986. 14.00 (ISBN 0-939660-17-2); pap. 8.00 (ISBN 0-939660-16-4). Threshold VT.

Unseen Revolution: How Pension Fund Socialism Came to America. Peter F. Drucker. LC 75-34795. 160p. 1976. 12.45i (ISBN 0-06-011097-X, HarpT). Har-Row.

Unseen Warfare. Lorenzo Scupoli. 280p. 1978. pap. 9.95 (ISBN 0-913836-52-4). St Vladimirs.

Unseen World. Julius Adewumi. 1986. 6.95 (ISBN 0-533-05824-4). Vantage.

Unseen World: A Spirited Guide to Using Crystals, Understanding Dreams, Reading Auras, Experiencing Past Lives, Fulfilling Your Karma, & Living Well in the New Age. Barbara Stabiner. LC 88-47526. (Illus.). 368p. 1988. pap. 9.95 (ISBN 0-553-34527-3). Bantam.

Unseen World: Catholic Theology & Spiritualism. A. M. Lepicier. 69.95 (ISBN 0-8490-1251-1). Gordon Pr.

Unselfishness of God & How I Discovered It. Hannah W. Smith. (Higher Christian Life Ser.). 312p. 1985. lib. bdg. 40.00 (ISBN 0-8240-6443-7). Garland Pub.

Unselfishness: The Role of the Vicarious Affects in Moral Philosophy & Social Theory. Nicholas Rescher. LC 75-9123. 1975. 12.95x (ISBN 0-8229-3308-X). U of Pittsburgh Pr.

Unsent Letters: Irreverent Notes from a Literary Life. Malcolm Bradbury. 1988. 16.95 (ISBN 0-670-82070-9). Viking.

Unsentimental Journey of Laurence Sterne. Ernest Dilworth. LC 75-75990. 1969. Repr. of 1948 ed. lib. bdg. 17.00x (ISBN 0-374-92185-7, Octagon). Hippocrene Bks.

UNSER: An American Family Portrait. Gorden Kirby. 176p. 1988. 29.95 (ISBN 0-916105-03-2). Anlon Pr.

Unsettling of America: Culture & Agriculture. Wendell Berry. LC 77-3729. 238p. 1977. 14.95 (ISBN 0-87156-194-8). Sierra.

Unsettling of America: Culture & Agriculture. rev. ed. Wendell Berry. LC 86-6426. (Paperback Library). 240p. 1986. pap. 7.95 (ISBN 0-87156-772-5). Sierra.

Unshakeable Kingdom. Ed. by Clarence M. Wagner. 90p. pap. 4.00 (ISBN 0-317-39376-6). Tru-Faith.

Unshakeable Kingdom see Reino Inconmovible.

Unshaken Friend: A Profile of Maxwell Perkins. Malcolm Cowley. 1985. 14.50 (ISBN 0-911797-15-7). R Rinehart Inc.

Unshared Care: Parents & Their Disabled Children. Carline Glendinning. (International Library of Social Policy). 370p. (Orig.). 1983. pap. 14.95x (ISBN 0-7100-9468-X). Routledge Chapman & Hall.

Unsheltered Woman: Women & Housing in the 80's. Ed. by Eugenie Ladner Birch. (Illus.). 346p. 1985. pap. text ed. 14.95x (ISBN 0-88285-104-7). Transaction Bks.

Unsilent Night. Tanith Lee. LC 81-80331. (Boskone BK.). 1981. 10.00 (ISBN 0-915368-18-8). New Eng SF Assoc.

Unsinkable Molly Brown. Al Hine. 13.95 (ISBN 0-8488-0166-0, Pub. by Amereon Hse). Amereon Ltd.

Unsinkable Mrs. Brown. Caroline Bancroft. 44p. 1963. pap. 3.50 (ISBN 0-933472-25-0). Johnson Bks.

Unsinkable Rock. Calvin Miller. (Bible Stories in Rhyme Ser.). (Illus.). 32p. (ps-4). 1988. 4.95 (ISBN 0-8407-6722-6). Nelson.

Untersuchungen Zu Den Prosaschriften Henry Vaughans. Gunther Wiese. Ed. by James Hogg. (Elizabethan & Renassaince Studies). 156p. (Orig.). 1978. pap. 15.00 (ISBN 3-7052-0716-4, Pub. by Salzburg Studies). Longwood Pub Group.

Untersuchungen zu Gorgias' Schrift Ueber das Nichtseiende. Hans-Joachim Newiger. 1973. 35.60x (ISBN 3-11-003432-8). De Gruyter.

Untersuchungen zum Einfluss von Rhizosphaeren-organismen der Fichte (Picea abies (L.) H. Karst.) auf den Rotfaeuleerreger Fomes Annosus (Fr.) B. Karst., sowie die Identifikation von Gliotoxin als Stoffwechselprodukt von Penicillium spinolosum Thom. Erich Falk. (Bibliotheca Mycologica Ser.: Vol. 111). (Illus.). 170p. (Ger.). 1987. text ed. 42.00x (ISBN 3-443-59012-8); pap. text ed. 42.00x (ISBN 3-443-59012-8). Lubrecht & Cramer.

Untersuchungen zum Humor in den Comedias Calderons unter Auschluss der Gracioso-Gestalten. Amelia Tejada. LC 73-88306. (Hamburger Romanistische Studien, Reihe B. Ibero-Amerikanische Reihe Calderoniana-Band 9). 1974. 33.60x (ISBN 3-11-004495-1). De Gruyter.

Untersuchungen Zum Serapiontischen Prinzip E.T.A. Hoffmans. Ilse Winter. (De Proprietatibus Litterarum: No. 111). 90p. (Orig.). 1976. pap. text ed. 11.60x (ISBN 90-2793-434-7). Mouton.

Untersuchungen Zum Sozlalverhatten Des Rindes. V. Reinhardt. (Tierhaltung: No. 10). (Illus.). 96p. (Ger.). 1980. pap. 22.95 (ISBN 0-8176-1138-X). Birkhauser.

Untersuchungen zum Spaetromischen Korporationswesen. Andreas Graeber. (European University Studies: No. 3, Vol. 196). 194p. (Ger.). 1983. 23.15 (ISBN 3-8204-7704-7). P Lang Pubs.

Untersuchungen zum Wasserhaushalt der Vegetation im Nordwestargentinischen Andenhochland. Erika Geyger. (Dissertationes Botanicae Ser.: 88). 228p. (Ger.). 1985. pap. text ed. 60.00x (ISBN 3-443-64002-8). Lubrecht & Cramer.

Untersuchungen zum Wasserhaushalt von Myrceugenia exsucca und Temu divaricatum in Relation zur Morphologie und Anatomie der Wurzel an Ueberflutungsstandorten. R. Debus. (Dissertationes Botanicae Ser.: Vol. 100). (Illus.). 154p. (Ger.). 1987. pap. text ed. 42.00x (ISBN 3-443-64012-5). Lubrecht & Cramer.

Untersuchungen zur Biologie der: Begleitflora Mediterraner Wein und Getreidekulturen im Westlichen Sizilien. Karl-Georg Bernhardt. (Dissertationes Botanica Ser.: Vol. 103). (Illus.). 138p. 1987. pap. 36.60x (ISBN 3-443-64015-X). Lubrecht & Cramer.

Untersuchungen zur Blueten-und Infloresz Enzmorphologie, Embryologie und Systematic der Restionaceen im Vergleich mit Gramineen und verwandten Familiem. Peter Kircher. (Dissertationes Botanicae Ser.: Vol. 94). (Illus.). 22p. 1986. 36.00X. Lubrecht & Cramer.

Untersuchungen zur Embryologie, Bluetenmorphologie und Systematik der Rapateaceen und der Xyridaceen-Gattung Abolboda: Monocotyledoneae. A. Tiemann. (Dissertatones Botanicae Ser.: No. 82). (Illus.). 202p. 1985. pap. text ed. 48.00x (ISBN 3-7682-1436-2). Lubrecht & Cramer.

Untersuchungen zur Entstehung und Stabilitaet der Panaschierungen bei Hedera. Garry Grueber. (Illus.). 112p. (Ger.). 1983. Color. pap. 85.00 (ISBN 0-937233-24-2); B&W. pap. 50.00 (ISBN 0-937233-23-4). Am Ivy Soc.

Untersuchungen zur Entwicklungsgeschichte der Cladoniaceen unter Besonderer Beruecksichtigung des Podetien-Problems. H. Martin Jahns. (Nova Hedwigia Ser.: No. 20). (Illus.). 178p. (Ger.). 1970. pap. text ed. 28.00x (ISBN 3-7682-0656-4). Lubrecht & Cramer.

Untersuchungen zur Fruhzeit des franzosischen Furstentums (9-10 Jahrhundert. Karl F. Werner. LC 79-8375. Repr. of 1960 ed. 18.50 (ISBN 0-404-18357-3). AMS Pr.

Untersuchungen Zur Genetik Des Fortpflanzungsverhaltens und der Fruchtkoerper-und Antibiotikabbildung Des Basidiomyceten Agrocybe Aegerita. F. Meinhardt. (Bibliotheca Mycologica: No. 75). (Illus.). 128p. (Ger.). 1981. pap. text ed. 24.00x (ISBN 3-7682-1275-0). Lubrecht & Cramer.

Untersuchungen Zur Geschichte Boiotiens In Der Zeit Alexanders Und Der Diadochen. Brigitte Gullath. (European University Studies: No. 3, Vol. 169). 249p. 1982. 30.55 (ISBN 3-8204-7026-3). P Lang Pubs.

Untersuchungen Zur Geschichte der Byzantinischen Verwaltung in Italien. Ludo M. Hartmann. 1889. 22.50 (ISBN 0-8337-1584-4). B Franklin.

Untersuchungen Zur Geschichte Des Kaisers Septimius Severus. Johannes Hasebroek. LC 75-7321. (Roman History Ser.). (Ger.). 1975. Repr. 17.00x (ISBN 0-405-07085-3). Ayer Co Pubs.

Untersuchungen zur Geschichte Einer Fragestellung. facsimile ed. Adolf Kleingunther. LC 75-13276. (History of Ideas in Ancient Greece Ser.). (Ger.). 1976. Repr. of 1933 ed. 11.00x (ISBN 0-405-07316-X). Ayer Co Pubs.

Untersuchungen Zur Jenaer Leiderhandschrift. Karl F. Bartsch. 18.00 (ISBN 0-384-03490-X); pap. 13.00 (ISBN 0-685-02216-1). Johnson Repr.

Untersuchungen Zur Konservierung der Frucht Koerper des Speisepilzes Pleurotus ostreatus (Jacqu. ex Fr.) Kummer in der Partiellen Autlyse von Pilzzellwaenden. Helga Schmitz. (Bibliothaca Mycologica: No. 77). (Illus.). 85p. (Ger.). 1980. pap. text ed. 18.00x (ISBN 3-7682-1278-5). Lubrecht & Cramer.

Untersuchungen zur Politik und Kriegfuehrung Roms im Osten Von 100-68 V. Chr. Rudolf K. Bulin. (European University Studies: No. 3, Vol. 177). 110p. (Ger.). 1983. 15.25 (ISBN 3-8204-7109-X). P Lang Pubs.

Untersuchungen zur Populationsdynamyk am Beginn von Sekundaersukzessionen. Beseutung von Samenbank und Samenniederschlag. Anton Fischer. (Dissertations Botanicae Ser.: Vol. 110). (Illus.). 234p. (Ger.). 1987. pap. text ed. 52.00x. Lubrecht & Cramer.

Untersuchungen zur Production und Reingung eines gelben Farbstoffes des Basidiomyceten: Pleurotus ostreatus (Jacq. ex Fr.) Kummer. Margraf Wolfgang. (Bibliotheca Mycologica Ser.). (Illus.). 95p. (Ger.). 1984. 28.00X (ISBN 3-7682-1412-5). Lubrecht & Cramer.

Untersuchungen zur Redaktionsgeschichte des Pentateuch. Peter Weimar. 1977. 34.40x (ISBN 3-11-006731-5). De Gruyter.

Untersuchungen Zur Reichskirchenpolitik Lothars III, 1125-1137: Zwischen Reichskirchlicher Tradition Und Reformkurie. Marie-Luise Crone. (European University Studies: No.3, Vol. 170). 398p. 1982. 40.55 (ISBN 3-8204-7019-0). P Lang Pubs.

Untersuchungen Zur Romischen Zenturienverfassung. Arthur Rosenberg. LC 75-7337. (Roman History Ser.). (Ger.). 1975. Repr. 11.00x (ISBN 0-405-07058-6). Ayer Co Pubs.

Untersuchungen zur Spaet- und Postglazialen Vegetationsgeschichte des Bayerischen Wald. H. Stalling. (Dissertationes Botanicae Ser.: Vol. 105). (Illus.). 201p. (Ger.). 1987. pap. 54.90x softbound (ISBN 3-443-64017-6). Lubrecht & Cramer.

Untersuchungen Zur Syntax Des Hindi Disputationes Rheno-Trajectinae, Vol. 2. Peter Gaeffke. 1967. pap. 22.00x (ISBN 0-686-21231-2). Mouton.

Untersuchungen zur Textkritischen Methode des Zenodotos von Ephesos. Klaus Nickau. (Untersuchungen Zur Antiken Literatur und Geschichte: Vol. 16). 1977. 41.20x (ISBN 3-11-001827-6). De Gruyter.

Untersuchungen Zur Ueberlieferung der Spruchdichtung Frauenlobs. Helmuth Thomas. 27.00 (ISBN 0-685-02052-5); pap. 22.00 (ISBN 0-384-60172-3). Johnson Repr.

Untersuchungen zur Vegetation Ostliguriens (Italien) Bernd Nowak. (Dissertationes Botanicae Ser.: Vol. 111). (Illus.). 264p. (Ger.). 1987. pap. text ed. 86.00x (ISBN 3-443-64023-0). Lubrecht & Cramer.

Untherapeutic Community: Organizational Behavior in a Failed Addiction Treatment Program. Robert S. Weppner. LC 83-1270. xvi, 269p. 1983. 22.95x (ISBN 0-8032-4723-0). U of Nebr Pr.

Unthinking Faith & Enlightenment: Nature & Politics in a Post-Hegelian Era. Jane Bennett. 192p. 30.00 (ISBN 0-8147-1095-6). NYU Pr.

Untidy Pilgrim. Date not set. pap. price not set (ISBN 0-413-55340-X). Heinemann Ed.

Untidy Pilgrim. Eugene Walter. Ed. by Bert Hitchcock. LC 87-5881. (Library of Alabama Classics). 264p. 1987. pap. 10.95 (ISBN 0-8173-0370-7). U of Ala Pr.

Untie the Winds. Jean Clark. 1978. pap. 2.25 (ISBN 0-89083-393-1). Zebra.

Until Christ Be Formed in You. James Alberione. 1988. 3.00 (ISBN 0-8198-7800-6, SP0785); pap. 2.00 (ISBN 0-8198-7801-4). Dghtrs St Paul.

Until Death & After: How to Live with a Dying Intimate. Jayne M. Murdock. Ed. by Dick Murdock & Jayne Murdock. LC 79-90348. (Illus.). 64p. 1979. pap. 4.00 (ISBN 0-932916-05-8). May-Murdock.

Until Death Do Us Part. Mary McMullen. pap. 2.95 (ISBN 0-515-08905-2). Jove Pubns.

Until Forever. Sally Garrett. (Superromances Ser.). 1983. pap. 2.95 (ISBN 0-373-70090-3, Pub. by Worldwide). Harlequin Bks.

Until I Return. Laura Simon. 480p. 1987. pap. 3.95 (ISBN 0-373-97051-X, Pub. by Worldwide). Harlequin Bks.

Until Justice & Peace Embrace. Nicholas Wolterstorff. 232p. (Orig.). 1983. 13.95 (ISBN 0-8028-3344-6). Eerdmans.

Until My Last Breath. Francis M. Seeger. 116p. 1980. pap. text ed. 5.50x (ISBN 0-932194-06-0). Health Comm.

Until Proven Guilty. J. A. Jance. 208p. 1988. pap. 3.50 (ISBN 0-380-89638-9). Avon.

Until Summer. Frances E. Wilson. (YA) (gr. 7 up). 1981. 9.95 (ISBN 0-686-84685-0, Avalon). Bouregy.

Until the Celebration. Zilpha K. Snyder. (Green Sky Trilogy: Vol. 3). 256p. 1985. pap. 2.95 (ISBN 0-8125-5480-9, Dist. by Warner Pub Services & St. Martin's Press). Tor Bks.

Until: The Coming of Messiah & His Kingdom. Robert Shank. LC 81-72098. 520p. 1982. pap. 11.95 (ISBN 0-911620-04-4). Westcott.

Until the Day Break. Louis Bromfield. 20.95 (ISBN 0-8488-0250-0). Amereon Ltd.

Until the End of Summer. Elisabeth Ogilvie. 192p. (Orig.). (gr. 7 up). 1981. pap. 1.95 (ISBN 0-590-31327-4). Scholastic Inc.

Until the Morning After: Selected Poems 1963-1985. Kofi Awoonor. LC 87-80177. 212p. (Orig.). 1987. pap. 10.95 (ISBN 0-912678-69-0). Greenfld Rev Pr.

Until the Sun Dies. Robert Jastrow. (Illus.). 1977. 12.95 (ISBN 0-393-06415-8). Norton.

Until the Sun Dies. Robert Jastrow. 224p. 1980. pap. 3.95 (ISBN 0-446-32195-8). Warner Bks.

Until the Whistle Blows: A Collection of Games, Dances & Activities for Eight to Twelve Year Olds. J. Tillman Hall et al. LC 76-55311. (Illus.). 1977. pap. 15.95 (ISBN 0-673-16211-7). Scott F.

Until There Was You. June M. Bacher. (Rhapsody Romance Ser.). 192p. 1984. 2.95 (ISBN 0-89081-419-8). Harvest Hse.

Until Tomorrow. Charlotte J. Long. 48p. (Orig.). 1983. pap. 3.95 (ISBN 0-88100-036-1). Marsh Creek.

Until Victory: Horace Mann & Mary Peabody. Louise H. Tharp. LC 77-6360. (Illus.). 1977. Repr. of 1953 ed. lib. bdg. 35.00x (ISBN 0-8371-9653-1, THUV). Greenwood.

Until We Are Free: Study Guide to South Africa's Moment of Truth. Patricia De Beer & John De Beer. 40p. 1988. pap. 3.95 (ISBN 0-377-00183-X). Friendship Pr.

Until We Are Six. Gary E. Stollak. LC 78-5723. 192p. 1978. text ed. 12.50 (ISBN 0-88275-939-6); pap. text ed. 7.50 (ISBN 0-88275-654-0). Krieger.

Until We Meet Again. Elena Poniatowska. Tr. by Magda Bogin. LC 87-43008. 256p. 1987. 16.45 (ISBN 0-394-54479-X). Pantheon.

Until We Reach the Valley. Ann Irwin & Bernice Reida. (Illus.). 173p. (gr. 4-7). 1979. pap. 1.50 (ISBN 0-380-43398-2, 43398-2, Camelot). Avon.

Until You Die. Bhagwan Shree Rajneesh. Ed. by Ma Yoga Anurag. LC 77-900984. (Sufi Ser.). (Illus.). 280p. (Orig.). 1976. 9.95 (ISBN 0-88050-165-0). Chidvilas Inc.

Untilled Field. George Moore. LC 70-125233. (Short Story Index Reprint Ser). 1903. 15.00 (ISBN 0-8369-3600-0). Ayer Co Pubs.

Untilled Field. George Moore. 1976. 21.00 (ISBN 0-900675-63-2, Pub. by Colin Smythe Ltd Britain). Dufour.

Untimely Guest. Marian Babson. 192p. 1987. 13.95 (ISBN 0-312-01103-2, Pub. by Thomas Dunne Bks). St Martin.

Untimely Meditations. Friedrich Nietzsche. Tr. by R. J. Hollingdale. LC 83-6604. (Texts in German Philosophy Ser.). 250p. 1984. 32.50 (ISBN 0-521-24740-3); pap. 10.95 (ISBN 0-521-28927-0). Cambridge U Pr.

Untimely Tracts. Roger Scruton. 256p. 1987. 19.95 (ISBN 0-312-00494-X). St Martin.

Untinears & Antennae for Maurice Pavel. Jonathan Williams. 60p. 1977. 4.00 (ISBN 0-916562-07-7). Truck Pr.

Untitled, Black - White. Janelle Reiring. (Illus.). 1978. pap. text ed. 4.95 (ISBN 0-931706-03-3). L Lawler.

Untitled Historical Romance. Joanna Hill. 1986. pap. 2.95 (ISBN 0-671-61743-5). PB.

Untitled Novel. Frank Deford. Date not set. 16.95 (ISBN 0-670-80649-8). Viking.

Untitled, Red - Blue, 2 vols. Louise Lawler. LC 78-59796. (Illus.). 1978. Set. pap. text ed. 7.95 (ISBN 0-931706-00-9). Vol. 1 (ISBN 0-931706-01-7). Vol. 2 (ISBN 0-931706-02-5). L Lawler.

Untitled Subjects. Richard Howard. LC 78-86548. 96p. (Orig.). 1983. pap. 6.95 (ISBN 0-689-10136-8). Atheneum.

Unto a Good Land. Vilhelm Moberg. 416p. 1983. pap. 4.95 (ISBN 0-446-31125-1). Warner Bks.

Unto a Perfect Man. 4th ed. Carl Coffman. 209p. 1982. pap. 8.95 (ISBN 0-943872-83-9). Andrews Univ Pr.

Unto Christ. H. L. Heijkoop. 47p. pap. 0.60 (ISBN 0-88172-087-9). Believers Bkshelf.

Unto Death. Amos Oz. LC 77-15963. (Illus.). 168p. 1978. pap. 3.95 (ISBN 0-15-693170-2, Harv). HarBraceJ.

Unto Dust You Shall Return. Norman Geller. (Illus.). 16p. (gr. 6-10). 1986. pap. 4.95 (ISBN 0-915753-11-1). N Geller Pub.

Unto God & Caesar: Religious Issues in the Emerging Commonwealth 1891-1906. R. Ely. 1976. 22.00x (ISBN 0-522-84093-0, Pub. by Melbourne U Pr). Intl Spec Bk.

Unto Him Be Glory. Paul Byers. 220p. 1974. 4.95 (ISBN 0-89114-047-6); pap. 2.95 (ISBN 0-89114-046-8). Baptist Pub Hse.

Unto Him Shall We Return: Selections from the Baha'i Writings on the Reality & Immortality of the Human Soul. Compiled by Hushidar Motlagh. 144p. 1985. pap. 9.95 (ISBN 0-87743-201-5). Baha'i.

Unto My Father. Clyde A. Kirby. LC 87-40256. 247p. 1988. pap. 10.95 (ISBN 1-55523-118-7). Winston-Derek.

Unto Our Times. Jerry Lackey. LC 79-160449. (Illus.). 128p. 1971. 5.00 (ISBN 0-933512-11-2). Pioneer Bk Tx.

Unto the Altar. John Tigges. 400p. (Orig.). 1985. pap. 3.75 (ISBN 0-8439-2225-7, Leisure Bks). Leisure NY.

Unto the Altar. John Tigges. 400p. 1988. pap. 3.95 Mass Market (ISBN 0-8439-2596-5). Leisure NY.

Unto the Beast. Richard Monaco. 480p. (Orig.). 1987. pap. 3.95 (ISBN 0-553-26144-4, Spectra). Bantam.

Unto the Churches: Jesus Christ, Christianity, & the Edgar Cayce Readings. Richard H. Drummond. 1978. pap. 7.95 (ISBN 0-87604-102-0). ARE Pr.

Unto the Generations. Daniel L. Marsh. LC 68-27392. 7.95 (ISBN 0-912806-25-7). Long Hse.

Unto the Hills. Sara Yoder. 1985. 2.95 (ISBN 0-87813-523-5). Christian Light.

Unto the Hills: A Devotional Treasury from Billy Graham. Billy Graham. 384p. 1986. 14.95 (ISBN 0-8499-0603-2). Word Bks.

Unto the Islands of the Sea: A History of the Latter-day Saints in the Pacific. R. Lanier Britsch. LC 85-27463. (Illus.). 599p. 1986. 16.95 (ISBN 0-87747-754-X). Deseret Bk.

Unto the Least of These: Special Education in the Church. Andrew Wood. LC 84-16077. 1984. pap. 4.95 (ISBN 0-87227-099-8). Reg Baptist.

Unto the Least Seattle Ryther Center. Cora G. Chase. 152p. pap. 5.95 (ISBN 0-8466-0283-0, S283). Shorey.

Unto the Uttermost. Mrs. Bob White. (Illus.). 80p. 1977. pap. 1.00 (ISBN 0-89114-079-4). Baptist Pub Hse.

Unto Thee I Grant. 32nd ed. Rev. by Sri Ramatherio. LC 49-15007. 96p. 1968. 8.95 (ISBN 0-912057-02-5, G-505). AMORC.

Unto This Hour. Tom Wicker. 752p. 1985. pap. 4.95 (ISBN 0-425-07583-4). Berkley Pub.

Unto This Last. John Ruskin. Incl. Political Economy of Art; Essays on Political Economy. 1979. Repr. of 1907 ed. 14.95x (ISBN 0-460-00216-3, Evman). Biblio Dist.

Unto this Last & Other Writings. John Ruskin. Ed. by Clive Wilmer. (Classics Ser.). 368p. 1986. pap. 6.95 (ISBN 0-14-043211-6). Penguin.

Unto This Last: Four Essays on the First Principles of Political Economy. John Ruskin. Ed. by Lloyd J. Hubenka. LC 67-12118. xlvi, 97p. 1967. pap. 6.95x (ISBN 0-8032-5165-3, BB 345, Bison). U of Nebr Pr.

Unto Us a Child is Born. Reuel Lemmons & John Bannister. Compiled by Rex Kyker. 126p. (Orig.). 1982. pap. 2.95 (ISBN 0-88027-109-4). Firm Foun Pub.

Unto You & to Your Children. Grace Wiens. (Illus.). 229p. (Orig.). 1976. pap. 5.95 (ISBN 0-912315-10-5). Word Aflame.

Unto You Is the Promise. Robert W. Cummings. 40p. pap. 0.79 (ISBN 0-88243-750-X, 02-0750). Gospel Pub.

Untold Decades. Robert Patrick. 160p. 1988. 14.95 (ISBN 0-312-02307-3). St Martin.

Untold Facts about the Small Business Game: How to Be Competent in Business. rev., abr. ed. Luanna C. Blagrove. (Illus.). 250p. 1988. 24.95 (ISBN 0-939776-14-6). Blagrove Pubns.

Untold History of Israel. Jacques Derogy & Hesi Carmel. LC 78-74552. Orig. Title: Histoire Secrete d'Israel. (Illus.). 396p. (Orig.). 1980. pap. 7.95 (ISBN 0-394-17651-0, E756, Ever). Grove.

Untold Legend of the Batman. Wein et al. 160p. 1982. pap. 1.95 (ISBN 0-523-49018-6, Dist. by Warner Pub Services & Saint Martin's Press). Tor Bks.

Untold Lives: The First Generation of American Women Psychologists. Elizabeth Scarborough & Laurel Furumoto. LC 86-20715. (Illus.). 224p. 1987. 27.50 (ISBN 0-231-05154-9). Columbia U Pr.

Untold Sequel of the Strange Case of Dr. Jekyll & Mr. Hyde. Francis H. Little. (Classics of Fantastic Literature Ser.: No. 1). 50p. Date not set. lib. bdg. 19.95x (ISBN 0-89370-832-1); pap. text ed. 9.95x (ISBN 0-89370-932-8). Borgo Pr.

Untold Sisters: Hispanic Nuns in Their Own Works. Electa Arenal & Stacey Schlau. Tr. by Amanda Powell from Span. (Illus.). 656p. Date not set. 39.95x (ISBN 0-8263-1105-9); pap. 19.95 (ISBN 0-8263-1106-7). U of NM Pr.

Untold Story: Jesus Son of God. Clarice Albritton. LC 83-73188. 1983. pap. 5.95 (ISBN 0-318-00817-3). W P Brownell.

Untold Story of Dr. Joseph Mengela. (Critic's Choice Paperbacks Ser.). 1988. pap. 3.95 (ISBN 1-55547-285-0, Univ Bks). Lyle Stuart.

Untold Story: The Life of Isadora Duncan 1921-1927. Mary Desti. LC 80-26739. (Series in Dance). (Illus.). 281p. 1981. Repr. of 1929 ed. lib. bdg. 35.00 (ISBN 0-306-76044-4). Da Capo.

Untouchability in India. R. K. Kshirsagar. 1986. 45.00 (ISBN 0-8364-1915-4, Pub. by Deep). South Asia Bks.

Untouchable. Mulk R. Anand. (Mayfair Paperbacks Ser.). 226p. 1983. pap. 5.00 (ISBN 0-86578-068-4). Ind-US Inc.

Untouchable: An Indian Life History. James M. Freeman. LC 78-55319. (Illus.). 1979. 39.50x (ISBN 0-8047-1001-5); pap. 10.00 (ISBN 0-8047-1103-8, SP40). Stanford U Pr.

Untouchable As Himself: Ideology, Identity & Pragmatism among the Lucknow Chamars. R. S. Khare. (Studies in Cultural Systems: No. 8). (Illus.). 208p. 1985. 39.50 (ISBN 0-521-26314-X); pap. cancelled (ISBN 0-521-26926-1). Cambridge U Pr.

Up & down Merton's Mountain: A Contemporary Spiritual Journey. Gerald Groves. Ed. by Herbert Lambert. 200p. (Orig.). 1988. pap. 12.95 (ISBN 0-8272-3801-0). CBP.

Up & down New Hampshire. Lillian Bailey. 1987. 7.95. Equity Pub NH.

Up & Down on the Merry-Go-Round. Bill Martin, Jr. & John Archambault. LC 87-28836. (Illus.). 32p. (gr. k-3). 1988. 12.95 (ISBN 0-8050-0681-8). H Holt & Co.

Up & Down the Blood Sugar Trail. Mary Payne. (Illus., Orig.). (gr. k-4). 1987. pap. 1.98 (ISBN 0-9619326-0-0). MstrWorks Pub.

Up & Running: A Case Study of Successful Systems Development. H. Dines Hansen. LC 83-51815. 152p. 1984. pap. 25.95 (ISBN 0-917072-41-3, Yourdon). P-H.

Up & Running in Fifteen Minutes. David T. Anderson & Charles Seiter. (Illus.). 200p. (Orig.). Date not set. pap. text ed. 12.95 (ISBN 0-915835-11-8). PC Software.

Up & Running in Real Estate Sales. P. J. Thompson. LC 87-16916. 200p. (Orig.). 1987. pap. 17.95 (ISBN 0-918785-02-2). Kricket.

Up & Running: Maintaining, Servicing & Enhancing the PC. John Woram. 320p. 1986. 19.95 (ISBN 0-933186-08-8). IBM Armonk.

Up & Running: Microcomputer Applications. Marilyn Popyk. LC 86-26620. 1987. pap. text ed. write for info. (ISBN 0-201-06274-7). Addison-Wesley.

Up & Up. Shirley Hughes. LC 85-24166. (Illus.). 32p. (gr. k-2). 1986. Repr. of 1979 ed. 10.25 (ISBN 0-688-06261-X). Lothrop.

Up at the Villa. W. Somerset Maugham. LC 75-25366. (Works of W. Somerset Maugham Ser.). 1977. Repr. of 1941 ed. 20.00x (ISBN 0-405-07824-2). Ayer Co Pubs.

Up at the Villa. W. Somerset Maugham. 1978. pap. 4.95 (ISBN 0-14-002670-3). Penguin.

Up Before Daylight: Life Histories from the Alabama Writers' Project, 1938-1939. Ed. by James S. Brown, Jr. LC 81-21988. 261p. 1982. pap. 10.95 (ISBN 0-8173-0099-6). U of Ala Pr.

Up Close & Personal: The Inside Story of Network Television Sports. Jim Spence & Dave Diles. 288p. 1988. 19.95 (ISBN 0-689-11943-7). Atheneum.

Up Country. (Illus.). 1987. 11.95 (ISBN 0-317-65228-1). Northword.

Up Country: Voices from the Midwestern Wilderness. Ed. by William J. Seno. LC 85-60995. (Voices from the Wilderness Ser.: No. 1). (Illus.). 256p. (Orig.). 1985. pap. 11.95 (ISBN 0-933437-00-5). Round River Pub.

Up Cutshin & Down Greasy. Leonard W. Roberts. LC 87-29600. 176p. 1988. 16.00 (ISBN 0-8131-1638-4); pap. 8.00 (ISBN 0-8131-0176-X). U Pr of Ky.

Up-Date. Dee H. Hadley. 112p. (YA) (gr. 9 up). 1988. pap. 3.95 (ISBN 0-87747-847-3). Deseret Bk.

Up-Date in Heart Valve. Ed. by F. Loogen & D. Horstkotte. 300p. 1985. 28.00 (ISBN 0-387-91266-5). Springer-Verlag.

Up, Down & All Around. Another Adventure Staff. (Teddy Ruxpin Answer Box Ser.). (Illus.). 22p. (ps). 1988. write for info. incl. pre-programmed audiotape (ISBN 0-934323-77-1). Alchemy Comms.

Up, Down, & Around the Raintree. Charlotte Graeber. LC 83-23155. (Cook's Early Readers Ser.). (Illus.). (gr. 1-4). 1984. 4.95 (ISBN 0-89191-840-X); pap. 3.95 (ISBN 0-89191-786-1). Cook.

Up Eel River. facs. ed. Margaret P. Montague. LC 77-150552. (Short Story Index Reprint Ser.). (Illus.). Repr. of 1928 ed. 17.00 (ISBN 0-8369-3849-6). Ayer Co Pubs.

Up for Grabs: A Trip Through Time & Space in the Sunshine State. John Rothchild. (Nonfiction Ser.). 224p. 1985. 15.95 (ISBN 0-670-74176-0). Viking.

Up for Grabs: Inquiries into Who Wants What. Daniel J. Chasan. LC 77-23881. 134p. 1977. 9.95 (ISBN 0-914842-18-8); pap. 5.95 (ISBN 0-914842-17-X). Madrona Pubs.

Up for None. Mick Mahoney & Melissa Murray. Ed. by Barrie Keefe. Bd. with Coming Apart. (New Theatrescripts Ser.). 64p. 1985. pap. 6.95 (ISBN 0-413-58930-7, 9655). Heinemann Ed.

Up from Agony: A Novel of Americanization. John Harms. 69.95 (ISBN 0-685-26305-3). Revisionist Pr.

Up from Apathy: A Study of Moral Awareness & Social Involvement. Richard A. Hoehn. LC 83-7057. 179p. (Orig.). 1983. pap. 10.95 (ISBN 0-687-43114-X). Abingdon.

Up from Captivity. 3.25 (ISBN 0-317-60929-7, 15-9630). Augsburg.

Up from Dependency: A New National Public Assistance Strategy. 62p. (Orig.). 1988. pap. 9.50 (S/N 040-000-00511-1). USGPO.

Up from Dependency: A New National Public Assistance Strategy, Supplement 1, The National Public Assistance System, V.1 - An Overview of the Current System. (Illus.). 111p. (Orig.). 1986. pap. 5.50 (ISBN 0-318-22440-2, S/N 040-000-00508-1). USGPO.

Up from Dependency: A New Public Assistance Strategy, Report. 77p. (Orig.). 1986. pap. 3.75 (ISBN 0-318-22473-9, S/N 040-000-00513-7). USGPO.

Up from Depression. Leonard Cammer. 1983. pap. 4.50 (ISBN 0-671-55768-8). PB.

Up from Eden. Ed. by Kendra Crossen. Date not set. pap. 14.95 (ISBN 0-87773-228-0). Shambhala Pubns.

Up from Eden: A Transpersonal View of Human Evolution. Ken Wilber. LC 82-42678. (New Science Library). (Illus.). 72p. 1981. pap. 14.95. Shambhala Pubns.

Up from Excellence: The Impact of the Excellence Movement on Schools. William W. Wayson et al. LC 87-63159. 215p. (Orig.). 1988. pap. 7.00 (ISBN 0-87367-435-9). Phi Delta Kappa.

Up from Grief. Bernardine Kreis & Alice Pattie. 292p. 1984. pap. 9.95 large print ed. (ISBN 0-8027-2486-8). Walker & Co.

Up from Grief: Patterns of Recovery. Bernadine Kreis & Alice Pattie. 160p. 1982. pap. 5.95 (ISBN 0-8164-2364-4, AY7442, HarpR). Har-Row.

Up from Jericho Tel. E. L. Konigsburg. LC 85-20061. 192p. (gr. 5 up). 1986. 13.95 (ISBN 0-689-31194-X, Atheneum Childrens Bks). Macmillan.

Up from Jericho Tel. E. L. Konigsburg. (gr. k-6). 1987. pap. 2.95 (ISBN 0-440-49142-8, YB). Dell.

Up from Puerto Rico. Elena Padilla. LC 58-7171. 317p. 1958. 29.00x (ISBN 0-231-02213-1). Columbia U Pr.

Up from Seltzer. Peter Hochstein. LC 80-54617. (Illus.). 96p. 1981. pap. 4.95 (ISBN 0-89480-145-7, 450). Workman Pub.

Up from Slavery. Booker T. Washington. (Airmont Classics Ser.). (gr. 5 up). pap. 1.95 (ISBN 0-8049-0157-0, CL-157). Airmont.

Up from Slavery. Booker T. Washington. 330p. 1971. Repr. of 1900 ed. 21.00 (ISBN 0-87928-021-2). Corner Hse.

Up from Slavery. Booker T. Washington. 15.95 (ISBN 0-89190-799-8, Pub. by Am Repr). Amereon Ltd.

Up From Slavery. Booker T. Washington. LC 85-16712. (Penguin Classics Ser.). 336p. 1986. pap. 3.95 (ISBN 0-14-039051-0). Penguin.

Up from Slavery see Three Negro Classics.

Up from the Ashes. Elaine H. Marze. 1987. 11.95 (ISBN 0-533-07201-8). Vantage.

Up from the Ashes: How to Survive & Grow Through Personal Crisis. Karl Slaikeu & Steve Lawhead. 240p. 1987. pap. 7.95 (ISBN 0-310-35541-9, 10255P). Zondervan.

Up from the Ashes: The Rise of the Steel Minimill in the United States. Donald F. Barnett & Robert W. Crandall. LC 85-48201. 135p. 1986. 26.95 (ISBN 0-8157-0834-3); pap. 9.95 (ISBN 0-8157-0833-5). Brookings.

Up from the Country; Infidelities; the Game of Love & Chance. Pierre C. De Marivaux. 384p. 1980. pap. 5.95 (ISBN 0-14-044303-7). Penguin.

Up from the Cradle of Jazz: New Orleans Music since World War II. Jason Berry et al. LC 85-29015. (Illus.). 272p. 1986. 35.00x (ISBN 0-8203-0853-6); pap. 15.95 (ISBN 0-8203-0854-4). U of GA Pr.

Up from the Earth: A Collection of Garden Poems. Ed. by Sylvia Spencer. 306p. 1981. Repr. of 1935 ed. lib. bdg. 40.00 (ISBN 0-8495-5411-X). Arden Lib.

Up from the Hardpan: The Biography of Rufus M. Utterback. Elizabeth U. Trent. (Illus.). 122p. 1985. pap. 8.95 (ISBN 0-9615438-0-9). South-West Pub.

Up from the Lizard. J. C. Trewin. 294p. 1982. pap. 7.50 (ISBN 0-907746-00-4, Pub. by A Mott Ltd). Longwood Pub Group.

Up from Uzam. Alta M. Rymer. (Tharma Lo Fairyland Ser.: Story 1). (Illus.). 28p. (Orig.). (gr. 2-4). 1987. pap. 11.50 (ISBN 0-9600792-8-9). Rymer Bks.

Up Front. Bill Mauldin. (Illus.). 1968. 8.95 (ISBN 0-393-08493-0). Norton.

Up Front. Bill Mauldin. 18.95 (ISBN 0-89190-896-X, Pub. by Am Repr). Amereon Ltd.

Up-Front Financing: The Entrepreneur's Guide. A. David Silver. LC 81-21985. (Wiley Series Small Business Management). 245p. 1982. 17.95 (ISBN 0-471-86386-6, Pub. by The Ronald Press). Wiley.

Up-Front MIP - How It Affects You. write for info. Mortgage Bankers.

Up Front Money: The Entrepreneur's Guide. A. David Silver. 1988. 24.95 (ISBN 0-471-63475-1). Wiley.

Up Front with U. S. Day by Day in the Life of a Combat Infantryman in General Patton's Third Army. Walter L. Brown. LC 79-54035. (Illus.). 744p. 1979. 14.95x (ISBN 0-9604822-0-2); lib. bdg. write for info. Brown's Studio.

Up Goes Mr. Downs. Jerry Smath. LC 84-1199. (Illus.). 48p. (ps-3). 1985. 5.95 (ISBN 0-8193-1137-5). Parents.

Up Goes Mr. Downs. Jerry Smath. (Parents Magazine Press Read Aloud Bks.). 48p. (ps-3). 1987. pap. 2.95 (ISBN 0-517-56623-0). Crown.

Up Goes the Skyscraper! Gail Gibbons. LC 85-16245. (Illus.). 32p. (gr. k-3). 1986. 12.95 (ISBN 0-02-736780-0, Four Winds). Macmillan.

Up Hatfield Holler. Lillie D. Chaffin. 40p. (Orig.). 1981. pap. 4.50 (ISBN 0-937992-04-6). Ashford Pr CT.

Up Here. Donald Schenker. Ed. by Orvis Burmaster. LC 88-71125. 50p. (Orig.). 1988. pap. 4.95 (ISBN 0-916272-36-2). Ahsahta Pr.

Up Hill, Down Dale: A Volume of Short Stories. facsimile 2nd ed. Eden Phillpotts. LC 79-150558. (Short Story Index Reprint Ser.). Repr. of 1925 ed. 18.00 (ISBN 0-8369-3855-0). Ayer Co Pubs.

Up in a Balloon. Leonard Cottrell. LC 69-17423. (Illus.). (gr. 8 up). 1970. 16.95 (ISBN 0-87599-142-4). S G Phillips.

Up in Arms: A Common Cause Guide to Understanding Nuclear Arms Policy. Sandra Secacca. (Illus.). 130p. 1984. pap. text ed. 3.50 (ISBN 0-914389-01-7). Common Cause.

Up in Bed. Stuart Friebert. LC 74-620108. (CSU Poetry Ser.: No. 1). 83p. 1974. pap. 4.95 (ISBN 0-914946-01-3). Cleveland St Univ Poetry Ctr.

Up in Heaven: Grove Press Victorian Library. 192p. 1986. pap. 3.95 (ISBN 0-394-62313-4, BC). Grove.

Up in Seth's Room. Norma F. Mazer. LC 79-2102. 208p. (gr. 7 up). 1979. pap. 7.95 (ISBN 0-385-29058-6). Delacorte.

Up in Seth's Room. Norma F. Mazer. 208p. (YA) (gr. 7 up). 1981. pap. 2.95 (ISBN 0-440-99190-0, LE). Dell.

Up in Smoke: A Business Guide to Fire & Life Safety. Robert Pessemier. Ed. by Carol C. Schneider. LC 86-62569. 144p. (Orig.). 1987. pap. 7.95 (ISBN 0-940383-07-1). Phoenix Pub Redmond.

Up in the Air. Mary W. Worthylake. (Illus.). 200p. 1984. pap. 8.95 (ISBN 0-89288-096-1). Maverick.

Up in the Air in a Balloon. N. Nosov. 16p. 1985. pap. 1.99 (ISBN 0-8285-3153-6, Pub. by Raduga Pubs USSR). Imported Pubns.

Up in the Air with Shelley Berman. Shelley Berman. 127p. 1986. 6.95 (ISBN 0-8431-1574-2). Price Stern.

Up in the Clouds. N. Nosov. 12p. 1985. pap. 1.99 (ISBN 0-8285-3152-8, Pub. by Raduga Pubs USSR). Imported Pubns.

Up Is Not the Only Way: A Guide for Career Development Practitioners see Guide for Career Development Practitioners: Up Is Not the Only Way.

Up Is the Mountain & Other Views. Erwin Rieger. LC 73-89240. (Illus.). 1973. 8.95 (ISBN 0-8323-0235-X). Binford-Metropolitan.

Up Jumped L. C. Furr. James Hulihan. 1987. 13.95 (ISBN 0-533-07340-5). Vantage.

Up Long's Peak in 1873 with Rocky Mountain Jim. Isabella L. Bird. Ed. by William R. Jones. (Illus.). 49p. 1977. pap. 2.95 (ISBN 0-89646-023-1). Outbooks.

Up-Lot Reveries: An Oral History of the North Fork. Maria Parson. 17.95 (ISBN 0-8488-0122-9, Pub. by Amereon Hse). Amereon Ltd.

Up Mountain One Time. Willie Wilson. LC 87-7624. (Illus.). 144p. (gr. 3-6). 1987. 12.95 (ISBN 0-531-05725-9); PLB 12.99 (ISBN 0-531-08325-X). Orchard Bks Watts.

Up My Coast. Joanne Kyger. (Illus.). 24p. (Orig.). 1981. pap. 3.00 (ISBN 0-912449-05-5). Floating Island.

Up North. Sam Cook. LC 86-62906. (Illus.). 192p. 14.95 (ISBN 0-938586-09-2, Pfeifer Hamilton). Whole Person.

Up North. John S. Wade. (W.N.J. Ser.: No. 12). 1980. signed ed. o.p. 20.00 (ISBN 0-685-60008-4); pap. 6.00 (ISBN 1-55780-061-8). Juniper Pr WI.

Up North in Winter. Deborah Hartley. (Illus.). 32p. (ps-3). 1986. 11.95 (ISBN 0-525-44268-5). Dutton.

Up North Is Down the Crick. Wallace D. McRae & Jeri D. Walton. LC 85-60892. (Illus.). 70p. (Orig.). 1985. pap. 6.95 (ISBN 0-933819-00-5). Museum Rockies.

Up North on the Mary. Tod Schacht. LC 87-92100. 1988. 17.50 (ISBN 0-87212-213-1). Libra.

Up Old Forge Way. limited ed. David H. Beetley. Bd. with West Canada Creek. (Illus.). 432p. 1984. 12.95 (ISBN 0-932052-14-2). North Country.

Up on Madison, Down on Seventy Fifth Street, Pt. 1. Jon F. Rice. (Illus.). 90p. 1982. 3.00 (ISBN 0-937352-03-9). Committee IL.

Up on the Downside. Layding L. Kaliba. (Illus.). 72p. (Orig.). 1982. 5.00 (ISBN 0-938887-02-5). Single Action Prod.

Up on the River: An Upper Missippi Chronicle. John Madson. (Illus.). 288p. 1986. pap. 7.95 (ISBN 0-14-008746-X). Penguin.

Up on the River: An Upper Mississippi Chronicle. John Madson. LC 84-23596. (Illus.). 288p. 1985. 17.95 (ISBN 0-8052-3966-9, Pub. by N Lyons Bks). Schocken.

Up Saskatchewan Way: An Anthology of Short Stories. J. Paul Loomis. (Illus.). 152p. 1985. 15.00 (ISBN 0-317-59459-1). G K Westgard.

Up Ship! U. S. Navy Rigid Airships, Nineteen Nineteen to Nineteen Thirty-Five. Charles L. Keller & Douglas H. Robinson. LC 82-6374. (Illus.). 360p. 1982. 29.95 (ISBN 0-87021-738-0). Naval Inst Pr.

Up South: Blacks in Chicago's Suburbs (1719-1983) James Dorsey. LC 86-50583. (Illus.). 113p. (Orig.). 1986. pap. text ed. 13.95x (ISBN 0-932269-93-1). Wyndham Hall.

Up Spake the Cabin Boy. 2nd ed. Robert Harbinson. 256p. 1988. pap. 10.95 (ISBN 0-85640-400-4, Pub. by Blackstaff Ireland). Irish Bks Media.

Up Stream: An American Chronicle. Ludwig Lewisohn. LC 24-11220. Repr. of 1923 ed. 29.00x (ISBN 0-403-00655-4). Scholarly.

Up the Chimney Down. Joan Aiken. LC 85-42642. (Charlotte Zolotow Bks.). 256p. (gr. 5 up). 1985. 12.70i (ISBN 0-06-020036-7); PLB 12.89g (ISBN 0-06-020037-5). HarpJ.

Up the Country: A Saga of Pioneering Days. Miles Franklin. (Illus.). 256p. 1987. 15.95 (ISBN 0-8253-0417-2). Beaufort Bks NY.

Up the Country: Letters Written to Her Sister from the Upper Provinces of India. Emily Eden. Ed. by Edward Thompson. (Illus.). 432p. 1982. text ed. 27.50x (ISBN 0-7007-0112-5, Pub. by Curzon Pr England). Apt Bks.

Up the Creek. John Harrison. 288p. 1986. pap. 11.95 (ISBN 0-87052-337-6). Hippocrene Bks.

Up the down Escalator: Development & the Economy, a Jamaican Case Study. Michael Manley. (Illus.). 320p. 1987. 19.95 (ISBN 0-88258-112-0). Howard U Pr.

Up the Down Staircase: Twenty-Fifth Anniversary Edition. Bel Kaufman. 1988. 19.95 (ISBN 0-13-939158-4). Prentice Hall Pr.

Up the EDP Pyramid: The Complete Job Hunting Manual for Computer Professionals. Jack French. LC 81-11605. 200p. (Orig.). 1981. 21.95 (ISBN 0-471-08925-7, Pub. by John Wiley). Krieger.

Up the Financial Ladder in a Downwardly Mobile Society. Dallas Whitney. LC 83-43154. 304p. 1984. 17.95 (ISBN 0-87951-953-3). Overlook Pr.

Up the Financial Ladder in a Downwardly Mobile Society. Dallas Whitney. LC 83-43154. 432p. 1986. pap. 9.95 (ISBN 0-87951-215-6). Overlook Pr.

Up the HRD Ladder: A Guide to Professional Growth. N. Chalofsky & C. I. Lincoln. 1983. text ed. write for info. (ISBN 0-201-04998-8). Addison-Wesley.

Up the I. R. A. Winifred Doyle. (Illus.). 289p. 1983. 15.50 (ISBN 0-682-49924-2). Exposition-Phoenix.

Up the Koyukuk. Alaska Geographic Staff. LC 83-15343. (Alaska Geographic Ser.: Vol. 10, no. 4). (Illus.). 152p. 1983. pap. 14.95 (ISBN 0-88240-200-5, Alaska Geographic Society). Alaska Northwest.

Up the Ladder. Thomas Friedman. 224p. (Orig.). 1987. pap. 4.50 (ISBN 0-446-34703-5). Warner Bks.

Up the Ladder: Coping with the Corporate Climb. Thomas Friedman. 203p. 1986. 17.95 (ISBN 0-446-51291-5). Warner Bks.

Up the Ladder in Foreign Missions. Lewis G. Jordan. Ed. by Edwin S. Gausted. LC 79-52596. (Baptist Tradition Ser.). (Illus.). 1980. Repr. of 1901 ed. lib. bdg. 27.50x (ISBN 0-405-12463-5). Ayer Co Pubs.

Up the Ladder-Women, Professionals & Clients in College Student Personnel. Beverly Gelwick. 1979. 3.00 (ISBN 1-55620-033-1, 72603C). Am Assn Coun Dev.

Up the Lake Road: The First Hundred Years of the Adirondack Mountain Reserve 1887-1987. Edith Pilcher. (Illus.). 208p. 1987. 35.00 (ISBN 0-9618456-0-0); pap. 17.50 (ISBN 0-9618456-1-9). Adk Mtn Reserve.

Up the Line. 4th ed. Robert Silverberg. (Del Rey Bks). 256p. 1978. pap. 2.95. Ballantine.

Up the Line. Robert Silverberg. 256p. (Orig.). 1985. pap. 3.95 (ISBN 0-345-32585-0). Ballantine.

Up the Road Slowly. Irene Hunt. (gr. 4-9). 1988. pap. 2.50. Scholastic Inc.

Up the Rough Side. Charles Perry. LC 85-61878. (Illus.). 96p. 1985. pap. 5.95 (ISBN 0-9615139-0-X). C Perry Pub.

Up There. Eric Hill. LC 82-60626. (Eric Hill's Baby Bear Bks). (Illus.). 14p. (ps). 1983. pap. 2.50 (ISBN 0-394-85635-X). Random.

Up They Rise: The Unfinished Works of Jamie Reid. Jamie Reid & Jon Savage. (Illus.). 144p. (Orig.). 1987. pap. 12.95 (ISBN 0-571-14762-3). Faber & Faber.

Up 'Til Now: A Memoir of the Decline of American Politics. Eugene McCarthy. 192p. 1987. 16.95 (ISBN 0-15-193170-4). HarBraceJ.

Up-to-Date Confectionery. 4th, rev. ed. A. R. Daniel. (Illus.). ix, 542p. 1978. 45.00 (ISBN 0-85334-791-3, Pub. by Elsevier Applied Sci England). Elsevier.

Up-to-Date Set of the Rules of the Superior Court, DC Court of Appeals, U. S. District Court, DC Circuit Court for the District of Columbia. LC 82-134872. 1987. 67.00. Rules Serv Co.

Up to Jerusalem. Richard E. Bauerle & Frederick W. Kemper. 1979. pap. 2.75 (ISBN 0-570-03795-6, 12-2777). Concordia.

Up to My Neck in Haiku. Liberty Campbell. 76p. 1982. 6.00 (ISBN 0-682-49922-6). Exposition-Phoenix.

Up to No Good. Rosemary Joyce. (Dream Girls Ser.: No.). (YA) (gr. 7 up). 1987. pap. 2.50 (ISBN 0-671-62115-7). Archway.

Up to Now. Martin Shaw. (Illus.). 218p. 1980. Repr. of 1929 ed. lib. bdg. 20.00 (ISBN 0-89984-404-9). Century Bookbindery.

Up to Ten & Down Again. Lisa C. Ernst. LC 84-21852. (Illus.). 40p. (ps). 1986. 10.95 (ISBN 0-688-04541-3); PLB 10.88 (ISBN 0-688-04542-1). Lothrop.

Up to the Front of the Line: The Black Man in the American Political System. Robert P. Turner. 1975. 23.95x (ISBN 0-8046-9097-9, 9097, Pub by Kennikat). Assoc Faculty Pr.

Up to the Lake. Tom Hegg. (Illus.). 50p. 1986. 9.95 (ISBN 0-931674-09-3). Waldman Hse Pr.

Up to the Mountains & Down to the Villages: The Transfer of Youth from Urban to Rural China. Thomas P. Bernstein. LC 77-76291. (Illus.). 1977. 37.50x (ISBN 0-300-02135-6). Yale U Pr.

Up to the Sky in Ships: In & Out of Quandry. A. Bertram Chandler & Lee Hoffman. Ed. by Charles J. Hitchcock. 172p. 1982. 13.00 (ISBN 0-915368-16-1). New Eng SF Assoc.

Up to There in Alligators. Patrick Oliphant. (Illus.). 176p. (Orig.). 1987. pap. 8.95 (ISBN 0-8362-2095-1). Andrews & McMeel.

Up, Up, & Away. Margaret Hillert. (Just Beginning-to-Read Ser.). (Illus.). 32p. (gr. 1-6). 1981. PLB 4.39 (ISBN 0-8136-5096-8, Dist. by Caroline Hse); pap. 1.95 (ISBN 0-8136-5596-X). Modern Curr.

Up Went the Goat. Barbara Gregorich. Ed. by Joan Hoffman. (Start to Read! Ser.). (Illus.). 16p. (Orig.). (gr. k-2). 1984. pap. 1.95 (ISBN 0-88743-002-3, 06002). Sch Zone Pub Co.

Up Where I Used to Live Stories: Stories. Max Schott. LC 78-11619. (Illinois Short Fiction Ser.). 144p. 1978. pap. 8.95 (ISBN 0-252-00720-4). U of Ill Pr.

Up with America see Faith for All Generations.

Up with Hope: A Biography of Jesse Jackson. Dorothy Chaplik. LC 86-11634. (People in Focus Ser.). (Illus.). 128p. (gr. 6 up). 1986. PLB 11.95 (ISBN 0-87518-347-6). Dillon.

Up with Math: Basic Skills Step by Step. Ron McCully. Ed. by Russell F. Jacobs. (Illus.). (gr. 5-12). 1979. pap. text ed. 6.00 (ISBN 0-918272-03-3); tchr's ed. 6.25 (ISBN 0-918272-04-1). Jacobs.

Up with Poetry. Ed. by Thomas L. Hakes. 10p. 1982. pap. 2.50x (ISBN 0-915020-15-7). Bardic.

Up-with-Wholesome, Down-with-Store-Bought Book of Recipes & Household Formulas. Yvonne Tarr. 1975. pap. 9.95 (ISBN 0-394-73140-9). Random.

Up with Worship. rev. ed. Anne Ortlund. LC 82-15063. 1982. pap. 5.95 (ISBN 0-8307-0867-7, 5417706). Regal.

Up Your Accountability: How to Up Your Financing Credibility by Upping Your Accounting Ability. Paul Bennett. LC 73-89364. (Nonprofit-Ability Ser.). (Illus.). 65p. 1973. pap. 14.95 (ISBN 0-914756-02-8). Taft Group.

Up Your Ante. Glen Chase. (Cherry Delight Ser.: No. 4). 1975. pap. 1.25 (ISBN 0-685-46896-8, LB4072K, Leisure Bks). Leisure NY.

Up Your Asteroid! A Science Fiction Farce. C. Everett Cooper. LC 77-866. 47p. 1977. lib. bdg. 16.95x (ISBN 0-89370-106-8); pap. 7.95x (ISBN 0-89370-206-4). Borgo Pr.

Up Your Career. 3rd ed. Dean C. Dauw. LC 79-57133. (Illus.). 256p. 1980. pap. text ed. 11.95x (ISBN 0-917974-40-9). Waveland Pr.

Up Your Cash Flow: Text & Accompanying Workbook. Harvey A. Goldstein. LC 84-82281. 176p. (Orig.). 1986. pap. 12.95 (ISBN 0-931349-04-4); 19.95 (ISBN 0-931349-02-8). Granville Pubns.

Up Your Equity: Build up Your Personal Net Worth. Victor I. Eber. LC 72-95079. (Illus.). 12.95 (ISBN 0-686-05084-3). Financial Pr.

Up Your Gas: Sixty-One Ways to Cut Gas Consumption, Increase Your Mileage, Chop Costs & Minimize Waiting in Gas Lines! Plus Eleven Ways to Find a Good Mechanic & Save Money! John V. Kamin. Incl. Sixty-One Ways to Cut Gas Consumption; Increase Your Mileage, Chop Costs & Minimize Waiting in Gas Lines; Eleven Ways to Find a Good Mechanic & Save Money. 52p. 1979. lib. bdg. 6.00 (ISBN 0-911353-07-0). Forecaster Pub Co.

Up Your Own Organization: A Handbook for Today's Entrepreneur. Donald M. Dible. Date not set. write for info. S&S.

Up Your Productivity. Kurt Hanks. 100p. 1988. 9.95 (ISBN 0-931961-49-1). Crisp Pubns.

Up Your Productivity. Kurt Hanks. 100p. Date not set. 9.95. Human Res Dev Pr.

Up Your Punctuation! An Almost Non-Grammatical Approach to Puntuation. Edgar C. Alward & E. Dale. 112p. (Orig.). (YA) (gr. 9-12). 1988. pap. 12.95 (ISBN 0-9620092-0-2). Pine Isl Pr.

Up Your Score: The Underground Guide to Psyching Out the SAT. Larry Berger et al. (Illus.). 224p. (Orig.). (YA) (gr. 11-12). 1987. pap. 9.95 (ISBN 0-942257-00-6). New Chapter Pr.

Up Your Visibility. Ellen Miller. Ed. by Jon Rappoport. LC 86-71829. 120p. (Orig.). 1987. pap. 6.95 (ISBN 0-317-56028-X). Authors Unltd.

Up Yours! Pierre Derriere. 1976. pap. 0.95 (ISBN 0-8439-0325-2, Leisure Bks). Leisure NY.

Up Yours: Guide to Advanced Revenge Techniques. G. Hayduke. 1986. lib. bdg. 79.95 (ISBN 0-8490-3732-8). Gordon Pr.

Up Yours! Guide to Advanced Revenge Techniques. George Hayduke. 220p. 1982. 16.95 (ISBN 0-87364-249-X). Paladin Pr.

Upa Gurus. David G. Eberhart. 10.00 (ISBN 0-89253-679-9). Ind-US Inc.

Upadesa Sahasri: A Thousand Teachings. Shankara. Tr. by Swami Jagadananda. (Sanskrit & Eng). pap. 4.95 (ISBN 0-87481-423-5). Vedanta Pr.

Upanayanam (Thread Marriage) Panduranga R. Malyala. (Illus.). 20p. 1983. pap. text ed. 2.00 (ISBN 0-938924-15-X). Sri Shirdi Sai.

Upanayanam: (Twice Born) 1983. pap. 2.00. Sri Shirdi Sai.

Upanisads. 2nd ed. Tr. by Srisa Chandra Vasu. LC 73-4980. (Sacred Books of the Hindus: No. 1). Repr. of 1911 ed. 34.50 (ISBN 0-404-57801-2). AMS Pr.

Upanisads: The Selections from 108 Upanisads. T. M. Mahadevan. Tr. by T. M. Mahadevan from Sanskrit. 240p. (Orig.). 1975. pap. 3.20 (ISBN 0-88253-985-X). Ind-US Inc.

Upanishads. Sri Aurobindo. 466p. (Sanskrit & Eng.). 1981. 46.00 (ISBN 0-89744-026-9, Pub. by Sri Aurobindo Ashram Trust India); pap. 30.00 (ISBN 0-89744-025-0). Auromere.

Upanishads. Tr. by Juan Mascaro. (Classics Ser.). (Orig.). 1965. pap. 3.50 (ISBN 0-14-044163-8). Penguin.

Upanishads, 2 Vols. F. Max Muller. 1963. Repr. of 1890 ed. text ed. 7.95 ea. Vol. 1 (ISBN 0-486-20992-X) (ISBN 0-486-20993-8). Dover.

Upanishads, 2 vols. F. Max Muller. 1974. lib. bdg. 250.00 (ISBN 0-8490-1252-X). Gordon Pr.

Upanishads, 2 vols. Tr. by Max Muller. lib. bdg. 250.00 (ISBN 0-87968-548-4). Krishna Pr.

Upanishads, 4 Vols. Tr. by Swami Nikhilananda. LC 49-9558. with notes (set) 32.00 (ISBN 0-911206-14-0); 8.50 ea.; Vol. I, 333p. (ISBN 0-911206-15-9); Vol. II, 400p. (ISBN 0-911206-16-7); Vol. III, 408p. (ISBN 0-911206-17-5); Vol. IV, 424p. (ISBN 0-911206-18-3). Ramakrishna.

Upanishads. 4th ed. Swami Paramananda. 1981. 6.50 (ISBN 0-911564-02-0); lexitone bdg. 4.00. Vedanta Ctr.

Upanishads: A Selection for the Modern Reader. Tr. & intro. by Eknath Easwaran. LC 87-14216. 1987. 18.00 (ISBN 0-915132-40-0); pap. 8.95 (ISBN 0-915132-39-7). Nilgiri Pr.

Upanishads: Breath of the Eternal. Swami Prabhavananda. Tr. by Frederick Manchester. pap. 2.95 (ISBN 0-451-62454-8, MJ2298, Ment). NAL.

Upanishads: Breath of the Eternal. Tr. by Swami Prabhavananda & Frederick Manchester. LC 48-5935. 6.95 (ISBN 0-87481-007-8); pap. 6.95 (ISBN 0-87481-040-X). Vedanta Pr.

Upanishads: Texts, Translations & Commentaries, Pt. 1. Sri Aurobindo. 466p. 1986. (Pub. by Sri Aurobindo Ashram India); pap. 12.00 (ISBN 0-89071-294-8). Aurobindo Assn.

Upanishads: The Crown of India's Soul. 1972. pap. 2.00 (ISBN 0-87847-012-3). Aum Pubns.

Upanishas: The Thirteen Principal Upanishads. 2nd ed. Tr. by R. E. Hume from Sanskrit. 1931. pap. 16.95x (ISBN 0-19-561641-3). Oxford U Pr.

Upasaka Two & One. Buddhadharma. 1981. pap. 3.95 (ISBN 0-87881-078-1). Mojave Bks.

Upchuck Summer. Joel L. Schwartz. LC 81-69670. (Illus.). 144p. (gr. 4-8). 9.95 (ISBN 0-440-09264-7); PLB 9.89 (ISBN 0-440-09269-8). Delacorte.

Upchuck Summer. Joel L. Schwartz. (Illus.). 144p. (gr. 3-7). 1983. pap. 2.75 (ISBN 0-440-49264-5, YB). Dell.

Upchuck Summer. Joel L. Schwartz. LC 81-65838. (Illus.). 144p. (gr. 4-6). 1982. 10.95 (ISBN 0-385-29099-3); pap. 10.95 (ISBN 0-385-29100-0). Delacorte.

UPCO's Review of Biology. 2nd ed. Sylvan Alcabes. (UPCO's Science Ser.). (Illus.). 288p. (YA) (gr. 9-12). 1988. pap. text ed. 3.00 (ISBN 0-937323-05-5). United Pub Co.

UPCO's Review of Chemistry. 2nd, rev. ed. (UPCO's Science Ser.). 256p. 1988. pap. text ed. 3.00 (ISBN 0-937323-04-7). United Pub Co.

UPCO's Review of Earth Science. Robert B. Sigda. Ed. by Freelance Editors Staff. (UPCO's Review Ser.). 1987. pap. text ed. 3.00 (ISBN 0-937323-03-9). United Pub Co.

UPCO's Review of Physics. Herbert H. Gottlieb. Ed. by Freelance Staff. (UPCO's Review Ser.). 1986. pap. text ed. 3.00 (ISBN 0-937323-02-0). United Pub Co.

Update. Fred Hartley. 160p. (gr. 7-12). 1982. pap. 2.95 (ISBN 0-8007-8431-6, Spire Bks). Revell.

Update--Belgium. rev. ed. Alison R. Lanier. LC 80-83924. (Country Orientation Ser.). 73p. 1988. pap. text ed. 27.50 (ISBN 0-933662-28-9). Intercult Pr.

Update--Britain. Alison R. Lanier. LC 80-83917. (Country Orientation Ser.). 1986. pap. text ed. 27.50 (ISBN 0-933662-35-1). Intercult Pr.

Update--Egypt. Alison R. Lanier. LC 80-83920. (Country Orientation Ser.). 94p. 1982. pap. text ed. 27.50 (ISBN 0-933662-32-7). Intercult Pr.

Update--France. Alison R. Lanier. LC 80-83928. (Country Orientation Ser.). 1984. pap. text ed. 27.50 (ISBN 0-933662-41-6). Intercult Pr.

Update--Germany. Alison R. Lanier. LC 80-83912. (Country Orientation Ser.). 1984. pap. text ed. 27.50 (ISBN 0-933662-40-8). Intercult Pr.

Update--Hong Kong. Alison R. Lanier. LC 80-83914. (Country Orientation Ser.). 1983. pap. 27.50 (ISBN 0-933662-38-6). Intercult Pr.

Update--Indonesia. Alison R. Lanier. LC 80-83915. (Counry Orientation Ser.). 1985. pap. text ed. 27.50 (ISBN 0-933662-37-8). Intercult Pr.

Update--Japan. Alison R. Lanier. LC 80-83913. (Country Orientation Ser.). 1984. pap. text ed. 27.50 (ISBN 0-933662-39-4). Intercult Pr.

Update--Kuwait. Alison R. Lanier. LC 80-83923. (Country Orientation Ser.). 1985. pap. text ed. 27.50 (ISBN 0-933662-29-7). Intercult Pr.

Update--Mexico. Alison R. Lanier. LC 80-83927. (Country Orientation Ser.). 150p. (Orig.). 1981. pap. text ed. 27.50 (ISBN 0-933662-25-4). Intercult Pr.

Update--Saudi Arabia. Alison R. Lanier. LC 80-83926. (Country Orientation Ser.). 150p. 1984. pap. text ed. 27.50 (ISBN 0-933662-26-2). Intercult Pr.

Update--South Korea. Alison R. Lanier. LC 80-83919. (Country Orientation Ser.). 1982. pap. text ed. 27.50 (ISBN 0-933662-33-5). Intercult Pr.

Update--Taiwan. Alison Lanier. LC 80-83922. (Country Orientation Ser.). 1982. pap. text ed. 27.50 (ISBN 0-933662-30-0). Intercult Pr.

Update--Venezuela. Alison R. Lanier. LC 80-83918. (Country Orientation Ser.). 1981. pap. text ed. 27.50 (ISBN 0-933662-34-3). Intercult Pr.

Update Eighty-Six: The PC's in Personnel Yearbook. Gary J. Meyer. 1986. pap. 39.95 (ISBN 1-55645-510-0). Busn Legal Reports.

Update for Tax Reform Act of 1984 to Accompany Introduction to "Taxation: A Decision-Making Approach". James E. Parker. 1984. write for info. instr's. edition of Update. West Pub.

Update: Guide to Kentucky Historical Highway Markers. rev., 2nd ed. 600p. (Orig.). 1985. pap. text ed. 11.00x (ISBN 0-916968-14-6). Kentucky Hist.

Update in Intensive Care & Emergency Medicine. Ed. by J. L. Vincent. (Anaesthesiology & Intensive Care Medicine Ser.: Vol. 178). (Illus.). xiv, 304p. 1985. pap. 34.00 (ISBN 0-387-15261-X). Springer-Verlag.

Update in Intensive Care & Emergency Medicine, 1986. J. L. Vincent. 588p. 1986. pap. 52.00 (ISBN 0-387-16508-8). Springer-Verlag.

Update: Manual of Clinical Nutrition. Paige. 1986. 17.95 (ISBN 0-8016-3880-1). Mosby.

Update Nineteen Eighty-Seven to Nineteen Eighty-Eight: Approaching the Automated Office. Walter A. Kleinschrod. 156p. 1987. pap. 19.95 (ISBN 0-916875-08-3). Admin Mgmt.

Update Nineteen Seventy-Nine. (Great Contemporary Issues Ser.). 1979. lib. bdg. 35.00x (ISBN 0-686-59848-2). Ayer Co Pubs.

Update of Guide to the Use of Standards: Version 3.1. Standards Promotion Application Group Staff. 316p. 1988. 79.00 (ISBN 0-444-70411-6, North Holland). Elsevier.

Update on Automotive Electronic Displays & Information Systems. 276p. 1983. pap. 50.00 (ISBN 0-89883-084-2, P123). Soc Auto Engineers.

Update on Christian Counseling, Vol. II. Jay E. Adams. 1981. pap. 2.75 (ISBN 0-87552-071-5). Presby & Reformed.

Update on Christian Counseling, 2 vols. Jay E. Adams. (Jay Adams Library). 288p. 1986. pap. 9.95 (ISBN 0-310-51051-1, 12117P). Zondervan.

Update on Christian Counseling, Vol. 1. Jay E. Adams. pap. 3.50 (ISBN 0-8010-0153-6). Baker Bk.

Update on Christian Counseling, Vol. 2. Jay E. Adams. 1981. pap. 2.75 (ISBN 0-8010-0180-3). Baker Bk.

Update on Healthy Aging: Reading Material on Health Topics for the New Reader & Tutor. 39p. (Orig.). 1986. pap. 6.95 (ISBN 0-910883-26-2, 131). Natl Coun Aging.

Update on Space, Vol. 1. Ed. by B. J. Bluth & S. R. McNeal. LC 80-52460. (Illus., Orig.). 1981. pap. 7.95 (ISBN 0-937654-00-0). Natl Behavior.

Update on State & Federal Regulation of Prepaid Legal Services: January Nineteen Eighty-One. 200p. 1981. 75.00 (ISBN 0-317-40263-3, 3-006); 4 tapes avail. Am Prepaid.

Update on the Liability Crisis. (Illus.). 1987. pap. 7.00 (ISBN 0-318-22580-8, S/N 027-000-01270-1). USGPO.

Update, Set One, 1981. New York Times Editors. (Great Contemporary Issues Ser.). 50.00 (ISBN 0-405-13941-1). Ayer Co Pubs.

Update, Set Two, 1980. New York Times Editors. (Great Contemporary Issues Ser.). 35.00 (ISBN 0-405-13781-8). Ayer Co Pubs.

Update Seven: Harrison's Principles of Internal Medicine. Ed. by Robert G. Petersdorf et al. 320p. 1986. text ed. 37.50 (ISBN 0-07-049618-8). McGraw.

Update: The University Gallery Collection. Ruth Beesch. 1988. pap. 8.00 (ISBN 0-8130-0898-0). U Presses Fla.

Update to the Response of Colleges & Universities to Calls for Divestment. Anne-Marea Griffin. 21p. (Orig.). 1986. pap. 25.00 (ISBN 0-931035-11-2). IRRC Inc DC.

Update 1980. Ed. by Arleen Kaylin & Douglas Bowen. LC 79-27511. (The Great Contemporary Issues Ser.). (Illus.). 1980. write for info. (ISBN 0-405-13086-4). Ayer Co Pubs.

Update 1987. Ed. by J. L. Vincent. (Update in Intensive Care & Emergency Medicine Ser.: Vol. 3). (Illus.). xvi, 494p. 1987. pap. 59.30 (ISBN 0-387-17576-8). Springer-Verlag.

Updated Devotion to the Sacred Heart. Walter Kern. LC 75-9277. (Illus.). 192p. 1975. pap. 2.95 (ISBN 0-8189-1124-7, Pub. by Alba Bks). Alba.

Updated ENT. 2nd, rev. ed. George G. Browning. (Illus.). 180p. 1987. pap. text ed. 22.95 (ISBN 0-407-00590-0). Butterworth.

Updated Guidebook on Biogas Development. (Energy Resources Development Ser.: No. 27). 178p. 17.50 (ISBN 92-1-119226-9, E.84.II.F.14). UN.

Updated Realistic Rock Drum Method. Carmine Appice. (Illus.). 76p. (Orig.). 1979. pap. 7.95 (ISBN 0-89705-012-6). Almo Pubns.

Updating Cutting Room Techniques. 79p. 1972. 20.00 (ISBN 0-318-13706-2). Clothing Mfrs.

Updating in Headache. Ed. by V. Pfaffenrath et al. (Illus.). 300p. 1985. pap. 49.00 (ISBN 0-387-15318-7). Springer-Verlag.

Updating Newsletters: A Directory. Update Publishing. LC 83-80145. 25p. 1983. pap. text ed. 8.95 (ISBN 0-686-38859-3, Pub. by Update Pub Co). Prosperity & Profits.

Updating of Subsurface Samplings of Soils & Rocks & their Insitu Testing. Ed. by Surendra K. Saxena. LC 85-70351. 516p. 1985. pap. 25.00 (ISBN 0-939204-25-8, 82-04). Eng Found.

Updating Supplemental of January, 1985. Irvin N. Gleim & Patrick R. Delancy. (CPA Examination Review Ser.). 1985. pap. write for info. (ISBN 0-471-82196-9). Wiley.

Updating Teachers for Tomorrow's Technology: A Strategy for Action. James B. Hamilton & Michael E. Wonacott. 71p. 1984. 4.95 (ISBN 0-318-22228-0, RD242). Natl Ctr Res Voc Ed.

Updating Teachers for Tomorrow's Technology: Programs & Practices. James B. Hamilton & Michael E. Wonacott. 66p. 1983. 5.75 (ISBN 0-318-22227-2, RD241). Natl Ctr Res Voc Ed.

Updating Your News Service. Ed. by Nancy S. Raley. 194p. 1980. incl. 8 tapes 65.00 (ISBN 0-89964-166-0). Coun Adv & Supp Ed.

Updike's Novels: Thorns Spell a Word. Jeff H. Campbell. 250p. 1987. 17.50x (ISBN 0-915323-02-8). Midwestern St U Pr.

Upgrade Your Italian: A Review Grammar. Gifford Orwen. 1983. pap. 8.50x (ISBN 0-913298-12-3). S F Vanni.

Upgrading & Refurbishing the Older Fiberglass Sailboat. William D. Booth. LC 84-46109. (Illus.). 292p. 1985. 24.50 (ISBN 0-87033-335-6). Cornell Maritime.

Upgrading Blue Collar & Service Workers. Charles Brecher. LC 79-186512. (Policy Studies in Employment & Welfare Ser.: No. 12). pap. 31.80 (ISBN 0-317-09670-2, 2020494). Bks Demand UMI.

Upgrading Coal Liquids. Ed. by Richard F. Sullivan. LC 81-1277. (ACS Symposium Ser.: No. 156). 1981. 31.95 (ISBN 0-8412-0629-5). Am Chemical.

Upgrading Existing Water Treatment Plants. American Water Works Association Staff. (AWWA Handbooks - Proceedings). (Illus.). 272p. 1974. pap. text ed. 12.60 (ISBN 0-89867-042-X). Am Water Wks Assn.

Upgrading Lecture Rooms. Peter H. Smith. (Illus.). 264p. 1979. 47.00 (ISBN 0-85334-849-9, Pub. by Elsevier Applied Sci England). Elsevier.

Upgrading Micro Hydro in Shri Lanka. Drummond Hislop. (Illus.). 63p. (Orig.). 1986. pap. 7.50 (ISBN 0-946688-62-1, Pub. by Intermediate Tech England). Intermediate Tech.

Upgrading of Low-Quality Aggregates for PCC & Bituminous Pavements. (National Cooperative Highway Research Program Report). 91p. 1979. 7.20 (ISBN 0-309-02915-5). Transport Res Bd.

Upgrading Residues & By-Products for Animals. J. T. Huber. 144p. 1981. 69.00 (ISBN 0-8493-5445-5). CRC Pr.

Upgrading Traditional Rural Technologies. Jeffrey James. 150p. 1988. text ed. 45.00x (ISBN 0-333-43711-X, Pub. by Macmillan London). Sheridan.

Upgrading Waste for Feeds & Food. Ed. by D. Ledward et al. (Illus.). 416p. 1983. text ed. 85.00 (ISBN 0-408-10837-1). Butterworth.

Upgrading Water Treatment Plants to Improve Water Quality. American Water Works Association Staff. (Handbooks-Proceedings). (Illus.). 132p. 1980. pap. text ed. 12.00 (ISBN 0-89867-245-7). Am Water Wks Assn.

Upgrading Your Airplane's Avionics. Timothy R. Foster. (Illus.). 112p. 1982. 9.95 (ISBN 0-8306-9620-2, 2301H). TAB Bks.

Upgrading Your College Reading: Study Skills. Harold Newman. 108p. (Orig.). 1984. pap. 15.00 (ISBN 0-9613577-0-3). Prestige Educ.

Upgrading Your Small Boat for Cruising. Paul Butler & Marya Butler. 224p. (Orig.). 1988. pap. 19.95 (ISBN 0-87742-960-X). Intl Marine.

Uphill All The Way. O. A. Battista. 1989. 24.95 (ISBN 0-915074-14-1). Knowledge TX.

Uphill All the Way. Lynn Hall. LC 83-20202. 128p. (gr. 7 up). 1984. 11.95 (ISBN 0-684-18066-9, Pub. by Scribner). Macmillan.

Uphill All the Way: A Documentary History of Women in Australia. Compiled by Kay Daniels & Mary Murnane. (Illus.). 335p. 1980. 32.50x (ISBN 0-7022-1476-0). U of Queensland Pr.

Uphill Both Ways. Marion Merritt. LC 85-13349. (Illus.). 100p. 1985. pap. 6.95 (ISBN 0-916897-05-2). Andrew Mtn Pr.

Uphill Both Ways: Hiking Colorado's High Country. Robert L. Brown. LC 73-83111. (Illus.). 1976. pap. 5.95 (ISBN 0-87004-249-1). Caxton.

Upholstering. 2nd ed. James E. Brumbaugh. LC 82-17781. (Illus.). 394p. 1984. 14.95 (ISBN 0-672-23372-X, Pub. by Audel). Macmillan.

Upholstering Methods. Fred W. Zimmerman. LC 80-25308. (Illus.). 192p. 1981. text ed. 14.96 (ISBN 0-87006-313-8). Goodheart.

Upholstery: A Practical Guide. David Broan & Freda Broan. (Illus.). 119p. 1987. 13.95 (ISBN 0-900873-48-5, Pub. by Bishopsgate Pr London); pap. 9.95 (ISBN 0-900873-49-3). Intl Spec Bk.

Upholstery Fact Book 1986. 1986. 1500.00x (ISBN 0-317-43728-3, Pub. by F I R A). State Mutual Bk.

Upholstery in America & Europe. Ed. by Edward S. Cooke, Jr. (Illus.). 1987. 35.00 (ISBN 0-393-02469-5, Barra Foundation Bk). Norton.

Upholstery Techniques Illustrated. W. Lloyd Gheen. (Illus.). 352p. 1986. pap. 17.95 (ISBN 0-8306-0402-2). Tab Bks.

Upjohn's Rural Architecture. Richard Upjohn. LC 74-16022. (Architecture & Decorative Art Ser.). (Illus.). 14p. 1975. Repr. of 1852 ed. lib. bdg. 49.50 (ISBN 0-306-70639-3). Da Capo.

Upland Field & Forest Wildflowers. J. E. Underhill. 64p. pap. 4.95 (ISBN 0-88839-174-9). Hancock House.

Upland Game Birds, Vol.1. (Illus.). 174p. 1982. pap. 9.95 (ISBN 0-686-47255-1). Rolfs Gall.

Upland Pasture: Poems. Theodore Holmes. LC 66-15289. 1966. 7.95 (ISBN 0-8265-1090-6). Vanderbilt U Pr.

Upland Pastures. Christina Rainsford. LC 75-93794. 1969. 4.00 (ISBN 0-8233-0133-8). Golden Quill.

Upland Rice. Rev. ed. (Better Farming Ser.: No. 20). 30p. 1977. pap. 7.50 (ISBN 92-5-100621-0, F78, FAO). UNIPUB.

Upland Rice: A Global Perspective. P. C. Gupta & J. C. O'Toole. 360p. (Orig.). 1986. pap. text ed. 11.70x (ISBN 971-104-172-3, Pub. by Intl Rice Res Philippines). Agribookstore.

Uplands of Dream. Edgar Saltus. Ed. by Charles Honce. LC 78-93776. Repr. of 1925 ed. 17.50 (ISBN 0-404-05550-8). AMS Pr.

Uplift Behavior of Anchor Foundations in Soil: Proceedings of a Session Sponsored by the Geotechnical Engineering Division. Ed. by Samuel P. Clemence. 126p. 1985. 16.00x (ISBN 0-87262-496-X). Am Soc Civil Eng.

Uplift War. David Brin. 656p. 1987. pap. 4.50 (ISBN 0-553-25121-X, Spectra). Bantam.

Uplift War. David Brin. 1987. 22.00 (ISBN 0-932096-44-1). Phantasia Pr.

Uplifted Atmospheres, Borrowed Taste. Howard Halle. (Illus.). 33p. (Orig.). 1986. pap. write for info. (ISBN 0-936739-04-5). Hallwalls Inc.

Uplifting the Race: The Black Minister in the New South 1865-1902. Edward L. Wheeler. 198p. (Orig.). 1986. lib. bdg. 26.00 (ISBN 0-8191-5161-0); pap. text ed. 12.50 (ISBN 0-8191-5162-9). U Pr of Amer.

Uplink Directory, 1986. Ed. by Mary A. Roybal & Virginia A. Ostendorf. 131p. (Orig.). 1986. pap. 125.00 (ISBN 0-937007-00-5). V A Ostendorf.

Uplink Directory, 1987, Vol. 2. Ed. by Mary A. Roybal & Virginia A. Ostendorf. 170p. (Orig.). 1987. pap. 125.00 (ISBN 0-317-56098-0). V A Ostendorf.

Upon a Moon-Dark Moor. Rebecca Brandewyne. 480p. (Orig.). 1988. pap. 4.95 (ISBN 0-446-32751-4). Warner Bks.

Upon a Quiet Landscape: The Photographs of Frank Sadorus. Ed. by Raymond Bial & Frederick A. Schlipf. LC 83-72993. (Champaign County Historical Archives Historical Publications Ser.: No. 6). (Illus.). 168p. 1983. 18.00 (ISBN 0-9609646-1-4). Urbana Free Lib.

Upon a Stone Altar: A History of the Island of Pohnpei to 1890. David Hanlon. LC 87-34288. (Pacific Island Monograph Ser.: No.5). 352p. 1988. text ed. 32.00x (ISBN 0-8248-1124-0). UH Pr.

Upon My Words. Alexander S. Kohanski. 1988. 29.95 (ISBN 0-8197-0553-5); pap. 19.95x (ISBN 0-8197-0550-0). Bloch.

Upon Some Midnights Clear. K C. Constantine. LC 84-48748. (Mario Balzic Mystery Ser.). 256p. 1985. 15.95 (ISBN 0-87923-570-5). Godine.

Upon Some Midnights Clear. K. C. Constantine. 232p. 1987. pap. 3.50 (ISBN 0-14-009404-0). Penguin.

Upon Such Sacrifices. P. Brockbank. (Shakespeare Lectures). 1976. pap. 5.50 (ISBN 0-85672-140-9, Pub. by British Acad). Longwood Pub Group.

Upon the Head of the Goat. Aranka Siegal. 192p. 1983. pap. 2.25 (ISBN 0-451-12084-1, Sig Vista). NAL.

Upon the Head of the Goat: A Childhood in Hungary, 1939-1944. Aranka Siegal. LC 81-12642. 214p. (gr. 7 up). 1981. 12.95 (ISBN 0-374-38059-7). FS&G.

Upon the Objects to Be Attained by the Establishment of a Public Library: Report of the Trustees of the Public Library of the City of Boston, 1852. Repr. 3.50 (ISBN 0-686-70431-2). Boston Public Lib.

Upon the Potter's Wheel. Ralph V. Reynolds. Ed. by Mary H. Wallace. LC 85-31583. 144p. (Orig.). 1981. pap. 4.95 (ISBN 0-912315-22-9). Word Aflame.

Upon the Shoulders of Giants: The Shaping of the Modern Mind. 2nd ed. Richard Hardison. 468p. 1988. lib. bdg. 34.25 (ISBN 0-8191-6737-1); pap. text ed. 17.50 (ISBN 0-8191-6738-X). U Pr of Amer.

Upon the Sweeping Flood. Joyce Carol Oates. LC 66-16632. 17.95 (ISBN 0-8149-0172-7). Vanguard.

Upon the Willows & Other Stories. Rowena T. Tiempo-Torrevillas. 192p. 1980. pap. 5.25x (ISBN 0-686-28650-2, Pub. by New Day Pub.). Cellar.

Upon This Rock, 3 vols. C. T. Davidson. 692p. 1973. Vol. 1. 11.95 (ISBN 0-934942-16-1); Vol. 2. 14.95 (ISBN 0-934942-17-X); Vol. 3. 17.95 (ISBN 0-934942-18-8). White Wing Pub.

Upon This Rock. Eric Godsen. pap. 4.95 (ISBN 0-87508-186-X). ChR Lit.

Upon This Rock. Valentine Long. 1983. 12.00 (ISBN 0-8199-0834-7). Franciscan Herald.

Upon This Rock. Walter Murphy. 1988. pap. 4.95. Ballantine.

Upon This Rock: A Centennial History of the First Baptist Church. Charlsie Little. 300p. 1985. write for info. (ISBN 0-914546-64-3). Rose Pub.

Upon This Rock: The Life of St. Peter. Walter F. Murphy. LC 87-15896. 520p. 1987. 19.95 (ISBN 0-02-588270-8). Macmillan.

Upon What Pretext? The Book & Literary History. Larzer Ziff. 29p. 1986. pap. 6.00 (ISBN 0-912296-81-X, Dist. by of U Pr of Va). Am Antiquarian.

Uppark & Its People. Margaret Meade-Fetherstonhaugh & Oliver Warner. (Century Classic Ser.). 128p. 1988. pap. 9.95 (ISBN 0-7126-1864-3, Pub. by Century Hutchinson). David & Charles.

Upper Arkansas: Rapids, History & Nature Mile by Mile. Frank Staub. (Fulcrum's Guide Ser.). (Illus.). 225p. 1988. pap. 14.95 (ISBN 1-55591-021-1). Fulcrum Inc.

Upper Atlantic (New Jersey, New York) Thomas G. Aylesworth & Virginia L. Aylesworth. (Let's Discover the States Ser.). (Illus.). 66p. 1987. lib. bdg. 14.95x (ISBN 1-55546-553-6). Chelsea Hse.

Upper Atmosphere. H. S. Massey & R. F. Boyd. 1959. 19.95 (ISBN 0-8022-1082-1). Philos Lib.

Upper Atmosphere & Solar. Hargreaves. 1979. pap. 34.95 (ISBN 0-442-30216-9). Van Nos Reinhold.

Upper Atmosphere in Motion. Ed. by C. O. Hines et al. LC 74-28234. (Geophysical Monograph Ser.: Vol. 18). (Illus.). 1027p. 1974. 29.00 (ISBN 0-87590-018-6). Am Geophysical.

Upper Atmosphere: Meteorology & Physics. Richard A. Craig. (International Geophysics Ser.: Vol. 8). 1965. 52.95 (ISBN 0-12-194850-1). Acad Pr.

Upper Atmosphere Research in Antarctica. Ed. by L. J. Lanzerotti & C. Park. (Illus.). 264p. 1977. 50.00 (ISBN 0-87590-141-7). Am Geophysical.

Upper Cervical Syndrome. Howard Vernon. (Illus.). 336p. 1988. 47.00 (ISBN 0-317-67381-5). Williams & Wilkins.

Upper Circle. Kitty Black. (Theatrical Chronical Ser.). (Illus.). 260p. 1985. text ed. 18.95 (ISBN 0-413-51040-9, 9687). Heinemann Ed.

Upper Class Amusements: House Party Games for the Titled Elite & Other Folks, Too. Andrew Melsom. LC 82-48831. (Illus.). 112p. 1987. pap. 6.95 (ISBN 0-06-097077-4, PL 7077, PL). Har-Row.

Upper Colorado Series see University of Utah Anthropological Papers.

Upper Columbia Rivers & the Great Plain of Columbia. enl. ed. Thomas Symons. (Illus.). 1967. 18.95 (ISBN 0-87770-025-7). Ye Galleon.

Upper Continental Margin Sedimentation off Brazil. Ed. by J. D. Milliman & C. P. Summerhays. (Contributions to Sedimentology Monograph: No. 4). (Illus.). 175p. 1975. pap. text ed. 50.00x (ISBN 3-510-57004-9). Lubrecht & Cramer.

Upper Cretaceous Foraminifera of the Gulf Coastal Region. J. A. Cushman. Repr. of 1946 ed. 21.80 (ISBN 0-934454-79-5). Lubrecht & Cramer.

Upper Cretaceous Spumellariina from the Great Valley Sequence, California Coast Ranges see Bulletins of American Paleontology.

Upper Crust: A Slice of the South. Johnson City Junior League High South Publications Staff. 323p. 1986. write for info. (ISBN 0-9616492-1-6). High South Pubns.

Upper Crust Cookbook. Sue Bennett-Ashcraft. LC 84-91700. 538p. (Orig.). 1984. spiral bdg. 24.95 (ISBN 0-9613757-0-1). Upper Crust.

Upper Crust: The Great American Sandwich Book. Brenda Bell. (Illus.). 80p. (Orig.). 1986. pap. 5.95 (ISBN 0-8092-4989-8). Contemp Bks.

Upper Damodar Valley: A Study in Settlement Geography. Jagadish Singh. (Illus.). xvii, 267p. 1986. text ed. 40.00x (ISBN 81-210-0037-8, Pub. by Inter India Pubns N Delhi). Apt Bks.

Upper Egypt Chief Temples, Six. Bertha Porter & Rosalind Moss. (Topographical Bibliography of Ancient Egyptian Hieroglyphic Texts, Reliefs & Paintings Ser.: Vol. 6). 264p. 1939. text ed. 38.50 (ISBN 0-900416-30-0, Pub. by Aris & Phillips UK). Humanities.

Upper Egypt: Historical Outline & Description Guide to the Ancient Sites. Jill Kamil. 224p. 1983. pap. text ed. 9.95 (ISBN 0-582-78314-3). Longman.

Upper Egypt: Its People & Its Products. Karl B. Klunzinger. LC 76-44747. 1984. Repr. of 1878 ed. 39.50 (ISBN 0-404-15866-8). AMS Pr.

Upper Elementary Social Studies Curriculum: Learning More About Black Americans. Montgomery County Public Schools Staff. LC 82-50375. (Illus.). 100p. 1982. pap. 7.95 (ISBN 0-88247-674-2). R & E Pubs.

Upper Eocene Flora of Hordle, Pts. 1-2. M. E. Chandler. 1925-26. Set. 20.00 (ISBN 0-384-08455-9). Johnson Repr.

Upper Eocene Foraminifera of the Southeastern U. S. J. A. Cushman. Repr. of 1935 ed. 15.20 (ISBN 0-934454-80-9). Lubrecht & Cramer

Upper Extremities Orthotics. photocopy ed. Miles H. Anderson. (Illus.). 476p. 1979. 48.00x (ISBN 0-398-00044-1). C C Thomas.

Upper Extremity: Guide to the Prosected Cadaver. Caryl E. Peterson. 110p. 1987. pap. text ed. 10.95 (ISBN 0-8403-4285-3). Kendall Hunt.

Upper Extremity in Sports Medicine. Nicholas. (Illus.). 900p. 1989. 99.95 (ISBN 0-8016-3943-3). Mosby.

Upper Extremity Orthotics: A Monograph. Ed. by Jacquelin Perry. 1978. pap. 5.00 (ISBN 0-912452-22-6). Am Phys Therapy Assn.

Upper Extremity Replantation: Basic Principles, Surgical Technique, & Strategy. Viktor E. Meyer. (Illus.). 119p. 1985. text ed. 40.00 (ISBN 0-443-08448-3). Churchill.

Upper Hand. Stuart Hood. 186p. 1987. 16.95 (ISBN 0-85635-719-7). Carcanet.

Upper House in Revolutionary America, 1763-1788. Jackson T. Main. LC 67-20753. pap. 80.80 (ISBN 0-317-09462-9, 2004974). Bks Demand UMI.

Upper Iowa University: Doc Dorman's Peacocks. Fred Breckner. LC 81-52627. (College Sports Ser.). 1981. 10.95 (ISBN 0-87397-195-7). Strode.

Upper Layers of Open Systems Interconnection. Ed. by Rainer W. Herbers. 1987. lib. bdg. 59.50 (ISBN 90-277-2447-4, Pub. by Reidel Holland). Kluwer Academic.

Upper Left-Hand Corner: A Writer's Guide for the Northwest. 2nd ed. E. Kernaghan et al. 122p. 1984. pap. 10.95 (ISBN 0-88908-596-X, 9534). ISC Pr.

Upper Limb see Jamieson's Illustrations of Regional Anatomy.

Upper Limb see Physiology of the Joints.

Upper-Limb Deficiencies in Children. Douglas W. Lamb & Law Hamish. 137p. 1987. text ed. 65.00. Little.

Upper Limb Deficiencies in Children. Douglas W. Lamb & Hamish Law. 152p. 1987. text ed. 58.50 (ISBN 0-316-51269-9, Little Med Div). Little.

Upper Main Sequence Stars with Anomalous Abundances. Ed. by C. R. Cowley et al. 1986. lib. bdg. 95.00 (ISBN 90-277-2296-X, Pub. by Reidel Holland). Kluwer Academic.

Upper Mississippi: Or, Historical Sketches of the Mound-Builder, the Indian Tribes, & the Progress of Civilization in the North-West. George Gale. 1975. Repr. of 1867 ed. 32.00 (ISBN 0-527-03220-4). Kraus Repr.

Upper Motor Neurons Functions & Dysfunctions. Ed. by John Eccles & M. R. Dimitrijevic. (Recent Achievements in Restorative Neurology Ser.: Vol. 1). (Illus.). xvii, 346p. 1985. 186.00 (ISBN 3-8055-4020-5). S Karger.

Upper New England. Peter Andrews et al. LC 79-22906. (Country Inns of America Ser.). (Illus.). 96p. (Orig.). 1980. pap. 9.95 (ISBN 0-03-043711-3). H Holt & Co.

Upper Northern California Counties Public Schools, 1988, Vol. 7. Lillian S. Clancy. (California Public Schools: How Are They Doing? Ser.). 400p. (Orig.). 1988. pap. 25.95 (ISBN 0-939580-51-9). Sindowilf Ltd.

Upper Northern California Counties Public Schools, Vol. 7. Lillian S. Clancy. (California Public Schools Ser.: How Are They Doing?). 400p. (Orig.). 1985. pap. 24.95 (ISBN 0-939580-34-9). Sindowilf Ltd.

Upper Northern California Countries Public Schools, 1987, Vol. 7. Lillian S. Clancy. (California Public Schools: How Are They Doing? Ser.). 400p. (Orig.). 1987. pap. 24.95 (ISBN 0-939580-43-8). Sindowilf Ltd.

Upper Ordovician Eurypterids of Ohio see Palaeontographica Americana.

Upper Ordovician Through Middle Silurian of the Eastern Great Basin: Part Two - Lithologic Descriptions. D. R. Budge & P. M. Sheehan. (Contributions in Biology & Geology Ser.: No. 29). 80p. 1980. 5.50 (ISBN 0-89326-041-X). Milwaukee Pub Mus.

Upper Ordovician Through Middle Silurian of the Eastern Great Basin: Part I--Introduction: Historical Perspective & Stratigraphic Synthesis. D. R. Budge & P. M. Sheehan. (Contributions in Biology & Geology Ser.: No. 28). 26p. 1980. 2.50 (ISBN 0-89326-040-1). Milwaukee Pub Mus.

Upper Palaeolithic Age in Britain. Dorothy A. Garrod. LC 76-44722. Repr. of 1926 ed. 29.50 (ISBN 0-404-15926-5). AMS Pr.

Upper Palaeolithic of Britain: A Study of Man & Nature in the Late Ice Age, Vols. I & II. John B. Campbell. (Illus.). 1978. Set. 89.00x (ISBN 0-19-813188-7). Oxford U Pr.

Upper Paleolithic of the Central Russian Plain. Olga Soffer. (Studies in Archaeology). 1985. 49.95 (ISBN 0-12-654270-8); pap. 24.95 (ISBN 0-12-654271-6). Acad Pr.

Upper Peninsula of Michigan. John S. Penrod. 1986. pap. 2.95 (ISBN 0-942618-02-5). Penrod-Hiawatha.

Upper Peninsula of Michigan. rev. ed. John S. Penrod. (YA) (gr. 7-12). 1988. pap. 2.95 (ISBN 0-942618-11-4). Penrod-Hiawatha.

Upper Pleistocene Prehistory of Western Eurasia. Ed. by Harold L. Dibble & Anta Montet-White. (University Museum Monograph, No. 54 - University Museum Symposium Ser.: No. 1). 500p. 1988. text ed. 50.00x (ISBN 0-934718-53-9). Univ Mus of U PA.

Upper Room. Bob Hughes. 1977. saddlewire 1.95 (ISBN 0-8054-9729-3). Broadman.

Upper Room. Mary Monroe. LC 84-18322. 304p. 1986. pap. 3.95 (ISBN 0-345-32913-9). Ballantine.

Upper Room. J. C. Ryle. 1983. pap. 10.95 (ISBN 0-85151-017-5). Banner of Truth.

Upper Room Disciplines, 1988. 382p. (Orig.). 1987. pap. 4.95 (ISBN 0-8358-0552-2). Upper Room.

Upper Room: Retreat Readings for Priests. Thomas Plassmann. (Spirit & Life Ser). 1954. 4.50 (ISBN 0-686-11565-1). Franciscan Inst.

Upper Room Worshipbook. Compiled by Elise S. Eslinger. 208p. (Orig.). 1985. pap. 8.95 (ISBN 0-8358-0515-8). Upper Room.

Upper Secondary School. L. Spolton. 1967. pap. 19.75 (ISBN 0-08-012496-8). Pergamon.

Upper Tertiary & Quaternary Depositional Systems, Central Coastal Plain, Texas--Regional Geology of the Coastal Aquifer & Potential Liquid-Waste Repositories. R. F. Solis. (Report of Investigations Ser.: No. 108). (Illus.). 89p. 1981. 3.00 (ISBN 0-318-03239-2). Bur Econ Geology.

Upper Tertiary Arcacea of the Mid-Atlantic Coastal Plain see Palaeontographica Americana.

Upper Thames Valley Today. Harry Knights. 80p. 1987. pap. 30.00x (ISBN 0-946163-02-2, Countryside Bks). State Mutual Bk.

Upper Valley: An Illustrated Tour along the Connecticut River Before the Twentieth Century. Jerold Wikoff. LC 85-4706. (Illus.). 192p. 1985. 29.95 (ISBN 0-930031-01-6). Chelsea Green Pub.

Upper Volta: Environmental Uncertainty & Livestock Production. Richard Vengroff. 147p. 1980. 10.95 (ISBN 0-318-14561-8, 80-1). Intl Ctr Arid & Semi-Arid.

Upper Waters of the Intertropical Pacific Ocean. Mizuki Tsuchiya. LC 68-9513. (Oceanographic Studies: No. 4). 50p. 1968. text ed. 12.00x (ISBN 0-8018-0636-4). Johns Hopkins.

Upper West Side. Robert M. Parker. 1988. 24.95 (ISBN 0-8109-1747-5). Abrams.

Upper Yukon Basin. Ed. by Alaska Geographic Staff. LC 72-92087. (Alaska Geographic Ser.: Vol. 14, No. 4). (Illus.). 120p. 1987. pap. 14.95 (ISBN 0-88240-183-1). Alaska Northwest.

Uppsala General Catalogue of Twelve Thousand Nine Hundred & Twenty-One Galaxies. Peter Nilson. 456p. (Orig.). 1973. pap. text ed. 85.00x (ISBN 91-554-0064-7, Pub. by Almqvist & Wiksell). Coronet Bks.

Uppsala, Universitetsbiblioteket, MS Vokalmusic i Handskrift 76a. Ed. by Howard M. Brown et al. (Renaissance Music in Facsimile Ser.). 175p. 1987. lib. bdg. 40.00 (ISBN 0-8240-1468-5). Garland Pub.

Upright Piano. Judith Jerome. Date not set. write for info. S&S.

Upright Pianos. J. Jerome. 1986. cancelled (ISBN 0-442-24434-7). Van Nos Reinhold.

Uprighting the Inclined Mandibular Molar in Preparation for Restorative Treatment. Robert L. Vanarsdall, Jr. Ed. by D. Walter Cohen. (Continuing Dental Education Series). 146p. 1980. pap. 20.00 (ISBN 0-931386-21-7). Quint Pub Co.

Uprising. David Irving. 1986. pap. 12.00 (ISBN 0-949667-91-9). Concord Bks.

Uprising. Liviu Rebreanu. 1964. 18.95 (ISBN 0-7206-9382-9). Dufour.

Uprising in East Germany & Other Stories. Jochen Ziem. Tr. by Jorn K. Bramann & Jeanette Axelrod. LC 84-71439. (Night Ser.: No. 5). 192p. (Orig.). 1985. pap. 8.95 (ISBN 0-913623-07-5, F379). Adler Pub Co.

Uprising of a Great People: The United States in 1861 to Which Is Added a Word of Peace Between England & the United States. facsimile ed. Agenor De Gasparin. Tr. by Mary L. Booth. LC 75-95066. (Select Bibliographies Reprint Ser). 1861. 27.50 (ISBN 0-8369-5068-2). Ayer Co Pubs.

Uprising of June Twentieth, 1792. Laura B. Pfeiffer. LC 78-115360. Repr. of 1913 ed. 21.00 (ISBN 0-404-05019-0). AMS Pr.

Uprising of the Twenty Thousand. Donna Ippolito. Ed. by Anne Pride. 29p. (Orig.). 1979. pap. 3.00 (ISBN 0-934238-00-6). Motheroot.

Uprising! One Nation's Nightmare: Hungary 1956. David Irving. (Illus.). 628p. 1986. 16.95 (ISBN 0-317-52998-6). Noontide.

Uprisings: The Whole Grain Bakers Book. Cooperative Whole Grain Educational Association Staff. LC 83-50137. 304p. (Orig.). 1983. pap. 9.95 (ISBN 0-9611600-0-4). Uprisings Pub Co.

Uproar on Hollercat Hill. Jean Marzollo. LC 79-22201. (Illus.). (ps-2). 1980. 8.95 (ISBN 0-8037-9027-9). Dial Bks Young.

Uproar on Hollercat Hill. Jean Marzollo. (Pied Piper Bk.). (Illus.). 32p. (ps-3). 1982. pap. 3.50 (ISBN 0-8037-9040-6). Dial Bks Young.

Uprooted Americans: The Japanese Americans & the War Relocation Authority During World War II. Dillon S. Myer. LC 76-125169. (Illus.). pap. 101.40 (ISBN 0-317-58772-2, 2029656). Bks Demand UMI.

Uprooted Children: The Early Life of Migrant Farm Workers. Robert Coles. LC 70-98270. (Horace Mann Lecture Ser). 1970. 17.95x (ISBN 0-8229-3192-3). U of Pittsburgh Pr.

Uprooted of the Western Sahel: Migrants' Quest for Cash in the Senegambia. Lucie G. Colvin et al. LC 81-5005. 400p. 1981. 52.95 (ISBN 0-275-90597-7, C0597). Praeger.
Uprooting & Development--Dilemmas of Coping with Modernization. Ed. by George V. Coelho et al. LC 81-16539. (Current Topics In Mental Health Ser.). 566p. 1980. 59.50x (ISBN 0-306-40509-1, Plenum Pr). Plenum Pub.
Uprooting & Integration in the Writings of Simone Weil. Betty McLane-Iles. (American University Studies VII-Theology & Religion: Vol. 20). 290p. 1987. text ed. 45.90 (ISBN 0-8204-0348-2). P Lang Pubs.
Uprooting & Surviving: Adaptation & Resettlement of Migrant Families. Richard C. Nann. 1982. 32.50 (ISBN 90-277-1339-1, Pub. by Reidel Holland). Kluwer Academic.
Uprooting Poverty: The Challenge in South Africa. Francis Wilson & Mamphela Ramphele. 1988. 27.50 (ISBN 0-393-02610-8). Norton.
Uprooting War. Brian Martin. 298p. (Orig.). 1984. pap. 9.50 (ISBN 0-900384-26-3). Left Bank.
Ups & Downs of an Unaccompanied Minor Refugee. Marie F. Portuondo. (Illus.). 31p. (Orig.). 1984. pap. 4.50 (ISBN 0-89729-352-5). Ediciones.
Ups & Downs of Drugs. Kathleen Elgin & John F. Osterritter. LC 75-168994. (Illus.). 72p. (gr. 4-7). 1972. Knopf.
Ups & Downs of Indo-U. S. Relations, 1948-1983. P. K. Goswami. 1984. 12.00x (ISBN 0-8364-1122-6, Pub. by Mukhopadhay India). South Asia Bks.
Ups & Downs of Jorie Jenkins. Betty Bates. (gr. 4-6). 1981. pap. 1.75 (ISBN 0-671-29950-6). Archway.
Ups & Downs of Life. Edward Sellon. Ed. by C. J. Scheiner & Dennis McMillan. (Illus.). 128p. 1987. Repr. of 1867 ed. ltd. ed. 35.00x (ISBN 0-939767-06-6). D McMillan.
Ups & Downs of Life in the Indies. P. A. Daum. Ed. by E. M. Beekman. Tr. by Elsje Sturtevant & Donald Sturtevant. LC 86-16807. (Library of the Indies). 216p. 1987. lib. bdg. 20.00x (ISBN 0-87023-551-6). U of Mass Pr.
Ups & Downs with Oink & Pearl. Kay Chorao. LC 85-45264. (Harper I Can Read Bks.). (Illus.). 64p. (gr. k-3). 1986. 9.95i (ISBN 0-06-021274-8); PLB 10.89 (ISBN 0-06-021275-6). HarpJ.
Upscaling Downtown: Stalled Gentrification in Washington, D. C. Brett Williams. LC 87-27350. (Anthropology of Contemporary Issues Ser.). 176p. 1988. 24.95x (ISBN 0-8014-2106-3); pap. 8.95x (ISBN 0-8014-9419-2). Cornell U Pr.
Upset: Australia Wins the America's Cup. Michael Levitt & Barbara Lloyd. LC 83-21910. (Illus.). 240p. (Orig.). 1983. pap. 8.95 (ISBN 0-89480-674-2, 674). Workman Pub.
Upset Book: A Guide for Dealing with Upset People. Pennie Myers & Don Nance. (Illus.). 222p. (Orig.). 1986. pap. 8.95 (ISBN 0-937647-01-2). Academic Pubns.
Upside-Down Boy. Janet Palazzo-Craig. LC 85-14067. (Illus.). 48p. (Orig.). (gr. 1-3). 1986. PLB 9.49 (ISBN 0-8167-0604-2); pap. text ed. 1.95 (ISBN 0-8167-0605-0). Troll Assocs.
Upside-Down Cat. Elizabeth Parsons. LC 80-13507. (Illus.). 48p. (gr. 3-6). 1981. 9.95 (ISBN 0-689-50187-0, M K McElderry). Macmillan.
Upside Down Circle: The Humor of Zen. Don Gilbert. Ed. by Paul M. Clemens. (Illus.). 176p. (Orig.). 1988. pap. 9.95 (ISBN 0-931892-18-X). B Dolphin Pub.
Upside Down Day. Mike Thaler. (Snuggle & Read Ser.). 32p. (gr. k-3). 1986. pap. 2.50 (ISBN 0-380-89999-X, Camelot). Avon.
Upside Down Eddie. Daniel Schantz. (Adventures with Eddie Ser.). 96p. (gr. 4-9). 1985. 2.50 (ISBN 0-87239-921-4, 2851). Standard Pub.
Upside-Down Kingdom. Donald B. Kraybill. LC 78-9435. (Christian Peace Shelf Ser.). 328p. 1978. pap. 6.95 (ISBN 0-8361-1860-X). Herald Pr.
Upside Down Rainbow. Jim Weekly. 1987. pap. 5.50 (ISBN 0-937172-66-9). JLJ Pubs.
Upside Down Riddle Book. Louis Phillips. LC 82-73. (Illus.). 32p. (gr. k up). 1982. 11.95 (ISBN 0-688-00931-X); PLB 11.88 (ISBN 0-688-00932-8). Lothrop.
Upside-Down Ship. Don Wulffson. Ed. by Ann Fay. (Illus.). 128p. (gr. 4 up). 1986. 9.75 (ISBN 0-8075-8346-4). A Whitman.
Upside down Tapestry Mosaic History. Leslie A. Reese. 53p. 1987. pap. 5.00 (ISBN 0-940713-00-4). Broadside Pr.
Upside-Downers. Mitsumasa Anno. (Illus.). (gr. k-4). 1988. 13.95 (ISBN 0-399-21522-0, Philomel Bks). Putnam Pub Group.
Upside-Downers: More Pictures to Stretch the Imagination. Mitsumasa Anno. Tr. by Meredith Weatherby & Suzanne Trumbull. LC 71-157269. (Illus.). 28p. (gr. k-3). 1971. 6.50 (ISBN 0-8348-2005-6). Weatherhill.
Upside-Downs of Jealousy, Possessiveness & Insecurity. Stuart J. Faber & Teddi Levison. 100p. 1975. pap. text ed. 4.95 (ISBN 0-89074-012-7). Charing Cross.
Upstaged. Jacqueline Shannon. 192p. 1987. pap. 2.50 (ISBN 0-380-75245-X, Flare). Avon.
Upstaged, No. 7. Kristi Andrews. (All That Glitters Ser.). 176p. (Orig.). (YA) (gr. 6 up). 1988. pap. 2.50 (ISBN 0-553-26704-3). Bantam.
Upstairs at the Office of the Future: Creating a High-Tech Office in Your Home. Judith Silberstein & Warren F. Benton. LC 84-19547. 202p. 1985. pap. 14.95 (ISBN 0-471-80018-X). Wiley.
Upstairs Downstairs. John Hawkesworth. 1973. pap. 3.95 (ISBN 0-440-19162-9). Dell.
Upstairs Room. Johanna Reiss. (Pathfinder Ser.). 176p. (gr. 5-8). 1973. pap. 2.50 (ISBN 0-553-24784-0). Bantam.
Upstairs Room. Johanna Reiss. LC 77-187940. 196p. (YA) (gr. 7 up). 1972. 12.70i (ISBN 0-690-85127-8, Crowell Jr Bks). HarpJ.
Upstairs Room. Johanna Reiss. LC 77-187940. 192p. (YA) (gr. 7 up). 1987. pap. 2.95 (ISBN 0-694-05610-3, Harper Keypoint). HarpJ.
Upstairs Room. Johanna Reiss. LC 77-187940. 196p. (YA) (gr. 7 up). 1987. PLB 12.89 (ISBN 0-690-04702-9, Crowell Jr Bks). HarpJ.
Upstairs to a Mine. Violet Boyce & Mabel Harmer. LC 76-28980. 189p. 1977. 7.95 (ISBN 0-87421-085-2). Utah St U Pr.
Upstart. Piers P. Read. 352p. 1980. pap. 2.25 (ISBN 0-380-49023-4, 49023-4). Avon.
Upstart Crow: An Introduction to Shakespeare's Plays. Gareth L. Evans. Ed. by Barbara L. Evans. 414p. 1982. text ed. 24.95x (ISBN 0-460-10256-7, BKA 04802, Pub. by J M Dent England); pap. text ed. 11.95x (ISBN 0-460-11256-2, 04803, Pub. by J M Dent England). Biblio Dist.
Upstart Earl: A Study of the Social & Mental World of Richard Boyle, First Earl of Cork, 1566-1643. Nicholas Canny. LC 81-21687. 208p. 1982. 37.50 (ISBN 0-521-24416-1). Cambridge U Pr.
Upstate. Dugan Gilman. LC 79-142724. (Wesleyan Poetry Program: Vol. 55). 1971. 12.00x (ISBN 0-8195-2055-1); pap. 8.95 (ISBN 0-8195-1055-6). Wesleyan U Pr.
Upstate. Edmund Wilson. (Illus.). 384p. 1971. 10.95 (ISBN 0-374-28189-0). FS&G.
Upstate Echos. Arch Merrill. (Arch Merrill's New York Ser.: No. 9). (Illus.). 168p. 1988. pap. 7.95 (ISBN 1-55787-003-9). Heart of the Lakes.
Upstate Literature: Essays in Memory of Thomas F. O'Donnell. Ed. by Frank Bergmann. LC 84-26853. (New York State Studies). 256p. 1985. pap. text ed. 11.95x (ISBN 0-8156-2331-3). Syracuse U Pr.
Upstate New York. Bradford B. Van Diver. (Geology Field Guide Ser.). (Illus.). 288p. 1980. pap. text ed. 15.95 (ISBN 0-8403-2214-3). Kendall-Hunt.
Upstate New York: Field Guide. 1986. 14.95. North Country.
Upstate Travels: British Views of Nineteenth-Century New York. Ed. by Roger M. Haydon. LC 82-3312. (York State Book). (Illus.). 320p. 1982. 21.00x (ISBN 0-8156-2270-8); pap. 11.95 (ISBN 0-8156-0175-1). Syracuse U Pr.
Upstream. Virginia L. Long. 1986. 2.95 (ISBN 0-934536-25-2). Merging Media.
Upstream: A Voyage on the Connecticut River. Ben Bachman. 1985. 15.95 (ISBN 0-395-34389-5). HM.
Upstream: A Voyage on the Connecticut River. Benjamin Bachman. 217p. 1988. pap. 10.95 (ISBN 0-87106-678-5). Globe Pequot.
Upstream Processes: Equipment & Techniques. Ed. by Avshalom Mizrahi. LC 83-644876. (Advances in Biotechnological Processes Ser.: Vol. 7). 254p. 1988. 64.00 (ISBN 0-8451-3206-7, 3207). A R Liss.
Uptake & Storage of Noradrenaline in Sympathetic Nerves. Leslie L. Iverson. LC 67-12318. pap. 66.80 (2027233). Bks Demand UMI.
Uptight. Gloria M. Guenther. (Contemporary Problems Reading Ser.). (Illus.). (gr. 7-12). 1976. pap. 4.95 (ISBN 0-914296-53-1). Ed Activities.
Uptight: The Velvet Underground Story. Victor Bockris & Gerard Malanga. LC 84-62393. (Illus.). 128p. 1985. pap. 7.95 (ISBN 0-688-03906-5, Quill). Morrow.
Upton-on-Severn Words & Phrases. Robert Lawson. (English Dialect Society Publications Ser.: No. 42). pap. 15.00 (ISBN 0-8115-0468-9). Kraus Repr.
Upton Sinclair. William Bloodworth, Jr. (United States Authors Ser.). 1977. lib. bdg. 17.95 (ISBN 0-8057-7197-2, Twayne). G K Hall.
Upton Sinclair. Jon A. Yoder. LC 74-78450. (Literature & Life Ser.). 160p. 1975. 16.95x (ISBN 0-8044-2989-8); pap. 7.95. Ungar.
Upton Sinclair: A Study in Social Protest. Floyd Dell. LC 73-133826. Repr. of 1927 ed. 24.50 (ISBN 0-404-02076-3). AMS Pr.
Upton Sinclair: An Annotated Checklist. Ronald Gottesman. LC 72-634010. (Serif Ser.: No. 24). pap. 141.00 (ISBN 0-8357-9375-3, 2014598). Bks Demand UMI.
Upton Sinclair: Biographical & Critical Opinions. 1973. lib. bdg. 17.00 (ISBN 0-8414-8858-4). Folcroft.
Upton Sinclair Presents William Fox. Upton Sinclair. LC 78-124037. (Literature of Cinema, Ser. 1). Repr. of 1933 ed. 17.00 (ISBN 0-405-01637-9). Ayer Co Pubs.
Upton Sinclair's The Jungle: The Lost First Edition. Intro. by Gene DeGruson. 320p. 1988. 21.95 (ISBN 0-918518-66-0, St Luke TN). Peachtree Pubs.
Upton's Heritage: The History of a Massachusetts Town. Donald B. Johnson. LC 84-16659. (Illus.). 280p. 1984. 20.00 (ISBN 0-914659-08-1). Phoenix Pub.
Uptown & Downtown. Fischler. pap. 12.95 (ISBN 0-8015-8196-6, Hawthorn). Dutton.
Uptown Down South. 198p. 1986. 10.95 (ISBN 0-9608172-1-2). Greenville SC Jr League.
Upward: A History of Norfolk State University. Lyman B. Brooks. LC 83-4328. 272p. 1983. 19.95 (ISBN 0-88258-084-1). Howard U Pr.
Upward Mobility of Young Managers. Phyllis A. Wallace. 224p. 1989. 26.95x (ISBN 0-88730-120-7). Ballinger Pub.
Upward Moving & Emergence Way: The Gishin Biye Version. Berard Haile. Ed. by Karl W. Luckert. LC 81-7441. (American Tribal Religions Ser.: Vol. 7). xvi, 239p. 1981. 21.95x (ISBN 0-8032-2320-X); pap. 11.95x (ISBN 0-8032-7212-X, BB 786, Bison). U of Nebr Pr.
Upward Path. Jim Lewis. LC 82-60277. 150p. (Orig.). 1982. pap. 7.95 (ISBN 0-942482-04-2). Unity Church Denver.
Upward Trend. 2nd ed ed. Harvey Jackins. LC 78-109407. 1977. 10.00 (ISBN 0-911214-57-7); pap. 7.50 (ISBN 0-911214-81-X). Rational Isl.
Ur 'of the Chaldees' A Revised & Updated Edition of Sir Leonard Woolley's Excavations at Ur by P. R. S. Moorey. Leonard Woolley. 1982. 29.95 (ISBN 0-8014-1518-7). Cornell U Pr.
Urach Geothermal Project: Swabian Alb, Germany. Ed. by Ralph Haenel. (Illus.). 419p. 1982. pap. text ed. 75.80x (ISBN 3-510-65107-3). Lubrecht & Cramer.
Ural-Altaische Jahrbucher - Ural-Altaic Yearbook, 1988, Vol. 60. Ed. by Gyula Decsy & A. J. Bodrogligeti. (Anniversary vol. with suppl.). 1988. 74.00 (ISBN 0-931922-30-5). Eurolingua.
Ural-Altaische Jahrbucher: Ural Altaic Yearbook, Vol. 58. Ed. by Gyula Decsy & A. D. Bodrogligeti. 172p. 1986. 48.00 (ISBN 0-931922-22-4). Eurolingua.
Ural-Altaische Jahrbucher: Ural-Altaic Yearbook, Vol. 59. Ed. by Gyula Decsy & A. D. Bodrogligeti. 172p. 1987. 48.00 (ISBN 0-931922-23-2). Eurolingua.
Ural-Altaische Jahrbucher: Ural Altaic Yearbook, 1980, Vol. 57. Ed. by Gyula Decsy & A. J. Bodrogligeti. 180p. 1980. 48.00 (ISBN 0-317-65405-5). Eurolingua.
Ural-Altaische Jahrbucher: Ural-Altaic Yearbook 1985, Vol. 58. Ed. by Gyula Decsy & A. J. Brodrogligeti. 180p. 1985. 48.00 (ISBN 0-931922-20-8). Eurolingua.
Ural-Altaische Jahrbucher: 1977, Vol. 49. Ed. by Gyula Decsy & A. J. Bodrogligeti. 177p. 1977. 48.00 (ISBN 3-447-01806-2). Eurolingua.
Ural-Altaische Jahrbucher: 1978, Vol. 50. Ed. by Gyula Decsy & A. J. Bodrogligeti. 207p. 1978. 48.00 (ISBN 3-447-01891-7). Eurolingua.
Ural-Altaische Jahrbucher: 1979, Vol. 51. Ed. by Gyula Decsy & A. J. Brodrogligeti. 183p. 1979. 48.00 (ISBN 0-931922-00-3). Eurolingua.
Ural-Altaische Jahrbucher: 1980, Vol. 52. Ed. by Gyula Decsy & A. J. Brodrogligeti. 191p. 1980. 48.00 (ISBN 0-931922-05-4). Eurolingua.
Ural-Altaische Jahrbucher: 1981, Vol. 53. Ed. by Gyula Decsy & A. J. Bodrogligeti. 172p. 1981. 48.00 (ISBN 0-931922-08-9). Eurolingua.
Ural-Altaische Jahrbucher: 1982, Vol. 54. Ed. by Gyula Decsy & A. J. Bodrogligeti. 172p. 1982. 48.00 (ISBN 0-931922-09-7). Eurolingua.
Ural-Altaische Jahrbucher: 1983, Vol. 55. Ed. by Gyula Decsy & A. J. Bodrogligeti. 174p. 1983. 48.00 (ISBN 0-931922-14-3). Eurolingua.
Ural-Altaische Jahrbucher: 1984, Vol. 56. Ed. by Gyula Decsy. 187p. 1984. 48.00 (ISBN 0-931922-17-8). Eurolingua.
Urania: A Choice Collection of Psalm-Tunes, Anthems & Hymns. James Lyon. LC 69-11667. (Music Reprint Ser.). 198p. 1974. Repr. of 1761 ed. lib. bdg. 37.50 (ISBN 0-306-71198-2). Da Capo.
Uranian Astrology Guide Plus Ephemeris. Sylvia Sherman & Jori F. Manske. LC 75-38487. 1976. 17.95 (ISBN 0-686-23112-0). Am Sch Astrol.
Uranian Astrology: Tools & Techniques. Martha P. Taub. (Illus., Orig.). 1981. pap. text ed. 32.50 (ISBN 0-9609700-0-2). Uranian Consult.
Uranian Transneptune Ephemeris Eighteen Fifty to Two Thousand. Neil Michelsen. 1978. 8.95 (ISBN 0-89159-001-3). Uranian Pubns.
Urania's Daughters: A Checklist of Women Science Fiction Writers, 1692-1982. Roger C. Schlobin. LC 83-2467. (Starmont Reference Guides Ser.: Vol. 1). (Illus., Orig.). 1983. text ed. 14.95x (ISBN 0-916732-57-6); pap. text ed. 6.95x (ISBN 0-916732-56-8). Starmont Hse.
Urania's Daughters: A Checklist of Women Science Fiction Writers, 1692-1982. Roger C. Schlobin. LC 83-25779. (Starmont Reference Guides Ser.: No. 1). 79p. 1983. Repr. lib. bdg. 16.95x (ISBN 0-89370-065-7). Borgo Pr.
Uraniia. Iosif Brodskii. 150p. (Rus.). 1987. 19.50 (ISBN 0-88233-840-4). Ardis Pubs.
Uranium. J. H. Gittus. LC 64-9713. (Metallurgy of the Rarer Metals Ser.: No. 8). pap. 159.30 (ISBN 0-317-42150-6, 2025762). Bks Demand UMI.
Uranium, Pt. C, Section 3. Max Planck Society for the Advancement of Science, Gmelin Institute for Inorganic Chemistry. (Illus.). 360p. 1975. 288.50 (ISBN 0-387-93290-9). Springer-Verlag.
Uranium & Nuclear Energy. 1981. text ed. 39.95 (ISBN 0-86103-041-9, Westbury Hse). Butterworth.
Uranium & Nuclear Energy: 1982. Ed. by Uranium Institute Staff. (Illus.). 384p. 1983. text ed. 125.00 (ISBN 0-408-22160-7). Butterworth.
Uranium Carbides, Nitrides & Silicides. Compiled by V. Maximov. (Bibliographical Ser.: No. 33). 110p. 1968. pap. 10.00 (ISBN 92-0-044368-0, ISP21 33, IAEA). UNIPUB.
Uranium Carbides, Nitrides & Silicides. Compiled by V. Maximov. (Bibliographical Ser.: No. 14). 175p. 1964. pap. 11.00 (ISBN 92-0-044064-9, ISP21 14, IAEA). UNIPUB.
Uranium Carbides, Nitrides & Silicides II, 1963-1965. Compiled by V. Maximov. (Bibliographical Ser.: No. 21). 172p. 1966. pap. 12.00 (ISBN 92-0-044166-1, ISP21 21, IAEA). UNIPUB.
Uranium-Carbon & Plutonium-Carbon Systems: A Thermochemical Assessment. (Technical Reports Ser.: No. 14). (Illus.). 44p. 1963. pap. 9.00 (ISBN 92-0-145063-X, IDC14, IAEA). UNIPUB.
Uranium Deposits in Africa: Geology & Exploration. (Panel Proceedings Ser.). (Illus.). 262p. 1980. pap. 42.00 (ISBN 92-0-041079-0, ISP509, IAEA). UNIPUB.
Uranium Deposits in Asia & the Pacific: Geology & Exploration. (Panel Proceedings Ser.). (Illus.). 341p. 1988. pap. 69.00 (ISP756, IAEA). UNIPUB.
Uranium Deposits in Latin America: Geology & Exploration. (Panel Proceedings Ser.). (Illus.). 625p. 1981. pap. 86.00 (ISBN 92-0-041081-2, ISP505, IAEA). UNIPUB.
Uranium Deposits in Metamorphic Environments. 1979. 78.70 (ISBN 0-942218-09-4). Minobras.
Uranium Deposits in Volcanic Rocks: Proceedings of a Technical Committee Meeting El Paso, Texas, April 2-5, 1984. (Panel Proceedings Ser.). 468p. 1986. pap. text ed. 73.75 (ISBN 92-0-041085-5, ISP690, IAEA). UNIPUB.
Uranium Deposits of Arizona, California & Nevada. 1978. 40.30 (ISBN 0-942218-10-8). Minobras.
Uranium Deposits of the Northern U. S. Region. 1977. 37.10 (ISBN 0-942218-11-6). Minobras.
Uranium Deposits: Origin, Evolution, & Present Characteristics. J. H. Tatsch. LC 75-9304. (Illus.). 303p. 1976. 96.00 (ISBN 0-912890-11-8). Tatsch.
Uranium Development in Less Developed Countries: A Handbook of Concerns. David M. Erickson. (Lincoln Institute Monograph: No. 81-4). 83p. 1981. pap. text ed. 14.00 (ISBN 0-686-30624-4). Lincoln Inst Land.
Uranium: Economic & Political Instability in a Strategic Commodity Market. Marian Radetzki. 1981. 35.00 (ISBN 0-312-83424-1). St Martin.
Uranium Enrichment. Ed. by S. Villani. (Topics in Applied Physics Ser.: Vol. 35). (Illus.). 1979. 59.00 (ISBN 0-387-09385-0). Springer-Verlag.
Uranium Enrichment & Nuclear Weapon Proliferation. A. S. Krass et al. LC 83-8486. 270p. 1983. 33.00x (ISBN 0-85066-219-2). Taylor & Francis.
Uranium Evaluation & Mining Techniques: Proceedings of an International Seminar Organized by the IAEA with the cooperation of the OECD Nuclear Energy Agency & held in Beunos Aires, 1-4 October 1979. 550p. 1981. pap. 77.00 (ISBN 92-0-040280-1, ISP524, IAEA). UNIPUB.
Uranium Exploration Case Histories: Proceedings of an Advisory Group Meeting, Vienna, 26-29 November 1979, Jointly Organized by IAEA & NEA (OECD) 407p. 1982. pap. 56.50 (ISBN 92-0-141081-6, ISP584, IAEA). UNIPUB.
Uranium Exploration Geology. (Panel Proceedings Ser.). (Illus., Orig.). 1971. pap. 25.75 (ISBN 92-0-041070-7, ISP277, IAEA). UNIPUB.
Uranium Exploration in Wet Tropical Environments. (Panel Proceedings Ser.). 162p. 1983. pap. text ed. 25.75 (ISBN 92-0-141183-9, ISP642, IAEA). UNIPUB.
Uranium Exploration Methods. 980p. (Orig., Eng. & Fr.). 1982. pap. 48.00x (ISBN 92-64-02350-X). OECD.
Uranium Exploration Methods. (Illus.). 320p. (Orig.). 1974. pap. 32.00 (ISBN 92-0-041073-1, ISP334, IAEA). UNIPUB.
Uranium Exploration: 1975. pap. 6.50 (SSC82, SSC). UNIPUB.
Uranium Extraction Technology. OECD Staff & NEA Staff. 270p. (Orig.). 1983. pap. 20.00 (ISBN 92-64-12397-0). OECD.
Uranium Fuel Supply: Proceedings, American Nuclear Society Executive Conference, Monterey CA, 23-26 January 1977. 456p. 34.00 (ISBN 0-89448-302-1, 650003). Am Nuclear Soc.
Uranium Geochemistry, Mineralogy, Geology, Exploration & Resources. Ed. by G. Capaldi et al. 201p. 1984. pap. text ed. 78.00X (ISBN 0-900488-70-0). Imm North Am.
Uranium Geology & Mines, South Texas. D. H. Eargle et al. (GB Ser.: No. 12). (Illus.). 59p. 1971. 1.75 (ISBN 0-686-29320-7). Bur Econ Geology.
Uranium Guidebook for the Paradox Basin: Utah-Colorado. 1978. 50.20 (ISBN 0-942218-12-4). Minobras.
Uranium in the Pine Creek Geosyncline: Proceedings. (Proceedings Ser.). (Illus.). 762p. 1980. pap. 120.00 (ISBN 92-0-140080-2, ISP555, IAEA). UNIPUB.
Uranium Mill Tailings. OECD Staff & NEA Staff. 238p. (Orig., Eng. & Fr.). 1982. pap. text ed. 16.00x (ISBN 92-64-02288-0). OECD.

Uranium Mill Tailings Management: Proceedings of the First Symposium, 1978, 2 vols. Set. 17.00 (ISBN 0-910069-11-5); Vol. 1; 172 pgs. write for info. (ISBN 0-910069-00-X); Vol. 2; 141 pgs. write for info. (ISBN 0-910069-01-8). Geotech Engineer Prog.

Uranium Mill Tailings Management: Proceedings of the Fourth Symposium, 1981. 729p. 1981. 28.00 (ISBN 0-910069-04-2). Geotech Engineer Prog.

Uranium Mill Tailings Management: Proceedings of the Fifth Symposium, 1982. 557p. 1982. 30.00 (ISBN 0-910069-06-9). Geotech Engineer Prog.

Uranium Mill Tailings Management: Proceedings of the Second Symposium, 1979. 331p. 1979. 20.00 (ISBN 0-910069-02-6). Geotech Engineer Prog.

Uranium Mill Tailings Management: Proceedings of the Third Symposium, 1980. 573p. 1980. 25.00 (ISBN 0-910069-03-4). Geotech Engineer Prog.

Uranium Nineteen Eighty. Emanuel Gordon. (Technical & Economic Reports: Nuclear Fuel Cycle). 61p. 1981. write for info. US Coun Energy Awareness.

Uranium, Nonproliferation & Energy Security. Steven J. Warnecke. (Atlantic Papers: No. 37). 121p. 1980. 6.50x (ISBN 0-916672-77-8, Pub. by Allanheld). Rowman.

Uranium, Nuclear Power, & Canada-U. S. Energy Relations. Hugh C. McIntyre. LC 78-54112. (Canadian-American Committee Ser.). 80p. 1978. 4.00 (ISBN 0-88806-035-1). Natl Planning.

Uranium Ore Processing. (Panel Proceedings Ser.). (Illus.). 238p. 1977. pap. 31.50 (ISBN 92-0-041176-2, ISP453, IAEA). UNIPUB.

Uranium Ores & Minerals. LC 81-80058. 1978. 33.50 (ISBN 0-942218-14-0). Minobras.

Uranium, Plutonium & the Transplutonic Elements. Ed. by H. C. Hodge et al. (Handbook of Experimental Pharmacology: Vol. 36). (Illus.). xxiii, 995p. 1973. 220.00 (ISBN 0-387-06168-1). Springer-Verlag.

Uranium Poems. Judith J. Sherwin. Repr. of 1969 ed. 18.00 (ISBN 0-404-53864-9, PS35). AMS Pr.

Uranium Prospecting Handbook. Ed. by S. H. Bowie et al. 346p. 1977. pap. text ed. 49.00x (ISBN 0-900488-15-8). IMM North Am.

Uranium, Resource Production & Demand. OECD Nuclear Energy Agency & International Atomic Energy Agency. 350p. 1984. pap. 32.00x (ISBN 92-64-12550-7). OECD.

Uranium Resources - an International Assessment: Proceedings of the American Nuclear Society Topical Symposium, Las Vegas, Sept., 1978. American Nuclear Society Staff. 445p. softcover 29.00 (ISBN 0-317-33084-5, 700034). Am Nuclear Soc.

Uranium Resources of the Central & Southern Rockies. 1979. 33.30 (ISBN 0-942218-15-9). Minobras.

Uranium Resources, Production & Demand. OECD. 194p. (Orig.). 1988. pap. 27.50x (ISBN 92-64-13090-X). OECD.

Uranium Resources, Production & Demand, 1986. OECD Staff. 414p. (Orig.). 1986. pap. 42.00x (ISBN 92-64-12842-5). OECD.

Uranium Seminar, 4th: Proceedings. LC 80-70454. (Uranium Seminars Ser.). 1980. pap. 5.00x (ISBN 0-89520-280-8). Soc Mining Eng.

Uranium-Series Disequilibrium: Applications to Environmental Problems. Ed. by M. Ivanovich & R. S. Harmon. (Illus.). 1982. 98.00x (ISBN 0-19-854423-5). Oxford U Pr.

Uranium Technology. J. E. Vance & J. C. Warner. (National Nuclear Energy Ser.: Div. VII, Vol. 2A). 231p. 1951. pap. 24.95 (ISBN 0-87079-227-X, TID-5231); microfilm 10.00 (ISBN 0-87079-463-9, TID-5231). DOE.

Uranium; the Real Facts: A Medical Response to the Marline Corporation's Uranium Fact Book. Eve Bargmann. 1982. pap. 2.00 (ISBN 0-937188-23-9). Pub Citizen Inc.

Uranium-234. V. V. Cherdyntsev. 240p. 1971. text ed. 46.00x (ISBN 0-7065-1104-2, Pub. by Keter Pub Jerusalem). Coronet Bks.

Uranometria. Joannes Bayer. (Mapping of the Stars Ser.). (Illus.). 216p. (Lat. & Gr.). 1987. Repr. of 1603 ed. 250.00 (ISBN 1-85297-021-9). Archival Facsimiles.

Uranometria Two Thousand Point Zero, Vol. 1. Wil Tirion & Barry Rappaport. (Illus.). 300p. 1987. text ed. 39.95 (ISBN 0-943396-14-X). Willmann-Bell.

URANTIA Book. URANTIA Foundation. LC 55-10554. 1955. 34.00 (ISBN 0-911560-02-5). URANTIA Foun.

Uranus. Seymour Simon. LC 86-31223. (Illus.). 32p. (ps-3). 1987. 13.00 (ISBN 0-688-06582-1, Morrow Junior Books); lib. bdg. 12.88 (ISBN 0-688-06583-X, Morrow Junior Books). Morrow.

Uranus & Neptune: The Distant Giants. Eric Burgess. (Illus.). 160p. 1988. 29.95 (ISBN 0-231-06492-6). Columbia U pr.

Uranus & the Outer Planets: Proceedings of the IAU-RAS Colloquium, No. 60. IAU-RAS Colloquium (60th: 1981: University of Bath) Staff. Ed. by Garry Hunt. LC 81-17047. pap. 82.50 (2031672). Bks Demand UMI.

Uranus: Freedom from the Known. Jeff Green. Ed. by Anne Holm. LC 87-46417. (Modern Astrology Library). 192p. (Orig.). 1988. pap. 7.95 (ISBN 0-87542-297-7). Llewellyn Pubns.

Uranus-Neptune-Pluto: The Spiritual Trinity. Ted George. LC 79-53906. 225p. 1980. 13.00 (ISBN 0-932782-01-9). Arthur Pubns.

Uranus: The Seventh Planet. Branklyn M. Branley. LC 87-35046. (Voyage into Space Book Ser.). (Illus.). 64p. (gr. 3-6). 1988. 11.95 (ISBN 0-690-04685-5, Crowell Jr Bks); PLB 11.89 (ISBN 0-690-04687-1, Crowell Jr Bks). HarpJ.

Uranus: The Sideways Planet. Isaac Asimov. LC 87-42594. (Isaac Asimov's Library of the Universe). (Illus.). 32p. (gr. 3-4). 1988. PLB 10.95 (ISBN 1-55532-324-3). Stevens Inc.

Uranus: The Topsy-Turvy Planet. Isaac Asimov. LC 87-42594. (Isaac Asimov's Library of the Universe). (Illus.). 32p. (gr. 2-3). 1988. PLB 9.95 (ISBN 0-317-66516-2). Stevens Inc.

Urashima Taro. Robert B. Goodman & Robert A. Spicer. Ed. by Ruth Tabrah. LC 73-79570. (Illus.). (gr. 1-7). 1973. 5.95 (ISBN 0-89610-013-8). Island Heritage.

Urashima Taro & Other Stories. Florence Sakade. (Illus.). (gr. 1-6). 1958. pap. 6.95 (ISBN 0-8048-0609-8). C E Tuttle.

Urashima, the Fisherman. (MacDonald Educational Ser.). (Illus., Arabic.). (gr. 5-12). 3.50x (ISBN 0-86685-242-5). Intl Bk Ctr.

Urban Aboriginals: A Celebration of Leathersexuality. Geoffrey Mains. (Illus.). 192p. (Orig.). 1984. pap. 8.95 (ISBN 0-917342-38-0); limited signed cloth ed. 30.00. Gay Sunshine.

Urban Accident Patterns, 5 reports. (Transportation Research Record Ser.). 56p. 1975. 2.60 (ISBN 0-309-02393-9). Transport Res Bd.

Urban Administration: Management, Politics & Change. Ed. by Alan E. Bent & Ralph A. Rossum. 1976. 27.00x (ISBN 0-8046-7106-0, Pub by Kennikat); pap. 14.50x (ISBN 0-8046-7109-5). Assoc Faculty Pr.

Urban Affair. Daniel Stern. 288p. (Orig.). 1986. pap. 2.75 (ISBN 0-380-57919-7, 57919). Avon.

Urban Affairs Subject Heading Comparisons. Jamie R. Graham. 184p. 1979. pap. 7.00 (ISBN 0-318-00030-X, INS 19). Inst for Urban & Regional.

Urban Affairs Subject Headings. Compiled by Edith Ward et al. LC 75-33026. vi, 34p. (Orig.). 1975. lib. bdg. 35.00x (ISBN 0-8371-8537-8, ICSH). Greenwood.

Urban Air Pollution Modeling. Michael M. Benarie. (Illus.). 1980. text ed. 65.00x (ISBN 0-262-02140-4). MIT Pr.

Urban Air Pollution: With Particular Reference to Motor Vehicles. WHO Expert Committee, Geneva, 1968. (Technical Report Ser: No. 410). 53p. 1969. pap. 2.00 (ISBN 92-4-120410-9, 64). World Health.

Urban Air Traffic & City Planning: Case Study of Los Angeles County. Melville C. Branch. LC 73-1090. (Special Studies in U. S. Economic, Social & Political Issues). 1973. 49.50x (ISBN 0-275-28701-7). Irvington.

Urban Alert: How to Survive in the City After Nuclear Explosion, Economic Disaster or Economic Collapse. B. Clayton & M. E. Clayton. 1986. lib. bdg. 79.95 (ISBN 0-8490-3699-2). Gordon Pr.

Urban Amenities & Economic Development, Vol. 2. Ed. by A. Tappan Wilder. (Livability Digest: No. 1). 80p. 1982. pap. 5.00 (ISBN 0-317-44279-1). Partners Livable.

Urban America: A Bibliography. Casper. 1985. lib. bdg. 34.00 (ISBN 0-8240-8815-8). Garland Pub.

Urban America & Public Policies. 2nd ed. Marian L. Palley & Howard A. Palley. 336p. 1981. pap. text ed. 14.00 (ISBN 0-669-04004-5). Heath.

Urban America & the Foreign Traveler, 1815-1855. Eugene P. Moehring. LC 73-13465. (Foreign Travelers in America, 1810-1935 Ser.). 334p. 1974. Repr. 23.00 (ISBN 0-405-05468-8). Ayer Co Pubs.

Urban America: Documenting the Planners. Elaine D. Engst & H. Thomas Hickerson. LC 85-73105. (Illus.). 44p. (Orig.). pap. 5.00 (ISBN 0-935995-00-5). Cornell Manu.

Urban America: From Downtown to No Town. David R. Goldfield & Blaine A. Brownell. LC 78-69562. (Illus.). 1979. pap. text ed. 28.76 (ISBN 0-395-27397-8). HM.

Urban America in the Modern Age, 1920 to the Present. Carl Abbott. Ed. by John H. Franklin & Abraham Eisenstadt. LC 86-6363. (American History Ser.). (Illus.). 192p. (Orig.). 1987. pap. text ed. 8.95 (ISBN 0-88295-840-2). Harlan Davidson.

Urban America: Institutions & Experience. Michael Lewis. LC 72-10944. pap. 131.50 (ISBN 0-317-07770-8, 2013723). Bks Demand UMI.

Urban American Catholicism: The Culture & Identity of the American Catholic People. Ed. by Timothy J. Meagher. (Heritage of American Catholicism Ser.). 368p. 1988. lib. bdg. 60.00 (ISBN 0-8240-4080-5). Garland Pub.

Urban Analysis for Branch Library System Planning. R. E. Coughlin et al. LC 71-133496. (Contributions in Librarianship & Information Science Ser.: No. 1). 1972. lib. bdg. 35.00 (ISBN 0-8371-5161-9, CLP/). Greenwood.

Urban Analytical Tools: A Handbook. Anthony Elipovitch. 198p. 1987. pap. text ed. 19.95 (ISBN 0-8403-4343-4). Kendall Hunt.

Urban & Metropolitan Economics. J. M. Levy. 448p. 1985. text ed. 34.95 (ISBN 0-07-037455-4). McGraw.

Urban & Regional Analysis for Development Planning. Richard Rhoda. (Replica Edition). 200p. 1982. softcover 29.50x (ISBN 0-86531-916-2). Westview.

Urban & Regional Development Planning: Policy & Administration. Dennis A. Rondinelli. LC 74-18539. 288p. 1975. 24.95x (ISBN 0-8014-0873-3). Cornell U Pr.

Urban & Regional Economics, Vol. 25. Compiled by Edward Tower. 194p. 1985. 14.00 (ISBN 0-88024-225-6). Eno River Pr.

Urban & Regional Economics: A Guide to Information Sources. Ed. by Jean A. Shackelford. LC 74-11556. (Economics Information Guide Ser.: Vol. 14). 190p. 1980. 68.00x (ISBN 0-8103-1303-0). Gale.

Urban & Regional Models in Geography & Planning. Alan G. Wilson. LC 73-8200. pap. 108.00 (ISBN 0-317-30329-5, 2024807). Bks Demand UMI.

Urban & Regional Planning. 2nd ed. Peter Hall. (Illus.). 336p. 1985. pap. text ed. 13.95x (ISBN 0-04-711014-7). Unwin Hyman.

Urban & Regional Planning for the Delhi-New Delhi Area: Capital for Conquerors & Country. Gerald Breese. 55p. 1974. pap. 3.50 (ISBN 0-686-09286-4). G Breese.

Urban & Regional Planning Glossary: English-French, Finnish-Russian. S. Heinonen & A. Kolm. 1984. pap. 25.00 (ISBN 951-682-092-1). Heinman.

Urban & Regional Planning in an Age of Austerity. Ed. by Pierre Clavel & William W. Goldsmith. LC 79-21416. (Policy Studies in Urban Affairs). 402p. 1980. text ed. 64.00 (ISBN 0-08-025539-6); pap. text ed. 12.00 (ISBN 0-08-025540-X). Pergamon.

Urban & Regional Planning in Canada. J. B. Cullingworth. 460p. 1987. 49.95 (ISBN 0-88738-135-9). Transaction Bks.

Urban & Regional Planning in India. K. V. Sundaram. 1979. text ed. 35.00x (ISBN 0-7069-0536-9, Pub. by Vikas India). Advent NY.

Urban & Regional Planning in Pakistan. Ghulam M. Samdani. (Working Papers Ser.: No. 74-6). 21p. 1979. pap. 6.00 (ISBN 0-686-78260-7, CRD041, UNCRD). UNIPUB.

Urban & Regional Policy Analysis In Developing Coutries. Lata Chatterjee & Peter Nijkamp. 270p. 1983. text ed. 37.90 (ISBN 0-566-00623-5). Gower Pub Co.

Urban & Regional Studies at United States Universities: A Report Based on a 1963 Survey of Urban & Regional Research. Ed. by Scott Keyes. pap. 35.30 (ISBN 0-317-26467-2, 2023803). Bks Demand UMI.

Urban & Regional Transformation of Britain. Ed. by J. B. Goddard & A. G. Champion. 1983. pap. 17.95x (ISBN 0-416-30900-3, NO. 3924). Routledge Chapman & Hall.

Urban & Rural Change in West Germany. Ed. by Trevor Wild. LC 83-6350. 272p. 1983. text ed. 27.50x (ISBN 0-389-20392-0). B&N Imports.

Urban & Rural Survival: Rural Home Modifications. CWL. (Security & Survival Ser.). (Illus.). 60p. (Orig.). 1985. pap. 20.00 (ISBN 0-939856-48-4). Tech Group.

Urban & Spatial Development in Mexico. Ian Scott. LC 80-8023. 416p. 1982. 32.50x (ISBN 0-8018-2498-2); pap. 12.95x (ISBN 0-686-86226-0). Johns Hopkins.

Urban Anthropology: A Research Bibliography, Nos. 944-945. William W. Pilcher. 1975. 10.50 (ISBN 0-686-20380-1). CPL Biblios.

Urban Areas, 4 pts. Incl. Pt. 1. Housing, 3 vols. Set. 343.00x (ISBN 0-7165-1463-X); Pt. 2. Planning, 10 vols. Set. 1196.00x (ISBN 0-7165-1464-8); Pt. 3. Sanitation, 7 vols. Set. 909.00x (ISBN 0-686-01166-X); Pt. 4. Water Supply, 9 vols. Set. 1172.00x (ISBN 0-7165-1466-4). (British Parliamentary Papers Ser.). 1971 (Pub. by Irish Academic Pr Ireland). Biblio Dist.

Urban Arena. J. Short. 202p. 1984. text ed. 25.00x (ISBN 0-333-36139-3, Pub. by Macmillan UK). Humanities.

Urban Atlanta: Redefining the Role of the City. Ed. by Andrew M. Hamer. LC 79-27699. (Research Monograph: No. 84). 1980. pap. 16.95 (ISBN 0-88406-125-6). Ga St U Busn Pub.

Urban Atmosphere. B. W. Atkinson. (Update Ser.). (Illus.). 80p. Date not set. pap. 6.95 (ISBN 0-521-31584-0). Cambridge U Pr.

Urban Atmosphere, Sydney: A Case Study. Ed. by J. N. Carras & G. M. Johnson. (Illus.). 654p. (Orig.). 1983. pap. text ed. 25.00 (ISBN 0-643-03479-X, Pub. by CSIRO). Intl Spec Bk.

Urban Australia: Planning Issues & Policies. Ed. by Stephen Hamnett. 208p. 1987. 65.00x (ISBN 0-7201-1843-3). Mansell.

Urban Black Politics. Ed. by John R. Howard & Robert C. Smith. LC 78-56922. (Annals: No. 439). 1978. 15.00 (ISBN 0-87761-230-7); pap. 7.95 (ISBN 0-87761-231-5). Am Acad Pol Soc Sci.

Urban Blight & Slums: Economic & Legal Factors in Their Origin, Reclamation & Prevention. Mabel L. Walker. LC 70-139943. (Illus.). 1971. Repr. of 1938 ed. 20.00x (ISBN 0-8462-1546-2). Russell.

Urban Blues. Charles Keil. LC 66-13876. (Illus.). 1966. 17.00x (ISBN 0-226-42959-8). U of Chicago Pr.

Urban Blues. Charles Keil. LC 66-13876. (Illus.). 1968. pap. 2.45 (ISBN 0-226-42960-1, P291, Phoen). U of Chicago Pr.

Urban Bosses, Machines & Progressive Reformers. 2nd ed. Bruce M. Stave & Sondra Stave. LC 79-27906. 272p. 1984. pap. 11.50 (ISBN 0-89874-119-X). Krieger.

Urban Builder: The Life & Times of Stanley Draper. James M. Smallwood. LC 77-9115. (Oklahoma Trackmaker Ser.: No. 5). (Illus.). 1978. 15.95 (ISBN 0-8061-1447-9). U of Okla Pr.

Urban Business Profiles. LC 79-14909. (Small-Business Library: Vol. 1). 400p. 1979. 95.00x (ISBN 0-8103-1027-9). Gale.

Urban Caldron: The Second Annual Donald Hagman Memorial Conference. Joseph DiMento et al. LC 85-21641. (Lincoln Institute of Land Policy). 160p. 1986. text ed. 35.00 (ISBN 0-89946-207-3). Oelgeschlager.

Urban Capitalists: Entrepreneurs & City Growth in Pennsylvania's Lackawanna & Lehigh Valleys, 1800-1920. Burton W. Folsom, Jr. LC 80-8864. (Studies in Industry & Society: No. 1). (Illus.). 208p. 1981. text ed. 24.50x (ISBN 0-8018-2520-2). Johns Hopkins.

Urban Challenge. Ed. by Larry L. Rose & C. Kirk Hadaway. LC 82-71026. 1982. pap. 5.95 (ISBN 0-8054-6238-4). Broadman.

Urban Change & Poverty. National Research Council. Ed. by Michael G. McGeary & Laurence E. Lynn, Jr. 350p. 1988. pap. text ed. 29.95x (ISBN 0-309-03837-5). Natl Acad Pr.

Urban Change & the Planning Syndrome. new ed. Ed. by George F. Mott & Richard D. Lambert. LC 72-93250. (Annals of the American Academy of Political & Social Science: No. 405). 250p. 1973. 15.00 (ISBN 0-87761-158-0, 87761); pap. 7.95 (ISBN 0-87761-157-2). Am Acad Pol Soc Sci.

Urban Change in China: Politics & Development in Tsinan, Shantung, 1890-1949. David D. Buck. (Illus.). 314p. 1978. 32.50x (ISBN 0-299-07110-3). U of Wis Pr.

Urban Christian. Raymond Bakke. LC 87-30861. 160p. 1987. pap. 6.95 (ISBN 0-87784-523-9). Inter-Varsity.

Urban Climate. Helmut Landsberg. LC 80-2766. (International Geophysics Ser.). 1981. 35.00 (ISBN 0-12-435960-4). Acad Pr.

Urban Community. Ed. by Ernest W. Burgess. LC 71-175038. (BCL Ser. I). Repr. of 1926 ed. 21.50 (ISBN 0-404-01235-3). AMS Pr.

Urban Community: A Guide to Information Sources. Ed. by Anthony Filipovitch & Earl Reeves. LC 78-13171. (Urban Studies Information Guide Ser.: Vol. 4). 296p. 1978. 68.00x (ISBN 0-8103-1429-0). Gale.

Urban Community Care for the Developmentally Disabled. Herbert J. Cohen & David Kligler. (Illus.). 360p. 1980. 38.25x (ISBN 0-398-03945-3). C C Thomas.

Urban Community: Housing & Planning in the Progressive Era. Roy Lubove. LC 81-6328. (American Historical Sources: Research & Interpretation Ser.). ix, 148p. 1981. Repr. of 1967 ed. lib. bdg. 35.00x (ISBN 0-313-22731-4, LUUC). Greenwood.

Urban Conservation. M. A. Muttalib. 64p. 1985. text ed. 15.00x (ISBN 0-86590-731-5, Pub. by Sterling Pubs India). Apt Bks.

Urban Cooperatives in India: On Behalf of National Federation of Urban Co-Operative Banks & Credit Societies, Ltd. (Illus.). 142p. 1987. text ed. 25.00x (ISBN 81-210-0176-5, Pub. by Inter India Pubns N. Delhi). Apt Bks.

Urban Crisis: A Symposium. J. V. Lindsay et al. LC 71-146555. (Symposia on Law & Society Ser). 1971. Repr. of 1969 ed. lib. bdg. 19.50 (ISBN 0-306-70115-4). Da Capo.

Urban Crucible: Social Change, Political Consciousness, & the Origins of the American Revolution. Gary B. Nash. LC 79-12894. 1979. pap. 11.95x (ISBN 0-674-93057-6). Harvard U Pr.

Urban Crucible: The Northern Seaports & the Origins of the American Revolution. Gary B. Nash. (Illus.). 296p. 1986. text ed. 37.00x (ISBN 0-674-93058-4). Harvard U Pr.

Urban Crucible: The Northern Seaports & the Origins of the American Revolution. Gary B. Nash. 296p. 1986. pap. text ed. 10.95x (ISBN 0-674-93059-2). Harvard U Pr.

Urban Danger: Life in a Neighborhood of Strangers. Sally E. Merry. 278p. 1981. 29.95 (ISBN 0-87722-219-3). Temple U Pr.

Urban Danger: Life in a Neighborhood of Strangers. Sally E. Merry. 278p. 1986. pap. 12.95 (ISBN 0-87722-425-0). Temple U Pr.

Urban Decay in India. R. S. Sharma. 1988. 40.00x (ISBN 81-215-0045-1, Munshiram Manoharial India). South Asia Bks.

Urban Decay in St. Louis. Institute for Urban & Regional Studies. 200p. 1972. pap. 10.00 (ISBN 0-318-00024-5, INS 10). Inst for Urban & Regional.

Urban Decision Making...a Guide to Information Sources. Ed. by Mark Drucker. LC 80-19252. (Urban Studies Information Guide Series. Part of the Gale Information Guide Library: Vol. 13). 208p. 1981. 68.00 (ISBN 0-8103-1481-9). Gale.

Urban Decline & the Future of American Cities. Katherine J. Bradbury & Anthony Downs. LC 82-70888. 309p. 1982. 31.95 (ISBN 0-8157-1054-2); pap. 11.95 (ISBN 0-8157-1053-4). Brookings.

Urban Guerilla, Module Fourteen. Ed. by Loren K. Wiseman. (Twilight Ser.: No. 2000). 49p. (Orig.). 1987. pap. 7.00 (ISBN 0-943580-46-3). Game Designers.

Urban Habitat: Past, Present & Future. Mary J. Huth. LC 77-7273. (Illus.). 320p. 1978. text ed. 24.95x (ISBN 0-88229-333-8). Nelson-Hall.

Urban Harvest. Roy Joslin. 1982. pap. 14.95 (ISBN 0-87552-920-8, Evangel Pr UK). Presby & Reformed.

Urban Health in America. Amasa B. Ford. (Illus.). 1976. 15.95x (ISBN 0-19-502003-0). Oxford U Pr.

Urban Historical Geography: Recent Progress in Britain & Germany. Ed. by Dietrich Denecke & Gareth Shaw. (Cambridge Studies in Historical Geography: No. 10). (Illus.). 416p. 1988. 59.50 (ISBN 0-521-34362-3). Cambridge U Pr.

Urban History: a Guide to Information Sources. Ed. by John Buenker et al. LC 80-19643. (American Government & History Ser., Part of the Gale Information Guide Library: Vol. 9). 464p. 1981. 68.00x (ISBN 0-8103-1479-7). Gale.

Urban History: Reviews of Recent Research. Ed. by Patricia J. Rosof et al. LC 80-27903. (Trends in History Ser.: Vol. 2, No. 1). 97p. 1981. text ed. 24.95 (ISBN 0-917724-26-7, B26). Haworth Pr.

Urban Homesteading: Nineteen Seventy-Five to Nineteen Eighty-Six. Azar Aryanpour. (Public Administration Ser.: P 2108). 8p. 1987. 3.00 (ISBN 1-55590-208-1). Vance Biblios.

Urban Hospital Location. Leslie Mayhew. LC 85-15820. (London Research Series in Geography: No. 4). (Illus.). 176p. 1985. text ed. 44.95x (ISBN 0-04-362054-X). Unwin Hyman.

Urban Housing--Public & Private: A Guide to Information Sources. Ed. by John E. Rouse, Jr. LC 79-100279. (Urban Studies Information Guide Ser.: Vol. 5). 336p. 1978. 68.00x (ISBN 0-8103-1398-7). Gale.

Urban Housing & Neighborhood Revitilization: Turning a Federal Program into Local Projects. Donald B. Rosenthal. LC 87-32259. (Contributions in Political Science Ser: No. 208). 240p. 1988. lib. bdg. 45.00 (ISBN 0-313-26148-2, RND/). Greenwood.

Urban Housing in India. Devendra B. Gupta et al. (Working Paper: No. 730). 252p. 1985. 10.00 (ISBN 0-8213-0554-9, WP 0730). World Bank.

Urban Housing in the Nineteen Eighties: Markets & Policies. Margery A. Turner & Raymond J. Struyk. LC 84-21942. 124p. 1984. text ed. 14.95x (ISBN 0-87766-371-8). Urban Inst.

Urban Housing Markets & Property Valuation. Ed. by C. F. Sirmans & Hugh O. Nourse. (Research in Real Estate Ser.: Vol. 2). 291p. 1982. 59.50 (ISBN 0-89232-270-5). Jai Pr.

Urban Housing Markets: Recent Directions in Research & Policy. Ed. by Larry S. Bourne & John R. Hitchcock. (Orig.). 1979. pap. 17.50x (ISBN 0-8020-2339-8). U of Toronto Pr.

Urban Hydrological Modeling & Catchment Research: International Summary. M. B. McPherson & F. C. Zuidema. (Technical Papers in Hydrology: No. 18). (Illus.). 48p. 1979. pap. 5.00 (ISBN 92-3-101691-1, U896, UNESCO). UNIPUB.

Urban Hydrology. M. J. Hall. 304p. 1984. 63.00 (ISBN 0-85334-268-7, I-217-84, Pub. by Elsevier Applied Sci England). Elsevier.

Urban Hydrology. Ed. by Harry C. Torno. 270p. 1983. pap. 23.00x (ISBN 0-87262-388-2). Am Soc Civil Eng.

Urban Idea in Colonial America. Sylvia D. Fries. LC 77-81333. (Illus.). 236p. 1977. 29.95 (ISBN 0-87722-103-0). Temple U Pr.

Urban Illusions: New Approaches to Inner City Unemployment. Michael Bernick. LC 87-7208. 256p. 1987. lib. bdg. 37.95 (ISBN 0-275-92804-7, C2804). Praeger.

Urban Impact of Federal Policies. Ed. by Norman J. Glickman. LC 79-2368. (Johns Hopkins Studies in Urban Affairs). pap. 160.00 (ISBN 0-317-41638-3, 2025837). Bks Demand UMI.

Urban Impact of Internal Migration. Ed. by James W. White. LC 79-16544. (Comparative Urban Studies Project: No. 5). 175p. 1979. pap. text ed. 5.50 (ISBN 0-89143-048-2). U NC Inst Res Soc Sci.

Urban Impact on American Protestantism, 1865-1900. Aaron I. Abell. x, 275p. 1962. Repr. of 1943 ed. 25.00 (ISBN 0-208-00587-0, Archon). Shoe String.

Urban India, Vol. 6. Ed. by Giri R. Gupta. (Main Currents In Indian Sociology Ser.: No. 6). 424p. 1984. text ed. 40.00x (ISBN 0-317-07654-X, Vikas India). Advent NY.

Urban Indians. Ed. by Center for the History of the American Indian Staff. (Library Center for the History of the American Indian: No. 4). 185p. 1981. text ed. 4.00 (ISBN 0-686-81346-4). Newberry.

Urban Indians. Ed. by Frank W. Porter, III. (Indians of North America Ser.). (Illus.). (gr. 5 up). 1989. 16.95 (ISBN 1-55546-732-6). Chelsea Hse.

Urban Indicators: A Guide to Information Sources. Ed. by Thomas P. Murphy. LC 80-13333. (Urban Studies Information Guide Ser.: Vol. 10). 256p. 1980. 68.00x (ISBN 0-8103-1451-7). Gale.

Urban Inequality & Housing Policy in Tanzania: The Problem of Squatting. Richard E. Stren. LC 75-620118. (Research Ser.: No. 24). (Illus.). 128p. 1975. pap. 2.95x (ISBN 0-87725-124-X). U of Cal Intl St.

Urban Influence on Farm Family Size. Nathan Keyfitz. Ed. by Harriet Zuckerman & Robert K. Merton. LC 79-9009. (Dissertations on Sociology Ser.). 1980. lib. bdg. 13.00x (ISBN 0-405-12977-7). Ayer Co Pubs.

Urban Informal Sector in an Urban Economy: A Study in Ahmedabad. T. S. Papola. 156p. 1981. text ed. 15.95x (ISBN 0-7069-1133-4, Pub by Vikas India). Advent NY.

Urban Informal Sector in Developing Countries: Employment, Poverty, & Environment. Ed. by S. V. Sethuraman. (WEP Study Ser.). xii, 225p. 1981. pap. 14.25 (ISBN 92-2-102591-8, ILO195, ILO). UNIPUB.

Urban Information Thesaurus: A Vocabulary for Social Documentation. Ed. by Paul Rosenberg. LC 76-52604. 1977. lib. bdg. 46.95 (ISBN 0-8371-9483-0, UTH). Greenwood.

Urban Innovation Abroad: Problem Cities In Search of Solutions. Ed. by Thomas L. Blair. 424p. 1984. 70.00x (ISBN 0-306-41492-9, Plenum Pr). Plenum Pub.

Urban Institutions & People of Indian Ancestry. Raymond Breton & Gail G. Akian. 52p. 1978. pap. text ed. 3.00x (ISBN 0-920380-14-X, Pub. by Inst Res Pub Canada). Brookfield Pub Co.

Urban Interaction on the Iranian Plateau: Excavations at Tepe Yahya, 1967-1973. C. C. Lambert-Karlovsky. (Albert Reckitt Archaeological Lectures). 1973. pap. 2.50 (ISBN 0-85672-099-2, Pub. by British Acad). Longwood Pub Group.

Urban Ireland: Development of Towns & Villages. Ed. by Curriculum Development Unit. (Illus.). 128p. 1982. 15.95 (ISBN 0-86278-017-9, XPub. by O'Brien Pr Ireland); pap. 7.95 (ISBN 0-86278-018-7, Pub. by O'Brien Pr Ireland). Irish Bks Media.

Urban Issues, Growth & the Economy, 1977-1982. LC 84-36415. 82p. (Orig.). 1984. pap. 3.25 (ISBN 0-87772-294-3). UCB IGS.

Urban Japanese Housewives: At Home & in the Community. Anne E. Imamura. LC 86-27262. 224p. 1987. text ed. 18.00x (ISBN 0-8248-1082-1). UH Pr.

Urban Jobless in Eastern Africa. Abel G. Ishumi. (Illus.). 112p. 1984. pap. 19.50 (ISBN 0-8419-9769-1, Africana). Holmes & Meier.

Urban Labor Market & Income Distribution. Dipak Mazumdar. (World Bank Research Publications Ser.). (Illus.). 1981. 29.95x (ISBN 0-19-520213-9); pap. 12.95x (ISBN 0-19-520214-7). Oxford U Pr.

Urban Labour in Informal Sector: A Case Study of Visakhaptnam City. Kudamala Sreeramamurty. xi, 140p. 1986. text ed. 25.00x (ISBN 81-7018-292-1, Pub. by B R Pub Corp Delhi). Apt Bks.

Urban Land & Shelter for the Poor. 1985. 6.00 (ISBN 0-905347-56-0). Intl Inst Environment.

Urban Land Economics. Michael A. Goldberg & Peter Chinloy. LC 83-23486. 566p. 1984. text ed. 38.95 (ISBN 0-471-09286-X). Wiley.

Urban Land Economics & Public Policy. Richard B. Andrews. LC 77-122281. 1971. 16.95 (ISBN 0-02-900710-0). Free Pr.

Urban Land Economics: Principles & Policy. Graham Hallett. LC 79-65820. (Illus.). xv, 274p. 1979. 27.50 (ISBN 0-208-01834-4, Archon). Shoe String.

Urban Land Markets: Price Indices, Supply Measures, & Public Policy Effects. Ed. by J. Thomas Black & James E. Hoben. LC 80-53134. (ULI Research Report: No. 30). (Illus.). 232p. 1980. pap. 20.00 (ISBN 0-87420-593-X); pap. 15.00 members. Urban Land.

Urban Land Nexus & the State. A. J. Scott. 256p. 1980. 24.00x (ISBN 0-85086-079-2, NO. 6390, Pub. by Pion England). Routledge Chapman & Hall.

Urban Land Policies & Land-Use Control Measures, 7 Vols. Incl. Vol. 1. Africa. pap. 3.00 (ISBN 0-686-93558-6, UN73/4/5); Vol. 2. Asia & the Far East. pap. 4.00 (ISBN 0-686-93559-4, UN73/4/6); Vol. 3. Western Europe. pap. 6.00 (ISBN 0-686-93560-8, UN73/4/7); Vol. 4. Latin America. pap. 3.00 (ISBN 0-686-93561-6, UN73/4/8); Vol. 5. Middle East. pap. 2.50 (ISBN 0-686-93562-4, UN73/4/9); Vol. 6. Northern America. pap. 5.00 (ISBN 0-686-93563-2, UN73/4/10); Vol. 7. Global Review. pap. 11.00 (ISBN 0-686-93564-0, UN73/4/11). UN.

Urban Land Policy: Issues & Opportunities. Harold B. Dunkerley & Christine M. E. Whitehead. LC 82-20247. 224p. 1983. 24.95 (OX 520403). World Bank.

Urban Land Policy: Issues & Opportunities. Ed. by Harold B. Dunkerley. (Illus.). 1983. 24.95x. Oxford U Pr.

Urban Land-Use & Transport Interaction: Policies & Models. F. V. Webster & P. H. Bly. 534p. 1988. text ed. 90.00 (ISBN 0-566-05726-3, Pub. by Gower Pub England). Gower Pub Co.

Urban Land Use Planning. 3rd ed. F. Stuart Chapin, Jr. & Edward J. Kaiser. LC 64-18666. (Illus.). 672p. 1979. 35.00 (ISBN 0-252-00580-5); wkbk 6.95 (ISBN 0-252-00791-3). U of Ill Pr.

Urban Land Use Planning. 3rd ed. F. Stuart Chapin, Jr. & Edward J. Kaiser. 672p. 1986. pap. 22.50 (ISBN 0-252-01257-7). U of Ill Pr.

Urban Land Use Policy. Ed. by Richard B. Andrews. LC 70-169230. 1972. 22.95 (ISBN 0-02-900700-3). Free Pr.

Urban Landscape Design. Garrett Eckbo. (Illus.). 1964. text ed. 41.50 (ISBN 0-07-018880-7). McGraw.

Urban Landscape: Historical Development & Management. Ed. by J. Whitehand. LC 81-68018. (Institute of British Geographer Special Publication: No. 13). 1982. 36.00 (ISBN 0-12-747020-4). Acad Pr.

Urban Landscapes: A New Jersey Portrait. George A. Tice. LC 75-30549. (Illus.). Repr. of 1975 ed. 28.00 (ISBN 0-8357-9529-2, 2050675). Bks Demand UMI.

Urban Law: A Guide to Information Sources. Ed. by Thomas P. Murphy & Robert D. Kline. (Urban Studies Information Guide: Vol. 11). 352p. 1980. 68.00x (ISBN 0-8103-1409-6). Gale.

Urban Legal Problems in Eastern Africa. Ed. by G. W. Kanyeihamba & J. P. McAuslan. (Studies of Law in Social Change & Development: No. 2). 298p. 1983. 39.50 (ISBN 0-8419-9748-9, Africana). Holmes & Meier.

Urban Life & the Struggle to Be Human. Albert J. Mayer & Leonard Gordon. 1979. pap. text ed. 15.95 (ISBN 0-8403-2035-3). Kendall-Hunt.

Urban Life in Contemporary China. Martin K. Whyte & William L. Parish. LC 83-7779. (Illus.). xii, 408p. 1984. lib. bdg. 32.50 (ISBN 0-226-89546-7); pap. 13.95. U of Chicago Pr.

Urban Life in Contemporary China. Martin K. Whyte & William L. Parish. LC 83-7779. xii, 412p. 1985. pap. 13.95x (ISBN 0-226-89549-1). U of Chicago Pr.

Urban Life in Kingston, Jamaica. Diane J. Austin. (Caribbean Studies: Vol. 3). 312p. 1984. 50.00 (ISBN 2-88124-006-2). Gordon & Breach.

Urban Life in Mediterranean Europe: Anthropological Perspectives. Ed. by Michael Kenny & David I. Kertzer. LC 82-1890. 352p. 1983. 29.95 (ISBN 0-252-00958-4); pap. 9.95 (ISBN 0-252-00990-8). U of Ill Pr.

Urban Life in Syria under the Early Mamluks. Nicola A. Ziadeh. Repr. of 1953 ed. lib. bdg. 35.00 (ISBN 0-8371-3162-6, ZILS). Greenwood.

Urban Life in Texas: A Statistical Profile & Assessment of the Largest Cities. Richard L. Cole et al. 95p. 1986. 25.00 (ISBN 0-292-76700-5). U of Tex Pr.

Urban Life in the Caribbean: A Study of a Haitian Urban Community. Michel S. Laguerre. 213p. 1982. 18.95 (ISBN 0-87073-734-1); pap. 11.95 (ISBN 0-87073-735-X). Schenkman Bks Inc.

Urban Life: Readings in Urban Anthropology. 2nd ed. Ed. by George Gmelch & Walter P. Zenner. (Illus.). 478p. 1988. pap. text ed. 17.95x (ISBN 0-88133-332-8). Waveland Pr.

Urban Living: The Individual in the City. D. J. Walmsley. 240p. 1988. pap. 23.95 (ISBN 0-470-20863-5). Wiley.

Urban Local Administration. Apurba Kumar Basiston. xv, 319p. 1986. text ed. 37.50x (ISBN 81-7018-291-3, Pub. by B R Pub Corp Delhi). Apt Bks.

Urban Low-Income Housing & Development: A Case Study in Peninsular Malaysia. E. A. Wegelin. 1978. lib. bdg. 23.00 (ISBN 90-207-0729-9, Pub. by Martinus Nijhoff Netherlands). Kluwer Academic.

Urban Management. Ed. by David R. Morgan. LC 72-8662. 183p. 1973. text ed. 34.50x (ISBN 0-8422-5065-4); pap. text ed. 9.95x (ISBN 0-8422-0249-8). Irvington.

Urban Management: A Guide to Information Sources. Ed. by Bernard H. Ross. LC 78-10310. (Urban Studies Information Guide Ser.: Vol. 8). 304p. 1979. 68.00x (ISBN 0-8103-1430-4). Gale.

Urban Mass Transit: A Guide to Organizations & Information Resources. Thomas N. Trzyna & Joseph R. Beck. LC 78-12497. (Who's Doing What Ser.: No. 5). 1979. pap. 25.00x (ISBN 0-912102-38-1). Cal Inst Public.

Urban Masses & Moral Order in America, 1820-1920. Paul Boyer. LC 78-15973. 1978. 30.00x (ISBN 0-674-93109-2). Harvard U Pr.

Urban Migrants in Developing Nations: Patterns & Problems of Adjustment. Ed. by Calvin Goldscheider. LC 83-10372. (Replica Edition Ser.). 288p. 1983. softcover 33.00x (ISBN 0-86531-974-X). Westview.

Urban Millennium: The City-Building Process from the Early Middle Ages to the Present. Josef W. Konvitz. 336p. 1985. text ed. 24.95x (ISBN 0-8093-1201-8). S Ill U Pr.

Urban Ministry. David Claerbaut. 224p. 1984. pap. 9.95 (ISBN 0-310-45961-3, 12605P). Zondervan.

Urban Minority Administrations: Politics, Policy, & Style. Ed. by Albert K. Karnig & Paula D. McClain. (Contributions in Political Science Ser.: No. 228). 1989. price not set (ISBN 0-313-25852-X, KUY/). Greenwood.

Urban Mission - God's Concern for the City: The Urbana '87 Compendium. LC 88-753. 192p. (Orig.). 1988. pap. 8.95 (ISBN 0-8308-1711-5). Inter-Varsity.

Urban Mission: Essays on the Building of a Comprehensive Model for Evangelical Urban Ministry. Craig Ellison. LC 82-23764. 230p. 1983. pap. text ed. 13.25 (ISBN 0-8191-2968-2). U Pr of Amer.

Urban Modelling. M. Batty. (Urban & Architectural Studies). (Illus.). 384p. 1976. 75.00 (ISBN 0-521-20811-4). Cambridge U Pr.

Urban Models. Janet R. Pack. (Monograph: No. 7). 12.50 (ISBN 0-686-32168-5). Regional Sci Res Inst.

Urban Mosaic: Towards a Theory of Residential Differentiation. Duncan Timms. LC 70-123665. (Cambridge Geographical Studies: No. 2). pap. 71.30 (2026354). Bks Demand UMI.

Urban Nation: Nineteen Twenty-Nineteen Eighty. rev. ed. George E. Mowry & Blaine A. Brownell. (Illus.). 360p. 1981. 12.50 (ISBN 0-8090-9541-6); pap. 9.95 (ISBN 0-8090-0148-9). Hill & Wang.

Urban Nationalism: A Study of Political Development in Trinidad. Alvin Magid. 314p. 1988. 25.00x (ISBN 0-8130-0853-0). U Presses Fla.

Urban Native Men & Women: Differences in Their Work Adaptations. new ed. Dorothy M. Jones. LC 76-620028. (ISEGR Occasional Paper: No. 12). 45p. 1976. pap. 1.00 (ISBN 0-88353-021-X). U Alaska Inst Res.

Urban Naturalist. Steven D. Garber. LC 87-2108. 242p. 1987. pap. 12.95 (ISBN 0-471-85793-9, Pub. by Wiley Science Ed.). Wiley.

Urban Needs: A Bibliography & Directory for Community Resource Centers. Paula Kline. LC 78-9265. 265p. 1978. 17.50 (ISBN 0-8108-1148-0). Scarecrow.

Urban Neighborhoods, Networks & Families. Peggy Wireman. LC 80-9016. 224p. 1984. 29.00x (ISBN 0-669-04503-9). Lexington Bks.

Urban Neighborhoods: Research & Policy. Ed. by Ralph B. Taylor. LC 85-28311. 397p. 1986. lib. bdg. 36.95 (ISBN 0-275-92017-8, C2017). Praeger.

Urban Nest. 162p. 1981. pap. 10.00 (ISBN 0-318-17836-2). Landscape Architecture.

Urban Networks in Russia, 1750-1800 & Premodern Periodization. T. Rozewicz. LC 75-3472. 344p. 1975. text ed. 39.00x (ISBN 0-691-09364-4). Princeton U Pr.

Urban Networks: The Structure of Activity Patterns see Progress in Planning.

Urban Notables & Arab Nationalism: The Politics of Damascus 1860-1920. Philip S. Khoury. LC 83-5289. (Cambridge Middle East Library). (Illus.). 192p. 1984. 39.50 (ISBN 0-521-24796-9). Cambridge U Pr.

Urban Notions. Stephen Marc. LC 84-180996. (Illus.). 70p. 1983. 15.00 (ISBN 0-915109-01-8); pap. 8.00 (ISBN 0-915109-02-6). Ataraxia.

Urban Oasis, Seventy-Five Years in a St. Louis Private Place. Parkview Historic Committee. (Illus.). 1979. pap. 11.95 (ISBN 0-932114-01-6). Boars Head.

Urban Open Spaces. Ed. by Lisa Taylor. (Illus.). 128p. 1980. pap. 9.95 (ISBN 0-8478-0304-X). Rizzoli Intl.

Urban Open Spaces. Ed. by Lisa Taylor. LC 81-655475. (Immovable Objects Ser.). (Illus.). 64p. (Orig.). 1979. Tabloid 2.50x (ISBN 0-910503-27-3). Cooper-Hewitt Museum.

Urban Operations Research. R. Larson & A. Odoni. 1981. write for info. (ISBN 0-13-939447-8). P-H.

Urban Options. William Pankey. LC 86-5965. 144p. 1986. 35.00 (ISBN 0-87833-533-1). Taylor Pub.

Urban Origins of Rural Revolution: Elites & the Masses in Hunan Province, China, 1911-1927. Angus W. McDonald, Jr. LC 76-7764. (Center for Chinese Studies, UC Berkeley: No. 21). 1978. 35.00x (ISBN 0-520-03228-4). U of Cal Pr.

Urban Outcomes: Schools, Streets, & Libraries. Frank S. Levy et al. (Oakland Project). 1974. 36.50x (ISBN 0-520-02546-6); pap. 11.95x (ISBN 0-520-03045-1). U of Cal Pr.

Urban Park Officer. Jack Rudman. (Career Examination Ser.: C-1995). (Cloth bdg. avail. on request). pap. 12.00 (ISBN 0-8373-1995-1). Natl Learning.

Urban Park Patrol Sergeant. Jack Rudman. (Career Examination Ser.: C-2541). (Cloth bdg. avail. on request). pap. 15.00 (ISBN 0-8373-2541-2). Natl Learning.

Urban Park Ranger. (Career Examination Ser.: C-3267). Date not set. pap. 15.00 (ISBN 0-8373-3267-2). Natl Learning.

Urban Parks & Recreation: Challenges of the 1970's. Richard Kraus. 1972. pap. 1.50 (ISBN 0-86671-006-X). Comm Coun Great NY.

Urban Pattern: City Planning & Design. 5th ed. Arthur Gallion & Simon Eisner. (Illus.). 512p. 1986. pap. 27.95 (ISBN 0-442-22731-0). Van Nos Reinhold.

Urban Patterns: Studies in Human Ecology. rev. ed. Ed. by George A. Theodorson. LC 81-83145. (Illus.). 475p. 1982. 26.75x (ISBN 0-271-00297-2). Pa St U Pr.

Urban Planner. Jack Rudman. (Career Examination Ser.: C-854). (Cloth bdg. avail. on request). pap. 14.00 (ISBN 0-8373-0854-2). Natl Learning.

Urban Planning. 2nd ed. Anthony J. Catanese & J. C. Synder. 416p. 1988. text ed. 39.95 (ISBN 0-07-010229-5). McGraw.

Urban Planning: A Guide to Information Sources. J. Alexander et al. LC 78-13462. (Urban Studies Information Guide Ser.: Vol. 2). 184p. 1979. 68.00x (ISBN 0-8103-1399-5). Gale.

Urban Southwest: A Profile History of Albuquerque, El Paso, Phoenix, Tucson. Bradford Luckingham. (Illus.). 196p. 1982. 18.00 (ISBN 0-87404-067-1); pap. 12.00 (ISBN 0-87404-068-X). Tex Western.

Urban Space. Rob Krier. LC 79-64347. (Illus.). 174p. 1979. pap. 27.50 (ISBN 0-8478-0236-1). Rizzoli Intl.

Urban Space: A Brief History of the City Square. 2nd ed. Jere S. French. (Illus.). 272p. 1986. pap. 25.95 (ISBN 0-8403-3109-6). Kendall Hunt.

Urban Spatial Traffic Patterns. Rodney Vaughan. 318p. 1987. 67.50 (ISBN 0-85086-122-5, 1162, Pub. by Pion England). Routledge Chapman & Hall.

Urban State Universities: An Unfinished National Agenda. Arnold B. Grobman. 140p. 1988. lib. bdg. 36.95 (ISBN 0-275-92934-5, C2934). Praeger.

Urban Statistical Surveys: An Original Anthology. United States Bureau of the Census General Statistics of Cities, 1909-1976 & 1916-1976. Ed. by United States Bureau of the Census Historical Statistics on State Local Government Finances, 1902-1953. (America in Two Centuries Ser.). 1976. 29.00 (ISBN 0-405-07750-5, 10174). Ayer Co Pubs.

Urban Storm Drainage. Ed. by P. R. Helliwell. LC 78-18235. 728p. 1978. 84.95x (ISBN 0-470-26461-6). Halsted Pr.

Urban Storm Drainage Management. Sheaffer. (Civil Engineering Ser.: Vol. 4). 368p. 1982. 59.75 (ISBN 0-8247-1351-6). Dekker.

Urban Stormwater Hydrology. D. K. Kibler. (Water Resources Monograph Ser.: Vol. 7). 271p. 1982. pap. 18.00 (ISBN 0-87590-308-8). Am Geophysical.

Urban Stormwater Management in Coastal Areas. Ed. by Chin Y. Kuo. LC 80-66949. 442p. 1980. pap. 32.00x (ISBN 0-87262-247-9). Am Soc Civil Eng.

Urban Stress: Experiments on Noise & Social Stressors. David C. Glass & Jerome E. Singer. LC 78-182640. (Social Psychology Ser.). 1972. 22.00 (ISBN 0-12-286050-0). Acad Pr.

Urban Structure. D. Lewis. LC 68-57502. 283p. (Orig.). 1968. 23.50 (ISBN 0-471-53375-0, JW). Krieger.

Urban Structure & Victimization. David L. Decker & David Shichor. LC 79-1865. 128p. 1982. 17.50x (ISBN 0-669-02951-3). Lexington Bks.

Urban Studies. W. Andrews et al. 1976. pap. text ed. 20.04 (ISBN 0-13-939280-7); tchr's guide 8.44 (ISBN 0-13-939454-0). P-H.

Urban Studies: An Introductory Reader. 2nd ed. Ed. by Louis K. Loewenstein. LC 76-19644. 1977. 22.50 (ISBN 0-02-919470-9); pap. text ed. 10.95 (ISBN 0-02-919440-7). Free Pr.

Urban Studies: Cumulative Index 1964-1975 (Volumes 1-12) 1983. 25.00 (ISBN 0-317-01054-9). Learned Info.

Urban-Suburban Problems. Bernard J. Frieden. (Task Force on the Eighties Ser.). 34p. 1981. pap. 2.50 (ISBN 0-87495-038-4). Am Jewish Comm.

Urban Surface Water Management. Stuart G. Walesh. 1988. 59.95 (ISBN 0-471-83719-9). Wiley.

Urban Survival Arsenal: The Best Guns for Self-Preservation. F. Rexer. 1986. lib. bdg. 79.95 (ISBN 0-8490-3817-0). Gordon Pr.

Urban Survival: Communications. (Security & Survival Ser.). (Illus.). 50p. (Orig.). 1985. pap. 10.00 (ISBN 0-939856-49-2). Tech Group.

Urban Survival: Home Modifications. CWL. (Security & Survival Ser.). (Illus.). 100p. (Orig.). 1985. pap. 25.00 (ISBN 0-939856-47-6). Tech Group.

Urban Survival: Vehicles. CWL. (Security & Survival Ser.). (Illus.). 48p. (Orig.). 1985. pap. 15.00 (ISBN 0-939856-46-8). Tech Group.

Urban System of a Developing Economy. H. N. Misra. 1988. 32.00x (ISBN 0-8364-2312-7, Pub. by Heritage). South Asia Bks.

Urban System Operation & Freeways. (Transportation Research Record Ser.). 115p. 1978. 6.40 (ISBN 0-309-02827-2). Transport Res Bd.

Urban Systems & Territorial Planning in Italy. Giancarlo Nuti. (UNCRD Working Paper: No. 85-2). 25p. (Orig.). 1986. pap. text ed. 5.00 (ISBN 0-318-21381-8, CRD183, CRD). UNIPUB.

Urban Systems: Contemporary Approaches to Modelling. Ed. by C. S. Bertuglia et al. 688p. 1987. 125.00 (ISBN 0-7099-3971-X, Pub. by Croom Helm UK). Routledge Chapman & Hall.

Urban Systems in a Dynamic Society. L. Van den Berg. 160p. 1986. text ed. 41.50 (ISBN 0-566-05251-2, Pub. by Gower Pub England). Gower Pub Co.

Urban Systems Models. Walter Helly. 1975. 34.50 (ISBN 0-12-339450-3). Acad Pr.

Urban Systems Operations. (Transportation Research Record Ser.). 116p. 1979. 6.20 (ISBN 0-309-02972-4). Transport Res Bd.

Urban Systems-Strategies for Regulation. L. S. Bourne. (Illus.). 1975. pap. 15.95x (ISBN 0-19-874055-7). Oxford U Pr.

Urban Technology: A Primer on Problems. Herbert Fox. LC 73-82700. (Urban Problems & Urban Technology Ser.: Vol. 1). pap. 47.80 (2027128). Bks Demand UMI.

Urban Technology Seminar: Proceedings. 152p. 1972. pap. 3.00 (ISBN 0-89940-054-X). LBJ Sch Pub Aff.

Urban Terrorism. Anthony M. Burton. LC 75-21937. 1976. 12.95 (ISBN 0-02-905000-6). Free Pr.

Urban Threshold: Growth & Change in a Nineteenth-Century American Community. Stuart M. Blumin. LC 75-27891. (Heritage of Sociology Ser.). 1976. pap. 10.00x (ISBN 0-226-06170-1, Midway Reprint). U of Chicago Pr.

Urban-to-Rural Return Migration in Korea. On-Jook Lee. 194p. 1980. text ed. 15.00x (ISBN 0-8248-0938-6). UH Pr.

Urban Transit Policy: An Economic & Political History. David Jones. (Illus.). 192p. 1985. text ed. 31.00 (ISBN 0-13-939257-2). P-H.

Urban Transit Systems: Guidelines for Examining Options. Alan Armstrong-Wright. (Technical Paper: No. 52). 92p. 1986. 5.00 (BK0765). World Bank.

Urban Transit: The Private Challenge to Public Transportation. Ed. by Charles A. Lave. LC 84-21529. (Illus.). 372p. 1985. 29.95 (ISBN 0-88410-969-0); pap. 12.95 (ISBN 0-88410-970-4). PRIPP.

Urban Transport. (Sector Policy Paper). 103p. 1975. 5.00 (ISBN 0-686-36222-5, PP-7504). World Bank.

Urban Transport. (World Bank Policy Study Ser.). 80p. (Eng., Fr. & Span.). 1986, Eng. Ed. 7.50 (BK0755); Fr. Ed. avail.; Span. Ed. avail. World Bank.

Urban Transport Economics. Ed. by David A. Hensher. LC 76-11061. 285p. pap. 74.10 (2030599). Bks Demand UMI.

Urban Transport Future. Ed. by Tony Young & Roy Cresswell. LC 81-19560. (Illus.). 214p. pap. 55.70 (2030326). Bks Demand UMI.

Urban Transport in Asean. V. Setty Pendakur. 68p. 1984. pap. 9.00 (ISBN 9971-902-78-8, Pub. by Inst Southeast Asian Stud). Gower Pub Co.

Urban Transport in South & Southeast Asia: An Annotated Bibliography. V. Setty Pendakur. 116p. 1985. pap. text ed. 8.50x (ISBN 9-971902-88-5, Pub. by Inst Southeast Asian Stud). Gower Pub Co.

Urban Transport in West Africa. Richard Barrett. (World Bank Technical Paper - Urban Transport Ser.: No. 81). 140p. 1988. 10.00 (ISBN 0-8213-1042-9, BK1042). World Bank.

Urban Transport Planning: Theory & Practice. John Black. LC 80-8860. pap. 62.00 (ISBN 0-317-41621-9, 2025831). Bks Demand UMI.

Urban Transport Planning: Theory & Practice. Ed. by John Black. LC 80-8860. (Illus.). 257p. 1981. pap. text ed. 10.95x (ISBN 0-8018-2604-7). Johns Hopkins.

Urban Transport Service Innovations. (Special Report). 142p. 1979. 7.80 (ISBN 0-309-02817-5). Transport Res Bd.

Urban Transportation Economics. (Special Report). 260p. 1978. 10.80 (ISBN 0-309-02663-6). Transport Res Bd.

Urban Transportation Efficiency. 442p. 1977. pap. 20.00x (ISBN 0-87262-174-X). Am Soc Civil Eng.

Urban Transportation Financing. LC 80-66290. 312p. 1980. pap. 26.00x (ISBN 0-87262-241-X). Am Soc Civil Eng.

Urban Transportation Financing: Theory & Policy in Ontario. Mark W. Frankena. (Ontario Economic Council Research Studies). 248p. 1982. pap. 4.95x (ISBN 0-8020-3380-6). U of Toronto Pr.

Urban Transportation Innovation. 445p. 1970. pap. 19.00x (ISBN 0-87262-044-1). Am Soc Civil Eng.

Urban Transportation Networks: Equilibrium Analysis with Mathematical Programming Methods. Yosef Sheffi. (Illus.). 400p. 1985. text ed. 52.00 (ISBN 0-13-939729-9). P-H.

Urban Transportation of Irradiated Fuels. Ed. by John Surrey. LC 83-40490. 300p. 1984. 25.95 (ISBN 0-312-83481-0). St Martin.

Urban Transportation Planning. M. Meyer & E. Miller. 544p. 1984. text ed. 49.95 (ISBN 0-07-041752-0). McGraw.

Urban Transportation Planning. 106p. 1968. pap. 9.00x (ISBN 0-87262-019-0). Am Soc Civil Eng.

Urban Transportation Planning, Evaluation, & Analysis. (Transportation Research Record Ser.). 53p. 1979. 3.40 (ISBN 0-309-02953-8). Transport Res Bd.

Urban Transportation Planning in the United States: An Historical Overview. Edward Weiner. LC 86-30343. 135p. 1987. 30.95 (ISBN 0-275-92493-9, C2493); pap. 9.95 (ISBN 0-275-92544-7, B2544). Praeger.

Urban Transportation Problem. John R. Meyer et al. LC 65-13848. (Rand Corporation Research Studies Ser.). (Illus.). 1965. 29.50x (ISBN 0-674-93120-3); pap. 9.95x (ISBN 0-674-93121-1). Harvard U Pr.

Urban Transportation System: Politics & Policy Innovation. Alan A. Altshuler et al. 1979. pap. 17.50x (ISBN 0-262-51023-5). MIT Pr.

Urban Transportation: The New Town Solution. Harry Dupree. 250p. 1987. text ed. 27.95 (ISBN 0-566-00839-4, Pub. by Gower Pub England). Gower Pub Co.

Urban Unemployment in Developing Countries: The Nature of the Problem & Proposals for Its Solution. 2nd ed. Paul Bairoch. 1976. 8.75 (ISBN 92-2-100998-X). Intl Labour Office.

Urban Unemployment in Developing Countries: The Nature of the Problem & Proposals for Its Solution. vi, 99p. (2nd Impression). 1976. pap. 8.75 (ISBN 92-2-100998-X, ILO1226, ILO). UNIPUB.

Urban University in America. Maurice R. Berube. LC 77-87917. 1978. lib. bdg. 35.00 (ISBN 0-313-20031-9, BUU/). Greenwood.

Urban Utopias in the Twentieth Century: Ebenezer Howard, Frank Lloyd Wright, Le Corbusier. Robert Fishman. (Illus.). 384p. 1982. pap. 9.95 (ISBN 0-262-56023-2). MIT Pr.

Urban Vegetation: A Review & Chicago Case Study. James A. Schmid. LC 74-84781. (Research Papers Ser.: No. 161). (Illus.). 266p. 1975. pap. 12.00 (ISBN 0-89065-068-3). U Chicago Comm Geo.

Urban Vigilantes in the New South: Tampa, 1882-1936. Robert P. Ingalls. LC 87-30077. (Illus.). 320p. 1988. text ed. 29.95x (ISBN 0-87049-571-2). U of Tenn Pr.

Urban Village: Community & Family in Germantown, Pennsylvania, 1683-1800. Stephanie G. Wolf. LC 76-3025. 376p. 1980. 42.00x (ISBN 0-691-04632-8); pap. 11.95x (ISBN 0-691-00590-7). Princeton U Pr.

Urban Villagers. Rev. Expanded ed. Herbert J. Gans. LC 82-8577. (Illus.). 456p. 1982. pap. text ed. 8.95 (ISBN 0-02-911240-0); 10.95 (ISBN 0-02-911250-8). Free Pr.

Urban Voter. C. P. Bhambri. 1973. 10.00 (ISBN 0-89684-532-X). Orient Bk Dist.

Urban Water Conservation: Increasing Efficiency-in-Use Residential Water Demand. J. Ernest Flack. LC 82-70113. 111p. 1982. pap. 13.00 (ISBN 0-87262-296-7). Am Soc Civil Eng.

Urban Water Infrastructure: Planning, Management & Operations. Neil S. Grigg. LC 85-26580. (Illus.). 328p. 1986. 39.95 (ISBN 0-471-82914-5). Wiley.

Urban Water Supply Alternatives: Perception & Choice in the Grand Basin, Ontario. Ian MacIver. LC 70-115926. (Research Papers Ser.: No. 126). 1970. pap. 12.00 (ISBN 0-89065-033-0). U Chicago Comm Geo.

Urban Waterfront. Bonnie Fisher & Boris Dramov. (Illus.). 144p. cancelled (ISBN 0-442-22496-6). Van Nos Reinhold.

Urban Waterfront Development. Douglas M. Wrenn & John A. Casazza. LC 82-84340. (Illus.). 224p. (Orig.). 1983. pap. 38.00 (ISBN 0-87420-619-7, W10); pap. 28.50 members. Urban Land.

Urban Waterfronts 1984: Toward New Horizons. Ann Breen & Dick Rigby. (Illus.). 100p. 1985. pap. 24.95 (ISBN 0-935957-00-6). Waterfront DC.

Urban Waterfronts '83. Ann Breen & Dick Rigby. (Illus.). 120p. 1984. pap. 17.95 (ISBN 0-317-61915-2). Waterfront DC.

Urban Waterfronts '85: Water Makes a Difference! Ann Breen & Dick Rigby. (Illus.). 134p. (Orig.). 1986. pap. 24.95 (ISBN 0-935957-02-2). Waterfront DC.

Urban Waterfronts '86: Developing Diversity. Ann Breen & Dick Rigby. (Illus.). 100p. (Orig.). 1987. pap. 24.95 (ISBN 0-935957-03-0). Waterfront DC.

Urban Waterfronts '87: Water - The Ultimate Amenity. Ann Breen & Dick Rigby. (Illus.). 100p. 1988. pap. 24.95 (ISBN 0-935957-04-9). Waterfront DC.

Urban Watershed Management: Flooding & Water Quality. Vanden Bosch et al. Ed. by Philip B. Bedient & Peter G. Rowe. (Rice University Studies: Vol. 65, No. 1). 205p. 1979. pap. 10.00x (ISBN 0-89263-240-2). Rice Univ.

Urban West. Ed. by Gerald D. Nash. (Illus.). 130p. 1979. pap. text ed. 9.95x (ISBN 0-89745-004-3). Sunflower U Pr.

Urban West at the End of the Frontier. Lawrence H. Larsen. LC 77-12019. xiv, 174p. 1978. 25.00x (ISBN 0-7006-0168-6). U Pr of KS.

Urban Woodland. Suzanne J. Price. (Illus.). 144p. 1986. 24.95 (ISBN 0-317-66036-5, Pub. by Lothian). Intl Spec Bk.

Urban Workers & Labor Unions in Chile, 1902-1927. Peter DeShazo. LC 82-70557. (Illus.). 384p. 1983. 32.50x (ISBN 0-299-09220-8). U of Wis Pr.

Urban Workers in the Industrial Revolution. Robert Glen. LC 83-43002. 256p. 1984. 30.00 (ISBN 0-312-83472-1). St Martin.

Urban Workers on Relief, 2 Vols. in 1. Gladys L. Palmer & Katherine D. Wood. LC 75-165688. (Research Monograph Ser.: Vol. 4). 1971. Repr. of 1936 ed. Set. lib. bdg. 59.50 (ISBN 0-306-70336-X). Da Capo.

Urban World. 2nd ed. J. John Palen. Ed. by Eric M. Munson. 480p. 1981. text ed. 34.95 (ISBN 0-07-048107-5). McGraw.

Urban World. 3rd ed. J. John Palen. 504p. 1987. text ed. 31.95 (ISBN 0-07-048111-3). McGraw.

Urban World. Larry L. Rose et al. LC 84-12649. 1984. pap. 8.95 (ISBN 0-8054-6339-9). Broadman.

Urbana Municipal Documents Center Manual. Jean E. Koch et al. LC 86-51179. (Illus.). 260p. 1987. 50.00x (ISBN 0-9609646-6-5). Urbana Free Lib.

Urbana Scripta: Studies of Fire Living Poets & Other Essays. Arthur H. Galton. text ed. 13.25 (ISBN 0-8369-8160-X, 8300). Ayer Co Pubs.

Urbane Thought: Culture & Class in an Andalusian City. J. R. Corbin & M. P. Corbin. (Studies in Spanish Anthropology: Vol. 2). 218p. 1987. text ed. 37.00x (ISBN 0-566-00668-5, Pub. by Gower Pub England). Gower Pub Co.

Urbane View: Life & Politics in Metropolitan America. Scott Greer. LC 71-182424. 1972. pap. 4.95 (ISBN 0-19-501728-5). Oxford U Pr.

Urbanidad y Buenas Maneras. Ed. by Maria E. Alvarez del Real. LC 84-182154. 432p. 1986. pap. 5.00 (ISBN 0-944499-10-4). Editorial Amer.

Urbanisation & Industrial Estates: The U. S. A., the U. K. & Indian Experience. K. K. Khakhar. 1985. 18.50x (ISBN 0-8364-1512-4, Pub. by Ashish India). South Asia Bks.

Urbanisation & Urban Centres under the Great Mughals, 1556-1707. Hameeda K. Naqvi. (Illus.). 210p. 1971. 11.25x (ISBN 0-89684-464-1). Orient Bk Dist.

Urbanisation in Ancient India. Vijay K. Thakur. 1981. 25.00x (ISBN 0-8364-0814-4, Pub. by Abhinav India). South Asia Bks.

Urbanisation in the Developing World. David Drakakis-Smith. 272p. 1986. 39.50 (ISBN 0-7099-0884-9, Pub. by Croom Helm Ltd). Routledge Chapman & Hall.

Urbanism: An Architectural Design Profile. David Gosling & Martland. (Illus.). 88p. 1984. pap. 14.95 (ISBN 0-312-83485-3). St Martin.

Urbanisme, Algiers & Other Buildings & Projects. Ed. by H. Allen Brooks & Alexander Tzonis. LC 83-5568. (Le Corbusier Archive Ser.). 1983. lib. bdg. 200.00 (ISBN 0-8240-5059-2). Garland Pub.

Urbanistica Contemporalis: Meeting of the European Capitals in Budapest, September 1972. Collets Staff. 542p. 1972. 59.25x (ISBN 0-317-53850-0, Pub. by Collets (UK)). State Mutual Bk.

Urbanitaet. Guenther Boehme. 116p. (Ger.). 1982. 10.00 (ISBN 3-8204-7025-5). P Lang Pubs.

Urbanities. Edward V. Lucas. LC 79-128272. (Essay Index Reprint Ser). 1921. 17.00 (ISBN 0-8369-1888-6). Ayer Co Pubs.

Urbanization & Cancer Mortality: The United States Experience, 1950-1975. Michael R. Greenberg. (Monographs in Epidemiology & Biostatistics). (Illus.). 1983. 45.00x (ISBN 0-19-503173-3). Oxford U Pr.

Urbanization & Community Building in Modern Norway. Joel S. Torstenson et al. (Illus.). 332p. (Orig.). 1985. pap. text ed. 34.00x (Pub. by Almqvist & Wiksell). Coronet Bks.

Urbanization & Counterurbanization. Ed. by Brian J. L. Berry. LC 76-15864. (Urban Affairs Annual Reviews: Vol. 11). (Illus.). 334p. 1976. 35.00 (ISBN 0-8039-0499-1). Sage.

Urbanization & Development: The Rural-Urban Transition in Taiwan. Alden Speare, Jr. et al. (Brown University Studies in Population & Development: No. 7). 220p. 1987. pap. 25.00 (ISBN 0-8133-7328-X). Westview.

Urbanization & Environmental Quality. T. R. Lakshmanan & Lata Chatterjee. Ed. by Salvatore Natoli. LC 76-57032. (Resource Papers for College Geography). 1977. pap. text ed. 5.00 (ISBN 0-89291-122-0). Assn Am Geographers.

Urbanization & Environmental Quality. Isao Orishimo. (Studies in Applied Regional Science). 192p. 1982. lib. bdg. 24.00 (ISBN 0-89838-080-4, Pub. by Kluwer-Nijhoff (Netherland)). Kluwer Academic.

Urbanization & Inequality: The Political Economy of Urban & Rural Development in Latin America. Ed. by Wayne A. Cornelius & Felicity M. Trueblood. LC 74-83000. (Latin American Urban Research Ser.: Vol. 5). (Illus.). pap. 79.50 (ISBN 0-317-08989-7, 2021879). Bks Demand UMI.

Urbanization & Kinship: The Domestic Domain on the Copperbelt of Zambia, 1950-6. A. L. Epstein. LC 81-67899. (Studies in Anthropology). 1982. 67.50 (ISBN 0-12-240520-X). Acad Pr.

Urbanization & Labor Markets in Developing Countries. Stuart W. Sinclair. LC 77-25913. 1978. 19.95x (ISBN 0-312-83492-6). St Martin.

Urbanization & Migration in Asean Development. Ed. by Philip M. Hauser & Daniel B. Suits. (Illus.). 400p. 1985. text ed. 25.00X (ISBN 0-8248-0996-3). UH Pr.

Urbanization & Migration in West Africa. Ed. by Hilda Kuper & California University at Los Angeles African Studies Center. LC 76-51201. (Illus.). 1977. Repr. of 1965 ed. lib. bdg. 25.00x (ISBN 0-8371-8762-1, KUUM). Greenwood.

Urbanization & Planning in the Third World: Spatial Perspectives & Public Participation. Robert Potter. LC 85-10924. 284p. 1985. 35.00 (ISBN 0-312-83497-7). St Martin.

Urbanization & Political Change: The Politics of Lagos, 1917-1967. Pauline H. Baker. LC 70-162001. 1974. 45.00x (ISBN 0-520-02066-9). U of Cal Pr.

Urbanization & Redistribution of Population in Regional Space: A Case Study of India. Moonis Raza & Aslam Mahmood. (Working Papers Ser.: No. 82-5). 27p. 1982. pap. text ed. 6.00 (ISBN 0-686-88356-X, CRD155, UNCRD). UNIPUB.

Urbanization & Settlement Systems: International Perspectives. Ed. by Bourne S. Larry et al. (Illus.). 1984. 49.95x (ISBN 0-19-823243-8). Oxford U Pr.

Urbanization & Urban Growth in the Caribbean. Malcolm Cross. LC 78-67307. (Urbanization in Developing Countries Ser.). pap. 46.50 (ISBN 0-317-26045-6, 2024438). Bks Demand UMI.

Urbanization & Urban Planning in Capitalist Societies. Michael J. Dear & Allen J. Scott. 1981. 37.50 (ISBN 0-416-74640-3, NO. 2869); pap. 18.00x (ISBN 0-416-74650-0, NO. 6382). Routledge Chapman & Hall.

Urkunde, Briefe und Actenstuecke Zur Geschichte der Habsburgischen Fuersten K. Ladislaus Posth: Erzherzog Albrecht Viherzog Siegmund Von Oesterreich. Ed. by Joseph Chmel. (Ger). Repr. of 1850 ed. 62.00 (ISBN 0-384-08898-8). Johnson Repr.

Urkunden der Ptolemaeerzeit (Aeltere Funde, 2 vols. Ulrich Wilcken. Incl. Vol. 1. Papyri aus Unteraegypten. x, 676p. Repr. of 1927 ed. 214.00x (ISBN 3-11-005711-5); Vol. 2. Papyri aus Oberaegypten. viii, 333p. Repr. of 1957 ed. 108.00x (ISBN 3-11-005712-3). (Illus.). 1977. De Gruyter.

Urkunden Des Cistercienser-Stiftes Heiligenkreuz Im Wiener Walde, 2 vols. Heiligenkreuz, Austria (Cistercian Abbey) Staff. 1856-1859. Vol. 11. pap. 23.00 (ISBN 0-384-22083-5); Vol. 16. pap. 62.00 (ISBN 0-685-27596-5). Johnson Repr.

Urkunden Dramatischer Auffuehrungen in Griechenland. Hans J. Mette. (Texte und Kommentare: Vol. 8). 1977. 53.60 (ISBN 3-11-006782-X). De Gruyter.

Urkunden Zur Geschichte der Mathematik Im Mittelalter & der Renaissance. Maximilian Curtze. (Bibliotheca Mathematica Teubneriana Ser: No. 45). (Ger). 1969. Repr. of 1902 ed. 45.00 (ISBN 0-384-10402-9). Johnson Repr.

Urkunden Zur Geschichte Der Nichteuklidischen Geometrie, 2 Vols. Friederich Engel & Paul Stackel. (Ger). Repr. of 1913 ed. Set. 95.00 (ISBN 0-384-63370-6). Johnson Repr.

Urkunden Zur Geschichte Von Oesterreich, Steiermark, Kaernten, Krain, Goerz, Triest, Istrien, Tirol Aus Den Jahren 1246-1300. Ed. by Joseph Chmel. (Ger). Repr. of 1849 ed. 23.00 (ISBN 0-384-08897-X). Johnson Repr.

Urkundenbuch Des Stiftes Klosterneuburg Bis Zum Ende Des Vierzehnten Jahrhunderts. Ed. by Hartmann Zeibig. (Ger). Repr. of 1857 ed. 62.00 (ISBN 0-384-29875-3). Johnson Repr.

Urkundenbuch Zur Geschichte Siebenburgens. Ed. by Georg D. Teutsch. lxxxiv, 204p. Repr. of 1857 ed. 23.00 (ISBN 0-384-59870-6). Johnson Repr.

Urn Burial. Patrick Ruell. 215p. 1987. pap. 4.95 (ISBN 0-88150-096-8). Countryman.

Urn Burial. Robert Westall. LC 87-23816. 160p. (YA) (gr. 7 up). 1988. 11.95 (ISBN 0-688-07595-9). Greenwillow.

Urn Models & Their Application: An Approach to Modern Discrete Probability Theory. Norman Johnson & Samuel Kotz. LC 76-58846. (Wiley Series in Probability & Mathematical Statistics). 402p. 1977. 53.50x (ISBN 0-471-44630-0, Pub. by Wiley-Interscience). Wiley.

Urn Models & their Application: An Approach to Modern Discrete Probability Theory. Norman L. Johnson & Samuel Kotz. LC 76-58846. (Wiley Series in Probability & Mathematical Statistics). pap. 103.80 (ISBN 0-317-55591-X, 2056343). Bks Demand UMI.

Urodynamics. P. H. Abrams. (Clinical Practice in Urology Ser.). (Illus.). 236p. 1983. 56.00 (ISBN 0-387-11903-5). Springer-Verlag.

Urodynamics: The Mechanics & Hydrodynamics of the Lower Urinary Tract. Derek J. Griffiths. (Medical Physics Handbooks: No. 4). 139p. 1980. 40.00x (ISBN 0-85274-507-9, Pub. by A Hilger UK). Taylor & Francis.

Urodynamics: Upper & Lower Urinary Tract II. Ed. by W. Lutzeyer & J. Hannappel. (Illus.). xi, 364p. 1985. 84.00 (ISBN 0-387-15357-8). Springer-Verlag.

Urogenital Infections. Ed. by A. Bondi et al. LC 87-14209. (Advances in Experimental Medicine & Biology Ser.: Vol. 224). (Illus.). 146p. 1988. 45.00x (ISBN 0-306-42799-0, Plenum Pr). Plenum Pub.

Urogential Trauma. Jack W. McAninch. (Trauma Management Ser.). (Illus.). 128p. 1985. text ed. 45.50 (ISBN 0-86577-128-6). Thieme Med Pubs.

Urohyal of Fishes. Takaya Kusaka. 320p. 1974. 74.50 (ISBN 0-86008-102-8, Pub. by U of Tokyo Japan). Columbia U Pr.

Uroki po Pastirskomu Bogosloviju. Basil Boshtchanovsky. 100p. 1961. pap. text ed. 5.00 (ISBN 0-317-30267-1). Holy Trinity.

Urokinase: Basic & Clinical Aspects. Ed. by P. M. Mannucci & A. D'Angelo. LC 81-68958. (Serono Symposium Ser.: Vol. 48). 276p. 1982. 50.50 (ISBN 0-12-469280-X). Acad Pr.

Urolithiasis. Ed. by R. A. Sutton. (Journal: Mineral & Electrolyte Metabolism: Vol. 13, No. 4, 1987). 96p. 1987. pap. 74.75 (ISBN 3-8055-4567-3). S Karger.

Urolithiasis & Related Clinical Research. Ed. by Paul O. Schwille et al. LC 85-3582. 1028p. 1985. 145.00x (ISBN 0-306-41931-9, Plenum Pr). Plenum Pub.

Urolithiasis: Theraphy, Prevention. Ed. by H. J. Schnieder. (Handbook of Urology Ser.: Vol 17, Pt. 2). (Illus.). 350p. 1986. 99.00 (ISBN 0-387-15789-1). Springer-Verlag.

Urologic Cancer: A Multidisciplinary Approach. Ed. by Marc Garnick & Jerome Richie. LC 83-17720. 288p. 1983. 49.00x (ISBN 0-306-41473-2, Plenum Med). Plenum Pub.

Urologic Cancer: Chemotherapeutic Principles & Management. Ed. by F. M. Torti. (Recent Results in Cancer Research Ser.: Vol. 85). (Illus.). 151p. 1983. 49.00 (ISBN 0-387-12163-3). Springer-Verlag.

Urologic Endocrinology. Jacob Rajfer. (Illus.). 448p. 1986. 68.00 (ISBN 0-7216-7426-7). Saunders.

Urologic Endoscopy: A Manual & Atlas. Demetrius H. Bagley et al. 336p. 1985. 99.00 (ISBN 0-316-07518-3). Little.

Urologic Imaging & Interventional Techniques. William H. Bush. 450p. 1989. price not set (ISBN 0-8067-2551-6). Urban & S.

Urologic Neoplasams: Proceedings of the Fiftieth Annual Anatomic Pathology Slide Seminar of the American Society of Clinical Pathologists. Myron R. Melamed & George M. Farrow. LC 86-32287. 150p. 1987. pap. text ed. 28.00 (ISBN 0-89189-222-2, 50-1-051-00); 24 glass slides 60.00 (ISBN 0-317-58150-3). Am Soc Clinical.

Urologic Oncology. Ed. by W. Catalona & T. Ratliff. (Cancer Treatment & Research Ser.). 1984. lib. bdg. 69.50 (ISBN 0-89838-628-4, Pub. by Martinus Nijhoff Netherlands). Kluwer Academic.

Urologic Oncology. Ed. by Sam D. Graham, Jr. (Illus.). 558p. 1986. text ed. 83.00 (ISBN 0-88167-144-4). Raven.

Urologic Oncology, Vol. 2. Richard D. Williams. 256p. 1989. text ed. 42.50 (ISBN 0-02-427940-4). Macmillan.

Urologic Pathology. Robert Peterson & Barry Stein. (Illus.). 700p. 1986. text ed. 95.00 (ISBN 0-397-50626-0, Lippincott Medical). Lippincott.

Urologic Pathology with Clinical & Radiologic Correlations. Ayten Someren. 784p. 1989. text ed. 165.00 (ISBN 0-02-413750-2). Macmillan.

Urologic Surgery. 3nd ed. Ed. by James F. Glenn. (Illus.). 1168p. 1983. text ed. 129.00 (ISBN 0-06-140922-7, 14-09234, Harper Medical). Lippincott.

Urologic Surgery: Diagnosis, Techniques, & Postoperative Treatment. Georges Mayor & Ernst J. Zingg. LC 75-36660. pap. 160.00 (ISBN 0-317-07965-4, 2016475). Bks Demand UMI.

Urologic Surgery in Neonates & Young Infants. Lowell King. (Illus.). 432p. 1988. 75.00 (ISBN 0-7216-2370-0). Saunders.

Urological Cancer. Ed. by Donald Skinner. 528p. 1983. 39.50 (ISBN 0-8089-1610-6, 794115). Grune.

Urological Complications in Gynecological Surgery & Radiotherapy. J. Kunz. (Contributions to Gynecology & Obstetrics Ser.: Vol. 11). (Illus.). viii, 220p. 1984. 90.00 (ISBN 3-8055-3759-X). S Karger.

Urological Products Market. Market Intelligence Research Company Staff. Ed. by Wilmoth Hammersley. 321p. (Orig.). pap. text ed. 995.00x. Market Res Co.

Urological Research: Papers Presented in Honor of William W. Scott. William W. Scott. LC 73-179757. pap. 59.00 (ISBN 0-317-30344-9, 2024716). Bks Demand UMI.

Urological System. 2nd ed. C. A. Charlton. (Penguin Library of Nursing Ser.). (Illus.). 1983. pap. text ed. 15.00 (ISBN 0-443-02606-8). Churchill.

Urology. Ed. by Elroy D. Kursh & Martin I. Resnick. (Problems in Primary Care Ser.). 352p. (Orig.). 1987. pap. 35.95 (ISBN 0-87489-419-0, 419-0). Med Economics.

Urology: A Core Textbook. Stephen N. Rous. 367p. 1985. pap. 34.95 (ISBN 0-8385-9317-8). Appleton & Lange.

Urology & Psychosocial Aspects of Chronic, Critical & Terminal Illness. John K. Lattimer et al. 252p. 1983. 26.25x (ISBN 0-398-04729-4). C C Thomas.

Urology & the Male Reproductive System. 2nd ed. (Medical Ser.). (Illus.). 1984. 12.95x (ISBN 0-935920-17-X, Pub. by Natl Medical Careers). Natl Pub Black Hills.

Urology Annual, 1987, Vol. 1. Stephen N. Rous. 288p. 1987. 65.00 (ISBN 0-8385-9318-6, Dist. by Prentice-Hall). Appleton & Lange.

Urology Annual, 1988, Vol. 2. 1988. text ed. 65.00 (A9319-3). Appleton & Lange.

Urology for the House Officer. Michael Macfarlane. (House Officer Ser.). (Illus.). 256p. (Orig.). 1988. pap. 14.95 (ISBN 0-683-05324-8). Williams & Wilkins.

Urology: From Antiquity to the 20th Century. Leonard P. Wershub. LC 71-78017. (Illus.). 320p. 1970. 18.50 (ISBN 0-87527-086-7). Green.

Urology Handbook for Nurses & Orology Technicians. Jan Lanners & Irving M. Bush. 1988. 26.50. Green.

Urology Illustrated. 2nd ed. R. Scott et al. (Illus.). 1975. pap. text ed. 34.00 (ISBN 0-443-02376-X). Churchill.

Urology in Childhood see Encyclopedia of Urology.

Uroradiology: An Integrated Approach, 2 vols. Gerald Friedland et al. (Illus.). 1983. text ed. 190.00 (ISBN 0-443-08037-2). Churchill.

Ursachen des Terrorismus in der Bundesrepublik Deutschland. (Sammlung Goeschen: Vol. 2806). 1978. 6.70x (ISBN 3-11-007702-7). De Gruyter.

Urschel's Guide to IBM Software. William Urschel. (Illus.). 384p. (Orig.). pap. cancelled (ISBN 0-915643-13-8). Santa Barb Pr.

Ursi's Amazing Fur Coat. (Beginning to Read Ser.). (gr. 2 up). 1988. PLB 5.95 (ISBN 0-8136-5186-7); pap. 2.95 (ISBN 0-8136-5686-9). Modern Curr.

Ursprunge der Lyrik: Eine Entwicklungspsychologische Untersuchung. Heinz Werner. (Ger). Repr. of 1924 ed. 28.00 (ISBN 0-384-66810-0). Johnson Repr.

Ursula K. Le Guin. Intro. by Harold Bloom. (Modern Critical Views Ser.). 266p. 1986. 27.50 (ISBN 0-87754-659-2). Chelsea Hse.

Ursula K. Le Guin. Charlotte Spivack. LC 81-18560. (United States Authors Ser.: No. 453). 182p. 1984. lib. bdg. 16.95 (ISBN 0-8057-7393-2, Twayne); pap. 7.95 (ISBN 0-8057-7430-0). G K Hall.

Ursula K. Le Guin: A Primary & Secondary Bibliography. Elizabeth C. Cogell. 248p. 1983. lib. bdg. 50.00 (ISBN 0-8161-8155-1, Hall Reference). G K Hall.

Ursula K. Le Guin's the Hand of Darkness. Intro. by Harold Bloom. (Modern Critical Interpretations Ser.). 152p. 1987. 19.95 (ISBN 1-55546-064-X). Chelsea Hse.

Ursula K. LeGuin. Ed. by Joseph D. Olander & Martin H. Greenberg. LC 77-76722. (Writers of the 21st Century Ser.). 1979. 12.95 (ISBN 0-8008-7943-0); pap. 5.95 (ISBN 0-8008-7942-2). Taplinger.

Ursula's Gift. Roger L. Disilvestro. 1988. 16.95 (ISBN 1-55611-108-8). D I Fine.

Ursule Mirouet. Honore De Balzac. (Folio Ser.: No. 1300). pap. 7.95 (ISBN 0-685-23960-8, 2449). Schoenhof.

Ursule Mirouet. Honore De Balzac. Tr. by Donald Adamson. (Classics Ser). 1976. pap. 5.95 (ISBN 0-14-044316-9). Penguin.

Ursule Mirouet. Honore De Balzac. write for info. (2449). French & Eur.

Urteil ohne Richter: Psychishe Integration oder Charakterentfaltung im Werke Franz Kafkas. Evelyn W. Asher. LC 83-48884. (Stanford German Studies: Vol. 20). 139p. (Ger.). 1984. pap. text ed. 14.75 (ISBN 0-8204-0062-9). P Lang Pubs.

Urth of the New Sun. Gene Wolfe. 384p. 1987. 17.95 (ISBN 0-312-93033-X, Dist. by Warner Pub Servs & St Martin Pr). Tor Bks.

Urth of the New Sun. Gene Wolfe. 384p. 1988. pap. 3.95 (ISBN 0-8125-5817-0). Tor Bks.

Urticaria. B. M. Czarnetzki. (Illus.). 200p. 1986. 84.00 (ISBN 0-387-15264-4). Springer-Verlag.

Urticarias. Ed. by R. H. Champion et al. LC 85-374. (Illus.). 237p. 1985. text ed. 49.95 (ISBN 0-443-03243-2). Churchill.

Uruguay. Rosa Q. Mesa. LC 73-180800. (Latin American Serial Documents Ser.: Vol. 11). pap. 48.30 (ISBN 0-317-10313-X, 2013553). Bks Demand UMI.

Uruguay. George Pendle. LC 85-24780. 136p. 1986. Repr. of 1965 ed. lib. bdg. 38.50x (ISBN 0-313-24981-4, PEUR). Greenwood.

Uruguay. (Let's Visit Places & Peoples - - Nations, Dependencies, & Sovereignties of the World Ser.). (Illus.). (gr. 5 up). 1988. 12.95 (ISBN 0-222-00953-5). Chelsea Hse.

Uruguay see Statements of the Laws of the OAS Member States in Matters Affecting Business.

Uruguay: A Historical Romance of South America. Jose B. Da Gama. Ed. by Frederick Garcia & Edward Stanton. Tr. by Richard F. Burton. LC 81-15920. 270p. (Port.). 1982. 35.00x (ISBN 0-520-04524-6). U of Cal Pr.

Uruguay & the United Nations. Uruguayan Institute Scholars. LC 74-8381. (National Studies on International Organization-Carnegie Endowment for International Peace). 129p. 1974. Repr. of 1958 ed. lib. bdg. 35.00x (ISBN 0-8371-7536-4, URUN). Greenwood.

Uruguay: Democracy at the Crossroads. Martin Weinstein. (Profiles - Nations of Contemporary Latin America Ser.). 160p. 1988. 29.95 (ISBN 0-86531-290-7). Westview.

Uruguay in Pictures. Nathan A. Haverstock. (Visual Geography Ser.). (Illus.). 64p. (gr. 5 up). 1987. PLB 9.95 (ISBN 0-8225-1823-6). Lerner Pubns.

Uruguay in Transition: From Civilian to Military Rule. Edy Kaufman. LC 78-55939. 200p. 1979. 26.95 (ISBN 0-87855-242-1). Transaction Bks.

Uruguay Round: A Handbook for the Multilateral Trade Negotiations. Michael Finger & Andrzej Olechowski. 1987. 22.95 (ISBN 0-8213-0975-7, BK0975). World Bank.

Uruguay: The End of a Nightmare? A Report on Human Rights in Uruguay. 1984. 6.00 (ISBN 0-934143-09-9). Lawyers Comm Intl.

Uruguayan Literature: A Selective Bibliographical Guide. Walter Rela. LC 86-15989. 85p. 1987. pap. 12.95 (ISBN 0-87918-060-9). ASU Lat Am St.

Uruguayan Paper Money. D. A. Seppa. (Illus.). 60p. 1974. pap. 5.00 (ISBN 0-916710-15-7). Obol Intl.

Uruguayans of To-Day. William B. Parker. (Illus.). 1921. 29.00 (ISBN 0-527-69830-X). Kraus Repr.

Uruguay's Tupamaros: The Urban Guerilla. Arturo C. Porzecanski. LC 73-13340. (Special Studies in International Politics & Government). 1973. 34.00x (ISBN 0-275-28802-1). Irvington.

Uruk Countryside: The Natural Setting of Urban Societies. Robert M. Adams & Hans J. Nissen. LC 78-179489. xii, 242p. 1972. 28.00x (ISBN 0-226-00500-3). U of Chicago Pr.

Uruk Document of the Time of Cambyses. Henry F. Lutz. (University of California Publications in Semitic Philology: Vol. 10, No. 8). pap. 20.00 (ISBN 0-317-10219-2, 2021479). Bks Demand UMI.

Urushi: Proceedings of the 1985 Urushi Group. (Illus.). 300p. 1988. pap. 40.00 (ISBN 0-89236-096-8). J P Getty Mus.

Us. Ralph Burns. (CSU Poetry Ser.: No. 12). 43p. (Orig.). 1983. pap. 4.50 (ISBN 0-914946-38-2). Cleveland St Univ Poetry Ctr.

U.S. - Japan Economic Relations: A Symposium on Critical Issues. James C. Abegglen et al. LC 80-620017. (Research Papers & Policy Studies: No. 1). 57p. 1980. pap. 5.00x (ISBN 0-912966-25-4). IEAS.

Us Against Them. Michael French. 160p. (YA) (gr. 7-12). 1987. 13.95 (ISBN 0-553-05440-6, Starfire). Bantam.

Us Against Them. Michael French. 160p. 1989. pap. 2.95 (ISBN 0-553-27647-6, Starfire). Bantam.

Us & Them: A Study of Group Consciousness. W. A. Elliott. 224p. 1986. text ed. 21.00 (ISBN 0-08-032438-X, Pub. by AUP). Pergamon.

Us & Them: Or Why America Is Like England, Why England Is Like America & How They Got That Way. Kevin Cobb. (Illus.). 144p. 1987. pap. 8.95 (ISBN 0-87833-565-X). Taylor Pub.

Us & Them: The Psychology of Ethnonationalism. Group for the Advancement of Psychiatry, Committee on International Relations. LC 87-17872. (Gap Report Ser.: No. 123). 160p. 1987. 20.00 (ISBN 0-87630-481-1); pap. 13.95 (ISBN 0-87630-480-3). Brunner-Mazel.

Us & Uncle Fraud. Lois Lowry. LC 84-12783. 192p. (gr. 5-9). 1984. 10.95. HM.

Us & Uncle Fraud. Lois Lowry. (gr. k-6). 1985. pap. 2.75 (ISBN 0-440-49185-1, YB). Dell.

U.S. Debate over Trade, Deficits, Protectionism & a New Era of International Competition. Don Wallace, Jr. 24p. 1986. pap. 5.00 (ISBN 0-317-65761-5). Japan Soc.

U.S. Foreign Trade Regulations: Monographs. Mary Vance. 1987. pap. 11.25 (ISBN 1-55590-455-6). Vance Biblios.

Us Four: A Senator, His Family, Their Brain-injured Child. Marion Menning. As told to Ruth Peterman. (Illus.). 160p. 1986. pap. write for info. (ISBN 0-9615632-0-6). Alpha Pub MN.

Us Henry Kids. Belle T. Hinther. (Illus.). 202p. (Orig.). 1986. pap. 10.95 (ISBN 0-9619970-1-X). Blue Sky Bks.

U.S.-Japan Economic Problem: The G-5 Plaza Agreement after Six Months. Fred Bergsten. 19p. 1986. pap. 3.00 (ISBN 0-317-65763-1). Japan Soc.

U.S.-Japan Relations in International Politics. Hisahiko Okazaki. 21p. 1980. pap. 1.50 (ISBN 0-317-65766-6). Japan Soc.

U.S. Progressive Periodicals Directory see Progressive Periodicals Directory.

Us Women. Marjorie Fletcher. LC 73-86245. (Illus.). 64p. 1973. pap. 7.95 (ISBN 0-914086-00-6). Alicejamesbooks.

Us 4 Ever Club. Joann Klusmeyer. (Illus.). 96p. (gr. 4-7). 1987. pap. 3.95 (ISBN 0-570-03644-5, 39-1128). Concordia.

USA: Readings, Documents, Activities. Philip Croisser & Sol Levine. (YA) (gr. 11-12). 1987. pap. 12.25 (ISBN 0-87720-649-X). AMSCO Sch.

USA, 1988. The Harvard Student Agencies, Inc. Staff. (Let's Go Ser.). (Illus.). 976p. 1988. pap. 11.95x (ISBN 0-312-01464-3). St Martin.

USAAF Fighters of World War Two in Action. Michael O'Leary. (Illus.). 480p. 1986. 39.95 (ISBN 0-7137-1839-0, Pub. by Blandford Pr England). Sterling.

Usable Knowledge. Charles E. Lindblom & Davis K. Cohen. 1979. 22.00x (ISBN 0-300-02335-9); pap. 7.95x (ISBN 0-300-02336-7). Yale U Pr.

Usable Past: Essays on Modern & Contemporary Poetry. Paul Mariani. LC 84-2613. 280p. 1984. lib. bdg. 24.00 (ISBN 0-87023-445-5). U of Mass Pr.

USAF Phantoms. Anthony Thornborough. (Illus.). 160p. 1988. 19.95 (ISBN 0-85368-887-7, Pub. by Arms & Armour). Sterling.

USAF Scientific Advisory Board: Its First Twenty Years, 1944-1964. Thomas A. Sturm. (Illus.). 194p. 1985. pap. write for info. (ISBN 0-912799-18-8). Off Air Force.

USAFE: A Primer of Modern Air Combat in Europe. rev. ed. Michael Skinner. (Presidio Power Ser.). (Illus.). 144p. (Orig.). 1988. pap. 12.95 (ISBN 0-89141-326-X). Presidio Pr.

Usage & Abusage: A Guide to Good English. Eric Partridge. 384p. 1963. pap. 7.95 (ISBN 0-14-051024-9). Penguin.

Usage in Dictionaries & Dictionaries of Usage. Thomas J. Creswell. Ed. by Virginia McDavid & James B. McMillan. (Publication of the American Dialect Society: Nos. 63-64). (Illus.). 219p. 1975. pap. 10.80 (ISBN 0-8173-0662-5). U of Ala Pr.

Usage of International Data Networks in Europe. OECD. (Information Computer Communications Policy Ser., No.2). 287p. (Orig.). 1979. pap. 20.00x (ISBN 92-64-11861-6). OECD.

Usage Sleuth. Linda Schwartz. (Language Arts Ser.). 24p. (gr. 4-7). 1978. 3.95 (ISBN 0-88160-055-5, LW 603). Learning Wks.

Usages of the American Constitution. Herbert W. Horwill. LC 68-8210. 1969. Repr. of 1925 ed. 23.50x (ISBN 0-8046-0216-6, Pub by Kennikat). Assoc Faculty Pr.

USAN & USP Dictionary of Drug Names, 1988. LC 72-88571. 1987. 60.00 (ISBN 0-913595-23-3). USPC.

Use of Artificial Satellites for Geodesy. Ed. by Soren Henriksen et al. LC 72-88669. (Geophysical Monographs Ser.: Vol. 15). (Illus.). 298p. 1972. 35.00 (ISBN 0-87590-015-1). Am Geophysical.

Use of Assessment Techniques by Applied Psychologists. Paula S. Wise. Date not set. pap. text ed. write for info. (ISBN 0-534-09750-2). Wadsworth Pub.

Use of Beneficial Organisms in the Control of Crop Pests: Proceedings of the Joint American-Soviet Conference. Ed. by Jack R. Coulson et al. 105p. 1981. 4.95 (ISBN 0-938522-08-6); 1985 Revision 18.50. Entomol Soc.

Use of Bioassay Procedures for Assessment of Internal Radionuclide Deposition. LC 86-33136. (NCRP Report Ser.: No. 87). 82p. 1987. pap. text ed. 16.00 (ISBN 0-913392-83-9). NCRP Pubns.

Use of Biological Specimens for the Assessment of Human Exposure to Environmental Pollutants. A. Berlin et al. 1979. lib. bdg. 50.00 (ISBN 90-247-2168-7, Pub. by Martinus Nijhoff Netherlands). Kluwer Academic.

Use of Books & Libraries. 10th ed. Raymond H. Shove et al. LC 63-16070. pap. 32.00 (ISBN 0-317-29481-4, 2055916). Bks Demand UMI.

Use of Both the Globes. Thomas Hood. LC 70-38111. (English Experience Ser.: No. 389). 54p. 1971. Repr. of 1592 ed. 20.00 (ISBN 90-221-0389-7). Walter J Johnson.

Use of Boundary Elements for the Determination of the Geometry Factor. Sandeep M. Vijayakar & Donald R. Houser. (Fall Technical Meeting Papers). (Illus.). 9p. 1986. pap. 30.00 (ISBN 1-55589-474-7, 86FTM10). AGMA.

Use of Calcium Antagonists in Cardiology: Proceedings of the 1st International Symposium on Tiapamil, Lausanne, April 1981. B. N. Singh. (Journal, Cardiology,: Vol. 69, Supplement 1, 1982). (Illus.). xii, 242p. 1982. pap. 50.00 (ISBN 3-8055-3588-0). S Karger.

Use of Calcium Carbonate in Patients with Chronic Renal Disease. Eduardo Slatopolsky & Jack Cowburn. 8p. 1986. write for info. medical monograph (ISBN 0-935404-51-1). Biomedical Info.

Use of Cannabis: Report. WHO Scientific Group. Geneva, 1970. (Technical Report Ser.: No. 478). (Also avail. in French & Spanish). 1971. pap. 2.00 (ISBN 92-4-120478-8). World Health.

Use of Ceramics in Surgical Implants. S. F. Hulbert & F. A. Young, Jr. LC 73-99078. 278p. 1978. 72.00 (ISBN 0-677-13870-9). Gordon & Breach.

Use of Charged Particles for Chemical Analysis. Albert et al. 1988. write for info. (ISBN 0-471-02944-0). Wiley.

Use of Civil Remedies in Organized Crime Control. 50p. 1977. 2.50 (ISBN 0-318-15237-1). Natl Attys General.

Use of Coal in Industry. OECD Staff. 445p. (Orig.). 1982. pap. 44.00x (ISBN 92-64-12308-3). OECD.

Use of Color. (Shorewood Art Programs for Education Ser.). 8p. 1974. tchr's. ed. 86.00 (ISBN 0-88185-021-7); mounted prints 119.00. Shorewood Fine Art.

Use of Color in the Verse of English Romantic Poets from Langland to Keats. Alice E. Pratt. (English Literature Ser., No. 33). 1970. pap. 39.95x (ISBN 0-8383-0061-8). Haskell.

Use of Comic Episodes in Tragedy. W. H. Hadow. LC 77-9470. 1915. lib. bdg. 16.00 (ISBN 0-8414-4916-3). Folcroft.

Use of Complexing Agents to Modify the Aging Behavior of Insulating Enamel on Copper Wire. 85p. 1983. write for info. (319). Intl Copper.

Use of Compounds & Archaic Diction in the Works of William Morris: Anglo-Saxon Language & Literature, Vol. 60. Linda Gallasch. (European University Studies: Ser. 14). 179p. 1979. pap. 20.15 (ISBN 3-261-03129-8). P Lang Pubs.

Use of Computers & Statistics in Toxicology. Ed. by M. J. Ord et al. 102p. 1985. 32.00x (ISBN 0-85066-977-4). Vol. 10. Taylor & Francis.

Use of Computers in Analysis of Experimental Data & the Control of Nuclear Facilities: Proceedings. Bernard I. Spinrad. LC 67-60057. (AEC Symposium Ser.). 306p. 1967. pap. 15.75 (ISBN 0-87079-214-8, CONF-660527); microfiche 6.50 (ISBN 0-87079-215-6, CONF-660527). DOE.

Use of Computers in External Beam Radiotherapy Procedures with High Energy Photons & Electrons. ICRU Staff. Ed. by ICRU Staff. LC 87-16975. (ICRU Reports: No. 42). 1987. 19.00. Intl Comm Rad Meas.

Use of Computers in High Schools. Joe E. Crick & Lawrence M. Stolurow. LC 74-121200. 172p. 1965. 25.00 (ISBN 0-403-04492-8). Scholarly.

Use of Computers in Home Study. Janice S. Ancarrow. (Education Department Publication Ser.: CS 86-403). (Illus.). 44p. 1987. pap. 2.25 (ISBN 0-318-22579-4, S/N 065-000-00279-5). USGPO.

Use of Computers in Litigation. LC 79-88511. 512p. 1979. 25.00 (ISBN 0-89707-007-0). Amer Bar Assn.

Use of Computers in Managing Material Property Data. Ed. by J. A. Graham. (MPC: No. 14). 64p. 1980. 18.00 (ISBN 0-686-69865-7, G00192). ASME.

Use of Computers in Perinatal Medicine. Thomas R. Harris. LC 82-7661. 416p. 1982. 56.95 (ISBN 0-275-91366-X, C1366). Praeger.

Use of Computers in Radiation Therapy: Proceedings of the 9th International Conference, Scheveningen, the Netherlands, 22-25 June, 1987. Ed. by I. A. Bruinvis et al. 590p. 1988. 131.50 (ISBN 0-444-70263-6, North Holland). Elsevier.

Use of Computers in the Coal Industry Conference, 2nd: Proceedings. Ed. by Thomas Novak et al. LC 85-70438. (Illus.). 475p. 1985. 15.00X (ISBN 0-89520-437-1, 437-1). Soc Mining Eng.

Use of Computers in the Coal Industry: Proceedings of the 3rd Conference on the Use of Computers in the Coal Industry, W. Virginia University, Morgantown, 28-30 July 1986. Ed. by Y. Wang et al. 342p. 1986. text ed. 48.50 (ISBN 90-6191-645-3, Pub. by A A Balkema). Brookfield Pub Co.

Use of Computers in the Fatigue Laboratory - STP 613. Ed. by H. Mindlin & R. W. Londgraf. 172p. 1976. 20.00 (ISBN 0-8031-0593-2, 04-613000-30). ASTM.

Use of Contempt to Enforce Child-Support Orders in North Carolina. Trudy Allen Ennis. LC 86-622604. 18p. 1986. 2.50 (ISBN 0-318-22529-8). U of NC Inst Gov.

Use of Contrast Coefficients: Supplement to McNeil, Kelly, & McNeil, "Testing Research Hypotheses Using Multiple Linear Regression". Ernest L. Lewis & John T. Mouw. LC 77-16406. 80p. 1978. pap. text ed. 2.95x (ISBN 0-8093-0868-1). S Ill U Pr.

Use of CPM in Construction. 192p. 1976. 12.00. Assn Gen Con.

Use of Creative Arts in Therapy: Art Therapy, Dance Therapy, Music Therapy, Psychodrama. American Psychiatric Association Staff. (Illus.). 80p. 1980. 5.00 (ISBN 0-89042-130-7, 42-130-7). Am Psychiatric.

Use of Credit Instruments in Payments in the United States. David Kinley. LC 68-27848. Repr. of 1910 ed. 27.50x (ISBN 0-678-00546-X). Kelley.

Use of Daniel in Jewish Apocalyptic Literature & in the Relevation of St. John. G. K. Beale. 364p. (Orig.). 1985. lib. bdg. 27.50 (ISBN 0-8191-4290-5); pap. text ed. 16.25 (ISBN 0-8191-4291-3). U Pr of Amer.

Use of Data in Social Discrimination Cases. Ed. by William Rosenthal & Bernard Yancey. LC 85-60833. (Institutional Research Ser.: No. 48). (Orig.). 1985. pap. text ed. 12.95x (ISBN 0-87589-754-1). Jossey-Bass.

Use of Debonded Strands in Pretensioned Bridge Members. (PCI Journal Reprints Ser.). 18p. pap. 5.00 (ISBN 0-318-19800-2, JR289). Prestressed Concrete.

Use of Definite & Indefinite Reference in Young Children: An Experimental Study of Semantic Acquisition. Michael P. Maratsos. pap. 39.50 (ISBN 0-317-27554-2, 2024500). Bks Demand UMI.

Use of Dental Services & Dental Health, 1986. Susan S. Jack & Barbara Bloom. Ed. by Mary Olmsted. LC 88-1593. (Series 10: No. 165). 150p. Date not set. pap. text ed. 2.75 (ISBN 0-8406-0398-3). Natl Ctr Health Stats.

Use of Devices for Collection of Skin Puncture Blood Specimens: Approved Guideline, Vol. 5. National Committee for Clinical Laboratory Standards. 1985. 20.00 (ISBN 0-318-19441-4, H14-A). Natl Comm Clin Lab Stds.

Use of Dictation in Ancient Book Production. T. C. Skeat. 1956. pap. 2.25 (ISBN 0-85672-647-8, Pub. by British Acad). Longwood Pub Group.

Use of Digital Computers in Process Control: An Independent Learning Module of the Instrument Society of America. Theodore J. Williams. LC 84-6649. 416p. 1984. text ed. 59.95x (ISBN 0-87664-638-0, 1638-0). Instru Soc.

Use of Direct Observation to Study Instructional-Learning Behaviors in School Settings. Ed. by Margaret C. Wang. 162p. 1974. 2.00 (ISBN 0-318-14746-7, ED 100 798). Learn Res Dev.

Use of Drugs in Psychiatry: A Handbook. Ed. by E. Persad & V. Rakoff. 200p. 1987. text ed. 29.90 (ISBN 0-920887-09-0, H Huber Canada). Hogrefe Intl.

Use of Early Release & Sentencing Guidelines to Ease Prison Crowding: The Shifting Sands of Reform. 8.00 (ISBN 0-318-21764-3). Natl Coun Crime.

Use of Economists in Antitrust Litigation. American Bar Association Staff. 81p. 1984. pap. 35.00 (ISBN 0-89707-145-X). Amer Bar Assn.

Use of English. Jones. 1985. tchr's. bk. 8.95 (ISBN 0-521-26977-6); student's bk. 5.95 (ISBN 0-521-26976-8). Cambridge U Pr.

Use of Essential Drugs: Model List of Essential Drugs, Fourth List. (Technical Report Ser.: No. 722). 50p. 1985. pap. 3.60 (ISBN 92-4-120722-1). World Health.

Use of Expert Witnesses. Massachusetts Continuing Legal Education Inc. LC 84-61760. (Illus.). 436p. write for info. Mass CLE.

Use of Experts by International Tribunals. Gillian White. (Procedural Aspects of International Law Ser.: Vol. 4). 1965. 20.00x (ISBN 0-8139-0837-X). U Pr of Va.

Use of Experts in Commercial Litigation: Discovery & Trial Techniques. (Litigation & Administrative Practice Ser.). 426p. 1988. 45.00 (H4-5042). PLI.

Use of Factory Statistics in the Investigation of Industrial Fatigue. Philip S. Florence. LC 76-76627. (Columbia University. Studies in the Social Sciences: No. 190). 1969. Repr. of 1918 ed. 16.50 (ISBN 0-404-51190-2). AMS Pr.

Use of Film Badges for Personnel Monitoring. (Safety Ser.: No. 8). pap. 7.75 (ISP43, IAEA). UNIPUB.

Use of First & Second Languages in Primary Education: Selected Case Studies. Nadine Dutcher. (World Bank Staff Working Paper: No. 504). iii, 62p. (Eng. & Span.). 1982. pap. 5.00 Eng. Ed. (ISBN 0-686-39727-4, WP-0504); pap. Span. Ed. avail. World Bank.

Use of Flocculants to Control Turbidity in Placer Mining Effluents. Yun-Hwei Shen. (MIRL Report: No 78). (Illus.). 50p. (Orig.). 1988. pap. 10.00 (ISBN 0-911043-07-1). UAKF Min Ind Res Lab.

Use of Force in Human Affairs. Laurance Labadie. (Men & Movements in the History & Philosophy of Anarchism Ser.). 1979. lib. bdg. 59.95 (ISBN 0-685-96418-3). Revisionist Pr.

Use of Force in International Relations. Ed. by F. S. Northedge. LC 74-10140. 1974. 20.50 (ISBN 0-02-923210-4). Free Pr.

Use of Force: International Politics & Foreign Policy. 2nd ed. Ed. by Robert J. Art & Kenneth N. Waltz. 674p. 1983. lib. bdg. 35.00 (ISBN 0-8191-3424-4); pap. text ed. 14.50 (ISBN 0-8191-3425-2). U Pr of Amer.

Use of Force: Military Power & International Politics. 3rd ed. Ed. by Robert J. Art & Kenneth N. Waltz. LC 88-17198. 740p. 1988. lib. bdg. 37.50 (ISBN 0-8191-7002-X); pap. text ed. 14.95 (ISBN 0-8191-7003-8). U Pr of Amer.

Use of Formal Specification of Software. Ed. by H. K. Berg & W. K. Giloi. (Informatik-Fachberichte Ser.: Vol. 36). 388p. 1980. pap. 22.10 (ISBN 0-387-10442-9). Springer-Verlag.

Use of Fragrance in Consumer Products. Joseph S. Jellinek. LC 75-2106. (Wiley-Interscience Publication Ser.). pap. 57.80 (ISBN 0-317-27938-6, 2055981). Bks Demand UMI.

Use of Fungi As Food & in Food Processing, Pt. 2. William D. Gray. LC 76-141883. (Monotopic Reprint Ser.). 1973. 22.00 (ISBN 0-8493-0118-1). CRC Pr.

Use of Glass in Architecture & Interior Design: Recent Periodical Literature. David K. Ballast. (Architecture Ser.: A 1876). 10p. 1987. 3.00 (ISBN 1-55590-426-2). Vance Biblios.

Use of Government Publications by Social Scientists. Peter Hernon. LC 79-16144. (Libraries & Librarianship Ser.). 1979. 35.00x (ISBN 0-89391-024-4). Ablex Pub.

Use of Grass Filters for Sediment Control in Strip Mine Drainage, Vol. III. Hayes & Barnhisel. 150p. 1982. pap. text ed. 8.00 (ISBN 0-86607-008-7). KY Energy Cabnt Lab.

Use of Group Services in Permanency Planning for Children. Ed. by Sylvia Morris. LC 82-23389. (Social Work with Groups Ser.: Vol. 5, No. 4). 110p. 1983. text ed. 26.95 (ISBN 0-86656-199-4, B199). Haworth Pr.

Use of Groups in Schools: A Practical Manual for Everyone Who Works in Elementary & Secondary Schools. Joy Johnson. 137p. 1977. pap. text ed. 10.00 (ISBN 0-8191-0099-4). U Pr of Amer.

Use of Hand Woodworking Tools. L. P. McDonnell & A. I. Kaumeheiwa. LC 76-48504. 301p. 1978. pap. 15.50 (ISBN 0-8273-1098-6); instr's. guide 5.00 (ISBN 0-8273-1099-4). Delmar.

Use of Health Care Resources: A Comparative Study of Two Health Plans. Ed. by Donald C. Reidel et al. LC 84-4616. (Illus.). 328p. 1984. text ed. 23.00x (ISBN 0-914904-96-5, 0797). Health Admin Pr.

Use of Health Services by Women Sixty-Five Years & Over. Ester Hing & Beulah K. Cypress. Ed. by Audrey Shipp. (Ser. 13: No. 59). 72p. 1981. pap. 4.75 (ISBN 0-8406-0228-6). Natl Ctr Health Stats.

Use of Health Services for Disorders of the Female Reproductive System: United States 1977-78. Beulah K. Cypress. Ed. by Klaudia Cox. (Series 13: No. 63). 52p. 1981. pap. 3.00 (ISBN 0-686-79386-2). Natl Ctr Health Stats.

Use of Heteroploid & Other Cell Substrates for the Production of Biologicals. Ed. by W. Hennessen. (Developments in Biological Standardization Ser.: Vol. 50). (Illus.). x, 402p. 1982. pap. 56.75 (ISBN 3-8055-3472-8). S Karger.

Use of High-Intensity Ultrasonics. A. Puskar. (Materials Science Monographs: Vol. 13). 304p. 1983. 92.00 (ISBN 0-444-99690-7). Elsevier.

Use of High Purity Oxygen in the Activated Sludge Process, 2 vols. Ed. by J. R. McWhirter. (Uniscience Ser.). 1978. Vol. 1, 296p. 79.00 (ISBN 0-8493-5101-4); Vol. 2, 292p. 79.00 (ISBN 0-8493-5102-2). CRC Pr.

Use of History. A. L. Rowse. Ed. by Robin W. Winks. LC 83-49152. (History & Historiography Ser.). 244p. 1985. lib. bdg. 25.00 (ISBN 0-8240-6376-7). Garland Pub.

Use of Human Beings in Research. Ed. by Stuart F. Spicker et al. 1988. lib. bdg. 59.00 (ISBN 1-55608-043-3, Pub. by Reidel Holland). Kluwer Academic.

Use of Human Cells for the Evaluation of Risk from Physical & Chemical Agents. Ed. by Amleto Castellani. LC 83-2429. (NATO ASI Series, Series A, Life Sciences: Vol. 60). 822p. 1983. 129.50x (ISBN 0-306-41274-8, Plenum Pr). Plenum Pub.

Use of Human Tissues & Organs for Therapeutic Purposes: A Survey of Existing Legislation. (International Digest of Health Legislation Reprint: Vol. 20, No. 1). (Also avail. in French). 1969. pap. 2.00 (ISBN 92-4-169201-4). World Health.

Use of Imagery in Wolfram's "Parzival" A Distributional Study. Patricia L. Kutzner. (Stanford German Studies: Vol. 8). 235p. 1976. pap. 24.15 (ISBN 3-261-01549-7). P Lang Pubs.

Use of In Situ Tests in Geotechnical Engineering. Ed. by Samuel P. Clemence. (Conference Proceedings Ser.). 1284p. 1986. 99.00x (ISBN 0-87262-541-9). Am Soc Civil Eng.

Use of Information in a Changing World: Proceedings of the FID Congress, 42nd, the Hague, Netherlands, Sept. 24-27, 1984. Ed. by A. Van Der Haan & A. A. Winters. 470p. 1984. 73.75 (ISBN 0-444-87554-9, I-301-84, North Holland). Elsevier.

Use of Instructional Television in Adult Education. R. Blakely. LC 73-13295. (Occasional Papers Ser.: No. 40). 1974. pap. text ed. 2.00 (ISBN 0-87060-064-8, OCP 40). Syracuse U Cont Ed.

Use of International Law. P. C. Jessup. LC 79-173670. 164p. 1971. Repr. of 1959 ed. lib. bdg. 27.50 (ISBN 0-306-70407-2). Da Capo.

Use of Ion Implantation to Modify the Para-Surface Properties of Copper. 74p. 1982. write for info. Intl Copper.

Use of Laboratory Animals in Biomedical & Behavioral Research. National Research Council. 72p. 1988. pap. text ed. 9.95x (ISBN 0-309-03839-1). Natl Acad Pr.

Use of LANDSAT Data in Forestry. Ed. by Josef Cihlar. (Remote Sensing Reviews Ser.: Vol. 1 Pt. 3). 256p. 1986. pap. text ed. 80.00 (ISBN 3-7186-0307-1). Harwood Academic.

Use of Lasers in Materials Processing Applications, Vol. 26. 90p. 1980. 15.00 (ISBN 0-912035-09-9). Laser Inst.

Use of Lateral Thinking. Edward De Bono. Date not set. price not set. Intl Ctr Creat Think.

Use of Less-Than-Fee Acquisition for the Preservation of Open Space. Robert E. Coughlin & Thomas Plaut. (Discussion Paper Ser.: No. 101). 1977. pap. 5.50 (ISBN 0-686-32267-3). Regional Sci Res Inst.

Use of Library Materials: University of Pittsburgh Study. Kent. (Books in Library & Information Science Ser.: Vol. 26). 1979. 65.00 (ISBN 0-8247-6807-8). Dekker.

Use of Line. (Shorewood Art Programs for Education Ser.). 8p. 1974. tchr's ed. 86.00 (ISBN 0-88185-022-5); mounted prints 119.00. Shorewood Fine Art.

Use of Local Minerals in the Treatment of Radioactive Waste. (Technical Reports Ser.: No. 136). (Illus.). 128p. (Orig.). 1973. pap. 16.00 (ISBN 92-0-125172-6, IDC136, IAEA). UNIPUB.

Use of Locks in Physical Crime Prevention. National Crime Prevention Institute. (Illus.). 104p. 1987. pap. text ed. 17.95 (ISBN 0-409-90092-3). Butterworth.

Use of Man. Aleksandar Tisma. Tr. by Bernard Johnson. 252p. 1988. 21.95 (ISBN 0-15-193203-4). HarBraceJ.

Use of Manuscripts in Literary Research: Problems of Access & Literary Property Rights. 2nd ed. James Thorpe. LC 79-87584. 40p. 1979. pap. 8.00x (ISBN 0-87352-085-8, S71). Modern Lang.

Use of Marking Data in Fish Population Analysis. Rodney Jones. (Fisheries Technical Papers: No. 153). (Illus.). 47p. 1976. pap. 7.50 (ISBN 92-5-100051-4, F886, FAO). UNIPUB.

Use of Massage in Facilitating Holistic Health. Robert H. Woody. (Illus.). 136p. 1980. 13.75 (ISBN 0-398-03954-2). C C Thomas.

Use of Mathematical Models. W. Thomas Lin & Paul R. Watkings. 72p. Date not set. 10.95 (ISBN 0-86641-116-X, 86187). Natl Assn Accts.

Use of Medical Evidence: Low-Back Permanent Disability Claims in Maryland. Leslie I. Boden. 60p. (Orig.). 1986. pap. 15.00 (ISBN 0-935149-02-3). Workers Comp Res Inst.

Use of Medical Literature: A Preliminary Survey. G. Ford et al. (R&D Report 5515). (Illus.). 137p. (Orig.). 1980. pap. 12.00 (ISBN 0-905984-51-X, Pub. by British Lib). Longwood Pub Group.

Use of Mercury & Alternative Compounds As Seed Dressings: Report of the FAO-WHO Meeting, Geneva, 1974. FAO-WHO Meeting Staff. (Technical Report Ser.: No. 555). (Also avail. in French & Spanish). 1974. pap. 2.00 (ISBN 92-4-120555-5). World Health.

Use of Microphones. 2nd ed. Alec Nisbett. (Media Manual Ser.). 168p. 1983. pap. 18.95 (ISBN 0-240-51199-9). Focal Pr.

Use of Microprocessors. Michel Aumiaux. LC 79-42904. (Wiley Series in Computing). pap. 54.10 (2031295). Bks Demand UMI.

Use of Micros in Fluid Engineering: Papers Presented at the International Conference. 326p. 1983. softcover 50.00 (ISBN 0-906085-81-0, Dist. by Air Science Co.). BHRA Fluid.

Use of the Ultrasonic Scaler by the Registered Dental Assistant. Joanne M. Noto. 74p. 1987. pap. text ed. 16.95 (ISBN 0-942801-00-8). Apogee Pr.

Use of the Upper Stage in Romeo & Juliet. Richard Hosley. LC 78-55117. 1954. lib. bdg. 16.00 (ISBN 0-8414-4767-5). Folcroft.

Use of Time. Godfrey M. Lebhar. 1958. 7.00 (ISBN 0-912016-00-0). Lebhar Friedman.

Use of Time & Resources by Provisioned Troops of Monkeys: Social Behaviour, Time & Energy in the Barbary Macaque (Macaca Sylanus L.) at Gibraltar. J. E. Fa. (Contributions to Primatology Ser.: Vol. 23). (Illus.). xii, 380p. 1986. 115.50 (ISBN 3-8055-4263-1). S Karger.

Use of Time: Daily Activities of Urban & Suburban Populations in Twelve Countries. Ed. by Alexander Szalai et al. 1972. text ed. 66.00x (ISBN 90-2797-146-3). Mouton.

Use of Tissue Culture & Photoplasts in Plant Pathology. Ed. by John P. Helgeson & B. J. Deverall. 208p. 1983. 33.00 (ISBN 0-12-338650-0). Acad Pr.

Use of Tora by Isaiah: His Debate with the Wisdom Tradition. Joseph Jensen. LC 73-83134. (Catholic Biblical Quarterly Monographs: No. 3). 3.00 (ISBN 0-915170-02-7). Catholic Biblical.

Use of Traditional Materials in Colossians: Their Significance for the Problem of Authenticity. George C. Cannon. LC 83-8181. viii, 253p. 1983. 17.95 (ISBN 0-86554-074-8, H51). Mercer Univ Pr.

Use of Transrectal Ultrasound in the Diagnosis & Management of Prostate Cancer. Ed. by Fred Lee & Richard D. McLeary. LC 87-4181. (Progress in Clinical & Biological Research: Vol. 237). 240p. 1987. 38.00 (ISBN 0-8451-5087-1, 5087). A R Liss.

Use of Tritiated Water in Studies of Production & Adaption in Ruminants: Five-Year Research Co-ordination Programme Organized by the Joint FAO-IAEA Division of Atomic Energy in Food and Agriculture. (Panel Proceedings Ser.). (Illus.). 218p. 1982. pap. 28.75 (ISBN 92-0-111082-0, ISP576, IAEA). UNIPUB.

Use of Troops in Civil Distrubances in the United States. A. Kenneth Pye. LC 82-70103. (Occasional Paper Ser.: No. 10). 42p. 1982. 5.00. Ctr Intl Stud Duke.

Use of Trust in Estate Planning 1985. 862p. 1985. pap. 15.00 (D4-5180). PLI.

Use of Trusts in Estate Planning, 1988, 2 vols. Malcolm A. Moore. 1289p. 1988. Set. pap. 45.00 (D4-5201). PLI.

Use of Underground Space to Achieve National Goals. 353p. 1972. pap. 22.00x (ISBN 0-87262-045-X). Am Soc Civil Eng.

Use of Variable Costing in Pricing Decisions. Thomas M. Brueggelmann et al. 61p. Date not set. 10.95 (ISBN 0-86641-130-5, 85176). Natl Assn Accts.

Use of Vernacular Languages in Education. United Nations Educational Scientific & Cultural Organization. Ed. by Francesco Cordasco. LC 77-90566. (Bilingual-Bicultural Education in the U. S. Ser.). 1978. Repr. of 1953 ed. lib. bdg. 19.00x (ISBN 0-405-11105-3). Ayer Co Pubs.

Use of Vibration Measurements in Structural Evaluation. Ed. by John R. Hall. 64p. 1987. 11.00x (ISBN 0-87262-586-9). Am Soc Civil Eng.

Use of Viruses for the Control of Insect Pests & Disease Vectors: Report of the FAO-WHO Meeting on Insect Viruses, Geneva, 1972. FAO-WHO Meeting on Insect Viruses Staff. (Technical Report Ser.: No. 531). (Also avail. in French & Spanish). 1973. pap. 1.60 (ISBN 92-4-120531-8). World Health.

Use of Viruses for the Control on Insect Pests & Disease Vectors. (Agricultural Planning Studies: No. 91). 48p. (Orig.). 1974. pap. 5.75 (ISBN 0-685-40246-0, F490, FAO). UNIPUB.

Use of Waste Materials & By-Products in Road Construction. OECD. (Road Research Ser.). 166p. (Orig.). pap. 7.50x (ISBN 92-64-11717-2). OECD.

Use of Waste Materials & Soil Stabilization. (Transportation Research Record Ser.). 69p. 1976. 3.00. Transport Res Bd.

Use of Welsh. Ed. by Martin Ball. 1988. 89.00x (ISBN 0-905028-99-6, Pub. by Multilingual Matters); pap. 32.00x (ISBN 0-905028-98-8, Pub. by Multilingual Matters). Taylor & Francis.

Use of Words in Context: The Vocabulary of College Students. John W. Black et al. (Cognition & Language: A Series in Pscyholinquistics). 276p. 1985. 50.00x (ISBN 0-306-42206-9, Plenum Pr). Plenum Pub.

Use of X-Ray Diffraction in the Study of Protein & Nucleic Acid Structure. rev. ed. K. C. Holmes & D. M. Blow. Ed. by D. Glick. LC 79-20293. 132p. 1979. lib. bdg. 12.50 (ISBN 0-89874-046-0). Krieger.

Use-Value Assessment in the United States. Robert J. Gloudemans. (Research & Information Ser.). 18p. 1979. 8.00 (ISBN 0-88329-127-4). IAAO.

Use-Value Farmland Assessments: Theory, Practice & Impact. Robert J. Gloudemans. LC 74-83299. (Studies in Property Taxation). 73p. 1974. pap. 14.00 (ISBN 0-88329-050-2). IAAO.

Use-Wear Analysis of Flaked Stone Tools. Patrick Vaughan. LC 85-989. 204p. 1985. text ed. 49.50x (ISBN 0-8165-0861-5). U of Ariz Pr.

Use Your Dictionary. Adrian Underhill. (Illus.). 1980. pap. text ed. 3.75x (ISBN 0-19-431104-X). Oxford U Pr.

Use Your Head, Dear. Aliki. LC 82-11911. (Illus.). 48p. (gr. k-3). 1983. 10.25 (ISBN 0-688-01811-4); PLB 10.88 (ISBN 0-688-01812-2). Greenwillow.

Use Your Head: How to Develop the Other Eighty Percent of Your Brain. Stuart Litvak. (Illus.). 154p. 1982. 11.95 (ISBN 0-13-939975-5); pap. 6.95 (ISBN 0-13-939967-4). P-H.

Use Your Head in Doubles. Bob Harmon. (Illus.). 1979. (ScribT). Scribner.

Use Your Head in Tennis. Bob Harman & K. Monroe. 1975. pap. 9.95x (ISBN 0-8046-9111-8, Pub by Kennikat). Assoc Faculty Pr.

Use Your Perfect Memory. 2nd ed. Tony Buzan. (Illus.). 256p. 1987. pap. 10.95 (ISBN 0-525-48284-9, 01063-320). Dutton.

Use Your Perfect Memory: A Complete Program of New Techniques for Remembering. Tony Buzan. (Illus.). 288p. 1984. pap. 9.95 (ISBN 0-525-48112-5, 0966-290). Dutton.

Used Book Price Guide: Five Year Edition, 2 vols. Ed. by Mildred S. Mandeville. Incl. Vol. 1. A-K May 1967 to May 1972. 376p; Vol. 2. L-Z May 1968 to May 1973. 368p. Repr. of 1973 ed (ISBN 0-911182-72-1). 1977. Set. 59.00 (ISBN 0-911182-73-X). Price Guide.

Used Book Price Guide: Five Year Edition, 1977 Supplement. Ed. by Mildred S. Mandeville. 479p. 1977. 49.00 (ISBN 0-911182-76-4). Price Guide.

Used Book Price Guide: Five Year, 1983 Edition. Ed. by Mildred S. Mandeville. 536p. 1983. 79.00. Price Guide.

Used Car Book. Consumer Automotive Press Staff & Don Fried. (Orig.). 1985. pap. 6.95 (ISBN 0-449-90144-0, Columbine). Fawcett.

Used Car Book - 1988: America's Most Helpful & Easy-to-Use- Guide to Buying a Safe, Reliable, & Economic Used Car. Jack Gillis. (Illus.). 160p. (Orig.). 1987. pap. 9.95 (ISBN 0-06-096225-9, PL/6225, PL). Har-Row.

Used Car Book: America's Most Helpful & Easy-to-Use Guide to Buying a Safe, Reliable & Economical Used Car, 1989. Jack Gillis. (Perennial Automobile Information Library). 160p. (Orig.). 1988. pap. 8.95 (ISBN 0-06-096299-2, PL 6299, PL). Har-Row.

Used Car Prices. rev. ed. Ed. by Michael L. Green. (Buyer's Guide Ser.). 1979. pap. 2.25 (ISBN 0-89552-055-9). DMR Pubns.

Used Car Prices. Ed. by Michael L. Green. 1978. pap. 1.95 (ISBN 0-89552-014-1). DMR Pubns.

Used Car Prices. rev. ed. (Vehicle Price Group Ser.). pap. 1.95 (ISBN 0-89552-001-X). DMR Pubns.

Used Cars: Finding the Best Buy. Jim Mateja. 1987. pap. 5.95 (ISBN 0-933893-27-2). Bonus Books.

Used Cars: Finding the Best Buy. 1988 ed. Jim Mateja. 245p. 1988. pap. 6.95 (ISBN 0-933893-52-3). Bonus Books.

Used Farm Equipment: Assessing Quality, Safety & Economics. James Garthe et al. (NRAES Small Farms Ser.). (Illus.). 40p. (Orig.). 1987. pap. 4.50 (ISBN 0-935817-04-2). NE Agri Engineer.

Used Future. 1988. 5.00. Inkblot Pubns.

Used Intercity Bus Pricing 1978-1986. Larry Plachno. Ed. by Jackie Plachno. LC 87-19189. (Illus.). 40p. 1987. pap. 20.00 (ISBN 0-933449-03-8). Transportation.

Used Math for the First Two Years of College Science. Clifford E. Swartz. (Illus.). 320p. 1973. pap. write for info. (ISBN 0-13-939736-1). P-H.

Used Oil: Disposal Options, Management Practices & Potential Liability. John T. Nolan et al. 145p. 1988. pap. text ed. 39.00 (ISBN 0-86587-744-0). Gov Insts.

Used-To-Be: A Compendium of Things that Used to be Called Something Else. Mario Milosevic. 200p. 1988. pap. price not set (ISBN 0-912087-03-X). Graham Conley.

Used Truck & Van Prices. rev. ed. Ed. by Michael L. Green. (Buyer's Guide Ser.). 1979. pap. 2.25 (ISBN 0-89552-056-7). DMR Pubns.

Used Truck & Van Prices. Ed. by Michael L. Green. 1978. pap. 1.95 (ISBN 0-89552-015-X). DMR Pubns.

Used Truck & Van Prices. rev. ed. (Vehicle Price Group Ser.). (Illus.). pap. 1.95 (ISBN 0-89552-005-2). DMR Pubns.

Used Tyres in Solid Waste Management. OECD Staff. (Illus., Orig.). 1981. pap. text ed. 6.00x (ISBN 92-64-12131-5, 97-80-07-1). OECD.

Useful & Instructive Poetry. Lewis Carroll. 1954. lib. bdg. 32.00 (ISBN 0-8414-3638-X). Folcroft.

Useful Arithmetic, Vol. 1. rev. ed. Raymond J. Bohn & John D. Wool. 64p. 1987. pap. 3.75 (ISBN 0-88323-239-1, 251); tchr's. key 1.25x (ISBN 0-88323-167-0, 252). Richards Pub.

Useful Arithmetic, Vol. 2. rev. ed. John D. Wool. 96p. 1981. pap. 3.75 (ISBN 0-88323-165-4, 253); tchr's. key 1.25 (ISBN 0-88323-168-9, 254). Richards Pub.

Useful Arts. Jacob Bigelow. LC 72-5034. (Technology & Society ser.). (Illus.). 762p. 1972. Repr. of 1840 ed. 42.00 (ISBN 0-405-04687-1). Ayer Co Pubs.

Useful Baskets. Mara Cary. 1977. 10.95 (ISBN 0-395-25707-7); pap. 10.70 (ISBN 0-395-25950-9). HM.

Useful Books of Reference for Designers (1926-1983) Held by the Science Reference Library: Pt 1 Units in Physics, Metrication, Mettallurgy, Computers in Engineering, Civil Engineering. M. M. Palyza. 168p. (Orig.). 1984. pap. 7.50 (ISBN 0-7123-0712-5, Pub. by British Lib). Longwood Pub Group.

Useful Books of Reference for Designers (1926-1983) Held by the Science Reference Library: Pt. 2 Electrical & Electronic Engineering. M. M. Palyza. 75p. (Orig.). 1984. pap. 7.50 (ISBN 0-7123-0713-3, Pub. by British Lib). Longwood Pub Group.

Useful Books of Reference for Designers (1926-1983) Held by the Science Reference Library: Pt. 3 Mechanical Engineering. M. M. Palyza. 125p. (Orig.). 1984. pap. 7.50 (ISBN 0-7123-0714-1, Pub. by British Pub). Longwood Pub Group.

Useful Economics. E. C. Harwood. 53p. 1970. 6.00 (ISBN 0-318-12796-2). Am Inst Econ Res.

Useful Gifts. Carole L. Glickfield. 1988. write for info. U of GA Pr.

Useful Knowledge. Gertrude Stein. 240p. 1988. Repr. of 1928 ed. 19.95 (ISBN 0-88268-075-7). Station Hill Pr.

Useful Measurements for Violin Makers: A Reference for Shop Use. Henry A. Strobel. LC 88-90888. (Illus.). 42p. (Orig.). 1988. pap. 10.00 (ISBN 0-9620673-0-X). H A Strobel.

Useful Orthopaedic Eponyms: A Group of Orthopaedic Terms, Their Origins, & Their Orginators. Richard B. Raney. 1987. 18.00 (ISBN 0-533-07152-6). Vantage.

Useful Plants of Brazil. Walter B. Mors & Carlos T. Rizzini. LC 66-17891. pap. 45.30 (ISBN 0-317-28317-0, 2016293). Bks Demand UMI.

Useful Procedures in Medical Practice. Ed. by Paul W. Roberts. LC 85-4534. (Illus.). 610p. 1986. pap. 34.50 (ISBN 0-8121-0985-6). Lea & Febiger.

Useful Procedures of Inquiry. Rollo Handy & E. C. Harwood. LC 72-93865. (Orig.). 1973. 15.00x (ISBN 0-913610-00-3). Behavioral Mass.

Useful Science. Jerry J. Danley. (Illus.). 92p. 1983. pap. 4.25 (ISBN 0-88323-181-6, 216); tchr's key 1.25 (ISBN 0-88323-132-8, 222). Richards Pub.

Useful Spanish for Medical & Hospital Personnel with a Bibliography on Hispanic Peoples in the United States. Francesco Cordasco & Pablo Rivera Alvarez. LC 77-16566. 1977. pap. 7.95 (ISBN 0-87917-062-X). Ethridge.

Useful Subroutines & Utilities for the Commodore 64. Ian Sinclair. (Illus.). 160p. (Orig.). 1985. pap. 17.95 (ISBN 0-00-383012-8, Pub. by Collins England). Sheridan.

Useful Toil: Autobiographies of Working People from the 1820s to the 1920s. Ed. & intro. by John Burnett. (Penguin Nonfiction Ser.). 368p. 1985. pap. 10.95 (ISBN 0-14-007346-9). Penguin.

Useful Wild Plants in Australia. A. B. Cribb & J. W. Cribb. (Illus.). 269p. 17.50x (ISBN 0-00-216441-8, Pub. by W Collins Australia); pap. 8.95x. Intl Spec Bk.

Usefulness & Necessity of a Liberal Education for Clergymen see Argument to Prove That the Tragedy of Douglas Ought to Be Publickly Burned by the Hands of the Hangman.

Usefulness of Classical Literature in the Eighteenth Century: Papers Presented at the 107th Annual Meeting of the American Philological Association. Ed. by Susan F. Wiltshire. (APA Pamphlets Ser.). 73p. 1974. pap. 8.50 (ISBN 0-89130-248-4, 40-06-05). Scholars Pr GA.

Usefulness of Mathematical Learning. Isaac Barrow. Tr. by J. Kirby. (Illus.). 458p. 1970. Repr. of 1734 ed. 32.50x (ISBN 0-7146-1591-9, F Cass Co). Biblio Dist.

Usefulness to Investors & Creditors of Information Provided by Financial Reporting: A Review of Empirical Accounting Research. Paul A. Griffin. LC 82-71093. (Financial Accounting Standards Board Research Report). (Illus.). 232p. (Orig.). 1982. pap. 20.00 (ISBN 0-910065-15-2). Finan Acct Found.

Useless Hands. Charles Bargone. LC 74-15969. (Science Fiction Ser). 300p. 1975. Repr. of 1926 ed. 25.50x (ISBN 0-405-06289-3). Ayer Co Pubs.

User & Geoscience Information: Proceedings, Geoscience Information Society Meeting, San Antonio, 1986, Vol. 17. Ed. by R. A. Bier, Jr. 1987. 35.00 (ISBN 0-934485-14-3). Geosci Info.

User Centered System Design. Donald A. Norman & Stephen Draper. (New Perspectives on Human-Computer Interaction Ser.). 1986. text ed. 39.95 (ISBN 0-89859-781-1); pap. 19.95 (ISBN 0-89859-872-9). L Erlbaum Assocs.

User Charges for Education: The Ability & Willingness To Pay in Malawi. Jee-Peng Tan et al. (Working Paper: No. 661). 116p. 1984. 5.00 (ISBN 0-8213-0405-4, WP 0661). World Bank.

User Charges in the Social Services: An Economic Theory of Need & Inability. Michael Krashinsky. (Ontario Economic Council Research Studies). 176p. 1981. pap. 4.95x (ISBN 0-8020-3381-4). U of Toronto Pr.

User Comparison of Quantitative Clinical Laboratory Methods Using Patient Samples: Proposed Guideline, Vol. 5. National Committee for Clinical Laboratory Standards. 1985. 20.00 (ISBN 0-318-19382-5, EP9-P). Natl Comm Clin Lab Stds.

User Education in Libraries. 2nd ed. Nancy Fjallbrant & Ian Malley. 190p. 1984. 22.50 (ISBN 0-85157-361-4, Pub. by Bingley England). ALA.

User Evaluation of Precision Performance of Clinical Chemistry Devices: Tentative Guideline, Vol. 4. National Committee for Clinical Laboratory Standards. 1984. 20.00 (ISBN 0-318-03271-6, EP5-T). Natl Comm Clin Lab Stds.

User Fees: A Practical Perspective. Miriam A. Drake. LC 81-6032. 142p. 1981. lib. bdg. 22.50 (ISBN 0-87287-244-0). Libs Unl.

User Friendliness of the Library Catalog. Danny P. Wallace. (Occasional Papers: No. 163). 41p. 1984. pap. 3.00 (ISBN 0-317-59015-4). U of Ill Lib Info Sci.

User Friendly Cookbook: Easy to Use Recipes for Busy People. Eleanor Copley. 200p. 1985. 14.95 (ISBN 0-943066-05-0). CareerTrack Pubns.

User Friendly Guide to Lap Portables: Featuring TRS Model 100 & Olivetti M-10. S. Redman & M. Standford. 256p. 1985. pap. text ed. 17.95 (ISBN 0-07-051388-0). McGraw.

User Friendly Systems. Murray. (Infotech Computer State of the Art Reports). 439p. 1981. 61.00x (ISBN 0-08-028557-0). Pergamon.

User Guide: The CCH State Blue Sky Law Library on LEXIS. Commerce Clearing House Staff. LC 85-222760. (Illus.). vi, 58p. Date not set. price not set. Commerce.

User Guide to Focus. R. P. Lipton. 272p. 1987. pap. text ed. 22.95 (ISBN 0-07-038006-6). McGraw.

User Guide to the UNIX System: Includes Berkeley & Bell System V. 2nd ed. Rebecca Thomas & Jean Yates. 520p. 1985. pap. text ed. 22.95 (ISBN 0-07-881109-0). Osborne-McGraw.

User Instruction in Academic Libraries: A Century of Selected Readings. Ed. by Larry L. Hardesty et al. LC 86-960. 326p. 1986. 29.50 (ISBN 0-8108-1881-7). Scarecrow.

User Interface Management Systems. Ed. by G. E. Pfaff. (Eurographic Seminars Ser.). (Illus.). 240p. 1985. 42.00 (ISBN 0-387-13803-X). Springer-Verlag.

User Interfaces: Gateway Or Bottleneck. Ed. by T. Berold. (GDI Technology Assessment & Management Ser.: Vol. 6). 234p. 1988. 79.00 (ISBN 0-444-70424-8). Elsevier.

User Manual for Portotype Proportionality Review System. National Center for State Courts Staff. 746p. 1984. manuscript 44.76 (NCSC-039). Natl Ctr St Courts.

User-Oriented Computer Languages. Melvin Klerer. LC 87-20359. 272p. 1988. 34.95 (ISBN 0-02-949911-9). Macmillan.

User-Oriented Decision Support Systems: Accent on Problem Finding. Robert J. Thierauf. (Illus.). 400p. 1988. text ed. 38.00 (ISBN 0-13-940412-0). P-H.

User Participation in Design: A Bibliography. Mary E. Huls. (Architecture Ser.: A 1662). 6p. 1986. 3.00 (ISBN 0-89028-992-1). Vance Biblios.

User Requirements & Staff Training. Ed. by Network Staff. 1982. 49.00x (ISBN 0-904999-18-1, Pub. by Network Events Ltd). State Mutual Bk.

User Requirements for Data Processing. British Computer Society Staff. 1978. pap. 44.95 (ISBN 0-471-25612-9, Wiley Heyden). Wiley.

User Studies. (SPEC Kit & Flyer Ser.: No. 101). 115p. 1984. 20.00 (ISBN 0-318-03455-7). OMS.

User Systems Analysis: A Guide to Computer Users' Conceptual Models & Attitudes for Systems Analysis & Design. A. P. Jagodzinski & D. D. Clarke. (Illus.). 220p. 1987. 20.00 (ISBN 0-85626-430-X). Abacus Pr.

User's Fuel Handbook. Ralph W. Ritchie. LC 81-90075. (Energy Conservation in the Crafts - a Craft Monograph: No. 7). (Illus., Orig.). 1981. pap. 4.50 (ISBN 0-939656-06-X). Studios West.

User's Guide. Laura Daly. (Literacy Volunteers of America Readers Ser.). (Orig.). 1983. pap. 9.50 (ISBN 0-8428-9625-2). Cambridge Bk.

Users Guide see Business.

User's Guide for Defining Software Requirements. Carolyn Shamlin. LC 83-72640. (Illus.). 139p. (Orig.). 1985. pap. 29.50 (ISBN 0-89435-071-4, DC 0714). QED Info Sci.

Users Guide for Seeds of Western Trees & Shrubs. William I. Stein & Rodger Danielson. (Forest Service General Technical Report PNW-193). (Illus.). 45p. 1986. pap. 4.25 (ISBN 0-318-21364-8, S/N 001-000-04465-6). USGPO.

User's Guide for the SVIB. Jo-Ida C. Hansen. LC 84-40087. 92p. (Orig.). 1984. pap. 12.00 (ISBN 0-89106-025-1, 8902). Consulting Psychol.

User's Guide for Voice & Data Communications Security Equipment. 75.00 (ISBN 0-686-32978-3). Info Gatekeepers.

User's Guide: Shareware, Freeware, & Public Domain Software. Bruce Jackson. 222p. (Orig.). 1987. pap. 25.00 (ISBN 0-939731-01-0). South Moulton Pr.

User's Guide to APPLE 1000, 2000. Consumer Guide Editors. (Orig.). 1983. pap. 3.95 (ISBN 0-671-49502-X). PB.

User's Guide to Atari, 400, 800, 1200XL. Consumer Guide Editors. (Orig.). 1983. pap. 3.95 (ISBN 0-671-49503-8). PB.

User's Guide to COBOL 85. P. R. Brown & V. Gwillim. 436p. 1985. 105.95 (ISBN 0-470-20170-3). Halsted Pr.

Usher's Passing. Robert R. McCammoon. 416p. 1985. pap. 3.95 (ISBN 0-345-32407-2). Ballantine.

Usher's Syndrome: What It Is, How to Cope, & How to Help. Earlene Duncan et al. (Illus.). 104p. 1988. text ed. 24.75x (ISBN 0-398-05481-9). C C Thomas.

Using a Computer in Church Ministry. James P. Emswiler. 1986. pap. 6.95 (ISBN 0-87193-248-2). Dimension Bks.

Using a Law Library. 2nd ed. HALT Staff. (Citizens Legal Manuals Ser.). 64p. 1983. pap. text ed. write for info. (ISBN 0-910073-04-X). HALT DC.

Using a Lawyer. Halt Staff. (Citizens Legal Manual Ser.). 103p. (Orig.). 1985. pap. text ed. write for info. (ISBN 0-910073-08-2). HALT DC.

Using a Microcomputer in the Classroom. Gary G. Bitter & Ruth A. Camuse. (gr. k-12). 1983. pap. text ed. 25.00 (ISBN 0-8359-8144-4, Reston). P-H.

Using a Microcomputer in the Classroom. 2nd ed. Gary G. Bitter & Ruth A. Camuse. (Illus.). 384p. 1988. pap. text ed. 30.00 (ISBN 0-13-938978-4). P-H.

Using a Multicultural Calendar. (Ethnic Studies Bulletins: No. 2). 14p. 1982. 2.00. I N Thut World Educ Ctr.

Using a Sanitary Napkin. Sunny Foster & Cynthia Billionis. (Project MORE Daily Living Skills Ser.). (Illus.). 48p. 1978. pap. text ed. 7.95 (ISBN 0-8331-1245-7). Hubbard Sci.

Using AACR2: A Diagrammatic Approach. Malcolm Shaw et al. 208p. 1981. lib. bdg. 45.00 (ISBN 0-912700-88-2). Oryx Pr.

Using Agenda. Mary Campbell. 400p. 1988. pap. text ed. 21.95 (ISBN 0-07-881409-X). Osborne-McGraw.

Using Aldus Pagemaker: Publish It Yourself. Roger C. Parker. (B. E. P. Ser.). 288p. 1987. pap. 19.95 (ISBN 0-553-34407-2). Bantam.

Using Aldus Pagemaker 3.0. Douglas Kramer & Roger Parker. 1988. pap. 22.95 (ISBN 0-553-34624-5). Bantam.

Using American Law Books. 2nd ed. Alfred J. Lewis. LC 82-83863. (Illus.). 208p. 1985. pap. text ed. 15.50 (ISBN 0-8403-3557-1). Kendall-Hunt.

Using AmigaDOS. Arlan Levitan & Sheldon Leemon. 18.95 (ISBN 0-87455-047-5). Compute Pubns.

Using an Impact Measurement System to Evaluate Land Development. Philip S. Schaenman. (Land Development Impact Ser.). 106p. 1976. pap. 6.50 (ISBN 0-87766-172-3, 15500). Urban Inst.

Using an Offshore Bank for Profit, Privacy & Tax Protection. Jerome Schneider. Ed. by Max Benavidez & Kate Vozoff. (Illus.). 259p. 1982. 15.00 (ISBN 0-933560-03-6). WFI Pub Co.

Using & Applying the Dow Jones Information Services. Donald R. Woodwell. 200p. 1985. pap. 19.95 (ISBN 0-87094-595-5). Dow Jones-Irwin.

Using & Programming Epson HX 20 PC. E. Balkan. 1985. pap. 24.95 (ISBN 0-442-30650-4). Van Nos Reinhold.

Using & Troubleshooting the MC68000. James W. Coffron. 1983. 19.95 (ISBN 0-8359-8159-2, Reston). P-H.

Using & Troubleshooting the Z-8000. James W. Coffron. 1982. text ed. 34.00 (ISBN 0-8359-8157-6, Reston); pap. text ed. 19.95 (ISBN 0-8359-8156-8). P-H.

Using & Understanding Engineering Service & Construction Contracts. Clark. 352p. 1986. 41.95 (ISBN 0-442-21804-4). Van Nos Reinhold.

Using & Understanding Medical Statistics. 2nd, rev. ed. D. E. Matthews & V. T. Farewell. (Illus.). xii, 228p. 1988. 26.75 (ISBN 3-8055-4719-6). S Karger.

Using & Understanding Medical Statistics. Ed. by D. E. Matthews & V. Farewell. (Illus.). xii, 200p. 1984. pap. 22.50 (ISBN 3-8055-3932-0). S Karger.

Using & Understanding Surveys. American Physical Therapy Association Staff. 1985. 11.50 (ISBN 0-912452-60-9). Am Phys Therapy Assn.

Using Anti-Shock Trousers (MAST) A Guide for the EMT. Steven C. Macdonald et al. 1982. 12.00 (ISBN 0-940432-03-X, Pub. by Emergency Training). Educ Direction.

Using Apple Works. 2nd ed. Keiko Pitter. 300p. 1989. pap. text ed. price not set (ISBN 0-394-39443-7). Mitchell Pub.

Using Apple Works: With Intro to Basic. Keiko Pitter. (YA) (gr. 7-12). 1986. pap. 14.50 (ISBN 0-394-39039-3). Mitchell Pub.

Using AppleWorks. 2nd ed. Arthur Aron & Elaine Aron. LC 86-63838. 460p. 1987. pap. 19.95 (ISBN 0-88022-280-8, 83). Que Corp.

Using Appleworks: The Complete Guide to Applications. Richard Loggins. Date not set. write for info. S&S.

Using Appleworks: The Complete Guide to Applications. Richard Loggins. 320p. 1985. pap. 17.95 (ISBN 0-89303-911-X). P-H.

Using Appleworks without Basic. Keiko Pitter. (YA) (gr. 7-12). 1986. pap. 12.00 (ISBN 0-394-39044-X). Mitchell Pub.

Using Application Software: PC Type, PC-Calc, PC-File, PC-DIAL. James Shuman. 256p. (Orig.). 1986. pap. text ed. 17.95 (ISBN 0-938188-43-7); data diskette avail. Mitchell Pub.

Using Applications Software. D. Beil. 355p. 1986. pap. text ed. 26.95 (ISBN 0-07-004427-9). McGraw.

Using Applications Software: An Introduction Featuring Framework. D. Beil & Ashton-Tate Staff. 355p. 1986. pap. text ed. 36.95 (ISBN 0-07-079651-3). McGraw.

Using Applied Psychology in Personnel Management. Daena Farrow. 1982. write for info. (ISBN 0-8359-8131-2, Reston). P-H.

Using Arbitration in Commercial Disputes. Norman Solovay & David R. Foley. LC 85-121262. (Business Law monographs). (Illus.). Set. 480.00. Bender.

Using Assembly Language. Allen L. Wyatt. 750p. (Orig.). 1988. pap. 22.95 (ISBN 0-88022-297-2). Que Corp.

Using Assessment Results in Career Counseling. 2nd ed. Vernon G. Zunker. LC 85-24323. 1986. pub net 11.25 (ISBN 0-534-05509-5, 81-18008). Brooks-Cole.

Using Astrology. Mae R. Wilson-Ludlam. LC 82-72553. 192p. 1985. 12.00 (ISBN 0-86690-287-2, 2649-01). Am Fed Astrologers.

Using Authoring in Education: Customizing Computer-Based Lessons for Students. Kristie Y. Davis & Milton Budoff. 255p. 1986. text ed. 22.95 (ISBN 0-914797-10-7); pap. text ed. 17.95 (ISBN 0-914797-20-4). Brookline Bks.

Using AutoCAD. Brenda L. Fouch. LC 87-60014. 550p. (Orig.). 1988. pap. 29.95 (ISBN 0-88022-288-3, 92). Que Corp.

Using AutoCAD. rev. ed. James E. Fuller. LC 86-2085. 258p. 1986. pap. text ed. 32.95 (ISBN 0-8273-2699-8); instr's. guide 8.00 (ISBN 0-8273-2672-6); chart 20.00 (ISBN 0-8273-2674-2). Delmar.

Using AutoCAD 2.5. James E. Fuller. LC 86-31909. 64p. 1986. pap. text ed. 20.00 (ISBN 0-8273-2949-0). Delmar.

Using AutoCAD 2.5. James E. Fuller. 1986. pap. 13.95 (ISBN 0-8273-2942-3). Delmar.

Using Bandages. Crystal Stevens & Ingo Keilitz. (Taking Care of Simple Injuries Ser.). (Illus.). 88p. (Orig.). 1978. pap. text ed. 10.25 (ISBN 0-8331-1249-X). Hubbard Sci.

Using BASIC. 2nd ed. Richard L. Didday & Rex Page. (Illus.). 510p. 1984. pap. text ed. 32.75 (ISBN 0-314-77885-3). West Pub.

Using BASIC. 3rd ed. Julien Hennefeld. 368p. 1985. pap. text ed. 23.50 (ISBN 0-87150-846-X, 37L8600, Prindle). PWS Kent Pub.

Using BASIC: An Introduction to Computer Programming. 2nd ed. Julien Hennefeld. LC 80-27465. 257p. 1981. pap. text ed. 15.00 (ISBN 0-87150-315-8, 2522, Prindle). PWS Kent Pub.

Using BASIC on the CYBER. Norman Sondak & Richard Hatch. 272p. 1982. pap. text ed. write for info. (ISBN 0-574-21395-3, 13-4395); instr's. guide avail. (ISBN 0-574-21396-1, 13-4396). SRA.

Using BASIC on the IBM Personal Computer. Norman E. Sondak & Richard A. Hatch. 384p. (Orig.). 1984. pap. text ed. write for info. (ISBN 0-574-21740-1, 13-4740); instr's. guide avail. (ISBN 0-574-21741-X, 13-4741). SRA.

Using BBC BASIC. P. J. Cockerell. 380p. 1984. pap. 27.95 (ISBN 0-471-90242-X). Wiley.

Using Biography. William Empson. 280p. 1985. 22.50x (ISBN 0-674-93160-2). Harvard U Pr.

Using Blackboard Drawing. Peter Shaw & Therese de Vet. (Practical Language Teaching Ser.). (Orig.). 1980. pap. text ed. 8.00x (ISBN 0-435-28969-1). Heinemann Ed.

Using Business BASIC. Wilson T. Price. 267p. 1983. pap. text ed. 23.95 (ISBN 0-03-063176-9). HR&W.

Using CADKEY. Paul J. Resetarits & Gary R. Bertoline. 320p. 1987. pap. text ed. 35.95 (ISBN 0-8273-2966-0); instr's. guide 6.00 (ISBN 0-8273-2967-9). Delmar.

Using Calculators for Business Problems: With Microcomputer Applications. 2nd ed. Gary A. Berg. Ed. by Richard E. Myers & Ann L. Meyer. (Illus.). 383p. 1987. pap. text ed. write for info. (ISBN 0-574-20890-9, 13-3890). SRA.

Using California Law Books. Alfred J. Lewis. LC 75-35385. 112p. 1983. perfect bdg. 10.50 (ISBN 0-8403-2982-2, 40298201). Kendall-Hunt.

Using Calligraphy: A Workbook of Alphabets, Projects, & Techniques. Margaret Shepherd. 1979. pap. 12.95 (ISBN 0-02-081970-6, Collier). Macmillan.

Using Cereal Boxes. Nancy Gill. (Illus.). 13p. (gr. 4-6). 1980. pap. 5.95 (ISBN 0-933358-73-3, 72203). Enrich.

Using Charts & Graphs: One Thousand Ideas for Getting Attention. Jan V. White. 208p. 1984. pap. 34.95 (ISBN 0-8352-1894-5). Bowker.

Using Children's Books in Social Studies: Early Childhood Through Primary Grades. Joan E. Schreiber. LC 83-63481. (Bulletin Ser.: No. 71). 44p. (Orig.). 1984. pap. text ed. 4.75 (ISBN 0-87986-047-2, 498-15314). Nat Coun Soc Studies.

Using Class Agents in Fund Raising. Paula J. Faust. 32p. 1985. pap. 9.50 (ISBN 0-89964-239-X). Coun Adv & Supp Ed.

Using Clipper. W. Edward Tiley. 500p. (Orig.). 1988. pap. 24.95 (ISBN 0-88022-379-0). Que Corp.

Using Coal & Wood Stoves Safely. 1974. pap. 2.00 (ISBN 0-685-58194-2, HS-8). Natl Fire Prot.

Using Commercial Fertilizers. 4th ed. Malcolm H. McVickar & William Walker. LC 76-53095. (Illus.). (gr. 9-12). 1978. 25.25 (ISBN 0-8134-1894-1); text ed. 18.95x. Inter Print Pubs.

Using Commercial Resources in Family Planning Communication Programs: The International Experience. Ed. by Michael McMillan. 144p. 1973. pap. 5.00x (ISBN 0-8248-0303-5, Eastwest Ctr). UH Pr.

Using Communication: A New Introduction for the Nineteen Eightys. Richard E. Crable. 336p. 1982. 37.00 (ISBN 0-205-07689-0, 487689). Allyn.

Using Communication Support in Projects: The World Bank's Experience. Heli E. Perret. (Working Paper: No. 551). 74p. 1983. 5.00 (ISBN 0-8213-0119-5, WP 0551). World Bank.

Using Community Resources. McVey & Associates. (Follett Coping Skills Ser.). 64p. pap. 3.75 (ISBN 0-8428-2328-X); tchr's. guide 1.50 (ISBN 0-8428-2324-7). Cambridge Bk.

Using Computer Color Effectively: An Illustrated Reference to Computer Color Interface. Lisa G. Thorell & Wanda J. Smith. (Illus.). 224p. 1988. 42.67; pap. 39.95 (ISBN 0-13-939852-X). P-H.

Using Computer Color Effectively: An Illustrated Reference to Computer Color Interface. Lisa G. Thorell & Wanda J. Smith. (Illus.). 224p. 1989. pap. 29.95. P-H.

Using Computer Graphics: Hangman. Mike Duck. (Write Your Own Program Bks.). (gr. 4 up). 1984. 12.40 (ISBN 0-531-03483-6). Watts.

Using Computer, No. One: An Introduction to Computers & Control. J. Arotsky et al. 130p. 1987. 160.00x (ISBN 1-85008-015-1, Pub. by Framework UK). State Mutual Bk.

Using Computers. Dorothy G. Dologite. (Illus.). 640p. 1987. text ed. write for info. (ISBN 0-13-939646-2). P-H.

Using Computers: A Manager's Guide. M. Peltu. 200p. 1980. pap. 18.60 (ISBN 0-471-89429-X). Wiley.

Using Computers: Human Factors in Information Systems. Raymond S. Nickerson. 22.50 (ISBN 0-317-42856-X). McGraw.

Using Computers: Human Factors in Information Systems. Raymond S. Nickerson. 456p. 1987. pap. 12.50 (ISBN 0-262-64022-8, Pub. by Bradford). MIT Pr.

Using Computers in Clinical Practice: Psychotherapy & Mental Health Applications. Ed. by Marc D. Schwartz. LC 83-18648. 510p. 1984. text ed. 39.95 (ISBN 0-86656-208-7, B208). Haworth Pr.

Using Computers in College Student Activities. Elliott Masie & Michele Stein. (National Student Leadership Center Ser.). 104p. 1984. pap. 12.95 (ISBN 0-913393-16-9). Sagamore.

Using Computers in English: A Practical Guide. Phil Moore. (Teaching Secondary English Ser.). 200p. 1986. pap. 11.95 (ISBN 0-416-36190-0, 9929). Routledge Chapman & Hall.

Using Computers in High School Student Activities. Elliott Masie & Michele Stein. (National Student Leadership Center Ser.). 104p. (Orig.). 1984. pap. 12.95 (ISBN 0-913393-15-0). Sagamore.

Using Computers in Nursing. Marion Ball & Kathryn Hannah. 1984. text ed. 21.95 (ISBN 0-8359-8130-4); pap. text ed. 19.95 (ISBN 0-8359-8129-0). Appleton & Lange.

Using Computers in Physics. John R. Merrill. LC 80-5681. 271p. 1980. pap. text ed. 14.25 (ISBN 0-8191-1134-1). U Pr of Amer.

Using Computers in Religious Education. E. V. Clemans. 80p. 1986. pap. 6.95 (ISBN 0-687-43120-4). Abingdon.

Using Computers in Teaching Foreign Languages. Geoffrey R. Hope et al. (Language in Education Ser.: No. 57). 138p. 1984. pap. 10.67 (ISBN 0-13-940289-6, Dist. by P-H). Ctr Appl Ling.

Using Computers in the Behavioral Sciences. Paul C. Cozby. 1984. 10.95 (ISBN 0-87484-714-1). Mayfield Pub.

Using Computers in the Classroom. William L. Callison. (Illus.). 192p. 1985. pap. 17.95 (ISBN 0-13-940214-4). P-H.

Using Computers in the Social Studies. Howard Budin et al. (Computers in the Curriculum Ser.: No. 1). 128p. (Orig.). 1986. pap. text ed. 11.95x (ISBN 0-8077-2781-4). Tchrs Coll.

Using Computers in the Teaching of Reading. Dorothy Strickland et al. (Computers & the Curriculum Ser.). 256p. 1987. pap. 16.95x (ISBN 0-8077-2823-3). Tchrs Coll.

Using Computers: Living & Working with Computers. Beth M. Buzby. 512p. (Orig.). 1985. pap. text ed. write for info. (ISBN 0-574-21455-0, 13-4455); write for info. wkbk (ISBN 0-574-21457-7, 13-4457); instr's. guide avail. (ISBN 0-574-21456-9, 13-4456). SRA.

Using Computers: Managing Change. Levi Reiss & Edwin Dolan. 752p. 1989. text ed. write for info. (ISBN 0-538-10760-X, J76). SW Pub.

Using Computers, No. Two: An Introduction to Information Systems. J. Arotsky et al. 127p. 1987. 160.00x (ISBN 1-85008-020-8, Pub. by Framework UK). State Mutual Bk.

Using Computers to Combat Welfare Fraud: The Operation & Effectiveness of Wage Matching. David Greenberg & Douglas Wolf. LC 85-30221. (Studies in Social Welfare Policies & Programs: No. 2). (Illus.). 279p. 1986. 38.95 (ISBN 0-313-24870-2, GRU/). Greenwood.

Using Computers to Create Art. Stephen Wilson. (Illus.). 416p. 1986. pap. text ed. 30.00 (ISBN 0-13-938341-7). P H.

Using Computers to Solve Reservoir Engineering Problems. 2nd ed. M. A. Nobles. LC 84-3759. 500p. 1984. 49.00x (ISBN 0-87201-899-7). Gulf Pub.

Using Computers to Teach Social Studies. Gene E. Rooze & Terry Northup. 225p. 1986. lib. bdg. 19.50 (ISBN 0-87287-500-8). Libs Unl.

Using Computers Today. David R. Sullivan et al. LC 85-80897. 640p. 1986. text ed. 37.76 (ISBN 0-395-40639-0); Apple II. text ed. 34.76 (ISBN 0-395-41065-7); IBM. text ed. 34.76 (ISBN 0-395-41066-5); instr's manual with test bank 3.16 (ISBN 0-395-40640-4); transparencies 53.56 (ISBN 0-395-40643-9); study guide 12.36 (ISBN 0-395-40641-2). HM.

Using Computers: With PASCAL Programming. Donald D. Spencer. LC 87-28935. 288p. (YA) (gr. 7 up). 1988. pap. 13.95 (ISBN 0-89218-093-5, NO. 3026); tchr's. manual 15.95 (ISBN 0-89218-159-1, NO. 3032); student wkbk. 6.95 (ISBN 0-89218-158-3, NO. 3035); test bank 12.95 (ISBN 0-89218-164-8, NO. 3040). Camelot Pub.

Using Concurrent PC DOS. Mark Dahmke. 160p. 1986. pap. text ed. 20.95 (ISBN 0-07-015073-7, BYTE Bks). McGraw.

Using Consultants: A Consumer's Guide for Managers. Thomas A. Easton & Ralph W. Conant. 192p. 1985. 17.95 (ISBN 0-917253-03-5). Probus Pub Co.

Using Consultants & Experts Effectively in Legal Services: A Desk Reference of Information Sources. Barbara Skolnick. 68p. 1983. 12.00 (ISBN 0-941077-09-8, 35,970); Set of four. 40.00. NCLS Inc.

Using Consultants for Materials Development. R. Soedharno & Nancy Bergau. (Technical Note Ser.: No. 19). (Illus.). 18p. (Orig.). 1982. pap. 2.00 (ISBN 0-932288-65-0). Ctr Intl Ed U of MA.

Using Copyrighted Videocassettes in Classrooms, Libraries, & Training Centers. 2nd ed. J. K. Miller. LC 83-20904. 1987. 19.95. Copyright Info.

Using Copyrighted Videocassettes in Classrooms, Libraries, & Training Centers. 2nd ed. Jerome K. Miller. LC 87-24572. (Copyright Information Bulletin Ser.: No. 3). 131p. 1988. 19.95 (ISBN 0-914143-14-X). Copyright Info.

Using Cream Antiseptic. James Lent & Crystal Stevens. (Taking Care of Simple Injuries Ser.). (Illus.). 32p. (Orig.). 1978. pap. text ed. 5.50 (ISBN 0-8331-1248-1). Hubbard Sci.

Using Credit & Banking Services & Understanding Income Tax. Northwest Regional Educational Laboratory Staff. (Lifeworks Ser.). (Illus.). 1979. pap. 12.96 (ISBN 0-07-047306-4). McGraw.

Using Credit to Sell More. Donald E. Miller. 109p. 1974. pap. 8.50 (ISBN 0-934914-13-3). NACM.

Using Data Processing Tools for Preparing Agricultural Development Projects. Michel Simeon. (Investment Centre Technical Papers: No. 2). 101p. 1985. pap. 23.75 (ISBN 92-5-102255-0, F2799, FAO). UNIPUB.

Using Data to Identify & Target Local Line Problems: Four Case Studies. 150p. 1982. 25.00 (ISBN 0-318-17359-X, DG/82-600). Pub Tech Inc.

Using dBASE II. Carl Townsend. 250p. (Orig.). 1983. pap. text ed. 19.95 (ISBN 0-07-881108-2, 108-2). Osborne-McGraw.

Using dBASE III. Edward Jones. 200p. (Orig.). 1985. pap. text ed. 17.95 (ISBN 0-07-881162-7). Osborne-McGraw.

Using dBASE III on the IBM PC. Darrell Davisson. Date not set. price not set. S&S.

Using dBASE III Plus. Intentional Educations Staff. 128p. 1987. pap. text ed. 12.95 (ISBN 0-07-031504-3). McGraw.

Using dBASE III Plus. Edward Jones. (Illus.). 530p. 1986. pap. text ed. 18.95 (ISBN 0-07-881252-6). Osborne-McGraw.

Using dBASE III Plus: Limited Use Version & Manual. Larry Metzelaar & Marianne Fox. 210p. 1987. pap. 15.95 (ISBN 0-8053-6742-X). Benjamin-Cummings.

Using dBase IV. Ed Jones. 700p. Date not set. 22.95 (ISBN 0-07-881475-8). Osborne-McGraw.

Using dBase IV. Wayne Ratliff et al. 400p. 1989. pap. 21.95 (ISBN 0-13-942814-3). Brady Comp Bks.

Using dBASE IV: Basics for Business. Mark Brownstein. (Illus.). 1988. pap. 19.95 (ISBN 0-471-61749-0). Wiley.

Using dBase Mac. Paul Springer & Ralph DeFranco. 400p. (Orig.). 1988. pap. 19.95 (ISBN 0-88022-337-5). Que Corp.

Using DEC Personal Computers: A Self-Teaching Guide. Romualdas Skvarcius. 1985. pap. 14.95 (ISBN 0-471-81150-5). Wiley.

Using Deluxe Paint II. Steven Anzovin. 1987. 19.95 (ISBN 0-87455-111-0). Compute Pubns.

Using Deodorant. Patricia Lewis & Casper Ferneti. (Project MORE Daily Living Skills Ser.). (Illus.). 32p. 1979. pap. text ed. 5.95 (ISBN 0-8331-1242-2). Hubbard Sci.

Using Desalination Technologies for Water Treatment, Background Paper. LC 86-600507. (Illus.). 74p. 1988. pap. 3.25 (S/N 052-003-01097-6). USGPO.

Using Digital & Analog Integrated Circuits. L. Shacklette & H. Ashworth. (Illus.). 1978. pap. text ed. 38.00 (ISBN 0-13-939488-5). P-H.

Using Minitab with Basic Statistics. Mark Soskin. (Orig.). 1987. pap. text ed. 13.95x (ISBN 0-393-95579-6); instr's. manual avail. (ISBN 0-393-95678-4). Norton.

Using Minitab with Statistics for Business & Economics. Mark Soskin. (Orig.). 1987. pap. text ed. 10.95x (ISBN 0-393-95581-8); instr's. manual avail. (ISBN 0-393-95679-2). Norton.

Using Money Series, 4 bks. rev. ed. John D. Wool. Incl. Bk. 1. Counting My Money (ISBN 0-88323-169-7, 171); Bk. 2. Making My Money Count. 64p (ISBN 0-88323-170-0, 172); Bk. 3. Buying Power (ISBN 0-88323-171-9, 173); Bk. 4. Earning, Spending & Saving (ISBN 0-88323-172-7, 174). 1987. pap. 3.75 ea.; tchr's answer key 1.50 (ISBN 0-88323-173-5, 224). Richards Pub.

Using MS-DOS. Kris Jamsa. 550p. 1988. pap. text ed. 22.95 (ISBN 0-07-881442-1). Osborne-McGraw.

Using Multi Mate Advantage II Work Book. Ashton-Tate. (Orig.). 1987. pap. text ed. 36.95 (ISBN 0-912677-95-3). Ashton-Tate Pub.

Using MultiMate Advantage. 2nd ed. Kate Barnes. LC 86-63836. 386p. 1987. pap. 19.95 (ISBN 0-88022-281-6, 78). Que Corp.

Using Multiplan. Robert Krumm. 320p. 1985. 16.95 (ISBN 0-89303-921-7). Brady Comp Bks.

Using Multivariate Statistics. Linda S. Fidell & Barbara G. Tabachnick. LC 82-11767. 509p. 1982. text ed. 39.50 scp (ISBN 0-06-042045-6, HarpC). Har-Row.

Using New Communications Technologies: A Guide for Organizations. The Media Institute. LC 85-63320. 70p. (Orig.). 1986. pap. 12.95 (ISBN 0-937790-30-3). Media Inst.

Using Newsroom at Home, School, & Work. Gregg Keizer. 1987. 19.95 (ISBN 0-87455-124-2). Compute Pubns.

Using Nonbroadcast Video in the Church. Daniel W. Holland et al. 128p. 1980. pap. 5.95 (ISBN 0-8170-0895-0). Judson.

Using Nursing Research: Discovery, Analysis & Interpretation. Patricia Trussel & Anne Brandt. LC 80-84150. 240p. 1981. 39.85 (ISBN 0-913654-70-1). Aspen Pub.

Using One-Two-Three: Special Edition. Que Corporation. 944p. 1987. pap. 24.95 (ISBN 0-88022-332-4). Que Corp.

Using Online Catalogs: A Nationwide Survey. Joseph R. Matthews & Gary S. Lawrence. LC 83-8061. (Illus.). 255p. 1983. pap. 35.00 (ISBN 0-918212-76-6). Neal-Schuman.

Using Oral History in Educational Studies. Frank A. Stone. 25p. 1977. 2.50 (ISBN 0-918158-87-7). I N Thut World Educ Ctr.

Using OS-2. Kris Jamsa. (Illus.). 600p. 1988. pap. text ed. 19.95 (ISBN 0-07-881306-9). Osborne-McGraw.

Using OS-2. Scott Mueller & David Gobel. 800p. (Orig.). 1988. pap. 19.95 (ISBN 0-88022-375-8). Que Corp.

Using Our Gifts. Hoyt E. Stone. 38p. (Orig.). 1981. pap. text ed. 1.00 (ISBN 0-87148-880-9). Pathway Pr.

Using Our Natural Resources: Nineteen Eighty-Three Yearbook of Agriculture. 611p. 1983. 7.00 (ISBN 0-318-11838-6, S/N 001-000-04387-1). USGPO.

Using PageMaker for the PC. Martin Matthews & Carole Matthews. (Illus.). 560p. (Orig.). 1987. pap. text ed. 22.95 (ISBN 0-07-881264-X). Osborne-McGraw.

Using PageMaker for the PC Version 3. 2nd ed. Martin S. Matthews & Carole B. Matthews. 560p. 1988. pap. text ed. 22.95 (ISBN 0-07-881422-7). Osborne-McGraw.

Using PageMaker on the IBM. Diane Burns & S. Venit. LC 86-63978. 400p. (Orig.). 1987. pap. 24.95 (ISBN 0-88022-285-9, 89). Que Corp.

Using Paradox. 2nd ed. George T. Chou. 500p. 1988. pap. 22.95 (ISBN 0-88022-362-6). Que Corp.

Using Paradox. Alfred Poor & Richard Ridington. 1986. pap. 21.95 (ISBN 0-89303-927-6). P-H.

Using Patent Literature: A Comprehensive Guide. Richard D. Walker. (Illus.). 208p. 1988. 67.50 (ISBN 0-89774-264-8). Oryx Pr.

Using PC DOS. 2nd ed. Chris DeVoney. 750p. 1987. pap. 22.95 (ISBN 0-88022-335-9, 807). Que Corp.

Using Performance Measurement in Urban Government. 250p. 1983. 40.00 (ISBN 0-318-17358-1, DG/83-202). Pub Tech Inc.

Using Personal Computers in Public Agencies. John R. Ottensmann. 208p. 1986. pap. 24.95 (ISBN 0-471-80706-0). Wiley.

Using Personal Software to Accompany an Introduction to Computers & Information Processing. 2nd ed. Robert A. Stern & Nancy Stern. (Illus.). 168p. 1985. pap. write for info. (ISBN 0-471-82993-5). Wiley.

Using Personality to Individualize Instruction. James A. Wakefield, Jr. LC 78-74138. 1979. 8.95 (ISBN 0-912736-21-6). EDITS Pubs.

Using Personnel Research. Ed. by Allan P. Williams. 258p. 1983. text ed. 35.50x (ISBN 0-566-02264-8). Gower Pub Co.

Using PFS... Professional File-Professional Write. Linda L. Rice. 248p. (Orig.). 1988. spiral-bound 17.95 (ISBN 0-317-67927-9). Custom Pub Co.

Using Phonics. Bearl Brooks. (Phonics Ser.). 24p. (gr. 1-4). 1978. wkbk. 5.00 (ISBN 0-8209-0334-5, P-6). ESP.

Using Photography to Preserve Evidence. Eastman Kodak Company. (Illus.). 49p. 1982. pap. 4.50 (ISBN 0-87985-166-X, M-2). Eastman Kodak.

Using Poetry to Teach Reading & Language Arts: A Handbook for Elementary School Teachers. Richard J. Smith. 1984. pap. text ed. 13.95x (ISBN 0-8077-2708-3). Tchrs Coll.

Using Policy Simulation Analysis to Guide Correctional Reform - Utah. 7.00 (ISBN 0-318-20317-0). Natl Coun Crime.

Using Political Ideas. Barbara Goodwin. LC 81-16009. 294p. 1982. 51.95 (ISBN 0-471-10115-X, Pub. by Wiley-Interscience); pap. 24.95x (ISBN 0-471-10116-8). Wiley.

Using Political Ideas. 2nd ed. Barbara Goodwin. 1987. pap. 11.30 (ISBN 0-471-91001-5). Wiley.

Using Polyethylene As a Coagulent for Reducing Turbidity from Placer Mining Discharge. Ray-Her Fan. (MIRL Report: No. 79). (Illus.). 50p. (Orig.). Date not set. pap. 10.00 (ISBN 0-911043-06-3). UAKF Min Ind Res Lab.

Using Prepositions & Particles. J. B. Heaton. (English As a Second Language Bk.). 1965. wkbk. 1 3.25x (ISBN 0-582-52122-X); wkbk. 2 3.25x (ISBN 0-582-52123-8); wkbk. 3 3.25x (ISBN 0-582-52124-6); key 3.25x (ISBN 0-582-52120-3). Longman.

Using Problem Solving in Teaching & Training. LeRoy Ford. LC 77-178060. (Multi-Media Teaching & Training Ser.). (Orig.). 1972. pap. 5.50 (ISBN 0-8054-3415-1). Broadman.

Using Process EM-26. Eastman Kodak Company. (Illus.). 130p. 1981. workbook 45.00 (ISBN 0-87985-289-5, Z-127). Eastman-Kodak.

Using Productivity Software. Wilson T. Price. 352p. 1986. pap. text ed. 13.95 (ISBN 0-03-006963-7, HoltC). HR&W.

Using Programmed Instruction see Educational Technology Reviews Ser.

Using Pronouns & Other Referents. Marcia Weinstein. Date not set. 3.95 (ISBN 0-87594-325-X). Book Lab.

Using Psychology: Principles of Behavior & Your Life. 3rd ed. Morris K. Holland. 1984. pap. text ed. write for info. (ISBN 0-673-39513-8); tchr's. ed. avail. Scott F.

Using Psychology to Teach Psychology. Thomas G. Carskadon. 1984. pap. 12.95 (ISBN 0-935652-11-6). Ctr Applications Psych.

Using Psychosocial Counselling Techniques in Primary Health Care. Ellen Jespersen & P. F. Pegg. 230p. 1987. text ed. 37.00 (ISBN 0-566-05463-9, Pub. by Gower Pub England). Gower Pub Co.

Using Published Data: Errors & Remedies. Herbert Jacob. LC 84-50250. (University Papers: No. 42). 63p. 1984. pap. 6.50 (ISBN 0-8039-2299-X). Sage.

Using Puppetry in the Church. Ed. by Everett Robertson. LC 78-72842. 1979. pap. 6.95 (ISBN 0-8054-7517-6). Broadman.

Using Q&A. David P. Ewing & Bill Langenes. LC 86-61153. 592p. (Orig.). 1986. pap. 19.95 (ISBN 0-88022-262-X, 61). Que Corp.

Using Q&A. 2nd ed. David P. Ewing & Bill Langenes. 600p. 1988. pap. 19.95 (ISBN 0-88022-382-0). Que Corp.

Using Quattro. David P. Gobel. 600p. 1988. pap. 21.95 (ISBN 0-88022-344-8). Que Corp.

Using Quattro: The Professional Spreadsheet. Stephen Cobb. 400p. 1988. pap. text ed. 21.95 (ISBN 0-07-881330-1). Osborne-McGraw.

Using Quick C. Werner Feibel. 375p. 1987. pap. text ed. 19.95 (ISBN 0-07-881292-5). Osborne-McGraw.

Using QuickBASIC. Don Inman & Bob Albrecht. 325p. 1987. pap. text ed. 19.95 (ISBN 0-07-881274-7). Osborne-McGraw.

Using QuickBASIC 4. Phil Feldman & Tom Rugg. 450p. (Orig.). 1988. pap. 19.95 (ISBN 0-88022-378-2). Que Corp.

Using R: Base 5000. Jonathan Erickson & Nicholas Baran. 250p. (Orig.). 1985. pap. text ed. 19.95 (ISBN 0-07-881129-5). Osborne-McGraw.

Using Reality Therapy. Robert E. Wubbolding. 192p. 1988. pap. 7.95 (ISBN 0-06-096266-6, PL-6266, PL). Har-Row.

Using Reflex. Mick Renner. LC 86-61156. 512p. (Orig.). 1986. pap. 19.95 (ISBN 0-88022-208-5, 119). Que Corp.

Using REFLEX: The Database Manager. Stephen Cobb. (Borland-Osborne-McGraw-Hill Business Ser.). 400p. 1987. pap. text ed. 21.95 (ISBN 0-07-881287-9). Osborne-McGraw.

Using Research: A Primer for Law Enforcement Managers. Police Executive Research Forum Staff & John E. Eck. LC 84-62330. (Illus.). 11.50. Police Exec Res.

Using Research for Strategic Planning. Ed. by Norman P. Uhl. LC 82-84191. (Institutional Research Ser.: No. 37). 1983. text ed. 12.95x (ISBN 0-87589-955-2). Jossey-Bass.

Using Research to Improve Nursing Practice: A Guide. Jo Anne Horsley. (Monographs in Applied Nursing). 1982. pap. 21.50 (ISBN 0-8089-1510-X, 792072). Grune.

Using Research to Improve Teacher Education: The Nebraska Consortium. Ed. by Robert L. Egbert & Mary M. Kluender. 1984. 6.50 (ISBN 0-89333-031-0). AACTE.

Using Research to Improve Teaching. Ed. by Janet G. Donald & Arthur M. Sullivan. LC 85-60840. (Teaching & Learning Ser.: No. 23). (Orig.). 1985. pap. text ed. 12.95x (ISBN 0-87589-773-8). Jossey-Bass.

Using Robots. C. Morgan. 250p. 1984. 45.00 (ISBN 0-387-12584-1). Springer Verlag.

Using Role Playing in the Classroom. John F. Thompson. LC 78-61318. (Fastback Ser.: No. 114). 1978. pap. 0.90 (ISBN 0-87367-114-7). Phi Delta Kappa.

Using Role Plays in Human Resource Development. J. William Pfeiffer & Arlette C. Ballew. LC 87-40534. (Training Technologies Set Ser.). 110p. (Orig.). 1988. pap. text ed. 16.95 (ISBN 0-88390-214-1). Univ Assocs.

Using Ropes, Chains, & Slings Safely. Center for Occupational Research & Development Staff. (Job Safety & Health Instructional Materials Ser.). (Illus.). 46p. 1981. pap. text ed. 3.50 (ISBN 1-55502-092-5). Ctr Res & Dev.

Using Self-Reports to Predict Student Performance. Leonard L. Baird. LC 76-4312. (Research Monographs: No. 7). 92p. 1976. pap. 5.00 (ISBN 0-87447-098-6, 251701). College Bd.

Using SI Units (Standard International Metric) in Heating, Air Conditioning, & Refrigeration. W. F. Stoecker. LC 74-26697. (Illus.). 1975. 3.75 (ISBN 0-912524-12-X). Busn News.

Using Sidekick Plus. Werner Feibel. 400p. 1988. pap. text ed. 21.95 (ISBN 0-07-881345-X). Osborne-McGraw.

Using Sidekick: The Desktop Organizer. Phillip R. Robinson. (Illus.). 300p. (Orig.). 1988. pap. text ed. 19.95 (ISBN 0-07-881296-8). Osborne McGraw.

Using Small Business Computers. Dorothy G. Dologite. (Illus.). 448p. 1984. text ed. 34.00 (ISBN 0-13-940156-3). P-H.

Using Small Business Computers with Lotus 1-2-3, dBASE II & WordStar. Dorothy G. Dologite. 1985. text ed. 34.00 (ISBN 0-13-940230-6). P-H.

Using Smart. Andrew N. Schwartz. LC 85-63881. 577p. 1986. pap. 22.95 (ISBN 0-88022-229-8, 197). Que Corp.

Using Social Science Research in Policy Making. Ed. by Carol H. Weiss. (Policy Studies Organization Ser.). 256p. 1977. 19.95 (ISBN 0-317-35635-6). Policy Studies.

Using Sociology: An Introduction from the Clinical Perspective. Ed. by Roger A. Straus. LC 84-81428. 200p. (Orig.). 1985. lib. bdg. 26.95x (ISBN 0-930390-58-X); pap. text ed. 12.95x (ISBN 0-930390-57-1). Gen Hall.

Using Sophisticated Models in Resolution Theorem Proving. D. M. Sandford. (Lecture Notes in Computer Science Ser.: Vol. 90). (Illus.). 239p. 1980. pap. 17.00 (ISBN 0-387-10231-0). Springer Verlag.

Using Space--Today & Tomorrow: Proceedings, Vol. 1. Luigi G. Napolitano & International Astronautical Congress, 28th, Prague, 1977. 1978. 93.00 (ISBN 0-08-023231-0). Pergamon.

Using Space, Today & Tomorrow, Vol. 2: Communications Satellite Symposium. L. G. Napolitano. 1978. 69.00 (ISBN 0-08-023232-9). Pergamon.

Using Spiritual Gifts. R. Wayne Jones. LC 83-70642. 1985. pap. 4.95 (ISBN 0-8054-6940-0). Broadman.

Using Sports & Physical Education to Strengthen Reading Skills. Lance M. Gentile. (IRA Reading Aids Ser.). (Illus.). 90p. (Orig.). 1980. pap. text ed. 5.00 (ISBN 0-87207-225-8, 225). Intl Reading.

Using Sports for Reading & Writing Activities, 2 vols. Lance Gentile. LC 82-6322. (Illus.). 232p. 1983. Vol. I: Elementary & Middle School Years, 200p. pap. 15.00x (ISBN 0-89774-023-8); Vol. II: Middle & High School Years, 230p. pap. 15.00x (ISBN 0-89774-098-X). Oryx Pr.

Using Sprint. Charles Ackerman. Date not set. pap. 19.95 (ISBN 0-673-38200-1). Scott F.

Using SPRINT: The Professional Word Processor. Kris Jamsa. (Borland-Osborne-McGraw-Hill Business Ser.). 350p. 1988. pap. text ed. 21.95 (ISBN 0-07-881291-7). Osborne-McGraw.

Using SQL. Joseph-David Carrabis. 500p. 1988. cancelled (ISBN 0-07-881429-4). Osborne-McGraw.

Using Standardized Tests in Education. 4th ed. William A. Mehrens & Irvin J. Lehmann. (Illus.). 529p. 1986. text ed. 25.95 (ISBN 0-582-29022-8). Longman.

Using Statistics in Classroom Instruction. Edward A. Townsend & Paul J. Burke. 1975. pap. write for info. (ISBN 0-02-421220-2). Macmillan.

Using Statistics in Psychological Research. James T. Walker. 620p. 1985. text ed. 28.95 (ISBN 0-03-063591-8, HoltC). HR&W.

Using Statistics to Solve Problems in Psychology. 4th ed. Eric F. Ward. 1985. pap. text ed. 7.50 (ISBN 0-89917-457-4). TIS Inc.

Using Stencils & Masks. (Airbrush Artist's Library). (Illus.). 144p. 1988. 12.95 (ISBN 0-89134-261-3). North Light Bks.

Using Storytelling in Christian Education. Patricia R. Griggs. LC 80-26468. 64p. (Orig.). 1981. pap. 7.25 (ISBN 0-687-43117-4). Abingdon.

Using Structured COBOL, Bk. 2. Judi N. Fernandez & Ruth Ashley. LC 84-17206. (Data Processing Training Ser.: No. 1-615). 256p. 1984. pap. 59.95x spiral bd. (ISBN 0-471-87185-0); tchr's. manual 1.00 (ISBN 0-471-81058-4). Wiley.

Using Structured Design: How to Make Programs Simple, Changeable, Flexible & Reusable. Wayne P. Stevens. LC 80-23481. 213p. 1981. 39.95 (ISBN 0-471-08198-1, Pub. by Wiley-Interscience). Wiley.

Using Structured Experiences in Human Resource Development. J. William Pfeiffer & Arlette C. Ballew. LC 87-40530. (Training Technologies Set Ser.). 110p. (Orig.). 1988. pap. text ed. 16.95 (ISBN 0-88390-212-5). Univ Assocs.

Using SuperCalc: The Next Generation. William J. Doyle, Jr. 406p. 1985. pap. 19.95 (ISBN 0-471-80828-8); Book with program disk. disk 46.95 (ISBN 0-471-82606-5). Wiley.

Using Supercalc 4: The New Generation. William J. Doyle, Jr. LC 87-13804. 382p. 1987. pap. 24.95 (ISBN 0-471-85992-3). Wiley.

Using SuperCalc4. James T. Perry & Joseph G. Lateer. LC 86-62531. 526p. 1987. pap. 19.95 (ISBN 0-88022-276-X, 81). Que Corp.

Using SuperProject Plus. Joan Knutson & Len Glauber. 250p. 1986. text ed. 17.95 (ISBN 0-07-881231-3). Osborne-Mcgraw.

Using Surveys to Value Public Goods: The Contingent Valuation Method. Robert C. Mitchell & Richard T. Carson. 240p. 1988. 25.00 (ISBN 0-915707-32-2). Resources Future.

Using Symphony. 2nd ed. David P. Ewing & Geoffrey T. LeBlond. 700p. 1988. pap. 24.95. Que Corp.

Using Systematic Observation Techniques in Evaluating Career Education. Ralph J. Kester. 64p. 1979. 4.50 (ISBN 0-318-15585-0, RD 169). Natl Ctr Res Voc Ed.

Using Systems Analysis to Implement Cost-Effectiveness & Program Budgeting in Education. John P. Van Gigch & Richard E. Hill. LC 71-153558. 64p. 1971. pap. 14.95 (ISBN 0-87778-007-2). Educ Tech Pubns.

Using Tear Sheets. Roy A. Frye. (Bridges for Ideas Handbook Ser.). 1963. pap. text ed. 6.00x (ISBN 0-913648-12-4). U Tex Austin Film Lib.

Using Technology for Education & Training. LC 83-81648. 248p. 1983. 25.00 (ISBN 0-317-36884-2); members 22.00 (ISBN 0-317-36885-0). Assn Ed Comm Tech.

Using Television in the Curriculum. Rosemary L. Potter. LC 83-83090. (Fastback Ser.: No. 208). 50p. (Orig.). 1984. pap. 0.90 (ISBN 0-87367-208-9). Phi Delta Kappa.

Using Ten-Key Electronic Desktop Calculators. John Kimmel. 207p. 1983. pap. text ed. 9.75 (ISBN 0-89420-235-9, 126520); cassette recordings 94.95 (ISBN 0-89420-242-1, 126500). Natl Book.

Using Tests & Other Information in Counseling: A Decision Model for Practitioners. James M. Schuerger & David G. Watterson. LC 77-71888. 1977. 4.40 (ISBN 0-918296-08-0). Inst Personality & Ability.

Using Tests in Counseling. Leo Goldman. LC 77-151115. (Orig.). 1971. text ed. write for info. (ISBN 0-673-16456-X, Appleton-Century-Crofts). Scott F.

Using the Access to Information Act. 135p. 1984. 5.95 (ISBN 0-88908-589-7). ISC Pr.

Using the Apple Computer. Stokes & Lukenbill. 196p. (Orig.). Date not set. 19.95x (ISBN 0-88725-047-5). Hunter Textbks.

Using the Bible in Groups. Roberta Hestenes. LC 84-15291. 118p. (Orig.). 1985. pap. 6.95 (ISBN 0-664-24561-7). Westminster John Knox.

Using the Biological Literature. Davis. (Books in Library & Information Science: Vol. 35). 272p. 1981. 49.75 (ISBN 0-8247-7209-1). Dekker.

Using the Case Study in Teaching & Training. LeRoy Ford. LC 71-105324. (Multi-Media Teaching & Training Ser.). (Illus.). 1970. pap. 5.50 (ISBN 0-8054-3413-5). Broadman.

Using the Census as a Creative Teaching Resource. Sandra M. Long. LC 82-60804. (Fastback Ser.: No. 184). 50p. 1982. pap. 0.90 (ISBN 0-87367-184-8). Phi Delta Kappa.

Using the Chemical Literature: A Practical Guide. Henry M. Woodburn. (Library & Information Science Ser.: Vol. 11). 312p. 1974. pap. 35.00 (ISBN 0-8247-7455-8). Dekker.

Using the Clinical Laboratory in Medical Decision Making. George D. Lundberg. LC 83-2801. 320p. (Orig.). 1983. text ed. 35.00 (ISBN 0-89189-164-1, 45-9-013-00). Am Soc Clinical.

Using the Commodore 64 in the Home. Hank Librach & William Behrendt. (Illus.). 100p. 1984. pap. 10.95; incl. disk o.p. 29.95 (ISBN 0-13-940099-0). P-H.

Using the Commodore 64 Without Learning BASIC. Tim Kelly. 1984. 15.95. P-H.

Using the Computer. Neil Ardley. (Action Science Ser.). 32p. (gr. 4-6). 1983. PLB 11.90 (ISBN 0-531-04518-8). Watts.

Using the Computer for Offensive Football Scouting. Charles Frazier & Alan Hatfield. (Illus.). 256p. 1984. 24.95 (ISBN 0-13-940198-9). P-H.

Using the Computer in Education: A Briefing for School Decision Makers. Paul G. Watson. LC 72-86779. 144p. 1972. pap. 19.95 (ISBN 0-87778-042-0). Educ Tech Pubns.

USSR Calendar of Events 1987. Joseph P. Mastro. 1988. 71.00 (ISBN 0-87569-104-8); pap. 91.00. Academic Intl.
USSR Facts & Figures Annual 1988, Vol. 12. Ed. by Alan P. Pollard. 1988. 71.00 (ISBN 0-87569-103-X); pap. 91.00. Academic Intl.
UST Cumulative Index, 1776-1949, 4 vols. Ed. by Igor I. Kavass & Mark A. Michael. LC 74-29385. 1975. Set. lib. bdg. 350.00 (ISBN 0-930342-02-X). W S Hein.
UST Cumulative Index: 1950-1970, Covering 1st to 21st UST, 4 vols. Ed. by Igor I. Kavass & Adolf Sprudzs. LC 72-92824. 1973. Set. lib. bdg. 650.00 incl. index supp. 1971-1975 (1977) 22nd-26th UST, service 1976-1979 27th-31st UST & current treaty index 1985 & Current Service (ISBN 0-930342-01-1). W S Hein.
USTA College Tennis Guide. 1988-1989. pap. 3.50 (ISBN 0-938822-81-0). USTA CERT.
USTA Guide to Forming a Community Tennis Association. 54p. 1985. pap. 2.00 (ISBN 0-938822-58-6). USTA Cert.
USTA Guide to Fund Raising for Community Tennis Associations. 56p. 1985: 2.00 (ISBN 0-938822-59-4). USTA-CERT.
USTA Official Yearbook. 1988. pap. 9.00 (ISBN 0-938822-82-9). USTA CERT.
USTA Recreational Tennis Programming Kit. 1981. 2.50 (ISBN 0-938822-16-0). USTA-CERT.
USTA Schools Program Tennis Curriculum. 73p. 1986. 3.50 (ISBN 0-938822-73-X). USTA-CERT.
USTA Scorebook for Coaches. 48p. 1984. 3.95 (ISBN 0-938822-42-X). USTA-CERT.
Ustad Allauddin Khan & His Music. Jatin Bhattacharya. 1983. 18.50x (ISBN 0-8364-1088-2, Pub. by BS Shah Delhi). South Asia Bks.
Usted Puede Tener lo Que Diga. Kenneth E. Hagin. (Span.). 1983. pap. 0.50 mini bk. (ISBN 0-89276-154-7). Hagin Ministries.
Usted y Yo: Primer Paso. Z. S. Da Silva. 1975. 25.68 (ISBN 0-02-270900-2). Macmillan.
Usteriosis Research: Present Situation & Perspective. B. Ralovich. 1984. text ed. 29.00 cancelled (ISBN 963-05-3657-9, Pub. by Akademiai Kaido Hungary). IPS.
Ustinov in Russia. Peter Ustinov. 160p. 1987. 49.00x (Pub. by M O'Mara UK). State Mutual Bk.
USTs Cumulative Index Supplement 1971-1979, 22nd to 26th UST: Supplement Two 27th to 31st UST, 1976-1979, 2 vols. Ed. by Igor I. Kavass & Adolf Sprudzs. LC 72-92824. (United States Treaties & Other International Agreements Cumulative Index Ser.). 1977. Set. lib. bdg. 180.00; Vol. 1. 95.00 (ISBN 0-930342-55-0); Vol. 2. 95.00 (ISBN 0-89941-314-5). W S Hein.
Usual Lunacy. D. G. Compton. LC 78-14953. (Illus.). 191p. 1978. lib. bdg. 17.95x (ISBN 0-89370-125-4); pap. 7.95x (ISBN 0-89370-225-0). Borgo Pr.
Usual Lunacy. D. G. Compton. 1983. pap. 2.75 (ISBN 0-441-84760-9, Ace Science Fiction). Ace Bks.
Usurper. Mark Smith & Jamie Thompson. (Way of the Tiger Ser.). Date not set. price not set (Pub. by Berkley-Pacer). Berkley Pub.
Usurper Jubg: Henry of Bolingbroke 1366-99. Marie-Louise Bruce. (Illus.). 288p. 1986. 29.95 (Rubicon Pr England). Intl Spec Bk.
Usurper King: Henry of Bolingbroke 1366-99. Marie L. Bruce. 1987. 75.00x (ISBN 0-948695-01-3, Pub. by Rubicon Pr). State Mutual Bk.
Usurpers. Francisco Ayala. Tr. by Carolyn Richmond from Span. LC 84-23602. 192p. 1987. 15.95 (ISBN 0-8052-3970-7). Schocken.
Usury & Consumer Credit Regulation. Kevin W. Brown & Kathleen E. Keest. (Consumer Credit & Sales Legal Practice Ser.). 340p. 1987. pap. 57.00 (ISBN 0-317-64903-5). Nat Consumer Law.
Usury & Usury Laws. F. W. Ryan. 1977. lib. bdg. 69.95 (ISBN 0-8490-2791-8). Gordon Pr.
Usury Debate after Adam Smith: Two Nineteenth Century Essays. LC 72-38472. (Evolution of Capitalism Ser.). 106p. 1972. Repr. 15.00 (ISBN 0-405-04139-X). Ayer Co Pubs.
Usury Debate in the Seventeenth Century: Three Arguments. LC 76-38473. (Evolution of Capitalism Ser.). 236p. 1972. Repr. 20.00 (ISBN 0-405-04140-3). Ayer Co Pubs.
USY Parshat HaShavuan Series. 10.00 (ISBN 0-686-96100-5). United Syn Bk.
Ut Austin: Traditions & Nostalgia. rev. ed. Margaret C. Berry. (Illus.). 136p. 1983. pap. 6.95 (ISBN 0-89015-410-4). Eakin Pr.
Ut Pictura Poesis Controversy in Eighteenth Century England & Germany. Niklaus R. Schweizer. (European University Studies 18: Vol. 2). 123p. 1972. 18.25 (ISBN 3-261-00222-0). P lang Pubs.
Ut Pictura Poesis: The Humanistic Theory of Painting. Rensselaer W. Lee. (Illus., Orig.). 1967. pap. 6.95 (ISBN 0-393-00399-X, Norton Lib.). Norton.
Utagawa Toyokuni und Seine Zeit Bank II. Friederich Succo. 198p. 1914. 320.00x (ISBN 0-317-68497-3, Pub. by Han-Shan Tang Ltd). State Mutual Bk.
Utah. new ed. Allan Carpenter. LC 79-12433. (New Enchantment of America State Bks.). (Illus.). 96p. (gr. 4 up). 1979. PLB 15.93 (ISBN 0-516-04144-4). Childrens.
Utah. Randy Collings. 1982. 7.95 (ISBN 0-933692-24-2). A R Collings.
Utah. Toby Olson. 1987. 17.95 (ISBN 0-671-63814-9, Linden Pr). S&S.
Utah. Toby Olson. 288p. 1988. pap. 8.95 (ISBN 0-02-098410-3, Collier). Macmillan.
Utah. Dana F. Ross. (Wagons West Ser.). 1984. pap. 4.50 (ISBN 0-553-26521-0). Bantam.
Utah. Turner Program Services, Inc. Staff & James I. Clark. (Portrait of America Library). 48p. (gr. 4 up). 1985. PLB 15.33 (ISBN 0-86514-446-X); pap. text ed. 9.27 (ISBN 0-86514-521-0); Beta video 113.33 (ISBN 0-86514-071-5); VHS video 113.33 (ISBN 0-86514-221-1); 3/4" video 136.00 (ISBN 0-86514-146-0); tchr's guide 13.27 (ISBN 0-86514-296-3); student activity bk. 6.60 (ISBN 0-86514-371-4); index 13.27. Raintree Pubs.
Utah. Nelson Wadsworth. (Illus.). 1984. 15.00 (ISBN 0-19-540602-8). Skyline Press.
Utah: A Family Travel Guide. Tom Wharton. 1987. pap. 8.50 (ISBN 0-915272-31-8). Wasatch Pubs.
Utah: A Guide to the State. Revised ed. Ward J. Roylance. 1982. 22.50 (ISBN 0-914740-23-7, 884P.); pap. 8.95 (ISBN 0-914740-25-3, PT. 2, TOUR SECTION, 400P.). Western Epics.
Utah: A History. Charles S. Peterson. (States & the Nation Ser.). (Illus.). 1977. 14.95 (ISBN 0-393-05629-5, Co-Pub. by AASLH). Norton.
Utah: A People's History. Dean May. LC 87-17898. (Bonneville Bks.). (Illus.). 1987. text ed. 25.00x (ISBN 0-87480-283-0); pap. 14.95x (ISBN 0-87480-284-9). U of Utah Pr.
Utah: A State Guide. Federal Writers' Project Staff. 1941. Repr. 59.00x (ISBN 0-403-02193-6). Somerset Pub.
Utah & the Mormons. B. G. Ferris. LC 77-134394. Repr. of 1856 ed. 40.00 (ISBN 0-404-08436-2). AMS Pr.
Utah & the Mormons. Donald W. Hemingway. (Illus.). 1979. pap. 2.50 (ISBN 0-686-30193-5). D W Hemingway.
Utah & the Mormons. Ed. by Donald W. Hemingway. (Colourpicture Travel Ser.). (Illus.). 32p. (gr. 7-8). 1983. pap. write for info. (ISBN 0-938440-47-0). Colourpicture.
Utah Appellate System: A Review. National Center for State Courts Staff. 82p. 1985. manuscript 5.00 (WRO-061). Natl Ctr St Courts.
Utah Beach to Cherbourg. Ed. by Historical Section European Theater of Operations Staff. (Combat Arms Ser.: No. 9). (Illus.). 214p. 1984. Repr. of 1946 ed. 26.50x (ISBN 0-317-05048-6, 0-89839796). Battery Pr.
Utah Bicentennial & History. 1984. 7.95 (ISBN 0-393-30221-0). Norton.
Utah Blaine. Louis L'Amour. 192p. 1982. pap. 2.50 (ISBN 0-449-12357-X, GM). Fawcett.
Utah Blaine. Louis L'Amour. 1984. pap. 2.95 (ISBN 0-553-24761-1). Bantam.
Utah Business & Industry Directory 1987-88. 274p. 1987. pap. 40.00 (ISBN 0-318-02874-3). Manufacturers.
Utah Canyon Country. F. A. Barnes. LC 85-52187. (Illus.). 120p. 1986. 24.95 (ISBN 0-936331-01-1); pap. 15.95 (ISBN 0-936331-00-3). Utah Geo Series.
Utah Census Index 1850. Ronald V. Jackson. LC 77-86077. (Illus.). lib. bdg. 28.00 (ISBN 0-89593-140-0). Accelerated Index.
Utah Census Index 1856. Ronald V. Jackson. (Illus.). lib. bdg. 75.00 (ISBN 0-317-17078-3). Accelerated Index.
Utah Census Index, 1856: An Every Name Index. Ed. by Bryan L. Dilts. LC 83-22660. xviii, 292p. 1984. lib. bdg. 99.00x (ISBN 0-914311-00-X); microfiche 67.00x (ISBN 0-914311-01-8). Index Pub.
Utah Census Index 1860. Ronald V. Jackson. (Illus.). lib. bdg. 60.00 (ISBN 0-317-17079-1). Accelerated Index.
Utah Census Index 1890 Union Veterans. Ronald V. Jackson. (Illus.). lib. bdg. 15.00 (ISBN 0-317-17080-5). Accelerated Index.
Utah Chronology & Factbook, Vol. 44. Robert I. Vexler. LC 78-21310. (Chronologies & Documentary Handbook of the States). 148p. 1978. 8.50 (ISBN 0-379-16169-9). Oceana.
Utah Civil Procedure, 4 vols. David A. Thomas. 1980. 150.00 (ISBN 0-911712-72-0). BYU Clark Law.
Utah Courts of Limited Jurisdiction: Analysis & Recommendations. National Center for State Courts Staff. 146p. 1976. manuscript 8.76 (WRO-003). Natl Ctr St Courts.
Utah Criminal Code. Loren D. Martin. (Orig.). plastic comb bdg. 12.50x (ISBN 0-9608244-3-X). Valiant Pubns.
Utah Dining Car. Junior League of Ogden, Utah Inc. Staff. Ed. by Many King. 300p. 1984. 12.95x (ISBN 0-9613453-0-6). Jr League Ogden.
Utah District Court Management Study. 222p. 1986. manuscript 14.00 (ISBN 0-317-59222-X, WRO-076). Natl Ctr St Courts.
Utah Expedition, Eighteen Fifty-Seven to Eighteen Fifty-Eight: A Documentary Account. Ed. by LeRoy R. Hafen & Ann W. Hafen. LC 58-11786. (Far West & Rockies Ser.: Vol.VIII). (Illus.). 375p. 1983. Repr. of 1958 ed. 27.50 (ISBN 0-87062-035-5). A H Clark.
Utah Handbook. Bill Weir. Ed. by Mark Morris. (Illus.). 400p. (Orig.). 1988. pap. 10.95 (ISBN 0-918373-19-0). Moon Pubns CA.
Utah Historical & Biographical Index, Vol. 1. Ronald Vern Jackson. LC 78-53720. (Illus.). 1984. lib. bdg. 30.00 (ISBN 0-89593-202-4). Accelerated Index.
Utah, Images of the Landscape. Tom Till. (Illus.). 160p. 1988. cancelled 35.00 (ISBN 0-942394-60-7). Westcliffe Pubs Inc.
Utah in Demographic Perspective: Regional & National Contrasts. Ed. by Thomas K. Martin et al. 304p. 1986. pap. 9.95 (ISBN 0-941214-44-3). Signature Bks.
Utah: In Words & Pictures. Dennis Fradin. LC 80-15177. (Young People's Stories of Our States Ser.). (Illus.). 48p. (gr. 2-5). 1980. PLB 13.27 (ISBN 0-516-03944-X). Childrens.
Utah Jazz. Jim Moore. (NBA Today Ser.). (Illus.). 48p. (gr. 4 up). 1984. PLB 10.45 (ISBN 0-87191-991-5). Creative Ed.
Utah Mountaineering Guide & the Best Canyon Hikes. 2nd ed. Michael R. Kelsey. (Illus.). 192p. 1986. pap. 7.95 (ISBN 0-9605824-5-2). Kelsey Pub.
Utah Photographs of George Edward Anderson. Rell G. Francis. LC 79-1123. (Illus.). xii, 155p. 1979. 24.95 (ISBN 0-8032-1952-0). U of Nebr Pr.
Utah Probate Handbook. Loren D. Martin. LC 82-50679. 352p. (Orig.). 1982. pap. 35.00 (ISBN 0-9608244-1-3). Valiant Pubns.
Utah Probate System. H. Reese Hansen & Stanley D. Neeleman. 1977. 60.00 (ISBN 0-686-40389-4). BYU Clark Law.
Utah Ski Country. Brooke Williams. LC 85-50488. (Illus.). 128p. 1986. 24.95 (ISBN 0-936331-03-8); pap. 15.95 (ISBN 0-936331-02-X). Utah Geo Series.
Utah Slaughter. Jon Sharpe. (Trailsman Ser.: No. 84). 1988. pap. 2.95 (ISBN 0-451-15719-2, Sig). NAL.
Utah Statistical Abstract 1983. 9th ed. Ed. by Bureau of Economic & Business Research Staff, University of Utah Staff. (Illus.). 396p. (Orig.). 1983. 25.00 (ISBN 0-942486-04-8). Univ Utah.
Utah Supreme Court Project Report. National Center for State Courts Staff. 78p. 1977. manuscript 4.68 (WRO-022). Natl Ctr St Courts.
Utah Survival. Betty L. Hall. 160p. (Orig.). (gr. 10-12). 1979. pap. text ed. 5.84 (ISBN 0-03-046981-3). Westwood Pr.
Utah Treasure Hunter's Ghost Town Guide. Theron Fox. (Illus.). 1983. pap. 1.95 (ISBN 0-913814-54-7). Nevada Pubns.
Utah: Unusual Beginning to Unique Present. Wayne K. Hinton. Ed. by Nora Perren. (Illus.). 192p. (YA) (gr. 7 up). 1988. 29.95 (ISBN 0-89781-247-6). Windsor Pubns Inc.
Utah Valley Trails. new ed. Shirley Paxman. LC 77-95049. (Illus.). 1978. pap. 2.50 (ISBN 0-915272-19-9). Wasatch Pubs.
Utah Vengeance. John E. Lewis. (YA) (gr. 7 up). 1981. 9.95 (ISBN 0-686-73961-2, Avalon). Bouregy.
Utah Wildlands. Stewart Aitchison. LC 86-50489. (Illus.). 112p. 1987. 24.95 (ISBN 0-936331-05-4); pap. 15.95 (ISBN 0-936331-04-6). Utah Geo Series.
Utah Women & the Law: A Resource Handbook. Compiled by Utah Governor's Commission on the Status of Women. LC 87-50075. (Bonneville Bks.). 176p. (Orig.). 1987. pap. 1.95 (ISBN 0-87480-301-2). U of Utah Pr.
Utah's High-Tech Directory 1987. Ed. by Jan E. Crispin. 28p. 1988. pap. 10.00 (ISBN 0-942486-06-4). Univ Utah.
Utah's Historic Architecture, 1847-1940: A Guide. Thomas Carter & Peter Goss. (Illus.). 192p. (Orig.). 1988. pap. text ed. 36.00x (ISBN 0-87480-276-8). U of Utah Pr.
Utah's History. Ed. by Richard D. Poll & Thomas G. Alexander. LC 77-20924. (Illus.). 1978. text ed. 17.95x (ISBN 0-8425-0842-2); pap. 15.95x (ISBN 0-8425-0838-4). Brigham.
Utah's Scenic San Rafael. Owen McClenahan. (Illus.). 128p. 1986. pap. 7.95 (ISBN 0-915272-28-8). Wasatch Pubs.
Utah's Wasatch Front. Ted Wilson. LC 86-51587. (Illus.). 112p. 1987. 24.95 (ISBN 0-936331-07-0); pap. 15.95 (ISBN 0-936331-06-2). Utah Geo Series.
Utamaro. Tadashi Kobayashi. Tr. by Mark A. Harbison. LC 81-20693. (Great Japanese Art Ser.). (Illus.). 48p. 1982. 24.95 (ISBN 0-87011-503-0). Kodansha.
Utamaro: Songs of the Garden. Ed. by Barbara Burn. Tr. by Yasuko Betchaku & Joan B. Mirviss. LC 84-60004. (Illus.). 48p. 16.95 (ISBN 0-87099-368-2). Metro Mus Art.
Utamaro: Songs of the Garden. Kitagawa Utamaro. Tr. by Yasuko Betchaku from Japanese. (Illus.). 1984. 19.95 (ISBN 0-670-39911-6). Viking.
UTC Instructor's Guide. Center for Occupational Research & Development Staff. (United Technical Concepts Ser.). 171p. 1986. pap. text ed. 20.00 (ISBN 1-55502-160-3). Ctr Res & Dev.
UTE Mountain Tribal Park: The Other Mesa Verde. Jean Akens. (Illus.). 113p. (Orig.). 1987. pap. 5.95 (ISBN 0-944123-00-7). Four Crnrs UT.
Ute Pass. new ed. Jan Pettit. (Illus.). 64p. (Orig.). 1979. pap. 3.50 (ISBN 0-936564-12-1). Little London.
Ute Revenge. Paul Ledd. 224p. 1986. pap. 2.50 (ISBN 0-8217-1957-2). Zebra.
Uterine Circulation. Ed. by Charles Rosenfeld. (Reproductive & Perinatal Medicine Ser.: No. X). 1989. price not set (ISBN 0-916859-30-4). Perinatology.
Uterine Physiology: Proceedings of the Brook Lodge Workshop. Ed. by Emanual A. Friedman et al. LC 79-332. (Illus.). 156p. 1979. text ed. 21.00 (ISBN 0-88416-263-X). PSG Pub Co.
Uterus. Henry J. Norris. LC 73-6905. (IAP Ser.: No. 14). 581p. 1973. 39.50 (ISBN 0-683-06563-7, WW). Krieger.
Utes: The Mountain People. Jan Pettit. (Illus.). 80p. 1982. pap. 6.95 (ISBN 0-937080-04-7). Century One.
Uthal. Etienne Mehul. Ed. by Philip Gossett & Charles Rosen. LC 76-49222. (Early Romantic Opera Ser.: Vol. 40). 1979. lib. bdg. 99.00 (ISBN 0-8240-2939-9). Garland Pub.
Utilice Su Casa para Evangelizar. Lee Baggett. 32p. 1987. Repr. of 1984 ed. 1.50 (ISBN 0-311-13832-2). Casa Bautista.
Utilisation des Methodes Manuelles dans les Programmes de Construction: Guide Pratique pour Organiser et Conduire les Travaux. World Bank Transportation Staff & Consultants & Basil Coukis. 406p. (Fr.). 1986. French. 14.95 (ISBN 0-8213-0821-1, BK0613); English. 14.95 (ISBN 0-317-57906-1, OX561512). World Bank.
Utilisation of Sewage Sludge on Land: Rates of Application & Long-Term Effects of Metals. Ed. by S. Berglund et al. 1984. lib. bdg. 39.00 (ISBN 90-277-1701-X, Pub. by Reidel Holland). Kluwer Academic.
Utilisation Regionale du Sol dans la Planification Agricole en Inde see Cahiers de l'Institut de Science Economique Appliquee.
Utilitarian Confucianism: Ch'en Liang's Challenge to Chu Hsi. Hoyt C. Tillman. (Harvard East Asian Monographs: No. 101). 300p. 1982. text ed. 22.50x (ISBN 0-674-93176-9). Harvard U Pr.
Utilitarian Jurisprudence in America: The Influence of Bentham & Austin on American Legal Thought in the 19th Century. Peter J. King. Ed. by Harold Hyman & Stuart Bruchey. (American Legal & Constitutional History Ser.). 460p. 1986. lib. bdg. 55.00 (ISBN 0-8240-8282-6). Garland Pub.
Utilitarian Logic & Politics: James Mill's 'Essay on Government', Macaulay's 'Critique' & the Ensueing Debate. James Mill. Ed. by Jack Lively & John Rees. 1978. pap. text ed. 12.95x (ISBN 0-19-827471-8). Oxford U Pr.
Utilitarianism. John S. Mill. Ed. by Oskar Piest. 1957. pap. 4.24 scp (ISBN 0-672-60164-8, LLA1). Bobbs.
Utilitarianism. John S. Mill. Ed. by George Sher. LC 78-74450. (HPC Philosophical Classics Ser.). 80p. 1979. pap. text ed. 2.95 (ISBN 0-915144-41-7). Hackett Pub.
Utilitarianism. John S. Mill. Ed. by Mary Warnock. Bd. with On Liberty; Essay on Bentham; Selected Writings of Jeremy Bentham & John Austin. pap. 6.95 (ISBN 0-452-00598-1, F598, Mer). NAL.
Utilitarianism. John S. Mill. LC 86-62704. pap. 3.95 (ISBN 0-87975-376-5). Prometheus Bks.
Utilitarianism & All That. Raghavan Iyer. xi, 132p. 1983. pap. 8.75 (ISBN 0-88695-003-1). Concord Grove.
Utilitarianism & Beyond. Ed. by Amartya Sen & Bernard Williams. LC 81-17981. 304p. 1982. pap. 17.95 (ISBN 0-521-28771-5). Cambridge U Pr.
Utilitarianism & Cooperation. Donald Regan. 1980. text ed. 39.95x (ISBN 0-19-824609-9); pap. 15.95x (ISBN 0-19-824636-6). Oxford U Pr.
Utilitarianism & Other Essays. John S. Mill & Jeremy Bentham. Ed. by Alan Ryan. 352p. 1987. pap. 5.95 (ISBN 0-14-043272-8). Penguin.
Utilitarianism & the Sense of Beauty. Carleton Randall. 139p. 1984. 87.55 (ISBN 0-89920-101-6). Am Inst Psych.
Utilitarianism: For & Against. J. J. Smart & B. Williams. LC 73-80487. 180p. 1973. 29.95 (ISBN 0-521-20297-3); pap. 9.95x (ISBN 0-521-09822-X). Cambridge U Pr.
Utilitarianism: Mill. Ed. by Oskar Piest. 1957. pap. text ed. write for info. (ISBN 0-02-395670-4). Macmillan.
Utilitarianism on Liberty, & Representative Government. John S. Mill. 1980. 14.95x (ISBN 0-460-10482-9, Evman); pap. 4.95x (ISBN 0-460-11482-4, Evman). Biblio Dist.
Utilities Desk Reference. 270p. 1981. 17.50 (32,615). NCLS Inc.
Utilities in Crisis: A Problem in Governance. Alvin L. Alm & Daniel A. Dreyfus. 64p. (Orig.). 1982. pap. text ed. 7.00 (ISBN 0-8191-5856-9, Pub. by Aspen Inst for Humanistic Studies). U Pr of Amer.
Utilities Service Worker. Jack Rudman. (Career Examination Ser.: C-3161). (Cloth bdg. avail. on request). 1988. pap. 14.00 (ISBN 0-8373-3161-7). Natl Learning.
Utility & Choice in Social Interaction. Lynne Ofshe & Richard Ofshe. LC 70-101539. (Illus.). 1970. 39.50x (ISBN 0-13-939645-4). Irvington.
Utility & Rights. Ed. by R. G. Frey. LC 83-27327. 1984. 29.50x (ISBN 0-8166-1319-2); pap. 13.95 (ISBN 0-8166-1320-6). U of Minn Pr.
Utility Gas Analysis by Gas Chromatography. D. V. Kniebes. (Technical Report Ser.: No. 4). vi, 32p. 1962. 1.00 (ISBN 0-317-56935-X). Inst Gas Tech.

Utopian Flight from Unhappiness: Freud Against Marx on Social Progress. Martin G. Kalin. (Quality Paperback: No. 314). 231p. 1975. pap. 3.50 (ISBN 0-8226-0314-4). Littlefield.

Utopian Flight from Unhappiness: Freud Against Marx on Social Progress. Martin G. Kalin. LC 73-80500. 244p. 1974. 21.95x (ISBN 0-911012-65-6). Nelson-Hall.

Utopian Function of Art & Literature: Selected Essays. Ernst Bloch. Tr. by Jack Zipes & Frank Mecklenburg. (Studies on Contemporary German Social Thought). 300p. 1987. text ed. 27.50x (ISBN 0-262-02270-2). MIT Pr.

Utopian Literature, 41 Bks. Ed. by Arthur O. Lewis, Jr. 1971. Set. 932.50 (ISBN 0-405-03510-1). Ayer Co Pubs.

Utopian Literature: A Bibliography with a Supplementary Listing of Works Influential in Utopian Thought. Glenn Negley. LC 77-8265. xxiv, 228p. 1978. 25.00x (ISBN 0-7006-0164-3). U Pr of KS.

Utopian Literature: A Selection. James Weldon Johnson. 1968. pap. text ed. write for info (ISBN 0-394-30996-0, RanC). Random.

Utopian Mind. Aurel Kolnai. Ed. by David Wiggins. 200p. 1988. text ed. 55.00 (ISBN 0-485-11232-9, Pub. by Athlone Pr UK). Humanities.

Utopian Moment in Contemporary American Poetry. Norman Finkelstein. LC 86-73242. 136p. 1988. 23.50x (ISBN 0-8387-5114-8). Bucknell U Pr.

Utopian Novel in America, 1865-1900. Robert L. Shurter. LC 72-2944. Repr. of 1973 ed. 36.00 (ISBN 0-404-10710-9). AMS Pr.

Utopian Novel in America, 1886-1896: The Politics of Form. Jean Pfaelzer. LC 84-40094. (Critical Essays in Modern Literature Ser.). 223p. 1985. 24.95x (ISBN 0-8229-3811-1). U of Pittsburgh Pr.

Utopian Novel in America, 1886-1896: The Politics of Form. Jean Pfaelzer. LC 84-40094. 223p. 1988. pap. 11.95x (ISBN 0-8229-5413-3). U of Pittsburgh Pr.

Utopian Studies I. Ed. by Gorman Beauchamp et al. 204p. (Orig.). 1987. lib. bdg. 24.50 (ISBN 0-8191-6164-0, Pub. by Soc for Utopian Studies); pap. text ed. 12.75 (ISBN 0-8191-6165-9, Pub. by Soc for Utopian Studies). U Pr of Amer.

Utopian Thought in the Western World. Frank E. Manuel & Fritzie P. Manuel. LC 79-12382. 912p. 1979. text ed. 40.00x (ISBN 0-674-93185-8, Belknap Pr); pap. 12.95 (ISBN 0-674-93186-6). Harvard U Pr.

Utopian Vision of Charles Fourier: Selected Texts on Work, Love & Passionate Attraction. Ed. by Jonathan Beecher & Richard Bienvenu. Tr. by Jonathan Beecher & Richard Bienvenu. LC 83-5897. 448p. 1985. text ed. 37.50 (ISBN 0-8262-0426-0); pap. text ed. 14.50 (ISBN 0-8262-0413-9). U of Mo Pr.

Utopian Vision of D. H. Lawrence. Eugene Goodheart. LC 63-22817. 1963. 12.00x (ISBN 0-226-30288-1). U of Chicago Pr.

Utopian Vision of Moholy-Nagy. Joseph H. Caton. Ed. by Diane Kirkpatrick. LC 83-18182. (Studies in Photography: No. 5). 200p. 1984. 42.95 (ISBN 0-8357-1528-0). UMI Res Pr.

Utopianism & Education: Robert Owen & the Owenites. Ed. by John F. Harrison. LC 68-54675. (Classics in Education Ser.). (Orig.). 1969. pap. text ed. 6.00x (ISBN 0-8077-1498-4). Tchrs Coll.

Utopianism & Marxism. Vincent Geoghegan. 176p. 1988. text ed. 37.50 (ISBN 0-416-08062-6); pap. text ed. 10.95 (ISBN 0-416-08072-3). Routledge Chapman & Hall.

Utopias. Ed. by E. Kamenka. (Australian Academy of Humanities Ser.). 204p. 1987. 39.95x (ISBN 0-19-554731-4). Oxford U Pr.

Utopias, Old & New. Madge A. Hart. LC 76-49623. 1977. Repr. of 1932 ed. lib. bdg. 37.00 (ISBN 0-8414-4944-9). Folcroft.

Utopias Old & New. Harry Ross. LC 73-181. 1973. lib. bdg. 37.50 (ISBN 0-8414-1388-6). Folcroft.

Utopias on Puget Sound, 1885-1915. Charles P. LeWarne. LC 74-13862. (Illus.). 340p. 1978. pap. 9.95 (ISBN 0-295-95611-9). U of Wash Pr.

Utopias; or Schemes of Social Improvement: From Sir Thomas More to Karl Marx. M. Kaufmann. 265p. 1984. Repr. of 1879 ed. lib. bdg. 30.00 (ISBN 0-918377-12-9). Russell Pr.

Utopias; or Schemes of Social Improvement. M. Kaufmann. 1897. lib. bdg. 29.00 (ISBN 0-8414-5552-X). Folcroft.

Utopias: Schemes of Social Improvement since Sir Thomas More. Moritz Kaufman. 59.95 (ISBN 0-8490-1253-8). Gordon Pr.

Utopismo Socialista. (Ayacucho Library Collection Ser: Vol. 26). (Span.). 1977. 25.00 (ISBN 0-317-56326-2, Pub. by Biblioteca Ayacucho); pap. 12.50 (ISBN 0-317-56327-0, Pub. by Biblioteca Ayacucho). Humanities.

Utopus Discovers America or Critical Realism in American Utopian Fiction 1798-1900. Ellene Ransom. LC 76-12358. 1947. lib. bdg. 20.50 (ISBN 0-8414-7356-0). Folcroft.

Utos Ng Hari at Iba Pang Kuwento. Jun C. Reyes. (Illus.). 130p. (Tagalog.). 1981. pap. 6.50x (ISBN 0-686-32578-8, Pub. by New Day Phillipines). Cellar.

Utrastructural Pathology of the Cell & Matrix, 2 vols, Vol. 2. 3rd ed. Feroze N. Ghadially. (Illus.). 600p. 1988. text ed. price not set (ISBN 0-407-01572-8). Butterworth.

Utrecht in Drawings-Utrecht Getekend. C. C. Wilmer. (Illus.). 1980. 35.00 (ISBN 90-247-9023-9). Heinman.

Utrillo. Alfred Werner. (Library of Great Painters Ser.). 1985. 45.00 (ISBN 0-8109-1725-4). Abrams.

Utstallningen Av Tibetansk Och Annan Ostasiatish Konst. Museet I. Kulturhist. 24p. 1931. pap. 20.00x (ISBN 0-317-68703-4, Pub. by Han-Shan Tang Ltd). State Mutual Bk.

Uttar Pradesh Bhoomi Prabandhak Samiti Niyam Sangraph (U.P. Gaon Samaj Manual in Hindi) B. N. Upadhyaya. 1980. 40.00x (ISBN 0-317-57747-6, Pub. by Eastern Bk India). State Mutual Bk.

Uttar Pradesh Bhoomi Vidhi (U.P. Land Laws in Hindi) R. P. Singh. 350p. 1974. 41.00x (ISBN 0-317-57689-5, Pub. by Eastern Bk India). State Mutual Bk.

Uttar Pradesh Dookan aur Vanijya Adhisthan Adhiniyam, 1962 (U.P Shop & Commercial Extablishments Act in English) K. D. Srivastava. 410p. 1984. 150.00x (ISBN 0-317-57726-3, Pub. by Eastern Bk India). State Mutual Bk.

Uttar Pradesh in Statistics. Kripa Shankar. 1986. 24.00 (ISBN 0-317-56193-6, Pub. by Ashish India). South Asia Bks.

Uttar Pradesh Industrial Disputes Act, 1947. Eastern Book Company Staff. 1987. 40.00x (ISBN 0-317-57727-1, Pub. by Eastern Bk India). State Mutual Bk.

Uttar Pradesh Land Revenue Act, 1901. S. M. Husain. 243p. 1983. 75.00x (ISBN 0-317-54673-2, Pub. by Eastern Bk India). State Mutual Bk.

Uttar Pradesh Local Acts, 12 vols. S. M. Husain. 800p. 270.00x (ISBN 0-317-54670-8, Pub. by Eastern Bk India). State Mutual Bk.

Uttar Pradesh (Nirmanya-Karya Viniyman) Adhiniyam, 1958 & Uttar Pradesh Nagar Yojna aur Vikas Adhiniyam, 1973. Uma Shanakar. 386p. 1983. 120.00x (ISBN 0-317-57739-5, Pub. by Eastern Bk India). State Mutual Bk.

Uttar Pradesh Sahkari Samiti Adhinyam, 1965 (Uttar Pradesh Co-operative Societies Act, 1965 in Hindi) Mahavir Singh. 1980. 240.00x (ISBN 0-317-57684-4, Pub. by Eastern Bk India). State Mutual Bk.

Uttaratantra, or Ratnagotravibhaga: Sublime Science of the Great Vehicle to Salvation. Aryasanga Maitreya. Tr. by E. Obermiller from Tibetan. 225p. 1984. Repr. of 1931 ed. lib. bdg. 22.50x (ISBN 0-88181-001-0). Canon Pubns.

Utter Nonsense. Barney Saltzberg. (Paperbacks Ser.). (Illus.). 80p. (Orig.). 1980. pap. text ed. 3.95 (ISBN 0-07-054486-7). McGraw.

Utterly Gross Jokes. Julius Alvin. 1984. pap. 2.50 (ISBN 0-8217-1350-7). Zebra.

Uttermost Farthing. R. Austin Freeman. 1974. 8.50 (ISBN 0-685-41690-9). Bookfinger.

Utuado Ceremonial Park. Ricardo E. Alegria. (Puerto Rico Ser.). 1979. lib. bdg. 59.95 (ISBN 0-8490-3013-7). Gordon Pr.

Utwory Poetyckie: Poems. Czesaw Milosz. 1976. 12.00 (ISBN 0-930042-22-0). Mich Slavic Pubns.

Utz. Bruce Chatwin. 1989. 16.95 (ISBN 0-670-82497-6). Viking.

UV-A: Biological Effects of Ultraviolet Radiation: With Emphasis on Human Response tO Longwave Ultraviolet. John A. Parrish et al. LC 78-14968. (Illus.). 272p. 1978. 42.50x (ISBN 0-306-31121-6, Plenum Pr). Plenum Pub.

UV-A: Biological Effects of Ultraviolet Radiation with Emphasis on Human Responses to Longwave Ultraviolet. John A. Parrish et al. LC 78-14968. pap. 68.00 (ISBN 0-317-26187-8, 2052076). Bks Demand UMI.

UV & EB Curing Formulations for Printing Inks, Coatings & Paint. 2nd ed. Ed. by R. Holman & P. Oldring. (Illus.). 239p. 1988. 95.00x (ISBN 0-947798-02-1, Selective Industrial Training Associates Ltd London). Rsrch Bks CT.

UV & EV Curing Formulation for Printing Inks, Coatings & Paints. Ed. by Portcullis Press Ltd. Staff. 1985. 130.00x (Pub. by Portcullis Pr UK). State Mutual Bk.

UV Curing in Screen Printing for Printed Circuits & the Graphic Arts. S. Wentink & S. Koch. LC 80-80985. 1981. 92.00 (ISBN 0-936840-00-5). Tech Marketing.

UV Curing: Science & Technology. Ed. by S. Peter Pappas. LC 78-56293. (Illus.). 1978. perfect bdg. 95.00 (ISBN 0-936840-04-8). Tech Marketing.

UV Curing: Science & Technology, Vol. II. Ed. by S. Peter Pappas. 360p. 1985. text ed. 99.00 (ISBN 0-936840-08-0). Tech Marketing.

Uveitis: A Clinical Approach to Diagnosis & Management. 2nd ed. Ronald E. Smith & Robert A. Nozik. 300p. 1988. 65.00 (ISBN 0-683-07769-4). Williams & Wilkins.

Uveitis: A Clinical Approach to Diagnosis & Management. Ronald E. Smith & Robert M. Nozik. (Illus.). 232p. 1983. lib. bdg. 59.50 (ISBN 0-683-07768-6). Williams & Wilkins.

Uveitis: A Colour Manual of Diagnosis & Treatment. Jack J. Kanski. (Illus.). 192p. 1987. text ed. 59.95 (ISBN 0-407-01640-6). Butterworth.

Uveitis: Pathophysiology & Therapy Revses & Enlarged Edition. 2nd ed. Ellen Kraus-MacKiw & G. R. O'Connor. (Illus.). 245p. 1986. text ed. 54.50 (ISBN 0-86577-256-8). Thieme Med Pubs.

Uveitis Update: Proceedings of the International Symposium on Uveitis, 1st, Held in Hanasaari, Espoo, Finland, 16-19 May 1984. Ed. by K. M. Saari. (International Congress Ser.: No. 651). 554p. 1985. 155.25 (ISBN 0-444-80644-X, Excerpta Medica). Elsevier.

Uvetis: Fundamental & Practice. Nussenblatt. 1988. 48.00 (ISBN 0-8151-6457-2). Year Bk Med.

Uwe Johnson. Mark Boulby. LC 73-82315. (Literature and Life Ser.). 1974. 16.95x (ISBN 0-8044-2062-9). Ungar.

Uxpanapa: Agricultural Development in the Mexican Tropics. Peter T. Ewell & Thomas T. Poleman. LC 80-12208. (Pergamon Policy Studies). 220p. 1980. 41.00 (ISBN 0-08-025967-7). Pergamon.

Uyun Al-Inba' Fi Tabakat Al-Atibba' Ahmed I. Kasim. 902p. Repr. of 1884 ed. text ed. 165.60x (ISBN 0-576-03131-3, Pub. by Gregg Intl Pubs England). Gregg Intl.

Uzbek-English Dictionary. Natalie Waterson. (Uzbek & Eng.). 1980. 55.00x (ISBN 0-19-713597-8). Oxford U Pr.

Uzbek Newspaper Reader. Nicholas Poppe, Jr. LC 62-62831. (U & A Ser.: Vol. 10). 247p. 1962. spiral bound 7.50 (ISBN 0-317-55076-4). Res Ctr Lang Semiotic.

Uzbek Texts from Afghan Turkestan. Gunnar Jarring. 246p. 1938. pap. 72.00x (ISBN 0-317-68737-9, Pub. by Han-Shan Tang Ltd). State Mutual Bk.

Uzbekistan. (Let's Visit Places & Peoples - - Nations, Dependencies, & Sovereignties of the World Ser.). (Illus.). (gr. 5 up). 1988. 12.95. Chelsea Hse.

Uzbeks. Edward A. Allworth. Ed. by Wayne S. Vucinich. (Studies of Nationalities in the U. S. S. R.). 500p. 1988. 39.95 (ISBN 0-8179-8731-2); pap. 24.95 (ISBN 0-8179-8732-0). Hoover Inst Pr.

U2. Winston Brandt. 160p. (Orig.). 1986. pap. 2.95 (ISBN 0-345-32892-2). Ballantine.

U2. Philip Kamin. (Illus.). 32p. (gr. 3 up). 1985. pap. cancelled (ISBN 0-88188-385-9, 00183796). H Leonard Pub Corp.

U2: In the Name of Love: A History from Ireland's Hot Press Magazine. Ed. by Niall Stokes. 1986. pap. 12.95 (ISBN 0-517-56215-4, Harmony). Crown.

U2 Portfolio. (Illus.). 96p. (Orig.). 1988. pap. 17.95 (ISBN 0-7119-0762-5, 00308526). H Leonard Pub Corp.

U2: Rattle & Hum. Peter Williams & Steve Turner. (Illus.). 1988. pap. 9.95 (ISBN 0-517-57214-1, Harmony). Crown.

U2: Touch the Flame. Geoff Parkyn. (Illus.). 96p. 1988. pap. 12.95 (ISBN 0-399-51469-4, Perigee Bks). Putnam Pub Group.

V

V. A. C. Crispin. 1984. lib. bdg. 13.95 (ISBN 0-8398-2840-3, Gregg). G K Hall.

V. Thomas Pynchon. 1968. pap. 4.95 (ISBN 0-553-24686-0). Bantam.

V. Thomas Pynchon. LC 85-45222. 496p. 1986. pap. 8.95 (ISBN 0-06-091308-8, PL 1308, PL). Har-Row.

V & A Album Four. (Illus.). 400p. (Orig.). 1985. pap. 7.95 (ISBN 0-948107-16-2, Pub. by Victoria & Albert Mus UK). Faber & Faber.

V & A Album 2. (Illus.). 400p. (Orig.). 1984. pap. 7.95 (ISBN 0-946345-03-1, Pub. by Victoria & Albert Mus UK). Faber & Faber.

V & A Album 3: Annual. (Illus.). 400p. (Orig.). 1985. pap. 7.95 (ISBN 0-905209-99-0, Pub. by Victoria & Albert Mus UK). Faber & Faber.

V & A Alphabet Book. Rachel Barnes. (Illus.). 32p. (Orig.). pap. cancelled (ISBN 0-948107-10-3, Pub. by Victoria & Albert Mus UK). Faber & Faber.

V: Below the Threshold. Alan Wold. 256p. 1988. pap. 3.50 (ISBN 0-8125-5732-8). Tor Bks.

V-Bombers. Bob Downey. (Warbirds Illustrated Ser.: No. 35). (Illus.). 72p. (Orig.). 1985. pap. 9.95 (ISBN 0-85368-740-4, Pub. by Arms & Armour). Sterling.

V D I Steam Tables up to Eight Hundred Degrees Centigrade & 1000 at Kcal. at. 7th rev ed. E. Schmidt. (Illus.). 1968. 28.40 (ISBN 0-387-04372-1). Springer-Verlag.

V. D. Venereal Disease & What You Should Do About It. rev. ed. Eric W. Johnson. LC 78-8666. (Illus.). (YA) (gr. 5-12) 1978. 12.70i (ISBN 0-397-31811-1, Lipp Jr Bks). HarpJ.

V-Discs: First Supplement. Compiled by Richard S. Sears. LC 86-19529. (Discographies: No. 25). 300p. 1986. 50.95 (ISBN 0-313-25421-4, SDN/). Greenwood.

V: East Coast Crisis. A. C. Crispin & Howard Weinstein. 1984. lib. bdg. 12.95 (ISBN 0-8398-2841-1, Gregg). G K Hall.

V-Eight Affair: An Illustrated History of the Pre-War Ford V-8. Ray Miller & Glenn Embree. LC 70-174898. (Ford Road Ser: Vol. 3). (Illus.). 303p. 1972. 39.95 (ISBN 0-913056-02-2). Evergreen Pr.

V for Victor: A Novel. Mark Childress. LC 88-45435. 320p. 1989. 18.95 (ISBN 0-394-56871-0). Knopf.

V. I. Lenin: An Annotated Bibliography of English-Language Sources to 1980. David R. Egan & Melinda A. Egan. LC 82-659. 516p. 1982. 39.50 (ISBN 0-8108-1526-5). Scarecrow.

V. I. P. Address Book. Ed. by James M. Wiggins. LC 87-33322. 800p. 1988. lib. bdg. 84.95 (ISBN 0-938731-07-6). Assoc Media Cos.

V. I. P. Strategy: Leadership Skills for Exceptional Performance. Art McNeil & Jim Clemmer. 288p. 1988. 24.95 (ISBN 1-55013-080-3, Pub. by Key Porter Canada). U of Toronto Pr.

V. K. Wellington Koo: A Case Study of China's Diplomat & Diplomacy of Nationalism, 1912-1966. Pao-chin Chu. xiii, 213p. 1981. text ed. 28.50x (ISBN 962-201-236-1, Pub. by Chinese U HK). Coronet Bks.

V. K. Wellington Koo's Foreign Policy: Some Selected Documents. V. K. Wellington. Ed. by Wuncz King. LC 75-32324. (Studies in Chinese History & Civilization). 141p. 1977. Repr. of 1931 ed. 16.00 (ISBN 0-89093-071-6). U Pubns Amer.

V Krugu Druzei J Muz. L. V. Timofeev. 288p. (Rus.). 1983. 39.00x (ISBN 0-317-40882-8, Pub. by Collets (UK)). State Mutual Bk.

V...-Mail: Letters of a World War II Combat Medic. Keith Winston. Ed. by Sarah Winston. (Illus.). 256p. 1985. 14.95 (ISBN 0-912697-28-8). Algonquin Bks.

V Mire Molitvi. Protopresbyer Michael Pomazansky. 148p. 1957. pap. 5.00 (ISBN 0-317-29096-7). Holy Trinity.

V Mire Otechestvennoi Klassiki. Sbornik Statei. 464p. 1984. 49.00x (ISBN 0-317-40829-1, Pub. by Collets (UK)). State Mutual Bk.

V. N. The Life & Art of Vladimir Nabokov. Andrew Field. (Illus.). 400p. 1986. 19.95 (ISBN 0-517-56113-1). Crown.

V O Science & Literature in the Nineteenth Century. J. A. Chapple. (Context & Commentary Ser.). (Illus.). 212p. 1986. text ed. 39.95 (ISBN 0-333-37586-6, Pub. by Macmillan UK); pap. text ed. 9.95 (ISBN 0-333-37587-4). Humanities.

V: Path to Conquest. Howard Weinstein. 288p. 1987. pap. 2.95 (ISBN 0-8125-5725-5). Tor Bks.

V. S. Naipaul. Peter Hughes. (Contemporary Writers Ser.). 96p. (Orig.). 1988. pap. text ed. 8.95 (ISBN 0-415-00654-6, Pub. by Routledge UK). Routledge Chapman & Hall.

V. S. Naipaul: A Materialist Reading. Selwyn R. Cudjoe. LC 87-35768. 304p. (Orig.). 1988. 32.50x (ISBN 0-87023-619-9); pap. text ed. 13.95x (ISBN 0-87023-620-2). U of Mass Pr.

V. S. Naipaul: A Study in Expatriate Sensibility. Sudha Rai. (Indian Writers Ser.: Vol. XIX). 136p. 1982. 12.00 (ISBN 0-86578-143-5). Ind-US Inc.

V. Sackville-West's Garden Book. Vita Sackville-West. LC 68-8261. (Illus.). 256p. 1983. pap. 10.95 (ISBN 0-689-70647-2, 295). Atheneum.

V-STOL: An Update & Overview. 1984. 30.00 (ISBN 0-89883-812-6, SP591). Soc Auto Engineers.

V-STOL: Key to Survival. Roy Braybrook. (Illus.). 224p. 1988. 39.95 (ISBN 0-85045-767-X, Pub. by Osprey England). Motorbooks Intl.

V-STOL-STOVL. 1986. 25.00 (ISBN 0-89883-951-3, SP680). Soc Auto Engineers.

V: Symphony of Terror. S. P. Somtow. 256p. 1988. pap. 3.50 (ISBN 0-8125-5482-5, Dist. by St Martin's Pr & Warner Pub Servs). Tor Bks.

V Teni Bol'Shogo Doma. Kirill Kostsinskii, pseud. Ed. by Gessen Elena. LC 87-22790. (Illus.). 135p. (Rus.). 1988. pap. 8.50 (ISBN 0-938920-91-X). Hermitage.

V: The Oregon Invasion. Jayne Tannhill. 1988. pap. 3.50 (ISBN 0-8125-5729-8, Dist. by St Martin's Pr & Warner Pub). Tor Bks.

V-Time: A New Way to Look. 76p. 1985. 25.00 (ISBN 0-940173-02-6). New Ways Work.

V: To Conquer the Throne. Tim Sullivan. 1987. pap. 2.95 (ISBN 0-8125-5727-1). Tor Bks.

V-Twin Thunder. Mike Arman & Carl McClanahan. (Illus.). 56p. (Orig.). 1984. pap. 9.00 (ISBN 0-933078-12-9). M Arman.

V Venke Iz Voska; Dirizhabl' Neizvestnogo Napravleniia. 2nd ed. Boris I. Poplavskii. Ed. by Simon Karlinsky. (Modern Russian Literature & Culture Studies & Texts: Vol. 9). (Illus.). 123p. 1981. pap. 7.50 (ISBN 0-933884-19-2). Berkeley Slavic.

V Was for Victory: Politics & American Culture During World War II. John M. Blum. LC 77-3426. 372p. 1977. pap. 7.95 (ISBN 0-15-693628-3, Harv). HarBraceJ.

V Zashchitu Pravoslavnoj Vjeri ot Sektantov. Michael Polsky. 1950. pap. 1.00 (ISBN 0-317-30261-2). Holy Trinity.

V-12 Program. James G. Schneider. (Education for Victory in World War II). (Illus.). 544p. 1987. text ed. 29.95 (ISBN 0-317-57602-X). HM.

V 29 den' mesiatsa avgusta slovo Ioanna Zlatoustogo na useknovenie glavy see Sermon on the Decollation of St. John the Baptist, & on Herodias, & on Good & Evil Women.

V-3. Ib Melchior. 352p. 1985. 16.95 (ISBN 0-396-08483-4). Dodd.

V-3. Ib Melchior. 400p. Date not set. pap. 3.95 (ISBN 0-441-84809-5, Pub. by Charter Bks). Ace Bks.

Va de Cuento. R. Charran & B. Maharaj. (Illus.). 1977. pap. text ed. 5.25 (ISBN 0-582-76616-8). Longman.

Va-Et-Vient see Comedies et Actes Divers.

Vagrant Memories. William Winter. LC 70-121514. (Essay Index Reprint Ser). 1915. 33.00 (ISBN 0-8369-1817-7). Ayer Co Pubs.

Vagrant Mood. W. Somerset Maugham. LC 71-86076. (Essay & General Literature Index Reprint Ser). 1969. Repr. of 1953 ed. 25.00x (ISBN 0-8046-0573-4, Pub by Kennikat). Assoc Faculty Pr.

Vagrant Mood: Six Essays. W. Somerset Maugham. LC 75-25378. (Works of W. Somerset Maugham Ser.). 1977. Repr. of 1953 ed. 20.00x (ISBN 0-405-07831-5). Ayer Co Pubs.

Vagrant Peasant: Agrarian Distress & Desertion in Bengal 1770-1830. C. N. Chowdhury-Zilly. xv, 196p. (Orig.). 1982. pap. text ed. 30.00x (ISBN 3-515-03855-8). Coronet Bks.

Vague Vacation. Joan M. Grant. 14.00 (ISBN 0-405-11793-0). Ayer Co Pubs.

Vahweh vs. Baal. Norman C. Habel. 128p. 1964. write for info. Concordia Schl Grad Studies.

Vail. Trevor Hoyle. (Orig.). 1984. pap. 7.95 (ISBN 0-7145-4055-2). Riverrun NY.

Vail Hiker & Ski Touring Guide. Mary E. Gilliland. (Illus.). 100p. (Orig.). 1988. pap. text ed. 9.95 (ISBN 0-9603624-6-0). Alpenrose Pr.

Vail Peak Day Survey. C. R. Goeldner & Jack Harrington. 130p. 25.00 (ISBN 0-686-64155-8). U CO Busn Res Div.

Vail Site: A Palaeo-Indian Encampment in Maine. Richard M. Gramly. LC 83-127191. (Natural Sciences Ser.: Vol. 30). (Illus.). 169p. (Orig.). 1982. pap. 12.95 (ISBN 0-944032-38-9). Buffalo SNS.

Vail Skier: (1975-76 Season) C. R. Goeldner et al. 121p. 1976. 10.00 (ISBN 0-686-64158-2). U CO Busn Res Div.

Vail Skier: (1976-77 Season) C. R. Goeldner & Nicola Phillips. 80p. 1977. 10.00 (ISBN 0-686-64157-4). U CO Busn Res Div.

Vail Skier: (1977-78 Season) C. R. Goeldner. 106p. 1978. 15.00 (ISBN 0-686-64156-6). U CO Busn Res Div.

Vailala Madness & Other Essays. Francis E. Williams. Ed. by Erik Schwimmer. LC 76-41133. 450p. 1977. text ed. 17.50x (ISBN 0-8248-0519-4). UH Pr.

Vailala Madness & the Destruction of Native Ceremonies in the Gulf Division. Francis E. Williams. LC 75-35166. (Territory of Papua. Anthropological Report: No. 4). Repr. of 1923 ed. 20.00 (ISBN 0-404-14180-3). AMS Pr.

Vailima Letters, 2 vols. Robert Louis Stevenson. LC 76-115278. 1983. Repr. of 1894 ed. Set. lib. bdg. 17.00x (ISBN 0-403-00283-4). Scholarly.

Vailima Letters: Being Correspondence Addressed to Sidney Colvin, November 1890-October 1894, 2 vols. Robert Louis Stevenson. 1970. Repr. of 1895 ed. Vol. 2. lib. bdg. 18.75 (ISBN 0-8371-1626-0, STVN). Greenwood.

Vain Endeavor: Robert Lansing's Attempts to End the American-Japanese Rivalry. Burton F. Beers. LC 61-16907. Repr. of 1962 ed. 54.80 (ISBN 0-8357-9119-X, 2017884). Bks Demand UMI.

Vain Glory. Jan Reid. 375p. 1986. 15.95 (ISBN 0-940672-37-5). Shearer Pub.

Vain Obligations. Katharine F. Gerould. 324p. 1980. Repr. of 1915 ed. lib. bdg. 25.00 (ISBN 0-89987-306-5). Century Bookbindery.

Vain Siecle Guerpir: A Literary Approach to Sainthood through Old French Hagiography of the Twelfth Century. Phyllis Johnson & Brigitte Cazelles. (Studies in the Romance Languages & Literatures: No.205). 320p. 1979. pap. 22.50x (ISBN 0-8078-9205-X). U of NC Pr.

Vairagya-Satakam: The Hundred Verses on Renunciation. Bhartrihari. (Sanskrit & Eng.). pap. 1.00 (ISBN 0-87481-070-1). Vedanta Pr.

Vaisesika Sutras of Kanada: With Commentary of Sankara Misra & Extracts from Gloss, of Jayanarayana & Notes from Commentary of Candrakanta. Kanada. Tr. & intro. by Nandalal Sinha. Incl. Notes from the Commentary of Chandrakanta. LC 73-3791. (Sacred Books of the Hindus: No. 6). 379p. Repr. of 1911 ed. 42.50 (ISBN 0-404-57806-3). AMS Pr.

Vaisesika Sutras of Kanada: With Commentary of Sankara Misra & Extracts from Gloss. of Jayanarayana & Notes from Commentary of Candrakanta. Tr. by Nandalal Sinha. 379p. 1986. Repr. 38.00 (ISBN 0-317-69977-6). Orient Bk Dist.

Vaisnava Behavior: Twenty-Six Qualities of a Devotee. Satsvarupa Das Goswami. Ed. by Mandalesvara Dasa. 201p. 1984. text ed. 10.95 (ISBN 0-911233-18-0). Gita Nagari.

Vaisnava Iconography in the Tamil Country. A. Champakalakshmi. 135p. 1981. text ed. 50.00x (ISBN 0-86131-216-3, Pub. by Orient Longman Ltd India). Apt Bks.

Vaisnava Iconography in the Tamil Country. R. Champakalakshmi. cancelled (ISBN 0-686-81463-0, Orient Longman). South Asia Bks.

Vaisnavism & Society in Northern India. Urmila Bhagowalia. 1980. 22.00x (ISBN 0-8364-0664-8, Pub. by Intellectual India). South Asia Bks.

Vaisnavism in Indian Arts & Culture. Ed. by R. Parimoo. (Illus.). 462p. 95.00x (ISBN 81-85016-18-6). Orient Bk Dist.

Vaisnavism Saivism & Minor Religious Systems. R. G. Bhandarkar. 238p. 1986. Repr. 14.00X (ISBN 0-8364-1704-6, Pub. by Minerva India). South Asia Bks.

Vaiyakarana Siddhanta Kaumudi of Bhattoji Diksita, Vol. I. P. V. Sastry. 1974. 17.50. Orient Bk Dist.

Vak: An Anthology of Australian, European & Indian Verse. Ed. by Sibnarayan Ray. 14.00 (ISBN 0-89253-623-3); pap. 8.00 (ISBN 0-86578-108-7). Ind-US Inc.

Vakataka - Gupta Age Circa 200-550 A.D. R. C. Majumdar & A. S. Altekar. 515p. 1986. 17.50 (ISBN 81-208-0026-5, Pub. by Motilal Banarsidass India); pap. 12.50 (ISBN 81-208-0043-5). South Asia Bks.

Vakyapadiya-Chapter Two. Tr. by K. A. Iyer. 1977. 11.25 (ISBN 0-8426-1032-4). Orient Bk Dist.

Vakyapadiya of Bharthari-Chapter Three. K. A. Iyer. 1974. 22.00 (ISBN 0-8426-0617-3). Orient Bk Dist.

Vakyavritti & Atmajnanopadeshavidhi. Shankara. (Sanskrit & Eng). pap. 1.95 (ISBN 0-87481-424-3). Vedanta Pr.

Val Verde. Judith Polley. 1974. pap. 6.95 (ISBN 0-440-06092-3). Delacorte.

Val Verde Winery. Robert C. Overfelt. (Southwestern Studies: No. 75). 76p. 1985. pap. 5.00 (ISBN 0-87404-151-1). Tex Western.

Valachi Papers. Date not set. pap. 3.95 (ISBN 0-671-63173-X). PB.

Valazquez: Painter & Courier. Jonathan Brown. LC 85-14234. 336p. 1988. Repr. of 1986 ed. 35.00 (ISBN 0-300-03894-1). Yale U Pr.

Valdepenas. Richard Lortz. LC 79-66114. 224p. 1984. pap. 15.95 (ISBN 0-933256-06-X); pap. 7.95 (ISBN 0-933256-07-8); rack 5.95 (ISBN 0-933256-49-3). Second Chance.

Valdes Leal, Spanish Baroque Painter. Elizabeth Du Gue Trapier. (Illus.). 1960. 10.00 (ISBN 0-87535-112-3). Hispanic Soc.

Valdes Leal: Spanish Baroque Painter. Elizabeth Trapier. (Illus.). 232p. 1960. 10.00 (ISBN 0-317-00607-X, Pub. by Hispanic Soc). Interbk Inc.

Valdes's Two Catechisms: The Dialogue on Christian Doctrine & the Christian Instruction for Children. Ed. by Jose Nieto. Tr. by William B. Jones & Carol D. Jones. (Illus.). 200p. 1981. 16.50x (ISBN 0-87291-151-9). Coronado Pr.

Valdez Creek Mining District Alaska. Clyde Ross. 56p. pap. 4.95 (ISBN 0-8466-0107-9, S107). Shorey.

Valdez Is Coming. Elmore Leonard. 144p. 1981. pap. 2.75 (ISBN 0-553-26304-8). Bantam.

Valdez Marriage. Violet Winspear. (Nightingale Ser.). 1985. pap. 9.95 (ISBN 0-8161-3856-7, Large Print Bks). G K Hall.

Valdika Mantras with Transliteration & Translation. Uma A. Saini. LC 85-52267. 288p. (Sanskrit.). 1986. text ed. 19.00 (ISBN 0-9616357-0-3). U & K Pub.

Vale of Love. Jean Howell. 400p. (Orig.). 1986. pap. 3.95 (ISBN 0-8439-2404-7, Leisure Bks). Leisure NY.

Vale of the Vole. Piers Anthony. 336p. 1988. pap. 3.95 (ISBN 0-380-75287-5). Avon.

Vale-Royall of England: Or, the County Palatine of Chester Illustrated. Daniel King. (Printed Sources of Western Art Ser.). (Illus.). 354p. 1981. pap. 60.00 slipcase (ISBN 0-915346-65-6). A Wofsy Fine Arts.

Valediction. Robert B. Parker. 1986. pap. 3.95 (ISBN 0-440-19246-3). Dell.

Valedictory Verses. A. G. Prys-Jones. 56p. 1985. 19.00x (ISBN 0-85088-840-9, Pub. by Gomer Pr). State Mutual Bk.

Valence Fluctuations. Ed. by E. Muller-Hartmann & B. Roden. 620p. 1986. 139.50 (ISBN 0-444-87000-8, North-Holland). Elsevier.

Valence Fluctuations in Solids: Proceedings of the International Conference at Santa Barbara, California, Jan. 27-30, 1981. Ed. by L. M. Falicov et al. 466p. 1981. 116.00 (ISBN 0-444-86204-8, North-Holland). Elsevier.

Valence Instabilities: Proceedings of the International Conference on Valence Instabilities, Zurich, Switzerland, April, 1982. Ed. by P. Wachter & H. Boppart. 598p. 1982. 66.00 (North Holland). Elsevier.

Valence Semantic Case & Grammatical Relations. Ed. by Werner Abraham. (Studies in Language Companion Ser.: No. 1). xiv, 729p. 1978. 60.00x (ISBN 90-272096-2-6). Benjamins North Am.

Valence Theory. 2nd ed. John N. Murrell et al. LC 70-129161. pap. 111.00 (2026688). Bks Demand UMI.

Valency. 2nd. ed. M. F. O'Dwyer et al. (Heidelberg Science Library). (Illus.). xii, 252p. 1985. pap. 19.50 (ISBN 0-387-90268-6). Springer-Verlag.

Valency see Physical Chemistry: An Advanced Treatise in Eleven Volumes.

Valency & Molecular Structure. 4th ed. E. Cartnell & G. W. A. Fowles. 1977. 22.95 (ISBN 0-408-70809-3). Butterworth.

Valency & the English Verb. D. J. Allerton. 1983. 42.50 (ISBN 0-12-052980-7). Acad Pr.

Valenge Women: The Social & Economic Life of the Valenge Women of Portuguese East Africa. new ed. E. Dora Earthy. (Illus.). 251p. 1968. 28.50x (ISBN 0-7146-1660-5, F Cass Co). Biblio Dist.

Valentin Aleksandrovich Serov: His Life & Work 1865-1911. Igor Grabar. (Illus.). 548p. 1980. 347.00x (ISBN 0-569-08673-6, Pub. by Collets (UK)). State Mutual Bk.

Valentin et Orson. (EETS, OS: No. 204). Repr. of 1937 ed. 55.00 (ISBN 0-527-00204-6). Kraus Repr.

Valentin Rasputin: Essays. N. Kotenko. 216p. 1988. pap. 3.95 (ISBN 0-8285-3589-2, Pub. by Raduga Pubs USSR). Imported Pubns.

Valentin Serov: Paintings, Graphic Works, Stage Designs. Dmitry Sarabyanov & Grigory Arbuzo. LC 80-68475. (Illus.). 328p. 1983. 45.00 (ISBN 0-8109-1605-3). Abrams.

Valentina. Fern Michaels. 1983. pap. 2.95 (ISBN 0-345-31126-4). Ballantine.

Valentina: Soul in Sapphire. Joseph H. Delaney & Marc Stiegler. 320p. 1984. pap. 3.50 (ISBN 0-671-55916-8, Pub. by Baen Bks). PB.

Valentine. George Sand. Tr. by George B. Ives from Fr. LC 77-28026. 336p. 1978. pap. 8.95 (ISBN 0-915864-59-2). Academy Chi Pubs.

Valentine. facsimile ed. Georges Sand. 363p. 1976. 37.50 (ISBN 0-686-54956-2). French & Eur.

Valentine Activity Book. Sarah S. Dietz & David Brokaw. (Stick-Out-Your-Neck Ser.). (Illus.). 32p. (gr. 4 up). 1984. pap. 1.98 (ISBN 0-88724-065-8, CD-8045). Carson-Dellos.

Valentine & Orson, a Study in Late Medieval Romance. Arthur Dickson. LC 75-153315. Repr. of 1929 ed. 22.50 (ISBN 0-404-02128-X). AMS Pr.

Valentine Bakfark: Lutenist from Transylvania. Istvan Homolya. (Illus.). 228p. 1982. 14.95x (ISBN 963-13-1802-8, Pub. by Corvina Kiado Hungary). Intl Spec Bk.

Valentine Bears. Eve Bunting. (Illus.). 32p. (gr. 3). 1983. 12.95 (ISBN 0-89919-138-X, Clarion). HM.

Valentine Bears. Eve Bunting. LC 82-9577. (Illus.). 32p. (ps-3). 1985. pap. 4.95 (ISBN 0-89919-313-7, Clarion). HM.

Valentine Box. Marjorie Thayer. LC 76-46543. (Holiday Play Books). (Illus.). 32p. (gr. k-4). 1977. PLB 13.27 (ISBN 0-516-08746-0, Golden Gate). Childrens.

Valentine Day Fun Book. Patti Carson & Janet Dellosa. (Stick-Out-Your-Neck Ser.). (Illus.). 32p. (ps-1). 1982. pap. 1.59 (ISBN 0-88724-054-2, CD-8009). Carson-Dellos.

Valentine Fantasy. Carolyn Haywood. LC 75-23083. (Illus.). 32p. (gr. k-3). 1976. PLB 11.88 (ISBN 0-688-32055-4). Morrow.

Valentine-February Primary Reading & Art Activities. Patti Carson & Janet Dellosa. (Stick-Out-Your-Neck Ser.). (Illus.). 32p. (gr. 1-3). 1984. pap. 1.98 (ISBN 0-88724-026-7, CD-8041). Carson-Dellos.

Valentine for a Dragon. Shirley R. Murphy. LC 83-17911. (Illus.). 48p. (gr. k-3). 1985. 11.95 (ISBN 0-689-31016-1, Atheneum Childrens Bks). Macmillan.

Valentine for Cousin Archie. Barbara Williams. LC 80-181. (Illus.). 32p. (gr. k-3). 1981. 8.95 (ISBN 0-525-41930-6). Dutton.

Valentine for Fuzzboom. True Kelley. LC 80-24284. (Illus.). 24p. (gr. k-3). 1981. PLB 5.95 (ISBN 0-395-30446-6); pap. 1.95 (ISBN 0-395-31888-2). HM.

Valentine for Noel. Emmett Williams. LC 73-78692. 1973. pap. 15.00 (ISBN 0-87110-107-6). Ultramarine Pub.

Valentine Foxes. Clyde Watson & Wendy Watson. 1988. price not set. Orchard Bks Watts.

Valentine Friends. Ann Schweninger. LC 87-22326. 32p. (ps-1). 1988. 9.95 (ISBN 0-670-81448-2). Viking.

Valentine Fun. Judith H. Corwin. LC 82-6047. (Messner Holiday Library). (Illus.). 64p. (gr. 3 up). 1982. PLB 10.29 (ISBN 0-671-45945-7); pap. 5.95 (ISBN 0-671-49755-3). Messner.

Valentine Generation & Other Stories see Longman Structural Readers.

Valentine Hill: Sparkplug of Early New England. Jean A. Sargent. (Illus.). 150p. (Orig.). 1981. pap. text ed. 18.00 (ISBN 0-9611502-1-1). J A Sargent.

Valentine Ideals '88. 1988. pap. 3.95 (ISBN 0-8249-1059-1). Ideals.

Valentine M'Clutchy, the Irish Agent: The Chronicles of Castle Cumber Property, with the Pious Aspirations of Solomon M'Slime, 3 vols. in 2. William Carleton. LC 79-8247. Repr. of 1845 ed. 84.50 set (ISBN 0-404-61807-3). AMS Pr.

Valentine Magic. James W. Baker. (Holiday Magic Ser.). (Illus.). 48p. (gr. 2-5). 1988. lib. bdg. 6.95 (ISBN 0-8225-2229-2). Lerner Pubns.

Valentine Mystery. Joan L. Nixon. Ed. by Kathleen Tucker. LC 79-7055. (First Read-Alone Mysteries Ser.). (Illus.). (gr. 1-3). 1979. PLB 7.95 (ISBN 0-8075-8450-9). A Whitman.

Valentine Poems. Myra C. Livingston. LC 85-31723. (Illus.). 32p. (gr. k-3). 1987. reinforced bdg. 12.95 (ISBN 0-8234-0587-7). Holiday.

Valentine Pontifex. Robert Silverberg. (Majipoor Trilogy Ser.: No. 3). 384p. (Orig.). Date not set. pap. 3.95 (ISBN 0-553-24494-9, Spectra). Bantam.

Valentine Preschool-K Practice. Patti Carson & Janet Dellosa. (Stick-Out-Your-Neck Ser.). (Illus.). 32p. (ps-k). 1984. pap. 1.98 (ISBN 0-88724-018-6, CD-8033). Carson-Dellos.

Valentine Rosey. Sheila Greenwald. (gr. k-6). 1986. pap. 2.50 (ISBN 0-440-49203-3, YB). Dell.

Valentine Rosy. Sheila Greenwald. LC 84-9694. (Illus.). 89p. (gr. 4 up). 1984. PLB 11.95 (ISBN 0-316-32708-5, Joy St Bks). Little.

Valentine Rosy. Sheila Greenwald. (gr. 3-7). 1986. pap. 2.50 (ISBN 0-317-43487-X, YB). Dell.

Valentine Star. Patricia R. Giff. (Kids of the Polk Street School Ser.: No. 6). (Illus.). 80p. (Orig.). (gr. k-6). 1985. pap. 2.50 (ISBN 0-440-49204-1, YB). Dell.

Valentine Star. Patricia R. Giff. (Kids of the Polk Street School Ser.). (Illus.). (ps-2). 1986. pap. 8.95 (ISBN 0-385-29497-2). Delacorte.

Valentine Star see Kids of the Polk Street School.

Valentines. Rod McKuen. LC 84-42578. 176p. 1986. 9.95 (ISBN 0-06-015501-9, HarpT). Har-Row.

Valentine's Day. Jayne Bauling. (Harlequin Presents Ser.). 192p. 1984. pap. 1.95 (ISBN 0-373-10663-7). Harlequin Bks.

Valentine's Day. Judy Beach & Kathleen Spencer. (Teachers' Holiday Helpers Ser.). (gr. 1-3). 1987. pap. 4.95 (ISBN 0-8224-6774-7). D S Lake Pubs.

Valentine's Day. Fern G. Brown. (First Bks.). (Illus.). 72p. (gr. 4 up). 1983. PLB 10.40 (ISBN 0-531-04533-1). Watts.

Valentine's Day. Gail Gibbons. LC 85-916. (Illus.). 32p. (ps-3). 1986. reinforced bdg. 12.95 (ISBN 0-8234-0572-9). Holiday.

Valentine's Day. Elizabeth Guilfoile. LC 65-10086. (Holiday Bks.). (Illus.). (gr. 2-5). 1965. PLB 7.56 (ISBN 0-8116-6556-9). Garrard.

Valentine's Day. Joyce K. Kessel. LC 81-3842. (Carolrhoda on My Own Bks.). (Illus.). 48p. (gr. k-3). 1981. PLB 8.95 (ISBN 0-87614-166-1, AACRZ). Carolrhoda Bks.

Valentine's Day. Nancy Reese. Ed. by Alton Jordan. (ARO Holidays Ser.). (Illus.). (gr. k-3). 1977. PLB 3.95 (ISBN 0-89868-029-8, Read Res); pap. text ed. 1.75 (ISBN 0-89868-062-X). ARO Pub.

Valentine's Day Grump. Rose Greydanus. LC 81-4712. (Illus.). 32p. (gr. k-2). 1981. PLB 9.89 (ISBN 0-89375-515-X); pap. text ed. 2.95 (ISBN 0-89375-516-8). Troll Assocs.

Valentine's Day in Strawberryland see Strawberry Shortcake's Holiday Library.

Valentine's Day: Things to Make & Do. Robyn Supraner. LC 80-23780. (Illus.). 48p. (gr. 1-5). 1981. PLB 9.49 (ISBN 0-89375-424-2); pap. 1.95 (ISBN 0-89375-425-0). Troll Assocs.

Valentine's Manuals: A General Index to the Manuals of the Corporation of the City of New York, 1841-1870. Hoe R. Lawrence & Otto Hufeland. LC 81-6437. 1981. 15.00 (ISBN 0-916346-42-0). Harbor Hill Bks.

Valentines to Make Yourself. Bill Cummings. (Illus.). 24p. (gr. 4-6). 1985. pap. 3.95 (ISBN 0-590-33675-4). Scholastic Inc.

Valentino. Andre L. Talley. (Illus.). 208p. 150.00 (ISBN 0-8478-5417-5). Rizzoli Intl.

Valentino & Sagittarius: Two Novellas. Natalia Ginzburg. Tr. by Avril Bardoni from Ital. LC 87-32349. 136p. 1988. 17.95 (ISBN 0-8050-0683-4). Seaver Bks.

Valentino & the Great Italians. Anthony Valerio. LC 86-7564. 248p. 1986. 17.95 (ISBN 0-88191-041-4). Freundlich.

Valentino: The Love God. Noel Botham & Peter Donnelly. 248p. 1976. 12.95 (ISBN 0-903925-49-4). Brown Bk.

Valentino's Hair: Poems by Yvonne Sapia. Yvonne Sapia. (Samuel French Morse Poetry Prize Ser.). 80p. (Orig.). 1987. pap. text ed. 7.95x (ISBN 1-55553-017-6). NE U Pr.

Valenz und Kongruenzbeziehungen. Monika Weissgerber. (European University Studies: No. 1, Vol. 652). 226p. (Ger.). 1983. 31.05 (ISBN 3-8204-7583-4). P Lang Pubs.

Valera: Pepita Jimenez. James Whiston. (Critical Guides to Spanish Texts Ser.: No. 22). 81p. (Orig.). 1977. pap. 4.95 (ISBN 0-7293-0051-X, Pub. by Grant & Cutler). Longwood Pub Group.

Valerian Persecution: A Study of the Relations Between Church & State in the Third Century A. D. Patrick J. Healy. LC 76-185943. xv, 285p. 1972. Repr. of 1905 ed. 21.00 (ISBN 0-8337-4169-1). B Franklin.

Valerie. Valerie Chronis. pap. 3.00 (ISBN 0-938078-11-9). Anhinga Pr.

Valerie & Mister Funderful. Harry Pearlman. (Illus.). 20p. (Orig.). (gr. 3-10). 1984. pap. 2.95 (ISBN 0-930451-00-7). Fundation.

Valerio Dorico: Music Printer in Sixteenth-Century Rome. Suzanne G. Cusick. LC 81-4745. (Studies in Musicology: No. 43). (Illus.). pap. 85.60 (2070262). Bks Demand UMI.

Valery Bryusov & the Riddle of Russian Decadence. Joan D. Grossman. LC 83-14470. 1985. 42.00x (ISBN 0-520-05141-6). U of Cal Pr.

Valery: Jeune Poete. Charles G. Whiting. (Yale Romantic Studies). 1960. pap. 39.50x (ISBN 0-685-69883-1). Elliots Bks.

Valery Larbaud et l'Italie. Ruggiero. 26.25 (ISBN 0-685-34263-8). French & Eur.

Valet's Tragedy & Other Studies. Andrew Lang. LC 75-112939. (Illus.). Repr. of 1903 ed. 11.00 (ISBN 0-404-03865-4). AMS Pr.

Valeur du Sol Urbain et la Propriete Fonciere: Le Marche Des Terrains a Paris. Jean-Jacques Granelle. (Recherche Urbain: No. 12). (Illus.). 240p. (Fr.). 1976. pap. text ed. 20.80x (ISBN 90-2797-892-1). Mouton.

Valeur et Socialisme see Cahiers de l'Institut de Science Economique Appliquee.

Valga Krusa. Charles Potts. LC 77-76164. 1977. pap. 7.77 (ISBN 0-915214-19-9). Litmus.

Valleys. Ed. by John Davies & Mike Jenkins. (Illus.). 141p. 1984. pap. 9.95 (ISBN 0-907476-31-7). Dufour.
Valleys of the Assassins. rev. ed. Freya Stark. (Illus.). 1972. 28.50 (ISBN 0-7195-2429-6). Transatl Arts.
Valleys of the Assassins. Freya Stark. LC 83-639. (Library of Travel Classics). (Illus.). 384p. 1983. 9.95 (ISBN 0-87477-261-3). J P Tarcher.
Valleys of Tirol: Their Traditions & Customs, & How to Visit Them. Rachel H. Busk. LC 77-87725. 488p. Repr. of 1874 ed. 43.50 (ISBN 0-404-16513-3). AMS Pr.
Valliere's Natural Cycles Almanac 1984. James T. Valliere et al. (Illus.). 44p. (Orig.). 1983. pap. 7.95 (ISBN 0-913637-02-5). Astrolabe SW.
Valliere's Natural Cycles Almanac 1985. James T. Valliere et al. (Illus.). 44p. (Orig.). 1984. pap. 7.95 (ISBN 0-913637-19-X). Astrolabe SW.
Valliere's Natural Cycles Almanac 1986. James T. Valliere et al. (Illus.). 44p. (Orig.). 1985. pap. 8.95 (ISBN 0-87199-038-5). Astrolabe SW.
Valliere's Natural Cycles Almanac 1987. James T. Valliere et al. (Illus.). 48p. (Orig.). pap. 8.95 (ISBN 0-87199-060-1). Astrolabe SW.
Valliere's Natural Cycles Almanac 1988. James T. Valliere et al. (Illus.). 48p. pap. 9.95 (ISBN 0-87199-062-8). Astrolabe SW.
Valliere's Natural Cycles Almanac, 1989. James T. Valliere et al. (Illus.). 48p. (Orig.). Date not set. pap. 9.95 (ISBN 0-87199-078-4). Astrolabe SW.
Vallingsby & Farsta - from Idea to Reality: The New Community Development Process in Stockholm. David Pass. 200p. 1973. 22.50x (ISBN 0-262-16034-X). MIT Pr.
Valmiki Ramayanan. V. Sitaramiah. 1982. Repr. 7.00x (ISBN 0-317-47015-9, Pub. by National Sahitya Akademi). South Asia Bks.
Valmouth. Ronald Firbank. 127p. 1977. 20.00 (ISBN 0-7156-1093-7, Pub. by Duckworth London); pap. 6.75 (ISBN 0-7156-1097-X). Longwood Pub Group.
Valmouth see Five Novels.
Valois Burgundy. Richard Vaughan. LC 74-34019. (Illus.). ix, 254p. (Orig.). 1975. 25.00 (ISBN 0-208-01511-6, Archon). Shoe String.
Valois Tapestries. Frances A. Yates. (Illus.). 232p. 1975. 25.00 (ISBN 0-7100-8244-4). Routledge Chapman & Hall.
Valor at Leyte. Lawrence Cortesi. (Orig.). 1983. pap. 3.25 (ISBN 0-8217-1213-6). Zebra.
Valor at Okinawa. Lawrence Cortesi. (Orig.). 1981. pap. 2.95 (ISBN 0-89083-904-2). Zebra.
Valor at Samar. Lawrence Cortesi. (World at War Ser.: No. 26). (YA) (gr. 7 up). 1981. pap. 2.75 (ISBN 0-89083-742-2). Zebra.
Valor at Samar. Lawrence Cortesi. (Orig.). 1983. pap. 2.75 (ISBN 0-8217-1226-8). Zebra.
Valor in the Bulge. Lawrence Cortesi. 288p. 1986. pap. 3.25 (ISBN 0-8217-1854-1). Zebra.
Valor in the Sky. Lawrence Cortesi. 1985. pap. 3.50 (ISBN 0-8217-1578-X). Zebra.
Valores de Puerto Rico: Spanish Text. Vincente Polanco. LC 74-14242. (Puerto Rican Experience Ser.). 178p. 1975. Repr. 14.00x (ISBN 0-405-06229-X). Ayer Co Pubs.
Valoric Fire & a Working Plan for Individual Sovereignty. The Valorian Society. LC 83-51820. 128p. (Orig.). 1984. pap. 5.00 (ISBN 0-914752-18-9). Sovereign Pr.
Valour Fore & Aft. Hope S. Rider. LC 76-17516. (Illus.). 280p. 1987. 17.00 (ISBN 0-934943-12-5); pap. 12.50 (ISBN 0-934943-11-7). Thirteen Colonies Pr.
Valperga: Or, the Life & Adventures of Castruccio, Prince of Lucca, 3 vols. in 1. Mary Wollstonecraft Shelley. LC 79-8199. Repr. of 1823 ed. 44.50 (ISBN 0-404-62122-8). AMS Pr.
Valse des Toreadors see Pieces Grincantes.
Valse Zilvermerken in Nederland. Citroen. Date not set. 21.50 (ISBN 0-686-94103-9). Elsevier.
Valserine & Other Stories. facsimile ed. Marguerite Audoux. LC 73-110178. (Short Story Index Reprint Ser.). 1912. 18.00 (ISBN 0-8369-3329-X). Ayer Co Pubs.
Valtat: The Complete Paintings. Jean Valtat. (Illus.). 367p. (Fr.). 1977. 525.00 (ISBN 1-55660-014-3). A Wofsy Fine Arts.
Valuable Nail: The Selected Poems of Gunter Eich. Gunter Eich. Tr. by David Walker et al from Ger. LC 80-85332. (Field Translation Ser.: No. 5). 150p. 1981. 9.95 (ISBN 0-932440-08-8); pap. 4.95 (ISBN 0-932440-09-6). Oberlin Coll Pr.
Valuable Repetitions for Brass Players. Robert D. Weast. 1986. 10.00 (ISBN 0-941084-11-6). McGinnis & Marx.
Valuable You. Adeline Kroll. (Illus.). 1972. pap. 2.50 (ISBN 0-87839-012-X). North Star.
Valuation & Distribution of Marital Property, 3 vols. Bender's Editorial Staff. 1984. Set, updates avail. looseleaf 250.00 (133); Update 1985 79.50; 1986 92.00. Bender.
Valuation & Property Taxation of Extractive Resources: A Bibliography. Robert M. Clatanoff. (Bibliographic Ser.). 47p. 1982. pap. 11.00 (ISBN 0-88329-114-2). IAAO.
Valuation & Property Taxation of Forests, Orchards, & Trees: A Bibliography. Robert M. Clatanoff. (Bibliographic Ser.: No. 4). 77p. 1982. pap. 14.00 (ISBN 0-88329-118-5). IAAO.
Valuation & Property Taxation of Nonrenewable Resources: An Annotated Bibliography. Robert M. Clatanoff. (CPL Bibliographies Ser.: No. 99). 53p. 1983. 8.00 (ISBN 0-86602-099-3). Coun Plan Librarians.
Valuation & Rate-Making. Robert L. Hale. LC 71-76710. (Columbia University Studies in the Social Sciences: No. 185). Repr. of 1918 ed. 16.50 (ISBN 0-404-51185-6). AMS Pr.
Valuation & Selection of Convertible Bonds: Based on Modern Option Theory. Stefan J. Gepts. LC 87-14606. 192p. 1987. lib. bdg. 37.95 (ISBN 0-275-92466-1, C2466). Praeger.
Valuation in Criticism & Other Essays. F. R. Leavis. Ed. by G. Singh. (Cambridge Paperback Library). 280p. 1986. 39.50 (ISBN 0-521-30966-2); pap. 13.95 (ISBN 0-521-31210-8). Cambridge U Pr.
Valuation; Its Nature & Laws: Being an Introduction to the General Theory of Value. Wilbur M. Urban. LC 75-3416. Repr. of 1909 ed. 49.50 (ISBN 0-404-59413-1). AMS Pr.
Valuation of a Closely Held Business. Pennsylvania Bar Institute. 96p. 1985. 50.00 (ISBN 0-318-19078-8, 307). PA Bar Inst.
Valuation of Commercial Sales Property: A Classified Annotated Bibliography. Robert M. Clatanoff. LC 84-29005. (Bibliographic Ser.: No. 10). 57p. 1985. pap. 14.00 (ISBN 0-88329-137-1). IAAO.
Valuation of Commercial Services Property: A Classified Annotated Bibliography. Robert M. Clatanoff. LC 85-89. (Bibliographic Ser.: No. 9). 101p. 1985. 18.00 (ISBN 0-88329-136-3). IAAO.
Valuation of Development Land in Hong Kong. Philip J. Roberts. LC 76-369546. pap. 24.30 (ISBN 0-317-27920-3, 2025128). Bks Demand UMI.
Valuation of Divorce Assets. Barth H. Goldberg. LC 84-20804. 689p. 1984. text ed. 80.00 (ISBN 0-314-87659-6). West Pub.
Valuation of Gasoline Jobberships in the United States, 1980 through 1983. David M. Nelson. 124p. 60.00 (ISBN 0-318-16175-3, F-2); members 45.00 (ISBN 0-318-16176-1). Petro Mktg Ed Found.
Valuation of Goods for Customs Purposes. Henk De Pagter & Richard Van Raan. 92p. 1982. 22.00 (ISBN 90-654-4023-2, Pub. by Kluwer Law Netherlands). Kluwer Academic.
Valuation of Hotels & Motels. American Institute of Real Estate Appraisers Staff & Stephen Rushmore. 120p. 18.00 (ISBN 0-318-15198-7, NO. 21-1022). Natl Assoc Realtors.
Valuation of Industrial Property: A Classified Annotated Bibliography. Robert M. Clatanoff. LC 87-22660. (Bibliography Ser.: No. 12). 75p. 1987. pap. 15.50 (ISBN 0-88329-144-4). IAAO.
Valuation of Intangible Assets & Intellectual Property. Smith. 1988. price not set (ISBN 0-471-61200-6). Wiley.
Valuation of Nationalized Property in International Law, Vol. 1. Ed. by Richard B. Lillich. LC 70-177376. pap. 47.00 (ISBN 0-317-26811-2, 2024314). Bks Demand UMI.
Valuation of Nationalized Property in International Law, Vol. 2. Ed. by Richard B. Lillich. LC 70-177376. (Virginia Legal Studies). 176p. 1973. 15.00x (ISBN 0-8139-0465-X). U Pr of Va.
Valuation of Nationalized Property in International Law, Vol. 3. Ed. by Richard B. Lillich. (Virginia Legal Studies). 212p. 1975. 15.00x (ISBN 0-8139-0384-X). U Pr of Va.
Valuation of Nationalized Property in International Law, Vol. 4. Ed. & contrib. by Richard B. Lillich. LC 70-17776. (Virginia Legal Studies). 230p. 1987. text ed. 30.00x (ISBN 0-8139-1119-2). U Pr of VA.
Valuation of Privately-Held Business: State-of-the-Art Techniques for Buyers, Sellers & Their Advisors. Irving L. Blackman. 360p. 1986. 40.00 (ISBN 0-917253-27-2). Probus Pub Co.
Valuation of Privately-Owned Businesses. Steven M. Reisinger. 155p. 1981. pap. 14.95 (ISBN 0-940694-00-X). Acquisition Plan.
Valuation of Property, 2 Vols. James C. Bonbright. 1965. Repr. 60.00x (ISBN 0-87215-014-3). Michie Co.
Valuation of Real Estate. Alfred A. Ring & James H. Boykin. 672p. 1986. text ed. 39.00 (ISBN 0-13-939935-6). P-H.
Valuation of Resort & Recreational Property: A Classified Annotated Bibliography. Robert M. Clatanoff. LC 84-15856. (Bibliographic Ser.: No. 6). 29p. 1984. pap. 11.50 (ISBN 0-88329-054-5). IAAO.
Valuation of Resort & Recreational Property: A Classified Annotated Biography. Robert M. Clatanoff. LC 87-30992. (Bibliography Ser.: No. 14). 54p. 1987. pap. 13.50 (ISBN 0-88329-065-0). IAAO.
Valuation of Used Capital Assets, Vol. 7. Carl Beidleman. (Studies in Accounting Research). 84p. 1973. 6.00 (ISBN 0-86539-019-3). Am Accounting.
Valuation of Utility & Transportation Property: A Classified Annotated Bibliography. 2nd ed. Robert M. Clatanoff. (Bibliographic Ser.: No. 13). 65p. 1986. pap. 14.50 (ISBN 0-88329-056-1). IAAO.
Valuation of Wildland Resource Benefits. George Peterson & Alan Randall. (Special Study Ser.). 315p. 1984. 35.00x (ISBN 0-8133-0018-5). Westview.
Valuation Strategies in Divorce. Ed. by Steven J. Shank & K. Richard Olson. 508p. 1986. pap. 45.00 (ISBN 0-941161-24-2). Pes Inc WI.
Valuation Theory. O. Endler. LC 72-92285. (Universitext). xii, 243p. 1972. pap. 18.50 (ISBN 0-387-06070-7). Springer-Verlag.
Valuation Under the Law of Eminent Domain, 2 Vols. 2nd ed. Lewis Orgel. 1953. 60.00x (ISBN 0-87215-037-2). Michie Co.
Valuations of Skew Fields & Projective Hjelmslev Spaces. K. Mathiak. (Lecture Notes in Mathematics). vii, 116p. 1986. pap. 11.60 (ISBN 0-387-16099-X). Springer-Verlag.
Value. Michael Allingham. LC 82-6018. 105p. 1983. 22.50x (ISBN 0-312-83611-2). St Martin.
Value Added Financial Management, 14 Vols. Incl. Management Guide to the PIA Ratios; All Printers by Sales Volume; All Printers by Product Specialty; All Printers by Geographic Area; Sheetfed Printers by Size and Geographic Area; Wed Offset Printers-Heatset; Wed Offset Printers-NonHeatset; Combination Offset--Sheetfed-Wed; Book Manufacturers' Ratios; Large Printers' Ratios; Typographers' Ratios; Preparatory Specialists' Ratios; Binders' Ratios; Quick Printers' Ratios. Set. 750.00 (ISBN 0-318-02606-6); 90.00 ea. (ISBN 0-318-02607-4); A Guide for Printers 50.00. Print Indus Am.
Value Added in Manufacturing, Mining, & Agriculture in the American Economy from 1809 to 1839. facsimile ed. Barry W. Poulson. LC 75-2592. (Dissertations in American Economic History). (Illus.). 1975. 18.00x (ISBN 0-405-07214-7). Ayer Co Pubs.
Value Added Networks. 580p. 1984. 1900.00 (ISBN 0-86621-626-X, E698). Frost & Sullivan.
Value-Added Processes in Information Systems. Robert S. Taylor. Ed. by Melvin J. Voigt. LC 85-18677. (Communication & Information Science Ser.). 272p. 1986. text ed. 39.50 (ISBN 0-89391-273-5). Ablex Pub.
Value Added Selling. Thomas P. Reilly. 192p. Date not set. cancelled (ISBN 0-89896-230-7). Larksdale.
Value Added Selling Techniques. Thomas P. Reilly. LC 87-90744. 1987. 19.95 (ISBN 0-944448-07-0). Motivation Pr.
Value-Added Tax & Other Tax Reforms. Richard W. Lindholm. LC 76-24827. (Illus.). 338p. 1976. 28.95x (ISBN 0-911012-87-7). Nelson-Hall.
Value-Added Tax in the EEC. D. A. Parkinson. 260p. 1980. 37.00 (ISBN 0-86010-190-8). Graham & Trotman.
Value-Added Tax in the Enlarged Common Market. Ed. by G. S. Wheatcroft. LC 73-2294. 140p. 1973. 24.95x (ISBN 0-470-93754-8). Halsted Pr.
Value-Added Tax: International Practice & Problems. Alan A. Tait. 430p. 1988. pap. write for info. (ISBN 1-55775-012-2). Intl Monetary.
Value Added Tax: Key to Deficit Reduction? Charles E. McLure, Jr. LC 86-28905. (Orig.). 1987. lib. bdg. 21.00 (ISBN 0-8447-3613-9); pap. 10.75 (ISBN 0-8447-3614-7). Am Enterprise.
Value Added Tax Law, Tax Exemption & Reduction Control Law, & Asset Revaluation Law & Enforcement Decrees see Tax Laws of Korea.
Value-Added Tax: Lessons from Europe. Ed. by Henry J. Aaron. LC 81-38475. (Studies of Government Finance). 107p. 1981. 22.95 (ISBN 0-8157-0028-8); pap. 8.95 (ISBN 0-8157-0027-X). Brookings.
Value-Added Taxation: The Experience of the United Kingdom. A. R. Prest. 1980. pap. 7.00 (ISBN 0-8447-3404-7). Am Enterprise.
Value Analysis. Robert E. Birdsong. (Aquarian Academy Monograph, Series A: Lecture No. 4). 1975. pap. 1.25 (ISBN 0-917108-14-0). Sirius Bks.
Value Analysis for Better Management. Warren J. Ridge. LC 75-96142. pap. 51.80 (ISBN 0-317-09939-6, 2050439). Bks Demand UMI.
Value & Capital: An Inquiry into Some Fundamental Principles of Economic Theory. 2nd ed. John R. Hicks. (Illus.). 1946. 13.50x (ISBN 0-19-828269-9). Oxford U Pr.
Value & Crisis: Essays on Marxian Economics in Japan. Makoto Itoh. LC 80-8084. 192p. 1980. 13.50 (ISBN 0-85345-556-2); pap. 7.00 (ISBN 0-85345-557-0). Monthly Rev.
Value & Destiny of the Individual. Bernard Bosanquet. LC 13-6278. (Gifford Lectures 1912). 1968. Repr. of 1913 ed. 32.00 (ISBN 0-527-10066-8). Kraus Repr.
Value & Distribution. Herbert J. Davenport. LC 64-17406. 1964. Repr. of 1908 ed. 45.00x (ISBN 0-678-00036-0). Kelley.
Value & Distribution in Capitalist Economies: An Introduction to Sraffian Economies. Lynn Mainwaring. LC 83-26228. (Illus.). 250p. 1984. 44.50 (ISBN 0-521-25904-5); pap. 13.95 (ISBN 0-521-27755-8). Cambridge U Pr.
Value & Ethics in Organization & Human Systems Development: An Annotated Bibliography. Ed. by Mark S. Frankel. 104p. 1987. pap. 5.00. AAAS.
Value & Meaning of Depression. M. Esther Harding. (Orig.). 1985. pap. 3.75 (ISBN 0-318-04660-1). Analytical Psych.
Value & Opportunity: Comparable Pay for Comparable Worth. Deborah Walker. Ed. by Steve Pejovich & Henry Dethloff. (Series On Public Issues: No. 10). 14p. 1984. pap. 2.00 (ISBN 0-86599-020-4). Ctr Educ Res.
Value & Price. 2nd. rev. ed. LC 73-81132. (Capital & Interest Extract Ser.). 246p. 1973. pap. 7.95 (ISBN 0-910884-01-3). Libertarian Press.
Value & Price in the Labor-Surplus Economy. Stephen A. Marglin. (Illus.). 1976. 37.50x (ISBN 0-19-828194-3). Oxford U Pr.
Value & Valuation: Axiological Studies in Honor of Robert S. Hartman. John W. Davis. LC 72-146661. Repr. of 1972 ed. 90.50 (2027564). Bks Demand UMI.
Value & Values in Evolution: A Symposium. E. Maziarz. (Current Topics of Contemporary Thought Ser.). 208p. 1979. 42.00 (ISBN 0-677-15240-X). Gordon & Breach.
Value & Virtue: Moral Education in the Public School. United States Catholic Conference Administrative Board. (Orig.). 1988. pap. 0.50 (ISBN 1-55586-189-X). US Catholic.
Value Areas & Their Development: Theory & Method of Self-Confrontation. Hubert J. Hermans. Tr. by Joseph A. Spiekerman from Dutch. 306p. 1975. text ed. 17.50 (ISBN 90-265-0225-7, Pub. by Swets & Zeitlinger Netherlands). Hogrefe Intl.
Value, Capital & Rent. Knut Wicksell. LC 68-58668. (Illus.). 1970. Repr. of 1954 ed. 27.50x (ISBN 0-678-00652-0). Kelley.
Value Change in Chinese Society. Richard W. Wilson et al. LC 77-83479. (Special Studies). 326p. 1979. 44.95 (ISBN 0-275-90437-7, C0437). Praeger.
Value Conflict in Study of Social Change in India. Girish C. Roy. 272p. 1983. 30.95. Asia Bk Corp.
Value Conflicts & Curriculum Issues. Jon Schaffarzick & Gary Sykes. LC 79-88125. 1980. 26.75x (ISBN 0-8211-1857-9); text ed. 24.75x in copies of 10. McCutchan.
Value Controversy in Sociology: A New Orientation for the Profession. Dennis C. Foss. LC 77-82915. (Jossey-Bass Series in Higher Education). pap. 38.30 (ISBN 0-317-41964-1, 2025672). Bks Demand UMI.
Value Development: A Practical Guide. Bruce Kalven et al. 1982. pap. 10.00 (ISBN 0-8091-2445-9); learning summaries 2.50 (ISBN 0-8091-2520-X); time diary 3.00 (ISBN 0-8091-2519-6). Paulist Pr.
Value Development As the Aim of Education. Ed. by Norman A. Sprinthall & Ralph L. Mosher. LC 78-68113. 1978. pap. 4.25 (ISBN 0-915744-10-4). Character Res.
Value Dimension. Ed. by Ben Fine. (Economy & Society Paperbacks Ser.). 224p. 1986. pap. 15.95 (ISBN 0-7102-0766-2, 07622, Pub. by Routledge UK). Routledge Chapman & Hall.
Value Distribution of Holomorphic Maps into Compact Complex Manifolds. W. Stoll. LC 75-121987. (Lecture Notes in Mathematics: Vol. 135). 1970. pap. 14.70 (ISBN 0-387-04924-X). Springer-Verlag.
Value Distribution on Parabolic Spaces. W. Stoll. (Lecture Notes in Mathematics: Vol. 600). 1977. 18.00 (ISBN 0-387-08341-3). Springer-Verlag.
Value Distribution: Proceedings, Joensuu, Finland, 1981. Ed. by I. Laine & S. Rickman. (Lecture Notes in Mathematics: Vol. 981). 245p. 1983. pap. 17.00 (ISBN 0-387-12003-3). Springer-Verlag.
Value Distribution Theory, Pt. A. Ed. by Robert O. Kujala & Albert L. Vitter, 3rd. (Pure & Applied Mathematics Ser.: Vol. 25). 288p. 1974. 49.75 (ISBN 0-8247-6124-3). Dekker.
Value Distribution Theory & Its Applications. Ed. by Chung-Chun Yang. LC 83-21465. (Contemporary Mathematics Ser.: Vol. 25). 253p. 1984. pap. text ed. 31.00 (ISBN 0-8218-5025-3). Am Math.
Value Distribution Theory: Deficit & Bezout Estimates, Pt. B. Ed. by Robert O. Kujala & Albert L. Vitter, III. (Pure & Applied Mathematics Ser.: Vol. 25). 288p. 1973. 49.75 (ISBN 0-8247-6125-1). Dekker.
Value Distribution Theory for Meromorphic Maps. W. Stoll. (Aspects of Mathematics Ser.: Vol. 7). 347p. 1985. pap. 28.00 (ISBN 3-528-08906-7, Pub. by Vieweg & Sohn). IPS.
Value Education for an Age of Crisis. Betty A. Sichel. LC 81-40642. 204p. (Orig.). 1982. lib. bdg. 29.75 (ISBN 0-8191-2361-7); pap. text ed. 13.25 (ISBN 0-8191-2362-5). U Pr of Amer.
Value, Exploitation & Class. John E. Roemer. (Fundamentals of Pure & Applied Economics Ser.: Vol. 1, pt. 4). 88p. 1985. pap. text ed. 28.00 (ISBN 3-7186-0278-4). Harwood Academic.
Value Exploration Through Role Playing. Robert C. Hawley. 124p. (Orig.). 1974. pap. 6.95 (ISBN 0-913636-03-7). Educ Res MA.
Value for Money in Health Services. Brian Abel-Smith. 1976. pap. text ed. 12.50x (ISBN 0-435-82006-0). Gower Pub Co.
Value for Money in the Public Sector: A Decision-Maker's Guide. Henry A. Butt & D. Robert Palmer. 200p. 1985. 45.00x (ISBN 0-631-14452-8); pap. 19.95x (ISBN 0-631-14453-6). Basil Blackwell.
Value for Money: The Hong Kong Budgetary Process. Alvin Rabushka. LC 75-27028. (Publications Ser.: No. 152). 152p. 1976. 10.95x (ISBN 0-8179-6521-1). Hoover Inst Pr.
Value for Value Psychotherapy: The Economic & Therapeutic Barter. Paul S. Rappoport. 208p. 1983. 35.00 (ISBN 0-275-91724-X, C1724). Praeger.

Values at Risk. Ed. by Douglas MacLean. (Maryland Studies in Public Philosophy). 192p. 1986. 28.50x (ISBN 0-8476-7414-2, Rowman & Allanheld). Rowman.

Values at War: Selected Tanner Lectures on the Nuclear Crisis. Freeman Dyson et al. 130p. (Orig.). 1983. pap. 5.95 (ISBN 0-87480-226-1). U of Utah Pr.

Values Auction see Kadima Kesher Series.

Values, Bureaucracy & Public Policy. Charles Sampson. (Illus.). 276p. (Orig.). 1983. lib. bdg. 28.50 (ISBN 0-8191-3482-1); pap. text ed. 14.00 (ISBN 0-8191-3483-X). U Pr of Amer.

Values Clarification: A Handbook of Practical Strategies for Teachers & Students. Sidney B. Simon et al. 400p. 1985. pap. 10.95 (ISBN 0-396-08470-2). Dodd.

Values Clarification for Counselors: How Counselors, Social Workers, Psychologists, & Other Human Service Workers Can Use Available Techniques. Gordon M. Hart. (Illus.). 104p. 1978. 15.25x (ISBN 0-398-03847-3). C C Thomas.

Values, Curriculum & the Elementary School. Alexander Frazier. LC 79-87862. 1980. pap. text ed. 20.95 (ISBN 0-395-26739-0). HM.

Values, Ethics & Aging, Vol. 4. Ed. by Gari Lesnoff-Caravaglia. (Frontiers in Aging Ser.). 196p. 1985. 29.95 (ISBN 0-89885-162-9). Human Sci Pr.

Values for Freedom. Harry E. Moore, Jr. LC 72-76584. 1972. 5.95 (ISBN 0-87212-026-0). Libra.

Values for Survival: Essays, Addresses, & Letters on Politics & Education. Lewis Mumford. LC 79-167387. (Essay Index Reprint Ser.). Repr. of 1946 ed. 19.50 (ISBN 0-8369-2704-4). Ayer Co Pubs.

Values for Tomorrow's Children. Ed. by John H. Westerhoff, III. LC 72-125961. 1979. pap. 6.95. Pilgrim NY.

Values, Identities, & National Integration: Empirical Research in Africa. John N. Paden. 400p. 1980. 49.95x (ISBN 0-8101-0467-9). Northwestern U Pr.

Values in Action: The Meaning of Executive Vignettes. Michael M. Lombardo. (Technical Report Ser.: No. 128). 36p. 1986. pap. 15.00 (ISBN 0-912879-26-2). Ctr Creat Leader.

Values in America. Ed. by Donald N. Barrett. 1961. pap. 6.95 (ISBN 0-268-00291-6). U of Notre Dame Pr.

Values in an Age of Confrontation: A Symposium Sponsored by the Religion in Education Foundation. Ed. by Jeremiah W. Canning. LC 72-109054. (Studies of the Person). pap. 41.10 (ISBN 0-317-09226-X, 2055239). Bks Demand UMI.

Values in an American Government Textbook: Three Appraisals. Michael Novak et al. Ed. by Ernest W. Lefever. LC 78-4586. 57p. 1978. pap. 6.75 (ISBN 0-89633-006-0). Ethics & Public Policy.

Values in Conflict: Blacks & the American Ambivalence Toward Violence. Charles A. Frye. LC 79-5516. 1980. pap. text ed. 11.25 (ISBN 0-8191-0899-5). U Pr of Amer.

Values in Conflict: Christianity, Marxism, Psychoanalysis & Existentialism. Ed. by Victor Comerchero. LC 74-111099. 986p. (Orig., Free booklet, "Suggestions for Instructors," available). 1970. pap. text ed. 19.95x (ISBN 0-89197-463-6). Irvington.

Values in Conflict: Contemporary Issues in Business & Society. Edward W. Wheatley. LC 76-6097. 1976. 6.95 (ISBN 0-916224-05-8). Banyan Bks.

Values in Conflict: Funding Priorities for Higher Education. Ed. by Mary P. McKeown & Kern Alexander. LC 86-20597. 360p. 1987. prof. ref. 34.95x (ISBN 0-88730-102-9). Ballinger Pub.

Values in Conflict: Life, Liberty & the Rule of Law. Burton M. Leiser. 1981. pap. text ed. write for info. (ISBN 0-02-369520-X). Macmillan.

Values in Conflict: Resolving Ethical Issues in Hospital Care. 120p. 1985. 15.00 (ISBN 0-87258-433-X). Am Hospital.

Values in Education & Society. Norman T. Feather. LC 75-2812. (Illus.). 1975. 14.95 (ISBN 0-02-910200-6). Free Pr.

Values in Geography. Anne Buttimer. LC 74-76634. (CCG Resource Papers Ser.: No. 24). (Illus.). 1974. pap. text ed. 5.00 (ISBN 0-89291-071-2). Assn Am Geographers.

Values in Geography. Annette Buttimer. 1987. Repr. 75.00x (ISBN 0-317-62325-7, Pub. by Scientific). State Mutual Bk.

Values in Medical Practice: A Statement of Philosophy for Physicians & Model for Teaching a Healing Science. Rudolph J. Napodano. LC 85-19742. 144p. 1986. text ed. 26.95 (ISBN 0-89885-268-4, Dist. by Independent Publishers Group). Human Sci Pr.

Values in Modern Medicine. William S. Middleton. LC 72-1379. (Illus.). 314p. 1972. 19.95x (ISBN 0-299-06220-1). U of Wis Pr.

Values in Selected Children's Books of Fiction & Fantasy. Ed. by Carolyn W. Field & Jaqueline S. Weiss. LC 87-3874. 240p. 1987. lib. bdg. 27.50 (ISBN 0-208-02100-0, Lib Prof Pubns). Shoe String.

Values in Social Policy: Nine Contradictions. Jean Hardy. (Radical Social Policy Ser.). 132p. (Orig.). 1981. pap. 15.95x (ISBN 0-7100-0782-5). Routledge Chapman & Hall.

Values in Social Work. Michael Horne. (Community Care Practice Handbooks Ser.: Vol. 26). 100p. 1988. pap. text ed. 30.00x (ISBN 0-7045-0581-9, Pub. by Gower Pub England). Gower Pub Co.

Values in Social Work: A Re-Examination. Intro. by Morton Teicher. LC 65-15322. 107p. (Orig.). 1967. pap. text ed. 5.95x (ISBN 0-87101-345-2). Natl Assn Soc Wkrs.

Values in the Electric Power Industry. Ed. by Kenneth M. Sayre. LC 76-51829. pap. 77.50 (ISBN 0-317-55791-2, 2029314). Bks Demand UMI.

Values, Neo-Kantianism, & the Development of Weberian Methodology. Thomas W. Segady. (American University Studies V: Philosophy: Vol. 41). 172p. 1987. text ed. 28.00 (ISBN 0-8204-0506-X). P Lang Pubs.

Values of New Type Examinations in the High School. Sterling G. Brinkley. LC 73-176589. (Columbia University. Teachers College. Contributions to Education: No. 161). Repr. of 1924 ed. 22.50 (ISBN 0-404-55161-0). AMS Pr.

Values of Non-Atomic Games. R. J. Aumann & L. S. Shapley. (Rand Corporation Research Study). 300p. 1972. 41.00x (ISBN 0-691-08103-4). Princeton U Pr.

Values of Social Science. rev. 2nd. ed. Ed. by Norman K. Denzin. LC 72-94545. 194p. 1973. 17.95x (ISBN 0-87855-054-2); pap. 11.95x (ISBN 0-87855-547-1). Transaction Bks.

Values of the American Heritage: Challenges, Case Studies & Teaching Strategies - 46th Yearbook. Ed. by Carl Ubbelohde & Jack R. Fraenkel. LC 76-7276. (Illus.). 214p. 1976. 4.25 (ISBN 0-87986-004-9, 490-15290); pap. 8.75 (ISBN 0-87986-037-5, 490-15288). Nat Coun Soc Studies.

Values Orientation in School. Johnnie McFadden & Joseph C. Rotter. 4.50 (ISBN 0-86548-045-1). R & E Pubs.

Values to Cherish. Helen R. Harrison. (Orig.). 1978. pap. 4.50 (ISBN 0-87881-071-4). Mojave Bks.

Valuing a Business: The Analysis & Appraisal of Closely Held Companies. Shannon Pratt. LC 80-85475. 424p. 1981. 55.00 (ISBN 0-87094-205-0). Dow Jones-Irwin.

Valuing a Business: The Analysis & Appraisal of Closely Held Companies. 2nd ed. 1988. 60.00 (ISBN 1-55623-127-X). Dow Jones-Irwin.

Valuing a Company: Practices & Procedures. George D. McCarthy & Robert E. Healy. 521p. 1971. 75.00 (ISBN 0-471-06542-0, Pub. by Ronald Pr). Wiley.

Valuing a Medical Practice: A Short Guide for Buyers & Sellers. American Medical Association Staff. (Orig.). 1987. pap. 6.00 (OP-117/7). AMA.

Valuing Assets in Estate Planning & Administration. 150p. 1987. pap. 26.00 (ES-49016). Cal Cont Ed Bar.

Valuing Closely Held Companies. Reilly. 1988. write for info. (ISBN 0-471-82594-8). Wiley.

Valuing Common Stock: The Power of Prudence. George Lasry. 1979. 17.95 (ISBN 0-8144-5491-7). AMACOM.

Valuing Common Stock: The Power of Prudence. George Lasry. LC 78-24023. pap. 67.50 (ISBN 0-317-27196-2, 2023930). Bks Demand UMI.

Valuing Environmental Goods: An Assessment of the Contingent Valuation Method. Ed. by Ronald G. Cummings et al. LC 85-14298. (Illus.). 288p. 1986. 49.50x (ISBN 0-8476-7448-7, Rowman & Allanheld). Rowman.

Valuing Professional Practises & Licenses: A Guide for the Matrimonial Practitioner. Ronald L. Brown. LC 87-12620. Date not set. price not set (ISBN 0-13-940669-7). P-H.

Valuing Small Businesses & Professional Practices. Shannon P. Pratt. 1985. 50.00 (ISBN 0-87094-598-X). Dow Jones-Irwin.

Valuing Suffering As a Christian: Some Psychological Perspectives. C. P. Simons. (Synthesis Ser.). 1976. pap. 0.75 (ISBN 0-8199-0708-1). Franciscan Herald.

Valuing the Self: What We Can Learn from Other Cultures. Dorothy Lee. (Illus.). 1986. pap. text ed. 6.95x (ISBN 0-88133-229-1). Waveland Pr.

Valuing the Timeshare Property. Kathleen Conroy. 97p. 1981. 17.00 (ISBN 0-911780-50-5). Am Inst Real Estate Appraisers.

Valuing Wildlife: Economic & Social Perspectives. Ed. by Daniel J. Decker & Gary R. Goff. (Westview Special Studies in National Resources & Energy Management). 426p. 1986. 35.00 (ISBN 0-8133-7120-1). Westview.

Valuings & Financing Information Companies. Ed. by Brad Henderson. 1987. 84.95 (ISBN 0-942774-26-4). Info Indus.

Valutare l'Anziano: Manuale de Riferimento dei Mezzi di Studio e di Misura delle Funzioni Mentali, 2 vols. Liliane Israel et al. (Limited Volume Ser.). xxviii, 668p. (Ital.). 1984. bound 249.50 (ISBN 3-8055-3835-9). S Karger.

Valve & Pipe Fittings Industry. 235p. 1985. 595.00 (ISBN 0-686-31541-3). Busn Trend.

Valve Design. G. H. Pearson. (SAE Technical Papers). 358p. 32.50 (ISBN 0-85298-404-9, MEP-88). Soc Auto Engineers.

Valve Manufacturers. Ed. by ICC Info. Group Staff. 1987. 695.00x (ISBN 1-85319-046-2, ICC Info Group Ltd UK). State Mutual Bk.

Valve Morphology in the Genus Cymbella: C. A. Agardh. Kurt Krammer. Ed. by J. G. Helmcke & Kurt Krammer. (Micromorphology of Datom Valves Ser.). (Illus.). 300p. (Orig.). 1982. Lubrecht & Cramer.

Valve Selection & Service Guide. John Mead. LC 85-25517. 240p. 1986. 39.95 (ISBN 0-912524-25-1). Busn News.

Valve Selection Handbook. 2nd ed. R. W. Zappe. 228p. 1987. 49.00 (ISBN 0-87201-918-7). Gulf Pub.

Valve Users Manual. Ed. by J. Kemplay. (SAE Technical Papers). 104p. 1980. 26.00 (ISBN 0-85298-428-6, MEP-115). Soc Auto Engineers.

Valves. Center for Occupational Research & Development Staff. (EUTEC Power Plant Operator Curriculum Ser.). (Illus.). 36p. 1985. pap. text ed. write for info. (ISBN 1-55502-222-7). Ctr Res & Dev.

Valves & Actuators Market. 311p. 1984. 1450.00 (ISBN 0-86621-555-7, E631). Frost & Sullivan.

Valvular Heart Disease. Greenberg. 328p. 1987. 48.00 (ISBN 0-88416-472-1). PSG Pub Co.

Valvular Heart Disease: Comprehensive Evaluation & Management. Ed. by William S. Frankl & Albert N. Brest. LC 70-6558. (Cardiovascular Clinics Ser.: Vol. 16, No. 2). (Illus.). 567p. 1986. text ed. 99.00 (ISBN 0-8036-3791-8). Davis Co.

Valvulas, Espitas y Tomas, Hechas de Hierro y Acero. (Productos Latinoamericanos Incluidos En el Sistema Generalizado De Preferencias De los Estados Unidos Ser.). 18p. 1977. pap. text ed. 3.00 (ISBN 0-8270-3495-4). OAS.

Vamos a Ver. Helena Valenti. 1972. pap. 5.95 (ISBN 0-912022-31-0, 70254). EMC.

Vamos: Bienvenidos al Mundo Hispanico. Kenneth Chastain. 576p. 1985. text ed. 32.50 (ISBN 0-8384-1277-7); instr's. ed. avail. (ISBN 0-8384-1280-7); wkbk. 16.75 (ISBN 0-8384-1279-3); tapes 125.00 (ISBN 0-8384-1281-5). Heinle & Heinle.

Vamos Caminando: A Peruvian Catechism. Pastoral Team of Bambamarca. Tr. by John Medcalf from Span. 383p. (Orig.). 1985. pap. 14.95 (ISBN 0-88344-526-3). Orbis Bks.

Vampire. Sydney Horler. 1974. 6.50 (ISBN 0-685-47865-3). Bookfinger.

Vampire Babies. Ed. by Jeanne Youngson. 18p. (Orig.). 1986. pap. 2.95 (ISBN 0-9611944-6-4). Dracula Pr.

Vampire Bat: A Field Study in Behavior & Ecology. Dennis C. Turner. LC 74-24396. (Illus.). 160p. 1975. 20.00x (ISBN 0-8018-1680-7). Johns Hopkins.

Vampire Bats. Laurence Pringle. 64p. (ps up). 1982. 12.95 (ISBN 0-317-68266-0); PLB 13.95. Enslow Pubs.

Vampire Express. Tony Koltz. (Choose Your Own Adventure Ser.: No. 31). 128p. (Orig.). (gr. 4-7). 1984. pap. text ed. 2.25 (ISBN 0-553-26185-1). Bantam.

Vampire in Europe. Montague Summers. 368p. 1981. pap. 35.00x (ISBN 0-85030-221-8, Pub. by Aquarian Pr England). State Mutual Bk.

Vampire in Fact, Legend, & Art. Basil Copper. 208p. 1974. 6.95 (ISBN 0-8065-0433-1, Pub. by Citadel Pr). Lyle Stuart.

Vampire in Nineteenth-Century England Literature. Carol Senf. LC 87-73508. 204p. 1988. 32.95 (ISBN 0-87972-424-2); pap. 15.95 (ISBN 0-87972-425-0). Bowling Green Univ.

Vampire in Verse: An Anthology. Ed. by Steven Moore. 196p. (Orig.). 1985. pap. 7.95 (ISBN 0-9611944-2-1). Dracula Pr.

Vampire Junction. S. P. Somtow. Ed. by Kay Reynolds. (Illus.). 280p. 15.95 (ISBN 0-89865-367-3, Starblaze); deluxe ed. 35.00 (ISBN 0-89865-368-1, Starblaze). Donning Co.

Vampire Junction. S. P. Somtow. 368p. 1985. pap. 3.95 (ISBN 0-425-09091-4). Berkley Pub.

Vampire Lestat. Anne Rice. LC 85-40123. (Chronicles of the Vampires Ser.: Bk. 2). 512p. 1985. 18.95 (ISBN 0-394-53443-3). Knopf.

Vampire Lestat. Anne Rice. 1986. pap. 4.50 (ISBN 0-345-31386-0). Ballantine.

Vampire Moves In. Angela Sommer-Bodenburg. LC 84-7062. (Illus.). (gr. 2-6). 1984. 9.95 (ISBN 0-8037-0077-6, 0966-290); PLB 9.89 (ISBN 0-8037-0078-4). Dial Bks Young.

Vampire Moves In. Angela Sommer-Bodenburg. (Illus.). (gr. 2-6). 1986. pap. 2.50 (ISBN 0-671-55422-0, Minstrel Bks). S&S.

Vampire of Sacramento: And Other Famous Cases of a Courtroom Psychiatrist. Ronald Markman & Dominick Bosco. 1989. 18.95 (ISBN 0-385-24427-4). Doubleday.

Vampire of Verdonia. Miranda Seymour. (Illus.). 100p. (gr. 3-6). 1988. 10.95 (ISBN 0-233-97867-4). Andre Deutsch.

Vampire on the Farm. Angela Sommer-Bodenburg. LC 87-2153. (Illus.). (gr. 2-6). Date not set. 10.95 (ISBN 0-8037-0326-0, 1063-320); PLB 10.89 (ISBN 0-8037-0327-9). Dial Bks Young.

Vampire Squadron: The Saga of the 44th Fighter Squadron. William H. Starke. LC 85-61542. (Illus.). xiv, 208p. 1985. 39.50 (ISBN 0-918837-02-2). Robinson Typos.

Vampire Takes a Trip. Angela Sommer-Bodenburg. LC 84-22995. (Illus.). 160p. (gr. 2-6). 1985. 9.95 (ISBN 0-8037-0199-3, 0966-290); PLB 9.89 (ISBN 0-8037-0201-9). Dial Bks Young.

Vampire Takes a Trip. Angela Sommer-Bodenburg. (Illus.). (gr. 3-7). 1987. pap. 2.50 (ISBN 0-671-64822-5, Minstrel Bks). S&S.

Vampire Tapestry. Suzy M. Charnos. 1981. pap. 2.75 (ISBN 0-671-83484-3, Timescape). PB.

Vampire Vacation. Thomas McKean. LC 85-48073. 1986. pap. 2.50 (ISBN 0-380-89808-X, Camelot). Avon.

Vampires. Colin Hawkins et al. LC 85-40424. (Illus.). 32p. (ps up). 1985. 7.45 (ISBN 0-382-09133-7). Silver.

Vampires. John Rechy. LC 70-155123. 1971. pap. 2.95 (ISBN 0-394-17817-3, B362, BC). Grove.

Vampires - Hammer Style. Robert G. Marrero. (Illus.). 100p. (Orig.). 1983. pap. 6.95 (ISBN 0-942436-02-4). RGM Pubns.

Vampires & Vampirism. Dudley Wright. 69.95 (ISBN 0-87968-093-8). Gordon Pr.

Vampires Are. Stephen Kaplan. LC 83-6515. 200p. 1984. 11.95 (ISBN 0-88280-102-3); pap. 6.95 (ISBN 0-88280-103-1). ETC Pubns.

Vampire's Honeymoon. Cornell Woolrich. 220p. 1985. pap. 3.50 (ISBN 0-88184-132-3). Carroll & Graf.

Vampires of the Andes. Henry Carew. Ed. by R. Reginald & Douglas Menville. LC 77-84206. (Lost Race & Adult Fantasy Ser.). 1978. Repr. of 1925 ed. lib. bdg. 26.50x (ISBN 0-405-10962-8). Ayer Co Pubs.

Vampires of the China Coast. J. Bok. (Illus.). 334p. 1932. 315.00x (Pub. by Han-Shan Tang Ltd). State Mutual Bk.

Vampires of the Nightworld. David Bischoff. (Orig.). 1981. pap. 2.25 (ISBN 0-345-28763-0, Del Rey). Ballantine.

Vampires, Spies & Alien Beings. R. G. Austin. (Which Way Bks.: No. 2). (Illus.). (gr. 3-6). 1982. pap. 1.95 (ISBN 0-671-45758-6). Archway.

Vampires Unearthed: The Vampire & Dracula Bibliography of Books, Articles, Movies, Records, & Other Material. Martin V. Riccardo. LC 82-49261. (Supernatural Studies). 150p. 1983. lib. bdg. 21.00 (ISBN 0-8240-9128-0). Garland Pub.

Vampirism in Literature: Shadow of a Shade. Margaret L. Carter. 1974. lib. bdg. 69.95 (ISBN 0-87968-225-6). Gordon Pr.

Vamps. Ed. by Greenburg & Waugh. 1987. pap. 3.50 (ISBN 0-88677-190-0). DAW Bks.

Vampyre. Retold by David Campton. (Fleshcreepers Ser.). 160p. (gr. 6 up). 1988. pap. 2.95 (ISBN 0-8120-4070-8). Barron.

Vampyre see Castle of Otranto (Three Gothic Novels).

Vampyre by Dr. Polidori. Polidori. Ed. by Donald K. Adams. 1968. 12.50 (ISBN 0-910330-14-X). Grant Dahlstrom.

Van. Trish Mylet & Antoinette Sheffield. Ed. by Barry W. Burton. (Phonetic Readers for the Short Vowels Ser.: Bk. 2). (Illus.). 16p. (ps-2). 1988. pap. text ed. 5.00 (ISBN 0-945590-02-4). Sizzy Bks.

Van Aaken Method. Ernst Van Aaken. Tr. by George Beinhorn from Ger. LC 75-20964. (Illus.). 135p. 1976. pap. 4.95 (ISBN 0-89037-070-2); 5.95 (ISBN 0-89037-071-0). Anderson World.

Van Alens: First Family of a Nation's First City. Samuel A. Schreiner, Jr. 1982. pap. 3.50 (ISBN 0-8217-1000-1). Zebra.

Van Arteveldes of Ghent: The Varieties of Vendetta & the Hero in History. David Nicholas. LC 88-3858. (Illus.). 232p. 1988. 23.50x. Cornell U Pr.

Van Bibber & Others, Vol. 1. Richard H. Davis. LC 72-5865. (Short Story Index Reprint Ser.). Repr. of 1892 ed. 21.00 (ISBN 0-8369-4208-6). Ayer Co Pubs.

Van Briggle Pottery: Price Guide, 1986. Scott H. Nelson. (NIA Ser.). 10p. (Orig.). 1986. pap. text ed. 3.00 (ISBN 0-317-52546-8). S H Nelson.

Van Buren County Genealogies. Shirley S. Howe. (Illus.). Date not set. Set. pap. text ed. write for info. (ISBN 0-9616538-0-9). S S Howe.

Van Buren County Genealogies, Vol. 1: Our Family Pioneers. Shirley S. Howe. (Illus.). 100p. 1986. pap. text ed. 10.00 (ISBN 0-9616538-1-7). S S Howe.

Van Buren County, Michigan 1860: Census Index. Ann Burton & Conrad Burton. (Illus.). 55p. (Orig.). 1986. pap. 6.50 (ISBN 0-937505-00-5). Glyndwr Resc.

Van Buren, Wizard of O.K. & 8th U. S. A. President. Ted Welles. Ed. by Mercy Johnson. LC 87-60750. (Illus.). 96p. (Orig.). (YA) (gr. 6 up). 1987. July 30, 1987. lib. bdg. 12.00 (ISBN 0-915189-04-6); June 30, 1987. pap. 5.95 (ISBN 0-915189-05-4). Oceanus.

Van Cleef & Arpels. Sylvie Raulet. LC 86-42721. (Illus.). 330p. 1987. 95.00 (ISBN 0-8478-0754-1). Rizzoli Intl.

Van Cookery. Betty Tucker. (Illus.). 1972. wrappers 1.00 (ISBN 0-910856-54-0). La Siesta.

Van Cortlandt Manor. Joseph T. Butler. LC 77-17531. (Sleepy Hollow Restorations Guidebook). (Illus.). 1978. pap. 1.95 (ISBN 0-912882-33-6). Sleepy Hollow.

Van de Velde Drawings: A Catalogue of Drawings in the National Maritime Museum Made by the Elder & the Younger William Van de Velde, Vol. 2: The Ingram Volume. National Maritime Museum. LC 58-14763. pap. 93.00 (ISBN 0-317-27097-4, 2024551). Bks Demand UMI.

Vanished. Fletcher Knebel. 368p. 1986. pap. 3.95 (ISBN 0-441-86038-9, Pub. by Charter Bks). Ace Bks.
Vanished. Mary M. Morris. 1988. 16.95 (ISBN 0-670-82216-7). Viking.
Vanished. Bill Pronzini. (Nameless Detective Mystery Ser.). 1984. pap. 4.95 (ISBN 0-88150-022-4, Foul Play). Countryman.
Vanished Arcadia. R. B. Cunningham Grahame & B. Cunningham. 1973. 59.95 (ISBN 0-8490-1254-6). Gordon Pr.
Vanished Arcadia: Being Some Account of the Jesuits in Paraguay 1607-1767. R. B. Graham. (Century Classic Ser.). 320p. 1988. pap. 13.95 (ISBN 0-7126-1887-2, Pub. by Century Hutchinson). David & Charles.
Vanished Arcadia: Being Some Account of the Jesuits in Paraguay. Robert B. Graham. LC 68-25238. (Studies in Spanish Literature, No. 36). 1969. Repr. of 1901 ed. lib. bdg. 50.95x (ISBN 0-8383-0949-6). Haskell.
Vanished Arizona: Recollections of the Army Life of a New England Woman. Martha Summerhayes. LC 78-26814. (Illus.). xxvi, 341p. 1979. 27.95x (ISBN 0-8032-4106-2); pap. 7.95 (ISBN 0-8032-9105-1, BB 683, Bison). U of Nebr Pr.
Vanished Dreams of a Poet: Poems from a Foreign Land. Elisabetta Denti. 56p. (Orig.). 1985. pap. write for info. (ISBN 0-9614723-0-8). Elisabetta Denti.
Vanished Empire. B. L. Weale. 379p. 1926. 96.00x (ISBN 0-317-68606-2, Pub. by Han-Shan Tang Ltd). State Mutual Bk.
Vanished Halls & Cathedrals of France. G. W. Edwards. 69.95 (ISBN 0-8490-1255-4). Gordon Pr.
Vanished Imam: Musa al Sadr & the Shia of Lebanon. Fouad Ajami. LC 85-48194. (Illus.). 228p. 1986. 19.95 (ISBN 0-8014-1910-7). Cornell U Pr.
Vanished Imam: Musa al Sadr & the Shia of Lebanon. Fouad Ajami. LC 85-48194. (Paperback Ser.). (Illus.). 228p. 1987. pap. 8.95 (ISBN 0-8014-9416-8). Cornell U Pr.
Vanished Messenger. E. Phillips Oppenheim. Repr. lib. bdg. 20.95x (ISBN 0-89190-416-6, Pub. by River City Pr). Amereon Ltd.
Vanished Present: The Memoirs of Alexander Pasternak. Alexander Pasternak. Tr. by Ann P. Slater. LC 84-6532. (Helen & Kurt Wolff Bk.). (Illus.). 240p. 1985. 17.95 (ISBN 0-15-193364-2). HarBraceJ.
Vanished Spendor III: Postcard Memories of Oklahoma City. Jim Edwards et al. LC 82-72945. (Illus.). 64p. 1985. write for info. Abalache Bkshop.
Vanished Splendor II: A Postcard Album of Oklahoma City. LC 82-72945. (Illus.). 88p. 1983. 19.95 (ISBN 0-910453-01-2). Abalache Bkshop.
Vanished Splendor: Postcard Views of Early Oklahoma City. Hal N. Ottaway & Jim L. Edwards. LC 82-72945. (Illus.). 64p. 1982. 17.95 (ISBN 0-910453-00-4). Abalache Bkshop.
Vanished Supremacies, Vol. 1. Collected Essays Of Sir Lewis Namier. facs. ed. Lewis B. Namier. LC 73-119603. (Select Bibliographies Reprint Ser). 1958. 12.50 (ISBN 0-8369-5195-6). Ayer Co Pubs.
Vanished World. Anne G. Sneller. LC 64-16923. (Illus.). 1964. 9.95 (ISBN 0-8156-0037-2). Syracuse U Pr.
Vanished World. Roman Vishniac. LC 83-16420. (Illus.). 192p. 1983. 65.00 (ISBN 0-374-28247-1). FS&G.
Vanished World. Roman Vishniac. (Illus.). 192p. 1986. pap. 19.95 (ISBN 0-374-52023-2). FS&G.
Vanishing. Kirby Wilkins. 136p. 1984. pap. 6.95 (ISBN 0-935330-01-1). Blackwells Pr.
Vanishing Adolescent. Edgar Z. Friedenberg. 223p. 1962. pap. 1.25 (ISBN 0-440-39276-4, LFL). Dell.
Vanishing Adolescent. Edgar Z. Friedenberg. LC 85-950. xxvi, 144p. 1985. Repr. of 1959 ed. lib. bdg. 35.00x (ISBN 0-313-24920-2, FRVA). Greenwood.
Vanishing Air. John C. Esposito. 328p. 1970. pap. 0.95 (ISBN 0-686-36549-6). Ctr Responsive Law.
Vanishing American Needle Arts. Denise Longhurst. LC 83-8722. (Illus.). 192p. 1984. 17.95 (ISBN 0-399-12850-6, Putnam). Putnam Pub Group.
Vanishing American: The Epic of the Indian. Zane Grey. (Orig.). 1984. pap. 3.50 (ISBN 0-671-55696-7). PB.
Vanishing American: White Attitudes & U. S. Indian Policy. Brian W. Dippie. LC 82-2804. (Illus.). 432p. 1982. pap. 12.95 (ISBN 0-8195-5056-6). Wesleyan U Pr.
Vanishing Animals. Andy Warhol & Kurt Benirschke. (Illus.). 110p. 1986. 29.95 (ISBN 0-387-96410-X). Springer-Verlag.
Vanishing Arctic: Alaska's National Wildlife Refuge. T. H. Watkins. (Illus.). 88p. 1988. 39.95; until 1/1989 29.95 (ISBN 0-89381-329-X). Aperture.
Vanishing Breed: Photographs of the Cowboy & the West. William A. Allard. (Illus.). 140p. 1984. pap. 14.45i (ISBN 0-8212-1565-5). NYGS.
Vanishing Child. Christopher C. Smith. 32p. 1988. 6.50 (ISBN 0-8062-3196-3). Carlton.
Vanishing Congress: Where Has All the Power Gone? David J. Muchow. 230p. 1976. 15.00 (ISBN 0-88265-005-X). North Am Intl.
Vanishing DeKalb. DeKalb Historical Society Staff. (Illus.). 240p. 1985. 30.00 (ISBN 0-9615459-0-9). DeKalb.
Vanishing Depot. Ranulph Bye. 1984. 35.00 (ISBN 0-910702-11-X). Bentley PA.
Vanishing Eagles. Philip Burton. (Illus.). 140p. 1983. 29.95 (ISBN 0-396-08168-1). Dodd.
Vanishing England. Gareth H. Davies & John Le Carre. (Illus.). 168p. 1987. 29.95 (ISBN 0-88162-247-8). Salem Hse Pubs.
Vanishing Farmland: A Legal Solution for the States. Sarah E. Redfield. 224p. 1984. 30.00x (ISBN 0-669-08233-3). Lexington Bks.
Vanishing Farmland Crisis: Critical Views of the Movement to Preserve Agricultural Land. Ed. by John Baden. LC 84-7472. (Studies in Government & Public Policy). x, 174p. 1984. 19.95x (ISBN 0-7006-0253-4). U Pr of KS.
Vanishing Fishes of North America. Dana R. Ono et al. LC 82-62896. (Illus.). 268p. 1983. 29.95 (ISBN 0-913276-43-X). Stone Wall Pr.
Vanishing Forest Reserves. Willard G. Van Name. Ed. by Stuart Bruchey. LC 78-56688. (Management of Public Lands in the U. S. Ser.). 1979. Repr. of 1929 ed. lib. bdg. 17.00x (ISBN 0-405-11356-0). Ayer Co Pubs.
Vanishing Forest: The Human Consequences of Deforestation. ICIHI Staff. (ICIHI Staff Report for the International Commission on International Humanitarian Issues Ser.). 128p. 1986. text ed. 18.50x (ISBN 0-86232-631-1, Pub. by Zed Pr England); pap. 6.95 (ISBN 0-86232-632-X). Humanities.
Vanishing Garden: A Conservation Guide to Garden Plants. Christopher Brickell & Fay Sharman. (Illus.). 261p. 1986. 24.95 (ISBN 0-88192-030-4). Timber.
Vanishing Georgia. LC 82-4764. (Illus.). 240p. 1982. 24.95 (ISBN 0-8203-0628-2). U of Ga Pr.
Vanishing Gwinnett County, Georgia. W. Dorsey Stancil. 240p. 1984. 25.00 (ISBN 0-914923-04-8). Gwinnett Hist.
Vanishing Habitats. Noel Simon. (Survival Ser.). (Illus.). 32p. (gr. 4-9). 1987. PLB 10.90 (ISBN 0-531-17062-4, Pub. by Gloucester Pr). Watts.
Vanishing Harvest: A Study of Food & its Conservation. R. K. Robinson. (Illus.). 1983. 39.95x (ISBN 0-19-854713-7). Oxford U Pr.
Vanishing Hero. facs. ed. Sean O'Faolain. LC 71-142686. (Essay Index Reprint Ser). 1957. 16.00 (ISBN 0-8369-2065-1). Ayer Co Pubs.
Vanishing Hitchhiker: American Urban Legends & Their Meanings. Jan H. Brunvand. (Orig.). 1981. 14.95 (ISBN 0-393-01473-8); pap. text ed. 7.95x (ISBN 0-393-95169-3). Norton.
Vanishing Holes Murder. Peter Chambers. 1985. 25.00x (ISBN 0-7090-1818-5, Pub. by R Hale Ltd UK). State Mutual Bk.
Vanishing Ireland. Edna O'Brien. (Illus.). 112p. 1987. 22.50 (ISBN 0-517-56508-0, C N Potter Bks). Crown.
Vanishing Lady, & Other Stories. English Language Services Staff. (English Readers Ser.). pap. 3.73 (ISBN 0-02-971310-2). Macmillan.
Vanishing Land. Hildegarde Flanner. 60p. (Orig.). 1980. pap. 6.00 (ISBN 0-931832-15-2). Fithian Pr.
Vanishing Land. Robert W. Howard. Ed. by Marc Jaffe. LC 84-40171. 352p. 1985. 15.45 (ISBN 0-394-53948-6, Pub. by Villard Bks). Random.
Vanishing Land. Robert W. Howard. 352p. 1986. pap. 4.50 (ISBN 0-345-32989-9). Ballantine.
Vanishing Land: The Corporate Theft of America. Frank Browning. 12.00 (ISBN 0-8446-5166-4). Peter Smith.
Vanishing Lands: A World Survey of Soil Erosion. Graham V. Jacks & Robert O. Whyte. LC 72-4280. (World Affairs Ser.: National & International Viewpoints). (Illus.). 384p. 1972. Repr. of 1939 ed. 25.50 (ISBN 0-405-04573-5). Ayer Co Pubs.
Vanishing Landscapes: Land & Life in the Tulare Lake Basin. William L. Preston. LC 80-6055. (Illus.). 290p. 1981. 27.50x (ISBN 0-520-04053-8). U of Cal Pr.
Vanishing Lives: Style & Self in Tennyson, D. G. Rossetti, Swinburne, & Yeats. James Richardson. LC 87-25269. (Virginia Victorian Studies). 325p. 1988. 32.50x (ISBN 0-8139-1165-6). U Pr of Va.
Vanishing Maharajas. Debesh Das. 1977. text ed. 28.50x. Coronet Bks.
Vanishing Old Castles in England. P. H. Ditchfield. (Philosophy of History Library). (Illus.). 109p. 1981. 85.50 (ISBN 0-86650-003-0). Gloucester Art.
Vanishing Paperclips America's Aerospace Secret. Hans H. Amtmann. Ed. by thomas H. Hitchcock. (Illus.). 128p. 1988. 25.95 (ISBN 0-914144-35-9). Monogram Aviation.
Vanishing Peasant: Innovation & Change in French Agriculture. Henri Mendras. Tr. by Jean Lerner from Fr. Orig. Title: Fin Des Paysans. 1971. 32.50x (ISBN 0-262-13065-3). MIT Pr.
Vanishing Point. Patricia Wentworth. 1976. Repr. of 1953 ed. lib. bdg. 17.95x (ISBN 0-88411-742-1, Pub. by Aeonian Bks). Amereon Ltd.
Vanishing Points. facsimile ed. Alice Brown. LC 71-106250. (Short Story Index Reprint Ser). 1913. 19.00 (ISBN 0-8369-3287-0). Ayer Co Pubs.
Vanishing Presence. Eugenia Janis & Max Kozloff. (Illus.). 160p. 1989. 35.00 (ISBN 0-8478-1006-2); pap. 19.95 (ISBN 0-8478-1007-0). Rizzoli Intl.
Vanishing Professor. Jack Long. (O'Reilly Mysteries Ser.). (Illus.). 24p. (ps-3). 1987. 3.95 (ISBN 0-02-688779-7, Checkerboard Pr). Macmillan.
Vanishing Pumpkin. Tony Johnston. LC 83-3122. (Illus.). (gr. k-4). 1983. 9.95 (ISBN 0-399-20991-3, Putnam). Putnam Pub Group.
Vanishing Pumpkin. Tony Johnston. (Illus.). 32p. (ps-5). 1984. pap. 4.95 (ISBN 0-399-20992-1, Putnam). Putnam Pub Group.
Vanishing Race & Other Illusions: Photographs of Indians by Edward S. Curtis. Christopher M. Lyman. (Illus.). 1982. pap. 14.95 (ISBN 0-394-71029-0). Pantheon.
Vanishing Race & Other Illusions: Photographs of Indians by Edward S. Curtis. Christopher M. Lyman. LC 81-607152. (Illus.). 158p. 1982. 24.95 (ISBN 0-87474-622-1, LYVR). Smithsonian.
Vanishing Race: Selection from Edward S. Curtis' The North American Indian. M. Gidley. (Illus.). 192p. 1987. pap. 14.95 (ISBN 0-295-96513-4). U of Wash Pr.
Vanishing Race: Selections from Edward S. Curtis' the North American Indian. Ed. by Mick Gidley. LC 76-23476. (Illus.). 1977. 9.95 (ISBN 0-8008-7945-7). Taplinger.
Vanishing Shadow. Margaret Sutton. (Judy Bolton Mysteries). 1976. Repr. of 1932 ed. lib. bdg. 15.95x (ISBN 0-88411-714-6, Pub. by Aeonian Pr). Amereon Ltd.
Vanishing Theorems on Complex Manifolds. Bernard Shiffman & Andrew J. Sommese. (Progress in Mathematics Ser.: Vol. 56). 183p. 1985. text ed. 22.50x (ISBN 0-8176-3288-3). Birkhauser.
Vanishing Tools. Robert Rohm. LC 78-730967. (Winnie the Witch: Stories About Values Ser.). (Illus.). (gr. k-3). 1979. pap. text ed. 24.95 (ISBN 0-89290-050-4); 6 bks. & one cassette incl. Soc for Visual.
Vanishing Tower. Michael Moorcock. (Elric of Melnibone Ser.). (Illus.). 200p. 1981. slipcased 25.00 (ISBN 0-915822-38-5). Archival Pr.
Vanishing Tower. Michael Moorcock. 176p. 1984. pap. 2.95. Berkley Pub.
Vanishing Tribes of Kenya: A Description of the Manners & Customs of the Primitive & Interesting Tribes Dwelling on the Vast Southern Slopes of Mount Kenya & Their Fast Disappearing Native Methods of Life. J. Orde Browne. 1925. 27.00 (ISBN 0-8115-3069-8). Kraus Repr.
Vanishing Tribes: Primitive Man On Earth. Alain Cheneviere. LC 86-29047. (Illus.). 240p. 1987. 35.00 (ISBN 0-385-23897-5, Dolp). Doubleday.
Vanishing Vector. John P. Evans & John B. Mannion. 256p. (Orig.). 1981. pap. 2.50 (ISBN 0-449-14409-7, GM). Fawcett.
Vanishing Village. Will Rose. 350p. 1970. 5.50 (ISBN 0-9600350-0-1). Catskill Art.
Vanishing Village: Danish Maritime Community. Robert T. Anderson & Barbara G. Anderson. LC 77-87704. (American Ethnological Soiciety Monographs: No. 39). Repr. of 1964 ed. 28.00 (ISBN 0-404-16498-6). AMS Pr.
Vanishing Western Ghost Towns with Lamentations. Thomas W. Moore. LC 86-60609. (Illus.). 160p. 1986. 12.00 (ISBN 0-9616501-0-9). Pony Pr.
Vanishing White Man. Stan Steiner. LC 86-28491. 322p. 1987. pap. 10.95 (ISBN 0-8061-2049-5). U of Okla Pr.
Vanishings. Philip Graham. LC 78-504343. (Illus.). 1978. pap. 3.00 (ISBN 0-913722-12-X, Pub. by Release). Small Pr Dist.
Vanitas. Jeffrey Ford. LC 87-20676. (Illus.). 184p. 1988. pap. 7.95 (ISBN 0-917053-07-9). Space And.
Vanitie & Downe-Fall of Superstitious Popish Ceremonies. Peter Smart. LC 77-7428. (English Experience Ser.: No. 894). 1977. Repr. of 1628 ed. lib. bdg. 20.00 (ISBN 90-221-0894-5). Walter J Johnson.
Vanities & Verities. R. H. Mottram. 1973. Repr. of 1958 ed. 20.00 (ISBN 0-8274-1196-0). R West.
Vanity & Mischief of the Old Letany see Letany of J. Bastwick.
Vanity Blade. Samantha Harte. Ed. by Nancy Parent. 384p. (Orig.). 1987. pap. 3.95 (ISBN 0-7701-0685-4). Paperjacks US.
Vanity Dies Hard. Ruth Rendell. 160p. 1985. pap. 2.95. Ballantine.
Vanity Dies Hard. Ruth Rendell. 15.95 (ISBN 0-89190-374-7, Pub. by Am Repr). Amereon Ltd.
Vanity Dies Hard. Ruth Rendell. 192p. 1987. pap. 3.50 (ISBN 0-345-34952-0). Ballantine.
Vanity Fair. William Makepeace Thackeray. (Classics Ser). (gr. 11 up). pap. 2.50 (ISBN 0-8049-0138-4, CL-138). Airmont.
Vanity Fair. William Makepeace Thackeray. (Literature Ser). (gr. 10-12). 1970. pap. text ed. 8.08 (ISBN 0-87720-741-0). AMSCO Sch.
Vanity Fair. William Makepeace Thackeray. 1979. (Evman); pap. 6.95x (ISBN 0-460-11298-8, Evman). Biblio Dist.
Vanity Fair. William Makepeace Thackeray. Ed. by Geoffrey Tillotson & Kathleen Tillotson. LC 63-3850. 1963. pap. 6.95 (ISBN 0-395-05161-4, RivEd). HM.
Vanity Fair. William Makepeace Thackeray. 1962. pap. 4.95 (ISBN 0-451-52041-6, CE1726, Sig Classics). NAL.
Vanity Fair. William Makepeace Thackeray. Ed. by J. M. Stewart. (English Library Ser.). 1969. pap. 4.95 (ISBN 0-14-043035-0). Penguin.
Vanity Fair. William Makepeace Thackeray. 1982. Repr. lib. bdg. 28.95 (ISBN 0-89966-406-7). Buccaneer Bks.
Vanity Fair. William Makepeace Thackeray. Ed. by John Sutherland. (World's Classics-Paperback Ser.). 1983. pap. 4.95 (ISBN 0-19-281642-X). Oxford U Pr.
Vanity Fair. William Makepeace Thackeray. (Illus.). 784p. 1985. 14.95 (ISBN 0-396-08534-2). Dodd.
Vanity Fair Caricature Lithographs: A Checklist. Jerold J. Savory. LC 78-104. (Reference Library of the Humanities: Vol. 120). 1978. lib. bdg. 28.00 (ISBN 0-8240-9824-2). Garland Pub.
Vanity Fair Gallery. Jerold J. Savory. 35.00 (ISBN 0-8453-2240-0, Cornwall Bks). Assoc Univ Prs.
Vanity Fair Gallery: A Collector's Guide to the Caricatures. Jerold J. Savory. LC 78-353. (Illus.). 209p. 1978. 35.00 (ISBN 0-87982-023-3). Art Alliance.
Vanity Fair Notes. Mildred R. Bennett. (Orig.). 1964. pap. 3.25 (ISBN 0-8220-1320-7). Cliffs.
Vanity Fur. Ilene Hochberg. 1988. pap. 9.95 (ISBN 0-671-67069-7). PB.
Vanity License PL8s. John Mahoney. (Illus.). 72p. 1988. pap. 6.95 (ISBN 0-87938-296-1). Motorbooks Intl.
Vanity of Existence. Arthur Schopenhauer. (Illus.). 123p. 1985. 117.85 (ISBN 0-89266-507-6). Am Classical Coll Pr.
Vanity of Power: American Isolationism & the First World War. John M. Cooper, Jr. LC 70-95508. (Contributions in American History: No. 3). 1969. lib. bdg. 35.00 (ISBN 0-8371-2342-9, COP/). Greenwood.
Vanity Square: A Story of Fifth Avenue Life. Edgar Saltus. LC 73-113267. Repr. of 1906 ed. 17.50 (ISBN 0-404-05538-9). AMS Pr.
Vanity Will Get You Somewhere. Joseph Cotten. 256p. 1988. pap. 4.50 (ISBN 0-380-70534-6). Avon.
Vanna Karenina. Frank Gannon. 1988. 15.95 (ISBN 0-670-82080-6). Viking.
Vanna Speaks. Vanna White. (Illus.). 208p. 1988. pap. 3.95 (ISBN 0-446-34669-1). Warner Bks.
Vanna Speaks. Vanna White & Bart Andrews. 256p. 1987. 15.95 (ISBN 0-446-34668-3). Warner Bks.
Vanna White. Marianne Robin-Tani. Date not set. pap. 2.95 (ISBN 0-317-59528-8). St Martin.
Vannes & Its Region: A Study of Town & Country in Eighteenth-Century France. T. J. Le Goff. (Illus.). 1981. 74.00x (ISBN 0-19-822515-6). Oxford U Pr.
Vanning Trends. Ed. by Spence Murray. LC 77-84297. (Pickups & Vans Ser.). (Illus., Orig.). 1977. pap. 3.95 (ISBN 0-8227-5015-5). Petersen Pub.
Vanport, Oregon: Life & Death of an Instant City. Manly Maben. (Illus., Orig.). 1987. pap. 10.95 (ISBN 0-87595-117-1). Oregon Hist.
Vanquished Hope: The Church in Russia on the Eve of the Revolution. James Cunningham. 1981. pap. 40.00x (Pub. by Mowbrays Pub Div). State Mutual Bk.
Vanquished Hope: The Movement for Church Renewal in Russia, 1905-1906. James W. Cunningham. LC 81-9077. 384p. 1981. pap. text ed. 10.95 (ISBN 0-913836-70-2). St Vladimirs.
Vanquished Nation, Broken Spirit: The Virtues of the Heart in Formative Judaism. Jacob Neusner. 208p. 1987. 24.95 (ISBN 0-521-32832-2). Cambridge U Pr.
Vans. Paul Dexler. LC 77-6181. (Superwheels & Thrill Sports Bks.). (Illus.). (gr. 4-9). 1977. PLB 8.95 (ISBN 0-8225-0415-4). Lerner Pubns.
Van't Hoff-LeBel Centennial. Ed. by O. Bertrand Ramsay. LC 75-9656. (ACS Symposium Ser.: No. 12). 1975. 21.95 (ISBN 0-8412-0247-8). Am Chemical.
Vantage Point. Charles Beard. 109p. 1988. 7.95 (ISBN 0-533-06238-1). Vantage.
Vanuatu (New Hebrides) (Let's Visit Places & Peoples - - Nations, Dependencies, & Sovereignties of the World Ser.). (Illus.). (gr. 5 up). 1989. 12.95 (ISBN 0-7910-0140-7). Chelsea Hse.
Vanuatu: Politics, Economics & Ritual in Island Melanesia. Ed. by Michael Allen. LC 81-65767. (Studies in Population). 425p. 1982. 44.00 (ISBN 0-12-051450-8). Acad Pr.
Vanya. Myrna Grant. LC 73-89729. 1974. pap. 5.95 (ISBN 0-88419-009-9, Creation Hse). Strang Comms Co.
Vanya. Myrna Grant. 208p. 1976. 3.25 (ISBN 0-88113-310-8). Edit Betania.
Vanya & the Clay Queen. Gary M. Prince. LC 74-9035. (Illus.). 32p. (gr. 2-5). 1975. PLB 4.95 (ISBN 0-87614-049-5). Carolrhoda Bks.
Vapheio Cups & Aegean Gold & Silver Ware. Ellen N. Davis. LC 76-23609. (Outstanding Dissertations in the Fine Arts). (Illus.). 492p. 1977. Repr. of 1973 ed. lib. bdg. 76.00 (ISBN 0-8240-2681-0). Garland Pub.
Vapor Deposition. Ed. by Carroll F. Powell et al. LC 66-13515. (Electrochemical Society Ser.). (Illus.). pap. 160.00 (ISBN 0-317-11088-8, 2051258). Bks Demand UMI.
Vapor Dreams in L.A. Terry Schoonhaven's Empty Stage. Museum Studies Class. (Illus.). 40p. 1982. pap. 9.00 (ISBN 0-936270-19-5). CA St U LB Art.

Variational Analysis: Critical Extremals & Sturmian Extensions. Marston Morse. LC 72-8368. (Pure & Applied Mathematics Ser.). Repr. of 1973 ed. 51.70 (ISBN 0-8357-9998-0, 2019523). Bks Demand UMI.

Variational & Hamiltonian Control Systems. P. E. Crouch & A. J. Van Der Schaft. (Lecture Notes in Control & Information Sciences: Vol. 101). vi, 121p. 1987. pap. 21.80 (ISBN 0-387-18372-8). Springer-Verlag.

Variational & Quasivariational Inequalities: Applications to Free Boundary Problems. Claudio Baiocchi & Antonio Capelo. Tr. by Lakshmi Jayakar. 462p. 1984. 83.95 (ISBN 0-471-90201-2, Pub. by Wiley-Interscience). Wiley.

Variational Calculations in Quantum Field Theory. Ed. by L. Polley & Del Pottinger. 316p. 1988. 55.00 (ISBN 9971-50-500-2); pap. 35.00 (ISBN 9971-50-501-0). World Scientific Pub.

Variational Calculus with Elementary Convexity. J. L. Troutman. (Undergraduate Texts in Mathematics). (Illus.). 364p. 1983. 36.00 (ISBN 0-387-90771-8). Springer-Verlag.

Variational Convergence for Functions & Operators. H. Attouch. (Pitman Applicable Mathematics Ser.). 352p. 1986. pap. 55.95 (ISBN 0-470-20405-2, Co-Pub. with Longman). Wiley.

Variational, Incremental & Energy Methods in Solid Mechanics & Shell Theory: IFIP World Congress. J. Mason. (Studies in Applied Mechanics: Vol. 4). 368p. 1980. 110.75 (ISBN 0-444-41899-7). Elsevier.

Variational Inequalities & Complementarity Problems: Theory & Applications. Ed. by Richard W. Cottle et al. LC 79-40108. 426p. pap. 110.80 (2029856). Bks Demand UMI.

Variational Inequalities & Flow in Porous Media. M. Chipot. (Applied Mathematical Sciences Ser.: Vol. 52). (Illus.). 120p. 1984. pap. 19.50 (ISBN 0-387-96002-3). Springer-Verlag.

Variational Method & Method of Monotone Operators in the Theory of Nonlinear Equations. M. M. Vainberg. 368p. 1974. text ed. 73.00x (Pub. by Keter Pub Jerusalem). Coronet Bks.

Variational Methods Applied to Problems of Diffusion & Reaction. R. Aris & W. C. Strieder. (Springer Tracts in Natural Philosophy: Vol. 24). (Illus.). 120p. 1973. 29.00 (ISBN 0-387-06311-0). Springer-Verlag.

Variational Methods for Eigenvalue Approximation. Hans F. Weinberger. (CBMS-NSF Regional Conference Ser.: No. 15). v, 160p. (Orig.). 1974. pap. text ed. 21.50 (ISBN 0-89871-012-X). Soc Indus-Appl Math.

Variational Methods for Free Surface Interfaces. Ed. by P. Concus & R. Finn. (Illus.). x, 204p. 1986. 36.00 (ISBN 0-387-96396-0). Springer-Verlag.

Variational Methods in Economics. G. Hadley & M. Kemp. (Advanced Textbooks in Economics: Vol. 1). 378p. 1971. 37.50 (ISBN 0-444-10097-0, North-Holland). Elsevier.

Variational Methods in Elasticity & Plasticity. 3rd ed. K. Washizu. (Illus.). 540p. 1982. text ed. 135.00 (ISBN 0-08-026723-8). Pergamon.

Variational Methods in Electron-Atom Scattering Theory. Robert K. Nesbet. (Physics of Atoms & Molecules Ser.). (Illus.). 236p. 1980. 45.00x (ISBN 0-306-40413-3, Plenum Pr). Plenum Pub.

Variational Methods in Engineering. Ed. by C. A. Brebbia. 750p. 1985. 98.00 (ISBN 0-387-15496-5). Springer-Verlag.

Variational Methods in Geosciences: Proceedings of the International Symposium on Variational Methods in Geosciences, University of Oklahoma, Norman, Ok., October 15-17, 1985. Ed. by Y. K. Sasaki. (Developments in Geomathematics Ser.: No. 5). 310p. 1986. 89.50 (ISBN 0-444-42697-3). Elsevier.

Variational Methods in Mathematics, Science & Engineering. Karel Rektorys. Tr. by Michael Basch from Czech. 572p. 1980. lib. bdg. 34.00 (ISBN 90-277-0561-5, Pub. by Reidel Holland). Kluwer Academic.

Variational Methods in Mathematics, Sciences & Engineering. new ed. Karel Rektorys. Ed. by SNTL. LC 74-80530. 1976. lib. bdg. 71.00 (ISBN 90-277-0488-0, Pub. by Reidel Holland). Kluwer Academic.

Variational Methods in Nonconservative Phenomena. Bozidar Vujanovic & Stanley E. Jonas. 500p. 1988. price not set (ISBN 0-12-728450-8). Acad Pr.

Variational Methods in Nuclear Reactor Physics. Weston M. Stacey, Jr. (Nuclear Science & Technology Ser.). 1974. 67.00 (ISBN 0-12-662060-1). Acad Pr.

Variational Methods in Optimum Control Theory. I. P. Petrov. Tr. by Morris D. Friedman. LC 68-18678. (Mathematics in Science & Engineering Ser.: Vol. 45). 1968. 71.00 (ISBN 0-12-552850-7). Acad Pr.

Variational Methods in the Mechanics of Solids: Proceedings of the UUTAM Symposium, Sept. 11-13, 1978. S Nemat-Nasser. LC 80-41529. (Illus.). 426p. 1980. 155.00 (ISBN 0-08-024728-8). Pergamon.

Variational Principles & Free-Boundary Problems. Avner Friedman. LC 87-29657. 720p. 1988. Repr. of 1982 ed. lib. bdg. 68.50 (ISBN 0-89464-263-4). Krieger.

Variational Principles. Benjamin L. Moiseiwitsch. LC 66-17233. (Interscience Monographs & Texts in Physics & Astronomy: Vol. 20). pap. 80.00 (ISBN 0-317-11049-7, 2016148). Bks Demand UMI.

Variational Principles for Nonpotential Operators. Filippov. (MMONO Ser.). 180p. Date not set. price not set. Am Math.

Variational Principles in Dynamics & Quantum Theory. 3rd ed. Wolfgang Yourgrau & Stanley Mandelstam. LC 78-73521. 1979. pap. text ed. 5.00 (ISBN 0-486-63773-5). Dover.

Variational Principles in Thermo- & Magneto-Elasticity: Proceedings of CISM, Department for Mechanics of Deformable Bodies, Technical Univ. of Vienna, 1970. CISM (International Center for Mechanical Sciences), Department for Mechanics of Deformable Bodies Staff. Ed. by H. Parkus. (CISM Pubns. Ser.: No. 58). 47p. 1973. pap. 9.50 (ISBN 0-387-81080-3). Springer-Verlag.

Variational Principles of Continuum Mechanics with Applications to Structural & Mechanical Engineering: Volume 1: Critical Points Theory. Vadim Komkov. 1986. lib. bdg. 59.00 (ISBN 90-277-2157-2, Pub. by Reidel Holland). Kluwer Academic.

Variational Principles of Continuum Mechanics with Engineering Applications: Vol. 2: Introduction to Optimal Design Theory. Vadim Komkov. 1988. lib. bdg. 69.00 (ISBN 90-277-2639-6, Pub. by Reidel Holland). Kluwer Academic.

Variational Principles of Mechanics. Cornelius Lanczos. 418p. 1986. pap. text ed. 10.00 (ISBN 0-486-65067-7). Dover.

Variational Principles of the Theory of Elasticity with Applications. Hu Haichang. 491p. 1985. text ed. 97.50 (ISBN 0-677-31330-6). Gordon & Breach.

Variational Semantics in Tibeto-Burman: The "Organic" Approach to Linguistic Comparison. James A. Matisoff. LC 77-28921. (Occasional Papers of the Wolfenden Society on Tibeto-Burman Linguistics Ser.: Vol. 6). (Illus.). 352p. 1978. text ed. 25.00 (ISBN 0-915980-85-1). ISHI PA.

Variational Technique in Electromagnetism. L. Cairo & T. Kahan. 168p. 1965. 58.00 (ISBN 0-677-10720-X). Gordon & Breach.

Variational Theory of Geodesics. M. M. Postnikov. Tr. by Scripta Technica Inc. 200p. 1983. pap. 7.00 (ISBN 0-486-63166-4). Dover.

Variationen in der Altgermanischen Alliterations Poesie. Walther Paetzel. pap. 22.00 (ISBN 0-384-44440-7). Johnson Repr.

Variationen uber ein Zahlenthroretisches Them von Carl Friedrich Gauss. H. Pieper. (Science & Civilization Ser.: No. 33). 160p. (Ger.). 1978. 16.95x (ISBN 0-8176-0959-8). Birkhauser.

Variations. Michael Hamburger. (Literary Ser.). 110p. 1983. 17.50 (ISBN 0-933806-14-0). Black Swan CT.

Variations. (Learning Science Program). (gr. 4). 6.30 (ISBN 0-02-656370-3, 65637); tchr's annotated ed. 9.36 (ISBN 0-02-656380-0, 65638). Benziger Pub Co.

Variations: An Anthology of Contemporary Poetry. Ed. by William C. Duncan. 1978. 10.00 (ISBN 0-930266-01-3). Contemp Lit Pr.

Variations: Five Los Angeles Painters. Susan C. Larsen. LC 80-69334. (Illus.). 51p. (Orig.). 1980. pap. write for info. (ISBN 0-911291-05-9). Fellows Cont Art.

Variations II: Seven Los Angeles Painters. Constance Mallinson. LC 83-80463. (Illus.). 52p. (Orig.). 1983. pap. write for info. (ISBN 0-911291-08-3). Fellows Cont Art.

Variations III: Emerging Artists in Southern California. Melinda Wortz. LC 87-80526. (Illus.). 79p. (Orig.). 1987. pap. write for info. (ISBN 0-911291-13-X). Fellows Cont Art.

Variations in Black & White Perceptions of the Social Environment. Ed. by Harry C. Triandis. LC 75-29056. 212p. 1976. 27.50 (ISBN 0-252-00515-5). U of Ill Pr.

Variations in C: Programming Techniques for Developing Efficient Professional Applications. Steve Schustack. 368p. 1985. pap. 19.95 (ISBN 0-914845-48-9). Microsoft.

Variations in Human Physiology. Ed. by R. M. Case. LC 84-11301. (Integrative Studies in Human Physiology). 241p. 1985. text ed. 29.00 (ISBN 0-7190-1086-1, Pub. by Manchester Univ Pr); pap. text ed. 15.00 (ISBN 0-7190-1732-7). St Martin.

Variations in Sexual Behavior. Frank S. Caprio. 1967. pap. 2.25 (ISBN 0-8065-0021-2, 257, Pub. by Citadel Pr). Lyle Stuart.

Variations in Susceptibility to inhaled Pollutants: Identification, Mechanisms, & Policy Implications. Ed. by Joseph D. Brain et al. LC 87-45484. (Environmental Toxicology Ser.). 528p. 1988. text ed. 65.00x (ISBN 0-8018-3503-8). Johns Hopkins.

Variations in Tectonic Styles in Canada. Ed. by Raymond A. Price & R. J. Douglas. LC 73-331222. (Geological Association of Canada. Special Paper: No. 11). pap. 160.00 (2027842). Bks Demand UMI.

Variations in the Global Water Budget. Street-Perrot & Beran. 1983. lib. bdg. 69.50 (ISBN 90-277-1364-2, Pub. by Reidel Holland). Kluwer Academic.

Variations in the Night. Emily Listfield. LC 87-941. 192p. 1987. pap. 6.95 (ISBN 0-553-34442-0). Bantam.

Variations of Real Wages & Profit Margins in Relation to the Trade Cycle. Sho-Chieh Tsiang. (London School of Economics & Political Science Studies in Economics & Commerce: Vol. 9). pap. 24.00 (ISBN 0-8115-3306-9). Kraus Repr.

Variations on a Garden. Robin L. Fox. LC 86-81687. (Illus.). 192p. 1987. 17.50 (ISBN 0-87923-657-4). Godine.

Variations on a Theme. Sr. Mary Francis. 1977. 5.00 (ISBN 0-8199-0664-6). Franciscan Herald.

Variations on a Theme. Alan Maley & Alan Duff. 171p. 1979. text ed. 7.95 (ISBN 0-521-22059-9); 13.95 (ISBN 0-521-22134-X). Cambridge U Pr.

Variations on a Theme: Embellished Elevations of the Carnegie Mansion. Ed. by Lisa Taylor. LC 83-71455. (Cooper-Hewitt Museum Exhibition Catalogue Ser.). (Illus.). 96p. (Orig.). 1983. pap. 15.95x (ISBN 0-910503-01-X). Cooper-Hewitt Museum.

Variations on a Theme: Figurative Painting. Georgia Coopersmith. (Illus.). 32p. 1985. pap. 8.00 (ISBN 0-942746-08-2). SUNYP R Gibson.

Variations on a Theme: World's Fairs of the Eighties: Knoxville, New Orleans, Tsukuba, Vancouver. Algimantas Kezys. (Illus.). 96p. (Orig.). 1987. pap. 15.00 (ISBN 0-9617756-0-2). Galerija.

Variations on Catastrophe: Some French Responses to the Great War. John Cruickshank. 1982. 34.95x (ISBN 0-19-212599-0). Oxford U Pr.

Variations on the Hermit. Hilary Ayer. 64p. 1973. pap. 5.00 (ISBN 0-87924-025-3). Membrane Pr.

Variations on the Imperial Theme: Studies in Ceremonial Art & Collecting in the Age of Maximilian II & Rudolf II. Thomas D. Kaufmann. LC 77-94699. (Outstanding Dissertations in the Fine Arts Ser.). 1978. lib. bdg. 29.00x (ISBN 0-8240-3231-4). Garland Pub.

Variations on the Theme of Man & Woman. Philip Metman. 1985. 10.00x (ISBN 0-317-62237-4, Guild of Pastoral Psych). State Mutual Bk.

Variations on Wayne Sleep. Wayne Sleep. (Illus.). 96p. 1983. pap. 12.95 (ISBN 0-434-70756-2, Pub. by W Heinemann Ltd). David & Charles.

Variations: Reading Skills-Oral Communication for Beginning Students of ESL. Patricia Duffy. (Illus.). 224p. 1986. pap. text ed. write for info (ISBN 0-13-940503-8). P-H.

Variations: The Systematic Design of Supports. N. John Habraken et al. 1976. pap. 20.00x (ISBN 0-262-58032-2). MIT Pr.

Variationsrechnung im Grossen. Herbert Seifert & W. Threlfall. LC 77-160837. (Ger.). 8.95 (ISBN 0-8284-0049-0). Chelsea Pub.

Varicocele & Male Infertility, II. Ed. by M. Glezerman & E. W. Jecht. (Illus.). 135p. 1984. pap. 19.00 (ISBN 0-387-12985-5). Springer Verlag.

Varicose Veins. Harold Ellis. LC 82-3975. (Positive Health Guide Ser.). (Illus.). 112p. 1983. pap. 7.95 (ISBN 0-668-05340-2, 5340). Arco.

Varicose Veins, Related Diseases & Sclerotherapy: A Guide for Practitioners. H. I. Biegeleisen. 255p. 1984. text ed. 35.00 (ISBN 0-920792-18-9). Eden Pr.

Varied Harvest. Ed. by Amy Loveman et al. LC 73-134109. (Essay Index Reprint Ser). 1953. 21.00 (ISBN 0-8369-1981-5). Ayer Co Pubs.

Varied Harvest: The Life & Works of Henry Blake Fuller. Kenneth Scambray. LC 86-30827. (Critical Essays in Modern Literature Ser.). 208p. 1987. 24.95x (ISBN 0-8229-3556-2). U of Pittsburgh Pr.

Varied Kitchens of India: Cuisines of the Anglo-Indians of Calcutta, Bengalis, Jews of Calcutta, Kashmiris, Parsis, & Tibetans of Darjeeling. Copeland Marks. (Illus.). 360p. 1986. 19.95 (ISBN 0-87131-476-2). M Evans.

Varied Occupations in String Work see Graded Lessons in Macrame, Knotting & Netting.

Varied Pattern: Studies in the 18th Century. Peter Hughes & David Williams. LC 70-159260. (McMaster 18th Century Studies). 457p. 1979. lib. bdg. 48.00 (ISBN 0-8240-4000-7). Garland Pub.

Varied Sociology of Paul Lazarsfeld. Ed. by Patricia K. Lazarsfeld. LC 81-24205. 400p. 1982. 45.50x (ISBN 0-231-05122-0); pap. 21.00 (ISBN 0-231-05123-9). Columbia U Pr.

Varied Types. facs. ed. Gilbert K. Chesterton. LC 68-16919. (Essay Index Reprint Ser). 1903. 17.00 (ISBN 0-8369-0300-5). Ayer Co Pubs.

Varied Verse: The Dreams of a Decade. rev. ed. Constance Fisher. Ed. & intro. by Jean Cornick. (Illus.). 32p. 1986. pap. 12.95 (ISBN 0-9615516-2-3). Cornick.

Variegated Verse. Carlota Trejos. 24p. 1987. pap. 3.95 (ISBN 0-939551-00-4). Trejos Lit Agy.

Varietes, 5 tomes. Paul Valery. Set. 34.75 (ISBN 0-685-36628-6). French & Eur.

Varietie of Lute Lessons. Robert Dowland. Ed. by Edgar Hunt. 1958. 24.00 (ISBN 0-901938-45-9, ST10441). Eur-Am Music.

Varietie of Lute Lessons. Robert Dowland. LC 79-84102. (English Experience Ser.: No. 921). 76p. 1979. Repr. of 1610 ed. lib. bdg. 20.00 (ISBN 90-221-0921-6). Walter J Johnson.

Varieties & Problems of Twentieth Century Socialism. Jack R. Thomas & Louis Patsouras. 214p. 1981. text ed. 20.95x (ISBN 0-88229-444-X); pap. text ed. 10.95x (ISBN 0-88229-743-0). Nelson-Hall.

Varieties: Essays. Jonathan Lieberson. 368p. 1988. 19.95 (ISBN 1-55584-059-0). Weidenfeld.

Varieties of Aesthetic Experience. Ed. by Earle J. Coleman. LC 83-6781. 268p. (Orig.). 1983. lib. bdg. 31.25 (ISBN 0-8191-3276-4); pap. text ed. 13.50 (ISBN 0-8191-3277-2). U Pr of Amer.

Varieties of American English: Essays by Raven I. McDavid, Jr. Raven I. McDavid, Jr. Ed. by Anwar S. Dil. LC 78-59374. (Language Science & National Development Ser). 400p. 1980. 32.50x (ISBN 0-8047-0982-3). Stanford U Pr.

Varieties of American Religion. facsimile ed. Ed. by Charles S. Braden. LC 76-156616. (Essay Index Reprint Ser). Repr. of 1936 ed. 15.50 (ISBN 0-8369-2307-3). Ayer Co Pubs.

Varieties of Anti-Americanism: Reflex & Response. Stephen Haseler. LC 85-27426. 72p. (Orig.). 1985. pap. 6.75 (ISBN 0-89633-098-2). Ethics & Public Policy.

Varieties of Attention. Raja Parasuraman & D. R. Davies. (Cognition & Perception Ser.). 1984. 69.50 (ISBN 0-12-544970-4). Acad Pr.

Varieties of Christian-Marxist Dialogue. Ed. by Paul Mojzes. 210p. (Orig.). 1978. pap. 3.00 (ISBN 0-931214-02-5). Ecumenical Phila.

Varieties of Civil Religion. Robert N. Bellah & Phillip E. Hammond. LC 80-7742. 224p. 1982. pap. 7.95 (ISBN 0-06-060769-6, RD-385, HarpR). Har-Row.

Varieties of Constructive Mathematics. Douglas Bridges & Fred Richman. LC 85-26904. (London Mathematical Society Lecture Notes Ser.: No. 97). 200p. 1987. pap. 19.95 (ISBN 0-521-31802-5). Cambridge U Pr.

Varieties of Contemporary Marxism. Thomas J. Blakeley & James J. O'Rourke. 1984. lib. bdg. 53.50 (ISBN 90-277-1636-6, Pub. by Reidel Holland). Kluwer Academic.

Varieties of Corporatism: Theory & Practice. Peter J. Williamson. (Illus.). 250p. 1985. 42.50 (ISBN 0-521-26805-2). Cambridge U Pr.

Varieties of Delinquent Youth, 2 Vols. William Sheldon. 1970. Repr. of 1949 ed. Set. 37.95x (ISBN 0-02-852190-0). Hafner.

Varieties of Economics: Documents, Examples & Manifestoes, 2 Vols. Robert Lekachman. 23.00 (ISBN 0-8446-2449-7). Peter Smith.

Varieties of Enchantment: Early Greek Views of the Nature & Function of Poetry. George B. Walsh. LC 83-6467. ix, 170p. 1988. pap. 8.95x (ISBN 0-8078-4206-0). U of NC Pr.

Varieties of Ethnic Experience: Kinship, Class, & Gender among California Italian-Americans. Micaela Di Leonardo. LC 83-45929. (Anthropology of Contemporary Issues Ser.). 262p. 1984. 31.95x (ISBN 0-8014-1632-9); pap. 9.95x (ISBN 0-8014-9278-5). Cornell U Pr.

Varieties of Experience: An Introduction to Philosophy. Albert W. Levi. LC 57-6807. pap. 134.30 (ISBN 0-317-08882-3, 2012555). Bks Demand UMI.

Varieties of Fascism: Doctrines of Revolution in the Twentieth Century. Eugen Weber. LC 81-20922. 1982. pap. 7.50 (ISBN 0-89874-444-X, Anvil). Krieger.

Varieties of Formal Languages. J. E. Pin. Tr. by J. A. Howie from Fr. (Foundations of Computer Science Ser.). 180p. 1986. 37.50x (ISBN 0-306-42294-8, Plenum Pr). Plenum Pub.

Varieties of Formal Semantics: Proceedings of the 4th Amsterdam Colloquium. Ed. by T. Landman & F. Veltman. (Groningen-Amsterdam Studies in Semantics). xii, 425p. 1985. write for info. (ISBN 90-6765-008-0); pap. write for info. (ISBN 90-6765-007-2). Foris Pubns.

Varieties of Groups. H. Neumann. (Ergebnisse der Mathematik und Ihrer Grenzgebiete: Vol. 37). 1967. 33.00 (ISBN 0-387-03779-9). Springer-Verlag.

Varieties of History: From Voltaire to the Present. Ed. by Fritz Stern. 1973. pap. 9.95 (ISBN 0-394-71962-X, Vin). Random.

Varieties of Human Habitation. R. Martin Helick. LC 73-19343. 1970. spiral 17.50x (ISBN 0-912710-02-0). Regent Graphic Serv.

Varieties of Human Value. Charles W. Morris. LC 56-6641. (Midway Reprint Ser.: 1973). Repr. of 1965 ed. 42.80 (ISBN 0-8357-9660-4, 2016989). Bks Demand UMI.

Varieties of Juvenile Delinquency. C. Frankenstein. 264p. 1970. 66.00 (ISBN 0-677-02820-2). Gordon & Breach.

Varieties of Literary Thematics. Theodore Ziolkowski. LC 83-42585. 264p. 1983. 29.50x (ISBN 0-691-06577-2). Princeton U Pr.

Varieties of Marxism. Avineri. (Van Leer Jerusalem Foundation Ser.). 1977. lib. bdg. 30.00 (ISBN 90-247-2024-9, Pub by Martinus Nijhoff Netherland). Kluwer Academic.

Varieties of Monetary Experience. Ed. by David M. Meiselman. LC 70-116027. (Economic Research Center Ser). 1971. 30.00x (ISBN 0-226-51930-9). U of Chicago Pr.

Varieties of Parable. Louis MacNeice. LC 66-10036. (Clark Lectures, 1963). pap. 41.30 (ISBN 0-317-20590-0, 2024498). Bks Demand UMI.

Vasari on Technique. Giorgio Vasari. Ed. by B. Baldwin Brown. (Illus.). 16.00 (ISBN 0-8446-3108-6). Peter Smith.
Vasarnap Farkaspusztan. Fury Lajos. 1978. casebd. 12.00 (ISBN 0-912404-11-6). Alpha Pubns.
Vasavadatta. Subandhu. Tr. by Louis H. Gray. LC 70-181070. (Columbia University. Indo-Iranian Ser.: No. 8). Repr. of 1913 ed. 20.00 (ISBN 0-404-50478-7). AMS Pr.
Vasco Da Gama. David Knight. LC 78-18057. (Illus.). 48p. (gr. 4-7). 1979. PLB 9.59 (ISBN 0-89375-175-8); pap. 1.95 (ISBN 0-89375-167-7). Troll Assocs.
Vasco de Quiroga & His Pueblo-Hospitals of Santa Fe. Fintan B. Warren. (Monograph Ser.). (Illus.). 1963. 10.00 (ISBN 0-88382-057-9). AAFH.
Vasco Pratolini: The Development of a Social Novelist. Frank Rosengarten. LC 65-16534. (Crosscurrents-Modern Critiques Ser.). 154p. 1965. 6.95x (ISBN 0-8093-0178-4). S Ill U Pr.
Vasconcelos of Mexico: Philosopher & Prophet. John H. Haddox. (Texas Pan American Ser.). 115p. 1967. 7.50x (ISBN 0-292-73688-6). U of Tex Pr.
Vasconselos: A Romance of the New World. W. Gilmore Simms. LC 70-116016. Repr. of 1885 ed. 10.00 (ISBN 0-404-06037-4). AMS Pr.
Vascular Access: A Practical Guide. Ed. by Moshe Haimov. (Illus.). 192p. 1987. 34.00 (ISBN 0-87993-242-2). Futura Pub.
Vascular Anatomy of the Spinal Cord. A. K. Thron. (Illus.). 150p. 1988. 59.50 (ISBN 0-387-82015-9). Springer-Verlag.
Vascular & Doppler Ultrasound. Ed. by C. Carl Jaffe. (Clinics in Diagnostic Ultrasound Ser: Vol. 13). (Illus.). 211p. 1984. text ed. 33.00 (ISBN 0-443-08295-2). Churchill.
Vascular & Neurologic Complications of Diabetes Mellitus. Ed. by F. Belfiore & G. M. Molinatti. (Frontiers in Diabetes Ser.: Vol. 8). (Illus.). xii, 256p. 1987. 132.00 (ISBN 3-8055-4452-9). S Karger.
Vascular & Neurological Changes in Early Diabetes see Advances in Metabolic Disorders: Supplements.
Vascular Aphasia. Joseph M. Tonkongy. (Illus.). 248p. 1986. text ed. 32.50x (ISBN 0-262-20054-6, Pub by Bradford). MIT Pr.
Vascular Birthmarks: Hemangiomas & Malformations. John B. Mulliken & Anthony E. Young. (Illus.). 560p. 1988. 150.00 (ISBN 0-7216-6601-9). Saunders.
Vascular Birthmarks: Pathogenesis & Management. Ed. by Terrence J. Ryan & George W. Cherry. (Illus.). 250p. 1987. 59.00 (ISBN 0-19-261628-5). Oxford U Pr.
Vascular Connection. Robert A. Gegan & Ray C. Wunderlich. (Illus.). 220p. (Orig.). Date not set. 16.95; pap. 8.95. Consumer Info Pubns.
Vascular Disease of the Gastrointestinal Tract. Adrian Marston. (Illus.). 186p. 1986. 51.95 (ISBN 0-683-05598-4). Williams & Wilkins.
Vascular Diseases: A Concise Guide to Diagnosis, Management, Pathogenesis, & Prevention. Sandor Friedman. (Illus.). 588p. 1982. 55.00 (ISBN 0-7236-7000-5). PSG Pub Co.
Vascular Diseases of the Nervous System see Handbook of Clinical Neurology.
Vascular Disorders of Childhood. Ed. by Richard H. Dean & James A. O'Neill, Jr. LC 82-191. (Illus.). 205p. 1983. text ed. 27.50 (ISBN 0-8121-0832-9). Lea & Febiger.
Vascular Disorders of the Upper Extremity. Ed. by Herbert I. Machleder. LC 82-84504. (Illus.). 304p. 1983. monograph 37.50 (ISBN 0-87993-193-0). Futura Pub.
Vascular Emergencies. Henry Haimovici. (Illus.). 656p. 1982. 72.00 (ISBN 0-8385-9361-5). Appleton & Lange.
Vascular Endothelium & Basement Membranes. Ed. by B. M. Altura. (Advances in Microcirculation Ser.: Vol. 9). (Illus.). 1979. 40.75 (ISBN 3-8055-3054-4). S Karger.
Vascular Endothelium in Hemostasis & Thrombosis. Ed. by Michael A. Gimbrone, Jr. (Contemporary Issues in Haemostasis & Thrombosis Ser.: Vol. 2). (Illus.). 250p. 1986. text ed. 90.00 (ISBN 0-443-03064-2). Churchill.
Vascular Flora of Georgia: An Annotated Checklist. Wilbur H. Duncan & John T. Kartesz. LC 80-22014. 158p. 1981. pap. 6.00x (ISBN 0-8203-0538-3). U of Ga Pr.
Vascular Flora of Glen Helen, Clifton Gorge, & John Bryan State Parks. Sture F. Anliot. 1973. 3.50 (ISBN 0-86727-064-0). Ohio Bio Survey.
Vascular Flora of Ohio, Vol. II: The Dicotyledoneae of Ohio, Pt. Three-Asteraceae. T. Richard Fisher. (Illus.). 320p. 1988. 65.00x (ISBN 0-8142-0446-5). Ohio St U Pr.
Vascular Flora of the Southeastern United States: Vol. 1-Asteraceae. Arthur Cronquist. Ed. by Albert E. Radford. LC 79-769. xv, 261p. 1980. 27.50x (ISBN 0-8078-1362-1). U of NC Pr.
Vascular Graft Update: Safety & Performance. Helen E. Kambic et al. LC 86-14077. (Special Technical Publications (STP) Ser.: No. 898). (Illus.). 360p. 1986. text ed. 54.00 (ISBN 0-8031-0462-6, 04-898000-54). ASTM.
Vascular Grafting: Clinical Applications & Techniques. Creighton B. Wright. (Illus.). 384p. 1983. text ed. 63.00 (ISBN 0-7236-7023-4). PSG Pub Co.
Vascular Injuries & Diseases of the Upper Limb. E. Shaw Wilgis. 183p. 1983. text ed. 49.00 (ISBN 0-316-94066-6). Little.
Vascular Injury & Atherosclerosis. Moore. (Biochemistry of Diseases Ser.: Vol. 9). 264p. 1981. 59.75 (ISBN 0-8247-1534-9). Dekker.
Vascular Malformations & Fistulas of the Brain. Ed. by Robert R. Smith et al. (Seminars in Neurological Surgery Ser.). 268p. 1982. text ed. 58.00 (ISBN 0-89004-683-2). Raven.
Vascular Mechanisms of the Brain. Georgii I. Mchedlishvili. LC 70-141241. pap. 31.80 (ISBN 0-317-07810-0, 2020684). Bks Demand UMI.
Vascular Neuroeffector Mechanisms: Proceedings. Symposium on Vascular Neuroeffector Mechanism, 2nd International, Odense, July-August 1975. (Illus.). 300p. 1976. 84.00 (ISBN 3-8055-2325-4). S Karger.
Vascular Neuroeffector Mechanisms: Proceedings of the 5th International Congress on Vascular Neuroeffector Mechanisms held in Paris, France, 6-8 August; 1984. Ed. by J. A. Bevan et al. 368p. 1985. 109.50 (ISBN 0-444-80667-9). Elsevier.
Vascular Neuroeffector Mechanisms: 4th International Symposium. Ed. by John A. Bevan et al. 456p. 1983. text ed. 115.50 (ISBN 0-89004-738-3). Raven.
Vascular Neuroeffector Systems, Physiology & Pharmacology: Proceedings. Symposium on the Physiology & the Pharmacology of Vascular Neuroeffector Systems, Interlaken, 1969. Ed. by J. A. Bevan et al. (Illus.). viii, 350p. 1971. 48.00 (ISBN 3-8055-1184-1). S Karger.
Vascular Nursing. Victoria Fahey. (Illus.). 512p. 1988. 60.00 (ISBN 0-7216-2656-4). Saunders.
Vascular Occlusion: Epidemiological, Pathophysiological & Therapeutic Aspects. Marcello Tesi & James Dormandy. (Serono Symposia Ser.: No. 37). 1981. 84.00 (ISBN 0-12-685380-0). Acad Pr.
Vascular Occlusive Disorders: Medical & Surgical Management. Ed. by George J. Collins, Jr. LC 81-66256. (Illus.). 480p. 1981. 49.50 (ISBN 0-87993-158-2). Futura Pub.
Vascular Perfusion in Cancer Therapy. Ed. by K. Schwemmle & K. Aigner. (Recent Results in Cancer Research: Vol. 86). (Illus.). 280p. 1983. 64.00 (ISBN 0-387-12346-6). Springer-Verlag.
Vascular Plant Families. James P. Smith, Jr. (Illus.). 320p. 1977. pap. 11.95x (ISBN 0-916422-11-9). Mad River.
Vascular Plant Taxonomy. 2nd ed. Dirk R. Walters. 272p. 1979. pap. text ed. 20.95 (ISBN 0-8403-1747-6). Kendall-Hunt.
Vascular Plants of Continental Northwest Territories. William J. Cody & A. Erling Porsild. (Illus.). 676p. 1980. lib. bdg. 85.00x (ISBN 0-660-00119-5, 56546-7, Pub. by Natl Mus Canada). U of Chicago Pr.
Vascular Plants of Illinois. G. Neville Jones & George D. Fuller. (Scientific Papers Ser.: Vol. VI). (Illus.). 593p. 1955. 10.00x (ISBN 0-89792-012-0). Ill St Museum.
Vascular Plants of Indiana: A Computer Based Checklist. Theodore J. Crovello et al. LC 83-10024. 160p. 1983. text ed. 15.00x (ISBN 0-268-01923-1). U of Notre Dame Pr.
Vascular Plants of South Dakota. 2nd ed. Theodore Van Bruggen. 476p. 1985. pap. text ed. 31.95x (ISBN 0-8138-0650-X). Iowa St U Pr.
Vascular Plants of the Leeward Island, Hawaii. E. Christophersen & E. L. Caum. (B M B Ser.). Repr. of 1931 ed. 12.00 (ISBN 0-527-02187-3). Kraus Repr.
Vascular Plants of the Medicine Bow Mountains, Wyoming. Burrell E. Nelson. 393p. 1984. pap. text ed. 12.00 (ISBN 0-936204-17-6). Jelm Mtn.
Vascular Plants of the Nevada Test Site & Central Southern Nevada: Ecologic & Geographic Distributions. ERDA Technical Information Center Staff & Janice C. Beatley. LC 76-21839. 316p. 1976. pap. 16.00 (ISBN 0-87079-033-1, TID-26881); microfiche 6.50 (ISBN 0-87079-216-4, TID-26881). DOE.
Vascular Plants of the Pacific Northwest, 5 pts. C. Leo Hitchcock et al. Incl. Pt. I. Vascular Cryptogams, Gymnosperms, & Monocotyledons. (Illus.). 925p. 1969. 40.00x (ISBN 0-295-73983-5); Pt. 2. Salicaceae to Saxifragaceae. (Illus.). 597p. 1964. 40.00x (ISBN 0-295-73984-3); Pt. 3. Saxifragaceae to Ericaceae. (Illus.). 614p. 1961. 40.00x (ISBN 0-295-73985-1); Pt. 4. Ericaceae Through Companulaceae. (Illus.). 516p. 1959. 40.00x (ISBN 0-295-73986-X); Pt. 5. Compositae. (Illus.). 349p. 1955. 40.00x (ISBN 0-295-73987-8). LC 56-62679. (Publications in Biology Ser.: No. 17). U of Wash Pr.
Vascular Plants of Unglaciated Ohio. Allison W. Cusick & Gene M. Silberhorn. 1977. 9.00 (ISBN 0-86727-081-0). Ohio Bio Survey.
Vascular Plants of Western Washington. Ed. by Irene Creso. LC 84-72043. (Illus.). 520p. (Orig.). 1984. pap. 14.95 (ISBN 0-9613916-0-X). Creso.
Vascular Problems in Musculoskeletal Disorders of the Limbs. D. I. Abramson & D. S. Miller. (Illus.). 404p. 1981. 65.00 (ISBN 0-387-90524-3). Springer-Verlag.
Vascular Problems in Urologic Surgery. Andrew C. Novick & Ralph A. Straffon. LC 81-50271. pap. 94.30 (ISBN 0-317-26417-6, 2024969). Bks Demand UMI.
Vascular Smooth Muscle in Culture, 2 vols. Ed. by Julie H. Campbell & Gordon R. Campbell. 1987. Set. 215.00 set (ISBN 0-8493-4325-9). Vol. I. Vol. II, 384. CRC Pr.
Vascular Smooth Muscle: Metabolic Ionic & Contractile Mechanisms. Ed. by Maurice Crass, 3rd. Charles Barnes. (Research Topics in Physiology Ser.). 1982. 49.00 (ISBN 0-12-195220-7). Acad Pr.
Vascular Surgery. Ed. by John B. Chang. LC 85-2319. 271p. 1985. text ed. 48.95 (ISBN 0-89335-232-2). PMA Pub Corp.
Vascular Surgery. 2nd ed. H. Haimovici. 1216p. 1984. 140.00 (ISBN 0-8385-9381-X). Appleton & Lange.
Vascular Surgery. Crawford W. Jamieson. (Illus.). 202p. 1985. 34.95 (ISBN 0-7216-0993-7). Saunders.
Vascular Surgery. 3rd ed. Rutherford. 1744p. 1989. price not set (ISBN 0-7216-2065-5). Saunders.
Vascular Surgery. 2nd ed. Robert B. Rutherford. (Illus.). 1660p. 1984. 195.00 (ISBN 0-7216-7856-4). Saunders.
Vascular Surgery. Ed. by S. E. Wilson & R. A. Williams. (Illus.). 992p. 1985. text ed. 125.00 (ISBN 0-07-070812-6). McGraw.
Vascular Surgery: A Comprehensive Review. 2nd ed. Wesley Moore. 1264p. 1986. 132.50 (ISBN 0-8089-1829-X, 792979). Grune.
Vascular Surgery (BIMR Surgery, Vol. 4) Ed. by Peter Bell & N. Tilney. 320p. 1984. text ed. 49.95 (ISBN 0-407-02320-8). Butterworth.
Vascular Surgery for the House Officer. Jon R. Cohen. LC 85-20305. (House Officer Ser.). 225p. 1985. pap. 14.95 (ISBN 0-683-02030-7). Williams & Wilkins.
Vascular Surgery: Guide & Handbook. Pratt. LC 75-27628. (Illus.). 416p. 1976. 32.50. Green.
Vascular Surgery of the Lower Extremity. Jarrett & Hirsch. 1985. 60.00 (ISBN 0-8016-2426-6). Mosby.
Vascular Surgical Emergencies. Ed. by John J. Bergan & James S. T. Yao. 560p. 1987. 99.50 (ISBN 0-8089-1843-5, 790565). Grune.
Vascular Surgical Techniques. Ed. by Roger M. Greenhalgh. (Illus.). 336p. 1984. text ed. 99.95 (ISBN 0-407-00351-7). Butterworth.
Vascular Systems of the Cerebral Cortex. T. Bear. (Advances in Anatomy, Embryology & Cell Biology: Vol. 59). (Illus.). 1980. pap. 26.00 (ISBN 0-387-09652-3). Springer-Verlag.
Vascular Technology Review. 2nd ed. Ed. by Barton A. Bean & Donna E. Cox. LC 86-14056. 225p. (Orig.). 1986. pap. text ed. 55.00 (ISBN 0-317-55218-X). Appleton Davies.
Vascularization & Tissue Differentiation. Kiss. 1975. 11.00 (ISBN 963-05-0394-8, Pub. by Akademiai Kaido Hungary). IPS.
Vascularization & Tissue Differentiation. F. A. Kiss. 168p. 1975. 34.00x (ISBN 0-569-08186-6, Pub. by Collets (UK)). State Mutual Bk.
Vasculature & Circulation: The Role of Myogenic Reactivity in the Regulation of Blood Flow. E. Basar & C. Weiss. 272p. 1981. 128.00 (ISBN 0-444-80271-1). Elsevier.
Vasculitides. Thomas R. Cupps & Anthony S. Fauci. (Major Problems in Internal Medicine: No.21). 1981. pap. write for info. (ISBN 0-7216-2794-3). Saunders.
Vasculogenic Impotence. A. W. Zorgniotti & G. Rossi. (Illus.). 344p. 1980. 43.75x (ISBN 0-398-03982-8). C C Thomas.
Vasculopathies of Childhood. Raquel V. Hicks. (Illus.). 372p. 1988. 45.00 (ISBN 0-88416-473-X). PSG Pub Co.
Vasectomy & Medicine: Guidebook for Reference & Research. Benard I. Valahos. LC 83-46111. 150p. 1985. 34.50 (ISBN 0-88164-156-1); pap. 26.50 (ISBN 0-88164-157-X). ABBE Pubs Assn.
Vasectomy Book: A Complete Guide to Decision Making. Marc Goldstein & Michael Feldberg. LC 81-1023. (Illus.). 192p. (Orig.). 1983. pap. 5.95 (ISBN 0-87477-274-5). J P Tarcher.
Vasectomy Counseling. S. D. Mumford. (Illus.). 1977. 10.00 (ISBN 0-911302-31-X); pap. 6.00 (ISBN 0-317-58585-1). San Francisco Pr.
Vasectomy: Immunologic & Pathophysiologic Effects in Animals & Man. Ed. by Irwin H. Lepow & Ruth Crozier. LC 79-13779. 1979. 65.50 (ISBN 0-12-444150-5). Acad Pr.
Vasectomy: The Decision-Making Process. S. D. Mumford. (Illus.). 1978. pap. 12.00 (ISBN 0-911302-33-6). San Francisco Pr.
Vases Communicants: Essai. Andre Breton. (Idees Ser.). pap. 7.95 (ISBN 0-685-37241-3). Schoenhof.
Vasile Alecsandri. Alexandre Cioranescu. LC 79-169637. (World Authors Ser.). 1973. lib. bdg. 17.95 (ISBN 0-8057-2020-0). Irvington.
Vasili & Vasilissa: Selected Stories. Ed. by Nina Kupreyanova. Tr. by Yuri Nemetsky et al from Rus. 389p. 1981. 9.95 (ISBN 0-8285-2358-4, Pub. by Progress Pubs USSR). Imported Pubns.
Vasilieff & His Art. St. Felicity Moore. (Illus.). 1982. 58.00x (ISBN 0-19-554324-6). Oxford U Pr.
Vasilikos Valley Project I: The Bronze Age Cemetery in Kalavasos Village. Ed. by Ian A. Todd. (Studies in Mediterranean Archaeology: Vol. 71-1). (Illus.). 308p. 1986. pap. text ed. 60.00 (ISBN 91-86098-38-1, Pub. by Astrom Pubs Sweden). Humanities.
Vasilikos Valley Project II: Middle Cypriote Bronze Age Tombs. Ian A. Todd et al. (Studies in Mediterranean Archaeology: Vol. 69-2). (Illus.). 200p. 1988. pap. 59.00x (Pub. by P Astrom Pubs Sweden). Humanities.
Vasilisa the Beautiful. Illus. by I. Bilibin. (Illus.). 16p. 1979. pap. 2.45 (ISBN 0-8285-1257-4, Pub. by Goznak Pubs USSR). Imported Pubns.
Vasiliy Pavlovich Aksenov: A Writer in Quest of Himself. Ed. by Edward Mozejko et al. (Illus.). 272p. 1987. 19.95 (ISBN 0-89357-141-5). Slavica.
Vasily Polenov Museum Estate. F. D. Polenov. 178p. 1982. 49.00x (ISBN 0-317-39523-8, Pub. by Collets (UK)). State Mutual Bk.
Vasily Shukshin: Articles. E. Yefimov & V. Shukshin. 247p. 1986. pap. 3.95 (ISBN 0-8285-3263-X, Pub. by Raduga Pubs USSR). Imported Pubns.
Vaslav Nijinsky. C. W. Beaumont. LC 74-1080. (Studies in Music, No. 42). 1974. lib. bdg. 75.00x (ISBN 0-8383-1752-9). Haskell.
Vasn Vardanay Ew Hayots Paterazmin: The History of Vartan & the Battle of the Armenians. Eghishse. Ed. by Peter Cow. (Classical Armenian Texts). 50.00 (ISBN 0-88206-034-1). Caravan Bks.
Vasoactive Intestinal Peptide. Ed. by Sami I. Said. (Advances in Peptide Hormone Research Ser.). 528p. 1982. text ed. 93.00 (ISBN 0-89004-443-0). Raven.
Vasoactive Renal Hormones. Ed. by G. M. Eisenbach & J. Brod. (Contributions to Nephrology Ser.: Vol. 12). (Illus.). 1978. pap. 45.50 (ISBN 3-8055-2839-6). S Karger.
Vasodepressor Hormones in Hypertension: Prostaglandins & Kallikrein-Kinins. Ed. by Gerd Bonner. (Agents & Actions Supplements Ser.: No. 22). 380p. 1987. 59.00 (ISBN 0-8176-1922-4). Birkhauser.
Vasodilatation. Ed. by Paul M. Vanhoutte & Isadore Leusen. 552p. 1981. 100.50 (ISBN 0-89004-602-6). Raven.
Vasodilatation: Vascular Smooth Muscle, Peptides, Autonomic Nerves, & Endothelium. Ed. by Paul M. Vanhoutte. (Illus.). 608p. 1988. text ed. 125.00 (ISBN 0-88167-408-7). Raven.
Vasodilator Mechanisms. Ed. by P. M. Vanhoutte & St. F. Vatner. (Bibliotheca Cardiologica Ser.: No. 38). (Illus.). viii, 284p. 1985. 92.00 (ISBN 3-8055-3903-7). S Karger.
Vasodilator Substances of Tissues. J. H. Gaddum. Intro. by F. C. MacIntosh. (Illus.). 288p. 1987. 44.50 (ISBN 0-521-30860-7). Cambridge U Pr.
Vasomotion & Quantitative Kapillaroskopie. Ed. by K. Messmer & F. Hammersen. (Progress in Applied Microcirculation Ser.: Vol. 3). (Illus.). viii, 152p. 1984. pap. 54.75 (ISBN 3-8055-3809-X). S Karger.
Vasopressin. Ed. by Robert W. Schrier. (Illus.). 602p. 1985. text ed. 108.50 (ISBN 0-88167-107-X). Raven.
Vasopressin: Cellular & Integrative Functions. Ed. by Allen W. Cowley, Jr. et al. (Illus.). 544p. 1988. text ed. 75.00 (ISBN 0-88167-446-X). Raven.
Vasopressin: Principles & Properties. Ed. by D. M. Gash & G. J. Boer. (Illus.). 626p. 1987. 89.50x (ISBN 0-306-42515-7, Plenum Pr). Plenum Pub.
Vassar: A Photographic Celebration. Mark C. Borton. (Illus.). 112p. 1984. 30.00 (ISBN 0-930527-01-1). Embassy Imp.
Vassar Stories. Grace M. Gallaher. LC 71-113663. (Short Story Index Reprint Ser.). 1899. 19.00 (ISBN 0-8369-3392-3). Ayer Co Pubs.
Vassi & Fideles in the Carolingian Empire. Charles E. Odegaard. 1971. lib. bdg. 16.00x (ISBN 0-374-96135-2, Octagon). Hippocrene Bks.
Vassilisa the Wise: A Tale of Medieval Russia. Adapted by Josepha Sherman. LC 87-8563. (Illus.). 32p. (gr. 5-8). 1988. 14.95 (ISBN 0-15-293240-2). HarBraceJ.
Vassouras, a Brazilian Coffee County, 1850-1900: The Roles of Planter & Slave in a Plantation Society. Stanley J. Stein. LC 85-42659. (Illus.). 340p. 1985. 41.50x (ISBN 0-691-07694-4); pap. 14.50x (ISBN 0-691-02236-4). Princeton U Pr.
Vast Design: Patterns in Yeats' Aesthetic. Edward Engelberg. LC 87-35101. 250p. 1988. pap. 12.95 (ISBN 0-8132-0643-X). Cath U Pr.
Vast Domain of Blood. Don Schellie. LC 68-29143. ixx, 268p. 9.95 (ISBN 0-686-74355-5). Westernlore.
Vast Majority. Michael Harrington. 1978. pap. 8.95 (ISBN 0-671-24407-8, Touchstone Bks). S&S.
Vast Venture: Hardy's Epic-Drama "The Dynasts". Chester A. Garrison. Ed. by James Hogg. (Poetic Drama & Poetic Theory ser.). 250p. (Orig.). 1973. pap. 15.00 (ISBN 3-7052-0845-4, Pub. by Salzburg Studies). Longwood Pub Group.
Vastness of Natural Languages. D. Terence Langendoen & Paul M. Postal. 224p. 1984. 45.00x (ISBN 0-631-13461-1). Basil Blackwell.
Vastness of Natural Languages. D. Terence Langendoen & Paul M. Postal. 208p. 1986. pap. text ed. 14.95x (ISBN 0-631-14756-X). Basil Blackwell.

Veblen's Theory of Social Change. Leonard A. Dente. Ed. by Stuart Bruchey. LC 76-39826. (Nineteen Seventy-Seven Disserataions Ser.). (Illus.). 1977. lib. bdg. 29.00x (ISBN 0-405-09906-1). Ayer Co Pubs.

Vebreitungsatlas der Farn- und Blutenpflanzen der Schweiz, 2 Vols. Ed. by Max Welten. 1982. Vol. 1, 704pp. text ed. 48.00; Vol. 2, 752pp. text ed. 103.95 (ISBN 0-8176-1308-0). Birkhauser.

Vecellio's Renaissance Costume Book. Cesare Vecellio. LC 76-55952. (Pictorialarchive Ser.). (Illus.). 1977. pap. 6.95 (ISBN 0-486-23441-X). Dover.

Vecher U Kler. Gaito Gazdanov. (Rus.). 1979. 12.00 (ISBN 0-88233-406-9); pap. 4.50 (ISBN 0-88233-407-7). Ardis Pubs.

Vector. Swigart. 1988. pap. 3.95 (ISBN 0-317-65475-6). St Martin.

Vector. Rob Swigart. 192p. 1986. 15.95 (ISBN 0-312-94446-2). Bluejay Bks.

Vector Analysis. D. Bourne & P. Kendall. 1977. pap. 23.95 (ISBN 0-442-30743-8). Van Nos Reinhold.

Vector Analysis. Jack C. Haldeman, II. 192p. 1984. pap. 2.50 (ISBN 0-441-86071-0). Ace Bks.

Vector Analysis & Cartesian Tensors: With Selected Applications. Karamcheti Krishnamurty. LC 67-13843. (Holden-Day Series in Mathematical Physics). pap. 67.00 (ISBN 0-317-09182-4, 2016290). Bks Demand UMI.

Vector Analysis for Mathematicians, Scientists & Engineers. 2nd ed. S. Simons. 1970. pap. text ed. 17.00 (ISBN 0-08-006895-2). Pergamon.

Vector Analysis Problem Solver. Research & Education Association Staff. LC 84-61811. (Illus.). 1280p. 1984. pap. text ed. 24.85 (ISBN 0-87891-554-0). Res & Educ.

Vector & Parallel Processors in Computational Science II: Proceedings of the Second International Conference Oxford, U. K., 28-31 August 1984. Ed. by I. S. Duff & J. K. Reid. 386p. 1985. Repr. 118.50 (ISBN 0-444-86974-3, North Holland). Elsevier.

Vector & Tensor Analysis. George E. Hay. 1953. pap. text ed. 5.00 (ISBN 0-486-60109-9). Dover.

Vector & Tensor Analysis. E. C. Young. (Pure & Applied Ser.: Vol. 48). 1978. 69.75 (ISBN 0-8247-6671-7). Dekker.

Vector & Tensor Analysis with Applications. A. I. Borisenko & I. E. Tarapov. LC 79-87809. 1979. pap. 6.00 (ISBN 0-486-63833-2). Dover.

Vector Bundles & Differential Equations. Ed. by A. Hirschowitz. (Progress in Math. Ser.: No. 7). 255p. 1980. pap. text ed. 28.50x (ISBN 0-8176-3022-8). Birkhauser.

Vector Bundles & Their Characteristic Classes: Vol. I, Vector Bundles & Stiefel-Whitney Classes. Howard Osborn. (Pure & Applied Mathematics Ser.). 1982. 65.50 (ISBN 0-12-529301-1). Acad Pr.

Vector Bundles on Algebraic Varieties: Papers Presented at the Bombay Colloquium 1984. M. F. Atiyah et al. 568p. 1987. pap. 35.00 (ISBN 0-19-562014-3). Oxford U Pr.

Vector Bundles on Complex Projective Spaces. Christian Okonek et al. (Progress in Mathematics Ser.: No. 3). 396p. 1980. pap. text ed. 49.00x (ISBN 0-8176-3000-7). Birkhauser.

Vector Calculus. Peter Baxandall & Hans Liebeck. (Applied Mathematics & Computing Science Ser.). (Illus.). 560p. 1987. 49.95 (ISBN 0-19-859652-9). Oxford U Pr.

Vector Calculus. 3rd ed. Jerrold E. Marsden & Anthony Tromba. LC 87-24595. (Illus.). 662p. 1988. text ed. 38.95 (ISBN 0-7167-1856-1). W H Freeman.

Vector Coherent State Method & Its Application to Problems of Higher Symmetries. K. T. Hecht. (Lecture Notes in Physics Ser.: Vol. 290). v, 154p. 1988. 20.60 (ISBN 0-387-18537-2). Springer-Verlag.

Vector Control. (WHO Bulletin Supplement: Vol. 29). (Also avail. in French). 1963. pap. 4.80 (ISBN 92-4-068291-0). World Health.

Vector Control in International Health. 144p. 1972. pap. 12.80 (ISBN 92-4-154016-8, 930). World Health.

Vector Control Supervisor. Jack Rudman. (Career Examination Ser.: C-2763). (Cloth bdg. avail. on request). 1988. pap. 14.00 (ISBN 0-8373-2763-6). Natl Learning.

Vector Ecology: Report. WHO Scientific Group. Geneva, 1972. (Technical Report Ser.: No. 501). (Also avail. in French & Spanish). 1972. pap. 1.60 (ISBN 92-4-120501-6). World Health.

Vector Field Theory with Applications. Leonard Sowerby. LC 73-90574. pap. 64.50 (ISBN 0-317-09319-3, 2019609). Bks Demand UMI.

Vector Fields. J. A. Shercliff. LC 76-8153. (Illus.). 1977. 67.50 (ISBN 0-521-21306-1); pap. 18.95x (ISBN 0-521-29092-9). Cambridge U Pr.

Vector Fields & Other Vector-Bundle Morphisms: A Singularity Approach. U. Koschorke. (Lecture Notes in Mathematics Ser.: Vol. 847). 304p. 1981. pap. 20.00 (ISBN 0-387-10572-7). Springer-Verlag.

Vector Handbook. George Burtt. LC 71-91981. 1969. pap. 3.50 (ISBN 0-913596-03-5). Vector Counsel.

Vector-Lee. Richard Cloke. LC 76-56063. 1977. pap. 5.25 (ISBN 0-917458-03-6). Kent Pubns.

Vector Measures. J. Diestel & J. J. Uhl. LC 77-9625. (Mathematical Surveys Ser.: No. 15). 322p. 1979. pap. 40.00 (ISBN 0-8218-1515-6, SURV15). Am Math.

Vector Mechanics for Engineers Combined. 3rd ed. Ferdinand P. Beer & E. Russell Johnston, Jr. 1977. text ed. 46.95 (ISBN 0-07-004277-2). McGraw.

Vector Mechanics for Engineers: Combined. 5th ed. Ferdinand P. Beer & Johnston E. Russell. 1088p. 1988. text ed. 58.95 (ISBN 0-07-079923-7). McGraw.

Vector Mechanics for Engineers: Combined Volume. 4th ed. Ferdinand P. Beer, Jr. & E. Russell Johnston. 1984. text ed. 58.95 (ISBN 0-07-004438-4). McGraw.

Vector Mechanics for Engineers: Dynamics. 3rd ed. Ferdinand P. Beer & E. Russell Johnston, Jr. 1977. text ed. 32.95 (ISBN 0-07-004281-0). McGraw.

Vector Mechanics for Engineers: Dynamics. 5th ed. Ferdinand P. Beer & Johnston E. Russell. 592p. 1988. text ed. 45.95 (ISBN 0-07-079926-1). McGraw.

Vector Mechanics for Engineers: Dynamics, Vol. 2. 4th ed. Ferdinand P. Beer & E. Russell Johnston. 1984. text ed. 45.95 (ISBN 0-07-004389-2). McGraw.

Vector Mechanics for Engineers: Statics. 3rd ed. Ferdinand P. Beer & E. Russell Johnston. 1977. text ed. 39.95 (ISBN 0-07-004278-0, C). McGraw.

Vector Mechanics for Engineers: Statics. 5th ed. Ferdinand P. Beer & Johnston E. Russell. 496p. 1987. 44.95 (ISBN 0-07-004507-0). McGraw.

Vector Mechanics for Engineers: Statics, Vol. 1. 4th ed. Ferdinand P. Beer & E. Russell Johnston. 1984. text ed. 45.95 (ISBN 0-07-004432-5). McGraw.

Vector Parallel Processing on Supercomputers: Applications Development for Scientists & Engineers. Campostrini et al. 1988. write for info. (ISBN 0-471-63841-2). Wiley.

Vector Putting: The Art & Science of Reading Greens & Computing Break. H. A. Templeton. LC 83-63158. (Illus.). 194p. 1984. 17.95 (ISBN 0-9613027-0-4); tchr's. ed. 14.95 (ISBN 0-9613027-1-2). Vector Golf.

Vector Space & Its Application in Crystal-Structure Investigation. Martin J. Buerger. LC 59-6760. pap. 91.30 (ISBN 0-317-08653-7, 2011964). Bks Demand UMI.

Vector Space Approach to Models & Optimization. C. Nelson Dorny. LC 80-12423. 622p. 1980. Repr. of 1975 ed. lib. bdg. 41.50 (ISBN 0-89874-210-2). Krieger.

Vector Space Measures & Applications I: Proceedings, Dublin, June 26-July 2, 1977. Ed. by R. M. Aron & S. Dineen. (Lecture Notes in Mathematics Ser.: Vol. 644). 1978. pap. 25.00 (ISBN 0-387-08668-4). Springer-Verlag.

Vector Space Measures & Applications II: Proceedings, Dublin, June 26-July 2, 1977. Ed. by R. M. Aron & S. Dineen. (Lecture Notes in Mathematics: Vol. 645). 1978. pap. 16.00 (ISBN 0-387-08669-2). Springer-Verlag.

Vector Valued Nevanlinna Theory. H. J. Ziegler. 244p. 1983. pap. 23.95 (ISBN 0-470-20623-3, Co-Pub. with Longman). Wiley.

Vector-Valued Optimization Problems in Control Theory. M. Salukvadze. Tr. by John Casti. LC 79-23364. (Mathematics in Science & Engineering Ser.). 1979. 59.00 (ISBN 0-12-616750-8). Acad Pr.

Vectoral Reactions in Electron & Ion Transport in Michondria & Bacteria. Ed. by F. Palmieri et al. (Developments in Bioenergetics & Biomembranes Ser.: Vol. 5). 430p. 1981. 114.25 (ISBN 0-444-80372-6, Biomedical Pr). Elsevier.

Vectorcardiography in Congenital Heart Disease: A Method for Estimating Severity. R. Curtis Ellison & Norma J. Restieaux. LC 75-183449. (Illus.). Repr. of 1972 ed. 55.30 (ISBN 0-8357-9561-6, 2013068). Bks Demand UMI.

Vectorial Astrometry. C. A. Murray. 1983. 84.00x (ISBN 0-85274-372-6, Pub. by A Hilger UK). Taylor & Francis.

Vectorization of Computer Programs with the Application of Computational Fluid Dynamics. W. Gentzsch. (Notes on Numerical Fluid Mechanics Ser.: Vol. 7). 1984. 33.00 (ISBN 3-528-08082-5, Pub. by Vieweg Publishing). IPS.

Vectors. Raymond A. Barnett & John N. Fujii. LC 75-12664. 140p. 1975. Repr. of 1963 ed. text ed. 12.50 (ISBN 0-88275-290-1). Krieger.

Vectors. Toby Olson. 1972. pap. 3.00 (ISBN 0-87924-017-2). Membrane Pr.

Vectors: A Survey of Molecular Cloning Vectors & Their Uses. Raymond Rodriguez & David T. Denhardt. (Biotechnology Ser.). (Illus.). 384p. 1987. text ed. 54.95 (ISBN 0-409-90042-7). Butterworth.

Vectors & Matrices. Pamela Liebeck. 192p. 1971. 37.00 (ISBN 0-08-015823-4). Pergamon.

Vectors & Smoothable Curves: Collected Essays of William Bronk. William Bronk. LC 83-61391. 240p. 1983. 20.00 (ISBN 0-86547-125-8); pap. 12.50 (ISBN 0-86547-126-6). N Point Pr.

Vectors & Tensors for Engineers & Scientists. F. A. Hinchey. LC 76-21725. 298p. 1976. 17.95x (ISBN 0-470-15194-3). Halsted Pr.

Vectors & Tensors for Engineers & Scientists. 1978. 3.00 (ISBN 0-471-63874-9). Wiley.

Vectors & Tensors in Crystallography. D. E. Sands. 1982. text ed. write for info. (ISBN 0-201-07147-9, Adv Bk Prog MSP). Addison-Wesley.

Vectors & Vector Operators. P. G. Dawber. (Student Monographs in Physics Ser.). 64p. 1987. pap. 10.00x (ISBN 0-85274-585-0). Taylor & Francis.

Vectors in Virus Biology. Ed. by Michael A. Mayo & K. A. Harrap. (Special Publications Society General Microbiology Ser.: No. 12). 1984. 41.00 (ISBN 0-12-481480-8). Acad Pr.

Vectors of Death: The Archaeology of European Contact. Ann F. Ramenofsky. LC 87-19232. (Illus.). 316p. 1987. 27.50x (ISBN 0-8263-0997-6). U of NM Pr.

Vectors of Disease Agents: Interactions with Plants, Animals, & Men. Ed. by John J. McKelvey, Jr. et al. LC 80-18676. 256p. 1981. 56.95 (ISBN 0-275-90521-7, C0521). Praeger.

Vectors of Diseases of Natural Foci. Ed. by P. A. Petrishcheva. 336p. 1965. text ed. 65.00x (ISBN 0-7065-0566-2, Pub. by Keter Pub Jerusalem). Coronet Bks.

Vectors of Plant Pathogens. Ed. by K. Harris & K. Maramorosch. 1980. 49.50 (ISBN 0-12-326450-2). Acad Pr.

Vectors, Tensors & Spinors in Relativity. Agacy. 1987. write for info. (ISBN 0-471-84543-4). Wiley.

Veda of the Black Yajus School: Taittiriya Sanhita, 2 vols. A. B. Keith. 1967. Repr. Set. 30.00 (ISBN 0-89684-334-3). Orient Bk Dist.

Veda Recitation in Varanasi. Wayne Howard. 1986. 42.00x (ISBN 0-8364-0872-1). South Asia Bks.

Veda Recitation in Varanasi. Wayne Howard. 401p. 1986. 38.00x (ISBN 81-208-0071-0, Pub. by Motilal Banarsidass India). Orient Bk Dist.

Vedanta & the Bengal Renaissance: Progress or Reaction. Niranjan Dhar. LC 76-52210. 1977. 11.00x (ISBN 0-88386-837-7). South Asia Bks.

Vedanta Doctrine of Sri Sankaracharya. A. Mahadeva Sastri. 245p. 1986. Repr. of 1899 ed. lib. bdg. 16.95 (ISBN 81-7030-029-0, Pub. by Sri Satguru Pubns India). Orient Bk Dist.

Vedanta for the Western World: A Symposium on Vedanta. Ed. by Christopher Isherwood. LC 46-25052. 1945. pap. 8.95 (ISBN 0-87481-000-0). Vedanta Pr.

Vedanta in Brief. Jyotir Maya Nanda. (Orig.). 1978. pap. 3.99 (ISBN 0-934664-37-4). Yoga Res Foun.

Vedanta in Practice. 3rd ed. Swami Paramananda. 1985. pap. 3.50 (ISBN 0-911564-04-7). Vedanta Ctr.

Vedanta Jnana Yoga. Swami Sivananda. Ed. by Swami Venkatesanda. (Life & Works of Swami Sivananda Ser.). 413p. (Orig.). 1986. pap. 11.95 (ISBN 0-949027-11-1). Integral Yoga Pubns.

Vedanta-Paribhasa. Dharmaraja Adhvarindra. Tr. by Swami Madhavananda. (English & Sanskrit). pap. 6.00 (ISBN 0-87481-072-8). Vedanta Pr.

Vedanta Philosophy. F. M. Muller. 182p. 1984. text ed. 27.00x. Coronet Bks.

Vedanta Philosophy. Max F. Muller. 173p. 1985. 29.95. Asia Bk Corp.

Vedanta-Sara-Sangraha. Anantendra-Yati. Tr. by T. M. Mahadevan. 1974. pap. 3.50 (ISBN 0-89744-124-9, Pub. by Ganesh & Co. India). Auromere.

Vedanta: Seven Steps to Samadhi. Bhagwan Shree Rajneesh. Ed. by Ma Yoga Pratima. LC 77-904425. (Upanishad Ser.). (Illus.). 518p. (Orig.). 1976. 9.95 (ISBN 0-88050-166-9). Chidvilas Inc.

Vedanta Sutras. Ed. by G. Thibaut. 1974. lib. bdg. 75.00 (ISBN 0-8490-1256-2). Gordon Pr.

Vedanta Sutras of Badarayana with the Commentary of Baladeva. Tr. by Srisa Chandra Vasu. LC 73-3790. (Sacred Books of the Hindus: Vol. 5). Repr. of 1912 ed. 74.50 (ISBN 0-404-57805-5). AMS Pr.

Vedanta: Voice of Freedom Swami Vivekananda. Ed. by Swami Chetanananda. LC 85-6464. (Illus.). 330p. 1986. 19.95 (ISBN 0-8022-2492-X). Philos Lib.

Vedantasara of Sadananda. Sadananda. pap. 3.00 (ISBN 0-87481-073-6). Vedanta Pr.

Vedantic Approaches to God. Eric Lott. LC 78-17886. (Library of Philosophy & Religion Ser.). 214p. 1980. text ed. 28.50x (ISBN 0-06-494365-8). B&N Imports.

Vedantic Buddhism of Buddha. J. G. Jennings. 1974. Repr. 28.00 (ISBN 0-8426-0683-1). Orient Bk Dist.

Vedas: Immortality's First Call. 1972. pap. 2.00 (ISBN 0-87847-018-2). Aum Pubns.

Vedas of Raja Rammohan Rai. rev. ed. J. L. Shastri. 1977. 7.95 (ISBN 0-89684-335-1). Orient Bk Dist.

Vedda Villages of Anuradhapura: The Historical Anthropology of a Community in Sri Lanka. James Brow. LC 77-16663. (Publications of the School of International Studies: No. 33). (Illus.). 288p. 1978. 30.00x (ISBN 0-295-95585-6). U of Wash Pr.

Veddas. Charles G. Seligman & Brenda Z. Seligman. LC 76-44787. Repr. of 1911 ed. 47.50 (ISBN 0-404-15970-2). AMS Pr.

Vedettes: A Collection of Stories. Edward Loomis. LC 64-16117. 112p. (Orig.). 1964. 6.50 (ISBN 0-8040-0309-2, Pub by Swallow); pap. 3.50 (ISBN 0-8040-0310-6, Pub by Swallow). Ohio U Pr.

Vedi. Ved Mehta. (Illus.). 1982. 18.95x (ISBN 0-19-503005-2). Oxford U Pr.

Vedi. Ved Mehta. (Illus.). 272p. 1987. pap. 7.95 (ISBN 0-393-30417-5). Norton.

Vedic Declension of the Type Vrkis: A Contribution to the Study of the Feminine Noun Declension in Indo-European. Ruth N. Albright. (LD: No.1). 1927. pap. 16.00 (ISBN 0-527-00747-1). Kraus Repr.

Vedic Experience. Raimundo Panniker. 937p. 1983. 28.50 (ISBN 0-89744-011-0). Auromere.

Vedic Grammar for Students. Arthur A. MacDonnell. 1916. pap. 11.95x (ISBN 0-19-560231-5). Oxford U Pr.

Vedic Hymns, 2 vols. F. Max Muller & H. Oldenberg. 1974. lib. bdg. 250.00. Gordon Pr.

Vedic India. G. S. Ghurye. 1979. 35.00x (ISBN 0-89684-061-1, Pub. by Motilal Banarsidass India). Orient Bk Dist.

Vedic Mathematics: Sixteen Simple Mathematical Formulae from the Vedas. Bharati K. Tirthaji. Ed. by V. S. Agrawala. 367p. 1986. 20.00 (ISBN 81-208-0163-6, Pub. by Motilal Banarsidass India); pap. 14.50 (ISBN 81-208-0164-4, Pub. by Motilal Banarsidass India). Orient Bk Dist.

Vedic Mathmatics. Bharati K. Tirthaji. 1986. Repr. 15.00 (ISBN 0-317-56417-X, Pub. by Motilal Banarsidass). South Asia Bks.

Vedic Metaphysics. Bharati K. Tirthaji. 1978. Repr. 16.95 (ISBN 0-89684-337-8). Orient Bk Dist.

Vedic Metaphysics. Bharati K. Tirthaji. 1983. 17.50x (ISBN 0-8364-2225-2, Pub. by Motilal Banarsidass). South Asia Bks.

Vedic Metre in Its Historical Development. E. V. Arnold. 1967. Repr. 25.00 (ISBN 0-89684-338-6). Orient Bk Dist.

Vedic Mythology, Vol. I. rev. 2nd ed. Alfred Hillebrandt. Tr. by Sreeramula R. Sarma from Ger. 472p. 1980. text ed. 19.50 (ISBN 0-89684-098-0, Pub. by Motilal Banarsidass India). Orient Bk Dist.

Vedic Mythology. A. A. Macdonell. 1974. Repr. 11.50. Orient Bk Dist.

Vedic Mythology. Arthur A. MacDonell. 69.95 (ISBN 0-87968-153-5). Gordon Pr.

Vedic Reader for Students. Arthur A. MacDonnell. 1917. pap. 7.95x (ISBN 0-19-519692-9). Oxford U Pr.

Vedic Religion. Abel Bergaigne. Tr. by V. G. Paranjpe. 1978. 55.00 (ISBN 0-89684-006-9, Pub. by Motilal Banarsidass India). Orient Bk Dist.

Vedic Religion & Philosophy. Swami Prabhavananda. 3.00 (ISBN 0-87481-411-1). Vedanta Pr.

Vedic Studies, Vol. 2. A. Venkatasubbiah. 5.25 (ISBN 0-8356-7447-9). Theos Pub Hse.

Vedic Symbolism. Aurobindo Ghose. Ed. by M. P. Pandit. LC 88-80999. 122p. (Orig.). 1988. pap. 6.95 (ISBN 0-941524-30-2). Lotus Light.

Vedic Tantrism: A Study of Rgvidhana of Saunaka. M. S. Bhat. 475p. 1987. 31.00x (ISBN 81-208-0197-0, Pub. by Motilal Banarsidass). South Asia Bks.

Vedic Vision. Ed. by John B. Alphonso-Karkala. 80p. 1980. pap. 4.50 (ISBN 0-86578-004-8). Ind-US Inc.

Vee-Dubb. Stephen Cosgrove. (Bugg Ser.). (Illus.). 32p. (gr. 2-7). 1983. 1.00 (ISBN 0-8431-1205-0). Price Stern.

Vee-Dubb. Stephen Cosgrove. (Bugg Bks.). (Orig.). (gr. 2-7). 1984. incl. cassette 3.95 (ISBN 0-8431-1229-8). Price Stern.

Veeck As in Wreck. Bill Veeck & Ed Linn. (Autographed Sports Classics Ser.). 1981. Repr. of 1962 ed. 19.95 (ISBN 0-941372-09-X). Holtzman Pr.

Veer Vinod, 2 pts. in 4 vols. Mahamahopadhyaya K. Shyamaldas. (Illus.). 1986. Set. 200.00x (ISBN 81-7018-358-8, Pub. by B. R. Pub Corp Delhi). Vol. 1 728p (ISBN 81-7018-359-6). Vol. 2, pt. I, 426p (ISBN 81-7018-360-X). Vol. 3, pt. II, 729p (ISBN 81-7018-361-8). Vol. 4, pt. III (ISBN 81-7018-362-6). Apt Bks.

Vega & Other Poems. Lawrence Durrell. LC 73-75122. 58p. 1974. 14.95 (ISBN 0-87951-009-9). Overlook Pr.

Vega Service, Repair Handbook 1971-1977 Models. 3rd ed. (Illus.). pap. 14.95 (ISBN 0-89287-130-X, A135). Clymer Pub.

Vegan Cookbook. Alan Wakeman & Gordon Baskerville. 1986. 8.95 (ISBN 0-571-13820-9). Faber & Faber.

Vegan Kitchen. 11th ed. Freya Dinshah. LC 87-70646. (Illus.). 64p. 1987. pap. 6.95 (ISBN 0-942401-08-5). Am Vegan Soc.

Vegan Nutrition: Pure & Simple. Michael Klaper. Ed. by Cynthia Klaper. 1987. 4.00 (ISBN 0-9614248-1-8). Gentle World.

Vega's English-Spanish Dictionary of Everyday Criminal & Legal Terms. Carlos B. Vega. LC 82-90393. 412p. 1982. pap. 30.00 (ISBN 0-88174-002-0). C B Vega.

Vega's Pocket English-Spanish, Spanish-English Dictionary of Today's Medical Terms: Diccionario de Bolsillo Ingles-Espanol, Espanol-Ingles de Terminologia Medica Actual. Carlos B. Vega & Pilar Sabater. 300p. (Span. & Eng.). pap. write for info. C B Vega.

Vegas Vendetta see Venganza en Las Vegas.

Vegemen's Revenge. Bertha Upton. 64p. (Orig.). (YA) (gr. 7-9). 1987. Repr. of 1897 ed. 9.95 (ISBN 0-88138-081-4). Green Tiger Pr.

Vegetable. F. Scott Fitzgerald. (Twentieth Century Classics Ser.). 224p. 1987. pap. 4.95 (ISBN 0-02-019880-9, Collier). Macmillan.

Vegetation Horizons & Related Phenomena: A Paeoecological-Micromorphological Study. J. F. Schoute. (Dissertationes Botanicae Ser.: vol. 81). (Illus.). 243p. 1984. lib. bdg. 66.00x (ISBN 3-7682-1429-X). Lubrecht & Cramer.

Vegetation in Civil & Landscape Engineering. David H. Bache & Ian A. MacAskill. (Illus.). 320p. 1984. text ed. 45.00x (ISBN 0-246-11507-6, Pub. by Granada England). Sheridan.

Vegetation in Gebiet des Messtischblattes 6434 Hersbruck. J Merkel. (Dissertationes Botanica Ser.: No. 51). (Illus.). 176p. (Ger.). 1980. pap. text ed. 27.50x (ISBN 3-7682-1235-1). Lubrecht & Cramer.

Vegetation Management of Freshwater Resources. Edward O. Gangstad. LC 85-52167. 350p. 35.00 (ISBN 0-913702-36-6). Thomson Pubns.

Vegetation Map of South America: Explanatory Notes. (Natural Resources Research Ser.: No. 17). 183p. 1981. pap. 35.00 (ISBN 92-3-001933-X, M131, UNESCO). UNIPUB.

Vegetation Mapping. A. W. Kuchler & I. S. Zonneveld. (Handbook of Vegetation Science Ser.). 1988. lib. bdg. 246.00 (ISBN 90-6193-191-6, Pub. by Junk Pubs Netherlands). Kluwer Academic.

Vegetation of Africa. (Natural Resources Research Ser.: No. 20). (Illus.). 356p. 1983. pap. text ed. 46.00 (ISBN 92-3-101955-4, M140, UNESCO). UNIPUB.

Vegetation of Australia. N. C. Beadle. LC 81-2662. (Illus.). 656p. 1981. 135.00 (ISBN 0-521-24195-2). Cambridge U Pr.

Vegetation of China, Vol. 1. Ed. by W. Cheng-Yih & H. Y. Hou. 1983. 95.50 (ISBN 0-677-31080-3). Gordon & Breach.

Vegetation of Europe, Its Conditions & Causes. Arthur Henfrey. Ed. by Frank N. Egerton, 3rd. LC 77-74227. (History of Ecology Ser.). 1978. Repr. of 1852 ed. lib. bdg. 30.00x (ISBN 0-405-10397-2). Ayer Co Pubs.

Vegetation of Hormoz, Queshm & Neighbouring Islands (Southern Persian Gulf Area, No. 6) G. Kunkel. (Flora et Vegetatio Mundi Ser.). (Illus.). 186p. 1977. text ed. 33.00x (ISBN 3-7682-1120-7). Lubrecht & Cramer.

Vegetation of North Point, San Salvador Island, Bahamas. Robert R. Smith & Kathleen Amatucci. (Occasional Papers: 1986, No. 6). (Illus.). 12p. 1986. pap. text ed. 2.50 (ISBN 0-935909-22-2). CCFL Bahamian.

Vegetation of North Stradbroke Island. H. T. Clifford & R. L. Specht. (Illus.). 1979. pap. 16.50x (ISBN 0-7022-1267-9). U of Queensland Pr.

Vegetation of Pacific Equatorial Islands. E. Christophersen. (BMB Ser.). Repr. of 1927 ed. 15.00 (ISBN 0-527-02147-4). Kraus Repr.

Vegetation of Peten. Cyrus L. Lundell. LC 77-11507. (Carnegie Institution of Washington. Publication: No. 478). Repr. of 1937 ed. 35.00 (ISBN 0-404-16270-3). AMS Pr.

Vegetation of the Districts of Hughli-Howrah & 24-Pergunnah. D. Prain. (Records of the Botanical Survey of India Ser.: Vol. 3). 1978. Repr. of 1904 ed. 24.00x (ISBN 0-89955-308-7, Pub. by Intl Bk Dist). Intl Spec Bk.

Vegetation of the Earth & Ecological Systems of the Geobiosphere. 3rd, rev. ed. H. Walter. Tr. by O. Muise from Ger. (Heidelberg Science Library). (Illus.). 340p. 1985. pap. 22.00 (ISBN 0-387-13748-3). Springer-Verlag.

Vegetation of the Mineral Springs Region of Adams County, Ohio. E. Lucy Braun. 1928. 3.00 (ISBN 0-86727-014-4). Ohio Bio Survey.

Vegetation of the Paramos of the Colombian Cordillera Oriental. A. M. Cleef. (Dissertationes Botanicae Ser.: Vol. 61). (Illus.). 320p. 1981. text ed. 33.00x (ISBN 3-7682-1302-1). Lubrecht & Cramer.

Vegetation of the Soviet Polar Deserts. Vera Aleksandrova. (Studies in Polar Research). (Illus.). 240p. 1988. 49.50 (ISBN 0-521-32998-1). Cambridge U Pr.

Vegetation of the Subantartic Islands & Prince Edward. N. J. Gremmen. 1982. lib. bdg. 49.00 (ISBN 90-6193-683-7, Pub. by Junk Pubs Netherlands). Kluwer Academic.

Vegetation of Wisconsin: An Ordination of Plant Communities. John T. Curtis. (Illus.). 672p. 1959. 29.50 (ISBN 0-299-01940-3). U of Wis Pr.

Vegetation Productivity. Gareth E. Jones. LC 78-40985. (Topics in Applied Geography Ser.). pap. 28.00 (ISBN 0-317-20789-X, 2025270). Bks Demand UMI.

Vegetation Surveys of Western Australia: Map & Memoir, No. 5. J. S. Beard & M. J. Webb. Incl. Pilbara. (Illus.). 1976. pap. 16.95x (ISBN 0-85564-092-8, Pub. by U of W Austral Pr). Intl Spec Bk.

Vegetation Surveys of Western Australia (1: 1,000,000 Scale Series), Memoir No. 3: Great Victoria Desert. J. S. Beard. (Illus.). xii, 136p. (Orig.). 1976. pap. 16.95 (ISBN 0-85564-085-5, Pub. by U of W Austral Pr). Intl Spec Bk.

Vegetation Surveys of Western Australia (1: 1,000,000 Scale Series), Memoir No. 4: Nullarbor. J. S. Beard. (Illus.). xx, 136p. 1975. pap. 16.95 (ISBN 0-85564-089-8, Pub. by U of W Austral Pr). Intl Spec Bk.

Vegetation Surveys of Western Australia (1: 1,000,000 Scale Series), Memoir No. 2: Great Sandy Desert. J. S. Beard & M. J. Webb. (Illus.). vii, 64p. 1976. pap. 16.95 (ISBN 0-85564-045-6, Pub. by U of W Austral Pr). Intl Spec Bk.

Vegetation und Flora im suedwestlichen Saudi-Arabien (Asir, Tihama) Peter Koenig. (Dissertationes Botanicae Ser.: Vol. 101). (Illus.). 258p. (Ger.). 1987. pap. text ed. 84.00 (ISBN 3-443-64013-3). Lubrecht & Cramer.

Vegetation von Afrika. R. Knapp. (Vegetationsmonographien: Vol. 3). (Illus.). 626p. 1973. text ed. 145.00x (ISBN 3-437-30131-4). Lubrecht & Cramer.

Vegetation von Nord: Und Mittelamarika und der Hawaii Inseln. R. Knapp. (Vegetationsmonographien: vol. 1). (Illus.). 373p. (Ger.). 1965. lib. bdg. 68.50x (ISBN 3-437-30084-9). Lubrecht & Cramer.

Vegetational & Climatic History of the High Plain of Bogota, Colombia: A Continuous Record of 3,5 Million Years. Henry Hooghiemstra. (Dissertationes Botanica Ser.: Vol. 79). (Illus.). 368p. 1984. lib. bdg. 82.50x (ISBN 3-7682-1404-4). Lubrecht & Cramer.

Vegetational History of the Oaxaca Valley see Prehistory & Human Ecology of the Valley of Oaxaca: Memoirs.

Vegetations Herbacees Basses Amphibies: Sytematique, Structuralisme, Synsytematique. Bruno De Foucault. (Dissertations Botanicae Ser.: Vol. 121). 150p. (Fr.). 1988. pap. text ed. 45.50x (ISBN 3-443-64033-8). Lubrecht & Cramer.

Vegetationsgeographische Untersuchungen im Dhaulagiri-und Annapurna-Himalaya, 2 vols. Georg. Miehe. (Dissertationes Botanica Ser.: No. 66). (Illus.). 500p. 1982. lib. bdg. 82.50x (ISBN 3-7682-1356-0). Lubrecht & Cramer.

Vegetationsgeschichtliche und Pflanzensoziologische Untersuchungen im Vicente Perez Nationalpark: Chile. M. C. Villagran. (Dissertationes Botanicae Ser.: No. 54). (Illus.). 166p. (Ger.). 1981. pap. text ed. 27.50x (ISBN 3-7682-1265-3). Lubrecht & Cramer.

Vegetationskundliche Untersuchungen in Hoehenlohe. Martin Nebel. (Dissertationes Botanicae Ser.: Vol. 97). (Illus.). 262p. (Ger.). 1986. pap. text ed. 71.50x (ISBN 3-443-64009-5). Lubrecht & Cramer.

Vegetationsmosaik im Nordschwarzwaelder Waldgebiet. Luise Murmann-Kristen. (Dissertationes Botanicae Ser.: Vol. 104). (Illus.). 290p. (Ger.). 1987. pap. 100.00x (ISBN 3-443-64016-8). Lubrecht & Cramer.

Vegetative Compatibility Responses in Plants. Ed. by Randy Moore. LC 83-72004. (Illus.). 163p. 1983. pap. 19.50 (ISBN 0-918954-40-1). Baylor Univ Pr.

Vegetative Key to the Genera of the Submersed & Floating Aquatic Vascular Plants of Michigan. (School of Library Science Ser.). 5.80. Campus.

Vegetative Propagation of Conifers. Carl G. Deuber. (Ct Academy of Arts & Science Transactions Ser.: Vol. 34). 1940. pap. 49.50x (ISBN 0-686-51323-1). Elliots Bks.

Vegetative Propagation of Trees in the 1980s. K. A. Longman. 1980. 30.00x (ISBN 0-85074-055-X, Pub. by For Lib Comm England). State Mutual Bk.

Vegetative Strukturen der Parmeliaceae und Ihre Entwicklung. H. A. Beltman. (Bibliotheca Lichenologica Ser.: No. 11). (Illus.). 1978. lib. bdg. 33.00x (ISBN 3-7682-1199-1). Lubrecht & Cramer.

Vehicle Aerodynamics Flow Visualization Techiques & Procedures. 1986. 40.00 (ISBN 0-89883-418-X, HSI15). Soc Auto Engineers.

Vehicle Aerodynamic Developments. 1983. 20.00 (ISBN 0-89883-316-7, SP545). Soc Auto Engineers.

Vehicle & Traffic Law Quizzer N.Y.S. write for info. Looseleaf Law.

Vehicle Body Building One. 75.00x (ISBN 0-85083-023-0, Pub. by Engineering Ind). State Mutual Bk.

Vehicle Body Building: Pt. 1. Ed. by B. Coombes et al. (Engineering Craftsmen: Pt. 2). (Illus.). 1968. 49.95x (ISBN 0-89563-035-4). Trans-Atl Phila.

Vehicle Body Building, Pt. 2, 2 vols. Ed. by B. Coombes. (Engineering Craftsmen: No. E22). (Illus.). 1969. Set. spiral bdg. 82.50x. Trans-Atl Phila.

Vehicle Body Building Two, 2 vols. Set. 75.00x (Pub. by Engineering Ind). State Mutual Bk.

Vehicle Fitting. Ed. by R. Aylen et al. (Engineering Craftsmen: No. H8). (Illus.). 1978. spiral bdg. 39.95x (ISBN 0-89563-036-2). Trans-Atl Phila.

Vehicle Fitting One. 50.00x (ISBN 0-85083-402-3, Pub. by Engineering Ind). State Mutual Bk.

Vehicle Fuel Emergency Preparedness: A Project Report. 65p. 1981. 15.00 (ISBN 0-318-17725-0, DG 81-314). Pub Tech Inc.

Vehicle Highway Infrastructure: Safety Compatibility. 1987. 55.00 (ISBN 0-89883-455-4, P194). Soc Auto Engineers.

Vehicle Identification: 1938-1968. Lee S. Cole. 75p. 1980. pap. 5.00 (ISBN 0-939818-03-5). Lee Bks.

Vehicle Identification: 1969-1982. Lee S. Cole. 136p. (Orig.). 1982. pap. 6.00 (ISBN 0-939818-05-1). Lee Bks.

Vehicle Identification, 1983. Lee S. Cole. (Illus.). 80p. (Orig.). 1983. pap. 6.50 (ISBN 0-939818-06-X). Lee Bks.

Vehicle Identification: 1984-1985. Lee S. Cole. 164p. (Orig.). 1984. pap. 15.00 (ISBN 0-939818-09-4). Lee Bks.

Vehicle Identification, 1986-1987. Lee S. Cole. 184p. (Orig.). 1986. pap. 15.00 (ISBN 0-939818-12-4). Lee Bks.

Vehicle Inspection Procedure Booklet & Forms. 1975. 3.50 (ISBN 0-686-31444-1); vehicle inspection forms 2.50 (ISBN 0-686-31445-X). Private Carrier.

Vehicle Laws of Pennsylvania. Gould Editorial Staff. (Supplemented annually). looseleaf 16.95 (ISBN 0-87526-233-3). Gould.

Vehicle Leasing. 2nd, rev. ed. James J. Larkin. 224p. 1985. text ed. 40.50 (ISBN 0-915260-18-2). Atcom.

Vehicle Lighting Trends. 1987. 30.00 (ISBN 0-89883-963-7, SP692). Soc Auto Engineers.

Vehicle Maintenance Facilities: A Planning Guide. 195p. 1984. 45.00 (ISBN 0-917084-45-4). Am Public Works.

Vehicle Management Four: Vehicles for Trade & Industry. F. Woodward. 1977. 40.00 (ISBN 0-85941-029-3). State Mutual Bk.

Vehicle Noise & Vibration. 1984. 56.00 (MEP198). Soc Auto Engineers.

Vehicle Noise Regulation & Reduction. LC 80-50123. 140p. 1980. Fifteen papers. pap. 34.00 (ISBN 0-89883-227-6, SP456). Soc Auto Engineers.

Vehicle Occupant Restraint Systems & Components. 1986. 35.00 (ISBN 0-317-47098-1, HS13). Soc Auto Engineers.

Vehicle Operating Costs: Evidence from Developing Countries. Andrew Chesher & Robert Harrison. LC 87-22178. (Highway Design & Maintenance Standards Ser.). 352p. (Orig.). 1988. pap. text ed. 18.95x (ISBN 0-8018-3588-7). Johns Hopkins.

Vehicle Painting, Pt. 1. Ed. by F. Brown et al. (Engineering Craftsmen: No. E1). (Illus.). 1968. spiral bdg. 45.00x. Trans-Atl Phila.

Vehicle Painting, Pt. 2. Ed. by F. Brown et al. (Engineering Craftsmen: No. E21). 1970. spiral bdg. 45.00x. Trans-Atl Phila.

Vehicle Painting One. 75.00x (Pub. by Engineering Ind). State Mutual Bk.

Vehicle Painting Two. 75.00x (Pub. by Engineering Ind). State Mutual Bk.

Vehicle Replacement. John E. Sussams. 102p. 1983. text ed. 44.50x (ISBN 0-566-02400-4). Gower Pub Co.

Vehicle Rescue. Harvey P. Grant. (Illus.). 1975. pap. 27.95 (ISBN 0-87618-137-X); instr's guide 7.95 (ISBN 0-87618-611-8) (ISBN 0-87618-610-X). P-H.

Vehicle Rescue. 1st ed. Harvey P. Grant & Robert H. Murray. (Illus.). 320p. pap. text ed. 24.95 (ISBN 0-89303-118-6). P-H.

Vehicle Routing: Methods & Studies. Ed. by B. L. Golden & A. A. Assad. (Studies in Management Science & Systems: Vol. 16). 480p. 1988. 105.25 (ISBN 0-444-70407-8, North Holland). Elsevier.

Vehicle Routing with Time-Window Constraints--Algorithmic Solutions. Ed. by Bruce L. Golden & Arjang A. Assad. LC 86-71927. (Mathematical & Management Sciences Ser.: Vol. 15). 1987. 49.75 (ISBN 0-935950-15-X). Am Sciences Pr.

Vehicle Safety Inspection Systems: How Effective? W. Mark Crain. 1980. pap. 7.00 (ISBN 0-8447-3361-X). Am Enterprise.

Vehicle Sizes & Weights Manual: Limitations, Oversize & Overweight Mobile Homes. rev ed. J. J. Keller & Associates, Inc. LC 74-31863. (1M). 586p. (Prog. Bk.). 1987. looseleaf 85.00 (ISBN 0-934674-21-3). J J Keller.

Vehicle Speeds & Operating Costs: Models for Road Planning & Management. Thawat Watanatada et al. LC 87-22176. (Highway Design & Maintenance Standards Ser.). 304p. (Orig.). 1988. pap. text ed. 16.95x (ISBN 0-8018-3589-5). Johns Hopkins.

Vehicle Stops Manual. August M. Yount, Jr. 1976. pap. text ed. 5.00x (ISBN 0-87563-123-1). Stipes.

Vehicle Structural Mechanics: Proceedings of the Sixth International Conference. 1986. 38.00 (ISBN 0-317-47100-7). Soc Auto Engineers.

Vehicle Structural Mechanics, 7th International Conference. 1988. 42.00 (ISBN 0-89883-470-8, P210). Soc Auto Engineers.

Vehicle Structures. Institute of Mechanical Engineers. 1984. 63.00 (MEP200). Soc Auto Engineers.

Vehicle Traction Mechanics. Ed. by R. N. Yong et al. (Developments in Agricultural Engineering Ser.: Vol. 3). 308p. 1984. 102.75 (ISBN 0-444-42378-8). Elsevier.

Vehicle Traffic Law. Edward C. Fisher & Robert H. Reeder. LC 74-77463. 360p. 1974. 12.50 (ISBN 0-912642-00-9). Traffic Inst.

Vehicles & Bridging. I. F. Tytler et al. (Battlefield Weapons Systems & Technology Ser.: Vol. 1). (Illus.). 256p. 1985. text ed. 29.00 (ISBN 0-08-028322-5); pap. text ed. 17.50 (ISBN 0-08-028323-3). Pergamon.

Vehicles: Experiments in Synthetic Psychology. Valentino Braitenberg. 168p. 1986. 17.50 (ISBN 0-262-02208-7, Pub. by Bradford); pap. 6.95 (ISBN 0-262-52112-1). MIT Pr.

Vehicles of the Air: A Popular Exposition of Modern Aeronautics with Working Drawings. Victor Lougheed. LC 75-169427. (Literature & History of Aviation Ser.). 1971. Repr. of 1909 ed. 27.00 (ISBN 0-405-03770-8). Ayer Co Pubs.

Vehicular Fuels-Additives for the Future. Business Communications Staff. 1988. 1950.00 (ISBN 0-89336-656-0, E-047). BCC.

Vehicular Structural Mechanics: Proceedings of the Fifth International Conference. 260p. 1984. 50.00 (ISBN 0-89883-700-6, P 144). Soc Auto Engineers.

Veho. Henry Tall Bull & Tom Weist. (Indian Culture Ser.). (gr. 2-6). 1971. 1.95 (ISBN 0-89992-007-1). Coun India Ed.

Veil. George C. Chesbro. 240p. 1986. 16.95 (ISBN 0-89296-159-7). Mysterious Pr.

Veil. Denis Johnson. LC 85-18383. 96p. 1987. 15.45 (ISBN 0-394-54127-8); pap. 8.95 (ISBN 0-394-74343-1). Knopf.

Veil. Robert Williams. 20p. 1976. pap. 3.95 (ISBN 0-89536-247-3, 2200). CSS of Ohio.

Veil & More Folklore of the Eastern Shore. Vernon O. Giffin. 1983. 5.50 (ISBN 0-9610674-0-3). McClain.

Veil Lifted. large type ed. J. Traill Taylor. (Illus.). pap. 4.95 (ISBN 0-910122-42-3). Amherst Pr.

Veil of Ignorance. Monica Quill. 208p. 1988. 15.95 (ISBN 0-312-02308-1). St Martin.

Veil of Iron. Ellen Glasgow. 462p. Repr. lib. bdg. 45.00 (ISBN 0-918377-37-4). Russell Pr.

Veil of Isis: A Series of Essays on Idealism. Thomas E. Webb. LC 72-8522. (Essay Index Reprint Ser.). 1972. Repr. of 1885 ed. 23.50 (ISBN 0-8369-7337-2). Ayer Co Pubs.

Veil of Mist. Scott Galloway. LC 87-43086. (Illus.). 136p. (Orig.). 1987. 8.95 (ISBN 0-941709-05-1); pap. 5.95 (ISBN 0-941709-04-3). Solo Pubns.

Veil of Shadow. Catherine Cooke. 288p. 1987. pap. 2.95 (ISBN 0-8125-3386-0, Dist. by St Martin's Pr & Warner Pub Servs). Tor Bks.

Veil of Veronica. Gertrud F. Von Lefort. Tr. by Conrad M. Bonacina. LC 70-126667. Repr. of 1933 ed. 21.45 (ISBN 0-404-03946-4). AMS Pr.

Veil: The Secret Wars of the C. I. A. 1981-1987. Bob Woodward. LC 87-20520. 543p. 1987. 21.95 (ISBN 0-671-60117-2). S&S.

Veil: The Secret Wars of the C. I. A., 1981-1987. Bob Woodward. (Illus.). 1988. pap. 4.95. PB.

Veil Too Thin: Reincarnation Out of Control. Betty Riley. LC 84-50090. 96p. 1984. pap. 2.95 (ISBN 0-911842-37-3). Valley Sun.

Veiled Being: On Kipling. J. M. Thomas. LC 74-23855. 1917. lib. bdg. 17.00 (ISBN 0-8414-8512-7). Folcroft.

Veiled Cliffs. Diane Yale. (YA) (gr. 7 up). 1983. 9.95 (ISBN 0-8034-8309-0, Avalon). Bouregy.

Veiled Gazelle: Seeing How to See. Idries Shah. 103p. 1977. 11.95 (ISBN 0-900860-58-8, Pub. by Octagon Pr England). Ins Study Human.

Veiled Images: Titian's Mythological Paintings for Philip II. Jane C. Nash. LC 83-45949. (Illus.). 120p. 1985. 30.00 (ISBN 0-87982-511-1). Art Alliance.

Veiled One: A New Inspector Wexford Novel. Ruth Rendell. LC 88-9926. 1988. 17.95 (ISBN 0-394-57206-8). Pantheon.

Veiled Sentiments: Honor & Poetry in a Bedouin Society. Lila Abu-Lughod. (Illus.). 317p. 1987. 35.00X (ISBN 0-520-05483-0); pap. 10.95 (ISBN 0-520-06327-9). U of Cal Pr.

Veiled Species of Hebeloma in the Western United States. Alexander H. Smith & Vera S. Evenson. (Illus.). 224p. 1983. text ed. 22.50x (ISBN 0-472-10036-X). U of Mich Pr.

Veils of Azlaroc. Fred Saberhagen. 224p. 1984. pap. 2.25 (ISBN 0-441-86065-6). Ace Bks.

Veils of Azlaroc. Fred Saberhagen. 224p. 1987. pap. 2.95 (ISBN 0-8125-5324-1, Dist. by St Martin's Pr & Warner Pub Servs). Tor Bks.

Vein of Iron. Ellen Glasgow. LC 35-27270. 416p. pap. 7.95 (ISBN 0-15-693476-0, Harv). HarBraceJ.

Vein-Type & Similar Uranium Deposits in Rocks Younger than Proterozoic: Proceedings of a Technical Committee Meeting Organized by the International Atomic Energy Agency & Held in Lisbon, Sept. 24-28, 1979. (Panel Proceedings Ser.). 395p. 1982. pap. 50.25 (ISBN 0-686-91858-4, ISP600, IAEA). UNIPUB.

Veins: Normal & Abnormal Function. James E. Wood. LC 65-25171. pap. 60.00 (ISBN 0-317-29845-3, 2051910). Bks Demand UMI.

Veins of Humor. Ed. by Harry Levin. LC 72-78425. (English Studies: No. 3). 1972. pap. 5.95x (ISBN 0-674-93280-3). Harvard U Pr.

Veins of the Posterior Fossa: Normal & Pathologic Findings. A. Wackenheim & Braun. LC 77-23953. (Illus.). 1978. 89.00 (ISBN 0-387-08337-5). Springer-Verlag.

Veinte Anos de Literatura Cubanoamericana. Ed. by Silvia Burunat & Ofelia Garcia. LC 87-70662. 224p. 1988. 20.00 (ISBN 0-916950-77-8); pap. 12.00 (ISBN 0-916950-78-6). Biling Rev-Pr.

Veinte Anos de Teatro Espanol (1960-1980) Juan E. Aragones. 280p. 1987. pap. 35.00 (ISBN 0-89295-043-9). Society Sp & Sp-Am.

Veinte Cuentistas Cubanos. Leonardo Fernandez-Marcane. LC 77-89099. 1978. pap. 6.00 (ISBN 0-89729-164-6). Ediciones.

Veinte Cuentos Breves de la Revolucion Cubana. Ricardo J. Aguiar. LC 87-80642. (Coleccione Caniqui). (Illus.). 84p. (Orig., Span.). 1987. pap. 9.95 (ISBN 0-89729-440-8). Ediciones.

Venetian Phoenix: Paolo Sarpi & Some of His English Friends, 1606-1700. John L. Lievsay. LC 73-6818. x, 262p. 1973. 29.95x (ISBN 0-7006-0108-2). U Pr of KS.

Venetian School of Painting. facsimile ed. Evelyn M. Phillipps. LC 70-37907. (Select Bibliographies Reprint Ser.). Repr. of 1912 ed. 24.00 (ISBN 0-8369-6745-3). Ayer Co Pubs.

Venetian Ships & Shipbuilders of the Renaissance. Frederic C. Lane. 1979. 25.50 (ISBN 0-405-10609-2). Ayer Co Pubs.

Venetian Tornesello: A Medieval Colonial Coinage. Alan M. Stahl. (Numismatic Notes & Monographs). (Illus.). 100p. 1986. 20.00x (ISBN 0-89722-209-1). Am Numismatic.

Venetian Vespers. Anthony Hecht. LC 79-52419. 1979. 10.00 (ISBN 0-689-11015-4); pap. 6.95 (ISBN 0-689-11019-7). Atheneum.

Venetian Villas. Michelangelo Muraro. LC 86-42731. (Illus.). 518p. 1986. 85.00 (ISBN 0-8478-0762-2, Dist. by Apollo). Rizzoli Intl.

Venetian Woods. Eamon Baeda. LC 88-81109. 62p. 1988. 10.95 (ISBN 0-9620529-0-6); pap. 5.95 (ISBN 0-9620529-1-4). Hellas.

Venetic see Mediterranean Studies.

Venetsianov & His School. Tatians Alekseeva. 240p. 1984. 154.00x (ISBN 0-317-61414-2, Pub. by Collets (UK)). State Mutual Bk.

Venetsianov & His School. T. Alexeyeva. 239p. 1984. 45.00 (ISBN 0-8285-2951-5, Pub. by Aurora Pubs USSR). Imported Pubns.

Venezia One-Hundred-One Disegni. Marie Z. Greene-Mercier. 111p. (Orig.). 1969. pap. 3.50x (ISBN 0-910790-18-3). Intl Bk Co IL.

Venezuela. L. Dalton. 1976. lib. bdg. 59.95 (ISBN 0-8490-2793-4). Gordon Pr.

Venezuela. Edwin Lieuwen. LC 85-24781. xi, 223p. 1986. Repr. of 1965 ed. lib. bdg. 38.50x (ISBN 0-313-24979-2, LIVE). Greenwood.

Venezuela. 2nd ed. J. Martz. 1985. 42.95 (ISBN 0-275-91815-7, C1815); pap. 17.95 (ISBN 0-275-92038-0, B2038). Praeger.

Venezuela. Rosa Q. Mesa. LC 73-180800. (Latin American Serial Documents Ser.: Vol. 12). pap. 84.30 (ISBN 0-317-10310-5, 2013554). Bks Demand UMI.

Venezuela. (Let's Visit Places & Peoples - - Nations, Dependencies, & Sovereignties of the World Ser.). (Illus.). (gr. 5 up). 1988. 12.95 (ISBN 1-55546-174-3). Chelsea Hse.

Venezuela see American Nations Past & Present.

Venezuela see Statements of the Laws of the OAS Member States in Matters Affecting Business.

Venezuela: A Century of Change. Judith Ewell. LC 83-40093. 272p. 1984. 25.00x (ISBN 0-8047-1213-1). Stanford U Pr.

Venezuela Alive. 3rd ed. Arnold Greenberg & Harriet Greenberg. (Alive Travel Ser.). (Illus.). 250p. pap. 9.95 (ISBN 0-935572-13-9). Alive Pubns.

Venezuela Alive. Harriet Greenberg & Arnold L. Greenberg. 1974. pap. 2.00 (ISBN 0-935572-04-X). Alive Pubns.

Venezuela & Its Ruler. N. Naranjo. 1976. lib. bdg. 59.95 (ISBN 0-8490-2794-2). Gordon Pr.

Venezuela at the Polls: The National Elections of 1978. Ed. by Howard R. Penniman. 287p. 1980. 23.00 (ISBN 0-8447-3418-7); pap. 13.50 (ISBN 0-8447-3391-1). Am Enterprise.

Venezuela-Guyana Border Dispute: Britain's Colonial Legacy in Latin America. Jacqueline A. Braveboy-Wagner. (Replica Edition Ser.). 200p. 1984. softcover 39.00x (ISBN 0-86531-953-7). Westview.

Venezuela in Pictures. Lerner Publications, Department of Geography Staff. (Visual Geography Ser.). (Illus.). 64p. (gr. 5 up). 1987. PLB 9.95 (ISBN 0-8225-1824-4). Lerner Pubns.

Venezuela: The Democratic Experience. Ed. by John D. Martz & David J. Myers. LC 77-7509. (Praeger Special Studies). 432p. 1977. pap. 18.95 (ISBN 0-275-91471-2, B1471). Praeger.

Venezuela: The Industrial Challenge. Sergio Bitar & Eduardo Troncoso. Tr. by Michael Shifter & Dorsey Vera. LC 86-19979. (Inter-American Politics Ser.: Vol. 7). 200p. 1987. text ed. 29.95 (ISBN 0-89727-070-3). ISHI PA.

Venezuela: The Search for Order, the Dream of Progress. John V. Lombardi. (Latin American Histories Ser.). (Illus.). 1982. 29.95x (ISBN 0-19-503013-3); pap. text ed. 9.95x (ISBN 0-19-503014-1). Oxford U Pr.

Venezuelan Economic Development: A Politico-Economic Analysis. Loring Allen. Ed. by Edward I. Altman & Ingo Walter. LC 76-10395. (Contemporary Studies in Economic & Financial Analysis: Vol. 7). 1977. lib. bdg. 52.50 (ISBN 0-89232-011-7). Jai Pr.

Venezuelan History: A Comprehensive Bibliography. John V. Lombardi. 1977. lib. bdg. 29.00 (ISBN 0-8161-7876-3, Hall Reference). G K Hall.

Venezuelan Law Governing Restrictive Business Practices. Gustavo Brillembourg. LC 85-82448. 398p. 1986. lib. bdg. 85.00 (ISBN 0-935328-35-1). Intl Law Inst.

Venezuelan Orchids Illustrated, Vol. 6. G. C. Dunsterville & L. A. Garay. 1975. 30.00 (ISBN 0-87544-001-0). Museum Bks.

Venezuelan Prose Fiction. Dillwyn F. Ratcliff. 286p. 2.60 (ISBN 0-318-14314-3). Hispanic Inst.

Venezuelan Vernacular. Federico Vegas. (Illus.). 96p. 1985. pap. 25.00 (ISBN 0-910413-05-3). Princeton Arch.

Venezuela's Movement Toward Socialism: From Guerilla Defeat to Innovative Politics. Steve Ellner. LC 87-30456. (Illus.). 310p. 1988. lib. bdg. 43.50 (ISBN 0-8223-0808-8). Duke.

Venezuela's Pursuit of Caribbean Basin Interests: Implications for United States National Security. David J. Myers. LC 83-19144. 1985. 4.00 (ISBN 0-8330-0527-8, R-2994-AF). Rand Corp.

Venezuela's Tutelary Pluralism: A Critical Approach to Venezuelan Democracy. Luis Oropeza. LC 83-176. (Harvard Studies in International Affairs Ser.: No. 46). 130p. 1981. 13.95x (ISBN 0-87674-052-2, 46); pap. 7.95x (ISBN 0-87674-053-0). U Pr of Amer.

Venganza de Tamar. Tirso De Molina. Ed. by A. K. Paterson. LC 69-10572. pap. 39.50 (ISBN 0-317-20843-8, 2024442). Bks Demand UMI.

Venganza en Las Vegas. Don Pendleton. Tr. by O. J. Blanco from Eng. (Compadre Collection: El Verdugo Ser. No. 9). Orig. Title: Vegas Vendetta. 160p. (Span.). 1974. pap. 0.75 (ISBN 0-88473-309-2). Fiesta Pub.

Vengeance. J. L. Bouma. 160p. 1981. pap. 1.75 (ISBN 0-8439-0991-9, Leisure Bks). Leisure NY.

Vengeance & Justice: Crime & Punishment in the 19th-Century American South. Edward L. Ayers. LC 83-17472. 353p. 1984. 32.00x (ISBN 0-19-503383-3). Oxford U Pr.

Vengeance & Justice: Crime & Punishment in the 19th Century American South. Edward L. Ayers. 353p. 1986. pap. 8.95x (ISBN 0-19-503988-2). Oxford U Pr.

Vengeance & Other Stories. Manoj Das. 106p. 1980. 8.95 (ISBN 0-86578-191-5). Ind-US Inc.

Vengeance Army. Axel Kilgore. (Call Me the Mercenary Ser.: No. 6). (Orig.). 1981. pap. 2.50 (ISBN 0-89083-872-0). Zebra.

Vengeance Breed. Charlie Barstow. 224p. (Orig.). 1982. pap. 2.25 (ISBN 0-505-51768-X, Pub. by Tower Bks). Leisure NY.

Vengeance Is Mine. Lynda R. Mealer. 96p. 1988. 8.95 (ISBN 0-8062-3280-3). Carlton.

Vengeance Is Mine. Mickey Spillane. pap. 2.50 (ISBN 0-451-13264-5, AE3264, Sig). NAL.

Vengeance Is Mine. Mickey Spillane. 14.95 (ISBN 0-89190-838-2, Pub. by Am Repr). Amereon Ltd.

Vengeance Is Mine. Michael Zuckerman. LC 87-5495. 320p. 1987. 19.95 (ISBN 0-02-633640-5). Macmillan.

Vengeance Man. Dan J. Marlowe. LC 87-72705. 160p. 1988. pap. 4.95 (ISBN 0-88739-040-4, Pub. by Black Lizard Bks). Creative Arts Bk.

Vengeance Mountain. R. C. House. 192p. 1984. pap. 2.25 (ISBN 0-8439-2130-7, Leisure Bks). Leisure NY.

Vengeance, My Love. E. G. Fulton. 320p. 1987. pap. 3.95 (ISBN 0-8125-0342-2, Dist. by St Martin's Pr & Warner Pub Servs). Tor Bks.

Vengeance of Felix. E. Albuquerque Medeiros. Ed. & tr. by Isaac Goldberg. (International Pocket Library). pap. 3.00 (ISBN 0-686-77244-X). Branden Pub Co.

Vengeance of Fortuna West. Ray Hogan. 192p. 1984. pap. 2.25 (ISBN 0-451-12919-9, Sig). NAL.

Vengeance of Orion. Ben Bova. 384p. 1988. 17.95x (ISBN 0-312-93049-6). Tor Bks.

Vengeance of Orion. Ben Bova. 352p. 1989. pap. 3.95 (ISBN 0-8125-3161-2). Tor Bks.

Vengeance of the Dancing Gods. Jack L. Chalker. (Dancing Gods Ser.). 1985. pap. 3.50 (ISBN 0-345-31549-9, Del Rey). Ballantine.

Vengeance of the God. Lewis Arriola. 206p. 1981. 9.50 (ISBN 0-682-49687-1). Exposition-Phoenix.

Vengeance of the Gods. Rex Warner. 192p. 1955. 3.50 (ISBN 0-87013-009-9). Mich St U Pr.

Vengeance of the Gods & Three Other Stories of Real American Color Line Life. William Pickens. LC 73-18564. Repr. of 1922 ed. 11.50 (ISBN 0-404-11376-1). AMS Pr.

Vengeance of the Gods; & Three Other Stories of Real American Color Line Life. William Pickens. LC 72-4612. (Black Heritage Library Collection Ser.). Repr. of 1922 ed. 14.25 (ISBN 0-8369-9120-6). Ayer Co Pubs.

Vengeance of the Lion. P. Danielson. (Children of the Lion Ser.: Bk. 3). 1985. lib. bdg. 12.95 (ISBN 0-8398-2871-3, Gregg). G K Hall.

Vengeance of the Lion. Peter Danielson. 432p. 1983. pap. 4.50 (ISBN 0-553-26769-8). Bantam.

Vengeance of the Victim: History & Symbol in Giorgio Bassani's Fiction. Marilyn Schneider. LC 85-28866. (Minnesota Publications in Humanities: Vol. 5). (Illus.). 250p. (Orig.). 1986. 35.00x (ISBN 0-8166-1512-8); pap. 14.95 (ISBN 0-8166-1513-6). U of Minn Pr.

Vengeance Spur. Tex Steele. 1980. pap. 1.75 (ISBN 0-8439-0833-5, Leisure Bks). Leisure NY.

Vengeance: The Fight Against Injustice. Pietro Marongiu & Graeme Newman. 176p. 1987. 27.50 (ISBN 0-317-56047-6). Rowman.

Vengeance: The True Story of an Israeli Counter-Terrorist Team. George Jonas. 376p. 1984. 17.95 (ISBN 0-671-50611-0). S&S.

Vengeance: The True Story of an Israeli Counter Terrorist Team. George Jonas. 384p. 1985. pap. 3.95 (ISBN 0-553-25058-2). Bantam.

Vengeance! The Vultee Vengeance Dive Bomber. Peter C. Smith. LC 87-61974. (Illus.). 188p. 1988. 24.95 (ISBN 0-87474-866-6). Smithsonian.

Vengeance Trail. Max Brand. 1987. pap. 2.75 (ISBN 0-671-64729-6). PB.

Vengeance Trail of Josey Wales. Forrest Carter. 1977. pap. 1.50 (ISBN 0-440-19344-3). Dell.

Vengeance Valley. Allen Appel. 240p. 1985. pap. 2.25 (ISBN 0-8439-2193-5, Leisure Bks). Leisure NY.

Vengeance Valley. J. D. Hardin. 192p. 1984. pap. 2.50 (ISBN 0-425-07114-6). Berkley Pub.

Vengeance Weapon 2: The V-2 Guided Missile. Gregory P. Kennedy. LC 82-600400. (Illus.). 88p. 1983. pap. text ed. 10.95x (ISBN 0-87474-573-X, KEVWP). Smithsonian.

Vengeful Flames. Alan Sewart. 1985. 24.95x (ISBN 0-7091-9874-4, Pub. by R Hale Ltd UK). State Mutual Bk.

Vengeful Men. Ray Gaulden. 1979. pap. 1.75 (ISBN 0-505-51449-4, Pub. by Tower Bks). Leisure NY.

Vengement Alixandre. Gui De Cambrai. Ed. by B. Edwards. (Elliott Monographs). 1928. 15.00 (ISBN 0-527-02626-3). Kraus Repr.

Vengerova System of Piano Playing. Robert D. Schick. LC 82-80454. (Illus.). 126p. 1982. 18.75x (ISBN 0-271-00313-8). Pa St U Pr.

Venice. Berlitz Editors. (Berlitz Travel Guide). 1987. pap. 6.95 (ISBN 0-02-965980-9, Berlitz). Macmillan.

Venice. Alta Macadam. (Blue Guide Ser.). (Illus.). 1982. 24.95 (ISBN 0-393-01555-6); pap. 13.95 (ISBN 0-393-30007-2). Norton.

Venice. 3rd ed. Alta Macadam. (Blue Guides Ser.). 1986. pap. 15.95 (ISBN 0-393-30080-3). Norton.

Venice. M. Muraro & A. Grabar. 39.95 (ISBN 0-517-62645-4). Outlet Bk Co.

Venice. (Panorama Bks.). (Illus., Fr.). 3.95 (ISBN 0-685-11615-8). French & Eur.

Venice. (Baedker's City Guides Ser.). 1986. pap. 10.95 (ISBN 0-13-058116-X). P-H.

Venice. (Berlitz Deluxe Guides). (Illus.). 336p. 1988. pap. 10.95 (ISBN 0-02-968230-4, Berlitz). Macmillan.

Venice. (Berlitz Deluxe Guide). (Illus.). 336p. 1989. 10.95 (ISBN 2-8315-0367-1, Berlitz). Macmillan.

Venice. Alvise Zorzi. LC 83-6432. (Illus.). 280p. 1983. 60.00 (ISBN 0-89659-406-8). Abbeville Pr.

Venice: A Maritime Republic. Frederic C. Lane. LC 72-12342. (Illus.). 518p. 1973. 45.00x (ISBN 0-8018-1445-6); pap. 14.95x (ISBN 0-8018-1460-X). Johns Hopkins.

Venice: A Thousand Years of Culture & Civilization. Peter Lauritzen. LC 78-2690. 1978. 12.95 (ISBN 0-689-10897-4); pap. 6.95 (ISBN 0-689-70603-0, 263). Atheneum.

Venice & History: The Collected Papers of Frederic C. Lane. Frederic C. Lane. LC 66-14160. pap. 145.50 (ISBN 0-317-30121-7, 2025304). Bks Demand UMI.

Venice & the Defense of Republican Liberty: Renaissance Values in the Age of the Counter Reformation. William J. Bouwsma. LC 68-14642. (Illus.). 1968. 47.50x (ISBN 0-520-00151-6); pap. 12.95x (ISBN 0-520-05221-8). U of Cal Pr.

Venice Beach. Photos by Claudio Edinger. LC 85-4015. (Illus.). 168p. 1985. pap. 16.95 (ISBN 0-89659-520-X). Abbeville Pr.

Venice: Birth of a City. Piero Ventura. (Illus.). 40p. (gr. 5 up). 1988. 13.95 (ISBN 0-399-21531-X). Putnam Pub Group.

Venice: Bride of the Adriatic. Fran Fanuele. Ed. by Leroy Ramsey. 210p. (Orig.). Date not set. pap. 12.95 (ISBN 0-930355-02-4). ELRAMCO Enter.

Venice, California: An Urban Fantasy. Horst Schmidt-Brummer. LC 72-11004. 1973. 6.95 (ISBN 0-670-74506-5). Viking.

Venice, Durer & the Oriental Mode. Julian Raby. (Hans Huth Memorial Studies: No. 1). (Illus.). 104p. 1983. text ed. 45.00 (ISBN 0-85667-162-2). Sotheby Pubns.

Venice for Pleasure. rev. ed. J. G. Links. (Illus.). 272p. 1985. pap. 9.95 (ISBN 0-374-51886-6). FS&G.

Venice: From the Earliest Beginnings to the Fall of the Republic, 2 vols. P. Molmenti. 1977. lib. bdg. 250.00 (ISBN 0-8490-2795-0). Gordon Pr.

Venice II. Photos by Fulvio Roiter. Olivier Bernier. (Illus.). 168p. 1985. 45.00 (ISBN 0-86565-056-X). Vendome.

Venice in Color see Travel Guides in Color.

Venice in the Eighteenth Century. Ed. by Henri Zerner. LC 67-17765. (Illus.). 1967. 1.75. Mus of Art RI.

Venice Italy: Cooking with Betty Evans. Betty Evans. (Illus.). 112p. 1986. pap. 6.96 (ISBN 0-931104-18-1). Sunflower Ink.

Venice: Its History-Art-Industries & Modern Life. Charles Yriate. 1978. lib. bdg. 35.00 (ISBN 0-8492-3111-6). R West.

Venice Observed. Mary McCarthy. LC 64-49016. 158p. 1963. pap. 4.95 (ISBN 0-15-693521-X, Harv). HarBraceJ.

Venice of America - 'Coney Island of the Pacific' Jeffrey Stanton. (Illus.). 176p. (Orig.). 1988. pap. 15.95 (ISBN 0-9619849-0-2). Donahue Pub.

Venice Preserved. Peter Lauritzen. LC 86-50108. (Illus.). 176p. 1986. 29.95 (ISBN 0-917561-17-1). Adler & Adler.

Venice Preserved. Thomas Otway. Ed. by Malcolm Kelsall. LC 69-12902. (Regents Restoration Drama Ser.). xxii, 116p. 1969. 11.95x (ISBN 0-8032-0366-7). U of Nebr Pr.

Venice Preserved see Restoration Plays.

Venice Rediscovered. Ronald S. Kennedy. 20.00 (ISBN 0-8453-1484-X, Cornwall Bks). Assoc Univ Prs.

Venice Rediscovered. Ronald Shaw-Kennedy. LC 73-22608. (Illus.). 136p. 1978. 20.00 (ISBN 0-87982-020-9). Art Alliance.

Venice Restored. 1979. pap. 5.50 (ISBN 92-3-101671-7, U1617, UNESCO). UNIPUB.

Venice Simplon Orient-Express: The Return of the World's Most Celebrated Train. Shirley Shirwood. (Illus.). 1984. 19.95 (ISBN 0-297-78261-4). Beaufort Bks NY.

Venice: The American View 1860-1920. Margaretta M. Lovell. LC 84-81857. (Illus.). 174p. 1984. pap. 19.95 (ISBN 0-88401-044-9). Fine Arts Mus.

Venice: The American View, 1860-1920. Margaretta M. Lovell. LC 84-81857. (Illus.). 170p. 1984. pap. 19.95 (ISBN 0-295-96288-7). U of Wash Pr.

Venice: The Hinge of Europe, 1081-1797. William H. McNeill. LC 73-84192. xviii, 334p. 1974. o.s.i 10.75x (ISBN 0-226-56148-8); pap. 18.00x (ISBN 0-226-56149-6). U of Chicago Pr.

Venice Train. Georges Simenon. Tr. by Alastair Hamilton. (Helen & Kurt Wolff Bk.). 160p. pap. 3.95 (ISBN 0-15-693523-6, Harv). HarBraceJ.

Venida del Senor. 2nd ed. Jorge Cutting. Ed. by Gordon H. Bennett. Tr. by Sara Bautista from Eng. (Serie Diamante). (Illus.). 48p. (Span.). 1982. pap. 0.85 (ISBN 0-942504-10-0). Overcomer Pr.

Venisamhara of Narayana Bhatta. Ed. by M. R. Kale. 1977. pap. 8.00 (ISBN 0-89684-339-4). Orient Bk Dist.

Venise. Jean Cocteau et al. 68p. 1951. 27.50 (ISBN 0-686-54561-3). French & Eur.

Venison Book: How to Dress, Cut up & Cook Your Deer. Audrey A. Gorton. LC 57-13401. (Illus.). 1957. pap. 4.95 (ISBN 0-8289-0001-9). Greene.

Venison Cookbook: More Than 200 Tested Recipes for Deer, Elk, Moose & Other Game. Jim Zumbo & Lois Zumbo. (Illus.). 208p. 1986. 17.95 (ISBN 0-13-941519-X). P-H.

Venison Handbook. Brad Sagstetter. LC 80-84354. (Illus.). 80p. (Orig.). 1981. 5.95 (ISBN 0-89896-075-4). Larksdale.

Venita. Georgette Heyer. Ed. by Joan Marlow. 320p. 1988. pap. 3.50 (ISBN 0-425-10719-1). Berkley Pub.

Venizelos: Patriot, Statesman, Revolutionary. Doros Alastos & S. Victor Papacosma. (CEES: 10). 1978. Repr. of 1940 ed. 22.00 (ISBN 0-87569-030-0). Academic Intl.

Venjance Alixandre. Jean Le Nevelon. Ed. by E. B. Ham. (Elliott Monographs: Vol. 27). 1931. 20.00 (ISBN 0-527-02630-1). Kraus Repr.

Venography of the Inferior Vena Cava & Its Branches. J. Chermet & J. M. Bigot. Tr. by A. Wackanheim from Fr. (Illus.). 280p. 1980. 116.90 (ISBN 0-387-09905-0). Springer-Verlag.

Venom. John Tigges. 368p. (Orig.). 1988. pap. 3.95 (ISBN 0-8439-2602-3, Pub. by Leisure Bks CT). Leisure NY.

Venom. Janet S. West. 256p. 1982. 12.95 (ISBN 0-89962-242-9). Todd & Honeywell.

Venom House. Arthur W. Upfield. 1988. pap. 4.50 (ISBN 0-02-025901-8, Collier). Macmillan.

Venom in My Veins: The Terry Jones Story. Terry L. Jones & David L. Nixon. 102p. (Orig.). 1985. pap. 3.95 (ISBN 0-8341-1078-4). Beacon Hill.

Venomous Animals & Their Toxins. G. Habermehl. (Illus.). 210p. 1981. pap. 17.50 (ISBN 0-387-10780-0). Springer-Verlag.

Venomous Animals & Their Venoms. Ed. by Wolfgang Bucherl et al. Incl. Vol. 1. 1968. 95.00 (ISBN 0-12-138901-4); Vol. 2. 1971. 95.00 (ISBN 0-12-138902-2); Vol. 3. 1971. 88.00 (ISBN 0-12-138903-0). Set (ISBN 0-686-66781-6). Acad Pr.

Venomous Creatures of Australia: A Field Guide with Notes on First Aid. 2nd ed. Struan Sutherland. (Illus.). 1985. pap. 24.95x (ISBN 0-19-554727-6). Oxford U Pr.

Venomous Snakes of Nicaragua. Jaime Villa. (Contributions in Biology & Geology Ser.: No. 59). 48p. 1984. 6.95 (ISBN 0-89326-107-6). Milwaukee Pub Mus.

Venomous Snakes of the World: A Checklist. Keith A. Harding & Kenneth R. Welch. 200p. 1980. 63.00 (ISBN 0-08-025495-0). Pergamon.

Venomous Woman: Fear of the Female in Literature. Margaret Hallissy. LC 87-10711. (Contributions in Women's Studies: No. 87). 192p. 1987. lib. bdg. 35.00 (ISBN 0-313-25919-4, HYV/). Greenwood.

Venoms of the Hymenoptera. Ed. by Tom Piek. 1986. 92.00 (ISBN 0-12-554770-6); pap. 39.95 (ISBN 0-12-554771-4). Acad Pr.

Venous Blood Pressure. Gail A. Rockford. 1978. 20.00 (ISBN 0-916750-72-8). Dayton Labs.

Venous Drainage of the Domestic Animals. Nani G. Ghoshal et al. LC 80-53898. pap. 69.50 (ISBN 0-317-26433-8, 2024989). Bks Demand UMI.

Venous Problems. Symposium on Venous Problems (1976: Northwestern University Medical School) Staff. Ed. by John J. Bergan & James S. Yao. LC 77-81529. pap. 160.00 (2030838). Bks Demand UMI.

TITLE INDEX

VENUS, NEAR NEIGHBOR OF

Venous Surgery in the Lower Extremity. Kenneth G. Swan. LC 74-2564. (Illus.). 442p. 1976. 37.50 (ISBN 0-87527-135-9). Green.
Venous Thromboembolism. Jack Hirsh et al. 1981. 46.50 (ISBN 0-8089-1408-1, 791992). Grune.
Venous Thromboembolism: Natural History, Diagnosis, & Management. Ed. by Jack Hirsh & Russell Hull. 192p. 1987. 113.00 (ISBN 0-8493-4761-0). CRC Pr.
Venous Thrombosis & Pulminary Embolism: Diagnostic Methods. Jack Hirsh. LC 86-18780. (Methods in Hematology Ser.: Vol. 18). (Illus.). 179p. 1987. text ed. 55.50 (ISBN 0-443-03311-0). Churchill.
Venous Thrombosis & Pulmonary Embolism. Michael Hume et al. LC 70-122215. (Commonwealth Fund Publications Ser). 1970. 30.00x (ISBN 0-674-93320-6). Harvard U Pr.
Venous Trauma: Pathophysiology Diagnosis & Surgical Management. Ed. by Robert W. Hobson, II. LC 81-71800. (Illus.). 256p. 1982. 32.50 (ISBN 0-87993-155-8). Futura Pub.
Venous Valves. R. Gottlob & R. May. (Illus.). 250p. 1985. 67.50 (ISBN 0-387-81898-7). Springer-Verlag.
Vent du Changement. Harold Kemp. Tr. by Yves D. Martin. (Illus.). 229p. (Orig., Fr.). 1983. pap. 5.95 (ISBN 0-914766-97-X). Illum Way Pub.
Ventana Press. Roger C. Parker. Orig. Title: Makeover Book. (Illus.). 275p. (Orig.). 1988. pap. 22.95 (ISBN 0-940087-20-0). Ventana Pr.
Ventana y Yo. 2nd ed. Jorge L. Morales. 98p. (Span.). 1973. pap. 6.00 (ISBN 0-318-03736-X). Edit Asol.
Ventanas al Paraiso. David Gooding. Orig. Title: Windows to Paradise. 160p. (Span.). 1983. pap. 4.50 (ISBN 0-8254-1276-5). Kregel.
Vente des Biens Nationaux Pendant la Revolution: Avec Etude Speciale des Ventes dans le Departement de la Gironde et du Cher. Marcel Marion. 466p. (Fr.). Repr. of 1908 ed. lib. bdg. 87.50x. Coronet Bks.
Ventilated Improved Pit Latrines: Recent Developments in Zimbabwe. D. D. Mara & Peter R. Morgan. (Technical Paper: No. 3). 48p. 1983. 5.00 (ISBN 0-8213-0078-4, BK 0078). World Bank.
Ventilation: A Bibliography. Mary Vance. (Architecture Ser.: A 1590). 26p. 1986. 7.50 (ISBN 0-89028-860-7). Vance Biblios.
Ventilation: A Practical Guide. Nancy Clark et al. LC 84-12680. (Illus.). 128p. (Orig.). 1984. text ed. 15.99 (ISBN 0-918875-03-X); pap. text ed. 7.95 (ISBN 0-918875-00-5). Ctr Occupational Hazards.
Ventilation: A Practical Guide for Artists, Craftspeople & Others in the Arts. Nancy Clark et al. 117p. (Orig.). Date not set. pap. text ed. 7.95 (ISBN 0-941130-44-4). N Lyons Bks.
Ventilation & Drainage Maintainer. Jack Rudman. (Career Examination Ser.: C-1528). (Cloth bdg. avail. on request). pap. 14.00 (ISBN 0-8373-1528-X). Natl Learning.
Ventilation: Blood Flow & Gas Exchange. 4th ed. West. 1986. pap. 15.50 (ISBN 0-632-01504-7, B-5433-5). Mosby.
Ventilation Effective Planning, Design & Operation in Business & Industry. Burgess et al. 1988. write for info. (ISBN 0-471-89219-X). Wiley.
Ventilation for Acceptable Indoor Air Quality, 1981. (ASHRAE Standards Ser.: No. 62). 36.00 (ISBN 0-317-58699-8). Am Heat Ref & Air Eng.
Ventilation in Relation to Mental Work. Edward L. Thorndike et al. LC 71-177714. (Columbia University. Teachers College. Contributions to Education: No. 78). Repr. of 1916 ed. 22.50 (ISBN 0-404-55078-9). AMS Pr.
Ventilation of Agricultural Structures. Ed. by Hellickson & Walker. LC 83-72691. 374p. 1983. 32.00 (ISBN 0-916150-56-9, M1083). Am Soc Ag Eng.
Ventilation of Coal Mines. Ed. by Hargraves. 350p. 1983. pap. text ed. 39.00x (ISBN 0-909520-62-3, Pub. by Australian Inst M & M). Brookfield Pub Co.
Ventilation of School Buildings: A Study of Present Practices & Costs in the Light of Experimental Research. John R. McLure. LC 72-177035. (Columbia University. Teachers College. Contributions to Education: No. 157). Repr. of 1924 ed. 22.50 (ISBN 0-404-55157-2). AMS Pr.
Ventilation of Wide-Span Schools in the Hot, Humid Tropics. (Educational Building Reports: No. 6). 1978. pap. 7.95 (ISBN 0-685-65235-1, UB65, UB). UNIPUB.
Ventilation '85: Proceedings of the First International Symposium on Ventilation for Contaminant Control, Toronto, Canada, 1-3 October 1985. Ed. by H. D. Goodfellow. (Chemical Engineering Monographs: Vol. 24). 870p. 1986. 260.75 (ISBN 0-444-42622-1). Elsevier.
Ventilations. Rev. ed. Wilmot Robertson. LC 74-20120. 115p. 1982. pap. 4.95 (ISBN 0-914576-06-2). Howard Allen.
Ventilator Concepts. 2nd ed. Neal Kelsey. 500p. 1988. pap. text ed. 27.50 (ISBN 0-933195-15-X). CA College Health Sci.
Ventilators & Muscular Dystrophy. Nancy C. Schock & Agatha P. Colbert. 40p. 1987. handbk. 6.00 (ISBN 0-931301-03-3). Gazette Intl.
Ventilators: Theory & Clinical Application. Dupuis. 1986. 39.95 (ISBN 0-8016-1420-1). Mosby.
Ventilatory Support in Respiratory Failure. Ed. by Micheal L. Nochomovitz & Hugo D. Montenegro. (Illus.). 240p. 1987. monograph 45.00 (ISBN 0-87993-297-X). Futura Pub.
Ventre de Paris. Emile Zola. (Coll. Diamant). 1957. 15.50 (ISBN 0-685-23942-X). French & Eur.
Ventricle: Basic & Clinical Aspects. Ed. by Herbert J. Levine & William H. Gaasch. LC 85-4976. 1985. lib. bdg. 92.50 (ISBN 0-89838-721-3, Pub. by Martinus Nijhoff Netherlands). Kluwer Academic.
Ventricular Function at Rest & During Exercise. Ed. by H. Roskamm & C. Hahn. 1976. pap. 21.30 (ISBN 0-387-07707-3). Springer-Verlag.
Ventricular Septum of the Heart. Ed. by Arnold C. Wenink et al. 1982. lib. bdg. 69.00 (ISBN 90-6021-486-2, Pub. by Martinus Nijhoff Netherlands). Kluwer Academic.
Ventricular Tachycardia: Mechanisms & Management. Mark E. Josephson. LC 82-83342. 320p. 1982. 49.50 (ISBN 0-87993-181-7). Futura Pub.
Ventricular Tachycardias. Ed. by Etienne Aliot & Ralph Lazzara. (Developments in Cardiovascular Medicine Ser.). 1987. lib. bdg. 121.50 (ISBN 0-89838-881-3, Pub. by Martinus Nijhoff Netherlands). Kluwer Academic.
Ventricular Vascular Coupling. Ed. by F. C. Yin. (Illus.). 480p. 1986. 65.00 (ISBN 0-387-96279-4). Springer-Verlag.
Ventricular Wall Motion. Ed. by R. Ulrich Sigwart et al. (Illus.). 327p. (Orig.). 1984. pap. text ed. 66.00 (ISBN 0-86577-146-4). Thieme Med Pubs.
Ventriloquism for the Total Dummy. Dan Ritchard & Kathleen Moloney. LC 87-40186. 96p. 1987. pap. 7.95 incl. puppet & mirror (ISBN 0-394-75638-X, Pub. by Villard Bks). Random.
Ventriloquism in a Nutshell. Clinton Detweiler. (Illus.). 1974. pap. 4.00 (ISBN 0-686-20905-2, 065). Maher Ventril Studio.
Ventriloquism: Magic with Your Voice. George Schindler. (Illus.). 1985. pap. 9.95 (ISBN 0-679-21025-3). McKay.
Ventriloquism: Magic with Your Voice. George Schindler. (Illus.). 1986. pap. 6.95 (ISBN 0-679-14127-8). McKay.
Ventriloquist: New & Selected Poems. Robert Huff. LC 77-1338. (Virginia Commonwealth University Series for Contemporary Poetry). 58p. 1977. 10.95x (ISBN 0-8139-0725-X). U Pr of Va.
Vents. Saint-John Perse, pseud. Bd. with Chronique. (Poesie Ser.). pap. 6.95 (ISBN 0-685-36547-6). Schoenhof.
Ventura County Companion. Tom Tuttle. (Illus.). 128p. (Orig.). 1988. pap. 8.95 (ISBN 0-945092-02-4). EZ Nature.
Ventura County Street Atlas 1987. Thomas Bros. Maps Staff. (Illus.). 94p. 1987. pap. 12.95 (ISBN 0-88130-212-0). Thomas Bros Maps.
Ventura County Thomas Guide 1988. Thomas Bros. Maps Staff. (Illus.). 98p. 1988. pap. 12.95 (ISBN 0-88130-274-0). Thomas Bros Maps.
Ventura Desktop Publishing Tips & Techniques. Robert Wolenik. 1988. pap. 18.95 (ISBN 0-673-38079-3). Scott F.
Ventura-Los Angeles Counties Street Atlas: 1988. Thomas Brothers Maps Staff. (Illus.). 384p. 1987. pap. 19.95. Thomas Bros Maps.
Ventura Publisher for the IBM PC: Mastering Desktop Publishing. Richard J. Jantz. LC 87-23755. (Illus.). 264p. 1987. pap. 19.95 (ISBN 0-471-62760-7). Wiley.
Ventura Publishers Handbook. Tony Bove & Cheryl Rhodes. (Computers Ser.). 400p. 1988. pap. 24.95 (ISBN 0-553-34504-4). Bantam.
Ventura Tips & Tricks. Ted Nace. (Illus.). 288p. (Orig.). 1987. pap. 18.95 (ISBN 0-938151-01-0). Peachpit Pr.
Ventura Tips & Tricks. 2nd ed. Ted Nace. (Illus.). 400p. 1988. pap. 22.95 (ISBN 0-938151-03-7). Peachpit Pr.
Venture Capital & Public Offering Negotiation. Ed. by Michael J. Halloran. 890p. 1983. Annual supplements avail. 95.00 (ISBN 0-15-004282-5, H42825, Law & Business). HarBraceJ.
Venture Capital & Small Business Financings, 2 Vols. Robert J. Haft. 1984. looseleaf 165.00 (ISBN 0-87632-447-2). Clark Boardman.
Venture Capital & Urban Development. Michael Kieschnick. Ed. by Michael Barker. LC 79-67385. (Studies in State Development Policy: Vol. 7). 59p. 1979. pap. 11.95 (ISBN 0-934842-06-X). CSPA.
Venture Capital: Context, Development & Policies. OECD. 66p. (Orig.). 1987. pap. 9.00x (ISBN 92-64-12901-4). OECD.
Venture Capital Financing: The Practical Aspects. (Commercial Law & Practice Ser.). 219p. 1988. 45.00 (A4-4220). PLI.
Venture Capital Handbook. rev. ed. David J. Gladstone. (Illus.). 416p. 1987. pap. 19.95 (ISBN 0-13-941501-7). P-H.
Venture Capital in Britain, America & Japan. Rodney Clark. LC 86-28001. 128p. 1987. 35.00 (ISBN 0-312-00505-9). St Martin.
Venture Capital in High-Tech Companies: The Electronics Business in Perspective. George Young. viii, 213p. 1985. lib. bdg. 32.95 (ISBN 0-89930-146-0, YVC/, Quorum). Greenwood.
Venture Capital in Information Technology. OECD. (ICCP Ser.). 54p. (Orig.). 1985. pap. 11.00x (ISBN 92-64-12696-1). OECD.
Venture Capital Inside Out: An Entrepreneur's Guide to How the System Works. Roy G. Helsing. LC 88-50083. 128p. (Orig.). 1988. pap. 17.00 (ISBN 0-945901-03-8). Transwest Ventures.
Venture Capital Investing: The Complete Handbook for Investing in Small Private Businesses for Outstanding Profits. David J. Gladstone. 512p. 1988. 39.95 (ISBN 0-13-941428-2). P-H.
Venture Capital: Law, Business Strategies, & Investment Planning. Joseph W. Bartlett. LC 87-30352. 514p. 1988. 95.00 (ISBN 0-471-85076-4). Wiley.
Venture Capital Markets for the Regeneration of Industry: Proceedings of the 4th Symposium on the Financing & Innovation, Held by the Commission of the European Communities, Luxembourg 23-25, Nov., 1983. Ed. by J. M. Gibb. 348p. 1984. 52.75 (ISBN 0-444-87567-0). Elsevier.
Venture Capital of Higher Education: The Private & Public Sources of Discretionary Funds. Martin Kramer. LC 80-65491. pap. 23.80 (ISBN 0-317-55386-0, 2029491). Bks Demand UMI.
Venture Capital Proposal Package. David B. Frigstad & Wyman N. Bravard. Ed. by Emmett Ramey. (Successful Business Library). 180p. 1984. 3-ring binder 33.95 (ISBN 0-916378-45-4, Oasis). PSI Res.
Venture Capital: The Complete Guide for Investors. A. David Silver. LC 84-19479. (Wiley Small Business Management Ser.: No. 1-471). 259p. 1985. 19.95 (ISBN 0-471-88029-9, Pub. by The Ronald Press). Wiley.
Venture Capital Today: A Guide to the Venture Capital Market in the United Kingdom. Tony Lorenz. LC 85-646. 214p. 1985. 41.25 (ISBN 0-85941-275-X, Pub. by Woodhead-Faullkner). Longwood Pub Group.
Venture Economics Guide to European Venture Capital Sources. Ed. by Stanley E. Pratt & Susan E. Lloyd. 320p. 1985. 125.00 (ISBN 0-914470-18-3, Dist. by Oryx Pr). Venture Econ Inc.
Venture Feasibility Planning Guide. Robert Ronstadt & Shuman. 150p. 1988. pap. 19.95 (ISBN 0-930204-21-2). Lord Pub.
Venture in History: The Production, Publication, & Sale of the Works of Hubert Howe Bancroft. Harry Clark. LC 72-173900. (UC Publications in Librarianship: Vol. 9). 1973. pap. 35.00x (ISBN 0-520-09417-4). U of Cal Pr.
Venture in the East. Bruce Lancaster. 1976. Repr. of 1951 ed. lib. bdg. 19.95x (ISBN 0-88411-684-0, Pub. by Aeonian Bks). Amereon Ltd.
Venture Inward: Edgar Cayce's Story & the Mysteries of the Unconscious Mind. Hugh L. Cayce. LC 85-42772. 256p. 1985. pap. 8.95 (ISBN 0-06-250131-3, HarpR). Har-Row.
Venture Magazine: Complete Guide to Venture Capital. Clinton Richardson. LC 87-5721. 260p. 1987. pap. 12.95 (ISBN 0-452-25918-5, Plume). NAL.
Venture Magazine's Guide to International Venture Capital. Venture Magazine Editors. 1985. 60.00 (ISBN 0-671-55698-3). S&S.
Venture of Form in the Novels of Virginia Woolf. Jean Alexander. LC 73-83260. 1974. 24.50x (ISBN 0-8046-9052-9, Pub by Kennikat). Assoc Faculty Pr.
Venture of Islam, 3 vols. Marshall G. Hodgson. Incl. Vol. 1. Classical Age of Islam. pap. 15.00x (ISBN 0-226-34683-8, P716); Vol. 2. Expansion of Islam in the Middle Period. pap. 18.00x (ISBN 0-226-34684-6, P717); Vol. 3. Gunpowder Empire & Modern Times. pap. 15.00x (ISBN 0-226-34685-4, P718). LC 73-87243. (Illus.). 716p. 1977 (Phoen). U of Chicago Pr.
Venture of Islam: Conscience & History in World Civilization, 3 vols. Marshall G. Hodgson. LC 73-87243. 1975. 30.00x ea.; Vol. 2. (ISBN 0-226-34680-3); Vol. 3. (ISBN 0-226-34681-1). U of Chicago Pr.
Venture to the Interior. Laurens Van Der Post. LC 79-10524. 253p. 1979. pap. 7.95 (ISBN 0-15-693529-5, Harv). HarBraceJ.
Venturers: The Hampton, Harrison & Earle Families of Virginia, South Carolina & Texas. Virginia G. Meynard. (Illus.). 1036p. 1981. 42.50 (ISBN 0-89308-241-4, BFH 14). Southern Hist Pr.
Ventures. Katharine Howard. 304p. 1985. pap. 3.50 (ISBN 0-8439-2304-0, Leisure Bks). Leisure NY.
Ventures & Adventures in Wall Street, 2 vols. Richard D. Wyckoff. (Illus.). 366p. 1987. Set. 227.45 (ISBN 0-86654-218-3). Inst Econ Finan.
Venture's Financing & Investing in Private Companies. rev. ed. Arthur Lipper, III. 400p. 1988. 32.50 (ISBN 0-917253-99-X). Probus Pub Co.
Ventures in Book Collecting. W. H. Arnold. 59.95 (ISBN 0-8490-1257-0). Gordon Pr.
Ventures in Common Sense. E. W. Howe. 1919. Repr. 20.00 (ISBN 0-8274-3668-8). R West.
Ventures in Common Sense. E. W. Howe. (Collected Works of E. W. Howe). 1988. Repr. of 1919 ed. lib. bdg. 59.00x. Am Biog Serv.
Ventures in Common Sense see Collected Works.
Ventures in Discipleship. John R. Martin. LC 84-19140. 304p. (Orig.). 1984. pap. 12.95 (ISBN 0-8361-3378-1). Herald Pr.
Ventures in Leisure-Time Christian Education. Norma E. Koenig. (Orig.). 1979. pap. 4.15 (ISBN 0-687-43670-2). Abingdon.
Ventures in Social Interpretation. Henry Winthrop. LC 68-24073. (Century Sociology Ser.). (Illus., Orig.). 1968. pap. text ed. 9.95x (ISBN 0-89197-465-2). Irvington.
Ventures in Thought. facs. ed. Francis B. Latymer. LC 67-23238. (Essay Index Reprint Ser). 1915. 18.00 (ISBN 0-8369-0610-1). Ayer Co Pubs.
Venturi Analysis. rev. ed. Ken Venturi & Al Barkow. (Classics of Golf Ser.). (Illus.). 160p. 17.95x (ISBN 0-940889-08-0). Classics Golf.
Venturi Analysis: Learning Better Golf from the Champions. Ken Venturi & Al Barkow. LC 80-69389. 160p. 1982. 9.95 (ISBN 0-689-11145-2); pap. 11.95 (ISBN 0-689-70633-2, 286). Atheneum.
Venturi, Rauch & Scott Brown. Ed. by Antonio Sanmartin. (Academy Architecture Ser.). (Illus.). 144p. 1987. pap. 29.95 (ISBN 0-312-00712-4). St Martin.
Venturi, Rauch, & Scott Brown. Stanislaus Von Moos. (Illus.). 336p. 1987. 60.00 (ISBN 0-8478-0743-6); pap. 37.50 (ISBN 0-8478-0745-2). Rizzoli Intl.
Venturi System. Ken Venturi & Al Barkow. LC 83-45088. (Illus.). 160p. 1983. 21.50 (ISBN 0-689-11414-1). Atheneum.
Venturing Abroad: Innovation by U. S. Multinationals. Frank C. Schuller. LC 87-37574. 184p. 1988. lib. bdg. 37.95 (ISBN 0-89930-129-0, SMT/, Quorum Bks). Greenwood.
Venturing: An Introduction to Sailing. Peter Burchard. (Illus.). 160p. (gr. 5 up). 1986. 17.95 (ISBN 0-316-11613-0). Little.
Venturing Beyond the Campus: Students Who Leave College. C. Hess Haagen. LC 77-2541. 1977. pap. 10.00x (ISBN 0-8195-8027-9). Wesleyan U Pr.
Venturing to Do Justice: Reforming Private Law. Robert E. Keeton. LC 69-18035. 1969. text ed. 16.95x (ISBN 0-674-93355-9). Harvard U Pr.
Venus. Ed. by Donald M. Hunten et al. LC 83-1064. 1143p. 1983. 49.95x (ISBN 0-8165-0788-0). U of Ariz Pr.
Venus After Forty: Sexual Myths, Men's Fantasies & Truths about Middle-Aged Women. Rita M. Ransohoff. 1987. 18.95 (ISBN 0-317-55895-1). New Horizon NJ.
Venus after Forty: Sexual Myths, Men's Fantasies, & Truths about Middle-Aged Women. Rita M. Ransohoff. 1987. 18.95 (ISBN 0-88282-034-6). New Horizon NJ.
Venus: An Errant Twin. Eric Burgess. LC 85-384. (Illus.). 176p. 1985. 29.95 (ISBN 0-231-05856-X). Columbia U Pr.
Venus & Adonis: A Study in Warwickshire Dialect. Ed. by James A. Morgan. LC 76-169261. (Shakespeare Society of New York. Publications: No. 2). Repr. of 1885 ed. 16.00 (ISBN 0-404-54202-6). AMS Pr.
Venus & Sothis: How the Ancient Near East Was Rediscovered. Wilbur D. Jones. LC 81-11130. 200p. 1981. text ed. 21.95x; pap. text ed. 10.95x (ISBN 0-88229-780-5). Nelson-Hall.
Venus & the Rain. Medbh McGuckian. 1984. pap. 8.95 (ISBN 0-19-211962-1). Oxford U Pr.
Venus Atmosphere. Ed. by R. Jastrow & S. I. Rasool. 616p. 1969. 175.00 (ISBN 0-677-13260-3). Gordon & Breach.
Venus Belt. L. Neil Smith. (Orig.). 1981. pap. 2.25 (ISBN 0-345-28721-5, Del Rey). Ballantine.
Venus Delights. 224p. 1986. pap. 3.95 (ISBN 0-88184-242-7). Carroll & Graf.
Venus d'Ille: Les Ames du Purgatoire. Prosper Merimee. (Illus.). 145p. 1974. 60.00 (ISBN 0-686-54763-2). French & Eur.
Venus Disposes. 240p. 1988. pap. 3.95 (ISBN 0-88184-426-8). Carroll & Graf.
Venus Equilateral. George O. Smith. Ed. by Lester Del Rey. LC 75-426. (Library of Science Fiction). 1975. lib. bdg. 21.00 (ISBN 0-8240-1431-6). Garland Pub.
Venus in Hollywood: The Continental Enchantress from Garbo to Loren. Michael Bruno. LC 71-90838. (Illus.). 1970. 6.95 (ISBN 0-8184-0091-9). Lyle Stuart.
Venus in India. Charles Devereaux. (Orig.). 1967. pap. 1.95 (ISBN 0-87067-611-3, BH611). Holloway.
Venus in India. 300p. 1987. pap. 3.95 (ISBN 0-88184-365-2). Carroll & Graf.
Venus in India: Love Adventures in Hindustan. Captain C. Devereaux. 352p. 1983. pap. 3.95 (ISBN 0-446-30789-0). Warner Bks.
Venus in Lace. Marcus Van Heller. 192p. 1984. pap. 3.95 (ISBN 0-88184-036-X). Carroll & Graf.
Venus in Paris. 224p. 1986. pap. 3.95 (ISBN 0-88184-284-2). Carroll & Graf.
Venus in the Country. LC 82-48000. (Grove Press Victorian Library). 224p. 1982. pap. 3.95 (ISBN 0-394-62420-3, B477, BC). Grove.
Venus Kit. Sherwood Harrington & Andrew Fraknoi. (Illus.). 40p. 1988. 11.00 (ISBN 0-937707-13-9). Astron Soc Pacific.
Venus Love: Potpourri. Scentouri Staff. (Orig.). 1985. pap. text ed. 1.75 (ISBN 0-318-04388-2, Pub. by Scentouri). Prosperity & Profits.
Venus, Near Neighbor of the Sun. Isaac Asimov. LC 80-26700. (Illus.). 224p. (gr. 5 up). 1981. 11.75 (ISBN 0-688-41976-3); PLB 11.88 (ISBN 0-688-51976-8). Lothrop.

Venus Numismatics Dictionary of Artists et al. Whose Works Were Commissioned by or Struck by the United States Mint, 1792-1977. Francis Pessolano-Filos. Ed. by Margaret M. Walsh. LC 82-90996. (Illus.). 214p. 1983. 45.00 (ISBN 0-911571-00-0). Eros Pub.

Venus Observed. Christopher Fry. 1950. 9.95x (ISBN 0-19-500395-0). Oxford U Pr.

Venus of Dreams, No. II. Pamela Sargent. 432p. (Orig.). 1988. pap. 3.95 (ISBN 0-553-27058-3, Spectra). Bantam.

Venus of Milo: An Archaeological Study of the Goddess of Womanhood. Paul Carus. 1977. lib. bdg. 59.95 (ISBN 0-8490-2796-9). Gordon Pr.

Venus of Shadows. Pamela Sargent. 1988. 19.95 (ISBN 0-385-24840-7, Foundation Bks). Doubleday.

Venus on the Half Shell. Kilgore Trout. 1975. pap. 2.95 (ISBN 0-440-16149-5). Dell.

Venus Plus X. Theodore Sturgeon. (Illus.). 224p. 1984. pap. 7.95 (ISBN 0-312-94447-0); cancelled ltd. ed. (ISBN 0-312-94448-9). Bluejay Bks.

Venus Plux X. Theodore Sturgeon. 224p. 1988. pap. 3.95 (ISBN 0-88184-387-3). Carroll & Graf.

Venus Remembered. 224p. 1985. pap. 3.95 (ISBN 0-88184-183-8). Carroll & Graf.

Venus School Mistress. LC 83-83037. (Victorian Library). 192p. 1984. pap. 3.95 (ISBN 0-394-62158-1, B499, BC). Grove.

Venus School Mistress. 1988. pap. 3.95 (ISBN 0-8216-5009-2). Blue Moon Bks.

Venus: The Gift of Love. Martin Schulman. LC 81-90119. (Illus.). 152p. (Orig.). 1981. pap. 7.95 (ISBN 0-940086-00-X). Golden Light.

Venus Tree: 1988 John Simmons Short Fiction Award. Michael Pritchett. 140p. 1988. 15.95 (ISBN 0-87745-220-2). U of Iowa Pr.

Venus Unbound. 200p. 1985. pap. 3.95 (ISBN 0-88184-159-5). Carroll & Graf.

Venus Unmasked. 160p. 1988. pap. 3.95 (ISBN 0-88184-381-4). Carroll & Graf.

Venus Venture. Hugh Zachary. 1986. 13.95 (ISBN 0-8149-0915-9). Vanguard.

Venuses Penuses. John Money. 659p. 1986. 30.95 (ISBN 0-87975-327-7). Prometheus Bks.

Venustiano Carranza's Nationalist Struggle, 1893-1920. Douglas W. Richmond. LC 83-3652. (Illus.). xxii, 328p. 1983. 28.45x (ISBN 0-8032-3863-0). U of Nebr Pr.

Vera & Her Friends. Marjolein Bastin. (Illus.). 28p. (ps-2). 1985. 2.95 (ISBN 0-8120-5689-2). Barron.

Vera Brittain. Hilary Bailey. (Illus.). 136p. 1987. pap. 4.95 (ISBN 0-14-008003-1). Penguin.

Vera Brown's Natural Beauty Book. Vera Brown & Pat Culligan. 220p. 1983. 15.95 (ISBN 0-89037-265-9). Anderson World.

Vera Storia Dei Bonobo Con Gli Occhiali see Real Story of the Bonobos Who Wore Spectacles.

Vera the Mouse. Marjolein Bastin. (ps-k). 1986. Four-bk. boxed set. 11.95 (ISBN 0-8120-7391-6); 2.95 ea. Barron.

Vera Zasulich: A Biography. Jay Bergman. LC 82-80927. 280p. 1983. 30.00x (ISBN 0-8047-1156-9). Stanford U Pr.

Veracious Imagination: Essays on American History, Literature & Biography. Cushing Strout. xiv, 301p. 1985. pap. 12.95 (ISBN 0-8195-6136-3). Wesleyan U Pr.

Veracruz. R. Wright. (Paperbacks Ser.). 624p. 1987. pap. text ed. 5.95 (ISBN 0-07-072077-0). McGraw.

Veracruz. Rosalind Wright. LC 84-47613. 480p. 1986. 18.45i (ISBN 0-06-015541-8, HarpT). Har-Row.

Veraenderungen der Moosflora von Berlin (West) Annemarie Schaeppe. (Bryophtorum Bibliotheca: No. 33). (Illus.). 392p. (Ger.). 1986. 82.50X (ISBN 3-443-62005-1). Lubrecht & Cramer.

Veraenderungen im-Gaswechsel bei Laubmoosen nach Experimentellen Belastungen mit Schwermetallverbingungen. H. P. Haseloff. (Bryohpytorum Bibliotheca 19). (Illus.). 1979. pap. text ed. 15.00x (ISBN 3-7682-1234-3). Lubrecht & Cramer.

Verandah. James P. Hennessy. (Century Classic Ser.). 313p. 1988. pap. 11.95 (ISBN 0-7126-0401-4, Pub. by Century Hutchinson). David & Charles.

Veranilda: A Romance. George Gissing. LC 68-54270. Repr. of 1904 ed. 15.00 (ISBN 0-404-02816-0). AMS Pr.

Verano. J. M. Parramon et al. (Four Seasons Ser.). (Span.). (ps). 1986. pap. 3.95 (ISBN 0-8120-3645-X). Barron.

Verano en Mexico. Robert Cabat & Louis Cabat. (Orig.). (gr. 7-12). 1975. pap. text ed. 8.50 (ISBN 0-87720-504-3). AMSCO Sch.

Verapaz in the Sixteenth & Seventeenth Centuries: A Contribution to the Historical Geography & Ethnography of Northeastern Guatemala. Karl Sapper. Tr. by Theodore E. Gutman from Ger. (Occasional Paper: 13). (Illus.). xviii, 53p. 1985. pap. 8.50x (ISBN 0-917956-46-X). UCLA Arch.

Verarbeitung von Nahrungsmitteln ohne Qualitaetseinbusse-Wunschtraum oder Wirklichkeit? Handling of Food without Change of Quality - Dream or Reality? Ed. by J. C. Somogyi. (Bibliotheca Nutritio et Dieta Ser.: No. 34). (Illus.). viii, 112p. 1984. 65.50 (ISBN 3-8055-3926-6). S Karger.

Vera's Dresses Up. Marjolein Bastin. 28p. (ps-2). 1985. 2.95 (ISBN 0-8120-5691-4). Barron.

Vera's Return: And Other Incidents in the Life of Frank Johnson. Leon Knight. LC 83-81706. 72p. (Orig.). 1983. pap. 4.50 (ISBN 0-940248-17-4). Guild Pr.

Vera's Special Hobbies. Marjolein Bastin. (Illus.). 28p. (ps-2). 1985. 2.95 (ISBN 0-8120-5692-2). Barron.

Verb Be & Its Synonyms. Incl. Part 1. Classical Chinese, Athapaskan, Mundari. Ed. by J. W. Verhaar. 100p. 1967. lib. bdg. 16.00 (ISBN 90-277-0032-X); Part 2. Eskimo, Hindi, Zuni, Modern Greek, Malayalam, Kurukh. Ed. by J. W. Verhaar. 148p. 1968. lib. bdg. 18.50 (ISBN 90-277-0033-8); Part 3. Japanese, Kashmiri, Armenian, Hungarian, Sumerian, Shona. Ed. by J. W. Verhaar. 125p. 1968. lib. bdg. 18.50 (ISBN 90-277-0034-6); Part 4. Twi, Modern Chinese, Arabic. Ed. by J. W. Verhaar. 125p. 1969. lib. bdg. 18.50 (ISBN 90-277-0035-4); Part 5. Urdu, Turkish, Beugali, Amharic, Indonesian, Telegu, Estonian. Ed. by J. W. Verhaar. LC 79-159659. 233p. 1972. lib. bdg. 31.50 (ISBN 90-277-0217-9); Part 6. Ancient Greek. Ed. by C. H. Kahn. LC 74-183367. 486p. 1973. lib. bdg. 63.00 (ISBN 90-277-0222-5); pap. 29.00 (ISBN 90-277-0313-2). (Foundations of Language Supplementary Ser., Pub. by Junk Pubs Netherlands). Kluwer Academic.

Verb Be in Ancient Greek. C. H. Kahn. LC 74-183367. (Foundations of Language Supplementary Ser: No. 16). 486p. 1973. lib. bdg. 63.00 (ISBN 90-277-0222-5, Pub. by Reidel Holland); pap. text ed. 29.00 (ISBN 90-277-0313-2). Kluwer Academic.

Verb Choices & Verb Forms. Alice C. Pack. (Dyad Learning Program Ser.). 1977. pap. text ed. 10.50 (ISBN 0-88377-079-2); tchr's. ed. incl. (ISBN 0-88377-080-6). Newbury Hse.

Verb Complementation in Written English. Evert Anderson. 292p. (Orig.). 1985. pap. text ed. 23.50x (ISBN 0-317-46432-9). Coronet Bks.

Verb-Intensifier Collocations in English. Sidney Greenbaum. (Janua Linguarum, Series Minor: No. 86). (Orig.). 1970. pap. text ed. 10.00x (ISBN 90-2790-711-0). Mouton.

Verb Second Phenomena in Germanic Languages. Ed. by H. Haider & M. Prinzhorn. (Publications in Language Sciences). vi, 207p. 1986. write for info. (ISBN 90-6765-133-8); pap. write for info. (ISBN 90-6765-134-6). Foris Pubns.

Verb Studies in Five New Guinea Languages. Ed. by Howard McKaughan et al. (Publications in Linguistics & Related Fields: No. 10). 182p. 1964. microfiche (2) 4.00 (ISBN 0-88312-314-2). Summer Inst Ling.

Verb Syntax in John Dryden's Prose, Pt. I. J. Soderlind. (Essays & Studies on English Language & Literature: Vol. 10). pap. 24.00 (ISBN 0-8115-0208-2). Kraus Repr.

Verb Syntax in John Dryden's Prose, Pt. 2. Johannes Soderlind. (Essays & Studies on English Language & Literature: Vol. 19). pap. 24.00 (ISBN 0-8115-0217-1). Kraus Repr.

Verb System of Present-Day American English. 2nd ed. Robert L. Allen. (Janua Linguarum, Series Practica: No. 24). (Orig.). 1983. pap. text ed. 29.25x (ISBN 90-2790-643-2). Mouton.

Verb "To Be" in Middle English: A Survey of the Forms. G. Forsstrom. (Lund Studies in English: Vol. 15). pap. 22.00 (ISBN 0-8115-0558-8). Kraus Repr.

Verbal & Analytical Review for the GRE, Workbook. Black. 203p. pap. 6.95 (ISBN 0-15-600025-3). HarbraceJ.

Verbal & Visual Art of Alfred Kubin. Phillip H. Rhein. (Studies in Austrian Literature, Culture, & Thought). (Illus.). 188p. 1988. 19.90 (ISBN 0-929497-01-5). Ariadne CA.

Verbal Art As Performance. Richard Bauman. 150p. 1984. pap. text ed. 7.95x (ISBN 0-88133-048-5). Waveland Pr.

Verbal Art of Jean Francois Regnard, Vol. 1. D. M. Medlin. 156p. 1966. pap. 7.00 (ISBN 0-912788-00-3). Tulane Romance Lang.

Verbal Art, Verbal Sign, Verbal Time. Roman Jakobson. Ed. by Krystyna Pomorska & Stephen Rudy. LC 84-7268. 232p. 1985. 29.50x (ISBN 0-8166-1358-3); pap. 13.95 (ISBN 0-8166-1361-3). U of Minn Pr.

Verbal Behavior. B. F. Skinner. 1957. 38.00 (ISBN 0-13-941591-2). P-H.

Verbal Behavior: Adaption & Psychopathology. Walter Weintraub. LC 80-27021. 224p. 1981. text ed. 23.95 (ISBN 0-8261-2660-X). Springer Pub.

Verbal Behavior & Politics. Doris A. Graber. LC 75-25830. 390p. 1976. 27.50 (ISBN 0-252-00262-8). U of Ill Pr.

Verbal Deficit: A Critique. John C. Gordon. 181p. 1981. 25.00 (ISBN 0-85664-990-2, Pub. by Croom Helm Ltd). Routledge Chapman & Hall.

Verbal Emphatic Responding. John Milnes & Harvey J. Bertcher. 1975. pap. 4.70 (ISBN 0-87506-054-4). Campus.

Verbal Expression. James T. Martinoff et al. (Language Rehabilitation Ser.). 352p. 1981. pkg. of 5 69.00x (ISBN 0-88120-126-X, 2366). Pro Ed.

Verbal Games of Pre-School Children. Susan Iwamura. LC 79-22384. 1979. 25.00x (ISBN 0-312-83877-8). St Martin.

Verbal Icon: Studies in the Meaning of Poetry. W. K. Wimsatt. LC 54-7479. 320p. 1954. pap. 8.00 (ISBN 0-8131-0111-5). U Pr of Ky.

Verbal Imagination: Coleridge & the Language of Modern Criticism. A. C. Goodson. 272p. 1988. 32.50 (ISBN 0-19-505450-4). Oxford U Pr.

Verbal Information Systems: A Comprehensive Guide to Writing Manuals. (Standards Ser.). 1974. 5.00 (ISBN 0-934356-18-1); member 4.00 (ISBN 0-686-00292-X). Assn Syst Mgmt.

Verbal Judo: Redirecting Behavior with Words. George J. Thompson & Michael J. Stroud. Ed. by Helen Moody. (Illus.). 110p. (Orig.). 1984. pap. 6.95 (ISBN 0-317-07520-9). Comm Strat Inc.

Verbal Judo: Words for Street Survival. George J. Thompson. (Illus.). 158p. 1983. 21.75x (ISBN 0-398-04879-7). C C Thomas.

Verbal Landscape-Dinosaur Sat Down. Nathan Lyons. (Illus.). 1987. pap. write for info. (ISBN 0-939784-16-5). CEPA Gall.

Verbal Landscapes - Dinosaur Sat Down. Nathan Lyons. (Illus.). 32p. 1987. pap. 6.50. Visual Studies.

Verbal Language & Communication. William D. Brooks et al. (Comm Comp Ser.). (Illus.). 32p. 1980. pap. text ed. 3.00x (ISBN 0-89787-306-8). Gorsuch Scarisbrick.

Verbal Pattern in Four Quartets: A Closing Reading of T. S. Eliot's Poem. Mary A. Weinig. 1982. 12.00x (ISBN 0-936968-04-4). Intl Bk Ctr.

Verbal Processes in Children: Progress in Cognitive Developmental Research. Ed. by C. J. Brainerd & M. Pressley. (Springer Series in Cognitive Development). (Illus.). 289p. 1982. 37.00 (ISBN 0-387-90648-7). Springer-Verlag.

Verbal Review & Workbook for the SAT. (Test Preparation Ser.). 282p. 1989. pap. 7.95 (ISBN 0-15-600088-1). HarBraceJ.

Verbal Review for Standardized Tests. William A. Covino & Peter Z. Orton. (Cliffs Test Preparation Ser.). (Illus.). 375p. 1986. pap. text ed. 7.95 (ISBN 0-8220-2034-3). Cliffs.

Verbal Skills' PSAT-SAT Preparation Guide. Elissa B. Sommerfield. LC 86-81902. 104p. 1986. pap. text ed. 13.95 (ISBN 0-9604058-0-1). Ed Skills Dallas.

Verbal Style & the Presidency: Computer Assisted Analysis of Persuasion. Roderick P. Hart. LC 83-21512. (Human Communication Research Ser.). 1984. 33.00 (ISBN 0-12-328420-1). Acad Pr.

Verbal System of Southern Agaw. Robert Hetzron. LC 70-14968. (University of California Publications. Near Eastern Studies: Vol. 12). pap. 33.50 (ISBN 0-317-10197-8, 2021379). Bks Demand UMI.

Verbal Workbook for the ACT. Joyce Lakritz. LC 82-11644. 256p. 1983. pap. 6.95 (ISBN 0-668-05348-8, 5348). Arco.

Verbal Workbook for the ACT. 2nd ed. Sally Martin. 224p. 1988. pap. 7.95 (ISBN 0-13-941832-6). P-H.

Verbal Workbook for the SAT. Walter J. Miller et al. 384p. 1987. pap. 7.95 (ISBN 0-668-06135-9). Arco.

Verbal Workbook for the S.A.T. College Entrance Examinations. Gabriel Freedman & M. A. Haller. LC 81-22751. 288p. 1981. pap. 6.00 (ISBN 0-668-04853-0, 4853). Arco.

Verbalism Among Blind Children: An Investigation & Analysis. Randall K. Harley. (Research Ser.: No. 10). 61p. 1963. pap. 2.40 (ISBN 0-89128-065-0, PER065). Am Foun Blind.

Verbalist. Alfred Ayers. 1911. 12.50 (ISBN 0-8274-3669-6). R West.

Verbally Charged Images. Nina Felshin. LC 84-80047. (Illus.). 50p. 1984. 2.50 (ISBN 0-317-66214-7). Ind Curators.

Verbatim, Vols. III & IV. 356p. 1981. 20.00 (ISBN 0-930454-12-X). Verbatim Bks.

Verbatim, Vols. V & VI. 385p. 1981. 20.00 (ISBN 0-930454-13-8). Verbatim Bks.

Verbatim, Vols. VII & VIII. Date not set. 20.00 (ISBN 0-930454-17-0). Verbatim Bks.

Verbatim: A Language Quarterly, 4 vols. Ed. by Laurence Urdang. 1100p. 1982. 24.00x ea. Vols. 3-4 (ISBN 0-8103-4358-4). Vols. 5-6 (ISBN 0-8103-4359-2). Gale.

Verbatim: Volumes I & II. LC 77-20392. 250p. 1979. 20.00 (ISBN 0-930454-04-9). Verbatim Bks.

Verbatim: Volumes I-VI Index. 128p. 1981. 20.00 (ISBN 0-930454-14-6). Verbatim Bks.

Verbe Francais: Five Tomes in One Volume. Jaime M. Tolentino. LC 78-14928. (Illus.). 1979. text ed. 12.00 (ISBN 0-8477-3322-X). U of PR Pr.

Verbes de Celine. Alphonse Juilland. (Stanford French & Italian Studies: Vol. 32). 160p. 1985. pap. 29.50 (ISBN 0-915838-05-2). Anma Libri.

Verbes de Mouvement en Francais et en Espagnol: Etude Comparee de Leurs Infinitives. Beatrice Lamiroy. (Linvisticae Investigationes Supplementa: No. 11). xiv, 323p. (Fr.). 1983. 38.00x (ISBN 90-272-3121-4). Benjamins North Am.

Verbiage. Mary Scandrett. (Educational Game Activity Ser.). 1987. 35.00 (ISBN 0-930599-12-8). Thinking Pubns.

Verbis non Factis: Words Meant to Influence Political Choices in the United States, 1800-1980. Fay M. Blake & H. Morton Newman. LC 84-1325. 143p. 1984. 15.00 (ISBN 0-8108-1688-1). Scarecrow.

Verbivocovisual. Thomasine Rose. (Illus.). 72p. 1982. 9.85 (ISBN 0-9606540-3-8). Classic Nonfic.

Verbivocovisual: The Presence of Bishop Berkeley in Finnegans Wake. Thomasine Rose. 1982. 9.95 (ISBN 0-930144-03-1). Mulford Colebrook.

Verbos Espanoles Regulares e Irregulares. Enrique G. Blanco. (Span.). 1966. pap. text ed. 1.30 (ISBN 0-8294-0133-4). Loyola.

Verbotzeit: A Number of the Nazi Party Leadership in Dissolution November 1923 to February 1925. David Jablonsky. 1988. 32.50 (ISBN 0-7146-3322-4, F Cass Co). Biblio Dist.

Verbreitungsatlas der Gattung Zygaena Fabricius, 1775: Lepidoptera, Zygaenidae. C. M. Naumann et al. (Theses Zoologicae Ser.: No. 5). (Illus.). 144p. 1985. lib. bdg. 29.00x (ISBN 3-7682-1405-2). Lubrecht & Cramer.

Verbs. Sheldon Tilkin. (Horizons II Ser.). (Illus.). 24p. (gr. 3-4). 1980. wkbk. 2.50 (ISBN 0-89403-598-3). EDC.

Verbs, Pt. 1. Joan M. Frazer & Cynthia J. Smith. (Shape up Your Language Ser.). 1982. spiral wire 24.95 (ISBN 0-88450-828-5, 7024-B). Communication Skill.

Verbs for a Specific Purpose. Sandra McKay. (Illus.). 256p. 1982. pap. text ed. write for info (ISBN 0-13-941617-X). P-H.

Verbs in Action. Linda Ferreira. LC 77-10886. 168p. 1978. pap. text ed. 9.50 (ISBN 0-88377-097-0). Newbury Hse.

Verbs, Nouns & Postpositives in Attic Prose. M. H. B. Marshall. Ed. by MacDowell. (Scottish Classical Ser.: Vol. 3). 208p. 1986. 20.00 (ISBN 0-7073-0477-6, Pub. by Scot Acad Pr). Longwood Pub Group.

Verbs of Eating. Harris Winitz. (Using Verbs Ser.). (Illus., Orig.). 1988. pap. text ed. 6.50 (ISBN 0-939990-55-5); incl. cassette 12.00. Intl Linguistics.

Verbs of Motion in Their Semantic Divergence. K. H. Collitz. (LM Ser.). 1931. pap. 16.00 (ISBN 0-527-00812-5). Kraus Repr.

Verbs of Placement. Harris Winitz. (Using Verbs Ser.). (Illus., Orig.). 1988. pap. text ed. 6.50 (ISBN 0-939990-56-3); incl. cassette 12.00. Intl Linguistics.

Verbs of Walking. Harris Winitz. (Using Verbs Ser.). (Illus., Orig.). 1988. pap. text ed. 6.50 (ISBN 0-939990-54-7); incl. cassette 12.00. Intl Linguistics.

Verbs Through Pictures. Harris Winitz. (Language Through Pictures Ser.). (Illus.). 62p. (gr. 2-12). 1982. pap. 4.75 (ISBN 0-939990-30-X). Intl Linguistics.

VerbtabellenDeutsch. Heinz F. Wendt. 71p. 3.50 (ISBN 3-468-34110-5). Langenscheidt.

Verbum ohne Pronominales Subjekt in der Aelteren Deutschen Sprache. Karl Held. 1967. o.o. 18.00 (ISBN 0-384-22176-9); pap. 13.00 (ISBN 0-384-22175-0). Johnson Repr.

Vercelli Book. Ed. by George P. Krapp. LC 32-10861. 152p. 1932. 27.50 (ISBN 0-231-08766-7). Columbia U Pr.

Vercelli Book see Early English Manuscripts in Facsimile.

Vercelli Book Poems, Done in a Normalized Orthography. Ed. by Francis P. Magoun, Jr. (Old English Ser: No. 4). 1960. pap. 4.95x (ISBN 0-674-93390-7). Harvard U Pr.

Vercelli Homilies Nine to Twenty-Three. Ed. by Paul E. Szarmach. (Toronto Old English Ser.). 192p. 1981. 30.00x (ISBN 0-8020-5528-1). U of Toronto Pr.

Vercoquin et le Plancton. Boris Vian. (Folio Ser.: No. 334). 192p. 1968. 5.95 (ISBN 0-686-55709-3). Schoenhof.

Vercors, Ecrivain et Dessinateur. Konstantinovic. (Bibliotheque Franc. et Romane. Et. Litter.). 10.95 (ISBN 0-685-36631-6). French & Eur.

Verdad sobre las Relaciones entre el Partido Marxista de los EUA y el Partido Communista del Canada (M-L) Marxist-Leninist Party, U. S. A. 86p. (Span.). 1981. pap. 1.00 (ISBN 0-86714-022-4). Marxist-Leninist.

Verdades que Cambian Vidas. Marcelino Ortiz. 96p. (Orig., Span.). 1981. pap. 2.50 (ISBN 0-89922-173-4). Edit Caribe.

Verdi. Ferruccio Bonavia. LC 78-66902. (Illus.). 1980. Repr. of 1947 ed. 18.00 (ISBN 0-88355-726-6). Hyperion Conn.

Verdi. Julian Budden. (Master Musicians Ser.). (Illus.). 416p. 1986. 26.95x (ISBN 0-460-03165-1, Pub. by J M Dent England). Biblio Dist.

Verdi. Julian Budden. 1987. 9.95 (ISBN 0-394-75280-5, Vin). Random.

Verdi. Pierre Petit. Tr. by Patrick Bowles from Fr. (Illustrated Composer Ser.). (Illus., Orig.). 1981. pap. 5.95 (ISBN 0-7145-0595-1). Riverrun NY.

Verdi. (Portraits of Greatness Ser.: No. I). (Eng.). 1987. pap. 7.50 (ISBN 0-918367-00-X). Elite.

Verdi. (Portraits of Greatness Ser.: No. I). (Ital.). 1987. pap. 7.50 (ISBN 0-317-57557-0). Elite.

Verdi. facs. ed. Ed. by Franz Werfel & Paul Stefan. Tr. by Edward Downes. LC 71-130565. (Select Bibliographies Reprint Ser.). 1942. 26.50 (ISBN 0-8369-5538-2). Ayer Co Pubs.

Verdi: A Life in the Theatre. Charles Osborne. LC 87-45205. (Illus.). 384p. 1988. 22.95 (ISBN 0-394-54110-3). Knopf.

Verdi: A Life in the Theatre. Charles Osborne. (Illus.). 1988. pap. 12.95 (ISBN 0-88064-106-1). Fromm Intl Pub.

Verdi Companion. Ed. by William Weaver & Martin Chusid. (Illus.). 1979. 22.95 (ISBN 0-393-01215-8). Norton.

Vermischte Schriften, 3 vols. Heinrich W. Von Gerstenberg. 1262p. Repr. of 1815 ed. 180.00 (ISBN 0-384-18220-8). Johnson Repr.
Vermont. new ed. Allan Carpenter. LC 79-829. (New Enchantment of America State Bks.). (Illus.). 96p. (gr. 4 up). 1979. PLB 15.93 (ISBN 0-516-04145-2). Childrens.
Vermont. Ed. by Richard Grossinger. (Illus.). 350p. 1974. pap. 10.00 (ISBN 0-913028-26-6). North Atlantic.
Vermont. Gary Irving & Charles Morrissey. (Illus.). 1985. 16.95 (ISBN 0-19-540607-9). Skyline Press.
Vermont. Charles T. Morrissey. (States & the Nation Ser.). (Illus.). 240p. 1981. 14.95 (ISBN 0-393-05625-2). Norton.
Vermont. Clyde Smith. Ed. by James Patrick. (Scenic Discovery Ser.). (Illus.). 128p. 1987. 35.00 (ISBN 0-89909-128-8). Yankee Bks.
Vermont. Turner Educational Services, Inc. Staff & James I. Clark. (Portrait of America Library). 48p. (gr. 4 up). 1986. PLB 15.33 (ISBN 0-86514-459-1); pap. text ed. 9.27 (ISBN 0-86514-534-2); Beta Video 113.33 (ISBN 0-86514-084-7); VHS Video 113.33 (ISBN 0-86514-159-2); 3-4" Video 136.00 (ISBN 0-86514-234-3); tchr. study guide 13.27 (ISBN 0-86514-309-9); student activity bk. 6.60 (ISBN 0-86514-384-6); Index 13.27. Raintree Pubs.
Vermont - Paris Odyssey. Esther. 12p. (Orig.). 1988. pap. text ed. 6.00 (ISBN 0-938885-05-7). Shu Pub.
Vermont: A Bibliography of Its History. T. D. Bassett. LC 83-19874. (No. 4). 427p. 1983. 45.00x (ISBN 0-87451-285-9). U Pr of New Eng.
Vermont: A Cultural Patchwork. Elise Guyette. (Illus.). 144p. (Orig.). (gr. 4-8). 1986. pap. text ed. 9.85 (ISBN 0-9607638-5-6). Cobblestone Pub.
Vermont: A Guide to the Green Mountain State. Federal Writers' Project Staff. 1937. Repr. 59.00x (ISBN 0-403-02194-4). Somerset Pub.
Vermont: A Special World. 7th ed. Ralph N. Hill et al. (Illus.). 168p. 21.95 (ISBN 0-936896-02-7). VT Life Mag.
Vermont: A Study of Independence. Rowland E. Robinson. LC 72-3751. (American Commonwealths: No. 14). Repr. of 1892 ed. 34.00 (ISBN 0-404-57214-6). AMS Pr.
Vermont: A Study of Independence. Rowland E. Robinson. LC 75-28714. 1976. pap. 4.95 (ISBN 0-8048-1167-9). C E Tuttle.
Vermont Adventure: Turn Left to E. Wallingford. A. F. Joy. (Illus.). 131p. (Orig.). 1985. pap. 4.95 (ISBN 0-934703-01-9). Saturscent Pubns.
Vermont Afternoons with Robert Frost. Vrest Orton. LC 70-134029. 64p. 1981. pap. 4.50 (ISBN 0-914960-34-2). Academy Bks.
Vermont: An Explorer's Guide. 3rd ed. Christina Tree & Peter S. Jennison. 400p. 1988. pap. 14.95 (ISBN 0-88150-110-7). Countryman.
Vermont Atlas & Gazetteer. rev. ed. Ed. by David DeLorme. (Atlas & Gazetteer Ser.). (Illus.). 88p. (Orig.). 1986. pap. 9.95 (ISBN 0-89933-005-3). DeLorme Map.
Vermont Bicentennial & History. 1984. 7.95 (ISBN 0-393-30223-7). Norton.
Vermont Blood. Barney Crosier. (Illus.). 128p. 1980. pap. 5.95 (ISBN 0-9603900-6-5). Lanser Pr.
Vermont Business Phone Book, 1987-88. 86p. 1987. pap. 15.00 (ISBN 0-318-02876-X). Manufacturers.
Vermont by Choice: The Earliest Years. Bertha S. Dodge. LC 87-62158. 160p. (Orig.). 1987. pap. 9.95 (ISBN 0-933050-50-X). New Eng Pr VT.
Vermont Census Index 1790. Ronald V. Jackson. (Illus.). lib. bdg. 22.00 (ISBN 0-317-17081-3). Accelerated Index.
Vermont Census Index, 1800. Ronald Vern Jackson. (Illus.). 1981. lib. bdg. 25.00 (ISBN 0-89593-214-8). Accelerated Index.
Vermont Census Index 1810. Ronald V. Jackson. LC 77-86067. (Illus.). lib. bdg. 23.00 (ISBN 0-89593-141-9). Accelerated Index.
Vermont Census Index 1820. Ronald V. Jackson. LC 77-86068. (Illus.). lib. bdg. 26.00 (ISBN 0-89593-142-7). Accelerated Index.
Vermont Census Index 1830. Ronald V. Jackson. LC 77-86069. (Illus.). lib. bdg. 32.00 (ISBN 0-89593-143-5). Accelerated Index.
Vermont Census Index 1840. Ronald V. Jackson. LC 77-86070. (Illus.). lib. bdg. 37.00 (ISBN 0-89593-144-3). Accelerated Index.
Vermont Census Index 1850. Ronald V. Jackson & Gary R. Teeples. LC 77-86071. (Illus.). lib. bdg. 53.00 (ISBN 0-89593-145-1). Accelerated Index.
Vermont Census Index, 1860: Heads of Households & Other Surnames in Households Index. Bryan L. Dilts. cancelled (ISBN 0-914311-46-8); cancelled (ISBN 0-914311-47-6). Index PUb.
Vermont Census Index, 1890: Union Veterans. Ronald V. Jackson. (Illus.). lib. bdg. 25.00 (ISBN 0-317-16990-4). Accelerated Index.
Vermont Chapbook. facs. ed. Compiled by Helen H. Flanders. LC 70-76935. (Granger Index Reprint Ser.). 1941. 13.00 (ISBN 0-8369-6016-5). Ayer Co Pubs.
Vermont Christmas. Text by Jay Parini. (Illus.). 128p. 1988. 29.95 (ISBN 0-316-11075-2). Little.
Vermont Chronology & Factbook. Robert I. Vexler. LC 78-26322. (Chronologies & Documentary Handbook of the States). 148p. 1978. 8.50 (ISBN 0-379-16170-2). Oceana.
Vermont Coinage see Colonial Coins of Vermont.
Vermont Country Cooking. Aristene Pixley. 1979. pap. 2.95 (ISBN 0-486-23803-2). Dover.
Vermont Court Rules Annotated, Vols. 1 & 2. 1987. Set. looseleaf 72.00. Equity Pub NH.
Vermont Diary: Language Arts in the Open Classroom. Marvin Hoffman. LC 78-16429. 180p. (Orig.). 1978. pap. 6.95 (ISBN 0-915924-22-6). Tchrs & Writers Coll.
Vermont Experience. Ed. by Susan B. Weber. (Illus.). 156p. 1987. 24.95 (ISBN 0-936896-08-6). VT Life Mag.
Vermont Fish & Wildlife Laws & Regulations. 1987. pap. write for info. Equity Pub NH.
Vermont Folk-Songs & Ballads. Helen H. Flanders & George Brown. LC 68-20768. iv, 264p. 1968. Repr. of 1931 ed. 40.00x (ISBN 0-8103-5010-6). Gale.
Vermont for Every Season. George D. Aiken et al. LC 80-23320. (Illus.). 160p. 1980. 30.00 (ISBN 0-936896-00-0). VT Life Mag.
Vermont General. Edward H. Ripley. Ed. by Otto Eisenschiml. (Illus.). 1959. 12.50 (ISBN 0-8159-7101-X). Devin.
Vermont Geography Book. Richard Allen et al. LC 86-63604. 1986. text ed. 5.95 (ISBN 0-317-53895-0, P112); tchr.guide & resource bk. 12.95 (P52). N Cartographic.
Vermont Golf Courses: A Player's Guide. Bob Labbance & David Cornwell. LC 87-61132. (Illus.). 144p. (Orig.). 1987. pap. 12.95 (ISBN 0-933050-47-X). New Eng Pr VT.
Vermont Historical & Biographical Index, Vol. 1. Ronald Vern Jackson. LC 78-53721. (Illus.). 1984. lib. bdg. 30.00 (ISBN 0-89593-203-2). Accelerated Index.
Vermont in the Making, 1750-1777. Matt B. Jones. xiv, 471p. 1968. Repr. of 1939 ed. 39.50 (ISBN 0-208-00620-6, Archon). Shoe String.
Vermont in the Victorian Age: Continuity & Change in the Green Mountain State, 1850-1900. LC 85-51147. 182p. 1985. 49.50 (ISBN 0-911853-06-5); limited edition 95.00 (ISBN 0-911853-07-3). Vermont Herit Pr.
Vermont: In Words & Pictures. Dennis Fradin. LC 79-22069. (Young People's Stories of Our States Ser.). (Illus.). 48p. (gr. 2-5). 1980. PLB 13.27 (ISBN 0-516-03946-6). Childrens.
Vermont Is Always with You. Marguerite H. Wolf. LC 83-62612. (Illus.). 132p. 1983. pap. 6.95 (ISBN 0-933050-20-8). New Eng Pr VT.
Vermont Is Where You Find It. Keith W. Jennison. (Illus.). 118p. 1987. pap. 7.95 (ISBN 0-88150-070-4). Countryman.
Vermont Landscape Images, 1776-1976. Ed. by William C. Lipke & Philip N. Grime. LC 76-19178. (Illus.). 119p. (Orig.). 1976. pap. 12.95 (ISBN 0-87451-991-8). U Pr of New Eng.
Vermont Law Review: 1976-1986, 11 vols. Bound set. 315.00x (ISBN 0-686-90087-1). Rothman.
Vermont Life's Guide to Fall Foliage. Gale Lawrence. LC 84-11890. (Illus.). 64p. 1984. pap. 3.95 (ISBN 0-936896-03-5). VT Life Mag.
Vermont Manufacturing Directory, 1988. Ed. by Tower Staff. 500p. (Orig.). 1988. pap. text ed. 35.00 (ISBN 0-89442-093-3). Tower Pub Co.
Vermont Manufacturing Directory 1988. 500p. 1988. pap. 35.00. Tower Pub Co.
Vermont Mind. Jeff Danziger. LC 86-60324. (Illus.). 65p. 1986. pap. 4.95 (ISBN 0-933050-34-8). New Eng Pr Vt.
Vermont Neighbors. Walter Hard. LC 60-3953. 122p. 1975. pap. 4.95 (ISBN 0-911570-14-4). Vermont Bks.
Vermont on Five Hundred Dollars a Day: More or Less. Peter S. Jennison. (Illus.). 128p. (Orig.). 1987. pap. 10.00 (ISBN 0-88150-082-8). Countryman.
Vermont Political Tradition. William T. Doyle. (Illus.). 1984. 20.00 (ISBN 0-9615486-0-6); pap. 12.50 (ISBN 0-9615486-1-4). W T Doyle.
Vermont: Portrait of the Land & Its People. George Wuerthner & Mollie Y. Matteson. (Vermont Geographic Ser.: No.1). 1987. pap. 15.95 (ISBN 0-938314-39-4). Am Geog Pub.
Vermont Prose. A. Peach & H. Rugg. 1977. Repr. of 1932 ed. 15.00 (ISBN 0-89984-088-4). Century Bookbindery.
Vermont Puzzle Book. Donna L. Pape et al. 96p. (Orig.). 1987. pap. 4.95 (ISBN 0-88150-092-5). Countryman.
Vermont Quiz Book. Frank Bryan & Melissa L. Bryan. LC 86-62544. (Illus.). 288p. (Orig.). 1986. pap. 9.95 (ISBN 0-933050-43-7). New Eng Pr VT.
Vermont Renaissance. Coral Crosman. (Illus.). 72p. 1976. pap. 2.50 (ISBN 0-913884-01-4). Porphyrion Pr.
Vermont Reports. 1987. write for info. Equity Pub NH.
Vermont River. W. D. Wetherell. (Illus.). 160p. 1987. 13.95 (ISBN 0-317-62720-1). N Lyons Bks.
Vermont River. W. D. Wetherell. 1989. 7.95 (ISBN 0-671-67344-0, Fireside). S&S.
Vermont Road Atlas. Edward Antczak et al. LC 85-61935. 96p. 1985. 8.95 (ISBN 0-9606738-8-1). N Cartographic.
Vermont Saints & Sinners: An Impressive Assortment of Geniuses, Nincompoops, Curmudgeons, Scurvy Knaves, & Characters. Lee D. Goodman. LC 85-72569. (Illus.). 172p. (Orig.). 1985. pap. 8.95 (ISBN 0-933050-32-1). New Eng Pr VT.
Vermont Seventeen Seventy-One Census. Jay M. Holbrook. LC 81-836773. 136p. 1982. lib. bdg. 25.00 (ISBN 0-931248-11-6). Holbrook Res.
Vermont Ski Trail Guide: Central Region. Stanton D. Allaben. 129p. 1983. pap. 5.00 (ISBN 0-913109-01-0). Stanton Production.
Vermont Ski Trail Guide: South Central Region. Allaben Stanton. 97p. 1982. pap. 5.00 (ISBN 0-913109-00-2). Stanton Production.
Vermont Statutes Annotated. 1987. write for info. casebound. Equity Pub NH.
Vermont Stone Chambers: An Inquiry into Their Past. Giovanna Neudorfer. LC 80-15808. 1980. pap. 4.50x (ISBN 0-934720-22-3). VT Hist Soc.
Vermont, the State with the Storybook Past. rev. ed. Cora Cheney. LC 86-60341. (Illus.). 272p. (gr. 5-9). 1986. pap. 12.95 (ISBN 0-933050-36-4). New Eng Pr VT.
Vermont Towns & Counties. Michael J. Denis. (New England Towns & Counties Ser.). 35p. 1983. pap. 4.50 (ISBN 0-935207-06-6). Danbury Hse Bks.
Vermont Townscape. Norman Williams, Jr. et al. 160p. 1987. 29.95 (ISBN 0-88285-120-9). Ctr Urban Pol Res.
Vermont Tradition: The Biography of an Outlook on Life. Dorothy C. Fisher. 496p. 1987. pap. 14.95 (ISBN 0-87797-153-6). Cherokee.
Vermont: Trusts, Vols. 1-2. suppl. 6.00 (ISBN 0-686-90911-9). Am Law Inst.
Vermont under Four Flags, a History of the Green Mountain State, Sixteen Thirty-Five to Nineteen Seventy-Five. Perry H. Merrill. (Illus.). ix, 325p. 1975. text ed. 10.95x (ISBN 0-9605806-1-1). P H Merrill.
Vermont Village Murder. B. Comfort. 192p. (Orig.). 1982. 4.00 (ISBN 0-9608726-0-4). Landgrove Pr.
Vermont Weather Book. David Ludlum. LC 85-6223. 320p. 1985. 16.95 (ISBN 0-934720-31-2); pap. 12.95 (ISBN 0-934720-30-4). VT Hist Soc.
Vermonters. Donald L. Tinney & Jon G. Fox. LC 85-450. 96p. 1985. pap. 9.95 (ISBN 0-88150-038-0). Countryman.
Vermonters & the State They're In. Keith Jennison. LC 85-61316. (Illus.). 96p. (Orig.). 1985. pap. 5.95 (ISBN 0-933050-30-5). New Eng Pr VT.
Vermonters at Their Craft: Vermont CraftsPeople Talk about Their Life & Work. Catharine Wright & Nancy M. Wright. LC 87-62334. (Illus.). 176p. (Orig.). 1987. pap. 19.95 (ISBN 0-933050-51-8). New Eng Pr VT.
Vermonters: Lively Oral Histories from Down Country to the Northeast Kingdom. Ron Strickland. LC 86-14738. (Illus.). 186p. (Orig.). 1986. pap. 12.95 (ISBN 0-87701-394-2). Chronicle Bks.
Vermont's Granite Raillroads: The Montpelier & Wells River & the Barre & Chelsea. Robert C. Jones & Whitney J. Maxfield. LC 85-16777. (Illus.). 277p. 1985. 34.95 (ISBN 0-87108-695-6). Pruett.
Vermont's Heritage: A Working Conference for Teachers - Plans, Proposals, & Needs. Intro. by Marshall True et al. (Illus.). 130p. (Orig.). 1983. pap. text ed. 5.00x (ISBN 0-944277-10-1). U VT Ctr Rsch VT.
Vermont's Historic Architecture: A Second Celebration. Paul Bruhn & Sanders Milens. (Illus.). 120p. Date not set. pap. 9.95 (ISBN 0-9615706-0-1). Preser Trust.
Vermont's Land & Resources. Harold A. Meeks. LC 86-50973. (Illus.). 336p. (Orig.). 1986. pap. 11.95 (ISBN 0-933050-40-2). New Eng Pr VT.
Vernacular Architecture in America: A Selective Bibliography. John A. Cuthbert & Barry J. Ward. 1984. lib. bdg. 39.95 (ISBN 0-8161-0436-0, Hall Reference). G K Hall.
Vernacular Architecture in Southern Illinois: The Ethnic Heritage. John M. Coggeshall & Jo Anne Nast. (Shawnee Bks). (Illus.). 148p. 1988. 19.95 (ISBN 0-8093-1462-2); pap. 12.95 (ISBN 0-8093-1463-0). S Ill U Pr.
Vernacular Architecture: Monographs Published 1976-1987. Mary Vance. (Architecture Ser.: A 1950). 54p. 1987. 13.50 (ISBN 1-55590-580-3). Vance Biblios.
Vernacular Christianity: Essays in the Social Anthropology of Religion. Ed. by Wendy James & Douglas H. Johnson. 196p. 1988. text ed. 45.00x (ISBN 0-936508-23-X). Barber Pr.
Vernacular Dreams. Angelo Loukakis. LC 85-14088. 228p. 1986. 16.95 (ISBN 0-7022-1897-9). U of Queensland Pr.
Vernacular Houses in the U. S. A. Lamia Doumato. (Architecture Ser.: A 1739). 18p. 1987. 5.00 (ISBN 1-55590-149-2). Vance Biblios.
Vernacular Language of Puerto Rico. Ed. by Raoul Gordon. 1976. lib. bdg. 59.95 (ISBN 0-8490-1258-9). Gordon Pr.
Vernacular Names for Texas Plants see Language Trends in Oil Field Jargon.
Vernacular Poetics in the Middle Ages. Lois Ebin. LC 83-23606. (Studies in Medieval Culture: No. 16). xvi, 293p. 1984. 24.95x (ISBN 0-918720-22-2); pap. 14.95x (ISBN 0-918720-19-2). Medieval Inst.
Vernacular Republic. Les Murray. 1982. pap. 8.95 (ISBN 0-89255-063-5). Persea Bks.
Vernacular Taxicabs: Jitneys & Gypsies in Urban America. Peter T. Suzuki. (Public Administration Ser.: Bibliography P-1608). 17p. 1985. pap. 2.25 (ISBN 0-89028-258-7). Vance Biblios.
Verna's Stained Glass in Fabric. Verna Holt. (Illus.). 32p. 1982. pap. 5.95 (ISBN 0-910585-00-8). Willcraft.
Verner's Law in Gothic, & Reduplicating Verbs in Germanic. Francis A. Wood. LC 73-173039. (Chicago University. Germanic Studies: No. 2). Repr. of 1895 ed. 18.00 (ISBN 0-404-50272-5). AMS Pr.
Verney Papers. Ralph Verney. Ed. by John Bruce. (Camden Society, London. Publications, First Ser.: No. 31). Repr. of 1845 ed. 28.00 (ISBN 0-404-50131-1). AMS Pr.
Verney Papers: Notes of Proceedings in the Long Parliament. Ralph Verney. Repr. of 1845 ed. 28.00 (ISBN 0-384-64365-5). Johnson Repr.
Vernon: An Anecdotal Novel. Osmond Beckwith. LC 81-65121. (Illus.). 204p. 1981. 10.00 (ISBN 0-917020-02-2). Breaking Point.
Vernon Lee Anthology. Violet Paget. LC 77-9906. 1977. Repr. of 1929 ed. lib. bdg. 32.00 (ISBN 0-8414-9613-7). Folcroft.
Vernon Lee Anthology: Selections from the Earlier Works Made by Irene Cooper Willis. Vernon Lee. 1929. 35.50 (ISBN 0-8274-3670-X). R West.
Vernon Lee: Violet Paget, 1856-1935. Peter Gunn. LC 75-12323. (Homosexuality Ser.). (Illus.). 1975. Repr. of 1964 ed. 14.00x (ISBN 0-405-07357-7). Ayer Co Pubs.
Vernon Manuscript: Bodleian Library MS. English Poet a.1. Intro. by I. A. Doyle. (Illus.). 704p. 1987. facsimile 810.00 (ISBN 0-85991-200-0, Pub. by Boydell & Brewer). Longwood Pub Group.
Vernon Ward: Child of the Guardian Era. Josephine Walpole. (Illus.). 200p. 1988. 49.50 (ISBN 1-85149-077-9). Antique Collect.
Vernon's Annotated Missouri Statutes. Missouri & Vernon Law Book Company. LC 52-19533. 1951. write for info. West Pub.
Vernon's Texas Code Forms Annotated: Uniform Commercial Code Forms, 2 vols. 2nd ed. 1344p. 1986. 85.00 (ISBN 0-317-52121-7). West Pub.
Vernunft und Welt. Marx. (Phaenomenologica Ser: No. 36). 1970. lib. bdg. 18.50 (ISBN 9-0247-5042-3, Pub. by Martinis Nijhoff Netherlands). Kluwer Academic.
Vernunftiges Denken. Ed. by Juergen Mittelstrass & Riedel Manfrd. 1978. 59.20 (ISBN 3-11-006956-3). De Gruyter.
Verona, Biblioteca Capitoare, Cod. DCCLVII. Ed. by Howard M. Brown et al. (Renaissance Music in Facsimile Ser.). 140p. 1987. lib. bdg. 55.00 (ISBN 0-8240-1473-1). Garland Pub.
Veronese's Drawings: With a "Catalogue Raisonne". Richard Cocke. LC 84-70788. (Illus.). 464p. 1984. 95.00x (ISBN 0-8014-1732-5). Cornell U Pr.
Veronica. Elisabeth Beresford. (Orig.). 1980. pap. 1.75 (ISBN 0-8439-8004-4, Tiara Bks). Leisure NY.
Veronica. Roger Duvoisin. (Illus.). (gr. k-3). 1961. lib. bdg. 11.99 (ISBN 0-394-91792-8). Knopf.
Veronica, No. 18. Jane C. Miner. 224p. (Orig.). (gr. 7 up). 1986. pap. 2.25 (ISBN 0-590-33933-8, Sunfire). Scholastic Inc.
Veronica & the Birthday Present. Roger Duvoisin. (ps-2). 1972. Knopf.
Veronica Ganz. Marilyn Sachs. (Illus.). 160p. (gr. 3-7). 1987. pap. 2.50 (ISBN 0-590-40405-9, Apple Paperbacks). Scholastic Inc.
Veronica Knows Best. Nancy K. Robinson. 128p. (gr. 4-6). 1987. 10.95 (ISBN 0-590-40509-8). Scholastic Inc.
Veronica My Daughter & Other Onitsha Plays & Stories. Ogali Ogali. Ed. by Reinhard W. Sander & Peter K. Ayers. LC 80-80886. 376p. (Orig.). 1980. 18.00x (ISBN 0-914478-61-3); pap. 7.00x (ISBN 0-914478-62-1). Three Continents.
Veronica the Show-Off. Nancy K. Robinson. LC 85-4483. (gr. 4-6). 1983. 10.95 (ISBN 0-02-777360-4, Four Winds). Macmillan.
Veronica the Show-Off. Nancy K. Robinson. (Illus.). 128p. (gr. 2-4). 1982. pap. 2.50 (ISBN 0-590-40305-2). Scholastic Inc.
Veronica's Smile. Roger Duvoisin. (Illus.). (gr. k-3). 1964. Knopf.
Veronique, Dialoque de L'Histoire et de l'Ame Charnelle. Charles Peguy. 12.75 (ISBN 0-685-37046-1). French & Eur.
Verordnungsvorschlag fuer eine Europaische Fusionskontrolle im Lichte der Erfahrungen des Deutschen Rechtes. Dimitrios Kutsukis. (European University Studies: No. 2, Vol. 338). 302p. (Ger.). 1983. 37.90 (ISBN 3-8204-7791-8). P Lang Pubs.
Verre en France, d'Emile Galle a Nos Jours. Janine Bloch-Dermant. (Illus.). 312p. (Fr.). 1983. 100.00 (ISBN 2-85917-029-4, Pub. by Editions de l'Amateur FR). Seven Hills Bks.
Verrine Orations, 2 Vols. Cicero. (Loeb Classical Library: No. 221, 293). 1935. Pt. 1. 13.95x (ISBN 0-674-99243-1); Pt. 2. 13.95x (ISBN 0-674-99323-3). Harvard U Pr.
Vers de la Mort. Helinandus. 1965. pap. 19.00 (ISBN 0-384-22200-5). Johnson Repr.
Vers de Societe & Parody. H. A. Page. 1973. Repr. of 1882 ed. lib. bdg. 35.00 (ISBN 0-8414-9238-7). Folcroft.
Vers de Societe Anthology. Ed. by Carolyn Wells. LC 7-37621. (Granger Poetry Library). 1976. Repr. of 1907 ed. 27.50x (ISBN 0-89609-055-8). Roth Pub Inc.
Vers le Renouveau (Mai 58-Juill. 62; see Discours et Messages.

Vertebrate Limb & Somite Morphogenesis: The Third Symposium of the British Society for Developmental Biology. British Society for Developmental Biology Staff. Ed. by D. A. Ede et al. LC 76-30451. (British Society for Developmental Biology. Symposium Ser.: No. 3). pap. 132.10 (2031644). Bks Demand UMI.

Vertebrate Limb & Somite Morphogenesis: The Third Symposium of the British Society for Developmental Biology. Ed. by D. A. Ede et al. LC 76-50312. (British Society for Developmental Biology Symposium: No. 3). 1978. 85.00 (ISBN 0-521-21552-8). Cambridge U Pr.

Vertebrate Limb Regeneration. Hugh Wallace. LC 80-40963. (Illus.). 288p. pap. 74.90 (2030446). Bks Demand UMI.

Vertebrate Locomotion. Ed. by M. H. Day. (Symposia of the Zoological Society of London Ser.: No. 48). 1981. 124.00 (ISBN 0-12-613348-4). Acad Pr.

Vertebrate Lung. rev. ed. G. M. Hughes. Ed. by J. J. Head. LC 77-75590. (Carolina Biology Readers Ser.). (Illus.). 16p. (gr. 10 up). 1979. pap. 1.60 (ISBN 0-89278-259-5, 45-9659). Carolina Biological.

Vertebrate Natural History. Mary F. Willson. 621p. 1984. text ed. 47.00 (ISBN 0-03-061804-5). SCP.

Vertebrate Neural Systems. Ulinski. (Neurobiology Ser.). 1985. write for info. (ISBN 0-471-87541-4); pap. write for info. (ISBN 0-471-87613-5). Wiley.

Vertebrate Neuromuscular Junction. Ed. by Miriam M. Salpeter. LC 86-15186. (Neurology & Neurobiology Ser.: Vol. 23). 454p. 1987. 96.00 (ISBN 0-8451-2725-X, 2725). A R Liss.

Vertebrate Ovary: Comparative Biology & Evolution. Ed. by Richard E. Jones. LC 78-16084. 876p. 1978. 110.00x (Plenum Pr). Plenum Pub.

Vertebrate Paleontology. 3rd ed. Alfred S. Romer. LC 66-13886. (Illus.). 1966. 45.00x (ISBN 0-226-72488-3). U of Chicago Pr.

Vertebrate Paleontology. Ed. by Robert M. Schoch. (Benchmark Papers in Geology). 384p. 1984. 54.95 (ISBN 0-442-28052-1). Van Nos Reinhold.

Vertebrate Paleontology & Evolution. Robert L. Carroll. LC 86-31808. (Geology Ser.). (Illus.). 640p. 1987. text ed. 52.95 (ISBN 0-7167-1822-7). W H Freeman.

Vertebrate Pest Control & Management Materials Second Conference: STP 680. 330p. 1979. 31.50x (ISBN 0-8031-0761-7, 04-680000-48). ASTM.

Vertebrate Pest Control & Management Materials: Third Conference - STP 752. Ed. by Schafer, Jr. & Walker. 206p. 1981. 23.00 (ISBN 0-8031-0760-9, 04-752000-48). ASTM.

Vertebrate Pest Control & Management Materials, 4th Symposium - STP 817. D. E. Kaukeinen. LC 83-70429. 305p. 1984. text ed. 44.00 (ISBN 0-8031-0213-5, 04-817000-48). ASTM.

Vertebrate Pest Control & Management Materials, Vol. 5. Ed. by Stephen A. Shumake & Roger W. Bullard. LC 87-37424. (Special Technical Publications: No. 974). (Illus.). 191p. 1988. text ed. 34.00 (ISBN 0-8031-0991-1, 04-974000-48). ASTM.

Vertebrate Photoreception. Ed. by H. B. Barlow. LC 76-55064. 1978. 86.00 (ISBN 0-12-078950-7). Acad Pr.

Vertebrate Photoreceptor Optics. Ed. by J. M. Enoch & F. L. Tobey. (Springer Series in Optical Sciences: Vol. 23). (Illus.). 520p. 1981. 53.00 (ISBN 0-387-10515-8). Springer-Verlag.

Vertebrate Reproduction. V. Blum. Tr. by A. C. Whittle from Ger. (Illus.). 400p. 1986. pap. 36.50 (ISBN 0-387-16314-X). Springer-Verlag.

Vertebrate Reproduction. Jameson. 1988. 49.50 (ISBN 0-471-62635-X). Wiley.

Vertebrate Retina: Principles of Structure & Function. R. W. Rodieck. LC 79-190434. (Biology Ser.). (Illus.). 1044p. 1973. text ed. 69.95x (ISBN 0-7167-0696-2). W H Freeman.

Vertebrate Visual System. Stephen Polyak. Ed. by Heinrich Kluver. LC 55-5153. (Illus.). 1957. 100.00x (ISBN 0-226-67494-0). U of Chicago Pr.

Vertebrates: Adaptation: Readings from Scientific American. Intro. by Norman K. Wessells. LC 80-188. (Illus.). 256p. 1980. pap. text ed. 13.95x (ISBN 0-7167-1168-0). W H Freeman.

Vertebrates: Comparative Anatomy, Function, Evolution. Kadong. (Illus.). 720p. 1990. 41.95 (ISBN 0-8016-2666-8). Mosby.

Vertebrates from the Barrier Islands of Tamaulipas, Mexico. Robert K. Selander et al. (Museum Ser.: Vol. 12, No. 7). 37p. 1962. pap. 2.00 (ISBN 0-686-79809-0). U of KS Mus Nat Hist.

Vertebrates of Arizona: With Major Section on Arizona Habitats. Ed. by Charles H. Lowe, Jr. LC 63-11981. 270p. 1964. pap. 8.95x (ISBN 0-8165-0348-6). U of Ariz Pr.

Vertebrates of Florida: Identification & Distribution. Henry M. Stevenson. LC 75-37723. 1976. 45.00x (ISBN 0-8130-0437-3). U Presses Fla.

Vertebrates, Phylogeny, & Philosophy. Jason A. Lillegraven et al. Ed. by K. Flanagan. LC 86-50857. (Illus.). 372p. 1986. lib. bdg. 30.00 (ISBN 0-941570-02-9). U of Wyoming.

Vertebrates: Their Forms & Functions. Charles G. Crispens, Jr. (Illus.). 224p. 1978. 26.00x (ISBN 0-398-03721-3). C C Thomas.

Vertebrobasilar Arterial Occlusive Disease: Medical & Surgical Management. Ed. by Ramon Berguer & Raymond B. Bauer. (Illus.). 352p. 1984. text ed. 68.00 (ISBN 0-89004-984-X). Raven.

Vertex Detectors. Ed. by F. Villa. LC 87-34301. (Ettore Majorana International Science Series, Physical Sciences: Vol. 34). (Illus.). 376p. 1988. 75.00x (ISBN 0-306-42798-2, Plenum Pr). Plenum Pub.

Vertex Operator Algebras & the Monster. Igor Frenkel et al. (Pure & Applied Mathematics Ser.: Vol. 134). 600p. 1989. price not set (ISBN 0-12-267065-5). Acad Pr.

Vertex Operators in Mathematics & Physics. Ed. by J. Lepowsky et al. (Mathematical Sciences Research Institute Publications Ser.: Vol. 3). (Illus.). xiv, 482p. 1985. 33.00 (ISBN 0-387-96121-6). Springer-Verlag.

Vertical Boring. 2nd ed. (Engineering Craftsmen: No. H28/1). (Illus.). 1976. spiral bdg. 37.50x. Trans-Atl Phila.

Vertical Boring. 1983. 50.00x (Pub. by Engineering Ind). State Mutual Bk.

Vertical Classification: A Study in Structuralism & the Sociology of Knowledge. Barry Schwartz. LC 80-24207. (Chicago Original Paperback Ser.). 244p. 1981. pap. 18.00x (ISBN 0-226-74208-3). U of Chicago Pr.

Vertical Drains. 166p. 1982. 34.75 (ISBN 0-7277-0147-9, Pub. by T Telford UK). Am Soc Civil Eng.

Vertical File & Its Satellites: A Handbook of Acquisition, Processing, & Organization. 2nd ed. Shirley Miller. LC 79-13773. (Library Science Text Ser.). 251p. 1979. lib. bdg. 22.50 (ISBN 0-87287-164-9). Libs Unl.

Vertical File Index. pap. 38.00 per year (ISBN 0-686-76913-9). Wilson.

Vertical Flight: The Age of the Helicopter. Ed. by Walter J. Boyne & Donald S. Lopez. LC 84-600107. (Illus., Orig.). 1984. pap. 19.95 (ISBN 0-87474-279-X). Smithsonian.

Vertical Gardening: Climbing Plants, Hanging Plants, Trellises, Wall Plantings, Terraces, Steep Banks, Window Boxes. Caroline Boisset. (Illus.). 1988. 24.95 (ISBN 1-55584-252-6). Weidenfeld.

Vertical Hold. Laurel Bauer. 320p. 1986. 16.95 (ISBN 0-312-83879-4). St Martin.

Vertical Integration & Joint Ventures in the Aluminum Industry. John A. Stuckey. (Harvard Economic Studies: No. 152). (Illus.). 360p. 1983. text ed. 30.00x (ISBN 0-674-93490-3). Harvard U Pr.

Vertical Integration in the Oil Industry. Ed. by Edward J. Mitchell. LC 76-20267. 1976. 22.50 (ISBN 0-8447-3218-4); pap. 7.25 (ISBN 0-8447-3215-X). Am Enterprise.

Vertical Loom: Principles & Construction. Kliot. 2.95 (ISBN 0-916896-09-9). Lacis Pubns.

Vertical Market - Optical Disk Market in the U. S. Frost & Sullivan, Inc. Staff. 264p. 1986. 1900.00 (ISBN 0-86621-472-0, A1545). Frost & Sullivan.

Vertical Markets for Electronic Mail. Market Intelligence Research Co. Staff. Ed. by Wilmoth Hammersley. 197p. (Orig.). 1987. pap. 995.00x (ISBN 0-317-58029-9). Market Res Co.

Vertical Milling Machine Explained. Leo Rizzo. LC 79-731074. (Orig.). 1978. wkbk. 6.00 (ISBN 0-8064-0241-5, 512); audio visual pkg. 299.00 (ISBN 0-8064-0242-3). Bergwall.

Vertical Mosaic: An Analysis of Social Class & Power in Canada. John Porter. LC 65-3947. 1965. pap. 15.95c (ISBN 0-8020-6055-2). U of Toronto Pr.

Vertical Poems. W. S. Merwin & Roberto Juarroz. 1976. 5.00 (ISBN 0-685-67046-5). Story Line.

Vertical Poetry. Roberto Juarroz. Tr. by W. S. Merwin from Span. LC 87-82591. 176p. 1988. 22.95 (ISBN 0-86547-306-4); pap. 10.95 (ISBN 0-86547-307-2). N Point Pr.

Vertical Restrictions upon Buyers Limiting Purchases of Goods from Others. Lynn H. Pasahow & American Bar Association. Section of Antitrust Law. LC 82-72695. xii, 99p. 1982. pap. 20.00 (ISBN 0-89707-081-X). Amer Bar Assn.

Vertical Seismic Profiling. E. I. Galperin. Tr. by A. J. Hermont. Ed. by J. E. White. LC 74-83416. 278p. 1974. 32.50 (ISBN 0-931830-06-0). Soc Expl Geophys.

Vertical Seismic Profiling & Its Exploration Potential. E. I. Galperin. 1985. lib. bdg. 69.00 (ISBN 90-277-1450-9, Pub. by Reidel Netherlands). Kluwer Academic.

Vertical Seismic Profiling: Technique, Applications, & Case Histories. A. H. Balch & Myung W. Lee. LC 84-547. (Illus.). 488p. 1984. 58.00 (ISBN 0-934634-47-5). Intl Human Res.

Vertical Transportation: Elevators & Escalators. 2nd ed. George R. Strakosch. LC 82-10866. 495p. 1983. 63.50 (ISBN 0-471-86733-0). Wiley.

Vertical Transportation for Buildings. Rodney R. Adler. LC 73-104976. (Elsevier Architectural Science Ser.). pap. 59.50 (ISBN 0-317-11060-8, 2007760). Bks Demand UMI.

Vertical Turbine, Mixed Flow, & Propeller Pumps. J. L. Dicmas. 416p. 1987. text ed. 47.50 (ISBN 0-07-016837-7). McGraw.

Vertical World of Yosemite. Ed. by Galen A. Rowell. LC 73-85908. (Illus.). 218p. (Orig.). 1974. pap. 17.95 (ISBN 0-911824-87-1). Wilderness Pr.

Verticals. Greg Kuzma. 1988. pap. 5.00 (ISBN 0-941179-17-6). Latitudes Pr.

Vertigo in Man. Gerald E. Smith. (Illus.). 1978. 20.00 (ISBN 0-916750-73-6). Dayton Labs.

Vertigo, Nausea, Tinnitus & Hearing Loss in Cardiovascular Diseases: Proceedings of the Scientific Meeting of the Neurobiological & Equilibriometric Society, 13th, Bad Kissingen, 21-23 March, 1986. Neurobiological & Equilibriometric Society. Ed. by C. F. Claussen & M. V. Kirtane. (International Congress Ser.: No. 708). 540p. 1986. 163.25 (ISBN 0-444-80825-6, Excerpta Medica). Elsevier.

Verts; or, the Three Creeds, 1876. Charles M. Davies. Ed. by Robert L. Wolff. LC 75-1506. (Victorian Fiction Ser.). 1975. lib. bdg. 66.00 (ISBN 0-8240-1580-0). Garland Pub.

Vertue XXXV. Humphrey Barton. 180p. 1985. 18.95 (ISBN 0-916025-05-5). Armchair Sail Pub.

Vertuose Boke of Distyllasyon. Von Braunschweig Hieronymus. Tr. by L. Andrewe. LC 72-6006. (English Experience Ser.: No. 532). 276p. 1973. Repr. of 1527 ed. 46.00 (ISBN 90-221-0532-6). Walter J Johnson.

Vertus de l'Enfer. Pierre Boulle. 272p. 1976. 14.95 (ISBN 0-686-54115-4); pap. 29.95 (ISBN 0-686-54116-2). French & Eur.

Verulamium: A Belgic & Two Roman Cities. Robert E. Wheeler & T. V. Wheeler. (Society of Antiquaries of London, Research Committee, Reports: No. 11). pap. 106.50 (ISBN 0-317-28843-1, 2020784). Bks Demand UMI.

Verus Israel. Marcal Simon. Tr. by H. McKeating. 592p. 1985. 57.00x (ISBN 0-19-710035-X). Oxford U Pr.

Veruschka: Trans-figurations. Vera Lehndorff & Holger Trulzsch. (Illus.). 1986. 35.00i (ISBN 0-8212-1637-6). NYGS.

Verve. Michael Anthonioz. Date not set. price not set. Abrams.

Vervoer voor Gehandicapten: Illusie of Realiteit? Ed. by J. B. Polak & G. Hupkes. 340p. (Dutch.). pap. 15.00x (ISBN 90-70176-62-9). Foris Pubns.

Verwandlung. Franz Kafka. Ed. by Marjorie L. Hoover. (Ger). 1960. pap. 4.95x (ISBN 0-393-09533-9, NortonC). Norton.

Verwendung des Konjunktivs im Altenglischen. Hans Glunz. Repr. of 1929 ed. 12.00 (ISBN 0-384-18965-2). Johnson Repr.

Very Amateur Guide to Antique Bottle Collecting. Bea Boynton. LC 65-22367. (Illus.). 1967. pap. 1.50 (ISBN 0-87004-017-0). Caxton.

Very Anxiously Engaged: A Cartoonist's View of Modern Courtship. Val C. Bagley. (Illus.). 96p. (Orig.). 1981. pap. 3.95 (ISBN 0-88290-157-5, 2042). Horizon Utah.

Very Bad Bunny. Marilyn Sadler. LC 84-3319. (Beginner Bks.). (Illus.). 48p. (ps-3). 1984. 5.95 (ISBN 0-394-86861-7, Pub. by BYR); lib. bdg. 6.99 (ISBN 0-394-96861-1). Beginner.

Very BASIC. (Computer Literacy Ser.). pap. 15.95 (ISBN 0-318-04030-1). UNISYS Corp.

Very Best Book of All. Fran Flournoy. LC 82-80032. (Happy Day Bks.). (Illus.). 24p. (Orig.). (ps-3). 1982. pap. 1.59 (ISBN 0-87239-545-6, 3591). Standard Pub.

Very Best Christmas Present. Jim Razzi. LC 87-83045. (Golden Look-Look Bks.). (Illus.). 24p. (Orig.). (ps-3). 1988. pap. 1.60 (ISBN 0-307-11711-1). Western Pub.

Very Best Christmas Tree. B. A. King. LC 84-47656. (Illus.). 24p. (gr. 2 up). 1984. 8.95 (ISBN 0-87923-539-X). Godine.

Very Best from Hallmark: Greetings Cards Through the Years. Ellen Stern. 1988. 29.95 (ISBN 0-8109-1745-9). Abrams.

Very Best Ice Cream & Where to Find It. Carol T. Robbins & Herbert Wolff. 1985. pap. 2.95 (ISBN 0-446-32564-3). Warner Bks.

Very Best: Mexican Restaurants & Where to Find Them. Herbert Wolff & Carol T. Robbins. LC 83-90979. 230p. (Orig.). 1983. pap. 7.95 (ISBN 0-911729-01-1). Very Best.

Very Best Name for Baby. Barbara S. Hazen. 96p. 1986. 7.95 (ISBN 0-8378-5088-6). Gibson.

Very Best of British. Nicholas Courtney. 160p. 1986. 12.95 (ISBN 0-312-83884-0). St Martin.

Very Best of Hagar the Horrible. Dik Browne. 128p. 1982. pap. 4.95 (ISBN 0-671-44732-7, Wallaby). S&S.

Very Best of Lee Greenwood. Lee Greenwood. (Piano-Vocal-Guitar, Personality Folio Ser.). (Illus.). 72p. 1986. pap. 8.95 (ISBN 0-88188-436-7, HL00356845). H Leonard Pub Corp.

Very Best of Ricky Skaggs. Ricky Skaggs. (Piano-Vocal-Guitar Ser.). (Illus.). 64p. 1986. pap. 8.95, perfect bdg. (ISBN 0-88188-435-9, HLOO358178). H Leonard Pub Corp.

Very Big Problem of Mr. & Mrs. Bumba. Pearl A. Harwood. LC 73-156354. (Mr. & Mrs. Bumba Bks.). (Illus.). (gr. k-3). 1971. PLB 3.95 (ISBN 0-8225-0130-9). Lerner Pubns.

Very Brief Season. Barbara Girion. LC 84-1217. (gr. 7 up). 1984. 11.95 (ISBN 0-684-18088-X, Pub. by Scribner). Macmillan.

Very Bumpy Bus Ride. Michaela Muntean. LC 81-16905. (Illus.). 48p. (ps-3). 1982. 5.95 (ISBN 0-8193-1079-4); 5.95 (ISBN 0-8193-1080-8). Parents.

Very Busy Spider. Eric Carle. LC 84-5907. (Illus.). 32p. (ps-2). 1984. 14.95 (ISBN 0-399-21166-7, Philomel). Putnam Pub Group.

Very Cagey Lady. Joyce Elbert. 1980. pap. 2.95 (ISBN 0-451-09936-2, E9936, Sig.). NAL.

Very Close & Very Slow. Judith Hemschemeyer. LC 74-20951. (Wesleyan Poetry Program: Vol. 76). 69p. 1975. 17.00x (ISBN 0-8195-2076-4); pap. 8.95 (ISBN 0-8195-1076-9). Wesleyan U Pr.

Very Cold for May. William P. McGivern. 254p. 1987. pap. 5.95 (ISBN 0-14-009368-0). Penguin.

Very Deadly Yours. Carolyn Keene. (Nancy Drew File Case Ser.: No. 20). 160p. (Orig.). (YA) (gr. 7 up). pap. 2.75 (ISBN 0-671-64226-X). Archway.

Very Dutiful Daughter. Elizabeth Mansfield. 256p. 1986. pap. 2.50 (ISBN 0-515-08740-8). Jove Pubns.

Very Easiest Exercises for Piano, Op. 190. Louis Kohler. (Carl Fischer Music Library: No. 381). 1905. pap. 3.00 (ISBN 0-8258-0117-6, L381). Fischer Inc NY.

Very Easy Death. Simone de Beauvoir. 1985. pap. 5.95 (ISBN 0-394-72899-8). Pantheon.

Very Eligible Place: An Illustrated History of Provo & Orem. Kenneth L. Cannon, 2nd. Ed. by Lane Powell. (Illus.). 128p. 1987. 24.95 (ISBN 0-89781-220-4). Windsor Pubns Inc.

Very Far Away. Maurice Sendak. LC 57-5356. (Illus.). (gr. k-3). 1957. PLB 10.89 (ISBN 0-06-025515-3); 11.25i (ISBN 0-06-025514-5). HarpJ.

Very Far Away from Anywhere Else. Ursula K. Le Guin. LC 76-4472. 96p. (gr. 6-9). 1976. 10.95 (ISBN 0-689-30525-7, Atheneum Childrens Bks). Macmillan.

Very Far Away from Anywhere Else. Ursula K. Le Guin. (YA) (gr. 9-12). 1982. pap. 2.50 (ISBN 0-553-25396-4). Bantam.

Very First Lucy Goose Book. Stephen Weatherill. (Illus.). (gr. 1-7). 1987. 9.95 (ISBN 0-13-941410-X). P-H.

Very First R: Teaching Children the Joy of Leisure Reading. Posy B. Lough. LC 79-89885. (Illus., Orig.). 1979. pap. 3.95 (ISBN 0-9603526-0-0). Posy VA.

Very First Stories with Brian Badger see Acorn Magic Readers.

Very Godly Defense, Defending the Marriage of Priests. Philip Melanchthon. Tr. by L. Beuchame. LC 76-25643. (English Experience Ser.: No. 199). 1969. Repr. of 1541 ed. 20.00 (ISBN 90-221-0199-1). Walter J Johnson.

Very Good Hater. Reginald Hill. 208p. 1988. pap. 3.50 (ISBN 0-451-15191-7, Sig). NAL.

Very Good, Jeeves. P. G. Wodehouse. Repr. lib. bdg. 17.95x (ISBN 0-89190-295-3, Pub. by River City Pr). Amereon Ltd.

Very Good, Jeeves. P. G. Wodehouse. 256p. 1975. pap. 3.95 (ISBN 0-14-001173-0). Penguin.

Very Good Land to Fall With: Scenes from the Life of an American Jew, Vol. 3. John Sanford. LC 87-20844. 300p. (Orig.). 1987. 20.00 (ISBN 0-87685-714-4); signed ltd. ed. 30.00 (ISBN 0-87685-715-2); pap. 12.50 (ISBN 0-87685-713-6). Black Sparrow.

Very Healthy Cat Book. W. O. Belfield & M. Zucker. 264p. 1983. text ed. 14.95 (ISBN 0-07-004367-1); pap. text ed. 6.95 (ISBN 0-07-004354-X). McGraw.

Very High Energy Gamma Ray Astronomy. Ed. by K. E. Turver. 1987. lib. bdg. 69.00 (ISBN 90-277-2459-8, Pub. by Reidel Holland). Kluwer Academic.

Very High Resolution Spectroscopy. Ed. by R. A. Smith. (Based upon a symposium). 1976. 76.00 (ISBN 0-12-651650-2). Acad Pr.

Very High Strength Cement-Based Materials, Vol. 42. Ed. by J. F. Young. LC 85-5144. (Materials Research Society Symposia Proceedings Ser.). 1985. text ed. 36.00 (ISBN 0-931837-07-3). Materials Res.

Very Hungry Caterpillar. Eric Carle. LC 70-82764. (Illus., Ger). (ps-2). 1981. 14.95 (ISBN 0-399-20853-4, Philomel). Putnam Pub Group.

Very Hungry Caterpillar. Eric Carle. (Illus.). 32p. (ps up). 1986. miniature ed. 3.95 (ISBN 0-399-21301-5, G&D). Putnam Pub Group.

Very Hungry Caterpillar. Eric Carle. 32p. (gr. k-3). pap. 2.95 (ISBN 0-590-03029-9). Scholastic Inc.

Very Idea: A Collection of Unusual Retail Advertising Ideas, Vol. 2. rev. ed. Arnold Fochs. 272p. (Orig.). 1980. pap. 19.95 (ISBN 0-914190-02-4). A J Pub.

Very Important Pregnancy Program: A Personal Approach to the Art & Science of Having a Baby. Gail S. Brewer. Ed. by Charlie Gerras. (Illus.). 320p. 1988. pap. 14.95 (ISBN 0-317-60733-2). Rodale Pr Inc.

Very Large Array: New Mexico Science Fiction & Fantasy. Ed. by Melinda M. Snodgrass. LC 87-19173. (Illus.). 270p. 1987. 16.95 (ISBN 0-8263-1013-3). U of NM Pr.

Very Large Consulate. Howard K. Simpson. (Crime Club Ser.). 1989. 12.95 (ISBN 0-385-24604-8). Doubleday.

Very Large Scale Integration (VLSI) Fundamentals & Applications. 2nd, updated ed. Ed. by B. F. Barbe. (Springer Series in Electrophysics: Vol. 5). (Illus.). 302p. 1982. 34.00 (ISBN 0-387-11368-1). Springer-Verlag.

Very Last First Time. Jan Andrews. LC 85-71606. (Illus.). 32p. (ps-4). 1986. 12.95 (ISBN 0-689-50388-1, M K McElderry). Macmillan.

Very Last Virgin at Hobeck High. Grace Williams. (YA) (gr. 7 up). 1986. pap. 2.50 (ISBN 0-451-14398-1, Sig Vista). NAL.

Very Messy Room. Elizabeth Stanton & Henry Stanton. Ed. by Caroline Rubin. LC 78-1031. (Albert Whitman Concept Bks.). (Illus.). 32p. (gr. 1-3). 1978. PLB 11.95 (ISBN 0-8075-5077-9). A Whitman.

Very Mice Joke Book. Karen J. Gounaud. (Illus.). (gr. 2-5). 1981. PLB 6.95 (ISBN 0-395-30445-8); pap. 12.95 (ISBN 0-395-30442-3). HM.

Very Much a Lady. Shana Alexander. 1986. pap. 4.95 (ISBN 0-440-19270-6). Dell.

Very Nice Work - If You Can Get It! The Socially Useful Production Debate. Ed. by Collective Design Staff. 200p. 40.00x (ISBN 0-85124-430-0, Pub. by Bertrand Russell Hse); pap. 29.00x (ISBN 0-85124-431-9). State Mutual Bk.

Very Old Money. Atanley Ellin. 320p. 1985. pap. 3.50 (ISBN 0-449-20915-6, Crest). Fawcett.

Very Old Money. Stanley Ellin. 1985. 18.95 (ISBN 0-8161-3916-4, Large Print Bks). G K Hall.

Very Ordinary Seaman. J. P. W. Mallalieu. 253p. pap. 5.95 (ISBN 0-583-12808-4). Academy Chi Pubs.

Very Parochial Murder. John Wainwright. 192p. 1988. 14.95 (ISBN 0-312-02309-X). St Martin.

Very Personal. Clara Saunders. (Illus.). 20p. 1981. pap. 7.50 (ISBN 0-933992-22-X). Coffee Break.

Very Poor & of a Lo Make: The Journal of Abner Sanger. Ed. by Lois K. Stabler. (Illus.). 660p. 1986. 30.00 (ISBN 0-914339-17-6). P E Randall Pub.

Very Practical Guide to Discipline with Young Children. Grace Mitchell. LC 82-16951. (Illus.). 160p. (Orig.). 1982. pap. text ed. 8.95 (ISBN 0-910287-00-7). TelShare Pub Co.

Very Practical Meditation. Serene West. LC 79-20249. 116p. (Orig.). 1981. pap. 4.95 (ISBN 0-89865-006-2, Unilaw). Donning Co.

Very Present Help. Guideposts Editors. LC 85-19521. 248p. 1985. pap. text ed. 9.95 (ISBN 0-89191-607-5). Cook.

Very Private Eye: An Autobiography in Diaries & Letters. Barbara Pym. Ed. by Hazel Holt & Hilary Holt. (Illus.). 352p. 1984. 19.95 (ISBN 0-525-24234-1). Dutton.

Very Private Eye: An Autobiography in Diaries & Letters. Barbara Pym. 1985. pap. 6.95 (ISBN 0-394-73106-9, Vin). Random.

Very Private Matter of Anorexia Nervosa. Sharon Christian & Margaret Johnson. Ed. by John Sloan. 176p. 1986. pap. 6.95 (ISBN 0-310-45841-2, 18140P). Zondervan.

Very Proper Widow. Laura Matthews. 224p. 1987. pap. 2.50 (ISBN 0-451-14812-6, Sig). NAL.

Very Quiet Place. Andrew Garve. (Black Dagger Crime Ser.). 200p. 1988. text ed. 14.95x (ISBN 0-86220-730-4, Pub. by Firecrest Pub Ltd). Prescott Pr NH.

Very Rare Glassware of the Depression Years. Gene Florence. (Illus.). 128p. 1988. 24.95 (ISBN 0-89145-366-0, 1848). Collector Bks.

Very Rich: A History of Wealth. Joseph J. Thorndike, Jr. 1976. 29.95 (ISBN 0-517-52810-X). Crown.

Very Rich Hours. Jean McGarry. LC 86-46290. (Johns Hopkins Poetry & Fiction Ser.). 144p. 1987. 15.95 (ISBN 0-8018-3504-6). Johns Hopkins.

Very Serious Thing: Women's Humor & American Culture. Nancy Walker. (American Culture Ser.). 224p. (Orig.). 1988. 39.50x (ISBN 0-8166-1702-3); pap. 14.95 (ISBN 0-8166-1703-1). U of Minn Pr.

Very Shy. Barbara S. Hazen. LC 81-6809. (Illus.). 32p. (ps-3). 1983. 13.95 (ISBN 0-89885-067-3); pap. 5.95 (ISBN 0-89885-203-X). Human Sci Pr.

Very Simple Grammar of English. Celia Blissett & Katherine Hallgarten. (Illus.). 112p. 1985. pap. text ed. 6.95 (ISBN 0-906717-43-4). Alemany Pr.

Very Slow Flows of Solids: Basics of Modeling in Geodynamics & Glaciology. Louis A. Lliboutry. 1987. lib. bdg. 145.00 (ISBN 90-247-3482-7, Pub. by Maritnus Nijhoff Netherlands). Kluwer Academic.

Very Small Aperture Terminals. 168p. 1985. 1850.00x (ISBN 0-88694-677-8). Intl Res Dev.

Very Small College. Joseph A. Kershaw. LC 76-7022. 24p. 1976. pap. 3.00 (ISBN 0-916584-02-X). Ford Found.

Very Small Garden. Martin Baxendale. 128p. 1987. 24.95 (ISBN 0-285-62736-8, Pub. by Souvenir Pr). Intl Spec Bk.

Very Small Insurance Policy: The Politics of Australian Involvement in Vietnam, 1954-1967. Glen S. Barclay. LC 86-27284. 199p. (Orig.). 1988. pap. text ed. 19.95x (ISBN 0-7022-2069-8). U of Queensland Pr.

Very Small Living Spaces. Beth Franks. (Illus.). 1988. 22.95 (ISBN 0-8050-0520-X). H Holt & Co.

Very Sneaky, Andy Capp. Reginald Smythe. (Illus.). 1983. pap. 1.95 (ISBN 0-449-12630-7, GM). Fawcett.

Very Special Baby. Carol Woodward. (gr. 3-7). 1960. pap. 1.95 (ISBN 0-8006-0420-2, 1-420). Fortress.

Very Special Baby-Jesus. Lynn Groth. (Cradle Roll Program Ser.). 8p. (Orig.). (ps). 1985. pap. 1.25 (ISBN 0-938272-76-4). Wels Board.

Very Special Child. Joan Hebden. (Illus.). 159p. 1987. pap. text ed. 10.95 (ISBN 0-285-65010-6, 0019). Demos Pubns Inc.

Very Special Christmas Tree. Linda Arnold. (Stick-On Activity & Coloring Bks.). 16p. (gr. k-3). 1983. pap. 1.50 (ISBN 0-87239-685-1, 2365). Standard Pub.

Very Special Day. Lois Rau. (Redwood Ser.). 1982. pap. 2.95 (ISBN 0-8163-0447-5). Pacific Pr Pub Assn.

Very Special Family: A Story Book to Color & Teach Your Child to Read. Ethyl R. Papa. (Illus.). 32p. (ps-2). 1983. saddle stitch, double stapled binding 9.95 (ISBN 0-915925-00-1). Innovative Educ Pub.

Very Special Family: Behavior Management System. Ethyl Papa & Randal Papa. (Illus.). 32p. (Orig.). 1987. 5.95 (ISBN 0-915925-02-8). Innovative Educ Pub.

Very Special Family: The Parts of Speech Family. Ethyl Papa & Randal Papa. (Illus.). 128p. (Orig.). 1987. tchr's ed. 34.95 (ISBN 0-915925-01-X). Innovative Educ Pub.

Very Special House. Ruth Krauss. LC 53-7115. (Illus.). (ps-1). 1953. PLB 11.89 (ISBN 0-06-023456-3). HarpJ.

Very Special Intelligence, No. 9. Patrick Beesly. 304p. 1981. pap. 2.75 (ISBN 0-345-29798-9). Ballantine.

Very Special Night. Ruth Odor. (Happy Day Bks.). (Illus.). 24p. (Orig.). (gr. k-2). 1980. 1.59 (ISBN 0-87239-405-0, 3637). Standard Pub.

Very Special Person. Lois Rau. (Sunshine Ser.). 1982. pap. 2.95 (ISBN 0-8163-0445-9). Pacific Pr Pub Assn.

Very Special Planet. Lois Rau. (Sunshine Ser.). 1982. pap. 2.95 (ISBN 0-8163-0446-7). Pacific Pr Pub Assn.

Very Special Promise. Lois Rau. (Sunshine Ser.). 1982. pap. 2.95 (ISBN 0-8163-0448-3). Pacific Pr Pub Assn.

Very Special Recipe Cookbook: A Cookbook to Fill with Special Recipes & Memories. (Illus.). 60p. 1986. GBC binding 9.95 (ISBN 0-935442-07-3). One Percent.

Very Special Relationship: Field Marshal Sir John Dill & Anglo-American Cooperation 1941-1944. A. Danchev. 224p. 1986. 28.00 (ISBN 0-08-031197-0, Pub. by BDP). Pergamon.

Very Special Yarmulka. 1982. pap. 2.95 (ISBN 0-87306-186-1). Feldheim.

Very Spirit of Cordiality: The Literary Uses of Alcohol... in the Tales of Edgar Allan Poe. Benjamin F. Fisher. Ed. by Averil Kadis. 1978. pap. 2.75 (ISBN 0-910556-10-5). Enoch Pratt.

Very Sure of God: Religious Language in the Poetry of Robert Browning. E. Leroy Lawson. LC 73-21617. xiii, 168p. 1974. 8.95x (ISBN 0-8265-1195-3). Vanderbilt U Pr.

Very Surprising Narrative of a Young Woman Discovered in a Rocky Cave after Having Been Taken by the Savage Indians of the Wilderness in the Year 1777. Abraham Panther. 1972. 6.95 (ISBN 0-87770-121-0); pap. 4.95 (ISBN 0-87770-095-8). Ye Galleon.

Very Touching Book. Jan Hindman. (Illus.). 56p. (Orig.). 1983. pap. 9.95 (ISBN 0-9611034-1-8). AlexAndria OR.

Very Touchy Subject. Todd Strasser. (gr. 6 up). 1986. pap. 2.75 (ISBN 0-440-98851-9, LFL). Dell.

Very Truly Yours. Jacob P. Rudin. 1971. 6.50x (ISBN 0-8197-0279-X). Bloch.

Very Truly Yours, Charles L. Dodgson, Alias Lewis Carroll. Lisa Bassett. LC 85-10972. (Illus.). 118p. (gr. 5 up). 1987. 15.95 (ISBN 0-688-06091-9). Lothrop.

Very Unusual: The Wonderful World of Mr. K. Nakamura. Manly P. Hall. 9.00 (ISBN 0-89314-537-8). Philos Res.

Very Very Slightly Imperfect. Ron Moody. LC 84-26492. 271p. 1985. 16.95 (ISBN 0-88186-425-0). Parkwest Pubns.

Very Worst Monster. Pat Hutchins. LC 84-5928. (Illus.). 32p. (gr. k-3). 1985. 11.75 (ISBN 0-688-04010-1); PLB 11.88 (ISBN 0-688-04011-X). Greenwillow.

Very Worst Monster. Pat Hutchins. (Illus.). 32p. (ps-3). 1988. pap. 3.95 (ISBN 0-688-07816-8, Mulberry Bks). Morrow.

Very Young Beginner. Nathan Bergenfeld. (Acorn Basic Lessons for Piano Ser.). 1977. pap. 2.95 (ISBN 0-8256-2683-8). Music Sales.

Very Young Circus Flyer. Jill Krementz. LC 78-20546. (Illus.). 1979. 10.95 (ISBN 0-394-50574-3). Knopf.

Very Young Circus Flyer. Jill Krementz. (gr. k-6). 1987. pap. 6.95 (ISBN 0-440-49216-5, YB). Dell.

Very Young Dancer. Jill Krementz. LC 76-13700. (gr. 4-6). 1976. 14.95 (ISBN 0-394-40885-3). Knopf.

Very Young Dancer. Jill Krementz. (gr. 3-6). 1986. pap. 6.95 (ISBN 0-440-49212-2, YB). Dell.

Very Young: Guiding Children from Infancy Through the Early Years. 3rd ed. George Maxim. 544p. 1988. 29.95 (ISBN 0-675-20861-0). Merrill.

Very Young Gymnast. Jill Krementz. LC 78-5502. (gr. 4-6). 1978. 14.95 (ISBN 0-394-50080-6). Knopf.

Very Young Gymnast. Jill Krementz. (gr. 3-6). 1986. pap. 6.95 (ISBN 0-440-49213-0, YB). Dell.

Very Young Rider. Jill Krementz. LC 77-74996. (gr. 5 up). 1977. 12.95 (ISBN 0-394-41092-0). Knopf.

Very Young Rider. Jill Krementz. (gr. k-6). 1987. pap. 6.95 (ISBN 0-440-49215-7, YB). Dell.

Very Young Skater. Jill Krementz. LC 79-2209. (Illus.). (gr. 4-6). 1979. 14.45 (ISBN 0-394-50833-5). Knopf.

Very Young Skater. Jill Krementz. (gr. 3-6). 1986. pap. 6.95 (ISBN 0-440-49214-9). Dell.

Verzeichnis der althochdeutschen und altsaechsischen Glossenhandschriften: Mit Bibliographie der Glosseneditionen, der Handschriftenbeschreibungen und der Dialektbestimmungen. Rolf Bergmann. LC 72-76056. (Arbeiten Zur Fruehmittelalterforschung Ser: Vol. 6). (Ger.). 1973. 31.60x (ISBN 3-11-003713-0). De Gruyter.

Verzeichnis der Nobelpreistrager Ni1901-1987: Mit Preisbegundungen, Kurzkommentaren, Literarischen, Werkbibliographien und einer Biographie Alfred Nobel. 2nd ed. Ed. by Werner Martin. xi, 382p. 1988. lib. bdg. 60.00 (ISBN 3-598-10721-8). K G Saur.

Verzeichnis der Nobelpreistrager 1901-1984. Ed. by Warner Martin. 362p. (Ger.). 1985. lib. bdg. 34.00 (ISBN 3-598-10578-9). K G Saur.

Verzeichnis der Nobelpreistrager, 1901-1984. Ed. by Werner Martin. 362p. 1985. 34.00 (ISBN 0-317-70031-6). K G Saur.

Verzeichnis Deutscher Datenbanken, Datenbankbetreiber und Informationsvermittlungsstellen. Gesellschaft fur Information und Dokumentation Editors. (Informationsdienste). 450p. 1985. lib. bdg. 30.00 (ISBN 3-598-10582-7). K G Saur.

Verzeichnis deutscher Informations-und Dokumentationsstellen: Bundesrepublik Deutschland und Berlin (West) 5. Auflage 1986. Gesellschaft fur Information und Dokumtation mbH (GID) Editors. 590p. (Ger.). 1988. lib. bdg. 20.00 (ISBN 3-598-10437-5). K G Saur.

Verzeichnis Medizinischer und Naturwissenschaftlicher Drucke 1472-1830: Reihe-A-D, 1-14. Ed. by Herzog August Bibliothek Wolfenbuttal. (Ger.). 1988. lib. bdg. 160.00 (ISBN 3-598-31680-1). K G Saur.

Verzeichnis von Programm-Aghandlungen Deutscher, Osterreichischer und Schweizerischer Schulen der Jahre 1825-1918: Alphabetisch Geordnet nach Verfassern, 4 vols. Franz Kossler. 2134p. (Ger.). 1987. lib. bdg. 500.00 (ISBN 3-598-10665-3). K G Saur.

Vesco: From Wall Street to Castro's Cuba, the Rise, Fall & Exile of White Collar Crime. Arthur Herzog. LC 87-7423. 384p. 1987. 18.95 (ISBN 0-385-24176-3). Doubleday.

Veselie Rusi. Evgeny Popov. 156p. (Rus.). 1981. pap. 7.50 (ISBN 0-88233-676-2). Ardis Pubs.

Vesennie Muzhskie Igry. Felix Roziner. LC 84-28882. 205p. 1985. pap. 8.50 (ISBN 0-938920-48-0). Hermitage.

Vesio de Bernat de So et le Debat entre Honor e Delit de Jacme March, Poemes Provenco-Catalans du 14ieme Siecle, Suivis du Sirventes de Joan de Castelnou. Bernat de So. (Bibliotheque Meridionale: 1 Ser., Tome 25). (Fr.). Repr. of 1945 ed. 17.00 (ISBN 0-384-04030-6). Johnson Repr.

Vesna Fialte: Spring in Fialte. Vladimir Nabokov. (Sobranie Rasskazov I Povestei: Vol. 3). (Rus.). 1978. pap. 8.95 (ISBN 0-88233-384-4). Ardis Pubs.

Vespasiano. Attilio Ariosti. Ed. by Howard M. Brown. LC 76-21078. (Italian Opera 1640-1770 Ser.). 1978. lib. bdg. 77.00 (ISBN 0-8240-2625-X). Garland Pub.

Vespasion Psalter see Early English Manuscripts in Facsimile.

Vesper Sparrows. Deborah Digges. LC 85-48124. 80p. 1986. 15.00 (ISBN 0-689-11767-1); pap. 8.95 (ISBN 0-689-11768-X). Atheneum.

Vessel Inspection & Maintenance. (Rotary Drilling Ser.: Unit V, Lesson 6). (Illus.). 37p. (Orig.). 1977. pap. text ed. 5.95 (ISBN 0-88698-074-7, 2.50610). PETEX.

Vessel Named Markings on United States Inland & Ocean Waterways 1810-1890. James W. Milgram et al. Ed. by Charless Hahn & Harold M. Stral. (Illus.). 832p. 1984. 99.00 (ISBN 0-916675-00-9). Collectors Club IL.

Vessel of Sadness. William Woodruff. LC 74-102075. 1969. 14.95 (ISBN 0-910824-12-6); pap. text ed. 5.95 (ISBN 0-910824-13-4). Kallman.

Vessel of Sadness. William Woodruff. LC 86-45709. 192p. 1987. 15.45i (ISBN 0-06-015709-7, HarpT). Har-Row.

Vessel Traffic Systems. Charles W. Koburger, Jr. LC 86-47713. (Illus.). 192p. 1986. text ed. 16.00x (ISBN 0-87033-360-7). Cornell Maritime.

Vessel Voyage Data Analysis: A Comparative Study. Kim J. Loroch. LC 65-20766. (Illus.). Repr. of 1966 ed. 40.00 (ISBN 0-8357-9075-4, 2016601). Bks Demand UMI.

Vessel Wall in Athero & Thrombogenesis: Studies in the U. S. S. R. Ed. by E. I. Chazov & V. N. Smirnov. (Illus.). 224p. 1982. pap. 64.00 (ISBN 0-387-11384-3). Springer-Verlag.

Vessels. Howard Schwartz. LC 76-13960. 1977. 10.00 (ISBN 0-87775-098-X); pap. 4.00 (ISBN 0-87775-099-8). Unicorn Pr.

Vessels. (Journal: Applied Pathology: Vol. 4, No. 4, 1986). (Illus.). iv, 88p. 1987. pap. 38.75 (ISBN 3-8055-4583-5). S Karger.

Vessels Unto Honor. Connie Broome. LC 76-22242. 1977. pap. 3.50 (ISBN 0-87148-879-5). Pathway Pr.

Vest Pocket Arabic. Institute for Language Study. LC 74-17006. (Illus.). 252p. (Arabic.). 1979. pap. 4.95 (ISBN 0-06-464907-5, BN 4907, B&N Bks). Har-Row.

Vest Pocket Bible Dictionary, Orig see Boyd's Bible Dictionary.

Vest-Pocket Business Fact Book. Information Please Almanac Editors Staff. 227p. 1988. pap. 2.25 (ISBN 0-395-47813-8). HM.

Vest Pocket Calorie Counter. (Dial Card Ser.). 1948. pap. 1.95 (ISBN 0-385-00174-6). Doubleday.

Vest-Pocket CPA. Nicky A. Dauber et al. 516p. 1988. flexi-cover 24.95 (ISBN 0-13-942293-5). P-H.

Vest Pocket English. Institute for Language Study. LC 58-59519. (Illus.). 188p. 1979. pap. 3.95 (ISBN 0-06-464908-3, BN 4908, B&N Bks). Har-Row.

Vest Pocket French. Institute for Language Study. (Illus.). 128p. (Fr.). 1979. pap. 2.95 (ISBN 0-06-464901-6, BN 4901, B&N Bks). Har-Row.

Vest Pocket German. Institute for Language Study. LC 58-8920. (Illus.). 128p. (Ger.). 1979. pap. 2.95 (ISBN 0-06-464902-4, BN 4902, B&N Bks). Har-Row.

Vest Pocket German Dictionary. rev. ed. Compiled by T. C. Appelt. LC 83-60677. 344p. 1975. pap. 2.95 (ISBN 0-8329-1533-5). New Century.

Vest Pocket Guide for Builders & Contractors. John E. Traister. (Illus.). 192p. 1988. pap. text ed. 12.95 (ISBN 0-13-941659-5). P-H.

Vest Pocket Guide for Electrical Engineers & Technicians. John E. Traister. (Illus.). 240p. 1986. text ed. 10.95 (ISBN 0-13-941600-5). P-H.

Vest Pocket Guide to Electrical Testing & Troubleshooting. John E. Traister. (Illus.). 144p. 1987. pap. 10.95 (ISBN 0-13-941584-X). P-H.

Vest Pocket Italian. Institute for Language Study. LC 58-8919. (Illus.). 128p. (Ital.). 1979. pap. 2.95 (ISBN 0-06-464903-2, BN 4903, B&N Bks). Har-Row.

Vest Pocket Japanese. Institute for Language Study. (Illus.). 240p. (Japanese.). 1979. pap. 3.95 (ISBN 0-06-464906-7, BN 4906, B&N Bks). Har-Row.

Vest-Pocket MBA. Jae K. Shim et al. 1986. 18.95 (ISBN 0-13-941627-7). P-H.

Vest-Pocket MBA. Jae K. Shim et al. (Illus.). 300p. 1987. pap. 8.95 (ISBN 0-13-941709-5). P-H.

Vest Pocket Modern Greek. Institute for Language Study. LC 60-53247. (Illus.). 184p. (Gr.). 1979. pap. 3.95 (ISBN 0-06-464904-0, BN4904, B&N Bks). Har-Row.

Vest Pocket Russian. Institute for Language Study. LC 60-9758. (Illus.). 182p. (Rus.). 1961. pap. 3.95 (ISBN 0-06-464905-9, BN4905, B&N Bks). Har-Row.

Vest Pocket Spanish. Institute for Language Study. (Illus.). 128p. (Span.). 1979. pap. 2.95 (ISBN 0-06-464900-8, BN 4900, B&N Bks). Har-Row.

Vest-Pocket Writer's Guide. LC 87-2768. 272p. 1987. pap. 2.25 (ISBN 0-395-44145-5). HM.

Vesta Boxes. Roger Fresco-Corbu. (Antique Pocket Guides). (Illus.). 64p. (Orig.). 1983. pap. 5.95 (ISBN 0-7188-2582-9, Pub. by Lutterworth Pr UK). Seven Hills Bks.

Vestal Vases: Sandy Rosen. Ruth K. Meyer. (Illus.). 12p. (Orig.). 1986. pap. 5.00 (ISBN 0-915577-08-9). Taft Museum.

Vestale. Mercadante Saverio. (Italian Opera II Ser.). 225p. 1985. lib. bdg. 85.00 (ISBN 0-8240-6571-9). Garland Pub.

Vestalische Ewige Feuer (Il Fuoco Eterno) Lodovico O. Burnacini. LC 68-21208. (Illus., Ger). 1969. Repr. of 1674 ed. 49.50 (ISBN 0-405-08333-5). Ayer Co Pubs.

Vested Interests. Ralph A. Raimi. xiv, 209p. 1982. 14.95 (ISBN 0-9609370-0-5). Raimi.

Vested Interests. Thorstein B. Veblen. LC 63-23513. 1964. Repr. of 1920 ed. 22.50x (ISBN 0-678-00053-0). Kelley.

Vested Rights: Balancing Public & Private Development Expectations. Charles L. Siemon & Wendy U. Larsen. LC 82-50897. 112p. (Orig.). 1982. pap. 50.00 (ISBN 0-87420-612-X, VO1); pap. 37.50 members. Urban Land.

Vestibular & Oculomotor Physiology: International Meeting of the Barany Society, Vol. 374. Ed. by Bernard Cohen. LC 81-14230. 892p. 1981. 177.00x (ISBN 0-89766-137-0); pap. 177.00x (ISBN 0-89766-138-9). NY Acad Sci.

Vestibular & Visual Control on Posture & Locomotor Equilibrium. M. Igarashi & O. F. Black. (Illus.). x, 366p. 1985. 126.00 (ISBN 3-8055-3951-7). S Karger.

Vestibular Disorders. Barber. 1988. 47.00 (ISBN 0-8151-0419-7). Year Bk Med.

Vestibular Neurotology. Ed. by P. Molina-Negro. (Advances in Oto-Rhino-Laryngology Ser.: Vol. 28). (Illus.). viii, 148p. 1982. 76.75 (ISBN 3-8055-3490-6). S Karger.

Vestibular Processing Dysfunction in Children. Ed. by Kenneth J. Ottenbacher & Margaret A. Short. LC 85-8636. (Physical & Occupational Therapy in Pediatrics: Vol. 5, Nos. 2-3). 152p. 1985. text ed. 27.95 (ISBN 0-86656-431-4); pap. text ed. 19.95 (ISBN 0-86656-432-2). Haworth Pr.

Vestibular System see Handbook of Sensory Physiology.

Vestibular System: Function & Morphology. Ed. by T. Gualtierotti. (Illus.). 560p. 1981. 120.00 (ISBN 0-387-90559-6). Springer-Verlag.

Vestibular System: Fundamental & Clinical Observations. Ed. by Jan Stahle. (Illus.). 296p. 1984. text ed. 87.50x (ISBN 91-22-00676-1, Pub. by Almqvist & Wiksell). Coronet Bks.

Vestibular System: Neurophysiologic & Clinical Research. Ed. by Malcolm D. Graham & John L. Kemink. (Illus.). 688p. 1987. text ed. 96.00 (ISBN 0-88167-206-8). Raven.

Vestibule. Jess E. Weiss. Ed. by Billie Young. LC 72-78506. 1972. 14.95 (ISBN 0-87949-004-7). Ashley Bks.

Vestibules of Heaven. Mid McKnight. 1982. pap. 3.95 (ISBN 0-89225-219-7). Gospel Advocate.

Vestiges of a Proud Nation. Raymond J. DeMallie et al. Ed. by Glenn E. Markoe. (Illus.). 176p. 1987. 37.50x (ISBN 0-934658-02-1); pap. 22.50 (ISBN 0-934658-01-3). R H Flem Mus.

Vestiges of Old Madras, 4 Vols. in 3. Henry D. Love. Repr. of 1913 ed. Set. 127.50 (ISBN 0-404-04060-8). Vol. 1 (ISBN 0-404-04061-6). Vol. 2 (ISBN 0-404-04062-4). Vol. 3 (ISBN 0-404-04063-2). AMS Pr.

Vestiges of the Venerable City: A Chronicle of Lexington, Kentucky. Clay Lancaster. LC 78-61797. (Illus.). 1978. 14.95 (ISBN 0-912839-01-5). Lexington-Fayette.

Vesting. Jeffrey Mamorsky & Leo Brown. (Requirements for Qualification of Plans Ser.). 27p. 1983. pap. 2.00 (ISBN 0-317-31160-3, B446). Am Law Inst.

Vesting. Jean Wells. (Illus., Orig.). 1985. pap. text ed. 9.00 (ISBN 0-932946-25-9). Burdett CA.

Vestments. Alfred Alcorn. 304p. 1988. 17.95 (ISBN 0-395-47042-0). HM.

Vestry Book & Register of St. Peter's Parish, New Kent & James City Counties, Virginia, 1684-1786. C. G. Chamberlayne. xxvi, 840p. 1973. Repr. of 1937 ed. 12.50 (ISBN 0-88490-037-1). VA State Lib.

Vestry Book of Blisland (Blissland) Parish, New Kent & James City Counties, Virginia, 1721-1786. Ed. by C. G. Chamberlayne. LC 79-16401. ixii, 277p. 1979. Repr. of 1935 ed. 10.00 (ISBN 0-88490-030-4). VA State Lib.

Vestry Book of Petsworth Parish, Glouster County, Virginia, 1670-1793. Ed. by C. G. Chamberlane. LC 79-13640. xv, 429p. 1979. Repr. of 1933 ed. 10.00 (ISBN 0-88490-032-0). VA State Lib.

Vestry Book of St. Paul's Parish, Hanover County, Virginia, 1706-1786. Ed. by C. G. Chamberlayne. xx, 672p. 1973. Repr. of 1940 ed. 12.50 (ISBN 0-88490-038-X). VA State Lib.

Vestry Book of Stratton Major Parish, King & Queen County, Virginia, 1729-1783. Ed. by C. G. Chamberlyne. LC 80-14672. xxi, 257p. 1980. Repr. of 1933 ed. 10.00 (ISBN 0-88490-087-8). VA State Lib.

Vestry Book of the Upper Parish, Nansemond County, Virginia, 1793-1943. Ed. by Wilmer L. Hall. LC 50-9492. ixxiv, 328p. 1949. 10.00 (ISBN 0-88490-039-8). VA State Lib.

Vestry Member's Guide. rev. ed. Van S. Bowen. 80p. 1983. pap. 3.95 (ISBN 0-8164-2464-0, HarpR). Har-Row.

Vestry Minute Book of the Parish of Stratford-on-Avon from 1617 to 1699. Ed. by George Arbuthnot. LC 72-142244. Repr. of 1899 ed. 18.00 (ISBN 0-404-00366-4). AMS Pr.

Vet Behind the Ears. Christopher Timothy. (Lythway Ser.). 1987. lib. bdg. 16.50x (ISBN 0-7451-0612-9, Pub. by Chivers Pr UK). G K Hall.

Vetera Analecta. Jean Mabillon. 620p. 1723. text ed. 124.20 (ISBN 0-576-72341-X, Pub. by Gregg Intl Pubs England). Gregg Intl.

Veteran & Vintage Aircraft. Leslie Hunt. LC 74-29025. 1975. pap. 3.95 encore ed. (ISBN 0-684-14895-1, SL 695, ScribT). Scribner.

Veteran & Vintage Cars. Ed. by Tony Curtis. (Illus.). 1978. 2.00 (ISBN 0-902921-53-3). Apollo.

Veteran & Vintage Cars of Australia. Malcolm Grant. LC 73-77577. (Illus.). 1973. 7.75 (ISBN 0-8048-1104-0). C E Tuttle.

Veteran Counselor. Jack Rudman. (Career Examination Ser.: C-2690). (Cloth bdg. avail. on request). pap. 14.00 (ISBN 0-8373-2690-7). Natl Learning.

Veteran's Administration. Glover E. Hopson. (Know Your Government Ser.). (Illus.). 96p. (gr. 5 up). 1988. lib. bdg. 12.95 (ISBN 1-55546-131-X). Chelsea Hse.

Veterans' Administration: Its History, Activities & Organization. Gustavus A. Weber & Laurence F. Schmeckebier. LC 72-3083. (Brookings Institution. Institute for Government Research. Service Monographs of the U. S. Government: No. 66). Repr. of 1934 ed. 56.00 (ISBN 0-404-57166-2). AMS Pr.

Veterans & Other Poems. Donagh MacDonagh. 52p. 1971. Repr. of 1941 ed. 15.00x (BBA 02066, Pub. by Cuala Press Ireland). Biblio Dist.

Veterans Claims Examiner. (Career Examination Ser.: C-3288). Date not set. pap. 14.00 (ISBN 0-8373-3288-5). Natl Learning.

Veterans Compensation: An American Scandal. Ronald L. Eisenberg. 309p. (Orig.). 1985. pap. 9.95 (ISBN 0-930883-01-2). Pierremont Press.

Veteran's Day. Jan Barry. 12p. 1983. pap. 1.00 (ISBN 0-686-46874-0). Samisdat.

Veteran's Day. Rod Kane. (Combat Bachelor: Part I). 55p. (Orig.). 1985. pap. 4.95 (ISBN 0-9618022-1-9). Combat Bachelor.

Veterans Flag List, Spencer & Halsey Valley New York (Tioga County) Laura C. Uhl. 1982. 2.00 (ISBN 0-943240-05-0). Uhls Pub.

Veterans Park. Don J. Snyder. Ed. by Ed Breslin. 272p. 1987. 16.95 (ISBN 0-531-15049-6). Watts.

Veterans Park. Don J. Snyder. 1988. pap. 3.95 (ISBN 0-317-67166-9). Ivy Books.

Veterans Pension: The Prospect for Advocacy by Legal Services Programs. Center on Social Welfare Policy & Law. 148p. 1981. 13.00 (31,685). NCLS Inc.

Veteran's Return to a Battlefield: Where 29th Division Fought near Aachen. Boyd Miller. (Illus.). 36p. 1985. 4.00 (ISBN 0-9615971-0-0). Wordpix Serv.

Veterinarian. Jack Rudman. (Career Examination Ser.: C-870). (Cloth bdg. avail. on request). pap. 29.95 (ISBN 0-8373-0870-4). Natl Learning.

Veterinarian Trainee. Jack Rudman. (Career Examination Ser.: C-1529). (Cloth bdg. avail. on request). pap. 22.95 (ISBN 0-8373-1529-8). Natl Learning.

Veterinarian's Guide to the Laboratory Diagnosis of Infectious Diseases. G. R. Carter. 326p. 1986. 29.95 (ISBN 0-935078-37-1). Veterinary Med.

Veterinarian's Puzzle Book: Continuing Education the Fun Way. Sherman J. Marcus. 140p. (Orig.). 1983. pap. 4.95 (ISBN 0-9610444-0-3). Cambita Bks.

Veterinarian's Treasury of Practice Tips II. Ed. by Seymour Glasofer & Lester Mandelker. 144p. 8.95 (ISBN 0-935078-14-2). Veterinary Med.

Veterinary Acupuncture. Alan M. Klide & Shiu H. Kung. LC 76-53193. 1977. 52.95x (ISBN 0-8122-7721-X). U of Pa Pr.

Veterinary Anaesthesia. 8th ed. L. W. Hall & K. W. Clarke. (Illus.). 432p. 1983. 58.00 (ISBN 0-7216-0809-4, Bailliere-Tindall). Saunders.

Veterinary Anatomy: Basic, Comparative, & Clinical. M. J. Shively. LC 84-40132. (Illus.). 592p. 1985. pap. 35.00x (ISBN 0-89096-202-2). Tex A&M Univ Pr.

Veterinary Anatomy: Volume II, the Horse. Ashdown & Done. LC 65-73315. 1988. text ed. 69.50 (ISBN 0-397-58304-4, Lippincott Medical). Lippincott.

Veterinary Anesthesia. 2nd ed. William V. Lumb & E. Wynn Jones. LC 83-18736. (Illus.). 693p. 1984. text ed. 69.50 (ISBN 0-8121-0906-6). Lea & Febiger.

Veterinary Annual. 25th ed. C. Grunsell & F. Hill. 1985. 39.00 (ISBN 0-85608-039-X). PSG Pub Co.

Veterinary Annual. 24th ed. C. S. Grunsell & F. W. Hill. (Illus.). 368p. 1984. 39.00 (ISBN 0-85608-038-1). PSG Pub Co.

Veterinary Annual. 26th ed. Ed. by C. S. Grunsell et al. (Illus.). 405p. 1986. 39.00 (ISBN 0-85608-041-1). PSG Pub Co.

Veterinary Annual 1987. 27th ed. C. S. Grunsell et al. 368p. 1987. 51.00 (ISBN 0-85608-042-X). PSG Pub Co.

Veterinary Annual, 1988. 28th ed. C. S. Grunsell et al. (Illus.). 336p. 1988. 60.00 (ISBN 0-85608-043-8). PSG Pub Co.

Veterinary Applied Pharmacology & Therapeutics. 4th ed. G. C. Brander et al. (Illus.). 582p. 1982. 69.00 (ISBN 0-7216-0780-2, Bailliere-Tindall). Saunders.

Veterinary Aptitude Test (VAT) Jack Rudman. (Admission Test Ser.: ATS-29). 25.95 (ISBN 0-8373-5129-4); pap. 15.00 (ISBN 0-8373-5029-8). Natl Learning.

Veterinary Aptitude Test (VAT) Student Guide. rev. ed. David M. Tarlow. (Illus.). 120p. 1986. pap. 14.95 (ISBN 0-931572-06-1). Datar Pub.

Veterinary Biology & Medicine of Captive Amphibians & Reptiles. Leonard C. Marcus. LC 80-24859. pap. 65.30 (2056518). Bks Demand UMI.

Veterinary Book for Farmers. R. W. Blowey. (Illus.). 395p. 1985. 28.95 (ISBN 0-85236-151-3, Pub. by Farming Pr UK). Diamond Farm Bk.

Veterinary Business Management: A Guide to an Effective & Profitable Practice. Mark Opperman. LC 82-25479. 1983. 18.95 (ISBN 0-932036-09-0, Harwal Pub Co). Wiley.

Veterinary Cancer Medicine. 2nd ed. Ed. by Gordon H. Theilen & Bruce R. Madewell. LC 86-21332. (Illus.). 676p. 1987. 85.00 (ISBN 0-8121-1049-8). Lea & Febiger.

Veterinary Clinical Diagnosis. 3rd ed. W. H. Kelly. (Illus.). 430p. 1984. pap. write for info. (ISBN 0-7216-0947-3, Bailliere-Tindall). Saunders.

Veterinary Clinical Immunology. Richard E. Halliwell & Neil T. Gorman. 496p. 1988. 50.00 (ISBN 0-7216-1197-4). Saunders.

Veterinary Clinical Parasitology. 5th ed. Margaret W. Sloss & Russell L. Kemp. LC 61-11865. (Illus.). 1978. 21.95x (ISBN 0-8138-1730-7). Iowa St U Pr.

Veterinary Clinical Pathology. 4th ed. Embert H. Coles. (Illus.). 486p. 1986. 41.95 (ISBN 0-7216-1828-6). Saunders.

Veterinary College Admissions: A Comprehensive Guide. James W. Morrison & Robert F. Wignall. LC 84-6251. 384p. (Orig.). 1984. pap. 10.00 (ISBN 0-668-05545-6). Arco.

Veterinary Contribution to Public Health Practice: Report of the FAO-WHO Expert Committee on Veterinary Public Health, Geneva, 1974. FAO-WHO Expert Committee on Veterinary Public Health. (Technical Report Ser.: No. 573). (Also avail. in French & Spanish). 1975. pap. 3.20 (ISBN 92-4-120573-3). World Health.

Veterinary Critical Care. Ed. by Fred P. Sattler et al. LC 80-27880. (Illus.). 549p. 1981. text ed. 45.00 (ISBN 0-8121-0702-0). Lea & Febiger.

Veterinary Dentistry. Erich Eisenmenger & Karl Zetner. LC 84-7908. (Illus.). 165p. 1985. text ed. 44.00 (ISBN 0-8121-0924-4). Lea & Febiger.

Veterinary Dentistry. Colin E. Harvey. (Illus.). 322p. 1985. 57.95 (ISBN 0-7216-1111-7). Saunders.

Veterinary Diagnostic Radiology. Donald E. Thrall. (Illus.). 563p. 1986. 49.95 (ISBN 0-7216-1199-0). Saunders.

Veterinary Dictionary: Russian-English. R. Mack. 104p. (Rus. & Eng.). 1972. pap. 35.00 (ISBN 0-686-92151-8, M-9710). French & Eur.

Veterinary Drug Formulary. David McBride. 200p. 1985. pap. text ed. 16.95 (ISBN 0-683-05743-X). Williams & Wilkins.

Veterinary Drug Index. Benjamin Lewis & Leon O. Wilkin, Jr. LC 78-64717. 600p. 1981. text ed. 50.00 (ISBN 0-7216-5764-8). Saunders.

Veterinary Drug Manufacturing Encyclopedia. Marshall Sittig. LC 81-16815. (Illus.). 507p. 1982. 64.00 (ISBN 0-8155-0870-0). Noyes.

Veterinary Endocrinology & Reproduction. 4th ed. Ed. by L. E. McDonald. LC 88-9015. (Illus.). 550p. 1989. text ed. price not set. Lea & Febiger.

Veterinary Epidemiology. M. V. Thrusfield. 300p. 1986. text ed. 84.95 (ISBN 0-408-10861-4). Butterworth.

Veterinary Epidemiology & Economics in Africa. S. N. Putt & A. P. Shaw. (ILCA Manual Ser.: No. 3). 130p. (Orig.). pap. 22.00 (ISBN 92-9053-076-6, Pub. by Intl Livestock Africa). Agribookstore.

Veterinary Epidemiology: Principles & Methods. S. Wayne Martin et al. 344p. 1987. text ed. 30.95x (ISBN 0-8138-1856-7). Iowa St U Pr.

Veterinary Eye Surgery. S. W. Petrick. (Illus.). 1986. text ed. 24.95 (ISBN 0-409-11265-8). Butterworth.

Veterinary Gastroenterology. 2nd ed. Ed. by Neil V. Anderson. (Illus.). 750p. 1988. text ed. price not set (ISBN 0-8121-1170-2). Lea & Febiger.

Veterinary Genetics. F. W. Nicholas. (Illus.). 500p. 1987. 57.50 (ISBN 0-19-857569-6). Oxford U Pr.

Veterinary Guide for Animal Owners: Cattle, Goats, Sheep, Horses, Pigs, Poultry, Rabbits, Dogs, Cats. C. E. Spaulding. LC 76-10641. (Illus.). 432p. 1976. 17.95 (ISBN 0-87857-118-3). Rodale Pr Inc.

Veterinary Helminthology. R. K. Reineke. (Illus.). 1986. text ed. 39.95 (ISBN 0-409-11262-3). Butterworth.

Veterinary Histology: An Outline Text-Atlas. Horst-Dieter Dellmann. LC 78-146030. pap. 82.20 (2056506). Bks Demand UMI.

Veterinary Immunology. P. M. Outteridge. 280p. 1986. pap. 22.50 (ISBN 0-12-531131-1). Acad Pr.

Veterinary Immunology. Peter M. Outteridge. (Monograph Ser.). 1985. 58.00 (ISBN 0-12-531130-3). Acad Pr.

Veterinary Immunology: An Introduction. 3rd ed. Ian Tizard. (Illus.). 424p. 1987. pap. 39.95 (ISBN 0-7216-2098-1). Saunders.

Veterinary Interpretive Clinical Pathology. Embert H. Coles & William E. Moore. (Illus.). 350p. Date not set. price not set (ISBN 0-7216-2654-8). Saunders.

Veterinary Laboratory Medicine: Clinical Pathology. 2nd ed. J. Robert Duncan & Keith W. Prasse. 286p. 1986. text ed. 29.95x (ISBN 0-8138-1916-4). Iowa St U Pr.

Veterinary Medical Mycology. Paul F. Jungerman & Robert Schwartzman. LC 78-157469. pap. 51.80 (ISBN 0-317-28598-X, 2055434). Bks Demand UMI.

Veterinary Medical Officer. Jack Rudman. (Career Examination Ser.: C-875). (Cloth bdg. avail. on request). pap. 27.95 (ISBN 0-8373-0875-5). Natl Learning.

Veterinary Medical School Admission Requirements in the United States & Canada, for enrollment in Academic Year: 1988-1989. 3rd ed. Association of American Veterinary Medical Colleges. Compiled by Marcia J. Sawyer. 160p. (Orig.). 1987. pap. 9.00. Betz Pub Co Inc.

Veterinary Medicine: A Textbook of the Diseases of Cattle, Pigs, Goats & Horses. 6th ed. D. C. Blood et al. (Illus.). 1328p. 1983. 73.00 (ISBN 0-7216-0817-5, Bailliere-Tindall). Saunders.

Veterinary Medicine & Human Health. 3rd ed. Calvin W. Schwabe. (Illus.). 848p. 1984. lib. bdg. 53.95 (ISBN 0-683-07594-2). Williams & Wilkins.

Veterinary Medicine: Subject, Reference & Research Guide. Max W. Denton. LC 87-47614. 160p. 1987. 34.50 (ISBN 0-88164-532-X); pap. 26.50 (ISBN 0-88164-533-8). ABBE Pubs Assn.

Veterinary Microbiology. Ed. by R. Pandey. (Progress in Veterinary Microbiology & Immunology Ser.: Vol. 2). (Illus.). x, 222p. 1985. 98.75 (ISBN 3-8055-4067-1). S Karger.

Veterinary Multilingual Thesaurus, 5 Vols. Ed. by Commission of the European Communities, Staff. (Thesauri Ser.). 122p. 1979. lib. bdg. 270.00 (ISBN 3-598-10109-0). K G Saur.

Veterinary Neuroanatomy & Clinical Neurology. 2nd ed. Alexander DeLahunta. LC 76-4246. (Illus.). 1983. text ed. 44.95 (ISBN 0-7216-3029-4). Saunders.

Veterinary Neurology: Diagnosis & Treatment. J. E. Oliver, Jr. et al. (Illus.). 576p. 1987. 78.95 (ISBN 0-7216-1314-4). Saunders.

Veterinary Neuropathology. Summers et al. (Illus.). 650p. 1991. 59.95 (ISBN 0-8016-5063-1). Mosby.

Veterinary Notes for Horse Owners. 15th ed. Horace M. Hayes. Ed. by J. F. Tutt. LC 64-12209. (Illus.). 1964. 19.95 (ISBN 0-668-00656-0). Arco.

Veterinary Notes for Horse Owners: An Illustrated Manual of Horse Medicine & Surgery. 17th, rev. ed. M. Horace Hayes. (Illus.). 688p. 1988. 26.95 (ISBN 0-13-941956-X). Prentice Hall Pr.

Veterinary Odyssey. Frank H. Manley. (Illus.). 1978. 7.50 (ISBN 0-682-49115-2). Exposition-Phoenix.

Veterinary Ophthalmology, Vol. I: Large Animal Ophthalmology. Lavach & Giddings. (Illus.). 475p. 1989. pap. 39.95 (ISBN 0-8016-2773-7). Mosby.

Veterinary Opthalmology, Vol. II: Small Animal Opthalmology. Lavach & Giddings. 1990. 39.95 (ISBN 0-8016-2774-5). Mosby.

Veterinary Parasitology. G. M. Urguhart et al. LC 85-19789. (Illus.). 1987. pap. text ed. 59.50 (ISBN 0-582-40906-3). Churchill.

Veterinary Pathology. 5th ed. Thomas C. Jones & Ronald D. Hunt. LC 81-20820. (Illus.). 1792p. 1983. text ed. 85.00 (ISBN 0-8121-0789-6). Lea & Febiger.

Veterinary Pharmaceuticals & Biologicals. 5th ed. LC 85-647677. 600p. 1986. 32.95 (ISBN 0-87489-843-9). Veterinary Med.

Veterinary Pharmacology & Therapeutics. 5th ed. Nicholas H. Booth & Leslie E. McDonald. (Illus.). 1134p. 1982. text ed. 63.95x (ISBN 0-8138-1740-4). Iowa St U Pr.

Veterinary Pharmacology & Therapeutics. 6th, rev. ed. Nicholas H. Booth & Leslie E. McDonald. (Illus.). 1168p. 1988. text ed. 79.95 (ISBN 0-8138-1739-0). Iowa St U Pr.

Veterinary Practice Management. McCurnin. LC 65-9467. Date not set. 45.00 (ISBN 0-397-50782-8, Lippincott Medical). Lippincott.

Veterinary Protozoology. Norman D. Levine. (Illus.). 414p. 1985. text ed. 43.50x (ISBN 0-8138-1861-3). Iowa St U Pr.

Veterinary Reproduction & Obstetrics. 5th ed. G. H. Arthur et al. (Illus.). 512p. 1983. 58.00 (ISBN 0-7216-0778-0, Bailliere-Tindall). Saunders.

Veterinary Science. (Illus.). 40p. (gr. 6-12). 1973. pap. 1.25x (ISBN 0-8395-3261-X, 3261). BSA.

Veterinary Science Officer. Jack Rudman. (Career Examination Ser.: C-871). (Cloth bdg. avail. on request). pap. 27.95 (ISBN 0-8373-0871-2). Natl Learning.

Veterinary Surgeon's Guide for Cat Owners. David Coffey. (Illus.). 216p. 1983. 16.95 (Pub. by Worlds Work). David & Charles.

Veterinary Surgeon's Guide to Dogs. David Coffey. (Illus.). 199p. 1980. 16.95 (ISBN 0-437-02500-4, Pub. by Worlds Work). David & Charles.

Veterinary Toxicology. Ed. by M. Bartik & A. Piskac. (Developments in Animal & Veterinary Science Ser.: Vol. 7). 346p. 1981. 100.00 (ISBN 0-444-99757-1). Elsevier.

Veterinary Toxicology. 2nd ed. Myra L. Clarke et al. 336p. 1981. write for info. (ISBN 0-7216-0785-3, Bailliere-Tindall). Saunders.

Veterinary Toxicology. Humphreys. 352p. 1988. write for info. Saunders.

Veterinary Toxicology. 2nd ed. Rudolph D. Radeleff. LC 74-85846. pap. 91.30 (ISBN 0-317-29245-5, 2055440). Bks Demand UMI.

Veterinary Trauma & Critical Care. Ira M. Zaslow. LC 83-22243. (Illus.). 584p. 1984. text ed. 58.50 (ISBN 0-8121-0868-X). Lea & Febiger.

Veterinary Viral Diseases: Their Significance in South-East Asia & the Western Pacific. Ed. by Antony J. Della-Porta. 1985. 47.50 (ISBN 0-12-208870-0). Acad Pr.

Veterinary Virology. Frank Fenner et al. 1987. 59.00 (ISBN 0-12-253055-1). Acad Pr.

Veterum Scriptorum et Monumentorum Historicorum, Dogmaticorum, Moralium, Amplissima Collectio, 9 Vols. Ed. by Edmund Martene. LC 68-56786. (Research & Source Works Ser: No. 275). 1969. Repr. of 1717 ed. Set. 735.00 (ISBN 0-8337-2263-8). B Franklin.

Veto Power of the Governor of Illinois. Niels H. Debel. (Illinois Studies in the Social Sciences: Vol. 6). 1917. 12.00 (ISBN 0-384-11165-3). Johnson Repr.

Vette Vues Factbook of the 1963-1967 Stingray. 7th ed. Ed. by M. F. Dobbins. (Vette Vues Factbook Ser.). (Illus.). 330p. 1986. 27.95x (ISBN 0-9607176-5-X). M F Dobbins.

Vette Vues Factbook of the 1968-1972 Stingray. 2nd ed. Dobbins M. F. (Vette Vues Factbook Ser.). (Illus.). 228p. 1982. 21.95x (ISBN 0-9607176-2-5). M F Dobbins.

Vetus Disciplina Canocorum Regularium & Saecularium ex Documentis Magna Parte Hucusque Ineditis a Temporibus Apostolicis ad Saeculum XVII. Eusebio Amort. 1112p. 1747. text ed. 248.40x (ISBN 0-576-99833-8, Pub. by Gregg Intl Pubs England). Gregg Intl.

Vibrations of Elastic Structural Members, No. 3. E. B. Magrab. (Mechanics of Structural Systems Ser.). 404p. 1979. 60.00x (ISBN 90-286-0207-0, Pub. by Sijthoff & Noordhoff). Kluwer Academic.
Vibrations of Engineering Structures. C. A. Brebbia et al. (Lecture Notes in Engineering Ser.: Vol. 10). 300p. 1985. pap. 29.50 (ISBN 0-387-13959-1). Springer-Verlag.
Vibrations of Soils & Foundations. F. E. Richart, Jr. et al. (Civil Engineering Ser.). 1970. 56.00 (ISBN 0-13-941716-8). P-H.
Vibrations: The Adventures & Musical Times of David Amram. David Amram. LC 79-24422. (Illus.). 469p. 1980. Repr. of 1968 ed. lib. bdg. 35.00x (ISBN 0-313-22230-4, AMVI). Greenwood.
Vibratory Compacting: Principles & Methods. Ed. by Henry H. Hausner et al. LC 65-24898. (Perspectives in Powder Metallurgy Series: Fundamentals, Methods & Applications: Vol. 2). (Illus.). pap. 78.00 (ISBN 0-317-08350-3, 2019458). Bks Demand UMI.
Vibrios in the Environment. Rita R. Colwell. LC 83-21720. (Environmental Science & Technology Ser.: 1-121). 634p. 1984. 54.50 (ISBN 0-471-87343-8). Wiley.
Vibromotors for Precision Microrobots. K. Ragulskis et al. (Applications of Vibration Ser.). 400p. 1988. 75.00 (ISBN 0-89116-549-5). Hemisphere Pub.
Vibronic Coupling. Gad Fischer. (Theoretical Chemistry Ser.). 1984. 57.00 (ISBN 0-12-257240-8). Acad Pr.
Vic & Blood: The Chronicles of a Boy & His Dog. Harlan Ellison. Adapted by Richard Corben & Jan Strnad. (Illus.). 120p. 1988. pap. 12.95 (ISBN 0-89865-604-4, Starblaze); ltd. ed. 40.00 (ISBN 0-89865-605-2, Starblaze). Donning Co.
Vic Braden's Quick Fixes: Expert Cures for Common Tennis Problems. Vic Braden & Bill Bruns. LC 87-26099. (Illus.). 224p. 1988. 17.95 (ISBN 0-316-10514-7). Little.
Vic Braden's Tennis for the Future. Vic Braden & Bill Bruns. 1977. 24.45i (ISBN 0-316-10510-4); pap. 14.95 (ISBN 0-316-10511-2). Little.
Vic Dunaway's Complete Book of Baits, Rigs & Tackle. 6th, rev. ed. Vic Dunaway. (Illus.). 224p. 1984. pap. 6.95 (ISBN 0-936240-02-4). Wickstrom.
Vic Dunaway's Complete Book of Baits, Rigs & Tackle. (Illus.). 224p. pap. 6.95 (ISBN 0-936240-00-8). Banyan Bks.
Vic Holyfield & the Class of 1957. William Heyen. 128p. (Orig.). 1986. pap. 4.95 (ISBN 0-345-32905-8, Pub. by Available Pr). Ballantine.
Vic Holyfield & the Class of 1957. William Heyen. 1988. pap. 3.50 (ISBN 0-345-34401-4). Ballantine.
VIC-20, Vol. 1. Robin Buxton. (Thinking-Learning-Creating: TLC for Growing Minds Ser.). 51p. (gr. 4-12). 1983. pap. text ed. 11.95 (ISBN 0-88193-061-X). Create Learn.
VIC-20, Vol. 2. Robin Buxton. (Thinking-Learning-Creating: TLC for Growing Minds Ser.). 59p. (gr. 4-12). 1983. pap. text ed. 11.95 (ISBN 0-88193-062-8). Create Learn.
VIC-20, Vol. 3. Robin Buxton. (Thinking-Learning-Creating: TLC for Growing Minds Ser.). 59p. (gr. 5-12). 1983. pap. text ed. 11.95 (ISBN 0-88193-063-6). Create Learn.
VIC-20, Vol. 4. Marilyn Buxton & Robin Buxton. (Thinking-Learning-Creating: TLC for Growing Minds Ser.). 63p. (gr. 5-12). 1983. pap. text ed. 11.95 (ISBN 0-88193-064-4). Create Learn.
VIC-20 & Commodore 64 Computer Program Writing Workbook. Howard Adler. 96p. 1983. 4.95 (ISBN 0-86668-811-0). ARCsoft.
VIC-20 BASIC Made Easy. David A. Gardner & Marianne L. Gardner. (Illus.). 256p. 1984. pap. text ed. 23.95 (ISBN 0-13-941972-1). P-H.
VIC-20 Computer Graphics Toolbox. Russell L. Schnapp & Irvin G. Stafford. (Prentice-Hall Personal Computing Ser.). (Illus.). 176p. 1984. pap. text ed. 14.95 (ISBN 0-13-941998-5); incl. cassette o.p. 29.95 (ISBN 0-13-942012-6); cassette 14.95 (ISBN 0-13-942004-5). P-H.
VIC-20 Interfacing Blue Book. V. J. Georgiou. (Illus.). 104p. 1983. pap. 14.95 (ISBN 0-912911-00-X). Microsignal.
Vicar of Bullhampton. Anthony Trollope. (Illus.). 1979. pap. 7.50 (ISBN 0-486-23824-5). Dover.
Vicar of Bullhampton. Anthony Trollope. Ed. by David Skilton. (World's Classics Ser.). 576p. 1988. pap. 8.95 (ISBN 0-19-282163-6). Oxford U Pr.
Vicar of Christ. Walter F. Murphy. 1980. pap. 4.95 (ISBN 0-345-32039-5). Ballantine.
Vicar of Morwenstow: A Life of Robert Stephen Hawker. S. Baring-Gould. 1973. 20.00 (ISBN 0-8274-1426-9). R West.
Vicar of Wakefield. Oliver Goldsmith. (Airmont Classics Ser.). (YA) (gr. 10 up). 1964. pap. 1.25 (ISBN 0-8049-0052-3, CL-52). Airmont.
Vicar of Wakefield. Oliver Goldsmith. 304p. 1982. Repr. lib. bdg. 30.00 (ISBN 0-8495-2126-2). Arden Lib.
Vicar of Wakefield. Oliver Goldsmith. 1976. 14.95x (ISBN 0-460-00295-3, Evman); pap. 4.50x (ISBN 0-460-01295-9, Evman). Biblio Dist.
Vicar of Wakefield. Oliver Goldsmith. pap. 2.50 (ISBN 0-451-52044-0, CE1723, Sig Classics). NAL.
Vicar of Wakefield. Oliver Goldsmith. Ed. by Arthur Friedman. (Oxford English Novels Ser.). 1974. 24.95x (ISBN 0-19-255345-3). Oxford U Pr.
Vicar of Wakefield. Oliver Goldsmith. 304p. 1980. Repr. of 1906 ed. lib. bdg. 35.00 (ISBN 0-8492-4950-3). R West.
Vicar of Wakefield. Oliver Goldsmith. 1982. Repr. lib. bdg. 19.95x (ISBN 0-89966-373-7). Buccaneer Bks.
Vicar of Wakefield. Oliver Goldsmith. 1982. pap. 2.50 (ISBN 0-14-043159-4). Penguin.
Vicar of Wakefield. Oliver Goldsmith. Ed. by Arthur Friedman. (World's Classics Paperback Ser.). 1981. pap. 2.50 (ISBN 0-19-281560-1). Oxford U Pr.
Vicar of Wakefield. W. Goldsmith & L. Rackham. 1986. 29.75X (ISBN 0-317-52513-1, Pub. by Harrap Ltd England). State Mutual Bk.
Vicar of Wrexhill. Frances Trollope. LC 70-162903. (Bentley's Standard Novels: No. 78). Repr. of 1840 ed. 27.50 (ISBN 0-404-54478-9). AMS Pr.
Vicarage Allsorts. Miles Kington & James Grainger. 44p. 1986. pap. 9.95 (ISBN 0-312-83903-0). St Martin.
Vicariance Biogeography: A Critique. Ed. by Gareth Nelson & Donn E. Rosen. LC 80-15351. (Illus.). 616p. 1981. 65.00x (ISBN 0-231-04808-4). Columbia U Pr.
Vicarious Image. Wanda Castle. Ed. by Steve Ingraham. 108p. (Orig.). 1985. pap. 1.45 (ISBN 0-916835-00-6, 600). C & I Pubns.
Vicarious Liability or Liability for the Acts of Others. J. B. Hodge. 48p. 1986. 68.00x (ISBN 0-948691-00-X, Pub. by Witherby & Co England). State Mutual Bk.
Vicarious Sacrifice. Ernest M. Ligon & Character Research Project Staff. Incl. Junior High Unit-Lesson Book. 2.00 (ISBN 0-915744-15-5); Junior High Unit-PLAN. 0.75 (ISBN 0-915744-17-1); Junior High Unit-Home Assignment Sheets. 0.75 (ISBN 0-915744-16-3). (Research Curriculum for Character Education Ser.). (Illus.). 1979. Character Res.
Vicar's Daughter. George MacDonald. 216p. 1985. 5.95 (ISBN 0-89693-330-X). Victor Bks.
Vicars of Christ: The Dark Side of the Papacy. Peter De Rosa. 1988. 18.95 (ISBN 0-517-57027-0). Crown.
Vice. Carla Harryman. 104p. (Orig.). 1987. pap. 7.50 (ISBN 0-937013-16-1). Potes Poets.
Vice & Virtue in Everyday Life. Christina H. Sommers. 653p. 1985. pap. text ed. 14.50 net (ISBN 0-15-594890-3, HC). HarBraceJ.
Vice Book. Alexander Communications, Inc. Staff. (Illus.). 165p. 1988. pap. 30.00 (ISBN 0-8230-5804-2). Alexander Comms.
Vice Chamberlain Coke's Theatrical Papers, 1706-1715. Ed. by Judith Milhous & Robert D. Hume. LC 81-5616. 319p. 1982. 28.95x (ISBN 0-8093-1024-4). S Ill U Pr.
Vice-Consul. Marguerite Duras. (Imaginaire Ser.). 216p. 1965. 8.95 (ISBN 0-686-55854-5). Schoenhof.
Vice-Consul. Marguerite Duras. Tr. by Eileen Ellenbogen. (Modern Writers Ser.). Date not set. 10.95 (ISBN 0-317-59513-X); pap. 6.95 (ISBN 0-317-59514-8). Pantheon.
Vice Czar Murders. Robert L. Bellem & Cleve F. Adams. (Classic Hard-Boiled Detective Ser.). 128p. 1988. pap. 6.95 (ISBN 0-939767-09-0). D McMillan.
Vice in a Vicious Society: Crime & Convicts in Mid-Nineteenth Century New South Wales. Michael Sturma. LC 82-8636. (Illus.). 224p. 1983. text ed. 32.50x (ISBN 0-7022-1911-8). U of Queensland Pr.
Vice in Chicago. Walter C. Reckless. LC 69-16243. (Criminology, Law Enforcement, & Social Problems Ser.: No. 84). 1969. Repr. of 1933 ed. 15.00x (ISBN 0-87585-084-7). Patterson Smith.
Vice in German Monasteries. Joseph McCabe. 35p. 1988. pap. 3.00 saddle-stitched (ISBN 0-911826-93-9). Am Atheist.
Vice of Verse & Other Slanderous Rhymes Concerning Famous Philosophers. Lamar H. Crosby, Jr. Ed. by Harrison B. Bell. (Illus.). 96p. (Orig.). 1984. pap. 9.95 (ISBN 0-916153-00-2). Ten-Thirty Pr.
Vice-President As Policy Maker: Rockefeller in the Ford White House. Michael Turner. LC 81-20301. (Contributions in Political Science Ser.: No. 78). xvii, 252p. 1982. lib. bdg. 35.00 (ISBN 0-313-23229-6, TUV/). Greenwood.
Vice-Presidential Power: Advice & Influence in the White House. Paul C. Light. LC 83-48050. 288p. 1983. text ed. 32.50x (ISBN 0-8018-3058-3). Johns Hopkins.
Vice-Presidents & Their Wives. George E. Ross & Barbara Novack. 1975. pap. 4.95 (ISBN 0-89036-052-9). Hawkes Pub Inc.
Vice-Presidents of the United States. John D. Feerick & Amalie P. Feerick. (First Books). (Illus.). (gr. 4-6). 1977. PLB 10.40 s&l (ISBN 0-531-02907-7). Watts.
Vice-Royalty & New Spain & Early Independent Mexico: A Guide to Original Manuscripts in the Collections of the Rosenbach Museum & Library. Ed. by David M. Szewczyk. LC 81-180741. 1981. 17.50 (Dist. by U Pr of Va). Rosenbach Mus & Lib.
Vice-Royalty of New Spain & Early Independent Mexico: A Guide to Original Manuscripts in the Collections of the Rosenbach Museum & Library. Compiled by David M. Szewczyk. 139p. 1980. 20.00x (ISBN 0-939084-00-7, Pub. by Rosenbach Mus & Lib). U Pr of Va.
Vice Versa. F. Anstey. LC 85-42968. (Puffin Classics Ser.). 302p. (gr. 6 up). 1985. pap. 2.25 (ISBN 0-14-035067-5, Puffin). Penguin.
Vicencio Caducho & Seventeenth Century Castilian Painting. Mary C. Volk. (Outstanding Dissertations in the Fine Arts Ser.). 1977. lib. bdg. 76.00 (ISBN 0-8240-2734-5). Garland Pub.
Vicente Aleixandre. Kessel Schwartz. LC 79-79209. (World Authors Ser.). 1970. lib. bdg. 17.95 (ISBN 0-8057-2024-3); pap. text ed. 4.95x (ISBN 0-8290-2047-0). Irvington.
Vicente Aleixandre: A Critical Appraisal. Ed. by Santiago Daydi-Tolson. LC 81-65036. (Studies in Literary Analysis). 330p. 1981. lib. bdg. 25.00x (ISBN 0-916950-21-2); pap. text ed. 16.00x (ISBN 0-916950-20-4). Biling Rev-Pr.
Vicente Blasco Ibanez: An Annotated Bibliography. Paul Smith. (Research Bibliography & Checklists Ser.: No. 14). 124p. (Orig.). 1976. pap. 11.95 (ISBN 0-7293-0015-3, Pub. by Grant & Cutler). Longwood Pub Group.
Vicente Espinel & Marcos de Obregon: A Life & Its Literary Representation. George Haley. LC 59-12056. (Brown University Studies). Repr. of 1959 ed. 67.50 (2027506). Bks Demand UMI.
Vicente Folch, Governor in Spanish Florida, Seventeen Eighty-Seven to Eighteen Eleven. David H. White. LC 80-5792. 120p. (Orig.). 1981. pap. text ed. 9.75 (ISBN 0-8191-1599-1). U Pr of Amer.
Vicente Silva: The Terror of Las Vegas. Carlos De Baca. (Wild & Woolly West Ser: No. 35). (Illus.). 1978. 8.00 (ISBN 0-910584-50-8); pap. 2.00 (ISBN 0-910584-93-1). Filter.
Viceregency of Antonio Maria Bucareli in New Spain, 1771-1779. Bernard E. Bobb. (Texas Pan American Ser.). (Illus.). 325p. 1962. 17.50x (ISBN 0-292-73425-5). U of Tex Pr.
Viceroy of Ouidah. Bruce Chatwin. LC 80-17896. 155p. 1980. 11.95 (ISBN 0-671-41253-1). Summit Bks.
Viceroy of Ouidah. Bruce Chatwin. pap. 5.15 (ISBN 0-671-41254-X). Summit Bks.
Viceroy of Ouidah. Bruce Chatwin. 1988. pap. 6.95 (ISBN 0-14-011290-1). Penguin.
Viceroys & Governors-General of India, 1757-1947. Clive B. Mersey. LC 70-160925. (Biography Index Reprint Ser.). Repr. of 1949 ed. 18.50 (ISBN 0-8369-8088-3). Ayer Co Pubs.
Vices & Virtues, Pt. I. Ed. by F. Holthausen. (EETS OS Ser.: Vol. 89). pap. 17.00 (ISBN 0-8115-3364-6). Kraus Repr.
Vices & Virtues, Pt. 2. Ed. by F. Holthausen. (EETS OS Ser.: Vol. 159). pap. 15.00 (ISBN 0-8115-3373-5). Kraus Repr.
Vichy France & the Jews. Michael R. Marrus & Robert O. Paxton. LC 82-16869. 432p. (Orig.). 1983. pap. 12.95 (ISBN 0-8052-0741-4). Schocken.
Vichy France & the Resistance: Ideology & Culture. Ed. by H. R. Kedward & Roger Austin. LC 85-6095. 304p. 1985. 27.50x (ISBN 0-389-20576-1). B&N Imports.
Vichy France: Old Guard & New Order, 1940-1944. Robert O. Paxton. LC 81-15221. (Morningside Book). 424p. 1982. 35.00x (ISBN 0-231-05426-2); pap. 13.00x (ISBN 0-231-05427-0). Columbia U Pr.
Vichy: Political Dilemma. Paul Farmer. 1977. Repr. of 1955 ed. lib. bdg. 29.00x (ISBN 0-374-92700-6, Octagon). Hippocrene Bks.
Vicia Faba: Agronomy Physiology & Breeding. Ed. by P. D. Hebblethwaite et al. LC 84-4181. (World Crops: Production, Utilization & Description Ser.). 380p. 1984. 53.50 (ISBN 90-247-2964-5, Pub. by Martinus Nijhoff Netherlands). Kluwer Academic.
Vicia Faba: Feeding Value, Processing & Viruses. Ed. by D. A. Bond. (World Crops: Production, Utilization, & Description Ser.: Vol. 3). x, 424p. 1980. lib. bdg. 50.00 (ISBN 9-0247-2362-0, Pub. by Martinus Nijhoff Netherlands). Kluwer Academic.
Vicious Circle. Imogen Howe. (Twilight Ser.: No. 13). (gr. 5-9). 1983. pap. 1.95 (ISBN 0-440-99318-0, LFL). Dell.
Vicious Circle Phenomenon: Our Battle for Self-Control - How to Win the War. Phyllis D. Brister & David M. Brister. (Illus.). 304p. 1987. 19.95 (ISBN 0-939977-69-9). Diadem Pub.
Vicious Circles. Maurice Blanchot. Tr. by Paul Auster from Fr. LC 84-8437. Orig. Title: Le Resassement Eternel. 80p. (Orig.). 1985. 13.95 (ISBN 0-930794-98-2); pap. 7.95 (ISBN 0-930794-97-4). Station Hill Pr.
Vicissitudes of Evangeline. Elinor Glyn. (Barbara Cartland's Library of Love: No. 8). 182p. 12.95 (ISBN 0-7156-1385-5, Pub. by Duckworth London). Longwood Pub Group.
Vicitrakarnika-Vadanoddhrta: A Collection of Buddhistic Legends. Ed. by Hans Jorgensen. LC 78-70134. Repr. of 1931 ed. 34.50 (ISBN 0-404-17404-3). AMS Pr.
Vickers Papers. Open Systems. 1984. pap. text ed. 16.50 (ISBN 0-06-318270-X). Har-Row.
Vicki. Marianne Dengler. 135p. (gr. 7 up). 1980. pap. 1.95 (ISBN 0-590-31324-X). Scholastic Inc.
Vicki. Joyce Milton & Ann L. Bardach. 352p. 1986. 16.95 (ISBN 0-312-83923-5, Pub. by Marek). St Martin.
Vicki. Joyce Milton & Ann L. Bardach. 1986. pap. 2.95 (ISBN 0-312-90829-6). St Martin.
Vicki Audette's Bargain Hunter's Guide to the Twin Cities. Vicki Audette. 197p. (Orig.). 1984. pap. 6.95 (ISBN 0-931674-06-9). Waldman Hse Pr.
Vicki Lansky's Kid's Cooking. Vicki Lansky. (Illus.). (gr. k-9). 1988. pap. 4.95. Scholastic Inc.
Vicki Lansky's Practical Parenting Tips. rev. ed. Vicki Lansky. Ed. by Kathryn Ring. LC 80-18646. (Illus.). 168p. 1982. pap. 6.95 (ISBN 0-671-54487-X). Meadowbrook.
Vicki Lansky's Sing Along as You Ride Along Travel Songs. Vicki Lansky. (ps-1). 1988. 5.95 (ISBN 0-590-63233-7). Scholastic Inc.
Vicksburg. John T. Foster. 1981. pap. 2.95 (ISBN 0-89083-789-9). Zebra.
Vicksburg Battlefield Monuments: A Photographic Record. Harold Young et al. LC 84-7386. (Illus.). 88p. 1984. pap. 10.95 (ISBN 0-87805-214-3). U Pr of Miss.
Vicksburg Campaign, Vol. I. Edwin C. Bearss. 37.50. Pr of Morningside.
Vicksburg Campaign, Vol. II. Edwin C. Bearss. 1986. 37.50 (ISBN 0-89029-313-9). Pr of Morningside.
Vicksburg Campaign, Vol. III. Edwin C. Bearss. 1986. 37.50 (ISBN 0-89029-516-6). Pr of Morningside.
Vicksburg: Southern City Under Siege. William L. Foster. Ed. by Kenneth T. Urquhart. LC 80-84685. (Illus.). xxvi, 82p. 1980. 15.95x (ISBN 0-917860-02-0). Historic New Orleans.
Vicksburg: Southern City Under Siege. William L. Foster. Ed. by Kenneth T. Urquhart. LC 80-84685. (Illus.). xxv, 82p. 1982. pap. text ed. 7.95 (ISBN 0-917860-12-8). Historic New Orleans.
Vicky. Catherine Storr. 160p. (gr. 6-9). 1981. 12.95 (ISBN 0-571-11762-7). Faber & Faber.
Vicky Lansky's Kids Cooking. Vicky Lansky. (Illus.). 48p. (gr. 4-6). 1987. spiral bnd. 4.95 (ISBN 0-590-40624-8). Scholastic Inc.
Vico. Peter Burke. (Past Masters Ser.). 128p. 1985. 13.95x (ISBN 0-19-287619-8); pap. 4.95 (ISBN 0-19-287618-X). Oxford U Pr.
Vico. Robert Flint. Ed. & intro. by J. P. Mayer. LC 78-67355. (European Political Thought Ser.). 1979. Repr. of 1901 ed. lib. bdg. 16.00x (ISBN 0-405-11697-7). Ayer Co Pubs.
Vico & Joyce. Ed. by Donald P. Verene. LC 86-23106. 256p. 1987. 49.50 (ISBN 0-88706-500-7); pap. 16.95 (ISBN 0-88706-501-5). State U NY Pr.
Vico & Providence. Maeve Albano. Ed. by Donald P. Verene. (Emory Vico Studies: Vol. 1). 198p. (Orig.). 1986. text ed. 37.50 (ISBN 0-8204-0331-8). P Lang Pubs.
Vico in the Tradition of Rhetoric. Michael Mooney. LC 84-42569. 336p. 1985. text ed. 29.00x (ISBN 0-691-05431-2). Princeton U Pr.
Vico: Le Droit Naturel, Expression de la Nature Commune des Nations see Cahiers de l'Institut de Science Economique Appliquee.
Vico: Selected Writings. Ed. & tr. by Leon Pompa. LC 81-12215. 280p. 1982. 39.50 (ISBN 0-521-23514-6); pap. 16.95 (ISBN 0-521-28014-1). Cambridge U Pr.
Vicomte de Bragelonne see Oeuvres Illustrees.
Vicomte de Bragelonne or Ten Years Later, 5 vols. Alexandre Dumas. 1981. Set. lib. bdg. 125.00 (ISBN 0-8495-1129-1). Arden Lib.
Vico's Science of Imagination. Donald P. Verene. LC 80-69828. 248p. 1981. 29.95x (ISBN 0-8014-1391-5). Cornell U Pr.
Victim. Saul Bellow. 264p. 1988. pap. 6.95 (ISBN 0-14-002493-X). Penguin.
Victim Aftershock: How to Get Results from the Criminal Justice System. James E. Morris. 256p. 1983. 13.95 (ISBN 0-531-09891-5). Watts.
Victim for Hire. Pablo Morales. 1979. pap. 1.50 (ISBN 0-8439-0625-1, Leisure Bks). Leisure NY.
Victim in International Perspective. Ed. by Hans Joachim Schneider. LC 82-1436. x, 513p. 1982. 97.25 (ISBN 3-11-007510-5). De Gruyter.
Victim Is Always the Same. I. S. Cooper. (Illus.). 160p. 1976. pap. 2.95 (ISBN 0-393-00817-7, Norton Lib). Norton.
Victim Must Be Found: A Benny Cooperman Mystery. Howard Engel. 288p. 1988. 16.95 (ISBN 0-312-02315-4). St Martin.
Victim No Longer. Dan Day. (Outreach Ser.). 30p. 1985. pap. 1.25 (ISBN 0-8163-0603-6). Pacific Pr Pub Assn.
Victim of Circumstance. Jannis E. MacVeigh. 32p. 1987. 6.50 (ISBN 0-8062-3148-3). Carlton.
Victim of Circumstances, & Other Stories. facsimile ed. George R. Gissing. LC 73-169551. (Short Story Index Reprint Ser.). Repr. of 1927 ed. 17.00 (ISBN 0-8369-4013-X). Ayer Co Pubs.
Victim of Love. Dyan Sheldon. (Contemporary American Fiction Ser.). 224p. 1984. pap. 5.95 (ISBN 0-14-007276-4). Penguin.
Victim of Rape: Institutional Reactions. Lynda L. Holmstrom & Ann W. Burgess. LC 83-678. 320p. 1983. pap. 14.95 (ISBN 0-87855-932-9). Transaction Bks.

Victorian Album: Julia Margaret Cameron & Her Circle. Ed. by Graham Ovenden. LC 75-18728. (Photography Ser.). (Illus.). 119p. 1975. lib. bdg. 45.00 (ISBN 0-306-70749-7). Da Capo.

Victorian Alphabets, Monograms & Names for Needle Workers. Godey's Lady's Book Staff & Peterson's Magazine Staff. LC 74-79939. 128p. 1974. pap. 4.50 (ISBN 0-486-23072-4). Dover.

Victorian America. Ed. by Daniel W. Howe. LC 76-20155. 1976. 23.95x (ISBN 0-8122-7713-9); pap. 12.95x (ISBN 0-8122-1090-5). U of Pa Pr.

Victorian American: Henry Wadsworth Longfellow. Herbert S. Gorman. 1979. Repr. of 1926 ed. lib. bdg. 35.00 (ISBN 0-8492-4933-3). R West.

Victorian American Wood Engraving. William J. Linton. LC 75-22525. (Athenaeum Library of 19th Century America). (Illus.). 1976. Repr. of 1882 ed. text ed. 25.00 (ISBN 0-89257-010-5). Am Life Foun.

Victorian & Edwardian Country House Life. Anthony J. Lambert. LC 80-26606. (Illus.). 120p. 1981. 29.50 (ISBN 0-8419-0684-X). Holmes & Meier.

Victorian & Edwardian Decor: From the Gothic Revival to Art Nouvean. Jeremy Cooper. (Illus.). 256p. 1987. 60.00 (ISBN 0-89659-768-7). Abbeville Pr.

Victorian & Edwardian Fashion: A Photographic Survey. Alison Gernsheim. (Illus.). 240p. 1982. pap. 6.00 (ISBN 0-486-24205-6). Dover.

Victorian & Edwardian London. John Betjeman. 1969. pap. 15.95 (ISBN 0-7134-2185-1, Pub. by Batsford England). David & Charles.

Victorian & Edwardian Theatres: An Architectural & Social Survey. Victor Glasstone. (Illus.). 192p. 1975. 21.00x (ISBN 0-674-93591-8). Harvard U Pr.

Victorian & Modern Poetics. Carol T. Christ. LC 83-18200. x, 178p. 1986. lib. bdg. 16.00x (ISBN 0-226-10458-3); pap. 7.95x (ISBN 0-226-10459-1). U of Chicago Pr.

Victorian Anthology, 1837 to 1895: Selections Illustrating the Editor's Critical Review of British Poetry in the Reign of Victoria. Edmund C. Stedman. 1973. lib. bdg. 39.50 (ISBN 0-8414-7955-0). Folcroft.

Victorian Anthology, 1837-1895, 2 Vols. Ed. by Edmund C. Stedman. LC 4-13936. 1969. Repr. of 1895 ed. Set. 29.00x. Scholarly.

Victorian Anthology, 1837-1895: Selections Illustrating the Editor's Critical Review of British Poetry in the Reign of Victoria. Ed. by Edmund C. Stedman. 1977. Repr. of 1896 ed. lib. bdg. 30.00 (ISBN 0-8495-4826-8). Arden Lib.

Victorian Anthropology. George W. Stocking, Jr. (Illus.). 429p. 1987. 27.50 (ISBN 0-317-57125-7). Free Pr.

Victorian Architectural Competitions: An Index to British & Irish Architectural Competitions in Builder 1843-1900. Roger H. Harper. 1983. 80.00X (ISBN 0-317-52176-4, Pub. by Pinhorns UK). State Mutual Bk.

Victorian Architectural Competitions: An Index to British & Irish Architectural Competitions in "The Builder", 1843-1900. Ed. by Roger H. Harper. 448p. 1983. 43.00 (ISBN 0-7201-1685-6). Mansell.

Victorian Architecture. Roger Dixon & Stefan Muthesius. (World of Art Ser.). (Illus.). 208p. 1985. text ed. 19.95 (ISBN 0-500-18163-2); pap. text ed. 9.95 (ISBN 0-500-20160-9). Thames Hudson.

Victorian Architecture: Four Studies in Evaluation. John Summerson. LC 74-89565. (Hampton Lectures in America Ser.: No. 19). 131p. 1969. 33.00x (ISBN 0-231-03261-7). Columbia U Pr.

Victorian Architecture: Four Studies in Evaluation see Victorian Architecture in England: Four Studies in Evaluation.

Victorian Architecture in Britain. Julian Orbach. (Blue Guides Ser.). 1988. pap. 19.95 (ISBN 0-393-30070-6). Norton.

Victorian Architecture in England: Four Studies in Evaluation. John Summerson. Orig. Title: Victorian Architecture: Four Studies in Evaluation. (Illus.). 1971. pap. 3.95x (ISBN 0-393-00577-1, Norton Lib). Norton.

Victorian Architecture: Monographs Published 1976-1987. Mary Vance. (Architecture Ser.: A 1938). 10p. 1987. 3.00 (ISBN 1-55590-548-X). Vance Biblios.

Victorian Arkansans: How They Lived, Played & Worked. Louise Bloom et al. Ed. by Mala Daggett. LC 81-67251. (Illus.). 208p. 1981. notebook 17.00 (ISBN 0-686-30547-7). AR Commemorative.

Victorian Army at Home: The Recruitment & Terms & Conditions of the British Regular, 1859-1899. Alan Skelley. (Illus.). 1977. lib. bdg. 32.95x (ISBN 0-7735-0304-8). McGill-Queens U Pr.

Victorian Art of Fiction: Essays on the Novel in British Periodicals, 1830-1900, 3 vols. John C. Olmsted. LC 77-83397. (Reference Library of Humanities). 677p. 1979. Vol. 1, 1830-1850. lib. bdg. 79.00 (ISBN 0-8240-9845-5); Vol. 2, 1851-1869. lib. bdg. 79.00 (ISBN 0-8240-9771-8); Vol. 3, 1870-1900. lib. bdg. 79.00 (ISBN 0-8240-9772-6). Garland Pub.

Victorian Art World in Photographs. Jeremy Maas. LC 83-40565. (Illus.). 224p. 1984. 35.00x (ISBN 0-87663-429-3). Universe.

Victorian Artists & the City: A Collection of Critical Essays. Ed. by Ira B. Nadel & F. S. Schwarzbach. LC 79-176. (Illus.). 1980. 64.00 (ISBN 0-08-023381-3). Pergamon.

Victorian at Bay. facs. ed. Anne K. Tuell. LC 67-22123. (Essay Index Reprint Ser). 1932. 13.00 (ISBN 0-8369-0952-6). Ayer Co Pubs.

Victorian Authority: The Daily Press in Late Nineteenth-Century Canada. Paul Rutherford. 316p. 1982. 37.50x (ISBN 0-8020-5588-5); pap. 13.95c (ISBN 0-8020-6459-0). U of Toronto Pr.

Victorian Autobiography: The Tradition of Self-Interpretation. Linda H. Peterson. LC 85-17964. 240p. 1986. 25.00x (ISBN 0-300-03563-2). Yale U Pr.

Victorian Ballet Girl: The Tragic Story of Clara Webster. Ivor Guest. LC 80-16216. (Series in Dance). 1980. Repr. of 1958 ed. 25.00 (ISBN 0-306-76043-6). Da Capo.

Victorian Best-Seller. Margaret Mare & Alicia C. Percival. LC 70-103202. 1970. Repr. of 1947 ed. 24.50x (ISBN 0-8046-0839-3, Pub by Kennikat). Assoc Faculty Pr.

Victorian Bibliomania: The Illuminated Book in 19th-Century Britain. Alice Beckwith. Ed. by Janet Phillips. LC 86-62734. (Illus.). 83p. (Orig.). 1987. pap. 18.00 (ISBN 0-911517-45-6). Mus of Art RI.

Victorian Biography: A Collection of Essays from the Period. Ed. by Ira B. Nadel. (Victorian Muse Ser.). 325p. 1986. lib. bdg. 40.00 (ISBN 0-8240-8629-5). Garland Pub.

Victorian Birthday Book. Florence Ward. 1987. 9.95 (ISBN 0-906671-16-7). Viking.

Victorian Bloomsbury: The Early Literary History of the Bloomsbury Group, Vol. 1. S. P. Rosenbaum. 298p. 1987. 24.95 (ISBN 0-312-84051-9). St Martin.

Victorian Book Illustration. Geoffrey Wakeman. LC 72-14042. (Illus.). 182p. 1973. 46.00x (ISBN 0-8103-2008-8). Gale.

Victorian Bookbindings: A Pictorial Survey. rev. ed. Sue Allen. LC 76-7420. 1976. 3 color fiches incl. 28.00 (ISBN 0-226-68787-2, Chicago Visual Lib). U of Chicago Pr.

Victorian Building Regulations: Summary Tables of English Building Acts & By-Laws, 1840-1914. Roger H. Harper. LC 84-26116. 137p. 1985. 33.00x (ISBN 0-7201-1751-8). Mansell.

Victorian Cabinet Maker: The Memoirs of James Hopkinson, 1819-1894. James Hopkinson. Ed. by Jocelyne B. Goodman. LC 69-17113. (Illus.). 1969. 25.00x (ISBN 0-678-06526-8). Kelley.

Victorian Cabinet-Maker's Assistant. Blackie & Son Staff. (Illus.). 1970. pap. 10.00 (ISBN 0-486-22353-1). Dover.

Victorian Cakes. Caroline B. King. Date not set. write for info. S&S.

Victorian Cakes. Caroline B. King. 240p. 1986. pap. 9.95 (ISBN 0-943186-26-9). Aris Bks Harris.

Victorian Canvas Work: Berlin Wool Work. Molly G. Procter. (Illus.). 160p. 1986. pap. 16.95 (ISBN 0-7134-5425-3, Pub. by Batsford England). David & Charles.

Victorian Cathedral Music in Theory & Practice. William J. Gatens. 300p. 1986. 42.50 (ISBN 0-521-26808-7). Cambridge U Pr.

Victorian Celebration of Death: The Architecture & Planning of the 19th-Century Necropolis. James S. Curl. LC 70-184048. 222p. 1972. 40.00x (ISBN 0-8103-2000-2). Gale.

Victorian Chaise Lounge. Marghanita Laski. 119p. 1984. pap. 3.95 (ISBN 0-89733-097-8). Academy Chi Pubs.

Victorian Childhood. Susan P. Casteras. (Illus.). 64p. 1987. pap. 14.95 (ISBN 0-8109-2340-8). Abrams.

Victorian Childhood: Themes & Variations. Thomas E. Jordan. LC 86-30184. (Illus.). 320p. 1987. 49.50x (ISBN 0-88706-544-9); pap. 16.95 (ISBN 0-88706-545-7). State U NY Pr.

Victorian Children. Eleanor Allen. (Junior Reference Ser.). (Illus.). 64p. (gr. 6 up). 1979. 13.95 (ISBN 0-7136-1324-6). Dufour.

Victorian Children Postcards. Shirley Buchholz. (Orig.). 1985. pap. 3.95 (ISBN 0-87588-261-7, 3112). Hobby Hse.

Victorian Christian Socialists. Edward Norman. 210p. 1987. 34.50 (ISBN 0-521-32515-3). Cambridge U Pr.

Victorian Christmas Crafts. Barbara Bruno. (Illus.). 128p. 1986. pap. 14.95 (ISBN 0-13-941758-3). P-H.

Victorian Christmas: 1876. Elspeth. 1974. pap. 1.50 (ISBN 0-87588-106-8, 2323). Hobby Hse.

Victorian Church Art. John Physick. (Illus.). 212p. (Orig.). 1984. pap. 12.95 (ISBN 0-901486-36-1, Pub. by Victoria & Albert Mus UK). Faber & Faber.

Victorian Church Building & Restoration in Suffolk. Anne Riches. (Illus.). 1982. 27.00 (ISBN 0-85115-176-0, Pub. by Boydell & Brewer). Longwood Pub Group.

Victorian City: Images & Realities, 2 vols. Ed. by H. J. Dyos & Michael Wolff. (Illus.). 1001p. 1973. Set. 110.00 (ISBN 0-7100-7384-4); Vol. 1. 60.00 (ISBN 0-7100-7374-7); Vol. 2. 60.00 (ISBN 0-7100-7383-6). Routledge Chapman & Hall.

Victorian City-Images & Realities, Vol. 1: Past & Present & Numbers of People. H. J. Dyos & Michael Wolff. (Illus.). 1978. pap. 14.95 (ISBN 0-7100-8458-7). Routledge Chapman & Hall.

Victorian City-Images & Realities, Vol. 2: Shapes on the Ground & a Change of Accent. Ed. by H. J. Dyos & Michael Wolff. (Illus.). 1978. pap. 14.95 (ISBN 0-7100-8812-4). Routledge Chapman & Hall.

Victorian Classics of San Francisco 1887. Ed. by Wayne Bonnett. (Illus.). 120p. 1987. 32.00 (ISBN 0-915269-05-8). Windgate Pr.

Victorian Clergy. Alan Haig. 380p. 1984. 33.00 (ISBN 0-7099-1230-7, Pub. by Croom Helm Ltd). Routledge Chapman & Hall.

Victorian Clerks. Gregory L. Anderson. (Illus.). 1976. lib. bdg. 27.50x (ISBN 0-678-06794-5). Kelley.

Victorian Colonial Wars. Philip Haythornthwaite. (Uniforms Illustrated Ser.: No. 21). (Illus.). 72p. (Orig.). 1988. pap. 9.95 (ISBN 0-85368-869-9, Pub. by Arms & Armour). Sterling.

Victorian Color Picture Books. Ed. by Jonathan Cott. (Illus.). 184p. 1983. 50.00x (ISBN 0-87754-398-4). Chelsea Hse.

Victorian Color Vignettes & Illustrations for Artists & Craftsmen: 344 Antique Chromolithographs. Carol B. Grafton. (Illus.). 48p. (Orig.). 1983. pap. 4.50 (ISBN 0-486-24477-6). Dover.

Victorian Colored Glass: Patterns & Prices, 1986-87, Vol. 1. rev. ed. William Heacock. (Illus.). 136p. (Orig.). 1987. pap. 9.95 (ISBN 0-915410-07-9). Antique Pubns.

Victorian Colored Glass: Patterns & Prices, 1986-87, Vol. 2. rev. ed. William Heacock. (Illus.). 120p. (Orig.). 1987. pap. 9.95 (ISBN 0-915410-13-3). Antique Pubns.

Victorian Conscience. Clarence R. Decker. LC 77-8021. 1977. Repr. of 1952 ed. lib. bdg. 35.00x (ISBN 0-8371-9684-1, DEVC). Greenwood.

Victorian Constitution. G. H. Le May. 1979. 27.50x (ISBN 0-312-84145-0). St Martin.

Victorian Conventions. John R. Reed. LC 73-92908. xiii, 561p. 1975. 25.00x (ISBN 0-8214-0147-5). Ohio U Pr.

Victorian Conventions. John R. Reed. LC 73-92908. xiii, 561p. 1985. pap. text ed. 15.95x (ISBN 0-8214-0828-3). Ohio U Pr.

Victorian Cookery Book. Ed. by Gordon Grimley. (Illus.). 132p. 1974. 9.50 (ISBN 0-200-72047-3). Transatl Arts.

Victorian Cottage Residences. Andrew J. Downing. Ed. by George E. Harney. (Illus.). 352p. 1981. pap. 6.95 (ISBN 0-486-24078-9). Dover.

Victorian Cottage Residences. Andrew J. Downing. 1982. 14.50 (ISBN 0-8446-5883-9). Peter Smith.

Victorian Country House. Mark Girouard. LC 79-64077. 1979. 50.00x (ISBN 0-300-02390-1). Yale U Pr.

Victorian Country House. rev. & enl. ed. Mark Girouard. LC 79-64077. (Illus.). 448p. 1985. pap. 17.95 (ISBN 0-300-03472-5, Y-547). Yale U Pr.

Victorian Country Parsons. Brenda Colloms. LC 77-82027. (Illus.). 284p. 1978. 23.95 (ISBN 0-8032-0981-9). U of Nebr Pr.

Victorian Countryside, 2 vols. Ed. by G. E. Mingay. (Illus.). 1986. Set. pap. 45.00 (88888). Vol. I, 380 pg (ISBN 0-7102-0884-7). Vol. II, 348 pg (ISBN 0-7102-0886-3). Routledge Chapman & Hall.

Victorian Critic & the Idea of History: Carlyle, Arnold, Pater. Peter Dale. 1977. 25.00x (ISBN 0-674-93581-0). Harvard U Pr.

Victorian Criticism of American Writers: A Study of British Criticism of American Writers in the Leading British Periodicals of the Victorian Period, 1824-1900. Arnella K. Turner. LC 87-807. (Literary Guides Ser.: No. 6). 224p. Date not set. lib. bdg. 24.95x (ISBN 0-89370-816-X); pap. 14.95x (ISBN 0-89370-916-6). Borgo Pr.

Victorian Criticism of the Novel. Ed. by Edwin M. Eigner & George J. Worth. (Cambridge English Prose Texts Ser.). 286p. 1985. o. p. 47.50 (ISBN 0-521-25515-5); pap. 15.95 (ISBN 0-521-27520-2). Cambridge U Pr.

Victorian Critics of Democracy. Benjamin E. Lippincott. 1964. lib. bdg. 20.00x (ISBN 0-374-95035-0, Octagon). Hippocrene Bks.

Victorian Crochet. Weldon & Company. LC 72-81611. Orig. Title: Weldon's Practical Crochet. (Illus.). 224p. 1974. pap. 8.95 (ISBN 0-486-22890-8). Dover.

Victorian Crochet. Weldon & Company. (Illus.). 16.00 (ISBN 0-8446-5096-X). Peter Smith.

Victorian Culture in America, 1865-1914. Ed. by H. Wayne Morgan. LC 72-89722. (Primary Sources in American History Ser.). 1973. pap. text ed. 6.95x (ISBN 0-88295-787-2). Harlan Davidson.

Victorian Delights: Reflections of Taste in the Nineteenth Century. John Hadfield. (Illus.). 128p. 1987. 19.95 (ISBN 0-941533-02-6). New Amsterdam Bks.

Victorian Devotional Poetry: The Tractarian Mode. G. B. Tennyson. LC 80-14416. 1980. text ed. 20.00x (ISBN 0-674-93586-1). Harvard U Pr.

Victorian Display Alphabets: One Hundred Complete Fonts. Daniel X. Solo. (Pictorial Archive Ser.). (Illus.). 112p. (Orig.). 1976. pap. 4.50 (ISBN 0-486-23302-2). Dover.

Victorian Divorce. Allen Horstman. LC 85-14491. 208p. 1985. 27.50 (ISBN 0-312-84156-6). St Martin.

Victorian Doll Family. rev. ed. Sandy Williams. (Illus.). 32p. 1985. pap. 3.95 (ISBN 0-87588-241-2, 2327). Hobby Hse.

Victorian Dollhouse. Illus. by Sheilah Beckett. (Illus.). (gr. k-7). 1982. pap. 6.95 (ISBN 0-394-85280-X). Random.

Victorian Domestic Architectural Plans & Details: Seven Hundred Thirty-Four Scale Drawings of Doorways, Windows, Staircases, Moldings, Cornices & Other Elements. William T. Comstock. (Illus.). 96p. 1987. pap. 5.95 (ISBN 0-486-25442-9). Dover.

Victorian Domesticity: Families in the Life & Art of Louisa May Alcott. Charles Strickland. LC 84-8654. xviii, 200p. 1985. 24.50 (ISBN 0-8173-0237-9). U of Ala Pr.

Victorian Dress in Photographs. Madeleine Ginsburg. (Illus.). 192p. 1983. 47.50 (ISBN 0-8419-0838-9). Holmes & Meier.

Victorian Economy. Francois Crouzet. Tr. by A. S. Forster. LC 82-1292. 400p. 1982. 45.00x (ISBN 0-231-05542-0); pap. 20.00x (ISBN 0-231-05543-9). Columbia U Pr.

Victorian Education & the Ideal of Womanhood. Joan N. Burstyn. (Illus.). 185p. 1980. 28.50x (ISBN 0-389-20103-0, 06877). B&N Imports.

Victorian Education & the Ideal of Womanhood. Joan N. Burstyn. 185p. 1984. pap. text ed. 12.00 (ISBN 0-8135-1031-7). Rutgers U Pr.

Victorian England: Aspects of English & Imperial History 1837-1901. L. C. Seaman. 500p. 1973. pap. 15.95x (ISBN 0-416-77550-0, NO. 2434). Routledge Chapman & Hall.

Victorian England: Portrait of an Age. 2nd ed. George M. Young. 1964. pap. 9.95 (ISBN 0-19-500259-8). Oxford U Pr.

Victorian Engravings. Hilary Beck. (Illus.). 188p. (Orig.). 1984. pap. 9.95 (ISBN 0-901486-64-7, Pub. by Victoria & Albert Mus UK). Faber & Faber.

Victorian Era: With Seventy-Five Illustrations & Two Maps. P. Anderson Graham. (Illus.). 1973. Repr. of 1897 ed. 25.00 (ISBN 0-8274-0738-6). R West.

Victorian Eureka & Ferndale. Bob Von Normann. Ed. by George Castaldo. 32p. (Orig.). 1988. 5.95 (ISBN 0-915687-02-X). FVN Corp.

Victorian Experience: The Novelists. Ed. by Richard A. Levine. LC 75-15338. 273p. 1976. 18.95x (ISBN 0-8214-0190-4). Ohio U Pr.

Victorian Experience: The Novelists. Intro. by Richard A. Levine. LC 75-15338. 273p. 1983. pap. 10.95x (ISBN 0-8214-0747-3). Ohio U Pr.

Victorian Experience: The Poets. Intro. by Richard A. Levine. LC 81-4020. 202p. 1982. text ed. 21.95x (ISBN 0-8214-0447-4). Ohio U Pr.

Victorian Experience: The Poets. Intro. by Richard A. Levine. LC 81-4020. x, 202p. 1983. pap. 12.00x (ISBN 0-8214-0748-1). Ohio U Pr.

Victorian Experience: The Prose Writers. Intro. by Richard A. Levine. LC 81-22493. x, 239p. 1983. pap. 12.00x (ISBN 0-8214-0707-4). Ohio U Pr.

Victorian Exterior Decoration: How to Paint Your 19th Century American House. Roger W. Moss & Gail C. Winkler. LC 86-15014. 1987. 29.95 (ISBN 0-8050-0376-2). H Holt & Co.

Victorian Fairy Tale Book. Michael P. Hearn. LC 87-36039. (Illus.). 1988. 19.95 (ISBN 0-394-56594-0). Pantheon.

Victorian Fairy Tales: The Revolt of the Fairies & the Elves. Jack Zipes. 1987. pap. 25.00 (ISBN 0-416-42080-X). Routledge Chapman & Hall.

Victorian Family, 3 vols. M. Vivian Hughes. 1979. pap. text ed. 13.95 boxed set (ISBN 0-19-281280-7). Oxford U Pr.

Victorian Fancies. 190p. 1988. pap. 3.95 (ISBN 0-88184-379-2). Carroll & Graf.

Victorian Farms. Roy Brigden. 1987. 32.00 (ISBN 0-946284-66-0, Pub. by Crowood Pr). Longwood Pub Group.

Victorian Fashions & Costumes from Harper's Bazar: 1898-1967. Stella Blum. (Illus.). 320p. (Orig.). 1974. pap. 10.95 (ISBN 0-486-22990-4). Dover.

Victorian Fashions, Volume I: 1880-1890. Hazel Ulseth & Helen Shannon. 130p. 1988. pap. 14.95 (ISBN 0-87588-309-5). Hobby Hse.

Victorian Fiction: A Collection of Essays from the Period. Ira B. Nadel. Ed. by W. E. Fredeman & J. F. Stasny. (Victorian Muse Ser.). 375p. 1986. lib. bdg. 45.00 (ISBN 0-8240-8628-7). Garland Pub.

Victorian Fiction: A Guide to Research. Ed. by Lionel Stevenson. LC 64-21246. (Reviews of Research Ser.). 440p. 1980. Repr. of 1964 ed. 32.00 (ISBN 0-87352-258-3, Z46). Modern Lang.

Victorian Fiction: A Second Guide to Research. Ed. by George H. Ford. xxv, 401p. 1978. 27.50x (ISBN 0-87352-254-0, Z43); pap. 15.00 (ISBN 0-87352-255-9, Z44). Modern Lang.

Victorian Floral Illustrations: Three Hundred Forty-Four Wood Engravings of Exotic Flowers & Plants. Carol B. Grafton. (Pictorial Archive Ser.). 112p. 1985. pap. 4.95 (ISBN 0-486-24822-4). Dover.

Victorian Florida: America's Last Frontier. Floyd Rinhart & Marion Rinhart. (Illus.). 224p. 1986. 29.95 (ISBN 0-934601-02-X). Peachtree Pubs.

Victorian Forerunner: The Later Career of Thomas Hood. John Clubbe. LC 68-28520. Repr. of 1968 ed. 52.30 (ISBN 0-8357-9120-3, 2017893). Bks Demand UMI.

Victorian Frame of Mind, 1830-1870. Walter E. Houghton. 1963. pap. 12.95 (ISBN 0-300-00122-3, Y99). Yale U Pr.

Victorian Prose. Frederick W. Roe. LC 47-12149. pap. 160.00 (ISBN 0-317-28653-6, 2055090). Bks Demand UMI.
Victorian Prose: A Guide to Research. Ed. by David J. DeLaura. LC 73-80586. (Reviews of Research). xvi, 576p. 1973. 27.50x (ISBN 0-87352-250-8, Z41); pap. 15.00x (ISBN 0-87352-251-6, Z42). Modern Lang.
Victorian Prose & Poetry. Ed. by Lionel Trilling & Harold Bloom. (Illus.). 1973. pap. 15.95x (ISBN 0-19-501616-5). Oxford U Pr.
Victorian Prose Masters. William C. Brownell. 59.95 (ISBN 0-8490-1260-0). Gordon Pr.
Victorian Prose Masters. William C. Brownell. LC 79-86000. 1969. Repr. of 1901 ed. 21.50x (ISBN 0-8046-0548-3, Pub by Kennikat). Assoc Faculty Pr.
Victorian Prose Masters: Thackeray-Carlyle-George Eliot-Matthew Arnold-Ruskin-George Meredith. William C. Brownell. LC 72-108771. (BCL Ser. I). Repr. of 1901 ed. 21.00 (ISBN 0-404-01142-X). AMS Pr.
Victorian Prose Writers after 1867. Ed. by William B. Thesing. LC 87-336. (Dictionary of Literary Biography Ser.: Vol. 57). 596p. 1987. 95.00x (ISBN 0-8103-1735-4). Gale.
Victorian Prose Writers Before 1867. Ed. by William B. Thesing. (Dictionary of Literary Biography Ser.: Vol. 55). 379p. 1986. 95.00x (ISBN 0-8103-1733-8). Gale.
Victorian Publisher's Bindings. Douglas Ball. (Illus.). 214p. 1985. 38.50 (ISBN 0-916271-01-3). BkPr Ltd.
Victorian Publishers' Book-Bindings in Paper. Ruari McLean. LC 83-40019. (Illus.). 200p. 1983. 48.00x (ISBN 0-520-05102-5). U of Cal Pr.
Victorian Publishers' Book-Bindings in Paper. Ruari MacLean. 200p. 1983. 150.00x (ISBN 0-86092-065-8, Pub. by Gordon Fraser). State Mutual Bk.
Victorian Pubs. Mark Girouard. LC 83-51291. (Illus.). 232p. 1984. text ed. 36.00 (ISBN 0-300-03199-8); pap. 17.95 (ISBN 0-300-03201-3, Y-492). Yale U Pr.
Victorian Radicalism. Paul Adelman. LC 83-17545. 1984. 13.95 (ISBN 0-582-49197-5). Longman.
Victorian Rebel: The Life of William Morris. Lloyd W. Eshleman. LC 74-168557. xiv, 386p. 1971. Repr. of 1940 ed. lib. bdg. 27.50x (ISBN 0-374-92627-1, Octagon). Hippocrene Bks.
Victorian Revival in Interior Design. Jim Kemp. LC 85-2232. (Illus.). 176p. 1985. 24.95 (ISBN 0-671-53061-5). S&S.
Victorian Revival in Interior Design. Jim Kemp. 1988. 15.95 (ISBN 0-671-66180-9, Fireside). S&S.
Victorian Revival in Interior Design. Jim Kemp. 1987. 39.00x (ISBN 0-86287-374-6, Pub. by Harrap Ltd England). State Mutual Bk.
Victorian Revolution: Government & Society in Victoria's Britain. Ed. by Peter Stansky. LC 73-2740. 417p. 1973. pap. text ed. 8.95x (ISBN 0-531-06482-4). Wiener Pub Inc.
Victorian Scene. Neil King. (Drama Ser.). pap. 11.95 (ISBN 0-7175-1235-5). Dufour.
Victorian School Manager: A Study in the Management of Education, 1800-1902. Peter Gordon. 337p. 1974. 27.50x (ISBN 0-7130-0125-9, Pub. by Woburn Pr England). Biblio Dist.
Victorian Schools Eighteen Thirty-Seven to Nineteen Hundred. Lawrence Burchell. (Colonial Government Architecture Ser.). 1980. 10.00 (ISBN 0-522-84160-0, Pub. by Melbourne U Pr Australia). Intl Spec Bk.
Victorian Science & Religion: A Bibliography of Works on Ideas & Institutions with Emphasis on Evolution, Belief & Unbelief, Published from 1900 to 1975. Ed. by Sydney Eisen & Bernard V. Lightman. LC 82-24497. xix, 696p. 1984. 55.00 (ISBN 0-208-02010-1, Archon Bks). Shoe String.
Victorian Science & Victorian Values: Literary Perspectives. Ed. by James Paradis & Thomas Postlewait. LC 80-29513. 362p. 1981. pap. 72.00x (ISBN 0-89766-110-9). NY Acad Sci.
Victorian Science & Victorian Values: Literary Perspectives. Ed. by James Paradis & Thomas Postlewait. 375p. 1985. text ed. 32.00 (ISBN 0-8135-1106-2); pap. text ed. 14.00 (ISBN 0-8135-1107-0). Rutgers U Pr.
Victorian Science Fiction in the U. K. The Discourses of Knowledge & of Power. Darko Suvin. 460p. 1983. lib. bdg. 55.00 (ISBN 0-8161-8435-6, Hall Reference). G K Hall.
Victorian Scrutinies: Reviews of Poetry, 1830-1870. Ed. by Isobel Armstrong. 344p. 1972. text ed. 38.50 (ISBN 0-485-11131-4, Pub. by Athlone Pr UK). Humanities.
Victorian Sculpture. Benedict Read. LC 81-70483. (Studies in British Art). (Illus.). 416p. 1982. 70.00x (ISBN 0-300-02506-8). Yale U Pr.
Victorian Sculpture. Benedict Read. LC 83-70483. (Paul Mellon Centre for Studies in British Art). (Illus.). 416p. 1984. pap. 24.95x (ISBN 0-300-03177-7). Yale U Pr.
Victorian Seaside Cookbook. Anne E. Bishop & Doris Simpson. LC 83-61979. (Illus.). 154p. (Orig.). pap. 8.95 (ISBN 0-911020-09-8). NJ Hist Soc.
Victorian Sextet. William D. Comstock. 96p. 1987. cancelled (ISBN 0-8062-3126-2). Carlton.
Victorian Sheet Music Covers. Ronald Pearsall. LC 72-6422. (Illus.). 116p. 1972. 16.00x (ISBN 0-8103-2001-0). Gale.
Victorian Shipping, Business & Imperial Policy: Donald Currie, the Castle Line & Southern Africa. Andrew Porter. LC 86-15619. (Royal Historical Society Studies in History). 352p. 1986. 35.00 (ISBN 0-312-84442-5). St Martin.
Victorian Shooting Days: East Anglia 1810-1910. Derek Johnson. (Illus.). 112p. 1981. 16.95 (ISBN 0-85115-156-6, Pub. by Boydell & Brewer). Longwood Pub Group.
Victorian Short Stories: An Anthology. Intro. by Harold Orel. 320p. 1987. pap. 6.95 (ISBN 0-460-01591-5, Evman). Biblio Dist.
Victorian Short Story: Development & Triumph of a Literary Genre. Harold Orel. (Illus.). 224p. 1986. 29.95 (ISBN 0-521-25899-5). Cambridge U Pr.
Victorian Sidelights. A. M. Stirling. 288p. 1980. Repr. lib. bdg. 39.50 (ISBN 0-89984-408-1). Century Bookbindery.
Victorian Sidelights. A. M. Stirling. 288p. 1980. Repr. lib. bdg. 25.00 (ISBN 0-89987-763-X). Darby Bks.
Victorian Silver: Hollow & Flatware, Sterling & Plated. Larry G. Freeman. LC 67-12052. (Victorian Culture Ser.). (Photos). 1967. 25.00 (ISBN 0-87282-056-4). Am Life Foun.
Victorian Sisters. Ina Taylor. LC 86-28766. (Illus.). 218p. 1987. 17.95 (ISBN 0-917561-34-1). Adler & Adler.
Victorian Sketchbook. Ranulph Bye & Margaret B. Richie. (Illus.). 128p. 1980. 35.00 (ISBN 0-910702-04-7). Bentley PA.
Victorian Snapshots. Paul Martin. LC 72-9219. (Literature of Photography Ser.). Repr. of 1939 ed. 16.00 (ISBN 0-405-04926-9). Ayer Co Pubs.
Victorian Social Medicine: The Ideas & Methods of William Farr. John M. Eyler. 1979. 34.50x (ISBN 0-8018-2246-7). Johns Hopkins.
Victorian Songs. Ed. & illus. by Edmund H. Garrett. LC 78-116404. (Granger Index Reprint Ser.). (Illus.). 1895. 18.00 (ISBN 0-8369-6145-5). Ayer Co Pubs.
Victorian Splendor: Re-creating America's Nineteenth-Century Interiors. Allison K. Leopold. LC 85-30267. (Illus.). 272p. 1986. 29.95 (ISBN 0-941434-69-9); pap. 18.95 (ISBN 0-941434-83-4). Stewart Tabori & Chang.
Victorian Splendour: Australian Interior Decoration, 1837-1901. Suzanne Forge. (Illus.). 1981. 75.00x (ISBN 0-19-554299-1). Oxford U Pr.
Victorian Spot Illustrations, Alphabets & Ornaments from Porret's Type Catalog. Ed. by Carol B. Grafton. (Illus.). 96p. (gr. 5 up). 1982. pap. 4.95 (ISBN 0-486-24271-4). Dover.
Victorian Staffordshire Figure. Anthony Oliver. (Illus.). 192p. 1980. 75.00 (ISBN 0-434-54390-X, Pub. by W Heinemann Ltd). David & Charles.
Victorian Stained Glass Pattern Book: 96 Designs for Workable Projects. Ed Sibbett, Jr. 1979. pap. 3.95 (ISBN 0-486-23811-3). Dover.
Victorian Stencils for Design & Decoration. Edmund V. Gillon, Jr. LC 68-26054. (Illus., Orig.). 1968. pap. 4.50 (ISBN 0-486-21995-X). Dover.
Victorian Sticker Postcard Book. Elke Droscher. (Illus.). 64p. (Orig.). pap. 6.95 (ISBN 0-89471-384-1). Running Pr.
Victorian Studies in Scarlet. Richard D. Altick. LC 70-103962. 1970. 7.95 (ISBN 0-393-08605-4). Norton.
Victorian Suicide: Mad Crimes & Sad Histories. Barbara T. Gates. (Illus.). 192p. 1989. 18.50 (ISBN 0-691-09437-3). Princeton U Pr.
Victorian Taste: A Study of the Arts & Architecture from 1830 to 1870. John Steegman. 1971. pap. 5.95x (ISBN 0-262-69028-4). MIT Pr.
Victorian Taste: The Complete Catalogue of Paintings at the Royal Hollaway College. Jeannie Chapel. (Illus.). 144p. 1983. pap. 25.00 (ISBN 0-8390-0302-1). Abner Schram Ltd.
Victorian Temper: A Study in Literary Culture. new ed. Jerome H. Buckley. (Illus.). 282p. 1966. 27.50x (ISBN 0-7146-2052-1, F Cass Co). Biblio Dist.
Victorian Temper: A Study in Literary Culture. Jerome H. Buckley. LC 81-6142. (Illus.). 282p. 1981. pap. 14.95 (ISBN 0-521-28448-1). Cambridge U Pr.
Victorian Temper: A Study in Literary Culture. Jerome H. Buckley. LC 74-89967. (Illus.). 1969. 20.00x (ISBN 0-674-93680-9). Harvard U Pr.
Victorian Theatre: 1792-1914. 2nd ed. G. Rowell. LC 78-2900. (Illus.). 1979. pap. 16.95 (ISBN 0-521-29346-4). Cambridge U Pr.
Victorian Toronto, 1850-1900: Pattern & Process of Growth. Peter G. Goheen. LC 76-137736. (Research Papers: No. 127). 278p. 1970. pap. 12.00 (ISBN 0-89065-034-9). U Chicago Comm Geo.
Victorian Types, Victorian Shadows: Biblical Typology in Victorian Literature, Art & Thought. George P. Landow. 256p. 1980. 27.95x (ISBN 0-7100-0598-9). Routledge Chapman & Hall.
Victorian Values. James Walvin. LC 87-28474. (Illus.). 183p. 1988. 20.00x (ISBN 0-8203-1012-3); pap. 9.95 (ISBN 0-8203-1013-1). U of Ga Pr.
Victorian Values: Secularism & the Smaller Family. J. A. Banks. 288p. 1981. 26.95x (ISBN 0-7100-0807-4). Routledge Chapman & Hall.
Victorian Viceroy. E. Neill Raymond. 346p. 1984. 39.00x (ISBN 0-7212-0599-2, Pub. by Regency Pr). State Mutual Bk.
Victorian Villainies. Graham Greene & Hugh Greene. 1985. 18.95 (ISBN 0-670-80046-5). Viking.
Victorian Villainies: The Great Tontine, the Rome Express, in the Fog, the Beetle. Graham Greene & Hugh Greene. 720p. 1986. pap. 7.95 (ISBN 0-14-006850-3). Penguin.
Victorian Visitors. Alfons L. Korn. 1958. text ed. 14.95x (ISBN 0-87022-421-2). UH Pr.
Victorian Voices. Anthony Thwaite. 1980. pap. 9.95 (ISBN 0-19-211937-0). Oxford U Pr.
Victorian Wallflowers. Malcolm Elwin. LC 78-58256. (Essay Index in Reprint Ser.). (Illus.). 1978. 27.25x (ISBN 0-8486-3018-1). Roth Pub Inc.
Victorian Wallpaper Design Book. Ramona Jablonski. (Internatinal Design Library). (Illus.). 48p. 1981. pap. 5.95 (ISBN 0-916144-89-5). Stemmer Hse.
Victorian Watercolors. Christopher Newall. (Illus.). 144p. 1988. 40.00 (ISBN 0-7148-2424-0, Pub. by Salem House-Phaidon). Salem Hse Pubs.
Victorian Wives. Katharine Moore. 242p. 1985. pap. 5.95 (ISBN 0-8052-8245-9, Pub. by Allison & Busby England). Schocken.
Victorian Woman: A Book of Days. Sally Fox. (Illus.). 1987. 12.95 (ISBN 0-8212-1646-5). NYGS.
Victorian Women: A Documentary Account of Women's Lives in Nineteenth-Century England, France, & the United States. Ed. by Erna O. Hellerstein et al. LC 79-67770. 544p. 1981. 35.00x (ISBN 0-8047-1088-0); pap. 12.95x (ISBN 0-8047-1096-1). Stanford U Pr.
Victorian Women in English: Social History. Barbara Kanner. LC 89-49189. (Women's History Ser.). 1200p. 1985. lib. bdg. 140.00 (ISBN 0-8240-9168-X). Garland Pub.
Victorian Women's Fiction: Marriage, Freedom & the Individual. Shirley Foster. 248p. 1986. pap. 11.95x (ISBN 0-389-20674-1). B&N Imports.
Victorian Woodblock Illustrators. Eric De Mare. (Illus.). 200p. 1982. 65.00 (ISBN 0-913720-32-1). Beil.
Victorian Woodblock Illustrators. Eric De Mare. 200p. 1980. 177.00x (ISBN 0-900406-58-5, Pub. by Gordon Fraser). State Mutual Bk.
Victorian Word-Painting & Narrative: Toward the Blending of Genres. Rhoda L. Flaxman. Ed. by Juliet McMaster. LC 86-30753. (Nineteenth-Century Studies). 160p. 1987. 39.95 (ISBN 0-8357-1787-9). UMI Res Pr.
Victorian Working Class: Selections from the "Morning Chronicle". Peter Razzell. Ed. by R. W Wainwright. (Illus.). 380p. 1973. 32.50x (ISBN 0-7146-2957-X, F. Cass Co). Biblio Dist.
Victorian Working Women. Michael Hiley. LC 79-92110. (Illus.). 144p. 1980. 18.95 (ISBN 0-87923-324-9). Godine.
Victorian Working Women. Michael Hiley. 144p. 1979. 65.00 (ISBN 0-86092-043-7, Pub. by Gordon Fraser); pap. 40.00 (ISBN 0-86092-033-X). State Mutual Bk.
Victorian Working Women. Wanda F. Neff. LC 77-181963. Repr. of 1929 ed. 16.45 (ISBN 0-404-04676-2). AMS Pr.
Victorian Writing & Working Women. Julia Swindells. LC 85-20821. (Feminist Perspectives Ser.). 240p. (Orig.). 1986. 35.00x (ISBN 0-8166-1476-8); pap. 14.95 (ISBN 0-8166-1477-6). U of Minn Pr.
Victorian Yearbook, 1983. cancelled. Intl Pubns Serv.
Victorians. Mary Azrael. LC 81-84759. 76p. (Orig.). 1982. pap. 4.95 (ISBN 0-87376-039-5). Red Dust.
Victorians. Ed. by Laurence Lerner. LC 78-15642. (Context of English Literature). 228p. 1978. 34.50 (ISBN 0-8419-0419-7); pap. 18.50 (ISBN 0-8419-0420-0). Holmes & Meier.
Victorians. Ed. by Arthur Pollard. LC 87-47750. (New History of Literature Ser.). 500p. 1987. 38.00 (ISBN 0-87226-130-1). P Bedrick Bks.
Victorians All. Flora Masson. LC 75-105806. 1970. Repr. of 1931 ed. 16.50x (ISBN 0-8046-0962-4, Pub by Kennikat). Assoc Faculty Pr.
Victorians & Ancient Greece. Richard Jenkyns. LC 79-25487. (Harvard Paperbacks Ser.). 400p. 1981. pap. 10.95 (ISBN 0-674-93687-6). Harvard U Pr.
Victorians & Ancient Greece. Richard Jenkyns. (Illus.). 400p. 1980. 32.00x (ISBN 0-674-93686-8). Harvard U Pr.
Victorians & Social Protest: A Symposium. Ed. by J. Butt & I. F. Clarke. 243p. 1973. 26.00 (ISBN 0-208-01329-6, Archon). Shoe String.
Victorians & the Machine: Literary Response to Technology. Herbert L. Sussman. LC 68-14274. (Illus.). Repr. of 1968 ed. 51.90 (ISBN 0-8357-9184-X, 2016540). Bks Demand UMI.
Victorians at Home & Away. Janet Phillips & Peter Phillips. (Illus.). 224p. 1978. 16.00 (ISBN 0-85664-688-1, Pub. by Croom Helm Ltd). Routledge Chapman & Hall.
Victorians in Japan. Hugh Cortazzi. 280p. 1987. 140.00x (ISBN 0-317-68609-7, Pub. by Han-Shan Tang Ltd). State Mutual Bk.
Victorians in Japan: In & Around the Treaty Ports. Hugh Cortazzi. 280p. 1987. text ed. 39.95 (ISBN 0-485-11312-0, Pub. by Athlone Pr UK). Humanities.
Victorians in the Harem: Grove Press Victorian Library. Ed. by Richard Manton. 224p. 1987. pap. 3.95 (ISBN 0-394-62312-6, BC). Grove.
Victorians Unbuttoned: Registered Designs for Clothing, Their Makers & Wearers, 1839-1900. Sarah Levitt. (Illus.). 246p. 1986. 34.95 (ISBN 0-04-391013-0). Unwin Hyman.
Victoria's Brown Coal: A Huge Fortune in Chancert. Ed. by J. T. Woodcock. 218p. 1984. text ed. 39.00x (ISBN 0-909520-79-8, Pub. by Australian Inst M & M). Brookfield Pub Co.
Victoria's Legacy: Tours of San Francisco Bay Area Architecture. Judith L. Waldhorn & Sally Woodbridge. LC 78-18350. (Illus.). 1978. pap. 5.95 (ISBN 0-89286-139-8). One Hund One Prods.
Victoria's Victories. Peter C. Smith. (Illus.). 192p. 1988. 29.95 (ISBN 0-87052-443-7). Hippocrene Bks.
Victoria's Walk. Caroline Gray. 1987. pap. 3.95 (ISBN 0-449-13015-0). Fawcett.
Victoria's World: An Exhibition from the Gernsheim Collection. 3rd ed. Intro. by Roy Flukinger. 1980. 2.50 (ISBN 0-87959-008-4). U of Tex H Ransom Ctr.
Victoria's Year: English Literature & Culture, 1837-1838. Richard L. Stein. (Illus.). 328p. 1988. 32.50 (ISBN 0-19-504922-5). Oxford U Pr.
Victories & Foibles: Some Western Haiku. David Seegal. LC 77-86327. 1977. 6.50 (ISBN 0-8048-1222-5). C E Tuttle.
Victories of the Saints. J. R. Young. 118p. 1987. pap. 4.95 (ISBN 0-917651-10-3). Holy Cross Orthodox.
Victories Without Violence. A. Ruth Fry. Ed. by Jenny Goodwin. (Liberty Literary Works: No. 1). 88p. (gr. 10 up). 1986. pap. 5.00 (ISBN 0-943734-06-1). Ocean Tree Bks.
Victorio & the Mimbres Apaches. Dan L. Thrapp. LC 72-9269. (Civilization of the American Indian Ser.: Vol. 125). (Illus.). 422p. 1980. pap. 12.95 (ISBN 0-8061-1645-5). U of Okla Pr.
Victorious Christ (Revelation) Leader's Guide. (New Horizons Bible Study Ser.). 48p. 1983. pap. 1.95 (ISBN 0-89367-089-8). Light & Life.
Victorious Christ (Revelation) Student Guide. 68p. 1983. pap. 2.50 (ISBN 0-89367-088-X). Light & Life.
Victorious Christian Faith. Alan Redpath. 192p. 9.95 (ISBN 0-8007-1208-0). Revell.
Victorious Christian Living: Studies in the Book of Joshua. Alan Redpath. 256p. 1955. 10.95 (ISBN 0-8007-0336-7). Revell.
Victorious Christian Service: Studies in the Book of Nehemiah. Alan Redpath. 192p. 9.95 (ISBN 0-8007-0337-5). Revell.
Victorious Christians You Should Know. Warren W. Wiersbe. 176p. 1984. pap. 4.95 (ISBN 0-8010-9667-7). Baker Bk.
Victorious Expression: A Study of Four Contemporary Spanish Poets, Unamuno, Machado, Jimenez, & Lorca. Howard T. Young. 1966. pap. 9.50x (ISBN 0-299-03144-6). U of Wis Pr.
Victorious Faith. Richard Wurmbrand. 1979. pap. 3.95 (ISBN 0-88264-120-4). Living Sacrifice Bks.
Victorious Journey: A Physician-Pilot Battles Cancer During a Worldwide Tour. John J. Fisher. (Illus.). 188p. 1983. 11.95 (ISBN 0-682-49978-1). Exposition-Phoenix.
Victorious Present. Ilija Poplasen. (Illus.). 255p. 1983. write for infor. (ISBN 0-935352-13-9). MIR PA.
Victorious Victorians: A Guide to the Major Architectural Styles. Peg Sinclair & Taylor Lewis. LC 85-7612. 80p. 1985. 15.95 (ISBN 0-03-004063-9). H Holt & Co.
Victors. Leslie Hardinge. (Anchor Ser.). 112p. 1982. pap. 1.99 (ISBN 0-8163-0490-4). Pacific Pr Pub Assn.
Victors & the Vanquished. Heda Kovaly & Erazim Kohak. 320p. 1973. 8.95 (ISBN 0-8180-1603-5). Horizon.
Victors & Vanquished: The German Influences on Army & Church in France after 1870. Allan Mitchell. LC 83-25917. xix, 169p. 1984. 35.00x (ISBN 0-8078-1603-5). U of NC Pr.
Victors Divided: America & the Allies in Germany, 1918-1923. Keith L. Nelson. (Illus.). 424p. 1975. 44.00x (ISBN 0-520-02315-3). U of Cal Pr.
Victors Divided: America & the Allies in Germany, 1918-1923. Keith L. Nelson. LC 72-87203. pap. 120.40 (2031308). Bks Demand UMI.
Victor's Wreath. Nina Johnson. 176p. (Orig.). 1988. pap. 3.95 (ISBN 0-88368-194-3). Whitaker Hse.
Victorverehrung Im Christlichen Altertum. Felix Rutten. Repr. of 1936 ed. 15.00 (ISBN 0-384-52655-1). Johnson Repr.
Victory. Howard Barker. 224p. (Orig.). 1984. pap. 4.95 (ISBN 0-7145-3986-4). Riverrun NY.
Victory. Joseph Conrad. LC 32-26954. 1971. pap. 5.95 (ISBN 0-385-09314-4, Anch). Doubleday.
Victory. LC 72-1874. (Black Heritage Library Collection-Prize Ser.). Repr. of 1866 ed. 16.75 (ISBN 0-8369-9051-X). Ayer Co Pubs.
Victory & Dominion Over Fear. Lester Sumrall. 104p. 1982. pap. 2.75 (ISBN 0-89274-233-X, HH-233). Harrison Hse.
Victory & Success Are Yours. Jerry Savelle. 41p. (Orig.). 1982. pap. text ed. 0.75 (ISBN 0-89274-236-4, HH-236). Harrison Hse.
Victory at C. Gerald N. Pitts. 1989. pap. text ed. write for info. (ISBN 0-538-10720-0, J72). SW Pub.
Victory at Guadalcanal. Robert E. Lee. (World-at-War Ser.). 1983. pap. 3.50 (ISBN 0-8217-1198-9). Zebra.
Victory at High Tide. Robert D. Heinl, Jr. LC 79-90111. (Illus.). 315p. 1979. Repr. of 1968 ed. 19.95 (ISBN 0-933852-03-7). Nautical & Aviation.

Victory at High Tide: The Inchon-Seoul Campaign. Robert D. Heinl. 16.95 (ISBN 0-405-13282-4). Ayer Co Pubs.

Victory at Sea. William S. Sims. (Classics of Naval Literature Ser.). 448p. 1984. Repr. of 1919 ed. 21.95 (ISBN 0-87021-745-3). Naval Inst Pr.

Victory Bible Reading Plan. James McKeever. 1984. 1.00 (ISBN 0-86694-102-9). Omega Pubns OR.

Victory Celebrations see Three Plays.

Victory Denied. Archibald E. Roberts. 300p. pap. 2.00 (ISBN 0-318-13714-3, Pub. by Betsy Ross Pr.). Comm Restore Const.

Victory Denied: The Rise of Air Power & the Defeat of Germany, 1920-45. Dudley Saward. Ed. by Jon Gillett. 376p. 1987. 18.95 (ISBN 0-531-15045-3). Watts.

Victory for Progress in Mental Medicine. Lloyd V. Briggs. Ed. by Gerald N. Grob. LC 78-22552. (Historical Issues in Mental Health Ser.). (Illus.). 1979. Repr. of 1924 ed. lib. bdg. 23.00x (ISBN 0-405-11906-2). Ayer Co Pubs.

Victory Garden Cookbook. Marian Morash. LC 81-48132. (Illus.). 352p. 1982. 29.95 (ISBN 0-394-50897-1); pap. 22.95 (ISBN 0-394-70780-X). Knopf.

Victory Garden Kids Book. Marjorie Waters. (Illus.). 160p. (gr. 6 up). Date not set. 21.95 (ISBN 0-395-42730-4); pap. 12.95 (ISBN 0-395-46560-5). HM.

Victory Garden Landscape Guide. Thomas Wirth. (Illus.). 360p. 1984. 29.95 (ISBN 0-316-94845-4); pap. 19.95 (ISBN 0-316-94846-2). Little.

Victory in Christ. Charles Trumbull. 1970. pap. 2.95 (ISBN 0-87508-533-4). Chr Lit.

Victory in Europe. D. Simons. LC 81-18315. (World War II Ser.). (gr. 7 up). lib. bdg. 22.60 (ISBN 0-8094-3404-0, Pub. by Time-Life). Silver.

Victory In Europe. Gerald Simons. (World War II Ser.). (Illus.). 208p. 1983. 14.95 (ISBN 0-8094-3403-2). Time Life.

Victory in Europe: The Fall of Hitler's Europe. Edward F. Dolan, Jr. Ed. by Margaret Ribaroff. (Illus.). 160p. (YA) (gr. 7-12). 1988. 12.90 (ISBN 0-531-10522-9). Watts.

Victory in Faith: Experiences of NSA Members. Ed. by George M. Williams. 100p. (Orig.). 1985. pap. text ed. 5.00 (ISBN 0-915678-14-4). World Tribune Pr.

Victory in Prayer. James McKeever. 32p. (Orig.). 1985. pap. 1.00 (ISBN 0-86694-103-7). Omega Pubns OR.

Victory in the Pacific. Albert Marrin. LC 82-6707. (Illus.). 224p. (gr. 5 up). 1983. 12.95 (ISBN 0-689-30948-1, Atheneum Childrens Bks). Macmillan.

Victory in the Voting Booth. Beatrice Kay. LC 78-31930. (Illus.). 1981. 17.95 (ISBN 0-88280-079-5); pap. 9.95 (ISBN 0-88280-078-7). ETC Pubns.

Victory: Life Maps. Chuck Swindoll. 64p. 1984. 5.95 (ISBN 0-8499-0442-0, 0442-0). Word Bks.

Victory Notes. J. M. Lybyer. (Orig.). 1963. pap. 3.95 (ISBN 0-8220-1339-8). Cliffs.

Victory Ode: An Introduction. Mary Lefkowitz. LC 76-11650. 186p. 1977. 18.00 (ISBN 0-8155-5045-6, NP). Noyes.

Victory of Connie Lee. Bess S. Aldrich. 20.95 (ISBN 0-8488-0160-1, Pub. by Amereon Hse). Amereon Ltd.

Victory of Light. Sam Stern. Ed. by Dorothy Stern. 144p. (Orig.). 1987. pap. 4.95 (ISBN 0-9619469-0-3). Hebrew Witness.

Victory of the Lamb. Bonnie B. O'Brien. 182p. 1982. pap. 9.95 (ISBN 0-311-72280-6). Casa Bautista.

Victory of the Papacy see Cambridge Medieval History.

Victory on Janus. Andre Norton. 1984. pap. 2.50 (ISBN 0-345-31625-8, Crest). Fawcett.

Victory on Janus. Andre Norton. 256p. 1984. pap. 2.50 (Del Rey). Ballantine.

Victory on Praise Mountain. Merlin Carothers. 1979. pap. 2.95 (ISBN 0-88270-378-1, Pub. by Logos). Bridge Pub.

Victory on Praise Mountain. Merlin R. Carothers. 175p. (Orig.). 1979. pap. 4.95 (ISBN 0-943026-04-0). Carothers.

Victory over Age. Jerome Ellison. 1980. pap. 6.95 (ISBN 0-8159-7103-6). Devin.

Victory over Death. Ronda Chervin. LC 85-8213. (Orig.). 1985. pap. 3.95 (ISBN 0-932506-43-7). St Bedes Pubns.

Victory over Depression. Frans M. Brandt. 304p. 1988. pap. 11.95 (ISBN 0-8010-0929-4). Baker Bk.

Victory over Diabetes. Dwight Kalita & William Philpott. 275p. 1983. text ed. 18.95 (ISBN 0-87983-318-1). Keats.

Victory over Europe: D-Day to VE Day. Max Hastings. (Illus.). 192p. 1985. 24.95 (ISBN 0-316-81334-6). Little.

Victory over Fear & Worry. Robert Russell. 132p. 1981. pap. 3.50 (ISBN 0-87516-439-0). DeVorss.

Victory over Japan: A Book of Stories. Ellen Gilchrist. 256p. 1984. 15.95 (ISBN 0-316-31303-3); pap. 7.95 (ISBN 0-316-31307-6). Little.

Victory over Sin & Self. David Wilkerson. 80p. 1982. pap. 2.95 (ISBN 0-8007-8434-0, Spire Bks). Revell.

Victory over the Devil. Jack R. Taylor. LC 72-96149. 128p. 1973. pap. 4.95 (ISBN 0-8054-5131-5). Broadman.

Victory over the Grand Depression: America & the World Saved from Imminent Economic Collapse. J. R. Estefania. (Victory Ser.). (Illus.). 210p. 1988. 19.95 (ISBN 0-945542-00-3). Park & Park Pub.

Victory over the Impossible. Elbert Willis. 1978. 1.25 (ISBN 0-89858-008-0). Fill the Gap.

Victory Over the World. Charles G. Finney. LC 66-24879. (Charles G. Finney Memorial Library). 124p. 1975. pap. 4.50 (ISBN 0-8254-2619-7). Kregel.

Victory Rode the Rails: The Strategic Place of the Railroads in the Civil War. George E. Turner. LC 73-184842. (Illus.). 419p. 1972. Repr. lib. bdg. 23.00x (ISBN 0-8371-6331-5, TUVR). Greenwood.

Victory: The Work of the Spirit. Pieter Potgieter. 42p. 1984. pap. 1.45 (ISBN 0-85151-430-8). Banner of Truth.

Victory Through Surrender: Self-Realization Through Self-Surrender. E. Stanley Jones. (Festival Ser.). 128p. 1980. pap. 1.50 (ISBN 0-687-43750-4). Abingdon.

Victory Through Word Confessions. Wadene C. Ward. 47p. 1985. pap. 1.95 (ISBN 0-88144-040-X). Christian Pub.

Victory Without Peace: American Foreign Relations in the 20th Century. David F. Trask. LC 75-11973. 232p. (Updated with supplementary material). 1975. Repr. of 1968 ed. 12.50 (ISBN 0-88275-304-5). Krieger.

Victuals & Vignettes. Herkimer County Historical Society Staff. (Illus.). 200p. 1984. spiral bdg. 12.95 (ISBN 0-317-39320-0). North Country.

Vida. Delacorta, pseud. Date not set. price not set. S&S.

Vida. Delacorta, pseud. Tr. by Victoria Reiter from Fr. 1985. 12.95 (ISBN 0-671-60424-4). Summit Bks.

Vida. Marge Piercy. 480p. 1985. pap. 4.50 (ISBN 0-449-20850-8, Crest). Fawcett.

Vida. Marge Piercy. 480p. 1981. 15.00 (ISBN 0-671-40110-6). Ultramarine Pub.

Vida. Marge Piercy. 480p. 1980. pap. 4.50 (ISBN 0-317-69921-0, Crest). Fawcett.

Vida. 1986. pap. 2.95 (ISBN 0-345-32941-4). Ballantine.

Vida a Plazos de Don Jacobo Lerner. Issac Goldemberg. 274p. (Span.). 1980. pap. 9.50 (ISBN 0-910061-00-9, 1101). Ediciones Norte.

Vida Abundante. Ray Baughman. Orig. Title: Abundant Life. 192p. (Span.). 1959. pap. 3.95 (ISBN 0-8254-1056-8). Kregel.

Vida & Poesia en Jose Antonio Davila. Adriana Ramos Mimoso. (Coleccion UPREX, Serie Estudios Literarios: No. 71). 1986. 6.00 (ISBN 0-8477-0071-2). U of PR Pr.

Vida Antes de la Vida. Fay D. De Montes. (Coleccion Aprender Ser.). (Illus.). 32p. (Orig., Span.). 1985. pap. 3.00 (ISBN 0-89729-359-2). Ediciones.

Vida Da Celula. OAS General Secretariat Department of Scientific & Technological Affairs. (Serie de Biologia: No. 5). (Illus.). 117p. (Orig.). Repr. of 1968 ed. 3.50 (ISBN 0-8270-1141-5). OAS.

Vida de Elias. A. W. Pink. 360p. (Span.). 1984. pap. 4.95 (ISBN 0-85151-424-3). Banner of Truth.

Vida de Jesucristo. James Stalker. 177p. (Span.). pap. 3.95. Edit Caribe.

Vida de Lazarillo de Tormes. Jones. 1987. pap. 11.00 (ISBN 0-7190-0210-9, Pub. by Manchester Univ Pr). St Martin.

Vida de Lazarillo de Tormes y de sus Fortunas y Adversidades. rev. ed. Ed. by Everett W. Hesse & Harry F. Williams. 104p. 1961. pap. text ed. 8.95x (ISBN 0-299-00545-3). U of Wis Pr.

Vida De Lenin. Maria Prilezhaeva. 190p. (Span.). 1974. 4.45 (ISBN 0-8285-1411-9, Pub. by Progress Pubs USSR). Imported Pubns.

Vida De los Animales Salvajes. (Span.). 9.95 (ISBN 84-241-5407-X). E Torres & Sons.

Vida De los Novios: The Life of Two Sweethearts. Martin Vinaver. (Illus.). 128p. 4.00 (ISBN 0-912528-05-2). John Muir.

Vida de San Millan de la Cogolla (Vol. 1 of the Obras Completas) rev. ed. Gonzalo De Berceo. (Serie A: Monagrafias, IV). (Illus.). 296p. (Span.). 1984. pap. 26.50 (ISBN 0-7293-0192-3, Pub. by Tamesis Bks Ltd). Longwood Pub Group.

Vida de San Pablo. James Stalker. 160p. (Span.). 1973. pap. 3.95 (ISBN 0-89922-025-8). Edit Caribe.

Vida de Santo Domingo de Silos: Estudio Y Edicion Critica por Brian Dutton (Vol. IV of the Obras Completas) Gonzalo De Berceo. Ed. by Brian Dutton. (Serie A: Monagrafias, LXXIV). 293p. (Orig., Span.). 1978. pap. 18.00 (ISBN 0-7293-0067-6, Pub. by Tamesis Bks Ltd). Longwood Pub Group.

Vida Disciplinada. Richard S. Taylor. 144p. 1979. 2.75 (ISBN 0-88113-341-8). Edit Betania.

Vida en Cristo. James J. Killgallon et al. Tr. by Manuel Pascual from Eng. LC 76-26451. 1978. pap. 2.50 (ISBN 0-914070-12-6). ACTA Pubns.

Vida en el Espiritu. Martyn Lloyd-Jones. 331p. 1987. pap. 7.00 (ISBN 0-939125-37-4). Evangelical Lit.

Vida en el Espiritu: Biblioteca de Doctrina Cristiana - Layman's Library of Christian Doctrine. Earl C. David. Tr. by Edna L. De Gutierrez from Eng. 143p. 1988. pap. 5.25 (ISBN 0-311-09121-0). Casa Bautista.

Vida En el Planta Tierra, 20 vols. 2864p. (Span.). 1979. Set. 695.00 (ISBN 84-274-0531-6, S-50494). French & Eur.

Vida en el Redil. Phillip Keller. Tr. by Carlos A. Vargas from Eng. LC 76-14500. 141p. (Span.). 1976. pap. 3.95 (ISBN 0-89922-073-8). Edit Caribe.

Vida en Espana. William H. Marshall & Elena L. De Martin. 1977. pap. text ed. 4.75x (ISBN 0-88334-105-0). Ind Sch Pr.

Vida Entera. Juan C. Martini. 284p. (Span.). 1981. pap. 9.50 (ISBN 84-02-07874-5, 3011). Ediciones Norte.

Vida es Sueno. Calderon. Ed. by A. E. Sloman. (Spanish Texts). 176p. (Span.). 1961. pap. text ed. 11.00 (ISBN 0-7190-0206-0, Pub. by Manchester Univ Pr). St Martin.

Vida es un Special. Roberto G. Fernandez. LC 81-69532. (Coleccion Caniqui). (Orig.). pap. 6.95 (ISBN 0-89729-303-7). Ediciones.

Vida Espanola. rev. ed. Diego Marin & Neale H. Tayler. LC 55-7036. (Illus., Span.). 1955. pap. text ed. 7.95x (ISBN 0-89197-973-5). Irvington.

Vida Maravillosa De los Animales, 2 vols. 6th ed. Cuspinera Jonch & Carlos Antonio y Bas Peired. 960p. (Span.). 1977. Set. leather 150.00 (ISBN 84-85009-32-0, S-50487). French & Eur.

Vida Maritima: Enciclopedia Ilustrada de los Animales Invertebrados del Mar. D. J. George. Ed. by R. Jordana. 288p. (Span.). 1979. 125.00 (ISBN 84-313-0624-6, S-37587). French & Eur.

Vida Matrimonial. (Span.). pap. 2.55 (ISBN 0-686-32335-1). Rod & Staff.

Vida Mistica de Jesus. 14th ed. H. Spencer Lewis. Tr. by AMORC Staff. (Illus.). 232p. (Orig., Span.). 1981. pap. 8.00 (ISBN 0-912057-63-7, GS 503). AMORC.

Vida Que Nace de la Muerte. T. A. Hegre. 272p. 1977. 2.95 (ISBN 0-88113-311-6). Edit Betania.

Vida Responsable: Orientacion Biblica Sobre Nuestro Estilo De Vivir. C. A. Ray. Tr. by Albert C. Lopez. Orig. Title: Living the Responsible Life. 160p. 1982. Repr. of 1980 ed. 3.75 (ISBN 0-311-46079-8). Casa Bautista.

Vida y Critica Literaria De Enrique Pineyro. Angela M. Aguirre. LC 81-51622. (Senda De Estudios y Ensayos). 274p. (Orig., Span.). 1981. pap. 11.95 (ISBN 0-918454-26-3). Senda Nueva.

Vida y Cultura Sefardita en los Poemas de "La Vara" (Del Ladino al Espanol) Berta Savariego & Jose Sanchez-Boudy. LC 87-81595. (Coleccion Polymita). 87p. (Orig., Span.). 1988. pap. 15.00 (ISBN 0-89729-447-5). Ediciones.

Vida y Ministerio de Cristo: Texto Programado. Weldon E. Viertel. Tr. by Ruben O. Zorzoli from Span. 192p. 1985. pap. text ed. write for info. (ISBN 0-311-04356-9). Casa Bautista.

Vida y Obra De Luis G. Inclan. Jorge L. Porras-Cruz. LC 76-1829. (Coleccion Mente y Palabra). 148p. (Orig., Span.). 1976. 6.00 (ISBN 0-8477-0536-6); pap. 5.00 (ISBN 0-8477-0537-4). U of PR Pr.

Vidal in Venice. Gore Vidal. 1985. 22.95 (ISBN 0-671-60691-3). Summit Bks.

Vidal in Venice. Gore Vidal. 1987. pap. 14.95 (ISBN 0-671-64536-6). Summit Bks.

Vidas Ejemplares. Mempo Giardinelli. 141p. (Span.). 1982. pap. 8.50 (ISBN 0-910061-11-4, 1110). Ediciones Norte.

Vidduy. 1982. pap. 2.95 (ISBN 0-686-76274-6). Feldheim.

Video. Helmkamp. 1987. pap. write for info. (ISBN 0-471-85367-4). Wiley.

Video. Gareth Renowden. (Inside Story Ser.). (Illus.). 40p. (gr. 4 up). 1983. PLB 12.40 (ISBN 0-531-04584-6). Watts.

Video. 1986. 17.50 (ISBN 0-87104-678-4, Branch Lib). NY Pub Lib.

Video. (Crayola Creativity Ser.). (Illus.). Date not set. 30.00 (ISBN 0-86696-215-8). Binney & Smith.

Video: A Guide for Lawyers. Ellen Miller. LC 83-80276. 142p. 1983. 29.75 (ISBN 0-88238-063-X). Law Arts.

Video: A Handbook of Classroom Ideas to Motivate Teaching Through the Use of Television. 1980. 8.95 (ISBN 0-89273-133-8). Educ Serv.

Video Age: Television Technology & Applications in the 1980s. LC 82-15177. (Video Bookshelf Ser.). 264p. 1982. professional 32.95 (ISBN 0-86729-033-1). Knowledge Indus.

Video & Cable Guidelines. 2nd ed. Ed. by Leslie Chamberlin Burk & Roberto Esteves. 461p. 1980. 9.75x (LITA). ALA.

Video & Electronic Displays: A User's Guide. Sol Sherr. LC 81-21915. 352p. 1982. 37.50x (ISBN 0-471-09037-9, Pub. by Wiley-Interscience). Wiley.

Video As a Second Language: How to Make a Video Documentary. rev. ed. Don Harwood. LC 79-63869. (Illus.). 1979. pap. 5.50 (ISBN 0-915146-06-1, V102). VTR Pub.

Video at Work in American Schools. Robert D. Carlisle. 65p. (Orig.). 1987. pap. text ed. 5.95 (ISBN 0-9603244-2-9). Agency Instr Tech.

Video-Based Information Systems: A Guide to Educational, Business, Library & Home Use. William Saffady. LC 84-21567. 230p. 1985. pap. text ed. 30.00x (ISBN 0-8389-0425-4). ALA.

Video Basics. John Yurko. LC 82-21543. (Illus.). 64p. (gr. 4-7). 1983. PLB 9.95 (ISBN 0-13-941781-8). P-H.

Video Blue Book, 1988. Ed. by Orion Research Corporation Staff. 280p. 1987. 99.50 (ISBN 0-317-62333-8). Orion Res.

Video Camcorder Handbook: How to Select & Use A Camcorder. Marjorie Costello & Michael Heiss. LC 87-12034. 160p. 1987. pap. 14.95 (ISBN 0-89586-590-4). Price Stern.

Video Camera Techniques. Gerald Millerson. (Media Manual Ser.). (Illus.). 160p. (Orig.). 1983. pap. 18.95 (ISBN 0-240-51225-1). Focal Pr.

Video Cameras: Theory & Servicing. Gerald P. McGinty. LC 84-50791. 264p. 1984. pap. 14.95 (ISBN 0-672-22382-1, 22382). Sams.

Video Capsule Reviews. Desmond Ryan. 350p. 1985. pap. 6.95 (ISBN 0-671-49182-2, Pub. by Fireside). S&S.

Video Cassette Recorders: Buying, Using & Maintaining. Bill Pasternak. (Illus.). 156p. (Orig.). 1983. pap. 8.95 (ISBN 0-8306-1490-7, 1490P). TAB Bks.

Video Classics: A Guide to Video Art & Documentary Tapes. Deirdre Boyle. LC 83-43239. (Illus.). 184p. 1986. pap. 20.00 (ISBN 0-89774-102-1). Oryx Pr.

Video-Clips. Stefano Tamburini et al. Ed. by Bernd Metz. Tr. by Tom Leighton from Fr. (Illus.). 70p. 1985. pap. 10.95 (ISBN 0-87416-015-4). Catalan Communs.

Video Companion: The Personal Video Reference. Randolph B. Welch. 64p. 1986. pap. 3.95 (ISBN 0-938207-08-3). Base Eight.

Video Computers: How to Select, Mix, & Operate Personal Computers & Home Video Equipment. Charles J. Sippl & Fred Dahl. (Illus.). 256p. 1981. 15.95 (ISBN 0-13-941856-3, Spec). P-H.

Video Connection: Integrating Video into Language Teaching. Charles Altman. 1989. pap. text ed. price not set (ISBN 0-395-48143-0). HM.

Video Culture: A Critical Investigation. Ed. & intro. by John Hanhardt. (Research, Visual Arts Ser.). 300p. 1986. 19.95 (ISBN 0-89822-044-0). Visual Studies.

Video Culture: A Critical Investigation. Intro. by John G. Hanhardt. 272p. 1986. 19.95 (ISBN 0-87905-222-8). Gibbs Smith Pub.

Video Culture: A Critical Investigation. Ed. & intro. by John G. Hanhardt. 304p. 1987. pap. 12.95 (ISBN 0-87905-279-1, Peregrine Smith). Gibbs Smith Pub.

Video Democracy: The Vote-from-Home Revolution. Richard Hollander. LC 85-81818. 161p. 1985. 24.95 (ISBN 0-912338-51-2); microfiche 9.95 (ISBN 0-912338-52-0). Lomond.

Video Display Terminals: Health & Safety Update, 1983. Mark Pinsky et al. (Excerpts from Microwave News). 29p. 1984. pap. 10.00 (ISBN 0-9610580-1-3). Microwave.

Video Display Terminals: Safety & Health (Excerpts from Microwave News) Louis Slesin & Martha Zybko. 84p. (Orig.). 1983. pap. 8.50 (ISBN 0-9610580-0-5). Microwave.

Video Displays, Work, & Vision. National Research Council. 273p. 1983. pap. 14.50x (ISBN 0-309-03388-8). Natl Acad Pr.

Video Editing: A Post-Production Primer. Browne. 1988. pap. 19.95 (ISBN 0-240-51791-1). Focal Pr.

Video Editing & Post-Production: A Professional Guide, 2nd Ed. Gary H. Anderson. LC 83-25124. (Video Bookshelf Ser.). 195p. 1988. professional 45.00 (ISBN 0-86729-257-1); pap. 27.95 students ed. (ISBN 0-86729-258-X). Knowledge Indus.

Video Editing & Post-Production Techniques. Schneider. 1989. 34.95 (ISBN 0-240-51799-7). Focal Pr.

Video Encyclopedia. Larry Langman. LC 83-47602. 250p. 1983. lib. bdg. 21.00 (ISBN 0-8240-9108-6). Garland Pub.

Video Family Portraits: The User Friendly Guide to Video Taping Your Family History, Stories, & Memories. Rob Huberman & Laura Janis. (Illus.). 151p. (Orig.). 1987. pap. 9.95 (ISBN 1-55613-074-0). Heritage Bk.

Video for Libraries: Special Interest Videos for Small & Medium-Sized Libraries. Sally Mason & James Scholtz. 240p. 1988. pap. text ed. 14.50x (ISBN 0-8389-0498-X). ALA.

Video Games. James I. Clark. LC 84-9790. (Look Inside Ser.). (Illus.). 48p. (gr. 4-12). 1984. PLB 15.99 (ISBN 0-8172-1410-0). Raintree Pubs.

Video Games. James I. Clark. LC 84-9790. (Look Inside Ser.). (Illus.). 48p. (gr. 4-12). 1985. pap. 9.27 (ISBN 0-8172-1436-4). Raintree Pubs.

Video Games. Jane M. Leder. Ed. by Howard Schroeder. LC 83-7674. (Technology (How Things are Made) Ser.). (Illus.). 48p. (gr. 4 up). 1983. PLB 9.95 (ISBN 0-89686-241-0). Crestwood Hse.

Video Games, Puzzles, & Quizzes. George Sullivan. 96p. (gr. 6 up). pap. 1.95 (ISBN 0-590-32956-1). Scholastic Inc.

Video Gift Book, Spring 1988. rev. ed. Jennifer Peters. (Illus.). 200p. 1988. pap. 4.95 (ISBN 0-942251-02-4). Videotakes.

Video Goals: Getting Results with Pictures & Sound. Tom Schroeppel. LC 86-91773. (Illus.). 120p. (Orig.). 1987. pap. 7.95 (ISBN 0-9603718-2-6). Schroeppel.

Video Guide. 3rd ed ed. Charles Bensinger. 1982. 18.95 (ISBN 0-318-04097-2). Timewindow Pubns.

Video Guide: Faces of Culture Study. John Young & Courtland L. Smith. 112p. 1986. pap. text ed. 8.95 (ISBN 0-8403-4113-X). Kendall-Hunt.

Video Handbook. 2nd ed. Ru Van Wezel. (Illus.). 432p. 1988. 65.00 (ISBN 0-434-92189-0, Pub. by W Heinemann Ltd). David & Charles.

Video in Language Teaching. Jack Lonergan. (New Directions in Language Teaching Ser.). (Illus.). 160p. 1984. pap. 9.95 (ISBN 0-521-27263-7). Cambridge U Pr.

Video in Mental Health Practice: An Activities Handbook. Ira Heilveil. 224p. 1983. 19.95 (ISBN 0-8261-4330-X). Springer Pub.

Video in the Language Classroom. Ed. by Marion Geddes & Gill Sturtridge. (Practical Language Teaching Ser.: No. 7). (Illus.). 192p. (Orig.). 1982. pap. text ed. 10.00x (ISBN 0-435-28971-3). Heinemann Ed.

Video Involvement for Libraries: A Current Awareness Package for Professionals. Ed. by Susan S. Cherry. LC 81-2337. 84p. 1981. pap. 6.00x (ISBN 0-8389-0323-1). ALA.

Video Magazine's Guide to Choosing & Using Your VCR. Jayne L. Schorn. (Illus.). 208p. 1985. pap. text ed. 9.95 (ISBN 0-07-051599-9). McGraw.

Video Magazine's Guide to Component TV. Ed. by Jayne L. Schorn. 208p. 1985. pap. text ed. 9.95 (ISBN 0-07-051600-6). McGraw.

Video Magazine's Guide to What's on Tape. Jayne L. Schorn. (Illus.). 352p. 1985. pap. text ed. 9.95 (ISBN 0-07-051598-0). McGraw.

Video Media Competition: Regulation, Economics & Technology. Ed. by Eli Noam. LC 85-435. (Columbia Studies in Business, Government, & Society). 416p. 1985. 42.00x (ISBN 0-231-06134-X). Columbia U Pr.

Video Microscopy. Shinya Inoue. LC 85-2852. 612p. 1986. 65.00x (ISBN 0-306-42120-8, Plenum Pr). Plenum Pub.

Video Movie Guide. Mick Martin & Marsha Porter. (Orig.). 1987. pap. 6.50. Ballantine.

Video Movie Guide for Kids. Mick Martin et al. (Orig.). 1987. pap. 3.95 (ISBN 0-345-33134-6). Ballantine.

Video Movie Guide 1987. Mick Martin & Marsha Potter. 256p. (Orig.). 1986. pap. 6.50. Ballantine.

Video Movie Guide 1988. Mick Martin & Marsha Porter. 1408p. 1987. pap. 6.50 (ISBN 0-345-34925-3). Ballantine.

Video Moviemakers Market. Frank Moore. 1984. pap. 12.95 (ISBN 0-452-25612-7, Plume). NAL.

Video Movies to Go. Murray Shukyn et al. 482p. 1986. pap. 12.95 (ISBN 0-919959-15-6, Pub. by Canada Wide). NY Zoetrope.

Video Nasties: Freedom & Censorship in the Media. Ed. by Martin Barker. 131p. (Orig.). 1984. pap. 5.25 (ISBN 0-86104-667-6, Pub. by Pluto Pr). Longwood Pub Group.

Video Night in Kathmandu: And Other Reports from the Not-So-Far East. Pico Iyer. LC 87-46006. 384p. 1988. 19.95 (ISBN 0-394-55027-7). Knopf.

Video Pencil: Cable Communications for Church & Community. Gene Jaberg & Louis G. Wargo, Jr. LC 80-7951. 156p. 1980. lib. bdg. 25.25 (ISBN 0-8191-1085-X); pap. text ed. 10.25 (ISBN 0-8191-1086-8). U Pr of Amer.

Video Pianist, Bk. 1. Walter Noona & Carol Noona. 48p. (Orig.). 1987. pap. 4.95 (ISBN 0-89328-100-X). Lorenz Corp.

Video Pictures of the Future. Ed. by Jeffrey B. Friedman. (Illus.). 296p. 1983. pap. text ed. 35.00 (ISBN 0-940690-07-1). Soc Motion Pic & TV Engrs.

Video Poems. Billy Collins. LC 79-50762. 1979. pap. 3.95 (ISBN 0-930090-05-5). Applezaba.

Video Poker. Tony Korfman & David Gerhardt. (Playing to Win). 76p. (Orig.). 1987. pap. 2.50 (ISBN 0-934047-08-1). Gaming Bks Intl.

Video Power: A Complete Guide to Writing, Planning, & Shooting Videos. Tom Shachtman & Harriet Shelare. LC 87-23681. (Illus.). 96p. (gr. 6-9). 1988. 15.95 (ISBN 0-8050-0338-X); pap. 7.95 (ISBN 0-8050-0414-9). H Holt & Co.

Video Primer. 3rd, rev. ed. Richard Robinson. (Illus.). 432p. 1983. pap. 10.95 (ISBN 0-399-50698-5, Perigee). Putnam Pub Group.

Video Production. Paul Huwiler. (Illus.). 114p. 1988. 13.95 (ISBN 0-944397-02-6). In-Time Pubns.

Video Production Guide. Charles Bensinger & McQuillin. 1983. 28.95 (ISBN 0-318-04098-0). Timewindow Pubns.

Video Production Guide. Lon McQuillin. Ed. by Charles Bensinger. (Illus.). 382p. 1983. pap. 28.95 (ISBN 0-672-22053-9). Sams.

Video Production Handbook. Gerald Millerson. (Illus.). 228p. (Orig.). 1987. pap. text ed. 21.95 (ISBN 0-240-51260-X). Focal Pr.

Video Production in Education & Training. Geoff Elliot. LC 84-45558. 150p. 1984. 26.00 (ISBN 0-7099-0930-6, Pub. by Croom Helm Ltd). Routledge Chapman & Hall.

Video Production: The Professional Way. Carl Caiati. (Illus.). 256p. (Orig.). 1985. 24.95 (ISBN 0-8306-0915-6, 1915); pap. 16.95 (ISBN 0-8306-1915-1). Tab Bks.

Video Purchasing Patterns in Schools. Quality Education Data Staff. (School Trend Ser.). 204p. 1988. pap. 49.95 (ISBN 0-88747-225-7, 2257Q). Quality Ed Data.

Video Reading Technics, Bk. 1. John A. Dwight & William J. Peel. 1976. pap. text ed. 5.30 (ISBN 0-934902-00-3); tchr's ed. 10.00 (ISBN 0-934902-04-6). Learn Concepts OH.

Video Register & Teleconferencing Resources Directory, 1988. Knowledge Industry Publications Staff. 650p. 1988. 74.50 (ISBN 0-86729-227-X). Knowledge Indus.

Video Resources in New York State. LC 75-11484. 64p. 1975. pap. 3.00 (ISBN 0-89062-015-6, Pub. by Film & Video Bureau). Pub Ctr Cult Res.

Video Revolution. Walter Oleksy. LC 85-30850. (New True Bks.). (Illus.). 48p. (gr. k-4). 1986. PLB 12.60 (ISBN 0-516-01285-1); pap. 3.95 (ISBN 0-516-41285-X). Childrens.

Video Rock Superstars. Chip Lovitt. LC 84-71680. (Illus.). 96p. (gr. 4-8). 1984. pap. 4.95 (ISBN 0-917657-03-9, Parachute Pr Bks). D I Fine.

Video Scrambling & Descrambling for Satellite & Cable TV. Rudolf F. Graf & William Sheets. 256p. 1986. pap. 19.95 (ISBN 0-672-22499-2). Sams.

Video Screams. 1983 ed. John McCarty. (Illus.). 300p. (Orig.). 1983. pap. 7.95x (ISBN 0-938782-02-9). Fantaco.

Video Security Systems. 2nd ed. Keith W. Bose. 210p. 1982. 21.95 (ISBN 0-409-95057-2). Butterworth.

Video Seminar Planbook for Dynamic Bible Teaching. Evangelical Teacher Training Association Staff. 64p. 1983. pap. 5.95 (ISBN 0-910566-60-7). Evang Tchr.

Video Source Book. 9th ed. The National Video Clearinghouse, Inc. Staff. 2500p. 1987. 199.00 (ISBN 0-935478-35-3). Natl Video.

Video Source Book. 10th ed. Ed. by David Weiner. 1988. 199.00 (ISBN 0-8103-4258-8). Gale.

Video Stars. Molly Albright. LC 88-15880. (Two of a Kind Ser.). (Illus.). 96p. (gr. 3-6). 1988. PLB 9.49 (ISBN 0-8167-1480-0); pap. text ed. 2.95 (ISBN 0-8167-1481-9). Troll Assocs.

Video Support in the Criminal Courts, 4 vols. 1974. Vol. I, 186 pgs. manuscript 11.16 (MAB-128); Vol. II, 82 pgs. manuscript 4.92 (MAB-129); Vol. III, 64 pgs. manuscript 3.84 (MAB-130); Vol. IV, 190 pgs. manuscript 1.40 (MAB-131). Natl Ctr St Courts.

Video Systems: Television Principles & Servicing. 2nd ed. Kamiran S. Badrkhan. LC 85-20348. 630p. 1986. write for info. (ISBN 0-471-81694-9). Wiley.

Video Tape & Disc Guide to Home Entertainment. 8th ed. National Video Clearinghouse, Inc. Staff. 1000p. (Orig.). 1987. pap. 13.95 (ISBN 0-935478-36-1). Natl Video.

Video Tape Recorders. 2nd ed. Harry Kybett. LC 78-51582. (Illus.). 400p. 1978. pap. 14.95 (ISBN 0-672-21521-7). Sams.

Video Taping Handbook: The Newest Systems, Cameras, & Techniques. Peter Lanzendorf. LC 82-19291. (Illus.). 240p. 1983. 16.95 (ISBN 0-517-54952-2, Harmony). Crown.

Video Technology: Its Use & Application in Law. (Litigation & Administrative Practice Course Handbook Ser.: Vol. 252). 250p. 1984. 45.00 (ISBN 0-317-11469-7, H4-4936). PLI.

Video Telephony Markets. International Resource Development Staff. 96p. 1986. 1650.00x (ISBN 0-88694-695-6). Intl Res Dev.

Video Texts. (Illus.). 45p. 1983. pap. 4.00 (ISBN 0-317-55960-5). Anthology Film.

Video: The Educational Challenge. Robin Moss. 160p. 1983. 25.25 (ISBN 0-7099-1747-3, Pub. by Croom Helm Ltd). Routledge Chapman & Hall.

Video to Online Reference Service & the New Technology. Ed. by Bill Katz & Ruth A. Fraley. LC 82-23292. (Reference Librarian: Nos. 5 & 6). 205p. 1983. text ed. 29.95 (ISBN 0-86656-202-8, B202). Haworth Pr.

Video Transformations. Lois Bianchi. LC 85-80971. (Illus.). 24p. 1986. 2.00 (ISBN 0-916365-18-2). Ind Curators.

Video User's Handbook. 2nd ed. Peter Utz. (Illus.). 1982. text ed. 24.95 (ISBN 0-13-941880-6, Spec); pap. 16.95 (ISBN 0-13-941872-5). P-H.

Video User's Handbook. 2nd ed. Peter Utz. 500p. 1982. pap. 19.95 (ISBN 0-86729-036-6). Knowledge Indus.

Video User's Handbook: Completely Revised & Expanded. 3rd ed. Peter Utz. 1988. pap. 19.95 (ISBN 0-13-941899-7). Prentice Hall Pr.

Video Violence & Children. Ed. by Geoffrey Barlow & Alison Hill. LC 85-14596. 192p. 1986. 19.95 (ISBN 0-312-84571-5). St Martin.

Video Wars. Stephen Manes. 256p. (YA) (gr. 7 up). 1983. pap. 2.25 (ISBN 0-380-83303-4, Flare). Avon.

Video Wizard Handbook. Keith Sobie et al. (Illus.). 196p. 1982. pap. 6.95 (ISBN 0-686-35866-X). Video Wizard.

Videocassette Recorders: Theory & Servicing. Gerald P. McGinty. (Illus.). 1979. pap. text ed. 20.35 (ISBN 0-07-044988-0). McGraw.

Videocassette Technology in American Education. George N. Gordon & Irving A. Falk. LC 72-81494. 176p. 1972. 26.95 (ISBN 0-87778-035-8). Educ Tech Pubns.

Videoconferencing Services & Systems: A Selective, Annotated Bibliography. James J. Sanchez. (Public Administration Ser.: P 2266). 6p. 1987. 3.00 (ISBN 1-55590-526-9). Vance Biblios.

Videodisc & Optical Digital Disk Technologies & Their Implications in Libraries. Judy McQueen & Richard W. Boss. 160p. 1986. pap. text ed. 25.00x (ISBN 0-8389-7041-9). ALA.

Videodisc & Optical Memory Technologies. Jordan Isailovic. (Illus.). 400p. 1985. text ed. 51.00 (ISBN 0-13-942053-3). P-H.

Videodisc & Related Technologies: A Glossary of Terms. Rockley Miller & John H. Sayers. 80p. (Orig.). 1986. pap. 7.95 (ISBN 0-938907-02-6). Future Syst.

Videodisc Hardware & Software for the Non-Consumer Market. (Marketing Research Reports). 1987. write for info. (ISBN 0-86621-845-9, A1665). Frost & Sullivan.

Videodisc-Microcomputer Courseware Design. Ed. by Michael L. DeBloois. LC 81-22161. 192p. 1982. 32.95 (ISBN 0-87778-183-4). Educ Tech Pubns.

Videodisc, Optical Disk & CD-ROM Conference Proceedings, Philadelphia, 1985. Judith P. Roth. 1985. pap. text ed. 30.00x (ISBN 0-88736-053-X). Meckler Corp.

Videodisc Systems: Theory & Applications. Jordan Isailovic. (Illus.). 400p. 1987. text ed. 51.00 (ISBN 0-13-941865-2). P-H.

Videodisc Training: A Cost Analysis: A Guide & Workbook for Choosing your Courseware Delivery System. Richard H. Brandt et al. (Monitor Report Ser.). 150p. 1987. pap. 49.95 (ISBN 0-938907-07-7); wkbk. 15.00 (ISBN 0-938907-08-5). Future Syst.

Videodiscs. Edward W. Schneider & Junius L. Bennion. Ed. by James E. Duane. LC 80-23563. (Instructional Media Library: Vol. 16). (Illus.). 128p. 1981. 23.95 (ISBN 0-87778-176-1). Educ Tech Pubns.

Videodiscs, Compact Discs & Digital Optical Disks. Tony Hendley. 208p. 1985. pap. 48.00 (ISBN 0-85267-245-4). Learned Info.

Videodiscs in Museums: A Project & Resource Directory. Roberta H. Binder et al. (The Monitor Report Ser.). 160p. (Orig.). 1987. pap. text ed. 49.95 (ISBN 0-938907-09-3). Future Syst.

Videodiscs in Voc Ed. William P. Olivier. 35p. 1985. 4.75 (IN299). Natl Ctr Res Voc Ed.

Videodrome. Jack Martin. pap. 2.95 (ISBN 0-8217-1166-0). Zebra.

Videogames & Electronic Toys. International Resource Development Inc. 185p. 1983. 1285.00x (ISBN 0-88694-550-X). Intl Res Dev.

Videogram, 1988: Sites, Services, Sources & Salaries for the New York State Television Commercial Producers. George Gilbert. (Illus.). 96p. (Orig.). 1988. pap. 9.00. G Gilbert Assocs.

Videos. L. Cridisque. 1977. pap. 1.50 (ISBN 0-686-20611-8). Ghost Dance.

Videoscope, 2 Vols. 64p. pap. 12.00xea. Vol. 1, No. 1. 1976 (ISBN 0-677-47015-0). Vol. 1, No. 2. 1977, 80p (ISBN 0-677-47025-8). Vol. 1, No. 3. 1977, 68p (ISBN 0-677-47035-5). Vol. 1, No. 4. 1977, 64p (ISBN 0-677-47045-2). Vol. 2, No. 1. 1978, 64p (ISBN 0-677-47055-X). Vol. 2, No. 2. 1978 (ISBN 0-677-47065-7). Gordon & Breach.

Videostyle in Senate Campaigns. Dorothy D. Nesbit. LC 88-2166. 192p. 1988. text ed. 24.95 (ISBN 0-87049-582-8). U of Tenn Pr.

Videotape in Legal Education: A Study of Its Implications & a Manual for its Users. Michael Botein. 70p. 1979. 20.00 (ISBN 0-941888-10-X). Comm Media.

Videotape on Trial: A View from the Jury Box. Gerald R. Miller & Norman E. Fontes. LC 79-18774. (People & Communication Ser.: Vol. 7). (Illus.). 224p. 1979. 35.00 (ISBN 0-8039-0967-5); pap. 16.95 (ISBN 0-8039-0968-3). Sage.

Videotape Profits: A Marketing Guide. Tom Guay. 71p. 1986. pap. 49.00 (ISBN 0-937925-40-3). Capitol VA.

Videotape Recording. 4th ed. Lowe. Date not set. price not set (ISBN 0-240-51227-8). Focal Pr.

Videotape Recording. 3rd ed. J. F. Robinson & Stephen Lowe. LC 80-41244. 1981. 45.00 (ISBN 0-240-51083-6). Focal Pr.

Videotape Rental Store: A Step by Step Guide to Setting up & Operating a Videotape Rental Store. 1986. lib. bdg. 79.95 (ISBN 0-8490-3814-6). Gordon Pr.

Videotape Techniques in Psychiatric Training & Treatment. 2nd ed. Ed. by Milton M. Berger. LC 78-1782. 1978. 45.00 (ISBN 0-87630-163-4). Brunner-Mazel.

Videotex & Electronic Publishing: A Legal, Regulatory & Economic Analysis. Michael Botein & Alan Pearce. 56p. (Orig.). 1982. pap. text ed. write for info. Comm Media.

Videotex & the Press. 1983. 30.00. Learned Info.

Videotex Business Markets. 167p. 1985. 1650.00x (ISBN 0-88694-654-9). Intl Res Dev.

Videotex in Europe: Proceedings of Videotex in Europe Conference, Luxembourg, July 1980. 1983. 90.00 (ISBN 0-317-01040-9). Learned Info.

Videotex Journalism: Teletext, Viewdata, & the News. David H. Weaver. 160p. 1983. text ed. 19.50x (ISBN 0-89859-263-1). L Erlbaum Assocs.

Videotex: Key to the Wired City. Michael Aldrich. 144p. 1982. 29.00x (ISBN 0-907621-12-0, Pub. by Quiller Pr England). State Mutual Bk.

Videotex: Key to the Wired City. Michael Aldrich. 128p. 1986. pap. 9.95 (ISBN 0-317-46214-8, Pub. by Quiller Pr England). Intl Spec Bk.

Videotex Marketplace. 200p. 1984. 150.00 (ISBN 0-317-55725-4). B Klein Pubns.

Videotex Systems: A Selective, Annotated Bibliography. James J. Sanchez. (Public Administration Ser.: P 2262). 17p. 1987. 5.00 (ISBN 1-55590-522-6). Vance Biblios.

Videotex-Teleservices Directory, Nineteen Eighty-Five. Ed. by Gary H. Arlen & Richard Adler. 272p. (Orig.). 1985. pap. text ed. 80.00 (ISBN 0-9609768-1-7). Arlen Comm Inc.

Videotex-Teletext: Principle & Practices. A. Alber. 416p. 1985. text ed. 43.95 (ISBN 0-07-000957-0). McGraw.

Videotex: Television - Telephone Information Services. Woolfe. 184p. 1980. 48.95 (ISBN 0-471-26089-4, Wiley Heyden). Wiley.

Videotex vs. Audiotex: The Competition for Home Information & Transactional Services. International Resource Development Inc. 204p. 1983. 1285.00x (ISBN 0-88694-560-7). Intl Res Dev.

Videotext: The Coming Revolution in Home-Office Information Retrieval. Ed. by Efrem Sigel. 1981. o. p. 14.95 (ISBN 0-517-54385-0, Harmony); pap. 2.98 (ISBN 0-517-54386-9, Harmony). Crown.

Vidhik Upchar (Legal Remedies in Hindi) V. M. Shukla. Tr. by Vijay Malik. 281p. 1978. 48.00x (Pub. by Eastern Bk India); pap. 37.50x (ISBN 0-317-54762-3). State Mutual Bk.

Vidotex & Teletext: New Online Resources for Libraries. M. B. Binder. LC 85-5246. (Foundations of Library & Information Science: Vol. 21). 160p. 1985. 52.50 (ISBN 0-89232-612-3). Jai Pr.

Vidrine-Vedrines Sixteen Hundred to Seventeen Fifty: Our Vedrines in France, Vol. 1. Jacqueline O. Vidrine. (Illus.). 246p. 1982. 25.00 (ISBN 0-937614-04-1). Acadiana Pr.

Viduy: Confession. Nosson Scherman. (ArtScroll Mesorah Ser.). 32p. 1986. pap. 2.95 (ISBN 0-89906-227-X). Mesorah Pubns.

Vie. Guy De Maupassant. (Folio Ser.: No. 544). 1959. pap. 7.95 (ISBN 0-685-11610-7, 478). Schoenhof.

Vie. Guy De Maupassant. 1959. write for info. (478). French & Eur.

Vie Americanie de Guillaume Merle d'Aubigne: Avec une Introd et des Notes par Gilbert Chinard. Merle Guillaume. 1979. 16.00 (ISBN 0-405-10591-6). Ayer Co Pubs.

Vie de Disraeli. Andre Maurois. (Coll. Leurs Figures). pap. 32.50 (ISBN 0-685-36967-6). French & Eur.

Vie de Haydn, de Mozart et de Metastase. Stendhal. 48.00 (ISBN 0-686-55083-8). French & Eur.

Vie De Henri Brulard, 2 tomes. Stendhal. (Folio Ser.: No. 447). 1961. Set. pap. 8.95 (ISBN 0-685-11617-4). Schoenhof.

Vie de Henri Brulard, 2 tomes. Stendhal. 1961. Set. write for info. French & Eur.

Vie de Henry Brulard. Stendhal & Beatrice Didier. 1973. write for info. French & Eur.

Vie De Jean-Arthur Rimbaud. Paterne Berrichon. LC 77-10252. (Symbolists Ser.). (Fr.). Repr. of 1897 ed. 27.50 (ISBN 0-404-16307-6). AMS Pr.

Vie de Jean Racine: Avec: Le Romancier et ses Personnages, L'Education ces Filles, Mes Grandes Hommes, Recontre avec Barres, Pascal. Francois Mauriac. (Illus.). 12.50 (ISBN 0-686-55480-9). French & Eur.

Vie de Jesus. Francois Mauriac. 9.95 (ISBN 0-685-34307-3). French & Eur.

Vie de la Princesse d'Angleterre. Marie-Madeleine de La Fayette. 264p. 1967. 17.50 (ISBN 0-686-54268-1). French & Eur.

Vie de Lord Byron en Italie, 9 vols. Teresa Guiccioli. Ed. by James Hogg. (Romantic Reassessment Ser.). 1746p. (Orig.). 1983. pap. 135.00 (ISBN 3-7052-0543-9, Pub. by Salzburg Studies). Longwood Pub Group.

Vie de Lord Byron en Italie, Introduction. Erwin A. Sturzl. Ed. by James Hogg. (Romantic Reassessment Ser.). (Orig.). 1985. pap. 15.00 (ISBN 3-7052-0544-7, Pub. by Salzburg Studies). Longwood Pub Group.

Vie de Mahomed. Henri Boulainvilliers. 416p. (Fr.). Repr. of 1730 ed. text ed. 41.40x (ISBN 0-576-12102-9, Pub. by Gregg Intl Pubs England). Gregg Intl.

Vie De Marianne. Pierre C. Marivaux. 1966. pap. 5.95 (ISBN 0-685-11618-2). French & Eur.

Vie de Monsieur Descartes, 2 Vols. Adrien Baillet. Ed. by Willis Doney. (Philosophy of Descartes Ser.). 1090p. (Fr.). 1987. Set. lib. bdg. 175.00 (ISBN 0-8240-4655-2). Garland Pub.

Vie de Napoleon. Stendhal, pseud. (Petite Bibliotheque Payot). pap. 5.95 (ISBN 0-685-35023-1). French & Eur.

Vie de Nostre Benoit Sauveur Ihesuscrist & la Saincte Vie de Nostre Dame. Millard Meiss & Elizabeth H. Beatson. LC 76-16657. (College Art Association Monograph Ser.: Vol. 32). (Illus.). 222p. (Fr.). 1985. Repr. of 1977 ed. 30.00x (ISBN 0-271-00403-7). Pa St U Pr.

Vie de Prophyre: Le Philosophe Neo-Platonicien. Joseph Bidez. 173p. Repr. of 1913 ed. lib. bdg. 42.00x (Pub. by G Olms BRD). Coronet Bks.

Vie De Pythagore De Diogene Laerce. Laertius Diogenes. Ed. by Gregory Vlastos. LC 78-19342. (Morals & Law in Ancient Greece Ser.). 1979. Repr. of 1922 ed. lib. bdg. 21.00x (ISBN 0-405-11537-7). Ayer Co Pubs.

Vie de Ramakrishna. Romain Rolland. 1978. 16.95 (ISBN 0-686-55279-2). French & Eur.

Vietnam & China, 1938-1954. King C. Chen. LC 78-83684. 1969. 49.50x (ISBN 0-691-03078-2). Princeton U Pr.

Vietnam & the Chinese Model: A Comparative Study of Nguyen & Ch'ing Civil Government in the First Half of the Nineteenth Century. Alexander B. Woodside. LC 76-119076. (East Asian Ser: No. 52). (Illus.). xii, 358p. 1971. 27.00x (ISBN 0-674-93720-1). Harvard U Pr.

Vietnam & the Chinese Model: A Comparative Study of Vietnamese & Chinese Government in the First Half of the Nineteenth Century. Alexander B. Woodside. (East Asian Monographs: No. 140). 360p. 1988. pap. text ed. 14.00 (ISBN 0-674-93721-X, Pub. by Coun East Asian Stud). Harvard U Pr.

Vietnam & the Soviet Union: Anatomy of an Alliance. Douglas Pike. 274p. 1987. 29.85 (ISBN 0-8133-0470-9). Westview.

Vietnam & the United States. Hans Morganthau. pap. 8.00 (ISBN 0-8183-0217-8). Pub Aff Pr.

Vietnam Anthology: American War Literature. Nancy Anisfield. LC 87-71030. 150p. 1987. 25.95 (ISBN 0-87972-395-5); pap. 11.95 (ISBN 0-87972-396-3). Bowling Green Univ.

Vietnam As History: Ten Years after the Paris Peace Accords. Ed. by Peter Braestrup. LC 83-21748. (Wilson Center Conference Report Ser.). (Illus.). 208p. (Orig.). 1984. lib. bdg. 20.75 (ISBN 0-8191-3653-0); pap. text ed. 9.50 (ISBN 0-8191-3654-9). U Pr of Amer.

Vietnam at War: The History, 1946-1975. Phillip B. Davidson. (Illus.). 848p. 1988. 27.50 (ISBN 0-89141-306-5). Presidio Pr.

Vietnam: Beyond the War. Joseph S. Salzburg. 250p. 1975. 12.50 (ISBN 0-317-60908-4). Sovereign MD.

Vietnam Blues. John B. Carn. (Orig.). 1988. pap. 3.25. Holloway.

Vietnam by Those Who Served. Ernest Miner. 48p. 1985. 7.95 (ISBN 0-89962-479-0). Todd & Honeywell.

Vietnam Choppers. Simon Dunstan. (Illus.). 200p. (Orig.). 1988. pap. 22.95 (ISBN 0-85045-572-3, Pub. by Osprey England). Motorbooks Intl.

Vietnam, Curse or Blessing. John L. Steer & Cliff Dudley. LC 82-82016. (Illus.). 192p. (Orig.). 1982. pap. 3.50 (ISBN 0-89221-091-5). New Leaf.

Vietnam Era: A Guide to Teaching Resources. Breakstone et al. (Illus.). 105p. (Orig.). (gr. 9-12). 1978. pap. text ed. 5.00 (ISBN 0-9607794-1-8). Indochina Curriculum Grp.

Vietnam Experience: Images of War. Julene Fischer the Picture Editors of Boston Publishing. 16.95 (ISBN 0-201-11274-4). Addison-Wesley.

Vietnam Experience: Ten Years of Reflections. James B. Stockdale. (Publication Ser.: No. 315). ix, 149p. 1984. lib. bdg. 19.95t (ISBN 0-8179-8151-9); pap. text ed. 9.95t (ISBN 0-8179-8152-7). Hoover Inst Pr.

Vietnam Experience: The Fall of the South, The False Peace 1972-74, The Aftermath 1975-85. Ed. by Robert Manning. Date not set. price not set. Addison-Wesley.

Vietnam Fact Book. Jeff Stein. (Orig.). 1987. pap. 3.95 (ISBN 0-440-19336-2). Dell.

Vietnam Forum Eight. Ed. by Huynh Sanh Thong. (Vietnam Forum Ser.: No. 8). 280p. 1986. pap. 5.00 (ISBN 0-317-64476-9). Yale U SE Asia.

Vietnam Forum Five. Ed. by Huynh Sanh Thong. (Vietnam Forum Ser.: No. 5). 259p. 1985. pap. 5.00 (ISBN 0-317-64472-6). Yale U SE Asia.

Vietnam Forum Four. Ed. by Huynh Sanh Thong. (Vietnam Forum Ser.: No. 4). 174p. 1984. pap. 5.00 (ISBN 0-317-64471-8). Yale U SE Asia.

Vietnam Forum Nine. Ed. by Huynh Sanh Thong. (Vietnam Forum Ser.: No. 9). 263p. 1987. pap. 5.00 (ISBN 0-317-64477-7). Yale U SE Asia.

Vietnam Forum One. Ed. by Huynh Sanh Thong. (Vietnam Forum Ser.: No. 1). 120p. 1983. pap. 5.00 (ISBN 0-317-64466-1). Yale U SE Asia.

Vietnam Forum Seven. Ed. by Huynh Sanh Thong. (Vietnam Forum Ser.: No. 7). 278p. 1986. pap. 5.00 (ISBN 0-317-64474-2). Yale U SE Asia.

Vietnam Forum Six. Ed. by Huynh Sanh Thong. (Vietnam Forum Ser.: No. 6). 273p. 1985. pap. 5.00 (ISBN 0-317-64473-4). Yale U SE Asia.

Vietnam Forum Ten. Ed. by Thong S. Huynh. (Vietnam Forum Ser.: No. 10). 266p. 1987. pap. 5.00. Yale U SE Asia.

Vietnam Forum Three. Ed. by Huynh Sanh Thong. (Vietnam Forum Ser.: No. 3). 169p. 1984. pap. 5.00 (ISBN 0-317-64469-6). Yale U SE Asia.

Vietnam Forum Two. Ed. by Huynh Sanh Thong. (Vietnam Forum Ser.: No. 2). 161p. 1983. pap. 5.00 (ISBN 0-317-64468-8). Yale U SE Asia.

Vietnam: Ground Zero. (Vietnam Ground Zero Ser.: No. 1). Date not set. pap. 2.75 (ISBN 0-317-64007-0, Pub. by Worldwide). Harlequin Bks.

Vietnam Heroes: A Tribute: An Anthology of Poems by Veterans & Their Friends. Joan M. Maiman et al. Ed. by J. Topham. LC 82-3955. 21p. 1982. lib. bdg. 12.95 (ISBN 0-933486-52-9); pap. 4.95 (ISBN 0-933486-34-0). Am Poetry & Lit.

Vietnam Heroes II: The Tears of a Generation; Poems & Prose on the Consequences of War. 2nd ed. John P. McAfee et al. Ed. by J. Topham. LC 82-11465. 40p. (Orig.). 1982. lib. bdg. 12.95 (ISBN 0-933486-51-0); pap. 4.95 (ISBN 0-933486-53-7). Am Poetry & Lit.

Vietnam Heroes IV: The Long Ascending Cry, an Anthology. Peter Hollenbeck et al. Ed. by J. Topham. LC 85-9008. (Illus.). 52p. 1985. lib. bdg. 12.95 (ISBN 0-933486-65-0); pap. 4.95 (ISBN 0-933486-66-9). Am Poetry & Lit.

Vietnam Heroes: That We Have Peace, Vol. III. Joyner et al. Ed. by J. Topham. LC 83-6400. 40p. (Orig.). 1983. lib. bdg. 12.95 (ISBN 0-933486-47-2); pap. 4.95 (ISBN 0-933486-44-8). Am Poetry & Lit.

Vietnam, Ho Quy Ly, & the Ming (Thirteen Seventy-One to Fourteen Twenty-One) John K. Whitmore. LC 85-51296. (Lac-Viet Ser.: No. 2). 205p. 1985. pap. 10.00 (ISBN 0-938692-22-4). Yale U SE Asia.

Vietnam in Prose & Film. James C. Wilson. LC 82-6635. 140p. (Orig.). 1982. pap. 18.95x (ISBN 0-89950-050-1). McFarland & Co.

Vietnam in Remission. Ed. by Harry A. Wilmer & James F. Veninga. LC 84-40560. (Published for the Texas Committee for the Humanities Ser.). (Illus.). 152p. 1985. 14.95 (ISBN 0-89096-213-8). Tex A&M Univ Pr.

Vietnam Legacy. Brian Freemantle. 384p. (Orig.). 1984. pap. 3.50 (ISBN 0-8125-0284-1, Dist. by Warner Pub Services & Saint Martin's Press). Tor Bks.

Vietnam Literature Anthology. rev. ed. Peter Hollenbeck et al. LC 85-3948. (Illus.). 76p. 1985. 13.95 (ISBN 0-933486-75-8); lib. bdg. 13.95 (ISBN 0-933486-77-4); pap. 7.95 (ISBN 0-933486-76-6). Am Poetry & Lit.

Vietnam Medal of Honor Heroes. Edward Murphy. 288p. (Orig.). 1987. pap. 8.95 (ISBN 0-345-33890-1). Ballantine.

Vietnam MiG Killers: Deadly Duel over Vietnam. Robert Dorr. (Illus.). 128p. 1988. 24.95 (ISBN 0-87938-286-4). Motorbooks Intl.

Vietnam: Nation in Revolution. William J. Duiker. LC 82-21946. (Illus.). 171p. 1983. 15.95x (ISBN 0-86531-731-3). Westview.

Vietnam Nineteen Sixty-Nine to Nineteen Seventy: A Company Commander's Journal. Michael L. Lanning. 320p. 1988. pap. 3.95 (ISBN 0-8041-0187-6, Pub. by Ivy). Ballantine.

Vietnam Nurse. Evelyn Hawkins. 1984. pap. 3.50 (ISBN 0-8217-1459-7). Zebra.

Vietnam Odyssey: 101st Airborne Division. 101 Airborne Division Staff. (Illus.). 112p. 1986. Repr. write for info. (ISBN 0-917231-06-6). Ferguson Comns Pubs.

Vietnam on Trial: Westmoreland vs. CBS. Bob Brewin & Sydney Shaw. LC 85-47595. 288p. 1987. 21.95 (ISBN 0-689-11610-1). Atheneum.

Vietnam: Peasant Land, Peasant Revolution. Nancy Wiegersma. LC 87-27352. 300p. 1988. 39.95 (ISBN 0-312-01358-2). St Martin.

Vietnam-Perkasie: A Combat Marine Memoir. W. D. Ehrhart. LC 83-9426. (Illus.). 328p. (Orig.). 1983. pap. 13.95x (ISBN 0-89950-076-5). McFarland & Co.

Vietnam Photo Book. Mark Jury. LC 86-40131. (Illus.). 144p. 1986. pap. 12.95 (ISBN 0-394-74661-9, Vin). Random.

Vietnam Poems. Nhat Hanh. Tr. by Helen Coutant from Vietnamese. (Keepsake Ser.: Vol. 1). 24p. 1972. 10.00 (ISBN 0-87775-030-0). Unicorn Pr.

Vietnam Primer. S. L. Marshal & David Hackworth. 58p. Date not set. pap. 5.95. Lancer.

Vietnam Reconsidered: Lessons from a War. Harrison E. Salisbury. LC 83-48382. 288p. 1984. pap. 9.95x (ISBN 0-06-132052-8, TB 2052, Torch). Har-Row.

Vietnam Remembered. Boston Publishing Co. Editors. Ed. by Robert Manning. (Vietnam Experience Ser.: Vol. 19). (Illus.). 192p. 1986. 16.95 (ISBN 0-939526-20-4). Boston Pub Co.

Vietnam Revisited: Covert Action to Invasion to Reconstruction. David Dellinger. 220p. (Orig.). 1986. 25.00 (ISBN 0-89608-320-9); pap. 9.00 (ISBN 0-89608-319-5). South End Pr.

Vietnam River Warfare. Victor Croizat. (Illus.). 160p. (Orig.). 1986. pap. 12.95 (ISBN 0-7137-1830-7, Pub. by Blandford Pr England). Sterling.

Vietnam Settlement: Why 1973 Not 1969? Abram Chayes et al. 1973. 19.50 (ISBN 0-8447-2038-0). Am Enterprise.

Vietnam since the Fall of Saigon. rev., 2nd ed. William Duiker. LC 82-90744. 300p. 1985. pap. text ed. 12.00x (ISBN 0-89680-133-0, Ohio U Ctr Intl). Ohio U Pr.

Vietnam: Strategy for a Stalemate. F. Charles Parker, IV. 224p. 1988. 19.95 (ISBN 0-88702-041-0). Paragon Hse.

Vietnam Ten Years After. Ed. by Robert E. Long. LC 86-1642. (Reference Shelf Ser.: Vol. 58, No. 2). 161p. 1986. pap. text ed. 10.00. Wilson.

Vietnam: Ten Years Later; What Have We Learned. (Illus.). 112p. 1985. pap. 4.00 (ISBN 0-318-11839-4, S/N 008-020-01023-5). USGPO.

Vietnam: The Definitive Documentation of Human Decisions, 2 vols. Ed. by George W. Johnson. 1979. 60.00 set (ISBN 0-685-87632-2). Vol. 1 (ISBN 0-930576-03-9). Vol. 2 (ISBN 0-930576-04-7). E M Coleman Ent.

Vietnam: the Endless War: From Monthly Review, 1954-1970. Paul M. Sweezy et al. LC 77-127927. pap. 40.90 (2030759). Bks Demand UMI.

Vietnam: The Habit of War. Robert Archer. 56p. 1983. 8.00x (ISBN 0-904393-68-2, Pub. by CIIR). State Mutual Bk.

Vietnam: The Heartland Remembers. Stanley W. Beesley. 208p. 1988. 16.95 (ISBN 0-8061-2062-2); pap. 7.95 (ISBN 0-8061-2162-9). U of Okla Pr.

Vietnam: The Naval Story. Ed. by Frank Uhlig, Jr. LC 86-16345. (Illus.). 288p. 1986. 28.95 (ISBN 0-87021-014-9). Naval Inst Pr.

Vietnam: The Other Side of Glory. William R. Kimball. LC 86-19948. 336p. 1987. 16.95 (ISBN 0-938936-57-3). Daring Bks.

Vietnam: The Other War. Charles R. Anderson. LC 81-15677. (Illus.). 244p. 1982. 13.95 (ISBN 0-89141-137-2). Presidio Pr.

Vietnam: The Valor & the Sorrow. Thomas D. Boettcher. (Illus.). 384p. 1985. 29.95 (ISBN 0-316-10083-8); pap. 16.95 (ISBN 0-316-10081-1). Little.

Vietnam: The View from Moscow, Peking, Washington. Daniel S. Papp. LC 80-20117. (Illus.). 263p. 1981. lib. bdg. 19.95x (ISBN 0-89950-010-2). McFarland & Co.

Vietnam, the War at Home: The Antiwar Movement, 1964-1968. Thomas Powers. 1984. pap. 7.95 (ISBN 0-8398-2855-1). G K Hall.

Vietnam: The War in the Air: A Pictorial History of the U. S. Air Forces in the Vietnam War: Air Force, Army, Navy, & the Marines. Gene Gurney. LC 84-11327. (Illus.). 277p. 1985. text ed. 17.95 (ISBN 0-517-55350-3). Crown.

Vietnam: The War Nobody Won. Stanley Karnow. LC 83-81891. (Headline Ser.: No. 263). (Illus.). 64p. (Orig.). 1983. pap. 4.00 (ISBN 0-87124-083-1). Foreign Policy.

Vietnam There & Here. Margot C. Mabie. LC 84-20518. (Illus.). 176p. (gr. 4 up). 1985. 11.95 (ISBN 0-8050-0545-5). H Holt & Co.

Vietnam There & Here. Margot C. Mabie. LC 84-20518. (Illus.). 11.95 (ISBN 0-03-072067-2). HR&W.

Vietnam: Three Battles. S. L. Marshall. (Quality Paperbacks Ser.). (Illus.). 242p. 1982. pap. 8.95 (ISBN 0-306-80174-4). Da Capo.

Vietnam Tracks: Armor in Battle, 1945-1975. Simon Dunstan. (Illus.). 192p. 1983. 20.00 (ISBN 0-89141-171-2). Presidio Pr.

Vietnam Trauma in American Foreign Policy, 1945-1975. Paul M. Kattenburg. LC 79-702. 354p. 1980. 19.95 (ISBN 0-87855-378-9); pap. 14.95 (ISBN 0-87855-903-5). Transaction Bks.

Vietnam: Trials & Tribulations of a Nation. D. R. SarDesai. LC 88-80065. (Illus.). 200p. 1988. 29.95 (ISBN 0-941910-04-0). Long Beach Pubns.

Vietnam under Communism. Nguyen Van Cahn & Earle Cooper. LC 83-10754. (Illus.). xvi, 312p. 1985. pap. 9.95x (ISBN 0-8179-7852-6). Hoover Inst Pr.

Vietnam Veteran: A History of Neglect. David E. Bonior & Steven M. Champlin. 222p. pap. 9.95 (ISBN 0-275-92026-7, B2026). Praeger.

Vietnam Veteran: A History of Neglect. David E. Bonior et al. 208p. 1984. 35.00 (ISBN 0-275-91733-9, C1733). Praeger.

Vietnam Veteran Redefined: Fact & Fiction. Ed. by Ghislaine Boulanger & Charles Kadushin. 200p. 1986. text ed. 22.50 (ISBN 0-89859-761-7). L Erlbaum Assocs.

Vietnam Veteran: Studies in Post-Traumatic Shock Disorders. Ed. by Wilfred Quaytman. (Journal of Contemporary Psychotherapy Ser.). 133p. 1987. pap. 12.95 (ISBN 0-89885-217-X). Human Sci Pr.

Vietnam Veterans Memorial. Michael Katakis. (Illus.). 96p. 1988. pap. 15.95 (ISBN 0-517-57019-X). Crown.

Vietnam Veterans Parade, Chicago, 1986. Tom Conroy & Kris Colt. LC 87-70018. (Illus.). 144p. (Orig.). 1987. pap. 22.00 (ISBN 0-9618111-0-2). Nam Vets Pub.

Vietnam Veterans: The Road to Recovery. Joel O. Brende & Erwin R. Parson. LC 84-26396. 300p. 1985. 17.95 (ISBN 0-306-41966-1, Plenum Pr). Plenum Pub.

Vietnam Vets: Road to Recovery. Brende & Parson. LC 86-13770. 320p. 1986. pap. 3.95 (ISBN 0-451-14724-3, Sig). NAL.

Vietnam Vets Sound Off, Part II. Thomas L. Hakes. 30p. 1986. pap. 6.75 (ISBN 0-915020-61-0). Bardic.

Vietnam Voices: Perspectives on the War Years, 1941-1982. John C. Pratt. LC 84-11172. 1984. pap. 12.95 (ISBN 0-14-006359-5). Penguin.

Vietnam War. E. B. Fincher. (gr. 7 up). 1980. PLB 11.90 (ISBN 0-531-04112-3, C07). Watts.

Vietnam War. (Flashpoints Ser.). (Illus.). (YA) (gr. 7 up). Date not set. write for info. Rourke Corp.

Vietnam War. LC 87-18224. (Illus.). 768p. (gr. 6 up). 1988. PLB 199.95x (ISBN 0-86307-852-4). Marshall Cavendish.

Vietnam War: A Study in the Making of American Policy. Michael P. Sullivan. LC 85-7497. 208p. 1985. 20.00 (ISBN 0-8131-1528-0). U Pr of Ky.

Vietnam War Almanac. Harry G. Summers, Jr. LC 83-14054. (Illus.). 416p. 1985. 24.95 (ISBN 0-8160-1017-X); pap. 12.95. Facts on File.

Vietnam War: An Almanac. Ed. by John S. Bowman. (Illus.). 512p. 1986. pap. 24.95 (ISBN 0-345-32631-8). Pharos Bks NY.

Vietnam War Bibliography: Selected from Cornell University's John M. Echols Collection of Southeast Asia. Christopher L. Sugnet et al. LC 83-47501. (Libraries & Librarianship). 592p. 1983. 45.00x (ISBN 0-669-06680-X). Lexington Bks.

Vietnam War Facts Quiz: The Truth & Drama of American Involvement. Erhard Konerding. LC 85-63489. (Illus.). 96p. (Orig.). 1986. pap. 6.95 (ISBN 0-913337-07-2). Southfarm Pr.

Vietnam War in American Literature. Nancy Anisfield. Ed. by Jerold M. Starr. (Lessons of the Vietnam War Ser.). (Illus.). 32p. 1988. pap. text ed. 3.00 (ISBN 0-945919-09-3). Ctr Social Studies.

Vietnam War in Retrospect. Martin F. Herz. LC 83-20600. (Illus.). 80p. 1984. pap. 5.75 (ISBN 0-934742-28-6). Geo U Sch For Serv.

Vietnam War in Retrospect. Martin F. Herz. 80p. 1985. pap. text ed. 6.25 (ISBN 0-8191-5062-2, Inst for Study Diplomacy). U Pr of Amer.

Vietnam War: Lessons from Yesterday for Today. George C. Herring & Kevin Simon. Ed. by Jerold M. Starr. (Lessons of the Vietnam War Ser.). (Illus.). 24p. 1988. pap. text ed. 3.00 (ISBN 0-945919-12-3). Ctr Social Studies.

Vietnam War Literature: An Annotated Bibliography of Imaginative Works About Americans Fighting in Vietnam. John Newman. LC 81-21509. 129p. 1982. 16.50 (ISBN 0-8108-1514-1). Scarecrow.

Vietnam War Literature: An Annotated Bibliography of Imaginative Works about Americans Fighting in Vietnam. 2nd ed. John Newman & Ann Hilfinger. LC 88-15747. 299p. 1988. 27.50 (ISBN 0-8108-2155-9). Scarecrow.

Vietnam War Memorials: An Illustrated Reference to Veterans Tributes Throughout the United States. Jerry L. Strait & Sandra S. Strait. LC 87-46385. 240p. 1988. lib. bdg. 29.95x (ISBN 0-89950-329-2). McFarland & Co.

Vietnam War: Opposing Viewpoints. Ed. by David L. Bender et al. LC 84-13628. (Opposing Viewpoints Ser.). (Illus.). 200p. (Orig.). 1984. lib. bdg. 13.95 (ISBN 0-89908-349-8); pap. text ed. 6.95 (ISBN 0-89908-324-2). Greenhaven.

Vietnam War: The Illustrated History of the Conflict in Southeast Asia. Bernard C. Nalty. 1979. 19.95 (ISBN 0-517-53612-9). Crown.

Vietnam: War Without Fronts. Thomas Thayer. (Special Studies). 1985. pap. 24.00x (ISBN 0-8133-7132-5). Westview.

Vietnam Weapons Handbook. Davis Rossner-Owen. (Illus.). 128p. (Orig.). 1986. pap. 7.99 (ISBN 0-85059-838-9, Pub. by PSL P Stephens England). Sterling.

Vietnam: Why Did We Go? Avro Manhattan. LC 84-70684. 192p. (Orig.). 1984. pap. 5.95 (ISBN 0-937958-19-0). Chick Pubns.

Vietnam Wives: Women & Children Surviving Life with Veterans Suffering Post Traumatic Stress Disorder. Aphrodite Matsakis. LC 87-51346. 310p. (Orig.). 1988. 16.95 (ISBN 0-933149-22-0). Woodbine House.

Vietnam Years: 1000 Questions & Answers. Michael Clodfelter & John Musgrave. LC 86-60205. (Illus.). 218p. Date not set. pap. 7.95 (ISBN 0-933341-38-5). Quinlan Pr.

Vietnam 1969-1970: A Company Commander's Journal. Michael L. Lanning. 1988. pap. 3.95 (ISBN 0-317-67158-8). Ivy Books.

Vietnamese AF - The South Vietnamese AF 1945-1975. (Illus.). 1987. pap. 8.95 (ISBN 0-89747-193-8, 6046). Squad Sig Pubns.

Vietnamese Air Force, Nineteen Fifty-One - Nineteen Seventy-Five: An Analysis of Its Role In Combat & Fourteen Hours At Kohn Tang. William W. Momyer & Louis L. Wilson, Jr. (USAF Southeast Asia Monograph Ser.: Vol. 3, Monograph 4 & 5). (Illus.). 161p. 1986. pap. write for info. (ISBN 0-912799-28-5). Off Air Force.

Vietnamese Anticolonialism, 1885-1925. David G. Marr. (Center for South & Southeast Asia Studies, UC Berkeley: No. 33). 1980. 28.00x (ISBN 0-520-04278-6); pap. 11.95x (ISBN 0-520-04277-8). U of Cal Pr.

Vietnamese Ceramics. Ed. by Carol M. Young & Marie-France Dupoizat. (Illus.). 1982. 55.00x (ISBN 0-19-582558-6). Oxford U Pr.

Vietnamese Communism: A Research Bibliography. Chau Phan Thien. LC 75-16961. 359p. 1975. lib. bdg. 67.95 (ISBN 0-8371-7950-5, CVC/). Greenwood.

Vietnamese Communism, 1925-1945. Huynh K. Khanh. LC 81-70696. (Paperback Ser.). 384p. 1982. 38.50x (ISBN 0-8014-1369-9). Cornell U Pr.

Vietnamese Communism, 1925-1945. Huynh K. Khanh. LC 81-70696. (Illus.). 384p. 1986. pap. 12.95x (ISBN 0-8014-9397-8). Cornell U Pr.

Vietnamese Cookery. Jill N. Miller. LC 68-13869. 1968. pap. 8.25 (ISBN 0-8048-1200-4). C E Tuttle.

Vietnamese Cooking: Recipes My Mother Taught Me. Anh T. Stuart. (Illus.). 104p. (Orig.). 1987. pap. 14.95 (ISBN 0-207-15472-4, Pub. by Angus & Robertson). Salem Hse Pubs.

Vietnamese-English Dictionary. Ed. by Nguyen-Dinh-Hoa. LC 66-17773. (Eng. & Vietnamese.). 1966. 17.95 (ISBN 0-8048-0618-7). C E Tuttle.

Vietnamese-English Dictionary Romanized. (Vietnamese & Eng.). 27.50 (ISBN 0-87559-014-4). Shalom.

Vietnamese-English, English Vietnamese Dictionary. Ed. by Le-Ba-Kong & Le-Ba-Khanh. (Vietnamese & Eng.). 45.00x (ISBN 0-8044-0310-4). Ungar.

Vietnamese-English Phrase Book of Everyday Language. Le Ngoc Diep. LC 75-27356. 1975. pap. 6.95x (ISBN 0-8044-6392-1). Ungar.

View of the State of Europe During the Middle Ages, 2 vols. Henry Hallam. 1979. Repr. of 1880 ed. Set. lib. bdg. 65.00 (ISBN 0-8495-2254-4). Arden Lib.
View of the State of Europe During the Middle Ages, 2 Vols. Henry Hallam. 1366p. Repr. of 1880 ed. Set. lib. bdg. 125.00 (ISBN 0-8414-5248-2). Folcroft.
View of the United States of America Between the Years 1787 & 1794. Tench Coxe. LC 64-24342. 1965. Repr. of 1794 ed. 57.50x (ISBN 0-678-00070-0). Kelley.
View of the Valley. Jean Curtis. 1985. 24.95x (ISBN 0-7090-1800-2, Pub. by R Hale Ltd UK). State Mutual Bk.
View of the Views about Hamlet. Albert Tolman. LC 73-9665. Repr. of 1898 ed. lib. bdg. 17.00 (ISBN 0-8414-2685-6). Folcroft.
View of the World: Selected Journalism. Norman Lewis. (Travel Classic Ser.). 288p. (Orig.). 1986. pap. 9.95 (ISBN 0-907871-41-0, Pub. by Eland Bks UK). Hippocrene Bks.
View of Washington Bottom: A Glance at Blennerhassett Island. Charles M. Bose. write for info. (ISBN 0-9612606-0-2). McClain.
View of Washington, D. C. Nita Scoggan. LC 86-60219. (Illus.). 48p. 1987. pap. 2.95 (ISBN 0-910487-07-3). Royalty Pub.
View of West Florida, Embracing Its Geography, Topography, & C., with an Appendix Treating of Its Antiquities, Land Titles, & Canals, & Containing a Map Exhibiting a Chart of the Coast, a Plan of Pensacola, & the Entrance of the Harbour. John L. Williams. Intro. by Herbert J. Doherty, Jr. LC 75-45282. (Floridiana Facsimile & Reprint Ser.). (Illus.). 1976. Repr. of 1827 ed. 8.50 (ISBN 0-8130-0375-X). U Presses Fla.
View the Land: Israel Today. Anne Dexter. LC 86-203335. 245p. 1986. pap. 4.50 (ISBN 0-88270-609-8). Bridge Pub.
View Vertical & Other Essays. Winifred M. Kirkland. LC 79-93350. (Essay Index Reprint Ser). 1920. 19.00 (ISBN 0-8369-1300-0). Ayer Co Pubs.
Viewdata Revolution. Sam Fedida & Rex Malik. LC 79-23869. 186p. 1980. 47.95 (ISBN 0-470-26879-4). Halsted Pr.
Viewdata Systems: A Practical Evaluation Guide. R. J. Firth. 100p. 1982. pap. 14.20 (ISBN 0-471-89431-1). Wiley.
Viewer's Guide to Film Theory & Criticism. Robert T. Eberwein. LC 79-9380. 243p. 1979. 18.50 (ISBN 0-8108-1237-1). Scarecrow.
Viewer's Guide to the Voyage of Charles Darwin. CBN-Graff. 48p. 1979. saddle stitch 8.95 (ISBN 0-8403-2167-8). Kendall-Hunt.
Viewer's Television Book: A Personal Guide to Understanding Television & Its Influence. Stanley J. Baran. LC 80-81369. 109p. (Orig.). 1980. pap. 6.95 (ISBN 0-936522-00-3). Penrith.
Viewfinders: Black Women Photographers, 1839-1985. Jeanne Moutoussamy-Ashe. LC 85-16233. (Illus.). 224p. 1986. 19.95 (ISBN 0-396-08609-8); pap. 12.95 (ISBN 0-396-08611-X). Dodd.
Viewgraphs on International Relations. Joseph D. Lowe. LC 88-91062. (Illus.). xii, 100p. 1988. 17.50 (ISBN 0-930325-10-9). Lowe Pub.
Viewing International Relations & World Politics. Richard H. Foster & Robert V. Edington. (Illus.). 192p. 1985. pap. text ed. write for info. (ISBN 0-13-942087-8). P-H.
Viewing the Past: An Interpretive Guidebook. 60p. 1977. pap. 2.00 (ISBN 0-910524-03-3). Eastern Wash.
Viewpoint. Ben Bova. (Boskone Bk.). (Illus.). 1977. 10.00 (ISBN 0-915368-14-5). New Eng SF Assoc.
Viewpoint on Nutrition: Featuring the Celebrity Way of Dieting & Keeping Fit. Arnold Pike. LC 80-24024. 221p. 1980. Repr. of 1973 ed. lib. bdg. 22.95x (ISBN 0-89370-621-3). Borgo Pr.
Viewpoints. Michael Baybak. 32p. pap. cancelled (ISBN 0-915598-09-4). Church of Scient Info.
Viewpoints: A Listening & Conversation Course in Russian. Donald K. Jarvis & Elena D. Lifschitz. iv, 66p. (Orig.). 1985. pap. text ed. 4.95 (ISBN 0-89357-152-0); pap. text ed. 3.95 tchr's. manual v, 37 p. (ISBN 0-89357-153-9). Slavica.
Viewpoints in Biology, 4 vols. Ed. by J. D. Carthy & C. L. Duddington. LC 63-4816. Vol. 1. pap. 75.00 (ISBN 0-317-42212-X, 2025766); Vol. 2. pap. 64.50 (ISBN 0-317-42213-8); Vol. 3. pap. 67.50 (ISBN 0-317-42214-6); Vol. 4. pap. 66.50 (ISBN 0-317-42215-4). Bks Demand UMI.
Viewpoints of a Commodity Trader. Roy W. Longstreet. 160p. 1986. Repr. of 1967 ed. 13.95x (ISBN 0-934380-14-7). Traders Pr.
Viewpoints on Folklife: Looking at the Overlooked. Warren E. Roberts. Ed. by Simon J. Bronner. LC 87-22710. (American Material Culture & Folklife Ser.). (Illus.). 350p. 1988. 44.95 (ISBN 0-8357-1849-2). UMI Res Pr.
Viewpoints on Supply Side Economics. Thomas J. Hailstones. 1983. pap. text ed. 27.00 (ISBN 0-8359-8386-2, Reston). P-H.
Viewpoints: Selections Worth Thinking & Writing About. W. Royce Adams. LC 88-81148. 416p. 1988. pap. text ed. 11.00 (ISBN 0-669-16129-2); instr's. ed. 2.00 (ISBN 0-669-20033-6). Heath.
Viewpoints: The Library of Congress Selection of Pictorial Treasures. new ed. Ed. by Alan Fern & Milton Kaplan. LC 76-5442. (Illus.). 1976. 12.00 (ISBN 0-405-08106-5). Ayer Co Pubs.
Viewpoints U. S. A., A Basic ESL Reader. Roberta J. Vann & Vivian P. Hefley. 286p. 1984. pap. 14.95 scp (ISBN 0-06-046791-6, HarpC). Har-row.
Viewport Technician: A Guide to Portable Software Design. Michael B. Bentley. 1987. pap. 24.95 (ISBN 0-673-18383-1). Scott F.
Views. Edward Dorn. Ed. by Donald Allen. LC 79-25498. (Writing 40 Ser.). 144p. 12.00 (ISBN 0-87704-050-8); pap. 5.95 (ISBN 0-87704-051-6). Four Seasons Foun.
Views. Enslin. 1973. 16.00 (ISBN 0-685-36866-1); pap. 8.00 (ISBN 0-685-36867-X). Elizabeth Pr.
Views About Hamlet & Other Essays. Albert H. Tolman. LC 78-177468. Repr. of 1904 ed. 16.00 (ISBN 0-404-06477-9). AMS Pr.
Views & Interviews on Journalism. Ed. by Charles F. Wingate. LC 78-125724. (American Journalists). 1970. Repr. of 1875 ed. 24.50 (ISBN 0-405-01707-3). Ayer Co Pubs.
Views & Reviews, 2 Vols in 1. facsimile ed. Havelock Ellis. LC 79-111829. (Essay Index Reprint Ser.). 1932. 29.00 (ISBN 0-8369-1606-9). Ayer Co Pubs.
Views & Reviews. Henry James. LC 79-98026. Repr. of 1908 ed. 15.00 (ISBN 0-404-03547-7). AMS Pr.
Views & Reviews. facs. ed. Henry James. LC 68-22101. (Essay Index Reprint Ser). 1908. 16.00 (ISBN 0-8369-0566-0). Ayer Co Pubs.
Views & Teachings on Architecture by John Ruskin. Martin H. Lenahan. (Illus.). 139p. 1982. 76.85 (ISBN 0-86650-015-4). Gloucester Art.
Views & Viewmakers of Urban America: Lithographs of Towns & Cities in the United States & Canada, Notes on the Artists & Publishers, & a Union Catalog of Their Work, 1825-1925. John W. Reps. LC 83-6495. (Illus.). 608p. 1984. text ed. 89.50x (ISBN 0-8262-0416-3). U of Mo Pr.
Views from a Many-Windowed Tower: Studies of Imagination in the Works of Gregory of Tours. Giselle De Nie. (Studies in Classical Antiquity). 360p. 1987. pap. text ed. 85.00 (ISBN 90-6203-719-4, Pub. by Rodopi Holland). Humanities.
Views from a Tuscan Vineyard. Julian More. LC 87-45096. (Illus.). 144p. 1987. 19.95 (ISBN 0-8050-0275-8). H Holt & Co.
Views from a Window: Conversations with Gore Vidal. Ed. by Robert J. Stanton & Gore Vidal. 320p. 1980. lib. bdg. 14.95 (ISBN 0-8184-0302-0). Lyle Stuart.
Views from Jade Terrace: Chinese Women Artists 1300-1912. Marsha Weidner et al. LC 88-80498. (Illus.). 256p. 1988. 45.00 (ISBN 0-8478-1003-8). Rizzoli Intl.
Views from the Bench: The Judiciary & Constitutional Politics. Ed. by Mark W. Cannon & David M. O'Brien. LC 85-9990. (Chatham House Series on Change in American Politics). 352p. 1985. 25.00 (ISBN 0-934540-34-9); pap. text ed. 14.95x (ISBN 0-934540-33-0). Chatham Hse Pubs.
Views from the Hollywood Hills. Julian & Careymore. LC 86-18335. 1987. 19.95 (ISBN 0-8050-0206-5). H Holt & Co.
Views from the Intersection. Virginia Mollencott & Catherine Barry. 112p. pap. 7.95 (ISBN 0-8245-0647-2). Crossroad NY.
Views from the Island. rev. ed. Charles E. Wadsworth. LC 78-52619. (Illus.). 10.00 (ISBN 0-930954-05-X); deluxe ed. 75.00 (ISBN 0-930954-06-8). Tidal Pr.
Views from the Real World: Early Talks, 1918-1934. G. I. Gurdjieff. 1975. pap. 11.95 (ISBN 0-525-48251-2). Dutton.
Views from the Top. Ed. by Jerome M. Rosow. 210p. 1986. 16.95x (ISBN 0-8160-1123-0). Facts on File.
Views from the Trade. Chicago Board of Trade, Education Department Staff. (Readings in Futures Markets Ser.: Bk. 3). pap. 12.00 (ISBN 0-317-46967-3, 52-37). Chicago Bd Trade.
Views from Thornhill: Of Family, Farm & Other Fancies. Dee Hardie. LC 87-31773. (Illus.). 288p. 1988. 17.95 (ISBN 0-689-11983-6). Atheneum.
Views from Valley Front. Beatrice J. Stubbs. LC 86-12904. 1986. pap. 6.95 (ISBN 0-89587-053-3). Blair.
Views in Texas, Eighteen Ninety-Five to Ninety-Six. Henry Stark. (Illus.). 120p. 1974. 15.00 (ISBN 0-88426-039-9). Encino Pr.
Views of a Vanishing Frontier. John C. Ewers et al. (Illus.). 150p. (Orig.). 1984. 29.95 (ISBN 0-936364-12-2); pap. 14.95 (ISBN 0-936364-13-0). Joslyn Art.
Views of American Constitutional Law: Its Bearing Upon American Slavery. facs. ed. William Goodell. LC 78-138337. (Black Heritage Library Collection Ser.). 1845. 15.25 (ISBN 0-8369-8729-2). Ayer Co Pubs.
Views of American Slavery, Taken a Century Ago. Anthony Benezet. LC 78-82171. (Anti-Slavery Crusade in America Ser.). 1969. Repr. of 1858 ed. 12.00 (ISBN 0-405-00610-1). Ayer Co Pubs.
Views of Berlin. Ed. by Gerhard Kirchhoff. 272p. 1988. 35.00 (ISBN 0-8176-3380-4). Birkhauser.
Views of Christian Nurture & Subjects Related Thereto. Horace Bushnell. LC 74-23297. 264p. 1975. Repr. of 1847 ed. lib. bdg. 40.00x (ISBN 0-8201-1147-3). Schol Facsimiles.
Views of Florence & Tuscany 11. rev. ed. Giuseppe Zocchi & Elaine E. Dee. LC 68-59110. (Illus.). 1971. pap. 7.00 (ISBN 0-88397-070-8, Pub. by Intl Exhibit Foun). C E Tuttle.
Views of Jeopardy. Jack Gilbert. LC 72-144762. (Yale Series of Younger Poets: No. 58). Repr. of 1962 ed. 18.00 (ISBN 0-404-53858-4). AMS Pr.
Views of Los Angeles. rev. ed. Ed. by William Burnett. (Illus.). 1979. 24.95 (ISBN 0-9602274-1-5); pap. 14.95 (ISBN 0-9602274-0-7). Portriga Pubns.
Views of Medieval Bhutan: The Diary & Drawings of Samuel Davis, 1783. Michael Aris. LC 81-85435. (Illus.). 124p. 1982. 39.95 (ISBN 0-87474-210-2, ARVM, Pub. by Serindia Pubs London). Smithsonian.
Views of Nature. Alexander Von Humboldt. Tr. by E. C. Otte & Henry G. Bohn. LC 74-26302. (History, Philosophy & Sociology of Science Ser). 1975. Repr. 36.50x (ISBN 0-405-06626-0). Ayer Co Pubs.
Views of Rome: From the Thomas Ashby Collection in the Vatican Library. Raymond Keaveney. Ed. by Leonard E. Boyle et al. LC 87-63617. (Illus.). 304p. 1988. 67.50 (ISBN 0-935748-89-X). Scala Books.
Views of Rome Then & Now. Giovanni B. Piranesi & Herschel Levit. (Illus.). 96p. (Orig.). 1976. pap. 8.95 (ISBN 0-486-23339-1). Dover.
Views of Salem History. Dale E. Shaffer. (Illus.). 75p. (Orig.). 1985. pap. 4.25 (ISBN 0-915060-22-1). D E Shaffer.
Views of Society & Manner in America. Francis D'Arusmont. 1988. Repr. lib. bdg. 75.00x. Am Biog Serv.
Views of Society & Manners in America. Frances W. D'Arusmont. Ed. by Paul R. Baker. LC 63-10878. pap. 79.30 (ISBN 0-317-10071-8, 2002996). Bks Demand UMI.
Views of Society & Manners in the North of Ireland: Letters Written in the Year 1818. John Gamble. LC 77-87688. 1977. Repr. of 1819 ed. 40.00 (ISBN 0-404-16487-0). AMS Pr.
Views of Spaceship Earth. Stan Proper. 1985. 3.00 (ISBN 0-932593-02-X). Black Bear.
Views of Texas, Eighteen Fifty-Two to Eighteen Fifty-Six. Ron Tyler. LC 88-70267. (Illus.). 80p. 1988. pap. 20.00 (ISBN 0-88360-061-7). Amon Carter.
Views of the Green: Presentations from New Directions for the Conservation of Parks; An International Working Conference. Ed. by Paul C. Pritchard. 154p. 1985. 14.95 (ISBN 0-940091-14-3); pap. 9.95 (ISBN 0-940091-13-5). Natl Parks & Cons.
Views of the Halls of the Hermitage & Winter Palace: In Watercolours & Drawings of the Mid-Nineteenth Century. Ed. by A. N. Voronikhin. (Illus.). 236p. (Rus. & Eng.). 1983. 135.00x (ISBN 0-317-57478-7, Pub. by Collets UK). State Mutual Bk.
Views of the Irish Peasantry, 1800-1916. Ed. by Daniel J. Casey & Robert E. Rhodes. LC 76-39913. (Illus.). 225p. 1977. 25.00 (ISBN 0-208-01630-9, Archon). Shoe String.
Views of the Past: Essays in Old World Prehistory & Paleoanthropology. Ed. by Leslie G. Freeman. (World Anthropology Ser.). (Illus.). xii, 466p. 1978. 49.25 (ISBN 90-279-7670-8). Mouton.
Views of the Past: Topographical Drawings in the British Library. Ann Payne. (Illus.). 1987. pap. 9.95 (ISBN 0-7123-0130-5, Pub. by British Lib). Longwood Pub Group.
Views of the Present...Visions of the Past. Randy M. Olson. Ed. by William N. Kremer. (Illus.). 225p. (Orig.). 1984. pap. text ed. 22.50 (ISBN 0-318-03518-9). Gazette Print.
Views of Trinidad. Michel J. Cazabon. (Illus.). Repr. of 1984 ed. 80.00x (ISBN 0-910938-92-X). McGilvery.
Views of Venice by Canaletto. Canaletto. (Illus.). 8.50 (ISBN 0-8446-0050-4). Peter Smith.
Views of Venice by Canaletto. Antonio Canaletto. (Illus.). pap. 7.95 (ISBN 0-486-22705-7). Dover.
Views on Henley-on-Thames. Margaret Shaida. 182p. 1985. 75.00x (ISBN 0-907349-80-3, Pub by Spindlewood). State Mutual Bk.
Views on Individualism: Presentations. Israel M. Kirzner et al. Ed. & intro. by Donna C. Charron. 92p. (Orig.). 1986. pap. 5.00 (ISBN 0-9616369-0-4). St Louis Human.
Views on Science, Technology & Development. Ed. by V. Rabinowitch & E. Rabinowitch. LC 74-32201. 300p. 1975. 55.00 (ISBN 0-08-018241-0). Pergamon.
Views on the News: The Developing Editorial Syndrome, 1500-1800. Jim A. Hart. LC 79-112388. (New Horizons in Journalism Ser). 251p. 1970. 8.95x (ISBN 0-8093-0455-4), S Ill U Pr.
Views on the Problems of Regional Planning in an Institutional & Systems Approach. (Working Papers Ser.: No. 78-24). 52p. 1978. pap. 6.00 (ISBN 0-686-75495-6, CRD065, UNCRD). UNIPUB.
Views on U. S. Economic & Business History: Molding the Mixed Enterprise Economy. Ed. by Jack Blicksilver. 350p. 1984. pap. 25.00 (ISBN 0-88406-165-5). Ga St U Busn Pub.
ViewText 'Eighty-One Conference. 50.00 (ISBN 0-686-33030-7). Info Gatekeepers.
Viga-Glum's Saga. Tr. by L. M. Hollander. LC 77-186718. (Library of Scandinavian Literature Ser.: Vol. 14). 1972. 7.50x (ISBN 0-89067-021-8). Am Scandinavian.
Viga-Glums Saga: With the Tales of Ogmund Bash & Thorvald Chatterbox. Tr. & intro. by John McKinnell. LC 87-71830. (New Saga Library Ser.). (Illus.). 160p. (Orig.). 1987. pap. 11.95 (ISBN 0-86241-084-3, Pub. by Canongate Pub Ltd). Dufour.
Vigeland: The Sculptor & His Works. Ragna Stang. (Tanum Token Ser.). (Illus.). 190p. 1980. pap. 20.00x (ISBN 82-518-0152-4, N400). Vanous.
Vigencia Politica & Literaria De Martin Morua Delgado. Aleyda T. Portuondo. (Coleccion Cuba & Sus Jueces). 1978. pap. 2.00 (ISBN 0-89729-205-7). Ediciones.
Vigesima Asambles De la Comision Interamericana De Mujeres Acta Final: Santo Domingo, Republica Dominicana del 26 de Octubre al 4de Noviembre de 1980. OAS, Inter-American Commission of Women. 110p. (Span.). 1980. pap. 8.00 (ISBN 0-686-74521-3). OAS.
Vigil. Swami Paramananda. 1923. 3.00 (ISBN 0-911564-19-5). Vedanta Ctr.
Vigil. Clay Reynolds. LC 87-43106. (Southwest Life & Letters Ser.). 232p. 1988. pap. 8.95 (ISBN 0-87074-269-8). SMU Press.
Vigil. R. C. Reynolds. 224p. 1985. 13.95 (ISBN 0-312-84639-8, Pub. by Marek). St Martin.
Vigil in Benicarlo. Manuel Azana. Ed. by Josephine Stewart & Paul Stewart. LC 81-65339. (Illus.). 136p. 1981. 16.50 (ISBN 0-8386-3093-6). Fairleigh Dickinson.
Vigil, Novel. Elisabeth Young-Bruehl. LC 82-17160. 167p. 1983. 16.95 (ISBN 0-8071-1075-2). La State U Pr.
Vigil of Prayer. Nolan P. Howington. (Orig.). 1987. pap. 4.95 (ISBN 0-8054-1505-X). Broadman.
Vigil of the Wounded. Philip Y. Minthorn. Ed. by Maurice Kenny & Josh Gosciak. (Illus.). 60p. (Orig.). 1987. pap. 5.95 (ISBN 0-936556-15-3). Contact Two.
Vigilance: The Problem of Sustained Attention. C. M. Stroh. 1971. 34.00 (ISBN 0-08-016711-X). Pergamon.
Vigilante. Gilbert Morris. 256p. (Orig.). 1988. pap. 4.50 (ISBN 0-8423-7811-1). Tyndale.
Vigilante Days & Ways, 2 Vols. Nathaniel P. Langford. LC 76-156021. Repr. of 1890 ed. Set. 72.50 (ISBN 0-404-09121-0). AMS Pr.
Vigilante Days & Ways. facsimile ed. Nathaniel P. Langford. LC 71-160979. (Select Bibliographies Reprint Ser). Repr. of 1890 ed. 38.50 (ISBN 0-8369-5847-0). Ayer Co Pubs.
Vigilante Days at Virginia City. facs. ed. Fred Lockley. 21p. pap. 2.95 (ISBN 0-8466-0146-X, SJS146). Shorey.
Vigilante Days: Frontier Justice Along the Niobrara. Harold Hutton. LC 76-17742. (Illus.). 365p. 1978. 15.95 (ISBN 0-8040-0738-1, SB). Ohio U Pr.
Vigilante Justice, No. 82. Jake Logan. 192p. 1985. pap. 2.75 (ISBN 0-425-10442-7). Berkley Pub.
Vigilantes. Alan Ansen. 60p. 1987. limited signed edition 15.00 (ISBN 0-934953-18-X); pap. 6.00 (ISBN 0-934953-17-1). Water Row Pr.
Vigilantes in Gold Rush San Francisco. Robert M. Senkewicz. LC 83-40284. (Illus.). 288p. 1985. 24.95 (ISBN 0-8047-1230-1). Stanford U Pr.
Vigilantes of Montana. Thomas J. Dimsdale. LC 53-9887. (Western Frontier Library: No. 1). 1985. pap. 6.95 (ISBN 0-8061-1379-0). U of Okla Pr.
Vigilantes on the Middle Border: A Study of Self-Appointed Law Enforcement in the States of the Upper Mississippi from 1840 to 1880. 02/1987 ed. Patrick B. Nolan. Ed. by Harold Hyman & Stuart Bruchey. (American Legal & Constitutional History Ser.). 256p. lib. bdg. 30.00 (ISBN 0-8240-8288-5). Garland Pub.
Vigilantes Ride in 1882. Herbert Stevens. 20p. 1979. Ye Galleon.
Vigilia & Cantico. Ramon R. D. Hoyos. (Poetry Ser.). 70p. 1982. pap. 6.00 (ISBN 0-686-37370-7). Edit Asol.
Vigner Dictionnaire des Chateaux de France. Bernard de Montgolfier. 250p. (Fr.). pap. 135.00 (ISBN 0-686-56837-0, M-6615). French & Eur.
Vigneron dans Sa Vigne see Oeuvres.
Vigneron Dans Sa Vigne see Oeuvres.
Vignettes. Thelma S. Crosby. 32p. 1987. 6.95 (ISBN 0-8062-3145-9). Carlton.
Vignettes from Indian War. George Macmun. (Illus.). 214p. 1984. Repr. of 1901 ed. text ed. 37.50x (ISBN 0-86590-356-5, Pub. by B R Pub Corp Delhi). Apt Bks.
Vignettes from the Life of Abdu'l-Baha. Annamarie Honnold. (Illus.). 224p. pap. 9.50 (ISBN 0-85398-129-9). G Ronald Pub.
Vignettes of Early Days in the Jewish Community of Great Barrington, Massachusetts. Shifra R. Deykin. (Illus.). 160p. 1987. 15.00 (ISBN 0-941583-12-0). Attic Rev Pr.
Vignettes of Legal History: Second Series. Julius J. Marke. (Illus.). xiv, 274p. 1977. lib. bdg. 15.00x (ISBN 0-8377-0833-8). Rothman.
Vignettes of Louisiana History. Louisiana Pen Women. 12.50 (ISBN 0-87511-068-1). Claitors.
Vignettes of Manhattan. facs. ed. Brander Matthews. LC 70-90587. (Short Story Index Reprint Ser.). 1894. 18.00 (ISBN 0-8369-3070-3). Ayer Co Pubs.
Vignettes of Mexico. William J. Conlen. 1937. 25.00 (ISBN 0-686-17227-2). Scholars Ref Lib.

Village "Contracts" in Tokugawa Japan: Fifty Specimens with English Translations & Comments. Dan F. Henderson. LC 74-31050. (Asian Law Ser.: No. 2). (Illus.). 220p. 1975. 30.00x (ISBN 0-295-95405-1). U of Wash Pr.

Village Creek. Gordon Baxter. 328p. 1981. pap. 7.95 (ISBN 0-940672-03-0). Shearer Pub.

Village Creek: An Architectural & Historical Resources Survey of Ensley, East Birmingham & East Lake. Marjorie L. White & Carter Hudgins. (Illus.). 151p. (Orig.). 1985. pap. 15.00 (ISBN 0-943994-05-5). Birmingham Hist Soc.

Village Daybook. August Derleth. (SAC Prairie Saga Ser.). 306p. 1947. 7.95 (ISBN 0-88361-072-8). Stanton & Lee.

Village Defense: Initial Special Forces Operations in Vietnam. Ronald A. Shackleton. LC 75-18573. (Illus.). 1975. 12.95 (ISBN 0-685-16409-8). Phoenix Assocs.

Village Development in India: A Sociological Approach. G. R. Madan. 1984. 18.50x (ISBN 0-8364-1173-0, Pub. by Allied India). South Asia Bks.

Village Diary. Miss Read. 255p. 1986. pap. 7.95 (ISBN 0-89733-212-1). Academy Chi Pubs.

Village Economy: Land & People of Huecorio. Michael H. Belshaw. LC 66-28489. (Institute of Latin American Studies). (Illus.). 421p. 1967. 42.00x (ISBN 0-231-02928-4). Columbia U Pr.

Village Education in India: The Report of a Commission of Enquiry. A. G. Fraser et al. 222p. 1986. Repr. of 1920 ed. 26.00 (ISBN 0-8364-1919-7, Pub. by Mittal). South Asia Bks.

Village England. Ed. by Peter Crookston. (Illus.). 256p. 1980. 16.95 (ISBN 0-09-142320-1, NO. 0216, Pub. by Hutchinson England). Routledge Chapman & Hall.

Village Entrepreneur: Change Agents in India's Rural Development. Wayne G. Broehl, Jr. LC 77-18880. 1978. 21.00x (ISBN 0-674-93915-8). Harvard U Pr.

Village Ethnoarchaeology: Rural Iran in Archaeological Perspective. Carol Kramer. (Studies in Archaeology). 302p. 1982. 29.95 (ISBN 0-12-425020-3). Acad Pr.

Village Fair at Cottage Corners. Cottage Corners Incorporated Staff et al. Ed. by Pamela Kephart. (Illus.). 32p. (Orig.). Date not set. pap. 7.95 (ISBN 0-938003-08-9). Pamela Pubns.

Village Flottante. Jules Verne. (Illus.). 8.95 (ISBN 0-686-55959-2). French & Eur.

Village Folk-Tales of Ceylon, 3 vols. Henry Parker. Ed. by Richard M. Dorson. LC 77-70614. (International Folklore Ser.). 1977. Repr. of 1914 ed. Set. lib. bdg. 99.00x (ISBN 0-405-10113-9); lib. bdg. 33.00x ea. Vol. 1 (ISBN 0-405-10114-7). Vol. 2 (ISBN 0-405-10115-5). Vol. 3 (ISBN 0-405-10116-3). Ayer Co Pubs.

Village Gods of South India. Henry Whitehead. (Illus.). 175p. 1986. Repr. 15.00X (ISBN 0-8364-1709-7, Pub. by Usha). South Asia Bks.

Village Government in British India. John Matthai. 211p. 1983. text ed. 27.95x (ISBN 0-86590-145-7). Apt Bks.

Village Handpump Technology: Research & Evaluation in Asia. Ed. by Donald Sharp & Michael Graham. 72p. (Eng., Fr. & Span.). 1983. pap. 5.00 (ISBN 0-88936-360-9, IDRC204, IDRC). UNIPUB.

Village Horse Doctor, West of the Pecos. Ben K. Green. LC 79-118716. 1971. 16.95 (ISBN 0-394-42922-2). Knopf.

Village in a Valley. Beverly Nichols. 1979. Repr. of 1934 ed. lib. bdg. 25.00 (ISBN 0-8495-4125-5). Arden Lib.

Village in England. Jane Fawcett & Graham Nicholson. LC 88-4395. (Illus.). 208p. 1988. 25.00 (ISBN 0-8478-0956-0). Rizzoli Intl.

Village in the Cevennes. Heather Willings. 1980. 19.95 (ISBN 0-575-02696-0, Pub. by Gollancz England). David & Charles.

Village in the Jungle. Leonard Woolf. 1982. pap. 6.95 (ISBN 0-19-281312-9). Oxford U Pr.

Village in the Treetops. Jules Verne. 4.95 (ISBN 0-87497-047-4). Assoc Bk.

Village in the Turkish Novel & Short Story 1920-1955. Carole Rathbun. (Near & Middle East Monographs Ser: No. 2). 192p. 1972. text ed. 24.60x (ISBN 90-2792-327-2). Mouton.

Village in the Vaucluse. 3rd ed. Laurence W. Wylie. (Illus.). 1974. 27.00x (ISBN 0-674-93937-9); pap. 9.95x (ISBN 0-674-93936-0). Harvard U Pr.

Village in Vietnam. Gerald C. Hickey. LC 64-20923. pap. 66.90 (ISBN 0-317-11300-3, 2016798). Bks Demand UMI.

Village India. Stephen Huyler. (Illus.). 272p. 1985. 37.50 (ISBN 0-8109-1728-9). Abrams.

Village India: Studies in the Little Community. Ed. by McKim Marriott. LC 55-9326. xx, 270p. 1986. pap. 15.00x (ISBN 0-226-50645-2). U of Chicago Pr.

Village Indians of the Upper Missouri: The Mandans, Hidatsas, & Arikaras. Roy W. Meyer. LC 77-4202. (Illus.). xvi, 354p. 1977. 27.50x (ISBN 0-8032-0913-4). U of Nebr Pr.

Village Industries & Agriculture in Changing Agrarian Situation. G. P. Mishra et al. 1985. 18.50x (ISBN 0-317-40626-4, Pub. by Ashish India). South Asia Bks.

Village Journey: The Report of the Alaska Native Review Commission. Thomas R. Berger. (Illus.). 288p. 1985. 16.95 (ISBN 0-8090-9624-2). Hill & Wang.

Village Journey: The Report of the Alaska Native Review Commission. Thomas R. Berger. (American Century Ser.). (Illus.). 288p. 1986. pap. 8.95 (ISBN 0-8090-0165-9). Hill & Wang.

Village Level Integrated Population Education: A Case Study of Bangladesh. Muhiuddin Haider. LC 81-43722. (Illus.). 184p. (Orig.). text ed. 29.25 (ISBN 0-8191-2489-3); pap. text ed. 12.50 (ISBN 0-8191-2490-7). U Pr of Amer.

Village Life & Labour. Ed. by Raphael Samuel. (History Workshop Ser.). (Illus.). 300p. 1983. pap. 10.95 (ISBN 0-7100-7500-6). Routledge Chapman & Hall.

Village Life in America, 1852-1872. C. C. Richards. 1977. lib. bdg. 59.95 (ISBN 0-8490-2798-5). Gordon Pr.

Village Life in America, 1852-1872: Diary of a School Girl. Caroline C. Richards. 225p. 1972. Repr. of 1913 ed. 17.95 (ISBN 0-87928-029-8). Corner Hse.

Village Life in China. Samuel S. Kung & Jeanne L. Kung. 96p. 1981. pap. text ed. 6.50x (ISBN 0-917974-62-X). Waveland Pr.

Village Life in China: A Study in Sociology. Arthur Smith. LC 68-25266. (World History Ser., No. 48). 1969. Repr. of 1899 ed. lib. bdg. 47.95x (ISBN 0-8383-0241-6). Haskell.

Village, Life in Colonial Times. James E. Knight. LC 81-23084. (Illus.). 32p. (gr. 5-9). 1982. PLB 9.79 (ISBN 0-89375-728-4); pap. text ed. 1.95 (ISBN 0-89375-729-2); cassette avail. Troll Assocs.

Village Life in Egypt, 2 vols. Bayle St. John. LC 73-6298. (Middle East Ser.). Repr. of 1852 ed. 39.00 (ISBN 0-405-05358-4). Ayer Co Pubs.

Village Life in India: Past & Present. Misra Bidyadhar. 1988. 22.50x (ISBN 81-202-0194-9, Pub. by Ajanta). South Asia Bks.

Village Life in Old China: A Community Study of Kao Yao Yhunnan. Cornelius Osgood. LC 63-19749. pap. 103.80 (ISBN 0-317-11315-1, 2012390). Bks Demand UMI.

Village Life Under the Soviets. Karl Borders. LC 72-12699. (Select Bibliographies Reprint Ser). 1973. Repr. of 1927 ed. 16.00 (ISBN 0-8369-7131-0). Ayer Co Pubs.

Village Life Under the Soviets. facsimile ed. Karl Borders. 200p. Repr. of 1927 ed. lib. bdg. 15.00 (ISBN 0-8290-0812-8). Irvington.

Village London, Pt. 1: West & North. (Village London Ser.). (Illus.). 296p. 1988. pap. 18.50 (ISBN 0-946619-11-5, Pub. by Alderman Pr London). Seven Hills Bks.

Village London, Pt. 2: North & East. (Village London Ser.). (Illus.). 279p. 1988. pap. 18.50 (ISBN 0-946619-12-3, Pub. by Alderman Pr London). Seven Hills Bks.

Village London, Pt. 3: South-East & South. (Village London Ser.). (Illus.). 271p. 1988. pap. 18.50 (ISBN 0-946619-13-1, Pub. by Alderman Pr London). Seven Hills Bks.

Village London, Pt. 4: South West. (Village London Ser.). (Illus.). 267p. 1988. pap. 18.50 (ISBN 0-946619-14-X, Pub. by Alderman Pr London). Seven Hills Bks.

Village Medical Manual. M. Vanderkooi. LC 85-62408. (Illus.). 365p. (Orig.). 1985. pap. 20.35x (ISBN 0-88312-650-8). Summer Inst Ling.

Village Memories. W. L. Stone. LC 84-72330. (Illus.). 176p. 1986. pap. 8.95 (ISBN 0-941216-24-1). Cay Bel.

Village: New & Selected Poems. Judson Jerome. Ed. by Richard Byrne et al. 192p. (Orig.). 1987. lib. bdg. 15.95 (ISBN 0-940475-61-8); pap. 8.95 (ISBN 0-940475-60-X). Dolphin-Moon.

Village Notables in Nineteenth Century France: Priests, Mayors, Schoolmasters. Barnett Singer. LC 82-3195. (European Social History Ser.). 199p. 1983. 59.50 (ISBN 0-87395-629-X); pap. 19.95 (ISBN 0-87395-630-3). State U NY Pr.

Village of Cockell: An Illustrated History of Pine Point, Maine. Robert A. Dominique. (Illus.). 140p. (Orig.). 1988. pap. 8.95 (ISBN 0-9620726-0-5). RAD Pub.

Village of Curers & Assassins: On the Production of Fala Kpelle Cosmological Categories. Beryl L. Bellman. LC 73-76893. (Approaches to Semiotics: No. 39). 196p. 1975. text ed. 33.00x (ISBN 90-2793-042-2). Mouton.

Village of Fools & Other Stories. Susan Moore. 1986. 34.00x (ISBN 0-86332-011-2, Pub. by Book Guild Ltd). State Mutual Bk.

Village of Parchanj: First English-Language Edition. Manoog Dzeron. 1984p. 1984. 20.00 (ISBN 0-914330-68-3). Panorama West.

Village of Round & Square Houses. Ann Grifalconi. (Illus.). 32p. (gr. k-3). 1986. 14.95 (ISBN 0-316-32862-6). Little.

Village of Stepanchikovo. Fyodor Dostoyevsky. Tr. by Ignat Avsey from Rus. 1983. 22.50 (ISBN 0-946162-06-9); pap. 12.95 (ISBN 0-946162-07-7). Dufour.

Village of Stepanchikovo & Its Inhabitants. Fyodor Dostoyevsky. Tr. by S. D. Cioran from Rus. Orig. Title: Selo Stepanchikovo. cancelled (ISBN 0-88233-975-3). Ardis Pubs.

Village of Stepanchikovo & Its Inhabitants. Fyodor Dostoyevsky. Tr. by Ignat Avsey from Rus. LC 86-47995. (Paperback Ser.). 256p. 1987. 24.95x (ISBN 0-8014-2051-2); pap. 6.95 (ISBN 0-8014-9457-5). Cornell U Pr.

Village of the Brothers. Rivka Guber. LC 78-54568. (Illus.). 1979. 10.00 (ISBN 0-88400-059-1). Shengold.

Village of the Vampire Cat: A Novel. Lensey Namioka. LC 80-68737. 224p. (YA) (gr. 8-12). 1981. 9.95 (ISBN 0-440-09377-5). Delacorte.

Village of Waiting. George Packer. LC 87-45912. (Departures Ser.). 352p. (Orig.). 1988. pap. 7.95 (ISBN 0-394-75754-8, Vin). Random.

Village on the Seine: Tradition & Change in Bonnieres, 1815-1914. Evelyn B. Ackerman. LC 78-58071. (Illus.). 188p. 1978. 29.95x (ISBN 0-8014-1178-5). Cornell U Pr.

Village ous l'Ancien Regime. 3rd rev. & enl. ed. Albert A. Babeau. LC 70-161721. Repr. of 1882 ed. 41.50 (ISBN 0-404-07509-6). AMS Pr.

Village Pantry's: Treasury of Homemade Liqueurs. rev. ed. Janet E. Reda. (Illus.). 115p. (Orig.). 1986. pap. 6.95 (ISBN 0-9618109-0-4). Village Pantry.

Village Poems. Man M. Singh. (Indian Poetry Ser.: No. 22). 1982. pap. 8.00 (ISBN 0-86578-275-X). Ind-US Inc.

Village Politician. John Buckmaster. 340p. 1982. 19.75 (ISBN 0-904573-37-0, Pub. by Caliban Bks); pap. 9.75 (ISBN 0-904573-76-1). Longwood Pub Group.

Village Republics: Economic Conditions for Collective Action in South India. Robert Wade. (Cambridge South Asian Studies: No. 40). (Illus.). 250p. 1988. 44.50 (ISBN 0-521-30146-7). Cambridge U Pr.

Village Revolts: Social Protest & Popular Disturbances in England, 1509-1640. Roger B. Manning. (Illus.). 368p. 1988. 74.00 (ISBN 0-19-820116-8). Oxford U Pr.

Village Romeo & Juliet. Gottfried Keller. Tr. by Paul B. Thomas. LC 55-8747. 6.00; pap. 5.95x (ISBN 0-8044-6353-0). Ungar.

Village School. Miss Read. 238p. 1986. pap. 7.95 (ISBN 0-89733-211-3). Academy Chi Pubs.

Village Schoolmaster. Joanne Hart. 1985. pap. 27.50x (ISBN 0-931460-23-9). Bieler.

Village So Small. Maude F. Zimmer. 1965. 8.95 (ISBN 0-8315-0006-9). Speller.

Village Song & Culture. M. Pickering. 192p. 1981. 27.50 (ISBN 0-7099-0059-7, Pub. by Croom Helm Ltd). Routledge Chapman & Hall.

Village Songs of Western India: Translations from Tukaram. Tr. by John S. Hoyland. 1980. pap. 2.50 (ISBN 0-932970-15-X). Prinit Pr.

Village sous l'Ancien Regime. Albert A. Barbeau. (Fr.). Repr. of 1878 ed. lib. bdg. 62.50x. Coronet Bks.

Village Studies in the Third World. Ed. by Biplab Dasgupta. 227p. 1977. 19.95. Asia Bk Corp.

Village Technology Handbook. rev. ed. Ed. by Margaret Crouch & Leonard Doak. 1987. write for info. (ISBN 0-86619-275-1). Vols Tech Asst.

Village Technology Handbook. 390p. (Eng., Fr. & Span.). 1970. perfect bdg. 9.95 (ISBN 0-317-36130-9); 10.95 (ISBN 0-86619-002-3, 1101); In French. 7.65 (ISBN 0-86619-003-1, 19001); In Spanish. 7.65 (ISBN 0-86619-004-X, 18001). Vols Tech Asst.

Village Texturer. Meals for Millions. 78p. 1977. saddle stitch 4.35 (ISBN 0-86619-051-1, 11034-BK). Vols Tech Asst.

Village Voice Guide to Manhattan's Hottest Shopping Neighborhoods. Mary Peacock & The Village Voice Editors. (Orig.). 1987. pap. 10.95 (ISBN 0-449-90206-4, Columbine). Fawcett.

Village War: Vietnamese Communist Revolutionary Activities in Dinh Tuong Province, 1960-1964. William R. Andrews. LC 73-80584. 168p. 1973. 18.00x (ISBN 0-8262-0150-4). U of Mo Pr.

Village Watch-Tower. Kate D. Wiggin. LC 74-113696. (Short Story Index Reprint Ser.). 1895. 15.00 (ISBN 0-8369-3425-3). Ayer Co Pubs.

Village Water Supply. (World Bank Paper). 98p. (Eng. & Fr. & Span.). 1976. Eng. Ed. 5.00 (ISBN 0-686-36161-X, BK9099); Fr. Ed. avail.; Span. Ed. avail. World Bank.

Village Water Supply: Economics & Policy in the Developing World. Robert J. Saunders & Jeremy J. Warford. LC 76-11758. (World Bank Research Publication Ser). 296p. 1976. 27.00x (ISBN 0-8018-1876-1). Johns Hopkins.

Village Water Supply in the Decade: Lessons From Field Experience. Colin Glennie. LC 82-23749. 152p. 1983. 42.95x (ISBN 0-471-10525-2, Pub. by Wiley-Interscience). Wiley.

Village Within a City: The Hessle Road Fishing Community of Hull. Alec Gill & Gary Sargeant. Ed. by Alan Bower. (Illus.). 72p. 1986. pap. 19.95 (ISBN 0-85958-450-X, Pub. by U of Hull UK). Humanities.

Village Without Solidarity: Polish Peasantry in Years of Crisis. C. M. Hann. LC 84-52242. (Illus.). 192p. 1985. 18.00x (ISBN 0-300-03353-2). Yale U Pr.

Village Woman in Ghana. Jette Bukh. (Centre for Development Research Studies: No. 1). (Illus.). 118p. 1983. pap. 12.50 (ISBN 0-8419-9756-X). Holmes & Meier.

Village Women of Bangladesh: Prospects for Change. T. Abdullah & S. Zeidenstein. (Women in Development Ser.: Vol. 4). (Illus.). 256p. 1981. text ed. 33.00 (ISBN 0-08-026795-5). Pergamon.

Village Yorkshire. Ed. by Maurice Colbeck. (Illus.). 176p. 1987. 29.95 (ISBN 0-7134-5032-0, Pub. by Batsford England). David & Charles.

Villagers. Jack Oleck. 5.95 (ISBN 0-8184-0117-6). Lyle Stuart.

Villagers (Huasipungo) A Novel. Jorge Icaza. Tr. by Bernard M. Dulsey from Span. LC 73-9551. (Arcturus Books Paperbacks). 238p. 1973. pap. 9.50x (ISBN 0-8093-0653-0). S Ill U Pr.

Villages. Richard Critchfield. LC 80-1721. (Illus.). 408p. 1983. pap. 10.95 (ISBN 0-385-18375-5, Anch). Doubleday.

Villages en Developpement: Contribution a une Sociologie Villageois. Ed. by Henri Desroche & Placide Rambaud. (Recherches Cooperatives: No. 4). (Illus.). 1972. pap. 14.00x (ISBN 0-686-21260-6). Mouton.

Villages in Indonesia. Ed. by Koentjaraningrat. LC 66-20014. (Illus.). 428p. 1967. 45.00x (ISBN 0-8014-0232-8). Cornell U Pr.

Villages of Edinburgh, Vol. 1: North Edinburgh. Malcolm Cant. (Illus.). 258p. 1986. text ed. 25.00x (ISBN 0-85976-147-9, Pub. by John Donald Pub UK). Humanities.

Villages of England. Brian Bailey. (Illus.). 1984. 14.95 (ISBN 0-517-55343-0, Harmony). Crown.

Villages of France. Photos by Charlie Waite. LC 87-43261. (Illus.). 160p. 1988. 25.00 (ISBN 0-8478-0927-7). Rizzoli Intl.

Villages of Hispanic New Mexico. Nancy H. Warren. LC 87-12715. (Illus.). 128p. (Orig.). 1987. 30.00 (ISBN 0-933452-19-5); pap. 14.95 (ISBN 0-933452-20-9). Schol Am Res.

Villages of Hispanic New Mexico. Nancy H. Warren. (Illus.). 136p. 1987. 30.00 (ISBN 0-295-96532-0); pap. 14.95 (ISBN 0-295-96533-9). U of Wash Pr.

Villages of the Algonquian, Siouan & Caddoan Tribes West of the Mississippi. David L. Bushnell. 1988. Repr. of 1922 ed. lib. bdg. 39.00x. Am Biog Serv.

Villages of the Algonquian, Siouan, & Caddoan Tribes West of the Mississippi. David L. Bushnell, Jr. Repr. of 1922 ed. 29.00x (ISBN 0-403-03724-7). Scholarly.

Villainage in England: Essays in English Medieval History. Paul Vinogradoff. 1968. Repr. of 1892 ed. 9.00x (ISBN 0-403-00048-3). Scholarly.

Villainage in England: Essays in English Medieval History. Paul Vinogradoff. 1988. Repr. of 1892 ed. lib. bdg. 98.00x. Am Biog Serv.

Villainy Victorious. L. Ron Hubbard. (Mission Earth Ser.: Vol. 9). 425p. 1987. 18.95 (ISBN 0-88404-215-4). Bridge Pubns Inc.

Villanelle: The Evolution of a Poetic Form. Ronald E. McFarland. 183p. 1987. pap. 14.95 (ISBN 0-89301-121-5). U of Idaho Pr.

Villanova Law School's Center for Continuing Legal Education Presents Transportation Labor Issues for the 1980s, May 18, 1982. Henry H. Perritt & Villanova University. Center for Continuing Legal Education. LC 82-196215. iii, 545p. Date not set. price not set. Villanova Law.

Villanova University. Nick Kelsh. (Illus.). 112p. 1987. 35.00 (ISBN 0-916509-20-6). Harmony Hse Pub LO.

Villas & Cottages. 2nd ed. Calvert Vaux. LC 68-29858. (Architecture & Decorative Art Ser). (Illus.). 1968. Repr. of 1857 ed. lib. bdg. 49.50 (ISBN 0-306-71044-7). Da Capo.

Villas & Cottages: A Series of Designs Prepared for Execution in the United States. 2nd ed. Calvert Vaux. (Illus.). 1970. pap. 6.50 (ISBN 0-486-22009-5). Dover.

Villas & Cottages: The Great Architectural Style-Book of the Hudson School. Calvert Vaux. (Illus.). 12.00 (ISBN 0-8446-0951-X). Peter Smith.

Villas at Table: A Passion for Food & Drink. James Villas. LC 88-45068. 288p. 1988. 19.95 (ISBN 0-06-015995-2, HarpT). Har-Row.

Villas of Frascati, 1650-1750. Carl L. Franck. (Illus.). 1966. 30.00 (ISBN 0-85458-669-5). Transatl Arts.

Villas of le Corbusier. Tim Benton. LC 86-51285. 224p. 1987. 50.00x (ISBN 0-300-03780-5). Yale U Pr.

Villas of Palladio. Photos by Philip Trager. (Illus.). 1986. 45.00 (ISBN 0-8212-1639-2). NYGS.

Villas of the Veneto. Text by Peter Lauritzen. 1988. 49.50 (ISBN 0-8109-1744-0). Abrams.

Villas on the Hudson: A Collection of Photo-Lithographs of Thirty-One Country Residences. LC 76-41854. (Architecture & Decorative Art Ser.). 1977. Repr. of 1860 ed. lib. bdg. 95.00 (ISBN 0-306-70800-0). Da Capo.

Villa's Rifles. Lewis B. Patten. 15.95 (ISBN 0-89190-420-4, Pub. by Am Repr). Amereon Ltd.

Villasandino y su Hablante Lirico. Yolanda Rosas. (American University Studies II Romance Languages & Literature: Vol. 53). 186p. 1987. text ed. 32.90 (ISBN 0-8204-0342-3). P Lang Pubs.

Villdemslekre Im Griechischen Recht. Richard Maschko. Ed. by Gregory Vlastos. LC 78-19369. (Morals & Law in Ancient Greece Ser.). 1979. Repr. of 1926 ed. lib. bdg. 16.00x (ISBN 0-405-11560-1). Ayer Co Pubs.

Ville. Paul Claudel. (Folio Ser.: No. 1345). 1967. 5.95 (ISBN 0-686-54442-0). Schoenhof.

Ville Dont le Prince Est un Enfant. Henry De Montherlant. (Folio Ser.: No. 293). 1963. pap. 7.95 (ISBN 0-685-11620-4). Schoenhof.

Ville Noire, 1861. facsimile ed. George Sand. 259p. 1976. 27.50 (ISBN 0-686-54948-1). French & Eur.

Ville ou Nul ne Meurt. Bernard B. Dadie. pap. 8.95 (ISBN 0-685-35633-7). French & Eur.

Ville Ouvriere au Temps du Socialisme Utopique: Toulon De 1815 a 1851. 2nd ed. Maurice Agulhon. (Civilisations et Societes: No. 18). 1977. pap. 16.80 (ISBN 90-2796-287-1). Mouton.

Ville sous l'Ancien Regime, 2 Vols. 2nd ed. Albert A. Babeau. Repr. of 1884 ed. Set. 65.00 (ISBN 0-404-07516-9). Vol. 1 (ISBN 0-404-07517-7). Vol. 2 (ISBN 0-404-07518-5). AMS Pr.

Villen Des Historismus in Basel. Rolf Broennimann. 132p. (Ger.). 1983. pap. 26.95 (ISBN 0-8176-1367-6). Birkhauser.

Villette. Charlotte Bronte. Ed. by Mark Lilly. Tr. by Tony Tanner. (English Library). 1980. pap. 5.95 (ISBN 0-14-043118-7). Penguin.

Villette. Charlotte Bronte. 1983. pap. text ed. 3.95x (ISBN 0-460-11351-8, Pub. by Evman England). Biblio Dist.

Villette. Charlotte Bronte. Ed. by Herbert Rosengarten & Margaret Smith. (Illus.). 768p. 1984. 92.00x (ISBN 0-19-812597-6). Oxford U Pr.

Villette. Charlotte Bronte. 1987. pap. 4.95 (ISBN 0-451-52083-1, Sig Classics). NAL.

Villette. Charlotte Bronte. 512p. 1986. pap. 3.95 (ISBN 0-553-21243-5). Bantam.

Villiane Petite Sorciere: The Horrible Impossible Bad Witch Child. Barbara Williams. (Illus.). 32p. (Fr.). (ps-3). 1983. pap. 2.25 (ISBN 0-380-85100-8, Camelot). Avon.

Villon: Poems. John Fox. (Critical Guides to French Texts Ser.: No. 37). 108p. 1984. pap. 4.95 (ISBN 0-7293-0185-0, Pub. by Grant & Cutler). Longwood Pub Group.

Vilna Goan Views Life. 1982. 4.00 (ISBN 0-686-76275-4). Feldheim.

Vilyatpur 1848-1968: Social & Economic Change in a North Indian Village. Tom G. Kessinger. LC 72-89788. (Center for South & Southeast Asia Studies, UC Berkeley: No. 19). (Illus.). 1974. 40.00x (ISBN 0-520-02340-4). U of Cal Pr.

Vim, a Very Important Mouse. Jane Weinberger. (Illus.). 40p. (ps-4). 1985. 4.95 (ISBN 0-932433-01-4). Windswept Hse.

Vin Blanc de la Villette. Jules Romains. 224p. 1923. 4.95 (ISBN 0-686-55293-8). French & Eur.

Vin de Paris. Marcel Ayme. (Folio Ser.: No. 1515). 1947. pap. 7.95 (ISBN 0-686-51908-6). Schoenhof.

Vin Est Tire. Robert Desnos. 208p. 1943. 9.95 (ISBN 0-686-56000-0). French & Eur.

Vin et Societe a Bergerac: Du Moyen Age Aux Temps Modernes. Jacques Beauroy. (Stanford French & Italian Studies: No. 4). (Illus.). 294p. (Fr.). 1977. pap. 29.50 (ISBN 0-915838-32-X). Anma Libri.

Vin Vignettes: Stories of Famous French Wines. Sarah J. English. 104p. 1984. 12.95 (ISBN 0-89015-452-X). Eakin Pr.

Vinasikhatantra: A Saiva Tantra of the Left Current. Teun Goudriaan. ix, 162p. 1986. 14.00x (ISBN 0-89581-766-7, Pub. by Motilal Banarsidass). South Asia Bks.

Vinatoarea Regala see Royal Hunt.

Vinaya Texts, 3 vols. Rhys Davids. lib. bdg. 300.00 (ISBN 0-87968-513-1). Krishna Pr.

Vinca Alkaloids: Botany, Chemistry, & Pharmacology. Ed. by William I. Taylor & Norman Farnsworth. LC 73-83859. pap. 94.30 (ISBN 0-317-28688-9, 2055284). Bks Demand UMI.

Vince: A Personal Biography of Vince Lombardi. Michael O'Brien. LC 87-12980. 352p. 1987. 19.95 (ISBN 0-688-07406-5). Morrow.

Vince Lombardi: Football Legend. Les Etter. LC 74-18076. (Garrard Sports Library). (Illus.). 96p. (gr. 3-6). 1975. PLB 7.12 (ISBN 0-8116-6670-0). Garrard.

Vince Lombardi Story. Dave Klein. LC 74-170971. (Illus.). 192p. (YA) 1971. 10.95; lib. bdg. 10.95 (ISBN 0-87460-257-2). Lion Bks.

Vincent. Bob Kunzinger. 160p. (Orig.). 1988. pap. 8.95 (ISBN 0-9618319-0-1). Public Garden Pub.

Vincent by Himself: A Selection of Van Gogh's Paintings & Drawings Together with Extracts from His Letters. Ed. by Bruce Bernard. 40.00 (ISBN 0-8212-1608-2). NYGS.

Vincent Crummles: His Theatre & His Times. F. Harvey Darton. LC 79-173157. Repr. of 1926 ed. 24.50 (ISBN 0-405-08431-5, Pub. by Blom). Ayer Co Pubs.

Vincent D'Indy, 1851-1931. Norman Demuth. LC 73-6259. (Illus.). 117p. 1974. Repr. of 1951 ed. lib. bdg. 25.00x (ISBN 0-8371-6895-3, DEVD). Greenwood.

Vincent from Nineteen Thirty-Eight: Road Test & Features from Motor Cycle & Motorcycling. Intro. by Cyril Ayton. (Illus.). 96p. 1988. pap. 17.95 (Pub. by Bay View Bks UK). Motorbooks Intl.

Vincent Lombardi-Pele. John N. Fago. (Pendulum Illustrated Biography Ser.). (Illus.). (gr. 4-12). 1979. text ed. 7.50 (ISBN 0-88301-370-3); pap. text ed. 2.95 (ISBN 0-88301-358-4); wkbk. 1.25 (ISBN 0-88301-382-7). Pendulum Pr.

Vincent Melzac Collection. (Illus.). 1971. 3.75 (ISBN 0-686-20543-X). Corcoran.

Vincent of Beauvais & Alexander the Great. W. J. Aerts et al. (Mediaevalia Groningana Ser.: Vol. VII). 187p. (Orig.). 1986. pap. 23.00x (ISBN 90-6980-009-8, Pub. by Egbert Forsten Holland). Benjamins North Am.

Vincent of Beauvais' 'De Eruditione Filiorum Nobilium' The Education of Women. Rosemary B. Tobin. LC 84-47531. (American University Studies XIV (Education): Vol. 5). 164p. 1984. text ed. 20.85 (ISBN 0-8204-0105-6). P Lang Pubs.

Vincent Price: Actor & Art Collector. Ed. by R. A. Lopez & Alan Curl. (Illus.). 48p. 1982. pap. 15.00 (ISBN 0-935661-08-5). Riverside Mus Pr.

Vincent Twins. (Super Profile MC Ser.). 8.95 (ISBN 0-85429-460-0, F460, Pub. by G T Foulis Ltd). Haynes Pubns.

Vincent Van Gogh. Sergio Bitossi. LC 86-42654. (Why They Became Famous Ser.). 64p. (gr. 5 up). 1986. PLB 13.96; pap. 6.95. Silver.

Vincent Van Gogh. Osjkar Hagen. 59.95 (ISBN 0-8490-1261-9). Gordon Pr.

Vincent Van Gogh. New York Museum of Modern Art. Ed. by Alfred H. Barr, Jr. LC 78-109811. (Illus.). 193p. 1971. Repr. of 1935 ed. lib. bdg. 35.00 (ISBN 0-8371-4302-0, NYVG). Greenwood.

Vincent Van Gogh. Ernest Raboff. LC 87-45300. (Trophy Nonfiction Art for Children). (Illus.). 32p. (gr. 1 up). 1988. pap. 5.95 (ISBN 0-06-446077-0, Trophy). HarpJ.

Vincent Van Gogh. Ernest Raboff. LC 87-45315. (Art for Children Ser.). (Illus.). 32p. (gr. 1 up). 1988. Repr. of 1973 ed. 11.95i (ISBN 0-397-32230-5, Lipp Jr Bks). HarpJ.

Vincent Van Gogh: A Biographical Study. Julius Meier-Graefe. Tr. by John Holroyd-Reece. 1970. Repr. of 1933 ed. lib. bdg. 35.00x (ISBN 0-8371-4278-4, MEVG). Greenwood.

Vincent Van Gogh: A Biography. Julius Meier-Graefe. 160p. 1987. pap. 3.95 (ISBN 0-486-25253-1). Dover.

Vincent Van Gogh: A Monograph. Alfred H. Barr, Jr. & Charles M. Brooks, Jr. LC 66-26121. (Museum of Modern Art Publications in Repr. Ser). Repr. of 1942 ed. 18.00 (ISBN 0-405-01514-3). Ayer Co Pubs.

Vincent Van Gogh: A Psychological Study. Humberto Nagera. (Illus.). 182p. 1967. text ed. 25.00x (ISBN 0-8236-6740-5). Intl Univs Pr.

Vincent Van Gogh: Art, Life & Letters. Bernard Zurcher. Tr. by Helga Harrison from Fr. LC 85-42914. (Illus.). 338p. 1985. 85.00 (ISBN 0-8478-0634-0). Rizzoli Intl.

Vincent Van Gogh, Eighteen Fifty-Three to Eighteen Ninety. Walter Pach. LC 78-99666. (Select Bibliographies Reprint Ser). 1936. 19.00 (ISBN 0-8369-5095-X). Ayer Co Pubs.

Vincent Van Gogh: Genius and Disaster. A. M. Hammacher. (Illus.). 208p. 19.95 (ISBN 0-8109-8067-3). Abrams.

Vincent Van Gogh in Creative Competition: Four Essays from Simiolus. E. V. Uitert. (Illus.). 1983. pap. 25.00. Heinman.

Vincent Van Gogh: Studies in the Social Aspects of His Work. Andre Krauss. (Illus.). 208p. 1987. pap. text ed. 25.00 (ISBN 0-391-03553-3). Humanities.

Vincent Van Gogh: Vision & Reality. Ingo F. Walther. (Illus.). 96p. (Orig.). 1987. pap. 7.95 (ISBN 3-8228-0041-4). Parkwest Pubns.

Vincente Espinel "Diversas Rimas". Dorothy C. Clark. 204p. Date not set. 4.50 (ISBN 0-318-22353-8). Hispanic Inst.

Vincente Huidobro & Creationism. H. A. Holmes. 1977. lib. bdg. 59.95 (ISBN 0-8490-2799-3). Gordon Pr.

Vincente Huidobro: The Careers of a Poet. Rene De Costa. (Illus.). 186p. 1984. 45.00x (ISBN 0-19-815789-4). Oxford U Pr.

Vincent's Word Studies in the New Testament, 4 vols. M. R. Vincent. 2720p. 49.95 (ISBN 0-917006-30-5). Hendrickson MA.

Vincenzo Bellini: His Life & His Operas. Herbert Weinstock. 1971. 20.00 (ISBN 0-394-41656-2). Knopf.

Vincenzo Capirola Lute Book. Vincenzo Capirola. Ed. by Otto Gombosi. (Music Ser.). 236p. 1983. Repr. of 1955 ed. lib. bdg. 75.00 (ISBN 0-306-76100-9). Da Capo.

Vincenzo Ruffo (c. 1508-1587) Madrigali a sei, sette e otto voci (Venice: Girolamo Scotto, 1554, Vol. 26. Ed. by Jessie A. Owens. (Italian Madrigal in the Sixteenth Century Ser.). 1988. lib. bdg. 75.00 (ISBN 0-8240-5528-4). Garland Pub.

Vincenzo Ruffo (c. 1508-1587) Primo Libro di madrigali a cinque voci (Venice: Girolamo Scotto 1533, Vol. 25. Ed. by Jessie A. Owens. (Italian Madrigal in the Sixteenth Century Ser.). 1988. lib. bdg. 75.00 (ISBN 0-8240-5527-6). Garland Pub.

Vincenzo Ruffo: Il Primo Livro de Motetti a Cinque Voci (Milan: Castillione, 1542) Motetti a Sei Voci (Venice: Scotto, 1955) Ed. by Richard Sherr. (Sixteenth-Century Motet Ser.: Vos. 19-20). 1988. lib. bdg. 75.00 (ISBN 0-8240-7919-1) (ISBN 0-8240-7920-5). Garland Pub.

Vincenzo Vela (Eighteen Twenty to Ninety-One) Nancy J. Scott. LC 78-74378. (Fine Arts Dissertations, Fourth Ser.). (Illus.). 1979. lib. bdg. 80.00 (ISBN 0-8240-3965-3). Garland Pub.

Vinculo see Aguilas.

Vindication of Absolute Idealism. Timothy Sprigge. 291p. 1983. 30.00x (ISBN 0-85224-455-X, Pub. by Edinburgh U Pr Scotland). Columbia U Pr.

Vindication of Commerce & the Arts. William Temple. (History of English Economic Thought Ser). Repr. of 1758 ed. 29.00 (ISBN 0-384-59800-5). Johnson Repr.

Vindication of Natural Diet. Percy Bysshe Shelley. LC 75-11886. (Illus.). 1975. Repr. of 1884 ed. lib. bdg. 17.00 (ISBN 0-8414-7822-8). Folcroft.

Vindication of Natural Diet: A New Edition. Percy Bysshe Shelley. LC 74-30288. (Shelley Society, Second Ser.: No. 4). Repr. of 1884 ed. 20.00 (ISBN 0-404-11506-3). AMS Pr.

Vindication of Natural Society. Edmund Burke. LC 81-84826. (Illus.). 130p. 1982. 8.50 (ISBN 0-86597-009-2, Liberty Clas); pap. text ed. 4.50 (ISBN 0-86597-010-6). Liberty Fund.

Vindication of Ruskin. John H. Whitehouse. LC 77-13453. 1977. Repr. lib. bdg. 25.00 (ISBN 0-8414-9638-2). Folcroft.

Vindication of the Captors of Major Andre. Egbert Benson. (American Revolutionary Ser.). Repr. of 1865 ed. lib. bdg. 29.50 (ISBN 0-8398-0187-4). Irvington.

Vindication of the Conduct of Captain Christopher Middleton, in a Late Voyage on Board His Majesty's Ship the Furnace. Christopher Middleton. (Illus.). Repr. of 1743 ed. 17.00 (ISBN 0-384-38831-0). Johnson Repr.

Vindication of the Government of New-England Churches. John Wise. Ed. by Perry Miller. LC 58-5422. Repr. of 1717 ed. 30.00x (ISBN 0-8201-1246-1). Schol Facsimiles.

Vindication of the Rights of Brutes. Thomas Taylor. LC 66-10010. 1966. Repr. of 1792 ed. 30.00x (ISBN 0-8201-1045-0). Schol Facsimiles.

Vindication of the Rights of Men. Mary Wollstonecraft. LC 60-5073. 192p. 1975. Repr. of 1790 ed. lib. bdg. 35.00x (ISBN 0-8201-1164-3). Schol Facsimiles.

Vindication of the Rights of Woman. Mary Wollstonecraft. Ed. by Miriam Kramnick. (English Library). 1982. pap. 4.95 (ISBN 0-14-043199-3). Penguin.

Vindication of the Rights of Woman. 2nd ed. Mary Wollstonecraft. Ed. by Carol H. Poston. (Critical Edition Ser.). 1987. pap. text ed. 8.95x (ISBN 0-393-95572-9). Norton.

Vindication of the Rights of Woman. 2nd ed. Mary Wollstonecraft. Ed. by Carol H. Poston. (Critical Edition Ser.). 1987. write for info. (ISBN 0-393-02427-X). Norton.

Vindication of the Rights of Woman & the Subjection of Women. Mary Wollstonecraft & John S. Mill. Incl. Subjugation of Women. 330p. 1983. Repr. of 1929 ed. 14.95x (ISBN 0-460-00825-0, Evman). Biblio Dist.

Vindication of the Rights of Woman & the Subjection of Women. Mary Wollstonecraft & John S. Mill. 330p. 1974. pap. text ed. 5.95x (ISBN 0-460-01825-6, Pub. by Evman England). Biblio Dist.

Vindication of the Stage see Collier Tracts 1698: Immorality of the English Pulpit.

Vindication of Tradition. Jaroslav Pelikan. LC 84-5132. 105p. 1984. 17.50t (ISBN 0-300-03154-8). Yale U Pr.

Vindication of Tradition. Jaroslav Pelikan. LC 84-5132. 128p. 1986. pap. 8.95x (ISBN 0-300-03638-8). Yale U Pr.

Vindication of William Prynne see Mr. William Prynn-His Defence of Stage-Plays: Retraction of a Former Book of His Called 'Histrio-Mastix'.

Vindications: Essays on Romantic Music. Deryck Cooke. LC 82-4295. 160p. 1982. 29.95 (ISBN 0-521-24765-9); pap. 9.95 (ISBN 0-521-28947-5). Cambridge U Pr.

Vindicators of Shakespeare. Granville G. Greenwood. LC 71-113367. 1970. Repr. of 1931 ed. 23.00x (ISBN 0-8046-1018-5, Pub. by Kennikat). Assoc Faculty Pr.

Vindiciae Epistolarum Sancti Ignatii, 2 Vols. John Pearson. LC 76-173936. (Library of Anglo-Catholic Theology: No. 16). Repr. of 1852 ed. Set. 57.50 (ISBN 0-404-52140-1). AMS Pr.

Vindictment. Merritt Clifton. 1977. pap. 1.00 (ISBN 0-686-23159-7). Samisdat.

Vine Remembers: French Vignerons Recall Their Past. Leo A. Loubere et al. LC 84-49. (SUNY Series in European Social History). 193p. 1985. 52.50 (ISBN 0-87395-913-2); pap. 17.95 (ISBN 0-87395-914-0). State U NY Pr.

Vine to Wine. Richards Lyon. LC 85-62333. (Illus.). 120p. (Orig.). 1985. pap. 9.95 (ISBN 0-9616004-0-3). Stonecrest Pr.

Vinegar Boy. Alberta Hawse. 1970. pap. 3.95 (ISBN 0-8024-9171-5). Moody.

Vinegar Pancakes & Vanishing Cream. Bonnie Pryor. LC 86-31085. (Illus.). 128p. (gr. 2-5). 1987. 11.75 (ISBN 0-688-06728-X, Morrow Junior Books). Morrow.

Vinegar Pie & Chicken Bread: A Woman's Diary of Life in the Rural South, 1890-1891. Ed. by Margaret J. Bolsterli. LC 82-4922. 144p. 1983. pap. 6.95 (ISBN 0-938626-25-6). U of Ark Pr.

Vinegar Pie & Other Tales of the Grand Traverse Region. Al Barnes. LC 58-12684. (Illus.). 184p. 1984. 14.50 (ISBN 0-915937-00-X). Hor Bks MI.

Vinegar Puss. S. J. Perelman. 16.95 (ISBN 0-89190-421-2, Pub. by Am Repr). Amereon Ltd.

Vinegar Use Poetry Pages. Alpha Pyramis Research Division Staff. 30p. 1984. pap. text ed. 1.50 (ISBN 0-913597-66-X, Pub. by Alpha Pyramis). Prosperity & Profits.

Vinegar Year. Lynne Dowell. Ed. by Clarinda H. Lott. (New Poets Ser.: Vol 7). (Illus.). 50p. 1980. pap. 2.95 (ISBN 0-932616-05-4). New Poets.

Vinegrowing in Britain. Gillian Pearkes. (Illus.). 336p. 1985. 19.95 (ISBN 0-460-04393-5, BKX 05269, Pub. by J M Dent England). Biblio Dist.

Vine's Expository Dictionary of Biblical Words. rev. ed. Ed. by W. E. Vine et al. 1100p. 1987. 19.95 (ISBN 0-8407-7559-8). Nelson.

Vines Expository Dictionary of New Testament Words. W. E. Vine. (Barbour Bks). 351p. 1985. 14.95 (ISBN 0-916441-31-8); pap. 10.95 (ISBN 0-916441-34-2). Barbour & Co.

Vine's Expository Dictionary of New Testament Words. William E. Vine. 1376p. Date not set. 14.95 (ISBN 0-917006-03-8). Hendrickson MA.

Vine's Expository Dictionary of Old & New Testament Words. W. E. Vine. 1568p. 1981. 19.95 (ISBN 0-8007-1282-X). Revell.

Vine's Expository Dictionary of Old & New Testament Words. W. E. Vine & F. F. Bruce. (Reference Library Edition). 1568p. 1987. Repr. text ed. 14.95 (ISBN 0-529-06374-3). World Bible.

Vines, Grapes & Wine. Jancis Robinson. LC 86-2844. 272p. 1986. 29.95 (ISBN 0-394-55598-8). Knopf.

Vines of Ferrara. Carolyn Coker. 224p. 1986. 14.95 (ISBN 0-396-08812-0). Dodd.

Vineyard. Fanny Howe. (Lost Roads Ser.: No. 33). 80p. (Orig.). 1988. pap. 7.95 (ISBN 0-918786-37-1). Lost Roads.

Vineyard of Liberty. James M. Burns. LC 83-3506. (Illus.). 768p. 1983. pap. 9.95 (ISBN 0-394-71629-9, Vin). Random.

Vineyard Seasons. Susan Branch. (Illus.). 160p. 1988. 19.95 (ISBN 0-316-10632-1). Little.

Vineyard Tales. Gale Huntington. LC 80-52793. 250p. (Orig.). 1980. pap. 7.95 (ISBN 0-932384-13-7). Tashmoo.

Vineyards & Wineries of America: A Traveler's Guide. Patrick W. Fegan. LC 82-15806. 1982. pap. 9.95 (ISBN 0-8289-0489-8). Greene.

Vineyards of France. Don Philpott. 441p. 1988. pap. 14.95 (ISBN 0-87106-687-4). Globe Pequot.

Vinganance & the Tree Toad. Verna Aardema. (Illus.). (gr. 3-8). 1988. pap. 4.95 (ISBN 0-14-050890-2, Puffin Bks). Penguin.

Vinganance & the Tree Toad. Retold by Verna Aardema. LC 82-13473. (Illus.). 48p. (gr. 1-4). 1983. 12.95 (ISBN 0-7232-6217-9). Warne.

Vingt Annees De Missions Dans le Nord-Ouest De L'amerique. Alexandre A. Tache. (Canadiana Before 1867 Ser). (Fr). Repr. of 1866 ed. 18.00 (ISBN 0-384-59425-5). Johnson Repr.

Vingt Annees De Missions Dans le Nord-Ouest De L'amerique Par Mgr. Alex. Tache Eveque De Saint-Boniface (Montreal, 1866) Alexandre A. Tache. (Canadiana Avant 1867: NO. 21). 1970. 16.80x (ISBN 90-2796-343-6). Mouton.

Vingt Ans Apres, 2 vols. Alexandre Dumas. (Folio Ser.: Nos. 682 & 683). 1975. Vol. 1. pap. 7.95; Vol. 2. pap. 9.95. Schoenhof.

Vingt Ans Apres. Alexandre Dumas. Ed. by Samaran. (Class. Garnier). pap. 12.95 (ISBN 0-685-34893-8). French & Eur.

Vingt Ans Apres. Alexandre Dumas. Ed. by Samaran. (Coll. Prestige). 12.95 (ISBN 0-685-34894-6). French & Eur.

Vingt ans Apres, 2 vols. Alexandre Dumas. 1975. write for info. French & Eur.

Vingt Ans Apres, 2 tomes. Alexandre Dumas, Sr. (Coll. GF). 1961. Set. pap. 9.00 (ISBN 0-685-11621-2). French & Eur.

Vingt-Deux Dessins sur le Theme du Desir. Jean-Paul Sartre & Andre Masson. (Illus.). 1250.00 (ISBN 0-686-55006-4). French & Eur.

Vingt Deuxiesme Livre. Ed. by Albert Seay. (Transcriptions Ser.: No. 4). iii, 67p. 1981. pap. 4.00 (ISBN 0-933894-07-4, Pub. by Attaingnant). Colo Coll Music.

Vingt et un Contes. 3rd ed. Leon P. Irvin & Donald L. King. 1964. pap. text ed. 17.95 scp (ISBN 0-06-043220-9, HarpC). Har-Row.

Vingt et une Recettes de Mort Violente. Vercors. (Illus.). 1977. 25.00 (ISBN 0-686-55144-3). French & Eur.

Vingt Mille Lieues sous les Mers. Jules Verne. pap. 8.50 (ISBN 0-685-37138-7). French & Eur.

Vingt Mille Lieues Sous les Mers, 2 vols. Jules Verne. 1977. 10.95 ea. French & Eur.

Vingt-Neuf Degres a l'Ombre. Eugene Labiche. 9.95 (ISBN 0-686-54257-6). French & Eur.

Vingt suites d'orchestre du XVIIe siecle francais, 2 vols. Ed. by Jules Ecorcheville. (Illus.). 384p. (Fr.). 1971. Repr. of 1906 ed. 185.00x (ISBN 0-8450-1005-0). Broude.

Vingtieme Siecle: La Problematique du Discours. Ed. by Roy Nelson. (Michigan Romance Studies: vol. 6). 127p. (Orig.). 1986. pap. 9.00 (ISBN 0-939730-05-7). Mich Romance.

Vingts Ans Apres see Oeuvres Illustrees.

Vinland Map Conference: Proceedings. Ed. by Wilcomb E. Washburn. LC 77-152380. 1971. 39.95x (ISBN 0-226-87394-3). U of Chicago Pr.

Vinland Sagas. Halldor Hermannsson. LC 45-1265. (Islandica Ser.: Vol. 30). 1944. 15.00 (ISBN 0-527-00361-1). Kraus Repr.

Vinland Sagas: & Norse Discovery of America. Tr. by Magnus Magnusson & Hermann Palsson. Incl. Graenlendinga Saga; Eirik's Saga. (Classics Ser.). (Orig.). 1965. pap. 5.95 (ISBN 0-14-044154-9). Penguin.

Vinland Sagas: The Norse Discovery of America. Pattr Groenlendinga. LC 66-31936. pap. 31.00 (ISBN 0-317-08208-6, 2050271). Bks Demand UMI.

Vinland Sagas: The Norse Discovery of America. Tr. by Magnus Magnusson. 125p. Date not set. 2.50 (ISBN 0-317-53192-1). Noontide.

Vinland Voyages. facsimile ed. Matthias Thordarson. Tr. by Thorstina J. Walters. LC 75-160996. (Select Bibliographies Reprint Ser.). Repr. of 1930 ed. 15.00 (ISBN 0-8369-5864-0). Ayer Co Pubs.

Vino E Pane. Ignazio Silone. (Easy Readers, Ser. B). 96p. (Ital.). 1976. pap. 4.95 (ISBN 0-88436-269-8, 55253). EMC.

Vino: The Wine & Winemakers of Italy. Burton Anderson. (Illus.). 416p. 1980. 22.50 (ISBN 0-316-03948-9, Pub. by Atlantic Monthly Pr). Little.

Vinoba on Gandhi. Vinoba Bhave. Ed. by K. Shah. 199p. 1983. 9.50 (ISBN 0-934676-38-0). Greenlf Bks.

Vintage. Evelyn Carlson et al. Ed. by Patricia Traxler. (Illus.). 104p. (Orig.). 1984. pap. 5.00 (ISBN 0-932199-00-3). Smoky Hill.

Vintage Aircraft Nose Art. G. Valant. (Illus.). 208p. 1987. 39.95 (ISBN 0-87938-266-X). Motorbooks Intl.

Vintage American & European Wrist Watch Price Guide, Bk. 1. rev. ed. Sherry Ehrhardt & Peter Planes. 1987. 19.95 (ISBN 0-913902-51-9). Heart Am Pr.

Vintage American & European Wrist Watch Price Guide, Bk. 2. Sherry Ehrhardt et al. (Illus.). 1988. pap. 20.00 (ISBN 0-913902-56-X). Heart Am Pr.

Vintage Bradbury. Ray Bradbury. 1965. pap. 4.95 (ISBN 0-394-74059-9, Vin, V294). Random.

Vintage Clothing 1880-1960. 2nd ed. Maryanne Dolan. (Illus.). 202p. 1984. pap. 16.95 (ISBN 0-89689-063-5, 1827). Bks Americana.

Vintage Fashions for Today. Eileen MacIntosh. LC 87-47979. (Creative Machine Arts & Crafts Ser.). (Illus.). 192p. 1988. pap. 12.95 (ISBN 0-8019-7799-1). Chilton.

Vintage Guildford. Hendon Publishing Co., Ltd. Staff. 1986. 18.20x (ISBN 0-317-54188-9, Pub. by Hendon Pub UK). State Mutual Bk.

Vintage King's Lynn: Second Impression. Hendon Publishing Co., Ltd. Staff. 1986. 21.00x (ISBN 0-317-54189-7, Pub. by Hendon Pub UK). State Mutual Bk.

Vintage Mad. (Mad Ser.: No. 41). (Illus.). (YA) 1988. pap. 2.95 (ISBN 0-446-35066-4). Warner Bks.

Vintage Mencken. H. L. Mencken. Ed. by Alistair Cooke. 1955. pap. 3.95 (ISBN 0-394-70025-2, Vin). Random.

Vintage Muggeridge: Religion & Society. Ed. by Geoffrey Barlow. 200p. (Orig.). 1986. pap. 7.95 (ISBN 0-8028-0181-1). Eerdmans.

Vintage Murder. Ngaio Marsh. 1976. Repr. of 1937 ed. lib. bdg. 17.95x (ISBN 0-88411-497-X, Pub. by Aeonian Bks). Amereon Ltd.

Vintage Murder. Ngaio Marsh. 272p. 1987. pap. 2.95 (ISBN 0-515-08084-5). Jove Pubns.

Vintage Places: A Connoisseur's Guide to North American Wineries & Vineyards. Suzanne Goldenson. LC 87-14110. (Illus.). 272p. (Orig.). 1985. 14.95 (ISBN 0-915590-76-X); pap. 8.95 (ISBN 0-915590-71-9). Main Street.

Vintage Racing Machine: Cars from the Collection of George Waterman Jr. Daniel Robbins. (Illus.). 1970. 5.00 (ISBN 0-911517-41-3). Mus of Art RI.

Vintage Radio: 1887-1929. 3rd ed. Morgan E. McMahon. (Illus.). 263p. 1981. pap. 11.95 (ISBN 0-914126-02-4). Vintage Radio.

Vintage Richmond Surrey: Third Impression. Hendon Publishing Co., Ltd. Staff. 1986. 22.40x (ISBN 0-317-54187-0, Pub. by Hendon Pub UK). State Mutual BK.

Vintage Scarborough: Second Impression. Hendon Publishing Co., Ltd. Staff. 1986. 21.00x (ISBN 0-317-54190-0, Pub. by Hendon Pub UK). State Mutual Bk.

Vintage Science Fiction Films, 1896-1949. Michael Benson. LC 83-42889. (Illus.). 231p. 1985. lib. bdg. 18.95x (ISBN 0-89950-085-4). McFarland & Co.

Vintage Station Wagon Shop Service. Ed. by Thomas B. Garrett. LC 76-57074. (Illus.). 160p. 1977. pap. 18.95 (ISBN 0-911160-85-X). Post-Era.

Vintage Stuff. Tom Sharpe. 1984. pap. 3.95 (ISBN 0-394-72417-8, Vin). Random.

Vintage Tractor Album, No. 1. Trent Valley Publications Staff. (Illus.). 96p. Date not set. 50.00x (Pub. by Trent Valley UK). State Mutual Bk.

Vintage Tractor Album, No. 2. Nick Baldwin. 96p. 1982. 40.00x (ISBN 0-7232-2895-7, Pub. by F Warne England). State Mutual Bk.

Vintage Tractor Album, No. 2. Trent Valley Publications Staff. 96p. Date not set. 50.00x (Pub. by Trent Valley UK). State Mutual Bk.

Vintage Vicksburg. Ed. by Natalie Bailess et al. 464p. 1985. 16.95 (ISBN 0-9614988-0-3). Vicksburg Jr Aux.

Vintage Views of Adams County, Ohio. Stephen Kelley. LC 85-90092. (Scenes from the Past Ser.: Vol. I). (Illus.). 52p. (Orig.). 1985. pap. 8.50 (ISBN 0-9614480-4-0). Kelley Pubns.

Vintage Volkswagens: An All-Color Album of Classic VW Bugs, Buses, Vans & Exotica. Photos by Flat 4 Project. (Illus.). 120p. 1985. pap. 12.95 (ISBN 0-87701-357-8). Chronicle Bks.

Vintage Whines. David Wechter & Cissy Wechter. 1988. pap. 2.95 (ISBN 0-317-67079-4). Price Stern.

Vintage Works by Patton. new ed. George S. Patton, Jr. Ed. by Charles M. Province. 395p. (Orig.). 1982. pap. 50.00 (ISBN 0-932348-17-3). C M Province.

Vintage Years: Growing Older with Meaning & Hope. William E. Hulme. LC 85-26399. 120p. (Orig.). 1986. pap. 8.95 (ISBN 0-664-24684-2). Westminster John Knox.

Vintner's Choice: California's Family Wineries Tell Their Stories, Present Their Wine, Share Their Favourite Recipes. Hilde G. Lee. LC 86-6037. (Illus.). 384p. 1986. 19.95 (ISBN 0-89815-174-0); pap. 13.95 (ISBN 0-89815-173-2). Ten Speed Pr.

Vinyl & Diene Monomers. Edward C. Leonard. (High Polymer Ser.: Vol. 24, Pt. 3). 432p. 1971. 36.00 (ISBN 0-471-39330-4, John Wiley). Krieger.

Vinyl & Diene Monomers see High Polymers.

Vinyl in Building & Construction: Regional Technical Conference, Sheraton Naperville Hotel, Naperville Illinois, Sept, 20-22, 1982. Society of Plastics Engineers. pap. 28.30 (ISBN 0-317-29842-9, 2019657). Bks Demand UMI.

Vinyl in Packaging: Regional Technical Conference, September 13 & 14, 1983, Ramada Inn, Airport West, Mississauga, Ontario, Canada. Society of Plastics Engineers. pap. 61.80 (ISBN 0-317-28107-0, 2022511). Bks Demand UMI.

Vinyl Polymerization. Ed. by G. E. Ham. (Kinetics & Mechanisms of Polymerization Ser.: Vol. 1, Pts. 1 & 2). 992p. Pt. 1, 1967. 115.00 (ISBN 0-8247-1292-7); Pt. 2, 1969. 110.00 (ISBN 0-8247-1294-3). Dekker.

Viola: Complete Guide for Teachers & Students. 2nd ed. Henry Barrett. LC 70-169498. 232p. 1978. 19.95 (ISBN 0-8173-6402-1). U of Ala Pr.

Viola d'Amore. rev. 2nd ed. Harry Danks. LC 79-313933. (Illus.). 128p. 1979. 52.00 (ISBN 0-900998-16-4, Pub. by S Bonner England). Theodore Front.

Viola Making, Plans. Harry S. Wake. 1975. 18.50 (ISBN 0-9607048-5-X). H S Wake.

Violation. Charlotte Lamb. (Bestsellers Ser.). 320p. 1983. pap. 3.50 (ISBN 0-373-97005-6, Pub. by Worldwide). Harlequin Bks.

Violation & Repair in the English Novel: The Paradigm of Experience from Richardson to Woolf. Steven Cohan. LC 86-1297. 254p. 1986. 26.50x (ISBN 0-8143-1794-4). Wayne St U Pr.

Violations de Frontieres. Jules Romains. 288p. 1951. 4.95 (ISBN 0-686-55294-6). French & Eur.

Violations of Free Speech & Rights of Labor: Proceedings of the Committee on Education & Labor, U. S. Senate, 76th Congress, 3rd Session, 3 vols. in 1. facsimile ed. Education & Labor Committee. Ed. by Dan C. McCurry & Richard E. Rubenstein. LC 74-30659. (American Farmers & the Rise of Agribusiness Ser.). 1975. Repr. of 1941 ed. 87.00x (ISBN 0-405-06836-0). Ayer Co Pubs.

Violations of Helsinki Accords, August 1983-September 1984. Helsinki Watch Staff. 208p. 1984. 8.00 (ISBN 0-938579-86-X). Fund Free expression.

Violations of the Helsinki Accords: Bulgaria. Helsinki Watch Staff. 33p. 1986. 5.00 (ISBN 0-938579-78-9). Fund Free Expression.

Violations of the Helsinki Accords: Czechoslovakia. Helsinki Watch Staff. 41p. 1986. 6.00 (ISBN 0-938579-79-7). Fund Free Expression.

Violations of the Helsinki Accords: East Germany. Helsinki Watch Staff. 43p. 1986. 6.00 (ISBN 0-938579-80-0). Fund Free Expression.

Violations of the Helsinki Accords: Hungary. Helsinki Watch Staff. 40p. 1986. 6.00 (ISBN 0-938579-81-9). Fund Free Expression.

Violations of the Helsinki Accords: Poland. Helsinki Watch Staff. 84p. 1986. 8.00 (ISBN 0-938579-82-7). Fund Free Expression.

Violations of the Helsinki Accords: Romania. Helsinki Watch Staff. 47p. 1986. 6.00 (ISBN 0-938579-83-5). Fund Free Expression.

Violations of the Helsinki Accords: Turkey. Helsinki Watch Staff. 91p. 1986. 8.00 (ISBN 0-938579-75-4). Fund Free Expression.

Violations of the Helsinki Accords: U. S. S. R. Helsinki Watch Staff. 343p. 1986. 12.00 (ISBN 0-938579-76-2). Fund Free Expression.

Violations of the Helsinki Accords: Yugoslavia. Helsinki Watch Staff. 51p. 1986. 6.00 (ISBN 0-938579-77-0). Fund Free Expression.

Violations of the Laws of War by Both Sides in Nicaragua, 1981-1985. Americas Watch Committee Staff. (Americas Watch Report). 97p. (Span.). 1985. 8.00 (Americas Watch). Fund Free Expression.

Violator. Lionel Webb. 1979. pap. 1.75 (ISBN 0-505-51335-8, Pub. by Tower Bks). Leisure NY.

Violence. Patrick Bizzaro. (Orig.). 1979. pap. 2.50 (ISBN 0-918092-12-4). Tamarack Edns.

Violence: A Guide for the Caring Professions. R. Glynn Owens & J. Barrie Ashcroft. LC 84-23865. 198p. 1985. 26.00 (ISBN 0-7099-1931-X, Pub. by Croom Helm Ltd); pap. 13.95 (ISBN 0-7099-1938-7). Routledge Chapman & Hall.

Violence Against Children: Physical Child Abuse in the United States. David G. Gil. LC 77-130809. (Commonwealth Fund Publications Ser). (Illus.). 1970. 13.00x (ISBN 0-674-93941-7); pap. 5.95 (ISBN 0-674-93942-5). Harvard U Pr.

Violence Against Wives. R. Emerson Dobash & Russell P. Dobash. LC 79-7181. 1979. 19.95 (ISBN 0-02-907320-0); pap. 11.95. Free Pr.

Violence Against Women: A Critique of the Sociobiology of Rape. Ed. by Ethel Tobach & Suzanne Sunday. (Genes & Gender Monograph). 176p. (Orig.). 1985. pap. 12.50x (ISBN 0-87752-231-6). Gordian.

Violence Against Women: An Annotated Bibliography. Carolyn F. Wilson. xiii, 111p. 1981. lib. bdg. 25.00 (ISBN 0-8161-8497-6, Hall Reference). G K Hall.

Violence Against Women & the Ongoing Challenge to Racism. Angela Y. Davis. (Freedom Organizing Pamphlet Ser.). 20p. (Orig.). 1987. pap. 3.50 (ISBN 0-913175-11-0). Kitchen Table.

Violence & Aggression: A Physiological Perspective. K. E. Moyer. LC 86-4987. 237p. 1986. cancelled; pap. 12.95 (ISBN 0-943852-19-6, Pub. by PWPA). Paragon Hse.

Violence & Aggression in the History of Ideas. Ed. by Philip P. Wiener & John Fisher. 288p. 1974. pap. 35.00x (ISBN 0-8135-0772-3). Rutgers U Pr.

Violence & Communication: Public Reactions to an Attempted Presidential Assasination. C. D. Mortensen. (Illus.). 232p. (Orig.). 1988. lib. bdg. 24.25 (ISBN 0-8191-6687-1); pap. text ed. 12.75 (ISBN 0-8191-6688-X). U Pr of Amer.

Violence & Crime in Cross National Perspective. Dane Archer & Rosemary Gartner. LC 83-21700. 416p. 1984. 35.00x (ISBN 0-300-03149-1). Yale U Pr.

Violence & Crime in Cross-National Perspectives. Dane Archer & Rosemary Gartner. LC 83-21700. 351p. 1987. pap. 11.95x (ISBN 0-300-04023-7). Yale U Pr.

Violence & Defiance. Herbert Lust. LC 83-81847. 184p. (Orig.). 1984. 12.95 (ISBN 0-930794-91-5); pap. 5.95 (ISBN 0-930794-90-7). Station Hill Pr.

Violence & Glory: Poems, Nineteen Sixty-Two to Nineteen Sixty-Eight. James Schevill. LC 76-75733. 148p. 1969. 7.95 (ISBN 0-8040-0313-0, Pub by Swallow); pap. 6.95 (ISBN 0-8040-0314-9, Pub by Swallow). Ohio U Pr.

Violence & Great Estates in the South of Italy: Apulia, 1900-1922. Frank M. Snowden. LC 85-11675. (Illus.). 257p. 1986. 42.50 (ISBN 0-521-30731-7). Cambridge U Pr.

Violence & Its Causes: Methodological & Theoretical Aspects of Recent Research on Violence. (Insights Ser.: No. 4). 269p. 1980. pap. 8.00 (ISBN 92-3-101809-4, U1088, UNESCO). UNIPUB.

Violence & Law in the Modern Age. Antonio Cassese. Tr. by S. J. Greenleaves. 210p. 1988. 29.95 (ISBN 0-691-07783-5). Princeton U Pr.

Violence & Nonviolence in South Africa: Jesus's Third Way. Walter Wink. 108p. (Orig.). 1987. 24.95 (ISBN 0-86571-116-X); pap. 6.95 (ISBN 0-86571-117-8). New Soc Pubs.

Violence & Oppression. James C. Dick. LC 78-2235. 224p. 1979. 17.00x (ISBN 0-8203-0446-8). U of Ga Pr.

Violence & Pathos of Verse. Donald J. Surincik. LC 83-91493. 162p. 1984. 7.50 (ISBN 0-9613231-0-8). Don Surincik.

Violence & Piety in Spanish Folklore. Timothy J. Mitchell. 256p. 1988. text ed. 24.95x (ISBN 0-8122-8093-8). U of Pa Pr.

Violence & Politics in Jamaica, 1960-1970: Internal Security in a Developing Country. Terrence J. Lacey. 184p. 1977. 28.50x (ISBN 0-7146-6002-7, F Cass Co). Biblio Dist.

Violence & Politics in Nigeria: A Case-Study of the Tiv & Yoruba. F. O. Anifowose. LC 79-88590. 1982. 22.95x; pap. 9.95 (ISBN 0-88357-084-X). NOK Pubs.

Violence & Religious Commitment: Implications of Jim Jones's People's Temple Movement. Ed. by Ken Levi. LC 81-83147. (Illus.). 224p. 1982. 22.50x (ISBN 0-271-00296-4). Pa St U Pr.

Violence & Repression in Latin America: A Quantitative & Historical Analysis. Ernest A. Duff & John F. McCamant. LC 75-16645. (Illus.). 1976. 22.95 (ISBN 0-02-907690-0). Free Pr.

Violence & Responsibility. John Harris. 1980. 20.00x (ISBN 0-7100-0448-6). Routledge Chapman & Hall.

Violence & Social Change. Henry Bienen. LC 68-56012. 1968. 6.50x (ISBN 0-226-04760-1); pap. 1.95x (ISBN 0-226-04762-8). U of Chicago Pr.

Violence & Social Change. (Great Contemporary Issues Ser.). 1979. lib. bdg. 35.00x (ISBN 0-686-59849-0). Ayer Co Pubs.

Violence & Terror in the Mass Media: An Annotated Bibliography. Compiled by Nancy Signorielli & George Gerbner. LC 87-29556. (Bibliographies & Indexes in Sociology: No. 13). 264p. 1988. lib. bdg. 39.95 (ISBN 0-313-26120-2, SVC/). Greenwood.

Violence & the Labor Movement. Robert Hunter. LC 71-90180. (Mass Violence in America Ser). Repr. of 1914 ed. 14.00 (ISBN 0-405-01320-5). Ayer Co Pubs.

Violence & the Latin American Revolutionaries. Ed. by Michael Radu. 246p. 1988. 24.95 (ISBN 0-88738-195-2). Transaction Bks.

Violence & the Police: An Analysis of Robbery-Related Assault Incidents. C. Kenneth Meyer et al. (Criminal Justice Policy & Administration Research Ser.). 76p. 1983. belo-bind 7.00 (ISBN 0-318-01369-X). Univ OK Gov Res.

Violence & the Politics of Research. Ed. by Willard Gaylin et al. LC 81-15900. (Hastings Center Series in Ethics). 272p. 1981. 32.50x (ISBN 0-306-40789-2, Plenum Pr). Plenum Pub.

Violence & the Sacred. Rene Girard. Tr. by Patrick Gregory. LC 77-4539. 1977. text ed. 32.50x (ISBN 0-8018-1963-6); pap. 10.95x (ISBN 0-8018-2218-1). Johns Hopkins.

Violence & the Violent Individual. Ed. by J. R. Hays et al. LC 80-24. (Illus.). 544p. 1981. text ed. 40.00 (ISBN 0-88331-210-7). Luce.

Violence & Truth: On the Work of Rene Girard. Ed. by Paul Dumouchel. LC 87-61959. 272p. 1988. text ed. 32.50x (ISBN 0-8047-1338-3). Stanford U Pr.

Violence & Vandalism. John Ban & Lewis Ciminillo. LC 77-87607. text ed. 6.95x (ISBN 0-8134-1981-6, 1981). Inter Print Pubs.

Violence As Communication: Insurgent Terrorism & the Western News Media. Alex Schmid & Janny De Graaf. (Illus.). 296p. 1982. 45.00 (ISBN 0-8039-9789-2); pap. 17.95 (ISBN 0-8039-9772-8). Sage.

Violence As Protest: A Study of Riots & Ghettos. Robert M. Fogelson. LC 80-36808. xviii, 265p. 1980. Repr. of 1971 ed. lib. bdg. 35.00x (ISBN 0-313-22642-3, FOVP). Greenwood.

Violence at Sundown. Frank O'Rourke. 1981. pap. 1.95 (ISBN 0-451-11134-6, Sig). NAL.

Violence at Sundown. Frank O'Rourke. 1987. pap. 2.75 (ISBN 0-671-63685-5). PB.

Violence, Civil Strife, & Revolution in the Classical City. Andrew Lintott. 288p. 1987. pap. text ed. 13.95x (Pub. by Croom Helm UK). Routledge Chapman & Hall.

Violence, Conflict, & Politics in Colombia. Paul Oquist. LC 79-6778. (Studies in Social Discontinuity). 1980. 19.95 (ISBN 0-12-527750-4). Acad Pr.

Violence Formula: Why People Lend Sympathy & Support to Terrorism. Terrell E. Arnold. LC 86-45292. 224p. 1988. 19.95 (ISBN 0-669-13153-9). Lexington Bks.

Violence in America, 16 Vols. Ed. by L. Friedman. (Illus.). 4783p. Set. pap. 143.20 (ISBN 0-87754-282-1). Chelsea Hse.

Violence in America. Stephen Goode. LC 83-25033. 192p. (YA) (gr. 7-12). 1984. lib. bdg. 9.79 (ISBN 0-671-45810-8). Messner.

Violence in America. Ed. by Annette Zimmern-Reed. (Conference Proceedings Ser.). 256p. 1987. 12.00 (ISBN 0-89940-100-7). LBJ Sch Pub Aff.

Violence in America: De Tocqueville's America Revisited. Joaquin De Alba. LC 70-75126. 1969. pap. 3.95 (ISBN 0-87491-120-6). Acropolis.

Violence in America: Historical & Comparative Perspectives. rev., college ed. Ed. by Hugh D. Graham & Ted R. Gurr. LC 78-21934. (Illus.). 528p. 1979. 35.00 (ISBN 0-8039-0963-2); pap. 16.95 (ISBN 0-8039-0964-0). Sage.

Violence in American Society. H. G. Nicholas. (Sarah Tryphena Phillips Lectures in American Literature & History). 1969. pap. 5.50 (ISBN 0-85672-302-9, Pub. by British Acad). Longwood Pub Group.

Violence in Animal & Human Societies. Arthur G. Neal et al. LC 76-21241. (Illus.). 240p. 1976. 24.95x (ISBN 0-88229-249-8). Nelson-Hall.

Violence in Early Renaissance Venice. Guido Ruggiero. 272p. 1980. 30.00x (ISBN 0-8135-0894-0). Rutgers U Pr.

Violence in Intimate Relationships. Ed. by Gordon Russell. LC 88-318. 312p. 1988. text ed. 45.00 (ISBN 0-89335-231-4). PMA Pub Corp.

Violence in Lincoln County, 1869-1881: A New Mexico Item. William A. Keleher. LC 82-1984. (Illus.). 416p. 1982. pap. 12.95 (ISBN 0-8263-0616-0). U of NM Pr.

Violence in Modern Literature. James A. Gould & John J. Iorio. LC 71-182676. 208p. 1972. pap. 8.00x (ISBN 0-87835-037-3). Boyd & Fraser.

Violence in Northern Ireland: Understanding Protestant Perspectives. John F. Galliher & Jerry L. DeGregory. 208p. 1985. 36.50 (ISBN 0-8419-1027-8). Holmes & Meier.

Violence in Politics: Terror & Political Assassination in Eastern Europe & Russia. Feliks Gross. Ed. by C. A. Van Nieuwenhuijze. LC 77-189701. (Studies in the Social Sciences: No. 13). 82p. 1973. pap. text ed. 11.20x (ISBN 0-686-22549-X). Mouton.

Violence in Recent Southern Fiction. Louise Y. Gossett. LC 65-13656. pap. 54.80 (ISBN 0-317-42186-7, 2026200). Bks Demand UMI.

Violence in the Arts. John Fraser. LC 73-84319. (Illus.). 236p. pap. 61.40 (2030594). Bks Demand UMI.

Viper of Milan. Marjorie Bowen. LC 65-25494. (gr. 4-8). 1965. 9.95 (ISBN 0-8023-1014-1). Dufour.
Viper Squad. J. B. Hadley. 288p. (Orig.). 1985. pap. 2.95 (ISBN 0-446-32328-4). Warner Bks.
Vipere. Guy Des Cars. 362p. 1969. 16.95 (ISBN 0-686-55665-8). French & Eur.
Viper's Bite. Jean D. Fitz. LC 72-87226. 1969. 4.95 (ISBN 0-87672-101-3). Geron-X.
Viper's Tangle. Francois Mauriac. 208p. 1987. pap. 8.95 (ISBN 0-88184-305-9). Carroll & Graf.
VIP's Directory of Giant Scale Plans, Vol. 1. John A. DeVries & Richard D. Phillips. (Illus.). 120p. 1987. pap. 11.95 (ISBN 0-934575-02-9). Vip Pubs.
Viracocha: The Nature & Antiquity of the Andean High God. Arthur A. Demarest. LC 81-80344. (Peabody Museum Monographs: No. 6). (Illus.). 102p. 1981. pap. 8.00x (ISBN 0-87365-906-6). Peabody Harvard.
Virago Book of Ghost Stories. 1988. 17.95 (ISBN 0-07-015133-4); pap. 8.95 (ISBN 0-07-015132-6). McGraw.
Virago! The Story of Ann Newport Royall (1769-1854) Alice S. Maxwell & Marion B. Dunlevy. LC 84-42731. (Illus.). 326p. 1985. lib. bdg. 19.95x (ISBN 0-89950-133-8). McFarland & Co.
Viraha-Bhakti: The Early History of Krsna Devotion in South India. Friedhelm E. Hardy. (Illus.). 1983. 55.00x (ISBN 0-19-561251-5). Oxford U Pr.
Viral & Bacterial Zoonoses. Christopher Andrewes & John R. Walton. (Illus.). 120p. 1983. pap. write for info. (ISBN 0-7216-0782-9, Bailliere-Tindall). Saunders.
Viral & Immunological Diseases in Non-Human Primates: Proceedings: Symposium, Viral & Immunological Disease, Febuary 28-March 3, 1982, San Antonio, Texas. S. S. Kalter. LC 83-5385. (Monographs in Primatology: Vol. 2). 278p. 1983. 33.00 (ISBN 0-8451-3401-9). A R Liss.
Viral & Mycoplasmal Infections of Laboratory Rodents. Ed. by Pravin N. Bhatt et al. 840p. 1986. 65.00 (ISBN 0-12-095785-X). Acad Pr.
Viral Carcinogenesis: Functional Aspects. Ed. by Niels O. Kjeldgaard & Jes Forchhammer. (Alfred Benzon Symposium Ser.: Vol. 24). 468p. 1987. text ed. 90.00 (ISBN 0-88167-150-9). Raven.
Viral Chemotherapy, Vol. 1. Ed. by D. Shugar. (International Encyclopedia of Pharmacology & Therapeutics Ser.: Section 111). (Illus.). 504p. 1984. 175.00 (ISBN 0-08-029821-4). Pergamon.
Viral Chemotherapy, Vol. 2. Ed. by D. Shugar. (International Encyclopedia of Pharmacology & Therapeutics, Section Ser.). 266p. 1985. 125.00 (ISBN 0-08-031985-8, Pub. by PPL). Pergamon.
Viral Cytopathology. H. H. Malherbe. 112p. 1980. 79.00 (ISBN 0-8493-5567-2). CRC Pr.
Viral Diseases in South East Asia & the Western Pacific. J. S. Mackenzie. 672p. 1983. 47.00 (ISBN 0-12-484820-6). Acad Pr.
Viral Diseases of Cattle. Robert F. Kahrs. (Illus.). 224p. 1981. text ed. 21.95x (ISBN 0-8138-0860-X). Iowa St U Pr.
Viral Diseases of the Eye. Ed. by Richard W. Darrell. LC 84-7897. (Illus.). 341p. 1985. text ed. 46.50 (ISBN 0-8121-0943-0). Lea & Febiger.
Viral Diseases of the Fetus & Newborn. 2nd ed. James B. Hanshaw et al. (Major Problems in Clinical Pediatrics Ser.). (Illus.). 308p. 1985. 48.95 (ISBN 0-7216-4501-1). Saunders.
Viral Etiology of Cervical Cancer. Ed. by Richard Peto & Harald Z. Hausen. LC 86-2227. (Banbury Report: No. 21). 362p. 1986. text ed. 68.00 (ISBN 0-87969-221-9). Cold Spring Harbor.
Viral Haemorrhagic Fevers. (Technical Report Ser.: No. 721). 126p. 1985. pap. 6.00 (ISBN 92-4-120721-3). World Health.
Viral Heart Disease. Ed. by H. D. Bolte. (Illus.). 190p. 1984. pap. 42.00 (ISBN 0-387-13112-4). Springer Verlag.
Viral Hepatitis. Ed. by F. Callea et al. (Proceedings in Life Sciences). (Illus.). 130p. 1986. 37.40 (ISBN 0-387-16730-7). Springer-Verlag.
Viral Hepatitis. Saul Krugman & David J. Gocke. LC 77-16974. (Major Problems in Internal Medicine Ser.: Vol. 15). pap. 30.60 (ISBN 0-317-08692-8, 2016671). Bks Demand UMI.
Viral Hepatitis: A Contemporary Assessment of Etiology, Epidemiology, Pathogenesis & Prevention. G. N. Vyas et al. (Illus.). 748p. 1979. 30.00 (ISBN 0-85626-182-3). Abacus Pr.
Viral Hepatitis & Delta Infection: Proceedings of a Symposium on Viral Hepatitis, Torino, Italy, June 10-11, 1983. Ed. by Giorgio Verme et al. LC 83-49050. (Progress in Clinical & Biological Research Ser.: Vol. 143). 448p. 1983. 60.00 (ISBN 0-8451-0143-9, 0143). A R Liss.
Viral Hepatitis & Liver Disease. Ed. by Girish N. Vyas et al. 784p. 1984. 79.50 (ISBN 0-8089-1678-5, 794711). Grune.
Viral Hepatitis & Liver Disease. Ed. by Arie J. Zuckerman. 1988. write for info. (ISBN 0-471-61270-7). Wiley.
Viral Hepatitis & Liver Disease. Ed. by Arie J. Zuckerman. LC 88-865. 1160p. 1988. 350.00 (ISBN 0-8451-4247-X, 4247). A R Liss.
Viral Hepatitis B Infection in the Western Pacific Region. Vaccine & Control Staff. Ed. by C. L. Lai et al. 304p. 1984. 58.00 (ISBN 9971-950-80-4). World Scientific Pub.
Viral Hepatitis: Biological & Clinical Features, Specific Diagnosis, & Prophylaxis. F. Blaine Hollinger et al. 222p. 1985. text ed. 37.50 (ISBN 0-88167-125-8). Raven.
Viral Hepatitis: Etiology, Epidemiology, Pathogenesis & Prevention. Ed. by Girish N. Vyas et al. LC 78-882. (Clinical Ser). (Illus.). 748p. (Orig.). 1978. 90.00 (ISBN 0-89859-738-2). L Erlbaum Assocs.
Viral Hepatitis: Laboratory & Clinical Science. Ed. by Friedrich Deinhardt & J. Deinhardt. (Liver: Normal Function & Disease Ser.: Vol. 3). 608p. 1983. 99.75 (ISBN 0-8247-1801-1). Dekker.
Viral Hepatitis: Report. WHO Meeting. Geneva, 1974. (Technical Report Ser.: No. 570). (Also avail. in French & Spanish). 1975. pap. 2.80 (ISBN 92-4-120570-9). World Health.
Viral Hepatitis: Report. WHO Scientific Group. Geneva, 1972. (Technical Report Ser.: No. 512). (Also avail. in French & Spanish). 1973. pap. 1.60 (ISBN 92-4-120512-1). World Health.
Viral Hepatitis: Standardization in Immunoprophylaxis of Infections by Hepatitis Viruses. Ed. by G. Papaevangelou & W. Hennessen. (Developments in Biological Standardization Ser.: Vol. 54). (Illus.). xviii, 590p. 1983. pap. 90.00 (ISBN 3-8055-3826-X). S Karger.
Viral Hepatitis Two. Ed. by Wolf Szmuness. 843p. 1982. 90.00 (ISBN 0-89859-737-4). L Erlbaum Assocs.
Viral Immunology & Immunopathology. Ed. by Abner L. Notkins. 1975. 65.50 (ISBN 0-12-522050-2). Acad Pr.
Viral Infections in Oral Medicine. Ed. by J. J. Hooks & G. W. Jordan. 352p. 1982. 78.25 (ISBN 0-444-00674-5, Biomedical Pr). Elsevier.
Viral Infections of Humans: Epidemiology & Control. 3rd ed. Ed. by A. S. Evans. (Illus.). 790p. Date not set. price not set (ISBN 0-306-42731-1, Plenum Med Bk). Plenum Pub.
Viral Infections of Humans: Epidemiology & Control. 2nd ed. Ed. by Alfred S. Evans. LC 82-1984. 758p. 1982. 69.50x (ISBN 0-306-40676-4, Plenum Med Bk). Plenum Pub.
Viral Infections of Humans: Epidemiology & Control. 2nd ed. Ed. by Alfred S. Evans. LC 84-1984. 758p. 1984. pap. 27.50x (ISBN 0-306-41635-2, Plenum Med Bk). Plenum Pub.
Viral Infections of the Nervous System. Richard T. Johnson. 446p. 1982. text ed. 90.00 (ISBN 0-89004-426-0). Raven.
Viral Insecticides for Biological Control. Ed. by Karl Maramorosch & K. E. Sherman. 1985. 82.50 (ISBN 0-12-470295-3). Acad Pr.
Viral Mechanisms of Immunosuppression. Norbert Gilmore & Mark A. Wainberg. LC 85-5788. (Progress in Leukocyte Biology Ser.: Vol. 1). 302p. 1985. 44.00 (ISBN 0-8451-4100-7). A R Liss.
Viral Messenger RNA. Ed. by Yechiel Becker. (Developments in Molecular Virology Ser.). 1985. lib. bdg. 62.50 (ISBN 0-89838-706-X, Pub. by Martinus Nijhoff Netherlands). Kluwer Academic.
Viral Oncology. Ed. by George Klein. 860p. 1980. text ed. 126.00 (ISBN 0-89004-390-6). Raven.
Viral Pathogenesis & Immunology. Cedric A. Mims & David O. White. (Illus.). 300p. 1984. pap. text ed. 37.00x (ISBN 0-632-01193-9, Pub. by Blackwell Sci UK). Blackwell Pubns.
Viral Pollution of the Environment. Ed. by Gerald Berg. 248p. 1983. 89.00 (ISBN 0-8493-6245-8). CRC Pr.
Viral Transformation & Endogenour Viruses. Ed. by Albert S. Kaplan. 1974. 41.50 (ISBN 0-12-397060-1). Acad Pr.
Viral Vaccines. P. B. Stones. (Essays in Applied Microbiology Ser.: No. 10). pap. 20.00 (2031942). Bks Demand UMI.
Viral Warts: Their Biology & Treatment. Mary H. Bunney. (Illus.). 1982. text ed. 21.95x (ISBN 0-19-261335-9). Oxford U Pr.
Virgen Insaciable. new ed. Jason Hytes. Tr. by Danilo Cesto from Eng. (Pimienta Collection Ser). Orig. Title: Part Time Virgin. (Illus.). 160p. (Span.). 1975. pap. 1.25 (ISBN 0-88473-244-4). Fiesta Pub.
Virgil. Ed. by Harold Bloom. (Modern Critical Views Ser.). 215p. 1986. 24.50 (ISBN 0-87754-728-9). Chelsea Hse.
Virgil. W. Lucas Collins. 1877. Repr. 27.00 (ISBN 0-8274-3674-2). R West.
Virgil. Jasper Griffin. 112p. 1986. 14.95x (ISBN 0-19-287655-4); pap. 4.95 (ISBN 0-19-287654-6). Oxford U Pr.
Virgil. George E. Woodberry. 1973. lib. bdg. 17.00 (ISBN 0-8414-9795-8). Folcroft.
Virgil. George E. Woodberry. LC 72-3495. (Studies in European Literature, No. 56). 1972. Repr. lib. bdg. 40.95x (ISBN 0-8383-1564-X). Haskell.
Virgil. see Roman Poets of the Augustan Age.
Virgil: Aeneid, Bk. VI. Ed. by F. M. Ahl. 200p. 1988. text ed. 49.95 (ISBN 0-85668-417-1, Pub. by Aris & Phillips UK); pap. text ed. 16.50 (ISBN 0-85668-418-X, Pub. by Aris & Phillips UK). Humanities.
Virgil: Aeneid, Vol. VI. Ed. by R. G. Austin. 316p. 1986. pap. 13.95x. Oxford U Pr.
Virgil Aeneid. Virgil. Ed. by R. D. Williams. (Classical Ser.). 1972. Bks. 1-6. 15.50 (ISBN 0-312-84735-1); Bks. 7-12. write for info. (ISBN 0-312-84340-2). St Martin.
Virgil: Aeneid Eight. H. Gould & J. Whiteley. 152p. 1979. Repr. of 1953 ed. 12.25 (ISBN 0-906515-39-4, Pub. by Bristol Classical UK). Focus Info Gr.
Virgil: Aeneid Five. R. D. Williams. 242p. 1981. Repr. of 1960 ed. 18.25 (ISBN 0-86292-000-0, Pub. by Bristol Classical UK). Focus Info Gr.
Virgil: Aeneid Four. H. Gould & J. Whiteley. 156p. 1981. Repr. of 1943 ed. 12.00 (ISBN 0-906515-93-9, Pub. by Bristol Classical UK). Focus Info Gr.
Virgil: Aeneid Nine. J. Whiteley. 156p. 1978. Repr. of 1955 ed. 12.25 (ISBN 0-906515-38-6, Pub. by Bristol Classical UK). Focus Info Gr.
Virgil: Aeneid One. H. Gould & J. Whiteley. 164p. 1984. Repr. of 1946 ed. 12.00 (ISBN 0-86292-167-8, Pub. by Bristol Classical UK). Focus Info Gr.
Virgil: Aeneid Seven & Eight. C. Fordyce. 340p. 1985. Repr. of 1977 ed. 21.00 (ISBN 0-86292-171-6, Pub. by Bristol Classical UK). Focus Info Gr.
Virgil: Aeneid Six. H. Gould & J. Whiteley. 164p. 1984. Repr. of 1946 ed. 12.00 (ISBN 0-86292-146-5, Pub. by Bristol Classical UK). Focus Info Gr.
Virgil: Aeneid Three. H. E. Gould & J. Whiteley. 156p. 1981. Repr. of 1943 ed. 12.00 (ISBN 0-906515-99-8, Pub. by Bristol Classical UK). Focus Info Gr.
Virgil: Aeneid Twelve. H. Gould & J. Whiteley. 202p. 1982. Repr. of 1950 ed. 12.25 (ISBN 0-86292-066-3, Pub. by Bristol Classical UK). Focus Info Gr.
Virgil: Aeneid Two. H. Gould & J. Whiteley. 164p. 1982. Repr. of 1943 ed. 12.00 (ISBN 0-86292-056-6, Pub. by Bristol Classical UK). Focus Info Gr.
Virgil: Aeneid XII. Ed. by W. S. Maguinness. (Classical Texts Ser.). 160p. pap. 9.95x (ISBN 0-631-13868-4). Basil Blackwell.
Virgil & His Influence, Bimillenial Studies. C. A. Martindale. 276p. 1984. 25.00 (ISBN 0-86292-083-3, Pub. by Bristol Classical UK). Focus Info Gr.
Virgil & Spenser. Merritt Y. Hughes. LC 79-118629. Repr. of 1929 ed. 12.50 (ISBN 0-404-07809-5). AMS Pr.
Virgil & Spenser. Merritt Y. Hughes. LC 73-91045. 1969. Repr. of 1929 ed. 21.50x (ISBN 0-8046-0655-2, Pub. by Kennikat). Assoc Faculty Pr.
Virgil: Eclogues. H. E. Gould. 132p. 1983. Repr. of 1967 ed. 12.25 (ISBN 0-86292-090-6, Pub. by Bristol Classical UK). Focus Info Gr.
Virgil Eclogues & a Special Vocabulary to Virgil. Virgil. Ed. by J. B. Greenough & G. L. Kittredge. (College Classical Ser.). 1977. lib. bdg. 30.00x (ISBN 0-89241-027-2). Caratzas.
Virgil, Eclogues & Georgics. Williams. 1984. write for info. (ISBN 0-312-84732-7). St Martin.
Virgil, Father of the West. Theodor Haecker. Tr. by A. Wheen. Repr. of 1934 ed. 14.00 (ISBN 0-384-20705-7). Johnson Repr.
Virgil Finlay: An Astrology Sketch Book. 15.00 (ISBN 0-937986-32-1). D M Grant.
Virgil: Georgics One & Four. H. H. Huxley. 272p. 1979. Repr. of 1963 ed. 15.25 (ISBN 0-906515-34-3, Pub. by Bristol Classical UK). Focus Info Gr.
Virgil: His Poetry Through the Ages. R. D. Williams & T. S. Pattie. LC 83-103578. (Illus.). 144p. 1982. 11.95 (ISBN 0-7123-0006-6, Pub. by British Lib); pap. 7.50 (ISBN 0-7123-0005-8). Longwood Pub Group.
Virgil in English Poetry. George S. Gordon. LC 74-19279. 1974. Repr. of 1931 ed. lib. bdg. 16.00 (ISBN 0-8414-4433-1). Folcroft.
Virgil in English Verse. Sir Charles Bowen. 1889. Repr. 35.00 (ISBN 0-8274-3676-9). R West.
Virgil Michel: American Catholic. Robert Spaeth & R. W. Franklin. 150p. 1988. pap. 7.95 (ISBN 0-8146-1584-8). Liturgical Pr.
Virgil: Moretum (The Ploughman's Lunch) E. J. Kenney. 128p. 1984. 15.25 (ISBN 0-86292-084-1, Pub. by Bristol Classical UK). Focus Info Gr.
Virgil, the Aeneid of Virgil. R. D. Williams. 152p. 1985. 11.00 (ISBN 0-86292-044-2, Pub. by Bristol Classical UK). Focus Info Gr.
Virgil Thomson. Virgil Thomson. LC 77-23407. (Quality Paperbacks Ser.). 1977. pap. 6.95 (ISBN 0-306-80081-0). Da Capo.
Virgil Thomson: A Bio-Bibliography. Michael Meckna. LC 86-14229. (Bio-Bibliographies in Music Ser.: No. 4). 217p. 1986. 35.00 (ISBN 0-313-25010-3, MVN/). Greenwood.
Virgil Thomson: His Life & Music. facsimile ed. Kathleen O. Hoover & John Cage. LC 70-119933. (Select Bibliographies Reprint Ser). Repr. of 1959 ed. 23.00 (ISBN 0-8369-5376-2). Ayer Co Pubs.
Virgil Thomson Reader. Virgil Thomson. 576p. 1981. 25.00 (ISBN 0-395-31330-9). HM.
Virgil Thomson's Musical Portraits. Anthony Tommasini. Ed. by Robert Kessler. LC 85-6297. (Thematic Catalogues Ser.: No. 13). 1986. lib. bdg. 42.00 (ISBN 0-918728-51-7). Pendragon NY.
Virgil: Vergil's Aeneid I & II. Waldo E. Sweet. 173p. 1983. Repr. of 1960 ed. 11.00 (ISBN 0-86516-023-6). Bolchazy-Carducci.
Virgil: Voyage of Aeneas. D. A. John & A. F. Turberfield. 278p. 1986. Repr. of 1968 ed. 15.25 (ISBN 0-86292-175-9, Pub. by Bristol Classical UK). Focus Info Gr.
Virgil's Aeneid. Intro. by Harold Bloom. (Modern Critical Interpretations Ser.). 1987. 24.50 (ISBN 0-87754-919-2). Chelsea Hse.
Virgil's Aeneid, 4 vols. Ed. by David F. Coldwell. Tr. by Gavin Douglas. 1964. Repr. of 1957 ed. 115.00 (ISBN 0-384-12439-9). Johnson Repr.
Virgil's Aeneid. Virgil. Tr. by John Dryden. (Airmont Classics Ser.). (gr. 11 up). 1968. pap. 1.95 (ISBN 0-8049-0177-5, CL-177). Airmont.
Virgil's Aeneid & the Tradition of Hellenistic Poetry. Wendell Clausen. (Sather-Classical Lectures: Vol. 51). 230p. 1986. text ed. 25.00x (ISBN 0-520-05791-0). U of Cal Pr.
Virgil's Aeneid: Cosmos & Imperium. Philip Hardie. 400p. 1986. 65.00x (ISBN 0-19-814036-3). Oxford U Pr.
Virgil's Eclogues: The Latin Text with a Verse Translation & Brief Notes. Guy Lee. (Liverpool Latin Texts (Classical & Medieval): No. I). 88p. 1980. pap. text ed. 6.50 (ISBN 0-905205-04-9, Pub. by F Cairns). Longwood Pub Group.
Virgil's Elements: Physics & Poetry in the Georgics. David O. Ross, Jr. 250p. 1987. text ed. 29.00 (ISBN 0-691-06699-X). Princeton U Pr.
Virgil's Gathering of the Clans. William W. Fowler. Ed. by Commager Steele. (Latin Poetry Ser.). 52.00 (ISBN 0-8240-2969-0). Garland Pub.
Virgil's Georgics: A Commentary. Virgil. Ed. by R. A. Mynors. 432p. 1988. 65.00 (ISBN 0-19-814445-8). Oxford U Pr.
Virgil's Georgics: A New Interpretation. Gary B. Miles. LC 78-64460. 1980. 33.00x (ISBN 0-520-03789-8). U of Cal Pr.
Virgil's Iliad: An Essay on Epic Narrative. K. W. Gransden. 232p. 1985. 44.50 (ISBN 0-521-24504-4); pap. 15.95 (ISBN 0-521-28756-1). Cambridge U Pr.
Virgil's Machines. Joel Sloman. (Orig.). 1966. pap. 1.95 (ISBN 0-393-04267-7). Norton.
Virgil's Mind at Work: An Analysis of the Symbolism of the Aeneid. Robert W. Cruttwell. LC 78-114505. 1971. Repr. of 1946 ed. lib. bdg. 35.00x (ISBN 0-8371-4733-6, CRVM). Greenwood.
Virgin. Geoffrey Ashe. 272p. 1988. pap. 12.95 (ISBN 1-85063-100-X). Routledge Chapman & Hall.
Virgin Anchorages. Simon Scott & Nancy Scott. (Illus.). 1988. pap. 24.95 (ISBN 0-944428-02-9). Cruising Guide.
Virgin & Martyr. Andrew M. Greeley. LC 84-40455. 448p. 1985. 17.50 (ISBN 0-446-51287-7). Warner Bks.
Virgin & Martyr. Andrew M. Greeley. 544p. 1987. pap. 4.95 (ISBN 0-446-32873-1). Warner Bks.
Virgin & the Gipsy. D. H. Lawrence. LC 84-50303. 128p. 1984. pap. 5.95 (ISBN 0-394-72666-9, Vin). Random.
Virgin & the Nightingale. Fleur Adcock. 1983. 22.50 (ISBN 0-906427-55-X, Pub. by Bloodaxe Bks); pap. 11.95 (ISBN 0-906427-56-8, Pub. by Bloodaxe Bks). Dufour.
Virgin & Whore: The Image of Women in the Poetry of William Carlos Williams. Audrey T. Rodgers. LC 86-43083. 176p. 1987. lib. bdg. 22.50x (ISBN 0-89950-279-2). McFarland & Co.
Virgin Birth in the Theology of the Ancient Church. Hans Campenhausen. LC 64-55217. (Studies in Historical Theology: No. 2). 1964. pap. 10.00x (ISBN 0-8401-0322-0). A R Allenson.
Virgin Birth of Christ. Robert G. Gromacki. 200p. 1981. pap. 5.95 (ISBN 0-8010-3765-4). Baker Bk.
Virgin Birth of Christ. J. Gresham Machen. 427p. 1958. Repr. of 1930 ed. 17.95 (ISBN 0-227-67630-0). Attic Pr.
Virgin Birth of Christ. J. Gresham Machen. (Twin Brooks Ser). 1967. pap. 10.95 (ISBN 0-8010-5885-6). Baker Bk.
Virgin Conception of Child. Pong Yui. 144p. 1982. 8.75 (ISBN 0-318-20497-5). Pong Yui.
Virgin Fish of Babughat. Lokenath Bhattacharya. Tr. by Meenakshi Mukherjee from Bengali. (Indian Novels Ser.). 160p. 1975. 5.95 (ISBN 0-89253-016-2). Ind-US Inc.
Virgin Guide to London. Ed. by Mark Williams. 1986. pap. 7.95 (ISBN 0-394-74421-7). Pantheon.
Virgin Guide to New York. Ed. by Mark Williams. 1986. pap. 7.95 (ISBN 0-394-74359-8). Pantheon.
Virgin in Flames. Sax Rohmer. 1978. 8.50 (ISBN 0-685-90567-5). Bookfinger.
Virgin Islands. Berlitz Editors. (Travel Guides for English Speakers Ser.). 1977. pap. 6.95 (ISBN 0-02-969700-X, Berlitz). Macmillan.
Virgin Islands. rev. ed. George T. Eggleston. LC 59-14615. 226p. 1973. 16.00 (ISBN 0-88275-087-9). Krieger.
Virgin Islands Alive. (Alive Ser.). (Illus.). 256p. (Orig.). 1988. pap. 10.95 (ISBN 1-55650-101-3). Hunter Pub NY.
Virgin Islands Bays: Modeling of Water Quality & Pollution Susceptibility. Maynard Nichols. (Illus.). 92p. 1979. 12.50 (ISBN 0-318-14619-3). Isl Resources.
Virgin Islands Code Annotated. 1987. write for info. Equity Pub NH.
Virgin Islands Corporation Laws. 1987. pap. 20.00. Equity Pub NH.
Virgin Islands National Park. updated ed. Ruth Radlauer. LC 80-22457. (Parks for People Ser.). (Illus.). 48p. (gr. 3 up). 1981. PLB 13.27 (ISBN 0-516-07741-4). Childrens.
Virgin Islands National Park: The Story Behind the Scenery. Alan H. Robinson. LC 74-81560. (Illus.). 48p. 1974. pap. 4.50 (ISBN 0-916122-14-X). KC Pubns.
Virgin Islands, Our New Possessions & the British Islands. Theodoor N. De Booy. LC 72-109318. (Illus.). 1970. Repr. of 1918 ed. 35.00x (ISBN 0-8371-3584-2, BVI&). Greenwood.
Virgin Islands Reports, 20 vols. 1987. 35.00 ea. Equity Pub NH.

Virginia Family & Its Plantation Houses. Elizabeth Langhorne et al. LC 86-28072. (Illus.). 176p. 1987. 27.50 (ISBN 0-8139-1127-3). U Pr of Va.
Virginia Family Law. 600p. 1987. write for info. D & S Pub.
Virginia Fishing Guide. Bob Gooch. LC 87-18906. (Illus.). 275p. (Orig.). 1988. pap. 10.95 (ISBN 0-8139-1141-9). U Pr of Va.
Virginia Football Mystery. Carole M. Longmeyer. (ACC (Pic-a-Point Sportsmystery) Ser.). (Illus.). 80p. (Orig.). (gr. 3 up). pap. 3.95 (ISBN 0-935326-35-9). Gallopade Pub Group.
Virginia Forms, Vol. III. Barbara G. Gallo. 411p. 1984. 75.00x (ISBN 0-87215-766-0). Michie Co.
Virginia Forms, Vol. IV. Barbara G. Gallo. 382p. 1984. 75.00x (ISBN 0-87215-786-5). Michie Co.
Virginia Forms, Vol. I. W. Clyde Gouldman & Amy M. Hess. 1978. 75.00x (ISBN 0-87215-205-7); 1983 supplement 10.00 (ISBN 0-87215-765-2). Michie Co.
Virginia Forms, Vol. II. George P. Smith & Barbara G. Gallo. 368p. 1982. 75.00x (ISBN 0-87215-527-7). Michie Co.
Virginia: Four Personal Narratives. LC 70-141100. (Research Library of Colonial Americana). 148p. 1971. Repr. of 1588 ed. 14.00 (ISBN 0-405-03310-9). Ayer Co Pubs.
Virginia Frontier, 1754-1763. Louis K. Koontz. LC 78-64117. (Johns Hopkins University. Studies in the Social Sciences. Forty-Third Ser. 1925: 2). Repr. of 1925 ed. 18.50 (ISBN 0-404-61232-6). AMS Pr.
Virginia Gazette Index, 2 vols. Lester J. Cappon & Stella F. Duff. LC 51-15336. 1314p. 1950. Inst Early Am.
Virginia Genealogical Research. 188p. 1983. pap. 9.00 (ISBN 0-913857-06-8). Genealog Sources.
Virginia Genealogies. Horace E. Hayden. LC 66-26936. (Illus.). 759p. 1979. Repr. of 1891 ed. 28.50 (ISBN 0-8063-0174-0). Genealog Pub.
Virginia Genealogies, Vol. 2. Stuart E. Brown et al. 351p. 1980. 30.00x (ISBN 0-686-64384-4). Va Bk.
Virginia Genealogies: A Trial List of Printed Books & Pamphlets. Stuart E. Brown, Jr. LC 67-7956. 310p. 1967. 30.00 (ISBN 0-685-65061-8). Va Bk.
Virginia Genealogy: A Guide to Resources in the University of Virginia Library. LC 82-8470. 1983. 5.95x (ISBN 0-8139-0958-9). U Pr of Va.
Virginia Gentleman & His Family. Natalie R. Boyer. 1978. Repr. of 1939 ed. lib. bdg. 35.00 (ISBN 0-8492-3712-2). R West.
Virginia Germans. Klaus Wust. LC 69-17334. Repr. of 1975 ed. 17.50x (ISBN 0-8139-0256-8). U Pr of Va.
Virginia Gleanings in England: Abstracts of 17th & 18th Century English Wills & Administrations Relating to Virginia & Virginians. Lothrop Withington. LC 79-90754. (Illus.). 745p. 1980. Repr. of 1903 ed. 25.00 (ISBN 0-8063-0869-9). Genealog Pub.
Virginia Goverment & Politics: Readings & Comments. Ed. by Morris R. Thomas & Larry Sabato. 231p. 1984. 13.50 (ISBN 0-318-04158-8). U Va Ctr Pub Serv.
Virginia Government & Politics: Readings & Comments. Weldon Cooper & Thomas R. Morris. LC 75-44333. 450p. 1976. 14.95x (ISBN 0-8139-0677-6). U Pr of Va.
Virginia Government & Politics: Readings & Comments. 2nd ed. Ed. by Thomas R. Morris & Larry Sabato. 231p. 1984. pap. 12.00 (ISBN 0-318-04190-1). U Va Ctr Pub Serv.
Virginia Gross State Product, 1958-1985. (Statistical Ser.). 1986. write for info. U Va Ctr Pub Serv.
Virginia Historical & Biographical Index, Vol. 1. Ronald Vern Jackson. LC 78-53722. (Illus.). 1984. lib. bdg. 30.00 (ISBN 0-89593-204-0). Accelerated Index.
Virginia Historical Index, 2 vols. in 4. Ed. by Earl G. Swem. 1934. Set. 168.00 (ISBN 0-8446-1431-9). Peter Smith.
Virginia Historical Register, 6 vols. in 3. Ed. by William Maxwell. LC 73-763. 1973. Repr. of 1853 ed. Vol. 1-2. 30.00 (ISBN 0-87152-118-0); Vol. 3-4. 30.00 (ISBN 0-87152-119-9); Vol. 5-6. 30.00 (ISBN 0-87152-120-2); Set. 90.00 (ISBN 0-686-66765-4). Reprint.
Virginia History & Whitfield Biographies. Vallie J. Whitfield. LC 77-357760. (Illus.). 1976. 35.00 (ISBN 0-930920-09-0); pap. 25.00 (ISBN 0-930920-10-4). Whitfield Bks.
Virginia History in Documents. 1621-1788. William H. Gaines, Jr. LC 73-94133. (Illus.). 1974. pap. 10.00 (ISBN 0-88490-000-2). VA State Lib.
Virginia Homes of the Lees. rev. ed. Eleanor L. Templeman. LC 73-81139. 1975. 2.50x (ISBN 0-911044-03-5). Templeman.
Virginia House: A Home for Three Hundred Years. Anne M. Faulconer. LC 83-51774. (Illus.). 176p. 1984. 25.00 (ISBN 0-88740-004-3). Schiffer.
Virginia House-Wife. Mary Randolph. Ed. by Karen Hess. LC 83-19869. 400p. 1984. 14.95 (ISBN 0-87249-423-3). U of SC Pr.
Virginia Hunting Guide. Bob Gooch. LC 84-21004. (Illus.). 236p. 1985. pap. 10.95 (ISBN 0-8139-1041-2). U Pr of VA.
Virginia in Our Century. Jean Gottmann. LC 68-8541. pap. 160.00 (ISBN 0-317-28909-8, 2020269). Bks Demand UMI.
Virginia in Words & Pictures. Dennis Fradin. LC 76-7387. (Young People's Stories of Four States). (Illus.). 48p. (gr. 2-5). 1976. PLB 13.27 (ISBN 0-516-03945-8). Childrens.
Virginia Industrial Directory: 1986-87. 17th ed. 350p. 1986. pap. 60.00 (ISBN 0-317-40524-1). VA Chamber Com.
Virginia Industrial Directory, 1988-89. 370p. 1988. pap. 70.00 (ISBN 0-318-02877-8). Manufacturers.
Virginia Jography: A Fun Run Through the Old Dominion State. Carole Marsh. (Carole Marsh Bks.). (Illus.). 50p. (Orig.). (gr. 3-12). 1986. pap. 7.95 (ISBN 0-935326-99-5). Gallopade Pub Group.
Virginia Journal of International Law: 1960-1986, 26 vols. Bound set. 850.00x (ISBN 0-686-90088-X). Rothman.
Virginia Journals of Benjamin Henry Latrobe, 1795-1798. Benjamin Latrobe. Ed. by Edward C. Carter. LC 77-76301. (Illus.). 1977. Set. 104.00x (ISBN 0-300-02198-4); Vol. 1. 52.00x (ISBN 0-300-02160-7); Vol. 2. 52.00x (ISBN 0-300-02176-3). Yale U Pr.
Virginia Land Office Inventory. rev. & enl. ed. Compiled by Daphne S. Gentry. xxx, 42p. (Orig.). 1981. pap. 5.00 (ISBN 0-88490-101-7). VA State Lib.
Virginia Land Office Inventory. Compiled by Daphne S. Gentry. 42p. 1988. pap. 5.00 (ISBN 0-88490-148-3). VA State Lib.
Virginia Land Records from The Virginia Magazine of History & Biography, the William & Mary College Quarterly, & Tyler's Quarterly. LC 82-81848. 888p. 1982. 40.00 (ISBN 0-8063-0992-X). Genealog Pub.
Virginia Landmarks Register. 3rd, rev. ed. Ed. by Calder Loth. LC 85-20374. (Illus.). 512p. 1986. 25.00 (ISBN 0-8139-1061-7). U Pr of Va.
Virginia Lands Grants. Fairfax Harrison. Ed. by Stuart Bruchey. LC 78-56669. (Management of Public Lands in the U. S. Ser.). 1979. Repr. of 1925 ed. lib. bdg. 14.00x (ISBN 0-405-11335-8). Ayer Co Pubs.
Virginia Law Reporters Before 1880. Ed. by William H. Bryson. LC 77-21451. 130p. 1977. 10.95x (ISBN 0-8139-0747-0). U Pr of Va.
Virginia Law Review: 1913-1986, 72 vols. Bound set. 2916.00x (ISBN 0-686-90089-8). Rothman.
Virginia Lawyer: A Basic Practice Handbook. Ed. by Joseph R. Mayes. 1979. with 1987 suppl. 70.00x (ISBN 0-87215-125-5); 1987 suppl. 30.00x (ISBN 0-87215-834-9). Michie Co.
Virginia Lawyer from Reconstruction to the Great Depression. Joseph G. Hylton, Jr. (American Social Experience Ser.: No. 10). 256p. 1988. 40.00x (ISBN 0-8147-3449-9). NYU Pr.
Virginia Legislative Petitions: Bibliography, Calendar, & Abstracts from Original Sources, 6 May 1776-21 June 1782. Intro. by Randolph W. Church. 508p. 1984. 35.00 (ISBN 0-88490-114-9). Va State Lib.
Virginia Life & Health. 1988. write for info. (ISBN 0-930868-26-9). Merritt Co.
Virginia Lineages, Letters & Memories. Alice J. Nelson. (Illus.). x, 302p. 21.50 (ISBN 0-9614497-0-5). A J Nelson.
Virginia Local History: A Bibliography. xxxvi, 46p. 1976. pap. 2.00 (ISBN 0-88490-026-6). VA State Lib.
Virginia Lover & Other Poems. John E. Sturm. Ed. by Jeanne Masson-Douglas. LC 82-81337. (Illus.). 56p. (Orig.). 1982. pap. 4.95 (ISBN 0-940282-01-1). Outermost Pr.
Virginia Magazine of History & Biography: Genealogies of Virginia Families from the Virginia Magazine of History & Biography, 5 vols. LC 80-83868. (Illus.). 4827p. 1981. 150.00 (ISBN 0-8063-0910-5). Genealog Pub.
Virginia Manufactory of Arms. Giles Cromwell. LC 74-8802. 1975. 20.00 (ISBN 0-8139-0573-7). U Pr of Va.
Virginia Marine: World War, Vol. 2. Robert K. Krick. (Illus.). 99p. 1987. 11.95 (ISBN 0-930919-38-6). H E Howard.
Virginia Marriage Records from the Virginia Magazine of History & Biography, William & Mary College Quarterly, & Tyler's Quarterly. LC 82-80465. 794p. 1984. 40.00 (ISBN 0-8063-0983-0). Genealog Pub.
Virginia Marriages in Rev. John Cameron's Register & Bath Parish Register, 1827-1897. Virginia Genealogical Society. 56p. 1963. pap. 10.00 (ISBN 0-89308-264-3, VA 28). Southern Hist Pr.
Virginia, Maryland & the Carolinas see English in America.
Virginia Military Institute Album, 1839-1910. Diane B. Jacob & Judith M. Arnold. LC 82-1865. (Illus.). 112p. 1982. 14.95x (ISBN 0-8139-0947-3). U Pr of Va.
Virginia Military Organizations in the World War with Supplement of Distinguished Service. Ed. by Arthur K. Davis. xx, 506p. 1927. 15.00 (ISBN 0-88490-124-6). VA State Lib.
Virginia Military Records from the Virginia Magazine of History & Biography, the William & Mary College Quarterly, & Tyler's Quarterly. LC 83-81466. 1017p. 1983. 45.00 (ISBN 0-8063-1044-8). Genealog Pub.
Virginia Military Surveys of Clermont & Hamilton Counties, Ohio, 1787-1849. Alma A. Smith. LC 85-90108. (Illus.). x, 253p. 1985. lib. bdg. 32.00 (ISBN 0-9614863-0-9); pap. 25.00 (ISBN 0-9614863-1-7). Alma Smith.
Virginia Militia in the Seventeenth Century. William L. Shea. LC 83-770. xi, 152p. 1983. text ed. 20.00x (ISBN 0-8071-1106-6). La State U Pr.
Virginia Model Jury Instructions--Criminal, 1985 Replacement Edition, 2 vols. rev. ed. Model Jury Instructions Committee. 1985. with 1987 suppl. 155.00x (ISBN 0-87215-928-0). Michie Co.
Virginia Model Jury Instructions: Civil, 2 vols. rev. ed. 1984. with 1987 suppl. 160.00x (ISBN 0-87215-851-9). Michie Co.
Virginia Occupational Demand, Supply, & Wage Information. 6th ed. 1986. write for info. U Va Ctr Pub Serv.
Virginia Occupational Safety & Health Standards for General Industry: 29 CFR Part 1910. LC 85-623098. 531p. Date not set. price not set. Commerce.
Virginia: Off the Beaten Path, A Guide to Unique Places. Judy Colbert & Ed Colbert. LC 85-45696. (Illus.). 176p. (Orig.). 1986. pap. 8.95 (ISBN 0-88742-067-2). Globe Pequot.
Virginia on Guard: Civilian Defense & the State Militia in the Second World War. Marvin W. Schlegel. LC 49-10538. (Illus.). 1949. 15.00 (ISBN 0-88490-040-1). VA State Lib.
Virginia One-Day Trip Book. Jane O. Smith. 224p. (Orig.). 1986. pap. 8.95 (ISBN 0-914440-93-4). EPM Pubns.
Virginia One Hundred Years Ago. Compiled by Skip Whitson. (Sun Historical Ser). (Illus., Orig.). 1976. pap. 3.50 (ISBN 0-89540-024-3, SB-024). Sun Pub.
Virginia Papers of the Presidency, Vol. V: The White Burkett Miller Center Forums, 1981, Pt. 1. Ed. by Kenneth W. Thompson. 91p. 1981. lib. bdg. 18.50 (ISBN 0-8191-1502-9); pap. text ed. 7.75 (ISBN 0-8191-1503-7). U Pr of Amer.
Virginia Papers on the Presidency, Vol. XV. Kenneth W. Thompson. (White Burkett Miller Center Forums, 1983 Ser.: Part. 4). 108p. (Orig.). 1984. lib. bdg. 21.50 (ISBN 0-8191-3866-5, Co-pub. by White Miller Center); pap. text ed. 7.75 (ISBN 0-8191-3867-3, Pub. by White Miller Center). U Pr of Amer.
Virginia Papers on the Presidency, Vol. XVI. Kenneth W. Thompson. LC 79-66241. (White Burkett Miller Center Fourms, 1984: Pt. I). 140p. (Orig.). 1984. lib. bdg. 19.75 (ISBN 0-8191-3983-1, Co-pub. by White Miller Center); pap. text ed. 7.75 (ISBN 0-8191-3984-X). U Pr of Amer.
Virginia Papers on the Presidency, Vol. XI. Ed. by Kenneth W. Thompson. LC 79-66241. (White Burkett Miller Center Forums: Pt. II, 1982). 102p. (Orig.). 1983. lib. bdg. 23.25 (ISBN 0-8191-3111-3); pap. text ed. 8.25 (ISBN 0-8191-3112-1). U Pr of Amer.
Virginia Papers on the Presidency, Vol. XII. Ed. by Kenneth W. Thompson. LC 79-66241. (White Burkett Miller Center Forums, 1983: Pt. 1). 110p. (Orig.). 1983. lib. bdg. 22.00 (ISBN 0-8191-3302-7); pap. text ed. 8.00 (ISBN 0-8191-3303-5). U Pr of Amer.
Virginia Papers on the Presidency, Vol. XIII. Ed. by Kenneth W. Thompson. LC 79-66241. (White Burkett Center Forums: Pt. II). 98p. (Orig.). 1984. lib. bdg. 20.75 (ISBN 0-8191-3622-0, Co-pub. by White Burkett Miller Center); pap. text ed. 7.25 (ISBN 0-8191-3623-9). U Pr of Amer.
Virginia Papers on the Presidency, Vol. XIV. Ed. by Kenneth W. Thompson. LC 79-66241. (White Burkett Miller Center Forums: Pt. III). 100p. (Orig.). 1984. lib. bdg. 19.50 (ISBN 0-8191-3647-6, Co-pub. by White Burkett Miller Center); pap. text ed. 6.75 (ISBN 0-8191-3648-4). U Pr of Amer.
Virginia Papers on the Presidency, Vol. XVII. Ed. by Kenneth W. Thompson. LC 79-66241. (White Burkett Miller Center Forums, 1984: Pt. II). 110p. (Orig.). 1985. lib. bdg. 20.75 (ISBN 0-8191-4255-7, Co-Pub. by White Miller Center); pap. text ed. 9.00 (ISBN 0-8191-4256-5). U Pr of Amer.
Virginia Papers on the Presidency, Vol. XVIII. Ed. by Kenneth W. Thompson. LC 79-66241. (White Burkett Miller Center Forums, 1984: Pt. III). 126p. (Orig.). 1985. lib. bdg. 20.75 (ISBN 0-8191-4315-4, Co-Pub. by White Miller Center); pap. text ed. 9.00 (ISBN 0-8191-4316-2). U Pr of Amer.
Virginia Papers on the Presidency, Vol. XIX. Ed. by Kenneth W. Thompson. LC 79-66241. (White Burkett Miller Center Forums, 1984 Ser.: Pt. IV). 122p. (Orig.). 1985. lib. bdg. 22.00 (ISBN 0-8191-4592-0, Co-pub. by White Miller Center); pap. text ed. 8.25 (ISBN 0-8191-4593-9, Co-pub. by White Miller Center). U Pr of Amer.
Virginia Papers on the Presidency, Vol. XXI. Ed. by Kenneth W. Thompson. LC 86-66241. (White Burkett Miller Center Forums Ser., 1985). 100p. (Orig.). 1986. lib. bdg. 22.75 (ISBN 0-8191-5489-X, Co-pub. by White Miller Center); pap. text ed. 9.25 (ISBN 0-8191-5490-3, Co-pub by White Miller Certer). U Pr of Amer.
Virginia Papers on the Presidency, Vol. XXII. Ed. by Kenneth W. Thompson. LC 79-66241. (White Burkett Miller Center Forums Ser., 1985-86, Part II). 108p. (Orig.). 1986. lib. bdg. 23.75 (ISBN 0-8191-5522-5, Co-pub. by White Miller Center); pap. text ed. 9.25 (ISBN 0-8191-5523-3, Cp-pub by White Miller Center). U Pr of Amer.
Virginia Papers on the Presidency, Vol. XXIII. Ed. by Kenneth W. Thompson. LC 79-66241. (White Burkett Miller Center Forums, 1986-87: Pt. 1). 112p. 1987. lib. bdg. 16.50 (ISBN 0-8191-6348-1, Co-pub. by White Miller Center); pap. text ed. 7.25 (ISBN 0-8191-6349-X, Co-pub. by White Miller Center). U Pr of Amer.
Virginia Papers on the Presidency: Tenth Anniversary Volume, Vol. XX. Ed. by Kenneth W. Thompson. LC 79-66241. (White Burkett Miller Center Forums 1985 Ser.). 164p. (Orig.). 1986. lib. bdg. 22.00 (ISBN 0-8191-5002-9, Co-pub. by White Miller Center); pap. text ed. 9.25 (ISBN 0-8191-5003-7). U Pr of Amer.
Virginia Papers on the Presidency: The White Burkett Miller Center Forums, 1980, Part II, Vol. IV. Ed. by Kenneth W. Thompson. LC 80-5576. 110p. 1980. lib. bdg. 19.75 (ISBN 0-8191-1201-1); pap. text ed. 8.25 (ISBN 0-8191-1202-X). U Pr of Amer.
Virginia Papers on the Presidency: The White Burkett Miller Center Forums, Nineteen Seventy-Nine, Vol. II. Ed. by Kenneth W. Thompson. LC 79-66241. 152p. 1980. 19.75 (ISBN 0-8191-0997-5); pap. 8.25 (ISBN 0-8191-0998-3). U Pr of Amer.
Virginia Papers on the Presidency: The White Burkett Miller Center Forums, 1979, Vol. 1. Kenneth W. Thompson. LC 79-66241. 1979. pap. text ed. 8.25 (ISBN 0-8191-0819-7). U Pr of Amer.
Virginia Papers on the Presidency, Volume IX: The White Burkett Miller Center Forums, 1981, Pt. V. Kenneth W. Thompson. LC 79-66241. 90p. (Orig.). 1982. lib. bdg. 18.00 (ISBN 0-8191-2425-7); pap. text ed. 7.25 (ISBN 0-8191-2426-5). U Pr of Amer.
Virginia Papers on the Presidency: Vol. III, The White Burkett Miller Center Forums, 1980, Pt. 1. Ed. by Kenneth W. Thompson. LC 79-66241. 133p. 1980. lib. bdg. 19.75 (ISBN 0-8191-1120-1); pap. text ed. 8.00 (ISBN 0-8191-1121-X). U Pr of Amer.
Virginia Papers on the Presidency: Vol. VI--The White Burkett Miller Center Forums, 1981, Part II. Ed. by Kenneth W. Thompson. LC 79-66241. 128p. 1981. lib. bdg. 18.50 (ISBN 0-8191-1544-4); pap. text ed. 8.00 (ISBN 0-8191-1604-1). U Pr of Amer.
Virginia Papers on the Presidency, Vol. VII: The White Burkett Miller Center Forums, 1981, Part III. Ed. by Kenneth W. Thompson. LC 79-66241. 104p. 1982. lib. bdg. 24.50 (ISBN 0-8191-1901-6); pap. text ed. 8.75 (ISBN 0-8191-1902-4). U Pr of Amer.
Virginia Papers on the Presidency, Vol. VIII: The White Burkett Miller Center Forums, 1981, Part IV. Ed. by Kenneth W. Thompson. LC 79-66241. 104p. 1982. lib. bdg. 24.50 (ISBN 0-8191-1951-2); pap. text ed. 8.75 (ISBN 0-8191-1952-0). U Pr of Amer.
Virginia Papers on the Presidency, Vol. XXIV: The White Burkett Miller Center Forums, 1986-87, Pt. II. Ed. by Kenneth W. Thompson. LC 79-66241. 138p. (Orig.). 1988. lib. bdg. 19.50 (ISBN 0-8191-6874-2, Co-pub. by White Miller Center); pap. text ed. 8.75 (ISBN 0-8191-6875-0, Co-pub. by White Miller Center). U Pr of Amer.
Virginia Papers on the Presidency, Vol. X: The White Burkett Miller Center Forums, 1982, Pt. 1. Ed. by Kenneth W. Thompson. LC 79-66241. 114p. (Orig.). 1983. lib. bdg. 22.00 (ISBN 0-8191-2823-6); pap. text ed. 8.00 (ISBN 0-8191-2824-4). U Pr of Amer.
Virginia Parks Guide. Margie McCarg. Ed. by Barbara McCarg & Chris Boyer. 100p. (Orig.). 1988. pap. text ed. 5.95 (ISBN 0-935201-30-0). Affordable Adven.
Virginia Probate Law, Vol. 2. 1987. 120.00 (ISBN 0-409-26581-0). D & S Pub.
Virginia Probate Practice. Brockenbrough Lamb. 1957. 25.00x (ISBN 0-87215-095-X). Michie Co.
Virginia Profile Nineteen Sixty to Two Thousand: Assessing Current Trends & Problems. Ed. by John V. Moeser. (Commonwealth Books Public Policy). (Illus.). 290p. (Orig.). 1981. pap. 12.95 (ISBN 0-940390-01-9). Comwealth Bks NJ.
Virginia Property & Casualty. 2nd ed. 1988. write for info. (ISBN 0-930868-39-0). Merritt Co.
Virginia Reels: Stories. William Hoffman. LC 78-16613. (Illinois Short Fiction Ser.). 150p. 1978. pap. 8.95 (ISBN 0-252-00703-4). U of Ill Pr.
Virginia Report of 1799-1800, Touching the Alien & Sedition Laws. James Madison. Bd. with Virginia Resolutions of December 21, 1789. LC 75-107626. (Civil Liberties in American History Ser.). 1970. Repr. of 1850 ed. lib. bdg. 35.00 (ISBN 0-306-71860-X). Da Capo.
Virginia Reports Annotated, Jefferson to 33 Grattan, 26 Vols. Ed. by Thomas J. Michie. 1900. Repr. write for info. (ISBN 0-87215-142-5). Michie Co.

Virgo. (Astroanalysis Ser.). 1987. pap. 8.95 (ISBN 0-317-63313-9, Charter Pub). Berkley Pub.
Virgo. pap. 3.50 (ISBN 0-515-09126-X). Jove Pubns.
Virgo. 1987. pap. 3.95 (ISBN 0-441-79362-2, Pub. by Charter Bks). Ace Bks.
Virgo. 1988. pap. 8.95 (ISBN 0-425-11211-X). Berkley Pub.
Virgo see Astroanalysis.
Virgo: Astro-Numerology. Michael J. Kurban. (Illus.). 50p. (Orig.). 1986. pap. 8.00 (ISBN 0-938863-14-2). Libra Press Chi.
Virgo-Astroanalysis. 360p. 1984. pap. 8.95. Ace BKs.
Virgo: Through the Numbers. Paul Rice & Valeta Rice. 40p. 1983. pap. 2.50 (ISBN 0-87728-570-5). Weiser.
Virgo 1987. Sydney Omarr. 1987. pap. 2.95 (ISBN 0-451-14408-2, Sig). NAL.
Virial Theorem in Stellar Astrophysics. George W. Collins, II. (Astronomy & Astrophysics Ser.: Vol. 7). 143p. 1978. pap. text ed. 19.00 (ISBN 0-912918-13-6, 0013). Pachart Pub Hse.
Viriconium Knights. M. John Harrison. 192p. 1987. pap. 2.75 (ISBN 0-441-86570-4, Pub. by Ace Science Fiction). Ace Bks.
Viroids. Ed. by T. O. Diener. LC 87-13017. (Viruses Ser.). (Illus.). 366p. 1987. 59.50x (ISBN 0-306-42523-8, Plenum Pr). Plenum Pub.
Viroids & Viroid Diseases. T. O. Diener. LC 78-21681. 270p. 1979. 37.50 (ISBN 0-471-03504-1, JW). Krieger.
Viroids & Viroid-Like Pathogens. Ed. by J. S. Semancik & S. M. Garnsey. 192p. 1987. 91.00 (ISBN 0-8493-6060-9). CRC Pr.
Virologie Medicale. Jacques Maurin. (Collection Traites). (Illus.). 930p. (Fr.). 1985. 150.00 (ISBN 2-257-10435-8). S M P F Inc.
Virology. 2nd ed. Renato Dulbecco & Harold S. Ginsberg. LC 65-10705. (Illus.). 425p. 1988. pap. text ed. 37.50 (ISBN 0-397-50905-7, Lippincott Medical). Lippincott.
Virology. Ed. by Bernard N. Fields et al. (Illus.). 1630p. 1985. text ed. 170.50 (ISBN 0-88167-026-X). Raven.
Virology. Heinz Fraenkel-Conrat & Paul C. Kimball. (Illus.). 432p. 1982. write for info. (ISBN 0-13-942144-0). P-H.
Virology. 2nd ed. Heinz Fraenkel-Conrat et al. (Illus.). 432p. 1988. text ed. 41.67 (ISBN 0-13-942186-6). P-H.
Virology. 2nd ed. Ed. by Wolfgang K. Joklik. 325p. 1985. 34.95 (ISBN 0-8385-9461-1). Appleton & Lange.
Virology: An Information Profile. Robin Nicholas & David Nicholas. 256p. 1983. 32.00x (ISBN 0-7201-1673-2). Mansell.
Virology & Immunology in Multiple Sclerosis: Rationale for Therapy. Ed. by C. L. Cazzullo et al. (Illus.). 250p. 1987. 81.20 (ISBN 0-387-18416-3). Springer-Verlag.
Virology in Agriculture. T. O. Diener. (Illus.). 293p. 1977. 28.00 (ISBN 0-85626-137-8). Abacus Pr.
Virology in Agriculture. John A. Romberger. LC 76-42139. (Beltsville Symposia in Agricultural Reasearch Ser.: No. 1). 320p. 1977. text ed. 26.50x (ISBN 0-916672-14-X, Pub. by Allanheld). Rowman.
Virology in Medicine. Ed. by Henry Rothschild & J. Craig Cohen. (Illus.). 1985. text ed. 45.00x (ISBN 0-19-503559-3); pap. text ed. 22.50x (ISBN 0-19-504017-1). Oxford U Pr.
Virology of Flowering Plants. W. A. Stevens. (Tertiary Level Biology Ser.). 1982. 39.95x (ISBN 0-412-00061-X, NO. 5011, Pub. by Chapman & Hall); pap. 19.95 (ISBN 0-412-00071-7, NO. 5012). Routledge Chapman & Hall.
Virology Review, Vol. 2. Ed. by V. M. Zhdanov. (Soviet Medical Reviews Ser.: Vol. 2). 394p. Date not set. Repr. of 1987 ed. text ed. 190.00 (ISBN 3-7186-0402-7). Harwood Academic.
Virology Reviews. Ed. by V. M. Zhdanov. (Soviet Medical Reviews Ser.: Section E). 78p. 1987. text ed. 180.00 (ISBN 3-7186-0314-4). Harwood Academic.
Virology Two: Proceedings. International Congress for Virology, 2nd, Budapest, 1971. Ed. by Joseph L. Melnick. 1972. 63.00 (ISBN 3-8055-1290-2). S Karger.
Virsuses of Potatoes & Seed-Potato Production. Ed. by J. A. De Bokx & J. P. Van der Want. 259p. 1987. text ed. 62.50 (ISBN 90-220-0859-2, PDC278, Pub. by PUDOC). UNIPUB.
Virtual Facsimile & PC Image Capture-Transmission-Processing. International Resource Development, Inc. Staff. 202p. 1986. 1850.00x (ISBN 0-88694-707-3). Intl Res Dev.
Virtual Memory Management. Richard W. Carr. Ed. by Harold Stone. LC 84-140. (Computer Science: Systems Programming: No. 20). 186p. 1984. 42.95 (ISBN 0-8357-1533-7). UMI Res Pr.
Virtual Storage. Bunyan. (Infotech Computer State of the Art Reports). 504p. 1976. 61.00x (ISBN 0-08-028516-3). Pergamon.
Virtue According to Love, in Chaucer. Eugene E. Slaughter. LC 72-949. Repr. of 1957 ed. 18.00 (ISBN 0-404-06098-6). AMS Pr.
Virtue, Commerce & History: Essays on Political Thought & History, Chiefly in the Eighteenth Century. J. G. Pocock. (Ideas in Context Ser.). 400p. 1985. 44.50 (ISBN 0-521-25701-8); pap. 14.95 (ISBN 0-521-27660-8). Cambridge U Pr.
Virtue Notagraph Manual. Constance Virtue. 1974. 6.00. Virtue Notagraph.
Virtue of Faith & Other Essays in Philosophical Theology. Robert M. Adams. 256p. 1987. 29.95x (ISBN 0-19-504145-3); pap. 12.95x (ISBN 0-19-504146-1). Oxford U Pr.
Virtue of Necessity: Inconclusiveness & Narrative Form in Chaucer's Poetry. Larry Sklute. LC 84-22825. 168p. 1985. 22.00 (ISBN 0-8142-0376-0); pap. 10.95 (ISBN 0-8142-0404-X). Ohio St U Pr.
Virtue of Selfishness. Ayn Rand. pap. 3.95 (ISBN 0-451-14839-8, AE2931, Sig). NAL.
Virtue of Sex. Jose de Vinck. LC 66-15236. 256p. 1966. 15.75 (ISBN 0-911726-14-4). Alleluia Pr.
Virtue: Public & Private. James Billington et al. Ed. by Richard J. Neuhaus. (Encounter Ser.). 96p. (Orig.). 1986. pap. 5.95 (ISBN 0-8028-0201-X). Eerdmans.
Virtue Under Fire: How World War II Changed Our Social & Sexual Attitudes. John Costello. 1986. 17.95 (ISBN 0-316-73968-5). Little.
Virtue under Fire: How World War II Changed Our Social & Sexual Attitudes. John Costello. LC 87-335. (Illus.). 336p. 1987. pap. 9.95 (ISBN 0-88064-070-7). Fromm Intl Pub.
Virtues. P. T. Geach. LC 76-19627. 1977. 29.95 (ISBN 0-521-21350-9). Cambridge U Pr.
Virtues & Values: An Introduction to Ethics. Joshua Halberstam. 384p. 1988. pap. text ed. price not set (ISBN 0-13-942202-1). P-H.
Virtues & Vices. James D. Wallace. LC 77-90912. (Contemporary Philosophy Ser.). 208p. 1986. pap. 8.95x (ISBN 0-8014-9372-2). Cornell U Pr.
Virtues & Vices. James D. Wallace. LC 77-90912. (Contemporary Philosophy Ser.). 208p. 1978. 27.50x (ISBN 0-8014-1142-4). Cornell U Pr.
Virtues & Vices see Athenian Constitution.
Virtues & Vices, & Other Essays in Moral Philosophy. Philippa R. Foot. LC 78-54794. 1979. 35.00x (ISBN 0-520-03686-7); pap. 9.95x (ISBN 0-520-04396-0). U of Cal Pr.
Virtues: Contemporary Essays on Moral Character. Ed. by Robert B. Kruschwitz & Robert C. Roberts. 263p. 1987. pap. text ed. write for info. (ISBN 0-534-06720-4). Wadsworth Pub.
Virtues: Die TuGenden. Herbert Witzenman. Tr. by Daisy Aldan. 1975. 4.50 (ISBN 0-913152-17-X). PLB 7.95 (ISBN 0-685-52245-8). Folder Edns.
Virtues of Aristotle. D. S. Hutchinson. 128p. 1986. 25.00 (ISBN 0-7102-0858-8, 08588). Routledge Chapman & Hall.
Virtues of Hell. Pierre Boulle. Tr. by Patricia Wolf from Fr. LC 74-81811. 224p. 1974. 12.95 (ISBN 0-8149-0744-X). Vanguard.
Virtues of Salat. M. Zakariya. 1970. 3.95x (ISBN 0-87902-193-4). Orientalia.
Virtuosa, a Book of Verse. Louise Owen. LC 75-144736. (Yale Series of Younger Poets: No. 29). Repr. of 1930 ed. 18.00 (ISBN 0-404-53829-0). AMS Pr.
Virtuosi: Classical Music's Great Performers from Paganini to Pavarotti. Harold C. Schonberg. 1988. 9.95 (ISBN 0-394-75532-4, Vin). Random.
Virtuoso. Thomas Shadwell. Ed. by Marjorie H. Nicolson & David S. Rodes. LC 65-19466. (Regents Restoration Drama Ser.). xxvi, 153p. 1966. 16.95x (ISBN 0-8032-0368-3). U of Nebr Pr.
Virtuoso Female Performer in the Italian Renaissance, 1600-1630: An Annotated Bibliography & Guide. Susan Cook & Thomasin LaMay. LC 82-49141. 150p. 1983. lib. bdg. 20.00 (ISBN 0-8240-9138-8). Garland Pub.
Virtuoso Goldsmiths & the Triumph of Mannerism, 1540-1620. J. F. Hayward. (Illus.). 798p. 1976. 95.00 (ISBN 0-85667-005-7). Sotheby Pubns.
Virtuoso: The Instrumentalist As Superstar. Harvey Sachs. LC 82-80491. (Illus.). 1982. 18.95 (ISBN 0-500-01286-5). Thames Hudson.
Virtuous Discourse: Sensibility & Community in Late Eighteenth-Century Scotland. John Dwyer. 212p. 1987. text ed. 55.00 (ISBN 0-85976-174-6, Pub. by Donald Pubs Ltd UK). Humanities.
Virtuous Journalist. Stephen Klaidman & Tom L. Beauchamp. 275p. 1987. 19.95 (ISBN 0-19-504205-0). Oxford U Pr.
Virtuous Journalist. Stephen Klaidman & Tom L. Beauchamp. 256p. 1988. pap. text ed. 9.95 (ISBN 0-19-505688-4). Oxford U Pr.
Virtuous Lady. Madeleine Ker. (Harlequin Presents Ser.). 192p. 1984. pap. 1.95 (ISBN 0-318-00043-1). Harlequin Bks.
Virtuous Men, Evil Men, Land & Money. Laurance Labadie. (Men & Movements in the History & Philosophy of Anarchism Ser.). 1979. lib. bdg. 59.95 (ISBN 0-685-96419-1). Revisionist Pr.
Virtuous Mistress. Pamela Frazier. Ed. by Mercer Warriner. 208p. (Orig.). 1988. pap. 2.75 (ISBN 0-425-10641-1). Berkley Pub.
Virtuous Octavia. Samuel Brandon. LC 73-133641. (Tudor Facsimile Texts. Old English Plays: No. 81). Repr. of 1912 ed. 49.50 (ISBN 0-404-53381-7). AMS Pr.
Virtuous Octavia. Samuel Brandon. LC 82-45749. (Malone Society Reprint Ser.: No. 15). Repr. of 1909 ed. 40.00 (ISBN 0-404-63015-4). AMS Pr.
Virtuous Orphan; or, the Life of Marianne, Countess of ---, 4 vols. Mary Collyer. Ed. by Ronald Paulson. LC 78-60843. (Novel 1720-1805 Ser.). 1979. Set. lib. bdg. 150.00 (ISBN 0-8240-3652-2). Garland Pub.
Virtuous Woman. Evelyn Edwards. 1978. 5.00 (ISBN 0-686-25538-0). Freedom Univ-FSP.
Virtuous Woman. Pat Strickland. LC 86-71360. 165p. 1986. 8.95 (ISBN 0-86690-321-6, 2360-01). Am Fed Astrologers.
Virtus et Fortuna. Ed. by Joseph P. Strelka & Jorg Jungmayr. 638p. (Ger.). 1983. 51.60 (ISBN 3-261-03223-5). P Lang Pubs.
Virulence Mechanisms of Bacterial Pathogens. Ed. by James A. Roth. (Illus.). 390p. 1988. text ed. 75.00 (ISBN 0-914826-99-9). Am Soc Microbio.
Virulence of Escherichia Coli: Reviews & Methods. Ed. by Max Sussman. 1985. 89.50 (ISBN 0-12-677520-6). Acad Pr.
Virus. OAS General Secretariat. (Serie De Biologia: No. 8). 72p. (Orig.). 1980. pap. text ed. 3.50 (ISBN 0-8270-1169-5). OAS.
Virus: A History of the Concept. Sally S. Hughes. LC 77-5120. (Illus.). 1977. 12.00 (ISBN 0-88202-168-0, Sci Hist). Watson Pub Intl.
Virus & the Liver. Ed. by L. Bianchi & W. Gerok. K. Sickinger. 1981. lib. bdg. 55.00 (ISBN 0-85200-350-1, Pub. by MTP Pr England). Kluwer Academic.
Virus-Associated Cancers in Africa. A. Olufemi Williams. (LARC Ser.). 806p. 1984. 36.00x (ISBN 0-19-723063-6). Oxford U Pr.
Virus Attachment & Entry Into Cells. Ed. by Richard L. Crowell & Karl Lonberg-Holm. (Illus.). 216p. 1986. pap. text ed. 28.00 (ISBN 0-914826-90-5). Am Soc Microbio.
Virus Chemotherapy. Ed. by F. E. Hahn. (Antibiotics & Chemotherapy Ser.: Vol. 27). (Illus.). vi, 310p. 1980. 126.75 (ISBN 3-8055-0263-X). S Karger.
Virus Diseases in Laboratory & Captive Animals. Ed. by Gholamreza Darai. (Developments in Veterinary Virology). 1987. lib. bdg. 139.95 (ISBN 0-89838-988-7, Pub. by M Nijhoff Boston MA). Kluwer Academic.
Virus Diseases of Food Animals: A World Geography of Epidemiology & Control, Vol. 1. Ed. by E. Paul Gibbs. LC 81-521. (International Perspectives Ser.). 1982. 91.00 (ISBN 0-12-282201-3). Acad Pr.
Virus Diseases of Food Animals: A World Geography of Epidemiology & Control, Vol. 2. Ed. by E. Paul Gibbs. LC 81-66681. (Disease Monographs). 1982. 109.00 (ISBN 0-12-282202-1). Acad Pr.
Virus Diseases of Small Fruits. (Agriculture Handbook Ser.: No. 631). (Illus., Orig.). 1987. pap. 20.00 (S/N 001-000-04483-4). USGPO.
Virus Diseases of Small Fruits & Grapevines. Ed. by N. W. Frazier. 1970. 7.50x (ISBN 0-931876-21-4, 4056). ANR Pubns CA.
Virus Hepatitis & Its Control. Yvonne E. Cossart. (Illus.). 1982. text ed. 25.95 (ISBN 0-7216-0714-4). Saunders.
Virus Inactivation in Plasma Products. Ed. by J. J. Morgenthaler. (Current Studies in Hematology & Blood Transfusion Ser.: No. 56). (Illus.). viii, 150p. 1989. 93.50 (ISBN 3-8055-4836-2). S Karger.
Virus-Induced Immunosuppression. Ed. by S. Specter et al. (Infectious Agents & Pathogenesis Ser.). (Illus.). 415p. Date not set. price not set (ISBN 0-306-43040-1, Plenum Pr). Plenum Pub.
Virus Infection & the Cell Surface. Ed. by G. Poste & G. Nicholson. (Cell Surface Reviews: Vol. 2). 342p. 1977. 144.25 (ISBN 0-7204-0598-X, Biomedical Pr). Elsevier.
Virus Infection & the Developing Nervous System. Ed. by G. Lyon. 1988. lib. bdg. 65.00 (ISBN 0-7462-0053-6, Pub. by MTP Pr England). Kluwer Academic.
Virus Infection in Pregnancy. Ed. by Marvin S. Amstey. (Monograph in Neonatology Ser.). 256p. 1984. 44.50 (ISBN 0-8089-1609-2, 790080). Grune.
Virus Infections & Diabetes Mellitus. Ed. by Yechiel Becker. (Developments in Medical Virology Ser.). 1987. lib. bdg. 75.00 (ISBN 0-89838-970-4, Pub. by Martinus Nijhoff). Kluwer Academic.
Virus Infections in Bats. S. E. Sulkin. Ed. by Rae Allen. (Mongraphs in Virology: Vol. 8). 100p. 1974. 46.00 (ISBN 3-8055-1696-7). S Karger.
Virus Infections: Modern Concepts & Status. Olson. (Microbiology Ser.: Vol. 6). 304p. 1982. 59.75 (ISBN 0-8247-1859-3). Dekker.
Virus Infections of Carnivores. Ed. by M. J. Appel. (Virus Infections of Vertabrates Ser.: Vol. 1). 516p. 1988. 189.50 (ISBN 0-444-42709-0). Elsevier.
Virus Infections of the Gastrointestinal Tract. Ed. by David A. Tyrell & Albert Z. Kapikian. (Infectious Diseases & Antimicrobial Agents Ser.: Vol. 3). (Illus.). 623p. 1982. 75.00 (ISBN 0-8247-1567-5). Dekker.
Virus-Inhibiting Factor: An Antiviral, Antibacterial & Antitumor Substance. Yasuiti Nagano. 250p. 1975. 25.00x (ISBN 0-86008-126-5, Pub. by Japan Sci Soc Japan). Intl Spec Bk.
Virus-Lymphocyte Interactions: Implications for Disease. Ed. by M. R. Profitt. LC 79-19984. (Developments in Immunology Ser.: Vol. 7). 319p. 1979. 65.75 (ISBN 0-444-00348-7, Biomedical Pr). Elsevier.
Virus, Mycoplasm & Rickettsia Diseases of Fruit Trees. M. Nemeth. (Forestry Sciences Ser.). 1986. lib. bdg. 161.00 (ISBN 90-247-2868-1, Pub. by Martinus Nijhoff Netherlands). Kluwer Academic.
Virus of Love & Other Tales of Medical Detection. Charles T. Gregg. LC 84-17204. 319p. 1985. pap. 12.95 (ISBN 0-8263-0793-0). U of NM Pr.
Virus Receptors, 2 pts. Ed. by K. Longberg-Holm et al. (Receptors & Recognition Ser. B: Vols. 7 & 8). Set. 90.00x (ISBN 0-686-80429-5, NO. 2170, Pub. by Chapman & Hall England). Routledge Chapman & Hall.
Virus Receptors, Part 1: Bacterial Viruses see Queues: Receptors & Recognition Series B.
Virus Receptors, Part 2: Animal Viruses see Queues: Receptors & Recognition Series B.
Virus Replication & Genome Interaction: The 7th John Innes Symposium. Ed. by J. W. Davies et al. (Journal of Cell Science Supplement: No. 7). 337p. 1987. text ed. 70.00x (ISBN 0-948601-10-8, Biochemical Society). Rsrch Bks CT.
Virus Structure. Robert W. Horne. 1974. 33.00 (ISBN 0-12-355750-X). Acad Pr.
Virus Structure & Assembly. Sherwood Casjens. 290p. 1985. text ed. 52.50 (ISBN 0-86720-044-8). Jones & Bartlett.
Viruses. S. Jane Flint. Ed. by J. J. Head. LC 87-70987. (Carolina Biology Readers Ser.: No. 194). (Illus.). 16p. (Orig.). (YA) (gr. 10 up). 1988. pap. text ed. 1.75 (ISBN 0-89278-094-0, 45-9794). Carolina Biological.
Viruses. rev. ed. Alan E. Nourse. (First Bk.). (Illus.). 72p. (gr. 4 up). 1983. PLB 10.40 (ISBN 0-531-04534-X). Watts.
Viruses. rev. ed. F. Kingsley Sanders. Ed. by J. J. Head. LC 77-94289. (Carolina Biology Readers Ser.). (Illus.). 32p. (gr. 10 up). 1981. pap. 2.10 (ISBN 0-89278-264-1, 45-9664). Carolina Biological.
Viruses Affecting Man & Animals. Murry Sanders & Morris Schaeffer. LC 75-117612. (Illus.). 478p. 1971. 27.50 (ISBN 0-87527-070-0). Green.
Viruses & Cancer. Ed. by P. W. Rigby & N. M. Wilkie. 325p. 1985. 70.00 (ISBN 0-521-26867-2). Cambridge U Pr.
Viruses & Cancer: A Report. WHO Scientific Group, Geneva, 1964. (Technical Report Ser: No. 295). 60p. (Eng., Fr., Rus. & Span.). 1965. pap. 2.00 (ISBN 92-4-120295-5). World Health.
Viruses & Demyelinating Diseases. Cedric Mims et al. 1984. 45.00 (ISBN 0-12-498280-8). Acad Pr.
Viruses & Environment. Edouard Kurstak & Karl Maramorosch. 1979. 29.95 (ISBN 0-12-429766-8). Acad Pr.
Viruses & Human Cancer. Ed. by Robert C. Gallo et al. LC 86-27526. (UCLA Symposia on Molecular & Cellular Biology, New Ser.: Vol. 43). 552p. 1987. 90.00 (ISBN 0-8451-2642-3, 2642). A R Liss.
Viruses & Human Cancer. Ed. by Yohei Ito. (Progress in Experimental Tumor Research Ser.: Vol. 21). (Illus.). 1977. 74.75 (ISBN 3-8055-2701-2). S Karger.
Viruses & Plasmids in Fungi. P. A. Lemke. (Mycology Ser.: Vol. 1). 1979. 99.75 (ISBN 0-8247-6916-3). Dekker.
Viruses & Reproduction: A Bibliography. Compiled by Ernest L. Abel. 1988. 45.00 (ISBN 0-313-26439-2, AVR/). Greenwood.
Viruses & the Environment. J. I. Cooper & F. O. MacCallum. (Illus.). 190p. 1984. 32.00x (ISBN 0-412-22870-X, NO. 6437); pap. 15.95x (ISBN 0-412-22880-7, NO. 6869). Routledge Chapman & Hall.
Viruses & Wastewater Treatment: Proceedings of International Symposium Held at the University of Surrey, Guilford, 15-17 September 1980. Ed. by M. Goddard & M. Butler. (Illus.). 316p. 1981. 81.00 (ISBN 0-08-026401-8). Pergamon.
Viruses As the Causative Agents of Naturally Occurring Tumors. Ed. by George Klein. (Advances in Viral Oncology Ser.: Vol. 5). 280p. 1985. text ed. 89.50 (ISBN 0-88167-053-7). Raven.
Viruses Associated with Human Cancer. Phillips. 896p. 1983. 99.75 (ISBN 0-8247-1738-4). Dekker.
Viruses: Catalogue, Characterization & Classification. Heinz Fraenkel-Conrat. LC 84-1984. 276p. 1985. 55.00x (ISBN 0-306-41766-9, Plenum Pr). Plenum Pub.
Viruses Causing Common Respiratory Diseases in Man. George G. Jackson & Robert L. Muldoon. LC 74-8430. (Studies in Infectious Diseases Research Ser). viii, 248p. 1975. lib. bdg. 17.95x (ISBN 0-226-38940-5). U of Chicago Pr.
Viruses from Space. Fred Hoyle et al. 118p. 1986. pap. 9.00 (ISBN 0-906449-93-6, Pub. by UC Cardiff Pr). Longwood Pub Group.
Viruses, Immunity, & Immunodeficiency. Ed. by Andor Szentivanyi & Herman Friedman. LC 86-3263. (University of South Florida International Biomedical Symposia Ser.). 380p. 1986. 55.00x (ISBN 0-306-42235-2, Pub. by Plenum Pr). Plenum Pub.
Viruses, Immunity & Mental Disorders. E. Kurstak et al. 425p. 1987. 65.00x (ISBN 0-306-42337-5, Plenum Med). Plenum Pub.
Viruses in Families. John P. Fox & Carrie E Hall. LC 75-12023. (Illus.). 462p. 1980. 47.00 (ISBN 0-88416-042-4). PSG Pub Co.
Viruses in Human Tumors. P. H. Hofschneider. Ed. by K. Munk. (Beitraege zur Onkologie; Contributions to Oncology Ser.: Vol. 24). (Illus.). viii, 216p. 1987. 44.75 (ISBN 3-8055-4354-9). S Karger.

Vision & Spirit: An Essay on Plato's Warrior Class. Joe Simmons. LC 88-1401. 74p. (Orig.). 1988. lib. bdg. 16.50 (ISBN 0-8191-6885-8); pap. text ed. 8.25 (ISBN 0-8191-6886-6). U Pr of Amer.

Vision & Sports: An Introduction. James R. Gregg. (Illus.). 188p. 1987. text ed. 29.95 (ISBN 0-409-90020-6). Butterworth.

Vision & Stagecraft in Sophocles. David Seale. LC 82-50459. 270p. 1982. lib. bdg. 27.50x (ISBN 0-226-74404-3). U of Chicago Pr.

Vision & Strategy for Church Growth. 2nd ed. Waldo J. Werning. 1983. pap. 4.50 (ISBN 0-8010-9658-8). Baker Bk.

Vision & Strategy: The Plan of Pastoral Action for Family Ministry. National Conference of Catholic Bishops, United States Catholic Conference. (Illus., Orig.). 1978. pap. 3.75 (ISBN 1-55586-961-0). US Catholic.

Vision & the Art of Drawing. Howard S. Hoffman. (Illus.). 256p. 1988. pap. 11.95 (ISBN 0-13-942285-4). P-H.

Vision & the Constant Star. Albert H. Hobbs. LC 56-9678. 5.75 (ISBN 0-912806-11-7). Long Hse.

Vision & the Dream. Marguerite Hargrove. 1980. pap. 2.25 (ISBN 0-8439-0811-4, Leisure Bks). Leisure NY.

Vision & the Reality: The Story of Home Missions in the General Conference Mennonite Church. Lois Barrett. LC 83-80402. 339p. (Orig.). 1983. pap. 8.95 (ISBN 0-87303-079-6). Faith & Life.

Vision & the Visual Arts in Galdos: A Study of the Novels & Newspaper Articles. Peter A. Bly. (Liverpool Monographs in Hispanic Studies: No. 6). 242p. 1986. text ed. 40.00 (ISBN 0-905205-30-8, Pub. by F Cairns). Longwood Pub Group.

Vision & Values in the Catholic School: Participant's Guide. 96p. 1981. 4.20 (ISBN 0-686-39942-0). Natl Cath Educ.

Vision & Vesture: A Study of William Blake in Modern Thought. Charles Gardner. LC 73-15646. 1916. lib. bdg. 25.00 (ISBN 0-8414-4470-6). Folcroft.

Vision, Brain & Cooperative Computation. Ed. by Michael A. Arbib. Allen R. Hanson. (Computational Model of Cognition & Perception Ser.). 512p. 1987. text ed. 65.00x (ISBN 0-262-01094-1). MIT Pr.

Vision Clara de Dios. Ed. by Eva Quinones de Dailey. (Span.). pap. 4.95 (ISBN 0-87148-884-1). Pathway Pr.

Vision, Composition, & Photography. Ernst A. Weber. (Illus.). 208p. 1980. 19.95 (ISBN 3-11-006903-2). De Gruyter.

Vision Conference Proceedings. 1985. 68.00 (ISBN 0-87263-173-7). SME.

Vision del Mundo en la Novela: Tiempo de silencio, de Luis Martin-Santos. Emilio Diaz-Valcarcel. 98p. (Orig., Span.). 1982. pap. 5.00 (ISBN 0-8477-3506-0). U of PR Pr.

Vision Du Passe. Pierre Teilhard De Chardin. 1957. 13.50 (ISBN 0-685-11622-0). French & Eur.

Vision Exchanged. Carolyn Bloor & Grace Seiberling. (Illus.). 48p. (Orig.). 1985. pap. 7.95 (ISBN 0-948107-05-7, Pub. by Victoria & Albert Mus UK). Faber & Faber.

Vision for America. Gerald R. Ford. 1981. Deluxe signed ed. 75.00 (ISBN 0-935716-08-4). Lord John.

Vision for Missions. Tom Wells. 157p. 1985. pap. 4.95 (ISBN 0-85151-433-2). Banner of Truth.

Vision for the Catechetical Ministry: An Instrument for Diocesan & Parish Planning. 1985. 5.30 (ISBN 0-318-18576-8); 4.00. Natl Cath Educ.

Vision for the Church. Mike Phillips. 110p. 1981. pap. 3.95 (ISBN 0-940652-02-1). Sunrise Bks.

Vision for the Future. Ann R. Colton. 139p. 1960. 5.95 (ISBN 0-917187-12-1). A R C Pub.

Vision Glorious: Themes & Personalities of the Catholic Revival in Anglicanism. Geoffrey Rowell. 280p. 1983. text ed. 27.00x (ISBN 0-19-826443-7). Oxford U Pr.

Vision: Human & Electronic. Ed. by Albert Rose. LC 73-97422. (Optical Physics & Engineering Ser.). (Illus.). 200p. 1974. 35.00x (ISBN 0-306-30732-4, Plenum Pr). Plenum Pub.

Vision in Action: The Art of Taking & Shaping Initiatives. Christopher Schaefer & Tijno Voors. 199p. (Orig.). 1986. pap. text ed. 12.95 (ISBN 0-88010-150-4). Anthroposophic.

Vision in Drosophila. M. Heisenberg & R. Wolf. (Studies of Brain Function: Vol. 12). (Illus.). 280p. 1984. 79.00 (ISBN 0-387-13685-1). Springer-Verlag.

Vision in Motion. Laszlo Moholy-Nagy. (Illus.). 1947. 21.50 (ISBN 0-911498-00-1). Theobald.

Vision in Spring. William Faulkner. Intro. by Judith L. Sensibar. (Illus.). 134p. 1984. 14.95 (ISBN 0-292-78712-X). U of Tex Pr.

Vision in the Animal World. R. H. Smythe. LC 75-13590. (Illus.). 175p. 1975. 27.50 (ISBN 0-312-84980-X). St Martin.

Vision: In the Eye of the Beholder. K. Cole. (Illus.). 106p. (Orig.). 1979. pap. 8.50 (ISBN 0-943451-04-3). Explorator.

Vision in Vehicles: Proceedings of the Conference, Nottingham, U. K., 9-13 September 1985. Ed. by A. G. Gale & M. H. Freeman. 465p. 1986. 110.75 (ISBN 0-444-87983-8). Elsevier.

Vision in Vertebrates. M. A. Ali & M. A. Klyne. LC 85-12191. 282p. 1985. 55.00x (ISBN 0-306-42065-1, Plenum Pr.). Plenum Pub.

Vision Is Fulfilled. Kay L. McDonald. 384p. 1984. pap. 3.50 (ISBN 0-451-12901-6, Sig). NAL.

Vision Obscured: Perceptions of Some Twentieth-Century Catholic Novelists. Ed. by Melvin J. Friedman. LC 72-126130. 1970. 25.00 (ISBN 0-8232-0890-7). Fordham.

Vision of a Contemporary University: A Case Study of Expansion & Development in American Higher Education, 1950-75. Russell M. Cooper & Margaret B. Fisher. LC 80-29022. (Illus.). xiv, 318p. 1981. 15.00 (ISBN 0-8130-0702-X). U Presses Fla.

Vision of an Artist & Writer. James J. Davidson. (Illus.). 1981. 6.95 (ISBN 0-533-04806-0). Vantage.

Vision of Anglo-America. H. B. Ryan. 240p. 1987. 34.50 (ISBN 0-521-32928-0). Cambridge U Pr.

Vision of Asia: An Interpretation of Chinese Art & Culture. L. Cranmer-Byng. 1979. Repr. of 1933 ed. lib. bdg. 30.00 (ISBN 0-8492-4025-5). R West.

Vision of Beasts: Creation Descending. Jack Lovejoy. (No. 1). 224p. (Orig.). 1984. pap. 2.95 (ISBN 0-8125-4500-1, Dist. by Warner Pub. Services & Saint Martin's Press). Tor Bks.

Vision of Beasts: The Brotherhood of Diablo, Bk. 3. Jack Lovejoy. 288p. 1985. pap. 2.95 (ISBN 0-8125-4504-4, Dist. by Warner Pub. Services & Saint Martin's Press). Tor Bks.

Vision of Beasts: The Second Kingdom, No. 2. Jack Lovejoy. (Orig.). 1984. pap. 2.95 (ISBN 0-8125-4502-8, Dist. by Warner Pub. Services & Saint Martin's Press). Tor Bks.

Vision of Color & Pattern. Gordon E. Legge & Fergus W. Campbell. Ed. by J. J. Head. LC 84-45835. (Biology Readers Ser.: No. 165). (Illus.). 16p. (Orig.). (YA) (gr. 10 up). 1987. pap. text ed. 1.65 (ISBN 0-89278-365-6, 45-9765). Carolina Biological.

Vision of Cosmic Order in the Vedas. Jeanine Miller. 320p. 1985. 39.95x (ISBN 0-7102-0369-1). Routledge Chapman & Hall.

Vision of Destiny. Whitney Stine. 1986. pap. 3.95 (ISBN 0-441-86458-9). Ace Bks.

Vision of Dhamma: The Buddhist Writings of Nyanaponika Thera. Nyanaponika Thera. Ed. by Bhikkhu Bodhi. 296p. (Orig.). 1986. pap. 12.50 (ISBN 0-87728-669-8). Weiser.

Vision of Doom. Mary Kirchoff. LC 86-90005. (Endless Quest Bks.: No. 35). 160p. (Orig.). (gr. 3-8). 1986. pap. 2.25 (ISBN 0-88038-307-0). TSR Inc.

Vision of Dynamic Space, Rudolf Laban. Compiled by Lisa Ullmann. (Illus.). 80p. 1984. 31.00x (ISBN 1-85000-008-5, Falmer Pr). Taylor & Francis.

Vision of God. Vladimir Lossky. 139p. 1963. 7.95 (ISBN 0-913836-19-2). St Vladimirs.

Vision of God. Nicholas Of Cusa. Tr. by Emma G. Satter. LC 60-9104. pap. 3.95x (ISBN 0-8044-6594-0). Ungar.

Vision of God & Man. Inayat Khan. (Sufi Message of Hazrat Inayat Khan Ser.: Vol. 12). 272p. 1979. 14.95 (ISBN 90-6325-100-9, Pub. by Servire BV Netherlands). Hunter Hse.

Vision of God: The Christian Doctrine of the Summum Bonum. abr. ed. Kenneth E. Kirk. Ed. by G. R. Dunstan. 223p. 1977. Repr. of 1934 ed. 17.50 (ISBN 0-227-67830-3). Attic Pr.

Vision of God's Dawn. Sri Chinmoy. 67p. 1974. pap. 2.00 (ISBN 0-685-53062-0). Aum Pubns.

Vision of Harmony: The Sculpture of Saul Baizerman. David Finn & Melissa Dabakis. (Contemporary Sculptors Ser.). (Illus.). 128p. 1988. 25.00 (ISBN 0-933806-53-1). Black Swan CT.

Vision of Hell. D. D. Owen. 1971. 17.50x (ISBN 0-7073-0160-2, Pub. by Scot Acad Pr). Longwood Pub Group.

Vision of Krishnamurti. R. K. Shringy. 140p. 1979. 6.95. Asia Bk Corp.

Vision of Life: A Photo Essay with Poetry by Breakthrough Foundation Youth at Risk Participants. Youth at Risk Participants. LC 87-32357. 72p. (Orig.). 1988. pap. 14.95 (ISBN 0-944296-01-7). Spirit Pr.

Vision of Light. Judith M. Riley. 1989. 19.95 (ISBN 0-440-50109-1). Delacorte.

Vision of Love. Elizabeth Graham. (Harlequin Presents Ser.). 192p. 1983. pap. 1.95 (ISBN 0-373-10583-5). Harlequin Bks.

Vision of Matthew: Christ, Church & Morality in the First Gospel. John P. Meier. LC 78-70820. 1979. pap. 8.95 (ISBN 0-8091-2171-9). Paulist Pr.

Vision of Modern Dance. Ed. by Jean M. Brown. LC 79-88382. (Illus.). 206p. 1979. pap. text ed. 12.95 (ISBN 0-916622-12-6). Princeton Bk Co.

Vision of Mohamed Omer Bushara. 1981. pap. 3.00 (ISBN 0-89192-318-7, Pub. by African Am Inst). Interbk Inc.

Vision of Order: A Study of Black South African Literature in English, 1914-1980. Ursula A. Barnett. LC 83-9296. 336p. 1983. lib. bdg. 22.50x (ISBN 0-87023-406-4). U of Mass Pr.

Vision of Piers Plowman. William Langland. 1978. 16.95x (ISBN 0-460-10571-X, Evman); pap. 6.95x (ISBN 0-460-11571-5, Evman). Biblio Dist.

Vision of Piers Plowman. William Langland. Tr. by Henry W. Wells. Repr. of 1959 ed. lib. bdg. 35.00x (ISBN 0-8371-0525-0, LAPP). Greenwood.

Vision of Piers Plowman: Text C, Pt. III. W. W. Skeat. (EETS OS Ser.: Vol. 54). Repr. of 1873 ed. 21.00 (ISBN 0-8115-3352-2). Kraus Repr.

Vision of Piers the Plowman. William Langland. Ed. by W. W. Skeat. LC 66-26827. (Medieval Library). Repr. of 1900 ed. 18.50x (ISBN 0-8154-0134-5). Cooper Sq.

Vision of Robert Flaherty: The Artist As Myth & Filmmaker. Richard Barsam. LC 87-45245. 160p. 1988. 27.50x (ISBN 0-253-32074-7); pap. 10.95 (ISBN 0-253-20460-7). Ind U Pr.

Vision of Self in Early Vedanta. W. Beidler. 1975. 18.50 (ISBN 0-8426-0990-3). Orient Bk Dist.

Vision of Tarot. Piers Anthony. 272p. 1984. pap. 3.50 (ISBN 0-425-09800-1). Berkley Pub.

Vision of the Aquarian Age. George Trevelyan. LC 84-50222. 166p. (Orig.). 1984. pap. 7.95 (ISBN 0-913299-03-0, Dist. by NAL). Stillpoint.

Vision of the Disinherited: The Making of American Pentecostalism. Robert M. Anderson. 1979. 24.95x (ISBN 0-19-502502-4). Oxford U Pr.

Vision of the Future: Twelve Ideas for a Better Life & a Better Society. Mortimer J. Adler. 272p. 1984. 14.95 (ISBN 0-02-500280-5). Macmillan.

Vision of the New Community: Public Ethics in the Light of Christian Eschatology. Lynn E. Mitchell. (American University Studies: Series VII: Theology & Religion, Vol. 29). 205p. 1988. text ed. 37.50 (ISBN 0-8204-0450-0). P Lang Pubs.

Vision of the Trinity. George H. Tavard. LC 80-5845. 166p. (Orig.). 1981. lib. bdg. 26.75 (ISBN 0-8191-1412-X); pap. text ed. 11.50 (ISBN 0-8191-1413-8). U Pr of Amer.

Vision of the Vedic Poets. J. Gonda. (Disputationes Rheno-Trajectinae Ser.: No. 8). (Orig.). 1963. pap. text ed. 28.80x (ISBN 90-2790-034-5). Mouton.

Vision of the Void: Theological Reflections on the Works of Elie Wiesel. Michael Berenbaum. xii, 240p. 1987. pap. 12.95 (ISBN 0-8195-6189-4). Wesleyan U Pr.

Vision of This Land: Studies of Vachel Lindsay, Edgar Lee Masters, & Carl Sandburg. Ed. by John E. Hallwas & Dennis J. Reader. LC 76-4350. 1976. pap. 5.00 (ISBN 0-934312-00-1). WIU Essays Lit.

Vision of Tragedy. rev. & enlarged ed. Richard B. Sewall. LC 79-24203. 1979. pap. 9.95x (ISBN 0-300-02489-4). Yale U Pr.

Vision of Unity. John Meyendorff. LC 87-23495. 192p. (Orig.). 1987. pap. 7.95 (ISBN 0-88141-068-3). St Vladimirs.

Vision of Unity: Adamovich in Exile. Roger Hagglund. 180p. 1985. 25.00 (ISBN 0-88233-410-7). Ardis Pubs.

Vision of Unity: The Bland Family in England & America, 1555-1900. Charles Bland. 610p. (Orig.). 1982. 74.95 (ISBN 0-9610804-0-X). C L Bland.

Vision of Unity: The History of the Bakery & Confectionery Workers International Union. Stuart B. Kaufman. (Illus.). 192p. 1987. 27.50 (ISBN 0-252-01422-7); pap. 10.95 (ISBN 0-252-01423-5). U of Ill Pr.

Vision of William Concerning Piers Plowman, Pt. 4. William Langland. Ed. by W. W. Skeat. (EETS, OS Ser.: No. 67). Repr. of 1877 ed. 62.00 (ISBN 0-527-00059-0). Kraus Repr.

Vision of William Concerning Piers the Plowman, in Three Parallel Texts, Together with Richard the Redeless, 2 Vols. William Langland. Ed. by W. W. Skeat. 1886. 98.00x (ISBN 0-19-811366-8). Oxford U Pr.

Vision of World Peace in Seventeenth & Eighteenth Century France. Elizabeth V. Souleyman. LC 76-118454. 1971. Repr. of 1941 ed. 27.00x (ISBN 0-8046-1585-3, Pub. by Kennikat). Assoc Faculty Pr.

Vision of Youth Ministry: Bilingual Edition. 48p. (Eng. & Span.). 1986. pap. text ed. 2.95 (ISBN 1-55586-107-5). US Catholic.

Vision on Fire: Emma Goldman on the Spanish Revolution. Ed. by David Porter. LC 82-74015. (Illus.). 383p. (Orig.). 1983. pap. 7.50 (ISBN 0-9610348-2-3). Commonground Pr.

Vision or Villainy: Origins of the Owens Valley-Los Angeles Water Controversy. Abraham Hoffman. LC 80-6111. (Environmental History Ser.: No.3). (Illus.). 328p. 1981. 22.50x (ISBN 0-89096-112-3). Tex A&M Univ Pr.

Vision Pathology in Education. Edith Kirk. (Illus.). 240p. 1981. 27.00x (ISBN 0-398-04504-6). C C Thomas.

Vision Problems in the United States. 80p. 10.00 (ISBN 0-318-15871-X, P10). Natl Soc Prevent Blindness.

Vision Quest & the Magic Meditation: The Quest of the Spirit; The Quest of the Universal Spirit; The Quest of the Higher Self. Gordon Banta. Ed. & illus. by Diane Martin. LC 86-63206. (Gordon Banta Vision Quest Bks.). (Illus.). 60p. (Orig.). 1987. pap. 9.95 (ISBN 0-931485-13-4). Scriptorium Pr.

Vision Quest Books. Gordon Banta. 1987. write for info. Scriptorium Pr.

Vision Quest of the Plains Indians: Its Spiritual Significance. Kathleen M. Dugan. LC 85-18768. (Studies in American Religion: Vol. 13). 272p. 1985. lib. bdg. 49.95x (ISBN 0-88946-659-9). E Mellen.

Vision Splendid (Hardy, Housman) Neville H. Watts. LC 74-16122. 1974. Repr. of 1946 ed. lib. bdg. 37.50 (ISBN 0-8414-9548-3). Folcroft.

Vision-Structure & Function. K. L. Chow & W. Mao. 624p. 1988. 62.00 (ISBN 9971-50-365-4). World Scientific Pub.

Vision Systems. 87.00 (ISBN 0-686-40543-9). C I M Systems.

Vision Therapy in a Primary Care Practice. Jerome Rosner & Joy Rosner. (Illus.). 160p. 1988. text ed. 40.00 (ISBN 0-87873-077-X). Prof Pr Bks NYC.

Vision Through the Atmosphere. William E. Middleton. pap. 66.00 (ISBN 0-317-08955-2, 2014366). Bks Demand UMI.

Vision, Tradition, Interpretation: Theology, Religion, & the Study of Religion. Eric J. Lott. (Religion & Reason Ser.: No. 35). 272p. 1988. text ed. 76.50x (ISBN 0-89925-347-4). De Gruyter.

Vision-Visual Perception. Ed. by Sam Weintraub & Robert J. Cowan. (Annotated Bibliography Ser.). 93p. (Orig.). 1982. pap. text ed. 4.50 (ISBN 0-87207-339-4, 339). Intl Reading.

Vision y Valores Manual del Participante. 96p. (Span.). 1982. 4.20 (ISBN 0-686-39943-9). Natl Cath Educ.

Vision '87 Conference Proceedings. Machine-Vision Association of the Society of Manufacturing Engineers. (Illus.). 981p. (Orig.). pap. write for info. (ISBN 0-87263-278-4). SME.

Visionaries. James G. Huneker. LC 78-116979. (Short Story Index Reprint Ser). 1905. 19.00 (ISBN 0-8369-3459-8). Ayer Co Pubs.

Visionaries & Seers: The People Who Saw Tomorrow. Charles Gattey. 288p. (Orig.). 1988. pap. 13.95 (ISBN 1-85327-020-2, Pub. by Prism Pr). Avery Pub.

Visionaries & Their Apocalypses. Ed. by Paul D. Hanson. LC 83-5488. (Issues in Religion & Theology Ser.). 176p. 1983. pap. 2.50 (ISBN 0-8006-1765-7). Fortress.

Visionary, 2 vols. in 1. Ursula K. Leguin. Bd. with Wonders Hidden. Scott R. Sanders. (Back-to-Back Ser.: Vol. 1). (YA) 7.50. McGraw.

Visionary. Walter Scott & Peter Garside. (Regency Reprints Ser.: No. I). 64p. (Orig.). 1984. pap. 6.75 (ISBN 0-906449-65-0, Pub. by UC Cardiff Pr). Longwood Pub Group.

Visionary & Dreamer: Two Poetic Painters, Samuel Palmer & Edward Burne-Jones. David Cecil. LC 68-57088. (Bollingen Ser.: No. 35). (Illus.). 177p. 1970. 50.00x (ISBN 0-691-09853-0); pap. 15.50x (ISBN 0-691-01858-8). Princeton U Pr.

Visionary & Other Poems. E. H. Meyerstein. 1977. Repr. of 1941 ed. 15.00 (ISBN 0-8274-4316-1). R West.

Visionary Apparatus: Michael Snow & Juan Geuer. Dana Friis-Hansen & Jeanne Randolph. LC 86-62271. (Illus.). 52p. (Orig.). 1986. pap. 5.00 (ISBN 0-938437-15-1). MIT List Visual Arts.

Visionary Appropriation. John D. McCurdy. LC 78-50530. 284p. 1978. 12.95 (ISBN 0-8022-2227-7). Philos Lib.

Visionary Architects: Boullee, Ledoux, Lequeu. Intro. by J. C. Lemagny & Dominique De Menil. (Illus.). 1968. pap. 8.00 (ISBN 0-914412-21-3). Inst for the Arts.

Visionary Betrayed: Aesthetic Discontinuity in Henry James's The American Scene. David L. Furth. (LeBaron Russell Briggs Prize Honors Essay in English). 1980. pap. text ed. 3.95x (ISBN 0-674-94085-7). Harvard U Pr.

Visionary Christian: One Hundred & Thirty-One Readings from C. S. Lewis. C. S. Lewis. 288p. 1984. 6.95 (ISBN 0-02-086730-1, Collier). Macmillan.

Visionary Christian: One Hundred Thirty-One Readings from C. S. Lewis. C. S. Lewis. Selected by Chad Walsh. 256p. 1981. 10.95 (ISBN 0-02-570540-7). Macmillan.

Visionary Closure in the Modern Novel. William R. Thickstun. 305p. 1987. 35.00 (ISBN 0-312-01339-6). St Martin.

Visionary Compacts: American Renaissance Writings in Cultural Context. Ed. by Donald E. Pease. LC 86-23371. (Wisconsin Project on American Writing Ser.). 320p. 1987. text ed. 32.50x (ISBN 0-299-11000-1); pap. 15.50x. U of Wis Pr.

Visionary Company: A Reading of English Romantic Poetry. rev. ed. Harold Bloom. LC 73-144032. (Paperback Ser.). 506p. 1971. pap. 14.95x (ISBN 0-8014-9117-7, CP117). Cornell U Pr.

Visionary Eye: Essays in the Arts, Literature, & Science. Jacob Bronowski. Ed. by Piero Ariotti & Rita Bronowski. 1978. pap. 7.95 (ISBN 0-262-52068-0). MIT Pr.

Visionary Film: The American Avant-Garde 1943-1978. 2nd ed. P. Adams Sitney. (Illus.). 1979. 27.50x (ISBN 0-19-502485-0); pap. 14.95 (ISBN 0-19-502486-9). Oxford U Pr.

Visionary Girls: Witchcraft in Salem Village. Marion Starkey. (gr. 7 up). 1973. 15.95 (ISBN 0-316-81087-8). Little.

Visionary Hand: Essays for the Study of William Blake's Art & Aesthetics. Ed. by Robert Essick. LC 72-96392. (Illus.). 600p. 1973. pap. 12.50 (ISBN 0-912158-41-7). Hennessey.

Visionary Leadership: Implementing Tomorrow's Strategy: Conference Proceedings. 344p. 1987. pap. 100.00 (ISBN 0-912841-28-1). Planning Forum.

Visionary Physics: Blake's Response to Newton. Donald D. Ault. LC 73-77128. (Midway Reprint Ser.). pap. 61.30 (2026762). Bks Demand UMI.

Visions: Stories & Photographs. Leonid Andreyev. Ed. by Olga Andreyev Carlisle. 1987. 21.95 (ISBN 0-15-193900-4). HarBraceJ.
Visions: 19 Short Stories by Outstanding Writers for Young Adults. Ed. by Donald R. Gallo. LC 87-6787. 224p. (YA) (gr. 7 up). 1987. pap. 16.95 (ISBN 0-385-29588-X). Delacorte.
Visit. T. Degens. LC 82-2600. 168p. (gr. 7 up). 1982. 11.95 (ISBN 0-670-74712-2). Viking.
Visit. Friedrich Durrenmatt. Tr. by Patrick Bowles from Ger. 1962. pap. 4.95 (ISBN 0-394-17239-6, E344, Ever). Grove.
Visit. Friedrich Durrenmatt. Tr. by Patrick Bowles. 109p. (Orig.). Date not set. pap. 6.95 (ISBN 0-8021-3066-6). Grove.
Visit. Diane Wolkstein. LC 76-54297. (Illus.). (ps-1). 1977. Knopf.
Visit from Dr. Katz. Ursula K. Le Guin. LC 87-1783. (Illus.). 32p. (gr. k-3). 1988. 12.95 (ISBN 0-689-31332-2, Atheneum Childrens Bks). Macmillan.
Visit from the Footbinder. Emily Prager. LC 87-40110. (Contemporaries Ser.). 208p. 1987. pap. 6.95 (ISBN 0-394-75592-8, Vin). Random.
Visit of Teshoo Lama to Peking. Ernest Ludwig. LC 78-70096. Repr. of 1904 ed. 18.50 (ISBN 0-404-17345-4). AMS Pr.
Visit of the French Frigate Sloop of War to the Sandwich Islands, 1836 see Unless Haste Is Made: A French Skeptic's Account of the Sandwich Islands in 1836.
Visit of the Rurik to San Francisco in 1816. August C. Mahr. LC 78-155606. (Stanford University. Stanford Studies in History, Economics, & Political Science: Vol. 2, Pt. 2). (Illus.). Repr. of 1932 ed. 22.00 (ISBN 0-404-50964-9). AMS Pr.
Visit of the Tomten. Barry L. Johnson. LC 81-70361. pap. 4.95x (ISBN 0-8358-0439-9). Upper Room.
Visit of the Wisemen. Martha Jander. 24p. 1987. pap. 1.29 (ISBN 0-570-09012-1, 59-1439). Concordia.
Visit to a Gnani. Edward Carpenter. 65p. 1971. Repr. of 1902 ed. 4.00 (ISBN 0-911662-44-8). Yoga.
Visit to Annabel Marie. Norbert Schiller. (Illus.). 1985. 2.50 (ISBN 0-943164-10-9). Geronima.
Visit to Ching-Te Chen. John Addis. 35p. 1975. 20.00x (ISBN 0-317-43969-3, Pub. by Han-Shan Tang Ltd). State Mutual Bk.
Visit to Europe in Eighteen Fifty-One, 2 vols. Benjamin Silliman. Ed. by I. Bernard Cohen. LC 79-8406. (Three Centuries in Science in America Ser.). (Illus.). 1980. Repr. of 1856 ed. lib. bdg. 75.00x (ISBN 0-405-12574-7); lib. bdg. 37.50x ea. Vol. 1 (ISBN 0-405-12684-0). Vol. 2 (ISBN 0-405-12575-5). Ayer Co Pubs.
Visit to Germany, Italy & Malta, 1840-1841. Hans Christian Andersen. Tr. by Grace Thornton from Danish. (Illus.). 182p. 1986. 27.50 (ISBN 0-7206-0636-5, Pub. by P Owen Ltd). Dufour.
Visit to New Orleans Coloring Book. Ruth Carvin. 28p. (gr. k-4). 1986. 3.50 (ISBN 0-9616390-0-8). Carvin Pub.
Visit to New Orleans: With Pictures to Color & Verses to Read. rev. ed. Ruth Carvin. (Illus.). 32p. (gr. k-4). 1988. coloring bk. 3.50 (ISBN 0-9616390-2-4). Carvin Pub.
Visit to Salt Lake. William Chandless. LC 76-134391. Repr. of 1857 ed. AMS Pr.
Visit to Some American Schools & Colleges. Sophia Jex-Blake. LC 74-33948. (Pioneers of the Woman's Movement: an International Perspective Ser.). xii, 250p. 1976. Repr. of 1867 ed. 21.45 (ISBN 0-88355-269-8). Hyperion Conn.
Visit to the Airport. Sandra Ziegler. LC 87-35470. (Field Trip Bks.). (Illus.). 32p. (gr. k-3). 1988. PLB 8.45 (ISBN 0-516-01488-9). Childrens.
Visit to the Bakery. Sandra Ziegler. LC 86-32647. (Field Trip Bks.). (Illus.). 32p. (gr. k-3). 1987. PLB 11.93 (ISBN 0-516-01495-1). Childrens.
Visit to the Barbary Regencies. R. Grosvenor. 112p. 1986. 200.00x (ISBN 1-85077-102-2, Pub. by Darf Pubs Ltd). State Mutual Bk.
Visit to the Cities of Cheese. Margaret Johnson. (Burning Deck Poetry Chapbooks). 40p. (Orig.). 1985. pap. 10.00 (ISBN 0-930901-37-1). Burning Deck.
Visit to the Dairy Farm. Sandra Ziegler. LC 87-19692. (Field Trip Bks.). (Illus.). 32p. (ps-3). 1987. PLB 11.93 (ISBN 0-516-01496-X); pap. 2.95 (ISBN 0-516-41496-8). Childrens.
Visit to the Doctor. Berger et al. (Illus.). (ps-1). pap. 2.95 (ISBN 0-448-14001-2, G&D). Putnam Pub Group.
Visit to the Doctor. D. Leb Tannenbaum. (New Feelings Activity Bks.). (Illus.). 64p. (ps-2). 1981. pap. 3.95 (ISBN 0-671-43205-2, Little Simon). S&S.
Visit to the Doctor. Illus. by Michael Twinn. (Nursery Ser.). (Illus., Orig.). (ps-2). 1977. 2.00 (ISBN 0-85953-067-1, Pub. by Child's Play England). Playspaces.
Visit to the Eagles' Nest. Tina Jordan. (Illus.). 20p. (gr. 3-5). 1980. PLB 2.25 (ISBN 0-938574-00-0). Cherubim.
Visit to the Fire Station. John Chao. (Illus.). (gr. k-3). Date not set. 14.95 (ISBN 0-590-40389-3, Scholastic Hardcover). Scholastic Inc.
Visit to the Fire Station. Dotti Hannum. LC 84-12155. (Field Trip Ser.). (Illus.). 32p. (gr. k-3). 1985. PLB 11.93 (ISBN 0-516-01491-9); pap. 2.95 (ISBN 0-516-41491-7). Childrens.
Visit to the Library. Cherry Gilchrist. (Cambridge Information Books for Children). (gr. 2-5). pap. 2.50 (ISBN 0-521-31931-5). Cambridge U Pr.
Visit to the Library. Sylvia R. Tester. LC 84-12637. (Field Trip Ser.). (Illus.). 32p. (gr. k-3). 1985. PLB 11.93x (ISBN 0-516-01492-7); pap. 2.95 (ISBN 0-516-41492-5). Childrens.
Visit to the Logos of Earth. George King et al. (Illus.). 125p. 1986. pap. 15.95 (ISBN 0-937249-11-4). Aetherius Soc.
Visit to the Missions of Southern California in February & March 1874. Henry L. Oak. Ed. by Ruth F. Axe et al. LC 81-52830. (Illus.). 87p. 1981. 20.00 (ISBN 0-916561-66-6). Southwest Mus.
Visit to the Police Station. Dotti Hannum. LC 84-12700. (Field Trip Ser.). (Illus.). 32p. (gr. k-3). 1985. PLB 11.93 (ISBN 0-516-01493-5); pap. 2.95 (ISBN 0-516-41493-3). Childrens.
Visit to the Province of Upper Canada in 1819. John Strachan. Repr. of 1820 ed. 21.00 (ISBN 0-384-58600-7). Johnson Repr.
Visit to the Sesame Street Firehouse. Dan Elliot. LC 83-4606. (Picturebacks Ser.). (Illus.). 32p. (ps-3). 1983. lib. bdg. 5.99 (ISBN 0-394-96029-7); pap. 1.95 (ISBN 0-394-86029-2). Random.
Visit to the Sesame Street Hospital. Deborah Hantzig. LC 84-17852. (Picturebacks Ser.). (Illus.). 32p. (ps-4). 1985. lib. bdg. 5.99 (ISBN 0-394-97062-4, BYR); pap. 1.95 (ISBN 0-394-87062-X). Random.
Visit to the Sesame Street Library. Deborah Hautzig. LC 85-18312. (Picturebacks Ser.). (Illus.). 32p. (ps-1). 1986. 1.95 (ISBN 0-394-87744-6); lib. bdg. 5.99 (ISBN 0-394-97744-0). Random.
Visit to the Sesame Street Museum. Liza Alexander. LC 87-1685. (Pictureback Book Ser.). (Illus.). 32p. (gr. 3-6). 1987. lib. bdg. 5.99 (ISBN 0-394-98715-2); pap. 1.95 (ISBN 0-394-88715-8). Random.
Visit to the Sesame Street Zoo. Ellen Weiss. LC 88-3201. (Picturebacks Ser.). (Illus.). 32p. (Orig.). (ps-1). 1988. PLB 5.99 (ISBN 0-394-90447-8, BYR); pap. 1.95 (ISBN 0-394-80447-3, BYR). Random.
Visit to the United States in Eighteen Forty-One. Joseph Sturge. LC 68-58023. 1969. Repr. of 1842 ed. 39.50x (ISBN 0-678-00583-4). Kelley.
Visit to the Vatican for Young People. Donald Wuerl & Michael Wilson. (Illus.). (gr. 3-7). 1980. 3.50 (ISBN 0-8198-8002-7). Dghtrs St Paul.
Visit to the Zoo. Illus. by San Diego Zoological Society. (San Diego Zoo Series of Picture Bks.). (Illus.). 12p. (ps-2). 1983. board 3.50 (ISBN 0-89346-219-5). Heian Intl.
Visit to the Zoo. Sylvia R. Tester. LC 84-12697. (Field Trip Bks.). (Illus.). 32p. (gr. k-3). 1987. PLB 11.93 (ISBN 0-516-01494-3); pap. 2.95 (ISBN 0-516-41494-1). Childrens.
Visit to Washington, D. C. Jill Krementz. LC 86-27973. (Illus.). 48p. (gr. 6 up). 1987. 13.95 (ISBN 0-590-40582-9, Scholastic Hardcover). Scholastic Inc.
Visit to William Blake's Inn. Nancy Willard. LC 80-27403. (Voyager Picture Bks.). (Illus.). 48p. (ps-3). 1987. pap. 3.95 (ISBN 0-15-293823-0, VoyB). HarBraceJ.
Visit to William Blake's Inn. Nancy Willard. (Illus.). (gr. k-3). 1988. 3.95 (VoyB). HarbraceJ.
Visit to William Blake's Inn: Poems for Innocent & Experienced Travelers. Nancy Willard. LC 80-27403. (Illus.). 44p. (ps-3). 1981. 12.95 (ISBN 0-15-293822-2, HJ). HarBraceJ.
Visit with Great-Grandma. Sharon H. Addy. Ed. by Ann Fay. (Illus.). 32p. (gr. 1-3). 1988. 11.95g (ISBN 0-8075-8497-5). A Whitman.
Visitable Past: Views of Venice by American Artists, 1860-1915. Margaretta M. Lovell. (Illus.). 250p. 1988. 39.95x (ISBN 0-226-49412-8). U of Chicago Pr.
Visitantes Del Mas Alla. new ed. Robert Tralins. Tr. by Juan A. Rios from Eng. (Compadre Collection Ser). Orig. Title: Weird People of the Unknown. 160p. (Span.). 1974. pap. 0.85 (ISBN 0-88473-706-3). Fiesta Pub.
Visitants. Randolph Stow. 192p. 1987. pap. 7.95 (ISBN 0-8008-8017-X). Taplinger.
Visitants. Miriam Waddington. 1981. pap. 9.95 (ISBN 0-19-540380-0). Oxford U Pr.
Visitants: A Novel. Randolph Stow. LC 80-53710. 192p. 1981. 12.95 (ISBN 0-8008-8018-8). Taplinger.
Visitation. Michele Roberts. 224p. (Orig.). 1984. pap. 6.95 (ISBN 0-7043-3903-X, Pub. by Quartet Bks). Salem Hse Pubs.
Visitation Evangelism Leader's Guide. rev. ed. Churches Alive, Inc. Staff. LC 84-73068. (Illus.). 112p. 1985. pap. text ed. 11.95 (ISBN 0-934396-40-X). Churches Alive.
Visitation Evangelism Member's Notebook. rev. ed. Churches Alive, Inc. Staff. (Illus.). 80p. 1985. pap. text ed. 9.95 (ISBN 0-934396-39-6). Churches Alive.
Visitation: Key to Church Growth. Gordon Lindsay. 1.25 (ISBN 0-89985-119-3). Christ Nations.
Visitation Made Easy. C. S. Lovett. 1959. pap. 2.95 (ISBN 0-938148-15-X). Personal Christianity.
Visitation of the County of Huntingdon. Nicholas Charles. 1849. 19.00 (ISBN 0-384-08525-3). Johnson Repr.
Visitation of the County of Huntingdon, Under the Authority of William Camden. Nicholas Charles. Ed. by Henry Ellis. LC 17-1223. (Camden Society, London. Publications, First Ser.: No. 43). Repr. of 1849 ed. 19.00 (ISBN 0-404-50143-5). AMS Pr.
Visitations. Jean Giraudoux. (Coll. Le Fleuron). pap. 14.95 (ISBN 0-685-33932-7). French & Eur.
Visitations. Mitch Sisskind. Ed. by Laurance Wieder. LC 84-71460. 96p. 1984. 10.95 (ISBN 0-918305-02-0). Brightwaters.
Visitations. 1982. 15.00x (ISBN 0-903653-71-0, Pub. by New Playwrights Network). State Mutual Bk.
Visitations: A Saga of Gods & Men, Vol. I. Ruth Norman. (Illus.). 578p. 1987. text ed. 75.00 (ISBN 0-932642-84-5). Unarius Pubns.
Visitations & Memorials of Southwell Minister. Southwell Cathedral. Ed. by Arthur F. Leach. Repr. of 1891 ed. 27.00 (ISBN 0-384-56770-3). Johnson Repr.
Visitations of the Diocese of Norwich, A. D. 1492-1532. Norwich England Diocese. Ed. by A. Jessopp. Repr. of 1888 ed. 30.00 (ISBN 0-384-41985-2). Johnson Repr.
Visiteurs du Soir. Jacques Prevert & Marcel Carne. (Illus.). 256p. 1974. 25.00 (ISBN 0-686-54920-1); pap. 5.95 (ISBN 0-686-54921-X). French & Eur.
Visiting a Museum. Althea. (Cambridge Information Books for Children). 26p. (gr. 2-5). 1983. pap. 2.50 (ISBN 0-521-27160-6). Cambridge U Pr.
Visiting a Museum. Althea. (Books for Children). (Illus.). 24p. (Orig.). (gr. 3 up). 1980. 1.50 (ISBN 0-907849-39-3, Pub. by Ashmolean Museum). State Mutual Bk.
Visiting a Museum. Althea. (Longwood Books for Children). (Illus.). 24p. (Orig.). (gr. 1 up). 1980. pap. 2.25 (ISBN 0-317-58716-1, Pub. by Ashmolean Mus). Longwood Pub Group.
Visiting: A Pastoral Care Ministry. Pastoral Care Office, Reorganized Church of Jesus Christ of Latter Day Saints. 186p. (Orig.). 1985. pap. 10.25 (ISBN 0-8309-0429-8). Herald Hse.
Visiting Boise: A Personal Guide. Dwight W. Jensen. LC 80-27098. (Illus.). 145p. 1981. pap. 7.95 (ISBN 0-87004-290-4). Caxton.
Visiting Captain Fibbur. A. Nekrasov. (Illus.). 21p. 1976. pap. 1.99 (ISBN 0-8285-1579-4, Pub. by Progress Pubs USSR). Imported Pubns.
Visiting Card: Ancient & Modern History of Script & Money. Ezra Pound. 1983. lib. bdg. 79.95 (ISBN 0-87700-458-7). Revisionist Pr.
Visiting Card Cases. Noel Riley. (Antique Pocket Guides). (Illus.). 64p. (Orig.). 1983. pap. 5.95 (ISBN 0-7188-2549-7, Pub. by Lutterworth Pr UK). Seven Hills Bks.
Visiting Cards of Painters. F. C. Schang. (Illus.). 115p. 1983. pap. 15.00 (ISBN 0-8390-0332-3). Abner Schram Ltd.
Visiting Cards of Pianists. F. C. Schang. LC 79-88628. (Illus.). 1979. pap. 7.50 (ISBN 0-915282-06-2). J Patelson Mus.
Visiting Cards of Violinists. F. C. Schang. LC 79-63411. (Illus.). 1979. pap. 6.50 (ISBN 0-915282-05-4). J Patelson Mus.
Visiting Day on the Psychiatric Ward. Alan Catlin. 1983. 3.50 (ISBN 0-318-04451-X). Pudding Hse Pubns.
Visiting Gig Harbor. Tanya Braumiller. (Color-A-Story Ser.). (Illus., Orig.). (gr. 1-4). 1983. pap. 2.75 (ISBN 0-933992-28-9). Coffee Break.
Visiting Grandpa. N. Nosov. 15p. 1980. 1.49 (ISBN 0-8285-1258-2, Pub. by Progress Pubs USSR). Imported Pubns.
Visiting Hours. 2.00 (ISBN 0-936672-49-8). Aerial Photo.
Visiting India. Allan Stacey. (Travel Bks.). (Illus.). 192p. 1986. 19.95 (ISBN 0-87052-286-8). Hippocrene Bks.
Visiting India. Allan Stacey. (Illus.). 192p. 1987. pap. 9.95 (ISBN 0-87052-463-1). Hippocrene Bks.
Visiting Judges in Federal District Courts. Donna Stienstra & Federal Judicial Center Staff. Date not set. price not set. Fed Judicial Ctr.
Visiting Junjun & Meimei in China. Janet Whitaker. (Illus.). 32p. (gr. 3-7). 1988. 9.95 (ISBN 0-521-34575-8). Cambridge U Pr.
Visiting Kashmir. Allan Stacey. (Illus.). 1988. 22.50 (ISBN 0-87052-568-9). Hippocrene Bks.
Visiting Kenya. John Brigden. (Illus.). 228p. (Orig.). 1988. pap. 8.95 (ISBN 0-87052-501-8). Hippocrene Bks.
Visiting Light. Jean Earle. LC 87-73293. 80p. 1988. pap. 12.50 (ISBN 0-907476-76-7, Pub. by Poetry Wales Pr UK). Dufour.
Visiting Miss Pierce. Pat Derby. LC 86-7559. 144p. (gr. 6 up). 1986. 11.95 (ISBN 0-374-38162-3). FS&G.
Visiting Mt. Rainier. David C. Helstrom. (Color-A-Story Ser.). (Illus.). 28p. (Orig.). (gr. 1-4). 1984. pap. 2.75 (ISBN 0-933992-37-8). Coffee Break.
Visiting Olympia. Val Dumond. (Color-A-Story Ser.). (Illus.). 24p. (Orig.). (gr. 1-4). 1983. pap. 2.75 (ISBN 0-933992-39-4). Coffee Break.
Visiting Our Past: America's Historylands. rev. ed. Ed. by Ross Bennett. (Illus.). 400p. 1986. 17.95 (ISBN 0-87044-646-0); deluxe ed. 27.95 (ISBN 0-87044-647-9). Natl Geog.
Visiting Our Western National Parks. George P. Perkins. Ed. by Carole Thickston. 1987. pap. 12.95 (ISBN 0-9613144-1-9). Perkins CA.
Visiting Pamela. Norma Klein. LC 78-72203. (Illus.). (ps-3). 1979. PLB 6.46 (ISBN 0-8037-9308-1). Dial Bks Young.
Visiting Rites. Phyllis Janowitz. (Princeton Series Contemporary Poets). 1982. 16.00x (ISBN 0-691-06523-3); pap. 7.50 (ISBN 0-691-01398-5). Princeton U Pr.
Visiting Russia. Dib Taylor. 51p. 1988. 6.95 (ISBN 0-533-07801-6). Vantage.
Visiting Tacoma. Carole Parkhurst. (Color-A-Story Ser.). (Illus.). 24p. (Orig.). (gr. 1-4). 1983. pap. 2.75 (ISBN 0-933992-38-6). Coffee Break.
Visiting Teacher. Jack Rudman. (National Teacher's Examination Ser.: NT-21). (Cloth bdg. avail. on request). pap. 13.95 (ISBN 0-8373-8431-1). Natl Learning.
Visiting Teaching: A Call to Serve. Johanna Flynn & Anita Canfield. 80p. (Orig.). 1984. pap. 3.95. Randall Bk Co.
Visiting the Art Museum. Laurence K. Brown & Mark Brown. (ps-4). 1986. 11.95 (ISBN 0-525-44233-2). Dutton.
Visiting the Father & Other Poems. David Pichaske. 1987. pap. 2.50 (ISBN 0-941127-02-8). Dacotah Terr Pr.
Visiting the Midwest's Historic Preservation Sites. Majory Grannis et al. 280p. 1988. 14.95 (ISBN 0-915463-53-9, Pub. by Jameson Bks). Green Hill.
Visiting the Shakers in 1857: Harper's New Monthly Magazine. Facsimile ed. Benson T. Lossing. (Illus.). 14p. 1975. pap. 2.50 (ISBN 0-937942-14-6). Shaker Mus.
Visiting Two-by-Two: Visitor's Guide. George E. Koehler. LC 86-70579. 72p. (Orig.). 1986. 2.95 (ISBN 0-88177-034-5, DR034B). Discipleship Res.
Visitor. Jack Hayford. 128p. 1986. pap. 4.95 (ISBN 0-8423-7802-2). Tyndale.
Visitor. Josephine Poole. LC 72-80367. (Story of Suspense Ser.). 160p. (YA) (gr. 7 up). 1972. PLB 11.89 (ISBN 0-06-024769-X). HarpJ.
Visitor see Three Little Friends Series.
Visitor Complains of My Disenfranchise. Charles Bukowski. (Tadbooks). (Orig.). 1987. pap. 10.00 (ISBN 0-89807-142-9); fifty copies signed & numbered o.p. 20.00 (ISBN 0-89807-143-7). Illuminati.
Visitor from Another Planet & Other Plays. George P. McCallum. (gr. 4-6). 1982. student's ed. 5.50x (ISBN 0-19-502743-4); tchr's. ed. 6.50x (ISBN 0-19-503167-9). Oxford U Pr.
Visitor: Jack Kerouac in Old Saybrook. John C. Holmes. 1981. limited edition, numbered & signed by the author 8.00 (ISBN 0-934660-04-2). TUVOTI.
Visitors. Walter De la Mare. LC 86-6244. (Creative's Classic Short Stories Ser.). 40p. (gr. 4 up). 1986. PLB 8.95 (ISBN 0-88682-070-7). Creative Ed.
Visitors. Peter T. Jones. (Poetry Wales Poet Ser.: Vol. 6). 54p. 1987. pap. 7.95 (ISBN 0-907476-61-9, Pub. by Poetry Wales Pr UK). Dufour.
Visitors. Clifford D. Simak. 1988. pap. 2.95 (ISBN 0-345-00761-1, Del Rey). Ballantine.
Visitors. John R. Townsend. LC 77-7197. 1977. 12.25 (ISBN 0-397-31752-2). Har-Row.
Visitors at Merville House. Sally Tyree Smith. (YA) (gr. 7 up). 1979. 9.95 (ISBN 0-685-93881-6, Avalon). Bouregy.
Visitor's Book. John Davies. LC 85-71576. 68p. 1985. pap. 10.95 (ISBN 0-907476-41-4, Pub. by Poetry Wales Pr UK). Dufour.
Visitors for Edward. Michaela Morgan. (Illus.). 24p. (ps-1). 1988. 8.95 (ISBN 0-525-44354-1, 0869-260). Dutton.
Visitors from Other Planets. Mark-Age. LC 73-90880. 334p. 1974. 15.00 (ISBN 0-912322-04-7). Mark-Age.
Visitors from Outer Space. R. G. Austin. (Which Way Secret Door Bks.: No. 5). (Illus.). 64p. (Orig.). (gr. 3 up). 1983. pap. 1.95 (ISBN 0-671-46983-5). Archway.
Visitors Guide to Cape Cod National Seashore. Margaret Koehler. LC 72-92014. (Illus.). 80p. (Orig.). 1973. pap. 6.95 (ISBN 0-85699-066-3). Chatham Pr.
Visitors Guide to Historic Yuma. Frank Love. pap. 2.95 (ISBN 0-936564-22-9). Little London.
Visitor's Guide to Planet Earth: An Astrological Primer. Celeste Longacre. (Orig.). 1984. pap. 5.00 (ISBN 0-930043-00-6). Flaming Arrow Pubns.
Visitor's Guide to Point Reyes National Seashore. Alice F. Dalbey. LC 73-89770. (Orig.). 1974. pap. 4.95 (ISBN 0-85699-098-1). Chatham Pr.
Visitor's Guide to the Dingle Peninsula. Steve MacDonogh & Pat Langan. (Illus.). 104p. (Orig.). 1985. pap. 5.95 (ISBN 0-86322-076-2, Pub. by Brandon Bks). Longwood Pub Group.
Visitor's Guide to the Everglades. Jeff Weber. LC 86-82931. (Illus.). 64p. 1986. pap. 3.95 (ISBN 0-9613236-7-1). Florida Flair Bks.
Visitor's Guide to the Serpent Mound. William F. Romain. (Illus.). 20p. (Orig.). 1988. pap. 4.00 (ISBN 0-9620741-0-1). Graphic Visns.
Visitors: The Stories of Ronald Blythe. Ronald Blythe. LC 85-8527. (Helen & Kurt Wolff Book). 256p. 1985. 16.95 (ISBN 0-15-193912-8). HarBracej.
Visitors to Arizona 1846 to 1980. James K. Ballinger & Andrea Rubinstein. LC 80-82651. (Illus.). 207p. (Orig.). pap. 12.00 (ISBN 0-910407-07-X). Phoenix Art.

Visual Field Symposium, Fifth International: Documenta Ophthalmoligica Proceedings. Ed. by E. L. Greve & A. Heijl. 1983. lib. bdg. 86.00 (ISBN 90-619-3731-0, Pub. by Junk Pubs Netherlands). Kluwer Academic.

Visual Fields: A Basis for Efficient Investigation. C. H. Bedwell. 1982. text ed. 55.00 (ISBN 0-407-00215-4). Butterworth.

Visual Fields: A Textbook & Atlas of Clinical Perimetry. 5th ed. David O. Harrington. LC 81-2558. (Illus.). 457p. 1981. text ed. 47.95 (ISBN 0-8016-2059-7). Mosby.

Visual Fields Examination. Norma R. Garber. Ed. by Candace Wolfe. LC 87-42949. (Ophthalmic Technical Skills Ser.). 150p. 1988. pap. 30.00 (ISBN 1-55642-025-0). Slack Inc.

Visual Fields Manual: A Practical Guide to Testing & Interpretation. Jonathan D. Trobe & Joel S. Glaser. (Illus.). 240p. (Orig.). 1983. pap. text ed. 17.95x (ISBN 0-937404-09-8). Triad Pub FL.

Visual Fields: Text & Atlas of Clinical Perimetry. 6th ed. Harrington. (Illus.). 515p. 1989. 52.95 (ISBN 0-8016-2073-2). Mosby.

Visual Forces: An Introduction to Design. Benjamin Martinez & Jacqueline Block. (Illus.). 256p. 1987. pap. text ed. write for info. (ISBN 0-13-942590-X). P-H.

Visual Form Detection in Three Dimensional Space. William R. Uttal. (MacEachram Lectures Ser.). 176p. 1983. text ed. 19.95x (ISBN 0-89859-289-5). L Erlbaum Assocs.

Visual Games. Franco Agostini. (Illus.). 192p. 1988. 27.50x (ISBN 0-8160-1979-7). Facts on File.

Visual Gourmet: A Calligraphic Treasury of International Vegetarian Recipes. Elizabeth Yasek. (Illus.). 160p. (Orig.). 1981. pap. 12.95 (ISBN 0-939212-00-5). Katahdin.

Visual Guide to Handwriting Analysis with Encyclopedic Dictionary. Ilyas M. Zeshan. (Illus.). 196p. (Orig.). 1988. pap. 14.95 (ISBN 0-9619922-3-9). Intl Inst Handwrit.

Visual Handbook. John Selby. 208p. 1988. pap. 14.95 (ISBN 1-85230-018-3, Pub. by Element Bks UK). Tempest Brookline.

Visual Handicap in Children. Ed. by John Keen & Vernon H. Smith. (Clinics in Developmental Medicine Ser.: Vol. 73). 182p. 1979. text ed. 29.00 (ISBN 0-433-30652-1, Pub. by Spastics Intl England). Lippincott.

Visual Handicaps & Learning. rev. ed. Natalie Barraga. (Orig.). 1983. pap. text ed. 10.95 (ISBN 0-935594-06-X). Exceptional Res.

Visual Histology. David T. Moran & J. Carter Rowley, III. LC 87-3835. (Illus.). 285p. 1988. text ed. 22.50 (ISBN 0-8121-1062-5). Lea & Febiger.

Visual History of Costume: The Eighteenth Century. Aileen Ribeiro. LC 83-14120. (Illus.). 144p. 1983. text ed. 19.95x (ISBN 0-89676-077-4). Drama Bk.

Visual History of Costume: The Fourteenth & Fifteenth Centuries. Margaret Scott. (Visual History of Costume Ser.). (Illus.). 152p. 1986. text ed. 19.95x (ISBN 0-7134-4857-1, Pub. by Batsford England). Drama Bk.

Visual History of Costume: The Nineteenth Century. Vanda Foster. LC 83-14120. (Visual History of Costume Ser.). (Illus.). 152p. 1984. text ed. 19.95x (ISBN 0-89676-079-0). Drama Bk.

Visual History of Costume: The Seventeenth Century. Valerie Cumming. LC 83-14120. (Visual History of Costume Ser.). (Illus.). 152p. 1984. text ed. 19.95x (ISBN 0-89676-078-2). Drama Bk.

Visual History of Costume: The Sixteenth Century. Jane Ashelford. LC 83-14120. (Visual History of Costume Ser.). (Illus.). 144p. 1983. text ed. 19.95x (ISBN 0-89676-076-6). Drama Bk.

Visual History of Costume: The Twentieth Century. Penelope Byrde. (Visual History of Costume Ser.). (Illus.). 152p. 1986. text ed. 19.95x (ISBN 0-7134-4859-8, Pub. by Batsford England). Drama Bk.

Visual I Ching: A New Approach to the Ancient Chinese Oracle. Oliver Perrottet. (Illus.). 96p. 1987. 24.95 (ISBN 0-88162-265-6). Salem Hse Pubs.

Visual Illusion of Motion During Eye Closure see Yale Psychological Studies, N.S,.

Visual Illusions: Their Causes, Characteristics & Applications. M. Luckiesh. (Illus.). 15.00 (ISBN 0-8446-0780-0). Peter Smith.

Visual Illusions: Their Causes, Characteristics & Applications. Matthew Luckiesh. (Illus.). 252p. 1965. pap. 4.95 (ISBN 0-486-21530-X). Dover.

Visual Imagination: An Introduction to Art. Bruce D. Kurtz. (Illus.). 448p. 1987. pap. text ed. write for info. (ISBN 0-13-942517-9). P-H.

Visual Impact in Print. Gerald D. Hurley & Angus McDougall. LC 71-176260. 1975. 32.00 (ISBN 0-913426-00-8); pap. 22.50x (ISBN 0-913426-01-6). Visual Impact.

Visual Impairment & Blindness: Education, Employment & Independent Living. Grace D. Napier. (Allied Health Professions Monograph Ser.). 1988. 24.50 (ISBN 0-87527-283-5). Green.

Visual Impairment in the Schools. 2nd ed. Randall K. Harley & G. Allen Lawrence. (Illus.). 204p. 1984. 24.00 (ISBN 0-398-05026-0). C C Thomas.

Visual Information Processing. Kathryn T. Spoehr & Stephen W. Lehmkuhle. (Illus.). 298p. 1982. text ed. 25.95x (ISBN 0-7167-1373-X); pap. text ed. 15.95 (ISBN 0-7167-1374-8). W H Freeman.

Visual Information Systems: The Power of Graphics & Video. Richard H. Veith. (Professional Librarian Ser.). 354p. 1988. lib. bdg. 36.50x (ISBN 0-8161-1861-2); pap. 36.50 (ISBN 0-317-69238-0). G K Hall.

Visual Introduction to Bucks Point Lace. Geraldine Stott. (Illus.). 96p. 1986. 25.95 (ISBN 0-7134-4371-5, Pub. by Batsford England). David & Charles.

Visual Keyboard Chord Progressions, Bk. I. William L. Fowler. LC 83-81908. (Illus.). 75p. 1983. pap. text ed. 10.00 (ISBN 0-943894-02-6). Fowler Music.

Visual Keyboard Chord Progressions, Bk. II. William L. Fowler. LC 83-81908. (Illus.). 76p. 1984. pap. text ed. 10.00 (ISBN 0-943894-03-4). Fowler Music.

Visual Keyboard Chord Progressions, Bk. III. William L. Fowler. LC 83-81908. (Illus.). 84p. 1985. pap. text ed. 10.00 (ISBN 0-943894-08-5). Fowler Music.

Visual Keyboard Chord Progressions, Bk. IV. William L. Fowler. LC 83-81908. (Illus.). 84p. 1986. pap. text ed. 10.00 (ISBN 0-943894-10-7). Fowler Music.

Visual Language Cookbook. new ed. Gayle Joyce & Laurene Gallimore. LC 79-92053. (Illus.). 60p. (gr. 6-12). 1979. 24.00 (ISBN 0-917002-41-5). Joyce Media.

Visual Languages. Ed. by Shi-Kuo Chang. (Management & Information Ser.). 452p. 1987. 69.50x (ISBN 0-306-42350-2, Plenum Pr). Plenum Pub.

Visual Learning, Thinking, & Communication. Ed. by Bikkar S. Randhawa & William E. Coffman. (Cognition & Perception Ser.). 1978. 24.95 (ISBN 0-12-579450-9). Acad Pr.

Visual Literacy Connections to Thinking, Reading & Writing. photocopy ed. Richard Sinatra. (Illus.). 326p. 1986. 37.00 (ISBN 0-398-05192-5). C C Thomas.

Visual Literature Criticism. Richard Kostelanetz. (Precisely: 3 4 5). 192p. (Orig.). 1979. pap. 6.00 (ISBN 0-317-17972-1). RK Edns.

Visual Literature Criticism: A New Collection. Ed. by Richard Kostelanetz. LC 79-18457. (Illus.). 194p. 1980. 13.95x (ISBN 0-8093-0950-5). S Ill U Pr.

Visual Masking: An Integrative Approach. Bruno G. Breitmeyer. (Oxford Psychology Ser.). (Illus.). 1984. 39.95x (ISBN 0-19-852105-7). Oxford U Pr.

Visual Masters for Teaching about Computers. 2nd ed. Donald D. Spencer. 64p. 1982. pap. 6.95 (ISBN 0-89218-050-1, NO. 1027). Camelot Pub.

Visual Masters for Teaching BASIC Programming. 2nd ed. Donald D. Spencer. 64p. 1982. pap. 6.95 (ISBN 0-89218-049-8, NO. 1026). Camelot Pub.

Visual Materials for the Language Teacher. Andrew Wright. (Longman Handbooks for Language Teachers). (Illus.). 152p. 1975. pap. text ed. 12.95 (ISBN 0-582-52267-6). Longman.

Visual Meditations on the Universe. James S. Perkins. LC 83-40233. (Illus.). 136p. 1984. 16.95 (ISBN 0-8356-0233-8). Theos Pub Hse.

Visual Merchandising. The National Retail Merchants Association's Visual Merchandising Board of Directors. LC 85-29885. (Illus.). 256p. 1986. 49.95 (ISBN 0-86636-014-X). PBC Intl Inc.

Visual Merchandising. 20.00 (ISBN 0-87102-055-6, 60-6656). Natl Ret Merch.

Visual Merchandising & Display. Martin Pegler. (Illus.). 250p. 1983. text ed. 20.00 (ISBN 0-87005-434-1). Fairchild.

Visual Merchandising: The Best Design from Leading Designers. 258p. 1986. 49.95 (ISBN 0-317-65517-5). Natl Ret Merch.

Visual Methods in Education. W. L. Sumner. 231p. 1957. 6.00 (ISBN 0-8022-1671-4). Philos Lib.

Visual Methods of Emission Spectroscopy. N. S. Sventitskii. 352p. 1965. text ed. 69.00x (ISBN 0-7065-0573-5, Pub. by Keter Pub Jerusalem). Coronet Bks.

Visual Modeling with Logo: A Structural Approach to Seeing. James Clayson. (Explorations in Logo Ser.). (Illus.). 400p. (Orig.). 1988. pap. 19.95x (ISBN 0-262-53069-4). MIT Pr.

Visual Narratives: Storytelling in Etruscan & Roman Art. Richard Brilliant. LC 83-18869. (Illus.). 208p. 1984. 39.95x (ISBN 0-8014-1558-6). Cornell U Pr.

Visual Narratives: Storytelling in Etruscan & Roman Art. Richard Brilliant. LC 83-18869. (Paperback Ser.). (Illus.). 208p. 1986. pap. 12.95x (ISBN 0-8014-9387-0). Cornell U Pr.

Visual Notes for Architects & Designers. Norman Crowe & Paul Laseau. (Illus.). 224p. 1986. pap. 19.95x (ISBN 0-442-29334-8). Van Nos Reinhold.

Visual Optics & Refraction: A Clinical Approach. 3rd ed. Michaels. 1985. 75.00 (ISBN 0-8016-3504-7). Mosby.

Visual Order: The Nature & Development of Pictorial Representation. Ed. by N. H. Freeman & M. V. Cox. (Illus.). 409p. 1985. 52.50 (ISBN 0-521-26668-8). Cambridge U Pr.

Visual Pathways. Ed. by H. Spekreijse & P. A. Apkarian. (Documenta Ophthalmologica Proceedings Ser.: No. 27). 472p. 1981. 99.00 (ISBN 90-6193-723-X, Pub. by Junk Pubs Netherlands). Kluwer Academic.

Visual Perception. Tom N. Cornsweet. 475p. 1970. text ed. 29.00 net (ISBN 0-15-594936-5, CORN, HC). HarBraceJ.

Visual Perception: Physiology, Psychology & Ecology. Vicki Bruce & Patrick Green. 384p. 1985. text ed. 39.95 (ISBN 0-86377-012-6); pap. 19.95 (ISBN 0-86377-013-4). L Erlbaum Assocs.

Visual Pigments in Man. W. Rushton. (Sherrington Lectures: Vol. VI). 48p. 1962. text ed. 7.95x (ISBN 0-85323-223-7, Pub. by Liverpool U Pr). Humanities.

Visual Play: A Green Dance in Three Acts. Elizabeth Cook. (Illus.). 30p. 1983. metalring bd. 10.00 (ISBN 0-915066-55-6). Assembling Pr.

Visual Preferences of Travelers along the Blue Ridge Parkway. Ed. by Francis P. Noe & William E. Hammitt. LC 88-600093. (Scientific Monograph Ser.: No. 18). (Illus., Orig.). 1988. pap. write for info. (ISBN 0-943475-00-7). Natl Park GA.

Visual Presentation of Information in COM Library Catalogues: A Survey, 2 vols. L. Reynolds. (R&D Report 5472). (Illus.). 126p. (Orig.). 1979. pap. 12.75 (ISBN 0-905984-34-X, Pub. by British Lib). Longwood Pub Group.

Visual Programming. Nan Shu. (Illus.). 320p. 1988. text ed. 32.95 (ISBN 0-442-28014-9). Van Nos Reinhold.

Visual Psychophysics see Handbook of Sensory Physiology.

Visual Quality in the Coastal Zone: Proceedings. 1975. 4.00 (ISBN 0-686-20723-8). SUNY Environ.

Visual Reading & Braille Reading: An Experimental Investigation of the Physiology & Psychology of Visual & Tactual Reading. T. Kusajima. 60p. 1974. pap. 3.00 (ISBN 0-89128-066-9, PPR066). Am Foun Blind.

Visual Reconstruction. Andrew Blake & Andrew Zisserman. (MIT Press Artificial Intelligence Ser.). (Illus.). 188p. 1987. text ed. 30.00x (ISBN 0-262-02271-0). MIT Pr.

Visual (Sampling) Scanning Processes. John W. Senders. 160p. 1983. pap. text ed. 19.95 (ISBN 0-89859-516-9). L Erlbaum Assocs.

Visual Science: Proceedings of the 1968 International Symposium. International Symposium on Visual Science, Indiana University, 1968. Ed. by John R. Pierce & John R. Levene. LC 78-150216. pap. 107.00 (ISBN 0-317-28585-8, 2055236). Bks Demand UMI.

Visual Skills. Ed. by Sharon Wheeler. (Preschool Express Ser.). (Illus.). (ps). 1984. wkbk. 1.95 (ISBN 0-916119-08-4). Creat Teach Pr.

Visual Skills Appraisal (VSA) Regina Richards & Gary S. Oppenheim. 80p. 1984. complete program test kit incl. manual, stimulus cards, forms, score sheets, & red-green glasses 44.00 (ISBN 0-87879-453-0, 453-0A). Acad Therapy.

Visual Solutions: A Workbook for Artists & Designers. Robin Landa. (Illus.). 256p. 1985. 22.95 (ISBN 0-13-942442-3); pap. 15.95. P-H.

Visual Solutions: Activities, Experiments, & Projects for Solving Art & Design Problems. Robin Landa. Date not set. write for info. S&S.

Visual Studies: A Foundation for Artists & Designers. Frank M. Young. (Illus.). 300p. 1985. pap. text ed. write for info (ISBN 0-13-942508-X). P-H.

Visual Symbolism, No. 3. Japan Typography Association Staff. 1988. pap. 59.95 (ISBN 4-947613-14-9). North Light Bks.

Visual Symphony: A Photographic Work in Four Movements. Photos by Bruce Barnbaum. LC 86-45288. (Illus.). 128p. 1987. 50.00 (ISBN 0-912383-30-5); Limited ed.; orig. signed photograph; slipcased. 400.00 (ISBN 0-912383-32-1). Van der Marck.

Visual System in Evolution in Vertebrates. A. Hughes. LC 77-4371. (Handbook of Sensory Physiology: Vol. 7, Pt. 5). 1977. 201.00 (ISBN 0-387-07908-4). Springer-Verlag.

Visual System in Meyelin Disorders. Ed. by A. Neetens et al. (Monographs in Ophthalmology Ser.). 1984. lib. bdg. 85.00 (ISBN 90-6193-807-4, Pub. by Junk Pubs Netherlands). Kluwer Academic.

Visual System: Proceedings of a Symposium in Honor of Edward F. MacNichol, Jr., Held in Woods Hole, MA, Dec. 2-3, 1983. Alan Fein & Joseph S. Levine. LC 84-21767. (MBL Lectures in Biology: Vol. 5). 208p. 1985. 44.00 (ISBN 0-8451-2204-5). A R Liss.

Visual Text of William Carlos Williams. Henry M. Sayre. LC 83-1395. (Illus.). 168p. 1983. 15.95 (ISBN 0-252-01059-0). U of Ill Pr.

Visual Thinking. Rudolf Arnheim. LC 71-76335. (Illus.). 1980. 30.00x (ISBN 0-520-01378-6); pap. 12.95 (ISBN 0-520-01871-0). U of Cal Pr.

Visual Thinking. Bob Eberle. (Illus.). 64p. (Orig.). 1981. pap. 5.95 (ISBN 0-88047-000-3, 8201). DOK Pubs.

Visual Thinking: Methods for Making Images Memorable. Henry Wolf. LC 88-70889. (Illus.). 184p. 1988. 45.00 (ISBN 0-8478-5518-X). Rizzoli Intl.

Visual Thinking: Methods for Making Images Memorable. Henry Wolf. LC 88-70889. (Illus.). 184p. 1988. 45.00 (ISBN 0-931144-47-7). Am Showcase.

Visual Thinking: Problems & Solutions. Richard Wilde. 224p. 1986. 44.95 (ISBN 0-442-29182-5). Van Nos Reinhold.

Visual Tracking. R. Robert Geake & Donald E. Smith. (Michigan Tracking Program Ser.). 1975. pap. 3.95x (ISBN 0-914004-43-3). Ulrich.

Visual Values for the Highway User. 118p. 5.00 (ISBN 0-318-17834-6). Landscape Architecture.

Visual Workouts: A Collection of Art-Making Problems. Mary F. Johnson. (Illus.). 160p. 1983. pap. text ed. 24.00 (ISBN 0-13-942664-7). P-H.

Visual World of the Child. Eliane Vurpillot. LC 75-790. 372p. 1976. text ed. 40.00x (ISBN 0-8236-6749-9). Intl Univs Pr.

Visualization: Breaking Through the Illusion of Problems. Stephen R. Schwartz. 64p. (Orig.). 1985. pap. write for info. (ISBN 0-936415-00-2). Riverrun Piermont.

Visualization: Directing the Movies of Your Mind. Adelaide Bry & Marjorie Bair. LC 77-3741. (Illus.). 192p. 1979. pap. 8.95 (ISBN 0-06-464033-7, BN4033, B&N Bks). Har-Row.

Visualization for Change. Patrick Fanning et al. 224p. 1988. pap. text ed. 10.95 (ISBN 0-934986-51-7). New Harbinger.

Visualization in Programming. Ed. by P. Gorny & M. J. Tauber. (Lecture Notes in Computer Science: Vol. 282). vii, 210p. 1987. pap. 21.80 (ISBN 0-387-18507-0). Springer-Verlag.

Visualization Techniques. Richard Leinbach. (Illus.). 208p. 1986. pap. text ed. 28.00 (ISBN 0-8359-8413-3). P-H.

Visualizations for an Easier Childbirth. Carl Jones. 110p. 1988. pap. 4.95. Meadowbrook.

Visualizations in the Realm of Historical Predictions in the Light of the Kondratieff Theory, 2 vols. Edoardo De Benedetti. (Illus.). 131p. 1983. 175.75 (ISBN 0-86722-041-4). Inst Econ Pol.

Visualize. Bobby G. Price. 58p. (Orig.). 1986. pap. 7.95 (ISBN 0-932662-60-9). St Andrews NC.

Visualized Flight Maneuvers Handbook for Instructors & Students. Haldon Books. (Illus.). 172p. 1980. ringbound softcover 20.00 (ISBN 0-940766-05-1, Pub. by Haldon). Aviation.

Visualizing & Verbalizing for Language Comprehension & Thinking. Nanci Bell. (Illus.). 197p. 1987. pap. 26.00 (ISBN 0-945856-00-8). Acad Reading.

Visualizing Deviance: A Study of News Organizations. Richard V. Ericson et al. 390p. 1987. 45.00; pap. 18.95. U of Toronto Pr.

Visualizing the Curriculum. Charles F. Hoban et al. 1979. Repr. of 1937 ed. lib. bdg. 20.00 (ISBN 0-8492-5337-3). R West.

Visualizing the Moral Life. Clifford Davidson. LC 88-47809. (AMS Studies in the Middle Ages: No. 16). 1988. 39.50 (ISBN 0-404-61446-9). AMS Pr.

Visually Handicapped Children & Young People. Elizabeth K. Chapman. (Special Needs in Education Ser.). 1978. 16.95x (ISBN 0-7100-8878-7). Routledge Chapman & Hall.

Visually Limited Child. R. Bonner et al. 1970. pap. text ed. 12.95x (ISBN 0-8422-0061-4). Irvington.

Visuals of the Clinical Histocompatibility Workshop: Palm Springs Invitational. Compiled by Paul I. Terasaki. LC 88-60350. (February 1988 Ser.). (Illus.). 173p. (Orig.). Date not set. pap. 10.00 (ISBN 0-945756-00-3, VIS88). One Lambda.

Visuddhimagga of Buddhaghosacariya. rev. ed. Buddhaghosa. Ed. by Henry C. Warren. LC 50-8905. (Oriental Ser.: No. 41). 1950. 37.50x (ISBN 0-674-94110-1). Harvard U Pr.

Viswambhara. C. Narayana Reddy. 66p. 1987. text ed. 15.95x (ISBN 81-207-0578-5, Pub. by Sterling Pubs India). Apt Bks.

Vita: A Bibliography of Vita Sackville-West. Victoria Glendinning. LC 84-62075. (Illus.). 464p. 1985. pap. 9.95 (ISBN 0-688-04111-6, Quill). Morrow.

Vita Christi of Ludolph of Saxony & Late Medieval Devotion Centered on the Incarnation: A Descriptive Analysis. Charles A. Conway, Jr. Ed. by James Hogg. (Analecta Cartusiana Ser.: No. 34). 153p. (Orig.). 1976. pap. 25.00 (ISBN 3-7052-0036-4, Pub. by Salzburg Studies). Longwood Pub Group.

Vita Haroldi: The Romance of the Life of Harold, King of England. Ed. by William D. Birch. Tr. by William D. Birch. LC 80-2232. Repr. of 1885 ed. 36.00 (ISBN 0-404-18753-6). AMS Pr.

Vita Laudanda-Essays in Memory of Ulrich S. Leupold. Ed. by Erich R. Schultz. 192p. 1976. pap. text ed. 6.95x (ISBN 0-88920-021-1, Pub. by Wilfrid Laurier Canada). Humanities.

Vita Nuova. Dante Alighieri. Tr. & intro. by Theodore Martin. Theodore Martin. LC 74-39195. (Select Bibliographies Reprint Ser). Repr. of 1861 ed. 15.00 (ISBN 0-8369-6797-6). Ayer Co Pubs.

Vita Nuova. Dante Alighieri. Tr. by Barbara Reynolds. (Classics Ser.). 128p. 1969. pap. 4.95 (ISBN 0-14-044216-2). Penguin.

Vita Patrum: The Life of the Fathers. St. Gregory of Tours. Ed. & tr. by Seraphim Rose. LC 88-60562. (Illus.). 325p. (Orig.). 1988. pap. 12.00 (ISBN 0-938635-23-9). St Herman AK.

Vita Quorundum Anglo-Saxonum: Original Lives of Anglo-Saxons Who Lived Before the Conquest. Ed. by John A. Giles. 1966. Repr. of 1854 ed. 24.00 (ISBN 0-8337-1349-3). B Franklin.

Vita Sancti Columbae. Saint Adamnan. Ed. by William Reeves. LC 79-174801. (Bannatyne Club, Edinburgh. Publications: No. 103). Repr. of 1857 ed. 45.00 (ISBN 0-404-52858-9). AMS Pr.

Vita Sexualis. Ogai Mori. Tr. by Kazuji Ninomiya & Sanford Goldstein. LC 72-79020. 1972. pap. 4.95 (ISBN 0-8048-1048-6). C E Tuttle.

Vitae. Cornelius Nepos. Ed. by E. O. Winstedt. (Oxford Classical Texts Ser). 1904. 16.95x (ISBN 0-19-814617-5). Oxford U Pr.

Vitae Dunkeldensis Ecclesiae Episcoporum, a Prima Sedis Foundatione, Ad Annum MDXV Ab Alexandro Myln, Eiusdem Ecclesiae Canonica Conscriptae, Repr. Of 1823 Ed. Alexander Mylne. Ed. by Thomas Thomson. Bd. with Compotum Magistri Fabrice Pontis Dunkeldensis, MDXIII-MDXVI. Ed. by Cosmo N. Innes. Repr. of 1831 ed. LC 78-173008. 20.00 (ISBN 0-404-52701-9). AMS Pr.

Vitae et Fragmenta. Cornelius Nepos. Ed. by P. K. Marshall. xvii, 122p. 1985. Repr. of 1977 ed. 15.00 (ISBN 0-89005-458-4). Ares.

Vitae Patrum in Old & Middle English Literature. Constance L. Rosenthal. LC 74-6161. 1936. Repr. lib. bdg. 39.00 (ISBN 0-8414-7303-X). Folcroft.

Vitae Summa Brevis: The Sum of My Short Life. Mike Gallatin. 496p. 1988. price not set (ISBN 0-943851-00-9, ProForma Bks). QED Pr Ann Arbor.

Vital & Important Appeal to the United Nations. Marie B. Hall. 1974. pap. 3.50 (ISBN 0-938760-05-X). Veritat Found.

Vital Approach. 2nd ed. Donald Mattam. 1973. pap. 9.25 (ISBN 0-08-017701-8). Pergamon.

Vital Balance: The Life Process in Mental Health & Illness. Karl Menninger. 1983. 21.25 (ISBN 0-8446-6077-9). Peter Smith.

Vital Business Connections: At Your Service via Mail Order. John Jaskiel. (Orig.). 1987. Directory. 24.95 (ISBN 0-938593-01-3). Goodlife Pubs.

Vital Business Secrets for New Companies. L. Joseph Schmoke & Richard R. Allen. 1988. 32.50 (ISBN 1-55623-124-5). Dow Jones-Irwin.

Vital Center. Arthur M. Schlesinger, Jr. (American Reform in the 20th Century Ser.). 274p. 1986. Repr. of 1962 ed. lib. bdg. 32.50 (ISBN 0-306-76280-3). Da Capo.

Vital Center: The Politics of Freedom. Arthur Schlesinger, Jr. (Quality Paperbacks Ser.). 1988. pap. 10.95 (ISBN 0-306-80323-2). Da Capo.

Vital Concept of Personal Growth. Manly P. Hall. pap. 2.50 (ISBN 0-89314-367-7). Philos Res.

Vital Continuum. rev. ed. Ed. by Eugene D. Fleharty & Gary K. Hulett. LC 80-50300. (Illus.). 500p. 1980. pap. 12.95 (ISBN 0-936352-00-0, B511). U of KS Cont Ed.

Vital Control: Forest Essays, First Series. Lynn H. Hough. LC 70-117809. (Essay Index Reprint Ser). 1934. 19.00 (ISBN 0-8369-1756-1). Ayer Co Pubs.

Vital Difference: Unleashing the Powers of Sustained Corporate Success. Frederick G. Harmon & Garry Jacobs. LC 85-47674. 288p. 1985. 18.95 (ISBN 0-8144-5569-7); pap. 8.95. AMACOM.

Vital Enthusiasm. James E. Melton. LC 82-81903. 232p. 1983. 12.95 (ISBN 0-9604752-1-4). Global Pubns CA.

Vital Few: The Entrepreneur & American Economic Progress. expanded ed. Jonathan Hughes. 576p. 1986. pap. 11.95 (ISBN 0-19-504038-4). Oxford U Pr.

Vital Force: A Study of Bioenergetics. Franklin M. Harold. LC 85-13640. (Illus.). 577p. 1986. text ed. 37.95 (ISBN 0-7167-1734-4). W H Freeman.

Vital Gesture: Franz Kline. Harry F. Gaugh. LC 85-7503. 192p. 1985. 55.00 (ISBN 0-89659-571-4). Abbeville Pr.

Vital Interests: The Soviet Issue in U. S. Central American Policy. Ed. by Bruce D. Larkin. LC 87-39458. 512p. 1988. lib. bdg. 38.50x (ISBN 1-55587-111-9); pap. text ed. 16.95x (ISBN 1-55587-112-7). Lynne Rienner.

Vital Involvement in Old Age. Erik H. Erikson et al. Date not set. pap. 8.95 (ISBN 0-393-30509-0). Norton.

Vital Involvement in Old Age: The Experience of Old Age in Our Time. Erik H. Erikson et al. 352p. 1986. 19.95 (ISBN 0-393-02359-1). Norton.

Vital Issues of the Constitution. Ed. by Robert H. Ratcliffe. (Trailmarks of Liberty Ser.). (Illus.). 150p. (gr. 11-12). 1975. pap. text ed. 10.08 (ISBN 0-395-20125-X); instructor's guide o.p. 3.00 (ISBN 0-395-20126-8). HM.

Vital Judo: Grappling Techniques. Isai Okano. pap. 11.95x (ISBN 0-685-70712-1). Wehman.

Vital Judo: Grappling Techniques. Isao Okano. LC 72-84814. (Illus.). 192p. 1983. 11.95 (ISBN 0-87040-517-9). Japan Pubns USA.

Vital Judo: Throwing Techniques. I. Okano & T. Sato. pap. 11.95x (ISBN 0-685-38458-6). Wehman.

Vital Judo: Throwing Techniques. Tetsuya Sato & Isao Okano. LC 74-84814. (Illus.). 192p. 1982. pap. 11.95 (ISBN 0-87040-516-0). Japan Pubns USA.

Vital Karate. Masutatsu Oyama. LC 67-19867. (Illus.). pap. 6.25 (ISBN 0-87040-143-2). Japan Pubns USA.

Vital Karate. Masutatsu Oyama. (Illus.). 1967. pap. 6.25x (ISBN 0-685-22152-0). Wehman.

Vital Lies, Simple Truths: The Psychology of Self-Deception. Daniel Goleman. 288p. 1986. pap. 9.95 (ISBN 0-671-62815-1, Touchstone Bks). S&S.

Vital Lies, Simple Truths: The Psychology of Self-Deception & Shared Illusions. Daniel Goleman. 1985. 17.95 (ISBN 0-671-45058-1). S&S.

Vital Maturity: Living Longer & Better. Morton Puner. LC 78-68919. 1979. 15.00x (ISBN 0-87663-232-0); pap. 6.95x (ISBN 0-87663-994-5). Universe.

Vital Network: A Theory of Communication & Society. Patrick Williams & Joan T. Pearce. LC 77-94757. (Contributions in Librarianship & Information Science Ser.: No 25). 1978. lib. bdg. 35.00x (ISBN 0-313-20324-5, WCS/). Greenwood.

Vital Parts. Chelsea Farraday. 1979. pap. 2.25 (ISBN 0-505-51444-3, Pub. by Tower Bks). Leisure NY.

Vital Past: Writings on the Uses of History. Ed. by Stephen Vaughn. LC 84-16204. 424p. 1985. 35.00x (ISBN 0-8203-0753-X); pap. 12.95x (ISBN 0-8203-0754-8). U of Ga Pr.

Vital Principles: The Molecular Mechanisms of Life. Andrew Scott. (Illus.). 256p. Date not set. 19.95 (ISBN 0-631-15398-5). Basil Blackwell.

Vital Probe: My Life As a Brain Surgeon. I. S. Cooper. (Illus.). 1981. 15.95 (ISBN 0-393-01469-X). Norton.

Vital Problems in Social Evolution: An Introduction to the Materialist Conception of History. Arthur M. Lewis. (Science for the Workers Ser.). 192p. 1984. 17.95 (ISBN 0-88286-089-5). C H Kerr.

Vital Provisions. Reynolds Price. LC 82-71255. 192p. 1982. 14.95 (ISBN 0-689-11322-6); pap. 7.95 (ISBN 0-689-11323-4). Atheneum.

Vital Record of Cranston, Johnston & North Providence, Rhode Island. James N. Arnold. (Vital Record of Rhode Island Ser.: Vol. 2, Pts. 2, 3 & 4). 138p. 1983. Repr. of 1892 ed. lib. bdg. 14.00 (ISBN 0-912606-12-6). Hunterdon Hse.

Vital Record of Providence, Rhode Island. James N. Arnold. (Vital Record of Rhode Island Ser.: Vol. 2, Pt. 1). 304p. 1988. lib. bdg. 21.00 (ISBN 0-912606-31-2). Hunterdon Hse.

Vital Record of Warwick, Rhode Island. James N. Arnold. (Vital Record of Rhode Island Ser.: Vol. 1, Pt. 1). 234p. 1983. Repr. of 1891 ed. lib. bdg. 16.00 (ISBN 0-912606-11-8). Hunterdon Hse.

Vital Records Handbook. Thomas J. Kemp. 231p. 1988. 19.95 (3140). Genealog Pub.

Vital Records of Charlestown, Massachusetts, to the Year 1850, Vol. 1. Ed. by Roger D. Joslyn. LC 84-25427. 919p. 1984. lib. bdg. 30.00 (ISBN 0-88082-009-8). New Eng Hist.

Vital Records of Hamilton, Massachusetts to 1849. Repr. of 1908 ed. 7.50 (ISBN 0-88389-075-5). Essex Inst.

Vital Records of Lynnfield, Massachusetts to 1849. Repr. of 1907 ed. 7.50 (ISBN 0-88389-077-1). Essex Inst.

Vital Records of Manchester, Massachusetts, to the End of the Year 1849. LC 4-9195. 298p. 1903. 10.00 (ISBN 0-88389-035-6). Essex Inst.

Vital Records of Marblehead, Massachusetts, to the End of the Year 1849, 2 vols. Incl. Vol. 1, Births. 564p. 1903; Vol. 2, Marriages & Deaths. 708p. 1904. LC 5-14241. 15.00 ea. (ISBN 0-88389-036-4). Essex Inst.

Vital Records of North Yarmouth Maine to the Year 1850. Ed. by Ruth W. Sherman. LC 80-11087. 421p. 1980. incl. addendum 16.00x (ISBN 0-930272-03-X). RI Mayflower.

Vital Records of Pepperell, Massachusetts, to the Year 1850. George A. Rice. LC 84-16660. 323p. 1985. 20.00 (ISBN 0-88082-008-X). New Eng Hist.

Vital Records of Saugus, Massachusetts to 1849. Repr. of 1907 ed. 10.00 (ISBN 0-88389-078-X). Essex Inst.

Vital Records of the Town of Lebanon (ME, Vol. 1: Births. 168p. 1986. pap. 18.50 (ISBN 0-935207-40-6). DanBury Hse Bks.

Vital Records of Wenham, Massachusetts, to the End of the Year 1849. LC 6-13929. 227p. 1904. 7.50 (ISBN 0-88389-045-3). Essex Inst.

Vital Records of Woodbridge, New Jersey. Joseph W. Dally. 56p. 1983. pap. 5.00 (ISBN 0-912606-14-2). Hunterdon Hse.

Vital Records, Town of Harwich Masschusetts, 1694 to 1850. Ed. by Louise H. Kelley & Dorothy Straw. 616p. 1982. write for info. (ISBN 0-88492-040-2). W S Sullwold.

Vital Role of Potassium Fertilizers in Tropical Agriculture: The Present Position, Future Potential & Constraints to Progress. T. Kaddar et al. Ed. by E. N. Roth & E. D. Frederick. LC 84-12971. (Technical Bulletin Ser.: T-29). (Illus.). 15p. (Orig.). 1984. pap. text ed. 4.00 (ISBN 0-88090-051-2). Intl Fertilizer.

Vital Science: Biology & the Literary Imagination 1860-1900. Peter Morton. LC 84-10991. 240p. 1984. text ed. 34.95x (ISBN 0-04-800025-6). Unwin Hyman.

Vital Signs. Ralph Burrows. 256p. 1982. pap. 2.75 (ISBN 0-449-14472-0, GM). Fawcett.

Vital Signs. Michael Weiner. LC 82-84738. (Illus.). 128p. (Orig.). 1983. pap. 8.95 (ISBN 0-932238-20-3, Pub. by Avant Bks). Slawson Comm.

Vital Signs. Barbara Wood. 1986. pap. 4.50 (ISBN 0-451-14218-7, Sig). NAL.

Vital Signs: A Young Doctor's Struggle with Cancer. Fitzhugh Mullan. 220p. 1983. 12.50 (ISBN 0-374-16864-4). FS&G.

Vital Signs: Mathematics in Everyday Life. Tina Levy. 326p. pap. text ed. 22.95 (ISBN 0-89863-113-0). Star Pub CA.

Vital Signs of Family Life & the YMCA: Resource Notebook. YMCA of the USA. (Illus.). 26p. (Orig.). 1983. pap. 19.95 3 ring Notebook (ISBN 0-88035-014-8, YMCA USA). Human Kinetics.

Vital Souls: Bororo Cosology, Natural Symbolism & Shamanism. J. Christopher Crocker. LC 85-1003. (Anthropology of Form & Meaning Ser.). 380p. 1985. 29.95x (ISBN 0-8165-0877-1). U of Ariz Pr.

Vital Statistics, Vol. 1. Ed. by Sandra Braman & Douglas Woolf. 1978. pap. 3.00 (ISBN 0-942296-04-4). Wolf Run Bks.

Vital Statistics, Vol. 2. Ed. by Sandra Braman & Douglas Woolf. 1978. pap. 3.00 (ISBN 0-942296-05-2). Wolf Run Bks.

Vital Statistics, Vol. 3. Ed. by Sandra Braman & Douglas Woolf. 1980. pap. 3.00 (ISBN 0-942296-06-0). Wolf Run Bks.

Vital Statistics: A Memorial Volume of Selections from the Reports & Writings of William Farr. William Farr. Ed. by Noel A. Humphreys & Sanitary Institute of Great Britain Staff. LC 75-38128. (Demography Ser.). (Illus.). 1976. Repr. of 1885 ed. 42.00x (ISBN 0-405-18600-2). Ayer Co Pubs.

Vital Statistics: American Folk Drawings & Watercolors from a Private Collection. Ed. by Philip M. Isaacson. LC 86-61948. (Illus.). 16p. (Orig.). 1986. pap. 5.00 (ISBN 0-916606-13-9). Bowdoin Coll.

Vital Statistics in Corrections. Ed. by Diana N. Travisono & Ann M. Ludwig. (Illus.). 62p. (Orig.). 1986. pap. 12.00 (ISBN 0-942974-74-3). Am Correctional.

Vital Statistics of the United States,1982: Mortality, Vol. 2, Pt. B. (DHHS Publication PHS Ser.: No. 86-1114). (Illus.). 753p. 1986. 36.00 (ISBN 0-318-21912-3, S/N 017-022-00975-7). USGPO.

Vital Statistics of the United States, 1984, Vol. 2. 756p. 1987. 35.00 (ISBN 0-318-23763-6, 017-022-01013-5). USGPO.

Vital Statistics of the United States: V. 2, Pt. B, Mortality, 1983. (DHHS Publication PHS 87-1102 Ser.). 752p. 1987. 37.00 (017-022-00997-8). USGPO.

Vital Statistics of the United States 1981: Mortality, Vol. 2, Pt. A. (DHHS Publication (PHS) 86-1101). 334p. 1986. text ed. 32.00 (ISBN 0-318-21322-2, S/N 017-022-00953-6). USGPO.

Vital Statistics of the United States 1981: Mortality, Vol. 2, Pt. B. (DHHS Publication PHS 86-1102). 691p. 1986. pap. 36.00 (ISBN 0-318-21323-0, S/N 017-022-00951-0). USGPO.

Vital Statistics of the United States, 1982: Mortality, Vol. 2, Pt. A. (DHHS Publication PHS 86-1122 Ser.). 510p. 1986. 32.00 (ISBN 0-318-21910-7, S/N 017-022-00971-4). USGPO.

Vital Statistics of the United States 1982: Vol. 1, Natality. (DHHS Publication PHS 87-1100). 426p. 1987. 29.00 (ISBN 0-318-22578-6, S/N 017-022-00984-6). USGPO.

Vital Statistics of the United States, 1983, Vol. 3: Marriage & Divorce. (DHHS Publication). (Illus.). 182p. 1987. 14.00 (ISBN 0-318-23852-7, S/N 017-022-01016-0). USGPO.

Vital Statistics on American Politics. Richard G. Niemi & Harold Stanley. 400p. 1988. 16.95 (ISBN 0-87187-472-5); pap. 11.95 (ISBN 0-87187-471-7). Congr Quarterly.

Vital Statistics on Congress, 1980. John F. Bibby et al. 1980. pap. 9.00 (ISBN 0-8447-3401-2). Am Enterprise.

Vital Statistics on Congress: 1984-85 Edition. Norman J. Ornstein et al. 261p. 1984. 23.00 (ISBN 0-8447-3560-4); pap. 12.50 (ISBN 0-8447-3564-7). Am Enterprise.

Vital Statistics on Congress, 1987-88. Ed. by Norman J. Ornstein. 275p. 1988. 16.95 (ISBN 0-87187-452-0). Congr Quarterly.

Vital Statistics Rates in the United States: 1940-1960. U. S. Dept of Health, Education & Welfare, Public Health Service et al. LC 75-37269. (Demography Ser.). (Illus.). 1976. Repr. of 1968 ed. 65.00x (ISBN 0-405-08001-8). Ayer Co Pubs.

Vital Statistics Rates in the United States: 1900-1940. U. S. Public Health Service, Federal Security Agency, National Office of Vital Statistics. LC 75-38136. (Demography Ser.). (Illus.). 1976. Repr. of 1947 ed. 77.00x (ISBN 0-405-07989-3). Ayer Co Pubs.

Vital Statistics Systems in Five Developing Countries. Hans A. Bruch & Luis M. Caviers. Ed. by Audrey Shipp. (Ser. 2: No. 79). 1979. pap. text ed. 1.95 (ISBN 0-8406-0169-7). Natl Ctr Health Stats.

Vital Tradition: The Catholic Novel in a Period of Convergence. Gene Kellogg. LC 74-108375. 1970. 8.35 (ISBN 0-8294-0192-X). Loyola.

Vital Years & Your Child. Audrey Bilski. 1977. 6.95 (ISBN 0-285-62088-6, Pub. by Souvenir Pr). Intl Spec Bk.

Vitale: Just Your Average Bald, One-Eyed Basketball Wacko Who Beat the Ziggy & Become a PTPer. Dick Vitale & Curry Kirkpatrick. (Illus.). 256p. 1988. 16.95 (ISBN 0-671-66040-3). S&S.

Vitalism of Hans Driesch: The Success & Decline of a Scientific Theory. Horst H. Freyhofer. (European University Studies: Series 20, Philosophy: Vol. 83). 250p. 1982. 24.20 (ISBN 3-8204-5703-8). P Lang Pubs.

Vitalist Reader: A Selection of the Poetry of Anthony L. Johnson, William Oxley & Peter Russell. James Hogg. Ed. by James Hogg. (Poetic Drama & Poetic Theory Ser.). 142p. (Orig.). 1982. pap. 15.00 (ISBN 3-7052-0906-X, Pub. by Salzburg Studies). Longwood Pub Group.

Vitalist Seminar: Studies in the Poetry of Peter Russell, Anthony L. Johnson, & William Oxley. James Hogg. Ed. by James Hogg. (Poetic Drama & Poetic Theory Ser.). (Orig.). 1984. pap. 15.00 (ISBN 3-7052-0911-6, Pub. by Salzburg Studies). Longwood Pub Group.

Vitality & Aging: Implications of the Rectangular Curve. James F. Fries & Lawrence M. Crapo. LC 81-4566. (Illus.). 172p. 1981. pap. text ed. 13.95 (ISBN 0-7167-1309-8). W H Freeman.

Vitality & Civilization. Griscom Morgan. 1971. pap. 1.00 (ISBN 0-910420-06-8). Comm Serv OH.

Vitality of the Christian Tradition. facsimile ed. Ed. by George F. Thomas. LC 70-134143. (Essay Index Reprint Ser). Repr. of 1944 ed. 22.00 (ISBN 0-8369-2378-2). Ayer Co Pubs.

Vitality of the Lyric Voice: Shih Poetry from the Late Han to the T'ang. Shuen-fu Lin & Stephen Owen. 400p. 1986. text ed. 50.00x (ISBN 0-691-03134-7). Princeton U Pr.

Vitality Old Testament Traditions. 2nd ed. Walter Brueggemann & Hans W. Wolff. LC 82-7141. pap. 8.95 (ISBN 0-8042-0112-9, John Knox). Westminster John Knox.

Vitalizing Intimacy in Marriage. Patricia Y. Travis & Robert P. Travis. LC 79-4374. 156p. 1979. 18.95 (ISBN 0-88229-398-2). Nelson-Hall.

Vitalizing Long-Term Care: The Teaching Nursing Home & Other Perspectives. Stuart F. Spicker & Stanley Ingman. 256p. 1984. 32.95 (ISBN 0-8261-4570-1). Springer Pub.

Vitam Alere, Franciscan Readings. Ed. by Marion A. Habig. (Tau Ser.). 1979. 5.95 (ISBN 0-8199-0769-3). Franciscan Herald.

Vitamin: A Deficiency & Its Control. J. Christopher Bauernfeind. (Nutrition: Basic & Applied Science). 1986. 89.00 (ISBN 0-12-082852-9). Acad Pr.

Vitamin & Carrier Functions of Polyprenoids. Ed. by G. H. Bourne & H. R. Cama. (World Review of Nutrition & Dietetrics Ser.: Vol. 31). (Illus.). 1978. 92.00 (ISBN 3-8055-2801-9). S Karger.

Vitamin & Health Encyclopedia. Jack Ritchason. Date not set. pap. 5.95 (ISBN 0-913923-52-4). Woodland UT.

Vitamin & Mineral Requirements in Preterm Infants. Tsang. (Clinical Disorders in Pediatric Nutrition Ser.). 240p. 1984. 55.00 (ISBN 0-8247-7317-9). Dekker.

Vitamin Assay: Tested Methods. 2nd ed. Rolf Strohecker & Heinz M. Henning. LC 65-22514. (Illus.). 360p. 1972. 33.60x (ISBN 3-527-25280-0). VCH Pubs.

Vitamin B: Requirements of Man. George R. Cowgill. 1934. 59.50x (ISBN 0-686-50034-2). Elliots Bks.

Vitamin B Six Catalysis. Ed. by T. Korpela & P. Christen. (Congress Reports: No. 1). 500p. 1987. 69.50 (ISBN 0-8176-1942-9). Birkhauser.

Vitamin B-Twelve: Proceedings of the European Symposium, 3rd, Zurich. European Symposium Staff. Ed. by B. J. Zayalak & W. Friedrich. 1979. 116.00x (ISBN 3-11-007668-3). De Gruyter.

Vitamin B-6: Its Role in Health & Disease. Robert D. Reynolds & James E. Leklem. LC 85-19702. (CTND Ser.: Vol. 13). 526p. 1985. 78.00 (ISBN 0-8451-1612-6). A R Liss.

Vitamin Book. Consumer Guide Editors. 1979. (Fireside). pap. 5.95 (ISBN 0-671-24819-7). S&S.

Vitamin Book: A No-Nonsense Consumer Guide. Harold Silverman et al. 368p. (Orig.). 1985. pap. 3.95 (ISBN 0-553-25060-4). Bantam.

Vitamin B12 & Folic Acid. Ruth Adams & Frank Murray. (Illus.). 176p. (Orig.). 1983. pap. 2.95 (ISBN 0-915962-31-4). Comm Channels.

Vitamin B3 (Niacin) Abram Hoffer. Ed. by Richard A. Passwater & Earl R. Mindell. (Good Health Guide Ser.). 32p. 1982. pap. 1.45 (ISBN 0-87983-266-5). Keats.

Vitamin B6 - Pyridoxal Phosphate: Chemical, Biochemical & Medical Aspects, 2 vols. Ed. by David Dolphin et al. LC 85-12350. (Coenzymes & Cofactors Ser.). 1986. Vol. 1, Pt. A. 99.95 (ISBN 0-471-09785-3); Vol. 1, Pt. B. 99.95 (ISBN 0-471-09783-7). Wiley.

Vitamin B6 - Pyridoxal Phosphate: Chemical, Biochemical & Medical Aspects, Vol. 1, Sets A & B. Ed. by David Dolphin et al. (Coenzymes & Cofactors Ser.). 1987. 199.90 (ISBN 0-471-83947-7). Wiley.

Vitamin B6 Book. Ruth Adams & Frank Murray. (Illus.). 176p. (Orig.). 1985. pap. 2.95 (ISBN 0-915962-30-6). Comm Channels.

Vitamin C & Thee. Susan B. Elder. (Illus.). 1978. 20.00 (ISBN 0-916750-74-4). Dayton Labs.

Vitamin C (Ascorbic Acid) J. N. Counsell & D. H. Horning. (Illus.). 383p. 1981. 83.00 (ISBN 0-85334-109-5, Pub. by Elsevier Applied Sci England). Elsevier.

Vitamin C Controversy: Questions & Answers. Emanuel Cheraskin. LC 87-71003. (Illus.). 221p. (Orig.). 1988. pap. 12.95 (ISBN 0-942333-01-2). Bio-Comns Pr.

Vitamin C: Its Molecular Biology & Medical Potential. S. Lewin. 1976. 61.00 (ISBN 0-12-446350-9). Acad Pr.

Vitamin C: Recent Aspects of Its Physiological & Technological Importance. G. G. Birch. (Illus.). 260p. 1974. 63.00 (ISBN 0-85334-606-2, Pub. by Elsevier Applied Sci England). Elsevier.

Vitamin C: Recent Aspects of Its Physiological & Technological Importance. Ed. by G. G. Birch & K. J. Parker. LC 74-16050. 259p. 1974. 64.95 (ISBN 0-470-07325-X). Halsted Pr.

Vitamin C, the Common Cold, & the Flu. Linus Pauling. LC 76-28516. (Illus.). 230p. 1976. pap. 10.95x (ISBN 0-7167-0361-0). W H Freeman.

Vitamin C-The Mysterious Redox-System: A Trigger of Life? Sylvia Nobile & Joan M. Woodhill. (Illus.). 185p. 1981. text ed. 29.00 (ISBN 0-85200-419-2, Pub. by MTP Pr England). Kluwer Academic.

Vitamin C Updated. Jack J. Challem. Ed. by Richard A. Passwater & Earl Mindell. (Good Health Guide Ser.). 32p. 1983. pap. text ed. 1.95 (ISBN 0-87983-285-1). Keats.

Vitamin Contents of Arterial Tissue. J. E. Kirk. (Monographs on Atherosclerosis: Vol. 3). 1973. 33.50 (ISBN 3-8055-1466-2). S Karger.

Vitamin Cookbook. Victor Lindlahr. 1972. pap. 5.95 (ISBN 0-87877-011-9, D-11). Newcastle Pub.

Vitamin D. Ed. by D. E. Lawson. 1978. 117.00 (ISBN 0-12-439850-2). Acad Pr.

Vitamin D - Chemical, Biochemical & Clinical Update: Proceedings of the 6th Workshop on Vitamin D, Italy, March 1985. Ed. by A. W. Norman et al. (Illus.). xxxxiii, 1249p. 1985. 220.00 (ISBN 3-11-010181-5). De Gruyter.

Vitamin D & Calcium Metabolism in the Renal Diseases. Ed. by J. Ono et al. (Contributions to Nephrology Ser.: Vol. 22). (Illus.). vi, 122p. 1980. soft cover 46.75 (ISBN 3-8055-0389-X). S Karger.

Vitamin D & Problems Related to Uremic Bone Diseases: Proceedings of the Workshop on Vitamin D, 2nd, Wiesbaden, West Germany, Oct. 1974. Ed. by A. W. Norman et al. xvi, 799p. 1975. 108.00x (ISBN 3-11-005775-1). De Gruyter.

Vitamin D: Basic & Clinical Aspects. Rajiv Kumar. 1984. lib. bdg. 95.00 (ISBN 0-318-00430-5, Pub. by Martinus Nijhoff Netherlands). Kluwer Academic.

Vitamin D: Biochemical, Chemical & Clinical Aspects Related to Calcium Metabolism: Proceedings of the Third Workshop on Vitamin D, Pacific Grove California, U. S. A., January 1977. 1977. 92.00x (ISBN 3-11-006918-0). De Gruyter.

Vitamin D: Chemical, Biochemical & Clinical Endocrinology of Calcium Metabolism. Ed. by A. W. Norman & K. Schaefer. (Illus.). 1288p. 1982. text ed. 184.00 (ISBN 3-11-008864-9). De Gruyter.

Vitamin D Fourth Workshop: Basic Research & Its Clinical Applications. A. W. Norman et al. 1979. 142.00 (ISBN 3-11-007712-4). De Gruyter.

Vitamin D: Metabolism & Function. H. F. DeLuca. (Monographs on Endocrinology: Vol. 13). (Illus.). 1979. 20.00 (ISBN 0-387-09182-3). Springer-Verlag.

Vitamin D: Molecular Biology & Clinical Nutrition. Norman. (Basic & Clinical Nutrition Ser.: Vol. 2). 760p. 1980. 110.00 (ISBN 0-8247-6891-4). Dekker.

Vitamin D: The Calcium Homeostatic Hormone. Anthony W. Norman. (Basic & Applied Science of Nutrition Ser.). 1979. 83.00 (ISBN 0-12-521050-7). Acad Pr.

Vitamin Deficiencies: Index of Modern Information with Bibliography. Michael J. Lichtenstein. LC 88-47794. 150p. 1988. 34.50 (ISBN 0-88164-888-4); pap. 26.50 (ISBN 0-88164-889-2). ABBE Pubs Assn.

Vitamin E. Ed. by L. Machlin. (Basic & Clinical Nutrition Ser.: Vol.1). 544p. 1980. 99.75 (ISBN 0-8247-6842-6). Dekker.

Vitamin E: Biochemical, Hematological, Clinical Aspects, Vol. 393. New York Academy of Sciences Annals, Nov. 11-13, 1981. Ed. by Bertram Lubin & Lawrence J. Machlin. 506p. 1982. 95.00x (ISBN 0-89766-176-1); pap. write for info. (ISBN 0-89766-177-X). NY Acad Sci.

Vitamin E Updated. Len Mervyn. Ed. by Richard A. Passwater & Earl R. Mindell. (Good Health Guide Ser.). 32p. (Orig.). 1983. pap. 1.45 (ISBN 0-87983-274-6). Keats.

Vitamin K-Dependent Biological Processes. Ed. by Maria B. Donati. (Journal: Haemostasis: Vol. 16, No. 2, 1986). (Illus.). 132p. 1986. pap. 55.50 (ISBN 3-8055-4270-4). S Karger.

Vitamin, Mineral Connection. Peggy Alderton. 30p. 1985. pap. 2.95 (ISBN 0-317-14757-9). Books World.

Vitamin Politics. John J. Fried. LC 83-62187. 238p. 1984. pap. 13.95 (ISBN 0-87975-222-X). Prometheus Bks.

Vitamin Power: A User's Guide to Nutritional Supplements & Botanical Substances That Can Change Your Life. Rita Aero & Stephanie Rick. 1987. 15.95 (ISBN 0-517-56428-9, Harmony). Crown.

Vitamin Power: Ten Power Programs for Nutritional Self-Defense. Rita Aero & Stephanie Rock. (Illus.). 1987. 15.95 (ISBN 0-317-56524-9, Harmony). Crown.

Vitamin Robbers. Earl R. Mindell. Ed. by Richard Passwater & Earl R. Mindell. (Good Health Guide Ser.). (Illus.). 1983. pap. 1.45 (ISBN 0-87983-275-4). Keats.

Vitamin Side Effects Revealed. exp. ed. Frank W. Cawood. 156p. 1984. pap. 9.95 (ISBN 0-915099-04-7). FC&A Pub.

Vitamin Side Effects Revealed. 2nd ed. Frank W. Cawood. 136p. 1984. pap. 5.99 (ISBN 0-915099-03-9). FC&A Pub.

Vitamin Tolerance of Animals. National Research Council. 108p. 1987. pap. text ed. 17.50x (ISBN 0-309-03728-X). Natl Acad Pr.

Vitamin Vitality. Patrick Holford. 208p. (Orig.). 1986. pap. 3.95 (ISBN 0-553-26230-0). Bantam.

Vitaminas y Otros Complementos Alimentarios y Su Salud. Carlson Wade. Orig. Title: Fact Book on Vitamins & Other Supplements. (Orig., Span.). 1980. pap. 4.95 (ISBN 0-87983-175-8). Keats.

Vitamins. Wihelm Friedrich. 1060p. 1988. lib. bdg. 246.00x (ISBN 3-11-010244-7). De Gruyter.

Vitamins see Nutrition & Environmental Health: The Influence of Nutritional Status on Pollutant Toxicity & Carcinogenicity.

Vitamins - What They Are, What They Do. Judith S. Seixas. LC 85-17761. (Greenwillow Read-Alone Bks.). (Illus.). 56p. (gr. 1-4). 1986. 10.25 (ISBN 0-688-06065-X); PLB 10.88 (ISBN 0-688-06066-8). Greenwillow.

Vitamins: A Practical Manual. J. Marks. 1985. lib. bdg. 32.50 (ISBN 0-85200-851-1, Pub. by MTP Pr England). Kluwer Academic.

Vitamins & Cancer. Ed. by Frank L. Meyskens, Jr. & Kedar Prasad. LC 85-27134. (Experimental Biology & Medicine Ser.). 504p. 1986. 69.50 (ISBN 0-89603-094-6). Humana.

Vitamins & Coenzymes. A. F. Wagner & K. Folkers. LC 74-30499. 552p. 1975. Repr. of 1964 ed. 37.50 (ISBN 0-88275-258-8). Krieger.

Vitamins & Health Foods the Great American Hustle. Victor Herbert & Stephen Barrett. LC 81-83596. 189p. 1985. pap. 9.95 (ISBN 0-89313-073-7). G F Stickley Co.

Vitamins & Hormones, Vol. 37. Ed. by Paul L. Munson et al. LC 43-10535. 1980. 71.00 (ISBN 0-12-709837-2). Acad Pr.

Vitamins & Hormones, Vol. 38. Ed. by P. L. Munson et al. (Serial Publication Ser.). 1981. 73.50 (ISBN 0-12-709838-0). Acad Pr.

Vitamins & Hormones, Vol. 39. 1982. 65.00 (ISBN 0-12-709839-9). Acad Pr.

Vitamins & Hormones, Vol. 40. Ed. by Donald D. McCormick. (Serial Publication). 1983. 75.00 (ISBN 0-12-709840-2). Acad Pr.

Vitamins & Hormones, Vol. 41. Ed. by Robert S. Harris & Kenneth V. Thimann. 1984. 75.00 (ISBN 0-12-709841-0). Acad Pr.

Vitamins & Hormones, Vol. 42. Ed. by Donald B. McCormick. 372p. 1985. 82.50 (ISBN 0-12-709842-9). Acad Pr.

Vitamins & Hormones: Adavances in Research & Applications, Vol. 43. Ed. by G. D. Aurbach & Donald M. McCormick. 316p. 1986. 59.00 (ISBN 0-12-709843-7). Acad Pr.

Vitamins & Hormones, Vol. 44: Advances in Research & Applications. Ed. by C. D. Aurbach & Donald B. McCormick. 350p. 1988. price not set (ISBN 0-12-709844-5). Acad Pr.

Vitamins & Medicine: Subject, Reference & Research Guide. Russell A. Rosness. LC 87-47633. 160p. 1987. 34.50 (ISBN 0-88164-568-0); pap. 26.50 (ISBN 0-88164-569-9). ABBE Pubs Assn.

Vitamins & Minerals. Ed. by Dale C. Garell & Solomon H. Snyder. (Encyclopedia of Health Ser.). (Illus.). (YA) (gr. 7-12). 1989. 17.95 (ISBN 0-7910-0032-X). Chelsea Hse.

Vitamins & Minerals. Martin Lushbough & Loretta L. Hood. 1983. pap. 2.00 (ISBN 0-933904-09-6). Gold Quill Pubs CA.

Vitamins & Minerals & What They Can Do for You. Peter L. Moore. 69p. (Orig.). 1985. pap. 6.95 (ISBN 0-9619829-0-X, TX 1-742-750). Sauk River Pr.

Vitamins & Minerals for a Healthy Pregnancy (And a Healthy Baby) Essential Nutrients for Each Stage of Your Pregnancy & Your Baby's Development. Richard Gerson. (Illus.). 160p. (Orig.). 1987. pap. 7.95 (ISBN 0-8092-4805-0). Contemp Bks.

Vitamins & Minerals: Help or Harm. Charles W. Marshall: 206p. 1985. pap. 11.95 (ISBN 0-89313-072-9). G F Stickley Co.

Vitamins & Minerals in Pregnancy & Lactation. Ed. by Heribert Berger. (Nestle Nutrition Workshop Ser.: Vol. 16). (Illus.). 472p. 1988. text ed. 49.00 (ISBN 0-88167-414-1). Raven.

Vitamins & Minerals: The Health Connection. Anni A. Lines. LC 85-7638. 188p. 1985. pap. 6.95 (ISBN 0-932090-14-1). Health Plus.

Vitamins & Nutrient Market. 220p. 1985. 595.00 (ISBN 0-318-00514-X). Busn Trend.

Vitamins & Over-the-Counter Nutritional Supplements. Business Communications Staff. 129p. 1987. pap. 1750.00 (ISBN 0-89336-523-8, GA-060). BCC.

Vitamins Explained Simply. Science of Life Books Editorial Committee. (Science of Life Ser.). 64p. 1984. pap. cancelled (ISBN 0-909911-68-1). Inner Tradit.

Vitamins in Animal Nutrition: Comparative Aspects to Human Nutrition. Lee R. McDowell. Ed. by Tony Cunha. (Animal Feeding & Nutrition Ser.). 650p. 1988. price not set (ISBN 0-12-483372-1). Acad Pr.

Vitamins in Human Biology & Medicine. M. H. Briggs. 272p. 1981. 99.00. CRC Pr.

Vitamins in Your Life. Erwin DiCyan. 1975. (Fireside); pap. 5.95 (ISBN 0-671-22010-1, Fireside). S&S.

Vitamins: Index of Modern Information. Vincent A. Spedding. LC 88-47631. 150p. 1988. 34.50 (ISBN 0-88164-792-6); pap. 26.50 (ISBN 0-88164-793-4). ABBE Pubs Assn.

Vitamins, Minerals & Food Supplements for Good Health. Estelle Rossen. 144p. 1988. 10.95 (ISBN 0-8059-3101-5). Dorrance.

Vitamins, Minerals, & Nutrition. Health Media of America Staff. (Health Media of America Nutrition Ser.). (Illus.). 80p. 1986. pap. 3.95 (ISBN 0-937325-02-3). Health Med Amer.

Vitamins, Minerals & Other Supplements. Carlson Wade. 148p. (Orig.). 1983. pap. 2.95 (ISBN 0-87983-333-5). Keats.

Vitamins, Nutrition & Cancer. Ed. by K. N. Prasad. (Illus.). xii, 320p. 1984. 132.00 (ISBN 3-8055-3846-4). S Karger.

Vitamins: Their Use & Abuse. Joseph V. Levy & Paul Bach-Y-Rita. 155p. 1976. 8.95 (ISBN 0-87140-616-0). Liveright.

Vita's Other World: A Gardening Biography of V. Sackville-West. Jane Brown. (Illus.). 208p. 1986. 20.00 (ISBN 0-670-80163-1). Viking.

Vita's Other World: A Gardening Biography of V. Sackville-West. Jane Brown. (Illus.). 256p. 1988. pap. 12.95 (ISBN 0-14-009354-0). Penguin.

Vitas Patrum. Henri D'Arci. Ed. by Basilides A. O'Connor. (Catholic University Studies in Romantic Languages & Literatures Ser.: No. 29). Repr. of 1949 ed. 30.00 (ISBN 0-404-50329-2). AMS Pr.

Vitas Patrum: The Lyff of the Olde Auncyent Fathers Hermytes. Saint Jerome. Tr. by W. Caxton. LC 77-7409. (English Experience Ser.: No. 874). 1977. Repr. of 1495 ed. lib. bdg. 99.00 (ISBN 90-221-0874-0). Walter J Johnson.

Vite de' pittori, scultori et architetti moderni. Giovanni P. Bellori. (Documents of Art & Architectural History, Ser. 1: Vol. 4). (Ital.). 1980. Repr. of 1672 ed. 47.50x (ISBN 0-89371-104-7). Broude Intl Edns.

Vite de piu Eccellenti Architetti, Pittori, et Scultori Italiani, 2 vols. Giorgio Vasari. (Documents of Art & Architectural History, Ser. 1: Vol. 1). (Ital.). 1980. Repr. of 1550 ed. Set. 97.50x (ISBN 0-89371-101-2). Broude Intl Edns.

Vite De' Piu Eccellenti Pittori see Lives of the Most Eminent Painters, Sculptors & Architects.

Vitez Voros Janos M. kir Vezerezredes Vezerkari Fonok Naploja see War Diary of the Chief of the General Staff, Janos Voros: From April 17 to October 15, 1944.

Vitezslav Nezval. 1981. pap. 5.00 (ISBN 92-3-201859-4, U1130, UNESCO). UNIPUB.

Viticultural Technique: Multilingual Illustrated Dictionary. H. Steinmetz. 320p. (Orig.). 1981. pap. text ed. 24.95x (Pub. by H Steinmetz). Agribookstore.

Vitiligo & Other Hypomelanoses of Hair & Skin. Jean-Paul Ortonne & David B. Mosher. LC 82-16490. (Topics In Dermatology Ser.). 700p. 1983. 95.00x (ISBN 0-306-40974-7, Plenum Med Bk). Plenum Pub.

Vito Acconci. Linda Shearer. (Illus.). 32p. (Orig.). 1988. pap. 9.95 (ISBN 0-87070-625-X). Museum Mod Art.

Vito Acconci: Dal Testo-Azione Al Corpo Come Testo. Mario Diacono. LC 75-22995. (Illus.). 245p. (Ital.). 1975. 9.95 (ISBN 0-915570-03-3). Oolp Pr.

Vito Marcantonio, Radical in Congress. Alan Schaffer. LC 66-29201. (Men & Movements Ser.). pap. 68.00 (ISBN 0-317-52021-0, 2027415). Bks Demand UMI.

Vito Marcantonio: Selected Debates, Speeches & Writings 1935-1950. Ed. by Annette T. Rubinstein et al. LC 73-12402. (Illus.). Repr. of 1956 ed. 45.00x (ISBN 0-678-01365-9). Kelley.

Vito Marcantonio y Puerto Rico. Ed. by Felix Ojeda. 156p. 1978. pap. 5.50 (ISBN 0-940238-40-3). Ediciones Huracan.

Vito Volterra Symposium on Mathematical Models in Biology: Proceedings. Ed. by Claudio Barigozzi. (LN in Biomathematics Ser.: Vol. 39). (Illus.). 417p. 1980. pap. 32.00 (ISBN 0-387-10279-5). Springer-Verlag.

Vitrectomy. 2nd ed. Robert Machemer & Thomas M. Aaberg. (Current Ophthalmology Monographs). 288p. 1979. 44.50 (ISBN 0-8089-1146-5, 792646). Grune.

Vitrectomy Techniques for the Anterior Segment Surgeon: A Practical Approach. Ed. by Walter H. Stern. (Current Opthamology Monographs). 169p. 1982. 35.50 (ISBN 0-8089-1520-7, 794347). Grune.

Vitreoretinal Disease: A Manual for Diagnosis & Treatment. 2nd ed. Peter H. Morse. 1988. 95.00 (ISBN 0-8151-5963-3). Year Bk Med.

Vitreoretinal Disorders: Diagnosis & Management. Felipe L. Tolentino et al. LC 73-81838. (Illus.). Repr. of 1976 ed. 120.00 (ISBN 0-8357-9562-4, 2012283). Bks Demand UMI.

Vitreous & Vitreoretinal Interface. Ed. by C. L. Schepens & A. Neetens. (Illus.). 350p. 1987. 57.00 (ISBN 0-387-96553-X). Springer-Verlag.

Vitreous Enamelling: A Guide to Modern Enamelling Practice. K. A. Maskall & D. W. White. 100p. 1986. text ed. 36.00 (ISBN 0-08-033428-8, Pub. by PPL); pap. text ed. 18.25 (ISBN 0-08-033429-6). Pergamon.

Vitreous Microsurgery. 2nd ed. Steve Charles. 265p. 1987. 52.95 (ISBN 0-683-01551-6). Williams & Wilkins.

Vitruvius & Later Roman Building Manuals. William H. Plommer. LC 72-90487. (Cambridge Classical Studies). pap. 31.30 (ISBN 0-317-27568-2, 2024512). Bks Demand UMI.

Vitruvius Architect & Engineer. A. MacKay. 88p. 1985. Repr. of 1978 ed. 11.00 (ISBN 0-86292-157-0, Pub. by Bristol Classical UK). Focus Info Gr.

Vitruvius Britannicus, 3 vols. Incl. Vol. 1. 1715-25 Ed. Colin Campbell; Vol. 2. 1739 & 1767-71 Eds. J. Badeslade et al; Vol. 3. 1802-08 Ed. George Richardson. LC 67-18052. 47.50 ea. Ayer Co Pubs.

Vittoria Colonna. Maud F. Jerrold. (Select Bibliographies Reprint Ser). 1906. 27.50 (ISBN 0-8369-5153-0). Ayer Co Pubs.

Vittoria Cottage. D. E. Stevenson. 350p. 1983. Repr. lib. bdg. 16.95x (ISBN 0-89966-163-7). Buccaneer Bks.

Vittorini Omnibus: The Twilight of the Elephant & Other Novels. Elio Vittorini. Tr. by Cinina Brescia et al from Ital. LC 73-78790. 320p. 1973. pap. 8.95 (ISBN 0-8112-0499-5, NDP366). New Directions.

Vittorio Alfieri. Franco Betti. (World Authors Ser.). 1984. lib. bdg. 20.95 (ISBN 0-8057-6579-4, Twayne). G K Hall.

Vittorio Alfieri, Forerunner of Italian Nationalism. Gaudens Megaro. LC 78-159246. 1971. Repr. of 1930 ed. lib. bdg. 18.50x (ISBN 0-374-95557-3, Octagon). Hippocrene Bks.

Vittorio de Sica: A Guide to References & Resources. John Darretta. 384p. (gr. 10-12). 1983. lib. bdg. 55.00 (ISBN 0-8161-8468-2, Hall Reference). G K Hall.

Vitus Bering. Peter Lauridsen. LC 70-94274. (Select Bibliographies Reprint Ser). 1889. 21.50 (ISBN 0-8369-5048-8). Ayer Co Pubs.

Viva. e. e. Cummings. LC 70-131279. 1970. 6.00 (ISBN 0-87140-528-8); pap. 2.95 (ISBN 0-87140-223-8). Liveright.

Viva Cristo Rey: The Cristero Rebellion & the Church-State Conflict in Mexico. David C. Bailey. (Illus.). 360p. 1974. 22.50x (ISBN 0-292-78700-6). U of Tex Pr.

Viva el Agua y el Jabon. Kornei Chukovski. (Illus.). 18p. (Span.). 1974. pap. 1.49 (ISBN 0-8285-1309-0, Pub. by Progress Pubs USSR). Imported Pubns.

Viva la Lengua. 2nd ed. Fransisco Jimenez et al. 124p. 1987. pap. text ed. 11.00 net (ISBN 0-15-594939-X, HC). HarBraceJ.

Viva la Muerta (Baal Babylone) Fernando Arrabal. 9.95 (ISBN 0-686-54477-3). French & Eur.

Viva Mad. Sergio Aragones. (Illus.). 192p. 1987. pap. 2.95 (ISBN 0-446-34545-8). Warner Bks.

Viva Mexico! A Traveller's Account of Life in Mexico. Claude M. Flandrau. (Eland Travel Classics Ser.). 294p. 1985. pap. 8.95 (ISBN 0-907871-20-8, Pub. by Eland Bks UK). Hippocrene Bks.

Viva Morelia. Eugenio Villicana. LC 72-159842. (Two Worlds Bks.). (Illus.). 64p. (gr. 4-6). 1972. 3.95 (ISBN 0-87131-098-8). M Evans.

Viva Nippon!? T. Ichikawa. Tr. by M. McDonald & S. McDonald. 300p. 1988. 35.00 (ISBN 9971-50-591-6). World Scientific Pub.

Viva Villa: A Recovery of the Real Pancho Villa, Peon, Bandit, Soldier, Patriot. Edgcumb Pinchon. LC 70-111729. (American Imperialism: Viewpoints of United States Foreign Policy, 1898-1941). 1970. Repr. of 1933 ed. 24.50 (ISBN 0-405-02045-7). Ayer Co Pubs.

Viva Vivas! Ed. by Henry Regnery. LC 76-9432. 1976. 7.95 (ISBN 0-913966-08-8, Liberty Clas). Liberty Fund.

Viva Vocab. Lucy Haagen. (gr. 7-9). 1983. pap. text ed. 6.95x (ISBN 0-317-02595-3); ans. key avail. Ind Sch Pr.

Viva! Zappa. Dominique Chevalier. (Illus.). 128p. 1986. pap. 12.95 (ISBN 0-312-00201-7). St Martin.

Vivacites du Capitaine Tic. Eugene Labiche. 9.95 (ISBN 0-686-54258-4). French & Eur.

Vivaldi. Michael Talbot. (Master Musicians Ser.). (Illus.). 275p. 1978. 17.95x (ISBN 0-460-03164-3, Pub. by J. M. Dent England). Biblio Dist.

Vivaldi in Early Fall. John Engels. LC 80-24571. (Contemporary Poetry Ser.). 112p. 1981. 9.95x (ISBN 0-8203-0543-X); pap. 5.95 (ISBN 0-8203-0552-9). U of Ga Pr.

Vivaldi Violin Concertos: A Handbook. Arlan S. Martin. LC 76-169698. 278p. 1972. 19.00 (ISBN 0-8108-0432-8). Scarecrow.

Vivamos En el Espiritu Cada Dia. Pat H. Carter. 160p. 1982. pap. 3.95 (ISBN 0-311-09089-3). Casa Bautista.

VLSI Specification, Verification & Synthesis. Ed. by Graham Birwistle & P. A. Subrahmanyam. 1987. lib. bdg. 65.00 (ISBN 0-89838-246-7). Kluwer Academic.

VLSI Support Technologies: Computer-Aided Design, Testing, & Packaging. Rex Rice. (Tutorial Texts Ser.). 450p. 1982. 30.00 (ISBN 0-8186-0386-0, Q386). IEEE Comp Soc.

VLSI System Design: When & How to Design Very Large Scale Integrated Circuits. S. Muroga. 300p. 1984. pap. 19.00 (ISBN 0-471-88697-1, EE25, Pub. by Wiley Interscience). Wiley.

VLSI Systems & Computations. Ed. by H. T. Kung et al. (Digital Systems Design Ser.). 415p. 1981. text ed. 39.95 (ISBN 0-914894-35-8, Computer Sci Pr). W H Freeman.

VLSI Systems Design for Digital Signal Processing, Vol. 1: Signal Processing & Signal Processors. B. A. Bowen & William R. Brown. (Illus.). 256p. 1982. text ed. 53.00 (ISBN 0-13-942706-6). P-H.

VLSI Systems Design: When & How to Design Very Large Scale Integrated Circuits. Saburo Muroga. LC 82-8598. 496p. 1982. 44.95 (ISBN 0-471-86090-5, Pub. by Wiley-Interscience). Wiley.

VLSI Technologies: Through the Eighties & Beyond. Denis J. McGreivy & Kenneth A. Pickar. (Tutorial Texts Ser.). 343p. 1982. 30.00 (ISBN 0-8186-0424-7, Q424). IEEE Comp Soc.

VLSI Technology. Ed. by Simon M. Sze. (Illus.). 608p. 1983. text ed. 48.95 (ISBN 0-07-062686-3). McGraw.

VLSI Technology. Ed. by Y. Tarui. (Springer Series in Electrophysics: Vol. 12). (Illus.). 460p. 1986. 69.00 (ISBN 0-387-12558-2). Springer-Verlag.

VLSI-Technology & Design. Ed. by D. G. Folberth & W. D. Grobman. LC 84-15848. 320p. 1984. 46.70 (ISBN 0-87942-180-0, PC01743). Inst Electrical.

VLSI Technology & Design. Edited Treatise ed. J. V. McCanny & John White. (Microelectronics & Signal Processing Ser.). 388p. 1987. 59.50 (ISBN 0-12-481840-4). Acad Pr.

VLSI Testing. Ed. by T. W. Williams. (Advances in CAD for VLSI Ser.: Vol. 5). 278p. 1986. 52.50 (ISBN 0-444-87895-5, North-Holland). Elsevier.

VLSI Testing & Validation Techniques. Hassan Reghbati. 603p. 1985. 45.00 (ISBN 0-8186-0668-1); microfiche 45.00 (ISBN 0-8186-4668-3). IEEE Comp Soc.

VLSI Theory. Ed. by Franco P. Preparata. (Advances in Computing Research Ser.: Vol. 2). 275p. 1985. 59.50 (ISBN 0-89232-461-9). Jai Pr.

VLSI '85. Ed. by E. Horbst. 440p. 1986. 81.75 (ISBN 0-444-87920-X, North Holland). Elsevier.

VM Applications Handbook. Ed. by Gary R. McClain. 320p. 1989. 44.95 (ISBN 0-07-044948-1). McGraw.

VM-CMS: Commands & Concepts. Steve Eckols. LC 87-62576. 288p. 1988. pap. 25.00 (ISBN 0-911625-44-5). M Murach & Assoc.

VM CMS Handbook. Howard Fosdick. 400p. 1987. pap. 32.95 (ISBN 0-672-46790-9). Sams.

VM-CMS: XEDIT Commands & Features. Steve Eckols. LC 88-60889. 213p. 1988. pap. 25.00 (ISBN 0-911625-47-X). M Murach & Assoc.

VMEbus Based Product Market. Frost & Sullivan, Inc. Staff. 229p. 1985. 1650.00 (ISBN 0-86621-497-6, A1570). Frost & Sullivan.

VN: The Life & Art of Vladimir Nabokov. Andrew Field. 1986. 19.95. Crown.

Vneshniai Torgovlia Rossii Cherez: Revel'skii Port V 1721-1756. A. A. Preobrazhenskii. (Illus.). 272p. (Rus. & Ger.). 1984. 59.00x (ISBN 0-317-40884-4, Pub. by Collets (UK)). State Mutual Bk.

Vneshniaia Politika Rossii KiK 1 Nachala XX Veka. Ed. by Collet's Holdings, Ltd. Staff. (Rus.). 1980. 79.00 (ISBN 0-317-40876-3, Pub. by Collets (UK)). State Mutual Bk.

VNR Concise Dictionary of Business & Finance. David M. Brownstone et al. 320p. 1980. 25.95 (ISBN 0-442-20949-5). Van Nos Reinhold.

VNR Concise Encyclopedia of Mathematics. Ed. by W. Gellert et al. (Illus.). 816p. 1977. 28.95 (ISBN 0-442-22646-2). Van Nos Reinhold.

VNR Concise Guide to Accounting & Control. Ed. by Carl Heyel. (VNR Concise Management Ser.). 1979. pap. 7.95x (ISBN 0-442-23407-4). Van Nos Reinhold.

VNR Concise Guide to Financial Management. Ed. by Carl Heyel. (VNR Concise Management Ser.). 1979. pap. 7.95 (ISBN 0-442-23406-6). Van Nos Reinhold.

VNR Concise Guide to Human Resources Development. Ed. by Carl Heyel. (VNR Concise Management Ser.). 213p. 1980. pap. 7.95 (ISBN 0-442-23401-5). Van Nos Reinhold.

VNR Concise Guide to Industrial Management. Ed. by Carl Heyel. (Van Nostrand Reinhold Concise Management Ser.). 1979. pap. 7.95 (ISBN 0-442-23403-1). Van Nos Reinhold.

VNR Concise Guide to Management Decision Making. Ed. by Carl Heyel. (VNR Concise Management Ser.). 227p. 1980. pap. 7.95 (ISBN 0-442-23400-7). Van Nos Reinhold.

VNR Encyclopedia of Chemistry. 4th ed. Ed. by Douglas M. Considine. (Illus.). 1168p. 1984. 99.95 (ISBN 0-442-22572-5). Van Nos Reinhold.

VNR Pocket Atlas. Ed. by Jiri Novotny & Marie Pankova. (Illus.). 233p. 1983. pap. 13.95 (ISBN 0-442-29661-4). Van Nos Reinhold.

Vnutrenee Osvoenie Zemel'Rossii V XVI v. L. I. Ivina. 272p. (Rus.). 1985. 39.00x (ISBN 0-317-42813-6, Pub by Collets (UK)). State Mutual Bk.

Vnutripoliticheskaia Bor'Ba 1970-1974. K. K. Khudolei. 158p. (Rus.). 1984. 39.00x (ISBN 0-317-40898-4, Pub. by Collets (UK)). State Mutual Bk.

Vo Dang Bat Quai Quyen Chuong. Hang-Thanh. LC 87-51680. (Illus.). 164p. 1988. pap. 8.00 (ISBN 0-944211-06-2). Vo Lam Pub.

Vo Lam Pham The. Hang-Thanh. LC 87-51561. (Illus.). 156p. pap. 8.00 (ISBN 0-944211-02-X). Vo Lam Pub.

Vo Slavu Otechestva Possiikogo. V. A. Zolotarev & M. N. Mexhevich. Ed. by D. E. Skorodumov. 336p. 1984. 49.00 (ISBN 0-317-40846-1, Pub. by Collets (UK)). State Mutual Bk.

Vocablos y Expresiones Medicos mas Usuales en Veinte Idiomas Vernaculos Peruanos. Ed. by Mary R. Wise. (Peruvian Working Papers: No. 2). 1973. pap. 5.75x (ISBN 0-88312-652-4); microfiche (2) 4.00 (ISBN 0-88312-315-0). Summer Inst Ling.

Vocabolarietto della Lingua Italiana. C. Grassi. (Ital.). write for info. French & Eur.

Vocabolario Latino-Italiano, Italiano-Latino. Ed. by G. Campanini & G. Carboni. 1500p. (Lat. & Ital.). 1982. 59.50x (ISBN 0-913298-76-X). S F Vanni.

Vocabolario Toscano Dell'arte del Disegno. Filippo Baldinucci. (Documents of Art & Architectural History, Ser. 1: Vol. 5). (Ital.). 1980. Repr. of 1681 ed. 42.50x (ISBN 0-89371-105-5). Broude Intl Edns.

Vocabulaire Barometre Dans le Langage Economique. 3rd ed. J. Delattre & G. DeVernisy. 160p. (Eng. & Fr.). 1967. pap. 29.95 (ISBN 0-686-56982-2, M-6109). French & Eur.

Vocabulaire Biblique. Ed. by Jean-Jacques Von Allmen. 320p. (Fr.). 1964. pap. 39.95 (ISBN 0-686-57248-3, M-6759). French & Eur.

Vocabulaire d'Astronomie. (Fr., Eng. & Ger.). 1978. pap. 49.95 (ISBN 0-686-57249-1, M-6555). French & Eur.

Vocabulaire de la Psychanalyse. 5th ed. Ed. by Jean Laplanche. Jean-Baptiste Pontalis. (Fr.). 1976. 85.00 (ISBN 0-686-57250-5, M-6558). French & Eur.

Vocabulaire De la Psychologie. 5th ed. Henri Pieron. 570p. (Fr.). 1973. 55.00 (ISBN 0-686-57078-2, M-6453). French & Eur.

Vocabulaire de la Publicite. Ed. by Conseil International de la Langue Francaise Staff. (Fr.). 1976. pap. 19.95 (ISBN 0-686-57251-3, M-6559). French & Eur.

Vocabulaire de la Radio & de la Television. 30p. (Fr.). 1977. pap. 9.95 (ISBN 0-7754-2273-8, M-9022). French & Eur.

Vocabulaire de la Vente Promotionelle: Anglais-Francais. M. Villiers et al. 30p. (Eng. & Fr.). 1975. pap. 7.95 (ISBN 0-7754-3244-X, M-9242). French & Eur.

Vocabulaire De L'astronautique. L. Guilbert. 361p. (Fr.). pap. 45.00 (ISBN 0-686-57265-3, F-137130). French & Eur.

Vocabulaire de L'astronautique: Enquete Linguistique a travers la Presse d'information a L'occasion De Cinq Exploits de Cosmonautes. Guilbert. (Publ. de l'Univ. de Rouen Fac. des Lettres et Sc. Hum.). (Fr.). 15.95 (ISBN 0-685-36683-9). French & Eur.

Vocabulaire De L'economie. Gilbert Mathieu. (Fr.). pap. 35.00 (ISBN 0-686-57041-3, M-6401). French & Eur.

Vocabulaire De L'Education. Gaston Mialaret. 488p. (Fr.). 1979. 95.00 (ISBN 0-686-57048-0, M-6410). French & Eur.

Vocabulaire de L'Environnement. Ed. by Conseil International de la Langue Francaise Staff. (Fr.). 1976. pap. 29.95 (ISBN 0-686-57283-1, M-4648). French & Eur.

Vocabulaire de l'Informatique de Gestion: Anglais-Francais. M. Villers. 31p. (Eng. & Fr.). 1980. pap. 7.95 (ISBN 2-551-03899-5, M-9228). French & Eur.

Vocabulaire De L'oceanologie. Ed. by Agence de Cooperation Culturelle et Technique. 431p. (Fr.). 1976. pap. 49.95 (ISBN 0-686-57252-1, M-6560). French & Eur.

Vocabulaire De Medecine & Des Sciences Connexes Anglais-Francais-Anglais. Gladstone. (Eng. & Fr.). 99.95 (ISBN 0-685-36682-0). French & Eur.

Vocabulaire De Medecine et Des Sciences Connexes: Francais-Anglais, Anglais-Francais. 298p. (Fr. & Eng.). 1971. 37.50 (ISBN 0-686-57281-5). French & Eur.

Vocabulaire De Psychopedagogie et De Psychiatrie De L'enfant. 3rd ed. Robert Lafon. 868p. (Fr.). 1973. 57.50 (ISBN 0-686-57282-3, F-19440). French & Eur.

Vocabulaire d'Ecologie. Ed. by Conseil International de la Langue Francaise Staff. (Fr.). 1974. pap. 9.95 (ISBN 0-686-57284-X, M-4641). French & Eur.

Vocabulaire des Assurances Sociales. G. Desrosiers & J. Boulay. 21p. (Fr.). 1971. pap. 9.95 (ISBN 0-7754-2274-6, M-9231). French & Eur.

Vocabulaire des assurances sur la vie. V. P. Grandpre. 14p. 1973. pap. 5.95 (ISBN 0-686-92148-8, M-9230). French & Eur.

Vocabulaire du Beton. Ed. by Conseil International de la Langue Francaise Staff. 192p. (Fr.). 1976. pap. 45.00 (ISBN 0-686-56961-X, M-6084). French & Eur.

Vocabulaire Du Droit Primaire Communautaire. Commission of the European Communities, Portuguese Translation Section. LC 86-156265. x, 416p. 1985. 20.00 (ISBN 9-282-55439-2). Comm Europe Comm.

Vocabulaire Economique et Financier: Coll. Points Economie. Yves Bernard & Jean-Claude Colli. 384p. (Fr.). 1976. pap. 14.95 (ISBN 0-686-56915-6, M-6031). French & Eur.

Vocabulaire Ethnologique. Armin Heymer. 237p. (Ger., Eng. & Fr.). 1977. 45.00 (ISBN 0-686-57329-3, M-6317). French & Eur.

Vocabulaire Fondamental de Technologie. Jacques Deweerdt. 272p. (Fr.). 1974. pap. 49.95 (ISBN 0-686-57280-7, M-4654). French & Eur.

Vocabulaire Francais-Anglais, Anglais-Francais D'archeologie Prehistorique. Roger Marois. 116p. (Fr.-Eng.). 1972. pap. 29.95 (ISBN 0-686-57039-1, M-6399). French & Eur.

Vocabulaire Francais-Anglais De la Machine a Coudre Industrielle. Francois Lanecki & Celine Dupre. 85p. (Fr. & Eng.). 1973. pap. 9.95 (ISBN 0-686-56991-1, M-6331). French & Eur.

Vocabulaire Francais-Anglais De L'automobile: Le Moteur. Anne-Marie Baudoin. 174p. (Eng. & Fr.). 1973. pap. 9.95 (ISBN 0-686-56909-1, M-6025). French & Eur.

Vocabulaire Francais-Anglais Des Relations Professionnelles. 2nd ed. Gerard Dion. 350p. (Fr. & Eng.). 1975. 37.50 (ISBN 0-686-57266-1, M-4655). French & Eur.

Vocabulaire Francais-Anglais Des Relations Professionnelles. Ed. by Ministre du Travail et de la Main d'Oeuvre. 302p. (Fr. & Eng.). 1972. pap. 37.50 (ISBN 0-686-57279-3, M-4655). French & Eur.

Vocabulaire Francais-Arabe De L'ingenieur et Du Technicien, 1: Eletricite. J. J. Schmidt. 136p. (Fr. & Arabic.). 1973. pap. 39.95 (ISBN 0-686-57215-7, M-6504). French & Eur.

Vocabulaire Franco-Anglo-Allemand De Geomorphologie. (Fr., Eng. & Ger.). 1970. pap. 49.95 (ISBN 0-686-57278-5, F-136940). French & Eur.

Vocabulaire International des Termes d'Urbanisme et d'Architecture. Jean-Henri Calsat & Jean P. Sydler. 350p. (Fr., Ger. & Eng.). 1970. 95.00 (ISBN 0-686-56935-0, M-6057). French & Eur.

Vocabulaire Latin Des Relations et Des Partis Politiques Sous la Republique. Jean Hellegouarc'H. (Fr.). 69.95 (ISBN 0-686-57327-7, M-6314). French & Eur.

Vocabulaire Medical De Base, 2 vols. Marie Bonvalot. 447p. (Fr.). 1972. Set. pap. 59.95 (ISBN 0-686-56925-3, M-6043). French & Eur.

Vocabulaire Oecumenique. Yves Congar & Gerard Siegwalt. 428p. (Fr.). pap. 39.95 (ISBN 0-686-56960-1, M-6083). French & Eur.

Vocabulaire Pratique De la Philosophie. Jean Miquel. 260p. (Fr.). 1974. pap. 12.95 (ISBN 0-686-57050-2, M-6412). French & Eur.

Vocabulaire Pratique des Sciences Sociales. Alain Birou. 384p. (Fr.). 49.95 (ISBN 0-686-57277-7, F-136960). French & Eur.

Vocabulaire Technique Allemand-Francais, Francais-Allemand. 8th ed. Francis Cusset. 474p. (Fr. & Ger.). 1977. 49.95 (ISBN 0-686-56970-9, M-6097). French & Eur.

Vocabulaire Technique Anglais-Francais, Francais-Anglais. 9th ed. Francis Cusset. 434p. (Fr. & Ger.). 1977. 69.95 (ISBN 0-686-56971-7, M-6098). French & Eur.

Vocabulaire Technique des Assurances sur la Vie, Vol. 1. L. Beguin et al. 309p. (Eng. & Fr.). 1979. pap. 14.95 (ISBN 0-7754-2396-3, M-9244). French & Eur.

Vocabulaire Technique des Assurances sur la Vie, Vol. 2. J. Beguin et al. 335p. (Eng. & Fr.). 1979. pap. 14.95 (ISBN 2-551-03302-0, M-9245). French & Eur.

Vocabulaire Technique et Critique de la Philosophie. 12th ed. Andre Lalande. (Fr.). 1972. 110.00 (ISBN 0-686-57275-0, F-18440). French & Eur.

Vocabulari Castella-Catala. 3rd ed. Eduard Artells. 224p. (Catalan & Span.). 1958. 9.95 (ISBN 84-7226-344-4, S-50355). French & Eur.

Vocabulari Catala De Matematica Basica. Claudi Alsina. 48p. (Catalan.). 1977. pap. 14.95 (ISBN 84-85008-06-5, S-50127). French & Eur.

Vocabulario Andaluz. A. Alcala. 676p. (Span.). 1980. 69.95 (ISBN 84-249-1364-7, S-32726). French & Eur.

Vocabulario Basico de la Arquitectura. J. R. Paniagua. 375p. (Span.). 1978. pap. 29.95 (ISBN 84-376-0134-7, S-37345). French & Eur.

Vocabulario Castellano-Mayo, Vol. 6. rev. ed. Howard Collard & Elizabeth Collard. (Vocabularios Indigenas Ser: No. 6). 225p. (Span.). 1974. pap. write for info. (ISBN 0-88312-657-5); microfiche (3) 6.00 (ISBN 0-88312-318-5). Summer Inst Ling.

Vocabulario Cayapa. John Lindskoog & Carrie Lindskoog. (Vocabularios Indigenas Ser.: No. 9). 129p. (Span.). 1964. microfiche (2) 4.00 (ISBN 0-88312-316-9). Summer Inst Ling.

Vocabulario Culto. 2nd ed. Gladys Neggers. 168p. (Span.). 1977. pap. 12.50 (ISBN 84-359-0034-7, S-50023). French & Eur.

Vocabulario de Artes de la Madera, Arquitectura y Decoracion. 152p. (Span.). 1975. pap. 22.50 (ISBN 84-236-1246-5, S-50084). French & Eur.

Vocabulario De Cine y Television En Espana. Maria V. Romero Gualda. 400p. (Span.). 1976. pap. 29.95 (ISBN 84-313-0234-8, S-50002). French & Eur.

Vocabulario De Romance En Latin: Antonio De Nebrija. Ed. by Gerald MacDonald. LC 72-96003. 214p. (Lat. & Span.). 1973. 19.95 (ISBN 0-87722-018-2). Temple U Pr.

Vocabulario de Teologila Biblica. 9th ed. Leon Dufour. 976p. (Span.). 1977. 35.95 (ISBN 84-254-0809-1, S-50205); pap. 29.95 (ISBN 84-254-0808-3, S-50204). French & Eur.

Vocabulario del Comercio Medieval. 2nd ed. Miguel Gual Camarena. 532p. (Span.). 1976. leather 75.00 (ISBN 84-7370-017-1, S-50115). French & Eur.

Vocabulario Galego-Castelan. Xose L. Franco Grande. 336p. (Span.). 1972. pap. 14.95 (ISBN 84-7154-283-8, S-50437). French & Eur.

Vocabulario General de Orientacion Cientifica y Sus Estratos. Victor Garcia Hoz. 432p. (Span.). 1976. pap. 45.00 (ISBN 84-00-04273-5, S-50108). French & Eur.

Vocabulario Huitoto Muinane. Eugene E. Minor & Dorothy Minor. (Peruvian Linguistic Ser: No. 5). 139p. (Span.). 1971. microfiche (2) 4.00 (ISBN 0-88312-362-2). Summer Inst LIng.

Vocabulario Ingles-Espanol De Electronica y Tecnica Nuclear. 2nd ed. John Markus. 196p. (Span. & Eng.). pap. 39.95 (ISBN 84-267-0247-3, S-30684). French & Eur.

Vocabulario Ingles-Espanol, Espanol-Ingles de Medicina. Francisco Ruiz Torres. 300p. (Eng. & Span.). 1979. pap. 23.95 (ISBN 84-205-0625-7, S-50091). French & Eur.

Vocabulario Ingles-Espanol, Espanol-Ingles. Jose Merino Bustamante. 186p. (Eng. & Span.). 1977. pap. 19.95 (ISBN 84-205-0565-X, S-50346). French & Eur.

Vocabulario Maritimo Ingles-Espanol y Espanol-Ingles. 5th ed. Juan Navarro Dagnino. 151p. (Span. & Eng.). 1976. pap. 19.95 (ISBN 84-252-0225-6, S-12239). French & Eur.

Vocabulario Mexicano de Tetelcingo Morelos. Forrest Brewer & Jean Brewer. (Vocabularios Indigenas Ser.: No. 8). 274p. (Span.). 1962. microfiche (3) 6.00 (ISBN 0-88312-363-0). Summer Inst Ling.

Vocabulario Mixe de Totontepec. Alvin Schoenhals & Louise Schoenhals. (Vocabularios Indigenas Ser.: No. 14). 353p. (Span.). 1965. pap. 11.95x (ISBN 0-88312-659-1); microfiche (4) 8.00 (ISBN 0-88312-319-3). Summer Inst Ling.

Vocabulario Mixteco de San Miguel el Grande. Anne Dyk & Betty Stoudt. (Vocabularios Indigenas Ser.: No. 12). 132p. (Span.). 1965. pap. 5.95 (ISBN 0-88312-660-5); microfiche (2) 4.00x (ISBN 0-88312-580-3). Summer Inst Ling.

Vocabulario Ocaina. Ilo M. Leach. (Peruvian Linguistic Ser: No. 4). 176p. (Span.). 1969. microfiche (2) 4.00 (ISBN 0-88312-364-9). Summer Inst Ling.

Vocabulario Politico Republicano y Franquista, 1931-1971. Miguel A. Rebollo Torio. 184p. (Span.). 1978. 24.95 (ISBN 84-7366-072-2, S-50122). French & Eur.

Vocabulario Popoluca de Sayula. Lawrence Clark & Nancy Clark. (Vocabularios Indigenas Ser.: No. 4). 165p. (Span.). 1960. microfiche (2) 4.00 (ISBN 0-88312-365-7). Summer Inst Ling.

Vocabulario Practico De la Biblia. Anton Grabner Haider. 892p. (Span.). 1975. 59.95 (ISBN 84-254-0964-0, S-50206). French & Eur.

Vocabulario Puertorriqueno. De Rosario. (Span.). 1966. 10.95 (ISBN 0-87751-010-5, Pub by Troutman Press). E Torres & Sons.

Vocabulario Quechua del Pastaza. Peter Landerman. (Peruvian Linguistic Ser.: No. 8). 114p. (Span.). 1973. pap. 3.00x (ISBN 0-88312-664-8); microfiche (2) 4.00 (ISBN 0-88312-366-5). Summer Inst Ling.

Vocabulario Sonorense. Horacio Sobrrzo. (Span.). 29.95 (ISBN 0-686-56691-2, S-12361). French & Eur.

Vocabulario Superior. Gaston Fernandez De La Torriente. 176p. (Span.). 1975. pap. 8.75 (ISBN 84-359-0124-6). French & Eur.

Vocabulario Tecnico De Contabilidad Moderna. Abiud Ramos-Ramos. LC 77-11200. (Span.). 1978. pap. 8.75 (ISBN 0-8477-2629-0). U of PR Pr.

Vocabulario Teologico del Evangelio de Saint Juan. J. Mateos Alvarez. 310p. (Span.). 1980. pap. 24.95 (ISBN 84-7057-270-9, S-33107). French & Eur.

Vocabulario Totonaco de la Sierra: Castellano-Totonaco, Totonaco-Castellano. Herman P. Aschmann. (Vocabularios Indigenas Ser.: No. 7). 171p. (Span.). 1962. pap. 11.95x (ISBN 0-88312-666-4); microfiche (2) 4.00 (ISBN 0-88312-568-4). Summer Inst Ling.

Vocabulario Tzeltal de Bachajon. Florence Gerdel & Marianna Slocum. (Vocabularios Indigenas Ser.: No. 13). 215p. (Span.). 1965. microfiche (3) 6.00 (ISBN 0-88312-589-7). Summer Inst Ling.

Vocabulario Vial. OAS General Secretariat. 368p. (Eng., Span., Fr. & Port.). 1979. text ed. 15.00 (ISBN 0-8270-1332-9). OAS.

Vocabulario y Refranero Criollo. Tito Saubidet. (Span.). 95.00 (ISBN 0-686-56666-1, S-33072). French & Eur.

Vocabularium Polyglottum Vitae Silvarum. R. Litschauer. 126p. (Lat., Eng., Ger., Fr., Span. & Romanian.). 1955. 55.00 (ISBN 0-686-56473-1, M-7679, Pub. by P. Parey). French & Eur.

Vocabularium Saxonicum. L. Nowell. Ed. by A. Marckwardt. (Lat.). Repr. of 1952 ed. 20.00 (ISBN 0-527-67800-7). Kraus Repr.

Vocabulary. Patricia Dunn-Rankin. (Illus.). 1978. text ed. 18.95 (ISBN 0-07-018268-X, C). McGraw.

Vocabulary. 2nd ed. Patricia Dunn-Rankin. 1984. text ed. 18.95 (ISBN 0-07-018278-7). McGraw.

Vocabulary. Lillian Lieberman. (Reading Superstar Ser.). 64p. (gr. 2-5). 1987. 6.95 (ISBN 0-912107-68-5). Monday Morning Bks.

Vocabulary. Jack Rudman. (Teachers License Examination Ser.: G-5). (Cloth bdg. avail. on request). pap. 13.95 (ISBN 0-8373-8195-9). Natl Learning.

Vocabulary Analysis of Gadda's "Pasticciaccio". Joan McConnell. LC 73-81570. (Romance Monographs: No. 2). 1973. 20.00x (ISBN 84-399-0685-4); pap. 15.00x (ISBN 0-686-31729-7). Romance.

Vocabulary & Composition Through Pleasurable Reading, Bk. 3. Harold Levine. (Orig.). (gr. 10-12). 1976. pap. text ed. 9.83 (ISBN 0-87720-377-6); wkbk. 11.00 (ISBN 0-87720-306-7). AMSCO Sch.

Vocabulary & Composition Through Pleasurable Reading, Bk. 4. Harold Levine. (gr. 11-12). 1978. pap. text ed. 9.83 (ISBN 0-87720-378-4); wkbk. 10.67 (ISBN 0-87720-376-8). AMSCO Sch.

Vocabulary & Composition Through Pleasurable Reading, Bk. 5. Harold Levine. (gr. 10-12). 1979. pap. text ed. 9.83 (ISBN 0-87720-385-7); wkbk. 10.67 (ISBN 0-87720-379-2). AMSCO Sch.

Vocabulary & Composition Through Pleasurable Reading, Bk. 6. Harold Levine. (gr. 11-12). 1979. pap. text ed. 9.83 (ISBN 0-87720-388-1); wkbk. 10.67 (ISBN 0-87720-387-3). AMSCO Sch.

Vocabulary & Notes to Ba Jin's Jia: An Aid for Reading the Novel. Cornelius C. Kubler. LC 76-369994. (East Asia Papers: No. 8). 300p. 1976. 7.00 (ISBN 0-939657-08-2). Cornell East Asia Pgm.

Vocabulary & Style of the Soliloquies & Dialogues of St. Augustine, Vol. 42. Mary Inez Bogan. (Patristic Studies). 238p. 1984. Repr. of 1935 ed. 28.00x (ISBN 0-939738-27-9). Zubal Inc.

Vocabulary & Syntax of the Old English Version in the Paris Psalter. John D. Tinkler. LC 68-29824. (Janua Linguarum, Ser. Practica: No. 67). (Illus.). 92p. (Orig., Anglo-Saxon.). 1971. pap. text ed. 12.80x (ISBN 90-2791-895-3). Mouton.

Vocabulary: Applied Linguistic Perspectives. Ronald Carter. (Aspects of English Ser.). 272p. 1987. text ed. 39.95x (ISBN 0-04-418007-1); pap. text ed. 14.95x (ISBN 0-04-418008-X). Unwin Hyman.

Vocabulary Arranged for the Instruction of the Deaf & Dumb. Wm. Vaughan. 69.95 (ISBN 0-8490-1265-1). Gordon Pr.

Vocabulary Boosters I. Nancy Gill. (gr. 3-6). 1985. pap. 5.95 (ISBN 0-8224-7280-5). D S Lake Pubs.

Vocabulary Boosters II. Nancy Gill. (gr. 3-6). 1985. pap. 5.95 (ISBN 0-8224-7281-3). D S Lake Pubs.

Vocabulary Builder & Verbal Aptitiude Test Guide. 6th ed. Walter J. Miller & Elizabeth Morse-Cluley. LC 83-3844. 224p. (Orig.). 1983. pap. 6.95 (ISBN 0-668-05807-2, 5807). Arco.

Vocabulary Builder for the SAT. Edward J. Deptula & Thomas H. Martinson. 1986. pap. 6.95 (ISBN 0-668-06369-6). P-H.

Vocabulary Builder: The Practicallly Painless Way to a Larger Vocabulary. Judi Kesselman-Turkel & Franklynn Peterson. 168p. 4.95 (ISBN 0-8092-5650-9). Contemp Bks.

Vocabulary Building: A Process Approach. Edgar Dale & Joseph O'Rourke. Ed. by Walter B. Barbe. 1986. 14.95 (ISBN 0-88309-122-4, 280199). Zaner Bloser.

Vocabulary Building & Word Study. Mary Lewick-Wallace. Ed. by Alton L. Raygor. (Communication Skills Ser.). 240p. (Orig.). 1981. pap. 19.95 (ISBN 0-07-067902-9). McGraw.

Vocabulary Building at the College Level. 2nd ed. Elton P. Henley. 256p. 1978. pap. text ed. 19.95 (ISBN 0-8403-1088-9). Kendall-Hunt.

Vocabulary Building in Indonesian: An Advanced Reader. Soenjono Dardjowidjojo. LC 82-90652. (Monographs in International Studies, Southeast Asia: No. 64). 660p. 1984. pap. text ed. 18.00x (ISBN 0-89680-118-7, Ohio U Ctr Intl). Ohio U Pr.

Vocabulary Building: Syllabus, Level III. Diana C. Watson & Hernan Hurtado. 1973. pap. text ed. 6.25 (ISBN 0-89420-007-0, 270043); cassette recordings 70.20 (ISBN 0-89420-194-8, 270000). Natl Book.

Vocabulary Building: Syllabus, Level IV. Diana C. Watson & Malcom Watson. 1975. pap. text ed. 6.25 (ISBN 0-89420-039-9, 270053); cassette recordings 69.80 (ISBN 0-89420-195-6, 270200). Natl Book.

Vocabulary Change: A Study of Variation in Regional Words in Eight of the Southern States. Gordon R. Wood. LC 76-86183. 407p. 1971. 19.50x (ISBN 0-8093-0433-3). S Ill U Pr.

Vocabulary Change in the Upper Midwest see Investigation of Urban Speech.

Vocabulary Control for Information Retrieval. 1st ed. F. Wilfrid Lancaster. LC 78-186528. (Illus.). xiv, 233p. 1972. text ed. 27.50 (ISBN 0-87815-006-4). Info Resources.

Vocabulary Control for Information Retrieval. 2nd ed. F. Wilfrid Lancaster. LC 84-82260. (Illus.). xvii, 270p. 1986. text ed. 27.50 (ISBN 0-87815-053-6). Info Resources.

Vocabulary de la Fonderie, Francais-Anglais. (Fr. & Eng., French-English Vocabulary of Foundries). pap. 19.95 (ISBN 0-686-56719-6, M-6557). French & Eur.

Vocabulary de la Fonderie, Francais-Anglais. (Fr. & Eng., French-English Vocabulary of Foundries). pap. 19.95 (ISBN 0-686-56720-X, M-6556). French & Eur.

Vocabulary Development. Gail Aemmer. (Stick-Out-Your-Neck Ser.). (Illus.). 20p. (gr. 5-6). 1985. pap. 5.95 (ISBN 0-88724-123-9, CD-0551). Carson-Dellos.

Vocabulary Development. Gail Aemmer. (Stick-Out-Your-Neck Ser.). (Illus.). 20p. (gr. 3-4). 1985. pap. 5.95 (ISBN 0-88724-122-0, CD-0550). Carson-Dellos.

Vocabulary Development. Gail Aemmer. (Stick-Out-Your-Neck Ser.). (Illus.). 20p. (gr. 1-2). 1985. pap. 5.95 (ISBN 0-88724-120-4, CD-0548). Carson-Dellos.

Vocabulary Development. Dale McMaster. (Language Arts Ser.). 24p. (gr. 6-9). 1976. wkbk. 5.00 (ISBN 0-8209-0312-4, VD-4). ESP.

Vocabulary Development. Anamary Slawter. (Let's Learn Ser.). (Illus.). 32p. (gr. 3-4). 1984. pap. 1.98 (ISBN 0-88724-073-9, CD-7016). Carson-Dellos.

Vocabulary Development in the Classroom. Lee C. Deighton. LC 59-8372. pap. 15.00 (ISBN 0-8357-9611-6, 2015778). Bks Demand UMI.

Vocabulary Development Through Language Awareness. Kristbjorg E. O'Harra. (Illus.). 192p. 1984. pap. text ed. write for info (ISBN 0-13-942946-8). P-H.

Vocabulary Drills, Middle Level. Edward Fry. (Illus.). 224p. 1986. pap. text ed. 7.20x (ISBN 0-89061-448-2). Jamestown Pubs.

Vocabulary Drills, Middle Level. Edward Fry. (Illus.). 224p. 1986. pap. text ed. 7.20x (ISBN 0-89061-447-4). Jamestown Pubs.

Vocabulary Expansion I. Dorothy Rubin. 416p. 1982. pap. text ed. write for info. (ISBN 0-02-404220-X). Macmillan.

Vocabulary Expansion II. Dorothy Rubin. 288p. 1982. pap. text ed. write for info. (ISBN 0-02-404240-4). Macmillan.

Vocabulary for Adults. Jack S. Romine. LC 75-17660. (Self-Teaching Guides Ser.). 221p. 1975. pap. text ed. 8.95 (ISBN 0-471-73285-0, Pub. by Wiley Pr). Wiley.

Vocabulary for Advanced Reading Comprehension: The Keyword Approach. John T. Crow. (Illus.). 288p. 1986. pap. text ed. write for info (ISBN 0-13-942988-3). P H.

Vocabulary for Annie Brigitte Gilles Tardos. Jackson MacLow. 1980. ltd. signed ed. 50.00 (ISBN 0-930794-73-7). Station Hill Pr.

Vocabulary for College Reading & Writing. Howard D. Peet & James E. Coomber. 176p. 1984. pap. text ed. write for info. (ISBN 0-574-23115-3, 13-6115); instr's. guide avail. (ISBN 0-574-23116-1, 13-6116); test bank avail. SRA.

Vocabulary for Enjoyment, Bk. III. Levine et al. (gr. 7-9). 1988. wkbk. 11.33 (ISBN 0-87720-670-8). Amsco Sch.

Vocabulary for Enjoyment, Bk. I. Levine et al. (gr. 6-7). 1986. wkbk. 8.33 (ISBN 0-87720-662-7). AMSCO Sch.

Vocabulary for Enjoyment, Bk. 2. Levine et al. (YA) (gr. 7-9). 1987. wkbk. 10.33 (ISBN 0-87720-663-5). AMSCO Sch.

Vocabulary for Fiber Optics & Lightwave Communications. 40.00 (ISBN 0-686-32964-3). Info Gatekeepers.

Vocabulary for the College-Bound Student. 2nd ed. Harold Levine. (Orig.). (gr. 11-12). 1982. wkbk. 9.75 (ISBN 0-87720-442-X). AMSCO Sch.

Vocabulary for the College-Bound Student. 2nd ed. Harold Levine. (gr. 11-12). 1983. text ed. 12.67 (ISBN 0-87720-447-0, 262H); pap. 8.08 (ISBN 0-87720-446-2, 262P); key 1.66 (ISBN 0-317-03340-9). AMSCO Sch.

Vocabulary for the High School Student. 2nd ed. Harold Levine. (gr. 10-12). 1982. wkbk. 9.75 (ISBN 0-87720-437-3). AMSCO Sch.

Vocabulary for the High School Student. 2nd ed. Harold Levine. (gr. 9-10). 1983. text ed. 12.67 (ISBN 0-87720-445-4, 255H); pap. 8.08 (ISBN 0-87720-444-6). AMSCO Sch.

Vocabulary Foundations for the College Student. Harold Levine & Robert T. Levine. (Orig.). 1980. pap. text ed. 11.25 (ISBN 0-87720-962-6). AMSCO Sch.

Vocabulary Growth in the First Two Years see Speech Development of a Bilingual Child.

Vocabulary Idea Book. Anthony D. Fredericks. 1986. pap. 8.95 (ISBN 0-673-18343-2). Scott F.

Vocabulary Improvement. 3rd ed. Nancy Davis. 1978. pap. text ed. 22.95 (ISBN 0-07-015543-7). McGraw.

Vocabulary in Context. English Language Institute Staff. (Intensive Course in English Ser.). 1964. pap. 7.95x (ISBN 0-472-08305-8). U of Mich Pr.

Vocabulary in Context: Getting the Precise Meaning. Walter Pauk. (Skill at a Time Ser). 64p. (gr. 9 up). 1975. pap. text ed. 4.00x (ISBN 0-89061-021-5, ST-1). Jamestown Pubs.

Vocabulary Made Easy. Visual Education Corporation Staff. (Illus.). 136p. (gr. 9 up). 1984. wkbk. 9.24 (ISBN 0-07-039665-5). McGraw.

Vocabulary Made Easy for Spanish Speakers. Muriel Hernandez De Prieto. LC 76-3732. 96p. (Orig., Prog. Bk.). 1976. pap. text ed. 3.75 (ISBN 0-8477-2622-3). U of PR Pr.

Vocabulary Made Easy for Spanish Speakers: Teacher's Guide. Muriel H. Prieto. LC 76-3732. 1978. pap. text ed. 3.00 (ISBN 0-8477-2635-5). U of PR Pr.

Vocabulary Mastery. Scott Bornstein. (Illus.). 272p. (YA) (gr. 9-12). 1982. 22.50 (ISBN 0-9602610-1-X); pap. 14.95 (ISBN 0-9602610-2-8). Bornstein Memory.

Vocabulary Norms for Deaf Children. George R. Guilfoyle & Toby Silverman-Dresner. LC 72-83498. (Lexington School Ser.: Book 7). 1972. softcover 8.00 (ISBN 0-88200-060-8, C2344). Alexander Graham.

Vocabulary of Anglo-Irish. James M. Clark. LC 73-12699. (Eng. & Irish.). 1917. lib. bdg. 27.00 (ISBN 0-8414-3394-1). Folcroft.

Vocabulary of Bernardin De Saint-Pierre & Its Relation to the French Romantic School. J. N. Ware. Repr. of 1927 ed. 14.00 (ISBN 0-384-65803-2). Johnson Repr.

Vocabulary of Common Japanese Words. A. Rose-Innes. (Japanese.). 3.95 (ISBN 0-88710-123-2). Yale Far Eastern Pubns.

Vocabulary of Common Terms for Direct Marketing of Training Programs. 2nd ed. Don M. Schrello. 32p. (Orig.). 1985. pap. 8.95 (ISBN 0-935823-05-0). Schrello Market.

Vocabulary of First-Grade Children. Alden J. Moe et al. 172p. 1982. 20.50 (ISBN 0-398-04623-9). C C Thomas.

Vocabulary of High School Latin. Gonzalez Lodge. LC 73-177003. (Columbia University. Teachers College. Contributions to Education: No. 9). (Lat.). Repr. of 1912 ed. 22.50 (ISBN 0-404-55009-6). AMS Pr.

Vocabulary of Intrigue in Roman Comedy. Blanche Brotherton. Ed. by Commager Steele. (Latin Poetry Ser.). 34.00 (ISBN 0-8240-2983-6). Garland Pub.

Vocabulary of Jewish Life. Abraham M. Heller. 366p. 1967. 8.95 (ISBN 0-88482-663-5). Hebrew Pub.

Vocabulary of Marble Playing. K. B. Harder. Bd. with Position of the Charleston Dialect. R. I. McDavid. (Publications of the American Dialect Society: No. 23). 61p. 1955. pap. 7.15 (ISBN 0-8173-0623-4). U of Ala Pr.

Vocabulary of Mental Aberration in Roman Comedy & Petronius. Dorothy M. Paschall. (Language Dissertations: No. 27). 1939. pap. 16.00 (ISBN 0-527-00773-0). Kraus Repr.

Vocabulary of Modern Spoken Greek (English-Greek & Greek-English) Donald C. Swanson. Ed. by Theofanis G. Stavrou. (Modern Greek History & Culture Ser.). 1982. 15.00 (ISBN 0-935476-11-3). Nostos Bks.

Vocabulary of Organic Chemistry. Milton Orchin et al. LC 79-25930. 609p. 1980. 51.95 (ISBN 0-471-04491-1, Pub. by Wiley-Interscience). Wiley.

Vocabulary of Race Relations in a Prison see Terms Used in Whitewater Kayaking in Colorado.

Vocabulary of Rotokas-Pidgin-English. Irwin Firchow & Jacqueline Firchow. 1973. microfiche (5) 10.00 (ISBN 0-88312-389-4). Summer Inst Ling.

Vocabulary of Six East African Languages. Ludwig Krapf. 74p. 1850. Repr. text ed. 24.84x (ISBN 0-576-11612-2, Pub by Gregg Intl England). Gregg Intl.

Vocabulary of Terms on Measurement & Instrumentation. Ed. by G. Hofmann. 202p. 1985. pap. text ed. 57.00 (ISBN 0-941743-33-0). Nova Sci Pubs.

Vocabulary of the Greek New Testament. James H. Moulton & George Milligan. (Gr.). 1949. 35.95 (ISBN 0-8028-2178-2). Eerdmans.

Vocabulary of the Greek Testament: Illustrated from the Papyri & Other Non-Literary Sources, 2 vols. J. H. Moulton & G. Milligan. 1977. lib. bdg. 250.00 (ISBN 0-8490-2800-0). Gordon Pr.

Vocabulary of the Institutiones of Cassiodorus with Special Advertence to the Technical Terminology & Its Sources, No. 9. Mary Gratia Ennis. (Studies in Medieval & Renaissance Latin). 186p. 1983. Repr. of 1939 ed. 38.00x (ISBN 0-939738-24-4). Zubal Inc.

Vocabulary of the Language of San Antonio Mission, California. Buenaventura Sitjar. LC 10-26367. (Library of American Linguistics: No. 7). (Span.). Repr. of 1861 ed. 28.50 (ISBN 0-404-50987-8). AMS Pr.

Vocabulary of the Lau Language, Big Mala, Solomon Islands. Walter G. Ivens. LC 75-35127. (Laotian.). Repr. of 1935 ed. 12.00 (ISBN 0-404-14143-9). AMS Pr.

Vocabulary of the Mangaian Language. F. W. Christian. (BMB Ser.). pap. 10.00 (ISBN 0-527-02114-8). Kraus Repr.

Vocabulary of the Shoshone Language. 2nd ed. George W. Hill. 40p. pap. 4.50 (ISBN 0-933046-05-7). Little Red Hen.

Vocabulary One Thousand: With Words in Context. 2nd ed. Morton J. Cronin. 180p. 1981. pap. text ed. 13.00 net (ISBN 0-15-594987-X, HC); test booklet avail. (ISBN 0-15-594988-8). HarBraceJ.

Vocabulary; or, Collection of Words & Phrases, Which Have Been Supposed to Be Peculiar to the United States of America; to Which Is Prefixed an Essay on the Present State of the English Language in the United States, 2 vols. in 1. John Pickering. Bd. with Letter to John Pickering on the Subject of His Vocabulary or Collection of Words & Phrases. Noah Webster. LC 70-178096. vii, 266p. 1972. Repr. of 1817 ed. lib. bdg. 24.00 (ISBN 0-8337-2752-4). B Franklin.

Vocabulary or Phrase Book of the Mutsun Language of Alta California. Felipe Arroyo De La Cuesta. (Library of American Linguistics: Vol. 8). (Catalan.). Repr. of 1862 ed. 28.50 (ISBN 0-404-50988-6). AMS Pr.

Vocabulary, Reading, & Reasoning. Martha Efurd & Margaret Newell. 101p. 1984. pap. text ed. 12.00x (ISBN 0-913507-03-2). New Forums.

Vocabulary Resources for the College Student. Harold Levine & Robert Levine. (Orig.). 1980. pap. 11.25 (ISBN 0-87720-961-8). AMSCO Sch.

Vocabulary Sampler. rev. ed. Beverly L. Ritter & Kim C. Davis. (Computer-Compatible Machine Shorthand for Expanding Careers Ser.). 116p. 1986. pap. text ed. 14.00 (ISBN 0-938643-06-1); tchr's. ed. 10.00 (ISBN 0-938643-08-8). Stenotype Educ.

Vocabulary, Spelling & Grammar. 10th ed. Walter J. Miller & Elizabeth Morse-Cluley. LC 83-3843. 240p. 1983. pap. 6.95 (ISBN 0-668-05806-4). Arco.

Vocabulary Strategies for Success. Lee A. Rinsky & Betty J. O'Brien. 180p. 1985. pap. text ed. 16.00x (ISBN 0-89787-514-1). Gorsuch Scarisbrick.

Vocabulary Study. Dale McMasters. (Language Arts Ser.). 24p. (gr. 5-7). 1976. wkbk. 5.00 (ISBN 0-8209-0311-6, VD-3). ESP.

Vocabulary Through Pleasurable Reading, Bk. 1. Harold Levine. (Orig.). (gr. 7-10). 1974. pap. text ed. 9.83 (ISBN 0-87720-373-3); wkbk. 11.00 (ISBN 0-87720-368-7). AMSCO Sch.

Vocabulary Through Pleasurable Reading, Bk. 2. Harold Levine. (gr. 7-12). 1974. pap. text ed. 9.83 (ISBN 0-87720-374-1); wkbk. 10.67 (ISBN 0-87720-369-5). AMSCO Sch.

Vocabulary Workbook: Prefixes, Roots & Suffixes for ESL Students. Anne Farid. 240p. 1985. pap. text ed. write for info (ISBN 0-13-942913-1). P-H.

Vocabulearn: Chinese (Mandarin) - English, Level I. Penton Overseas, Inc. Staff. Tr. by Linguatheque of L. A. 36p. 1986. incl. 2 cass. 14.95 (ISBN 0-939001-60-8). Penton Overseas.

Vocabulearn: Chinese (Mandarin) - English, Level II. Penton Overseas, Inc. Staff. Tr. by Linguatheque of L. A. 36p. 1987. incl. 2 cass. 14.95 (ISBN 0-939001-62-4). Penton Overseas.

Vocabulearn: French - English, Level I. Penton Overseas, Inc. Staff. Tr. by Linguatheque of L. A. 36p. 1986. incl. 2 cass. 14.95 (ISBN 0-939001-01-2). Penton Overseas.

Vocabulearn: French - English, Level II. Penton Overseas, Inc. Staff. Tr. by Linguatheque of L. A. 36p. 1987. incl. 2 cass. 14.95 (ISBN 0-939001-55-1). Penton Overseas.

Vocabulearn: French - Spanish, Level I. Penton Overseas, Inc. Staff. Tr. by Linguatheque of L. A. 36p. 1986. incl. 2 cass. 14.95 (ISBN 0-939001-02-0). Penton Overseas.

Vocabulearn: French-Spanish Level II. rev. ed. Penton Overseas, Inc. Staff. Ed. by Linguatheque of L.A. Staff. (Vocabulearn Ser.). (Illus.). 36p. 1987. pap. 14.95 (ISBN 0-939001-65-9). Penton Overseas.

Vocabulearn: German - English, Level I. Penton Overseas, Inc. Staff. Tr. by Linguatheque of L. A. 36p. 1986. incl. 2 cass. 14.95 (ISBN 0-939001-30-6). Penton Overseas.

Vocabulearn: German - English, Level II. Penton Overseas, Inc. Staff. Tr. by Linguatheque of L. A. 36p. 1987. incl. 2 cass. 14.95 (ISBN 0-939001-58-6). Penton Overseas.

Vocabulearn: Italian - English, Level I. Penton Overseas, Inc. Staff. Tr. by Linguatheque of L. A. 36p. 1986. incl. 2 cass. 14.95 (ISBN 0-939001-20-9). Penton Overseas.

Vocabulearn: Italian - English, Level II. Penton Overseas, Inc. Staff. Tr. by Linguatheque of L. A. 36p. 1987. incl. 2 cass. 14.95 (ISBN 0-939001-57-8). Penton Overseas.

Vocabulearn: Japanese - English, Level I. Penton Overseas, Inc. Staff. Tr. by Linguatheque of L. A. 36p. 1986. incl. 2 cass. 14.95 (ISBN 0-939001-40-3). Penton Overseas.

Vocabulearn: Japanese - English, Level II. Penton Overseas, Inc. Staff. Tr. by Linguatheque of L. A. 36p. 1987. incl. 2 cass. 14.95 (ISBN 0-939001-59-4). Penton Overseas.

Vocabulearn: Korean - English, Level I. Penton Overseas, Inc. Staff. Tr. by Lingutheque of L. A. 36p. 1986. incl. 2 cass. 14.95 (ISBN 0-939001-50-0). Penton Overseas.

Vocabulearn: Korean - English, Level II. Penton Overseas, Inc. Staff. Tr. by Linguatheque of L. A. 36p. 1987. incl. 2 cass. 14.95 (ISBN 0-939001-61-6). Penton Overseas.

Vocabulearn: Portugese (South American)-English Level II. rev. ed. Penton Overseas, Inc. Staff. Ed. by Linguatheque of L. A. Staff. (Vocabulearn Ser.). 36p. 1987. pap. 14.95 (ISBN 0-939001-64-0). Penton Overseas.

Vocabulearn: Portugese (South American)-English Level I. rev. ed. Penton Overseas, Inc. Staff. Ed. by Linguatheque of L. A. Staff. (Vocabulearn Ser.). 36p. 1987. pap. 14.95 (ISBN 0-939001-80-2). Penton Overseas.

Vocabulearn: Russian - English, Level I. Penton Overseas, Inc. Staff. Tr. by Linguatheque of L. A. 1986. incl. 2 cass. 14.95 (ISBN 0-939001-70-5). Penton Overseas.

Vocabulearn: Russian - English, Level II. Penton Overseas, Inc. Staff. Tr. by Linguatheque of L. A. 36p. 1987. incl. 2 cass. 14.95 (ISBN 0-939001-63-2). Penton Overseas.

Vocabulearn: Spanish - English, Level I. Penton Overseas, Inc. Staff. Tr. by Linguatheque of L. A. 36p. 1986. incl. 2 cass. 14.95 (ISBN 0-939001-10-1). Penton Overseas.

Vocabulearn: Spanish - English, Level II. Penton Overseas, Inc. Staff. Tr. by Linguatheque of L. A. 36p. 1987. incl. 2 cass. 14.95 (ISBN 0-939001-56-X). Penton Overseas.

Vocal & Literary Interpretation of the Bible. S. E. Curry. 1979. Repr. of 1903 ed. 37.00 (ISBN 0-8414-9988-8). Folcroft.

Vocal & Literary Interpretation of the Bible. S. S. Curry. 1909. 37.50 (ISBN 0-8274-3677-7). R West.

Vocal Chamber Music: A Selected Bibliography. Virginia Dunlap & Barbara Winchester. LC 83-49309. (Library of the Humanities). 178p. 1985. lib. bdg. 26.00 (ISBN 0-8240-9003-9). Garland Pub.

Vocal Development Through Organic Imagery. 2nd, rev., enl. ed. William D. Leyerle. LC 78-103579. (Illus.). 189p. 1986. pap. 11.95 (ISBN 0-9602296-6-3). Leyerle Pubns.

Vocal Expression. Katherine J. Everts. 330p. 1979. Repr. lib. bdg. 20.00 (ISBN 0-89987-201-8). Darby Bks.

Vocal Fold Histopathology: A Symposium. Ed. by John A. Kirchner. LC 86-8208. (Illus.). 138p. 1986. text ed. 45.00 (ISBN 0-316-49456-9, 494569). College-Hill.

Vocal Fold Physiology. Ed. by Kenneth N. Stevens & Minoru Hirano. 421p. 1981. 24.50 (ISBN 0-86008-281-4, Pub. by U of Toyko Japan). Columbia U Pr.

Vocal Fold Physiology: A Laryngeal Function in Phonation & respiration. Ed. by Thomas Baer et al. LC 86-24512. (Vocal Fold Physiology Ser.). (Illus.). 598p. (Orig.). 1987. pap. text ed. 49.50 (ISBN 0-316-34828-7, 348287). College-Hill.

Vocal Fold Physiology: Biomechanics, Acoustics & Phonatory Control Conference Proceedings. Pref. by Ingo R. Titze & Ronald C. Scherer. 327p. 1985. 39.50 (ISBN 0-936947-53-5). Denver Ctr Performing Arts.

Vocal Fold Physiology: Contemporary Research & Clinical Issues. Ed. by Diane M. Bless & James H. Abbs. LC 83-1899. (Illus.). 482p. 1983. pap. 47.00 (ISBN 0-316-09956-2). College-Hill.

Vocal Gymnastics for the Pop Singer. Al Berkman. 1979. 10.00 (ISBN 0-934972-07-9). Melrose Bk Co.

Vocal Melodies. Bartok. (Rumanian Folk Music Ser: Vol. 2). lib. bdg. 53.00 (ISBN 90-247-0624-6, Pub. by Martinus Nijhoff Netherlands). Kluwer Academic.

Vocal Music. Philip L. Miller. LC 78-94. (Guide to Long-Playing Records Ser.: Vol. 2). 1978. Repr. of 1955 ed. lib. bdg. 26.25x (ISBN 0-313-20295-8, GULP02). Greenwood.

Vocal Music Education. Kenneth E. Miller. (Illus.). 352p. 1988. text ed. 32.00 (ISBN 0-13-942996-4). P-H.

Vocal Music from Fifteen Twelve to Sixteen Fifty, Vol. 2: Of the Hague Municipal Museum Catalogue of the Music Library. Marie Charbon. Ed. by C. C. Von Gleich. LC 73-18245. (Music Ser.). 1974. Repr. lib. bdg. 39.50 (ISBN 0-306-77222-1). Da Capo.

Vocal Physiology: Voice Production, Mechanisms & Functions. Ed. by Osamu Fujimura. (Vocal Fold Physiology Ser.: Vol. 2). (Illus.). 524p. 1988. text ed. 95.00 (ISBN 0-88167-389-7). Raven.

Vocal Resonance: Its Source & Command. M. Barbereux-Parry. 1979. Repr. of 1941 ed. 9.50 (ISBN 0-8158-0380-X). Chris Mass.

Vocal Sight Reading Tests for Treble Voices. Stuart Wade. pap. 1.50 (ISBN 0-8008-8021-8, Crescendo). Taplinger.

Vocal Solos for Christian Churches: A Descriptive Reference of Solo Music for the Church Year. 3rd ed. Noni Espina. LC 84-51398. 256p. 25.00 (ISBN 0-8108-1730-6). Scarecrow.

Vocal Sound. Barbara K. Sable. (Illus.). 224p. 1982. pap. 24.00 ref. ed. (ISBN 0-13-942979-4). P-H.

Vocal Trax: All My Loving & Other Beatles Hits. (Orig.). 1988. pap. 9.95 (ISBN 0-88188-919-9, 00367040). H Leonard Pub Corp.

Vocal Trax: Let It Be & Other Beatles Hits. (Orig.). 1988. pap. 9.95 (ISBN 0-88188-920-2, 00368285). H Leonard Pub Corp.

Vocal Trax: Madonna Hits. (Orig.). 1988. pap. 9.95 (ISBN 0-88188-924-5, 00368460). H Leonard Pub Corp.

Vocal Trax: Pop Hits. (Orig.). 1988. pap. 9.95 (ISBN 0-88188-923-7, 00368865). H Leonard Pub Corp.

Vocal Trax: Sounds of Madonna. (Orig.). 1988. pap. 9.95 (ISBN 0-88188-921-0, 00369810). H Leonard Pub Corp.

Vocal Trax: Yesterday & Other Beatles Hits. (Orig.). 1988. pap. 9.95 (ISBN 0-88188-922-9, 00369935). H Leonard Pub Corp.

Vocal Truth: Some of the Things I Teach. E. Herbert-Caesari. 1979. 6.95 (ISBN 0-8008-8027-7, Crescendo). Taplinger.

Vocal Wisdom. William E. Brown & Giovanni B. Lamperti. Ed. by Lillian Strongin. 1957. (Crescendo); pap. 5.95 (ISBN 0-8008-8023-4, Crescendo). Taplinger.

Vocalian Organ. New York Organ Co. (Illus.). 1888. pap. 5.00x. Organ Lit.

Vocalised Talmudic Manuscripts in the Cambridge Genizah Collections: Taylor-Schechter Old Series, Vol. 1. Shelomo Morag. (Cambridge University Library Genizan Ser.: No. 4). 60p. 1988. Vol. I: Taylor-Schechter Old Series. 49.50 (ISBN 0-521-26863-X). Cambridge U Pr.

Vocalism of Romantic Words in Chaucer. Ruben Nojd. LC 74-23653. 1974. Repr. of 1919 ed. lib. bdg. 30.50 (ISBN 0-8414-6274-7). Folcroft.

Vocalism of Romantic Words in Chaucer. Ruben Nojd. 30.00 (ISBN 0-8274-3678-5). R West.

Vocalisme et le Consonantisme Francais. Donahue-Gaudet. 14.95 (ISBN 0-685-36654-5). French & Eur.

Vocalization of the Egyptian Syllabic Orthography. William F. Albright. (American Orient Ser.). 1934. pap. 16.00. Kraus Repr.

Vocalization Systems of Arabic, Hebrew & Aramaic: Their Phonetic & Phonemic Principles. Shelomo Morag. (Janua Linguarum, Ser. Minor: No. 13). 1972. pap. text ed. 8.80x (ISBN 0-686-22534-1). Mouton.

Vocation & Mission of the Laity in the Church & in the World Twenty Years after the Second Vatican Council (Instrumentum Laboris) General Secretariat of the Synod of Bishops. 72p. (Orig.). 1987. pap. 2.95 (ISBN 1-55586-165-2). US Catholic.

Vocation & Spirituality of the Director of Religious Education. 25p. 1980. 4.20 (ISBN 0-686-29244-8). Natl Cath Educ.

Vocation & Spirituality of the DRE. 25p. 1980. 4.20 (ISBN 0-318-20610-2). Natl Cath Educ.

Vocation of Man. Johann G. Fichte. Tr. by William Smith. LC 56-44104. 1956. pap. 5.99 scp (ISBN 0-672-60220-2, LLA50). Bobbs.

Vocation of Man. Johann G. Fichte. Tr. by Peter Preuss from Ger. (Hackett Classics Ser.). 1987. lib. bdg. 18.50 (ISBN 0-87220-038-8); pap. text ed. 5.45 (ISBN 0-87220-037-X). Hackett Pub.

Vocation of Man: Fichte. Ed. by Roderick M. Chisholm. 1956. pap. text ed. write for info. (ISBN 0-02-322530-0). Macmillan.

Vocation of Pearl Duncan. Moira Duff. 180p. (Orig.). 1984. pap. 6.95 (ISBN 0-7043-3897-1, Pub. by Quartet Bks). SAlem Hse Pubs.

Vocation of the Theologian. Ed. by Theodore W. Jennings, Jr. LC 84-48722. 160p. 1985. pap. 1.00 (ISBN 0-8006-1838-6, 1-1838). Fortress.

Vocational Adjustment of Disabled Persons. Brian Bolton. LC 82-7058. 272p. 1982. pap. 19.00x (ISBN 0-89079-122-8, 1195). Pro Ed.

Vocational & Personal Adjustments in Practical Nursing. 6th ed. Becker. (Illus.). 200p. 1990. pap. 15.95 (ISBN 0-8016-0393-5). Mosby.

Vocational & Personal Adjustments in Practical Nursing. 5th ed. Becker & Fendler. 1985. 15.95 (ISBN 0-8016-0573-3). Mosby.

Vocational & Technical Audiovisuals: A Teacher's Sourcebook. NICEM Staff. Ed. by J. C. Johnstone. 450p. (Orig.). 1986. pap. 49.95 (ISBN 0-89320-100-6). Natl Info Ctr NM.

Vocational Aspiration Levels of Adults. Harold A. Wren. LC 71-177619. (Columbia University. Teachers College. Contributions to Education: No. 855). Repr. of 1942 ed. 22.50 (ISBN 0-404-55855-0). AMS Pr.

Vocational Assessment & Work Preparation Centers for the Disabled. 3rd ed. 1974. 5.60 (ISBN 92-2-100993-9). Intl Labour Office.

Vocational Astrology: Personality & Potential. Sue Ann. LC 82-70041. 7.50 (ISBN 0-86690-028-4). Am Fed Astrologers.

Vocational Counseling: An Introduction for the Practitioner. Patricia M. Raskin. (Guidance & Counseling Ser.). 176p. 1987. pap. text ed. 15.95x (ISBN 0-8077-2860-8). Tchrs Coll.

Vocational Counselling & Guidance in the Federal Republic of Germany. Rev. ed. FESC. 1983. 24.00x (ISBN 0-907659-23-3, Pub. by FESC). State Mutual Bk.

Vocational Counselor. Jack Rudman. (Career Examination Ser.: C-1530). (Cloth bdg. avail. on request). pap. 14.00 (ISBN 0-8373-1530-1). Natl Learning.

Vocational Counselor Trainee. Jack Rudman. (Career Examination Ser.: C-1531). (Cloth bdg. avail. on request). pap. 14.00 (ISBN 0-8373-1531-X). Natl Learning.

Vocational Curriculum for Developmentally Disabled Persons. Paul Wehman & Philip J. McLaughlin. LC 79-16433. (Illus.). 253p. 1980. pap. 19.00x (ISBN 0-89079-118-X, 1156). Pro Ed.

Vocational Decision Workbook. Richard Z. Glerum & Donna J. Blake. 1977. 4.50x (ISBN 0-910328-14-5); guide 2.50. Carroll Pr.

Vocational Development & Guidance. W. Wesley Tennyson et al. 1974. 29.50x (ISBN 0-8422-7160-0). Irvington.

Vocational Development of Welfare-Supported Youth. Rea T. Alsup. LC 74-28606. 1975. soft bdg. 11.95. R & E Pubs.

Vocational Education: A Look into the Future. Richard Ruff & Bruce Shylo. 78p. 1981. 5.50 (ISBN 0-318-15588-5, RD207). Natl Ctr Res Voc Ed.

Vocational Education & Economic Development. National Center for Research in Vocational Education Staff. 44p. 1984. 4.95 (ISBN 0-318-22231-0, BB73). Natl Ctr Res Voc Ed.

Vocational Education & Economic Growth: Connections & Conundrums. Stuart Rosefeld. 22p. 1986. 3.00 (ISBN 0-318-22232-9, OC 112). Natl Ctr Res Voc Ed.

Vocational Education & the Public Schools: A Chief State School Officer's Perspective. Franklin B. Walter. 12p. 2.75 (ISBN 0-318-22233-7, OC117). Natl Ctr Res Voc Ed.

Vocational Education & Training in Denmark. FESC. 1985. 25.00x (ISBN 0-907659-28-4, Pub. by FESC). State Mutual Bk.

Vocational Education & Training in Sweden. FESC. 1984. 25.00x (ISBN 0-907659-03-9, Pub. by FESC). State Mutual Bk.

Vocational Education & Training in the Federal Republic of Germany. FESC. 1985. 25.00x (ISBN 0-907659-04-7, Pub. by FESC). State Mutual Bk.

Vocational Education & Training in the German Democratic Republic. FESC. 1985. 25.00x (ISBN 0-907659-21-7, Pub. by FESC). State Mutual Bk.

Vocational Education & Training in the Republic of Ireland. FESC. 1984. 25.00x (ISBN 0-907659-02-0, Pub. by FESC). State Mutual Bk.

Vocational Education & Youth Employment. George H. Copa. 73p. 1984. 7.25 (ISBN 0-318-22236-1, IN274). Natl Ctr Res Voc Ed.

Vocational Education: Concepts & Operations. 2nd ed. Calfrey C. Calhoun & Alton V. Finch. 352p. 1982. text ed. write for info. (ISBN 0-534-00996-4). Wadsworth Pub.

Vocational Education Evaluation & Assessment Process (VEEAP) Procedures & Training Handbook. Pennsylvania Department of Education Staff. 62p. (Orig.). 1983. pap. 6.50x (ISBN 0-317-06014-7). Material Dev.

Vocational Education Evaluation: Problems, Alternatives, Recommendations. William W. Stevenson. 61p. 1979. 4.50 (ISBN 0-318-15590-7, RD 182). Natl Ctr Res Voc Ed.

Vocational Education for a Changing Society. Harry Knutton. 19p. 1982. 2.20 (ISBN 0-318-22237-X, OC81). Natl Ctr Res Voc Ed.

Vocational Education for Gifted & Talented Students. Bruce G. Milne. 52p. 1982. 4.95 (ISBN 0-318-22238-8, IN236). Natl Ctr Res Voc Ed.

Vocational Education for High Technology. ERIC Clearinghouse on Adult, Career, & Vocational Education Staff. 69p. 1983. 4.95 (ISBN 0-318-22239-6, BB68). Natl Ctr Res Voc Ed.

Vocational Education for Immigrant & Minority Youth. Peggy Reubens. 42p. 1983. 4.25 (ISBN 0-318-22240-X, IN257). Natl Ctr Res Voc Ed.

Vocational Education for Migrant Youth. J. Steven Picou. 29p. 1982. 3.75 (ISBN 0-318-22241-8, IN238). Natl Ctr Res Voc Ed.

Vocational Education for Multihandicapped Youth with Cerebral Palsy. Paul Wehman et al. LC 88-7318. 256p. 1988. pap. text ed. 25.00 (ISBN 1-55766-003-4, 334). P H Brookes.

Vocational Education for Persons with Handicaps. Robert Gaylord-Ross. 480p. 1988. text ed. 27.95 (ISBN 0-87484-757-5). Mayfield Pub.

Vocational Education for Youth & Adults. Michael N. Sugarman & Albert J. Pautler. 147p. 1974. pap. text ed. 7.95x (ISBN 0-8422-0459-8). Irvington.

Vocational Education in Agriculture in Federally-Aided Secondary Schools: A Study of Its Instructional & Training Phases. Gustavus A. Schmidt. LC 75-177802. (Columbia University. Teachers College. Contributions to Education: No. 534). Repr. of 1932 ed. 22.50 (ISBN 0-404-55534-9). AMS Pr.

Vocational Education in an Information Age: Society at Risk? Anne Campbell. 20p. 1984. 3.00 (ISBN 0-318-22242-6, OC99). Natl Ctr Res Voc Ed.

Vocational Education in Corrections. Sherman R. Day & Mel R. McCane. 37p. 1982. 4.25 (ISBN 0-318-22243-4, IN237). Natl Ctr Res voc Ed.

Vocational Education in the Industrialization of Japan. 267p. 1988. pap. 30.00 (ISBN 92-808-0584-3, E.87.III.A.1). UN.

Vocational Education in the United States: Retrospect & Prospect. Robert M. Worthington. 26p. 1984. 3.00 (ISBN 0-318-22244-2, OC101). Natl Ctr Res Voc Ed.

Vocational Education: Teaching the Handicapped in Regular Classes. Ed. by Robert A. Weisgerber. LC 78-68174. 96p. 1978. pap. text ed. 4.25 (ISBN 0-86586-093-9). Coun Exc Child.

Vocational Education, Washington 1938. John D. Russell. Ed. by Sheila M. Rothman & David J. Rothman. (Women & Children First Ser.). 325p. 1986. lib. bdg. 40.00 (ISBN 0-8240-7672-9). Garland Pub.

Vocational Entry-Skills for Secondary Students. W. Washburn. 1975. pap. 5.00x wkbk (ISBN 0-87879-129-9); pap. 10.00x manual (ISBN 0-87879-128-0). Acad Therapy.

Vocational ESL Handbook. Joan Friedenberg & Curtis Bradley. 96p. 1984. pap. text ed. 10.95 (ISBN 0-88377-415-1). Newbury Hse.

Vocational Evaluation in Special Education. Norman C. Hursh & Allen F. Kerns. (Orig.). 1988. pap. text ed. 24.50 (ISBN 0-316-38331-7, 383317). College-Hill.

Vocational Evaluation, Work Adjustment & Independent Living for Severely Disabled People. Robert A. Lassiter et al. (Illus.). 458p. 1983. 41.25x (ISBN 0-398-04695-6). C C Thomas.

Vocational Guidance & Human Development. Ed. by Edwin L. Herr. LC 81-40850. 608p. 1982. lib. bdg. 40.50 (ISBN 0-8191-1955-5); pap. text ed. 23.50 (ISBN 0-8191-1956-3). U Pr of Amer.

Vocational Guidance Counselor. Jack Rudman. (Career Examination Ser.: C-1532). (Cloth bdg. avail. on request). pap. 14.00 (ISBN 0-8373-1532-8). Natl Learning.

Vocational Guidance in Catholic Secondary Schools: A Study of Developments & Present Status. Teresa G. Murray, Sr. LC 77-177098. (Columbia University. Teachers College. Contributions to Education: No. 754). Repr. of 1938 ed. 22.50 (ISBN 0-404-55754-6). AMS Pr.

Vocational Guidance of Youth. Meyer Bloomfield. LC 70-89151. (American Education: Its Men, Institutions & Ideas Ser). 1969. Repr. of 1911 ed. 13.00 (ISBN 0-405-01389-2). Ayer Co Pubs.

Vocational Guidance: Theory & Practice. W. P. Gothard. LC 84-23780. 198p. 1985. 29.00 (ISBN 0-7099-1161-0, Pub. by Croom Helm Ltd). Routledge Chapman & Hall.

Vocational Guidance Theory & Practice: Theory & Practice. W. P. Gothard. 208p. 1987. pap. text ed. 18.95x (ISBN 0-7099-1195-5, Pub. by Croom Helm UK). Routledge Chapman & Hall.

Vocational Habilitation of Severely Retarded Adults. G. Thomas Bellamy et al. LC 78-10161. (Illus.). 256p. 1979. pap. text ed. 19.00x (ISBN 0-936104-81-3, 1133). Pro Ed.

Vocational Interest Patterns. M. Irene Wightwick. LC 74-177641. (Columbia University. Teachers College. Contributions to Education: No. 900). Repr. of 1945 ed. 22.50 (ISBN 0-404-55900-X). AMS Pr.

Vocational Interests of High School Girls As Inventoried by the Strong & Manson Blanks. Grace E. Laleger. LC 76-176970. (Columbia University. Teachers College. Contributions to Education: No. 857). Repr. of 1942 ed. 22.50 (ISBN 0-404-55857-7). AMS Pr.

Vocational Interests of Men & Women. Edward K. Strong, Jr. 1943. 45.00x (ISBN 0-8047-0375-2). Stanford U Pr.

Vocational Mainstreaming. Winifred Y. Washburn. 1979. pap. 6.00x (ISBN 0-87879-204-X). Acad Therapy.

Vocational Mathematics for Business. Marie E. Martinka & James L. Southam. 394p. 1984. write for info. (ISBN 0-538-13181-0, M18U). SW Pub.

Vocational Objectives Within the U. S. Education System. FESC. 1985. 25.00x (ISBN 0-907659-00-4, Pub. by FESC). State Mutual Bk.

Vocational Personalities: An Application of the Rorschach Group Method. Goldie R. Kaback. LC 74-176924. (Columbia University. Teachers College. Contributions to Education: No. 924). Repr. of 1946 ed. 22.50 (ISBN 0-404-55924-7). AMS Pr.

Vocational Plumbing. Gerald B. Sherry. (Illus.). 256p. 1982. 26.00 (ISBN 0-13-943019-9). P-H.

Vocational Preparation of Handicapped Individuals. 2nd ed. Donn E. Brolin & James C. Brolin. 368p. 1982. pap. text ed. 33.95 (ISBN 0-675-09878-5). Merrill.

Vocational Psychology. John O. Crites. 1969. text ed. 46.95 (ISBN 0-07-013780-3). McGraw.

Vocational Psychology & Character Analysis. H. L. Hollingworth. 409p. 1980. Repr. of 1929 ed. lib. bdg. 35.00 (ISBN 0-89987-355-3). Darby Bks.

Vocational Psychology: Its Problems & Methods. H. L. Wollingworth. 308p. 1980. Repr. of 1920 ed. lib. bdg. 30.00 (ISBN 0-89987-354-5). Darby Bks.

Vocational Rehabilitation & Feder. Garth L. Mangum. 63p. 20.00 (ISBN 0-317-03968-7). U of Mich Inst Labor.

Vocational Rehabilitation & Supported Employment. Ed. by Paul Wehman & M. Sherril Moon. LC 88-7315. 432p. 1988. text ed. 43.00 (ISBN 0-933716-98-2, 982). P H Brookes.

Vocational Rehabilitation & the Employment of the Disabled: A Glossary. 182p. 1981. pap. 10.50 (ISBN 92-2-002571-X). Intl Labour Office.

Vocational Rehabilitation & the Employment of the Disabled: A Glossary. 182p. (Eng., Fr. & Span.). 1981. pap. 8.75 (ISBN 92-2-002571-X, ILO177, ILO). UNIPUB.

Voice Crying in the Wilderness: Essays on the Problem of Science & World Affairs. Bernard T. Feld. (Illus.). 1980. 46.00 (ISBN 0-08-023106-3); pap. 17.50 (ISBN 0-08-026065-9). Pergamon.

Voice-Data Telecommunications Systems: An Introduction to Technology. Michael Gurrie & Patrick J. O'Connor. (Illus.). 416p. 1986. text ed. 42.00 (ISBN 0-13-943283-3). P-H.

Voice Development Hints see Your Voice: Methods for Strengthening & Developing the Voice.

Voice Disorders & Their Management. Ed. by Margaret Fawcus. 304p. (Orig.). 1986. pap. 24.00 (ISBN 0-7099-1070-3, Pub. by Croom Helm Ltd). Routledge Chapman & Hall.

Voice Disorders: Current Therapy of Communication Disorders, Vol. 4. Ed. by William H. Perkins. 160p. 1983. 17.50 (ISBN 0-86577-101-4). Thieme Med Pubs.

Voice for Princess. John Morressy. 224p. 1986. pap. 2.95 (ISBN 0-441-84800-1, Pub. by Ace Science Fiction). Ace Bks.

Voice for the Theatre. Harry Hill & Robert Barton. 270p. 1985. text ed. 18.95 (ISBN 0-03-063636-1, HoltC). HR&W.

Voice from Colorado's Past for the Present: Selected Writings of George Norlin. George Norlin. Ed. by Ralph Ellsworth. LC 85-72909. 1986. 15.00x (ISBN 0-87081-157-6). Colo Assoc.

Voice from Germany: Speeches by Richard von Weizsacker. Richard Von Weizsacker. Tr. by Karin Von Abrams from Ger. LC 86-11177. 120p. 1987. 12.95 (ISBN 1-55584-016-7). Weidenfeld.

Voice from Harper's Ferry. Osborne P. Anderson. LC 72-8569. (Black Heritage Library Collection). 1972. Repr. of 1861 ed. 15.50 (ISBN 0-8369-9182-6). Ayer Co Pubs.

Voice from Heaven. Ralph W. Neighbour, Sr. 1986. pap. 5.95 (ISBN 0-937931-04-7). Global TN.

Voice from Japan: An Outsider Looks In. Carolyn Meyer. (Illus.). 240p. (gr. 5 up). 1988. 14.95 (ISBN 0-15-200633-8, Gulliver Bks). HarBraceJ.

Voice from South Carolina. facsimile ed. John A. Leland. LC 72-37310. (Black Heritage Library Collection). Repr. of 1879 ed. 17.50 (ISBN 0-8369-8947-3). Ayer Co Pubs.

Voice from the Chorus. Abram Tertz, pseud. LC 76-7526. 352p. 1976. 10.00 (ISBN 0-374-28500-4). FS&G.

Voice from the Chorus. Abram Tertz. 339p. (Rus.). 1974. Repr. lib. bdg. 23.00x (ISBN 0-374-97854-9, Octagon). Hippocrene Bks.

Voice from the Dumb: A Memoir of John William Lashford. W. Sleight. 59.95 (ISBN 0-8490-1266-X). Gordon Pr.

Voice from the Forest. Nahum Kohn & Howard Roiter. LC 80-81685. (Illus.). 256p. (Orig.). 1985. 16.95 (ISBN 0-89604-020-8); pap. 10.95 (ISBN 0-89604-021-6). Holocaust Pubns.

Voice from the Forest: Memoirs of a Jewish Partisan. Nahum Kohn & Howard Roiter. LC 80-81685. (Illus.). 288p. 1980. 16.95 (ISBN 0-8052-5021-2, Pub. by Holocaust Library); pap. 10.95 (ISBN 0-8052-5020-4). Schocken.

Voice from the Forest: Memoirs of a Jewish Partisan. Nahum Kohn & Howard Roiter. (Illus.). 288p. 5.95 (ISBN 0-686-95099-2). ADL.

Voice from the Grave-A Documented True Life Happening. Carol Mercado & O. A. Mercado. 171p. (Orig.). 1979. pap. 2.25 (ISBN 0-940542-00-5). Carolando.

Voice from the Hump. John Wheatcroft. 8.95 (ISBN 0-8453-1909-4, Cornwall Bks). Assoc Univ Prs.

Voice from the South. Anna J. Cooper. (Schomburg Library of Nineteenth-Century Black Women Writers). 368p. 1988. 19.95 (ISBN 0-19-505246-3). Oxford U Pr.

Voice from Waterloo. Edward Cotton. (Illus.). 1977. Repr. of 1949 ed. 15.95x (ISBN 0-85409-957-3). Charles River Bks.

Voice in Her Tribe: A Navajo Woman's Own Story. Irene Stewart. (Ballena Press Anthropological Papers: No. 17). (Illus.). 1980. pap. 8.95 (ISBN 0-87919-088-4). Ballena Pr.

Voice in the Closet. Raymond Federman. 80p. 1986. pap. 6.95 (ISBN 0-930956-05-2). Station Hill Pr.

Voice in the Dark. Claire Lorrimer. 256p. 1988. 18.95 (ISBN 0-7126-0949-0, Pub. by Century Hutchinson). David & Charles.

Voice in the Darkness. Colin Hamer. 1985. 18.95x (ISBN 0-901976-45-8, Pub. by United Writers Pubns England). State Mutual Bk.

Voice in the Night. Velda Johnston. 192p. 1984. 12.95 (ISBN 0-396-08379-X). Dodd.

Voice in the Night. Velda Johnston. 224p. 1987. pap. 3.50 (ISBN 0-445-20202-5, Pub. by Popular Lib). Warner Bks.

Voice in the Night. Velda Johnston. 1985. 13.95 (ISBN 0-8161-3786-2, Large Print Bks). G K Hall.

Voice in the Night. Velda Johnston. 224p. 1987. pap. 3.50 (ISBN 0-446-34499-0). Warner Bks.

Voice in the Wilderness. Grace L. Hill. Repr. lib. bdg. 21.95 (ISBN 0-89190-031-4, Pub. by River City Pr). Amereon Ltd.

Voice in the Wilderness. Grace L. Hill. (Grace Livingston Hill Classic Ser.). 264p. 1984. Repr. of 1916 ed. 8.95 (ISBN 0-8007-1209-9). Revell.

Voice in the Wilderness. Allan May. LC 77-28519. (Illus.). 204p. 1978. 18.95x (ISBN 0-88229-309-5). Nelson-Hall.

Voice in the Wilderness: A History of the Cumberland Presbyterian Church in Texas. R. Douglas Brackenridge. LC 68-20136. (Illus.). 192p. 1968. 4.00 (ISBN 0-911536-03-5). Trinity U Pr.

Voice in the Wilderness: Collected Essays of Corliss Lamont. Corliss Lamont. LC 74-75351. 344p. 1974. 18.95 (ISBN 0-87975-044-8); pap. 13.95 (ISBN 0-87975-060-X). Prometheus Bks.

Voice in Three Mirrors: Poems. Mary Low. 48p. 1983. pap. 5.95 (ISBN 0-941194-21-3). Black Swan Pr.

Voice Manual. George A. Brouillet. LC 74-14145. 1974. pap. 2.00 (ISBN 0-8008-8024-2, Crescendo). Taplinger.

Voice of a Nation. Rowland Lucas. 233p. 1981. 40.50x (ISBN 0-85088-745-3, Pub. by Gomer Pr). State Mutual Bk.

Voice of Africa, 2 vols. Leo Frobenius. LC 68-56516. (Illus.). 1969. Repr. of 1913 ed. 73.00 (ISBN 0-405-08536-2, Blom Pubns); 37.50 ea. Vol. 1 (ISBN 0-405-08537-0). Vol. II (ISBN 0-405-08538-9). Ayer Co Pubs.

Voice of America. new ed. Robert W. Pirsein. Ed. by Christopher H. Sterling. LC 78-21733. (Dissertations in Broadcasting Ser.). 1979. lib. bdg. 40.00x (ISBN 0-405-11770-1). Ayer Co Pubs.

Voice of America at the Crossroads. Media Institute. 65p. (Orig.). 1982. 10.00 (ISBN 0-937790-13-3). Media Inst.

Voice of America: From Detente to the Reagan Doctrine. Laurien Alexandre. Ed. by Brenda Dervin. (Communication & Information Science Ser.). 224p. 1988. text ed. 32.50 (ISBN 0-89391-465-7). Ablex Pub.

Voice of Asia. James A. Michener. 1951. 18.00 (ISBN 0-394-45077-9). Random.

Voice of Black Theology in South Africa. Louise Kretzschmar. 136p. 1986. pap. 10.95 (ISBN 0-86975-269-3, Pub. by Ravan Pr). Ohio U Pr.

Voice of Books. Julius Moldenhawer. LC 70-121491. (Essay Index Reprint Ser). 1940. 17.00 (ISBN 0-8369-1766-9). Ayer Co Pubs.

Voice of Cecil Harwood: A Miscellany. A. Cecil Harwood. Ed. by Owen Barfield. (Illus.). 320p. 1979. 20.00 (ISBN 0-85440-329-9, Pub. by Steinerbooks). Anthroposophic.

Voice of Christian & Jewish Dissenters in America: U. S. Internal Revenue Service Hearings, December 1978. Martin P. Claussen & Evelyn B. Claussen. xv, 591p. 1982. pap. 25.00. Piedmont.

Voice of Conscience. Krikor Zohrab. Tr. by Jack Antreassian from Armenian. 164p. 1983. 10.00 (ISBN 0-934728-09-7). D O A C.

Voice of Cyprus. Ed. by Adonis Decavalles et al. 1966. 8.50 (ISBN 0-8079-0132-6). October.

Voice of Doom. Steve Perrin. 32p. (Orig.). (YA) (gr. 10-12). 1987. pap. 6.00 (ISBN 0-915795-80-9). Iron Crown Ent Inc.

Voice of Emma Sachs. D. M. Fraser. 137p. 1983. pap. 7.95 (ISBN 0-88978-138-9). Left Bank.

Voice of England: A History of English Literature. Charles G. Osgood. 627p. 1985. Repr. of 1935 ed. lib. bdg. 35.00 (ISBN 0-89987-677-3). Darby Bks.

Voice of Eros, Vol. 2. 2nd ed. Ernest L. Norman. (Pulse of Creation Ser.). (Illus.). 1958. 9.95 (ISBN 0-932642-01-2). Unarius Pubns.

Voice of Experience. R. D. Laing. 1982. 12.00 (ISBN 0-394-51552-8). Pantheon.

Voice of Her Own. Nancy M. Tischler. 196p. 1987. pap. 10.95 (ISBN 0-310-33951-0, 11330P). Zondervan.

Voice of Hermes. Ernest L. Norman. (Pulse of Creation Ser). (Illus.). 1959. 9.95 (ISBN 0-932642-02-0). Unarius Pubns.

Voice of Human Justice. George Jordac. Tr. by M. Fazal Haq. 508p. 1984. 25.00 (ISBN 0-941724-24-7). Islamic Seminary.

Voice of Illness: A Study of Therapy and Prophecy. Aarne Siirala. LC 81-38338. 225p. 1981. Repr. of 1964 ed. 49.95 (ISBN 0-88946-995-4). E Mellen.

Voice of Isis. H. A. Curtiss & F. H. Curtiss. 472p. Date not set. pap. 24.00 (ISBN 0-89540-130-4, SB-130). Sun Pub.

Voice of Jerusalem. Israel Zangwill. 1976. lib. bdg. 59.95 (ISBN 0-8490-2801-9). Gordon Pr.

Voice of Labor. Symmes Jelley. LC 72-114813. (Research & Source Works: No. 428). 1970. Repr. of 1888 ed. text ed. 24.00 (ISBN 0-8337-1835-5). B Franklin.

Voice of Labor. Symmes M. Jelley. LC 78-89740. (American Labor, from Conspiracy to Collective Bargaining Ser., No. 1). 401p. 1969. Repr. of 1888 ed. 24.50 (ISBN 0-405-02129-1). Ayer Co Pubs.

Voice of Muse, Unarius, Elysium, Vol. 5. Ernest L. Norman. (Pulse of Creation Ser). 1964. 9.95 (ISBN 0-932642-04-7). Unarius Pubns.

Voice of Neurosis. Paul J. Moses. LC 54-8213. (Illus.). 140p. 1954. 49.50 (ISBN 0-8089-0334-9, 792985). Grune.

Voice of Norway. Halvdan Koht & Sigmund Skard. LC 75-181941. Repr. of 1944 ed. 24.00 (ISBN 0-404-03769-0). AMS Pr.

Voice of Okharon. Ed. by Society of Metaphysicians Staff. (Esoteric Ser.). 15.00x (ISBN 0-317-43562-0, Pub. by Soc of Metaphysicians). State Mutual Bk.

Voice of Omoldon, Bk. 11. Ed. by Society of Metaphysicians Staff. (Esoteric Ser.). 15.00x (ISBN 0-317-43561-2, Pub. by Soc of Metaphysicians). State Mutual Bk.

Voice of Orion, Vol. 4. Ernest L. Norman. (Pulse of Creation Ser.). 1961. 9.95 (ISBN 0-932642-03-9). Unarius Pubns.

Voice of Our Shadow. Johnathan Carroll. pap. 2.75 (ISBN 0-441-86584-4, Pub. by Ace Science Fiction). Ace Bks.

Voice of Ozoldon. Ed. by Society of Metaphysicians Staff. (Esoteric Ser.). 15.00x (ISBN 0-317-43563-9, Pub. by Soc of Metaphysicians). State Mutual Bk.

Voice of Prose: Early Prose & Autobiography. Boris Pasternak. Ed. & intro. by Christopher Barnes. 272p. 1986. 19.95 (ISBN 0-394-55604-6, Ever); pap. 9.95 (ISBN 0-394-62285-5). Grove.

Voice of Reason! Essays in Objectivist Thought. Ayn Rand. 304p. 1988. 18.95 (ISBN 0-453-00634-5). NAL.

Voice of Reform: Essays by Tat'iana I. Zaslavskaia. Tat'iana I. Zaslavskaia. Tr. by Arlo Schultz & Michel Vale. 192p. 1988. pap. 25.00 (ISBN 0-87332-505-2). M E Sharpe.

Voice of Revelation. Lillian De Waters. 5.95 (ISBN 0-686-05714-7). L De Waters.

Voice of Silence. 5th ed. Starr Farish. (Illus.). 119p. 1983. pap. 6.95 (ISBN 0-9605492-2-6). Touch Heart.

Voice of Terror. Betty C. Mowery. (YA) (gr. 7 up). 1983. 9.95 (ISBN 0-317-17584-X, Avalon). Bouregy.

Voice of Terror: A Biography of Johann Most. Frederic Trautmann. LC 79-8279. (Contributions in Political Science Ser.: No. 42). (Illus.). xxv, 288p. 1980. lib. bdg. 35.00 (ISBN 0-313-22053-0, TVT/). Greenwood.

Voice of the Beech Oracle: A Shaman Song. W. Inman. 1977. pap. 1.00 (ISBN 0-686-19036-X); signed ed. 3.00 (ISBN 0-686-28599-9). Man-Root.

Voice of the Blood. William J. O'Malley. LC 79-90055. (Five Christian Martyrs of Our Time Ser.: No. 633). 195p. (Orig.). 1980. pap. 1.99 (ISBN 0-88344-539-5). Orbis Bks.

Voice of the Buddha: The Beauty of Compassion, 2 vols. Lalitavistara Sutra. Tr. by Gwendolyn Bays from Fr. LC 83-15024. (Translation Ser.: Vol 1.). (Illus.). 704p. 1983. Set. 75.00; Vol. I. pap. 35.00 (ISBN 0-913546-84-4). Vol. II (ISBN 0-913546-85-2). Dharma Pub.

Voice of the Corpse. Max Murray. 224p. 1985. pap. 4.50 (ISBN 0-486-24905-0). Dover.

Voice of the Coyote. J. Frank Dobie. LC 49-8879. (Illus.). xx, 386p. 1961. pap. 8.95 (ISBN 0-8032-5050-9, BB 109, Bison). U of Nebr Pr.

Voice of the Democracy: A Critical Biography of David Graham Phillips, Journalist, Novelist, Progressive. Louis Filler. LC 77-13893. 1978. 22.50x (ISBN 0-271-00528-9). Pa St U Pr.

Voice of the Desert: A Naturalist's Interpretation. Joseph W. Krutch. (Illus.). 1971. pap. 8.95 (ISBN 0-688-07715-3). Morrow.

Voice of the Gawain Poet. Lynn S. Johnson. LC 83-12401. 256p. 1983. text ed. 32.50x (ISBN 0-299-09540-1). U of Wis Pr.

Voice of the Gewein-Poet. Lynn S. Johnson. LC 83-12401. pap. cancelled (2026566). Bks Demand UMI.

Voice of the Heart. Barbara Taylor Bradford. LC 81-47863. 744p. 1983. 17.95 (ISBN 0-385-15323-6). Doubleday.

Voice of the Heart. Barbara Taylor Bradford. 784p. 1984. pap. 4.95 (ISBN 0-553-26253-X). Bantam.

Voice of the Heart. Barbara Taylor Bradford. (Large Print Bks.). 1096p. 1988. lib. bdg. 21.95x (ISBN 0-8161-4465-6, Large Print Bks); pap. 13.95x (ISBN 0-8161-4466-4, Large Print Bks). G K Hall.

Voice of the Hive. rev. ed. Ric Masten. LC 78-59786. (Orig.). 1978. pap. 6.00 (ISBN 0-931104-02-5). Sunflower Ink.

Voice of the Master. Kahlil Gibran. 1963. pap. 3.95 (ISBN 0-8065-0022-0, 150, Pub. by Citadel Pr). Lyle Stuart.

Voice of the Master. 2nd ed. Eva B. Werber. 1970. pap. 3.25 (ISBN 0-87516-105-7). DeVorss.

Voice of the Masters: Writing & Authority in Modern Latin American Literature. Roberto E. Gonzalez. 207p. 1988. pap. 8.95 (ISBN 0-292-78709-X). U of Tex Pr.

Voice of the Masters: Writing & Authority in Modern Latin American Literature. Roberto Gonzalez-Echevarria. (Latin American Monographs: No. 64). 207p. 1985. text ed. 20.00x (ISBN 0-292-78716-2). U of Tex Pr.

Voice of the Muse: A Study of the Role of Inspiration in Musical Composition. Louise Duchesneau. (European University Studies: Series 36, Musicology: Vol 19). 211p. 1986. pap. 26.85 (ISBN 3-8204-9394-8). P Lang Pubs.

Voice of the Negro, 1919. Robert T. Kerlin. LC 68-54163. (American Negro: His History & Literature Ser., No. 1). 1968. Repr. of 1920 ed. 11.00 (ISBN 0-405-01825-8). Ayer Co Pubs.

Voice of the New West: John G. Jackson, His Life & Times. Stephen W. Brown. LC 85-4991. xxvi, 262p. 1985. 22.95 (ISBN 0-86554-162-0, MUP/H152). Mercer Univ Pr.

Voice of the Nightingale in Middle English Poems & Bird Debates. Josepha E. Gellinek-Schellekens. LC 84-47905. 191p. (Orig.). 1984. pap. text ed. 19.00 (ISBN 0-8204-0161-7). P Lang Pubs.

Voice of the Past: Oral History. Paul Thompson. (Oxford Paperback University Ser.). 1978. pap. text ed. 8.95x (ISBN 0-19-289102-2). Oxford U Pr.

Voice of the Past: Oral History. 2nd ed. Paul Thompson. 336p. 1988. 29.95 (ISBN 0-19-219230-2); pap. text ed. 12.95 (ISBN 0-19-289216-9). Oxford U Pr.

Voice of the People. Ellen Glasgow. Repr. lib. bdg. 24.95 (ISBN 0-89190-151-5, Pub. by River City Pr). Amereon Ltd.

Voice of the People. Ellen Glasgow. Ed. by W. L. Godshalk. (Masterworks of Literature Ser.). 1972. 12.95 (ISBN 0-8084-0030-4); pap. 8.95x (ISBN 0-8084-0031-2). New Coll U Pr.

Voice of the People. Ellen Glasgow. LC 71-96882. 444p. lib. bdg. 19.50 (ISBN 0-8398-0662-0). Irvington.

Voice of the People. Ellen Glasgow. Tr. by Henry Troth. 444p. Repr. of 1902 ed. lib. bdg. 45.00 (ISBN 0-918377-36-6). Russell Pr.

Voice of the People. Ellen Glasgow. 444p. 1986. Repr. of 1904 ed. lib. bdg. 49.50 (ISBN 0-89984-668-8). Century Bookbindery.

Voice of the Plains: Selected Radio Commentaries. John Cogswell. (Illus., Orig.). 1987. pap. 9.95 (ISBN 0-944720-01-3). Greenridge Pr.

Voice of the Poor: Essays in Economic & Political Persuasion. John Kenneth Galbraith. 96p. 1983. 9.95 (ISBN 0-674-94295-7). Harvard U Pr.

Voice of the Poor: Essays in Economic & Political Persuasion. John Kenneth Galbraith. LC 82-18732. 96p. 1984. pap. 3.95 (ISBN 0-674-94296-5). Harvard U Pr.

Voice of the S. S. A History of the S. S. Journal "Das Schwarze Korps". William L. Combs. (Amercan University Studies IX, History: Vol. 1). 350p. 1987. text ed. 89.00 (ISBN 0-8204-0083-1). P Lang Pubs.

Voice of the Saints. Ed. by Francis W. Johnston. LC 86-50851. 150p. 1986. pap. 4.00 (ISBN 0-89555-304-X). TAN Bks Pubs.

Voice of the Silence. Helena P. Blavatsky. LC 73-7619. 1970. pap. 2.50 (ISBN 0-8356-0380-6, Quest). Theos Pub Hse.

Voice of the Silence: Chosen Fragments from the Book of the Golden Precepts. Tr. & intro. by Helena P. Blavatsky. iv, 110p. 1928. Repr. of 1889 ed. 3.00 (ISBN 0-938998-06-4). Theosophy.

Voice of the Silence: Verbatim with 1889 ed. Helena P. Blavatsky. LC 76-25345. 1976. 6.00 (ISBN 0-911500-04-9); pap. 3.50 (ISBN 0-911500-05-7). Theos U Pr.

Voice of the Stranger. Madge Reinhardt. LC 81-65402. (Illus.). 477p. 1982. pap. 8.50 (ISBN 0-917162-06-4). Back Row Pr.

Voice of the Tambaran: Truth & Illusion in Ilahita Arapesh Religion. Donald F. Tuzin. 350p. 1980. 38.00x (ISBN 0-520-03964-5). U of Cal Pr.

Voice of the Turtle. John Ankenbruck. 1976. pap. 1.95 (ISBN 0-686-15471-1). Lions Head.

Voice of the Universe: Building the Jodrell Bank Telescope. Bernard Lovell. (Convergence Ser.). 336p. 1987. pap. 14.95 (ISBN 0-275-92679-6, B2679). Praeger.

Voice of the Universe: Building the Jodrell Bank Telescope. rev. & updated ed. Bernard Lovell. 331p. 1987. lib. bdg. 37.95 (ISBN 0-275-92678-8, C2678). Praeger.

Voice of the Voiceless. CIIR Staff. 208p. 1986. 54.00x (ISBN 0-946848-53-X, Pub. by CIIR). State Mutual Bk.

Voice of the Voiceless: The Four Pastoral Letters & Other Statements. Oscar Romero. Tr. by Michael J. Walsh from Span. LC 84-14722. 208p. (Orig.). 1985. pap. 9.95 (ISBN 0-88344-525-5). Orbis Bks.

Voice of the Whaleman: With an Account of the Nicholson Whaling Collection. Stuart C. Sherman. LC 65-18564. pap. 54.00 (ISBN 0-317-28766-4, 2020627). Bks Demand UMI.

Voice of the Whirlwind. Walter J. Williams. 320p. 1987. 16.95 (ISBN 0-312-93013-5, Dist by St. Martin's Pr & Warner Pub Servs). Tor Bks.

Voice of the Whirlwind. Walter J. Williams. 288p. 1988. pap. 3.95 (ISBN 0-8125-5785-9). Tor Bks.

Voice of Thy Brother's Blood. Mary Balazs. LC 76-18590. 1976. pap. 3.00 (ISBN 0-936014-02-4). Dawn Valley.

Voice of Vengeance. Junita T. Osborne. (YA) (gr. 7 up). 1985. 9.95 (ISBN 0-8034-8514-X, Avalon). Bouregy.

Voice of Venus, Vol. 1. 5th ed. Ernest L. Norman. (Pulse of Creation Ser). (Illus.). 177p. 1956. 8.95 (ISBN 0-932642-00-4). Unarius Pubns.

Voice on an Anthill. Jonas Zdanys. 1981. pap. 4.00 (ISBN 0-87141-063-X). Manyland.

Voice on the Southwind. Betty Dickens. Ed. by Barbara Holley. (Illus., Orig.). 1982. pap. 3.50 (ISBN 0-933494-15-7). Earthwise Pubns.

Voice Out of Ramah. Lee Killough. 1979. pap. 1.75 (ISBN 0-345-28021-0, Del Rey Bks). Ballantine.

Voice over the Water. William Breault. LC 84-73051. 128p. (Orig.). 1985. pap. 4.95 (ISBN 0-87793-281-6). Ave Maria.

Voice Placing & Training Exercise, 2 vols. George Dodds. Incl. Contralto & Baritone (ISBN 0-19-322141-1); Soprano & Tenor (ISBN 0-19-322140-3). (YA) (gr. 9up). 1927. pap. 9.95 ea. Oxford U Pr.

Voices of Children. Edward Candy. 1980. 13.95 (ISBN 0-575-02735-5, Pub. by Gollancz England). David & Charles.
Voices of Christmas. Norma Leary. (Orig.). 1983. pap. 3.50 (ISBN 0-937172-55-3). JLJ Pubs.
Voices of Combat: A Century of Liberty & War Songs, 1765-1865. Kent A. Bowman. LC 86-25724. (Contributions to the Study of Music & Dance Ser.: No. 10). 181p. 1987. lib. bdg. 29.95 (ISBN 0-313-25408-7, BVC/). Greenwood.
Voices of Conflict: Teenagers Themselves. Ed. by Howard Spanogle. 272p. 1987. 16.95 (ISBN 0-915361-94-9, Dist. by Watts). Adama Pubs Inc.
Voices of Conscience: Essays on Medieval & Modern French Literature in Memory of James D. Powell & Rosemary Hodgins. Ed. by Raymond J. Cormier. LC 76-15343. 282p. 1977. 34.95 (ISBN 0-87722-090-5). Temple U Pr.
Voices of Czecholslovak Socialists. Ed. by Tamara Deutscher et al. 134p. (Orig.). 1977. pap. 3.35 (ISBN 0-85036-228-8, Pub. by Merlin Pr UK). Longwood Pub Group.
Voices of Deliverance: Interviews with Quebec & Acadian Writers. Donald Smith. Tr. by Larry Shouldice. 365p. 1986. pap. 14.95 (ISBN 0-88784-148-1, Pub. by Hse Anansi Pr Canada). U of Toronto Pr.
Voices of Dissent. Dissent (Periodical) LC 77-99630. (Essay Index Reprint Ser.). 1958. 27.50 (ISBN 0-8369-1405-8). Ayer Co Pubs.
Voices of Earth & Sky. Vinson Brown. LC 76-41761. (Illus.). 177p. 1976. pap. 6.95 (ISBN 0-87961-060-3). Naturegraph.
Voices of Elderly Black Women: An Historical Perspective. Gwendolyn Starlard. (Illus.). 120p. pap. text ed. 20.00 (ISBN 0-938991-20-5). Colonial Pr AL.
Voices of Emergency: An All India Anthology of Protest Poetry of the 1975-77 Emergency, India. Ed. by John O. Perry. 1983. 28.50x (ISBN 0-317-05076-1, Pub. by Popular Prakashan). South Asia Bks.
Voices of Eternity. Sarah W. Estep. 1988. pap. 3.95 (ISBN 0-449-13424-5, GM). Fawcett.
Voices of Experience: Fifteen Hundred Retired People Talk about Retirement. rev. ed. Mario A. Milletti. 208p. 1987. pap. 3.00 (ISBN 0-9613704-1-6). Tchrs Insurance.
Voices of French Pacifism. Incl. La Paix et l'Enseignement Pacifiste, Lecons Professees a l'Ecole des Hautes Etudes Sociales. Estournelles De Constant et al; International Peace: Speeches. Estournelles De Constant et al; Le Mensonge du Pacifisme. Ferdinand Brunetiere; A Propos du Pacifisme. Frederic Passy et al. LC 71-147705. (Library of War & Peace; Problems of the Organized Peace Movement: Selected Documents). 1973. lib. bdg. 46.00 (ISBN 0-8240-0239-3). Garland Pub.
Voices of German Pacifism. Incl. Das Personliche Wirken und Werben. Arthur Muller; German Pacifism During the War. Caroline E. Playne; Die Fuhrer der Deutschen Friedensbewegung, 1890-1923. Hans Wehberg; Hans Wehberg Als Pazifist in Weltkrieg. Hans Wehberg. LC 71-147710. (Library of War & Peace; Problems of the Organized Peace Movement: Selected Documents). 1973. lib. bdg. 46.00 (ISBN 0-8240-0241-5). Garland Pub.
Voices of Hope: Teenagers Themselves, Pt. III. Compiled by Glenard East Echo Staff & Howard Spanogle. (Illus.). (YA) (gr. 12 up). 1988. 16.95 (ISBN 1-55774-012-7, Dist. by Watts). Adama Pubs Inc.
Voices of Independence: New Black Writing from Papua New Guinea. Ed. by Ulli Beier. LC 80-10818. 1980. 20.00 (ISBN 0-312-85084-0). St Martin.
Voices of Inspiration. Renee Arrington et al. 34p. 1982. pap. 3.50 (ISBN 0-939296-04-7). Bond Pub Co.
Voices of Ireland. Donncha O. Dulaing. (Illus.). 176p. 1984. (Pub. by O'Brien Pr Ireland); pap. 8.95 (ISBN 0-86278-065-9). Irish Bks Media.
Voices of Jacob, Hands of Esau: Jews in American Life & Thought. Stephen J. Whitfield. LC 83-25720. x, 322p. 1984. 27.50 (ISBN 0-208-02024-1, Archon Bks). Shoe String.
Voices of Japan. Carolyn Meyer. 240p. (YA) (gr. 7 up). 1988. 14.95 (Gulliver Bks). HarBraceJ.
Voices of Julie. Joan Oppenheimer. (YA) (gr. 7 up). 1979. pap. 1.95 (ISBN 0-590-32201-X, Wildfire). Scholastic Inc.
Voices of Love. Roseann Cervelli. 286p. (Orig.). 1986. pap. 10.00 (ISBN 0-87418-024-4, 159). Coleman Pub.
Voices of Love. Doris Stokes & Linda Dearsley. (Lythway Ser.). 256p. 1988. lib. bdg. 18.50x (ISBN 0-7451-0671-4, Pub. by Chivers Pr UK). G K HAll.
Voices of Man. Mario A. Pei. LC 71-173940. Repr. of 1962 ed. 15.00 (ISBN 0-404-07928-8). AMS Pr.
Voices of Marrakesh: A Record of a Visit. Elias Canetti. Tr. by J. A. Underwood from Ger. 104p. 1984. pap. 6.95 (ISBN 0-374-51823-8). FS&G.
Voices of Matthew Arnold. W. Stacy Johnson. LC 72-12313. 146p. 1973. Repr. of 1961 ed. lib. bdg. 35.00x (ISBN 0-8371-6693-4, JOMA). Greenwood.
Voices of Melancholy: Studies in Literary Treatments of Melancholy in Renaissance England. Bridget G. Lyons. 224p. 1975. pap. 3.45x (ISBN 0-393-00755-3, Norton Lib). Norton.
Voices of Modern Greece: Cavafy, Sikelianos, Seferis, Elytis & Gatsos. rev. & expanded ed. Ed. by Edmund Keeley & Phillip Sherrard. LC 81-47282. (Lockert Library of Poetry in Translation). 210p. 1981. 26.50x (ISBN 0-691-06473-3); pap. 9.50 (ISBN 0-691-01382-9). Princeton U Pr.
Voices of Negritude: The Expression of Black Experience in the Poetry of Senghor, Cesaire & Dramas. Edward A. Jones. LC 75-152062. Repr. of 1971 ed. 31.30 (ISBN 0-8357-9357-5, 2012606). Bks Demand UMI.
Voices of Negro Protest in Amercia. William H. Burns. LC 80-21197. 88p. 1980. Repr. of 1963 ed. lib. bdg. 35.00x (ISBN 0-313-22219-3, BUVN). Greenwood.
Voices of Northern Ireland: Growing up in a Troubled Land. Carolyn Meyer. LC 87-199. (Illus.). 212p. (YA) (gr. 7 up). 1987. 14.95 (ISBN 0-15-200635-4, Gulliver Bks). HarBraceJ.
Voices of Our Ancestors: Cherokee Teachings from the Wisdom Fire. Dhyani Ywahoo. LC 87-9711. (Illus.). 294p. (Orig.). 1987. pap. 9.95 (ISBN 0-87773-410-0, Dist. by Random). Shambhala Pubns.
Voices of Our Elders. Sandra Simons. (Illus.). 35p. (Orig.). 1982. pap. 8.95 (ISBN 0-915347-16-4). Pueblo Acoma Pr.
Voices of Our Kind. rev. ed. Ed. by Alexander Scott. 128p. 1986. 20.00x (ISBN 0-550-20495-4, Pub. by Saltire Soc). State Mutual Bk.
Voices of Our Kind: An Anthology of Contemporary Scottish Verse. Ed. by Moven Cameron. 80p. 1975. 25.00x (ISBN 0-85411-000-3, Pub. by Saltire Soc). State Mutual Bk.
Voices of Praise. Mary V. Reilly & Margaret K. Wetterer. (Illus., Orig.). 1980. pap. 4.95 (ISBN 0-8192-1276-8). Morehouse.
Voices of Protest: Huey Long, Father Coughlin, & the Great Depression. Alan Brinkley. LC 81-48121. 1982. 18.00 (ISBN 0-394-52241-9). Knopf.
Voices of Protest: Huey Long, Father Coughlin & the Great Depression. Alan Brinkley. LC 83-3496. 1983. pap. 8.95 (ISBN 0-394-71628-0, Vin). Random.
Voices of Readers: How We Come to Love Books. G. Robert Carlsen & Anne Sherrill. (Illus.). 180p. 1988. pap. write for info. (ISBN 0-8141-5639-8). NCTE.
Voices of Resurgent Islam. Ed. by John L. Esposito. 1983. 27.00x (ISBN 0-19-503339-6); pap. 12.95x (ISBN 0-19-503340-X). Oxford U Pr.
Voices of Robby Wilde. Elizabeth Kytle. 336p. 1987. 17.95 (ISBN 0-932020-45-3). Seven Locks Pr.
Voices of Rural Practitioners: Self-Analysis of Local Rural Development Initiatives World-Wide. Institute of Cultural Affairs International Editors. (IERD Ser.: Vol. 2). 500p. 1987. lib. bdg. 95.00 (ISBN 3-598-21042-6). K G Saur.
Voices of Silence. Andre Malraux. Tr. by Stuart Gilbert from Fr. LC 77-92101. (Bollingen Ser.: Vol. XXIV: A). (Illus.). 661p. 1978. 67.50x (ISBN 0-691-09941-3); pap. 17.50x (ISBN 0-691-01821-9). Princeton U Pr.
Voices of Silent: English Translation of Hali's Majalis Un-Nissa & Chup Di Dad. Ed. by Gail Minault. 1986. 18.50x (ISBN 81-7001-018-7, Pub. by Chanakya India). South Asia Bks.
Voices of South Africa: Growing up in a Troubled Land. Carolyn Meyer. LC 86-45059. 224p. (gr. 7 up). 1986. 14.95 (ISBN 0-15-200637-0). HarBraceJ.
Voices of Spirit. Charles H. Hapgood. 1975. pap. 8.95 (ISBN 0-440-05983-6, Sey Lawr). Delacorte.
Voices of Spirit. Charles H. Hapgood. 1976. pap. 1.75 (ISBN 0-685-73462-5, LB404, Leisure Bks). Leisure NY.
Voices of Strength & Hope for a Friend with AIDS. Joseph Gallagher. LC 87-61464. (Illus.). 53p. (Orig.). 1987. pap. 2.95 (ISBN 1-55612-073-7). Sheed & Ward MO.
Voices of Survival in the Nuclear Age. Ed. by Dennis Paulson. (Illus.). 288p. (Orig.). 1986. pap. 8.95 (ISBN 0-88496-249-0). Capra Pr.
Voices of Survival in the Nuclear Age. Ed. by Dennis Paulson. 288p. 1988. Repr. lib. bdg. 22.95x (ISBN 0-8095-4024-X). Borgo Pr.
Voices of the American Revolution. 2nd ed. Ed. by Harry C. Boyte. 224p. pap. cancelled (ISBN 0-8298-0478-1). Pilgrim NY.
Voices of the Americas: Traditional Music & Dance from North, South, & Central America, & the Caribbean. R. Allen et al. Ed. by Ray Allen. LC 87-51358. (Orig.). 1988. pap. 5.00 (ISBN 0-945017-00-6). World Mus Inst.
Voices of the Civil Rights Movement: Black American Freedom Songs, 1960-66. (Smithsonian Collection of Recordings Ser.). incl. 3-LP boxed set 19.95 (ISBN 0-252-01009-4). U of Ill Pr.
Voices of the Dead: A Novel. Autran Dourado. Tr. by John M. Parker from Port. LC 81-4470. Orig. Title: Opera Dos Mortos. 248p. 1981. 10.95 (ISBN 0-8008-8030-7). Taplinger.
Voices of the French Revolution. Ed. by Richard Cobb & Colin Jones. (Illus.). 256p. 1988. 29.95 (ISBN 0-88162-338-5). Salem Hse Pubs.
Voices of the Game: The First Full-Scale Overview of Baseball Broadcasting, 1921 to the Present. Curt Smith. LC 86-24189. (Illus.). 1987. 22.95 (ISBN 0-912083-21-2). Diamond Communications.
Voices of the Industrial Revolution: Selected Readings from the Liberal Economists & Their Critics. Ed. by John Bowditch & Clement Ramsland. 1961. pap. 8.95 (ISBN 0-472-06053-8, 53, AA). U of Mich Pr.
Voices of the Majestic Sage. Sal St. John Buttaci & Susan L. Gerstle. 140p. 1984. 17.98 (ISBN 0-917398-13-0). New Worlds.
Voices of the Old Sea. Norman Lewis. 208p. 1986. pap. 5.95 (ISBN 0-14-007780-4). Penguin.
Voices of the Past: Key Documents in the History of American Journalism. Pickett. 1986. pap. write for info. (ISBN 0-471-84134-X). Wiley.
Voices of the Past: Key Documents in the History of American Journalism. Calder M. Pickett. LC 76-19674. (Advertising & Journalism Ser.). 496p. 1977. pap. text ed. write for info. (ISBN 0-02-395790-5, Pub. by Grid). Macmillan.
Voices of the People: The Politics & Life of "La Sociale" at the End of the Second Empire. John Moore et al. (History Workshop Ser.). 376p. 1988. text ed. 65.00 (ISBN 0-7102-1308-5, Pub. by Routledge UK). Routledge Chapman & Hall.
Voices of the Poor: Selections from the "Morning Chronicle"; "Labour & the Poor", 1849-1950. Henry Mayhew. Ed. by Anne Humphreys. (Illus.). 280p. 1971. 29.50x (ISBN 0-7146-2929-4, F Cass Co). Biblio Dist.
Voices of the Rainbow. Kenneth Rosen. LC 80-52071. 232p. 1980. pap. 4.95 (ISBN 0-8050-0187-5). Seaver Bks.
Voices of the Red Giants. James W. Markham. (Illus.). 1967. 10.50x (ISBN 0-8138-1085-X). Iowa St U Pr.
Voices of the Storyteller: Cuba's Lino Novas Calvo. Lorraine E. Roses. LC 85-27148. (Contributions to the Study of World Literature Ser.: No. 14). 170p. 1986. lib. bdg. 35.00 (ISBN 0-313-25077-4, RVS). Greenwood.
Voices of the Wineland. Ed. by Michael Dow & Carl T. Endemann. (Illus.). 48p. (Orig.). 8.50 (ISBN 0-931926-09-2); pap. 4.75 (ISBN 0-931926-08-4). Alta Napa.
Voices of Time: A Cooperative Survey of Man's Views of Time As Expressed by the Sciences & by the Humanities. 2nd ed. Ed. by J. T. Fraser. LC 81-3025. (Illus.). 772p. 1981. pap. text ed. 19.95x (ISBN 0-87023-337-8). U of Mass Pr.
Voices of Tomorrow: Critical Studies of the New Spirit in Literature. Edwin A. Bjorkman. LC 74-98818. Repr. of 1913 ed. lib. bdg. 35.00x (ISBN 0-8371-2962-1, BJVT). Greenwood.
Voices of Tomorrow, Critical Studies of the New Spirit in Literature. Edwin A. Bjorkman. Repr. of 1913 ed. 25.00 (ISBN 0-384-04540-5). Johnson Repr.
Voices of Two Women. Florence J. Goodman & Shelley Adler. 1974. 9.95x (ISBN 0-917232-01-1). Gee Tee Bee.
Voices of Verse. Grace C. Williams. LC 84-90505. 1984. 6.50 (ISBN 0-8233-0399-3). Golden Quill.
Voices of Wisdom. Francine Klagsbrun. 594p. 1986. 16.95 (ISBN 0-8246-0320-6). Jonathan David.
Voices of Women: Three Critics on Three Poets on Three Heroines. Ed. by Cynthia Navaretta. LC 80-80281. (Illus.). 1980. pap. text ed. 5.50 (ISBN 0-9602476-1-0). Midmarch Arts-WAN.
Voices on a Cold Day: Collected Columns. Bill Easterling. Ed. by Mike Kaylor. LC 86-82553. 220p. (Orig.). 1986. pap. text ed. 5.00 (ISBN 0-916039-02-1). Kaylor Christ Co.
Voices on Fire: A Book of Meditations. John Walchars. LC 81-7767. 250p. 1981. pap. 7.95 (ISBN 0-8245-0094-6). Crossroad NY.
Voices on the Wind. Evelyn Anthony. 288p. 1985. 16.95 (ISBN 0-399-13067-5). Putnam Pub Group.
Voices on the Wind. Palani Vaughan. (Illus.). 176p. 1987. 24.95 (ISBN 0-935180-59-1). Mutual Pub HI.
Voices-The Walls. M. Basheer. 1977. 4.00x (ISBN 0-88386-211-5). South Asia Bks.
Voices Under the Ground: Themes & Images in the Early Poetry of Gunnar Ekelof. Ross Shideler. LC 70-171620. (U. C. Publ. in Modern Philology: Vol. 104). Repr. of 1973 ed. 31.40 (ISBN 0-8357-9640-X, 2013809). Bks Demand UMI.
Voices under the Window. John Hearne. LC 85-1568. 168p. 1985. pap. 6.95 (ISBN 0-571-09985-8). Faber & Faber.
Voices, Visions, & a New Reality: Mexican Fiction Since 1970. J. Ann Duncan. LC 85-40853. (Pitt Latin American Ser.). 280p. 1986. 26.95x (ISBN 0-8229-3815-4). U of Pittsburgh Pr.
Voices Within the Ark. Ed. by Howard Schwartz & Anthony Rudolf. 1983. pap. 15.95 (ISBN 0-380-76109-2, 80119). Avon.
Voices Within the Ark: The Modern Jewish Poets. Ed. by Howard Schwartz & Anthony Rudolf. 1980. slipcased ed. 50.00 (ISBN 0-686-77603-8). Pushcart Pr.
Voices 1870-1914. Peter Vansittart. 1986. pap. 4.95 (ISBN 0-380-69857-9, Discus). Avon.
Void: A Psychodynamic Investigation of the Relationship Between Mind & Space. A. H. Almaas. LC 85-82559. (Diamond Mind Ser.: Bk. 1). 175p. (Orig.). 1986. pap. 8.00 (ISBN 0-936713-00-3). Almaas Pubns.
Void Captain's Tale. Norman Spinrad. LC 81-21334. 250p. 1983. 15.00 (ISBN 0-671-43483-7). Ultramarine Pub.
Void in Hearts. Willian G. Tapply. (Brady Coyne Mystery Ser.: No. 7). 224p. 1988. 15.95 (ISBN 0-684-18793-0). Scribner.
Void Indigo. Steve Gerber & Val Mayerik. (Marvel Graphic Novel Ser.: No. 11). 4.95 (ISBN 0-87135-059-9). Marvel Comics.
Voidism. Edward Echols. 1981. pap. 3.00 (ISBN 0-682-49813-0). Exposition-Phoenix.
Voie d'Enfer et de Paradis. Jean de la Mote. Ed. by Sr. M. Aquiline Pety. (Catholic University of America. Studies in Romance Languages & Literatures: No. 20). Repr. of 1940 ed. 25.00 (ISBN 0-404-50320-9). AMS Pr.
Voie Royale. Andre Malraux. (Coll. Soleil). 1954. 12.50 (ISBN 0-685-11623-9). French & Eur.
Voie Royale, La Condition Humaine see Oeuvres.
Voies de la Pragmatique. Sandra Golopentia. (Stanford French & Italian Studies: No. 51). 224p. (Orig., Fr.). 1988. pap. 29.50 (ISBN 0-915838-67-2). Anma Libri.
Voies Moyennes et Logique du Capitalisme see Cahiers de l'Institut de Science Economique Appliquee.
Voightlander & I. James F. Ryder. LC 72-9235. (Literature of Photography Ser.). Repr. of 1902 ed. 21.00 (ISBN 0-405-04940-4). Ayer Co Pubs.
Voila! An Introduction to French. Laura Heilenman et al. 576p. 1988. text ed. 35.50t (ISBN 0-06-042758-2, HarpC). Har-Row.
Voila! Lafayette Centennial Cookbook 1884-1984 from Open Fire to Microwave. Jean K. Durkee. LC 83-91087. (Illus.). 264p. 1983. 11.95 (ISBN 0-9605362-2-1). Tout de Suite.
Voix dans la Foule. Stuart Merrill. 59.95 (ISBN 0-8490-1267-8). Gordon Pr.
Voix du Siecle. Ed. by Eunice C. Smith & John K. Savacool. 276p. (Orig., Fr.). 1960. pap. text ed. 11.00 net (ISBN 0-15-595006-1, HC). HarBraceJ.
Voix et le Regard see Voice & the Eye: The Analysis of Social Movements.
Voix et silences: Les Meilleures pieces radiophoniques francaises. Ed. by Anna Otten. Incl. Silences de Paris. Albert Camus & V. Vedres; Une L'arme. Jean Forest & Rene Clair; C'est vrai mais il ne faut pas le croire. Claude Aveline; Frederic General. Jacques Constant; Interview. Robert Pinget. LC 68-11212. (Illus., Fr.). 1968. pap. text ed. 8.95x (ISBN 0-89197-466-0). Irvington.
Voix Francaises du Monde Noir: Anthologie d'Auteurs Noirs Francophones. Ed. by Keith Q. Warner. (Illus.). 158p. (Fr.). 1984. pap. text ed. 11.50 (ISBN 0-8191-3687-5). U Pr of Amer.
Voix Humaine. Jean Cocteau. pap. 18.95 (ISBN 0-685-37277-4). French & Eur.
Voix sur Israel. Paul Claudel. 46p. 1950. 8.95 (ISBN 0-686-54445-5). French & Eur.
Vokabular der Psychoanalyse, 2 vols. Jean Laplanche. (Ger.). 1973. pap. 49.95 (ISBN 3-518-07607-8, M-7680, Pub. by Suhrkamp). French & Eur.
Vokabular Farn Onheyber Klas. Israel Steinbaum et al. LC 45-12914. 78p. (Yiddish.). 1944. pap. 5.00 (ISBN 0-914512-28-5). Yivo Inst.
Vol de la Joconde. Huguette Zahller. (YA) (gr. 8-11). 1987. pap. 6.25 (ISBN 0-87720-483-7). AMSCO Sch.
Vol de Nuit. Antoine De Saint-Exupery. 1972. write for info. French & Eur.
Vol de Nuit. Antoine de Saint-Exupery. (Folio Ser.: No. 4). 1972. 5.95 (ISBN 0-686-55420-5). Schoenhof.
Vol d'Icare. Raymond Queneau. 260p. 1968. 10.95 (ISBN 0-686-54687-3). French & Eur.
Vol D'Icare see Flight of Icarus.
Vol. 8: Vol. 8 see Growth of Crystals.
Volatile Halogenated Anaesthetics: Post Graduate Course. Proceedings of International Meeting of Anaesthesiology & Resuscitation, C. H. U. PetieSalpetriere, Paris, 1980. Ed. by C. Conseiller et al. 242p. 1981. 75.25 (ISBN 90-219-0474-8, Excerpta Medica). Elsevier.
Volcan d'Or. Jules Verne. 1972. 10.95 (ISBN 0-686-55960-6). French & Eur.
Volcan: Poems from Central America. Ed. by Alejandro Murguia & Barbara Paschke. LC 83-20936. 159p. 1984. pap. 5.95 (ISBN 0-87286-153-8). City Lights.
Volcanic Activity & Human Ecology. Ed. by Payson D. Sheets & Donald K. Grayson. LC 79-51701. 1979. 49.95 (ISBN 0-12-639120-3). Acad Pr.
Volcanic Ash. Grant Heiken & Kenneth Wohletz. (Los Alamos Series in Basic & Applied Sciences: No. 6). 1985. 48.00x (ISBN 0-520-05241-2). U of Cal Pr.
Volcanic Firearms & Their Successors. James Edsall. 2.50 (ISBN 0-913150-28-2). Pioneer Pr.
Volcanic Hazards: A Sourcebook on the Effects of Eruptions. R. J. Blong. 440p. 1984. 78.00 (ISBN 0-12-107180-4). Acad Pr.
Volcanic History of Honduras. Howel Williams & A. R. McBirney. LC 79-627247. (University of California Publications in Geological Sciences: vol. 85). pap. 27.80 (2015001). Bks Demand UMI.

Voltage & Patch Clamping with Microelectrodes. Ed. by Thomas G. Smith, Jr. et al. (American Physiological Society Book). (Illus.). 268p. 1985. pap. 39.50 (ISBN 0-19-520700-9). Oxford U Pr.
Voltaire. Richard Aldington. LC 77-21922. 1977. Repr. of 1925 ed. lib. bdg. 35.00 (ISBN 0-8414-1738-5). Folcroft.
Voltaire. Richard Aldington. 278p. 1980. Repr. of 1925 ed. lib. bdg. 39.50 (ISBN 0-8492-3202-3). R West.
Voltaire. Wayne Andrews. LC 80-29565. (Illus.). 1981. 13.95 (ISBN 0-8112-0800-1); pap. 6.95 (ISBN 0-8112-0802-8, NDP519). New Directions.
Voltaire. A. J. Ayer. LC 86-6757. 224p. 1986. 19.45 (ISBN 0-394-54798-5). Random.
Voltaire. 3rd ed. Theodore Besterman. (Illus.). 1977. lib. bdg. 33.00x (ISBN 0-226-04430-0). U of Chicago Pr.
Voltaire. Henry N. Brailsford. 256p. 1981. Repr. of 1935 ed. lib. bdg. 20.00 (ISBN 0-8495-0473-2). Arden Lib.
Voltaire. Henry N. Brailsford. 1963. pap. 6.95x (ISBN 0-19-281021-9). Oxford U Pr.
Voltaire. Edward Hamley. 1877. Repr. 20.00 (ISBN 0-8274-3681-5). R West.
Voltaire. Andre Maurois. Tr. by Hamish Miles. 1978. Repr. lib. bdg. 30.00 (ISBN 0-8492-6744-7). R West.
Voltaire. A. Meyer. 59.95 (ISBN 0-8490-1268-6). Gordon Pr.
Voltaire. John Morley. LC 72-82326. 384p. 1973. Repr. of 1903 ed. lib. bdg. 23.50 (ISBN 0-8337-4293-0). B Franklin.
Voltaire. John Morley. 30.00 (ISBN 0-8274-0145-0). R West.
Voltaire. John Morley. 365p. 1982. Repr. of 1913 ed. lib. bdg. 40.00 (ISBN 0-89984-803-6). Century Bookbindery.
Voltaire. Alfred Noyes. 646p. 1983. Repr. of 1936 ed. lib. bdg. 45.00 (ISBN 0-89987-612-9). Darby Bks.
Voltaire. Peyton Richter & Ilona Ricardo. (World Authors Ser.). 1980. 16.95 (ISBN 0-8057-6425-9, Twayne). G K Hall.
Voltaire. J. M. Robertson. 122p. 1981. Repr. of 1922 ed. lib. bdg. 25.00 (ISBN 0-8495-4643-5). Arden Lib.
Voltaire. J. M. Robertson. 1922. Repr. 27.50 (ISBN 0-8274-3682-3). R West.
Voltaire. Colwyn E. Vulliamy. LC 76-113328. 1970. Repr. of 1930 ed. 24.00x (ISBN 0-8046-1004-5, Pub. by Kennikat). Assoc Faculty Pr.
Voltaire: A Biography. Haydn Mason. LC 80-8868. (Illus.). 224p. 1981. 22.50x (ISBN 0-8018-2611-X). Johns Hopkins.
Voltaire & Beccaria As Reformers in Criminal Law. Marcello Maestro. LC 72-5741. xii, 178p. 1972. Repr. of 1942 ed. lib. bdg. 16.50x (ISBN 0-374-95257-4, Octagon). Hippocrene Bks.
Voltaire & Catherine the Great: Selected Correspondence. Ed. by A Lentin. (Illus.). 196p. 1974. 16.00 (ISBN 0-89250-099-9). Orient Res Partners.
Voltaire & English Critics of Shakespeare. George R. Havens. LC 77-932. 1973. lib. bdg. 17.00 (ISBN 0-8414-4945-7). Folcroft.
Voltaire & Jean Meslier. Andrew R. Morehouse. LC 72-1716. (Yale Romanic Studies: No. 9). Repr. of 1936 ed. 22.00 (ISBN 0-404-53209-8). AMS Pr.
Voltaire & Madame Du Chatelet: An Essay on the Intellectual Activity at Cirey. Ira O. Wade. 1967. Repr. lib. bdg. 17.00x (ISBN 0-374-98132-9, Octagon). Hippocrene Bks.
Voltaire & Sensibility. Ronald S. Ridgway. LC 72-94539. pap. 77.00 (ISBN 0-317-29412-1, 2023845). Bks Demand UMI.
Voltaire & the Century of Light. A. Owen Aldridge. LC 75-2978. 472p. 1975. 56.50x (ISBN 0-691-06287-0). Princeton U Pr.
Voltaire & the Cowboy: The Letters of Thurman Arnold. Ed. by Gene M. Gressley. LC 76-15772. (Illus.). 1977. 22.50x (ISBN 0-87081-073-1). Colo Assoc.
Voltaire & the State. Constance Rowe. 1968. lib. bdg. 18.50x (ISBN 0-374-96992-2, Octagon). Hippocrene Bks.
Voltaire As an Historian of Seventeenth-Century French Drama. Robert Lowenstein. 1973. Repr. of 1935 ed. 19.00 (ISBN 0-384-33853-4). Johnson Repr.
Voltaire Bibliographie de ses Oeuvres: Paris, 1882-1890, 4 Vols. G. Bengesco. 176.00 (ISBN 0-318-23472-6). Kraus Repr.
Voltaire, Biographical Fantasy. Laura Riding. LC 77-23088. 1927. lib. bdg. 25.50 (ISBN 0-8414-7353-6). Folcroft.
Voltaire dans ses contes. Van Den Heuvel. 27.95 (ISBN 0-685-34066-X). French & Eur.
Voltaire: Dictionnaire Philosophique. Christopher Todd. (Critical Guides to French Texts Ser.). 72p. 1980. pap. 3.50 (ISBN 0-7293-0101-X, Pub. by Grant & Cutler). Longwood Pub Group.
Voltaire, Dryden & Heroic Tragedy. Trusten W. Russell. LC 46-5389. Repr. of 1946 ed. 12.50 (ISBN 0-404-05467-6). AMS Pr.
Voltaire Essays, & Another. Theodore Besterman. LC 80-17075. (Illus.). 181p. 1980. Repr. of 1962 ed. lib. bdg. 35.00x (ISBN 0-313-22527-3, BEVO). Greenwood.
Voltaire in America: 1744-1800. Mary M. Barr. Repr. of 1941 ed. 14.00 (ISBN 0-384-03441-1). Johnson Repr.
Voltaire in His Letters. facsimile ed. Tr. by S. G. Tallentyre. LC 77-150205. (Select Bibliographies Reprint Ser). Repr. of 1919 ed. 20.00 (ISBN 0-8369-5718-0). Ayer Co Pubs.
Voltaire in Love. Nancy Mitford. Repr. of 1957 ed. lib. bdg. 35.00x (ISBN 0-8371-2307-0, MIVL). Greenwood.
Voltaire: Lettres Philosophiques. Dennis Fletcher. Ed. by Roger Little et al. (Critical Guides to French Texts Ser.). 75p. 1986. pap. 4.95 (ISBN 0-7293-0222-9, Pub. by Grant & Cutler). Longwood Pub Group.
Voltaire, Montesquieu & Rousseau in England. J. Churton Collins. 293p. 1980. Repr. of 1908 ed. lib. bdg. 37.00 (ISBN 0-8414-3032-2). Folcroft.
Voltaire Musicien. Edmond V. Straeten. LC 76-43943. (Music & Theatre in France in the 17th & 18th Centuries). Repr. of 1878 ed. 27.00 (ISBN 0-404-60197-9). AMS Pr.
Voltaire, Pascal & Human Destiny. Mina Waterman. LC 70-120676. 1970. Repr. lib. bdg. 14.50x (ISBN 0-374-98279-1, Octagon). Hippocrene Bks.
Voltaire Smile & Other Stories. Ron Harvie. 196p. (Orig.). 1982. pap. 6.95 (ISBN 0-9604724-1-X). Gay Pr NY.
Voltaire: The Incomparable Infidel. 91p. 1982. Repr. of 1929 ed. lib. bdg. 35.00 (ISBN 0-89987-522-X). Darby Bks.
Voltaire's Binary Masterpiece: L'Ingenu Reconsidered. John S. Clouston. (European University Studies XIII - French Language & Literature: Vol. 111). 364p. 1986. text ed. 33.00 (ISBN 3-261-03593-5). P Lang Pubs.
Voltaire's Essay on Epic Poetry: A Study & Edition. Ed. by Florence White. LC 74-90363. 167p. 1970. Repr. of 1915 ed. 20.00x (ISBN 0-87753-044-0). Phaeton.
Voltaire's Essay on Milton. Desmond Flower. LC 77-918. 1954. lib. bdg. 17.00 (ISBN 0-8414-4186-3). Folcroft.
Voltaire's Faceties. D. Guiragossian. 140p. (Orig.). 1963. pap. text ed. 18.00x (ISBN 0-317-56058-1, Pub. by Droz Switzerland). Coronet Bks.
Voltaire's Marginalia on the Pages of Rousseau: A Comparative Study of Ideas. George Havens. LC 68-762. (Studies in French Literature, No. 45). 1969. Repr. of 1933 ed. lib. bdg. 49.95x (ISBN 0-8383-0695-0). Haskell.
Voltaire's Marginalia on the Pages of Rousseau; a Comparative Study of Ideas. Ed. by George R. Havens. LC 73-171515. (Research & Source Works Ser: No. 869). 210p. (Philosophy Monographs, No. 84). 1972. Repr. of 1933 ed. lib. bdg. 19.00 (ISBN 0-8337-4167-5). B Franklin.
Voltaire's Old Testament Criticism. B. E. Schwartzbach. 275p. (Orig.). 1970. pap. text ed. 24.00x (ISBN 0-317-56059-X, Pub. by Droz Switzerland). Coronet Bks.
Voltaire's Philosophy on Matters Earthly & Divine. Voltaire. (Illus.). 141p. 1988. 137.75 (ISBN 0-89901-364-3). Found Class Reprints.
Voltaire's Politics: The Poet As Realist. Peter Gay. LC 87-51375. 448p. 1988. text ed. 40.00 (ISBN 0-300-04096-2); pap. 15.95x (ISBN 0-300-04095-4). Yale U Pr.
Voltaire's Stylistic Transformation of Rabelaisian Satirical Devices. Ruth C. Flowers. LC 72-94182. (Catholic University of America. Studies in Romance Languages & Literatures: No. 41). 1969. Repr. of 1951 ed. 21.00 (ISBN 0-404-50341-1). AMS Pr.
Voltaire's Visit to England, Seventeen Twenty-Six to Seventeen Twenty-Nine. Archibald Ballantyne. (Works of Archibald Ballantyne). 338p. 1985. Repr. of 1919 ed. lib. bdg. 49.00 (Pub. by Am Repr Serv). Am Biog Serv.
Voltairian Narrative Devices As Considered in the Author's Contes Philosophiques. Dorothy M. McGhee. LC 72-84997. (Illus.). 192p. 1973. Repr. of 1933 ed. 15.00x (ISBN 0-8462-1675-2). Russell.
Voltairiens, 8 Vols. Compiled by Jeroom Vercruysse. (Series I). 1978. lib. bdg. 360.00 (ISBN 3-262-00190-2). Kraus Intl.
Voltairiens: Series 2, a Collection of 125 pamphlets about Voltaire Published Between 1719-1749, 7 vols. Jeroom Vercruysse. LC 82-49005. 1983. Set. lib. bdg. 375.00 (ISBN 0-527-93364-3). Kraus Intl.
Voltairine de Cleyre: A Chronology. V. Munoz. Tr. by W. Scott Johnson. (Libertarian & Anarchist Chronology Ser.). 1979. lib. bdg. 59.95 (ISBN 0-8490-3036-6). Gordon Pr.
Voltammetry in the Neurosciences. Ed. by Joseph B. Justice, Jr. LC 86-20105. (Contemporary Science Ser.). 416p. 1987. 64.50 (ISBN 0-89603-103-9). Humana.
Volterra & Functional Differential Equations. Ed. by Kenneth B. Hannsgen & Terry L. Herdman. (Lecture Notes in Pure & Applied Mathematics Ser.: Vol. 81). (Illus.). 352p. 1982. 65.00 (ISBN 0-8247-1721-X). Dekker.
Volterra Equations: Proceedings, Helsinki Symposium, Finland, August 11-14, 1978. Ed. by S. O. Londen & O. J. Staffan. (Lecture Notes in Mathematics: Vol. 737). 1979. pap. 20.00 (ISBN 0-387-09534-9). Springer-Verlag.
Volterra Integral & Differential Equations. T. A. Burton. LC 82-18932. (Mathematics in Science & Engineering Ser.). 328p. 1983. 58.50 (ISBN 0-12-147380-5). Acad Pr.
Volterra Integral Equations & Topological Dynamics. Richard K. Miller & George R. Sell. LC 52-42839. (Memoirs: No. 102). 1979. pap. 14.00 (ISBN 0-8218-1802-3, MEMO-102). Am Math.
Volterra-Stieltjes Integral Equations & Generalized Ordinary Differential Expressions. A. B. Mingarelli. (Lecture Notes in Mathematics: Vol. 989). 318p. 1983. pap. 19.50 (ISBN 0-387-12294-X). Springer-Verlag.
Voltmeier: Or, the Mountain Men. William G. Simms. Ed. by John C. Guilds. LC 68-9190. (Centennial Edition of the Writings of William Gilmore Simms: Vol. 1). (Illus.). xxxii, 448p. 1969. 35.95x (ISBN 0-87249-140-4). U of SC Pr.
Volts to Hertz: The Rise of Electricity. Sanford P. Bordeau. LC 82-17702. (Illus.). 308p. 1982. write for info. (ISBN 0-8087-4908-0). Burgess MN Intl.
Volume & Delay in Appellate Courts: Preliminary Findings from a National Study. National Center for State Courts. 185p. 1979. manuscript 11.10 (NERO-091). Natl Ctr St Courts.
Volume & Delay in State Appellate Courts: Problems & Responses. Stephen L. Wasby & Thomas B. Marvell. 131p. 1979. manuscript 7.86 (ISBN 0-89656-040-6, R-048). Natl Ctr St Courts.
Volume & Delay in the Colorado Court of Appeals. National Center for State Courts Staff. 100p. 1980. manuscript 6.00 (NERO-055). Natl Ctr St Courts.
Volume & Delay in the Florida District Court of Appeals; First District. National Center for State Courts Staff. 98p. 1980. manuscript 5.88 (NERO-054). Natl Ctr St Courts.
Volume & Delay in the Illinois Appellate Court, First District. National Center for State Courts Staff. 107p. 1980. manuscript 6.42 (NERO-058). Natl Ctr St Courts.
Volume & Delay in the Indiana Court of Appeals. National Center for State Courts Staff. 107p. 1980. manuscript 6.42 (NERO-074). Natl Ctr St Courts.
Volume & Delay in the Montana Supreme Court. National Center for State Courts Staff. 98p. 1980. manuscript 5.88 (NERO-053). Natl Ctr St Courts.
Volume & Delay in the Nebraska Supreme Court. National Center for State Courts Staff. 97p. 1980. manuscript 5.82 (NERO-057). Natl Ctr St Courts.
Volume & Delay in the New Jersey Superior Court, Appellate Division. National Center for State Courts Staff. 97p. 1980. manuscript 5.82 (NERO-056). Natl Ctr St Courts.
Volume & Delay in the Ohio Court of Appeals, Eighth District. National Center for State Courts Staff. 103p. 1980. manuscript 6.18 (NERO-059). Natl Ctr St Courts.
Volume & Delay in the Oregon Court of Appeals. National Center for State Courts Staff. 92p. 1980. manuscript 5.52 (ISBN 0-317-59223-8, NERO-052). Natl Ctr St Courts.
Volume & Delay in the Virginia Supreme Court. National Center for State Courts Staff. 101p. 1980. manuscript 6.06 (NERO-075). Natl Ctr St Courts.
Volume Cycles in the Stock Market. Richard W. Arms, Jr. LC 82-73619. 200p. 1983. 50.00 (ISBN 0-87094-405-3). Dow Jones-Irwin.
Volume di Tutta L'Arte della Trombetta see Entire Art of Trumpet Playing.
Volume Holography & Volume Gratings. L. Solymar & D. J. Cooke. LC 81-66394. 1981. 67.50 (ISBN 0-12-654580-4). Acad Pr.
Volume International Discography of the New Wave. Ed. by B. George. (Illus.). 264p. (Orig.). (YA) (gr. 8 up). 1980. pap. 7.95 (ISBN 0-9605778-0-7). One Ten Records.
Volume-International Discography of the New Wave, Vol. 2. Ed. by B. George & Martha DeFoe. (Illus.). 736p. 1982. pap. 12.95 (ISBN 0-7119-0050-7, Co-Pub. by Omnibus Press). One Ten Records.
Volume of Memorial Essays. Fritz Saxl. Ed. by D. Gordon. 1957. 19.50 (ISBN 0-8337-3131-9). B Franklin.
Volume of Payments & the Informal Economy in the Netherlands 1965-82. W. C. Boeschoten & M. M. Fase. 1984. pap. 12.50 (ISBN 90-247-3095-3, Pub. by Martinus Nijhoff Netherlands). Kluwer Academic.
Volume Reduction of Low-Activity Solid Wastes. (Technical Reports Ser.: No. 106). (Illus., Orig.). 1970. pap. 10.50 (ISBN 92-0-125170-X, IDC106, IAEA). UNIPUB.
Volume Requirements for Air & Gas Drilling. R. R. Angel. (Air & Gas Drilling Technology Ser.: Vol. 2). 94p. (Orig.). 1958. 27.00x (ISBN 0-87201-890-3). Gulf Pub.
Volume Theory of Stock Market Prices as an Infallible Barometer for the Anticipation of the Future of the Market. Frederick O. Olmstead. (Illus.). 142p. 1983. 117.75 (ISBN 0-86654-085-7). Inst Econ Finan.
Volume 3: From the Protestant Reformation to the Twentieth Century see History of Christian Thought.
Volumes, Limits & Extensions of Analytic Varieties. G. Stolzenberg. (Lecture Notes in Mathematics: Vol. 19). (Orig.). 1966. pap. 10.70 (ISBN 0-387-03602-4). Springer-Verlag.
Volumezero. Ed. by David H. Bell. (Illus.). 76p. (Orig.). 1986. pap. 15.00 (ISBN 0-937919-00-4). RPI Schl Arch.
Volumina Legum, 11 vols. Repr. of 1859 ed. Set. 2000.00 (ISBN 0-318-23366-5). Szwede Slavic.
Voluntarism & Social Work Practice: A Growing Collaboration. Ed. by Florence S. Schwartz. LC 83-21749. 248p. (Orig.). 1984. lib. bdg. 39.50 (ISBN 0-8191-3677-8); pap. text ed. 23.25 (ISBN 0-8191-3678-6). U Pr of Amer.
Voluntarism in Organized Labor in the United States, 1930-40. George C. Higgins. LC 76-89737. (American Labor: From Conspiracy to Collective Bargaining Ser., No. 1). 1969. Repr. of 1944 ed. 13.00 (ISBN 0-405-02126-7). Ayer Co Pubs.
Voluntary Agencies & Rural Development. I. S. Sundaram. xii, 311p. 1986. text ed. 45.00x (ISBN 81-7018-328-6, Pub by B R Pub Corp Delhi). Apt Bks.
Voluntary Agencies in the Welfare State. Ralph M. Kramer. LC 80-5918. 400p. 1981. 40.00x (ISBN 0-520-04290-5). U of Cal Pr.
Voluntary Agency As an Instrument of Social Change: Effective Advocacy on Behalf of the Aging. Ed. by Charlotte Nusberg. (Orig.). 1976. pap. text ed. 2.00 (ISBN 0-910473-01-3). Intl Fed Ageing.
Voluntary Approaches to Debt Relief. John Williamson. 1988. write for info (ISBN 0-88132-075-7). Inst Intl Eco.
Voluntary Associations. Donato J. Pugliese. LC 82-49155. 300p. 1986. lib. bdg. 42.00 (ISBN 0-8240-9156-6). Garland Pub.
Voluntary Associations among Mexican Americans in San Antonio, Texas: Organizational & Leadership Characteristics. John H. Lane, Jr. Ed. by Carlos E. Cortes. LC 76-1292. (Chicano Heritage Ser.). 1976. 18.00x (ISBN 0-405-09510-4). Ayer Co Pubs.
Voluntary Associations & the Urban Public Life in Bengal. Sanyal Rajat. 1983. 16.50x (ISBN 0-8364-0980-9, Pub. by Riddhi India). South Asia Bks.
Voluntary Associations: Perspectives on the Literature. Constance Smith & Anne Freedman. LC 72-75404. 432p. 1972. pap. 15.00x (ISBN 0-674-94310-4). Harvard U Pr.
Voluntary Associations: Socio-cultural Analyses & Theological Interpretation. James L. Adams. Ed. by J. Ronald Engel. LC 86-80304. 410p. 1986. text ed. 27.95x (ISBN 0-913552-34-8); pap. text ed. 14.95X (ISBN 0-913552-35-6). Exploration Pr.
Voluntary Associations: Structure & Process. James C. Peterson et al. 272p. 1986. 26.95t (ISBN 0-03-061756-1). Praeger.
Voluntary Controls. Jack Schwarz. pap. 8.95 (ISBN 0-525-48321-7). Dutton.
Voluntary Controls: Exercises for Creative Meditation & for Activating the Potential of the Chakras. Jack Schwarz. 1978. pap. 7.95 (ISBN 0-525-47494-3). Dutton.
Voluntary Corporate Liquidations. Ronald J. Kudla. LC 87-32282. 160p. 1988. lib. bdg. 35.00 (ISBN 0-89930-275-0, KCR/, Quorum Bks). Greenwood.
Voluntary Efforts in Decentralized Management: Opportunities & Constraints in Rural Development. Lenore Ralston et al. LC 83-324. (Research Ser.: No. 53). x, 175p. 1983. pap. 10.00x (ISBN 0-87725-153-3). U of Cal Intl St.
Voluntary Euthanasia: A Comprehensive Bibliography. Gretchen Johnson. 318p. 1987. 29.95 (ISBN 0-9606030-6-9). Hemlock Soc.
Voluntary Export Restriction As a Foreign Commercial Policy with Special Reference to Japanese Cotton Textiles, 1930-1962. Kenneth L. Bauge. (Foreign Economic Policy of the United States Ser.). 277p. 1987. lib. bdg. 45.00 (ISBN 0-8240-8072-6). Garland Pub.
Voluntary Food Intake of Farm Animals. Michael Forbes. 220p. 1986. text ed. 75.00 (ISBN 0-408-11154-2). Butterworth.
Voluntary Health & Welfare Organizations. (American Institute of CPAs Audit Guides Ser.). 1988. pap. 10.50 (ISBN 0-87051-027-4). Am Inst CPA.
Voluntary Health Organizations: A Guide to Patient Services. Labe Scheinberg & Diana M. Schneider. LC 86-72099. 122p. 1987. text ed. 31.95 (ISBN 0-939957-00-0, 0002). Demos Pubns Inc.
Voluntary Isolation of Control in a Natural Muscle Group. J. C. Barnes. Bd. with Psycho-Motor Norms for Practical Diagnosis. J. E. Wallin. Repr. of 1916 ed; Apparatus & Experiments on Sound Intensity. A. P. Weiss. Repr. of 1916 ed; No. 2. Wellesley College Studies in Psychology. Ed. by E. A. Gamble. Repr. of 1916 ed; Children's Association Frequency Tables. H. Woodrow. Repr. of 1916 ed. (Psychology Monographs General & Applied: Vol. 22). pap. 29.00 (ISBN 0-8115-1421-8). Kraus Repr.
Voluntary Nonprofit Enterprise Management. David E. Mason. (Nonprofit Management & Finance Ser.). 206p. 1985. 34.50x (ISBN 0-306-41582-8, Plenum Pr). Plenum Pub.
Voluntary Organisations: An NCVO Directory 1985-1986. 208p. 1985. pap. text ed. 11.95x (ISBN 0-7199-1137-0, Pub. by Bedford England). Brookfield Pub Co.
Voluntary Political Government: Letters from Charles Lane. Charles Lane. 104p. (Orig.). 1982. pap. 5.95 (ISBN 0-9602574-3-8). M E Coughlin.

Voodoo in New Orleans. Robert Tallant. 248p. 1983. pap. 3.50 (ISBN 0-88289-336-X). Pelican.
Voodoo Lost Arts & Sciences. abr. ed. Luanna C. Blagrove. (Illus.). 250p. 1988. 24.95 (ISBN 0-939776-22-7). Blagrove Pubns.
Voodoo, McDonnell Douglas F-101. (Modern Military Aircraft Ser.). (Illus.). 64p. 1986. pap. 6.95 (ISBN 0-89747-162-8, 5002). Squad Sig Pubns.
Voodoo Planet. Andre Norton. Bd. with Star Hunter. (Solar Queen Ser.: Bk. No. 3). 1983. pap. 2.75 (ISBN 0-441-78196-9, Ace Science Fiction). Ace Bks.
Voodoo Queen. Robert Tallant. 314p. 1983. pap. 3.50 (ISBN 0-88289-332-7). Pelican.
Voodoo Science, Twisted Consumerism. Peter Harnik & Michael F. Jacobson. 67p. (Orig.). 1982. pap. 4.00 (ISBN 0-89329-095-5). Ctr Sci Public.
Voodoo Tales As Told among the Negroes of the Southwest. facs. ed. Mary A. Owen. LC 70-149874. (Black Heritage Library Collection). (Illus.). 1893. 17.00 (ISBN 0-8369-8754-3). Ayer Co Pubs.
Voodoo: Treasure in Bootle Bay, Vol. 1. Allan Campbell. (Illus.). 200p. 1985. 14.95 (ISBN 0-9613326-0-3). C I L Inc.
Voodooism in Music, & Other Essays. facs. ed. Richard R. Terry. LC 68-16978. (Essay Index Reprint Ser). 1934. 17.00 (ISBN 0-8369-0930-5). Ayer Co Pubs.
Voodoos & Obeahs. Joseph J. Williams. LC 74-11170. 1970. Repr. of 1932 ed. 23.00 (ISBN 0-404-06986-X). AMS Pr.
Voodoos & Obeahs: Phases of West India Witchcraft. Joseph J. Williams. 257p. 1984. Repr. of 1932 ed. lib. bdg. 85.00 (ISBN 0-89987-880-6). Darby Bks.
Voorloper. Andre Norton. 272p. 1981. pap. 2.75 (ISBN 0-441-86611-5). Ace Bks.
Vor Dem Nichts. Peter Henke. (Theologischo Bibliothek Toepelmann: Vol. 34). (Illus.). 1978. 26.80 (ISBN 3-11-007254-8). De Gruyter.
Voragine. Jose E. Rivera. (Ayacucho Library Collection Ser: Vol. 4). (Span.). 1985. 19.95 (ISBN 0-317-56236-3, Pub. by Biblioteca Ayacucho); pap. 8.50 (ISBN 0-317-56237-1, Pub. by Biblioteca Ayacucho). Humanities.
Vorchristliche Judische Gnosticismus. M. Friedlander. 134p. (Ger.). Repr. of 1898 ed. text ed. 41.40x (ISBN 0-576-80172-0, Pub. by Gregg Intl Pubs England). Gregg Intl.
Vorentwurfe der Redaktoren zun BGB: Die Vorlagen der Radaktoren fur die erste Kommission zur Ausarbeitung des Entwurfs eines Burgerlichen Gesetzbuches, 3 pts. Ed. by Werner Schubert. 1983. Pt. I, 1176 ps. 106.00 (ISBN 3-11-009766-4); Pt. II, 1280 ps. 106.00 (ISBN 3-11-009767-2); Pt. III, 1172 ps. 106.00 (ISBN 3-11-009768-0). De Gruyter.
Vorformen der Schriftexegese innerhalb des Alten Testaments. Ina Willi-Plein. 286p. 1971. 43.20x (ISBN 3-11-001897-7). De Gruyter.
Vorlesungen I: Schrift fuer die Kandidatur Am College De France: Lob der Philosophie; Vorlesungszusammenfassungen (College De France 1952-1960) Die Humanwissenschaften und die Phaenomenologie. Maurice Merleau-Ponty. Tr. by Alexandre Metraux from Fr. (Phaenomenologisch-Psychologische Forschungen 9). (Ger.). 1972. 46.40 (ISBN 3-11-001823-3). De Gruyter.
Vorlesungen Uber Continuierliche Gruppen Mit Geometrischen und Anderen Anwendungen. 2nd ed. Sophus Lie. LC 66-12879. (Ger). 1971. text ed. 39.95 (ISBN 0-8284-0199-3). Chelsea Pub.
Vorlesungen Uber Differential und Integralrechnung, 3 vols. A. Ostrowski. Incl. Vol. 1. Funktionen Einer Variablen. 3rd ed. 330p. 1965 (ISBN 0-8176-0287-9); Vol. 2. Differentialrechnung Auf Dem Gebiete Mehrerer Variablen. 3rd ed. 382p. 1968 (ISBN 0-8176-0288-7); Vol. 3. Integralrechnung auf dem Gebiete Mehrerer Variablen. 396p. 1967 (ISBN 0-8176-0289-5). (Mathematische Reihe Ser.: Nos. 4, 5 & 7). (Illus.). 41.95x ea. Birkhauser.
Vorlesungen Uber Funktionalgleichungen und Ihre Anwendungen. J. Aczel. (Mathematische Reihe Ser.: No. 25). (Illus.). 331p. (Ger.). 1961. 44.95x (ISBN 0-8176-0002-7). Birkhauser.
Vorlesungen Uber Nichtlineare Funktionalanalysis 111: Variationsmethoden und Optimierung. E. Zeidler. 240p. 1977. pap. 35.00x (ISBN 0-317-52969-2, Pub. by Collets (UK)). State Mutual Bk.
Vorlesungen Uber Numerische Mathematik, 2 vols. H. Rutishauser. Ed. by M. Gutknecht & Martin. Incl. Vol. 1. Gleichungssysteme, Interpolation und Approximation. 164p. 1976. pap. 34.95 (ISBN 0-8176-0810-9); Vol. 2. Differentialgleichungen und Eigenwertprobleme. 228p. 1976. pap. 41.95 (ISBN 0-8176-0850-8). (Mathematische Reihe Ser.: Nos. 50 & 57). Birkhauser.
Vorlesungen uber Partielle und pfaffsche Diggerentialgleichungen. W. Haack & W. Wendland. (Mathematische Reihe Ser.: No. 3). (Illus.). 555p. (Ger.). 1969. 92.95x (ISBN 0-8176-0159-7). Birkhauser.
Vorlesungen Uber Zahlen & Funktionenlehre, 2 Vols. Alfred Pringsheim. (Bibliotheca Mathematica Teubneriana Ser: Nos. 28-29). (Ger). 1969. Repr. of 1916 ed. Set. 145.00 (ISBN 0-384-47885-9). Johnson Repr.
Vorlesungen uber Zalentheorie. H. Luneburg. (Elemente der Mathematik Von Hoeheren Standpunkt Aus: Vol. 8). 108p. (Ger.). 1978. pap. 21.95x (ISBN 0-8176-0932-6). Birkhauser.
Vorlesungen ueber die Juedischen Philosophen des Mittelalters, 3vols in 2. Moritz Eisler. 1965. Repr. of 1884 ed. 39.50 (ISBN 0-8337-4086-5). B Franklin.
Vorlesungen Ueber Geometrie Mit Besonderer Benutzung der Vortrage Von Clebsch, 2 Vols. in 3 Pts. Tr. by Rudolph F. Clebsch. (Bibliotheca Mathematica Teubneriana Ser. 43-44). (Ger). 1969. Repr. Set. 140.00 (ISBN 0-384-09295-0). Johnson Repr.
Vorlesungen Ueber Hoehere Geometrie. 3rd ed. Felix Klein. LC 51-3040. 1976. text ed. 9.95 (ISBN 0-8284-0065-2). Chelsea Pub.
Vorlesungen Ueber Natuerliche Geometrie. Ernesto Cesaro. (Bibliotheca Mathematica Teubneriana Ser: No. 36). (Ger). 1969. Repr. of 1921 ed. 33.00 (ISBN 0-384-08090-1). Johnson Repr.
Vorlesungen Ueber Reelle Funktionen. 3rd ed. Constantin Caratheodory. LC 63-11321. (Ger). 1968. 17.95 (ISBN 0-8284-0038-5). Chelsea Pub.
Vorlesungen Ueber Variationsrechnung. Oskar Bolza. LC 62-8228. 29.50 (ISBN 0-8284-0160-8). Chelsea Pub.
Vorlesungen Ueber Zahlentheorie, 3 Vols. in One. Edmund Landau. LC 49-235. (Ger). 45.00 (ISBN 0-8284-0032-6). Chelsea Pub.
Vormundschaft Mach Attischem Recht. Otto Schulthess. Ed. by Gregory Vlastos. LC 78-19379. (Morals & Law in Ancient Greece Ser.). 1979. Repr. of 1886 ed. lib. bdg. 21.00x (ISBN 0-405-11573-3). Ayer Co Pubs.
Voroshilograd Art Museum. Collet's Staff. 1982. 11.00x (ISBN 0-317-57370-5, Pub. by Collets UK). State Mutual Bk.
Vorster's Gamble for Africa. Colin Legum. (Current Affairs Ser.). 127p. 1976. pap. 5.95 (ISBN 0-8419-6501-3, Africana). Holmes & Meier.
Vortex. Jon Land. 1984. pap. 3.50 (ISBN 0-8217-1469-4). Zebra.
Vortex: A Personal Quest into the Nature of What Is. Olivia Orfield. LC 80-90007. 228p. (Orig.). 1981. pap. 7.95 (ISBN 0-938774-00-X). Prism Pr.
Vortex Flow in Nature & Technology. Hans J. Lugt. LC 82-23903. 297p. 1983. 60.00 (ISBN 0-471-86925-2, Pub. by Wiley-Interscience). Wiley.
Vortex Methods in Two-Dimensional Fluid Dynamics. C. Marchioro et al. (Lecture Notes in Physics Ser.: Vol. 203). iii, 137p. 1984. pap. 10.00 (ISBN 0-387-13352-6). Springer-Verlag.
Vortex Motion. Ed. by H. G. Hornung & E. A. Mueller. (Illus.). 172p. 1982. pap. 25.00 (ISBN 3-528-08536-3, Pub. by Vieweg & Sohn). IPS.
Vortex Points: A Complete Muscular Relaxation. Oscar Ichazo. (Illus.). 32p. 1978. pap. 20.00 (ISBN 0-686-44140-0). Arica Inst Pr.
Vortex: Pound, Eliot, & Lewis. Timothy Materer. LC 79-13009. (Illus.). 208p. 1979. 24.95x (ISBN 0-8014-1225-0). Cornell U Pr.
Vortex Universe. Mario Priletta. 1985. 10.00 (ISBN 0-533-06555-0). Vantage.
Vortices & Hell. Rudell Coursey. 1968. pap. 1.50 (ISBN 0-686-14909-2). Goliards Pr.
Vortices & Monopoles: Structure of Static Gauge Theories. Arthur Jaffe & Clifford Taubes. (Progress in Physics Ser.: No. 2). 275p. 1980. text ed. 22.95x (ISBN 0-8176-3025-2). Birkhauser.
Vorticism & Abstract Art in the First Machine Age, 2 vols. Richard Cork. Incl. Vol. 1. Origins & Development. 1976; Vol. 2. Synthesis & Decline. 1977 (ISBN 0-520-03269-1). LC 75-37227. 95.00 ea. U of Cal Pr.
Vorticism & Abstract Art in the First Machine Age, Vol. 1. Richard Cork. 344p. 1976. 240.00x (Pub. by Gordon Fraser). State Mutual Bk.
Vorticism & Abstract Art in the First Machine Age, Vol. 2. Richard Cork. 320p. 1976. 240.00x (ISBN 0-900406-25-9, Pub. by Gordon Fraser). State Mutual Bk.
Vorticism & Abstract Art in the First Machine Age, Vol. 1: Origins & Development. Richard Cork. 344p. 1976. 160.00 (ISBN 0-900406-24-0, Pub. by Gordon Fraser). State Mutual Bk.
Vorticism & the English Avant-Garde. Willaim C. Wees. LC 73-185744. (Illus.). pap. 77.80 (ISBN 0-317-10209-5, 2014454). Bks Demand UMI.
VOS Story Bible, 3 vols. Set. pap. 30.95 (ISBN 0-85151-442-1). Banner of Truth.
VOS Story Bible: New Testament. pap. 10.95 (ISBN 0-85151-237-2). Banner of Truth.
VOS Story Bible: Old Testament (Genesis-Ruth) pap. 10.95 (ISBN 0-85151-250-X). Banner of Truth.
VOS Story Bible: Old Testament (Samuel-Malachi) pap. 10.95 (ISBN 0-85151-251-8). Banner of Truth.
Vosges: French Edition-Regions of France. (Michelin Green Guides). pap. 12.95 (ISBN 0-686-56428-6). French & Eur.
Voskhishchenie: Roman. Ilia M. Zdanevich. 252p. (Rus.). 1984. pap. 8.00. Berkeley Slavic.
Vos'migrannik. Vadim Kreyd. LC 85-81524. 90p. (Rus.). 1986. 7.00 (ISBN 0-911971-19-X). Effect Pub.
Vospominaniia. Afanasii Fet. 494p. 1983. 49.00 (ISBN 0-317-40697-3, Pub. by Collets UK). State Mutual Bk.
Vospominaniia. T. I. Ivanova. 130p. (Rus.). 1984. cancelled (ISBN 0-88233-918-4). Ardis Pubs.
Vospominaniia I. Razmyshleniia, 3 vols. G. K. Zhukov. 984p. (Rus.). 1983. 95.00x (ISBN 0-317-40839-9, Pub. by Collets (UK)). State Mutual Bk.
Vospominaniia O Kornee Chukovskom. Ed. by Collet's Holdings, Ltd. Staff. 480p. 1983. 59.00x (ISBN 0-317-40840-2, Pub. by Collets (UK)). State Mutual Bk.
Vospominaniia O Litinstitute. Ed. by Collet's Holdings, Ltd. Staff. 480p. 1983. 49.00x (ISBN 0-317-40845-3, Pub. by Collets (UK)). State Mutual Bk.
Vospominaniia O Neproshedshem Vremeni. Raisa Orlova. 310p. (Rus.). 1983. 27.50 (ISBN 0-88233-725-4); pap. 13.50 (ISBN 0-88233-726-2). Ardis Pubs.
Vospominanija O Fevral'skoj Revoljucii, 2 vols. I. G. Cereteli. (Etudes Sur L'histoire L'economie et la Sociologie Des Pays Slaves: No. 7). 1963. pap. 50.40x (ISBN 90-2796-127-1). Mouton.
Voss. Patrick White. 448p. 1984. pap. 7.95 (ISBN 0-14-001438-1). Penguin.
Voss. Patrick White. 1957. 13.95 (ISBN 0-670-74807-2). Viking.
Vostaas: The Story of Montana's Indian Nations. Maxine Ruppel. (Indian Culture Ser.). (gr. 3-11). 1970. 2.95 (ISBN 0-89992-001-2). Coun India Ed.
Vostochnye Ottsy IV-Go Veka: Iz Chtenii v Pravoslavnom Bogoslovskom Institute v Parizhe. G. V. Florovsky. 240p. Repr. of 1931 ed. text ed. 49.68x (ISBN 0-576-99231-3, Pub. by Gregg Intl Pubs England). Gregg Intl.
Vote for Love. Dana Gregory. (Sweet Dreams Ser.: No. 129). 160p. (Orig.). 1987. pap. 2.50 (ISBN 0-553-26672-1). Bantam.
Vote For Me...& It Serves You Right, or Left. Dick Locher. (Orig.). 1988. pap. 5.95 (ISBN 0-933893-55-8). Bonus Books.
Vote Motive. Gordon Tullock. (Institute of Economic Affairs Hobart Paperback Ser.: No. 9). 1977. pap. 5.95 technical (ISBN 0-255-36085-1). Transatl Arts.
Vote of the People: Initiated & Referred Measures in North Dakota from Statehood Through 1984. LC 85-622756. Date not set. price not set. U ND Pr.
Vote Yes on September 23rd. Ed. by Mark Melnicove. (Illus.). 56p. (Orig.). 1980. pap. 5.00 (ISBN 0-937966-02-9). Dog Ear.
Voter Decides. Angus Campbell et al. LC 73-138211. 242p. 1971. Repr. of 1954 ed. lib. bdg. 45.00x (ISBN 0-8371-5566-5, CAVD). Greenwood.
Voter Mobilization & the Politics of Race: The South & Universal Suffrage, 1952-1984. Harold W. Stanley. LC 87-15080. 208p. 1987. lib. bdg. 35.00 (ISBN 0-275-92673-7, C2673). Praeger.
Voter Registration: A Handbook for Local Organizing. Ed. by Sherrill Marcus. 1975. pap. write for info. Voter Ed Proj.
Voter Registration & the States: Effective Policy Approaches to Increasing Participation. Ed. by Farley Peters et al. 150p. 1986. 8.95 (ISBN 0-89788-094-3). NCPa Washington.
Voter Registration in Eleven Southern States, by Race: 1960-1980, in U. S. Bureau of the Census: Statistical Abstract of the United States: 1981. Richard A. Hudlin. 1981. 0.10 ea. Voter Ed Proj.
Voters Begin to Choose: From Closed-Class to Open Elections in Britain. Richard Rose & Ian McAllister. 192p. (Orig.). 1986. text ed. 45.00 (ISBN 0-8039-9743-4); pap. text ed. 17.50 (ISBN 0-8039-9744-2). Sage.
Voters' Choice: Varieties of American Electoral Behavior. Gerald M. Pomper. (Illus.). 276p. 1983. pap. text ed. 9.75 (ISBN 0-8191-3188-1). U Pr of Amer.
Voters, Elections & Parties: The Practice of Democratic Theory. Gerald M. Pomper. 320p. 1988. 29.95 (ISBN 0-88738-160-X). Transaction Bks.
Voter's Guide to the Nineteen Eighty-Four Special Legislative Session on Education & Taxes. Tom Whatley. LC 85-117866. xi, 43p. Date not set. price not set. Tex Gov.
Voter's Guide to the Sixty-Ninth Legislature. Tom Whatley. LC 86-105987. xviii, 133p. Date not set. price not set. Tex Gov.
Voters' Money. Deane B. Caldwell. LC 85-52236. (Illus.). 130p. (Orig.). 1986. pap. 9.95 (ISBN 0-937409-00-6). Truth Cons Pub.
Votes & More for Women: Suffrage & After in Connecticut. Carole Nichols. LC 83-8405. (Women & History, No. 5). 92p. 1983. text ed. 24.95 (ISBN 0-86656-192-7, B192). Haworth Pr.
Votes for Women: The Women's Fight in Portsmouth. Sarah Peacock. (Illus.). 1983. 42.00x (ISBN 0-317-43799-2, Pub. by City of Portsmouth). State Mutual Bk.
Voting: A Study of Opinion Formation in a Presidential Campaign. Bernard R. Berelson et al. LC 54-11205. (Illus.). 1954. 20.00x (ISBN 0-226-04350-9); pap. 10.00x (ISBN 0-226-04349-5). U of Chicago Pr.
Voting & Elections. Dennis B. Fradin. LC 85-7715. (New True Bks.). (Illus.). 45p. (gr. k-4). 1985. PLB 12.60 (ISBN 0-516-01274-6); pap. 3.95 (ISBN 0-516-41274-4). Childrens.
Voting & Registration in the Election of November 1986. (Current Population Reports Series P-20, Population Characteristics: No. 414). (Illus.). 61p. 1987. pap. 3.25 (ISBN 0-318-23853-5, S/N 803-005-00007-9). USGPO.
Voting & the Handling of Disputes in the Security Council. Eduardo Jimenez de Arechaga. LC 78-3780. (Carnegie Endowment for International Peace, United Nations: No. 5). 1978. Repr. of 1950 ed. lib. bdg. 22.50x (ISBN 0-313-20332-6, ARVH). Greenwood.
Voting Behavior II. Ed. by Samuel Long. (Research in Micropolitics Ser.: Vol. II). 304p. 1987. 54.50 (ISBN 0-89232-562-3). Jai Pr.
Voting Behavior in a Tri-Ethnic Community. Gabino Rendon. LC 75-36553. 1977. soft bdg. 10.95 (ISBN 0-88247-464-2). R & E Pubs.
Voting Behavior in the South Dakota Legislature: An Exploratory Investigation into Divisible Roll Calls. Alan L. Clem. 1966. 1.00 (ISBN 1-55614-014-2). U of SD Gov Res Bur.
Voting by Institutional Investors on Corporate Governance Questions: 1987 Proxy Season. Sharon Marcil. LC 86-108877. (Corporate Governance Service). 120p. 1987. 100.00. IRRC Inc DC.
Voting Districts of the Roman Republic: The Thirty-Five Urban & Rural Tribes. Lily R. Taylor. LC 62-2896. (American Academy in Rome. Papers & Monographs: Vol. 20). pap. 97.50 (2026732). Bks Demand UMI.
Voting for President: The Electoral College & the American Political System. Wallace S. Sayre & Judith H. Parris. LC 78-139815. (Studies in Presidential Selection). 169p. 1970. pap. 9.95 (ISBN 0-8157-7719-1). Brookings.
Voting in Provincial America: A Study of Elections in the Thirteen Colonies, 1689-1776. Robert J. Dinkin. LC 77-71861. (Contributions in American History: No. 64). (Illus.). 1977. lib. bdg. 35.00 (ISBN 0-8371-9543-8, DIV/). Greenwood.
Voting in Revolutionary America: A Study of Elections in the Original Thirteen States, 1776-1789. Robert J. Dinkin. LC 81-13266. (Contributions in American History Ser.: No. 99). (Illus.). x, 184p. 1982. lib. bdg. 35.00 (ISBN 0-313-23091-9, DVR/). Greenwood.
Voting in the Security Council. Sydney D. Bailey. LC 69-15990. Repr. of 1969 ed. 54.20 (ISBN 0-8357-9252-8, 2013017). Bks Demand UMI.
Voting Patterns in the United States: Recent Writings, 1980-1984. Dale E. Casper. (Public Administration Ser.: P 1716). 9p. 1985. 2.00 (ISBN 0-89028-466-0). Vance Biblios.
Voting Procedure in International Political Organizations. Wellington Koo, Jr. LC 79-137253. Repr. of 1947 ed. 26.45 (ISBN 0-404-03774-7). AMS Pr.
Voting Procedures. Michael Dummett. (Illus.). 1985. 36.00X (ISBN 0-19-876188-0). Oxford U Pr.
Voting Rights Act & Black Electoral Participation. Kenneth H. Thompson. (Illus.). 50p. (Orig.). 1982. pap. 4.95 (ISBN 0-941410-24-2). Jt Ctr Pol Studies.
Voting Rights Act: Consequences & Implications. Lorn S. Foster. LC 85-6600. 224p. 1985. 36.95 (ISBN 0-275-90101-7, C0101). Praeger.
Voting Rights Act: Questions & Answers. Richard A. Hudlin & Brimah K. Farouk. 1981. 1.00 (ISBN 0-686-38020-7). Voter Ed Proj.
Voting Trusts: A Chapter in Modern Corporate History. Harry A Cushing. LC 27-22631. (Business Enterprises Reprint Ser.). 257p. 1983. Repr. of 1927 ed. lib. bdg. 40.00 (ISBN 0-89941-273-4). W S Hein.
Votive & Historical Texts from Babylonia & Assyria. Ferris J. Stephens. LC 78-63538. (Yale Oriental Series: Babylonian Texts: No. 9). (Illus.). 160p. Repr. of 1937 ed. 31.00 (ISBN 0-404-60259-2). AMS Pr.
Votive Offerings Among Greek-Philadelphians: A Ritual Perspective. Robert T. Teske. Ed. by Richard M. Dorson. LC 80-735. (Folklore of the World Ser.). 1980. lib. bdg. 33.50x (ISBN 0-405-13325-1). Ayer Co Pubs.
Votive Sculpture of Hellenistic Cyprus. Joan B. Connelly. (Illus.). 170p. 1988. 30.00x (ISBN 0-8147-1416-1). NYU Pr.
Votive Tablets: Studies Chiefly Appreciative of English Authors & Books. facs. ed. Edmund C. Blunden. LC 67-26716. (Essay Index Reprint Ser). 1932. 20.00 (ISBN 0-8369-0219-X). Ayer Co Pubs.
Votive Terracottas of Gujarat. Haku Shah. LC 85-222060. (Living Traditions of India Ser.). (Illus.). 160p. 1985. 22.50 (ISBN 0-295-96249-6, Pub. by U of Tokyo Japan). U of Wash Pr.
Votre Force Spirituelle et Emotionnelle. Richard D. Dobbins. Ed. by Annie L. Cosson. Tr. by Valerie Chardenal from Eng. 188p. (Fr.). 1985. pap. text ed. 2.25 (ISBN 0-8297-0703-4). Life Pubs Intl.
Voucher Examiner. Jack Rudman. (Career Examination Ser.: C-3265). (Cloth bdg. avail. on request). 1988. pap. 12.00 (ISBN 0-8373-3265-6). Natl Learning.
Voudoun Fire: The Living Reality of the Mystical Religions. Melita Denning & Osborne Phillips. LC 79-3375. (Mystery Religions Series: No. 1). (Illus.). 172p. (Orig.). 1979. pap. 9.95 (ISBN 0-87542-699-9). Llewellyn Pubns.

Voyage into Levant. Henry Blount. LC 77-6850. (English Experience Ser.: No. 850). 1977. Repr. of 1636 ed. lib. bdg. 25.00 (ISBN 90-221-0850-3). Walter J Johnson.
Voyage into Substance: Art, Science, Nature & the Illustrated Travel Account 1760-1840. Barbara M. Stafford. (Illus.). 650p. 1984. text ed. 45.00x (ISBN 0-262-19223-3). MIT Pr.
Voyage into the Past: Continuous Life in Thirty Five Centuries. Carl T. Endemann. LC 81-81554. 1981. 9.95. Gondwana Bks.
Voyage into the Past: Continuous Life Through 35 Centuries. Carl T. Endemann. LC 81-81554. (Illus.). 1981. 9.95 (ISBN 0-931926-10-6). Alta Napa.
Voyage into Violence. Frances Lockridge & Richard Lockridge. 1975. Repr. of 1956 ed. lib. bdg. 16.95x (ISBN 0-89190-908-7, Pub. by River City Pr). Amereon Ltd.
Voyage Litteraire de Deux Benedictins de la Congregation de Saint-Maur, 2 vols. Edmond Martene & Ursin Durand. 1042p. Repr. of 1717 ed. text ed. 207.00x (ISBN 0-576-99707-2, Pub. by Gregg Intl Pubs England). Gregg Intl.
Voyage Musical Aux Pays du Passe. facsimile ed. Romain Rolland. (Illus.). 271p. 1976. 22.50 (ISBN 0-686-55282-2). French & Eur.
Voyage Musicale en Allemagne & en Italie, 2 vols. Hector Berlioz. 802p. Date not set. Repr. of 1844 ed. text ed. 104.00x (ISBN 0-576-28419-X, Pub. by Gregg Intl Pubs England). Gregg Intl.
Voyage of Alexander Mackenzie. facs. ed. 42p. pap. 5.75 (ISBN 0-8466-0182-6, S182). Shorey.
Voyage of Argo. Appollonius of Rhodes. Tr. by Emil V. Rieu. (Classics Ser.). (Orig.). 1959. pap. 5.95 (ISBN 0-14-044085-2). Penguin.
Voyage of Bran, Son of Febal, to the Land of the Living, 2 Vols. Imran Brain. Tr. by Kuno Meyer. LC 70-144520. (Grimm Library: Nos. 4, 6). Repr. of 1897 ed. Set. 54.50 (ISBN 0-404-53580-1). AMS Pr.
Voyage of Captain Don Felipe Gonzalez to Easter Island in 1770-1771. Ed. by Bolton G. Corney. (Hakluyt Society Works Ser.: No. 2, Vol. 13). (Illus.). Repr. of 1903 ed. 38.00 (ISBN 0-8115-0335-6). Kraus Repr.
Voyage of Captain John Saris to Japan in 1613. Ed. by Ernest M. Satow. (Hakluyt Society Works Series 2: Vol. 5). (Illus.). Repr. of 1900 ed. 48.00 (ISBN 0-8115-0328-3). Kraus Repr.
Voyage of Captain Luke Foxe of Hull & Captain Thomas James of Bristol, in Search of a Northwest Passage, in 1631-32. Ed. by Miller Christy. (Hakluyt Society. Publications: Nos. 88-89). (Illus.). 1966. Repr. of 1894 ed. 63.00 (ISBN 0-8337-0568-7). B Franklin.
Voyage of Charles Darwin. Charles Darwin. Ed. by Christopher Ralling. LC 79-916. (Illus.). 1980. 12.50 (ISBN 0-8317-9212-4, Mayflower Bks). Smith Pubs.
Voyage of Charles Darwin: His Autobiographical Writings. Selected by Christopher Ralling. LC 85-19111. (Illus.). 182p. (Orig.). 1986. 17.95 (ISBN 0-88186-426-9); pap. 4.95 (ISBN 0-88186-925-2). Parkwest Pubns.
Voyage of Death. write for info. Sri Shirdi Sai.
Voyage of Desire. Ben Westfield. 304p. (Orig.). 1980. pap. 2.50 (ISBN 0-89083-622-1). Zebra.
Voyage of Discovery. Hilda Nickson. (Romances Ser.: No. 2859). 192p. Date not set. pap. 1.95 (ISBN 0-317-63916-1). Harlequin Bks.
Voyage of Discovery & Research in the Southern & Antarctic Regions 1839-43, 2 Vols. James C. Ross. LC 69-10852. (Illus.). 1969. Repr. of 1847 ed. 87.50xset (ISBN 0-678-05624-2). Kelley.
Voyage of Discovery: George Deacon 70th Anniversary Volume. new ed. Ed. by Martin V. Angel. LC 76-57958. 1977. 175.00 (ISBN 0-08-021380-4). Pergamon.
Voyage of Discovery to the Strait of Magellan. Jose De Vargas Y Ponce. LC 77-88580. 1977. Repr. of 1820 ed. lib. bdg. 12.50 (ISBN 0-89341-286-4). Longwood Pub Group.
Voyage of Doctor Dolittle. Hugh Lofting. (gr. 4-7). 1988. pap. 3.50 (ISBN 0-440-40002-3, YB). Dell.
Voyage of Francois Pyrard of Laval to the East Indies, the Maldives, the Moluccas & Brazil, 2 vols in 3. Francois Pyrard. Ed. by Albert Gray. (Hakluyt Ser.: No. 80). 1971. Repr. of 1890 ed. lib. bdg. 92.00 (ISBN 0-8337-1431-7). B Franklin.
Voyage of J. Huyghen Van Linschoten to the East Indies, 2 Vols. Jan H. Van Linschoten. Ed. by Arthur C. Burnell & P. A. Tiele. 1967. Repr. of 1598 ed. 59.00 (ISBN 0-8337-2117-8). B Franklin.
Voyage of Life on a Paper Boat, No. 12. Arnold C. Westphal. pap. 3.95 (ISBN 0-915398-22-2). Visual Evangels.
Voyage of Nicholas Downton to the East Indies, 1614-1615. Ed. by William Foster. (Hakluyt Society Works Ser.: No. 2 Vol. 82). (Illus.). Repr. of 1938 ed. 32.00 (ISBN 0-8115-0382-8). Kraus Repr.
Voyage of Odysseus. Homer. Adapted by I. M. Richardson. LC 83-14235. (Tales from the Odyssey Ser.). (Illus.). 32p. (gr. 4-8). 1984. lib. bdg. 10.79 (ISBN 0-8167-0005-2); pap. text ed. 2.50 (ISBN 0-8167-0006-0). Troll Assocs.
Voyage of Odysseus: Homer's Odyssey. Retold by James Reeves. LC 86-10869. (Children's Classics from World Literature Ser.). 192p. (gr. 4 up). 1986. pap. 6.95 (Bedrick Blackie); 12.95. P Bedrick Bks.
Voyage of Pedro Alvares Cabral to Brazil & India. Compiled by William B. Greenlee. (Hakluyt Society Works Ser.: No. 2, Vol. 81). (Illus.). Repr. of 1937 ed. 38.00 (ISBN 0-8115-0381-X). Kraus Repr.
Voyage of Pleasure: The Log of Bernard Gilboy's Transpacific Cruise in the Boat "Pacific," 1882. John B. Tompkins. LC 56-12045. (Illus.). 77p. 1956. pap. 6.00 (ISBN 0-87033-004-7). Cornell Maritime.
Voyage of Re-Discovery: The Veneration of St. Vincent. Anne F. Francis. 1978. 15.00 (ISBN 0-682-48429-6, University). Exposition-Phoenix.
Voyage of Robert Dudley: Afterwards Styled Earl of Warwick & Leicester & Duke of Northumberland, to the West Indies, 1594-1595. Ed. by G. F. Wagner. (Hakluyt Society Works Series 2: Vol. 3). Repr. of 1899 ed. 25.00 (ISBN 0-8115-0326-7). Kraus Repr.
Voyage of St. Brendan. Tr. by John J. O'Meara. 1981. write for info. (Pub. by Colin Smythe Ltd Britain). Dufour.
Voyage of Seventeen Eighty-Nine to the Northwest Coast. George Mortimer. 1988. 22.95. Ye Galleon.
Voyage of Sir Henry Middleton to the Moluccas: 1604-1606. Compiled by William Foster. (Hakluyt Society Works Ser.: No. 2, Vol. 88). (Illus.). Repr. of 1943 ed. 32.00 (ISBN 0-8115-0386-0). Kraus Repr.
Voyage of Terror. J. H. Brennan. (Grailquest Ser.: No. 4). (Orig.). (gr. k-12). 1987. pap. 2.50 (ISBN 0-440-99324-5, LFL). Dell.
Voyage of the Armada. David Howarth. 1982. pap. 7.95 (ISBN 0-14-006315-3). Penguin.
Voyage of the "Beagle". Charles Darwin. 1979. 10.95x (ISBN 0-460-00104-3, Evman); pap. 6.95x (ISBN 0-460-01104-9, Evman). Biblio Dist.
Voyage of the Beagle. Charles Darwin. LC 62-2990. 1962. 6.95 (ISBN 0-385-02767-2, Anchor). Natural Hist.
Voyage of the Beagle. Charles Darwin. LC 62-2990. 6.95. Doubleday.
Voyage of the Beagle. Charles Darwin. 1988. pap. 4.95 (ISBN 0-451-62620-6, Mentor). NAL.
Voyage of the Damned. Gordon Thomas & Max M. Witts. 19.95 (ISBN 0-88411-897-5, Pub. by Aeonian Pr). Amereon Ltd.
Voyage of the "Dawn Treader". C. S. Lewis. LC 52-4219. (Illus.). 224p. (gr. 4 up). 1969. 11.95 (ISBN 0-02-758800-9); pap. 2.95 (ISBN 0-02-044260-2, Collier). Macmillan.
Voyage of the "Dawn Treader". C. S. Lewis. (Chronicles of Narnia Ser.: Vol. 3). 284p. (gr. 4-8). 1986. lib. bdg. 13.95x (ISBN 0-8161-4091-X, Large Print Bks.). G K Hall.
Voyage of the "Dawn Treader". C. S. Lewis. LC 85-29979. (Chronicles of Narnia Ser.). (Illus.). 224p. (gr. 4 up). 1986. pap. 5.95 (ISBN 0-02-044440-0, Collier). Macmillan.
Voyage of the Dawn Treader. C. S. Lewis. LC 52-4219. (Chronicles of Narnia Ser.). (Illus.). 224p. (gr. 4 up). 1988. 12.95 (ISBN 0-02-758820-3). Macmillan.
Voyage of the Discovery, 2 vols. Robert F. Scott. LC 68-55218. (Illus.). 1970. Repr. of 1905 ed. Vol. 1. lib. bdg. 31.25 (ISBN 0-8371-1334-2, SCDJ); Vol. 2. lib. bdg. 31.25 (ISBN 0-8371-1335-0, SCDK). Greenwood.
Voyage of the 'Discovery' Robert S. Scott. (Illus.). 1951. 18.00 (ISBN 0-685-20649-1). Transatl Arts.
Voyage of the Flying Bird. Margaret Titcomb. LC 74-94023. (Illus.). (gr. 7-9). 1970. 4.35 (ISBN 0-8048-0723-X). C E Tuttle.
Voyage of the Iceberg: The Story of the Iceberg That Sank the Titanic. Richard Brown. (Illus.). 1984. 13.95 (ISBN 0-8253-0187-4). Beaufort Bks NY.
Voyage of the Jolly Boat. Margret Rettich. Tr. by Olive Jones from Ger. (Illus.). 32p. (gr. k-4). 1981. 9.95 (ISBN 0-416-30791-4, NO. 0227). Routledge Chapman & Hall.
Voyage of the Komagata Maru: The Sikh Challenge to Canada's Colour Bar. Hugh Johnston. (Illus.). 1979. 19.95x (ISBN 0-19-561164-0). Oxford U Pr.
Voyage of the Liberdade see Sailing Alone Around the World.
Voyage of the Lucky Dragon. Jack Bennett. 156p. (gr. 7 up). 1982. 9.95 (ISBN 0-13-944165-4). P-H.
Voyage of the Lucky Dragons. Jack Bennett. 156p. (gr. 5 up). 1985. pap. 5.95 (ISBN 0-13-944158-1). P-H.
Voyage of the Ludgate Hill: A Journey with Robert Louis Stevenson. Nancy Willard et al. LC 86-19502. (Illus.). 32p. (gr. 5-8). 1987. 14.95 (ISBN 0-15-294464-8). HarBraceJ.
Voyage of the Mistral. Madeleine Ker. (Harlequin Romances Ser.). 192p. 1984. pap. 1.75 (ISBN 0-373-02595-5). Harlequin Bks.
Voyage of the New Hazard to the Northwest Coast, Hawaii & China, 1810-1813. Stephen Reynolds. 1970. 14.95 (ISBN 0-87770-076-1). Ye Galleon.
Voyage of the Planetslayer. Jefferson Swycaffer. 1988. pap. 3.50 (ISBN 0-425-11341-8). Berkley Pub.
Voyage of the "Pourquoi Pas?" in the Antarctic: The Journal of the Second French South Polar Expedition, 1908-1910. Jean Charcot. LC 77-20265. (Illus.). vi, 315p. 1978. Repr. of 1911 ed. 35.00 (ISBN 0-208-01644-9, Archon). Shoe String.
Voyage of the Ruslan: The First Manned Exploration of Mars. Joshua Stoff. LC 85-28803. (Illus.). 96p. (gr. 4 up). 1986. 12.95 (ISBN 0-689-31191-5, Atheneum Childrens Bks). Macmillan.
Voyage of the Sonora in the Second Bucareli Expedition to Explore the Northwest Coast. Francisco A. Mourelle. Tr. by Daines Barrington from Span. LC 20-13605. Repr. of 1920 ed. 39.00 (ISBN 0-527-03237-9). Kraus Repr.
Voyage of the Starfire to Atlantis. Edwin Mumford. 1973. 4.00 (ISBN 0-682-47692-7). Exposition-Phoenix.
Voyage of the Water Witch: A Scientific Expedition to Paraguay & the La Plata Region (1853-1856) Robert D. Wood. LC 85-50095. (Illus.). 114p. 1985. pap. 13.00x (ISBN 0-911437-15-0). Labyrinthos.
Voyage of Thomas Best to the East Indies, 1612-1614. Ed. by William Foster. (Hakluyt Society Works Ser.: No. 2, Vol. 75). (Illus.). Repr. of 1934 ed. 50.00 (ISBN 0-8115-0377-1). Kraus Repr.
Voyage of Vengeance. L. Ron Hubbard. (Mission Earth Ser.: Vol. 7). 1987. 18.95 (ISBN 0-88404-213-8). Bridge Pubns Inc.
Voyage of Verrazzano. facs. ed. Henry C. Murphy. LC 72-126244. (Select Bibliographies Reprint Ser). 1875. 23.50 (ISBN 0-8369-5471-8). Ayer Co Pubs.
Voyage Out. Virginia Woolf. LC 31-141. 375p. 1968. pap. 6.95 (ISBN 0-15-693625-9, Harv). HarBraceJ.
Voyage Perilous: Willa Cather's Romanticism. Susan J. Rosowski. LC 86-4341. xviii, 284p. 1986. 23.95x (ISBN 0-8032-3874-6). U of Nebr Pr.
Voyage Pittoresque en Algerie, 1845. Theophile Gautier. 302p. 1973. 35.00 (ISBN 0-686-55914-2). French & Eur.
Voyage Round My Father - The Dock Brief - What Shall We Tell Caroline? John Mortimer. 186p. 1983. pap. 5.95 (ISBN 0-14-048169-9). Penguin.
Voyage Round the World in H. M. S. Resolution 1772-1775, 2 vols. George Forster. (Illus.). 300p. 1986. 49.00 (ISBN 0-904573-38-9, Pub. by Caliban Bks). Longwood Pub Group.
Voyage Round the World in the Years Eighteen Hundred & Three, Eighten Hundred & Four, Eighteen Hundred & Five & Eighteen Hundred & Six: By Order of His Imperial Majesty Alexander the First, 2 vols. Adam J. Krusenstern. (Illus.). 718p. 1968. Repr. of 1813 ed. Set. 32.50 (ISBN 0-8398-1060-1). Parnassus Imprints.
Voyage Round the World in the Years 1785, 1786, 1787, & 1788. William C. Lauder. 150p. 1985. Repr. of 1789 ed. 14.95 (ISBN 0-87770-325-6). Ye Galleon.
Voyage Round the World in the Years 1740-1744. Lord Anson. Ed. by Ernest Rhys. 384p. 1981. Repr. lib. bdg. 20.00. Century Bookbindery.
Voyage That Never Ends see Malcolm Lowry.
Voyage: The Discovery of Hawaii. Herb K. Kane. LC 76-1503. (Illus.). 1976. 12.95 (ISBN 0-89610-031-6). Island Heritage.
Voyage: The First Galway Hooker to America. Paddy Barry. (Illus.). 157p. (Orig.). 1986. pap. 11.95 (ISBN 0-7171-1441-4, Pub. by Gill & Macmillan Ireland). Irish Bks Media.
Voyage to Abyssinia. Samuel Johnson. Ed. by Joel J. Gold. LC 57-11918. (Works of Samuel Johnson Ser.: Vol. XV). 400p. 1985. text ed. 45.00t (ISBN 0-300-03003-7). Yale U Pr.
Voyage to Abyssinia. Jeronymo Lobo. Tr. by Samuel Johnson. LC 74-15064. Repr. of 1789 ed. 40.00 (ISBN 0-404-12105-5). AMS Pr.
Voyage to Abyssinia & Travels into the Interior of That Country. H. Salt. (Illus.). 600p. 1967. 55.00x (ISBN 0-7146-1015-1, F Cass Co). Biblio Dist.
Voyage to America in Eighteen Forty-Seven: The Diary of a Bohemian Jew on His Voyage from Hamburg to New York in 1847. S. E. Rosenbaum. (Studies in Judaica & the Holocaust: No. 3). 60p. 1989. lib. bdg. 19.95x (ISBN 0-89370-371-0); pap. text ed. 9.95x (ISBN 0-89370-471-7). Borgo Pr.
Voyage to America, 1783-1786. Grigorii I. Shelikhov. Ed. by Richard A. Pierce. Tr. by Marina Ramsay. (Alaska History Ser.: No. 19). (Illus.). 1981. 16.50x (ISBN 0-919642-67-5). Limestone Pr.
Voyage To Arcturus. David Lindsay. 248p. 1985. pap. 5.95 (ISBN 0-8065-0944-9, Pub. by Citadel Pr). Lyle Stuart.
Voyage to Cacklagallinia see Virgin Seducer.
Voyage to Cacklogallinia see Gulliveriana, No. 4.
Voyage to Dauphin Island in 1720: The Journal of Bertet De la Clue. Ed. by Francis Escoffier & Jay Higginbotham. Tr. by Francis Escoffier & Jay Higginbotham. LC 73-91909. (Illus., Fr.). 1974. 7.95 (ISBN 0-914334-02-6). Museum Mobile.
Voyage to Freedom: An Episode in the Illegal Immigration to Palestine. Ze'ev V. Hadari & Ze'ev Tsahor. (Illus.). 224p. 1985. 18.50x (ISBN 0-85303-208-4, Vallentine Mitchell England); pap. 11.50x (ISBN 0-85303-217-3, Vallentine Mitchell England). Biblio Dist.
Voyage to Freedom: Story of the Pilgrim Fathers. David Gay. pap. 6.95 (ISBN 0-85151-384-0). Banner of Truth.
Voyage to Gondwana: The Third "Lost Continent". Carl T. Endemann. LC 78-5699. (Illus., Orig.). 1979. pap. 13.39 (ISBN 0-931926-06-8). Alta Napa.
Voyage to Guinea, Brasil, & the West Indies, with Remarks on the Gold, Ivory & Slave Trade. John Atkins. LC 70-99333. 265p. 1972. Repr. of 1735 ed. lib. bdg. 16.50 (ISBN 0-8411-0004-7). Metro Bks.
Voyage to Hudson's Bay, by the Dobbs Galley & California, in the Years 1746 & 1747, for Discovering a North West Passage. Henry Ellis. 1748. 32.00 (ISBN 0-384-14200-1). Johnson Repr.
Voyage to Illyria: A New Study of Shakespeare. facsimile ed. Kenneth Muir & Sean O'Loughlin. LC 79-128891. (Select Bibliographies Reprint Ser). Repr. of 1937 ed. 17.00 (ISBN 0-8369-5511-0). Ayer Co Pubs.
Voyage to Inishneefa. John P. Brady. 112p. (Orig.). 1987. pap. 8.95 (ISBN 0-936784-31-8). J Daniel.
Voyage to Inner Mongolia & Tibet: 1985-86. Christine De Weck. 1988. 10.95 (ISBN 0-533-07379-0). Vantage.
Voyage to Jupiter. David Morrison & Jane Samz. (NASA SP 439 Ser.). 211p. 1980. pap. 9.00 (ISBN 0-318-11840-8, S/N 033-000-00797-3). USGPO.
Voyage to Louisiana: 1803-1805. C. C. Robin. 1966. Repr. of 1807 ed. 20.00 (ISBN 0-911116-20-6). Pelican.
Voyage to Madagascar & the East Indies. Alexis M. De Rochon. Repr. of 1792 ed. 42.00 (ISBN 0-384-51590-8). Johnson Repr.
Voyage to Marege' Macassan Trepangers in Northern Australia. C. C. MacKnight. (Illus.). 1976. 30.00x (ISBN 0-522-84088-4, Pub. by Melbourne U Pr). Intl Spec Bk.
Voyage to Northwest America, Eighteen Twenty-Seven. Frederick Luetke. Ed. by Richard A. Pierce. Tr. by Renee Marshall from Fr. (Alaska History Ser.: No. 29). (Illus.). 1986. 32.00x (ISBN 0-919642-97-7). Limestone Pr.
Voyage to Pagany. William Carlos Williams. LC 76-122108. 1970. pap. 8.25 (ISBN 0-8112-0237-2, NDP307). New Directions.
Voyage to Pagany. William Carlos Williams. LC 71-145373. 338p. 1972. Repr. of 1928 ed. 39.00x (ISBN 0-403-01278-3). Scholarly.
Voyage to Pagany. William Carlos Williams. 1988. Repr. of 1928 ed. lib. bdg. 49.00x. Am Biog Serv.
Voyage to South America, 2 vols. H. M. Brackenridge. 250.00 (ISBN 0-8490-1269-4). Gordon Pr.
Voyage to South America, 2 vols. in 1. Henry M. Brackenridge. LC 70-128425. Repr. of 1820 ed. 27.50 (ISBN 0-404-00922-0). AMS Pr.
Voyage to South America. George Juan & Don Antonio De Ulloa. LC 77-88573. 1977. Repr. of 1807 ed. lib. bdg. 65.00 (ISBN 0-89341-280-5). Longwood Pub Group.
Voyage to the City of the Dead. Alan D. Foster. (Commonwealth Ser.). 256p. (Orig.). 1984. pap. 3.50 (ISBN 0-345-35061-8, Del Rey). Ballantine.
Voyage to the First of December. Carlisle. 1987. pap. 3.95 (ISBN 0-312-90050-3). St Martin.
Voyage to the New World: An Adventure into Unlimitedness. Ramtha Mahr & Douglas J. Mahr. LC 85-4865. 275p. 1985. 5.95 (ISBN 0-317-61697-8). Masterwrks Inc.
Voyage to the New World: An Adventure into Unlimitedness. Ramtha & Douglas J. Mahr. 256p. (Orig.). 1987. pap. 3.95 (ISBN 0-449-13185-8, GM). Fawcett.
Voyage to the North Pacific. John D'Wolf. 148p. 1968. Repr. of 1861 ed. 14.95 (ISBN 0-87770-011-7). Ye Galleon.
Voyage to the Otherworld Island in Early Irish Literature. Christa Maria Loffler. Ed. by James Hogg. (Elizabethan & Renaissance Studies). 96p. (Orig.). 1983. pap. 30.00 (ISBN 3-7052-0770-9, Pub. by Salzburg Studies). Longwood Pub Group.
Voyage to the Planets: Proceedings of the Goddard Memorial Symposium, 5th, 1967. (Science & Technology Ser.: Vol. 16). 20.00x (ISBN 0-87703-044-8, Pub. by Am Astronaut). Univelt Inc.
Voyage to the South Seas. William Bligh. 1980. 29.00 (ISBN 0-09-135440-4, NO. 0219, Pub. by Hutchinson England). Routledge Chapman & Hall.
Voyage to the Southern Ocean: The Letters of Lieutenant William Reynolds from the U. S. Exploring Expedition, 1838-1842. Ed. by Anne H. Cleaver & E. Jeffrey Stann. (Illus.). 384p. 1988. 24.95 (ISBN 0-87021-300-8). Naval Inst Pr.
Voyage to Windward. J. C. Furnas. 478p. 1980. Repr. lib. bdg. 30.00 (ISBN 0-8492-4649-0). R West.
Voyage up the Persian Gulf, & a Journey Overland from India to England in 1817. William Heude. 262p. Repr. of 1819 ed. text ed. 49.68x (ISBN 0-576-03324-3, Pub. by Gregg Intl Pubs England). Gregg Intl.
Voyage with Columbus. Seymour Reit. (Time Traveler Ser.: No. 1). 96p. (Orig.). 1986. pap. 2.50 (ISBN 0-553-15431-1). Bantam.
Voyager. Janice M. Barkan. LC 84-73411. (Illus.). 64p. 1985. 8.00 (ISBN 0-8233-0406-X). Golden Quill.
Voyager. Don Hinkle. 1988. 11.95 (ISBN 0-943718-14-7). Kipling Pr.
Voyager. Jeana Yeager et al. LC 86-46163. (Illus.). 256p. 1987. 19.95 (ISBN 0-394-55266-0). Knopf.

VSAM for the COBOL Programmer. Doug Lowe. (Illus.). 150p. 1982. pap. 15.00 (ISBN 0-911625-12-7). M Murach & Assoc.
VSAM for the COBOL Programmer. rev. ed. Doug Lowe. LC 88-60035. 200p. Date not set. pap. 17.50 (ISBN 0-911625-45-3). M Murach & Assoc.
VSAM Performance & System Fine-Tuning Quick Reference Handbook. Treva L. Thompson. LC 82-83606. 150p. 1984. (list price) 17.50x (ISBN 0-942898-02-8); (net price) 10.25x. Halpern & Simon.
VSAM: Performance, Design, & Fine-Tuning. Jay Renade. (Database & Data Communications Ser.). 300p. 1987. 36.95 (ISBN 0-02-948631-9). Macmillan.
VSAM: Services & Programming Techniques. James Martin & Joe Leben. (Illus.). 432p. 1987. text ed. 48.00 (ISBN 0-13-944174-3). P-H.
VSAM Techniques: System Concepts & Programming Procedures. Boris Musteata & Robert Lesser. LC 86-610. (Illus.). 424p. 1987. pap. 39.95 (ISBN 0-89435-181-8). QED Info Sci.
Vse of the Two Mathematicall Instruments, the Crosse Staffe & the Iacobs Staffe, Newly Reviewed & the Second Time Imprinted, 2 pts. Thomas Hood. LC 75-38202. (English Experience Ser.: No. 468). 40p. 1972. Repr. of 1596 ed. 25.00 (ISBN 90-221-0468-0). Walter J Johnson.
Vsjenoshchnoje Bdjenije see Tserkovno-Pjevcheskiji Sbornik.
VSLI Image Processing. Offen. 1986. text ed. 38.95 (ISBN 0-07-047771-X). McGraw.
VTAM-SNA Reference Handbook. Date not set. 75.00 (ISBN 0-317-52330-9). OSI Pubns.
VTC--Vocational Training Continuum for the Disabled. Bruno J. D'Alonzo & Allen A. Mori. 240p. 1985. 3-ring binding 25.00 (ISBN 0-87562-088-4). Spec Child.
VTR Workshop: Small Format Video. Loretta J. Atienza. (Monographs on Communication Technology & Utilization: No. 4). (Illus.). 114p. (2nd Printing 1979). 1977. pap. text ed. 5.00 (ISBN 92-3-101467-6, U748, UNESCO). UNIPUB.
Vu-Calc & Vu-File (The Organizer) Robert B. Masters. LC 83-22489. 176p. 1984. pap. 19.95 (ISBN 0-89303-941-1). P-H.
Vue de la Terre Promise see Chronique des Pasquier.
Vue d'Ensemble sur les Methodes de Projection de la Production Agricole see Cahiers de l'Institut de Science Economique Appliquee.
Vue d'Ensemble sur les Problemes du Developpement Agricole en Martinique see Cahiers de l'Institut de Science Economique Appliquee.
Vuela del Triunfador. Ed. by Armida O. De Hernandez Carrera. (Span.). Date not set. pap. 3.95 (ISBN 0-87148-306-8). Pathway Pr.
Vuelo, Level 3. Z. S. Da Silva. 1971. 30.72 (ISBN 0-02-270770-0). Macmillan.
Vuelo 714 para Sidney. Herge. (Illus.). 62p. (Span.). 15.95 (ISBN 0-686-54348-3). French & Eur.
Vuelta a la Galia. R. Goscinny & M. Uderzo. (Illus., Span.). 15.95 (ISBN 0-686-56226-7). French & Eur.
Vuelta a la Galia. Rene Goscinny & Albert Uderzo. (Asterix the Gaul Ser.). (Illus.). 48p. 7.95. Dargaud Pub.
Vuelta a la Manzana. Rene Ariza. Ed. by Carlota Caulfield. 76p. (Span.). Date not set. pap. cancelled (ISBN 0-932367-09-7). Ed El Gato Tuerto.
Vues sur Rimbaud. Georges Duhamel. 256p. 1952. 25.00 (ISBN 0-686-55203-2). French & Eur.
Vuillard. Stuart Preston. (Masters of Art Ser.). (Illus.). 128p. 1985. 19.95 (ISBN 0-8109-1706-8). Abrams.
Vuillard. Belinda Thomson. (Illus.). 160p. Date not set. 45.00 (ISBN 0-89659-883-7). Abbeville Pr.
Vuillard, His Life & Work. Claude Roger-Marx. LC 75-41229. Repr. of 1946 ed. 25.00 (ISBN 0-404-14718-6). AMS Pr.
Vulcan. 1962. pap. 3.00 (ISBN 0-317-11780-7). Southern U Pr.
Vulcan. (Super Profile SC Ser.). 8.95 (ISBN 0-85429-436-8, F436, Pub. by G T Foulis Ltd). Haynes Pubns.
Vulcan Academy Murders. Jean Lorrah. (Star Trek Ser.: No. 20). (Orig.). 1987. pap. 3.95 (ISBN 0-671-64744-X). PB.
Vulcan: The Making of a Prairie Community. Paul Voisey. 368p. 1988. 37.50x (ISBN 0-8020-6676-3); pap. 18.95. U of Toronto Pr.
Vulcanization of Elastomers: Principles & Practice of Vulcanization of Commercial Rubbers. Ed. by G. Alliger & I. J. Sjothun. LC 78-8167. 416p. 1978. Repr. of 1964 ed. lib. bdg. 28.50 (ISBN 0-88275-686-9). Krieger.
Vulgar Boatman. William G. Tapply. (Brady Coyne Mystery Ser.). 240p. 1988. 14.95 (ISBN 0-684-18792-2). Scribner.
Vulgar Streak. Wyndham Lewis. LC 85-6099. 273p. 1985. 20.00 (ISBN 0-87685-629-6); deluxe ed. 30.00 (ISBN 0-87685-630-X); pap. 12.50 (ISBN 0-87685-628-8). Black Sparrow.
Vulgaria of J. Stanbridge & the Vulgaria of Robert Whittinton. J. Stanbridge. (EETS, OS Ser.: No. 187). Repr. of 1932 ed. 35.00 (ISBN 0-527-00187-2). Kraus Repr.
Vulgaria Uiri Doctissimi Guil. Hormani Caesarisburgensis. William Horman. LC 74-28865. (English Experience Ser.: No. 745). 1975. Repr. of 1519 ed. 46.00 (ISBN 90-221-0745-0). Walter J Johnson.
Vulgate Version of the Arthurian Romances, 8 Vols. in 7. Ed. by H. Oskar Sommer. LC 78-19691. Repr. of 1916 ed. Set. 612.50 (ISBN 0-404-17630-5); 87.50 ea. AMS Pr.
Vulnerabilities to Delinquency. Ed. by Dorothy O. Lewis. 343p. 1981. text ed. 37.95 (ISBN 0-88331-211-5). Luce.
Vulnerability, Coping, & Growth: From Infancy to Adolescence. Lois B. Murphy & Alice E. Moriarty. 488p. 1976. 50.00x (ISBN 0-300-01901-7); pap. 16.95x (ISBN 0-300-02355-3). Yale U Pr.
Vulnerability of S & Ls to Rising Market Interest Rates. 76p. 1979. 6.25 (ISBN 0-317-32428-4, 186100); members 5.00 (ISBN 0-317-32429-2). Am Bankers.
Vulnerable Age Phenomenon. Michael Inbar. LC 76-23365. (Social Science Frontiers Ser.). 59p. 1976. pap. 4.95x (ISBN 0-87154-397-4). Russell Sage.
Vulnerable Country: Civil Resources in the Defence of Australia. Ed. by J. O. Langtry & D. Ball. 704p. 1986. 46.00 (ISBN 0-08-033045-2, K122,K120,K115). Pergamon.
Vulnerable Infants: A Psychosocial Dilemma. new ed. Jane T. Schwartz & Lawrence H. Schwartz. (Illus.). 1977. pap. 23.95 (ISBN 0-07-055764-0). McGraw.
Vulnerable People: A View of American Fiction Since 1945. Josephine Hendin. 1978. pap. 7.95 (ISBN 0-19-502620-9). Oxford U Pr.
Vulnerable Six Hundred. Documentary Publications Staff. Date not set. write for info. (ISBN 0-89712-208-9). Documentary Pubns.
Vulnerable Social Worker: Liability for Serving Children & Families. Douglas J. Besharov. 288p. 1985. 16.95 (ISBN 0-87101-136-0). Natl Assn Soc Wkrs.
Vulnerable Text: Essays on Renaissance Literature. Thomas M. Greene. 256p. 1986. 32.50 (ISBN 0-231-06246-X). Columbia U Pr.
Vulture. Sidney Simon. (Illus.). 72p. 1977. pap. 3.95 (ISBN 0-317-60035-4). Tabor Pub.
Vulture & the Bull: Religious Responses to Death. Antonio R. Gualtieri. 194p. (Orig.). 1984. lib. bdg. 27.50 (ISBN 0-8191-3963-7); pap. text ed. 12.50 (ISBN 0-8191-3964-5). U Pr of Amer.
Vulture Biology & Management. Ed. by Sandford R. Wilbur & Jerome A. Jackson. LC 82-45912. (Illus.). 554p. 1983. text ed. 42.00x (ISBN 0-520-04755-9). U of Cal Pr.
Vulture Gather, the Fig Tree Blooms. Thomas E. Mails. (Illus.). 100p. 1972. pap. 8.00 (ISBN 0-913856-00-2). Hayfield Pub.
Vultures. Robert E. Howard. (Illus., Also including "Showdown at Hell's Canyon). 1973. 8.50 (ISBN 0-87707-115-2). Fictioneer Bks.
Vultures & the Phoenix. Robert W. Millett. LC 81-65877. (Illus.). 168p. 1983. 28.50 (ISBN 0-87982-039-X). Art Alliance.
Vultures in the Sun. Brian Garfield. 160p. 1987. pap. 2.50 (ISBN 0-553-26331-5). Bantam.
Vultures of the Horn. (S.O.B. Ser.: No. 10). Date not set. pap. 2.50 (Pub. by Worldwide). Harlequin Bks.
Vultures of the Void: A History of British Science Fiction Publishing, 1946-1956. Philip Harbottle & Stephen Holland. LC 87-748. (I. O. Evans Studies in the Philosophy & Criticism of Literature: No. 13). 144p. Date not set. lib. bdg. 19.95x (ISBN 0-89370-315-X); pap. text ed. 9.95x (ISBN 0-89370-415-6). Borgo Pr.
Vultures on Horseback. Paul E. Lehman. 1979. pap. 1.25 (ISBN 0-8439-0645-6, Leisure Bks). Leisure NY.
Vulture's Vengeance. (Executioner Ser.). 192p. 1983. pap. 1.95 (ISBN 0-373-61051-3, Pub. by Worldwide). Harlequin Bks.
Vulvar Disease. 2nd ed. Eduard G. Friedrich, Jr. (Major Problems in Obstetrics & Gynecology Ser.: Vol. 9). (Illus.). 272p. 1983. 83.00 (ISBN 0-7216-1096-X). Saunders.
Vulvovaginal Candidosis. W. Mendling. (Illus.). 185p. 1988. pap. 21.90 (ISBN 0-387-18704-9). Springer-Verlag.
Vunshnata Politika na Bulgaria. 151p. (Orig., Bulgarian.). 1986. pap. 10.00 (ISBN 0-937785-11-3). Sliabhair.
Vuta Kamba: The Development of Trade Unions in Tanganyika. William H. Friedland. LC 74-81689. (Publications Ser.: No. 84). 1969. 11.95x (ISBN 0-8179-1841-8); pap. 7.95x (ISBN 0-8179-1842-6). Hoover Inst Pr.
Vvedenie v Sviatootecheskoe Bogoslovia. rev. ed. John Meyendorff. Tr. by Larisa Volokhonsky from Eng. LC 85-61006. 359p. (Rus.). 1985. pap. 16.00 (ISBN 0-934927-00-6). RBR.
Vvedenije vo Khram Presvjatija Bogoroditsi. M. Skaballanovitch. 115p. pap. 4.00 (ISBN 0-317-29157-2). Holy Trinity.
VW Beetle. Jonathan Wood. (Collector's Guide Ser.). (Illus.). 128p. 1983. 29.95 (ISBN 0-900549-67-X, Pub. by Motor Racing Pubns England). Motorbooks Intl.
VW Beetle: An Illustrated History. (Illus.). 160p. 1987. 29.95 (ISBN 0-85429-591-7, Pub. by GT Foulis Ltd). Haynes Pubns.
VW FWD Nineteen Seveny-Four to Eighty-Seven. Chilton's Automotives Editorial Staff. LC 86-47776. 264p. 1987. pap. 13.95 (ISBN 0-8019-7754-1). Chilton.
VW Kubelwagen, Nineteen Forty to Nineteen Seventy-Five. Konrad F. Schreier, Jr. 100p. 1986. pap. 13.95 (ISBN 0-948207-56-6). Portrayal.
VW Rabbit Tune-up & Repair. Ed. by Spence Murray. LC 79-53095. (Tune-up & Repair Ser.). (Illus.). 1979. pap. 4.95 (ISBN 0-8227-5045-7). Petersen Pub.
VW Treasures by Karmann. Jan Norbye. LC 85-15575. (Illus.). 176p. (Orig.). 1985. pap. 14.95 (ISBN 0-87938-202-3). Motorbooks Intl.
VW Vanagon: 1980-1982 Shop Manual. Alfred A. Pegal. (Illus., Orig.). 1982. pap. 14.95 (ISBN 0-89287-351-5, A123). Clymer Pub.
Vyacheslav Ivanov: Poet, Critic & Philosopher. Ed. by Robert L. Jackson & Lowry Nelson, Jr. LC 85-51637. (Yale Russian & East European Publications: No. 8). 455p. 1986. 32.00 (ISBN 0-936586-08-7). Yale Russian.
Vybor. Vladimir Voinovich. (Rus.). 1983. cancelled (ISBN 0-88233-912-5). Ardis Pubs.
Vybor V Adu: Zhizneutverzhdenie solzhenitsynskikh geroev. Rita Brackman. LC 83-26381. 144p. (Rus.). 1984. pap. 7.50 (ISBN 0-938920-20-0). Hermitage.
Vybrani Lysty Panteleimona Kulisha. Panteleimon Kulish & G. Luckyj. 360p. (Ukrainian.). 1984. 20.00 (ISBN 0-916381-01-3). Ukrainian Arts Sci.
Vygotsky & the Social Formation of Mind. James V. Wertsch. (Illus.). 288p. 1985. text ed. 25.00x (ISBN 0-674-94350-3). Harvard U Pr.
Vygotsky & the Social Formation of Mind. James V. Wertsch. 280p. 1988. pap. text ed. 12.95 (ISBN 0-674-94351-1). Harvard U Pr.
Vykhovannia i navchannia, zbirka stattei i lektsii. Wasyl O. Luciw. 175p. (Ukrainian.). 1986. pap. 10.00 (ISBN 0-317-47658-0). Slavia Lib.
Vystrel V. Serdtse Revoliutsii. Ed. by Collet's Holdings, Ltd. Staff. 288p. (Rus.). 1983. 29.00 (ISBN 0-317-40880-1, Pub. by Collets (UK)). State Mutual Bk.
Vzaimosviazi Russkoi I Zarubezhnoi Literatur. Ed. by Collet's Holdings, Ltd. Staff. 332p. 1983. 49.00x (ISBN 0-317-40850-X, Pub. by Collets (UK)). State Mutual Bk.

W

W. Georges Perec. Tr. by David Bellos. 1988. 16.95. Godine.
W. A. Mozart. Eric Roseberry. LC 60-3144. (Great Masters Ser.). 1960. pap. 3.75 (ISBN 0-913932-20-5). Boosey & Hawkes.
W. A. Mozart: Die Entfuhrung aus dem Serail. Thomas Bauman. (Cambridge Opera Handbooks Ser.). (Illus.). 160p. 1988. 39.50 (ISBN 0-521-32545-5); pap. 12.95 (ISBN 0-521-31060-1). Cambridge U Pr.
W. A. Mozart: Don Giovanni. Julian Rushton. (Cambridge Opera Handbooks Ser.). (Illus.). 1981. 27.95 (ISBN 0-521-22826-3); pap. 9.95 (ISBN 0-521-29663-3). Cambridge U Pr.
W. A. Mozart: Le Nozze di Figaro. Tim Carter. (Cambridge Opera Handbooks Ser.). (Illus.). 180p. 1988. 39.50 (ISBN 0-521-30267-6); pap. 12.95 (ISBN 0-521-31606-5). Cambridge U Pr.
W. A. Mozart: Sa Vie Musicale & Son Oeuvre, 2 vols. T. De Wyzewa & G. De Saint-Foix. (Music Reprint Ser.). 2274p. 1980. Repr. of 1936 ed. Set. lib. bdg. 125.00 (ISBN 0-306-79561-2). Da Capo.
W. A. P Martin: Pioneer of Progress in China. Ralph Covell. LC 77-13321. Repr. of 1978 ed. 59.10 (ISBN 0-8357-9133-5, 2012723). Bks Demand UMI.
W Algebras. Jacob T. Schwartz. (Notes on Mathematics & Its Applications Ser.). 266p. 1967. 86.00 (ISBN 0-677-00670-5). Gordon & Breach.
W. B. Yeats. Intro. by Harold Bloom. (Modern Critical Views Ser.). 224p. 1986. 24.50 (ISBN 0-87754-700-9). Chelsea Hse.
W. B. Yeats. Michael MacLiammoir & Eavan Boland. (Literary Lives Ser.). (Illus.). 1986. pap. 9.95 (ISBN 0-500-26022-2, Dist. by W. W. Norton & Co). Thames Hudson.
W. B. Yeats. B. P. Misra. LC 76-42484. 1962. lib. bdg. 19.50 (ISBN 0-8414-6161-9). Folcroft.
W. B. Yeats. Moriarty & Sweeney. (Junior Biography Library). (Illus.). 64p. (Orig.). (gr. 5-10). 1988. pap. 8.95 (ISBN 0-317-69932-6, Pub. by O'Brien Pr Ireland). Irish Bks Media.
W. B. Yeats. Humbert Wolfe. 1982. 42.50 (ISBN 0-686-81930-6). Bern Porter.
W. B. Yeats. C. L. Wrenn. 1982. 42.50 (ISBN 0-686-81935-7). Bern Porter.
W. B. Yeats. William B. Yeats. 49p. 1980. Repr. of 1927 ed. lib. bdg. 15.50 (ISBN 0-8495-6126-4). Arden Lib.
W. B. Yeats: A Classified Bibliography of Criticism Including Additions to Allan Wade's Bibliography of the Writings of W.B. Yeats and a Section of the Irish Literary & Dramatic Revival. Ed. by K. P. Jochum. LC 77-10346. 816p. 1977. 49.95 (ISBN 0-252-00577-5). U of Ill Pr.
W. B. Yeats: A Critical Study. Forrest Reid. LC 72-1317. (Studies in Irish Literature, No. 16). 1972. Repr. of 1915 ed. lib. bdg. 75.00x (ISBN 0-8383-1434-1). Haskell.
W. B. Yeats: A Literary Study. C. L. Wrenn. LC 73-11392. 1920. lib. bdg. 17.50 (ISBN 0-8414-9383-9). Folcroft.
W. B. Yeats: A Literary Study. Charles L. Wrenn. 50p. 1980. Repr. of 1920 ed. lib. bdg. 17.50 (ISBN 0-8492-2998-7). R West.
W. B. Yeats: An Indian Approach. Naresh Guha. 1978. Repr. of 1968 ed. lib. bdg. 27.00 (ISBN 0-8495-1916-0). Arden Lib.
W. B. Yeats & His Contemporaries. Ian Fletcher. LC 84-40573. 224p. 1987. 27.50 (ISBN 0-312-85306-8). St Martin.
W. B. Yeats & His World. Micheal MacLiammoir & Eavan Boland. LC 77-90492. (Illus.). 1978. 10.95 (ISBN 0-684-15573-7, ScribT). Scribner.
W. B. Yeats & Irish Folklore. Mary H. Thuente. 286p. 1981. 28.50x (ISBN 0-389-20161-8). B&N Imports.
W. B. Yeats & T. Sturge Moore: Their Correspondence, 1901-1937. William B. Yeats. Ed. by Ursula Bridge. LC 78-6910. 1978. Repr. of 1953 ed. lib. bdg. 35.00 (ISBN 0-313-20489-6, YEYM). Greenwood.
W. B. Yeats & the Anti-Democratic Tradition. Grattan Freyer. 154p. 1981. 27.50x (ISBN 0-389-20166-9, 06936). B&N Imports.
W. B. Yeats & the Craft of Verse. Malati Ramratnam. (Illus.). 146p. (Orig.). 1986. lib. bdg. 26.25 (ISBN 0-8191-5017-7); pap. text ed. 10.00 (ISBN 0-8191-5018-5). U Pr of Amer.
W. B. Yeats & the Creation of a Tragic Universe. Maeve Good. LC 86-10891. 160p. 1986. 25.00x (ISBN 0-389-20642-3). B&N Imports.
W. B. Yeats & the Emergence of the Irish Free State, 1918-1939: Living in the Explosion. Bernard G. Krimm. LC 80-51875. 324p. 1981. 20.00x (ISBN 0-87875-200-5). Whitston Pub.
W. B. Yeats & the Tribes of Danu: Three Views of Ireland's Fairies. Peter A. Smith. (Irish Literary Studies: No. 27). 340p. 1986. 28.95x (ISBN 0-389-20696-2). B&N Imports.
W. B. Yeats Dramatist of Vision. A. S. Knowland. LC 83-12274. (Irish Literary Studies: No. 17). 272p. 1983. 29.50x (ISBN 0-389-20407-2, 07292). B&N Imports.
W. B. Yeats Eighteen Sixty-Five to Nineteen Thirty-Nine. Joseph Hone. 504p. 1985. Repr. of 1942 ed. lib. bdg. 50.00 (ISBN 0-8414-5200-8). Folcroft.
W. B. Yeats: Images of a Poet. Donald J. Gordon. LC 79-9441. 1980. Repr. of 1961 ed. lib. bdg. 35.00x (ISBN 0-313-22069-7, GOWBY). Greenwood.
W. B. Yeats: Man & Poet. A. Norman Jeffares. 365p. 1949. 22.50 (ISBN 0-7100-1607-7). Routledge Chapman & Hall.
W. B. Yeats, Manuscripts & Printed Books, Exhibited in the Library of Trinity College, Dublin. R. O. Dougan. 50p. 1980. Repr. of 1956 ed. lib. bdg. 27.50 (ISBN 0-8492-4216-9). R West.
W. B. Yeats Manuscripts & Printed Books. R. O. Dougan. LC 73-16227. 1956. lib. bdg. 25.00 (ISBN 0-8414-3699-1). Folcroft.
W. B. Yeats: Metaphysician As Dramatist. Heather C. Martin. 136p. 1986. 25.00x (ISBN 0-88920-192-7, Pub. by Wilfrid Laurier Canada). Humanities.
W. B. Yeats: Poetic Theory & Practice. Rama Nand Rai. Ed. by James Hogg. (Poetic Drama & Poetic Theory). 210p. 1983. pap. 15.00 (ISBN 3-7052-0887-X, Pub. by Salzburg Studies). Longwood Pub Group.
W. B. Yeats (The Augustan Books of English Poetry) Humbert Wolfe. 1973. lib. bdg. 17.50 (ISBN 0-8414-9780-X). Folcroft.
W. B. Yeats: The Critical Heritage. Ed. by A. Norman Jeffares. (Critical Heritage Ser.). 1977. 34.00x (ISBN 0-7100-8480-3). Routledge Chapman & Hall.
W. B. Yeats: The Writing of Sophocles' King Oedipus. David Clark & James B. McGuire. LC 86-72889. (Memoir Ser.: Vol. 175). (Illus.). 1988. write for info. (ISBN 0-87169-175-2). Am Philos.
W. B. Yeats: The Writing of "The Player Queen". Compiled by Curtis B. Bradford. LC 73-18798. 483p. 1977. 35.00 (ISBN 0-87580-048-3). N Ill U Pr.
W. C. Fields: A Bio-Bibliography. Wes D. Gehring. LC 84-4454. (Popular Culture Bio-Bibliographies Ser.). (Illus.). xv, 233p. 1984. lib. bdg. 36.95 (ISBN 0-313-23875-8, GWC/). Greenwood.
W. C. Fields: A Life in Film. Ronald Fields. (Illus.). 288p. 1984. pap. 14.95 (ISBN 0-312-85312-2). St Martin.
W. C. Fields: His Follies & Fortunes. R. L. Taylor. 18.95 (ISBN 0-89190-109-4, Pub. by Am Repr). Amereon Ltd.
W. C. Fields: His Follies & Fortunes. Robert L. Taylor. (Illus.). 1967. pap. 1.25 (ISBN 0-451-50653-7, CY653, Sig Classics). NAL.
W. C. Fields in French Light. Rochelle Owens. Ed. by Josh Gosciak & Maurice Kenny. LC 86-16843. 60p. (Orig.). 1986. pap. 4.50 (ISBN 0-936556-14-5). Contact Two.

Wading Birds. Ed. by Alexander Sprunt et al. LC 77-26723. (Research Reports: No. 7). (Illus.). 1978. pap. 11.50 (ISBN 0-930698-00-2). Natl Audubon.
Wads: True Homosexual Experiences from STH Writers, Vol. 6. Ed. by Boyd McDonald. (Illus.). 192p. (Orig.). 1985. pap. 12.00 (ISBN 0-917342-11-9). Gay Sunshine.
Wadsworth Anaerobic Bacteriology Manual. 4th ed. Vera L. Sutter et al. (Illus.). 160p. 1986. lib. bdg. 25.95 (ISBN 0-89863-100-9); pap. 15.95 (ISBN 0-317-39903-9). Star Pub CA.
Wadsworth Atheneum Paintings: The Netherlands & German Speaking Countries; Fifteenth Through Nineteenth Centuries. LC 77-82219. (Illus.). 208p. 1978. 25.00 (ISBN 0-317-13588-0); pap. 12.00 (ISBN 0-317-13589-9). Wadsworth Atheneum.
Wadsworth-Longfellow House. Nathan Goold. (Illus.). 1969. pap. 3.00 (ISBN 0-915592-04-5). Maine Hist.
Wadsworth-Longfellow House: Longfellow's Old Home. Nathan Goold. Repr. of 1915 ed. lib. bdg. 17.50 (ISBN 0-8492-4907-4). R West.
Wadsworth's Review of Nursing. Carol R. Kneisl. LC 84-25601. (Nursing Ser.). 600p. 1985. pap. text ed. 20.00 (ISBN 0-534-04362-3). Jones & Bartlett.
Wafer Scale Integration. Ed. by Chris Jesshope et al. (Illus.). 256p. 1986. 79.00x (ISBN 0-85274-497-8, Pub. by A Hilger UK). Taylor & Francis.
Wafer Scale Integration. Ed. by G. Saucier & J. Trilhe. 354p. 1986. 79.00 (ISBN 0-444-70103-6, North-Holland). Elsevier.
Wafer's Secret Report (1699; see New Voyage & Description of the Isthmus of America.
Waffen -- SS. Brian L. Davis. (Illus.). 96p. (Orig.). 1986. (Pub. by Blandford Pr England); pap. 12.95 (ISBN 0-7137-1545-6). Sterling.
Waffen SS. John Keegan. pap. 4.95 (ISBN 0-345-32641-5). Ballantine.
Waffen SS: Hitler's Elite Guard at War, 1939-1945. George H. Stein. LC 66-11049. (Paperback Ser.). 366p. 1984. pap. 11.95 (ISBN 0-8014-9275-0). Cornell U Pr.
Waffen SS in Action. (Weapons in Action Ser.). (Illus.). 50p. 1984. pap. 5.95 (ISBN 0-89747-053-2, 3003). Squad Sig Pubns.
Waffen SS in Russia: World War Two Photo Album Ser. Bruce Quarrie. (Illus.). 96p. (Orig.). 1988. pap. 7.99 (ISBN 1-85260-155-8, Pub. by PSL P Stephens England). Sterling.
Waffle Cookbook. D. Stone. 1986. cancelled (ISBN 0-442-28170-6). Van Nos Reinhold.
Waffles & Wafers: Traditional Recipes for Today's Kitchen. Mary Barile. (Illus.). 66p. 1987. pap. 6.00 (ISBN 0-937213-01-2). Heritage Margaretville.
Wag-by-Wall. Beatrix Potter. (Illus.). (ps-3). 1987. 4.95 (ISBN 0-7232-3448-5). Warne.
Wage & Employment Patterns in Labor Contracts: Microfoundations & Macroconmics Implications. Russell W. Cooper. (Fundamentals of Pure & Applied Economics Ser.: Vol. 19). 80p. 1987. pap. text ed. 20.00 (ISBN 3-7186-0378-0). Harwood Academic.
Wage & Hour Law Handbook for the Lodging & Food Service Industry. Branch & Swann. LC 80-65115. 1980. 34.95 (ISBN 0-86730-236-4). Lebhar Friedman.
Wage & Hour Manual: For California Employers. 4th. ed. Richard J. Simmons. 548p. 1988. 55.00 (ISBN 0-943178-06-1). Castle Pubns.
Wage & Pension Cuts: A Bibliography. Mary Vance. (Public Administration Ser.: P 2102). 12p. 1987. 3.75 (ISBN 1-55590-202-2). Vance Biblios.
Wage & Salary. Ad Wittemann. 11p. 1983. pap. 25.00 (ISBN 0-938481-11-8). Camelot Consult.
Wage & Salary Administration. Lawrence Aft. 1985. text ed. 35.00 (ISBN 0-8359-8528-8, Reston); instr's. manual avail. (ISBN 0-8359-8529-6). P-H.
Wage & Salary Administration. (Personnel Policies Forum Surveys Ser.: No. 131). 56p. 1981. 30.00 (ISBN 0-87179-981-2). BNA.
Wage & Salary Administration in a Changing Economy. William Davidson. 250p. 1984. manual 61.95 (ISBN 0-85013-145-6). Dartnell Corp.
Wage & Salary Administration: Pay & Benefits. Leonard Burgess. 480p. 1984. text ed. 34.95 (ISBN 0-675-20080-6). Merrill.
Wage & Salary Administration: Total Compensation Systems. J. D. Dunn & F. Rachel. 1970. text ed. 39.95 (ISBN 0-07-018291-4). McGraw.
Wage & Salary Audit. A. Schofield & T. Husband. 126p. 1977. text ed. 34.50x (ISBN 0-566-02008-4). Gower Pub Co.
Wage & Salary Program Based on Position Evaluation for Administrative & Supervisory Staff. Rhone. 1980. 8.95 (ISBN 0-910170-15-0). Assn Sch Busn.
Wage Bargain & the Labor Market. H. M. Douty. 160p. 1980. 18.50x (ISBN 0-8018-2393-5). Johns Hopkins.
Wage Bargain & the Labor Market. Harry M. Douty. LC 79-3720. (Policy Studies in Employment & Welfare: No. 37). pap. 40.00 (ISBN 0-317-42310-X, 2025806). Bks Demand UMI.
Wage Behavior in the Postwar Period. William Bowen. LC 73-10582. (Princeton University Industrial Relations Ser.). (Illus.). 137p. 1973. Repr. of 1960 ed. lib. bdg. 35.00x (ISBN 0-8371-7013-3, BOWB). Greenwood.
Wage Control & Inflation in the Soviet Bloc Countries. Ed. by Jan Adam. 266p. 1980. 42.95 (ISBN 0-275-90442-3, C0442). Praeger.
Wage Controls in Canada, 1975-78. A. Maslove & G. Swimmer. 182p. 1980. pap. text ed. 11.95x (ISBN 0-920380-50-6, Pub. by Inst Res Pub Canada). Brookfield Pub Co.
Wage Cost Control. William L. Kahrl. LC 80-81945. 1980. 6.95 (ISBN 0-86730-233-X). Lebhar Friedman.
Wage Determination & Comparable Worth for Librarians: A Checklist of Materials. Lorna Peterson. (Public Administration Ser.: Bibliography P 1635). 1985. pap. 2.25 (ISBN 0-89028-305-2). Vance Biblios.
Wage Determination & Incomes Policy in Open Economies. Anne R. Braun. LC 86-10414. (Illus.). xix, 380p. 1986. pap. 18.50 (ISBN 0-939934-75-2). Intl Monetary.
Wage Determination & Incomes Policy in Open Economies. Anne R. Braun. LC 86-10414. pap. 100.00 (ISBN 0-317-55518-9, 2029549). Bks Demand UMI.
Wage Determination in Asia & the Pacific: The Views of Employers' Organisations-Reports & Documents Submitted to an ILO-DANIDA Regional Seminar (Singapore, October 8-12, 1979) (Labour-Management Relations Ser.: No. 58). ii, 169p. (Orig.). 1983. pap. 14.00 (ISBN 92-2-102492-X). Intl Labour Office.
Wage Determination in Asia & the Pacific: The Views of Employers' Organisations. (Labour-Management Relations Ser.: No. 58). ii, 169p. 1981. pap. 14.00 (ISBN 92-2-102492-X, ILO157, ILO). UNIPUB.
Wage Determination in English-Speaking Caribbean Countries: Record of, Proceedings of, & Documents Submitted to, an ILO/DANIDA Regional Seminar (Kingston, Jamaica, 1-7 March 1978. (Labour-Management Relations Ser.: No. 57). 121p. 1979. pap. 12.25 (ISBN 92-2-102021-5, ILO1244, ILO). UNIPUB.
Wage Determination: Market or Power Forces? Ed. by Richard Perlman. LC 76-56370. (Illus.). 1977. Repr. of 1964 ed. lib. bdg. 22.50x (ISBN 0-8371-9423-7, PEWD). Greenwood.
Wage Determination under Trade Unions. John T. Dunlop. LC 50-58147. Repr. of 1944 ed. 27.50x (ISBN 0-678-00137-5). Kelley.
Wage Differentials. Carrie Glasser. LC 77-76638. (Columbia University Studies in the Social Sciences: No. 476). (Illus.). 1969. Repr. of 1940 ed. 16.50 (ISBN 0-404-51476-6). AMS Pr.
Wage Differentials: A Bibliography. Mary Vance. (Public Administration Ser.: P 2101). 23p. 1987. 6.25 (ISBN 1-55590-201-4). Vance Biblios.
Wage Differentials & Economic Growth. Pasquale M. Sgro. 147p. 1980. 28.50x (ISBN 0-389-20002-6). B&N Imports.
Wage Earners' Budgets: A Study of Standards & Cost of Living in New York City. Louise B. More. LC 73-137178. (Poverty U. S. A. Historical Record Ser.). 1971. Repr. of 1907 ed. 20.00 (ISBN 0-405-03116-5). Ayer Co Pubs.
Wage-Earning Pittsburgh, Vol. 6. Ed. by Paul U. Kellogg. LC 73-11906. (Metropolitan America Ser.). (Illus.). 726p. 1974. Repr. 49.50x (ISBN 0-405-05398-3). Ayer Co Pubs.
Wage-Earning Women. Annie M. MacLean. LC 74-3962. (Women in America Ser). (Illus.). 218p. 1974. Repr. of 1910 ed. 22.00x (ISBN 0-405-06111-0). Ayer Co Pubs.
Wage-Earning Women: Industrial Work & Family Life in the U. S., 1900-1930. Leslie Tentler. 1979. 25.00x (ISBN 0-19-502627-6). Oxford U Pr.
Wage-Earning Women: Industrial Work & Family Life in the United States, 1900-1930. Leslie W. Tentler. 1982. pap. 9.95 (ISBN 0-19-503211-X). Oxford U Pr.
Wage Employment Programmes in Rural Development. Indira Hirway. 1986. 11.00 (ISBN 81-204-0072-0, Pub. by Oxford IBH). South Asia Bks.
Wage-Fixing Revsited. J. E. Meade. (Occasional Paper Ser.: No. 72). 48p. (Orig.). 1985. pap. text ed. 5.95x (ISBN 0-255-36180-7, Pub. by Inst Econ Affairs UK). Transatl Arts.
Wage Flexibility & Full Employment. R. D. Gupta. 1971. 4.50x (ISBN 0-686-20323-2). Intl Bk Dist.
Wage-Hour & Employment Practices Manual for the Multihousing Industry. Harry Weisbrod et al. Ed. by Peggy J. Schleker. LC 78-70825. 210p. 1979. 25.95 (ISBN 0-912104-36-8, 807). Inst Real Estate.
Wage-Hour Guide. (Information Services Ser.). Date not set. price not set ring bound l'leaf. P-H.
Wage Incentive Systems. P. Shwinger. 220p. 1975. text ed. 44.00x (ISBN 0-7065-1526-9, Pub. by Keter Pub Jerusalem). Coronet Bks.
Wage-Labor & Capital. Karl Marx. Tr. & intro. by Friedrich Engels. 59p. lib. bdg. 17.95; pap. 3.95 (ISBN 0-88286-052-6). C H Kerr.
Wage, Labour & Capital. Karl Marx. 1978. pap. 1.95 (ISBN 0-8351-0547-4). China Bks.
Wage-Labour & Capital & Value, Price & Profit. Karl Marx. LC 76-10456. 110p. 1976. pap. 1.50 (ISBN 0-7178-0470-4). Intl Pubs Co.
Wage Patterns & Wage Policy in Modern China, 1919-1972. Christopher Howe. LC 72-97875. (Cambridge Studies in Chinese History, Literature & Institutions Ser.). pap. 46.80 (ISBN 0-317-29416-4, 2024473). Bks Demand UMI.
Wage Policies & Collective Bargaining Developments in Finland, Ireland & Norway. 110p. 1979. 7.25x (ISBN 92-64-11915-9). OECD.
Wage Policies of Labor Organizations in a Period of Industrial Depression. Vertrees J. Wyckoff. LC 78-64121. (Johns Hopkins University. Studies in the Social Sciences. Forty-Fourth Ser. 1926: 3). Repr. of 1926 ed. 24.50 (ISBN 0-404-61235-0). AMS Pr.
Wage Policies of Labor Organizations in a Period of Industrial Depression. Vertrees J. Wyckoff. LC 77-89772. (American Labor, from Conspiracy to Collective Bargaining Ser., No. 1). 119p. 1969. Repr. of 1926 ed. 14.00 (ISBN 0-405-02159-3). Ayer Co Pubs.
Wage Policy & European Integration. Bernhard Seidel. 304p. 1983. text ed. 58.00x (ISBN 0-566-00357-0). Gower Pub Co.
Wage Policy Issues in Economic Development. Ed. by Anthony D. Smith. LC 69-13690. (International Institute for Labour Studies). 1969. 35.00 (ISBN 0-312-85330-0). St Martin.
Wage-Price Controls & Labor Market Distortions. Daniel J. Mitchell & Ross E. Azevedo. (Monograph & Research Ser.: No.16). 109p. 1976. 6.00 (ISBN 0-89215-056-4). U Cal LA Indus Rel.
Wage-Price Issue: A Theoretical Analysis. William G. Bowen. LC 72-90471. Repr. of 1960 ed. lib. bdg. 35.00x (ISBN 0-8371-2286-4, BOWP). Greenwood.
Wage, Price, Productivity & Industrial Planning. Basudeb Sahoo. 1985. 32.50x (ISBN 0-8364-1463-2, Pub. by Ashish India). South Asia Bks.
Wage-Price Standards & Economic Policy. Jack A. Meyer. 80p. 1982. pap. 7.00 (ISBN 0-8447-3490-X). Am Enterprise.
Wage Rates in Philadelphia, Seventeen Ninety to Eighteen Thirty. facsimile ed. Donald R. Adams, Jr. LC 75-2572. (Dissertations in American Economic History). (Illus.). 1975. Repr. of 1975 ed. 29.00x (ISBN 0-405-07253-8). Ayer Co Pubs.
Wage Restraint & the Control of Inflation: An International Survey. Ed. by Beth Bilson. LC 86-22575. 208p. 1987. 32.50 (ISBN 0-312-00374-9). St Martin.
Wage Restraint & the Control of Inflation: An International Survey. Ed. by Beth Wilson. 208p. 1986. 40.00 (ISBN 0-7099-3929-9, Pub. by Croom Helm UK). Routledge Chapman & Hall.
Wage Restraint by Consensus: Britain's Search for an Income Policy Agreement, 1965-1979. Warren H. Fishbein. 300p. 1984. 35.00x (ISBN 0-7102-0074-9). Routledge Chapman & Hall.
Wage Rigidity & Unemployment. Ed. by Wilfred Beckerman. LC 86-45446. 240p. 1986. text ed. 30.00x (ISBN 0-8018-3400-7). Johns Hopkins.
Wage the Energy War at Home. Joseph C. Davis & Claxton Walker. LC 78-51121. (Illus.). 1978. 11.95 (ISBN 0-87523-191-8). Emerson.
Wage War on Silence. Vassar Miller. LC 60-13157. (Wesleyan Poetry Program: Vol. 8). (Orig.). 1960. 17.00x (ISBN 0-8195-2008-X). Wesleyan U Pr.
Wage Worth of School Training: An Analytical Study of Six Hundred Women-Workers in Textile Factories. Anna Charlotte Hedges. LC 74-176853. (Columbia University. Teachers College. Contributions to Education: No. 70). Repr. of 1915 ed. 22.50 (ISBN 0-404-55070-3). AMS Pr.
Wager. Steven Linder. 192p. 1986. 14.95 (ISBN 0-8027-4061-8). Walker & Co.
Wager & Other Stories. Daniel Corkery. (Illus.). 1950. 8.50 (ISBN 0-8159-7200-8). Devin.
Wager for Love. Rachelle Edwards. 1980. pap. 1.75 (ISBN 0-449-50021-7, Coventry). Fawcett.
Wager on Love. Prudence Martin. 256p. 1986. pap. 2.50 (ISBN 0-8217-1577-1). Zebra.
Wager with the Wind: The Don Sheldon Story. James Greiner. (Illus.). 256p. 1982. pap. 8.95 (ISBN 0-312-85337-8). St Martin.
Wagered Weekend. Jayne Castle. (Candlelight Ecstacy Ser.: No. 17). (Orig.). 1986. pap. 1.50 (ISBN 0-440-19413-X). Dell.
Wagered Widow. Patricia Veryan. 256p. 1985. pap. 2.50 (ISBN 0-449-20740-4, Crest). Fawcett.
Wages. Maurice H. Dobb. LC 82-994. (Cambridge Economic Handbooks). (Illus.). xv, 201p. 1982. Repr. of 1966 ed. lib. bdg. 35.00x (ISBN 0-313-23483-3, DOWA). Greenwood.
Wages - Fog or Facts? David Layton. (Institute of Economic Affairs, Eaton Papers Ser.: No. 7). pap. 2.50 technical (ISBN 0-255-69581-0). Transatl Arts.
Wages: A Bibliography of Statistical Sources. Marian Dworaczek. (Public Administration Ser.: Bibliography P 1631). 1985. pap. 4.50 (ISBN 0-89028-301-X). Vance Biblios.
Wages: A Workers' Education Manual. 3rd ed. xii, 179p. (Orig.). 1982. pap. 10.50 (ISBN 92-2-102961-1). Intl Labour Office.
Wages & Earnings. Andrew Dean. (Reviews of United Kingdom Statistical Sources Ser.: Vol. XIII). 1980. 65.00 (ISBN 0-08-024060-7). Pergamon.
Wages & Earnings in the United States, 1860-1890. Clarence D. Long. LC 75-19725. (National Bureau of Economic Research Ser.). (Illus.). 1975. Repr. 16.00x (ISBN 0-405-07603-7). Ayer Co Pubs.
Wages & Earnings of the Working Class. Leone Levi. (Development of Industrial Society Ser.). 208p. 1971. Repr. of 1885 ed. 27.50x (ISBN 0-7165-1792-2, BBA 03064, Pub. by Irish Academic Pr). Biblio Dist.
Wages & Economic Control in Norway, 1945-1957. Mark W. Leiserson. LC 59-5565. (Wertheim Publications in Industrial Relations Ser). 1959. 12.50x (ISBN 0-674-94470-4). Harvard U Pr.
Wages & Employment Policy Nineteen Thirty-Six to Nineteen Eighty-Six. Russell Jones. 230p. 1986. text ed. 34.95x (ISBN 0-04-331110-5); pap. text ed. 16.95x (ISBN 0-04-331111-3). Unwin Hyman.
Wages & Exchange Rates: Nordic Reactions to Foreign Disturbances, 1973-1981. Dag Linkskog. 1985. text ed. 33.50 (ISBN 0-566-00974-9). Gower Pub Co.
Wages & Hours. (Labor Relations Reporter Ser.). looseleaf 368.00. BNA.
Wages & Hours: Labor & Reform in Twentieth-Century America. Ronnie Steinberg. (Illus.). 296p. 1982. 35.00 (ISBN 0-8135-0916-5). Rutgers U Pr.
Wages & Payroll Statistics. Bd. with Methods of Family Living Studies; Methods of Labour Productivity Statistics. Repr. of 1951 ed. (I.L.O. Studies & Reports New Ser.: Nos. 16-18). Repr. of 1949 ed. 51.00 (ISBN 0-8115-3337-9). Kraus Repr.
Wages & Prices in a Mixed Economy. James E. Meade. (Institute of Economic Affairs, Occasional Papers Ser.: No. 35). 1972. pap. 2.50 technical (ISBN 0-255-36022-3). Transatl Arts.
Wages & Salaries. Tom Lupton & Angela Bowey. 192p. 1983. text ed. 33.00x (ISBN 0-566-02368-7). Gower Pub Co.
Wages & Salaries Paid Support Personnel in Public Schools, 1987-88. 74p. 1988. 36.00. Ed Research.
Wages & the Working Day. John Keracher. 1946. pap. 1.25 (ISBN 0-88286-039-9). C H Kerr.
Wages & Wants of Science-Workers. Richard A. Proctor. 270p. 1970. Repr. of 1876 ed. 28.50x (ISBN 0-7146-1627-3, F Cass Co). Biblio Dist.
Wages & Whitlam: The Wages Policy of the Whitlam Government. P. A. McGavin. 280p. 1987. 42.50 (ISBN 0-19-554732-2). Oxford U Pr.
Wages, Hours & Strikes: Labor Panaceas in the Twentieth Century. Ed. by Leon Stein & Philip Taft. LC 79-89743. (American Labor, from Conspiracy to Collective Bargaining Ser., No. 1). 528p. 1969. 40.00 (ISBN 0-405-02152-6). Ayer Co Pubs.
Wages in Eighteenth Century England. Elizabeth L. Gilboy. LC 79-81457. 1969. Repr. of 1934 ed. 11.00x (ISBN 0-8462-1362-1). Russell.
Wages in Practice & Theory. John W. Rowe. LC 70-76356. 1969. Repr. of 1928 ed. 35.00x (ISBN 0-678-06502-0). Kelley.
Wages in Practice & Theory: McCormick & International Harvestor, 1860-1960. Robert Ozanne. 196p. 1968. text ed. 27.50X (ISBN 0-299-04790-3). U of Wis Pr.
Wages in the Business Cycle: An Empirical & Methodological Analysis. Jonathan Michie. 194p. 1987. 27.50 (ISBN 0-86187-686-5, Pub. by Pinter Pubs UK). Columbia U Pr.
Wages in the United Kingdom in the Nineteenth Century. Arthur L. Bowley. LC 68-55489. 1972. Repr. of 1900 ed. 25.00x (ISBN 0-678-00870-1). Kelley.
Wages of Farm & Factory Laborers. Daniel J. Ahearn, Jr. LC 78-76649. (Columbia University Studies in the Social Sciences: No. 518). 1969. Repr. of 1945 ed. 20.00 (ISBN 0-404-51518-5). AMS Pr.
Wages of Sin. Gerald Haslam. Ed. by Kirk Robertson. LC 80-65780. (Windriver Ser.). (Illus.). 88p. (Orig.). 1980. pap. 4.00 (ISBN 0-916918-11-4). Duck Down.
Wages of Sin. Schmidt. 1988. pap. 3.95 (ISBN 0-312-90146-1). St Martin.
Wages of Unskilled Labor in Manufacturing Industries in the United States, 1890-1924. Whitney Coombs. LC 76-76686. (Columbia University Studies in the Social Sciences: No. 283). Repr. of 1926 ed. 16.50 (ISBN 0-404-51283-6). AMS Pr.
Wages of War, Eighteen Sixteen to Nineteen Sixty-Five. J. David Singer & Melvin Small. 1974. codebk. write for info. (ISBN 0-89138-068-X). ICPSR.
Wages of Writing. Paul W. Kingston & Jonathan R. Cole. LC 85-25543. 224p. 1986. 29.50 (ISBN 0-231-05786-5). Columbia U Pr.
Wages of Zen. James Melville. 224p. 1985. pap. 2.95 (ISBN 0-449-20838-9, Crest). Fawcett.
Wages, Price & Profit. Karl Marx. 1965. pap. 1.95 (ISBN 0-8351-0422-2). China Bks.
Wages, Prices, Profits & Productivity. Ed. by Charles A. Myers. LC 59-12574. 1959. pap. 2.00 (ISBN 0-936904-07-0). Am Assembly.
Wages, Productivity, & Industrialization in Puerto Rico. Lloyd G. Reynolds & Luz M. Torruellas. LC 65-12407. (Yale University, Economic Growth Center, Publications). pap. 93.30 (ISBN 0-317-29718-X, 2022034). Bks Demand UMI.

Waiting. Jody Sorenson. (Cheerleaders Ser.: No. 15). 176p. (Orig.). (gr. 7 up). 1986. pap. 2.25 (ISBN 0-590-40047-9). Scholastic Inc.
Waiting. Karen Van der Zee. (Harlequin Presents Ser.). 192p. 1982. pap. 1.75 (ISBN 0-373-10544-4). Harlequin Bks.
Waiting & Loving: Thoughts Occasioned by the Illness & the Death of a Parent. Martha H. Hickman. LC 83-51399. 160p. (Orig.). 1984. pap. 5.95 (ISBN 0-8358-0483-6). Upper Room.
Waiting at the Gate: Creativity & Hope in the Nursing Home. Susan L. Sandel & David R. Johnson. Ed. by Phyllis Foster. LC 87-8713. (Activities, Adaption & Aging Ser.). 120p. 1987. 22.95 (ISBN 0-86656-631-7). Haworth Pr.
Waiting Father. Helmut Thielicke. Tr. by J. W. Doberstein from Ger. 192p. 1978. Repr. 17.95 (ISBN 0-227-67634-3). Attic Pr.
Waiting Father. Helmut Thielicke. LC 75-12284. 192p. 1981. 7.95 (ISBN 0-06-067991-3, RD-364, HarpR). Har-Row.
Waiting for a Hero: Poems. Penelope Austin. LC 87-26354. 80p. (Orig.). 1988. pap. 6.95 (ISBN 0-8262-0673-5). U of Mo Pr.
Waiting for a "Pearl Harbor" Japan Debates Defense. Tetsuya Kataoka. (Publication Ser.: No. 232). 95p. (Orig.). 1981. pap. 7.95x (ISBN 0-8179-7322-2). Hoover Inst Pr.
Waiting for an Army to Die: The Tragedy of Agent Orange. Fred A. Wilcox. LC 82-42791. 256p. 1983. pap. 6.95 (ISBN 0-394-71518-7, Vin). Random.
Waiting for Childhood. Summer L. Elliott. LC 86-46306. 256p. 1987. 16.95i (ISBN 0-06-015797-6, HarpT). Har-Row.
Waiting for Childhood. Sumner L. Elliott. LC 86-46306. 256p. 1988. pap. 7.95 (ISBN 0-06-091506-4, PL 1506, Perennial Fiction Lib). Har-Row.
Waiting for Christmas: Stories & Activities for Advent. Carol Greene. LC 87-70474. (Illus.). 32p. (Orig.). (ps-5). 1987. pap. 4.95 (ISBN 0-8066-2264-4, 10-6915). Augsburg.
Waiting for Death: A Diary. Philip Mechanicus. Tr. by Irene R. Gibbons from Dutch. 228p. 1983. pap. 8.95 (ISBN 0-7145-0605-2, Dist. by Kampmann & Co). M Boyars Pubs.
Waiting for Death: The Philosophical Significance of Beckett's En Attendant Godot. Ramona Cormier & Janis L. Pallister. LC 76-10218. (Studies in Humanities: No. 19). 176p. 1979. 14.25 (ISBN 0-8173-7605-4). U of Ala Pr.
Waiting for Disaster: Earthquake Watch in California. Ralph H. Turner et al. LC 85-8447. 375p. 1986. text ed. 40.00x (ISBN 0-520-05550-0). U of Cal Pr.
Waiting for Five O Five: Terminal, Station, & Depot in America. Ed. by Clay Lancaster & Lawrence Grow. LC 76-56632. (Illus.). 1977. (Main Street); pap. 8.95 (ISBN 0-87663-957-0). Universe.
Waiting for Garbo: 44 Ghazals. Robert Peterson. LC 87-71660. 52p. (Orig.). 1987. pap. 7.95 (ISBN 0-933525-30-3). Black Dog Pr.
Waiting for God. Simone Weil. pap. 6.95 (ISBN 0-06-090295-7, CN295, PL). Har-Row.
Waiting for Godot. Samuel Beckett. Tr. by Samuel Beckett from Fr. 1970. 10.00 (ISBN 0-394-47529-1, GP640). Grove.
Waiting for Godot. Samuel Beckett. Tr. by Samuel Beckett from Fr. 1954. pap. 4.50 (ISBN 0-394-17204-3, E33, Ever). Grove.
Waiting for Godot. Samuel Beckett. 68p. (Orig.). Date not set. pap. 4.95 (ISBN 0-8021-3034-8). Grove.
Waiting for Jennifer. Kathryn O. Galbraith. LC 87-4151. (Illus.). 32p. (ps-3). 1987. 12.95 (ISBN 0-689-50430-6, M K McElderry). Macmillan.
Waiting for Johnny Miracle. Alice Bach. LC 79-2813. 256p. (YA) (gr. 7 up). 1980. PLB 12.89 (ISBN 0-06-020349-8). HarpJ.
Waiting for Lunch. Greta Rasmussen. LC 81-82797. (Illus.). 63p. (Orig.). (gr. 2-6). 1981. pap. 5.95 (ISBN 0-936110-02-3). Tin Man Pr.
Waiting for Mama. Beatrice S. De Regniers. LC 83-14982. (Illus.). 32p. (ps-2). 1984. PLB 9.95 (ISBN 0-89919-222-X, Clarion). HM.
Waiting for Mom. Linda W. Tyler. LC 86-26760. (Illus.). (ps-1). 1987. 10.95 (ISBN 0-670-81408-3, Viking Kestrel). Viking.
Waiting for My Baby. Barbara O. Webb. 80p. 1985. 6.95 (ISBN 0-570-04219-4, 15-2180). Concordia.
Waiting for Next Week. Michele Orwin. LC 87-25125. 1988. 17.95 (ISBN 0-8050-0517-X). H Holt & Co.
Waiting for Nothing & Other Writings. Tom Kromer. Ed. by Arthur D. Casciato & James L. West, III. LC 85-8610. (Illus.). 312p. 1986. 24.00x (ISBN 0-8203-0797-1); pap. 9.95 (ISBN 0-8203-0798-X). U of GA Pr.
Waiting for Pegasus: Studies of the Presence of Symbolism & Decadence in Hispanic Letters. Ed. by Roland Grass & William R. Risley. LC 79-64810. 1979. pap. 5.00 (ISBN 0-934312-02-8). WIU Essays Lit.
Waiting for Prime Time: The Women of Television News. Marlene Sanders & Marcia Rock. (Illus.). 248p. 1988. 19.95 (ISBN 0-252-01435-9). U of Ill Pr.
Waiting for Sheila. John Braine. LC 79-24757. 1977. 9.95 (ISBN 0-416-00571-3, NO. 0183). Routledge Chapman & Hall.
Waiting for Something to Happen. Gregory X. Gorman. 80p. 1984. pap. 4.00 (ISBN 0-942582-05-5). Erie St Pr.
Waiting for Spring. R. P. Jones. LC 78-52925. 1978. pap. 4.00 (ISBN 0-931594-00-6). Circinatum Pr.
Waiting-for-Spring Stories. Bethany Roberts. LC 83-49486. (Illus.). 32p. (ps-3). 1984. 11.70i (ISBN 0-06-025061-5); PLB 11.89 (ISBN 0-06-025062-3). HarpJ.
Waiting for Surabiel. Raja Proctor. (Asian & Pacific Writing Ser.). 238p. 1981. pap. 12.50 (ISBN 0-7022-1567-8). U of Queensland Pr.
Waiting for the Apocalypse: Doomsday Deferred. rev. ed. Daniel Cohen. LC 83-62189. (Illus.). 262p. 1983. pap. 11.95 (ISBN 0-87975-223-8). Prometheus Bks.
Waiting for the Apples. Ed. by Kathleen R. Leo et al. LC 82-62746. (Illus.). 100p. (Orig.). (gr. k up). 1983. pap. 6.50 (ISBN 0-9606678-2-2). Sylvan Pubns.
Waiting for the Barbarians. J. M. Coetzee. 156p. 1982. pap. 5.95 (ISBN 0-14-006110-X). Penguin.
Waiting for the Boat. Dennis Potter. LC 83-25374. 256p. (Orig.). 1984. pap. 8.50 (ISBN 0-571-13081-X). Faber & Faber.
Waiting for the Curtain to Fall. Ved Vatuk. LC 78-17102. 1978. 2.50 (ISBN 0-914476-79-3). Thorp Springs.
Waiting for the Dawn: Mircea Eliade in Perspective. Ed. by David Carrasco & Jane M. Swanberg. (Academy of Independent Scholars Retrospective Ser.). 128p. 1985. 20.00x (ISBN 0-8133-0148-3). Westview.
Waiting for the End of the World. Madison S. Bell. LC 85-2743. 1985. 16.95 (ISBN 0-89919-377-3). Ticknor & Fields.
Waiting for the End of the World. Madison S. Bell. 324p. 1986. pap. 6.95 (ISBN 0-14-009330-3). Penguin.
Waiting for the End of the World. Andrew Taylor. (Crime Monthly Ser.). 192p. 1986. pap. 3.95 (ISBN 0-14-008063-5). Penguin.
Waiting for the Galactic Bus. Parke Godwin. LC 87-33069. 216p. 1988. pap. 17.95 (ISBN 0-385-24635-8, Foundation Bks). Doubleday.
Waiting for the Lame Horse. Joan Burstyn. LC 87-73262. 65p. 1987. pap. 8.00 (ISBN 0-9610346-8-8). Belle Mead Pr.
Waiting for the Lord: A Season of Anticipation. William J. Carl, III. 64p. 1988. pap. 5.95 (ISBN 0-687-43980-9). Abingdon.
Waiting for the Mahatma. R. K. Narayan. vii, 241p. 1955. 6.00 (ISBN 0-87013-012-9). Mich St U Pr.
Waiting for the Mahatma. R. K. Narayan. LC 81-3075. 256p. 1981. lib. bdg. 15.00x (ISBN 0-226-56826-1); pap. 4.50 (ISBN 0-226-56828-8). U of Chicago Pr.
Waiting for the Morning Train: An American Boyhood. Bruce Catton. LC 87-10613. (Great Lakes Bks.). (Illus.). 270p. 1987. 24.50x (ISBN 0-8143-1884-3); pap. 12.95x (ISBN 0-8143-1885-1). Wayne St U Pr.
Waiting for the Rain. Sheila Gordon. LC 87-7638. 224p. (gr. 7 up). 1987. 12.95 (ISBN 0-531-05726-7); PLB 12.99 (ISBN 0-531-08326-8). Orchard Bks Watts.
Waiting for the Rain. Charles Mungoshi. (African Writers Ser.). 1975. pap. text ed. 7.00 (ISBN 0-435-90170-2). Heinemann Ed.
Waiting for the Soothsayer. Guy Beining. 1981. pap. 1.50 (ISBN 0-686-47954-8). Ghost Dance.
Waiting for the Spring Freshet. Paul Corrigan. 1984. pap. 3.00 (ISBN 0-942396-33-2). Blackberry ME.
Waiting for the Unicorn: Poems & Lyrics of China's Last Dynasty, 1644-1911. Ed. by Irving Y. Lo & William Schultz. LC 85-42816. (Chinese Literature in Translation Ser.). (Illus.). 416p. 1986. 27.50x (ISBN 0-253-36321-7). Ind U Pr.
Waiting for the Verdict. facsimile ed. Rebecca H. Davis. LC 68-57520. (Illus.). 361p. Repr. of 1867 ed. lib. bdg. 49.50 (ISBN 0-8398-0354-0). Irvington.
Waiting for the Virgin. Gavin Dillard. LC 85-2145. 75p. (Orig.). 1985. pap. 5.95 (ISBN 0-933322-22-4). Sea Horse.
Waiting for Willa. Dorothy Eden. 1980. pap. 1.95 (ISBN 0-449-23187-9, Crest). Fawcett.
Waiting Game. Eve Bunting. LC 80-8793. 64p. (YA) (gr. 7 up). 1981. 11.70i (ISBN 0-397-31941-X, Lipp Jr Bks). HarpJ.
Waiting Game. Alexander Fullerton. 160p. 1980. pap. 3.95 (ISBN 0-583-11758-9, Pub. by Granada England). Academy Chi Pubs.
Waiting Game: Photographs of the Oakland A's. John Krich & Debra Heimerdinger. (Illus.). 136p. 1982. 25.00 (ISBN 0-913028-92-4); pap. 8.95 (ISBN 0-913028-93-2). North Atlantic.
Waiting Games. Bruce Hart & Carol Hart. 320p. (Orig.). (YA) (gr. 7 up). 1981. pap. 2.95 (ISBN 0-380-79012-2, Flare). Avon.
Waiting Gun. Wayne C. Lee. 1986. 9.95 (ISBN 0-8034-8605-7, Avalon). Bouregy.
Waiting in Joyful Hope: Aids to the Daily Prayer Based on the Readings of the Day. Gregory Manly & Anneliese Reinhard. 138p. (Orig.). 1985. pap. 7.95 (ISBN 0-86786-086-3, Pub. by Spectrum Pubns). ANZ Religious Pubns.
Waiting in Line: Stories. David Walton. (Ardis Fiction Ser.: No. 1). 150p. 1975. 6.95 (ISBN 0-88233-088-8). Ardis Pubs.
Waiting in Style: A Maternity Wardrobe That Works. Alyson Fendel. LC 85-4035. 196p. 1983. 14.95 (ISBN 0-87491-553-8); pap. 9.95 (ISBN 0-87491-702-6). Acropolis.
Waiting in the Wings: A Larger Audience for the Arts & How to Develop It. Bradley G. Morison & Julie G. Dalgleish. (Illus.). 176p. (Orig.). 1987. text ed. 21.95 (ISBN 0-915400-53-7); pap. 14.95 (ISBN 0-915400-54-5). Am Council Arts.
Waiting Land: A Spell in Nepal. Dervla Murphy. (Illus.). 1969. 12.50 (ISBN 0-7195-1745-1). Transatl Arts.
Waiting Land: A Spell in Nepal. Dervla Murphy. LC 85-5736. 216p. 1987. 17.95 (ISBN 0-87951-251-2). Overlook Pr.
Waiting on God. Andrew Murray. 1961. pap. 2.95 (ISBN 0-87508-399-4). Chr Lit.
Waiting on God. Andrew Murray. (Andrew Murray Ser.). pap. 3.95 (ISBN 0-8024-0026-4). Moody.
Waiting on God. Andrew Murray. 160p. 1981. pap. 2.95 (ISBN 0-88368-101-3). Whitaker Hse.
Waiting on God: Daily Readings on Knowing God. Andrew Murray. (Andrew Murray Classics). 110p. 1987. pap. 3.95 (ISBN 0-310-55142-0, 19014P). Zondervan.
Waiting on the Outside. Kathy Royer. LC 87-21104. 64p. (Orig.). 1987. pap. 3.50 (ISBN 0-8361-3454-0). Herald Pr.
Waiting Out the Rain. Tony Petrosky. 1974. saddlestitched in wrappers 1.50 (ISBN 0-685-78966-7, Pub. by Ironwood Pr). Small Pr Dist.
Waiting Room. T. M. Wright. 352p. (Orig.). 1986. pap. 3.95 (ISBN 0-8125-2760-7, Dist. by Warner Pub. Services & St. Martin's Press). Tor Bks.
Waiting Room Cartoons. 2nd ed. William Armstrong. (Armstrong Cartoon Ser.). (Illus.). 48p. (ps up). 1971. pap. 1.00 (ISBN 0-913452-10-6). Jesuit Bks.
Waiting Sands. Susan Howatch. 224p. 1986. pap. 2.95 (ISBN 0-449-20997-0, Crest). Fawcett.
Waiting Spirits. Bruce Coville. (Dark Forces Ser.: No. 11). 160p. (Orig.). (gr. 8-10). 1984. pap. text ed. 2.25 (ISBN 0-553-26004-9). Bantam.
Waiting: The Hope & Frustrations of a Childless Couple. Joan Y. McGowan. 1983. 10.95 (ISBN 0-533-05705-1). Vantage.
Waiting to Live. Mewa Ramgobin. 1986. pap. 8.95 (ISBN 0-394-74432-2, Vin). Random.
Waiting to Vanish. Ann Hood. (New Fiction Ser.). 1988. pap. 7.95 (ISBN 0-553-34521-4). Bantam.
Waiting to Waltz: A Childhood. Cynthia Rylant. LC 84-11030. (Illus.). 48p. (gr. 6-8). 1984. 10.95 (ISBN 0-02-778000-7). Bradbury Pr.
Waiting Tree & Other Poems: Sonnets. G. W. Sherman. (Orig.). 1966. pap. 3.00 (ISBN 0-685-00355-8). Cobra Pr.
Waiting with Alistair. Alistair Sampson. (Illus.). 176p. 1978. 9.95. Schiffer.
Waiting Years. Fumiko Enchi. Tr. by John Bester from Japanese. LC 72-15864. 203p. 1971. 12.95x (ISBN 0-87011-159-0). Kodansha.
Waiting Years. Fumiko Enchi. Tr. by John Bester from Japanese. LC 72-15864. 203p. 1980. pap. 5.95 (ISBN 0-87011-424-7). Kodansha.
Waiting Years: Essays on American Negro Literature. Blyden Jackson. LC 74-82001. 216p. 1976. 27.50 (ISBN 0-8071-0173-7). La State U Pr.
Waitress: America's Unsung Heroine. Leon Elder & Lin Rolens. (Illus.). 128p. (Orig.). 1985. pap. 8.95 (ISBN 0-88496-235-0). Capra Pr.
Waitress: America's Unsung Heroine. Leon Elder & Lin Rolens. 128p. 1988. Repr. lib. bdg. 22.95x (ISBN 0-8095-4025-8). Borgo Pr.
Waitress! Oh, Waitress. Eloh Pantone. LC 81-84725. 196p. 1982. 10.00 (ISBN 0-937894-04-4); pap. 5.00 (ISBN 0-937894-05-2). Life Arts.
Waitresses Handbook: A Guide to the Legal Rights of Waitresses & Other Restaurant Workers. (Women's Legal Defense Fund Staff). 80p. 1986. pap. 7.00 (ISBN 0-932689-17-5). Women's Legal Defense.
Waitressing: Inside Tips for Better Tips. Marcia Love-Jackson. (Illus.). 52p. (Orig.). pap. 4.95 (ISBN 0-9614315-0-4). Love-Jackson.
Wait'Till Your Father Gets Home: A Collection Reasonable Threats & Sayings. Connie Wallace. 70p. (Orig.). 1988. pap. 5.95 (ISBN 1-55618-032-2). Brunswick Pub.
Waiver, Transfer, Certification of Juveniles to Criminal Court: 1981 Statutes Analysis. John L. Hutzler. 8p. 1981. 2.00. Natl Juv & Family Ct Judges.
Wakabayashi Mineral Collection at the University Museum of the University of Tokyo. Ed. by Ryoichi Sadanaga & Michiaki Bunno. 177p. 1974. 44.50 (ISBN 0-86008-115-X, Pub. by U of Tokyo Japan). Columbia U Pr.
Wake Forest. Kenneth Garrett. (Illus.). 112p. 1987. 35.00 (ISBN 0-916509-17-6); deluxe ed. 125.00. Harmony Hse Pub LO.
Wake Forest Football Mystery. Carole M. Longmeyer. (ACC (Pic-a-Point Sportsmystery) Ser.). (Illus.). 80p. (Orig.). (gr. 3 up). pap. 3.95 (ISBN 0-935326-34-0). Gallopade Pub Group.
Wake Forest Law Review: 1965-1985, Vols. 1-21, index 1-15. Bound set. 725.00x (ISBN 0-686-90090-1). Rothman.
Wake in Darkness. Donald E. McQuinn. 1984. pap. 3.95 (ISBN 0-8125-8552-6, Dist. by Warner Pub. Services & Saint Martin's Press). Tor Bks.
Wake in Ybor City. Jose Yglesias. 28.50 (ISBN 0-405-13172-0). Ayer Co Pubs.
Wake Kitten. Emanuel Schongut. Ed. by Kate Klimo. (Kitten Board Bks.). (Illus.). 14p. 1983. 3.95 (ISBN 0-671-46383-7, Little Simon). S&S.
Wake Me up When I'm a Size Five. Cathy Guisewite. (Illus.). 128p. (Orig.). 1985. pap. 6.95 (ISBN 0-8362-2069-2). Andrews & McMeel.
Wake Me When the Band Starts Playing. Nancy Hopper. LC 87-22898. 160p. (YA) (gr. 7 up). 1988. 13.95 (ISBN 0-525-67244-3, 01258-370). Lodestar Bks.
Wake of Imagination: Toward a Postmodern Culture. Richard Kearney. LC 88-1311. 500p. (Orig.). 1988. 45.00x (ISBN 0-8166-1713-9); pap. 19.95 (ISBN 0-8166-1714-7). U of Minn Pr.
Wake of the Bounty. C. S. Wilkinson. 1953. 30.00 (ISBN 0-8274-3685-8). R West.
Wake of the Coasters. 2nd, rev. ed. John F. Leavitt. LC 75-120265. (American Maritime Library: Vol. 2). (Illus.). xvii, 201p. 1970. pap. 19.00 (ISBN 0-913372-34-X). Mystic Seaport.
Wake of the Electron. Donald Finkel. LC 86-47699. 64p. (Orig.). 1987. 13.95 (ISBN 0-689-11857-0); pap. 7.95 (ISBN 0-689-11858-9). Atheneum.
Wake of the Gods: Melville's Mythology. H. Bruce Franklin. 1963. pap. 16.95x (ISBN 0-8047-0137-7). Stanford U Pr.
Wake of the Prairie Schooner. 3rd ed. Irene D. Paden. (Illus.). 24.95 (ISBN 0-935284-40-0); pap. 12.95 (ISBN 0-935284-38-9). Patrice Pr.
Wake-Pick Poems. Kristjana Gunnars. (House of Anansi Poetry Ser.: No. 40). 85p. (Orig.). 1981. pap. 6.95 (ISBN 0-88784-089-2, Pub. by Hse Anansi Pr Canada). U of Toronto Pr.
Wake Up, America: World War I & the American Poster. Walton Rawls. Date not set. price not set. Abbeville Pr.
Wake up & Goodnight. Charlotte Zolotow. LC 75-135187. (Illus.). (ps-3). 1971. PLB 10.89 (ISBN 0-06-027042-X). HarpJ.
Wake Up & Preach. James F. Finley. LC 85-26667. 111p. (Orig.). 1986. pap. 5.95 (ISBN 0-8189-0492-5). Alba.
Wake Up Bear. Lynley Dodd. LC 86-42798. (Gold Star First Readers Ser.). (Illus.). 32p. (gr. 1-2). 1988. PLB 9.95 (ISBN 1-55532-124-0). Stevens Inc.
Wake up Bear, Its Christmas. Stephen Gammell. (Picture Puffins Ser.). 32p. (ps-k). 1984. pap. 3.95 (ISBN 0-14-050475-3, Puffin). Penguin.
Wake up, Bear...It's Christmas! Stephen Gammell. LC 81-5019. (Illus.). 32p. (ps-3). 1981. 11.75 (ISBN 0-688-00692-2); PLB 11.88 (ISBN 0-688-00693-0). Lothrop.
Wake Up, Busy Bears! Julia Killingback. (Busy Bears Ser.). 24p. (ps-1). 1987. 4.95 (ISBN 0-19-520601-0). Oxford U Pr.
Wake up Dead Man: Afro-American Worksongs from Texas Prisons. Bruce Jackson. LC 70-169857. (Illus.). 416p. 1972. text ed. 24.50x (ISBN 0-674-94546-8); pap. 9.95x (ISBN 0-674-94547-6). Harvard U Pr.
Wake up Detroit! The EVs Are Coming. Albert C. Smith, Jr. Ed. by Albert Smith, 3rd. LC 81-68726. (Illus., Orig.). 1982. pap. 3.95 (ISBN 0-933086-03-2). Cromwell-Smith.
Wake up, Jeremiah. Ronald Himler. LC 77-25679. (Illus.). (ps-1). 1979. PLB 12.89 (ISBN 0-06-022324-3). HarpJ.
Wake Up O' Sleeping World. 48p. 1983. 9.95 (ISBN 0-89962-315-8). Todd & Honeywell.
Wake up, Poor American People. Mae Wilson. 48p. 1985. pap. 5.00 (ISBN 0-682-40227-3). Exposition-Phoenix.
Wake up, Sam! Ski Michaels. LC 85-14115. (Illus.). 48p. (Orig.). (gr. 1-3). 1986. PLB 9.49 (ISBN 0-8167-0580-1); pap. text ed. 1.95 (ISBN 0-8167-0581-X). Troll Assocs.
Wake up, Small Bear. Adelaide Holl. LC 76-44318. (Small Bear Adventures Ser.). (Illus.). 48p. (gr. k-4). 1977. PLB 6.69 (ISBN 0-8116-4450-2). Garrard.
Wake up! Spirituality for Today. Anthony De Mello. 20p. 1987. pap. 5.95 (ISBN 0-89505-558-9). Tabor Pub.
Wake up, Stupid. Mark Harris. 1983. pap. text ed. 5.95 (ISBN 0-07-026841-X). McGraw.
Wake up, Sun. David Harrison. LC 85-30053. (Step into Reading Bks.). (Illus.). 32p. (ps-1). 1986. lib. bdg. 6.99 (ISBN 0-394-98256-8, BYR); pap. 2.95 (ISBN 0-394-88256-3, BYR). Random.
Wake up, Vladimir. Felicia Bond. LC 84-45342. (Illus.). 32p. (ps-3). 1987. 12.70i (ISBN 0-690-04452-6, Crowell Jr Bks); PLB 12.89 (ISBN 0-690-04453-4). HarpJ.
Wake up, William! Anita Riggio. LC 86-25866. (Illus.). 32p. (ps-1). 1987. PLB 12.95 (ISBN 0-689-31344-6, Atheneum Childrens Bks). Macmillan.
Wake up World! Jesus Is Coming Soon! George B. Eager. 40p. (Orig.). (gr. 7-12). 1980. pap. 1.00 (ISBN 0-9603752-3-6). Mailbox.
Wake up, World-We're People Too. Edward J. Kerneckel, Jr. 53p. 1985. 7.95 (ISBN 0-533-06255-1). Vantage.
Wake up! You Can Heal Yourself. Bo-In Lee. 139p. (Orig.). 1985. pap. text ed. 6.95 (ISBN 0-9615731-0-4). Intl Mahayana.

TITLE INDEX WALFORD'S GUIDE TO REFERENCE

Wake up Your Creative Genius. Kurt Hanks & Jay Perry. LC 83-6247. (Illus.). 142p. (Orig.). 1983. pap. 9.95 (ISBN 0-86576-051-9). W Kaufmann.
Wake up! You're Alive. Arnold Fox & Barry Fox. 1988. pap. 8.95 (ISBN 0-932194-66-4). Health Comm.
Wakefield Family. G. T. Ridlon. LC 73-746526. (Saco Valley Settlements Ser). 1970. pap. 1.50 (ISBN 0-8048-0851-1). C E Tuttle.
Wakefield Mystery Plays. Ed. by Martial Rose. 1969. pap. 10.95x (ISBN 0-393-00483-X, Norton Lib). Norton.
Wakefield Pageants in the Towneley Cycle. Ed. by A. C. Cawley. (Old & Middle English Texts). 187p. 1975. pap. 12.95x (ISBN 0-06-491013-X, 06392). B&N Imports.
Wakefield Plays. Israel Horovitz. 1985. pap. 3.50 (ISBN 0-380-42903-9, Bard). Avon.
Wakefulness. Bruce Renner. LC 78-71828. 78p. (Orig.). 1978. pap. 3.75 (ISBN 0-934332-10-X). L'Epervier Pr.
Wakemap Mound & Nearby Sites on the Long Narrows of the Columbia River. 2nd ed. Ed. by Emory Strong. (Illus.). 1977. pap. 2.00 (ISBN 0-8323-0137-X). Binford-Metropolitan.
Waking. Eva Figes. 1982. pap. 4.95 (ISBN 0-394-72227-2). Pantheon.
Waking a Sleeping Giant. Theodore F. Kouba. 1987. 14.95 (ISBN 0-533-07267-0). Vantage.
Waking at the Bottom of the Dark. Jan Clausen. LC 78-71983. 1979. pap. 3.00 (ISBN 0-9602284-0-3). Long Haul.
Waking Brain. 2nd ed. Horace W. Magoun. (Illus.). 196p. 1969. 13.00x (ISBN 0-398-01201-6). C C Thomas.
Waking Dream. Carol M. Wallace. LC 87-15555. 210p. 1987. 15.95 (ISBN 0-312-01108-3). St Martin.
Waking, Dream & Deep Sleep. Swami Jyotir Maya Nanda. (Illus.). 1974. pap. 2.99 (ISBN 0-934664-10-2). Yoga Res Foun.
Waking Dream Therapy: Dream Process As Imagination. Gerald Epstein. LC 80-25925. 237p. 1981. 29.95 (ISBN 0-89885-018-5). Human Sci Pr.
Waking Dreams. 3rd, rev. ed. Mary Watkins. LC 83-20435. viii, 174p. 1984. pap. 12.00 (ISBN 0-88214-324-7). Spring Pubns.
Waking Dreams. new ed. Mary M. Watkins. (Psychic Studies Ser.). 186p. 1976. 42.00 (ISBN 0-677-05100-X). Gordon & Breach.
Waking from the American Dream: What to Do When Success Fails. Donald McCullough. 182p. (Orig.). 1988. pap. 7.95 (ISBN 0-8308-1702-6). Inter-Varsity.
Waking from the Dream: America in the Sixties. Toby Goldstein. LC 87-14016. (Illus.). 160p. (YA) (gr. 7 up). 1988. 10.29 (ISBN 0-671-63709-6); pap. price not set (ISBN 0-671-66051-9). Messner.
Waking Giant: Gorbachev's Russia. Martin Walker. 298p. 1987. 17.45 (ISBN 0-394-55239-3). Pantheon.
Waking Giant: Gorbachev's Russia. Martin Walker. LC 86-42928. 336p. 1988. pap. 8.95 (ISBN 0-679-73954-8). Pantheon.
Waking in Seoul. Rob Wilson. 140p. 1988. 15.00 (ISBN 0-8248-1210-7). UH Pr.
Waking of the Human Soul & the Forming of Destiny - The Need for Understanding Christ. Rudolf Steiner. Tr. by Olin D. Wannamaker. 25p. (Ger.). 1983. pap. 3.00 (ISBN 0-919924-19-0, Pub by Steiner Book Centre Canada). Anthroposophic.
Waking Passenger. Charles Black. Ed. by Maxine Cassin. (New Orleans Poetry Journal Press Bks). 80p. 1983. pap. 5.00 (ISBN 0-938498-03-7). New Orleans Poetry.
Waking Rooms. Richard Downing. 176p. (Orig.). 1986. text ed. 19.95x (ISBN 0-936111-03-8); pap. text ed. 9.95x (ISBN 0-936111-04-6). Persun & Berlin.
Waking the Dead. Scott Spencer. LC 85-45600. 1986. 17.95 (ISBN 0-394-54356-4). Knopf.
Waking the Dead. Scott Spencer. 448p. 1987. pap. 4.95 (ISBN 0-345-34073-6). Ballantine.
Waking Their Neighbors Up: The Nashville Agrarians Rediscovered. Thomas D. Young. LC 81-14736. (Mercer University Lamar Memorial Lecture Ser.). 96p. 1982. 8.50x (ISBN 0-8203-0600-2). U of Ga Pr.
Waking to My Name: New & Selected Poems. Robert Pack. LC 79-3651. 272p. 1980. 25.00x (ISBN 0-8018-2357-9). Johns Hopkins.
Waking Up. Charles T. Tart. LC 86-11844. (New Science Library). 300p. 1986. 17.45 (ISBN 0-87773-374-0). Shambhala Pubns.
Waking up a Rainbow. Theodore Taylor. LC 85-16239. 275p. (YA) (gr. 7 up). 1986. pap. 14.95 (ISBN 0-385-29435-2). Delacorte.
Waking up Dry: How to End Bedwetting Forever. Martin Scharf. LC 86-19029. 112p. (Orig.). 1986. pap. 8.95 (ISBN 0-89879-229-0). Writers Digest.
Waking up in the Nuclear Age: A Vision for Survival. Chellis Glendinning. LC 86-32109. 160p. 1987. 14.95 (ISBN 0-688-06937-1, Pub. by Beech Tree Bks). Morrow.
Waking up, Late. Gary Eddy. 1977. pap. 2.00 (ISBN 0-918366-04-6). Slow Loris.
Waking Up: Overcoming the Obstacles to Human Potential. Charles T. Tart. LC 86-11844. 223p. 1987. pap. 14.95 (ISBN 0-87773-426-7). Shambhala Pubns.
Waking up the Ducks. Wally Swist. 18p. (Orig.). 1987. pap. 5.00 ltd. ed. (ISBN 0-938566-33-4). Adastra Pr.
Waking up Together. Paul Williams. (Illus.). 202p. 1985. 12.50 (ISBN 0-934558-13-2). Entwhistle Bks.
Walahfrid Strabo's Visio Wettini: Text, Translation & Commentary. David A. Traill. (Lateinische Sprache und Literatur des Mittelalters: Vol. 2). 223p. 1974. pap. 25.05 (ISBN 3-261-00942-X). P Lang Pubs.
Walapai Ethnography. Alfred L. Kroeber. LC 35-6835. (Amer Anthro Assn Memoirs). 1935. 34.00 (ISBN 0-527-00541-X). Kraus Repr.
Walbiri Iconography: Graphic Representation & Cultural Symbolism in a Central Australian Society. Nancy D. Munn. LC 86-4320. (Illus.). 244p. 1986. pap. 11.95x (ISBN 0-226-55110-5). U of Chicago Pr.
Waldara Answers: Lecture at Lakemont, Bk. 1. 1974. pap. 1.95 (ISBN 0-934258-04-X). S F Learnard.
Waldara Answers: Lecture Questions, Bk. 2. 1975. pap. 1.95 (ISBN 0-934258-09-0). S F Learnard.
Waldara Answers: Lecture Questions, Bk. 3. 1975. pap. 1.95 (ISBN 0-934258-10-4). S F Learnard.
Waldeck-Rousseau, Combes, & the Church: The Politics of Anticlericalism, 1899-1905. Malcolm O. Partin. LC 74-76167. pap. 77.80 (ISBN 0-317-20441-6, 2023432). Bks Demand UMI.
Waldeck-Rousseau, Combes, & the Church, 1899-1905: The Politics of Anticlericalism. Malcolm O. Partin. LC 74-76167. (Duke Historical Publication Ser). xi, 299p. 1969. 27.75 (ISBN 0-8223-0130-X). Duke.
Walden. Henry David Thoreau. Bd. with On Civil Disobedience. (Airmont Classics Ser.). (gr. 10up). pap. 1.50 (ISBN 0-8049-0083-3, CL-83). Airmont.
Walden, 2 vols. Henry David Thoreau. Ed. by F. B. Sanborn. LC 80-2685. Repr. of 1909 ed. Set. 58.50 (ISBN 0-404-19080-4). AMS Pr.
Walden. Henry David Thoreau. (Literature Ser.). (gr. 7-12). 1969. pap. text ed. 7.17 (ISBN 0-87720-719-4). AMSCO Sch.
Walden. Henry David Thoreau. 1960. pap. 4.95 (ISBN 0-385-09503-1, C10, Anch). Doubleday.
Walden. Henry David Thoreau. Bd. with Civil Disobedience. (Classics Edition). pap. 1.50 (ISBN 0-06-080615-X, HC615, PL). Har-Row.
Walden. Henry David Thoreau. Ed. by Paul Sherman. Bd. with Civil Disobedience. LC 60-16148. (YA) (gr. 9 up). 1960. pap. 6.50 (ISBN 0-395-05113-4, RivEd). HM.
Walden. Henry David Thoreau. Bd. with On the Duty of Civil Disobedience. 1962. pap. 3.95 (ISBN 0-02-054720-X, 05472, Collier). Macmillan.
Walden. Henry David Thoreau. 1966. 5.95 (ISBN 0-88088-566-1). Peter Pauper.
Walden. Henry David Thoreau. 367p. 1983. Repr. lib. bdg. 18.95x (ISBN 0-89966-466-0). Buccaneer Bks.
Walden. Henry David Thoreau. LC 86-63620. (Running Press Classics Ser.). 248p. 1987. lib. bdg. 12.90 (ISBN 0-89471-496-1); pap. 3.95 (ISBN 0-89471-495-3). Running Pr.
Walden see Week, Walden, Maine Woods, Cape Cod.
Walden see Writings of Henry D. Thoreau.
Walden: A Concordance. Marlene A. Ogden & Clifton Keller. (Reference Library of the Humanities). 302p. 1984. lib. bdg. 42.00 (ISBN 0-8240-8786-0). Garland Pub.
Walden & Civil Disobedience. Henry David Thoreau. 256p. 1973. pap. 2.25 (ISBN 0-451-52121-8, Sig Classics). NAL.
Walden & Civil Disobedience. Henry David Thoreau. Ed. by Owen Thomas. (Critical Editions). (Annotated). (gr. 9-12). 1966. pap. text ed. 7.95x (ISBN 0-393-09665-3, Nortonc). Norton.
Walden & Civil Disobedience. Henry David Thoreau. (Penguin American Library). 440p. (Orig.). 1983. pap. 2.95 (ISBN 0-14-039044-8). Penguin.
Walden & Other Writings. New ed. Henry David Thoreau. Ed. by Brooks Atkinson. 1981. pap. 4.00x (ISBN 0-394-32666-0, T35, Mod LibC). Modern Lib.
Walden & Other Writings. Henry David Thoreau. 435p. (YA) (gr. 9-12). 1981. pap. 1.95 (ISBN 0-553-21139-0, Bantam Classics). Bantam.
Walden & Other Writings. Henry David Thoreau. Ed. & intro. by Brooks Atkinson. LC 50-13711. 1937. 8.95 (ISBN 0-394-60421-0). Modern Lib.
Walden & Other Writings. Henry David Thoreau. Ed. by William Howarth. (Modern Library College Edition). 743p. 1981. pap. text ed. write for info (RanC). Random.
Walden & Other Writings. Henry David Thoreau. (Classics Ser.). 448p. 1983. pap. 2.25 (ISBN 0-553-21246-X, Bantam Classics). Bantam.
Walden Notes. Joseph McElrath. (Orig.). 1971. pap. 3.25 (ISBN 0-8220-1358-4). Cliffs.
Walden Pond Caper. James Magorian. LC 83-71263. 148p. 1983. pap. 6.00 (ISBN 0-930674-11-1). Black Oak.
Walden Revisited. George F. Whicher. 93p. 1973. pap. 4.45 (ISBN 0-87532-063-5). Hendricks House.
Walden: Selected Essays. Henry David Thoreau. Ed. by George F. Whicher. 492p. 1973. pap. 5.95 (ISBN 0-87532-109-7). Hendricks House.
Walden (Thoreau) Milton. (Book Notes Ser.). 1984. pap. 2.50 (ISBN 0-8120-3447-3). Barron.
Walden Three. Ruben Ardila. 144p. 1988. 10.75 (ISBN 0-8062-3309-5). Carlton.
Walden Three. Jack Catran. 432p. (Orig.). 1988. pap. 14.95 (ISBN 0-936162-30-9). Jade Pubns.
Walden Two. B. F. Skinner. 1980. Repr. text ed. cancelled (ISBN 0-8290-0128-X). Irvington.
Walden Two. B. F. Skinner. 1976. write for info.; pap. 3.95 (ISBN 0-02-411510-X). Macmillan.
Walden Two Notes. Cynthia C. McGowan. (gr. 10-12). 1979. pap. 3.50 (ISBN 0-8220-1361-4). Cliffs.
Walden West. August Derleth. LC 61-14127. (SAC Prairie Saga Ser.). 262p. 1961. 8.95 (ISBN 0-88361-073-6). Stanton & Lee.
Walden with Reader's Guide. Henry David Thoreau. (Literature Program Ser.). (Orig.). (gr. 7-12). 1973. text ed. 12.50 (ISBN 0-87720-826-3); pap. text ed. 8.75 (ISBN 0-87720-818-2); tchr's. ed. 8.33 (ISBN 0-87720-918-9). AMSCO Sch.
Walden Zero: A Novella. Jorn K. Bramann. LC 87-63331. 140p. (Orig.). 1988. pap. 9.00 (ISBN 0-945073-07-0). Nightsun MD.
Walden's Post Card Enthusiast Revisited. Ed. by Orville C. Walden. LC 82-70058. (Illus.). 224p. 1982. 7.95 (ISBN 0-913782-09-2). Deltiologists Am.
Walden's Stove Trade Directory, 1892-93. 52p. Repr. 10.00 (ISBN 0-9612204-2-2). Autonomy Hse.
Waldgesellschaften der Neiderrheinischen Sandplatten, No. 64. Wolfgang Dinter. (Dissertationes Botanicae). (Illus.). 112p. 1982. pap. text ed. 30.00x (ISBN 3-7682-1325-0). Lubrecht & Cramer.
Waldgesellschaften im Noerdlichen Steigerwald. W. Welss. (Dissertationes Botanicae Ser.: Vol. 83). (Illus.). 173p. (Ger.). 1985. pap. 30.00x (ISBN 3-7682-1438-9). Lubrecht & Cramer.
Waldheim. Luc Rosenzweig & Bernard Cohen. Tr. by Josephine Bacon from Fr. (Illus.). 224p. 1987. 17.95 (ISBN 1-55774-010-0, Dist. by Watts). Adama Pubs Inc.
Waldheim & Austria. Richard Bassett. 1989. 19.95 (ISBN 0-670-82173-X). Viking.
Waldheim Case: An Analysis of Austria's Nazi Past. Gerhard Botz. 180p. 1989. 35.00 (ISBN 0-8133-0654-X). Westview.
Waldheim: The Missing Years. Robert E. Herzstein. LC 87-34928. (Illus.). 1988. 18.95 (ISBN 0-87795-959-5, Arbor Hse). Morrow.
Waldingfield. Janine French. LC 87-27691. (Starlight Romance Ser.). 192p. 1988. 12.95 (ISBN 0-385-24342-1). Doubleday.
Waldo & Magic, Inc. Robert A. Heinlein. 1986. pap. 3.95 (ISBN 0-345-33015-3, Del Rey). Ballantine.
Waldo County: The Way It Was. Frank Claes. (Illus.). 192p. 1985. pap. 16.95 (ISBN 0-89272-176-6). Down East.
Waldo Emerson. Fay W. Allen. (Illus.). 782p. 1982. pap. 10.95 (ISBN 0-14-006278-5). Penguin.
Waldo Emerson: A Biography. Gay W. Allen. LC 81-65275. (Illus.). 696p. 1981. 25.00 (ISBN 0-670-74866-8). Viking.
Waldo Frank. Paul J. Carter. (Twayne's United States Authors Ser.). 1967. pap. 8.95x (ISBN 0-8084-0313-3, T125, Twayne). New Coll U Pr.
Waldo Frank: A Study. Gorham B. Munson. LC 75-23023. 1975. lib. bdg. 20.00 (ISBN 0-8414-6124-4). Folcroft.
Waldo Frank in America Hispana. 249p. 2.80 (ISBN 0-318-14317-8). Hispanic Inst.
Waldo: Pioneer Aviator. Waldo D. Waterman & Jack Carpenter. (Illus.). 502p. (Orig.). 1988. pap. 18.95 (ISBN 0-9600736-0-4). Arsdalen Bosch.
Waldo Point Syndrome. Brigitta Tofferi. 174p. (Orig.). 1987. pap. 8.95 (ISBN 0-935539-32-8). Heroica Bks.
Waldo, Tell Me about Christ. Hans Wilhelm. (Waldo, Tell Me Ser.). (Illus.). 40p. (ps-3). 1988. 4.95 (ISBN 0-8378-1812-5). Gibson.
Waldo, Tell Me about God. Hans Wilhelm. (Waldo, Tell Me Ser.). (Illus.). 40p. (ps-3). 1988. 4.95 (ISBN 0-8378-1809-5). Gibson.
Waldo, Tell Me about Guardian Angels. Hans Wilhelm. (Waldo Tell Me Ser.). (Illus.). 40p. (ps-3). 1988. 4.95 (ISBN 0-8378-1811-7). Gibson.
Waldo, Tell Me about Me. Hans Wilhelm. (Waldo, Tell Me Ser.). (Illus.). 40p. (ps-3). 1988. 4.95 (ISBN 0-8378-1810-9). Gibson.
Waldo, the Goat Dog. Jean Ebeling. Ed. by Melissa Roberts. (Illus.). 48p. (gr. 4-7). 1987. 8.95 (ISBN 0-89015-588-7). Eakin Pr.
Waldo the Tortoise. David Lloyd. (Great Escapes Ser.). (Illus.). 32p. (gr. k-3). 1986. 3.95 (ISBN 0-590-33654-1). Scholastic Inc.
Waldo Trench. Henry B. Fuller. (Collected Works of Henry B. Fuller). 1988. Repr. of 1908 ed. lib. bdg. 59.00x. Am Biog Serv.
Waldorf Education for Adolescence. Rudolf Steiner. 1980. pap. 15.50 (ISBN 0-906492-37-8, Pub. by Kolisko Archives). St George Bk Serv.
Waldorf Parenting Handbook: Useful Information on Child Development & Education from Anthroposophical Sources. 2nd, rev. ed. Lois Cusick. 1988. pap. 10.95 (ISBN 0-916786-75-7). St George Bk Serv.
Waldorf School Approach to History. Rev. ed. Werner Glas. 102p. 1981. pap. 6.95 (ISBN 0-88010-004-4). Anthroposophic.
Waldpilzzucht Fuer Jedermann. Erfolgsanleitung Fuer den Anbau von Waldpilzen auf Stroh Oder Holz. W. J. Hawlik. (Illus.). 64p. (Ger.). 1983. pap. text ed. 5.00x (ISBN 3-923090-07-2). Lubrecht & Cramer.
Waldron Phoenix Belknap, Jr., Collection of Portraits & Silver. Ed. by John M. Phillips et al. LC 55-14415. (Illus.). 1955. 13.50x (ISBN 0-674-94560-3). Harvard U Pr.
Waldron's Continuation see Sad Shepherd.
Waldschaeden Durch Immissionen? Gottlieb Duttweiler Institut Staff. 227p. (Ger.). 1983. pap. 13.00 (ISBN 0-89192-365-9). Interbk Inc.
Waldstein Woolen Mill. Herman Freudenberger. (Kress Library Publications: No. 18). (Illus.). 1963. pap. 8.95x (ISBN 0-678-09912-X, Baker Lib). Kelley.
Wales. Compiled by Jan Morris. (Small Oxford Bks.). (Illus.). 1982. 14.95 (ISBN 0-19-214118-X). Oxford U Pr.
Wales. Dorothy B. Sutherland. LC 86-29954. (Enchantment of the World Ser.). (Illus.). 128p. (gr. 5-9). 1987. PLB 22.60 (ISBN 0-516-02794-8). Childrens.
Wales. (AA Road Map Ser.). 1988. pap. 8.95 (ISBN 0-86145-522-3, Pub. by British Tour). Salem Hse Pubs.
Wales. (Let's Visit Places & Peoples - - Nations, Dependencies, & Sovereignties of the World Ser.). (Illus.). (gr. 5 up). 1988. 12.95 (ISBN 0-222-01029-0). Chelsea hse.
Wales: A New Study. Ed. by David Thomas. 1977. 24.95 (ISBN 0-7153-7414-1). David & Charles.
Wales: An Archaeological Guide. Christopher Houlder. LC 74-81539. (Illus.). 1975. 15.00 (ISBN 0-8155-5030-8, NP). Noyes.
Wales & Her Language. John E. Southall. LC 77-7289. 1977. Repr. of 1893 ed. lib. bdg. 45.00 (ISBN 0-89341-150-7). Longwood Pub Group.
Wales & Medicine. John Cule. 249p. 1984. 28.00x (ISBN 0-85088-260-5, Pub. by Gomer Pr). State Mutual Bk.
Wales & the Marches. John Tomes. (Blue Guides). (Illus.). 22.95 (ISBN 0-393-01556-4); pap. 16.95 (ISBN 0-393-30008-0). Norton.
Wales & the Quest for Peace. Goronwy J. Jones. 187p. 1970. text ed. 12.50x (ISBN 0-900768-34-7, Pub. by U of Wales). Humanities.
Wales at Westminster: A History of the Parliamentary Representation of Wales, 1800-1979. Arnold J. James & John E. Thomas. 284p. 1981. 58.50x (ISBN 0-85088-684-8, Pub. by Gomer Pr). State Mutual Bk.
Wales: Bed & Breakfast. 112p. 1987. pap. 5.95 (ISBN 1-85013-022-1, Pub. by British Tour). Salem Hse Pubs.
Wales Between the Wars. Ed. by Trevor Herbert & Gareth E. Jones. (Welsh History & Its Sources Ser.). 1988. pap. text ed. 19.95 (ISBN 0-7083-0989-5, Pub. by U of Wales). Humanities.
Wales England Wed. Ernest Rhys. 1973. Repr. of 1940 ed. 30.00 (ISBN 0-8274-0959-1). R West.
Wales: Going Places. (Illus.). 72p. 1985. pap. 4.95 (ISBN 1-85013-001-9, Pub. by Automobile Assn Brit). Salem Hse Pubs.
Wales in British Politics 1868-1922. 3rd ed. Kenneth O. Morgan. 360p. 1980. text ed. 22.50x (ISBN 0-7083-0743-4, Pub. by U of Wales). Humanities.
Wales in the Reign of James I. G. Dyfnallt Owen. 1988. 45.00 (ISBN 0-86193-210-2, Pub. by Boydell & Brewer). Longwood Pub Group.
Wales the Imagined Nation: Essays in Cultural & National Identity. Ed. by Tony Curtis. (Illus.). 306p. 1986. pap. 15.95 (ISBN 0-907476-54-6, Pub. by Poetry Wales Pr UK). Dufour.
Wales: The Shaping of a Nation. David Thomas & Prys Morgan. (Illus.). 256p. 1984. 35.95 (ISBN 0-7153-8418-X). David & Charles.
Wales Today. Don Dale-Jones & W. Randal Jenkins. 144p. 1986. 25.00x (ISBN 0-85088-377-6, Pub. by Gomer Pr). State Mutual Bk.
Wales Tourist Map. rev. ed. pap. 2.95 (ISBN 1-85013-003-5, Pub. by Automobile Assn Brit). Salem Hse Pubs.
Wales! Wales! Dai Smith. (Illus.). 200p. 1984. 17.95x (ISBN 0-04-942185-9). Unwin Hyman.
Wales: Walking. 108p. (Orig.). 1984. pap. 4.95 (ISBN 0-900784-97-0, Pub. by Automobile Assn Brit). Salem Hse Pubs.
Wales' Work. Robert Walshe. 1986. 16.95 (ISBN 0-89919-430-3). Ticknor & Fields.
Wales, 1880-1914. Trevor Herbert. Ed. by Trevor Herbert. (Welsh History & Its Sources Ser.). 160p. 1988. pap. text ed. 15.00 (ISBN 0-7083-0967-4, Pub. by U of Wales Pr). Humanities.
Wales: 1937-1940, Nos. 1-11. new ed. Ed. by Keidrych Rhys. 310p. 1969. 55.00x (ISBN 0-7146-2117-X, F Cass Co). Biblio Dist.
Walford's Concise Guide to Reference Material. A. J. Walford. 444p. 1981. 50.00x (ISBN 0-85365-882-X, Pub. by Library Assn Pub London). ALA.
Walford's Guide to Current British Periodicals in the Humanities & Social Sciences. A. J. Walford. 479p. 1985. 55.00x (ISBN 0-85365-676-2, 0-8389-L676-2). ALA.
Walford's Guide to Reference Material: Generalities, Languages, the Arts, & Literature, Vol. III. 4th ed. A. J. Walford. 768p. 1986. 80.00x (ISBN 0-85365-836-6, L836-6). ALA.
Walford's Guide to Reference Material: Social & Historical Sciences, Philosophy & Religion, Vol. 2. 4th ed. A. J. Walford. 822p. 1982. 80.00 (ISBN 0-85365-564-2, Pub. by Library Assn Pub London). ALA.

Walford's Guide to Reference Material: Science & Technology, Vol. 1. 4th ed. A. J. Walford. 708p. 1980. 80.00 (ISBN 0-85365-611-8, Pub. by Library Assn Pub London). ALA.

Walg: A Novel of Australia. B. Wongar. 192p. 1983. 14.95 (ISBN 0-396-08189-4). Dodd.

Walgenbach, Hanson, Dittrich: Principles of Accounting: Transparencies. 4th ed. Walgenbach et al. 85p. 1988. net 25.00 (ISBN 0-15-571391-4). HarBraceJ.

Walhachin: Catastrophe or Camelot? Joan Weir. (Illus.). 104p. (Orig.). 1984. pap. 7.95 (ISBN 0-88839-982-0). Hancock House.

Walid & His Friends: An Umayyad Tragedy. Robert Hamilton. (Studies in Islamic Art). (Illus.). 176p. 1988. 55.00 (ISBN 0-19-728011-0). Oxford U Pr.

Waling in God's Way: Studies in Ruth & Esther. Ruth M. Bathauer & Doris W. Greig. Ed. by Mary Beckwith. (Joy of Living Bible Study). 180p. 1988. pap. 5.95 (ISBN 0-8307-1284-4, 5417474). Regal.

Walk According to the Spirit. Pope John Paul II. 6.00 (ISBN 0-8198-8220-8); 5.00 (ISBN 0-8198-8221-6). Dghtrs St Paul.

Walk Across Africa. James A. Grant. LC 74-15042. Repr. of 1864 ed. 30.00 (ISBN 0-404-12049-0). AMS Pr.

Walk Across America. Peter Jenkins. 336p. (Orig.). 1983. pap. 3.95 (ISBN 0-449-20455-3, Crest). Fawcett.

Walk Across America. Peter Jenkins. LC 78-10320. (Illus.). 1979. 22.95 (ISBN 0-688-03427-6). Morrow.

Walk & Pray. Faye Field. 111p. 1982. pap. 3.50 (ISBN 0-8341-0785-6). Beacon Hill.

Walk Around the Downs. Roy Chapman. 64p. 1987. pap. 30.00x (ISBN 0-905392-00-0, Countryside Bks). State Mutual Bk.

Walk Back in Time Around Coseley. C. Beryl Wilkes. 1987. pap. 20.00x (Pub. by K A F Brewin Bks UK). State Mutual Bk.

Walk-Behind Lawn Mower Service Manual. 3rd ed. Intertec Publishing Corporation Staff. LC 86-83162. (Illus.). 152p. 1987. pap. 11.95 (ISBN 0-87288-272-1, WLMS-3). Intertec Pub.

Walk Beside Me, Be My Friend. Joan Oppenheimer. (gr. 7 up). 1982. pap. 1.95 (ISBN 0-590-32450-0, Wishing Star Bks). Scholastic Inc.

Walk by My Side. Sandra Field. (Harlequin Presents Ser.). 192p. 1983. pap. 1.75 (ISBN 0-373-10568-1). Harlequin Bks.

Walk Cheerfully Friends. Seth B. Hinshaw. (Illus.). 152p. (Orig.). 1978. pap. 4.50x (ISBN 0-942727-06-1). NC Yrly Pubns Bd.

Walk Cheerfully over the Earth. James O. Bond. LC 85-81076. (Illus.). 360p. 1985. text ed. 15.00 (ISBN 0-9608520-1-8). JOB Pubns.

Walk Don't Die. Fred A. Stutman. 356p. 1988. pap. 3.95 (ISBN 1-55785-038-0). Bart Books.

Walk, Don't Die: How to Stay Fit, Trim & Healthy Without Killing Yourself. Fred A. Stutman. LC 85-63360. (Illus.). 256p. (Orig.). 1986. 18.95 (ISBN 0-934232-06-7); pap. 9.95 (ISBN 0-934232-05-9). Med Manor Bks.

Walk Don't Run. Elvira Monroe. LC 79-63351. 1979. pap. 3.95 (ISBN 0-933174-04-7). Wide World-Tetra.

Walk, Don't Run: The Doctor's Book of Walking. Fred A. Stutman. LC 79-84815. 97p. 1979. pap. 6.95 (ISBN 0-934232-00-8). Med Manor Bks.

Walk Down Main Street. Ruth Moore. 386p. 1988. pap. 8.95 (ISBN 0-942396-56-1). Blackberry ME.

Walk Easy on the Earth. James Kavanaugh. (Illus.). 1979. 9.95 (ISBN 0-525-93078-7). Dutton.

Walk Gently This Good Earth. Margaret Craven. 192p. (gr. 7 up). 1981. pap. 2.25 (ISBN 0-440-39484-8). Dell.

Walk! Get into Shape the Easy Way. Othniel J. Seiden. (Illus.). 112p. (Orig.). 1985. pap. 6.95 (ISBN 0-8306-1934-8, 1934P). TAB Bks.

Walk in Dread: Twelve Classic Eerie Tales. Ed. by Dorothy Tomlinson. LC 72-2204. 285p. 1972. 6.95 (ISBN 0-8008-8037-4). Taplinger.

Walk in East Berkshire. Mick Tapp. 64p. 1987. pap. 30.00x (ISBN 0-905392-28-0, Countryside Bks). State Mutual Bk.

Walk in Love. Carmeline Koller. 10.50 (ISBN 0-8199-0843-6). Franciscan Herald.

Walk in My Footsteps. Martha Grooms. Ed. by Suzanne Hartman. 160p. (Orig.). (YA) (gr. 9-12). 1985. pap. 8.95 (ISBN 0-913678-15-5). New Day Pr.

Walk in My Soul. Lucia St. Clair Robson. LC 84-91666. 608p. (Orig.). 1987. pap. 8.95 (ISBN 0-345-30789-5). Ballantine.

Walk in Other Worlds in Dante. Marion S. Bainbrigge. 253p. 1982. Repr. of 1914 ed. lib. bdg. 30.00 (ISBN 0-686-98149-9). Darby Bks.

Walk in Other Worlds with Dante. Marion S. Bainbrigge. LC 73-101024. 1969. Repr. of 1914 ed. 23.50x (ISBN 0-8046-0691-9, Pub. by Kennikat). Assoc Faculty Pr.

Walk in the Light. Anna M. Cottrell. Ed. by Nancy Wikingstad. LC 87-15821. (Illus.). 128p. (Orig.). 1987. pap. 9.95 (ISBN 0-931892-12-0). B Dolphin Pub.

Walk in the Night & Other Stories. Alex La Guma. 1967. 17.95 (ISBN 0-8101-0399-0); pap. 8.95 (ISBN 0-8101-0139-4). Northwestern U Pr.

Walk in the Rain. Ursel Scheffler. (Illus.). 32p. (ps-2). 1986. 7.95 (ISBN 0-399-21267-1, G&D). Putnam Pub Group.

Walk in the Sky: Climbing Hidden Peak. Nicholas Clinch. (Illus.). 232p. 1982. 18.95 (ISBN 0-89886-042-3). Mountaineers.

Walk in the Sun. Harry Brown. 192p. Repr. of 1970 ed. lib. bdg. 15.95x (ISBN 0-88411-075-3, Pub. by Aeonian Bks). Amereon Ltd.

Walk in the Sun. Harry Brown. 187p. 1985. pap. 3.95 (ISBN 0-88184-117-X). Carroll & Graf.

Walk in the White Horse Country. Nigel Hammond. 80p. 1987. 30.00x (ISBN 0-905392-14-0, Countryside Bks). State Mutual Bk.

Walk in the Woods. Lee Blessing. 1988. pap. 6.95 (ISBN 0-452-26199-6, Plume). NAL.

Walk in Wolf Wood. rev. ed. Mary Stewart. LC 80-13010. (Illus.). 160p. (gr. 5up). 1984. 10.25 (ISBN 0-688-03679-1). Morrow.

Walk in Your Soul: Love Incantations of the Oklahoma Cherokees. Jack F. Kilpatrick & Anna G. Kilpatrick. LC 65-24931. 176p. 1965. pap. 6.95 (ISBN 0-87074-186-1). SMU Press.

Walk into April. Sam Ragan. 1986. 10.00 (ISBN 0-932662-62-5). St Andrews NC.

Walk into Awareness: A Gestalt Approach to Growth. Julia Crawford. LC 85-52116. (Illus.). 88p. (Orig.). 1985. pap. 9.95 (ISBN 0-934955-05-0). Watercress Pr.

Walk into My Parlor. Ed. & compiled by Betty Bandel. LC 76-158783. (gr. 6 up). 1972. 5.00 (ISBN 0-8048-0920-8). C E Tuttle.

Walk Me to the Distance. Percival Everett. LC 84-8845. 240p. 1985. 14.95 (ISBN 0-89919-321-8). Ticknor & Fields.

Walk My Way. Paige Dixon. LC 79-23291. 156p. (gr. 6-9). 1980. 7.95 (ISBN 0-689-30738-1, Atheneum Childrens Bk). Macmillan.

Walk On! Christmas Humphreys. LC 74-139270. pap. 4.50 (ISBN 0-8356-0419-5, Quest). Theos Pub Hse.

Walk on a Snowy Night. Judy Delton. LC 81-48660. (Illus.). 32p. (gr. k-3). 1982. PLB 12.89 (ISBN 0-06-021593-3). HarpJ.

Walk On: A Tool Kit for Building Your Own Walking Fitness Program. Nike Staff. (Illus.). 76p. 1987. pap. 7.95 (ISBN 0-87857-709-2). Rodale Pr Inc.

Walk on in Peace. Dorothy Edgerton. LC 82-73133. 64p. (Orig.). 1982. pap. 1.45 (ISBN 0-87029-187-4, 20278-8). Abbey.

Walk on the Great Barrier Reef. Caroline Arnold. (Nature Watch Ser.). (Illus.). 48p. (gr. 2-5). 1988. PLB 12.95 (ISBN 0-87614-285-4). Carolrhoda Bks.

Walk on the Wild Side. Nelson Algren. 352p. 1977. pap. 6.95 (ISBN 0-14-003565-6). Penguin.

Walk on the Wild Side: A Guide to Edible Wild Flowers & Plants of the Northeast. Nicholas Fish. 1987. write for info. Scriptorium Pr.

Walk on Water. Don Thornton. 44p. (Orig.). 1985. pap. 4.00 (ISBN 0-933727-00-3). Cajun Pubs.

Walk Out a Brother. Thomas Baird. LC 82-48859. 288p. (YA) (gr. 7 up). 1983. 12.70i (ISBN 0-06-020355-2); PLB 12.89g (ISBN 0-06-020356-0). HarpJ.

Walk Out of the World. Ruth Nichols. 144p. 1986. pap. 2.95 (ISBN 0-441-87133-X, Pub. by Ace Science Fiction). Ace Bks.

Walk Out of Worry. Janice Wise. (Enrichment Bible Study Ser.). 64p. (Orig.). 1988. pap. 2.95 (ISBN 0-932305-49-0, 522008). Aglow Pubns.

Walk Quietly Through the Night & Cry Softly. new ed. Burniece Avery. LC 77-2891. (Illus.). 1977. 7.00 (ISBN 0-913642-08-8). Balamp Pub.

Walk, Run, or Retreat: The Modern School Administrator. Neil V. Sullivan et al. LC 71-135013. Repr. of 1971 ed. 48.00 (ISBN 0-8357-9253-6, 2017642). Bks Demand UMI.

Walk Slowly: Poems & Drawings. John Campos. LC 86-83186. (Illus.). 80p. (Orig.). 1987. pap. 5.00 (ISBN 0-917021-02-9). Lighthouse Pr.

Walk Tall, Ride Tall. Burt Arthur & Budd Arthur. 128p. 1988. pap. 2.25 (ISBN 0-451-15140-2, Sig). NAL.

Walk the Dark Streets: A Sam Birge Mystery. William Krasner. 1985. pap. 3.95 (ISBN 0-684-18361-7, Collier). Macmillan.

Walk the Distant Hills: The Story of Longri Ao. Richard G. Beers. (Bold Believers Ser.). 1969. pap. 0.95 (ISBN 0-377-84171-4). Friendship Pr.

Walk the Edge of Panic. Karl Goodman. LC 85-51447. 192p. 1985. 9.95 (ISBN 0-88290-309-8, 1962). Horizon Utah.

Walk the Moons Road. Jim Aikin. 352p. 1985. pap. 2.95 (ISBN 0-345-32169-3, Del Rey). Ballantine.

Walk the Path of the Hills. Carmel Pritt. 1975. 8.95 (ISBN 0-87012-201-0). McClain.

Walk the World's Rim. Betty Baker. LC 65-11458. 192p. (gr. 5 up). 1965. PLB 12.89 (ISBN 0-06-020381-1). HarpJ.

Walk This Way Please: On Foot on the Monterey Peninsula, Carmel, Carmel Valley & Big Sur. Irene Gaasch. (Illus.). 96p. (Orig.). 1984. pap. 6.95. Hummbird Pr.

Walk Through Cold Fire. Lin Forshay-Lunsford. (gr. 6 up). 1986. pap. 2.95 (ISBN 0-440-99322-9, LFL). Dell.

Walk Through Graceland Cemetery: A Chicago Architecture Foundation Walking Tour. 3rd ed. Barbara Lanctot. (Illus.). 68p. 1988. write for info. Chi Arch Fndtn.

Walk Through Our Kitchen Garden. Judy Walter. 60p. (Orig.). 1985. pap. 6.95 (ISBN 0-9614650-1-8). Herb Farm Pr.

Walk Through the Cloisters. Bonnie Young. (Illus.). 144p. (Orig.). 1979. 14.95 (ISBN 0-670-74922-2, Pub by Metro Mus Art). Viking.

Walk Through the Cloisters. Text by Bonnie Young. (Illus.). 144p. 1988. pap. 7.95 (ISBN 0-8109-2383-1). Abrams.

Walk Through the Shire: Wherein We Discover Some Rare Drawings of Hobbit Life. Michael Green. LC 80-52955. (Illus., Orig.). 1980. lib. bdg. 12.90 (ISBN 0-89471-114-8); pap. 5.95 (ISBN 0-89471-115-6). Running Pr.

Walk Through the Wilderness. Emma S. Etuk. 240p. 1988. 12.95 (ISBN 0-8062-3225-0). Carlton.

Walk Through the Year. Edwin W. Teale. (Edwin Way Teale Library of Nature Classics). 1987. 17.95 (ISBN 0-396-09019-2); pap. 9.95 (ISBN 0-396-09020-6). Dodd.

Walk Through the Yellow Pages. Agha S. Ali. (Illus.). 32p. (Orig.). 1987. pap. 4.50 (ISBN 0-933313-07-1); Hand-sewn wrappers. 20.00 (ISBN 0-933313-06-3). Sun-Gemini Pr.

Walk Through Time: Seven Walking Tours of Howell, Michigan. David Andersen et al. (Illus.). 120p. (Orig.). 1988. pap. 8.00 (ISBN 0-9620432-0-6). City Howell Historic Preservation.

Walk to Grow On. Louise Plummer. (Care Bear Cousins Ser.). (Illus.). 40p. (ps-3). 1985. 5.95 (ISBN 0-910313-85-7). Parker Bros.

Walk to Rome. Dennis Larkin. (Illus.). 300p. (Orig.). 1987. 14.95 (ISBN 0-937495-20-4); pap. 9.94 (ISBN 0-937495-21-2). Trinity Comns.

Walk to the Pole: To the Heart of Antarctica in the Footsteps of Scott. Roger Mear & Robert Swan. (Illus.). 288p. 1987. 24.95 (ISBN 0-517-56611-7). Crown.

Walk to Win: Easy 4-Day Diet & Fitness Plan. Fred A. Stutman. LC 85-63311. (Illus.). 256p. 1988. 19.95 (ISBN 0-934232-08-3); pap. 10.95 (ISBN 0-934232-07-5). Med Manor Bks.

Walk Together Children. Ashley Bryan. (Illus.). (gr. 2 up). 1981. pap. 2.95 (ISBN 0-689-70485-2, Aladdin). Macmillan.

Walk Together, Talk Together. Katharine T. Kinkead. (Illus.). 1962. 3.95 (ISBN 0-393-07384-X). Norton.

Walk under the Rainbow. Ivan Gantschev. LC 85-30286. (Illus.). 28p. (ps-2). 1986. 5.75 (ISBN 0-382-09181-7). Silver.

Walk upon the Earth. Mary Talken. (Illus.). 192p. (Orig.). 1987. pap. 3.95 (ISBN 0-9619510-0-1). M Talken.

Walk West. Peter Jenkins & Barbara Jenkins. LC 81-11177. 320p. 1981. 19.95 (ISBN 0-688-00666-3). Morrow.

Walk West: A Walk Across America 2. Peter Jenkins & Barbara Jenkins. 1982. pap. 3.95 (ISBN 0-449-20022-1, Crest). Fawcett.

Walk When the Moon Is Full. Frances Hamerstrom. LC 75-33878. (Illus.). 64p. (gr. 3-8). 1975. 14.95 (ISBN 0-912278-69-2); pap. 6.95 (ISBN 0-912278-84-6). Crossing Pr.

Walk Where Jesus Walked: A Pilgrim's Guide with Prayer & Song. Willard F. Jabusch. LC 86-71224. (Illus.). 200p. (Orig.). 1986. pap. 6.95 (ISBN 0-87793-339-1). Ave Maria.

Walk with a Shadow. Juanita T. Osborne. 1982. 9.95 (ISBN 0-686-84187-5, Avalon). Bouregy.

Walk with a White Bushman. Laurens Van der Post. LC 87-1622. 320p. 1987. 18.95 (ISBN 0-688-07264-X). Morrow.

Walk with Me. Hazel G. Bremm. 76p. 1987. 6.95 (ISBN 0-533-07073-2). Vantage.

Walk with Me in White. Elmer T. Church. LC 86-81184. 154p. 1986. perfect bdg. 5.98 (ISBN 0-318-21723-6). E T Church.

Walk with Me: Prayers & Meditations. Large Print ed. Marilyn R. Riddle. (Illus.). 40p. (Orig.). 1982. pap. 3.00 (ISBN 0-9603748-2-5). Sandpiper OR.

Walk with Praise. Janet Van Rys. (Devotional Ser.). (Illus.). 200p. (Orig.). 1986. pap. 4.95 (ISBN 0-9616989-0-X). Jan Van Pubns.

Walk with Raschid & Other Stories. Josephine Jacobsen. LC 78-4584. 1978. 11.00 (ISBN 0-917492-08-0). Jackpine Pr.

Walk with Tom Jefferson. Philip Levine. LC 87-46080. 80p. 1988. 16.95 (ISBN 0-394-57038-3); pap. 8.95 (ISBN 0-394-75859-5). Knopf.

Walk Without Feet, Fly Without Wings, & Think Without Mind. Bhagwan Shree Rajneesh. Ed. by Ma Yoga Anurag. LC 83-181337. (Questions & Answers Ser.). (Illus.). 384p. (Orig.). 1979. 9.95 (ISBN 0-88050-167-7). Chidvilas Inc.

Walk Your Way to Better Dancing. L. Hostetler. (Ballroom Dance Ser.). 1985. 79.95 (ISBN 0-87700-680-6). Revisionist Pr.

Walk Your Way to Better Dancing. L. Hostetler. (Ballroom Dance Ser.). 1986. lib. bdg. 79.95 (ISBN 0-8490-3354-3). Gordon Pr.

Walkabout Woman. Michaela Roessner. 272p. (Orig.). 1988. pap. 3.95 (ISBN 0-553-27545-3, Spectra). Bantam.

Walkalong Model Railroad Track Plans. Don Mitchell. Ed. by Bob Hayden. (Illus., Orig.). 1989. pap. price not set (ISBN 0-89024-081-7). Kalmbach.

Walker & Other Poems. Arturo Giovannitti. (Poets of Revolt Ser.: No. 3). 64p. 1985. 13.95 (ISBN 0-88286-175-1); pap. 3.95 (ISBN 0-88286-150-6). C H Kerr.

Walker County, TX: A History. Ed. by Walker County Genealogical Society Staff & Walker County Historical Commission Staff. (Illus.). 964p. 1986. 65.00 (ISBN 0-88107-057-2). Curtis Media.

Walker Evans. John Szarkowski. LC 71-146835. (Illus.). 1971. 19.95 (ISBN 0-87070-312-9, 918040, Pub. by Museum Mod Art); pap. 12.50 (ISBN 0-87070-313-7, 918059). NYGS.

Walker Evans: American Photographs. Walker Evans. (Illus.). 1988. 40.00 (ISBN 0-87070-237-8, Pub. by Museum Mod Art); pap. 18.95 (ISBN 0-87070-238-6, Pub. by Museum Mod Art). NYGS.

Walker Evans at Work. Walker Evans. LC 79-1661. 256p. 1982. 18.45i (ISBN 0-06-011104-6, HarpT). Har-Row.

Walker Evans at Work. Walker Evans. LC 79-1661. (Illus.). 240p. 1985. pap. 15.95 (ISBN 0-06-091248-0, CN 1248, PL). Har-Row.

Walker Evans: Photographs for the Farm Security Admininistration, 1935-1938. Walker Evans. LC 74-149598. (Photography Ser.). 1974. Repr. of 1970 ed. lib. bdg. 39.50 (ISBN 0-306-70099-9). Da Capo.

Walker Evans: Photographs for the Farm Security Administration, 1935-1938. Walker Evans. LC 74-23992. (Illus.). 1975. pap. 15.95 (ISBN 0-306-80008-X). Da Capo.

Walker Evans: Photographs from the "Let Us Now Praise Famous Men Project". Compiled by William Stott. (Illus.). 1974. pap. 3.50 (ISBN 0-87959-016-5). U of Tex H Ransom Ctr.

Walker Expedition to Quebec, 1711. Ed. by Gerald S. Graham. LC 69-14509. 1969. Repr. of 1953 ed. lib. bdg. 26.75x (ISBN 0-8371-5072-8, GRWE). Greenwood.

Walker Family. G. T. Ridlon. LC 77-146527. (Saco Valley Settlements Ser). 1970. pap. 2.00 (ISBN 0-8048-0852-X). C E Tuttle.

Walker in Jerusalem. Samuel Heilman. 380p. 1986. 18.95 (ISBN 0-671-54433-0). Summit Bks.

Walker in the City. Alfred Kazin. LC 53-18408. 176p. 1969. pap. 6.95 (ISBN 0-15-694176-7, Harv). HarBraceJ.

Walker in the City. Alfred Kazin. 14.25 (ISBN 0-8446-6216-X). Peter Smith.

Walker in the Shadows. Barbara Michaels. 224p. 1981. pap. 2.50 (ISBN 0-449-24450-4). Fawcett.

Walker Percy. Intro. by Harold Bloom. (Modern Critical Views Ser.). 167p. 1986. 19.95 (ISBN 0-87754-714-9). Chelsea Hse.

Walker Percy. Jac Tharpe. (United States Authors Ser.). 1983. lib. bdg. 17.95 (ISBN 0-8057-7389-4, Twayne). G K Hall.

Walker Percy: A Comprehensive, Descriptive Bibliography. Linda W. Hobson. (Illus.). 125p. 1988. 35.00 (ISBN 0-917905-06-7). Faust Pub Co.

Walker Percy: A Southern Wayfarer. William R. Allen. LC 86-5647. 230p. 1986. 22.50x (ISBN 0-87805-296-8). U Pr of Miss.

Walker Percy & the Old Modern Age: Reflections on Language, Argument, & the Telling of Stories. Patricia Lewis Poteat. LC 84-10005. (Southern Literary Studies). 177p. 1985. text ed. 22.50 (ISBN 0-8071-1187-2). La State U Pr.

Walker Percy & the Postmodern World. Mary K. Sweeny. 1987. 8.95 (ISBN 0-8294-0541-0). Loyola.

Walker Percy: Art & Ethics. Ed. by Jac L. Tharpe. LC 80-12227. (Southern Quarterly Ser.). 168p. 1980. pap. 5.00 (ISBN 0-87805-120-1). U Pr of Miss.

Walker Percy, Nineteen Thirty to Nineteen Eighty-Four: A Bibliography. Stuart Wright. 1987. lib. bdg. 29.50x (ISBN 0-88736-046-7). Meckler Corp.

Walker Revised: Being a Revision of John Walker's Sufferings of the Clergy During the Grand Rebellion, 1642-60. Ed. by A. G. Matthews. 492p. 1988. 88.00 (ISBN 0-19-821264-X). Oxford U Pr.

Walker: The True Story of the First American Invasion of Nicaragua. Rudy Wurlitzer. LC 87-45824. (Illus.). 256p. Date not set. 19.45 (ISBN 0-06-055122-4). Har-Row.

Walker: The True Story of the First American Invasion of Nicaragua. Rudy Wurlitzer. LC 87-45824. (Illus.). 256p. Date not set. pap. 8.95 (ISBN 0-06-096258-5, PL6258, PL). Har-Row.

Walker Washington Guide. John Walker & Katharine Walker. (Illus.). 288p. 1987. pap. 6.95 (ISBN 0-914440-96-9). EPM Pubns.

Walkers. Gary Brandner. 1981. pap. 2.50 (ISBN 0-449-14319-8, GM). Fawcett.

Walker's Appeal & Garnet's Address to the Slaves of the United States of America. David Walker & Henry H. Garnet. LC 78-77508. (American Negro: His History & Literature Ser., No. 2). 1969. Repr. 14.50 (ISBN 0-405-01901-7). Ayer Co Pubs.

Walker's Britain. Andrew Duncan. (Illus.). 336p. (Orig.). 1986. pap. 12.95 (ISBN 0-935161-54-6). Hunter Pub NY.

Walker's Building Estimator's Reference Book. 22nd ed. William H. Spradlin, Jr. (Illus.). 1270p. 1986. 39.95 (ISBN 0-911592-22-9). F R Walker.

Walkers Guide to Harpers Ferry, West Virginia. Dave Gilbert. LC 82-63068. (Illus.). 80p. 1983. pap. 4.95 (ISBN 0-933126-28-X). Pictorial Hist.

Walker's Guidebook: Serendipitous Outings Near New York City Including a Section for Birders. Marina Harrison & Lucy D. Rosenfeld. (Illus.). 192p. (Orig.). 1988. pap. 12.95 (ISBN 0-935576-27-4). Kesend Pub Ltd.

Walker's Insulation Techniques & Estimating Handbook. 2nd, rev. ed. Harry Hardenbrook. Ed. by Gary D. Cook. (Illus.). 131p. 1983. pap. text ed. 12.95. F R Walker.

Walker's Insulation Techniques & Estimating Handbook. Harry Hardenbrook. (Illus.). 128p. pap. 12.95 (ScribT). Scribner.

Walker's Journal. Robert J. Sweetgall & John Dignam. (Illus.). 128p. 1986. pap. 7.95 (ISBN 0-939041-02-2). Creative Walking.

Walker's Mammals of the World, 2 vols. 4th ed. Ed. by Ronald M. Nowak & John L. Paradiso. LC 82-49056. (Illus.). 1472p. 1983. 75.00x set (ISBN 0-8018-2525-3). Johns Hopkins.

Walker's Manual for Construction Cost Estimating. Vick S. Crespin et al. Ed. by Frank R. Walker Company. (Illus.). 128p. 1981. pap. 14.95 (ISBN 0-911592-85-7). F R Walker.

Walker's Manual Incorporated. 78th, annual ed. National Standards Association Staff. LC 10-19951. 1950p. 1986. 345.00 (ISBN 0-916234-11-8). Cambridge MD.

Walker's Manual of Western Corporations, 2 vols. 74th annual ed. Walker's Manual Incorporated Editors. LC 10-19951. 1700p. 1982. (ISBN 0-916234-07-X). Cambridge MD.

Walker's Manual of Western Corporations, 2 vols. 75th annual ed. Walker's Manual Incorporated Editors. LC 10-19951. 1850p. 1983. Set. 260.00 (ISBN 0-916234-08-8). Cambridge MD.

Walker's Manual of Western Corporations, 2 vols. 76th annual ed. Walker's Manual Incorporated Editors. LC 10-19951. 1850p. 1984. Set. 295.00 (ISBN 0-916234-09-6). Cambridge MD.

Walker's Manual of Western Corporations, 2 vols. 77th annual ed. Walker's Manual Incorporated Editors. LC 10-19951. 1950p. 1985. 335.00 (ISBN 0-916234-10-X). Cambridge MD.

Walkers of Hanningfield: Surveyors & Mapmakers Extraordinary. A. C. Edwards & K. C. Newton. 152p. 1986. 125.00x (ISBN 0-7212-0614-X, Pub. by Regency Pr). State Mutual Bk.

Walker's Pocket Estimator. 22nd ed. Ed. by William H. Spradlin, Jr. 240p. 1986. pap. 7.95 (ISBN 0-911592-41-5). F R Walker.

Walker's Quantity Surveying & Basic Construction Estimating. G. Patrick Bourgeois et al. Ed. by Walker, Frank R., Company Staff. (Illus.). 128p. 1981. pap. 14.95 (ISBN 0-911592-75-X). F R Walker.

Walker's Remodeling Estimators Reference Book. 2nd ed. Harry Hardenbrook. Ed. by Robert Siddens & P. J. Sammartino. (Illus.). 340p. 1987. text ed. 23.95 (ISBN 0-911592-61-X). F R Walker.

Walker's Rhyming Dictionary of the English Language: In Which the Whole Language Is Arranged According to Its Terminations. rev. & enl. ed. J. Walker. 558p. 1983. Repr. of 1924 ed. 16.95 (ISBN 0-7100-9306-3). Routledge Chapman & Hall.

Walker's RR Routes - 1853. facsimile ed. Joseph R. Walker. Ed. by Pat Adler & Walt Wheelock. 1965. 4.50 (ISBN 0-910856-18-4). La Siesta.

Walkies. Barbara Woodhouse. (Illus.). 32p. 1983. 7.95 (ISBN 0-671-46892-8). Summit Bks.

Walkin' Matilda. Clayton R. Graham. LC 84-19413. 249p. (Orig.). 1985. pap. 6.95 (ISBN 0-915175-08-8). Knights Pr.

Walking. John Pleas. 150p. 1987. 12.95 (ISBN 0-393-02446-6). Norton.

Walking. Henry David Thoreau. 48p. (Orig.). Date not set. pap. 5.95 (ISBN 1-55709-100-5). Applewood.

Walking. Henry David Thoreau. 41p. 1988. Repr. of 1863 ed. price not set (ISBN 0-9614597-5-1). Ninja Pr.

Walking a Thin Line: Anorexia & Bulimia, the Battle Can Be Won. Pam W. Vredevelt & Joyce R. Whitman. LC 85-18916. (Touch of Grace Ser.). 1985. pap. 7.95 (ISBN 0-88070-117-X). Multnomah.

Walking Across Egypt. Clyde Edgerton. 218p. 1987. 14.95 (ISBN 0-912697-51-2). Algonquin Bks.

Walking Across Egypt. Clyde Edgerton. (Large Print Bks.). 260p. 1988. lib. bdg. 16.95x (ISBN 0-8161-4379-X, Large Print Bks). G K Hall.

Walking Across Egypt. Clyde Edgerton. 240p. 1988. pap. 3.95 (ISBN 0-345-34649-1). Ballantine.

Walking after Midnight. Maureen McCoy. LC 85-9506. 223p. 1985. 15.95 (ISBN 0-671-55423-9, Poseidon). PB.

Walking after Midnight. Maureen McCoy. pap. 5.95. WSP.

Walking after Midnight. Maureen McCoy. pap. 5.95. PB.

Walking Along the Missouri River. John McKernan. LC 77-8920. (Lost Roads Poetry Ser.: No. 5). 1978. pap. 3.00 (ISBN 0-918786-09-6). Lost Roads.

Walking Among the Unseen. Hannah Hurnard. 1977. pap. 3.95 (ISBN 0-8423-7805-7). Tyndale.

Walking Ancient Trackways. Michael Dunn. (Illus.). 232p. 1986. 30.95 (ISBN 0-7153-8640-9). David & Charles.

Walking & Leaping. Merlin R. Carothers. 129p. (Orig.). 1974. pap. 4.95 (ISBN 0-943026-05-9). Carothers.

Walking & Working Surfaces. Center for Occupational Research & Development Staff. (Job Safety & Health Instructional Materials Ser.). (Illus.). 24p. 1981. pap. text ed. 2.00 (ISBN 1-55502-084-4). Ctr Res & Dev.

Walking Around in South Street: Discoveries in New York's Old Shipping District. Ellen F. Rosebrock. (Illus., Orig.). 1974. pap. 3.95 (ISBN 0-913344-17-6). South St Sea Mus.

Walking Austria's Alps: Hut to Hut. Jonathan Hurdle. (Illus.). 240p. (Orig.). 1988. pap. 10.95 (ISBN 0-89886-159-4). Mountaineers.

Walking Away. H. R. Coursen. 1977. pap. 1.50 (ISBN 0-686-23157-0). Samisdat.

Walking Away. Elizabeth Winthrop. LC 72-9869. (Illus.). 240p. (gr. 5 up). 1973. PLB 11.89 (ISBN 0-06-026534-5). HarpJ.

Walking Beside Jesus in the Holy Land. Isabelle W. Bacon. 100p. (Orig.). 1987. pap. 6.95 (ISBN 0-915597-53-5). Amana Bks.

Walking Black & Tall. rev. ed. Omar Fletcher. (Orig.). 1984. pap. 2.25 (ISBN 0-87067-241-X, BH241). Holloway.

Walking Canals. Ronald Russell. (Illus.). 144p. 1984. 14.95 (ISBN 0-7153-8350-7). David & Charles.

Walking Cure. Bernard Macfadden. (Illus.). 179p. 1984. pap. text ed. 15.00 (ISBN 0-87556-391-0). Saifer.

Walking Dead. Peter Dickinson. (International Crime Ser.). 1985. pap. 3.95 (ISBN 0-394-74173-0). Pantheon.

Walking Dead. Pat Holliday. 124p. (Orig.). 1982. pap. 3.95 (ISBN 0-937408-29-8). GMI Pubns Inc.

Walking Delegate. facsimile ed. Leroy Scott. LC 68-57549. 372p. Repr. of 1905 ed. lib. bdg. 29.50 (ISBN 0-8398-1853-X). Irvington.

Walking Delegate. Leroy Scott. 372p. 1986. pap. text ed. 7.95x (ISBN 0-8290-1950-2). Irvington.

Walking Distance. Anthony Backes. 40p. 1987. limited edition 6.00 (ISBN 0-89018-022-9); pap. 4.00 (ISBN 0-89018-021-0). Lionhead Pub.

Walking Distance. Marian Thurm. LC 86-27947. 272p. 1987. 16.45 (ISBN 0-394-55147-8). Random.

Walking Distance. Marian Thurm. 1988. pap. 6.95 (ISBN 0-14-010756-8). Penguin.

Walking Doll: Or, the Asters & Disasters of Society. Robert H. Newell. LC 74-171061. Repr. of 1872 ed. 23.50 (ISBN 0-404-03664-3). AMS Pr.

Walking Down Jerusalem Ridge. Wanda M. Thomason. LC 84-90409. 109p. 1984. 7.50 (ISBN 0-8233-0392-6). Golden Quill.

Walking Down the Stairs. Galway Kinnell. Ed. by Donald Hall. LC 77-23752. (Poets on Poetry Ser.). pap. 8.95 (ISBN 0-472-52530-1). U of Mich Pr.

Walking Drum. Louis L'Amour. pap. 4.50 (ISBN 0-553-24923-1). Bantam.

Walking Europe from Top to Bottom. Susanna Margolis & Ginger Harmon. LC 85-18469. (Adventure Travel Guide Ser.). (Illus.). 320p. (Orig.). 1986. pap. 10.95 (ISBN 0-87156-752-0, Dist. by Random). Sierra.

Walking for Fitness & Pleasure. Ronald E. Walker. 112p. 1988. 8.75 (ISBN 0-8062-3230-7). Carlton.

Walking for Health & Fitness. Consumer Guide Editors. 256p. 1988. pap. 6.95 (ISBN 0-451-82194-7, Sig). NAL.

Walking for Health & Fitness. Ann Ward & James M. Rippe. LC 65-10200. (Illus.). 32p. 1988. pap. 11.50x (ISBN 0-397-50855-7, Lippincott Medical). Lippincott.

Walking for the Health of It: The Easy & Effective Exercise for People over Fifty. Jeannie Ralston. (Illus.). 221p. 1986. pap. 6.95 (ISBN 0-673-24826-7). Am Assn Retire.

Walking Four Ways in the Wind. John Allman. LC 79-83974. (Princeton Series of Contemporary Poets). 1979. 15.00x (ISBN 0-691-06402-4); pap. 7.50x (ISBN 0-691-01359-4). Princeton U Pr.

Walking from Inn to Inn: The San Francisco Bay Area. Jacqueline Kudler & Arlene Stark. LC 85-45697. (Illus.). 288p. 1986. pap. 8.95 (ISBN 0-88742-068-0). Globe Pequot.

Walking Guide to the Caribbean: From the Virgin Islands to Martinique. Leonard M. Adkins. 200p. (Orig.). 1988. pap. 7.95 (ISBN 1-55566-020-7). Johnson Bks.

Walking Guides. Colin Speakman. 208p. 1985. pap. 19.00x (ISBN 0-7090-2166-6, Pub. by R Hale Ltd UK). State Mutual Bk.

Walking Home from the Ice-House. Vern Rutsala. LC 80-70566. (Poetry Ser.). 1980. 12.95 (ISBN 0-915604-47-7); pap. 4.95 (ISBN 0-915604-48-5). Carnegie-Mellon.

Walking in Austria. B. Spencer. (Illus.). 192p. (Orig.). 1987. pap. 10.95 (ISBN 1-55650-023-8). Hunter Pub NY.

Walking in France. Rob Hunter. (Illus.). 224p. pap. 9.95 (ISBN 0-902280-83-X, P138, Pub. by Oxford Ill Pr). Haynes Pubns.

Walking in France. Rob Hunter. (Illus.). 218p. 1986. pap. 9.95 (ISBN 0-946609-38-1, Pub. by Oxford Ill Pr). Haynes Pubns.

Walking in God's Light. Jim Larson. LC 84-9963. 1984. pap. 4.95 (ISBN 0-8307-0953-3, S181216). Regal.

Walking in Hampshire. 64p. 1987. 30.00x (ISBN 0-905392-33-7, Countryside Bks). State Mutual Bk.

Walking in Missionary Shoes. Lima L. Williams. 1986. pap. 14.95 (ISBN 0-87162-417-6, D8750). Warner Pr.

Walking in Northern France. (Visitor's Guides Ser.). (Illus.). 192p. (Orig.). 1987. pap. 8.95 (ISBN 0-935161-63-5). Hunter Pub NY.

Walking in Old Shoes: Love Is Comfortable. Ray Runde. 208p. 1986. pap. text ed. 12.95 (ISBN 0-8403-3943-7). Kendall-Hunt.

Walking in Switzerland. Brian Spencer. (Illus.). 192p. 1986. pap. 9.95 (ISBN 0-935161-20-1). Hunter Pub NY.

Walking in the Alps. Brian Spencer. (Illus.). 192p. 1986. pap. 9.95 (ISBN 0-935161-23-6). Hunter Pub NY.

Walking in the Garden: Inner Peace from the Flowers of God. Paula Connor. (Illus.). 170p. 1984. 14.95 (ISBN 0-13-944280-4); pap. 5.95 (ISBN 0-13-944264-2). P-H.

Walking in the Light. Joyce M. Smith. 1980. pap. 2.95 (ISBN 0-8423-7813-8). Tyndale.

Walking in the Light. R. Pearsall Smith. 128p. 1987. pap. 5.95 (ISBN 0-310-20921-8, 12510P). Zondervan.

Walking in the National Parks in Britain. Alan Mattingly. (Illus.). 192p. 1982. 18.95 (ISBN 0-7153-8144-X). David & Charles.

Walking in the Spirit. Zenas J. Bicket. LC 76-51000. 96p. 1977. pap. 1.25 (ISBN 0-88243-611-2, 02-0611). Gospel Pub.

Walking in the Spirit. Michael Harper. 112p. (Orig.). 1983. pap. 3.95 (ISBN 0-87123-614-1, 210614). Bethany Hse.

Walking in the World. Marjorie Von Harten. 1978. 4.95 (ISBN 0-900306-46-7, Pub. by Coombe Springs Pr). Claymont Comm.

Walking in Tower Grove Park: A Victorian Strolling Park. 2nd, rev. ed. Robert E. Knittel. LC 83-82822. (Illus.). 105p. 1984. 12.95 (ISBN 0-933038-05-4); pap. 8.95 (ISBN 0-933038-03-8). Grass Hooper Pr.

Walking in Two Worlds: Paper Doll Book for Girls, Bk. 50. (ps-3). write for info. (ISBN 0-931363-50-0). Celia Totus Enter.

Walking in Two Worlds: Paper Doll Book for Boys, Bk. 51. (ps-3). write for info. (ISBN 0-931363-51-9). Celia Totus Enter.

Walking in Wisdom: A Woman's Workshop on Ecclesiastes. Barbara Bush. (Woman's Workshop Ser.). 128p. (Orig.). 1982. pap. 2.95 (ISBN 0-310-43041-0, 12014P). Zondervan.

Walking in Zen, Sitting in Zen. Bhagwan Shree Rajneesh. Ed. by Rajneesh Foundation International. LC 82-24025. (Questions & Answers Ser.). 444p. (Orig.). 1982. pap. 10.95 (ISBN 0-88050-668-7). Chidvilas Inc.

Walking into Darkness: The Experience of Spinal Cord Injury. M. J. Oliver et al. 150p. 1988. text ed. 45.00x (ISBN 0-333-44360-8, Pub. by Macmillan England); pap. text ed. 23.50x (ISBN 0-333-44361-6, Pub. by Macmillan England). Sheridan Med Bks.

Walking into Light. David Winter. 160p. 1986. pap. 3.50 (ISBN 0-87788-916-3). Shaw Pubs.

Walking into the Dawn: A Celebration see Two by Terry Plus One: An Anthology of Plays by Women.

Walking into the Morning. Margaret Walpole. 48p. 1986. pap. 7.95 (ISBN 0-8378-5093-2). Gibson.

Walking Is Wild, Weird & Wacky. Karen Kerber. LC 85-50701. (ps-3). 1985. 12.95 (ISBN 0-933849-01-X). Landmark Edns.

Walking Larder: Patterns of Domestication Pastoralism, & Predation. Juliet C. Brock. (One World Archaeology Ser.: No. 2). (Illus.). 384p. 1988. text ed. 60.00 (ISBN 0-04-445013-3). Unwin Hyman.

Walking Liberty Half Dollars. A. Swiatek. LC 83-71497. 1984. soft cover 18.00 (ISBN 0-317-27386-8); lib. bdg. 17.00 (ISBN 0-942666-23-2). S J Durst.

Walking London's Waterways. Bryan Fairfax. (Illus.). 192p. 1985. 18.95 (ISBN 0-7153-8584-4). David & Charles.

Walking Machines: A Introduction to Legged Robots. D. J. Todd. (Advanced Industrial Technology Ser.). 240p. 1985. text ed. 39.50 (ISBN 0-412-01131-X, 9661, Pub. by Chapman & Hall England New York). Routledge Chapman & Hall.

Walking Old Railways. Christopher Somerville. LC 78-74078. 1979. 17.95 (ISBN 0-7153-7681-0). David & Charles.

Walking on Air. Pierre Delattre. 243p. 1987. pap. 8.00 (ISBN 0-915308-95-9). Graywolf.

Walking on Air. Helen E. McLaughlin. Ed. by Beverly Gandy. (Orig.). 1986. pap. 19.95 (ISBN 0-930161-04-1). State of the Art Ltd.

Walking on Air. Helen E. McLaughlin. (Illus.). 224p. 1986. pap. 19.95 (ISBN 0-317-57844-8). Aviation.

Walking on Borrowed Land. William A. Owens. LC 87-40266. (Texas Tradition Ser.: No. 9). 323p. 1988. pap. 11.95 (ISBN 0-87565-028-7). Tex Christian.

Walking on Glass. Ian Banks. 239p. 1985. 15.95 (ISBN 0-395-40048-1). HM.

Walking on the Edge of the World: A Journey of Discovery Through the Sixties & Beyond. George Leonard. (Illus.). 384p. 1988. 19.95 (ISBN 0-395-48311-5). HM.

Walking on the North & South Downs. Mark Chapman. 192p. 1985. 24.95x (ISBN 0-7090-1866-5, Pub. by R Hale Ltd UK). State Mutual Bk.

Walking on Thorns: The Call to Christian Obedience. Allan Boesak. 80p. (Orig.). 1984. pap. 4.95 (ISBN 0-8028-0041-6). Eerdmans.

Walking on Water. Leo Booth. 180p. (Orig.). 1985. pap. 8.95 (ISBN 0-932194-28-1). Health Comm.

Walking on Water: Reflections on Faith & Art. Madeleine L'Engle. LC 80-21066. (Wheaton Literary Ser.). 198p. 1980. pap. 7.95 (ISBN 0-87788-919-8). Shaw Pubs.

Walking Out the Dark. Shirley Buettner. (W.N.J. Ser.: No. 20). pap. 6.00 (ISBN 1-55780-069-3). Juniper Pr WI.

Walking Papers. Jay Cronley. LC 87-43234. 320p. 1988. 16.95 (ISBN 0-394-56947-4). Random.

Walking Point: American Narratives of Vietnam. Thomas Myers. 272p. 1988. 24.95 (ISBN 0-19-505351-6). Oxford U Pr.

Walking Shadows. Fred Taylor. 1986. pap. 3.95 (ISBN 0-312-90377-4). St Martin.

Walking Softly in the Wilderness: The Sierra Club Guide to Backpacking. rev. ed. John Hart. LC 83-19592. (Outdoor Activities Guides Ser.). (Illus.). 448p. 1984. pap. 9.95 (ISBN 0-87156-813-6). Sierra.

Walking-Stick Papers. Robert C. Holland. 1973. Repr. of 1918 ed. 15.00 (ISBN 0-8274-0253-8). R West.

Walking Sticks. Edward Hart. (Illus.). 96p. 1986. 10.95 (ISBN 0-946284-52-0, Pub. by Crowood Pr). Longwood Pub Group.

Walking Straight in a Crooked World. Don M. Aycock. (Orig.). 1987. pap. 3.95 (ISBN 0-8054-5034-3). Broadman.

Walking Switzerland - the Swiss Way: From Vacation Apartments, Mountain Hotels, Inns & Huts. Marcia Lieberman & Philip Lieberman. (Illus.). 260p. (Orig.). 1987. pap. 10.95 (ISBN 0-89886-137-3). Mountaineers.

Walking the Beach to Bellingham. Harvey Manning. LC 86-21516. 272p. 1986. 18.95 (ISBN 0-88089-018-5). Madrona Pubs.

Walking the Boundaries. Peter Davison. LC 73-93708. 128p. 1974. 6.95 (ISBN 0-689-10608-4). Atheneum.

Walking the Cotswold Way. June R. Lewis. (Illus.). 192p. 1986. 19.95 (ISBN 0-7153-8715-4). David & Charles.

Walking the Dartmoor Waterways. Eric Hemery. (Illus.). 128p. 1986. 14.95 (ISBN 0-7153-8627-1). David & Charles.

Walking the Dead Diamond River. Edward Hoagland. LC 85-60857. 352p. 1985. pap. 10.00 (ISBN 0-86547-208-4). N Point Pr.

Walking the Dog & Other Stories. Marian Eldridge. LC 83-12884. 220p. 1985. pap. 8.95 (ISBN 0-7022-1785-9). U of Queensland Pr.

Walking the Maine Coast. Gibson. (Illus.). 1977. pap. 4.50 (ISBN 0-89272-028-X). Down East.

Walking-the Pleasure Exercise: A 60-Day Walking Program. Mort Malkin. (Illus.). 208p. 1986. 16.95 (ISBN 0-87857-614-2); pap. 8.95 (ISBN 0-87857-608-8). Rodale Pr Inc.

Walking the Road to Freedom: A Story about Sojourner Truth. Jeri Ferris. (Creative Minds Bks.). (Illus.). (gr. 3-6). 1988. lib. bdg. 9.95 (ISBN 0-87614-318-4). Carolrhoda Bks.

Walking the Tops: Dartmoor to Scotland. Rex Bellamy. (Illus.). 208p. 1984. 22.95 (ISBN 0-7153-8419-8). David & Charles.

Walking Though Northern England. Charlie Emett & Mick Hutton. (Illus.). 192p. 1982. 16.95 (ISBN 0-7153-8285-3). David & Charles.

Walking Through Israel. Daniel Gavron. 448p. 1980. 12.95 (ISBN 0-395-27777-9). HM.

Walking Through Northern England. Charlie Emmett & Mike Hutton. (Illus.). 208p. (Orig.). 1987. pap. 10.95 (ISBN 1-55650-002-5). Hunter Pub NY.

Walking Through Scotland. David MacInnes & Kathleen MacInnes. (Illus.). 192p. (Orig.). 1987. pap. 10.95 (ISBN 1-55650-003-3). Hunter Pub NY.

Walking Through the Bible with H. M. S. Richards. Ken Richards. 384p. 1983. 9.95 (ISBN 0-8163-0433-5). Pacific Pr Pub Assn.

Walking Through the Dark. Phyllis R. Naylor. LC 75-23039. 224p. (gr. 5-9). 1976. 6.95 (ISBN 0-689-30509-5, Atheneum Childrens Bks). Macmillan.

Walking Through the Lake District. Michael Dunn. (Illus.). 224p. 1984. 18.95 (ISBN 0-7153-8443-0). David & Charles.

Walking Through the Lake District. 224p. (Orig.). 1987. pap. 10.95 (ISBN 1-55650-012-2). Hunter Pub NY.

Walking Through the Mist of Life. Arthur L. Conway. LC 82-61883. 56p. 1983. pap. 4.95 (ISBN 0-938232-18-5). Winston-Derek.

Walking Through Wales. David MacInnes & Kathleen MacInnes. (Illus.). 172p. (Orig.). 1987. pap. 10.95 (ISBN 1-55650-004-1). Hunter Pub NY.

Walking to Jesus: Scenes from My Journey. Mark Shutts. LC 84-91288. (Illus.). 80p. (Orig.). 1984. pap. 3.98 (ISBN 0-9614077-1-9). Shutts Minist.

Walking To New Orleans see Rhythm & Blues in New Orleans.

Walking to Sleep: New Poems & Translations. Richard Wilbur. LC 69-20054. 81p. 1971. pap. 4.95 (ISBN 0-15-694185-6, Harv). HarBraceJ.

Walking to Where the River Ends. Wang Fang-Yu et al. (Illus.). 96p. 1980. pap. 17.50 (ISBN 0-208-01882-4, Archon). Shoe String.

Walking to Work: Tramps in America, 1790-1935. Ed. by Eric H. Monkkonen. LC 83-21807. vi, 253p. 1984. 21.95x (ISBN 0-8032-3087-7). U of Nebr Pr.

Walking Together: A Book of Growth & Caring. Ken Greene & Bonnie Greene. (Illus.). 140p. (Orig.). 1981. pap. text ed. 11.28 (ISBN 0-933419-01-5). Quest Intl.

Walking Tour of Historic Cooperstown. David O'Connor. (Illus.). 48p. (Orig.). 1983. pap. 2.95 (ISBN 0-931308-13-5). Molly Yes.

Walking Tour of Sykesville. Healan Barrow. Ed. by Linda Greenberg & Samuel J. Baum. (Illus.). 86p. (Orig.). 1987. pap. 7.95 (ISBN 0-89778-018-3). Greenberg Pub Co.

Walking Tours of Historic Philadelphia. John F. Marion. LC 84-575. (Illus.). 224p. 1984. pap. 7.95 (ISBN 0-89727-055-X). ISHI PA.

Walking Tours of New York City. Leslie Gourse. (Illus.). 1989. pap. price not set (ISBN 0-87106-637-8). Globe Pequot.

Walking Tours of Old Washington & Alexandria. Paul Hogarth. (Illus., Orig.). 1985. pap. 24.95 (ISBN 0-914440-85-3). EPM Pubns.

Walking up a Rainbow. Theodore Taylor. (gr. k-12). 1988. pap. 2.95 (ISBN 0-440-99326-1, LFL). Dell.

Walking Up & Down in the World: Memories of a Mountain Rambler. Smoke Blanchard. LC 84-5380. (Illus.). 288p. 1985. 15.95 (ISBN 0-87156-827-6). Sierra.

Walking Up Rainbow. Theodore Taylor. (gr. 5 up). 1988. pap. 2.95 (ISBN 0-440-20039-3, LFL). Dell.

Walking Wellness. Robert J. Sweetgall. Ed. by Robert E. Neeves. (Illus.). 96p. (gr. 4-8). 1986. wkbk. 5.25 (ISBN 0-939041-00-6); tchr's. curriculum guidebk. 12.95 (ISBN 0-939041-01-4). Creative Walking.

Walking What You're Talking: Principles of James. rev. ed. Harold L. Fickett. Ed. by Margaret Rosenberger. (Bible Commentary for Laymen Ser.). 128p. 1988. pap. 5.95 (ISBN 0-8307-1298-4, S418175). Regal.

Walking with a Hero: Children's Bible Studies for Children's Church. Ruth Powell. 96p. (Orig.). 1982. pap. 7.95 (ISBN 0-87239-593-6, 3375). Standard Pub.

Walking with Contemplation: A Walker's Guide. Ed. by P. K. Colleran. (Illus.). 230p. (Orig.). 1983. pap. 4.95 (ISBN 0-9609102-0-4). CAFH Found Inc.

Walking with God. W. Phillip Keller. 160p. 1980. pap. 5.95 (ISBN 0-8007-5187-6). Revell.

Walking with God. J. C. Metcalfe. 1960. pap. 3.25 (ISBN 0-87508-924-0). Chr Lit.

Walking with God. 8.95 (ISBN 0-318-18183-5). WCTU.

Walking with Jesus. V. Gilbert Beers & Ronald A. Beers. (Illus.). 192p. (gr. 1-6). 1984. 14.95 (ISBN 0-89840-069-4). Heres Life.

Walking with Jesus under the Blood. Janette Rauen. 33p. 1988. lib. bdg. 3.95 large type (ISBN 0-9619268-4-8); pap. 5.95 (ISBN 0-9619268-3-X). J Rauen Pubns.

Walking with Loneliness. Paula Ripple. LC 82-73048. 176p. (Orig.). 1982. pap. 4.95 (ISBN 0-87793-259-X). Ave Maria.

Walking with Loneliness. Paula Ripple. 318p. 1985. pap. 9.95 large print ed. (ISBN 0-8027-2490-6). Walker & Co.

Walking with Spring. 160p. 1983. pap. 6.95 (ISBN 0-917953-11-8, 505). Appalachian Trail.

Walking with the Giants: A Minister's Guide to Good Reading & Great Preaching. Warren W. Wiersbe. LC 76-22989. 304p. 1976. 14.95 (ISBN 0-8010-9578-6). Baker Bk.

Walking with the River. Bob Boldman. 32p. 1980. 10.00 (ISBN 0-913719-15-3); pap. 3.50 (ISBN 0-913719-14-5). High-Coo Pr.

Walking with the Walkers. Edward R. Walker, III. 128p. 1981. 10.00 (ISBN 0-932807-08-9). Overmountain Pr.

Walking with Trees, Poems. Leonard Clark. 1970. pap. 4.50 (ISBN 0-685-01019-8, Pub. by Enitharmon Pr). Small Pr Dist.

Walking Workouts: How to Use Your Walking Body As the Ultimate Exercise Machine. Gary Yanker. 288p. 1985. pap. 9.95 (ISBN 0-446-38267-1). Warner Bks.

Walking Wounded. Beverly Barbo. LC 87-72944. (Illus.). 248p. (Orig.). 1987. 13.95 (ISBN 0-944996-00-0); pap. 6.95 (ISBN 0-944996-01-9). Carlsons.

Walking Wounded. Murphy & Sapir. (Destroyer Ser.: No. 74). 1988. pap. 3.50 (ISBN 0-451-15600-5, Sig). NAL.

Walks Among the Poor of Belfast. W. M. O'Hanlon. 1971. Repr. of 1853 ed. 14.00x (ISBN 0-8464-0961-5). Beekman Pubs.

Walks & Climbs in the Engadine. 192p. (Orig.). 1988. pap. 12.95 (ISBN 1-55650-081-5). Hunter Pub NY.

Walks & Climbs in the Pyrenees. Kev Reynolds. 206p. (Orig.). 1988. pap. 12.95 (ISBN 1-55650-082-3). Hunter Pub NY.

Walks & Rambles in Rhode Island: A Guide to the Natural & Historic Wonders of the Ocean State. rev. ed. Ken Weber. LC 85-26843. (Walks & Rambles Ser.). (Illus.). 176p. 1986. pap. 8.95 (ISBN 0-942440-28-5). Backcountry Pubns.

Walks & Rambles in Westchester & Fairfield Counties: A Nature Lover's Guide to Thirty Parks & Sanctuaries. Katherine S. Anderson. LC 85-28570. (Walks & Rambles Ser.). (Illus.). 144p. (Orig.). 1986. pap. 7.95 (ISBN 0-942440-29-3). Backcountry Pubns.

Walks & Rambles on the Delmarva Peninsula: A Guide for Hikers & Naturalists. Jay Abercrombie. LC 85-15813. (Walks & Rambles Ser.). (Illus.). 208p. (Orig.). 1985. pap. 8.95 (ISBN 0-942440-27-7). Backcountry Pubns.

Walks Around London: Celebration of the Capital. Ian Norrie & Dorothy Bohm. (Illus.). 160p. 1986. pap. 14.95 (ISBN 0-233-97853-4, Pub. by A Deutsch England). David & Charles.

Walks in Gertrude Stein's Paris: Five Walking Tours for the Literary Traveller. Mary E. Jordan Haight. (Illus.). 160p. 1988. pap. 11.95 (ISBN 0-87905-268-6). Gibbs Smith Pub.

Walks in Rome. F. T. Prince. 32p. 1988. pap. text ed. 7.95 (ISBN 0-935296-72-7). Sheep Meadow.

Walks in South Lancashire & on Its Borders. Samuel Bamford. LC 72-80019. 288p. 1972. Repr. of 1844 ed. lib. bdg. 37.50x (ISBN 0-678-08023-2). Kelley.

Walks in the Cairngorms. E. L. Cross. 86p. 1986. pap. 11.00x (ISBN 0-946487-09-X, Pub. by Luath Pr UK). State Mutual Bk.

Walks in the Catskills. John Bennet & Seth Masia. LC 74-81304. (Illus.). 204p. 1974. pap. 7.95 (ISBN 0-914788-00-0). Globe Pequot.

Walks in the Great Smokies. Rod Albright & Priscilla Albright. LC 79-4898. (Illus.). 192p. 1979. pap. 7.95 (ISBN 0-914788-14-0). Globe Pequot.

Walks of California. Gary Ferguson. (Illus.). 280p. (Orig.). 1987. pap. 11.95 (ISBN 0-13-944257-X). P-H.

Walks of the Rockies. Gary Ferguson. (Illus.). 240p. 1988. pap. 12.95 (ISBN 0-13-944489-0). Prentice Hall Pr.

Walks of Usefulness: Or Reminiscenes of Mrs. Margaret Prior. Sarah R. Ingraham. Ed. by Carolyn Gifford & Donald Dayton. (Women in American Protestant Religion 1800-1930 Ser.). 324p. 1987. lib. bdg. 45.00 (ISBN 0-8240-0666-6). Garland Pub.

Walks Two Worlds. Robert B. Fox. LC 83-513. (Illus.). 62p. (Orig.). (gr. 4-6). 1983. pap. 6.95 (ISBN 0-86534-015-3). Sunstone Pr.

Walks, Walls & Fences. James E. Russell. Ed. by Marilyn M. Auer. LC 81-65752. (Illus., Orig.). 1981. pap. 7.95 (ISBN 0-932944-36-1). Creative Homeowner.

Walks, Walls, & Patio Floors. 3rd ed. Sunset Editors. LC 72-92521. (Illus.). 96p. 1973. pap. 5.95 (ISBN 0-376-01706-6, Sunset Bks.). Sunset-Lane.

Walks With Nature in Rocky Mountain National Park see Short Hikes in Rocky Mountain National Park.

Walkure: Complete Vocal & Orchestral Score. Richard Wagner. LC 77-84850. (Music Scores Ser.). 1978. pap. 19.95 (ISBN 0-486-23566-1). Dover.

Walkway Clause. 256p. 1986. pap. 2.95 (ISBN 0-8125-3475-1, Dist. by Warner Pub Services & St. Martin's Press). Tor Bks.

Walkway Surfaces: Measurement of Slip Resistance - STP 649. Ed. by C. Anderson & J. Senne. 117p. 1978. pap. 8.00 (ISBN 0-8031-0596-7, 04-649000-47). ASTM.

Wall. William R. Gardiner. (Illus.). 87p. (Orig.). 1987. pap. 6.95 (ISBN 0-9619400-0-X). Gardiner Pub.

Wall. John Hersey. Ed. by Carolyn Reidy. LC 87-45944. 644p. 1988. pap. 9.95 (ISBN 0-394-75696-7, Vin). Random.

Wall. John R. Hersey. 1961. 24.50 (ISBN 0-394-45092-2). Knopf.

Wall. Ardath Mayhar. LC 86-31453. (Illus.). 136p. (Orig.). 1987. pap. 6.95 (ISBN 0-917053-06-0). Space And.

Wall & Floor Systems: Design & Performance of Light Frame Structures. 263p. 1983. 20.00 (ISBN 0-8403-2949-0). Forest Prod.

Wall Around a Star. Frederik Pohl & Jack Williamson. 288p. (Orig.). 1983. pap. 2.95 (ISBN 0-345-28995-1, Del Rey). Ballantine.

Wall Art. Photos by Stefan Merken. (Illus.). 128p. 1987. 14.95 (ISBN 0-89471-572-0). Running Pr.

Wall Between Church & State. Ed. by Dallin H. Oaks. LC 63-20897. 1963. pap. 1.95X (ISBN 0-226-61429-8, P137, Phoen). U of Chicago Pr.

Wall Book. Stanley Schuler. LC 73-87709. (Illus.). 176p. 1974. 8.95 (ISBN 0-87131-143-7); pap. 4.95 (ISBN 0-87131-150-X). M Evans.

Wall, Ceilings & Woodwork. Time-Life Books Editors. (Fix-It-Yourself Ser.). 144p. 1987. 17.27 (ISBN 0-8094-6212-5); lib. bdg. 21.27 (ISBN 0-8094-6213-3). Time-Life.

Wall Charts: Overview of Corporate Planning Process & Unique Elements of Corporate Planning. (Illus.). 1978. pap. 2.00 (ISBN 0-88441-434-5, 26-162). Girl Scouts USA.

Wall Construction & Finishing. Elizabeth Williams & Robert Williams. (Illus.). 192p. 1989. 23.95 (ISBN 0-8306-9087-5, 3087); pap. 14.95 (ISBN 0-8306-9387-4, 3087). TAB Bks.

Wall Coverings. Sunset Editors. LC 82-81370. (Illus.). 96p. (Orig.). 1982. pap. 6.95 (ISBN 0-376-01719-8, Sunset Bks). Sunset-Lane.

Wall-Eyed Caesar's Ghost & Other Sketches. facsimile ed. Jane Cotton. LC 77-106281. (Short Story Index Reprint Ser.). 1925. 18.00 (ISBN 0-8369-3315-X). Ayer Co Pubs.

Wall Framing. Elizabeth Williams & Robert Williams. (Illus.). 192p. 1989. 23.95 (ISBN 0-8306-9097-2, 3097); pap. 14.95 (ISBN 0-8306-9397-1, 3097). TAB Bks.

Wall: Images & Offerings from the Vietnam Memorial. Sal Lopes. Intro. by Micheal Norman. 24.95 (ISBN 0-00-217974-1, Pub. by Collins Pub England). Greene.

Wall: Intimacy. 3rd ed. Jean-Paul Sartre. Tr. by Lloyd Alexander. LC 73-88731. 1969. pap. 5.95 (ISBN 0-8112-0190-2, NDP272). New Directions.

Wall Jumper. Peter Schneider. Tr. by Leigh Hafrey. 1985. pap. 6.95. Pantheon.

Wall of Controversy. Francis G. Lee. LC 85-19697. 132p. 1986. pap. 6.50 (ISBN 0-89874-828-3). Krieger.

Wall of Eyes. Margaret Millar. 224p. 1986. pap. 4.95 (ISBN 0-930330-42-0). Intl Polygonics.

Wall of Flames: The Minnesota Forest Fire of 1894. Lawrence H. Larsen. LC 84-61133. 187p. 1984. 9.85 (ISBN 0-911042-29-6). N Dak Inst.

Wall of Glass. Walter Satterthwait. 256p. 1988. 16.95x (ISBN 0-312-01530-5, Pub. by Thomas Dunne Bks). St Martin.

Wall of Paradise: Essays on Milton's Poetics. John M. Steadman. LC 85-9671. 156p. 1985. text ed. 20.00 (ISBN 0-8071-1230-5). La State U Pr.

Wall of Separation: The Constitutional Politics of Church & State. Frank J. Sorauf. LC 75-3476. 420p. 1976. 42.00x (ISBN 0-691-07574-3). Princeton U Pr.

Wall of the Plague. Andre Brink. LC 84-16325. 447p. 1985. 17.95 (ISBN 0-671-54189-7). Summit Bks.

Wall Paintings from Central India. R. A. Agarwala. (Illus.). 1987. 74.95x (ISBN 0-317-66132-9). Asia Bk Corp.

Wall Paintings from Central India. R. A. Agarwala. 1987. 78.50x (ISBN 0-8364-2203-1, Pub. by Sundeep). South Asia Bks.

Wall Paintings of Punjab & Haryana. Kanwarjit S. Kang. (Illus.). 193p. 1985. 105.00. Asia Bk Corp.

Wall Paintings of the Dogra Hills. Mira Seth. (Illus.). 1983. 59.00x (ISBN 0-19-561549-2). Oxford U Pr.

Wall Paintings of the Tomb of Nefertari: Scietific Studies for Their Conservation. (Illus.). 140p. 1987. pap. 25.00 (ISBN 0-89236-129-8). J P Getty Mus.

Wall Paintings of the Western Himalayas. Mira Seth. 1976. 55.00 (ISBN 0-940500-96-5, Pub. by Pubns Div India). Asia Bk Corp.

Wall Paper. Ed. by Frank Endersby. (Choices Ser.). 12p. (ps). 1984. 3.50 (ISBN 0-85953-188-0, Child's Play England). Playspaces.

Wall People: In Search of a Home. Joseph Di Certo. LC 84-21535. (Illus.). 168p. (gr. 3 up). 1985. 11.95 (ISBN 0-689-31090-0, Atheneum Childrens Bks). Macmillan.

Wall Quilts. Marsha R. McCloskey. (Illus.). 76p. 1983. pap. 8.00 (ISBN 0-943574-22-6). That Patchwork.

Wall Reliefs of Joe Goode. Helene Winer. (Illus.). 8p. 1971. 1.00 (ISBN 0-915478-22-6). Galleries Coll.

Wall Scenes from the Tomb of Amenhotep (Huy) Governor of Bahria Oasis. Charles C. Van Siclen, III. (Illus.). ii, 46p. 1981. pap. text ed. 11.00x (ISBN 0-933175-00-0). Van Siclen Bks.

Wall Shadows: A Study in American Prisons. Frank Tannenbaum. LC 70-156033. Repr. of 1922 ed. 12.50 (ISBN 0-404-09183-0). AMS Pr.

Wall Street. Ken Lipper. 1987. pap. 3.50 (ISBN 0-317-65129-3). Berkley Pub.

Wall Street. Kenneth Lipper. Ed. by Jayne Pliner. 256p. (Orig.). 1988. pap. 3.50 (ISBN 0-425-11062-1). Berkley Pub.

Wall Street. William C. Moore. LC 66-19018. 1969. Repr. of 1841 ed. flexible cover 7.00 (ISBN 0-87034-041-7). Fraser Pub Co.

Wall Street---How It Works. Jeffrey Little. (Basic Investors Library). (Illus.). 48p. 1987. lib. bdg. 9.95x (ISBN 1-55546-621-4). Chelsea Hse.

Wall Street & Regulation. Ed. by Samuel L. Hayes, III. 206p. 1987. 24.95 (ISBN 0-87584-183-X). Harvard Busn.

Wall Street & the Rise of Hitler. Antony C. Sutton. LC 76-14011. (Orig.). 1976. 12.95 (ISBN 0-89245-004-5). Concord Bks.

Wall Street & the Security Markets, 58 vols. facsimile ed. Ed. by Vincent P. Carosso. 1975. Repr. Vols. 1-29. 2103.00x (ISBN 0-405-12493-7); Vols. 30-58. 770.00x (ISBN 0-405-19007-7). Ayer Co Pubs.

Wall Street: Asset or Liability? facsimile ed. Compiled by James G. Hodgson. LC 75-2641. (Wall Street & the Security Market Ser.). 1975. Repr. of 1934 ed. 24.50x (ISBN 0-405-06966-9). Ayer Co Pubs.

Wall Street Blues. Jerome Tuccille. 224p. 1988. 15.95 (ISBN 0-8184-0455-8). Lyle Stuart.

Wall Street Bull: A Humorous Guide to Investment Jargon. rev. ed. Bruce Lansky. (Illus.). 120p. 1987. pap. 4.95 (ISBN 0-88166-100-7). Meadowbrook.

Wall Street Diet & Reducing Guidebook. Spencer Fleming. 79p. 1987. pap. text ed. 8.45 (ISBN 0-86654-225-6). Inst Econ Finan.

Wall Street Gurus: How You Can Profit from Investment Newsletters. Peter Brimelow. LC 85-28153. 256p. 1986. 19.95 (ISBN 0-394-54202-9). Random.

Wall Street Insiders' Joke Book: Over 500 Tasteless Jokes from Triumph to Disaster. Buffy Bluechip. 128p. 1988. pap. 5.95 (ISBN 0-517-56953-1). Crown.

Wall Street Journal. Murray & Birnbaum. 1987. write for info. Random.

Wall Street Journal Access: A Guide to the Financial Pages. (Financial Reference Guidebook Ser.). (Illus.). 120p. 1989. pap. price not set. Access Pr.

Wall Street Journal of Management: Best of Managers Journal. Asman. 1986. 12.95 (ISBN 0-256-03745-0). Irwin.

Wall Street Journal on Management. 246p. 1985. 19.95 (ISBN 0-317-66111-6, 390). Bank Admin Inst.

Wall Street Journal on Management: The Best of the Manager's Journal. Ed. by David Asman & Adam Meyerson. 200p. 1985. 19.95 (ISBN 0-87094-685-4). Dow Jones-Irwin.

Wall Street Journal on Management: The Best of the "Manager's Journal". Ed. by David Asman & Adam Meyerson. 240p. 1988. pap. 4.95 (ISBN 0-451-62654-0, Ment). NAL.

Wall Street Journal on Management: The Best of the "Manager's Journal". Ed. by David Asman & Adam Myerson. 264p. 1986. pap. 8.95 (ISBN 0-452-25862-6, Plume). NAL.

Wall Street Journal on Marketing. Ronald Alsop & Bill Abrams. 250p. 1986. 19.95 (ISBN 0-87094-896-2). Dow Jones-Irwin.

Wall Street Journal on Marketing. Ronald Alsop & Bill Abrams. 1987. 12.95x (ISBN 0-256-05679-X); 11.95. Irwin.

Wall Street Journal on Marketing. Ed. by Ronald Alsop & Bill Abrams. LC 87-11248. 264p. 1987. pap. 8.95 (ISBN 0-452-25988-6, Plume). NAL.

Wall Street Journal Views America Tomorrow. Ed. by Donald Moffitt. LC 76-52501. pap. 47.50 (ISBN 0-317-27197-0, 2023931). Bks Demand UMI.

Wall Street Journal's Pepper... & Salt Cartoons: CEO's & Other Kings. Ed. by Charles Preston. 128p. 1986. pap. 5.95 (ISBN 0-452-25863-4, Plume). NAL.

Wall Street Journal's Pepper & Salt Cartoons: Man's New Best Friend. Charles Preston. 128p. (Orig.). 1988. pap. 5.95 (ISBN 0-399-51492-9, Perigee Bks). Putnam Pub Group.

Wall Street Library, 3 vols. Ed. by C. M. Flumiani. (New Stock Market Library Book). (Illus.). Set. deluxe ed. 175.00x (ISBN 0-918968-26-7). Inst Econ Finan.

Wall Street Manual for Teenagers. C. M. Flumiani. LC 72-89684. (Illus.). 80p. (gr. 7-12). 1973. 27.75 (ISBN 0-913314-24-2). Am Classical Coll Pr.

Wall Street Maximal Physical Fitness Handbook. Vilfred Eschenbach. (Illus.). 109p. 1983. 75.75x (ISBN 0-86654-065-2). Inst Econ Finan.

Wall Street on Twenty Dollars a Month: How To Profit from an Investment Club. Phyllis A. Humphrey. LC 85-22503. 172p. 1986. pap. 12.95 (ISBN 0-471-84038-6). Wiley.

Wall Street Point of View. Henry Clews. LC 68-28620. (Illus.). 1968. Repr. of 1900 ed. lib. bdg. 25.00x (ISBN 0-8371-0048-8, CLWS). Greenwood.

Wall Street Speculation: Its Tricks & Tragedies. Franklin C. Keyes. 1979. Repr. of 1904 ed. flexible cover 7.00 (ISBN 0-87034-053-0). Fraser Pub Co.

Wall Street Stories. facsimile ed. Edwin Lefevre. LC 75-150478. (Short Story Index Reprint Ser.). Repr. of 1901 ed. 17.00 (ISBN 0-8369-3819-4). Ayer Co Pubs.

Wall Street Talk: How to Understand Your Broker. Barbara Quint. (Illus.). 1983. 11.95 (ISBN 0-8027-0754-8); pap. 5.95 (ISBN 0-8027-7232-3). Walker & Co.

Wall Street, the Other Las Vegas. Nicolas Darvas. 1962. 4.95 (ISBN 0-8184-0092-7). Lyle Stuart.

Wall Street: The Other Las Vegas. Nicolas Darvas. 192p. 1986. pap. 7.95 (ISBN 0-8184-0398-5). Lyle Stuart.

Wall Street: The Story of a Street. Frederick T. Hill. 1977. lib. bdg. 69.95 (ISBN 0-8490-2804-3). Gordon Pr.

Wall Street Thesaurus. Paul Sarnoff. 1963. 19.95 (ISBN 0-8392-1127-9). Astor-Honor.

Wall Street Trivia. Douglas Grunther & Tad Richards. LC 85-63180. (Illus.). 178p. 1986. pap. 7.95 (ISBN 0-933341-30-X). Quinlan Pr.

Wall Street Ventures & Adventures Through Forty Years. Richard D. Wyckoff. 400p. 1986. Repr. of 1930 ed. 19.95x (ISBN 0-934380-13-9). Traders Pr.

Wall Street Ventures & Adventures Through 40 Years. Richard D. Wyckoff. LC 85-70938. 313p. 1985. pap. text ed. 17.00 (ISBN 0-87034-078-6). Fraser Pub Co.

Wall Street Waltz: Ninety Visual Perspectives. Kenneth L. Fisher. 224p. 1987. 30.00 (ISBN 0-8092-4797-6). Contemp Bks.

Wall Street Words. David L. Scott. 1989. pap. 8.95 (ISBN 0-395-46777-2). HM.

Wall Street Words: Over 3600 Investment Terms Explained with Tips from Experts. David L. Scott. Ed. by Anne Soukhanov. LC 87-21444. (Illus.). 416p. 1988. 18.95 (ISBN 0-395-43747-4). HM.

Wally Hunt's Vermont. Ed. by James Hayford. 56p. (Orig.). 1983. pap. 4.00 (ISBN 0-9610860-0-9). Orleans.

Wally Phillips People Book. Wally Phillips. LC 79-88664. (Illus.). 1979. 7.95 (ISBN 0-89803-012-9, Dist. by Kampmann). Green Hill.

Wally, the Hiccupping Whale. Donald Keefe. Ed. by Marjorie Oelerich. (Baker Street Great Big Bks.). (Illus.). 16p. (gr. k-2). 1986. 14.95 (ISBN 0-914867-29-6). Baker St Prod.

Wally the Whale Who Loved Balloons. Yuichi Watanabe. Tr. by D. T. Ooka from Japanese. (Illus.). 32p. (ps-4). 1982. 9.95 (ISBN 0-89346-150-4). Heian Intl.

Wally the Wordworm. Clifton Fadiman. LC 83-9181. (Illus.). (gr. 3 up). 1984. 12.95 (ISBN 0-88045-038-X); cassette & bk. 21.90 (ISBN 0-88045-101-7); cassette only 8.95 (ISBN 0-88045-098-3). Stemmer Hse.

Wally Wooluf & Other Stories: A Young Person's Guide to Humor. Tom Mooney. pap. 3.00 (ISBN 0-317-28510-6). Mooney.

Wally's Cat. Marilyn B. Cannon. 32p. 1987. 6.95 (ISBN 0-8062-3150-5). Carlton.

Wally's Stories. Vivian G. Paley. LC 80-21882. 208p. 1981. text ed. 16.00x (ISBN 0-674-94592-1). Harvard U Pr.

Wally's Stories: Conversations in the Kindergarten. Vivian Paley. LC 80-21882. 232p. 1987. pap. text ed. 8.95x (ISBN 0-674-94593-X). Harvard U Pr.

Walnut Canyon: On the Edge of the Past. Scott Thybony. Ed. by T. J. Priehs. LC 87-63545. 48p. (Orig.). 1988. pap. write for info. (ISBN 0-911408-75-4). SW Pks Mnmts.

Walnut Creek. George Emanuels. LC 84-70073. (Illus.). 1984. 20.00 (ISBN 0-9607520-2-1). Diablo Bks.

Walnut Creek Learns the Alphabet: From Settlement to Suburbia - a History of Walnut Creek Through the Great Depression. 2nd ed. Jeane Elder. LC 74-84514. (Illus.). 144p. 1974. pap. 4.95 (ISBN 0-914974-01-7). Holmgangers.

Walnut Orchard Management. David E. Ramos. LC 84-73509. (Illus.). 200p. (Orig.). 1985. pap. 25.00x (ISBN 0-931876-71-0, 21410). ANR Pubns CA.

Walnut Pickles to Watermelon Cake: A Century of Michigan Cooking. Larry B. Massie & Priscilla Massie. (Illus.). 400p. 1988. 25.00x (ISBN 0-8143-1939-4). Wayne St U Pr.

Walnut Street Prison Workshop. John L. Cotter et al. (Illus.). 1988. pap. 7.50 (ISBN 0-916530-12-4). Athenaeum Phila.

Walpole. Syd Hoff. LC 76-41514. (Early I Can Read Bks.). (Illus.). 32p. (gr. k-3). 1977. 8.70i (ISBN 0-06-022543-2); PLB 9.89 (ISBN 0-06-022544-0). HarpJ.

Walpole. John Morley. 1973. lib. bdg. 25.50 (ISBN 0-8414-6648-3). Folcroft.

Walpole. John M. Morley. LC 76-110858. 1971. Repr. of 1889 ed. lib. bdg. 35.00x (ISBN 0-8371-4527-9, MOHW). Greenwood.

Walpole & the Robinocracy. Paul Langford. LC 85-6609. (The English Satirical Print Ser.). 252p. 1986. lib. bdg. 65.00 (ISBN 0-85964-175-9). Chadwyck-Healey.

Walpole & the Wits: The Relation of Politics to Literature, 1722-1742. Bertrand A. Goldgar. LC 76-6809. viii, 256p. 1976. 21.00x (ISBN 0-8032-0893-6). U of Nebr Pr.

Walrasian Microeconomics: An Introduction to the Economic Theory of Market Behavior. Donald W. Katzner. LC 86-26622. (Illus.). 500p. 1987. text ed. write for info. (ISBN 0-201-10461-X). Addison-Wesley.

Walras's Economics. M. Morishima. LC 76-40833. 1977. pap. 15.95 (ISBN 0-521-28522-4). Cambridge U Pr.

Walrus. Carl R. Green & William R. Sanford. Ed. by Howard Schroeder. LC 85-17509. (Wildlife (Habits & Habitat) Ser.). (Illus.). 48p. (gr. 4-5). 1986. PLB 10.95 (ISBN 0-89686-273-9). Crestwood Hse.

Walrus & the Carpenter. Lewis Carroll. LC 85-7591. (Illus.). 32p. (gr. 2-4). 1986. 13.95 (ISBN 0-8050-0071-2). H Holt & Co.

Walrus & the Carpenter & Other Remarkable Rhymes. Lewis Carroll. LC 86-61021. (Illus.). 42p. 1986. bds. 12.95 laminated (ISBN 0-88162-218-4). Salem Hse Pubs.

Walrus & the Carpenters. Jack Boswell. 1982. 15.00x (ISBN 0-906660-13-0, Pub. by New Playwrights Network). State Mutual Bk.

Walrus & the Warwolf. Hugh Cook. 1988. 21.00 (ISBN 0-86140-294-4, Pub. by Colin Smythe Ltd Britain). Dufour.

Walsh & Hoyt's Clinical Neuro-Ophthalmology, Vol. 1. 4th ed. Neil Miller. (Illus.). 382p. 1982. lib. bdg. 69.95 (ISBN 0-683-06020-1). Williams & Wilkins.

Walsh & Hoyt's Clinical Neuro-Opthalmology, Vol. III. 4th ed. Ed. by Neil Miller. 720p. 1987. 102.00 (ISBN 0-683-06022-8). Williams & Wilkins.

Walsh & Hoyt's Clinical Neuro-Opthalmology, Vol. 2. 4th ed. Neil R. Miller. 400p. 1984. 99.50 (ISBN 0-683-06021-X). Williams & Wilkins.

Walsh Functions in Signal & Systems Analysis & Design. Ed. by Spyros G. Tzafestas. (Illus.). 368p. 1985. 64.95 (ISBN 0-442-28298-2). Van Nos Reinhold.

Walsh Heritage-Walsh Co. Historical Society, 4 vols. 50.00 set (ISBN 0-686-30746-1); Vols. 1 & 2. 20.00 (ISBN 0-686-30747-X); Vols. 3 & 4. 30.00 (ISBN 0-686-30748-8). Assoc Print.

Walt: Backstage Adventures with Walt Disney. Charles Shows. (Illus.). 1980. 10.95 (ISBN 0-934846-01-4). Windsong.

Walt Bellamy: The Saturnine Center. Ronald L. Thomas. 1985. pap. 8.95 (ISBN 0-933085-00-1). Antaeus Pr.

Walt Disney: A Guide to References & Resources. Gartley Lynn & Elizabeth Leebron. 1979. lib. bdg. 34.50 (ISBN 0-8161-8004-0, Hall Reference). G K Hall.

Walt Disney: An American Original. Bob Thomas. Date not set. pap. 4.50 (ISBN 0-671-62870-4). PB.

Walt Disney & Assorted Other Characters: An Unauthorized Account of the Early Years at Disney's. Jack Kinney. (Illus.). 176p. 1988. 16.95 (ISBN 0-517-57057-2, Harmony). Crown.

Walt Disney Choose Your Own Adventure. (ps-1). 1985. write for info. Bantam.

Walt Disney Fun to Learn Library. 1985. write for info. Bantam.

Walt Disney: Master of Make-Believe. Elizabeth R. Montgomery. LC 71-146705. (Americans All Ser.). (Illus.). 96p. (gr. 3-6). 1971. PLB 7.12 (ISBN 0-8116-4568-1). Garrard.

Walt Disney Productions Presents Brer Rabbit & His Friends. (Disney's Wonderful World of Reading Ser.: No. 13). (Illus.). (ps-3). 1974. 5.95 (ISBN 0-394-82774-0, BYR); lib. bdg. 4.99 (ISBN 0-394-92774-5). Random.

Walt Disney Productions Presents Goofy's Gags. Walt Disney Productions. LC 74-2043. (Disney's Wonderful World of Reading Ser: No. 19). (Illus.). 48p. (ps-3). 1974. (BYR). Random.

Walt Disney Productions Presents Robin Hood & the Great Coach Robbery. (Disney's Wonderful World of Reading Ser.: No. 15). (Illus.). (ps-3). 1974. 4.95 (ISBN 0-394-82554-3). Random.

Walt Disney Productions Presents "The Black Hole". Walt Disney Productions. LC 79-10622. (Walt Disney's Wonderful World of Reading: No. 47). (Illus.). (ps-3). 1979. 4.95 (ISBN 0-394-84279-0, BYR); lib. bdg. 4.99 (ISBN 0-394-94279-5). Random.

Walt Disney Productions Presents The Love Bug. (Disney's Wonderful World of Reading Ser.: No. 45). (Illus.). (ps-3). 1979. 4.95 (ISBN 0-394-84139-5). Random.

Walt Disney Productions Presents "the Rescuers". Walt Disney Productions. LC 76-54412. (Disney's Wonderful World of Reading: No. 37). (Illus.). (ps-2). 1977. 5.95 (ISBN 0-394-83456-9, BYR); lib. bdg. 4.99 (ISBN 0-394-93456-3). Random.

Walt Disney Productions Presents "The Small One". Walt Disney Productions. LC 78-20718. (Walt Disney's Wonderful World of Reading: No. 46). (Illus.). (ps-3). 1979. 3.95 (ISBN 0-394-84232-4, BYR). Random.

Walt Disney Productions Presents "The Haunted House". Walt Disney Productions. LC 75-16430. (Disney's Wonderful World of Reading Ser.: No. 33). (Illus.). 48p. (ps-3). 1976. 5.95 (ISBN 0-394-82570-5, BYR); lib. bdg. 4.99 (ISBN 0-394-92570-X). Random.

Walt Disney Productions Presents "The Mystery of the Missing Peanuts". Walt Disney Productions. LC 75-1088. (Disney's Wonderful World of Reading Ser: No. 30). (Illus.). 48p. (gr. 1-2). 1975. 4.95 (ISBN 0-394-82572-1, BYR); lib. bdg. 4.99 (ISBN 0-394-92572-6). Random.

Walt Disney Productions Presents Tod & Copper from The Fox & the Hound. Walt Disney Productions. LC 81-2619. (Walt Disney's Wonderful World of Reading Ser.: No. 50). (Illus.). 48p. (ps-3). 1981. 4.95 (ISBN 0-394-84819-5); lib. bdg. 4.99 (ISBN 0-394-94819-X). Random.

Walt Disney Productions Presents Tod & Vixey from The Fox & the Hound. Walt Disney Productions. LC 81-5209. (Walt Disney's Wonderful World of Reading Ser.: No. 51). (Illus.). 48p. (ps-3). 1981. 4.95 (ISBN 0-394-84904-3); lib. bdg. 4.99 (ISBN 0-394-94904-8). Random.

Walt Disney Story. Maxine P. Fisher. Ed. by Jennie Rakos. (First Bk.). (Illus.). 72p. (YA) (gr. 7 up). 1988. 9.90 (ISBN 0-531-10493-1). Watts.

Walt Disney Story Land. 1987. 11.95 (ISBN 0-317-66556-1, Golden Bks). Western Pub.

Walt Disney: The Master of Animation. Gerald Kurland. Ed. by D. Steve Rahmas. LC 70-185664. (Outstanding Personalities Ser.: No. 8). 32p. 1972. lib. bdg. 3.75 incl. catalog cards (ISBN 0-87157-508-6); pap. 2.50 vinyl laminated covers (ISBN 0-87157-008-4). SamHar Pr.

Walt Disney World Nineteen Eighty-Seven. Steve Birnbaum. (Illus.). 192p. 1986. pap. 8.95 (ISBN 0-395-42719-3). HM.

Walt Disney World, 1988. Steve Birnbaum. (Illus.). 192p. 1987. pap. 8.95 (ISBN 0-395-44529-9). HM.

Walt Disney's America. Christopher Finch. LC 78-16863. (Illus.). 1978. 29.95 (ISBN 0-89659-000-3). Abbeville Pr.

Walt Disney's Bambi. (Big Golden Storybooks). (Illus.). 24p. (ps-k). 1986. 2.95 (ISBN 0-307-10380-3, Pub. by Golden Bks). Western Pub.

Walt Disney's Bambi: A Disney Read-Aloud Film Classic. (Illus.). (gr. 3-5). 1982. pap. 5.95 o. p. (ISBN 0-517-54463-6, Harmony); 10.95 (ISBN 0-517-54462-8). Crown.

Walt Disney's Bambi Album. Carl Barks. (Gladstone Comic Album Ser.: Vol. 9). (Illus.). 48p. (Orig.). (ps up). 1988. pap. 5.95 (ISBN 0-944599-08-7). Gladstone Pub.

Walt Disney's Bambi Comic Album. Felix Salten. (Comic Album Ser.: No. 10). (Illus.). 48p. (Orig.). (ps up). 1988. pap. 5.95 (ISBN 0-944599-09-5). Gladstone Pub.

Walt Disney's Bambi Gets Lost. A. G. Miller. (Disney's Wonderful World of Reading Ser: No. 2). (ps-3). 1973. 5.95 (ISBN 0-394-82520-9, BYR); lib. bdg. 4.99 (ISBN 0-394-92520-3). Random.

Walt Disney's Bambi's Fragrant Forest. LC 74-33127. (Golden Scratch & Sniff Bks.). (Illus.). 32p. (ps-2). 1988. 4.95 (ISBN 0-317-70040-5). Western Pub.

Walt Disney's Christmas Treasury. LC 78-14209. (Illus.). (YA) (gr. 7 up). 1978. 19.95 (ISBN 0-89659-004-6). Abbeville Pr.

Walt Disney's Cinderella. Walt Disney Productions. LC 74-22325. (Disney's Wonderful World of Reading Ser.: No. 16). (Illus.). 48p. (ps-3). 1974. 5.95 (ISBN 0-394-82552-7, BYR); lib. bdg. 4.99 (ISBN 0-394-92552-1). Random.

Walt Disney's Cinderella. (Big Golden Storybooks). (Illus.). 24p. (ps-k). 1986. 2.95 (ISBN 0-307-10200-9, Pub. by Golden Bks). Western Pub.

Walt Disney's Cinderella. (Super Shape Bks.). (Illus.). 24p. (gr. 2-5). 1987. pap. write for info. (ISBN 0-307-10056-1, Pub. by Golden Bks). Western Pub.

Walt Disney's Classic Cinderella. Jan Carr. (Walt Disney Classics-Media Ser.). (Illus.). 80p. (Orig.). (gr. 4-6). 1987. pap. 2.50 (ISBN 0-590-41171-3). Scholastic Inc.

Walt Disney's Donald & Daisy Comic Album. Carl Barks. (Comic Album Ser.). (Illus.). 52p. (Orig.). (ps up). 1988. pap. 5.95 (ISBN 0-944599-11-7). Gladstone Pub.

Walt Disney's Donald Duck Adventures Album. Carl Barks. (Comic Album Ser.: No. 14). (Illus.). 48p. (Orig.). (ps up). 1988. pap. 5.95 (ISBN 0-944599-13-3). Gladstone Pub.

Walt Disney's Donald Duck Adventures Comic Album. Carl Barks. (Gladstone Comic Album Ser.: Vol. 5). (Illus.). 48p. (Orig.). (ps up). 1988. pap. 5.95 (ISBN 0-944599-04-4). Gladstone Pub.

Walt Disney's Donald Duck Album. Carl Barks. (Gladstone Comic Album Ser.: Vol. 7). (Illus.). 48p. (Orig.). (ps up). 1988. pap. 5.95 (ISBN 0-944599-06-0). Gladstone Pub.

Walt Disney's Donald Duck Album. Carl Barks. (Gladstone Comic Album Ser.: No. 16). (Illus.). 48p. (Orig.). (ps up). 1989. pap. 5.95 (ISBN 0-944599-15-X). Gladstone Pub.

Walt Disney's Donald Duck Comic Album. Carl Barks. (Gladstone Comic Album Ser.: Vol. 2). (Illus.). 48p. (Orig.). (ps up). 1987. pap. 5.95 (ISBN 0-944599-01-X). Gladstone Pub.

Walt Disney's Donald Duck: Fifty Years of Happy Frustration. (Illus.). 96p. 1987. 7.98 (ISBN 0-89471-530-5, Pub. by Courage Bks). Running Pr.

Walt Disney's Duck Tales: The Road to Riches. LC 86-72394. (Big Little Golden Bks.). (Illus.). 24p. (gr. k-3). 1987. text ed. price not set (ISBN 0-307-10278-5, Pub. by Golden Bks). Western Pub.

Walt Disney's Dumbo. Adapted by Teddy Slater. LC 88-80740. (Big Golden Storybook Ser.). (Illus.). 24p. (ps-1). 1988. 2.95 (ISBN 0-307-11994-7). Western Pub.

Walt Disney's Dumbo. (Golden Super Shape Bks.). (Illus.). 24p. (ps-k). 1977. pap. write for info (ISBN 0-307-10076-6, Pub. by Golden Bks). Western Pub.

Walt Disney's Dumbo. LC 87-81495. (Disney Movie Greats Ser.). (Illus.). 36p. (ps-2). 1988. pap. 1.95 (ISBN 0-307-11051-6, Pub. by Golden Bks). Western Pub.

Walt Disney's Dumbo: On Land, on Sea, in the Air. Jerry Walters. (Disney's Wonderful World of Reading Ser.: No. 1). (Illus.). (ps-3). 1973. 5.95 (ISBN 0-394-82518-7, BYR); lib. bdg. 4.99 (ISBN 0-394-92518-1). Random.

Walt Disney's Fantasia. John Culhane. (Illus.). 224p. 1987. 19.95 (ISBN 0-8109-8078-9, Abradale Pr). Abrams.

Walt Disney's Goofy. Walt Disney Productions. 96p. 14.95 (ISBN 0-89586-414-2). Price Stern.

Walt Disney's Happy, Healthy Pooh Book. Mary Carey. (Look-Look Ser.). (Illus.). 24p. (ps-3). 1977. pap. 1.50 (ISBN 0-307-11832-0, Golden Bks). Western Pub.

Walt Disney's Mickey Mouse Comic Album. Floyd Gottfredson. (Gladstone Comic Album Ser.: Vol. 3). (Illus.). 48p. (Orig.). (ps up). 1987. pap. 5.95 (ISBN 0-944599-03-6). Gladstone Pub.

Walt Disney's Mickey Mouse Comic Album. Floyd Gottfredson. (Gladstone Comic Album Ser.: Vol. 8). (Illus.). 48p. (Orig.). (ps up). 1988. pap. 5.95 (ISBN 0-944599-07-9). Gladstone Pub.

Walt Disney's Mickey Mouse Comic Album. Floyd Gottfredson. (Comic Album Ser.: No. 13). (Illus.). 48p. (Orig.). (ps up). 1988. pap. 5.95 (ISBN 0-944599-12-5). Gladstone Pub.

Walt Disney's Mickey Mouse: His Life & Times. Richard Hollis & Brian Sibley. LC 86-45115. 96p. 1986. 14.95i (ISBN 0-06-015619-8, HarpT). Har-Row.

Walt Disney's Mickey Mouse in Color. 192p. 1988. 39.95 (ISBN 0-394-57519-9). Pantheon.

Walt Disney's Mickey Mouse Memorabilia: The Vintage Years 1928-1938. Ed. by Bevis Hillier. (Illus.). 176p. 1986. 29.95 (ISBN 0-8109-1439-5). Abrams.

Walt Disney's One Hundred & One Dalmatians. Walt Disney Productions. LC 74-10829. (Disney's Wonderful World of Reading: No. 23). (Illus.). 48p. (ps-3). 1975. 5.95 (ISBN 0-394-82571-3, BYR); lib. bdg. 4.99 (ISBN 0-394-92571-8). Random.

Walt Disney's One Hundred & One Dalmatians. LC 87-81496. (Disney Movie Greats Ser.). (Illus.). 36p. (ps-2). 1988. pap. 1.95 (ISBN 0-307-11052-4, Pub. by Golden Bks). Western Pub.

Walt Disney's Peter & the Wolf. Walt Disney Productions. LC 74-6423. (Disney's Wonderful World of Reading Ser.: No. 20). (Illus.). 48p. (ps-3). 1974. 5.95 (ISBN 0-394-82563-2, BYR); lib. bdg. 5.99 (ISBN 0-394-92563-7). Random.

Walt Disney's Peter Pan. (Vocal Selection Ser.). (Illus.). 32p. (gr. 4-12). 1985. 5.95 (ISBN 0-88188-414-6). H Leonard Pub Corp.

Walt Disney's Peter Pan. (Big Golden Storybooks). (Illus.). 24p. (gr. 3-6). 1987. Repr. of 1952 ed. 2.95 (ISBN 0-307-10409-5, Pub. by Golden Bks). Western Pub.

Walt Disney's Peter Pan. LC 87-81497. (Disney Movie Greats Ser.). (Illus.). 36p. (ps-2). 1988. pap. 1.95 (ISBN 0-307-11053-2, Pub. by Golden Bks). Western Pub.

Walt Disney's Peter Pan & Captain Hook. Mary Carey. (Disney's Wonderful World of Reading Ser.: No. 4). (Illus.). (ps-3). 1973. 5.95 (ISBN 0-394-82517-9, BYR); lib. bdg. 4.99 (ISBN 0-394-92517-3). Random.

Walt Disney's Peter Pan in Tinkerbell & the Pirates. (Big Little Golden Bks.). (Illus.). 24p. (gr. k-3). 1986. write for info. (ISBN 0-307-10259-9, Pub. by Golden Bks). Western Pub.

Walt Disney's Pinocchio. Walt Disney Productions. (Disney's Wonderful World of Reading Ser: No. 10). (Illus.). (ps-3). 1973. 5.95 (ISBN 0-394-82626-4, BYR); lib. bdg. 4.99 (ISBN 0-394-92626-9). Random.

Walt Disney's Pinocchio. (Big Golden Storybooks). (Illus.). 24p. (ps-1). 1987. Repr. of 1984 ed. 2.95 (ISBN 0-307-10381-1, Pub. by Golden Bks); (Pub. by Golden Bks). Western Pub.

Walt Disney's Pinocchio. LC 87-81498. (Disney Movie Greats Ser.). (Illus.). 36p. (ps-2). 1988. pap. 1.95 (ISBN 0-307-11054-0, Pub. by Golden Bks). Western Pub.

Walt Disney's Pinocchio. (Golden Super Shape Bks.). (Illus.). 24p. (ps-k). 1988. pap. 1.30 (ISBN 0-307-10093-6, Pub. by Golden Bks). Western Pub.

Walt Disney's Pinocchio: A Disney Read-Aloud Film Classic. (Illus.). (gr. 3-5). 1982. 10.95 (ISBN 0-517-54460-1, Harmony); pap. 5.95 (ISBN 0-517-54461-X). Crown.

Walt Disney's Sleeping Beauty. (Big Golden Storybooks). (Illus.). 24p. (ps-1). 1986. 2.95 (ISBN 0-307-10408-7, Pub. by Golden Bks). Western Pub.

Walt Disney's Snow White. LC 87-81499. (Disney Movie Greats Ser.). (Illus.). 36p. (ps-2). 1988. pap. 1.95 (ISBN 0-307-11055-9, Pub. by Golden Bks). Western Pub.

Walt Disney's Snow White & the Seven Dwarfs & the Making of the Classic Film. Richard Holliss & Brian Sibley. (Illus.). (ps up). Date not set. 14.95 (ISBN 0-671-64439-4). S&S.

Walt Disney's Snow White & the Seven Dwarfs. Walt Disney Productions. (Disney's Wonderful World of Reading Ser: No. 8). (Illus.). (ps-3). 1973. 5.95 (ISBN 0-394-82625-6, BYR); lib. bdg. 5.99 (ISBN 0-394-92625-0). Random.

Walt Disney's Snow White & the Seven Dwarfs. (Golden Melody Bks.). (Illus.). 32p. (ps-2). 1983. write for info. (ISBN 0-307-12249-2, 12276, Golden Bks). Western Pub.

Walt Disney's Snow White & the Seven Dwarfs. (Big Golden Storybooks). (Illus.). 24p. (ps-k). 1986. 2.95 (ISBN 0-307-10205-X, Pub. by Golden Bks). Western Pub.

Walt Disney's Story Land. Walt Disney Studio. (Illus.). 320p. (gr. 1-5). 1987. 11.95 (ISBN 0-307-16547-7, Golden Bks). Western Pub.

Walt Disney's the Adventures of Mr. Toad Adapted from the Wind in the Willows. Walt Disney Productions. LC 81-2783. (Walt Disney's Wonderful World of Reading Ser.: No. 49). (Illus.). 48p. (ps-3). 1981. 4.95 (ISBN 0-394-84818-7). Random.

Walt Disney's The Bambi Book. (Super Shape Bks.). (Illus.). 24p. (gr. 2-5). 1987. pap. write for info. (ISBN 0-307-10055-3, Pub. by Golden Bks). Western Pub.

Walt Disney's the Mickey Mouse Book. (Golden Super Shape Books). (Illus.). 24p. (ps-k). 1965. pap. write for info (ISBN 0-307-10077-4, Pub. by Golden Bks). Western Pub.

Walt Disney's The Penguin That Hated the Cold. Barbara Brenner. (Disney's Wonderful World of Reading Ser.: No. 7). (Illus.). (ps-3). 1973. (BYR); lib. bdg. 4.99 (ISBN 0-394-92628-5). Random.

Walter Burley Griffin, Marion Mahoney Griffin: Architectural Drawings in the Burnham Library of Architecture. John Zukowsky. (Illus.). 16p. (Orig.). 1981. pap. 4.00 (ISBN 0-86559-047-8). Art Inst Chi.
Walter Burley: On the Lives & Characters of the Philosophers. Paul Theiner. LC 80-8957. (Garland Library of Medieval Literature). 1985. lib. bdg. 35.00 (ISBN 0-8240-9445-X). Garland Pub.
Walter Camp, the Father of American Football. facs. ed. Harford. Powel, Jr. LC 70-126246. (Select Bibliographies Reprint Ser.). (Illus.). 1926. 18.00 (ISBN 0-8369-5473-4). Ayer Co Pubs.
Walter Clinton Jackson Essays in the Social Sciences. University of North Carolina Woman's College Faculty. Ed. by Vera Largeut. LC 79-167431. (Essay Index Reprint Ser.). Repr. of 1942 ed. 19.00 (ISBN 0-8369-2725-7). Ayer Co Pubs.
Walter D. Edmonds, Storyteller. Lionel D. Wyld. LC 82-10443. (York State Bks.). (Illus.). 168p. 1982. text ed. 20.00x (ISBN 0-8156-0180-8). Syracuse U Pr.
Walter Darby Bannard. Jane H. Cone. LC 73-87987. (Illus.). 1973. pap. 2.98 (ISBN 0-912298-34-0). Baltimore Mus.
Walter De la Mare. John Atkins. LC 73-16197. 1973. lib. bdg. 12.00 (ISBN 0-8414-2931-6). Folcroft.
Walter De la Mare. David Cecil. 1978. 42.50 (ISBN 0-685-87742-6). Bern Porter.
Walter De la Mare: A Biography & Critical Study. R. L. Megroz. LC 72-145175. 305p. 1972. Repr. of 1924 ed. 39.00 (ISBN 0-403-01103-5). Scholarly.
Walter De La Mare: A Biography & Critical Study. R. L. Megroz. 1988. Repr. of 1924 ed. lib. bdg. 49.00x. Am Biog Serv.
Walter De La Mare, a Checklist. David Cecil. 1956. lib. bdg. 15.00 (ISBN 0-8414-3636-3). Folcroft.
Walter De La Mare: A Critical Study. Forrest Reid. LC 73-131813. 1970. Repr. of 1929 ed. 39.00x (ISBN 0-403-00700-3). Scholarly.
Walter De La Mare, a Study of His Poetry. H. C. Duffin. LC 71-95424. (Studies in Poetry, No. 38). 1970. Repr. of 1949 ed. lib. bdg. 48.95x (ISBN 0-8383-0972-0). Haskell.
Walter De La Mare, a Study of His Poetry. Henry C. Duffin. (Select Bibliographies Reprint Ser.). 1949. 21.00 (ISBN 0-8369-5043-7). Ayer Co Pubs.
Walter De La Mare, A Study of His Poetry. Henry C. Duffin. 1973. lib. bdg. 16.00 (ISBN 0-8414-3866-8). Folcroft.
Walter De la Mare: An Exploration. J. Atkins. LC 75-22359. (Studies in Poetry, No. 38). 1975. lib. bdg. 46.95x (ISBN 0-8383-2105-4). Haskell.
Walter de la Mare & the Traveller. (Warton Lectures on English Poetry). 1953. pap. 5.50 (ISBN 0-85672-008-9, Pub. by British Acad). Longwood Pub Group.
Walter Dusenbery: Classical Echoes. Daniel E. Stetson & Tim Threlfall. Ed. by Kevin Boatright. LC 85-73204. (Illus.). 20p. (Orig.). 1985. pap. text ed. 5.00 (ISBN 0-932660-10-X). U of NI Dept Art.
Walter F. Isaacs: An Artist in America, 1886-1964. Spencer Moseley & Gervais Reed. LC 74-28489. (Index of Art in the Pacific Northwest Ser.: No. 8). (Illus.). 124p. 1982. 17.50x (ISBN 0-295-95950-9). U of Wash Pr.
Walter Farley's Black Stallion Books, 4 bks. Walter Farley. Incl. Black Stallion. LC 41-21882; Black Stallion Returns. LC 45-8763; Black Stallion & Satan. LC 49-6117; Black Stallion Mystery. LC 57-7527. (gr. 4-9). 1979. Boxed Set. pap. 11.80 (ISBN 0-394-84176-X, BYR). Random.
Walter Farley's Black Stallion Books, 4 bks. Walter Farley. 768p. (gr. 5-9). 1987. pap. 12.95 boxed set (ISBN 0-394-89137-6, BYR). The Black Stallion. The Black Stallion Mystery. The Black Stallion Returns. The Black Stallion & Satan. Random.
Walter Flex, ein Deuter Des Weltkrieges. J. Klein. 1929. pap. 9.00 (ISBN 0-384-29750-1). Johnson Repr.
Walter Frye & the Contenance Angloise. Sylvia W. Kenney. (Music Reprint Ser.). 1980. Repr. of 1964 ed. 35.00 (ISBN 0-306-76011-8). Da Capo.
Walter George Smith. Thomas A. Bryson. LC 77-9967. pap. 59.80 (2029500). Bks Demand UMI.
Walter Goodwin Davis: A Scholar's Unique Contribution to New England Geneology. Danny D. Smith. LC 85-61390. (Special Publications of Maine Genealogical Society: No. 1). 80p. 1985. pap. text ed. 11.00 (ISBN 0-9615551-0-6). Me Geneal Soc.
Walter Griffin: American Impressionist (1861-1935) Richard H. Love. (Illus.). 25p. 1975. pap. 5.00 (ISBN 0-940114-01-1). Haase-Mumm Pub Co.
Walter Gropius: Selected Journal Articles Published 1970-1986. Mary Vance. (Architecture Ser.: A 1830). 10p. 1987. 3.00 (ISBN 1-55590-340-1). Vance Biblios.
Walter Hammond. David B. James. 192p. 1986. 65.00x (ISBN 0-946771-51-0, Pub. by Spellmount Ltd Pubs). State Mutual Bk.
Walter Hard's Vermont People. Walter Hard. Intro. by J. Kevin Graffagnino. 96p. 1981. pap. 5.95 (ISBN 0-911570-18-7). Vermont Bks.
Walter Hasenclever's Humanitarianism: Themes of Protest in His Work. Alfred Hoelzel. LC 83-48134. (American University Studies, Ser. I: Germanic Languages & Literature: Vol. 11). 260p. 1983. pap. text ed. 28.40 (ISBN 0-8204-0014-9). P Lang Pubs.
Walter Hilton: An English Spiritual Guide. V. White. 1985. 10.00x (ISBN 0-317-62247-1, Guild of Pastoral Psych). State Mutual Bk.
Walter Hilton's Latin Writings, 2 vols. John P. Clark & Cheryl Taylor. (Lat. & Eng.). 1987. pap. 50.00 (ISBN 3-7052-0208-1, Pub. by Analecta). Longwood Pub Group.
Walter Hilton's Mixed Life. Ogilvie Thomson. Ed. by James Hogg. (Elizabethan & Renaissance Studies). (Orig.). 1985. pap. 15.00 (ISBN 3-7052-0756-3, Pub. by Salzburg Studies). Longwood Pub Group.
Walter Hines Page & the World's Work: 1900-1913. Robert J. Rusnak. LC 81-40929. 154p. (Orig.). 1982. lib. bdg. 25.50 (ISBN 0-8191-2604-7); pap. text ed. 10.00 (ISBN 0-8191-2605-5). U Pr of Amer.
Walter Hines Page: The Southerner As American, 1855-1918. John M. Cooper, Jr. LC 77-4390. (Fred W. Morrison Series in Southern Studies). xxx, 457p. 1977. 37.50x (ISBN 0-8078-1298-6). U of NC Pr.
Walter Holtkamp: American Organ Builder. John A. Ferguson. LC 78-26500. (Illus.). 140p. 1979. 12.50x (ISBN 0-87338-217-X). Kent St U Pr.
Walter Knott - Keeper of the Flame. Helen Kooiman. LC 73-83770. (Illus.). 224p. 1973. 7.95x (ISBN 0-916434-07-9). Plycon Pr.
Walter Lantz Story. Joe Adamson. LC 85-3665. (Illus.). 240p. 1985. 19.95 (ISBN 0-399-13096-9). Putnam Pub Group.
Walter Launt Palmer. 35.00 (ISBN 0-317-47636-X). Schiffer.
Walter Launt Palmer: Poetic Reality. Maybelle Mann & Alvin Mann. LC 84-50506. (Illus.). 176p. 1984. 35.00x (ISBN 0-88740-001-9); catalogue raisonne incl. ALM Assocs.
Walter Legge: A Discography. Compiled by Alan Sanders. LC 84-8991. (Discographies Ser.: No. 11). xx, 452p. 1984. lib. bdg. 36.95 (ISBN 0-313-24441-3, SDW/). Greenwood.
Walter Lippmann, a Study in Personal Journalism. David E. Weingast. Repr. of 1949 ed. lib. bdg. 35.00x (ISBN 0-8371-2970-2, WEWL). Greenwood.
Walter Lippmann & the American Century. Ronald Steel. (Illus.). 640p. 1980. 25.00 (ISBN 0-316-81190-4, Pub. by Atlantic Monthly Pr). Little.
Walter Lippmann & the American Century. Ronald Steel. LC 81-40077. (Illus.). 704p. 1981. pap. 12.95 (ISBN 0-394-74731-3, Vin). Random.
Walter Lippmann: Cosmopolitanism in the Century of Total War. D. Steven Blum. LC 84-7041. 208p. 1984. 22.50x (ISBN 0-8014-1676-0). Cornell U Pr.
Walter Lippmann, Philosopher-Journalist. Edward Schapsmeier & Frederick Schapsmeier. 1969. 15.00 (ISBN 0-8183-0218-6). Pub Aff Pr.
Walter McElreath: An Autobiography. Albert B. Saye. LC 84-20542. xxxvi, 226p. 1984. 21.95 (ISBN 0-86554-146-9, MUP/H137). Mercer Univ Pr.
Walter Muir Whitehill, Director & Librarian, Boston Athenaeum, 1946-1973: A Bibliography & Verses by Friends Presented on His Retirement. Compiled by Marez E. D'Orbessan. (Illus.). 36p. (Orig.). 1974. pap. 0.50 (ISBN 0-934552-30-4). Boston Athenaeum.
Walter Murdoch: A Biographical Memoir. John La Nauze. 1977. 20.00x (ISBN 0-522-84119-8, Pub. by Melbourne U Pr). Intl Spec Bk.
Walter Murdoch's Alfred Deakin on Books & Men: Letters & Comments, 1900-1918. new ed. J. A. La Nauze & Elizabeth Nurser. 1974. 17.50x (ISBN 0-522-84056-6, Pub. by Melbourne U Pr). Intl Spec Bk.
Walter Northway. Ed. by Yvonne Yarber & Curt Madison. Tr. by Della Northway et al. (Illus.). x, 56p. (Orig.). 1987. pap. 7.00 (ISBN 1-55500-030-4). Alaska Native.
Walter of Aquitaine: Materials for the Study of His Legend. Tr. by F. P. Magoun, Jr. & H. M. Smyser. 62p. 1983. Repr. of 1950 ed. lib. bdg. 30.00 (ISBN 0-89984-017-5). Century Bookbindery.
Walter Pater. A. C. Benson. 1973. lib. bdg. 17.50 (ISBN 0-8414-1638-9). Folcroft.
Walter Pater. Arthur C. Benson. LC 67-23876. (Library of Lives & Letters: British Writers Ser.). 240p. 1968. Repr. of 1906 ed. 30.00x (ISBN 0-8103-3054-7). Gale.
Walter Pater. Intro. by Harold Bloom. (Modern Critical Views Ser.). 174p. 1985. 19.95 (ISBN 0-87754-612-6). Chelsea Hse.
Walter Pater. F. Greenslet. LC 73-21634. (English Literature Ser., No. 33). 1974. lib. bdg. 33.95x (ISBN 0-8383-1798-7). Haskell.
Walter Pater. Gerald C. Monsman. LC 76-58511. (Twayne's English Authors Ser.). 213p. 1977. lib. bdg. 17.95 (ISBN 0-8057-6676-6). Irvington.
Walter Pater. F. Olivero. 1939. Repr. 75.00 (ISBN 0-8274-3690-4). R West.
Walter Pater: A Critial Study. Edward Thomas. LC 74-23816. 1973. lib. bdg. 32.00 (ISBN 0-8414-8520-8). Folcroft.
Walter Pater: A Study in Methods & Effects. J. Gordon Eaker. LC 74-4450. 1933. lib. bdg. 15.00 (ISBN 0-8414-3930-3). Folcroft.
Walter Pater: An Annotated Bibliography of Writings about Him. Ed. by Franklin E. Court. LC 78-56125. (Annotated Secondary Bibliography Series on English Literature in Transition: 1880-1920). 411p. 1980. 25.00 (ISBN 0-87580-072-6). N Ill U Pr.
Walter Pater: An Imaginative Sense of Fact. Ed. by Philip Dodd. 104p. 1981. 17.50x (ISBN 0-7146-3183-3, F Cass Co). Biblio Dist.
Walter Pater & the French Tradition. John J. Conlon. LC 81-65458. 180p. 1982. 21.50 (ISBN 0-8387-5016-8). Bucknell U Pr.
Walter Pater & the Gods of Disorder. Robert Keefe & Janice A. Keefe. 216p. 1988. text ed. 24.95x (ISBN 0-8214-0892-5). Ohio U Pr.
Walter Pater As a Critic of English Literature. Albert J. Farmer. LC 73-9788. 1931. lib. bdg. 16.50 (ISBN 0-8414-1970-1). Folcroft.
Walter Pater L'Homme et L'Oeuvre, 2 vols. Germain D'Hangest. 404p. 1983. Repr. of 1961 ed. Set. lib. bdg. 200.00. Darby Bks.
Walter Pater: Scholar Artist. David Cecil. 1955. lib. bdg. 15.00 (ISBN 0-8414-3632-0). Folcroft.
Walter Pater: The Aesthetic Moment. Wolfgang Iser. Tr. by David H. Wilson. (European Studies in English Literature). 224p. 1987. 34.50 (ISBN 0-521-30962-X). Cambridge U Pr.
Walter Pater: The Critical Heritage. Ed. by R. M. Seiler. (Critical Heritage Ser.). 1980. 32.50x (ISBN 0-7100-0380-3). Routledge Chapman & Hall.
Walter Pater: Three Major Texts, (The Renaissance, Appreciations & Imaginary Portraits) Ed. by William E. Buckler. LC 85-29738. 576p. 1986. 50.00x (ISBN 0-8147-1088-3); pap. 20.00x (ISBN 0-8147-1089-1). NYU Pr.
Walter Pater's Art of Autobiography. Gerald Monsman. LC 80-11941. 176p. 1980. 24.00x (ISBN 0-300-02533-5). Yale U Pr.
Walter Pater's Renaissance. Paul Barolsky. LC 85-43561. 228p. 1987. 23.50x (ISBN 0-271-00436-3). Pa St U Pr.
Walter Payton. Jane M. Leder. Ed. by Howard Schroeder. LC 86-16526. (Sports Close-up Ser.). (Illus.). 48p. (gr. 5-6). PLB 10.95 (ISBN 0-89686-318-2). Crestwood Hse.
Walter Payton: Record-Breaking Runner. Conrad R. Stein. LC 87-13241. (Sports Stars Ser.). (Illus.). 48p. (gr. 2 up). 1987. PLB 11.27 (ISBN 0-516-04363-3); pap. 2.95 (ISBN 0-516-44363-1). Childrens.
Walter Peter: The Idea in Nature. Anthony Ward. 220p. 1981. Repr. of 1966 ed. lib. bdg. 30.00 (ISBN 0-89984-513-4). Century Bookbindery.
Walter Prescott Webb: In Stephens County. Mike Kingston. (Illus.). 128p. 1985. 9.95 (ISBN 0-89015-503-8). Eakin Pr.
Walter P38 Auto Pistol Caliber 9mm Parabellum. 1986. lib. bdg. 79.95 (ISBN 0-8490-3483-3). Gordon Pr.
Walter Rathenau; Industralist, Banker, Intellectual, & Politian: Notes & Diaries 1907-1922. Walter Rathenau. Ed. by Harmut P. Von Strandmann. Tr. by Hilary Von Strandmann & Caroline Pinder-Cracraft. 1985. 72.00x (ISBN 0-19-822506-7). Oxford U Pr.
Walter Rauscenbusch: Selected Writings. Ed. by Winthrop S. Hudson. (Sources of American Spirituality Ser.). 252p. 1985. text ed. 14.95 (ISBN 0-8091-0356-7). Paulist Pr.
Walter Rauschenbusch. Paul M. Minus. (Illus.). 336p. 1988. 19.95 (ISBN 0-02-896470-5). Macmillan.
Walter Reed: A Biography. William B. Bean. LC 81-16123. (Illus.). 1982. 16.95x (ISBN 0-8139-0913-9). U Pr of Va.
Walter Reuther. (Labor Studies Ser.). (gr. 7 up). 1972. 2.00 (ISBN 0-89550-028-0). Stevens & Shea.
Walter Reuther & the Rise of the Autoworkers. John Barnard. 1983. pap. text ed. write for info. (ISBN 0-673-39320-8). Scott F.
Walter Reuther: Modern Leader of the United Automobile Workers Union. Gerald Kurland. Ed. by D. Steve Rahmas. LC 72-89213. (Outstanding Personalities Ser.: No. 52). 32p. 1972. lib. bdg. 3.75 incl. catalog cards (ISBN 0-87157-545-0); pap. 2.50 vinyl laminated covers (ISBN 0-87157-045-9). SamHar Pr.
Walter Rodney, Revolutionary & Scholar: A Tribute. Ed. by Edward A. Alpers & Pierre-Michel Fontaine. LC 82-4509. (CAAS Special Publication Ser.). (Illus.). 200p. (Orig.). 1983. pap. 10.95x (ISBN 0-934934-08-8). UCLA CAAS.
Walter S. Landor. Ernest Dillworth. (Twayne's English Authors Ser.). 198p. 1968. lib. bdg. 17.95 (ISBN 0-8057-1312-3); pap. text ed. 4.95x (ISBN 0-8290-1951-0). Irvington.
Walter Savage Landor: A Biography, 2 vols. John Forster. 1979. Repr. of 1869 ed. lib. bdg. 100.00 (ISBN 0-8492-4612-1). R West.
Walter Savage Landor: A Biography, 8 Bks. John Forster. LC 79-115241. 1971. Repr. of 1869 ed. 59.00x (ISBN 0-403-00407-1). Scholarly.
Walter Savage Landor: A Critical Study. Edward W. Evans. LC 74-22322. 1974. Repr. of 1907 ed. lib. bdg. 17.00 (ISBN 0-8414-3929-X). Folcroft.
Walter Savage Landor: A Critical Study. Edward W. Evans, Jr. LC 74-103186. 1970. Repr. of 1892 ed. 21.50x (ISBN 0-8046-0823-7, Pub. by Kennikat). Assoc Faculty Pr.
Walter Savage Landor: Studies of Italian Life & Literature. Felice Elkin. LC 74-8062. 1934. lib. bdg. 15.00 (ISBN 0-8414-3938-9). Folcroft.
Walter Scott. Thomas Crawford. Ed. by David Daiches. (Scottish Writers Ser.). 130p. (Orig.). 1983. pap. text ed. 6.50x (ISBN 0-7073-0305-2, Pub. by Scot Acad Pr). Longwood Pub Group.
Walter Scott. Robin Mayhead. LC 72-88622. (British Authors Ser.). 128p. 1973. pap. 8.95 (ISBN 0-521-09781-9). Cambridge U Pr.
Walter Scott. Robin Mayhead. LC 72-88622. (British Authors-Introductory Critical Studies). pap. 35.50 (2026348). Bks Demand UMI.
Walter Scott. Daniel D. Schantz. (Restoration Booklets Ser.). (Illus.). 16p. (Orig.). 1984. pap. 0.75 (ISBN 0-87239-777-7, 3297). Standard Pub.
Walter Scott: His Life & Personality. Hesketh Pearson. 308p. 1987. pap. 15.95 (ISBN 0-241-12005-5, Pub. by Hamish Hamilton). David & Charles.
Walter Scott Operas. Jerome Mitchell. LC 76-7406. 415p. 1977. 24.75 (ISBN 0-8173-6401-3). U of Ala Pr.
Walter Scott: The Making of the Novelist. Jane Millgate. 223p. 1984. write for info.; pap. 14.95 (ISBN 0-8020-6692-5). U of Toronto Pr.
Walter Sickert: A Conversation. Virginia S. Woolf. LC 77-24047. 1977. Repr. of 1934 ed. lib. bdg. 35.00 (ISBN 0-8414-9620-X). Folcroft.
Walter Spies & Balinese Art. H. Rhodius & J. Darling. Ed. by John Stowell. (Illus.). 1980. 17.50 (ISBN 90-6255-079-7). Heinman.
Walter, the Homing Pigeon. Nathaniel Benchley. LC 79-2696. (Illus.). 32p. (gr. 1-4). 1981. PLB 11.89g (ISBN 0-06-020508-3). HarpJ.
Walter Van Tilburg Clark. L. L. Lee. LC 73-8337. (Western Writers Ser: No. 8). 1973. pap. 2.95x (ISBN 0-88430-007-2). Boise St Univ.
Walter Van Tilburg Clark: Critiques. Ed. by Charlton Laird. (Illus.). 296p. 1983. 16.00 (ISBN 0-87417-077-X). U of Nev Pr.
Walter White: Political Activist. Ed. by Nathan I. Huggins. (Black Americans of Achievement Ser.). (Illus.). 1989. 16.95 (ISBN 1-55546-617-6). Chelsea Hse.
Walteri Abbatis Dervensis Epistolae. Gualterus, Abbot of Montier-En-der. Ed. by C. Messiter. 1850. 24.00 (ISBN 0-8337-3679-5). B Franklin.
Waltham Book of Dog & Cat Nutrition. 2nd ed. Ed. by A. T. B. Edney. 130p. 1988. text ed. 36.00 (ISBN 0-08-035730-X); pap. text ed. 18.00 (ISBN 0-08-035729-6). Pergamon.
Waltham Pocket Watch Identification & Price Guide, with Serial Numbers. Roy Ehrhardt. (Illus.). 1976. Repr. ring bdg. 10.00_plastic (ISBN 0-913902-17-9). Heart Am Pr.
Waltharius. Gernot Wieland. (Latin Commentaries Ser.). 109p. (Orig.). 1986. pap. text ed. 8.00. Bryn Mawr Commentaries.
Waltharius & Ruodlieb. Dennis M. Kratz. Ed. by James Wilhelm et al. LC 80-8958. (Library of Medieval Literature). 195p. 1984. lib. bdg. 43.00 (ISBN 0-8240-9444-1). Garland Pub.
Walther Rathenau, His Life & Work. Harry K. Kessler. LC 70-181937. Repr. of 1930 ed. 9.00 (ISBN 0-404-03665-1). AMS Pr.
Walther Rathenau: His Life & Work. Harry K. Kessler. LC 68-9663. 1970. Repr. 9.00x (ISBN 0-86527-203-4). Fertig.
Walthers Decal Catalog & Reference Manual, 1985. (Illus.). 176p. 1985. pap. 4.95 (ISBN 0-941952-17-7, 913-637). W K Walthers.
Walther's Orthodontic Notes. 4th ed. W. Houston. 288p. 1983. 16.00 (ISBN 0-7236-0670-6). PSG Pub Co.
Walthers the World of O Scale, 1983: A Walthers Catalog & Reference Manual. Wm. K. Walthers, Inc. (Illus.). 368p. 1983. pap. 12.50 (ISBN 0-941952-13-4, 913-635). W K Walthers.
Walton & Some Earlier Writers on Fish & Fishing. R. B. Marston. 1894. Repr. 30.00 (ISBN 0-8274-3691-2). R West.
Waltz Across Texas. Max Crawford. LC 74-26604. 393p. 1975. 8.95 (ISBN 0-374-28628-0). FS&G.
Waltz (American) Earl Atkinson. (Ballroom Dancing Ser.). 1983. lib. bdg. 79.95 (ISBN 0-87700-479-X). Revisionist Pr.
Waltz in Marathon. Charles Dickinson. 1984. pap. 6.95 (ISBN 0-452-25593-7, Plume). NAL.
Waltz Kings of Old Vienna. facsimile ed. Ada B. Teetgen. LC 78-107833. (Select Bibliographies Reprint Ser). 1939. 22.00 (ISBN 0-8369-5198-0). Ayer Co Pubs.
Waltz Made Easy. (Ballroom Dance Ser.). 1985. lib. bdg. 78.00 (ISBN 0-87700-673-3). Revisionist Pr.
Waltz of the Shadows. Magda Herzberger. 121p. 1983. 12.00 (ISBN 0-8022-2428-8). Philos Lib.
Waltz (Viennese) Earl Atkinson. 1983. lib. bdg. 79.95 (ISBN 0-87700-486-2). Revisionist Pr.
Waltzer. Henry J. Ambers. LC 76-114002. 320p. 1970. 9.95 (ISBN 0-9600874-4-3). Edelweiss Pr.
Waltzes & Scherzos, Vols. IX, XII, V. Frederic Chopin. (Music Scores Ser.). (Illus.). 208p. 1983. pap. 7.95 (ISBN 0-486-24316-8). Dover.
Waltzes for Piano. Frederic Chopin. (Carl Fischer Music Library: No. 309). 80p. 1902. pap. 6.00 (ISBN 0-8258-0103-6, L 309). Fischer Inc NY.
Waltzing Matilda. Alice Notley. 7.00x (ISBN 0-317-17176-3); pap. 3.50x (ISBN 0-317-17177-1). Kulchur Foun.

Wanted: A Date for Saturday Night. Janet Quin-Harkin. 160p. (gr. 5 up). 1985. 11.95 (ISBN 0-448-47752-1). Putnam Pub Group.

Wanted: A Girl for the Horses. Betty Cavanna. LC 83-19289. 224p. (gr. 7 up). 1984. 12.95 (ISBN 0-688-02757-1). Morrow.

Wanted: A Little Love. Stephanie G. Tessler. (Caprice Ser.: No. 49). 144p. 1985. pap. 2.25 (ISBN 0-441-87169-0). Ace Bks.

Wanted-A Wedding Ring. Barbara Cartland. (Camfield Ser.: No. 48). 176p. 1987. pap. 2.75 (ISBN 0-515-09111-1). Jove Pubns.

Wanted Alive. Erin Moure. (House of Anansi Poetry Ser.: No. 42). 111p. 1983. pap. 8.95 (ISBN 0-88784-097-3, Pub. by Hse Anansi Pr Canada). U of Toronto Pr.

Wanted & Unwanted Childbearing in the United States: National Natality Surveys 1968-1969 & 1972. Robert H. Weller & Robert L. Heuser. Ed. by Taloria Stevenson. (Series 21: No. 32). 1978. pap. text ed. 1.75 (ISBN 0-8406-0140-9). Natl Ctr Health Stats.

Wanted Child: A Childrens Book on Adoption. Linda A. Sands. (Illus.). 29p. (ps-3). 1988. 14.95 (ISBN 0-945961-00-6). Aarid Pub Co.

Wanted: Date for Saturday Night. Janet Quin-Harkin. 160p. (YA) 1986. pap. 2.50 (ISBN 0-425-08448-5, Pub by Berkley-Pacer). Berkley Pub.

Wanted Dead or Alive: The Story of Harriet Tubman. Ann McGovern. (gr. 4-6). 1977. pap. 1.95 (ISBN 0-590-40259-5). Scholastic Inc.

Wanted: Liberal Arts Graduates. Martin L. Salzman. LC 87-8846. 360p. 1987. pap. 9.95 (ISBN 0-385-24008-2, Anchor Pr). Doubleday.

Wanted Man. Regan Forest. pap. 2.50 (ISBN 0-373-25276-5). Harlequin Bks.

Wanted: The Search for Nazis in America. Howard Blum. 1978. pap. 1.95 (ISBN 0-449-23409-6, Crest). Fawcett.

Wanted to Buy. 200p. 1988. pap. 9.95 (ISBN 0-89145-384-9). Collector Bks.

Wanted: World Christians. J. Herbert Kane. 204p. 1986. pap. 9.95 (ISBN 0-8010-5474-5). Baker Bk.

Wanted Your Daily Life. M. B. Room. 1976. pap. 2.50 (ISBN 0-87508-011-1). Chr Lit.

Wanting. Campbell Black. 272p. 1986. text ed. 15.95 (ISBN 0-07-005564-5). McGraw.

Wanting. Campbell Black. 320p. 1987. pap. 3.95 (ISBN 0-515-09177-4). Jove Pubns.

Wanting. Angela Huth. 240p. 1985. 15.95 (ISBN 0-02-557800-6). Macmillan.

Wanting a Job. Richard H. Turner. (Follet Success Skills Ser.). 48p. pap. 3.75 (ISBN 0-8428-2271-2). Cambridge Bk.

Wanting It All. Susan B. Pfeffer. (Make Me a Star Ser.: No. 3). 176p. 1985. pap. 2.25 (ISBN 0-425-08413-2, Pub by Berkley-Pacer). Berkley Pub.

Wanting It All. Susan B. Pfeffer. 176p. 1987. 2.50 (ISBN 0-425-10113-4). Berkley Pub.

Wanting Seed. Anthony Burgess. 288p. 1976. pap. 7.95 (ISBN 0-393-00808-8, Norton Lib). Norton.

Wanton. Rosemary Rogers. 336p. 1985. pap. 3.95 (ISBN 0-380-86165-8, 86165-8). Avon.

Wanton. Rosemary Rogers. 505p. 1986. lib. bdg. 18.95 (ISBN 0-8161-4009-X, Large Print Bks). G K Hall.

Wanton Angel. Linda L. Miller. 352p. 1987. pap. 3.95 (ISBN 0-671-62197-1). PB.

Wanton Summer Air. Samuel Hazo. LC 82-81479. 224p. 1982. 15.50 (ISBN 0-86547-085-5). N Point Pr.

Wanton Wenches & Wayward Wives: Peasants & Illicit Sex in Early Seventeenth Century England. G. R. Quaife. 1979. 32.00x (ISBN 0-8135-0890-8). Rutgers U Pr.

Wantons. 210p. 1986. pap. 3.95 (ISBN 0-88184-262-1). Carroll & Graf.

Wants, Decisions & Human Action: A Praxeological Investigation. Andrew B. Schoedinger. LC 78-62705. 1978. pap. text ed. 13.00 (ISBN 0-8191-0591-0). U Pr of Amer.

Want's Federal-State Court Directory, 1986. Want Publishing Company Staff. LC 84-51847. (Know Your Government Ser.). 130p. 1986. pap. 16.95 (ISBN 0-942008-36-7). Want Pub.

Wapiti Wilderness: The Life of Olaus & Margaret Murie in Jackson Hole, Wyoming. Margaret Murie & Olaus Murie. (Illus.). 302p. 1985. pap. 9.95 (ISBN 0-87081-155-X). Colo Assoc.

Wappatomaka. Charles Morrison. (Illus.). 150p. 1971. 6.50 (ISBN 0-87012-107-3). McClain.

Wappo: A Report. Yolande S. Beard. 1979. pap. 7.50 (ISBN 0-939046-26-1). Malki Mus Pr.

Wapshot Scandal. John Cheever. 224p. 1983. pap. 3.50 (ISBN 0-345-34323-9). Ballantine.

War. Marguerite Duras & Barbara Bray. LC 86-43435. 192p. 1987. pap. 6.95 (ISBN 0-394-75039-X). Pantheon.

War. Gwynne Dyer. (Illus.). 320p. 1985. 17.95 (ISBN 0-517-55615-4). Crown.

War. Gwynne Dyer. 1985. pap. 21.00x (ISBN 0-256-03645-4). Dorsey.

War. Ludwig Renn. Tr. by Willa Muir & Edwin Muir. 1988. 35.00x (ISBN 0-86527-324-3). Fertig.

War. Ludwig Renn. 364p. 1984. pap. 7.50 (Pub. by A Mott Ltd). Longwood Pub Group.

War: A Call to the Inner Land. Eberhard Arnold. 144p. (Orig.). 1987. pap. 5.95 (ISBN 0-8091-2851-9). Paulist Pr.

War: A Call to the Innerland. Eberhard Arnold. Ed. by Hutterian Brethren. 144p 1986. pap. 5.95 (Pub. by Paulist Pr). Plough.

War: A Medical, Psychological & Scientific Subject Analysis with Research Index & Bibliography. John C. Bartone. LC 83-71661. 160p. 1984. 34.50 (ISBN 0-941864-91-X); pap. 26.50 (ISBN 0-941864-90-1). ABBE Pubs Assn.

War: A Memoir. Marguerite Duras. Tr. by Barbara Bray. LC 85-43435. 183p. (Fr.). 1986. 13.45 (ISBN 0-394-55236-9). Pantheon.

War According to Anna. Kamilla C. Chadwick. 132p. (Orig.). 1986. pap. 8.95 (ISBN 0-940249-00-6). Seven Stones Pr.

War Against Children: South Africa's Youngest Victims. Lawyers Committee for Human Rights Staff. 94p. (Orig.). 1986. pap. 10.00 (ISBN 0-934143-00-5). Lawyers Comm Intl.

War Against East Timor. Carmel Budiardjo & Liem S. Liong. (Asia Ser.). (Illus.). 272p. 1984. 29.95x (ISBN 0-86232-228-6, Pub. by Zed Pr); pap. 10.50 (ISBN 0-86232-229-4, Pub. by Zed Pr). Humanities.

War Against Japan. Sbrega. 1985. lib. bdg. 50.00 (ISBN 0-8240-8940-5). Garland Pub.

War Against Nuclear Power. Eric N. Skousen. (Illus.). 211p. (Orig.). 1981. pap. 7.95 (ISBN 0-88080-002-X). Natl Ctr Constitutional.

War Against Paris, 1871. Robert Tombs. LC 80-42024. (Illus.). 272p. 1981. 54.50 (ISBN 0-521-23551-0); pap. 18.95 (ISBN 0-521-28784-7). Cambridge U Pr.

War Against Poetry. Russell Fraser. LC 71-113001. 1970. 28.00x (ISBN 0-691-06190-4). Princeton U Pr.

War Against Population: The Economics & Ideology of Population Control. Jacqueline Kasun. LC 87-83505. 225p. (Orig.). 1988. pap. 14.95 (ISBN 0-89870-191-0). Ignatius Pr.

War Against Proslavery Religion: Abolitionism & the Northern Churches, 1830-1865. John R. McKivigan. LC 83-45933. 328p. 1984. 32.50x (ISBN 0-8014-1589-6). Cornell U Pr.

War Against Terrorism. Neil C. Livingstone. 304p. 1982. pap. 16.95 (ISBN 0-669-09551-6). Lexington Bks.

War Against the Amazons. A. W. Kleinbaum. 293p. 1983. text ed. 18.95 (ISBN 0-07-035033-7). McGraw.

War Against the Chtorr: Vol. 1-A Matter for Men. David Gerrold. Date not set. 16.50 (ISBN 0-671-46493-0, Timescape); pap. 6.75 (ISBN 0-671-46494-9, Timescape). PB.

War Against the Idols: The Reformation of Worship from Erasmus to Calvin. Carlos M. Eire. 320p. 1986. 39.50 (ISBN 0-521-30685-X). Cambridge U Pr.

War Against the Jews: 1933-1945. Lucy S. Dawidowicz. 640p. 1976. pap. 10.95 (ISBN 0-553-34302-5). Bantam.

War Against the Jews, 1933-1945. Lucy S. Dawidowicz. 496p. 1986. 22.95 (ISBN 0-02-908030-4). Free Pr.

War Against the Press: Politics, Pressure & Intimidation in the 80's. Peter Stoler. 256p. 1987. 17.95 (ISBN 0-396-08757-4). Dodd.

War Against the Seals: A History of the North American Seal Fishery. Briton C. Busch. (Illus.). 432p. 1985. 32.95x (ISBN 0-7735-0578-4, Dist. by Univ. of Toronto Pr); pap. 15.95 (ISBN 0-7735-0610-1, Dist. by Univ. of Toronto Pr). McGill-Queens U Pr.

War Against the Terrorists: How to Win It. Gayle Rivers. 272p. pap. 3.95 (ISBN 0-441-87187-9, Pub. by Charter Bks). Ace Bks.

War Against War. Ernst Friedrich. (Illus.). 276p. 1987. 18.95 (ISBN 0-941104-19-2); pap. 9.95 (ISBN 0-941104-18-4). Real Comet.

War Against War: British & German Radical Movements in the First World War. F. L. Carsten. LC 81-69812. 300p. 1982. 30.00x (ISBN 0-520-04581-5). U of Cal Pr.

War Against Women: Overcoming Female Abuse. Hal Ackerman. 28p. (Orig.). 1985. pap. 1.75 (ISBN 0-89486-282-0). Hazelden.

War All the Time: Poems, 1981-1984. Charles Bukowski. LC 84-20390. 285p. 1984. 20.00 (ISBN 0-87685-638-5); pap. 12.50 (ISBN 0-87685-637-7). Black Sparrow.

War, an Essay. Jonathan Dymond. LC 72-147433. (Library of War & Peace; Proposals for Peace: a History). 1980. lib. bdg. 46.00 (ISBN 0-8240-0480-9). Garland Pub.

War, an Essay. Jonathan Dymond. 59.95 (ISBN 0-8490-1275-9). Gordon Pr.

War & Administration: The Significance of the Crimean War for the British Army. John Sweetman. (Illus.). 208p. 1984. 20.00x (ISBN 0-7073-0332-X, Pub. by Scot Acad Pr). Longwood Pub Group.

War & American Thought: From the Revolution to the Monroe Doctrine. Reginald C. Stuart. LC 81-19358. 250p. 1982. 19.50x (ISBN 0-87338-267-6). Kent St U Pr.

War & an Irish Town. rev. 2nd ed. Eamonn McCann. 176p. 1981. pap. 7.50 (ISBN 0-86104-302-2, Pub. by Pluto Pr). Longwood Pub Group.

War & Breed. David S. Jordan. 70p. 1986. pap. 3.50 (ISBN 0-317-53021-6). Noontide.

War & Change in World Politics. Robert Gilpin. LC 81-2885. (Illus.). 288p. 1983. pap. 13.95 (ISBN 0-521-27376-5). Cambridge U Pr.

War & Children. Anna Freud & Dorothy T. Burlingham. Ed. by Philip R. Lehrman. LC 73-7699. 191p. 1973. Repr. of 1943 ed. lib. bdg. 41.50x (ISBN 0-8371-6942-9, FRWC). Greenwood.

War & Chivalry: Warfare & Aristocratic Culture in England, France, & Burgundy at the End of the Middle Ages. Malcolm Vale. LC 81-3046. (Illus.). 236p. 1981. 27.50x (ISBN 0-8203-0571-5). U of Ga Pr.

War & Christian Ethics. Arthur F. Holmes. LC 75-14602. pap. 13.95 (ISBN 0-8010-4170-8). Baker Bk.

War & Christianity. Elliott Coues. 250.00 (ISBN 0-8490-1276-7). Gordon Pr.

War & Cinema: The Logics of Perception. Paul Virilio. Tr. by Patrick Camiller. 200p. 1988. text ed. 35.00 (ISBN 0-86091-214-0, Pub. by Verso); pap. text ed. 13.95 (ISBN 0-86091-928-5, Pub. by Verso). Routledge Chapman & Hall.

War & Conscience. Allen C. Isbell. 12.95 (ISBN 0-89112-061-0). Abilene Christ·U.

War & Conscience in the Nuclear Age. Sydney D. Bailey. LC 87-18755. 200p. 1987. 32.50 (ISBN 0-312-01345-0). St Martin.

War & Democracy. R. W. Seton-Watson. Ed. by Dover Wilson. LC 70-110922. 1970. Repr. of 1915 ed. 31.50 (ISBN 0-8046-0904-7, Pub. by Kennikat). Assoc Faculty Pr.

War & Diplomacy Across the Pacific, 1919-1952. Ed. by A. Hamish & Barry D. Hunt. 192p. 1988. text ed. 29.95 (ISBN 0-88920-973-1, Pub. by Wilfrid Laurier Canada). Humanities.

War & Diplomacy in the French Republic: An Inquiry into Political Motivations & the Control of Foreign Policy. Frederick L. Schuman. LC 68-9635. 1970. Repr. of 1931 ed. 19.50x (ISBN 0-86527-204-2). Fertig.

War & Diplomacy in the French Republic. Frederick L. Schuman. LC 71-11468. 1970. Repr. of 1931 ed. 29.50 (ISBN 0-404-05623-7). AMS Pr.

War & Economy: In the Age of William III & Marlborough. D. W. Jones. (Illus.). 320p. 1988. text ed. 60.00x (ISBN 0-631-16069-8). Basil Blackwell.

War & Education. Porter E. Sargent. 1975. lib. bdg. 69.95 (ISBN 0-87700-244-4). Revisionist Pr.

War & Government in the Middle Ages: Essays in Honour of J. O. Prestwich. Ed. by John Gillingham & J. C. Holt. LC 84-423. (Illus.). 210p. 1984. 45.00x (ISBN 0-389-20475-7, 08037). B&N Imports.

War & Hope: The Case for Cambodia. Nordom Sihanouk. Tr. by Mary Fenney. 1980. 10.95 (ISBN 0-394-51115-8). Pantheon.

War & Human Nature: Opposing Viewpoints. Ed. by David L. Bender & Bruno Leone. LC 85-8008. (Opposing Viewpoints Ser.). (Illus.). 160p. 1983. lib. bdg. 13.95 (ISBN 0-89908-341-2); pap. text ed. 6.95 (ISBN 0-89908-316-1). Greenhaven.

War & Imperialism in Republican Rome, 327-70 B. C. William V. Harris. 312p. 1985. pap. 16.95x (ISBN 0-19-814866-6). Oxford U Pr.

War & Insurance. Norman Hill et al. (Economic & Social History of the World War, British Ser.). (Ger.). 1927. 90.00x (ISBN 0-317-27648-4). Elliots Bks.

War & Insurance. Josiah Royce. LC 75-3336. Repr. of 1914 ed. 22.50 (ISBN 0-404-59339-9). AMS Pr.

War & International Ethics: Tradition & Today. W. L. LaCroix. 316p. (Orig.). lib. bdg. 28.50 (ISBN 0-8191-6707-X); pap. text ed. 15.25 (ISBN 0-8191-6708-8). U Pr of Amer.

War & Intervention in Lebanon: The Israeli-Syrian Deterrence Dialogue. Yair Evron. LC 87-2851. 350p. 1987. text ed. 39.50x (ISBN 0-8018-3569-0). Johns Hopkins.

War & Its Alleged Benefits. Jacques Novicow. LC 75-147482. (Library of War & Peace; the Character & Causes of War). 1972. lib. bdg. 46.00 (ISBN 0-8240-0274-1). Garland Pub.

War & Its Alleged Benefits. Jakov A. Novikov. Tr. by Thomas Seltzer. 1969. Repr. of 1911 ed. 19.50 (ISBN 0-8337-2591-2). B Franklin.

War & Justice. Robert L. Phillips. LC 84-40278. (Illus.). 160p. 1984. 16.95 (ISBN 0-8061-1893-8). U of Okla Pr.

War & Military Courts: Judicial Interpretation of Its Meaning. Dorothy Schaffter. 184p. 1980. 20.00 (ISBN 0-682-49570-0, University). Exposition-Phoenix.

War & Military Reform in the Roman Republic: 578-589 B.C. John M. Carter. 95p. (Orig.). 1980. pap. 9.50x (ISBN 0-89126-096-X). MA-AH Pub.

War & Moral Responsibility. Ed. by M. Cohen et al. (Philosophy & Public Affairs Reader). 1974. pap. 8.50x (ISBN 0-691-01980-0). Princeton U Pr.

War & Morality. Ed. by Richard A. Wasserstrom. 136p. 1970. pap. text ed. write for info. (ISBN 0-534-00681-7). Wadsworth Pub.

War & Order: Reflections on Vietnam & History. George Liska. LC 68-9697. (Washington Center of Foreign Policy Research. Studies in International Affairs: No. 11). pap. 31.80 (ISBN 0-317-19922-6, 2023126). Bks Demand UMI.

War & Other Essays. William G. Sumner. Ed. & intro. by Albert G. Keller. LC 78-108124. 1970. Repr. of 1911 ed. 15.00 (ISBN 0-404-06304-7). AMS Pr.

War & Other Essays. William G. Sumner. Ed. by Albert G. Keller. LC 76-93379. (Essay Index Reprint Ser.). 1911. 26.50 (ISBN 0-8369-1530-5). Ayer Co Pubs.

War & Peace. Leo Tolstoy. Tr. by Garnett Constance. LC 83-4572. 1931. 13.95 (ISBN 0-394-60475-X). Modern Lib.

War & Peace. Leo Tolstoy. Tr. by Ann Dunnigan. (Orig.). 1968. pap. 5.95 (ISBN 0-451-52116-1, Sig Classics). NAL.

War & Peace. Leo Tolstoy. Ed. by George Gibian. (Critical Editions Ser.). (Annotated). (gr. 9-12). 1966. pap. text ed. 16.95x (ISBN 0-393-09672-6, NortonC). Norton.

War & Peace. Leo Tolstoy. 1982. pap. 8.95 (ISBN 0-14-044417-3). Penguin.

War & Peace, 2 vols. Leo Tolstoy. Ed. by Henry Gifford. Tr. by Louise Maude & Aylmer Maude. (World's Classics-Paperback Ser.). 1983. pap. 5.95 Vol. 1 (ISBN 0-19-281582-2); pap. 5.95 Vol. 2 (ISBN 0-19-281614-4). Oxford U Pr.

War & Peace: A Christian Foreign Policy. John W. Robbins. (Trinity Papers: No. 21). 250p. (Orig.). 1988. pap. 8.95 (ISBN 0-940931-21-4). Trinity Found.

War & Peace from Genesis to Revelation. Vernard Eller. LC 80-26280. (Christian Peace Shelf Ser.). 232p. 1981. pap. 9.95 (ISBN 0-8361-1947-9). Herald Pr.

War & Peace in an Age of Upheaval, 1793-1830 see Cambridge New Modern History.

War & Peace in Europe, 1815-1970. new ed. E. L. Woodward. 292p. 1963. 29.50x (ISBN 0-7146-1530-7, F Cass Co). Biblio Dist.

War & Peace in Jalemo: The Management of Conflict in Highland New Guinea. Klaus-Friedrich Koch. LC 73-92579. 288p. 1974. text ed. 17.50x (ISBN 0-674-94590-5). Harvard U Pr.

War & Peace in Literature. Lucy Dougall. 128p. 1981. 5.00 (ISBN 0-318-16880-4). World Without War Pubns.

War & Peace in Nagaland. Y. D. Gundevia. LC 75-908123. 1975. 12.50x (ISBN 0-88386-580-7). South Asia Bks.

War & Peace in Soviet Diplomacy. Timothy A. Taracouzio. LC 74-10081. (Russian Studies: Perspectives on the Revolution Ser.). x, 354p. 1975. Repr. of 1940 ed. 30.25 (ISBN 0-88355-188-8). Hyperion Conn.

War & Peace in the Law of Islam. Majid Khadduri. LC 77-2418. Repr. of 1955 ed. 24.50 (ISBN 0-404-10925-X). AMS Pr.

War & Peace in the Nuclear Age. John Newhouse. 1989. 24.95 (ISBN 0-394-56217-8). Knopf.

War & Peace in the World's Religions. John Ferguson. 1978. pap. 5.95 (ISBN 0-19-520074-8). Oxford U Pr.

War & Peace News. Glasgow Media Group Staff. LC 85-11594. 354p. 1985. 59.00x (ISBN 0-335-15071-3, Open Univ Pr); pap. 21.00x (ISBN 0-335-10598-X, Open Univ Pr). Taylor & Francis.

War & Peace Notes. Marianne Sturman. (Orig.). 1967. pap. 3.75 (ISBN 0-8220-1366-5). Cliffs.

War & Peace: Series One, Volume V. Ed. by Lynchburg College Faculty Staff. LC 82-45154. (Classical Selections on Great Issues, Symposium Readings). 648p. (Orig.). 1982. lib. bdg. 24.00 (ISBN 0-8191-2470-2); pap. text ed. 9.25 (ISBN 0-8191-2471-0). U Pr of Amer.

War & Peace: The Evils of the First, & a Plan for Preserving the Last. William Jay. LC 70-137547. (Peace Movement in America Ser.). xiv, 69p. 1972. Repr. of 1919 ed. lib. bdg. 11.95x (ISBN 0-89198-075-X). Ozer.

War & Peace: The Views from Moscow & Beijing. Banning N. Garrett & Bonnie S. Glaser. LC 84-80320. (Policy Papers in International Affairs: No. 20). 160p. 1984. pap. 7.95x (ISBN 0-87725-520-2). U of Cal Intl St.

War & Peas. Michael Foreman. LC 74-10368. (Illus.). (ps-3). 1974. (Crowell Jr Bks); PLB 12.89 (ISBN 0-690-00629-2). HarpJ.

War & Politics. Bernard Brodie. 514p. 1974. write for info. (ISBN 0-02-315020-3); pap. write for info. (ISBN 0-685-28575-8). Macmillan.

War & Politics in Cambodia: A Communications Analysis. LC 73-81737. pap. 46.50 (ISBN 0-317-26848-1, 2023450). Bks Demand UMI.

War & Politics in China. facsimile ed. John T. Pratt. LC 78-146869. (Select Bibliographies Reprint Ser). Repr. of 1943 ed. 22.00 (ISBN 0-8369-5636-2). Ayer Co Pubs.

War & Politics in Ireland, 1649-1730. J. G. Simms. 335p. 1986. 40.00 (ISBN 0-907628-72-9). Hambledon Press.

War & Politics in Twentieth Century Europe: Essays in Military & Diplomatic History. R. H. Haigh & D. S. Morris. 1982. Vol. 1. 32.00x (ISBN 0-89126-105-2); Vol. 2. 37.00x (ISBN 0-89126-106-0); Vol. 3. 18.00x (ISBN 0-89126-114-1); Vol. 4. 27.00x (ISBN 0-89126-115-X); Vol. 5. 35.00x (ISBN 0-89126-116-8); Vol. 6. 18.00x (ISBN 0-89126-117-6); complete set 118.00. MA-AH Pub.

War & Presidential Power: A Chronicle of Congressional Surrender. Thomas F. Eagleton. 1974. 8.95 (ISBN 0-87140-581-4). Liveright.

War Diaries of Jean-Paul Sartre: November 1939 - March 1940. Tr. by Quinn Hoare. 1986. pap. 10.95 (ISBN 0-394-74422-5). Pantheon.
War Diaries of Jean-Paul Sartre: November 1939 to March 1940. Jean-Paul Sartre. LC 84-18947. 1985. 17.45 (ISBN 0-394-53813-7). Pantheon.
War Diaries of Kenneth Slessor: Official Australian Correspondent 1940-1944. Ed. by Clement Semmler. 1986. 42.50 (ISBN 0-317-46037-4). U of Queensland Pr.
War Diaries: Politics & War in the Mediterranean, January 1943-May 1945. Harold MacMillan. LC 84-50454. (Illus.). 800p. 1984. 29.95 (ISBN 0-312-85566-4). St Martin.
War Diary: Eastern Sea Frontier Dec., 1941-July 1942. 500p. 1987. 22.00 (ISBN 0-317-61261-1). Shellback Pr.
War Diary of the Chief of the General Staff, Janos Voros: From April 17 to October 15, 1944. Hungarian Historical Research Society Staff. LC 77-95242. Orig. Title: Vitez Voros Janos M. kir Vezerezredes Vezerkari Fonok Naploja. 297p. 1979. pap. 14.95 (ISBN 0-935484-03-5). Universe Pub Co.
War Diary of the Emperor Frederick III, 1870-1871. Frederick III. Tr. by A. R. Allinson from Ger. (Illus.). viii, 356p. 1988. Repr. of 1926 ed. lib. bdg. 40.00x (ISBN 0-86527-376-6). Fertig.
War, Diplomacy, & History: Papers & Reviews. Raymond G. O'Connor. LC 79-88951. 1979. pap. text ed. 14.50 (ISBN 0-8191-0790-5). U Pr of Amer.
War Dispatches of Kenneth Slessor Official Australian Correspondent 1940-1944. Kenneth Slessor. Intro. by Clement Semmler. LC 87-10457. (Illus.). 493p. 1988. text ed. 47.50x (ISBN 0-7022-2076-0). U of Queensland Pr.
War Dispatches of Stephen Crane. Ed. by R. W. Stallman & E. R. Hagemann. LC 77-2994. (Illus.). 1977. Repr. of 1964 ed. lib. bdg. 35.00x (ISBN 0-8371-9549-7, CRWD). Greenwood.
War Dogs. Nik Uhernik. 1984. pap. 3.50 (ISBN 0-8217-1474-0). Zebra.
War Dogs, No. 2: M-16 Jury. Nik-Uhernik. 272p. 1985. pap. 2.75 (ISBN 0-8217-1539-9). Zebra.
War Drums. Donald C. Porter. (White Indian Ser.: No. 13). 353p. (Orig.). 1986. pap. 3.95 (ISBN 0-553-25868-0). Bantam.
War Drums & Wagon Wheels: The Story of Russell, Majors & Waddell. Raymond W. Settle & Mary L. Settle. LC 65-18414. (Illus.). x, 268p. 1966. 21.95x (ISBN 0-8032-0172-9). U of Nebr Pr.
War Drums at Eden Prairie. Gladys T. Nelson. (Illus.). (gr. 5-9). 1977. 5.95 (ISBN 0-87839-023-5). North Star.
War Eagle: A Life of General Eugene A. Carr. James T. King. LC 63-14694. (Illus.). x, 324p. 1964. 27.95x (ISBN 0-8032-0092-7). U of Nebr Pr.
War Eagle: A Story of Auburn Football. Rev. & enl. ed. Clyde Bolton. LC 73-83502. (College Sports Ser.). 1979. 9.95 (ISBN 0-87397-023-3). Strode.
War Eagle: The Story of Auburn Football. rev. ed. Clyde Bolton. (College Sports Book Ser.). (Illus.). 358p. 1987. pap. 10.95 (ISBN 0-87397-302-X). Strode.
War Eagles. James S. Childers. Ed. by James A. Gray. 369p. Repr. 20.00 (ISBN 0-941624-71-4). Eagle Pub.
War, Economy & Society: 1939-1945. Alan S. Milward. LC 76-40823. (History of World Economy in the Twentieth Century: Vol. 5). 1977. pap. 11.95x (ISBN 0-520-03942-4). U of Cal Pr.
War Eighteen Twelve. George May. (Illus.). 43p. (Orig.). 1962. pap. 1.50 (ISBN 0-911872-28-0). Mackinac Island.
War: Ends & Means. Paul Seabury & Angelo Codevilla. LC 88-48797. 304p. 1989. 19.95 (ISBN 0-465-09067-2). Basic.
War Everyone Lost - & Won. Timothy Lomperis. 192p. 1987. pap. 10.95 (ISBN 0-87187-409-1). Congr Quarterly.
War Everyone Lost-And Won: America's Intervention in Viet Nam's Twin Struggles. Timothy J. Lomperis. LC 83-11989. x, 192p. 1984. text ed. 25.00 (ISBN 0-8071-1104-X). La State U Pr.
War, Famine & Our Food Supply. Robert B. Marston. LC 75-26308. (World Food Supply Ser). (Illus.). 1976. Repr. of 1897 ed. 21.00x (ISBN 0-405-07787-4). Ayer Co Pubs.
War Flying in France. George A. Vaughn, Jr. (Illus.). 160p. (Orig.). 1980. pap. 23.00x (ISBN 0-89126-082-X). MA-AH Pub.
War for Eternity. Christopher B. Rowley. 352p. 1985. pap. 2.95 (ISBN 0-345-31052-7, Del Rey). Ballantine.
War for Independence: A Military History. Howard H. Peckham. LC 58-5685. (Chicago History of American Civilization Ser). 1958. pap. 8.00X (ISBN 0-226-65316-1, CHAC15). U of Chicago Pr.
War for Independence: The Story of the American Revolution. Albert Marrin. LC 87-13711. (Illus.). 288p. (gr. 5 up). 1988. 14.95 (ISBN 0-689-31390-X, Atheneum Childrens Bks). Macmillan.
War for Lebanon: 1970-1985. rev. ed. Itamar Rabinovich. LC 83-45935. (Paperback Ser.). 243p. 1985. 31.50x (ISBN 0-8014-1870-4); pap. 9.95x (ISBN 0-8014-9313-7). Cornell U Pr.
War for the World see No Break Here.
War, Foreign Affairs, & Constitutional Power, 1829-1901. American Bar Association Staff & Henry B. Cox. LC 76-15392. 440p. 1984. prof. ref. 35.00x (ISBN 0-88410-956-9). Ballinger Pub.
War: Four Christian Views. Herman A. Hoyt et al. Ed. by Robert G. Clouse. 216p. (Orig.). 1981. pap. 7.95 (ISBN 0-88469-097-0). BMH Bks.
War from the Inside. Frederick L. Hitchcock. LC 84-16142. (Collector's Library of the Civil War). 1985. kivar bdg 26.60 (ISBN 0-8094-4475-5, Pub. by Time-Life). Silver.
War from Within. Sophie Goetzel-Leviathan. Ed. by Rebecca Fromer. LC 86-62879. 89p. 1987. pap. 7.95 (ISBN 0-943376-29-7). Magnes Mus.
War Gallery of the Winter Palace. Voennaia Galereia & Dvortsa Zimnego. 240p. 1981. 60.00x (ISBN 0-317-14332-8, Pub. by Collets (UK)). State Mutual Bk.
War Gallery of the Winter Palace: Voennaia Galereia Zimnego Dvortsa. V. M. Glinka & A. V. Pomarnatsii. 240p. 1981. 66.00x (ISBN 0-317-57480-9, Pub. by Collets UK). State Mutual Bk.
War Game. Anthony Price. 256p. Date not set. pap. 4.95 (ISBN 0-445-40238-5). Mysterious Pr.
War Game: A Critique of Military Problem Solving. Garry Brewer & Martin Shubik. (Illus.). 404p. 1979. text ed. 29.95x (ISBN 0-674-94600-6). Harvard U Pr.
War Games. Thomas B. Allen. LC 86-27498. 368p. 1987. text ed. 19.95 (ISBN 0-07-001195-8). McGraw.
War Games. Wright Morris. LC 78-5603. x, 164p. 1978. 16.50x (ISBN 0-8032-0950-9); pap. 3.95 (ISBN 0-8032-5878-X, BB 657, Bison). U of Nebr Pr.
War Generation: Veterans of the First World War. Ed. by Stephen R. Ward. 1975. 21.50 (ISBN 0-8046-9101-0, Pub. by Kennikat). Assoc Faculty Pr.
War Government, Federal & State, 1861-65. William B. Weeden. LC 75-87685. (Law, Politics & History Ser.). 1972. Repr. of 1906 ed. lib. bdg. 45.00 (ISBN 0-306-71707-7). Da Capo.
War Governors in the American Revolution. Margaret B. Macmillan. 1943. 13.25 (ISBN 0-8446-1295-2). Peter Smith.
War Hangover. Gregory W. Bitz. LC 87-71864. (Illus.). 272p. (Orig.). 1988. pap. 11.95 (ISBN 0-944357-67-9). Angel Wing Pr.
War History of American Railroads. Walker D. Hines. LC 74-75240. (United States in World War 1 Ser). xviii, 327p. 1974. Repr. of 1928 ed. lib. bdg. 20.95x (ISBN 0-89198-104-7). Ozer.
War History of American Railroads. Walker D. Hines. (Economic & Social History of the World War, American Ser.). 1928. 17.50x (ISBN 0-317-27572-0). Elliots Bks.
War Horses. Bill Bragg. (Orig.). 1980. pap. 1.75 (ISBN 0-505-51511-3, Pub. by Tower Bks). Leisure NY.
War Hound & the World's Pain. Michael Moorcock. 1983. pap. 2.95 (ISBN 0-671-60409-0, Timescape). PB.
War Hound & the World's Pain: A Fable. Michael Moorcock. LC 81-9030. 239p. 1981. 15.00 (ISBN 0-671-43708-9). Ultramarine Pub.
War in Afghanistan. Mark Urban. LC 87-14375. 240p. 1988. 45.00 (ISBN 0-312-01205-5). St Martin.
War in Afghanistan, 1879-80: The Personal Diary of Major General Sir Charles Metcalfe MacGregor. Ed. by William Trousdale. LC 85-13921. (Illus.). 252p. 1986. 29.95x (ISBN 0-8143-1783-9). Wayne St U Pr.
War in an Empty House. Don Domanski. (House of Anansi Poetry Ser.: No. 41). 72p. (Orig.). 1982. pap. 6.95 (ISBN 0-88784-094-9, Pub. by Hse Anansi Pr Canada). U of Toronto Pr.
War in Ancient India. V. R. Ramachandra Dikshitar. 1987. Repr. of 1948 ed. 26.00x (ISBN 81-208-0382-5, Pub. by Motilal Banarsidass). South Asia Bks.
War in China: America's Role in the Far East. Varian Fry. LC 76-111741. (American Imperialism: Viewpoints of United States Foreign Policy, 1898-1941). 1970. Repr. of 1938 ed. 11.00 (ISBN 0-405-02021-X). Ayer Co Pubs.
War in Clare Nineteen Eleven-Nineteen Twenty-One: Personal Memoirs of the Irish War of Independence. Michael Brennan. 112p. 1980. 15.00x (ISBN 0-906127-26-2, Pub. by Irish Academic Pr Ireland). Biblio Dist.
War in Cuba, Being a Full Account of Her Great Struggle for Freedoms. Gonzalo De Quesada. LC 79-111731. (American Imperialism: Viewpoints of United States Foreign Policy, 1898-1941). 1970. Repr. of 1896 ed. 37.50 (ISBN 0-405-02047-3). Ayer Co Pubs.
War in El Salvador: Current Situation & Outlook for the Future. Joaquin Villalobos. Ed. by David Loeb. Tr. by C. Courtright from Span. Orig. Title: Estado Actual de la Guerra y sus Perspectivas. 30p. (Orig.). 1986. pap. 2.50 (ISBN 0-942638-15-8, 32L). New Amer Pr.
War in European History. Michael Howard. 1976. pap. text ed. 9.95x (ISBN 0-19-289095-6, Opus). Oxford U Pr.
War in Heaven. Charles Williams. 290p. Repr. of 1949 ed. lib. bdg. 40.00 (ISBN 0-8495-5919-7). Arden Lib.
War in Heaven see Novels.
War in Heaven: "Paradise Lost" & the Tradition of Satan's Rebellion. Stella P. Revard. LC 79-23297. (Illus.). 320p. 1980. 34.50x (ISBN 0-8014-1138-6). Cornell U Pr.
War in International Society. Evan Luard. LC 87-8175. 472p. 1987. 32.50x (ISBN 0-300-04016-4). Yale U Pr.
War in Kansas. facsimile ed. G. Douglas Brewerton. LC 74-164381. (Black Heritage Library Collection). Repr. of 1856 ed. 17.00 (ISBN 0-8369-8840-X). Ayer Co Pubs.
War in Modern World. Theodore Ropp. 1985. pap. 8.95 (ISBN 0-02-036390-7, Collier). Macmillan.
War in Nicaragua. William Walker. LC 84-22224. 448p. 1985. pap. 11.95 (ISBN 0-8165-0882-8). U of Ariz Pr.
War in Peace: Conventional & Guerilla Warfare since 1945. updated ed. Ed. by Robert Thompson. 328p. 1985. 25.00 (ISBN 0-517-55817-3). Crown.
War in Peace: The Marshall Cavendish Illustrated Encyclopedia of Postwar Conflict, 12 vols, Vols. 1-12. Ed. by Ashley Brown & Mark Dartford. (Illus.). 3000p. 1984. Set. lib. bdg. 499.95x (ISBN 0-86307-293-3). Marshall Cavendish.
War in Slow Motion. Ed. by Zelle Andrews. 128p. (Orig.). 1985. pap. 6.95 (ISBN 0-8298-0553-2). Pilgrim Ny.
War in Slow Motion: The Economic & Social Impact of Militarism. Zelle W. Andrews. 1985. 6.95 (ISBN 0-377-00155-4). Friendship Pr.
War in South Africa. Prussia. Tr. by Hubert Du Cane. LC 69-19361. (Ger). Repr. of 1906 ed. 35.00x (ISBN 0-8371-5089-2, PRW&). Greenwood.
War in South Africa: Its Causes & Effects. J. A. Hobson. LC 68-9620. 1970. Repr. of 1900 ed. 29.50x (ISBN 0-86527-208-5). Fertig.
War in Southwest Virginia 1861-65. Gary C. Walker. Date not set. 24.95 (ISBN 0-317-67961-9). A & W Enterprises.
War in Space. Christopher Lee. (Illus.). 248p. 1987. 24.95 (ISBN 0-241-11591-4, Pub. by Hamish Hamilton England). David & Charles.
War in Texas (1836) see Life Travels & Opinions of Benjamin Lundy: Including His Journeys to Texas.
War in the Air, Nineteen Fourteen to Nineteen Eighteen. 96p. 1981. 25.00x (ISBN 0-85153-266-7, Pub. by D B Barton England). State Mutual Bk.
War in the Desert. Richard Collier. LC 77-81945. (World War II Ser.). (gr. 7 up). 1977. lib. bdg. 22.60 (ISBN 0-8094-2475-4, Pub. by Time-Life). Silver.
War in the Desert. Richard Collier. (World War II Ser.). 1977. 14.95 (ISBN 0-8094-2474-6). Time-Life.
War in the Desert: An R. A. F. Frontier Campaign. John B. Glubb. LC 80-1929. Repr. of 1961 ed. 38.00 (ISBN 0-404-18964-4). AMS Pr.
War in the Desert: The Eighth Army at El Alamein. James Lucas. (Illus.). 288p. 1983. 16.95 (ISBN 0-8253-0153-X). Beaufort Bks NY.
War in the Falklands: The Full Story. Linklater & Sunday Times of London Insight Team. LC 82-48612. (Illus.). 320p. 1982. 14.45 (ISBN 0-06-015082-3, HarpT). Har-Row.
War in the Far East. Fiona Reynolds. 80p. (Orig.). 1983. pap. text ed. 6.50x (ISBN 0-435-31882-9). Heinemann Ed.
War in the Mediterranean, 1803 to 1810. Piers Mackesy. LC 81-6457. (Illus.). xviii, 430p. 1981. Repr. of 1957 ed. lib. bdg. 41.50x (ISBN 0-313-22913-9, MAWM). Greenwood.
War in the Middle Ages. Philippe Contamine. Tr. by Michael Jones. 420p. 1986. pap. 14.95 (ISBN 0-631-14469-2). Basil Blackwell.
War in the Modern Great Power System, 1495-1975. Jack S. Levy. LC 83-10249. 232p. 1983. 24.00x (ISBN 0-8131-1497-7); pap. 8.00 (ISBN 0-8131-0164-6). U Pr of Ky.
War in the Modern World. Theodore Ropp. LC 81-6448. xv, 400p. 1981. Repr. of 1959 ed. lib. bdg. 45.50x (ISBN 0-313-22844-2, ROWM). Greenwood.
War in the Modern World. Theodore Ropp. LC 60-5274. pap. 104.00 (ISBN 0-317-08033-4, 2010250). Bks Demand UMI.
War in the Outposts. Simon Rigge. LC 80-8532. (World War II Ser.). (gr. 7 up). 22.60 (ISBN 0-8094-3380-X, Pub. by Time-Life). Silver.
War in the Outposts. Simon Rigge. Ed. by Time-Life Books Editors. (World War II Ser.). (Illus.). 208p. 1981. 14.95 (ISBN 0-8094-3379-6). Time-Life.
War in the Pacific. John Winton. (Illus.). 1979. 12.50 (ISBN 0-8317-9300-7, Mayflower Bks). Smith Pubs.
War in the Pacific: A Study of Navies, Peoples, & Battle Problems. Sutherland Denlinger & Charles B. Gary. LC 77-111752. (American Imperialism: Viewpoints of United States Foreign Policy, 1898-1941). 1970. Repr. of 1936 ed. 20.00 (ISBN 0-405-02011-2). Ayer Co Pubs.
War in the Painted Buttes. Peter Field. 176p. 1988. pap. 2.75 (ISBN 0-380-70423-4). Avon.
War in the Poetry of George Seferis. Carmen Capri-Karka. LC 85-62597. 232p. 1986. 25.00 (ISBN 0-918618-28-2); pap. 11.00 (ISBN 0-918618-27-4). Pella Pub.
War in the Shadows. Ed. by Robert Manning. Boston Publishing Co. Editors. LC 87-73527. (Vietnam Experience Ser.: Vol. 25). (Illus.). 192p. 1988. 16.95 (ISBN 0-939526-38-7). Boston Pub Co.
War in the Third Dimension: Essays in Contemporary Airpower. Ed. by Mason. 236p. 1986. text ed. 30.00 (ISBN 0-08-031187-3); pap. text ed. 16.95 (ISBN 0-08-031188-1). Pergamon.
War in the Twentieth Century. Willard Waller. 79.95 (ISBN 0-87700-201-0). Revisionist Pr.
War in the West. LC 76-42074. (Civil War Monographs). 1977. lib. bdg. 44.00 (ISBN 0-527-17556-0); pap. 36.00 (ISBN 0-527-17557-9). Kraus Repr.
War in the Yemen. Edgar O'Ballance. LC 79-21058. 218p. 1971. 23.00 (ISBN 0-208-01038-6, Archon). Shoe String.
War in Val D'Orcia: An Italian War Diary, 1943-1944. Iris Origo. LC 82-49344. 256p. 1984. 14.95 (ISBN 0-87923-500-4); pap. 8.95 (ISBN 0-87923-476-8). Godine.
War in Vietnam. Don Lawson. (First Bks.). (Illus.). 96p. (gr. 4 up). 1981. lib. bdg. 10.40 (ISBN 0-531-04331-2). Watts.
War in Vietnam: The Religious Connection. Madalyn M. O'Hair. 83p. (Orig.). 1982. pap. 4.00 (ISBN 0-911826-28-9). Am Atheist.
War Inconsistent with the Religion of Jesus Christ. David L. Dodge. LC 75-137540. (Peace Movement in America Ser). xxiv, 168p. 1972. Repr. of 1905 ed. lib. bdg. 15.95x (ISBN 0-89198-067-9). Ozer.
War Industries Board: Business-Government Relations during World War 1. Robert D. Cuff. LC 72-4002. 320p. 1973. 37.50x (ISBN 0-8018-1360-3). Johns Hopkins.
War Injuries of the Upper Extremity. Ed. by J. Engel & I. Kessler. (Progress in Surgery Ser.: Vol. 16). (Illus.). 1979. pap. 65.50 (ISBN 3-8055-2900-7). S Karger.
War Is a Dinosaur, & Other Songs of Hope, Love & Weltschmerz. Teddy Milne. LC 86-64053. 96p. 1987. pap. 8.95 (ISBN 0-938875-04-3). Pittenbruach Pr.
War Is a Racket. Smedley Butler. 59.95 (ISBN 0-87700-153-7). Revisionist Pr.
War Is Good for Babies & Other Young Children. Deborah Dwork. 300p. 1987. write for info. (ISBN 0-422-60660-X, 1200, Pub. by Tavistock England). Routledge Chapman & Hall.
War is the Enemy. A. J. Muste. 1942. pap. 2.50x (ISBN 0-87574-015-4, 015). Pendle Hill.
War is Their Business. G. Tsagalov. 292p. 1985. pap. 4.95 (ISBN 0-8285-3019-X, Pub. by Progress Pubs USSR). Imported Pubns.
War, Its Causes & Correlates. Ed. by Martin A. Nettleship et al. (World Anthropology Ser.). (Illus.). xviii, 814p. 1975. 69.50 (ISBN 90-279-7659-7). Mouton.
War Journey. Wade Hawsey. Ed. by Bette G. Wahlfeldt. (Illus.). 30p. (Orig.). 1986. pap. 4.95 (ISBN 0-9616280-0-6). BW Enterprises.
War, Justice & Public Order: England & France in the Late Middle Ages. Richard W. Kaeuper. 464p. 1988. 78.00 (ISBN 0-19-822873-2). Oxford U Pr.
War, Law, & Labor: The Munitions Acts, State Regulation, & the Unions 1915-1921. G. Rubin. 308p. 1988. 55.00 (ISBN 0-19-825538-1). Oxford U Pr.
War Ledger. A. F. Organski & Jacek Kugler. LC 79-23366. (Illus.). xii, 292p. 1981. pap. 11.00x (ISBN 0-226-63280-6). U of Chicago Pr.
War Ledger. A. F. Organski & Jacek Kugler. LC 79-23366. (Illus.). 1980. lib. bdg. 25.00x (ISBN 0-226-63279-2). U of Chicago Pr.
War Lords. A. G. Gardiner. (Wayfarer's Library). 328p. lib. bdg. 32.50. Century Bookbindery.
War Lords. Sima Qian. Tr. by William Dolby & John Scott. 168p. 1974. 12.95 (ISBN 0-900025-08-5); pap. 10.95 (ISBN 0-900025-09-3). Dufour.
War Lords. A. J. Taylor. (Illus.). 1979. pap. 6.95 (ISBN 0-14-004638-0). Penguin.
War Lords of Washington. Bruce Catton. LC 70-90481. 1969. Repr. of 1948 ed. lib. bdg. 35.00 (ISBN 0-8371-2149-3, CAWL). Greenwood.
War-Lyrics & Other Poems. Henry H. Brownell. LC 72-4953. (Romantic Tradition in American Literature Ser.). 256p. 1972. 19.00 (ISBN 0-405-04625-1). Ayer Co Pubs.
War Machine. William Marshall. 1988. 15.95 (ISBN 0-89296-198-8). Mysterious Pr.
War Machine: German Weapons & Manpower. Ed. by W. Victor Madej. LC 84-80626. (Illus.). 180p. 1984. 13.95 (ISBN 0-941052-58-3, 68); pap. 9.95 (ISBN 0-941052-21-4, 8). Valor Pub.
War Machine: The Case Against the Arms Race. James A. Joyce. 14.95 (ISBN 0-7043-2254-4, Pub. by Quartet England). Charles River Bks.
War Machine: The Case Against the Arms Race. James A. Joyce. 240p. 1982. pap. 3.95 (ISBN 0-380-59915-5, 59915-5, Discus). Avon.
War Magician. David Fisher. 256p. 1983. 16.95 (ISBN 0-698-11140-0, Coward). Putnam Pub Group.
War Making Powers of the President. Ann Van Wynen Thomas & A. J. Thomas, Jr. LC 82-10541. 192p. 1982. 15.00x (ISBN 0-87074-185-3). SMU Press.
War Managers. Douglas Kinnard. 226p. pap. 9.95 (ISBN 0-89529-281-5). Avery Pub.

War Maps. Simon Goodenough. (Illus.). 192p. 1983. 18.95 (ISBN 0-312-85584-2). St Martin.

War Memoirs. Jubal A. Early. Ed. by Frank E. Vandiver. LC 60-11858. (Indiana University Civil War Centennial Ser.). (Illus.). 1968. Repr. of 1960 ed. 47.00 (ISBN 0-527-26150-5). Kraus Repr.

War Memoirs of David Lloyd George, 6 vols. D. Lloyd George. LC 75-41179. Repr. of 1936 ed. 295.00 set (ISBN 0-404-15040-3). AMS Pr.

War Memoirs of Robert Lansing, Secretary of State. Robert Lansing. 1971. Repr. of 1935 ed. lib. bdg. 35.00x (ISBN 0-8371-4520-1, LAWM). Greenwood.

War Memorials As Political Landscape: The American Experience & Beyond. James M. Mayo. LC 87-22328. 219p. 1988. lib. bdg. 42.95 (ISBN 0-275-92812-8, C2812). Praeger.

War Moon. Tom Cooper. 384p. 1987. pap. 3.50 (ISBN 0-373-97031-5, Pub. by Worldwide). Harlequin Bks.

War, Morality, & the Military Profession. 2nd, rev. ed. Ed. by Malham H. Wakin. 521p. 1986. 46.00 (ISBN 0-8133-0359-1); pap. 23.00 (ISBN 0-8133-0360-5). Westview.

War Movies: The Complete Viewer's Guide. Brock Garland. (Illus.). 240p. 1987. 22.95 (ISBN 0-8160-1206-7). Facts on File.

War Music: An Account of Books 16 to 19 of Homer's Iliad. Christopher Logue. 96p. 1987. 12.95 (ISBN 0-374-28648-5). FS&G.

War Music: An Account of Books 16 to 19 of Homer's Iliad. Christopher Logue. 192p. 1988. pap. 7.95 (ISBN 0-374-52089-5). FS&G.

War Myth in U. S. History see Propaganda & Myth in Time of War.

War Neuroses. Roy R. Grinker & John P. Spiegel. Ed. by Richard H. Kohn. LC 78-22381. (American Military Experience Ser.). 1979. Repr. of 1945 ed. lib. bdg. 12.00x (ISBN 0-405-11858-9). Ayer Co Pubs.

War Nurses. Sharon Cosner. (American History Series for Young People). (YA) (gr. 7 up). Date not set. 17.95. Walker & Co.

War of a Jewish Partisan: A Youth Imperiled by His Russian Comrades & Nazi Conquerors. Yechiel Granatstein. (ArtScroll History Ser.). (Illus.). 256p. 1986. 14.95 (ISBN 0-89906-476-0); pap. 11.95 (ISBN 0-89906-477-9). Mesorah Pubns.

War of American Independence. R. E. Evans. (Cambridge Introduction to World History Topic Bks.). (Illus.). 48p. (YA) (gr. 7 up). 1976. pap. 4.95 (ISBN 0-521-20903-X). Cambridge U Pr.

War of American Independence: Military Attitudes, Policies & Practice, 1763-1789. Don Higginbotham. LC 83-2374. 521p. 1983. text ed. 29.95x (ISBN 0-930350-43-X); pap. 9.95x (ISBN 0-930350-44-8). NE U Pr.

War of Chupas (Civil Wars of Peru) Pedro D. Cieza de Leon. Ed. by Clements Markham. (Hakluyt Society Works Ser.: Vol. 2, Vol. 42). (Illus.). Repr. of 1917 ed. 60.00 (ISBN 0-8115-0351-8). Kraus Repr.

War of Conquest: How It Was Waged Here in Mexico. As told to Bernardino de Sahagun. Tr. by Arthur J. Anderson & Charles E. Dibble. (Illus.). 1978. pap. 7.95 (ISBN 0-87480-192-3). U of Utah Pr.

War of Dreams. Angela Carter. 1983. pap. 1.95 (ISBN 0-380-00933-1, 31948-9, Bard). Avon.

War of Eighteen Twelve. Harry L. Coles. LC 65-17283. (Chicago History of American Civilization Ser: No. 22). (Illus.). 1965. pap. 10.00x (ISBN 0-226-11350-7, CHAC22). U of Chicago Pr.

War of Eighteen Twelve. rev. ed. Richard B. Morris. (American History Topic Bks.). (Illus.). 72p. (gr. 5-10). 1985. PLB 8.95 (ISBN 0-8225-1705-1). Lerner Pubns.

War of Eighteen Twelve. (Massachusetts Historical Society Picture Books Ser.). 16p. 1962. pap. 2.00 (ISBN 0-934909-18-0). Mass Hist Soc.

War of Eighteen Twelve: An Annotated Bibliography. Dwight L. Smith. LC 84-48071. (Reference Library of Social Science Wars of the U. S.). 364p. 1984. lib. bdg. 54.00 (ISBN 0-8240-8945-6). Garland Pub.

War of Eighteen Twelve Genealogy. 88p. 1987. pap. 7.00 (ISBN 0-913857-07-6). Genealog Sources.

War of Eighteen Twelve in the Champlain Valley. Allan S. Everest. (New York State Study). (Illus.). 264p. 1981. 19.95x (ISBN 0-8156-2240-6). Syracuse U Pr.

War of Eighteen-Twelve in the Old Northwest. Alec R. Gilpin. (Illus.). vii, 286p. 1958. 6.50 (ISBN 0-87013-032-3). Mich St U Pr.

War of Eighteen-Twelve on the Chesapeake Bay. Gilbert Byron. (Illus.). 94p. 1964. 5.00 (ISBN 0-686-36633-6). Md Hist.

War of Eighteen Twelve: Virginia Land & Pension Applicants: A Quick Reference Guide to Ancestors Having War of 1812 Service Who Served, Lived, Died, or Married in Virginia or West Virginia. Patrick G. Wardell. iv, 402p. (Orig.). 1987. pap. 15.00 (ISBN 1-55613-055-4). Heritage Bk.

War of Eyes & Other Stories. Wanda Coleman. LC 88-14714. 200p. 1988. 20.00 (ISBN 0-87685-736-5); deluxe ed. 30.00 (ISBN 0-87685-737-3); pap. 10.00 (ISBN 0-87685-735-7). Black Sparrow.

War of Fools: The Letters of Obscure Men - A Study of the Satire & the Satirized. Reinhard P. Becker. (New York University Ottendorfer Series Neue Folge: Vol. 12). 190p. 1981. pap. 21.60 (ISBN 3-261-04727-5). P Lang Pubs.

War of Ideas: American Intellectuals & the World Crisis, 1938 -1945. Ed. by Frank Feidel & Ernest May. (Harvard Dissertations in American History & Political Science Ser.). 484p. 1988. lib. bdg. 80.00 (ISBN 0-8240-5141-6). Garland Pub.

War of Ideas: America's International Identity Crisis. George N. Gordon & Irving Falk. (Communication Arts Bks.). 1973. 9.00x (ISBN 0-8038-8064-2). Hastings.

War of Ideas in Spain: Philosophy, Politics & Education. Jose Castilejo. 1976. lib. bdg. 59.95 (ISBN 0-8490-2806-X). Gordon Pr.

War of Invention: Science in the Great War, 1914-18. G. Hartcup. (Illus.). 208p. 1988. 43.00 (ISBN 0-08-033591-8). Pergamon.

War of Quito, by Pedro de Cieza de Leon, & Other Inca Documents. Ed. by Clements Markham. (Hakluyt Society Works Ser.: No. 2, Vol. 31). Repr. of 1913 ed. 35.00 (ISBN 0-8115-0347-X). Kraus Repr.

War of Shadows. Jack L. Chalker. 320p. 1984. pap. 2.95 (ISBN 0-441-87197-6, Pub. by Ace Science Fiction). Ace Bks.

War of Steel & Gold: A Study of the Armed Peace. Henry N. Brailsford. (Development of the Industrial Society Ser.). 340p. 1971. Repr. of 1915 ed. 27.50x (ISBN 0-7165-1767-1, Pub. by Irish Academic Pr). Biblio Dist.

War of the American Revolution: A Selected, Annotated Bibliography of Published Sources. Richard L. Blanco. LC 82-49168. (Wars of the U. S.: Vol. 1). 654p. 1983. lib. bdg. 49.00 (ISBN 0-8240-9171-X). Garland Pub.

War of the Classes. Jack London. (Illus.). 278p. 1982. pap. 6.95 (ISBN 0-932458-11-4). Star Rover.

War of the Dispossessed: Honduras & El Salvador, 1969. Thomas P. Anderson. LC 80-24080. (Illus.). xiv, 203p. 1981. 19.95x (ISBN 0-8032-1009-4). U of Nebr Pr.

War of the Doomed: Jewish Armed Resistance in Poland, 1942-1944. Shmuel Krakowski. LC 83-18537. 340p. 1984. 44.50 (ISBN 0-8419-0851-6). Holmes & Meier.

War of the Dots. Robert B. Irwin. 56p. 1970. pap. 4.00 (ISBN 0-89128-069-3, PIP069). Am Foun Blind.

War of the End of the World. Mario V. Llosa. Tr. by Helen R. Lane. 1985. 9.95 (ISBN 0-380-69987-7). Avon.

War of the End of the World. Mario Vargas-Llosa. Tr. by Helen Lane from Span. 624p. 1984. 18.95 (ISBN 0-374-28651-5); ltd. ed. 75.00. FS&G.

War of the Flea: A Study of Guerrilla Warfare. Robert Taber. (Theory & Practise Ser). 1970. pap. 1.95 (ISBN 0-8065-0225-8, Pub. by Citadel Pr). Lyle Stuart.

War of the Gaedhil with Gaill, or the Invasion of Ireland by the Danes & Other Norsemen: Irish Text with Translation. Ed. by James Todd. (Rolls Ser.: No. 48). Repr. of 1867 ed. 44.00 (ISBN 0-8115-1107-3). Kraus Repr.

War of the Generations: The Revolt of Eleven Seventy-Three to Seventy-Four. Thomas M. Jones. LC 80-18411. (Monograph Publishing; Sponsor Ser.). pap. 60.50 (ISBN 0-317-28156-9, 2022592). Bks Demand UMI.

War of the Gods: The Social Code in Indo-European Mythology. Jarich G. Oosten. (International Library of Anthropology). 240p. 1985. 32.50x (ISBN 0-7102-0289-X). Routledge Chapman & Hall.

War of the Maelstrom. Jack L. Chalker. 1988. pap. 3.95 (ISBN 0-441-10268-9). Ace Bks.

War of the Moonrhymes. Calvin Miller. LC 83-48428. (Singreale Chronicles Ser.: Vol. 3). (Illus.). 224p. (Orig.). 1984. pap. 7.95 (ISBN 0-06-250579-3, CN 4086, HarpR). Har-Row.

War of the Nations: A Pictorial Portfolio of World War I. 38.50 (ISBN 0-405-09858-8, 19527). Ayer Co Pubs.

War of The Ninja Masters, No. 2: The Shibo Discipline. Wade Barker. 288p. Date not set. pap. 2.95 (ISBN 0-446-34709-4). Warner Bks.

War of the Ninja Masters, No. 3: The Himitsu Attack. Wade Barker. Date not set. pap. 3.50 (ISBN 0-446-34711-6). Warner Bks.

War of the Rebellion Official Records of the Union & Confederate Armies, 128 vols. 1985. Repr. of 1880 ed. Set. 2200.00 (ISBN 0-918678-07-2). Historical Times.

War of the Roses. Warren Adler. LC 80-23036. 272p. (Orig.). 1981. 10.95 (ISBN 0-446-51220-6). Warner Bks.

War of the Salinas (Civil Wars of Peru) Pedro D. Cieza de Leon. Ed. by Clements Markham. (Hakluyt Society Works Ser.: No. 2, Vol. 54). Repr. of 1923 ed. 45.00 (ISBN 0-8115-0358-5). Kraus Repr.

War of the Springing Tigers. Gerard H. Corr. 200p. 1979. 12.95. Asia Bk Corp.

War of the Star Lords. Hegstad & Munson. 34p. 1983. pap. 2.50 (ISBN 0-8163-0517-X). Pacific Pr Pub Assn.

War of the Theatres. Josiah Penniman. 1897. lib. bdg. 29.50 (ISBN 0-8414-9220-4). Folcroft.

War of the Theatres. Josiah H. Penniman. LC 73-126649. Repr. of 1897 ed. 16.50 (ISBN 0-404-04992-3). AMS Pr.

War of the Twins. Margaret Weis & Tracy Hickman. LC 85-52462. (Dragonlance Legends Ser.: Vol. 2). 400p. (Orig.). 1986. pap. 3.95 (ISBN 0-88038-266-X). TSR Inc.

War of the Two Emperors: The Confrontation Between Napoleon & Tzar Alexander. Curtis Cate. LC 84-42506. (Illus.). 423p. 1985. pap. 24.45 (ISBN 0-394-53670-3). Random.

War of the Wenuses. C. L. Graves & E. V. Lucas. LC 74-15979. (Science Fiction Ser). (Illus.). 140p. 1975. Repr. of 1898 ed. 16.00x (ISBN 0-405-06293-1). Ayer Co Pubs.

War of the Wizards. Carol Gaskin. LC 84-2663. (Forgotten Forest Ser.). (Illus.). 128p. (gr. 3-7). 1985. PLB 9.49 (ISBN 0-8167-0318-3); pap. text ed. 2.95 (ISBN 0-8167-0319-1). Troll Assocs.

War of the Wizards. Ian Page & Joe Dever. (World of Lone Wolf Ser.). pap. 2.50 (ISBN 0-317-62827-5, Pub. by Berkley-Pacer). Berkley Pub.

War of the Worlds. (Guild Books Classics Illustrated Ser.). (Illus.). pap. 0.59 (ISBN 0-685-74097-8, 124). Guild Bks.

War of the Worlds. H. G. Wells. (Airmont Classics Ser.). (gr. 8 up). 1964. 1.75 (ISBN 0-8049-0045-0, CL-45). Airmont.

War of the Worlds. H. G. Wells. (Literature Ser). (gr. 7-12). 1970. pap. text ed. 6.83 (ISBN 0-87720-742-9). AMSCO Sch.

War of the Worlds. H. G. Wells. pap. 2.50 (ISBN 0-425-08624-0). Berkley Pub.

War of the Worlds. H. G. Wells. (gr. 3 up). 1978. 6.95 (ISBN 0-448-41106-7, G&D). Putnam Pub Group.

War of the Worlds. H. G. Wells. Ed. by Naunerle Farr. (Now Age Illustrated Ser., No. 2). (Illus.). 64p. (Orig.). (gr. 5-10). 1974. 7.50 (ISBN 0-88301-223-5); pap. 2.95 (ISBN 0-88301-136-0). Pendulum Pr.

War of the Worlds. H. G. Wells. (Looking Glass Library: No. 21). (gr. 3 up). 1960. lib. bdg. 5.39 (ISBN 0-394-90471-0). Random.

War of the Worlds. H. G. Wells. (gr. 7-12). 1972. pap. 2.25 (ISBN 0-590-10112-9). Scholastic Inc.

War of the Worlds. H. G. Wells. 1981. Repr. lib. bdg. 16.95x (ISBN 0-89966-376-1). Buccaneer Bks.

War of the Worlds. H. G. Wells. Date not set. price not set. S&S.

War of the Worlds. H. G. Wells. 14.95 (ISBN 0-89190-424-7, Pub. by Am Repr). Amereon Ltd.

War of the Worlds. H. G. Wells. 176p. 1988. pap. 1.95 (ISBN 0-553-21338-5). Bantam.

War of the Worlds. H. G. Wells. 224p. 1988. pap. 2.95 (ISBN 0-8125-5754-9). Tor Bks.

War of the Worlds see Seven Science Fiction Novels.

War of the Worlds: Student Activity Book. Marcia Sohl & Gerald Dackerman. (Now Age Illustrated). (Illus.). (gr. 4-10). 1976. wkbk 1.25 (ISBN 0-88301-198-0). Pendulum Pr.

War of the Worlds: The Resurrection. J. M. Dillard. 1988. pap. 3.95. PB.

War of Titans: Blake's Critique of Milton & the Politics of Religion. Jackie DiSalvo. LC 82-11136. 403p. 1983. 39.95x (ISBN 0-8229-3804-9). U of Pittsburgh Pr.

War of Truth: Milhemet Ha-Emet. N. Kalomiti. Ed. by P. Doron. 25.00x (ISBN 0-87068-441-8). Ktav.

War of Wits: The Anatomy of Espionage & Intelligence. Ladislas Farago. LC 75-31362. (Illus.). 379p. 1976. Repr. of 1954 ed. lib. bdg. 32.50x (ISBN 0-8371-8518-1, FAWW). Greenwood.

War of Words: Chicano Protest in the 1960's & 1970's. John C. Hammerback et al. LC 85-5598. (Contributions in Ethnic Studies: No. 12). x, 187p. 1985. lib. bdg. 35.00 (ISBN 0-313-24825-7, JWW/). Greenwood.

War Office at War. Sir Sam Fay. 1976. Repr. 15.00x (ISBN 0-85409-883-6). Charles River Bks.

War on Charity Ross. Jack M. Bickham. 1976. pap. 2.25 (ISBN 0-441-87263-8). Ace Bks.

War on Christ in America: The Christian Fortress America under Siege Christophobes of the Media & of the Supreme Court in Action - Demonic Maladies of the Western Culture, Freud, Marx, Skinner & Other Ugly Pagans. Ratibor-Ray Jurjevich. 538p. 1985. pap. 22.95 (ISBN 0-930711-01-7). Ichthys Bks.

War on Drugs: Heroin, Cocaine, Crime & Public Policy. James A. Inciardi. 240p. 1986. pap. text ed. 9.95 (ISBN 0-87484-743-5). Mayfield Pub.

War on Films: The American Cinema & World War I, 1914-1941. Michael T. Isenberg. LC 76-19835. 400p. 1981. 27.50 (ISBN 0-8386-2004-3). Fairleigh Dickinson.

War on Gold. Antony C. Sutton. 1977. 12.95 (ISBN 0-89245-008-8). Concord Bks.

War on Light: The Destruction of the Image of God in Man Through Modern Art. Margaret E. Stucki. 1975. 25.00 (ISBN 0-686-23419-7). Birds' Meadow Pub.

War on Light: The Destruction of the Image of God in Man Through Modern Art. Margaret E. Stucki. 5.95 (ISBN 0-686-18059-3). Freedom Univ-FSP.

War on Powder River. Helena H. Smith. LC 65-28734. (Illus.). xiv, 328p. 1967. pap. 9.95 (ISBN 0-8032-5188-2, BB 375, Bison). U of Nebr Pr.

War on the Bank of the United States. Thomas F. Gordon. (Research & Source Works Ser.: No. 1622). 1966. Repr. of 1834 ed. 18.50 (ISBN 0-8337-1389-2). B Franklin.

War on the Bank of the United States. Thomas F. Gordon. LC 68-18219. 1968. Repr. of 1834 ed. 27.50x (ISBN 0-678-00380-7). Kelley.

War on the Cimarron. Luke Short. (Orig.). 1986. pap. 2.75 (ISBN 0-553-26236-X). Bantam.

War on the Frontier. (Civil War Ser.). 175p. 1986. 14.95 (ISBN 0-8094-4780-0). Time-Life.

War on the Line. Peter Hay. 1986. 34.75x (ISBN 0-906520-10-X, Pub. by Middleton Pr UK). State Mutual Bk.

War on the Mississippi. Jerry Korn. LC 84-16206. (Civil War Ser.). lib. bdg. 19.94 (ISBN 0-8094-4745-2, Pub. by Time-Life). Silver.

War on the Nile: Britain, Egypt & the Sudan 1882-1898. Michael Barthorp. (Illus.). 190p. 1986. pap. 14.95 (ISBN 0-7137-1858-7, Pub. by Blandford Pr England). Sterling.

War on the Saints. rev. ed. Jessie Penn-Lewis. 1964. pap. 3.95 (ISBN 0-87508-958-5). Chr Lit.

War on the Saints. 9th ed. Jessie Penn-Lewis & Evan Roberts. 1988. Repr. of 1912 ed. 11.50. T E Lowe.

War on the Short Waves see Propaganda by Short Wave.

War on the Webfoot Saloon & Other Tales of Feminine Adventures. Malcolm Clark, Jr. & Kenneth W. Porter. (Illus.). 54p. 1969. pap. 2.95 (ISBN 0-87595-023-X). Oregon Hist.

War on Villa Street. Harry Mazer. 128p. (YA) (gr. 7 up). Date not set. pap. price not set (ISBN 0-440-99062-9, LFL). Dell.

War on War. Lowell Jaeger. 70p. 1988. pap. price not set (ISBN 0-87421-138-7). Utah St U Pr.

War on Wishbone Range. Charles A. Seltzer. 303p. 1975. Repr. of 1932 ed. lib. bdg. 19.95x (ISBN 0-88411-106-7, Pub. by Aeonian Bks). Amereon Ltd.

War on World Poverty: An Appeal to the Conscience of Mankind. Harold Wilson. LC 54-19767. 1969. Repr. of 1953 ed. 20.00 (ISBN 0-527-97100-6). Kraus Repr.

War or Peace in the Twentieth Century. Roosevelt Eleanor Institute Staff. Ed. by Sue R. Roff. (Illus.). 270p. (gr. 8-12). 1984. binder 49.95 (ISBN 0-89908-502-4). Greenhaven.

War Outside Ireland. Michael Joyce. LC 82-80497. 192p. (Orig.). 1982. pap. 8.50 (ISBN 0-943608-01-5). Tinkers Dam Pr.

War Party. John Benteen. (Sundance Ser.: No. 14). 1974. pap. 1.50 (ISBN 0-8439-1009-7, Leisure Bks). Leisure NY.

War Party. Max Brand. LC 81-38502. 224p. 1982. Repr. of 1972 ed. 12.50x (ISBN 0-8376-0460-5). Bentley.

War Party. Louis L'Amour. 160p. (Orig.). 1982. pap. 2.95 (ISBN 0-553-25393-X). Bantam.

War Party. William O. Steele. LC 78-52815. (gr. k-3). 1978. 4.95 (ISBN 0-15-294789-2, HJ). HarBraceJ.

War, Peace, & International Politics. 4th ed. David W. Ziegler. 1987. pap. write for info. (ISBN 0-673-39501-4). Scott F.

War, Peace & Nonresistance. rev. ed. Guy F. Hershberger. LC 53-7586. (Christian Peace Shelf Ser.). 375p. 1969. 15.95 (ISBN 0-8361-1449-3). Herald Pr.

War, Peace & Revolution: International Socialism at the Crossroads, 1914-1918. David Kirby. LC 86-11895. 340p. 1986. 32.50 (ISBN 0-312-85587-7). St Martin.

War, Peace, & the Future. Ellen Key. LC 78-147728. (Library of War & Peace; the Character & Causes of War). 1973. lib. bdg. 46.00 (ISBN 0-8240-0507-4). Garland Pub.

War, Peace & the Presidency. Henry Paolucci. LC 68-8774. 20.00. Griffon Hse.

War, Peace, Survival: Global Politics & Conceptual Synthesis. Robert C. North. 448p. 1988. pap. 14.95 (ISBN 0-8133-0683-3). Westview.

War Period of American Finance, 1908-1925. A. D. Noyes. 1973. Repr. of 1926 ed. 32.50 (ISBN 0-384-42130-X). Johnson Repr.

War Pictures from the South. Bela Estvan. LC 74-179516. (Select Bibliographies Reprint Ser). Repr. of 1863 ed. 22.00 (ISBN 0-8369-6645-7). Ayer Co Pubs.

War Pilot of Orange. Bob Vanderstok. LC 87-62612. 242p. (Orig.). 1987. pap. 10.95 (ISBN 0-933126-89-1). Pictorial Hist.

War Planet. James Soutar. LC 83-90992. 232p. 1986. 12.95 (ISBN 0-533-05989-5). Vantage.

War Plans of the Great Powers, 1880-1914. Ed. by Paul M. Kennedy. (Illus.). 280p. 1985. pap. text ed. 14.95x (ISBN 0-04-940082-7). Unwin Hyman.

War Play Dilemma: Balancing Needs & Values in the Early Childhood Classroom. Nancy Carlsson-Paige & Diane Levin. (Early Childhood Education Ser.). 120p. 1987. pap. text ed. 9.95x (ISBN 0-8077-2875-6). Tchrs Coll.

War Plays, Vol. II, Pt. 3. Date not set. pap. price not set. Heinemann Ed.

War Plays: A Trilogy. Edward Bond. (Methuen New Theatrescripts Ser.). 56p. (Orig.). 1985. pap. 5.95 (ISBN 0-413-57240-4, 9381). Heinemann Ed.

War Poems & After. G. Lewis Cook. 51p. 1986. 9.00x (ISBN 0-7223-2043-4, Pub. by A H Stockwell England). State Mutual Bk.

War Poems of Siegfried Sassoon. Siegfried Sassoon. Ed. by Rupert Hart-Davis. LC 82-24202. 160p. 1983. 11.95 (ISBN 0-571-13010-0); pap. 6.95. Faber & Faber.
War Poetry of the South. Ed. by William G. Simms. LC 72-4974. (Romantic Tradition in American Literature Ser.). 494p. 1972. Repr. of 1866 ed. 36.50 (ISBN 0-405-04644-8). Ayer Co Pubs.
War Poets: The Lives & Writings of Rupert Brooke, Siegfried Sassoon, Wilfred Owen, Robert Graves, Edmund Blunden & the Other Great Poets of the 1914-1918 War. Robert Giddings. (Illus.). 192p. 1988. 24.95 (ISBN 0-317-66927-3, Orion Bks). Crown.
War, Politics & Power. Karl Von Clausewitz. Tr. by Edward M. Collins. 304p. 1962. pap. 9.95 (ISBN 0-89526-999-6). Regnery Gateway.
War Pony. Donald E. Worcester. LC 83-40486. (Chaparral Bks.). (Illus.). 95p. (gr. 4 up). 1984. Repr. of 1961 ed. 10.95 (ISBN 0-912646-85-3). Tex Christian.
War Potential of Nations. Klaus Knorr. LC 78-13603. (Illus.). 1978. Repr. of 1956 ed. lib. bdg. 35.00x (ISBN 0-313-21049-7, KNWA). Greenwood.
War, Poverty, Freedom: The Christian Response. Franz Bockle. (Concilium Ser.: Vol. 15). 7.95 (ISBN 0-8091-0154-8). Paulist Pr.
War Powers & the Constitution. Dick Cheney et al. 29p. 1984. pap. 5.00 (ISBN 0-8447-2248-0). Am Enterprise.
War Powers of the Executive in the United States. Clarence A. Berdahl. LC 21-12280. Repr. of 1921 ed. lib. bdg. 22.00 (ISBN 0-384-03970-7). Johnson Repr.
War Powers of the President & Congress: Who Holds the Arrow & Olive Branch? W. Taylor Reveley. LC 80-29046. 394p. 1981. 27.50x (ISBN 0-8139-0808-6). U Pr of Va.
War Powers Resolution: Its Implementation in Theory & Practice. Robert F. Turner. LC 82-24192. (Philadelphia Policy Papers). (Orig.). 1983. pap. 4.95 (ISBN 0-910191-06-9). For Policy Res.
War Powers Resolution: The Role of Congress in U. S. Armed Intervention. Pat M. Holt. 1978. pap. 5.00 (ISBN 0-8447-3299-0). Am Enterprise.
War Powers Under the Constitution of the United States. William Whiting. LC 70-169640. (American Constitutional & Legal History Ser). 1971. Repr. of 1871 ed. lib. bdg. 69.50 (ISBN 0-306-70361-0). Da Capo.
War Prayer. Mark Twain. LC 68-29574. (Illus.). 96p. 1984. pap. 4.95 (ISBN 0-06-091113-1, CN 1113, PL). Har-Row.
War, Presidents & Public Opinion. John E. Mueller. LC 85-5352. (Illus.). 326p. 1985. pap. text ed. 13.50 (ISBN 0-8191-4649-8). U Pr of Amer.
War Propaganda & the U. S. Harold Lavine & James Wechsler. 59.95 (ISBN 0-8490-1277-5). Gordon Pr.
War Propaganda & the United States. Harold Lavine & James Wechsler. LC 72-4668. (International Propaganda & Communications Ser.). (Illus.). 389p. 1972. Repr. of 1940 ed. 19.00 (ISBN 0-405-04753-3). Ayer Co Pubs.
War Propaganda & the United States. Harold Lavine & James Wechsler. 1940. 17.50x (ISBN 0-686-50035-0). Elliots Bks.
War Propoganda & the United States. James Wechsler & Harold Lavine. LC 72-147476. (Library of War & Peace; the Character & Causes of War). 1972. lib. bdg. 46.00 (ISBN 0-8240-0268-7). Garland Pub.
War, Prosperity & Depression: The U.S. Economy, 1917-1945. Peter Fearon. LC 87-21571. x, 294p. 1987. 35.00x (ISBN 0-7006-0348-4); pap. 17.95x (ISBN 0-7006-0349-2). U Pr of KS.
War Remembered. Clark Dougan et al. write for info. (ISBN 0-201-11275-2). Addison-Wesley.
War Report: D-Day to VE-Day. Compiled by Desmond Hawkins. 368p. 1986. pap. 7.95 (ISBN 0-563-20421-4, Pub. by BBC). Parkwest Pubns.
War Report: The War Correspondent's View of Battle from the Crimea to the Falklands. Trevor Royle. 224p. 1987. 65.00x (ISBN 1-85158-064-6, Pub. by Mainstream Scotland). State Mutual Bk.
War Resistance in Historical Perspective. Larry Gara. 1970. pap. 2.50x (ISBN 0-87574-171-1, 171). Pendle Hill.
War, Revolution & Peace: Essays in Honor of Charles B. Burdick. Ed. by Joachim Remak. (Illus.). 298p. 1987. lib. bdg. 26.75 (ISBN 0-8191-6342-2). U Pr of Amer.
War, Revolution, & Society in Romania: The Road to Independence. Ilie Ceausescu. (East European Monographs: No. 135). 298p. 1983. 30.00x (ISBN 0-88033-023-6). East Eur Quarterly.
War, Revolution & the Ku Klux Klan: A Study of Intolerance in a Border City. Shawn Lay. LC 85-90937. 224p. 1985. 20.00 (ISBN 0-87404-094-9). Tex Western.
War Secrets in the Ether, 2 vols. Wilhelm F. Flicke. LC 77-88801. (Cryptographic Ser.). 1977. Vol. 1. 18.80 (ISBN 0-89412-021-2); Vol. 2. 18.80 (ISBN 0-89412-023-9). Aegean Park Pr.
War Since Nineteen Forty-Five. Michael Carver. (Illus.). 336p. 1980. 17.95x (ISBN 0-297-77846-3, GWN 04977, Pub. by Weidenfeld & Nicolson England). Biblio Dist.
War since Nineteen Forty-Five. updated ed. Michael Carver. Date not set. pap. text ed. 17.50 (ISBN 0-948660-12-0, Pub. by Ashfield Pr UK). Humanities.
War so Terrible: Sherman & Atlanta. James L. McDonough & James P. Jones. (Illus.). 1987. 19.95 (ISBN 0-393-02497-0). Norton.
War Song. M. J. Naparsteck. (Orig.). 1980. pap. 1.75 (ISBN 0-8439-0729-0, Leisure Bks). Leisure NY.
War Stars: The Superweapon & the American Imagination. H. Bruce Franklin. (Illus.). 272p. 1988. 22.95 (ISBN 0-19-505295-1). Oxford U Pr.
War, State & Society. Ed. by Martin Shaw. LC 83-40167. 272p. 1984. 25.95 (ISBN 0-312-85593-1). St Martin.
War: Stonewall Jackson's Campaigns & Battles. James B. Wood. 70p. 1988. pap. 15.00 (ISBN 0-87556-357-0). Saifer.
War Stories: Poems. H. R. Coursen. Ed. by Lewis Turco. LC 84-72827. (Illus.). 48p. 1984. 4.00 (ISBN 0-910380-05-8). Cider Mill.
War Stories: Poems about Long Ago & Now. Howard Nemerov. LC 87-5097. 72p. 1987. 10.95 (ISBN 0-226-57242-0). U of Chicago Pr.
War Story. Jim Morris. 1985. pap. 4.50 (ISBN 0-440-19362-1). Dell.
War Story. Derek Robinson. LC 87-45445. 416p. 1988. 18.95 (ISBN 0-394-56389-1). Knopf.
War Story Guide: An Annotated Bibliography of Military Fiction. Myron J. Smith, Jr. LC 79-26740. 449p. 1980. lib. bdg. 27.50 (ISBN 0-8108-1281-9). Scarecrow.
War, Strategy & Maritime Power. B. Mitchell Simpson, 3rd. 1977. 40.00x (ISBN 0-8135-0842-8). Rutgers U Pr.
War System of the Commonwealth of Nations. Charles Sumner. LC 70-137552. (Peace Movement in America Ser). 71p. 1972. Repr. of 1849 ed. lib. bdg. 12.95x (ISBN 0-89198-082-2). Ozer.
War, Taxation & Rebellion in Early Tudor England: Henry VIII, Wolsey & the Amicable Grant of 1525. G. W. Bernard. LC 86-13065. 208p. 1986. 32.50 (ISBN 0-312-85611-3). St Martin.
War, Technology, & Society in the Middle East. V. J. Parry & M. E. Yapp. (Illus.). 1975. 35.00x (ISBN 0-19-713581-1). Oxford U Pr.
War That Hitler Won: Goebbels & the Nazi Media Campaign. Robert E. Herzstein. LC 86-20471. (Illus.). 491p. 1986. pap. 9.95 (ISBN 0-913729-47-7). Paragon Hse.
War, The West, & The Wilderness. Kevin Brownlow. LC 78-54934. 1979. 27.50 (ISBN 0-394-48921-7). Knopf.
War Through Children's Eyes: The Soviet Occupation of Poland & the Deportations, 1939-1941. Ed. by Irena Grudzenska-Gross & Jan. T. Gross. LC 80-83832. (Archival Documentaries). 1985. pap. 7.95x (ISBN 0-8179-7472-5). Hoover Inst Pr.
War-Time Journal of a Georgia Girl. Eliza F. Andrews. Ed. & intro. by Spencer B. King. LC 75-39489. 416p. 1981. Repr. of 1960 ed. bds. 14.95 (ISBN 0-87797-033-5). Cherokee.
War-Time Strikes & Their Adjustment. Alexander M. Bing. LC 79-156405. (American Labor Ser., No. 2). 1971. Repr. of 1921 ed. 23.50 (ISBN 0-405-02915-2). Ayer Co Pubs.
War to End All Wars: The American Military Experience in World War I. Edward M. Coffman. LC 86-15918. 440p. 1986. 35.00x (ISBN 0-299-10960-7); pap. 12.50 (ISBN 0-299-10964-X). U of Wis Pr.
War Today: East vs. West: Battlefield Europe. Date not set. price not set. S&S.
War Today: East vs. West: The Machinery of Destruction. Date not set. price not set. S&S.
War Today: East vs. West: The Nuclear Duel. Date not set. price not set. S&S.
War Today: East vs. West: The Strategy of Combat. Date not set. price not set. S&S.
War: Toward a Solution. Tom Mooney. pap. 2.00 (ISBN 0-317-28513-0). Mooney.
War Toys. Jesse Ramage. LC 81-84846. 1982. 8.95 (ISBN 0-87212-160-7). Libra.
War Trails of the Blue Ridge. Shepherd M. Dugger. (Illus.). 1974. 6.00 (ISBN 0-686-15219-0). Puddingstone.
War Trap. Bruce Bueno De Mesquita. LC 80-24631. (Illus.). 238p. 1981. 35.00x (ISBN 0-300-02558-0); pap. 10.95 (ISBN 0-300-03091-6, Y-469). Yale U Pr.
War Under the Pacific. Keith Wheeler. Ed. by Time-Life Books Editors. (World War Two Ser.). (Illus.). 208p. 1980. 14.95 (ISBN 0-8094-3375-3). Time-Life.
War Vehicles. Christopher Maynard. LC 79-5063. (Lerner Question & Answer Bks.). (Illus.). 36p. (gr. 3-6). 1980. PLB 8.95 (ISBN 0-8225-1185-1). Lerner Pubns.
War, Violence & Children in Uganda. Ed. by Cole P. Dodge & Magne Raundalen. 160p. 1987. pap. 14.95 (ISBN 82-00-18408-0). Oxford U Pr.
War! War! War! rev. ed. Cincinnatus. Frwd. by Eustace Mullins. 291p. 1984. pap. 6.00 (ISBN 0-89562-100-2). Sons Lib.
War-Wasted Asia: Letters, 1945-46. Otis Cary et al. LC 75-11395. (Illus.). 322p. 16.95x (ISBN 0-87011-257-0). Kodansha.
War Weapons. Craig Sargent. 176p. (Orig.). 1987. pap. 2.95 (ISBN 0-445-20434-6, Pub. by Popular Lib). Warner Bks.
War, Weimar, & Literature: The Story of the Neue Merkur, 1914-1925. Guy Stern. LC 71-136960. (Illus.). 1971. 24.95x (ISBN 0-271-01147-5). Pa St U Pr.
War-What for? George Kirkpatrick. LC 78-147519. (Library of War & Peace; Labor, Socialism & War). 1973. lib. bdg. 46.00 (ISBN 0-8240-0307-1). Garland Pub.
War-What for? George R. Kirkpatrick. 1981. lib. bdg. 75.00 (ISBN 0-686-71635-3). Revisionist Pr.
War Will Not Take Place: The French Parliamentary Elections March, 1978. J. C. Frears & Jean-Luc Parodi. LC 79-527. (Illus.). 148p. 1979. 24.50x (ISBN 0-8419-0478-2). Holmes & Meier.
War Winners. Ronald W. Clark. (Illus.). 154p. 1980. 14.95 (ISBN 0-283-98503-8, Pub. by Sidgwick & Jackson England). Presidio Pr.
War with Catiline, War with Jugurtha, Etc. Sallust. (Loeb Classical Library: No. 116). 13.95x (ISBN 0-674-99128-1). Harvard U Pr.
War with Crime: Being a Selection of Reprinted Papers on Crime, Reformation, Etc. Thomas B. Baker. LC 83-49246. (Crime & Punishment in England, 1850-1922 Ser.). 299p. 1984. lib. bdg. 35.00 (ISBN 0-8240-6215-9). Garland Pub.
War with Empty Hands: Self-Defense Against Aggression. Lenox Cramer. (Illus.). 210p. (Orig.). 1987. pap. 14.95 (ISBN 0-939427-40-0). Alpha Pubns OH.
War with Germany. Leonard P. Ayres. Ed. by Richard H. Kohn. LC 78-22374. (American Military Experience Ser.). (Illus.). 1979. Repr. of 1919 ed. lib. bdg. 12.00x (ISBN 0-405-11852-X). Ayer Co Pubs.
War with Grandpa. Robert K. Smith. LC 83-14366. (Illus.). 128p. (gr. 4-8). 1984. pap. 12.95 (ISBN 0-385-29312-7); pap. 12.95 (ISBN 0-385-29314-3). Delacorte.
War with Grandpa. Robert K. Smith. (Illus.). 128p. (gr. 5-9). 1984. pap. 2.95 (ISBN 0-440-49276-9, YB). Dell.
War with Hannibal. Livy. Tr. by Aubrey De Selincourt. (Classics Ser.). (Orig.). 1965. pap. 6.95 (ISBN 0-14-044145-X). Penguin.
War with Mexico, 2 Vols. Roswell S. Ripley. 1849. 55.50 (ISBN 0-8337-3000-2). B Franklin.
War with Mexico, 2 vols. Justin H. Smith. (Illus.). 36.00 set (ISBN 0-8446-1413-0). Peter Smith.
War with Mexico Reviewed. Abiel A. Livermore. Ed. by Carlos E. Cortes. LC 76-1287. (Chicano Heritage Ser.). 1976. Repr. of 1850 ed. 24.50x (ISBN 0-405-09511-2). Ayer Co Pubs.
War with Mexico, 1846-1848. Henry E. Haferkorn. 1970. Repr. of 1914 ed. 21.50 (ISBN 0-8337-1529-1). B Franklin.
War with Mexico 1846-1848: A Select Bibliography on the Causes, Conduct & the Political Aspect of the War with Annotations & an Index. Henry E. Haferkorn. 1970. Repr. of 1848 ed. lib. bdg. 14.95x (ISBN 0-89712-000-0). Documentary Pubns.
War with Military & Civil Aspects: Subject Analysis with Bibliography. John C. Bartone. LC 87-47631. 160p. 1987. 34.50 (ISBN 0-88164-542-7); pap. 26.50 (ISBN 0-88164-543-5). ABBE Pubs Assn.
War with Mr. Wizzle. Gordon Korman. (Bruno & Boots Ser.). 240p. (gr. 4-6). 1982. pap. 2.50 (ISBN 0-590-40378-8, Apple Paperbacks). Scholastic Inc.
War with Spain. Henry C. Lodge. LC 70-111702. (American Imperialism: Viewpoints of United States Foreign Policy, 1898-1941). 1970. Repr. of 1899 ed. 22.00 (ISBN 0-405-02035-X). Ayer Co Pubs.
War with Spain in Eighteen Ninety-Eight. David F. Trask. Ed. by Louis Morton. LC 80-2314. (Macmillan Wars of the United States Ser.). (Illus.). 775p. 1981. 37.95x (ISBN 0-02-932950-7). Macmillan.
War with the Evil Power Master. R. A. Montgomery. (Choose Your Own Adventure Ser.: No. 37). 128p. (Orig.). (gr. 4). 1984. pap. 2.25 (ISBN 0-553-25778-1). Bantam.
War with the Newts. Karel Capek. Tr. by M. Weatherall & R. Weatherall. LC 75-41049. (BCL Ser. II). Repr. of 1937 ed. 19.00 (ISBN 0-404-14649-X). AMS Pr.
War with the Newts. Karel Capek. 360p. 1985. 29.95x (ISBN 0-8101-0700-7); pap. 9.95. Northwestern U Pr.
War with the Newts. Karel Capek. 346p. 1985. 29.95x (ISBN 0-8101-0663-9); pap. 9.95. Northwestern U Pr.
War with Two Voices. Laurence Deonna. 240p. 1988. 24.00 (ISBN 0-89410-638-4); pap. 12.00 (ISBN 0-89410-639-2). Three Continents.
War with Words: Stucture & Transcendence. Harley C. Shands. LC 77-144009. (Approaches to Semiotics Ser: No. 12). 1971. text ed. 14.00x (ISBN 90-2791-603-9). Mouton.
War Within & Without: Diaries & Letters, Nineteen Thirty-Nine to Nineteen Forty-Four. Anne M. Lindbergh. LC 79-21614. 536p. 1980. 14.95 (ISBN 0-15-194661-2). HarBraceJ.
War Within: From Victorian to Modernist Thought in the South, 1919-1945. Daniel J. Singal. LC 81-16358. (Fred. W. Morrison Series in Southern Studies). (Illus.). xvi, 455p. 1982. 30.00x (ISBN 0-8078-1505-5); pap. 15.95x (ISBN 0-8078-4087-4). U of NC Pr.
War Within: Making a Science of Communication in America's Success System. Lester Pazol. (Skill Builder Ser.). (Illus.). 194p. (Orig.). 1989. 17.95 (ISBN 0-943920-58-2); pap. 9.95 (ISBN 0-943920-59-0). Metamorphous Pr.
War Within You: A Study of the Believer's Two Natures. 2nd ed. Craig Massey. 1987. pap. 5.95 (ISBN 0-8024-0483-9). Moody.
War Without End. D. Dobson Payne. 1986. 49.75X (ISBN 0-245-54354-6, Pub. by Harrap Ltd England). State Mutual Bk.
War Without End: Michael T. Halbouty's Fight for American Energy Security. Jack Donahue. 226p. 1987. 19.95 (ISBN 0-87201-921-7). Gulf Pub.
War Without Fighting & The Oil that Multiplied. Joann Knox. (Junior Adventure Ser.). 68p. (gr. 4-8). 1973. pap. 1.00 (ISBN 0-88243-772-0, 02-0772). Gospel Pub.
War Without Fronts: The American Experience in Vietnam. Thomas C. Thayer. 276p. 1986. pap. 29.50. Westview.
War Without Men: Robots on the Future Battlefield. S. M. Shaker & A. R. Wise. (Illus.). 200p. 1988. 19.95 (ISBN 0-08-034216-7, Pub. by Pergamon-Brasseys). Pergamon.
War Without Mercy: Race & Power in the Pacific War. John Dower. 1986. 22.50 (ISBN 0-394-50030-X). Pantheon.
War Without Mercy: Race & Power in the Pacific War. John Dower. LC 85-43462. 416p. 1987. pap. 9.95 (ISBN 0-394-75172-8). Pantheon.
War Without Victory: The Downfall of Pitt, 1799-1802. Piers Mackesy. (Illus.). 1984. 45.00x (ISBN 0-19-822495-8). Oxford U Pr.
War Without Windows: The Personal Account of a Young Officer in Vietnam Trapped in the U. S. Intelligence Cover-Up. Bruce E. Jones. 320p. 1987. 18.95 (ISBN 0-8149-0934-5). Vanguard.
War World. William C. Dietz. 256p. 1986. pap. 2.95 (ISBN 0-441-87346-4, Pub. by Ace Science Fiction). Ace Bks.
War Year. Joe Haldeman. (Vietnam Ser.). 128p. 1984. pap. 2.95 (ISBN 0-380-67975-2, 67975). Avon.
War Years, 1939-1945. I. F. Stone. (Nonconformist History of Our Times Ser.). 353p. 1988. 18.95 (ISBN 0-316-81771-6). Little.
War Zone. Richard Austin. (Guardians Ser.: No. 6). pap. 2.75 (ISBN 0-515-08723-8). Jove Pubns.
War Zone. Alexander Stuart. 1989. 16.95 (ISBN 0-385-24953-5). Doubleday.
War Zones: Voices from the World's Killing Grounds. Jon L. Anderson & Scott Anderson. 352p. 1988. 21.95 (ISBN 0-396-08915-1). Dodd.
Waratah. Paul Nixon. (Illus.). 80p. 1987. 19.95 (ISBN 0-86417-160-9, Pub. by Kangaroo Pr). Intl Spec Bk.
Warbirds. Richard Herman, Jr. 1988. 18.95. D I Fine.
Warbirds. Mike Jerram. (Osprey Color Ser.). (Illus.). 126p. 1984. pap. 14.95 (ISBN 0-85045-578-2, Pub. By Osprey England). Motorbooks Intl.
Warbirds Worldwide, Issue No. 1. (Illus.). 47p. 1987. pap. 9.95 (ISBN 1-870601-00-9, Midland Counties). Motorbooks Intl.
Warbirds Worldwide, Issue No. 2. (Illus.). 47p. 1987. pap. 9.95 (ISBN 1-870601-01-7, Midland Counties). Motorbooks Intl.
Warbirds Worldwide, Issue No. 3. (Illus.). 47p. 1988. pap. 9.95 (ISBN 1-870601-02-5, Midland Counties). Motorbooks Intl.
Warble Fly Control in Europe: A Symposium in the EC Programme of Coordination of Research on Animal Pathology, Brussels, 16-17 September 1982. Ed. by Chantal Boulard & H. Thornberry. 168p. 1984. text ed. 28.00 (ISBN 90-6191-529-5, Pub. by A A Balkema). Brookfield Pub Co.
Warbler's Song in the Dusk: The Life & Writings of Otomo Yakamochi (718-785) Paula Doe. LC 80-29236. 180p. 1982. 37.50x (ISBN 0-520-04346-4). U of Cal Pr.
Warbots. G. Harry Stine. 1988. pap. 4.50 (ISBN 1-55817-111-8). Windsor NY.
Warbots, No. 2: Operation Steel Band. G. Harry Stine. 432p. 1988. pap. 3.95 (ISBN 1-55817-061-8). Windsor NY.
Warbots, No. 3: The Bastaard Rebellion. G. Harry Stine. 432p. 1988. pap. 3.95 (ISBN 1-55817-089-8). Windsor NY.
Warbots, No. 4: Sierra Madre. G. Harry Stine. 432p. 1988. pap. 3.95 (ISBN 1-55817-132-0). Windsor NY.
Warchild. Richard Bowes. 208p. (Orig.). 1986. pap. 3.50 (ISBN 0-445-20177-0, Pub. by Popular Library). Warner Bks.
Ward Clerk Skills. B. J. Rambo. LC 77-1819. (Nursing & Allied Health Ser.). 1977. pap. 24.95 (ISBN 0-07-051176-4). McGraw.
Ward Eight. Joseph Dinneen. LC 76-6335. (Irish Americans Ser). 1976. Repr. of 1936 ed. 26.50 (ISBN 0-405-09331-4). Ayer Co Pubs.
Ward Management & Teaching. 2nd ed. Ellen L. Perry. (Illus.). 304p. 1983. 22.95 (ISBN 0-7216-0822-1, Bailliere-Tindall). Saunders.
Ward Number Six & Other Stories. Anton Chekhov. Tr. by Ronald Hingley. (World's Classics Ser.). 272p. 1988. pap. 3.95 (ISBN 0-19-282174-1). Oxford U Pr.

Ward Perkins, John Bryan, Nineteen Twelve to Nineteen Eighty-One. J. J. Wilkes. (Memoirs of the Fellows of the British Academy). (Illus.). 24p. 1985. pap. 5.50 (ISBN 0-85672-507-2, Pub. by British Acad). Longwood Pub Group.

Ward Ritchie, Printer & Designer. Photos by Amanda Blanco. (Illus.). 1988. portfolio 250.00 (ISBN 0-937048-40-2). CSUN.

Ward Sister: Role & Preparation. Hazel O. Allen. 192p. 1982. pap. 18.95 (ISBN 0-7216-0800-0, Bailliere-Tindall). Saunders.

Ward Six & Other Short Novels. Anton Chekhov. Tr. by Ann Dunnigan. (Orig.). 1965. pap. 3.95 (ISBN 0-451-51895-0, Sig Classics). NAL.

Ward Six & Other Stories. Anton Chekhov. 384p. 1986. Repr. lib. bdg. 18.95x (ISBN 0-89966-523-3). Buccaneer Bks.

Ward Six & Other Stories. Anton Chekhov. Date not set. pap. 4.95 (ISBN 0-452-00826-3, Mer). NAL.

Warday. Whitley Strieber & James Kunetka. 528p. Date not set. pap. 4.95 (ISBN 0-446-35036-2). Warner Bks.

Warday. Whitley Strieber & James W. Kunetka. 528p. (Orig.). 1987. pap. 4.95 (ISBN 0-446-32630-5). Warner Bks.

Wardell Buffalo Trap Forty Eight SU Three Hundred & One: Communal Procurement in the Upper Green River Basin, Wyoming. George C. Frison. (Anthropological Papers: No. 48). 1973. pap. 3.00x (ISBN 0-932206-46-8). U Mich Mus Anthro.

Warden. Jack Rudman. (Career Examination Ser.: C-894). (Cloth bdg. avail. on request). pap. 18.00 (ISBN 0-8373-0894-1). Natl Learning.

Warden. Anthony Trollope. 1975. 14.95x (ISBN 0-460-00182-5, Evman); pap. 3.95x (ISBN 0-460-01182-0, Evman). Biblio Dist.

Warden. Anthony Trollope. (World's Classics Ser.). (Illus.). 1980. pap. 3.95 (ISBN 0-19-281506-7). Oxford U Pr.

Warden. Anthony Trollope. 1983. pap. 2.50 (ISBN 0-451-51815-2, Sig Classics). NAL.

Warden. Anthony Trollope. Ed. by Robin Gilmour. (English Library). 320p. 1984. pap. 3.95 (ISBN 0-14-043214-0). Penguin.

Warden see Barchester Towers.

Wardove. L. Neil Smith. 100p. 1987. pap. 2.95 (ISBN 0-425-09207-0). Berkley Pub.

Wardrobe see Lion, the Witch & the Wardrobe.

Wardrobe for a Little Girl 1900-1910. Susan B. Sirkis. (Wish Bklets: Vol. 10). 44p. 1972. pap. 5.50x (ISBN 0-913786-10-1). Wish Bklets.

Wardrobe from the King. Berit Kjos. 96p. 1988. pap. text ed. 4.95 (ISBN 0-89693-419-5). Victor Bks.

Wardrobes at Work: A Woman's Professional Dress Guide. Carol L. Reed. (Illus.). 64p. (Orig.). 1983. pap. 6.25 (ISBN 0-910347-02-6). Chatham Comm Inc.

Ward's Automotive Yearbook. Ed. by Harry A. Stark. 1980. 60.00x (ISBN 0-686-18833-0). Wards Comm.

Ward's Automotive Yearbook. Ed. by Harry A. Stark. LC 40-33639. 1982. 75.00 (ISBN 0-686-35855-4). Wards Comm.

Ward's Automotive Yearbook 1983. 45th ed. Ed. by Harry A. Stark. LC 40-33639. (Illus.). 400p. 1983. 85.00 (ISBN 0-910589-00-3). Wards Comm.

Ward's History of Coffee County. Warren P. Ward. LC 78-13236. 1978. Repr. of 1930 ed. 25.00 (ISBN 0-87152-290-X). Reprint.

Ward's Natural Sign Language Thesaurus of Useful Signs N' Synonyms. Jill Ward. Ed. by John Joyce. LC 77-93547. (Illus.). 1978. 29.95 (ISBN 0-917002-18-0, 446). Joyce Media.

Wards of Armageddon. J. N. Williamson & John Maclay. 400p. (Orig.). 1986. pap. 3.95 (ISBN 0-8439-2393-8, Leisure Bks). Leisure NY.

Wards of Liberty. facs. ed. Myra Kelly. LC 74-140332. (Short Story Index Reprint Ser). (Illus.). 1907. 18.00 (ISBN 0-8369-3724-4). Ayer Co Pubs.

Ward's Who's Who Among U. S. Motor Vechicle Manufacturers. Ed. by David C. Smith. 1977. 29.75x (ISBN 0-686-18832-2). Wards Comm.

Wardship: The Law & Practice. Nasreen Pearce. 126p. 1986. 104.00x (ISBN 0-906840-97-X, Pub. by Fourmat England). State Mutual Bk.

Ware Aus Dem Teufelsland. 272p. 1981. 140.00x (ISBN 0-317-69467-7, Pub. by Han-Shan Tang Ltd). State Mutual Bk.

Ware Hawk. Andre Norton. 272p. 1984. pap. 2.75 (ISBN 0-345-31685-1, Del Rey). Ballantine.

Wareham's Basic Business Types: Sorting Winners from Losers & Managing People for Profit. John Wareham. LC 86-47686. 256p. 1987. 15.95 (ISBN 0-689-11756-6). Atheneum.

Wareham's Way: Escaping the Judas Trap. John Wareham. LC 82-73036. 160p. 1983. 10.95 (ISBN 0-689-11367-6). Atheneum.

Warehouse Accounting & Control: Guidelines for Distribution & Financial Management. Ernst & Whinney. 268p. Date not set. 50.00 (ISBN 0-86641-106-2, 84158). Natl Assn Accts.

Warehouse Accounting & Control: Guidelines for Distribution & Financial Managers. Ernst & Whinney Staff & Cleveland Consulting Associates Staff. 1985. 50.00 (ISBN 0-318-03941-9); members 25.00 (ISBN 0-318-03942-7). Coun Logistics Mgt.

Warehouse Examiner. Jack Rudman. (Career Examination Ser.: C-895). (Cloth bdg. avail. on request). pap. 14.00 (ISBN 0-8373-0895-X). Natl Learning.

Warehouse Management Handbook. J. A. Tompkins & J. D. Smith. 800p. 1988. text ed. 69.95 (ISBN 0-07-064952-9). McGraw.

Warehouse Operations. Stephen L. Frey. 295p. 1983. 25.95 (ISBN 0-930206-14-2). Weber Systems.

Warehouse Operations Planning & Management. Andrew J. Briggs. LC 78-15299. 320p. 1979. Repr. of 1960 ed. 24.50 (ISBN 0-88275-715-6). Krieger.

Warehouse Sanitation Manual. 144p. soft bound 12.50 (ISBN 0-318-12793-8). Am Inst Baking.

Warehouse Supervisor. Jack Rudman. (Career Examination Ser.: C-926). (Cloth bdg. avail. on request). pap. 14.00 (ISBN 0-8373-0926-3). Natl Learning.

Warehouseman. Jack Rudman. (Career Examination Ser.: C-890). (Cloth bdg. avail. on request). pap. 12.00 (ISBN 0-8373-0890-9). Natl Learning.

Warehousing: Analysis for Effective Operations. Victor G. Powell. 240p. 1976. text ed. 36.75x (ISBN 0-220-66301-7, Pub. by Busn Bks England). Brookfield Pub Co.

Warehousing Storage & Retrieval Safety. Center for Occupational Research & Development Staff. (Job Safety & Health Instructional Materials Ser.). (Illus.). 40p. 1981. pap. text ed. 3.00 (ISBN 1-55502-125-5). Ctr Res & Dev.

Warenford, V. C. The First Naval Airman to be Awarded the V. C. Mary Gibson. 128p. 1987. 54.00x (ISBN 0-902633-91-0, Pub. by Picton UK). State Mutual Bk.

Wares of the Ming Dynasty. R. L. Hobson. 240p. 1923. 625.00x (ISBN 0-317-44238-4, Pub. by Han-Shan Tang Ltd); deluxe ed. 1250.00 (ISBN 0-317-44239-2, Pub. by Han Shan Tang Ltd.). State Mutual Bk.

Wares of the Ming Dynasty. R. L. Hobson. 208p. 1962. Repr. of 1923 ed. 150.00x (ISBN 0-317-44241-4, Pub. by Han-Shan Tang Ltd). State Mutual Bk.

Wares of the Ming Dynasty. Robert L. Hobson. LC 62-18358. (Illus.). 1962. Repr. of 1923 ed. 39.50 (ISBN 0-8048-0623-3). C E Tuttle.

Wares of the Transitional Period Between the Ming & the Ch'ing 1623-1683. Soame R. Jenyns. 1955. 40.00x (ISBN 0-317-44242-2, Pub. by Han-Shan Tang Ltd). State Mutual Bk.

Warfare. Robert Harrison. LC 73-82852. (Basic Concepts in Anthropology Ser.). pap. 15.00 (ISBN 0-8357-9056-8, 2015880). Bks Demand UMI.

Warfare: A Study of Military Methods from the Earliest Times. Oliver L. Spaulding et al. LC 72-4301. (World Affairs Ser.: National & International Viewpoints). 616p. 1972. Repr. of 1925 ed. 34.00 (ISBN 0-405-04592-1). Ayer Co Pubs.

Warfare along the Mississippi. Ed. by Norman E. Clarke, Sr. (Illus.). 153p. 1961. 7.50 (ISBN 0-915056-19-4, Pub. by Clarke Hist Collect Central MI Univ). Hardscrabble Bks.

Warfare & Welfare: Integrating Security Policy into Socio-Economic Policy. Jan Tinbergen & Dietrich Fischer. LC 87-9625. 203p. 1987. 35.00 (ISBN 0-312-00957-7). St Martin.

Warfare As a Whole. Frank Kitson. 192p. 1987. 14.95 (ISBN 0-571-14693-7). Faber & Faber.

Warfare, Culture, & Environment. R. Brian Ferguson. LC 83-21452. (Studies in Anthropology). 1984. 44.00 (ISBN 0-12-253780-7). Acad Pr.

Warfare, Diplomacy & Politics: Essays in Honour of A. J. P. Taylor. Ed. by Chris Wrigley. 247p. 1987. 35.95 (ISBN 0-241-11789-5, Pub. by Hamish Hamilton England). David & Charles.

Warfare for Wealth: Early Indian Perspective. Ranabir Chakravarti. 1986. 34.00x (ISBN 0-8364-1570-1, Pub. by KL Mukhopadhyay). South Asia Bks.

Warfare in a Fragile World: Military Impact on the Human Environment. Ed. by Taylor & Francis, Ltd. 250p. 1980. 45.00x (ISBN 0-85066-187-0). Taylor & Francis.

Warfare in Ancient Greece. Pierre Ducrey. LC 86-6704. (Illus.). 320p. 1986. 55.00 (ISBN 0-8052-3959-6). Schocken.

Warfare in England. Hilaire Belloc. 254p. 1983. Repr. of 1912 ed. lib. bdg. 35.00 (ISBN 0-89987-094-5). Darby Bks.

Warfare in Feudal Europe, 730-1200. John Beeler. LC 74-148018. (Paperback Ser.). (Illus.). 288p. 1973. pap. 7.95x (ISBN 0-8014-9120-7). Cornell U Pr.

Warfare in the Classical World: An Illustrated Encyclopedia of Weapons, Warriors & Warfare in the Ancient Civilizations of Greece & Rome. John Warry. LC 80-54639. (Illus.). 224p. 1981. 24.95 (ISBN 0-312-85614-8). St Martin.

Warfare in the Sokoto Caliphate: Historical & Sociological Perspectives. Joseph P. Smaldone. LC 75-27795. (African Studies Ser.: No. 19). 240p. pap. 62.40 (2030620). Bks Demand UMI.

Warfare in the Twentieth Century: Theory & Practice. Ed. by Colin J. McInnes & Gary D. Sheffield. 256p. 1988. text ed. 49.95 (ISBN 0-04-355034-7); pap. text ed. 16.95 (ISBN 0-04-355035-5). Unwin Hyman.

Warfare of a Nation. Friedrich Meinecke. 1977. 59.95 (ISBN 0-8490-2807-8). Gordon Pr.

Warfare: The Relation of War to Society. facsimile ed. Ludwig Renn. Tr. by Edward Fitzgerald. LC 79-160989. (Select Bibliographies Reprint Ser). Repr. of 1939 ed. 20.00 (ISBN 0-8369-5857-8). Ayer Co Pubs.

Warfare with Satan. Jessie Penn-Lewis. 1962. pap. 4.50 (ISBN 0-87508-999-2). Chr Lit.

Wargamer. Richard Neebel. 320p. 1987. pap. 3.95 (ISBN 0-8125-1221-9, Dist. by St Martin's Pr & Warner Pub Servs). Tor Bks.

Warhaven. M. Elayn Harvey. 224p. 1987. 15.95 (ISBN 0-531-15068-2). Watts.

Warhawks: American Interventionists Before Pearl Harbor. Mark L. Chadwin. Orig. Title: Hawks of World War Two. 1970. pap. 1.95x (ISBN 0-393-00546-1, Norton Lib). Norton.

Warhol: Conversations about the Artist. Patrick S. Smith. Ed. by Stephen C. Foster. LC 87-28565. (Studies in the Fine Arts: The Avant-Garde: No. 59). 392p. 1987. 44.95 (ISBN 0-8357-1836-0). UMI Res Pr.

Warhorse. Wayne Barton & Stan Williams. 256p. (Orig.). Date not set. pap. 2.75 (ISBN 0-671-65215-X). PB.

Warhunter, No. 3: The Great Salt Lake Massacre. Scott Siegel. 1981. pap. 2.25 (ISBN 0-89083-785-6). Zebra.

Warily We Roll Along. Irene Warsaw. 1979. 5.00 (ISBN 0-8233-0301-2). Golden Quill.

Waring Papers: The Collected Works of Antonio J. Waring. Jr. Ed. by Stephen Williams. LC 67-27476. (Peabody Museum Papers: Vol. 58). 1977. pap. 22.50x (ISBN 0-87365-169-3). Peabody Harvard.

Warkis of the Famous & Worthie Knicht, Schir David Lyndesay. Newly Correctit & Augmentit. Lindsay, David, 1490-1555. LC 75-171797. (English Experience Ser.: No. 352). 362p. 1971. Repr. of 1574 ed. 44.00 (ISBN 90-221-0352-8). Walter J Johnson.

Warleggan. Winston Graham. (Poldark Ser.: No. 4). 1977. pap. 2.25 (ISBN 0-345-27734-1). Ballantine.

Warlock. Oakley Hall. LC 79-25080. viii, 471p. 1980. 32.50x (ISBN 0-8032-2311-0); pap. 8.95 (ISBN 0-8032-7206-5, BB 737, Bison). U of Nebr Pr.

Warlock. Jim Harrison. 1988. pap. 8.95 (ISBN 0-440-55019-X, Delta). Dell.

Warlock. Ernest J. Martin. LC 82-61712. (Illus.). 296p. (Orig.). 1983. pap. 4.95. Mars Pubns.

Warlock at the Wheel & Other Stories. Diana W. Jones. LC 84-18661. 156p. (gr. 7up). 1985. reinforced 10.25 (ISBN 0-688-04305-4). Greenwillow.

Warlock Enraged. Christopher Stasheff. 1987. pap. 3.50 (ISBN 0-441-87334-0, Pub. by Ace Science Fiction). Ace Bks.

Warlock Heretical. Christopher Stasheff. 224p. 1987. pap. 2.95 (ISBN 0-441-87286-7, Pub. by Ace Science Fiction). Ace Bks.

Warlock in Spite of Himself. Christopher Stasheff. Ed. by Lester Del Ray. LC 75-433. (Library of Science Fiction). 1975. lib. bdg. 21.00 (ISBN 0-8240-1436-7). Garland Pub.

Warlock in Spite of Himself. Christopher Stasheff. 1987. pap. 3.95 (ISBN 0-441-87337-5, Pub. by Ace Science Fiction). Ace Bks.

Warlock Is Missing. Christopher Stasheff. 1987. pap. 2.95 (Pub. by Ace Science Fiction). Ace Bks.

Warlock of Firetop Mountain. Steve Jackson & Ian Livingstone. (Fighting Fantasy Gamebooks: No. 1). (YA) (gr. 5 up). 1983. pap. 1.95 (ISBN 0-440-99381-4, LFL). Dell.

Warlock of Rhada. Robert C. Gilman. 176p. 1985. pap. 2.95 (ISBN 0-441-87310-3). Ace Bks.

Warlock Unlocked. Christopher Stasheff. 1987. pap. 3.50 (ISBN 0-441-87332-4, Pub. by Ace Science Fiction). Ace Bks.

Warlock Wandering. Christopher Stasheff. 1987. pap. 3.50 (ISBN 0-441-87362-6, Pub. by Ace Science Fiction). Ace Bks.

Warlock: Western Ser. Oakley Hall. 464p. (Orig.). 1988. pap. 4.50 (ISBN 0-553-27114-8). Bantam.

Warlord. Malcolm Bosse. LC 82-19696. 717p. 1983. 17.95 (ISBN 0-671-44332-1). S&S.

Warlord. Malcolm Bosse. Ed. by Linda Grey. 768p. (Orig.). 1984. pap. 4.95 (ISBN 0-553-26523-7). Bantam.

Warlord. Jason Frost. 1983. pap. 3.50 (ISBN 0-8217-1189-X). Zebra.

Warlord! Janet Morris. 1987. pap. 3.95 (ISBN 0-671-61923-3). PB.

Warlord, No. 3: Badland. Jason Frost. 1984. pap. 2.50 (ISBN 0-8217-1437-6). Zebra.

Warlord, No. 46: Killer's Keep. Jason Frost. 1987. pap. 2.50 (ISBN 0-8217-2214-X). Zebra.

Warlord of Antares. Dray Prescott. (Dray Prescott Ser.: No. 37). 1988. pap. 3.50 (ISBN 0-88677-269-9). DAW Bks.

Warlord of Azatlan. Robert Payne. (Able Team Ser.). 192p. 1983. pap. 2.25 (ISBN 0-373-61206-0, Pub. by Worldwide). Harlequin Bks.

Warlord of Mars. Edgar Rice Burroughs. 1976. Repr. of 1919 ed. lib. bdg. 16.95x (ISBN 0-89966-045-2). Buccaneer Bks.

Warlord of Mars. Edgar Rice Burroughs. pap. 2.25 (ISBN 0-345-32453-6, Del Rey). Ballantine.

Warlord Politics in China, 1916-1928. Hsi-sheng Ch'i. LC 75-7482. xiv, 282p. 1976. 27.50x (ISBN 0-8047-0894-0). Stanford U Pr.

Warlord Soldiers: Chinese Common Soldiers, 1911-1935. Diana Lary. (Contemporary China Institute Publications Ser.). 192p. 1985. 32.50 (ISBN 0-521-30270-6). Cambridge U Pr.

Warlords, 2 bks. David Cook. LC 86-90221. (One-On-One Adventure Gamebook: No. 7). (Orig.). 1986. pap. 5.95 (ISBN 0-88038-304-6). TSR Inc.

Warlords & Muslims in Chinese Central Asia: A Political History of Republican Sinkiang, 1911-1949. Andrew D. W. Forbes. 220p. 1986. 59.50 (ISBN 0-521-25514-7). Cambridge U Pr.

Warlords & Muslims in Chinese Central Asia. Andrew D. Forbes. 392p. 1985. 228.00x (Pub. by Han-Shan Tang Ltd). State Mutual Bk.

Warlords, Artists, & Commoners: Japan in the Sixteenth Century. Ed. by George Elison & Bardwell L. Smith. LC 80-24128. (Illus.). 373p. 1981. 20.00x (ISBN 0-8248-0692-1); pap. text ed. 12.00x (ISBN 0-8248-1109-7). UH Pr.

Warlords of Crime: The New Mafia. Gerald L. Posner. (Illus.). 288p. 1988. 18.95 (ISBN 0-07-050600-0). McGraw.

Warlords of Nin, Bk. II. Stephen R. Lawhead. LC 82-73974. (Dragon King Trilogy Ser.). 488p. 1983. pap. 8.95 (ISBN 0-89107-278-0, Crossway Bks). Good News.

Warlove, the Hipocrite II. Thomas K. Siemer. 276p. 1986. pap. 9.95 (ISBN 0-940157-02-0). Abbeyhills O C.

Warm Air Heating & Air Conditioning System. (Eighty-Ninety Ser). 1973. pap. 6.00 (ISBN 0-685-58162-4, 90B). Natl Fire Prot.

Warm Air Heating for Climate Control. W. Cooper. 1980. 38.00 (ISBN 0-13-944231-6). P-H.

Warm & Cold. David Mamet & Donald Sultan. 32p. 1988. 19.95 (ISBN 0-8021-1084-3). Grove.

"Warm & Zealous Spirit" John J. Zubly & the American Revolution, a Selection of His Writings. Ed. by Randall M. Miller. LC 81-22367. xii, 211p. 1982. 14.95x (ISBN 0-86554-028-4, MUP-H29). Mercer Univ Pr.

Warm-Blooded Animals. Maurice Burton. (World of Science Ser.). (Illus.). 64p. (YA) (gr. 4-7). 1985. 12.95 (ISBN 0-8160-1059-5). Facts on File.

Warm-Blooded Animals. Charles Fishman. (Juniper Bk.: No. 22). 1977. 5.00. Juniper Pr WI.

Warm-Blooded Animals. (Let's Discover Library). (Illus.). 80p. (gr. k-3). 1983. pap. 13.27 (ISBN 0-8172-2080-1). Raintree Pubs.

Warm Bloods, Cold Bloods. Joanne De Longchamps. (Illus.). 44p. (Orig.). 1982. pap. text ed. 10.00 (ISBN 0-915596-25-3). West Coast.

Warm Brown Sand. Michael D. Parker. (Illus.). 200p. (Orig.). pap. 4.95 (ISBN 0-9611048-0-5). Parker Engine Pub.

Warm December. Jaqueline Topaz. Ed. by Joan Marlow. (Second Chance at Love Ser.: No. 435). 192p. (Orig.). 1988. pap. 2.50 (ISBN 0-425-10683-7). Berkley Pub.

Warm Desert Environment. Andrew Goudie & John Wilkinson. LC 76-9731. (Cambridge Topics in Geography Ser.). pap. 24.00 (ISBN 0-317-26407-9, 2024463). Bks Demand UMI.

Warm Flesh, Hot Lead. Robert E. Mills. (Kansan Ser.: No. 5). 176p. 1981. pap. 1.95 (ISBN 0-8439-0978-1, Leisure Bks). Leisure NY.

Warm Fuzzies. Joan E. Pickart. (Loveswept Ser.: No. 259). 192p. 1988. pap. 2.50 (ISBN 0-553-21902-2). Bantam.

Warm Fuzzy Tale. Claude Steiner. LC 77-77981. (Illus., Orig.). (ps). 1977. 5.95 (ISBN 0-915190-08-7). Jalmar Pr.

Warm Hearts & Cold Noses: A Common Sense Guide to Understanding the Family Dog. Ernie Smith. LC 87-10173. (Illus.). 96p. (Orig.). 1987. pap. 10.95 (ISBN 0-86534-109-5). Sunstone Pr.

Warm Hug Book. William Coleman. 128p. (Orig.). (ps). 1985. pap. 4.95 (ISBN 0-87123-794-6, 210794). Bethany Hse.

Warm in Winter, Cold in Summer. Maud Johnson. 270p. (YA) (gr. 7 up). 1978. pap. 2.25 (ISBN 0-590-11913-3). Scholastic Inc.

Warm Nest. (Color-a-Story Bks.). (Illus.). (ps-3). 1985. pap. 0.99 (ISBN 0-89191-997-X, 59972). Cook.

Warm Rooms & Cold. Lars Gustafsson. Tr. by Yvonne Sandstroem from Swedish. (Orig.). 1975. pap. 3.50 (ISBN 0-914278-05-3). Copper Beech.

Warm Rooms & Cold. Lars Gustafsson. Tr. by Yvonne L. Sandstroem from Swedish. 64p. 1975. pap. 3.50 (Pub. by Copper Beech). Small Pr Dist.

Warm Side of the Island. Zoe Dozier. (YA) (gr. 7 up). 1978. 9.95 (ISBN 0-685-53394-8, Avalon). Bouregy.

Warm Smiles, Happy Faces. Charlie Daniel & Becky Daniel. (gr. k-4). 1978. 5.95 (ISBN 0-916456-24-2, GA79). Good Apple.

Warm Snuggles & Cold Ouchies: A Parable for Children Over & Under 21. Jim Ballard. LC 75-25393. (Mandala Ser. in Education). 1975. pap. 4.50 (ISBN 0-916250-05-9). Irvington.

Warm-Soft Village: Chinese Essays on Love. Tr. by Howard S. Levy. (Illus.). 1964. 10.00x (ISBN 0-686-00727-1). Oriental Bk Store.

Warm Tones & Tiny Miracles, Vol. I. Don J. Black. LC 78-186682. 136p. (Orig.). 1972. pap. 4.50 (ISBN 0-8425-1409-0, 8782). Pubs Bk Sales.

Warm-Up Exercises, Bk. I. Rita Kisner & Brooke Knowles. 100p. 1984. spiral-wire 12.00x (ISBN 0-9610370-8-3). Thinking Pubns.

Warm-up Exercises, Bk. II. Rita Kisner & Brooke Knowles. 100p. 1985. wire spiral 12.00x (ISBN 0-9610370-9-1). Thinking Pubns.

Warm up for Little League Baseball. rev. ed. Morris A. Shirts. (Illus.). (gr. 3-5). 1988. pap. 2.50. Archway.

Warm up for Little League Baseball. Morris A. Shirts. (Illus.). 208p. (gr. 3 up). 1984. pap. 2.25 (ISBN 0-671-47198-8). Archway.

Warm-Up to Creativity. Bob Eberle. (Illus.). 64p. (gr. 5-12). 1985. wkbk. 6.95 (ISBN 0-86653-275-7). Good Apple.

Warm Ups for Meeting Leaders. Susan Bianchi & Jan Butler. Ed. by Jean Parcher & Cathy Lewis. LC 84-61535. (Illus.). 138p. (Orig.). 1984. 14.95x (ISBN 0-930733-00-2). Quality Groups Pub.

Warm Weather Dishes. Feingold. 1983. 5.95 (ISBN 0-8120-5531-4). Barron.

Warm Welcomes. Joan Zeigler. (Illus.). 28p. (Orig.). 1986. pap. 4.50 (ISBN 0-933491-12-3). Hot Off Pr.

Warm Winds, Cold Winds: Intellectual Life in China Today. Judith Shapiro & Liang Heng. x, 198p. 1987. 17.95 (ISBN 0-8195-5162-7); pap. 12.95 (ISBN 0-8195-6168-1). Wesleyan U Pr.

Warman's Americana & Collectibles. 3rd ed. Ed. by Harry L. Rinker. LC 84-643834. (Price Key Ser.). (Illus.). 560p. (Orig.). 1988. pap. 13.95 (ISBN 0-911594-12-4). Warman.

Warman's Antique American Games: 1840-1940. Lee Dennis. LC 85-50969. (Warman's Price Key Ser.). (Illus.). 232p. (Orig.). 1985. pap. 14.95 (ISBN 0-911594-08-6). Warman.

Warman's Antiques & Their Prices: The Standard Reference for Antiques & Collectibles. 22nd ed. Ed. by Harry L. Rinker. LC 82-643542. (Illus.). 728p. 1988. pap. 11.95 (ISBN 0-911594-13-2). Warman.

Warman's English & Continental Pottery & Porcelain: An Illustrated Price Guide. Susan Bagdade & Al Bagdade. LC 86-51232. (Price Key Ser.). (Illus.). 480p. (Orig.). 1987. pap. 18.95 (ISBN 0-911594-11-6). Warman.

Warmed by Love. Leonard Nimoy. 150p. 1983. text ed. 14.95 (ISBN 0-88396-200-4). Blue Mtn Pr Co.

Warmed by Memories. Dallas A. Sall. (Illus.). 80p. (Orig.). 1981. pap. 4.95 (ISBN 0-9604344-3-7). Sunrise Pub OR.

Warmed: Over Flavor of Meat. Ed. by Allen J. St. Angelo & Milton E. Bailey. 294p. 1987. 59.00 (ISBN 0-12-661605-1). Acad Pr.

Warmeleitung see Heat Conduction.

Warmer Season. J. Olshan. 288p. 1987. text ed. 15.95 (ISBN 0-07-083641-8). McGraw.

Warmer Season. Joseph Olshan. 1988. pap. 3.95. Ballantine.

Warmest Witches To You. MaryAnn Farmer. (Illus.). 12p. 1982. pap. 4.00 (ISBN 0-943574-18-8). That Patchwork.

Warming Up for the GED. 2nd ed. Ed. by Chuck Herring. 103p. 1980. write for info. (ISBN 0-937128-00-7). GED Inst.

Warmth Dimension. Ronald P. Rohner. LC 85-19623. (New Perspectives on the Family Ser.: Vol. 5). 248p. 1986. text ed. 25.00 (ISBN 0-8039-2353-8). Sage.

Warmth of Life. Carol A. Vercz. Date not set. 3.75 (ISBN 0-910119-15-5). SOCO Pubns.

Warmwater Streams Symposium. Ed. by Louis A. Krumholz. 422p. 1981. pap. 10.00 (ISBN 0-913235-21-0). AM Fisheries Soc.

Warner Bros. Television: Major Shows of the Fifties & Sixties Episode-by-Episode. Lynn M. Woolley et al. LC 84-43217. 304p. 1985. lib. bdg. 25.95x (ISBN 0-89950-144-3). McFarland & Co.

Warner Brother Story: The Complete History of Hollywood's Greatest Studio. Ed. by Clive Hirschorn. (Illus.). 1979. 17.95 (ISBN 0-517-53834-2). Crown.

Warner Brothers. M. Freedland. 1986. 44.75X (ISBN 0-317-56254-5, Pub. by Harrap Ltd England); pap. 29.75X (ISBN 0-245-54316-3). State Mutual Bk.

Warner Brothers Cartoons. Will Friedwald & Jerry Beck. LC 80-27839. 287p. 1981. 17.50 (ISBN 0-8108-1396-3). Scarecrow.

Warner Collector's Guide to American Clocks. Anita Schorsch. (Illus., Orig.). 1981. pap. 9.95 (ISBN 0-446-97633-4). Warner Bks.

Warner Collector's Guide to American Longarms. H. Michael Madaus. (Illus., Orig.). 1981. pap. 9.95 (ISBN 0-446-97628-8). Warner Bks.

Warner Collector's Guide to American Pottery & Porcelain. Bert Denker & Ellen Denker. (Illus.). 256p. (Orig.). 1982. pap. 9.95 (ISBN 0-446-97631-8). Warner Bks.

Warner Collector's Guide to American Quilts. Phyllis Haders. (Illus., Orig.). 1981. pap. 9.95 (ISBN 0-446-97636-9). Warner Bks.

Warner Collector's Guide to American Toys. William Ayres. (Illus., Orig.). 1981. pap. 9.95 (ISBN 0-446-97632-6). Warner Bks.

Warner Collector's Guide to Pressed Glass. Lawrence Grow. (Illus.). 256p. (Orig.). 1982. pap. 9.95 (ISBN 0-446-97709-8). Warner Bks.

Warner Collector's Guide to Sterling Silver & Silverplated Holloware. James H. Burke. (Illus.). 256p. (Orig.). 1982. pap. 9.95 (ISBN 0-446-97634-2). Warner Bks.

Warner: Selected Poems. Sylvia T. Warner. 128p. 1986. 14.95 (ISBN 0-670-80850-4). Viking.

Warning. Harrison Arnston. 384p. 1987. pap. 3.95 (ISBN 0-8217-2231-X). Zebra.

Warning. Dorothy Francis. 192p. (Orig.). (gr. 7-12). 1984. pap. 1.95 (ISBN 0-590-33250-3, Windswept Bks). Scholastic Inc.

Warning. George Hirthler. LC 81-17225. 144p. (Orig.). 1981. pap. 4.95 (ISBN 0-87784-841-6). Inter-Varsity.

Warning: Accident at Three Mile Island. Mike Gray & Ira Rosen. (Illus.). 1982. 14.95 (ISBN 0-393-01522-X). Norton.

Warning & Response to Mount St. Helen Eruption. Thomas F. Saarinen & James L. Sell. LC 84-46. (SUNY Series in Environmental Public Policy). 240p. 1985. 59.50 (ISBN 0-87395-915-9); pap. 19.95 (ISBN 0-87395-916-7). State U NY Pr.

Warning: Anthology of Poetry from Prisoners of Oklahoma. Ed. by Mary McAnally. 1980. pap. 5.00 (ISBN 0-931350-03-4). Moonlight Pubns.

Warning Bell. Lynne R. Banks. 352p. 1987. 17.95 (ISBN 0-312-00017-0). St Martin.

Warning Call. Robert G. Keller. 1981. pap. 1.95 (ISBN 0-8439-0890-4, Leisure Bks). Leisure NY.

Warning! Dating May Be Hazardous to Your Health! Claudette McShane. LC 88-60718. 192p. (Orig.). 1988. pap. 9.95 (ISBN 0-941300-08-0). Mother Courage.

Warning for Fair Women. LC 70-133757. (Tudor Facsimile Texts. Old English Plays Ser.: No. 84). Repr. of 1912 ed. 49.50 (ISBN 0-404-53384-1). AMS Pr.

Warning for Fair Women: A Critical Edition. Charles D. Cannon. LC 73-81080. (Studies in English Literature: No. 86). 241p. 1975. text ed. 27.20 (ISBN 90-2793-134-8). Mouton.

Warning from the West Indies. facsimile ed. William M. Macmillan. LC 73-160982. (Select Bibliographies Reprint Ser). Repr. of 1936 ed. 19.00 (ISBN 0-8369-5850-0). Ayer Co Pubs.

Warning of Danger. Lorena Ann Olmsted. (YA) (gr. 7 up). 1979. 9.95 (ISBN 0-685-93882-4, Avalon). Bouregy.

Warning Out in New England. facs. ed. Josiah H. Benton. LC 70-137370. (Select Bibliographies Reprint Ser). 1911. 13.00 (ISBN 0-8369-5571-4). Ayer Co Pubs.

Warning: Psychotherapists May Be Harmful to Your Mental Health. Judi Striano. LC 87-7364. 43p. (Orig.). 1987. pap. 9.95 (ISBN 0-943659-02-7). Professional SBCA.

Warning: Sex May Be Hazardous to Your Health. Edwin Flatto. 1975. pap. 9.95 (ISBN 0-935540-07-5). Plymouth Pr.

Warning Signs. Andre Bustonoby. 224p. 1988. 12.95 (ISBN 0-8007-1607-8). Revell.

Warning Signs: A Parent's Guide to In-Time Intervention in Drug & Alcohol Abuse. William C. Van Ost & Elaine Van Ost. 128p. (Orig.). Date not set. pap. 7.95 (ISBN 0-446-38727-4). Warner Bks.

Warning: The Coming Great Crash in the Stock Market. Joseph Granville. 402p. 1985. 18.95 (ISBN 0-88191-034-1). Freundlich.

Warning: the Media May be Harmful to Your Health! A Consumers' Guide to Medical News & Advertising. Ralph C. Heussner, Jr. & Marla E. Salmon. 224p. 1988. text ed. 16.95 (ISBN 0-8362-2425-6). Andrews & McMeel.

Warning to Conquerors. Donagh MacDonagh. LC 68-26023. 1968. 12.95 (ISBN 0-8023-1167-9). Dufour.

Warning to the West. Aleksandr I. Solzhenitsyn. 146p. 1976. 7.95 (ISBN 0-374-26758-8); pap. 6.95 (ISBN 0-374-51334-1). FS&G.

Warning Tract: A Guide to Good Writing from Sports Stories. Michael Paul. 54p. 1986. pap. 3.00 (ISBN 0-9616367-0-X). Michael Paul.

Warning: Willy 'N' Ethel. Joe Martin. (Illus.). 114p. 1984. pap. 4.95 (ISBN 0-943084-15-6). Turnbull & Willoughby.

Warning: Writer at Work: The Best Collectibles of Larry L. King. Larry L. King. LC 84-24013. (Illus.). 290p. 1985. 17.95 (ISBN 0-87565-004-X); pap. 10.95 (ISBN 0-87565-016-3). Tex Christian.

Warnings: An Annotated Bibliography with Topical Index, 2 vols, Vol. II. Mark R. Lehto et al. (Warnings Ser.). (Illus.). 288p. 1987. Set. 90.00 (ISBN 0-940537-02-8); Vol. 2. 35.00 (ISBN 0-317-59090-1). Fuller Tech.

Warnings: An Anthology on the Nuclear Peril. Ed. by John Witte. LC 84-14761. (Illus.). 210p. 1984. pap. 8.00 (ISBN 0-918402-08-5). NW Review Bks.

Warnings: Fundamentals, Design & Evaluation Methodologies, Vol. I. Mark R. Lehto & James M. Miller. (Illus.). 287p. 1986. 55.00 (ISBN 0-940537-00-1). Fuller Tech.

Warnock's Eighteen Percent: Children with Special Needs in the Primary School. Caroline Gipps et al. 200p. 1987. 31.00x (ISBN 1-85000-139-1, Falmer Pr); pap. 15.00 (ISBN 1-85000-140-5, Falmer Pr). Taylor & Francis.

Warp: A Weaving Reference. Blair Tate. (Illus.). 133p. (Orig.). 1987. pap. 14.95 (ISBN 0-937274-33-X, Dist. by Sterling Publishing Co.). Lark Bks.

Warp & Weft: A Dictionary of Textile Terms. Dorothy K. Burnham. (Illus.). 240p. 1982. 35.00 (ISBN 0-684-17332-8, ScribT). Scribner.

Warp & Woof of the General Manager's Job. Robert E. Kaplan. (Technical Report Ser.: No. 27). 34p. 1986. pap. 15.00 (ISBN 0-912879-25-4). Ctr Creat Leader.

Warp Weighted Loom. Marta Hoffmann. pap. 16.95 (ISBN 82-00-08094-3). Robin & Russ.

Warpath. Oliver Payne. (Northwest Territory Ser.: No. 1). 432p. (Orig.). 1984. pap. 3.95 (ISBN 0-425-08006-4). Berkley Pub.

Warpath: The True Story of the Fighting Sioux Told in a Biography of Chief White Bull. Stanley Vestal. LC 84-3557. (Illus.). xxxviii, 311p. 1984. 26.95x (ISBN 0-8032-4653-6); pap. 7.95 (ISBN 0-8032-9601-0, BB 854, Bison). U of Nebr Pr.

Warped Vision: British Foreign Policy, 1933-1939. Margaret George. LC 83-18493. xxiii, 238p. 1983. Repr. of 1965 ed. lib. bdg. 38.50x (ISBN 0-313-24257-7, GEWV). Greenwood.

Warping All by Yourself. Cay Garrett. 192p. 1974. 6.00 (ISBN 0-930670-01-9). Interweave.

Warping Calculations. Ed. by Wira Staff. 30.00x (ISBN 0-317-43588-4, Pub. by Wira Tech Group). State Mutual Bk.

Warping Equipment: Its Choice & Design, with Descriptions of Certain Machines. Ed. by Wira Staff. 30.00x (ISBN 0-317-43591-4, Pub. by Wira Tech Group). State Mutual Bk.

Warplanes of the Third Reich. William Green. LC 86-80568. (Illus.). 1970. 37.50 (ISBN 0-88365-666-3). Kraus Repr.

Warrant for Genocide. Norman Cohn. LC 80-21733. 1981. pap. 18.75 (ISBN 0-89130-423-1, 14 00 23). Scholars Pr GA.

Warrant for X. Philip MacDonald. LC 83-5732. 288p. 1983. pap. 3.95 (ISBN 0-394-71660-4, Vin). Random.

Warranties in the Sale of Business Equipment & Consumer Products 1985: Vol. 346. 382p. 1985. pap. 15.00 (ISBN 0-317-27436-8, #A4-4113). PLI.

Warranties in Weapon System Procurement: An Analysis of Practice & Theory. Robert E. Kuenne et al. (Westview Special Studies in National Security & Defense Policy). 200p. 1988. 35.00 (ISBN 0-8133-7592-4). Westview.

Warrants: Analysis & Investment Strategy. Donald T. Mesler. 250p. 1985. 35.00 (ISBN 0-917253-25-6). Probus Pub Co.

Warrants for Highway Lighting. (National Cooperative Highway Research Project Report). 117p. 1974. 6.40 (ISBN 0-309-02303-3). Transport Res Bd.

Warrants for Lands in South Carolina, 1672-1711. Ed. by A. S. Salley & R. Nicholas Olsberg. LC 73-9542. 724p. 1973. 34.95x (ISBN 0-87249-938-3). U of SC Pr.

Warren-Adams Letters, Being Chiefly a Correspondence among John Adams, Samuel Adams, & James Warren, 2 Vols. John Adams et al. LC 79-158225. 1917-25. Repr. of 1925 ed. Set. 85.00 (ISBN 0-404-06854-5). Vol. 1 (ISBN 0-404-06855-3). Vol. 2 (ISBN 0-404-06856-1). AMS Pr.

Warren Akin Candler: The Conservative As Idealist. Mark K. Bauman. LC 80-22230. 290p. 1981. 20.00 (ISBN 0-8108-1368-8). Scarecrow.

Warren-Ballard Debate. Thomas B. Warren & L. S. Ballard. 1979. pap. 9.00 (ISBN 0-934916-39-X). Natl Christian Pr.

Warren-Barnhart Debate on Ethics. Thomas B. Warren & Joe Barnhart. 1981. pap. 13.00 (ISBN 0-934916-47-0). Natl Christian Pr.

Warren Beatty & Desert Eyes: A Life & a Story. David Thomson. LC 86-19707. (Illus.). 408p. 1987. 17.95 (ISBN 0-385-18707-6). Doubleday.

Warren Beatty & Desert Eyes: A Life & a Story. David Thomson. Ed. by Rebecca Saletan. LC 87-45934. 480p. 1988. pap. 7.95 (ISBN 0-394-75756-4, Vin). Random.

Warren Brandt. Nicholas F. Weber. LC 87-32372. (Illus.). 120p. 1988. 50.00 (ISBN 0-933920-98-9, Dist. by Rizzoli). Hudson Hills.

Warren County, Kentucky, 1810-1840 Censuses. Rowena Lawson. iv, 97p. (Orig.). 1986. pap. 10.00 (ISBN 1-55613-026-0). Heritage Bk.

Warren County Marriages, Eighteen Thirty-Six to Eighteen Fifty. John Vogt & T. William Kethley, Jr. (Virginia Historic Marriage Register Ser.). (Illus.). viii, 48p. (Orig.). 1983. pap. 3.50 (ISBN 0-935931-20-1). Iberian Pub.

Warren County Marriages, Eighteen Thirty-Six to Eighteen Fifty. John Vogt & T. William Kethley, Jr. (Virginia Historic Marriage Register Ser.). 48p. 1988. Repr. lib. bdg. 15.95x (ISBN 0-8095-8234-1). Borgo Pr.

Warren County North Carolina Census 1790. Courtney York & Gerlene York. (Orig.). 1972. pap. 12.00x (ISBN 0-916660-09-5). Hse of York.

Warren County North Carolina Census 1810. Courtney York & Gerlene York. (Orig.). 1970. pap. 12.00x (ISBN 0-916660-14-1). Hse of York.

Warren County, North Carolina, Records: Abstracted Records of Colonial Bute County, North Carolina, 1764-1779, & Bute County Marriages, Vol. I. Mary H Kerr. LC 82-20498. 104p. 1983. Repr. of 1967 ed. 27.50 (ISBN 0-87152-366-3). Reprint.

Warren County, Ohio, Apprenticeship & Indenture Records, 1824-1832, 1864-1867. W. Louis Phillips. vi, 51p. (Orig.). 1987. pap. 6.00 (ISBN 1-55613-039-2). Heritage Bk.

Warren Court: A Critical Analysis. Ed. by Richard H. Sayler et al. LC 73-85196. 270p. 1980. pap. 7.95 (ISBN 0-87754-136-1). Chelsea Hse.

Warren Court & Its Critics. Clifford M. Lytle. LC 66-28788. pap. 37.30 (ISBN 0-317-28216-6, 2022756). Bks Demand UMI.

Warren Court & the Constitution: A Critical View of Judicial Activism. John D. Carter. LC 73-7828. 176p. 1972. 10.00 (ISBN 0-911116-98-2). Pelican.

Warren Court: Constitutional Decision As an Instrument of Reform. Archibald Cox. LC 68-21971. 1968. pap. 5.95x (ISBN 0-674-94742-8). Harvard U Pr.

Warren Court, 1953-1969. Arnold S. Rice. LC 86-7973. (Supreme Court in American Life Ser.: Vol. 8). 1987. 35.00x (ISBN 0-86733-063-5). Assoc Faculty Pr.

Warren Court's Conceptions of Democracy: An Evaluation of the Supreme Court's Apportionment Opinions. Howard Ball. LC 70-149826. 256p. 1971. 24.50 (ISBN 0-8386-7913-7). Fairleigh Dickinson.

Warren Family. G. T. Ridlon. LC 70-146528. (Saco Valley Settlements Ser). 1970. pap. 3.50 (ISBN 0-8048-0853-8). C E Tuttle.

Warren Family: One Thousand Years of History. 1982. 75.00x (ISBN 0-946095-00-0, Pub. by Gresham Bks); pap. 50.00 (ISBN 0-946095-01-9, Pub. by Gresham England). State Mutual Bk.

Warren-Flew Debate on the Existence of God. Ed. by Thomas B. Warren & A. G. N. Flew. 1977. pap. 14.00 (ISBN 0-934916-40-3). Natl Christian Pr.

Warren G. Harding. Ed. by Carol B. Fitzgerald. (Meckler's Bibliographies of the Presidents of the United States, 1789-1989 Ser.: No. 28). (Illus.). 1988. lib. bdg. 45.00x (ISBN 0-88736-142-0). Meckler Corp.

Warren G. Harding Papers: An Inventory to the Microfilm Edition. Andrea D. Lentz. 283p. 1970. 4.00 (ISBN 0-318-03212-0). Ohio Hist Soc.

Warren G. Harding, 1865-1923: Chronology, Documents, Bibliographical Aids. Ed. by P. Moran. LC 78-95013. (Presidential Chronology Ser). 120p. 1970. 8.00 (ISBN 0-379-12064-X). Oceana.

Warren Harding: President Betrayed by Friends. Gerald Kurland. Ed. by D. Steve Rahmas. LC 72-185662. (Outstanding Personalities Ser.: No. 6). 32p. (Orig.). (YA) (gr. 7-12). 1972. lib. bdg. 3.75 incl. catalog cards (ISBN 0-87157-506-X); pap. 2.50 vinyl laminated covers (ISBN 0-87157-006-8). SamHar Pr.

Warren Hastings. facsimile ed. Alfred Lyall. LC 73-140364. (Select Bibliographies Reprint Ser). Repr. of 1889 ed. 18.00 (ISBN 0-8369-5607-9). Ayer Co Pubs.

Warren Hastings: Volume Six of Rulers of India. L. J. Trotter. Ed. by William W. Hunter. LC 70-39407. (Select Bibliographies Reprint Ser.). 1972. Repr. of 1890 ed. 17.00 (ISBN 0-8369-9922-3). Ayer Co Pubs.

Warren-Matson Debate on the Existence of God. Thomas B. Warren & Wallace I. Matson. LC 78-64546. 1979. 14.00; pap. 11.00 (ISBN 0-934916-45-4). Natl Christian Pr.

Warren R. Austin at the U. N. 1946-1953. George T. Mazuzan. LC 76-52990. 233p. 1977. 15.00x (ISBN 0-87338-202-1). Kent St U Pr.

Warren's Forms of Agreements, 4 vols. Oscar Leroy Warren & Gloria C. Markuson. 1954. Set, updates avail. looseleaf 360.00 (770); Updates 1985. 309.50; Supplement 1986. 298.00. Bender.

Warren's Forms of Agreements - Business Forms: Desk Edition. Amelia C. Greenhill. 1975. looseleaf 95.00 (771); Updates 1985. 81.00; Supplement 1986. 89.00. Bender.

Warren's Health on Surrogates' Court Practice, 20 vols. 6th ed. Ed. by Willis Edgar Heaton et al. LC 40-3521. 1940. Set. 870.00 (ISBN 0-317-67441-2). Bender.

Warren's Heaton on Surrogates' Court Practice, 20 vols. 6th ed. Oscar L. Warren & Gloria C. Markuson. 1940. Set. looseleaf 830.00 (780); Updates 1985. 512.50; Supplement 1986. 546.50. Bender.

Warren's Heaton SCPA, EPTL: Greenbook. 1967. Annual replacement volume. pap. 25.50 (781). Bender.

Warren's Minstrel. J. S. Warren, Jr. Ed. by John L. Brasher. LC 82-2382. xxxvii, 161p. 1984. Repr. of 1857 ed. text ed. 29.95x (ISBN 0-8214-0681-7). Ohio U Pr.

Warren's Movie Poster Price Guide. Jon R. Warren. 1986. pap. 12.95 (ISBN 0-517-56167-0, Harmony). Crown.

Warren's Negligence in the New York Courts, 22 vols. 3rd ed. Oscar L. Warren et al. LC 67-9319. 1985 470.00; 1985 334.50; 1986 335.00. Bender.

Warren's Negligence in the New York Courts, 22 vols. 3rd ed. Oscar L. Warren et al. 1966. 470.00 set (790); Updates avail. 1985 334.50; 1984 75.00. Bender.

Warren's Operation. G. P. Marzoli & S. Versontini. (Illus.). 90p. 1982. 43.00 (ISBN 0-387-10785-1). Springer-Verlag.

Warren's Weed New York Real Property, 14 vols. 4th ed. Oscar L. Warren & Gloria C. Markuson. 1950. looseleaf set 750.00 (800); Updates. 1985 467.50; 1986 467.50. Bender.

Warrick. Marilyn Harris. 1987. pap. 4.95 (ISBN 0-345-32923-6). Ballantine.

Warrick County. Peyton Autry. (Illus.). 144p. 1986. 21.95 (ISBN 0-9617663-1-X); pap. 14.95 (ISBN 0-9617663-0-1). McDowell Pubns.

Warship, Vol. VII. Ed. by John Roberts. LC 78-55455. (Illus.). 292p. 1984. 24.95 (ISBN 0-87021-982-0). Naval Inst Pr.
Warship, Vol. II. (Illus.). 287p. 1980. 24.95 (ISBN 0-87021-976-6). Naval Inst Pr.
Warship, Vol. VIII. (Illus.). 288p. 1985. 24.95 (ISBN 0-87021-983-9). Naval Inst Pr.
Warshipbuilding on the Clyde: Naval Orders & the Prosperity of the Clyde Shipbuilding Industry 1889-1939. Hugh B. Peebles. 208p. 1987. text ed. 45.00 (ISBN 0-85976-193-2, Pub. by John Donald UK). Humanities.
Warships. C. J. Norman. LC 85-51458. (Picture Library). 32p. (gr. 1-6). 1986. PLB 10.90 (ISBN 0-531-10093-6). Watts.
Warships & Their Story. R. A. Fletcher. 1977. lib. bdg. 69.95 (ISBN 0-8490-2808-6). Gordon Pr.
Warships Associated with World War 2 in the Pacific. Harry A. Butowsky. (National Historic Landmark Theme Study). (Illus.). 756p. (Orig.). 1985. pap. 22.00 (ISBN 0-318-18869-4, S/N 024-005-00961-2). USGPO.
Warship's Battle Damage 1: USS Hornet CV-8. Ed. by Robert Sumrall. LC 85-63164. (Illus.). 32p. 1985. pap. text ed. 5.95 (ISBN 0-933126-65-4). Pictorial Hist.
Warship's Data No. 2: USS Missouri (BB-63) Ed. by Robert Sumrall. (Illus.). 42p. (Orig.). 1986. pap. 7.95 (ISBN 0-933126-67-0). Pictorial Hist.
Warship's Data: U. S. S. Iowa, No. 3. Robert F. Sumrall. LC 86-61291. (Illus.). 54p. 1987. pap. text ed. 7.95 (ISBN 0-933126-77-8). Pictorial Hist.
Warships of the Imperial Japanese Navy, 1869-1945. Hansgeorg Jentschura & Dieter Jung. Tr. by David Brown & Antony Preston. LC 75-43861. (Illus.). 220p. 1976. 29.95 (ISBN 0-87021-893-X); bulk rates avail. Naval Inst Pr.
Warships of the Royal Navy. John E. Moore. (Illus.). 136p. 1979. 12.95 (ISBN 0-87021-978-2); bulk rates avail. Naval Inst Pr.
Warships of the World: An Illustrated Encyclopedia. Gino Galluppini. (Illus.). 320p. 1986. 69.45 (ISBN 0-8129-1129-6). Times Bks.
Warships of the World: Escort Vessels. Bernard Ireland. (Illus.). 1979. encore ed. 4.95 (ISBN 0-684-17235-6, ScribT). Scribner.
Wart, Son of Toad. Alden R. Carter. 208p. (gr. 7 up). 1985. 12.95 (ISBN 0-448-47770-X, Putnam). Putnam Pub Group.
Wart, Son of Toad. Alden R. Carter. 100p. 1987. pap. 2.50 (ISBN 0-425-08885-5, Pub. by Berkley-Pacer). Berkley Pub.
Wart Toad. Don Bush. LC 82-60482. (Illus.). 40p. 1982. 4.50x (ISBN 0-943978-00-9). Rolling Hills Pr.
Wartburg Und Ihre Sammlungen. Werner Noth. 212p. (Ger.). 1972. 38.00x (ISBN 0-317-57372-1, Pub. by Collets UK). State Mutual Bk.
Wartime. Milovan Djilas. LC 80-16174. 496p. 1980. pap. 7.95 (ISBN 0-15-694712-9, Harv). HarBraceJ.
Wartime Agriculture in Australia & New Zealand, 1939-50. John G. Crawford et al. (Illus.). 1954. 35.00x (ISBN 0-8047-0455-4). Stanford U Pr.
Wartime Children, Nineteen Thirty-Nine to Nineteen Forty-Five. Eleanor Allen. (Junior Reference Ser.). (Illus.). 64p. (gr. 6 up). 1978. 13.95 (ISBN 0-7136-1503-6). Dufour.
Wartime Correspondence: Between President Roosevelt & Pope Pius 12th. Ed. by Myron Taylor. (FDR & the Era of the New Deal Ser). 1975. Repr. of 1947 ed. lib. bdg. 22.50 (ISBN 0-306-70709-8). Da Capo.
Wartime Economic Planning in Agriculture. Bela Gold. LC 68-58580. (Columbia University. Studies in the Social Sciences: No. 551). Repr. of 1949 ed. 34.50 (ISBN 0-404-51551-7). AMS Pr.
Wartime Exile, the Exclusion of the Japanese Americans from the West Coast see U. S. War Relocation Authority.
Wartime Farm & Food Policy. Iowa State College, Economics & Sociology Department Staff. LC 75-26304. (World Food Supply Ser). (Illus.). 1976. Repr. of 1943 ed. 41.00x (ISBN 0-405-07783-1). Ayer Co Pubs.
Wartime Handling of Evacuee Property see U. S. War Relocation Authority.
Wartime Journalism, Nineteen Forty to Nineteen Forty-Two. Paul de Man. Ed. by Werner Hamacher et al. 308p. 1988. 35.00x (ISBN 0-8032-1684-X); pap. 15.95x (ISBN 0-8032-6576-X). U of Nebr Pr.
Wartime Journals of Charles A. Lindbergh. Charles A. Lindbergh. LC 78-124830. 1038p. 1970. 19.95 (ISBN 0-15-194625-6). HarBraceJ.
Wartime Labour Conditions & Reconstruction Planning in India see War & Women's Employment: The Experience of the U. K. & the U. S. A. 1946.
Wartime Letters of Rainer Maria Rilke, 1914-1921. Rainer M. Rilke. Tr. by M. D. H. Norton. 1964. pap. 6.45 (ISBN 0-393-00160-1, Norton Lib). Norton.
Wartime Mission in Spain. Carlton Hayes. LC 76-18191. (Politics & Strategy of World War II Ser.). 1976. Repr. of 1945 ed. lib. bdg. 37.50 (ISBN 0-306-70771-3). Da Capo.
Wartime Origins of the Berlin Dilemma. Daniel J. Nelson. 256p. 1978. 19.95 (ISBN 0-8173-4727-5). U of Ala Pr.
Wartime Papers of Robert E. Lee. Ed. by Clifford Dowdey & Louis H. Manarin. (Quality Paperbacks Ser.). (Illus.). xiv, 994p. 1987. pap. 16.95 (ISBN 0-306-80282-1). Da Capo.
Wartime Production Controls. David Novick et al. LC 76-5795. (FDR & the Era of the New Deal Ser). 1976. Repr. of 1949 ed. lib. bdg. 49.50 (ISBN 0-306-70818-3). Da Capo.
Wartime Relations of the Federal Government & the Public Schools, 1917-1918. Lewis P. Todd. LC 76-165743. (American Education, Ser. 2). 1971. Repr. of 1945 ed. 20.00 (ISBN 0-405-03614-0). Ayer Co Pubs.
Wartime Shipyard: A Study in Social Disunity. Katherine Archibald. LC 76-7621. (FDR & the Era of the New Deal Ser.). 1976. Repr. of 1947 ed. 27.50 (ISBN 0-306-70802-7). Da Capo.
Wartime Shipyard: Study in Social Disunity. Katherine Archibald. Ed. by Leon Stein. LC 77-70478. (Work Ser.). (Illus.). 1977. Repr. of 1947 ed. lib. bdg. 23.50x (ISBN 0-405-10152-X). Ayer Co Pubs.
Wartime Strikes. Martin Glaberman. (Illus., Orig.). 1980. pap. 6.00 (ISBN 0-935590-11-0). Bewick Edns.
Wartime Technological Developments, 2 vols. in one. United States Bureau of Labor Statistics, U. S. Congress, Senate Committee on Military Affairs, Subcommittee on War Moblization. LC 78-22407. (American Military Experience Ser.). 1979. Repr. of 1945 ed. lib. bdg. 42.00x (ISBN 0-405-11882-1). Ayer Co Pubs.
Wartime Washington: The Secret OSS Journal of James Grafton Rogers. Ed. by Thomas F. Troy. LC 86-28184. (Foreign Intelligence Book Ser.). 400p. 1987. 25.00 (ISBN 0-89093-491-6). U Pubns Amer.
Wartime Women: Sex Roles, Family Relations & the Status of Women During World War II. Karen Anderson. LC 80-1703. (Contributions in Women's Studies: No. 20). 198p. 1982. pap. text ed. 12.95 (ISBN 0-313-23607-0, AWWPB). Greenwood.
Wartime Writings Nineteen Thirty-Nine to Nineteen Forty-Four. Antoine de Saint-Exupery. LC 85-30566. 1986. 12.95 (ISBN 0-15-194680-9). HarBraceJ.
Warton & the Contest. Russell E. Erickson. LC 86-102. (Illus.). 96p. (ps-4). 1986. 10.25 (ISBN 0-688-05818-3); PLB 10.88 (ISBN 0-688-05819-1). Lothrop.
Warton on Pope see Popeiana.
Warton's History of English Poetry. David N. Smith. Repr. of 1929 ed. lib. bdg. 17.00 (ISBN 0-8414-1582-X). Folcroft.
Wartville Wizard. Don Madden. LC 85-23159. (Illus.). 32p. (gr. k up). 1986. 12.95 (ISBN 0-02-762100-6). Macmillan.
Warum Gibt Es in Den Vereinigten Staaten Keinen Sozialismus see Why Is There No Socialism in the United States.
Warum Ich Sagen Kann: Ich Bin Gott. Herbert L. Beierle. 1981. 1.00 (ISBN 0-940480-15-8). U of Healing.
Warwick Atlas of World History. Jane Olliver. Ed. by JV-Warwick Press Staff. (Illus.). 96p. (gr. 4-9). 1988. 15.50 (ISBN 0-531-19037-4, Warwick). Watts.
Warwick Mountain Series. Photos by Philip Perkis. LC 78-61647. (Illus.). 1978. 24.00x (ISBN 0-932526-01-2). Nexus Pr.
Warwick the Kingmaker. Paul M. Kendall. (Illus.). 416p. 1987. pap. 9.95 (ISBN 0-393-30380-2). Norton.
Warwick the Kingmaker. facsimile ed. Charles W. Oman. LC 79-137383. (Select Bibliographies Reprint Ser). Repr. of 1891 ed. 16.00 (ISBN 0-8369-5584-6). Ayer Co Pubs.
Warwickshire Grazier & London Skinner, 1532 to 1555: The Account Book of Peter Temple & Thomas Heritage. Ed. by N. W. Alcock. (Records of Social & Economic History Ser.). (Illus.). 1981. 98.00x (ISBN 0-19-726008-X). Oxford U Pr.
Warwickshire Word-Book Comprising Obsolescent & Dialect Words, Colloquialisms, Etc. G. T. Northall. (English Dialect Society Publications Ser.: No. 79). pap. 31.00 (ISBN 0-8115-0497-2). Kraus Repr.
Warwords: U. S. Militarism the Catholic Right & the Bulgarian Connection. David Eisenhower & John Murray. Ed. by Betty Smith. LC 86-21016. 138p. 1987. pap. 3.95 (ISBN 0-7178-0650-2). Intl Pubs Co.
Warworld, Vol. 1: The Burning Eye. Ed. by Jerry Pournelle. (Warworld Ser.). 384p. (Orig.). 1988. pap. text ed. 3.95 (ISBN 0-671-65420-9). Baen Bks.
Wary Fugitives: Four Poets & the South. Louis D. Rubin, Jr. LC 77-25479. (Walter Lynwood Fleming Lectures Ser.). 408p. 1978. 37.50 (ISBN 0-8071-0360-8); pap. 10.95 (ISBN 0-8071-0454-X). La State U Pr.
Wary Spinster. April Kihlstrom. 224p. 1988. pap. 2.75 (ISBN 0-451-15190-9, Sig). NAL.
Wary Widow. Sheila Walsh. 1985. pap. 2.50 (ISBN 0-451-13805-8, Sig). NAL.
Was Christ God? Spiros Zodhiates. 1966. 7.95 (ISBN 0-89957-504-8). AMG Pubs.
Was Christopher Columbus a Jew? Walter F. McEntire. 1976. lib. bdg. 59.95 (ISBN 0-8490-1278-3). Gordon Pr.
Was Einstein Right? Putting General Relativity to the Test. Clifford Will. LC 85-73877. (Illus.). 304p. 1988. pap. 8.95 (ISBN 0-465-09087-7, PL 5218). Basic.
Was Einstein Right? Putting General Relativity to the Test. Clifford M. Will. LC 85-73877. (Illus.). 272p. 1986. 18.95 (ISBN 0-465-09088-5). Basic.
Was It Good for You, Too? Jack Wohl. 1988. pap. 4.95 (ISBN 0-317-67078-6). Price Stern.
Was It Good for You, Too? Quotations on Love & Sex. Bob Chieger. LC 83-45061. 256p. 1983. pap. 8.95 (ISBN 0-689-70650-2). Atheneum.
Was It Murder? James Hilton. LC 78-74115. 1979. pap. 4.95 (ISBN 0-486-23774-5). Dover.
Was It Murder (Centralia Massacre) William C. Smith. 48p. pap. 3.95 (ISBN 0-8466-0127-3, S127). Shorey.
Was It Something I Said? Jean Thesman. 160p. 1988. pap. 2.50 (ISBN 0-380-75462-2, Flare). Avon.
Was Jesus Christ a Negro? The African Origin of the Myths & Legends of the Garden of Eden. John G. Jackson. LC 87-80245. 50p. 1987. pap. 3.95 (ISBN 0-938818-11-2). ECA Assoc.
Was Jesus Crucified? A. Deedat. pap. 1.50 (ISBN 0-686-63916-2). Kazi Pubns.
Was Jesus Married? The Distortion of Sexuality in the Christian Tradition. William E. Phipps. LC 85-32319. 250p. 1986. pap. text ed. 12.50 (ISBN 0-8191-5191-2). U Pr of Amer.
Was Lady Godiva Involved in a Cover-Up: And Other Logic Puzzles. Roger Hufford. 176p. 1988. pap. 7.95. Prentice Hall Pr.
Was Mary Also Redeemed. Ignatius Haryono. 32p. 1989. 6.95 (ISBN 0-89962-768-4). Todd & Honeywell.
Was Poet William Shakespeare a Cuckoo Imposter, 2 vols. Horace Deluscar. (Vol. 1 61pp; Vol. 2 57pp.). 1981. Repr. of 1913 ed. Set. lib. bdg. 100.00 (ISBN 0-89987-160-7). Darby Bks.
Was Pythagoras Chinese? Frank J. Swetz & T. I. Kao. LC 76-41806. (Illus.). 75p. 1977. pap. 7.00. NCTM.
Was Pythagoras Chinese? An Examination of Right Triangle Theory in Ancient China. Frank Swetz & T. I. Kao. LC 76-41806. (Penn State Studies: No. 40). (Illus.). 1977. pap. 5.95x (ISBN 0-271-01238-2). Pa St U Pr.
Was Roosevelt Pushed into War? Harry E. Barnes. 59.95 (ISBN 0-87700-285-1). Revisionist Pr.
Was Shakespeare Shakespeare? A Lawyer Reviews the Evidence. Milward W. Martin. LC 65-16143. 1965. 20.00x (ISBN 0-8154-0147-7). Cooper Sq.
Was That a Real Poem & Other Essays. Robert Creeley. Ed. by Donald Allen. LC 78-16254. (Writing: 39). 150p. 1979. pap. 5.00 (ISBN 0-87704-042-7). Four Seasons Foun.
Was the Vietnam War Legal? Steven Cohen & Millard Clements. Ed. by Jerold M. Starr. (Lessons of the Vietnam War Ser.). (Illus.). 32p. 1988. pap. text ed. 3.00 (ISBN 0-945919-03-4). Ctr Social Studies.
Was There a Fifth Man? Quintessential Recollections. Wilfrid B. Mann. (Illus.). 128p. 1981. 23.00 (ISBN 0-08-027445-5). Pergamon.
Was There Vitamin B-12 in the Wedding Cake? Jim Weekly. 1987. pap. 4.95 (ISBN 0-937172-65-0). JLJ Pubs.
Was Thomas Lodge an Actor? An Exposition Touching the Social Status of the Playwright in the Time of Queen Elizabeth. C. M. Ingleby. Repr. of 1868 ed. lib. bdg. 15.00 (ISBN 0-8414-5077-3). Folcroft.
Wasafiri-ATCAL Journal, Vol. 1, No. 1. Ed. by Susheila Nasta. 32p. 1984. pap. 7.50 (ISBN 0-317-38703-0, Pub. by Assoc Carib Stud). Three Continents.
Wasatch Hiking Map: Provo Area. Thomas Patterson. (Illus.). 1984. pap. 4.95 (ISBN 0-87480-241-5). U of Utah Pr.
Wasatch Hiking Map: Salt Lake City Area. Thomas Patterson. 1983. pap. 4.95 (ISBN 0-87480-220-2). U of Utah Pr.
Wasatch Quartzite. John W. Gottman. (Illus.). 1979. pap. 3.00 (ISBN 0-915272-23-7). Wasatch Pubs.
Wasatch Savage. Lee Nelson. 135p. pap. 6.95 (ISBN 0-936860-20-0). Liberty Pr.
Wasatch Tours. Alexis Kelner & David Hanscom. LC 76-28112. 1976. pap. 6.50 (ISBN 0-915272-06-7). Wasatch Pubs.
Wasatch Trails. Betty Bottcher & Mel Davis. (Illus.). 77p. 1973. pap. 2.00 (ISBN 0-915272-00-8). Wasatch Pubs.
Wasatch Trails, Vol. 2. Daniel Geery. (Illus., Orig.). 1977. pap. 2.50 (ISBN 0-915272-10-5). Wasatch Pubs.
WASCO. Martel Scroggin. LC 87-71308. 264p. 1987. pap. 8.95 (ISBN 0-8323-0457-3). Binford-Metropolitan.
Wash & Be Healed: The Wate-Cure Movement & Women's Health. Susan E. Cayleff. LC 86-23027. (Health, Society, & Policy Ser.). (Illus.). 1987. 29.95 (ISBN 0-87722-462-5). Temple U Pr.
Wash & Brush up. Eleanor Allen. (Junior Reference Ser.). (Illus.). 64p. (gr. 7 up). 1977. 13.95 (ISBN 0-7136-1639-3). Dufour.
Wash & Gouache: A Study of the Development of the Materials of Watercolor. Marjorie B. Cohn. LC 77-176. 120p. 1980. pap. 7.50 (ISBN 0-916724-06-9). Harvard Art Mus.
Wash Me on Home Mama. Peter Najarian. 86p. (Orig.). 1978. pap. 3.00 (ISBN 0-917658-10-8). BPW & P.
Wash Tubbs, Vol. 1. Roy Crane. Ed. by Bill Blackbeard. LC 87-62174. 192p. 1987. 32.50x (ISBN 0-918348-43-9, Pub. by Flying Buttress Classics); pap. 16.95x (ISBN 0-918348-44-7, Pub. by Flying Buttress Classics). NBM.
Wash Tubbs, Vol. 2. Roy Crane. Ed. by Bill Blackbeard. LC 87-62174. 192p. 1988. 32.50x (ISBN 0-918348-45-5, Pub. by Flying Buttress Classics); pap. 16.95x (ISBN 0-918348-46-3, Pub. by Flying Buttress Classics). NBM.
Wash Tubbs, Vol. 3. Roy Crane & Bill Blackbeard. LC 87-62174. (Illus.). 192p. 1988. 32.50x (ISBN 0-918348-52-8, Pub by Flying Buttress Classics); pap. 16.95x (ISBN 0-918348-51-X, Pub. by Flying Buttress Classics). NBM.
Wash Tubbs, Vol. 4. Roy Crane. Ed. by Bill Blackbeard. LC 87-62174. 192p. 1988. 32.50x (ISBN 0-918348-54-4, Pub. by Flying Buttress Classics); pap. 16.95x (ISBN 0-918348-53-6, Pub. by Flying Buttress Classics). NBM.
Washaki: An Account of Indian Resistance of the Covered Wagon & Union Pacific Railroad Invasion of Their Territory. Grace R. Hebard. LC 76-43733. Repr. of 1930 ed. 29.00 (ISBN 0-404-15575-8). AMS Pr.
Washburn, a Town History: Settlers of Salmon Brook, Maine. Ray H. Carter. (Illus.). 192p. 1987. 25.00 (ISBN 0-933858-18-3); pap. 17.50 (ISBN 0-933858-10-8). Kennebec River.
Washburn College Bible. Ed. by Bradbury Thompson. 1980. 75.00 (ISBN 0-19-502786-8). Oxford U Pr.
Washburn Reader. Ed. by Robert Stein. (Illus.). 238p. 1984. pap. 6.95 (ISBN 0-939391-02-3). B Woodley Pr.
Washburne Trade School: Its Future in the Chicago Metropolitan Labor Market. Edward A. Marciniak. LC 86-72488. (Urban Insights Ser.: No. 16). (Illus.). 74p. (Orig.). 1987. pap. 5.00 (ISBN 0-911531-18-1). Loyola U ctr Urban.
Washburne's Tables 1986. Randel Washburne. 16p. (Orig.). 1985. pap. 4.95 (ISBN 0-935727-01-9). Weatherly Pr.
Washburn's Yellowstone Expedition, Parts 1 & 2: Extracts. facs. ed. 18p. pap. 2.95 (ISBN 0-8466-2041-3, S41). Shorey.
Washi: The World of Japanese Paper. Sukey Hughes. LC 75-55094. (Illus.). 1981. deluxe ed. 300.00 (ISBN 0-317-39993-4). Kodansha.
Washi: The World of Japanese Paper. Sukey Hughes. 452p. 1978. deluxe ed. 1500.00x (Pub. by Han-Shan Tang Ltd). State Mutual Bk.
Washing & Dressing Prayers with Jesus. Shirley Lamb. 1983. pap. 1.50 (ISBN 0-910709-41-6). PTL Repro.
Washing Away of Wrongs: Forensic Medicine in Thirteenth-Century China. Sung Tz'u. Tr. by Brian E. McKnight from Chinese. LC 81-6195. (Science, Medicine, & Technology in East Asia Ser.: No. 1). (Illus.). 200p. (Orig.). 10.00 (ISBN 0-89264-801-5); pap. 7.00 (ISBN 0-89264-800-7). U of Mich Ctr Chinese.
Washing of Pulp. (Bibliographic Ser.: No. 250). 115p. 1972. 14.00 (ISBN 0-317-34465-X). Inst Paper Chem.
Washing of the Spears: The Rise & Fall of the Zulu Nation. Donald R. Morris. 688p. 1986. 25.00 (ISBN 0-671-63108-X, Touchstone Bks); pap. 13.95 (ISBN 0-671-62822-4). S&S.
Washing Silk: The Life & Selected Poetry of Wei Chung, (834?-910) Robin D. Yates. LC 87-29642. (Harvard-Yenching Institute Monographs: No. 26). 280p. 1987. text ed. 23.00x (ISBN 0-674-94775-4, Pub. by Coun East Asian Stud). Harvard U Pr.
Washing the Cow's Skull: Texas Poetry in Translation. bilingual ed. Ed. by Dave Oliphant & Luis Ramos-Garcia. 400p. (Eng. & Span.). 1981. pap. 15.00 (ISBN 0-933384-05-X). Prickly Pear.
Washing Your Hair. Patricia Lewis & Casper Ferneti. (Project MORE Daily Living Skills Ser.). (Illus.). 32p. 1978. pap. text ed. 5.95 (ISBN 0-8331-1244-9). Hubbard Sci.
Washing Your Hands. Crystal Stevens & Casper Ferneti. (Project MORE Daily Living Skills Ser.). (Illus.). 32p. 1979. pap. text ed. 5.95 (ISBN 0-8331-1241-4). Hubbard Sci.
Washington. Allan Carpenter. LC 79-13390. (New Enchantment of America State Bks.). (Illus.). 96p. (gr. 4 up). 1979. PLB 15.93 (ISBN 0-516-04147-9). Childrens.
Washington. Norman H. Clark. (States & the Nation Ser). (Illus.). 1976. 14.95 (ISBN 0-393-05587-6, Co-Pub by AASLH). Norton.
Washington. Photos by John Marshall. (Illus.). 160p. (Text by Ruth Kirk). 1988. 35.00 (ISBN 0-932575-64-1). GR Arts Ctr Pub.
Washington! Dana F. Ross. (Wagons West Ser.). 1984. pap. 4.50 (ISBN 0-553-26163-0). Bantam.
Washington. Turner Educational Services, Inc. Staff & James I. Clark. (Portrait of America Library). 48p. (gr. 4 up). 1986. PLB 15.33 (ISBN 0-86514-470-2); pap. text ed. 9.27 (ISBN 0-86514-545-8); Beta Video 113.33 (ISBN 0-86514-097-9); VHS Video 113.33 (ISBN 0-86514-172-X); 3-4" Video 136.00 (ISBN 0-317-47591-6); tchr. study guide 13.27 (ISBN 0-86514-322-6); student activity bk. 6.60 (ISBN 0-86514-397-8); Index 13.27. Raintree Pubs.

Washington Information Workbook see How to Find Business Intelligence in Washington.
Washington: I.O.U. see Deuda De Sangre.
Washington Iron Works of Franklin County, Virginia, 1773 - 1850. John S. Salmon. (Illus.). 1986. 25.00 (ISBN 0-88490-137-8). VA State Lib.
Washington Irving. Mary W. Bowden. (United States Authors Ser.). 1981. lib. bdg. 16.95 (ISBN 0-8057-7314-2, Twayne). G K Hall.
Washington Irving. William R. Langfeld. 90p. 1980. Repr. of 1933 ed. lib. bdg. 25.00 (ISBN 0-8495-3253-1). Arden Lib.
Washington Irving. Henry A, Pochman. 1988. Repr. lib. bdg. 75.00x. Am Biog Serv.
Washington Irving. Henry A. Pochmann. 389p. 1981. Repr. of 1934 ed. lib. bdg. 49.00 (ISBN 0-8495-4404-1). Arden Lib.
Washington Irving. Henry A. Pochmann. 389p. 1980. Repr. lib. bdg. 30.00 (ISBN 0-8492-2187-0). R West.
Washington Irving. Charles D. Warner. LC 80-23548. (American Men & Women of Letters Ser.). 310p. 1981. pap. 4.95 (ISBN 0-87754-153-1). Chelsea Hse.
Washington Irving. Charles D. Warner. 304p. 1983. Repr. of 1892 ed. lib. bdg. 30.00 (ISBN 0-89987-889-X). Darby Bks.
Washington Irving, a Bibliography. William R. Langfeld. LC 72-194090. 1933. lib. bdg. 22.00 (ISBN 0-8414-5711-5). Folcroft.
Washington Irving: A Reference Guide. Haskell S. Springer. 1976. lib. bdg. 29.00 (ISBN 0-8161-1101-4, Hall Reference). G K Hall.
Washington Irving: A Sketch. George W. Curtis. LC 76-28379. 1976. Repr. of 1901 ed. lib. bdg. 25.50 (ISBN 0-8414-3489-1). Folcroft.
Washington Irving: A Tribute. Ed. by Andrew B. Myers. LC 77-189961. (Illus.). 86p. 1972. pap. 2.95 (ISBN 0-912882-05-0). Sleepy Hollow.
Washington Irving: An American Study, 1802-1832. William L. Hedges. LC 80-23564. (Goucher College Ser.). xiv, 274p. 1980. Repr. of 1965 ed. lib. bdg. 41.50x (ISBN 0-313-21159-0, HEWI). Greenwood.
Washington Irving & Other Essays. Charles A. Ingraham. 1978. Repr. of 1922 ed. lib. bdg. 35.00 (ISBN 0-8495-2601-9). Arden Lib.
Washington Irving & Other Essays. Charles A. Ingraham. LC 73-14933. 1922. Repr. lib. bdg. 35.00 (ISBN 0-8414-5054-4). Folcroft.
Washington Irving & the House of Murray: Geoffrey Crayon Charms the British, 1817-1856. Washington Irving. Ed. by Ben H. McClary. LC 73-77843. pap. 71.80 (ISBN 0-317-29308-7, 2022219). Bks Demand UMI.
Washington Irving: His Life & Work. George H. Putnam. LC 78-10597. 1978. Repr. of 1903 ed. lib. bdg. 18.00 (ISBN 0-8414-6819-2). Folcroft.
Washington Irving: Representative Selections. Washington Irving. Ed. by Henry A. Pochmann. 1971. 59.00x (ISBN 0-403-01039-X). Scholarly.
Washington Irving: The Western Works. Richard Cracroft. LC 74-1973. (Western Writers Ser: No. 14). 1974. pap. 2.95x (ISBN 0-88430-013-7). Boise St Univ.
Washington Irving's Tales of the Supernatural. Washington Irving. Ed. by Edward Wagenknecht. LC 80-29313. (Illus.). 288p. (gr. 6 up). 1982. 17.95 (ISBN 0-916144-64-X). Stemmer Hse.
Washington Is Leaking. Art Buchwald..1978. pap. 2.95 (ISBN 0-449-23294-8, Crest). Fawcett.
Washington Itself: An Informal Guide to the Capital of the United States. E. J. Applewhite. LC 81-47484. 384p. 1981. pap. 9.95 (ISBN 0-394-74875-1). Knopf.
Washington Land Use & Environmental Law & Practice. Richard L. Settle. LC 83-71948. 378p. 1984. 65.00 (ISBN 0-409-20359-9). Butterworth WA.
Washington Law of Wills & Intestate Succession. Mark Reutlinger & William C. Oltman. LC 84-70030. 592p. 1985. 45.00. Butterworth WA.
Washington Law Review: 1925-1986, 61 vols. Bound set. 2013.00x (ISBN 0-686-90096-0). Rothman.
Washington Lawyer. Edward Howrey. LC 83-310390. (Illus.). xi, 503p. 1984. write for info. U Iowa Law.
Washington Lawyer: A Series of Lectures Delivered under the Auspices of the Julius Rosenthal Foundation at Northwestern University School of Law in April, 1952. Charles A. Horsky. LC 81-646. viii, 179p. 1981. Repr. of 1952 ed. lib. bdg. 35.00x (ISBN 0-313-22736-5, HOWL). Greenwood.
Washington, Library of Congress, MS M21.M185 Case. Ed. by Alexander Silbiger. (Seventeenth-Century Keyboard Music). 225p. 1987. lib. bdg. 60.00 (ISBN 0-8240-8020-3). Garland Pub.
Washington Life & Health. 6th ed. 1984. write for info. (ISBN 0-930868-27-7). Merritt Co.
Washington Lobby. 5th ed. LC 86-29030. 212p. 1987. pap. 12.95 (ISBN 0-87187-408-3). Congr Quarterly.
Washington Lobbyists Survey, 1956-1957. Lester Milbrath. 1972. codebk. write for info. (ISBN 0-89138-054-X). ICPSR.
Washington Manufacturers Register, 1986-1987. 5th ed. Ed. by Terry Gutirrez. LC 78-643574. 300p. 1986. 70.00 (ISBN 0-911510-92-3). Times Mirror.
Washington Manufacturers Register, 1988-1989. 300p. 1988. pap. 90.00 (ISBN 0-318-02838-7). Manufacturers.
Washington Manufactures Register, 1988-89. 5th ed. Terry Gutierrez. LC 78-643574. 300p. 1988. 75.00 (ISBN 0-911510-97-4). TMP Pub.
Washington Medal. Howard P. Arnold. 1976. 3.00 (ISBN 0-89073-040-7). Boston Public Lib.
Washington Merry-Go-Round of Libel Actions. Douglas A. Anderson. LC 79-18126. 352p. 1980. 24.95x (ISBN 0-88229-547-0); pap. 12.95 (ISBN 0-88229-746-5). Nelson-Hall.
Washington Motor Vehicle Accident Deskbook - Insurance. 1988. price not set (ISBN 0-88129-222-2). Wash Bar CLE.
Washington Motor Vehicle Accident Deskbook. LC 87-51491. 1987. looseleaf 120.00 (ISBN 0-88129-218-4). Wash Bar CLE.
Washington Motor Vehicle Accident Insurance Deskbook. 1988. price not set looseleaf. Wash Bar CLE.
Washington Notary Law Primer. The National Notary Magazine Editors. LC 86-60899. 1986. pap. 8.75 (ISBN 0-933134-19-3). Natl Notary.
Washington on Foot. 3rd, rev. ed. Ed. by John J. Protopappas & Lin Brown. LC 83-12880. (Illus.). 224p. 1984. pap. 5.95 (ISBN 0-87474-765-1, PRWFP). Smithsonian.
Washington on Forty Dollars a Day. Rena Bulkin. 312p. 1986. pap. 11.95 (ISBN 0-671-55630-4). S&S.
Washington One-Day Trip Book: One Hundred One Offbeat Excursions in & Around the Nation's Capital. Jane O. Smith. LC 83-25417. 240p. 1984. pap. 7.95 (ISBN 0-914440-70-5). EPM Pubns.
Washington Parks Guide. Chris Boyce. Ed. by Barbara McCaig. 100p. (Orig.). 1988. pap. text ed. 5.95 (ISBN 0-317-67996-1). Affordable Adven.
Washington Partnership Law & Practice Handbook. 735p. 1984. looseleaf 95.00 (ISBN 0-88129-083-1); Supplement. write for info. (ISBN 0-88129-227-3). Wash Bar CLE.
Washington Past & Present. Richard Striner & Donald Kennon. Ed. by Paul Martin. LC 83-3582. (Illus.). 144p. 1983. pap. 5.00 (ISBN 0-916200-05-1). US Capitol Hist.
Washington Past & Present: A Guide to the Nation's Capital. 2nd ed. Donald R. Kennon & Richard Striner. LC 83-3582. (Illus.). 143p. 1983. pap. 6.00 (ISBN 0-317-56351-3, S/N 066-001-00003-2). US Capitol Hist.
Washington Pattern Forms. National Center for State Courts Staff. 448p. 1978. manuscript 26.88 (WRO-021). Natl Ctr St Courts.
Washington Playland. Edmund Griffen & Daniel Dodge. 1976. pap. 1.95 (LB403, Leisure Bks). Leisure NY.
Washington Plenary Meeting of the Trilateral Commission. write for info. Trilateral Comm.
Washington Politics: Published under the Auspices of the Citizenship Clearing House. Daniel M. Ogden, Jr. & Hugh A. Bone. LC 80-25647. (Illus.). vi, 77p. 1981. Repr. of 1960 ed. lib. bdg. 35.00x (ISBN 0-313-22803-5, OGWP). Greenwood.
Washington: Portrait of a City. Photos by Steven Gottlieb. Frank Getlein. LC 85-4035. (Illus.). 160p. 1985. 38.00 (ISBN 0-87491-771-9). Acropolis.
Washington: Portrait of the Land. Robert U. Steelquist. (Washington Geographic Ser.: No. 3). (Orig.). 1988. pap. 14.95 (ISBN 0-938314-33-5). Am Geog Pub.
Washington Post Deskbook on Style. Ed. by Robert A. Webb. 1978. (ISBN 0-07-068397-2); pap. text ed. 5.95 (ISBN 0-07-068398-0). McGraw.
Washington Post National Weekly Edition Index. Research Publications Inc. Staff. Incl. Index for 1984. 125p. 1986. 70.00 (ISBN 0-89235-114-4); Index for 1985. 125p. 1987. lib. bdg. 70.00 (ISBN 0-89235-115-2); Index for 1986. 125p. 1986. lib. bdg. 70.00 (ISBN 0-89235-116-0). Res Pubns CT.
Washington Postcard Catalog. James L. Lowe. LC 74-30734. (Illus.). 128p. 1986. pap. 5.95 (ISBN 0-913782-06-8). Deltiologists Am.
Washington Potatoes: Guide to Quality. Washington State Potato Commission Staff. (Illus.). 80p. 1984. pap. 9.95 (ISBN 0-9609940-1-7). Storypole.
Washington: Property, Vols. 1-2. Set. 8.50 (ISBN 0-686-90923-2); suppl. 6.00 (ISBN 0-686-90924-0). Am Law Inst.
Washington Property & Casualty Supplement. (State License Examination Study Manuals Ser.). 380p. 1985. write for info. (ISBN 0-930868-28-5). Merritt Co.
Washington Property Law Reporter. 1980. ann. subscr. 40.00 (ISBN 0-409-20342-4). Butterworth Legal Pubs.
Washington Public Shore Guide: Marine Waters. James W. Scott et al. LC 85-40976. (Illus.). 342p. 1986. 25.00x (ISBN 0-295-96334-4); pap. 14.95 (ISBN 0-295-96335-2). U of Wash Pr.
Washington: Readings in the History of the Evergreen State. Ed. by Burton J. Williams. 1977. pap. 12.50x (ISBN 0-87291-090-3). Coronado Pr.
Washington Real Estate Review Questions. N. R. E. I. 225p. (Orig.). 1982. pap. 19.95x wkbk. (ISBN 0-915799-01-4). Natl Real Estate Inst.
Washington Real Property Deskbook. 2nd ed. LC 86-50423. 1986. looseleaf 185.00 (ISBN 0-88129-215-X). Wash Bar CLE.
Washington Redskins. Julian May. (NFL Today Ser.). (Illus.). (gr. 3-6). 1977. PLB 10.45 (ISBN 0-87191-597-9). Creative Ed.
Washington Redskins. James R. Rothaus. (NFL Today Ser.). (gr. 4 up). 1986. PLB 10.45 (ISBN 0-88682-051-0). Creative Ed.
Washington Redskins: A Pictorial History. David Slattery. LC 77-15328. (Illus.). 168p. 1977. 14.95 (ISBN 0-686-84393-2). JCP Corp VA.
Washington Reporters. Stephen Hess. LC 80-70077. 174p. 1981. 26.95 (ISBN 0-8157-3594-4); pap. 9.95 (ISBN 0-8157-3593-6). Brookings.
Washington Representatives. 264p. 50.00 (ISBN 0-317-57046-3). B Klein Pubns.
Washington Representatives, 1979. 3rd ed. Ed. by Craig Colgate, Jr. & Arthur C. Close. LC 76-21152. 1979. pap. 30.00x (ISBN 0-910416-31-1). Columbia Bks.
Washington Representatives, 1980. 4th ed. Ed. by Arthur C. Close & Craig Colgate, Jr. LC 76-21152. 1980. pap. 30.00x (ISBN 0-910416-33-8). Columbia Bks.
Washington Representatives, 1982. 6th annual ed. Ed. by Arthur C. Close & Laurie A. Evans. LC 76-21152. 583p. 1982. pap. 35.00 (ISBN 0-910416-40-0). Columbia Bks.
Washington Representatives, 1983. 7th ed. Ed. by Arthur C. Close & Stephany J. Freedman. LC 76-21152. 611p. 1983. pap. 40.00 (ISBN 0-910416-42-7). Columbia Bks.
Washington Representatives, 1985. 9th ed. Ed. by Arthur C. Close & Jody Curtis. LC 76-21152. 650p. 1985. pap. 45.00 (ISBN 0-910416-54-0). Columbia Bks.
Washington Representatives, 1986. 10th ed. Ed. by Arthur C. Close. LC 76-21152. 650p. 1986. pap. 45.00 (ISBN 0-910416-59-1). Columbia Bks.
Washington Representatives, 1986. 11th ed. 640p. 1986. 50.00 (ISBN 0-317-55728-9). B Klein Pubns.
Washington Representatives, 1987. Ed. by Arthur C. Close & John P. Gregg. LC 76-21152. 650p. 1987. pap. 50.00 (ISBN 0-910416-65-6). Columbia Bks.
Washington Representatives 1988. 12th ed. Intro. by Arthur C. Close & Gregory Bologna. LC 76-21152. 685p. 1988. pap. 50.00 (ISBN 0-910416-72-9). Columbia Bks.
Washington Rock: A Climbing Guide. Don Brooks. (Illus., Orig.). 1982. pap. 8.95 (ISBN 0-89886-046-6). Mountaineers.
Washington Silhouttes. N. Yakovlev. 157p. 1985. pap. 3.95 (ISBN 0-8285-3094-7, Pub. by Progress Pubs USSR). Imported Pubns.
Washington Songs & Lore. Compiled by Linda Allen & Chrystle L. Snider. (Illus.). 164p. (gr. 1-12). 1988. pap. 15.95 (ISBN 0-9616441-3-3); Abriged ed. pap. 9.95 (ISBN 0-9616441-4-1). Melior Pubns.
Washington Square. Henry James. (Airmont Classics Ser.). (gr. 10 up). 1969. pap. 1.50 (ISBN 0-8049-0210-0, CL-210). Airmont.
Washington Square. Henry James. (Literature Ser). (gr. 10-12). 1970. pap. text ed. 6.83 (ISBN 0-87720-743-7). AMSCO Sch.
Washington Square. Henry James. pap. 2.50 (ISBN 0-451-51990-6, Sig Classics). NAL.
Washington Square. Henry James. Ed. by Mark Le Fanu. (World's Classics Ser.). 1982. pap. 2.50 (ISBN 0-19-281611-X). Oxford U Pr.
Washington Square. Henry James. Ed. by Brian Lee. (English Library). 224p. 1984. pap. 2.50 (ISBN 0-14-043226-4). Penguin.
Washington Square. Henry James. 192p. 1986. Repr. lib. bdg. 17.95x (ISBN 0-89966-532-2). Buccaneer Bks.
Washington Square see Novels Eighteen Eighty-One to Eighteen Eighty-Six.
Washington Square Ensemble. Madison S. Bell. 352p. 1984. pap. 6.95 (ISBN 0-14-007025-7). Penguin.
Washington Square Press: Handbook of Good English. Edward D. Johnson. Orig. Title: Grammar Book. 320p. (Orig.). 1983. pap. 4.95 (ISBN 0-671-44294-5). WSP.
Washington Star Garden Book: The Encyclopedia of Gardening for the Chesapeake & Potomac Region. rev. ed. Deborah Fialka. Ed. by Nancy C. Modrak. (Illus.). 250p. 1988. pap. 9.95 (ISBN 0-915168-08-1). Wash Bk Trad.
Washington State. Charles P. LeWarne. LC 85-40977. (Illus.). 464p. 1986. text ed. 35.00x (ISBN 0-295-96341-7); tchr's manual 25.00 (ISBN 0-295-96390-5). U of Wash Pr.
Washington State & Cities Revenue Catalog. M. E. Matesen. (Illus.). 27p. (Orig.). 1973. pap. 4.00 (ISBN 0-934939-03-9). State Revenue Soc.
Washington State Atlas: A Political & Economic View of the Evergreen State. rev. ed. Richard Yates & Charity Yates. (Illus.). 64p. (Orig.). 1987. pap. 6.95 (ISBN 0-911927-09-3). Info Oregon.
Washington State Coloring Guide. Seth H. Seablom. (Great Five Star Coloring Bks.). (Illus.). 32p. (gr. 1-6). 1978. pap. 2.50 (ISBN 0-918800-03-X). Seablom.
Washington State Employers' Guide for Small Business. Reed Swanson & Renee Swanson. 315p. 1987. 49.95 (ISBN 0-9617974-0-1). Persona Ltd.
Washington State Environmental Policy Act, a Legal & Policy Analysis. Richard L. Settle. 456p. 1987. looseleaf 65.00. Butterworth WA.
Washington State Fishing Guide. 6th, rev. ed. Stan Jones. (Illus.). 334p. (Orig.). 1984. pap. 7.95 (ISBN 0-939936-02-X). Jones Pub.
Washington State Gold Mines. Roy F. Mayo. 92p. 1983. comb bound 10.95 (ISBN 0-931461-00-6). Nugget Ent.
Washington State International Trade Directory. Howard S. Hirshman. 394p. 1983. 58.00 (ISBN 0-318-00151-9). Robinson Pub.
Washington State: National Parks, Historic Sites, Recreation Areas, & Natural Landmarks. Ruth Kirk. LC 74-6020. (Illus.). 64p. 1974. pap. 3.95 (ISBN 0-295-95323-3). U of Wash Pr.
Washington State Place Names. rev. ed. James W. Phillips. LC 73-159435. (Illus.). 186p. 1971. pap. 8.95 (ISBN 0-295-95498-1). U of Wash Pr.
Washington State Yearbook, Nineteen Eighty-Eight: A Guide to Government in the Evergreen State. Ed. by Richard Yates & Charity Yates. (Illus.). 224p. 1988. pap. 14.95 (ISBN 0-911927-11-5). Info Oregon.
Washington Steam Locomotives. Kenneth G. Johnsen. (Illus.). 80p. 4.75 (ISBN 0-89685-036-6). Chatham Pub CA.
Washington Story: Behind the Scenes in the Federal Government - An Official under Civil Service Describes His Experiences. A. C. Rosander. LC 85-227965. xiii, 546p. 1985. 7.95 (ISBN 0-9615168-0-1). Natl Directions.
Washington Studies Program: Activity Manual. 1st ed. D. P. Superka & L. R. Singleton. Ed. by Eunice B. Combs. (Illus.). 153p. (gr. 4). 1982. duplication Masters 49.00 (ISBN 0-943068-71-1); tchr's Guide 5.00 (ISBN 0-943068-70-3). Graphic Learning.
Washington Superior Court Weighted Caseload Project. National Center for State Courts Staff. 74p. 1977. manuscript 4.44 (WRO-012). Natl Ctr St Courts.
Washington Supplement for Modern Real Estate Practice. Richard Duce & Olive Ziegler. 1978. pap. 9.95 (ISBN 0-88462-331-9, 1510-33, Real EState Ed). Longman Finan.
Washington Survival. Betty L. Hall & Ken Holmes. 160p. (Orig.). (gr. 10-12). 1981. pap. text ed. 5.84 (ISBN 0-936159-05-7). Westwood Pr.
Washington Territory. E. Meeker. 56p. pap. 3.95 (ISBN 0-8466-0194-X, S194). Shorey.
Washington, The Capital. Photos by Robert Llewellyn. LC 81-69086. (Illus.). 120p. 1981. 18.98 (ISBN 0-934738-02-5). Thomasson-Grant.
Washington: The Indispensable Man. James T. Flexner. LC 74-7235. (Illus.). 1974. 22.95 (ISBN 0-316-28605-2). Little.
Washington: The Indispensable Man. James T. Flexner. 1979. pap. 3.95 (ISBN 0-451-62213-8, ME2213, Ment). NAL.
Washington: The Indispensable Man. James T. Flexner. pap. 8.95 (ISBN 0-452-25542-2, Plume). NAL.
Washington, the Indispensable Man. James T. Flexner. 1984. pap. 3.95 (ISBN 0-451-14698-0, Sig). NAL.
Washington Times & Trails. rev. ed. Joan Olson & Gene Olson. LC 75-83521. (Illus.). (gr. 7-12). 1983. pap. 8.97x (ISBN 0-913366-01-3). Windyridge.
Washington Travel Guide. LC 86-82773. (Illus.). 128p. 1987. 8.95 (ISBN 0-376-06847-7). Sunset-Lane.
Washington Trial Courts, Statistical Reporting System Report. National Center for State Courts Staff. 68p. 1978. manuscript 4.08 (WRO-008). Natl Ctr St Courts.
Washington University in St. Louis: Its Design & Architecture. Buford Pickens & Margarett J. Darnall. (Illus.). 88p. 1978. pap. 5.00 (ISBN 0-936316-06-3). Wash U Gallery.
Washington University Papyri I: Non-Literary Texts, Nos. 1-16. Verne B. Schuman. LC 79-14199. (American Society of Papyrologists Ser.: No. 310017). 1981. 15.00 (ISBN 0-89130-286-7, 310017). Scholars Pr GA.
Washington Used & Rare, Notes on a Weekend in Washington's Antiquarian Bookshops. Henry Turlington. viii, 39p. (Orig.). 1979. pap. 4.95 (ISBN 0-938768-01-8). Oak Knoll.
Washington V. 600p. 1986. 45.00 (ISBN 0-317-57045-5). B Klein Pubns.
Washington Week in Review. Paul Duke et al. LC 86-1508. 338p. 1986. pap. 9.95 (ISBN 0-446-37019-3). Warner Bks.
Washington, Westminster & Whitehall. Walter Williams. (Illus.). 268p. Date not set. price not set (ISBN 0-521-35185-5). Cambridge U Pr.
Washington Whitewater I: A Guide to 17 of Washington's Most Popular Whitewater Trips. 2nd ed. Douglass North. (Washington Whitewater Ser.). (Illus.). 176p. (Orig.). 1988. pap. 10.95 (ISBN 0-89886-158-6). Mountaineers.
Washington Whitewater Two: A Guide to Seventeen of Washington's Lesser-Known Whitewater Trips. Douglass North. (Illus.). 176p. (Orig.). 1987. pap. 10.95 (ISBN 0-89886-134-9). Mountaineers.
Washington Wilderness: The Unfinished Work. Harvey Manning & Pat O'Hara. (Illus.). 120p. 1985. pap. 20.00 (ISBN 0-89886-116-0). Mountaineers.
Washington Wildlife. Loralie Cecotti. (Color-A-Story Ser.). (Illus.). 24p. (Orig.). (gr. k-5). 1984. pap. text ed. 2.75 (ISBN 0-318-04105-7). Coffee Break.
Washington Wind & Wisdom. Dick Hyman. 44p. 1988. pap. 6.95 (ISBN 0-8289-0698-X). Greene.

Wasted Land. facsimile ed. Gerald W. Johnson. LC 78-130556. (Select Bibliographies Reprint Ser). Repr. of 1937 ed. 14.00 (ISBN 0-8369-5529-3). Ayer Co Pubs.

Wasted Lives: A Clinician's Indictment of Traditional Psychiatry. Daniel D. DeSole. (Traditional Healing Ser.). 300p. Date not set. cancelled (ISBN 0-932426-13-1). Trado-Medic.

Wasted Lives: A Study of Children in Mental Hospitals & Their Families. Lillian C. Kovar. 1979. text ed. 23.95 (ISBN 0-89876-051-8). Gardner Pr.

Wasted Lives: A Study of Children in Mental Hospitals & Their Families. Lillian C. Kovar. LC 78-23248. 213p. 1979. 19.95x (ISBN 0-470-26564-7). Halsted Pr.

Wasted Manpower: The Challenge of Unemployment. Corrington Gill. LC 72-2371. (FDR & the Era of the New Deal Ser). 316p. 1973. Repr. of 1939 ed. lib. bdg. 39.50 (ISBN 0-306-70467-6). Da Capo.

Wasted Space. Judie Gulley. 1988. 11.95 (ISBN 0-687-44060-2). Abingdon.

Wasted Water Pressure & Potential Energy Generation: Tech Info. Proj. 1980. 15.00 (ISBN 0-686-73448-3). Tech Info Proj.

Wasted Wealth: The Participation of Women in Public Life. Ed. by Claudia Bernadoni & Verena Werner. Tr. by Ruth Stanley & Mary Hess. 238p. 1985. pap. 20.00 (ISBN 3-598-10603-3). K G Saur.

Wasteland. Jo Sinclair. (Gems of American Jewish Literature Ser.). 348p. 1987. pap. 9.95 (ISBN 0-8276-0280-4). JPS Phila.

Wastelands & Afforestation. Irshad Khan. 176p. 1987. 12.75x (ISBN 81-204-0212-X, Pub. by Oxford IBH). South Asia Bks.

Wasteless Chemical Processing. V. V. Kafarov. 251p. 1985. 9.95 (ISBN 0-8285-3114-5, Pub. by Mir Pubs USSR). Imported Pubns.

Wastemaker: Nineteen Twenty-Six to Nineteen Sixty-One. Bern Porter. 300p. pap. 42.50 (ISBN 0-686-74432-2). Bern Porter.

Wastepaper Theater Anthology. Edwin Honig & James Schevill. (Pourboire Ser.). 1979. pap. 5.00 (ISBN 0-930900-56-1). Burning Deck.

Wastes. Christina G. Miller & Louise A. Berry. (First Books Ser.). 72p. (gr. 4-9). 1986. lib. bdg. 10.40 (ISBN 0-531-10130-4). Watts.

Wastes for Imported Fill. Philip Sherwood. 48p. 1987. 6.00 (ISBN 0-7277-0378-1, Pub. by T Telford UK). Am Soc Civil Eng.

Wastes in the Ocean: Deep-Sea Waste Disposal, Vol. 5. Ed. by Dana R. Kester et al. P. Kilho Park. LC 84-27147. (Environmental Science & Technology Ser.). 346p. 1985. 89.95 (ISBN 0-471-89331-5, Pub. by Wiley Interscience). Wiley.

Wastes in the Ocean: Near-Shore Waste Disposal, Vol. 6. Ed. by Bostwick H. Ketchum et al. LC 84-25697. (Environmental Science & Technology Ser.). 534p. 1985. 105.00 (ISBN 0-471-89330-7, Pub. by Wiley-Interscience). Wiley.

Wastes in the Ocean, Vol. 1: Industrial & Sewage Wastes in the Ocean. Ed. by Iver W. Duedall et al. LC 82-13695. (Environmental Science & Technology Ser.). 431p. 1983. 80.00 (ISBN 0-471-09772-1, Pub. by Wiley-Interscience); Set, 3 vols. 200.00 (ISBN 0-471-82054-7). Wiley.

Wastes in the Ocean, Vol. 2: Dredge Material Disposal in the Ocean. Dana R. Kester et al. Ed. by Iver W. Duedall. LC 82-17370. (Environmental Science & Technology Ser.). 299p. 1983. 63.00 (ISBN 0-471-09771-3). Wiley.

Wastes in the Ocean, Vol. 3: Radioactive Wastes & the Ocean. Ed. by Kilho P. Park et al. State University of New York, Stony Brook. (Environmental Science & Technology Ser.: No. 1-121). 522p. 1983. 99.50 (ISBN 0-471-09770-5). Wiley.

Wastes to Resources: Appropiate Technologies for Sewage Treatment & Conversation. 28p. 1983. 5.00 (ISBN 0-317-53921-3). NCAT.

Wasteside Development, Nineteen Eighty-Eight. John M. Bennett et al. Ed. by Mike Miskowski. (Wasteside Development Ser.: No. 2). (Illus.). 40p. (Orig.). 1988. pap. 4.00 (ISBN 0-938309-10-2). Bomb Shelter Prop.

Wasteside Development: 1987. Ll Dunn et al. Ed. by Mike Miskowski. (Illus.). 40p. (Orig.). 1987. pap. 3.00 (ISBN 0-938309-01-3). Bomb Shelter Prop.

Wastewater Conference Proceedings. Eighth Conference. 1981 see Wastewater Conference Proceedings. (1974) First Conference.

Wastewater Conference Proceedings. Fifth Conference. 1978 see Wastewater Conference Proceedings. (1974) First Conference.

Wastewater Conference Proceedings. Fourth Conference. 1977 see Wastewater Conference Proceedings. (1974) First Conference.

Wastewater Conference Proceedings. Second Conference. 1975 see Wastewater Conference Proceedings. (1974) First Conference.

Wastewater Conference Proceedings. Seventh Conference. 1980 see Wastewater Conference Proceedings. (1974) First Conference.

Wastewater Conference Proceedings. Sixth Conference. 1979 see Wastewater Conference Proceedings. (1974) First Conference.

Wastewater Conference Proceedings. Third Conference. 1976 see Wastewater Conference Proceedings. (1974) First Conference.

Wastewater Conference Proceedings. (1974) First Conference. Incl. Wastewater Conference Proceedings. Second Conference. 1975. 214p. 30.00 (ISBN 0-317-36359-X); Wastewater Conference Proceedings. Third Conference. 1976. 213p. 30.00 (ISBN 0-317-36360-3); Wastewater Conference Proceedings. Fourth Conference. 1977. 232p. 30.00 (ISBN 0-317-36361-1); Wastewater Conference Proceedings. Fifth Conference. 1978. 295p. 30.00 (ISBN 0-317-36362-X); Wastewater Conference Proceedings. Sixth Conference. 1979. 514p. 30.00 (ISBN 0-317-36363-8); Wastewater Conference Proceedings. Seventh Conference. 1980. 355p. 30.00 (ISBN 0-317-36364-6); Wastewater Conference Proceedings. Eighth Conference. 1981. 350p. 30.00 (ISBN 0-317-36365-4). 163p. 30.00 (ISBN 0-317-36358-1). Natl Sanit Foun.

Wastewater Disinfection. Water Pollution Control Federation Staff. (Manual of Practice Ser.: MFD10). 165p. 1986. pap. 40.00 (ISBN 0-943244-64-1). Water Pollution.

Wastewater Disinfection: A State-of-the Art Report. Water Pollution Control Federation Staff. (Manual of Practice Ser.: P0050). 78p. 1984. pap. 29.50 (ISBN 0-943244-54-4). Water Pollution.

Wastewater Engineering: Collection & Pumping of Wastewater. Metcalf & Eddy, Inc. Staff & George Tchobanoglous. (Water Resources & Engineering Ser.). (Illus.). 448p. 1981. text ed. 52.95 (ISBN 0-07-041680-X). McGraw.

Wastewater Engineering: Collection, Treatment, Disposal & Reuse. 2nd ed. Metcalf & Eddy, Inc. Staff. Ed. by George Tchobanoglous. (Illus.). 1978. text ed. 52.95 (ISBN 0-07-041677-X). McGraw.

Wastewater Engineering Design for Unsewered Areas. 2nd, rev. ed. Rein Laak. LC 86-50173. 181p. 1986. 39.00 (ISBN 0-87762-462-3). Technomic.

Wastewater Irrigation in Developing Countries: Health Effects & Technical Solutions. Hillel I. Shuval et al. (Technical Paper: No. 51). 360p. 1986. 20.00 (BK0763). World Bank.

Wastewater Management: A Guide to Information Sources. Ed. by George Tchobanoglous et al. LC 74-11570. (Man & the Environment Information Guide Ser.: Vol. 2). 216p. 1976. 68.00x (ISBN 0-8103-1338-3). Gale.

Wastewater Management for Coastal Cities: The Ocean Disposal Option. Ed. by Charles C. Gunnerson. (Technical Paper Ser.: No. 77). 426p. 1988. 23.00 (ISBN 0-8213-0989-7, BK0989). World Bank.

Wastewater Renovation & Reuse: Proceedings of the International Conference on the Renovation & Reuse of Wastewater Through Aquatic & Terrestrial Systems. Ed. by Frank M. D'Itri. LC 76-54588. (Pollution Engineering & Technology: Vol. 3). pap. 120.00 (ISBN 0-317-08391-0, 2055036). Bks Demand UMI.

Wastewater Resource Manual. 500p. 60.00 (ISBN 0-317-34786-1); members 50.00 (ISBN 0-317-34787-X). Irrigation.

Wastewater Sampling for Process & Quality Control, 1980: Manual of Practice, Operation & Maintenance-I. Water Pollution Control Federation. 103p. 1980. pap. 15.00 (ISBN 0-943244-21-8, M0M1). Water Pollution.

Wastewater Stabilization Lagoon Design, Performance & Upgrading. Joe E. Middlebrooks et al. (Illus.). 320p. 1982. text ed. 49.00x (ISBN 0-02-949500-8). Macmillan.

Wastewater Technician. (Career Examination Ser.: C-3412). Date not set. pap. 16.00 (ISBN 0-8373-3412-8). Natl Learning.

Wastewater Treatment. R. E. Bartlett. (Illus.). xii, 326p. 1971. 61.00 (Pub. by Elsevier Applied Sci England). Elsevier.

Wastewater Treatment. Donald W. Sundstrom & Herbert E. Klei. LC 78-13058. (Illus.). 1979. 56.00 (ISBN 0-13-945832-8). P-H.

Wastewater Treatment & Disposal. Arceivala. (Pollution Engineering & Technology Ser.: Vol. 15). 920p. 1981. 115.00 (ISBN 0-8247-6973-2). Dekker.

Wastewater Treatment & Resource Recovery: Report of a Workshop on High-Rate Algae Ponds, Singapore, 27-29 Feb. 1980. 47p. 1980. pap. 5.00 (ISBN 0-88936-260-2, IDRC154, IDRC). UNIPUB.

Wastewater Treatment by Ion Exchange. B. A. Bolto & L. Pawlowski. 250p. 1987. 55.00 (ISBN 0-419-13320-8, 2968, Pub. by E & FN Spon England). Routledge Chapman & Hall.

Wastewater Treatment Plant Design. Compiled by American Society of Civil Engineers Staff. (Manual & Report on Engineering Practice Ser.: No. 36). 574p. 1982. 20.00x (ISBN 0-87262-213-4). Am Soc Civil Eng.

Wastewater Treatment Plant Design. Water Pollution Control Federation Staff. (Manual of Practice Ser.: M0008). 550p. pap. 23.00. Water Pollution.

Wastewater Treatment Plant Design ('77) Manual of Practice, No. 8. (Illus.). 550p. 20.00 (ISBN 0-943244-08-0, M0008). Water Pollution.

Wastewater Treatment Plant Maintenance Supervisor. Jack Rudman. (Career Examination Ser.: C-3064). 1988. pap. 14.00 (ISBN 0-8373-3064-5). Natl Learning.

Wastewater Treatment Plants. Syed R. Qasim. 704p. 1985. text ed. 42.95 (ISBN 0-03-062449-5, HoltC). HR&W.

Wastewater Treatment: Public Health Engineering Design in Metric. Ed. by R. B. Bartlett. 326p. 1971. 39.00 (ISBN 0-85334-504-X, Pub. by Elsevier Applied Sci England). Elsevier.

Wasting of the British Economy. Sidney Polland. LC 81-21325. 1982. 27.50 (ISBN 0-312-85650-4). St Martin.

Wat Haripunjaya: A Study of the Royal Temple of the Buddha's Relic, Lamphun, Thailand. Donald K. Swearer. LC 75-33802. (American Academy of Religion. Studies in Religion). 1976. pap. 9.95 (ISBN 0-89130-052-X, 010010). Scholars Pr GA.

Watanabe Kyosai Shitae. Koysai Memorial Museum Staff. 182p. 1984. 80.00x (ISBN 0-317-68714-X, Pub. by Han-Shan Tang Ltd). State Mutual Bk.

Watch & Clock Encyclopedia. Donald DeCarle. (Illus.). 1959. 19.95x (ISBN 0-685-22155-5). Wehman.

Watch & Clock Encyclopedia. 3rd ed. Donald De Carle. 328p. 1985. 60.00x (ISBN 0-7198-0170-2, Pub. by Tiptree Bk. Serv.). State Mutual Bk.

Watch & Clock Information, Please. Orville R. Hagans. 1981. 30.00 (ISBN 0-918845-03-3). Am Watchmakers.

Watch & Clock Making. David Glasgow. (Illus.). 1977. Repr. of 1885 ed. 25.00 (ISBN 0-7158-1215-7). Charles River Bks.

Watch & Clockmakers' Handbook. F. J. Britten. (Illus.). 1976. 29.50 (ISBN 0-902028-46-4). Apollo.

Watch & Clockmakers' Handbook, Dictionary & Guide. F. J. Britten. (Illus.). 499p. 1976. Repr. of 1907 ed. 29.50. Antique Collect.

Watch & Ward see Novels Eighteen Seventy-One to Eighteen Eighty.

Watch Escapement. Henry B. Fried. 1984. 8.00 (ISBN 0-317-17086-4). Am Watchmakers.

Watch for a Cloud of Dust: Memories of a Dixie Veterinarian. John E. McCormack. LC 85-81587. 193p. (Orig.). 1985. pap. 4.95 (ISBN 0-932147-01-1). Hoard & Sons Co.

Watch for the Fox, Poems. William Mills. LC 73-90863. 62p. 1974. pap. 6.95 (ISBN 0-8071-0071-4). La State U Pr.

Watch Guard Dogs. Matthew Newman. Ed. by Howard Schroeder. LC 85-19542. (Working Dogs Ser.). (Illus.). 48p. (gr. 5-6). 1985. 9.95 (ISBN 0-89686-287-9). Crestwood Hse.

Watch Harry Grow! Demi. LC 84-60109. (Follow-Me Bks.). (Illus.). 26p. (ps-1). 1984. bds. 3.50 (ISBN 0-394-86857-9, Pub. by BYR). Random.

Watch It Come Down. John Osborne. 58p. 1975. 5.95 (ISBN 0-571-10854-7). Faber & Faber.

Watch It, Mr. Contractor. Coert Engelsman. 1986. cancelled (ISBN 0-442-22314-5). Van Nos Reinhold.

Watch-Making in England: 1760-1820. Leonard Weiss. (Illus.). 304p. 1982. 39.95x (ISBN 0-7091-9725-X, Pub. by Robert Hale). Trans-Atl-Phila.

Watch Officer's Guide. 11th ed. Kenneth C. Jacobson. LC 79-87470. (Illus.). 275p. 1979. 11.50x (ISBN 0-87021-749-6). Naval Inst Pr.

Watch Officers Guide. 12th ed. Seamanship Department, U. S. Naval Academy Staff. (Illus.). 120p. 1986. 14.95x (ISBN 0-87021-757-7). Naval Inst Pr.

Watch Out! Richard Hefter. LC 83-2190. (Stickybear Bks.). (Illus.). 32p. (ps-1). 1983. 5.95 (ISBN 0-911787-03-8). Optimum Res Inc.

Watch Out, Busy Bears! Julia Killingback. (Illus.). 24p. (ps up). 1988. bds. 4.95 laminated (ISBN 0-19-520651-7). Oxford U Pr.

Watch Out for the Chicken Feet in Your Soup. Tomie De Paola. LC 74-8201. (Illus.). (ps-3). 1974. PLB 9.95 (ISBN 0-13-945782-8, Pub. by Treehouse); pap. 3.95 (ISBN 0-13-945766-6). P-H.

Watch Out for the Foreign Guests! China Encounters the West. Orville Schell. 1981. pap. 3.95 (ISBN 0-394-74899-9). Pantheon.

Watch Out for the Golly Whompers. Dorothy D. Corrigan. (Illus.). 35p. (gr. k-3). 1988. 6.95 (ISBN 1-55523-149-7). Winston-Derek.

Watch Out for the Turkey! Yvon Le Gall & Genevieve Le Gall. Tr. by Didi Charney from Fr. LC 88-16700. (Aladdin Storybooks Ser.). (Illus.). 36p. (Orig.). (gr. 1-3). Date not set. pap. 2.95 (ISBN 0-689-71283-9, Aladdin Bks). Macmillan.

Watch Out for the Wind. C. J. Mize. (Orig.). 1980. pap. 2.25 (ISBN 0-505-51555-5, Pub. by Tower Bks). Leisure NY.

Watch Out for the Wolf on the Car Lot! Robert Cord. LC 85-63669. (Illus.). 144p. 1986. 14.95 (ISBN 0-937541-01-X); pap. 7.95 (ISBN 0-937541-00-1). Panda Bks Pubs.

Watch Out for Zoo Robbers. (First Reading Bks.). (Illus.). 32p. (gr. 1). Date not set. pap. 0.99 (2001). Garrard.

Watch Out! I'm Peeking in Your Window! Shirley Lueth. (Orig.). 1986. pap. 5.95 (ISBN 0-937911-00-3). Lueth Hse Pubs.

Watch Out! Man Eating Snake. Patricia R. Giff. (New Kids at the Polk Street School Ser.: No. 1). (Orig.). (gr. k-6). 1988. pap. 2.50 (ISBN 0-440-40085-6, YB). Dell.

Watch out, Ronald Morgan. Patricia Giff. LC 84-19623. (Illus.). 24p. (gr. k-3). 1985. 9.95 (ISBN 0-670-80433-9). Viking.

Watch Out, Ronald Morgan. Patricia R. Giff. (Picture Puffins Ser.). (Illus.). 32p. (gr. k-4). 1986. pap. 3.95 (ISBN 0-14-050638-1, Puffin). Penguin.

Watch Out, the Tide. May Devenport. LC 86-91602. 84p. (Orig.). (YA) (gr. 7-12). 1987. 13.25 (ISBN 0-943864-49-6); pap. 3.95 (ISBN 0-943864-48-8). Pogosticks by Andrea Ross. Ginger: Poof! Bam! Growl! by Andrea Ross. Poems by Kay Garrard. Davenport.

Watch Out! Word Bird. Jane B. Moncure. (Word House Words for Early Birds Ser.). (Illus.). (ps-2). lib. bdg. 7.95 (ISBN 0-89565-219-6). Childs World.

Watch Out! Word Bird. Jane B. Moncure. LC 81-21570. (Word Birds for Early Birds Ser.). (ps-2). 1982. 11.93 (ISBN 0-516-06556-4). Childrens.

Watch Repairer's Manual. 4th, rev. ed. Henry B. Fried. (Illus.). 27.00 (ISBN 0-918845-11-4). Am Watchmakers.

Watch Repairing As a Hobby. D. W. Fletcher. LC 84-24607. (Illus.). 64p. 1985. pap. 6.95 (ISBN 0-930163-24-9). Arlington Bk.

Watch: Stories. Rick Bass. 1989. 16.95 (ISBN 0-393-02623-X). Norton.

Watch That Made the Dollar Famous: With 1983 Price Guide. George Townsend. 1974. 8.00 (ISBN 0-913702-39-0). Heart Am Pr.

Watch the Flame. Eleni Fourtouni. (Greek Women Poets Ser.). (Orig.). 1983. pap. 6.95 (ISBN 0-915017-04-0). Thelpini Pr.

Watch the North Wind Rise. Robert Graves. 290p. 1949. pap. 7.95 (ISBN 0-374-51679-0). FS&G.

Watch the Stars Come Out. Riki Levinson. LC 84-28672. (Illus.). 32p. (ps-3). 1985. 13.95 (ISBN 0-525-44205-7). Dutton.

Watch the Stars Come Out. Riki Levinson. (Reading Rainbow Library). 64p. (gr. 1-5). 1987. pap. 4.95 (ISBN 0-02-688766-5, Checkerboard Pr). Macmillan.

Watch with Both Eyes: Anthology. (Orig.). 1988. pap. 4.95 (ISBN 0-937172-81-2). JLJ Pubs.

Watch-Word!!! Argus J. Tresidder. 110p. 1981. Repr. 2.50 (ISBN 0-940328-00-3). Marine Corps.

Watch Your Child's Weight. Jennifer J. Ashcroft & R. Glynn Owens. 160p. 1987. pap. 10.95 (ISBN 0-19-261645-5). Oxford U Pr.

Watch Your Dreams. Ann R. Colton. LC 72-90911. (Illus.). 414p. 1973. 10.00 (ISBN 0-917187-02-4). A R C Pub.

Watch Your Language. Theodore M. Bernstein. LC 58-12309. 1965. pap. 7.95 (ISBN 0-689-70531-X, 220). Atheneum.

Watch Your Language. Salvatore Parlato. 1986. pap. 7.95x (ISBN 0-932666-29-9). T J Pubs.

Watch Your Language: Bk. 1. Ed. by Brian Schenk et al. 1984. pap. 3.95 grammar text, 192 pgs. (ISBN 0-8428-9700-3); pap. 2.65 wkbk. suppl. exercise, 96 pgs. (ISBN 0-8428-9706-2); pap. text ed. 1.00 student ans. bk., 96 pgs. (ISBN 0-8428-9701-1); pap. 1.00 student ans. bk. 96 pgs. (ISBN 0-8428-9707-0). Cambridge Bk.

Watch Your Language: Bk. 2. Ed. by Brian Schenk et al. 192p. 1984. pap. 3.95 grammar text, 192 pgs. (ISBN 0-8428-9702-X); pap. 2.85 suppl. exercise bk. 96 pgs. (ISBN 0-8428-9708-9); pap. 1.00 student ans. bk. 96 pgs. text (ISBN 0-8428-9709-7); pap. 1.00 student ans. bk. 96 pgs. (ISBN 0-8428-9703-8). Cambridge Bk.

Watch Your Language Diagnostic-Prescriptive Locator Test. Ed. by Brian Schenk et al. 24p. 1984. pap. 1.50 (ISBN 0-8428-9712-7). Cambridge Bk.

Watch Your Language Evaluative Test. Ed. by Brian Schenk et al. 24p. 1984. pap. 1.50 (ISBN 0-8428-9713-5). Cambridge Bk.

Watch Your Step. Y. Cherepanov. 140p. 1979. pap. 4.95 (ISBN 0-8285-1589-1, Pub. by Progress Pubs USSR). Imported Pubns.

Watch Your Step, Andy Capp. Reginald Smythe. (Andy Capp Ser.). (Illus.). (gr. 4 up). 1979. pap. 1.25 (ISBN 0-449-13562-4, P3562, GM). Fawcett.

Watch 1988 - The Year of Climax! Charles R. Taylor. (Illus.). 112p. (Orig.). 1988. pap. 4.95 (ISBN 0-937682-09-8). Today Bible.

Watchboy, What of the Night? Turner Cassity. LC 66-23920. (Wesleyan Poetry Program Ser.: Vol. 31). (Orig.). 1966. 17.00x (ISBN 0-8195-2031-4); pap. 8.95. Wesleyan U Pr.

Watchdog. Faith Sullivan. 1982. pap. 11.95 (ISBN 0-07-062355-4). Mcgraw.

Watchdog on the Potomac: A Study of the Comptroller General of the United States. Joseph Pois. LC 78-66276. 1979. pap. text ed. 16.25 (ISBN 0-8191-0691-7). U Pr of Amer.

Watchdogs of Terror. Peter Deriabin. LC 84-11873. (Foreign Intelligence Bk.). 469p. 1984. 24.00x (ISBN 0-89093-674-9). U Pubns Amer.

Watchdogs of Wall Street. facsimile ed. Hillel Black. LC 75-2621. (Wall Street & the Security Market Ser.). 1975. Repr. of 1962 ed. 20.00x (ISBN 0-405-06948-0). Ayer Co Pubs.

Watcher. Charlotte Eldridge. (Orig.). 1981. pap. write for info. Shamar Bk.

Watcher. Robert Kammen. 160p. 1985. pap. 2.50 (ISBN 0-345-32215-0). Ballantine.

Watcher. Charles Maclean. 350p. 1983. 14.95 (ISBN 0-671-25531-2). S&S.

Watcher. Jane Palmer. 178p. 1988. pap. 5.95 (ISBN 0-7043-4038-0, Pub. by Women's Press). Salem Hse Pubs.

Watcher & Other Stories. Italo Calvino. Tr. by William Weaver & Archibald Colquhoun. LC 75-9829. 181p. 1975. pap. 3.95 (ISBN 0-15-694952-0, Harv). HarBraceJ.

Watcher & Other Weird Stories. Joseph S. Le Fanu. Ed. by Devendra P. Varma. LC 76-5279. (Collected Works Ser.). (Illus.). 1977. Repr. of 1894 ed. 24.00x (ISBN 0-405-09241-5). Ayer Co Pubs.

Watcher at the Nest. M. M. Nice. (Illus.). 11.25 (ISBN 0-8446-2656-2). Peter Smith.

Watcher Bee. Mary Melwood. (Illus.). 272p. (gr. 9 up). 1983. 9.95 (ISBN 0-233-97432-6). Andre Deutsch.

Watcher by the Threshold. John Buchan. 1971. Repr. of 1918 ed. 39.00x (ISBN 0-403-00880-8). Scholarly.

Watcher by the Threshold. John Buchan. 1988. Repr. of 1918 ed. lib. bdg. 49.00x. Am Biog Serv.

Watcher in the Dark. Beverly Hastings. 160p. (YA) 1986. pap. 2.50 (ISBN 0-425-10131-2, Pub by Berkley-Pacer). Berkley Pub.

Watcher in the Dark. Beverly Hastings. (gr. 7 up). 1986. 2.50. Putnam Pub Group.

Watcher in the Garden. Joan Phipson. LC 82-3960. 228p. (YA) (gr. 12 up). 1982. 10.95 (ISBN 0-689-50246-X, Argo). Atheneum.

Watcher in the Mist. Norma Johnston. 208p. 1986. pap. 2.95 (ISBN 0-553-26032-4, Starfire). Bantam.

Watcher in the Shadows. Geoffrey Household. 1985. 20.00x (ISBN 0-86025-196-9, Pub. by Ian Henry Pubns England). State Mutual Bk.

Watcher of Windcliff. J. H. Rhodes. (YA) (gr. 7 up). 1980. 9.95 (ISBN 0-686-76781-0, Avalon). Bouregy.

Watcher on the Cast Iron Balcony. Hal Porter. 255p. (Orig.). 1986. pap. 7.95. Faber & Faber.

Watcher Within. William Appel. 192p. (Orig.). 1987. pap. 3.50 (ISBN 0-7701-0552-1). Paperjacks US.

Watchers. Frank Frate. 12p. 1983. pap. 1.00 (ISBN 0-686-89394-8). Samisdat.

Watchers. Dean R. Koontz. 352p. 1987. 17.95 (ISBN 0-399-13263-5, Putnam). Putnam Pub Group.

Watchers. Dean R. Koontz. 1988. pap. 4.95 (ISBN 0-425-11203-9). Berkley Pub.

Watchers & Seekers. Ed. by Rhonda Cobham & Merle Collins. LC 87-33357. 1988. 17.95 (ISBN 0-87226-178-6, Dist. by Harper & Row); pap. 8.95 (ISBN 0-87226-202-2, Dist. by Harper & Row). P Bedrick Bks.

Watchers at the Pond. Franklin Russell. LC 80-83963. (Illus.). 272p. 1981. pap. 7.95 (ISBN 0-87923-390-7, Nonpareil Bks). Godine.

Watchers at the Strait Gate: Mystical Tales. Russell Kirk. LC 84-267. (Illus.). 256p. 1984. 14.95 (ISBN 0-87054-098-X). Arkham.

Watchers of Space. Nancy Etchemendy. (Illus.). 124p. (Orig.). (gr. 3-7). 1985. pap. 2.50 (ISBN 0-380-78220-0, Camelot). Avon.

Watchers of the Dark. Lloyd Biggle, Jr. 1975. pap. 0.95 (ISBN 0-685-53128-7, LB275NK, Leisure Bks). Leisure NY.

Watchers of the Sky. Alfred Noyes. LC 72-131790. 1971. Repr. of 1922 ed. 29.00x (ISBN 0-403-00677-5). Scholarly.

Watchers of the Sky. Alfred Noyes. 1988. Repr. of 1922 ed. lib. bdg. 29.00x. Am Biog Serv.

Watchers Out of Time & Others. H. P. Lovecraft & August Derleth. 1974. 14.95 (ISBN 0-87054-033-5). Arkham.

Watches: A Complete History of the Technical & Decorative Development of the Watch. 3rd, rev. & enl. ed. Cecil Clutton & George Daniels. (Illus.). 312p. 1979. 85.00 (ISBN 0-85667-058-8). Sotheby Pubns.

Watches & Clocks. 185p. 1985. 595.00 (ISBN 0-318-00526-3). Busn Trend.

Watches & Clocks in the Sir David Salomons Collection. George Daniels & Ohannes Markarian. (Illus.). 320p. 1983. 65.00 (ISBN 0-85667-074-X). Sotheby Pubns.

Watches, Prayers, Arguments. Ed. by Mary Baker Eddy & Gilbert C. Carpenter. 100p. 1985. pap. 14.00 (ISBN 0-930227-01-8). Pasadena Pr.

Watches: Their History, Decoration & Mechanism. G. H. Baillie. 408p. 1987. 120.00x (ISBN 0-7198-0140-0, Pub. by E Bruton Assocs Ltd UK). State Mutual Bk.

Watchfires. Louis Auchincloss. 368p. 1982. 13.95 (ISBN 0-395-31546-8). HM.

Watchful Stork. Eno Raud. Tr. by Evi Mannermaa. 16p. 1984. pap. 1.99 (ISBN 0-8285-2701-6, Pub. by Perioodika Tallinn). Imported Pubns.

Watching. Todd Moore. 36p. 1985. pap. 3.00 (ISBN 0-935390-10-3). Wormwood Rev.

Watching & Wondering: Observing & Recording Child Development. Judith G. Isaksen. 240p. 1986. pap. 10.95 (ISBN 0-87484-755-9). Mayfield Pub.

Watching Birds. rev. ed. James Fisher & James Flegg. (Illus.). 1974. 10.00 (ISBN 0-85661-005-4, Pub. by T & A D Poyser). Buteo.

Watching Birds: An Introduction to Ornithology. Roger F. Pasquier. 1980. pap. 11.95 (ISBN 0-395-29068-6). HM.

Watching Dallas: Soap Opera & the Melodramatic Imagination. Ien Ang. 224p. 1986. lib. bdg. 25.00 (ISBN 0-416-41630-6, 9778); pap. 8.95 (ISBN 0-416-41640-3, 9781). Routledge Chapman & Hall.

Watching Fishes: Life & Behavior on Coral Reefs. Roberta Wilson & James Q. Wilson. LC 84-48205. (Illus.). 224p. 1985. 24.50i (ISBN 0-06-015371-7, HarpT). Har-Row.

Watching for Dolphins. David Constantine. Date not set. pap. 11.95 (ISBN 0-906427-54-1, Pub. by Bloodaxe Bks). Dufour.

Watching Foxes. Jim Arnosky. LC 84-20157. (Illus.). 24p. (ps-3). 1984. PLB 11.88 (ISBN 0-688-04260-0); 11.75 (ISBN 0-688-04259-7). Lothrop.

Watching How or Why. Larry Eigner. 1977. bound in boards, slipcased 10.00 (ISBN 0-685-88993-9); in wraps 5.00 (ISBN 0-685-88994-7). Elizabeth Pr.

Watching Orangutans. Joyce Hunt & Irwin Hunt. LC 83-7009. (Watching Animals in the Wild Ser.). (Illus.). 64p. (gr. 2-5). 1983. PLB 12.85 (ISBN 0-8027-6509-2). Walker & Co.

Watching Sea Birds. Richard Perry. LC 75-904. (Illus.). 240p. 1975. 10.95 (ISBN 0-8008-8047-1). Taplinger.

Watching Shakespeare: A Playgoer's Guide. Anthony B. Dawson. LC 87-24166. 272p. 1988. 29.95 (ISBN 0-312-01563-1). St Martin.

Watching Television. Ed. by Todd Gitlin. LC 86-42640. 256p. 1987. 19.45 (ISBN 0-394-54496-X); pap. 9.95 (ISBN 0-394-74651-1). Pantheon.

Watching the Body Burn: A Novel. Thomas Glynn. LC 88-80772. 304p. 1989. 18.95 (ISBN 0-394-57176-2). Knopf.

Watching the Dragon. C. Hadfield & J. Hadfield. 1986. 44.75X (ISBN 0-245-54390-2, Pub. by Harrap Ltd England). State Mutual Bk.

Watching the World. Raymond Clapper. (FDR & the Era of the New Deal Ser.). 1975. Repr. of 1944 ed. 45.00 (ISBN 0-306-70730-6). Da Capo.

Watching the World Go by. Willis J. Abbot. (American Newspapermen 1790-1933 Ser.). (Illus.). 358p. 1974. 17.50x (ISBN 0-8464-0033-2). Beekman Pubs.

Watching Through Tall Windows. DiIorio. 144p. 1982. 7.50 (ISBN 0-682-49841-6, Banner). Exposition-Phoenix.

Watching Washington Butterflies. Robert M Pyle. LC 73-94500. (Trailside Ser). (Illus.). 1974. pap. 4.50 (ISBN 0-914516-03-5). Seattle Audubon Soc.

Watching Wildlife. Ian Russell & Alan Major. (Illus.). 192p. 1983. 16.95 (ISBN 0-7153-8469-4). David & Charles.

Watchmakers & Clockmakers of the World, 2 vols. 3rd ed. G. H. Baillie & Brian Loomes. (Illus.). 1976. 75.00x ea. (ISBN 0-89563-046-X, Pub. by Tiptree Bk Serv). Vol. 1, 400p (ISBN 0-7198-0040-4, Pub. by Tiptree Bk Serv). Vol. 2, 278p (ISBN 0-7198-0080-3). State Mutual Bk.

Watchmaker's Lathe. Donald De Carle. 192p. 1987. 24.95x (ISBN 0-7090-2186-0, Pub. by R Hale Ltd UK). State Mutual Bk.

Watchmakers of Massachusetts. August C. Bolino. 276p. 1987. 22.00 (ISBN 0-939133-01-6). Kensington Hist.

Watchmaking. rev. ed. George Daniels. (Illus.). 448p. 1981. 75.00 (ISBN 0-85667-150-9). Sotheby Pubns.

Watchman. Jack Rudman. (Career Examination Ser.: C-891). (Cloth bdg. avail. on request). pap. 12.00 (ISBN 0-8373-0891-7). Natl Learning.

Watchman see Collected Works of Samuel T. Coleridge.

Watchman in Babylon: A Study Guide to Ezekiel. John Job. 112p. (Orig.). pap. 6.95 (ISBN 0-85364-339-3). Attic Pr.

Watchman Tell Us of the Night. A. B. Paulson. 320p. 1987. 17.95 (ISBN 0-670-80323-5). Viking.

Watchman's Flute. John Heath-Stubbs. 64p. 1978. pap. 8.50 (ISBN 0-85635-245-4). Carcanet.

Watchmen. Alan Moore & Dave Gibbons. 384p. (Orig.). 1987. pap. 14.95 (ISBN 0-446-38689-8). Warner Bks.

Watchmen in the Night: Presidential Accountability after Watergate. Theodore C. Sorensen. LC 75-1273. 1975. 24.00x (ISBN 0-262-19133-4). MIT Pr.

Watchmen of Eternity: Blake's Debt to Jacob Boehme. Bryan Aubrey. (Illus.). 208p. (Orig.). 1986. PLB 28.50 (ISBN 0-8191-5220-X); pap. text ed. 14.00 (ISBN 0-8191-5221-8). U Pr of Amer.

Watchtower. Elizabeth A. Lynn. (Chronicles of Terror Ser.: Bk. 1). 240p. 1986. pap. 2.95 (ISBN 0-425-08660-7). Berkley Pub.

Watchtower Files. Duane Magnani & Arthur Barrett. 340p. (Orig.). 1985. pap. 7.95 (ISBN 0-87123-816-0, 210816). Bethany Hse.

Watchwords of Liberty: A Pageant of American Quotations. Robert Lawson. (Illus.). 117p. (gr. 4 up). 1986. 7.95 (ISBN 0-316-51754-2). Little.

Water Figure in Medieval Tradition. Winder McConnell. (Stanford German Studies: Vol. 13). 129p. 1978. pap. 14.55 (ISBN 3-261-03058-5). P Lang Pubs.

Water. Rae Bains. LC 84-2718. (Illus.). 32p. (gr. 3-6). 1985. PLB 8.45 (ISBN 0-8167-0194-6); pap. text ed. 1.95 (ISBN 0-8167-0195-4). Troll Assocs.

Water. Jacqueline Dineen. (World's Harvest Ser.). 32p. (gr. 4-8). 1988. lib. bdg. 9.95 (ISBN 0-89490-225-3). Enslow Pubs.

Water. Cyril S. Fox. LC 75-138233. (Illus.). 148p. 1972. Repr. of 1951 ed. lib. bdg. 35.00x (ISBN 0-8371-5590-8, FOWA). Greenwood.

Water. Bill Gunston. LC 82-50389. (Visual Science Ser.). 48p. (gr. 6 up). 1982. PLB 14.96 (ISBN 0-382-06659-6). Silver.

Water. Alfred Leutscher. LC 82-14749. (Illus.). 32p. (ps-4). 1983. 9.95 (ISBN 0-8037-9390-1, 0966-290). Dial Bks Young.

Water. Alfred Leutscher. LC 82-14749. (Pied Piper Bk.). (Illus.). (gr. k-3). 1984. pap. 3.95 (ISBN 0-8037-9394-4, 0383-120). Dial Bks Young.

Water. Lewis. (gr. 4-6). 1980. PLB 9.40 (ISBN 0-531-04176-X). Watts.

Water, 4 bks. Bessie Love & Paul Newey. Incl. Bk. 1. Source of Life; Bk. 2. Destroyer; Bk. 3. Sustainer; Bk. 4. Transformer. (Illus., Orig.). (gr. 6-7). 1974. Set. pap. 3.50x (ISBN 0-8192-4041-9); leaders guide 2.75x (ISBN 0-8192-4042-7). Morehouse.

Water. J. M. Parramon et al. (Four Elements Ser.). 32p. (ps). 1985. pap. 3.95 (ISBN 0-8120-3599-2). Barron.

Water. Diane Tippell. LC 86-42827. (Where Does It Come From Ser.). (Illus.). 20p. (gr. k-4). 1986. 6.95 (ISBN 0-382-09365-8). Silver Burdett Pr.

Water. Brenda Walpole. (Fun with Science Ser.). (Illus.). 40p. (gr. 4-6). 1987. lib. bdg. 12.90 (ISBN 0-531-19025-0, Glouster Pr). Watts.

Water, 2 Vols. (Class B, Class C). 1984. Class B. 126P. loose-leaf ed. 10.00 (ISBN 0-318-15039-5); Class C. 118P. loose-leaf ed. 6.00 (ISBN 0-318-15040-9). NARUC.

Water. Angela Webb. (Talk Abouts Ser.). (Illus.). 32p. (gr. k-3). 1987. PLB 9.90 (ISBN 0-531-10372-2). Watts.

Water - Nineteen Seventy-Five. LC 74-93783. 448p. 1975. pap. 27.00 (ISBN 0-8169-0090-6, S-151). Am Inst Chem Eng.

Water - Nineteen Seventy-Four, Part One: Industrial Wastewater Treatment. LC 74-27534. 400p. 1974. pap. 27.00 (ISBN 0-8169-0086-8, S-144). Am Inst Chem Eng.

Water - Nineteen Seventy-Four, Part Two: Municipal Wastewater Treatment. LC 74-29199. 400p. 1975. pap. 27.00 (ISBN 0-8169-0087-6, S-145). Am Inst Chem Eng.

Water - Nineteen Seventy-One. 536p. 1972. pap. 27.00 (ISBN 0-8169-0076-0, S-124). Am Inst Chem Eng.

Water - Nineteen Seventy-Seven. LC 74-93783. 315p. 1978. pap. 27.00 (ISBN 0-8169-0107-4, S-178). Am Inst Chem Eng.

Water - Nineteen Sixty-Nine. 315p. 1969. pap. 24.00 (ISBN 0-8169-0279-8, S-97). Am Inst Chem Eng.

Water- What It Is, What It Does. Judith S. Seixas. LC 86-14926. (A Greenwillow Read-alone Book). (Illus.). 56p. (gr. 1-4). 1987. 10.25 (ISBN 0-688-06607-0); lib. bdg. 10.88 (ISBN 0-688-06608-9). Greenwillow.

Water: A Comprehensive Treatise, 6 vols. Ed. by Felix Franks. Incl. Vol. 1. Physics & Physical Chemistry of Water. LC 78-165694. 596p. 1972. 85.00x (ISBN 0-306-37181-2); Vol. 2. Water in Crystalline Hydrates. LC 78-165694. 682p. 1973. 85.00x (ISBN 0-306-37182-0); Vol. 3. Aqueous Solutions of Simple Electrolytes. LC 78-165694. 472p. 1973. 85.00x (ISBN 0-306-37183-9); Vol. 4. Aqueous Solutions of Amphiphiles & Macromolecules. LC 74-17244. 840p. 1975. 95.00x (ISBN 0-306-37184-7); Vol. 5. Water in Disperse Systems. LC 74-17190. 366p. 1975. 69.50x (ISBN 0-306-37185-5); Vol. 6. Recent Advances. LC 78-165694. 466p. 1979. 79.50x (ISBN 0-306-40139-8); Vol. 7. Water & Aqueous Solutions at Subzero Temperatures. 400p. 1982. 79.50x (ISBN 0-306-40710-8). (Illus., Plenum Pr). Plenum Pub.

Water: A Source of Energy for Today & Tomorrow. Kenneth L. Smallwood. Ed. & illus. by Arthur F. Ide. LC 82-6059. (E Equals MC Squared Ser.: Vol. 3). (Illus.). 60p. (Orig.). 1982. 12.95 (ISBN 0-86663-802-4); unbound 1.00. Ide Hse.

Water Activity & Food. John A. Troller & J. H. Christian. (Food Science & Technology Ser.). 1978. 47.00 (ISBN 0-12-700650-8). Acad Pr.

Water Activity: Influences on Food Quality: Proceedings of Second International Symposium on Properties of Water Affecting Food Quality. Ed. by Louis B. Rockland & George F. Stewart. LC 79-26632. 1981. 89.50 (ISBN 0-12-591350-8). Acad Pr.

Water Activity: Theory & Applications. Rockland & Beuchat. 448p. 1987. 59.75 (ISBN 0-8247-7759-X). Dekker.

Water Allocation in California: Legal Rights & Reform Needs. Harrison C. Dunning. LC 82-6110. (IGS Research Papers). 62p. 1982. pap. 4.50x (ISBN 0-87772-288-9). UCB IGS.

Water Analysis. Ed. by W. Fresenius & K. Quentin. (Illus.). 850p. 1987. 85.00 (ISBN 0-387-17723-X). Springer-Verlag.

Water Analysis, Vol. 2. Keith Minear. LC 82-1755. 1984. 77.00 (ISBN 0-12-498302-2). Acad Pr.

Water Analysis, Vol. 3. Keith Minear. LC 82-1755. 1984. 82.00 (ISBN 0-12-498303-0). Acad Pr.

Water Analysis: A Practical Treatise on the Examination of Potable Water. J. Alfred Wanklyn & Ernest T. Chapman. Ed. by Barbara G. Rosenkrantz. LC 76-40651. (Public Health in America Ser.). (Illus.). 1977. Repr. of 1884 ed. lib. bdg. 17.00x (ISBN 0-405-09834-0). Ayer Co Pubs.

Water Analysis & the Quality of Water. Taylor. (Chemical Analysis Ser.). 1988. write for info. (ISBN 0-471-84558-2). Wiley.

Water Analysis: Some Revised Methods for Limnologists. F. J. Mackereth et al. 1978. 25.00x (ISBN 0-900386-31-2, Pub. by Freshwater Bio). State Mutual Bk.

Water Analysis, Vol. 1: Solution Control Parameters & Analysis Techniques of Inorganic Species. Ed. by Roger Minear & L. H. Keith. 1982. 52.50 (ISBN 0-12-498301-4). Acad Pr.

Water & Aqueous Solutions. Ed. by G. W. Neilson & J. E. Enderby. (Colston Papers: No. 37). (Illus.). 362p. 1986. 102.00x (ISBN 0-85274-576-1, Pub. by A Hilger UK). Taylor & Francis.

Water & Aqueous Solutions at Subzero Temperatures. see Water: A Comprehensive Treatise.

Water & Aqueous Solutions: Introduction to a Molecular Theory. Arieh Ben-Naim. LC 74-7325. (Illus.). 474p. 1974. 75.00x (ISBN 0-306-30774-X, Plenum Pr). Plenum Pub.

Water & Baptismal Fonts Through the Ages: A Bibliography of Scholarship Dealing with Stylistic, Design, & Iconographic Aspects. Carole Cable. (Architecture Ser.: A 1484). 8p. 1985. 2.00 (ISBN 0-89028-614-0). Vance Biblios.

Water & Bread. Alfred Cordes. LC 87-50263. 71p. 1987. 6.95 (ISBN 1-55523-069-5). Winston-Derek.

Water & Dreams: An Essay on the Imagination of Matter. Gaston Bachelard. Tr. by Edith R. Farrell from Fr. LC 83-23641. (Bachelard Translation Ser.). 213p. 1983. 25.00 (ISBN 0-911005-01-3). Dallas Inst Pubns.

Water & Electrolytes in Pediatrics: Physiology, Pathophysiology & Treatment. Laurence Finberg et al. (Illus.). 272p. 1982. 48.95 (ISBN 0-7216-3625-X). Saunders.

Water & Energy Demand & Effects: Prepared for the International Hydrological Programme by the U. S. National Committee on Scientific Hydrology. George H. Davis. (Studies & Reports in Hydrology: No. 42). 129p. 1986. pap. text ed. 14.00 (ISBN 92-3-102328-4, U1502, Pub. by Unesco). UNIPUB.

Water & Energy: Technical & Policy Issues. Ed. by F. Kilpatrick & D. Matchett. LC 82-71351. 668p. 1982. pap. 52.00x (ISBN 0-87262-308-4). Am Soc Civil Eng.

Water & Environmental Technology: Volume 11.03, Atmospheric Analysis; Occupational Health & Safety. 766p. 1986. 50.00 (ISBN 0-8031-0904-0). ASTM.

Water & Environmental Technology: Volume 11.04, Pesticides; Resource Recovery; Hazardous Substances & Oil Spill Response; Waste Disposal; Biological Effects. 1028p. 1986. 62.00 (ISBN 0-8031-0905-9). ASTM.

Water & Environmental Technology: Volume 11.01, Water (I) 844p. 1986. 52.00 (ISBN 0-8031-0902-4). ASTM.

Water & Environmental Technology: Volume 11.02, Water (II) 1192p. 1986. 73.00 (ISBN 0-8031-0903-2). ASTM.

Water & Grass: Study in the Pastoral Economy of Southern Europe. Else H. Carrier. LC 77-87717. Repr. of 1932 ed. 41.50 (ISBN 0-404-16579-6). AMS Pr.

Water & Ions in Biological Systems. Ed. by Alberte Pullman et al. LC 85-3438. 840p. 1985. 125.00x (ISBN 0-306-41921-1, Plenum Pr). Plenum Pub.

Water & Ions in Biological Systems. Ed. by V. Vasilescu. (Congress Reports: No. 2). 500p. 1987. 72.50 (ISBN 0-8176-1941-0). Birkhauser.

Water & Land-Use Development & the Aquatic Environment: Problems & Solutions. W. A. Dill et al. (Fisheries Technical Papers: No. 141). 12p. (2nd Printing 1976). 1975. pap. 7.50 (ISBN 92-5-101908-8, F871, FAO). UNIPUB.

Water & Landscape: An Aesthetic Overview of the Role of Water in the Landscape. R. Burton Litton, Jr. et al. LC 74-79147. (Illus.). 314p. 1974. pap. text ed. 20.00 (ISBN 0-912394-10-2). Water Info.

Water & Life: Poetry in English & Italian. Adolph Caso. 1976. pap. 5.00 (ISBN 0-8283-1682-1). Branden Pub Co.

Water & Metal Cations in Biological Systems. Ed. by Bernard Pullman & K. Yagi. 270p. 1980. 42.00x (ISBN 0-89955-335-4, Pub. by Japan Sci Soc Japan). Intl Spec Bk.

Water & Metropolitan Man. 94p. 1969. pap. 8.00 (ISBN 0-87262-011-5). Am Soc Civil Eng.

Water & Politics: A Study of Water Policies & Administration in the Development of Los Angeles. Vincent Ostrom. Repr. of 1953 ed. 28.00 (ISBN 0-384-43860-1). Johnson Repr.

Water & Poverty in the Southwest: Conflict, Opportunity & Challenge. F. Lee Brown & Helen M. Ingram. LC 87-19217. 226p. 1987. 19.95x (ISBN 0-8165-1038-5); pap. 12.95x (ISBN 0-8165-1039-3). U of Ariz Pr.

Water & Power Resources of West Pakistan, A Study in Sector Planning. Pieter Lieftinck. Incl. Vol. 1. The Main Report. 310p. 1968. 24.00x (ISBN 0-8018-1004-3); Vol. 2. The Development of Irrigation & Agriculture. 419p. 1969. 24.00x (ISBN 0-8018-1005-1); Vol. 3. Background & Methodology. 386p. 1969 (ISBN 0-8018-1006-X). (World Bank Ser). 1968. 24.00x ea. Johns Hopkins.

Water & Power: The Conflict over Los Angeles' Water Supply in the Owens Valley. William L. Kahrl. (Illus.). 584p. 1982. 24.95 (ISBN 0-520-04431-2); pap. 12.95 (ISBN 0-520-05068-1). U of Cal Pr.

Water & Related Land Resource Systems: Proceedings. Y. Haimes. Ed. by J. Kindler. LC 80-41690. (IFAC Proceedings Ser.). (Illus.). 550p. 1981. 160.00 (ISBN 0-08-027307-6). Pergamon.

Water & Salt Regimes of Soils; Modelling & Management. Ed. by E. A. Sokolenko. Tr. by R. K. Mishra from Rus. 254p. 1984. text ed. 41.50 (ISBN 90-6191-425-6, Pub. by A A Balkema). Brookfield Pub Co.

Water & Sewer Rates in Virgina. Ed. by Mary J. Fields. (Virginia Municipal League Survey Ser.). 1988. pap. 15.00 (ISBN 0-932993-02-8). VA Muni League.

Water & Shadows. Brown Miller. 1969. pap. 2.50 (ISBN 0-912136-15-4); pap. 10.00x signed ed. (ISBN 0-685-01074-0). Twowindows Pr.

Water & Society, Conflicts in Development: Water Conflicts & Research Priorities, Part 2. (Water Development, Supply & Management Ser.: Vol. 8). (Illus.). 260p. 1980. 63.00 (ISBN 0-08-023422-4). Pergamon.

Water & Society: The Social & Ecological Effects of Water Exploitation in Developing Countries, Part 1. C. G. Widstrand et al. 1982. flexi-cover 26.00 (ISBN 0-08-028751-4). Pergamon.

Water & Soil Repellents for Fabrics. Charles S. Sodano. LC 79-13241. (Chemical Technology Review Ser.: No. 134). (Illus.). 395p. 1979. 39.00 (ISBN 0-8155-0761-5). Noyes.

Water & Steam: Their Properties & Current Industrial Applications: Proceedings. International Conference on the Properties of Steam, 9th, Munich, West Germany, Sep. 10-14, 1979 & Straub. (Illus.). 704p. 1980. 180.00 (ISBN 0-08-025431-4). Pergamon.

Water & Survival in an Island Environment: Challenge of Okinawa. Nobuya Miwa et al. LC 87-50463. 176p. 1988. text ed. 25.00x (ISBN 0-8248-1174-7, Pub. by UH WRRC). UH Pr.

Water & the Arid Lands of the Western United States. Ed. by Mohamed T. El-Ashry & Diana C. Gibbons. (Illus.). 475p. Date not set. price not set (ISBN 0-521-35040-9). Cambridge U Pr.

Water & the Cycle of Life. Joseph Cocannouer. 10.95 (ISBN 0-8159-7202-4). Devin.

Water & the Leaf: Oriental Poems for Meditation. Angela Lobo-Cobb. (Illus.). Date not set. pap. price not set. Bloomsberry Pr.

Water & the West: The Colorado River Compact & the Politics of Water in the American West. Norris Hundley, Jr. LC 73-93054. (Illus.). 432p. 1975. 42.00x (ISBN 0-520-02700-0). U of Cal Pr.

Water & Waste-Water Technology. 2nd ed. Mark J. Hammer. LC 86-5563. 550p. 1986. write for info. (ISBN 0-471-05650-2); S.I. Version. write for info. (ISBN 0-471-82961-7). Wiley.

Water & Waste-Water Technology, SI Version. Mark J. Hammer. LC 77-9243. 504p. 1977. 35.95 (ISBN 0-471-03787-7); solutions manual 6.50 (ISBN 0-471-03819-9). Wiley.

Water & Wastewater Engineering, 2 vols. Gordon M. Fair & Daniel A. Okun. LC 66-16139. Vol. 1, Water Supply & Wastewater Removal. pap. 128.00 (ISBN 0-317-11201-5, 2055401); Vol. 2, Water Purification & Wastewater Treatment & Disposal. pap. 160.00 (ISBN 0-317-11202-3). Bks Demand UMI.

Water & Wastewater Treatment: Calculations for Chemistry & Physical Processes. M. J. Humenick. (Pollution Engineering & Technology Ser.: Vol. 4). 1977. pap. 59.75 (ISBN 0-8247-7280-6). Dekker.

Water & Wastewater Treatment Chemicals (U. S.) 208p. 1985. 1700.00 (ISBN 0-86621-420-8, A1495). Frost & Sullivan.

Water & Wastewater Treatment Market. Frost & Sullivan Inc., Staff. 340p. 1986. 1550.00 (ISBN 0-86621-764-9, A1581). Frost & Sullivan.

Water & Water Policy in World Food Supplies. Ed. by Wayne R. Jordan. LC 86-23065. (Illus.). 466p. 1987. lib. bdg. 69.50x (ISBN 0-89096-278-2). Tex A&M Univ Pr.

Water & Water Pollution Handbook, Vol. 1. Ed. by Leonard L. Ciaccio. 1971. 95.00 (ISBN 0-8247-1104-1). Dekker.

Water & Water Pollution Handbook, Vol. 2. Ed. by Leonard L. Ciaccio. 400p. 1971. 95.00 (ISBN 0-8247-1116-5). Dekker.

Water & Water Pollution Handbook, Vol. 3. Ed. by Leoanrd L. Ciaccio. 1972. 95.00 (ISBN 0-8247-1117-3). Dekker.

Water & Water Pollution Handbook, Vol. 4. Ed. by Leoanrd L. Ciaccio. 548p. 1973. 95.00 (ISBN 0-8247-1118-1). Dekker.

Water & Water Treatment in Nuclear Power Plants. A. A. Kot. 320p. 1966. text ed. 63.00x (ISBN 0-7065-0401-1, Pub. by Keter Pub Jerusalem). Coronet Bks.

Water & Wildlife. Douglas Hey. (Illus.). 321p. 1987. pap. 15.00 (ISBN 0-86978-280-0, Pub. by Timmins S Africa). Intl Spec Bk.

Water & Windfall. Marilyn A. Francis. (Illus.). 48p. 1982. 20.00 (ISBN 0-88014-039-9). Mosaic Pr OH.

Water As a Productive Environment. C. F. Hickling. LC 75-4394. 200p. 1975. 25.00 (ISBN 0-312-85680-6). St Martin.

Water at the Surface of the Earth: An Introduction to Ecosystem Hydrodynamics. D. H. Miller. 1977. 82.00 (ISBN 0-12-496750-7). Acad Pr.

Water at the Surface of the Earth: Student Edition. David H. Miller. LC 82-13769. (International Geophysics Ser.). 1982. 29.00 (ISBN 0-12-496752-3). Acad Pr.

Water Atlas of the U. S. 3rd ed. Geraghty, Miller, Van der Leeden, & Troise Staff. LC 73-76649. 1973. 60.00 (ISBN 0-912394-03-X). Water Info.

Water Babies. Charles Kingsley. (Madhuban Abridged Classics Ser.). x, 130p. 1983. text ed. 6.95x (ISBN 0-7069-1818-5, Pub. by Vikas India). Advent NY.

Water Babies. Charles Kingsley. (Puffin Classics Ser.). 192p. (gr. 5 up). 1986. pap. 2.25 (ISBN 0-14-035035-7, Puffin). Penguin.

Water Babies. Charles Kingsley. Ed. by G. Mercer Adam. (Illus.). (gr. k-4). Repr. of 1905 ed. 12.95 (ISBN 0-940561-09-3). White Rose Pr.

Water Babies. (gr. k-6). 1986. 8.98 (ISBN 0-517-61817-6). Outlet Bk Co.

Water Babies: A Fairy-Tale for a Land Baby. Charles Kingsley. (Dent's Illustrated Children's Classics Ser.). (Illus.). 254p. (gr. 4 up). 1982. Repr. of 1957 ed. 13.95x (ISBN 0-460-05037-0, Pub. by J M Dent England). Biblio Dist.

Water Babies: The Igor Tjarkovsky Method for Delivery in Water. Erik Sidenbladh. Tr. by Wendy Croton. LC 83-60344. (Illus.). 156p. 1983. 12.95 (ISBN 0-312-85688-1). St Martin.

Water Balance in Land Arthropods. E. B. Edney. (Zoophysiology & Ecology Ser.: Vol. 9). 1977. 49.00 (ISBN 0-387-08084-8). Springer-Verlag.

Water Balance of Monsoon Asia: A Climatological Approach. Ed. by Masatoshi M. Yoshino. (Illus.). 308p. 1971. text ed. 25.00x (ISBN 0-87022-895-1). UH Pr.

Water Banking: How to Stop Wasting Agricultural Water. Eugene Bardach & Sotirios Angelides. LC 78-50766. 56p. 1978. pap. 2.00 (ISBN 0-917616-26-X). ICS Pr.

Water Baptism. Perry A. Gaspard. 1983. pap. 1.50 (ISBN 0-931867-01-0). Abundant Life Pubns.

Water Baptism. Guy B. Giovanni. 24p. (Orig.). 1983. pap. 1.00 (ISBN 0-912981-05-9). Hse Bon Giovanni.

Water Baptism. Jack Hayford. 96p. (Orig.). cancelled (ISBN 0-8423-7814-6). Tyndale.

Water Baptism: Sealed by Christ, the Lord. Jack W. Hayford. LC 84-80750. (Orig.). 1984. pap. 2.95 (ISBN 0-916847-01-2). Living Way.

Water Bears No Scars. David K. Reynolds. LC 87-7036. 192p. (Orig.). 1987. pap. 6.95 (ISBN 0-688-07448-0). Morrow.

Water Beetle. Nancy Mitford. LC 85-48119. 160p. 1986. pap. 6.95 (ISBN 0-689-70703-7, 340). Atheneum.

Water Beetles & Other Things (Half a Century's Work) F. Balfour-Browne. 226p. 1962. 37.00x (ISBN 0-317-07182-3, Pub. by FW Classey UK). State Mutual Bk.

Water Birds of California. Howard L. Cogswell. (Natural History Guides Ser.: No. 40). 1977. 22.00 (ISBN 0-520-02994-1); pap. 8.95 (ISBN 0-520-02699-3). U of Cal Pr.

Water Birds of North America, 2 vols. in one. S. F. Baird et al. (Natural Sciences in America Ser). (Illus.). 1974. 74.00 (ISBN 0-405-05716-4). Ayer Co Pubs.

Water Book: Where It Came from & Where It Goes. Ira M. Freeman & Sean Morrison. (Pop-Up Science Bks.: No. 1). (Illus.). (gr. 1-5). 1970. 3.50 (ISBN 0-394-80842-8). Random.

Water Boundaries. George Cole. (Riparian Boundaries: No. 1). (Illus.). 68p. 1984. pap. 10.00 (ISBN 0-910845-13-1, 645). Landmark Ent.

Water Boundaries for Land Surveyors. Roy Minnick. 145p. (Orig.). 1985. pap. 50.00 (ISBN 0-910845-24-7). Landmark Ent.

Water Break Its Neck. Frederick Grice. 112p. (YA) (gr. 7 up). 1987. 13.95 (ISBN 0-19-271535-6). Oxford U Pr.

Water Buffalo. (No. 4). (Illus.). 283p. (Animal Production & Health Ser.). 1977. pap. 19.50 (ISBN 92-5-100108-1, F1391, FAO). UNIPUB.

Water Bugs & Dragonflies: Explaining Death to Children. Doris Stickney. (Illus.). 24p. 1982. pap. 1.25 (ISBN 0-8298-0609-1). Pilgrim NY.

Water-Bug's Mittens. James Dickey. 1980. ltd. ed. 30.00 (ISBN 0-89723-021-3). Bruccoli.

Water Can Do Wonders. Wesley T. Runk. Ed. by Michael L. Sherer. (Orig.). 1986. pap. 1.75 (ISBN 0-89536-816-1, 6826). CSS of Ohio.

Water Can Undermine Your Health. N. W. Walker. (Illus.). 106p. 1974. pap. 4.95 (ISBN 0-89019-037-2). Norwalk Pr.

Water: Canadian Needs & Resources. 3rd ed. J. S. Cram. LC 74-171154. (International Ser.). pap. 55.00 (ISBN 0-317-28411-8, 2022290). Bks Demand UMI.

Water Carriers in Hades: A Study of Catharsis Through Toil in Classical Antiquity. E. Keuls. (Illus.). 179p. 1974. pap. text ed. 54.00x (ISBN 0-317-54499-3, Pub. by A. M. Hakkert). Coronet Bks.

Water Castle. Ingeborg Lauterstein. 416p. 1981. 12.95 (ISBN 0-395-29471-1). HM.

Water Charges for Private Fire Protection. (Twenty Ser). 1974. pap. 2.00 (ISBN 0-685-58113-6, 292M). Natl Fire Prot.

Water Chemicals Codex. National Research Council. 1982. pap. text ed. 7.25x (ISBN 0-309-03338-1). Natl Acad Pr.

Water Chemistry. Vernon L. Snoeyink & David Jenkins. LC 79-21331. (SPE Monographs). 183p. 1980. 49.95 (ISBN 0-471-05196-9); pap. write for info. (ISBN 0-471-06272-3). Wiley.

Water Chemistry & Corrosion in Steam Systems. Jonas. 400p. 1988. price not set (ISBN 0-471-88408-1). Wiley.

Water Chemistry & Corrosion Problems in Nuclear Power Plants: Proceedings of a Symposium, Vienna, 22-26 November 1982. (Proceedings Ser.). 516p. (Eng., Fr. & Rus.). 1984. pap. 98.00 (ISBN 92-0-050783-2, ISP630, IAEA). UNIPUB.

Water Chemistry of Nuclear Reactor Systems 3: Proceedings of an International Conference Organized by the British Nuclear Energy Society, 2 vols. 541p. 1983. Set. 115.00 (ISBN 0-7277-0202-5, Pub. by T Telford UK). Am Soc Civil Eng.

Water Chlorination: Chemistry, Environmental Impact & Health Effects, Vol. 5. Robert L. Jolley. LC 86-20139. (Illus.). 1575p. 1985. 89.95 (ISBN 0-87371-005-3). Lewis Pubs Inc.

Water Chlorination: Environmental Impact & Health Effects, 2 vols. Ed. by Robert L. Jolley et al. LC 77-92588. (Illus.). 1200p. 1980. 65.00 (ISBN 0-250-40342-0). Butterworth.

Water Chlorination: Environmental Impact & Health Effects, Vol. 1. Ed. by Robert L. Jolley. LC 77-92588. 1978. 34.95 (ISBN 0-250-40200-9). Butterworth.

Water Chlorination: Environmental Impact & Health Effects, Vol. 2. Ed. by Robert L. Jolley et al. LC 77-92588. 1978. 34.95 (ISBN 0-250-40201-7). Butterworth.

Water Chlorination Principles & Practices - M20. (AWWA Manuals Ser.). (Illus.). 92p. 1973. pap. text ed. 8.40 (ISBN 0-89867-078-0). Am Water Wks Assn.

Water Circulation in the Arctic Basin. A. F. Treshnikov & G. I. Baranov. 160p. 1973. text ed. 35.00x (ISBN 0-7065-1310-X, Pub. by Keter Pub Jerusalem). Coronet Bks.

Water Clarification Processes: Practical Design & Evaluation. H. E. Hudson, Jr. (Environmental Engineering Ser.). 272p. 1981. 38.95 (ISBN 0-442-24490-8). Van Nos Reinhold.

Water Color... Lets Think About. Judi Betts. 114p. 1984. pap. 15.00 (ISBN 0-317-67945-7). Aquarelle Pr.

Water Colors. Hale Chatfield. LC 78-11143. (Illus.). 1979. cloth 20.00 (ISBN 0-916906-11-6); signed ed. 50.00 (ISBN 0-916906-12-4); pap. 12.00 (ISBN 0-916906-10-8). Konglomerati.

Water-Colourist. Sebastian Barry. 1983. pap. 9.95 (ISBN 0-85105-412-9, Pub. by Colin Smythe Ltd Britain). Dufour.

Water Conditioning Technical Manual. 98p. 6.25 (ISBN 0-318-15927-9). Natl Water Well.

Water Conservance & Irrigation in China. E. B. Vermeer. 1977. lib. bdg. 45.00 (ISBN 90-6021-410-2, Pub. by Leiden Univ Holland). Kluwer Academic.

Water Conservation in Landscape Design & Management. Environmental Design Press Staff. 1984. 31.95 (ISBN 0-442-22204-1). Van Nos Reinhold.

Water Conservation Management. (American Water Works Association Handbooks-General). (Illus.). 76p. 1981. text ed. 10.75 (ISBN 0-89867-264-3). Am Water Wks Assn.

Water Conservation: Needs & Implementing Strategies. 277p. 1979. pap. 20.00x (ISBN 0-87262-198-7). Am Soc Civil Eng.

Water Conservation Strategies. (AAWA Handbooks - General Ser.). (Illus.). 108p. 1980. pap. text ed. 12.00 (ISBN 0-89867-240-6). Am Water Wks Assn.

Water Control in Tokugawa Japan: Irrigation Organization in a Japanese River Basin, 1600-1870. William W. Kelly. LC 83-126822. (East Asia Papers: No. 31). 260p. 1982. 7.00 (ISBN 0-939657-31-7). Cornell East Asia Pgm.

Water Coolant Technology of Power Reactors. Paul Cohen. Ed. by Diane Wallin. LC 79-57306. (Monograph Ser.). 250p. 1980. Repr. of 1969 ed. 32.00 (ISBN 0-89448-020-0, 300016). Am Nuclear Soc.

Water-Cooling Towers. National Fire Protection Association Staff. 1983. 10.50 (ISBN 0-317-63332-5, 214-83). Natl Fire Prot.

Water-Cooling Towers. (Two Hundred Ser). 1971. pap. 2.00 (ISBN 0-685-58033-4, 214). Natl Fire Prot.

Water Crisis: Ending the Policy Drought. Terry L. Anderson. LC 83-48046. 136p. 1983. text ed. 17.50x (ISBN 0-8018-3087-7); pap. text ed. 8.95x (ISBN 0-8018-3088-5). Johns Hopkins.

Water Current Turbines: A Fieldworkers Guide. Peter Garman. (Illus.). 113p. (Orig.). 1986. pap. 20.50x (ISBN 0-946688-27-3, Pub. by Intermediate Tech England). Intermediate Tech.

Water Customer Information. American Water Works Association Staff. (AWWA Handbooks Proceedings Ser.). (Illus.). 56p. 1979. pap. text ed. 7.20 (ISBN 0-89867-222-8). Am Water Wks Assn.

Water Cycle. Eleanor Keats. LC 85-73376. 102p. (Orig.). 1986. pap. 8.50 (ISBN 0-936014-16-4). Dawn Valley.

Water Dancer. Jenifer Levin. 1983. pap. 3.95 (ISBN 0-671-46764-6). PB.

Water Deficits & Plant Growth, 5 vols. Ed. by Theodore T. Kozlowski. LC 68-14658. Vol. 1 1968. 78.00 (ISBN 0-12-424150-6); Vol. 2 1968. 66.50 (ISBN 0-12-424152-2); Vol. 3 1972. 66.50 (ISBN 0-12-424153-0); Vol. 4 1976. 73.50 (ISBN 0-12-424154-9); Vol. 5, 1978. 59.50 (ISBN 0-12-424155-7). Acad Pr.

Water Deficits & Plant Growth, Vol. 6: Woody Plant Communities. T. T. Kozlowski. LC 68-14658. 1981. 89.00 (ISBN 0-12-424156-5). Acad Pr.

Water Deficits & Plant Growth, Vol. 7: Additional Woody Crop Plants. T. T. Kozlowski. Ed. by A. J. Riker. 1983. 44.00 (ISBN 0-12-424157-3). Acad Pr.

Water Demand for Steam Electric Generation: An Economic Projection Model. Paul H. Cootner & George O. Lof. LC 65-27669. pap. 39.00 (ISBN 0-317-09080-1, 2020959). Bks Demand UMI.

Water Development & Management, 4 vols. United Nations. Incl. Part 1. 1978. 140.00 (ISBN 0-08-023402-X); 50.00 (ISBN 0-08-023403-8); Part 2. 1978. 220.00 (ISBN 0-08-023404-6); 70.00 (ISBN 0-08-023405-4); Part 3. 1978. 250.00 (ISBN 0-08-023406-2); 90.00 (ISBN 0-08-023407-0); Part 4. 1978. 325.00 (ISBN 0-08-023408-9); 110.00 (ISBN 0-08-023409-7). 1978. 880.00 set (ISBN 0-08-021987-X). Pergamon.

Water Disinfection with Ozone, Chloramines, or Chlorine Dioxide. (Handbooks-Proceedings Ser.). (Illus.). 224p. 1980. pap. text ed. 11.40 (ISBN 0-89867-244-9). Am Water Wks Assn.

Water Distribution Operator Training Handbook. (AWWA Handbooks - General Ser.). (Illus.). 232p. 1976. pap. text ed. 14.40 (ISBN 0-89867-013-6). Am Water Wks Assn.

Water District Clerk. (Career Examination Ser.: C-3378). Date not set. pap. 14.00 (ISBN 0-8373-3378-4). Natl Learning.

Water District Superintendent. (Career Examination Ser.: C-3342). Date not set. pap. 18.00 (ISBN 0-8373-3342-3). Natl Learning.

Water District Supervisor. Jack Rudman. (Career Examination Ser.: C-2625). (Cloth bdg. avail. on request). pap. 14.00 (ISBN 0-8373-2625-7). Natl Learning.

Water Divining & Other Dowsing: A Practical Guide. Ralph Whitlock. (Illus.). 144p. 1982. 16.95 (ISBN 0-7153-8220-9). David & Charles.

Water Dog. Richard A. Wolters. 1964. 14.95 (ISBN 0-525-24430-1). Dutton.

Water Dog's Tale. Melissa Zink. (Illus.). 32p. (Orig.). 1985. pap. 6.25 (ISBN 0-917270-04-5). Finn Hill.

Water, Earth, & Fire: Land Use & Environmental Planning in the New Jersey Pine Barrens. Jonathan Berger & John W. Sinton. LC 84-47963. (Illus.). 248p. 1985. text ed. 25.00x (ISBN 0-8018-2398-6). Johns Hopkins.

Water, Earth & Man. Ed. by Richard J. Chorley. 1969. 66.00x (ISBN 0-416-12030-X, NO. 2138). Routledge Chapman & Hall.

Water Ecology. Jennifer Cochrane. (Project Ecology Ser.). (Illus.). 48p. (gr. 4-9). 1987. lib. bdg. 11.40 (ISBN 0-531-18152-9, Pub. by Bookwright Pr). Watts.

Water Economy of a Fictive Crop. (Agricultural Research Reports: No. 817). 1979. pap. 5.00 (ISBN 90-220-0511-9, PDC121, PUDOC). UNIPUB.

Water, Energy & Economic Alternatives: Proceedings Irrigation Association. 331p. 1982. 15.00 (ISBN 0-935030-03-4); members 12.00 (ISBN 0-317-36871-0). Irrigation.

Water Engine & Mr. Happiness. David Mamet. LC 78-3118. 1978. 10.00 (ISBN 0-394-50120-9, GP811); pap. 7.95 (ISBN 0-394-17043-1). Grove.

Water Environment: Algal Toxins & Health. Ed. by Wayne W. Carmichael. (Environmental Science Research Ser.: Vol. 20). 504p. 1981. 85.00x (ISBN 0-306-40756-6, Plenum Pr). Plenum Pub.

Water Escapes in the Northeast. Betsy Wittemann & Nancy Webster. Ed. by Richard Woodworth. (Illus.). 420p. (Orig.). 1987. pap. 12.95 (ISBN 0-934260-62-1). Wood Pond.

Water: Examination, Assessment, Conditioning, Chemistry, Bacteriology, Biology. Karl Hoell et al. 1972. 40.00 (ISBN 3-11-003728-9). De Gruyter.

Water Exercises for All Ages. Jaye Slater. (Illus.). 44p. (Orig.). 1981. 5.00 (ISBN 0-9607454-0-8). Slater Pub.

Water Flow. Elementary Science Study Staff. 1971. tchr's guide 18.40 (ISBN 0-07-017733-3). McGraw.

Water Fluoridation Principles & Practices - M4. (AWWA Manuals Ser.). (Illus.). 120p. 1977. pap. text ed. 9.60 (ISBN 0-89867-062-4). Am Water Wks Assn.

Water for a City: A History of New York City's Problem from the Beginning to the Delaware River System. Charles H. Weidner. LC 72-4204. pap. 93.80 (ISBN 0-317-11234-1, 2050689). Bks Demand UMI.

Water: No Longer Taken for Granted. Ed. by Mark A. Siegel et al. (Information Aids Ser.). 104p. 1987. pap. text ed. 16.95 (ISBN 0-936474-73-4). Info Plus TX.

Water of Kane. O. A. Bushnell. LC 80-5463. 468p. 1980. 12.95 (ISBN 0-8248-0714-6). UH Pr.

Water of Life. John W. Armstrong. 136p. 1971. pap. 4.75x (ISBN 0-8464-1060-5). Beekman Pubs.

Water of Life. John W. Armstrong. 1980. 17.50x (ISBN 0-85032-194-8, Pub. by Daniel Co England). State Mutual Bk.

Water of Life. John Bunyan. pap. 1.50 (ISBN 0-685-88397-3). Reiner.

Water of Life. Glenn Clark. 1979. pap. 5.95 (ISBN 0-910924-86-4). Macalester.

Water of Life. Ed. by Alma Gilleo. LC 74-734825. (Fairy Tales of the Brothers Grimm Book Cassettes). (Illus.). 1976. Set. 6 bks. & one cassette 24.95 (ISBN 0-89290-006-7). Soc for Visual.

Water of Life. Retold by Barbara Rogasky. LC 84-19226. (Illus.). 40p. (gr. k-3). 1986. reinforced bdg. 14.95 (ISBN 0-8234-0552-4). Holiday.

Water of Life: A Treatise on Urine Therapy. 2nd ed. John W. Armstrong. 136p. 1957. pap. text ed. 11.95 (ISBN 0-88697-016-4). Life Science.

Water of the Hills: Jean de Florette & Manon of the Springs. Marcel Pagnol. Tr. by W. E. van Heyningen. (Illus.). 440p. 1988. cancelled (ISBN 0-317-70127-4); pap. cancelled (ISBN 0-317-70128-2). N Point Pr.

Water of Thought. Fred Saberhagen. 256p. (Orig.). 1985. pap. 2.95 (ISBN 0-8125-5290-3, Dist. Warner Pub. Services & Saint Martin's Press). Tor Bks.

Water on the Brain. Denys Gamblin. 96p. 1979. 6.00 (ISBN 0-7277-0070-7, Pub. by T Telford UK). Am Soc Civil Eng.

Water on the Plateau, Vol. 53, No. 3. 32p. 1981. pap. 3.00 (ISBN 0-686-94116-0). Mus Northern Ariz.

Water over the Dam. 1986. 13.50 (ISBN 0-317-43198-6). North Country.

Water over the Dam at Mountain View in the Adirondacks. Floy S. Hyde. LC 73-126350. 1984. 13.50 (ISBN 0-317-56106-5). F S Hyde.

Water Over the Road see **NEA Series.**

Water, Pine & Stone Retreat Collection. Hugh Moss. (Illus.). 1987. 39.00x (Pub. by Han-Shan Tang Ltd). State Mutual Bk.

Water Planet: A Celebration of the Wonder of Water. Lyall Watson. (Illus.). 224p. 1988. 30.00 (ISBN 0-517-56504-8). Crown.

Water Planet: Poems. Mary Rudge. LC 85-51148. (Illus.). 96p. (Orig.). 1986. pap. 5.00 (ISBN 0-935327-00-2). Gateway Arts.

Water Planning in Arid Sudan. Andrew Shepherd et al. (Middle East Science Policy Studies: Vol. 10). 228p. 1987. 39.95 (ISBN 0-86372-082-X, Pub. by Ithaca Pr); pap. 19.95 (ISBN 0-86372-072-2, Pub. by Ithaca Pr). Humanities.

Water Planning in Britain. Dennis J. Parker & Edmund C. Penning-Rowsell. (Resource Management Ser.: No. 1). (Illus.). 288p. (Orig.). 1980. text ed. 45.00x (ISBN 0-04-711006-6). Unwin Hyman.

Water Plant Instrumentation & Automation. (AWWA Handbooks-Proceedings Ser.). (Illus.). 304p. 1976. pap. text ed. 14.40 (ISBN 0-89867-049-7). Am Water Wks Assn.

Water Plant Operator. Jack Rudman. (Career Examination Ser.: C-897). (Cloth bdg. avail. on request). pap. 14.00 (ISBN 0-8373-0897-6). Natl Learning.

Water Plant Operator Trainee. Jack Rudman. (Career Examination Ser.: C-886). (Cloth bdg. avail. on request). pap. 12.00 (ISBN 0-8373-0886-0). Natl Learning.

Water Plant Supervisor. Jack Rudman. (Career Examination Ser.: C-2445). (Cloth bdg. avail. on request). pap. 14.00 (ISBN 0-8373-2445-9). Natl Learning.

Water Plants in the Aquarium. Ines Scheurmann. (Illus.). 1987. pap. 3.95 (ISBN 0-8120-3926-2). Barron.

Water Plants of the World. C. D. Cook. (Illus.). 1974. 125.00 (ISBN 9-0619-3024-3). Heinman.

Water Plants: Study of Aquatic Angiosperms. Agnes Arber. (Illus.). 1963. Repr. of 1920 ed. 44.00x (ISBN 3-7682-0157-0). Lubrecht & Cramer.

Water Policy Initiatives: Positions of the National Water Policy Committee of ASCE on the President's June 1978 Statements. 280p. 1979. pap. 20.00x (ISBN 0-87262-193-6). Am Soc Civil Eng.

Water Pollutants: Medical Subject Analysis & Research Index. Henry B. Chogue. LC 87-47662. 150p. 1987. 34.50 (ISBN 0-88164-674-1); pap. 26.50 (ISBN 0-88164-675-X). Abbe Pubs Assn.

Water Pollution: A Guide to Information Sources. Ed. by Allen W. Knight & Mary Ann Simmons. LC 73-17537. (Man & the Environment Information Guide Ser.: Vol. 9). 288p. 1980. 68.00x (ISBN 0-8103-1346-4). Gale.

Water Pollution & Fish Physiology. Alan G. Heath. 272p. 1987. 149.00 (ISBN 0-8493-4649-5). CRC Pr.

Water Pollution & Management. 1984. 10.00 (ISBN 0-471-63914-1). Wiley.

Water Pollution Assessment: Automatic Sampling & Measurement - STP 582. 126p. 1975. pap. 6.50 (ISBN 0-8031-0597-5, 04-582000-16). ASTM.

Water Pollution by Fertilizers & Pesticides. OECD Staff. 145p. (Orig.). 1986. pap. 12.00x (ISBN 92-64-12856-5). OECD.

Water Pollution: Causes & Effects in Australia & New Zealand. 2nd ed. D. W. Connell. (Australian Environment Ser.: Vol. 2). (Illus.). 203p. 1981. pap. text ed. 12.95x (ISBN 0-7022-1781-6). U of Queensland Pr.

Water Pollution Control. BNA's Environment & Safety Services Staff. (Policy & Practice Ser.). looseleaf 416.00 (ISBN 0-87179-913-8). BNA.

Water Pollution Control. W. W. Eckenfelder & D. Ford. (Illus.). 17.50 (ISBN 0-8363-0099-8). Jenkins.

Water Pollution Control: Guidelines for Project Planning & Financing. Ralph C. Palange & Alfonso Zavala. (Technical Paper: No. 73). 1987. 12.00 (ISBN 0-8213-0967-6, BK0967). World Bank.

Water Pollution Control in Developing Countries: Report. WHO Meeting. Geneva, 1972. (Technical Report Ser.: No. 404). (Also avail. in Russian). 1968. pap. 2.00 (ISBN 92-4-120404-4). World Health.

Water Pollution Control in Developing Countries. E. A. Ouano et al. 1978. 230.00 (ISBN 0-08-023567-0). Pergamon.

Water Pollution Control in Low Density Areas: Proceedings. Conference on Rural Environmental Engineering. Ed. by William J. Jewell & Rita Swan. LC 74-82975. (Illus.). 518p. 1975. 50.00x (ISBN 0-87451-105-4). U Pr of New Eng.

Water Pollution Control Technology. J. K. Bewtra. (Theoretical & Applied Environmental Reviews Ser.: Vol. 1). Date not set. price not set (ISBN 3-7186-0027-7). Harwood Academic.

Water Pollution: Disposal & Reuse, Vol. 1. James E. Zajic. LC 70-163919. pap. 101.30 (2027129). Bks Demand UMI.

Water Pollution: Disposal & Reuse, Vol. 2. J. E. Zajic. 272p. 1971. 75.00 (ISBN 0-8247-1816-X). Dekker.

Water Pollution: Economic Aspects & Research Needs. Allen V. Kneese. (Resources for the Future Ser). 120p. 1962. pap. 6.95x (ISBN 0-8018-0343-8). Johns Hopkins.

Water Pollution: Economic Aspects & Research Needs. Allen V. Kneese. 107p. 1962. pap. 6.95 (ISBN 0-317-60305-1). RFF Assocs.

Water Pollution in the Greater New York Area. A. A. Johnson. 232p. 1970. 58.00 (ISBN 0-677-14470-9). Gordon & Breach.

Water Pollution Microbiology. Ed. by Ralph Mitchell. LC 73-168641. pap. 106.50 (ISBN 0-317-26263-7, 2055711). Bks Demand UMI.

Water Pollution Monitoring. Ed. by Frank L. Cross, Jr. LC 74-33841. (Environmental Monograph). (Illus.). 38p. 1976. 14.95 (ISBN 0-87762-180-2). Technomic.

Water Pollution Research & Control, Amsterdam 1984: Proceedings of the 12th Biennial Conference of the International Association on Water Pollution Research & Control Held in Amsterdam, The Netherlands, 17-20 September 1984. Ed. by L. Lijklema et al. 1985. 330.00 (ISBN 0-08-033657-4, Pub. by PPL). Pergamon.

Water Pollution Research & Control: Proceedings of the Eleventh Biennial Conference of the International Association on Water Pollution Research, Capetown, March 29-April 2, 1982, Vol. 14, No. 11. Ed. by S. H. Jenkins. (Illus.). 1500p. 1983. 215.00 (ISBN 0-08-029689-0). Pergamon.

Water Pollution Research & Control, Rio de Janeiro, 1986: Proceedings of the Thirteenth Biennial Conference of the International Association on Water Pollution Research & Control Held in Rio de Janeiro, Brazil, 1986, 4 vols. L. Lijklema. LC 82-645900. (Water Science & Technology Ser.: No. 19). (Illus.). 1302p. 1988. Set. 380.00 (ISBN 0-08-035589-7). Pergamon.

Water Pollution Research & Development: Proceedings of the IAWPR International Conference on Water Pollution Research, 10th, Toronto, June, 1980. IAWPR International Conference Staff. Ed. by S. H. Jenkins. (Water Science & Technology Ser.). (Illus.). 1388p. 1981. 235.00 (ISBN 0-08-026025-X). Pergamon.

Water Pollution Research: Proceedings of the Second International Conference. 2nd ed. Ed. by O. Jaag et al. 1966. Set. 270.00 (ISBN 0-08-011438-5). Pergamon.

Water Polo. Charles F. Cicciarella. 108p. 1981. pap. text ed. 3.95x (ISBN 0-89641-066-8). American Pr.

Water Potential Relations in Soil Microbiology. Ed. by J. F. Parr et al. 151p. 1981. pap. 6.25 (ISBN 0-89118-767-7). Soil Sci Soc Am.

Water Power. Ed Catherall. LC 81-86272. (Fun with Science Ser.). 12.68 (ISBN 0-382-06630-8). Silver.

Water Power Engineering. M. M. Dandekar & N. K. Sharma. 451p. 1983. pap. text ed. 18.95x (ISBN 0-7069-2362-6, Pub. by Vikas India). Advent NY.

Water Power Workout. Linda Huey & R. R. Knudsen. 208p. (Orig.). 1986. pap. 8.95 (ISBN 0-452-25828-6, Plume). NAL.

Water (Prevention & Control of Pollution) Act, 1974. Vijay Malik. 147p. 1984. Repr. of 1982 ed. 90.00x (ISBN 0-317-54576-0, Pub. by Eastern Bk India). State Mutual Bk.

Water Problems of Urbanizing Areas. 358p. 1979. pap. 20.00x (ISBN 0-87262-145-6). Am Soc Civil Eng.

Water Production Functions for Irrigated Agriculture. Roger W. Hexem & Earl O. Heady. 1978. text ed. 14.50x (ISBN 0-8138-1785-4). Iowa St U Pr.

Water Production Using Nuclear Energy. Ed. by Roy G. Post & Robert L. Seale. LC 66-24303. (Illus.). pap. 98.00 (ISBN 0-317-10713-5, 2055358). Bks Demand UMI.

Water Program Specialist. (Career Examination Ser.: C-3488). Date not set. pap. 16.00 (ISBN 0-8373-3488-8). Natl Learning.

Water Publications of State Agencies, 2 vols. Gerald J. Giefer & David K. Todd. LC 72-75672. 1976. Set. 60.00 (ISBN 0-912394-04-8). Water Info.

Water Publications of State Agencies - First Supplement. Ed. by Gerald J. Giefer & David K. Todd. LC 72-75672. 1976. 30.00 (ISBN 0-912394-17-X). Water Info.

Water-Pumping Devices: A Handbook for Users & Choosers. Peter Fraenkel. (Illus.). 176p. (Orig.). 1986. pap. 22.50 (ISBN 0-946688-85-0, Pub. by Intermediate Tech England). Intermediate Tech.

Water Purification Control. 4th ed. Edward S. Hopkins & Elwood L. Bean. LC 74-21712. 346p. 1975. Repr. of 1966 ed. 19.50 (ISBN 0-88275-248-0). Krieger.

Water Purification Market. Ed. by Peter Allen. 300p. 1987. pap. 1250.00 (ISBN 0-941285-09-X). FIND-SVP.

Water Quality & Its Control. James C. Lamb. LC 84-20945. 384p. 1985. write for info. (ISBN 0-471-80047-3). Wiley.

Water Quality & Treatment: A Handbook for Public Water Supplies. 3rd ed. American Water Works Association Staff. 1971. text ed. 67.00 (ISBN 0-07-001539-2). McGraw.

Water Quality & Treatment: A Handbook of Public Water Supplies. 3rd ed. (General References Ser.). (Illus.). 654p. 1971. text ed. 42.60 (ISBN 0-89867-005-5). Am Water Wks Assn.

Water Quality, Conduits & Geometrics: Four Reports. (Transportation Research Record Ser.). 51p. 1975. 4.00 (ISBN 0-309-02463-3). Transport Res Bd.

Water Quality Control Specialist. (Career Examination Ser.: C-3337). Date not set. pap. 16.00 (ISBN 0-8373-3337-7). Natl Learning.

Water Quality Criteria. American Society for Testing & Materials Staff. LC 67-14533. (American Society for Testing & Materials. Special Technical Publication Ser.: 416). pap. 31.80 (ISBN 0-317-10923-5, 2000707). Bks Demand UMI.

Water Quality Criteria for European Freshwater Fish: Report on the Effect of Zinc & Copper Pollution on the Salmonid Fisheries in a River & Lake System in Central Norway. (European Inland Fisheries Advisory Commission (EIFAC): Technical Papers: No. 29). 40p. (Eng. & Fr.). 1977. pap. 7.50 (ISBN 92-5-100296-7, F770, FAO). UNIPUB.

Water Quality Criteria for European Freshwater Fish: Report on Cadmium & Freshwater Fish. (European Inland Fisheries Advisory Commission (EIFAC): Technical Papers: No. 30). 32p. (Eng. & Fr.). 1977. pap. 7.50 (ISBN 92-5-002056-2, F771, FAO). UNIPUB.

Water Quality Criteria for European Freshwater Fish Rpt on Zinc & Freshwater. (European Inland Fisheries Advisory Commission (EIFAC): Technical Papers: No. 21). 22p. 1973. pap. 7.50 (ISBN 0-686-93195-5, F761, FAO). UNIPUB.

Water Quality Criteria for European Freshwater Fish: Report on Copper & Freshwater Fish. pap. 7.50 (F768, FAO). UNIPUB.

Water Quality Criteria for European Freshwater Fish: Report on Nickel & Freshwater Fish. (EIFAC Technical Papers: No. 45). 20p. 1985. pap. 7.50 (ISBN 92-5-102176-7, F2739, FAO). UNIPUB.

Water Quality Criteria for European Freshwater Fish: Revised Report on Combined Effects on Freshwater Fish & Other Aquatic Life of Mixtures of Toxicants in Water. (EIFAC Technical Paper: No. 37). (Illus.). 75p. 1987. pap. text ed. 6.00 (ISBN 92-5-102556-8, F3092, FAO). UNIPUB.

Water Quality Criteria for Fresh Water Fish. Ed. by Richard Lloyd & J. S. Alabaster. LC 79-41350. 1980. text ed. 59.95 (ISBN 0-408-10673-5). Butterworth.

Water Quality Deterioration in a Suburbanizing Basin: Brandywine Creek, Pennsylvania. Thomas B. Hammer. (Discussion Paper Ser.: No. 78). 1974. pap. 6.50 (ISBN 0-686-32244-4). Regional Sci Res Inst.

Water-Quality Impacts of Unsewered Housing. William T. Howard & Thomas R. Hammer. (Discussion Paper Ser.: No. 66). 1973. pap. 6.50 (ISBN 0-686-32232-0). Regional Sci Res Inst.

Water Quality Improvement Seminar, 2nd: Proceedings of 1968. 50p. 1968. 8.00 (ISBN 0-317-33235-X, PO268). Am Soc Ag Eng.

Water Quality in Catchment Ecosystems. A M. Gower. LC 79-42907. (Institution of Environmental Sciences Ser.). 335p. 1980. 87.95x (ISBN 0-471-27692-8, Pub. by Wiley-Interscience). Wiley.

Water Quality in Catchment Ecosystems. Ed. by Anthony M. Gower. LC 79-42907. (Institution of Environmental Sciences Ser.). 347p. pap. 90.30 (2030391). Bks Demand UMI.

Water Quality in Hydroelectric Projects: Considerations for Planning in Tropical Forest Regions. Camilo E. Garzon. 48p. 1985. 5.00 (ISBN 0-8213-0363-5, BK0363). World Bank.

Water Quality in Warmwater Fish Ponds. Claude E. Boyd. (Illus.). 359p. 1979. pap. 9.95 (ISBN 0-8173-0055-4, Pub. by Ag Experiment). U of Ala Pr.

Water Quality Investigations in the Mackenzie Basin with Special Reference to the Potential for Impairment of Water Quality by Pipeline or Road Construction. 1979. pap. 5.00 (SSC128, SSC). UNIPUB.

Water Quality Issues at Fossil Fuel Plants: Proceedings of a Symposium Sponsored by the Energy Division. Ed. by William G. Dinchak & Michael J. Mathis. 90p. 1985. 13.00x (ISBN 0-87262-490-0). Am Soc Civil Eng.

Water Quality Management. Peter A. Krenkel & Vladimir Novotny. LC 80-516. 1980. 77.00 (ISBN 0-12-426150-7). Acad Pr.

Water Quality Management: A Review of the Development & Application of Mathematical Models. M. B. Beck. (Lecture Notes in Engineering Ser.: Vol. 11). viii, 107p. 1985. pap. 13.50 (ISBN 0-387-13986-9). Springer-Verlag.

Water Quality Management: An Introduction. George Tchobanoglous & Edward D. Schroeder. (Illus.). 1985. write for info. (ISBN 0-201-05433-7); solutions manual avail. (ISBN 0-201-05434-5). Addison-Wesley.

Water Quality: Management & Pollution Control Problems see **Progress in Water Technology.**

Water Quality Management for Pond Fish Culture. C. E. Boyd. (Developments in Aquaculture & Fisheries Science Ser.: Vol. 9). 318p. 1982. 89.50 (ISBN 0-444-42054-1). Elsevier.

Water Quality Management for the Metals & Minerals Industries, a Short Course (In Conjunction with the 104th AIME Annual Meeting, New York, 1975) The Metallurgical Society of AIME. pap. 36.80 (ISBN 0-317-10692-9, 2004307). Bks Demand UMI.

Water Quality Management Under Conditions of Scarcity: Israel As a Case Study. Ed. by Hillel I. Shuval. LC 79-8848. (Water Pollution Ser.). 1980. 54.50 (ISBN 0-12-641280-4). Acad Pr.

Water Quality Measurement. Mark & Mattson. (Pollution Engineering & Technology Ser.: Vol. 18). 496p. 1981. 75.00 (ISBN 0-8247-1334-6). Dekker.

Water Quality Parameters - STP 573. 590p. 1975. 29.50 (ISBN 0-8031-0598-3, 04-573000-16). ASTM.

Water Quality, Planning & Management. Ed. by D. Ouazar et al. (Computer Methods & Water Resources Ser.: Vol. 6). 310p. 1988. 71.50 (ISBN 0-387-18858-4). Springer-Verlag.

Water Quality: Proceedings of an International Symposium. Ed. by Frederick Coulston & E. Mrak. (Ecotoxicology & Environmental Quality Ser.). 1977. 33.00 (ISBN 0-12-193150-1). Acad Pr.

Water Quality Technology Conference - 1979: Advances in Laboratory Techniques for Quality Control. (AWWA Handbooks Proceedings Ser.). (Illus.). 350p. 1980. pap. text ed. 14.40 (ISBN 0-89867-231-7). Am Water Wks Assn.

Water Quality Technology Conference, 1981: Advances in Laboratory Techniques for Quality Control. (AWWA Handbooks-Proceedings Ser.). (Illus.). 1982. pap. text ed. 18.60 (ISBN 0-89867-267-8). Am Water Wks Assn.

Water Quality Technology Conference, 1980: Advances in Laboratory Techniques for Quality Control. (AWWA Handbooks-Proceedings Ser.). (Illus.). 1981. pap. text ed. 18.00 (ISBN 0-89867-251-1). Am Water Wks Assn.

Water Quality Technology Conference: 1975-Laboratory Tools for Safe Water. (AWWA Handbooks-Proceedings Ser.). (Illus.). 1976. pap. text ed. 12.00 (ISBN 0-89867-045-4). Am Water Wks Assn.

Water Quality Technology Conference: 1978-New Laboratory Tools for Quality Control in Water Treatment & Distribution. (AWWA Handbooks-Proceedings Ser.). (Illus.). 1979. pap. text ed. 12.00 (ISBN 0-89867-175-2). Am Water Wks Assn.

Water Quality Technology Conference: 1976, the Water Laboratory - Key to Process & Quality Control. (AWWA Handbooks-Proceedings Ser.). (Illus.). 342p. 1977. pap. text ed. 12.00 (ISBN 0-89867-051-9). Am Water Wks Assn.

Water Quality Technology Conference: 1973-Water Quality. (AWWA Handbooks-Proceedings Ser.). (Illus.). 272p. 1974. pap. text ed. 12.00 (ISBN 0-89867-041-1). Am Water Wks Assn.

Water Quality Technology Conference: 1974-Water Quality. (AWWA Handbooks-Proceedings Ser.). (Illus.). 248p. 1975. pap. text ed. 12.00 (ISBN 0-89867-043-8). Am Water Wks Assn.

Water Quality Technology Conference: 1977-Water Quality in the Distribution System. (AWWA Handbooks-Proceedings Ser.). (Illus.). 320p. 1978. pap. text ed. 12.00. Am Water Wks Assn.

Water Tanks for Private Fire Protection. National Fire Protection Association Staff. 58p. 1984. 13.50 (ISBN 0-317-63060-1, 22-84). Natl Fire Prot.
Water Tanks for Private Fire Protection. (Twenty Ser.). 137p. 1974. pap. 4.00 (ISBN 0-685-46065-7, 22). Natl Fire Prot.
Water Tender. Jack Rudman. (Career Examination Ser.: C-1649). (Cloth bdg. avail. on request). 1988. pap. 14.00 (ISBN 0-8373-1649-9). Natl Learning.
Water: The Fountain of Opportunity. H. G. Deming. Ed. by W. S. Gillam & W. S. McCoy. (Illus.). 1975. 25.00x (ISBN 0-19-501841-9). Oxford U Pr.
Water, the Life Sustaining Resource. Robert Gardner. LC 82-2231. 192p. (gr. 7 up). 1982. PLB 9.79 (ISBN 0-671-43655-4). Messner.
Water: The Nature, Uses, & Future of Our Most Precious & Abused Resource. Fred Powledge. 384p. 1982. 13.95 (ISBN 0-374-28660-4); pap. 7.95 (ISBN 0-374-51798-3). FS&G.
Water: The Next Great Resource Battle. Laurence Pringle. LC 81-23694. (Science for Survival Ser.). (Illus.). 144p. (gr. 6 up). 1982. 10.95 (ISBN 0-02-775400-6). Macmillan.
Water: The Web of Life. Cynthia A. Hunt & Robert M. Garrels. LC 78-152663. (Illus.). 1972. text ed. 9.95 (ISBN 0-393-06386-0); pap. 3.95x (ISBN 0-393-09407-3). Norton.
Water Today & Tomorrow: Proceedings of a Specialty Conference Sponsored by the Irrigation & Drainage Division. Ed. by John A. Replogle & Kenneth G. Renard. 740p. 1984. 57.00x (ISBN 0-87262-408-0). Am Soc Civil Eng.
Water: Too Much, Too Little, Too Polluted. Augusta Goldin. LC 82-48760. (Illus.). 224p. (gr. 7 up). 1983. 12.95 (ISBN 0-15-294819-8, HJ). HarBraceJ.
Water Towers. Bernd Becher & Hilla Becher. Commentary by Weston J. Naef. (Illus.). 224p. 1988. 50.00 (ISBN 0-262-02277-X). MIT Pr.
Water Trails of Washington. rev. ed. Werner Furrer. (Illus., Orig.). 1979. pap. 5.95 (ISBN 0-913140-31-7). Signpost Bk Pub.
Water Transfer from Soil to the Atmosphere As Related to Climate & Soil Properties. Charles Wendt. LC 73-136103. 101p. 1970. 19.00 (ISBN 0-403-04546-0). Scholarly.
Water Transfers: Economic Efficiency & Alternative Institutions. Loyal M. Hartman & Don Seastone. LC 70-108382. pap. 36.00 (ISBN 0-317-28863-6, 2020963). Bks Demand UMI.
Water Treatment. Center for Occupational Research & Development Staff. (EUTEC Environmental & Chemical Analysis Curriculum Ser.). (Illus.). 222p. 1985. pap. text ed. 26.00 (ISBN 1-55502-206-5). Ctr Res & Dev.
Water Treatment. (Illus.). 410p. 1984. looseleaf 79.50x (ISBN 0-87683-368-7); 195.00x (ISBN 0-87683-369-5). GP Pub.
Water Treatment. (Principles of Steam Generation Ser.: Module 2). (Illus.). 80p. 1982. spiral bdg. 17.50x (ISBN 0-87683-252-4). GP Pub.
Water Treatment, Vol. 2, Pt. 14. J. D. Skelly. (Marine Engineering Practice Ser.). 1977. pap. 11.50x (ISBN 0-900976-66-7, Pub. by Inst Marine Eng). Intl Spec Bk.
Water Treatment & Sanitation. H. Mann & D. Williamson. 92p. 1982. 4.50 (ISBN 0-317-36540-1, 91015-BK). Vols Tech Asst.
Water Treatment & Sanitation: Simple Methods for Rural Areas. 3nd ed. H. T. Mann & D. Williamson. (Illus.). 92p. (Orig.). 1982. pap. 9.75x (ISBN 0-903031-23-X, Pub. by Intermediate Tech England). Intermediate Tech.
Water Treatment Basics: From Pretreatment to Wastewater Seminar, 1986: The Peabody, Memphis, TN, October 15-17. Technical Association of the Pulp & Paper Industry Staff. (TAPPI Notes Ser.). (Illus.). pap. 22.10 (ISBN 0-317-58158-9, 2029694). Bks Demand UMI.
Water Treatment: Calculations, Examples, Problems. F. Belan. 293p. 1984. pap. 6.95 (ISBN 0-317-07272-2, Pub. by Mir Pubs USSR). Imported Pubns.
Water Treatment Handbook. 5th ed. Degremont Company Editors. LC 79-87503. 1186p. 1979. 100.00 (ISBN 0-470-26749-6). Halsted Pr.
Water Treatment Handbook. Degremont Company Editors. LC 72-96505. (Illus.). 1116p. 1973. 40.00 (ISBN 0-686-02503-2). Scholarly Bk Ctr.
Water Treatment: Industrial-Commercial-Municipal. 2nd ed. D. C. Brandvold. (Illus.). 1982. pap. 5.00 (ISBN 0-9610178-0-5). Branchemco.
Water Treatment Plant Design. (General References Ser.). (Illus.). 362p. 1969. text ed. 18.00 (ISBN 0-89867-004-7). Am Water Wks Assn.
Water Treatment Plant Design for Practicing Engineers. Ed. by Robert L. Sanks. LC 77-76914. 1978. 59.95 (ISBN 0-250-40183-5). Butterworth.
Water Treatment Principles & Design. James M. Montgomery. LC 85-5344. 696p. 1985. 58.00 (ISBN 0-471-04384-2, Pub. by Wiley-Interscience). Wiley.
Water Treatment Specification Manual. F. Rosa. 224p. 1985. text ed. 39.50 (ISBN 0-07-053606-6). McGraw.
Water Treatment Waste Disposal. (AWWA Handbooks-Proceedings Ser.). (Illus.). 136p. 1978. pap. text ed. 10.20 (ISBN 0-89867-058-6). Am Water Wks Assn.
Water under the Bridge. Margarette De Andrade. LC 85-52408. (Illus.). 250p. 1988. 17.50 (ISBN 0-8048-1430-9). C E Tuttle.
Water Usage in Wet Processing & Problems Associated with Treatment & Re-use of Effluents. Ed. by Wira Staff. 30.00x (ISBN 0-317-43603-1, Pub. by Wira Tech Group). State Mutual Bk.
Water Use Inspector. Jack Rudman. (Career Examination Ser.: C-898). (Cloth bdg. avail. on request). pap. 14.00 (ISBN 0-8373-0898-4). Natl Learning.
Water Use Seminar: Report of the FAO-UNDP Regional Seminar on Effective Use of Irrigation Water at the Farm Level, Damascus, Syria, Dec. 7-13, 1971. (Irrigation & Drainage Papers: No. 13). 318p. (Eng. & Fr.). 1972. pap. 23.75 (ISBN 0-686-92947-0, F982, FAO). UNIPUB.
Water Utility Accounting. 2nd ed. (General References Ser.). (Illus.). 288p. 1980. text ed. 33.60 (ISBN 0-89867-237-6). Am Water Wks Assn.
Water Utility Management Practices - M5. (AWWA Manuals Ser.). (Illus.). 1980. pap. text ed. 16.80 (ISBN 0-89867-063-2). Am Water Wks Assn.
Water Utility Operating Data, 1981. (AWWA Handbooks - General). (Illus.). 1981. pap. text ed. 30.00. Am Water Wks Assn.
Water Utilization Studies in the Dry Lands: Proceedings of Frontiers of the Semi-Arid World. Ed. by Robert M. Sweazy. 64p. 1976. 3.00 (ISBN 0-318-14563-4, 76-5). Intl Ctr Arid & Semi-Arid.
Water Vapour Line Parameters from Microwave to Medium Infrared: An Atlas of H2 to the Sixteenth, O; H2 to the Seventeenth, O; H2 to the Eighteenth, O; Line Positions & Intensities Between O & 4350 Cm to the -1. J. M. Flaud & C. Camy-Peyret. (International Tables of Constants Ser.: Vol. 19). xvi, 259p. 1981. 100.00 (ISBN 0-08-026181-7). Pergamon.
Water Virology: Water Science & Technology, Vol. 15, No. 5. Ed. by W. Grabow. (Illus.). 166p. 1983. pap. 44.00 (ISBN 0-08-030440-0). Pergamon.
Water Virology 1984: Proceedings of an IAWPRC Seminar Held in Amsterdam & Bilthoven, The Netherlands, 19-21 September 1984. Ed. by W. O. Grabow. 1985. pap. 48.00 (ISBN 0-08-033659-0, Pub. by PPL). Pergamon.
Water, Wastes & Health in Hot Climates. Ed. by Richard Feachem et al. LC 76-18946. 399p. 1977. 82.95x (ISBN 0-471-99410-3, Pub. by Wiley-Interscience). Wiley.
Water, Water! Tom Johnston. LC 87-42750. (Science in Action Ser.). (Illus.). 32p. (gr. 4-5). 1988. PLB 9.95 (ISBN 1-55532-407-X). Stevens Inc.
Water, Water Everywhere. David J. Gerick. (Illus.). 1978. 20.00 (ISBN 0-916750-75-2). Dayton Labs.
Water, Water, Water. Ed. by O. B. Leigh. 203p. (Orig.). 1978. write for info. (ISBN 0-9618633-0-7). Leighton Pub.
Water Wave Mechanics for Engineers & Scientists. Robert G. Dean & Robert A. Dalrymple. (Illus.). 384p. 1984. text ed. 52.00 (ISBN 0-13-946038-1). P-H.
Water Waves. N. F. Barber & G. Ghey. (Wykeham Science Ser.: No. 5). 152p. 1969. 18.00x (ISBN 0-8448-1107-6, Pub. by Crane Russak & Co). Taylor & Francis.
Water Waves. James J. Stoker. LC 56-8228. (Pure & Applied Mathematics Ser.). (Illus.). 595p. 1957. 61.95x (ISBN 0-470-82863-3, Pub. by Wiley-Interscience). Wiley.
Water Waves & Ship Hydrodynamics: An Introduction. R. Timman et al. LC 85-18807. 1985. lib. bdg. 35.50 (ISBN 90-247-3218-2, Pub. by Martinus Nijhoff Netherlands). Kluwer Academic.
Water Waves: The Mathematical Theory with Applications. James J. Stoker. LC 56-8228. (Pure & Applied Mathematics Ser.: No. 4). pap. 141.80 (ISBN 0-317-55626-6, 2056353). Bks Demand UMI.
Water Well Drillers Beginning Training Manual. 84p. 10.00 (ISBN 0-318-15931-7). Natl Water Well.
Water Well Drillers Beginning Training Manual. 2nd ed. 1985. 10.00 (ISBN 0-318-23053-4). Natl Water Well.
Water Well Drilling Cost Survey. 1979. 10.75 (ISBN 0-318-23052-6). Natl Water Well.
Water Well Manual: A Practical Guide for Locating & Constructing Wells for Individual & Small Community Water Supplies. Ulric P. Gibson & Rexford D. Singer. LC 71-153696. (Illus.). 156p. 1971. pap. 13.00 (ISBN 0-912722-00-2). Prem Press.
Water Well Specifications: A Manual of Technical Standards & General Contractual Conditions for Construction of Water Wells. National Water Well Association, Committee on Waterwell Standards. LC 80-80552. (Illus.). 156p. 1981. 13.00 (ISBN 0-912722-04-5). Prem Press.
Water Well Technology. Michael D. Campbell & Jay H. Lehr. 681p. 43.75 (ISBN 0-318-15933-3). Natl Water Well.
Water Well Technology: Field Principles of Exploration & Drilling for Ground Water & Other Selected Minerals. National Water Well Association Staff. 600p. 1973. text ed. 67.00 (ISBN 0-07-046097-3). McGraw.
Water: Where Water Comes From. (Better Farming Ser.: No. 28). 31p. 1981. pap. 7.50 (ISBN 92-5-101086-2, F2265, FAO). UNIPUB.
Water-Witch. James Fenimore Cooper. (BCL Ser.). Repr. of 1896 ed. 14.50 (ISBN 0-404-00629-9). AMS Pr.
Water Witch. Cynthia Felice & Connie Willis. 224p. (Orig.). 1984. pap. 2.75 (ISBN 0-441-87380-4). Ace Bks.
Water Witch. Janece Hudson. (Loveswept Ser.: No. 293). 192p. (Orig.). 1988. pap. 2.50 (ISBN 0-553-21945-6). Bantam.
Water-Witch: Or, the Skimmer of the Seas. James F. Cooper. LC 4-15437. 1896. 13.00x (ISBN 0-403-00244-3). Scholarly.
Water Witching. Kathleene West. LC 84-71254. 64p. 1984. pap. 7.00 (ISBN 0-914742-82-5). Copper Canyon.
Water Witching U. S. A. 2nd ed. Evon Z. Vogt & Ray Hyman. LC 79-240. xii, 260p. 1979. pap. 10.95 (ISBN 0-226-86297-6, P814, Phoen). U of Chicago Pr.
Water Wizard. Edith Fine & Judith Josephson. (Learning Works Preschool Ser.). 24p. (ps). 1982. 2.95 (ISBN 0-88160-093-8, LW 129). Learning Wks.
Water Workout: One Hundred Twenty Water Exercises for Swimmers & Nonswimmers. Bill Reed & Murray Rose. 1986. pap. 9.95 (ISBN 0-517-56183-2, Harmony). Crown.
Water Workout Recovery Program. Robert G. Watkins et al. (Orig.). 1988. 12.95 (ISBN 0-8092-4636-8). Contemp Bks.
Water World. Mary L. Settle. LC 83-16598. 144p. (gr. 5-9). 1984. 11.95 (ISBN 0-525-66777-6, 01160-350). Lodestar Bks.
Water, 1980. Ed. by Gary F. Bennett. LC 81-93783. (AIChE Symposium Ser.: Vol. 77, No. 201). 344p. 1981. pap. 38.00 (ISBN 0-8169-0217-8, S-209). Am Inst Chem Eng.
Waterbird & Mammal Censuses at Siuslaw Estuary, Lane County, Oregon. Range D. Bayer & Roy W. Lowe. LC 87-83287. (Studies in Oregon Ornithology: No. 4). (Illus.). x, 101p. 1988. pap. 6.50x (ISBN 0-939819-03-1). Gahmken Pr.
Waterborne Coatings: Emulsion & Water-Soluble Paints. Charles R. Martens. 384p. 1980. 36.95 (ISBN 0-442-25137-8). Van Nos Reinhold.
Waterborne Commerce of British Columbia & Washington, 1850-1870. Hitchman. (Occasional Papers: No. 7). 1986. pap. 4.00 (ISBN 0-318-23326-6). WWU CPNS.
Waterborne Diseases in the United States. Ed. by Gunther F. Craun. 336p. 1986. 125.00 (ISBN 0-8493-5937-6). CRC PR.
Waterbuffalo Theology. Kosuke Koyama. LC 74-80980. (Illus.). 250p. (Orig.). 1974. pap. 8.95 (ISBN 0-88344-702-9). Orbis Bks.
Waterbury Clock Company 1867. 1976. pap. 7.95 (ISBN 0-915706-09-1). Am Reprints.
Waterbury Clocks: The Complete Illustrated Catalog of 1983. 2nd ed. Waterbury Clock Co. (Illus.). 128p. 1983. pap. 6.95 (ISBN 0-486-24460-1). Dover.
Waterchild. Judith Bolinger & Jane English. LC 80-80650. (Orig.). 1980. pap. 6.95 (ISBN 0-89793-023-1). Hunter Hse.
Waterchild: Poems from a Pregnant Year. Judith Bolinger & Jane English. LC 85-21317. 53p. 1985. Repr. of 1980 ed. lib. bdg. 19.95x (ISBN 0-89370-592-6). Borgo Pr.
Watercise While You Wait: The Complete Prenatal Water Workout Book. Helga Hughes. (Illus.). 96p. (Orig.). 1988. pap. 8.95 (ISBN 0-89529-306-4). Avery Pub.
Watercolor. enl. ed. John Pike. (Illus.). 224p. 1973. 27.50 (ISBN 0-8230-5651-1). Watson-Guptill.
Watercolor. Simon. (Grosset Art Introduction Ser.: Vol. 42). pap. 3.95 (ISBN 0-399-50784-1, G&D). Putnam Pub Group.
Watercolor: A Painting Study Guide. Pat Regan. (Illus.). 68p. pap. 12.95 (ISBN 0-9615826-0-X). P Regan.
Watercolor & Collage Workshop. Gerald Brommer. (Illus.). 144p. 1986. 24.95 (ISBN 0-8230-5652-X). Watson-Guptill.
Watercolor Bold & Free. Lawrence C. Goldsmith. (Illus.). 160p. 1980. 27.50 (ISBN 0-8230-5654-6). Watson-Guptill.
Watercolor Bright & Beautiful. Richard C. Karwoski. (Illus.). 144p. 1988. 27.50 (ISBN 0-8230-5653-8). Watson-Guptill.
Watercolor Day by Day. Michael Crespo. (Illus.). 144p. 1987. 27.50 (ISBN 0-8230-5668-6). Watson-Guptill.
Watercolor Energies. Frank Webb. (Illus.). 176p. 1985. pap. 17.95 (ISBN 0-89134-055-6). North Light Bks.
Watercolor Fast & Loose. Ron Ranson. (Illus.). 128p. 1988. 21.95 (ISBN 0-89134-225-7). North Light Bks.
Watercolor for All Seasons. Elaine Wentworth & Murray Wentworth. LC 84-25445. (Illus.). 176p. 1984. 21.95 (ISBN 0-89134-095-5, North Light). Writers Digest.
Watercolor for Illustration. Jacqui Morgan. (Illus.). 144p. 1986. 24.95 (ISBN 0-8230-5658-9). Watson-Guptill.
Watercolor Handbook: Learning from the Masters. Ettore Maiotti. (Illus.). 160p. 1986. bds. 10.95 (ISBN 0-517-56306-1, C N Potter Bks). Crown.
Watercolor Interpretations. John Blockley. (Illus.). 160p. 1987. pap. 19.95 (ISBN 0-89134-196-X). North Light Bks.
Watercolor: Let the Medium Do It. Valfred Thelin & Patricia Burlin. (Illus.). 144p. 1988. 27.50 (ISBN 0-8230-5667-8). Watson-Guptill.
Watercolor Options. Ray Loos. LC 84-27227. (Illus.). 176p. 1985. 22.50 (ISBN 0-89134-115-3). North Light Bks.
Watercolor Painter's Solution Book. Angela Gair. (Illus.). 144p. 1988. 24.95 (ISBN 0-89134-233-8). North Light Bks.
Watercolor Painting. Wendon Blake & Claude Croney. (Artist's Painting Library). (Illus.). 80p. 1979. pap. 8.95 (ISBN 0-8230-5673-2). Watson-Guptill.
Watercolor Painting. Hubert Gautier. (Printed Sources of Western Art Ser.). 154p. (Fr.). 1981. pap. 20.00 slipcase (ISBN 0-915346-63-X). A Wofsy Fine Arts.
Watercolor Painting on Location. El Meyer. LC 83-25449. (Illus.). 160p. 1984. 19.95 (ISBN 0-89134-068-8, North Light); pap. write for info cancelled (ISBN 0-89134-077-7). Writers Digest.
Watercolor Painting Techniques: Learn How to Master Watercolor Working Techniques to Create Your Own Successful Paintings. John Blockley & Richard Bolton. Ed. by Wendon Blake. (Illus.). 144p. 1983. pap. 16.95 (ISBN 0-8230-5669-4). Watson-Guptill.
Watercolor Painting: The Ron Ranson Technique. Ron Ranson. (Illus.). 192p. 1985. 19.95 (ISBN 0-7137-1396-8, Pub. by Blandford England); pap. 14.95 (ISBN 0-7137-1991-5). Sterling.
Watercolor Portraiture: A Practical Guide. Phoebe Flory et al. 192p. 1985. pap. 4.95 (ISBN 0-486-24972-7). Dover.
Watercolor-the Creative Experience. Barbara Nechis. LC 79-9334. (Illus.). 160p. 1984. pap. 16.95 (ISBN 0-89134-066-1, North Light). Writers Digest.
Watercolor Tricks & Techniques. Cathy Johnson. (Illus.). 176p. 1987. 24.95 (ISBN 0-89134-221-4). North Light Bks.
Watercolor U. S. A. National Invitational Exhibition, 1976. Allen S. Weller. (Watercolor U. S. A. Ser.). (Illus., Orig.). 1976. pap. text ed. 5.00x (ISBN 0-934306-00-1). Springfield.
Watercolor U. S. A. 1986: The Monumental Image. William C. Landwehr. LC 86-61583. (Illus.). 80p. (Orig.). 1986. pap. text ed. 15.00 (ISBN 0-934306-06-0). Springfield.
Watercolor, Wax & Wool: The Art of Janet Shook LaCoste. Intro. by Amy F. Lee & Al Lowman. LC 80-82780. (Illus.). 96p. (Orig.). 1980. pap. 3.95 (ISBN 0-933164-81-5). U of Tex Inst Tex Culture.
Watercolor Workbook. Bud Biggs & Lois Marshall. (Illus.). 160p. 1987. pap. 18.95 (ISBN 0-89134-203-6). North Light Bks.
Watercolor: You Can Do It! Tony Couch. LC 86-23597. (Illus.). 176p. 1987. 25.95 (ISBN 0-89134-188-9). North Light Bks.
Watercolorist's Guide to Painting Skies. Photos by John Shaw. (Illus.). 144p. 1984. 27.50 (ISBN 0-8230-5691-0). Watson-Guptill.
Watercolorist's Guide to Painting Trees. Ed. by Elizabeth Leonard. (Illus.). 144p. 1984. 27.50 (ISBN 0-8230-2159-9). Watson-Guptill.
Watercolorist's Guide to Painting Water. Illus. by Ferdinand Petrie. (Illus.). 144p. 1985. 27.50 (ISBN 0-8230-5693-7). Watson-Guptill.
Watercolors. J. M. Parramon & G. Fresquet. LC 80-82381. (Art Ser.). (Orig.). 1980. pap. 5.95 (ISBN 0-89586-074-0). Price Stern.
Watercolors: A Concise History. Graham Reynolds. (World of Art Ser). (Illus.). 1986. pap. 11.95 (ISBN 0-500-20109-9). Thames Hudson.
Watercolors: From Durer to Balthus. Jean Leymarie & Skira-Rizzoli. (Illus.). 142p. 1984. 37.50 (ISBN 0-8478-0557-3). Rizzoli Intl.
Watercolors of David Levine. David Levine. LC 81-127264. (Illus.). 24p. 1981. pap. 9.00 (ISBN 0-295-95817-0, Pub. by Phillips). U of Wash Pr.
Watercolors of Dixie. Ben E. Looney. 1974. 13.95 (ISBN 0-87511-075-4). Claitors.
Watercolors of the Rio Grande. Michael Frary. LC 84-40128. (Illus.). 134p. 1984. 29.95 (ISBN 0-89096-207-3). Tex A&M Univ Pr.
Watercolours & Drawings: Akvareli i Risunki v Gosudarstvennom Russkom Muzee. V. A. Pushkarev. (Illus.). 1982. 116.00x (ISBN 0-317-57493-0, Pub. by Collets UK). State Mutual Bk.
Watercolours & Drawings of Russian & Soviet Artists in the Pushkin Fine Arts Museum. A. Alexandrova. (Illus., Rus. & Eng.). 1982. 53.00x (ISBN 0-317-57489-2, Pub. by Collets UK). State Mutual Bk.
Watercolours & Drawings of the Eighteenth & First Half of the Nineteenth Century in the Tretysakov Gallery. M. A. Nemirovskaias. (Illus.). 162p. (Rus. & Eng.). 1982. 173.00x (ISBN 0-317-57485-X, Pub. by Collets UK). State Mutual Bk.
Watercolours & Drawings of Thomas Bewick & His Workshop Apprentices, 2 vols. Lain Bain. 1981. Set; Vol. 1, 240 pgs.; Vol. 2, 323 pgs. 750.00x (ISBN 0-86092-057-7, Pub. by Gordon Fraser). State Mutual Bk.

Watershed Management 1980, 2 vols. LC 80-66952. 1122p. 1980. Set. pap. 68.00x (ISBN 0-87262-250-9). Am Soc Civil Eng.
Watershed of Empire. Ed. by James J. Martin & Leonard Liggio. 219p. Date not set. pap. 7.00 (ISBN 0-317-53208-1). Noontide.
Watershed of Empire: Essays on New Deal Foreign Policy. Ed. by Leonard P. Liggio & James J. Martin. LC 76-4291. 1976. pap. 3.95 (ISBN 0-87926-020-3). R Myles.
Watershed of Juvenile Justice. 7.00 (ISBN 0-318-20318-9). Natl Coun Crime.
Watershed of Two Eras: Europe in 1900. Jan Romein. Tr. by Arnold Pomerans from Dutch. LC 77-14841. 1978. pap. 12.95x (ISBN 0-8195-6066-9). Wesleyan U Pr.
Watershed Planning: A Selected Research Bibliography, No. 1014. Frank L. Kudrna. 1976. 5.50 (ISBN 0-686-20391-7). CPL Biblios.
Watershed Resources Management: An Integrated Framework with Studies from Asia & the Pacific. Ed. by K. William Easter et al. (Westview Special Studies in Water Policy & Management). 260p. 1986. pap. 24.00 (ISBN 0-8133-7300-X). Westview.
Watersheds. Betty Gray. 64p. (Orig.). 1987. pap. 1.95 (ISBN 1-85239-003-4). Greenwood.
Watershed's. Robert Lauer & Jeannette Lauer. 1988. 8.95 (ISBN 1-55525-202-8). Nightingale-Conant.
Watersheds: Mastering Life's Unpredictable Crises. Robert H. Lauer & Jeanette C. Lauer. 272p. 1988. 16.95 (ISBN 0-316-51629-5). Little.
Watership Down. Richard Adams. LC 73-6044. 444p. (YA) (gr. 8 up). 1974. 24.95 (ISBN 0-02-700030-3, 70003). Macmillan.
Watershots: How to Take Better Photos on & Around the Water. Bruce Brown. (Illus.). 160p. 1988. pap. 17.95 (ISBN 0-87742-966-9). Intl Marine.
Waterskiing. (Illus.). 48p. (gr. 6-12). 1984. pap. 1.25x (ISBN 0-8395-3357-8, 3357). BSA.
Waterskiing Is for Me. Carole S. Briggs. (Sports for Me Bks.). (Illus.). 48p. (gr. 2-5). 1986. lib. bdg. 7.95 (ISBN 0-8225-1140-1). Lerner Pubns.
Watersmeet. Nancy Garden. LC 83-11512. 202p. (gr. 5 up). 1983. 13.95 (ISBN 0-374-38244-1). FS&G.
Watersong. Mary Caraker. 224p. (Orig.). 1987. pap. 2.95 (ISBN 0-445-20512-1, Pub. by Popular Lib). Warner Bks.
Watersplash. Patricia Wentworth. 256p. 1987. pap. 3.50 (ISBN 0-446-34448-6). Warner Bks.
Watertrips: A Guide to East Coast Cruise Ships, Ferryboats, & Island Excursions. Theodore Scull. (Illus.). 192p. 1987. pap. 14.95 (ISBN 0-87742-239-7). Intl Marine.
Watervliet Shaker Cemetery, Albany, N. Y. Elizabeth D. Shaver. 1986. pap. 2.50 (ISBN 0-317-56377-7). Shaker Her Soc.
Watervliet Shaker Meeting House. Elizabeth Shaver. 6p. 1986. pap. 2.50 (ISBN 0-317-56375-0). Shaker Her Soc.
Waterway. Berard Haile. LC 79-66605. (American Tribal Religions Ser.: Vol. 5). (Illus.). vi, 153p. 1979. pap. 12.95x (ISBN 0-89734-030-2, Pub. by Mus Northern Ariz). U of Nebr Pr.
Waterway: A Navajo Ceremonial Myth Told by Black Moustache Circle. Berard Haile. LC 79-66605. (Illus.). 6p. 1977. pap. 12.95x. Mus Northern Ariz.
Waterway Industrial Sites: A Chicago Case Study. David M. Solzman. LC 66-29231. (Research Papers: No. 107). 138p. 1967. pap. 12.00 (ISBN 0-89065-016-0). U Chicago Comm Geo.
Waterways see Historic Highways of America.
Waterways Management Supervisor. (Career Examination Ser.: C-3414). Date not set. pap. 16.00 (ISBN 0-8373-3414-4). Natl Learning.
Waterways: Poetry in the Mainstream Cumulative Index 1979-1986. Ed. by Barbara Fisher & Richard Spiegel. (Illus.). 45p. 1987. pap. 10.00 (ISBN 0-934830-40-1). Ten Penny.
Waterways: Poetry in the Mainstream, 1987. Ed. by Barbara Fisher & Richard Spiegel. (Illus.). 16p. 1988. pap. 5.00 (ISBN 0-934830-41-X). Ten Penny.
Waterweed. Jo Merrill. LC 76-9285. 1976. perfect bdg. 2.00 (ISBN 0-915214-13-X). Litmus.
Waterworks & Water Pumping Stations: Periodical Literature, 1970-1985. Mary E. Huls. (Architecture Ser.: A 1615). 5p. 1986. 3.00 (ISBN 0-89028-905-0). Vance Biblios.
Waterworks in the Athenian Agora. Mabel Lang. LC 69-22670. (Excavations of the Athenian Agora Picture Bks.: No. 11). (Illus.). 1968. pap. 3.00x (ISBN 0-87661-611-2). Am Sch Athens.
WATFIV. James D. Moore. 1975. pap. write for info. (ISBN 0-87909-876-7, Reston). P-H.
WATFIV for Humans. Rex L. Page & Richard L. Didday. LC 76-3433. (Illus.). 491p. 1976. pap. text ed. 32.25 (ISBN 0-8299-0100-0). West Pub.
WATFIV-S Fundamentals & Style. Walt Brainerd et al. 448p. (Orig.). 1986. pap. text ed. 22.00 (ISBN 0-87835-174-4); write for info. instr's manual (ISBN 0-87835-175-2). Boyd & Fraser.
WATFIV S: Language & Style. Michael J. Merchant. 449p. 1985. pap. text ed. write for info. (ISBN 0-534-04728-9). Wadsworth Pub.
Wath upon Dearne As It Was. Hendon Publishing Co., Ltd. Staff. 1986. 20.30x (ISBN 0-317-54192-7, Pub. by Hendon Pub UK). State Mutual BK.
Watling Operator's Companion. Ed. by Dan R. Post. LC 79-53627. (Slot Machines of Yesteryear Ser.). (Illus.). 1979. 21.95 (ISBN 0-911160-74-4). Post-Era.
Watson-Jones Fractures & Joint Injuries, 2 vols. 6th ed. J. N. Wilson. (Illus.). 1304p. 1983. Set. text ed. 260.00 (ISBN 0-443-02082-5). Churchill.
Watson vs. Jones: The Walnut Street Presbyterian Church & the First Amendment. Ronald W. Eades. 144p. 1982. 18.50 (ISBN 0-89097-023-8). Archer Edns.
Watsons. Jane Austen. LC 72-9808. 318p. 1973. Repr. of 1958 ed. lib. bdg. 35.00x (ISBN 0-8371-6598-9, AUTW). Greenwood.
Watsons. Jane Austen. Ed. by R. W. Chapman. (Jane Austen Library: vol. 4). 164p. 1985. Repr. of 1927 ed. 18.95 (ISBN 0-485-10503-9, Pub. by Athlone Pr). Humanities.
Watsons see Northanger Abbey.
Watson's Apology. Beryl Bainbridge. 224p. 1988. pap. text ed. write for info. (ISBN 0-07-003255-6). McGraw.
Watson's Choice Collection of Comic & Serious Poems. James Watson. 120p. 1983. Repr. of 1706 ed. lib. bdg. 30.00 (ISBN 0-8492-3050-0). R West.
Watson's Classic Book on the Play of the Hand at Bridge. Louis H. Watson. Ed. by Sam Fry, Jr. LC 75-5240. 1959. pap. 7.95 (ISBN 0-06-463209-1, EH 209, B&N Bks). Har-Row.
Watsons: Jane Austen's Fragment Continued & Completed by John Coates. John Coates. 1978. Repr. of 1958 ed. lib. bdg. 25.00 (ISBN 0-8495-0724-3). Arden Lib.
Watsonville: Memories That Linger, Vol. 1. Betty Lewis. write for info. (ISBN 0-9617681-0-X). Otter B Bks.
Watsonville: Memories That Linger, Vol. 2. Betty Lewis. LC 76-41500. (Illus.). 154p. 1980. 11.95 (ISBN 0-934136-08-4, Valley Calif). Western Tanager.
Watt. Samuel Beckett. 29.95 (ISBN 0-685-37202-2). French & Eur.
Watt. Samuel Beckett. 1970. 12.50 (ISBN 0-394-47530-5, GP652). Grove.
Watt. Samuel Beckett. (Orig.). 1959. pap. 10.95 (ISBN 0-394-17216-7, E152, Ever). Grove.
Watt Got You Started, Mr. Fulton? Robert Quackenbush. (Famous Inventor Ser.). (Illus.). 39p. (gr. 1-4). 1982. 7.95 (ISBN 0-13-944397-5). P-H.
Watteau. Donald Posner. LC 83-45154. (Illus.). 288p. 1983. 75.00x (ISBN 0-8014-1571-3). Cornell U Pr.
Watteau & the North Studies in the Dutch & Flemish Baroque Influence on French Rocco Painting. Oliver Banks. LC 76-23602. (Outstanding Dissertations in the Fine Arts Ser.). 1977. lib. bdg. 76.00 (ISBN 0-8240-2676-4). Garland Pub.
Watteau Drawings: Forty-Four Plates. Antoine Watteau. 43p. (Orig.). 1985. pap. 3.50 (ISBN 0-486-24958-1). Dover.
Watteau's Drawings: Their Use & Significance. Martin Eidelberg. LC 76-23616. (Outstanding Dissertations in the Fine Arts - 18th Century). (Illus.). 1977. Repr. of 1965 ed. lib. bdg. 68.00 (ISBN 0-8240-2687-X). Garland Pub.
Watteau's Shepherds: The Detective Novel in Britain 1914-1940. Leroy Panek. 1979. 13.95 (ISBN 0-87972-131-6); pap. 6.95 (ISBN 0-87972-132-4). Bowling Green Univ.
Watts & Woodstock: Identity & Culture in the United States & South Africa. James O'Toole. (George & Louise Spindler-Case Studies in Cultural Anthropology Ser.). (Illus.). 162p. 1983. pap. cancelled (ISBN 0-8290-0586-2). Irvington.
Watts Family. G. T. Ridlon. LC 74-146529. (Saco Valley Settlements Ser). 1970. pap. 1.50 (ISBN 0-8048-0854-6). C E Tuttle.
Watts Riots. Clayton D. Clingan. 1987. 10.95 (ISBN 0-533-06968-8). Vantage.
Watty Piper's Trucks. (Platt & Munk Cricket Bks.). (Illus.). 24p. (ps-3). 1978. pap. 2.50 (ISBN 0-448-46526-4, G&D); PLB 3.59 (ISBN 0-448-13068-8). Putnam Pub Group.
Watunna: An Orinoco Creation Cycle. Marc De Civrieux. Ed. by David Guss. LC 80-82440. (Illus.). 216p. 1980. pap. 12.50 (ISBN 0-86547-003-0). N Point Pr.
Wau-Bun: The Early Day in the Northwest. Juliette Kinzie. (Illus.). xxii, 395p. (YA) (gr. 9-12). 1987. pap. 20.00 (ISBN 1-55613-054-6). Heritage Bk.
Waugh on Women. Jacqueline McDonnell. LC 85-22323. 250p. 1986. 25.00 (ISBN 0-312-85815-9). St Martin.
Waupaca County: Seven A. M. Jerry McGinley. 46p. 1986. 20.00 (ISBN 0-9616222-0-2); pap. 5.50 (ISBN 0-9616222-1-0). Indian Crossing Bks.
Wausau in Nineteen Hundred. rev. ed. George A. Martin. Ed. by John Janke & Jane J. Johnson. (Illus.). 140p. 1987. 19.95 (ISBN 0-9617780-1-6). Birch Lake Pr.
Wave. John Ashbery. LC 83-40217. 112p. 1984. 15.95 (ISBN 0-670-75176-6). Viking.
Wave. John Ashbery. (Poetry Ser.). 96p. 1985. pap. 7.95 (ISBN 0-14-042343-5). Penguin.
Wave. Morton Rhue. LC 81-70394. 144p. (gr. 7 up). 1981. 10.95 (ISBN 0-440-09822-X). Delacorte.
Wave. Morton Rhue. 143p. (YA) (gr. 7 up). 1981. pap. 2.95 (ISBN 0-440-99371-7, LFL); tchr's. guide by Lou Stanek 0.50. Dell.
Wave. Evelyn Scott. 624p. 1986. pap. 9.95 (ISBN 0-88184-209-5). Carroll & Graf.
Wave & the Flame. M. Bradley Kellogg. (Lear's Daughters Ser.: Pt. 1). 1986. pap. 3.50 (ISBN 0-451-14269-1, Sig). NAL.
Wave & Wind Directionality: Applications to the Design of Offshore Structures. 574p. (Orig.). 1983. 95.00x (ISBN 0-87201-906-3). Gulf Pub.
Wave Breaking, Turbulent Mixing & Radio Probing. Y. Toba & H. Mitsuyasu. 1985. lib. bdg. 69.00 (ISBN 0-318-04570-2, Pub. by Riedel Netherlands). Kluwer Academic.
Wave Climate Study, Great Lakes & Gulf of St. Lawrence. 218p. 1971. 17.00 (ISBN 0-317-35947-9, 2-17); members 11.75 (ISBN 0-317-35948-7). Soc Naval Arch.
Wave Crest, Glass of C. F. Monroe. Wilfred Cohen. (Illus.). 240p. 1987. 29.95 (ISBN 0-89145-352-0, 1814). Collector Bks.
Wave Deep. Rebecca Holland. LC 87-91336. 69p. 1987. pap. 5.95 (ISBN 0-9619028-0-9). Neptune Pr.
Wave Dynamics & Radio Probing of the Ocean Surface. Ed. by O. M. Phillips & Klaus Hasselmann. 687p. 1986. 95.00x (ISBN 0-306-41992-0, Plenum Pr). Plenum Pub.
Wave Energy. Tony Lewis. (Illus.). 149p. 1985. pap. 46.00 (ISBN 0-86010-793-0). Graham & Trotman.
Wave Energy: A Design Challenge. Ronald Shaw. LC 82-11780. (Ellis Horwood Series in Energy & Fuel Science). 202p. 1982. 59.95 (ISBN 0-470-27539-1). Halsted Pr.
Wave Equation on a Curved Space-Time. F. G. Friedlander. LC 74-14435. (Cambridge Monographs on Mathematical Physics). (Illus.). 328p. 1976. 82.50 (ISBN 0-521-20567-0). Cambridge U Pr.
Wave Functions: An Explanatory Hypothesis. James S. Hughes. (Illus.). 70p. 1976. 50.00 (ISBN 0-915386-02-X). Arctinurus Co.
Wave Heating & Current Drive in Plasmas. Ed. by V. L. Granatstein & P. L. Colestock. LC 85-12634. 506p. 1985. text ed. 94.00 (ISBN 2-88124-057-7). Gordon & Breach.
Wave Instabilities in Space Plasmas. Ed. by Peter J. Palmadesco & K. Papadopoulos. (Astrophysics & Space Science Library: No. 74). 1979. lib. bdg. 39.50 (ISBN 90-277-1028-7, Pub. by Reidel Holland). Kluwer Academic.
Wave Interactions & Fluid Flows. Alex D. Craik. (Cambridge Monographs on Mechanics & Applied Mathematics). (Illus.). 336p. 1986. 65.00 (ISBN 0-521-26740-4). Cambridge U Pr.
Wave Interactions & Fluid Flows. Alex D. Craik. (Cambridge Monographs on Mechanics & Applied Mathematics). (Illus.). 336p. 1988. pap. 24.95 (ISBN 0-521-36829-4). Cambridge U Pr.
Wave Length: A History of the International Federation of Societies for Electroenephalography & Clinical Neurophysiology. W. A. Cobb. 104p. 1985. 30.00 (ISBN 0-444-80708-X). Elsevier.
Wave Mechanics & Its Applications. P. Gombas & D. Kisdi. LC 73-5789. 250p. 1973. text ed. 34.00 (ISBN 0-08-016979-1). Pergamon.
Wave Motion & Vibration Theory: Proceedings. Symposium in Applied Mathematics, Carnegie Institute of Technology, 1952. Ed. by A. E. Heins. LC 50-1183. (Vol. 5). 169p. 1954. 27.00 (ISBN 0-8218-1305-6, PSAPM-5). Am Math.
Wave Motion: Theory, Modelling, & Computation. Ed. by A. Chorin & A. J. Majda. (Mathematical Science Research Institute Publications: Vol. 7). (Illus.). 350p. 1987. 32.00 (ISBN 0-387-96594-7). Springer Verlag.
Wave of Fury. William J. Harllee. 176p. 1988. 12.50 (ISBN 0-8062-3294-3). Carlton.
Wave Phenomena: Modern Theory & Applications. C. Rogers & T. B. Moodie. (Mathematical Studies: Vol. 97). 1984. 100.00 (ISBN 0-444-87586-7, North-Holland). Elsevier.
Wave Physics. R. E. Newton. (Illus.). 320p. 1988. pap. text ed. 24.95 (ISBN 0-7131-2656-6). Routledge Chapman & Hall.
Wave Principle, 2 vols. Ralph N. Elliott. (Illus.). 1979. deluxe ed. 287.75x (ISBN 0-86722-183-6). Inst Econ Pol.
Wave Propagation: An Invariant Imbedding Approach. R. Bellman & R. Vasudevan. 1985. lib. bdg. 54.50 (ISBN 90-277-1766-4, Pub. by Reidel Holland). Kluwer Academic.
Wave Propagation & Group Velocity. Leon Brillouin. (Pure & Applied Physics Ser.: Vol. 8). 1960. 33.50 (ISBN 0-12-134968-3). Acad Pr.
Wave Propagation & Scattering. Ed. by B. J. Uscinski. (Institute of Mathematics & Its Applications Conference Ser.: No. 5). (Illus.). 360p. 1986. 59.00 (ISBN 0-19-853607-0). Oxford U Pr.
Wave Propagation & Scattering in Random Media: Multiple Scattering Turbulence, Rough Surfaces & Remote Sensing, Vol. 2. A. Ishimaru. 1978. 68.50 (ISBN 0-12-374702-3). Acad Pr.
Wave Propagation & Scattering in Varied Media. Ed. by Varadan. 1988. 50.00 (ISBN 0-89252-962-8, 927). SPIE.
Wave Propagation & Turbulent Media. Roy N. Adams & Eugene D. Denman. LC 66-30179. (Modern Analytic & Computational Methods in Science & Mathematics Ser.). pap. 33.50 (ISBN 0-317-08452-6, 2007766). Bks Demand UMI.
Wave Propagation in Elastic Solids. J. D. Achenbach. (Applied Mathematics & Mechanics Ser.: Vol. 16). 400p. 1973-75. 110.75 (ISBN 0-444-10465-8, North-Holland); pap. 47.50 (ISBN 0-444-10840-8). Elsevier.
Wave Propagation in Solids. Ed. by Julius Miklowitz. LC 72-101230. pap. 47.30 (ISBN 0-317-08536-0, 2010125). Bks Demand UMI.
Wave Propagation Theory. James R. Wait. LC 80-23286. 400p. 1981. 66.00 (ISBN 0-08-026345-3); pap. 35.00 (ISBN 0-08-026344-5). Pergamon.
Wave Resistance: The Low Speed-Limit. T. Francis Ogilvie. (University of Michigan Dept. of Naval Archicture & Marine Engineering Report Ser.). pap. 20.00 (ISBN 0-317-28265-4, 2022627). Bks Demand UMI.
Wave the Flag for Hudson High. John Behee & Tom Saylor. LC 77-89960. (Illus.). 1977. pap. 9.95x (ISBN 0-914464-02-7). J & J Bks.
Wave Theory & Applications. D. R. Bland. (Applied Mathematics & Computing Science Ser.). (Illus.). 256p. 1988. 57.95 (ISBN 0-19-859654-5); pap. 27.95 (ISBN 0-19-859669-3). Oxford U Pr.
Wave Theory Flow of Speculative Matter into the Active Cylinder Theory Stream. C. M. Flumiani. (Illus.). 1980. deluxe ed. 117.75 (ISBN 0-918968-48-8). Inst Econ Finan.
Wave Theory of Light & Spectra. Ed. by I. Bernard Cohen. LC 80-2102. (Development of Science Ser.). (Illus.). 1981. lib. bdg. 35.00x (ISBN 0-405-13867-9). Ayer Co Pubs.
Wave Without a Shore. C. J. Cherryh. (Science Fiction Ser.). 176p. 1981. pap. 2.95 (ISBN 0-88677-101-3). DAW Bks.
Waveform Quantization & Coding. Ed. by N. S. Jayant. LC 75-44651. 624p. 1976. 55.50 (ISBN 0-87942-073-1, PC00687). Inst Electrical.
Waveforms: A History of Early Oscillography. V. J. Phillips. 272p. 1987. 95.00x (ISBN 0-85274-274-6, Pub. by A Hilger UK). Taylor & Francis.
Waveforms: A Modern Guide to Nonsinusoidal Waves & Nonlinear Processes. Homer B. Tilton. LC 85-12427. 245p. 1986. 33.95 (ISBN 0-13-946096-9, Busn). P-H.
Wavefunctions & Mechanisms from Electron Scattering Processes. Ed. by F. A. Gianturco & G. Stefani. (Lecture Notes in Chemistry Ser.: Vol. 35). ix, 279p. 1984. 27.00 (ISBN 0-387-13347-X). Springer-Verlag.
Waveguide Handbook. Ed. by N. Marcuvitz et al. (Electromagnetic Waves Ser.). 448p. 1986. casebound 52.00 (ISBN 0-86341-058-8, EW021). Inst Elect Eng.
Waveguide Tapers, Transitions & Couplers. Hans-Georg Unger. Ed. by Frank Sporleder. (IEE Electromagnetic Waves Ser.: No. 6). (Illus.). 320p. 1979. casebound 58.00 (ISBN 0-906048-16-8, EW006). Inst Elect Eng.
Wavelengths of X-Ray Emission Lines & Absorption Edges. Ed. by Y. Cauchois et al. LC 78-40419. 1978. 230.00 (ISBN 0-08-022448-2); pap. text ed. 80.00. Pergamon.
Wavering Friendship: Russia & Austria 1876-1878. George H. Rupp. LC 76-8455. (Perspectives in European History Ser.: No. 11). xiv, 599p. 1976. Repr. of 1941 ed. lib. bdg. 49.50x (ISBN 0-87991-617-6). Porcupine Pr.
Waverley. Walter Scott. 1976. (Evman); pap. 5.95x (ISBN 0-460-01075-1, Evman). Biblio Dist.
Waverley. Walter Scott. Ed. & intro. by Claire Lamont. (World's Classics Ser.). 480p. 1986. pap. 5.95 (ISBN 0-19-281722-1). Oxford U Pr.
Waverley Anecdotes. Walter Scott. LC 74-12342. 1974. Repr. of 1887 ed. lib. bdg. 55.00 (ISBN 0-8414-7788-4). Folcroft.
Waverley Dictionary. May Rogers. 75.00 (ISBN 0-8490-1279-1). Gordon Pr.
Waverley Novels. Charles A. Young. 136p. 1980. Repr. of 1907 ed. lib. bdg. 22.50 (ISBN 0-8495-6100-0). Arden Lib.
Waverley: Or 'Tis Sixty Years Since. Walter Scott. Ed. by Claire Lamont. 1981. 72.00x (ISBN 0-19-812643-3). Oxford U Pr.
Waverley Pageant: The Best Passages from the Novels of Sir Walter Scott. Ed. by Hugh Walpole. 1973. Repr. of 1932 ed. 17.50 (ISBN 0-8274-0579-0). R West.
Waverly. Walter Scott. (English Library). 608p. 1981. pap. 5.95 (ISBN 0-14-043071-7). Penguin.
Waverly Dictionary. 2nd ed. May Rogers. LC 66-27850. 358p. 1967. Repr. of 1885 ed. 37.00x (ISBN 0-8103-3222-1). Gale.
Waverly Manual, or Hand-Book of the Chief Characters, Incidents & Descriptions. 1978. Repr. of 1871 ed. lib. bdg. 57.00 (ISBN 0-8414-9683-8). Folcroft.
Waverly Novels. Charles A. Young. LC 72-194988. 1907. lib. bdg. 35.00 (ISBN 0-8414-9952-7). Folcroft.
Wavertree: An Ocean Wanderer. George Spiers. (Illus.). 134p. 1969. 4.50 (ISBN 0-913344-01-X). South St Sea Mus.
Waves. Shin-Jae Kang. Tr. by Tina Sallee from Korean. 160p. 1988. pap. 19.95 (ISBN 0-7103-0281-9, Kegan Paul). Routledge Chapman & Hall.
Waves. Virginia Woolf. LC 77-92142. 297p. 1978. pap. 5.95 (ISBN 0-15-694960-1, Harv). HarBraceJ.
Waves. Virginia Woolf. 1983. 15.25 (ISBN 0-8446-6078-7). Peter Smith.
Waves see Berkeley Physics Course.

Way of Faith. Ed. by James M. Pitts. 176p. (Orig.). 1985. pap. 8.95 (ISBN 0-913029-10-6). Stevens Bk Pr.

Way of God's Will. Sun M. Moon. 418p. (Orig.). Date not set. pap. 6.95 (ISBN 0-910621-31-4). HSA Pubns.

Way of Happiness: A Reading of Wordsworth. Henry C. Duffin. LC 72-192021. 1947. lib. bdg. 17.00 (ISBN 0-8414-3726-2). Folcroft.

Way of Harmony. Howard Reid. 1989. 29.95 (ISBN 0-671-67010-7, Fireside); pap. 12.95 (ISBN 0-671-66632-0, Fireside). S&S.

Way of Healing. Hannah Hurnard. 210p. 1986. pap. 7.95 (ISBN 0-06-064092-8). Har-Row.

Way of Heaven. Manly P. Hall. 7.95 (ISBN 0-89314-527-0). Philos Res.

Way of Heaven: An Introduction to the Confucian Religious Life. R. L. Taylor. (Iconography of Religions XII Ser.: No. 3). (Illus.). xi, 37p. 1986. pap. 32.75 (ISBN 90-04-07423-6, Pub. by E J Brill). Heinman.

Way of Herbs. Michael Tierra. 1983. pap. 4.95. WSP.

Way of Herbs. Michael Tierra. Date not set. pap. 4.95. PB.

Way of His Own. T. A. Dyer. (gr. 5-8). 1981. 7.95 (ISBN 0-395-30443-1). HM.

Way of Holiness. Samuel L. Brengle. 1966. Repr. of 1902 ed. 3.95 (ISBN 0-86544-008-5). Salv Army Suppl South.

Way of Holiness. John H. Noyes. LC 75-337. (Radical Tradition in America Ser.). 230p. 1975. Repr. of 1838 ed. 21.50 (ISBN 0-88355-240-X). Hyperion Conn.

Way of Hope: An Autobiography. Lech Walesa. 1987. 19.95 (ISBN 0-8050-0668-0). H Holt & Co.

Way of Illumination, Vol. 1: The Sufi Message. Hazrat I. Khan. 1988. 17.00x (ISBN 81-208-0497-X, Pub. by Motilal Banarsidass). South Asia Bks.

Way of Individuation. Jolande Jacobi. 1983. pap. 9.95 (ISBN 0-452-00866-2, Mer). NAL.

Way of Karate. George E. Mattson. LC 62-14116. (Illus.). 1963. 19.50 (ISBN 0-8048-0624-1). C E Tuttle.

Way of Karate. George E. Mattson. 19.50x (ISBN 0-685-22157-1). Wehman.

Way of Knowing. William P. Montague. 1962. Repr. of 1978 ed. text ed. 19.95x (ISBN 0-391-00568-5). Humanities.

Way of Korean Zen. Kusan Sunim. Tr. by Martine Fages. (Illus.). 182p. pap. 12.50 (ISBN 0-8348-0201-5). Weatherhill.

Way of Language: An Introduction. Fred West. 250p. (Orig.). 1975. pap. text ed. 11.00 net (ISBN 0-15-595130-0, HC). HarBraceJ.

Way of Lao Tzu. Wing-Tsit Chan. 1963. pap. text ed. write for info. (ISBN 0-02-320700-0). Macmillan.

Way of Lao Tzu: Tao-Te Ching. Lao Tzu. Tr. by Wing-Tsit Chan. LC 62-21266. (Orig.). 1963. pap. 8.40 scp (ISBN 0-672-60350-0, LLA139). Bobbs.

Way of Liberation: Essays & Lectures on the Transformation of the Self. Alan Watts. Ed. by Mark Watts & Rebecca Shropshire. LC 82-21917. 120p. 1983. pap. 8.95 (ISBN 0-8348-0181-7). Weatherhill.

Way of Life. Charles Hodge. 1978. pap. 5.95 (ISBN 0-85151-273-9). Banner of Truth.

Way of Life. H. Glyn Joner & Barbara Collins. (Illus.). 192p. 1987. 25.95 (ISBN 0-85236-166-1, Farming Press UK). Diamond Farm Bk.

Way of Life. Jim Kinter. Ed. by Joseph E. Walker. LC 74-29188. (Lancaster County During the American Revolution Ser.). (Illus.). 64p. 1975. pap. 2.00 (ISBN 0-915010-04-6). Sutter House.

Way of Life. Lao Tzu. 1988. pap. 3.95 (ISBN 0-451-62674-5, Ment). NAL.

Way of Life. William Osler. 1937. 6.75x (ISBN 0-06-141860-9, Harper Medical). Lippincott.

Way of Life. D. E. Pohren. (Illus.). 194p. (Orig.). 1980. 15.95 (ISBN 0-317-56900-7, Pub. by Soc Sp Studies Madrid); pap. 11.95 (ISBN 0-933224-03-6, Pub. by Soc Sp Studies Madrid). Bold Strummer Ltd.

Way of Life. Hendrik Roehrman. LC 70-144677. Orig. Title: Marlow & Shakespeare. Repr. of 1952 ed. 5.00 (ISBN 0-404-05386-6). AMS Pr.

Way of Life. M. L. Sexton. (Series Outlines). 2.95 (ISBN 0-89315-352-4). Lambert Bk.

Way of Life. Arthur J. Vincellette. 160p. 1983. 7.95 (ISBN 0-89962-312-3). Todd & Honeywell.

Way of Life According to Lao Tzu. Ed. by Witter Bynner. (Illus.). 112p. 1986. pap. 4.95 (ISBN 0-399-51298-5, Perigee). Putnam Pub Group.

Way of Life: An Address Delivered to Yale Students Sunday Evening, April 20, 1913. William Osler. (Illus.). 56p. 1969. 12.00 (ISBN 0-398-01433-7). C C Thomas.

Way of Life & Death: Three Centuries of Prussian-German Militarism, An Anthropological Approach. Emilio Willems. LC 85-22488. 256p. (Orig.). 1986. pap. text ed. 12.95x (ISBN 0-8265-1214-3). Vanderbilt U Pr.

Way of Life: Being a Catholic Today. Ed. by David M. Board. (Illus.). 208p. 1986. 9.95 (ISBN 0-00-599705-4, Collins Liturgical). HarpR.

Way of Life: Kettle's Yard. Jim Ede. 1984. 54.50 (ISBN 0-521-25062-5). Cambridge U Pr.

Way of Life, Only a Memory. Iva M. Dickson. 1986. 7.95 (ISBN 0-533-06858-4). Vantage.

Way of Life: Tao Te Ching. Lao Tzu. Tr. by R. B. Blakney. 1955. pap. 3.95 (ISBN 0-451-62563-3, Ment). NAL.

Way of Living Faith: A Spirituality of Liberation. Segundo Galilea. LC 85-45352. 160p. 1988. 14.45 (ISBN 0-06-063082-5, HarpR). Har-Row.

Way of Looking at Things: Selected Papers of Erik H. Erikson 1930-1980. Ed. by Stephen P. Schlein. 1987. 29.95 (ISBN 0-393-02267-6). Norton.

Way of Love. Ed. by E. Rozanne Elder. (Cistercian Fathers Ser.: No. 16). (Illus.). 1977. 7.95 (ISBN 0-87907-616-X); pap. 4.50 (ISBN 0-87907-966-5). Cistercian Pubns.

Way of Love. John B. Glubb. LC 75-44945. 1976. 7.95x (ISBN 0-916624-00-5); pap. 2.95x (ISBN 0-916624-01-3). Troy State Univ.

Way of Love: A Thought & a Prayer a Day at a Time. Denis Duncan. LC 81-15925. 96p. 1982. Westminster John Knox.

Way of Love, a Way of Life: A Young Person's Introduction to What It Means to Be Gay. Frances Hanckel & John Cunningham. LC 79-2424. (Illus.). (YA) (gr. 9-12). 1979. PLB 11.88 (ISBN 0-688-51907-5). Lothrop.

Way of Man. Martin Buber. 1966. pap. 2.95 (ISBN 0-87574-106-1, 106, Pub. by Citadel Pr). Lyle Stuart.

Way of Man. Martin Buber. 44p. 1985. pap. 3.95 (ISBN 0-8065-0024-7, Pub. by Citadel Pr). Lyle Stuart.

Way of Man, 1959. Martin Buber. 2.50x (ISBN 0-317-66540-5). Pendle Hill.

Way of Microwave Cooking - Como Trabajo el Microonda. Claudette Harshberger. Tr. by Alfredo Borunda. 120p. (Orig., Span. & Eng.). 1981. pap. 7.50 (ISBN 0-9606100-0-6). Pan Prods.

Way of My Cross: The Masses & Homilies of Father Jerzy Popieluszko. Jerzy Popieluszko. Tr. by Michael Wren from Pol. & Fr. 200p. pap. 9.95 (ISBN 0-89526-806-X). Regnery Gateway.

Way of Mysticism. Joseph James. 256p. 1981. pap. 14.50 (ISBN 0-89540-086-3, SB-086). Sun Pub.

Way of Mysticism: An Anthology. Joseph James. 1977. lib. bdg. 59.95 (ISBN 0-8490-2810-8). Gordon Pr.

Way of Non-Attachment. Dhiravamsa. pap. 8.99 (ISBN 0-85500-210-7, Pub. by Turnstone Pr England). Sterling.

Way of Our People. Arnold Griese. LC 74-23086. (Illus.). 90p. (gr. 2-5). 1975. (Crowell Jr Bks); PLB 12.89 (ISBN 0-690-00707-8). HarpJ.

Way of P. D. N. The Ultimate Vegetarian Athletic Nutrition Program. rev. ed. Donald Thomas. 156p. 1986. pap. 9.93 (ISBN 0-939380-01-3). PDN Pub Bklyn.

Way of Paradox: Spiritual Life As Taught by Meister Eckhart. Cyprian Smith. 144p. 1988. pap. 7.95 (ISBN 0-8091-2948-5). Paulist Pr.

Way of Peace. J. C. Wenger. LC 77-86349. (Mennonite Faith Ser.: No. 3, Christian Peace Shelf Ser). 72p. 1977. pap. text ed. 1.95 (ISBN 0-8361-1835-9). Herald Pr.

Way of Peace & Blessedness. 3rd ed. Swami Paramananda. 1961. 4.50 (ISBN 0-911564-06-3). Vedanta Ctr.

Way of Peace: Essays & Addresses. Algernon Cecil. LC 68-15818. 1968. Repr. of 1938 ed. 21.00 (ISBN 0-8046-0073-2, Pub. by Kennikat). Assoc Faculty Pr.

Way of Perfection. St. Teresa of Avila. 1964. pap. 5.95 (ISBN 0-385-06539-6, D176, Im). Doubleday.

Way of Poetry. facs. ed. Ed. by John Drinkwater. LC 73-116399. (Granger Index Reprint Ser.). 1922. 16.00 (ISBN 0-8369-6140-4). Ayer Co Pubs.

Way of Power. Nicholas A. Roderey. LC 69-14358. 187p. 1969. 6.95 (ISBN 0-8022-2298-6). Philos Lib.

Way of Response: Selections from His Writings. Martin Buber. Ed. by Nahum N. Glatzer. LC 66-26977. 1971. pap. 6.95 (ISBN 0-8052-0292-7). Schocken.

Way of St. Francis: The Challenge of Franciscan Spirituality for Everyone. Murray Bodo. LC 83-14066. 1985. pap. 7.95 (ISBN 0-385-19913-9, Im). Doubleday.

Way of St. James, 3 vols. Georgianna G. King. LC 78-63469. Repr. of 1920 ed. Set. 140.00 (ISBN 0-404-17160-5). AMS Pr.

Way of Salvation N. T. 1982. pap. 3.95 (ISBN 0-89225-220-0). Gospel Advocate.

Way of Seeing. Helen Levitt. (Illus.). 1981. 27.50 (ISBN 0-8180-1422-9); ltd, signed ed 75.00 (ISBN 0-686-86069-1). Horizon.

Way of Seeing. Helen Levitt. (Illus.). Date not set. lib. bdg. 27.50 (ISBN 0-8223-0733-2, Dist. by Duke). Horizon.

Way of Seeing. Helen Levitt. LC 81-82838. (Illus.). xv, 68p. 1987. lib. bdg. 27.50 (ISBN 0-317-59257-2). Duke.

Way of Seeing. Philip Rusten. (Illus.). 96p. 1978. 23.00 (ISBN 0-686-29711-3). Way of Seeing.

Way of Seeing. Edith Schaeffer. 256p. 1977. pap. 6.95 (ISBN 0-8007-5036-5, Power Bks). Revell.

Way of Seeing: A Critical Study of James Agee. Alfred T. Barson. LC 75-181365. 232p. 1971. 17.50x (ISBN 0-87023-094-8). U of Mass Pr.

Way of Sequestered Places. Ewing Campbell. LC 79-87889. 6.95 (ISBN 0-918722-10-1). Nefertiti.

Way of Shalom: Jesus Christ, Giver of Peace. Elizabeth Caldwell. (Vacation Ventures Series 1988). 48p. 1987. administrative manual 4.15 (ISBN 0-664-24040-2). Westminster John Knox.

Way of Siddhartha: A Life of the Buddha. David J. Kalupahana & Indrani Kalupahana. 242p. 1987. pap. text ed. 11.75 (ISBN 0-8191-6066-0). U Pr of Amer.

Way of Silence: The Prose & Poetry of Basho. Richard Lewis. LC 74-102828. (Illus.). 111p. 1970. 7.50 (ISBN 0-89062-120-9, Pub. by Touchstone). Pub Ctr Cult Res.

Way of Spider. W. Michael Gear. (Spider Trilogy Ser.: No. 2). 1989. pap. 3.95 (ISBN 0-88677-318-0). DAW Bks.

Way of Spiritual Direction. Francis K. Nemeck & Marie T. Coombs. LC 84-81254. 1985. pap. 8.95 (ISBN 0-89453-447-5). M Glazier.

Way of Suffering: A Geography of Crisis. Jerome Miller. 1988. 22.95 (ISBN 0-317-68137-0). Georgetown U Pr.

Way of Tao: Part II. Bhagwan S. Rajneesh. Tr. by Dolli Didi. 1979. 15.50 (ISBN 0-89684-056-5, Pub. by Motilal Banarsidass India). Orient Bk Dist.

Way of Tea. Rand Castile. LC 70-157271. (Illus.). 332p. 1971. 27.50 (ISBN 0-8348-0059-4). Weatherhill.

Way of Tenderness. Kevin O'Shea. LC 78-61728. (Orig.). 1978. pap. 2.95 (ISBN 0-8091-2166-2). Paulist Pr.

Way of the Actor: A Path to Knowledge & Power. Brian Bates. LC 86-31332. 216p. 1987. 15.95 (ISBN 0-87773-384-8); 9.95 (ISBN 0-87773-441-0). Shambhala Pubns.

Way of the Ascetics. Tito Colliander. 130p. Repr. of 1960 ed. cancelled 5.95 (ISBN 0-913026-22-0). St Nectarios.

Way of the Ascetics: The Ancient Tradition of Discipline & Inner Growth. Ed. by Tito Colliandor. Tr. by Katharine Ferre from Swedish. LC 85-83900. 110p. 1985. pap. 5.95 (ISBN 0-88141-049-7). St Vladimirs.

Way of the Black Messiah: The Hermeneutical Challenge of Black Theology. Theo Witvliet. 352p. 1987. 39.95 (ISBN 0-940989-09-3); pap. 19.95 (ISBN 0-940989-04-2). Meyer Stone Bks.

Way of the Brush. Fritz Van Briessen. 329p. 1962. 210.00x (ISBN 0-317-69290-9, Pub. by Han-Shan Tang Ltd). State Mutual Bk.

Way of the Brush: Painting Techniques of China & Japan. Fritz Van Briessen. LC 62-14119. (Illus.). 1962. 47.50 (ISBN 0-8048-0625-X). C E Tuttle.

Way of the Buddha. C. A. Burland. (Way Ser.). (gr. 3-7). pap. 5.95 (ISBN 0-7175-0590-1). Dufour.

Way of the Bull. Leo Buscaglia. 1988. 8.95 (ISBN 1-55525-167-6). Nightingale-Conant.

Way of the Bull. Leo F. Buscaglia. LC 73-83777. 176p. 1973. 9.95 (ISBN 0-913590-08-8). Slack Inc.

Way of the Bull. Leo F. Buscaglia. LC 73-83777. 192p. 1982. 9.95 (ISBN 0-03-062882-2, Pub by Slack Inc). H Holt & Co.

Way of the Child. David Patterson. LC 86-83410. 280p. (Orig.). 1988. pap. 8.95 (ISBN 0-89896-316-8). Larksdale.

Way of the Christian. J. Catling Allen. (Way Ser.). (gr. 3-7). pap. 5.95 (ISBN 0-7175-0782-3). Dufour.

Way of the Cross. Ed Carley. (gr. 4-6). 1985. 9.95 (ISBN 0-89837-101-5, Pub. by Pflaum Press). Pflaum Pr.

Way of the Cross. Josemaria Escriva. (Illus.). 123p. 1983. 10.95 (ISBN 0-906138-05-1); pap. 6.95 (ISBN 0-906138-06-X); pocket size 3.95 (ISBN 0-906138-07-8). Scepter Pubs.

Way of the Cross. Roy Hession. 1974. pap. 1.95 (ISBN 0-87508-238-6). Chr Lit.

Way of the Cross. Tolbert McCarroll. LC 84-61025. 128p. (Orig.). 1985. pap. 4.95 (ISBN 0-8091-2653-2). Paulist Pr.

Way of the Cross. Mary C. Morrison. LC 85-60516. 32p. (Orig.). 1985. pap. 2.50x (ISBN 0-87574-260-2). Pendle Hill.

Way of the Cross. Anthony Sketch. (Illus.). 32p. (Orig.). 1988. pap. 2.95 (ISBN 0-00-599088-2, Pub. by Collins Liturgical). Har Row.

Way of the Cross: According to the Method of St. Alphonsus Liguori. Alphonsus Ligouri. 1987. pap. 0.60 (ISBN 0-89555-313-9). TAN Bks Pubs.

Way of the Cross for Congregational Use. Ed. by Jeremy Harrington. (Illus.). 28p. (Orig.). 1976. pap. text ed. 0.65 (ISBN 0-912228-24-5). St Anthony Mess Pr.

Way of the Cross for the Separated & Divorced. Anajean Hauber. (Illus.). 45p. (Orig.). 1985. pap. text ed. 2.95 (ISBN 0-86716-050-0). St Anthony Mess Pr.

Way of the Cross: Giant Print Edition. rev. ed. Fulton J. Sheen. (Illus.). 64p. 1982. pap. 2.50 (ISBN 0-87973-659-3, 659); roncote pocket-size 2.50 (ISBN 0-87973-660-7, 660). Our Sunday Visitor.

Way of the Cross in the Light of the Holy Shroud. Giulio Ricci. (Illus.). 117p. 1988. pap. 9.95 (ISBN 0-8198-8228-3). Dghtrs St Paul.

Way of the Cross in Time of Revolt. Robert McGovern. 22p. 1971. pap. 1.00 (ISBN 0-912592-04-4). Ashland Poetry.

Way of the Cross: The Pilgrimage at Jerusalem. Ade Bethune. (Illus.). 30p. (Orig.). 1986. pap. 1.00 (ISBN 0-934134-94-4). Sheed & Ward MO.

Way of the Cross: Way of Justice. Leonardo Boff. Tr. by John Drury from Port. LC 79-23776. 144p. (Orig.). 1980. pap. 7.95 (ISBN 0-88344-701-0). Orbis Bks.

Way of the Dead Indians: Guajiro Myths & Symbols. Michel Perrin. Tr. by Michael Fineberg from Fr. (Texas Press Sourcebooks in Anthropology Ser.: No. 13). (Illus.). 229p. 1987. text ed. 30.00x (ISBN 0-292-79032-5); pap. 12.95 (ISBN 0-292-79039-2). U of Tex Pr.

Way of the Dictators. Lewis Broad & Leonard Russell. LC 71-112796. (Illus.). 1970. Repr. of 1935 ed. 24.50 (ISBN 0-8046-1063-0, Pub. by Kennikat). Assoc Faculty Pr.

Way of the Disciple. Codd. 5.00 (ISBN 0-8356-7049-X). Theos Pub Hse.

Way of the Drama. Bruce Carpenter. 1975. Repr. of 1929 ed. 25.00 (ISBN 0-8274-4108-8). R West.

Way of the Eagle. Jerry Fankhauser. 133p. (Orig.). 1987. pap. write for info. (ISBN 0-9617006-4-5). J Fankhauser.

Way of the Fussbudget Is Not Easy. Charles M. Schulz. 192p. 1986. pap. 5.95 (ISBN 0-03-005619-5, Owl Bks). H Holt & Co.

Way of the Goddess: A Manual for Wiccan Initiation. Ly Warren-Clarke. 160p. pap. 10.95 (ISBN 1-85327-006-7, Pub. by Prism Pr). Avery Pub.

Way of the Greeks. Frank R. Earp. LC 75-136393. Repr. of 1929 ed. 21.50 (ISBN 0-404-02234-0). AMS Pr.

Way of the Grizzly. Dorothy H. Patent. LC 86-17562. (Illus.). 64p. (gr. 4 up). 1987. 12.95 (ISBN 0-89919-383-8, Pub. by Clarion). Ticknor & Fields.

Way of the Heart. Henri J. Nouwen. (Epiphany Bks.). 1983. pap. 2.95 (ISBN 0-345-32959-7). Ballantine.

Way of the Heart: Desert Spirituality & Contemporary Ministry. Henri J. Nouwen. 96p. 1981. 10.45 (ISBN 0-86683-913-5, AY7443, HarpR). Har-Row.

Way of the Heart: The Rajneesh Movement. Judith Thompson & Paul Heelas. LC 87-29792. (New Religious Movements Ser.: No. 3). 142p. 1988. Repr. lib. bdg. 19.95x (ISBN 0-8095-7038-6). Borgo Pr.

Way of the Hindu. Swami Yogeshananda. (Way Ser.). (gr. 3-7). pap. 5.95 (ISBN 0-7175-0626-6). Dufour.

Way of the Hummingbird: In Legend, History & Today's Gardens. Virginia Holmgren. (Illus.). 176p. (Orig.). 1986. pap. 8.95 (ISBN 0-88496-250-4). Capra Pr.

Way of the Hummingbird: In Legend, History & Today's Gardens. Virginia C. Holmgren. 160p. 1988. Repr. lib. bdg. 22.95x (ISBN 0-8095-4026-6). Borgo Pr.

Way of the Hunter: The Art & Spirit of Modern Hunting. Thomas McIntyre. Ed. by William Doerflinger. (Illus.). 256p. 1988. 18.95 (ISBN 0-525-24718-1). Dutton.

Way of the Hunters: An Illustrated Commentary & Prehistoric Record. Raoul M. Dixon. (Illus.). 256p. 1987. 14.95 (ISBN 0-8062-2864-4). Carlton.

Way of the Immortal Threefold Self: The Straight Path. Robert E. Birdsong. (Aquarian Academy Monograph: Ser. E, No. 4). 1980. pap. 1.45 (ISBN 0-917108-29-9). Sirius Bks.

Way of the Jews. Louis Jacobs. (Way Ser.). (gr. 3-7). pap. 5.95 (ISBN 0-7175-0875-7). Dufour.

Way of the Kabbalah. Z'ev Ben Shimon Halevi. 1976. pap. 12.50 (ISBN 0-87728-305-2). Weiser.

Way of the Lawless. Max Brand. 1980. pap. 2.50 (ISBN 0-446-32665-8). Warner Bks.

Way of the Makers. Marguerite Wilkinson. 316p. 1980. Repr. of 1925 ed. lib. bdg. 30.00 (ISBN 0-8492-8820-7). R West.

Way of the Masks. Claude Levi-Strauss. Tr. by Sylvia Modelski from Fr. LC 82-2723. (Illus.). 276p. 1982. 19.95 (ISBN 0-295-95929-0). U of Wash Pr.

Way of the Masks. Claude Levi-Strauss. (Illus.). 1988. pap. 14.95 (ISBN 0-295-96636-X). U of Wash Pr.

Way of the Muslim. Muhammad Iqbal. (Way Ser.). (gr. 3-7). pap. 5.95 (ISBN 0-7175-0632-0). Dufour.

Way of the Mystics. H. C. Graef. 1977. lib. bdg. 59.95 (ISBN 0-8490-2811-6). Gordon Pr.

Way of the Mystics: The Early Christian Mystics & the Rise of the Sufis. Margaret Smith. 1978. pap. 6.95 (ISBN 0-19-519967-7). Oxford U Pr.

Way of the Peaceful Warrior: A Book That Changes Lives. rev. ed. Dan Millman. LC 83-83240. 216p. 1984. pap. 9.95 (ISBN 0-915811-00-6). H J Kramer Inc.

Way of the Physician. Jacob Needleman. LC 84-48776. 224p. 1985. 15.95 (ISBN 0-06-250644-7, HarpR). Har-Row.

Way of the Pilgrim. Gordon R. Dickson. 1987. 16.95 (ISBN 0-441-87486-X, Pub. by Ace Science Fiction). Ace Bks.

Way of the Pilgrim. Gordon R. Dickson. 1988. pap. 4.50 (ISBN 0-441-87487-8). Ace Bks.

Way of the Preacher. Simon Tugwell. (Orig.). 1979. pap. 7.95 (ISBN 0-87243-093-6). Templegate.

Way of the Righteous see Science - The False Messiah.

Way of the Ronin: A Guide to Career Strategy. Beverly A. Potter. LC 84-45203. 192p. (Orig.). 1984. 17.95 (ISBN 0-8144-5798-3). AMACOM.

Way of the Ronin: Riding the Waves of Changes at Work. Beverly A. Potter. (Illus.). 227p. 1988. pap. 9.95 (ISBN 0-914171-26-7). Ronin Pub.

TITLE INDEX WAY TO LOCATE ACU-POINTS.

Way of the Rosycross in Our Times. 3rd ed. De Rozekruis Pevs Staff. 51p. 1986. pap. 1.75 (ISBN 90-70196-46-8). Rozekruis Pr.
Way of the Sacred Tree. Edna Hong. LC 82-72643. 208p. 1983. pap. 11.95 (ISBN 0-8066-1949-X, 10-6958). Augsburg.
Way of the Saints: The Collected Short Writings of Kirpal Singh. Kirpal Singh. Ed. by Russell Perkins. LC 76-21987. 402p. 1978. 8.00 (ISBN 0-89142-026-6). Sant Bani Ash.
Way of the Samurai. Yukio Mishima. 166p. 1983. pap. 7.95 (ISBN 0-399-50907-0, Wideview). Putnam Pub Group.
Way of the Samurai. Minoru Tanaka. 88p. 1975. pap. 7.50 (ISBN 0-89540-009-X, SB-009). Sun Pub.
Way of the Scarlet Pimpernel. E. Orczy. 318p. 1983. Repr. lib. bdg. 18.95x (ISBN 0-89966-461-X). Buccaneer Bks.
Way of the Sea. Norman Duncan. LC 76-121537. (Short Story Index Reprint Ser). 1903. 20.00 (ISBN 0-8369-3493-8). Ayer Co Pubs.
Way of the Sea. H. J. Fleure & Harold Peake. (Corridors of Time Ser.: No. 6). 1929. 39.50x (ISBN 0-686-83850-5). Elliots Bks.
Way of the Sea see Corridors of Time: New Haven & London, 1927-1956.
Way of the Shaman. Michael Harner. 214p. 1982. pap. 4.50 (ISBN 0-553-25982-2). Bantam.
Way of the Shepherd: Courage & Contentment from the 23rd Psalm. Don Baker. Ed. by Larry R. Libby. LC 87-5699. 1987. pap. 5.95 (ISBN 0-88070-193-5). Multnomah.
Way of the Sikh. W. H. McLeod. (Way Ser.). (gr. 4-8). pap. 5.95 (ISBN 0-7175-0731-9). Dufour.
Way of the Soul: The "Heart Path" to Human Perfection. Robert E. Birdsong. (Aquarian Academy Monograph: Ser. D, No. 2). 1980. pap. 1.45 (ISBN 0-917108-28-0). Sirius Bks.
Way of the Spirit: The "Head Path" to Human Perfection, Ser. C, No. 2. Robert E. Birdsong. (Aquarian Academy Monograph). 1980. pap. 1.45 (ISBN 0-917108-27-2). Sirius Bks.
Way of the Stars: Greek Legends of the Constellations. Ghislaine Vautier. Adapted by Kenneth McLeish. (Illus.). 32p. (gr. 3-7). 1983. 11.95 (ISBN 0-521-25061-7). Cambridge U Pr.
Way of the Storyteller. rev. ed. Ruth Sawyer. 1977. pap. 5.95 (ISBN 0-14-004436-1). Penguin.
Way of the Sufi. Idries Shah. 1970. pap. 8.95 (ISBN 0-525-47261-4). Dutton.
Way of the Sufi. Idries Shah. 1983. 18.95 (ISBN 0-900860-80-4, Pub. by Octagon Pr England). Ins Study Human.
Way of the Sun. White Eagle. 112p. 1982. 5.95 (ISBN 0-85487-055-5). DeVorss.
Way of the Sword: The Tengu-geijutsu-ron of Chozan Shissai. Reinhard Kammer. Tr. by Betty J. Fitzgerald from Japanese. 144p. 1986. pap. 5.95 (ISBN 1-85063-043-7). Routledge Chapman & Hall.
Way of the Tiger: Assassin! Mark Smith & Jamie Thomson. 1988. pap. 3.50 (ISBN 0-425-11101-6, Pub. by Berkley-Pacer). Berkley Pub.
Way of the Tiger: Avenger! Mark Smith & Jamie Thomson. 1988. pap. 3.50 (ISBN 0-425-11052-4). Berkley Pub.
Way of the Urban Samurai. Deborah Minkin. (Illus.). 128p. (Orig.). 1988. pap. 8.95 (ISBN 0-88089-031-2). Madrona Pubs.
Way of the Warrior. Howard Reid & Michael Croucher. 1987. pap. 12.95 (ISBN 0-671-64674-5, Fireside). S&S.
Way of the WAVES: Women in the Navy. Marie B. Alsmeyer. LC 81-81450. 186p. 1981. pap. 12.50x (ISBN 0-9606152-0-2). Hamba Bks.
Way of the West: The Formation of Modern Society, Vol. B. Arthur J. Slavin. LC 72-91059. 648p. 1973. pap. 21.95 (ISBN 0-536-00908-2, JW). Krieger.
Way of the West: Tradition & Innovation, Prehistory-1650, Vol. A. Arthur J. Slavin. LC 72-91059. 704p. 1975. pap. 21.95 (ISBN 0-536-00907-4, JW). Krieger.
Way of the White Clouds. Bhagwan Shree Rajneesh. (Illus.). 1979. pap. 9.95 (ISBN 0-394-17089-X, E729, Ever). Grove.
Way of the Wind. Paul J. Lederer. (Indian Heritage Ser.: No. 5). 1986. pap. 3.50 (ISBN 0-451-14038-9, Pub. by Sig). NAL.
Way of the Wise. Compiled by T. O. Tollett. 64p. 1970. pap. 1.00 (ISBN 0-89114-061-1). Baptist Pub Hse.
Way of the Wolf. Martin Bell. (Epiphany Ser.). 144p. 1983. pap. 2.95 (ISBN 0-345-30522-1). Ballantine.
Way of the Wolf: The Gospel in New Images. Martin Bell. LC 77-120366. (Illus.). 128p. 1970. pap. 8.95 (ISBN 0-8164-0202-7, AY6445, HarpR); 2 records 8.95 ea. Har-Row.
Way of the World. William Congreve. Ed. by Henry T. Perry. LC 51-6756. (Crofts Classics Ser.). 1951. pap. text ed. 3.95x (ISBN 0-88295-024-X). Harlan Davidson.
Way of the World. William Congreve. Ed. by Brian Gibbons. (New Mermaid Ser.). 1976. pap. 5.95x (ISBN 0-393-90004-5). Norton.
Way of the World. William Congreve. Ed. by Kathleen M. Lynch. LC 65-10543. (Regents Restoration Drama Ser.). xxii, 136p. 1965. pap. 3.50x (ISBN 0-8032-5354-0, BB 251, Bison). U of Nebr Pr.
Way of the World see Restoration Plays.
Way of the World: The Bildungsroman in European Culture. Franco Moretti. 288p. 1987. 34.95 (ISBN 0-86091-159-4, Pub. by Verso); pap. write for info. (ISBN 0-86091-872-6). Routledge Chapman & Hall.
Way of the World: The Bildungsroman in European Culture. Franco Moretti. Tr. by Albert Sbragia. 264p. 1988. text ed. 16.95 (ISBN 0-86091-891-2, Pub. by Verso). Routledge Chapman & Hall.
Way of Theology in Karl Barth: Essays & Comments. Ed. by H. Martin Rumscheidt. LC 86-15069. (Princeton Theological Monograph Ser.: No. 8). 1986. pap. 13.90 (ISBN 0-915138-61-1). Pickwick.
Way of Things. Kathleen Iddings. 60p. (Orig.). 1984. pap. 4.95x (ISBN 0-942424-06-9). W Anglia Pubns.
Way of Things: A Philosophy of Knowledge, Nature & Value. William P. Montague. LC 75-3283. Repr. of 1940 ed. 49.50 (ISBN 0-404-59271-6). AMS Pr.
Way of Thinking in Traditional Philosophy: Prospects & Limits. 26p. 1979. pap. 5.00 (ISBN 92-808-0121-X, TUNU050, UNU). UNIPUB.
Way of Torah: An Introduction to Judaism. 4th ed. Jacob Neusner. (Religious Life of Man Ser.). 194p. 1988. pap. text ed. write for info. (ISBN 0-534-08040-5). Wadsworth Pub.
Way of Tradition I. Sun M. Moon. 326p. (Orig.). Date not set. pap. 6.95 (ISBN 0-910621-22-5). HSA Pubns.
Way of Tradition II. Sun M. Moon. 295p. Date not set. pap. 6.95 (ISBN 0-910621-23-3). HSA Pubns.
Way of Tradition III. Sun M. Moon. 541p. Date not set. pap. 6.95 (ISBN 0-910621-24-1). HSA Pubns.
Way of Tradition IV. Sun M. Moon. 462p. 1980. pap. 8.00 (ISBN 0-910621-35-7). HSA Pubns.
Way of Transformation. Karlfried G. Durckheim. (Unwin Paperbacks). 112p. 1980. pap. 10.95 (ISBN 0-04-291014-5). Unwin Hyman.
Way of True Riches. Milo Kaufman. LC 79-83505. (Mennonite Faith Ser: No. 6). 64p. 1979. pap. 1.95 (ISBN 0-8361-1885-5). Herald Pr.
Way of Vaisnava Sages: A Medieval Story of South Indian Sadhus. N. S. Narasimha & Ramananda Babaji. LC 86-28251. (Sanskrit Notes of Visnu-vijay Swami). 422p. (Orig.). 1987. lib. bdg. 35.25 (ISBN 0-8191-6060-1); pap. text ed. 18.75 (ISBN 0-8191-6061-X). U Pr of Amer.
Way of Western Art, Seventeen Seventy-Six to Nineteen Fourteen. Edgar P. Richardson. LC 73-79604. (Illus.). 1969. Repr. of 1939 ed. 28.50x (ISBN 0-8154-0287-2). Cooper Sq.
Way of Widsom. R. B. Scott. 1972. pap. 7.95 (ISBN 0-02-089280-2, Collier). Macmillan.
Way of Working: The Spiritual Dimension of Craft. Ed. by D. M. Dooling. xiv, 127p. 1986. pap. text ed. 8.95 (ISBN 0-930407-01-6). Parabola Mag.
Way of Wyrd. Brian Bates. 1988. pap. 3.95 (ISBN 0-425-11059-1). Berkley Pub.
Way of Wyrd: The Book of a Sorcerer's Apprentice. Brian Bates. LC 83-48417. 224p. 1984. 12.45 (ISBN 0-06-250040-6, HarpR). Har-Row.
Way of Zen. Alan W. Watts. 1974. pap. 4.95 (ISBN 0-394-70298-0, Vin). Random.
Way Out. A. R. Bailey & D. G. Hull. (Illus.). 85p. 1980. pap. text ed. 6.95x (ISBN 0-920380-62-X, Pub. by Inst Res Pub Canada). Brookfield Pub Co.
Way Out. Jeanne Guyon. (Orig.). 1985. pap. 6.95 (ISBN 0-940232-20-0). Christian Bks.
Way Out. pap. 4.00 (ISBN 0-87516-302-5). DeVorss.
Way Out: A Story of the Cumberland Today. Emerson Hough. 1976. lib. bdg. 14.75x (ISBN 0-89968-048-8). Lightyear.
Way Out: Anarchist, Mutualist & Individualist Essays. Laurance Labadie. (Men & Movements in the History & Philosophy of Anarchism Ser.). 1980. lib. bdg. 59.95 (ISBN 0-686-60065-7). Revisionist Pr.
Way Out Book. John-Roger. 1980. pap. 8.00 (ISBN 0-914829-23-8). Mandeville LA.
Way Out: Federalist Options for South Africa. Ed. by Michael Briand. 100p. 1987. pap. 5.95 (ISBN 0-917616-90-1). ICS Pr.
Way Out Here! Hawaii's Own Love Story. Jean MacKellar. (Illus.). 344p. (Orig.). 1988. pap. 7.50 (ISBN 0-9603518-6-8). Glen Pr.
Way Out: Libertarian & Mutualist Essays on Free Banking, Free Land & Individualism. Vardis Fisher et al. 1979. lib. bdg. 59.95 (ISBN 0-87700-267-3). Revisionist Pr.
Way Out Must Lead In: Life Histories in the Civil Rights Movement. rev. ed. William R. Beardslee. LC 82-12054. 224p. 1983. 14.95 (ISBN 0-88208-153-5); pap. 7.95 (ISBN 0-88208-120-9). Chicago Review.
Way Out of Agnosticism: Or the Philosophy of Free Religion. Francis E. Abbot. LC 75-3014. (Philosophy in America Ser.). Repr. of 1890 ed. 20.00 (ISBN 0-404-59000-4). AMS Pr.
Way Out of Alcoholism. John R. Hackl & Alphons J. Hackl. (Illus.). 48p. 30.00 (ISBN 0-87491-762-X); pap. 2.50 (ISBN 0-87491-761-1). Acropolis.
Way Out of the Dead End: A Plea for Peace. Huschmand Sabet. Tr. by Patricia Crampton from Ger. 1986. 13.50 (ISBN 0-85398-245-7); pap. 7.95 (ISBN 0-85398-240-6). G Ronald Pub.
Way Out of Vietnam. Patricia. 166p. (Orig.). 1980. pap. 3.00 (ISBN 0-935146-21-0). Morningland.
Way-Paver. Anne Devlin. 151p. 1988. 14.95 (ISBN 0-571-14597-3); pap. 4.95 (ISBN 0-571-14816-6). Faber & Faber.
Way Prepared: Arabic & Islamic Studies in Honor of Bayly Winder. Ed. by Farhad Kazemi & Robert D. McChesney. (Illus.). 352p. 1987. 50.00x (ISBN 0-8147-4591-1). NYU Pr.
Way Society Develops. E. Plimak & A. Volodin. (Library of Political Knowledge: No. 1). 144p. 1983. 7.50x (ISBN 0-317-53797-0, Pub. by Collets (UK)). State Mutual Bk.
Way Station. Clifford D. Simak. LC 79-20182. 1980. Repr. of 1963 ed. lib. bdg. 12.50x (ISBN 0-8376-0440-0). Bentley.
Way Station. Clifford D. Simak. 240p. 1986. pap. 2.95 (ISBN 0-345-33246-6, Del Rey). Ballantine.
Way That I Teach. Da Free John. LC 77-94503. 1978. 24.95 (ISBN 0-913922-38-2). Dawn Horse Pr.
Way: The Discovery of the Grail of Immortality. Rhuddlwm Gawr. LC 85-73759. (Illus., Orig.). 1987. 18.95 (ISBN 0-931760-50-X, CP 10128); pap. 15.95 (ISBN 0-931760-28-3). Camelot GA.
Way the Earth Works: An Introduction to the New Global Geology & Its Revolutionary Development. Peter J. Wyllie. LC 75-23197. 296p. 1976. pap. text ed. write for info. (ISBN 0-471-96896-X). Wiley.
Way the Future Was: A Memoir. Frederik Pohl. 1979. pap. 1.95 (ISBN 0-345-26059-7, Del Rey). Ballantine.
Way, the Truth, & the Life: An Introduction to Lutheran Christianity. Duane W. Arnold & C. George Fry. (Illus.). 204p. (Orig.). 1982. pap. 9.95 (ISBN 0-8010-0189-7). Baker Bk.
Way the World Is. John C. Polkinghorne. LC 84-1527. Repr. of 1984 ed. 35.00 (2027549). Bks Demand UMI.
Way the World Works: How Economics Fail & Succeed. rev. ed. Jude Wanniski. 1983. pap. 7.75 (ISBN 0-671-43862-X, Touchstone Bks). S&S.
Way the World Works: How Economies Fail & Succeed. Jude Wanniski. LC 77-20412. 1978. 18.95x (ISBN 0-465-09095-8). Basic.
Way There. Michael Rothberg. 16p. 1981. pap. 2.50 (ISBN 0-938370-09-X). Wildflower.
Way They Died. Leslie Ernenwein. 1978. pap. 1.50 (ISBN 0-505-51275-0, Pub. by Tower Bks). Leisure NY.
Way They Play, Bk. 1. Samuel Applebaum & Sada Applebaum. (Illus.). 380p. (gr. 9-12). 1972. 12.95 (ISBN 0-87666-437-0, Z-1). Paganiniana Pubns.
Way They Play, Bk. 2. Samuel Applebaum & Sada Applebaum. (Illus.). 384p. (gr. 9-12). 1983. 12.95 (ISBN 0-87666-438-9, Z-4). Paganiniana Pubns.
Way They Play, Bk. 3. Samuel Applebaum & Sada Applebaum. (Illus.). 320p. (gr. 9-12). 1975. 12.95 (ISBN 0-87666-447-8, Z-7). Paganiniana Pubns.
Way They Play, Bk. 4. Samuel Applebaum & Sada Applebaum. (Illus.). 320p. (gr. 9-12). 1975. 12.95 (ISBN 0-87666-448-6, Z-8). Paganiniana Pubns.
Way They Play, Bk. 5. Samuel Applebaum & Henry Roth. (Illus.). 320p. (gr. 9-12). 1978. 12.95 (ISBN 0-87666-449-4, Z-11). Paganiniana Pubns.
Way They Play, Bk. 6. Samuel Applebaum & Henry Roth. (Illus.). 352p. (gr. 9-12). 1978. 12.95 (ISBN 0-87666-615-2, Z-29). Paganiniana Pubns.
Way They Play, Bk. 7. Samuel Applebaum & Henry Roth. (Illus.). 288p. (gr. 9-12). 1980. 12.95 (ISBN 0-87666-619-5, Z-33). Paganiniana Pubns.
Way They Play, Bk. 8. Samuel Applebaum & Henry Roth. (Illus.). 288p. (gr. 9-12). 1980. 12.95 (ISBN 0-87666-622-5, Z-34). Paganiniana Pubns.
Way They Play, Bk. 9. Samuel Applebaum & Henry Roth. (Illus.). 285p. (gr. 9-12). 1981. 12.95 (ISBN 0-87666-586-5, Z-56). Paganiniana Pubns.
Way They Play, Bk. 10. Samuel Applebaum & Henry Roth. (Illus.). 253p. (YA) (gr. 9-12). 1982. 12.95 (ISBN 0-87666-595-4, Z-65). Paganiniana Pubns.
Way They Play, Bk. 11. Samuel Applebaum et al. (Illus.). 253p. (gr. 9-12). 1983. 12.95 (ISBN 0-87666-799-X, Z-74). Paganiniana Pubns.
Way They Play, Bk. 12. Samuel Applebaum et al. (Illus.). 283p. (gr. 9-12). 1983. 12.95 (ISBN 0-87666-798-1, Z-75). Paganiniana Pubns.
Way They Play, Bk. 13. Samuel Appelbaum et al. (Illus.). 288p. (gr. 9-12). 12.95 (ISBN 0-86622-009-7, Z-76). Paganiniana Pubns.
Way They Play, Bk. 14. Samuel Appelbaum et al. (Illus.). (gr. 9-12). 1986. 12.95 (ISBN 0-86622-010-0). Paganiniana Pubns.
Way Things Are. Phillip Corwin. 96p. (Orig.). 1985. pap. 5.95 (ISBN 0-933515-06-5). Exile Pr.
Way Things Were. Ruby D. Cook. 1988. 11.95 (ISBN 0-533-07721-4). Vantage.
Way Things Work. David Macaulay. (Illus.). 400p. (ps up). 1988. 24.95 (ISBN 0-395-42857-2). HM.
Way Things Work: An Encyclopedia of Modern Technology, Vol. 1. (gr. 7 up). 1967. 19.25 (ISBN 0-671-22621-5). S&S.
Way Things Work: An Encyclopedia of Modern Technology, Vol. 2. 1971. 19.95 (ISBN 0-671-21086-6). S&S.
Way Things Work: Book of the Body. 1979. 18.95 (ISBN 0-671-22454-9). S&S.
Way: Three Hundred Sixty-Four Adventures in Daily Living. E. Stanley Jones. 368p. (Orig.). 1984. pap. 4.35 (ISBN 0-687-44099-8). Abingdon.
Way Through for the Damned. W. Inman. 1984. pap. 5.50 (ISBN 0-936204-32-X). Jelm Mtn.
Way to a Man's Heart. Candy Coleman. (Illus.). 32p. (Orig.). 1979. pap. text ed. 3.00 (ISBN 0-943768-02-0). C Coleman.
Way to a Man's Heart. Ed. by Sadie Levine. (Illus.). 192p. 1985. Repr. of 1971 ed. 12.50x (ISBN 0-318-21778-3, Pub. by Vallentine Mitchell England). Biblio Dist.
Way to a Man's Heart. Adrienne F. Lund. 323p. 1987. pap. 14.95 (ISBN 0-938400-09-6). Donahoe Pubs.
Way to a New Life. J. C. Wenger. LC 77-86326. (Mennonite Faith Ser.: No. 2). 72p. 1977. pap. 1.95 (ISBN 0-8361-1834-0). Herald Pr.
Way to Be Free. J. G. Bennett. 1980. pap. 6.95 (ISBN 0-87728-491-1). Weiser.
Way to Chaeronea: Foreign Policy, Decision-Making, & Political Influence in Demosthenes' Speeches. Hugo Montgomery. (Illus.). 132p. 1984. pap. 16.00x (ISBN 82-00-06443-3). Oxford U Pr.
Way to Chinese Painting. Sze Mai-Mai. (Illus.). 1959. pap. 6.95 (ISBN 0-394-70166-6, Vin). Random.
Way to Christianity: The Pilgrim. Richard W. Chilson. 1980. pap. 8.95 (ISBN 0-03-053426-7, HarpR). Har-Row.
Way to Contemplation: Encountering God Today. Willigis Jager. Tr. by Matthew J. O'connell. 1987. pap. 7.95 (ISBN 0-8091-2876-4). Paulist Pr.
Way to Danish. 3rd ed. E. Norlev & H. A. Koefoed. 1976. pap. 25.00 (ISBN 8-7160-0998-3). Heinman.
Way to Dawnworld: A Farstar & Son Novel. Bill Starr. 1979. 2.50 (ISBN 0-345-30948-0, Del Rey Bks). Ballantine.
Way to Durable Peace. M. N. Roy. 1986. 6.50x (ISBN 0-8364-2198-1, Pub. by Minerva India). South Asia Bks.
Way to Dusty Death. Alistair MacLean. 1985. pap. 2.95 (ISBN 0-449-21053-7, Crest). Fawcett.
Way to Escape: How You Can Have Victory over Temptation - Temptations of the Spirit-Filled Christ. Donald Gee. 64p. 1966. pap. 0.95 (ISBN 0-88243-613-9, 02-0613). Gospel Pub.
Way to Get What You Want. W. M. Davis. 1941. pap. 3.50 (ISBN 0-88027-022-5). Firm Foun Pub.
Way to Go: A Woman's Guide to Careers in Travel. Elaine Lerner & C. B. Abbott. 208p. 1982. pap. 6.95 (ISBN 0-446-37022-3). Warner Bks.
Way to Go: Academic Travel Pack. Gloria M. Prather & Alfred G. Prather. Ed. by Arden C. Prather & Ellen Smith. (Illus.). 48p. (gr. k-2). 1987. write for info. wkbk. (ISBN 0-9619655-0-9). Academic Packs Co.
Way to Go Home. Eric Pendry. 1978. 8.95 (ISBN 0-393-08834-0). Norton.
Way to God. D. L. Moody. pap. 3.95 (ISBN 0-8024-9231-2). Moody.
Way to God. D. L. Moody. 160p. 1983. pap. text ed. 2.95 (ISBN 0-88368-131-5). Whitaker Hse.
Way to God see Camino Hacia Dios.
Way to God According to the Rule of Saint Benedict. Emmanuel Heufelder. Tr. by Luke Eberle from Ger. (Cistercian Studies: No. 49). 1983. 25.95 (ISBN 0-87907-849-9); pap. 8.00 (ISBN 0-87907-949-5). Cistercian Pubns.
Way to God, Peace & Prosperity. R. E. McMaster, Jr. Date not set. price not set. Reaper Pub.
Way to Greece. Harold Melcher & Joan Melcher. LC 84-18400. (Illus.). 113p. (Orig.). 1984. pap. 7.95 (ISBN 0-87233-077-X). Bauhan.
Way to Happiness. L. Ron Hubbard. 1984. gift edition 13.95 (ISBN 0-317-03443-X); pap. 9.00. Bridge Pubns Inc.
Way to Happiness. Alfred A. Montapert. LC 77-13678. 1978. pap. 2.95 (ISBN 0-9603174-3-0). Bks of Value.
Way to Happiness. Alfred A. Montapert. (Eternal Quest of Mankind Ser.). pap. 2.95 (ISBN 0-13-946228-7). Borden.
Way to Happiness. Iverna Tompkins. 176p. 1983. pap. text ed. 2.50 pocket ed. (ISBN 0-9611260-0-0). I Tompkins.
Way to Happiness in Your Home: Bible Study on Family Living. Jack Terry. 36p. 1982. pap. 3.50 (ISBN 0-939298-06-6). J M Prods.
Way to Heaven: Matthew 7, 13-29. John MacArthur, Jr. (John MacArthur's Bible Studies). 1988. pap. 3.95 (ISBN 0-8024-5357-0). Moody.
Way to Independence: Memories of a Hidatsa Indian Family, 1840-1920. Carolyn Gilman et al. LC 87-11152. (Illus.). 371p. (Orig.). 1987. 40.00; pap. 24.95. Minn Hist.
Way to Liberation: Moksha Dharma of Mahabharata, 2 vols. Swami Jyotir Maya Nanda. (Illus.). 1976. Ea. pap. 4.99 (ISBN 0-934664-11-0). Yoga Res Foun.
Way to Life. Helmut Gollwitzer. Tr. by David Cairns from Ger. 232p. 1981. 26.95 (ISBN 0-567-09322-0, Pub. by T&T Clark Ltd UK); pap. 14.95 (ISBN 0-567-29322-X). Fortress.
Way to Life & Immortality. R. Swinburne Clymer. 244p. 1948. 7.95 (ISBN 0-932785-48-4). Philos Pub.
Way to Life: At the Heart of the Tao Te Ching. Benjamin Hoff. LC 80-18309. (Illus.). 88p. 1981. 17.50 (ISBN 0-8348-0156-6). Weatherhill.
Way to Live. Donald B. Clark. 1978. pap. 10.95 (ISBN 0-8403-1915-0). Kendall Hunt.
Way to Locate Acu-Points. Ed. by Yang Jiasan. Tr. by Meng Xiankun & Li Xuewu. (Illus.). 72p. (Orig.). 1982. pap. 13.95 (ISBN 0-8351-1028-1). China Bks.

Way to Modern Man: An Introduction to Human Evolution. Fred T. Adams. LC 68-28011. (Anthropology & Education Ser.). pap. 74.00 (ISBN 0-317-41948-X, 2025986). Bks Demand UMI.

Way to Natural Beauty. Cheryl Tiegs. (Illus.). 288p. 1983. pap. 9.95 (ISBN 0-671-47245-3, Fireside). S&S.

Way to Nirvana: Six Lectures on Ancient Buddhism As a Discipline of Salvation. Louis de La Vallee Poussin. LC 77-27154. (Hibbert Lectures Ser.: 1916). Repr. of 1917 ed. 24.50 (ISBN 0-404-60417-X). AMS Pr.

Way to Oneness. 4th ed. Disciples of Morningland. 1979. pap. 3.95 (ISBN 0-935146-00-8). Morningland.

Way to Peace. 11.95 (ISBN 0-87418-037-6). Coleman Pub.

Way to Peace: Liberation Through the Bible. John Topel. LC 78-9148. 208p. (Orig.). 1979. pap. 7.95 (ISBN 0-88344-704-5). Orbis Bks.

Way to Pentecost. Samuel Chadwick. 1960. pap. 2.95 (ISBN 0-87508-096-0). Chr Lit.

Way to Perfection. Joseph F. Smith. 365p. 1972. 8.95 (ISBN 0-87747-300-5). Deseret Bk.

Way to Poetry: An Anthology of English Verse from Chaucer to Sidney Keyes. Ed. by E. E. Herron. 708p. 1981. Repr. lib. bdg. 40.00 (ISBN 0-89987-381-2). Darby Bks.

Way to Power & Poise. E. Stanley Jones. (Festival Bks). 1978. pap. 2.25 (ISBN 0-687-44190-0). Abingdon.

Way to Rainy Mountain. N. Scott Momaday. LC 69-19154. (Illus.). 90p. 1976. pap. 8.95 (ISBN 0-8263-0436-2). U of NM Pr.

Way to Remember. Susan Davis. Ed. by Tom Davis. 32p. (ps up). 1980. pap. 2.95 (ISBN 0-8280-0023-9). Review & Herald.

Way to Sattin Shore. Philippa Pearce. LC 83-14152. (Illus.). 192p. (gr. 5-9). 1984. reinforced 10.25 (ISBN 0-688-02319-3). Greenwillow.

Way to Sattin Shore. Philippa Pearce. LC 84-23729. 176p. (gr. 5-9). 1985. pap. 3.50 (ISBN 0-14-031644-2, Puffin). Penguin.

Way to Sketch: With Special Reference to Water Color. Vernon Blake. (Illus.). 144p. (Unabridged replication of 2nd ed.). 1981. pap. 3.50 (ISBN 0-486-24119-X). Dover.

Way to Ski! The Official Method. Stu Campbell et al. Ed. by Carol Worth. LC 86-62074. 160p. (Orig.). 1986. 19.95 (ISBN 0-89586-485-1, HP Bks); lib. bdg. 19.95 (ISBN 0-317-66144-2); pap. 12.95 (ISBN 0-89586-444-4). Price Stern.

Way to Start a Day. Byrd Baylor. LC 78-113. (Illus.). (gr. 1-4). 1978. 12.95 (ISBN 0-684-15651-2, Pub. by Scribner). Macmillan.

Way to Start a Day. Byrd Baylor. LC 85-28802. (Illus.). 32p. (gr. 1-4). 1986. pap. 3.95 (ISBN 0-689-71054-2, Aladdin). Macmillan.

Way to Survive the AIDS Epidemic: Based on the Metaphysical Teachings of the Ancient Masters. Thomas A. Berg. LC 84-108491. 84p. 1984. pap. 4.95 (ISBN 0-9613110-0-2). Palm Pubns.

Way to the Kingdom. 2nd ed. 345p. 1972. pap. 7.95 (ISBN 0-87516-164-2). DeVorss.

Way to the Labyrinth: Memories of East & West. Alain Danielou. Tr. by Marie-Claire Cournand from Fr. LC 86-28660. 352p. 1987. 23.95 (ISBN 0-8112-1014-6); pap. 13.95 (ISBN 0-8112-1015-4, NDP634). New Directions.

Way to the North. Gordon Ward. 320p. 1988. pap. 3.95 (ISBN 0-8125-1256-1). Tor Bks.

Way to the Sun: A Guide to Celestial Living. David F. Barrus. 104p. 1972. 5.95 (ISBN 0-88290-008-0). Horizon Utah.

Way to the Uncle Sam Hotel. William D. Brown. (Orig.). 1966. pap. 2.75 (ISBN 0-940556-00-6). Coyote.

Way to the Western Sea: Lewis & Clark Across the Continent. David Lavender. LC 88-45040. (Illus.). 416p. 1988. 22.95 (ISBN 0-06-015982-0, HarpT). Har-Row.

Way to the Zoo: Poems about Animals. Ed. by David Jackson. (Illus.). 128p. (ps-6). 1987. 12.95 (ISBN 0-19-276045-9). Oxford U Pr.

Way to Transfiguration: Mi Primera Transfiguracion. Francisco E. Harvide. 1986. 10.00 (ISBN 0-533-06623-9). Vantage.

Way to Vibrant Health. Alexander Lowen & Leslie Lowen. (Orig.). 1977. pap. 9.95 (ISBN 0-06-090542-5, CN 542, PL). Har-Row.

Way to Wealth. Benjamin Franklin. 32p. Date not set. 6.95 (ISBN 0-918222-88-5); leather 14.95 (ISBN 0-918222-99-0). Applewood.

Way to Wealth, Wherein Is Plainly Taught a Remedy for Sedicion. Richard Crowley. LC 74-28843. (English Experience Ser.: No. 724). 1975. Repr. of 1550 ed. 3.50 (ISBN 90-221-0724-8). Walter J Johnson.

Way to Wear'Em: One Hundred & Fifty Years of Punch on Fashion. Christina Walkley. (Illus.). 190p. 1985. 32.50 (ISBN 0-317-61362-6, Pub. by P Owen Ltd). Dufour.

Way to Winning Golf. David Graham & Larry Dennis. Date not set. write for info. S&S.

Way to Wisdom: An Introduction to Philosophy. Karl Jaspers. Tr. by Ralph Manheim. 1954. pap. 7.95x 1960 (ISBN 0-300-00134-7, Y27). Yale U Pr.

Way to Write for Children. Joan Aiken. 112p. 1982. 10.95 (ISBN 0-312-85839-6); pap. 4.95 (ISBN 0-312-85840-X). St Martin.

Way to Write for Television. Eric Paice. 96p. 1982. pap. 15.95 (ISBN 0-241-10650-8, Pub. by Hamish Hamilton England, Pub. by Hamish Hamilton England). David & Charles.

Way to Write Radio Drama. William Ash. 160p. 1985. 20.95 (ISBN 0-241-11445-4, Pub. by Hamish Hamilton England); pap. 14.95 (ISBN 0-241-11446-2, Pub. by Hamish Hamilton England). David & Charles.

Way to Write Short Stories. Michael Baldwin. 96p. 1987. 20.95 (ISBN 0-241-11767-4, Pub. by Hamish Hamilton England); pap. 14.95 (ISBN 0-241-11766-6, Pub. by Hamish Hamilton England). David & Charles.

Way to Wyoming. Dan Parkinson. 432p. 1988. pap. 3.95 (ISBN 0-8217-2411-8). Zebra.

Way Towards the Blessed Life see Characteristics of the Present Age.

Way up from Down: A Safe, New Program That Relieves Low Moods & Depression with Amino Acids & Vitamin Supplements. Priscilla Slagle. LC 86-28062. 224p. 1987. 17.95 (ISBN 0-394-55194-X). Random.

Way Ward Pokey. Ann Bischoff. 40p. 1986. 5.75 (ISBN 0-8062-2843-1). Carlton.

Way We Build Now. Andrew Orton. (Illus.). 530p. 1988. pap. 49.95 (ISBN 0-7476-0011-2). Van Nos Reinhold.

Way We Come Home. Gail White. (Sparrow Poverty Pamphlets Ser.: No. 48). 28p. (Orig.). 1985. 2.50x (ISBN 0-935552-20-0). Sparrow Pr.

Way We Die: An Investigation of Death & Dying in America Today. David K. Dempsey. LC 76-51356. (McGraw-Hill Paperback Ser.). 1977. pap. text ed. 5.95 (ISBN 0-07-016340-5). McGraw.

Way We Die Now. Charles Willeford. LC 87-27226. 256p. 1988. 15.95 (ISBN 0-394-56525-8). Random.

Way We Live. Kathleen Jamie. LC 87-73050. 64p. (Orig.). 1988. pap. 11.95 (ISBN 1-85224-034-2, Pub. by Bloodaxe Bks). Dufour.

Way We Live, 3 Bks. Neena Kaushal & Satya Uberoi. 335p. 1983. Bk. 1. pap. text ed. 3.95x (ISBN 0-86131-364-X, Pub. by Orient Longman Ltd India); Bk. 2. pap. text ed. 3.95x (ISBN 0-86131-365-8). Apt Bks.

Way We Live Now. Anthony Trollope. (Illus.). 416p. 1982. pap. 7.95 (ISBN 0-486-24360-5). Dover.

Way We Live Now. Anthony Trollope. Ed. by John Sutherland. (World's Classics Ser.). 1982. pap. 9.95 (ISBN 0-19-281576-8). Oxford U Pr.

Way We Live Now. Anthony Trollope. LC 84-4659. 825p. 1984. 11.95 (ISBN 0-394-60512-8). Modern Lib.

Way We Live Now: Design for Interiors 1950 to the Present Day. Margaret Timmers. (Illus.). 40p. (Orig.). 1984. pap. 1.95 (ISBN 0-317-02564-3, Pub. by Victoria & Albert Mus UK). Faber & Faber.

Way We Lived. Rems Nna Umeasiegbu. (African Writers Ser.). 1969. pap. text ed. 6.00 (ISBN 0-435-90061-7). Heinemann Ed.

Way We Lived: California Indian Reminiscences, Stories and Songs. Ed. by Malcolm Margolin. LC 81-81383. 1981. pap. 6.95 (ISBN 0-930588-04-5). Heyday Bks.

Way We Lived: Durham, 1900-1920. James G. Leyburn. Ed. by Lon K. Savage. 220p. 1987. 16.95 (ISBN 0-9617256-1-3). Northcross Hse.

Way We Lived: Essays & Sources in American Social History, 2 vols. Frederick M. Binder & David M. Reimers. LC 87-81182. 1988. Vol. I, 320pgs. pap. text ed. 12.00 (ISBN 0-669-09030-1); Vol. II, 328pgs. pap. text ed. 12.00 (ISBN 0-669-09031-X). Heath.

Way We Lived in North Carolina, 5 vols. Ed. by Sydney Nathans. write for info. U of NC Pr.

Way We Look: A Framework for Visual Analysis of Dress. Marilyn R. DeLong. 172p. 1987. text ed. 23.95x (ISBN 0-8138-1906-7). Iowa St U Pr.

Way We Looked: The Meaning & Magic of Family Photographs. Catherine Noren. (Illus.). 96p. (gr. 7 up). 1983. 10.95 (ISBN 0-525-66738-5, 01063-320). Lodestar Bks.

Way We Pray. Leonel L. Mitchell. 96p. (Orig.). 1984. pap. 1.15 (ISBN 0-88028-039-5). Forward Movement.

Way We Really Live. Sam B. Warner. 1978. 8.00 (ISBN 0-89073-053-9). Boston Public Lib.

Way We Were. Ken Bell. (Illus.). 256p. Date not set. 39.95 (ISBN 0-8020-3990-1). U of Toronto Pr.

Way We Were. Arthur Laurents. 17.95 (ISBN 0-88411-446-5, Pub. by Aeonian Pr). Amereon Ltd.

Way We Were: The Year Kennedy Was Shot. Robert MacNeil. (Illus.). 1988. 39.95 (ISBN 0-88184-433-0). Carroll & Graf.

Way We Wore: Fashion Illustrations of Children's Wear 1870-1970. Linda Martin. LC 78-17243. (Illus.). 1978. (ScribT); (ScribT). Scribner.

Way We Work. Andrew Hepworth & Michael Osbaldeston. 208p. 1979. text ed. 36.95x (ISBN 0-566-00212-4). Gower Pub Co.

Way with Words. Bob Eberle. (Illus.). 96p. (gr. 4-7). 1987. pap. 7.95 (ISBN 0-86653-377-X, GA1009). Good Apple.

Way with Words: A Guide for Writers. Thomas Whissen. 1982. pap. 6.95 (ISBN 0-19-503041-9). Oxford U Pr.

Way with Words: How to Improve Your Relationships Through Better Communications. Toni Brougher. LC 81-18841. 352p. 1982. text ed. 23.95x (ISBN 0-88229-645-0); pap. text ed. 12.95x (ISBN 0-88229-810-0). Nelson-Hall.

Way with Words: On Creative Writing. Edna Gilbert. 95p. 1968. pap. 3.25 (ISBN 0-85225-533-0). Ed Solutions.

Wayang Wong: The State Ritual Dance Drama in the Court of Yogyakarta. Soedarsono. LC 82-95123. (Illus.). xxiii, 386p. 1984. pap. text ed. 16.50x (ISBN 0-8214-0813-5, Pub by Gadjah Mada Univ Pr). Ohio U Pr.

Wayfarer. James Dickey. 1988. 40.00 (ISBN 0-8487-0691-9). Oxmoor Hse.

Wayfarer. Natsume Soseki. Tr. by Beongcheon Yu. LC 66-26974. 326p. 1967. 25.00x (ISBN 0-8143-1318-3). Wayne St U Pr.

Wayfarer. Natsume Soseki. Tr. by Beongcheon Yu from Japanese. (Perigee Japanese Library). 324p. 1982. pap. 6.95 (ISBN 0-399-50612-8, Perigee). Putnam Pub Group.

Wayfarer in China. Elizabeth Kendall. 338p. 1913. 60.00x (ISBN 0-317-68718-2, Pub. by Han-Shan Tang Ltd). State Mutual Bk.

Wayfarer in the Land. Watchman Nee. 1975. pap. 3.50 (ISBN 0-8423-7823-5). Tyndale.

Wayfarers. Knut Hamsun. Tr. by James W. McFarlane from Norwegian. 460p. 1980. pap. 10.95 (ISBN 0-374-51592-1). FS&G.

Wayfarers in Arcady. Charles Vince. LC 71-90688. (Essay Index Reprint Ser). 1922. 17.00 (ISBN 0-8369-1236-5). Ayer Co Pubs.

Wayfarer's Words, 3 vols. C. Rhys Davids. LC 78-72414. Repr. of 1942 ed. Set. 125.00 (ISBN 0-404-17600-3). AMS Pr.

Wayfaring Pilgrim. Mary of Carmel. 1988. 18.95 (ISBN 0-533-07829-6). Vantage.

Wayfaring Stranger. Jackie Black. (Orig.). (YA) 1989. pap. price not set (ISBN 0-440-20335-X). Dell.

Wayfaring Tree. W. H. Hudson. (Illus.). 1978. Repr. of 1945 ed. lib. bdg. 17.50 (ISBN 0-8495-0361-2). Arden Lib.

Wayfaring with Birds. Ina Griffin. (Illus.). 288p. (Orig.). 1987. pap. 9.95 (ISBN 0-936784-23-7). J Daniel.

Wayfinders: For Believers & Non-Believers. Lucille J. Plewe. LC 77-78794. 1977. pap. 5.00 (ISBN 0-89555-028-8). TAN Bks Pubs.

Wayfinding in Architecture. Romedi Passini. 234p. 1984. 38.95 (ISBN 0-442-27590-0). Van Nos Reinhold.

Waylon: A Biography. R. Serge Denisoff. (Illus.). 375p. 1984. pap. 10.95 (ISBN 0-312-85848-5). St Martin.

Waylon: A Biography. R. Serge Denisoff. LC 82-24786. Repr. of 1983 ed. 97.30 (2027556). Bks Demand UMI.

Waymarks: The Notre Dame Inaugural Lectures in Anthropology. Kenneth Moore. LC 86-40339. 157p. 1988. pap. text ed. 7.95x (ISBN 0-268-01941-X). U of Notre Dame Pr.

Waymarks: The Notre Dame Inaugural Lectures in Anthropology. Ed. by Kenneth Moore. LC 86-40339. 160p. 1987. text ed. 15.95x (ISBN 0-268-01939-8). U of Notre Dame Pr.

Wayne County Court Financing Study: Executive Summary. National Center for State Courts Staff. 15p. 1980. manuscript 0.90 (NCRO-044). Natl Ctr St Courts.

Wayne County Court Financing Study: Final Report. National Center for State Courts Staff. 204p. 1980. manuscript 12.24 (NCRO-043). Natl Ctr St Courts.

Wayne County, Kentucky, Censuses, 1810-1840. Rowena Lawson. iv, 73p. (Orig.). 1988. pap. 11.00 (ISBN 1-55613-095-3). Heritage Bk.

Wayne County Mediation Program in the Eastern District of Michigan. Federal Judicial Center Staff & Kathy L. Shuart. LC 85-602028. (Innovations in the Courts Ser.). (Illus.). v, 60p. Date not set. price not set. Fed Judicial Ctr.

Wayne County, Missouri. Rose F. Cramer. (Illus.). 734p. 1972. 11.00 (ISBN 0-911208-22-4). Ramfre.

Wayne County: The Aesthetic Heritage of a Rural Area. Stephen W. Jacobs. LC 79-64132. (Architecture Worth Saving Ser.). (Illus.). 288p. 1979. 45.00x (ISBN 0-89062-044-X, Pub. by Wayne County Hist Soc); pap. 20.00x (ISBN 0-89062-041-5). Pub Ctr Cult Res.

Wayne Gretzky. Gelfand. (Sports Superstars Ser.). (Illus.). 32p. (gr. 4 up). 1985. PLB 8.95 (ISBN 0-317-31206-5). Creative Ed.

Wayne Gretzky. Jane M. Leder. Ed. by Howard Schroeder. (Sports Close-up Ser.). (Illus.). 48p. (gr. 5-6). 1985. PLB 10.95 (ISBN 0-89686-255-0). Crestwood Hse.

Wayne Gretzky: Portrait of a Hockey Player. Craig T. Wolff. (Illus.). 80p. (gr. 3-7). 1983. pap. 1.95 (ISBN 0-380-82420-5, 82420-5, Camelot). Avon.

Wayne Gretzky: Profil d'un Joueur de Hockey. Craig T. Wolff. (Illus.). 64p. (Fr.). (ps-5). pap. 2.25 (ISBN 0-380-85753-7, Camelot). Avon.

Wayne Gretzky: The Great Gretzky. Bert Rosenthal. LC 82-19752. (Sports Stars Ser.). (Illus.). 48p. (gr. 2-8). 1983. PLB 11.27 (ISBN 0-516-04330-7); pap. 2.95 (ISBN 0-516-44330-5). Childrens.

Wayne Morse: A Bio-Bibliography. Lee Wilkins. LC 85-10028. (Bio-Bibliographies in Law & Political Science: No. 1). xiv, 115p. 1985. lib. bdg. 35.00 (ISBN 0-313-24268-2, WIM/). Greenwood.

Wayne Thiebaud. Karen Tsujimoto. LC 85-40351. (Illus.). 208p. (Orig.). 1985. 40.00x (ISBN 0-295-96251-8); pap. 24.95 (ISBN 0-295-96269-0). U of Wash Pr.

Wayne Thiebaud, Paintings & Works on Paper. Douglas McClellan. (Illus.). 8p. (Orig.). 1976. pap. 1.00 (ISBN 0-939982-00-5). Sesnon Art Gall.

Wayne Thiebaud: Private Drawings, the Artist's Sketchbook. Intro. by Constance Glenn. (Facsimile Reproduction Sketchbook Ser.). (Illus.). 44p. 1987. slipcased 85.00 (ISBN 0-8109-1665-7); deluxe ed. 275.00 ltd 100 copies, slipcased (ISBN 0-8109-4994-6). Abrams.

Wayne Wheeler, Dry Boss. Justin Steuart. LC 75-100207. (Illus.). 304p. 1971. Repr. of 1928 ed. lib. bdg. 35.00x (ISBN 0-8371-4033-1, STWW). Greenwood.

Waynesburg College Story, 1849-1974. William H. Dusenberry. LC 74-27386. (Illus.). 489p. 1975. 12.50x (ISBN 0-87338-173-4). Kent St U Pr.

Waynesburg: Prosperous & Beautiful. Fred High. 1973. Repr. 10.00 (ISBN 0-87012-156-1). McClain.

Waynflete Lectures on Physics: Selected Topics in Contemporary Physics & Astrophysics. V. L. Ginzburg & P. N. Lebedev. Tr. by D. ter Haar. LC 82-24619. (International Series in Natural Philosophy: Vol. 106). (Illus.). 133p. 1983. 34.00 (ISBN 0-08-029147-3). Pergamon.

Ways & Crossways. facs. ed. Paul Claudel. Tr. by Fr. J. O'Conner. LC 67-28732. (Essay Index Reprint Ser.). 1933. 20.00 (ISBN 0-8369-0313-7). Ayer Co Pubs.

Ways & Crossways. Paul Claudel. LC 68-15820. 1968. Repr. of 1933 ed. 21.50 (ISBN 0-8046-0079-1, Pub. by Kennikat). Assoc Faculty Pr.

Ways & Means of Payment. Stephen Colwell. LC 65-23212. Repr. of 1859 ed. 49.50x (ISBN 0-678-00110-3). Kelley.

Ways & Means of Using Birds in Combating Noxious Insects. Ed. by L. P. Poznanin. 138p. 1956. text ed. 26.50x (ISBN 0-317-46490-6, Pub. by Keter Pub Jerusalem). Coronet Bks.

Ways Animals Sleep, 4 vols. Jane R. McCauley. LC 83-13189. (Books for Young Explorers: Set 10). 32p. (ps-3). 1983. Set. 10.95 (ISBN 0-87044-489-1); PLB 12.95 (ISBN 0-87044-494-8). Natl Geog.

Ways Children Learn: What Do Experts Say? Geeta R. Lall & Bernard M. Lall. 88p. 1983. 15.25x (ISBN 0-398-04754-5). C C Thomas.

Ways In: Analyzing & Responding to Literature. Leo Rockas. 208p. 1984. pap. text ed. 12.50x (ISBN 0-86709-075-8). Boynton Cook Pubs.

Ways of a Judge: Reflections from the Federal Apellate Bench. Frank Coffin. 288p. 1980. 10.95 (ISBN 0-395-29461-4). HM.

Ways of Approaching. John Riley. 1973. signed 4.00 (ISBN 0-685-78924-1, Pub. by Grosseteste); sewn in wrappers 2.00 (ISBN 0-685-78925-X). Small Pr Dist.

Ways of Art: Literature, Music, Painting in France: A Critical Work, II. Robert G. Cohn. (Stanford French & Italian Studies: Vol. 40). 384p. 1986. pap. 29.50 (ISBN 0-915838-52-4). Anma Libri.

Ways of Being. Herbert W. Schneider. LC 72-9832. 116p. 1974. Repr. of 1962 ed. lib. bdg. 35.00x (ISBN 0-8371-6149-5, SCWB). Greenwood.

Ways of Being Religious: Readings for a New Approach to Religion. Frederick J. Streng et al. (Illus.). 608p. 1973. 34.67 (ISBN 0-13-946277-5). P-H.

Ways of Darkness. Joseph Hayes. LC 84-29497. 1985. 16.95 (ISBN 0-688-04289-9). Morrow.

Ways of Darkness. Joseph Hayes. 1987. pap. 3.95 (ISBN 0-451-40019-4, Onyx). NAL.

Ways of Desire: New Essays in Philosophical Psychology on the Concept of Wanting. Ed. by Joel Marks. 1986. 29.95 (ISBN 0-913750-44-1, Dist. by Transaction Bks). Precedent Pub.

Ways of Escape. Graham Greene. 288p. 1982. pap. 3.95 (ISBN 0-671-43820-4). WSP.

Ways of Escape. Graham Greene. 13.50 (ISBN 0-8446-6289-5). Peter Smith.

Ways of Escape & a Sort of Life. Graham Greene. (Uniform Editions Ser.). 320p. 20.00 (ISBN 0-670-75262-2). Viking.

Ways of God: Paths into the New Testament. Harry C. Griffith. 149p. 1986. pap. 7.95 (ISBN 0-8192-1377-2). Morehouse.

Ways of Imperfection. Simon Tugwell. 252p. 1985. 10.95 (ISBN 0-87243-164-9). Templegate.

Ways of Indian Magic. Teresa Van Etten. LC 85-2722. (Illus.). 96p. (Orig.). 1985. pap. 8.95 (ISBN 0-86534-061-7). Sunstone Pr.

Ways of Indian Wisdom. Teresa VanEtten. LC 86-5924. 117p. (Orig.). 1987. pap. 10.95 (ISBN 0-86534-090-0). Sunstone Pr.

Ways of Life. (Hungarian Sociological Studies). 404p. 1977. 13.75x (ISBN 0-317-53848-9, Pub. by Collets (UK)). State Mutual Bk.

Ways of Life in Finland & Poland: Comparative Studies on Urban Population. J. P. Roos & Andrzej Sicinski. 200p. 1987. text ed. 31.50 (ISBN 0-566-05342-X, Pub. by Gower Pub England). Gower Pub Co.

We Are Not Afraid: The Murder of Goodman, Schwerner & Chaney & the Civil Rights Campaign for Mississippi. Seth Cagin & Philip Dray. (Illus.). 320p. 1988. 22.50 (ISBN 0-02-520260-X). Macmillan.

We Are Not Alone. James Hilton. 13.95 (ISBN 0-88411-843-6, Pub. by Aeonian Pr). Amereon Ltd.

We Are Not Alone: Learning to Live with Chronic Illness. Sefra Pitzele. LC 84-16378. (Illus.). 320p. 1985. pap. 14.95 (ISBN 0-918351-01-4). Thompson Co Inc.

We Are Not Alone: Learning to Live with Chronic Illness. Sefra K. Pitzele. LC 86-40200. (Illus.). 331p. (Orig.). 1986. pap. 8.95 (ISBN 0-89480-139-2). Workman Pub.

We Are Not in This Together. William Kittredge. LC 83-82866. 131p. 1984. write for info.; pap. 8.00 (ISBN 0-915308-44-4). Graywolf.

We Are One Another: A Record of Group Reincarnation. Arthur Guirdham. LC 86-33425. 227p. 1986. Repr. of 1974 ed. lib. bdg. 19.95x (ISBN 0-8095-7034-3). Borgo Pr.

We Are One in the Lord: Developing Caring Groups in the Church. Dennis Denning. LC 81-14958. 96p. (Orig.). 1982. pap. 5.50 (ISBN 0-687-44281-8). Abingdon.

We Are Ordinary Women: A Chronicle of the Puget Sound Women's Peace Camp. Puget Sound Women's Peace Camp Participants. LC 85-8221. (Illus.). 115p. (Orig.). 1985. pap. 5.95 (ISBN 0-931188-27-X). Seal Pr Feminist.

We Are Proud to Announce. Redbook Editors. 1978. 4.95 (ISBN 0-8027-0617-7). Walker & Co.

We Are Talking about Homes: A Great University Against Its Neighbors. Lynne S. Schwartz. LC 85-42735. 175p. 1985. 15.45i (ISBN 0-06-015479-9, HarpT). Har-Row.

We Are Ten. facsimile ed. Fannie Hurst. LC 72-178442. (Short Story Index Reprint Ser.). Repr. of 1937 ed. 33.00 (ISBN 0-8369-4043-1). Ayer Co Pubs.

We Are the Aggies: The Texas A&M University Association of Former Students. John A. Adams, Jr. LC 78-21782. (Centennial Series of the Association of Former Students, Texas A&M University: No. 7). (Illus.). 244p. 1979. 18.50 (ISBN 0-89096-062-3). Tex A&M Univ Pr.

We Are the Church: The Book. John J. Weigand. 128p. (Orig.). 1986. pap. 12.95 (ISBN 0-941850-16-1). Liturgical Pubns.

We Are the Church: The Manual. John Weigand. 80p. (Orig.). 1986. pap. 2.50 (ISBN 0-941850-17-X). Liturgical Pubns.

We Are the Fire: A Selection of Poems. Toby Olson. LC 84-4772. 128p. 1984. 14.95 (ISBN 0-8112-0913-X); pap. 7.50 (ISBN 0-8112-0914-8, NDP580). New Directions.

We Are the Lord's. Jean A. Vis. 3.50 (ISBN 0-686-23479-0). Rose Pub MI.

We Are the Mainstream. Jenefer Ellingston. Ed. by Constance McKenna. (Illus.). 16p. 1981. pap. 1.00 (ISBN 0-915365-02-2). Cath Free Choice.

We Are the Masters of Our Fate. Stephen Tarver. 140p. 1984. 8.00 (ISBN 0-9614237-1-4). Powder River.

We Are the Shakers. A. F. Joy. Orig. Title: Queen of the Shakers. (Illus.). 130p. (Orig.). 1985. pap. 5.00 (ISBN 0-934703-00-0). Saturscent Pubns.

We Are the Shakers. rev., & abr. ed. A. F. Joy. (Illus.). 130p. 1985. pap. 5.50 (ISBN 0-318-18279-3). A F Joy.

We Are the Targets: Environmental Impacts. Harold McKenna, Jr. (Student Scientist Ser.). (Illus.). 115p. (gr. 7-12). 1980. PLB 10.97 (ISBN 0-8239-0474-1). Rosen Group.

We Are the Way We Are. Sondra A. Barnes. LC 86-72759. (Illus.). 85p. (Orig.). 1986. pap. 5.00 (ISBN 0-9602534-1-6). Brason Sargar.

We Are the World: The Photos, Music, & Inside Story of One of the Most Historic Events in American Popular Music. (Illus.). 1985. pap. 5.95 (ISBN 0-399-51172-5, Perigee). Putnam Pub Group.

We Are Thy Children. Heini Arnold. 36p. 1985. pap. 1.50 (ISBN 0-87486-193-4). Plough.

We Are Your Sisters: Black Women in the Nineteenth Century. Ed. by Dorothy Sterling. (Illus.). 560p. 1985. pap. 10.95 (ISBN 0-393-30252-0). Norton.

We Are Your Sons: The Legacy of Ethel & Julius Rosenberg. 2nd ed. Robert Meeropol & Michael Meeropol. LC 85-30892. (Illus.). 508p. 1986. 27.50 (ISBN 0-252-01263-1). U of Ill Pr.

We Ask Only a Fair Trial: A History of the Black Community of Evansville, Indiana. Darrel E. Bigham. LC 86-45892. (Midwestern History & Culture & Blacks in the Dialpora Ser.). (Illus.). 302p. 1987. 20.00 (ISBN 0-253-36326-8). Ind U Pr.

We Ate Gooseberries: Growing up on a Minnesota Farm During the Depression. Vernon J. Schaefer. 1974. 8.50 (ISBN 0-682-47836-9). Exposition-Phoenix.

We Bake Cookies. Faith Carlson. (Illus.). 28p. (Orig.). (ps-2). 1987. pap. 5.00 (ISBN 0-932591-06-X). Baggeboda Pr.

We Band of Brothers. R. E. Peppy Blount. 393p. 1984. 16.95 (ISBN 0-89015-443-0). Eakin Pr.

We Be Brethen. J. D. Thomas. 1958. 13.95 (ISBN 0-89112-001-7). Abilene Christ U.

We Be Here When the Morning Comes. Bryan Woolley. LC 75-18285. pap. 42.00 (ISBN 0-317-26724-8, 2024362). Bks Demand UMI.

We Be Here When the Morning Comes: The Brookside Mine Strike, 1973-1974. Bryan Woolley. LC 75-18285. (Illus.). 168p. 1975. 15.00x (ISBN 0-8131-1337-7). U Pr of Ky.

We Became Flying Tigers. Jack S. Carroll. 1986. 7.95 (ISBN 0-533-06840-1). Vantage.

We Began at Jamestown. Guy Friddell. (Illus.). 1968. 5.95 (ISBN 0-87517-046-3). Dietz.

We Beheld His Glory. Nicolai S. Arsen'ev. Tr. by Mary A. Ewer. LC 76-113545. Repr. of 1936 ed. 18.00 (ISBN 0-404-00407-5). AMS Pr.

We Beheld His Glory. Marleigh G. Eakes. Ed. by David Bernard. LC 87-16075. (Illus.). 112p. (Orig.). 1987. pap. 4.95 (ISBN 0-932581-20-X). Word Aflame.

We Believe. Sr. Mary D. Bothwell. (Christ Our Life Ser.). (Illus.). (gr. 4). 1987. pap. text ed. 4.60 (ISBN 0-8294-0551-8); tchr's ed. 12.95 (ISBN 0-8294-0575-5). Loyola.

We Believe. Paul Erb. LC 69-15831. 112p. (Orig.). 1969. pap. 4.95 (ISBN 0-8361-1587-2). Herald Pr.

We Believe. Douglas Leroy. (Illus.). 56p. (gr. 7-12). 1975. pap. 3.95 (ISBN 0-87148-906-6). Pathway Pr.

We Believe. Ralph M. Riggs. 184p. 1954. 3.50 (ISBN 0-88243-780-1, 02-0780). Gospel Pub.

We Believe - Teacher's Guide. rev. ed. Riley B. Case & Charles W. Keysor. Ed. by James V. Heidinger, II et al. 60p. 1988. 2.95 (ISBN 0-917851-21-8, Bristol Bks). Forum Script.

We Believe... A Guide to a Better Understanding of the Bible As a Source Book for the Humanities. school ed. School ed. 0.75 (ISBN 0-89942-247-0, 247.05-SD). Catholic Bk Pub.

We Believe: A Study of the Book of Confessions for Church Officers. Harry W. Eberts, Jr. LC 87-2097. 118p. (Orig.). 1987. pap. 5.95 (ISBN 0-664-24063-1, A Geneva Press Publication). Westminster John Knox.

We Believe & Teach. Martin J. Heinecken. Ed. by Harold W. Rast. LC 80-16363. (Lead Book). 128p. (Orig.). 1980. pap. 4.95 (ISBN 0-8006-1387-2, 1-1387). Fortress.

We Believe in God. John Taylor. 184p. 1987. pap. 7.95 (ISBN 0-8192-1407-8). Morehouse.

We Believe in One God: Creed & Scripture. Frank E. Eakin, Jr. LC 85-51755. 165p. 1985. pap. text ed. 21.95 (ISBN 0-932269-64-8). Wyndham Hall.

We Believe: Jr. High. rev. ed. Riley B. Case & Charles W. Keysor. Ed. by James V. Heidinger, II et al. (Illus.). 60p. (YA) (gr. 6-9). 1988. wkbk. 3.95 (ISBN 0-917851-20-X, Bristol Bks). Forum Script.

We Believe: Junior High Edition 88. write for info.; write for info. tchr's ed. Forum Script.

We Belong to the Land: Memories of a Midwesterner. Beulah M. Pelton. (Illus.). 212p. 1984. 16.95 (ISBN 0-8138-1143-0). Iowa St U Pr.

We Belong Together. Bruce Milne. LC 78-13882. 1979. pap. 2.95 (ISBN 0-87784-455-0). Inter-Varsity.

We Break Bread in Loving Thanksgiving. (gr. 5). 2.85 (ISBN 0-02-649450-7, 64945); tchr's manual 2.52 (ISBN 0-02-649460-4, 64946). Benziger Pub Co.

We Break Bread in Loving Thanksgiving see Word & Worship: CCD Ed.

We Build a Climber. Ruth Phang & Susan Roth. LC 85-20053. (Illus.). 32p. (ps-2). 1986. 11.95 (ISBN 0-689-31183-4, Atheneum Childrens Bks). Macmillan.

We Built Jerusalem: Tales of Pioneering Days. Arye Lipshitz. Tr. by Misha Louvish. LC 84-45016. 176p. 1985. 14.95 (ISBN 0-8453-4787-X, Cornwall Bks). Assoc Univ Prs.

We Buried Him Twice. Annie M. Howard. 80p. 1987. 7.95 (ISBN 0-8062-3104-1). Carlton.

We Call It Gravy: A No-Effort Cookbook, Italian Style. Edythe V. Piccione. 72p. 1985. pap. 6.95 (ISBN 0-8059-2972-X). Dorrance.

We Call Ourselves Disciples. 2nd ed. Kenneth L. Teegarden. LC 82-24455. 116p. 1983. pap. 5.95 (ISBN 0-8272-4215-8). CBP.

We Called a Strike & No One Came: Comics. Kalamazoo Black & Red. 1.50x (ISBN 0-934868-10-7). Black & Red.

We Called Him Casper. James E. Vincent. Ed. by Frank Cannon. (Psychic Phenomena Series: A History). (Illus., Orig.). 1987. 6.00. RAPCOM Enter.

We Called It Music. Eddie Condon & Thomas Sugrue. (Roots of Jazz Ser.). (Illus.). 341p. 1987. Repr. of 1947 ed. lib. bdg. 35.00 (ISBN 0-306-76267-6). Da Capo.

We Came from Vietnam. Muriel Stanek. Ed. by Ann Fay. (Illus.). 48p. (gr. 1-6). 1985. PLB 9.95 (ISBN 0-8075-8699-4). A. Whitman.

We Came to Australia. Thomas Jenkins. LC 78-448322. (Illus.). 186p. pap. 70.00 (ISBN 0-317-11339-9, 2019383). Bks Demand UMI.

We Came to Town. Ed. by Caroline Kerfoot. (Illus.). 74p. 1986. pap. 12.95 (ISBN 0-86975-251-0, Pub. by Ravan Pr). Ohio U Pr.

We Can, 2 vols. Robin R. Star. (gr. 4 up). 1980. Set. PLB 4.95. Vol. 1 88 pgs (ISBN 0-88200-135-3, C2670). Vol. 2 98 pgs (ISBN 0-88200-136-1, C2786). Alexander Graham.

We Can Always Call Them Bulgarians: The Emergence of Lesbians & Gay Men on the American Stage. Kaier Curtin. (Illus.). 340p. 1987. 18.95 (ISBN 0-932870-36-8). Alyson Pubns.

We Can Avert a Nuclear War. Ed. by William Epstein & Lucy Webster. LC 82-7974. 192p. 1983. pap. 12.50 (ISBN 0-89946-204-9). Oelgeschlager.

We Can Break the Cycle of Child Abuse. Virginia Kent. LC 85-72114. 116p. (Orig.). 1985. pap. 5.75 (ISBN 0-88177-021-3, DR021B). Discipleship Res.

We Can Fly: Stories of Katherine Stinson & Other Gutsy Texas Women. Mary B. Rogers & Sherry A. Smith. LC 82-80441. (Illus.). 184p. (Orig.). (gr. 7up). 1983. 19.95 (ISBN 0-936650-02-8); pap. 12.95 (ISBN 0-936650-03-6). E C Temple.

We Can Implement Cost-Effective Information Systems NOW: Proceedings. 126p. 12.00 (ISBN 0-318-14034-9); members 6.00 (ISBN 0-318-14035-7). Educom.

We Can Make It...Together. Joseph A. Jordan. (Illus.). 64p. 1984. 5.50 (ISBN 0-682-40157-9). Exposition-Phoenix.

We Can Make It...Together. Joseph A. Jordan. (Illus.). 112p. 1985. Repr. of 1984 ed. 5.50. Exposition-Phoenix.

We Can Make It...Together: A Daring Vision of the Future for Black Americans. Jordan. LC 84-234729. 1984. 5.50. Jordan Enter.

We Can Minister with Dying Persons. Joseph P. Dulany. LC 86-50872. (Orig.). 1986. pap. 5.95 (ISBN 0-88177-029-9, DRO29B). Discipleship Res.

We Can Prevent World War III. Samuel Cohen. LC 85-5785. 140p. 1985. 16.95 (ISBN 0-915463-10-5, Pub. by Jameson Bks, Dist. by Kampmann). Green Hill.

We Can Read: Story Pack-54 Little Stories. Priscilla L. McQueen. 1973. pap. 18.66 (ISBN 0-685-47089-X). McQueen.

We Can Save Ourselves...How to Live Better on Fewer Energy Dollars, Vol. 4. 68p. 1978. 2.50 (ISBN 0-317-34114-6, 017811). Edison Electric.

We Can Share God's Love. Jean Richards. 80p. (ps up). 1984. pap. 2.95 (ISBN 0-8170-1010-6). Judson.

We Cannot Find Words. Tad Dunne. pap. 6.95 (ISBN 0-87193-138-9). Dimension Bks.

We Cannot Find Words. Tad Dunne. pap. 6.95 (ISBN 0-87193-262-8). Dimension Bks.

We Can't All Be Heroes, You Know. Linda Anderson. LC 84-16359. 208p. 1985. 14.95 (ISBN 0-89919-333-1). Ticknor & Fields.

We Can't Pay? We Won't Pay! Dario Fo. 72p. (Orig.). 1981. pap. 4.95 (ISBN 0-86104-204-2). Routledge Chapman & Hall.

We Can't Sleep. James Stevenson. LC 81-20307. (Illus.). 32p. (gr. k-3). 1982. 11.75 (ISBN 0-688-01213-2); PLB 11.88 (ISBN 0-688-01214-0). Greenwillow.

We Care: A Preschool Curriculum for Children Ages 2-5. Bertie W. Kingore & Glenda M Higbee. 1988. pap. 26.95 (ISBN 0-673-18574-5). Scott F.

We Care Cookbook. Robert D. Reed & Kathy Reed. pap. 3.00 (ISBN 0-88247-181-3). R & E Pubs.

We Celebrate Our Marriage. John Van Bemmel & Dolores Van Bemmel. (Greeting Book Line Ser.). 32p. (Orig.). 1986. pap. 1.50 (ISBN 0-89622-304-3). Twenty-Third.

We Charge Genocide: The Historic Petition to the United Nations for Relief from a Crime of the United States Government Against the Negro People. Civil Rights Congress Staff. Ed. by William L. Patterson. LC 76-140208. pap. 64.00 (ISBN 0-317-28065-1, 2025547). Bks Demand UMI.

We Choose Peace. V. Fedosov & A. Fyodorov. 200p. 1985. pap. 1.95 (ISBN 0-8285-3092-0, Pub. by Progress Pubs USSR). Imported Pubns.

We Chose Cape Cod. Scott Corbett. LC 52-13127. 1970. pap. 6.95 (ISBN 0-85699-007-8). Chatham Pr.

We Chose Cape Cod. Scott Corbett. 320p. 1984. pap. 8.95 (ISBN 0-940160-27-7). Parnassus Imprints.

We Christians & Jews. Paul J. Kirsch. 160p. pap. 3.95 (ISBN 0-686-95187-5). ADL.

We Christians & Jews. Paul J. Kirsch. LC 74-26332. pap. 40.00 (2026838). Bks Demand UMI.

We Come to Object: The Peasants of Morelos & the National State. Arturo Warman. Tr. by Stephen K. Ault from Span. LC 80-8092. (Johns Hopkins Studies in Atlantic History & Culture). 328p. 1981. text ed. 34.50x (ISBN 0-8018-2170-3). Johns Hopkins.

We Confess: The Church, Vol. 3. Hermann Sasse. Tr. by Norman Nagel. 160p. 1987. pap. 11.95 (ISBN 0-570-03990-8, 12-3018). Concordia.

We Confess: The Sacraments. Herman Sasse. (We Confess Ser.: Vol. II). 160p. 1985. 11.95 (ISBN 0-570-03982-7, 12-2899). Concordia.

We Confess, Vol. 1: Jesus Christ. Herman Sasse. Tr. by Norman Nagel. 1984. pap. 10.95 (ISBN 0-570-03941-X, 12-2877). Concordia.

We Could Have Finished Last Without You. Bill Borst. 48p. (Orig.). 1986. pap. 3.95 (ISBN 0-9612260-3-X). Krank Pr.

We Cried Together. Apurba Maitra. 1983. 11.00x (ISBN 0-8364-0952-3, Pub. by Mukhopadhyay India). South Asia Bks.

We Deliver. Joan Lisante. LC 87-46262. 1988. pap. 7.95 (ISBN 1-55611-079-0). D I Fine.

We Did Not Plummet into Space. Ernest N. Brookings. (Illus.). 1983. pap. 7.50 (ISBN 0-911623-01-9). I Klang.

We Didn't Ask Utopia: A Quaker Family in Soviet Russia. Harry Timbres & Rebecca Timbres. LC 76-115590. (Russia Observed, Ser., No. 1). 1970. Repr. of 1939 ed. 17.00 (ISBN 0-405-03067-3). Ayer Co Pubs.

We Didn't Have Much, But We Sure Had Plenty. Sherry Thomas. LC 80-956. (Illus.). 185p. 1984. pap. 5.95 (ISBN 0-385-14951-4). Spinsters Aunt Lute.

We Didn't Know They Were Angels. Doris W. Greig. Ed. by Mary Beckwith. 300p. (Orig.). 1987. pap. 8.95 (ISBN 0-8307-1145-7, 5418802). Regal.

We Didn't Mean to. Sharon Addy. LC 80-24976. (Life & Living from a Child's Point of View Ser.). (Illus.). 32p. (gr. k-5). 1981. PLB 15.33 (ISBN 0-8172-1370-8). Raintree Pubs Ltd.

We Die Before We Live: Talking with the Very Ill. Daniel Berrigan. 160p. 1980. 11.95 (ISBN 0-8164-0462-3, HarpR). Har-Row.

We Discovered Alien Bases on the Moon. Fred Steckling. LC 81-90609. (Illus.). 192p. 1981. pap. 9.95 (ISBN 0-942176-00-6). GAF Intl.

We Dissent. Ed. by Hoke Norris. LC 73-6210. 211p. 1973. Repr. of 1962 ed. lib. bdg. 35.00x (ISBN 0-8371-6889-9, NOWD). Greenwood.

We Do It Every Day: The Story Behind the Success of Levitz Furniture. Wight Martindale, Jr. LC 72-86727. 1972. text ed. 12.00 (ISBN 0-87005-139-3). Fairchild.

We Do It for Jesus - Mother Teresa & Her Missionaries. E. Le. Joly. 182p. 1977. 6.95. Asia Bk Corp.

We Don't Buy Sickness, It Just Comes: Health, Illness & Health Care in the Lives of Black People in London. Jenny Donovan. 1986. text ed. 42.00 (ISBN 0-566-05201-6, Pub. by Gower Pub England). Gower Pub Co.

We Don't Die: George Anderson's Conversations with the Other Side. Joel Martin & Patricia Romanowski. 304p. 1988. 17.95 (ISBN 0-399-13323-2, Putnam). Putnam Pub Group.

We Don't Have Any Here. Toby Gould et al. 52p. 1986. pap. 4.95 (ISBN 0-88177-030-2, DR030B). Discipleship Res.

We Don't Know How: An Independent Audit of What They Call Success in Foreign Assistance. William Paddock & Elizabeth Paddock. 1973. pap. 8.95x (ISBN 0-8138-1755-2). Iowa St U Pr.

We Don't Live Here Anymore. Andre Dubus. 279p. 1984. pap. 7.95 (ISBN 0-517-55362-7). Crown.

We Dont't Look Like Our Mom & Dad. Harriet L. Sobol. (Illus.). 32p. (gr. 4-7). 1984. 11.95 (ISBN 0-698-20608-8, Coward). Putnam Pub Group.

We Dream of Honour: John Berryman's Letters to His Mother. John Berryman. Ed. by Richard J. Kelly. (Illus.). 1988. 22.50 (ISBN 0-393-02477-6). Norton.

We Drink from Our Own Wells: The Spiritual Journey of a People. Gustavo Gutierrez. Tr. by Matthew J. O'Connell from Span. LC 83-22008. Orig. Title: Beber en Supropio Pozo: En el Itinerario Espiritual de un Pueblo. 208p. (Orig.). 1984. pap. 7.95 (ISBN 0-88344-707-X). Orbis Bks.

We Drive an Eighteen Wheeler. Compiled by David Enlow. 136p. 1981. pap. 2.49 (ISBN 0-87509-305-1). Transport Chr.

We Each Have a Dream. (Shorewood Art Programs for Education Ser.). 12p. 1974. tchr's ed. 86.00 (ISBN 0-88185-050-0); mounted prints 119.00. Shorewood Fine Art.

We Eat the Mines & the Mines Eat Us: Dependency & Exploitation in Bolivian Tin Mines. June Nash. LC 79-11623. 1979. 35.00x (ISBN 0-231-04710-X); pap. 16.00x (ISBN 0-231-04711-8). Columbia U Pr.

We Endeavor. C. H. Spurgeon. 1975. pap. 2.25 (ISBN 0-686-16835-6). Pilgrim Pubns.

We Europeans. Julian S. Huxley & A. C. Haddon. Repr. of 1935 ed. 23.00 (ISBN 0-527-43830-8). Kraus Repr.

We Europeans: A Survey of "Racial" Problems. Julian S. Huxley & A. C. Haddon. 1979. Repr. of 1935 ed. lib. bdg. 30.00 (ISBN 0-8495-2285-4). Arden Lib.

We Fed Them Cactus. Fabiola C. De Baca. (Illus.). 200p. pap. 10.95 (ISBN 0-8263-1119-9). U of NM Pr.

We Fight for Oil. Ludwell Denny. 1979. lib. bdg. 59.95 (ISBN 0-8490-3014-5). Gordon Pr.

We Fight for Oil. Ludwell Denny. LC 75-6468. (History & Politics of Oil Ser.). 297p. 1976. Repr. of 1928 ed. 21.50 (ISBN 0-88355-287-6). Hyperion Conn.

We Fished All Night. Willard Motley. LC 73-18875. Repr. of 1951 ed. 32.50 (ISBN 0-404-11370-2). AMS Pr.

We Follow Jesus. (gr. 3). 2.82 (ISBN 0-02-649490-6, 64949); tchr's manual 2.52 (ISBN 0-02-649500-7, 64950). Benziger Pub Co.

We Follow Jesus see Word & Worship: CCD Ed.

We Gather, Remember, & Eat. Joan Mitchell. (gr. 2). 1986. tchr's. ed. 4.50 (ISBN 0-89837-110-4); wkbk. 5.25 (ISBN 0-89837-109-0). Pflaum Pr.

We Must March, My Darlings. Diana Trilling. LC 76-54566. 320p. 1977. 10.00 (ISBN 0-15-195599-9). HarBraceJ.

We Must March, My Darlings. Diana Trilling. 315p. 1985. pap. 3.95 (ISBN 0-15-695706-X). HarBraceJ.

We Need Each Other. Guy Greenfield. 1984. pap. 7.95 (ISBN 0-8010-3800-6). Baker Bk.

We Need One Another. D. H. Lawrence. LC 74-1421. (Studies in D. H. Lawrence, No. 20). 1974. lib. bdg. 75.00x (ISBN 0-8383-2031-7). Haskell.

We Need to Dream All This. Bernard Pomerance. 1987. 15.95 (ISBN 0-670-81551-9). Viking.

We Need to Dream All This Again: An Account of Crazy Horse, Custer, & the Battle for the Black Hills. Bernard Pomerance. 96p. 1988. pap. 8.95 (ISBN 0-14-011004-6). Penguin.

We Never Get to Do Anything. Martha Alexander. LC 78-121575. (Pied Piper Bk.). (Illus.). (ps-2). 1978. pap. 1.75 (ISBN 0-8037-9781-8). Dial Bks Young.

We Never Get to Do Anything. Martha Alexander. (Illus.). (ps-3). 1970. PLB 7.89 (ISBN 0-8037-9416-9). Dial Bks Young.

We Never Make Mistakes. Aleksandr Solzhenitsyn. Tr. by Paul W. Blackstock from Rus. 1971. pap. 6.95 (ISBN 0-393-00598-4, Norton Lib). Norton.

We Never Said Goodbye: The Tragedy of Alzheimer's Disease. Isobelle Gidley & Richard Shears. 191p. 1985. 14.95x (ISBN 0-86861-551-X). Unwin Hyman.

We of the Never-Never & the Little Black Princess. Aeneas Gunn. 256p. 1984. pap. 3.95 (ISBN 0-380-87791-0, Discus). Avon.

We Offer Ourselves As Evidence: Toward Workers' Control of Occupational Health. Bennett M. Judkins. LC 85-24775. (Contributions in Labor Studies: No. 61). 272p. 1986. lib. bdg. 36.95 (ISBN 0-313-24898-2, JWO/). Greenwood.

We Owed You One! The Uphill Struggle of the Philadelphia 76'ers. Pat Williams & Bill Lyon. LC 84-167343. (Illus.). 224p. 1983. 17.95 (ISBN 0-914663-00-3). TriMark Pub Co.

We Own It: Starting & Managing Co-Ops, Collectives & Employee Owned Ventures. 165 ed. Peter J. Honigsberg et al. 1982. 14.00 (ISBN 0-917510-02-X); pap. 9.00 (ISBN 0-917510-03-8). Bell Springs Pub.

We Own It: Starting & Managing Co-ops, Collectives & Employee-Owned Ventures. Peter Jan Honigsberg & Bernard Kamoroff. 165p. 1982. 9.00 (ISBN 0-318-17055-8, Pub. by Bell Springs Publishing). NASCO.

We Planned It That Way. Frank Knox. LC 77-37889. (Select Bibliographies Reprint Ser.). Repr. of 1938 ed. 13.00 (ISBN 0-8369-6726-7). Ayer Co Pubs.

We Please God. Cathy Falk. (Bible Activities for Little People Ser.: Bk. 4). 24p. (Orig.). (ps-k). 1983. pap. 1.50 (ISBN 0-87239-679-7, 2454). Standard Pub.

We Pointed Them North: Recollections of a Cowpuncher. E. C. Abbott. 1976. pap. 7.95 (ISBN 0-8061-1366-9). U of Okla Pr.

We Praise You, O Lord! Patricia Fritz. 2.95 (ISBN 0-8091-2518-8). Paulist Pr.

We Pray at Mass: A Mass Book for Young Children. Illus. by Ferelith E. Williams. (Illus.). 32p. (Orig.). (gr. k-2). 1986. pap. 1.25 (ISBN 0-00-599532-9, Collin Liturgical). HarpR.

We Pray to the Lord: General Intercessions Based on the Scriptural Readings for Sundays & Holy Days. Richard Mazziotta. LC 84-71135. 208p. (Orig.). 1984. pap. 9.95 (ISBN 0-87793-323-5). Ave Maria.

We Preach Jesus. Compiled by T. O. Tollett. 40p. 1971. pap. 1.00 (ISBN 0-89114-063-8). Baptist Pub Hse.

We Protest: The Public Order Debates. Peter Thornton. 1985. 20.00x (ISBN 0-946088-21-7, Pub. by NCCL UK). State Mutual Bk.

We Read: A to Z. Donald Crews. LC 83-25453. (Illus.). 64p. (ps-1). 1984. 11.50 (ISBN 0-688-03843-3); PLB 10.51 (ISBN 0-688-03844-1). Greenwillow.

We Read More Stories. pap. 10.62 set (ISBN 0-917186-11-7); tchrs guide 4.72 (ISBN 0-917186-12-5). McQueen.

We Really Do Need Each Other. Reuben Welch. 112p. 1982. pap. 5.95 (ISBN 0-310-70221-6, 14012P). Zondervan.

We Receive the Spirit of Jesus (Confirmation Program) Brian A. Haggerty & Thomas P. Walters. wkbk. 3.50 (ISBN 0-8091-9532-1); parent's notes 2.45 (ISBN 0-8091-9533-X); celebration's bk. 9.95 (ISBN 0-8091-9531-3); director's manual 7.50 (ISBN 0-8091-9530-5). Paulist Pr.

We Receive the Spirit of Jesus Filmstrips. Brian A. Haggerty & Thomas P. Walters. with guidebook & cassette 49.95 (ISBN 0-8091-7664-5). Paulist Pr.

We Rejoice in the Light: Candlelighting Ceremonies for Advent. Sandra J. Dixon. Ed. by Herbert Lambert. 64p. Date not set. pap. 5.95 (ISBN 0-8272-4223-9). CBP.

We Remember the Holocaust. David A. Adler. LC 87-21139. (Illus.). 96p. (gr. 4-7). 1988. 12.95 (ISBN 0-8050-0434-3). H Holt & Co.

We Ride the Gale. Emilie Loring. Repr. lib. bdg. 19.95x (ISBN 0-88411-374-4, Pub. by Aeonian Pr). Amereon Ltd.

We Rode the Wind: Recollections of 19th-Century Tribal Life. Ed. by Jane B. Katz. LC 74-11909. (Voices of the American Indian Ser.). (Illus.). 112p. (gr. 7 up). 1975. PLB 8.95 (ISBN 0-8225-0639-4). Lerner Pubns.

We Sagebrush Folks. Annie P. Greenwood. (Illus.). 496p. 1988. pap. 17.95 (ISBN 0-89301-122-3). U of Idaho Pr.

We Saw Brother Francis. Francis De Beer. 1983. 12.00 (ISBN 0-8199-0803-7). Franciscan Herald.

We Saw Him Act: A Symposium on the Art of Sir Henry Irving. Ed. by Harry A. Saintsbury & Cecil Palmer. LC 78-113453. (Illus.). 1939. 22.00 (ISBN 0-405-08909-0). Ayer Co Pubs.

We Say We Love Each Other. Minnie B. Pratt. LC 85-50991. 120p. (Orig.). 1985. pap. 5.95 (ISBN 0-933216-16-5). Spinsters Aunt Lute.

We See All. Bruce Bailey. 281p. 1983. 35.00 (ISBN 0-317-69293-3). B M Bailey.

We Seized Our Rifles. Eugene L. Silliman. LC 81-14106. (Illus.). 200p. 1982. pap. 7.95 (ISBN 0-87842-116-5). Mountain Pr.

We Shall Be All: A History of the Industrial Workers of the World. Melvyn Dubofsky. LC 87-16725. 1988. 39.95 (ISBN 0-252-01408-1). U of Ill Pr.

We Shall Be Heard: Women Speakers in America. Patricia Kennedy & Gloria O'Shields. 384p. 1983. 23.95 (ISBN 0-8403-2975-X). Kendall-Hunt.

We Shall Fight in the Streets. S. J. Cuthbert. (Illus.). 68p. 1972. pap. 7.00 (ISBN 0-87364-049-7). Paladin Pr.

We Shall Live Again: The 1870 & 1890 Ghost Dance Movements As Demographic Revitalization. Russell Thornton. (ASA Rose Monographs). (Illus.). 112p. 1986. 24.95 (ISBN 0-521-32894-2). Cambridge U Pr.

We Shall Not Overcome: Populism & Southern Blue-Collar Workers. Robert E. Botsch. LC 80-11567. xv, 237p. 1981. 22.50x (ISBN 0-8078-1444-X). U of NC Pr.

We Shall Not Sleep. Clyde O. Jackson. (Illus.). 1985. 8.00 (ISBN 0-682-40219-2). Exposition-Phoenix.

We Shall Return! MacArthur's Commanders & the Defeat of Japan. Ed. by William M. Leary. LC 88-2731. 320p. 1988. 25.00 (ISBN 0-8131-1654-6). U Pr of Ky.

We Shall Return: Women of Palestine. Ingela Bendt & Jim Downing. (Illus.). 144p. (Orig.). 1982. 16.95 (ISBN 0-88208-154-3); pap. 8.50 (ISBN 0-88208-155-1). Chicago Review.

We Share New Life (Baptism Program) Brian A. Haggerty et al. Reflections & Activities for Families. 2.95 (ISBN 0-8091-9183-0); Activities for Children. 2.75 (ISBN 0-8091-9182-2); director's manual 7.95 (ISBN 0-8091-9181-4); celebrations bk. 4.95 (ISBN 0-8091-9184-9). Paulist Pr.

We Should Be Thankful. Swartzentruber. (God Is Good Ser.). 1976. 2.45 (ISBN 0-686-18188-3). Rod & Staff.

We Sing Our Struggle: A Tribute to Us All. Ed. by Mary McAally. (Illus.). 82p. (Orig.). 1982. pap. 5.00 (ISBN 0-943594-03-0). Cardinal Pr.

We Sing Out. Illus. by Cristina Ong. LC 86-60289. (Gymboree Board Bks.). (Illus.). 12p. (ps-1). 1986. 2.95 (ISBN 0-394-88202-4, BYR). Random.

We Speak for Ourselves: Experiences in Homosexual Counselling. Jack Babuscio. LC 77-78623. pap. 40.00 (2026837). Bks Demand UMI.

We Speak in Code. Melanie Kaye. (Illus.). 106p. (Orig.). 1980. pap. 4.75 (ISBN 0-934238-02-2). Motheroot.

We Speak No Treason, Bk. 1. Rosemary H. Jarman. 272p. 1985. pap. 3.50 (ISBN 0-515-08338-0). Jove Pubns.

We Speak No Treason, Bk. 2. Rosemary H. Jarman. 336p. 1986. pap. 3.95 (ISBN 0-515-08567-7). Jove Pubns.

We Still Love You, Bob. Dorothea Nyberg. 144p. 1984. pap. 6.95 (ISBN 0-87178-925-6). Brethren.

We Survived: Fourteen Histories of the Hidden & Hunted of Nazi Germany. 3rd ed. Eric H. Boehm. 320p. 1985. lib. bdg. 21.00 (ISBN 0-87436-429-9). ABC-Clio.

We Swam the Grand Canyon: The True Story of a Cheap Vacation That Got a Little Out of Hand. Bill Beer. (Illus.). 276p. 1988. 15.95 (ISBN 0-89886-151-9). Mountaineers.

We Talk of Christ, We Rejoice in Christ. Neal A. Maxwell. LC 84-71873. 180p. 8.95 (ISBN 0-87747-762-0). Deseret Bk.

We Tell It to Our Children: The Story of Passover: A Haggadah for Seders with Young Children. MaryAnn B. Wark. LC 87-63604. (Illus.). 150p. (Orig.). (ps-6). 1988. pap. 11.95 wire-o (ISBN 0-9619880-9-6). Mensch Makers Pr.

We, the Accused. TV tie-in ed. Ernest Raymond. 512p. 1983. pap. 4.95 (ISBN 0-14-006220-3). Penguin.

We, the American Women: A Documentary History. rev. ed. Beth M. Kava & Jeanne Bodin. LC 75-28344. (Illus.). xii, 362p. 1977. lib. bdg. 24.95 (ISBN 0-574-01058-0); pap. text ed. 15.95 (ISBN 0-574-01055-6). Ozer.

We the Bereaved. Anna Clarke. 1988. pap. 2.95 (ISBN 1-55773-026-1, Charter Bks). Berkley Pub.

We the Creators of Heavens & Earths. Frank R. Wallace. 1987. 17.50 (ISBN 0-911752-51-X). I & O Pub.

We, the Divided Self. John G. Watkins & Rhonda J. Johnson. 140p. 1982. text ed. 18.95x (ISBN 0-8290-1011-4); One hr. audio cassette (for prof. use only) 12.00x (ISBN 0-8290-1412-8). Irvington.

We, the Homeless. Stephenie Hollyman. (Illus.). 250p. 1988. 45.00 (ISBN 0-8022-2542-X). Philos Lib.

We the Living. Ayn Rand. pap. 4.50 (ISBN 0-451-14146-6, Sig). NAL.

We the Living. Ayn Rand. 1959. 19.95 (ISBN 0-394-45124-4). Random.

We, the Navigators: The Ancient Art of Landfinding in the Pacific. David Lewis. LC 72-82139. (Illus.). 363p. 1975. pap. 9.95 (ISBN 0-8248-0394-9). UH Pr.

We, the One. Unohu. 1977. 6.00 (ISBN 0-87881-060-9). Mojave Bks.

We, the Other People: Alternative Declarations of Independence, by Labor Groups, Farmers, Woman's Rights Advocates, Socialists, & Blacks, 1829-1975. Ed. by Philip S. Foner. LC 76-10736. 224p. 1976. 22.95 (ISBN 0-252-00623-2); pap. 8.95 (ISBN 0-252-00624-0). U of Ill Pr.

We, the People. Lonnelle Aikman. LC 81-52034. text ed. 5.00 (ISBN 0-916200-00-0); pap. 4.00 (ISBN 0-916200-14-0). US Capitol Hist.

We the People. Richard Halverson. LC 87-4808. 128p. 1987. 15.95 (ISBN 0-8307-1220-8, 5111709). Regal.

We, the People. Leo Huberman. (Illus.). 384p. 1970. pap. 8.00 (ISBN 0-85345-134-6). Monthly Rev.

We the People. Frances H. Stephens. 80p. 1987. text ed. 19.95 (ISBN 0-944377-00-9). Facts Pubns.

We the People: A Family Guide to Constitution City. The Philadelphia Inquirer & Jonathan Storm. (Illus.). 80p. (Orig.). 1987. pap. 4.95 (ISBN 0-912608-41-2). Mid Atlantic.

We the People: A Good News Odyssey. John Rayburn. (Illus.). 288p. 1987. 16.95 (ISBN 0-917895-13-4). Cordillera CO.

We the People: A Pictorial Celebration of America. Illus. by Parade-Fuji National Photo Contest Winners. (Illus.). 144p. 1988. 24.95 (ISBN 0-8264-0405-7). Crossroad NY.

We the People: A Story of Internment in America. Mary Tsukamoto & Elizabeth Pinkerton. LC 87-205205. (Illus.). 324p. 1988. 30.00 (ISBN 0-944665-41-1); pap. 15.00 (ISBN 0-944665-42-X). Laguna Pubs.

We the People: An Atlas of America's Ethnic Diversity. James P. Allen & Eugene J. Turner. LC 87-28194. xii, 315p. 1988. 105.00 (ISBN 0-02-901420-4). Macmillan.

We the People: An Atlas of America's Ethnic Diversity. Eugene J. Turner & James P. Allen. 1987. 85.00. Scribner.

We the People & Others: Duality & America's Treatment of Its Racial Minorities. Benjamin B. Ringer. 1178p. 1986. pap. text ed. 27.00 (ISBN 0-422-60160-8, 9677, Pub. by Tavistock England). Routledge Chapman & Hall.

We the People & Others: Duality & America's Treatment of the Racial Minorities. Benjamin Ringer. 1165p. 1983. 75.00x (ISBN 0-422-78180-0, NO. 3734, Pub. by Tavistock). Routledge Chapman & Hall.

We the People: Bits, Bytes & Highlights of the U. S. Constitution & Bill of Rights from Honey Bees Tye & Sy. D. M. Wolf. (Illus.). 32p. (Orig.). (gr. 3-5). 1987. pap. 4.95 (ISBN 0-9617057-1-X). Storyviews Pub.

We the People: Community Forums on the Constitution. 1986. pap. 10.00. Amer Bar Assn.

We the People: Indiana & the United States Constitution: Lectures in Observance of the Bicentennial of the Constitution. Patrick J. Furlong. LC 86-27175. 1987. 4.00 (ISBN 0-87195-007-3). Ind Hist Soc.

We the People of Montana. James Lopach et al. LC 83-8072. 320p. 1983. 22.00 (ISBN 0-87842-154-8); pap. 10.95 (ISBN 0-87842-159-9). Mountain Pr.

We the People of the United States. Lynne Glasner & Marylin Thypin. (Government Ser.: Bk. 2). (Illus.). 96p. (Orig.). (gr. 7-12). 1984. Bk. 2. pap. text ed. 5.45 (ISBN 0-941342-10-7, 1042). Entry Pub.

We the People: The Constitution in American Life. Robert S. Peck. (Illus.). 176p. 1987. 29.95 (ISBN 0-8109-1789-0). Abrams.

We the People: The Story of the United States Capitol. 13th ed. Lonnelle Aikman. Ed. by National Geographic Society Staff. LC 85-51287. (Illus.). 144p. 1985. pap. 4.50 (ISBN 0-916200-06-X). US Capitol Hist.

We the People: The Story of the U. S. Constitution. Peter Spier. LC 86-24205. (Illus.). 48p. (gr. k-3). 1987. pap. 13.95 (ISBN 0-385-23589-5); pap. 13.95 (ISBN 0-385-23789-8). Doubleday.

We, the People: The Story of the United States Capitol. (Illus.). 144p. 1985. pap. 6.95 (ISBN 0-317-61450-9). Natl Geog.

We the People: The Story of the United States Constitution since 1787. Harold Faber & Doris Faber. LC 86-31404. (Illus.). 256p. (YA) (gr. 12 up). 1987. 13.95 (ISBN 0-684-18753-1, Pub. by Scribner). Macmillan.

We the People: The Way We Were 1783-1793. Suzanne Hilton. LC 81-11392. (A Junior Literary Guild Selection). (Illus.). 206p. (gr. 6-9). 1981. 12.95 (ISBN 0-664-32685-4). Westminster John Knox.

We, the Puerto Rican People: A Story of Oppression & Resistance. Juan A. Silen. Tr. by Cedric Belfrage from Span. LC 70-158926. (Illus.). 144p. 1971. pap. 6.00 (ISBN 0-85345-217-2). Monthly Rev.

We, the Teachers. Terry Herndon. 192p. 1983. 7.95 (ISBN 0-8106-1427-8). NEA.

We, the Tikopia: A Sociological Study of Kinship in Primitive Polynesia. abr. ed. Raymond Firth. LC 83-42540. (Illus.). xxviii, 497p. 1963. 37.50x (ISBN 0-8047-1201-8); pap. 11.95x (ISBN 0-8047-1202-6). Stanford U Pr.

We the Unreconciled. Sujatha Modayil. (Redbird Ser.). 52p. 1975. 10.00 (ISBN 0-88253-672-9); pap. text ed. 4.80 (ISBN 0-88253-671-0). Ind-US Inc.

We the Victors. Curtis B. Pepper. 416p. 1985. pap. 4.50 (ISBN 0-451-13408-7, Sig). NAL.

We the Women: Career Firsts in Nineteenth-Century America. Madeleine B. Stern. 1977. pap. 7.95 (ISBN 0-89102-093-4). B Franklin.

We the Women: Career Firsts in Nineteenth-Century America. new ed. Madeleine B. Stern. LC 74-11307. 1975. 23.50 (ISBN 0-8337-5535-8). B Franklin.

We Think the World of You. Joe R. Ackerley. 1961. 11.95 (ISBN 0-685-06622-3). Astor-Honor.

We Thought at Least the Roof Would Fall. Leslie Mellichamp. LC 87-2231. (Illus.). 128p. (Orig.). 1987. pap. 5.95 (ISBN 0-936015-07-1). Pocahontas Pr.

We Three Came West. Ed. by Helen Raitt & Mary C. Wayne. LC 74-81909. (Illus.). 272p. 1974. 10.00 (ISBN 0-914488-03-1). Rand-Tofua.

We Three Came West. rev. 2nd ed. Ed. by Helen Raitt & Mary C. Wayne. LC 74-81909. (Illus.). 272p. 1975. pap. 4.95 (ISBN 0-914488-08-2). Rand-Tofua.

We Tibetans. Pinchen Lhamo. 228p. 1985. pap. 42.00x (ISBN 0-317-69451-0, Pub. by Han-Shan Tang Ltd). State Mutual Bk.

We Too Are Drifting. Gale Wilhelm. LC 75-12359. (Homosexuality). 1975. Repr. 11.00x (ISBN 0-405-07380-1). Ayer Co Pubs.

We Too Are Drifting. Gale Wilhelm. 128p. 1985. pap. 6.95 (ISBN 0-930044-61-4). Naiad Pr.

We Too Are the People. Louise V. Armstrong. LC 78-137155. (Poverty U. S. A. Historical Record Ser.). 1971. Repr. of 1938 ed. 28.00 (ISBN 0-405-03093-2). Ayer Co Pubs.

We Too Are the People. Louise V. Armstrong. LC 74-168679. (FDR & the Era of the New Deal Ser.). 1972. Repr. of 1938 ed. lib. bdg. 55.00 (ISBN 0-306-70367-X). Da Capo.

We Took a Ride. Alan Benjamin & Theresa Woodward. (Little Ones Ser.). (Illus.). (ps). 1986. bds. 2.95 (ISBN 0-671-62922-0, Little Simon). S&S.

We Took to the Woods. Louise D. Rich. (Illus.). 1975. pap. 8.95 (ISBN 0-89272-016-6). Down East.

We Took to the Woods. Louise D. Rich. 19.95 (ISBN 0-89190-858-7, Pub. by Am Repr). Amereon Ltd.

We Travel an Appointed Way. A. W. Tozer. Selected by Harry Verploegh. LC 88-70130. 145p. (Orig.). 1988. pap. 5.95 (ISBN 0-87509-407-4). Chr Pubns.

We: Understanding the Psychology of Romantic Love. Robert A. Johnson. LC 83-47725. 224p. 1985. pap. 7.95 (ISBN 0-06-250436-3, HarpR). Har-Row.

We Walk the Back of the Tiger. Patricia A. Murphy. 256p. 1988. pap. 8.95 (ISBN 0-941483-13-4). Pergamon.

We Walk the Way of the New World. Don L. Lee. 1970. 6.00 (ISBN 0-910296-26-X); tapes o.p. 5.00 (ISBN 0-685-07556-7). Broadside Pr.

We Walked, Then Ran. Alice M. Shipley. Ed. by Mary E. Hawkins. (Illus.). 300p. 1984. 9.00 (ISBN 0-9610918-0-0); pap. 7.95 (ISBN 0-9610918-3-5). A M Shipley.

We Walked to Moscow. Jerry Lehmann. Ed. by Arthur Harvey. 100p. (Orig.). 1966. pap. 5.00 (ISBN 0-934676-07-0). Greenlf Bks.

We Walked Very Warily: A History of Women at McGill. Margaret Gillett. (Illus.). 496p. 1981. 18.95 (ISBN 0-920792-08-1). Eden Pr.

We Wanna Boogie: An Illustrated History of the American Rockabilly Movement. Randy McNutt. (Illus.). 288p. 1988. 19.95 (ISBN 0-940152-05-3). McNutt Pubns.

We Were Children Then: More Stories from the Yarns of Yester-Year Project, Vol. II. Ed. by Clarice Dunn & Gen Lewis. LC 76-22961. (Illus.). 249p. 1982. pap. 10.95 (ISBN 0-88361-085-X). Stanton & Lee.

We Were Children Then: Ninety Yarns of Yester-Year Writers, Age Sixty to Ninety-Six. Ed. by Robert E. Gard et al. LC 76-22961. 187p. 1976. pap. 9.95 (ISBN 0-88361-041-8). Stanton & Lee.

We Were Dreamers. James Lehrer. 224p. 1986. pap. 6.95 (ISBN 0-689-70710-X, 342). Atheneum.

We Were Hooked. As told to Harold Flender. (gr. 6 up). 1972. Random.

We Were Once Beautiful Butterflies. Maria Kavanagh. (Orig.). 1982. pap. 2.95 (ISBN 0-89083-968-9). Zebra.

We Were That Young. Irene Ruthbone. 500p. 1988. 29.95 (ISBN 1-55861-001-4); pap. 10.95 (ISBN 1-55861-002-2). Feminist Pr.

Wealth Weapon: U. S. Foreign Policy & Multinational Corporations. Ben J. Wattenberg & Richard J. Whalen. LC 79-66448. 127p. 1980. 21.95 (ISBN 0-87855-340-1); pap. 8.95 (ISBN 0-87855-820-9). Transaction Bks.

Wealth Without Risk: How to Develop a Personal Fortune Without Going Out on a Limb. Charles J. Givens. 352p. 1988. 18.95 (ISBN 0-671-61938-1). S&S.

Wealth Without Work: Keys to More Thru Management. Clifton M. Whitley. Date not set. price not set (ISBN 0-935497-02-1). Fountainhead.

Wealthy Citizens of New York. Moses Y. Beach. LC 73-1992. (Big Business; Economic Power in a Free Society Ser.). Repr. of 1973 ed. 8.00 (ISBN 0-405-05117-4). Ayer Co Pubs.

Wealthy Corinth: A History of the City to 338 BC. J. B. Salmon. (Illus.). 464p. 1984. 67.00x (ISBN 0-19-814833-X). Oxford U Pr.

Wealthy Women. Lynda Logan-Frank et al. 1985. 14.95 (ISBN 0-910019-35-5). Regency Bks.

Weaning & Human Development. Gordon R. Forrer. LC 72-79731. 1969. 5.95 (ISBN 0-87212-020-1). Libra.

Weaning: Why, What, & When? Ed. by Angel Ballabriga & Jean Rey. (Nestle Nutrition Workshop Ser.: Vol. 10). (Illus.). 240p. 1987. text ed. 31.00. Raven.

Weapon Masters of Okinawa: An Informal History of the Ryukyu Kobudo (Ancient Weapon Ways) Sid Campbell. (Audio Cassette Book Ser.). (Illus.). 25p. 1988. audio-book 15.95. Gong Prods.

Weapon of Prayer. E. M. Bounds. (Direction Bks.). 57p. 1975. pap. 3.95 (ISBN 0-8010-0634-1). Baker Bk.

Weapon of Prayer. Basilea Schlink. 1974. Gift ed. 0.95 (ISBN 3-87209-658-3). Evang Sisterhood Mary.

Weapon on the Wall. Murray Dyer. 1979. 25.50 (ISBN 0-405-10599-1). Ayer Co Pubs.

Weapon Retention Techniques for Officer Survival. Robert J. Downey & Jordan T. Roth. (Illus.). 120p. 1981. 19.25x (ISBN 0-398-04108-3). C C Thomas.

Weaponeer: An Encyclopedia of Weapons. K. Saxon. 1986. lib. bdg. 79.95 (ISBN 0-8490-3613-5). Gordon Pr.

Weaponless Control: For Law Enforcement & Security Personnel. Jeff Cope & Kenneth Goddard. (Illus.). 302p. 1979. photocopy ed. 36.75x (ISBN 0-398-03902-X). C C Thomas.

Weaponless Defense: A Law Enforcement Guide to Non-Violent Control. Jack Hibbard & Bryan A. Fried. (Illus.). 184p. 1980. spiral bdg. 17.50x (ISBN 0-398-03936-4). C C Thomas.

Weaponless Warriors. Richard Kim. Ed. by John Scurra. LC 74-21218. (History & Philosophy Ser.). (Illus.). 1974. pap. text ed. 9.95x (ISBN 0-89750-041-5, 313, Dist. by Wehman). Ohara Pubns.

Weaponry in Space: The Dilemma of Security. Ed. by Y. Velikhov. 147p. 1986. 8.95 (ISBN 0-8285-3428-4, Pub. by Mir Pubs USSR). Imported Pubns.

Weaponry in Space: The Dilemma of Security. Ed. by Y. Velikhov et al. 174p. 1987. 22.95 (ISBN 0-08-034752-5, Pub. by BDP). Pergamon.

Weapons. The Diagram Group. (Illus.). 320p. 1980. 27.50 (ISBN 0-312-85946-5). St Martin.

Weapons Acquisition Process: Economic Incentives. Frederic M. Scherer. LC 64-12400. (Illus.). 468p. 1964. 24.95t (ISBN 0-87584-034-5, Dist. by Harper & Row Pubs., Inc.). Harvard Busn.

Weapons Against Chaos. Mary Ewald. 1986. 14.95 (ISBN 0-8159-7225-3). Devin.

Weapons & Armor: A Pictorial Archive of Woodcuts & Engravings. Harold H. Hart. 1983. 14.50 (ISBN 0-8446-5937-1). Peter Smith.

Weapons & Armor: A Pictorial Archive of Woodcuts & Engravings. Ed. by Harold H. Hart. (Illus.). 192p. pap. 7.95 (ISBN 0-486-24242-0). Dover.

Weapons & Equipment of Counter-Terrorism. Michael Dewar. (Illus.). 240p. 1988. 29.95 (ISBN 0-85368-841-9, Pub. by Arms & Armour). Sterling.

Weapons & Hope. Freeman J. Dyson. LC 82-48675. (Cornelia & Michael Bessie Bk.). 320p. 1984. 17.45 (ISBN 0-06-039031-X). Har-Row.

Weapons & Hope. Freeman J. Dyson. LC 83-48343. 341p. 1985. pap. 7.95 (ISBN 0-06-039039-5). Har-Row.

Weapons & Tactics of the Soviet Army. 2nd ed. David Isby. (Illus.). 512p. 1988. 45.00 (ISBN 0-7106-0352-5). Janes Info Group.

Weapons & Warfare: Conventional Weapons & Their Roles in Battle. Ed. by K. Perkins. (Illus.). 264p. 1987. 39.50 (ISBN 0-08-033615-9, Pub. by BDP). Pergamon.

Weapons & Warfare in Ancient Times. Rivka Gonen. LC 72-10802. (Archaeology Ser.). (Illus.). (gr. 5 up). 1976. PLB 7.95 (ISBN 0-8225-0832-X). Lerner Pubns.

Weapons Demonstration. Tadashi Yamashita. Ed. by Mike Lee. LC 87-63018. (Weapons Ser.). 192p. (Orig.). 1987. pap. 8.95 (ISBN 0-89750-114-4, 454). Ohara Pubns.

Weapons for the World Update: The U. S. Corporate Role in International Arms Transfer. Steve Lydenberg. 72p. 1977. 2.00. CEP.

Weapons in Space. Ed. by Franklin A. Long et al. 1986. 16.95 (ISBN 0-393-01989-6); pap. text ed. 9.95x (ISBN 0-393-95527-3). Norton.

Weapons Kumite: Fighting with Traditional Weapons. Takayuki Kubota. Ed. by James Gierman. LC 83-80055. (Illus.). 200p. (Orig.). 1983. pap. 8.95 (ISBN 0-86568-042-6, 307). Unique Pubns.

Weapons Law. J. B. Hill. (Waterlow Practitioner's Library). 96p. (Orig.). 1988. pap. 12.51 (ISBN 0-08-033104-1, Pub. by Waterlow). Pergamon.

Weapons of Chaos Book I: Echoes of Chaos. Robert E. Vardeman. 192p. (Orig.). 1986. pap. 2.95 (ISBN 0-425-09295-X). Berkley Pub.

Weapons of Criticsm: Marxism in America & the Literary Tradition. Ed. by Norman Rudich. LC 74-9178. (Illus.). 389p. 1976. 14.00 (ISBN 0-87867-056-4); pap. 4.95 (ISBN 0-87867-057-2). Ramparts.

Weapons of Happiness. Howard Brenton. 79p. 1976. pap. 6.95 (ISBN 0-413-36650-2, NO. 2995). Heinemann Ed.

Weapons of Mass Destruction & the Environment. 108p. 1977. 21.00x (ISBN 0-85066-132-3, Pub. by A Hilger UK). Taylor & Francis.

Weapons of Okinawa: A Devastating Kobudo Arsenal. Sid Campbell. (Illus.). 168p. 1987. pap. text ed. 12.00 (ISBN 0-87364-429-8). Paladin Pr.

Weapons of Our Warfare: Help for Troubled Minds. (Illus.). 144p. 1987. pap. 3.95 (ISBN 0-936369-06-X). Son-Rise Pubns.

Weapons of the Weak. James C. Scott. LC 85-51779. 414p. 1987. pap. 14.95x (ISBN 0-300-03641-8, Y-665). Yale U Pr.

Weapons of the Weak: Everyday Forms of Peasant Resistance. James C. Scott. 1986. 40.00 (ISBN 0-300-03336-2). Yale U Pr.

Weapons of Tomorrow. Brian Beckett. 160p. 1983. 14.95 (ISBN 0-306-41383-3, Plenum Pr). Plenum Pub.

Weapons Systems & Political Stability: A History. Carroll Quigley. LC 82-21791. 1064p. 1983. lib. bdg. 48.25 (ISBN 0-8191-2947-X). U Pr of Amer.

Weaponsmakers: Personal & Professional Crisis During the Vietnam War. Jeffrey Schevitz. LC 78-21046. 224p. 1979. text ed. 18.95 (ISBN 0-87073-932-8); pap. text ed. 11.95 (ISBN 0-87073-933-6). Schenkman Bks Inc.

Wear & Fracture Prevention: Proceedings of a Conference Held May 21-22, 1980, Peoria, Illinois. American Society for Metals Staff. LC 81-67226. (Materials-Metalworking Technology Ser.). pap. 79.80 (ISBN 0-317-26752-3, 2024351). Bks Demand UMI.

Wear & Tear; or, Hints for the Overworked. 5th ed. S. Weir Mitchell. LC 73-2407. (Mental Illness & Social Policy; the American Experience Ser.). Repr. of 1887 ed. 13.50 (ISBN 0-405-05217-0). Ayer Co Pubs.

Wear Control Handbook. Ed. by M. Peterson & W. Winer. 1500p. 85.00 (ISBN 0-317-33640-1, G00169); members 68.00 (ISBN 0-317-33641-X). ASME.

Wear in Pipeline Engines & Compressors: Methods of Measurement. D. V. Kniebes. iv, 35p. 1959. 18.00 (ISBN 0-317-56934-1). Inst Gas Tech.

Wear in Slurry Pipelines. Lavinia Gittins. (BHRA Information Ser.). (Illus.). 173p. (Orig.). 1980. pap. 41.00x (ISBN 0-906085-45-4). BHRA Fluid.

Wear, Lubrication & Repair: Proceedings of the Europort Conference, 1973. Europort Conference Staff. 40p. 1973. limp bdg. 9.00 (ISBN 0-900976-36-5, Pub. by Inst Marine Eng). Intl Spec Bk.

Wear of Agricultural Machine Parts. Ed. by M. Severnev. Tr. by S. Kaila from Rus. 271p. 1985. text ed. 33.50 (ISBN 90-6191-454-X, Pub. by A A Balkema). Brookfield Pub Co.

Wear of Metals. A. D. Sarkar. 1976. 36.00 (ISBN 0-08-019738-8); pap. 15.25 (ISBN 0-08-019737-X). Pergamon.

Wear Tests for Plastics: Selection & Use- STP 701. Ed. by R. G. Bayer. 106p. 1980. pap. 12.75x (ISBN 0-8031-0599-9, 04-701000-19). ASTM.

Wearing Dad's Head: A Collection of Short-Short Stories. Barry Yourgrau. 128p. (Orig.). 1987. pap. 7.95 (ISBN 0-87905-283-X, Peregrine Smith). Gibbs Smith Pub.

Wearing the Edged Weapons of the Third Reich. Thomas M. Johnson. LC 77-82820. (Illus.). 1977. pap. 10.00. Johnson Ref Bks.

Weary & the Wary: U. S. & Japanese Security Policies in Transition. Robert Osgood. LC 71-186510. (Washington Center of Foreign Policy Research. Studies in International Affairs: No. 16). pap. 26.50 (ISBN 0-317-19919-6, 2023132). Bks Demand UMI.

Weary Road: A Recollection of a Subaltern of Infantry. Charles Douie. 240p. 1988. 75.00x (ISBN 1-871048-00-1, Pub. by S P A Bks Ltd). State Mutual Bk.

Weary Sons of Freud. Catherine Clement. Tr. by Nicole Ball. 115p. Date not set. 29.95 (ISBN 0-86091-177-2, Pub. by Verso); pap. 11.95 (ISBN 0-86091-888-2, Pub. by Verso). Routledge Chapman & Hall.

Weary Titan: Britain & the Experience of Relative Decline, 1895-1905. Aaron L. Friedberg. (Illus.). 376p. 1988. 29.95 (ISBN 0-691-05532-7). Princeton U Pr.

Weasel School of Education. James Willard. LC 85-62439. (Illus.). 80p. Date not set. text ed. 12.50 (ISBN 0-915053-05-5). Chiron Pub Co.

Weasel Words. Philip Howard. 1979. 21.95x (ISBN 0-19-520107-8). Oxford U Pr.

Weasel's Luck. Michael Williams. LC 88-50060. (Dragonlance Saga Heroes Ser.). 392p. 1988. pap. 3.95 (ISBN 0-88038-625-8). TSR Inc.

Weather. B. W. Atkinson & Alan Gadd. LC 86-19073. (Mitchell Beazley Earth Science Handbook Ser.). (Illus.). 160p. 1987. 12.95 (ISBN 1-55584-028-0). Weidenfeld.

Weather. 2nd ed. Louis J. Battan. (Illus.). 160p. 1985. text ed. write for info. (ISBN 0-13-947698-9); pap. text ed. write for info. (ISBN 0-13-947680-6). P-H.

Weather. Martyn Bramwell. Ed. by Franklin Watts Ltd. (Earth Science Ser.). (Illus.). 32p. (YA) (gr. 7 up). 1988. 9.90 (ISBN 0-531-10357-9). Watts.

Weather. rev. ed. Herta S. Breiter. LC 87-23226. (Read About Science Ser.). (Illus.). 48p. (gr. 3). 1987. PLB 15.33 (ISBN 0-8172-3265-6). Raintree Pubs.

Weather. Illus. by Claude D'Ham. (Moments Ser.). (Illus., Orig.). (ps-2). 1975. pap. 2.00 (ISBN 0-85953-037-X, Pub. by Child's Play England). Playspaces.

Weather. Terry Jennings. Ed. by Franklin Watts Ltd. (Junior Science Ser.). (Illus.). 28p. (gr. k-3). 1988. 9.90 (ISBN 0-531-17088-8, Gloucester Pr). Watts.

Weather. Pierre Kohler. (Focus on Science Ser.). (gr. 6 up). 1988. 4.95 (ISBN 0-8120-3833-9). Barron.

Weather. David Lambert. (Easy-Read Fact Bks.). (Illus.). 32p. (gr. k-3). 1983. PLB 9.90 (ISBN 0-531-04621-4). Watts.

Weather. Paul E. Lehr & R. Will Burnett. (Golden Guides Ser.). (Illus.). 160p. 1987. pap. 3.95 (ISBN 0-307-24051-7, Pub. by Golden Bks). Western Pub.

Weather. Antonio Padial & Winifred H. Roderman. (Science in Action Ser.). (Illus.). 48p. (gr. 9 up). 1982. pap. text ed. 2.95 (ISBN 0-915510-79-0). Janus Bks.

Weather. Mark Pettigrew. (Science Today Ser.). (Illus.). 32p. (gr. 1-6). 1987. lib. bdg. 10.90 (ISBN 0-531-17060-8, Gloucester Pr). Watts.

Weather. Jan Pienkowski. Ed. by Kate Klimo. (Concept Bks.). (Illus.). 32p. (ps-k). 1983. 3.95 (ISBN 0-671-46245-8, Little Simon). S&S.

Weather. Jan Pienkowski. (Illus.). 32p. (ps). 1983. 7.97 (ISBN 0-671-46934-7). Messner.

Weather. Raintree Publishers Inc. LC 87-28715. (Science & Its Secrets Ser.). (Illus.). 64p. (Orig.). (gr. 5-6). 1988. lib. bdg. 18.65 (ISBN 0-8172-3079-3); pap. 11.93 (ISBN 0-8172-3096-3). Raintree Pubs.

Weather. Louis Sabin. LC 84-2706. (Illus.). 32p. (gr. 3-6). 1985. PLB 8.45 (ISBN 0-8167-0200-4); pap. text ed. 1.95 (ISBN 0-8167-0201-2). Troll Assocs.

Weather. 64p. (gr. 6-12). 1963. pap. 1.25x (ISBN 0-8395-3274-1, 3274). BSA.

Weather. LC 79-798. (Spotter's Guide). (Illus.). 1979. 3.95 (ISBN 0-8317-9393-7, Mayflower Bks); pap. 1.95 (ISBN 0-8317-9394-5). Smith Pubs.

Weather. (Science Adventures Ser.). 48p. (gr. 2-7). 1987. pap. 2.95 (ISBN 0-8431-2655-8). Price Stern.

Weather. Harris Winitz. (All about Language Ser.). (Illus.). 50p. (gr. 7 up). 1986. pap. text ed. 4.75 (ISBN 0-317-46316-0); cassette tape 12.00 (ISBN 0-939990-47-4). Intl Linguistics.

Weather. rev. 1987 ed. Herbert S. Zim et al. (Golden Guide Ser). (Illus.). 1957. pap. 3.95 (Golden Pr). Western Pub.

Weather: A User's Guide to the Atmosphere. Ti Sanders. (Illus.). 280p. 1985. 16.95 (ISBN 0-89651-906-6); pap. 11.95 (ISBN 0-89651-907-4). B L Pub.

Weather Almanac. 5th ed. Ed. by James A. Ruffner & Frank E. Bair. 811p. 1986. 110.00 (ISBN 0-8103-1497-5). Gale.

Weather Almanac. 6th ed. Ed. by James A. Ruffner & Frank E. Bair. 800p. 1988. 110.00 (ISBN 0-8103-2843-7). Gale.

Weather & Bird Behaviour. Norman Elkins. (Illus.). 320p. 1983. 37.50 (ISBN 0-85661-035-6, Pub. by T & A D Poyser England). Buteo.

Weather & Climate. Paul E. Lydolph. LC 84-18080. (Illus.). 230p. 1985. 24.95x (ISBN 0-86598-120-5, Rowman & Allanheld). Rowman.

Weather & Climate. Seymour Simon. (Science Library: No. 7). (gr. 4-6). 1969. lib. bdg. 4.99 (ISBN 0-394-90804-X); pap. 1.50 (ISBN 0-394-80805-3). Random.

Weather & Climate. Reginald C. Sutcliffe. (Advancement of Science Ser.). (Illus.). 1967. 5.95x (ISBN 0-393-06329-1). Norton.

Weather & Climate Modification: Problems & Progress. Intro. by Thomas F. Malone. LC 79-22479. 288p. 1980. Repr. of 1973 ed. 55.00x (ISBN 0-8103-1017-1). Gale.

Weather & Climate of the Antarctic. W. Schwerdtfeger. (Developments in Atmospheric Science Ser.: Vol. 15). 1984. 71.00 (ISBN 0-444-42293-5, I-092-84). Elsevier.

Weather & Climate of the Great Lakes Region. Val Eichenlaub. LC 78-51526. (Illus.). 1979. text ed. 21.95x (ISBN 0-268-01929-0); pap. text ed. 8.95 (ISBN 0-268-01930-4). U of Notre Dame Pr.

Weather & Climate on Planets. K. Y. Kondratyev & G. E. Hunt. (Illus.). 750p. 1981. 140.00 (ISBN 0-08-026493-X). Pergamon.

Weather & Climate Responses to Solar Variations. Ed. by Billy M. McCormac. LC 82-73247. pap. 159.00 (2027297). Bks Demand UMI.

Weather & Climate: Text-Exercises-Weather Maps. John J. Hidore. LC 84-61956. 238p. 1984. pap. 15.95 (ISBN 0-941226-05-0). Park Pr Co.

Weather & Energy. Bruce Schwoegler & Michael McClintock. 224p. 1982. text ed. 27.95 (ISBN 0-07-055746-2). McGraw.

Weather & Forecasting. (Field Guide Ser.). 160p. 1987. pap. 8.95 (ISBN 0-02-013700-1). Macmillan.

Weather & Its Work. David Lambert & Ralph Hardy. (World of Science). (Illus.). 64p. (gr. 7 up). 1985. 12.95 (ISBN 0-87196-987-4). Facts on File.

Weather & Rice: Proceedings of the International Workshop on the Impact of Weather Parameteters on Growth & Yield of Rice 7-10 April, 1986. 323p. (Orig.). 1987. pap. text ed. 11.00 (ISBN 971-104-178-2). Agribookstore.

Weather & Water. B. W. Atkinson et al. LC 85-6594. (Reviews of U. K. Statistical Sources Ser.: Vol. 7). (Illus.). 240p. 1985. 53.00 (ISBN 0-08-031844-4, Pub. by PPI). Pergamon.

Weather & Weather Maps. Ed. by Gosta H. Liljequist. (Contributions to Current Research in Geophysics: 10). 265p. 1982. text ed. 52.95x (ISBN 0-8176-1192-4). Birkhauser.

Weather & Women Treat Me Fair. Percival Everett. LC 87-11424. 116p. 1987. pap. 6.95 (ISBN 0-87483-013-3). August Hse.

Weather at Sea. David Houghton & Fred Sanders. 128p. (Orig.). 1988. pap. 12.95 (ISBN 0-87742-959-6). Intl Marine.

Weather Atlas of the United States. U. S. Environmental Data Service. LC 74-11931. 272p. 1975. 95.00x (ISBN 0-8103-1048-1). Gale.

Weather Book. Janet Kauffman. 71p. (Orig.). 1981. 9.95 (ISBN 0-89672-090-X); pap. 4.95 (ISBN 0-89672-089-6). Tex Tech Univ Pr.

Weather Bureau: Its History, Activities & Organization. Gustavus A. Weber. LC 72-3022. (Brookings Institution. Institute for Government Research. Service Mongraphs of the U. S. Government: No. 9). Repr. of 1922 ed. 21.50 (ISBN 0-404-57109-3). AMS Pr.

Weather, Climate & Human Affairs. Hubert H. Lamb. 416p. 1988. text ed. 89.95 (ISBN 0-415-00674-0). Routledge Chapman & Hall.

Weather Companion: An Album of Meteorological History, Science, Legend, & Folklore. Gary Lockhart. (Illus.). 1989. pap. 12.95 (ISBN 0-471-62079-3). Wiley.

Weather Company. Bernie Fass & Rosemary Caggiano. 48p. (gr. k-8). 1978. pap. 8.95 (ISBN 0-86704-004-1). Clarus Music.

Weather Conspiracy: The Coming of the New Ice Age. The Impact Team. pap. 1.95 (ISBN 0-345-27209-9). Ballantine.

Weather, Electricity, Environmental Investigations. Sandra Markle. (Gifted & Talented Ser.). 112p. (gr. 4-6). 1982. 8.95 (ISBN 0-88160-082-2, LW 902). Learning Wks.

Weather Experiments. Vera Webster. LC 81-17062. (New True Bks.). (Illus.). 48p. (gr. k-4). 1982. PLB 12.60 (ISBN 0-516-01662-8). Childrens.

Weather Eyes in the Sky: America's Meteorological Satellites. Joseph G. Vaeth. LC 65-12760. pap. 33.50 (ISBN 0-317-09224-3, 2012372). Bks Demand UMI.

Weather Factor: Fascinating Accounts of How Weather Shaped America's Battles, Sports, & History. David M. Ludlum. 225p. 1984. 17.95 (ISBN 0-395-27604-7). HM.

Weather-Fear: New & Selected Poems, 1958-1982. John Engels. LC 82-13591. (Contemporary Poetry Ser.). 144p. 1983. pap. 6.95 (ISBN 0-8203-0655-X). U of Ga Pr.

Weather Flying. 3rd, rev. & enl. ed. Robert N. Buck. (Eleanor Friede Bk.). (Illus.). 1988. 19.95 (ISBN 0-02-518021-5). Macmillan.

Weather for Poetry: Essays, Reviews & Notes on Poetry, 1977-1981. Donald Hall. LC 82-8544. (Poets on Poetry Ser.). 304p. 1982. pap. 8.95 (ISBN 0-472-06340-5). U of Mich Pr.

Weather for the Mariner. 3rd. ed. William J. Kotsch. LC 83-13084. 1983. 17.95 (ISBN 0-87021-756-9). Naval Inst Pr.

Weather Forecast For Utopia & Vicinity: Poems Nineteen Sixty-Seven to Nineteen Eighty-Two. Charles Simic. LC 83-527. 56p. (Orig.). 1983. pap. 4.95 (ISBN 0-930794-83-4); ltd. signed ed. 30.00 (ISBN 0-88268-030-7). Station Hill Pr.

Weather Forecasting. Gail Gibbons. LC 86-7602. (Illus.). 32p. (gr. k-3). 1987. 12.95 (ISBN 0-02-737250-2, Four Winds). Macmillan.

Weather Forecasting for Agriculture & Industry: A Symposium. Ed. by James A. Taylor. LC 72-6550. (Illus.). 250p. 1973. 24.50 (ISBN 0-8386-1260-1). Fairleigh Dickinson.

Weather Forecasting: Rules, Techniques & Procedures. George Elliott. 154p. 1988. pap. text ed. 11.95x (ISBN 0-89641-171-0). American Pr.

Weather Handbook. rev. ed. Ed. by H. McKinley Conway & Linda L. Liston. LC 79-54253. (Illus.). 255p. 1974. 14.95 (ISBN 0-910436-00-2). Conway Data.

Weather, Health & Biomedicine: Subject Analysis Index with Research Bibliography. American Health Research Institute Staff. LC 85-47846. 150p. 1987. 34.50 (ISBN 0-88164-354-8); pap. 26.50 (ISBN 0-88164-355-6). ABBE Pubs Assn.

Weather in Africa. Martha Gellhorn. 240p. 1981. pap. 3.50 (ISBN 0-380-55855-6, 55855-6, Bard). Avon.

Web of Progress: Private Values & Public Styles in Boston & Charleston, 1828-1843. William H. Pease & Jane H. Pease. (Illus.). 353p. 1987. pap. 12.95 (ISBN 0-19-505105-X). Oxford U Pr.

Web of Silk. Yvonne Whittal. (Harlequin Presents Ser.). 192p. 1983. pap. 1.95 (ISBN 0-373-10582-7). Harlequin Bks.

Web of Southern Social Relations: Women, Family, & Education. Ed. by Walter J. Fraser, Jr. et al. LC 85-1054. 280p. 1985. 25.00x (ISBN 0-8203-0787-4). U of Ga Pr.

Web of Southern Social Relations: Women, Family, & Education. Ed. by Walter J. Fraser, Jr. et al. LC 85-1054. 280p. 1987. pap. 12.95x (ISBN 0-8203-0942-7). U of Ga Pr.

Web of the Chozen. Jack L. Chalker. 1987. pap. 2.95 (ISBN 0-345-33959-2, Del Rey). Ballantine.

Web of the City. Harlan Ellison. 224p. 1983. pap. 2.75 (ISBN 0-441-87718-4). Ace Bks.

Web of the Romulans. M. S. Murdock. 256p. (Orig.). 1985. pap. 3.50 (ISBN 0-671-60549-6, Timescape). PB.

Web of the Witch World. Andre Norton. 192p. 1983. pap. 2.75 (Pub. by Ace Science Fiction). Ace Bks.

Web of the Witch World, No. 2. Andre Norton. pap. 2.75 (ISBN 0-441-87879-2). Ace Bks.

Web of Their Lives: Macbeth & Human Greatness. Arthur T. Levinson. 120p. 1984. pap. 7.95. Byrnam Pr.

Web of Urban Housing. Frank de Leeuw et al. 231p. 1975. 16.95x (ISBN 0-87766-151-0, 12900); pap. 6.95x (ISBN 0-87766-150-2, 12700). Urban Inst.

Web of Victory: Grant at Vicksburg. Earl S. Miers. LC 84-9717. (Illus.). 320p. 1984. pap. 9.95 (ISBN 0-8071-1199-6). La State U Pr.

Web of Violence: A Study of Violence in the Family. Jean Renvoizie. 1978. 19.95x (ISBN 0-7100-8804-3). Routledge Chapman & Hall.

Web of Wind. J. F. Rifkin. 192p. (Orig.). 1987. pap. 2.95 (ISBN 0-441-87883-0, Pub. by Ace Science Fiction). Ace Bks.

Web of Wizardry. Juanita Coulson. 1984. pap. 2.95 (ISBN 0-345-31788-2, Del Rey Bks). Ballantine.

Web Offset Press Operating. 2 ed. David B. Crouse et al. LC 83-83335. (Illus.). 304p. 1984. 48.00 (ISBN 0-88362-066-9, 1516). Graphic Arts Tech Found.

Web Offset Press Troubles. 3rd ed. Robert F. Reed & David B Crouse. LC 77-94463. (Illus.). 198p. 1979. 48.00 (1518) (ISBN 0-88362-023-5). Graphic Arts Tech Found.

Web Processing & Converting Technology & Equipment. Ed. by Don Satas. (Illus.). 560p. 1984. 52.95 (ISBN 0-442-28177-3). Van Nos Reinhold.

Web She Weaves: An Anthology of Mystery & Suspense Stories by Women. Ed. by Marcia Muller & Bill Pronzini. 1985. pap. 9.95 (ISBN 0-688-04831-5, Quill). Morrow.

Web: Stories by Argentine Women. Ed. by Ernest H. Lewald. LC 81-51646. 135p. 1983. 20.00 (ISBN 0-89410-085-8); pap. 10.00 (ISBN 0-89410-086-6). Three Continents.

Web That Has No Weaver: Understanding Chinese Medicine. Ted J. Kaptchuk. LC 82-2511. 432p. 1984. 19.95 (ISBN 0-312-92932-3); pap. 12.95 (ISBN 0-312-92933-1). Congdon & Weed.

Webb Society Deep-Sky Observer's Handbook: Galaxies, Vol. 4. Ed. by Webb Society Staff & Kenneth G. Jones. LC 77-359099. 256p. 1981. pap. 17.95x (ISBN 0-89490-050-1). Enslow Pubs.

Webb Society Deep-Sky Observer's Handbook: Clusters of Galaxies, Vol. 5. Ed. by Kenneth G. Jones & Webb Society. LC 78-31260. 256p. 1982. pap. 17.95x (ISBN 0-89490-066-8). Enslow Pubs.

Webb Society Deep-Sky Observer's Handbook: Open & Globular Clusters, Vol. 3. Webb Society Staff. Ed. by Kenneth G. Jones. LC 78-31260. (Illus.). 224p. 1980. pap. 15.95x (ISBN 0-89490-034-X). Enslow Pubs.

Webb Society Deep-Sky Observer's Handbook: Planetary & Gaseous Nebulae, Vol. 2. Ed. by Webb Society Staff & Kenneth G. Jones. LC 78-31260. 160p. 1979. pap. 11.95x (ISBN 0-89490-028-5). Enslow Pubs.

Webb Society Deep-Sky Observer's Handbook, Volume 1: Double Stars. 2nd ed. Webb Society Staff. Ed. by Kenneth G. Jones. LC 85-20553. (Illus.). 192p. 1986. pap. 14.95x (ISBN 0-89490-122-2). Enslow Pubs.

Webb Society Deep-Sky Observer's Handbook, Vol. 6: Anonymous Galaxies. Webb Society Staff. Ed. by Kenneth G. Jones. LC 78-31260. 160p. 1987. pap. 12.95 (ISBN 0-89490-133-8). Enslow Pubs.

Webb Society Deep-Sky Observer's Handbook, Vol. 7: The Southern Sky. Webb Society Staff. Ed. by Kenneth G. Jones. LC 78-31260. (Illus.). 224p. 1987. pap. 16.95 (ISBN 0-89490-134-6). Enslow Pubs.

Webber Quartet, 4 Vols. Helen Webber. (gr. k-6). Set. deluxe slipcase 35.00 (ISBN 0-8392-3070-2). Astor-Honor.

Webbing. Drummond Hadley. LC 67-20765. (Writing Ser: No. 15). 38p. (Orig.). 1967. pap. 2.00 (ISBN 0-87704-006-0). Four Seasons Foun.

Webbs & Their Work. Ed. by Margaret I. Cole. LC 84-22459. (Illus.). xvi, 304p. 1985. Repr. of 1949 ed. lib. bdg. 41.50 (ISBN 0-313-24677-7, COWW). Greenwood.

Webelos Den Activities. (Illus.). 66p. 1969. pap. 1.10x (ISBN 0-8395-3853-7, 3853). BSA.

Webelos Scout Book. rev. ed. Boy Scouts of America. (Illus.). 416p. (gr. 4-6). 1987. pap. 3.50 (ISBN 0-8395-3235-0, 3235). BSA.

Weber. 2nd ed. William Saunders. LC 69-11670. (Music Reprint Ser.). 1970. Repr. of 1940 ed. lib. bdg. 42.50 (ISBN 0-306-71200-8). Da Capo.

Weber & Islam: A Critical Study. Bryan S. Turner. 1978. pap. 9.95x (ISBN 0-7100-8942-2). Routledge Chapman & Hall.

Weber & Rickert: Concept Formation in the Cultural Sciences. Guy Oakes. (Studies in Contemporary German Social Thought). 200p. 1988. text ed. 20.00x (ISBN 0-262-15034-4). MIT Pr.

Weber & the Marxist World. Johannes Weiss. Tr. by Elizabeth King-Utz & Michael J. King. (International Library of Sociology). 320p. 1986. text ed. 62.50 (ISBN 0-7100-9981-9, 99819). Routledge Chapman & Hall.

Weber Carburetors: Select, Install & Tune Weber Sidedraft & Downdraft Carburetors for Performance or Economy. Pat Braden. LC 87-21266. 160p. 1987. pap. 12.95 (ISBN 0-89586-377-4). Price Stern.

Weber in London. Ed. by David Reynolds. (Illus.). 64p. (Orig.). 1976. pap. 9.95 (ISBN 0-85496-403-7, Pub. by Berg Pubs). St Martin.

Weber-Marx Dialogue. Ed. by Robert J. Antonio & Ronald M. Glassman. LC 85-3148. xxii, 336p. 1985. 29.95x (ISBN 0-7006-0265-8); pap. 14.95x (ISBN 0-7006-0312-3). U Pr of KS.

WEBER! The American Adventure of Captain Charles M. Weber. James M. Shebl. (Illus.). 150p. 1988. write for info. Sn Joaquin Cty Hist Soc.

Weber, the Ideal Type, & Contemporary Social Theory. Susan Hekman. LC 82-40381. 223p. 1983. pap. 9.95 (ISBN 0-268-01932-0). U of Notre Dame Pr.

Weberian Sociological Theory. Randall Collins. (Illus.). 320p. 1986. 44.50 (ISBN 0-521-30698-1); pap. 15.95 (ISBN 0-521-31426-7). Cambridge U Pr.

Webfoot Volunteer: The Diary of William M. Hilleary, 1864-1866. William M. Hilleary. Ed. by Herbert B. Nelson & Preston E. Onstad. LC 65-65228. (Studies in History: No. 5). (Illus.). 248p. 1965. 11.95 (ISBN 0-87071-075-3). Oreg St U Pr.

Webs. Scott Baker. 336p. 1989. pap. price not set. Tor Bks.

Webs & Wardrobes: Humanist & Religious World Views in Children's Literature. Ed. by Joseph O'Beirne Milner & Lucy F. Milner. 170p. (Orig.). 1987. lib. bdg. 24.50 (ISBN 0-8191-6545-X); pap. text ed. 11.75 (ISBN 0-8191-6546-8). U Pr of Amer.

Webs of Everywhere. John Brunner. 192p. 1983. pap. 2.25 (ISBN 0-345-30680-5, Del Rey). Ballantine.

Webster & Arnold & the Giant Box. P. K. Roche. LC 80-11595. (Easy-to-Read Bks.). (Illus.). 56p. (ps-3). 1980. PLB 5.89 (ISBN 0-8037-9436-3). Dial Bks Young.

Webster & Arnold Go Camping. P. K. Roche. LC 88-1485. 32p. (ps-3). 1988. 12.95 (ISBN 0-670-81993-X, Viking Kestrel). Viking.

Webster & Hayne's Speeches in the United States Senate. facsimile ed. Daniel Webster & Robert Y. Hayne. LC 71-37318. (Black Heritage Library Collection). Repr. of 1850 ed. 12.75 (ISBN 0-8369-8955-4). Ayer Co Pubs.

Webster & the Witch. Graham Marks. (Illus.). 40p. (gr. k-3). 1987. 15.95 (ISBN 0-340-35564-6, Pub. by Hodder & Stoughton UK). David & Charles.

Webster Bible. Noah Webster. 928p. 1987. 29.95 (ISBN 0-8010-9684-7). Baker Bk.

Webster Comprehensive Dictionary: International Edition, 2 Vols. 1514p. 1987. write for info (ISBN 0-89434-080-8). Ferguson.

Webster Dictionary. 448p. pap. 5.95 (ISBN 0-317-68268-7). Book Essentials.

Webster Illustrated Contemporary Dictionary. 1122p. 1987. write for info. (ISBN 0-89434-081-6). Ferguson.

Webster, Massachusetts Vital Records to Eighteen Fifty. Jay M. Holbrook. LC 78-60365. 336p. 1980. lib. bdg. 35.00 (ISBN 0-931248-08-6). Holbrook Res.

Webster 'Reformed' A Study of Post-Restoration Versions of John Webster's Plays, 2 vols. James Hogg. (Jacobean Drama Studies). (Orig.). 1986. pap. 30.00 (ISBN 3-7052-0323-1, Pub. by Salzburg Studies). Longwood Pub Group.

Webster: The Critical Heritage. Don Moore. (Critical Heritage Ser.). 172p. 1982. 26.95x (ISBN 0-7100-0773-6). Routledge Chapman & Hall.

Webster: Three Plays. John Webster. Ed. by D. C. Gunby. (English Library). 1973. pap. 6.95 (ISBN 0-14-043081-4). Penguin.

Webster's American Biographies. LC 74-6341. 1248p. 1975. 18.95 (ISBN 0-87779-253-4). Merriam-Webster Inc.

Webster's American Military Biographies. Ed. by Robert McHenry. LC 84-8004. 548p. 1984. pap. 11.95 (ISBN 0-486-24758-9). Dover.

Webster's American Military Biographies. Ed. by Robert McHenry. 18.25 (ISBN 0-8446-6143-0). Peter Smith.

Webster's Basic Reference Collection. 1987. pap. 10.40 (ISBN 0-446-11259-3). Warner Bks.

Webster's Beginning Book of Facts. (Illus.). (ps-2). 1978. 9.95 (ISBN 0-87779-074-4). Merriam-Webster Inc.

Webster's Collegiate Thesaurus. Ed. by Merriam-Webster Editorial Staff. 1976. 12.95 (ISBN 0-87779-069-8); brown leather-look 13.95 (ISBN 0-87779-070-1). Merriam-Webster Inc.

Webster's Compact Dictionary. Ed. by Merriam-Webster Editorial Staff. 432p. 1987. 5.95 (ISBN 0-87779-488-X). Merriam-Webster Inc.

Webster's Compact Dictionary of Synonyms. Merriam-Webster Editorial Staff. 384p. 1987. 4.95 (ISBN 0-87779-186-4). Merriam-Webster Inc.

Webster's Compact Rhyming Dictionary. Merriam-Webster Editorial Staff. 400p. 1987. 4.95 (ISBN 0-87779-185-6). Merriam-Webster Inc.

Webster's Compact Writers Guide. Merriam-Webster Editorial Staff. 336p. 1987. 4.95 (ISBN 0-87779-187-2). Merriam-Webster Inc.

Webster's Concise Dictionary of Modern English. LC 87-1589. 608p. 1987. pap. 5.95 (ISBN 0-8407-3110-8). Nelson.

Webster's Concise Family Dictionary. Ed. by Merriam-Webster Editorial Staff. 848p. 1975. 8.95 (ISBN 0-87779-039-6). Merriam-Webster Inc.

Webster's Desk-Top Reference. 1987. Set. pap. 20.90 (ISBN 0-446-11257-7). Warner Bks.

Webster's Dictionary. Ottenheimer Publishers. 288p. 1987. pap. 2.95 (ISBN 0-06-461005-5, DI/5, B&N Bks). Har-Row.

Webster's Dictionary for Everyday Use. Compiled by John G. Allee. LC 83-48346. 446p. 1981. pap. 5.95 (ISBN 0-06-463330-6, CN 1142, B&N Bks). Har-Row.

Webster's Dictionary Game. Wilbur Webster. 200p. 1987. pap. 5.95 (ISBN 0-671-64172-7). Meadowbrook.

Webster's Elementary Dictionary. Merriam-Webster Editorial Staff. (Illus.). (gr. 1-6). 1980. 11.95 (ISBN 0-87779-475-8). Merriam-Webster Inc.

Webster's First New Intergalactic Wickedary of the English Language. Mary Daly. Ed. by Jane Caputi. LC 87-1133. (Illus.). 288p. 1987. 35.00 (ISBN 0-8070-6706-7); pap. 14.95 (ISBN 0-8070-6733-4, BP770). Beacon Pr.

Webster's Guide to Abbreviations. Ed. by Merriam-Webster Editorial Staff. 1985. 4.95 (ISBN 0-87779-072-8). Merriam-Webster Inc.

Webster's II New Riverside Children's Dictionary. (Illus.). 800p. 1985. pap. 8.95 (ISBN 0-395-37884-2). HM.

Webster's II New Riverside Dictionary. 832p. 1985. pap. 3.95 (ISBN 0-425-08298-9). Berkley Pub.

Webster's II: New Riverside Dictionary. 1536p. 1984. 15.95 (ISBN 0-395-33957-X); pap. 3.95 (ISBN 0-395-36341-1). HM.

Webster's II New Riverside Pocket Dictionary. prepack 10 copy 22.50 (ISBN 0-395-41822-4). HM.

Webster's II New Riverside Student's Notebook Dicitionary. 100p. 1987. pap. 2.50 (ISBN 0-425-09168-6). Berkley Pub.

Webster's II New Riverside Student's Notebook Dictionary. 64p. Date not set. pap. 2.50 (ISBN 0-317-64611-7). HM.

Webster's II New Riverside University Dictionary. Ed. by Marion Severynse. 1984. write for info. HM.

Webster's II New Riverside Y. A. Dicitionary. 100p. 1987. pap. 3.95 (ISBN 0-425-09169-4). Berkley Pub.

Webster's Instant Word Guide. Ed. by Merriam-Webster Reference Editor. 384p. 1980. 3.95 (ISBN 0-87779-273-9). Merriam-Webster Inc.

Webster's Intermediate Dictionary. Ed. by Merriam Company. (Illus.). 960p. (gr. 7-9). 1986. 10.95 (ISBN 0-87779-379-4). Merriam-Webster Inc.

Webster's Legal Secretaries Handbook. Ed. by Coleen K. Withgott & Austin G. Anderson. (Illus.). 1981. 12.95 (ISBN 0-87779-034-5). Merriam-Webster Inc.

Webster's Legal Speller. Merriam-Webster Editorial Staff. 1978. 4.95 (ISBN 0-87779-038-8). Merriam-Webster Inc.

Webster's Medical Desk Dictionary. Ed. by Merriom Webster Staff. 816p. 1986. 18.95 (ISBN 0-87779-025-6). Merriam-Webster Inc.

Webster's Medical Secretaries Handbook. Merriam-Webster Editorial Staff. 1979. 12.95 (ISBN 0-87779-135-X). Merriam-Webster Inc.

Webster's Medical Speller. Ed. by Merriam-Webster Editorial Staff. 400p. 1975. 4.95 (ISBN 0-87779-037-X). Merriam-Webster Inc.

Webster's New Biographical Dictionary. Merriam-Webster Editorial Staff. 1983. 21.95 (ISBN 0-87779-543-6). Merriam-Webster Inc.

Webster's New Compact Dictionary. LC 84-4798. 1979. 2.95 (ISBN 0-8407-4081-6); pap. 1.95 (ISBN 0-8407-5846-4). Nelson.

Webster's New Dictionary & Roget's Thesaurus. Ed. by William Morris. 1008p. 1984. 11.95 (ISBN 0-8407-4115-4). Nelson.

Webster's New Dictionary of Synonyms. Merriam-Webster Editorial Staff. 942p. 1984. thumb-indexed 14.95 (ISBN 0-87779-241-0). Merriam-Webster Inc.

Websters New Elementary Dictionary. 624p. (gr. 3-8). 1981. pap. 9.95 (ISBN 0-671-62515-2). PB.

Webster's New Geographical Dictionary. rev. ed. Merriam-Webster Editorial Staff. (Illus.). 1568p. 1984. 19.95 (ISBN 0-87779-446-4). Merriam-Webster Inc.

Webster's New Ideal Dictionary. Ed. by Merriam Company Staff. (Illus.). 1984. 7.95 (ISBN 0-87779-249-6). Merriam-Webster Inc.

Webster's New Reference Library. (Illus.). 1341p. 17.98. Smith Pubs.

Webster's New Thesaurus. (gr. 4 up). 1988. pap. 3.95. Scholastic Inc.

Webster's New Word Dictionary of Synonyms. Ed. by New World Dictionary Editors. 1984. pap. 4.95 (ISBN 0-671-50403-7). S&S.

Webster's New World Atlas. (Illus.). 320p. (YA) (gr. 7-12). 1987. 39.95 (ISBN 0-13-948134-6). P-H.

Webster's New World Atlas. 320p. 1988. 39.95. Prentice Hall Pr.

Webster's New World Best Book of Aphorisms. Auriel Douglas & Micheal Strumpf. 352p. 1989. pap. 5.95 with vinyl jacket (ISBN 0-13-947128-6). Prentice Hall Pr.

Webster's New World Bible Dictionary. Websters New World Staff. 1986. pap. text ed. 5.95 (ISBN 0-671-60436-8). P-H.

Webster's New World Collins Italian-English, English-Italian Dictionary. 1985. 12.95 (ISBN 0-671-44505-7). S&S.

Webster's New World Compact Dictionary of Computer Terms. 416p. 1984. pap. 4.95 vinyl (ISBN 0-671-49692-1). S&S.

Webster's New World Compact Japanese-English, English-Japanese Dictionary. Date not set. price not set. S&S.

Webster's New World Compact School & Office Dictionary. 8.95 (ISBN 0-671-41822-X); pap. 5.95 (ISBN 0-671-44882-X). S&S.

Webster's New World Crossword Puzzle Dictionary. 1983. pap. 6.95 (ISBN 0-671-46870-7); thumb indexed 13.95 (ISBN 0-671-41832-7); 12.95 (ISBN 0-671-41831-9). S&S.

Webster's New World Crossword Puzzle Dictionary. Jane S. Whitfield. 1980. pap. 4.95 (ISBN 0-671-53268-5). PB.

Webster's New World Dictionary. 2nd college ed. 1983. leatherkraft bdg. 17.95 (ISBN 0-671-47035-3). S&S.

Webster's New World Dictionary. 1987. 16.95 (ISBN 0-671-41809-2). S&S.

Webster's New World Dictionary & Thesaurus. 1982. Boxed Set. 32.95 (ISBN 0-671-93033-8). S&S.

Webster's New World: Dictionary & Thesaurus. 1987. Boxed set, includes Webster's New World Dictionary: 2nd college edition & Webster's New World Thesaurus, rev. ed. 32.95 (ISBN 0-671-92375-7). P-H.

Webster's New World Dictionary & Thesaurus: Leather-Kraft Boxed Set. 1984. Set. 35.00 (ISBN 0-671-93463-5). S&S.

Webster's New World Dictionary: Basic School Edition. Ed. by David B. Gurainik. 1976. 15.00 (ISBN 0-13-944652-4). P-H.

Webster's New World Dictionary: College Edition. 3rd ed. thumb-indexed 17.95 (ISBN 0-13-947169-3); plain-edged 16.95 (ISBN 0-13-949280-1); leatherkraft thumb-indexed 18.95 (ISBN 0-13-949314-X). P-H.

Webster's New World Dictionary for Young Readers. 14.95 (ISBN 0-671-41821-1). S&S.

Webster's New World Dictionary of Acronyms & Abbreviations. Auriel Douglas & Micheal Strumpf. 352p. 1989. pap. 5.95 with vinyl jacket (ISBN 0-13-947136-7). Prentice Hall Pr.

Webster's New World Dictionary of Business Terms. Ed. by William W. Cook. 256p. 1985. pap. 6.95 (ISBN 0-671-50286-7). S&S.

Webster's New World Dictionary of Computer Terms. Compiled by Laura Darcy. Date not set. price not set. S&S.

Webster's New World Dictionary of Computer Terms. 1983. 5.95 (ISBN 0-671-46866-9). S&S.

Webster's New World Dictionary of Computer Terms. Webster's New World Editorial Staff. (Webster's New World-Collins Foreign Language Dictionaries Ser.). 1988. pap. 6.95 (ISBN 0-13-949231-3). Prentice Hall Pr.

Webster's New World Dictionary of Quotable Definitions. Eugene F. Brussel. (Webster's New World). 1988. pap. 14.95 (ISBN 0-13-948159-1). Prentice Hall Pr.

Webster's New World Dictionary of the American Language. Ed. by David Guralink. Date not set. pap. 3.95 (ISBN 0-446-31450-1). Warner Bks.

Webster's New World Dictionary of the American Language. rev. ed. Ed. by David B. Guralnik. 704p. 1982. pap. 9.95 (ISBN 0-446-38240-X); pap. 3.50 (ISBN 0-446-31299-1). Warner Bks.

Webster's New World Dictionary of the American Language. (Illus.). 1988. pap. 3.95 (ISBN 0-446-31475-7); pen incl. Warner Bks.

Webster's New World Dictionary of the American Language: 100,000 Entry Edition. pap. 9.95 (ISBN 0-452-00619-8, F619, Mer). NAL.

Webster's New World Dictionary: Second College Edition. 1728p. plain-edged 15.95 (ISBN 0-671-41807-6). S&S.

Webster's New World Dictionary: Student Edition. 15.95 (ISBN 0-671-41815-7). S&S.

Webster's New World German Dictionary: A Collins Concise Dictionary. 1987. 16.95 (ISBN 0-671-63815-7). P-H.

Wedge of Words. 2nd ed. Frederic Will. LC 61-15828. (Tower Poetry Ser.: No. 1). (Illus.). 1963. Repr. of 1962 ed. 5.95 (ISBN 0-87959-055-6). U of Tex H Ransom Ctr.
Wedge: The Extraordinary Communications of an Earthbound Spirit. Margaret Moon & Maurine. (Illus.). 113p. 1975. pap. 3.95 (ISBN 0-87542-497-X). Llewellyn Pubns.
Wedges & Wings: The Patterning of Paradise Regained. Burton J. Weber. LC 74-20703. (Literary Structure Ser.). 144p. 1975. 10.00x (ISBN 0-8093-0673-5). S Ill U Pr.
Wedgewood & Bentley Pottery from the Kadison Collection. LC 83-16635. (Illus.). 71p. 1983. 15.00 (ISBN 0-87328-081-4). Huntington Lib.
Wedging Oaks into Acorns. David Henson. 1979. pap. 1.50 (ISBN 0-930600-08-8). Uzzano Pr.
Wedgwood. Gene Garrison. (Illus.). 48p. 1982. 24.00 (ISBN 0-88014-061-5). Mosaic Pr OH.
Wedgwood. John M. Graham, II & Hensleigh C. Wedgwood. LC 71-128384. (Brooklyn Museum Publications in Reprint Ser.). (Illus.). 122p. Repr. of 1948 ed. 17.00 (ISBN 0-405-00878-3). Ayer Co Pubs.
Wedgwood. F. Rathbone. 1968. Repr. of 1898 ed. 10.00 (ISBN 0-912014-54-7). Buten Mus.
Wedgwood ABC but Not Middle E. 2nd ed. Harry M. Buten. (Illus.). 112p. 1981. pap. 7.95 (ISBN 0-912014-58-X). Buten Mus.
Wedgwood & America, Wedgwood Bas-Relief Ware. David Buten & Patricia Pelehach. LC 77-83634. (Monographs in Wedgwood Studies). (Illus.). 1977. pap. text ed. 5.00 (ISBN 0-912014-51-2). Buten Mus.
Wedgwood & His Imitators. 2nd & rev. ed. Hannah H. Moore. LC 76-2888. (Illus.). 1978. 19.95 (ISBN 0-89344-005-1). Ars Ceramica.
Wedgwood Ceramics 1846-1959: A New Appraisal. Maureen Batkin. (Illus.). 244p. 85.00 (ISBN 0-317-55061-6). Apollo.
Wedgwood Chats. Harry Barnard. 1970. Repr. of 1924 ed. 7.50 (ISBN 0-912014-07-5). Buten Mus.
Wedgwood Circle: 1730-1897; Four Generations of Wedgwoods & Their Friends. Barbara Wedgwood & Hensleigh Wedgwood. LC 80-65213. (Illus.). 408p. 1980. 22.50 (ISBN 0-89860-038-3). Eastview.
Wedgwood Handbook. Eliza Meteyard. 75.00 (ISBN 0-8490-1281-3). Gordon Pr.
Wedgwood in the Collection of the R. W. Norton Art Gallery. (Illus.). 101p. 1980. pap. 10.00x (ISBN 0-913060-18-6). Norton Art.
Wedgwood: Its Competitors & Imitators, 1800-1830. 1977. 27.50 (ISBN 0-89344-021-3). Ars Ceramica.
Wedgwood Trio. Eliza Meteyard. 1967. Repr. of 1867 ed. 10.00 (ISBN 0-912014-57-1). Buten Mus.
Wedlock. Jacob Wassermann. 1961. 6.95 (ISBN 0-87140-815-5). Liveright.
Wedlock's the Devil: Eighteen Fourteen to Eighteen Fifteen see Byron's Letters & Journals.
Wednesday Game. Martin Yoseloff. LC 87-47860. 240p. 1988. 15.95 (ISBN 0-8453-4808-6, Cornwall Bks). Assoc Univ Prs.
Wednesday Midweek Winners. Thomas J. Palumbo. (Illus.). 64p. (gr. 3-8). 1985. wkbk. 6.95 (ISBN 0-86653-310-9). Good Apple.
Wednesday's Child. Deborah Shlian & Joel Shlian. 1986. 3.95 (ISBN 0-317-52123-3). PB.
Wee Bit O'Scotland: Growing up in Lonaconing, Md., at the Turn of the Century. Ruth B. Levy. LC 83-50562. (Illus.). 80p. (Orig.). 1983. pap. 8.00 (ISBN 0-938420-26-7). Md Hist.
Wee Color Wee Sing. Pamela C. Beall & Susan H. Nipp. (Wee Color Ser.). (Illus.). 48p. (ps-3). 1985. pap. 1.95 (ISBN 0-8431-1423-1). Price Stern.
Wee Color Wee Sing America. Pam Beall & Susan Nipp. (Illus.). 48p. (ps-2). Date not set. pap. 1.95 (ISBN 0-8431-2277-3); pap. 7.95 incl. cass. (ISBN 0-8431-2299-4). Price Stern.
Wee Color Wee Sing Australia. Pam Beall & Susan Nipp. (Wee Color Wee Sing Ser.). 48p. (ps-2). 1988. pap. 1.95 (ISBN 0-8431-4725-3); audio pkg. 7.95. Price Stern.
Wee Color Wee Sing Bible. Pam Beall & Susan Nipp. (Wee Sing Ser.). (Illus.). Date not set. pap. 1.95 (ISBN 0-317-62153-X) (ISBN 0-317-62154-8). Price Stern.
Wee Color Wee Sing Bible Songs. Pamela C. Beall & Susan H. Nipp. (Illus.). 48p. (ps-2). 1987. pap. 1.95 (ISBN 0-8431-4703-2); incl. cass., 6 markers 6.95 (ISBN 0-8431-4708-3). Price Stern.
Wee Color Wee Sing Dinosaurs. Pam Beall & Susan Nipp. (Wee Color Wee Sing Ser.). 48p. (ps-2). 1988. pap. 1.95 (ISBN 0-8431-4726-1); audio pkg. 7.95. Price Stern.
Wee Color Wee Sing for Christmas. Pamela C. Beall & Susan H. Nipp. (Wee Color Ser.). (Illus.). 48p. (ps-2). 1986. pap. 1.95 (ISBN 0-8431-1781-8); book & cassette 6.95 (ISBN 0-8431-1782-6). Price Stern.
Wee Color Wee Sing King Cole's Party. Pam Beall & Susan Nipp. (Wee Color Wee Sing Ser.). 48p. (ps-2). 1988. pap. 1.95 (ISBN 0-8431-4728-8); audio pkg. 7.95. Price Stern.
Wee Color Wee Sing Nursery Rhymes & Lullabies. Pamela C. Beall & Susan H. Nipp. (Wee Color Wee Sing Ser.). (Illus.). 48p. (ps-7). 1987. pap. 1.95 (ISBN 0-8431-1900-4); bk, cassette & markers 7.95 (ISBN 0-8431-1925-X). Price Stern.
Wee Color Wee Sing Together. Pam Beall & Susan Nipp. (Wee Color Wee Sing Ser.). 48p. (ps-2). 1988. pap. 1.95 (ISBN 0-8431-4727-X); audio pkg. 7.95. Price Stern.
Wee Cookbook. 4th ed. Irish Children's Fund Families & Friends. (Illus.). 300p. pap. 7.95 (ISBN 0-9614331-2-4). Irish Childs Fund.
Wee Folks Legends: Ghosts, Gremlins, etc. Johnny Young. Ed. by Tom Hakes. 28p. 1985. pap. 3.95 (ISBN 0-915020-57-2). Bardic.
Wee Gillis. Illus. by Robert Lawson. (Illus.). 72p. (ps-3). 1938. lib. bdg. 12.95 (ISBN 0-670-75608-3, Viking Kestrel). Viking.
Wee Green Witch. Mary Leister. LC 78-12380. (Illus.). 44p. (ps up). 1978. 9.95 (ISBN 0-916144-30-5). Stemmer Hse.
Wee Kitten Who Sucked Her Thumb. Mary L. Tufts. (All Aboard Bks.). (Illus.). 32p. (ps-2). 1986. pap. 1.95 (ISBN 0-448-19076-1, G&D). Putnam Pub Group.
Wee Kitten Who Sucked Her Thumb. Mary L. Tufts. (Illus.). (ps-2). 1988. incl. audio cassette 5.95 (ISBN 0-448-19091-5). Platt.
Wee Peter Puffin. 3rd ed. Jane Weinberger. (Illus.). 40p. (gr. k-8). 1984. 9.95 (ISBN 0-932433-03-0). Windswept Hse.
Wee Scot Book - A Greenberg Guide. Aileen Campbell. (Illus.). 64p. 1987. text ed. 25.00 (ISBN 0-89778-067-1, 10-6965). Greenberg Pub Co.
Wee Sing. Pamela Beall & Susan Nipp. (Wee Sing Ser.). (ps-2). 1982. pap. 2.25 (ISBN 0-8431-0676-X). Price Stern.
Wee Sing America. Pamela C. Beall & Susan H. Nipp. (Illus.). 64p. (ps-2). 1987. pap. 2.25 (ISBN 0-8431-4702-4); incl. cass. 8.95 (ISBN 0-8431-1983-7). Price Stern.
Wee Sing & Play. Pamela Beall & Susan Nipp. (Wee Sing Ser.). (Illus.). (ps-6). 1983. pap. 8.95 (ISBN 0-8431-0743-X); cassette incl. Price Stern.
Wee Sing Around the Campfire. Pamela Beall & Susan Nipp. (Wee Sing Ser.). (Illus.). 64p. (ps-6). 1983. pap. 8.95 (ISBN 0-8431-0742-1); cassette incl. Price Stern.
Wee Sing Australia. (Wee Color Ser.). (Illus.). (ps-2). 1988. pap. 7.95 (ISBN 0-8431-2320-6); audiocassette incl. Price Stern.
Wee Sing Bible Songs. Pamela C. Beall & Susan H. Nipp. (Wee Sing Ser.). (Illus.). 64p. (ps-2). 1986. pap. 2.25 (ISBN 0-8431-1566-1); book & cassette 8.95 (ISBN 0-8431-1780-X). Price Stern.
Wee Sing Campfire Songs. Pamela Beall. (Wee Sing Ser.). (Illus.). 64p. (Orig.). (ps-2). 1982. pap. 2.25 (ISBN 0-8431-0311-6). Price Stern.
Wee Sing: Childrens' Songs & Fingerplays. Pamela Beall & Susan Nipp. (Wee Sing Ser.). (ps-2). pap. 8.95 (ISBN 0-8431-0522-4); cassette incl. Price Stern.
Wee Sing Dinosaurs. (Wee Color Ser.). (Illus.). 48p. (ps-2). 1988. pap. 7.95 (ISBN 0-8431-2321-4); audiocassette incl. Price Stern.
Wee Sing for Christmas. Pam Beall & Susan Nipp. (Wee Sing Ser.). (Illus.). 64p. (Orig.). (ps-2). 1984. pap. 2.25 (ISBN 0-8431-1197-6). Price Stern.
Wee Sing for Christmas. (Wee Sing Ser.). (ps-2). 1984. incl. cassette 8.95 (ISBN 0-8431-1071-6). Price Stern.
Wee Sing Nursery Rhymes & Lullabies. Pamela C. Beall & Susan H. Nipp. (Wee Sing Ser.). (Illus.). 64p. (Orig.). (ps-2). 1985. pap. 8.95 incl. cassette (ISBN 0-8431-1422-3); pap. 2.25 (ISBN 0-8431-1438-X). Price Stern.
Wee Sing over in the Meadow. Pamela C. Beall et al. (Wee Sing Ser.). (Illus.). 64p. (ps). Date not set. 10.95 (ISBN 0-8431-1949-7); incl. cass. 14.95 (ISBN 0-8431-1978-0). Price Stern.
Wee Sing Silly Songs. Pamela C. Beall & Susan H. Nipp. (Wee Sing Ser.). (Illus.). 64p. (ps-6). 1983. pap. 8.95 incl. cass. (ISBN 0-8431-0310-8). Price Stern.
Wee Sing Together. Pamela C. Beall & Susan H. Nipp. (We Sing Ser.). (Illus.). (ps-2). 1987. 21.95 (ISBN 0-8431-1444-4); incl. audiocassette soundtrack 24.94 (ISBN 0-8431-1831-8). Price Stern.
Wee Sing Together. (Wee Color Ser.). (Illus.). 48p. (ps-2). 1988. pap. 7.95 (ISBN 0-8431-2322-2); audiocassette incl. Price Stern.
Wee TV - Black Children & Television, Prime Time & Daytime: A History & Bibliography. George Hill. 60p. 1987. text ed. 12.00 (ISBN 0-933650-10-8); pap. text ed. 7.50 (ISBN 0-933650-11-6). Daystar Co Carson.
Wee Willie Winkie. Rudyard Kipling. Intro. by Hugh Haughton. 432p. 1988. pap. 5.95 (ISBN 0-14-043303-1). Penguin.
Wee Wonders of Nature. Blonder. (Wee Pudgy Board Bks.). (gr. 2 up). 1988. 2.50 (ISBN 0-448-09254-9, G&D). Putnam Pub Group.
Wee Workout. Illus. by Cristina Ong. LC 86-60288. (Gymboree Board Bks.). (Illus.). 12p. (ps-1). 1986. 2.95 (ISBN 0-394-88203-2, BYR). Random.
Weed: Adventures of a Dope Smuggler. Jerry Kamstra. LC 73-18665. (Illus.). 352p. 1983. pap. 9.95 (ISBN 0-915520-62-1). Ross-Erikson.
Weed: Adventures of a Dope Smuggler. rev. ed. Jerry Kamstra. (Illus.). 352p. (YA) (gr. 12). pap. text ed. 10.00 (ISBN 0-9617715-0-X). Peer Amid Pr.
Weed & the Winter Solstice: Confessions of a Soul Apart. Howard Cook. LC 88-80845. 384p. 1988. 18.50 (ISBN 0-938212-02-8). Friendly City.
Weed Control. 3.95 (ISBN 0-686-21165-0). Bklyn Botanic.
Weed Control Economics. Ed. by B. A. Auld et al. (Applied Botany & Crop Science Ser.). 177p. 1987. 44.00 (ISBN 0-12-068278-8). Acad Pr.
Weed Control in Limited-Tillage Systems. Ed. & intro. by A. F. Wiese. 298p. 1985. text ed. 22.50. Weed Sci Soc.
Weed Control Methods for Public Health Applications. Edward O. Gangstad. 320p. 1980. 99.00 (ISBN 0-8493-5326-2). CRC Pr.
Weed Control Methods for Recreation Facility Management. Edward O. Gangstad. 312p. 1982. 99.00 (ISBN 0-8493-5330-0). CRC Pr.
Weed Control Methods for Rights of Way Management. Ed. by Edward O. Gangstad. 1981. 99.00 (ISBN 0-8493-5329-7). CRC Pr.
Weed Control Methods for River Basin Management. Ed. by Edward O. Gangstad. 232p. 1978. 79.00 (ISBN 0-8493-5328-9). CRC Pr.
Weed Control on Vine & Soft Fruits: Proceedings. Ed. by R. Cavalloro & D. W. Robinson. 176p. 1987. text ed. 33.50 (ISBN 90-6191-691-7, Pub. by A A Balkema). Brookfield Pub Co.
Weed Eaters Cook Book. rev., 2nd ed. Cora G. Chase. (Illus.). 66p. 1981. pap. 5.95 (ISBN 0-933992-18-1). Coffee Break.
Weed Ecology: Implications for Vegetation Management. Steven R. Radosevich & Jodie S. Holt. LC 83-23249. 265p. 1984. 44.50 (ISBN 0-471-87674-7, Pub. by Wiley-Interscience). Wiley.
Weed Flora of Egypt: A Practical Guide. Loutfy Boulos & M. Nabil El-Hadidi. 1985. pap. 17.00x (ISBN 977-424-038-3, Pub. by Am Univ Cairo Pr). Columbia U Pr.
Weed Flora of Kashmir Valley. M. K. Srinagar. 422p. 1886. 120.00x (ISBN 81-85046-28-X, Pub. by Scientific). State Mutual Bk.
Weed for Burning. Conrad Detrez. Tr. by Lydia Davis. LC 83-22844. 256p. 1984. 13.95 (ISBN 0-15-195596-4). HarbraceJ.
Weed Garden. Lewis Turco. 1973. pap. 2.50 (ISBN 0-317-43230-3). Mathom.
Weed Identification Handbook. University of California Staff. (Illus.). 231p. 3-ring binder 65.00 (ISBN 0-317-54019-X). Thomson Pubns.
Weed Is a Flower: The Life of George Washington Carver. Aliki. (Illus.). 32p. (ps-3). 1988. PLB 12.95 (ISBN 0-671-66118-3, Juveniles); pap. 5.95 (ISBN 0-671-66490-5, Juveniles). S&S.
Weed King & Other Stories. Jack Conroy. LC 85-5438. 312p. 1985. 17.95 (ISBN 0-88208-185-3); pap. 9.95 (ISBN 0-88208-186-1). Chicago Review.
Weed Management in Agroecosystems: Ecological Approaches, 2 vols. Ed. by Miguel Altieri & Matthew Z. Liebman. 1988. Vol. I, 192p. 185.00 (ISBN 0-8493-6816-2, 6816); Vol. II, 176p. cancelled (ISBN 0-8493-6817-0, 6817). CRC Pr.
Weed Physiology. Ed. by Stephen O. Duke. 1985. Vol. I: Reproduction & Ecophysiology, 176p. 79.00 (ISBN 0-8493-6313-6); Vol. II: Herbicide Physiology, 272p. 89.00 (ISBN 0-8493-6314-4). CRC Pr.
Weed Science & Weed Control in Southeast Asia. J. T. Swarbrick & B. L. Mercado. (Plant Production & Protection Paper: No. 81). 203p. (Orig.). 1987. pap. 20.25 (ISBN 92-5-102588-6, F3138, FAO). UNIPUB.
Weed Science in the Tropics. I. Okezie Akobundu et al. LC 87-8128. 1988. 90.00 (ISBN 0-471-91544-0). Wiley.
Weed Science: Principles. 2nd ed. Wood P. Anderson. (Illus.). 655p. 1983. text ed. 49.25 (ISBN 0-314-69632-6). West Pub.
Weed Science: Principles & Practices. 2nd ed. Glenn C. Klingman & Floyd M. Ashton. LC 82-2750. 449p. 1982. text ed. 26.50x (ISBN 0-471-08487-5, Pub. by Wiley-Interscience). Wiley.
Weeding & Sowing: Preface to a Science of Mathematical Education. Hans Freudenthal. ix, 314p. 1980. lib. bdg. 47.50 (ISBN 90-277-0789-8, Pub. by Reidel Holland); pap. 15.00 (ISBN 90-277-1072-4). Kluwer Academic.
Weeding Library Collections II. 2nd, rev. ed. Stanley J. Slote. LC 81-20724. 198p. 1982. text ed. 23.50 (ISBN 0-87287-283-1). Libs Unl.
Weeding of Collections in Sci-Tech Libraries. Ed. by Ellis Mount. LC 85-27010. (Science & Technology Libraries: Vol. 6, No. 3). 164p. 1986. text ed. 24.95 (ISBN 0-86656-552-3). Haworth Pr.
Weeding of Covent Garden & the Sparagus Garden. Richard Brome. Ed. by Donald S. McClure & Stephen Orgel. LC 79-54351. (Renaissance Drama Second Ser.). 438p. 1980. lib. bdg. 61.00 (ISBN 0-8240-4468-1). Garland Pub.
Weeding Out the Target Population: The Law of Accountability in a Manpower Program. James Latimore. LC 84-8952. (Contributions in Sociology Ser.: No. 54). (Illus.). x, 176p. 1985. lib. bdg. 35.00 (ISBN 0-313-24495-2, LWT/). Greenwood.
Weeding the Duchess. Sarah Maclay. 1979. pap. 5.00 (ISBN 0-686-71066-5). Black Stone.
Weeds. Edith S. Kelley. 372p. 1982. pap. 8.95 (ISBN 0-935312-01-3). Feminist Pr.
Weeds. Edith S. Kelley. LC 72-75333. (Lost American Fiction Ser.). 349p. 1972. 7.95 (ISBN 0-8093-0587-9). S Ill U Pr.
Weeds. Alexander C. Martin. (Golden Guide Ser.). (Illus.). 160p. (gr. 7 up). 1973. pap. 3.95 (ISBN 0-307-24353-2, Golden Pr). Western Pub.
Weeds. 2nd ed. Walter C. Muenscher. LC 79-48017. (Illus.). 560p. 1980. 39.95x (ISBN 0-8014-1266-8, Comstock Pub). Cornell U Pr.
Weeds. 2nd ed. Walter C. Muenscher. LC 79-48017. (Illus.). 560p. 1987. pap. 16.95x (ISBN 0-8014-9417-6, Comstock Pub). Cornell U Pr.
Weeds: A Guide for Dyers & Herbalists. Anne Bliss. LC 78-59236. (Illus.). 1978. pap. 6.00x (ISBN 0-931870-01-1). Juniper Hse.
Weeds among the Wheat: Discernment: Where Prayer & Action Meet. Thomas Green. LC 84-70663. 208p. (Orig.). 1984. pap. 4.95 (ISBN 0-87793-318-9). Ave Maria.
Weeds: An Illustrated Botanical Guide to the Weeds of Australia. B. A. Auld & R. W. Medd. (Illus.). 264p. 1986. 65.00x (ISBN 0-909605-37-8, Pub. by Inkata Pr Australia). Intl Spec Bk.
Weeds & Poisonous Plants of Wyoming & Utah. Ed. by Thomas D. Whitson. (Illus.). 284p. (Orig.). 1987. pap. 13.50x (ISBN 0-941570-06-1). U of Wyoming.
Weeds & What They Tell. E. E. Pfeiffer. 96p. 3.50 (ISBN 0-938250-04-3). Bio-Dynamic Farm.
Weeds & Wild Flowers. Illa Podendorf. LC 81-7737. (New True Bks.). (Illus.). 48p. (gr. k-4). 1981. PLB 12.60 (ISBN 0-516-01661-X); pap. 3.95 (ISBN 0-516-41661-8). Childrens.
Weeds & Wildflowers of Eastern North America. T. Merrill Prentice & Elizabeth O. Sargent. 1973. 30.00 (ISBN 0-87577-063-0). Peabody Mus Salem.
Weeds & Words: The Etymology of the Scientific Names of Weeds & Crops. Robert L. Zimdahl. 136p. 1988. text ed. 19.95xt (ISBN 0-8138-0128-1). Iowa St U Pr.
Weeds: Guardians of the Soil. Joseph Cocannouer. (Illus.). pap. 9.95 (ISBN 0-8159-7205-9). Devin.
Weeds in Tropical Crops: Review of Abstracts on Constraints in Production Caused by Weeds in Maize, Rice, Sorghum-Millet, Groundnuts, & Cassava, 1952-1980. Jacqueline M. Benson. (Plant Production & Protection Papers: No. 32, Suppl. 1). 68p. 1982. pap. 7.50 (ISBN 92-5-101206-7, F2333, FAO). UNIPUB.
Weeds in Tropical Crops: Selected Abstracts on Constraints on Production Caused by Weeds in Maize, Rice, Sorghum-Millet, Groundnuts & Cassava, 1952-1980. (Plant Production & Protection Papers: No. 32). 94p. 1981. pap. 7.50 (ISBN 92-5-101146-X, F2288, FAO). UNIPUB.
Weeds in Winter. Lauren Brown. (Illus.). 1986. pap. 7.95 (ISBN 0-393-30348-9). Norton.
Weeds of Canada. Gerald Mulligan & Clarence Frankton. (Illus.). 224p. (Orig.). 1987. pap. 16.95 (ISBN 1-55021-016-5, Pub. by NC Press Ltd). U of Toronto Pr.
Weeds of Lebanon. Winnie Edgecombe. (Illus.). 1970. pap. 20.00x (ISBN 0-8156-6001-4, Am U Beirut). Syracuse U Pr.
Weeds of the United States & Their Control. Harri J. Lorenzi & Larry S. Jeffery. LC 87-2062. (Illus.). 1987. 74.95 (ISBN 0-442-25884-4). AVI.
Weeds? or Wildflowers! Dori J. Somers. LC 87-72456. (Illus.). 110p. (Orig.). 1987. pap. 6.50 (ISBN 0-318-23571-4). Choice Fullerton.
Weegee. Pantheon Photo Library. LC 86-42651. (Illus.). 144p. 1986. pap. 7.95 (ISBN 0-394-74785-2). Pantheon.
Weegee by Weegee: An Autobiography. Weegee & Mel Harris. LC 75-4885. (Photography Ser.). (Illus.). 224p. 1975. Repr. of 1961 ed. lib. bdg. 27.50 (ISBN 0-306-70737-3). Da Capo.
Weegee's New York: Photographs, Nineteen Thirty-Five to Nineteen Sixty. (Illus.). 334p. 1984. 60.00 (ISBN 0-394-53875-7). Grove.
Weegee's People. Weegee, pseud. LC 75-4846. (Illus.). 242p. 1975. Repr. of 1946 ed. lib. bdg. 27.50 (ISBN 0-306-70723-3). Da Capo.
Weegee's People. Weegee, pseud. (Quality Paperbacks Ser.). (Illus.). 242p. 1985. pap. 13.50 (ISBN 0-306-80242-2). Da Capo.
Weehawken Ferry. Ed Ochester. (W.N.J. Ser.: No. 21). 1985. Signed Edition. 20.00 (ISBN 1-55780-088-X); pap. 7.00 (ISBN 1-55780-070-7). Juniper Pr WI.
Week. Francis H. Colson. LC 73-7697. 126p. 1974. Repr. of 1926 ed. lib. bdg. 40.00x (ISBN 0-8371-6940-2, CTHW). Greenwood.
Week-End Athletes' Guide to Sports Medicine: Lower Body. James. Key. Ed. by Ellington Darden. LC 77-76073. (Physical Fitness & Sports Medicine Ser). (Illus.). 1978. pap. 4.95 (ISBN 0-89305-015-6). Anna Pub.
Week-End Athletes' Guide to Sports Medicine: Upper Body. James D. Key. Ed. by Ellington Darden. LC 77-76073. (Physical Fitness & Sports Medicine Ser.). (Illus.). 1978. pap. 3.95 (ISBN 0-89305-016-4). Anna Pub.
Week-End Book of Humor. facs. ed. Ed. by P. G. Wodehouse & Scott Meredith. LC 71-134162. (Essay Index Reprint Ser.). 1952. 17.00 (ISBN 0-8369-2094-5). Ayer Co Pubs.
Week-End Gold Miner. 1987. 2.50 (ISBN 0-935182-03-9). Gembooks.
Week-End Pilot. Frank K. Smith. LC 74-5195. 1974. pap. 4.95 (ISBN 0-394-71069-X, Vin). Random.
Week in South Dakota. Gary Gildner. (Bright Leaf Short Fiction Ser.: No. IV). 208p. 1987. 14.95 (ISBN 0-912697-43-1). Algonquin Bks.

TITLE INDEX

WEIGHT GROUP THERAPIST: SPIRITUAL

Week in the Life of Best Friends. Beatrice Schenk de Regniers. (Illus.). 48p. (gr. 2-7). 1988. pap. 2.50 (ISBN 0-590-41461-5). Scholastic Inc.
Week in the Life of Best Friends: And Other Poems of Friendship. Beatrice S. De Regniers. LC 85-28680. (Illus.). 47p. (gr. 4-6). 1986. 11.95 (ISBN 0-689-31179-6, Atheneum Childrens Bks). Macmillan.
Week in the Middle East: An Arabic Language Reader. F. A. Pragnell. 208p. (Arabic & Eng.). 1984. pap. text ed. 19.95 (ISBN 0-85331-473-X, Pub. Lund Humphries Pubs UK). Humanities.
Week in the Woods. Heather S. Thomas. Ed. by Raymond H. Woolsey. 64p. (gr. 2-4). 1988. pap. price not set (ISBN 0-8280-0435-8). Review & Herald.
Week Is a Long Time. Pat Barton. (Illus.). 28p. 1.95 (ISBN 0-200-72464-9). Academy Chi Pubs.
Week Mom Unplugged the TVs. Terry W. Phelan. (Illus.). 48p. (gr. 2-5). 1988. pap. 3.95 (ISBN 0-936915-09-9). McDonald Shoe Tree Pr.
Week of Dream Horses. Dorothy Fletcher. (Envelope Bks.). (Illus.). (YA) (gr. 7-9). 1984. pap. 2.50 (ISBN 0-88138-017-2). Green Tiger Pr.
Week of Lullabies. Helen Plotz. LC 86-18458. (Illus.). 32p. (ps-3). 1988. 11.95 (ISBN 0-688-06652-6); lib. bdg. 11.88 (ISBN 0-688-06653-4). Greenwillow.
Week of Raccoons. Gloria Whelan. LC 87-16800. (Illus.). 40p. (ps-1). 1988. 11.95 (ISBN 0-394-88396-9); lib. bdg. 12.99 (ISBN 0-394-98396-3). Knopf.
Week on the Concord & Merimack Rivers. Henry David Thoreau. 504p. 1987. pap. 9.95 (ISBN 0-940160-36-6). Parnassus Imprints.
Week on the Concord & Merrimack Rivers see Week, Walden, Maine Woods, Cape Cod.
Week on the Concord & Merrimack Rivers see Writings of Henry D. Thoreau.
Week That Changed the World. Ernest C. Wilson. 1968. 5.95 (ISBN 0-87159-170-7). Unity School.
Week, Walden, Maine Woods, Cape Cod. Henry David Thoreau. Ed. by Robert Sayre. Incl. Week on the Concord & Merrimack Rivers; Walden; Maine Woods; Cape Cod. LC 85-5175. 1114p. 1985. 27.50 (ISBN 0-940450-27-5). Library of America.
Weekday Early Education: Art Idea Book. Patricia Elkins. LC 77-87252. (Illus.). 1978. spiral bdg 8.50 (ISBN 0-8054-4919-1, 4249-19). Broadman.
Weekday Prayer Book. expanded ed. Morris Silverman & United Synagogue. 8.95x (ISBN 0-87677-071-5). Prayer Bk.
Weekday Prayerbook. 6.25 (ISBN 0-686-96031-9). United Syn Bk.
Weekday Speech Activities to Promote Carryover. Roberta Fehling. 41p. 1986. text ed. 11.95x (ISBN 0-8134-2500-X). Inter Print Pubs.
Weekend. Christopher Pike. 230p. (Orig.). (gr. 7 up). 1986. pap. 2.50 (ISBN 0-590-40753-8, Point). Scholastic Inc.
Weekend. Marlene F. Shyer. Date not set. pap. 3.95. Warner Bks.
Weekend Adventures for City-Weary People: Overnight Trips in Northern California. rev. ed. Carole T. Meyers. LC 83-26139. (Weekend Adventures for City-Weary People in the U. S. A. Ser.). (Illus.). 1984. pap. 11.95 (ISBN 0-917120-07-8). Carousel Pr.
Weekend Adventures for City-Weary People: Overnight Trips in Northern California. 4th, rev. ed. Carole T. Meyers. (Illus.). 250p. 1988. pap. 10.95 (ISBN 0-917120-09-4). Carousel Pr.
Weekend Afghans. Jean Leinhauser & Rita Weiss. (Illus.). 128p. 1987. 19.95 (ISBN 0-8069-6486-3). Sterling.
Weekend at Muskrat Lake. Nicki Weiss. LC 83-20789. (Illus.). 32p. (gr. k-3). 1984. 11.50 (ISBN 0-688-03767-4); PLB 10.51 (ISBN 0-688-03768-2). Greenwillow.
Weekend Athlete. Time-Life Books Editors. (Fitness, Health & Nutrition Ser.). (Illus.). 144p. 1989. 17.27 (ISBN 0-8094-6138-2); lib. bdg. 21.27 (ISBN 0-8094-6139-0). Time-Life.
Weekend Dog. Myrna M. Milani. 1985. pap. 3.50 (ISBN 0-451-13570-9, Sig). NAL.
Weekend Entertainer Cookbook. Carolyn Schlemme. LC 86-51110. (Great American Cookbook Ser.). 184p. 1987. pap. 5.95 (ISBN 0-89914-020-3). Third Party Pub.
Weekend Fathers. Gerald A. Silver & Myrna Silver. 224p. 1986. pap. 3.95 (ISBN 0-425-08740-9). Berkley Pub.
Weekend for Love. Glenna Finley. 1984. pap. 2.25 (ISBN 0-451-12971-7, Sig). NAL.
Weekend Galley. Charlene McCaull. (Illus.). 56p. 1984. pap. 6.95 (ISBN 0-916669-01-7). Alcyone Pubns.
Weekend Gardener. Peter McHoy. LC 86-12059. 192p. 1987. 19.95i (ISBN 0-06-015674-0, HarpT). Har-Row.
Weekend in Dinlock. Clancy Sigal. 1976. pap. 1.65 (ISBN 0-380-01463-7, 12229, Bard). Avon.
Weekend in September. John E. Weems. LC 79-7415. (Illus.). 192p. 1980. pap. 12.95 (ISBN 0-89096-097-6). Tex A&M Univ Pr.
Weekend in the Country. Lee Lorenz. (Illus.). 32p. (gr. k-3). 1985. 11.95 (ISBN 0-13-947961-9). P-H.
Weekend in the Country. Lee Lorenz. (Illus.). 32p. (ps-3). 1987. pap. 4.95 (ISBN 0-13-948191-5, Juveniles). S&S.
Weekend in the Country. Lee Lorenz. (Illus.). (gr. k-4). 1988. pap. 4.95 (ISBN 0-317-69450-2, Little Simon). S&S.
Weekend in the Dunes. H. R. Sheffer. Ed. by Howard Schroeder. LC 80-28624. (Teamates Ser.). (Illus.). 48p. (gr. 3 up). 1981. PLB 7.95 (ISBN 0-89686-109-0). Crestwood Hse.
Weekend Journeys. The Philadelphia Inquirer Staff. (Illus.). 336p. (Orig.). 1988. pap. 9.95 (ISBN 0-912608-59-5). Mid Atlantic.
Weekend Mechanic's Handbook: Complete Auto Repairs You Can Make. rev. ed. Paul Weissler. LC 82-3992. (Illus.). 480p. 1982. 19.95 (ISBN 0-668-05379-8); pap. 12.95 (ISBN 0-668-05384-4). Arco.
Weekend Mechanic's Handbook: Complete Auto Repairs You Can Make. rev. ed. Paul Weissler. (Illus.). 480p. 1987. pap. 15.95 (ISBN 0-13-948100-1). P-H.
Weekend Navigator. Bruce Fraser. 1981. 18.50 (ISBN 0-8286-0090-2). J De Graff.
Weekend of Fear. Virginia Nielsen. 176p. (Orig.). (gr. 7 up). 1984. pap. 2.25 (ISBN 0-590-41815-7, Windswept Bks). Scholastic Inc.
Weekend Prospecting. Roy Lagal. Ed. by Hal Dawson. LC 88-60012. (Illus.). 82p. (Orig.). 1988. pap. 3.95 (ISBN 0-915920-48-4). Ram Pub.
Weekend Quilter. Leslie Linsley. (Illus.). 160p. 1986. 19.95 (ISBN 0-312-86016-1). St Martin.
Weekend Real Estate Investor. Weston P. Hatfield. (McGraw-Hill Paperback Ser.). 228p. 1982. pap. text ed. 5.95 (ISBN 0-07-027024-4). McGraw.
Weekend Real Estate Investor: The New Low-Risk Team Approach That Transforms Everyday Opportunities into Big Profits. Weston P. Hatfield. 1978. text ed. 9.95 (ISBN 0-07-027023-6). McGraw.
Weekend Sisters. Hila Coleman. (gr. 6 up). 1988. pap. 2.95 (ISBN 0-449-70206-5, Juniper). Fawcett.
Weekend Sisters. Hila Colman. LC 85-5665. 192p. (gr. 7 up). 1985. 10.25 (ISBN 0-688-05785-3, Morrow Junior Books). Morrow.
Weekend Tennis: How to Have Fun & Win at the Same Time. Bill Talbert. pap. 3.00 (ISBN 0-87980-277-4). Wilshire.
Weekend Vacation. Ken Girard. 58p. 1987. pap. 3.95 (ISBN 0-8224-2336-7). D S Lake Pubs.
Weekend Visit. LC 84-73542. 1985. pap. 5.95 (ISBN 0-394-62014-3, E-986, Ever). Grove.
Weekend Visit. 1988. pap. 4.50 (ISBN 0-8216-5031-9). Blue Moon Bks.
Weekend Walking: A Selection of 50 Fully Planned Routes for Exploring Britain on Foot. Roger Smith. 254p. (Orig.). 1984. pap. 6.95 (ISBN 0-600-20443-X, Pub. by Automobile Assn Brit). Salem Hse Pubs.
Weekend Warriors: Alcohol in a Micronesian Culture. Mac Marshall. Ed. by Robert B. Edgerton & L. L. Langness. LC 78-64597. 1979. pap. 9.95 (ISBN 0-87484-455-X). Mayfield Pub.
Weekend Was Murder: Homicide As Entertainment. Susan Casey. 240p. (Orig.). 1987. pap. 5.95 (ISBN 0-15-695300-5, Harv). HarBraceJ.
Weekend Wings: The Complete Adventures of the Original Weekend Pilot. Frank K. Smith. 1982. 13.45 (ISBN 0-394-52527-2). Random.
Weekend with Claude. Beryl Bainbridge. LC 81-17965. 152p. 1982. 10.95 (ISBN 0-8076-1031-3). Braziller.
Weekend with Wendell. Kevin Henkes. LC 85-24822. (Illus.). 32p. (ps-3). 1986. 11.75 (ISBN 0-688-06325-X); PLB 11.88 (ISBN 0-688-06326-8). Greenwillow.
Weekend with Wendell. Kevin Henkes. (ps-3). 1987. pap. 3.95 (ISBN 0-14-050728-0, Puffin Bks). Penguin.
Weekend Wood Project for Toymakers. Jeff Burke et al. (Illus.). 144p. 1987. 18.95 (ISBN 0-8069-6602-5); pap. 9.95 (ISBN 0-8069-6494-4). Sterling.
Weekender's Gardening Manual: Easy-Care Gardens in Two Hours (Or Less!) a Week. Patricia A. Taylor. LC 85-21856. (Illus.). 144p. 1986. 19.95 (ISBN 0-03-006329-9). H Holt & Co.
Weekender's Guide to the Four Seasons. 8th ed. Robert Shosteck. Ed. by Susan C. Dore. 1988. pap. 11.95 (ISBN 0-88289-701-2). Pelican.
Weekending in New England. Betsy Wittemann & Nancy Webster. LC 80-80817. (Illus.). 242p. 1984. pap. 8.95 (ISBN 0-934260-58-3). Wood Pond.
Weekends for Two. June H. Marquis. LC 84-80984. 128p. 1984. pap. 5.95 (ISBN 0-89709-135-3). Liberty Pub.
Weekly Occidental, Nevada's First Literary Journal. Ed. by Dave Basso. 36p. 1988. text ed. 169.00 (ISBN 0-936332-09-3). Falcon Hill Pr.
Weekly on the Wabash. Wheeler McMillen. LC 69-15328. (New Horizons in Journalism Ser.). 256p. 1969. 5.95x (ISBN 0-8093-0364-7). S Ill U Pr.
Weekly Political Intelligence Summaries, 1939-1947: Great Britain, Foreign Office, 16 vols. LC 82-49004. (Orig.). 1983. Set. lib. bdg. 1050.00x (ISBN 0-527-35749-9). Kraus Intl.
Weekly Quiz Bowl Questions 1986: With Emphasis on the News. John Campbell. Ed. by Rinda Brewbaker. 452p. (Orig.). (YA) (gr. 7-8). 1987. pap. 15.95 (ISBN 0-9609412-9-0). Patricks Pr.
Weekly Reader: Sixty Years of News for Kids. Ed. by Weekly Reader Editors. (Illus.). 256p. (ps-6). 1988. 21.95 (ISBN 0-88687-373-8); pap. 11.95 (ISBN 0-88687-365-7). Pharos Bks NY.
Weekly Review, Vols. 1-8, No. 27. 1969. Repr. of 1943 ed. Vols. 1-3. lib. bdg. 47.00 (ISBN 0-313-21958-3, WR01); Vol. 4. lib. bdg. 47.00 (ISBN 0-313-21959-1, WR04); Vol. 5. lib. bdg. 91.00 (ISBN 0-313-21960-5, WR05); Vol. 6. lib. bdg. 91.00 (ISBN 0-313-21961-3, WR06); Vol. 7. lib. bdg. 91.00 (ISBN 0-313-21962-1, WR07); Vol. 8. lib. bdg. 91.00 (ISBN 0-313-21963-X, WR08). Greenwood.
Weekly Wages by Direct Credit. British Computer Society Staff. 1979. pap. 44.95 (ISBN 0-471-25613-7, Wiley Heyden). Wiley.
Weeks Hall Tapes. Morris Raphael. LC 83-91286. 90p. (Orig.). pap. 7.95 (ISBN 0-9608866-2-1). M Raphael.
Weeks Hall: The Master of the Shadows. Morris Raphael. LC 81-90439. (Illus.). 207p. (gr. 5-12). 1981. 14.95 (ISBN 0-9608866-1-3). M Raphael.
Weeks Tramp in Dickens Land: Together with Personal Reminiscences of the 'Inimitable Box' Therein Collected. William R. Hughes. (Illus.). 432p. 1982. Repr. of 1891 ed. lib. bdg. 100.00 (ISBN 0-89987-382-0). Darby Bks.
WEEKSA Electronic Data Communications. McKay. (What Every Engineer Should Know Ser.). 248p. 1988. 39.75 (ISBN 0-8247-8008-6). Dekker.
Weeny Witch. Ida DeLage. LC 68-10173. (Old Witch Bks.). (Illus.). (gr. k-4). 1968. PLB 6.69 (ISBN 0-8116-4052-3). Garrard.
Weep, Moscow, Weep. (Phoenix Force Ser.: No. 27). Date not set. pap. 2.25 (Pub. by Worldwide). Harlequin Bks.
Weep No More, My Brother. Sterling Watson. 1989. pap. 7.95 (ISBN 0-440-55025-4, Delta). Dell.
Weep No More, My Lady. Mary H. Clark. 1987. 17.95 (ISBN 0-671-55664-9). S&S.
Weep No More, My Lady. Mary Higgins Clark. 1988. pap. 4.95 (ISBN 0-440-20098-9). Dell.
Weep Not Child. Ngugi. (African Writers Ser.). 1964. pap. text ed. 7.00 (ISBN 0-435-90830-8). Heinemann Ed.
Weep Not for Me. Moultrie Guerry. viii, 43p. 1984. pap. 2.95 (ISBN 0-918769-14-0). Univ South.
Weep Not for Me. John V. Taylor. LC 86-71639. 64p. 1987. pap. 3.95 (ISBN 0-89622-313-2). Twenty-Third.
Weep Not for Me: Meditations on the Cross & the Resurrection. John V. Taylor. (Risk Book Ser.). 56p. 1986. pap. 3.50 (ISBN 2-8254-0850-6). Wrld Coun Churches.
Weep Some More, My Lady. Sigmund Spaeth. LC 80-11295. (Music Reprint Ser.). (Illus.). xv, 268p. 1980. Repr. of 1927 ed. lib. bdg. 35.00 (ISBN 0-306-76003-7). Da Capo.
Weepeeple: A Unique Adventure in Crafts in America. Ed Baldwin & Stevie Baldwin. (Illus.). 160p. 1983. 17.95 (ISBN 0-399-12813-1, Putnam). Putnam Pub Group.
Weeping & the Laughter. Noel Barber. 384p. 1988. 17.95 (ISBN 0-07-003657-8). McGraw.
Weeping Church: Confronting the Crisis of Church Polity. Clayton Nuttall. LC 85-10760. 1985. pap. 5.95 (ISBN 0-87227-104-8). Reg Baptist.
Weeping Crab. Iefke Goldberger. 36p. (Orig.). 1984. pap. 4.95 (ISBN 0-913370-16-9, Sol Press). Wisconsin Bks.
Weeping Ghost. Evelyn Wray. (YA) (gr. 9-12). 1985. 9.95 (ISBN 0-8034-8509-3, Avalon). Bouregy.
Weeping in Ramah. J. R. Lucas. LC 85-70477. 250p. (Orig.). 1985. pap. 7.95 (ISBN 0-89107-357-4, Crossway Bks). Good News.
Weeping in the Playtime of Others: The Plight of Incarcerated Children. Kenneth Wooden. 1976. pap. text ed. 6.95 (ISBN 0-07-071643-9). McGraw.
Weeping Mist. Jenna Mallow. 1985. 24.95x (ISBN 0-7090-1841-X, Pub. by R Hale Ltd UK). State Mutual Bk.
Weeping Season. Gauri Pant. (Redbird Bk.). 36p. 1975. 4.80 (ISBN 0-88253-717-2); pap. 4.00 (ISBN 0-88253-847-0). Ind-US Inc.
Weeping Woman: Encounters with La Llorona. Ed. by Edward G. Kraul & Judith Beatty. LC 88-50347. (Illus.). 120p. (Orig.). 1988. pap. 9.95 (ISBN 0-945937-06-7). Word Process.
Weepy. Ted Carroll. LC 87-62713. 112p. 1987. pap. 7.95 (ISBN 0-934040-26-5). Quality Ohio.
WEESKA Engineering Information Resources. Schenk & Webster. (What Every Engineer Should Know Ser.). 176p. 1984. 29.75 (ISBN 0-8247-7244-X). Dekker.
WEESKA Engineering Work Stations. Harlow. (What Every Engineer Should Know Ser.). 224p. 1986. 29.75 (ISBN 0-8247-7509-0). Dekker.
WEESKA Patenets. Konold et al. (What Every Engineer Should Know Ser.). 168p. 1988. 39.75 (ISBN 0-8247-8010-8). Dekker.
WEESKA Quality Control. (What Every Engineer Should Know Ser.). 248p. 1988. 39.75 (ISBN 0-8247-7966-5). Dekker.
Weetman Pearson, First Viscount Cowdray, 1856-1927. John A. Spender. Ed. by Mira Wilkins. LC 76-40616. (European Business Ser.). (Illus.). 1977. Repr. of 1930 ed. lib. bdg. 29.00 (ISBN 0-405-09801-4). Ayer Co Pubs.
Weeuns Journey of Two Cousins. Beatrice Tallarico & S. Callis Stone. (Illus.). 39p. (gr. 2-8). 1984. 12.95 (ISBN 0-936191-13-9). Tallstone Pub.
Weevils. Georgianne Heymann. (Nature Close-Ups Ser.). (Illus.). 32p. (gr. 3-4). 1986. PLB 15.33 (ISBN 0-8172-2713-X); pap. text ed. 9.27 (ISBN 0-8172-2731-8). Raintree Pubs.
Weevils in the Wheat: Interviews with Virginia Ex-Slaves. Ed. by Charles L. Perdue, Jr. et al. LC 79-65433. (Midland Bks.: No. 237). (Illus.). 456p. 1980. pap. 8.95x (ISBN 0-253-20237-X). Ind U Pr.
Weft Twining. Virginia I. Harvey & Harriet Tidball. LC 76-24017. (Shuttle Craft Guild Monograph: No. 28). (Illus.). 39p. 1969. pap. 7.45 (ISBN 0-916658-28-7). Shuttle Craft.
Weg der Mathematischen Grundlagenforschung. Heinz Bachmann. 240p. (Ger.). 1985. 16.50 (ISBN 3-261-05089-6). P Lang Pubs.
Weg Zum Lesen. Van Horn Vail & Kimberly Sparks. 288p. (Ger.). 1986. pap. text ed. 14.00 net (ISBN 0-15-517351-0, Pub. by HC); net cassettes 32.00 (ISBN 0-15-517352-9). HarBraceJ.
Wege ins Alte Testament - und Zurueck: Vom Sinn und den Moeglichkeiten einer "Theologie mit dem Alten Testament" in der Arbeit mit Erwachsenen, Vol 211. Heinrich Dickerhoff. (European University Studies: No. 23). 409p. (Ger.). 1983. 40.55 (ISBN 3-8204-7734-9). P Lang Pubs.
Wei Shih Er Shih Lun: Or, the Treatise in Twenty Stanzas on Representation Only. Vasu-Bandhu. (American Oriental Ser.: Vol. 13). 1938. pap. 16.00 (ISBN 0-527-02687-5). Kraus Repr.
Wei Yuan & China's Rediscovery of the Maritime World. Jane K. Leonard. (Harvard East Asian Monographs: No. 111). (Illus.). 300p. 1983. 20.00x. Harvard E Asian.
Weibliche Muse: Sechs Essays uber kunstlerisch Schaffende Frauen der Goethezeit. Helene Kastinger-Riley. LC 81-69883. (Studies in German Literature, Linguistics, & Culture: Vol. 8). (Illus.). 300p. 1986. 29.00x (ISBN 0-938100-05-X). Camden Hse.
Weider Body Book. Betty Weider & Joe Weider. (Illus.). 224p. (Orig.). 1984. pap. 12.95 (ISBN 0-8092-5429-8). Contemp Bks.
Weider Book of Bodybuilding for Women. Betty Weider & Joe Weider. (Illus.). 160p. (Orig.). 1981. pap. 8.95 (ISBN 0-8092-5906-0). Contemp Bks.
Weider System of Bodybuilding. Joe Weider. Ed. by Bill Reynolds. (Illus.). 224p. (Orig.). 1983. pap. 12.95 (ISBN 0-8092-5559-6). Contemp Bks.
Weiga of Temagami. facs. ed. Cy Warman. LC 76-140346. (Short Story Index Reprint Ser.). 1908. 17.00 (ISBN 0-8369-3738-4). Ayer Co Pubs.
Weigher. Jack Rudman. (Career Examination Ser.: C-2674). (Cloth bdg. avail. on request). pap. 12.00 (ISBN 0-8373-2674-5). Natl Learning.
Weighing. (Tops Cards Ser.: No. 5). 1978. pap. 8.30 (ISBN 0-941008-05-3). Tops Learning.
Weighing an Elephant. 1981. pap. 3.95 (ISBN 0-8351-0893-7). China Bks.
Weighing & Proportioning of Bulk Solids. 2nd ed. Hendrik Colijn. LC 74-77792. (Bulk Materials Handling Ser.: Vol. 3). (Illus.). 362p. 1983. 60.00 (ISBN 0-87849-047-7, Trans Tech Germany). Trans Tech.
Weighing & Proportioning of Bulk Solids. 2nd ed. Hendrik Colijn. LC 83-81909. (Illus.). 412p. 1984. 60.00x (ISBN 0-87201-914-4). Gulf Pub.
Weighing the Planets. Olivia Parker. LC 87-81294. (Untitled Ser.: No. 44). (Illus.). 56p. (Orig.). 1987. pap. 22.00 (ISBN 0-933286-49-X). Friends Photography.
Weighing the Planets. Olivia Parker. (Illus.). 1987. 40.00 (ISBN 0-8212-1667-8). NYGS.
Weight. Henry Pluckrose. Ed. by Franklin Watts Ltd. (Knowabouts Ser.). (Illus.). 32p. (ps-6). 1988. 9.90 (ISBN 0-531-10525-3). Watts.
Weight & Height of Adults 18-74 Years of Age: United States, 1971-1974. Sidney Abraham et al. Ed. by Karen Akers. (Series II: No. 211). 1978. pap. text ed. 1.75 (ISBN 0-8406-0142-5). Natl Ctr Health.
Weight & Weightlessness. Franklyn M. Branley. LC 70-132292. (Let's-Read-&-Find-Out Science Bks.). (Illus.). (gr. k-3). 1972. PLB 12.89 (ISBN 0-690-87329-8, Crowell Jr Bks). HarpJ.
Weight by Height & Age for Adults, 18-74 Years, United States, 1971-1974. Sidney Abraham et al. Ed. by Klaudia Cox. (Ser. 11: No. 208). 1978. pap. text ed. 1.75 (ISBN 0-8406-0141-7). Natl Ctr Health Stats.
Weight Control. Robert F. Allen. (Lifegain Program for Changing Our Health Cultures Ser.). 31p. 1981. pap. 5.95 (ISBN 0-318-03837-4). Human Res Inst.
Weight Control: A Guide for Counselors & Therapists. Ed. by Aaron M. Atlschul. LC 87-11725. 305p. 1987. lib. bdg. 45.00 (ISBN 0-275-92697-4, C2697). Praeger.
Weight Control: A Nutritional Approach. Louise Tenney. (Todays Health Ser.: No. 6). Date not set. pap. 3.95 (ISBN 0-913923-33-8). Woodland UT.
Weight Control: The Behavioural Strategies. Michael D. LeBow. LC 79-41728. (Illus.). 358p. pap. 93.10 (2030527). Bks Demand UMI.
Weight Control with Asian Foods. Kay Shimizu. (Illus.). 92p. 1975. pap. 6.50 (ISBN 4-07-972252-4, Pub. by Shufunotomo Co Ltd Japan). C E Tuttle.
Weight Group Therapist: Spiritual Gifts. large type ed. Prophet Pearl. 32p. 1984. pap. 6.00 (ISBN 0-914009-16-8). VHI Library.

Weight Lifting & Progressive Resistance Exercise. Jim Murray. pap. 23.80 (ISBN 0-317-28592-0, 2055167). Bks Demand UMI.
Weight Loss & Nutrition. Health Media of America. (Health Media of America Nutrition Ser.). (Illus.). 80p. 1986. pap. 3.95 (ISBN 0-937325-07-4). Health Med Amer.
Weight Loss for the Middle-Aged Athlete. Bruce C. Vandre. (How to Succeed in Fitness). 192p. (Orig.). 1987. pap. 10.95 (ISBN 0-942223-00-4). VanPress.
Weight Loss from the Inside Out: Help for the Compulsive Eater. Marion Bilich. LC 83-633. 192p. (Orig.). 1983. pap. 9.95 (ISBN 0-8164-2485-3, HarpR). Har-Row.
Weight Loss to Super Wellness. 2nd ed. Ted L. Edwards, Jr. LC 87-31863. (Illus.). 161p. 1988. pap. 11.95 (ISBN 0-87322-924-X, LEDW0924, Life Enhancement). Human Kinetics.
Weight Loss to Super Wellness. Ted L. Edwards, Jr. & Barbara Lau. (Illus.). 176p. (Orig.). 1982. pap. text ed. 8.95 (ISBN 0-938934-07-4). Hills Med.
Weight Machines. Michael T. Cannell & Judith Zimmer. Ed. by Susan Wallach. LC 84-40602. (At Home Gym Ser.). 64p. 1985. pap. 2.95 (ISBN 0-394-72974-9, Pub. by Villard Bks). Random.
Weight No Longer. William G. Johnson & Peter Stalonas. 188p. 1981. 12.95 (ISBN 0-88289-261-4). Pelican.
Weight No More. Karen Darling. 120p. 1984. pap. 5.95 (ISBN 0-931432-18-9). New Wrld Lib.
Weight of Glory & Other Addresses. rev. ed. C. S. Lewis. 96p. 1980. pap. 4.95 (ISBN 0-02-095980-X). Macmillan.
Weight of Numbers. Judith Baumel. viii, 72p. 1988. 17.50x (ISBN 0-8195-2144-2); pap. 9.95 (ISBN 0-8195-1145-5). Wesleyan U Pr.
Weight of the Historical Inevitabilities at the End of the 20th Century & the Future of Humanity. Lorenzo G. Grant. (Illus.). 141p. 1981. 145.50x (ISBN 0-930008-76-6). Inst Econ Finan.
Weight of the World. Peter Handke. Tr. by Ralph Manheim from Ger. 288p. 1984. 16.95 (ISBN 0-374-28745-7). FS&G.
Weight, Sex, & Marriage. Richard B. Stuart & Barbara Jacobsen. 1989. 6.95 (ISBN 0-671-67008-5, Fireside). S&S.
Weight, Sex & Marriage: A Delicate Balance. Richard B. Stuart & Barbara Jacobson. 1987. 15.95 (ISBN 0-393-02466-0). Norton.
Weight Training. E. G. Bartlett. (Illus.). 96p. 1984. 14.95 (ISBN 0-7153-8512-7). David & Charles.
Weight Training. James Hesson. (Illus.). 208p. 1985. pap. 7.95x (ISBN 0-89582-129-X). Morton Pub.
Weight Training. 4th ed. Philip J. Rasch. (P. E. Activity Ser.). 120p. 1982. pap. text ed. write for info. (ISBN 0-697-07190-1). Wm C Brown.
Weight Training & Body Building for Young Athletes. Franco Columbu & Dick Tyler. (Illus.). (gr. 4-8). 1979. pap. 6.95 (ISBN 0-671-33006-3). Wanderer Bks.
Weight Training & Conditioning for Basketball. Robert V. Wilcox. LC 86-71206. (Illus.). 88p. (Orig.). (YA) (gr. 10 up). 1986. pap. 8.00 (ISBN 1-55618-006-3). Brunswick Pub.
Weight Training Everyone. Rich Tuten & Clancy Moore. (Illus.). 236p. (Orig.). 1982. pap. text ed. 8.95 (ISBN 0-88725-000-9). Hunter Textbks.
Weight Training for Baseball. Robert V. Wilcox. LC 87-72624. (Illus.). 120p. (Orig.). 1987. pap. 8.00 (ISBN 1-55618-029-2). Brunswick Pub.
Weight Training for Beginners. Bill Reynolds & Lou Ferrigno. (Illus.). 96p. 1982. cancelled (ISBN 0-8092-5729-7); pap. 6.95 (ISBN 0-8092-5728-9). Contemp Bks.
Weight Training for Cyclists. Fred Matheny et al. LC 87-115125. (Illus.). 78p. (Orig.). 1986. pap. 7.95 (ISBN 0-941950-11-5). Velo-News.
Weight Training for Fitness & Sports. Thomas P. McHugh. 144p. 1984. pap. 13.95 (ISBN 0-8403-3438-9). Kendall-Hunt.
Weight Training for Football. Robert V. Wilcox. LC 86-70138. (Illus.). 98p. (Orig.). (YA) (gr. 10-12). 1986. pap. 8.00 (ISBN 0-931494-88-5). Brunswick Pub.
Weight Training for Gifted Athletes. William J. Maitland. (Illus.). 150p. (Orig.). 1986. pap. 16.95 (ISBN 0-936759-01-1). Maitland Enter.
Weight Training for the over Thirty-Fives. E. G. Bartlett & Mary Southall. (Illus.). 96p. 1987. pap. 14.95 (ISBN 0-7153-8957-2). David & Charles.
Weight Training for the Young Athlete. Frederick C. Hatfield. LC 79-55614. (Illus.). 120p. (gr. 5 up). 1982. pap. 6.95 (ISBN 0-689-70632-4, 285). Atheneum.
Weight Training for Women. Mary Southall & E. G. Bartlett. (Illus.). 96p. 1986. pap. 14.95 (ISBN 0-7153-8842-8). David & Charles.
Weight Training in Athletics. Rev. ed. Jim Murray & Peter Karpovich. (Illus.). 216p. 1983. pap. 7.95 (ISBN 0-13-948000-5). P-H.
Weight Training in Sports: A Bibliography with Special Reference to Body-Building & Olympic Power Lifting. Donald D. Macchia. LC 83-48256. 108p. 1984. lib. bdg. 18.00 (ISBN 0-8240-9103-5). Garland Pub.
Weight Watchers Fast & Fabulous Cookbook. Jean Nidetch. LC 83-12097. 384p. 1984. 15.50 (ISBN 0-453-01008-3). NAL.
Weight Watchers Fast & Fabulous Cookbook. Weight Watchers International, Inc. Staff. 1985. pap. 8.95 (ISBN 0-452-25727-1, Plume). NAL.
Weight Watchers Favorite Recipes. Weight Watchers International, Inc. Staff. 1988. pap. 9.95 (ISBN 0-452-26055-8, Plume). NAL.
Weight Watchers Favorite Recipes: Over 280 Winning Dishes from Weight Watchers Members & Staff. Weight Watchers International, Inc. Staff. LC 86-16174. 384p. 1986. 17.95 (ISBN 0-453-01012-1). NAL.
Weight Watchers Food Plan Diet Cookbook. Jean Nidetch. LC 82-12417. 384p. 1982. 13.95 (ISBN 0-453-01007-5, TE7). NAL.
Weight Watchers International Cookbook. Jean Nidetch. 1977. 11.95 (ISBN 0-453-01004-0, TE4). NAL.
Weight Watchers International Cookbook. Intro. by Jean Nidetch. LC 80-80067. (Illus.). 400p. 1980. pap. 8.95 (ISBN 0-452-25780-8, Z5416, Plume). NAL.
Weight Watchers New International Cookbook. Weight Watchers International, Inc. Staff. LC 85-13443. (Illus.). 400p. 1985. 18.95 (ISBN 0-453-01011-3). NAL.
Weight Watchers New International Cookbook. 1987. pap. 9.95 (ISBN 0-452-25951-7, Plume). NAL.
Weight Watchers New Program Cookbook. Weight Watchers International, Inc. Staff. 1980. 9.95 (ISBN 0-453-01003-2, TE 3). NAL.
Weight Watchers Party & Holiday Cookbook. Ed. by Jean Nidetch. 1984. pap. 3.95 (ISBN 0-451-13299-8, Sig). NAL.
Weight Watcher's Party & Holiday Cookbook. Weight Watchers International, Inc. Staff. LC 80-15245. 1982. 12.95 (ISBN 0-453-01005-9); pap. 7.95 (ISBN 0-452-25324-1, Plume). NAL.
Weight Watchers Quick & Easy Menu Cookbook. Weight Watchers International, Inc. Staff. LC 87-20426. 320p. 1987. 17.95 (ISBN 0-453-01015-6). NAL.
Weight Watchers Quick Start Plus Program Cookbook. Jean Nidetch. 496p. 1986. 17.95 (ISBN 0-453-01014-8). NAL.
Weight Watchers Quick Start Plus Program Cookbook. Jean T. Nidetch. 1986. pap. 9.95 (ISBN 0-452-25831-6, Plume). NAL.
Weight Watchers Quick Start Program Cookbook: Including the Full Exchange Plan. Jean Nidetch. (Illus.). 416p. 1984. 18.50 (ISBN 0-453-01010-5). NAL.
Weight Watchers Quick Success Program Cookbook. Jean Nidetch. 448p. 1989. 18.95 (ISBN 0-453-01016-4). NAL.
Weight Watchers Three Hundred & Sixty-Five Day Menu Cookbook. 1983. pap. 9.95 (ISBN 0-452-25958-4, Plume). NAL.
Weight Watchers Three Hundred Sixty-Five Day Menu Cookbook. Ed. by Weight Watchers International, Inc. Staff. LC 81-11183. 368p. 1981. 15.95 (ISBN 0-453-01009-1). NAL.
Weighted Energy Methods in Fluid Dynamics & Elasticity. G. P. Galdi & S. Rionero. LC 85-12662. (Lecture Notes in Mathematics: Vol. 1134). vii, 126p. 1985. pap. 11.00 (ISBN 0-387-15645-3). Springer-Verlag.
Weighted Expansions for Canonical Desingularization. S. S. Abhyanker. (Lecture Notes in Mathematics Ser.: Vol. 910). 236p. 1982. pap. 16.00 (ISBN 0-387-11195-6). Springer-Verlag.
Weighted Inequalities & Degenerate Elliptic Partial Differential Equations. E. W. Stredulinsky. (Lecture Notes in Mathematics Ser.: Vol. 1074). iii, 143p. 1984. pap. 11.00 (ISBN 0-387-13370-4). Springer-Verlag.
Weighted Norm Inequalities & Related Topics. Garcia-Cuerva & J. L. Rubio De Francia. LC 85-12925. (Mathematics Studies: Vol. 116). 604p. 1985. 97.50 (ISBN 0-444-87804-1, North-Holland). Elsevier.
Weighted Sobolev Spaces. A. Kufner. 130p. 1985. 37.00 (ISBN 0-471-90367-1). Wiley.
Weightier Matters of the Law Essays on Law & Religion: A Tribute to Harold J. Berman. John Witte, Jr. & Frank S. Alexander. LC 87-28845. (Studies in Religion). 450p. 1988. 39.95 (ISBN 1-55540-179-1, 01-11-51). Scholars Pr GA.
Weighting for Baudot & Other Problems for You & Your Computer. Francis Federighi & Edward D. Reilly. (Illus.). 1978. 11.95 (ISBN 0-89529-061-8). Avery Pub.
Weighting Game: The Truth about Weight Control. Lawrence E. Lamb. 196p. 1988. 15.95 (ISBN 0-8184-0487-6). Lyle Stuart.
Weightlessness: Physical Phenomena & Biological Effects. special vol ed. Ed. by E. T. Benedikt. 1960. 20.00x (ISBN 0-87703-000-6, Pub. by Am Astronaut). Univelt Inc.
Weightlifting & Bodybuilding: Total Fitness for Men & Women. Donald Macchia. 200p. 1987. 23.95 (ISBN 0-8304-1124-0); pap. 13.95 (ISBN 0-8304-1183-6). Nelson-Hall.
Weightlifting & Weight Training. George W. Kirkley. LC 63-17653. (Illus., Orig.). 1966. pap. 1.50 (ISBN 0-668-01098-3). Arco.
Weightlifting Handbook, Nineteen Seventy-Nine to Nineteen Eighty. cancelled (ISBN 0-686-43041-7). AAU Pubns.
Weights & Measures. Paul Christensen. LC 85-70444. 64p. 1985. pap. 5.00 (ISBN 0-916383-01-6, Univ Edtns). Aegina Pr.
Weighty Word Book. Paul M. Levitt et al. LC 85-62731. (Illus.). 112p. 1985. 15.95 (ISBN 0-917665-13-9). Bookmakers Guild.
Weil Representation I: Intertwining Distributions & Discrete Spectrum. Stephen Rallis & Gerard Schiffmann. LC 80-12191. (Memoirs of the American Mathematical Society Ser.: No. 231). 203p. 1980. pap. 12.00 (ISBN 0-8218-2231-4, MEMO-231). Am Math.
Weil Representation, Maslov Index & Theta Series. Ed. by Gerard Lion & Michele Vergne. (Progress in Mathematics Ser.: No. 6). 346p. 1980. pap. text ed. 28.50x (ISBN 0-8176-3007-4). Birkhauser.
Weimar: A Cultural History. Walter Laqueur. LC 74-16605. (Illus.). 295p. 1976. 8.95 (ISBN 0-399-50346-3, Perigee). Putnam Pub Group.
Weimar & the Rise of Hitler. 2nd ed. A. J. Nicholls. LC 79-10134. (Making of the Twentieth Century Ser.). 1980. pap. text ed. write for info. (ISBN 0-312-86067-6). St Martin.
Weimar & the Vatican, 1919-1933. Stewart A. Stehlin. LC 83-42544. (Illus.). 512p. 1986. pap. 19.95x (ISBN 0-691-10195-7); text ed. 58.50x (ISBN 0-691-05399-5). Princeton U Pr.
Weimar Chronicle: Prelude to Hitler. Alex De Jonge. 1979. pap. 8.95 (ISBN 0-452-00868-9, Mer). NAL.
Weimar Culture: The Outsider As Insider. Peter Gay. LC 81-2046. (Illus.). xv, 205p. 1981. Repr. of 1968 ed. lib. bdg. 27.50x (ISBN 0-313-22972-4, GAWC). Greenwood.
Weimar Culture: The Outsider As Insider. Peter Gay. 1970. pap. 7.95x (ISBN 0-06-131482-X, TB1482, Torch). Har-Row.
Weimar Dilemma: Intellectuals in the Weimar Republic. Anthony Phelan. LC 84-25031. 224p. 1985. 32.50 (ISBN 0-7190-0949-9, Pub. by Manchester Univ Pr); pap. 14.00 (ISBN 0-7190-1833-1). St Martin.
Weimar Etudes. Henry Pachter. Ed. by Steven Bronner. LC 82-1122. (Illus.). 360p. 1982. 27.50 (ISBN 0-231-05360-6). Columbia U Pr.
Weimar Germany: Germany 1918-33. Ed. by Josh Brooman. (Twentieth Century History Ser.). (Illus.). 32p. (Orig.). 1985. pap. text ed. 5.75 (ISBN 0-582-22372-5). Longman.
Weimar Germany: Writers & Politics. Ed. by Alan Bance. 183p. 1983. pap. 16.00x (ISBN 0-7073-0291-9, Pub. by Scot Acad Pr). Longwood Pub Group.
Weimar Intellectuals & the Threat of Modernity. Dagmar Barnouw. LC 87-45246. 352p. 1988. 27.50 (ISBN 0-253-36427-2). Ind U Pr.
Weimar Prussia, Nineteen Eighteen to Nineteen Twenty-Five: The Unlikely Rock of Democracy. Dietrich Orlow. LC 85-1187. (Illus.). 376p. 1986. 34.95x (ISBN 0-8229-3519-8). U of Pittsburgh Pr.
Weimar Republic: A Historical Bibliography. LC 83-21522. (Research Guides Ser.: No. 9). 285p. 1984. lib. bdg. 34.00 (ISBN 0-87436-378-0). ABC-Clio.
Weimar Republic & Nazi Germany. Warren B. Morris. LC 81-14179. 400p. 1982. 26.95x (ISBN 0-88229-336-2); pap. 13.95 (ISBN 0-88229-797-X). Nelson-Hall.
Weimar Years: A Culture Cut Short. John Willet. Ed. by Mark Magowan. LC 83-7243. (Illus.). 160p. 35.00 (ISBN 0-89659-409-2); pap. 24.95 (ISBN 0-89659-410-6). Abbeville Pr.
Weimaraner. Anna K. Nicholas. (Illus.). 288p. 1986. 16.95 (ISBN 0-86622-156-5, PS-821). TFH Pubns.
Weimaraner Champions, 1952-1987. Camino E. E. & B. Co. Staff. (Illus.). 150p. (YA) (gr. 7 up). 1988. pap. 29.95 (ISBN 0-940808-81-1). Camino E E & B.
Weimaraners. Anna K. Nicholas. (Illus.). 128p. 1983. pap. 9.95 (ISBN 0-87666-731-0, KW-096). TFH Pubns.
Weinberg, Schumaker & Oltman's Statistics: An Intuitive Approach, Study Guide. 4th ed. Debra Oltman. 250p. (Orig.). 1982. pap. text ed. 8.00 pub net (ISBN 0-8185-0442-0). Brooks-Cole.
Weiner Werkstatte: Design in Vienna. Werner J. Schweiger. LC 84-6244. (Illus.). 272p. 1984. 75.00 (ISBN 0-89659-440-8). Abbeville Pr.
Weiner Werkstatte-the Registered Trade Marks: Vol. I, Rose Mark & Trade Name. Waltraud Neuwirth. (Illus.). 240p. (Ger. & Eng.). 1985. 45.00 (ISBN 3-900282-23-4, Pub. by Waltraud Neuwirth). Seven Hills Bks.
Weinstein, Korn & Miller CPLR Manual. 2nd ed. Oscar G. Chase. 1980. looseleaf set 90.00 (802); Updates. 1985 45.00; 1986 45.00. Bender.
Weinstein's Evidence manual. Jack B. Weinstein & Margaret A. Berger. 1987. looseleaf 90.00. Bender.
Weinstein's Evidence: United States Rules, 7 vols. Jack B. Weinstein & Margaret A. Berger. 1975. Set, updates avail. looseleaf 750.00 (803); Updates 1985. 521.50; Supplement 1986. 580.00. Bender.
Weir. Ruth Moore. 1986. pap. 8.50 (ISBN 0-942396-48-0). Blackberry ME.
Weir Mitchell: His Life & Works. Anna R. Burr. 1973. Repr. of 1930 ed. 45.00 (ISBN 0-8274-1423-4). R West.
Weir of Hermiston: An Unfinished Romance. facs. ed. Robert Louis Stevenson. LC 78-150563. (Short Story Index Reprint Ser.). Repr. of 1896 ed. 16.00 (ISBN 0-8369-3861-5). Ayer Co Pubs.
Weir of Hermiston & Other Stories. Robert Louis Stevenson. Ed. by Paul Binding. (English Library). 1980. pap. 4.95 (ISBN 0-14-043138-1). Penguin.
Weird & the Beautiful. Richard Headstrom. LC 81-67780. (Illus.). 240p. 1984. 14.95 (ISBN 0-8453-4727-6, Cornwall Bks). Assoc Univ Prs.
Weird & Wonderful. (Amazing Mini Bks.). (Illus.). 96p. (gr. 2-5). 1988. pap. 2.95 (ISBN 0-8431-2272-2). Price Stern.
Weird & Wonderful Ants. Lynn Poole & Gray Poole. (Illus.). (gr. 5 up). 1961. 8.95 (ISBN 0-8392-3041-9). Astor-Honor.
Weird & Wonderful Science Facts. Magnus Pyke. LC 83-24288. (Illus.). 128p. (gr. 5 up). 1984. 10.95 (ISBN 0-8069-4688-1). Sterling.
Weird & Wonderful Science Facts. Magnus Pyke. LC 83-24288. (Illus.). 128p. (gr. 5 up). 1985. pap. 3.95 (ISBN 0-8069-6254-2). Sterling.
Weird & Wonderful Wildlife: A Gallery of Nature's Most Unusual Creations. Rosemary Taylor et al. LC 82-25245. (Illus.). 224p. 1983. pap. 16.95 (ISBN 0-87701-295-4). Chronicle Bks.
Weird Disappearance of Jordan Hall. Judie Angell. LC 87-7781. 128p. (gr. 6-8). 1987. 11.95 (ISBN 0-531-05727-5); PLB 11.99 (ISBN 0-531-08327-6). Orchard Bks Watts.
Weird Gathering & Other Tales. Ed. by Ronald Curran. 1979. pap. 2.50 (ISBN 0-449-23994-2, Crest). Fawcett.
Weird Henry Berg. Sarah Sargent. 160p. (gr. 5 up). 1981. pap. 2.25 (ISBN 0-440-49346-3, YB). Dell.
Weird of the White Wolf, Bk. 3. Michael Moorcock. (Elric Saga Ser.). 160p. 1984. pap. 2.95 (ISBN 0-425-10407-9). Berkley Pub.
Weird People of the Unknown see Visitantes Del Mas Alla.
Weird Tales, 2 Vols. in 1. Ernst T. Hoffman. Tr. by J. T. Bealby from Ger. LC 74-125218. (Short Story Index Reprint Ser.). 1923. 32.00 (ISBN 0-8369-3586-1). Ayer Co Pubs.
Weird Tales, No. 1. Ed. by Lin Carter. 288p. (Orig.). 1981. pap. 2.50 (ISBN 0-89083-714-7). Zebra.
Weird Tales, No. 2. Ed. by Lin Carter. 288p. (Orig.). 1981. pap. 2.50 (ISBN 0-89083-715-5). Zebra.
Weird Tales, Vol. 4. Ed. by Lin Carter. 1983. pap. 2.95 (ISBN 0-8217-1238-1). Zebra.
Weird Tales from Northern Seas, from the Danish of Jonas Lie. facs. ed. Jonas L. Lie. LC 79-81272. (Short Story Index Reprint Ser.). (Illus.). 1893. 17.00 (ISBN 0-8369-3024-X). Ayer Co Pubs.
Weird Tales, No. 3. Ed. by Lin Carter. (YA) (gr. 7 up). 1981. pap. 2.50 (ISBN 0-89083-803-8). Zebra.
Weird Tales of Roscoe Funye. Robert S. Perry. LC 84-90060. 112p. 1987. 8.95 (ISBN 0-533-06144-X). Vantage.
Weird Things & Other Oddities about Pennsylvania. Patrick M. Reynolds. (Pennsylvania Profiles Ser.: Vol. 3). (Illus.). 1979. pap. 3.25 (ISBN 0-932514-03-0). Red Rose Studio.
Weird Wonderful America: The Nation's Most Offbeat & Off-the-Beaten-Path Tourist Attractions. Laura A. Bergheim. (Illus.). 1988. pap. 8.95 (ISBN 0-02-030630-X, Collier). Macmillan.
Weirdest Is the Sphere. Marion Cohen. (Poetry Chapbooks: No. 3). 32p. 1979. pap. 2.50 (ISBN 0-913282-15-4). Seven Woods Pr.
Weirdos, Winos & Defrocked Priests. Ludlow Porch. 180p. 1986. 9.95 (ISBN 0-934601-05-4). Peachtree Pubs.
Weirds: A Facsimile Selection of Fiction from the Era of the Shudder Pulps. Ed. by Sheldon Jaffery. (Starmont Popular Culture Ser.: No. 1). 173p. 1987. lib. bdg. 19.95x (ISBN 0-8095-5502-6). Borgo Pr.
Weirds: Annotated Facsimile Examples of the Weird Menace Stories of the 1930's. Ed. by Sheldon Jaffery. (Starmont Popular Culture Studies: Vol. 1). (Illus.). 1987. 17.95x (ISBN 0-930261-93-3); pap. text ed. 9.95x (ISBN 0-930261-92-5). Starmont Hse.
Weirdstone of Brinsingamen. Alan Garner. 1981. pap. 1.95 (ISBN 0-345-29043-7, Del Rey). Ballantine.
Weirs & Fumes for Flow Measurement. P. Ackers et al. LC 78-317. 327p. 1978. 112.00 (ISBN 0-471-99637-8). Wiley.
Weisheit in Israel see Wisdom in Israel.
Weissenberger's Federal Evidence. Glen Weissenberger. 1987. text ed. 80.00 (ISBN 0-87084-923-9); pap. text ed. 30.00 (ISBN 0-87084-924-7). Anderson Pub Co.
Weizmann & Smuts: A Study in Zionist-South African Cooperation. Richard P. Stevens. 1978. French. pap. 6.00 (ISBN 0-88728-125-7). Inst Palestine.
Weland: Smith of the Gods. Ursula Synge. LC 73-5945. (Illus.). 94p. (gr. 7 up). 1973. 14.95 (ISBN 0-87599-200-5). S G Phillips.
Welborn Beeson on the Oregon Trail in 1853. Ed. by Bert Webber. LC 85-31464. (Illus.). 80p. (Orig.). 1986. pap. 6.95 (ISBN 0-936738-15-4). S S S Pub Co.
Welborn Beeson on the Oregon Trail in 1853 see Oregon & California Trail Diary of Welborn Beeson in 1853.
Welch Report, Allegheny Portage RR, 1833. Ed. by W. H. Shank. 1983. 2.00 (ISBN 0-933788-23-1). Am Canal & Transport.
Welchman's Hose. Robert Graves. LC 76-30507. Repr. of 1925 ed. lib. bdg. 35.00 (ISBN 0-8414-4508-7). Folcroft.

Welding Fundamentals. R. Madsen. 300p. 1982. 15.96 (ISBN 0-8269-3095-6). Am Technical.

Welding: Fundamentals & Procedures. Jerry Galyen et al. LC 83-10438. 273p. 1984. write for info. (ISBN 0-471-06079-8). Wiley.

Welding Guidelines with Aircraft Supplement. William Kielhorn. (IAP Training Ser.). (Illus.). 187p. 1978. pap. text ed. 10.95 (ISBN 0-89100-076-3, EA-WB-1). IAP.

Welding Handbook. Incl. Vol. 1. Fundamentals of Welding. 7th ed. 373p. 1976. 38.00 (ISBN 0-686-95566-8); Vol. 2. Welding Processes-Arc & Gas Welding & Cutting, Brazing, & Soldering. 7th ed. 592p. 1978. 38.00 (ISBN 0-686-95567-6); Vol. 3. Welding Processes-Resistance & Solid-State Welding & Other Joining Processes. 7th ed. 459p. 1980. 38.00 (ISBN 0-686-95568-4); Vol. 4. Metals & Their Weldability. 7th ed. 656p. 1982. 38.00 (ISBN 0-686-95569-2); Vol. 5. Applications of Welding. 6th ed. 603p. 1973. Am Welding.

Welding Health & Safety: Resources Manual. American Industrial Hygiene Association Staff. 40p. 1984. 25.00 (ISBN 0-932627-17-X). Am Indus Hygiene.

Welding, Heating, Air Conditioning see Plumbers & Pipe Fitters Library.

Welding, Heating, Air Conditioning see Plumbers & Pipefitters Library.

Welding Inspection, Course 28. (Illus.). 410p. 1979. looseleaf 95.00x (ISBN 0-87683-104-8). GP Pub.

Welding Inspection & Quality Control: The Welding Handbook. Vol. 2 225.00, 14 wkbks (ISBN 0-686-95803-9). Am Welding.

Welding Inspection WI. 222p. 1980. 30.00 (ISBN 0-87171-177-X, WI). Am Welding.

Welding Metallurgy of Stainless & Heat-Resisting Steels. Rene Castro & J. J. De Cadenet. LC 74-76582. pap. 50.00 (ISBN 0-317-26032-4, 2024434). Bks Demand UMI.

Welding Metallurgy of Structural Steels. Ed. by Jay Y. Koo. LC 87-42882. 537p. 1987. 98.00 (ISBN 0-87339-025-3). Metal Soc.

Welding Occupations 1981: Equipment Planning Guides for Vocational & Technical Training & Education Programmes, Vol. 3. pap. 28.00 (ISBN 92-2-101887-3, ILO237, ILO). UNIPUB.

Welding of HSLA Structural Steels: Proceedings of an International Conference. American Society for Metals Staff. Ed. by A. B. Rothwell & J. Malcolm Gray. LC 78-18220. (Materials Metalworking Technology Ser.). pap. 160.00 (ISBN 0-317-27699-9, 2019490). Bks Demand UMI.

Welding of Line Pipe Steels. 1977. 20.00 (ISBN 0-318-18633-0). Welding Res Coun.

Welding of Open Web Steel Joists. (Technical Digest Ser.: No. 8). 10.00 (ISBN 0-318-01793-8). Steel Joist Inst.

Welding of Sand Cast Incramet 800. British Welding Research Association Staff. 75p. 1965. 11.25 (ISBN 0-317-34556-7, 57). Intl Copper.

Welding of Tubular Structures. International Institute of Welding. (Illus.). 574p. 1984. 145.00 (ISBN 0-08-031156-3). Pergamon.

Welding of Tubular Structures: WTS. 500p. 1984. 50.00 (ISBN 0-317-17734-6). Am Welding.

Welding Power Handbook, WPH. A. F. Manz. 208p. 1973. 13.00 (ISBN 0-914096-04-4, WPH). Am Welding.

Welding Practice: Standards for Terms-Definitions, Graphical Representation & Electric Welding Equipment, Pt. 3. (DIN Standards Ser.). write for info (ISBN 0-686-31851-X, 11296-4/145). IPS.

Welding Practices & Procedures. Richard Carr & Robert O'Con. (Illus.). 416p. 1983. text ed. write for info. (ISBN 0-13-948059-5). P-H.

Welding: Principles & Applications. Larry Jeffus & Harold Johnson. LC 83-71046. 1984. text ed. 29.95 (ISBN 0-8273-1806-5); instr's. guide 7.95 (ISBN 0-8273-1807-3); wkbk. 7.50 (ISBN 0-8273-1822-7). Delmar.

Welding: Principles & Practice. Raymond Sacks. (gr. 10-12). 1981. text ed. 30.60 (ISBN 0-02-666140-3); student guide 7.12 (ISBN 0-02-666120-9); tchr's guide 6.00 (ISBN 0-02-666110-1). Bennett IL.

Welding Print Reading. Robert Putnam. (Illus.). 384p. 1986. pap. text ed. 24.00 (ISBN 0-8359-8609-8). P-H.

Welding Procedure & Performance Qualification. 97p. 1977. 18.00 (ISBN 0-686-95771-7). Am Welding.

Welding Procedures: Oxyacetylene. Frank R. Schell. LC 76-4306. 1977. Delmar.

Welding Process Technology. Peter Thomas Houldcroft. LC 76-47408. (Illus.). 1977. 52.50 (ISBN 0-521-21530-7). Cambridge U Pr.

Welding Processes. 3rd ed. I. H. Griffin et al. 400p. 1984. text ed. 23.95 (ISBN 0-8273-2133-3); instr's. guide 8.00 (ISBN 0-8273-2136-8). Delmar.

Welding Processes & Power Sources. 3rd ed. Edwards R. Pierre. (Student Study Guide). (Illus.). 416p. 1984. text ed. write for info. (ISBN 0-8087-3369-9); write for info. (ISBN 0-8087-3370-2). Burgess MN Intl.

Welding Processes & Practices. Leonard Koellhoffer et al. 482p. 1988. write for info. (ISBN 0-471-81671-X); wkbk. avail. (ISBN 0-471-81668-X). Wiley.

Welding Processes-Arc & Gas Welding & Cutting, Brazing, & Soldering see Welding Handbook.

Welding Processes-Resistance & Solid-State Welding & Other Joining Processes see Welding Handbook.

Welding Projects: A Design Approach. J. A. Pender & J. Masson. 1976. text ed. 34.95 (ISBN 0-07-077330-0). McGraw.

Welding Research: The State of the Art. 204p. 1986. 68.00 (ISBN 0-87170-255-X, 6624). ASM.

Welding Safety. Gary Hutchinson. LC 81-730682. 1982. wkbk. 5.00 (ISBN 0-8064-0247-4, 515); audio visual pkg. 129.00 (ISBN 0-8064-0248-2). Bergwall.

Welding Safety & Health: WSH. incl. study text & workbook 235.00 (ISBN 0-317-37070-7). Am Welding.

Welding Skills. J. W. Giachino & W. Weeks. (Illus.). 424p. 1985. 21.96 (ISBN 0-8269-3001-8). Am Technical.

Welding Skills & Practices. Joseph W. Giachino et al. LC 77-123471. pap. 108.00 (ISBN 0-317-10910-3, 2012979). Bks Demand UMI.

Welding Skills & Techniques. Robert P. Schmidt. 1982. text ed. 27.00 (ISBN 0-8359-8611-X, Reston); instr's. manual avail. (ISBN 0-8359-8612-8). P-H.

Welding Structural Steels. Earl Kent. 1977. pap. text ed. 10.00 (ISBN 0-918782-01-5). E Kent.

Welding Technology. 2nd ed. J. W. Giachino et al. (Illus.). 489p. 1973. pap. 19.96 (ISBN 0-8269-3063-8). Am Technical.

Welding Technology. 2nd ed. Gower A. Kennedy. 598p. 1982. text ed. 33.28 scp (ISBN 0-672-97778-8); scp student manual 12.04 (ISBN 0-672-97990-X); scp ans. key 1.11 (ISBN 0-672-97136-4). Bobbs.

Welding Technology for the Aerospace Industry: Proceedings of the AWS conference on Welding for the Aerospace Industry, October, 1980. AWS Conference Staff. (Welding Technology Ser.). 176p. 1981. 25.00 (ISBN 0-686-95643-5). Am Welding.

Welding Technology in Japan, Pt. I & II. 1982. 25.00 (ISBN 0-318-18640-3). Welding Res Coun.

Welding Terms & Definitions: A3.O. 80p. 1980. 22.00 (ISBN 0-87171-189-3); members 16.50. Am Welding.

Welding's Engineering Data Sheets. 9th ed. (Monticello Bks.). 188p. 1978. soft cover 12.00 (ISBN 0-686-12001-9). Jefferson Pubns.

Weldments: Physical Metallurgy & Failure Phenomena - Proceedings of the Bolton Conference, 5th. Bolton Conference Staff. Ed. by R. J. Christoffel et al. LC 79-14269. (Illus.). 436p. 1979. 55.75 (ISBN 0-931690-07-2). Genium Pub.

Weldon Kees. William T. Ross. (United States Author Ser.). 1985. lib. bdg. 20.95 (ISBN 0-8057-7437-8, Twayne). G K Hall.

Weldon Kees: A Critical Introduction. Ed. & intro. by Jim Elledge. LC 85-14170. 263p. 1985. 21.00 (ISBN 0-8108-1830-2). Scarecrow.

Weldon Kees & the Midcentury Generation: Letters, 1935-1955. Weldon Kees. Ed. by Robert E. Knoll. LC 86-1288. (Illus.). viii, 253p. 1987. 19.95x (ISBN 0-8032-2709-4). U of Nebr Pr.

Weldon Kees: Reviews & Essays, Nineteen Thirty-Six - Fifty-Five. Ed. by James Reidel. (Poets on Poetry Ser.). (Orig.). 1988. 24.95 (ISBN 0-472-09383-5); pap. 8.95 (ISBN 0-472-06383-9). U of Mich Pr.

Weldon's Practical Crochet see Victorian Crochet.

Welfare: A Handbook for Friend & Foe. Timothy J. Sampson. LC 72-8551. 1972. pap. 5.95 (ISBN 0-8298-0255-X). Pilgrim NY.

Welfare: a National Policy: Proceedings. Conference of the Institute of Industrial Relations. 64p. 1973. 3.00 (ISBN 0-89215-041-6). U Cal LA Indus Rel.

Welfare Abroad: An Introduction to Social Welfare in Seven Countries. Ed. by Roslyn Ford & Mono Chakrabarti. (Illus.). 212p. 1987. 30.00 (ISBN 0-7073-0479-2, Pub. by Scot Acad Pr); pap. 9.95 (ISBN 0-7073-0507-1). Longwood Pub Group.

Welfare Activities among the Greek People in Los Angeles: Thesis. Mary Antoniou. LC 74-7650. 1974. Repr. of 1939 ed. soft bdg. 10.95 (ISBN 0-88247-283-6). R & E Pubs.

Welfare Activities of Federal, State, & Local Governments in California, 1850-1934. Frances Cahn & Valeska Bary. LC 75-17212. (Social Problems & Social Policy Ser.). 1976. Repr. of 1936 ed. 33.00x (ISBN 0-405-07484-0). Ayer Co Pubs.

Welfare Analysis of Policies Affecting Prices & Products. Robert D. Willig. LC 78-75051. (Outstanding Dissertations in Economics). 1980. lib. bdg. 24.00 (ISBN 0-8240-4129-1). Garland Pub.

Welfare & Efficiency in Public Economics. Ed. by D. Bos et al. (Illus.). 440p. 1988. 84.90 (ISBN 0-387-18824-X). Springer-Verlag.

Welfare & Efficiency: Their Interactions in Western Europe & Implications for International Economic Relations. Theodore Geiger & Frances M. Geiger. LC 78-63434. 160p. 1978. 7.00 (ISBN 0-89068-045-0). Natl Planning.

Welfare & Husbandry of Calves. Ed. by J. P. Signoret. 1982. lib. bdg. 34.50 (ISBN 90-247-2680-8, Pub. by Martinus Nijhoff Netherlands). Kluwer Academic.

Welfare & Pension Plans Disclosure Act of 1958: Legislative History. U. S. Solicitor of the Department of Labor. LC 63-26. xxxvi, 568p. 1978. Repr. of 1962 ed. lib. bdg. 45.00 (ISBN 0-930342-97-6). W S Hein.

Welfare & Poverty. National Center for Policy Analysis Staff. 1983. 10.00 (ISBN 0-943802-08-3). Natl Ctr Pol.

Welfare & the Poor in the Nineteenth Century City: Philadelphia, 1800-1854. Priscilla F. Clement. LC 83-49357. (Illus.). 224p. 1985. 27.50 (ISBN 0-8386-3216-5). Fairleigh Dickinson.

Welfare & Worker Participation: Eight Case Studies. Patrick Kerans et al. LC 87-11878. 260p. 1988. 55.00 (ISBN 0-312-00908-9). St Martin.

Welfare Aspects of Industrial Markets. Ed. by A. P. Jacquemin & H. W. DeJong. (Nijenrode Studies in Economics: No. 2). 1977. lib. bdg. 40.00 (ISBN 90-207-0625-X, Pub. by Martinus Nijhoff Netherlands). Kluwer Academic.

Welfare Assessment of Transport Deregulation: The Case of the Express Coach Market in 1980. N. J. Douglas. (Institute for Transport Studies: Vol. 2). 360p. 1987. text ed. 47.50 (ISBN 0-566-05350-0, Pub. by Gower Pub England). Gower Pub Co.

Welfare Bind. Naomi Gottlieb. LC 73-17259. 206p. 1974. 27.50x (ISBN 0-231-03762-7). Columbia U Pr.

Welfare Bureaucracies: Their Design & Changes in Response to Social Problems. David Billis. 252p. 1985. pap. text ed. 23.95x (ISBN 0-435-82059-1). Gower Pub Co.

Welfare Connection. S. Taylor-Moore. 64p. 1982. pap. 4.95x (ISBN 0-938758-14-4). MTM Pub Co.

Welfare Debate of Nineteen Seventy-Eight. Gordon L. Weil. LC 78-19555. 134p. 1978. 8.00 (ISBN 0-915312-08-5). Inst Socioecon.

Welfare, Democracy & the New Deal. William R. Brock. 300p. 1988. 49.50 (ISBN 0-521-33379-2). Cambridge U Pr.

Welfare Economic Theory. John O'Connell. 206p. 1982. pap. 15.00 (ISBN 0-86569-074-X). Auburn Hse.

Welfare Economics: A Liberal Restatement. C. K. Rowley & A. T. Peacock. LC 75-22430. 198p. 1975. 34.95x (ISBN 0-470-74362-X). Halsted Pr.

Welfare Economics & Social Choice Theory. Allan M. Feldman. 1980. lib. bdg. 26.00 (ISBN 0-89838-033-2, Pub. by Martinus Nijhoff Netherlands); pap. text ed. 12.00 (ISBN 0-89838-034-0, Martimus Nijhoff Pubs). Kluwer Academic.

Welfare Economics & the Elements of Socialism. Maurice Dobb. LC 69-16280. (Illus.). 1969. 49.50 (ISBN 0-521-07462-2); pap. 17.95 (ISBN 0-521-09937-4). Cambridge U Pr.

Welfare Economics & Urban Problems. Bruce Walker. 400p. 1981. 29.95x (ISBN 0-312-86149-4). St Martin.

Welfare Economics of the Second Best. Ed. by D. Bos & C. Seidl. (Journal of Economics Ser.: Supplementum 5). (Illus.). viii, 280p. 1986. pap. 71.50 (ISBN 0-387-81942-8). Springer-Verlag.

Welfare Economics: Theory & Applications. Robin Boadway & Neil Bruce. 336p. 1984. 45.00x (ISBN 0-631-13326-7); pap. 19.95x (ISBN 0-631-13327-5). Basil Blackwell.

Welfare Employment Programs: The Utah Experience. (Innovations Reports). 8p. 1985. 4.00 (ISBN 0-317-45870-1, RM 753). Coun State Govts.

Welfare for the Well-to-Do. Gordon Tullock. LC 83-80789. (Illus.). 75p. 1983. text ed. 9.95 (ISBN 0-933028-21-0). Fisher Inst.

Welfare Fraud Investigation. Gary W. Hutton. (Illus.). 330p. 1985. 38.00x (ISBN 0-398-05140-2). C C Thomas.

Welfare Fraud: Possibilities for Advocacy by Legal Services Programs. Howard Zwickel & Shirley Brown. 80p. 1981. 7.75 (31,486). NCLS Inc.

Welfare Housing Consultant. (Career Examination Ser.: C-3331). Date not set. pap. 16.00 (ISBN 0-8373-3331-8). Natl Learning.

Welfare in Rural Areas: The North Carolina-Iowa Income Maintenance Experiment. Ed. by John L. Palmer & Joseph A. Pechman. LC 77-91826. (Studies in Social Experimentation). 273p. 1978. 28.95 (ISBN 0-8157-6896-6); pap. 10.95 (ISBN 0-8157-6895-8). Brookings.

Welfare in Transition: Living Conditions in Sweden 1968-1981. Robert Erikson & Rune Aberg. (Illus.). 292p. 1987. 55.00 (ISBN 0-19-828516-7). Oxford U Pr.

Welfare Industry. Charles D. Hobbs. LC 75-52899. (Policy Studies). 1978. pap. text ed. 3.00 (ISBN 0-89195-022-2). Heritage Found.

Welfare, Justice, & Freedom. Scott Gordon. LC 80-14571. 256p. 1980. 29.50x (ISBN 0-231-04976-5); pap. 13.00x (ISBN 0-231-04977-3). Columbia U Pr.

Welfare Law: Structure & Entitlement in a Nutshell. Arthur B. LaFrance. LC 78-23544. (Nutshell Ser.). 455p. 1979. pap. text ed. 11.95 (ISBN 0-8299-2020-X). West Pub.

Welfare Management System Coordinator. Jack Rudman. (Career Examination Ser.: C-3024). 1988. pap. 16.00 (ISBN 0-8373-3024-6). Natl Learning.

Welfare Medical Care: An Experiment. Charles H. Goodrich et al. LC 77-85075. (Illus.). 1970. 24.50x (ISBN 0-674-94895-5). Harvard U Pr.

Welfare Medicine in America: A Case Study of Medicaid. Robert Stevens & Rosemary Stevens. LC 74-2870. 1974. 16.95 (ISBN 0-02-931520-4). Free Pr.

Welfare Mother. Susan Sheehan. 144p. 1977. pap. 2.95 (ISBN 0-451-62537-4, Ment). NAL.

Welfare Mothers Movement: A Decade of Change for Poor Women? Susan H. Hertz. LC 81-40358. (Illus.). 200p. (Orig.). 1981. lib. bdg. 27.50 (ISBN 0-8191-1780-3); pap. text ed. 12.25 (ISBN 0-8191-1781-1). U Pr of Amer.

Welfare of Pigs: Current Topics in Veterinary Medicine & Animal Science, No. 11. Ed. by Watse Sybesma. x, 334p. 1981. 49.00 (ISBN 90-247-2521-6, Pub. by Martinus Nijhoff Netherlands). Kluwer Academic.

Welfare of the Elderly: An Economic Analysis & Policy Prescription. W. Kip Viscusi. LC 78-31223. (Wiley Series in Urban Research). pap. 62.80 (ISBN 0-317-09193-X, 2055533). Bks Demand UMI.

Welfare of the Poor. Mary B. Sanger. LC 79-20923. 1979. 26.50 (ISBN 0-12-618650-2). Acad Pr.

Welfare or Bureaucracy: Problems of Matching Social Services to Clients' Needs. Ed. by Dieter Grunow & Friedhart Hegner. LC 80-20631. (Research on Service Delivery Ser.: Vol. 2). 256p. 1980. text ed. 35.00 (ISBN 0-89946-060-7). Oelgeschlager.

Welfare, Planning, & Employment: Selected Essays in Economic Theory. Abram Bergson. 288p. 1982. 39.50x (ISBN 0-262-02175-7). MIT Pr.

Welfare Politics in Mexico. Peter M. Ward. (London Research Series in Geography: No. 9). (Illus.). 192p. 1986. text ed. 34.95x (ISBN 0-04-361058-7). Unwin Hyman.

Welfare, Power, & Juvenile Justice: The Social Control of Delinquent Youth. Robert Harris & David Webb. LC 86-23148. Date not set. price not set (ISBN 0-422-60460-7, Tavistock Pubns). Routledge Chapman & Hall.

Welfare Reform, No. 28. Incl. Vol. II. Income Maintenance Policy: An Analysis of Historical & Legislative Precedents. 145p. 3.00 (ISBN 0-89940-622-X); Vol. III. Analyses of Contemporary Welfare Reform Issues. 98p. 3.00 (ISBN 0-89940-623-8); Vol. IV. Family Independence Project: An Alternative Welfare Reform Approach. 130p. 3.00 (ISBN 0-89940-624-6). (Policy Research Project Reports). 1978. LBJ Sch Pub Aff.

Welfare Reform & the Carter Public Service Employment Program: A Critique. David I. Meiselman. LC 77-95219. 1978. pap. 2.50 (ISBN 0-916770-05-2). Law & Econ U Miami.

Welfare Reform: Consensus or Conflict? Ed. by James S. Denton. (Illus.). 136p. (Orig.). 1988. lib. bdg. 21.50 (ISBN 0-8191-6902-1, Pub. by Natl Forum Found); pap. text ed. 9.75 (ISBN 0-8191-6903-X, Pub. by Natl Forum Found). U Pr of Amer.

Welfare Reform in America. Ed. by Paul M. Sommers. (Middlebury College Conference Ser. on Economic Issues). 256p. 1982. lib. bdg. 29.00 (ISBN 0-89838-079-0). Kluwer Academic.

Welfare Reform: State & Federal Roles. Wilbur J. Cohen & W. Joseph Heffernan. (Policy Research Project Report Ser.: No. 59). 163p. 1984. 9.95 (ISBN 0-89940-661-0). LBJ Sch Pub Aff.

Welfare Representative. Jack Rudman. (Career Examination Ser.: C-899). (Cloth bdg. avail. on request). pap. 14.00. Natl Learning.

Welfare Resources Supervisor. (Career Examination Ser.: C-3332). Date not set. pap. 14.00 (ISBN 0-8373-3332-6). Natl Learning.

Welfare Rights. Ruth Cohen & Andree Rushton. Ed. by Martin Davies. (Community Care Practice Handbook Ser.: No. 10). viii, 117p. (Orig.). 1982. pap. text ed. 6.50x (ISBN 0-435-82175-X). Gower Pub Co.

Welfare Rights. Carl Wellman. LC 82-3728. (Philosophy & Society Ser.). 228p. 1982. text ed. 26.50 (ISBN 0-8476-6759-6). Rowman.

Welfare Rights Handbook. Arenia Edwards. 45p. 1985. 4.00 (40,755). NCLS Inc.

Welfare State. Christopher Wright. (Illus.). 72p. (gr. 9-12). 1981. 17.95 (ISBN 0-7134-2375-7, Pub. by Batsford England). David & Charles.

Welfare State & Beyond: Success & Problems in Scandinavia. Gunnar Heckscher. LC 83-21883. 283p. 1984. 29.50x (ISBN 0-8166-0930-6); pap. 12.95 (ISBN 0-8166-0933-0). U of Minn Pr.

Welfare State & Canadian Federalism. Keith G. Banting. 260p. 1987. 32.00 (ISBN 0-7735-0630-6); pap. 14.95 (ISBN 0-7735-0631-4). McGill-Queens U Pr.

Welfare State & Equality: Structural & Ideological Roots of Public Expenditures. Harold L. Wilensky. 1975. pap. 9.95x (ISBN 0-520-02908-9). U of Cal Pr.

Welfare State & Its Aftermath. S. N. Eisenstadt & Ora Ahimeir. (Illus.). 340p. 1985. 28.50x (ISBN 0-389-20529-X, 08091). B&N Imports.

Welfare State & Its Clients. Ed. by New Society Staff. 24p. 1985. pap. text ed. 6.00 (ISBN 0-566-00858-0). Gower Pub co.

Welfare State & Woman Power: Essays in State Feminism. Ed. by Helga Hernes. 180p. 1988. 37.50 (ISBN 82-00-18495-1, Norwegian University Press Publication). Oxford U Pr.

Well-Tempered Sentence: A Punctuation Handbook for the Innocent, the Eager & the Doomed. Karen E. Gordon. LC 82-19704. (Illus.). 96p. (gr. 7 up). 1983. 8.95 (ISBN 0-89919-170-3). Ticknor & Fields.
Well-Tempered Tongue: The Politics of Standard English in the High School. John Willinsky. LC 84-47530. (American University Studies XIV (Education): Vol. 4). 183p. 1984. text ed. 23.15 (ISBN 0-8204-0108-0). P Lang Pubs.
Well-Tempered Tongue: The Politics of Standard English in the High School. John Willinsky. 184p. 1988. pap. text ed. 9.95x (ISBN 0-8077-2925-6). Tchrs Coll.
Well Testing. John Lee. 150p. 1982. 40.00x (ISBN 0-89520-317-0). Soc Petrol Engineers.
Well Testing Analysis. Muhammed Aruna. (Illus.). 150p. 1987. notebook 200.00 (ISBN 0-934355-03-7). Huddleston-Brown Pubs.
Well Testing in Heterogeneous Formations. Tatian D. Streltsova. LC 87-21669. (Exxon Monographs). 1988. 59.95 (ISBN 0-471-63169-8). Wiley.
Well, This Is Another Fine How Do You Do. Johnny Hart & Brant Parker. 128p. 1984. pap. 1.95 (ISBN 0-449-12623-4, GM). Fawcett.
We'll to the Woods No More. Edouard Dujardin. Tr. by Stuart Gilbert. LC 67-13317. 1957. 5.00 (ISBN 0-8112-0268-2). New Directions.
Well-Trained Computer: Designing Systematic Instructional Materials for the Classroom Microcomputer. Mynga K. Futrell & Paul Geisert. LC 84-1629. (Illus.). 290p. 1984. 32.95 (ISBN 0-87778-190-7). Educ Tech Pubns.
Well Traveled Rabbits. Muriel Miller. LC 84-81275. (Woodlander Ser.: No. 3). (Illus.). 32p. (gr. 1-4). Date not set. pap. 7.95 (ISBN 0-915677-16-4). Roundtable Pub.
Well-Tuned Harp. Geraldine C. Little. LC 87-28838. (Illus.). 72p. (Orig.). 1988. pap. 7.00 (ISBN 0-938158-09-0). Saturday Pr.
Well Tuned Word: Musical Interpretations of English Poetry, 1597-1651. Elise B. Jorgens. LC 81-13090. (Illus.). 320p. 1982. 29.50x (ISBN 0-8166-1029-0). U of Minn Pr.
Well Water & Daisies. John S. Wade. (Juniper Bk.: No. 13). 1973. 5.00 (ISBN 1-55780-012-X). Juniper Pr WI.
Well-Wishers. Edward Eager. LC 85-5247. (Illus.). 191p. (gr. 3-7). 1985. pap. 4.95 (ISBN 0-15-294992-5, VoyB). HarBraceJ.
Well Wrought Urn: Studies in the Structure of Poetry. Cleanth Brooks. LC 47-3143. 300p. (Orig.). (YA) (gr. 7 up). 1956. pap. 8.95 (ISBN 0-15-695705-1, Harv). HarBraceJ.
Wellcome Institute for the History of Medicine, London: Subject Catalogue of the History of Medicine & Related Sciences, 18 Vols. in 3 Sections. 1980. Set. 2400.00; subject section, 9 vols. 1276.00; bibliographical section, 5 vols. 847.00; topographical section, 4 vols. 517.00. Kraus Intl.
Wellensittiche-Mein Hobby see Budgerigars.
Weller-Strawser Scales of Adaptive Behavior for the Learning Disabled Manual (WSSAB) Carol Weller & Sherri Strawser. (Orig.). 1981. pap. 33.00 test kit elementary (ISBN 0-87879-258-9, 258-9-AN); test kit-secondary 33.00 (258-9-BN); individual components 15.00 (258-9); elementary forms 15.00 (259-7N); secondary forms 14.00 (260-ON); specimen set 15.00 (258-9-S). Acad Therapy.
Weller Way: The Story of the Weller Streets Housing Cooperative. Alan McDonald. 240p. 1986. pap. cancelled (ISBN 0-571-13963-9). Faber & Faber.
Wellesley. Photos by Dan Dry. (First Edition Ser.). (Illus.). 112p. 1988. 35.00 (ISBN 0-916509-42-7); deluxe ed. 125.00 slipcased. Harmony Hse Pub LO.
Wellesley Affair: Richard Marquess Wellesley & the Conduct of Anglo-Spanish Diplomacy, 1809-1812. John K. Severn. LC 80-25416. xii, 291p. 1981. 25.00x (ISBN 0-8130-0684-8). U Presses Fla.
Wellesley College Studies in Psychology see Voluntary Isolation of Control in a Natural Muscle Group.
Wellesley Cookie Exchange Cookbook. Susan M. Peery. 1986. 15.95 (ISBN 0-396-08832-5). Dodd.
Wellesley Cookie Exchange Cookbook. Susan M. Peery. (Illus.). 256p. 1988. pap. 8.95 (ISBN 0-671-66588-X, Fireside). S&S.
Wellesley Index to Victorian Periodicals, 1824-1900, 3 vols. Ed. by Walter E. Houghton. Incl. Vol. 1. 1966; Vol. 2. 1972. 150.00x (ISBN 0-8020-1910-2); Vol. 3. 1978. 150.00x (ISBN 0-8020-2253-7). LC 66-5405. U of Toronto Pr.
Wellfleet Whale & Companion Poems. Stanley Kunitz. LC 83-61493. 1983. ltd deluxe 50.00 (ISBN 0-935296-37-9); 20.00 (ISBN 0-935296-48-4); pap. 6.95 (ISBN 0-935296-36-0). Sheep Meadow.
Wellin Magic. (Wellinworld Tapes & Books for Children: 2-9). 36p. (ps-4). 1985. 8.95 (ISBN 0-88684-180-1); cassette tape avail. Listen USA.
Wellington. Philip Guedella. 1979. Repr. of 1931 ed. lib. bdg. 30.00 (ISBN 0-8495-2007-X). Arden Lib.
Wellington. William O. Morris. LC 73-14459. (Heroes of the Nations Series). Repr. of 1904 ed. 30.00 (ISBN 0-404-58277-X). AMS Pr.
Wellington. A. Scott & C. Scott. (Clarendon Biography Ser.). (Illus.). 1973. pap. 3.50 (ISBN 0-912728-81-7). Newbury Bks.
Wellington after Waterloo. Neville Thompson. 304p. 1986. 45.00 (ISBN 0-7102-0747-6, 07476, Pub. by Routledge UK). Routledge Chapman & Hall.
Wellington Commander: The Iron Duke's Generalship. Paddy Griffith et al. 224p. 1986. 45.00 (ISBN 0-907319-08-4). Faber & Faber.
Wellington in Action. (Illus.). 1987. pap. 5.95 (ISBN 0-89747-183-0, 1076). Squad Sig Pubns.
Wellington Pelican. Bob Reese. LC 82-23587. (Critterland Ocean Adventures Ser.). (Illus.). 24p. (ps-2). 1983. PLB 9.27 (ISBN 0-516-02316-0); pap. 1.95 (ISBN 0-516-42316-9). Childrens.
Wellington: Pillar of State. Elizabeth Longford. (Illus.). 547p. 1982. pap. 6.95 (ISBN 0-586-04155-9, Pub. by Granada England). Academy Chi Pubs.
Wellington's Men: Some Soldier Autobiographies. Ed. by W. H. Fitchett. 1977. Repr. of 1900 ed. 27.00 (ISBN 0-7158-1151-7). Charles River Bks.
Wellington's Surgeon General, Sir James McGrigor. Richard L. Blanco. LC 74-75477. pap. 64.30 (ISBN 0-317-28968-3, 2023759). Bks Demand UMI.
Welliver Winter Rainbow Print: Special Edition of Neil Welliver Print. Ed. by Mark Strand. 150p. 1983. 800.00 (ISBN 0-517-55153-5). Crown.
Wellness see Wellness: Your Invitation to Full Life.
Wellness: A Context for Living. Jerry A. Johnson. LC 85-71770. 144p. 1986. pap. text ed. 19.95 (ISBN 0-943432-50-2). Slack Inc.
Wellness: An Arthritis Reality. Beth Ziebell. LC 80-84001. 144p. 1981. pap. text ed. 7.95 (ISBN 0-8403-2329-8). Kendall-Hunt.
Wellness & Health Promotion for the Elderly. Ken Dychtwald. 416p. 1985. 45.50 (ISBN 0-87189-238-3). Aspen Pub.
Wellness at Work. Robert M. Cunningham, Jr. LC 81-15500. 137p. 1982. pap. text ed. 7.95 (ISBN 0-914818-08-2, Inquiry Bk). Blue Cross & Shield.
Wellness Media: An Audiovisual Sourcebook for Health & Fitness. Ed. by NICEM Staff & J. C. Johnstone. 330p. (Orig.). 1986. pap. 49.95 (ISBN 0-89320-107-3). Natl Info Ctr NM.
Wellness Medicine. Robert A. Anderson. LC 87-70316. (Illus.). 520p. 1987. lib. bdg. 34.95 (ISBN 0-942767-00-4). Amer Health Pr.
Wellness Nursing: Concepts, Theory, Research & Practice. Carolyn C. Clark. 384p. 1986. pap. text ed. 25.95 (ISBN 0-8261-5150-7); student text 19.95. Springer Pub.
Wellness R.S.V.P. Robert F. Valois et al. 1986. 9.95 (ISBN 0-8053-2297-3). Benjamin-Cummings.
Wellness Spirituality. John J. Pilch. 112p. 1985. pap. 7.95 (ISBN 0-8245-0710-X). Crossroad NY.
Wellness, Spirituality & Sports. Thomas Ryan. LC 86-4923. 224p. 1986. pap. 8.95 (ISBN 0-8091-2801-2). Paulist Pr.
Wellness: The Revolution in Health Care. St. Vincent Hospital Staff & Theresa Peck. LC 82-23581. 1983. pap. 6.50 (ISBN 0-87125-079-9). Cath Health.
Wellness Workbook. 2nd ed. John W. Travis & Regina S. Ryan. LC 86-6052. 256p. 1986. pap. 11.95 (ISBN 0-89815-179-1). Ten Speed Pr.
Wellness Workbook: A Guide to Attaining High Level Wellness. Regina S. Ryan & John W. Travis. 15.95 (ISBN 0-89815-033-7); pap. 9.95 (ISBN 0-89815-032-9). Ten Speed Pr.
Wellness: Your Invitation to Full Life. John J. Pilch. Ed. by Miriam Frost. Orig. Title: Wellness. 128p. (Orig.). 1981. pap. text ed. 5.95 (ISBN 0-86683-758-2, HarpR). Har-Row.
Wells Coates. Sherban Cantacuzino. 112p. 1978. 48.00x (ISBN 0-900406-59-3, Pub. by Gordon Fraser). State Mutual Bk.
Wells Fargo & Co. in Idaho Territory. W. Turrentine Jackson. (Illus.). iv, 120p. (Orig.). 1984. pap. 5.95 (ISBN 0-931406-05-6). Idaho State Soc.
Wells, Fargo Detective: A Biography of James B. Hume. Richard Dillon. (Illus.). 320p. 1986. pap. 8.95 (ISBN 0-87417-113-X). U of Nev Pr.
Wells Fargo in Arizona Territory. John Theobald & Lillian Theobald. Ed. by Bert M. Fireman. LC 78-67555. 1978. pap. 10.00 (ISBN 0-910152-10-1). AZ Hist Foun.
Wells Fargo Stagecoaching in Montana Territory. W. Turrentine Jackson. (Illus.). 64p. (Orig.). 1979. pap. 2.75 (ISBN 0-917298-03-9). MT Hist Soc.
Wells of Abundance. E. V. Ingraham. 1938. pap. 2.25 (ISBN 0-87516-028-X). DeVorss.
Wells of Discontent. Charles G. Daughters. Ed. by Stuart Bruchey & Vincent P. Carosso. LC 78-18959. (Small Business Enterprise in America Ser.). (Illus.). 1979. Repr. of 1937 ed. lib. bdg. 27.50x (ISBN 0-405-11463-X). Ayer Co Pubs.
Wells of Hell. Masterton. 2.95 (ISBN 0-523-48042-3, Dist. by Warner Pub Services & Saint Martin's Press). Tor Bks.
Wells of Hell. Graham Masterton. 320p. 1989. pap. 3.95 (ISBN 0-8125-2211-7). Tor Bks.
Wells of Power: The Oil Fields of South-Western Asia. Olaf Caroe. (Middle East in the 20th Century Ser.). 1976. Repr. of 1951 ed. lib. bdg. 29.50 (ISBN 0-306-70825-6). Da Capo.
Wells of Power: The Oilfields of South-Western Asia. Olaf Caroe. LC 75-6465. (History & Politics of Oil Ser.). (Illus.). xx, 240p. 1976. Repr. of 1951 ed. 23.65 (ISBN 0-88355-284-1). Hyperion Conn.
Wells of Salvation. Edmund E. Wells. (Orig.). pap. 2.00 (ISBN 0-686-30400-4). WOS.
Wells of Salvation: Meditations of Isaiah. Charles Ellis & Norma Ellis. 224p. (Orig.). 1986. pap. 7.50 (ISBN 0-85151-457-X). Banner of Truth.
Wells of Williamsburg: Colonial Time Capsules. Ivor Noel Hume. LC 71-109382. (Archaeological Ser.: No. 4). (Illus.). 48p. (Orig.). 1969. pap. 3.95 (ISBN 0-910412-09-X). Williamsburg.
Wellspring. Janice H. Giles. LC 75-15989. 272p. 1975. 8.95 (ISBN 0-395-20731-2). HM.
Wellspring. Edward Hawkins. 1978. text ed. 9.95 (ISBN 0-07-027295-6). McGraw.
Wellspring. Donna Keene & Dathy Keene. Ed. by Faren Bachelis. (Illus.). 64p. (gr. 5-8). 1982. 8.00 (ISBN 0-931724-19-8). Dandy Lion.
Wellspring: A Story from the Deep Country. Barbara Dean. LC 79-2606. (Illus.). 208p. 1979. pap. 8.95 (ISBN 0-933280-01-7). Island CA.
Wellspring of Guidance: Messages 1963-1968. rev. ed. The Universal House of Justice. LC 76-129996. 1976. 9.95 (ISBN 0-87743-032-2, 225-005); pap. 4.95 (ISBN 0-87743-033-0, 225-006). Baha'i.
Wellspring of Worship. Jean Corbon. 1988. pap. 12.95 (ISBN 0-8091-2968-X). Paulist Pr.
Wellspring: On the Myth & Source of Culture. Robert P. Armstrong. LC 73-85781. (Illus.). 100p. 1975. 30.00x (ISBN 0-520-02571-7). U of Cal Pr.
Wellsprings. Harry Lewis. LC 81-16762. lib. bdg. 12.50 (ISBN 0-917672-18-6); pap. 5.95 (ISBN 0-917672-17-8). Momos.
Wellsprings: A Book of Spiritual Exercises. Anthony DeMello. LC 84-13655. 216p. 1985. 12.95 (ISBN 0-385-19616-4). Doubleday.
Wellsprings: A Book of Spiritual Exercises. Anthony DeMello. LC 86-4478. 240p. 1986. pap. 7.95 (ISBN 0-385-19617-2, Im). Doubleday.
Wellsprings of a Nation: America Before 1801. Rodger D. Parker. LC 77-72082. (Illus.). 1977. pap. 10.00x (ISBN 0-912296-13-5, Dist. by U Pr of Va). Am Antiquarian.
Wellsprings of Literary Creation. Ursula R. Mahlendorf. LC 84-72198. (Studies in German Literature, Linguistics, & Culture: Vol. 18). (Illus.). 292p. 1985. 29.00x (ISBN 0-938100-34-3). Camden Hse.
Wellsprings of Music. Curt Sachs. Ed. by Jaap Kunst. LC 77-23410. 1977. pap. 6.95 (ISBN 0-306-80073-X). Da Capo.
Wellsprings of the American Spirit. Ed. by F. Ernest Johnson. (Religion & Civilization Series of the Institute for Religious & Social Studies). 241p. 1964. Repr. of 1948 ed. 26.50x (ISBN 0-8154-0121-3). Cooper Sq.
Wellsprings of the Pentecostal Movement. David Womack. 96p. 1968. pap. 1.50 (ISBN 0-88243-628-7, 02-0628). Gospel Pub.
Wellsprings of Torah. Alexander Z. Friedman. Tr. by Gertrude Hirschler from Yiddish. 584p. 1980. slipcased 18.95 (ISBN 0-910818-20-7); pap. 16.95 (ISBN 0-910818-04-5). Judaica Pr.
Welsh Administrative & Territorial Units, Medieval & Modern. Melville Richards. 324p. 1969. text ed. 25.00 (ISBN 0-900768-08-8, Pub. by U of Wales). Humanities.
Welsh Airs. R. S. Thomas. LC 87-60982. 56p. 1987. 19.95 (ISBN 0-907476-72-4, Pub. by Poetry Wales Pr UK); pap. 9.95 (ISBN 0-907476-75-9, Pub. by Poetry Wales Pr UK). Dufour.
Welsh Ambassadors: Powys Lives & Letters. Louis Marlow. LC 73-157126. 1971. 16.00x (ISBN 0-912568-04-6). Colgate U Pr.
Welsh Borders. Lawrence Garner. (Visitor's Guides Ser.). (Illus.). 144p. 1986. pap. 8.95 (ISBN 0-935161-35-X). Hunter Pub NY.
Welsh Castles of Edward I. Arnold Taylor. 129p. 1986. pap. 12.00 (ISBN 0-907628-71-0). Hambledon Press.
Welsh Cattle Drovers. Richard J. Colyer. 55p. 1976. text ed. 17.50x (ISBN 0-7083-0592-X, Pub. by U of Wales). Humanities.
Welsh Church from Conquest to Reformation. Glanmor Williams. 612p. 1976. text ed. 28.50x (ISBN 0-7083-0651-9, Pub. by U of Wales). Humanities.
Welsh Classics: The Law of Hywel Dda, Vol. 2. Dafydd Jenkins. 1985. 75.00x (ISBN 0-317-54070-X, Pub. by Gomer Pr). State Mutual Bk.
Welsh Dylan. John Ackerman. (Illus.). 143p. 1982. pap. 6.95 (ISBN 0-586-08350-2, Pub. by Granada England). Academy Chi Pubs.
Welsh Elizabethan Catholic Martyrs. D. Aneurin Thomas. 331p. 1971. text ed. 28.50 (ISBN 0-900768-97-5, Pub. by U of Wales). Humanities.
Welsh Embassador. Thomas Dekker. LC 82-45779. (Malone Society Reprint Ser.: No. 48). Repr. of 1920 ed. 40.00 (ISBN 0-404-63048-0). AMS Pr.
Welsh-English, English-Welsh Dictionary. H. Meurig Evans & W. O. Thomas. (Welsh & Eng.). 42.50 (ISBN 0-87557-091-7, 091-7). Saphrograph.
Welsh Fever: Welsh Activities in the United States & Canada Today. David Greenslade. (Illus.). 344p. 1986. text ed. 16.95 (ISBN 0-905928-56-3). B Hirsch.
Welsh Folk Lore. Elias Owen. xii, 359p. 1980. Repr. of 1896 ed. lib. bdg. 47.00 (ISBN 0-8414-6548-7). Folcroft.
Welsh Folk-Lore: A Collection of Folk-Tales & Legends of North Wales. Elias Owen. 1977. Repr. of 1896 ed. 29.00x (ISBN 0-7158-1179-7). Charles River Bks.
Welsh Folklore & Folk-Custom. Thomas G. Jones. LC 77-3195. 1977. lib. bdg. 39.00 (ISBN 0-8414-5319-5). Folcroft.
Welsh Folklore & Folk-Custom. Thomas G. Jones. 255p. 1980. Repr. of 1930 ed. lib. bdg. 37.00 (ISBN 0-8492-1366-5). R West.
Welsh Folklore & Legends. L. A. Simmonds. 2.00 (ISBN 0-913714-10-0). Legacy Bks.
Welsh Ghosts. Jeannette Dixon. 2.00 (ISBN 0-913714-11-9). Legacy Bks.
Welsh Heirs. Glyn Jones. 158p. 1985. 22.50x (ISBN 0-317-54073-4, Pub. by Gomer Pr). State Mutual Bk.
Welsh: History, Charter & By-Laws. Edward G. Hartmann. 57p. 1981. 2.00 (ISBN 0-318-16861-8). Welsh Soc Phila.
Welsh History Review, December 1988, Vol. 14, No. 2. Ed. by Trevor Herbert & Gareth E. Jones. 1988. pap. text ed. 9.95 (Pub. by U of Wales). Humanities.
Welsh History Review, June 1988, Vol. 14, No. 1. Ed. by Trevor Herbert & Gareth E. Jones. 1988. pap. text ed. 9.95 (Pub. by U of Wales). Humanities.
Welsh History Review, Vol. 13: December 1987, Nos. 3 & 4. Ed. by Kenneth O. Morgan. 128p. 1987. pap. text ed. 9.95 ea. (Pub. by U of Wales). Humanities.
Welsh in Fun. Heini Gruffudd & Edwyn Loan. 20.00X (ISBN 0-9500178-4-1, Pub. by Y Lolfa Wales). State Mutual Bk.
Welsh in Fun-Tastic. Heini Gruffudd & Edwyn Loan. 20.00X (ISBN 0-9500178-7-6, Pub. by Y Lolfa Wales). State Mutual Bk.
Welsh in Their History. Gwyn A. Williams. (Illus.). 218p. 1982. (Pub. by Croom Helm Ltd); pap. 11.95 (ISBN 0-7099-3651-6). Routledge Chapman & Hall.
Welsh Is Fun. Heini Gruffudd & Elwyn Ioan. 1987. pap. 7.95 (ISBN 0-317-59609-8). British Am Bks.
Welsh Knight: Paradoxicality in Chretien's Conte del Graal. Rupert T. Pickens. LC 76-47499. (French Forum Monographs: No. 6). 163p. (Orig.). 1977. pap. 10.95x (ISBN 0-917058-05-4). French Forum.
Welsh Language 1961-1981: An Interpretative Atlas. J. Aitchison & H. Carter. 84p. 1985. pap. text ed. 9.95x (ISBN 0-7083-0906-2, Pub. by U of Wales). Humanities.
Welsh Latin Chronicles Annales Cambriae & Related Texts. K. Hughes. (Sir John Rhys Memorial Lectures in Celtic Studies). 1973. pap. 5.50 (ISBN 0-85672-609-5, Pub. by British Acad). Longwood Pub Group.
Welsh Law of Women. Ed. by D. Jenkins & M. Owen. 253p. 1980. text ed. 28.50x (ISBN 0-7083-0771-X, Pub. by U of Wales). Humanities.
Welsh Legends & Fairy Lore. Daniel Parry-Jones. LC 76-10823. 1976. Repr. of 1963 ed. lib. bdg. 39.00 (ISBN 0-8414-6724-2). Folcroft.
Welsh Legends & Folklore. D. Parry-Jones. 59.95 (ISBN 0-8490-1282-1). Gordon Pr.
Welsh Life of St. David. D. Simon Evans. 176p. 1988. text ed. 35.00 (ISBN 0-7083-0995-X, Pub. by U of Wales). Humanities.
Welsh Metrical Treatise Attributed to Einion Offeiriad. T. Parry. (Sir John Rhys Memorial Lectures in Celtic Studies). 1961. pap. 5.50 (ISBN 0-902732-79-X, Pub. by British Acad). Longwood Pub Group.
Welsh Metrics. J. Glyn Davies. LC 78-72625. (Celtic Language & Literature: Goidelic & Brythonic). Repr. of 1911 ed. 14.50 (ISBN 0-404-17547-3). AMS Pr.
Welsh Nationalist Party, 1925-1945: A Call to Nationhood. Hywel D. Davies. LC 83-11221. 300p. 1983. 27.50 (ISBN 0-312-86190-7). St Martin.
Welsh People. John Rhys & David B. Jones. LC 68-25263. (British History Ser., No. 30). 1969. Repr. of 1906 ed. lib. bdg. 62.95x (ISBN 0-8383-0233-5). Haskell.
Welsh Personal Names. Haini Gruffudd. pap. 8.95 (ISBN 0-317-06852-0). British AM Bks.
Welsh Personal Names. heini Gruffudd. 20.00 (ISBN 0-904864-99-5, Pub. by Y Lolfa Wales). State Mutual Bk.
Welsh Phonology. Ed. by Martin Ball & G. Jones. 296p. 1984. text ed. 40.00x (ISBN 0-7083-0861-9, Pub. by U of Wales). Humanities.
Welsh Poems & Ballads. George H. Borrow. LC 78-72620. (Celtic Language & Literature: Goidelic & Brythonic). Repr. of 1915 ed. 20.00 (ISBN 0-404-17537-6). AMS Pr.
Welsh Poems: Sixth-Century to 1600. Ed. & tr. by Gwyn Williams. 1974. 22.50x (ISBN 0-520-02603-9). U of Cal Pr.
Welsh Proverbs. H. H. Vaughan. 59.95 (ISBN 0-8490-1283-X). Gordon Pr.
Welsh Proverbs with English Translations. Henry H. Vaughan. LC 74-8296. 1974. Repr. of 1889 ed. lib. bdg. 45.00 (ISBN 0-8414-9162-3). Folcroft.
Welsh Proverbs with English Translations. Henry H. Vaughan. LC 68-17945. 386p. (Eng. & Welsh.). 1969. Repr. of 1889 ed. 43.00x (ISBN 0-8103-3205-1). Gale.

Werewolves: A Collection of Original Stories. Ed. by Jane Yolen & Martin H. Greenberg. LC 87-45863. 288p. (gr. 5 up). 1988. 13.95i (ISBN 0-06-026798-4); PLB 13.89 (ISBN 0-06-026799-2). HarpJ.

Werkbund. Lucius Burckhardt. 118p. 1987. 90.00x (ISBN 0-85072-108-3, Design Council Bks). State Mutual Bk.

Werke, 3 vols. Adelbert Von Chamisso. LC 75-41053. (BCL Ser.: No. II). 1976. Repr. of 1908 ed. 72.50 set (ISBN 0-404-14850-6). AMS Pr.

Werke, 5 vols. Leopold Kronecker. LC 66-20394. 1969. Repr. Set. 150.00 (ISBN 0-8284-0224-8). Chelsea Pub.

Werke, 2 Vols. in 1. P. G. Lejeune-Dirichlet. Ed. by L. Kronecker. LC 68-54716. (Ger). 1969. Repr. 49.50 (ISBN 0-8284-0225-6). Chelsea Pub.

Werke, 43 Vols. Karl Marx & Frederick Engels. write for info. Adlers Foreign Bks.

Werke, 5 vols. Paracelsus. (Ger.). Repr. of 1591 ed. Set. 277.25x (ISBN 3-7965-0471-X). Adlers Foreign Bks.

Werke, Vol. 2. Johannes von Paltz. (Illus.). 504p. 1983. 79.20 (ISBN 3-11-004955-4). De Gruyter.

Werke fuer Pianoforte, 7 vols. Johann Strauss, Sr. Ed. by Johann Strauss, Jr. Incl. Vol.1. Walzer 1-38. 176p (ISBN 0-89371-001-6); Vol. 2. Walzer 39-68. 184p (ISBN 0-89371-002-4); Vol. 3. Walzer 69-96. 184p (ISBN 0-89371-003-2); Vol. 4. Walzer 97-122. 168p (ISBN 0-89371-004-0); Vol. 5. Walzer 123-150. 176p (ISBN 0-89371-005-9); Vol. 6. Polkas, Galoppe, Maersche. 144p (ISBN 0-89371-006-7); Vol. 7. Quadrillen. 160p (ISBN 0-89371-007-5). (Ger.). 1976. Repr. of 1889 ed. 325.00x set (ISBN 0-89371-000-8); 45.00x ea. Broude.

Werke und Briefe. Historisch-kritische Ausgabe (Hamburger Klopstock-Ausgabe) Friedrich G. Klopstock. Ed. by Elisabeth Hopker-Herberg et al. Incl. Section Briefe I. Briefe 1738-1750. 1978. 136.00 (ISBN 3-11-007257-2); Section Briefe II. Briefe 1751-1752. 1985. 199.00 (ISBN 3-11-010552-7); Section Briefe VII. Briefe 1776-1782 (1) Text. 1982. 94.00 (ISBN 3-11-008128-8); Section Briefe VII. Briefe 1776-1782 (2) Apparat-Kommentar (Nr. 1-131) 1982. 146.00 (ISBN 3-11-008932-7); Section Briefe VII. Briefe 1776-1782 (3) Apparat-Kommentar (Nr. 132-244) Anhang. 1982. 146.00 (ISBN 3-11-008933-5); Section Werke II. Epigramme. Text und Apparat. 1982. 157.00 (ISBN 3-11-008735-9). (Ger.). De Gruyter.

Werke und Briefe. Historisch-kritische Ausgabe (Hamburger Klopstock-Ausgabe) Friedrich G. Klopstock. Ed. by Elisabeth Hopker-Herberg et al. Incl. Section Werke IV, Bd. 4. Der Messias. Band 4 Apparat. 1984. 210.00 (ISBN 3-11-008898-3); Section Addenda, Bd. 2. Klopstock, Arbeitstagebuch. 1977. 130.00 (ISBN 3-11-005713-1); Section Addenda, Bd. 3. Die Zeitgenossischen Drucke von Klopstocks Werken. Band 1 Bibliographie. 1981. 146.00 (ISBN 3-11-008119-9); Section Addenda, Bd. 3. Die zeitgenossischen Drucke von Klopstocks Werken. Band 2 Bibliographie. 1981. 146.00 (ISBN 3-11-008570-4). (Ger.). De Gruyter.

Werner: A Tragedy. George Gordon Byron. Bd. with Facsimile of the Acting Version of William Charles Macready. 232p. 1970. soft cover 32.50x (ISBN 3-7705-0360-0). Adlers Foreign Bks.

Werner Bergengreun's Das Buch Rodenstein: A Detailed Analysis. David J. Parent. 1974. pap. text ed. 17.60x (ISBN 90-2792-622-0). Mouton.

Werner Heisenberg: A Bibliography of His Writings. Compiled by Martha Baker-Cassidy & David Cassidy. LC 82-60498. (Berkeley Papers in History of Science: No. 9). 200p. (Orig.). 1984. pap. 10.00x (ISBN 0-918102-10-3). U Cal Hist Sci Tech.

Werner Herzog: Images at the Horizon. Ed. by Gene Walsh. Roger Ebert. (Facets Multimedia Ser.). (Illus., Orig.). 1980. pap. 4.50 (ISBN 0-918432-26-X). NY Zoetrope.

Werner Krauss. W. Goetz. 1976. lib. bdg. 59.95 (ISBN 0-8490-2814-0). Gordon Pr.

Wernerian Theory of the Neptunian Origin of Rocks: A Facsimile Reprint of Elements of Geognosy, 1808. Robert Jameson. Ed. by George W. White. LC 75-43364. (Contributions to the History of Geology Ser.). (Illus.). 1976. Repr. of 1808 ed. 31.95x (ISBN 0-02-847160-1). Hafner.

Werner's Syndrome & Human Aging. Ed. by Darrell Salk et al. (Advances in Experimental Medicine & Biology Ser.: Vol. 190). 672p. 1985. 110.00x (ISBN 0-306-42101-1, Plenum Pr). Plenum Pub.

Werner's the Thyroid: A Fundamental & Clinical Text. 5th ed. Ed. by Sidney H. Ingbar & Lewis E. Braverman. LC 65-9673. (Illus.). 1526p. 1986. text ed. 137.50 (ISBN 0-397-50802-6, Lippincott Medical). Lippincott.

Wernher der Gartenaere: Meier Helmbrecht. Ed. by Ulrich Seelbach. Tr. by Linda B. Parshall. 200p. 1986. lib. bdg. 25.00 (ISBN 0-8240-8954-5). Garland Pub.

Wernher von Braun. Christopher Lampton. Ed. by Maury Solomon. (Impact Bio Ser.). (Illus.). 160p. (YA) (gr. 7 up). 1988. 12.90 (ISBN 0-531-10606-3). Watts.

WERT & Psychogram: Projective-Objective Character Tests. W. John Weilgart. (Illus.). 1979. pap. 5.00 cancelled (ISBN 0-912038-03-9). Cosmic Comm.

Werther see Sorrows of Young Werther.

Wertmuller: Artist & Immigrant Farmer. Franklin D. Scott. 1963. 1.00 (ISBN 0-318-03685-1). Swedish Am.

Wes Montgomery. Adrian Ingram. 128p. (Orig.). 1987. pap. 9.95 (ISBN 0-9506224-9-4, HL 00183830, Pub. by Ashley Mark Pub). H Leonard Pub Corp.

Wes Weatherby, Gunfighter. Merle M. Funk. (YA) (gr. 7 up). 1979. 9.95 (ISBN 0-685-93883-2, Avalon). Bouregy.

Wes Wyatt's Seminar Selling System. Wes Wyatt. LC 80-67857. 1980. 19.95 (ISBN 0-87863-018-X, Farnsworth Pub Co). Longman Finan.

Wesen der Repraesentation und der Gestaltwandel der Demokratie im 20. Jahrhundert see Repraesentation in der Demokratie.

Wesen der Sprachielichen Gebilde. Ludwig Sutterlin. 1902. 20.00 (ISBN 0-8274-3693-9). R West.

Wesen und Sinn Des Spiels: The Essence & Meaning of Games. Jacobus J. Buytendijk. LC 75-35064. (Studies in Play & Games). (Illus., Ger.). 1976. Repr. 17.00x (ISBN 0-405-07915-X). Ayer Co Pubs.

Wesker on File. Compiled by Glenda Leeming & Simon Trussler. (Writers on File Ser.). 96p. 1985. pap. 6.50 (ISBN 0-413-53660-2, 9391). Heinemann Ed.

Wesker: The Playwright. Glenda Leeming. 224p. 1982. pap. 11.95 (ISBN 0-413-49240-0, NO. 3649). Heinemann Ed.

Wesley & Methodism. F. J. Snell. 243p. 1983. Repr. of 1900 ed. lib. bdg. 43.50 (ISBN 0-8495-4977-9). Arden Lib.

Wesley & Sanctification. Harald Lindstrom. LC 83-17025. 256p. (Orig.). 1984. 10.95 (ISBN 0-310-75011-3, 17025P). Zondervan.

Wesley Hymns: As a Guide to Scriptural Teaching. John Lawson. 224p. 1988. Repr. 14.95 (ISBN 0-310-75290-6, 17184). Zondervan.

Wesley Speaks on Christian Vocation. Paul W. Chilcote. LC 86-72494. 104p. (Orig.). 1987. pap. 6.95 (ISBN 0-88177-041-8, DR041B). Discipleship Res.

Wesleyan & Tractarian Worship. Trevor Dearing. LC 66-72190. 1966. text ed. 15.00x (ISBN 0-8401-0531-2). A R Allenson.

Wesleyan Bible Commentary, 6 vols. Charles W. Carter. 4484p. 1986. 149.50 (ISBN 0-913573-33-7). Hendrickson MA.

Wesleyan Bible Commentary, 2 vols. Ed. by Charles W. Carter. 808p. 1986. 24.95 (ISBN 0-913573-36-1). Hendrickson MA.

Wesleyan Bible Commentary, Vol. 1. Charles W. Carter. 1060p. 1986. 27.95 (ISBN 0-913573-34-5). Hendrickson MA.

Wesleyan Bible Commentary, Vol. 2. Charles W. Carter. 660p. 1986. 27.95 (ISBN 0-913573-35-3). Hendrickson MA.

Wesleyan Bible Commentary, Vol. 4. Charles W. Carter. 752p. 1986. 27.95 (ISBN 0-913573-37-X). Hendrickson MA.

Wesleyan Bible Commentary, Vol. 5. Charles W. Carter. 676p. 1986. 27.95 (ISBN 0-913573-38-8). Hendrickson MA.

Wesleyan Bible Commentary, Vol. 6. Charles W. Carter. 528p. 1986. 27.95 (ISBN 0-913573-39-6). Hendrickson MA.

Wesleyan Movement in the Industrial Revolution. Wellman J. Warner. LC 66-24768. 1967. Repr. of 1930 ed. 8.00x (ISBN 0-8462-0960-8). Russell.

Wesleyan Photographs. Philip Trager et al. Ed. by Vincent Scully & Samuel Green. LC 81-21853. 72p. 1982. 42.50x (ISBN 0-8195-5063-9); Ltd. ed. 250.00x; pap. 19.95 (ISBN 0-8195-6073-1). Wesleyan U Pr.

Wesleyan Theology: A Sourcebook. Thomas A. Langford. 318p. 1984. lib. bdg. 30.00 (ISBN 0-939464-40-3); pap. 14.95 (ISBN 0-939464-41-1). Labyrinth Pr.

Wesleyan Theology Today. Ed. by Theodore Runyon. 1983. pap. 19.95 (ISBN 0-687-44452-7). Abingdon.

Wesley's Christology: An Interpretation. John Deschner. LC 85-2274. 244p. 1985. pap. 12.95x (ISBN 0-87074-200-0). SMU Press.

Wesley's Christology: An Interpretation. John Deschner. 240p. 1988. pap. 11.95 (ISBN 0-310-36861-8, 17114P). Zondervan.

Wesley's Fifty-Two Standard Sermons. 9.95 (ISBN 0-686-12929-6). Schmul Pub Co.

Wesley's New Testament Notes. 14.95 (ISBN 0-686-12927-X). Schmul Pub Co.

Wesley's Notes on the Bible. G. Roger Schoenhals. 624p. text ed. 27.95 (ISBN 0-310-36410-8, 17098). Zondervan.

Wesley's Old & New Testament Notes. 200.00 (ISBN 0-686-12928-8). Schmul Pub Co.

Wesley's Veterans, 7 vols. pap. 5.95 ea. Schmul Pub Co.

Wesley's Works, 14 vols. 125.00 set (ISBN 0-686-23581-9). Schmul Pub Co.

Wesleys World Parish. 3.50 (ISBN 0-686-27780-5). Schmul Pub Co.

Wesner Conjectures. R. Wesner. LC 82-21421. 128p. 1985. pap. 4.95 (ISBN 0-88437-070-4). Psych Dimensions.

Wessex. Patricia Beer & Fay Godwin. (Illus.). 224p. 1985. 30.95 (ISBN 0-241-11550-7, Pub. by Hamish Hamilton England). David & Charles.

Wessex. (AA Beautiful Britain Ser.). 160p. 1988. 29.95 (ISBN 0-86145-517-7, Pub. by British Tour). Salem Hse Pubs.

Wessex. (AA-OS Leisure Guides). (Illus.). 120p. 1988. pap. 19.95 (ISBN 0-86145-658-0, Pub. by British Tour). Salem Hse Pubs.

Wessex - C. (AA-OS Leisure Guides). (Illus.). 120p. 1988. 24.95 (ISBN 0-86145-668-8, Pub. by British Tour). Salem Hse Pubs.

Wessex & England from Alfred to Edgar. David N. Dumville. 256p. 1988. 63.00 (ISBN 0-85115-430-1, Pub. by Boydell & Brewer). Longwood Pub Group.

Wessex & Old English Poetry. Cecilia A. Hotchner. LC 73-5980. 1939. Repr. lib. bdg. 35.50 (ISBN 0-8414-2093-9). Folcroft.

Wessex from A. D. One Thousand. J. H. Bettey. (Regional History of England Ser.). 352p. 1986. text ed. 42.95 (ISBN 0-582-49207-6); pap. text ed. 32.95 (ISBN 0-582-49208-4). Longman.

Wessex Novels of Thomas Hardy. Randall Williams. LC 74-31361. 1924. lib. bdg. 35.00 (ISBN 0-8414-9374-X). Folcroft.

Wessex of Romance. Wilkinson Sherren. 1973. Repr. of 1903 ed. 30.00 (ISBN 0-8274-0450-6). R West.

Wessex of Thomas Hardy. Bertram C. Windle. LC 78-610. 1906. lib. bdg. 35.50 (ISBN 0-8414-9586-6). Folcroft.

Wessex Tales. Thomas Hardy. LC 77-79927. (Hardy New Wessex Editions). 1978. pap. 3.95 (ISBN 0-312-86276-8). St Martin.

West. Eliot Porter. (Illus.). 1988. 60.00 (ISBN 0-8212-1711-9). NYGS.

West: A Trivia Quiz Book. Allen C. Kupfer & David L. Sheenan, III. 192p. (Orig.). 1985. pap. 2.50 (ISBN 0-446-32525-2). Warner Bks.

West Africa: A Travel Survival Kit. Alex Newton. (Illus.). 480p. (Orig.). 1988. pap. 12.95 (ISBN 0-86442-028-5). Lonely Planet.

West Africa: An Introduction to Its History. Michael Crowder. (Illus.). 1977. pap. text ed. 10.95 (ISBN 0-582-60003-0). Longman.

West Africa Fertilizer Study: Chad, Vol. VI. R. B. Diamond et al. (Technical Bulletin - T-8). (Illus.). 55p. (Orig.). 1977. pap. 4.00 (ISBN 0-88090-007-5). Intl Fertilizer.

West Africa Fertilizer Study: Mali, Vol. III. R. B. Diamond et al. (Technical Bulletin T-5). (Illus.). 64p. (Orig.). 1976. pap. 4.00 (ISBN 0-88090-004-0). Intl Fertilizer.

West Africa Fertilizer Study: Mauritania, Vol. VII. R. B. Diamond et al. (Technical Bulletin T-9). (Illus.). 39p. (Orig.). 1978. pap. 4.00 (ISBN 0-88090-008-3). Intl Fertilizer.

West Africa Fertilizer Study: Niger, Vol. V. R. B. Diamond et al. (Technical Bulletin - T-7). (Illus.). 47p. (Orig.). 1978. pap. 4.00 (ISBN 0-88090-006-7). Intl Fertilizer.

West Africa Fertilizer Study: Regional Overview, Vol. I. R. B. Diamond et al. (Technical Bulletin Ser.: T-3). 79p. (Orig.). 1977. pap. 4.00 (ISBN 0-88090-039-3). Intl Fertilizer.

West Africa Fertilizer Study: Senegal, Vol. II. R. B. Diamond et al. (Technical Bulletin, T-4). (Illus.). 64p. (Orig.). pap. 4.00 (ISBN 0-88090-003-2). Intl Fertilizer.

West Africa Fertilizer Study: Upper Volta, Vol. IV. R. B. Diamond et al. (Technical Bulletin - T-6). (Illus.). 60p. (Orig.). 1977. pap. 4.00 (ISBN 0-88090-005-9). Intl Fertilizer.

West Africa: Introduction Geologique et Termes Stratigraphiques-Geological Introduction & Stratigraphic Terms. Ed. by J. Fabre. LC 83-13418. (Lexique Stratigraphique International: Nouvelle Series No. 1). (Illus.). 426p. 1984. 87.00 (ISBN 0-08-030267-X). Pergamon.

West Africa Partitioned: The Elephants & the Grass, Vol. 2. John D. Hargreaves. LC 74-10451. 240p. 1985. text ed. 35.00x (ISBN 0-299-09990-3). U of Wis Pr.

West Africa Portraits: A Biographical Dictionary of West African Personalities, 1947-1977. Ed. by A. H. Kirk-Greene. 1983. 35.00x (ISBN 0-7146-3112-4, F Cass Co). Biblio Dist.

West Africa: Regional Cooperation & Development. Ed. by Julius Okolo & Stephen Wright. 250p. 1988. pap. 27.50 (ISBN 0-8133-7354-9). Westview.

West African Christianity: The Religious Impact. Lamin Sanneh. 304p. (Orig.). 1983. pap. 11.95 (ISBN 0-88344-703-7). Orbis Bks.

West African City: A Study of Tribal Life in Freetown. Michael Banton. (International African Institute Ser.). 1957. 29.95x (ISBN 0-19-724102-6). Oxford U Pr.

West African Countries & Peoples, British & Native. James A. Horton. 1868. 38.00 (ISBN 0-8115-2962-2). Kraus Repr.

West African Culture Dynamics: Archaeological & Historical Perspectives. Ed. by B. K. Schwartz, Jr. (World Anthropology Ser.). (Illus.). xiv, 630p. 1980. text ed. 77.50 (ISBN 90-279-7920-0). Mouton.

West African Folk-Tales. W. H. Barker. (Illus.). 1917. 18.00 (ISBN 0-8115-2992-4). Kraus Repr.

West African Folk-Tales. William H. Barker. LC 72-99339. (Illus.). 209p. 1972. Repr. of 1917 ed. lib. bdg. 12.50 (ISBN 0-8411-0010-1). Metro Bks.

West African Kingdoms in the Nineteenth-Century. Ed. by Daryll Forde & P. M. Kaberry. 1967. pap. 14.95x (ISBN 0-19-724187-5). Oxford U Pr.

West African Leadership. Magnus J. Sampson. 160p. 1969. 29.50x (ISBN 0-7146-1766-0, F Cass Co). Biblio Dist.

West African Marine Fisheries: Alternatives for Management. James A. Crutchfield & Rowena Lawson. LC 73-10843. (Program of International Studies of Fishery Arrangements Ser.: Paper No. 3). pap. 20.00 (ISBN 0-317-28865-2, 2020960). Bks Demand UMI.

West African Monetary Union: An Analytical Review. Rattan J. Bhatia. (Occasional Papers: No. 35). 59p. 1985. pap. 7.50 (ISBN 0-317-19912-9). Intl Monetary.

West African Narrow Strip Weaving. Venice Lamb & Alastair Lamb. Ed. by Patricia Fiske. (Illus.). 48p. 1975. pap. 6.00 (ISBN 0-685-56285-9). Textile Mus.

West African Oil: Will It Matter? David C. Underwood. LC 83-16359. (Significant Issues Ser.: Vol. 5, No. 6). 57p. 1983. 5.95 (ISBN 0-89206-046-8). CSI Studies.

West African Oil: Will It Matter? David C. Underwood. (Significant Issues Ser.: Vol. V, No. 6). 64p. (Orig.). 1983. pap. text ed. 6.95 (ISBN 0-8191-5921-2, Pub. by CSIS). U Pr of Amer.

West African Passage: A Journey Through Nigeria, Chad & the Cameroons. Margery Perham. Intro. by A. H. Kirk-Greene. 245p. 1983. 26.00 (ISBN 0-7206-0609-8, Pub. by P Owen Ltd). Dufour.

West African Poetry: A Critical History. Robert Fraser. (Illus.). 352p. 1986. 42.50 (ISBN 0-521-30993-X); pap. 15.95 (ISBN 0-521-31223-X). Cambridge U Pr.

West African Psychology. Edward G. Parrinder. LC 74-15076. Repr. of 1951 ed. 27.50 (ISBN 0-404-12125-X). AMS Pr.

West African Resistance: The Military Response to Colonial Occupation. Ed. by Michael Crowder. LC 73-127106. (Illus.). 314p. 1971. 49.50 (ISBN 0-8419-0049-3, Africana). Holmes & Meier.

West African Sahel: Human Agency & Environmental Change. Jeffrey A. Gritzner. (Research Papers: No. 226). (Illus., Orig.). 1988. pap. 12.00 (ISBN 0-89065-130-2). U Chicago Comm Geo.

West African Secret Societies: Their Organizations, Officials & Teaching. Frederick W. Butt-Thompson. 1969. Repr. of 1929 ed. 20.00 (ISBN 0-87266-003-6). Argosy.

West African Secret Societies, Their Organizations, Officials & Teaching. Frederick W. Butt-Thompson. LC 70-109320. (Illus.). 1970. Repr. of 1929 ed. 35.00x (ISBN 0-8371-3585-0, BWA&). Greenwood.

West African States. Ed. by John Dunn. LC 77-80832. (African Studies Ser.). (Illus.). 1978. o. p. 42.50 (ISBN 0-521-21801-2); pap. 15.95 (ISBN 0-521-29283-2). Cambridge U Pr.

West African Studies. 3rd ed. Mary Kingsley. (Illus.). 507p. 1964. 35.00x (F Cass Co). Biblio Dist.

West African Sufi: The Religious Heritage & Spiritual Quest of Cerno Bokar Saalif Taal. Louis Brenner. LC 83-4803. 215p. 1984. lib. bdg. 28.00x (ISBN 0-520-05008-8). U of Cal Pr.

West African Trade. Peter T. Bauer. LC 67-19585. 1967. Repr. of 1954 ed. 45.00x (ISBN 0-678-06510-1). Kelley.

West African Urbanization: A Study of Voluntary Associations in Social Change. Kenneth L. Little. LC 65-14349. pap. 46.80 (ISBN 0-317-20625-7, 2024579). Bks Demand UMI.

West African Village Novel, Vol. 8. George Nyamndi. (European University Studies: No. 27). 241p. 1983. pap. 23.70 (ISBN 3-261-05077-2). P Lang Pubs.

West African Wager: Houphouet Versus Nkrumah. Jon Woronoff. LC 72-5155. 371p. 1972. 22.50 (ISBN 0-8108-0523-5). Scarecrow.

West Against the Wind. Lisa K. Murrow. (YA) (gr. 7 up). Date not set. pap. 2.50. Troll Assocs.

West Against the Wind. Liza K. Murrow. LC 87-45337. 248p. (YA) (gr. 7 up). 1987. 13.95 (ISBN 0-8234-0668-7). Holiday.

West American Cenozoic Echinoidea. Ulysses S. Grant, 4th & L. G. Hertlein. 1967. Repr. of 1938 ed. 23.00 (ISBN 0-384-09680-8). Johnson Repr.

West & Other Plays. Steven Berkoff. LC 85-14834. 96p. (Orig.). 1985. 22.50 (ISBN 0-394-55017-X). Grove.

West & Other Plays. Steven Berkoff. LC 85-14834. 96p. 1985. pap. 7.95 (ISBN 0-394-62084-4, Ever). Grove.

West & Reconstruction. Eugene H. Berwanger. LC 80-26357. (Illus.). 304p. 1981. 24.95 (ISBN 0-252-00868-5). U of Ill Pr.

West & South Africa. Christopher Hill & James Barber. (Chatham House Papers on Foreign Policy). (Orig.). 1983. pap. 10.95x (ISBN 0-7100-9232-6). Routledge Chapman & Hall.

West & the Rest of Us: White Predators, Black Slavers & the African Elite. Chinweizu. 544p. 1978. text ed. 21.95x (ISBN 0-88357-015-7); pap. 9.95 (ISBN 0-88357-016-5). Nok Pubs.

West & the World: A History of Civilization, Vol. 1. 2nd ed. Kevin Reilly. 384p. 1988. pap. text ed. 16.95t (ISBN 0-06-045346-X, HarpC). Har-Row.

West & the World: A History of Civilization, Vol. 2. 2nd ed. Kevin Reilly. 432p. 1988. pap. text ed. 16.95t (ISBN 0-06-045347-8, HarpC). Har-Row.

TITLE INDEX WEST GERMANY.

West & the World: A Topical History of Civilization, 2 vols. Kevin Reilly. (Illus.). 1980. One Vol. Ed. pap. text ed. 26.95 scp (ISBN 0-06-045345-1, HarpC); Vol. 1. pap. text ed. 18.50 scp (ISBN 0-06-045343-5); Vol. 2. pap. text ed. 18.50 scp (ISBN 0-06-045344-3). Har-Row.

West & World since Nineteen Forty-Five. Glenn Blackburn. LC 84-51149. 150p. 1984. pap. text ed. write for info. (ISBN 0-312-86280-6). St Martin.

West (Arizona, Nevada, Utah) Thomas G. Aylesworth & Virginia L. Aylesworth. (Let's Discover the States Ser.). (Illus.). 66p. (gr. 5 up). 1988. lib. bdg. 14.95x (ISBN 1-55546-563-3). Chelsea Hse.

West As Romantic Horizon. William H. Goetzmann & Joseph C. Porter. LC 81-12424. (Illus.). 128p. 1981. o. p. 34.50x (ISBN 0-936364-04-1); pap. 18.95. U of Nebr Pr.

West As Romantic Horizon. William H. Goetzmann et al. LC 81-12424. 128p. (Orig.). 1981. pap. 17.95 (ISBN 0-936364-05-X). Joslyn Art.

West Asia & North Africa: A Documentary Study of Major Crises, 1974-78. Krishan Gopal & Kokila K. Gopal. 434p. 1981. 37.50x (ISBN 0-86590-012-4). Apt Bks.

West Asia on a Shoestring. 5th ed. Tony Wheeler. 368p. (Orig.). 1986. pap. 8.95 (ISBN 0-908086-68-7). Lonely Planet.

West Asia: Problems & Prospects. N. Bhaktavatsalam. 1985. text ed. 15.00x (ISBN 0-86590-594-0, Pub. by Sterling Pubs India). Apt Bks.

West Bank & Gaza: Toward the Making of a Palestinian State. Emile A. Nakhleh. 1979. pap. 7.00 (ISBN 0-8447-3335-0). Am Enterprise.

West Bank & the Rule of Law. Raja Shehadeh & Jonathan Kuttab. 128p. 1980. pap. 5.50 (Pub. by Intl Commission of Jurists). Interbk Inc.

West Bank Data Base 1987 Report: Demographic, Economic, Legal, Social, & Political Developments in the West Bank. Meron Benvenisti. (West Bank Data Base Project Ser.). (Illus.). 94p. 1987. pap. 18.95 (ISBN 0-8133-0688-4). Westview.

West Bank Data Project: A Survey of Israel's Policies. Meron Benvenisti. LC 84-2984. (AEI Studies: No. 398). 97p. 1984. 25.00 (ISBN 0-8447-3545-0); pap. 15.00 (ISBN 0-8447-3544-2). Am Enterprise.

West Bank-East Bank: The Palestinians in Jordan, 1949-1967. Shaul Mishal. LC 77-20692. (Illus.). 1978. 18.00x (ISBN 0-300-02191-7). Yale U Pr.

West Bank-Gaza Strip. Rebecca Stetoff. (Places & Peoples of the World Ser.). (Illus.). 104p. (gr. 5 up). 1988. lib. bdg. 12.95x (ISBN 1-55546-782-2). Chelsea Hse.

West Bank Handbook: A Political Lexicon. Meron Benvenisti et al. 248p. 1986. pap. 28.00 (ISBN 0-8133-0473-3). Westview.

West Bank: History, Politics, Society & Economy. Don Peretz. 1986. pap. 26.50x (ISBN 0-8133-0297-8). Westview.

West Bank Palestinian Family. Ibrahim W. Ata. 250p. 1987. text ed. 55.00 (ISBN 0-7103-0186-3, Kegan Paul). Routledge Chapman & Hall.

West Bank Story: An Israeli Arab's View of Both Sides of a Tangled Conflict. rev. ed. Rafik Halabi. Tr. by Ina Friedman. (Illus.). 324p. 1985. pap. 7.95 (ISBN 0-15-695724-8, Harv). HarBraceJ.

West Bengal & the Federalizing Process in India. Marcus F. Franda. LC 68-10391. 1968. 33.00x (ISBN 0-691-03068-5). Princeton U Pr.

West Berlin: History of the Nineteen Seventy-One Agreement. V. Vysotsky. (Illus.). 355p. 1975. 17.95 (ISBN 0-8464-0964-X). Beekman Pubs.

West Berlin: The City Museums for the Cultural Patrimony of Prussia, 15 vols. (Illus.). 1980. Set. 140.00. Kraus Repr.

West Berlin: The City Museums for the Cultural Patrimony of Prussia: Egyptian Museum (Agyptisches Museum) (Illus., Ger.). 1980. 10.00 (ISBN 3-7630-2000-4). Kraus Repr.

West Berlin: The City Museums for the Cultural Patrimony of Prussia: Museum of Classical Antiques (Antiken Museum) (Illus., Ger.). 1980. 10.00 (ISBN 3-7630-2001-2). Kraus Repr.

West Berlin: The City Museums for the Cultural Patrimony of Prussia: Museum for Islamic Art (Museum fur Islamische Kunst) (Illus., Ger.). 1980. 10.00 (ISBN 3-7630-2002-0). Kraus Repr.

West Berlin: The City Museums for the Cultural Patrimony of Prussia: Museum for Indian Art (Museum fur Indische Kunst) (Illus., Ger.). 1980. 10.00 (ISBN 3-7630-2004-7). Kraus Repr.

West Berlin: The City Museums for the Cultural Patrimony of Prussia: Sculpture Gallery (Skulpturegalerie) (Illus., Ger.). 1980. 10.00 (ISBN 3-7630-2005-5). Kraus Repr.

West Berlin: The City Museums for the Cultural Patrimony of Prussia: Picture Gallery (Gemaldegalerie) (Illus., Ger.). 1980. 10.00 (ISBN 3-7630-2006-3). Kraus Repr.

West Berlin: The City Museums for the Cultural Patrimony of Prussia: National Gallery (Nationalgalerie) (Illus., Ger.). 1980. 10.00 (ISBN 3-7630-2007-1). Kraus Repr.

West Berlin: The City Museums for the Cultural Patrimony of Prussia: Cabinet of Prints & Engravings (Kupferstichkabinett) (Illus., Ger.). 1980. 10.00 (ISBN 3-7630-2008-X). Kraus Repr.

West Berlin: The City Museums for the Cultural Patrimony of Prussia: Museum of Handicrafts (Kunstgewerbe Museum) (Illus., Ger.). 1980. 10.00 (ISBN 3-7630-2009-8). Kraus Repr.

West Berlin: The City Museums for the Cultural Patrimony of Prussia: Art Library (Kunstbibliothek) (Illus., Ger.). 1980. 10.00 (ISBN 3-7630-2010-1). Kraus Repr.

West Berlin: The City MUseums for the Cultural Patrimony of Prussia: Museum of Prehistory & Early History (Museum fur Vor-und Frugeshichte) (Illus., Ger.). 1980. 10.00 (ISBN 3-7630-2011-X). Kraus Repr.

West Berlin: The City Museums for the Cultural Patrimony of Prussia: Ethnological Museum I (Museum fur Volkerkunde Band 1) (Illus., Ger.). 1980. 10.00 (ISBN 3-7630-2012-8). Kraus Repr.

West Berlin: The City Museums for the Cultural Patrimony of Prussia: Ethnological Museum II (Museum fur Volkerkunde Band 2) (Illus., Ger.). 1980. 10.00 (ISBN 3-7630-2013-6). Kraus Repr.

West Berlin: The City Museums for the Cultural Patrimony of Prussia: Museum of German Folklore (Museum fur Deutsche Volkskunde) (Illus., Ger.). 1980. 10.00 (ISBN 3-7630-2014-4). Kraus Repr.

West Berlin: The City Museums for the Cultural Patrimony Prussia: Museum for East Asian Art (Museum fur Oastasiatische Kunst) (Illus., Ger.). 1980. 10.00 (ISBN 3-7630-2003-9). Kraus Repr.

West Branch of the Penobscot & the Kennebec Gorge Flip Map. Ron Rathnow. LC 87-34978. (Great American Rivers Flip Map Ser.). (Illus.). 56p. 1989. pap. 4.95 (ISBN 0-89732-081-6). Menasha Ridge.

West Branch Trolleys: Street Railways of Lycoming & Clinton Counties, Pennsylvania. Paul J. Schieck & Harold E. Cox. (Illus., Orig.). 1978. pap. 10.00 (ISBN 0-911940-29-4). Cox.

West Broadway Neighborhood, Newport, Rhode Island. John F. Herzan. (Statewide Preservation Report). (Illus.). 59p. (Orig.). 1977. pap. 5.95 (ISBN 0-917012-95-X). RI Pubns Soc.

West by East: The American West in the Gilded Age. Gene M. Gressley. (Charles Redd Monographs in Western History: No. 1). 54p. 1972. pap. 2.50 (ISBN 0-941214-30-3, Dist. by Signature Bks). C Redd Ctr.

West Canada Creek see Up Old Forge Way.

West Coast Bed & Breakfast Guide: California-Oregon-Washington. Courtia Worth & Terry Berger. 1986. pap. 12.95 (ISBN 0-671-62946-8). P-H.

West Coast Chinese Boy. Sing Lim. (Illus.). 64p. (gr. 6-12). 1979. 6.95 (ISBN 0-88776-121-6). Tundra Bks.

West Coast Plays, 13 & 14. Alan Finneran et al. Ed. by Rick Foster. (Illus.). 300p. (Orig.). 1983. pap. 12.50 (ISBN 0-934782-13-X). CA Thea-Westcoast.

West Coast Plays: A Collection of Complete Scripts of New One Act Plays, Vol. 19-20. Ed. by Robert Hurwitt. 340p. 1986. pap. 12.95 (ISBN 0-317-43009-2, 9900). CA Thea-WestCoast.

West Coast Plays: A Collection of Complete Scripts of New Plays. Ed. by Rick Foster. (Illus.). 186p. (Orig.). 1981. pap. 6.00 (ISBN 0-934782-09-1). CA Thea-Westcoast.

West Coast Plays: A Collection of Complete Scripts of New Plays, No. 1. 1977. 4.95 (ISBN 0-934782-00-8). CA Thea-Westcoast.

West Coast Plays: A Collection of Complete Scripts of New Plays, No. 3. (Illus.). 1978. pap. 6.00 (ISBN 0-934782-02-4). CA Thea-Westcoast.

West Coast Plays: A Collection of Complete Scripts of New Plays, No. 4. (Illus., Orig.). 1979. pap. text ed. 6.00 (ISBN 0-934782-03-2). CA Thea-Westcoast.

West Coast Plays: A Collection of Complete Scripts of New Plays, No. 6. (Illus.). 1980. pap. 6.00 (ISBN 0-934782-05-9). CA Thea-Westcoast.

West Coast Plays: A Collection of Complete Scripts of New Plays, No. 7. (Illus.). 1980. pap. 6.00 (ISBN 0-934782-06-7). CA Thea-Westcoast.

West Coast Plays: A Collection of Complete Scripts of New Plays, No. 8. (Illus.). 160p. (Orig.). 1981. pap. 6.00 (ISBN 0-934782-07-5). CA Thea-Westcoast.

West Coast Plays: A Collection of Eight Complete Scripts of New Plays, Nos. 11 & 12. Ed. by Rick Foster. (Illus.). 369p. (Orig.). 1982. pap. 9.95 (ISBN 0-934782-11-3). CA Thea-Westcoast.

West Coast Plays: A Collection of Eight Complete Scripts of New Plays, Nos. 13 & 14. Ed. by Rick Foster. (Illus.). 300p. (Orig.). 1982. pap. 12.95 (ISBN 0-317-18251-X). CA Thea-Westcoast.

West Coast Plays: A Collection of Eight Complete Scripts of New Plays, Nos. 15 & 16. Ed. by Rob Hurwitt. (Illus.). 327p. (Orig.). 1983. pap. 12.95 (ISBN 0-934782-15-6). CA Thea-Westcoast.

West Coast Plays: A Collection of Eight Complete Scripts of New Plays, No. 17 & 18. Ed. by Rob Hurwitt. 320p. 1985. pap. 12.95 (ISBN 0-934782-17-2). CA Thea-Westcoast.

West Coast Plays: A Collection of New Plays, from California, No. 21 & 22. Ed. by Rob Hurwitt. 328p. 1988. 12.95 (ISBN 0-934782-21-0). CA Thea-Westcoast.

West Coast Plays 10. Ed. by Rick Foster. (Illus.). 185p. (Orig.). 1981. pap. 6.00 (ISBN 0-317-18245-5). CA Thea-Westcoast.

West Coast Theatre Directory Nineteen Eighty-Four to Eighty-Five. Ed. by Patti Johns. 60p. (Orig.). 1984. pap. 6.00 (ISBN 0-317-18254-4). CA Thea-Westcoast.

West Coast Theatre Directory, 1987. 136p. 1987. pap. 10.00 (ISBN 0-934782-18-0). CA Thea Westcoast.

West Coast Trail & Nitinat Lakes. 5th ed. Sierra Club of British Columbia. (Illus.). 96p. 1980. pap. 8.95 (ISBN 0-88894-275-3, Pub. by Douglas & McIntyre Ltd England). Signpost Bk Pub.

West Coast Victorians: A Nineteenth Century Legacy. Kenneth Naversen. LC 87-17426. (Illus.). 256p. 1988. 34.95 (ISBN 0-89802-495-1); pap. 26.95 (ISBN 0-89802-494-3). Beautiful Am.

West Collection. West Publishing Staff. (Illus.). 224p. 1986. pap. text ed. 60.00 (ISBN 0-314-95791-X); ltd. ed. 75.00 (ISBN 0-317-45599-0). West Pub.

West Country. (AA Regional Touring Guides). (Illus.). 152p. 1988. pap. 19.95 (ISBN 0-86145-501-0, Pub. by British Tour). Salem Hse Pubs.

West Country. (AA Holiday Guides). (Illus.). 192p. 1988. pap. 11.95 (ISBN 0-86145-644-0, Pub. by British Tour). Salem Hse Pubs.

West Country Fly Fishing. Anne V. Bark. (Illus.). 140p. 1987. pap. 20.95 (ISBN 0-7134-1883-4, Pub. by Batsford England). David & Charles.

West Country Historic Houses & Their Families, Vol. 2: Dorset, Wiltshire & N. Somerset. Eric R. Delderfield. 16.95 (ISBN 0-7153-4910-4). David & Charles.

West-Country Historical Studies. H. P. Finberg. LC 69-11235. (Illus.). 1969. 27.50x (ISBN 0-678-05515-7). Kelley.

West Country Passenger Steamers. Grahame Farr. LC 67-103343. (Illus.). 1967. 29.95x (ISBN 0-678-05656-0). Kelley.

West Countrymen in Prince Edward's Isle: A Fragment of the Great Migration. Basil Greenhill & Ann Giffard. LC 67-113574. pap. 62.00 (2026521). Bks Demand UMI.

West County Tithe Barns. M. J. Beacham. 1987. pap. 30.00x (Pub. by K A F Brewin Bks UK). State Mutual Bk.

West Door. Alfred Corn. 1988. 17.95 (ISBN 0-670-81956-5). Viking.

West Eighty-Five: Art & the Law. West Publishing Company Staff. LC 85-50908. (Illus.). 120p. 1985. pap. text ed. write for info. (ISBN 0-314-93133-3). West Pub.

West End Horror. Nicholas Meyer. 1980. pap. 2.50 (ISBN 0-345-30592-2). Ballantine.

West Europa Auf Dem Weg in die Informationsgesellschaft. Christian Lutz. 148p. (Orig., Ger.). 1984. pap. text ed. 20.00. Interbk Inc.

West European City: A Social Geography. P. White. 280p. 1984. pap. 24.95 (ISBN 0-470-20613-6, Co-Pub. with Longman). Wiley.

West European City: A Social Geography. Paul White. LC 83-9382. (Illus.). 1984. pap. text ed. 16.95 (ISBN 0-582-30047-9). Wiley.

West European Communism & American Foreign Policy. Michael Ledeen. 310p. 1987. 34.95 (ISBN 0-88738-140-5). Transaction Bks.

West European Economic Handbook. (Economic Handbook Ser.). 300p. 1987. 80.00x (ISBN 0-86338-142-1, Pub. by Euromonitor Pubns). Gale.

West European Integration: It's Policies & International Relations. Vsevolod Kniazhinsky. 426p. 1984. 18.75x (ISBN 0-317-53827-6, Pub. by Collets (UK)). State Mutual Bk.

West European Integration: Policies & International Relations. V. Kniazhinsky. 426p. 1985. 6.95 (ISBN 0-8285-2814-4, Pub. by Progress Pubs USSR). Imported Pubns.

West European Pacifism & the Strategy for Peace. Ed. by Peter Van den Dungen. LC 84-11585. 208p. 1985. 29.95 (ISBN 0-312-86284-9). St Martin.

West European Politics Today. Geoffrey K. Roberts & Jill Lovecy. LC 83-18702. 224p. 1984. 25.00 (ISBN 0-7190-0983-9, Pub. by Manchester Univ Pr); pap. 8.00 (ISBN 0-7190-0909-X). St Martin.

West European Population Change. Allan Findlay & Paul White. 304p. 1986. 43.00 (ISBN 0-7099-3667-2, Pub. by Croom Helm Ltd). Routledge Chapman & Hall.

West European Security Policy: Asserting European Priorities. Reinhardt Rummel. (Westview Special Studies in West European Politics & Society: No. 34). 200p. 1988. pap. 25.00 (ISBN 0-8133-7534-7). Westview.

West Federal Taxation: Comprehensive Volume, 1988. William H. Hoffman, Jr. 1100p. 1987. text ed. 51.00 (ISBN 0-314-34511-6); write for info. tchrs.' ed. (ISBN 0-314-35089-6); study guide 16.50 (ISBN 0-314-35090-X). West Pub.

West Federal Taxation: Corporations, Partnerships, Trusts & Estates, 1988. William H. Hoffman, Jr. 900p. 1987. text ed. 43.72 (ISBN 0-314-34512-4); write for info. tchrs.' ed. (ISBN 0-314-35083-7); study guide 16.50 (ISBN 0-317-59697-7). West Pub.

West Federal Taxation: Individual Income Tax, 1988. William H. Hoffman, Jr. 975p. 1987. text ed. 44.50 (ISBN 0-314-34513-2); write for info. tchrs.' ed. (ISBN 0-314-35079-9); study guide 17.25. West Pub.

West Florida & Its Relations to the Historical Cartography of the United States. Henry E. Chambers. 1973. pap. 9.00 (ISBN 0-384-08451-6). Johnson Repr.

West Florida Cookbooks & a Random Selection of Early Recipes. Ed. by James A. Servies. 60p. 1984. write for info. (ISBN 0-933776-15-2). Perdido Bay.

West Florida in Relation to the Historical Cartography of the United States. Henry E. Chambers. LC 78-63863. (Johns Hopkins University. Studies in the Social Sciences. Sixteenth Ser. 1898: 5). Repr. of 1898 ed. 11.50 (ISBN 0-404-61119-2). AMS Pr.

West from Abilene. Al Cody. (Gunsmoke Western Ser.). 176p. 1988. text ed. 12.95x (ISBN 0-85997-852-4, Pub. by Firecrest Pub Ltd). Prescott Pr NH.

West from Deadwood. Al Cody. 1980. pap. 1.95 (ISBN 0-8439-0850-5, Leisure Bks). Leisure NY.

West from Fort Pierre: The World of Scotty Philip. James M. Robinson. (Great West & Indian Ser: Vol. 43). (Illus.). 1974. 9.50 (ISBN 0-87026-032-4). Westernlore.

West from Home: Letters of Laura Ingalls Wilder, San Francisco 1915. Laura I. Wilder. Ed. by Roger L. MacBride. LC 73-14342. 176p. (YA) (gr. 7 up). 1974. 13.95i (ISBN 0-06-024110-1); PLB 13.89 (ISBN 0-06-024111-X). HarpJ.

West from Home: Letters of Laura Ingalls Wilder, San Francisco 1915. Laura I. Wilder. Ed. by Roger L. MacBride. LC 73-14342. (Trophy I Can Read Bks.). (Illus.). 168p. (YA) (gr. 7 up). 1974. pap. 3.50 (ISBN 0-06-440081-6, Trophy). HarpJ.

West from Singapore. Louis L'Amour. pap. 2.95 (ISBN 0-317-58106-6). Bantam.

West Futuna Aniwa: An Introduction to a Polynesian Outlier Language. Janet W. Dougherty. LC 82-7005. (UC Publications in Linguistics: Vol. 102). 732p. 1984. pap. text ed. 40.00x (ISBN 0-520-09657-6). U of Cal Pr.

West German Cinema since 1945: A Reference Handbook. Richard C. Helt & Marie Helt. LC 87-16429. (Illus.). 758p. 1987. 52.50 (ISBN 0-8108-2053-6). Scarecrow.

West German Economy. Eric Owen Smith. LC 83-8630. 350p. 1983. 32.50 (ISBN 0-312-86290-3). St Martin.

West German Elite Views on National Security & Foreign Policy Issues. Dietmar Schoessler & Erich Weede. 128p. pap. text ed. 30.00 (ISBN 3-7610-8207-X). Oelgeschlager.

West German Film in the Course of Time: Reflections on the Twenty Years since Oberhausen. Eric Rentschler. v, 260p. (Orig.). 1984. pap. 14.95 (ISBN 0-913178-00-4). Redgrave Pub Co.

West German Filmmakers on Film: Visions & Voices. Ed. by Eric Rentschler. (Modern German Voices Ser.). 300p. 1988. 45.00 (ISBN 0-8419-0984-9); pap. 19.50 (ISBN 0-8419-0985-7). Holmes & Meier.

West German Foreign Aid, Nineteen Fifty-Six to Nineteen Sixty-Six. Karel Holbik & Henry Allen Myers. LC 68-58498. 1968. 7.95 (ISBN 0-8419-8716-5, Pub. by Boston U Pr). Holmes & Meier.

West German Foreign Policy: The Domestic Setting. Gebhard Schweigler. (Washington Papers: No. 106). 136p. 1984. pap. 9.95 (ISBN 0-275-91635-9, B1635). Praeger.

West German Hospitals & European Medical Care Services. W. A. Farndale et al. 136p. 1983. 89.00x (ISBN 0-901812-18-8, Pub. by Ravenswood Pubns UK); pap. 69.00x (ISBN 0-901812-55-2). State Mutual Bk.

West German Lay Judges: Recruitment & Representativeness. John P. Richert. LC 82-20251. 1984. 22.00x (ISBN 0-8130-0701-1). U Presses Fla.

West German Model: Perspectives on a Stable State. Ed. by William E. Paterson & Gordon Smith. (Illus.). 184p. 1981. 27.50x (ISBN 0-7146-3180-9, F Cass Co); pap. 12.50x (ISBN 0-7146-4034-4, F Cass Co). Biblio Dist.

West German Peace Movement & the National Question. Kim R. Holmes. LC 84-3745. (Foreign Policy Report Ser.). 73p. 1984. 7.50 (ISBN 0-89549-058-7). Inst Foreign Policy Anal.

West German Poets on Society & Politics. Karl H. Van D'Elden. LC 78-20793. 252p. 1979. 25.00x (ISBN 0-8143-1628-X). Wayne St U Pr.

West German Politics. Lewis J. Edinger. LC 85-11703. (Illus.). 350p. 1985. 32.50x (ISBN 0-231-06090-4); pap. 11.00x (ISBN 0-231-06091-2). Columbia U Pr.

West German Politics. Geoffrey K. Roberts. LC 77-185875. 206p. 1972. 10.95 (ISBN 0-8008-8151-6); pap. 5.95 (ISBN 0-8008-8152-4). Taplinger.

West German Social Democrats, 1969-1982: Profile of a Party in Power. Gerard Braunthal. LC 82-3464. (Replica Edition Ser.). 350p. 1983. softcover 37.00x (ISBN 0-86531-958-8). Westview.

West Germanic Inflection, Derivation & Compounding. Joseph B. Voyles. LC 72-94456. (Janua Linguarum, Ser. Practica: No. 145). 204p. (Orig.). 1974. pap. text ed. 27.60x (ISBN 90-2792-711-1). Mouton.

West Germany. Donald S. Detwiler & Ilse E. Detwiler. (World Bibliography Ser.: No. 72). 300p. 1988. lib. bdg. 45.00 (ISBN 1-85109-017-7). ABC-Clio.

West Germany. Barbara Einhorn. Ed. by Janet Caulkins. (Countries of the World Ser.). (Illus.). 48p. (gr. 1-6). 1988. 11.90 (ISBN 0-531-18187-1, Pub. by Bookwright Pr). Watts.
West Germany. Martin Hintz. LC 82-17882. (Enchantment of the World Ser.). (Illus.). 128p. (gr. 5-9). 1983. PLB 22.60 (ISBN 0-516-02793-X). Childrens.
West Germany. George Morey. LC 75-44866. (Silver Burdett Countries Ser.). (Illus.). 64p. (gr. 7 up). 1976. PLB 14.96 (ISBN 0-382-06105-5). Silver.
West Germany. Valerie Schloredt. (Countries Ser.). (Illus.). 48p. (YA) (gr. 5-10). 1988. PLB 14.96 (ISBN 0-382-09471-9); pap. 6.95 (ISBN 0-382-09478-6). Silver.
West Germany. Waite. 1978. 22.95 (ISBN 0-7134-1087-6, Pub. by Batsford England). David & Charles.
West Germany. (Economist Business Traveller's Guides). (Illus.). 1988. 17.95 (ISBN 0-13-234956-6). Prentice Hall Pr.
West Germany. (Let's Visit Places & Peoples - - Nations, Dependencies, & Sovereignties of the World Ser.). (Illus.). (gr. 5 up). 1988. 12.95 (ISBN 0-222-00913-6). Chelsea Hse.
West Germany: A European & Global Power. Wilfied L. Kohl & Giorgio Basevi. (Illus.). 240p. 1980. 22.00x (ISBN 0-669-03162-3). Lexington Bks.
West Germany: A Geography of Its People. Trevor Wild. LC 79-55698. (Illus.). 255p. 1980. text ed. 27.50x (ISBN 0-06-497658-0). B&N Imports.
West Germany & the European Community: Changing Interests & Competing Policy Objectives. Werner J. Feld. LC 81-8599. 160p. 1981. 35.00 (ISBN 0-275-90621-3, C0621). Praeger.
West Germany: Internal Structures & External Relations: Foreign Policy of the Federal Republic of Germany. Frank R. Pfetsch. LC 87-29129. 288p. 1988. lib. bdg. 45.00 (ISBN 0-275-92868-3, C2868). Praeger.
West Germany: Politics & Society. David Childs & Jeffrey Johnson. 1981. 26.00 (ISBN 0-312-86300-4). St Martin.
West Germany: Politics of Non-Planning. Hans J. Arndt. LC 66-17524. (National Planning Ser.: No. 8). pap. 46.50 (ISBN 0-317-28999-3, 2020394). Bks Demand UMI.
West Germany's Foreign Plicy in the Era of Brandt & Schmidt, 1969-1982: An Introduction. Michael Wolffsohn. 95p. pap. 16.55 (ISBN 3-8204-8616-X). P Lang Pubs.
West Germany's Foreign Policy Agenda. Roger Morgan. (Washington Papers: Vol. VI, No. 54). 80p. (Orig.). 1978. pap. text ed. 7.95 (ISBN 0-8191-6003-2, Pub. by CSIS). U Pr of Amer.
West Germany's Foreign Policy: Nineteen Forty-Nine to Nineteen Seventy-Nine. Ed. by Wolfram F. Hanrieder. (Special Study in West European Politics & Society). 1979. lib. bdg. 42.00 (ISBN 0-89158-579-6). Westview.
West Germany's Foreign Policy: The Impact of the Social Democrats & the Greens. Diane Rosolowsky. LC 87-12017. (Contributions in Political Science Ser.: No. 192). 168p. 1987. lib. bdg. 35.00 (ISBN 0-313-25672-1, RWG/). Greenwood.
West Germany's Trade with the East: Hypotheses & Perspectives. Frank D. Weiss. 120p. 1983. lib. bdg. 44.50x (ISBN 3-16-344677-9, Pub. by J C B Mohr BRD). Coronet Bks.
West Goes East: Paul Georg von Mollendorff & Great Power Imperialism in Late Yi Korea. Yur-Bok Lee. (Illus.). 288p. 1988. text ed. 29.00x (ISBN 0-8248-1150-X). UH Pr.
West Greenlandic. Michael Fortesque. LC 84-19862. (Descriptive Grammars Ser.). 384p. 1984. 52.50 (ISBN 0-7099-1069-X, Pub. by Croom Helm Ltd). Routledge Chapman & Hall.
West Ham: A Study in Social & Industrial Problems. Edward G. Howarth & Mona Wilson. LC 79-56958. (English Working Class Ser.). 1980. lib. bdg. 46.00 (ISBN 0-8240-0111-7). Garland Pub.
West Ham United: A Complete Record, 1900-1987 - Includes Thames Ironworks, 1895-1900. John Northcutt & Roy Shoesmith. 432p. 1987. 60.00x (ISBN 0-907969-29-1, Pub. by Breedon Bks Pub UK). State Mutual Bk.
West Ham United: The Making of a Football Club. Charles Korr. (Sport & Society Ser.). (Illus.). 272p. 1987. 24.95 (ISBN 0-252-01405-7). U of Ill Pr.
West Haven: Classroom Culture & Society in a Rural Elementary School. Norris B. Johnson. LC 84-17371. 420p. 1985. 32.00x (ISBN 0-8078-1630-2). U of NC Pr.
West Highland Cattle! The Grand Olde Breed. John M. Anderson. (Illus.). 96p. 1985. 8.50 (ISBN 0-318-19047-8). J Mac Anderson.
West Highland Railway. John Thomas. (Illus.). 198p. 1984. 24.95 (ISBN 0-946537-14-3). David & Charles.
West Highland Railway: History of the Railways of the Scottish Highlands, Vol. 1. John Thomas. (Illus.). 224p. 1986. pap. 12.95 (ISBN 0-946537-22-4). David & Charles.
West Highland Steam. Picton Publishing Staff. 1987. 32.00x (Pub. by Picton UK). State Mutual Bk.
West Highland White Terriers. Martin Weil. (Illus.). 128p. 1983. 9.95 (ISBN 0-87666-732-9, KW-113). TFH Pubns.
West Highlands of Scotland. W. H. Murray. (Companion Guides Ser.). (Illus.). 1984. pap. 11.95 (ISBN 0-13-154782-8); 11.95 (ISBN 0-13-154774-7). P-H.
West in Russia & China, 2 vols. Donald W. Treadgold. Incl. Vol.1. Russia 1472-1917. 324p. pap. 30.00x (ISBN 0-8133-0254-4); Vol. 2. China 1582-1949. 252p. pap. 25.00x (ISBN 0-8133-0255-2). (Westview Encore Edition Ser.). 1985. Westview.
West in Russia & China: Religious & Secular Thought in Modern Times, 2 vols. Donald W. Treadgold. Incl. Vol. 1. Russia, 1472-1917. pap. 91.00; Vol. 2. China, 1582-1949. pap. 68.50. LC 72-78886. pap. (2022474). Bks Demand UMI.
West in the Diplomacy of the American Revolution. Paul C. Phillips. Repr. of 1913 ed. 19.00 (ISBN 0-384-46390-8). Johnson Repr.
West in the Life of the Nation. Arrell M. Gibson. 640p. 1976. pap. text ed. 19.00 (ISBN 0-669-08407-7). Heath.
West India Colonies. James MacQueen. LC 72-88416. 1970. Repr. of 1825 ed. 25.00x (ISBN 0-8371-1829-8, MAI&). Greenwood.
West India Pickles. William P. Talboys. text ed. 18.75 (ISBN 0-8369-9255-5, 9108). Ayer Co Pubs.
West Indian Amphibians & Reptiles: A Checklist. Albert Schwartz & Robert W. Henderson. (Contributions in Biology & Geology Ser.: No. 74). (Illus.). 176p. 1988. pap. text ed. 14.95 (ISBN 0-89326-156-4). Milwaukee Pub Mus.
West Indian Community of Greater Hartford: Connecticut. rev. ed. Lynroy A. Grant & Frank A. Stone. 52p. 1985. 5.00 (ISBN 0-317-65372-5). I N Thut World Educ Ctr.
West Indian Constitutions: Post-Independence Reform. Sir Fred Phillips. LC 84-63092. 370p. 1985. lib. bdg. 50.00 (ISBN 0-379-20834-2). Oceana.
West Indian Family Structure. Michael G. Smith. LC 84-45531. (American Ethnological Society Monographs: No. 36). 1988. Repr. of 1962 ed. 35.00 (ISBN 0-404-62935-0). AMS Pr.
West Indian Folk Tales. Philip Sherlock. (Illus.). 151p. (gr. 3 up). 1988. pap. 6.95 (ISBN 0-19-274127-6). Oxford U Pr.
West Indian Folk Tales. Philip M. Sherlock. (Oxford Myths & Legends Ser.). (Illus.). (gr. 6-12). 1978. Repr. of 1966 ed. 14.95 (ISBN 0-19-274116-0). Oxford U Pr.
West Indian Green Monkeys: Problems in Historical Biogeography. W. W. Denham. (Contributions to Primatology Ser.: Vol. 24). (Illus.). viii, 80p. 1987. 32.00 (ISBN 3-8055-4518-5). S Karger.
West Indian Islands. Hans W. Hannau. (Illus.). 1977. 7.95 (ISBN 0-912458-85-2). E A Seemann.
West Indian Literature. Ed. by Bruce King. LC 79-1255. 247p. 1980. 23.00 (ISBN 0-208-01814-X, Archon). Shoe String.
West Indian Literature: An Index to Criticism, 1930-1975. Jeannette B. Allis. (Reference Bks.). 1981. lib. bdg. 36.50 (ISBN 0-8161-8266-3, Hall Reference). G K Hall.
West Indian Novel & Its Background. 2nd ed. Kenneth Ramchand. (Studies in Caribbean Literature). xii, 310p. 1984. 17.50x (ISBN 0-435-98665-1). Heinemann Ed.
West Indian Poetry. 2nd. Ed. ed. Lloyd W. Brown. (Studies in Caribbean Literature). 202p. (Orig.). 1984. pap. text ed. 16.50x (ISBN 0-435-91830-3). Heinemann Ed.
West Indian Societies. David Lowenthal. 1972. pap. 9.95x (ISBN 0-19-501559-2). Oxford U Pr.
West Indian Stories. Ed. by Andrew Salkey. 224p. (Orig.). 1968. pap. 4.95 (ISBN 0-571-08630-6). Faber & Faber.
West Indian Stories. Ed. by Andrew Salkey. 224p. 1986. Repr. of 1960 ed. PLB 50.00 (ISBN 0-8495-4980-9). Arden Lib.
West Indian Tales of Old. Algernon E. Aspinall. LC 69-18650. (Illus.). 1969. Repr. of 1915 ed. 25.00x (ISBN 0-8371-4977-0, ASW&). Greenwood.
West Indians. Miriam Klevan. (The Peoples of North America Ser.). (Illus.). 112p. Date not set. lib. bdg. 16.95 (ISBN 1-55546-140-9). Chelsea Hse.
West Indians & Their Language. P. Roberts. 224p. 1988. 39.50 (ISBN 0-521-35136-7); pap. 10.95 (ISBN 0-521-35955-4). Cambridge U Pr.
West Indies. Don Brothers. (Places & Peoples of the World Ser.). (Illus.). 96p. (gr. 5 up). 1989. lib. bdg. 12.95x (ISBN 1-55546-793-8). Chelsea Hse.
West Indies. C. Washington Eves. 1976. lib. bdg. 59.95 (ISBN 0-8490-2815-9). Gordon Pr.
West Indies see Coins of the British Commonwealth of Nations to the End of the Reign of George VI.
West Indies & the Spanish Main. Anthony Trollope. 352p. 1985. pap. 5.95 (ISBN 0-87052-210-8, Pub. by Allan Sutton England). Hippocrene Bks.
West Indies Before & since Emancipation Compromising the Windward & Leeward Islands' Military Command. John Davy. 1971. Repr. of 1854 ed. 45.00x (ISBN 0-7146-1935-3, F Cass Co). Biblio Dist.
West Indies in Eighteen Thirty-Seven. Joseph Sturge & Thomas Harvey. 475p. 1968. Repr. of 1838 ed. 34.00x (ISBN 0-7146-1900-0, F Cass Co). Biblio Dist.
West Indies in Twenty-Two Days. Cyndy Morreale & Sam Morreale. Ed. by Richard Harris. (Twenty-Two Days Ser.). (Illus.). 136p. (Orig.). 1987. pap. 6.95 (ISBN 0-912528-74-5). John Muir.
West Indies Island Arcs. Ed. by Peter H. Mattson. (Benchmark Papers in Geology Ser.: Vol. 33). 1977. 81.00 (ISBN 0-12-787060-1). Acad Pr.
West Indies: Patterns of Development, Culture & Environmental Change since 1492. David Watts. (Cambridge Studies in Historical Geography: No. 8). (Illus.). 512p. 1987. 49.50 (ISBN 0-521-24555-9). Cambridge U Pr.
West Irian & Jakarta Imperialism. Kees Lagerberg. LC 79-11232. 1980. 22.50x (ISBN 0-312-86322-5). St Martin.
West Irish Folk-Tales & Romances. Compiled by William Larminie. LC 72-4191. (Select Bibliographies Reprint Ser.). 1972. Repr. of 1893 ed. 17.00 (ISBN 0-8369-6888-3). Ayer Co Pubs.
West Is West: Rudyard Kipling in San Francisco. Lois Rather. (Illus.). 1976. ltd. ed. 20.00 (ISBN 0-686-20624-X). Rather Pr.
West, Japan, & Cape Route Imports: The Oil & Non-Fuel Mineral Trades. Charles Perry. LC 82-80947. (Special Report Ser.). 88p. 1982. 7.50 (ISBN 0-89549-042-0). Inst Foreign Policy Anal.
West Loch Story: Hawaii's Second Greatest Disaster in Terms of Lives Lost. William L. Johnson. LC 86-50525. (Illus.). 176p. (Orig.). 1986. pap. 10.95 (ISBN 0-9616964-0-0). Westloch Pubns.
West Main School, a History Book: The Story of a School in Ravenna, Ohio, U. S. A. Lois F. Lewis. (Illus., Orig.). (gr. 5). 1988. pap. text ed. 2.00 (ISBN 0-9620136-0-9). L F Lewis.
West Malaysia & Singapore: A Selected Bibliography. Karl J. Pelzer. LC 72-87853. (Bibliographies Ser.). 400p. 1971. 25.00x (ISBN 0-87536-235-4). HRAFP.
West: Manhattan to Oregon. Conrad Pendleton. LC 82-72254. 72p. 1966. 5.95 (ISBN 0-8040-0318-1, Pub by Swallow). Ohio U Pr.
West Meets East. Japan Creative Association Staff. 1988. 79.95 (ISBN 4-931154-11-5). North Light Bks.
West Midlands. (AA Day Trips Ser.). 120p. 1988. pap. 14.95 (ISBN 0-86145-509-6, Pub. by British Tour). Salem Hse Pubs.
West Midlands from AD One Thousand. Marie B. Rowlands. (Regional History of England Ser.). 480p. 1987. pap. text ed. 32.95 (ISBN 0-582-49216-5). Longman.
West of Apache Pass. Charles A. Seltzer. 309p. 1975. Repr. of 1934 ed. lib. bdg. 19.95x (ISBN 0-88411-108-3, Pub. by Aeonian Pr). Amereon Ltd.
West of Chicago. Dave Etter. 81p. (Orig.). 1982. 4.50. Spoon Riv Poetry.
West of Childhood, Poems Nineteen Fifty to Nineteen Sixty-Five. Isabella Gardner. LC 65-18491. 1965. sewn in wrappers 4.00 (ISBN 0-685-79015-0). Small Pr Dist.
West of Eden. Harry Harrison. 528p. (Orig.). 1985. pap. 4.50 (ISBN 0-553-26551-2). Bantam.
West of Eden: A History of Art & Literature of Yosemite. David Robertson. (Illus.). 1984. 15.95 (ISBN 0-939666-40-5); pap. 9.95 (ISBN 0-939666-41-3). Yosemite Assn.
West of Eden: A History of the Art & Literature of Yosemite. David Robertson. LC 83-51539. (Illus.). 200p. 1984. 19.95 (ISBN 0-89997-035-4); pap. 9.95 (ISBN 0-89997-043-5). Wilderness Pr.
West of Fifth: The Rise & Fall & Rise of Manhattan's West Side. James Trager. LC 86-47665. (Illus.). 320p. 1987. 22.50 (ISBN 0-689-11775-2). Atheneum.
West of Hayle River. Gerald Priestland & Sylvia Priestland. 1985. 25.00x (ISBN 0-317-58008-6, Pub. by Dyllansow & Truran). State Mutual Bk.
West of Hell's Fringe: Crime, Criminals, & the Federal Peace Officer in Oklahoma Territory, 1889-1907. Glenn Shirley. LC 77-9112. (Illus.). 1978. 21.95 (ISBN 0-8061-1444-4). U of Okla Pr.
West of Hollywood: Poems from a Hermitage. Jack Butler. LC 80-65468. 60p. 1980. 9.95 (ISBN 0-935304-10-X); pap. 4.95 (ISBN 0-935304-09-6). August Hse.
West of Honor. Jerry Pournelle. (Orig.). 1980. pap. 2.25 (ISBN 0-671-41137-3). PB.
West of Honor. Jerry Pournelle. 1987. pap. 2.95 (ISBN 0-671-65347-4). Baen Bks.
West of Morning. August Derleth. LC 60-16459. 64p. 1960. 4.95 (ISBN 0-88361-075-2). Stanton & Lee.
West of Owen Wister: Selected Short Stories. Owen Wister. LC 74-175805. xviii, 247p. 1972. 21.00x (ISBN 0-8032-0808-1); pap. 4.50 (ISBN 0-8032-5760-0, BB 546, Bison). U of Nebr Pr.
West of Rome. John Fante. LC 86-12995. 192p. (Orig.). 1986. 20.00 (ISBN 0-87685-678-4). pap. 10.00 (ISBN 0-87685-677-6). Black Sparrow.
West of the Great Divide: Norwegian Migration to the Pacific Coast, 1847-1893. Kenneth O. Bjork. LC 58-4511. (Publications of the Norwegian-American Historical Association Ser.). pap. 160.00 (ISBN 0-317-27953-X, 2056021). Bks Demand UMI.
West of the Imagination. William H. Goetzmann & William N. Goetzmann. (Illus.). 1986. 34.95 (ISBN 0-393-02370-2). Norton.
West of the Law. William M. Raine. Date not set. pap. 2.95 (ISBN 0-445-20265-3, Pub. by Popular Lib). Warner Bks.
West of the Mad Coyote: Poems. Larry K. Jacobson. LC 84-1094. 90p. (Orig.). 1984. pap. 9.95 (ISBN 0-916447-02-2). Edit Review.
West of the Moon. Jonathan Nasaw. 224p. 1987. 16.95 (ISBN 0-531-15064-X). Watts.
West of the Pecos. Zane Grey. 1981. pap. 1.95 (ISBN 0-671-43949-9). PB.
West of Wall Street. George Angell & Barry Haigh. 1987. 21.95 (ISBN 0-88462-623-7). Longman Finan.
West of Warsaw. Frank Serafino. LC 82-73450. 248p. 1983. 13.95 (ISBN 0-910977-00-3). Avenue Pub.
West of Wichita: Settling the High Plains of Kansas, 1865-1890. Craig Miner. LC 85-26013. (Illus.). viii, 304p. 1986. 19.95x (ISBN 0-7006-0286-0). U Pr of KS.
West of Wichita: Settling the High Plains of Kansas, 1865-1890. Craig Miner. (Illus.). 312p. pap. 9.95 (ISBN 0-7006-0364-6). U Pr of KS.
West of Wild Bill Hickok. Joseph G. Rosa. LC 81-21945. (Illus.). 201p. 1982. 24.95 (ISBN 0-8061-1604-8). U of Okla Pr.
West of Yesterday East of Tomorrow. O. Ray Dodson. Ed. by Iona R. Hoeppner & Ruth Snider. (Illus.). Date not set. 17.95 (ISBN 0-940129-08-6). Highlighter.
West on Wood: Antique Wood Engravings of the Old West, 8 vols. Kelly Choda. Incl. Vol. 1. Southwestern Indians (ISBN 0-86541-015-1); Vol. 2. Plains Indians (ISBN 0-86541-016-X); Vol. 3. Scenic Mountains (ISBN 0-86541-017-8); Vol. 4. Scenic Southwest (ISBN 0-86541-018-6); Vol. 5. Railroads (ISBN 0-86541-019-4); Vol. 6. Mining Camps & Miners (ISBN 0-86541-020-8); Vol. 7. Ancient Pueblos Ruins (ISBN 0-86541-021-6); Vol. 8. National Parks (ISBN 0-86541-022-4). (Illus.). 1983. Set. pap. 12.00 (ISBN 0-86541-014-3); pap. 2.00 ea. Filter.
West Parker Remembers When. Elizabeth B. Kelley. (Illus.). 67p. (Orig.). 1988. pap. 12.50 (ISBN 0-945677-03-0). Riverby Bks.
West Pier. Patrick Hamilton. (Modern Classics Ser.). 256p. 1986. pap. 6.95 (ISBN 0-14-007499-6). Penguin.
West Point Wooing & Other Stories. facsimile ed. Clara L. Burnham. LC 79-94709. (Short Story Index Reprint Ser.). 1899. 18.00 (ISBN 0-8369-3088-6). Ayer Co Pubs.
West Portals of Chartres Cathedral, I: The Iconology of the Creation. Jan Van der Meulen & Nancy W. Price. LC 80-5586. 1981. lib. bdg. 29.75 (ISBN 0-8191-1402-2); pap. text ed. 14.00 (ISBN 0-8191-1403-0). U Pr of Amer.
West: Resources Issues & the Soviet Union in the Third World. 281p. Date not set. pap. text ed. 50.00 (ISBN 1-55813-009-8, HI-3739). Hudson Inst.
West River Voting Patterns. Alan L. Clem. 1965. 5.00 (ISBN 1-55614-016-9). U of SD Gov Res Bur.
West Rock to the Barndoor Hills: The Traprock Ridges of Connecticut. Cara Lee. (Illus.). 60p. 1985. pap. 5.00 (ISBN 0-942081-00-5). CT DEP CGNHS.
West Saxony Four Hundred Fifty-Two America 1982, 3 vols. Richard Patterson. Set. 200.00 (ISBN 0-317-27997-1); vol. 80.00 ea. R Patterson.
West Side Story. Leonard Bernstein et al. 1958. 13.95 (ISBN 0-394-40788-1). Random.
West Side Story. Irving Shulman. (Orig.). (gr. 8 up). 1961. pap. 2.95 (ISBN 0-671-50448-7). PB.
West Side Studies, 2 vols. Ed. by Richard C. Wade. Incl. Vol. 1. Boyhood & Lawlessness & the Neglected Girl. Ruth S. True; Vol. 2. The Middle West Side by Ortho G Cartwright & Mothers Who Must Earn by Katharine Anthony. LC 73-11932. (Metropolitan America Ser.). (Illus.). 778p. 1974. Repr. Set. 49.50x (ISBN 0-405-05434-3). Ayer Co Pubs.
West Somerset Word-Book: East Devon. Frederic T. Elworthy. (English Dialect Society Publications Ser.: No. 50). pap. 86.00 (ISBN 0-8115-0473-5). Kraus Repr.
West Sussex Probate Inventories, Fifteen Twenty-One to Eighteen Thirty-Four. Timothy J. McCann. 1981. 95.00x (ISBN 0-86260-005-7). State Mutual Bk.
West Sussex Village Book. Tony Wales. 224p. 1987. 30.00x (ISBN 0-905392-34-5, Countryside Bks). State Mutual Bk.
West Sussex Waterways. Peter Hay. 1986. 34.75x (ISBN 0-906520-24-X, Pub. by Middleton Pr. UK). State Mutual Bk.
West Texas Natural Resources: Economic Perspectives for the Future, Proceedings of the Conference. Ed. by Idris R. Traylor & J. R. Goodin. 73p. 1983. 3.00 (ISBN 0-318-17671-8, 83-3). Intl Ctr Arid & Semi-Arid.
West That Was: Featuring the Writings of Michael P. Jones & the Artwork of Will Lehnen. Michael P. Jones. (Illus.). 8p. (Orig.). 1984. pap. text ed. write for info. (ISBN 0-89904-087-X). Crumb Elbow Pub.
West That Was: From Texas to Montana. John Leakey & Nellie S. Yost. LC 58-14110. (Illus.). xii, 287p. 1965. pap. 9.95 (ISBN 0-8032-5117-3, Bison). U of Nebr Pr.
West to Cambodia. S. L. Marshall. 240p. 1986. pap. 3.50 (ISBN 0-515-08890-0). Jove Pubns.

Western Christian Thought in the Middle Ages. Sydney H. Mellone. 1977. lib. bdg. 59.95 (ISBN 0-8490-2816-7). Gordon Pr.

Western Church in the Later Middle Ages. Francis Oakley. LC 79-7621. (Paperback Ser.). 346p. 1985. 33.95x (ISBN 0-8014-1208-0); pap. 9.95x (ISBN 0-8014-9347-1). Cornell U Pr.

Western Circuit Assize Orders, 1629-48. Ed. by Royal Historical Society, Camden Society Staff. (Camden Fourth Ser.: No. 17). 200p. 1970. 27.00 (ISBN 0-901050-29-6, Pub. by Boydell & Brewer). Longwood Pub Group.

Western Circus. Rene de Goscinny. (Lucky Luke Series). (Fr.). 1976. 7.95x (ISBN 2-205-00425-5). Intl Learn Syst.

Western Civilization. Gerson Antell & Walter Harris. (Orig.). (gr. 10-12). 1983. text ed. 23.25 (ISBN 0-87720-632-5); pap. text ed. 18.25 (ISBN 0-87720-631-7). AMSCO Sch.

Western Civilization, 2 vols. 2nd ed. William L. Langer et al. Incl. Vol. 1. Prehistory to the Peace of Utrecht. 526p (ISBN 0-06-043844-4); Vol. 2. The Expansion of Empire to Europe in the Modern World. 485p (ISBN 0-06-043846-0). 1975. pap. text ed. 21.95 ea. scp; test item to accompany vol. 1 avail. (ISBN 0-06-363843-6); test item to accompany vol. 2 2.00 (ISBN 0-06-363844-4). Har-Row.

Western Civilization. Jack Rudman. (College Level Examination Ser.: CLEP-29). 25.95 (ISBN 0-8373-5379-3); pap. 13.95 (ISBN 0-8373-5329-7). Natl Learning.

Western Civilization. Jack Rudman. (College Proficiency Examination Ser.: CPEP-16). 25.95 (ISBN 0-8373-5466-8); pap. 13.95 (ISBN 0-8373-5416-1). Natl Learning.

Western Civilization, 2 vols. 4th ed. F. Roy Willis. LC 84-81086. 1985. Vol. I, From Ancient Times Through the Seventeenth Century, 683pgs. pap. text ed. 20.00 (ISBN 0-669-07215-X); test ques. 2.00 (ISBN 0-669-12782-5); Vol. II, From the Seventeenth Century to the Contemporary Age, 559pgs. pap. text ed. 20.00 (ISBN 0-669-07216-8); test ques. 2.00 (ISBN 0-669-12783-3); Both Vols. instr's guide 2.00 (ISBN 0-669-07217-6). Heath.

Western Civilization, Vol. 1. William Hughes. LC 82-645823. (Annual Editions Ser.). (Illus.). 224p. 1987. pap. text ed. 9.95 (ISBN 0-87967-678-7). Dushkin Pub.

Western Civilization, Vol. 2. 4th ed. William Hughes. (Annual Editions Ser.). (Illus.). 224p. 1987. pap. text ed. 9.95 (ISBN 0-87967-679-5). Dushkin Pub.

Western Civilization: A Brief History. 2nd ed. Robin W. Winks. 495p. 1988. pap. text ed. 22.00 (ISBN 0-939693-05-4). Collegiate Pr.

Western Civilization: A Brief Introduction. F. Roy Willis. 962p. 1987. pap. write for info. (ISBN 0-02-428110-7). Macmillan.

Western Civilization Condemned by Itself, 2 vols. M. Jameelah. pap. 35.00 set (ISBN 0-686-18564-1). Kazi Pubns.

Western Civilization: Ideas, Politics. 2nd ed. Marvin Perry et al. LC 84-61367. 920p. 1985. Set. pap. text ed. 36.76 (ISBN 0-395-35957-0); Vol. I; to 1789. pap. text ed. 25.56 (ISBN 0-395-36538-4); Vol. II; From 1600's. pap. text ed. 25.56 (ISBN 0-395-36539-2); instr's. manual with test items 2.36 (ISBN 0-395-36540-6). HM.

Western Civilization: Ideas, Politics, & Society. 3rd ed. Marvin Perry et al. LC 88-81355. 1989. pap. price not set (ISBN 0-395-36935-5); instr's. manual, tests avail. HM.

Western Civilization: Ideas, Politics, & Society. 3rd ed. Marvin Perry et al. LC 88-81356. Date not set. Vol. I, To 1789 (Chapters 1-18) pap. price not set (ISBN 0-395-36936-3); Vol. II, From the 1600s (Chapters 16-37) pap. price not set (ISBN 0-395-36937-1). HM.

Western Civilization: Ideas, Politics, & Society - from the 1400s, Chapters 13-37. 3rd ed. Marvin Perry et al. LC 88-81370. Date not set. price not set (ISBN 0-395-48647-5). HM.

Western Civilization: Images & Interpretations, 2 vols. 2nd ed. Dennis Sherman. 1987. Vol. 1, 280p. pap. text ed. 10.00 (ISBN 0-394-35206-8, KnopfC); Vol. 2, 280p. pap. text ed. 10.00 (ISBN 0-394-35207-6). Knopf.

Western Civilization in Biological Perspective: Patterns in Biohistory. Stephen Boyden. (Illus.). 384p. 1987. 60.00 (ISBN 0-19-857672-2). Oxford U Pr.

Western Civilization in the Near East. Hans Kohn. Tr. by E. W. Dickes. LC 37-23489. Repr. of 1936 ed. 10.00 (ISBN 0-404-03739-9). AMS Pr.

Western Civilization, Islam & Muslims. A. H. Nadvi. 16.50 (ISBN 0-686-18563-3). Kazi Pubns.

Western Civilization: Recent Interpretations. Incl. Bk. 1. Earliest Times to 1715. Ed. by Charles D. Hamilton (ISBN 0-88295-724-2); Bk. 2. From 1715 to the Present. Ed. by C. Stewart Doty (ISBN 0-88295-725-2). LC 72-13456. 1973. pap. 12.95x. Harlan Davidson.

Western Civilization since Fifteen Hundred. 2nd ed. Walther Kirchner. 1975. pap. 8.95 (ISBN 0-06-460111-0, CO 111, B&N Bks). Har-Row.

Western Civilization Through Muslim Eyes. Sayyed M. Musavi. Tr. by F. J. Goulding from Persian. 146p. 1977. 4.95 (ISBN 0-941722-20-1); pap. 3.95 (ISBN 0-941722-06-6). Book-Dist-Ctr.

Western Civilization to Fifteen Hundred. Walther Kirchner. 1960. pap. 7.50 (ISBN 0-06-460110-2, CO 110, B&N Bks). Har-Row.

Western Civilization, 1789-1919. John S. Jackson. 1988. pap. 16.50 (ISBN 0-911337-01-6). Intell Pr CA.

Western Civilizations, 2 vols. 9th ed. Edward M. Burns et al. (Illus.). 1980. instr's manual pap. 2.95x (ISBN 0-393-95099-9); study guide o.p. 7.95x (ISBN 0-393-95091-3). Norton.

Western Civilizations. 10th ed. Edward M. Burns et al. 1984. Complete ed. 32.95x (ISBN 0-393-95315-7); Vol. I. pap. 21.95x (ISBN 0-393-95319-X); Vol. II. pap. 21.95x (ISBN 0-393-95323-8); tchr's. ed. o.p. 4.95x (ISBN 0-393-95328-9); Vol. I. study guide 8.95x (ISBN 0-393-95433-1); Vol. II. study guide 8.95x (ISBN 0-393-95422-6). Norton.

Western Civilizations. 11th ed. Robert E. Lerner et al. (Illus.). 1090p. 1988. Vol. I. pap. text ed. 21.95; Vol. II. pap. text ed. 21.95; instr's. manual avail.; Vol. I. study guide 8.95 (ISBN 0-393-95660-1); Vol. II. study guide 8.95 (ISBN 0-393-95662-8); computer test item file & map transparencies avail. Norton.

Western Clearings. Caroline Kirkland. 1972. Repr. of 1845 ed. lib. bdg. 29.00 (ISBN 0-8422-8088-X). Irvington.

Western Clearings. Caroline Kirkland. 1986. pap. text ed. 7.95x (ISBN 0-8290-1948-0). Irvington.

Western Coinages of Nero. David W. MacDowall. LC 74-82869. (Numismatic Notes & Monographs: No. 161). (Illus.). 281p. (Orig.). 1979. pap. 40.00 (ISBN 0-89722-176-1). Am Numismatic.

Western Coloured Township: Problems of an Urban Slum. Marianne Brindley. (Illus.). 110p. 1976. pap. text ed. 9.95x (ISBN 0-86975-049-6, Pub. by Ravan Pr). Ohio U Pr.

Western Contribution to Buddhism. William Peiris. 372p. 1974. lib. bdg. 79.95 (ISBN 0-87968-550-6). Krishna Pr.

Western Contribution to Buddhism. William Peiris. 1973. 8.50 (ISBN 0-8426-0537-1). Orient Bk Dist.

Western Crisis Over Southern Africa. Colin Legum. LC 79-9723. (Current Affairs Ser.). (Illus.). 1979. 24.50 (ISBN 0-8419-0492-8, Africana); pap. 16.50 (ISBN 0-8419-0496-0). Holmes & Meier.

Western Customs. Edna Goo. 132p. 1980. 1.95 (ISBN 0-89955-151-3, Pub. by Mei Ya China). Intl Spec Bk.

Western Defences of Portsmouth Harbour, 1400-1800. G. H. Williams. 1979. 42.00x (ISBN 0-317-43740-2, Pub. by City of Portsmouth). State Mutual Bk.

Western Diseases: Their Emergence & Prevention. Ed. by H. C. Trowell & D. P. Burkitt. LC 80-28917. (Illus.). 480p. 1981. text ed. 42.00x (ISBN 0-674-95020-8). Harvard U Pr.

Western Echoes. Earl F. Moore. LC 23-939860. (Illus.). 198p. (gr. 4-12). 1980. 12.95 (ISBN 0-939860-00-7). Tremaine Graph & Pub.

Western Economic Statecraft in East-West Relations Embargoes, Sanctions, Linkage, Economic Warfare & Detente. Philip Hanson. 96p. 1988. text ed. 12.95 (ISBN 0-7102-1443-X, Pub. by Routledge UK). Routledge Chapman & HAll.

Western Economics in Non-Western Economies. Lloyd G. Reynold. (Tenth Edward Shann Memorial Lecture in Economics Ser.). (Illus.). 1971. pap. 2.50x (ISBN 0-85564-046-4, Pub. by U of W Austral Pr). Intl Spec Bk.

Western Economists & Eastern Societies: Agents of Change in South Asia, 1950-1970. George Rosen. LC 84-4370. (Studies in Development). 296p. 1985. text ed. 34.50x (ISBN 0-8018-3187-3). Johns Hopkins.

Western Edible Wild Plants. H. D. Harrington. LC 77-190061. (Illus.). 1972. pap. 7.95 (ISBN 0-8263-0218-1). U of NM Pr.

Western Energy Policy. Douglas Evans. LC 78-23315. 1979. 10.95x (ISBN 0-312-86392-6). St Martin.

Western Enterprise in Far Eastern Economic Development, China & Japan. George C. Allen & Audrey G. Donnithorne. LC 54-1323. pap. 72.80 (ISBN 0-317-28695-1, 2055254). Bks Demand UMI.

Western Enterprise in Late Ch'ing China: A Selective Survey of Jardine, Matheson & Company's Operations, 1842-1895. Edward LeFevour. LC 73-386. (East Asian Monographs Ser: No. 26). 1968. pap. 11.00x (ISBN 0-674-95010-0). Harvard U Pr.

Western Europe. Leslie Gardiner. (Illus.). 64p. 1985. pap. 4.95 (ISBN 0-933521-16-2). AGT Pub.

Western Europe. Ed. by Richard Mayne. (Handbooks to the Modern World Ser.). 700p. 1986. 45.00x. Facts On File.

Western Europe: A Survey of Holdings at the Hoover Institution on War, Revolution & Peace. Agnes F. Peterson. LC 72-142950. (Library Survey Ser.: No. 1). 60p. 1970. pap. 3.00x (ISBN 0-8179-5012-5). Hoover Inst Pr.

Western Europe: A Systematic Geography. Allan Bealt. (Illus.). 192p. 1977. pap. text ed. 16.95 (ISBN 0-8464-0965-8). Beekman Pubs.

Western Europe: A Systematic Human Geography. 2nd ed. Brian W. Ilbery. (Illus.). 220p. 1986. text ed. 42.00x (ISBN 0-19-823278-0); pap. text ed. 15.95x (ISBN 0-19-823277-2). Oxford U Pr.

Western Europe after Hitler. B. J. Elliot. (Modern Times Ser.). (Illus.). 162p. (Orig.). (gr. 9-12). 1968. pap. text ed. 4.95 (ISBN 0-582-20436-4). Longman.

Western Europe & Japan Between the Superpowers. Wolf Mendl. LC 84-40047. 192p. 1984. 25.00 (ISBN 0-312-86401-9). St Martin.

Western Europe & the Crisis in U. S.-Soviet Relations. Ed. by Richard H. Ullman & Mario Zucconi. LC 86-30625. 144p. 1987. lib. bdg. 36.95 (ISBN 0-275-92584-6, C2584). Praeger.

Western Europe & the Development of the Law of the Sea: National Legislation, 4 binders set closed. Francesco Durante & Walter Rodino. LC 79-55008. 1979. looseleaf 300.00 (ISBN 0-379-20286-7). Oceana.

Western Europe & the New International Economic Order: Representative Samples of European Perspectives. Ed. by Ervin Laszlo & Joel Kurtzman. LC 80-16620. (Pergamon Policy Studies). 120p. 1980. 28.00 (ISBN 0-08-025114-5). Pergamon.

Western Europe & the United States: The Uncertain Alliance. Michael Smith. (Studies in Contemporary Europe: No. 6). 1984. text ed. 34.95X (ISBN 0-04-327071-9); pap. text ed. 11.95x (ISBN 0-04-327072-7). Unwin Hyman.

Western Europe: Economic & Social Studies. Hudson & Williams. 1986. pap. text ed. 10.00 (ISBN 0-317-63011-3, Pub. by Har-Row Ltd England). Har-Row.

Western Europe: Geographic Perspectives. H. Clout et al. 288p. 1986. pap. 24.95 (ISBN 0-470-20443-5, Co-Pub. with Longman). Wiley.

Western Europe: Geographical Perspectives. H. Clout et al. (Illus.). 1984. pap. text ed. 17.95 (ISBN 0-582-30060-6). Wiley.

Western Europe in Color. Alice F. Mutton. (Illus.). 279p. 1972. pap. 7.50 (ISBN 0-7137-0555-8). Transatl Arts.

Western Europe in Kissinger's Global Strategy. Argyris G. Andrianopoulos. LC 87-26528. 270p. 1988. 47.50 (ISBN 0-312-01544-5). St Martin.

Western Europe in Soviet Global Strategy. Ed. by Ray S. Cline et al. (Special Studies on the Soviet Union & Eastern Europe). 176p. 1987. pap. 16.95 (ISBN 0-8133-7480-4). Westview.

Western Europe in the Middle Ages: A Short History. 3rd ed. Joseph R. Strayer. 1982. pap. text ed. write for info. (ISBN 0-673-16052-1). Scott F.

Western Europe in the Middle Ages, 300-1475. 4th ed. Brian Tierney & Sidney Painter. 1982. text ed. 25.00 (ISBN 0-394-33060-9, RanC). Random.

Western Europe in World Affairs: Continuity, Change, & Challenge. Guy De Carmoy. 208p. 1986. 38.95 (ISBN 0-275-92057-7, C2057). Praeger.

Western Europe since Nineteen Forty-Five: A Short Political History. 3rd ed. W. Urwin. 416p. 1982. pap. text ed. 15.95 (ISBN 0-582-49071-5). Longman.

Western Europe: Technology & the Future. Stanley Woods. (Atlantic Paper: No. 63). 128p. 1987. pap. 12.95 (ISBN 0-7099-5220-1, Pub. by Croom Helm UK). Routledge Chapman & Hall.

Western Europe, 1983. 2nd rev. ed. Wayne C. Thompson. Ed. by Pierre E. Dostert. (World Today Ser.). (Illus.). 404p. 1983. pap. text ed. 9.50 (ISBN 0-943448-11-5). Stryker-Post.

Western Europe, 1988. 6th, rev. ed. Wayne C. Thompson. (World Today Ser.). (Illus.). 485p. 1988. pap. 13.50 (ISBN 0-943448-45-X). Stryker-Post.

Western Europe, 1989: A Political & Economic Survey. 1988. 190.00 (ISBN 0-946653-47-X, Pub. by Europa England). Gale.

Western European Adjustment to Structural Economic Problems. Marie J. Drouin et al. Ed. by Catherine Albrecht & Adrienne Kearny. (Illus.). 282p. (Orig.). 1987. lib. bdg. 27.50 (ISBN 0-8191-6527-1, Pub. by Hudson Inst); pap. text ed. 14.75 (ISBN 0-8191-6528-X). U Pr of Amer.

Western European Art in the Hermitage: Paintings, Drawings, Sculpture. B. Asvarishch & N. Kosareva. 1977. 110.00x (ISBN 0-317-14333-6, Pub. by Collets (UK)). State Mutual Bk.

Western European Censuses, Nineteen Sixty. Judith Blake & Jerry J. Donovan. LC 76-4558. (Population Monograph Ser.: No. 8). 1976. Repr. of 1971 ed. lib. bdg. 48.50x (ISBN 0-8371-8831-8, BLWE). Greenwood.

Western European Costume & Its Relation to the Theatre. Iris Brooke. Incl. Vol. 1. 13th to 17th Centuries (ISBN 0-87830-511-4); Vol. 2. 17th Through 19th Centuries. 1963 (ISBN 0-87830-514-9). LC 63-18334. (Illus., Orig.). pap. 7.95 ea. Theatre Arts.

Western European Economy: A Geography of Post-War Development. Allan M. Williams. 368p. 1988. 28.50 (ISBN 0-389-20772-1). Rowman.

Western European Embroidery in the Collection of the Cooper-Hewitt Museum: The Smithsonian Institution's National Museum of Design. Milton Sonday & Gillian Moss. LC 78-62366. (Cooper-Hewitt Museum Collection Handbook Ser.). (Illus.). 32p. (Orig.). 1978. pap. 3.95x (ISBN 0-910503-03-6). Cooper-Hewitt.

Western European Energy Policies: A Comparative Study. Nigel Lucas. 1985. 36.00x (ISBN 0-19-828488-8). Oxford U Pr.

Western European Idea in Education. V. Mallinson. (Illus.). 1980. 57.00 (ISBN 0-08-025208-7). Pergamon.

Western European Labor & the American Corporation. Ed. by Alfred Kamin. LC 72-83775. pap. 143.50 (ISBN 0-317-29811-9, 2016699). Bks Demand UMI.

Western European Painting in the Hermitage, 19th-20th Centuries. Ed. by A. Kostenevich. 360p. 1987. 75.00 (ISBN 0-8285-3749-6, Pub. by Aurora Pubs USSR). Imported Pubns.

Western European Painting in the Latvian Museum of Western Art, Riga. M. Kachalova & V. Sproge. 1977. 39.00x (ISBN 0-317-14334-4, Pub. by Collets (UK)). State Mutual Bk.

Western European Painting of the Renaissance. Frank J. Mather. LC 65-28209. (Illus.). Repr. of 1939 ed. 37.50x (ISBN 0-8154-0148-5). Cooper Sq.

Western European Party Systems: Continuity & Change. Ed. by Hans Daalder & Peter Mair. 466p. 1983. 45.00 (ISBN 0-8039-9769-8); pap. 16.50 (ISBN 0-8039-9702-7). Sage.

Western European Party Systems: Trends & Prospects. Ed. by Peter H. Merkl. LC 78-22783. (Illus.). 1980. 55.00 (ISBN 0-02-920060-1). Free Pr.

Western Europe's Global Reach: Regional Cooperation & Worldwide Aspirations. Ed. by Werner J. Feld. (Policy Studies). 1980. 48.00 (ISBN 0-08-025130-7). Pergamon.

Western Expansion & Indigenous People: The Heritage of Las Casas. Ed. by Elias Sevilla-Casas. (World Anthropology Ser.). xiv, 308p. 1977. 33.75 (ISBN 90-279-7510-8). Mouton.

Western Experience. 3rd ed. Mortimer Chambers et al. LC 82-17096. 1982. text ed. 25.00 (ISBN 0-394-33086-2, KnopfC); Vol. 1, to 1715. pap. text ed. 16.00 (ISBN 0-394-33085-4); Vol. 2, since 1600. pap. text ed. 16.00 (ISBN 0-394-33096-X); Vol. 1, to 1500. pap. text ed. 14.00 (ISBN 0-394-33084-6); Vol. 2, 1300-1815. pap. text ed. 13.50 (ISBN 0-394-33098-6); Vol. 3, 1789-Present. pap. text ed. 13.50 (ISBN 0-394-33097-8); Vol. 1. net study guide 6.00 (ISBN 0-394-33225-3); Vol. 2. study guide 6.00 (ISBN 0-394-33226-1). Knopf.

Western Experience, Vol. 1. 4th ed. Mortimer Chambers et al. 1986. text ed. write for info. (ISBN 0-394-36232-2, KnopfC); pap. text ed. write for info. (ISBN 0-394-36432-5, KnopfC); write for info. wkbk. (ISBN 0-394-36436-8). Knopf.

Western Experience, Vol. 2. 4th ed. Mortimer Chambers et al. 1200p. 1987. pap. text ed. 17.50 (ISBN 0-394-36434-1, KnopfC); wkbk. 6.00 (ISBN 0-394-36440-6, KnopfC). Knopf.

Western Experiment: New England Transcendentalists in the Ohio Valley. Elizabeth R. McKinsey. LC 72-83467. (Essays in History & Literature Ser.). 80p. 1973. pap. 5.95x (ISBN 0-674-95040-2). Harvard U Pr.

Western Fertilizer Handbook. 7th ed. California Fertilizer Association Staff. 312p. 1985. pap. text ed. 10.95x (ISBN 0-8134-2490-9, 2490). Inter Print Pubs.

Western Fertilizer Handbook. rev., 7th ed. 1986. pap. 12.50 (ISBN 0-318-19714-6). Thomson Pubns.

Western Fiction in the Library of Congress Classification Scheme. Michael Burgess & Beverly A. Ryan. LC 87-6309. (Borgo Cataloging Guides Ser.: No. 3). 70p. 1988. lib. bdg. 22.95x (ISBN 0-89370-822-4); pap. text ed. 12.95x (ISBN 0-89370-922-0). Borgo Pr.

Western Films: A Brief History. Ed. by Richard W. Etualin. (Illus.). 96p. 1983. pap. text ed. 9.95x (ISBN 0-89745-048-5). Sunflower U Pr.

Western Films: A Complete Guide. Brian Garfield. (Quality Paperbacks Ser.). (Illus.). 400p. 1988. pap. 16.95 (ISBN 0-306-80333-X). Da Capo.

Western Films: An Annotated Critical Bibliography. John Nachbar. LC 75-6696. (Reference Library of Humanities: Vol. 17). 110p. 1975. lib. bdg. 25.00 (ISBN 0-8240-1086-8). Garland Pub.

Western Films of John Ford. J. A. Place. (Illus.). 226p. 1974. text ed. 12.00 (ISBN 0-8065-0445-5, Pub. by Citadel Pr). Lyle Stuart.

Western Films of John Ford. J. A. Place. 1977. pap. 7.95 (ISBN 0-8065-0594-X, Pub. by Citadel Pr). Lyle Stuart.

Western Fly Fishing Guide. Dave Hughes. (Illus.). 88p. (Orig.). 1987. pap. 5.95 (ISBN 0-936608-50-1). F Amato Pubns.

Western Fly-Fishing Vacations: A Selective Guide. Nanci Reynolds & Kirk Reynolds. LC 88-6603. (Illus.). 1988. pap. 12.95 (ISBN 0-87701-425-6). Chronicle Bks.

Western Forest Industry: An Economic Outlook. John A. Guthrie & George R. Armstrong. LC 61-9914. pap. 88.00 (ISBN 0-317-28864-4, 2020962). Bks Demand UMI.

Western Forests. Stephen Whitney. Ed. by Charles Elliott. LC 84-48670. (Audubon Society Nature Guides Ser.). (Illus.). 671p. 1985. pap. 14.95 (ISBN 0-394-73127-1). Knopf.

Western Fruit, Berries & Nuts: How to Select, Grow & Enjoy. Robert L. Stebbins & Lance Walheim. LC 81-82134. (Illus.). 192p. (Orig.). pap. 9.95 (ISBN 0-89586-078-3). Price Stern.

Western Garden Book. 5th ed. Sunset Magazine & Book Editors. LC 88-80952. 592p. 1988. pap. 16.95 (ISBN 0-376-03891-8); pap. text ed. 22.95 (ISBN 0-376-03853-5). Sunset Lane.

TITLE INDEX WESTERN POPULAR THEATRE.

Western Garden Calendar. Sunset Editors. 96p. 1988. text ed. 14.95 (ISBN 0-376-03900-0). Sunset Lane.
Western Gazetteer: Or Emigrant's Directory. Samuel R. Brown. LC 79-146380. (First American Frontier Ser). (Illus.). 1971. Repr. of 1817 ed. 23.00 (ISBN 0-405-02831-8). Ayer Co Pubs.
Western Geopolitical Thought in the Twentieth Century. Geoffrey Parker. LC 85-14546. 208p. 1985. 27.50 (ISBN 0-312-86404-3). St Martin.
Western Grasses: A Grazier's Guide to the Grasses of South West Queensland. B. R. Roberts & R. G. Silcock. 118p. 1982. 22.95x (ISBN 0-909306-28-1, Pub. by Darling Downs Inst Pr Australia). Intl Spec Bk.
Western Grazing Grounds & Forest Ranges. William C. Barnes. Ed. by Stuart Bruchey. LC 78-56685. (Management of Public Lands in the U. S. Ser.). (Illus.). 1979. Repr. of 1913 ed. lib. bdg. 26.50x (ISBN 0-405-11317-X). Ayer Co Pubs.
Western Great Lakes (Illinois, Iowa, Minnesota, Wisconsin) Thomas G. Aylesworth & Virginia L. Aylesworth. (Let's Discover the States Ser.). (Illus.). 66p. 1987. lib. bdg. 14.95x (ISBN 1-55546-560-9). Chelsea Hse.
Western Greek Land: Use & City-Planning in the Archaic Period. Guy P. Metraux. LC 77-94709. (Outstanding Dissertations in the Fine Arts Ser.). 1978. lib. bdg. 25.00 (ISBN 0-8240-3241-1). Garland Pub.
Western Greeks. T. J. Dunbabin. 504p. 1979. 40.00 (ISBN 0-89005-300-6). Ares.
Western Gulf of Alaska: A Socio-Economic Study. David T. Kresge et al. LC 74-620053. (Illus.). 200p. 1974. pap. write for info (ISBN 0-88353-014-7). U Alaska Inst Res.
Western Hemisphere Idea: Its Rise & Decline. Ed. by Arthur P. Whitaker. (Paperback Ser.). 204p. 1965. pap. 5.95x (ISBN 0-8014-9001-4). Cornell U Pr.
Western Heritage. 3rd ed. Donald Kagan & Steven Ozment. (Illus.). 1987. Vol. A, to 1527. pap. write for info. (ISBN 0-02-363230-5); Vol. B, 1300-1815. pap. write for info. (ISBN 0-02-363240-2); Vol. C, since 1789. pap. write for info. (ISBN 0-02-363250-X). Macmillan.
Western Heritage, 2 vols. 3rd ed. Donald Kagen & Steven Ozment. (Illus.). 1987. Vol. 1, to 1715. pap. write for info. (ISBN 0-02-363210-0); Vol. 2, since 1648. pap. write for info. (ISBN 0-02-363220-8). Macmillan.
Western Heritage: A Study of the Colonial Architecture of Perth, Western Australia. Ray Oldham & John Oldham. LC 79-670392. 1979. 18.95 (ISBN 0-85564-134-7, Pub. by U of W Austral Pr). Intl Spec Bk.
Western Heritage & American Values: Law, Theology & History. Alberto R. Coll. Ed. by Kenneth W. Thompson. LC 81-43761. (American Values Projected Abroad Ser.: Vol. I). 126p. 1982. lib. bdg. 25.25 (ISBN 0-8191-2526-1); pap. text ed. 8.75 (ISBN 0-8191-2527-X). U Pr of Amer.
Western Heritage: Man's Encounter with Himself & the World, a Journey for Meaning. Ed. by Francis R. Gendreau & Angelo Caranfa. LC 84-17268. 418p. (Orig.). 1985. lib. bdg. 33.25 (ISBN 0-8191-4251-4); pap. text ed. 14.50 (ISBN 0-8191-4252-2). U Pr of Amer.
Western Heritage Part 2: George Temple-Pool, Architect of the Golden Years 1885-1897. Ray Oldham & John Oldham. 227p. 1981. 39.95x (ISBN 0-85564-173-8, Pub. by U of W Austral Pr). Intl Spec Bk.
Western Heritage: Since Sixteen Forty-Eight, Vol.II. 3rd ed. Anthony M. Brescia. 278p. 1987. pap. text ed. write for info. study guide (ISBN 0-02-363530-4). Macmillan.
Western Heritage: Since Thirteen Hundred. 3rd ed. Donald Kagan & Steven Ozment. (Illus.). 1987. write for info. (ISBN 0-02-363260-7). Macmillan.
Western Heritage: To Seventeen Fifteen, Vol. I. 3rd ed. Anthony M. Brescia. 212p. 1987. pap. text ed. write for info. study guide (ISBN 0-02-363520-7). Macmillan.
Western Hero in Film & Television: Mass Media Mythology. Rita Parks. LC 81-21826. (Studies in Cinema: No. 10). pap. 51.00 (ISBN 0-8357-1287-7, 2070307). Bks Demand UMI.
Western Hero in Film & Television: Mass Media Mythology. Rita Parks. (Studies in Cinema: No. 10). 198p. 1988. 19.95 (ISBN 0-8357-1914-6). UMI Res Pr.
Western Himalayas & Tibet. Thomas Thomson. 501p. 1978. Repr. of 1852 ed. 22.00 (ISBN 0-89684-155-3, Pub. by Cosmo Pubns India). Orient Bk Dist.
Western Histories of Linguistic Thought: An Annotated Chronological Bibliography, 1822-1976. E. Konrad Koerner. (Studies in the History of Linguistics Ser.: No. 11). x, 113p. 1978. 22.00x (ISBN 90-272-0952-9). Benjamins North Am.
Western Home Landscaping. Ken Smith. LC 86-27094. (Illus.). 1978. pap. 12.95 (ISBN 0-89586-003-1). Price Stern.
Western Horse. John A. Gorman. LC 66-12997. (Illus.). (gr. 9-12). 1967. 19.95 (ISBN 0-8134-0126-7); text ed. 14.95x. Inter Print Pubs.
Western Horse: Advice & Training. Dave Jones. LC 73-7422. (Illus.). 184p. 1982. 16.95 (ISBN 0-8061-1130-5). U of Okla Pr.
Western Horse Behavior & Training. Robert W. Miller. 336p. 1975. pap. 10.95 (ISBN 0-385-08181-2, Dolp). Doubleday.
Western Horsemanship. Richard Shrake. Ed. by Pat Close. (Illus.). 144p. (Orig.). 1987. pap. 9.95 (ISBN 0-911647-09-0). Western Horseman.
Western Illinois University 13th Annual Spring Transportation-Physical Distribution Seminar Proceedings: Just in Time: New Dimensions in Logistics. Ed. by David J. Bloomberg. 100p. 1986. pap. 10.50 (ISBN 0-931497-03-5). WIU CBER.
Western Impact on World Music Change, Adaption, & Survival. Bruno Nettl. 232p. 1985. 22.95x (ISBN 0-317-46649-6). Macmillan.
Western Impact upon Tsarist Russia. Melvin C. Wren. LC 74-23545. (Berkshire Ser.). 266p. 1976. pap. 8.50 (ISBN 0-88275-241-3). Krieger.
Western Impressions of Nature & Landscape in Southeast Asia. Victor Savage. 456p. 1984. text ed. 26.95x (ISBN 9971-69-080-2, Pub. by Singapore U Pr). Ohio U Pr.
Western India Before & During the Mutinies. George L. Jacob. 262p. 1985. Repr. of 1872 ed. text ed. 45.00x (ISBN 0-86590-714-5, Pub. by Mayur Pubns India). Apt Bks.
Western Influence in Iqbal. TC Rastogi. 1987. 34.00x (ISBN 81-7024-080-8, Pub. by Ashish India). South Asia Bks.
Western Influences on Political Parties to Eighteen Twenty-Five. H. C. Hockett. LC 75-87650. (American Scene Ser.). 1970. Repr. of 1917 ed. lib. bdg. 24.50 (ISBN 0-306-71777-8). Da Capo.
Western Inner Workings. William G. Gray. LC 82-62846. (Sangreal Sodality Ser.: Vol. 1). 188p. 1983. pap. 8.95 (ISBN 0-87728-560-8). Weiser.
Western Intellectual Tradition: From Leonardo to Hegel. facsimile ed. Jacob Bronowski & Bruce Mazlish. LC 70-167315. (Essay Index Reprint Ser.). Repr. of 1960 ed. 37.00 (ISBN 0-8369-2448-7). Ayer Co Pubs.
Western Intellectual Tradition: From Leonardo to Hegel. Jacob Bronowski & Bruce Mazlish. pap. 10.95x (ISBN 0-06-133001-9, TB 3001, Torch). Har-Row.
Western Intellectual Tradition: Greece Through the Middle Ages, Vol. 1. David C. Riede & J. Wayne Baker. 208p. 1980. pap. text ed. 14.95 (ISBN 0-8403-2259-3). Kendall-Hunt.
Western Intellectual Tradition: The Renaissance of Modern Times, Vol. 2. 2nd ed. David C. Riede & J. Wayne Baker. 256p. 1980. pap. text ed. 13.95 (ISBN 0-8403-2171-6). Kendall-Hunt.
Western Interests & U. S. Policy Options in the Caribbean Basin. Atlantic Council's Working Group on Western Interest & U. S. Policy Options in the Caribbean Basin Staff. Ed. by James R. Greene & Brent Scowcroft. LC 84-3571. 290p. 1984. text ed. 30.00 (ISBN 0-89946-181-6); pap. 12.50 (ISBN 0-89946-183-2). Oelgeschlager.
Western Interests in the Pacific Realm. T. R. Adam. 10.00 (ISBN 0-8446-1507-2). Peter Smith.
Western Invasions of the Pacific & Its Continents: A Study of Moving Frontiers & Changing Landscapes, 1513-1958. Archibald G. Price. LC 80-14037. (Illus.). xi, 236p. 1980. Repr. of 1963 ed. lib. bdg. 35.00x (ISBN 0-313-22433-1, PRWE). Greenwood.
Western Iowa Prehistory. Facsimile ed. Duane Anderson. (Illus.). 86p. 1975. 6.95x (ISBN 0-8138-2223-8). Iowa St U Pr.
Western Island or the Great Basket. Robin Flower. (Oxford Paperbacks Ser.). (Illus.). 1978. pap. 6.95x (ISBN 0-19-281234-3). Oxford U Pr.
Western Isles Today. Judith Ennew. LC 79-13643. (Changing Cultures Ser.). (Illus.). 1980. o. p. 34.50 (ISBN 0-521-22590-6); pap. 10.95 (ISBN 0-521-29572-6). Cambridge U Pr.
Western Jerusalem: University of California Studies on Tasso. Ed. by Luisa Del Giudice. LC 84-20560. (Italian Literary Studies). 150p. (Orig.). 1985. pap. 12.95 (ISBN 0-915570-22-X). Oolp Pr.
Western Jewish History Center: Guide to Archival & Oral History Collections. Ruth K. Rafael. LC 86-50102. (Illus.). 1987. pap. 24.95 (ISBN 0-943376-35-1). Magnes Mus.
Western Journal. Thomas Wolfe. LC 51-5284. 1968. pap. 4.95 (ISBN 0-8229-5121-5). U of Pittsburgh Pr.
Western Journal of Isaac Mayer Wise, 1877. Ed. by William K. Kramer. 1974. pap. 5.00 (ISBN 0-943376-05-X). Magnes Mus.
Western Journey with Mr. Emerson. James B. Thayer. LC 70-122665. 1971. Repr. of 1884 ed. 20.50 (ISBN 0-8046-1314-1, Pub. by Kennikat). Assoc Faculty Pr.
Western Junior League Cookbook. Ed. by Anne Seranne. (Illus.). 1979. 12.95 (ISBN 0-679-51454-6). McKay.
Western Kentucky University. Lowell H. Harrison. LC 86-32456. (Illus.). 384p. 1987. 33.00 (ISBN 0-8131-1620-1). U Pr of Ky.
Western Landmarks: Historic Buildings of Western Australia. Ronald P. Wright. (Illus., Orig.). 1979. pap. 6.95 (ISBN 0-85564-109-6, Pub. by U of W Austral Pr). Intl Spec Bk.
Western Lands. William S. Burroughs. 1987. 18.95 (ISBN 0-670-81352-4). Viking.
Western Lands. William S. Burroughs. 272p. 1988. pap. 7.95 (ISBN 0-14-009456-3). Penguin.
Western Lawmen. Frank Surge. LC 68-30568. (Pull Ahead Bks.). (Illus.). 64p. (gr. 5-10). 1969. PLB 5.95 (ISBN 0-8225-0451-0). Lerner Pubns.
Western Life & Adventure, 1889-1970 see Western Life & Adventures in the Great Southwest.
Western Life & Adventures in the Great Southwest. Elliott S. Barker. LC 74-15149. Orig. Title: Western Life & Adventure, 1889-1970. (Illus.). 328p. 1974. Repr. of 1970 ed. 9.95 (ISBN 0-913504-19-X). Lowell Pr.
Western Life in the Stirrups. Ed. by Dwight L. Smith. 1965. 25.00 (ISBN 0-940550-01-6). Caxton Club.
Western Literature, 3 vols. A. Bartlett Giamatti. Incl. Vol. 1. Ed. by Heinrich Von Staden. 550p. pap. (ISBN 0-15-595276-5); Vol. 2. The Middle Ages, Renaissance, Enlightenment. Ed. by Robert Hollander. 550p. pap. (ISBN 0-15-595277-3); Vol. 3. The Modern World. Ed. by Peter Brooks. 552p. pap. (ISBN 0-15-595278-1). 1971. 11.50net ea. (HC); instr's. manual avail. (ISBN 0-15-595279-X, HC). HarBraceJ.
Western Man. Janet Dailey. pap. 2.95 (ISBN 0-671-62064-9). PB.
Western Man & the Modern World, 5 vols. Leonard F. James et al. Incl. Vol. 1. Origins of Western Civilization. 1973. text ed. 13.60 (ISBN 0-08-017198-2); pap. text ed. 9.00 (ISBN 0-08-017199-0); student primary source re 3.00 (ISBN 0-08-017728-X); Vol. 2. Rivalry, Reason & Revolution. 1973. text ed. 13.60 (ISBN 0-08-017200-8); pap. 9.00 (ISBN 0-08-017201-6); student primary source re 3.00 (ISBN 0-08-017729-8); Vol. 3. Industrialism, Imperialism & War. 1973. text ed. 13.60 (ISBN 0-08-017202-4); pap. text ed. 9.00 (ISBN 0-08-017203-2); student primary source re 3.00 (ISBN 0-08-017730-1); Vol. 4. The Western World Today. 2nd ed. 1984. text ed. 17.00 (ISBN 0-08-021975-6); pap. text ed. 13.00 (ISBN 0-08-022614-0); student primary source re 3.00 (ISBN 0-08-022618-3); Vol. 5. Africa, Latin America & the East. 1984. text ed. 16.00 (ISBN 0-08-021976-4); pap. text ed. 12.00 (ISBN 0-08-022616-7); student primary source readings 2.20 (ISBN 0-08-022619-1); Teaching Resource Book. 1973. pap. 12.00 (ISBN 0-08-017208-3). 1979. pap. write for info. Pergamon.
Western Mandala: A Survey of the Mandala in the Western Esoteric Tradition. Adam McClean. (Illus.). 1987. pap. 15.00 (ISBN 0-317-57173-7). Phanes Pr.
Western Manuscripts from Classical Antiquity to the Renaissance: A Handbook. Laurel N. Braswell. LC 79-7908. 404p. 1985. lib. bdg. 61.00 (ISBN 0-8240-9541-3). Garland Pub.
Western Maryland: A Profile. Thomas H. Hattery. LC 79-65634. 208p. 1980. 19.75 (ISBN 0-912338-21-0). Lomond.
Western Maryland in the Revolution. Bernard C. Steiner. LC 78-63885. (Johns Hopkins University. Studies in the Social Sciences. Twentieth Ser. 1902: 1). Repr. of 1902 ed. 11.50 (ISBN 0-404-61140-0). AMS Pr.
Western Massachusetts in the Revolution. Robert J. Taylor. 1954. 26.00 (ISBN 0-527-89075-8). Kraus Repr.
Western Masters. Jean Stern. LC 81-83939. (Illus.). 124p. 1981. lib. bdg. 21.00 (ISBN 0-8227-8040-2, Dist. by DeRu's Fine Art). Petersen Pub.
Western Medical Pioneers in Feudal Japan. John Z. Bowers. LC 73-86098. (Josiah Macy Foundation Ser). 256p. 1970. 28.50x (ISBN 0-8018-1081-7). Johns Hopkins.
Western Medieval Civilization. Deno J. Geanakoplos. 1979. text ed. 24.00 (ISBN 0-669-00868-0). Heath.
Western Mediterranean. Ed. by R. Margalef. (Key Environments Ser.). 275p. 1985. text ed. 37.95 (ISBN 0-08-028870-7). Pergamon.
Western Mediterranean Europe: A Historical Geography of Italy, Spain & Southern France Since the Neolithic. Catherine Delano-Smith. 1979. 91.00 (ISBN 0-12-210450-1). Acad Pr.
Western Mediterranean World: An Introduction to Its Regional Landscapes. James M. Houston. LC 65-87641. (Geographies for Advanced Study Ser.). pap. 160.00 (ISBN 0-317-27875-4, 2025261). Bks Demand UMI.
Western Military Frontier 1815-1846. Henry P. Beers. LC 75-25798. (Perspectives in American Hist. Ser.: No. 35). (Illus.). vi, 227p. 1975. Repr. of 1935 ed. lib. bdg. 25.00x (ISBN 0-87991-359-2). Porcupine Pr.
Western Mining: An Informal Account of Precious-Metals Prospecting, Placering, Lode Mining, & Milling on the American Frontier from Spanish Times to 1893. Otis E. Young, Jr. LC 76-108800. (Illus.). 1970. pap. 12.95 (ISBN 0-8061-1352-9). U of Okla Pr.
Western Montana: A Portrait of the Land & Its People. John A. Alwin. (Montana Geographic Ser.: No. 5). (Illus.). 152p. (Orig.). 1983. pap. 13.95 (ISBN 0-938314-07-6). Am Geog Pub.
Western Movies: A TV & Video Guide to 4200 Genre Films. Michael R. Pitts. LC 85-31014. 635p. 1986. lib. bdg. 39.95x (ISBN 0-89950-195-8). McFarland & Co.
Western Mystery Tradition. Christine Hartley. 160p. 1986. pap. 11.95 (ISBN 0-85030-561-6, Pub. by Thorsons UK). Weiser.
Western Mystical Tradition: An Intellectual History of Western Civilization, Vol. 1. Thomas Katsaros & Nathaniel Kaplan. 1969. 15.95x (ISBN 0-8084-0316-8); pap. 11.95x (ISBN 0-8084-0317-6). New Coll U Pr.
Western Mysticism: A Guide to the Basic Works. Compiled by Mary Ann Bowman. LC 78-18311. vi, 114p. 1979. pap. 9.00x (ISBN 0-8389-0266-9). ALA.
Western Mysticism: Neglected Chapters in the History of Religion. C. Butler. 69.95 (ISBN 0-87968-244-2). Gordon Pr.
Western Nevada Jeep Trails. Roger Mitchell. (Illus.). 1985. wrappers 1.50 (ISBN 0-910856-50-8). La Siesta.
Western New York Exhibition, No. 39. LC 82-70389. (Illus.). 40p. 1982. pap. 4.00 (ISBN 0-914782-44-4). Buffalo Acad.
Western North Atlantic, Vol. M. Ed. by P. R. Vogt & B. E. Tucholke. (DNAG Geology of North America Ser.). (Illus.). 1986. 47.50 (ISBN 0-8137-5202-7). Geol Soc.
Western North Carolina: A History from 1730 to 1913. John P. Arthur. LC 73-1945. (Illus.). 710p. 1973. Repr. of 1914 ed. 35.00 (ISBN 0-87152-126-1). Reprint.
Western North Carolina: Its Mountains & Its People to 1880. 2nd ed. Ora Blackmun. LC 76-53030. (Illus., Orig.). 1977. 13.95 (ISBN 0-913239-32-1); pap. 9.95 (ISBN 0-913239-31-3). Appalach Consortium.
Western North Carolina since the Civil War. Ina Van Noppen & John Van Noppen. LC 73-1241. 1973. 13.95 (ISBN 0-913239-33-X); pap. 9.95 (ISBN 0-913239-34-8). Appalach Consortium.
Western Ocean Packets. Basil Lubbock. (Illus.). 192p. 1988. pap. 5.95 (ISBN 0-486-25684-7). Dover.
Western Oil World: Rocky Mountain Petroleum Directory. 34th ed. Ed. by Dori Harrell. 900p. (Orig.). 1988. pap. text ed. 35.00 (ISBN 0-912553-12-X). Hart Pubns.
Western Oregon. Photos by Greg Lawson. LC 81-71871. (Illus.). 64p. (Eng., Span., Fr., Ger. & Japanese.). Date not set. pap. 8.95 (ISBN 0-9606704-4-0). First Choice.
Western Oregon: Portrait of the Land & Its People. Marnie McPhee. (Oregon Geographic Ser.). (Orig.). 1987. pap. 14.95 (ISBN 0-938314-34-3). Am Geog Pub.
Western Outlaws: The "Good Badman" in Fact, Film & Folklore. Kent L. Steckmesser. (Topics in American History & Culture Ser.). 161p. 1983. 18.95x (ISBN 0-941690-07-5); pap. 11.95x (ISBN 0-941690-08-3); pap. text ed. 7.75x. Regina Bks.
Western Pacific Trade, Vol. 1. W. F. Gossling. 1985. 16.00x (ISBN 0-904870-19-7, Pub. by Input-Output UK). State Mutual Bk.
Western Pacific Trade, Vol. 2. W. F. Gossling. 1986. 16.00x (ISBN 0-904870-20-0, Pub. by Input-Output UK). State Mutual Bk.
Western Pacific's Diesel Years. Joseph A. Strapac. LC 80-68133. (Overland Railbook Ser.). (Illus.). 208p. 1980. pap. 18.50 (ISBN 0-916160-08-4). G R Cockle.
Western Paradise of Amitabha. Manly P. Hall. pap. 2.50 (ISBN 0-89314-369-3). Philos Res.
Western Peace Officer: The Legacy of Law & Order. Frank R. Prassel. LC 71-39627. 304p. 1981. pap. 12.95 (ISBN 0-8061-1694-3). U. of Okla Pr.
Western Perspectives of Soviet Education in the 1980s. Ed. by J. J. Tomiak. LC 85-22252. 304p. 1986. 29.95 (ISBN 0-312-86420-5). St Martin.
Western Philosophy: An Introduction. R. J. Hollingdale. LC 79-63624. 158p. 1983. pap. 5.95 (ISBN 0-8008-8130-3). Taplinger.
Western Philosophy: From Antiquity to the Middle Ages. James N. Jordan. 887p. (YA) (gr. 9 up). 1987. pap. write for info. (ISBN 0-02-361450-1). Macmillan.
Western Pioneer: Or, Incidents of the Life & Times of Rev. Alfred Brunson.., 2 vols. in 1. facsimile ed. Alfred Brunson. LC 75-89. (Mid-American Frontier Ser.). 1975. Repr. of 1872 ed. 60.50x (ISBN 0-405-06856-5). Ayer Co Pubs.
Western Poetics & Eastern Thought. Gurbachan Singh. 1987. 10.00x (ISBN 81-202-0103-5, Pub. by Ajanta). South Asia Bks.
Western Policies on East-West Trade. Stephen Woolcock. (Chatham House Papers: No. 15). 96p. (Orig.). 1982. pap. 10.95x (ISBN 0-7100-9314-4). Routledge Chapman & Hall.
Western Political Theory from Its Origins to the Present, 3 vols. Lee C. McDonald. Incl. Vol. 1. Ancient & Medieval. 243p. pap. text ed. 9.50 net (ISBN 0-15-595297-8); Vol. 2. From Machiavelli to Burke. 297p. pap. text ed. 9.50 net (ISBN 0-15-595298-6); Vol. 3. Nineteenth & Twentieth Centuries. 239p. pap. text ed. 9.50 net (ISBN 0-15-595299-4). 1970. pap. 9.50 ea. net (HC). HarBraceJ.
Western Political Theory in the Face of the Future. John Dunn. LC 78-25625. (Themes in the Social Sciences Ser.). 1979. o. p. 32.50 (ISBN 0-521-22619-8); pap. 11.95 (ISBN 0-521-29578-5). Cambridge U Pr.
Western Political Thought. R. P. Sharma. 340p. 1984. pap. text ed. 10.95x (ISBN 0-86590-316-6, Sterling Pubs India). Apt Bks.
Western Political Thought: From Theory & Ideology. Brian Nelson. 352p. 1982. write for info. (ISBN 0-13-951640-9). P-H.
Western Popular Theatre. Ed. by David Mayer & Kenneth Richards. 1980. pap. 11.95x (ISBN 0-416-73150-3, NO. 6507). Routledge Chapman & Hall.

Western Populism: Studies in an Ambivalent Conservatism. Karel D. Bicha. (Illus.). 1976. 8.50 (ISBN 0-87291-085-7). Coronado Pr.
Western Portal of Saint-Loup-De-Naud. Clark Maines. LC 78-74373. (Fine Arts Dissertations, Fourth Ser.). (Illus.). 511p. 1979. lib. bdg. 53.00 (ISBN 0-8240-3960-2). Garland Pub.
Western Prices Before Eighteen Sixty-One: A Study of the Cincinnati Market. Thomas Berry. (Harvard Economic Studies: Vol. 74). Repr. of 1943 ed. 38.00 (ISBN 0-384-04075-6). Johnson Repr.
Western Prices Before Eighteen Sixty-One: A Study of the Cincinnati Market. Thomas Berry, Sr. 1943. 35.00x (ISBN 0-317-27656-5). Elliots Bks.
Western Psychotherapy & Hindu-Sadhana: A Contribution to Comparative Studies in Psychology & Metaphysics. Hans Jacobs. LC 61-3343. (Illus.). pap. 60.50 (ISBN 0-317-10274-5, 2010706). Bks Demand UMI.
Western Public Lands: The Management of Natural Resources in a Time of Declining Federalism. Ed. by John G. Francis & Richard Ganzel. LC 83-19067. 320p. 1984. 39.50x (ISBN 0-86598-147-7, Rowman & Allanheld). Rowman.
Western Pulp Hero. Compiled by Nick Carr. (Popular Culture Studies: No. 3). 1988. 21.95; pap. 11.95. Starmont Hse.
Western Question in Greece & Turkey: A Study in the Contrast of Civilizations. 2nd ed. Arnold J. Toynbee. LC 68-9598. (Illus., Maps). 1970. Repr. of 1922 ed. 40.00x (ISBN 0-86527-209-3). Fertig.
Western Races & the World. Unity Ser. 5. facs. ed. Ed. by Francis S. Marvin. LC 68-22929. (Essay Index Reprint Ser). 1968. Repr. of 1922 ed. 17.00 (ISBN 0-8369-0684-5). Ayer Co Pubs.
Western Range. U. S. Senate. Ed. by Stuart Bruchey. LC 78-53570. (Development of Public Land Law in the U. S. Ser.). (Illus.). 1979. Repr. of 1936 ed. lib. bdg. 43.00x (ISBN 0-405-11390-0). Ayer Co Pubs.
Western Range Livestock Industry. Marion Clawson. Ed. by Stuart Bruchey. LC 78-56713. (Management of Public Land Law in the U. S. Ser.). (Illus.). 1979. Repr. of 1950 ed. lib. bdg. 28.50x (ISBN 0-405-11326-9). Ayer Co Pubs.
Western Religion: A Country by Country Sociological Inquiry. Ed. & intro. by Hans Mol. (Religion & Reason Ser.: No. 2). (Illus.). 642p. 1972. text ed. 59.00x (ISBN 90-2797-004-1). Mouton.
Western Reports on the Taiping: A Selection of Documents. Ed. by Prescott Clarke & J. S. Gregory. LC 81-68942. 484p. 1982. text ed. 25.00x (ISBN 0-8248-0807-X); pap. text ed. 15.95x (ISBN 0-8248-0809-6). UH Pr.
Western Reserve & the Fugitive Slave Law: A Prelude to the Civil War. William C. Cochran. LC 71-127273. 1972. Repr. of 1920 ed. 29.50 (ISBN 0-306-71212-1). Da Capo.
Western Reserve's Experiment in Medical Education & Its Outcome. Greer Williams. 1980. 35.00x (ISBN 0-19-502679-9). Oxford U Pr.
Western Response to State-Supported Terrorism. Geoffrey M. Levitt. LC 86-418. (Washington Papers: No. 134). (Illus.). 160p. 1988. lib. bdg. 32.95 (ISBN 0-275-93021-1, C3021); pap. 9.95 (ISBN 0-275-93022-X, B3022). Praeger.
Western Response to Zoroaster. J. Duchesne-Guillemin. LC 72-9593. 112p. 1973. Repr. of 1958 ed. lib. bdg. 35.00x (ISBN 0-8371-6590-3, DUWR). Greenwood.
Western Responses to Tanzanian Socialism 1967-83. Susan C. Crouch. 300p. 1987. text ed. 39.00x (ISBN 0-566-05455-8, Pub. by Gower Pub England). Gower Pub Co.
Western River Transportation: The Era of Early Internal Development, 1810-1860. Erik F. Haites et al. LC 75-12568. (Studies in Historical & Political Science: Ninety-Third Series (1975)). (Illus.). 224p. 1975. 24.50x (ISBN 0-8018-1681-5). Johns Hopkins.
Western Rocks & Minerals. Stan Leaming & Chris Leaming. (Illus.). 33p. (Orig.). 1980. pap. 3.00 (ISBN 0-88839-053-X). Hancock House.
Western Roots in Japan. Neil Pedlar. 1985. 35.00x (ISBN 0-904404-51-X, Pub. by Norbury Pubns Ltd). State Mutual Bk.
Western Sahara. David L. Price. (Washington Papers: Vol. VII, No. 63). 80p. (Orig.). 1979. pap. text ed. 7.95 (ISBN 0-8191-6012-1, Pub. by CSIS). U Pr of Amer.
Western Sahara: A Comprehensive Bibliography. Lynn F. Sipe. LC 82-49258. (Reference Library of Social Science). 500p. 1984. lib. bdg. 54.00 (ISBN 0-8240-9125-6). Garland Pub.
Western Sahara: Roots of a Desert War. Tony Hodges. LC 83-8565. 400p. (Orig.). 1984. 19.95 (ISBN 0-88208-151-9); pap. 14.95 (ISBN 0-88208-152-7). Chicago Review.
Western Saharans: Background to Conflict. Virginia Thompson & Richard Adloff. LC 80-41164. 348p. 1980. 28.50x (ISBN 0-389-20148-0). B&N Imports.
Western Samoa: The Experience of Slow Growth & Resource Imbalance. Shadid Yusef & R. Kyle Peters, Jr. (Working Paper: No. 754). 34p. 1985. 3.50 (ISBN 0-8213-0622-7, WP 0754). World Bank.
Western Science in the Arab World: The Impact of Darwinism, 1860-1930. Adel A. Ziadat. LC 85-27929. 256p. 1986. 29.95x (ISBN 0-312-86433-7). St Martin.
Western Sculpture: Definitions of Man. Ruth Butler. LC 79-1912. (Illus.). 1979. pap. 12.95x (ISBN 0-06-430098-6, IN-98, HarpT). Har-Row.
Western Security: The Formative Years. Ed. by Olav Riste. LC 85-7795. 410p. 1985. 42.00x (ISBN 0-231-06168-4). Columbia U Pr.
Western Septet: Seven Stories of the American West. new ed. Henryk Sienkiewicz. Ed. by Marion M. Coleman. LC 72-96321. (Illus.). 175p. 1973. pap. 5.00 (ISBN 0-910366-15-2). Alliance Coll.
Western Series & Sequels: A Reference Guide. Bernard A. Drew & Martin H. Waugh. (Reference of the Humanities Ser.: Vol. 625). 160p. 1986. lib. bdg. 25.00 (ISBN 0-8240-8657-0). Garland Pub.
Western Sexuality. Philippe Aries & Andre Bejin. 224p. 1985. 24.95 (ISBN 0-631-13476-X). Basil Blackwell.
Western Sexuality: Practice & Precept in Past & Present Times. Ed. by Philippe Aries & Andre Bejin. Tr. by Anthony Forster from Fr. 232p. 1986. pap. 9.95 (ISBN 0-631-14989-9). Basil Blackwell.
Western Sierra Jeep Trails. Roger Mitchell. (Jeep Trails Ser.). (Illus.). 1977. pap. 2.95 (ISBN 0-910856-63-X). La Siesta.
Western Slave Coast & Its Rulers: European Trade & Administration among the Yoruba & Adja-Speaking Peoples of Southwestern Nigeria, Southern Dahomey & Togo. Colin W. Newbury. LC 83-12619. ix, 234p. 1983. Repr. of 1961 ed. lib. bdg. 38.50x (ISBN 0-313-23967-3, NEWE). Greenwood.
Western Societies: A Documentary History, 2 vols. Brian Tierney & Joan Scott. 480p. 1983. Vol. 1. pap. text ed. 10.00 (ISBN 0-394-32691-1, KnopfC); Vol. 2. pap. text ed. 10.00 (ISBN 0-394-32692-X). Knopf.
Western Society after the Holocaust. Ed. by Lyman H. Letgers. (Replica Editon Ser.). 200p. 1984. 20.00x (ISBN 0-86531-985-5). Westview.
Western Society & the Church in the Middle Ages. R. W. Southern. (History of the Church). (Orig.). 1970. pap. 6.95 (ISBN 0-14-020503-9, Pelican). Penguin.
Western Somoa. (Let's Visit Places & Peoples - - Nations, Dependencies, & Sovereignties of the World Ser.). (Illus.). (gr. 5 up). 1988. 12.95 (ISBN 0-7910-0141-5). Chelsea Hse.
Western Spirituality: Historical Roots, Ecumenical Routes. Matthew Fox. LC 81-67364. 448p. 1981. pap. 12.95 (ISBN 0-939680-01-7). Bear & Co.
Western Stars of Country Music. Bonnie Lake. LC 77-90149. (Country Music Bks.). (Illus.). (gr. 5 up). 1978. PLB 5.95 (ISBN 0-8225-1407-9). Lerner Pubns.
Western State: Some of Its People & Ports. 3rd, facsimile ed. John P. Stokes. LC 76-375777. (Illus.). 1976. pap. 7.00x (ISBN 0-85564-119-3, Pub. by U of W Austral Pr). Intl Spec Bk.
Western State University Law Review: 1972-1986, 13 vols. Bound set. 390.00x (ISBN 0-686-90098-7). Rothman.
Western Story: The Recollections of Charley O'Kieffe, 1884-1898. Charley O'Kieffe. LC 60-5381. (Pioneer Heritage Ser: Vol. 2). (Illus.). xvi, 223p. 1960. 21.00x (ISBN 0-8032-0134-6); pap. 5.50 (ISBN 0-8032-5796-1, BB 585, Bison). U of Nebr Pr.
Western Strategic Interests in Saudi Arabia. Anthony Cordesman. 320p. 1986. 52.50 (ISBN 0-7099-4823-9, Pub. by Croom Helm UK). Routledge Chapman & Hall.
Western Streamside Guide. Dave Hughes. (Illus.). 160p. (Orig.). 1987. pap. 9.95 (ISBN 0-936608-59-5). F Amato Pubns.
Western Sunrise: The Genesis & Growth of Britain's Major High Tech Corridor. P. Hall et al. 192p. 1987. text ed. 34.95x (ISBN 0-04-338142-1). Unwin Hyman.
Western Swing. Tim Sandlin. LC 87-23601. 1988. 19.95 (ISBN 0-8050-0458-0). H Holt & Co.
Western Systems of Juvenile Justice. Malcolm W. Klein. LC 83-19150. 1983. 25.95 (ISBN 0-8039-2125-X). Sage.
Western Taste for Japanese Prints. Jack Hillier. 120p. 1976. pap. 42.00x (Pub. by Han-Shan Tang Ltd). State Mutual Bk.
Western Technology & Soviet Economic Development, 1930 to 1945. Vol. 2 see Western Technology & Soviet Economic Development, 1917-1930.
Western Technology & Soviet Economic Development, 1945 to 1965. Vol. 3 see Western Technology & Soviet Economic Development, 1917-1930.
Western Technology & Soviet Economic Development, 1917-1930, Vol. 1. Antony C. Sutton. Incl. Western Technology & Soviet Economic Development, 1930 to 1945. Vol. 2. Antony C. Sutton. LC 68-2442. (Publications Ser.: No. 90). 1971. 15.00x (ISBN 0-8179-1901-5); Western Technology & Soviet Economic Development, 1945 to 1965. Vol. 3. LC 68-24442. (Publications Ser.: No. 113). (Illus.). 482p. 1973. 18.00x (ISBN 0-8179-6131-3). LC 68-24442. (Publications Ser.: No. 76). (Illus.). 1968. Set. 36.95x. Hoover Inst Pr.
Western Territories in the Civil War. Ed. by Leroy H. Fischer. 1977. pap. 8.00 (ISBN 0-686-00373-X). AG Pr.
Western Territories in the Civil War. Ed. by LeRoy H. Fischer. (Illus.). 113p. 1977. pap. text ed. 9.95x (ISBN 0-89745-000-0). Sunflower U Pr.
Western Theatre: Revolution & Revival. Patti P. Gillespie & Kenneth M. Cameron. (Illus.). 608p. 1984. text ed. write for info. (ISBN 0-02-343050-8). Macmillan.
Western Theology. Wes Seeliger. LC 72-96685. 103p. 1985. pap. 6.95 (ISBN 0-915321-00-9). Pioneer Vent.
Western Tradition: From the Ancient World to Louis 14th, Vol. 1. 3rd ed. Eugen Weber. LC 72-172911. 1972. pap. text ed. 15.50 (ISBN 0-669-81166-1). Heath.
Western Tradition: From the Renaissance to the Present, Vol. 2. 3rd ed. Eugen Weber. LC 72-172911. 1971. pap. text ed. 15.00 (ISBN 0-669-81141-6). Heath.
Western Tradition: Study Guide, Semester I & II. WGBH Educational Foundation Staff & Ray Boggis. 384p. 1989. pap. text ed. write for info. (ISBN 0-02-426620-5). Macmillan.
Western Tradition: Study Guide, Semester II. WGBH Educational Foundation Staff & Jay Boogis. 372p. 1989. pap. write for info. (ISBN 0-02-426600-0). Macmillan.
Western Trails: A Collection of Short Stories by Mary Austin. Selected by Melody Graulich. 300p. 1987. 22.50 (ISBN 0-87417-127-X). U of Nev Pr.
Western Trainer. Dave Jones. LC 73-92075. (Illus.). 1979. pap. 5.95 (ISBN 0-668-04791-7, 4791). Arco.
Western Transition: Economic Council Report. Canadian Government Publishing Centre Staff. 260p. (ps-2). 1985. pap. 18.50 (ISBN 0-660-11693-6, SSC178, SSC). UNIPUB.
Western Travel Books from Wagner-Camp. John H. Jenkins. (Illus.). 5.00 (ISBN 0-685-83966-4). Jenkins.
Western Tree Book. George Palmer & Martha Stuckey. Ed. by Ken Bierly. (Illus.). 144p. 1987. pap. 8.95 (ISBN 0-911518-75-4). Touchstone Oregon.
Western Trips & Trails. rev. ed. E. M. Sterling. (Illus.). 360p. 1987. pap. 12.95 (ISBN 0-87108-727-8). Pruett.
Western Turkey. (Michael's Guides Ser.). (Illus.). 224p. (Orig.). 1988. pap. text ed. 7.95. Hunter Pub NY.
Western Union. Zane Grey. 1986. pap. 2.50 (ISBN 0-671-83537-8). PB.
Western Union Directory & Buyer's Guide, 1986-87 (including Easy Link, Telex I-II & Teletex, 2 Vols. rev. ed. Ed. by Jonathan F. Zimman & Frances Poff. 3000p. 1986. Set. pap. 30.00 (ISBN 0-938899-00-7). Vol. I (ISBN 0-938899-01-5). Vol. II (ISBN 0-938899-02-3). Vol. III (ISBN 0-938899-03-1). Western Union.
Western University on Trial. Ed. by John W. Chapman. LC 82-20120. 256p. 1983. text ed. 30.00x (ISBN 0-520-04940-3). U of Cal Pr.
Western Views of Islam in the Middle Ages. R. W. Southern. LC 62-13270. 1978. 13.50x (ISBN 0-674-95055-0). Harvard U Pr.
Western Wall. Meir Ben-Dov et al. Tr. by Raphael Posner from Hebrew. LC 86-70788. (Illus.). 248p. 1986. 19.95 (ISBN 0-915361-51-5, Dist. by Watts). Adama Pubs Inc.
Western Wall. Menachem Kasher. 172p. 1972. 6.95 (ISBN 0-910818-03-7). Judaica Pr.
Western Waltz. (Ballroom Dance Ser.). 1985. lib. bdg. 58.00 (ISBN 0-87700-752-7). Revisionist Pr.
Western Waltz. (Ballroom Dance Ser.). 1986. lib. bdg. 59.95 (ISBN 0-8490-3298-9). Gordon Pr.
Western Washington Treaty Proceedings. Robert B. Lane & Barbara Lane. (Treaty Manuscripts Ser.: No. 2). 67p. 12.50 (ISBN 0-944253-24-5). Inst Dev Indian Law.
Western Water Flows to the Cities. John A. Folk-Williams et al. Ed. by Anna Deardorff. (Water in the West Ser.). (Illus.). 184p. (Orig.). 1985. pap. 25.00x (ISBN 0-933280-28-9). Island CA.
Western Way: A Practical Guide to the Western Mystery Tradition. Caitlin Matthews & John Matthews. (Hermetic Tradition Ser.: Vol. II). 261p. 1986. pap. 11.95 (ISBN 1-85063-017-8). Routledge Chapman & Hall.
Western Way: A Practical Guide to the Western Mystery Tradition. Catlin Matthews & John Matthews. 160p. (Orig.). 1985. pap. 8.95 (ISBN 1-85063-012-7, Ark Paperbks). Routledge Chapman & Hall.
Western Ways to the Center: An Introduction to Western Religions. Denise L. Carmody & John T. Carmody. 252p. 1983. pap. text ed. write for info. (ISBN 0-534-01328-7). Wadsworth Pub.
Western Wild Harvest: Edible Plants of The Pacific Northwest. Terry Domico. (Illus.). 88p. 1979. pap. 6.95 (ISBN 0-88839-022-X). Hancock House.
Western Wind American Tune-Book. Ed. by Lawrence Bennett. 1977. pap. 12.50x (ISBN 0-8450-0076-4). Broude.
Western Wind: An Introduction to Poetry. 2th ed. John F. Nims. 1983. pap. text ed. write for info (ISBN 0-394-33070-6, RanC). Random.
Western Window in the Arab World. Leon B. Blair. LC 78-131423. pap. 91.00 (2030736). Bks Demand UMI.
Western Women in Colonial Africa. Caroline Oliver. LC 81-24194. (Contributions in Comparative Colonial Studies: No. 12). xv, 201p. 1982. lib. bdg. 35.00 (ISBN 0-313-23388-8, OWA/). Greenwood.
Western Women in Eastern Lands: An Outline Study of Fifty Years of Women's Work in Foreign Missions. Helen B. Montgomery. Ed. by Carolyn Gifford & Donald Dayton. (Women's American Protestant Religion 1800-1930 Ser.). 286p. 1987. lib. bdg. 40.00 (ISBN 0-8240-0670-4). Garland Pub.
Western Women: Their Land, Their Lives. Ed. by Lillian Schlissel et al. (Illus.). 368p. 1988. 27.50x (ISBN 0-8263-1089-3); pap. 14.95 (ISBN 0-8263-1090-7). U of NM Pr.
Western Woods Use Book: incl. 1987 update package. 3rd ed. LC 73-77089. (Illus.). 314p. 1983. 35.00 (ISBN 0-9600912-2-X). Western Wood.
Western World, 2 vols. Wallace E. Adams et al. 1968. Vol. 1. pap. text ed. 22.95 scp (ISBN 0-06-040165-6, HarpC); Vol. 2. pap. text ed. 22.95 scp (ISBN 0-06-040166-4). Har-Row.
Western World & Japan: A Study in the Interaction of European & Asiatic Cultures. G. B. Sansom. LC 86-50704. (Cresset Historical Ser.). (Illus.). 532p. pap. 12.95 (ISBN 0-8048-1510-0). C E Tuttle.
Western World: Or, Travels in the United States in 1846-47. Alexander Mackay. LC 68-55900. 1969. Repr. of 1849 ed. 15.90x (ISBN 0-8371-0549-8, MAWF). Vol. 2. 15.90 (ISBN 0-8371-0823-3, MAWG); Vol. 3. 15.90 (ISBN 0-8371-0824-1, MAWH). Greenwood.
Western Writer's Handbook. Ed. by James L. Collins. 250p. (Orig.). 1987. 12.95 (ISBN 1-55566-023-1); pap. 7.95 (ISBN 1-55566-013-4). Johnson Bks.
Western Yesterdays, 12 Vols. Forest Crossen. 1972. 44.95 set (ISBN 0-913730-09-2). Robinson Pr.
Westerners among the Figurines of the Tang Dynasty of China. Jame G. Mahler. 220p. 1959. 630.00x (ISBN 0-317-44243-0, Pub. by Han-Shan Tang Ltd). State Mutual Bk.
Westernization of Asia: A Comparative Political Analysis. Frank C. Darling. 500p. 1980. pap. text ed. 11.95x (ISBN 0-87073-971-9). Schenkman Bks Inc.
Westernized Yankee: The Story of Cyrus Woodman. Larry Gara. LC 56-14602. (Illus.). 254p. 1956. 7.50 (ISBN 0-87020-032-1). State Hist Soc Wis.
Westerns. Richard Dankleff. LC 83-21979. 96p. 1984. pap. 5.95 (ISBN 0-87071-340-X). Oreg St U Pr.
Westerns. 2nd ed. Philip French. 1977. pap. 6.95 (ISBN 0-19-519987-1). Oxford U Pr.
Westfaelischen Fabrikengerichtsdeputationen: Vorbilder, Werdegang und Scheitern. Karl-Hans Schlosstein. (Rechtshistorische Reihe: Vol. 20). 219p. (Ger.). 1982. 25.80 (ISBN 3-8204-7111-1). P Lang Pubs.
Westfalians. Walter D. Kamphoefner. (Illus.). 240p. 1987. text ed. 29.00 (ISBN 0-691-04746-4). Princeton U Pr.
Westgermanische Bodenfunde des Ersten bis Dritten Jahrhunderts N. Ch. aus Mittel-und Westdeutschland, 2 vols. Rafael Von Uslar. (Illus.). 1978. 112.00x (ISBN 3-11-002250-8). De Gruyter.
Westghosts: The Psychic World of California. Hans Holzer. LC 77-88693. Orig. Title: Ghosts of the Golden West. xiv, 233p. 1980. pap. 5.95 (ISBN 0-8040-0759-4, Pub by Swallow). Ohio U Pr.
Westhampton Beach Chronicles. Circe K. Fraguadas. (Illus.). 130p. 1986. pap. 5.95 (ISBN 0-939820-04-8). Lindon Ent.
Westies: From Head to Tail. Ruth Faherty. (Illus.). 232p. 1981. 19.98 (ISBN 0-931866-08-1). Alpine Pubns.
Westing Game. Ellen Raskin. (Illus.). 188p. (YA) (gr. 7 up). 1980. pap. 2.75 (ISBN 0-380-67991-4, Camelot). Avon.
Westing Game. Ellen Raskin. (gr. 5-9). 1978. 14.95 (ISBN 0-525-42320-6). Dutton.
Westinghouse Electric Railway Transportation: Bulletin No. 118. LC 78-74493. (Illus.). 384p. 1979. 23.00 (ISBN 0-915348-18-7). Central Electric.
Westinghouse Equipped Cars. 1984. 6.95 (ISBN 0-912113-08-1). Railhead Pubns.
Westinghouse Equipped Diesel-Electric. 100p. 10.95 (ISBN 0-912113-11-1). Railhead Pubns.
Westlaw Access Guide for the IBM 3101 Terminal: Basic User Training. Westlaw-West Publishing Company. 28p. 1981. write for info. (ISBN 0-314-62803-7). West Pub.
Westlaw for Law Students. 2nd ed. West Publishing Company. LC 85-228463. 1985. write for info. (ISBN 0-314-95833-9). West Pub.
Westlaw Reference Manual. Westlaw-West Publishing Company. 60p. 1981. pap. text ed. write for info. (ISBN 0-314-62801-0). West Pub.
Westliche Hunsrueck-Eifel-Kultur: Text-Vol. & Vol. with Plates. A. Haffner. (Roemisch-Germanische Forschungen, Vol. 36). (Illus.). 1976. 178.00x (ISBN 3-11-004889-2). De Gruyter.
Westmark. Lloyd Alexander. 192p. (gr. 5-9). 1982. pap. 2.95 (ISBN 0-440-99731-3, LFL). Dell.
Westmark. Lloyd Alexander. LC 80-22242. (gr. 5 up). 1981. 14.95 (ISBN 0-525-42335-4). Dutton.
Westminister Pulpits, 10 vols. Campbell G. Morgan. 1983. Set. deluxe ed. 99.95 (ISBN 0-8010-6155-5). Baker Bk.

Wet Strength of Paper. 2nd ed. Jack Weiner. LC 52-26053. (Bibliographic Ser.: No. 168, Supp. 3). 1977. pap. 20.00 (ISBN 0-87010-052-1). Inst Paper Chem.

Wet Watercolor. Wilfred Ball. (Illus.). 160p. 1987. 24.95 (ISBN 0-89134-204-4). North Light Bks.

Wet Wishing Stump: A Muffin Miniature. V. Gilbert Beers. LC 88-80701. 32p. (Orig.). (gr. 1-6). 1988. 3.95 (ISBN 0-89081-691-3). Harvest Hse.

W.E.T. Workout: Water Exercise Techniques to Help You Tone Up & Slim Down Aerobically. Ed. by Jane Katz. LC 83-20829. (Illus.). 192p. 1985. 16.95 (ISBN 0-8160-1159-1); pap. 10.95 (ISBN 0-8160-1032-3). Facts on File.

Wetherby. David Hare. (Illus.). 128p. (Orig.). 1985. pap. 8.95 (ISBN 0-571-13489-0). Faber & Faber.

Wetherel Affair. John W. De Forest. (Collected Works of John W. De Forest). 1988. Repr. of 1873 ed. lib. bdg. 59.00x. Am Biog Serv.

Wetherel Affair see Collected Works.

Wetherills of the Mesa Verde. Benjamin A. Wetherill. Ed. by Maurine S. Fletcher. LC 86-14606. (Illus.). 333p. 1987. pap. 9.95 (ISBN 0-8032-9719-X, Bison). U of Nebr Pr.

Wetland Conservation: A Bibliography. Mary Vance. (Public Administration Ser.: P 2058). 20p. 1986. 5.00 (ISBN 1-55590-118-2). Vance Biblios.

Wetland Drainage in Europe. 1984. 7.50 (ISBN 0-905347-52-8). Intl Inst Environment.

Wetland Ecology. John R. Etherington. (Studies in Biology: No. 154). 64p. 1983. 69.00x (ISBN 0-7131-2865-8, Pub. by Arnold-Heinemann). State Mutual Bk.

Wetland Functions & Values: The State of Our Understanding, Proceedings of the National Symposium of Wetlands Held in Disneyworld Village, Lake Buena Vista, Florida, November 7-10. National Symposium on Wetlands (1978: Lake Buena Vista, FL) LC 79-93316. (American Water Resources Technical Publication Ser.: TPS 79-2). pap. 160.00 (2027149). Bks Demand UMI.

Wetland Heritage: The Louisiana Duck Decoy. Charles W. Frank, Jr. 192p. 1985. 49.95 (ISBN 0-88289-398-X). Pelican.

Wetland Modelling. Ed. by W. J. Mitsch et al. (Developments in Environmental Modelling: Vol. 12). 238p. 1988. 97.25 (ISBN 0-444-42936-0). Elsevier.

Wetland Soils: Characterization, Classification, & Utilization. International Rice Research Institute Staff. 559p. 1985. text ed. 31.30x (ISBN 971-104-139-1, Pub. by Intl Rice Res Philippines). Agribookstore.

Wetlands. William J. Mitsch & James G. Gosselink. (Illus.). 560p. 1986. 44.95x (ISBN 0-442-26398-8). Van Nos Reinhold.

Wetlands. William A. Niering. Ed. by Charles Elliott. LC 84-48672. (Audubon Society Nature Guides Ser.). (Illus.). 638p. 1985. pap. 15.95 (ISBN 0-394-73147-6). Knopf.

Wetlands & Water Quality: A Citizen's Handbook on How to Review & Comment on Section 404 Permits. Gerald A. Paulson. 47p. 1985. 3.00 (ISBN 0-318-18950-X). Lake Mich Fed.

Wetlands of Bottomland Hardwood Forests: Proceedings at Lake Lanier, Georgia, June 1-5, 1980. Ed. by J. H. Clark & J. Benforado. (Developments in Agricultural & Managed-Forest Ecology Ser.: Vol. 11). 402p. 1981. 139.50 (ISBN 0-444-42020-7). Elsevier.

Wetlands of the Chesapeake: Conference Proceedings, 1985. Ed. by Erik Meyers & Timothy Henderson. 600p. 1985. 18.00 (ISBN 0-911937-19-6). Environ Law Inst.

Wets & Drys of Springdale. Rose M. Brown. (Illus.). 136p. (Orig.). 1987. pap. 9.95 (ISBN 0-940151-01-4). Statesman Exam.

Wetting Agents. National Fire Protection Association Staff. 1986. 10.50 (ISBN 0-317-63057-1, 18-86). Natl Fire Prot.

Wetting Agents. (Ten Ser). 1972. pap. 6.50 (ISBN 0-685-58125-X, 18). Natl Fire Prot.

Wetting Our Lines Together: An Anthology of Recent American Fishing Poems. Ed. by Allen Hoey. 200p. (Orig.). 1982. pap. 7.50 (ISBN 0-918092-26-4). Tamarack Edns.

Wetware. Rudy Rucker. 192p. 1988. pap. 2.95 (ISBN 0-380-70178-2). Avon.

We've All Got Scars: What Boys & Girls Learn in Elementary School. Raphaela Best. LC 82-49198. 192p. 1983. 15.00x (ISBN 0-253-36420-5). Ind U Pr.

We've Been Framed! Cartoons by Dan Wasserman. Dan Wasserman. (Illus.). 128p. 1987. pap. 8.95 (ISBN 0-317-60425-2). Faber & Faber.

We've Been Had! Writings on Men's Issues. Roy W. Schenk. 60p. (Orig.). 1988. pap. 5.00 (ISBN 0-9613177-1-X). Bioenergetics Pr.

We've Got a Hit. Thomas W. McCarthy. LC 86-62422. (Illus.). 184p. 1986. pap. 24.95 (ISBN 0-933341-63-6). Quinlan Pr.

We've Got to Start Meeting Like This: A Guide to Successful Business Meeting Management. Roger K. Mosvick & Robert B. Nelson. 1986. 18.95 (ISBN 0-673-18468-4). Scott F.

We've Got to Stop Meeting Like This. Johnny Hart & Brant Parker. (Wizard of Id Ser.). (Illus.). 1984. pap. 1.95 (ISBN 0-449-12743-5, GM). Fawcett.

We've Laughed a Lot Together. Perry Tanksley. 2.50 (ISBN 0-686-15442-8). Allgood Bks.

We've Only Just Begun. Nancy L. Van Pelt. Ed. by Richard W. Coffen. (Subscription Ser.). 240p. 1986. 26.00 (ISBN 0-8280-0306-8). Review & Herald.

Wexford Carols. Diarmuid O Muirithe. 1982. pap. 13.95 (ISBN 0-85105-376-9, Pub. by Colin Smythe Ltd Britain). Dufour.

Weyerhaeuser: Northwest Loggers, Vol. 2. Jim Spencer. (Illus.). 150p. 1985. write for info. Darwin Pubns.

Weyer's Warships of the World 1988-89: Flottentaschenbuch. Ed. by G. Albrecht. LC 46-43961. (Weyer's Warships of the World Flottentaschenbuch Ser.). (Illus.). 736p. 1988. 78.95 (ISBN 0-933852-75-4). Nautical & Aviation.

Weymouth. Samuel T. Ragan. (Illus.). 152p. (Orig.). 1987. 14.00 (ISBN 0-932662-71-4); pap. price not set. St Andrews Pr.

WFF: Beginner's Game of Modern Logic. Layman Allen. 2.50 (ISBN 0-911624-01-5). Wffn Proof.

Wffn Proof: Game of Modern Logic. Layman Allen. 15.00 (ISBN 0-911624-36-8). Wffn Proof.

WGBH-Vietnam: Anthology & Guide to a Television History. Steven Cohen. 520p. 1983. pap. text ed. 10.50 (ISBN 0-394-33251-2, KnopfC). Knopf.

Whack on the Side of the Head: How to Unlock Your Mind for Innovation. Roger Von Oech. 160p. 1988. pap. 10.95 (ISBN 0-446-38908-0). Warner Bks.

Whack Your Porcupine & Other Drawings. B. Kliban. LC 76-52861. (Illus.). 160p. 1977. pap. 3.95 (ISBN 0-911104-92-5). Workman Pub.

Whaddaya Say? Nina Weinstein. (Orig.). 1982. pap. text ed. 2.95 (ISBN 0-87789-214-8, 1605); cassettes 14.95 (ISBN 0-87789-218-0, 1606). ELS Educ Servs.

Whakairo: Maori Tribal Art. David Simmons. (Illus.). 1985. 34.95x (ISBN 0-19-558119-9). Oxford U Pr.

Whale. Paula Z. Hogan. LC 79-13379. (Life Cycles Bks.). (Illus.). 32p. (gr. k-3). 1979. PLB 14.65 (ISBN 0-8172-1500-X). Raintree Pubs.

Whale. Paula Z. Hogan. LC 79-13379. (Life Cycles Clippers Ser.). (Illus.). 32p. (gr. k-3). 1981. PLB 27.99 incl. cassette (ISBN 0-8172-1847-5); cassette 14.00. Raintree Pubs.

Whale & Dolphin. Vincent Serventy. LC 84-15118. (Animals in the Wild Ser.). (Illus.). 24p. (gr. k-3). 1985. PLB 11.33 (ISBN 0-8172-2401-7). Raintree Pubs.

Whale & Dolphin. Vincent Serventy. (Animals in the Wild Ser.). (Illus.). 24p. (gr. k-3). 1986. pap. 1.95 (ISBN 0-590-40227-7). Scholastic Inc.

Whale & Other Uncollected Translations. Tr. by Richard Wilbur. (New American Translation Ser.: No. 3). 56p. 1982. 12.95 (ISBN 0-918526-32-9); pap. 6.95 (ISBN 0-918526-33-7). Boa Edns.

Whale & the Reactor: A Search for Limits in an Age of High Technology. Langdon Winner. LC 85-8718. xiv, 200p. 1986. lib. bdg. 17.50 (ISBN 0-226-90210-2). U of Chicago Pr.

Whale & the Reactor: A Search for Limits in an Age of High Technology. Langdon Winner. xiv, 200p. 1988. pap. 8.95 (ISBN 0-226-90211-0). U of Chicago Pr.

Whale Brother. Barbara Steiner. (Illus.). (ps-3). Date not set. 12.95. Walker & Co.

Whale Called Trouble. Mary Ann Brittain. (Illus.). 24p. (gr. 1-12). 1985. pap. 1.50 (ISBN 0-917134-08-7). NC Natl Sci.

Whale for the Killing. Farley Mowat. 224p. 1984. pap. 3.95 (ISBN 0-553-26752-3). Bantam.

Whale for the Killing. Farley Mowat. 16.95 (ISBN 0-89190-822-6, Pub. by Am Repr). Amereon Ltd.

Whale in the Sky. Anne Siberell. LC 82-2483. (Illus.). 32p. (ps-3). 1982. pap. 11.95 (ISBN 0-525-44021-6). Dutton.

Whale in the Sky. Anne Siberell. (Unicorn Paperback Ser.). (Illus.). (ps-3). 1985. pap. 3.95 (ISBN 0-525-44197-2). Dutton.

Whale Lake see Arctic Adventure.

Whale Nation. Heathcote Williams. (Illus.). 1988. 25.00 (ISBN 0-517-56932-9, Harmony). Crown.

Whale of a Rescue. Eleanor Hudson. Ed. by Jane Gerver. LC 82-61014. (Sea World Mini-Storybooks). (Illus.). 32p. (gr. 1-5). 1983. pap. 1.25 (ISBN 0-394-85642-2). Random.

Whale on Copyright. R. F. Whale & Jeremy J. Phillips. 1987. 125.00x (ISBN 0-906214-18-1, Pub. by ESC Ltd UK); pap. 95.00x (ISBN 0-906214-17-3, Pub. by ESC Ltd UK). State Mutual Bk.

Whale Problem: A Status Report. Ed. by William E. Schevill. LC 73-88056. 384p. 1974. text ed. 29.95x (ISBN 0-674-95075-5). Harvard U Pr.

Whale Sharks. S. Palmer. (Shark Discovery Library). (Illus.). 24p. (gr. k-5). Date not set. PLB 11.33 (ISBN 0-86592-463-5). Rourke Corp.

Whale Ships & Whaling. George F. Dow. (Illus.). 1967. Repr. of 1925 ed. 35.00 (ISBN 0-87266-007-9). Argosy.

Whale Ships & Whaling: A Pictorial History. George F. Dow. (Antiques Ser.: Transportation). 288p. 1985. pap. 8.95 (ISBN 0-486-24808-9). Dover.

Whale Song. Tony Johnston. (Illus.). (ps-3). 1987. 12.95 (ISBN 0-399-21402-X). Putnam Pub Group.

Whale Songs & Wasp Maps: The Mystery of Animal Thinking. Joseph Mortenson. 1987. 17.95 (ISBN 0-525-24442-5). Dutton.

Whale Tale. John Stevenson. LC 81-5042. (Muppet Show Bks.). (Illus.). 32p. (gr. 1-5). 1981. pap. 1.95 (ISBN 0-394-84875-6). Random.

Whale War. David Day. LC 87-4833. (Illus.). 224p. 1987. 19.95 (ISBN 0-87156-775-X); pap. 9.95 (ISBN 0-87156-778-4). Sierra.

Whale Watch. Ada Graham & Frank Graham. LC 77-20531. (Audubon Readers Ser.: No. 1). (Illus.). (gr. 5 up). 1978. 7.95 (ISBN 0-440-09505-0); pap. 6.46 (ISBN 0-440-09506-9). Delacorte.

Whale Watchers' Guide. Robert Gardner. LC 83-17425. (Illus.). 170p. (YA) (gr. 7 up). 1984. lib. bdg. 10.79 (ISBN 0-671-45811-6); pap. 5.95 (ISBN 0-671-49807-X). Messner.

Whale-Watcher's Handbook. Erich Hoyt. LC 83-45167. (Illus.). 192p. 1984. pap. 12.95 (ISBN 0-385-19036-0). Doubleday.

Whale Who Wanted to Be Small. Gill McBarnet. (Illus.). 32p. (gr. k-2). 1985. 6.95 (ISBN 0-9615102-0-X). Ruwanga Trad.

Whaleboat: A Study of Design, Construction & Use from 1850-1970. 2nd rev. ed. Willits D. Ansel. (Illus.). vi, 147p. 1983. pap. 12.00 (ISBN 0-913372-40-4). Mystic Seaport.

Whalebone Whales of the Western North Atlantic. Frederick W. True. LC 82-600395. (Illus.). 380p. 1983. Repr. of 1904 ed. text ed. 37.50 (ISBN 0-87474-922-0, TRWW). Smithsonian.

Whaleghost. Howard L. Hipp. LC 87-71717. 141p. (Orig.). 1988. text ed. 8.00 (ISBN 0-916383-35-0). Aegina Pr.

Whalehead, Tales of Corolla N.C. Suzanne Tate. As told by Norris Austin. LC 87-90489. (Illus.). 52p. 1987. pap. 5.95 (ISBN 0-9616344-1-3). Nags Head Art.

Whalemen & Whaleships of Maine. Kenneth R. Martin. LC 74-28773. (Illus.). 72p. 1976. pap. 5.95 (ISBN 0-88448-030-5). Harpswell Pr.

Whalemen's Paintings & Drawings: Selections from the Kendall Whaling Museum Collection. Kenneth Martin. LC 81-50343. (Illus.). 176p. 1982. 30.00. U Delaware Pr.

Whalemen's Paintings & Drawings: Selections from the Kendall Whaling Museum Collection. Kenneth R. Martin. LC 81-50343. (Illus.). 172p. 1983. 29.95 (ISBN 0-87413-191-X). Kendall Whaling.

Whalers. A. B. Whipple. LC 78-31228. (Seafarers Ser.). (Illus.). (gr. 7 up). 1979. lib. bdg. 21.27 (ISBN 0-8094-2671-4, Pub. by Time-Life). Silver.

Whalers & Whaling: The Story of the Whaling Ships up to the Present Day. E. Keble Chatterton. LC 79-178626. (Illus.). 248p. 1975. Repr. of 1925 ed. 40.00x (ISBN 0-8103-4028-3). Gale.

Whales. Lionel Bender. Ed. by Franklin Watts Ltd. (First Sight Ser.). (Illus.). 32p. (gr. k-9). 1988. 10.90 (ISBN 0-531-17078-0, Gloucester Pr). Watts.

Whales. Gilda Berger. LC 86-16500. (Illus.). 48p. (gr. k-3). 1987. pap. 9.95 (ISBN 0-385-23420-1); pap. 9.95 (ISBN 0-385-23421-X). Doubleday.

Whales. Althea Braithwaite. (Save Our Wildlife Bks.). (ps-6). 1988. PLB 7.95; pap. 2.95. Longman Crown.

Whales. Althea Braithwaite & Carolyn Rubin. (Save Our Wildlife Ser.). (Illus.). (gr. k-3). Date not set. pap. 2.95. Longman Trade.

Whales. Susan Harris. (gr. 2-4). PLB 9.40 (ISBN 0-531-00444-9). Watts.

Whales. Tom Hill. 1973. pap. 1.75 (ISBN 0-685-37098-4). Twowindows Pr.

Whales. Michael P. Jones. LC 86-74418. (Sealife Ser.: No. 1). (Illus.). 76p. 1984. signed ed. 25.00 (ISBN 0-89904-000-4); 15.00; pap. text ed. 10.00 (ISBN 0-89904-096-9). Crumb Elbow Pub.

Whales. L. Martin. (Wildlife in Danger Ser.). (Illus.). 24p. (gr. k-5). Date not set. PLB 11.33 (ISBN 0-86592-988-2). Rourke Corp.

Whales. rev. ed. Kate Petty. Ed. by FS-Aladdin Staff. (Small World Ser.). (Illus.). 32p. (gr. 1-3). 1988. 9.90 (ISBN 0-531-17124-8, Gloucester Pr). Watts.

Whales. Noel Simon. (Animal Families Ser.). (Illus.). 47p. (gr. 4 up). 1985. 6.50x (ISBN 0-460-06957-8, BKA 05283, Pub. by J M Dent England). Biblio Dist.

Whales. Wildlife Education, Ltd. (Zoobooks). (Illus.). 20p. (Orig.). 1983. pap. 1.95 (ISBN 0-937934-10-0). Wildlife Educ.

Whales--The Gentle Giants: Calendar 1988. Michael P. Jones. (Illus., Orig.). ltd. ed. 25.00 (ISBN 0-89904-213-9); text ed. 10.00 (ISBN 0-89904-211-2); pap. text ed. 5.00 (ISBN 0-89904-212-0). Crumb Elbow Pub.

Whales Alive: Report of Global Conference on the Non-Consumptive Utilization of Cetacean Resources. Ed. by Robbins Barstow. (Illus., Orig.). 1983. pap. 10.00 (ISBN 0-9618858-0-7). Cetacean Society.

Whales: An Educational Coloring Book. Spizzirri Publishing Co. Staff. Ed. by Linda Spizzirri. (Illus.). 32p. (gr. 1-8). 1982. pap. 1.49 (ISBN 0-86545-039-0). Spizzirri.

Whales & Dolphins. Francene Sabin. LC 84-2709. (Illus.). 32p. (gr. 3-6). 1985. PLB 8.45 (ISBN 0-8167-0286-1); pap. text ed. 1.95 (ISBN 0-8167-0287-X). Troll Assocs.

Whales & Dolphins. Everhard J. Slijper. Tr. by John Drury from Ger. LC 73-90889. (Ann Arbor Science Library). (Illus.). 1976. 9.95x (ISBN 0-472-00122-1). U of Mich Pr.

Whales & Dolphins. Everhard J. Slijper. Tr. by John Drury from Ger. LC 73-90889. (Ann Arbor Science Library). (Illus.). 1975. pap. 7.95 (ISBN 0-472-05022-2, AA). U of Mich Pr.

Whales & Man: Adventures with the Giants of the Deep. Tim Dietz. Ed. by Dougald MacDonald. (Illus.). 192p. 1987. 18.95 (ISBN 0-89909-120-2). Yankee Bks.

Whales & Other Sea Mammals. Elsa Posell. LC 82-4451. (New True Bks.). (gr. k-4). 1982. 12.60 (ISBN 0-516-01663-6); pap. 3.95 (ISBN 0-516-41663-4). Childrens.

Whales & Seals: A Guide to Coastal & Offshore Mammals. Al Kidwell. (Maine Geographic Ser.). (Illus.). 48p. 1983. pap. 2.95 (ISBN 0-89933-051-7). Delorme Map.

Whales & Sharks. Suzanne S. Miller. Ed. by Kate Klimo. (Illus.). 48p. 1982. text ed. 8.95 (ISBN 0-671-45148-0, Little Simon). S&S.

Whales & Sharks & Other Creatures of the Deep. Susanne S. Miller. LC 82-8201. (Illus.). 48p. (gr. k-3). 1982. PLB 9.97g (ISBN 0-671-46006-4); pap. 7.95. Messner.

Whales & Whale Strandings. Marjorie Orr. (Illus.). 39p. (Orig.). 1984. pap. 5.95 (ISBN 0-86868-060-5, Pub. by J McIndoe Ltd New Zealand). Intl Spec Bk.

Whales, Dolphins & Porpoises. Richard Harrison et al. 240p. 1988. 35.00 (ISBN 0-8160-1977-0). Facts on File.

Whales, Dolphins & Porpoises of the Pacific. Peter C. Howorth. LC 84-81847. (Shorelines of America Ser.). (Illus.). 48p. (Orig.). 1985. pap. 4.95 (ISBN 0-916122-98-0). KC Pubns.

Whales, Dolphins, & Porpoises of the Eastern North Pacific & Adjacent Arctic Waters: A Guide to Their Identification. Stephen Leatherwood et al. (Illus.). 256p. 1988. pap. 17.95t (ISBN 0-486-25651-0). Dover.

Whales, Dolphins & Porpoises of the Western North Atlantic: A Guide to Their Identification. Stephen Leatherwood et al. (NOAA Technical Report NMFS Circular: No. 396). 180p. (Orig.). 1976. pap. 7.00 (ISBN 0-318-18871-6, S/N 003-020-00119-0). USGPO.

Whale's Footprints. Rick Boyer. 288p. 1988. 17.95 (ISBN 0-395-42738-X). HM.

Whales: Giants of the Deep. Dorothy H. Patent. LC 84-729. (Illus.). 96p. (gr. 3-7). 1984. reinforced 14.95 (ISBN 0-8234-0530-3). Holiday.

Whales, Ice, & Men: The History of Whaling in the Western Arctic. John R. Bockstoce. LC 85-91266. (Illus.). 400p. 1986. 29.95 (ISBN 0-295-96318-2). U of Wash Pr.

Whales of Capistrano Bay. Doris Walker. (Illus.). 1982. 2.95 (ISBN 0-9606476-2-7). To-the-Point.

Whales of Hawaii: Including All Species of Marine Mammals in Hawaiian & Adjacent Waters. Kenneth C. Balcomb, III & Stanley M. Minasian. (Illus.). 114p. (Orig.). (YA) (gr. 9 up). 1987. pap. 9.95 (ISBN 0-9617803-0-4). Marine Mammal Fund.

Whales of the World. June Behrens. LC 87-8046. (Selected Easy Reading Picture Bks.). (Illus.). 48p. (gr. 1-4). 1987. PLB 13.27 (ISBN 0-516-08877-7); pap. 3.95 (ISBN 0-516-48877-5). Childrens.

Whales of the World. Spencer W. Tinker. LC 87-70063. (Illus.). 320p. 1988. pap. 19.95 (ISBN 0-935848-47-9). Bess Pr.

Whale's Scars. Brian Swann. 1974. signed ed. o.p. 10.00 (ISBN 0-685-56669-2); pap. 2.50 (ISBN 0-912284-64-1); 5.00 (ISBN 0-912284-65-X). New Rivers Pr.

Whale's Tale. Deborah Evans-Smith. LC 85-51791. (Illus.). 25p. (gr. 2-6). 1986. 8.95 (ISBN 0-917507-02-9). Sea Fog Pr.

Whales, the Nomads of the Sea. Helen R. Sattler. LC 86-10397. (Illus.). 128p. (gr. 3 up). 1987. 14.00 (ISBN 0-688-05587-7). Lothrop.

Whales: Their Life in the Sea. Faith McNulty. LC 74-20395. (Illus.). 96p. (gr. 5 up). 1975. PLB 11.89 (ISBN 0-06-024169-1). HarpJ.

Whale's Wake. Harry Morton. (Illus.). 396p. 1982. text ed. 32.50x (ISBN 0-8248-0830-4). UH Pr.

Whalesong. Robert Siegel. LC 81-66610. 144p. 1981. 9.95 (ISBN 0-89107-219-5, Crossway Bks). Good News.

Whalesong. Robert Siegel. 144p. 1985. pap. 2.95 (ISBN 0-425-09175-9). Berkley Pub.

Whalesong. Robert Siegel. pap. 4.95 (ISBN 0-425-06573-1). Berkley Pub.

Whalesong. MacKinnon Simpson & Robert Goodman. 1987. 29.50 (ISBN 0-941831-10-8); incl. cassette or album 39.50 (ISBN 0-941831-06-X). Beyond Words Pub.

WhaleSong: A Pictorial History of Whaling & Hawaii. Simpson MacKinnon. Ed. by Robert Goodman. 24.95. Island Heritage.

Whalewatch! June Behrens. LC 78-7338. (Illus.). (gr. 1-4). 1978. PLB 10.60 (ISBN 0-516-08873-4, Golden Gate); pap. 2.95 (ISBN 0-516-48873-2). Childrens.

Whaling & Old Salem: A Chronicle of the Sea. Frances D. Robotti. (Illus.). 292p. 1983. Repr. 17.95x (ISBN 0-685-41738-7). Fountainhead.

Whaling City: A History of New London. Robert O. Decker. LC 74-30794. (Illus.). 413p. 1976. 15.00 (ISBN 0-87106-053-1). New London County.

Whaling Days in Old Hawaii see Hawaii's Whaling Days.

What Are They Saying about Peace & War? Thomas A. Shannon. (WATSA Ser.). 128p. 1983. pap. 4.95 (ISBN 0-8091-2499-8). Paulist Pr.
What Are They Saying about Salvation? Denis Edwards. 100p. 1986. pap. 4.95 (ISBN 0-8091-2793-8). Paulist Pr.
What Are They Saying about Scripture & Ethics? William C. Spohn. (WATSA Ser.). (Orig.). 1984. pap. 4.95 (ISBN 0-8091-2624-9). Paulist Pr.
What Are They Saying about Sexual Morality? James Hanigan. (WATSA Ser.). 128p. (Orig.). 1982. pap. 4.95 (ISBN 0-8091-2451-3). Paulist Pr.
What Are They Saying about the End of the World? Zachary Hayes. (WATSA Ser.). 80p. (Orig.). 1983. pap. 4.95 (ISBN 0-8091-2550-1). Paulist Pr.
What Are They Saying about the Grace of Christ? Brian O. McDermott. (WATSA Ser.). 1984. pap. 4.95 (ISBN 0-8091-2584-6). Paulist Pr.
What Are They Saying about the Prophets? David P. Reid. LC 80-80869. 112p. (Orig.). 1980. pap. 3.95 (ISBN 0-8091-2304-5). Paulist Pr.
What Are They Saying about the Social Setting of the New Testament? Carolyn Osiek. (WATSA Ser.). (Orig.). 1984. pap. 4.95 (ISBN 0-8091-2625-7). Paulist Pr.
What Are They Saying about Theological Method? J. J. Mueller. LC 84-61031. (WATSA Ser.). 88p. (Orig.). 1985. pap. 4.95 (ISBN 0-8091-2657-5). Paulist Pr.
What Are They Saying about Virtue. John W. Crossin. (WATSA Ser.). pap. 4.95 (ISBN 0-8091-2674-5). Paulist Pr.
What Are They Saying about Wisdom Literature? Dianne Bergant. LC 83-82027. (WATSA Ser.). (Orig.). 1984. pap. 4.95 (ISBN 0-8091-2605-2). Paulist Pr.
What Are They Teaching Our Children? Mel Gabler & Norma Gabler. 192p. 1985. pap. 6.95 (ISBN 0-317-60081-8). Victor Bks.
What Are We Afraid Of? An Assessment of the "Communist Threat" in Central America. John Lamperti. Ed. by NARMIC-AFSC Staff. 100p. (Orig.). 1988. 25.00 (ISBN 0-89608-339-X); pap. 8.00 (ISBN 0-89608-338-1). South End Pr.
What Are We Doing Here? Associated Women's Organization, Mars Hill Bible School. 1972. pap. 4.95 (ISBN 0-89137-404-3). Quality Pubns.
What Are We Doing in Gym Today? New Games & Activities for the Elementary Physical Education Class. Kenneth G. Tillman & Patricia R. Toner. LC 82-24606. 202p. 1983. 19.95 (ISBN 0-13-951822-3, Parker). P-H.
What Are We Going to Do about Andrew? Marjorie W. Sharmat. LC 88-3357. (Illus.). 32p. (gr. k-4). Date not set. pap. 3.95 (ISBN 0-689-71264-2, Aladdin Bks). Macmillan.
What Are We Living for? A Practical Philosophy, 3 vols. Chauncey D. Leake. Incl. Vol. 1. Ethics. 1973 (ISBN 0-9600290-2-8); Vol. 2. Logics. 1974 (ISBN 0-9600290-5-2); Vol. 3. Esthetics. 1976 (ISBN 0-9600290-6-0). LC 72-95448. 12.75 ea.; Set. 30.00 (ISBN 0-685-76504-0). PJD Pubns.
What Are We Up to, Herman? Jim Unger. 1985. pap. 1.95 (ISBN 0-451-13823-6, Sig). NAL.
What Are You Afraid of? An Illustrated Dictionary of Fearful Words Ending in Phobia. Sam Goldstein. (Weirdictionaries Ser.). (Illus.). 72p. (Orig.). pap. 3.95 cancelled (ISBN 0-938338-05-6). Winds World Pr.
What Are You Doing? Ed. by Naomi Glasser. LC 80-7586. 340p. 1982. pap. 8.95 (ISBN 0-06-090947-1, CN 947, PL). Har-Row.
What Are You Doing? Robert D. Hoeft. 28p. (Orig.). 1987. pap. 3.00 (ISBN 0-916155-03-X). Trout Creek.
What Are You Doing in My Universe? Chuck Hillig. 1983. pap. 5.95 (ISBN 0-87877-065-8). Newcastle Pub.
What Are You Doing in My Universe? Chuck Hillig. LC 83-6426. 224p. 1983. lib. bdg. 19.95x (ISBN 0-89370-665-5). Borgo Pr.
What Are You Doing with the Rest of Your Life: Cerebral Palsy. Schumacker. text ed. 16.95 (ISBN 0-938550-30-6). Acad Guild.
What Are You Doing Wrong with Your Automatic Camera. Dennis Curtin & Barbara London. (Your Automatic Camera Ser.). (Illus.). 144p. (Orig.). 1980. pap. 6.95 (ISBN 0-930764-20-X). Curtin & London.
What Are You Figuring Now? A Story about Benjamin Banneker. Jeri Ferris. (Creative Minds Ser.). (Illus.). 56p. (gr. 3-6). 1988. PLB 9.95 (ISBN 0-87614-331-1). Carolrhoda Bks.
What Are You Going to Do about It? Aldous Huxley. LC 77-3406. Repr. of 1936 ed. lib. bdg. 18.00 (ISBN 0-8414-4914-7). Folcroft.
What Are You Meowing about Now? Dorothy T. Haag. 1987. 6.95 (ISBN 0-533-07186-0). Vantage.
What Are You Waiting for? Jill Medvedow & Clive Phillpot. LC 84-9777. (Illus.). 32p. 1984. pap. 6.00 (ISBN 0-941104-11-7). Real Comet.
What Are You Worth? Edward M. Hallowell & William J. Grace, Jr. 1989. 18.95 (ISBN 1-55584-089-2). Weidenfeld.
What Are You Worth? And How to Be Worth More. Thomas W. Moffitt. 1988. pap. 12.95 (ISBN 0-673-38191-9). Scott F.
What Are Your Dreams Telling You? 2nd, rev., & expanded ed. A La Lansun, pseud. (Solar Ser.: Bk. I). 136p. 1986. pap. 8.95 (ISBN 0-935861-00-9). Solarium Analy.
What Astrology Can Do for You. Llewellyn Publications Staff. Ed. by Terry Buske. (Llewellyn Educational Guide Ser.). 32p. (Orig.). 1986. pap. 2.00 (ISBN 0-87542-375-2, L-375). Llewellyn Pubns.
What Asylums Were, Are, & Ought to Be: Being the Substance of Five Lectures Delivered Before the Managers of the Montrose Royal Lunatic Asylum. W. A. Browne. LC 75-16691. (Classics in Psychiatry Ser.). 1976. Repr. 19.00x (ISBN 0-405-07421-2). Ayer Co Pubs.
What Auditors Should Know about Data Processing. Donald L. Dawley. Ed. by Richard N. Farmer. LC 83-17879. (Research for Business Decisions Ser.: No. 63). 250p. 1983. 44.95 (ISBN 0-8357-1483-7). UMI Res Pr.
What Augustine Says. Aurelius Augustine. Ed. by Norman L. Geisler. 204p. (Orig.). 1982. pap. 8.95 (ISBN 0-8010-0185-4). Baker Bk.
What Automation Does to Human Beings. George Soule. Ed. by Leon Stein. LC 77-70534. (Work Ser.). 1977. Repr. of 1956 ed. lib. bdg. 20.00x (ISBN 0-405-10202-X). Ayer Co Pubs.
What Baptists Believe. Herschel H. Hobbs. LC 64-12411. 1963. bds. 4.25 (ISBN 0-8054-8101-X). Broadman.
What Became of Them & Other Stories from Franco-America. Denis Ledoux. 120p. (Orig.). 1988. pap. 9.95 (ISBN 0-9619373-0-0). Soleil Pr.
What Beckoning Ghost. Douglas G. Browne. 265p. 1986. pap. 4.95 (ISBN 0-486-25055-5). Dover.
What Beckoning Ghost? Kenneth Lillington. 128p. (YA) (gr. 7 up). 1983. 10.95 (ISBN 0-571-11959-X). Faber & Faber.
What Becomes of Pollution? Adversary Science & the Controversy on the Self-Purification of Rivers in Britain, 1850-1900. Christopher Hamlin. Ed. by William H. McNeill & Peter Stansky. (Modern European History Ser.). 650p. 1987. lib. bdg. 95.00 (ISBN 0-8240-7812-8). Garland Pub.
What Being Responsible Means to Me. Donna Brook. 1988. 15.00 (ISBN 0-914610-50-3); pap. 7.00. Hanging Loose.
What Belongs? (Turn the Dials Learning Picture Bks.). (Illus.). 12p. (ps-1). 1988. 5.95 (ISBN 0-8431-2662-0). Price Stern.
What Belongs: A Book-in-a-Book. (Learning Curves Bks.). (Illus.). 10p. (ps-1). 1987. pap. 5.95 (ISBN 0-553-18356-7). Bantam.
What Belongs to Caesar? Donald D. Kaufman. LC 70-109939. 128p. 1969. pap. 5.95 (ISBN 0-8361-1621-6). Herald Pr.
What Belongs? Understanding Classification. (Golden Activity Book 'n' Tapes). (Illus.). (ps-3). pap. write for info. incl. cassette (ISBN 0-307-13791-0, Golden Bks). Western Pub.
What Big Teeth You Have! Patricia Lauber. LC 85-47902. (Illus.). 64p. (gr. 2-6). 1986. 11.25i (ISBN 0-690-04506-9, Crowell Jr Bks); PLB 10.89 (ISBN 0-690-04507-7). HarpJ.
What Bird Is This? Henry H. Collins, Jr. (Illus.). 1961. pap. 3.50 (ISBN 0-486-21490-7). Dover.
What Black Librarians Are Saying. E. J. Josey. LC 72-5372. 324p. 1972. 17.50 (ISBN 0-8108-0530-8). Scarecrow.
What Blenders Do Best. Ann Seranne. 256p. 1985. 16.95 (ISBN 0-312-92938-2). Congdon & Weed.
What Bloody Man Is That? Simon Brett. 196p. 1987. 14.95 (ISBN 0-684-18824-4). Scribner.
What Bloody Man Is That? Simon Brett. (Nightingale Ser.). 297p. 1988. pap. 12.95 (ISBN 0-8161-4398-6, Large Print Bks). G K Hall.
What Books & Records Should I Get for My Preschooler? Norma Rogers. (Micromonograph Ser.). 1972. 1.50 (ISBN 0-87207-872-8). Intl Reading.
What Books for Children? Guideposts for Parents. Josette Frank. 363p. 1981. Repr. of 1937 ed. lib. bdg. 25.00 (ISBN 0-89987-266-2). Darby Bks.
What Bounces? Kate Duke. LC 84-73138. (Guinea Pig Board Bks.). (Illus.). 12p. (ps). 1986. 2.95 (ISBN 0-525-44209-X). Dutton.
What Business Can Get from the Government. N. H. Mager & S. K. Mager. LC 81-24210. 657p. 1982. 75.00 (ISBN 0-932648-21-5). Boardroom.
What Can a Free Man Believe. E. Haldeman-Julius. 55p. pap. cancelled (ISBN 0-911826-99-8). Am Atheist.
What Can a Man Do? A Selection of His Most Challenging Writings. Milton S. Mayer. Ed. by W. Eric Gustafson. LC 64-15801. pap. 38.40 (ISBN 0-317-09760-1, 2020118). Bks Demand UMI.
What Can a Mother Do? Finding Significance at Home & Beyond. Judy D. Douglass. 192p. 1988. pap. 6.95 (ISBN 0-89840-201-8). Heres Life.
What Can a Police Officer Do: A Comparative Study: U. S. A. - German Federal Republic - Israel - Italy. (New York University Criminal Law Education & Research Center Monograph: Vol. 7). (Illus.). xiii, 272p. (Orig.). 1974. pap. text ed. 12.50x (ISBN 0-8377-0417-0). Rothman.
What Can a Woman Do; Or, Her Position in the Business & Literary World. Martha L. Rayne. LC 74-3970. (Women in America Ser). (Illus.). 584p. 1974. Repr. of 1893 ed. 40.00x (ISBN 0-405-06118-8). Ayer Co Pubs.
What Can Be Automated? Computer Science & Engineering Research Study. Ed. by Bruce W. Arden. 933p. 1980. 50.00x (ISBN 0-262-01060-7); pap. 20.00x (ISBN 0-262-51026-X). MIT Pr.
What Can Children Learn in Geography? A Review of Research. Marion J. Rice & Russell L. Cobb. 130p. 1979. 9.95 (ISBN 0-89994-235-0). Soc Sci Ed.
What Can I Be? A Guide to Five Hundred Twenty-Five Liberal Arts & Business Careers. Leo Lieberman. LC 75-26001. 1976. 18.50 (ISBN 0-935198-03-2). M M Bruce.
What Can I Bring? Yvonne Baker. (Illus.). 352p. 1988. 17.95 (ISBN 0-8007-1577-2). Revell.
What Can I Do? Tom Watson. LC 73-85896. 1974. pap. 1.25 (ISBN 0-88270-067-7, Pub. by Logos). Bridge Pub.
What Can I Do: My Loved One Has Cancer. Rosa Dotson. 1986. pap. 1.25 (ISBN 0-89137-325-X). Quality Pubns.
What Can I Do Today? A Treasury of Crafts for Children. Joan F. Klimo. LC 73-15110. (Illus.). 64p. (gr. k-3). 1971. Pantheon.
What Can I Do When I Am Sorry? Joan Mitchell. (gr. 2). 1986. tchr's. ed. 4.50 (ISBN 0-89837-112-0); wkbk. 5.25 (ISBN 0-89837-111-2). Pflaum Pr.
What Can I Do with a Major In...? How to Choose & Use Your College Major. Lawrence R. Malnig & Anita Malnig. LC 83-73269. 250p. 1984. 24.95x (ISBN 0-9612678-1-X); pap. 17.95x (ISBN 0-9612678-0-1). Abbott Pr.
What Can I Do with My Microwave? Ruth Spear. (Orig.). 1988. pap. 3.95 (ISBN 0-440-50085-0, Dell Trade Pbks). Dell.
What Can I Dream About? Arnold Shapiro. (Illus.). 32p. (ps-1). 1987. 8.95 (ISBN 0-8431-4701-6). Price Stern.
What Can I Learn? Mary L. George. (Illus.). 128p. (Orig.). 1983. pap. 5.25 (ISBN 0-9610930-0-5). Sisters.
What Can I Say? Roger F. Miller. Ed. by Herbert Lambert. LC 86-26868. 96p. (Orig.). 1987. pap. 4.95 (ISBN 0-8272-4220-4). CBP.
What Can I Say to a Friend with Cancer. Randy Becton. 160p. 1988. pap. 6.95 (ISBN 0-89225-320-7). Gospel Advocate.
What Can I Say to You, God? Elspeth Murphy. (David & I Talk to God Ser.). (Illus.). (gr. k-2). 1980. pap. 2.95 (ISBN 0-89191-276-2). Cook.
What Can I Write About? Seven Thousand Topics for High School Students. David Powell. LC 81-9675. (Orig.). 1981. pap. 8.00 (ISBN 0-8141-5656-8). NCTE.
What Can the Matter Be? Phoebe Hesketh. 136p. 1985. 34.00x (ISBN 0-901976-95-4, Pub. by United Writers Pubns England). State Mutual Bk.
What Can We Believe. Vergilius Ferm. 1952. 5.95 (ISBN 0-8022-0497-X). Philos Lib.
What Can We Do? Food & Hunger: How You Can Make a Difference. William Valentine. (Illus.). 60p. (Orig.). 1980. pap. 2.95 (ISBN 0-935028-06-4). Inst Food & Develop.
What Can We Do Today? Janet Hopkins. 1981. 3.00 (ISBN 0-937684-12-0). Tradd St Pr.
What Can We Play Today? Jane B. Moncure. (Magic Castle Readers Ser.). (Illus.). 32p. (ps-2). 1987. 11.93 (ISBN 0-516-05742-1). Childrens.
What Can We Play Today? Jane B. Moncure. LC 87-32565. (Magic Castle Readers Ser.). (Illus.). 32p. (ps-2). 1987. PLB 7.75 (ISBN 0-89565-412-1). Childs World.
What Can We Share? A Lutheran-Episcopal Resource & Study Guide. Ed. by William Norgren et al. (Lutheran-Episcopal Dialogue Ser.). 88p. (Orig.). 1985. pap. 2.00 (ISBN 0-88028-047-6). Forward Movement.
What Can You..., 4 bks. Angela Littler & Maureen Galvani. (Illus.). (ps-1). Date not set. 3.95 ea. What Can You See? What Can You Hear? What Can You Feel? What Can You Do? Messner.
What Can You Believe in the Bible. Robert Ingersoll. 106p. 1988. 4.00 (ISBN 0-911826-70-X). Am Atheist.
What Can You Do? Bill Gillham. LC 85-28137. (Look & Talk Bks.). (Illus.). 24p. (ps-1). 1986. 5.95 (ISBN 0-399-21324-4, Putnam). Putnam Pub Group.
What Can You Do with a Shoe? Beatrice S. de Regniers. LC 55-6429. (Illus.). 32p. (ps-k). 1955. 9.70i (ISBN 0-06-024849-1); PLB 10.89 (ISBN 0-06-024850-5). HarpJ.
What Can't Be Cured Must Be Endured. Sylvia Firestone. 1988. 12.95 (ISBN 0-533-07602-1). Vantage.
What Catholics Believe. Lawrence G. Lovasik. (Illus.). 1977. pap. 3.50 (ISBN 0-89555-027-X). TAN Bks Pubs.
What Catholics Believe: A Primer of the Catholic Faith. Josef Pieper & Heinrich Raskop. Tr. by Jan Van Heurck. LC 82-1411. 116p. 1983. 8.50 (ISBN 0-8199-0796-0). Franciscan Herald.
What Cheer? Merry Stories for All Occasions. Ralph Frost. 1977. Repr. of 1929 ed. lib. bdg. 25.00 (ISBN 0-8495-1603-X). Arden Lib.
What Child Is This? Martha Marshall. (gr. 1-3). 1982. text ed. 5.95 (Sonflower Bks). SP Pubns.
What Child Is This? Martha Marshall. LC 82-7239. (Illus.). (gr. 1-2). 1982. lib. bdg. 6.95 (ISBN 0-89693-204-4). Dandelion Hse.
What Child Is This? Readings & Prayers for Advent-Christmas. Samuel H. Miller. LC 82-5084. (Illus.). 64p. (Orig.). 1982. pap. 0.95 (ISBN 0-8006-1638-3, 1-1638). Fortress.
What Children Need to Know When Parents Get Divorced. William L. Coleman. 91p. (gr. k-5). 1983. pap. 3.95 (ISBN 0-87123-612-5, 210612). Bethany Hse.
What Children Read in School. Ed. by Sara G. Zimet. LC 75-178589. 154p. 1972. 41.50 (ISBN 0-8089-0743-3, 794965). Grune.
What Christ Thinks of the Church. John R. Stott. 1972. pap. 5.95 (ISBN 0-8028-1451-4). Eerdmans.
What Christians Believe. John Balchin. (Manuals Ser.). 128p. (Orig.). Date not set. pap. 6.95 (ISBN 0-85648-566-7). Lion USA.
What Christians Believe. Creemos Esto. 128p. 1981. pap. 3.25 (ISBN 0-8254-1216-1). Kregel.
What Christians Believe. Richard Harries. 176p. 1982. pap. 4.95 (ISBN 0-86683-677-2, HarpR). Har-Row.
What Christians Believe. Moody Press Editors. 1951. pap. 3.95 (ISBN 0-8024-9378-5). Moody.
What Christians Believe. Hans Schwarz. LC 86-45923. 112p. 1987. pap. 4.95 (ISBN 0-8006-1959-5). Fortress.
What Christians Believe: A Biblical & Historical Summary. Alan F. Johnson & Robert E. Webber. 448p. 1988. pap. write for info. (ISBN 0-310-36721-2). Zondervan.
What Christians Believe about the Bible. Donald K. McKim. LC 85-18846. 183p. 1985. pap. 8.95 (ISBN 0-8407-5968-1). Nelson.
What Christians Believe in Simple English. Wes Eby. 52p. (Orig.). Date not set. pap. 2.00 (ISBN 0-8341-1245-0). Beacon Hill.
What Christians Believe Workbook. John Balchin. (Manuals Ser.). 32p. (Orig.). Date not set. pap. 1.95 (ISBN 0-85648-854-2). Lion USA.
What Citizens Know about Their Schools. William H. Todd. LC 70-177700. (Columbia University. Teachers College. Contributions to Education: No. 279). Repr. of 1927 ed. 22.50 (ISBN 0-404-55279-X). AMS Pr.
What Civilization Owes to Italy. J. J. Walsh. 250.00 (ISBN 0-87968-361-9). Gordon Pr.
What Clients Really Think About Consultants: 160 Turn-Ons & 169 Turn-Offs in 4 Phases of the Engagement. Ed. by James H. Kennedy. 1985. 3-ringbound 49.00 (ISBN 0-317-46177-X). Consultants News.
What Coleridge Thought. Owen Barfield. 1983. pap. 10.95 (ISBN 0-8195-6084-7). Wesleyan U Pr.
What College Students Know About Their World. Thomas S. Barrows et al. LC 80-69768. 56p. (Orig.). 1981. pap. 8.95x (ISBN 0-915390-30-2, Pub. by Change Mag). Transaction Bks.
What Color? Fiona Pragoff. LC 87-645. (Illus.). 20p. (gr. k-3). 1987. pap. 5.95 (ISBN 0-385-24173-9). Doubleday.
What Color Are You? Darwin Walton. (Ebony Jr. Bks.). (Illus.). 64p. (gr. 5 up). 1973. 10.95 (ISBN 0-87485-045-2). Johnson Chi.
What Color Are You? The Way to Health Through Color. Annie Wilson & Lilla Bek. (Illus.). 160p. (Orig.). 1987. pap. 6.99 (ISBN 0-85030-616-7, Pub. by Aquarian Pr). Sterling.
What Color Are Your Eyes? Hale Chatfield. (WNJ Ser.: No. 9). 1977. signed ed. 20.00 (ISBN 1-55780-089-8); pap. 6.00 (ISBN 1-55780-058-8). Juniper Pr WI.
What Color Is It. Elisabeth Ivanovsky. (Picture-Word Boards Bks.). (Illus.). (ps). 1985. bds. 3.98 (ISBN 0-517-47342-9). Outlet Bk Co.
What Color Is It? Deborah Manley. LC 78-26525. (Ready, Set, Look Ser.). (Illus.). 32p. (gr. k-3). 1979. PLB 13.31 (ISBN 0-8172-1300-7). Raintree Pubs.
What Color Is Your Aura? Barbara Bowers. 1989. 7.95. PB.
What Color Is Your Balloon? Wesley Runk. (Orig.). 1987. pap. 5.75 (ISBN 0-89536-883-8, 7869). CSS of Ohio.
What Color Is Your God? Black Consciousness & the Christian Faith. Christopher Salley & Ronald Behm. LC 81-6758. 132p. (Orig.). 1981. pap. 4.50 (ISBN 0-87784-791-6). Inter-Varsity.
What Color Is Your God? Black Consciousness & the Christian Faith. Columbus Salley & Ronald Behm. 1988. pap. 5.95 (ISBN 0-8065-1111-7, Citadel Pr). Lyle Stuart.
What Color Is Your Parachute? 1987. updated ed. Richard N. Bolles. LC 84-649334. (Illus.). 416p. 1987. 16.95; pap. 8.95 (ISBN 0-89815-176-7). Ten Speed Pr.
What Color Is Your Parachute?, 1989: 1988. rev. ed. Richard N. Bolles. LC 84-649334. 352p. 1988. 16.95 (ISBN 0-89815-229-1); pap. 9.95 (ISBN 0-89815-228-3). Ten Speed Pr.
What Color Is Your Swimming Pool? The Guide to Trouble-Free Pool Maintenance. John O'Keefe. Ed. by Sarah M. Clarkson. LC 85-61479. 150p. (Orig.). 1987. pap. 9.95 (ISBN 0-88266-408-5, Storey Pub). Storey Comm Inc.
What Color Is Your Toothbrush. Kate Kelly et al. 1985. pap. 5.95 (ISBN 0-671-54337-7, Wallaby). PB.
What Color Is Your World. Bob Gill. (Illus.). (gr. k-3). 1963. 10.95 (ISBN 0-8392-3042-7). Astor-Honor.

What Does Christmas Sound Like? Ruth S. Odor. (Happy Day Bks.). (Illus.). 32p. (gr. k-2). 1987. 1.59 (ISBN 0-87403-282-2, 3782). Standard Pub.

What Does God Do? Hans Wilhelm. LC 87-42782. (Illus.). 32p. (YA) (ps-7). 1987. 9.95 (ISBN 0-8344-0150-9, 150). Worthy TX.

What Does God Do All Day? Joseph R. Swain. 1977. 7.00 (ISBN 0-682-48919-0, Testament). Exposition-Phoenix.

What Does God Want Me to Do with My Life? How to Decide about School, Job, Friends, Sex, Marriage. Steve Swanson. LC 79-50086. 104p. 1979. pap. 4.95 (ISBN 0-8066-1722-5, 10-7046). Augsburg.

What Does He Mean by "A Little While?". Ralph J. Wallace. (Orig.). 1981. pap. 6.25 (ISBN 0-937172-30-8). JLJ Pubs.

What Does It All Mean? Sarah A. Fifield. Ed. by Susan Carlton. (Illus.). 103p. (Orig.). 1983. pap. 2.50 (ISBN 0-686-45384-0). SarSan Pub.

What Does It All Mean? A Very Short Introduction to Philosophy. Thomas Nagel. 120p. 1987. 14.95 (ISBN 0-19-505292-7). Oxford U Pr.

What Does It All Mean? A Very Short Introduction to Philosophy. Thomas Nagel. 128p. 1987. pap. 5.95 (ISBN 0-19-505216-1). Oxford U Pr.

What Does It Feel Like to Have Diabetes: A Diary of Events in the Life of a Diabetic. Denise J. Bradley. 190p. 1987. 26.75x (ISBN 0-398-05367-7). C C Thomas.

What Does It Mean? Bill Loader. 64p. (Orig.). 1985. pap. 7.95 (ISBN 0-85819-472-4, Pub. by JBCE). ANZ Religious Pubns.

What Does It Mean to Believe in Jesus. Lois B. Sovenson. (Cornerstone Ser.). 32p. 1981. pap. 2.00 (ISBN 0-930756-64-9, 533004). Aglow Pubns.

What Does It Mean to Grow Old: Reflections from the Humanities. Ed. by Thomas R. Cole & Sally A. Gadow. LC 85-27406. (Illus.). xiv, 302p. 1986. text ed. 39.50 (ISBN 0-8223-0545-3); pap. 14.95 (ISBN 0-8223-0817-7). Duke.

What Does It Profit...? Christian Dialogue on the U. S. Economy. Shantilal P. Bhagat & T. Wayne Rieman. LC 83-3687. 144p. (Orig.). 1983. pap. 6.95 (ISBN 0-87178-927-2). Brethren.

What Does Revelation Mean for the Modern Jew? Michael Oppenheim. LC 85-18929. (Symposium Ser.: Vol. 17). 152p. 1985. lib. bdg. 39.95x (ISBN 0-88946-708-0). E Mellen.

What Does Santa Bring? Illus. by Cathy Beylon. (Cuddle Doll Books). (Illus.). 12p. (gr. 1-4). 1985. 3.95 (ISBN 0-394-87510-9, BYR). Random.

What Does Sunny Bunny Love? McQueen. (Wee Pudgy Board Bks.). (gr. 2 up). 1988. 2.50 (ISBN 0-448-09252-2, G&D). Putnam Pub Group.

What Does the Bible Mean? Scripture Interpretations Through the Centuries. Carl Savage. LC 84-72433. 96p. (Orig.). 1985. DR018B. pap. 4.75 (ISBN 0-88177-018-3). Discipleship Res.

What Does the Bible Say About...? Howard Sugden & Lucile Sugden. LC 87-33869. 221p. (Orig.). 1987. pap. text ed. 8.95 (ISBN 0-8254-3759-8). Kregel.

What Does the Charpy Test Really Tell Us? Proceedings of a Symposium Held at the Annual Meeting of the American Institute of Mining, Metallurgical & Petroleum Engineers, 1978. Ed. by A. R. Rosenfield et al. LC 78-10109. pap. 60.00 (ISBN 0-317-26236-X, 2052145). Bks Demand UMI.

What Does the Lord Require? The Old Testament Call to Social Witness. Bruce C. Birch. LC 85-610. 120p. 1985. pap. 8.95 (ISBN 0-664-24630-3). Westminster John Knox.

What Does Woman Want. rev. ed. Timothy Leary. LC 87-83574. (Future History Ser.). (Illus.). 275p. 1987. 17.95 (ISBN 0-941404-76-5); pap. 9.95 (ISBN 0-941404-62-5). Falcon Pr Az.

What Does Word Bird See? Jane B. Moncure. LC 81-21594. (Word House Words for Early Birds Ser.). (Illus.). (ps-2). 1982. lib. bdg. 7.95 (ISBN 0-89565-220-X). Childs World.

What Does Word Bird See? Jane B. Moncure. LC 81-21594. (Word Birds for Early Birds Ser.). (ps-2). 1982. 11.93 (ISBN 0-516-06557-2). Childrens.

What Does Your Name Mean? Roberta F. Hitt. 1984. 9.95 (ISBN 0-87012-467-6). McClain.

What Does Your Soul Look Like. Gail Northe. LC 74-86554. 136p. 1970. 7.95 (ISBN 0-8022-2304-4). Philos Lib.

What Doth the Lord Require of Thee? Mildred B. Young. 1966. pap. 2.50x (ISBN 0-87574-145-2, 145). Pendle Hill.

What Dread Hand? Sarah Kemp. (Lythway). 280p. 1988. lib. bdg. 19.50 (ISBN 0-7451-0665-X, Pub. by Chivers Pr UK). G K HAll.

What Dread Hand. Sarah Kemp. 224p. Date not set. pap. 3.50 (ISBN 0-373-26005-9, Pub. by Worldwide). Harlequin Bks.

What Drives Third World City Growth. Allen C. Kelley & Jeffrey G. Williamson. LC 84-2070. 272p. 1984. text ed. 44.50x (ISBN 0-691-04240-3); pap. 16.50x (ISBN 0-691-10164-7). Princeton U Pr.

What Educators Should Know about Copyright. Virginia M. Helm. LC 85-63688. (Fastback Ser.: No. 233). 50p. (Orig.). 1986. pap. 0.75 (ISBN 0-87367-233-X). Phi Delta Kappa.

What Eight Million Women Want. R. L. Dorr. LC 10-28964. Repr. of 1910 ed. 37.00 (ISBN 0-527-24600-X). Kraus Repr.

What Else Can You Do with Your TRS-80 Color Computer. Peter Lear et al. (Illus.). 64p. (gr. 4-9). 1985. PLB 10.69 (ISBN 0-88625-121-4). C Hayes Pr.

What Else You Can Do with Your Micro Computer. Peter Lear. (Illus.). 63p. (gr. 4-9). 1984. PLB 10.69 (ISBN 0-88625-078-1). C Hayes Pr.

What Eric Knew. James Howe. 144p. 1986. pap. 2.50 (ISBN 0-380-70171-5, Flare). Avon.

What Eric Knew: A Sebastian Barth Mystery. James Howe. 156p. (gr. 4-6). 1985. 10.95 (ISBN 0-689-31159-1, Atheneum Childrens Bks). Macmillan.

What Europe Means to Me. George A. Effinger. 188p. 1989. pap. 3.50 (ISBN 1-55785-077-1). Bart Books.

What Ever Happened to Commitment? Edward R. Dayton. 224p. 1983. pap. 6.95 (ISBN 0-310-23161-2, 10748P). Zondervan.

What Ever Happened to Sunday Best. Joyce Irwin. (Illus.). 1986. 32.00x (ISBN 0-86332-028-7, Pub. by Book Guild Ltd). State Mutual Bk.

What Every Adventist Should Know about 1988. Arnold V. Wallenkampf. Ed. by Raymond H. Woolsey. 96p. 1988. pap. 5.95 (ISBN 0-8280-0442-0). Review & Herald.

What Every American Should Know about Islam & the Muslims. Muhammad A. Nu'man. 74p. (Orig.). 1985. pap. 5.00 (ISBN 0-933821-04-2). New Mind Prod.

What Every Baby Knows. T. Berry Brazelton. (Illus.). 224p. 1987. 14.95 (ISBN 0-201-09262-X). Addison-Wesley.

What Every Baby Knows. T. Berry Brazelton. (Illus.). 288p. 1988. pap. 8.95 (ISBN 0-345-34455-3). Ballantine.

What Every Banker Should Know about Broker-Dealers. 1988. 67.00 (ISBN 0-9603592-6-5). MTA Financial Servs.

What Every Businesswoman Needs to Know to Get Ahead. Peggy Van Hulsteyn. 224p. 1985. pap. 8.95 (ISBN 0-396-08422-2). Dodd.

What Every Child Must Know about Grownups. Gail Elbek. Ed. by Jo Jaworski. LC 86-40333. (Illus.). 65p. (gr. k-4). 1987. 5.95 (ISBN 1-55523-015-6). Winston-Derek.

What Every Child Would Like His Parents to Know to Help Him with the Emotional Problems of Everyday Life. Lee Salk. 224p. 1984. pap. 8.95 (ISBN 0-671-49219-5, Fireside). S&S.

What Every Christian Should Know about God: A Study Manual. Rick Yohn. LC 76-20396. 80p. 1976. 3.95 (ISBN 0-89081-054-0). Harvest Hse.

What Every Christian Should Know about the Supernatural. McCandlish Phillips. 228p. 1988. pap. 7.95 (ISBN 0-317-60084-2). Victor Bks.

What Every Christian Should Know about Growing. LeRoy Eims. LC 75-44842. 168p. 1976. pap. 6.50 (ISBN 0-88207-727-9). Victor Bks.

What Every Church Member Should Know about Clergy. Robert G. Kemper. 180p. 1985. pap. 7.95 (ISBN 0-8298-0728-4). Pilgrim NY.

What Every Cook Should Know. Jessie Lindsay & Helen Tress. 1974. lib. bdg. 69.95 (ISBN 0-685-51386-6). Revisionist Pr.

What Every Employer Should Be Doing About Sexual Harassment. Susan M. Omilian. 1986. pap. 24.95 (ISBN 1-55645-443-0). Busn Legal Reports.

What Every Engineer Should Know about Artificial Intelligence. William A. Taylor. 350p. 1988. text ed. 25.00x (ISBN 0-262-20069-4). MIT Pr.

What Every Engineer Should Know about Computer Modeling & Simulation. Ingels. (What Every Engineer Should Know Ser.). 256p. 1985. 29.75 (ISBN 0-8247-7444-2). Dekker.

What Every Engineer Should Know about Data Communications. Clifton. (What Every Engineer Should Know Ser.). 216p. 1986. 29.75 (ISBN 0-8247-7566-X). Dekker.

What Every Engineer Should Know about Economic Decision Analysis. Dean S. Shupe. (What Every Engineer Should Know Ser.: Vol. 4). (Illus.). 152p. 1980. 29.75 (ISBN 0-8247-1019-3). Dekker.

What Every Engineer Should Know about Finite Analysis. Brauer. (What Every Engineer Should Know about Ser.). 232p. 1988. 39.75 (ISBN 0-8247-7832-4). Dekker.

What Every Engineer Should Know about Human Resources Management. Martin & Shell. (What Every Engineer Should Know Ser.: Vol. 5). 264p. 1980. 29.75 (ISBN 0-8247-1130-0). Dekker.

What Every Engineer Should Know about Manufacturing. Malstrom. (What Every Engineer Should Know Ser.: Vol. 6). 208p. 1981. 29.75 (ISBN 0-8247-1511-X). Dekker.

What Every Engineer Should Know about Microcomputers: Hardware-Software Design: a Step by Step Example. William S. Bennet & Carl F. Evert, Jr. (What Every Engineer Should Know Ser.: Vol. 3). (Illus.). 192p. 1980. 29.75 (ISBN 0-8247-6909-0). Dekker.

What Every Engineer Should Know about Micrcomputer Program Design. Keith R. Wehmeyer. (What Every Engineer Should Know Ser.: Vol. 14). (Illus.). 184p. 1984. 29.75 (ISBN 0-8247-7275-X). Dekker.

What Every Engineer Should Know about Microcomputer System Design & Debugging. Bill Wray & Bill Crawford. (What Every Engineer Should Know Ser.: Vol. 12). (Illus.). 200p. 1984. 29.75 (ISBN 0-8247-7160-5). Dekker.

What Every Engineer Should Know about Product Liability. James F. Thorpe & Middendorf. (What Every Engineer Should Know Ser.: Vol. 2). 120p. 1979. 29.75 (ISBN 0-8247-6876-0). Dekker.

What Every Engineer Should Know about Project Management. Ruskin. Ed. by Estes. (What Every Engineer Should Ser.). 184p. 1982. 29.75 (ISBN 0-8247-1718-X). Dekker.

What Every Engineer Should Know about Corrosion. Schweitzer. (What Every Engineer Should Know Ser.). 160p. 1987. 29.75 (ISBN 0-8247-7755-7). Dekker.

What Every Engineer Should Know about Inventing. Middendorf. (What Every Engineer Should Know Ser.: Vol. 7). 192p. 1981. 29.75 (ISBN 0-8247-7497-3). Dekker.

What Every Engineer Should Know about Lasers. Winburn. (What Every Engineer Should Know Ser.). 272p. 1987. 32.50 (ISBN 0-8247-7748-4). Dekker.

What Every Engineer Should Know about Patents. Konold et al. (What Every Engineer Should Know Ser.: Vol. 1). 1979. 29.75 (ISBN 0-8247-6805-1). Dekker.

What Every Engineer Should Know about Robots. Maurice Zeldman. (What Every Engineer Should Know Ser.: Vol. II). (Illus.). 208p. 1984. 29.75 (ISBN 0-8247-7123-0). Dekker.

What Every Engineer Should Know about Threaded Fasteners. Blake. (What Every Engineer Should Know Ser.). 216p. 1986. 29.75 (ISBN 0-8247-7554-6). Dekker.

What Every Engineer Should Know about Technology Transfer & Innovation. Mogavero & Shane. (What Every Engineer Should Know Ser.: Vol. 8). 168p. 1982. 29.75 (ISBN 0-8247-1863-1). Dekker.

What Every Executive Better Know about the Law. Michael G. Trachtman. 256p. 1987. 17.95 (ISBN 0-671-60046-X). S&S.

What Every Executive Should Know about Chapter 11. Benjamin Weintraub. Ed. by James J. Andover. LC 85-18949. 254p. 1985. pap. 19.95 (ISBN 0-934914-64-8). NACM.

What Every Family Needs or Whatever Happened to Mom, Dad, & the Kids. Carl Brecheen & Paul Faulkner. LC 78-68726. (Journey Bks.). 190p. 1979. pap. 3.95 (ISBN 0-8344-0104-5, 104). Worthy TX.

What Every Hospital Employee Should Know about DRGs: Diagnosis Related Groups. Karen Sandrick. (Orig.). 1983. pap. 2.00 (ISBN 0-916499-04-9). Care Comm Inc.

What Every Husband & Wife Should Know Before It's Too Late. Alvin B. Baranov & Esther Sirkin. 165p. pap. 3.00 (ISBN 0-686-36142-3). Legal Pubns CA.

What Every Husband Should Know. Jack R. Taylor. LC 81-65389. 1981. 9.95 (ISBN 0-8054-5642-2). Broadman.

What Every Husband Should Know About Having a Baby: The Psychoprophylactic Way. Jeannette L. Sasmor. LC 72-75633. 232p. 1972. pap. 9.95 (ISBN 0-88229-496-2). Nelson-Hall.

What Every Investor Should Know: A Handbook from the United States Securities & Exchange Commission. (Illus.). 36p. 1986. pap. 1.25 (ISBN 0-318-21914-X, S/N 046-000-00137-1). USGPO.

What Every Jehovah's Witness Should Know. Arthur M. Bowser. 1975. micro book 1.95 (ISBN 0-916406-35-0). Accent Bks.

What Every Kid Should Know. Jonah Kalb & David Viscott. LC 75-45123. (Illus.). 128p. (gr. 5-9). 1976. 12.95 (ISBN 0-395-24386-6). HM.

What Every Lawyer Needs to Know about Bankruptcy. Pennsylvania Bar Institute. 1985. 50.00 (ISBN 0-318-19079-6, 325). PA Bar Inst.

What Every Man Should Know about His Prostate. rev. ed. Monroe Greenberger & Mary-Ellen Siegel. 1988. 18.95 (ISBN 0-8027-1023-9). Walker & Co.

What Every Man Should Know about His Prostate. Monroe E. Greenberger & Mary-Ellen Siegel. (Illus.). 1983. 13.95 (ISBN 0-8027-0725-4). Walker & Co.

What Every Man Should Know about the "New Woman" A Survival Guide. S. Carter. 208p. 1984. pap. text ed. 7.95 (ISBN 0-07-010163-9). McGraw.

What Every Manager Needs to Know about Manufacturing. Ed. by Richard G. Brandenburg. 192p. 1987. pap. 9.95 (ISBN 0-8144-7686-4). AMACOM.

What Every Manager Needs to Know about Quality Circles & Participative Management. John T. Allen. 32p. 1985. pap. 2.50 (ISBN 0-937670-34-0). Quality Circle.

What Every Manager Needs to Know about Finance. Ed. by Hurbert D. Vos & William K. Fallon. LC 86-47626. 208p. 1986. 10.95 (ISBN 0-8144-7667-8). AMACOM.

What Every Manager Needs to Know about Marketing. Ed. by David J. Freiman & William K. Fallon. LC 86-47625. 272p. 1986. 10.95 (ISBN 0-8144-7666-X). AMACOM.

What Every Mormon Should Know. Edmond C. Gruss. (Orig.). 1975. micro book 1.95 (ISBN 0-916406-34-2). Accent Bks.

What Every Nurse Should Know about Computers. Walker. LC 64-4420. (Illus.). 150p. 1984. pap. 12.50 (ISBN 0-397-54502-9, Lippincott Nursing). Lippincott.

What Every Pastor Needs to Know about Music, Youth, & Education. Garth Bolinder et al. (Leadership Library). 192p. 1986. 9.95 (ISBN 0-917463-09-9). Chr Today.

What Every Pastor's Wife Should Know. Ruthe White. 176p. (Orig.). 1986. pap. 5.95 (ISBN 0-8423-7932-0). Tyndale.

What Every Person Should Know About God: Bible Study for New Christians. John A. Ishee. 36p. 1982. pap. 3.50 (ISBN 0-939298-05-8). J M Prods.

What Every Personnel Assistant Should Know About EEO Law. S. E. Parnes. 1984. pap. 21.95 (ISBN 1-55645-418-X). Busn Legal Reports.

What Every Personnel Assistant Should Know About Interviewing. Stephen D. Bruce. 1985. pap. text ed. 21.95 (ISBN 1-55645-544-5). Busn Legal Reports.

What Every Personnel Assistant Should Know About Recruiting & Employment. Stephen D. Bruce. 1985. pap. 21.95 (ISBN 1-55645-545-3). Busn Legal Reports.

What Every Piano Pupil Should Know. Clarence G. Hamilton. LC 74-27349. Repr. of 1928 ed. 11.50 (ISBN 0-404-12951-X). AMS Pr.

What Every Pregnant Woman Should Know: The Truth about Diets & Drugs in Pregnancy. Gail S. Brewer & Tom Brewer. 256p. 1985. pap. 6.95 (ISBN 0-14-007974-2). Penguin.

What Every Pregnant Woman Should Know: The Truth About Diet & Drugs in Pregnancy. Gail S. Brewer & Tom Brewer. 1977. 9.95 (ISBN 0-394-41117-X). Random.

What Every Supervisor Should Know. 5th ed. Lester R. Bittel. 672p. 1985. text ed. 37.65 (ISBN 0-07-005574-2); Skills development Portfolio. 16.45 (ISBN 0-07-005575-0). McGraw.

What Every Supervisor Should Know: The Basics of Supervisory Management. 5th ed. Lester R. Bittel. 1985. text ed. 38.95 (ISBN 0-07-005577-7). McGraw.

What Every Teacher Should Know about Student Rights. Eve Cary. LC 75-19038. pap. 20.00 (ISBN 0-317-29208-0, 2022231). Bks Demand UMI.

What Every Trucking Executive Needs to Know about Tax Reform. American Trucking Associations, Inc. Staff & Arthur Andersen & Co. 40p. 1986. pap. text ed. 8.00 (ISBN 0-88711-074-6). Am Trucking Assns.

What Every Union Free Supervisor Should Know About Unions. Gordon E. Jackson & Ted M. Yeiser, Jr. 1978. pap. text ed. 3.95 (ISBN 0-9607826-3-X). Management Pr.

What Every Veteran Should Know: 1987. 1987. 6.00 (ISBN 0-346-32464-5). Veterans Info.

What Every Well-Informed Person Should Know about Drug Addiction. David P. Ausubel. LC 79-16961. 1980. 18.95x (ISBN 0-88229-566-7); pap. 9.95 (ISBN 0-88229-721-X). Nelson-Hall.

What Every Woman Knows & Other Plays see Works of J. M. Barrie.

What Every Woman Needs to Know: Facts & Fears about Pregnancy, Childbirth, & Womanhood. Ed. by Penny Junor. (Illus.). 203p. 1989. pap. 13.95 (ISBN 0-7126-1623-3, Pub. by Century Hutchinson). David & Charles.

What Every Woman Ought to Know about Love & Marriage. Joyce Brothers. 335p. 1984. 15.45 (ISBN 0-671-44159-0). S&S.

What Every Woman Ought to Know about Love & Marriage. Joyce Brothers. 1985. pap. 3.95 (ISBN 0-345-32113-8). Ballantine.

What Every Woman Should Know about Child Support, Getting It! Mark A. Simpkins. LC 82-22597. 1985. pap. 10.95 (ISBN 0-87949-226-0). Ashley Bks.

What Every Woman Should Know about Men. Joyce Brothers. 288p. 1985. pap. 3.95 (ISBN 0-345-35372-2). Ballantine.

What Every Writer Should Know about Publishing His Own Book. 21st ed. Edward Uhlan et al. 1976. pap. 3.00 (ISBN 0-682-48674-4, Banner). Exposition-Phoenix.

What Every Young Christian Should Know. William S. Deal. 1982. 1.95. Crusade Pubs.

What Every Young Girl Should Know Before She Marries a Naval Architect. Harry Benford. 48p. (Orig.). 1985. pap. text ed. 6.00 (ISBN 0-931781-01-9). Jennings Pr.

What Every Young Wizard Should Know. Cal Roy. (Illus.). (gr. 2 up). 1963. 8.95 (ISBN 0-8392-3043-5). Astor-Honor.

What Everyone Should Know about Homosexuality. Tim LaHaye. 1980. pap. 3.50 (ISBN 0-8423-7933-9). Tyndale.

What Everyone Should Know about Islam & Muslims. S. Haneef. pap. 12.50 (ISBN 0-686-63919-7). Kazi Pubns.

What Everyone Should Know about the U. S. S. R. An Eyewitness Report of a Three-Year Visit. Joseph North. 1976. pap. 0.50 (ISBN 0-87898-121-7). New Outlook.

What Faith Is. 2nd ed. Kenneth E. Hagin. 1966. pap. 1.00 (ISBN 0-89276-002-8). Hagin Ministries.

What Faith Really Means. Henry G. Graham. LC 82-74243. 94p. 1982. pap. 2.50 (ISBN 0-89555-204-3). TAN Bks Pubs.

What Farrar Saw: A Novel & Short Stories. James Hanley. 296p. 1984. 14.95 (ISBN 0-8180-0641-2). Horizon.

What I Did for Roman. Pam Conrad. LC 86-45497. 192p. (YA) (gr. 7 up). 1987. 12.95i (ISBN 0-06-021331-0); PLB 12.89 (ISBN 0-06-021332-9). HarpJ.
What I Did Last Summer. Jack Prelutsky. LC 83-11561. (Greenwillow Read-Alone Bks.). (Illus.). 48p. (gr. 1-3). 1984. 10.25 (ISBN 0-688-01754-1); PLB 10.88 (ISBN 0-688-01755-X). Greenwillow.
What I Do Not Believe, & Other Essays. N. R. Hanson. Ed. by S. Toulminland & H. Woolf. LC 74-154738. (Synthese Library: No. 38). 390p. 1971. lib. bdg. 47.50 (ISBN 90-277-0191-1, Pub. by Reidel Holland). Kluwer Academic.
What I Don't Know for Sure. Phil Demise. (Burning Deck Poetry Ser.). 1978. pap. 10.00 signed ed (ISBN 0-930900-55-3). Burning Deck.
What I Have Learned: Thinking about the Future Then & Now. Ed. by Michael Marien & Lane Jennings. LC 86-14958. 219p. 1987. lib. bdg. 29.95 (ISBN 0-313-25071-5, MWL/). Greenwood.
What I Heard. Mark Geller. LC 86-45494. (Charlotte Zolotow Bks.). 128p. (gr. 5 up). 1987. 11.25i (ISBN 0-06-022160-7); PLB 11.89 (ISBN 0-06-022161-5). HarpJ.
What I Know of Farming. facsimile ed. Horace Greeley. LC 74-30631. (American Farmers & the Rise of Agribusiness Ser.). 1975. Repr. of 1871 ed. 30.00x (ISBN 0-405-06800-X). Ayer Co Pubs.
What I Know of Farming: A Series of Brief & Plain Expositions of Practical Agriculture As an Art Based upon Science. Horace Greeley. LC 72-89058. (Rural America Ser.). 1973. Repr. of 1871 ed. 31.00 (ISBN 0-8420-1484-5). Scholarly Res Inc.
What I Know So Far: Short Stories. Gordon Lish. (Signature Editions Ser.). 176p. 1986. pap. 4.95 (ISBN 0-684-18644-6). Scribner.
What I Like About. George Vandeman. 108p. 1986. pap. 1.95 (ISBN 0-8163-0668-0). Pacific Pr Pub Assn.
What I Like: Eating. Marcia Leonard. 24p. (Orig.). (ps-1). 1988. pap. 3.95 (ISBN 0-553-05463-5). Bantam.
What I Like: Getting Dressed. Marcia Leonard. 24p. (Orig.). (ps-1). 1988. pap. 3.95 (ISBN 0-553-05467-8). Bantam.
What I Like: Going to Bed. Marcia Leonard. 24p. (Orig.). (ps-1). 1988. pap. 3.95 (ISBN 0-553-05468-6). Bantam.
What I Like: Taking a Bath. Marcia Leonard. 24p. (Orig.). (ps-1). 1988. pap. 3.95 (ISBN 0-553-05464-3). Bantam.
What I Love: Selected Poems of Odysseus Elytis 1939-1978. Odysseus Elytis. Tr. by Olga Broumas. LC 85-73081. 64p. 1985. 15.00 (ISBN 0-914742-95-7); pap. 9.00 (ISBN 0-914742-91-4). Copper Canyon.
What I Owe to My Father. facsimile ed. Ed. by Sydney D. Strong. LC 69-17590. (Essay Index Reprint Ser). Repr. of 1931 ed. 18.00 (ISBN 0-8369-2672-2). Ayer Co Pubs.
What I Own. Tim Longville & John Riley. 1973. signed 10.00 (ISBN 0-685-78928-4, Pub. by Grosseteste); sewn in wrappers 4.00 (ISBN 0-685-78929-2). Small Pr Dist.
What I Really Think of You. M. E. Kerr. LC 81-47735. (Charlotte Zolotow Bks.). 224p. (YA) (gr. 7 up). 1982. 12.70i (ISBN 0-06-023188-2); PLB 12.89 (ISBN 0-06-023189-0). HarpJ.
What I Really Think of You. M. E. Kerr. 160p. (YA) (gr. 7 up). 1983. pap. 2.50 (ISBN 0-451-12254-2, Sig Vista). NAL.
What I Remember. Millicent Fawcett. LC 74-33939. (Pioners of the Woman's Movement Ser.). (Illus.). 272p. 1975. Repr. of 1925 ed. 21.45 (ISBN 0-88355-261-2). Hyperion-Conn.
What I Saw - Chto Ya Videl. Boris Zhitkov. Ed. by Richard L. Leed & Lora Paperno. (Illus.). 128p. (Orig., Rus. & Eng.). 1988. pap. text ed. 11.95 (ISBN 0-89357-183-0). Slavica.
What I Saw in America. 2nd ed. G. K. Chesterton. LC 68-16226. (American Scene Ser). 1968. Repr. of 1922 ed. 37.50 (ISBN 0-306-71009-9). Da Capo.
What I Saw in California. Edwin Bryant. 1967. Repr. 12.50 (ISBN 0-87018-004-5). Ross.
What I Saw in California. Edwin Bryant. LC 84-28003. xxii, 455p. 1985. pap. 9.95 (ISBN 0-8032-6070-9, BB 887, Bison). U of Nebr Pr.
What I Tell You Three Times Is False. Sam Holt. 256p. 1987. 14.95. Tor Bks.
What I Tell You Three Times Is False. Samuel Holt. 256p. 1987. 14.95 (ISBN 0-312-93004-6). St Martin.
What I Tell You Three Times Is False. Samuel Holt. 256p. 1988. pap. 3.95 (ISBN 0-8125-0465-8, Dist. by St Martin's Pr & Warner Pub Servs). Tor Bks.
What I Think. Adlai E. Stevenson. LC 74-12647. 240p. 1974. Repr. of 1956 ed. lib. bdg. 35.00x (ISBN 0-8371-7738-3, STIT). Greenwood.
What I Want to Be. Mark A. Taylor. (Happy Day Bks.). (Illus.). 24p. (ps-2). 1986. 1.59 (ISBN 0-87403-031-5, 3491). Standard Pub.
What I Wish I'd Learned in Seminary. John Guest. 192p. 1987. 9.95 (ISBN 0-8499-0518-4). Word Bks.
What I Wish My Parents Knew about Sexuality. Josh McDowell. 1987. pap. 6.95 (ISBN 0-317-57148-6). Heres Life.
What If...? Joan P. Berry. 1985. 3.50 (ISBN 0-89536-729-7, 5813). CSS of Ohio.
What If... Earl N. Jenkins. 1988. 6.95 (ISBN 0-533-07891-1). Vantage.
What If? Else H. Minarik. LC 86-7649. (Illus.). 24p. (ps-2). 1987. 11.75 (ISBN 0-688-06473-6); PLB 11.88 (ISBN 0-688-06474-4). Greenwillow.
What If. LC 85-80646. (Illus.). 672p. (Orig.). 1985. pap. 13.95 (ISBN 0-935541-00-4). N C Hinds Pub.
What If...? A Guide to Computer Modelling. Thomas Simondi. (Illus.). 251p. 1983. pap. 19.95 (ISBN 0-912003-00-6). Bk Co.
What If...? A Selection of Social-Science Fiction. Ed. by Nelson W. Polsby. LC 82-18759. 224p. 1982. 12.95 (ISBN 0-86616-018-3). Greene.
What If? A User's Guide to Spreadsheets on the IBM-PC. Andrew T. Williams. (IBM Personal Computer Ser.: Nos. 1-646). 281p. (Orig.). 1984. pap. text ed. 16.95 (ISBN 0-471-89218-1, Pub. by Wiley Pr). Wiley.
What If? Fifty Discoveries That Changed the World. Seli Groves & Dian D. Buchman. 96p. (gr. 5-9). 1988. 1.95 (ISBN 0-590-41009-1). Scholastic Inc.
What If I Were a Clown. Graham Round. 24p. (ps-1). 1987. 3.95 (ISBN 0-8120-5774-0). Barron.
What If I Were an Astronaut? Graham Round. (Illus.). 24p. (ps-1). 1987. 3.95 (ISBN 0-8120-5773-2). Barron.
What If? (Middle School) 1987. 3.95 (ISBN 0-88047-050-X). DOK Pubs.
What If: Poems, 1969-1987. Andrew Hoyem. (Illus.). 92p. 1987. pap. 10.00 (ISBN 0-910457-14-X). Arion Pr.
What If the Teacher Calls on Me? Alan Gross. LC 79-18560. (Illus.). 32p. (ps-3). 1980. PLB 11.93 (ISBN 0-516-03671-8); pap. 2.95 (ISBN 0-516-43671-6). Childrens.
What If They Knew. Patricia Hermes. 128p. (gr. k-6). 1981. pap. 2.25 (ISBN 0-440-49515-6, YB). Dell.
What If They Knew. Patricia Hermes. LC 79-90033. (gr. 4-6). 1980. 10.95 (ISBN 0-15-295317-5, HJ). HarBraceJ.
What If They Saw Me Now? Jean Ure. LC 83-14981. 160p. (gr. 7 up). 1984. 13.95 (ISBN 0-385-29317-8). Delacorte.
What If...I Say No. rev. ed. Jill Haddad & Lloyd Martin. (Illus.). 26p. (gr. k-6). 1981. pap. text ed. 3.50 (ISBN 0-911375-00-7). M H Cap.
What I'm Going to Do, I Think. Larry Woiwode. LC 69-13735. 309p. 1969. 5.95 (ISBN 0-374-28792-9). FS&G.
What in Blazes. Glenhall Taylor. 1980. pap. 1.75 (ISBN 0-686-37155-0). Eldridge Pub.
What in the World Is a Christian? John Blanchard. 1987. pap. 6.95 (ISBN 0-310-20101-2, 11678P). Zondervan.
What in the World is Rolfing? Ida P. Rolf. pap. 4.00 (ISBN 0-930422-05-8). Dennis Landman.
What in the World Will Happen Next? Ivor C. Powell. LC 85-7579. 176p. (Orig.). 1985. pap. 5.95 (ISBN 0-8254-3524-2). Kregel.
What Investing Is All About. 3rd ed. John Barnes. 1984. write for info. wkbk. (ISBN 0-538-14570-6, N57). SW Pub.
What Is A. A.? 6p. 1980. pap. 0.35 (ISBN 0-89486-109-3). Hazelden.
What Is a Bird. Rev. ed. Jenifer W. Day. (Golden Look-Look Bks.). (Illus.). 24p. (Orig.). (ps-3). 1986. pap. 1.50 (ISBN 0-307-11805-3, Pub. by Golden Bks). Western Pub.
What Is a Bird? Ron Hirschi. (Illus.). (ps-4). 1987. 10.95 (ISBN 0-8027-6720-6); PLB 11.85 (ISBN 0-8027-6721-4). Walker & Co.
What Is a Butterfly? Chris Arvetis. (Just Ask Ser.). 32p. (ps-3). pap. 3.95 (ISBN 0-02-689001-1, Checkerboard Pr). Macmillan.
What Is a California Sea Otter? Jack A. Graves. (Illus.). (gr. 3 up). 1977. pap. 3.50 (ISBN 0-910286-61-2). Boxwood.
What Is a Cat? Bill Adler. LC 87-12376. (Illus.). 64p. 1987. 6.95 (ISBN 0-688-07528-2). Morrow.
What Is a Christian? Carolyn Nystrom. (Children's Bible Basics Ser.). 32p. (gr. 2). 1981. pap. 4.95 (ISBN 0-8024-6155-7). Moody.
What Is a Church: The Dilemma of the Parachurch. Center for Law & Religious Freedom Staff. 73p. (Orig.). 1979. pap. text ed. 3.00 (ISBN 0-944561-00-4). Chr Legal.
What Is a City: A Multi-Media Guide on Urban Living. Ed. by Rose Moorachian. 1969. 2.00 (ISBN 0-89073-016-4). Boston Public Lib.
What Is a City: Young People Reply. Compiled by Dianne Farrell & Ruth M. Hayes. (Illus.). 1969. 1.00 (ISBN 0-89073-017-2). Boston Public Lib.
What Is a Classic? T. S. Eliot. LC 74-4089. (Studies in T. S. Eliot, No. 11). 1974. lib. bdg. 75.00x (ISBN 0-8383-2059-7). Haskell.
What Is a Computer. Marion J. Ball. (Illus.). 92p. (gr. 4-12). 1972. pap. text ed. 8.88 (ISBN 0-395-13772-1). HM.
What Is a Crime? Mark V. Hansel. (Literacy Volunteers of America Readers Ser.). 32p. (Orig.). 1983. pap. 1.95 (ISBN 0-8428-9612-0). Cambridge Bk.
What Is a Desert? Chris Arvetis. (Just Ask Ser.). 32p. (ps-3). 1987. pap. 3.95 (ISBN 0-02-689003-8, Checkerboard Pr). Macmillan.
What Is a Doctor? Alex Comfort. LC 80-51834. 232p. 1980. 10.95 (ISBN 0-89313-022-2). G F Stickley Co.
What Is a Family? Elaine Moore. (Illus.). 32p. 1987. 4.95 (ISBN 0-570-04171-6, 56-1628). Concordia.
What Is a Family? Edith Schaeffer. 256p. 1982. pap. 7.95 (ISBN 0-8007-5088-9, Power Bks). Revell.
What Is a Fish? David Eastman. LC 81-11373. (Now I Know Ser.). (Illus.). 32p. (gr. k-2). 1982. lib. bdg. 9.89 (ISBN 0-89375-660-1); pap. text ed. 2.95 (ISBN 0-89375-661-X). Troll Assocs.
What Is a Flood? Barbara King. 61p. 1981. pap. 3.00 (ISBN 0-317-20874-8). CSA Pr.
What Is a Flower? Jennifer W. Day. (Golden Look-Look Bks.). (Illus.). 24p. (ps-3). 1987. Repr. of 1975 ed. 1.50 (ISBN 0-307-11800-2, Pub. by Golden Bks). Western Pub.
What Is a Freckle? Carol H. Schramm. 1975. pap. 1.25 (ISBN 0-8198-0484-3). Dghtrs St Paul.
What Is a Horoscope? J. I. Cox. 166p. 1985. 14.00 (ISBN 0-86690-238-4). Am Fed Astrologers.
What Is a Jew? Israel Ministry. 1975. 30.00 (ISBN 0-379-13904-9). Oceana.
What Is a Jew. rev. ed. Morris N. Kertzer. LC 73-77280. 217p. 1973. Repr. of 1953 ed. 8.95x (ISBN 0-8197-0299-4). Bloch.
What Is a Jew? 4th ed. Morris N. Kertzer. 1978. pap. 5.95 (ISBN 0-02-086350-0, Collier). Macmillan.
What Is a Jungle? Chris Arvetis & Carole Palmer. (Just Ask Ser.). (Illus.). 32p. (ps-3). 1984. Repr. 3.95 (ISBN 0-317-65120-X, Checkerboard Pr). Macmillan.
What Is a Kiss? Love Riddles. Ed. by Lois L. Kaufman. LC 87-60947. (Illus.). 64p. 1987. 5.95 (ISBN 0-88088-571-8). Peter Pauper.
What Is a Law of Nature? D. M. Armstrong. (Cambridge Studies in Philosophy). 190p. 1985. pap. 11.95 (ISBN 0-521-31481-X). Cambridge U Pr.
What Is a Law of Nature? David M. Armstrong. LC 83-5130. (Cambridge Studies in Philosophy). pap. cancelled (2026330). Bks Demand UMI.
What Is a Mammal? Rev. ed. Jenifer W. Day. (Golden Look-Look Bks.). (Illus.). 24p. (Orig.). (ps-3). 1986. pap. 1.50 (ISBN 0-307-11802-9, Pub. by Golden Bks). Western Pub.
What Is a Man? What Is a Woman? Morton Hunt. LC 79-1202. 176p. (gr. 7 up). 1979. 10.95 (ISBN 0-374-38299-9). FS&G.
What Is a Masterpiece? Kenneth Clark. (Illus.). 1981. pap. 4.95 (ISBN 0-500-27206-9). Thames Hudson.
What Is a Masterpiece? Kenneth Clark. 1983. 14.50 (ISBN 0-8446-5991-6). Peter Smith.
What Is a Miracle? Barbara King. 61p. 1981. pap. 3.00 (ISBN 0-317-20876-4). CSA Pr.
What Is a Monster? Sylvia R. Tester. LC 78-23642. (Magic Monsters Ser.). (Illus.). (ps-3). 1979. PLB 7.95 (ISBN 0-89565-055-X). Childs World.
What Is a Monster? Sylvia R. Tester. LC 78-23642. (Magic Monsters Ser.). (Illus.). 32p. (ps-3). 1979. PLB 11.93 (ISBN 0-516-06189-5). Childrens.
What Is a Mountain? Chris Arvetis. (Just Ask Ser.). 32p. (ps-3). 1987. pap. 3.95 (ISBN 0-02-689004-6, Checkerboard Pr). Macmillan.
What Is a New Mexico Santo? Eluid L. Martinez & James C. Smith, Jr. LC 77-78519. (Illus.). 1978. pap. 2.95 (ISBN 0-913270-76-8). Sunstone Pr.
What Is a Patent? 2nd ed. 14p. 1982. pap. 1.00 (ISBN 0-317-31333-9). Amer Bar Assn.
What Is a Person? Intro. by Michael Goodman. LC 86-21487. (Contemporary Issues in Biomedicine, Ethics, & Society Ser.). 320p. 1988. 29.50 (ISBN 0-89603-117-9). Humana.
What Is a Poet? Hank Lazer. LC 86-19234. (Illus.). 288p. 1987. 25.95 (ISBN 0-8173-0325-1); pap. 17.95 (ISBN 0-8173-0326-X). U of Ala Pr.
What Is a Rainbow? Chris Arvetis. (Jusk Ask Ser.). (Illus.). 32p. (ps-3). 1988. pap. 1.95 (ISBN 0-02-688810-6, Checkerboard Pr). Macmillan.
What Is a Reptile? Susan Kuchalla. LC 81-11364. (Now I Know Ser.). (Illus.). 32p. (gr. k-2). 1982. PLB 9.89 (ISBN 0-89375-672-5). Troll Assocs.
What Is a SAM? A Layman's Guide to Social Accounting Matrices. Benjamin B. King. (Working Paper: No. 463). 59p. 1981. pap. 5.00 (ISBN 0-686-39656-1, WP-0463). World Bank.
What Is a Scientist? Memorial Issue for Professor Oscar Bodansky. Ed. by Stacey B. Day. (Journal: Biosciences Communications Ser.: Vol. 4, No. 5). 1978. pap. 12.75 (ISBN 3-8055-2967-8). S Karger.
What Is a Share of Stock? Jeffrey Little. (Basic Investors Library). (Illus.). 48p. 1987. lib. bdg. 9.95x (ISBN 1-55546-620-6). Chelsea Hse.
What Is a Spiritual Master? Omraam M. Aivanhov. (Izvor Collection Ser.: Vol. 207). 185p. 1984. pap. 5.95 (ISBN 2-85566-300-8, Pub. by Prosveta France). Prosveta USA.
What Is a Thing? Martin Heidegger. Tr. by W. B. Barton, Jr. & Vera Deutsch. LC 67-31050. 310p. 1968. pap. 5.95 (ISBN 0-89526-979-1). Regnery Gateway.
What Is a Thing? Martin Heidegger. Tr. by W. B. Barton & Vera Deutsch. 320p. 1985. pap. text ed. 9.25 (ISBN 0-8191-4545-9). U Pr of Amer.
What Is a Volcano? Chris Arvetis & Carole Palmer. (Just Ask Ser.). (Illus.). (ps-3). 1987. Repr. 3.95 (ISBN 0-528-82434-1, Checkerboard Pr). Macmillan.
What Is a Wife Worth? A Leading Expert Places a High Dollar Value on Homemaking. Michael H. Minton & Jean L. Block. 292p. 1984. pap. text ed. 6.95 (ISBN 0-07-042414-4). McGraw.
What Is a Woman. 2nd ed. William H. Graham. (Illus.). 1967. 12.50 (ISBN 0-910550-16-6). Elysium.
What Is Acupuncture? How Does It Work? Eric H. Stiefvater. 1980. 15.00x (ISBN 0-85032-170-0, Pub. by Daniel Co England). State Mutual Bk.
What Is Acupuncture? How Does It Work? Eric H. Stievater. 48p. 1971. pap. 3.00x (ISBN 0-8464-1061-3). Beekman Pubs.
What Is America Eating? National Research Council. 173p. (Orig.). 1986. pap. text ed. 14.95x (ISBN 0-309-03635-6). Natl Acad Pr.
What Is an Editor? Saxe Commins at Work. Dorothy Commins. LC 77-81716. 256p. pap. 5.95 (ISBN 0-226-11428-7, Phoen). U of Chicago Pr.
What Is an Emotion? Classic Readings in Philisophical Psychology. Ed. by Cheshire Calhoun & Robert C. Solomon. 1984. 26.00x (ISBN 0-19-503355-8); pap. 10.95x (ISBN 0-19-503304-3). Oxford U Pr.
What Is an Iceberg? Chris Arvetis. (Just Ask Ser.). (Illus.). 32p. (ps-3). 1987. 3.95 (ISBN 0-02-689009-7, Pub. by Checkerboard Pr). Macmillan.
What Is an Insect? Jennifer W. Day. (Golden Look-Look Bks.). (Illus.). 24p. (ps-3). 1987. Repr. of 1975 ed. 1.50 (ISBN 0-307-11803-7, Pub. by Golden Bks). Western Pub.
What Is & What Ought to Be Done: An Essay on Ethics & Epistemology. Morton White. 1981. 14.95x (ISBN 0-19-502916-X). Oxford U Pr.
What Is Anglicanism? Urban T. Holmes, 3rd. LC 81-84715. 112p. (Orig.). 1982. pap. 5.95 (ISBN 0-8192-1295-4). Morehouse.
What Is Anthroposophy? Otto Frankl-Lundborg. Tr. by Joseph Wetzl. 1977. pap. 2.95 (ISBN 0-916786-14-5). St George Bk Serv.
What Is Archaeology? An Essay on the Nature of Archaeological Research. Paul Courbin. Tr. by Paul Bahn. (Illus.). 232p. 1988. 24.95X (ISBN 0-226-11656-5). U of Chicago Pr.
What Is Art? Hugh Curtler. (World of Art Ser.). (Illus.). 220p. (Orig.). 1983. pap. text ed. 25.00 (ISBN 0-930586-17-4). Haven Pubns.
What Is Art. Leo Tolstoy. Tr. by Aylmer Maude. LC 60-9557. 1960. pap. 7.87 scp (ISBN 0-672-60221-0, LLA51). Bobbs.
What Is Art? An Introduction to Painting, Sculpture & Architecture. John Canaday. 1980. text ed. 22.00 (ISBN 0-394-32450-1). Knopf.
What Is Art? And Essays on Art. Len N. Tolstoi. LC 33-5715. 339p. 1959. Repr. 29.00x (ISBN 0-403-04330-1). Somerset Pub.
What Is Art? And Essays on Art. Leo N. Tolstoy. 1988. Repr. of 1959 ed. lib. bdg. 29.00x. Am Biog Serv.
What Is Art For? Ellen Dissanayake. LC 87-40553. (Illus.). 240p. 1988. 20.00 (ISBN 0-295-96612-2). U of Wash Pr.
What Is Art History? Mark Roskill. LC 75-34872. (Icon Editions). (Illus.). 192p. 1977. (HarpT); pap. 8.95xi (ISBN 0-06-430074-9, IN-74, HarpT). Har-Row.
What Is Art? Studies in the Technique & Criticism of Painting. John C. Van Dyke. 154p. 1982. Repr. of 1910 ed. lib. bdg. 30.00 (ISBN 0-8495-5523-X). Arden Lib.
What Is Art: Tolstoy. Almyer Maude & Vincent Tomas. 1960. pap. text ed. write for info. (ISBN 0-02-377400-2). Macmillan.
What Is Astrology? Colin Bennett. 124p. 1981. 10.00 (ISBN 0-89540-113-4, SB-113). Sun Pub.
What Is Balance? Marima F. D'Arcier & Volker Theinhardt. (Viking Kestrel Science Bks.). (Illus.). 32p. (ps-3). 1986. 3.95 (ISBN 0-670-81198-X, Viking Kestrel). Viking.
What Is Behavioralism? Thoughts on the Crisis in the Social Sciences. W. J. Stankiewicz. 1971. chroma ed. 8.50 (ISBN 0-686-09044-6); art parchment ed. 25.00 (ISBN 0-686-09045-4). Girs Pr.
What Is Beyond the Hill? Ernst A. Ekker. LC 85-45446. (Illus.). 28p. (ps-1). 1986. 8.95i (ISBN 0-397-32166-X, Lipp Jr Bks); PLB 8.89 (ISBN 0-397-32167-8). HarpJ.
What Is Calculus About? W. W. Sawyer. LC 61-6227. (New Mathematical Library: No. 2). 118p. 1961. pap. 9.90 (ISBN 0-88385-602-6). Math Assn.
What Is Called Logic: A Diachronic Study of the Laws of Thought. Percy Johnston. (Dasein-Jupiter Hammen Ser.). 180p. 1985. pap. text ed. 10.95 (ISBN 0-915833-48-4). Drama Jazz Hse Inc.
What Is Called Thinking? Martin Heidegger. Tr. by J. Glenn Gray & Fred D. Wieck. 272p. 1972. pap. 8.95 (ISBN 0-06-090528-X, CN528, PL). Har-Row.
What Is Chanukah? A Programmed Text. Louis Nulman. text ed. 2.25 (ISBN 0-914131-73-7, B30). Torah Umesorah.
What Is Christian Doctrine? John P. Newport. LC 83-71266. (Layman's Library of Christian Doctrine Ser.). 1984. 5.95 (ISBN 0-8054-1631-5). Broadman.
What Is Christianity. John W. Alexander. pap. 0.75 (ISBN 0-87784-133-0). Inter-Varsity.
What Is Christianity? Michael Green. 64p. 1982. 10.95 (ISBN 0-687-44650-3). Abingdon.
What Is Christianity? Adolf Harnack. LC 78-15359. 1978. Repr. lib. bdg. 40.00 (ISBN 0-8414-4869-8). Folcroft.

What Is Periodontal Disease? Joel M. Berns. (Illus.). 64p. (Orig.). 1982. pap. text ed. 18.00 (ISBN 0-86715-109-9). Quint Pub Co.
What Is Philosophy? Archie J. Bahm. 28p. 1984. pap. 1.00 (ISBN 0-911714-13-8, World Bks). Bahm.
What Is Philosophy. Martin Heidegger. 1956. pap. 5.95x (ISBN 0-8084-0319-2). New Coll U Pr.
What Is Philosophy. G. Korolenko & L. Korshunova. 350p. 1985. pap. 1.95 (ISBN 0-8285-3360-1, Pub. by Progress Pubs USSR). Imported Pubns.
What Is Philosophy. Jose Ortega Y Gasset. 1964. pap. 6.95 (ISBN 0-393-00126-1, Norton Lib). Norton.
What Is Philosophy? Dietrich Von Hilderbrand. LC 73-9988. pap. 63.00 (ISBN 0-317-09325-8, 2019098). Bks Demand UMI.
What Is Philosophy: A Short Introduction. Elmer Sprague. (Orig.). 1961. pap. 6.95x (ISBN 0-19-501061-2). Oxford U Pr.
What Is Political Economy. S. Ilyin & A. Motylev. 350p. 1987. pap. 1.95 (ISBN 0-8285-3284-2, Pub. by Progress Pubs USSR). Imported Pubns.
What Is Political Economy. Martin Staniland. LC 84-13193. 240p. 1987. pap. 9.95 (ISBN 0-300-03936-0, Y-630). Yale U Pr.
What Is Political Economy? Ed. by David K. Whynes. 250p. 1984. 34.95x (ISBN 0-85520-746-9); pap. 11.95 (ISBN 0-85520-747-7). Basil Blackwell.
What Is Political Economy? A Study of Social Theory & Underdevelopment. Martin Staniland. LC 84-13193. 240p. 1985. 27.50t (ISBN 0-300-03295-1). Yale U Pr.
What Is Political Philosophy? Leo Strauss. LC 73-1408. 315p. 1973. Repr. of 1959 ed. lib. bdg. 25.00x (ISBN 0-8371-6802-3, STPP). Greenwood.
What Is Political Philosophy? And Other Studies. Leo Strauss. 318p. 1988. pap. 12.95 (ISBN 0-226-77713-8). U of Chicago Pr.
What Is Politics? The Activity & Its Study. Ed. by Adrian Leftwich. 192p. 1984. 24.95x (ISBN 0-631-13486-7); pap. 9.95x (ISBN 0-631-13553-7). Basil Blackwell.
What Is Post-Modernism? Charles Jencks. (Illus.). 48p. 1986. pap. 12.95 (ISBN 0-312-86603-8). St Martin.
What Is Post-Modernism? 2nd, rev. & enl. ed. Charles Jencks. (Academy Editions Ser.). (Illus.). 56p. 1988. pap. 12.95 (ISBN 0-312-01699-9). St Martin.
What Is Pragmatism? James B. Pratt. LC 75-3327. Repr. of 1909 ed. 23.00 (ISBN 0-404-59322-4). AMS Pr.
What Is Prayer? Carolyn Nystrom. (Children's Bible Basics Ser.). 32p. (ps-2). 1980. pap. 3.95 (ISBN 0-8024-6156-5). Moody.
What Is Property. P. J. Proudhon. 75.00 (ISBN 0-8490-1287-2). Gordon Pr.
What Is Property? M. Suvorova & B. Romanov. 189p. 1987. pap. 1.95 (ISBN 0-8285-3204-4, Pub. by Progress USSR). Imported Pubns.
What Is Psychoanalysis? Isador H. Coriat. LC 73-2393. (Mental Illness & Social Policy; the American Experience Ser.). Repr. of 1917 ed. 11.50 (ISBN 0-405-05201-4). Ayer Co Pubs.
What Is Psychoanalysis? Ernest Jones. LC 72-11478. 126p. 1973. Repr. of 1948 ed. lib. bdg. 35.00x (ISBN 0-8371-6670-5, JOWP). Greenwood.
What Is Psychoanalysis? rev. & enl. ed. Ernest Jones. LC 48-2924. pap. 31.50 (ISBN 0-317-10263-X, 2010707). Bks Demand UMI.
What Is Psychotherapy? Sidney Bloch. 1982. text ed. 18.95x (ISBN 0-19-219154-3). Oxford U Pr.
What Is Psychotherapy? Sidney Bloch. 1982. pap. 8.95 (ISBN 0-19-289142-1). Oxford U Pr.
What Is Psychotherapy? Proceedings: International Congress of Psychotherapy, 9th, Oslo, June 1973, 3 pts. Ed. by T. E. Mogstad & F. Magnussen. (Journal: Psychotherapy & Psychosomatic Ser.: Vol. 24, Nos. 4-6). 600p. 1975. Repr. 98.75 (ISBN 3-8055-2057-3). S Karger.
What Is Pure French; see Preliminary Announcement.
What Is Quakerism? A Primer. George Peck. (Orig.). 1988. pap. 2.50 (ISBN 0-87574-277-7). Pendle Hill.
What Is Quality Child Care? Bettye M. Caldwell & Asa G. Hilliard, III. 33p. 1985. 2.50 (ISBN 0-912674-89-X, NAEYC #117). Natl Assn Child Ed.
What Is Reading Readiness? Norma Rogers. (Micromonograph Ser.). 1971. pap. 1.50 (ISBN 0-87207-870-1). Intl Reading.
What Is Redaction Criticism? Norman Perrin. Ed. by Dan O. Via, Jr. LC 72-81529. (Guides to Biblical Scholarship). 96p. (Orig.). 1969. pap. 4.50 (ISBN 0-8006-0181-5, 1-181). Fortress.
What Is Religion? Rubem Alves. Tr. by Don Vinzant from Port. LC 83-19398. Orig. Title: O Que E Religiao. 96p. (Orig.). 1984. pap. 4.95 (ISBN 0-88344-705-3). Orbis Bks.
What Is Religion? An Inquiry for Christian Theology, Concilium 136. Ed. by Mircea Eliade & David Tracy. (New Concilium 1980). 128p. 1980. pap. 5.95 (ISBN 0-8164-2278-8, HarpR). Har-Row.
What Is Religious Life? Thomas Dubay. 5.95 (ISBN 0-87193-116-8). Dimension Bks.
What Is Remembered. Alice B. Toklas. LC 84-62304. 224p. 1985. 9.50 (ISBN 0-86547-180-0). N Point Pr.
What Is Revelation? Frederick D. Maurice. LC 76-173061. Repr. of 1859 ed. 37.50 (ISBN 0-404-04276-7). AMS Pr.
What Is Revolution. A. Sertsova et al. 191p. 1986. pap. 1.95 (ISBN 0-8285-3439-X, Pub. by Progress Pubs USSR). Imported Pubns.
What Is Romanticism? Henri Peyre. Tr. by Roda P. Roberts from Fr. LC 75-42374. 1977. 15.50 (ISBN 0-8173-7003-X). U of Ala Pr.
What Is Sacrament? Richard McBrien. 20p. 1987. pap. 4.95 (ISBN 0-89505-557-0). Tabor Pub.
What Is Safe: Corporate Aviation Safety Seminar Proceedings, 28th Annual Meeting, April 17-19, 1983, Fairmont Hotel, New Orleans, Louisiana. Flight Safety Foundation. pap. 53.00 (ISBN 0-317-29629-9, 2021549). Bks Demand UMI.
What Is Science? Norman R. Campbell. 1921. pap. 4.50 (ISBN 0-486-60043-2). Dover.
What Is Science? An Introduction to the Structure & Methodology of Science. V. James Mannoia, Jr. LC 79-47988. (Illus.). 149p. 1980. pap. text ed. 8.25 (ISBN 0-8191-0989-4). U Pr of Amer.
What Is Scientific Communism. L. Selezhnev. 173p. 1985. pap. 1.95 (Pub. by Progress Pubs USSR). Imported Pubns.
What Is Scientology? L. Ron Hubbard. 50.00 (ISBN 0-686-30807-7). Church Scient NY.
What Is Scientology? Taken from the Works of L. Ron Hubbard. 1978. 47.16 (ISBN 0-88404-061-5). Bridge Pubns Inc.
What Is Secular Humanism? Why Humanism Became Secular & How It Is Changing Our World. James Hitchcock. (Illus.). 158p. 1982. pap. 6.95 (ISBN 0-89283-163-4). Servant.
What Is Sex. Abraham Smith. 100p. (Orig.). 1986. write for info. (ISBN 0-9615763-0-8). Pussy Willow.
What Is Sex Education All About? A Guide for Parents. Sidney S. Ross. LC 78-64612. 1979. pap. 6.95 (ISBN 0-9602028-0-3). Sidney Scott Ross.
What Is Shakespeare? L. A. Sherman. 1974. Repr. of 1912 ed. lib. bdg. 29.00 (ISBN 0-8414-8085-0). Folcroft.
What Is Social Case Work: An Introductory Description. Mary E. Richmond. LC 70-137185. (Poverty U. S. A. Historical Record Ser.). 1971. Repr. of 1922 ed. 20.00 (ISBN 0-405-03123-8). Ayer Co Pubs.
What Is Socialism. D. Klementyev & T. Vassilyeva. 192p. 1986. pap. 1.95 (ISBN 0-8285-3440-3, Pub. by Progress Pubs USSR). Imported Pubns.
What Is Sociology? Norbert Elias. LC 78-2386. 187p. 1978. 24.00x (ISBN 0-231-04550-6); pap. 11.00x (ISBN 0-231-04551-4). Columbia U Pr.
What Is Soviet Power? Vladimir I. Lenin. 103p. 1973. pap. 0.95 (ISBN 0-8285-0179-3, Pub. by Progress Pubs USSR). Imported Pubns.
What Is Spirituality? Paul Bjorklund. 16p. (Orig.). 1983. pap. 0.95 (ISBN 0-89486-182-4). Hazelden.
What Is Structural Exegesis? Daniel Patte. Ed. by Dan O. Via, Jr. LC 75-36454. (Guides to Biblical Scholarship: New Testament Ser.). 96p. (Orig.). 1976. pap. 4.50 (ISBN 0-8006-0462-8, 1-462). Fortress.
What Is Sufism? Martin Lings. 136p. 1988. pap. 9.95 (ISBN 0-04-297039-3). Unwin Hyman.
What Is Surplus Value? T. Volkova & F. Volkov. 301p. 1986. pap. 1.95 (ISBN 0-8285-3241-9, Pub. by Progress Pubs USSR). Imported Pubns.
What Is Surrealism. Andre Breton. LC 74-6446. (Studies in Comparative Literature, No. 35). 1973. Repr. of 1936 ed. lib. bdg. 75.00x (ISBN 0-8383-1709-X). Haskell.
What Is Surrealism? Selected Writings. Andre Breton. Ed. by Franklin Rosemont. LC 71-186691. (Illus.). 1978. lib. bdg. 35.00x (ISBN 0-913460-59-1); pap. 18.95 (ISBN 0-913460-60-5). Anchor Found.
What Is Symbolism? Henri Peyre. Tr. by Emmett Parker from Fr. LC 79-4686. 224p. 1980. 16.50 (ISBN 0-8173-7004-8). U of Ala Pr.
What Is Taoism? And Other Studies in Chinese Cultural History. Herrlee G. Creel. LC 77-102905. (Midway Reprint Ser.). viii, 192p. 1982. pap. text ed. 12.95x (ISBN 0-226-12047-3). U of Chicago Pr.
What Is the Appropriate Role of Testing in the Teaching Profession? Gregory R. Anrig et al. 88p. 1987. 8.95 (ISBN 0-8106-1460-X). NEA.
What Is the Baha'i Faith. Rene Derkse. (Illus.). 176p. 1987. 9.50 (ISBN 0-85398-257-0). G Ronald Pub.
What Is the Best Way to Avoid Divorce? Hisanori Kontani. 80p. 1988. 7.95 (ISBN 0-89962-767-6). Todd & Honeywell.
What Is the Bible? Carolyn Nystrom. (Children's Bible Basics Ser.). 32p. (gr. 2). 1982. pap. 4.95 (ISBN 0-8024-0157-0). Moody.
What Is the Bible? A Nazareth Book. Robert R. Barr. 128p. (gr. 7-12). 1984. pap. 4.95 (ISBN 0-86683-727-2, HarpR). Har-Row.
What Is the Christian's Hope? W. J. Ouweneel. 53p. pap. 2.95 (ISBN 0-88172-166-6). Believers Bkshelf.
What Is the Church? Charles P. Conn & Charles W. Conn. 1977. pap. 1.99 (ISBN 0-87148-907-4). Pathway Pr.
What Is the Church, Bk. 3. Bruce L. Shelly. Tr. by Lorna Y. Chao. (Basic Doctrine Ser.). (Chinese.). 1985. pap. write for info. (ISBN 0-941598-25-X). Living Spring Pubns.
What Is the Church? Leader's Guide. S. P. Publications Editors. Tr. by Lorna Y. Chao. (Basic Doctrine Ser.). 1986. pap. write for info. (ISBN 0-941598-35-7). Living Spring Pubns.
What Is the Connection Between Religious & Schizophrenic Experience? J. L. Birley. 1985. 10.00x (ISBN 0-317-62252-8, Guild of Pastoral Psych). State Mutual Bk.
What Is the Conscious Process? Da Free John. LC 83-73637. 1983. pap. 8.95 (ISBN 0-913922-82-X). Dawn Horse Pr.
What Is the Difference? see Cual Es la Diferencia?.
What Is the Iona Community? Date not set. 20.00x (ISBN 0-947988-07-6, Pub. by Wild Goose Pubns Scotland). State Mutual Bk.
What Is the Matter with Mother? Patricia Berry. 1985. 10.00x (ISBN 0-317-62256-0, Guild of Pastoral Psych). State Mutual Bk.
What Is the Moon? Chris Arvetis. (Just Ask Ser.). (Illus.). 32p. (ps-3). 1987. 3.95 (ISBN 0-02-689007-0, Pub. by Checkerboard Pr). Macmillan.
What Is the Moon? Japanese Haiku Sequence. Ruby Lytle. LC 65-12861. (Illus., Orig.). (gr. 7 up). 1965. pap. 3.00 (ISBN 0-8048-0626-8). C E Tuttle.
What Is the Name of This Book? The Riddle of Dracula & Other Logical Puzzles. Raymond Smullyan. LC 77-18692. 1978. pap. 5.95 (ISBN 0-13-955062-3). P-H.
What Is the Name of This Book? The Riddle of Dracula & Other Puzzles. Raymond Smullyan. 256p. 1986. pap. 7.95 (ISBN 0-671-62832-1, Touchstone Bks). S&S.
What Is the Reformed Faith? John R. DeWitt. (Orig.). 1981. pap. text ed. 1.45 (ISBN 0-85151-326-3). Banner of Truth.
What Is the Sign for Friend? Judith E. Greenberg. LC 84-26986. (Illus.). 32p. (gr. k-6). 1986. lib. bdg. 9.40 (ISBN 0-531-04939-6). Watts.
What Is the Sonship of Christ? W. J. Ouweneel. pap. 2.25 (ISBN 0-88172-167-0). Believers Bkshelf.
What Is the Soviet Union Up To? 1977. write for info. Comm Present Danger.
What Is the State. G. Belov. 156p. 1986. pap. 1.95 (ISBN 0-317-60493-7, Pub. by Progress Pubs USSR). Imported Pubns.
What Is the Theory of Relativity? L. Landau & Yu Rumer. 62p. 1981. 11.00x (ISBN 0-317-46754-9, Pub. by Collets (UK)). State Mutual Bk.
What Is the Theory of Relativity? L. Landau & Yuri Rumer. 61p. 1961. 7.95 (ISBN 0-8464-1150-4). Beekman Pubs.
What Is the Transition Period? V. Kashin & N. Cherkasov. 173p. 1987. pap. 1.95 (ISBN 0-8285-3548-5, Pub. by Progress USSR). Imported Pubns.
What Is the World Socialist System? G. Pirogov. 159p. 1987. pap. 1.95 (ISBN 0-8285-3805-0, Pub. by Progress Pubs USSR). Imported Pubns.
What Is Theatre? Incorporating - the Dramatic Event. Eric Bentley. LC 86-5693. 512p. 1984. pap. 10.95 (ISBN 0-87910-012-5). Limelight Edns.
What Is Theosophy? A General View of Occult Doctrine. rev. ed. Charles J. Ryan. Ed. by W. Emmett Small & Helen Todd. (Theosophical Manual: No. 1). 92p. 1975. pap. 2.25 (913004-18-9). Point Loma Pub.
What Is This? Myrna Perkins. (Illus.). 36p. (Orig.). (ps-3). 1986. pap. 4.95 (ISBN 0-937729-01-9). Markins Enter.
What Is This For. Lawrence Henry. Ed. by Kate Klimo. (Learn with E.T. Ser.). (Illus.). 24p. 1982. pap. 1.95 (ISBN 0-671-46444-2, Little). S&S.
What Is This Madness? Bud Johns. LC 85-12710. (Illus.). 192p. (Orig.). 1985. pap. 7.95 (ISBN 0-912184-05-1). Synergistic Pr.
What Is This Power That Heals. Frederick Bailes. pap. 1.00 (ISBN 0-87516-171-5). DeVorss.
What Is This Thing Called Love. Nelson M. Smith. 1970. 8.75 (ISBN 0-89137-505-8); pap. 4.95 (ISBN 0-89137-504-X). Quality Pubns.
What Is This Thing Called Science? Alan Chalmers. (Paperbacks Ser.). 179p. 1985. pap. 9.95 (ISBN 0-7022-1831-6). U of Queensland Pr.
What Is This Thing Called Science? An Assessment of the Nature & Status of Science & Its Methods. A. F. Chalmers. 1976. pap. text ed. 19.95x (ISBN 0-7022-1341-1). Humanities.
What Is Thought? James H. Stirling. LC 83-48631. (Philosophy of Hegel Ser.). 432p. 1984. lib. bdg. 50.00 (ISBN 0-8240-5638-8). Garland Pub.
What Is to Be Done? Nikolai Chernyshevsky. Ed. & tr. by K. Feuer. 482p. 1986. pap. 6.95 (ISBN 0-87501-017-2). Ardis Pubs.
What Is to Be Done? Lenin. 253p. 1973. pap. 3.95 (ISBN 0-8351-0426-5). China Bks.
What Is to Be Done? V. I. Lenin. Intro. by Robert Service. 272p. 1988. pap. 7.95 (ISBN 0-14-044499-8). Penguin.
What Is To Be Done? Burning Questions of Our Movement. Vladimir I. Lenin. Ed. by James S. Allen. LC 69-18884. 200p. 1969. pap. 3.75 (ISBN 0-7178-0218-3). Intl Pubs Co.
What Is to be Done: Russian Reader. N. G. Chernyshevsky. 432p. 1987. 10.95 (ISBN 0-8285-3473-X, Pub. by Rus Lang Pubs USSR). Imported Pubns.
What Is to Be Done: The Enlightened Thinkers & an Islamic Renaissance. Ali Shari'ati. Ed. & tr. by Farhang Rajaee. A. Alidust & Ali Behzadnia. 200p. 1987. 25.95 (ISBN 0-932625-04-5); pap. text ed. 11.95 (ISBN 0-932625-01-0). Inst Res Islam.
What Is to Be Done with Our Criminals? A Letter to the Right Honorable the Lord Mayor. Charles Pearson. LC 83-49228. (Crime & Punishment in England 1850-1922 Ser.). 134p. 1984. lib. bdg. 33.00. Garland Pub.
What Is Total Quality Control? The Japanese Way. Kaoru Ishikawa. LC 84-26265. 215p. 1985. 24.95 (ISBN 0-13-952433-9). P-H.
What Is Total Quality Control? The Japanese Way. Kaoru Ishikawa. Tr. by David J. Lu. 215p. 1985. pap. 22.95 (PH100, PH). UNIPUB-Kraus Intl.
What Is Transfiguration? Jan Van Rijckenborgh. 40p. 1987. pap. 1.50 (ISBN 0-317-56232-0). Rozekruis Pr.
What Is Transylvania? S. Mehedinti. 124p. 1986. write for info. (ISBN 0-937019-02-X); pap. 15.00 (ISBN 0-937019-03-8). Romanian Hist.
What Is Truth? Christopher J. Williams. LC 75-23533. 118p. pap. 30.70 (2030629). Bks Demand UMI.
What Is User Friendly? Ed. by F. Wilfred Lancaster. (Proceedings of the 1986 Clinic on Library Applications of Data Processing). 1988. text ed. 15.00 (ISBN 0-87845-076-9). U of Ill Lib Info Sci.
What Is Veterans Day? Margot Parker. LC 86-11732. (Understanding Holidays Ser.). (Illus.). 48p. (ps-3). 1986. PLB 11.93 (ISBN 0-516-03782-X). Childrens.
What Is Wisdom? Cyril Upton. 148p. 1959. 15.00 (ISBN 0-8464-0967-4). Beekman Pubs.
What Is Wisdom? The World's Oldest Question Posed in the Light of Contemporary Perplexity. Cyril. Upton. pap. 61.80 (ISBN 0-317-08824-6, 2015627). Bks Demand UMI.
What Is Working Peoples' Power. D. Dmiterko & V. Pugachov. 228p. 1986. pap. 1.95 (ISBN 0-8285-3318-0, Pub. by Progress Pubs USSR). Imported Pubns.
What Is World & Family Enlightenment? Marie B. Hall. 1977. 4.50 (ISBN 0-938760-04-1). Veritat Found.
What Is Written in the Wind. Roger Finch. (Sparrow Poverty Pamphlet Ser.: No. 47). 32p. 1984. pap. 2.50x (ISBN 0-935552-19-7). Sparrow Pr.
What Is Wrong with the European Communities? Juergen B. Donges. (Institute of Economic Affairs, Occasional Papers Ser.: No. 59). pap. 4.25 technical (ISBN 0-255-36139-4). Transatl Arts.
What Is Wrong with the Truth? Helen W. Crounse, pseud. 1971. 14.95x (ISBN 0-8084-0357-5). New Coll U Pr.
What Is Your Cat Saying? Michael W. Fox & Wende D. Gates. LC 81-4884. (Illus.). 80p. (ps-1). 1982. 9.95 (ISBN 0-698-20443-3, Coward). Putnam Pub Group.
What Is Your Dream? pap. 3.95 (ISBN 0-317-46977-0). CSA Pr.
What Is Your Name? Sophy Moody. (International Library of Names). Date not set. Repr. of 1863 ed. text ed. cancelled (ISBN 0-8290-1228-1). Irvington.
What Is Your Name: A Popular Account of the Meaning & Derivations of Christian Names. Sophy Moody. LC 73-5523. 324p. 1975. Repr. of 1863 ed. 45.00x (ISBN 0-8103-4250-2). Gale.
What Islam Gave to Humanity? A. H. Siddiqui. pap. 2.50 (ISBN 0-686-63918-9). Kazi Pubns.
What Isn't Culture? Ed. by Brian Durrans. 250p. 1989. pap. 12.95 (ISBN 0-88477-033-8). Intl General.
What It Costs. 1987. 18.00 (ISBN 0-942326-35-0, 30179). Rough Notes.
What It Feels Like to Be a Building. rev. ed. Forrest Wilson. (Landmark Reprint Ser.). (Illus.). 80p. (gr. 2 up). 1988. Repr. of 1969 ed. 15.95 (ISBN 0-89133-142-5). Preservation Pr.
What It Is? Frank S. Jenkins. LC 81-90546. (Illus.). 48p. (Orig.). 1982. pap. 4.00 (ISBN 0-942048-00-8). Shockley Pr.
What It Is. Robert Long. 28p. 1981. pap. 3.00 (ISBN 0-935252-30-4); pap. 10.00 o. p. (ISBN 0-686-86778-5). Street Pr.
What It Is & What It Is Not see Notes on Nursing.
What It Is That Heals. Vance Cheney. 1980. 18.50x (ISBN 0-686-64693-2, Pub. by Daniel Co England). State Mutual Bk.
What It Means to Be a Christian. Stuart Briscoe & Jill Briscoe. 128p. 1987. pap. 4.95 (ISBN 1-55513-803-9). Cook.
What It Means to Be a Christian. William L. Ludlow. 1986. 7.95 (ISBN 0-8158-0434-2). Chris Mass.
What It Means to Be a Church Leader: A Biblical Point of View. Norman Shawchuck. (Illus.). 71p. (Orig.). 1984. pap. 7.95 (ISBN 0-938180-13-4). Org Resources Pr.
What It Means to Forgive. Ivan A. Beals. (Christian Living Ser.). 32p. (Orig.). 1987. pap. 1.50 (ISBN 0-8341-1185-3). Beacon Hill.
What It Takes: Good News from 100 of America's Top Professional & Business Women. Lee Gardenschwartz. LC 87-13657. (Illus.). 216p. 1987. pap. 16.95 (ISBN 0-385-23820-7, Dolp). Doubleday.
What It Takes to Get to the Top...& Stay There. Charles W. Golding. LC 82-24035. 208p. 1983. 13.95 (ISBN 0-399-12817-4, Putnam). Putnam Pub Group.
What It Was Like Flying for Ike. Laurence Hansen. pap. 5.95 (ISBN 0-912522-73-9). Aero Medical.

What Now, Charlie Brown? Selected Cartoons from "the Unsinkable Charlie Brown", Vol. 1. Charles M. Schulz. (Peanuts Ser.). (Illus.). 128p. (gr. 7 up). 1985. pap. 1.95 (ISBN 0-449-20589-4, Crest). Fawcett.
What Now McBride? Gary Davis. 99p. 1982. 7.95 (ISBN 0-934126-22-4). Randall Bk Co.
What Now My Life - How I Handled Cancer Plus. Glendola Skaggs. 64p. 1988. 6.95 (ISBN 0-8062-3372-9). Carlton.
What Number Now? Grahame Corbett. LC 82-70034. (Very First Bks.). (Illus.). 14p. (ps-k). 1982. bds. 3.50 (ISBN 0-8037-9735-4). Dial Bks Young.
What Nursery School Teachers Ask Us About: Psychoanalytic Consultations in Preschools. Erna Furman. LC 86-4346. (Emotions & Behavior Monographs: No. 5). 250p. 1986. 27.50x (ISBN 0-8236-6830-4, BN#6830). Intl Univs Pr.
What Nurses Should Know about DRG. Karen Sandrick. (Orig.). 1983. pap. 2.00 (ISBN 0-916499-02-2). Care Comm Inc.
What Odd Expedients & Other Poems. Robinson Jeffers. Ed. by Robert I. Scott. LC 80-26821. vii, 125p. 1981. 20.00 (ISBN 0-208-01885-9, Archon). Shoe String.
What of Tomorrow. Challoner. 3.95 (ISBN 0-8356-5300-5). Theos Pub Hse.
What on Earth Are You Doing? Michael Griffiths. 1983. pap. 4.95 (ISBN 0-8010-3792-1). Baker Bk.
What on Earth Is an Atheist? Madalyn M. O'Hair. LC 71-88701. (Fifty-Two Programs from the American Atheist Radio Ser.). 282p. 1969. pap. 6.00 (ISBN 0-911826-00-9). Am Atheist.
What on Earth Is an Atheist. Madalyn M. O'Hair. LC 74-161339. (Atheist Viewpoint Ser). 288p. 1972. Repr. of 1969 ed. 18.00 (ISBN 0-405-03802-X). Ayer Co Pubs.
What on Earth Is God Doing? Satan's Conflict with God. Renald E. Showers. LC 73-81551. 1973. pap. 3.95 (ISBN 0-87213-784-8). Loizeaux.
What on Earth Is God Doing? Satan's Conflict with God: Study Guide. Renald E. Showers. 48p. 1983. pap. 3.50 (ISBN 0-87213-785-6). Loizeaux.
What On Earth? Making Personal Decisions on Controversial Issues. Harvey Seifert. (Orig.). 1986. pap. 7.25 (ISBN 0-9613222-1-7, CS1014); pap. text ed. 7.25. General Board.
What Only a Mother Can Tell You about Having a Baby. K. C. Cole. 320p. 1986. pap. 3.95 (ISBN 0-425-09688-2). Berkley Pub.
What Order? Barbara Gregorich. Ed. by Joan Hoffman. (Get Ready! Bks.). (Illus.). 32p. (ps). 1983. wkbk. 1.95 (ISBN 0-938256-61-0). Sch Zone Pub Co.
What Parents Need to Know about Marijuana. 24p. pap. 1.50 (ISBN 0-89486-171-9). Hazelden.
What Paul Really Said about Women. John T. Bristow. LC 87-46200. 112p. 1988. 12.95 (ISBN 0-317-67244-4, HarpR). Har-Row.
What People Say. 5th ed. Kathryn A. Ordman & Mary P. Ralli. LC 76-6143. 1976. pap. text ed. 9.75 (ISBN 0-88200-073-X, B0990). Alexander Graham.
What People Say They Do with Words. Jef Verschueren. Ed. by Roy O. Freedle. LC 85-6211. (Advances in Discourse Processes Ser.: Vol. 14). 224p. 1985. text ed. 45.00 (ISBN 0-89391-196-8); pap. text ed. 29.50 (ISBN 0-89391-197-6). Ablex Pub.
What Pet Will I Get? Susan M. Drawbaugh. LC 77-83881. (gr. 1-3). 1977. 7.95 (ISBN 0-89430-017-2). Palos Verdes.
What Philosophy Can Do. John Wilson. LC 86-3413. 220p. 1986. 23.50x (ISBN 0-389-20622-9); pap. 9.95x (ISBN 0-389-20623-7). B&N Imports.
What Philosophy Is. A. O'Hear. 320p. 1985. text ed. 32.50x (ISBN 0-391-03354-9); pap. text ed. 9.95x (ISBN 0-391-03355-7). Humanities.
What Plato Said. Paul Shorey. LC 33-11964. (Midway Reprint Ser.). pap. 160.00 (2026743). Bks Demand UMI.
What Poetry Is. Harry Mulisch. Ed. by Stanley H. Barkan. Tr. by Claire Nicolas White. (Cross-Cultural Review Chapbook 9). 40p. (Dutch & Eng.). 1981. pap. 3.50 (ISBN 0-89304-808-9). Cross Cult.
What Political Economy Is All about: An Exposition & Critique. Ezra Mishan. LC 82-12880. 256p. 1982. 42.50 (ISBN 0-521-25072-2); pap. 12.95 (ISBN 0-521-27195-9). Cambridge U Pr.
What Present-Day Theologians Are Thinking. rev. ed. Daniel D. Williams. LC 78-16410. 1978. Repr. of 1959 ed. lib. bdg. 35.00 (ISBN 0-313-20587-6, WIWP). Greenwood.
What Price Compensation, Vol. 9. GAP Committee on Psychiatry in Industry. LC 77-80351. (Report: No. 99). 1977. pap. 8.95 (ISBN 0-87630-367-X, Pub. by GAP). Brunner-Mazel.
What Price Democracy? Politics, Markets, & America's Schools. John E. Chubb & Terry M. Moe. 196p. 1988. 28.95t (ISBN 0-8157-1410-6); pap. 10.95t (ISBN 0-8157-1409-2). Brookings.
What Price Food? Agricultural Price Policies in Developing Countries. Paul Streeten. 200p. 1987. 35.00 (ISBN 0-312-00739-6). St Martin.
What Price Food? Agricultural Price Policies in Developing Countries. Paul Streeten. LC 88-47773. 128p. 1988. pap. 7.95x (ISBN 0-8014-9533-4). Cornell U Pr.
What Price Glory? Helen Morgan. 1971. pap. 2.50 (ISBN 0-87508-598-9). Chr Lit.
What Price Incentives? Economists & the Environment. Steven Kelman. LC 81-7883. 170p. 1981. 24.95 (ISBN 0-86569-082-0). Auburn Hse.
What Price Israel? Alfred M. Lilienthal. 274p. 1969. Repr. of 1953 ed. 9.00 (ISBN 0-88728-092-7). Inst Palestine.
What Price Love. Alice L. Covert. (Orig.). 1979. pap. 2.25 (ISBN 0-89083-491-1). Zebra.
What Price Mink? Edward J. Ohanian. (Illus.). 240p. (Orig.). 1983. pap. 9.95 (ISBN 0-317-13105-2). Ohanian.
What Price PACS? Frank J. Sorauf. (Report of the Twentieth Century Fund on Political Action Committees). 129p. (Orig.). 1984. pap. text ed. 10.00x (ISBN 0-87078-152-9). Priority Pr Pubns.
What Price Revolution. David J. Krichevsky. LC 76-18448. 175p. (YA) (gr. 9-12). 1976. 8.95 (ISBN 0-87881-052-8). Mojave Bks.
What Price Unemployment? Robert Miller & John B. Wood. (Institute of Economic Affairs, Hobart Papers Ser.: No. 92). pap. 6.95 technical (ISBN 0-255-36149-1). Transatl Arts.
What Price Vigilance? The Burdens of National Defense. Bruce M. Russett. LC 75-119475. (Yale Fastback Ser.: No. YF-5). (Illus.). pap. 68.50 (ISBN 0-317-09345-2, 2022036). Bks Demand UMI.
What Printers Need to Know about Digitization. 36p. Date not set. 50.00 (ISBN 0-318-21982-4, P211). NAPL.
What Prize Awaits Us: Letters from Guatemala. Bernice Kita. 200p. (Orig.). 1988. 17.95 (ISBN 0-88344-374-0); pap. 8.95 (ISBN 0-88344-273-6). Orbis Bks.
What Process Is Due? Courts & Science-Policy Disputes. David M. O'Brien. LC 87-43100. 190p. 1987. text ed. 18.50 (ISBN 0-87154-623-X). Russell Sage.
What 'Progress & Poverty' Did for Me. Francis Neilson. 1979. lib. bdg. 39.00 (ISBN 0-685-96647-X). Revisionist Pr.
What Prometheus Began: Challenge of Technology in the Third World. D. E. Palaith. LC 75-14395. 1975. 4.00 (ISBN 0-686-11967-3). Bks Intl DH-TE.
What Proper Person? H. H. Huxley. 64p. 1984. 12.50 (ISBN 0-86292-109-0, Pub. by Bristol Classical UK). Focus Info Gr.
What Psychology Knows That. Coleman & Freedman. 1986. pap. 6.95 (ISBN 0-86616-011-6). Greene.
What Real Socialism Means to the People. R. Belousov. 261p. 1982. pap. 2.95 (ISBN 0-8285-2300-2, Pub. by Progress Pubs USSR). Imported Pubns.
What Real Socialism Means to the People. R. Belousov. 262p. 1982. 7.50x (ISBN 0-317-53801-2, Pub. by Collets (UK)). State Mutual Bk.
What Really Happened to the Class of '65. Michael Medved & David Wallechinsky. 1976. 10.00 (ISBN 0-394-40074-7). Random.
What Really Happened to the Dinosaurs? Mark Dinsmore. (Illus.). 24p. (ps-2). 1988. pap. 5.95 (ISBN 0-89051-142-X). Master Bks.
What Really Happened When Christ Died. M. H. Dinsmore. LC 79-52539. 1979. pap. 4.95 (ISBN 0-89636-025-3). Accent Bks.
What Really Helps (Or Hurts) the Company's Bottom Line? 1983. incl. audio tape 30.00 (ISBN 0-318-19180-6). Assn Equip Distrs.
What Really Matters. Eugenia Price. 160p. 1985. pap. 2.95 (ISBN 0-515-08989-3). Jove Pubns.
What Reason Was. John Riley. 1970. 4.00 (ISBN 0-685-78922-5, Pub. by Grosseteste); sewn in wrappers 2.00 (ISBN 0-685-78923-3). Small Pr Dist.
What Religion Is in the Words of Vivekananda. Swami Vivekananda. Ed. by John Yale. pap. 5.95 (ISBN 0-87481-213-5). Vedanta Pr.
What Research Says to the Middle Level Practitioner. J. Howard Johnston & Glenn C. Markle. 103p. 1986. 8.00 (ISBN 0-318-23123-9). Natl Middle Schl.
What Research Says to the Science Teacher, Vol. 1. Ed. by Mary B. Rowe. Incl. What Research Says to the Science Teacher, Vol. 2. Ed. by Mary B. Rowe. (Orig.). 1979. pap. 7.00 (ISBN 0-87355-013-7); What Research Says to the Science Teacher, Vol. 3. Ed. by Norris C. Harms & Robert E. Yager. (Orig.). 1981. pap. 7.00 (ISBN 0-87355-018-8); What Research Says to the Science Teacher, Vol. 4. Ed. by Robert E. Yager. 107p. 1982. pap. 7.00. 1978. pap. 7.00 (ISBN 0-87355-009-9). Natl Sci Tchrs.
What Research Says to the Science Teacher, Vol. 2 see What Research Says to the Science Teacher.
What Research Says to the Science Teacher, Vol. 3 see What Research Says to the Science Teacher.
What Research Says to the Science Teacher, Vol. 4 see What Research Says to the Science Teacher.
What Return Can I Make? The Dimensions of the Christian Experience. M. Scott Peck et al. LC 85-11945. 96p. 1985. 24.95 (ISBN 0-317-38030-3). S&S.
What Rhymes With Cancer? Harry Brander. LC 82-81363. (Illus.). 54p. 1982. pap. 3.00 (ISBN 0-89823-038-1). New Rivers Pr.
What Right to Strike? Arthur Shenfield. (Hobart Paperback Ser.: No. 106). 64p. (Orig.). 1986. pap. text ed. 7.50x (ISBN 0-255-36190-4, Pub. by Inst Econ Affairs UK). Transatl Arts.
What Role for Government? Lessons from Policy Research. Ed. by Richard F. Zeckhauser & Derek Leebaert. LC 82-21074. (Duke Press Policy Studies). (Illus.). x, 365p. 1983. 38.75 (ISBN 0-8223-0481-3). Duke.
What Roosevelt Thought: The Social & Political Ideas of Franklin D. Roosevelt. Thomas H. Greer. xv, 244p. 1958. 5.00 (ISBN 0-87013-034-X). Mich St U Pr.
What Rules America? James W. Lamare. 203p. 1988. pap. text ed. 16.50 (ISBN 0-314-64228-5). West Pub.
What Sadie Sang. Eve Rice. LC 75-33244. (Illus.). 32p. (ps-1). 1983. 10.25 (ISBN 0-688-02179-4); PLB 10.88 (ISBN 0-688-02181-6). Greenwillow.
What Sayeth the Law: The Treatment of Slaves & Free Blacks in the State & Local Courts of Tennessee. Arthur F. Howington. LC 86-4652. (American Legal & Constitutional History Ser.). 1986. 45.00 (ISBN 0-8240-8273-7). Garland Pub.
What Schools Are For. John I. Goodlad. LC 79-54644. (Foundation Monograph Ser.). 136p. 1979. pap. 5.50 (ISBN 0-87367-422-7). Phi Delta Kappa.
What Science Stands For. J. B. Orr et al. LC 72-134157. (Essay Index Reprint Ser). 1937. 12.00 (ISBN 0-8369-1938-6). Ayer Co Pubs.
What Scripture Says about Healing. David E. Rosage. 72p. (Orig.). 1988. pap. 5.95 (ISBN 0-89283-600-8). Servant.
What Seas What Shores. Cornelia Veenendaal. LC 84-51671. (Chapbook Ser.: No. 6). 64p. (Orig.). 1984. pap. 5.95 (ISBN 0-937672-15-7). Rowan Tree.
What Shall I Be? V. Mayakovsky. 32p. 1981. pap. 2.70 (ISBN 0-8285-2139-5, Pub. by Progress Pubs USSR). Imported Pubns.
What Shall I Do with This? Margaret Hutchings. (gr. 4-7). 1965. 3.95 (ISBN 0-8008-8231-8). Taplinger.
What Shall the Public Schools Do for the Feeble Minded? G. P. Davies. (Harvard Studies in Education: Vol. 10, Pt. 1). 1927. pap. 19.00 (ISBN 0-384-11005-3). Johnson Repr.
What Shall This Man Do? Watchman Nee. 1965. pap. 2.95 (ISBN 0-87508-427-3). Chr Lit.
What Shall This Man Do? Watchman Nee. 1978. pap. 4.50 (ISBN 0-8423-7910-X). Tyndale.
What Shall We Defend? Denham Sutcliffe. Ed. by Harley Henry. 92p. 1973. pap. 1.50 (ISBN 0-911028-24-2). Newberry.
What Shall We Do in a Hungry World? Robert Parham. 96p. (Orig.). 1988. pap. 4.95 (ISBN 0-936625-46-5, New Hope AL). Womans Mission Union.
What Shall We Do Today? Delphine Evans. (Illus.). 128p. (ps). 1987. 13.95 (ISBN 0-09-160400-1, Pub. by Century Hutchinson). David & Charles.
What Shall We Do with Our Daughters? Boston 1883. Mary A. Livermore. Ed. by Sheila M. Rothman & David J. Rothman. (Women & Children First Ser.). 208p. 1986. 30.00 (ISBN 0-8240-7663-X). Garland Pub.
What Shall We Do with the Children? Catherine Kiddle. 109p. 1985. 25.00x (ISBN 0-907349-05-6, Pub by Spindlewood); pap. 19.00x (ISBN 0-907349-10-2). State Mutual Bk.
What Shall We Do Without Us? The Voice & Vision of Kenneth Patchen. Kenneth Patchen. LC 84-4891. (Illus.). 112p. (Orig.). 1984. 25.00 (ISBN 0-87156-843-8); pap. 12.95 (ISBN 0-87156-818-7). Sierra.
What Shall We Draw? Adrian Hill. (Illus.). 80p. (Orig.). 1986. pap. 7.95 (ISBN 0-7137-1829-3, Pub. by Blandford Pr England). Sterling.
What Shall We Name the Baby. Ed. by Winthrop Ames. (Illus.). 1959. pap. 5.95 (ISBN 0-671-81210-6, Fireside). S&S.
What Shall We Name the Baby? Ed. by Winthrop Ames. pap. 3.50 (ISBN 0-671-54152-8). PB.
What Shape Is She In? A Guide to the Surveying of Boats. Alan Vaitses. LC 84-48689. (Illus.). 176p. 1985. 12.95 (ISBN 0-87742-192-7). Intl Marine.
What She Means. Clayton Eshleman. LC 78-7502. 180p. 1978. pap. 6.00 (ISBN 0-87685-346-7). Black Sparrow.
What She Told Him. Carolyn Doty. 312p. 1985. 16.95 (ISBN 0-670-71087-3). Viking.
What Should Banks Do? Robert E. Litan. LC 87-18235. 207p. 1987. 26.95 (ISBN 0-8157-5270-9); pap. 9.95t (ISBN 0-8157-5269-5). Brookings.
What Should Be Taxed: Income or Expenditure? Ed. by Joseph A. Pechman. LC 79-22733. (Studies of Government Finance). 332p. 1980. 31.95 (ISBN 0-8157-6966-0); pap. 11.95 (ISBN 0-8157-6965-2). Brookings.
What Should Economists Do? James Buchanan. LC 79-19511. 1979. 8.00 (ISBN 0-913966-64-9, Liberty Pr); pap. 3.50 (ISBN 0-913966-65-7). Liberty Fund.
What Should I Do? Learning to Make Choices. Roxane B. Kunz & Judy H. Swenson. LC 85-25344. (Understanding Pressure Ser.). (Illus.). 48p. (gr. 2-6). 1986. lib. bdg. 8.95 (ISBN 0-87518-325-5). Dillon.
What Should I Do? Safety & Emergency Care Handbook. rev. ed. Judith K. Schneider et al. (Competent Caregiver Ser.). (Illus.). 63p. 1986. pap. text ed. 6.95 (ISBN 0-944454-00-3); wkbk. 3.95 (ISBN 0-944454-07-0); evaluation exercises 2.95 (ISBN 0-944454-08-9). CAPE Center.
What Should I Eat? (Nutrition Information Resource Ser.). 8p. (Avail. in Span.). 1975. pap. 1.00 (ISBN 0-686-35883-X). Soc Nutrition Ed.
What Should I Teach? The Challenge & Demands of Authentic Catechesis. Thomas M. Martin. 1988. pap. 8.95 (ISBN 0-8091-2957-4). Paulist Pr.
What Should Political Theory Be Now? Ed. by John S. Nelson. LC 82-19167. (SUNY Series in Political Theory: Contemporary Issues). 607p. 1984. 49.50 (ISBN 0-87395-694-X); pap. 16.95 (ISBN 0-87395-695-8). State U NY Pr.
What Should We Be Teaching in the Social Studies? Ed. by Richard E. Gross & Thomas L. Dynneson. LC 83-61786. (Fastback Ser.: No. 199). 50p. 1983. pap. 0.90 (ISBN 0-87367-199-6). Phi Delta Kappa.
What Should We Do about Davey? Julius Fast. 248p. 1988. 16.95x (ISBN 0-312-00698-5, Pub. by Thomas Dunne Bks). St Martin.
What Should We Teach & How Should We Teach It? Aims & Purpose of Higher Learning. Patrick Nuttgens. 100p. 1988. text ed. 20.00 (ISBN 0-7045-3092-9, Pub. by Gower Pub England). Gower Pub Co.
What Should You Do When...? Amy C. Bahr. LC 85-80574. (It's OK to Say No Picture Bks.). (Illus.). 32p. (ps-2). 1986. 4.95 (ISBN 0-448-15327-0, G&D). Putnam Pub Group.
What So Proudly We Hail: All about Our American Flag, Monuments & Symbols. Maymie R. Krythe. LC 68-15993. (YA) 1968. (HarpT); lib. bdg. 9.97 (ISBN 0-06-012464-4). Har-Row.
What So Proudly We Hailed. Raymond Holden. 72p. 1976. 7.95 (ISBN 0-914378-17-1). Countryman.
What Social Classes Owe to Each Other. William G. Sumner. LC 70-172234. (Right Wing Individualist Tradition in America Ser). 1972. Repr. of 1883 ed. 17.00 (ISBN 0-405-00443-5). Ayer Co Pubs.
What Social Classes Owe to Each Other. William G. Sumner. 1947. pap. 4.95 (ISBN 0-87004-166-5). Caxton.
What Social Classes Owe to Each Other. William G. Sumner. 1925. 16.00x (ISBN 0-686-83855-6). Elliots Bks.
What Socrates Began: An Examination of the Intellect, Vol. 1. Libby G. Cohen. (Orig.). 1988. pap. write for info. (ISBN 0-939561-01-8). Univ South ME.
What Sort of People Should There Be? Jonathan Glover. 192p. 1984. pap. 6.95 (ISBN 0-14-022224-3, Pelican). Penguin.
What Southern Catholics Need to Know about Evangelical Religion. Richard Tristano. 1984. pap. 3.00x (ISBN 0-914422-14-6). Glenmary Res Ctr.
What Spot? Crosby Bonsall. LC 63-8005. (Trophy I Can Read Bks.). (Illus.). 64p. (gr. k-3). 1980. pap. 3.50 (ISBN 0-06-444027-3, Trophy). HarpJ.
What Spot? Crosby N. Bonsall. LC 63-8005. (Harper I Can Read Bks.). (Illus.). 64p. (gr. k-3). 1963. PLB 10.89 (ISBN 0-06-020611-X). HarpJ.
What Stanley Knew. Hiawyn Oram. (Illus.). 32p. (gr. k-3). 1987. 12.95 (ISBN 0-86264-044-X, Pub. by Century Hutchinson). David & Charles.
What Stories Are: Narrative Theory & Interpretation. Thomas M. Leitch. LC 85-43559. 232p. 1986. 22.95x (ISBN 0-271-00431-2). Pa St U Pr.
What Style Is It? A Guide to American Architecture. 2nd ed. John Poppeliers et al. LC 83-19278. (Building Watchers Ser.). (Illus.). 112p. 1984. pap. 7.95 (ISBN 0-89133-116-6). Preservation Pr.
What Tabbit the Rabbit Found. Jean L. Latham. LC 73-20395. (Easy Venture Ser.). (Illus.). 32p. (gr. k-2). 1974. PLB 6.69 (ISBN 0-8116-6052-4). Garrard.
What Teenagers Are Saying about Drugs & Alcohol. Chris Lutes. 256p. (YA) (gr. 7 up). 1988. pap. 6.95 (ISBN 0-8423-7939-8). Tyndale.
What Teenagers Want to Know. Shideler Harpe & Wesley W. Hall. (Illus.). 1988. pap. 2.99. Budlong.
What Teenagers Want to Know about Sex. Boston Children's Hospital. LC 87-36680. 181p. (gr. 7 up). 1988. 16.95 (ISBN 0-316-25063-5). Little.
What the AFS Literature Says About...Gating & Risering of Copper-Base Alloys. 137p. 1987. looseleaf binder 60.00 (ISBN 0-317-59873-2, LS5). Am Foundrymen.
What the AFS Literature Says About...Gas Defects in Gray & Ductile Iron Castings. 243p. 1987. looseleaf binder 100.00 (ISBN 0-317-59871-6, LS4). Am Foundrymen.
What the AFS Literature Says About...Gas Porosity in Aluminum Castings. 131p. 1987. looseleaf binder 60.00 (ISBN 0-317-59870-8, LS3). Am Foundrymen.
What the AFS Literature Says About...Inclusions in Cast Iron. 112p. 1987. looseleaf binder 50.00 (ISBN 0-317-59866-X, LS1). Am Foundrymen.
What the AFS Literature Says About...Inclusions in Steel. 159p. 1987. looseleaf binder 70.00 (ISBN 0-317-59868-6, LS2). Am Foundrymen.
What the AFS Literature Says About...Sand Reclamation. 142p. 1987. 70.00 (ISBN 0-317-59876-7, LS7). Am Foundrymen.

What They Said in 1970: The Standard Source Book for the World's Spoken Opinion. Ed. by Alan F. Pater & Jason R. Pater. LC 74-111080. (Second Annual Vol.). 1971. 17.50 (ISBN 0-9600252-3-5). Monitor.

What They Said in 1971: The Standard Source Book for the World's Spoken Opinion. Ed. by Alan F. Pater & Jason R. Pater. LC 74-111080. (Third Annual Vol.). 1972. 17.50 (ISBN 0-9600252-4-3). Monitor.

What They Said in 1972: The Standard Source Book for the Worlds Spoken Opinion. Ed. by Alan F. Pater & Jason R. Pater. LC 74-111080. (Fourth Annual Vol.). 1973. buckram bdg. 17.50 (ISBN 0-9600252-5-1). Monitor.

What They Said in 1973: The Standard Source Book for the World's Spoken Opinion. Ed. by Alan F. Pater & Jason R. Pater. LC 74-111080. (Fifth Annual Vol.). 1974. 17.50 (ISBN 0-9600252-6-X). Monitor.

What They Said in 1974. Ed. by Alan F. Pater & Jason R. Pater. LC 74-111080. (Sixth Annual Vol.). 640p. 1975. lib. bdg. 17.50 (ISBN 0-9600252-7-8). Monitor.

What They Said in 1975. Ed. by Alan F. Pater & Jason R. Pater. LC 74-111080. (Seventh annual vol.). 1976. 17.50 (ISBN 0-9600252-8-6). Monitor.

What They Said in 1976. Ed. by Alan F. Pater & Jason R. Pater. LC 74-111080. (Eighth Annual Vol.). 1977. 19.50 (ISBN 0-9600252-9-4). Monitor.

What They Said in 1977. Ed. by Alan F. Pater & Jason R. Pater. LC 74-111080. (Ninth Annual Vol.). 1978. lib. bdg. 19.50 (ISBN 0-917734-01-7). Monitor.

What They Said in 1978. Ed. by Alan F. Pater & Jason R. Pater. LC 74-111080. (Tenth Annual Vol.). 1979. 19.50 (ISBN 0-917734-02-5). Monitor.

What They Said in 1981: The Yearbook of Spoken Opinion. Ed. by Alan F. Pater & Jason R. Pater. LC 74-111080. (Thirteenth Annual Vol.). 1982. 27.50 (ISBN 0-917734-06-8). Monitor.

What They Said in 1982: The Yearbook of World Opinion, Vol. 14. Ed. by Alan F. Pater & Jason R. Pater. LC 74-111080. 1983. 27.95 (ISBN 0-917734-08-4). Monitor.

What They Said in 1985: The Yearbook of World Opinion, Vol. 17. Ed. by Alan F. Pater & Jason R. Pater. LC 74-111080. 1986. 35.00 (ISBN 0-917734-13-0). Monitor.

What They Said in 1987: The Yearbook of World Opinion, Vol. 19. Ed. by Alan F. Pater & Jason R. Pater. LC 74-111080. 600p. 1988. 37.50 (ISBN 0-917734-17-3). Monitor.

What Time Does. Klaus Wagn. 1976. 4.50 (ISBN 0-686-17603-0). Caann Verlag.

What Time Is Grandma Coming? (Surprise Bks.). (Illus.). 22p. (ps-1). 1984. 5.95 (ISBN 0-8431-0645-X). Price Stern.

What Time Is It? Judith Grey. LC 81-5113. (Illus.). 32p. (gr. k-2). 1981. PLB 9.89 (ISBN 0-89375-509-5); pap. text ed. 1.95 (ISBN 0-89375-510-9). Troll Assocs.

What Time Is It? Elisabeth Ivanovsky. (Picture-Word Boards Bks.). (Illus.). (ps). 1985. bds. 3.98 (ISBN 0-517-47343-7). Outlet Bk Co.

What Time Is It? Illus. by Tadasu Izawa & Shigemi Hijikata. (Puppet Storybooks). (Illus.). 18p. (gr. k-2). 1981. (G&D); PLB 2.99 (ISBN 0-448-03701-7). Putnam Pub Group.

What Time Is It? Ralph C. Martin. 32p. (Orig.). 1984. pap. text ed. 1.25 (ISBN 0-89283-256-8). Servant.

What Time Is It? Lizzy Pearl. LC 87-9093. (Turn the Dial Board Bk.). (Illus.). 10p. (ps-k). 1988. 4.95 (ISBN 0-8037-0480-1, 0481-140). Dial Bks Young.

What Time Is It? Tony Tallarico. (Tote Bks.). (Illus.). 12p. (gr. 3-8). 1982. pap. 3.50 (ISBN 0-89828-302-7). Tuffy Bks.

What Time Is It Around the World? Hans Baumann. LC 75-24710. (Illus.). (gr. k-5). 1979. 6.95 (ISBN 0-87592-061-6). Scroll Pr.

What Time Is It, Little Rabbit? J. P. Miller. LC 85-2225. (Knee-High Books). (Illus.). 24p. (ps-1). 1985. 3.95 (ISBN 0-394-87533-8, BYR); lib. bdg. 4.99 (ISBN 0-394-97533-2). Random.

What Time Is It, Mrs. Bear? Julia Killingback. LC 84-6664. (Illus.). 24p. (ps-k). 1985. 6.25 (ISBN 0-688-04076-4, Morrow Junior Books). Morrow.

What Time Is It, Nana? Beverly Andrews. 136p. 1982. 7.50 (ISBN 0-682-49795-9). Exposition-Phoenix.

What Time Is This Place? Kevin Lynch. LC 72-7059. 1972. pap. 11.95x (ISBN 0-262-62032-4). MIT Pr.

What Time of Night Is It? Mary Stolz. LC 80-7917. (Ursula Nordstrom Bks.). 224p. (gr. 6 up). 1981. PLB 12.89 (ISBN 0-06-026062-9). HarpJ.

What Time's the Midnight Buffet? 2nd ed. Ken Noyle. LC 81-82179. (Illus.). 72p. (Orig.). 1982. pap. 4.00 (ISBN 0-940324-00-8). One Thousand Ways.

What to Do about AIDS: Physicians & Mental Health Professionals Discuss the Issues. Ed. by Leon McKusick. 224p. 1986. 20.00 (ISBN 0-520-05935-2); pap. 9.95 (ISBN 0-520-05936-0). U of Cal Pr.

What to Do about Equal Pay for Women in the United Kingdom. G. L. Buckingham. 144p. 1973. 17.95 (ISBN 0-8464-0968-2). Beekman Pubs.

What to Do about Japan. C. Fred Bergsten. 35p. 1982. pap. 1.50 (ISBN 0-317-65769-0). Japan Soc.

What to Do about Performance Appraisal. Rev. ed. Marion S. Kellogg. LC 75-8604. pap. 55.30 (ISBN 0-317-26907-0, 2023555). Bks Demand UMI.

What to Do about Performance Appraisal. rev. ed. Marion S. Kellogg. LC 75-8604. 224p. 1975. 14.95 (ISBN 0-8144-5389-9). AMACOM.

What to Do about Worry. J. Adams. 1972. pap. 0.75 (ISBN 0-87552-065-0); pap. 7.50 set of 12 (ISBN 0-87552-084-7). Presby & Reformed.

What to do about Youth Dropouts? A Summary of Solutions. Margaret T. Orr. Ed. by Mary L. O'Connor. 32p. (Orig.). 1987. pap. 5.00 (ISBN 0-943567-00-9). SeedCo.

What to Do after You Turn off the TV: Fresh Ideas for Enjoying Family Time. Frances M. Lappe. (Orig.). 1985. pap. 7.95 (ISBN 0-345-31660-6). Ballantine.

What to Do Before the Books Arrive. Jean D. Maculaitis & Mona Scheraga. (Illus.). 173p. 1981. pap. text ed. 8.95x (ISBN 0-88084-008-0). Alemany Pr.

What to Do? Creative Problem-Solving Level A. Kathryn T. Hegeman. (gr. 1-2). 1984. pap. 12.95 tchr's. manual (ISBN 0-89824-045-X); PLB 4.95 wkbk (ISBN 0-89824-043-3). Trillium Pr.

What to Do? Creative Problem-Solving Level B. Kathryn T. Hegeman. (gr. 3-4). 1985. pap. 12.95 tchr's. manual (ISBN 0-89824-088-3); PLB 4.95 wkbk (ISBN 0-89824-089-1). Trillium Pr.

What to Do for the Gifted Few. Judith S. Wooster. (Illus.). 1978. 2.95 (ISBN 0-914634-56-9). DOK Pubs.

What to Do If You or Someone You Know Is under 18 & Pregnant. Arlene K. Richards & Irene Willis. LC 82-12698. (Illus.). 256p. 1983. 10.88 (ISBN 0-688-51961-X); pap. 7.00 (ISBN 0-688-01044-X). Lothrop.

What to Do in & Around Dublin. Hugh Oram. (Illus.). 72p. (Orig.). 1984. pap. 5.95 (ISBN 0-86281-134-1, Pub. by Appletree Pr). Irish Bks Media.

What to Do, Know & Expect When a Loved One Dies. Susan K. Thomas. 138p. (Orig.). 1984. pap. 5.95 (ISBN 0-9613660-0-1). S K Thomas.

What to Do on a Jewish Holiday? Sol Scharfstein. (gr. 3-5). 1985. 6.95 (ISBN 0-88125-170-4). Ktav.

What to Do on Thursday. Jay E. Adams. 1982. pap. 3.95 (ISBN 0-87552-074-X). Presby & Reformed.

What to Do on Thursday: A Layman's Guide to the Practical Use of the Scriptures. Jay E. Adams. 144p. 1982. pap. 3.95 (ISBN 0-8010-0188-9). Baker Bk.

What to Do till Jesus Comes. Knofel Staton. LC 81-14594. 112p. 1983. pap. 2.25 (ISBN 0-87239-481-6, 41016). Standard Pub.

What to Do until the Counselor Comes. rev. ed. S. Norman Feingold & Shirley Levin. (Careers in Depth Ser.). 1983. 9.97. Rosen Group.

What to Do until the Doctor Calls Back. Gloria Dawley & James Sorger. Ed. by Kathleen M. Guindon. (Illus.). 96p. (Orig.). 1982. 10.95 (ISBN 0-942696-01-8); pap. 5.95 (ISBN 0-942696-00-X). Transmediacom.

What to Do When & Why: At Parties, at Home, at School, in Your Growing World. Marjabelle Y. Stewart & Ann Buchwald. 1988. 12.95 (ISBN 0-88331-105-4). Luce.

What to Do When Cable Comes to Town: A Handbook for Local Officials. 115p. 1980. spiral 50.00 (ISBN 0-941888-06-1). Comm Media.

What to Do When Cable Comes to Town: Some Guidelines for Citizen Action. Ben Park. 30p. 1980. pap. write for info. Comm Media.

What to Do When Faith Seems Weak & Victory Lost. Kenneth E. Hagin. 1979. pap. 3.50 (ISBN 0-89276-501-1). Hagin Ministries.

What to Do When Gravity Fails. Dan Rattiner. LC 83-63248. (Illus.). 64p. 1984. pap. 4.95 (ISBN 0-932966-55-1). Permanent Pr.

What to Do When He Won't Change. Dan Kiley. 1988. pap. 4.95 (ISBN 0-449-21616-0, Crest). Fawcett.

What to Do When He Won't Change: Getting What You Need from the Man You Love. Dan Kiley. 244p. 1987. 16.95 (ISBN 0-399-13324-0, Putnam). Putnam Pub Group.

What to Do When Leaded Fuel Becomes Extinct. Timothy P. Banse. (Illus.). 64p. 1986. pap. 4.95 (ISBN 0-934523-21-5). Middle Coast Pub.

What to Do When Mom or Dad Says "Get Good Grades!". Joy W. Berry. LC 81-83789. (Living Skills Survival Series for Kids). (Illus.). 48p. (gr. 3-7). 1982. 4.98 (ISBN 0-941510-01-8). Living Skills.

What to Do When the Dot Hazardous Materials Inspector Calls. Lawrence W. Bierlein. 1986. 24.95 (ISBN 0-940394-20-0). Intereg.

What to Do When the Lights Go On: A Comprehensive Guide to Sixteen Millimeter Films & Related Activities for Children. Maureen Gaffney & Gerry B. Laybourne. (Illus.). 292p. 1981. lib. bdg. 36.00x (ISBN 0-912700-65-3); pap. 30.00x (ISBN 0-912700-69-6). Oryx Pr.

What to Do When the Numbers Are In. Joan DiLeonardi & Patrick Curtis. (Illus.). 175p. 1988. pap. text ed. 11.95 (ISBN 0-8304-1145-3). Nelson-Hall.

What to Do When There's Nothing to Do. Boston Children's Medical Center Staff & Elizabeth Gregg. 1970. pap. 1.25 (ISBN 0-440-19471-7). Dell.

What to Do When You Pray. Lucille Walker. LC 78-60948. 181p. 1983. pap. text ed. 6.95 (ISBN 0-87148-920-1). Pathway Pr.

What to Do When Your Friends Reject Christ. C. S. Lovett. 1966. pap. 4.25 (ISBN 0-938148-06-0). Personal Christianity.

What to Do When Your Mom or Dad Says "Be Prepared". Joy W. Berry. LC 81-83790. (Living Skills Survival Series for Kids). (Illus.). 48p. (gr. 3-7). 1982. 4.98 (ISBN 0-941510-02-6). Living Skills.

What to Do When Your Mom or Dad Says: "Be Careful!". Joy W. Berry. Ed. by Orly Kelley. LC 83-80837. (Living Skills Survival Series for Kids). (Illus.). 48p. (gr. k-6). 4.98 (ISBN 0-941510-12-3). Living Skills.

What to Do When Your Mom or Dad Says: "Be Good!". Joy W. Berry. Ed. by Orly Kelley. LC 83-80509. (Living SKills Survival Series for Kids). (Illus.). 48p. (gr. k-6). 4.98 (ISBN 0-941510-15-8). Living Skills.

What to Do When Your Mom or Dad Says: "Get Dressed!". Joy W. Berry. Ed. by Orly Kelley. LC 83-80839. (Living Skills Survival Series for Kids). (Illus.). 48p. (gr. k-6). 4.98 (ISBN 0-941510-17-4). Living Skills.

What to Do When Your Mom or Dad Says: "Go to Bed!". Joy W. Berry. Ed. by Orly Kelley. LC 83-80508. (Living Skills Survival Series for Kids). (Illus.). 48p. (gr. k-6). 4.98 (ISBN 0-941510-16-6). Living Skills.

What to Do When Your Mom Or Dad Says..."Be Good!". Joy W. Berry. LC 83-80000509. (Survival Series for Kids). (Illus.). 48p. (gr. 3 up). 1983. 11.93 (ISBN 0-516-02578-3). Childrens.

What to Do When Your Mom or Dad Says..."Be Prepared!". Joy W. Berry. LC 81-83790. (Survival Series for Kids). (Illus.). 48p. (gr. 3 up). 1982. lib. bdg. 11.93 (ISBN 0-516-02566-X). Childrens.

What to Do When Your Mom or Dad Says..."We Can't Afford It!". Joy W. Berry. Ed. by Orly Kelley. LC 83-80845. (Living Skills Survival Series for Kids). (Illus.). 48p. (gr. k-6). 4.98 (ISBN 0-941510-24-7). Living Skills.

What to Do When Your Mom or Dad Says..."Take Care of Your Clothes!". Joy W. Berry. LC 82-81201. (Living Skills Survival Series for Kids). (Illus.). 48p. (gr. 3-7). 1982. 4.98 (ISBN 0-941510-05-0). Living Skills.

What to Do When Your Mom or Dad Says..."Take Care of Your Clothes!". Joy W. Berry. LC 82-81201. (Surivial Series for Kids). (Illus.). 48p. (gr. 3 up). 1982. PLB 11.93 (ISBN 0-516-02573-2). Childrens.

What to Do When Your Mom or Dad Says..."Get the Phone!". Joy W. Berry. LC 83-80000507. (Survival Series for Kids). (Illus.). 48p. (gr. 3 up). 1983. 11.93 (ISBN 0-516-02579-1). Childrens.

What to Do When Your Mom or Dad Says..."Get the Phone!". Joy W. Berry. Ed. by Orly Kelley. LC 83-80507. (Living Skills Survival Series for Kids). (Illus.). 48p. (gr. k-6). 4.98 (ISBN 0-941510-13-1). Living Skills.

What to Do When Your Mom or Dad Says..."Get Good Grades!". Joy W. Berry. LC 81-83789. (Survival Series for Kids). (Illus.). 48p. (gr. 3 up). 1982. lib. bdg. 11.93 (ISBN 0-516-02569-4). Childrens.

What to Do When Your Mom or Dad Says..."Go to Bed!". Joy W. Berry. LC 83-80000508. (Survival Series for Kids). (Illus.). 48p. (gr. 3 up). 1983. 11.93 (ISBN 0-516-02580-5). Childrens.

What to Do When Your Mom or Dad Says..."Be Good While You're There". Joy W. Berry. LC 82-81202. (Living Skills Survival Series for Kids). (Illus.). 48p. (gr. 3-7). 1982. 4.98 (ISBN 0-941510-07-7). Living Skills.

What to Do When Your Mom or Dad Says..."Be Good While You're There". Joy W. Berry. LC 82-81202. (Survival Series for Kids). (Illus.). 48p. (gr. 3 up). 1982. PLB 11.93 (ISBN 0-516-02570-8). Childrens.

What to Do When Your Mom or Dad Says..."Don't Hang Around with the Wrong Crowd!". Joy W. Berry. Ed. by Orly Kelly. LC 32-82086. (Living Skills Survival Series for Kids). (Illus.). 48p. (gr. k-6). 1982. 4.98 (ISBN 0-941510-10-7). Living Skills.

What to Do When Your Mom or Dad Says..."Don't Hang Around with the Wrong Crowd!". Joy W. Berry. LC 82-82000086. (Survival Series for Kids). (Illus.). 48p. (gr. 3 up). 1983. 11.93 (ISBN 0-516-02574-0). Childrens.

What to Do When Your Mom or Dad Says..."Help!". Joy W. Berry. Ed. by Orly Kelly. LC 32-32088. (Living Skills Survival Series for Kids). (Illus.). 48p. (gr. k-6). 1982. 4.98 (ISBN 0-941510-09-3). Living Skills.

What to Do When Your Mom or Dad Says..."Help!". Joy W. Berry. LC 82-82000088. (Survival Series for Kids). (Illus.). 48p. (gr. 3 up). 1983. 11.93 (ISBN 0-516-02577-5). Childrens.

What to Do When Your Mom or Dad Says..."Behave in Public!". Joy W. Berry. Ed. by Orly Kelley. LC 83-80842. (Living Skills Survival Series for Kids). (Illus.). 48p. (gr. k-6). 4.98 (ISBN 0-941510-22-0). Living Skills.

What to Do When Your Mom or Dad Says..."Be Kind to Your Guest". Joy W. Berry. LC 82-81203. (Living Skills Survival Series for Kids). (Illus.). 48p. (gr. 3-7). 1982. 4.98 (ISBN 0-941510-06-9). Living Skills.

What to Do When Your Mom or Dad Says..."Be Kind to Your Guest!". Joy W. Berry. LC 82-81203. (Survival Series for Kids). (gr. 3 up). 1982. 11.93 (ISBN 0-516-02571-6). Childrens.

What to Do When Your Mom or Dad Says..."Turn Off the Water & Lights!". Joy W. Berry. Ed. by Orly Kelley. LC 83-80844. (Living Skills Survival Series for Kids). (Illus.). 48p. (gr. k-6). 4.98 (ISBN 0-941510-23-9). Living Skills.

What to Do When Your Mom or Dad Says..."Don't Overdo with Video Games!". Joy W. Berry. Ed. by Orly Kelley. (Living Skills Survival Series for Kids). (Illus.). 48p. (gr. k-6). 4.98 (ISBN 0-941510-25-5). Living Skills.

What to Do When Your Mom or Dad Says..."Do Something Besides Watching TV". Joy W. Berry. Ed. by Orly Kelly et al. LC 82-82087. (Living Skills Survival Series for Kids). (Illus.). 48p. (gr. k-6). 1982. 4.98 (ISBN 0-941510-11-5). Living Skills.

What to Do When Your Mom or Dad Says..."Do Something Besides Watching TV!". Joy W. Berry. LC 82-82000087. (Survival Series for Kids). (Illus.). 48p. (gr. 3 up). 11.93 (ISBN 0-516-02575-9). Childrens.

What to Do When Your Mom or Dad Says..."Don't Slurp Your Soup!". Joy W. Berry. Ed. by Orly Kelley. LC 83-80838. (Living Skills Survival Series for Kids). (Illus.). 48p. (gr. k-6). 4.98 (ISBN 0-941510-20-4). Living Skills.

What to Do When Your Mom or Dad Says..."What Should You Say Dear?" Proper Verbal Responses. Joy W. Berry. LC 83-80000506. (Survival Series for Kids). (Illus.). 48p. (gr. 3 up). 1983. 11.93 (ISBN 0-516-02581-3). Childrens.

What to Do When Your Mom or Dad Says..."Write to Grandma!". Joy W. Berry. Ed. by Orly Kelley. LC 83-80841. (Living Skills Survival Series for Kids). (Illus.). 48p. (gr. k-6). 4.98 (ISBN 0-941510-21-2). Living Skills.

What to Do When Your Mom or Dad Says..."Stand Up Straight!". Joy W. Berry. Ed. by Orly Kelly. LC 83-80843. (Living Skills Survival Series for Kids). (Illus.). 48p. (gr. k-6). 4.98 (ISBN 0-941510-19-0). Living Skills.

What to Do When Your Mom or Dad Says: "What Should You Say, Dear?". Joy W. Berry. Ed. by Orly Kelley. LC 83-80506. (Living Skills Survival Series for Kids). (Illus.). 48p. (gr. k-6). 4.98 (ISBN 0-941510-14-X). Living Skills.

What to Do When Your Mom or Dad Says..."Earn Your Allowance". Joy W. Berry. LC 81-83791. (Living Skills Survival Series for Kids). (Illus.). 48p. (gr. 3-7). 1982. 4.98 (ISBN 0-941510-03-4). Living Skills.

What to Do When Your Mom or Dad Says..."Earn Your Allowance!". Joy W. Berry. LC 81-83791. (Survival Series for Kids). (Illus.). 48p. (gr. 3 up). 1982. lib. bdg. 11.93 (ISBN 0-516-02568-6). Childrens.

What to Do When Your Mom or Dad Says..."Make Your Breakfast & Lunch!". Joy W. Berry. Ed. by Orly Kelley. LC 83-80840. (Living Skills Survival Series for Kids). (Illus.). 48p. (gr. k-6). 4.98 (ISBN 0-941510-18-2). Living Skills.

What to Do When Your Mom or Dad Says..."Do Your Homework!". Joy W. Berry. LC 82-82089. (Living Skills Survival Series for Kids). (Illus.). 48p. (gr. k-6). 1982. 4.98 (ISBN 0-941510-08-5). Living Skills.

What to Do When Your Mom or Dad Says..."Do Your Homework!". Joy W. Berry. LC 82-82000089. (Survival Series for Kids). (Illus.). 48p. (gr. 3 up). 1983. 11.93 (ISBN 0-516-02576-7). Childrens.

What to Do When Your Mom or Dad Says..."Clean Your Room!". Joy W. Berry. LC 82-81200. (Living Skills Survival Series for Kids). (Illus.). 48p. (gr. 3-7). 1982. 4.98 (ISBN 0-941510-00-X). Living Skills.

What to Do When Your Mom or Dad Says..."Clean Your Room!". Joy W. Berry. LC 81-83788. (Survival Series for Kids). (Illus.). 48p. (gr. 3 up). 1982. lib. bdg. 11.93 (ISBN 0-516-02567-8). Childrens.

What to Do When Your Mom or Dad Says..."Clean Yourself Up!". Joy W. Berry. (Living Skills Survival Series for Kids). (Illus.). 48p. (gr. 3-7). 1981. 3.95 (ISBN 0-941510-04-2). Living Skills.

What to Do When Your Mom or Dad Says..."Clean Yourself Up!". Joy W. Berry. LC 82-81200. (Survival Series for Kids). (gr. 3 up). 1982. 11.93 (ISBN 0-516-02572-4). Childrens.

What to Do When Your Son or Daughter Divorces. Inez B. Gottlieb et al. 192p. (Orig.). 1988. pap. 7.95 (ISBN 0-553-34447-1). Bantam.

What to Do With a Squirt of Glue: And Paper, Paint & Scissors, Too! Lori A. Howard. (Illus.). 96p. (gr. k-6). 1987. pap. text ed. 7.95 (ISBN 0-86530-086-0, IP 86-0). Incentive Pubns.

What to Do with Sunday Morning. Harold M. Daniels. LC 78-21040. 132p. 1979. softcover 4.95 (ISBN 0-664-24237-5). Westminster John Knox.

What to Do with the Kids This Year: One Hundred Family Vacation Places with Time Off for You! Jane Wilford & Janet Tice. LC 85-45698. 272p. (Orig.). 1986. pap. 9.95 (ISBN 0-88742-064-8). Globe Pequot.

What to Do with the Rest of Your Life. Catalyst Staff. 1981. pap. 13.95 (ISBN 0-671-25071-X, Touchstone Bks). S&S.

What You Aren't Supposed to Know about Writing & Publishing: An Expose of Editors, Agents, Publishing Houses & More: An Insider's Report. Laurens R. Schwartz. 1988. 14.95 (ISBN 0-944007-03-1). Shapolsky Pubs.
What You Can Believe About Drugs: An Honest & Unhysterical Guide for Teens. Daniel Cohen & Susan Cohen. 156p. (YA) (gr. 7 up). 1988. 12.95 (ISBN 0-87131-527-0). H Holt & Co.
What You Can Do about Health Costs. 10p. 1985. pap. 12.50 pkg. of 10 copies (ISBN 0-89970-263-5, OP-397). AMA.
What You Can Do to Prevent Cancer. Oliver Alabaster. 1985. 17.45 (ISBN 0-671-49537-2). S&S.
What You Can Do with a Word. Dorothy Raymond. 144p. (Orig.). 1981. pap. 8.00 (ISBN 0-87879-269-4). Acad Therapy.
What You Can Say When You Don't Know What to Say: Reaching out to Those Who Hurt. Lauren Littauer Briggs. 176p. (Orig.). 1985. pap. 5.95 (ISBN 0-89081-465-1). Harvest Hse.
What You Can See, You Can Be! David A. Anderson. (Illus.). 48p. (Orig.). (gr. 3-8). 1988. pap. 8.95 (ISBN 0-87516-603-2). DeVorss.
What You Didn't Think to Ask Your Obstetrician: All Your Questions Answered. Raymond Poliakin. (Illus.). 128p. 1987. pap. 7.95 (ISBN 0-8092-4721-6). Contemp Bks.
What You Do If... Jane B. Moncure. LC 85-10418. (Illus.). 32p. (ps-k). 1985. PLB 4.95 (ISBN 0-89693-227-3). Dandelion Hse.
What You Don't Know Can Hurt You. Lester Markel. 1972. 9.50 (ISBN 0-8183-0221-6). Pub Aff Pr.
What You Don't Know Can Hurt You: A Guide to the Medical Literature. A. J. Longley. (Orig.). 1981. pap. 3.00 (ISBN 0-937038-00-8). Star Pr.
What You Get When You Go for It: Startling Accounts from Professional Women about Their Male Colleagues. Beth Milwid. 1987. 17.95 (ISBN 0-396-08905-4). Dodd.
What You Know Might Not be So: Two Hundred Twenty Misinterpretations of Bible Texts Explained. Compiled by David C. Downing. 1987. pap. 8.95 (ISBN 0-8010-2975-9). Baker Bk.
What You Must Know about Home Lenders: Seventeen Answers - the Answer Book, Vol. I. Larry Oxenham. (Illus.). 40p. (Orig.). 1987. pap. 4.75 (ISBN 0-943813-00-X). Page One Pub.
What You Must Know about Social Security & Medicare. Eric Kingson. 112p. 1986. pap. 4.95 (ISBN 0-345-34397-2). Newspaper Ent.
What You Must Know about Social Security & Medicare. Eric R. Kingson. (Illus.). 112p. 1987. pap. 4.95. Pharos Bks NY.
What You Must Know to Get the Job You Want. Kenneth H. Kuehne. LC 83-90472. (Illus.). 160p. 1983. pap. 10.00 (ISBN 0-916041-84-0). Kenco Pub Co.
What You Need to Know about Business, Money & Power. Michael Kidron & Ronald Siegel. 1987. 22.95 (ISBN 0-671-54113-7); pap. 12.95 (ISBN 0-671-54114-5). S&S.
What You Need to Know about Moving--So You Won't Be Misled. Bert C. Kelton. LC 82-72463. (Illus.). 73p. (Orig.). 1982. pap. 5.95 (ISBN 0-9608674-0-6). B & B Pubs.
What You Need to Know about Your Gold & Silver. O. T. Branson. (Illus.). 56p. (Orig.). 1980. pap. 4.95 (ISBN 0-918080-44-4). Treasure Chest.
What You Need to Know When You Buy a Franchise (Plus a Listing of the World's Leading Franchising Companies) 264p. 1987. 4.95 (ISBN 0-317-66127-2). Intl Franchise Assn.
What You Say Is What You Get. Don Gossett. 192p. 1976. pap. 3.95 (ISBN 0-88368-066-1). Whitaker Hse.
What You See Is What You Get. Berneth N. McKercher. (Illus.). 99p. 1972. pap. 3.00x (ISBN 0-87013-166-4). Mich St U Pr.
What You See Is What You Get. Valjean McLenighan. (Illus.). 32p. (gr. 2). 1980. PLB 4.39 (ISBN 0-8136-5084-4, Dist. by Caroline Hse); pap. 1.95 (ISBN 0-8136-5584-6). Modern Curr.
What You Should Know about Acquisitions & Mergers. Milton B. Burstein. LC 72-5483. (Business Almanac Ser.: No. 19). 128p. 1973. lib. bdg. 5.95 (ISBN 0-379-11219-1). Oceana.
What You Should Know about Advertising. I. Joel Amstell. LC 69-19797. (Business Almanac Ser.: No. 17). (Illus.). 83p. 1969. 5.95 (ISBN 0-379-11217-5). Oceana.
What You Should Know about Building Your Mailing Lists. Paul Crown. LC 72-13927. (Business Almanac Ser.: No. 20). 121p. 1973. 5.95 (ISBN 0-379-11220-5). Oceana.
What You Should Know about Business Writing. Robert Koch. LC 67-10893. (Business Almanac Ser.: No. 9). 92p. 1967. 5.95 (ISBN 0-379-11209-4). Oceana.
What You Should Know about Customer Relations. Arthur Einstein & A. W. Einstein, Jr. LC 65-22173. (Busiess Almanac Ser.: No. 4). 1966. 5.95 (ISBN 0-379-11204-3). Oceana.
What You Should Know about Data Processing. John E. Cook. LC 69-19799. (Business Almanac Ser.: No. 15). 90p. 1969. text ed. 5.95 (ISBN 0-379-11215-9). Oceana.
What You Should Know about Direct Mail. H. Hoke. LC 65-22171. (Business Almanac Ser.: No. 2). 91p. 1966. 5.95 (ISBN 0-379-11202-7). Oceana.
What You Should Know about Earthquakes: It Could Save Your Life. Joseph W. Foraker. (Illus.). 64p. (Orig.). 1983. pap. 5.95 (ISBN 0-912287-00-4). SJB Pub Co.
What You Should Know about Emotions & Mental Health. Ed. by Paul R. Keating. LC 74-75985. 128p. 1975. pap. 1.50 (ISBN 0-87983-082-4). Keats.
What You Should Know about Federal Taxes When You Sell Your House. 32p. 1983. 2.00. P-H.
What You Should Know about Gambling. William J. Petersen. LC 74-75984. 128p. 1974. pap. 1.50 (ISBN 0-87983-081-6). Keats.
What You Should Know about Generic Drugs Before You Buy. American Allergy Association Staff. 8p. (Orig.). 1987. pap. 3.00 (ISBN 0-9616708-5-1). Allergy Pubns.
What You Should Know about Ghosts...But Were Afraid to Ask. Norma Edwards. LC 87-72592. 256p. 1988. 16.95 (ISBN 0-944534-00-7). Diamond Stockton.
What You Should Know about Jewish Religion, History, Ethics, & Culture. Sidney L. Markowitz. 226p. 1973. pap. 5.95 (ISBN 0-8065-0028-X, Pub. by Citadel Pr). Lyle Stuart.
What You Should Know about Labor Relations. Julius Spivack. LC 66-24434. (Business Almanac Ser.: No. 8). 89p. 1966. 5.95 (ISBN 0-379-11208-6). Oceana.
What You Should Know about Marriage, Divorce, Annulment, Separation & Community Property in Louisiana. R. Lee Eddy, III. LC 73-91094. 1974. 10.00 (ISBN 0-682-47861-X); pap. 6.00 (ISBN 0-682-47862-8). Exposition-Phoenix.
What You Should Know about Personnel Management. Howard Falberg. LC 68-23567. (Business Almanac Ser.: No. 12). 89p. 1968. 5.95 (ISBN 0-379-11212-4). Oceana.
What You Should Know about Prophecy. C. M. Ward. LC 75-22610. (Radiant Life Ser.). 128p. 1975. pap. 2.50 (ISBN 0-88243-890-5, 02-0890); teacher's guide 3.95 (ISBN 0-88243-164-1, 32-0164). Gospel Pub.
What You Should Know about Public Relations. Edward Starr. LC 68-21536. (Business Almanac Ser.: No. 13). 92p. 1968. 5.95 (ISBN 0-379-11213-2). Oceana.
What You Should Know about Reducing Credit Losses. John H. Burns & John E. Cook. LC 66-25579. (Business Almanac Ser.: No. 10). 96p. 1966. 5.95 (ISBN 0-379-11210-8). Oceana.
What You Should Know about Research Techniques for Retailers. Howard Eilenberg. LC 67-28901. (Business Almanac Series No. 14). 1968. 5.95 (ISBN 0-379-11214-0). Oceana.
What You Should Know about Scientific Management for Small Business. R. Y. Lim. LC 73-1806. (Business Almanac Ser.: No. 22). 128p. 1973. lib. bdg. 5.95 (ISBN 0-379-11222-1). Oceana.
What You Should Know about Selling & Salesmanship. Milton B. Burstein. LC 69-19798. (Business Almanac Ser.: No. 18). 85p. 1969. 5.95 (ISBN 0-379-11218-3). Oceana.
What You Should Know about Small Business Credit & Finance. Eugene H. Fram. LC 65-27748. (Business Almanac Ser.: No. 5). 96p. 1966. 5.95 (ISBN 0-379-11205-1). Oceana.
What You Should Know about Small Business Marketing. Eugene H. Fram. LC 67-28902. (Business Almanac Ser.: No. 11). 96p. 1968. 5.95 (ISBN 0-379-11211-6). Oceana.
What You Should Know about Small Business Management. Donald Grunewald. LC 66-25580. (Business Almanac Ser.: No. 6). 96p. 1966. 5.95 (ISBN 0-379-11206-X). Oceana.
What You Should Know about Taxes & Marital Split-Ups. 36p. 1983. 2.15x. P-H.
What You Should Know about Teaching & Learning Styles. Claudia E. Cornett. LC 82-63062. (Fastback Ser.: No. 191). 50p. 1983. pap. 0.90 (ISBN 0-87367-191-0). Phi Delta Kappa.
What You Should Know about the American Flag. Earl P. Williams, Jr. LC 87-61317. (Illus.). 75p. 1987. pap. 9.95 (ISBN 0-917882-25-3); pap. 5.95 (ISBN 0-317-59836-8). MD Hist Pr.
What You Should Know about the Bible: A Practical Guide to Bible Basics. Stanford Herlick. LC 85-82137. (Illus.). 255p. 1985. 12.50 (ISBN 0-9616026-0-0). FBF Pubns.
What You Should Know about the Foundations of Management. Roy A. Lindberg. LC 73-3319. (Business Almanac Ser.: No. 21). 128p. 1973. lib. bdg. 5.95 (ISBN 0-379-11221-3). Oceana.
What You Should Know about the Golden Dawn. 5yh, rev. ed. Israel Regardie. LC 83-81663. 208p. 1983. pap. 9.95 (ISBN 0-941404-15-3). Falcon Pr Az.
What You Should Know about the Holy Spirit. J. W. Jepson. LC 85-81719. 160p. 1986. pap. 3.95 (ISBN 0-88243-639-2, 02-0639). Gospel Pub.
What You Should Know about Women's Lib. Ed. by Miriam G. Moran. LC 74-75980. 128p. 1974. pap. 1.50 (ISBN 0-87983-084-0). Keats.
What You Should Know about Your Child. Maria Montessori. (Illus.). 155p. 1986. 137.50 (ISBN 0-89920-144-X). Am Inst Psych.
What You Should Know about Your Social Security. 112p. pap. 6.50. Res Inst Am.
What You Should Know Before Going into the Hospital. Opal W. Nelson. pap. 2.95 (ISBN 0-8217-1361-2). Zebra.
What You Should Know If You're Accused of a Crime. Joyce B. David. 32p. (Orig.). 1986. pap. 4.00 (ISBN 0-9617121-0-4). Balaban Pub.
What You Think of Me Is None of My Business. Cole Cole-Whittaker. 1988. pap. 3.95 (ISBN 0-317-68101-X). Berkley Pub.
What You Think of Me Is None of My Business. Terry Cole-Whittaker. LC 79-21739. 1979. 9.95 (ISBN 0-916392-39-2). Oak Tree Pubns.
What You Think of Me Is None of My Business. Terry Cole-Whittaker. 194p. (Orig.). 1982. pap. 9.95 (ISBN 0-86679-002-0). Oak Tree Pubns.
What You Want to Know about Budgerigars. E. Johns. LC 75-12412. (Illus.). 1975. 12.00 (ISBN 0-7091-7058-0). Newbury Bks.
What You Were Never Told about Controlling Your Printer from the TI99-4A. Robert M. McKechnie. 34p. (Orig.). (gr. 8). 1986. pap. text ed. 9.95 (ISBN 0-939577-01-1). McWare Products.
What You Were Never Told about Controlling Your Printer from the Commodore Plus 4. Robert M. McKechnie. 31p. (Orig.). 1987. pap. 9.95 (ISBN 0-939577-07-0). McWare Products.
What Your Astrologer Never Told You. Maxine Taylor. 56p. 1976. 4.50 (ISBN 0-86690-216-3). Am Fed Astrologers.
What Your Boss Can't Tell You. Kent L. Straat. 196p. 1988. 16.95 (ISBN 0-8144-7704-6). AMACOM.
What Your Car is Trying To Tell You. Peter Novellino. LC 81-730689. 1982. wkbk. 5.00 (ISBN 0-8064-0153-2, 445); audio visual pkg. 179.00 (ISBN 0-8064-0154-0). Bergwall.
What Your Doctor Didn't Learn in Medical School...& What You Can Do about It! Stuart M. Berger. Ed. by Pat Golbitz. LC 87-36562. (Illus.). 384p. 1988. 18.95 (ISBN 0-688-06553-8). Morrow.
What Your Dreams Mean. Alan Davis. 1984. pap. 3.95 (ISBN 0-553-25909-1). Bantam.
What Your Dreams Mean. Polly Strong. 1988. pap. 9.95 (ISBN 0-934791-14-7). W Mulvey Inc.
What Your Handwriting Reveals. Margaret Gullan-Whur. LC 86-33428. 256p. 1986. Repr. of 1984 ed. lib. bdg. 22.95x (ISBN 0-8095-7035-1). Borgo Pr.
What Your Handwriting Reveals. Margaret Gullan-Whur. pap. 8.99 (ISBN 0-85030-378-8, Pub. by Aquarian Pr England). Sterling.
What Your Handwriting Reveals. Albert E. Hughes. 1978. 3.00 (ISBN 0-87980-365-7). Wilshire.
What Your Horoscope Doesn't Tell You. Charles R. Strohmer. 128p. 1988. pap. 4.95 (ISBN 0-8423-7936-3). Tyndale.
What Your Lenses Can Do. Herb Taylor et al. LC 81-71225. (Modern Photo Guides). (Illus.). 120p. (Orig.). 1982. pap. 7.95 (ISBN 0-385-18146-9). Avalon Comm.
What Your Nose Knows! Jane B. Moncure. LC 82-9464. (Five Senses Ser.). (Illus.). 32p. (ps-3). 1982. PLB 11.93 (ISBN 0-516-03255-0); pap. 2.95 (ISBN 0-516-43255-9). Childrens.
What Your Wedding Can Be. William J. Peters. LC 80-65402. 136p. (Orig.). 1980. pap. 2.95 (ISBN 0-87029-163-7, 20350-5). Abbey.
What You've Always Wanted to Know about Nutrition. Charles F. Berg. 1987. 10.95 (ISBN 0-533-07172-0). Vantage.
What'cha Gonna Do with What'cha Got? A Study in Christianomics. James W. Jackson. LC 87-72005. (Christianomics Ser.). 165p. (Orig.). 1988. pap. 5.95 (ISBN 1-55513-835-7, 68353). Cook.
What'cha Gonna Do with What'cha Got? A 13-session Study in Christianomics Adult Leader's Guide. James W. Jackson. (Christianomics Ser.). 55p. (Orig.). 1988. tchr's. ed. 7.95 (ISBN 1-55513-836-5, 68361). Cook.
What'cha Gonna Do with What'cha Got? Christianomics for Young People Leader's Guide. James W. Jackson. (Christianomics Ser.). 52p. (Orig.). 1988. tchr's. ed. 5.95 (ISBN 1-55513-837-3, 68379). Cook.
Whatcha' Want, Boy? Clifford F. Smith. 96p. 1988. 8.95 (ISBN 0-8062-3250-1). Carlton.
Whatcom County Bike Book. Patrick Vala. (Illus.). 1977. pap. 2.95 (ISBN 0-913140-22-8). Signpost Bk Pubns.
Whatcom County in Maps, 1932-1937, No. 2. Scott & Turbeville. 1986. pap. 9.95 (ISBN 0-318-23341-X). WWU CPNS.
Whatcom Images. Koert & Scott. 1986. pap. 12.50 (ISBN 0-318-23344-4). WWU CPNS.
Whatcom Scenes. Koert. 1986. pap. 9.95 (ISBN 0-318-23343-6). WWU CPNS.
Whatever Became of Atlanta? Norman Shavin. (Illus.). 84p. 1984. 8.95 (ISBN 0-910719-09-8). Capricorn Corp.
Whatever Became of...? Ninth Series. Richard Lamparski. (Illus.). 224p. 1984. pap. 9.95 (ISBN 0-517-55541-7). Crown.
Whatever Became of Sin? Karl Menninger. 288p. 1988. pap. 3.95 (ISBN 0-553-27368-X). Bantam.
Whatever Became of...? Tenth Series--100 Profiles of the Most Asked about Movie Stars & TV Personalities. Richard Lamparski. (Illus.). 224p. 1986. 15.95 (ISBN 0-517-56228-6); pap. 9.95 (ISBN 0-517-56229-4). Crown.
Whatever Happened to Amelia Earhart? Melinda Blau. LC 77-22173. (Great Unsolved Mysteries Ser.). (Illus.). (gr. 4-5). 1977. PLB 15.33 (ISBN 0-8172-1057-1). Raintree Pubs.
Whatever Happened to Amelia Earhart? Melinda E. Blau. LC 77-22173. (Great Unsolved Mysteries Ser.). (Illus.). 48p. (gr. 4up). 1983. pap. 9.27 (ISBN 0-8172-2170-0). Raintree Pubs.
Whatever Happened to Britain? The Economics of Decline. John Eatwell. (Illus.). 1984. pap. 7.95 (ISBN 0-19-520443-3). Oxford U Pr.
Whatever Happened to Divine Grace? Ramon Stevens. (Alexander Bks.). 560p. (Orig.). 1988. pap. 14.95 (ISBN 0-913299-46-4, Dist. by NAL). Stillpoint.
Whatever Happened to Epperson Springs? Vernon Roddy. 1974. pap. 5.50 (ISBN 0-686-40797-0). Upper Country.
Whatever Happened to Friday? & Other Questions Catholics Ask. Joseph C. Gibbons. LC 79-91275. (Orig.). 1980. pap. 3.95 (ISBN 0-8091-2278-2). Paulist Pr.
Whatever Happened to Gloomy Gus of the Chicago Bears. Robert Coover. 160p. 1987. 16.95 (ISBN 0-671-63813-0, Linden Pr). S&S.
Whatever Happened to Happily Ever After? Sandra Fujita. (Uplook Ser.). 1981. pap. 0.99 (ISBN 0-8163-0378-9). Pacific Pr Pub Assn.
Whatever Happened to Heaven? Dave Hunt. LC 88-81256. 224p. (Orig.). 1988. pap. 8.95 (ISBN 0-89081-698-0). Harvest Hse.
Whatever Happened to Hope. Roy H. Hicks. 1978. mini book 0.75 (ISBN 0-89274-074-4). Harrison Hse.
Whatever Happened to Lady Chatterley's Lover? Martin Levin. (Illus.). 128p. (Orig.). 1985. pap. 6.95 (ISBN 0-8362-7960-3). Andrews & McMeel.
Whatever Happened to Ordinary Christians. Jim Smoke. 1987. pap. 5.95 (ISBN 0-89081-605-0). Harvest Hse.
Whatever Happened to Planning? Peter Ambrose. 224p. 1987. text ed. 55.00x (ISBN 0-416-37100-0, 1121). Routledge chapman & Hall.
Whatever Happened to Productivity. Graham Hutton. (Institute of Economic Affairs, Occasional Papers Ser.: No. 56). pap. 4.25 technical (ISBN 0-255-36128-9). Transatl Arts.
Whatever Happened to Sandy Fowler? Gary Gabriel. Ed. by Jean McConochie. (Regents Readers Ser.). 80p. (gr. 7-12). 1983. pap. text ed. 3.00 (ISBN 0-13-952052-X, 20987). Prentice ESL.
Whatever Happened to Shell's New Philosophy of Management? F. H. Blackler & C. A. Brown. 192p. 1980. text ed. 37.00 (ISBN 0-566-00306-6). Gower Pub Co.
Whatever Happened to Susie? Mary Brittain. 32p. (ps up). 1988. 6.95 (ISBN 0-8062-3347-8). Carlton.
Whatever Happened to the Dinosaurs? William Jaber. LC 78-15939. (Illus.). 160p. (gr. 7 up). 1978. PLB 8.79 (ISBN 0-671-32872-7). Messner.
Whatever Happened to the Dinosaurs? Bernard Most. LC 84-3779. (Illus.). 40p. (ps-1). 1984. PLB 12.95 (ISBN 0-15-295295-0, HJ). HarBraceJ.
Whatever Happened to the Dinosaurs? Bernard Most. (Illus.). (gr. 1-4). 1988. 3.95 (VoyB). HarBraceJ.
Whatever Happened to the Dinosaurs? LC 84-37795. (Voyager Picture Bks.). (Illus.). 32p. (Orig.). (ps-3). 1987. pap. 3.95 (ISBN 0-15-295296-9, VoyB). HarBraceJ.
Whatever Happened to the Human Race? C. Everett Koop & Francis A. Schaeffer. LC 83-70955. 168p. 1983. pap. 7.95 (ISBN 0-89107-291-8, Crossway Bks). Good News.
Whatever Happened to the Kids from Pierce? Delores Stacy. 1985. pap. 4.95. Delcy Bks.
Whatever Happened to Uncle Albert? Sue Alexander. (Illus.). 128p. (gr. 3-6). 1980. 8.95 (ISBN 0-395-29104-6, Clarion); pap. 3.95 (ISBN 0-395-30061-4). HM.
Whatever Happened to Worship? A. W. Tozer. Ed. by Gerald B. Smith. LC 85-71185. 128p. (Orig.). 1985. pap. 5.95 (ISBN 0-87509-367-1). Chr Pubns.
Whatever It Is, I'm Against It. Ed. by Nat Shapiro. 1984. 17.95 (ISBN 0-671-49748-0); pap. 8.95 (ISBN 0-671-50837-7). S&S.
Whatever It Takes: Decision Makers at Work. Morgan McCall, Jr. & Robert K. Kaplan. (Illus.). 144p. 1985. text ed. 27.00 (ISBN 0-13-952086-4); pap. 19.00 (ISBN 0-13-952078-3). P-H.
Whatever Time We Live. Sheila Moon. 1982. 6.50 (ISBN 0-8233-0347-0). Golden Quill.
What'll You Have: Fifty Plus Non-Alcoholic Drinks for Brunch, Lunch & Dinner. Ed. by Cynthia Parsons. 52p. (Orig.). 1986. pap. 5.00 (ISBN 0-9617872-0-1). VT Schoolhse Pr.
What's a Body to Do? Ruth S. Odor. LC 81-17031. (Successful Living Ser.). (Illus.). 112p. (gr. 2-6). 1981. PLB 8.95 (ISBN 0-89565-209-9). Childs World.
What's a Body to Do? Ruth S. Odor. Ed. by Jane Buerger. LC 80-17584. (Illus.). 112p. (gr. k-4). 1980. 5.95 (ISBN 0-89565-176-9, 4933). Standard Pub.
What's a Body to Do? Schurr. (Choose-a-Card Ser.). 32p. (gr. 4-6). 1979. pap. text ed. 6.95 (ISBN 0-913916-87-0, IP87-0). Incentive Pubns.

What's Mite Might? Homophone Riddles to Boost Your Word Power! Giulio Maestro. LC 86-2665. (Illus.). 64p. (gr. 2-5). 1986. 11.95 (ISBN 0-89919-434-6, Pub. by Clarion); pap. 4.95 (ISBN 0-89919-435-4). Ticknor & Fields.
What's Music All about? Libby Hobson. (Music Ser.). 24p. (gr. 3-6). 1977. wkbk. 5.00 (ISBN 0-8209-0272-1, MU-1). ESP.
What's New in Allergy. Stephen Astor. (What's New in Medicine Ser.). 128p. (Orig.). 1985. pap. 6.50 (ISBN 0-915001-02-0). Two A's.
What's New in Anesthesiology. Ed. by T. H. Stanley. (Developments in Critical Care Medicine & Anesthesiology). 1988. lib. bdg. 70.00 (ISBN 0-89838-367-6, Pub. by Martinus Nojhoff). Kluwer Academic.
What's New in Electrocardiography. Ed. by Hein J. Wellens & Henri E. Kulbertus. 1981. lib. bdg. 57.50 (ISBN 90-247-2450-3); pap. text ed. 38.00 (ISBN 0-686-37016-3). Kluwer Academic.
What's New in Religion? A Critical Study of New Theology, New Morality & Secular Christianity. Kenneth Hamilton. 176p. 1969. pap. 3.95 (ISBN 0-85364-092-0). Attic Pr.
What's New in Wedding Food. Beth Tartan. 102p. 1985. 7.95 (ISBN 0-933193-00-9). TarPar.
What's News: A Game Simulation of TV News, Participant's Manual. William A. Gamson. 1984. text ed. 9.95 (ISBN 0-02-911110-2); coordinator's manual avail. (ISBN 0-02-911200-1); pap. 10.95. Free Pr.
What's News: The Media in American Society. Ed. by Eli Abel. 300p. 1981. 24.95; pap. 7.95. Transaction Bks.
What's News: The Media in American Society. Ed. by Elie Abel. LC 81-81414. 296p. 1981. pap. text ed. 7.95. ICS Pr.
What's Next? Becky Daniel & Charlie Daniel. (gr. k-6). 1979. 6.95 (ISBN 0-916456-41-2, GA116). Good Apple.
What's Next? Robert Wood. (Illus.). (ps-2). 1982. PLB 8.95 (ISBN 0-395-31611-1). HM.
What's Next? Career Strategies after 35. Jack Falvey. Ed. by Susan Williamson. 192p. (Orig.). 1987. pap. 9.95 (ISBN 0-913589-26-8). Williamson Pub Co.
What's Next for Facility Management, 2 vols. Ed. by Clark Malcolm. LC 86-21854. 100p. 1986. Set. pap. 25.00. Vol. 1 (ISBN 0-936658-22-3). Vol. 2 (ISBN 0-936658-23-1). H Miller Res.
What's Next? How to Prepare Yourself for the Crash of 1989 & Profit in the 1990s. Paul Erdman. 1988. 14.95 (ISBN 0-385-24698-6). Doubleday.
What's Next? New Life in Christ Guidebook for Children. Ralph W. Harris. 25p. 1971. pap. 0.40 (ISBN 0-88243-559-0, 02-0559). Gospel Pub.
What's Novel in the Novel. (YFS Ser.: No. 8). 1951. pap. 16.00 (ISBN 0-527-01716-7). Kraus Repr.
What's Nude? Fred Gwynne & Peter Basch. (Illus.). 1960. pap. 10.95 (ISBN 0-8392-1129-5). Astor-Honor.
What's O'Clock. Amy Lowell. 240p. 1985. 25.00 (ISBN 0-8495-3419-4). Arden Lib.
What's on Tap. Kent C. DeHaven & Charlotte DeHaven. (Illus., Orig.). 1982. pap. 4.95 (ISBN 0-910879-00-1). Trends & Custom.
What's on the Worker's Mind: By One Who Put on Overalls to Find Out. Whiting Williams. LC 73-156441. (American Labor Ser., No. 2). 1971. Repr. of 1920 ed. 22.00 (ISBN 0-405-02949-7). Ayer Co Pubs.
What's on Top, Head? Nancy Bentley. (Illus.). 16p. (ps). Date not set. 3.95 (ISBN 0-8431-2234-X). Price Stern.
What's on Your Mind. Merlin R. Carothers. 1984. 4.95 (ISBN 0-943026-13-X). Carothers.
What's on Your Plate? Norah Smaridge. LC 81-17684. (Illus.). 32p. (gr. k-3). 1982. 8.25 (ISBN 0-687-44911-1). Abingdon.
What's One More? Margaret Poynter. LC 84-21545. (Illus.). 160p. (gr. 6 up). 1985. 11.95 (ISBN 0-689-31083-8, Atheneum Childrens Bks). Macmillan.
What's Opposite? Illus. by Tony Tallarico. (Tiny Bks.). (Illus.). 28p. (ps-1). 1984. bds. 3.50 (ISBN 0-89828-054-0). Tuffy Bks.
What's Past Is Prologue. Ed. by S. Bacarisse et al. 208p. 1984. 16.00x (ISBN 0-7073-0344-3, Pub. by Scot Acad Pr). Longwood Pub Group.
What's Past Is Prologue. Mary B. Gilson. Ed. by Annette K. Baxter. LC 79-8793. (Signal Lives Ser.). 1980. Repr. of 1940 ed. lib. bdg. 32.50x (ISBN 0-405-12842-8). Ayer Co Pubs.
What's Promising: New Approaches to Dropout Prevention for Girls. 1988. 6.00. NASBE.
What's Published about Colorado. C. R. Goeldner & James Manire. 1985. 25.00 (ISBN 0-89478-079-4). U CO Busn Res Div.
What's Published about Colorado. C. R. Goeldner et al. 139p. 1978. 15.00 (ISBN 0-686-64142-6). U CO Busn Res Div.
What's Really Wrong with Phenomenalism. J. L. Mackie. (Philosophical Lectures (Henriette Hertz Trust)). 1969. pap. 5.50 (ISBN 0-85672-307-X, Pub. by British Acad). Longwood Pub Group.
What's Remembered: L-N Score. Lampert & Rotman. (EPC Ser.). 231p. 1986. pap. write for info. (ISBN 0-932582-46-X). Dance Notation.
What's Right? Eugene Baker. Ed. by Jane Buerger. LC 80-17552. (Illus.). 112p. (gr. k-4). 1980. 5.95 (ISBN 0-89565-175-0, 4932). Standard Pub.
What's Right? Eugene H. Baker. LC 81-16999. (Successful Living Ser.). (Illus.). 112p. (gr. 2-6). 1981. lib. bdg. 8.95 (ISBN 0-89565-208-0). Routledge Chapman & Hall.
What's Right? A Teenager's Guide to Christian Living. Jim Auer. 96p. 1987. pap. 3.25 (ISBN 0-89243-265-9). Liguori Pubns.
What's Right What's Wrong in an Upside-Down World. Fred Hartley. 1988. pap. 6.95 (ISBN 0-8407-9518-1). Nelson.
What's Right with Feminism? Elaine Storkey. 192p. (Orig.). 1986. pap. 8.95 (ISBN 0-8028-0177-3). Eerdmans.
What's Right with the Church. William H. Willimon. LC 84-48233. 160p. 1985. 13.95 (ISBN 0-06-069531-5, HarpR). Har-Row.
What's Skin For? Pat Blakely. (Creative Question & Answer Library). (Illus.). 32p. (ps-4). 1981. PLB 8.95 (ISBN 0-87191-745-9). Creative Ed.
What's So Funny? A Foreign Student's Introduction to American Humor. Elizabeth Claire. (Illus.). 160p. 1984. pap. 7.95 (ISBN 0-937630-01-2). Eardley Pubns.
What's So Funny about Business? Sidney Harris. (Illus.). 128p. 1986. pap. 7.95 (ISBN 0-86576-100-0). W Kaufmann.
What's So Funny about Computers? Sidney Harris. LC 82-21227. (Illus.). 128p. 1983. pap. 6.95 (ISBN 0-86576-049-7). W Kaufmann.
What's So Funny about Microbiology? Joachim Czichos. Tr. by Jane A. Phillips. LC 87-12792. (Illus.). 160p. (Orig.). 1987. pap. 6.95 (ISBN 0-910239-12-6). Sci Tech Pubs.
What's So Funny about Science? Cartoons from American Scientist. Sidney Harris. LC 77-82638. (Illus.). 128p. 1977. 8.95x (ISBN 0-913232-39-4); pap. 5.95 (ISBN 0-913232-42-4). W Kaufmann.
What's So Funny, Ketu? Verna Aardema. LC 82-70195. (Illus.). 32p. (ps-2). 1982. 9.95 (ISBN 0-8037-9364-2); PLB 9.89 (ISBN 0-8037-9370-7). Dial Bks Young.
What's So Special about Fall? I'm Going to School. Jane B. Moncure. LC 88-2868. (What's So Special Ser.). (Illus.). 32p. (ps-2). 1988. PLB 7.95 (ISBN 0-89565-420-2). Childs World.
What's So Special about Lauren? She's My Baby Sister. Jane B. Moncure. LC 87-21927. (What's So Special Ser.). (Illus.). 32p. (ps-2). 1988. PLB 7.95 (ISBN 0-89565-413-X). Childs World.
What's So Special about Me? I'm One of a Kind. Janet McDonnell & Sandra Ziegler. LC 88-2872. (What's So Special Ser.). (Illus.). 32p. (ps-2). 1988. PLB 7.95 (ISBN 0-89565-419-9). Childs World.
What's So Special about Today? It's My Birthday. Jane B. Moncure. LC 87-21907. (What's So Special Ser.). (Illus.). 32p. (ps-2). 1988. PLB 7.95 (ISBN 0-89565-414-8). Childs World.
What's Teddy Bear Doing? (Folding Bks.). 12p. (ps). 1983. 2.50 (ISBN 0-8431-0945-9). Price Stern.
What's That Color? Kate Petty. (What's That Ser.). (Illus.). 24p. (gr. 1-3). 1986. PLB 10.40 (ISBN 0-531-10257-2). Watts.
What's That I Feel? Kate Petty. (What's That Ser.). (Illus.). 24p. (gr. k-3). 1987. lib. bdg. 10.40 (ISBN 0-531-10280-7). Watts.
What's That I Hear? Listening Activities for Young Children. Sam E. Brown. 128p. (Orig.). 1986. pap. text ed. 9.95 (ISBN 0-88450-958-3, 7282-B). Communication Skill.
What's That I Smell? Kate Petty. (What's That Ser.). (Illus.). 24p. (gr. k-3). 1987. lib. bdg. 10.40 (ISBN 0-531-10283-1). Watts.
What's That Noise? Michele Lemieux. LC 84-16631. (Illus.). 32p. (ps-1). 1985. 10.25 (ISBN 0-688-04139-6, Morrow Junior Books); PLB 10.88 (ISBN 0-688-04140-X, Morrow Junior Books). Morrow.
What's That Noise? Kate Petty. (What's That... Ser.). (Illus.). 32p. (gr. k-3). 1986. lib. bdg. 10.40 (ISBN 0-531-10175-4). Watts.
What's That Number? Kate Petty. (What's That Ser.). (Illus.). 32p. (gr. k-3). 1986. lib. bdg. 10.40 (ISBN 0-531-10176-2). Watts.
What's That on My Plate. Gilson Henry. Ed. by Ron Hansen. (Illus.). 24p. (ps-4). 1988. pap. 3.95 (ISBN 0-943925-04-5). Purple Turtle Pub.
What's That Room For? Betsy James. LC 87-24462. (Illus.). 32p. (ps-1). 1988. 11.95 (ISBN 0-525-44382-7, 01160-350). Dutton.
What's That Shape? Kate Petty. (What's That Ser.). (Illus.). 24p. (gr. k-3). 1987. lib. bdg. 10.40 (ISBN 0-531-10281-5). Watts.
What's That Size? Kate Petty. (What's That Ser.). (Illus.). 24p. (gr. k-3). 1987. lib. bdg. 10.40 (ISBN 0-317-53452-1). Watts.
What's That Taste? Kate Petty. (What's That Ser.). (Illus.). 24p. (gr. 1-3). 1986. PLB 10.40 (ISBN 0-531-10258-0). Watts.
What's That You're Eating? Food Label Language & What it Means to you. C. D. King. Ed. by Mary L Grubb & John D. Grubb. LC 82-90187. (Illus.). 62p. 1982. pap. 3.95 (ISBN 0-9608862-0-6). C King.
What's the Best Way to Deal with Hyperactivity? New Update on the Attention Deficit Disorders. C. Thomas Wild. LC 83-71951. (Illus.). 52p. (Orig.). 1983. pap. 3.95 (ISBN 0-9606990-1-5). ASA.
What's the Big Idea, Ben Franklin? Jean Fritz. (Illus.). 48p. (gr. 2-6). 1982. 9.95 (ISBN 0-698-20365-8, Coward); pap. 5.95 (ISBN 0-698-20543-X, Coward). Putnam Pub Group.
What's the Difference? Ellen Barnes et al. 1978. 6.50 (ISBN 0-937540-08-0, HPP-11). Human Policy Pr.
What's the Difference? Bill Gillham. LC 85-28138. (Look & Talk Bks.). (Illus.). (gr. 3-6). 1986. 5.95 (ISBN 0-399-21321-X). Putnam Pub Group.
What's the Difference? How Men & Women Compare. Jane B. Stump. LC 85-502. 247p. 1986. pap. 7.95 (ISBN 0-688-06263-6, Quill). Morrow.
What's the Difference: How Men & Women Compare. Jane B. Stumpp. LC 84-20569. 252p. 1985. 12.95 (ISBN 0-688-04192-2). Morrow.
What's the Fair Ward? Psychiatric Humor. Edwin Mumford. (Illus.). 1979. pap. 3.00 (ISBN 0-682-49422-4). Exposition-Phoenix.
What's the Funny Ward? Or My Last Ten Years with Snooksie the Guinea Pig. Edwin Mumford. (Illus.). 1979. pap. 4.00 (ISBN 0-682-49522-0). Exposition-Phoenix.
What's the Good Word? William Safire. LC 81-52568. 320p. 1982. 15.45 (ISBN 0-8129-1006-0). Times Bks.
What's the Good Word. William Safire. 1983. pap. 5.95 (ISBN 0-380-64550-5, 64550). Avon.
What's the Hurry. Anne Rogovin & Christine Z. Cataldo. LC 82-13450. (Illus.). 220p. 1983. text ed. 19.00x (ISBN 0-8391-1761-2, 1242). Pro-Ed.
What's the Joke, Beetle Bailey. Mort Walker. 1987. pap. 2.25 (ISBN 0-441-05279-7, Pub. by Charter Bks). Ace Bks.
What's the Matter, Girl? Elizabeth Brochmann. LC 79-2022. 128p. (YA) (gr. 7 up). 1980. PLB 12.89 (ISBN 0-06-020678-0). HarpJ.
What's the Matter, Little Frog? Lucille Hammond. LC 86-22081. (Tough Enough for Toddlers Ser.). (Illus.). 24p. (ps-k). 1987. 3.95 (ISBN 0-394-88865-0, BYR). Random.
What's the Matter, Sylvie, Can't You Ride? Karen B. Andersen. LC 80-12514. (Illus.). 32p. (ps-3). 1981. 9.95 (ISBN 0-8037-9607-2, 0966-290); PLB 9.89 (ISBN 0-8037-9621-8). Dial Bks Young.
What's the Matter with Carruthers? James Marshall. LC 72-75607. (Illus.). 32p. (gr. k-3). 1972. PLB 14.95 (ISBN 0-395-13895-7). HM.
What's the Matter with Carruthers? James Marshall. LC 72-75607. (Sandpipers Ser.). (Illus.). 32p. (gr. k-3). 1987. pap. 3.95 (ISBN 0-395-45358-5). HM.
What's the Matter with Christy? Ruth Allen. LC 82-8036. 110p. (Orig.). 1982. pap. 3.95 (ISBN 0-87123-629-X, 210629). Bethany Hse.
What's the Matter with Dog. (Easy Readers Ser.). (gr. k-3). 1.25 (ISBN 0-8431-4323-1). Wonder.
What's the Matter with Herbie Jones? Suzy Kline. (Illus.). (gr. 2-6). 1986. 11.95 (ISBN 0-399-21315-5, Putnam). Putnam Pub Group.
What's the Matter with Herbie Jones? Suzy Kline. (Illus.). (gr. 3-7). Date not set. pap. 3.95 (ISBN 0-317-62246-3, Puffin Bks). Penguin.
What's the Matter with Miss Taylor. Evelyn Witter. Ed. by Patricia McKissack & Fredrick McKissack. (Reading Well Ser.). (Illus.). 30p. (Orig.). (gr. 1-3). 1987. text ed. 9.95 (ISBN 0-88335-728-3); pap. text ed. 4.95 (ISBN 0-88335-748-8). Milliken Pub Co.
What's the Matter with the Dobsons. Hila Colman. (gr. 5-7). 1982. pap. 1.95 (ISBN 0-671-43143-9). Archway.
What's the Next Move? George Kane. LC 74-12618. (Encore Editions). (Illus.). (gr. 4-6). 1974. 1.79 (ISBN 0-684-15841-8, ScribT). Scribner.
What's the Object: A Way to Reach Them, Vol. I. Neil W. Decker. (Illus.). 149p. (Orig.). 1980. pap. 6.95 (ISBN 0-942241-10-X, 8785). Pubs Bk Sales.
What's the Object: A Way to Reach Them, Vol. II. Neil W. Decker. (Illus.). 124p. (Orig.). 1986. pap. 6.95 (ISBN 0-942241-11-8, 8786). Pubs Bk Sales.
What's the Point? Norman Warren. 80p. 1987. pap. 2.50 (ISBN 0-7459-1224-9). Lion USA.
What's the Problem Here. Michael Sanderson. 1981. text ed. 24.95 (ISBN 0-917386-51-5). Exec Ent Pubns.
What's the Score? Devotions for Sports Lovers. Rolf E. Aaseng. 1987. pap. 4.95 (ISBN 0-8010-0207-9). Baker Bk.
What's the Story? Photographs for Language Practice, 4 bks. Linda Markstein & Dorien Grunbaum. (English As a Second Language Bk.). 1981. pap. text ed. 4.95 ea. Bk. 1: Beginning (ISBN 0-582-79783-7). Bk. 2: Low-Intermediate (ISBN 0-582-79784-5). Bk. 3: High-Intermediate (ISBN 0-582-79785-3). Bk. 4: Advanced (ISBN 0-582-79786-1). tchr's manual 4.95 (ISBN 0-582-79787-X); wall charts 49.50 (ISBN 0-582-79788-8). Longman.
What's This? Ellin B. Church. 64p. (gr. k-3). 1984. 6.95 (ISBN 0-912107-14-6). Monday Morning Bks.
What's This World Coming To? Stan Campbell. 144p. (YA) (gr. 8 up). 1988. pap. text ed. 4.95 (ISBN 0-89693-865-4). Victor Bks.
What's This World Coming To? Ray C. Stedman. LC 86-6439. 1986. pap. 5.95 (ISBN 0-8307-1154-6, 5418825). Regal.
What's to Become of the Boy? Heinrich Boll. Tr. by Leila Vennewitz. LC 83-49087. 96p. 1984. 11.45 (ISBN 0-394-53016-0). Knopf.
What's to Become of the Boy. Heinrich Boll. (Nonfiction Ser.). 96p. 1985. pap. 5.95 (ISBN 0-14-008321-9). Penguin.
What's to Eat? Edith Down. 1981. text ed. 16.60 (ISBN 0-02-666150-0); tchr's. ed. 9.32 (ISBN 0-02-666160-8). Bennett IL.
What's under My Bed? James Stevenson. LC 83-1454. (Illus.). 32p. (gr. k-3). 1983. 12.95 (ISBN 0-688-02325-8); PLB 11.88 (ISBN 0-688-02327-4). Greenwillow.
What's under My Bed. James Stevenson. (Illus.). 1984. pap. 3.95 (ISBN 0-14-050485-0, Puffin). Penguin.
What's under That Rock? Stephen M. Hoffman. LC 84-21643. (Illus.). 96p. (gr. 4 up). 1985. 11.95 (ISBN 0-689-31081-1, Atheneum Childrens Bks). Macmillan.
What's under the Ocean. Janet Craig. LC 81-11425. (Now I Know Ser.). (Illus.). 32p. (gr. k-2). 1982. PLB 9.89 (ISBN 0-89375-652-0). Troll Assocs.
What's under the Sea? Solveig P. Russell. LC 81-20521. (Illus.). 48p. (gr. 2-4). 1982. 9.95 (ISBN 0-687-44913-8). Abingdon.
What's Up? Ellin B. Church. 64p. (gr. k-3). 1983. 6.95 (ISBN 0-912107-09-X). Monday Morning Bks.
What's up, Doc? Doctor & Dentist Jokes. Charles Keller. LC 84-6821. (Illus.). 64p. (gr. 3-7). 1984. 9.95 (ISBN 0-13-954967-6). P-H.
What's up Duck? Mike Thaler. (Illus.). 128p. (gr. 3-7). 1981. pap. 1.95 (ISBN 0-380-53363-4, 53363-4, Camelot). Avon.
What's up There? Dinah Moche. (gr. 4-6). 1976. pap. 1.50 (ISBN 0-590-04850-3). Scholastic Inc.
What's What. Arlene D. Miller. Ed. by Carol Gilbert. (Illus.). 21p. (Orig.). (ps-6). 1985. pap. 4.00 (ISBN 0-9614209-0-1). Adam Pub Co.
What's What: A Reference Book about World Politics. E. M. Primakov & A. I. Vlasov. 463p. 1987. 14.95 (ISBN 0-8285-3770-4, Pub. by Progress Pubs USSR). Imported Pubns.
What's What: A Visual Glossary of the Physical World. Reg Bragonier & David Fisher. LC 81-7149. (Illus.). 576p. 1981. 30.00 (ISBN 0-8437-3329-2); printed cover 19.95 (ISBN 0-8437-3331-4). Hammond Inc.
What's What: A Visual Glossary of the Physical World. Ed. by David Fisher & Reginald Bragonier, Jr. (Illus.). 574p. 1982. pap. 9.95 (ISBN 0-345-30302-4). Ballantine.
What's What in American Business: Facts & Figures about the Biggest & the Best. George Kurian. 224p. 1985. 14.95 (ISBN 0-917253-17-5). Probus Pub Co.
What's What in Japanese Restaurants. Robb Satterwhite. LC 87-82865. (Illus.). 144p. 1988. pap. 9.95 (ISBN 0-87011-867-6). Kodansha.
What's What in Sports: The Visual Glossary of the Sports World. Ed. by David Fisher & Reginald Bragonier, Jr. LC 84-9082. (Illus.). 256p. 1984. 19.95 (ISBN 0-8437-3528-7); lexotone 14.95 (ISBN 0-8437-3529-5). Hammond Inc.
What's What in the Nineteen Eighty's: A Dictionary of Contemporary History, Literature, Arts, Technology, Medicine, Cinema, Theatre, Controversies, Fads, Movements & Events, Vol. 1. Ed. by Christopher Pick. 399p. 1982. 58.00x (ISBN 0-8103-2035-5). Gale.
What's Whole in Whole Language? Kenneth Goodman. LC 85-27154. 80p. (Orig.). 1986. pap. 7.50x (ISBN 0-435-08254-X). Heinemann Ed.
What's Wildlife Worth? 1982. 5.50 (ISBN 0-905347-35-8). Intl Inst Environment.
What's Worth Teaching? Selecting, Organizing, & Integrating Knowledge. Marion Brady. (Philosophy of Education Ser.). 224p. 1988. 39.50x (ISBN 0-88706-815-4); pap. 12.95x (ISBN 0-88706-816-2). State U NY Pr.
What's Wrong? Ellin B. Church. 64p. (gr. k-3). 1983. 6.95 (ISBN 0-912107-08-1). Monday Morning Bks.
What's Wrong Here? Illus. by John Wallner. (Illus.). 12p. (ps-2). 1988. 7.95 (ISBN 0-448-19067-2, G&D). Putnam Pub Group.
What's Wrong: Poems. Laurel Blossom. LC 87-26803. xii, 55p. 1987. 15.00 (ISBN 0-944125-02-6). Cobham Hatherton.
What's Wrong? What's Wrong? Carol Hamoy. (Illus.). (gr. k-3). 1965. 8.95. Astor-Honor.
What's Wrong, Who's Right in Central America: A Citizen's Guide. Richard Nuccio & Kelly A. McBride. LC 85-31093. 160p. 1986. 15.95 (ISBN 0-8160-1374-8). Facts on File.
What's Wrong, Who's Right in Central America? Richard Nuccio. 1988. write for info. (ISBN 0-8419-1177-0). Holmes & Meier.
What's Wrong with a Van? Franz Brandenberg. (Illus.). (ps-3). 1987. 11.75 (ISBN 0-688-06773-5); PLB 11.88 (ISBN 0-688-06775-1). Greenwillow.
What's Wrong with Being Crabby? Charles M. Schulz. 1976. pap. 4.95 (ISBN 0-03-017486-4). H Holt & Co.
What's Wrong with Daddy? Alida E. Young. 176p. (gr. 5-8). 1986. 2.95 (ISBN 0-87406-066-4). Willowisp Pr.
What's Wrong with Eating Meat? Barbara Parham. LC 79-52319. (Illus., Orig.). 1979. pap. 2.05 (ISBN 0-88476-009-X). Ananda Marga.
What's Wrong with Formalization in Economics? An Epistemological Critique. Henry K. Woo. 130p. 1985. pap. 11.95 (ISBN 0-9613204-2-7). Victoria Pr.

What's Wrong with God. T. Steeman. Ed. by Fantan McNamee. (Synthesis Ser.). pap. 0.75 (ISBN 0-8199-0391-4). Franciscan Herald.

What's Wrong with Human Rights. T. Robert Ingram. LC 78-68732. (Orig.). 1979. pap. 3.50 (ISBN 0-686-24267-X). St Thomas.

What's Wrong with Melissa? Marilyn Hamalainen. LC 82-82670. (Illus.). 96p. (Orig.). (YA) (gr. 7-11). 1983. pap. 1.95 (ISBN 0-88243-641-4, 02-0641). Gospel Pub.

What's Wrong with My Child? R. Gattozi. 384p. 1986. text ed. 19.95 (ISBN 0-07-038781-8). McGraw.

What's Wrong with Our Technological Society - & How to Fix It. Simon Ramo. LC 83-696. 320p. 1983. text ed. 23.95 (ISBN 0-07-051169-1). McGraw.

What's Wrong with Public Education - From A to Z. Carl W. Salser, Jr. LC 78-68114. 1978. pap. 8.95 (ISBN 0-89420-049-6, 110060, Halcyon). Natl Book.

What's Wrong with the Mental Health Movement. K. Edward Renner. LC 74-26831. 272p. 1975. 22.95x (ISBN 0-88229-180-7). Nelson-Hall.

What's Wrong with the Movies? Tamar Lane. LC 78-160237. (Moving Pictures Ser.). 254p. 1971. Repr. of 1923 ed. lib. bdg. 16.95x (ISBN 0-89198-038-5). Ozer.

What's Wrong with the U. S. Economy. Institute for Labor Education & Research. (Illus.). 350p. 1982. 25.00 (ISBN 0-89608-011-0); pap. 10.00 (ISBN 0-89608-010-2). South End Pr.

What's Wrong with This Picture? Cheryl G. Bartholomew. 64p. 1988. 7.95 (ISBN 0-8062-3319-2). Carlton.

What's Wrong with Wall Street: Short-Term Gain & the Absentee Shareholder. Louis Lowenstein. 1988. 17.95 (ISBN 0-201-17169-4). Addison-Wesley.

What's Wrong with Your Sun Sign? Barbara Watters. LC 74-126771. 316p. 1978. 3.50 (ISBN 0-86690-170-1, 1513-02). Am Fed Astrologers.

What's Your Beef. Marion Hodgson. (Illus.). pap. 1.50 (ISBN 0-912848-03-0). Coll Kids Cook.

What's Your Diet Sign? A New Method for Losing Weight & Eating Well. Jennifer Michaels & Joyce Jack. 1985. pap. text ed. 8.95 (ISBN 0-07-009613-9). McGraw.

What's Your Game Plan? Creating Business Strategies That Work. Milton Lauenstein. 1985. 19.95 (ISBN 0-87094-593-9). Dow Jones-Irwin.

What's Your Name, Again? More Jokes about Names. Rick Walton & Ann Walton. (Make Me Laugh! Joke Bks.). (Illus.). (gr. 1-4). 1987. PLB 5.95 (ISBN 0-8225-0997-0). Lerner Pubns.

What's Your Name? Jokes about Names. Scott K. Peterson. (Make Me Laugh! Joke Bks.). (Illus.). 32p. (gr. 1-4). 1987. PLB 5.95 (ISBN 0-8225-0994-6); pap. 2.95 (ISBN 0-8225-9520-6). Lerner Pubns.

What's Your Point? A Proven Method for Giving Crystal-Clear Presentations. Bob Boylan. Ed. by Norine Larson. (Illus.). 160p. 1988. pap. 12.95 (ISBN 0-941755-01-0). Point Pubns MN.

What's Your Problem? Karen Dockrey. 96p. (YA) (gr. 7 up). 1987. pap. 11.95 (ISBN 0-89693-381-4); pap. 1.95 student bk. (ISBN 0-317-60085-0). Victor Bks.

What's Your S. Q.? (Spiritual Quotient) Maralene Wesner & MIles Wesner. LC 86-71133. 100p. 1986. pap. 4.95 (ISBN 0-936715-04-9). Diversity Okla.

Whatsoever Things Are True. Compiled by Harold Whaley. LC 79-67283. 64p. 1980. 5.95 (ISBN 0-87159-100-6). Unity School.

Whattizit? Nature Pun Quizzes. Allan Eckert. (Illus.). 48p. (Orig.). 1981. pap. 2.95 (ISBN 0-913428-30-2). Landfall Pr.

Wheare, Kenneth Clinton, Nineteen Seven to Nineteen Seventy-Nine. G. Marshall. (Memoirs of the Fellows of the British Academy). (Illus.). 17p. 1983. pap. 5.50 (ISBN 0-85672-378-9, Pub. by British Acad). Longwood Pub Group.

Wheat among Bones. Mary Baron. LC 79-90839. 94p. 1980. 9.95 (ISBN 0-935296-04-2); pap. 4.95 (ISBN 0-935296-05-0). Sheep Meadow.

Wheat & Chaff. Mitterand. (Seaver Bks); pap. 7.95 (ISBN 0-8050-0185-9). H Holt & Co.

Wheat & Politics. facsimile ed. J. W. Brinton. Ed. by Dan C. McCurry & Richard E. Rubenstein. LC 74-30621. (American Farmers & the Rise of Agribusiness Ser.). 1975. Repr. of 1931 ed. 24.50x (ISBN 0-405-06768-2). Ayer Co Pubs.

Wheat & the AAA. Joseph S. Davis. LC 76-172868. (FDR & the Era of the New Deal Ser.). 468p. 1973. Repr. of 1935 ed. 59.50 (ISBN 0-306-70375-0). Da Capo.

Wheat & the Chaff, 2 pts. in 1. Francois Mitterand. Tr. by Richard Woodward & Concilia Hayter. 1982. 16.95. Seaver Bks.

Wheat & the Chaff. Francois Mitterrand. Tr. by Richard Woodward & Concilia Hayter. 352p. 1983. pap. 7.95. Seaver Bks.

Wheat & Wheat Improvement. Ed. by K. S. Quisenberry & L. P. Reitz. (Illus.). 1967. 10.00 (ISBN 0-89118-014-1). Am Soc Agron.

Wheat & Woman. Georgina Binnie-Clark. (Social History of Canada Ser.). 1979. 11.95 (ISBN 0-8020-2354-1); pap. 10.95 (ISBN 0-8020-6386-1). U of Toronto Pr.

Wheat & Women. Georgina Binnie-Clark. LC 80-463250. (Social History of Canada: No. 30). pap. 91.00 (2026424). Bks Demand UMI.

Wheat Breeding & Its Scientific Basis. F. G. Lupton. 580p. 1988. lib. bdg. 145.00 (ISBN 0-412-24470-5, Pub. by Chapman & Hall England). Routledge Chapman & Hall.

Wheat Diseases & Pests: A Guide to Field Identification. J. M. Prescott et al. (Illus.). 140p. (Orig.). 1986. pap. text ed. 10.00 (ISBN 0-318-20347-2, Pub. by Intl Maize & Wheat Mexico). Agribookstore.

Wheat Flour Messiah: Eric Jansson of Bishop Hill. Paul Elmen. LC 76-28380. (Illus.). 239p. 1976. 8.95x (ISBN 0-8093-0787-1). S Ill U Pr.

Wheat Flour Messiah: Eric Jansson of Bishop Hill. Paul Elmen. LC 76-28380. 222p. 1976. 7.95 (ISBN 0-318-16626-7). Swedish-Am.

Wheat Flowers. 3rd ed. Printer Bowler & Mac Schaffer. LC 83-83012. 94p. pap. 6.95 (ISBN 0-915945-00-2). Heartland Image.

Wheat Growth & Modeling. Ed. by W. Day & R. K. Atkin. LC 85-3691. (NATO ASI Series A, Life Sciences: Vol. 86). 420p. 1985. 75.00x (ISBN 0-306-41933-5, Plenum Pr). Plenum Pub.

Wheat: Humor & Wisdom of J. Golden Kimball. Mikal Lofgren. LC 80-81556. 95p. 1980. 6.50 (ISBN 0-936718-04-8). Moth Hse.

Wheat in the Third World. Haldore Hanson & Norman Borlaug. (IADS Development Oriented Literature Ser.). 192p. 1982. lib. bdg. 21.00x (ISBN 0-86531-357-1). Westview.

Wheat Market & the Farmer in Minnesota, 1858-1900. Henrietta M. Larson. LC 70-82232. (Columbia University. Studies in the Social Sciences: No. 269). Repr. of 1926 ed. 21.00 (ISBN 0-404-51269-0). AMS Pr.

Wheat, Millet & Other Grains. Beatrice T. Hunter. (Good Health Guide Ser.). 1982. pap. 1.45 (ISBN 0-87983-289-4). Keats.

Wheat of Christ. Dmitry Mishetski. (Orig.). 1988. pap. price not set (ISBN 0-913026-68-9). St Nectarios.

Wheat Plant: Its Origin, Culture, Growth, Development, Composition, Varieties Together with Information on Corn & Its Culture, 2 vols. John H. Klippart. 1980. Set. lib. bdg. 200.00 (ISBN 0-8490-3119-2). Gordon Pr.

Wheat Problem. William Crookes. LC 75-27633. (World Food Supply Ser.). (Illus.). 1976. Repr. of 1900 ed. 23.50x (ISBN 0-405-07775-0). Ayer Co Pubs.

Wheat Science-Today & Tomorrow. Ed. by L. T. Evans & W. J. Peacock. LC 80-41871. (Illus.). 300p. 1981. 47.50 (ISBN 0-521-23793-9). Cambridge U Pr.

Wheat Stalk. Tr. by I. Zheleznova. 78p. 1981. 6.00 (ISBN 0-8285-2166-2, Pub. by Malysh Pubs USSR). Imported Pubns.

Wheat Studies: Retrospects & Prospects, The Birthplace of Genetical Research on Wheat. H. Kihara. (Developments in Crop Science: Vol. 3). 308p. 1982. 94.75 (ISBN 0-444-99695-8). Elsevier.

Wheat That Springeth Green. J. F. Powers. LC 87-46104. 352p. 1988. 18.95 (ISBN 0-394-49609-4). Knopf.

Wheat Trap: Bread & Underdevelopment in Nigeria. Gunilla Andrae & Bjorn Beckman. 256p. 1985. 32.50 (ISBN 0-86232-520-X, Pub. by Zed Pr); pap. 11.50 (ISBN 0-86232-521-8, Pub. by Zed Pr). Humanities.

Wheat Varieties for Kansas: Your Best Choices for 1989. Steve Watson. Ed. by Bobbie Rasor. 92p. (Orig.). 1988. pap. 9.95. Lone Tree.

Wheatberry Cookbook Ecology of Food. (Illus.). 156p. (Orig.). 1986. pap. 7.20 (ISBN 0-938281-00-3). Span Inc.

Wheaten Years: The History of Ireland's Soft Coated Wheaten Terrier. Maureen Holmes. LC 77-88422. 130p. 14.95x (ISBN 0-9606448-0-6). B P Reynolds.

Wheatgrass Book. Ann Wigmore. LC 84-24194. 144p. (Orig.). 1985. pap. 7.95 (ISBN 0-89529-234-3). Avery Pub.

Wheatgrass Juice-Gift of Nature. rev. ed. Ed. by Besty Russell-Manning. 1988. pap. 2.95. Greensward Pr.

Wheatheart Chronicles, 4 bks. Set. 17.95 (ISBN 0-89693-700-3). Victor Bks.

Wheatless Cooking. Lynette Coffey. LC 85-17289. (Illus.). xxx, 96p. 1986. pap. 8.95 (ISBN 0-89815-156-2). Ten Speed Pr.

Wheatley, Banneker & Horton. facs. ed. William G. Allen. LC 77-133145. (Black Heritage Library Collection Ser). 1849. Repr. of 1849 ed. 7.00 (ISBN 0-8369-8657-1). Ayer Co Pubs.

Wheatley Manuscript: A Collection of Middle English Verse & Prose. (EETS, OS: No. 155). 1932. Repr. of 1921 ed. 29.00 (ISBN 0-527-00152-X). Kraus Repr.

Wheaton Book of Animal Stories. Martha Robinson. (Illus.). (YA) (gr. 9-12). 1981. text ed. 8.90 (ISBN 0-08-026421-2). Pergamon.

Wheaton Book of Science Fiction Stories. Robert Swindells. (Illus.). (YA) (gr. 9-12). 1982. text ed. 8.90 (ISBN 0-08-026425-5). Pergamon.

Wheaton College Collection of Greek & Roman Coins. David Bishop & R. Ross Holloway. (Ancient Coins in North American Collections 3). (Illus.). 64p. 1981. 30.00 (ISBN 0-89722-190-7). Am Numismatic.

Wheats for More Tropical Environments. Ed. by Reynaldo L. Villareal & Arthur R. Klatt. 354p. (Orig.). 1985. pap. text ed. 25.15 (Pub. by Intl Maize & Wheat Mexico). Agribookstore.

Wheats of Classical Antiquity. Naum Jasny. LC 78-64196. (Johns Hopkins University. Studies in the Social Sciences. Sixty-Second Ser. 1944: 3). Repr. of 1944 ed. 24.50 (ISBN 0-404-61302-0). AMS Pr.

Whedon Commentary: Psalms. boards 13.95 (ISBN 0-686-27779-1). Schmul Pub Co.

Whedon's Commentary on First Corinthians, Vol. 4. 13.95 (ISBN 0-686-13331-5). Schmul Pub Co.

Whedon's Commentary on Luke, Vol. 2. 13.95 (ISBN 0-686-13330-7). Schmul Pub Co.

Whedon's Commentary on Matthew, Vol. 1. 13.95 (ISBN 0-686-13329-3). Schmul Pub Co.

Whedon's Commentary on Titus & Revelations, Vol. 5. 13.95 (ISBN 0-686-13332-3). Schmul Pub Co.

Whedon's Commentary Revised, 2 vols. D. D. Whedon. 1981. Vol. Matthew Mark. 7.65 (ISBN 0-87813-917-6); Vol. Luke John. 7.65 (ISBN 0-87813-918-4). Christian Light.

Whee! We, Wee All the Way Home: A Guide to a Sensual, Prophetic Spirituality. Matthew Fox. LC 81-67365. 266p. 1981. pap. 9.95 (ISBN 0-939680-00-9). Bear & Co.

Wheedle on the Needle. (gr. 1-6). 1975. pap. 2.50 (ISBN 0-8431-0564-X). Price Stern.

Wheel & Handwriting Analysis. Joseph Zmuda. (Illus.). 48p. (Orig.). 1985. pap. text ed. 20.00 (ISBN 0-941572-02-1). Z Graphic Pubns.

Wheel & Rim out of Service Guide. American Trucking Associations, Inc. Maintenance Council. 60p. 1987. updated loose-leaf 50.00 (ISBN 0-88711-097-5). Am Trucking Assns.

Wheel, Camel, Fish & Plow: Yoga for You. Rachel Carr. (Illus.). (gr. 5 up). 1981. 9.95 (ISBN 0-13-956045-9). P-H.

Wheel of Becoming: Personal Growth Through the Liturgical Year. Augustin Belisle. (Orig.). 1987. pap. 6.95 (ISBN 0-932506-57-7). St Bedes Pubns.

Wheel of Destiny. Wilhelmina McKerron. 1981. 20.00x (ISBN 0-7223-1408-6, Pub. by A H Stockwell England). State Mutual Bk.

Wheel of Fire: Interpretations of Shakespearean Tragedy. 4th ed. G. Wilson Knight. 350p. 1949. pap. 13.95x (ISBN 0-416-50930-4, NO. 2276). Routledge Chapman & Hall.

Wheel of Fortune. Willard Anderson. 1985. 11.95 (ISBN 0-317-28984-5). Vantage.

Wheel of Fortune. Susan Howatch. 1184p. 1984. 19.95 (ISBN 0-671-49989-0). S&S.

Wheel of Fortune. Susan Howatch. 1280p. 1985. pap. 4.95 (ISBN 0-449-20624-6, Crest). Fawcett.

Wheel of Fortune. Sams. 1988. pap. 3.95 (ISBN 0-312-90833-4). St Martin.

Wheel of Fortune: How to Control Your Future. David Line & Julia Line. (Illus.). 304p. (Orig.). 1988. pap. 16.95 (ISBN 0-85030-618-3, Pub. by Aquarian Pr England). Sterling.

Wheel of God. George Egerton, pseud. LC 79-8263. Repr. of 1898 ed. 44.50 (ISBN 0-686-63604-X). AMS Pr.

Wheel of Life. Ellen Glasgow. 474p. Repr. of 1906 ed. lib. bdg. 45.00 (ISBN 0-918377-35-8). Russell Pr.

Wheel of Life. Dorothy M. Lyon. 1987. 35.00x (ISBN 0-7223-2167-8, Pub. by A H Stockwell). State Mutual Bk.

Wheel of Life & Death: A Practical & Spiritual Guide to Death, Dying & Beyond. Philip Kapleau. 1989. 18.95 (ISBN 0-385-23413-9). Doubleday.

Wheel of Life: The Autobiography of a Western Buddhist. John Blofeld. (Dragon Editions Ser.). (Illus.). 305p. 1988. pap. 12.95 (ISBN 0-87773-034-2). Shambhala Pubns.

Wheel of Servitude: Black Forced Labor after Slavery. Daniel A. Novak. LC 77-76334. 144p. 1978. 13.00 (ISBN 0-8131-1371-7). U Pr of Ky.

Wheel of Stars. Andre Norton. 320p. (Orig.). 1984. pap. 3.50 (ISBN 0-8125-4725-X, Dist. by Warner Pub. Services & Saint Martin's Press). Tor Bks.

Wheel of the Law: Buddhism Illustrated from Siamese Sources. Henry Alabaster. 384p. Repr. of 1871 ed. text ed. 49.68x (ISBN 0-576-03126-7, Pub. by Gregg Intl Pubs England). Gregg Intl.

Wheel of the Winds. M. J. Engh. 384p. 1988. 18.95. Tor Bks.

Wheel of Time. David Patt. 1983. pap. write for info. Deer Park Bks.

Wheel on the Chimney. Margaret W. Brown. LC 84-48379. (Illus.). 32p. (ps-3). 1985. 13.70i (ISBN 0-397-30288-6, Lipp Jr Bks); PLB 13.89 (ISBN 0-397-30296-7). HarpJ.

Wheel on the School. Meindert DeJong. LC 54-8945. (Illus.). (gr. 3-6). 1954. 13.95i (ISBN 0-06-021585-2); PLB 13.89 (ISBN 0-06-021586-0). HarpJ.

Wheel on the School. Meindert DeJong. LC 54-8945. (Trophy I Can Read Bks.). (Illus.). (gr. 3-6). 1954. pap. 3.50 (ISBN 0-06-440021-2, Trophy). HarpJ.

Wheel: Poems. Wendell Berry. LC 82-81482. 72p. 1982. 10.00 (ISBN 0-86547-078-2); pap. 6.95 (ISBN 0-86547-079-0). N Point Pr.

Wheel Turning on the Hub of the Sun see Reasons for Going It on Foot.

Wheelchair Batteries. Betty Garee. 32p. (Orig.). 1987. pap. 3.50 (ISBN 0-915708-22-1). Cheever Pub.

Wheelchair Book: Mobility for the Disabled. Herman L. Kamenetz. (Illus.). 288p. 1969. photocopy ed. 31.50x (ISBN 0-398-00965-1). C C Thomas.

Wheelchair Child: How Handicapped Children Can Enjoy Life to Its Fullest. Philippa Russell. (Illus.). 272p. 1984. 18.95 (ISBN 0-13-956020-3); pap. 9.95 (ISBN 0-13-956012-2). P-H.

Wheelchair Gourmet: A Cookbook for the Disabled. Mary E. Blakeslee. LC 81-4547. 192p. 1981. spiralbound 8.95 (ISBN 0-8253-0063-0). Beaufort Bks NY.

Wheelchair Posture & Pressure Sores. Dennis Zacharkow. (Illus.). 108p. 1984. 18.50 (ISBN 0-398-04892-4). C C Thomas.

Wheelchair Recipes from the Collection of Momma Wheels. Maxine Smolen. Ed. by Debbie Hammond. LC 80-11153. Date not set. pap. 9.95 (ISBN 0-87949-171-X). Ashley Bks.

Wheelchair Summer see Summer Dreams.

Wheelchair Willie & Other Plays: Brown Ale with Gertie & O'Conner. Alan Brown. (Orig.). 1980. pap. 4.95 (ISBN 0-7145-3655-5). Riverrun NY.

Wheelchairs: A Prescription Guide. A. Bennett Wilson, Jr. & Samuel R. McFarland. (Illus.). 48p. 1986. pap. 14.95 spiral bdg. (ISBN 0-317-69658-0, 000001). Demos Pubns Inc.

Wheeler & Goldhor's Practical Administration of Public Libraries. rev. ed. Ed. by Carlton Rochell. LC 79-3401. (Illus.). 480p. 1981. 29.45i (ISBN 0-06-013601-4, HarpT). Har-Row.

Wheeler: Trail in the Dust. new braille ed. Richard G. Hubler. LC 70-91859. 772p. 1970. 9.95 (ISBN 0-685-24689-2). Creek Hse.

Wheeler's Atlas of Tooth Form. 5th ed. Major M. Ash, Jr. (Illus.). 158p. 1984. 29.00 (ISBN 0-7216-1277-6). Saunders.

Wheeler's Big Break. Daniel Schantz. (Wheeler's Adventures Ser.). (Illus.). 96p. (Orig.). (gr. 3-6). 1988. pap. 2.98 (ISBN 0-87403-451-5, 24-02911). Standard Pub.

Wheeler's Big Catch. Daniel Schantz. (Wheeler Ser.). (Illus.). 96p. (gr. 3-5). 1987. pap. 2.95 (ISBN 0-87403-318-7, 2927). Standard Pub.

Wheeler's Campaign. Daniel Schantz. (Wheeler's Adventures Ser.). (Illus.). 96p. (Orig.). (gr. 3-6). pap. 2.98 (ISBN 0-87403-454-X, 24-02914). Standard Pub.

Wheeler's Deal. Daniel Schantz. (Wheeler Ser.). (Illus.). 96p. (gr. 3-5). 1987. pap. 2.95 (ISBN 0-87403-317-9, 2926). Standard Pub.

Wheeler's Dental Anatomy, Physiology & Occlusion. 6th ed. Major M. Ash. (Illus.). 464p. 1984. 34.95 (ISBN 0-7216-1429-9). Saunders.

Wheeler's Freedom. Daniel Schantz. (Wheeler's Adventures Ser.). (Illus.). 96p. (Orig.). (gr. 3-6). 1988. pap. 2.98 (ISBN 0-87403-453-1, 24-02913). Standard Pub.

Wheeler's Ghost Town. Daniel Schantz. (Wheeler Ser.). (Illus.). 96p. (gr. 3-5). 1987. pap. 2.95 (ISBN 0-87403-319-5, 2928). Standard Pub.

Wheeler's Good Time. Daniel Schantz. (Wheeler Ser.). (Illus.). 96p. (gr. 3-5). 1987. pap. 2.95 (ISBN 0-87403-320-9, 2929). Standard Pub.

Wheeler's Photographic Survey of the American West, 1871-1873: With Fifty Landscape Photographs by Timothy O'Sullivan & Willia Bell. Ed. by George M. Wheeler. LC 82-19773. (Illus.). 50p. 1983. pap. 6.95 (ISBN 0-486-24466-0). Dover.

Wheelers RV Resort & Campground Guide. rev. ed. Gloria S. Telander et al. 848p. 1986. pap. 10.95 (ISBN 0-942398-04-1). Print Med Serv Ltd.

Wheelers RV Resort & Campground Guide. rev. ed. Gloria S. Telander et al. 848p. (Orig.). 1987. pap. 10.95 (ISBN 0-942398-05-X). Print Med Serv Ltd.

Wheelers RV Resort & Campground Guide. Gloria S. Telander et al. 848p. (Orig.). 1988. pap. 10.95 (ISBN 0-942398-06-8). Print Med Serv Ltd.

Wheeler's RV Resort & Campground Guide. 854p. 1988. 10.95. RV Indus Assn.

Wheeler's Site: A Specialized Shellfish Processing Station on the Merrimack River. Russell J. Barber. LC 82-62726. (Peabody Museum Monographs: No. 7). (Illus.). 96p. 1983. pap. 12.00x (ISBN 0-87365-907-4). Peabody Harvard.

Wheeler's Vacation. Daniel Schantz. (Wheeler's Adventures Ser.). (Illus.). 96p. (Orig.). (gr. 3-6). 1988. pap. 2.98 (ISBN 0-87403-452-3, 24-02912). Standard Pub.

Wheeling & Dealing: An Ethnography of an Upper-Level Drug Dealing & Smuggling Community. Patricia A. Adler. LC 85-2644. 1985. 30.00 (ISBN 0-231-06060-2). Columbia U Pr.

Wheeling & Dealing: An Ethnography of an Upper-Level Drug Dealing & Smuggling Community. Patricia A. Adler. LC 85-2644. 192p. 1987. pap. text ed. 13.00 (ISBN 0-231-06061-0). Columbia U Pr.

Wheeling: Options for Industries. 25p. 1984. 10.00. Elec Consumers Res.

Wheels. Byron Barton. LC 78-20541. (Illus.). (ps-3). 1979. o. p. 9.57i (ISBN 0-690-03951-4, Crowell Jr Bks); PLB 12.89 (ISBN 0-690-03952-2). HarpJ.

Wheels. Julie Fitzpatrick. (Science Spirals Ser.). (Illus.). 32p. (gr. 3-5). 1987. PLB 8.96 (ISBN 0-382-09534-0). Silver.

Wheels. Arthur Hailey. 1986. pap. 4.50 (ISBN 0-440-19414-8). Dell.

Wheels. David Squire. LC 79-5064. (Lerner Question & Answer Bks.). (Illus.). (gr. 3-6). 1980. PLB 8.95 (ISBN 0-8225-1186-X). Lerner Pubns.

Wheels. Jane R. Thomas. (ps-3). 1986. 12.95 (ISBN 0-317-39001-5). HM.

Wheels. Jane R. Thomas. LC 85-13291. (Illus.). 32p. (ps-3). 1986. 12.95 (ISBN 0-89919-410-9, Pub. by Clarion). Ticknor & Fields.
Wheels: A Pictorial History. Edwin Tunis. LC 76-25809. (Illus.). (gr. 6 up). 1977. 19.70 (ISBN 0-690-01282-9, Crowell Jr Bks). HarpJ.
Wheels & Deals: Buying a Car. Marilyn Thypin & Lynne Glasner. LC 78-12466. (Consumer Education Ser.). 1979. pap. text ed. 3.95 (ISBN 0-88436-506-9, 30253). EMC.
Wheels & Looms: Making Equipment for Spinning & Weaving. David Bryant. (Illus.). 1988p. 34.95 (ISBN 0-7134-4828-8, Pub. by Batsford England). David & Charles.
Wheels & Paddles in the Sudan: Nineteen Twenty-Three to Nineteen Forty-Six. C. R. Williams. 1986. 45.00x (ISBN 0-946270-24-4, Pub. by Pentland Pr UK). State Mutual Bk.
Wheels & Wings. Ed. by Gakken Co. Ltd. Editors. Tr. by Time-Life Books Inc. Editors. (Child's First Library of Learning). (Illus.). 90p. (gr. k-3). 1988. price not set (ISBN 0-8094-4861-0); PLB price not set (ISBN 0-8094-4862-9). Time-Life.
Wheels at Work. Bernie Zubrowski. LC 86-12500. (Illus.). 112p. (gr. 3-7). 1986. lib. bdg. 10.88 (ISBN 0-688-06348-9, Morrow Junior Books); pap. 5.95 (ISBN 0-688-06349-7, Morrow Junior Books). Morrow.
Wheels for Walking. Sandra Richmond. Ed. by Melanie Kroupa. LC 85-70855. 196p. (gr. 6 up). 1985. 13.95 (ISBN 0-316-74439-5, Joy St Bks). Little.
Wheels for Walking. Sandra Richmond. 176p. 1988. pap. 2.50 (ISBN 0-451-15235-2, Sig). NAL.
Wheels Go Round. (Poke & Look Bks.). (Illus.). 24p. (gr. k-2). 1982. 6.95 (ISBN 0-448-01452-1, G&D). Putnam Pub Group.
Wheel's Kick & the Wind's Song. 3rd ed. A. G. Course. LC 68-23816. 1968. 27.95x (ISBN 0-678-05592-0). Kelley.
Wheels, Life & Other Mathematical Amusements. Martin Gardner. LC 83-11592. (Illus.). 350p. 1983. pap. 12.95 (ISBN 0-7167-1589-9). W H Freeman.
Wheels of a Soul. Philip S. Berg. 224p. 1984. 15.95 (ISBN 0-943688-12-4); pap. 9.95 (ISBN 0-943688-13-2). Res Ctr Kabbalah.
Wheels of a Soul. Philip S. Berg. 256p. 1987. 14.95 (ISBN 0-943688-45-0); pap. 9.95 (ISBN 0-943688-46-9). Res Ctr Kabbalah.
Wheels of a Soul. Philip S. Berg. 288p. (Fr.). 1987. 14.95 (ISBN 0-943688-71-X); pap. 9.95 (ISBN 0-943688-72-8). Res Ctr Kabbalah.
Wheels of a Soul. Philip S. Berg. 160p. 1986. 14.95 (ISBN 0-943688-41-8); pap. 9.95 (ISBN 0-943688-42-6). Res Ctr Kabbalah.
Wheels of Commerce, Vol. 2: Civilization & Capitalism 15th-18th Century. Fernand Braudel. LC 81-47653. (Illus.). 720p. 1986. pap. 16.95 (ISBN 0-06-091295-2, PL 1295, PL). Har-Row.
Wheels of Commerce Vol. 2: Civilization & Capitalism, 15th-18th Century, No. 2. Fernand Braudel. Tr. by Sian Reynolds from Fr. LC 82-48109. (Illus.). 720p. 1983. 34.50i (ISBN 0-06-015091-2, HarpT). Har-Row.
Wheels of Farm Progress. Marvin McKinley. (Illus.). 160p. 1980. 11.95 (ISBN 0-916150-24-0, HO680). Am Soc Ag Eng.
Wheels of Fortune. Francis A. Seufert. Ed. by Thomas Vaughan. LC 80-81719. (Illus.). 284p. 1981. 19.95 (ISBN 0-87595-083-3); pap. 12.95 (ISBN 0-87595-069-8). Oregon Hist.
Wheels of Life: A User's Guide to the Chakra System. Anodea Judith. Ed. by Phyllis Galde. (New Age Ser.). (Illus.). 544p. 1987. pap. 12.95 (ISBN 0-87542-320-5); audio tape 9.95 (ISBN 0-87542-321-3). Llewellyn Pubns.
Wheels of Misfortune: The Rise & Fall of the British Motor Industry. Jonathan Wood. 280p. Date not set. write for info. Wayne St U Pr.
Wheels of Progress? Motor Transport, Pollution & the Environment. Ed. by Rose. 170p. 1973. pap. 35.00 (ISBN 0-677-15425-9). Gordon & Breach.
Wheels on Ice. Ed. by Terrence Cole. LC 84-2861. (Northern History Library). (Illus.). 64p. 1985. 6.95 (ISBN 0-88240-272-2). Alaska Northwest.
Wheels on the Bus. Maryann Kovalski. (Illus.). 32p. (ps-k). 1987. 11.95 (ISBN 0-316-50256-1, Joy St Bks). Little.
Wheels on the Bus. Illus. by Sylvie K. Wickstrom. (Raffi Songs to Read Ser.). (Illus.). 32p. (ps-2). 1988. PLB 9.95 (ISBN 0-517-56784-9). Crown.
Wheels on the Mountains. James E. Craft. (Illus.). 1969. 8.00 (ISBN 0-87012-072-7). McClain.
Wheels Rolling-West. Dave Styffe & Ted Benson. LC 79-63044. (Illus.). 1979. 17.50 (ISBN 0-9602466-0-6). Westrail Pubns.
Wheels That Work. (Chubby Board Bks.). (Illus.). 16p. (ps-k). 1988. 2.95 (ISBN 0-671-64872-1, Little Simon). S&S.
Wheels to Adventure: Bill Rishel's Western Routes. Virginia Rishel. LC 83-10823. (Illus.). 160p. 1983. 00.00; pap. 9.95 (ISBN 0-935704-16-7). Howe Brothers.
Wheelwork. Marilyn R. Rosenberg. 14p. 1986. pap. 100.00 (ISBN 0-913615-11-0). M Rosenberg.
Wheelwright's Shop. George Sturt. 42.50 (ISBN 0-521-06570-4); pap. 15.95 (ISBN 0-521-09195-0). Cambridge U Pr.
Wheezy. Michael Charlton. (Illus.). 30p. (ps-2). 1988. 10.95 (ISBN 0-370-31150-7). Knopf.
Wheezy. Michael Charlton. (ps-2). 1988. 10.95. Random.
Wheldon's Business Statistics. 9th ed. G. L. Thirkettle. (Illus.). 1981. pap. text ed. 23.50x (ISBN 0-7121-2331-8, Pub. by Macdonald & Evans England). Trans-Atl Phila.
Wheldon's Cost Accounting. 15th ed. L. W. Owler & J. L. Brown. (Illus.). 706p. 1984. 37.50x (ISBN 0-7121-2327-X). Trans-Atl Phila.
Wheldon's Costing Simplified. 5th ed. L. W. Owler & J. L. Brown. (Illus.). 336p. 1978. pap. text ed. 20.00x (ISBN 0-7121-2309-1, Pub. by Macdonald & Evans England). Trans-Atl Phila.
Whelping & Rearing of Puppies: A Complete & Practical Guide. Muriel P. Lee. (Illus.). 126p. 1984. pap. 9.95 (ISBN 0-9612546-0-2). Plantin Pr.
When. Laura Alden. LC 83-7305. (Question Bks). (Illus.). 32p. (gr. k-2). 1983. 11.93 (ISBN 0-516-06592-0); pap. 2.95 (ISBN 0-516-46592-9). Childrens.
When? Margaret W. Hudson. 1965. 1.50 (ISBN 0-88323-081-X, 178). Richards Pub.
When? Leo Lionni. LC 83-4100. (Four Board Bks.). 14p. (ps). 1983. 3.95 (ISBN 0-394-86032-2, Pant Bks Young). Pantheon.
When a Baby Dies: A Handbook for Healing & Helping. Rana K. Limbo & Sara R. Wheeler. 168p. 1986. pap. 8.95 (ISBN 0-9612310-3-3). Harsand Pr.
When A Bough Breaks. Mary Y. Nilsen. 220p. (Orig.). 1985. pap. 5.95 (ISBN 0-89486-338-X). Hazelden.
When a Caring Family Faces Crises. Charles W. Stewart. LC 80-69089. (When Bks.). (Illus.). 96p. (Orig.). pap. 2.45 (ISBN 0-87029-169-6, 20264-8). Abbey.
When a Child Dies. Lisl A. Der Heide. (Illus., Orig.). 1987. pap. 6.00 (ISBN 0-9618036-3-0). Hospice Santa Barbara.
When a Child Is Born: A Guide to Natural Mothering, Pregnancy, Birth & Early Childhood. Wilhelm Z. Linden. 222p. (Orig.). 1984. pap. 8.95 (ISBN 0-7225-0956-1). Inner Tradit.
When a Christian Sins. John R. Rice. 1954. pap. 3.95 (ISBN 0-8024-9434-X). Moody.
When a College Works with a Public School: A Case Study of School-College Collaboration. Sidney Trubowitz et al. (Orig.). 1984. pap. 8.50 (ISBN 0-917754-22-0, 20C). Inst Responsive.
When a Congregation Cares. Abraham Schmitt & Dorothy Schmitt. LC 84-19294. 128p. (Orig.). 1984. pap. 6.95 (ISBN 0-8361-3410-9). Herald Pr.
When a Doctor Hates a Patient: And Other Chapters in a Young Physician's Life. Richard E. Peschel & Enid R. Peschel. Date not set. pap. 9.95. U of Cal Pr.
When a Doctor Hates a Patient: Chapters from a Young Physicians Life. Richard E. Peschel & Enid R. Peschel. 1986. 18.95 (ISBN 0-520-05755-4); pap. 8.95. U of Cal Pr.
When a Duo Becomes Single see Survival Tips for a Single Parent.
When a Family Loses a Loved One. Paul F. Wilczak. LC 81-68846. (WHEN Bk. Ser.). 96p. (Orig.). 1981. pap. 2.45 (ISBN 0-87029-179-3, 20272-1). Abbey.
When a Father Is Hard to Honor. Elva McAllaster. 126p. (Orig.). 1984. pap. 6.95 (ISBN 0-87178-930-2). Brethren.
When a Good God Lets Bad Things Happen. Duane Kelderman. 1983. 3.25 (ISBN 0-89536-583-9, 2333). CSS of Ohio.
When a Good Man Falls. Erwin W. Luzer. 132p. 1985. pap. 4.95 (ISBN 0-89693-361-X). Victor Bks.
When a Great Tradition Modernizes: An Anthropological Approach to Indian Civilization. Milton Singer. LC 79-26490. (Midway Reprint Ser.). 1980. pap. text ed. 21.00x (ISBN 0-226-76102-9). U of Chicago Pr.
When a Jew Celebrates. Harry Gersh. LC 70-116678. (Jewish Values Ser.). (Illus.). 256p. (gr. 5-6). 1971. pap. text ed. 7.95x (ISBN 0-87441-091-6); tchr's guide 14.95; student activity bk. 3.95; tchr's cassette 5.95. Behrman.
When a Jew Prays. Seymour Rossel. Ed. by Eugene B. Borowitz & Hyman Chanover. LC 73-1233. (Illus.). 192p. (gr. 4-6). 1973. pap. text ed. 7.95x (ISBN 0-87441-093-2); tchr's guide 14.95; tchr's cassette 5.95; student encounter bk. 3.95. Behrman.
When a Jew Seeks Wisdom: The Sayings of the Fathers. Seymour Rossel. LC 75-14119. (Jewish Values Ser.). (gr. 7). pap. 7.95x (ISBN 0-87441-089-4); student's encounter bk. 3.95; tchr's guide 14.95. Behrman.
When a Lady: Prose - 1982. Mark Insingel et al. Tr. by Dixon et al. 95p. (Dutch, Fr., Ger. & Rus.). 1982. 8.95 (ISBN 0-87376-038-7). Red Dust.
When a Lawyer Divorces: How to Value a Professional Practice. American Bar Association, Economics of Law Practice & Family Law Staffs. LC 86-72153. 150p. 1986. pap. 34.95 (ISBN 0-89707-266-9). Amer Bar Assn.
When a Loved One Dies. Philip W. Williams. LC 75-22713. 96p. 1976. pap. 5.95 (ISBN 0-8066-1520-6, 10-7056). Augsburg.
When a Man Loves a Woman: How to Love a Woman of the Eighties. Claude M. Steiner. LC 85-71164. 256p. 1986. 19.50 (ISBN 0-394-54945-7). Grove.
When a Man Loves a Woman: How to Love a Woman of the Eighties. Claude M. Steiner. LC 85-71164. 256p. 1986. pap. 8.95 (ISBN 0-394-62076-3, Ever). Grove.
When a Man's Single see Works of J. M. Barrie.
When a Member of the Family Needs Counseling. John A. Larsen. LC 79-51274. (When Bk.). (Illus.). 1979. pap. 2.45 (ISBN 0-87029-147-5, 20234-1). Abbey.
When a Parent Imposes Limits: Discipline, Authority, & Freedom in Today's Family. Beth Michel. LC 81-68517. (WHEN Bk.). 96p. (Orig.). 1981. pap. 2.45 (ISBN 0-87029-178-5, 20269-7). Abbey.
When a Parent Is Mentally Ill: What to Say to Your Child. Helene S. Arnstein. 36p. 1974. pap. 1.50 (ISBN 0-686-12282-8). Jewish Bd Family.
When a Parent Is Very Sick. Eda LeShan. (Illus.). 112p. (gr. 3-7). 1986. 12.95 (ISBN 0-316-52162-0, Joy St Bks). Little.
When a Pastor Search Committee Comes... or Doesn't. J. William Harbin. LC 85-13541. 1985. pap. 4.95 (ISBN 0-8054-2545-4). Broadman.
When a Person Dies: Pastoral Theology in Death Experiences. Robert L. Kinast. LC 84-11431. 160p. (Orig.). 1984. pap. 9.95 (ISBN 0-8245-0657-X). Crossroad NY.
When a Pet Dies. Fred Rogers. (First Experience Bks.). (Illus.). (ps-4). 1988. 12.95 (ISBN 0-399-21504-2); pap. 5.95 (ISBN 0-399-21529-8). Putnam Pub Group.
When a Place Becomes a Person. Anees Jung. 1977. 11.00x (ISBN 0-7069-0526-1). Intl Bk Dist.
When a Story Would Help: An Approach to Creative Parenting. Lucie W. Barber. LC 80-70550. (When Bk.). (Illus.). 88p. (Orig.). 1981. pap. 2.45 (ISBN 0-87029-173-4, 20267-1). Abbey.
When a Writer Can't Write: Studies in Writer's Block & Other Composing Problems. Ed. by Mike Rose. LC 84-19304. (Perspectives in Writing Research Ser.). 272p. 1985. text ed. 35.00 (ISBN 0-89862-251-4); pap. 15.00 (ISBN 0-89862-904-7). Guilford Pr.
When AAs go to OA. Judi Hollis. 24p. (Orig.). 1986. pap. 1.50 (ISBN 0-89486-347-9). Hazelden.
When Adam Clarke Preached, People Listened. Wesley Tracy. 238p. (Orig.). 1981. pap. 4.95 (ISBN 0-8341-0714-7). Beacon Hill.
When Age Grows Young. Clare H. Kirk. Ed. by Robert Kastenbaum. LC 78-22204. (Aging & Old Age Ser.). 1979. Repr. of 1888 ed. lib. bdg. 21.00x (ISBN 0-405-11819-8). Ayer Co Pubs.
When AIDS Comes to the Church. William E. Amos, Jr. LC 87-30875. 132p. 1988. pap. 9.95 (ISBN 0-664-25009-2). Westminster John Knox.
When Alaska Was Free. Knut D. Peterson. Ed. by Sylvia Ashton. LC 77-70299. 1977. 15.95 (ISBN 0-87949-081-0). Ashley Bks.
When All Hell Breaks Loose. C. E. Douglas. 1974. pap. 4.95 (ISBN 0-9601124-0-5). Tusayan Gospel.
When All Is Said & Done. David Bergelson. Tr. by Bernard Martin from Yiddish. LC 76-25614. xxi, 310p. 1971. 18.95x (ISBN 0-8214-0360-5); pap. 10.00 (ISBN 0-8214-0392-3). Ohio U Pr.
When All the Wild Summer. Gene Detro. (Kestrel Ser.: No. 7). 28p. 1983. pap. 3.00 (ISBN 0-914974-39-4). Holmgangers.
When All You've Ever Wanted Isn't Enough. Harold Kushner. (Large Print Bks). 255p. 1987. lib. bdg. 17.95x (ISBN 0-8161-4202-5, Large Print Bks). G K Hall.
When All You've Ever Wanted Isn't Enough. Harold Kushner. pap. 4.50. PB.
When All You've Ever Wanted Isn't Enough. Harold S. Kushner. 1986. 16.95 (ISBN 0-671-54342-3). Summit Bks.
When All You've Ever Wanted Isn't Enough: The Search for a Life That Matters. Harold Kushner. 272p. 1987. pap. 10.95 (ISBN 0-8161-4203-3, Large Print Bks). G K Hall.
When Am I Going to Be Happy? How to Break the Emotional Bad Habits That Make You Miserable. Penelope Russianoff. LC 88-47645. 272p. 1988. 19.95 (ISBN 0-553-05054-0). Bantam.
When America Does It Right. Ed. by Jay Spechlere. 1988. price not set (ISBN 0-89806-097-4). Inst Indus Eng.
When America Was Young. Mabel A. Murphy. LC 72-38326. (Biography Index Reprint Ser.). (Illus.). Repr. of 1948 ed. 19.75 (ISBN 0-8369-8126-X). Ayer Co Pubs.
When an Angel Dies. Kent Cahill & Kathleen Cahill. Ed. by Bob Moog. (Murder Mystery Party Ser.). 50p. 1986. 8.00 (ISBN 0-935145-05-2). Univ Games.
When & How to Choose an Attorney. 2nd ed. Cameron K. Wehringer. LC 78-21138. (Legal Almanac Ser.: No. 63). 1978. 6.95 (ISBN 0-379-11113-6). Oceana.
When & Where I Enter: The Impact of Black Women on Race & Sex in America. Paula Giddings. LC 84-60089. 403p. 1984. 17.95 (ISBN 0-688-01943-9). Morrow.
When & Where I Enter: The Impact of Black Women on Race & Sex in America. Paula Giddings. LC 85-47761. 408p. 1985. pap. 8.95 (ISBN 0-553-34225-8). Bantam.
When Angels Appear. Hope MacDonald. 128p. (Orig.). 1982. pap. 6.95 (ISBN 0-310-28531-3, 10047P). Zondervan.
When Antibiotics Fail: Restoring the Ecology of the Body. 2nd, rev. ed. Marc Lappe. 288p. 1987. 25.00 (ISBN 0-938190-75-X); pap. 12.95 (ISBN 0-938190-74-1). North Atlantic.
When Baby Comes Home. Erma Brenner. (Illus.). 128p. 1984. pap. text ed. 5.95 (ISBN 0-88102-038-9); tchr's guide 6.95 (ISBN 0-88102-039-7). Janus Bks.
When Baby Makes Two. Helen Duran. LC 86-83412. (Illus.). 260p. (Orig.). 1988. pap. 9.95 (ISBN 0-89896-341-9). Larksdale.
When Bad Happens to God's People. Richard Rice. 1984. pap. 6.95 (ISBN 0-8163-0570-6). Pacific Pr Pub Assn.
When Bad Things Happen, God Still Loves. Joe Blair. LC 85-13240. 1986. pap. 4.95 (ISBN 0-8054-5010-6). Broadman.
When Bad Things Happen to Good People. Harold S. Kushner. LC 81-40411. 160p. 1981. 13.95 (ISBN 0-8052-3773-9). Schocken.
When Bad Things Happen to Good People. Harold S. Kushner. 160p. 1983. pap. 6.95 (ISBN 0-380-67033-X, 67033X). Avon.
When Bad Things Happen to Good People. Harold S. Kushner. (General Ser.). 1982. lib. bdg. 13.95 (ISBN 0-8161-3465-0, Large Print Bks). G K Hall.
When Bad Things Happen to Good People. Harold S. Kushner. 160p. 1963. pap. 3.95 (ISBN 0-380-60392-6). Avon.
When Bad Things Happen to Good People. Harold S. Kushner. LC 81-40411. 160p. 1987. Deluxe boxed gift edition. deluxe ed. 19.95 (ISBN 0-8052-4039-X). Schocken.
When Basildon Was Farms & Fields. Jessie K. Payne. 1988. 30.00x (ISBN 0-86025-416-X, Pub. by Ian Henry Pubns England). State Mutual Bk.
When Batistine Made Bread. Treska Lindsey. LC 84-42988. (Illus.). 48p. (gr. k-3). 1985. 9.95 (ISBN 0-02-759120-4). Macmillan.
When Battered Women Kill. Angela Browne. 1987. 19.95 (ISBN 0-02-903880-4). Free Pr.
When Battle Rages How Can Law Protect? H. S. Levie. Ed. by John Carey. LC 78-123998. (Hammarskjold Forum Ser.: No. 14). 115p. 1971. 10.00 (ISBN 0-379-11814-9). Oceana.
When Bear Bakes a Cake. Jasper Tomkins. 60p. (Orig.). (ps-2). 1987. 8.95 (ISBN 0-88138-082-2). Green Tiger Pr.
When Bikehood Was in Flower. 2nd ed. Irving A. Leonard. LC 83-61026. (Illus.). 151p. 1983. pap. 7.95 (ISBN 0-912593-02-4). Seven Palms.
When Biology Became Destiny: Women in Weimar & Nazi Germany. Renate Bridenthal et al. (New Feminist Library). 416p. 1984. 27.50 (ISBN 0-85345-642-9); pap. 12.00 (ISBN 0-85345-643-7). Monthly Rev.
When Birds Change Their Feathers. Roma Gans. LC 78-20627. (Let's Read & Find Out Science Bks.). (Illus.). 40p. (gr. k-3). 1980. (Crowell Jr Bks); PLB 12.89 (ISBN 0-690-03948-4). HarpJ.
When Blind Eyes Pierce the Darkness: A Mother's Insights. Tr. & compiled by Peter A. Angeles. (Golden Age Bks.). 130p. 1988. 17.95 (ISBN 0-87975-472-9). Prometheus Bks.
When Bonding Fails: Clinical Assessment of High Risk Families, Vol. 151. Frank G. Bolton, Jr. (Sage Library of Social Research). 224p. 1983. 35.00 (ISBN 0-8039-2079-2); pap. 16.95 (ISBN 0-8039-2080-6). Sage.
When Borders Don't Divide: Labor Migration & Refugee Movements in the Americas. Ed. by Patricia R. Pessar. 1988. 17.50 (ISBN 0-934733-26-0); pap. 12.95 (ISBN 0-934733-27-9). Ctr Migration.
When Breaks the Dawn. Janette Oke. 250p. (Orig.). (gr. 6). 1986. pap. 5.95 (ISBN 0-87123-882-9, 210882). Bethany Hse.
When Brooklyn Was the World 1920-1957. Elliot Willensky. (Illus.). 1986. 19.95 (ISBN 0-517-55858-0, Harmony). Crown.
When Buffalo Ran. George B. Grinnell. LC 66-13429. (Western Frontier Library: No. 31). (Illus.). 1966. pap. 4.95 (ISBN 0-8061-1271-9). U of Okla Pr.
When Burdens Become Bridges. Henry G. Bosch. (Solace Ser.). 1984. pap. 1.50 (ISBN 0-8010-0867-0). Baker Bk.
When California was an Island. Barbara Haas. 156p. (Orig.). 1987. 15.00 (ISBN 0-934257-11-6); pap. 8.00 (ISBN 0-934257-10-8). Story Line.
When Calls the Heart. Janette Oke. LC 82-24451. 221p. (Orig.). 1983. pap. 5.95 (ISBN 0-87123-611-7, 210611). Bethany Hse.
When Calls the Heart. Large type ed. Janette Oke. (Canadian West Ser.). 221p. (Orig.). 1986. pap. 7.95 (ISBN 0-87123-885-3). Bethany Hse.
When Can a Child Believe? Chamberlain. LC 73-80778. pap. 5.95 (ISBN 0-8054-6208-2). Broadman.
When Can Daddy Come Home? Martha W. Hickman. (Illus.). 48p. (gr. 1-3). 1983. 9.50 (ISBN 0-687-44969-3). Abingdon.
When Can I Say, "I Love You"? Max M. Rice & Vivian B. Rice. LC 76-54926. 1977. pap. 4.95 (ISBN 0-8024-9436-6). Moody.
When Cancer Strikes: A Book for Patients, Families & Friends. John A. MacDonald. 132p. 1982. pap. 4.95 (ISBN 0-13-956086-6). P-H.

When Governments Come to Washington: Governors, Mayors, & Intergovernmental Lobbying. Donald H. Haider. LC 73-17643. (Illus.). 1974. 15.95 (ISBN 0-02-913370-X). Free Pr.
When Grandmama Fell Off the Boat: The Best of Harry Graham, Inventor of Ruthless Rhymes. Harry Graham. (Illus.). 160p. 1988. laminated bds. 12.95 (ISBN 0-88162-357-1). Salem Hse Pubs.
When Grandpa Came to Stay. Judith Caseley. LC 85-12616. (Illus.). 32p. (gr. k-2). 1986. 11.75 (ISBN 0-688-06128-1); PLB 11.88 (ISBN 0-688-06129-X). Greenwillow.
When Grandpa Died. Margaret Stevens. LC 78-12360. (Social Values Ser.). (Illus.). 32p. (ps-3). 1979. PLB 11.93 (ISBN 0-516-02025-0); pap. 3.95 (ISBN 0-516-42025-9). Childrens.
When Grandpa Was a Boy. Oscar Cooley. LC 84-29177. (Illus.). 32p. 1984. pap. 4.95 (ISBN 0-934720-29-0). VT Hist Soc.
When Grapes Turn to Wine. Rumi Jelaluddin. Tr. by Robert Bly. (Illus., Persian, Modern.). 1986. pap. 4.00 (ISBN 0-938756-16-8). Yellow Moon.
When Gravity Fails. George A. Effinger. 256p. (Orig.). 1988. pap. 3.95 (ISBN 0-553-25555-X, Spectra). Bantam.
When Gravity Fails. George A. Effinger. 1987. 16.95 (ISBN 0-87795-851-3). Morrow.
When Great Aunt Zelda Comes. Carol A. Marron. LC 84-17733. (Family Bks.). (Illus.). 32p. (ps-3). 1985. PLB 14.65 (ISBN 0-940742-42-X). Raintree Pubs.
When Greek Meets Greek. George Demetrios. LC 76-116949. (Short Story Index Reprint Ser). (Illus.). 1947. 18.00 (ISBN 0-8369-3452-0). Ayer Co Pubs.
When Grover Moved to Sesame Street. Jocelyn Stevenson. (Golden Story Book 'n' Tapes). (Illus.). 24p. (ps-3). 1987. pap. write for info incl. cassette (Pub. by Golden Bks). Western Pub.
When Grover Moved to Sesame Street. Jocelyn Stevenson. (Sesame Street Growing-Up Bks.). (Illus.). 32p. (ps-k). 1985. 2.95 (ISBN 0-307-12017-1, Pub. by Golden Bks). Western Pub.
When Grownups Drive You Crazy. Eda LeShan. LC 87-22005. 144p. (gr. 3-7). 1988. PLB 11.95 (ISBN 0-02-756340-5). Macmillan.
When Half-Gods Go. Hannelore Valencak. Tr. by Patricia Crampton from Ger. LC 76-6140. 192p. (Orig.). (gr. 7 up). 1976. PLB 11.88 (ISBN 0-688-32077-5). Morrow.
When Hamtramck & I Were Friends. Arthur J Majewski. LC 86-62351. 120p. 1987. 10.00 (ISBN 0-9617557-0-9). Maryt Pub.
When Harlem Was in Vogue. David L. Lewis. LC 80-2704. (Illus.). 400p. 1981. 22.00 (ISBN 0-394-49572-1). Knopf.
When Harlem Was Jewish, Eighteen Seventy to Nineteen Thirty. Jeffrey Gurock. LC 79-14768. 216p. 1979. 29.50x (ISBN 0-231-04666-9). Columbia U Pr.
When Harley Heard from Heaven. Harley W. Vail. LC 82-72633. 84p. 1982. pap. 2.95 (ISBN 0-9609096-0-5). Bethel Pub Or.
When Harlie Was One. David Gerrold. 288p. 1988. pap. 3.95 (ISBN 0-553-26465-6, Spectra). Bantam.
When Harlie Was Two. David Gerrold. (Spectra Ser.). 240p. 1987. pap. 3.50 (ISBN 0-553-26466-4, Spectra). Bantam.
When He Is Come. A. W. Tozer & G. B. Smith. Orig. Title: Tozer Pulpit, Vol. 2: Ten Sermons on the Ministry of the Holy Spirit. 146p. (Orig.). 1980. pap. 3.45 (ISBN 0-87509-221-7). Chr Pubns.
When Health Care Employees Strike: A Guide for Planning & Action. Norman Metzger et al. LC 84-2870. 300p. 1984. 53.50 (ISBN 0-89443-588-4). Aspen Pub.
When Hearts Are Light Again. Emilie Loring. 1976. Repr. of 1943 ed. lib. bdg. 18.95x (ISBN 0-88411-365-5, Pub. by Aeonian Pr). Amereon Ltd.
When Hearts Awaken. June M. Bacher. 192p. 1988. pap. 5.95 (ISBN 0-89081-610-7). Harvest Hse.
When Hearts Dream. Laurel Pace. (American Romance Ser.: No. 220). 245p. Date not set. pap. 2.50. Harlequin Bks.
When Hell Laughs. David C. Smith & Richard L. Tierney. (Red Sonja Ser.: No. 3). 1985. pap. 2.95 (ISBN 0-317-31733-4) (ISBN 0-317-31734-2). Ace Bks.
When Hello Means Goodbye: A Guide for Parents Whose Child Dies Before Birth, at Birth or Shortly after Birth. rev. 2nd ed. Pat Schwiebert & Paul Kirk. Ed. by Perinatal Loss Project. 48p. 1985. Eng. pap. 1.75 (ISBN 0-9615197-0-3); Span. pap. 1.75 (ISBN 0-9615197-1-1). Perinatal Loss.
When Helping You Is Hurting Me: Escaping the Messiah Trap. Carmen R. Berry. LC 87-45685. 128p. 1988. 12.95 (ISBN 0-06-060788-2, HarpR). Har-Row.
When Hippo Was Hairy & Other Tales from Africa. Nick Greaves. (Illus.). 144p. (gr. 3-12). 1988. 12.95 (ISBN 0-8120-4131-3). Barron.
When Hitler Stole Pink Rabbit. Judith Kerr. (Illus.). (gr. 6 up). 1972. 8.95 (ISBN 0-698-20182-5, Coward). Putnam Pub Group.
When Hitler Stole Pink Rabbit. Judith Kerr. (gr. 3 up). 1987. pap. 3.25 (ISBN 0-440-49017-0, YB). Dell.
When Hollywood Ruled the Skies. Bruce W. Orriss. (Illus.). 220p. (Orig.). 1984. 27.95; pap. 18.95. Aviation.
When Hollywood Ruled the Skies: The Aviation Film Classics of WWII. Bruce W. Orriss. LC 83-73551. (Illus.). 236p. 1984. 27.95 (ISBN 0-87910-056-7); pap. 18.95 (ISBN 0-9613088-0-X). Aero Assocs.
When Hope Springs New. Janette Oke. 224p. (Orig.). 1986. pap. 5.95 (ISBN 0-87123-657-5, 210657). Bethany Hse.
When Horses Pulled Boats. Alvin S. Harlow. Ed. by W. H. Shank. 1983. Repr. of 1936 ed. 5.00 (ISBN 0-933788-43-6). Am Canal & Transport.
When Humans Began. John Stidworthy. LC 86-60986. (Creatures from the Past Ser.). 37p. (gr. 4-9). 1986. pap. 6.75 (ISBN 0-382-09322-4). Silver.
When I Am an Old Woman I Shall Wear Purple. Ed. by Sandra K. Martz. 180p. (Orig.). 1987. pap. 10.00 (ISBN 0-918949-02-5). Papier-Mache Press.
When I Am Sick. Christine Tangvald. (I Am Special Bks.). (Illus.). 20p. (ps). 1985. 3.95 (ISBN 0-89191-908-2, 59089). Cook.
When I Become a Functionnaire-School Knowledge in French Colonial Africa. Gail P. Kelly. (Special Studies in Comparative Education: No. 11). 76p. (Orig.). 1984. pap. text ed. 5.00 (ISBN 0-937033-01-4). SUNY Compar Educ Ctr.
When I Celebrate His Birthday. Robin J. Gunn. (Jesus Is with Me Ser.). (Illus.). (ps). 1988. bds. 3.95 (ISBN 1-55513-567-6, Chariot Bks). Cook.
When I Cross the Street. Dorothy Chlad. LC 81-18108. (Safety Town Bks.). (Illus.). (gr. k-3). 1982. PLB 11.93 (ISBN 0-516-01985-6); pap. 2.95 (ISBN 0-516-41985-4). Childrens.
When I Do, I Learn: A Guide to Creative Planning for Teachers & Parents of Preschool Children. rev. ed. Barbara J. Taylor. LC 74-2122. (Illus.). 250p. 1977. pap. 9.95x (ISBN 0-8425-1023-0). Brigham.
When I Eat I Hurt. James P. Gould. 168p. (Orig.). 1980. pap. 5.95 (ISBN 0-89288-029-5). Maverick.
When I Eat I Hurt: Freedom from Abdominal Pain. rev. ed. James P. Gould. Ed. by Joyce Moyer. (Illus.). 149p. 1987. pap. 7.95 (ISBN 0-9602506-0-3). Keller-Burns & McGuirk.
When I Get Bigger. Mercer Mayer. (Golden Look-Look Bks.). (Illus.). 24p. (ps-3). 1985. pap. 2.50 (ISBN 0-307-11943-2, Pub. by Golden Bks). Western Pub.
When I Get Old, This Will Be Funny: A Nostalgic Look at the One-Room School. Robert Haney. (Illus.). 247p. 1979. 12.95x (ISBN 0-9609552-0-8). Haney Bks.
When I Go to the Park. Robin J. Gunn. (Jesus Is with Me Ser.). (Illus.). (ps). 1988. bds. 3.95 (ISBN 1-55513-589-7, Chariot Bks). Cook.
When I Go Visiting. Anne Rockwell & Harlow Rockwell. LC 83-17586. (Illus.). 24p. (ps-k). 1984. 8.95 (ISBN 0-02-777740-5). MacMillan.
When I Grew up Long Ago. Alvin Schwartz. LC 78-8719. (Illus.). (gr. 6-12). 1978. 11.70i (ISBN 0-397-31726-3, Lipp Jr Bks). HarpJ.
When I Grow Too Old to Dream: A Journal on Alzheimer's Disease. Clare Bauer. 1987. 10.95 (ISBN 0-533-06833-9). Vantage.
When I Grow Up. Harry Bornstein. (Signed English Ser.). 46p. 1974. pap. 5.95 (ISBN 0-913580-35-X, Clerc Bks). Gallaudet Univ Pr.
When I Grow Up... Heidi Goennel. (ps-3). 1987. 12.95 (ISBN 0-316-31838-8). Little.
When I Grow Up: Structured Experiences for Expanding Male & Female Roles, Vol. II. new ed. Michelle Kavanaugh. LC 78-56486. (Illus.). 200p. 1978. pap. 14.95 (ISBN 0-89334-017-0). Humanics Ltd.
When I Grow Up: Structured Experiences for Expanding Male & Female Roles, Vol. I. new ed. Michelle Kavanaugh. LC 78-56486. (Illus.). 206p. 1978. pap. 14.95 (ISBN 0-89334-016-2). Humanics Ltd.
When I Have a Babysitter. Robin J. Gunn. (Jesus Is with Me Ser.). (Illus.). (ps). 1988. bds. 3.95 (ISBN 1-55513-573-0, Chariot Bks). Cook.
When I Have a Little Boy. Reissue. ed. Charlotte Zolotow. LC 67-14072. (Illus.). 32p. (gr. k-3). 1987. PLB 12.89 (ISBN 0-06-027044-6). HarpJ.
When I Have a Little Boy. Charlotte Zolotow. LC 67-14072. (Trophy Picture Bk.). (Illus.). 32p. (ps-3). 1988. pap. 2.95 (ISBN 0-06-443176-2, Trophy). HarpJ.
When I Have a Little Girl. Charlotte Zolotow. LC 65-24656. (Illus.). (gr. k-3). 1965. 12.95 (ISBN 0-06-027045-4); PLB 8.89 (ISBN 0-06-027046-2). HarpJ.
When I Have a Little Girl. Charlotte Zolotow. LC 65-24656. (Trophy Picture Bk.). (Illus.). 32p. (ps-3). 1988. pap. 2.95 (ISBN 0-06-443175-4, Trophy). HarpJ.
When I Help My Mommy. Robin J. Gunn. (Jesus Is with Me Ser.). (Illus.). (ps). 1988. bds. 3.95 (ISBN 1-55513-566-8, Chariot Bks). Cook.
When I Know the Power of My Black Hand. Lance Jeffers. 1975. 4.95 (ISBN 0-910296-04-9); pap. 2.50. Broadside Pr.
When I Lead, Why Don't They Follow? 2nd ed. Roger Plachy. LC 78-58718. 1978. pap. text ed. 11.95 (ISBN 0-931028-07-8). Teach'em.
When I Lead Why Don't They Follow? Roger Plachy. 1986. 14.95 (ISBN 0-933893-21-3). Bonus Books.
When I Left God in Heaven. Sri Chinmoy. 50p. (Orig.). 1975. pap. 2.00 (ISBN 0-88497-223-2). Aum Pubns.
When I Listen: A Listener's Little Book. Marilyn Gatlin & Mary L. Cook. LC 85-60794. (Printery Edition: No. 1). (Illus.). 68p. 1985. pap. 6.50 (ISBN 0-943734-03-7). Ocean Tree Bks.
When I Relax I Feel Guilty. Tim Hansel. LC 78-73460. 1979. pap. 6.95 (ISBN 0-89191-137-5). Cook.
When I Relax I Feel Guilty: Leader's Kit. Tim Hansel. Date not set. 19.50 (ISBN 1-55513-501-3, LifeJourney). Cook.
When I Ride in a Car. Dorothy Chlad. LC 83-7382. (Safety Town Ser.). (Illus.). 32p. (ps-2). 1983. lib. bdg. 11.93 (ISBN 0-516-01987-2); pap. 2.95 (ISBN 0-516-41987-0). Childrens.
When I Saw Him. Roy Hession. 1975. pap. 2.95 (ISBN 0-87508-239-4). Chr Lit.
When I Say No, I Feel Guilty. Manuel J. Smith. 352p. 1985. pap. 4.95 (ISBN 0-553-26390-0). Bantam.
When I See My Dentist. Susan Kuklin. LC 87-25695. (Illus.). 32p. (ps-k). 1988. 12.95 (ISBN 0-02-751231-2). Bradbury Pr.
When I See My Doctor. Susan Kuklin. LC 87-25621. (Illus.). 32p. (ps-k). 1988. 12.95 (ISBN 0-02-751232-0). Bradbury Pr.
When I Sleep, Then I See Clearly: Selected Poems of J. V. Foix. Tr. & intro. by David H. Rosenthal. (Illus.). 1988. pap. 12.95 (ISBN 0-89255-130-5). Persea Bks.
When I Talk to God. Linda S. Chandler. LC 84-4967. (Illus.). (gr. k-3). 1984. 5.95 (ISBN 0-8054-4291-X, 4242-91). Broadman.
When I Think about You, My Friend. Ed. by Susan P. Schutz. (Illus.). 93p. 1983. text ed. 13.95 (ISBN 0-88396-196-2). Blue Mtn Pr Co.
When I Visit Yosemite. Mary Arrigo & Connie Hargreaves. (Illus.). 43p. (Orig.). (ps). Date not set. pap. 2.95 (ISBN 0-318-21253-6). Arrigo CA.
When I Walk I Change the Earth. Ruth Krauss. (Burning Deck Poetry Ser). 1978. pap. 20.00 signed ed. (ISBN 0-930900-51-0). Burning Deck.
When I Was a Boy in Boston. facs. ed. Charles Angoff. LC 70-132111. (Short Story Index Reprint Ser.). (Illus.). 1947. 14.50 (ISBN 0-8369-3668-X). Ayer Co Pubs.
When I Was a Boy in Palestine. Mousa J. Kaleel. LC 77-876440. (Illus.). Repr. of 1914 ed. 27.50 (ISBN 0-404-16429-3). AMS Pr.
When I Was a Boy in Persia. Youel B. Mirza. LC 77-87650. (Illus.). Repr. of 1920 ed. 20.00 (ISBN 0-404-16419-6). AMS Pr.
When I Was a Boy in Turkey. Ahmed Sabri. LC 77-87624. (Illus.). Repr. of 1924 ed. 18.50 (ISBN 0-404-16450-1). AMS Pr.
When I Was a Child. Charles Shaw. 258p. 1980. pap. 7.50 (ISBN 0-904573-42-7, Pub. by Caliban Bks). Longwood Pub Group.
When I Was a Father. Alvaro Cardona-Hine. LC 82-80604. (Minnesota Voices Project Ser.: No. 7). (Illus.). 73p. 1982. pap. 4.00 (ISBN 0-89823-036-5). New Rivers Pr.
When I Was a Girl, I Used to Scream & Shout. Sharman Macdonald. LC 85-6838. 72p. (Orig.). 1985. pap. 8.95 (ISBN 0-571-13725-3). Faber & Faber.
When I Was Comin' Up: An Oral History of Aged Blacks. Ed. by Audrey Faulkner et al. LC 82-8738. 221p. 1982. 25.00 (ISBN 0-208-01952-9, Archon). Shoe String.
When I Was Little. Meryl Doney. (Illus.). 16p. 1983. pap. 0.99 (ISBN 0-86683-704-3, AY8301, HarpR). Har-Row.
When I Was Nine. James Stevenson. LC 85-9777. (Illus.). 32p. (gr. k-3). 1986. 12.95 (ISBN 0-688-05942-2); PLB 12.88 (ISBN 0-688-05943-0). Greenwillow.
When I Was Otherwise. Stephen Benatar. 272p. 1984. 13.95 (ISBN 0-312-86664-X, Pub. by Marek). St Martin.
When I Was Twelve. Noemi Weygant. (Illus., Orig.). pap. 8.00 (ISBN 0-318-01123-9). Priory Bks.
When I Was Young in the Mountains. Cynthia Rylant. LC 81-5359. (Illus.). 32p. (ps-3). 1982. 12.95 (ISBN 0-525-42525-X, 0966-290). Dutton.
When I Was Young in the Mountains. Cynthia Rylant. (Unicorn Paperback Ser.). (Illus.). (ps-3). 1985. pap. 3.95 (ISBN 0-525-44198-0). Dutton.
When I Was Your Age. Joan Malerba-Foran. 52p. (Orig.). 1984. pap. 4.50 (ISBN 0-89486-231-6). Hazelden.
When I Whistle. Shusaku Endo. Tr. by Van C. Gessel from Japanese. LC 79-13183. Orig. Title: Kuchibue wo Fuku Toki. 273p. 1980. pap. 6.95 (ISBN 0-8008-8244-X). Taplinger.
When I Whistle. Shusaku Endo. Tr. by Van C. Gessel from Japanese. LC 79-13183. 1979. 8.95 (ISBN 0-8008-8243-1). Taplinger.
When I'm a Daddy. Ginger A. Fulton. 1985. pap. 3.25 (ISBN 0-8024-0387-5). Moody.
When I'm a Mommy: A Little Girl's Paraphrase of Proverbs 31. Ginger A. Fulton. (Illus.). (gr. 1-4). 1984. pap. 3.25 (ISBN 0-8024-0367-0). Moody.
When I'm Afraid. Sylvia Tester. (Child's World Books of Understanding). (Illus.). (gr. 1-3). 1985. PLB 5.95 (ISBN 0-89565-071-1, R4900). Standard Pub.
When I'm Alone. Ron DelBene et al. 24p. 1988. pap. 2.95 (ISBN 0-8358-0579-4). Upper Room.
When I'm Big. Dick Bruna. (Dick Bruna Bks.). 1984. 2.95 (ISBN 0-8431-1546-7). Price Stern.
When I'm Sleepy. Jane R. Howard. LC 84-25895. (Illus.). 24p. (ps-3). 1985. 11.95 (ISBN 0-525-44204-9). Dutton.
When in France: A Serendipitous Visit Touching on Paris, the Chateaux, the Wines & Waters the Food, the Morals, the Cliches, & "La Gloire". Christopher Sinclair-Stevenson. (Illus.). 208p. 1987. 15.95 (ISBN 0-671-41644-8). S&S.
When in France... An Insider's Guide to the Hotels & Restaurants of France. Roland Escaig & Maurice Beaudon. 1988. pap. price not set. Warner Bks.
When in Rome. Ngaio Marsh. 1976. lib. bdg. 18.95x (ISBN 0-88411-498-8, Pub. by Aeonian Pr). Amereon Ltd.
When in Rome. Ngaio Marsh. 224p. 1987. pap. 2.95 (ISBN 0-515-07504-3). Jove Pubns.
When in Rome. Ngaio Marsh. (Portway Ser.). 336p. 1988. lib. bdg. 18.50x (ISBN 0-7451-7098-6, Pub. by Chivers Pr UK). G K Hall.
When in Rome: An Introduction to Relativism & Knowledge. N. L. Gifford. LC 82-10374. (SUNY Series in Philosophy). 159p. 1983. 34.50x (ISBN 0-87395-667-2); pap. 8.95x (ISBN 0-87395-668-0). State U NY Pr.
When Information Counts: Grading the Media. Bernard Rubin. 256p. 1985. pap. text ed. 19.95x (ISBN 0-669-10162-1). Lexington Bks.
When Is an Example Binding? Thomas B. Warren. (Biblical Hermeneutics Ser.). 1975. pap. 7.00 (ISBN 0-934916-43-8). Natl Christian Pr.
When Is It Right to Fight? Robert A. Morey. 160p. (Orig.). 1985. pap. 4.95 (ISBN 0-87123-810-1, 210810). Bethany Hse.
When Is My Birthday? Ray Sipherd. LC 88-80284. (Sesame Street Growing-Up Books Ser.). (Illus.). 32p. (ps-1). 1988. 2.95 (ISBN 0-307-12028-7). Western Pub.
When Is Something Fiction? Thomas J. Roberts. LC 79-188698. (Crosscurrents-Modern Critiques Ser.). 157p. 1972. 6.95x (ISBN 0-8093-0578-X). S Ill U Pr.
When Is the Singing Part? (ps-6). 1985. 2.50 (ISBN 0-89837-096-5, Pub. by Pflaum Press). Pflaum Pr.
When Is Tomorrow? Nancy D. Watson. (Illus.). (ps). 1963. 2.75 (ISBN 0-394-81813-X). Knopf.
When It Comes to Bugs. Aileen Fisher. LC 85-45248. (Charlotte Zolotow Bks.). (Illus.). 32p. (gr. k-3). 1986. 12.70i (ISBN 0-06-021819-3); PLB 12.89 (ISBN 0-06-021822-3). HarpJ.
When It Hits the Fan. Gerald C. Meyers. 288p. 1987. pap. 4.95 (ISBN 0-451-62604-4, Ment). NAL.
When It Hits the Fan: Managing the Nine Crises of Business. Gerald C. Meyers & John Holusha. 1986. 17.95 (ISBN 0-395-41171-8). HM.
When It Hurts to Be Single. Randy Petersen & Anita Palmer. LC 88-70290. (Helping Others in Crisis Ser.). 96p. (Orig.). 1988. pap. 6.95 (ISBN 1-55513-883-7, 68833). Cook.
When It Hurts Too Much to Wait: Understanding God's Timing. Larry Richards. 160p. 1985. 9.95 (ISBN 0-8499-0489-7, 0489-7). Word Bks.
When it Rains: Papago & Pima Poetry. Ed. by Ofelia Zepeda. LC 82-10967. (Sun Tracks, An American Indian Literary Ser.: Vol. 7). pap. 22.00 (ISBN 0-317-28046-5, 2025557). Bks Demand UMI.
When It's Time to Move: A Guide to Changing Churches. Paul D. Robbins. (Leadership Library). 160p. 1985. 9.95 (ISBN 0-917463-07-2). Chr Today.
When Its Time to Talk about Sex. Gordon J. Lester. LC 81-65691. (When Bk.). 96p. (Orig.). 1981. pap. 2.45 (ISBN 0-87029-176-9, 20268-9). Abbey.
When James Allen Whitaker's Grandfather Came to Stay. Martha W. Hickman. (Illus.). 48p. (gr. 2-4). 1985. 12.95 (ISBN 0-687-45016-0). Abingdon.
When Jesus Comes. Nancee Berry. (Come Unto Me Library). 1979. pap. 1.95 (ISBN 0-8127-0210-7). Review & Herald.
When Jesus Comes. Charles R. Taylor. (Illus.). 76p. (Orig.). 1985. pap. 4.95 (ISBN 0-937682-08-X). Today Bible.
When Jesus Confronts the World: An Exposition of Matthew 8-10. D. A. Carson. 240p. 1987. pap. 7.95 (ISBN 0-8010-2522-2). Baker Bk.
When Jesus Cried. Thora H. Seaton. 1955. 5.95 (ISBN 0-8022-1527-0). Philos Lib.
When Jesus Holds Our Hand. Audrey Carli. 72p. (Orig.). 1987. pap. 3.95 (ISBN 0-9618664-0-3). AMC Pub.
When Jesus Was a Baby. Dan Burow. LC 84-70244. (Augsburg Open Window Bks.). (Illus.). 12p. (Orig.). (ps-1). 1984. pap. 4.95 (ISBN 0-8066-2078-1, 10-7082). Augsburg.
When Jesus Was a Boy. Joann Scheck. (Illus.). 10p. (ps-1). 1978. text ed. 3.95 (ISBN 0-8066-1602-4, 10-7064). Augsburg.
When Jesus Was a Boy. Frances T. Stewart & Charles P. Stewart, III. (Orig.). (gr. k-3). 1987. pap. 6.95 (ISBN 0-8054-4188-3). Broadman.
When Jesus Was a Lad. R. Oetting. LC 68-56816. (Illus.). 32p. (gr. 2-3). 1968. PLB 9.95x (ISBN 0-87783-047-9). Oddo.
When Jesus Was a Lad. Rae Otting. (Illus.). (gr. 1-2). 1978. pap. 1.25 (ISBN 0-89508-055-9). Rainbow Bks.
When Jesus Was a Little Boy. 32p. 1981. pap. 2.95 (ISBN 0-8249-8009-3). Ideals.
When Jesus Was Born. Daughters of St. Paul. (Illus.). 1973. plastic bdg. 2.00 (ISBN 0-8198-0326-X); pap. 1.25 (ISBN 0-8198-0327-8). Dghtrs St Paul.

When She Was the Good Time Girl. Katharyn M. Aal. 24p. (Orig.). 1987. pap. 2.00 (ISBN 0-936563-11-7). Signpost.
When Sheep Cannot Sleep. Satoshi Kitamura. LC 86-45000. (Illus.). 32p. (ps up). 1986. 9.95 (ISBN 0-374-38311-1). FS&G.
When Sheep Cannot Sleep. Satoshi Kitamura. (Illus.). 32p. (ps up). 1988. pap. 3.95 (ISBN 0-374-48359-0, Sunburst). FS&G.
When Shlemiel Went to Warsaw & Other Stories. Isaac Bashevis Singer. Tr. by Elizabeth Shub from Yiddish. LC 68-30932. (Illus.). 128p. (gr. 4 up). 1968. 10.95 (ISBN 0-374-38316-2). FS&G.
When Shlemiel Went to Warsaw & Other Stories. Isaac Bashevis Singer. (Illus.). 161p. (gr. 3-7). 1986. pap. 3.45 (ISBN 0-374-48365-5, Sunburst). FS&G.
When Silence Becomes Singing. Helen Kylin. LC 84-61827. 32p. (Orig.). 1984. pap. 2.50x (ISBN 0-87574-258-0). Pendle Hill.
When Sky Lets Go. Madeline DeFrees. LC 76-55838. (Braziller Series of Poetry). 1978. 6.95 (ISBN 0-8076-0844-0); pap. 3.95 (ISBN 0-8076-0845-9). Braziller.
When Small Is Tall: And Other Read-Together Tales. Seymour V. Reit et al. LC 83-9811. (Pictureback Ser.). (Illus.). 32p. (ps-1). 1985. lib. bdg. 5.99 (ISBN 0-394-95836-5, BYR); pap. 1.95 (ISBN 0-394-85836-0). Random.
When Smart People Fail & Reinventing Yourself after Defeat. Carole Hyatt & Linda Gottlieb. 240p. 1987. 17.95 (ISBN 0-671-61941-1). S&S.
When Smart People Fail: Rebuilding Yourself for Success. Carole Hyatt & Linda Gottlieb. 240p. 1988. pap. 7.95 (ISBN 0-14-010727-4). Penguin.
When Social Services Are Local. Roger Hadley & Morag McGrath. 1984. 40.00x (ISBN 0-317-40564-0, Pub. by Natl Soc Work). State Mutual Bk.
When Society Becomes an Addict. Anne W. Schaef. 1987. 15.95 (ISBN 0-06-254812-3, HarpR). Har-Row.
When Society Becomes an Addict. Anne W. Schaef. LC 86-46828. 176p. 1988. pap. 8.95 (ISBN 0-06-254854-9, HarpR). Har-Row.
When Someone Asks for Help: A Practical Guide to Counseling. Everett L. Worthington, Jr. LC 82-81. (Illus.). 239p. (Orig.). 1982. pap. 9.95 (ISBN 0-87784-375-9). Inter-Varsity.
When Someone Dies. Edgar N. Jackson. Ed. by William E. Hulme. LC 76-154488. (Pocket Counsel Bks). 58p. (Orig.). 1971. pap. 2.95 (ISBN 0-8006-1103-9, 1-1103). Fortress.
When Someone Very Special Dies: Children Can Learn to Cope with Grief. Marge E. Heegaard. (Illus.). 32p. (gr. 1-6). 1988. wkbk. 4.95 (ISBN 0-9620502-0-2). Woodland Pr.
When Someone Wants to Die. S. J. Anderson. (Pathfinder Pamphlets Ser.). 32p. (Orig.). 1988. pap. 1.95 (ISBN 0-87784-220-5). Inter Varsity.
When Someone You Know Has AIDS: A Practical Guide. Leonard J. Martelli et al. 256p. 1987. 15.97 (ISBN 0-317-52879-3); pap. 9.95. Crown.
When Someone You Love Dies. Lawrence Ruegg. 1984. 0.95 (ISBN 0-89536-659-2, 2355). CSS of Ohio.
When Someone You Love Has AIDS: A Book of Hope for Family & Friends. Bettyclare Moffatt. 160p. (Orig.). 1986. pap. 9.95 (ISBN 0-9616605-0-3). IBS Press.
When Someone You Love Has AIDS: A Book of Hope for Family & Friends. BettyClare Moffatt. LC 87-721. 154p. 1986. Repr. lib. bdg. 24.95x (ISBN 0-8095-6551-X). Borgo Pr.
When Someone You Love Has AIDS: A Book of Hope for Family & Friends. Bettyclare Moffatt. LC 87-7723. 176p. 1987. pap. 8.95 (ISBN 0-452-25945-2, Plume). NAL.
When Someone You Love Has AIDS: A Practical Guide. Leonard J. Martelli et al. LC 86-29276. 1987. 15.95 (ISBN 0-517-56555-2); pap. 9.95 (ISBN 0-517-56556-0). Crown.
When Someone You Love Is Dying. Norma S. Upson. 192p. 1986. pap. 6.95 (ISBN 0-671-61079-1, Fireside). S&S.
When Someone You Love Is Dying: A Handbook for Counselors & Those Who Care. 2nd ed. Ruth Kopp & Stephen Sorenson. 240p. 1985. pap. 9.95 (ISBN 0-310-41601-9, 11165P). Zondervan.
When Sorrow-Song Descends on You. Vinoko Akpalu. Ed. by Stanley H. Barkan. Tr. by Kofi Awoonor. (Cross-Cultural Review Chapbook 14: African Ghanaian Poetry 1). 16p. (Ewe & Eng.). 1981. pap. 2.00 (ISBN 0-89304-813-5). Cross Cult.
When Spirits Walk. Christine Gentry. 288p. (Orig.). 1988. pap. 3.95 (ISBN 1-55547-227-3). Critics Choice Paper.
When Stars Came Down to Earth: Cosmology of the Skidi Pawnee Indians of North America. Von Del Chamberlain. LC 82-16390. (Ballena Press Anthropological Papers: No. 26). (Illus.). 260p. (Orig.). 1982. pap. 17.95 (ISBN 0-87919-098-1). Ballena Pr.
When Summer Came. Gertrude Errington-Kerr. 1985. 18.95x (ISBN 0-901976-44-X, Pub. by United Writers Pubns England). State Mutual Bk.
When Sweet Birds Sing. Robert A. Bowen. (Illus.). 1967. pap. 2.00x (ISBN 0-912462-03-5). Foun Hist Rest.
When Talk Is Not Cheap: Or, How to Find the Right Therapist When You Don't Know Where to Begin. Mandy Aftel & Robin T. Lakoff. LC 85-684. 224p. 1985. 17.50 (ISBN 0-446-51309-1). Warner Bks.
When Talk Is Not Cheap: Or, How to Find the Right Therapist When You Don't Know Where to Begin. Mandy Aftel & Robin T. Lakoff. 224p. 1986. pap. 4.50 (ISBN 0-446-30070-5). Warner Bks.
When Teachers Face Themselves. Arthur T. Jersild. LC 55-12176. 1955. pap. text ed. 9.95x (ISBN 0-8077-1575-1). Tchrs Coll.
When Teddy Woke Early. Jan Mogensen. LC 85-26096. (Teddy Tales Ser.). (Illus.). 28p. (ps-2). 1985. PLB 9.95 (ISBN 1-55532-006-6). Stevens Inc.
When Teenagers Work: The Psychological & Social Costs of Adolescent Employment. Ellen Greenberger & Laurence Steinberg. LC 85-73885. 1986. 17.95 (ISBN 0-465-09180-6). Basic.
When Teenagers Work: The Psychological & Social Costs of Adolescent Employment. Ellen Greenberger & Laurence Steinberg. LC 85-73885. 304p. 1988. pap. 9.95 (ISBN 0-465-09177-6, PL 5219). Basic.
When Telephones Reach the Village. Heather Hudson. Ed. by Melvin J. Voigt. LC 84-18409. (Communication & Information Science Ser.). 1985. text ed. 29.50 (ISBN 0-89391-207-7). Ablex Pub.
When the Aardvark Parked on the Ark. Calvin Miller. LC 84-47894. (Illus.). 192p. 1984. 13.45i (ISBN 0-06-065748-0, HarpR). Har-Row.
When the Angels Go Away. Jon L. Joyce. (Orig.). 1980. pap. 4.95 (ISBN 0-937172-14-6). JLJ Pubs.
When the Animals Leave. Peggy Rambach. LC 86-70220. 48p. 1986. pap. 4.00 (ISBN 0-935331-00-X). Ampersand RI.
When the Answer Is No. Dandi D. Knorr. 1985. pap. 4.95 (ISBN 0-8054-5801-8). Broadman.
When the Baby Went to Bed. Susan Pearson. (Illus.). (ps-k). 1987. 2.95 (ISBN 0-670-81300-1, Viking Kestrel). Viking.
When the Bear & the Eagle Meet. James R. Barbour. 1988. 13.95 (ISBN 0-533-07486-X). Vantage.
When the Bell Sounded: The Evolution of Schools. LC 72-88112. 5.95 (ISBN 0-685-37751-2); pap. 2.95 (ISBN 0-685-37752-0). F M McCarty.
When the Birds Fly South. Stanton A. Coblentz. Ed. by R. Reginald & Douglas Melville. LC 77-84212. (Lost Race & Adult Fantasy Ser.). 1978. Repr. of 1945 ed. lib. bdg. 20.00x (ISBN 0-405-10967-9). Ayer Co Pubs.
When the Birds Fly South. Stanton A. Coblentz. Ed. by R. Reginald & Douglas Menville. LC 80-23935. (Newcastle Forgotten Fantasy Library Ser.: Vol. 23). 223p. 1980. Repr. lib. bdg. 19.95x (ISBN 0-89370-522-5). Borgo Pr.
When the Birds Fly South. Stanton A. Coblentz. (Newcastle Forgotten Fantasy Library: Vol. 23). 1980. pap. 5.95 (ISBN 0-87877-122-0). Newcastle Pub.
When the Bottom Drops: How Any Business Can Survive & Thrive in the Coming Hard Times. A. David Silver. 300p. 1988. 18.95 (ISBN 0-914629-46-8). Prima Pub Comm.
When the Bough Breaks. Jonathan Kellerman. LC 84-16805. 304p. 1985. 15.95 (ISBN 0-689-11519-9). Atheneum.
When the Bough Breaks. Jonathan Kellerman. 1986. pap. 4.50 (ISBN 0-451-14870-3, Sig). NAL.
When the Bough Breaks, & Other Stories. facsimile ed. Naomi M. Mitchison. LC 71-160944. (Short Story Index Reprint Ser.). Repr. of 1924 ed. 18.00 (ISBN 0-8369-3923-9). Ayer Co Pubs.
When the Boys Ran the House. Joan Carris. LC 82-47762. (Illus.). 160p. (gr. 4-7). 1982. 10.70i (ISBN 0-397-32019-1, Lipp Jr Bks); PLB 12.89 (ISBN 0-397-32020-5). HarpJ.
When the Boys Ran the House. (Illus.). 160p. (gr. 3-7). 1983. pap. 2.75 (ISBN 0-440-49450-8, YB). Dell.
When the Brave Ones Cried. Lee Dalton. LC 86-81778. 176p. 1986. 8.95 (ISBN 0-88290-282-2). Horizon Utah.
When the Buffalo Fight. Lex McAulay. 240p. 1987. pap. 3.50 (ISBN 0-553-26448-6). Bantam.
When the Cat's Away. Kinky Friedman. 224p. 1988. 16.95 (ISBN 0-688-07555-X, Pub. by Beech Tree Bks). Morrow.
When the Changewinds Blow. Jack L. Chalker. 1988. pap. 3.50 (ISBN 0-441-88081-9). Ace Bks.
When the Cheering Stopped: The Last Years of Woodrow Wilson. Gene Smith. (Illus.). 1964. pap. 7.70 (ISBN 0-688-06011-0). Morrow.
When the Clock Strikes Thirteen. David Hanna. 1976. pap. 1.50 (ISBN 0-685-73464-1, LB387, Leisure Bks). Leisure NY.
When the Coast Was Wild & Lonely: Early Settlers of The Sur. Rosalind S. Wall. (Illus.). 190p. 1987. pap. 9.95 (ISBN 0-940168-03-0). Boxwood.
When the Cold Came & Other Stories see Night of the Sphinx & Other Stories.
When the Comforter Came. Albert B. Simpson. pap. 2.95 (ISBN 0-87509-042-7). Chr Pubns.
When the Crew Matter Most. Erroll Bruce. (World of Cruising Ser.: No. 2). 192p. 1987. pap. 12.95 (ISBN 0-85177-421-0, Pub. by Nautical Bks England). Sheridan.
When the Dark Comes Dancing: A Bedtime Poetry Book. Nancy Larrick. LC 81-428. (Illus.). (ps-2). 1983. 17.95 (ISBN 0-399-20807-0, Philomel). Putnam Pub Group.
When the Doctor Says "It's Cancer". abr. ed. Mary B. Moster. (Pocket Guides Ser.). 96p. 1986. 1.95 (ISBN 0-8423-7981-9). Tyndale.
When the Dolls Woke. Marjorie Stover. Ed. by Abby Levine. (Illus.). 128p. (gr. 3-6). 1985. PLB 8.95 (ISBN 0-8075-8882-2). A Whitman.
When the Dolls Woke. Marjorie F. Stover. (Illus.). 144p. (gr. 4-6). 1987. pap. 2.50 (ISBN 0-590-40419-9, Apple Paperbacks). Scholastic Inc.
When the Drumbeat Changes. Ed. by Carolyn Parker & Stephen Arnold. 293p. (Orig.). 1981. 22.00x (ISBN 0-89410-262-1); pap. 14.00x (ISBN 0-89410-263-X). Three Continents.
When the Earth Quakes. James B. Macelwane. LC 76-29402. Repr. of 1947 ed. 23.50 (ISBN 0-404-15340-2). AMS Pr.
When the Elephants Came. Nima Yushij. Ed. by Mariam Evans & M. Batamaglij. Tr. by Mariam Evans from Eng. (Illus.). 32p. (Persian.). (gr. 4 up). 1988. 18.50 (ISBN 0-934211-15-9); English-Persian Version. 18.50 (ISBN 0-934211-09-4). Mage Pubs Inc.
When the Fat Man Sings. William Murray. LC 87-47564. 224p. 1987. 14.95 (ISBN 0-553-05216-0). Bantam.
When the French Were Here. Stephen Bonsal. LC 68-26261. 1968. Repr. of 1945 ed. 24.00 (ISBN 0-8046-0034-1, Pub. by Kennikat). Assoc Faculty Pr.
When the French Were Here. Fritz Reuter. Tr. by Carl F. Bayerschmidt. 200p. 1984. 24.50 (ISBN 0-8386-3230-0). Fairleigh Dickinson.
When the Gods Are Silent. Mikhail Soloviev. Tr. by Harry C. Stevens from Rus. LC 74-27185. 506p. 1975. Repr. of 1952 ed. lib. bdg. 48.50x (ISBN 0-8371-7891-6, SOGS). Greenwood.
When the Gods Returned. Charles Beamer. 240p. 1986. pap. 2.95 (ISBN 0-345-32676-8, Del Rey). Ballantine.
When the Going Gets Tough. D. Stuart Briscoe. LC 82-11205. (YA) (gr. 7-12). 1982. 7.95 (ISBN 0-8307-0802-2, 5417507). Regal.
When the Grass was Taller: Autobiography & the Experience of Childhood. Richard N. Coe. LC 84-3517. 352p. 1984. 29.50x (ISBN 0-300-03210-2). Yale U Pr.
When the Grass Was Taller: The Autobiography of Childhood & Adolescence Considered as a Form of Literature. Richard N. Coe. 1979. 65.00x (ISBN 0-900000-95-3, Pub. by Centaur Bks). State Mutual Bk.
When the Guayacans Were in Bloom. Nelson E. Bass. Tr. by Henry J. Richards from Span. LC 87-72081. 230p. (Orig.). 1987. pap. 15.00 (ISBN 0-939423-01-4). Afro Hispanic Inst.
When the Handwriting on the Wall Is in Brown Crayon. Susan Lenzkes. 1986. pap. 5.95 (ISBN 0-310-43631-1, 6891P). Zondervan.
When the Holy Ghost Is Come. Samuel L. Brengle. 1980. pap. 3.95 (ISBN 0-86544-009-3). Salv Army Suppl South.
When the Honeymoon's Over. David Mace & Vera Mace. 1988. pap. 5.95. Abingdon.
When the Hurt Won't Go Away. Paul Powell. 144p. 1986. pap. 5.95 (ISBN 0-89693-365-2). Victor Bks.
When the Idols Walked. John Jakes. (Brak Ser.: No. 4). 176p. 1981. pap. 2.25 (ISBN 0-505-51660-8, Pub. by Tower Bks). Leisure NY.
When the Job Seems Too Big, Take a Lesson from Joshua. Gene A. Getz. Ed. by Earl Roe. LC 87-12790. 176p. 1987. pap. 6.95 (ISBN 0-8307-1206-2, 5419100). Regal.
When the Journey Seems Too Great. Charles E. Blair. 192p. 1988. pap. 5.95 (ISBN 0-8423-7997-5). Tyndale.
When the Killing Starts. Ted Wood. 224p. 1989. 15.95 (ISBN 0-684-18331-5). Scribner.
When the King Loses His Head, & Other Stories. facs. ed. Leonid N. Andreev. Tr. by Archibald J. Wolfe. LC 74-116927. (Short Story Index Reprint Ser.). 1919. 19.00 (ISBN 0-8369-3429-6). Ayer Co Pubs.
When the Ku Klux Rode. facsimile ed. Eyre Damer. LC 79-37588. (Black Heritage Library Collection). Repr. of 1912 ed. 13.25 (ISBN 0-8369-8964-3). Ayer Co Pubs.
When the Latch Is Lifted. Frances J. Roberts. 1970. 3.95 (ISBN 0-932814-18-2). Kings Farspan.
When the Legends Die. Hal Borland. 224p. (YA) (gr. 6-12). 1984. pap. 2.95 (ISBN 0-553-25738-2). Bantam.
When the Legends Die. Center for Learning Staff. (YA) (gr. 9-12). 1988. pap. text ed. 14.95 (ISBN 0-697-02597-7). Wm C Brown.
When the Lights Go Down. Pauline Kael. LC 79-19067. 608p. (Orig.). 1983. (Owl Bks.); pap. 9.95 (ISBN 0-03-056842-0). H Holt & Co.
When the Lights Go Out. Margaret R. MacDonald. (Illus.). 176p. 1988. 30.00 (ISBN 0-8242-0770-X). Wilson.
When the Man You Love Is an Alcoholic. Jean Klewin & Thomas Klewin. LC 79-51276. (When Bks). (Illus.). 1979. pap. 2.45 (ISBN 0-87029-149-1, 20232-5). Abbey.
When the Many Become One: Three Lectures. 2nd ed. Swami Ashokananda. 104p. 1987. pap. 4.95 (ISBN 0-9612388-1-X). Vedanta Soc N Cal.
When the Marching Stopped: The Politics of Civil Rights Regulatory Agencies. Hanes Walton, Jr. (Afro-American Studies). 320p. 1988. 52.50x (ISBN 0-88706-687-9); pap. 19.95x (ISBN 0-88706-688-7). State U NY Pr.
When the Master Relents: The Neglected Short Fictions of Henry James. George Bishop. Ed. by A. Walton Litz. LC 87-25543. (Studies in Modern Literature: No. 80). 128p. 1987. 34.95 (ISBN 0-8357-1826-3). UMI Res Pr.
When the Mental Patient Comes Home. George Bennett. LC 79-23809. (Christian Care Bks.). 118p. 1980. pap. 7.95 (ISBN 0-664-24295-2). Westminster John Knox.
When the Mind Hears: A History of the Deaf. Harlan Lane. LC 83-43201. 608p. 1984. 27.95 (ISBN 0-394-50878-5). Random.
When the Mockingbird Sings. Ed. by Richard S. Danbury, III. 100p. (Orig.). 1986. 19.95x (ISBN 0-89754-059-X); pap. 9.95x (ISBN 0-89754-058-1). Dan River Pr.
When the Moon Rises. Tony Davies. 165p. 1987. 25.95 (ISBN 0-436-12450-5, Pub. by Secker & Warburg UK). David & Charles.
When the Moon Shines Brightly on the House. Hans Poppel & Ilona Bodden. 24p. (ps). 1985. 5.95 (ISBN 0-8120-5669-8). Barron.
When the Movies Were Young. Linda A. Griffith. 1972. 18.00 (ISBN 0-405-09119-2, 1724). Ayer Co Pubs.
When the Music Mattered: Rock in the 1960s. Bruce Pollack. LC 83-10853. (Illus.). 214p. 1983. 15.95 (ISBN 0-03-060426-5); pap. 9.95 (ISBN 0-03-060421-4). H Holt & Co.
When the New Baby Comes, I'm Moving Out. Martha Alexander. LC 79-4275. (Pied Piper Bk.). (Illus.). 32p. (gr. k-3). 1981. pap. 3.95 (ISBN 0-8037-9563-7, 0286-090). Dial Bks Young.
When the New Baby Comes, I'm Moving Out. Martha Alexander. LC 79-4275. (Illus.). (ps-2). 1979. 8.95 (ISBN 0-8037-9557-2); PLB 8.89 (ISBN 0-8037-9558-0, 0869-260). Dial Bks Young.
When the Night Wind Howls. Pamela F. Service. LC 86-10851. 160p. (gr. 4-8). 1987. 12.95 (ISBN 0-689-31306-3, Atheneum Childrens Bks). Macmillan.
When the Night Wind Howls. Pamela F. Service. 1988. pap. 2.50 (ISBN 0-449-70279-0, Juniper). Fawcett.
When the Nightmare Ends. Geoffrey Nash. (Orig.). 1988. pap. 11.95 (ISBN 0-933770-54-5). Kalimat.
When the Owl Cries, Indians Die. J. W. Rivers. LC 85-47624. 112p. 1986. 14.95x (ISBN 0-8453-4509-5). Va Ctr Creative Arts.
When the Phone Rang. Harry Mazer. LC 84-6098. (Illus.). 192p. (gr. 7 up). 1985. 11.95 (ISBN 0-590-32167-6, Scholastic Hardcover). Scholastic Inc.
When the Phone Rang. Harry Mazer. 240p. (gr. 7 up). 1986. pap. 2.50 (ISBN 0-590-40383-4, Point). Scholastic Inc.
When the Pieces Don't Fit... God Makes the Difference. Glaphre. 176p. 1984. pap. 6.95 (ISBN 0-310-45341-0, 12239P). Zondervan.
When the Plow Cuts. Katherine Andraski. 64p. (Orig.). 1988. pap. 5.95 (ISBN 0-939395-11-8). Thorntree Pr.
When the Pressure Is on see Vivendo Sob Pressao.
When the Pressure's On. Gene A. Getz. LC 83-21119. (Take a Lesson from... Ser.). 1984. pap. 6.95 (ISBN 0-8307-0923-1, 5418100). Regal.
When the Revolution Really. Peter Michelson. LC 83-9189. 160p. (Orig.). 1984. 14.95 (ISBN 0-938410-17-2); pap. 6.95 (ISBN 0-938410-16-4). Thunder's Mouth.
When the Road Gets Rough. Edward Hindson & Walter Byrd. 160p. 1986. 9.95 (ISBN 0-8007-1495-4). Revell.
When the Roof Caves in. (In Living Testimony: No. 2). 1985. pap. 3.95 (ISBN 9971-972-31-X). OMF Bks.
When the Root Children Wake Up. Helen D. Fish. (Illus.). 24p. Date not set. Repr. of 1976 ed. 12.95 (ISBN 0-88138-103-9). Green Tiger Pr.
When the Sacred Ginmill Closes. Lawrence Block. 361p. 1987. lib. bdg. 18.95 (ISBN 0-8161-4244-0, Large Print Bks). G K Hall.
When the Sacred Ginmill Closes. Lawrence Block. 272p. 1987. pap. 3.95 (ISBN 0-441-88097-5, Pub. by Charter Bks). Ace Bks.
When the Sad One Comes to Stay. Florence P. Heide. LC 75-9747. (gr. 5-8). 1975. 11.70i (ISBN 0-397-31651-8, Lipp Jr Bks). HarpJ.
When the Saints Come Storming In. Leslie Flynn. 180p. 1988. pap. 6.95 (ISBN 0-89693-471-3). Victor Bks.
When the Saints Go Marching Out. Chuck Murphy & Anne Murphy. 1987. pap. 5.95 (ISBN 0-8007-9101-0, Chosen Bks). Revell.
When the Scot Smiles. A. H. Charteris. lib. bdg. 17.50 (ISBN 0-8495-0702-2). Arden Lib.
When the Shoe Fits. Bhagwan Shree Rajneesh. Ed. by Ma Prema Veena. LC 76-904914. (Zen Masters Ser.). (Illus.). 388p. (Orig.). 1976. 9.95 (ISBN 0-88050-171-5). Chidvilas Inc.
When the Shooting Stops... The Cutting Begins: A Film Editor's Story. Ralph Rosenblum & Robert Karen. (Illus.). 304p. 1986. pap. 9.95 (ISBN 0-306-80272-4). Da Capo.
When the Sirens Wailed. Noel Streatfeild. LC 75-38326. (Illus.). (gr. 4-6). 1976. (BYR). Random.

When You Are the Headline: Managing a Major News Story. Robert B. Irvine. 250p. 1987. 19.95 (ISBN 0-87094-926-8). Dow Jones-Irwin.
When You Buy or Sell a Company. rev. ed. Paul B. Baron. 396p. 1986. 3-ring binder 85.00 (ISBN 0-317-57775-1). Ctr Busn Info.
When You Call upon the Lord. rev. ed. Charles A. Cook. 384p. 1987. Repr. of 1900 ed. 9.95 (ISBN 0-8007-1486-5). Revell.
When You Can Walk on Water, Take the Boat: A Transformational Journey. John Harricharan. LC 86-63449. 160p. (Orig.). 1988. pap. 9.95 (ISBN 0-943477-01-8). New World GA.
When You Can't Find Time for Each Other. Wayne E. Oates. LC 81-71999. (WHEN Bks). 96p. (Orig.). 1982. pap. 2.45 (ISBN 0-87029-182-3, 20274-7). Abbey.
When You Can't Pay Your Taxes! How to Deal with the IRS. Robert S. Schriebman. 200p. 1986. pap. 14.95 (ISBN 0-87094-752-4); 19.95 (ISBN 0-87094-906-3). Dow Jones-Irwin.
When You Can't See a Way. Theta Burke. LC 85-72772. 80p. (Orig.). 1987. pap. 5.95 (ISBN 0-916872-08-4). Delafield Pr.
When You Don't Agree. James G. T. Fairfield. LC 77-3133. 240p. 1977. pap. text ed. 4.95 (ISBN 0-8361-1819-7). Herald Pr.
When You Don't Know Where to Turn: A Self-Diagnosing Guide to Conseling & Therapy. Steven J. Bartlett. 256p. 1987. pap. 11.95 (ISBN 0-8092-4829-8). Contemp Bks.
When You Face the Chemically Dependent Patient: A Practical Guide for Nurses. Judy Bluhm. (Illus.). 210p. 1986. pap. 22.50 (ISBN 0-912791-38-1). Ishiyaku Euro.
When You Feel Like a Failure. rev. ed. Gene A. Getz. LC 77-99282. (Take a Lesson from...Ser.). 160p. 1984. pap. 6.95 (ISBN 0-8307-0977-0, 5418319). Regal.
When You Feel Like a Failure. Margaret Parker. (Study & Grow Electives). 64p. 1985. pap. 3.95 leader's guide (ISBN 0-8307-1036-1, 6102073). Regal.
When You Feel Like Screaming: Help for Frustrated Mothers. Pat Holt & Grace Ketterman. 128p. (Orig.). 1988. pap. 6.95 (ISBN 0-87788-940-6). Shaw Pubs.
When You Feel You Haven't Got It. rev. ed. Gene A. Getz. LC 86-540. (Biblical Renewal Ser.). 160p. 1986. pap. 6.95 (ISBN 0-8307-1123-6, 5418757). Regal.
When You Fight the Tiger. Joan Hewett. (Illus.). 96p. (gr. 5 up). 1984. 14.95 (ISBN 0-316-35956-4). Little.
When You Go Back to Work. Robert I Ward. 20p. (Orig.). 1984. pap. 0.85 (ISBN 0-89486-235-9). Hazelden.
When You Go to Kindergarten. James Howe. LC 85-18055. (Illus.). 48p. (ps-k). 1986. lib. bdg. 8.99 (ISBN 0-394-97303-8); pap. 5.95 (ISBN 0-394-87303-3). Knopf.
When You Go to the Tax Court: Practice & Procedure. 512p. 1986. 30.00 (ISBN 0-317-04242-4, 5457). Commerce.
When You Go to Tonga. Edward Tremblay. (Illus.). 1954. 3.25 (ISBN 0-8198-0173-9). Dghtrs St Paul.
When You Graduate. Charles L. Allen & Mouzon Biggs. 64p. 1972. 7.95 (ISBN 0-8007-0527-0). Revell.
When You Graduate. Steve Swanson. LC 85-1214. 128p. (Orig.). 1985. pap. 6.95 (ISBN 0-8066-2157-5, 10-7086). Augsburg.
When You Have to Draw the Line. Les Christie. 132p. (YA) (gr. 8 up). 1988. pap. text ed. 5.95 (ISBN 0-89693-439-X). Victor Bks.
When You Hear Hoofbeats, Think of a Zebra Talks on Sufism. Shems Friedlander. LC 86-45657. 128p. (Orig.). 1987. pap. 5.95 (ISBN 0-06-096128-7, PL 6128, PL). Har-Row.
When You Hurt. Ann Lunde. (Encourager Bible Study Ser.). 32p. (Orig.). 1987. pap. 2.25 (ISBN 0-932305-48-2, 523003). Aglow Pubns.
When You Live Alone: More Things Dedicated Singles Do. Don-Paul Benjamin. (Illus., Orig.). 1983. pap. 5.00 (ISBN 0-932624-06-5). Elevation Pr.
When You Live Alone: Things Dedicated Singles Do. Don-Paul Benjamin. (Illus.). 1979. pap. 5.00 (ISBN 0-932624-00-6). Elevation Pr.
When You Look in the Mirror, What Do You See? Joan Malerba-Foran. 24p. (Orig.). (YA) (gr. 7 up). 1985. pap. 1.50 (ISBN 0-89486-262-6). Hazelden.
When You Lose a Child. Laird J. Stuart. 20p. (Orig.). 1988. pap. 1.25 (ISBN 0-914733-11-7). Desert Min.
When You Lose a Loved One. Charles L. Allen. 64p. 1959. 7.95 (ISBN 0-8007-0347-2). Revell.
When You Lose a Loved One-Life Is Forever. Charles L. Allen & Helen S. Rice. 128p. 1979. pap. 5.95 (ISBN 0-8007-5031-4, Power Bks). Revell.
When You Need a Special Sermon Series. 1981. pap. 5.95 (ISBN 0-570-03836-7, 12-2801). Concordia.
When You Owe the IRS. Jack W. Wade, Jr. 256p. 1985. pap. 8.95 (ISBN 0-14-046638-X). Penguin.
When You Pray - Things Happen. Bob Fitts. LC 82-82018. 144p. 1982. 2.95 (ISBN 0-89221-089-3). New Leaf.
When You Pray: Thinking Your Way Into God's World. Douglas J. Hall. 176p. 1987. pap. 9.95 (ISBN 0-8170-1105-6). Judson.
When You Preside. 5th ed. John D. Lawson. 1979. 13.95x (ISBN 0-8134-2036-9, 2036). Inter Print Pubs.
When You Receive a Child. Judy B. Hull. LC 79-55859. (When Books). (Illus., Orig.). 1980. pap. 2.45 (ISBN 0-87029-159-9, 20261-4). Abbey.
When You See Me You Know Me. Samuel Rowley. LC 70-133730. (Tudor Facsimile Texts. Old English Plays: No. 106). Repr. of 1913 ed. 49.50 (ISBN 0-404-53406-6). AMS Pr.
When You See Me You Know Me, or the Famous Chronicle History of King Henry the Eighth. Samuel Rowley. LC 82-45700. (Malone Society Reprint Ser.: No. 97). Repr. of 1952 ed. 40.00 (ISBN 0-404-63097-9). AMS Pr.
When You Teach English As a Second Language. Constance Jolly & Robert Jolly. LC 74-84601. (Illus.). 144p. 1974. 6.95 (ISBN 0-87594-118-4). Book-Lab.
When You Think You're in Love. Sandra Drescher & John Drescher. LC 81-65208. (When Bks.). 96p. 1981. pap. 2.45 (ISBN 0-87029-174-2, 20270-5). Abbey.
When You Walk Through the Fire. Warren McWilliams. (Orig.). 1986. pap. 7.95 (ISBN 0-8054-1621-8). Broadman.
When You Went Away. Gladys W. DuRapau. LC 84-90174. (Illus.). 51p. 1985. 5.95 (ISBN 0-533-06232-2). Vantage.
When You Were a Baby. Ann Jonas. LC 81-12800. (Illus.). 24p. (ps-1). 1982. 13.00 (ISBN 0-688-00863-1); PLB 12.88 (ISBN 0-688-00864-X). Greenwillow.
When You Were a Baby. Ann Jonas. (Illus.). (ps). 1982. 13.00; PLB 12.88. Greenwillow.
When You Were a Baby. Ann Jonas. (Picture Puffins Ser.). (Illus.). 32p. (ps-1). 1986. pap. 3.95 (ISBN 0-14-050574-1, Puffin). Penguin.
When You Were a Baby: Yellow Ladder Books for Toddlers Through 4 Years. Katharine Ross. LC 87-37464. (Learning Ladders Ser.). (Illus.). 32p. (ps). 1988. 5.95 (ISBN 0-394-89897-4, BYR); PLB 5.99 (ISBN 0-394-99897-9, BYR). Random.
When You Were Young: A Memory Book. Illus. by Emily Boland. (Illus.). 64p. 1985. 14.95 (ISBN 0-89659-603-6). Abbeville Pr.
When You Wish Upon a Star. Ned Washington. (Illus.). 36p. (ps-1). 1987. 15.95 (ISBN 0-88138-087-3). Green Tiger Pr.
When Your Child... John M. Drescher et al. LC 86-4831. 144p. (Orig.). 1986. pap. 7.95 (ISBN 0-8361-3416-8). Herald Pr.
When Your Child Becomes Your Friend. Marion Duckworth. LC 81-71998. (When Bk.). 96p. (Orig.). 1982. pap. 2.45 (ISBN 0-87029-183-1, 20275-4). Abbey.
When Your Child Drives You Crazy. Eda LeShan. 385p. 1985. 14.95 (ISBN 0-312-86678-X). St Martin.
When Your Child Drives You Crazy. Eda LeShan. 1988. pap. 4.50 (ISBN 0-312-90387-1). St Martin.
When Your Child Grows up Too Fast. Alan Yellin & Penelope B. Grenoble. 1988. pap. 5.95 (ISBN 0-8092-4669-4). Contemp Bks.
When Your Child Has Been Molested: A Parent's Guide to Healing & Recovery. Kathyrn B. Hagans & Joyce Case. LC 87-46364. 160p. 1988. 18.95 (ISBN 0-669-17980-9). Lexington Bks.
When Your Child Is Gone. Francine Toder. 1987. pap. 3.50 (ISBN 0-317-56908-2). Fawcett.
When Your Child Is Gone: Learning to Live Again. Francine A. Toder. LC 85-72304. (Illus.). 215p. (Orig.). 1986. pap. 12.95 (ISBN 0-9615703-7-7). Capital Pub Co.
When Your Child Is Hyperactive. Kenneth Heiting. LC 78-73015. (When Bk). (Illus., Orig.). 1978. pap. 2.45 (ISBN 0-87029-142-4, 20227-5). Abbey.
When Your Child Is Ill. rev. ed. Samuel Karelitz. LC 69-16463. 1972. Random.
When Your Child Is Overweight. Leslie-Jane Maynard. LC 79-55863. (When Books). (Illus.). 96p. (Orig.). 1980. pap. 2.45 (ISBN 0-87029-162-9, 20263-0). Abbey.
When Your Child Isn't Doing Well in School. Penelope B. Grenoble et al. (Parentbooks That Work Ser.). 128p. (Orig.). 1988. pap. 5.95 (ISBN 0-8092-4670-8). Contemp Bks.
When Your Child Learns to Choose. Andrew D. Thompson. LC 78-73018. (When Bk). (Illus.). 1978. pap. 2.45 (ISBN 0-87029-145-9, 20228-3). Abbey.
When Your Child Needs a Hug. Larry Losoncy. LC 78-73016. (When Bk). (Illus.). 1978. pap. 2.45 (ISBN 0-87029-141-6, 20226-7). Abbey.
When Your Child Needs You: A Parents' Guide through the Early Years. Eleanor Weisberger. LC 86-14197. 216p. 1987. 16.95 (ISBN 0-917561-31-7); pap. 7.95 (ISBN 0-917561-33-3). Adler & Adler.
When Your Daughter Marries. Rayburn W. Ray & Rose Ann Ray. 96p. (Orig.). 1982. pap. 7.95 (ISBN 0-939298-14-7, 147). J M Prods.
When Your Friend Gets Cancer: How You Can Help. Amy Harwell & Kristine Tomasik. (Heart & Hand Ser.). 128p. (Orig.). 1987. pap. 6.95 (ISBN 0-87788-934-1). Shaw Pubs.
When Your Friend Needs You. abr. ed. Paul Welter. (Pocket Guides Ser.). 96p. 1986. mass 1.95 (ISBN 0-8423-7998-3). Tyndale.
When Your Goals Seem Out of Reach: Take a Lesson from Nehemiah. Gene A. Getz. LC 87-12791. 180p. 1988. pap. 6.95 (ISBN 0-8307-1141-4, 5418793). Regal.
When Your Lover Leaves. Susan Trott. LC 86-46233. 224p. 1987. pap. 6.95 (ISBN 0-06-097107-X, PL 7107, PL). Har-Row.
When Your Marriage Goes Stale. James Kenny & Mary Kenny. LC 79-51277. (When Bks). (Illus.). 1979. pap. 2.45 (ISBN 0-87029-150-5, 20236-6). Abbey.
When Your Mind Goes Blank: A Resource Book of Word Lists & Activities. Nancy M. Allen. (Orig.). 1984. pap. text ed. 15.95 (ISBN 0-913956-15-5). EBSCO Ind.
When Your Money Fails. Mary S. Relfe. 234p. (Orig.). 1981. pap. text ed. 5.95 (ISBN 0-9607986-0-9). League Prayer.
When Your Parent Drinks Too Much. Eric Ryerson. 192p. 1987. pap. 3.95 (ISBN 0-446-34692-6). Warner Bks.
When Your Parent Drinks Too Much: A Book for Teenagers. Eric Ryerson. LC 85-12961. 144p. 1985. 14.95x (ISBN 0-8160-1259-8). Facts on File.
When Your Parents Divorce, Vol. 1. William V. Arnold. LC 79-20055. (Christian Care Bks.). 118p. 1980. pap. 7.95 (ISBN 0-664-24294-4). Westminster John Knox.
When Your Parents Grow Old. Florence D. Shelley. LC 88-45059. 416p. 1988. 22.95 (HarpT). Har-Row.
When Your Patient Dies. William G. Justice, Jr. LC 83-15064. 60p. 1983. pap. 8.75 (ISBN 0-87125-091-8). Cath Health.
When Your Pet Dies: How to Cope with Your Feelings. Jamie Quackenbush & Denise Graveline. Date not set. write for info. S&S.
When Your Relationship Ends. Bruce Fisher. (Illus.). 1981. pap. text ed. 8.00 (ISBN 0-9607250-0-8). Family Relations.
When Your Rope Breaks. Stephen Brown. 1988. 12.95 (ISBN 0-8407-7612-8). Nelson.
When Your Son or Daughter Plans for the Future. Thomas D. Bachhuber. LC 78-73014. (When Bk). (Illus.). 1978. pap. 2.45 (ISBN 0-87029-144-0, 20230-9). Abbey.
When Your Teenager Stops Going to Church. James Di Giacomo. LC 80-65401. (When Books). (Illus.). 96p. (Orig.). 1980. pap. 2.45 (ISBN 0-87029-165-3, 20260-6). Abbey.
When Your Wife Wants to Work. Mary Shivanandan. LC 79-51278. (When Bks). (Illus.). 1980. pap. 2.45 (ISBN 0-87029-151-3, 20237-4). Abbey.
When You're Confused & Uncertain. rev. ed. Gene A. Getz. LC 86-477. (Biblical Renewal Ser.). 160p. 1986. pap. 6.95 (ISBN 0-8307-1122-8, 5418749). Regal.
When You're Divorced & Catholic. James J. Young. LC 80-69090. (When Bk). 96p. 1980. pap. 2.45 (ISBN 0-87029-172-6, 20265-5). Abbey.
When You're in You're Out. Mollie Thompson. LC 86-10977. (Illus.). 192p. (Orig.). 1986. pap. 5.95 (ISBN 0-932581-50-1). Word Aflame.
When You're Ready: A Woman's Healing from Childhood Physical & Sexual Abuse by Her Mother. Kathy Evert. LC 87-82076. 194p. 1987. pap. 9.95 (ISBN 0-9613205-4-0). Launch Pr.
When You're Teaching Adults. rev. ed. Intro. by James R. Dorland. LC 59-15148. 1970. pap. text ed. 1.00 (ISBN 0-686-00786-7, 751-00798). A A A C E.
When You're the News. Rick Taylor. 112p. 1987. pap. 5.95 (ISBN 0-87403-225-3, 3185). Standard Pub.
When You're up to Your Ass in Alligators: More Urban Folklore from the Paperwork Empire. Alan Dundes & Carl R. Pagter. LC 87-3056. (Illus.). 272p. 1987. 25.00x (ISBN 0-8143-1866-5); pap. 9.95x (ISBN 0-8143-1867-3). Wayne St U Pr.
When You've Done Your Best. Marcia A. Neese. Ed. by Marjorie Oelerich. LC 83-22424. (Boulder Gang Ser.). (Illus.). 32p. (gr. k-4). 1984. lib. bdg. 9.95 (ISBN 0-914867-03-2). Baker St Prod.
Whence & Whither. Paul Carus. 59.95 (ISBN 0-8490-1289-9). Gordon Pr.
Whence Comes the Rain. Bethany Chaffin. LC 83-81724. 114p. 1983. 6.95 (ISBN 0-88290-230-X). Horizon-Utah.
Whence the Power? The Artistry & Humanity of Saul Bellow. M. Gilbert Porter. LC 74-791252. 221p. 1974. 25.00x (ISBN 0-8262-0165-2). U of Mo Pr.
Whence? Where? Whither? & Occasional Verse. Hugh R. Lupton. 120p. 1984. 29.00 (ISBN 0-7212-0678-6, Pub. by Regency Pr). State Mutual Bk.
When's Later, Daddy? Bil Keane. (Family Circus Ser.). (Illus.). 1986. pap. 2.25 (ISBN 0-449-13035-5, GM). Fawcett.
Where? Margaret W. Hudson. 1965. 1.50 (ISBN 0-88233-082-8, 179). Richards Pub.
Where? Leo Lionni. LC 83-4079. (Four Board Bks.). 14p. (ps). 1983. 3.95 (ISBN 0-394-86033-0, Pant Bks Young). Pantheon.
Where? Jane B. Moncure. LC 83-7307. (Question bks). (Illus.). 32p. (gr. k-2). 1983. 11.93 (ISBN 0-516-06593-9); pap. 2.95 (ISBN 0-516-46593-7). Childrens.
Where. Bernard H. Porter. 1975. 24.50 (0-911156-13-9). Bern Porter.
Where All the Ladders Start. Ron Loewinsohn. Ed. by Upton B. Brady. 240p. 1987. 17.95 (ISBN 0-87113-151-X). Atlantic Monthly.
Where Am I? Sylvia Caveny & Rosemary Giesen. LC 76-22476. (Lerner First Facts Bks.). (Illus.). (gr. k-3). 1977. PLB 4.95 (ISBN 0-8225-1365-X). Lerner Pubns.
Where Am I? ADF & OMNI Instruction Manual. Ed. by Ken Stremming & Harold J. Holmes. 1976. 13.95 (ISBN 0-940766-07-8, Pub. by Haldon Bks). Aviation.
Where America's Large Foundations Make Their Grants: 1983-1984 Edition. Ed. by Joseph Dermer. 1983. pap. 44.50 (ISBN 0-686-37909-8). Public Serv Materials.
Where & How to Find the Law. Frank H. Childs. LC 85-60261. (Legal Bibliographic & Research Reprint Ser.: Vol. 4). vi, 119p. 1985. Repr. of 1929 ed. lib. bdg. 32.00 (ISBN 0-89941-397-8). W S Hein.
Where & How to Sell Your Photographs. 9th ed. Amphoto Editors & Arvel Ahlers. (Illus.). 1979. (Amphoto); pap. 12.95 (ISBN 0-8174-2166-1). Watson-Guptill.
Where & Why. Susan S. Swartz. (The Illustrator Is....Ser.). (Illus.). 24p. (Orig.). (ps-6). 1987. pap. 4.50 wkbk. (ISBN 0-943901-00-6). Creare Pubns.
Where Angels Fear to Trade. Eve Smith. 1971. 5.95 (ISBN 0-8065-0234-7, Pub. by Citadel Pr). Lyle Stuart.
Where Angels Fear to Tread. E. M. Forster. Ed. by Oliver Stallybrass. (Abinger Edition of E. M. Forster Ser.). 200p. 1978. 29.50 (ISBN 0-8419-5803-3). Holmes & Meier.
Where Angels Fear to Tread. E. M. Forster. 1958. pap. 3.95 (ISBN 0-394-70061-9, V61, Vin). Random.
Where Angels Fear to Tread. E. M. Forster. 1986. Repr. lib. bdg. 18.95x (ISBN 0-89968-224-3). Lightyear.
Where Angels Fear to Tread. O. S. Hawkins. LC 83-24022. 1984. pap. 4.95 (ISBN 0-8054-5538-8). Broadman.
Where Angels Fear to Tread, & Other Tales of the Sea. Morgan Robertson. LC 79-122733. (Short Story Index Reprint Ser). 1899. 14.50 (ISBN 0-8369-3566-7). Ayer Co Pubs.
Where Animals Live, 8 vols. (Illus.). (gr. 2-3). 1988. Set. 79.60 (ISBN 1-55532-157-7). Stevens Inc.
Where Animals Live, 4 vols. (Illus.). (gr. 2-3). 1987. Set. PLB 39.80 (ISBN 0-317-66534-0). Stevens Inc.
Where Are All the Kittens? Jennifer Perryman. LC 83-63492. (Cuddle Shape Bks.). (Illus.). 14p. (ps-1). 1984. bds. 3.95 (ISBN 0-394-86793-9, Pub. by BYR). Random.
Where Are the Boys? Janet A. Bloss. 128p. (gr. 6-8). 1986. 2.50 (ISBN 0-87406-065-6). Willowisp Pr.
Where Are the Children? Mary Higgins Clark. 256p. 1976. pap. 4.95 (ISBN 0-440-19593-4). Dell.
Where Are the Customers Yachts? Fred Schwed, Jr. LC 85-70937. 256p. 1985. pap. 10.00 (ISBN 0-87034-077-8). Fraser Pub Co.
Where Are the Dead? Arnold Bennett. LC 74-17034. (Collected Works of Arnold Bennett: Vol. 87). 1976. Repr. of 1928 ed. 18.75 (ISBN 0-518-19168-0). Ayer Co Pubs.
Where Are the Dead? see Donde Estan los Muertes?.
Where Are the Love Poems for Dictators? E. Ethelbert Miller. (Illus., Orig.). 1987. pap. 7.95 (ISBN 0-940880-16-4). Open Hand.
Where Are the Lutherans? 368p. pap. 8.95 (ISBN 0-8066-2102-8, 10-7095). Augsburg.
Where Are the Mothers? Dorothy Marino. LC 59-12894. (Illus.). 32p. 1959. lib. bdg. 11.89 (ISBN 0-397-31622-4, Lipp Jr Bks). HarpJ.
Where Are the Twins? Rosemary Breckler. LC 79-10390. (Hiway Bk.: A High Interest-Low Reading Level Book). 96p. (gr. 7 up). 1979. hardcover 8.95 (ISBN 0-664-32651-X). Westminster John Knox.
Where Are the Victors? Donald Richie. LC 86-50706. (Illus.). 317p. 1986. pap. 7.25 (ISBN 0-8048-1512-7). C E Tuttle.
Where Are They Now? Don Kearney. 1977. pap. 1.25 (ISBN 0-8439-0431-3, Leisure Bks). Leisure NY.
Where Are They Now; see Albert's Bridge & Other Plays.
Where Are They Now? Human Rights Monitors in the U. S. S. R.: Ten years after Helsinki. Helsinki Watch Organization (U. S.) LC 86-157512. Date not set. price not set (Helsinki Watch). Fund Free Expression.
Where Are They? The After-Life of a Figure of Speech. J. S. Cunningham. (Warton Lectures on English Poetry). 1979. pap. 5.50 (ISBN 0-85672-205-7, Pub. by British Acad). Longwood Pub Group.
Where Are They Today? Great Sports Stars of Yesteryear. John Devaney. LC 84-17475. (Illus.). 288p. 1985. 16.95 (ISBN 0-517-55344-9); pap. 9.95 (ISBN 0-517-55345-7). Crown.
Where Are We Going? Deborah Manley. LC 78-31860. (Ready, Set, Look Ser.). (Illus.). 32p. (gr. k-3). 1979. PLB 13.31 (ISBN 0-8172-1305-8). Raintree Pubs.
Where Are We Going in Space? David J. Darling. LC 84-12672. (Discovering Our Universe Ser.). (Illus.). 64p. (gr. 4 up). 1984. PLB 10.95 (ISBN 0-87518-265-8). Dillon.
Where Are We Running? June Strong. LC 78-26271. (Orion Ser.). 1979. pap. 3.95 (ISBN 0-8127-0207-7). Review & Herald.

Where I'm Bound. Sidonie Smith. LC 73-20973. 194p. 1974. lib. bdg. 35.00 (ISBN 0-8371-7337-X, SPS/). Greenwood.

Where I'm Calling From: New & Selected Stories. Raymond Carver. 416p. 1988. 19.95 (ISBN 0-87113-216-8); deluxe ltd. signed ed. 75.00 (ISBN 0-87113-235-4). Atlantic Monthly.

Where in the World Is God? God's Presence in Every Moment of Our Lives. Robert Brizee. 160p. 1987. pap. 6.95 (ISBN 0-8358-0556-5). Upper Room.

Where in the World, When in the World? Ben George. (Illus.). 125p. (Orig.). 1988. pap. text ed. 15.00 (ISBN 0-935920-37-4). Natl Pub Black Hills.

Where Industry Failed: Water-Powered Mills at Harpers Ferry, W. Va. Dave T. Gilbert. LC 84-60831. (Illus.). 92p. 1984. pap. 6.95 (ISBN 0-933126-49-2). Pictorial Hist.

Where Is Baby Bear? Jane B. Moncure. (Magic Castle Readers Ser.). (Illus.). 32p. (ps-2). 1987. 11.93 (ISBN 0-516-05739-1). Childrens.

Where Is Baby Bear? Jane B. Moncure. LC 87-12840. (Magic Castle Readers Ser.). (Illus.). 32p. (ps-2). 1987. PLB 7.75 (ISBN 0-89565-405-9). Childs World.

Where Is Baby Twinkle? Michael Teitelbaum. (Illus.). (ps-1). 1986. pap. 1.95 (ISBN 0-448-48594-X); bk. & audio cassette 5.95 (ISBN 0-448-48598-2). Putnam Pub Group.

Where Is Bernardino? A. L. Staveley. (Illus.). 96p. 1982. 8.95 (ISBN 0-89756-011-6). Two Rivers.

Where Is Bobby Now? Marvin Moore. (Flame Ser.). 1976. pap. 1.25 (ISBN 0-8127-0106-2). Review & Herald.

Where Is Bone? Palmer & Weinert. (Illus.). 1980. pap. 1.50 (ISBN 0-380-75242-5, 75242-5, Camelot). Avon.

Where Is Crystal Martin? C. Cambray. 288p. (Orig.). 1988. pap. 3.95 (ISBN 0-671-64155-7). PB.

Where Is Daddy? The Story of a Divorce. Beth Goff. LC 69-14608. (Illus.). 32p. (ps-k). 1969. pap. 4.95 (ISBN 0-8070-2305-1, BP 694). Beacon Pr.

Where Is Duckling Three? I. Green. LC 68-16402. (Illus.). 32p. (gr. 1-2). 1967. PLB 9.95 (ISBN 0-87783-048-7). Oddo.

Where Is Freddy? Laura J. Allen. LC 85-45275. (Harper I Can Read Bks.). (Illus.). 64p. (gr. k-3). 1986. 9.70i (ISBN 0-06-020098-7); PLB 10.89 (ISBN 0-06-020099-5). HarpJ.

Where Is God In My Praying? Biblical Responses to Eight Searching Questions. Daniel J. Simundson. LC 86-22294. 96p. (Orig.). 1986. pap. 5.95 (ISBN 0-8066-2241-5, 10-7096). Augsburg.

Where Is God in My Suffering? Biblical Responses to Seven Searching Questions. Daniel J. Simundson. LC 83-72108. 80p. 1983. pap. 5.95 (ISBN 0-8066-2052-8, 10-7071). Augsburg.

Where Is God Now? Nuclear Terror, Feminism & the Search for God. Juliana Casey. LC 86-63341. 160p. (Orig.). 1987. pap. 7.95 (ISBN 1-55612-053-2). Sheed & Ward MO.

Where Is God When a Child Suffers: Faith & Suffering in the Family. Penny R. Giesbrecht. (Illus.). 180p. 1988. pap. 8.95 (ISBN 0-929292-02-2). Hannibal Bks.

Where Is God When It Hurts? Philip Yancey. 1977. pap. 6.95 (ISBN 0-310-35411-0, 9992P). Zondervan.

Where Is God When It Hurts. Phillip Yancey. 6.95 (9992P). Zondervan.

Where Is Grandma Potamus. Stephanie Calmenson. (Ready Readers). (Illus.). 32p. (gr. 1-3). 1983. pap. 3.50 (ISBN 0-448-21706-6, G&D). Putnam Pub Group.

Where Is Here? Phylliss Adams et al. (BTR Ser.). (Illus.). 32p. (gr. k-3). 1982. PLB 4.95 (ISBN 0-8136-5405-X, Dist. by Caroline Hse); pap. 2.25 (ISBN 0-8136-5905-1). Modern Curr.

Where Is History Going? John W. Montgomery. LC 69-11659. 256p. 1969. 7.95 (ISBN 0-87123-640-0, 210640). Bethany Hse.

Where Is Home? Basic Elements. Louise Neaderland. (Illus.). 1986. 10.00 (ISBN 0-942561-09-0). Bone Hollow.

Where Is It? Barbara Gregorich. Ed. by Joan Hoffman. (Get Ready Bk.). (Illus.). 32p. (ps). 1983. wkbk. 1.95 (ISBN 0-938256-51-3). Sch Zone Pub Co.

Where Is It? Tana Hoban. LC 73-8573. (Illus.). 32p. (ps-1). 1974. 9.95 (ISBN 0-02-744070-2). Macmillan.

Where Is It? Dee Lillegard. LC 84-7005. (Rookie Readers Ser.). (Illus.). 32p. (ps-2). lib. bdg. 9.93 (ISBN 0-516-02065-X); pap. 2.50 (ISBN 0-516-42065-8). Childrens.

Where Is It, Dainty Dinosaur? (Beginning to Read Ser.). (gr. 2 up). 1988. PLB 5.95 (ISBN 0-8136-5224-3); pap. 2.95 (ISBN 0-8136-5724-5). Modern Curr.

Where Is It Written? An Introductory, Annotated Bibliography in Spirituality. John Weborg. 1978. 0.75 (ISBN 0-8199-0739-1). Franciscan Herald.

Where Is Janice Gantry? John D. MacDonald. 1980. pap. 1.95 (ISBN 0-449-14224-8, GM). Fawcett.

Where Is Jeffrey's Yo-Yo? Mildred S. Smith. (Illus.). 56p. (ps-12). 1988. 8.50 (ISBN 0-9612296-5-9). Williams SC.

Where Is Jesus? Joyce Morse. (Books I Can Read). 32p. (gr. 2). 1980. pap. 1.95 (ISBN 0-8127-0280-8). Review & Herald.

Where Is Joey? Lost among the Hare Krishnas. Morris Yanoff. LC 81-11280. x, 260p. 1982. 15.95 (ISBN 0-8040-0414-5, Pub by Swallow). Ohio U Pr.

Where Is Maria? Louise Gunther. LC 79-11733. (For Real Ser.). (Illus.). 32p. (gr. 1-5). 1979. PLB 6.69 (ISBN 0-8116-4311-5). Garrard.

Where Is Mouse? (Folding Bks.). 12p. (ps). 1983. pap. 2.50 (ISBN 0-8431-0944-0). Price Stern.

Where Is My Daddy? Shigeo Watanabe. (I Can Do It All By Myself Ser.). (Illus.). 32p. 1985. pap. 3.95 (ISBN 0-399-21049-0, Philomel). Putnam Pub Group.

Where Is My Dinner? Harriet Ziefert. (Hide & Peek Game Bks.). (Illus.). 24p. (ps). 1985. 3.95 (ISBN 0-448-19129-6, G&D). Putnam Pub Group.

Where Is My Family? Harriet Ziefert. (Hide & Peek Game Bks.). (Illus.). 24p. (ps). 1985. 3.95 (ISBN 0-448-19128-8, G&D). Putnam Pub Group.

Where Is My Friend? Marcus Pfister. LC 85-63301. (Illus.). 12p. (ps-k). 1986. 3.95 (ISBN 0-03-008033-9, North South Bks). H Holt & Co.

Where Is My Friend? Harriet Ziefert. (Hide & Peek Game Bks.). (Illus.). 24p. (ps). 1985. 3.95 (ISBN 0-448-19127-X, G&D). Putnam Pub Group.

Where Is My Friend? A Word Concept Book. Betsy Maestro. LC 75-15902. (Illus.). 32p. (ps-1). 1976. PLB 12.95 (ISBN 0-517-52436-8). Crown.

Where Is My Friend? A Word Concept Book. Betsy Maestro & Giulio Maestro. (Illus.). 32p. (ps-6). 1987. pap. 2.50 (ISBN 0-517-55304-X). Crown.

Where Is My God? Neal Thomas. 32p. 1987. 6.95 (ISBN 0-8062-3167-X). Carlton.

Where Is My House? Harriet Ziefert. (Hide & Peek Game Bks.). (Illus.). 24p. (ps). 1985. 3.95 (ISBN 0-448-19126-1, G&D). Putnam Pub Group.

Where Is My Little Joey? Donna L. Pape. LC 78-1022. (Imagination Ser.). (Illus.). (gr. k-4). 1978. PLB 6.69 (ISBN 0-8116-4411-1). Garrard.

Where Is Nicaragua? Peter Davis. 272p. 1987. 19.95 (ISBN 0-671-54618-X). S&S.

Where Is Nicaragua? Peter Davis. 1988. pap. 8.95 (ISBN 0-671-65720-8, Touchstone Bks). S&S.

Where Is Palestine? The Arabs in Israel. Shannee Marks. 114p. 1984. pap. 7.50 (ISBN 0-86104-754-0, Pub. by Pluto Pr). Longwood Pub Group.

Where Is Science Going? Max Planck. Tr. by James Murphy from Ger. LC 80-84974. 224p. 1981. 20.00 (iSBN 0-918024-21-8); pap. 10.00 (ISBN 0-918024-22-6). Ox Bow.

Where Is Science Going? Max K. Planck. Tr. by James Murphy. LC 75-41215. (Prologue by Albert Einstein). Repr. of 1932 ed. 18.50 (ISBN 0-404-14696-1). AMS Pr.

Where is the Afikomen? Judye Groner & Madeline Wikler. LC 85-80781. (Illus.). 12p. (ps). 1985. bds. 4.95 (ISBN 0-930494-52-0). Kar Ben.

Where Is the Bear? Richard Hefter. LC 83-6296. (Stickybear Books). (Illus.). 32p. (gr. 3-6). 1983. 5.95 (ISBN 0-911787-06-2). Optimum Res Inc.

Where Is the Bear? Bonnie L. Nims. Ed. by Ann Fay. LC 87-25321. (Illus.). 24p. (ps-2). 1988. PLB 9.95 (ISBN 0-8075-8933-0). A Whitman.

Where Is the Light. Dorothy M. Arnold. 244p. 32.00x (ISBN 0-85335-236-4, Pub. by Maclellan Sales Ltd). State Mutual Bk.

Where Is the Lost Ark? Doug Wead. LC 82-71755. 122p. (Orig.). 1982. pap. 2.95 (ISBN 0-87123-628-1, 200628). Bethany Hse.

Where Is the North? B. Vassilevsky. 286p. 1977. pap. 3.95 (ISBN 0-8285-1264-7, Pub. by Progress Pubs USSR). Imported Pubns.

Where Is the Rainbow? Nancy R. Vaughn & Johnny W. Sloan. LC 84-52691. (Illus.). 144p. (Orig.). 1985. pap. 5.95 (ISBN 0-318-04447-1). Vaughn Pub KY.

Where Is the Wilderness? Pat Bridges. (Illus.). 28p. (Orig.). 1984. pap. 4.00 (ISBN 0-916897-00-1); ltd. ed. 10.00 (ISBN 0-916897-01-X). Andrew Mtn Pr.

Where Is Willie Worm? Demi. LC 80-53680. (Follow-Me Bks.). (Illus.). 24p. (ps-1). 1981. 3.95 (ISBN 0-394-84759-8). Random.

Where Is Your Nose? Where Are Your Toes? Illus. by Kathy Wilburn. LC 86-72423. (Baby's First Golden Bks.). (Illus.). 12p. (ps). 1988. pap. price not set (ISBN 0-307-06059-4, Pub. by Golden Bks). Western Pub.

Where It Stops, Nobody Knows. Amy Ehrlich. 192p. (YA) (gr. 6 up). 1988. 14.95 (ISBN 0-8037-0575-1, 01451-440). Dial Bks Young.

Where It's At: Geography for the Quick. (gr. 4-8). 1.95. Trillium Pr.

Where Jesus Walked. William H. Stephens. LC 80-67422. 1981. soft cover 14.95 (ISBN 0-8054-1138-0). Broadman.

Where Jesus Walked: Through the Holy Land with the Master. Frank M. Field. Ed. by Moshe Davis. LC 77-70681. (America & the Holy Land Ser.). (Illus.). 1977. Repr. of 1951 ed. lib. bdg. 20.00x (ISBN 0-405-10244-5). Ayer Co Pubs.

Where Judaism Differed. Abba H. Silver. LC 87-71337. 318p. 1987. Repr. of 1956 ed. 25.00 (ISBN 0-87668-957-5). Aronson.

Where Kings & Gods Meet: The Royal Centre at Vijayanagara India. John Fritz et al. LC 85-1117. (Illus.). 158p. 1985. 28.95x (ISBN 0-8165-0927-1). U of Ariz Pr.

Where Land & Water Interwine: An Architectural History of Talbot County, Maryland. Ed. by Christopher Weeks. LC 84-7186. (Illus.). 280p. (Orig.). 1984. pap. 14.95 (ISBN 0-8018-3165-2). Johns Hopkins.

Where Land Meets Sea. Clare Leighton. LC 54-7922. 208p. 1984. pap. 8.95 (ISBN 0-87923-424-5). Godine.

Where Land Meets Sea: The Enduring Cape Cod. Clare Leighton. LC 54-7922. (Illus.). 208p. 1973. pap. 9.95 (ISBN 0-85699-056-6). Chatham Pr.

Where Late the Sweet Birds Sang. Kate Wilhelm. 1981. pap. 2.95 (ISBN 0-671-49409-0, Timescape). PB.

Where Laughter Stops: Pinter's Tragicomedy. Bernard F. Dukore. LC 76-15590. (Literary Frontiers Ser.). 80p. 1976. pap. 7.95 (ISBN 0-8262-0208-X). U of Mo Pr.

Where Lawyers Fear to Tread. Lia Matera. 1987. pap. 3.50 (ISBN 0-553-27588-7). Bantam.

Where Legends Live. Douglas A. Rossman. (Illus.). 48p. (Orig.). 1988. pap. 5.00 (ISBN 0-935741-10-0). Cherokee Pubns.

Where Life Begins. Barry Callen. 128p. 1973. pap. 2.50 (ISBN 0-87162-146-0, D9026). Warner Pr.

Where Lilith Dances. Darl M. Boyle. LC 70-144713. (Yale Ser. of Younger Poets: No. 6). Repr. of 1920 ed. 18.00 (ISBN 0-404-53806-1). AMS Pr.

Where Living Waters Flow. Claire Lynn. (Illus.). 99p. (Orig.). 1979. pap. 2.00 (ISBN 0-89323-002-2, 339). Bible Memory.

Where Love & Friendship Dwelt: Hilaire Belloc, Daudet, Zola, George Moore. Mrs. Belloc Lowndes. 1944. 20.00 (ISBN 0-8274-3698-X). R West.

Where Love Begins. Carol B. York. 128p. 1983. pap. 1.95 (ISBN 0-448-15682-2). Ace Bks.

Where Love Has Gone. Harold Robbins. 416p. 1987. pap. 4.50 (ISBN 0-671-55866-8). PB.

Where Love is Found. Marion K. Rich. 154p. (Orig.). 1984. pap. 5.95 (ISBN 0-8341-0922-0). Beacon Hill.

Where Love Is, There Is God Also. large type ed. Leo Tolstoy. Ed. by Marilyn R. Riddle. (Illus.). 36p. (Orig.). 1987. pap. 3.00 (ISBN 0-9603748-4-1). Sandpiper OR.

Where Love Rules. Elizabeth N. Dubus. 544p. 1987. pap. 3.95 (ISBN 0-441-88279-X, Pub. by Charter Bks). Ace Bks.

Where Medicine Fails. Carol E. McMahon. 300p. 1986. 19.95x (ISBN 0-932426-37-9); text ed. 19.95x. Trado-Medic.

Where Medicine Fails. 4th ed. Ed. by Anselm L. Strauss. 400p. 1984. pap. text ed. 14.95x (ISBN 0-87855-951-5). Transaction Bks.

Where Memories Begin. Elizabeth Glenn. pap. 2.50 (ISBN 0-373-25275-7). Harlequin Bks.

Where Men Only Dare to Go! The Story of a Boy Company, Parker's Battery C. S. A. Royall W. Figg. Repr. of 1885 ed. 23.95 (ISBN 0-317-13714-X). Zenger Pub.

Where Mist Clothes Dream & Song Runs Naked. Sara. LC 75-3982. 200p. 1976. Repr. of 1965 ed. lib. bdg. 35.00x (ISBN 0-8371-7413-9, BLWM). Greenwood.

Where Moth & Rust Do Not Consume. A. M. Coniaris. 1983. pap. 5.95 (ISBN 0-937032-30-1). Light&Life Pub Co MN.

Where Mountains Live: Twelve Great Treks of the World. Leo Le Bon. (Illus.). 144p. 1988. 40.00 (ISBN 0-89381-242-0). Aperture.

Where Mountains Meet the Sea: Alaska's Gulf Coast. Ed. by Alaska Geographic Staff. LC 72-92087. (Alaska Geographic Ser.: Vol. 13, No. 1). (Illus.). 192p. (Orig.). pap. 14.95 (ISBN 0-88240-175-0). Alaska Northwest.

Where Mountains Meet the Sea: An Illustrated History of Puget Sound. James R. Warren. (Illus.). 288p. 1986. 24.95 (ISBN 0-89781-175-5). Windsor Pubns Inc.

Where Mystery Dwells: A Psychiatrist Studies Psychical Phenomena. B. J. Laubscher. 272p. 1972. 11.50 (ISBN 0-227-67801-X). Attic Pr.

Where Nature Ends: The Designation of Landscape in Arnold, Swinburne, Hardy, Conrad & Woolf. Susan E. Lorsch. LC 81-72056. 240p. 1983. 22.50 (ISBN 0-8386-3162-2). Fairleigh Dickinson.

Where Nights Are Longest: Travels by Car Through Western Russia. Colin Thubron. Ed. by Gary Fisketjon. (Travel Ser.). 224p. 1987. pap. 7.95 (ISBN 0-87113-167-6). Atlantic Monthly.

Where Nobody Dies. Carolyn Wheat. 288p. 1986. 15.95 (ISBN 0-312-86700-X). St Martin.

Where Nobody Dies. Carolyn Wheat. 240p. 1988. pap. 3.50 (ISBN 0-553-27369-8). Bantam.

Where on Earth? Irol W. Balsley. 144p. (gr. 4-8). 1986. wkbk. 9.95 (ISBN 0-86653-336-2). Good Apple.

Where One Is Gathered in His Name. Dan R. Crawford. LC 85-19519. 1986. 7.95 (ISBN 0-8054-5025-4). Broadman.

Whe're (One Issue; see Work (Four Issues).

Where Our Lives Touch. Mary H. Johnson. 35p. (Orig.). 1985. pap. 3.00 (ISBN 0-914631-00-4). Questpr.

Where Passion Leads. Lisa Kleypas. 1987. pap. 3.95 (ISBN 0-451-40049-6, Onyx). NAL.

Where People & Nature Meet: A History of the West Virginia State Parks. Ed. by Debra Patterson. LC 88-60471. (Illus.). 176p. 1988. pap. text ed. 9.95 (ISBN 0-933126-91-3). Pictorial Hist.

Where Peoples Meet: Racial & Ethnic Frontiers. Everett C. Hughes & Helen M. Hughes. LC 80-27901. 204p. 1981. Repr. of 1952 ed. lib. bdg. 35.00x (ISBN 0-313-22785-3, HUWP). Greenwood.

Where Prosperity Appears. 2nd, rev. ed. Harvest Economic Research Department Staff. 1988. pap. 17.95 (ISBN 0-939074-13-3). Harvest Pubns.

Where Ravens Fly. Vincent Marzilli, II. (Illus.). 64p. (Orig.). (gr. k-6). 1987. pap. 7.95 (ISBN 0-9617809-0-8). Vincent Marzilli.

Where Robot Mice & Robot Men Run Round in Robot Towns. Ray Bradbury. 1977. 6.95 (ISBN 0-394-42206-6). Knopf.

Where Rolls the Oregon. Rick Steber & Jerry Gildemeister. (Illus.). 1985. 42.50 (ISBN 0-936376-03-1). Bear Wallow Pub.

Where Shadows Fall. Judith Kelman. 288p. 1987. pap. 3.95 (ISBN 0-425-10181-9). Berkley Pub.

Where Shakespeare Set His Stage. Elise Lathrop. LC 70-128571. (Studies in Shakespeare, No. 24). 1970. Repr. of 1906 ed. lib. bdg. 49.95x (ISBN 0-8383-0907-0). Haskell.

Where Shall We Eat in Marin? Ed. by Susan Shaffer et al. (Where Shall We Eat, Restaurant Finders for the San Francisco-Bay Area Ser.: No.1). (Illus., Orig.). 1987. pap. 6.95 (ISBN 0-9617297-0-8). Mdwsweet Pr.

Where Shall We Go This Summer? 2nd ed. Anita Desai. 157p. 1982. pap. 4.50 (ISBN 0-86578-125-7). Ind-US Inc.

Where She Danced... American Dancing, 1880-1930. Elizabeth Kendall. LC 78-20544. (Illus.). 1979. 14.95 (ISBN 0-394-40029-1). Knopf.

Where She Danced: The Birth of American Art-Dance. Elizabeth Kendall. (Illus.). 254p. 1984. pap. 8.95 (ISBN 0-520-05173-4). U of Cal Pr.

Where She Was. Anderson Ferrell. LC 85-40225. 141p. 1985. 13.45 (ISBN 0-394-53521-9). Knopf.

Where She Was. Anderson Ferrell. 1986. pap. 6.95 (ISBN 0-671-62438-5). WSP.

Where Should the Money Go? Paula J. Bussard. (Critter County Ser.). (Illus.). 32p. (gr. k-6). 1986. 1.29 (ISBN 0-87403-105-2, 3435). Standard Pub.

Where Silence Reigns: Selected Prose. Rainer M. Rilke. LC 78-9079. 1978. pap. 6.95 (ISBN 0-8112-0697-1, NDP464). New Directions.

Where Sparrows Work Hard. Gary Soto. LC 81-50635. (Pitt Poetry Ser.). 75p. 1981. 16.95x (ISBN 0-8229-3446-9); pap. 8.95 (ISBN 0-8229-5332-3). U of Pittsburgh Pr.

Where Stands a Winged Sentry. Margaret Kennedy. 1941. 39.50x (ISBN 0-685-69832-7). Elliots Bks.

Where Stands Democracy? facs. ed. Fabian Society - London Staff. LC 76-117788. (Essay Index Reprint Ser). 1940. 14.00 (ISBN 0-8369-1651-4). Ayer Co Pubs.

Where Still the Source Endures. Pearl N. Rook. 64p. 1987. 7.50 (ISBN 0-8233-0426-4). Golden Quill.

Where Texas Meets the Sea: A Coastal Portrait. Bryan Woolley & Skeeter Hagler. (Illus.). 70p. (Orig.). 1985. pap. 24.95 (ISBN 0-939722-25-9). Pressworks.

Where the Action Is. Glen Chase. (Cherry Delight Ser.). 1977. pap. 1.50 (ISBN 0-8439-0495-X, Leisure Bks). Leisure NY.

Where the Air Is Clear. Carlos Fuentes. Tr. by Sam Hileman from Span. 376p. 1971. pap. 9.95 (ISBN 0-374-50919-0). FS&G.

Where the American Presidents Lived: Including a Guide to the Homes That Are Open. Ellyn R. Kern. LC 81-70751. (Illus.). 120p. (Orig.). 1982. pap. 10.95 (ISBN 0-942124-00-6). Cottontail Pubns.

Where the Bald Eagles Gather. Dorothy H. Patent. LC 83-20852. (Illus.). 64p. (gr. 3-6). 1984. PLB 12.95 (ISBN 0-89919-230-0, Clarion). HM.

Where the Bluebonnets Grow. Virginia Hurlburt & Billie Matthews. Ed. by Edwin M. Eakin. (Illus.). 128p. (gr. 4-6). 1987. 8.95 (ISBN 0-89015-619-0). Eakin Pr.

Where The Brave Dare Not Go. Lela Gilberts. LC 87-14664. 1987. pap. 6.95 (ISBN 1-55513-898-5, Life Journey). Cook.

Where the Bright Lights Shine. Anne N. Stallworth. LC 75-25145. 1978. 10.95 (ISBN 0-8149-0770-9). Vanguard.

Where the Buffaloes Begin. Olaf Baker. LC 80-23319. (Illus.). 48p. (gr. 2-5). 1981. 10.95 (ISBN 0-7232-6195-4); pap. 4.95 (ISBN 0-7232-6257-8). Warne.

Where the Buffaloes Begin. Olaf Baker. LC 85-5682. (Illus.). 48p. (ps-4). 1985. pap. 5.95 (ISBN 0-14-050560-1, Puffin). Penguin.

Where the Children Live. Thomas B. Allen. (Illus.). 27p. 1981. 10.95 (ISBN 0-13-957126-4). P-H.

Where the Chill Came From: Cree Windigo Tales & Journeys. Tr. by Howard Norman. LC 81-81506. 144p. 1982. 17.50 (ISBN 0-86547-047-2); pap. 9.00 (ISBN 0-86547-048-0). N Point Pr.

Where the Creeks Meet. Lael J. Littke. 1987. 8.95 (ISBN 0-87579-092-5). Deseret Bk.

Where the Dai People Live. Ed. by An Chunyang & Liu Bohua. (Illus.). 117p. (Orig.). 1985. pap. 19.95 (ISBN 0-8351-1187-3). China Bks.

Where the Dark Streets Go. Dorothy S. Davis. 192p. 1986. pap. 2.95 (ISBN 0-380-70131-6). Avon.

Where to Go in Britain. (Illus.). 1983. pap. 13.95 (ISBN 0-86145-152-X, Pub. by Automobile Assn Brit). Salem Hse Pubs.

Where to Go in Greece. 2nd, rev. ed. Trevor Webster. (Illus.). 130p. 1987. pap. 8.95 (ISBN 0-87052-355-4). Hippocrene Bks.

Where to Go in Los Angeles. Ed. by Jeffrey Kaufman. (Illus.). 656p. (Orig.). 1985. pap. 17.95 (ISBN 0-912785-01-2). Where To Go.

Where to Go in Minneapolis & St. Paul. 2nd ed. Ed. by Jeffrey Kaufman. (Illus.). 352p. 1985. pap. 14.95 (ISBN 0-317-27038-9). Where To Go.

Where to Go in Spain. (Where to Go Ser.). 1988. 11.95 (ISBN 0-317-67731-4). Hippocrene Bks.

Where to Go in the Southwest of Ireland. Hugh Oram. (Pocket Bk.). (Illus.). 72p. (Orig.). 1985. pap. 5.95 (ISBN 0-86281-149-X, Pub. by Appletree Pr). Irish Bks Media.

Where to Go in the West of Ireland. Hugh Oram. (Illus.). 70p. (Orig.). 1984. pap. 5.95 (ISBN 0-86281-135-X, Pub. by Appletree Pr). Irish Bks Media.

Where to Go in Turkey. (Where to Go Ser.). 1988. 11.95 (ISBN 0-317-67730-6). Hippocrene Bks.

Where to Go Really Four-Wheelin' in California. Casey Smith. Ed. by Lori Smith. (Illus.). 122p. (Orig.). 1988. pap. 9.95 (ISBN 0-945294-00-X). Cloud Nine Pubns.

Where to Go? Short Stories. Bernard Gadd. 72p. (Orig.). 1983. pap. 3.45x (ISBN 0-86863-687-8, Pub. by Heinemann Pub New Zealand). Intl Spec Bk.

Where to Go with Kids in the Capital District. Patricia Dahl & Laura Degenhart. (Illus.). 50p. (Orig.). 1982. pap. text ed. 2.50 (ISBN 0-9611292-0-4). With Kids.

Where to Go with Your Troubles. William F. Burton. 80p. 1969. pap. 1.00 (ISBN 0-88243-627-9, 02-0627). Gospel Pub.

Where to Learn English in Great Britain. 64p. 1984. 25.00x (ISBN 0-317-43549-3, Pub. by Truman & Knightley). State Mutual Bk.

Where to Next? Whitney M. Moore. (The BLR Career Development & Outplacement Workshop Ser.). 1986. pap. 21.95 (ISBN 1-55645-538-0). Busn Legal Reports.

Where to Put Your Money, 1985. Peter Passell. 1985. pap. 3.95 (ISBN 0-446-38201-9). Warner Bks.

Where to Put Your Money 1986. Peter Passell. 1986. pap. 3.95 (ISBN 0-446-38369-4). Warner Bks.

Where to Put Your Money 1987. Peter Passell. 96p. (Orig.). 1987. pap. 3.95 (ISBN 0-446-38497-6). Warner Bks.

Where to Put Your Money 1988. Peter Passell. 1988. pap. 3.95 (ISBN 0-446-38753-3). Warner Bks.

Where to Put Your Money, 1989. Peter Passell. 1989. price not set. Warner Bks.

Where to Retire on a Small Income. 24th, rev. ed. Norman D. Ford. (Illus.). 327p. 1985. pap. text ed. 6.95 (ISBN 0-686-46668-3). Harian.

Where to Sell Anything & Everything. Rev. ed. Henry A. Hyman. 288p. (Orig.). 1985. pap. 8.95 (ISBN 0-345-32188-X). Pharos Bks NY.

Where to Sell Anything & Everything Book. Henry A. Hyman. 288p. 1986. pap. 8.95 (World Almanac). Newspaper Ent.

Where-to-Sell-It Directory. rev. ed. Margaret A. Boyd. LC 78-31582. 64p. 1988. pap. 3.95 (ISBN 0-87576-078-3). Pilot Bks.

Where to Start: Essential Resource Guide for Career Planning & Job Hunting, 1987-1989. 6th ed. 296p. (Orig.). 1987. pap. 14.95 (ISBN 0-87866-597-8). Petersons Guides.

Where to Stay in London. 100p. 1987. pap. 6.95 (ISBN 0-948880-00-7, Pub. by British Tour). Salem Hse Pubs.

Where to Stay in Wales. 384p. 1987. pap. 9.95 (ISBN 1-85013-021-3, Pub. by British Tour). Salem Hse Pubs.

Where to Stay U. S. A. From Three Dollars to Thirty Dollars a Night. CIEE Staff. 1988. pap. 10.95 (ISBN 0-13-957234-1). Prentice Hall Pr.

Where to Stay U. S. A., 1984-85. Council on International Educational Exchange Staff & Marjorie A. Cohen. 448p. 1984. 8.95 (ISBN 0-671-47604-1). Prentice Hall Pr.

Where to Take the Kids: The Parents' Guide to the Orlando Area. Luanne Napoli. (Illus.). 176p. (Orig.). Date not set. pap. price not set (ISBN 0-941263-06-1). Sentinel Comns.

Where to, Tarapada-Babu? Tarapada Roy. Tr. by Shyamasree Devi & P. Lal. (Saffronbird Bk.). 51p. 1975. 10.00 (ISBN 0-88253-839-X); pap. 4.80 (ISBN 0-88253-840-3). Ind-US Inc.

Where to Turn for Help for Older Persons: A Guide for Action on Behalf of an Older Person. 55p. 1986. pap. 1.75 (ISBN 0-318-21668-X, S/N 017-062-00139-1). USGPO.

Where to Turn: The Directory of Health, Welfare & Community Services in Allegheny County. rev. ed. Ed. by Anne Walsh-Fogoros. 598p. (Orig.). 1987. pap. 35.00x (ISBN 0-930053-01-X). HelpLine.

Where to Watch Birds in Europe. John Gooders. LC 77-84451. (Illus.). 1978. 10.95 (ISBN 0-8008-8246-6). Taplinger.

Where to Watch Birds in Southern Africa. A. Berruti & J. C. Sinclair. (Illus.). 302p. 1985. 24.95 (ISBN 0-88072-066-2). Longwood Pub Group.

Where to Write for Vital Records: Births, Death, Marriages, & Divorces. National Center for Health Statistics Staff. Ed. by Klaudia Cox. 73p. Date not set. pap. text ed. 2.00 (ISBN 0-8406-0375-4). Natl Ctr Health Stats.

Where Town Meets Country: Problems of Peri-Urban Areas of Scotland, Royal Scottish Geographical Society Symposium May 1981. Ed. by A. B. Cruickshank. (Illus.). 140p. 1982. 18.75 (ISBN 0-08-028442-6, R130); pap. 13.00 (ISBN 0-08-028443-4, R145). Pergamon.

Where Two or Three Are Gathered. Leonard Mann. 1986. 6.25 (ISBN 0-89536-791-2, 6809). CSS of Ohio.

Where Two or Three Are Gathered, Someone Spills the Milk. Tom Mullen. 126p. 1986. pap. 3.50 (ISBN 0-913408-95-6). Friends United.

Where Two Ways Met. Grace L. Hill. 18.95 (ISBN 0-8488-0089-3, Pub. by Amereon Hse). Amereon Ltd.

Where Two Worlds Meet: The Great Lakes Fur Trade. Carolyn Gilman. LC 82-2089. (Museum Exhibit Ser.: No. 2). (Illus.). 148p. (Orig.). 1982. pap. 18.95 (ISBN 0-87351-156-5). Minn Hist.

Where War Lives. Dick Durrance, II. 160p. 1988. 35.00 (ISBN 0-8090-9692-7); pap. 14.95 (ISBN 0-374-52129-8). FS&G.

Where Was Patrick Henry on the 29th of May? Jean Fritz. (Illus.). 48p. (gr. 3-5). 1975. 9.95 (ISBN 0-698-20307-0, Coward). Putnam Pub Group.

Where Was Patrick Henry on the 29th of May? Jean Fritz. (Illus.). (gr. 3-5). 1982. pap. 5.95 (ISBN 0-698-20544-8, Coward). Putnam Pub Group.

Where Was the Sexual Revolution When I Needed It? Lew Riley. (Orig.). 1984. pap. text ed. 6.00 (ISBN 0-88734-204-3). Players Pr.

Where Water Comes Together with Other Water. Raymond Carver. 1985. 13.45 (ISBN 0-394-54470-6). Random.

Where We Are: American Catholics in the 1980's. Ed. by Michael Glazier. LC 85-45549. 1985. pap. 7.95 (ISBN 0-89453-471-8). M Glazier.

Where We Are At. Thomas H. Barber. (Right Wing Individualist Tradition in America Ser). 1972. Repr. of 1950 ed. 19.00 (ISBN 0-405-00412-5, 71-172202). Ayer Co Pubs.

Where We Got the Bible... Our Debt to the Catholic Church. Henry G. Graham. 153p. 1977. pap. 4.00 (ISBN 0-89555-137-3). TAN Bks Pubs.

Where We Live. Peter Makuck. (New Poets of America Ser.). 80p. 1982. 12.95 (ISBN 0-918526-40-X); pap. 6.95 (ISBN 0-918526-41-8). Boa Edns.

Where We Live: The American Home & the Social, Political, & Economic Landscape, from Slums to Suburbs. Irving Welfeld. (Illus.). 288p. 1988. 17.95 (ISBN 0-671-63869-6). S&S.

Where We Live: The Residential Districts of Minneapolis & St. Paul. Judith A. Martin & David Lanegran. LC 82-11064. (Illus.). 144p. 1983. 29.50x (ISBN 0-8166-1093-2); pap. 14.95 (ISBN 0-8166-1094-0). U of Minn Pr.

Where We Sleep. Nancy Tafuri. LC 86-27115. (Illus.). (ps). pap. 3.95 (ISBN 0-688-07189-9). Greenwillow.

Where We Stand on Arms Control. 87p. 1986. write for info. Comm Present Danger.

Where We Stand: Services for Sexually Active, Pregnant & Parenting Adolescents in New York City, Vol. 2. Leslie Ancrum et al. (Illus.). 180p. (Orig.). 1987. write for info. Ctr Pub.

Where Were You When I Was Hurting? (Orig.). 1986. pap. 6.95 (ISBN 0-910311-41-2). Huntington Hse Inc.

Where We've Been. William Greenway. LC 87-888. 80p. 1987. 14.95 (ISBN 0-932576-45-1); pap. 7.95 (ISBN 0-932576-46-X). Breitenbush Bks.

Where Will the Animals Stay? Stephanie Calmenson. LC 83-13479. (Illus.). 48p. (ps-3). 1984. 5.95 (ISBN 0-8193-1119-7). Parents.

Where Will the Animals Stay? Stephanie Calmenson. (Read Aloud Bks.). (Illus.). 48p. (ps-2). 1988. pap. 2.95 (ISBN 0-517-56854-3). Crown.

Where Will You Run To? James Donald. 1988. 11.95 (ISBN 0-533-07671-4). Vantage.

Where Women Work: A Study of Yoruba Women in the Marketplace & in the Home. Niara Sudarkasa. LC 74-175945. (University of Michigan Museum of Anthropology Anthropological Papers Ser.: No. 53). pap. 46.50 (ISBN 0-317-29764-3, 2017305). Bks Demand UMI.

Where You First Saw the Eyes of Coyote. Linda Noel. 16p. (Orig.). 1983. pap. 2.00 (ISBN 0-936574-09-7). Strawberry Pr NY.

Where You'll Find Me. Ann Beattie. 192p. 1987. pap. 7.95 (ISBN 0-02-016560-9, Collier). Macmillan.

Where You'll Find Me: And Other Stories. Ann Beattie. 1986. 14.95 (ISBN 0-671-62220-X, Linden Pr). S&S.

Where Your Heart Is: The Story of Harvey Dunn, Artist. Robert F. Karolevitz. LC 78-125992. (Illus.). 208p. 1970. 15.00 (ISBN 0-87970-118-8). North Plains.

Whereabouts: Notes on Being a Foreigner. Alastair Reid. LC 86-60997. 1987. 16.95 (ISBN 0-86547-258-0). N Point Pr.

Whereas... a Judge's Premises: Essays in Judgement, Ethics, & the Law. Charles E. Wyzanski. LC 76-43310. xvi, 312p. 1976. Repr. of 1965 ed. lib. bdg. 35.00 (ISBN 0-8371-9298-6, WYWH). Greenwood.

Whereby We Thrive: A History of American Farming, 1607 to 1972. John T. Schlebecker. LC 74-19455. pap. 88.00 (2026658). Bks Demand UMI.

Where's Al. Byron Barton. LC 78-171866. (Illus.). 32p. (ps-3). 1972. 7.95 (ISBN 0-395-28765-0, Clarion). HM.

Where's Baby? Illus. by Toni Scribner. LC 86-43148. (Peek-a-Board Bks.). (Illus.). 14p. (ps). 1987. bds. 2.95 (ISBN 0-394-89071-X, BYR). Random.

Where's Baby Mickey. (Disney Babies Pockets). (Illus.). (ps). 1986. 3.95 (ISBN 0-671-62931-X, Little Simon). S&S.

Where's Bear? Colin Hawkins & Jacqui Hawkins. LC 85-48301. (Illus.). 14p. (ps). 2.95 (ISBN 0-316-35103-2, Joy St Bks). Little.

Where's Buddy. Ron Roy. (Illus.). 64p. (gr. 3-6). 1982. 8.95 (ISBN 0-89919-076-6, Clarion). HM.

Where's Buddy? Ron Roy. (Illus.). 96p. (gr. 4-6). 1986. pap. 2.50 (ISBN 0-590-41120-9, Apple Paperbacks). Scholastic Inc.

Where's Chimpy? Berniece Rabe. Ed. by Kathleen Tucker. LC 88-37259. (Illus.). 32p. (ps-2). 1988. PLB 11.95 (ISBN 0-8075-8928-4). A Whitman.

Where's Dad Now That I Need Him? Surviving Away from Home. Betty R. Frandsen. (Illus.). 1987. write for info. (ISBN 0-9615390-2-X). Aspen West Pub.

Where's Dinah When You Need Her? Southern Traditions for High Tech Kitchens. Sara Pitzer. LC 88-1992. 160p. 1989. 16.95 (ISBN 0-918518-61-X, St Luke TN). Peachtree Pubs.

Where's Grandma? Daughters of St. Paul. (gr. k-2). write for info. Dghtrs St Paul.

Where's Julius? John Burningham. (ps-1). 1987. PLB 9.95 (ISBN 0-517-56511-0); pap. 9.95 (ISBN 0-517-56476-9). Crown.

Where's Mom Now That I Need Her? Surviving Away from Home. Betty R. Frandsen et al. (Illus.). 1983. 21.95 (ISBN 0-9615390-0-3, TX 1-504-973). Aspen West Pub.

Where's My Baby? H. A. Rey. (Illus.). (gr. k-3). 1943. pap. 1.95 (ISBN 0-395-07069-4, Sandpiper). HM.

Where's My Blankie? Anna H. Dickson. LC 83-83278. (Sesame Street Growing-Up Bks.). (Illus.). 32p. (ps). 1984. 2.95 (ISBN 0-307-12013-9, 12013, Golden Bks). Western Pub.

Where's My Cheese? Stan Mack. LC 76-3443. (Illus.). (ps-1). 1977. Pantheon.

Where's My Daddy? Shigeo Watanabe. LC 79-19347. (I Can Do It All by Myself Bks.). (Illus.). 32p. (ps-1). 1982. PLB 8.95 (ISBN 0-399-20899-2, Philomel). Putnam Pub Group.

Where's My Easter Egg? Harriet Ziefert. LC 84-62004. (Illus.). (gr. 2-6). 1985. pap. 4.95 (ISBN 0-14-050537-7, Puffin). Penguin.

Where's My Hat? Neil Morris & Ting Morris. (Mystery Picture Bks.). (Illus.). 24p. (gr. k-3). 1983. PLB 6.95 (ISBN 0-316-58378-2). Little.

Where's My Lamb. Elspeth C. Murphy. LC 87-70608. (Brenda Learns about God Ser.). 1987. 3.95 (ISBN 1-55513-248-0, Chariot Bks). Cook.

Where's My Mommy? Colin Hawkins & Jacqui Hawkins. LC 85-13208. (It's Great to Read Ser.). (Illus.). 32p. (ps-1). 1986. 5.95 (ISBN 0-517-55974-9). Crown.

Where's My Monkey. Dieter Schubert. LC 86-16578. (Illus.). 32p. (ps-2). 10.95 (ISBN 0-8037-0069-5, 01063-320). Dial Bks Young.

Where's My Truck? Anne S. O'Brien. LC 85-5579. (Illus.). 14p. (gr. k). 1985. 3.95 (ISBN 0-03-005013-8). H Holt & Co.

Where's Ours? Natalie McKelvy. 192p. 1987. 16.95 (ISBN 0-89733-278-4); pap. 7.95 (ISBN 0-89733-277-6). Academy Chi Pubs.

Where's Peter? Edith Kunhardt. LC 86-27061. (Illus.). 24p. (ps-3). 1988. 11.95 (ISBN 0-688-07204-6); lib. bdg. 11.88 (ISBN 0-688-07205-4). Greenwillow.

Where's Peter Rabbit? Beatrix Potter. (Illus.). (ps-3). 1988. 6.95 (ISBN 0-7232-3519-8). Warne.

Where's PJ? Bil Keane. (Family Circus Ser.). (Illus.). 1985. pap. 2.25 (ISBN 0-449-12974-8, GM). Fawcett.

Where's Prancer? Syd Hoff. LC 60-9450. (Illus.). (gr. k-3). 1960. PLB 12.89 (ISBN 0-06-022546-7). HarpJ.

Where's Sarah. Bob Graham. (Illus.). (ps-1). 1988. 4.95 (ISBN 0-316-32306-3). Little.

Where's Spot? Eric Hill. 1980. 10.95 (ISBN 0-399-20758-9, Putnam). Putnam Pub Group.

Where's Spot. Ed. by Eric Hill. (Lift-the-Flap Ser.). (Illus.). 22p. (Arabic & Eng.). (ps-2). 1988. 10.95 (ISBN 0-940793-04-0, Pub. by Crocodile Bks). Interlink Pub.

Where's Spot? A Lift-the-Flap Book. Eric Hill. LC 87-13866. (Illus.). 22p. (ps-1). 1987. 11.95 (ISBN 0-399-21478-X). Putnam Pub Group.

Where's Teddy? Michael J. Pellowski. (Illus.). 24p. (gr. k-3). 1986. 1.50 (ISBN 0-87406-140-7). Willowisp Pr.

Where's That Duck? Mary Blocksma. LC 85-15001. (Just One More Bks.). 24p. (gr. 1-2). 1985. PLB 10.60 (ISBN 0-516-01587-7); pap. 2.95 (ISBN 0-516-41587-5). Childrens.

Where's The Baby? Pat Hutchins. LC 86-33566. (Illus.). 32p. (ps-3). 1988. 11.95 (ISBN 0-688-05933-3); lib. bdg. 11.88 (ISBN 0-688-05934-1). Greenwillow.

Where's the Bear? Charlotte Pomerantz. LC 83-1697. (Illus.). 32p. (ps-1). 1984. 10.25 (ISBN 0-688-01752-5); PLB 10.88 (ISBN 0-688-01753-3). Greenwillow.

Where's the Bear? Charlotte Pomerantz. LC 84-17928. (Illus.). 32p. (ps-1). 1985. pap. 3.95 (ISBN 0-14-050514-8, Puffin). Penguin.

Where's the Cat? Harriet Ziefert. LC 86-45953. (Illus.). 14p. (ps). 1987. 3.50 (ISBN 0-694-00185-6). HarpJ.

Where's the Dog? Harriet Ziefert. LC 86-45952. (Illus.). 14p. (ps). 1987. 3.50 (ISBN 0-694-00184-8). HarpJ.

Where's the Fire? Warren Fuchs, Jr. LC 85-71760. (Illus.). 180p. 1985. pap. 19.95 (ISBN 0-933341-12-1). Quinlan Pr.

Where's the Fish? Taro Gomi. LC 85-15282. (Illus.). 32p. (ps-k). 1986. 10.25 (ISBN 0-688-06241-5, Morrow Junior Books); lib. bdg. 10.88 (ISBN 0-688-06242-3). Morrow.

Where's the Glory? Eric L. Salander. 476p. (Orig.). 1984. pap. 5.95 (ISBN 0-943472-03-2, TXU 89-806). Delgren Bks.

Where's the Guinea Pig? Harriet Ziefert. LC 86-45950. (Illus.). 14p. (ps). 1987. 3.50 (ISBN 0-694-00182-1). HarpJ.

Where's the Halloween Treat? Harriet Ziefert. LC 85-3632. (Illus.). 20p. (ps). 1985. pap. 4.95 (ISBN 0-14-050556-3, Puffin). Penguin.

Where's the Kids, Herman? Jim Unger. (Illus.). 96p. 1984. pap. 1.95 (ISBN 0-451-12922-9, Sig). NAL.

Where's the Me in Museum: Going to Museums with Children. Mildred Waterfall & Sarah Grusin. (Illus.). 1988. write for info.; pap. 6.95 (ISBN 0-918339-08-1). Vandamere.

Where's the Melody? A Listener's Introduction to Jazz. Martin Williams. LC 82-23644. (Quality Paperbacks Ser.). 224p. 1983. pap. 8.95 (ISBN 0-306-80183-3). Da Capo.

Where's the Party? An Assessment of Changes in Party Loyalty & Party Coalitions in the 1980s. Warren E. Miller & John R. Petrocik. LC 87-70304. (Alternatives for the 1980s Ser.). 64p. (Orig.). 1987. pap. text ed. 9.75 (ISBN 0-944237-15-0, Ctr National Policy). U Pr of Amer.

Where's the Turtle? Harriet Ziefert. LC 86-45951. (Illus.). 14p. (ps). 1987. 3.50 (ISBN 0-694-00183-X). HarpJ.

Where's Waldo? Martin Handford. (ps up). 1987. 9.95 (ISBN 0-316-34293-9). Little.

Where's Wallace? Hilary Knight. LC 64-19717. (Illus.). (gr. k-3). 1964. 12.95i (ISBN 0-06-023170-X); PLB 12.89 (ISBN 0-06-023171-8). HarpJ.

Where's Wallace? Hilary Knight. LC 64-19717. (Trophy Picture Bks.). (Illus.). 48p. (ps-3). 1986. pap. 4.95 (ISBN 0-06-443094-4, Trophy). HarpJ.

Where's War-Time Journal. Dolly S. Lunt. 68p. 1987. 7.95 (ISBN 0-87797-148-X); pap. 3.95 (ISBN 0-317-62652-3). Cherokee.

Where's Your License' W. Joseph Hickmott. (Illus.). 1950. 7.00 (ISBN 0-87282-074-2). Am Life Foun.

Wherever Dreams Live. Peter Harris. (Illus.). 88p. (Orig.). 1982. pap. 7.95 (ISBN 0-943510-00-7). Lifesigns.

Wherever He Leads I'll Go: The Story of B. B. McKinney. Paul Powell. 50p. (Orig.). 1974. pap. 2.00 (ISBN 0-914520-04-0). Insight Pr.

Wherever I Go, I Go to Jerusalem. Hillel Goldberg. 240p. 1986. 12.95 (ISBN 0-940646-09-9); pap. 8.95 (ISBN 0-940646-10-2). Rossel Bks.

Wherever I Went: Translations from the German Originals in Japanese Senryu Forms Maintained in English. Carl H. Kurz. 50p. 1982. perf. bd. 4.95 (ISBN 0-931926-17-3). Alta Napa.

Wherever Love Leads. Regan Forest. (Temptation Ser.: No. 152). 224p. Date not set. pap. 2.25 (ISBN 0-317-63841-6). Harlequin Bks.

Wherever Men Trade: The Romance of the Cash Register. Isaac F. Marcosson. LC 72-5062. (Technology & Society Ser.). (Illus.). 310p. 1972. Repr. of 1945 ed. 19.00 (ISBN 0-405-04713-4). Ayer Co Pubs.

Wherever We Step the Land Is Mined. Natalie Scott. 240p. 1980. 8.95 (ISBN 0-531-09939-3). Watts.

Wheston's Commentaries on Acts, Romans, Vol. 3. 13.95 (ISBN 0-686-13906-2). Schmul Pub Co.

Whether or Not. Marie L. Kaschnitz. Tr. by Lisel Mueller. (Juniper Bks.: No. 46). 1984. pap. 5.00 (ISBN 1-55780-040-5). Juniper Pr WI.

Whether White or Black, a Man. facsimile ed. Edith S. Davis. LC 77-37590. (Black Heritage Library Collection). (Illus.). Repr. of 1898 ed. 17.25 (ISBN 0-8369-8966-X). Ayer Co Pubs.

Whethlow an Seyth Den Fur a Rom. A. S. Smith. 1985. 5.00x (ISBN 1-85022-016-6, Pub. by Dyllansow & Truran). State Mutual Bk.

Whetstone. John Knoepfle. LC 81-670240. 1972. 1.00 (ISBN 0-933532-29-6). BkMk.

Which Ad Pulled Best? 5th ed. Philip W. Burton. LC 80-70202. 136p. 1981. pap. text ed. 12.95 (ISBN 0-8442-3160-6, Crain Bks). Natl Textbk.

Which Ad Pulled Best? 5th ed. Philip W Burton & Scott C. Purvis. (Illus.). 156p. 1987. pap. 12.95 (ISBN 0-8442-3139-8, NTC Busn Bks); answer key 3.50 (ISBN 0-8442-3140-1). Natl Textbk.

Which Babies Shall Live? Ed. by Thomas H. Murray & Arthur L. Caplan. LC 85-18058. (Contemporary Issues in Biomedicine, Ethics, & Society Ser.). 240p. 1985. 24.50 (ISBN 0-89603-086-5). Humana.

Whiplash Injuries: The Cervical Acceleration-Deceleration Syndrome. Steve Foreman & Arthur Croft. (Illus.). 448p. 1988. 64.95 (ISBN 0-683-03314-X). Williams & Wilkins.
Whiplash on the Couch. John Bennett. Ed. by Kirk Robertson. LC 77-73210. (Orig.). 1979. pap. 3.00 (ISBN 0-916918-06-8). Duck Down.
Whipman Is Watching. T. A. Dyer. (gr. 5-9). 1979. 7.95 (ISBN 0-395-28581-X). HM.
Whipperginny. Robert Graves. LC 76-39795. Repr. of 1923 ed. lib. bdg. 35.00 (ISBN 0-8414-4512-5). Folcroft.
Whippet. Bo Bengtson. (Illus.). 208p. 1985. 25.95 (ISBN 0-7153-8499-6). David & Charles.
Whippet Champions, 1952-1980. Jan L. Pata. (Illus.). 187p. 1987. pap. 29.95 (ISBN 0-940808-03-X). Camino E E & B.
Whippet Champions: 1981-1986. Camino E. E. & B. Co. Staff. (Illus.). 158p. 1984. pap. 24.95 (ISBN 0-940808-29-3). Camino E E & B.
Whipping Boy. Sid Fleischman. LC 85-17555. (Illus.). 96p. (gr. 2-6). 1986. reinforced bdg. 11.95 (ISBN 0-688-06216-4). Greenwillow.
Whipping Boy. Sid Fleischman. (Illus.). (gr. 2-5). 1987. pap. 2.95 (ISBN 0-8167-1038-4). Troll Assocs.
Whipping Star. Frank Herbert. 192p. 1985. pap. 2.95 (ISBN 0-425-09962-8). Berkley Pub.
Whipping Star see Worlds Beyond Dune: The Best of Frank Herbert.
Whipple & Black: Commercial Photographers in Boston. Sally Pierce. (Illus.). 132p. 1987. 45.00 (ISBN 0-934552-49-5); pap. 18.00 (ISBN 0-934552-50-9). Boston Athenaeum.
Whipple's Castle. Thomas Williams. LC 87-16111. 552p. 1988. pap. 9.95 (ISBN 0-385-24249-2, Anchor Pr). Doubleday.
Whipple's Disease. William O. Dobbins, III. (Illus.). 254p. 1987. 44.75 (ISBN 0-398-05317-0). C C Thomas.
Whips & Whipmaking: With a Practical Introduction to Braiding. David Morgan. LC 72-78240. (Illus.). 144p. 1972. pap. 7.95 (ISBN 0-87033-270-8). Cornell Maritime.
Whirligigs. 2nd ed. Lunde. LC 86-47607. 96p. 1986. pap. 10.95 (ISBN 0-8019-7707-X). Chilton.
Whirling Ecstasy. Aflaki. Tr. by C. Huart. (Illus.). 30p. (Orig.). 1973. pap. 1.95 (ISBN 0-915424-02-9, Prophecy Pressworks). Sufi Islamia-Prophecy.
Whirlpool. Aleister Crowley. 1973. lib. bdg. 79.95 (ISBN 0-87968-507-7). Krishna Pr.
Whirlpool. George Gissing. LC 71-80632. Repr. of 1897 ed. 18.00 (ISBN 0-404-02812-8). AMS Pr.
Whirlpool. George Gissing. Ed. by Patrick Parinder. LC 77-80329. 467p. 24.50 (ISBN 0-8386-2172-4). Fairleigh Dickinson.
Whirlpool. George Gissing. Ed. by Patrick Parrinder. 496p. (Orig.). 1985. pap. 7.95 (ISBN 0-416-01081-4, NO. 9281). Routledge Chapman & Hall.
Whirlpool. Marguerite Henry. (Misty Ser.). 24p. (ps-3). 1987. pap. 1.95 (ISBN 0-02-688783-5, Checkerboard Pr). Macmillan.
Whirlpool of Torment: The Oppressive Presence of God in Ancient Israel. James L. Crenshaw. LC 83-18479. (Overtures to Biblical Theology Ser.). 144p. 1984. pap. 2.50 (ISBN 0-8006-1536-0, 1-1536). Fortress.
Whirlwind. Marolyn Caldwell-Wilson. (Judy Sullivance Romance Ser.). 1985. 14.95 (ISBN 0-8027-0850-1). Walker & Co.
Whirlwind. James Clavell. LC 86-11293. (Illus.). 1152p. 1986. 22.95 (ISBN 0-688-06663-1). Morrow.
Whirlwind. James Clavell. 1280p. 1987. pap. 5.95 (ISBN 0-380-70312-2). Avon.
Whirlwind Courtship. Jayne Taylor. (Orig.). 1980. pap. 1.75 (ISBN 0-8439-8012-5, Tiara Bks). Leisure NY.
Whirlwind Courtship. Jayne A. Taylor. 192p. 1987. pap. 2.75 (ISBN 0-8439-2537-X). Leisure NY.
Whirlwind in Culture: Frontiers in Theology. Ed. by Donald W. Musser & Joseph L. Price. LC 88-42731. 288p. (Orig.). 1988. lib. bdg. 39.95 (ISBN 0-940989-43-3); pap. 19.95 (ISBN 0-940989-39-5). Meyer Stone Bks.
Whirlwind in Dublin: The Plough & the Stars Riots. Ed. by Robert G. Lowery. LC 83-22652. (Contributions to Drama & Theatre Studies: No. 11). xiii, 121p. 1984. lib. bdg. 35.00 (ISBN 0-313-23764-6, LOW/). Greenwood.
Whirlwinds in the Plain: Ludwig Leichardt - Friends, Foes & History. E. M. Webster. 484p. 1980. 44.00x (ISBN 0-522-84181-3, Pub. by Melbourne U Pr Australia). Intl Spec Bk.
Whiskers, a Kitten's Story. Roma N. Burke. LC 87-62417. 120p. (gr. 3-8). 1988. pap. 8.95 (ISBN 0-88100-058-2). Natl Writ Pr.
Whiskers & Rhymes. Arnold Lobel. LC 83-25424. (Illus.). 48p. (gr. k-3). 1985. 13.00 (ISBN 0-688-03835-2); lib. bdg. 12.88 (ISBN 0-688-03836-0). Greenwillow.
Whiskers & Rhymes. Arnold Lobel. 48p. (gr. k-3). 1987. pap. 2.95 (ISBN 0-590-40712-0). Scholastic Inc.
Whiskers & Rhymes. Arnold Lobel. Date not set. pap. 3.95 (ISBN 0-688-08291-2). Morrow.
Whiskers Once & Always. Doris Orgel. LC 86-5468. (Viking Kestrel Illustrated Bks.). (Illus.). 80p. (gr. 2-5). 1986. 9.95 (ISBN 0-670-80959-4, Viking Kestrel). Viking.
Whiskers, the Bank Mouse. Claudia E. Wells. LC 77-10823. (Illus.). (gr. 1-4). 1981. pap. write for info. (ISBN 0-930506-01-4). Popcorn Pubs.
Whiskers, the Bank Mouse. Claudia E. Wells. LC 77-10823. (Illus.). (gr. 1-4). 1977. 4.50 (ISBN 0-930506-00-6). Popcorn Pubs.
Whiskers the Rabbit. Rebecca Anders. Tr. by Dyan Hammarberg from Fr. LC 76-1236. (Animal Friends Bks). (Illus.). 24p. (Eng.). (gr. k-4). 1976. PLB 5.95 (ISBN 0-87614-070-3). Carolrhoda Bks.
Whiskey Bottles of the Old West. John Thomas. (Illus.). 88p. (Orig.). 1978. pap. 8.95 (ISBN 0-89288-014-7). Maverick.
Whiskey Rebellion: Frontier Epilogue to the American Revolution. Thomas P. Slaughter. LC 85-3095. (Illus.). 288p. 1986. 21.95 (ISBN 0-19-503899-1). Oxford U Pr.
Whiskey Rebellion: Frontier Epilogue to the American Revolution. Thomas P. Slaughter. 304p. 1988. pap. 7.95 (ISBN 0-19-505191-2). Oxford U Pr.
Whiskey Rebellion: Past & Present Perspectives. Ed. by Steven R. Boyd. LC 84-22437. (Contributions in American History Ser.: No. 109). (Illus.). xii, 212p. 1985. lib. bdg. 36.95 (ISBN 0-313-24534-7, BWH/). Greenwood.
Whiskey Rebels: The Story of a Frontier Uprising. Leland D. Baldwin. LC 39-11763. (Illus.). 1968. pap. 8.95 (ISBN 0-8229-5151-7). U of Pittsburgh Pr.
Whiskey's Song. Mitzi Chandler. 1987. pap. 6.95 (ISBN 0-932194-42-7). Health Comm.
Whiskies of Scotland. R. J. S. McDowall. Rev. by William Waugh. (Illus.). 192p. 1987. pap. 9.95 (ISBN 0-941533-06-9). New Amsterdam Bks.
Whisky Distilleries of the United Kingdom: The Centenary Edition. Alfred Barnard. 528p. 1987. 100.00x (ISBN 1-85158-087-5, Pub. by Mainstream Scotland). State Mutual Bk.
Whisky Distillers of Scotland, 1887. Picton Publishing Staff & Alfred Barnard. (Illus.). 160p. 1987. Repr. 20.00x (Pub. by Picton UK). State Mutual Bk.
Whisky Murders. Richard Grindal. 192p. 1987. 15.95 (ISBN 0-8027-5661-1). Walker & Co.
Whisper. William Marshall. 1988. 15.95 (ISBN 0-670-81959-X). Viking.
Whisper. Gina Wilson. LC 83-25298. 160p. (gr. 6 up). 1984. 11.95 (ISBN 0-571-11930-1). Faber & Faber.
Whisper Again. Dorothy N. Morrison. LC 87-924. 208p. (gr. 4-8). 1987. 12.95 (ISBN 0-689-31348-9, Atheneum Childrens Bks). Macmillan.
Whisper Again. Dorothy N. Morrison. (gr. 2-9). Date not set. pap. 2.95. Troll Assocs.
Whisper Behind the Wind. Walkin J. Stoltz. 52p. (Orig.). 1988. pap. 6.00 (ISBN 0-9620228-0-2). Lone Coyote Pubns.
Whisper, Curse of the Dragon. Christopher Brown. (In-between Bks). (Illus.). 32p. (gr. 4). 1985. pap. 2.95 (ISBN 0-89954-401-0). Antioch Pub Co.
Whisper Goodbye. Dorothy N. Morrison. LC 84-21626. 192p. (gr. 4-8). 1985. 12.95 (ISBN 0-689-31109-5, Atheneum Childrens Bks). Macmillan.
Whisper Goodbye. Dorothy N. Morrison. (gr. 4-8). Date not set. pap. 2.95 (ISBN 0-8167-1045-7). Troll Assocs.
Whisper in His Ear. Liane Gardner. (Orig.). 1984. pap. 3.50 (ISBN 0-671-50348-0). PB.
Whisper in the Gloom: A Nigel Strangeways Mystery. Nicholas Blake. LC 87-46117. 336p. 1988. pap. 3.95 (ISBN 0-317-67400-5, P-418, PL). Har-Row.
Whisper in the Night. Joan Aiken. (gr. k-12). 1988. pap. 3.25 (ISBN 0-440-20185-3, LFL). Dell.
Whisper in the Wind. B. J. Hoff. LC 87-70529. (Dalton Saga Trilogy: Bk. II). 180p. (Orig.). 1987. pap. 5.95 (ISBN 0-87029-200-5). Abbey.
Whisper Love in the Wind. Adrian C. Van Dyk, Jr. (Illus.). 40p. (Orig.). 1975. pap. 3.95 (ISBN 0-686-19010-6). Van Dyk.
Whisper My Name. Ernest Hebert. LC 83-40685. 276p. 1984. 15.95 (ISBN 0-670-76200-8). Viking.
Whisper My Name. Ernest Hebert. LC 85-9417. (Contemporary American Fiction Ser.). 256p. 1985. pap. 6.95 (ISBN 0-14-008403-7). Penguin.
Whisper of Christmas: Reflections for Advent & Christmas. Joe E. Pennel, Jr. LC 84-50839. 128p. (Orig.). 1984. pap. 4.95 (ISBN 0-8358-0492-5). Upper Room.
Whisper of Dreams: A Collection of Poetry. Ed. by Rebecca S. Bell & C. S. Severin. (CSS Collection of National Poetry Ser.). (Illus.). 232p. 1982. pap. 9.95 (ISBN 0-942170-04-0). CSS Pubns.
Whisper of Evil. J. H. Rhodes. 1985. 9.95 (ISBN 0-8034-8519-0, Avalon). Bouregy.
Whisper of Glocken. Carol Kendall. LC 85-17634. (Illus.). 256p. (Orig.). (gr. 3 up). 1986. 4.95 (ISBN 0-15-295699-9, VoyB). HarBraceJ.
Whisper of His Grace: A Fresh Look at Suffering Through the Eyes of Job & Jesus. David McKenna. 192p. 1987. 12.95 (ISBN 0-8499-0560-5). Word Bks.
Whisper of Lace. Gillian Cross. 144p. (gr. 3-6). 1987. 13.95 (ISBN 0-19-271447-3). Oxford U Pr.
Whisper of Scandal. Janis Laden. 448p. 1988. pap. 3.95 (ISBN 0-8217-2407-X). Zebra.
Whisper of Stars: A Siberian Journey. Stan Grossfeld. Date not set. price not set. Globe Pequot.
Whisper of the Axe. Richard Condon. 1983. pap. 2.25 (ISBN 0-345-28296-5). Ballantine.
Whisper of the Cat. Norma Johnston. 192p. (Orig.). (YA) 1988. pap. 2.95 (ISBN 0-553-26947-X, Starfire). Bantam.
Whisper of the Muse: The Overstone Album & Other Photographs by Julia Margaret Cameron. Michael Weaver. (Illus.). 104p. 1986. 25.00 (ISBN 0-89236-088-7). J P Getty Mus.
Whisper of the River. Ferrol Sams. LC 84-42777. 528p. 1984. 14.95 (ISBN 0-931948-60-6). Peachtree Pubs.
Whisper of the River. Ferrol Sams. (Contemporary Americn Fiction Ser.). 544p. 1986. pap. 6.95 (ISBN 0-14-008387-1). Penguin.
Whisper: Shadow of the Hawk. Christopher Brown. (Whisper Collector Sticker Bks.). (Illus.). 24p. (gr. 3-7). 1985. pap. 1.95 (ISBN 0-89954-414-2). Antioch Pub Co.
Whisper the Winged Unicorn. Karen Stiles. (Whisper the Winged Unicorn Ser.). (Illus.). 24p. (gr. 2-6). 1983. pap. 1.95 (ISBN 0-89954-220-4). Antioch Pub Co.
Whisper the Winged Unicorn in Flying Is Fun. Christopher Brown. (Whisper the Winged Unicorn Ser.). (Illus.). 22p. (ps-2). 1985. 2.95 (ISBN 0-89954-327-8). Antioch Pub Co.
Whisper the Winged Unicorn: Rescue from Rainbow Forest. (gr. 2-3). 1.95 (ISBN 0-89954-366-9). Antioch Pub Co.
Whisper to the Earth. David Ignatow. 1981. 10.95 (ISBN 0-316-41494-8, Pub. by Atlantic Monthly Pr); pap. 6.95 (ISBN 0-686-96773-9). Little.
Whispered Meanings: Selected Essays of Simon O. Lesser. Simon O. Lesser. Ed. by Robert W. Sprich & Richard Noland. LC 77-73480. 248p. 1977. 17.50x (ISBN 0-87023-243-6); pap. 9.95x (ISBN 0-87023-244-4). U of Mass Pr.
Whispering Cabin. J. H. Rhodes. 1985. 9.95 (ISBN 0-8034-8559-X, Avalon). Bouregy.
Whispering Gallery. Richard H. Francis. 251p. 1984. 13.95 (ISBN 0-393-01926-8). Norton.
Whispering Gallery: Being Leaves from the Diary of an Ex-Diplomat. 1978. Repr. of 1926 ed. lib. bdg. 15.00 (ISBN 0-8495-0121-0). Arden Lib.
Whispering Gallery: W. B. Yeats, Lytton Strachey, Stephen Spender, George Orwell, Etc. John Lehmann. 1954. 35.00 (ISBN 0-8274-3699-8). R West.
Whispering Gate. Mary Wibberley. (Nightingale Paperbacks). 1985. pap. 9.95 (ISBN 0-8161-3871-0, Large Print Bks). G K Hall.
Whispering Land. Gerald Durrell. (Illus.). 224p. 1975. pap. 4.95 (ISBN 0-14-002083-7). Penguin.
Whispering Land. Gerald Durrell. 1983. 12.75 (ISBN 0-8446-6072-8). Peter Smith.
Whispering Mezuzah. Carol K. Hubner. (Judaica Youth Series: Devorah Doresh Mysteries). (Illus.). (gr. 3-9). 1979. 6.95 (ISBN 0-910818-18-5). Judaica Pr.
Whispering Noll. Catherine Wittler. LC 87-70943. 200p. Date not set. price not set (ISBN 0-937239-02-X). B & C Pub.
Whispering River. A. Westcott & C. Symons. LC 78-108727. (Illus.). 48p. (gr. 3-5). 1970. PLB 10.95 (ISBN 0-87783-049-5); pap. 3.94 deluxe ed (ISBN 0-87783-116-5). Oddo.
Whispering Smith. Frank H. Spearman. 1979. pap. 1.75 (ISBN 0-8439-0620-0, Leisure Bks). Leisure NY.
Whispering Statue. Carolyn Keene. LC 72-106316. (Nancy Drew Ser.: Vol. 14). (Illus.). (gr. 4-7). 1937. 4.50 (ISBN 0-448-09514-9, G&D); PLB 3.29. Putnam Pub Group.
Whispering Surgeon. 2nd ed. Edward Mycue & Vincent Spina. Ed. by Joseph A. Uphoff, Jr. (Illus.). 32p. pap. text ed. 2.00 (ISBN 0-943123-01-1). Arjuna Lib Pr.
Whispering Terror. Betty C. Mowery. (YA) (gr. 7 up). 1984. 9.95 (ISBN 0-8034-8449-6, Avalon). Bouregy.
Whispering to Fool the Wind. Alberto Rios. LC 82-3269. 1982. 13.95 (ISBN 0-935296-30-1); pap. 7.95 (ISBN 0-935296-31-X). Sheep Meadow.
Whispering Veils: Poems on Christo's Art. Cyril Christo. (Illus.). 24p. 1988. 15.00 (ISBN 0-88363-023-0). H L Levin.
Whispering Voices. Doris Stokes. (Lythway Ser.). 1987. lib. bdg. 17.50x (ISBN 0-7451-0595-5, Pub. by Chivers Pr UK). G K Hall.
Whispering Wind. Marion H. Freeman. 96p. 1982. 6.00 (ISBN 0-682-49880-7). Exposition-Phoenix.
Whispering Wood: Practice Set, No. 2. Wiley Staff. (Practice Set Series for Principles of Accounting). 1988. pap. price not set (ISBN 0-471-61953-1). Wiley.
Whisperings of My Soul. Henry Kotschorek. (Illus.). 40p. (Orig.). 1987. pap. 2.95 (ISBN 0-9604342-7-5). Ransom Hill.
Whisperings of Self. 6th ed. Validivar. LC 68-57028. 86p. 1986. 7.95 (ISBN 0-912057-40-8, G-510). AMORC.
Whisperings with Love. Edward Kane. (Illus.). 64p. 1983. 6.95 (ISBN 0-89962-316-6). Todd & Honeywell.
Whisperings Within. David P. Barash. 288p. 1981. pap. 7.95 (ISBN 0-14-005699-8). Penguin.
Whispers. Dorothy Fletcher. 432p. (Orig.). 1980. pap. 2.50 (ISBN 0-89083-675-2). Zebra.
Whispers. Dorothy Fletcher. 432p. 1987. pap. 3.95 (ISBN 0-8217-2236-0). Zebra.
Whispers. B. H. Friedman. LC 73-151219. (Ithaca House Fiction Ser.). 154p. 1972. 3.95 (ISBN 0-87886-021-5). Greenfld Rev Pr.
Whispers. Dean R. Koontz. 512p. 1987. pap. 4.95 (ISBN 0-425-09760-9). Berkley Pub.
Whispers. Donna H. Miesbach. LC 88-90791. (Illus.). 60p. (Orig.). 1988. pap. 8.95 (ISBN 0-945157-03-7). Peak Output Unltd.
Whispers along the Mission Trail. Gail Faber & Michele Lasagna. (California History Ser.). (Illus., Orig.). 1986. permabound student's 15.95 (ISBN 0-936480-04-1); pap. text ed. 12.95 student's ed. 216p. (ISBN 0-936480-03-3); tchr's. ed. 3-ring binder 331p. 27.95 (ISBN 0-936480-05-X). Magpie Pubns.
Whispers at Night. Andrea Parnell. 272p. 1987. pap. 2.95 (ISBN 0-451-14880-0, Sig). NAL.
Whisper's Christmas in Rainbow Forest. Jill Wolf. (Illus.). 24p. (gr. 3-7). 1985. pap. 1.95 (ISBN 0-89954-461-4). Antioch Pub Co.
Whispers from Eternity. 9th ed. Paramahansa Yogananda. LC 86-60584. (Illus.). 239p. 1986. 7.95 (ISBN 0-87612-103-2); pap. 3.50x Span. ed. (ISBN 0-87612-101-6); German ed. 10.00x (ISBN 3-85399-034-7). Self Realization.
Whispers from Eternity. Paramahansa Yogananda. LC 85-71375. 1978. pap. 12.95 (ISBN 0-937134-03-1). Amrita Found.
Whispers from Eternity, First Vision. Paramahansa Yogananda. 1977. 6.95 (ISBN 0-87612-102-4). Self Realization.
Whispers from Old Genesee & Echoes of the Salmon River. John A. Platt. (Illus.). 184p. 1975. 14.95 (ISBN 0-87770-143-1). Ye Galleon.
Whispers from the First Californians. 2nd ed. Gail Faber & Michele Lasagna. (California History Ser.). (Illus.). 1981. permabound student's ed. 15.95 (ISBN 0-936480-02-5); pap. text ed. 12.95 student's ed., 223p. (ISBN 0-936480-00-9); Tchr's ed., 240p. 3-ring binder 27.95 (ISBN 0-936480-01-7). Magpie Pubns.
Whispers from the Other Shore. Ravi Ravindra. LC 84-40164. 170p. (Orig.). 1984. pap. 6.50 (ISBN 0-8356-0589-2, Quest). Theos Pub Hse.
Whispers from the Woods. Peter Curto. 3.75 (ISBN 0-533-00121-8). Vantage.
Whispers from Within, Vol. II. Madeleine S. Gary. Ed. by Stephen M. Stigler. 150p. 1986. pap. 7.95 (ISBN 0-913459-04-6). New Writers Guild.
Whisper's Golden Friend. Jill Wolf. (Collector Sticker Bks.). (Illus.). 24p. (gr. 3-7). 1986. pap. 1.95 (ISBN 0-89954-426-6). Antioch Pub Co.
Whispers I. Ed. by Stuart D. Schiff. pap. 3.50 (ISBN 0-515-08881-1). Jove Pubns.
Whispers II. Ed. by Stuart D. Schiff. 1987. pap. 3.95 (ISBN 0-515-09252-5). Jove Pubns.
Whispers III. Stuart D. Schiff. 272p. 1988. pap. 3.95 (ISBN 0-515-09363-7). Jove Pubns.
Whispers in the Dark. Sam Goldenberg. (Illus.). 140p. 1988. 12.95 (ISBN 0-88400-130-X). Shengold.
Whispers in the Wind, Vol. I. Madeleine S. Gary. Ed. by Stephen M. Stigler. 150p. (Orig.). 1986. pap. 7.95 (ISBN 0-913459-03-8); Set. pap. write for info. (ISBN 0-913459-05-4). New Writers Guild.
Whispers Near Niagara. S. Santhi. 5.00 (ISBN 0-89253-731-0); flexible cloth 4.00 (ISBN 0-89253-732-9). Ind-US Inc.
Whispers of God: Liturgical Resources for Year B. Lavon Bayler. 272p. 1987. pap. 10.95 (ISBN 0-8298-0758-6). Pilgrim NY.
Whispers of His Power. Amy Carmichael. 256p. 1985. pap. 6.95 (ISBN 0-8007-5206-6, Power Bks). Revell.
Whispers of Love & Other Poems. Esther Potack. 64p. 1988. 7.95 (ISBN 0-8062-3114-9). Carlton.
Whispers of Love on Wings of Light. Ruth E. Norman. (Tesla Speaks Ser.: No. 10). (Illus.). 1975. 10.95 (ISBN 0-932642-33-0); pap. 6.95 (ISBN 0-932642-44-6). Unarius Pubns.
Whispers of Nature. Vijay. (Orig.). pap. 9.00 (ISBN 0-89744-009-9). Auromere.
Whispers of Passion. Sandra DuBay. 416p. 1984. pap. 3.75 (ISBN 0-8439-2101-3, Leisure Bks). Leisure NY.
Whispers of the Angel (Nawa-E-Sarosh) Mirza A. Ghalib. (Illus.). 56p. 1969. 3.00 (ISBN 0-88253-384-3). Ind-US Inc.
Whispers of the Heart. Jillian Fayre. 192p. 1981. pap. 2.95 (ISBN 0-671-43867-0, Wallaby). S&S.
Whispers of the Heart. Dale R. Olen. LC 86-60623. 180p. 1987. pap. 8.95 (ISBN 0-89390-100-8). Resource Pubns.
Whispers of the Unchained Heart. Ed. by Sal St. John Buttaci & Susan L. Gerstle. LC 77-75496. 1977. 10.95 (ISBN 0-917398-05-X); pap. 8.95 (ISBN 0-917398-06-8). New Worlds.
Whispers on the Wind. Richard Heasler. 84p. 1979. pap. 4.00 (ISBN 0-686-38083-5). Jelm Mtn.
Whisper's Secret Dream. Peter Mandel. (Illus.). 24p. (gr. 3-7). 1986. pap. 1.95 (ISBN 0-89954-635-8). Antioch Pub Co.
Whistle Blower. John Hale. LC 85-3860. 240p. 1985. 12.95 (ISBN 0-689-11605-5). Atheneum.
Whistle Blower. John Hale. (Spymasters Ser.). (Illus.). 240p. 1988. pap. 4.95 (ISBN 0-02-028851-4, Collier). Macmillan.
Whistle: Chapter One of a Work-in-Progress. James Jones. 1974. 30.00 (ISBN 0-89723-017-5). Bruccoli.

White Collar: The American Middle Classes. C. Wright Mills. 1951. 27.95x (ISBN 0-19-500024-2). Oxford U Pr.

White-Collar Trade Unions: Contemporary Developments in Industrialized Societies. Ed. by Adolf Sturmthal. LC 66-10059. (Illus.). 427p. 1967. pap. 12.95 (ISBN 0-252-74535-3). U of Ill Pr.

White Collar Union: The Story of the OPEIU & Its People. Joseph E. Finley. 288p. 1975. lib. bdg. 14.00x (ISBN 0-374-92742-1, Octagon). Hippocrene Bks.

White-Collar Workers & the UAW. Carl D. Snyder. LC 72-88954. 211p. 1973. 19.95 (ISBN 0-252-00286-5). U of Ill Pr.

White Collar Workers in Transition: The Boom Years, 1940-1970. Mark McColloch. LC 83-5546. (Contributions in Labor History Ser.: No. 15). xii, 193p. 1983. lib. bdg. 35.00 (ISBN 0-313-23785-9, MCW/). Greenwood.

White Collar Workers, Trade Unions & Class. Peter Armstrong et al. 224p. 1986. 34.50 (ISBN 0-7099-0571-8, Pub. by Croom Helm Ltd). Routledge Chapman & Hall.

White Columns in Hollywood: Reports from the GWTW Sets. Susan Myrick. LC 82-18881. (Illus.). 345p. 1982. pap. 14.95 (ISBN 0-86554-245-7, P37). Mercer Univ Pr.

White Company. Arthur Conan Doyle. 1986. Repr. lib. bdg. 22.95x (ISBN 0-89966-517-9). Buccaneer Bks.

White Company. Arthur Conan Doyle. LC 87-62625. (Books of Wonder). (Illus.). 362p. 1988. 17.00 (ISBN 0-688-07817-6). Morrow.

White Conquest, 2 Vols. facsimile ed. William H. Dixon. LC 70-138335. (Black Heritage Library Collection Ser.). 1876. Set. 38.25 (ISBN 0-8369-8727-6). Ayer Co Pubs.

White Corp. James Benjamin & Stanley Kratchman. 1988. pap. 7.95 (ISBN 0-256-06498-9). Irwin.

White Crochet. Better Homes & Gardens Editors. (Illus.). 80p. 1988. pap. 7.95 (ISBN 0-696-01631-1). BH&G.

White Crochet Lace. Ondori Publishing Company Staff. (Illus.). 96p. 1982. pap. 8.50 (ISBN 0-87040-521-7). Japan Pubns USA.

White Cutter. David Pownall. 1989. 18.95 (ISBN 0-670-82579-4). Viking.

White Darkness: & Other Stories of the Great Northwest. facsimile ed. Lawrence Mott. LC 74-150554. (Short Story Index Reprint Ser.). (Illus.). Repr. of 1906 ed. 20.00 (ISBN 0-8369-3851-8). Ayer Co Pubs.

White Death. Georges Bettembourg & Michael Brame. (Illus.). 300p. 1981. 13.95 (Reynard Hse). Noit Amrofer.

White Death. Georges Bettembourg & Michael Brame. 13.95. Reynard Hse.

White Death, No. 203. Nick Carter. 208p. 1985. pap. 2.50 (ISBN 0-441-88568-3) (ISBN 0-317-31719-9). Ace Bks.

White Deer. James Thurber. LC 45-35191. (Illus.). 115p. 1968. pap. 3.95 (ISBN 0-15-696264-0, Harv). HarBraceJ.

White Deer. 20p. 1979. pap. 1.49 (ISBN 0-8285-1266-3, Pub. by Progress Pubs USSR). Imported Pubns.

White Devil. John Webster. Ed. by Elizabeth M. Brennan. (New Mermaid Ser.). 1976. pap. 5.95x (ISBN 0-393-90037-1). Norton.

White Devil. John Webster. Ed. by J. R. Mulryne. LC 68-20771. (Regents Renaissance Drama Ser). xxviii, 158p. 1969. 17.50x (ISBN 0-8032-0287-3); pap. 5.95x (ISBN 0-8032-5288-9, BB 233, Bison). U of Nebr Pr.

White Devil. John Webster. Ed. by John R. Brown. (Revels Plays Ser.). 205p. 1979. pap. 11.00 (ISBN 0-7190-1611-8, Pub. by Manchester Univ Pr). St Martin.

White Devil. John Webster. (Illus.). 144p. 1986. pap. 4.50 (ISBN 0-413-57030-4, 9349). Heinemann Ed.

White Devil. John Webster. (Study Texts Ser.). (YA) (gr. 7 up). Date not set. pap. 5.95. Longman Trade.

White Devil. John Webster. (Study Texts Ser.). 1988. pap. 5.95 (ISBN 0-582-33188-9). Longman.

White Devil & The Duchess of Malfi. Richard A. Cave. (Text & Performance Ser.). 72p. 1988. pap. text ed. 8.50 (ISBN 0-333-39577-8, Pub. by Macmillan UK). Humanities.

White Devil & the Duchess of Malfy. John Webster. Ed. by Martin W. Sampson. 422p. 1981. Repr. of 1906 ed. lib. bdg. 35.00 (ISBN 0-89987-867-9). Darby Bks.

White Devil Discover'd: Backgrounds & Foregrounds to Webster's Tragedy. Frederick O. Waage. LC 83-48766. (American University Studies IV (English Language & Literature): Vol. 5). 185p. (Orig.). 1984. pap. text ed. 19.70 (ISBN 0-8204-0055-6). P Lang Pubs.

White Doe of Rylstone. Arthur H. Quinn & William Wordsworth. LC 76-44498. 1976. Repr. of 1889 ed. lib. bdg. 47.00 (ISBN 0-8414-6914-8). Folcroft.

White Doe of Rylstone. William Wordsworth. 102p. 1980. Repr. of 1889 ed. lib. bdg. 29.50 (ISBN 0-8495-4439-4). Arden Lib.

White Doe of Rylstone: Or, The Fate of the Nortons. William Wordsworth. Ed. by Kristine Dugas. LC 87-9265. (Wordsworth Ser.). (Illus.). 392p. 1988. 35.00x (ISBN 0-8014-1946-8). Cornell U Pr.

White Doe: The Fate of Virginia Dare, an Indian Legend. Sallie S. Cotten. (Illus.). 94p. (gr. 8-12). 1975. Repr. of 1901 ed. 6.50 (ISBN 0-930230-30-2). Johnson NC.

White Dog. Feodor Sologub. Ed. by Isaac Goldberg. Tr. by John Cournos. (International Pocket Library). pap. 2.00 (ISBN 0-686-77249-0). Branden Pub Co.

White Dog see Modern Russian Classics.

White Dove. Rosie Thomas. 640p. 1986. 18.95 (ISBN 0-670-80013-9). Viking.

White Dove. Rosie Thomas. 640p. 1987. pap. 4.95 (ISBN 0-553-26457-5). Bantam.

White Dove Review, Nos. 1-5. Ed. by Ron Padgett. (Avant-Garde Mags). Repr. of 1959 ed. 15.00 (ISBN 0-405-01757-X). Ayer Co Pubs.

White Dragon. Anne McCaffrey. 1981. 15.00 (ISBN 0-345-27567-5). Ultramarine Pub.

White Dragon, No. 3. Anne McCaffrey. 1980. pap. 3.95 (ISBN 0-345-34167-8, Del Rey). Ballantine.

White Dress. Brenda Hillman. (Wesleyan New Poets Ser.). vi, 58p. 1985. 17.00 (ISBN 0-8195-2121-3); pap. 8.95 (ISBN 0-8195-1122-6). Wesleyan U Pr.

White Dwarf: Proceedings of the I.A.U. Symposium, No. 42, Fife, Scotland, Aug. 11-13, 1970. International Astronomical Union Staff. Ed. by S. J. Luythen. LC 75-146966. (I.A.U. Symposia). 164p. 1971. lib. bdg. 21.00 (ISBN 90-277-0180-6, Pub. by Reidel Holland). Kluwer Academic.

White Dwarfs. Vanhorn. 1988. write for info. (ISBN 0-471-02100-8). Wiley.

White Dwarfs-Black Holes: An Introduction to Realistic Astrophysics. Roman Sexl & Hannelore Sexl. LC 79-23307. 1979. 17.50 (ISBN 0-12-637350-7). Acad Pr.

White Dynamite & Curly Kidd. Bill Martin, Jr. & John Archambault. LC 85-27214. (Illus.). 32p. (gr. k-2). 1986. 11.95 (ISBN 0-8050-0658-3). H Holt & Co.

White Eagle Inheritance. Ingrid Lind. 96p. 1984. pap. 8.95 (ISBN 0-85500-186-0, Pub. by Thorsons UK). Weiser.

White Eagle Lodge Book of Health & Healing. Joan Hodgson. 240p. 1983. pap. 9.95 (ISBN 0-85487-063-6). DeVorss.

White Eagle, Red Star: Polish Soviet War 1919-1920. Norman Davies. (Illus.). 308p. 1987. pap. 14.95 (ISBN 0-901149-23-3, Pub. by Orbis Bks Ltd England). Hippocrene Bks.

White Eagles Over Serbia. Lawrence Durrell. LC 58-7779. 1958. 14.95 (ISBN 0-87599-030-4). S G Phillips.

White Egret. Shingi Itoh. (Illus.). 1988. pap. 18.95 (ISBN 0-87701-523-6); 35.00 (ISBN 0-87701-584-8). Chronicle Bks.

White Embroidery Story: Candlewicking. Etsuko Inoue. (Illus.). 74p. (Orig.). 1986. pap. 7.50 (ISBN 0-87040-704-X). Japan Pubns USA.

White Face. Carl R. Offord. LC 73-18596. Repr. of 1943 ed. 24.50 (ISBN 0-404-11407-5). AMS Pr.

White Faculty, Black Students: Exploring Assumptions & Practices. Carolyn D. Spatta. (Illus.). 23p. 1984. pap. 4.00 (ISBN 0-911696-37-7). Assn Am Coll.

White Falcon: The House of Godeffroy & Its Commercial & Scientific Role in the Pacific. Florence M. Spoehr. LC 63-18693. (Illus.). 1963. 10.95 (ISBN 0-87015-119-3). Pacific Bks.

White Fang. Jack London. (Airmont Classics Ser.). (gr. 6 up). 1964. pap. 1.75 (ISBN 0-8049-0036-1, CL-36). Airmont.

White Fang. new & abr. ed. Jack London. Ed. by Naunerle Farr. (Now Age Illustrated III Ser.). (Illus.). (gr. 4-12). 1977. text ed. 7.50 (ISBN 0-88301-283-9); pap. text ed. 2.95 (ISBN 0-88301-271-5). Pendulum Pr.

White Fang. Jack London. (gr. 7 up). 1972. pap. 2.50 (ISBN 0-590-40523-3, Apple Classics). Scholastic Inc.

White Fang. Jack London. (Dent's Illustrated Children's Classics Ser.). (Illus.). 238p. (gr. 4 up). 1975. Repr. of 1967 ed. 11.00x (ISBN 0-460-05073-7, BKA 01609, Pub. by J M Dent England). Biblio Dist.

White Fang. Jack London. LC 85-4297000001. (Puffin Classics Ser.). 272p. (gr. 4-6). 1985. pap. 2.25 (ISBN 0-14-035045-4, Puffin). Penguin.

White Fang see Call of the Wild.

White Fang see Novels & Stories.

White Fang: Student Activity Book. Marcia Sohl & Gerald Dackerman. (Now Age Illustrated Ser.). (Illus.). (gr. 4-12). 1976. wkbk. 1.25 (ISBN 0-88301-295-2). Pendulum Pr.

White Feather. Ruth Eitzen. LC 86-31786. (Illus.). 64p. (gr. 3-4). 1987. 9.95 (ISBN 0-8361-3439-7). Herald Pr.

White Fire: The Life & Works of Jessie Sampter. Bertha Badt-Strauss. Ed. by Moshe Davis. LC 77-70663. (America & the Holy Land Ser.). (Illus.). 1977. Repr. of 1956 ed. lib. bdg. 20.00x (ISBN 0-405-10224-0). Ayer Co Pubs.

White Flag. Gene Stratton-Porter. 1976. Repr. of 1923 ed. lib. bdg. 25.95x (ISBN 0-89190-943-5, Pub. by River City Pr). Amereon Ltd.

White Flag. Gene Stratton-Porter. 483p. 1981. Repr. of 1923 ed. lib. bdg. 35.00 (ISBN 0-89984-448-0). Century Bookbindery.

White Flower. Grace L. Hill. Repr. lib. bdg. 19.95x (ISBN 0-89190-051-9, Pub. by River City Pr). Amereon Ltd.

White Flowers in the Snow. Penny Harter. LC 81-80549. (Illus.). 95p. 1981. pap. 3.00 (ISBN 0-89823-024-1). New Rivers Pr.

White Forest Battle. Harold Calin. (Inflation Fighter). 208p. 1982. pap. 1.50 (ISBN 0-8439-1150-6, Leisure Bks). Leisure NY.

White Fox of Andhra. Donald S. Fox. 216p. 1978. 6.95 (ISBN 0-8059-2432-9). Dorrance.

White Gamma. David Chacko. 208p. 1988. 15.95 (ISBN 0-312-02317-0). St Martin.

White Generals: An Account of the White Movement & the Russian Civil War. Richard Luckett. 428p. 1988. text ed. 25.00 (ISBN 0-416-01991-9, Pub. by Routledge UK). Routledge Chapman & Hall.

White German Shepherd. Vicki Hearne. LC 87-19536. 228p. 1988. 16.95 (ISBN 0-87113-196-X). Atlantic Monthly.

White German Shepherd Book. Paul D. Strang et al. (Illus.). 119p. 17.50 (ISBN 0-911039-00-7). Medea DC.

White Gloves & Party Manners. Marjabelle Young & Ann Buchwald. LC 65-25830. (Illus.). (gr. 1-7). 1965. 12.95 (ISBN 0-88331-054-6). Luce.

White God & Other Poems. Thomas C. Chubb. LC 76-144712. (Yale Ser. of Younger Poets: No. 5). Repr. of 1920 ed. 18.00 (ISBN 0-404-53805-3). AMS Pr.

White God & Other Poems. Thomas C. Chubb. 1920. pap. 9.50x (ISBN 0-686-51325-8). Elliots Bks.

White Goddess: A Historical Grammar of Poetic Myth. rev. & enl. ed. Robert Graves. 511p. 1966. pap. 9.95 (ISBN 0-374-50493-8). FS&G.

White Goddess (amended & enlarged edition) Robert Graves. 1983. 18.00 (ISBN 0-8446-5983-5). Peter Smith.

White Gold: The Story of African Ivory. Derek Wilson & Peter Ayerst. LC 76-363. (Illus.). (YA) (gr. 10 up). 1976. 9.95 (ISBN 0-8008-8251-2). Taplinger.

White Gold Wielder. Stephen R. Donaldson. 1984. pap. 4.95 (ISBN 0-345-34870-2, Del Rey). Ballantine.

White Grubs & Their Allies: A Study of North American Scarabaeoid Larvae. Paul O. Ritcher. LC 66-63008. (Studies in Entomology: No. 4). (Illus.). 216p. 1966. 21.95x (ISBN 0-87071-054-0). Oreg St U Pr.

White Guard. Mikhail Bulgakov. 288p. 1987. pap. 8.95 (ISBN 0-89733-246-6). Academy Chi Pubs.

White Haired Girl. He & Ying. Date not set. 4.95 (ISBN 0-8351-1562-3). China Bks.

White Hand. Jean Warmbold. LC 87-60782. 224p. 1988. 18.95 (ISBN 0-932966-79-9). Permanent Pr.

White Hand. Jean Warmbold. LC 87-60782. 224p. 1988. 18.95. Permanent Pr.

White Hannah. D. M. Wallace. Ed. by Rodger Moody. (Illus.). 32p. 1983. 3.00 (ISBN 0-9610508-0-2). Silverfish Rev Pr.

White-Headed Eagle: John McLoughlin, Builder of an Empire. facsimile ed. Richard G. Montgomery. LC 76-164616. (Select Bibliographies Reprint Ser). Repr. of 1934 ed. 24.50 (ISBN 0-8369-5900-0). Ayer Co Pubs.

White Heat. Chuck Bainbridge. (Hard Corps Ser.: No. 3). 1987. pap. 2.95 (ISBN 0-515-09083-2). Jove Pubns.

White Heat. Ed. by Patrick McGilligan. LC 83-40257. (Wisconsin-Warner Brothers Screenplay Ser.). 1984. 18.95x (ISBN 0-299-09670-X); pap. 8.95t (ISBN 0-299-09674-2). U of Wis Pr.

White Hell. Jon Sharpe. (Trailsman Ser.: No. 74). 176p. 1988. pap. 2.75 (ISBN 0-451-15193-3, Sig). NAL.

White Hell. Gar Wilson. (Phoenix Force Ser.: No. 6). 192p. 1983. pap. 2.25 (ISBN 0-373-61306-7, Pub. by Worldwide). Harlequin Bks.

White Heron. Sarah O. Jewett. LC 83-71791. (Creative's Classic Short Stories Ser.). 40p. (gr. 6 up). 1983. PLB 8.95 (ISBN 0-87191-966-4). Creative Ed.

White Heron & Other Stories. Sarah O. Jewett. (Collected Works of Sarah O. Jewett). 1988. Repr. of 1886 ed. lib. bdg. 59.00x. Am Biog Serv.

White Heron & Other Stories see Collected Works.

"White Heron" & the Question of Minor Literature. Louis A. Renza. LC 84-40157. (Wisconsin Project on American Writers Ser.: No. 1). 256p. 1984. text ed. 19.95x (ISBN 0-299-09960-1); pap. text ed. 9.95x (ISBN 0-299-09964-4). U of Wis Pr.

White-Hmong English Dictionary. rev. ed. Compiled by Ernest E. Heimbach. (Linguistic Ser.: No. IV). 497p. 1979. 6.50 (ISBN 0-87727-075-9, DP 75). Cornell SE Asia.

White Hoods: Canada's Ku Klux Klan. Julian Sher. 250p. 1983. lib. bdg. 17.95; pap. 7.95 (ISBN 0-317-18556-X). Left Bank.

White Horse Cafe. Roberta Smoodin. 256p. 1988. pap. 6.95 (ISBN 0-14-009838-0). Penguin.

White Horse of Alih & Other Stories. Mig A. Enriquez. 110p. (Orig.). 1986. pap. text ed. 6.25 (ISBN 971-10-0233-7, Pub. by New Day Philippines). Cellar.

White Horse of Zennor. Michael Morpurgo. 128p. (gr. 3-7). 1985. 14.95 (ISBN 0-7182-3981-4, Pub. by Kaye & Ward). David & Charles.

White Hotel. D. M. Thomas. 336p. 1982. pap. 4.95 (ISBN 0-671-62731-7). PB.

White Hotel. D. M. Thomas. LC 80-52004. 256p. 1981. 13.95 (ISBN 0-670-76292-X). Viking.

White Hotel. D. M. Thomas. pap. 4.50 (ISBN 0-317-56805-1). WSP.

White Hound of the Mountain. Thomas J. Kiernan. (Illus.). 1962. 9.95 (ISBN 0-8159-7208-3). Devin.

White House: An Historic Guide. 160p. 1982. 5.50 (ISBN 0-912308-17-6); pap. 3.75 (ISBN 0-912308-16-8). White House Hist.

White House: An Historic Guide. LC 79-64879. (Illus.). 161p. 1979. 9.50 (ISBN 0-912308-11-7, S/N 066-000-00006-1). USGPO.

White House: An Historic Guide. 160p. 1987. pap. 6.95 (ISBN 0-317-61451-7). Natl Geog.

White House & Capitol Hill. Nigel Bowles. 300p. 1987. 42.00 (ISBN 0-19-827478-5). Oxford U Pr.

White House Autumn. Ellen E. White. (Orig.). (gr. 7 up). 1985. pap. 2.95 (ISBN 0-380-89780-6, Flare). Avon.

White House Conference on Small Business: A Report to the President of the United States. 82p. (Orig.). 1986. pap. 5.50 (ISBN 0-318-22477-1, S/N 040-000-00506-4). USGPO.

White House Ethics: The History of the Politics of Conflict of Interest Regulation. Robert N. Roberts. LC 87-24962. (Contributions in Political Science Ser.: No. 204). 224p. 1988. lib. bdg. 37.95 (ISBN 0-313-25934-8, RWH/). Greenwood.

White House Family Cookbook. Henry Haller & Virginia Aronson. LC 87-9674. (Illus.). 464p. 1987. 19.95 (ISBN 0-394-55657-7). Random.

White House Gang. Earle Looker. 15.95 (ISBN 0-89190-546-4, Pub. by Am Repr). Amereon ltd.

White House Hand-Book of Oratory. Ed. by Charles E. Chadman. LC 77-88075. (Granger Poetry Library Ser.). 1977. Repr. of 1889 ed. 22.50x (ISBN 0-89609-062-0). Roth Pub Inc.

White House Mess. Christopher Buckley. 256p. 1986. 16.45 (ISBN 0-394-54940-6). Knopf.

White House Mess. Christopher Buckley. 1987. pap. 4.50 (ISBN 0-14-009793-7). Penguin.

White House Mess. Christopher Buckley. 373p. 1987. lib. bdg. 18.95x (ISBN 0-8161-4194-0, Large Print Bks). G K Hall.

White House News Photographers' Best. Ed. by Beverly Jackson. LC 77-13227. (Illus.). 116p. 1977. 12.50 (ISBN 0-87491-191-5). Acropolis.

White House Operations: The Johnson Presidency. Emmette S. Redford & Richard T. McCulley. (Administrative History of the Johnson Presidency Ser.). 261p. 1986. text ed. 30.00x (ISBN 0-292-79033-3). U of Tex Pr.

White House: Organization & Operations. R. Gordon Hoxie. LC 72-160151. 218p. 1971. 10.00 (ISBN 0-317-39576-9). Ctr Study Presidency.

White House Pantry Murder. Elliott Roosevelt. 224p. 1988. pap. 3.95 (ISBN 0-380-70404-8). Avon.

White House Pantry Murder: An Eleanore Roosevelt Mystery. Elliott Roosevelt. 224p. 1987. 15.95 (ISBN 0-312-00202-5, Pub. by Thomas Dunne Bks). St Martin.

White House Press on the Presidency: News Management & Co-option. Frank Cormier & James Deakin. Ed. by Kenneth W. Thompson. LC 83-6708. (Presidency & the Press Ser.: Vol. IV). 92p. (Orig.). 1983. lib. bdg. 22.00 (ISBN 0-8191-3254-3, Pub. by White Miller Center); pap. text ed. 8.25 (ISBN 0-8191-3255-1). U Pr of Amer.

White House Sucks. Chris Musun. (Orig.). 1986. pap. 8.95 (ISBN 0-936729-00-7). Dare Co.

White House Years. Henry Kissinger. (Illus.). 1979. 29.95 (ISBN 0-316-49661-8). Little.

White Hunter, Black Heart. Peter Viertel. 1987. pap. 4.95 (ISBN 0-440-39809-6, LE). Dell.

White Indian. Donald C. Porter. 1984. pap. 3.95 (ISBN 0-553-24650-X). Bantam.

White Indian Boy. Duane R. Lund. 1981. 7.95 (ISBN 0-934860-17-3). Adventure Pubns.

White Indian Boy. Charles A. Wilson. Ed. by John Stewart & Trilba N. Redding. Bd. with Return of the White Indian. LC 86-127837. (Illus.). 395p. 1985. 32.50 (ISBN 0-9616261-0-0). C A Wilson.

White Indian Boy. rev ed. Ed. by Charles A. Wilson & Trilba N. Redding. Bd. with Return of the White Indian. LC 86-127837. (Illus.). 395p. 1988. 32.50. C A Wilson.

White Indians of Colonial America. James Axtell. 38p. pap. 3.00. Ye Galleon.

White Is the Color of Death. J. N. Catanach. 320p. 1988. 16.95 (ISBN 0-88150-104-2). Countryman.

White Jacket. Herman Melville. 1979. pap. 3.95 (ISBN 0-451-51732-6, CE1732, Sig Classics). NAL.

White-Jacket. Herman Melville. Ed. by Harrison Hayward. LC 67-21603. (Writings of Herman Melville Ser.). 1970. 36.95x (ISBN 0-8101-0257-9); pap. 12.95 (ISBN 0-8101-0258-7). Northwestern U Pr.

White-Jacket. Herman Melville. (Classics of Naval Literature Ser.). 736p. 1988. Repr. of 1970 ed. 21.95 (ISBN 0-87021-788-7). Naval Inst Pr.

White-Jacket; Or the World in a Man-of-War see Redburn, White-Jacket, Moby-Dick.

White Jade Fox. Andre Norton. 1980. pap. 1.95 (ISBN 0-449-24005-3, Crest). Fawcett.

White Jaguar. William Appel. 272p. 1985. 16.95 (ISBN 0-931933-02-1). Richardson & Steirman.

White Jaguar. William Appel. 288p. 1986. pap. 3.95 (ISBN 0-7701-0493-2). Paperjacks US.

White Jazz. Charles Newman. LC 86-46072. 213p. (Orig.). 1984. pap. 7.95 (ISBN 0-385-18863-3). Ultramarine Pub.

TITLE INDEX

WHITE SANDS, OF WIND

White Junk of Love, Again. Sibyl James. LC 86-20772. 75p. (Orig.). 1986. 13.95 (ISBN 0-934971-05-6); pap. 6.95 (ISBN 0-934971-03-X). Calyx Bks.

White Knight: (Lewis Carroll) Alexander L. Taylor. 1978. Repr. of 1952 ed. lib. bdg. 37.50 (ISBN 0-8495-5116-1). Arden Lib.

White Knight. (Lewis Carroll) Alexander L. Taylor. LC 74-3131. 1974. Repr. of 1952 ed. lib. bdg. 35.00 (ISBN 0-8414-8570-4). Folcroft.

White Knuckles: Getting over the Fear of Flying. Layne Ridley. LC 86-24397. (Illus.). 168p. 1987. pap. 5.95 (ISBN 0-385-23793-6). Doubleday.

White Knuckles Log. Don McAlpine. Ed. by Melba McAlpine. LC 86-71127. (Illus.). 192p. 1986. 14.95 (ISBN 0-933031-05-X). Coun Oak Bks.

White Labyrinth: A Guide to the Health Care System. 2nd ed. David B. Smith & Arnold D. Kaluzny. LC 86-9859. 276p. 1986. text ed. 26.00 (ISBN 0-910701-13-X, 0790). Health Admin Pr.

White Lace, Red Flowers: A Question of Morality. Curtis W. Smith. LC 87-63427. 128p. (Orig.). 1988. pap. 6.95 (ISBN 0-944208-02-9). Seventh-Wing Pubns.

White Lady. Grace L. Hill. 1976. Repr. of 1930 ed. lib. bdg. 18.95 (ISBN 0-89190-025-X, Pub. by River City Pr). Amereon Ltd.

White Lady, No. 72. Grace L. Hill. (Romance Ser.). 208p. 1986. pap. 2.95 (ISBN 0-553-25573-8). Bantam.

White Land, Black Labor: Caste & Class in Late Nineteenth-Century Georgia. Charles L. Flynn, Jr. LC 83-721. xi, 196p. 1983. text ed. 25.00 (ISBN 0-8071-1097-3). La State U Pr.

White Law: Racism in the Police, Courts & Prisons. Paul Gordon. 159p. 1983. pap. 7.50 (ISBN 0-86104-706-0, Pub. by Pluto Pr). Longwood Pub Group.

White Leopard. Inglis Fletcher. 304p. 1976. Repr. of 1931 ed. lib. bdg. 21.95x (ISBN 0-89244-013-9). Queens Hse-Focus Serv.

White Liberals, Moderates & Radicals in Rhodesia 1953-1980. Ian Hancock. LC 84-40041. 256p. 1984. 25.00 (ISBN 0-312-86778-6). St Martin.

White Lie. Walter T. Rea. (Illus.). 409p. (Orig.). 1982. 15.95 (ISBN 0-9607424-0-9); pap. 12.95 (ISBN 0-9607424-1-7). M & R Pubns.

White Lies. Lane Jennings et al. (Black Buzzard Illustrated Poetry Chapbook Ser.). (Illus.). 28p. 1984. pap. text ed. 3.50 (ISBN 0-938872-06-0). Black Buzzard.

White Lies. Julie Salamon. 224p. (Orig.). 1988. 16.95 (ISBN 0-940595-08-7). Hill & Co Pubs.

White Light. Campbell Armstrong. 1988. pap. 18.45. Morrow.

White Light. Patricia Volk. LC 87-17122. 256p. 1987. 18.95 (ISBN 0-689-11868-6). Atheneum.

White-Light Optical Signal Processing. Francis T. Yu. LC 84-29154. (Pure & Applied Optics Ser.). 316p. 1985. 49.95 (ISBN 0-471-80954-3). Wiley.

White Limbo: The First Australian Climb of Mt. Everest. Lincoln Hall. (Illus.). 262p. 1987. 35.00 (ISBN 0-89886-135-7). Mountaineers.

White Logic: Jack London's Short Stories. James I. McClintock. LC 74-84862. (Monograph Ser.: No. 2). (Illus.). 208p. 1976. 15.00 (ISBN 0-915046-22-9). Wolf Hse.

White Lotus. Bhagwan Shree Rajneesh. Ed. by Ma Prem Asha. LC 81-903266. (Zen Ser.). (Illus.). 430p. 1981. 17.95 (ISBN 0-88050-172-3); pap. 9.95 (ISBN 0-88050-672-5). Chidvilas Inc.

White Lotus: At the Feet of the Mother. Ravindra. (Illus.). 1978. 12.50x (ISBN 0-89684-466-8). Orient Bk Dist.

White Magic. Faith Baldwin. 1976. Repr. of 1939 ed. lib. bdg. 19.95x (ISBN 0-88411-615-8, Pub. by Aeonian Pr). Amereon Ltd.

White Magic. David C. Phillips. (Collected Works of David G. Phillips). 1988. Repr. of 1981 ed. lib. bdg. 59.00x. Am Biog Serv.

White Magic. David G. Phillips. (American Author Ser.). 1981. Repr. lib. bdg. 29.00 (ISBN 0-686-71946-8). Scholarly.

White Magic & English Renaissance Drama. David Woodman. LC 72-423. 148p. 1973. 16.50 (ISBN 0-8386-1125-7). Fairleigh Dickinson.

White Man: A Study of the Attitudes of Africans to Europeans in Ghana before Independence. Gustav Jahoda. LC 83-5655. xii, 144p. 1983. Repr. of 1961 ed. lib. bdg. 35.00x (ISBN 0-313-23963-0, JAWH). Greenwood.

White Man Appears on Southern California Beach. Richard Martin. 88p. (Orig.). 1988. pap. 7.95 (ISBN 0-910829-07-1). First East.

White Man of God. Kenjo Jumbam. (African Writers Ser.). (Orig.). 1981. pap. text ed. 6.00 (ISBN 0-435-90231-8). Heinemann Ed.

White Man Problem. Merritt Clifton & Jack Powers. 12p. 1985. 1.00 (ISBN 0-317-19193-4). Samisdat.

White Man, We Want to Talk to You. Denis Herbstein. LC 78-26133. 270p. 1979. 24.50 (ISBN 0-8419-0455-3, Africana). Holmes & Meier.

White Mandarin. Dan Sherman. pap. 3.50 (ISBN 0-345-30895-6). Ballantine.

White Man's Bible. Ben Klassen. 453p. 1986. pap. 8.00 (ISBN 0-317-53279-0). Noontide.

White Man's Burden: A Satirical Forecast. Roger S. Tracy, pseud. LC 72-4597. (Black Heritage Library Collection Ser.). Repr. of 1915 ed. 20.00 (ISBN 0-8369-9130-3). Ayer Co Pubs.

White Man's Burden: Historical Origins of Racism in the United States. Winthrop D. Jordan. 1974. pap. 7.95x (ISBN 0-19-501743-9). Oxford U Pr.

White Man's Country: Racism in British Politics. Robert Miles & Annie Phizacklea. 184p. 1984. pap. 9.50 (ISBN 0-86104-765-6, Pub. by Pluto Pr). Longwood Pub Group.

White Man's Dilemma: Climax of the Age of Imperialism. Nathaniel Peffer. LC 72-4288. (World Affairs Ser.: National & International Viewpoints). 320p. 1972. Repr. of 1927 ed. 20.00 (ISBN 0-405-04580-8). Ayer Co Pubs.

White Man's Indian: Images of the American Indian from Columbus to the Present. Robert F. Berkhofer, Jr. LC 78-11047. (Illus.). 1979. pap. 5.95 (ISBN 0-394-72794-0, V-794, Vin). Random.

White Man's Justice: Black Man's Grief. Donald Goines. 224p. (Orig.). 1973. pap. 2.25 (ISBN 0-87067-027-1, BH027). Holloway.

White Man's Road. Benjamin Capps. LC 88-42633. (Southwest Life & Letters Ser.). 328p. 1988. text ed. 22.50x (ISBN 0-87074-281-7); pap. 10.95 (ISBN 0-87074-272-8). SMU Press.

White Man's Road. 1988. pap. 2.75 (ISBN 0-515-09576-1). Jove Pubns.

White Marble. Charlotte Zolotow. LC 81-43131. (Illus.). 32p. (gr. k-3). 1982. 11.70i (ISBN 0-690-04152-7, Crowell Jr Bks); PLB 11.89 (ISBN 0-690-04151-9). HarpJ.

White Mare, Red Stallion. Diana L. Paxson. 240p. 1986. pap. 2.95 (ISBN 0-425-08531-7). Berkley Pub.

White Meat. Peter Corris. 1986. pap. 2.95 (ISBN 0-449-13027-4, GM). Fawcett.

White Mercedes. Sandra Agricola. (Ohio Review Bks.). 72p. 1988. 11.95 (ISBN 0-942148-09-6); pap. 7.95 (ISBN 0-942148-08-8). Ohio Review.

White Metal Universe: Navajo Silver from the Fred Harvey Collection. E. Wesley Jernigan & Gary Whiterspoon. LC 81-171386. (Heard Museum Ser.). (Illus.). 54p. 1981. pap. 10.00 (ISBN 0-295-95861-8, Pub. by Heard Mus). U of Wash Pr.

White Mischief. James Fox. 1984. pap. 4.95 (ISBN 0-394-72366-X, Vin). Random.

White Mischief: The Murder of Lord Erroll. James Fox. Ed. by Martha Levin. LC 87-40272. 304p. 1988. pap. 4.95 (ISBN 0-394-75687-8, Vin). Random.

White Monkey King: A Chinese Fable. Sally Wriggins. LC 76-44281. (Illus.). (gr. 1-5). 1977. Pantheon.

White Monkeys. Bin Ramke. LC 80-24582. (Contemporary Poetry Ser.). 104p. 1981. 9.95x (ISBN 0-8203-0544-8); pap. 5.95 (ISBN 0-8203-0551-0). U of Ga Pr.

White Moon, Black Sea. Roberta Latow. 384p. 1989. pap. 4.50 (ISBN 0-553-27704-9). Bantam.

White Mountains. John Christopher. LC 67-10362. 192p. (gr. 5-9). 1967. 12.95 (ISBN 0-02-718360-2); pap. 3.95 (ISBN 0-02-042710-7, Collier). Macmillan.

White Mountains. 2nd ed. John Christopher. LC 88-16119. (Illus.). 224p. (YA) (gr. 7 up). Date not set. pap. 3.95 (ISBN 0-02-042711-5, Collier). Macmillan.

White Mountains of New Hampshire. Alan Nyiri. (Illus.). 84p. (Orig.). 1987. pap. 9.95 (ISBN 0-89272-241-X). Down East.

White Mountains: Place & Perceptions. Donald D. Keyes et al. LC 80-68935. (Illus.). 150p. 1980. pap. 14.95 (ISBN 0-87451-190-9). U Pr of New Eng.

White Mountains; the City of Gold & Lead see Tripods Trilogy.

White Mountains-West. Philip Preston & Jonathan A. Kannair. LC 79-66098. (Illus., Orig.). 1979. pap. 7.50 (ISBN 0-9603106-0-6). Waumbek.

White Mule. William Carlos Williams. LC 37-11249. (Stecher Trilogy: Vol. 1). 1967. pap. 9.95 (ISBN 0-8112-0238-0, NDP226). New Directions.

White Museum. Lynne Dreyer. LC 86-6180. (Roof Bks.). 125p. (Orig.). 1986. pap. 7.50 (ISBN 0-937804-21-5). Segue NYC.

White Mutiny. Edwin Hirschmann. 1980. 24.00x (ISBN 0-8364-0639-7). South Asia Bks.

White, New York Corporations, 8 vols. 13 ed. Isidore Kantrowitz & Sol Slutsky. 1963. Set. looseleaf 360.00 (812); Updates 1985. 300.00; Supplement 1986. 190.00. Bender.

White Niggers of America: The Precocious Autobiography of a Quebec Terrorist. Pierre Vallieres. Tr. by Joan Pinkham from Fr. LC 76-142986. 288p. 1971. pap. 4.50 (ISBN 0-85345-198-2). Monthly Rev.

White Nights. Dee Norman. (Silhouette Special Edition Ser.). pap. 2.75 (ISBN 0-373-09417-5). Harlequin Bks.

White Nights. Boris Sokoloff. 9.95 (ISBN 0-8159-7209-1). Devin.

White Nights, Red Dawn. Frederick Nolan. 1983. pap. 3.95 (ISBN 0-8217-1277-2). Zebra.

White Nile. Alan Moorehead. LC 82-48896. (Illus.). 254p. 1983. pap. 15.95 (ISBN 0-394-71445-8, Vin). Random.

White Nile Arabs: Political Leadership & Economic Change. Abbas A. Mohamed. (London School of Economic Monographs on Social Anthropology: No. 53). (Illus.). 193p. 1980. 42.50 (ISBN 0-485-19553-4, Pub. by Athlone Pr UK). Humanities.

White Noise. Don DeLillo. LC 84-40375. 352p. 1985. 16.95 (ISBN 0-670-80373-1, E Sifton Bks). Viking.

White Noise. Don DeLillo. (Contemporary American Fiction Ser.). 336p. 1986. pap. 7.95 (ISBN 0-14-007702-2). Penguin.

White Notebook. Andre Gide. LC 64-16975. 1964. 5.95 (ISBN 0-8022-0590-9). Philos Lib.

White of Selborne. Walter S. Scott. 1950. Repr. 20.00 (ISBN 0-8274-3700-5). R West.

White on Black on White. Coleman Dowell. LC 83-7205. 251p. 1983. 14.95 (ISBN 0-88150-000-3). Countryman.

White on Red: Images of the American Indian. Ed. by Nancy B. Black & Bette S. Weidman. 1976. 26.50 (ISBN 0-8046-9084-7, Pub. by Kennikat). Assoc Faculty Pr.

White Orchids. Grace L. Hill. 18.95 (ISBN 0-8488-0090-7, Pub. by Amereon Hse). Amereon Ltd.

White Over Black: American Attitudes Toward the Negro, 1550-1812. Winthrop D. Jordan. 1977. pap. 12.95x (ISBN 0-393-00841-X, Norton Lib). Norton.

White over Black: American Attitudes Toward the Negro, 1550-1812. Winthrop D. Jordan. LC 68-13295. (Institute of Early American History & Culture Ser.). (Illus.). xx, 651p. 1968. 37.50x (ISBN 0-8078-1055-X). U of NC Pr.

White Pages of the Radio & Record Industries. Jeffrey Green. 350p. 1987. pap. 19.95 (ISBN 0-939735-01-6). Prof Desk Ref.

White Palace. Glenn Savan. (New Fiction Ser.). 304p. (Orig.). 1987. pap. 7.95 (ISBN 0-553-34419-6). Bantam.

White Paper for the New Hampshire Judicial Council. National Center for State Courts Staff. 15p. 1982. manuscript 0.90 (NERO-123). Natl Ctr St Courts.

White Paper on International Trade - Japan 1983. Japan External Trade Organization. 1984. 100.00 (ISBN 0-444-86854-2, I-083-84). Elsevier.

White Paper on International Trade, Japan 1985. Ed. by Japan External Trade Organization (JETRO) Staff. 412p. 1986. 92.75 (ISBN 0-444-87979-X). Elsevier.

White Paper on International Trade: Japan 1986. JETRO. 426p. 1987. 131.75 (ISBN 0-444-70172-9, North Holland). Elsevier.

White Paper on NLRB. 4.00. Natl Lawyers Guild.

White Paper on Science Museums. Howard Learner. 53p. (Orig.). 1979. pap. 2.50 (ISBN 0-89329-025-4). Ctr Sci Public.

White Paper Whitewash: Philip Agee on the CIA & El Salvador. Philip Agee. Ed. by Warner Poelchau. 220p. 1981. casebound 12.95 (ISBN 0-940380-01-3); pap. 6.50 (ISBN 0-940380-00-5). Sheridan Square Pubns.

White Papers for White Americans. Calvin C. Hernton. LC 82-6101. x, 155p. 1982. Repr. of 1966 ed. lib. bdg. 35.00x (ISBN 0-313-22325-4, HEWP). Greenwood.

White Pass & Yukon Routes: A Pictorial History. Stan B. Cohen. LC 79-90884. (Illus.). 112p. 1980. pap. text ed. 8.95 (ISBN 0-933126-08-5). Pictorial Hist.

White Pass: Gateway to the Klondike. Roy Minter. (Illus.). 394p. 1987. 24.95 (ISBN 0-912006-26-9). U Of Alaska Pr.

White Paternoster, & Other Stories. facsimile ed. Theodore F. Powys. LC 70-178455. (Short Story Index Reprint Ser.). Repr. of 1930 ed. 16.00 (ISBN 0-8369-4056-3). Ayer Co Pubs.

White Peacock. D. H. Lawrence. (Cambridge Edition Texts Ser.). 416p. 1985. 22.50 (ISBN 0-670-76358-6). Viking.

White People. Frances H. Burnett. 72p. 1987. pap. 5.50. Select Bks.

White Pine & Blue Water. Henry Beston. 1974. pap. 8.95 (ISBN 0-89272-013-1). Down East.

White Pine Empire: The Life of a Lumberman. John E. Nelligan. Ed. by Charles M. Sheridan. 1969. Repr. of 1927 ed. 7.50 (ISBN 0-87839-001-4). North Star.

White Pipes. Nancy Kress. 224p. 1985. 14.95 (ISBN 0-312-94451-9, Dist. by St. Martin). Bluejay Bks.

White Pipes. Nancy Kress. 100p. 1987. pap. 2.95 (ISBN 0-425-09107-4). Berkley Pub.

White Plague. Frank Herbert. 528p. 1983. pap. 4.50 (ISBN 0-425-09050-7). Berkley Pub.

White Plague. Frank Herbert. 512p. 1987. pap. 4.50 (ISBN 0-441-88569-1, Pub. by Ace Science Fiction). Ace Bks.

White Plague: Tuberculosis, Man, & Society. Ed. by Rene Dubos & Jean Dubos. 277p. 1987. text ed. 27.00 (ISBN 0-8135-1223-9); pap. text ed. 12.00 (ISBN 0-8135-1224-7). Rutgers U Pr.

White Planet. Frank E. Stranges. 24p. 1985. pap. text ed. 2.00 (ISBN 0-933470-04-5). Intl Evang.

White Porcelain of Ding Yao. Nezu Institute of Fine Arts Staff. 169p. 1983. 75.00x (ISBN 0-317-45330-0, Pub. by Han-Shan Tang Ltd). State Mutual Bk.

White Press & Black America. Carolyn Martindale. LC 85-27219. (Contributions in Afro-American & African Studies: No. 97). 215p. 1986. 35.00 (ISBN 0-313-25103-7, MWP/). Greenwood.

White Problem in America. Ebony Editors. 1966. 3.50 (ISBN 0-87485-020-7). Johnson Chi.

White Python: Adventure & Mystery in Tibet. Mark Channing. Ed. by R. Reginald & Douglas Melville. LC 77-84208. (Lost Race & Adult Fantasy Ser.). 1978. Repr. of 1934 ed. lib. bdg. 26.50x (ISBN 0-405-10964-4). Ayer Co Pubs.

White Rabbit. Ethel Marbach. (Illus.). 20p. (Orig.). (gr. 3-6). 1985. pap. 3.95 (ISBN 0-86716-070-5). St Anthony Mess Pr.

White Rabbit. Bruce Marshall. LC 87-8663. 256p. 1987. Repr. of 1952 ed. lib. bdg. 39.75x (ISBN 0-313-25322-6, MRWR). Greenwood.

White Rabbit: A Woman Doctor's Story of Addiction & Recovery. Martha Morrison. (Illus.). 288p. 1988. 17.95 (ISBN 0-517-56816-0). Crown.

White Racism. Joel Kovel. LC 83-20961. 301p. 1984. 35.00 (ISBN 0-231-05796-2); pap. 13.00 (ISBN 0-231-05797-0). Columbia U Pr.

White Rat: A Life in Baseball. Whitey Herzog & Kevin Horrigan. LC 86-45660. (Illus.). 240p. 1988. pap. 3.95 (ISBN 0-06-080910-8, P-910, PL). Har-Row.

White Rat: The Whitey Herzog Story. Whitey Herzog & Kevin Horrigan. LC 86-45660. 256p. 1987. 16.95i (ISBN 0-06-015694-5, HarpT). Har-Row.

White Raven. Mary M. Holmes. Date not set. pap. 3.95 (ISBN 0-445-20660-8, Pub. by Popular Lib). Warner Bks.

White Raven. Diana Paxson & Adrian Zackheim. 320p. 1988. 18.95 (ISBN 0-688-07496-0). Morrow.

White, Red, Black, 2 Vols. in One. Ferencz A. Pulszky. LC 72-107853. 1971. Repr. of 1853 ed. 48.00 (ISBN 0-384-48250-3). Johnson Repr.

White, Red, Black, Sketches of Society in the United States During the Visit of Their Guest, 3 vols. Ferencz A. Pulszky & Terezia W. Pulszky. LC 68-58066. 1969. Repr. of 1853 ed. Vol. 1. 12.50 (ISBN 0-8371-1593-0, PUX&); Vol. 2. 13.50 (ISBN 0-8371-0834-9, PUY&); Vol. 3. 12.25 (ISBN 0-8371-0835-7, PUZ&). Greenwood.

White Reflections on Black Power. Charles E. Fager. LC 67-13982. pap. 29.50 (ISBN 0-317-10004-1, 2012961). Bks Demand UMI.

White River, Brown Water: A Record-Making Kayak Journey Down the Amazon. Alan Holman. (Illus.). 192p. 1985. 13.95 (ISBN 0-89886-113-6). Mountaineers.

White River Junction. Pat Schneider. (Amherst Writers & Artists Chapbook Ser.). 34p. (Orig.). 1987. pap. 4.95 (ISBN 0-941895-00-9). Amherst Wri Art.

White River Poems: Conversations, Pronouncements, Testimony, Recollections & Mediations on the Subject of the White River Massacre, Sept. 29, 1879. Alan Stephens. 115p. 1975. 6.95 (ISBN 0-8040-0774-8, Pub by Swallow). Ohio U Pr.

White Road. Claude Esteban. Tr. by David Cloutier. LC 78-64433. 1979. 7.50 (ISBN 0-910350-04-3). Charioteer.

White Robed Monk. 3rd, rev. & enl. ed. Ira Progoff. LC 79-1553. (Entrance Meditation Ser.). 111p. 1983. pap. 3.95 (ISBN 0-87941-007-8); pap. 12.50 incl. cassette. Dialogue Hse.

White Rocks: A Woodland Rockshelter in Monroe County, Ohio. Dana E. Ormerod. LC 82-21378. (Research Papers in Archaeology). 100p. 1983. pap. 7.00x (ISBN 0-87338-285-4). Kent St U Pr.

White Romance. Virginia Hamilton. 200p. (YA) (gr. 8 up). 1987. 14.95 (ISBN 0-399-21213-2, Philomel Bks). Putnam Pub Group.

White Room. Christopher Butters. 20p. 1987. pap. 1.00 (ISBN 0-318-23496-3). Samisdat.

White Roots: A Nichols Genealogy. M. Q. Nichols. (Illus.). 377p. 1983. 25.00 (ISBN 0-9612516-0-3). M Q Nichols.

White Roots & the Mysteries of God. Lena E. Rudder. (Illus.). 144p. (Orig.). 1986. pap. write for info. (ISBN 0-937581-00-3). Zarathustrotemo Pr.

White Roots & the Mysteries of God. rev. ed. Lena E. Rudder. (Illus.). 144p. (Orig.). Date not set. price not set (ISBN 0-937581-01-1). Zarathustrotemo Pr.

White Roots & the Mystery of Babylon. Lena E. Rudder. (Orig.). Date not set. price not set (ISBN 0-937581-02-X). Zarathustrotemo Pr.

White Roots of Peace. Paul A. Wallace. LC 84-72986. (Illus.). 104p. 1986. 12.95 (ISBN 0-918517-07-9); pap. 8.95 (ISBN 0-918517-04-4). Chauncy Pr.

White Rose. Glen Cook. (Black Company Trilogy Ser.: Vol. 3). 320p. 1985. pap. 2.95 (ISBN 0-8125-3374-7, Dist. by Warner Pub Services & Saint Martin's Press). Tor Bks.

White Rose. Alanna Knight. 1977. pap. 1.25 (ISBN 0-8439-0465-8, Leisure Bks). Leisure NY.

White Rose. B. Traven. LC 78-24774. 224p. 1980. pap. 8.95 (ISBN 0-88208-176-4). Chicago Review.

White Rose: Munich 1942-1943. 2nd ed. Inge Scholl. Tr. by Arthur R. Schultz. LC 83-16828. (Illus.). xiv, 162p. 1983. pap. 9.95 (ISBN 0-8195-6086-3). Wesleyan U Pr.

White Saddle. Ethel H. Miller. 1934. 5.95 (ISBN 0-912142-02-2); lib. bdg. 6.95 (ISBN 0-912142-01-4); pap. 3.95 (ISBN 0-912142-03-0). White S Bks.

White Sahibs in India. Reginald Reynolds. 1970. Repr. of 1937 ed. lib. bdg. 35.00x (ISBN 0-8371-4320-9, REWS). Greenwood.

White Sands, of Wind, Sand & Time. Richard Atkinson. LC 76-57523. (Popular Ser.: No. 21). (Illus.). 1977. pap. 3.95 (ISBN 0-911408-46-0). SW Pks Mnmts.

White Satin. Audrey Evans. 1984. 15.00x (ISBN 0-86319-023-5, Pub. by New Playwrights Network). State Mutual Bk.

White Savannahs. William E. Collin. LC 73-92516. (Literature of Canada, Poetry & Prose in Reprint: No. 15). pap. 95.80 (ISBN 0-317-26932-1, 2023604). Bks Demand UMI.

White Screen. John M. Bennett. 1975. signed ed. o.p. 7.50 (ISBN 0-685-79003-7); perfect bound in wrappers 3.00 (ISBN 0-912284-73-0). New Rivers Pr.

White Screen, Poetry & Graphics. John M. Bennett. 1976. 6.00 (ISBN 0-686-73442-4). Luna Bisonte.

White Seahorse. Eleanor Fairburn. 288p. 1985. pap. 7.95 (ISBN 0-86327-075-1, Pub. by Wolfhound Pr Ireland). Irish Bks Media.

White Seal. Rudyard Kipling. (Illus.). (ps-3). 1982. PLB 13.27 (ISBN 0-516-09224-3). Childrens.

White Seal. Rudyard Kipling. 1985. 5.95 (ISBN 0-8249-8118-9). Ideals.

White Sects & Black Men in the Recent South. David E. Harrell, Jr. LC 72-157742. 1971. 9.95x (ISBN 0-8265-1171-6). Vanderbilt U Pr.

White Serpent. Tanith Lee. 1988. pap. 3.95 (ISBN 0-88677-267-2). DAW Bks.

White Servitude in Colonial America: An Economic Analysis. David Galenson. LC 81-7682. (Illus.). 320p. 1984. pap. 10.95 (ISBN 0-521-27379-X). Cambridge U Pr.

White Servitude in Colonial South Carolina. Warren B. Smith. LC 60-53017. (Illus.). x, 156p. 1970. 9.95x (ISBN 0-87249-078-5); pap. 9.95x (ISBN 0-87249-177-3). U of SC Pr.

White Servitude in Maryland, 1634-1820. Eugene I. McCormac. LC 78-63901. (Johns Hopkins University. Studies in the Social Sciences. Twenty-Second Ser. 1904: 3-4). Repr. of 1904 ed. 15.00 (ISBN 0-404-61154-0). AMS Pr.

White Servitude in Pennsylvania: Indentured & Redemption Labor in Colony & Commonwealth. facsimile ed. Cheesman A. Herrick. LC 78-124238. (Select Biographies Reprint Ser.). Repr. of 1926 ed. 24.50 (ISBN 0-8369-5426-2). Ayer Co Pubs.

White Servitude in Pennsylvania: Indentured & Redemption Labor in Colony & Commonwealth. Cheesman A. Herrick. LC 70-99480. Repr. of 1926 ed. 35.00x (ISBN 0-8371-2373-9, HWS&). Greenwood.

White Servitude in the Colony of Virginia: A Study of the System of Indentured Labor in the American Colonies. J. C. Ballagh. 11.00 (ISBN 0-384-03146-3). Johnson Repr.

White Servitude in the Colony of Virginia: A Study of the System of Indentured Labor in the American Colonies. James C. Ballagh. LC 78-63840. (Johns Hopkins University. Studies in the Social Sciences. Thirteenth Ser. 1895: 6-7). Repr. of 1895 ed. 11.50 (ISBN 0-404-61098-6). AMS Pr.

White Servitude in the Colony of Virginia. James C. Ballagh. LC 71-101987. 1970. Repr. of 1898 ed. 15.00 (ISBN 0-8337-0158-4). B Franklin.

White Settlers & Native Peoples: An Historical Study of Racial Contacts Between English-Speaking Whites & Aboriginal Peoples in the United States, Canada, Australia, & New Zealand. Archibald G. Price. LC 71-142320. (Illus.). 232p. 1972. Repr. of 1950 ed. lib. bdg. 35.00x (ISBN 0-8371-5923-7, PRWH). Greenwood.

White Settlers in the Tropics. Archibald G. Price. LC 75-41217. Repr. of 1939 ed. 47.50 (ISBN 0-404-14731-3). AMS Pr.

White Settlers in Tropical Africa. Lewis H. Gann & Peter Duignan. LC 76-49445. 1977. Repr. of 1962 ed. lib. bdg. 48.50x (ISBN 0-8371-9394-X, GAWH). Greenwood.

White Shadows. Carroll Yoder. LC 86-51308. 180p. (Orig.). 1989. 26.00 (ISBN 0-914478-78-8); pap. 14.00 (ISBN 0-914478-79-6). Three Continents.

White Ship: Estonian Tales. facsimile ed. Aino J. Kallas. Tr. by Alex Matson from Finnish. LC 73-163034. (Short Story Index Reprint Ser.). Repr. of 1924 ed. 17.00 (ISBN 0-8369-3948-4). Ayer Co Pubs.

White Shroud. Allen Ginsberg. LC 86-45104. 128p. 1986. 14.95i (ISBN 0-06-015714-3, HarpT). Har-Row.

White Shroud: Poems 1980-1985. Allen Ginsberg. LC 86-45104. (Illus.). 112p. 1987. pap. 8.95 (ISBN 0-06-091429-7, PL/1429, PL). Har-Row.

White Silk Dress. Peter Simonds. (Illus.). 304p. 1985. 13.00 (ISBN 0-682-40163-3). Exposition-Phoenix.

White Slave. Richard Owen. LC 86-23920. 320p. 1987. 16.95t (ISBN 0-688-06939-8). Morrow.

White Slave. Richard Owen. 352p. (Orig.). 1988. pap. 4.50 (ISBN 0-451-15395-2, Sig). NAL.

White Slave Market. A. Mackirdy & W. N. Willis. 59.95 (ISBN 0-8490-1291-0). Gordon Pr.

White Slave: Or, Memoirs of a Fugitive. Richard Hildreth. LC 71-82200. (Anti-Slavery Crusade in America Ser). (Illus.). 1969. Repr. of 1852 ed. 16.00 (ISBN 0-405-00639-X). Ayer Co Pubs.

White Slave Trade & the Immigrants: A Chapter in American Social History. Francesco Cordasco & Thomas M. Pitkin. LC 80-25556. 1981. 16.50 (ISBN 0-87917-077-8); pap. 6.95 (ISBN 0-87917-076-X). Ethridge.

White Slave Traffic. Emma Goldman. 69.95 (ISBN 0-8490-1292-9). Gordon Pr.

White Slavery in the Barbary States. facs. ed. Charles Sumner. LC 74-89443. (Black Heritage Library Collection Ser). 1847. 7.00 (ISBN 0-8369-8663-6). Ayer Co Pubs.

White Slaves of England: Compiled from Official Documents. J. C. Cobden. (Development of Industrial Society Ser.). 498p. 1971. Repr. of 1860 ed. 37.50x (ISBN 0-7165-1585-7, Pub. by Irish Academic Pr). Biblio Dist.

White Smoke. Robert Herz. LC 77-92110. 50p. 1977. perfect bound in wrappers 3.75 (ISBN 0-934332-01-0). L'Epervier Pr.

White Snow Bright Snow. Alvin Tresselt. (Illus.). Date not set. pap. 3.95 (ISBN 0-688-08294-7). Morrow.

White Society in Black Africa: The French of Senegal. Rita C. O'Brian. LC 74-183533. pap. 80.00 (ISBN 0-317-11345-3, 2006875). Bks Demand UMI.

White Society in the Antebellum South. Bruce Collins. (Studies in Modern History Ser.). 256p. 1985. pap. text ed. 14.95 (ISBN 0-582-49194-0). Longman.

White Song & a Black One. Joseph S. Cotter. LC 73-18568. Repr. of 1909 ed. 11.50 (ISBN 0-404-11382-6). AMS Pr.

White Southerners. rev. ed. Lewis Killian. LC 85-5844. 216p. (Orig.). 1986. lib. bdg. 25.00x (ISBN 0-87023-487-0); pap. text ed. 10.95x (ISBN 0-87023-488-9). U of Mass Pr.

White Spaces. Paul Auster. 1980. pap. 3.50 (ISBN 0-930794-27-3). Station Hill Pr.

White Spaces in Shakespeare. Paul Bertram. 112p. 1981. 12.50x (ISBN 0-934958-01-7); pap. 8.50x (ISBN 0-934958-02-5). Bellflower.

White Spider. Joyce Wolf. 400p. (Orig.). 1987. pap. 3.95 (ISBN 0-8439-2513-2). Leisure NY.

White Squaw, No. 11: Hot-Handed Heathen. E. J. Hunter. 224p. 1986. pap. 2.50 (ISBN 0-8217-1882-7). Zebra.

White Squaw, No. 12: Ball & Chain. E. J. Hunter. 224p. 1986. pap. 2.50 (ISBN 0-8217-1930-0). Zebra.

White Squaw, No. 13: Track Tramp. E. J. Hunter. 224p. 1987. pap. 2.50 (ISBN 0-8217-1995-5). Zebra.

White Squaw, No. 14: Red Top Tramp. E. J. Hunter. 224p. 1987. pap. 2.50 (ISBN 0-8217-2075-9). Zebra.

White Squaw, No. 17: Bullwhipped Beauty. E. J. Hunter. 224p. 1988. pap. 2.50 (ISBN 0-8217-2461-4). Zebra.

White Squaw, No. 4: Hot Texas Tail. E. J. Hunter. pap. 2.50 (ISBN 0-8217-1359-0). Zebra.

White Squaw, No. 5: Buckskin Bombeshell. E. J. Hunter. 224p. 1984. pap. 2.50 (ISBN 0-8217-1410-4). Zebra.

White Squaw, No. 7: Abilene Tight Spot. E. J. Hunter. (Illus.). 224p. 1985. pap. 2.50 (ISBN 0-8217-1562-3). Zebra.

White Stag. Kate Seredy. (Story Bks. Ser.). (gr. 4-7). 1979. pap. 3.95 (ISBN 0-14-031258-7, Puffin). Penguin.

White Stag. Kate Seredy. (Illus.). (gr. 7 up). 1937. 12.95 (ISBN 0-670-76375-6). Viking.

White Stallion. Elizabeth Shub. LC 81-20308. (Greenwillow Read-Alone Bks.). (Illus.). 56p. (gr. 1-3). 1982. 9.00 (ISBN 0-688-01210-8); PLB 8.88 (ISBN 0-688-01211-6). Greenwillow.

White Stallion. Elizabeth Shub. (Illus.). 64p. (gr. 1-4). 1984. pap. 2.50 (ISBN 0-553-15244-0, Skylark). Bantam.

White Stallion of Lipizza. Marguerite Henry. LC 64-17445. (Illus.). 112p. (gr. 3-8). 9.95 (ISBN 0-528-82041-9, Checkerboard Pr). Macmillan.

White Stallion of Lipizza. Marguerite Henry. LC 64-17445. (Illus.). 112p. (gr. 3-8). 1979. pap. 2.95 (ISBN 0-528-87050-5). Macmillan.

White Steed. Ed. by V. A. Smirnov. 159p. 1985. pap. 2.95 (Pub. by Rus Lang Pubs USSR). Imported Pubns.

White Stone. Wilfred H. Weeks. LC 85-51932. (Illus.). 37p. (Orig.). (gr. 4-9). 1988. pap. price not set (ISBN 0-9615677-0-8). Three River Ctr.

White Stones & Fir Trees: An Anthology of Contemporary Slavic Literature. Ed. by Vasa D. Mihailovich. LC 74-32519. 603p. 1977. 35.00 (ISBN 0-8386-1194-X). Fairleigh Dickinson.

White Supremacy: A Comparative Study in American & South African History. George M. Fredrickson. 1981. pap. 10.95 (ISBN 0-19-503042-7). Oxford U Pr.

White Supremacy: A Comparative Study of American & South African History. George M. Fredrickson. (Illus.). 1981. 39.95x (ISBN 0-19-502759-0). Oxford U Pr.

White Sweaters. Nihon Vogue Staff. (Illus.). 61p. (Orig.). 1985. pap. 6.95 (ISBN 0-87040-652-3). Japan Pubns USA.

White Tablecloths. Lynne McMahon. (Riverstone International Poetry Chapbook Competition Ser.). 11p. (Orig.). 1984. pap. 4.00 (ISBN 0-936600-04-7). Riverstone Foothills.

White Tail: The Story of an African Buffalo. Ed Naylor. 1986. 37.00x (ISBN 0-86332-014-7, Pub. by Book Guild Ltd). State Mutual Bk.

White-Tailed Deer: Ecology & Management. Ed. by Lowell K. Halls. 864p. 1984. 44.95 (ISBN 0-8117-0486-6). Stackpole.

White-Tails & Whooping Cranes: A Smithsonian Magazine Wildlife Collection. Ed. by Alexis Doster. (Illus.). Date not set. postponed 27.50 (ISBN 0-89599-011-3). Norton.

White Talk, Black Talk: Inter-Racial Friendship & Communication Amongst Adolescents. Roger Hewitt. (Comparative Ethnic & Race Relations Ser.). 272p. 1986. 42.50 (ISBN 0-521-26239-9); pap. 15.95 (ISBN 0-521-33824-7). Cambridge U Pr.

White Teacher. Vivian G. Paley. LC 78-9841. 1979. text ed. 13.50 (ISBN 0-674-95185-9). Harvard U Pr.

White Teacher, Black School: The Professional Growth of a Ghetto Teacher. Forrest W. Parkay. 240p. 1983. 35.00 (ISBN 0-275-91056-3, C1056). Praeger.

White Teacher in a Black School. Robert Kendall. 1980. 9.95 (ISBN 0-8159-7210-5). Devin.

White Terror & the Political Reaction After Waterloo. Daniel P. Resnick. LC 66-18254. (Historical Studies: No. 77). 1966. 10.00x (ISBN 0-674-95190-5). Harvard U Pr.

White Terror & the Red: A Novel of Revolutionary Russia. facsimile ed. Abraham Cahan. LC 74-27969. (Modern Jewish Experience Ser.). 1975. Repr. of 1905 ed. 34.50x (ISBN 0-405-06699-6). Ayer Co Pubs.

White Thighs. 240p. 1986. pap. 3.95 (ISBN 0-88184-244-3). Carroll & Graf.

White Thunder. Dane Rudhyar. 1976. pap. 3.50 (ISBN 0-916108-07-4). Seed Center.

White Tie Tales. John H. Morecraft. 101p. 1981. 15.00x (ISBN 0-561-00236-3, Pub. by Bailey Bros & Swinfen Ltd). State Mutual Bk.

White Tiger. Robert S. Nathan. 1987. 18.95 (ISBN 0-671-63338-4). S&S.

White Tiger. Robert S. Nathan. 432p. Date not set. pap. 4.95 (ISBN 0-446-35206-3). Warner Bks.

White Towers. Paul Hirshorn & Steven Izenour. (Illus.). 1979. pap. 12.50 (ISBN 0-262-58051-9). MIT Pr.

White Town Drowsing. Ron Powers. 320p. 1987. pap. 7.95 (ISBN 0-14-010409-7). Penguin.

White Town Drowsing. Ron Powers. (Large Print Bks.). 450p. 1988. lib. bdg. 19.95x (ISBN 0-8161-4401-X, Large Print Bks). G K Hall.

White Trash: An Anthology of Contemporary Southern Poets. 2nd ed. Nancy Stone & Robert W. Grey. 123p. 1984. pap. 7.95 (ISBN 0-917990-06-4). New South Co.

White Trash: An Anthology of Contemporary Southern Poets. Ed. by Nancy Stone & Robert W. Grey. (Illus.). 128p. 1986. 25.00 (ISBN 0-917990-01-3). New South Co.

White Trash Cooking. Ernest M. Mickler. 100p. 1986. pap. 12.95 spiralbound (ISBN 0-912330-59-7). Jargon Soc.

White Trash Cooking. Ernest M. Mickler. 1986. 14.95 (ISBN 0-89815-207-0); spiral bdg. 12.95 (ISBN 0-89815-189-9). Ten Speed Pr.

White Trash: The Eugenics Family Studies, 1877-1919. Intro. by Nicole H. Rafter. 428p. 1988. 40.00x (ISBN 1-55553-030-3). NE U Pr.

White Tribe Dreaming: Apartheid's Bitter Roots as Witnessed by Eight Generations of an Afrikaner Family. Marc De Villiers. 1988. 21.95 (ISBN 0-670-81794-5). Viking.

White Tribe of Africa: South Africa in Perspective. David Harrison. (Perspectives on Southern Africa Ser.: No. 31). (Illus.). 315p. 1982. 25.00x (ISBN 0-520-04690-0); pap. 10.95 (ISBN 0-520-05066-5). U of Cal Pr.

White Umbrella: Indian Political Thought from Manu to Ghandi. Donald M. Brown. LC 81-13391. (Illus.). xii, 204p. 1982. Repr. of 1953 ed. lib. bdg. 35.00x (ISBN 0-313-23210-5, BRWU). Greenwood.

White Violence & Black Response: From Reconstruction to Montgomery. Herbert Shapiro. LC 87-6009. (Illus.). 584p. 1988. lib. bdg. 35.00x (ISBN 0-87023-577-X); pap. text ed. 14.95x (ISBN 0-87023-578-8). U of Mass Pr.

White Waits. Robert Ronnow. LC 83-71219. 64p. (Orig.). 1984. pap. 6.95 (ISBN 0-935306-27-7). Barnwood Pr.

White Wall of Spain: The Mysteries of Andalusian Culture. Allen Josephs. 188p. 1983. text ed. 21.95x (ISBN 0-8138-1921-0). Iowa St U Pr.

White Water. Joyce R. Kornblatt. 1987. pap. 3.95 (ISBN 0-440-39324-8, LE). Dell.

White Water Handbook for Canoe & Kayak. 2nd ed. John T. Urban. (Illus.). 198p. (Orig.). 1981. pap. 6.95 (ISBN 0-910146-28-4). Appalach Mtn.

White Water, Pebbles & Love. Faith T. Allum. (Illus.). 48p. (Orig.). (gr. 6 up). 1984. pap. 3.00 (ISBN 0-9613349-0-8). F T Allum.

White-Water River Book: A Guide to Techniques, Equipment, Camping, & Safety. Ron Watters. LC 82-2164. (Illus.). 208p. (Orig.). 1982. pap. 12.95 (ISBN 0-914718-66-5). Pacific Search.

White Water Terror: The Nancy Drew Files, Case 6. Carolyn Keene. 149p. (YA) (gr. 7-10). 1988. Repr. of 1986 ed. 9.50 (ISBN 0-942545-37-0); lib. bdg. 10.50 (ISBN 0-942545-32-X). Grey Castle.

White Waters & Black. Gordon MacCreagh. LC 85-8745. (Illus.). xxxii, 336p. 1985. pap. 11.95 (ISBN 0-226-50016-0). U of Chicago Pr.

White Wave. Kate Daniels. LC 83-40341. (Pitt Poetry Ser.). 61p. 1984. 16.95x (ISBN 0-8229-3493-0); pap. 8.95 (ISBN 0-8229-5359-5). U of Pittsburgh Pr.

White Wave: A Chinese Tale. Diane Wolkstein. LC 78-4781. (Illus.). (gr. 2 up). 1979. 12.70 (ISBN 0-690-03893-3, Crowell Jr Bks); PLB 12.89 (ISBN 0-690-03894-1). HarpJ.

White Wealth & Black Poverty: American Investments in Southern Africa. Barbara Rogers. LC 75-35353. (Studies in Human Rights: No. 2). 288p. 1976. lib. bdg. 35.00 (ISBN 0-8371-8277-8, RWW/). Greenwood.

White Wife, with Other Stories Supernatural, Romantic, & Legendary. Edward Bradley. LC 76-49836. 1976. Repr. of 1865 ed. lib. bdg. 35.00 (ISBN 0-8414-1757-1). Folcroft.

White Wing. Gordon Kendall. 320p. (Orig.). 1985. pap. 2.95 (ISBN 0-8125-4297-5, Dist. by Warner Pub Services & St. Martin's Press). Tor Bks.

White Witch. Elizabeth Ashton. (Harlequin Romances Ser.). 192p. 1982. pap. 1.50 (ISBN 0-373-02503-3). Harlequin Bks.

White Witch Doctor. Louise A. Stinetorf. (Illus.). 286p. (gr. 7 up). 1950. Westminster John Knox.

White Witch of Agusta. Frances L. Banker. 176p. 1988. 12.95 (ISBN 0-89962-756-0). Todd & Honeywell.

White Wolf Calling & Others: The Year's Best Horror Stories IV. Ed. by Gerald W. Page. (Hardcover Collection Ser.: No. 5). Date not set. 19.95. Starmont Hse.

White Wolf: Living with an Arctic Legend. Jim Brandenburg. 176p. 1988. 40.00 (ISBN 0-942802-95-0). Northword.

White Woman & Her Valley. Arch Merrill. LC 87-434. (Arch Merrill's New York Series: Volume 14). (Illus.). 228p. 1987. pap. 7.95 (ISBN 0-932334-88-1, Empire State Bks). Heart of the Lakes.

White Women, Coloured Men. H. Champly. 59.95 (ISBN 0-8490-1293-7). Gordon Pr.

White Women's Protection Ordinance. Amirah Inglis. 1975. 10.00x (ISBN 0-85621-049-8, Pub. by Scot Acad Pr). Longwood Pub Group.

White Women's Protection Ordinance: Sexual Anxiety & Politics in Papua, 1920-1934. Amirah Inglis. LC 74-32646. 300p. 1975. 9.95 (ISBN 0-312-86800-6). St Martin.

White Words. Baron Wormser. 1983. 12.95 (ISBN 0-395-33109-9); pap. 6.95 (ISBN 0-395-33110-2). HM.

White Work Embroidery. Barbara Dawson. (Illus.). 240p. 1987. 42.50 (ISBN 0-7134-3950-5). Branford.

White Work: Techniques & 180 Designs. Ed. by Carter Houck. (Illus.). 1979. pap. 2.95 (ISBN 0-486-23695-1). Dover.

White Workers & Black Trainees: An Outline of Some of the Issues Raised by Special Training Programs for the Disadvantaged. Joe Shedd. (Key Issues Ser.: No. 13). 40p. 1973. pap. 2.00 (ISBN 0-87546-243-X). ILR Pr.

White World: Life & Adventures Within the Arctic Circle. Ed. by Rudolf Kersting. LC 74-5851. Repr. of 1902 ed. 27.50 (ISBN 0-404-11658-2). AMS Pr.

White Wreath. Louis Kish. (Illus.). 160p. 1984. 8.95 (ISBN 0-89962-374-3). Todd & Honeywell.

White Writing. J. M. Coetzee. LC 87-21568. 208p. 1988. 19.95x (ISBN 0-300-03974-3). Yale U Pr.

Whiteboy. Stan Rice. 1975. pap. 3.00 (ISBN 0-685-52155-9). Mudra.

Whitefella Business: Aborigines in Australian Politics. Ed. by Michael C. Howard. LC 77-28757. (Illus.). 176p. 1978. text ed. 17.50 (ISBN 0-915980-48-7). ISHI PA.

Whitefield & Wesley on the New Birth. Timothy L. Smith. 544p. 1986. pap. 8.95 (ISBN 0-310-75151-9, 17072P). Zondervan.

Whitehall & the Colonial Service. Charles Jeffries. (Commonwealth Papers: No. 15). 109p. 1972. pap. 26.50 (ISBN 0-485-17615-7, Pub. by Athlone Pr UK). Humanities.

Whitehall & the Labour Problem in Late Victorian & Edwardian Britain: A Study in Official Statistics & Social Control. Roger Davidson. LC 84-21424. 294p. 1985. 32.50 (ISBN 0-7099-0832-6, Pub. by Croom Helm Ltd). Routledge Chapman & Hall.

Whitehall & the Wilderness: The Middle West in British Colonial Policy, 1760 to 1775. Jack M. Sosin. LC 80-21061. (Illus.). xi, 307p. 1981. Repr. of 1961 ed. lib. bdg. 38.50x (ISBN 0-313-22678-4, SOWW). Greenwood.

Whitehall, Cheam. C. Bradley. 24p. 20.00x (ISBN 0-9503224-4-X, Pub. by Sutton Lib & Arts). State Mutual Bk.

Whitehall Sanction. Jack Gerson. 320p. 1985. pap. 3.50 (ISBN 0-8125-0364-3, Dist. by Warner Pub Services & St. Martin's Press). Tor Bks.

Whitehall: Tragedy & Farce. Clive Ponting. 190p. 1987. 24.95 (ISBN 0-241-11835-2, Pub. by Hamish Hamilton England). David & Charles.

Whitehaven. Richard Holland. Ed. by Paula Cunningham. (Illus.). 200p. 1987. write for info. (ISBN 0-913383-07-4). McClanahan Pub.

Whitehead & the Modern World: Science, Metaphysics, & Civilization. Victor Lowe et al. LC 72-5738. (Essay Index Reprint Ser.). Repr. of 1950 ed. 15.00 (ISBN 0-8369-7281-3). Ayer Co Pubs.

WHO Activities in Nutrition, 1948-1964. (WHO Chronicle Reprint: Vol. 19, Nos. 10-12). (Also avail in French & Spanish). 1965. pap. 1.20 (ISBN 92-4-156019-3). World Health.

Who Am I. Lillian DeWaters. 5.95 (ISBN 0-686-17825-4). L De Waters.

Who Am I? Norman P. Grubb. 1975. pap. 3.50 (ISBN 0-87508-227-0). Chr Lit.

Who Am I? Barry Head & Jim Sequin. (I Am, I Can, I Will Ser.). (Illus.). 36p. (Orig.). (ps-4). 1975. pap. 3.95 (ISBN 0-8331-0035-1). Hubbard Sci.

Who Am I? Sesame Street Staff. (Golden Sturdy Bks.). 22p. (ps). 1978. 3.50 (ISBN 0-307-12124-0, Golden Bks). Western Pub.

Who Am I? Illus. by Tony Tallarico. (Tiny Bks.). (Illus.). 28p. (ps-1). 1984. bds. 3.50 (ISBN 0-89828-053-2). Tuffy Bks.

Who Am I? Paul L. Walker & Charles P. Conn. LC 74-82934. 1974. pap. 1.99 (ISBN 0-87148-905-8). Pathway Pr.

Who Am I? (Art Programs for Education Ser.). 8p. tchr's. ed. 86.00 (ISBN 0-88185-023-3); mounted prints 119.00. Shorewood Fine Art.

Who Am I? (Golden Sturdy Books Ser.). (Illus.). 22p. (ps). Date not set. 3.50 (ISBN 0-317-64894-2, Pub. by Golden Bks). Western Pub.

Who Am I? A Book of Baby Animals. (Illus.). 22p. (ps-3). 1983. 2.50 (ISBN 0-89954-213-1). Antioch Pub Co.

Who Am I? A Genealogical Study of the Bower, Taylor, & Related Families. Mary Carpenter. 208p. 1986. 11.95 (ISBN 0-9617470-0-5). McClain.

Who Am I? A Look in the Mirror. Carolyn Nystrom & Mathew Floding. (Young Fisherman Bible Studyguide Ser.). 64p. (Orig.). (YA) (gr. 7 up). 1987. pap. 4.95 tchr's. ed. (ISBN 0-87788-933-3); pap. 2.95 student ed. (ISBN 0-87788-932-5). Shaw Pubs.

Who Am I & What Am I Doing Here. Mark W. Lee. 1986. pap. 5.95 (ISBN 0-8010-5643-8). Baker Bk.

Who Am I & What Difference Does It Make? David L. Hocking. LC 85-8810. (Living Theology Ser.). 1985. pap. 7.95 (ISBN 0-88070-102-1). Multnomah.

Who Am I? Asks the Alcoholic: A Study Based on Concepts a Recovering Alcoholic Heard, Heeded & Now Teaches. Ivan Lackey. LC 74-34514. 1975. 10.00 (ISBN 0-682-48199-8, Banner). Exposition-Phoenix.

Who Am I in the Lives of Children? An Introduction to Teaching Young Children. Stephanie Feeney & Doris Christensen. 416p. 1983. 31.95 (ISBN 0-675-20056-3). Additional supplements may be obtained from publisher. Merrill.

Who Am I in the Lives of Children? An Introduction to Teaching Young Children. 3rd ed. Stephanie Feeney et al. 448p. 1987. 31.95 (ISBN 0-675-20567-0). Merrill.

Who Am I, Lord? Betty S. Everett. LC 82-72645. (Augsburg Young Readers Ser.). 112p. (Orig.). (gr. 3-6). 1983. pap. 4.50 (ISBN 0-8066-1951-1, 10-7072). Augsburg.

Who Am I Lord... & Why Am I Here? William Hulme & Dale Hulme. LC 83-25175. 1984. pap. 4.95 (ISBN 0-570-03926-6, 12-2860). Concordia.

Who Am I Now That I Am Alone? 2nd ed. James L. Ramsey. (Orig.). 1987. pap. 29.95 leader's guide 70 pgs. (ISBN 0-941697-00-2); pap. 7.95 wkbk. guide 39 pgs. (ISBN 0-941697-01-0). ABT Inc.

Who Am I, Really? Carolyn Jones. LC 87-72022. 196p. 1987. pap. 7.95 (ISBN 0-88419-202-4, Creation Hse). Strang Comms Co.

Who Am I... Really? An Autobiographical Exploration on Becoming Who You Are. Sheldon Kopp. Ed. by Ted Mason. 256p. (Orig.). 1987. pap. 10.95 (ISBN 0-87477-429-2). J P Tarcher.

Who Am I? Refugee Voices. Gloria Christen-Morris. 1986. 12.50 (ISBN 0-533-07049-X). Vantage.

Who Am I This Time? For Romeos & Juliets. Kurt Vonnegut, Jr. (Prefect Presents Ser.). (Illus.). 32p. pap. 5.95 (ISBN 1-55628-027-0). Redpath Pr.

Who Am I This Time? The Power of Fictions in Our Lives. Jay Martin. 1988. 18.95 (ISBN 0-393-02525-X). Norton.

Who Am I? What Am I? A Christian View of Working. Calvin Redekop & Urie A. Bender. 352p. 1988. pap. 14.95 (ISBN 0-310-35581-8, 18090P). Zondervan.

Who Am I? What Am I? Where Do I Belong? The Story of the Little Unknown Creature. Shinan N. Barclay. (Illus.). 32p. (ps-4). 1988. text ed. price not set; pap. price not set (ISBN 0-945086-08-3). Sunlight Prodns.

Who Am I? Who Are You? Kathy London & Frank Caparulo. 144p. 1983. pap. 8.95 (ISBN 0-201-10813-5). Addison-Wesley.

Who & How in Planning for Large Companies: Generalizations from the Experiences of Oil Companies. Leslie E. Grayson. 256p. 1987. 37.50 (ISBN 0-312-87005-1). St Martin.

Who Are My Brothers? Cleric-Lay Relationships in Men's Religious Communities. Ed. by Philip Armstrong. LC 88-6351. 229p. 1988. pap. 12.95 (ISBN 0-8189-0533-6). Alba.

Who Are Our Educators? A Study of Gender Roles in Elementary School Teaching 1850-1920. Helen Corr. 1988. 30.00 (ISBN 0-7130-0173-9, Pub. by Woburn Pr England). Biblio Dist.

Who Are the Amish? Merle Good. LC 85-70283. (Illus.). 128p. (Orig.). 1985. 24.95 (ISBN 0-934672-28-8); pap. 15.95 (ISBN 0-934672-26-1). Good Bks PA.

Who Are the Anglicans? Charles H. Long et al. (Orig.). 1988. pap. 2.75 (ISBN 0-88028-080-8). Forward Movement.

Who Are the Best? The Sports Survey Book. 2nd ed. Bob McMahon & Jay Leopold. (Illus.). 144p. 1984. pap. 8.95 (ISBN 0-88011-256-5, PMCM0256). Leisure Pr.

Who Are the Chinese Texans? Marian Martinello & William T. Field, Jr. (University of Texas Institute of Texan Culture Young Readers Ser.). (Illus.). 84p. (Orig.). (gr. 5-8). 8.95 (ISBN 0-933164-36-X); pap. 5.95 (ISBN 0-933164-46-7). U of Tex Inst Tex Culture.

Who Are the Finns? A Study in Prehistory. Robert E. Burnham. LC 76-44701. Repr. of 1946 ed. 20.00 (ISBN 0-404-15913-3). AMS Pr.

Who Are the Guilty? A Study of Education & Crime. David Abrahamsen. LC 70-143306. 340p. 1972. Repr. of 1952 ed. lib. bdg. 35.00x (ISBN 0-8371-5807-9, ABWG). Greenwood.

Who Are "The Jews" Today? D. Lutzweiler. 1984. lib. bdg. 79.95 (ISBN 0-87700-568-0). Revisionist Pr.

Who Are the Major American Writers? Jay B. Hubbell. LC 72-172020. xvi, 344p. 1972. 34.50 (ISBN 0-8223-0289-6). Duke.

Who Are the Mennonite Brethren? Katie F. Wiebe. LC 84-82049. 107p. (Orig.). 1984. pap. 5.95 (ISBN 0-919797-31-8). Kindred Pr.

Who Are the Poor? The Beatitudes As a Call to Community. John S. Pobee. (Risk Bk.: No. 32). 74p. (Orig.). 1987. pap. 5.50 (ISBN 2-8254-0884-0). Wrld Coun Churches.

Who Are the Unchurched? An Exploratory Study. J. Russell Hale. LC 77-81922. 1977. pap. 2.00x (ISBN 0-914422-06-5). Glenmary Res Ctr.

Who Are the Urban Poor? rev ed. Anthony Downs. LC 77-133484. 64p. 1970. pap. 1.50 (ISBN 0-87186-226-3). Comm Econ Dev.

Who Are They? (Contemporary Vedic Library Series Based on the Teachings of A. C. Bhaktivedanta Swami Prabhupada). 1.50 (ISBN 0-89213-111-X). Bhaktivedanta.

Who Are We Americans? Josephine McConnell. 80p. 1986. 9.95 (ISBN 0-8062-2865-2). Carlton.

Who Are You? Diagram Group Staff. (Illus.). 160p. 1988. pap. 8.95 (ISBN 0-345-33699-2). Ballantine.

Who Are You? William Hornaday. 1972. pap. 1.25 (ISBN 0-87516-146-4). DeVorss.

Who Are You? Jon L. Joyce. (Orig.). 1985. pap. 3.75 (ISBN 0-937172-61-8). JLJ Pubs.

Who Are You? Sidney Lecker. 1979. 4.95 (ISBN 0-686-66206-7, Fireside). S&S.

Who Are You & Why Are You Here? Peter D. Francuch. LC 83-51781. 256p. (Orig.). 1984. pap. 4.95 (ISBN 0-939386-07-0). TMH Pub.

Who Are You? Discovering Your Real Identity. Chris Butler. LC 83-80825. (Who are You? Ser.: Vol. 1). 489p. 1985. 12.95 (ISBN 0-912093-00-5). Identity Inst.

Who Are You Monsieur Gurdjieff? Rene Zuber. Tr. by Jenny Koralek. 80p. 1980. pap. 4.95 (ISBN 0-7100-0674-8). Routledge Chapman & Hall.

Who Are You: The Life of St. Cecilia. Marie C. Buehrle. LC 70-158918. 85p. 1971. pap. 2.95 (ISBN 0-913382-07-8, 101-7). Prow Bks-Franciscan.

Who Are Your Today? A Survivors Handbook for Substitute Teachers. Tom Quinlan. (Illus.). vi, 82p. 1985. pap. 6.95 (ISBN 0-9615691-0-7). Queue Pubns.

Who Audits America. Compiled by Spencer P. Harris. (Corporations & Accountants Ser.). 1982. 62.00 (ISBN 0-933088-03-5); pap. 54.00 (ISBN 0-685-90844-5). Data Financial.

Who Audits Singapore. Sebastian Chong et al. 62p. 1987. pap. text ed. 13.50 (ISBN 9971-69-106-X, Pub. by Gower Pub England). Gower Pub Co.

Who Audits the World: Trends in the Worldwide Accounting Profession. Vinod B. Bavishi & Harold E. Wyman. 900p. 1983. pap. 75.00 (ISBN 0-913795-01-1). Ctr Trans Acct Fin.

Who Bears the Tax Burden? Joseph A. Pechman & Benjamin A. Okner. LC 74-280. (Studies of Government Finance). 119p. 1974. 26.95 (ISBN 0-8157-6968-7). Brookings.

Who Becomes a Bishop? A Study of Priests Who Become Bishops in the Episcopal Church (1960 to 1980) John H. Morgan. 65p. (Orig.). 1985. pap. 6.95x (ISBN 0-932269-28-1). Wyndham Hall.

Who Belongs? (Turn the Dials Learning Picture Bks.). (Illus.). 12p. (ps-1). 1988. 5.95 (ISBN 0-8431-2661-2). Price Stern.

Who Benefits from Federal Education Dollars: The Development of ESEA Title 1 Allocation Policy. James J. Vanecko et al. 220p. 1984. Repr. of 1980 ed. lib. bdg. 31.50 (ISBN 0-8191-4067-8). U Pr of Amer.

Who Benefits from Federal Education Dollars? The Development of ESEA Title I Allocation Policy. Ed. by James J. Vanecko et al. LC 79-55777. (Illus.). 1980. text ed. 30.00 (ISBN 0-89011-541-9). Abt Bks.

Who Benefits from Government Expenditure? A Case Study of Colombia. Marcello Selowsky. (World Bank Research Publication Ser.). 1979. 19.95x (ISBN 0-19-520098-5); pap. 8.95x (ISBN 0-19-520099-3). Oxford U Pr.

Who Broke the Baby? Jean S. Garton. LC 79-22683. 112p. (Orig.). 1979. pap. 4.95 (ISBN 0-87123-608-7, 210608). Bethany Hse.

Who Burned the Hartley House? Carole Smith. Ed. by Abby Levine. (High-Low Mysteries Ser.). (Illus.). 128p. (gr. 3-9). 1985. 8.95 (ISBN 0-8075-8993-4). A Whitman.

Who Can Be Educated? Milton Schwebel. 1968. pap. 3.45 (ISBN 0-394-17274-4, E494, Ever). Grove.

Who Can Be Happy & Free in Russia. Nikolai A. Nekrasov. LC 72-120571. Repr. of 1917 ed. 21.50 (ISBN 0-404-04677-0). AMS Pr.

Who Can Be Happy & Free in Russia ? Nikolai A. Nekrasov. Tr. by Juliet Soskice from Rus. LC 76-23891. (Classics of Russian Literature). 1977. pap. 10.00 (ISBN 0-88355-505-0). Hyperion Conn.

Who Can Fix the Dragon's Wagon? R. Eugene Jackson. 52p. 1966. pap. 2.50 (ISBN 0-88680-202-4); royalty 35.25 (ISBN 0-317-03603-3). I E Clark.

Who Can Fix the Dragon's Wagon? R. Eugene Jackson. (Illus.). 76p. (Director's Production Script). 1966. pap. 10.00 (ISBN 0-88680-203-2). I E Clark.

Who Can Kill the Lion. Adele DeLeeuw. LC 66-20137. (Fantasy Ser.). (Illus.). 48p. (gr. k-4). 1966. PLB 6.69 (ISBN 0-8116-4051-5). Garrard.

Who Can Touch These Knots: New & Selected Poems. Simon Perchik. LC 85-2092. (Poets Now Ser.: No. 9). 173p. 1985. 13.50 (ISBN 0-8108-1803-5). Scarecrow.

Who Can We Trust? Mary Bernard. LC 80-80531. 128p. 1980. 2.50 (ISBN 0-89221-075-3). New Leaf.

Who Can't Follow an Ant? Michael J. Pellowski. LC 85-14009. (Illus.). 48p. (Orig.). (gr. 1-3). 1986. PLB 9.49 (ISBN 0-8167-0592-5); pap. text ed. 1.95 (ISBN 0-8167-0593-3). Troll Assocs.

Who Cares. John Chambers. 1984. 15.00x (ISBN 0-86319-045-6, Pub. by New Playwrights Network). State Mutual Bk.

Who Cares? A Handbook of Christian Counselling. Evelyn H. Peterseon. 181p. 1982. pap. text ed. 11.95 (ISBN 0-85364-272-9). Attic Pr.

Who Cares? A Handbook of Christian Counselling. Evelyn Peterson. LC 82-60447. (Illus.). 192p. 1982. pap. 7.95 (ISBN 0-8192-1317-9). Morehouse.

Who Cares about Apathy? Ludlow Porch. LC 87-80972. 121p. 1987. 9.95 (ISBN 0-934601-30-5). Peachtree Pubs.

Who Cares about Health? Caleb Gattegno. 166p. 1979. pap. text ed. 12.50 (ISBN 0-87825-149-9). Ed Solutions.

Who Cares? An Economic & Ethical Analysis of Private Charity & the Welfare State. Robert Sugden. (Occasional Papers: No. 67). 48p. 1983. pap. 5.95 technical (ISBN 0-255-36167-X, Pub. by Inst Econ Affairs). Transatl Arts.

Who Cares Nineteen Eighty-Eight? Butch Meyer. 64p. 1989. 7.95 (ISBN 0-89962-800-1). Todd & Honeywell.

Who Censored Roger Rabbit? Gary Wolf. 224p. 1982. pap. 3.50 (ISBN 0-345-30325-3). Ballantine.

Who Changes into What? (Changing Picture Bks.). (Illus.). 10p. (gr. k-3). 1986. 3.95 (ISBN 0-8431-1558-0). Price Stern.

Who Commits Crimes: A Survey of Prison Inmates. Mark A. Peterson et al. LC 81-9478. 298p. 1981. text ed. 30.00 (ISBN 0-89946-103-4). Oelgeschlager.

Who Controls Me? A Psychotheological Reflection. Thomas A. Kane. LC 74-22261. 1974. 4.50 (ISBN 0-682-48186-6). Exposition-Phoenix.

Who Controls Our Schools? American Values in Conflict. Michael W. Kirst. LC 84-25881. (Illus.). 183p. 1985. case 20.95 (ISBN 0-7167-1719-0); pap. text ed. 13.95 (ISBN 0-7167-1720-4). W H Freeman.

Who Controls the Schools. NCCE Staff & Carl Marburger. 1978. pap. 3.50 (ISBN 0-934460-06-X). NCCE.

Who Crucified Jesus? Solomon Zeitlin. 1976. pap. write for info. (ISBN 0-8197-0013-4). Bloch.

Who Dares Wins. Ed. by Rory McGrath & Denise O'Donoghue. LC 85-20434. (Orig.). 1986. pap. 9.95 (ISBN 0-571-13774-1). Faber & Faber.

Who Decides? Conflicts of Rights in Health Care. Ed. by Nora K. Bell. LC 81-83908. (Contemporary Issues in Biomedicine, Ethics & Society Ser.). 240p. 1982. 34.50 (ISBN 0-89603-034-2). Humana.

Who Defends America? Ed. by Edwin Dorn. 1987. 5.95 (ISBN 0-941410-40-4). Jt Ctr Pol Studies.

Who Did It, Jenny Lake? Jean D. Okimoto. 143p. (gr. 6-10). 1984. pap. 2.25 (ISBN 0-399-21104-7, Putnam). Putnam Pub Group.

Who Did this, Dainty Dinosaur? (Beginning to Read Ser.). (gr. 2 up). 1988. PLB 5.95 (ISBN 0-8136-5221-9); pap. 2.95 (ISBN 0-8136-5721-0). Modern Curr.

Who Dies: An Investigation of Conscious Living & Dying. Stephen Levine. LC 81-43214. 336p. 1982. pap. 9.95 (ISBN 0-385-17010-6, Anch). Doubleday.

Who Dies There? Henry Kane. Date not set. price not set. Maxim Bks.

Who Discovered America? Settlers & Explorers of the New World Before the Time of Columbus. (Illus.). (gr. 5-9). 1970. Random.

Who Discriminates Against Women? Ed. by Florence Denmark. LC 74-78560. (Sage Contemporary Social Science Issues Ser.: No. 15). (Illus.). pap. 36.00 (ISBN 0-317-08953-6, 2021887). Bks Demand UMI.

Who Do Americans Say That I Am? George Gallup, Jr. & George O'Connell. LC 85-26383. 130p. (Orig.). 1986. pap. 9.95 (ISBN 0-664-24685-0). Westminster John Knox.

Who Do People Say I Am? The Interpretation of Jesus in the New Testament Gospels. Marvin W. Meyer. LC 82-24229. pap. 23.80 (ISBN 0-317-30155-1, 2025337). Bks Demand UMI.

Who Do You Say? Jesus Christ in Latin American Theology. Claus Bussmann. Tr. by Robert Barr from Ger. LC 84-16476. 192p. (Orig.). 1985. pap. 9.95 (ISBN 0-88344-711-8). Orbis Bks.

Who Do You Say That I Am? Joseph E. Monti. LC 83-82023. (Orig.). 1984. pap. 4.95 (ISBN 0-8091-2598-6). Paulist Pr.

Who Do You Say That I Am? An Adult Inquiry into the First Three Gospels. Edward J. Ciuba. LC 74-10808. 155p. 1974. pap. 5.95 (ISBN 0-8189-0295-7). Alba.

Who Do You Say You Are? Christ's Love for Us. George A. Maloney. (Orig.). 1986. pap. 4.95 (ISBN 0-914544-64-0). Living Flame Pr.

Who Do you Think You Are. Sue Armstrong. 1983. 24.00x (ISBN 0-86334-046-6, Pub. by Macdonald Pub UK). State Mutual Bk.

Who Do You Think You Are, Charlie Brown: Selected Cartoons from "Peanuts Every Sunday", Vol. 1. Charles M. Schulz. (Peanuts Ser.). (Illus.). 1982. pap. 1.95 (ISBN 0-449-20255-0, Crest). Fawcett.

Who Does Pay the Taxes? Helen Tarasov. (Social Research Suppl.: No. 4). 1942. pap. 10.00 (ISBN 0-527-00864-8). Kraus Repr.

Who Does What? Eric Hill. (Peek-A-Bks.). 20p. (ps-k). 1982. 4.95 (ISBN 0-8431-0909-2). Price Stern.

Who Done Did It? A Crime Reader for Students of English. Carlos A. Yorio & L. A. Morse. 192p. 1981. pap. text ed. write for info (ISBN 0-13-958207-X). P-H.

Who Eats What? (Changing Picture Bks.). (Illus.). 10p. (gr. k-3). 1986. 3.95 (ISBN 0-8431-1559-9). Price Stern.

Who Eats Whom: The Struggle for Life in the Animal World. (Illus.). 475p. 1989. price not set. Facts on File.

Who Ever Heard of a Tiger in a Tree. John McInnes. LC 72-155571. (Garrard Venture Ser.). (Illus.). 40p. (gr. k-3). 1971. PLB 6.69 (ISBN 0-8116-6706-5); pap. 1.19 (9029). Garrard.

WHO Expert Committee on Biological Standardization: Report. WHO Expert Committee. Geneva, 1971, 24th. (Technical Report Ser.: No. 486). (Also avail. in French, Russian & Spanish). 1972. pap. 2.00 (ISBN 92-4-120486-9). World Health.

WHO Expert Committee on Biological Standardization: Report. WHO Expert Committee. Geneva, 1973, 25th. (Technical Report Ser.: No. 530). (Also avail. in French & Spanish). 1973. pap. 2.00 (ISBN 92-4-120530-X). World Health.

WHO Expert Committee on Biological Standardization: Report. WHO Expert Committee. Geneva, 1974, 26th. (Technical Report Ser.: No. 565). (Also avail. in French & Spanish). 1975. pap. 2.80 (ISBN 92-4-120565-2). World Health.

WHO Expert Committee on Biological Standardization: Thirty-Fifth Report. (Technical Report Ser.: No. 725). 140p. 1985. pap. 6.60 (ISBN 92-4-120725-6). World Health.

WHO Expert Committee on Biological Standardization Thirty Sixth Report. (Technical Report: No. 745). 149p. 1987. pap. 12.00 (ISBN 9-2412-0745-0). World Health.

WHO Expert Committee on Drug Dependence: Report. WHO Expert Committee. Geneva, 1969, 17th. (Technical Report Ser.: No. 437). (Also avail. in French, Russian & Spanjsh). 1970. pap. 2.00 (ISBN 92-4-120437-0). World Health.

WHO Expert Committee on Drug Dependence: Report. WHO Expert Committee. Geneva, 1970, 18th. (Technical Report Ser.: No. 460). (Also avail. in French, Russian & Spanish). 1970. pap. 2.00 (ISBN 92-4-120460-5). World Health.

WHO Expert Committee on Drug Dependence: Report. WHO Expert Committee. Geneva, 1972, 19th. (Technical Report Ser.: No. 526). (Also avail. in French & Spanish). 1973. pap. 1.60 (ISBN 92-4-120526-1). World Health.

WHO Expert Committee on Drug Dependence: Report. WHO Expert Committee. Geneva, 1973, 20th. (Technical Report Ser.: No. 551). (Also avail. in French & Spanish). 1974. pap. 2.80 (ISBN 92-4-120551-2). World Health.

WHO Expert Committee on Drug Dependence: Twenty-Second Report. (Technical Report Ser.: No. 729). 31p. 1985. pap. 2.40 (ISBN 92-4-120729-9). World Health.

WHO Expert Committee on Drug Dependence Twenty-Third Report. (Technical Report: No. 741). 64p. 1987. pap. 5.40 (ISBN 9-2412-0741-8). World Health.

WHO Expert Committee on Filariasis: Report. WHO Expert Committee. Athens, 1973, 3rd. (Technical Report Ser.: No. 542). (Also avail. in French & Spanish). 1974. pap. 2.00 (ISBN 92-4-120542-3). World Health.

WHO Expert Committee on Insecticides: Report. WHO Expert Committee. Geneva, 1971, 19th. (Technical Report Ser.: No. 475). (Also avail. in French & Spanish). 1971. pap. 1.20 (ISBN 92-4-120475-3). World Health.

WHO Expert Committee on Leprosy: Report. WHO Expert Committee. Geneva, 1970, 4th. (Technical Report Ser.: No. 459). (Also avail. in French & Spanish). 1970. pap. 2.00 (ISBN 92-4-120459-1). World Health.

WHO Expert Committee on Malaria: Eighteenth Report. (Technical Report: No. 735). 104p. 1986. pap. 8.40 (ISBN 92-4-120735-3). World Health.

WHO Expert Committee on Malaria: Report. WHO Expert Committee. Geneva, 1973, 16th. (Technical Report Ser.: No. 549). (Also avail. in French & Spanish). 1974. pap. 2.80 (ISBN 92-4-120549-0). World Health.

WHO Expert Committee on Medical Rehabilitation: Report. WHO Expert Committee. Geneva, 1968, 2nd. (Technical Report Ser.: No. 419). (Also avail. in French). 1969. pap. 1.20 (ISBN 92-4-120419-2). World Health.

WHO Expert Committee on Onchocerciasis Third Report. (Technical Report: No. 752). 167p. 1987. pap. 14.40 (ISBN 9-2412-0752-3). World Health.

WHO Expert Committee on Plague: Report. WHO Expert Committee. Geneva, 1969, 4th. (Technical Report Ser.: No. 447). (Also avail. in Russian & Spanish). 1970. pap. 1.20 (ISBN 92-4-120447-8). World Health.

WHO Expert Committee on Rabies: Report. WHO Expert Committee. Geneva, 1972, 6th. (Technical Report Ser.: No. 523). (Also avail. in French & Spanish). 1973. pap. 1.60 (ISBN 92-4-120523-7). World Health.

WHO Expert Committee on Specifications for Pharmaceutical Preparations: Report. WHO Expert Committee. Geneva, 1968, 22nd. (Technical Report Ser.: No. 418). (Also avail. in French, Russian & Spanish). 1969. pap. 2.00 (ISBN 0-686-16796-1). World Health.

WHO Expert Committee on Specifications for Pharmaceutical Preparations: Report. WHO Expert Committee. Geneva, 1971, 24th. (Technical Report Ser.: No. 487). (Also avail. in French & Spanish). 1972. pap. 2.40 (ISBN 92-4-120487-7). World Health.

WHO Expert Committee on Specifications for Pharmaceutical Preparations: Report. WHO Expert Committee. Geneva, 1974, 25th. (Technical Report Ser.: No. 567). (Also avail. in French & Spanish). 1975. pap. 3.60 (ISBN 92-4-120567-9). World Health.

WHO Expert Committee on Specifications for Pharmaceutical Preparations Thirtieth Report. (Technical Report: No. 748). 50p. 1987. pap. 5.40 (ISBN 9-2412-0748-5). World Health.

WHO Expert Committee on Tuberculosis: Report. WHO Expert Committee. Geneva, 1973, 9th. (Technical Report Ser.: No. 552). (Also avail. in French & Spanish). 1974. pap. 2.00 (ISBN 92-4-120552-0). World Health.

WHO Expert Committee on Venereal Diseases & Treponematoses: Sixth Report. (Technical Report: No. 736). 141p. 1986. pap. 10.80 (ISBN 92-4-120736-1). World Health.

Who Farted? Phil Cammarata. (Orig.). 1984. pap. 5.95 (ISBN 0-671-55300-3, Long Shadow Bks). PB.

Who First Discovered America? A Critique of Writings on Pre-Colombian Voyages. Eugene R. Fingerhut. (Guides to Historical Issues Ser.: No. 1). 147p. 1984. 17.95x (ISBN 0-941690-10-5); pap. 10.95x (ISBN 0-941690-09-1); pap. text ed. 7.75x. Regina Bks.

Who Fought for the U. S. Jerold M. Starr. (Lessons of the Vietnam War Ser.). (Illus.). 32p. 1988. pap. text ed. 3.00 (ISBN 0-945919-04-2). Ctr Social Studies.

Who Framed Roger Rabbit: A Different Toon. Justine Korman. LC 87-83194. (Golden Look-Look Bks.). (Illus.). 24p. (gr. k-3). 1988. write for info. (ISBN 0-307-11733-2). Western Pub.

Who Framed Roger Rabbit: Make the World Laugh. Adapted by Justine Korman. LC 87-83195. (Golden Look-Look Bks.). (Illus.). 24p. (Orig.). (gr. k-3). 1988. pap. 1.60 (ISBN 0-307-11734-0). Western Pub.

Who Framed Roger Rabbit Movie Storybook. Adapted by Justine Korman. LC 87-83487. (Illus.). 48p. (ps-3). 1988. 6.95 (ISBN 0-307-15847-0). Western Pub.

Who from Their Labours Rest? Conflict & Practice in Rural Tourism. Mary Bouquet & Michael Winter. 160p. 1987. text ed. 41.50 (ISBN 0-566-05330-6, Pub. by Gower Pub England). Gower Pub Co.

Who Gains from Deep Ocean Mining? Simulating the Impact of Regimes for Regulating Nodule Exploitation. Ian G. Bulkley. LC 79-87567. (Research Ser.: No. 40). (Illus.). 1979. pap. 3.50x (ISBN 0-87725-140-1). U of Cal Intl St.

Who Gathered & Whispered Behind Me. Albert Goldbarth. LC 80-21309. 53p. (Orig.). 1980. pap. 4.25 (ISBN 0-934332-27-4). L'Epervier Pr.

Who Gets In? A Guide to College Selection - 1988. Ed. by Dan Tyson. 120p. 1988. pap. 37.50x (ISBN 0-945871-34-1). Graphic Pub KS.

Who Gets It When You Go? Wills, Probate & Inheritance Taxes for the Hawaii Resident. rev. ed. David C. Larsen. LC 86-11258. (Illus.). 128p. 1987. pap. 8.50 (ISBN 0-8248-1089-9). UH Pr.

Who Gets Sick: How Thoughts, Moods, & Beliefs Can Affect Your Health. Blair Justice. 416p. 1988. Repr. of 1987 ed. 17.95 (ISBN 0-87477-467-5). J P Tarcher.

Who Gets Sick: Thinking & Health. Blair Justice. LC 86-61576. 408p. 1987. 17.95 (ISBN 0-9605376-1-9). Peak Pr.

Who Gets the Antelope's Liver? W. George Bourland. 12.95 (ISBN 0-686-37633-1). Harp & Thistle.

Who Gets the Business? A Guide to Passing on a Closely Held Business Interest. Herbert Chasman. LC 83-80632. 200p. 1983. 14.95 (ISBN 0-910580-73-1, Farnsworth Pub Co). Longman Finan.

Who Gets to the Top? Gloria L. Lee. 176p. 1981. text ed. 33.00x (ISBN 0-566-00497-6). Gower Pub Co.

Who Gets to the Top? Executive Suite Discrimination in the Eighties. Richard L. Zweigenhaft. LC 84-70044. 48p. 1984. pap. 3.00 (ISBN 0-87495-059-7). Am Jewish Comm.

Who Gets What from Government. Benjamin I. Page. LC 82-13454. 264p. 1983. 25.00x (ISBN 0-520-04702-8); pap. 10.95x (ISBN 0-520-04703-6). U of Cal Pr.

Who Gives a Toot? Illus. by John E. Johnson. (Whistle While You Learn Book Ser.). (Illus.). 12p. (gr. k-1). 1983. 3.95 (ISBN 0-394-85518-3). Random.

Who Goes First? The Story of Self-Experimentation in Medicine. Lawrence K. Altman. LC 84-18807. 416p. 1987. 22.50 (ISBN 0-394-50382-1). Random.

Who Goes Home? 192p. 1987. 15.95 (ISBN 0-8027-5675-1). Walker & Co.

Who Goes Out in the Midday Sun? An Englishman's Trek Through the Amazon Jungle. Benedict Allen. LC 85-40778. (Illus.). 272p. 1986. 18.95 (ISBN 0-670-81032-0). Viking.

Who Goes There? Seven Tales of Science Fiction. John W. Campbell. LC 75-28850. (Classics of Science Fiction Ser.). 230p. 1986. 22.00 (ISBN 0-88355-365-1). Hyperion-Conn.

Who Goes There: The Search for Intelligent Life in the Universe. Edward Edelson. (Illus.). 228p. 1980. pap. text ed. 4.95 (ISBN 0-07-018986-2). McGraw.

Who Goes to School? Margaret Hillert. (Just Beginning-to-Read Ser.). (Illus.). (gr. 1). 1980. PLB 4.39 (ISBN 0-8136-5075-5, Dist. by Caroline Hse); pap. 1.95 (ISBN 0-8136-5575-7). Modern Curr.

Who Goes to the Park. Warabe Aska. (Illus.). 32p. (ps up). 1984. pap. 9.95 (ISBN 0-88776-187-9). Tundra Bks.

Who Got Einstein's Office? Eccentricity & Genius at the Institute for Advanced Study. Ed Regis. LC 87-11568. (Illus.). 320p. 1987. 17.95 (ISBN 0-201-12065-8). Addison-Wesley.

Who Got Einstein's Office: Eccentricity & Genius at the Institute for Advanced Study. Edward Regis. (Illus.). 1988. pap. 10.95 (ISBN 0-201-12278-2). Addison-Wesley.

Who Governs: Democracy & Power in an American City. Robert A. Dahl. LC 61-16913. (Studies in Political Science: No. 4). (Illus.). 1961. 37.00x (ISBN 0-300-00395-1); pap. 10.95x (ISBN 0-300-00051-0, Y73). Yale U Pr.

Who Guards the Guardians: Judicial Control of Administration. Martin M. Shapiro. LC 87-5927. (Richard B. Russell Lectures: No. 6). 208p. 1988. 20.00x (ISBN 0-8203-0963-X); pap. 10.00 (ISBN 0-8203-1028-X). U of GA Pr.

Who Guards the Prince? Reginald Hill. 1982. 12.45 (ISBN 0-394-52077-7). Pantheon.

Who Guards the Prince. Reginald Hill. 1983. pap. 2.95 (ISBN 0-394-71337-0). Pantheon.

WHO Handbook for Standardized Cancer Registries. (Offset Pub.: No. 25). (Also avail. in French). 1976. pap. 4.00 (ISBN 92-4-170025-4). World Health.

Who Has the Lucky-Duck in Class 4-B? Maggie Twohill. LC 83-15719. 112p. (gr. 3-5). 1984. 9.95 (ISBN 0-02-789690-0). Bradbury Pr.

Who Has the Lucky Duck in Class 4-B. Maggie Twohill. (gr. k-6). 1986. pap. 2.50 (ISBN 0-440-49533-4, YB). Dell.

Who Has the Nine-Thirty Appointment? Robert M. Miller. (Illus.). 192p. 1979. 24.50 (ISBN 0-939674-12-2). Am Vet Pubns.

Who Has the Say in the Church, Vol. 148. Ed. by Hans Kung & Jurgen Moltman. (Concilium 1981). 128p. (Orig.). 1981. pap. 6.95 (ISBN 0-8164-2348-2, HarpR). Har-Row.

Who Helps. Bernard Palmer & Marjorie Palmer. (Illus.). 32p. (Orig.). (ps-k). 1982. pap. 3.95 (ISBN 0-934998-08-6). Bethel Pub.

Who Hides in the Park. Warabe Aska. (Illus.). 36p. (gr. 3 up). 1986. text ed. 17.95 (ISBN 0-88776-182-8, Dist. by U of Toronto Pr). Tundra Bks.

Who Hold the Balance? Michael Hurry. 1984. pap. 4.25 (ISBN 0-949667-58-7). Concord Bks.

Who Hold the Balance. 62p. 1986. pap. 4.00 (ISBN 0-317-53293-6). Noontide.

Who I Am. Julius Lester. LC 73-15447. (Illus.). 64p. (gr. 7 up). 1974. 5.95 (ISBN 0-8037-8758-8). Dial Bks Young.

Who I Am in Jesus. Sarah Hornsby. (Illus.). 160p. 1986. 8.95 (Pub by Chosen Bks). Revell.

Who I Will Be: Is There Joy & Suffering in God? Robert Wild. 5.95 (ISBN 0-87193-089-7). Dimension Bks.

Who If I Cry Out. Gustavo Corcao. Tr. by Clotilde Wilson from Port. (Texas Pan American Ser). 229p. 1967. 9.95x (ISBN 0-292-73669-X). U of Tex Pr.

Who in the World in Christ Are You? Bill Kaiser. 231p. (Orig.). 1983. pap. text ed. 6.95 (ISBN 0-914307-12-6, Dist. by Harrison Hse). Word Faith.

Who in the Zoo? Wilma Shore. LC 76-10272. (Illus.). (ps-2). 1976. 4.95 (ISBN 0-397-31701-8, JBL-J). Lippincott.

Who in Their Own Words. Compiled by Steve Clarke. (Illus.). 1982. pap. 6.95 (ISBN 0-399-41006-6, Perigee). Putnam Pub Group.

Who Invented It & What Makes It Work. (Illus.). 48p. (gr. 1-7). 1978. 5.95 (ISBN 0-448-47612-6, G&D); PLB 5.99 (ISBN 0-448-13037-8). Putnam Pub Group.

Who Is a Campbell? Jack Campbell. 1988. pap. write for info. Deertrail Bks.

Who Is a Campbell? More Than Most Campbells Ever Learn about Their Famous (and Infamous) Scottish Family. Jack Campbell. (Illus.). 144p. (Orig.). 1988. 17.00 (ISBN 0-945508-00-X); pap. 12.00 (ISBN 0-945508-01-8). DeerTrail Bks.

Who Is a Christian? 24.95 (ISBN 0-87193-188-5). Dimension Bks.

Who Is a Stranger & What Should I Do? Linda W. Girard. Ed. by Abby Levine. LC 84-17313. (Albert Whitman Concept Bks.). (Illus.). 32p. (gr. 2-6). 1985. PLB 10.50 (ISBN 0-8075-9014-2). A Whitman.

Who Is Bruce Simonds. Virginia Gaburo. 44p. 1978. saddle stitched plus boxed recording 13.95 (ISBN 0-939044-22-6). Lingua Pr.

Who Is Bugs Potter? Gordon Korman. 192p. (Orig.). (gr. 4-6). 1984. pap. 2.50 (ISBN 0-590-40376-1, Apple Paperbacks). Scholastic Inc.

Who Is Carla Hart? Joanna Barnes. 1986. pap. 3.95 (ISBN 0-671-60130-X). PB.

Who Is Carrie? James L. Collier & Christopher Collier. LC 83-23947. 192p. (gr. 4-6). 1984. 14.95 (ISBN 0-385-29295-3). Delacorte.

Who Is Carrie? James Lincoln Collier & Christopher Collier. (gr. k-6). 1987. pap. 3.25 (ISBN 0-440-49536-9, YB). Dell.

Who Is Chauncey Spencer? Chauncey E. Spencer. 1975. 7.95. Broadside Pr.

Who Is Christ. Bill Kaiser. 152p. (Orig.). 1983. pap. text ed. 4.95 (ISBN 0-914307-01-0, Dist. by Harrison Hse). Word Faith.

Who Is Christ? A Theology of the Incarnation. Galot. Tr. by M. Angeline Bouchard. 423p. 1981. 10.00 (ISBN 0-8199-0813-4). Franciscan Herald.

Who Is Coming? Patricia McKissack. LC 86-11805. (Rookie Readers Ser.). (Illus.). 32p. (ps-2). 1986. PLB 9.93 (ISBN 0-516-02073-0); pap. 2.50 (ISBN 0-516-42073-9). Childrens.

Who Is Coming to Our House? Joseph Slate. (Illus.). 32p. (ps-1). 1988. PLB 13.95 (ISBN 0-399-21537-9, Putnam). Putnam Pub Group.

Who Is David? The Story of an Adopted Adolescent & His Friends. LC 85-3837. 1985. pap. 15.00 (ISBN 0-87868-233-3, 2333). Child Welfare.

Who Is Father Christmas? Shirley Harrison. (Illus.). 64p. 1983. 8.95 (ISBN 0-7153-8222-5). David & Charles.

Who Is Felix the Great? Ronald Kidd. LC 82-7298. 160p. (gr. 7 up). 1983. 10.95 (ISBN 0-525-66778-4, 01063-320). Lodestar Bks.

Who Is for Liberty. H. R. Williamson. 59.95 (ISBN 0-8490-1294-5). Gordon Pr.

Who Is For Life? Francis A. Schaffer et al. LC 83-62685. 64p. 1984. pap. 2.95 (ISBN 0-89107-305-1, Crossway Bks). Good News.

Who Is God? Carolyn Nystrom. (Children's Bible Basics Ser.). 32p. (ps-2). 1980. pap. 4.95 (ISBN 0-8024-6158-1). Moody.

Who Is in Control? R. Devenish. 1981. pap. 4.95 (ISBN 0-87552-916-X, Evangel Pr UK). Presby & Reformed.

Who Is in the House: A Psychological Study of Two Centuries of Women's Fiction in America, 1795 to Present. McNall. 25.00 (ISBN 0-444-99081-X, MWH/, Pub. by Elsevier). Greenwood.

Who Is in the Water? (Changing Picture Bks.). (Illus.). 10p. (gr. k-3). 1986. 3.95 (ISBN 0-8431-1560-2). Price Stern.

Who Is Insane? Stephen Smith. Ed. by Gerald N. Grob. LC 78-22590. (Historical Issues in Mental Health Ser.). 1979. Repr. of 1916 ed. lib. bdg. 21.00x (ISBN 0-405-11941-0). Ayer Co Pubs.

Who Is Jesus. Bruce A. Demarest. Tr. by Ruth T. Chen. (Basic Doctrine Ser.: Bk. 1). 1985. pap. write for info. (ISBN 0-941598-26-8). Living Spring Pubns.

Who Is Jesus? Carolyn Nystrom. (Children's Bible Basics Ser.). 32p. (ps-2). 1980. pap. 4.95 (ISBN 0-8024-6159-X). Moody.

Who Is Jesus? Pope Paul VI. LC 72-80446. pap. 2.25 (ISBN 0-8198-0325-1). Dghtrs St Paul.

Who Is Jesus? R. C. Sproul. 96p. 1983. pap. 2.95 (ISBN 0-8423-8216-X). Tyndale.

Who Is Jesus? A Woman's Workshop on Mark. Carolyn Nystrom. (Woman's Workshop Ser.). 144p. 1987. pap. 4.95 (ISBN 0-310-42001-6, 11289P). Zondervan.

Who Is Jesus Christ? William L. Hendricks. LC 83-71265. (Layman's Library of Christian Doctrine Ser.). 1985. 5.95 (ISBN 0-8054-1632-3). Broadman.

Who Is Jesus? Leader's Guide. Robert Clark. Tr. by Lorna Y. Chao. (Basic Doctrine Ser.). 1986. pap. write for info. (ISBN 0-941598-33-0). Living Spring Pubns.

Who Is Kissinger? Henry Paolucci. 1980. pap. 4.00 (ISBN 0-918680-13-1). Griffon Hse.

Who Is Man. Abraham J. Heschel. LC 65-21491. 1965. 12.50x (ISBN 0-8047-0265-9); pap. 6.95 (ISBN 0-8047-0266-7, SP64). Stanford U Pr.

Who Is My Doll? Romy Roeder. (Illus.). 128p. (Orig.). 1985. pap. 8.95 (ISBN 0-86417-055-6, Pub. by Kangaroo Pr). Intl Spec Bk.

Who Is My Mother? Mary T. Malone. 144p. 1984. pap. 7.25 (ISBN 0-697-02019-3). Wm C Brown.

Who Is Next? Grahame Corbett. LC 82-70036. (Very First Bks.). (Illus.). 14p. (ps-k). 1982. bds. 3.50 (ISBN 0-8037-9759-1). Dial Bks Young.

Who Is Padre Pio? Tr. by Laura C. White. (Illus.). 44p. 1974. pap. 1.00 (ISBN 0-89555-101-2). TAN Bks Pubs.

Who Is Polluting Our Country? Herbert J. Kauders. (Illus.). 158p. 1987. 15.95 (ISBN 0-8059-3053-1). Dorrance.

Who Is Responsible for Sickness. Elbert Willis. 1978. 1.25 (ISBN 0-89858-010-2). Fill the Gap.

Who Is Root Beer? Norma Q. Hare. LC 76-16015. (Imagination Ser.). (Illus.). (gr. 1). 1977. PLB 6.69 (ISBN 0-8116-4400-6). Garrard.

Who Is She? Images of Women in Australian Fiction. Ed. by Shirley Walker. LC 83-47740. 320p. 1983. 29.95x (ISBN 0-312-87015-9). St Martin.

Who Is She That Looketh Forth As the Morning. Antoninus. 1970. ltd signed ed. 45.00 (ISBN 0-685-29879-5). Small Pr Dist.

Who Is Simon Warwick? Patricia Moyes. LC 78-53951. 1979. pap. 3.95 (ISBN 0-03-059783-8). H Holt & Co.

Who Is Sun Myung Moon? Paul Duncan. 21p. (Orig.). 1981. pap. text ed. 1.25 (ISBN 0-87148-914-7). Pathway Pr.

Who Is Sylvia? Tom Clark. LC 79-19070. 1979. 19.95 (ISBN 0-912652-54-3); pap. 6.95 (ISBN 0-912652-53-5); signed & numbered ed. 29.95x (ISBN 0-912652-55-1). Blue Wind.

Who Is Tapping at My Window? A. G. Deming. (Illus.). 24p. (ps-k). 1988. 10.95 (ISBN 0-525-44383-5, 01063-320). Dutton.

Who Is Teddy Villanova? Thomas Berger. 1978. pap. 3.95 (ISBN 0-385-29149-3, Delta). Dell.

Who Is Teresa Neumann? Charles M. Carty. 1974. pap. 1.25 (ISBN 0-89555-093-8). TAN Bks Pubs.

Who Is That? Warren B. Meyers. (Illus.). 1976. pap. 3.95 (ISBN 0-8065-0535-4, Pub. by Citadel Pr). Lyle Stuart.

Who Is the Antichrist? John L. Benson. LC 78-2426. 1978. pap. 2.50 (ISBN 0-87227-058-0). Reg Baptist.

Who Is the Master Omraam Mikhael Aivanhov. (Testimonials Ser.). (Illus.). 156p. (Orig.). 1982. pap. 9.95 (ISBN 2-85566-190-0, Pub. by Prosveta France). Prosveta USA.

Who Is the Minister's Wife? A Search for Personal Fulfillment. Charlotte Ross. LC 79-24027. 132p. 1980. pap. 6.95 (ISBN 0-664-24302-9). Westminster John Knox.

Who Is the Mona Lisa. Ruth E. Norman & Vaughn Spaegal. 1973. pap. 4.95 (ISBN 0-932642-18-7). Unarius Pubns.

Who Is the Next. Henry K. Webster. LC 75-46005. (Crime Fiction Ser). 1976. Repr. of 1931 ed. lib. bdg. 21.00 (ISBN 0-8240-2397-8). Garland Pub.

Who Is the Strongest? V. Suslov. 16p. 1974. pap. 0.99 (ISBN 0-8285-1268-X, Pub. by Progress Pubs USSR). Imported Pubns.

Who Is the True Guru. Roy E. Davis. 192p. 1981. pap. 4.95 (ISBN 0-317-20864-0). CSA Pr.

Who Is the Woman of the Apocalypse? John M. Haffert. 104p. 1982. pap. 1.95 (ISBN 0-911988-47-5). AMI Pr.

Who Is There to Mourn for Logan? Boen Hallum. (Illus.). 144p. (Orig.). 1982. pap. 6.95. B Hallum.

Who Is This Christ? Gospel Christology & Contemporary Faith. Reginald Fuller & Pheme Perkins. LC 82-48590. 176p. 1983. pap. 8.95 (ISBN 0-8006-1706-1, 1-1706). Fortress.

Who Is This God You Pray To. Bernard Hayes. 96p. (Orig.). 1981. pap. 2.95 (ISBN 0-914544-41-1). Living Flame Pr.

Who Is This Guy, Anyway? Phillip Turk & Bob Degroot. (Leonardo the Genius Ser.). 48p. 1984. pap. 4.95 (ISBN 2-205-06580-7). Dargaud Pub.

Who Is to Be Master of the World? an Introduction to the Philosophy of Friedrich Nietzsche. A. M. Ludovici. 59.95 (ISBN 0-8490-1295-3). Gordon Pr.

Who Is to Blame? A. Herzen. 275p. 1978. 7.45 (ISBN 0-8285-1620-0, Pub. by Progress Pubs USSR). Imported Pubns.

Who Is to Blame? A. I. Herzen. 252p. 1985. pap. 5.95 (ISBN 0-8285-3026-2, Pub. by Rus Lang Pubs USSR). Imported Pubns.

Who Is to Blame, 2 pts. Alexander Herzen. Tr. by Michael R. Katz from Rus. LC 84-7666. 288p. 1984. 35.00x (ISBN 0-8014-1460-1); pap. 9.95x (ISBN 0-8014-9286-6). Cornell U Pr.

Who Is Who? Patricia McKissack. LC 83-7361. (Rookie Reader Ser.). (Illus.). 32p. (ps-2). 1983. PLB 9.93 (ISBN 0-516-02042-0); pap. 2.50 (ISBN 0-516-42042-9). Childrens.

Who Is Who? A Directory of Agricultural Engineers Available for Work in Developing Countries. 209p. 1985. pap. 25.00 (ISBN 0-916150-68-2, C0685). Am Soc Ag Eng.

Who Is Who in Latin America: Government & Politics, Banking & Industry. 2nd ed. 1988. 85.00 (ISBN 0-910365-05-9). Decade Media.

Who Is Worth Following. Spiros Zodhiates. 1982. pap. 4.95 (ISBN 0-89957-514-5). AMG Pubs.

Who Is Your Doctor & Why? Alonzo J. Shadman. LC 80-82320. 446p. 1980. pap. 3.95 (ISBN 0-87983-227-4). Keats.

Who Judges the Judges? A Study of Procedures for Removal & Retirement. American Bar Foundation Staff. 185p. 1971. pap. 5.00 (ISBN 0-910058-45-8, 765-0039-01). Amer Bar Assn.

Who Keeps America Clean? Barbara Steinberg. LC 76-102. (Adventures in the World of Work). (Illus.). (gr. 5 up). 1977. pap. 2.50 (ISBN 0-394-83283-3, BYR). Random.

Who Kidnapped Princess Saralinda. Megan Stine & H. William Stine. (Wizards, Warriors & You Ser.: Bk. 3). 112p. (Orig.). (gr. 4 up). 1984. pap. 2.25 (ISBN 0-380-89268-5). Avon.

Who Kidnapped the Sheriff? Larry Callen. (Illus.). 176p. (gr. 4 up). 1985. 13.95 (ISBN 0-316-12499-0, Joy St Bks). Little.

Who Killed Adam? A Look at the Major Types of Fossil Man. Edward Lugenbeal. LC 78-8513. (Flame Ser.). 1978. pap. 1.25 (ISBN 0-8127-0186-0). Review & Herald.

Who Killed Amandela Delapina? Arthur De Lima. 1987. 13.95 (ISBN 0-533-07161-5). Vantage.

Who Killed Carlo Tresca? Norman Thomas & Edmund Wilson. Ed. by Warren Hope. 36p. 1983. pap. 3.95x (ISBN 0-911687-00-9). Mountain Laurel.

Who Killed CBS? How America's Number One News Network Went Down the Tubes. Peter J. Boyer. LC 87-42650. (Illus.). 384p. 1987. 18.95 (ISBN 0-394-56034-5). Random.

Who Killed Harlowe Thrombey, No. 9. Edward Packard. (Choose Your Own Adventure Ser.). 121p. (gr. 2-7). 1987. Repr. of 1981 ed. 8.95 (ISBN 0-942545-13-3); lib. bdg. 9.95 (ISBN 0-942545-18-4). Grey Castle.

Who Killed Jim Crow? The Story of the Civil Rights Movement & Its Lessons for Today. Peter Camejo. pap. 0.75 (ISBN 0-87348-343-X). Path Pr NY.

Who Killed Joe McCarthy? William B. Ewald, Jr. 1984. 17.95 (ISBN 0-671-44946-X). S&S.

Who Killed Karen Silkwood? Howard Kohn. 440p. 1981. pap. 8.95 (ISBN 0-671-43654-6). Summit Bks.

Who Killed Merblyn Henderson? Philip E. Donkor. 81p. 1987. 7.95 (ISBN 0-533-06072-9). Vantage.

Who Killed Mujib? A. L. Khatib. 250p. 1981. text ed. 17.95x (ISBN 0-7069-1514-3, Pub. by Vikas India). Advent NY.

Who Killed Palomino Molero? Mario Vargas-Llosa. Tr. by Alfred MacAdam from Span. 1987. 14.95 (ISBN 0-374-28978-6). FS&G.

Who Killed Palomino Molero? Mario Vargas Llosa. 1988. pap. 6.95 (ISBN 0-02-022570-9, Collier). Macmillan.

Who Killed Robert Prentice? Dennis Wheatley & Jay Links. 117p. 1980. 17.95 (ISBN 0-686-64567-7, Mayflower Bks). Smith Pubs.

Who Killed Sack Annie? Dana Brookins. 160p. (gr. 4-7). 1983. 9.95 (ISBN 0-89919-137-1, Clarion). HM.

Who Killed Sal Mineo? Susan Braudy. 1982. 14.95 (ISBN 0-671-61009-0, Wyndham Bks). S&S.

Who Killed Sal Mineo? Susan Braudy. 1984. pap. 3.95 (ISBN 0-671-46736-0). PB.

Who Killed the Congo? Philippa Schuyler. (Illus.). 1962. 9.50 (ISBN 0-8159-7212-1). Devin.

Who Killed the Constitution: The Judges vs. the Law. William Eaton. 1988. 16.95 (ISBN 0-89526-560-5); pap. 10.95 (ISBN 0-89526-776-4). Regnery Gateway.

Who Killed the Robins Family? Bill Adler & Thomas Chastin. 192p. 1984. pap. 3.50 (ISBN 0-446-32314-4). Warner Bks.

Who Killed Virginia Woolf? A Psychobiography. Alma H. Bond. 168p. 1989. 19.95 (ISBN 0-89885-427-X). Human Sci Pr.

Who Knew There'd Be Ghosts? Bill Brittain. LC 84-48496. (Illus.). 128p. (gr. 4-7). 1985. 12.95i (ISBN 0-06-020699-3); PLB 12.89g (ISBN 0-06-020700-0). HarpJ.

Who Knew There'd Be Ghosts? Bill Brittain. LC 84-48496. (Trophy Book). (Illus.). 128p. (gr. 4-7). 1988. pap. 2.95 (ISBN 0-06-440224-X, Trophy). HarpJ.

Who Knows. Remy Hall. 168p. (Orig.). 1987. pap. 4.00 (ISBN 0-937815-04-7). Hanuman Bks.

Who Knows: A Guide to Washington Experts. 8th ed. Washington Researchers, Limited Staff. (Business Research Ser.: Vol. 5). 425p. (Orig.). 1986. pap. 125.00 (ISBN 0-934940-32-0). Wash Res Pub.

Who Knows: A Guide to Washington Experts. 9th ed. Washington Researchers Publishing Staff. (Business Research Ser.: Vol. 5). Orig. Title: Researcher's Guide to Washington Experts. (Orig.). 1988. pap. 125.00 (ISBN 0-934940-55-X). Wash Res Pub.

Who Knows about Foreign Industries & Markets: Country Experts in the Federal Government. 9th ed. Washington Researchers Publishing Staff. (Briefcase Ser.). 1987. pap. 50.00 (ISBN 0-934940-57-6). Wash Res Pub.

Who Knows about Foreign Industries & Markets. VIII ed. Washington Researchers Staff. (Briefcase Ser.: Vol. 3). 70p. 1986. pap. 50.00 (ISBN 0-934940-34-7). Wash Res Pub.

Who Knows about Foreign Industries & Markets. 10th ed. (Briefcase Ser.: Bk. 3). 1988. pap. 50.00 (ISBN 0-934940-65-7). Wash Res Pub.

Who Knows about Industries & Markets: Industry Analysts in the Federal Government. 9th ed. Washington Researchers Publishing Staff. (Briefcase Ser.). 1987. pap. 50.00 (ISBN 0-934940-58-4). Wash Res Pub.

Who Knows about Industries & Markets. 10th ed. Washington Researchers Publishing Staff. (Briefcase Ser.: Bk. 4). 1988. pap. 50.00 (ISBN 0-934940-66-5). Wash Res Pub.

Who Knows about Industries & Markets. VIII ed. Washington Researchers Staff. (Briefcase Ser.: Vol. 4). 54p. (Orig.). 1986. pap. 50.00 (ISBN 0-934940-33-9). Wash Res Pub.

Who Knows Better Must Say So! Elmer Berger. 113p. 1970. Repr. of 1955 ed. 6.50 (ISBN 0-88728-094-3). Inst Palestine.

Who Knows: Information in the Age of the Fortune 500. Herbert I. Schiller. LC 81-3572. (Communications & Information Science Ser.). 150p. 1981. text ed. 29.50x (ISBN 0-89391-069-4); pap. 17.95. Ablex Pub.

Who Knows One? A Book of Jewish Numbers. Yaffa Ganz. (gr. k-4). 1981. 8.95 (ISBN 0-87306-285-X). Feldheim.

Who Knows Ten: Children's Tales of the Ten Commandments. Molly Cone. LC 65-24639. (Illus.). (gr. 3-5). 1968. text ed. 6.00 (ISBN 0-8074-0080-7, 102551); record o.p. 5.95 (ISBN 0-8074-0081-5, 102552). UAHC.

Who Knows the Little Man? Walburga Attenberger. (Illus.). (ps-1). 1972. Random.

WHO Laboratory Manual for the Examination of Human Semen & Semen-Cervical Mucus Interaction. WHO Special Programme of Research, Development & Research Training in Human Reproduction Staff. (Illus.). 80p. 1987. plastic cover 14.95 (ISBN 0-521-33647-3). Cambridge U Pr.

Who Laughs Last. Rosalind E. Dickenson. 64p. 1982. 5.00 (ISBN 0-682-49847-5). Exposition-Phoenix.

Who Let Muddy Boots into the White House. Robert Quackenbush. (Illus.). 40p. 1986. pap. 11.95 (ISBN 0-13-958257-6). P-H.

Who Like the Water God Made? Elspeth Murphy. (Tubable Hugable Ser.). (Illus.). (gr. 1-5). 1984. pap. 3.50 soft cover (ISBN 0-89191-817-5). Cook.

Who Lived Where in Europe. John Eastman. (Illus.). 400p. 1985. 35.00 (ISBN 0-87196-749-9). Facts on File.

Who Lives Here? Dot Barlowe & Sy Barlowe. LC 79-27494. (Picturebacks Ser.). (Illus.). 32p. (ps-3). 1980. pap. 1.95 (ISBN 0-394-83740-1). Random.

Who Lives Here? Jean L. Latham. LC 73-22080. (Easy Venture Ser.). (Illus.). 32p. (gr. k-2). 1974. PLB 6.69 (ISBN 0-8116-6063-X). Garrard.

Who Lives Here? (Changing Picture Bks.). (Illus.). 10p. 1986. 3.95 (ISBN 0-8431-1557-2). Price Stern.

Who Lives in the Igloo? Coby Lund et al. (Illus.). 52p. (Orig.). (gr. 4-9). 1984. 5.95 (ISBN 0-88047-046-1, 8402). DOK Pubs.

Who Lives in the Warm Sea? S. Sakharnov. 15p. 1975. pap. 0.99 (ISBN 0-8285-1269-8, Pub. by Progress Pubs USSR). Imported Pubns.

Who Lives in the Woods? (Platt & Munk Cricket Bk.). (ps-1). 1987. 3.50 (ISBN 0-448-46537-X). Putnam Pub Group.

Who Loves Sam Grant? Delores Beckman. LC 82-18211. 160p. (gr. 5-9). 1983. 10.95 (ISBN 0-525-44055-0). Dutton.

Who Made God. Emmy L. Murphy. (ps-3). 1978. pap. 2.25 (ISBN 0-915374-07-2, 07-2). Rapids Christian.

Who Made Me? Malcolm Doney & Meryl Doney. (Illus.). 38p. (ps-3). 1987. 9.95 (ISBN 0-310-55660-0, 19064). Zondervan.

Who Made Stevie Cry? Michael Bishop. (Illus.). 325p. 1984. 15.95 (ISBN 0-87054-099-8, Arkham House). Arkham.

Who Made the Lamb. Charlotte Painter. LC 64-23637. 208p. (Orig.). 1988. pap. 8.95 (ISBN 0-88739-063-3). Creative Arts Bk.

Who Made These Things? Joyce W. Crapps. LC 86-18773. (Bible-&-Me Ser.). (ps). 1987. 5.95 (ISBN 0-8054-4178-6). Broadman.

Who Makes Our Money. F. J. Irsigler. 164p. 1986. pap. 6.00 (ISBN 0-317-53296-0). Noontide.

Who Makes Our Money: How Our Financial System Creates Poverty & War. F Irsigler. 1982. lib. bdg. 69.95 (ISBN 0-87700-447-1). Revisionist Pr.

WHO Manual on Environmental Management for Mosquito Control. 283p. 1982. 13.50 (ISBN 92-4-170066-1). Am Mosquito.

WHO Manual on Larval Control Operations in Malaria Programmes. 199p. 1973. 20.00 (ISBN 0-318-12865-9). Am Mosquito.

Who: Maximum R&B. Richard Barnes. (Illus.). 168p. 1982. pap. 13.95 (ISBN 0-312-86989-4). St Martin.

Who, Me? Ely J. Kahn. LC 77-179731. (Biography Index Reprint Ser). Repr. of 1949 ed. 15.75 (ISBN 0-8369-8099-9). Ayer Co Pubs.

Who Me? A Missionary? Daniel W. Bacon. 1985. pap. 1.25 (ISBN 9971-972-32-8). OMF Bks.

Who, Me, Give a Speech? Handbook for Christian Woman. Nancy I. Alford. 160p. (Orig.). 1987. pap. 7.95 (ISBN 0-8010-0211-7). Baker Bk.

Who, Me Lead a Group? Jean I. Clarke. 128p. (Orig.). 1983. pap. 3.95 (ISBN 0-86683-724-8, AY8284, HarpR). Har-Row.

Who, Me Teach My Child Religion? rev. ed. Dolores Curran. 156p. 1981. pap. 6.95 (ISBN 0-86683-619-5, HarpR). Har-Row.

Who Moved the Stone? Frank Morison. pap. 7.95 (ISBN 0-310-29561-0, 10373P). Zondervan.

Who Needs a Bear? Barbara Dillon. LC 80-26530. (Illus.). 64p. (gr. k-3). 1981. PLB 10.88 (ISBN 0-688-00446-6). Morrow.

Who Needs a Bratty Brother? Linda Gondosch. (Illus.). 112p. (gr. 4-6). 1985. 11.95 (ISBN 0-525-67170-6, 01063-320). Lodestar Bks.

Who Needs a Bratty Brother? Linda Gondosch. (Illus.). (gr. 3-7). 1987. pap. 2.50 (ISBN 0-671-62777-5, Minstrel Bks). S&S.

Who Needs a Bratty Brother. Linda Gondosch. (gr. k-9). 1988. pap. 2.50. Scholastic Inc.

Who Needs Alligators? Patricia Lauber. LC 73-22102. (Good Earth Ser.). (Illus.). 64p. (gr. 2-6). 1974. PLB 7.22 (ISBN 0-8116-6100-8). Garrard.

Who Needs Care? Social Work Decisions about Children. Jean Packman. 224p. 1986. text ed. 45.00x (ISBN 0-631-14374-2). Basil Blackwell.

Who Needs Enemies? Alan D. Foster. 1984. pap. 2.95 (ISBN 0-345-31657-6, Del Rey). Ballantine.

Who Needs Glamour Anyway? Marion Schultz. 144p. (YA) (gr. 7 up). 1988. pap. 2.75 (ISBN 0-449-70255-3, Juniper). Fawcett.

Who Needs Her? Lorraine Hare. LC 82-13899. (Illus.). 32p. (gr. 2-5). 1983. 9.95 (ISBN 0-689-50268-0, M K McElderry). Macmillan.

Who Needs the Family? O. R. Johnston. LC 80-7780. 152p. (Orig.). 1980. pap. 5.95 (ISBN 0-87784-588-3). Inter-Varsity.

Who Needs the Wages Councils? 56p. 7.50x (ISBN 0-317-43612-0, Pub. by Bertrand Russell Hse). State Mutual Bk.

Who Needs Theatre. Robert Brustein. Ed. by Gary Fishetjon. 336p. (Orig.). 1987. pap. 18.95 (ISBN 0-87113-206-0). Atlantic Monthly.

Who Offers Part-Time Degree Programs? 2nd ed. LC 84-22744. 423p. (Orig.). 1985. pap. 7.95 (ISBN 0-87866-285-5). Petersons Guides.

Who, or What, Is God? Parker L. Johnstone. 212p. 1984. 7.95 (ISBN 0-917802-12-8). Theoscience Found.

Who Owns America. facs. ed. Ed. by Herbert Agar & Allen Tate. LC 71-99616. (Essay Index Reprint Ser). 1936. 23.00 (ISBN 0-8369-1540-2). Ayer Co Pubs.

Who Owns America? Edmund B. Bolles. (Illus.). 288p. 1984. pap. 8.95 (ISBN 0-87131-450-9). M Evans.

Who Owns America? A New Declaration of Independence. Ed. by Herbert Agar & Allen Tate. LC 82-24752. 352p. 1983. pap. text ed. 15.25 (ISBN 0-8191-2767-1). U Pr of Amer.

Who Owns Appalachia. (Southern Exposure Studies). 88p. 1982. 3.00 (ISBN 0-318-14481-6). Inst Southern Studies.

Who Owns Appalachia? Landownership & Its Impact. Appalachian Land Ownership Task Force Staff. LC 82-40173. (Illus.). 272p. 1983. 25.00x (ISBN 0-8131-1476-4). U Pr of Ky.

Who Owns the Blue Chips in Great Britain. R. A. Vernon et al. 200p. 1973. 24.00 (ISBN 0-8464-0971-2). Beekman Pubs.

Who Owns the Children? Compulsory Education & the Dilemma of Ultimate Authority. 3rd, rev. ed. Blair Adams et al. LC 84-50087. (Education As Religious War Ser.: Vol. 5). 514p. 1986. pap. 12.95 (ISBN 0-916387-07-0). Truth Forum.

Who Owns the Children? Compulsory Education & the Dilemma of Ultimate Authority. 4th ed. Blair Adams et al. (Education as Religous War Ser.: Bk. 5). 620p. (Orig.). 1988. pap. 12.95 (ISBN 0-916387-11-9). Truth Forum.

Who Owns the Corporation? Management vs. Shareholders. Edward J. Epstein. (Twentieth Century Fund Paper). 69p. (Orig.). 1986. pap. text ed. 8.00x (ISBN 0-87078-208-8). Priority Pr Pubns.

Who Owns the Earth? James Ridgeway. 1980. 15.95 (ISBN 0-02-603300-3); pap. 8.95 (ISBN 0-02-081220-5). Macmillan.

Who Owns the Family? God or the State? Ray Sutton. write for info. (ISBN 0-930462-16-5). Am Bur Eco Res.

Who Owns the Moon? Sonia Levitin. (Illus.). (gr. k-3). 1973. Repr. HM.

Who Owns the Past? Papers from the Annual Symposium of the Australian Academy of the Humanities. Ed. by Isabel McBryde. (Illus.). 1985. 32.50x (ISBN 0-19-554565-6). Oxford U Pr.

Who Owns the Sun? Stacy Chbosky. LC 88-12694. (Illus.). 26p. (gr. 3-12). 1988. lib. bdg. 12.95 (ISBN 0-933849-14-1). Landmark Edns.

Who Owns the Unicorn. Katherine Lucas & Louise Lucas. (Illus., Orig.). (gr. 4-12). 1980. pap. text ed. 5.95 (ISBN 0-914634-69-0, 7918). DOK Pubs.

Who Owns the Wildlife? The Political Economy of Conservation in Nineteenth-Century America. James A. Tober. LC 80-23482. (Contributions in Economics & Economic History Ser.: No. 37). (Illus.). 300p. 1981. lib. bdg. 35.00 (ISBN 0-313-22597-4, TOW/). Greenwood.

Who Owns Whom: Australasia & the Far East, 1986. 1400p. 1986. 245.00 (ISBN 0-8002-4066-9). Intl Pubns Serv.

Who Owns Whom: Continental Europe, 1986, 2 vols. 1986. 290.00 (ISBN 0-8002-4065-0). Intl Pubns Serv.

Who Owns Whom: North America, 1985. 17th ed. 1985. 240.00 (ISBN 0-8002-3950-4). Intl Pubns Serv.

Who Owns Whom: North America, 1986. 1640p. 1986. 295.00 (ISBN 0-8002-4049-9). Intl Pubns Serv.

Who-Paddled-Backward-with-Trout. Howard Norman. (Illus.). 32p. (ps-3). 1987. 13.95 (ISBN 0-316-61182-4, Joy St Bks). Little.

Who Paid the Taxes, 1966-85? Joseph A. Pechman. LC 84-45845. (Studies of Government Finance). 84p. 1985. 22.95 (ISBN 0-8157-6998-9); pap. 8.95 (ISBN 0-8157-6997-0). Brookings.

Who Pays Hawaii's Taxes? A Study of the Incidence of State & Local Taxes in Hawaii for 1970. Robert D. Ebel & Robert M. Kamins. 135p. 1975. pap. 5.00x (ISBN 0-8248-0403-1). UH Pr.

Who Pays State & Local Taxes? Donald Phares. LC 80-15454. 288p. 1980. text ed. 30.00 (ISBN 0-89946-026-7). Oelgeschlager.

Who Pays the Cost. Louis R. Rivera. (Illus.). 40p. (Orig.). 1977. pap. 2.00x (ISBN 0-917886-03-8). Shamal Bks.

Who Pays the Property Tax? A New View. Henry J. Aaron. LC 75-19270. (Studies of Government Finance). 110p. 1975. (ISBN 0-8157-0021-0); pap. 9.95. Brookings.

Who Profits: Winners, Losers, & Government Regulations. Robert A. Leone. LC 85-47992. 208p. 1986. 17.95 (ISBN 0-465-09183-0). Basic.

Who Profits: Winners, Losers & Government Regulation. Robert A. Leone. LC 85-47992. 272p. 1987. pap. 8.95 (ISBN 0-465-09184-9, PL 5200). Basic.

Who Put All These Cucumbers in My Garden? Patricia F. Wilson. LC 83-51398. 144p. (Orig.). 1984. pap. 6.95 (ISBN 0-8358-0475-5). Upper Room.

Who Put Jesus on the Cross. A. W. Tozer. 1976. pap. 3.45 (ISBN 0-87509-212-8). Chr Pubns.

Who Put That Hair in My Toothbrush? Jerry Spinelli. LC 83-20716. (gr. 5-9). 1984. 14.95 (ISBN 0-316-80712-5). Little.

Who Put That Hair in My Toothbrush? Jerry Spinelli. (gr. 5-9). 1986. pap. 2.95 (ISBN 0-440-99485-3, LFL). Dell.

Who Put the Cannon in the Courthouse Square: A Guide to Uncovering the Past. Kay Cooper. LC 84-17251. (Illus.). (gr. 4 up). 1984. cancelled (ISBN 0-8027-6547-5); PLB 11.85 set (ISBN 0-8027-6561-0). Walker & Co.

Who Put the Con in Consumer? David Sanford. 1972. 5.95 (ISBN 0-87140-550-4); pap. 2.95 (ISBN 0-87140-270-X). Liveright.

Who Puts the Water in the Taps? 1983. 5.50 (ISBN 0-905347-47-1). Intl Inst Environment.

Who Reads What? facs. ed. Charles H. Compton. LC 69-18923. (Essay Index Reprint Ser). 1934. 14.00 (ISBN 0-8369-0012-X). Ayer Co Pubs.

Who Reads What When: Literature Selections for Children Ages Three Through Thirteen. Jane A. Williams. 60p. (Orig.). 1988. pap. 3.95 (ISBN 0-942617-01-0). Blstckng Pr.

Who Really Discovered America. Stephen Krensky. (Illus.). 64p. (Orig.). (gr. 4-6). 1987. pap. 2.50 (ISBN 0-590-40854-2). Scholastic Inc.

Who Really Discovered America? Stephen Krensky. Ed. by Judy Donnelly. (Illus.). 64p. (gr. 3-7). 1987. 12.95 (ISBN 0-8038-9306-X). Hastings.

Who Really Rules? New Have & Community Power Reexamined. G. William Domhoff. 190p. 1978. text ed. 29.95 (ISBN 0-87855-228-6). Transaction Bks.

Who Really Starves? Women & World Hunger. Lisa Leghorn & Mary Roodkowsky. (Orig.). 1977. pap. 1.25 (ISBN 0-377-00066-3). Friendship Pr.

Who Remembers the Sea. Mohammed Dib. Tr. by Louis Tremaine from Fr. LC 85-50529. 122p. 1985. 18.00 (ISBN 0-89410-444-6); pap. 8.00 (ISBN 0-89410-445-4). Three Continents.

Who Rules America? J. McConaughey. 1980. lib. bdg. 59.95 (ISBN 0-8490-3205-9). Gordon Pr.

Who Rules America Now? G. Domhoff Domhoff. 1986. pap. 9.95 (ISBN 0-671-62235-8, Touchstone Bks). S&S.

Who Rules America Now? A View for the Eighties. G. William Domhoff. 230p. (Orig.). (YA) (gr. 9-12). 1983. (Spec); pap. 7.95 (ISBN 0-13-958405-6, Spec). P-H.

Who Was Who on Screen. abridged ed. Evelyn M. Truitt. (Illus.). 438p. 1984. pap. 29.95 (ISBN 0-8352-1867-8). Bowker.

Who We Are Is How We Pray: Matching Personality & Spirituality. Dr. Charles J. Keating. LC 86-50245. 144p. (Orig.). 1987. 13.95 (ISBN 0-89622-292-6); pap. 7.95 (ISBN 0-89622-321-3). Twenty-Third.

Who We Are: What Some Educators Say About Their Characteristics, Competencies & Roles. A. Charters & R. Hilton. (MS Ser.). 1977. 5.00 (ISBN 0-686-52212-5, MSS 5). Syracuse U Cont Ed.

Who We Like, Why We Like Them, & What We Do with Them. Letty C. Pogrebin. (Paperbacks Ser.). 432p. 1988. pap. text ed. 7.95 (ISBN 0-07-050413-X). McGraw.

Who Were the Fascists? Social Roots of European Fascism. Ed. by Stein U. Larsen. 1981. 48.00x (ISBN 8-20005-331-8). Oxford U Pr.

Who Were the Israelites? Gosta W. Ahlstrom. x, 134p. 1986. text ed. 12.50x (ISBN 0-931464-24-2). Eisenbrauns.

Who Were You? The Diagram Group & J. Maya Pilkington. 1988. pap. 8.95 (ISBN 0-345-35264-5). Ballantine.

Who, What & Where in Communications Security. Marketing Consultants International, Inc. Ed. by J. Michael Nye. (Illus.). 124p. 1986. pap. 75.00 (ISBN 0-937195-25-1). Mktg Consult Intl.

Who, What, When, Where Bible Busy Book. William Coleman. 32p. (gr. 2-8). 1984. pap. 2.50 (ISBN 0-89191-853-1). Cook.

Who, What, When, Where Book about the Bible. William Coleman. (Illus.). (gr. 1-5). 1980. 11.95 (ISBN 0-89191-291-6). Cook.

Who' Who in American Politics. 12th ed. Ed. by Bowker, R. R., Staff. 1800p. 1989. price not set (ISBN 0-8352-2577-1). Bowker.

Who Will Be My Friends? Syd Hoff. (Early I Can Read Bks.). (Illus.). (gr. k-2). 1960. PLB 9.89 (ISBN 0-06-022556-4). HarpJ.

Who Will Be My Friends? Syd Hoff. LC 60-14096. (Trophy Early I Can Read Bks.). (Illus.). 32p. (ps-2). 1985. pap. 2.95 (ISBN 0-06-444072-9, Trophy). HarpJ.

Who Will Be My Teacher? The Christian Way to Stronger Schools. Marti W. Garlett. 256p. 1985. 12.95 (ISBN 0-8499-0471-4, 0471-4). Word Bks.

Who Will Be the Sun? A North American Indian Folk Tale. Retold by & illus. by Joanna Troughton. LC 85-15074. (Folk-Tales of the World Ser.). (Illus.). 28p. (gr. k-4). 1986. 12.95 (ISBN 0-87226-038-0, Dist. by Har-Row). P Bedrick Bks.

Who Will Benefit from Psychotherapy. Lester Luborsky. LC 88-47762. 272p. 1988. text ed. 22.95 (ISBN 0-465-09189-X). Basic.

Who Will Deliver Us? Paul Zahl. 170p. 1985. pap. 7.95 large print ed. (ISBN 0-8027-2487-6). Walker & Co.

Who Will Deliver Us? Paul F. Zahl. 96p. (Orig.). 1983. pap. 5.95 (ISBN 0-8164-2468-3, HarpR). Har-Row.

Who Will Fly with Butterfly? Lorice Hartmann. (Illus.). (gr. k-3). 1978. pap. 4.95 (ISBN 0-912760-51-6). Valkyrie Pub Hse.

Who Will Lead Kiddush? Barbara Pomerantz. (Illus.). 32p. (Orig.). (gr. 1-3). 1985. pap. 6.00 (ISBN 0-8074-0306-7, 102000). UAHC.

Who Will Listen to Me? Prayer Thoughts for High School Girls. Judith Mattison. LC 77-72450. (Illus.). 1977. pap. 4.95 (ISBN 0-8066-1596-6, 10-7085). Augsburg.

Who Will Make Us Wise? How the Churches Are Failing Higher Education. Eric O. Springsted. 162p. (Orig.). 1988. pap. 8.95 (ISBN 0-936384-63-8). Cowley Pubns.

Who Will Remember the People... Jean Raspail. Tr. by Jeremy Leggatt from Fr. 288p. 1988. 18.95 (ISBN 0-916515-42-7). Mercury Hse Inc.

Who Will Rise Up? Jed Smock. LC 84-62777. 203p. (Orig.). 1985. pap. 5.95 (ISBN 0-910311-25-0). Huntington Hse Inc.

Who Will Stop the Bomb? A Primer on Nuclear Proliferation. Roger Molander & Robbie Nichols. LC 85-10362. 160p. 12.95 (ISBN 0-8160-1283-0). Facts on File.

Who Will Take Care of Me? Patricia Hermes. LC 82-48757. 128p. (gr. 3-7). 1983. PLB 11.95 (ISBN 0-15-296265-4, HJ). HarBraceJ.

Who Will Take Our Children? The Story of the Evacuation of Britain 1939-1945. Carlton Jackson. (Illus.). 224p. 1985. 17.95 (ISBN 0-413-58130-6, 9526). Heinemann Ed.

Who Will Take the Children? A New Custody Option for Divorced Mothers & Fathers. Susan Meyers & Joan Lakin. LC 82-17847. 228p. 1983. 13.95 (ISBN 0-672-52739-1). Bobbs.

Who Will Teach Me? Joseph F. Girzone. 87p. 1987. Repr. of 1982 ed. 6.95 (ISBN 0-911519-00-9). Richelieu Court.

Who Won What When: The Nineteen Eighty Edition of the Record Book of Winners. Ed. by Sandra L. Stuart. 1980. 12.00 (ISBN 0-8184-0295-4); pap. 8.95 (ISBN 0-8184-0293-8). Lyle Stuart.

Who Would Be the Most Compatible Man or Woman for You? Dionisio C. Bolloso. 1988. 7.95. Vantage.

Who Would Want to Kill Hallie Panky's Cat? G. Majors. 160p. (gr. 4-7). 1981. 8.95g (ISBN 0-8038-8094-4). Hastings.

Who Writes What - 1988 Edition. Ed. by Price Gaines. 291p. 1988. plastic spiral 17.25 (ISBN 0-87218-058-1). Natl Underwriter.

Who Wrote It? William A. Wheeler. Ed. by C. G. Wheeler. (English Literary Reference Ser). Repr. of 1881 ed. 14.00 (ISBN 0-384-67860-2). Johnson Repr.

Who Wrote That Song? Dick Jacobs. LC 88-19351. (Illus.). 312p. (Orig.). 1988. 29.95 (ISBN 1-55870-108-7); pap. 17.95 (ISBN 1-55870-100-1). Betterway Pubns.

Who Wrote That Song: Popular Songs in America & Their Composers. W. Colbert. 1974. lib. bdg. 69.95 (ISBN 0-87700-216-9). Revisionist Pr.

Who Wrote the Bible? Richard E. Friedman. 1987. 18.95 (ISBN 0-671-63161-6). Summit Bks.

Who Wrote the Bible? Richard E. Friedman. (Illus.). 192p. 1988. text ed. price not set (ISBN 0-13-958513-3). P-H.

Who Wrote the Bible? A Book for the People. Washington Gladden. LC 72-5435. (Select Bibliographies Reprint Ser.). 1972. Repr. of 1891 ed. 22.00 (ISBN 0-8369-6909-X). Ayer Co Pubs.

Who Wrote the Book of Love? Thomas Farber. LC 84-45096. 127p. 1984. pap. 6.95 (ISBN 0-916870-69-3, A Donald S. Ellis Book). Creative Arts Bk.

Who Wrote the Mozart Four-Wind Concertante? Authenticity, Origin & Reconstruction. Robert D. Levin. LC 84-26365. 1988. 48.00x (ISBN 0-918728-31-2). Pendragon NY.

Who Wrote What? W. A. Wheeler. 69.95 (ISBN 0-87968-367-8). Gordon Pr.

Who You Are When No One's Looking: Christian Character for All of Life. Bill Hybels. LC 87-16856. 128p. (Orig.). 1987. pap. 5.95 (ISBN 0-87784-945-5). Inter-Varsity.

Whoa - Long Ago. Robert C. Sieg. 260p. (Orig.). 1988. pap. 12.95 (ISBN 1-55618-040-3). Brunswick Pub.

Whoa...Yuh Sonsabitches. Edgar R. Potter. (Illus.). 1977. pap. 6.95 (ISBN 0-918292-00-X). Griggs Print.

Whobody There? Charles Morse & Ann Morse. 1977. pap. 6.95x (ISBN 0-8358-0350-3). Upper Room.

Who'd Be a Missionary? Helen Morgan. 1972. pap. 1.50 (ISBN 0-87508-365-X). Chr Lit.

Who'd Hire Brett? John Brett. (Orig.). 1989. pap. 3.50 (ISBN 0-553-27714-6). Bantam.

Who'd Stay a Missionary? Helen Morgan. 1972. pap. 1.95 (ISBN 0-87508-366-8). Chr Lit.

Whoever Finds This: I Love You. Faye Mosokovitz. 1988. 15.95 (ISBN 0-87923-746-5). Godine.

Whoever Said Life Is Fair? A Guide to Growing Through Life's Injustices. Sara K. Cohen. 1988. pap. 3.95 (ISBN 0-425-10888-0). Berkley Pub.

Whole Again. Lee Whipple. LC 80-81034. 232p. 1980. 9.95 (ISBN 0-89803-023-4, Dist. by Kampmann). Green Hill.

Whole Again Resource Guide. Tim Ryan. LC 83-641044. 380p. 1986. pap. 24.95 (ISBN 0-915051-01-X). Sourcenet.

Whole Air Weather Guide. Walter F. Dabberdt. (Illus.). 1976. pap. 4.50 (Pub. by Solstice). Aviation.

Whole Armor. Rhoda L. Seoane. 1965. 6.95 (ISBN 0-8315-0023-9). Speller.

Whole Armor & the Secret Ladder. Wilson Harris. 260p. 1973. pap. 5.95 (ISBN 0-571-10231-X). Faber & Faber.

Whole Art of the Stage. Francois H. Aubignac. LC 68-21218. 33.00 (ISBN 0-405-08227-4, Pub. by Blom). Ayer Co Pubs.

Whole Art Thing. Justin Spring. 192p. 1987. 13.95 (ISBN 0-312-00204-1, J Kahn). St Martin.

Whole Arts Directory. Cynthia Navaretta. LC 87-62789. (Arts Guide Ser.). (Illus.). 176p. (Orig.). 1987. pap. text ed. 12.95 (ISBN 0-9602476-7-X). Midmarch Arts WAN.

Whole Ball of Wax & Other Colloquial Phrases. Laurence Urdang. 160p. 1988. pap. 8.95 (ISBN 0-399-51436-8, Perigee Bks). Putnam Pub Group.

Whole Birth Catalogue. Joy Overbeck. pap. 6.95 (ISBN 0-671-61876-8). PB.

Whole-Body Autoradiography. Christopher Curtis et al. (Biological Techniques Ser.). 1981. 48.00 (ISBN 0-12-199660-3). Acad Pr.

Whole Body Computerized Tomography. O. H. Wegener. (Illus.). 396p. 1983. 54.75 (ISBN 3-8055-2773-X). S Karger.

Whole Body Healing. Carl Lowe & Jim Nechas. (Illus.). 440p. 1983. 21.95 (ISBN 0-87857-441-7, 05-024-0). Rodale Pr Inc.

Whole Brain Thinking: Working from Both Sides of the Brain to Achieve Peak Job Performance. Jacquelyn Wonder & Priscilla Donovan. 320p. 1985. pap. 3.95 (ISBN 0-345-32204-5). Ballantine.

Whole Car Catalog. Consumer Guide Editors. (Illus.). 1978. pap. 7.95 (ISBN 0-671-23022-0, Fireside). S&S.

Whole Child: Early Education for the Eighties. 3rd ed. Joanne Hendrick. 608p. 1984. text ed. 31.95 (ISBN 0-675-20600-6). Merrill.

Whole Child: The Developmental Education for the Early Years. 4th ed. Joanne Hendrick. 624p. 1988. case bound 31.95 (ISBN 0-675-20761-4); supplements avail. Merrill.

Whole Child-Whole Parent. Polly B. Berends. (Illus.). 384p. 1987. pap. 10.95 (ISBN 0-06-091427-0, PL1427, PL). Har-Row.

Whole Christ. E. Mersch. 638p. 1981. 39.00x (ISBN 0-234-77051-1, Pub. by Dobson Bks England). State Mutual Bk.

Whole Christmas Catalog. rev. ed. (Illus.). 224p. 1988. pap. 15.95 (ISBN 0-89586-740-0). Price Stern.

Whole Christmas Catalog for Kids. (Illus.). 160p. 1988. pap. 12.95 (ISBN 0-89586-742-7). Price Stern.

Whole Christmas Catalogue. Ed. by Naomi Black. LC 85-82487. 192p. 1987. pap. 12.95 (ISBN 0-89586-636-6). Price Stern.

Whole Cloth. M. Constantine. 1986. cancelled. Van Nos Reinhold.

Whole Cloth: A History of the Greater Boston Council of Girl Scouts, 1913-1969. Nancy H. Hannan. 136p. (Orig.). 1987. pap. 12.95 (ISBN 0-913553-04-2). Albert Hse Pub.

Whole Computer Catalog. Narda L. Schwartz. 1984. pap. 35.00 (ISBN 0-9609254-0-6). Designs Three.

Whole Cosmos Catalog of Science Activities for Kids of All Ages. Joe Abruscato & Jack Hassard. LC 76-46463. (Illus.). 1977. pap. 12.95 (ISBN 0-673-16459-4). Scott F.

Whole Counsel of God. Carl E. Braaten. LC 73-88345. pap. 44.00 (2026840). Bks Demand UMI.

Whole Craft of Spinning from the Raw Material to the Finished Yarn. Carol Kroll. 1981. pap. 2.95 (ISBN 0-486-23968-3). Dover.

Whole Days in the Trees. Marguerite Duras. Tr. by Anita Barrows from Fr. (Orig.). 1984. pap. 6.95 (ISBN 0-7145-3854-X). Riverrun NY.

Whole Earth Access Mail Order Catalog. rev. ed. LC 84-51170. (Illus.). 480p. 1985. pap. 14.95 (ISBN 0-89815-132-5). Ten Speed Pr.

Whole Earth Atlas: New Census Edition. Ed. by Martin A. Bacheller. LC 82-83211. (Illus.). 256p. 1986. pap. 8.95 (ISBN 0-8437-2499-4). Hammond Inc.

Whole Earth Cookbook 2. Sharon Cadwallader. LC 75-23317. 1975. 7.95 (ISBN 0-395-21984-1, Co-Pub. by San Francisco Bk. Co.). HM.

Whole Earth Holiday Book. Linda Polon & Aileen Cantwell. 1983. pap. 12.95 (ISBN 0-673-16585-X). Scott F.

Whole-Earth Security: Geopolitics of Peace. Daniel Deudney. LC 83-50619. (Worldwatch Papers Ser.). 1983. 4.00 (ISBN 0-916468-54-2). Worldwatch Inst.

Whole Earth Shall Cry Glory. George F. MacLeod. 1987. 35.00x (ISBN 0-947988-04-1, Pub. by Wild Goose Pubns Scotland); pap. 21.00x (ISBN 0-947988-01-7, Pub. by Wild Goose Pubns Scotland). State Mutual Bk.

Whole Emergency Department Catalog. Michael S. Jastremski. (Illus.). 416p. 1985. pap. 38.95 (ISBN 0-7216-1175-3). Saunders.

Whole Enchilada: A Spicy Collection of Sylvia. Nicole Hollander. 208p. 1986. pap. 11.95 (ISBN 0-312-87757-9). St Martin.

Whole Europe Escape Manual: France, Holland, Belgium, with Luxembourg. Kerry Green & Charles Leocha. Ed. by W. A. Demers. LC 85-150460. (Escape Manual Ser.). Orig. Title: Escape Manual: France, Holland, Belgium, with Luxembourg. (Illus.). 160p. (Orig.). 1985. pap. 6.95 (ISBN 0-915009-02-1). World Leis Corp.

Whole Europe Escape Manual: Germany, Austria, Switzerland. James Kitfield & William Walker. Ed. by W. A. Demers. LC 85-150468. (Escape Manual Ser.). Orig. Title: Escape Manual: Germany, Austria, Switzerland. (Illus.). 160p. 1985. pap. 6.95 (ISBN 0-915009-01-3). World Leis Corp.

Whole Europe Escape Manual: U. K., Ireland. Kerry Green & Charles A. Leocha. Ed. by W A. Demers. LC 83-51834. (Escape Manual Ser.). Orig. Title: Escape Manual: U. K., Ireland. (Illus.). 160p. 1984. pap. 6.95 (ISBN 0-915009-00-5). World Leis Corp.

Whole Family: A Novel by Twelve Authors. Henry James et al. (Illus.). 350p. 1986. pap. 9.95 (ISBN 0-8044-6036-1). Ungar.

Whole Film Sourcebook. Ed. by Leonard Maltin. 464p. 1982. pap. 8.95 (ISBN 0-452-25361-6, Z5361, Plume). NAL.

Whole Film Sourcebook. Ed. by Leonard Maltin. LC 82-84314. 476p. 1983. 14.95x (ISBN 0-87663-416-1). Universe.

Whole Food Facts. Evelyn Roehl. (Illus.). 192p. 1988. pap. 10.95 (ISBN 0-89281-231-1, Healing Arts Pr). Inner Tradit.

Whole Foods Encyclopedia: A Shopper's Guide. Rebecca Wood. (Illus.). 256p. 1988. pap. 14.95 (ISBN 0-13-958554-0). Prentice Hall Pr.

Whole Foods Experience. Ellen S. Spivack. (Illus.). 248p. 1985. pap. 9.95 (ISBN 0-89496-042-3). Ross Bks.

Whole Foods for the Whole Family. Ed. by Roberta Johnson. LC 81-81988. (Illus.). 352p. 1981. pap. 12.50 spiral bound (ISBN 0-912500-09-3). La Leche.

Whole Foods for the Whole Family: La Leche League International Cookbook. Ed. by Roberta B. Johnson. LC 84-2128. (Illus.). 340p. 1984. pap. 10.95 (ISBN 0-452-25503-1, Plume). NAL.

Whole Foods for Whole People. Lucy Fuller. (Illus.). 92p. 1986. comb bdg. 9.95 (ISBN 0-912145-10-2). MMI Pr.

Whole Garden Catalog. Marliss Johnston. (Illus.). 1980. lib. bdg. 17.50 (ISBN 0-933474-13-X, Gabriel Bks); pap. 12.95 (ISBN 0-933474-17-2, Gabriel Bks). Media Mktg Group.

Whole Grain Baking. Diana S. Greene. LC 84-16971. (Cookbook Ser.). (Illus.). 200p. (Orig.). 1984. 20.95 (ISBN 0-89594-148-1); pap. 8.95 (ISBN 0-89594-147-3). Crossing Pr.

Whole-Grain Baking Sampler. Beatrice T. Hunter. LC 74-190457. 320p. 1972. 6.95 (ISBN 0-87983-013-1). Keats.

Whole-Grain Health Saver Cookbook. Miriam Polunin. LC 81-84465. (Illus.). 1982. pap. 2.95 (ISBN 0-87983-270-3). Keats.

Whole Health Catalog see Issues & Trends in Stealth.

Whole Health Manual. Patrick Holford. (Illus.). 144p. (Orig.). 1988. pap. 5.99 (ISBN 0-7225-1682-7, Pub. by Thorsons (England)). Sterling.

Whole Horse Catalog. Ed. by Steven D. Price et al. (Illus.). 288p. 1983. (Fireside); pap. 12.95 (ISBN 0-671-54196-X). S&S.

Whole House Catalog. Rev ed. Consumer Guide Editors. 384p. 1981. pap. 9.95 (ISBN 0-671-43640-6, Fireside). S&S.

Whole in the Head. Lewis Nuckols. 64p. 1987. 7.95 (ISBN 0-89962-641-6). Todd & Honeywell.

Whole Internal Universe: Imitation & the New Defense of Poetry in British Criticism, 1660-1830. John L. Mahoney. LC 85-80479. x, 166p. 1985. 25.00 (ISBN 0-8232-1122-3); pap. 10.00 (ISBN 0-8232-1123-1). Fordham.

Whole Internist Catalog: A Compendium of Clues to Diagnosis & Management. Arlan J. Gottlieb et al. LC 79-66034. (Illus.). 509p. 1980. pap. text ed. 30.95 (ISBN 0-7216-4179-2). Saunders.

Whole Journey: Shakespeare's Power of Development. C. L. Barber & Richard P. Wheeler. LC 85-20712. 425p. 1986. text ed. 37.50x (ISBN 0-520-05432-6). U of Cal Pr.

Whole Language Approach to Reading. Gordon S. Anderson. LC 84-13229. (Illus.). 642p. (Orig.). 1984. lib. bdg. 43.75 (ISBN 0-8191-4196-8); pap. text ed. 26.75 (ISBN 0-8191-4197-6). U Pr of Amer.

Whole Language Language. Kenneth Gaburo. (Illus.). 41p. Date not set. softcover 8.75 (ISBN 0-939044-21-8). Lingua Pr.

Whole Language: Theory in Use. Ed. by Judith M. Newman. LC 85-17636. x, 204p. (Orig.). 1985. pap. text ed. 15.00x (ISBN 0-435-08244-2). Heinemann Ed.

Whole Lay Ministry Catalog. Barbara Kuhn. (Orig.). 1979. pap. 8.95 (ISBN 0-8164-2187-0, HarpR). Har-Row.

Whole Life Diet: An Integrated Program of Nutrition & Exercise for a Lifestyle of Total Health. Thomas J. Bassler & Robert E. Burger. LC 79-19375. 204p. 1979. 9.95 (ISBN 0-87131-305-7). M Evans.

Whole Man & a Half Century, 1890-1940. Rockwell Hereford. (Illus.). 1985. 19.50 (ISBN 0-910286-97-3). Boxwood.

Whole Man: Body Mind is Sprit. Roscoe Van Nuys. LC 77-145467. 134p. 1971. 6.95 (ISBN 0-8022-2050-9). Philos Lib.

Whole Meal Book with Practical Recipes. Ettie Hornibook. 1974. lib. bdg. 69.95 (ISBN 0-685-51358-0). Revisionist Pr.

Whole Meal Salad Book. Frances S. Goulart. LC 84-73450. 208p. 1985. 12.95 (ISBN 0-917657-24-1). D I Fine.

Whole Meals: Wholefood Recipes for Cookery & Nutrition. Marcea Weber. (Illus.). 176p. (Orig.). 1988. pap. 9.95 (ISBN 0-89529-388-9). Avery Pub.

Whole Mna. Alexander Duddington. 1985. 10.00x (ISBN 0-317-62258-7, Guild of Pastoral Psych). State Mutual Bk.

Whole Mystery of Art: Pattern into Poetry in the Work of W. B. Yeats. Giorgio Melchiori. LC 72-12553. (Illus.). 1978. lib. bdg. 35.00x (ISBN 0-8371-6719-1, MEMA). Greenwood.

Whole, New & Vital Permanent Weight Loss Program. Neil L. Erickson, II & Virginia B. Noble. LC 84-72981. (Illus.). 117p. 1985. pap. 5.95 (ISBN 0-931979-20-X). Algonquin Enter.

Whole New Ball Game: An Interpretation of American Sports. Allen Guttmann. LC 87-26131. x, 233p. 1988. 24.95x (ISBN 0-8078-1786-4); pap. 10.95 (ISBN 0-8078-4220-6). U of NC Pr.

Whole Nine Yards. Dallin Malmgren. (YA) (gr. 7 up). 1987. pap. 2.95 (ISBN 0-440-99575-2, LFL). Dell.

Whole Numbers - Addition. (Programmed Math Ser.). (Illus.). 30p. (Orig.). (gr. 3-12). 1986. pap. text ed. 3.95 (ISBN 0-945915-02-0). Programmed Lrn.

Whole Numbers - Division. Allan D. Suter. (Programmed Math Ser.). (Illus.). 30p. (Orig.). (gr. 3-12). 1986. pap. text ed. 3.95 (ISBN 0-945915-05-5). Programmed Lrn.

Whole Numbers - Multiplication. Allan D. Suter. (Programmed Math Ser.). (Illus.). 30p. (Orig.). (gr. 3-12). 1986. pap. text ed. 3.95 (ISBN 0-945915-04-7). Programmed Lrn.

Whole Numbers - Subtraction. Allan D. Suter. (Programmed Math Ser.). (Illus.). 30p. (Orig.). (gr. 3-12). 1986. pap. text ed. 3.95 (ISBN 0-945915-03-9). Programmed Lrn.

Whole Nurse Catalog. Jane C. Jackson. (Illus.). 743p. 1980. pap. 23.95 (ISBN 0-7216-5065-1). Saunders.

Whole Ocean Catalog. Ed. by Craig Lockwood. 272p. 1987. pap. 7.95 (ISBN 0-89586-599-8). Price Stern.

Whore's Rhetorick. Ferrante Pallavicino. 1961. 10.95 (ISBN 0-8392-1132-5). Astor-Honor.

Whores Rhetorick, Calculated to the Meridian of London, & Conformed to the Rules of Art. LC 79-17643. 1979. 40.00x (ISBN 0-8201-1338-7). Schol Facsimiles.

Whoreson. Donald Goines. (Orig.). 1971. pap. 2.25 (ISBN 0-87067-046-8, BH046). Holloway.

Who's a Friend of the Water-Spurting Whale? Sanna A. Baker. (Illus.). (ps-2). 1987. 7.95 (ISBN 0-89191-587-7). Cook.

Who's a Pest? Crosby Bonsall. LC 62-13310. (Trophy I Can Read Bks.). (Illus.). 64p. (gr. k-3). 1986. pap. 3.50 (ISBN 0-06-444099-0, Trophy). HarpJ.

Who's a Pest? Crosby N. Bonsall. LC 62-13310. (Harper I Can Read Bks.). (Illus.). 64p. (gr. k-3). 1962. PLB 10.89 (ISBN 0-06-020621-7). HarpJ.

Who's a Silly Egg? Bob Reese. Ed. by Alton Jordan. (Buppet Ser.). (Illus.). (gr. k-3). 1981. PLB 5.95 (ISBN 0-89868-092-1, Read Res); pap. text ed. 1.95 (ISBN 0-89868-103-0). ARO Pub.

Who's Afraid? & Other Strange Stories. Philippa Pearce. LC 86-14299. 160p. (gr. 5-9). 1987. 10.25 (ISBN 0-688-06895-2). Greenwillow.

Who's Afraid of Big Blue? How Companies Are Challenging IBM-& Winning. Regis McKenna. 1989. 17.95 (ISBN 0-201-15574-5). Addison-Wesley.

Who's Afraid of Ernestine? Marjorie W. Sharmat. LC 85-14911. (Break-of-Day Beginning Reading Ser.). (Illus.). 48p. (gr. 1-4). 1985. lib. bdg. 7.99 (ISBN 0-698-30746-1, G&D). Putnam Pub Group.

Who's Afraid of Ghosts? Richard Carlisle. (Who's-Afraid Ser.). (Illus.). 24p. (gr. k up). 1987. 2.95 (ISBN 0-86679-045-4). Oak Tree Pubns.

Who's Afraid of Ghosts? Richard Carlisle. (Who's Afraid Ser.). (Illus.). 24p. (gr. 3-8). Date not set. Incl. cassette. pap. 7.49 (ISBN 0-86679-072-1). Oak Tree Pubns.

Who's Afraid of Haggerty House. Linda Gondosch. LC 86-24265. (gr. 4-6). 1987. 11.95 (ISBN 0-525-67198-6, 01160-350). Lodestar Bks.

Who's Afraid of Monsters? Richard Carlisle. (Who's Afraid Ser.). (Illus.). 24p. (gr. 3-8). Date not set. Incl. cassette. pap. 7.49 (ISBN 0-86679-073-X). Oak Tree Pubns.

Who's Afraid of Monsters? Richard Carlisle & David Anstey. (Who's-Afraid Ser.). 24p. (gr. k up). 1987. 2.95 (ISBN 0-86679-044-6). Oak Tree Pubns.

Who's Afraid of Sixth Grade? Janet A. Bloss. 128p. (gr. 5-8). 1985. 2.50 (ISBN 0-317-61033-3). Willowisp Pr.

Who's Afraid of Spiders? Richard Carlisle. (Who's-Afraid Ser.). (Illus.). 24p. (gr. k up). 1987. 2.95 (ISBN 0-86679-043-8). Oak Tree Pubns.

Who's Afraid of Spiders? Richard Carlisle. (Who's Afraid Ser.). (Illus.). 24p. (gr. 3-8). Date not set. Incl. cassette. pap. 7.49 (ISBN 0-86679-074-8). Oak Tree Pubns.

Who's Afraid of the Big Bad Worm? Joyce M. Burkes. (Funny Flippin's Ser.: Bk. 5). (Illus.). 8p. (ps-6). 1987. book & cassette 4.95 (ISBN 0-931218-54-3, 4605). Joybug.

Who's Afraid of the Dark? Crosby Bonsall. LC 79-2700. (Trophy Early I Can Read Bks.). (Illus.). 32p. (ps-2). 1985. pap. 3.50 (ISBN 0-06-444071-0, Trophy). HarpJ.

Who's Afraid of the Dark? Crosby N. Bonsall. LC 79-2700. (Early I Can Read Bk.). (Illus.). 32p. (ps-3). 1980. 8.70i (ISBN 0-06-020598-9); PLB 9.89 (ISBN 0-06-020599-7). HarpJ.

Who's Afraid of the Dark? Richard Carlisle. (Whos-Afraid Ser.). (Illus.). 24p. (gr. k up). 1987. 2.95 (ISBN 0-86679-042-X). Oak Tree Pubns.

Who's Afraid of the Dark? Richard Carlisle. (Who's Afraid Ser.). (Illus.). 24p. (gr. 3-8). Date not set. Incl. cassette. pap. 7.49 (ISBN 0-86679-075-6). Oak Tree Pubns.

Who's Afraid of the Dark? Morse Hamilton. 32p. (gr. 3-7). 1983. pap. 2.25 (ISBN 0-380-82883-9, 82883-9, Camelot). Avon.

Who's Afraid of the IRS. 2nd ed. Lynn Johnston. 320p. 1985. pap. 12.95 (ISBN 0-930073-03-7). Libertarian Rev Found.

Who's Afraid of Virginia Woolf? Edward Albee. LC 62-17691. 1962. pap. text ed. 5.95x (ISBN 0-689-70565-4). Atheneum.

Who's Afraid of Virginia Woolf? Edward Albee. 256p. 1983. pap. 3.95 (ISBN 0-451-14079-6, Sig). NAL.

Who's Afraid of Virginia Woolf? (Book Notes Ser.). 1985. pap. 2.50 (ISBN 0-8120-3549-6). Barron.

Who's Afraid of Virginia Woolf? Notes. Cynthia C. McGowan. (Orig.). 1979. pap. text ed. 3.25 (ISBN 0-8220-1383-5). Cliffs.

Who's Afraid? The Phobic's Handbook. rev. ed. Barbara Fried. (Illus.). 100p. 1985. Repr. of 1972 ed. 14.95 (ISBN 0-89876-104-2). Gardner Pr.

Who's Behind Our Farm Policy. Wesley McCune. LC 75-14699. 374p. 1975. Repr. of 1957 ed. lib. bdg. 35.00x (ISBN 0-8371-8238-7, MCWB). Greenwood.

Who's Boss? Training Your Pre-Schooler in Self-Management. Francis H. Wise. Ed. & intro. by Joyce M. Wise. LC 82-91074. (Illus.). 220p. (Orig.). 1982. pap. 5.95 (ISBN 0-915766-58-2). Wise Pub.

Who's Bugging You? Brendan Munnelly. 120p. (Orig.). 1987. pap. 9.95 (ISBN 0-85342-784-4, Pub. by Mercier Pr Ireland). Irish Bks Media.

Who's Cooking in Laguna Beach. Arline Isaacs. LC 77-74324. (Illus.). 347p. 1980. 15.95 (ISBN 0-930052-01-3). SunBox.

Who's Counting? Nancy Tafuri. LC 85-17702. (Illus.). 24p. (ps-1). 1986. 11.75 (ISBN 0-688-06130-3); PLB 11.88 (ISBN 0-688-06131-1). Greenwillow.

Who's Counting. (Little Remembrance Gift Editions). 5.95 (ISBN 0-87741-006-2). Makepeace Colony.

Who's Following Directions? Bev Armstrong. (Skill Builder Ser.). (Illus.). 32p. (gr. 4-7). 1979. wkbk. 3.95 (ISBN 0-88160-072-5, LW 805). Learning Wks.

Who's Gonna Cover 'Em Up? Chapel Hill Uncovered Since 1950. Roland Giduz. LC 85-72908. (Illus.). 224p. 1985. 14.95x (ISBN 0-9615867-0-2). Citizen Pub.

Who's Gonna Love Me? Don Kimball. 160p. (Orig.). (YA) (gr. 9-12). 1988. pap. 6.95 (ISBN 0-89505-769-7). Tabor Pub.

Who's Got a Secret. Susan Saunders. (Bad News Bunny Ser.: No. 4). (gr. 2-5). 1987. pap. 2.50 (ISBN 0-671-62716-3, Minstrel Bks). S&S.

Who's Haunting the Eighth Grade, No. 13. Kate Kenyon. (Junior High Ser.). 176p. (gr. 5-9). 1988. pap. 2.50 (ISBN 0-590-41787-8). Scholastic Inc.

Who's He When He's at Home: A James Joyce Directory. Shari Benstock & Bernard Benstock. LC 79-17947. 252p. 1980. 22.95 (ISBN 0-252-00756-5); pap. 9.95 1983 (ISBN 0-252-00757-3). U of Ill Pr.

Who's Hiding? Children's Television Workshop Staff. LC 84-81602. (Golden Touch & Feel Books). (Illus.). 14p. (ps-k). 1986. comb binding 5.95 (ISBN 0-307-12157-7, Pub. by Golden Bks). Western Pub.

Who's Hiding Here? Yoshi. LC 86-25455. (Illus.). 36p. (ps up). 1987. 14.95 (ISBN 0-88708-041-3). Picture Bk Studio.

Who's Hiring in Hospitality. Joe Witzman & Jack Block. (Illus.). 200p. (Orig.). 1987. pap. write for info. (ISBN 0-935423-02-8). Educ Pubns.

Who's Hiring Who. 3rd, rev. ed. Richard Lathrop. LC 75-44412. (Illus.). 272p. 1977. 9.95 (ISBN 0-913668-82-6); pap. 7.95 (ISBN 0-913668-55-9). Ten Speed Pr.

Who's Hu? Lensey Namioka. LC 80-20062. 124p. (gr. 4 up). 1981. 12.95 (ISBN 0-8149-0843-8). Vanguard.

Who's Important: Communication & Self Awareness Activities. Julie Strand & Juanita Boggs. (Illus.). 72p. (Orig.). 1983. pap. text ed. 5.50 (ISBN 0-910817-02-2). Collaborative Learn.

Who's in Charge. Harvey Jackins. 1965. pap. 0.50 (ISBN 0-911214-10-0). Rational Isl.

Who's in Charge? Philip Seib. LC 87-28810. 192p. 1988. 14.95 (ISBN 0-87833-583-8). Taylor Pub.

Who's in Charge Here - 1988. Gerald Gardner. 96p. 1988. pap. 3.95 (ISBN 0-553-34522-2). Bantam.

Who's In Charge Here, Beetle Bailey, No. 23. Mort Walker. 128p. 1982. pap. 1.75 (ISBN 0-448-16932-0). Ace Bks.

Who's in Charge of Mediation? 60p. 1982. pap. 5.00 (ISBN 0-686-47774-X). Amer Bar Assn.

Who's in Control? A Parent's Guide to Discipline. Susan Isaacs. 1986. pap. 6.95 (ISBN 0-399-51239-X, Perigee). Putnam Pub Group.

Who's in Control? Dr. Balter's Guide to Discipline Without Combat. Lawrence Balter & Anita Shreve. 1988. 16.95 (ISBN 0-671-62507-1, Poseidon Pr). PB.

Who's in Rabbit's House? Retold by Verna Aardema. LC 77-71514. (Illus.). 32p. (gr. k-3). 1977. 14.95 (ISBN 0-8037-9550-5); PLB 14.89 (ISBN 0-8037-9551-3). Dial Bks Young.

Who's in Rabbit's House? Retold by Verna Aardema. LC 77-71514. (Pied Piper Bk.). (Illus.). 32p. (ps-3). 1979. pap. 4.95 (ISBN 0-8037-9549-1, 0481-140). Dial Bks Young.

Who's in the Box, Bobby? Illus. by Pat Paris. (Illus.). 28p. (ps). 1987. 9.95 (ISBN 0-8431-1906-3). Price Stern.

Who's in the Mirror? Phoebe Erickson. (gr. 1-3). Repr. of 1965 ed. PLB 4.95 (ISBN 0-317-13837-5). P Erickson.

Who's Inside? Grahame Corbett. LC 82-70033. (Very First Bks.). (Illus.). 14p. (ps-k). 1982. bds. 3.50 (ISBN 0-8037-9726-5). Dial Bks Young.

Who's Listening? Bev Armstrong. (Skill Builders Ser.). (Illus.). 32p. (gr. 1-3). 1981. wkbk. 3.95 (ISBN 0-88160-079-2, LW 812). Learning Wks.

Who's Listening? Leonard E. Read. 208p. 1973. 3.00 (ISBN 0-910614-48-2). Foun Econ Ed.

Who's Listening - Handbook of the Listening Activity. Franklin H. Ernst, Jr. LC 73-84380. 1973. 15.95x (ISBN 0-916944-15-8). Addresso'set.

Who's Lost a Mitten. Elspeth C. Murphy. LC 87-70615. (Brenda Learns about God Ser.). 1987. 3.95 (ISBN 1-55513-578-1, Chariot Bks). Cook.

Who's Mining the Farm: A Report on the Energy Corporation's Ownership of Illinois Land & Coal Reserves & its Implications for Rural People & Their Communities. Janet M. Smith & David Ostendorf. 76p. (Orig.). 1978. 4.00 (ISBN 0-943724-02-3). Illinois South.

Who's My Friend? Alan T. Dale. (Rainbow Books (Bible Story Books for Children)). 16p. 1978. pap. 1.00 (ISBN 0-8192-1236-9). Morehouse.

Who's New at the Zoo. Jack Winder. Ed. by Dan Wasserman. (Ten Word Bks.). (Illus.). (gr. k-1). 1979. PLB 5.95 (ISBN 0-89868-074-3); pap. 1.95 (ISBN 0-89868-085-9). Aro Pub.

Who's New Wave in Music: An Illustrated Encyclopedia, 1976-1982. Ed. by David Bianco. LC 84-61228. (Rock & Roll Reference Ser.: No. 14). (Illus.). 430p. 1985. 29.50 (ISBN 0-87650-173-0). Pierian.

Who's News! World Personalities. Wendy Dunn & Janet Morey. LC 85-13753. (Illus.). 128p. (gr. 5 up). 1985. pap. 9.79 (ISBN 0-671-54436-5). Messner.

Who's Number One. Joe White. 144p. 1986. pap. 4.95 (ISBN 0-8423-8215-1). Tyndale.

Who's on First. William F. Buckley, Jr. 288p. 1981. pap. 3.95 (ISBN 0-380-52555-0). Avon.

Who's on Third? The Chicago White Sox Story. Richard Lindberg. (Illus.). 1983. pap. 3.95 (ISBN 0-89651-904-X). B L Pub.

Who's on Time? Donald J. Lehnus. LC 79-17330. 177p. 1980. lib. bdg. 17.50 (ISBN 0-379-20684-6). Oceana.

Who's Raising Whom? A Parent's Guide to Effective Child Discipline. Larry Waldman. LC 87-13759. (Illus.). 144p. (Orig.). 1987. pap. 6.95 (ISBN 0-943247-00-4). UCS Press.

Who's Reading Darci's Diary? Martha Tolles. 128p. (gr. 4-6). 1984. 10.95 (ISBN 0-525-67153-6, 01063-330). Lodestar Bks.

Who's Reading Darci's Diary? Martha Tolles. 128p. (gr. 4-6). 1985. pap. 2.50 (ISBN 0-590-41224-8, Apple Paperbacks). Scholastic Inc.

Who's Running America: The Conservative Years. 4th ed.,Thomas R. Dye. (Illus.). 304p. 1986. pap. text ed. 22.67 (ISBN 0-13-958505-2). P-H.

Who's Running Your Life: A Look at Young People's Rights. Jules Archer. (Illus.). (YA) (gr. 7 up). 1979. PLB 7.95 (ISBN 0-15-296058-9, HJ). HarBraceJ.

Who's Scared? Not Me! Judith St. George. 160p. (gr. 5 up). 1987. 13.95 (ISBN 0-399-21481-X). Putnam Pub Group.

Who's Scaring Alfie Atkins? Gunilla Bergstrom. Tr. by Joan Sandin from Swedish. (Illus.). 32p. (ps up). 1987. 6.95 (ISBN 91-29-54857-8, R & S Bks). FS&G.

Who's Searching for Whom: 1986. Victoria Wilson. 10p. (Orig.). 1986. pap. 2.00x (ISBN 0-940133-01-6). Kinseeker Pubns.

Who's Searching for Whom: 1987. Victoria Wilson. 1987. pap. text ed. 3.00 (ISBN 0-940133-05-9). Kinseeker Pubns.

Who's Searching for Whom, 1988. 65p. 1988. pap. 5.00 (ISBN 0-940133-17-2). Kinseeker Pubns.

Who's Sick. W. B. Park. LC 83-8429. (Illus.). 32p. (gr. k-3). 1983. PLB 9.95 (ISBN 0-395-33229-X). HM.

Who's Sick Today? Lynne Cherry. LC 87-22185. (Illus.). 24p. (ps-1). 1988. 11.95 (ISBN 0-525-44380-0, 01160-350). Dutton.

Who's Sorry Now? Connie Francis. (Illus.). 400p. 1985. pap. 3.95 (ISBN 0-312-90386-3). St Martin.

Who's Sorry Now? Connie Francis Tells Her Own Story. Connie Francis. LC 84-11759. (Illus.). 352p. 1984. 14.95 (ISBN 0-312-87088-4). St Martin.

Who's Squeaking? (Surprise Bks.). (Illus.). 22p. (ps-1). 1984. 5.95 (ISBN 0-8431-0646-8). Price Stern.

Who's Stealing Your Business: How to Identify & Prevent Business Espionage. William M. Johnson & Jack Maguire. 236p. 1988. 17.95 (ISBN 0-8144-5903-X). AMACOM.

Who's Teaching? Who's Learning? Active Learning in Elementary Schools. Dale Brubaker. LC 77-20894. 1979. pap. 12.95 (ISBN 0-673-16152-8). Scott F.

Who's That? S. Pynina. 16p. 1987. pap. 4.95 (ISBN 0-8285-3555-8, Pub. by Malysh Pubs USSR). Imported Pubns.

Who's That Girl with the Gun? Story of Annie Oakley. Robert Quackenbush. LC 87-11545. (Illus.). 40p. 11.95 (ISBN 0-13-957671-1). P-H.

Who's That in the Photo? Me? A Story of Posture & Poise. Raymond Moore & Dorothy Moore. (Schoolhouse Gang Adventures Ser.). (Illus.). 32p. (gr. 1-5). Date not set. cancelled. Nelson.

Who's That Knocking at My Door? Tilde Michels. (Illus.). 28p. (ps-3). 1986. 7.95 (ISBN 0-8120-5732-5). Barron.

Who's That Stepping on Plymouth Rock? Jean Fritz. LC 74-30593. (Illus.). 32p. (gr. 2-6). 1975. 8.95 (ISBN 0-698-20325-9, Coward). Putnam Pub Group.

Who's the Boss? Love, Authority & Parenting. Gerald E. Nelson & Richard W. Lewak. LC 85-8184. Orig. Title: One-Minute Scolding. (Illus.). 164p. 1985. pap. 6.95 (ISBN 0-87773-342-2, 74223-0). Shambhala Pubns.

Who's the Boss? Love, Authority, & Parenting. Gerald E. Nelson & Richard W. Lewak. pap. 6.95 (ISBN 0-394-74223-0). Shambhala Pubns.

Who's the Funny-Looking Kid with the Big Nose? Charles M. Schulz. 1976. pap. 5.70 (ISBN 0-03-017491-0). H Holt & Co.

Who's the Junior High Hunk? Kate Kenyon. (Junior High Ser.: No. 9). 160p. (gr. 5-9). 1988. pap. 2.50 (ISBN 0-590-41388-0). Scholastic Inc.

Who's the Matter with Me? Alice T. Steadman. (Illus.). 1977. pap. 6.95 (ISBN 0-87516-225-8). DeVorss.

Who's the New Girl? Emily Chase. (Girls of Canby Hall Ser.: No. 12). 176p. (Orig.). (YA) (gr. 7 up). 1985. pap. 2.25 (ISBN 0-590-40381-8). Scholastic Inc.

Who's the Next President? Ken Lawless. 96p. 1988. pap. 4.95 (ISBN 0-399-51411-2, Preigee Bks). Putnam Pub Group.

Who's the Savage? Ed. by David R. Wrone & Russell S. Nelson. LC 81-17167. 186p. (Orig.). 1982. lib. bdg. 18.50 (ISBN 0-89874-452-0). Krieger.

Who's Uptown: Harlem 'Eighty-Seven. Ed. by Glenderlyn Johnson. (Illus.). 56p. (Orig.). 1988. special signed, limited ed. 50.00x (ISBN 0-87104-407-2); pap. 12.50 (ISBN 0-87104-406-4). NY Pub Lib.

Who's Wearing My Baseball Cap? Donald Smith. LC 86-23957. (Peep Through Board Bks.). (Illus.). 12p. (ps-k). 1987. 3.95 (ISBN 0-8037-0396-1). Dial Bks Young.

Who's Wearing My Bow Tie? Donald Smith. (Peep Through Board Bks.). (Illus.). 12p. (ps-k). 1987. 3.95 (ISBN 0-8037-0395-3). Dial Bks Young.

Who's Wearing My Sneakers? Donald Smith. LC 86-23954. (Peep Through Board Bks.). (Illus.). 12p. (ps-k). 1987. 3.95 (ISBN 0-8037-0398-8). Dial Bks Young.

Who's Wearing My Sunglasses? Donald Smith. LC 86-23959. (Peep Through Board Bks.). 12p. (ps-k). 1987. 3.95 (ISBN 0-8037-0399-6). Dial Bks Young.

Who's What & Where: A Directory & Reference Book on America's Minority Journalists. Ben Johnson & Mary Bullard-Johnson. (Illus.). 600p. (Orig.). 1988. pap. text ed. 34.95 (ISBN 0-9614418-2-8). Who's What Where.

Who's What & Where: A Directory of America's Black Journalists. Ben Johnson & Mary Bullard-Johnson. (Illus.). 480p. (Orig.). 1985. pap. 24.95x (ISBN 0-9614418-0-1). Who's What Where.

Who's Who. Loretta Minn. (Illus.). 48p. (gr. 3-7). 1983. wkbk. 5.95 (ISBN 0-86653-102-5, GA 472). Good Apple.

Who's Who among American High School Students, 1985-1986, 10 vols. 20th ed. LC 68-43796. 1986. 10-vol. set 28.50 ea. (ISBN 0-930315-12-X). Vol. 1 (ISBN 0-930315-13-8). Vol. 2 (ISBN 0-930315-14-6). Vol. 3 (ISBN 0-930315-15-4). Vol. 4 (ISBN 0-930315-16-2). Vol. 5 (ISBN 0-930315-17-0). Vol. 6 (ISBN 0-930315-18-9). Vol. 7 (ISBN 0-930315-19-7). Vol.8,9 & 10 (ISBN 0-930315-20-0). Educ Comm.

Who's Who among American High School Students, 1986-87, 12 vols. 21st ed. Incl. Vol. 1 (ISBN 0-930315-28-6); Vol. 2 (ISBN 0-930315-29-4); Vol. 3 (ISBN 0-930315-30-8); Vol. 4 (ISBN 0-930315-31-6); Vol. 5 (ISBN 0-930315-32-4); Vol. 6 (ISBN 0-930315-33-2); Vol. 7 (ISBN 0-930315-34-0); Vol. 8 (ISBN 0-930315-35-9); Vol. 9 (ISBN 0-930315-36-7); Vol. 10 (ISBN 0-930243-37-5); Vol. 11 (ISBN 0-930315-41-3); Vol. 12 (ISBN 0-930315-42-1). LC 68-43796. 1987. Set. write for info. (ISBN 0-930315-27-8); 28.50 ea. Educ Comm.

Who's Who among American High School Students, 1987-88, Vols. 1-6. 22nd annual ed. LC 68-43796. 1988. Set of 12 Volumes. 30.00 (ISBN 0-930315-43-X). Vol. 1 (ISBN 0-930315-44-8). Vol. 2 (ISBN 0-930315-45-6). Vol. 3 (ISBN 0-930315-46-4). Vol. 4 (ISBN 0-930315-47-2). Vol. 5 (ISBN 0-930315-48-0). Vol. 6 (ISBN 0-930315-49-9). Educ Comm.

Who's Who among American High School Students, 1987-88, Vols. 7-12. 22nd annual ed. LC 68-43796. 1988. Set of 12 Volumes. 30.00. Vol. 7 (ISBN 0-930315-50-2). Vol. 8 (ISBN 0-930315-51-0). Vol. 9 (ISBN 0-930315-52-9). Vol. 10 (ISBN 0-930315-53-7). Vol. 11 (ISBN 0-930315-54-5). Vol. 12 (ISBN 0-930315-55-3). Educ Comm.

Who's Who among American Law Students. 4th. ed. Ed. by Joanne R. Desotelle. LC 81-645742. 364p. 1984. 35.00 (ISBN 0-317-19181-0). Summa Pub Bur.

Who's Who among American Law Students. 5th ed. Ed. by Joanne R. Desotelle. 366p. 1985. 35.00 (ISBN 0-317-52484-4). Summa Pub Bur.

Who's Who among American Law Students. 6th ed. Ed. by Joanne R. Desotelle. 350p. 1986. 35.00 (ISBN 0-317-52485-2). Summa Pub Bur.

Who's Who among American Law Students, 1983. Ed. by Joanne R. Desotelle. LC 81-645742. 160p. 1982. 30.00. Summa Pub Bur.

Who's Who among American Law Students, 1984. 3rd ed. Ed. by Joanne R. Desotelle. LC 81-645742. 321p. 1983. 35.00. Summa Pub Bur.

Who's Who among Bible Women. Peggy Musgrove. LC 81-81126. (Radiant Life Ser.). 128p. (Orig.). 1981. 2.50 (ISBN 0-88243-883-2, 02-0883); teacher's guide 3.95 (ISBN 0-88243-193-5, 32-0193). Gospel Pub.

Who's Who among Black Americans. 1st ed. Ed. by William C. Matney. LC 75-42841. 900p. 1976. 45.00 (ISBN 0-915130-05-X). Who's Who Black Am.

Who's Who among Black Americans. 2nd ed. Ed. by William C. Matney. LC 76-643293. 1978. 49.95 (ISBN 0-915130-16-5). Who's Who Black Am.

Who's Who among Black Americans, 1980-1981. 3rd ed. Ed. by William C. Matney. LC 76-643293. 1981. 59.95 (ISBN 0-915130-33-5). Who's Who Black Am.

Who's Who among Black Americans, 1985. 4th ed. LC 76-643293. 1985. 90.00 (ISBN 0-915130-96-3). Who's Who Black Am.

Who's Who among Black Americans, 1988. 5th, rev. ed. LC 76-643293. 1987. 99.50 (ISBN 0-930315-26-X). Educ Comm.

Who's Who among Free Will Baptists. Ed. by H. D. Harrison. 1978. 18.95 (ISBN 0-89265-052-4). Randall Hse.

Who's Who among Human Service Professionals: 1986-1987. Ed. by Jeffrey Franz. 656p. 1986. 69.95 (ISBN 0-940863-01-4). Soc Nursing Prof.

Who's Who among Living Authors of Older Nations. A. Lawrence. 59.95 (ISBN 0-8490-1297-X). Gordon Pr.

Who's Who among Living Authors of Older Nations. LC 28-28492. 488p. 1966. Repr. of 1931 ed. 47.00x (ISBN 0-8103-3022-9). Gale.

Who's Who among the Colored Baptists of the United States. Samuel W. Bacote. Ed. by Edwin S. Gaustad. LC 79-52588. (Baptist Tradition Ser.). (Illus.). 1980. Repr. of 1913 ed. lib. bdg. 28.50x (ISBN 0-405-12455-4). Ayer Co Pubs.

Who's Who & Why of Successful Florida Women. Beth Brennan. (Premier Edition Ser.). 512p. 1985. 85.00 (ISBN 0-930507-00-2). Currier-Davis.

Who's Who at the Frankfurt Book Fair 1988: An International Publishers' Guide. Compiled by Karl H. Strasser. 1988. 36.00 (ISBN 3-598-21888-5). K G Saur.

Who's Who at the Zoo! Janet Palazzo-Craig. LC 85-14123. (Illus.). 48p. (Orig.). (gr. 1-3). 1986. PLB 9.49 (ISBN 0-8167-0658-1); pap. text ed. 1.95 (ISBN 0-8167-0659-X). Troll Assocs.

Who's Who European Communities & Other European Organizations: 1986. 3rd ed. 1987. pap. 65.00 (ISBN 2-8029-0060-9, ED19, ED). UNIPUB.

Who's Who in African Heritage Book Publishing. Ed. by E. Curtis Alexander. LC 87-82649. 150p. 1988. pap. 11.95 (ISBN 0-938818-12-0). ECA Assoc.

Who's Who in African Heritage Book Publishing. Ed. by E. Curtis Alexander. LC 87-82649. 150p. 1988. 21.95 (ISBN 0-938818-13-9). ECA Assoc.

Who's Who in AI - Update 'Eighty-Eight. Ed. by Di Schwartz. 200p. 1988. 87.95 (ISBN 0-937287-04-0). WWAI.

Who's Who in AI-A Guide to People, Products, Companies, Resources, Schools & Jobs. Ed. by Alan Kernoff. 330p. (Orig.). 1986. lib. bdg. 125.00 (ISBN 0-937287-01-6); pap. 95.00 (ISBN 0-937287-00-8). WWAI.

Who's Who in Alaskan Politics: A Biographical Dictionary of Alaskan Political Personalities, 1884-1974. Compiled by Evangeline Atwood. LC 77-76025. 1977. 10.00 (ISBN 0-8323-0287-2). Binford-Metropolitan.

Who's Who in America Classroom Project Book, 1983: A Useful New Addition to Classroom Studies for Teachers & Students. write for info. classroom project bk., 33 pgs. (ISBN 0-8379-6101-7); write for info. tchr's ed., 63 pgs. (ISBN 0-8379-6102-5); of 10 project books & tchrs' ed. 10.00 set (ISBN 0-317-03694-7, 030338). Marquis.

Who's Who in America Geographic: Professional Index 1986-1987. rev. ed. 520p. 1986. 72.00x (ISBN 0-8379-1504-X). Marquis.

Who's Who in America: Professional Geographic Index. 43rd ed. 520p. 1984. 72.00x (ISBN 0-8379-1503-1). Marquis.

Who's Who in America, 1984-1985, 2 vols. 43rd ed. LC 84-16934. 1984. 250.00 (ISBN 0-8379-0143-X, 030293). Marquis.

Who's Who in America: 1986-1987. 44th, rev. ed. 3900p. 1986. 250.00 (ISBN 0-8379-0144-8). Marquis.

Who's Who in American Art, 1989-90. 18th ed. Ed. by Bowker, R. R., Staff. 1989. lib. bdg. 129.95 (ISBN 0-8352-2477-5). Bowker.

Who's Who in American Chiropractic: Comprehensive Referral Directory. Ed. by Heritage Publishers Services Staff. 500p. 1988. 59.95 (ISBN 0-939379-07-4). Herit Pubs Servs.

Who's Who in American Film Now. rev. ed. James Monaco. (Illus.). 600p. 1987. 39.95 (ISBN 0-918432-63-4). NY Zoetrope.

Who's Who in American Film Now. rev. ed. James Moraeo. (Orig.). 1987. pap. 19.95 (ISBN 0-918432-62-6). NY Zoetrope.

Who's Who in American Law. 4th, rev. ed. 880p. 1985. 165.00x (ISBN 0-8379-3504-0, 030396). Marquis.

Who's Who in American Law 1987-88. rev., 5th ed. 1987. 165.00x (ISBN 0-8379-3505-9, 030460). Marquis.

Who's Who in American Music: Classical. 2nd ed. Ed. by Bowker, R. R., Staff. 1200p. 1985. 124.95 (ISBN 0-8352-2074-5). Bowker.

Who's Who in American Nursing, 1984. Ed. by Jeffrey Franz. 392p. 1984. 59.95 (ISBN 0-940863-00-6). Soc Nursing Prof.

Who's Who in American Nursing, 1986-1987. Ed. by Jeffrey Franz. 750p. 1987. 69.95 (ISBN 0-940863-03-0). Soc Nursing Prof.

Who's Who in American Nursing 1988-1989. 3rd ed. Ed. by Jeffrey Franz. 656p. 1989. 69.95 (ISBN 0-940863-14-6); leather bdg. 125.00 (ISBN 0-940863-16-2). Soc Nursing Prof.

Who's Who in American Politics, 1987-1988. 11th ed. Ed. by Bowker, R. R., Staff. 1811p. 1987. 149.95 (ISBN 0-8352-2219-5). Bowker.

Who's Who in America's Restaurants: New York & Eastern States Limited, 1983 - 1984. Sheldon Landwehr & Associates. Ed. by Sheldon Landwehr. LC 82-645944. (Illus.). 272p. 1983. 129.50 (ISBN 0-910297-01-0); softcover 14.95 (ISBN 0-910297-02-9). Whos Who Rest.

Who's Who in America's Restaurants 1985. Sheldon Landwehr & Associates. Ed. by Sheldon Landwehr. LC 82-645944. (Illus.). 435p. 1984. 49.95 (ISBN 0-910297-03-7); pap. 14.95 (ISBN 0-910297-04-5). Whos Who Rest.

Who's Who in America's Restaurants 1986-1987. Sheldon Landwehr & Associates. LC 82-645944. (Illus.). 401p. 1985. 49.95 (ISBN 0-910297-05-3); pap. 14.95 (ISBN 0-910297-06-1). Whos Who Rest.

Who's Who in Antiques. Ed. by Cheryl Gorder. (Illus.). 1986. pap. 14.95 (ISBN 0-933025-02-5). Blue Bird Pub.

Who's Who in Art. 22nd ed. 600p. 1986. 90.00x (ISBN 0-8103-0533-X, Pub. by Art Trade Pr). Gale.

Who's Who in Art. 23rd ed. 600p. 1988. 90.00 (ISBN 0-8103-2744-9). Gale.

Who's Who in Australia, 1985. 25th ed. 1985. 95.00 (ISBN 0-8002-3977-6). Intl Pubns Serv.

Who's Who in Austria. 1983. 240.00x (ISBN 3-921-22044-0). Adlers Foreign Bks.

Who's Who in Aviation & Aerospace. 1415p. 1983. 95.00 (ISBN 0-317-02406-X). Grey Hse Pub.

Who's Who in Banking in Europe, 1984-85. 3rd ed. 1984. 225.00 (ISBN 0-8002-3832-X). Intl Pubns Serv.

Who's Who in Biblical Studies & Archaeology, 1986-1987. LC 86-72710. 272p. 1986. 23.95 (ISBN 0-9613089-3-1). Biblical Arch Soc.

Who's Who in Bloomsbury. Alan Palmer & Victoria Palmer. LC 87-28467. 225p. 1988. 29.95 (ISBN 0-312-01630-1). St Martin.

Who's Who in Boswell. Louis L. Smith-Dampier. 1935. lib. bdg. 52.50 (ISBN 0-8414-1594-3). Folcroft.

Who's Who in Burns. John D. Ross. LC 75-144480. Repr. of 1927 ed. 18.00 (ISBN 0-404-08547-4). AMS Pr.

Who's Who in California. 16th ed. Sarah Vitale. LC 56-1715. 500p. text ed. 135.00 (ISBN 0-9603166-5-5). Who's Who Hist Soc.

Who's Who in California. 17th ed. Sarah Vitale. 545p. 1987. text ed. 135.00 (ISBN 0-9603166-6-3). Who's Who Hist Soc.

Who's Who in California. 14th ed. Ed. by Sarah Vitale. LC 56-1715. 600p. 1983. text ed. 87.50x (ISBN 0-9603166-3-9). Who's Who Hist Soc.

Who's Who in California. 13th ed. Ed. by Sarah Vitale. LC 56-1715. 606p. 1981. text ed. 74.50x (ISBN 0-9603166-2-0). Who's Who Hist Soc.

Who's Who in California. 12th ed. Ed. by Sarah A. Vitale. LC 56-1715. 1979. text ed. 50.00x (ISBN 0-9603166-0-4). Who's Who Hist Soc.

Who's Who in Canvas & Fabrics. 40.00 (ISBN 0-318-01511-0, 12040). Indus Fabrics.

Who's Who in China. 6th ed. LC 78-38093. Repr. of 1950 ed. 25.00 (ISBN 0-404-56968-4). AMS Pr.

Who's Who in Chiropractic International. 2nd ed. Fern L. Dzaman. Ed. by Sidney Scheiner et al. LC 80-51366. 1980. 55.00 (ISBN 0-918336-02-3). Chiropractic.

Who's Who in Chiropractic, International 1976-78. Ed. by Fern L. Dzaman et al. LC 77-79754. (Illus.). 1977. 49.50 (ISBN 0-918336-01-5). Chiropractic.

Who's Who in Computer Education & Research: U. S. Edition. U. S. ed. Ed. by T. C. Hsiao. LC 74-18169. 330p. 1975. 35.00x (ISBN 0-912291-01-X). Sci & Tech Pr.

Who's Who in Consulting: A Reference Guide to Professional Personnel Engaged in Consultation for Business, Industry & Government. 2nd ed. Ed. by Paul Wasserman & Janice McLean. LC 73-16373. 216p. 1973. 180.00x (ISBN 0-8103-0360-4). Gale.

Who's Who in Consumer Electronics: North American Edition. Ed. by Martin Porter. 255p. (Orig.). 1985. pap. 100.00 (ISBN 0-935305-00-9). Who's Who Electro.

Who's Who in D. H. Lawrence. Graham Holderness. LC 75-34782. (Who's Who in Literature Ser.). 128p. 1976. 8.95 (ISBN 0-8008-8272-5). Taplinger.

Who's Who in Dickens. Thomas A. Fyfe. 352p. Repr. of 1913 ed. lib. bdg. 45.50 (ISBN 0-8495-1713-3). Arden Lib.

Who's Who in Dickens. Thomas A. Fyfe. LC 72-190886. Repr. of 1913 ed. lib. bdg. 45.50 (ISBN 0-8414-0820-3). Folcroft.

Who's Who in Dickens: A Complete Dickens Repertory in Dickens Own Words. T. Fyfe. LC 75-152551. (Studies in Dickens, No. 52). 1971. Repr. of 1913 ed. lib. bdg. 75.00x (ISBN 0-8383-1236-5). Haskell.

Who's Who in Dickens: A Complete Dickens Repertory in Dickens' Own Words. Compiled by Thomas A. Fyfe. 355p. 1982. Repr. of 1912 ed. lib. bdg. 49.50 (ISBN 0-89987-278-6). Darby Bks.

Who's Who in Direct Marketing Creative Services--1988: Writers--Designers--Consultants Direct Mail, Space, Telemarketing, Television, Radio. Ed. by Denison Hatch. 400p. (Orig.). 1987. pap. 85.00 (ISBN 0-9619436-0-2). Whos Mailing What.

Who's Who in Economics: A Biographical Dictionary of Major Economists, 1700-1984. 2nd ed. Mark Blaug. 800p. 1986. text ed. 115.00x (ISBN 0-262-02256-7). MIT Pr.

Who's Who in Electronics. 1100p. 1986. 100.00 (ISBN 0-317-55730-0). B Klein Pubns.

Who's Who in Electronics 1988. Ed. by Kathi Graeser. 1988. 129.50 (ISBN 1-55600-051-0). Harris Pub.

Who's Who in Engine & Component Markets 1981 - Companies. 400p. 1981. lib. bdg. 89.95x (ISBN 0-906237-19-X, Pub. by Martin Pub England). Marlin.

Who's Who in Engineering. 7th ed. Gordon Davis. 1988. 200.00 (ISBN 0-87615-015-6). AAES.

Who's Who in Espionage. Christopher Dobson & Ronald Payne. 240p. 1985. 15.95 (ISBN 0-312-87432-4). St Martin.

Who's Who in Exposition Management. 294p. 1988. write for info. Nat Assn Expo Mgrs.

Who's Who in Fashion. 2nd. ed. Ann Stegemeyer. (Illus.). 1988. text ed. 22.50 (ISBN 0-87005-574-7). Fairchild.

Who's Who in Fashion (Europe, 3 Vols. Ed. by Karl Strute & Dr. Theodor Doelken. Incl. Vol. 1. Fashion. UNIPUB; Vol. 2. Beauty. UNIPUB; Vol. 3. Jewelry. UNIPUB. (International Red Ser.). 1763p. 1982. Set 160.00 (ISBN 3-921220-32-7, WWIR103, WWIR). UNIPUB.

Who's Who in Federal Government Prime Contractors. 1986. 65.00 (ISBN 0-317-55733-5). B Klein Pubns.

Who's Who in Finance & Industry: 1985-1986. 24th ed. LC 70-616550. 1985. 165.00 (ISBN 0-8379-0324-6, 30358). Marquis.

Who's Who in Finance & Industry 1987-1988. rev., 25th ed. 1987. 165.00x (ISBN 0-8379-0325-4, 030454). Marquis.

Who's Who in Foreign Trade. 150p. 1987. pap. 15.00 (ISBN 0-318-14134-5). Foreign Trade.

Who's Who in Frontier Science & Technology. 1st. ed. LC 82-82015. 846p. 1984. 99.50 (ISBN 0-8379-5701-X, 030290). Marquis.

Who's Who in Frontier Science & Technology. 2nd, rev. ed. 800p. 1985. 99.50x (ISBN 0-8379-5702-8). Marquis.

Who's Who in Genealogy. Ed. by Mary K. Meyer & P. William Filby. LC 81-69203. 1982. 70.00x (ISBN 0-8103-1630-7). Gale.

Who's Who in George Eliot. Phyllis Hartnoll. LC 76-39621. (Who's Who in Literature Ser.). 1977. 9.50 (ISBN 0-8008-8273-3). Taplinger.

Who's Who in Germany, 2 vols. 1983. deluxe ed. 395.00x set (ISBN 3-921220-47-5). Adlers Foreign Bks.

Who's Who in Gerontology. 175p. 1986. pap. 5.00 (ISBN 0-318-20326-X). Gerontological Soc.

Who's Who in Greek & Roman Mythology. David Kravitz. 256p. 1977. (C N Potter Bks); pap. 5.95 (ISBN 0-517-52747-2). Crown.

Who's Who in Health Care. 2nd ed. Ed. by Elliot A. Sainer. LC 77-79993. 612p. 1982. text ed. 79.95 (ISBN 0-89443-092-0). Aspen Pub.

Who's Who in Hearing Aids. California ed. Steven J. Mihaly, Jr. LC 85-51278. (Illus.). 1985. text ed. 24.95 (ISBN 0-934725-00-4). Vanguard Inst.

Who's Who in Henry James. Glenda Leeming. LC 75-34783. (Who's Who in Literature Ser.). 224p. 1976. 7.95 (ISBN 0-8008-8268-7). Taplinger.

Who's Who in Horror & Fantasy Fiction. Mike Ashley. LC 77-4608. 1978. pap. 4.95 (ISBN 0-8008-8278-4). Taplinger.

Who's Who in Intellectual Property. Pref. by Eric D. Offner & Gary Offner. (Annual Ser.). 400p. 1988. text ed. 199.00 (ISBN 0-929432-00-2). WWIP NY.

Who's Who in International Banking: 1986/87. 3rd ed. 1986. 150.00 (ISBN 0-8002-4110-X). Intl Pubns Serv.

Who's Who in Israel, 1985-86. 20th ed. 1985. 118.00X (ISBN 0-8002-3946-6). Intl Pubns Serv.

Who's Who in Isshinryu Karate. Harold Long & Allen Wheeler. 110p. (Orig.). 1981. pap. 3.95 (ISBN 0-89826-007-8). Natl Paperback.

Who's Who in Italy. Ed. & pref. by John C. Dove. (Sutter's International Red Ser.). 1671p. 1986. text ed. 120.00 (ISBN 88-85246-02-8, WWIR112). Europa.

Who's Who in Jane Austen & the Brontes. Glenda Leeming. LC 73-17674. (Who's Who in Literature Ser.). 192p. 1974. 6.95 (ISBN 0-8008-8267-9). Taplinger.

Who's Who in Japan. Ed. by Japan Travel Bureau. (JTB's Illustrated Japin in Your Pocket Ser.: No. 9). (Illus.). 192p. 1987. pap. 9.95 (ISBN 4-53300-79-88, Japan Trvl Bur). Bks Nippan.

Who's Who in Japan, 1987-88. 1083p. 1988. 210.00x (ISBN 962-7191-01-9, Pub. by Inter Culture Inst). Gale.

Who's Who in Karate: 1982-83. Ed. by Dale Brooks. (Illus.). 112p. 1983. pap. 17.95 (ISBN 0-931981-00-X). Am Martial Arts Pub.

Who's Who in Labor. LC 75-7962. 1976. 65.00 (ISBN 0-405-06651-1). Ayer Co Pubs.

Who's Who in Lebanon, 1986-87. 9th ed. Charles Gedeon. 667p. 1986. lib. bdg. 95.00 (ISBN 2-903188-04-1, Pub. by Publitec Publications & the Middle East Commercial Information Center). ABC-Clio.

Who's Who in Library & Information Services. Joel Lee. LC 81-20480. xiv, 559p. 1982. 150.00x (ISBN 0-8389-0351-7). ALA.

Who's Who in Library Service: A Biographical Directory of Professional Librarians in the United States & Canada. 4th ed. Ed. by Lee Ash et al. 776p. 1966. 59.50 (ISBN 0-208-00598-6). Shoe String.

Who's Who in Mail Order: A Directory of Longtime & Reputable Publishers. Ed. by S. Diane Bogus. 50p. (Orig.). Date not set. pap. 7.00 (ISBN 0-934172-18-8). WIM Pubns.

Who's Who in Malaysia & Singapore, 1983-1984: Singapore, Vol. II. 263p. 1983. text ed. 49.50x (ISBN 0-317-13133-8, Pub. by Exec Pubns). Gower Pub Co.

Who's Who in Malaysia & Singapore, 1983. 15th ed. 144.00 (ISBN 0-317-12279-7). Intl Pubns Serv.

Who's Who in Marketing in Great Britain. Ed. by Gower Publications Staff. 500p. 1974. 40.00 (ISBN 0-8464-0972-0). Beekman Pubs.

Who's Who in Medicine, 2 Vols.set. 5th ed. Ed. by Karl Strute & Theodor Dr. Doelken. (International Red Ser.). 1981. pap. 120.00 set (ISBN 3-921220-40-8, WWIR101, WWIR). UNIPUB.

Who's Who in Medicine: Austria, Germany, Switzerland, 2 vols. 5th ed. LC 78-641400. 1505p. 1983. cancelled (WWIR 101). Intl Pubns Serv.

Who's Who in MetroOrlando. George J. Mauer, pseud. 96p. (Orig.). 1986. pap. 3.95 (ISBN 0-9616803-0-X). G J Mauer.

Who's Who in Mexico Today. Roderic A. Camp. (Special Studies on Latin America & the Caribbean). 250p. 1988. 45.00 (ISBN 0-8133-7397-2). Westview.

Who's Who in Microcomputing. Datapro Research Corporation Staff. 1983. pap. text ed. 42.95 (ISBN 0-07-015405-8, Pub. by Datapro). McGraw.

Who's Who in Modern Japanese Prints. Frances Blakemore. LC 74-28174. (Illus.). 264p. 1975. 15.00 (ISBN 0-8348-0101-9). Weatherhill.

Who's Who in Mozart's Operas: From Don Alfonso to Zerlina. Joachim Kaiser. Tr. by Charles Kessler. (Illus.). 304p. 1987. 19.95 (ISBN 0-02-873380-0). Schirmer Bks.

Who's Who in Nobel Prize Winners. Ed. by Bernard S. Schlessinger et al. LC 86-42784. 208p. 1986. 35.00 (ISBN 0-89774-193-5). Oryx Pr.

Who's Who in Ocean & Freshwater Science. Ed. by Allen Varley. LC 79-301729. pap. 84.00 (ISBN 0-317-27839-8, 2025251). Bks Demand UMI.

Who's Who In Oceania: 1980-1981. Compiled by Robert D. Craig & Russell T. Clement. 1981. 12.95 (ISBN 0-939154-13-7); pap. 7.95 (ISBN 0-939154-14-5). Inst Polynesian.

Who's Who in Opera: An International Biographical Directory of Singers, Conductors, Directors, Designers & Administers. Maria F. Rich. 1976. 71.50 (ISBN 0-405-06652-X, 19119). Ayer Co Pubs.

Who's Who in Oz. Jack Snow. 1988. 15.95. P Bedrick Bks.

Who's Who in Pennsylvania Management & Related Professions. Institute for Effective Management. 230p. 36.75 (ISBN 0-914804-01-4). Inst Effect Mgmt.

Who's Who in Philosophy, Vol. 1. Ed. by Dagobert D. Runes. 1969. Repr. of 1942 ed. lib. bdg. 35.00 (ISBN 0-8371-2095-0, WWIP). Greenwood.

Who's Who in Polish America: A Biographical Directory of Polish-American Leaders & Distinguished Poles Resident in the Americas. Ed. by Francis Bolek. LC 75-129390. (American Immigration Collection, Ser. 2). 1970. Repr. of 1943 ed. 31.50 (ISBN 0-405-00545-8). Ayer Co Pubs.

Who's Who in Popular Music in Britain. Sheila Tracy. (Illus.). 128p. 1984. 16.95 (ISBN 0-437-17601-0, Pub. by Worlds Work). David & Charles.

Who's Who in Prepaid Legal Services: 1987 Membership Directory. 83p. 1986. 15.00 (ISBN 0-317-55970-2). Am Prepaid.

Who's Who in Professional Speaking. 320p. 1987. 25.00 (ISBN 0-318-15873-6). Natl Speakers.

Who's Who in Public Relations. 5th ed. LC 62-4348. 1976. 35.00 (ISBN 0-914016-25-3). P R Pub Co.

Who's Who in Real Estate. 903p. 1983. 75.00 (ISBN 0-939300-14-1). Grey Hse Pub.

Who's Who in Rock Music. rev. ed. William York. LC 81-21368. 624p. 1982. pap. 29.95 (ISBN 0-684-17342-5, ScribT); encore ed. 4.50 (ISBN 0-684-17343-3). Scribner.

Who's Who in Rodeo. Willard H. Porter. (Illus.). 224p. (Orig.). 1982. pap. 15.95 (ISBN 0-932154-12-3). Natl Cowboy Hall of fame.

Who's Who in Romanian America. Serban Andronescu. LC 76-46879. 1976. 35.00 (ISBN 0-917944-01-1). Am Inst Writing Res.

Who's Who in Saudi Arabia. 3rd ed. 350p. 1984. 65.00x (ISBN 0-686-78116-3, Pub. by Europa England). Gale.

Who's Who in Science Fiction. Brian Ash. LC 76-11667. 1978. pap. 4.95 (ISBN 0-8008-8279-2). Taplinger.

Who's Who in Science in Europe, 3 vols. 4th ed. 2500p. 1984. 500.00 (ISBN 0-582-90109-X). Intl Pubns Serv.

Who's Who in Science in Europe, 3 vols. 5th ed. 1300p. 1987. Set. 695.00x (ISBN 0-582-90114-6, Pub. by Longman). Gale.

Who's Who in Shakespeare. Robin May. LC 73-5334. (Who's Who in Literature Ser). 190p. 1973. o. s. i. 6.50 (ISBN 0-8008-8269-5). Taplinger.

Who's Who in Shakespeare's England. Alan Palmer & Veronica Palmer. (Illus.). 350p. 1981. 32.50x (ISBN 0-312-87096-5). St Martin.

Who's Who in Shaw. Phyllis Hartnoll. LC 74-21719. (Who's Who in Literature Ser.). 256p. 1975. 8.95 (ISBN 0-8008-8270-9). Taplinger.

Who's Who in Sherlock Holmes. Scott R. Bullard & Michael Collins. LC 79-66638. 1980. 14.95 (ISBN 0-8008-8281-4); pap. 7.95 (ISBN 0-8008-8282-2). Taplinger.

Who's Who in Socialist Countries of Europe: Albania, Bulgaria, CSSR, Hungary, Poland, Romania & Yugoslavia. Ed. by Juliusz Stroynowskij. (A Biographical Encyclopedia of More than 14,000 Leading Personalities). 2000p. 1988. lib. bdg. 325.00 (ISBN 3-598-10636-X). K G Saur.

Who's Who in Society. LC 87-648094. 1071p. 1986. 109.00 (ISBN 0-940789-01-9). Amer Pub FL.

Who's Who in South African Politics. Shelagh Gastrow. 150p. 1986. pap. text ed. 13.95x (ISBN 0-86975-280-4, Pub. by Ravan Pr). Ohio U Pr.

Who's Who in South African Politics. 2nd ed. Shelagh Gastrow. 400p. 1988. pap. text ed. 19.95x (ISBN 0-86975-336-3, Pub. by Ravan Pr). Ohio U Pr.

Who's Who in Southern California Real Estate. Linda M. Lowson. 285p. 1988. pap. text ed. 195.00 (ISBN 0-944354-00-9). Database Resources.

Who's Who in Space: The First Twenty-Five Years. Michael Cassutt. (Illus.). 336p. 1987. lib. bdg. 35.00 (ISBN 0-8161-8801-7, Hall Reference). G K Hall.

Who's Who in Spain. (Sutter's International Red Ser.). 1050p. 1987. text ed. 140.00 (ISBN 88-85246-04-4, WWIR113, WWIR). UNIPUB.

Who's Who in Special Libraries, 1987-88. Special Libraries Association. 296p. pap. 25.00 (ISBN 0-87111-331-7). SLA.

Who's Who in Stained Glass. Carl Hungness. 284p. 1983. pap. 9.95 (ISBN 0-915088-34-7). C Hungness.

Who's Who in Stained Glass. 2nd ed. LC 83-80082. 224p. 1984. pap. 14.95 (ISBN 0-915088-37-1). C Hungness.

Who's Who in Technology, 7 vols. 5th ed. Research Publications Staff. 1986. Set. 545.00 (ISBN 0-89235-106-3). Res Pubns CT.

Who's Who in Technology, 3 Vols. (International Red Ser.). 1984. Set. pap. 160.00 (WWIR102, WWIR). UNIPUB.

Who's Who in Technology: Austria, Germany, Switzerland. 2nd ed. 1984. 240.00 (ISBN 0-8002-3837-0). Intl Pubns Serv.

Who's Who in Technology: Master Index of Expertise, Master Index of Names, Vol. 7. 150.00 (ISBN 0-89235-113-6). Res Pubns CT.

Who's Who in Technology: Who's Who in Biotechnology, Vol. 6. 95.00 (ISBN 0-89235-112-8). Res Pubns CT.

Who's Who in Technology: Who's Who in Chemistry & Plastics, Vol. 3. 95.00 (ISBN 0-89235-109-8). Res Pubns CT.

Who's Who in Technology: Who's Who in Civil Engineering, Earth Sciences & Energy, Vol. 4. 95.00 (ISBN 0-89235-110-1). Res Pubns CT.

Who's Who in Technology: Who's Who in Electronics & Computer Science, Vol. 1. 95.00 (ISBN 0-89235-107-1). Res Pubns CT.

Who's Who in Technology: Who's Who in Mechanical Engineering & Materials, Vol. 2. 95.00 (ISBN 0-89235-108-X). Res Pubns CT.

Who's Who in Technology: Who's Who in Physics & Optics, Vol. 5. 95.00 (ISBN 0-89235-111-X). Res Pubns CT.

Who's Who in Television & Cable. Steven Scheuer. LC 82-12045. (Illus.). 608p. 1983. 49.95x (ISBN 0-87196-747-2). Facts on File.

Who's Who in the Ancient World. Betty Radice. (Reference Ser.). (Orig.). 1973. pap. 7.95 (ISBN 0-14-051055-9). Penguin.

Who's Who in the Arab World, 1986-1987. 8th ed. Charles Gedeon. 1432p. 1986. lib. bdg. 155.00 (ISBN 2-903188-03-3, Pub. by Publitec-Butterworth & the Middle East Commercial Information Center). ABC-Clio.

Who's Who in the Arab World 1986-1987. 8th ed. 1432p. 1986. 155.00 (ISBN 2-90318-803-3). ABC-Clio.

Who's Who in the Bible. Frank S. Mead. (Christian Library). 250p. Repr. of 1934 ed. 6.95 (ISBN 0-916441-56-3). Barbour & Co.

Who's Who in the Bible. Albert E. Sims & George Dent. 1979. pap. 2.95 (ISBN 0-8065-0705-5, Pub. by Citadel Pr). Lyle Stuart.

Who's Who in the Bible. Albert E. Sims & George Dent. 1982. pap. 4.95 (ISBN 0-8022-1577-7). Philos Lib.

Who's Who in the Commonwealth. 3rd ed. 1985. cancelled (ISBN 0-8002-3891-5). Intl Pubns Serv.

Who's Who in the East, 1985-1986. 20th ed. 828p. 1984. 165.00 (ISBN 0-8379-0620-2, 030366). Marquis.

Who's Who in the East: 1986-1987. 21st, rev. ed. 828p. 1986. 165.00x (ISBN 0-8379-0621-0). Marquis.

Who's Who in the Film World of 1914. Fred C. Justice & T. R. Smith. 1976. lib. bdg. 59.95 (ISBN 0-8490-2820-5). Gordon Pr.

Who's Who in the History of Philosophy. Thomas Kiernan. LC 65-20325. 195p. 1966. 10.00 (ISBN 0-8022-0854-1). Philos Lib.

Who's Who in the Jewelry Industry. Ed. by Donald S. McNeil. LC 79-27501. 231p. 1980. 24.95 (ISBN 0-931744-02-4). Jewelers Bk Club.

Who's Who in the Martial Arts. Ed. by Dale Brooks. (Illus.). 180p. (Orig.). 1985. pap. 12.95 (ISBN 0-931981-04-2). Am Martial Arts Pub.

Who's Who in the Martial Arts & Directory of Black Belts. Bob Wall. LC 75-22880. (Illus.). 275p. (Orig.). 1975. pap. 7.95 (ISBN 0-685-62677-6). R A Wall.

Who's Who in the Middle East Banking & Trade, 2 vols. 2nd ed. 1053p. 1984. Set. cancelled. Marquis.

Who's Who in the Midwest, 1986-1987. 20th, rev. ed. 609p. 1985. 165.00 (ISBN 0-8379-0720-9, 030407). Marquis.

Who's Who in the Midwest, 1988-1989. 21st, rev ed. 1987. 165.00x (ISBN 0-8379-0721-7, 030466). Marquis.

Who's Who in the Motion Picture Industry: 1988-89. 6th ed. 180p. 1988. pap. 18.95. Packard.

Who's Who in the People's Republic of China. Wolfgang Bartke. LC 80-27599. (Illus.). 729p. 1981. 150.00 (ISBN 0-87332-183-9). M E Sharpe.

Who's Who in the People's Republic of China. 2nd ed. Ed. by Wolfgang Bartke. (Illus.). ix, 786p. 1987. lib. bdg. 175.00 (ISBN 3-598-10610-6). K G Saur.

Who's Who in the South & Southwest, 1984-1985. 19th ed. LC 50-58231. 928p. 1984. 165.00 (ISBN 0-8379-0819-1, 030292). Marquis.

Who's Who in the South & Southwest: 1986-1987. 20th ed. 800p. 1986. 165.00x (ISBN 0-8379-0820-5). Marquis.

Who's Who in the Soviet Union: A Biographical Encyclopedia of 5,000 Leading Personalities in the Soviet Union. 2nd ed. Ed. by Borys Lewytzkyj. 428p. 1984. lib. bdg. 150.00x (ISBN 3-598-10467-7). K G Saur.

Who's Who in the Super Bowls: The Performance of Every Player in Super Bowls I to XX. Mark J. Sabljak & Martin H. Greenberg. LC 86-6208. (Illus.). 1986. 22.50 (ISBN 0-934878-80-3); pap. 14.95 (ISBN 0-934878-81-1). Dembner Bks.

Who's Who in the Talmud. rev. ed. Alfred J. Kolatch. LC 64-24891. 228p. 1981. Repr. 9.95 (ISBN 0-8246-0263-3). Jonathan David.

Who's Who in the Theatre, 2 vols. 17th ed. Ed. by Ian Herbert. 768p. 1981. Set. 120.00x (ISBN 0-8103-0234-9). Gale.

Who's Who in the United Nations & Related Agencies. LC 75-4105. 1975. 65.00 (ISBN 0-405-06490-X). Ayer Co Pubs.

Who's Who in the United Nations & Related Agencies. 71.50 (ISBN 0-405-00490-7, 19120). Ayer Co Pubs.

Who's Who in the West 1987-1988. rev., 21st ed. 1987. 165.00x (ISBN 0-8379-0921-X, 030457). Marquis.

Who's Who in the World Zionist Conspiracy. J. Combs. 1982. lib. bdg. 75.00 (ISBN 0-87700-327-0). Revisionist Pr.

Who's Who in the World, 1984-1985. 7th ed. LC 79-139215. 1110p. 1984. 199.00 (ISBN 0-8379-1107-9, 030337). Marquis.

Who's Who in the World: 1987-1988. 8th, rev. ed. 1138p. 1986. 199.00x (ISBN 0-8379-1108-7, 030430). Marquis.

Who's Who in Thomas Hardy. Glenda Leeming. LC 74-24527. (Who's Who in Literature Ser). 144p. 1975. 8.95 (ISBN 0-8008-8271-7). Taplinger.

Who's Who in Typesetting. 72p. cancelled (ISBN 0-318-17399-9); cancelled (ISBN 0-318-17400-6). Print Indus Am.

Who's Who in U. S. Business in Australia. 302p. 1986. pap. 48.50 (ISBN 0-318-19485-6, Pub. by Am Chamber Commerce Australia). A M Newman.

Who's Who in U. S. Writer's, Editors & Poets, 1988. 2nd ed. Ed. by Curt Johnson. LC 87-648220. 704p. 1988. 92.00x (ISBN 0-913204-21-8). December Pr.

Who's Who in U. S. Writers, Editors & Poets; 1986-87. 1st ed. Ed. by Curt Johnson. 600p. 1987. 35.00 (ISBN 0-913204-18-8). December Pr.

Who's Who in Venture Capital. A. David Silver. LC 83-19802. (Small Business Management Ser.: I-471). 378p. 1984. 90.00x (ISBN 0-471-89125-8, Pub. by Ronald Pr.). Wiley.

Who's Who in Venture Capital. 2nd ed. A. David Silver. LC 85-31502. 548p. 1986. pap. 24.95 (ISBN 0-471-83059-3). Wiley.

Who's Who in Venture Capital. 3rd ed. A. David Silver. LC 86-28974. 468p. 1987. pap. 29.95 (ISBN 0-471-85639-8). Wiley.

Who's Who in Wodehouse. Daniel Garrison. (Illus.). 175p. 1987. text ed. 32.50 (ISBN 0-8204-0517-5). P Lang Pubs.

Who's Who (Internationally) at ABA. Date not set. price not set. AAP.

Who's Who of American Women: 1986-1987. 15th. rev. ed. 900p. 1986. 165.00X (ISBN 0-8379-0415-3, 030427). Marquis.

Who's Who of Australian & New Zealand Film Actors: The Sound Era. Scott Palmer. LC 87-32215. 179p. 1988. 20.00 (ISBN 0-8108-2090-0). Scarecrow.

Who's Who of Ballooning: 1783-1983. Robert J. Rechs. 362p. (Orig.). 1982. 35.00 (ISBN 0-937568-26-0); pap. text ed. 20.00 (ISBN 0-937568-27-9). Rechs Pubns.

Who's Who of Black Millionaires. Frank J. Johnson. LC 83-82591. (Illus.). 182p. 1984. pap. 9.95 (ISBN 0-915021-00-5). Who's Black Mill.

Who's Who of British Engineers 1980. 352p. 1981. 55.00x (ISBN 0-312-87413-8). St Martin.

Who's Who of British Scientists 1980-81. 650p. 1981. 75.00x (ISBN 0-312-87433-2). St Martin.

Who's Who of California Executive Women, 1983-1984. 1st ed. Ed. by Diane Livingstone. 160p. 1984. write for info. (ISBN 0-9614609-0-3). Intl Woman Ctr.

Who's Who of Emerging Leaders in America. 960p. 1987. 165.00x (ISBN 0-8379-7200-0, 030507). Marquis.

Who's Who of Heaven: Saints for All Seasons. John P. Kleinz. 220p. (Orig.). 1987. pap. 12.95 (ISBN 0-87061-136-4). Chr Classics.

Who's Who of Horrors. David J. Hogan. LC 79-17606. 1980. 14.95 (ISBN 0-498-02591-8). A S Barnes.

Who's Who of Invention, 1617-1980: 1617-1899. British Library, Science Reference Library Staff. 1985. diazo microfiche 450.00 (ISBN 0-317-26889-9, Pub. by British Lib). Longwood Pub Group.

Who's Who of Invention, 1617-1980: 1900-1980. British Library, Science Reference Library Staff. 1985. diazo microfiche 360.00 (ISBN 0-317-26888-0, Pub. by British Lib). Longwood Pub Group.

Who's Who of Jazz. 4th ed. John Chilton. LC 84-20062. (Roots of Jazz Ser.). (Illus.). 362p. 1985. 29.50 (ISBN 0-306-76271-4); pap. 11.95 (ISBN 0-306-80243-0). Da Capo.

Who's Who of Manchester United, 1945-1985. Tony Matthews. 104p. 1987. 29.00x (ISBN 0-907969-09-7, Pub. by Breedon Bks Pub UK). State Mutual Bk.

Who's Who on British Television. (Illus.). 255p. 1981. pap. 5.95 (ISBN 0-900727-72-1, Pub. by ITV Bks). NY Zoetrope.

Who's Who on the Postage Stamps of Eastern Europe. Paul G. Partington. LC 79-22183. (Illus.). viii, 498p. 1979. lib. bdg. 42.50 (ISBN 0-8108-1266-5). Scarecrow.

Who's Who on the Screen. C. D. Fox & Milton L. Silver. 95.00 (ISBN 0-87968-277-9). Gordon Pr.

Who's Who on TV Soaps, Mini Serials Movies & Lots More. Doris F. Plott. 112p. 1986. 8.95 (ISBN 0-8062-2971-3). Carlton.

Who's Who Regional Library: A Library of Biographies of Distinct Regional Interest...Cross Indexed with Who's Who in America. 1986. cancelled. Marquis.

Who's Who Television: Writers, Directors, Producers & the Networks. Ed. by Rodman W. Gregg. 170p. 1987. pap. 17.95x (ISBN 0-941710-11-4). Packard.

Who's Who, 1975-1976. LC 4-16933. 3511p. 1975. 52.50x (ISBN 0-312-87430-8). St Martin.

Who's Who 1976-1977. 2656p. 1976. 62.50 (ISBN 0-312-87465-0). St Martin.

Who's Who 1978-1979. 1978. 67.50 (ISBN 0-312-87467-7). St Martin.

Who's Who 1979-1980. 131st ed. 1979. 69.95x (ISBN 0-312-87468-5). St Martin.

Who's Who 1980-1981. 132nd ed. 1980. 99.50x (ISBN 0-312-87469-3). St Martin.

Who's Who 1982-1983. 134th ed. 99.50x (ISBN 0-312-87471-5). St Martin.

Who's Who 1984-1985. 136th ed. LC 84-16933. 2600p. 1984. 110.00x (ISBN 0-312-87473-1). St Martin.

Who's Who, 1985-1986. 137th ed. LC 4-16933. 2143p. 1985. 115.00 (ISBN 0-312-87474-X). St Martin.

Who's Who 1986-1987. LC 4-16933. 2140p. 1986. 115.00 (ISBN 0-312-87475-8). St Martin.

Who's Who, 1987-1988. 139th ed. 1950p. 1987. 125.00x (ISBN 0-312-00236-X). St Martin.

Who's Who 1988. 140th ed. LC 4-16933. 1950p. 1988. 130.00 (ISBN 0-312-01556-9). St Martin.

Who's Whodunit. Lenore S. Gribbin. LC 71-627563. (North CArolina University Library Studies: No. 5). pap. 46.00 (ISBN 0-317-09228-6, 2004350). Bks Demand UMI.

Who's your Furry Friend? write for info. (ISBN 0-8431-0635-2). Price Stern.

Whose Baby? Masayuki Yabuuchi. LC 84-1088. (First Book of Nature Study Ser.). (Illus.). 32p. (gr. k-1). 1985. 8.95 (ISBN 0-399-21210-8, Philomel). Putnam Pub Group.

Whose Baby Are You. LC 86-62382. (Matchem Board Bks). (Illus.). 18p. (ps). 1987. 4.95 (ISBN 0-394-88629-1, BYR). Random.

Whose Body? Dorothy L. Sayers. LC 86-45146. 256p. 1987. 17.45i (ISBN 0-06-055036-8, HarpT). Har-Row.

Whose Body? Dorothy L. Sayers. LC 86-45146. 256p. 1987. pap. 4.50 (ISBN 0-06-080829-2, P829, PL). Har-Row.

Whose Business? Brian Griffiths & Hugh Murray. (Hobart Paperback Ser.: No. 102). 88p. (Orig.). 1985. pap. text ed. 9.25x (ISBN 0-255-36182-3, Pub. by Inst Econ Affairs UK). Transatl Arts.

Whose Child Am I? Adults' Recollections of Being Adopted. John Y. Powell. LC 84-52530. (Illus.). 127p. 1985. casebound 12.95 (ISBN 0-913292-41-9). Tiresias Pr.

Whose Child? Children's Rights, Parental Authority, & State Power. Ed. by William Aiken & Hugh LaFollette. LC 79-29741. (Quality Paperbacks: No. 358). 310p. 1980. pap. 10.95 (ISBN 0-8226-0358-6). Littlefield.

Whose Child? Children's Rights, Parental Authority, & State Power. Ed. by William Aiken & Hugh LaFollette. LC 79-27577. 310p. 1980. 27.50x (ISBN 0-8476-6282-9). Rowman.

Whose Child Cries: Children of Gay Parents Talk about Their Lives. Joe Gantz. LC 83-81973. (Creative Parenting Ser.). 272p. 1983. 16.95 (ISBN 0-915190-40-0, JP9040-0KK); pap. 8.95 (ISBN 0-915190-39-7, JP9039-7KK). Jalmar Pr.

Whose Church Is This Anyway? Robert Versteeg. LC 85-13282. 1985. 6.95 (ISBN 0-89536-767-X, 5874). CSS of Ohio.

Whose Constitution? An Inquiry into the General Welfare. Henry A. Wallace. Repr. of 1936 ed. lib. bdg. 35.00x (ISBN 0-8371-3157-X, WAWC). Greenwood.

Whose Energy. cancelled (ISBN 0-442-23882-7). Van Nos Reinhold.

Whose Experience Counts in Theological Reflection? Monika Hellwig. LC 82-80331. (Pere Marquette Lecture Ser.). 112p. 1982. 7.95 (ISBN 0-87462-537-8). Marquette.

Whose FBI? Ed. by Richard O. Wright. LC 74-60. 405p. 1974. 9.95 (ISBN 0-87548-148-5). Open Court.

Whose File Is It Anyway. Ruth Cohen. 1982. 20.00x (ISBN 0-901108-97-9, Pub. by NCCL UK). State Mutual Bk.

Whose Footprints? Masayuki Yabuuchi. LC 84-1087. (First Look of Nature Study Ser.). (Illus.). 32p. (gr. k-1). 1985. 8.95 (ISBN 0-399-21209-4, Philomel). Putnam Pub Group.

Whose Furry Nose? Henrik Drescher. LC 87-45151. (Illus.). 32p. (gr. k-3). 1987. 11.70i (ISBN 0-397-32236-4, Lipp Jr Bks); PLB 11.89 (ISBN 0-397-32243-7). HarpJ.

Whose Hat? Margaret Miller. LC 86-18324. (Illus.). 40p. (ps-1). 1988. 11.95 (ISBN 0-688-06906-1); lib. bdg. 11.88 (ISBN 0-688-06907-X). Greenwillow.

Whose Hat Is That? Ron Roy. LC 86-17553. 40p. (ps-2). 1987. 12.95 (ISBN 0-89919-446-X, Pub. by Clarion). Ticknor & Fields.

Whose House Is This? Carol Loelling. (Surprise Bk). (Illus.). 22p. (ps-4). 1978. 5.95 (ISBN 0-8431-0444-9). Price Stern.

Whose Is the Hidden Hand? J. Schoeman. 1984. lib. bdg. 79.95 (ISBN 0-87700-604-0). Revisionist Pr.

Whose Is the Sun? Y. Avernikov. 16p. 1973. pap. 0.99 (ISBN 0-8285-1270-1, Pub. by Progress Pubs USSR). Imported Pubns.

Whose Justice? Which Rationality? Alasdair MacIntyre. LC 87-40354. 432p. 1988. text ed. 22.95x (ISBN 0-268-01942-8). U of Notre Dame Pr.

Whose Language: A Study in the Linguistic-Pragmatics, No. 3. Jacob L. Mey. LC 85-6123. (Pragmatics and beyond Companion Ser.: Vol. 3). ix, 412p. 1985. 52.00x (ISBN 0-915027-61-5); pap. 19.95x. Benjamins North Am.

Whose Life Is It Anyway? Brian Clark. 160p. 1980. pap. 2.95 (ISBN 0-380-52407-4, 64808-3, Bard). Avon.

Whose Little Boy Are You? A Memoir of the Broun Family. Heywood H. Broun. (Illus.). 224p. 1983. 14.95 (ISBN 0-312-87765-X, Pub. by Marek). St Martin.

Whose Mess Is This? Carol Roth. LC 87-81757. (Golden Look-Look Bks.). (Illus.). 24p. (ps-3). 1988. pap. 1.60 (ISBN 0-307-11749-9, Pub. by Golden Bks). Western Pub.

Whose Mouse Are You? Robert Kraus. LC 70-89931. (Illus.). (ps-2). 1972. pap. 4.95 (ISBN 0-02-044160-6, Aladdin Bks). Macmillan.

Whose Mouse Are You? Robert Kraus. LC 70-89931. (Illus.). 32p. (ps-2). 1970. 11.95 (ISBN 0-02-751190-1). Macmillan.

Whose Needs Count? Community Action for Health. Charmian Kenner. 110p. 1986. pap. text ed. 9.90x (ISBN 0-7199-1163-X, Pub. by Bedford England). Brookfield Pub Co.

Whose Promised Land? Colin Chapman. 256p. (Orig.). Date not set. pap. 7.95 (ISBN 0-85648-956-5). Lion USA.

Whose Revolution? Ed. by Irving D. Talmadge. LC 75-346. (Radical Tradition in America Ser). 314p. 1975. Repr. of 1941 ed. 23.65 (ISBN 0-88355-250-7). Hyperion Conn.

Whose Scaly Tail? Henrik Drescher. LC 87-45152. (Illus.). 32p. (gr. k-3). 1987. 11.95i (ISBN 0-397-32237-2, Lipp Jr Bks); PLB 11.89 (ISBN 0-397-32244-5). HarpJ.

Whose School Is It Anyway? Parent-Teacher Conflict Over an Innovative School. Barry A. Gold & Matthew B. Miles. LC 81-8562. 416p. 1981. 44.95 (ISBN 0-275-90633-7, C0633). Praeger.

Why Do Grown-Ups Have All the Fun? Marisabina Russo. LC 86-4644. (Illus.). 24p. (ps-3). 1987. 11.75 (ISBN 0-688-06625-9); PLB 11.88 (ISBN 0-688-06626-7). Greenwillow.
Why Do I Daydream? Betty R. Wright. LC 80-25561. (Life & Living from a Child's Point of View Ser.). (Illus.). 32p. (gr. k-5). 1981. PLB 15.33 (ISBN 0-8172-1371-6). Raintree Pubs Ltd.
Why Do I Do Things Wrong? Carolyn Nystrom. (Children's Bible Basics Ser.). 32p. (gr. 2). 1981. pap. 3.95 (ISBN 0-8024-5996-X). Moody.
Why Do I Do What I Don't Want to Do? William Backus & Marie Chapian. LC 84-6336. 144p. 1984. pap. 5.95 (ISBN 0-87123-625-7, 210625). Bethany Hse.
Why Do I Drink More Than I Want? Five Came Back; Three Did Not. Juanita M. Ferrey. LC 88-72476. 200p. (Orig.). 1987. pap. 13.00 (662-4680). AFCOM Pub.
Why Do I Eat More Than I Want Diet Book. Juanita M. Ferrey. LC 88-72476. 214p. (Orig.). 1987. pap. 13.00 (662-4680). AFCOM Pub.
Why Do I Feel So Bad (When the Doctor Says I'm O.K.)? 2nd ed. Howard E. Hagglund. Ed. by Pam Mauldin. (Illus.). 48p. 1984. pap. 6.00 (ISBN 0-9614173-0-7). HEH Med Pubns.
Why Do I Shout at My Wife? Dick Jewett. (Uplook Ser.). 1978. pap. 0.99 (ISBN 0-8163-0300-2, 23617-4). Pacific Pr Pub Assn.
Why Do I Think I Am Nothing Without a Man? Penelope Russianoff. 1983. pap. 4.50 (ISBN 0-553-26678-0). Bantam.
Why Do I Write? Elizabeth Bowen. 57p. 1980. Repr. of 1948 ed. lib. bdg. 15.00 (ISBN 0-8492-3776-9). R West.
Why Do I Write? Elizabeth Bowen & V. Pritchett. LC 75-22190. (English Literature Ser., No. 33). 1975. lib. bdg. 75.00x (ISBN 0-8383-2094-5). Haskell.
Why Do I Write. V. S. Pritchett. LC 77-4324. 1948. lib. bdg. 18.00 (ISBN 0-8414-6788-9). Folcroft.
Why Do Juveniles Start Smoking? 37p. 1986. 10.00 (ISBN 0-318-22259-0). Intl Advertising Assn.
Why Do Leaves Change Color. Chris Arvetis & Carole Palmer. (Just Ask Ser.). (Illus.). 32p. (ps-3). 1984. 3.95 (ISBN 0-317-65115-3, Checkerboard Pr). Macmillan.
Why Do Men Fight & Destroy One Another? Laurance Labadie. (Men & Movements in the History & Philosophy of Anarchism Ser.). 1979. lib. bdg. 59.95 (ISBN 0-685-96421-3). Revisionist Pr.
Why Do Mullet Jump? And Other Puzzles & Possibilities of God's Creation. Gene Zimmerman. 128p. (Orig.). 1986. pap. 6.95 (ISBN 0-935311-01-7). Post Horn Pr.
Why Do Our Bodies Stop Growing? Philip Whitfield & Ruth Whitfield. (ps up). 1988. 15.95 (ISBN 0-670-82331-7, Viking Kestrel). Viking.
Why Do People Do Bad Things in the Name of Religion? Richard E. Wentz. LC 86-28605. 96p. (Orig.). 1987. pap. 9.95 (ISBN 0-86554-257-0, MUP P-43). Mercer Univ Pr.
Why Do People Fall under the Power? Kenneth E. Hagin. 1981. pap. 0.50 mini bk (ISBN 0-89276-254-3). Hagin Ministries.
Why Do People Take Drugs? Judith Hemming. Ed. by FS-Aladdin Staff. (Let's Talk about...Ser.). (Illus.). 32p. (gr. 1-3). 1988. 9.90 (ISBN 0-531-17113-2, Gloucester Pr). Watts.
Why Do Research? 50p. 2.00 (ISBN 0-317-34985-6). Natl Assn Broadcasters.
Why Do Some People Get Fat? Jane Claypool. (Creative's Little Question Books). (Illus.). 32p. (ps-4). 1982. PLB 8.95 (ISBN 0-87191-898-6). Creative Ed.
Why Do Some Urban Schools Succeed? The Phi Delta Kappa Study of Exceptional Urban Elementary Schools. LC 80-81869. 225p. 1980. pap. 7.00 (ISBN 0-87367-773-0). Phi Delta Kappa.
Why Do the Jews Need a Land of Their Own? Ed. by Joseph Leftwich & Mordecai S. Chertoff. LC 83-45297. 242p. 1984. 19.95 (ISBN 0-8453-4774-8, Cornwall Bks). Assoc Univ Prs.
Why Do the Right Words Always Come Out of the Wrong Mouth? Cathy Guisewite. (Illus.). 128p. (Orig.). 1988. pap. 6.95 (ISBN 0-8362-1808-6). Andrews & McMeel.
Why Do the Righteous Suffer? Gordon Lindsay. (Divine Healing & Health Ser.). 1.50 (ISBN 0-89985-032-4). Christ Nations.
Why Do the Seasons Change? Questions on Nature's Rhythms & Cycles Answered by the Natural History Museum. Philip Whitfield & Joyce Pope. LC 87-40133. 96p. (ps up). 1987. 15.95 (ISBN 0-317-62526-8, Viking Kestrel). Viking.
Why Do They Do It? Gordon Lindsay. 1.00 (ISBN 0-89985-120-7). Christ Nations.
Why Do They Dress That Way? Stephen Scott. LC 86-81058. (People's Place Booklet Ser.: No. 7). (Illus.). 160p. (Orig.). 1986. pap. 5.50 (ISBN 0-934672-18-0). Good Bks PA.
Why Do Wars Happen? Judith Hemming. Ed. by FS-Aladdin Staff. (Let's Talk about...Ser.). (Illus.). 32p. (gr. 1-3). 1988. 9.90 (ISBN 0-531-17114-0, Gloucester). Watts.
Why Do We Age? Hilton Hotema. 65p. 1959. pap. text ed. 7.95 (ISBN 0-88697-018-0). Life Science.
Why Do We Eat? Pamela Espeland. (Creative's Questions & Answers Library). (Illus.). 32p. (ps-4). 1981. PLB 8.95 (ISBN 0-87191-747-5). Creative Ed.
Why Do We Have Earthquakes? Norita D. Larson. (Creative's Little Question Bks.). (Illus.). 32p. (ps-4). 1982. PLB 8.95 (ISBN 0-87191-879-X). Creative Ed.
Why Do We Have Hair? Pat Blakely. (Creative's Little Question Bks.). (Illus.). 32p. (ps-4). 1982. PLB 8.95 (ISBN 0-87191-881-1). Creative Ed.
Why Do We Have Skeletons? Pat Blakely. (Creative Questions & Answers Ser.). (Illus.). 32p. (ps-4). 1982. PLB 7.95 (ISBN 0-87191-750-5). Creative Ed.
Why Do We Laugh? A. A. Redpath. (Creative's Questions & Answers Ser.). (Illus.). 32p. (ps-4). 1981. PLB 7.95 (ISBN 0-87191-751-3). Creative Ed.
Why Do We Not See Little People, Miss Wintergreen? see Magga Birds of Ranatan.
Why Do We Say...? Nigel Rees. 224p. 1988. 17.95 (ISBN 0-7137-1944-3, Pub. by Blandford Pr England). Sterling.
Why Do You Act the Way You Do? Carl H. Peterson & Karla Von Ehrenkrook. 210p. (Orig.). 1988. pap. write for info. Creative AZ.
Why Doctrines? Charles Hefling. LC 82-83553. 196p. (Orig.). 1984. pap. 8.00 (ISBN 0-936384-09-3). Cowley Pubns.
Why Does Everybody Always Tell You You Talk Too Much When You Know Darn Well It Isn't True? Barbara Bishop. (Illus.). 200p. (Orig.). 1985. pap. 8.95 (ISBN 0-9615772-0-7). Priority GA.
Why Does It Float? Chris Arvetis & Carole Palmer. (Just Ask Ser.). (Illus.). 32p. (ps-3). 1984. Repr. 3.95 (ISBN 0-317-65118-8, Checkerboard Pr). Macmillan.
Why Does It Fly? Chris Arvetis & Carole Palmer. (Just Ask Ser.). (Illus.). 32p. (ps-3). 1984. Repr. 3.95 (ISBN 0-317-65117-X, Checkerboard Pr). Macmillan.
Why Does It Rain? Chris Arvetis & Carole Palmer. (Just Ask Ser.). (Illus.). 32p. (ps-3). 1984. Repr. 3.95 (ISBN 0-317-65119-6, Checkerboard Pr). Macmillan.
Why Does It Snow? Chris Arvetis & Carole Palmer. (Just Ask Ser.). (Illus.). 32p. (ps-3). 1984. 3.95 (ISBN 0-317-65116-1, Checkerboard Pr). Macmillan.
Why Does It Thunder & Lightning. Chris Arvetis. (Jusk Ask Ser.). (Illus.). 32p. (ps-3). 1988. pap. 1.95 (ISBN 0-02-688813-0, Checkerboard Pr). Macmillan.
Why Does It Thunder & Lightning? Chris Arvetis & Carole Palmer. LC 85-60559. (Just Ask Ser.). 32p. (ps-3). 1985. 3.95 (ISBN 0-528-82671-9). Macmillan.
Why Does Language Matter to Philosophy. Ian Hacking. LC 75-19432. 180p. 1975. 34.50 (ISBN 0-521-20923-4); pap. 11.95x (ISBN 0-521-09998-6). Cambridge U Pr.
Why Does My Mother's Day Potted Plant Always Die? Janene W. Baadsgaard. LC 88-482. 130p. 1988. 9.95 (ISBN 0-87579-144-1). Deseret Bk.
Why Does My Nose Run? & Other Questions Kids Ask about Their Bodies. Joanne Settel & Nancy Baggett. LC 84-21549. (Illus.). 80p. (gr. 4-6). 1985. 9.95 (ISBN 0-689-31078-1, Atheneum Childrens Bks). Macmillan.
Why Does That Man Have Such a Big Nose? Mary Beth Quinsey. LC 85-63760. (Illus.). 32p. (Orig.). (ps). 1986. lib. bdg. 11.95 (ISBN 0-943990-25-4); pap. 4.95 (ISBN 0-943990-24-6). Parenting Pr.
Why Does Your Dog Do That. Goran Bergman. LC 73-165560. (Illus.). 160p. 1973. 14.95 (ISBN 0-87605-808-X). Howell Bk.
Why Doesn't God Do Something? Phoebe Cranor. LC 78-118. 144p. (YA) (gr. 7-12). 1978. pap. 3.50 (ISBN 0-87123-605-2, 200605). Bethany Hse.
Why Doesn't God Do Something? Edwin Settle. 142p. 1988. 13.95 (ISBN 0-533-07618-8). Vantage.
Why Doesn't God Intervene? Basilea Schlink. Tr. by Evangelical Sisterhood of Mary. 32p. 1982. pap. 0.50 (ISBN 3-87209-629-X). Evang Sisterhood Mary.
Why Doesn't She Go Home! Bonnie Towne. 96p. (gr. 4-6). 1986. 1.95 (ISBN 0-87406-119-9). Willowisp Pr.
Why Doesn't the Earth Fall Up? And Other Not Such Dumb Questions about Motion. Vicki Cobb. (Illus.). 40p. (gr. 2-5). 1988. 12.95 (ISBN 0-525-67253-2). Lodestar Bks.
Why Don't Teachers Teach Like They Used To. Rachel Pinder. 1987. pap. 10.95 (ISBN 0-948096-04-7, Pub. by Hilary Shipman Ltd). Longwood Pub Group.
Why Don't You Believe What We Tell You. 39p. 1983. pap. 1.00. Noontide.
Why Don't You Get a Horse, Sam Adams? Jean Fritz. (Illus.). 48p. (gr. 2-6). 1974. 9.95 (ISBN 0-698-20292-9, Coward). Putnam Pub Group.
Why Don't You Get a Horse, Sam Adams? Jean Fritz. (Illus.). 48p. (gr. 3-7). 1982. pap. 5.95 (ISBN 0-698-20545-6, Coward). Putnam Pub Group.
Why Don't You Love Yourself: Some Information on Dealing with Yourself & Others. Maryetta Lucero. LC 75-46072. 1976. pap. 3.50 (ISBN 0-89016-021-X). Lightning Tree.
Why Duchamp: An Essay on Aesthetic Impact. Gianfranco Baruchello & Henry Martin. LC 85-11544. 160p. 1985. 20.00 (ISBN 0-914232-71-1); pap. 10.00 (ISBN 0-914232-73-8); deluxe ed. 200.00 (ISBN 0-914232-72-X). McPherson & Co.
Why Economic Policies Change Course: Eleven Case Studies. OECD. 122p. (Orig.). 1988. pap. 13.50x (ISBN 92-64-13099-3). OECD.
Why Economics Is Not Yet a Science. Ed. by Alfred S. Eichner. LC 83-12859. 264p. 1983. 35.00 (ISBN 0-87332-249-5); pap. 14.95 (ISBN 0-87332-265-7). M E Sharpe.
Why Education in the Later Years? Louis Lowy & Darlene O'Connor. LC 82-47966. 288p. 1986. 30.00x (ISBN 0-669-05721-5). Lexington Bks.
Why ERA Failed: Politics, Women's Rights, & the Amending Process of the Constitution. Mary F. Berry. LC 85-45985. (Everywoman: Studies in History, Literature & Culture). 286p. 1986. 22.50 (ISBN 0-253-36537-6). Ind U Pr.
Why ERA Failed: Politics, Women's Rights, & the Amending Process of the Constitution. Mary F. Berry. LC 85-45985. 160p. 1988. pap. 8.95 (ISBN 0-253-20459-3). Ind U Pr.
Why Europe Leaves Home: a True Account of the Reasons Which Cause Central Europeans to Overrun America. Kenneth L. Roberts. Ed. by Gerald Grob. LC 76-46100. (Anti-Movements in America). 1977. Repr. of 1922 ed. lib. bdg. 31.00x (ISBN 0-405-09971-1). Ayer Co Pubs.
Why Even Competent Businessmen Fail when Managing Their Own Businesses: The Negatives You Ought to Know. Vittorio De Aureliani. (Illus.). 102p. 1984. 117.75 (ISBN 0-86654-103-9). Inst Econ Finan.
Why Exercise? Bruce Davies & David Ashton. 240p. (Orig.). 1986. text ed. 29.95 (ISBN 0-631-14174-X); pap. 8.95 (ISBN 0-631-14175-8). Basil Blackwell.
Why Explore? 1986. 0.25 (ISBN 0-939418-59-2). Ferguson-Florissant.
Why Families Move. 2nd ed. Peter H. Rossi. LC 79-25370. (Illus.). 243p. 1980. 32.00 (ISBN 0-8039-1348-6); pap. 16.95 (ISBN 0-8039-1349-4). Sage.
Why Farm Wives Age Fast, Vol. II. Ed. by Eleanor Jacobs. LC 86-61012. 64p. 1986. pap. 4.95 (ISBN 0-89821-074-7). Reiman Assocs.
Why Farm Wives Age Fast. Ed. by Ann Kaiser. LC 83-60741. 64p. 1983. pap. 4.95 (ISBN 0-89821-050-X). Reiman Assocs.
Why Farmers Are Poor: The Agricultural Crisis in the United States. facsimile ed. Anne Rochester. Ed. by Dan C. McCurry & Richard E. Rubenstein. LC 74-30649. (American Farmers & the Rise of Agribusiness Ser.). 1975. Repr. of 1940 ed. 29.00 (ISBN 0-405-06821-2). Ayer Co Pubs.
Why Fascism? Ellen C. Wilkinson & Edward Conze. LC 78-177843. Repr. of 1934 ed. 29.50 (ISBN 0-404-56169-1). AMS Pr.
Why Flannery O'Connor Stayed Home. Marion Montgomery. (Prophetic Poet & the Spirit of the Age Ser.: Vol. I). 486p. 1981. 19.95 (ISBN 0-89385-013-6). Sugden.
Why Foreign Aid. facs. ed. Ed. by Robert A. Goldwin. LC 71-134083. (Essay Index Reprint Ser). 1963. 14.00 (ISBN 0-8369-2036-8). Ayer Co Pubs.
Why Frau Frohman Raised Her Prices & Other Stories. Anthony Trollope. Ed. by N. John Hall. LC 80-1900. (Selected Works of Anthony Trollope Ser.). 1981. Repr. of 1882 ed. lib. bdg. 45.00 (ISBN 0-405-14189-0). Ayer Co Pubs.
Why Frau Frohmann Raised Her Prices. Anthony Trollope. Ed. by John K. Shannon. (Harting Grange Library Ser.). (Illus.). 1978. lib. bdg. 9.95 (ISBN 0-932282-06-7); pap. 5.95 (ISBN 0-932282-05-9). Caledonia Pr.
Why Friends Are Friends. Jack L. Willcuts. 90p. (Orig.). 1984. pap. 3.95 (ISBN 0-913342-45-9). Barclay Pr.
Why Frogs Are Wet. Judy Hawes. LC 85-43009. (Trophy Let's-Read-&-Find-Out Book). (Illus.). 40p. (ps-3). 1987. pap. 4.95 (ISBN 0-06-445043-0, Trophy). HarpJ.
Why Gaelic Matters. Derick Thomson. 36p. 1986. 15.00x (ISBN 0-85411-028-3, Pub. by Saltire Soc.). State Mutual Bk.
Why Girls Ride Sidesaddle. Dennis Lynds. LC 79-50801. (Illus.). 115p. 1980. pap. 7.50x (ISBN 0-913204-13-7). December Pr.
Why God? Burton Z. Cooper. LC 87-21499. 132p. 1988. pap. 9.95 (ISBN 0-8042-0731-3, John Knox). Westminster John Knox.
Why God Allows Trials & Disappointments. Gerald R. Nash. (Uplook Ser.). 31p. 1972. pap. 0.99 (ISBN 0-8163-0082-8, 23618-2). Pacific Pr Pub Assn.
Why God Became Man & the Virgin Conception & Original Sin. Anselm of Canterbury. Tr. & intro. by Joseph M. Colleran. LC 71-77166. 256p. (Orig.). 1982. pap. text ed. 4.95x (ISBN 0-87343-025-5). Magi Bks.
Why God Gave Me Pain. Shirley Holdren. 128p. 1984. pap. 4.95 (ISBN 0-8294-0469-4). Loyola.
Why God Loves Me So Much. Dana Carvey. 1987. pap. 6.95. PB.
Why God Permits Accidents. Spiros Zodhiates. LC 79-51340. 1982. pap. 2.25 (ISBN 0-89957-537-4). AMG Pubs.
Why God Permits Evil, Poems. Miller Williams. LC 77-8711. 59p. 1977. 13.95x (ISBN 0-8071-0377-2); pap. 6.95 (ISBN 0-8071-0378-0). La State U Pr.
Why Gone Those Times? James W. Schultz. Ed. by Lee Silliman. LC 72-9262. (Civilization of the American Indian Ser.: Vol. 127). 271p. 1981. pap. 7.95 (ISBN 0-8061-1639-0). U of Okla Pr.
Why Good Parents Have Bad Kids: How to Make Sure Your That Your Child Grows up Right. E. Kent Hayes. 1989. 16.95 (ISBN 0-385-24352-9). Doubleday.
Why Good People Suffer: A Practical Treatise on the Problem of Evil. Bartholomew Gottemoller. 1987. 9.95 (ISBN 0-533-07107-0). Vantage.
Why Government Programs Fail: Improving Policy Implementation. James S. Larson. LC 79-26917. 140p. 1980. 35.00 (ISBN 0-275-90511-X, C0511). Praeger.
Why Governments Grow: Measuring the Public Sector: Explanations of Size & Growth. Charles L. Taylor. LC 83-14390. (Advances in Political Science Ser.: No. 3). 1983. 29.95 (ISBN 0-8039-2124-1). Sage.
Why Growth Rates Differ: Postwar Experience in Nine Western Countries. Edward F. Denison. LC 67-27682. 1967. 34.95 (ISBN 0-8157-1806-3); pap. 14.95 (ISBN 0-8157-1805-5). Brookings.
Why Has Japan Succeeded? Western Technology & the Japanese Ethos. Michio Morishima. (Illus.). 219p. 1984. pap. 11.95 (ISBN 0-521-26903-2); 39.50. Cambridge U Pr.
Why Have I Accepted Islam? A. Chattopadhya. pap. 1.75 (ISBN 0-686-18476-9). Kazi Pubns.
Why Hawthorne Was Melancholy. Marion Montgomery. (Prophetic Poet & the Spirit of the Age Ser.: Vol. III). 576p. (Orig.). 1984. 24.95 (ISBN 0-89385-027-6). Sugden.
Why Her Why Now: A Man's Journey Through Love & Death & Grief. Lon Elmer. LC 87-62939. (Illus.). 228p. 1987. pap. 10.00 (ISBN 0-944844-47-2). Signal Elm Pr.
Why Hitler Came into Power. Theodore Abel. 352p. 1986. pap. text ed. 9.95x (ISBN 0-674-95200-6). Harvard U Pr.
Why Humans Vary in Intelligence. Seymour W. Itzkoff. LC 87-8861. (Evolution of Human Intelligence Ser.: Vol. 3). 400p. 1987. 18.00 (ISBN 0-913993-09-3). Paideia MA.
Why I Am a Conscientious Objector. John M. Drescher. LC 82-894. (Christian Peace Shelf Ser.). 73p. (Orig.). 1982. pap. 3.95 (ISBN 0-8361-1993-2). Herald Pr.
Why I Am a Jew. 2nd facsimile ed. Edmond Fleg. Tr. by Louise W. Wise from Fr. LC 74-27984. (Modern Jewish Experience Ser.). (Eng.). 1975. Repr. of 1945 ed. 13.00 (ISBN 0-405-06711-9). Ayer Co Pubs.
Why I Am a Jew. Edmond Fleg. Tr. by Louise W. Wise from Fr. LC 75-4124. 1985. pap. 4.95 (ISBN 0-8197-0009-6). Bloch.
Why I Am a Jew. Joseph R. Narot. pap. 0.95 (ISBN 0-686-15802-4). Rostrum Bks.
Why I Am a Mennonite: Essays on Mennonite Identity. Ed. by Harry Loewen. LC 87-62522. 312p. (Orig.). 1988. pap. 14.95 (ISBN 0-8361-3463-X). Herald Pr.
Why I Am a Preacher: A Plain Answer to an Oft-Repeated Question. Uldine Utley. Ed. by Carolyn D. Gifford & Donald Dayton. (Women in American Protestant Religion 1800-1930 Ser.). 152p. 1987. lib. bdg. 25.00 (ISBN 0-8240-0680-1). Garland Pub.
Why I Am a Separatist. Marcel Chaput. Tr. by Robert Taylor from Fr. LC 75-9634. 101p. 1975. Repr. of 1962 ed. lib. bdg. 48.50x (ISBN 0-8371-8107-0, CHWI). Greenwood.
Why I Am a Seventh-Day Adventist. William G. Johnsson. Ed. by Richard W. Coffen. (Better Living Ser.). 32p. (Orig.). 1986. pap. 0.75 (ISBN 0-8280-0352-1). Review & Herald.
Why I Am an Anarchist. Benjamin R. Tucker. 59.95 (ISBN 0-87700-232-0). Revisionist Pr.
Why I Am An Atheist. rev. ed. Madalyn O'Hair. 39p. 1980. Repr. of 1966 ed. 3.25 (ISBN 0-911826-12-2). Am Atheist.
Why I Am an Atheist. Carl Shapiro. 14p. (Orig.). 1979. write for info. (ISBN 0-914937-02-2); incl. cassette 10.00 (ISBN 0-317-18464-4). Ind Pubns.
Why I Am Not a Christian & Other Essays on Religion & Related Subjects. Bertrand Russell. 1967. pap. 8.95 (ISBN 0-671-20323-1, Touchstone Bks). S&S.
Why I Am Still a Christian. Hans Kung. 112p. 1987. 13.95 (ISBN 0-687-45358-5). Abingdon.
Why I Became a Buddhist. William Constandse. 130p. (Orig.). 1985. pap. 6.95 (ISBN 0-911527-02-8). Utama Pubns Inc.
Why I Believe. D. James Kennedy. 1980. 6.95 (ISBN 0-8499-2943-1). Word Bks.
Why I Believe in the Baptism with the Holy Spirit. Stanford E. Linzey. 12p. 1962. pap. 0.75 (ISBN 0-88243-764-X, 02-0764). Gospel Pub.
Why I Came to Judevine. David Budbill. 1987. 7.00. White Pine.
Why I Can Say I Am God. Herbert L. Beierle. 1978. 1.00 (ISBN 0-940480-04-2). U of Healing.

Why Nothing Works: The Anthropology of Daily Life. Marvin Harris. Orig. Title: America Now: The Anthropology of a Changing Culture. 7.95 (ISBN 0-317-55900-1, Touchstone Bks). S&S.

Why Nurnberg. Meredyth Goethe. (Illus.). 256p. 1981. text ed. 12.95 (ISBN 0-9606714-0-4). Goethe Pubs.

Why, O Lord? Psalms & Sermons from Namibia. Zephania Kameeta. LC 86-45211. 80p. 1987. pap. 3.95 (ISBN 0-8006-1923-4, 1-1923). Fortress.

Why O Lord? The Inner Meaning of Suffering. Carlo Carretto. Tr. by Robert R. Barr from Ital. LC 85-29874. 128p. (Orig.). 1986. 10.95 (ISBN 0-88344-224-8); pap. 6.95 (ISBN 0-88344-222-1). Orbis Bks.

Why on Earth. rev. ed. Joan Hodgson. 144p. 1979. pap. 4.95 (ISBN 0-85487-043-1). DeVorss.

Why Pacifists Should Be Socialists. George Lansbury. LC 72-147520. (Library of War & Peace; Labor, Socialism & War). 1972. lib. bdg. 46.00 (ISBN 0-8240-0454-X). Garland Pub.

Why Papa Went Away & Other Stories. Phyllis Marten. 112p. (YA) (gr. 8 up). 1987. pap. 3.95 (ISBN 0-317-64776-8). Herald Pr.

Why Pascal? D. J. DesChamps. 125p. 1984. pap. cancelled (ISBN 0-88056-302-8). Dilithium Pr.

Why Pay an Attorney? Settle Your Own Bodily Injured Claim. Daniel Kushner. 103p. (Orig.). 1985. pap. 7.95 (ISBN 0-9615694-0-9). D Kushner Ltd.

Why People Buy. John O'Shaughnessy. 207p. 1987. 19.95 (ISBN 0-19-504086-4). Oxford U Pr.

Why People Intend to Move: Individual & Community-Level Factors of Out-Migration in the Philippines. Sun-Hee Lee. 195p. 1985. pap. 21.00x (ISBN 0-8133-7102-3). Westview.

Why People Kill Themselves: A 1980's Summary of Research Findings on Suicidal Behavior. 2nd ed. David Lester. 172p. 1983. 19.75x (ISBN 0-398-04826-6). C C Thomas.

Why People Lack Confidence in Chairs. Norman Fischer. (Morning Coffee Chapbook Ser.). (Illus.). 20p. (Orig.). 1984. pap. 7.50 (ISBN 0-918273-07-2). Coffee Hse.

Why People Move: Comparative Perspectives on the Dynamics of Internal Migration. Jorge Balan. (Illus.). 342p. 1981. pap. 15.75 (ISBN 92-3-101909-0, U1186, UNESCO). UNIPUB.

Why People Recreate: An Overview of Research. David H. Smith & Nancy Theberge. LC 82-83933. 192p. 1987. text ed. 24.00x (ISBN 0-87322-902-9, LSMI0902, Life Enhancement). Human Kinetics.

Why Persimmons & Other Poems. Stanley R. Hopper. LC 86-13913. (Scholars Press Studies in the Humanities). 192p. 1987. 23.95 (ISBN 1-55540-043-4, 00-01-12). Scholars Pr GA.

Why Poe Drank Liquor. Marion Montgomery. (Prophetic Poet & the Spirit of the Age Ser.: Vol. II). 442p. 1982. 19.95 (ISBN 0-89385-026-8). Sugden.

Why Policies Succeed or Fail. Ed. by Helen M. Ingram & Dean E. Mann. LC 79-26317. (Sage Yearbooks in Politics & Public Policy: Vol. 8). (Illus.). 312p. 1980. pap. 16.95 (ISBN 0-8039-1417-2). Sage.

Why Poor People Stay Poor: Urban Bias in World Development. Michael Lipton. 1977. 25.00x (ISBN 0-674-95238-3). Harvard U Pr.

Why Potocki? R. T. Risk. (Illus.). 60p. 1981. 40.00x (ISBN 0-930126-07-6). Typographeum.

Why Pray? Spiros Zodhiates. LC 82-71266. (Luke Trio Ser.). 1982. pap. 5.95 (ISBN 0-89957-554-4). AMG Pubs.

Why Preach? Why Listen? William Muehl. LC 86-45216. 96p. 1986. pap. 4.95 (ISBN 0-8006-1928-5, 1-1928). Fortress.

Why Preserve Natural Variety? Bryan G. Norton. 296p. 1988. text ed. 30.00 (ISBN 0-691-07762-2). Princeton U Pr.

Why Presidents Succeed. Dean K. Simonton. LC 86-28088. 304p. 1987. 22.50x (ISBN 0-300-03836-4). Yale U Pr.

Why? Psychic Development & How! Ed. by Mystic Jhamom Staff. (Conversations with a Mystic Ser.: No. 2). (Illus.). 176p. 1985. pap. 11.75 (ISBN 0-933961-05-7). Mystic Jhamom.

Why? Psychic Development & How! Illustration Booklet, Supplement. Ed. by Mystic Jhamom Staff. (Conversations Mystic Ser.: No. 2). (Illus.). 12p. 1985. pap. 1.75 (ISBN 0-933961-06-5). Mystic Jhamom.

Why Psychotherapists Fail. Richard Chessick. LC 84-45108. 203p. 1983. 20.00x (ISBN 0-87668-700-1). Aronson.

Why Punish the Children? A Study of Children of Women Prisoners. Brenda G. McGowan & Karen L. Blumenthal. 124p. 1978. 6.50 (ISBN 0-318-15376-9). Natl Coun Crime.

Why Pupils Fail in Reading. Helen M. Robinson. (LC A46-5912). 1946. 6.75x (ISBN 0-226-72210-4). U of Chicago Pr.

Why Race Riots? Earl L. Brown. LC 74-22734. (Labor Movement in Fiction & Non-Fiction). Repr. of 1944 ed. 20.00 (ISBN 0-404-58486-1). AMS Pr.

Why Racism Is Used Against Welfare Programs: Why Workers Should Join Welfare Recipients' Struggles. Julia Barnes. 1971. pap. 0.10 (ISBN 0-87898-068-7). New Outlook.

Why Rainbows? And Other Wonders of the Natural World Explained. Ira Flatow. (Illus.). 256p. 1988. 15.95 (ISBN 0-688-06705-0). Morrow.

Why Read Aloud to Children? Julie M. Chan. (Micromonograph Ser.). 12p. 1974. pap. 1.50 (ISBN 0-87207-877-9). Intl Reading.

Why Reaganomics & Keynesian Economics Failed. James E. Sawyer. LC 87-9578. 256p. 1987. 29.95 (ISBN 0-312-00532-6). St Martin.

Why Recall? An Example of Politics in the Public Schools. Vera W. Fredrickson. (Orig.). 1987. pap. 9.95 (ISBN 0-9619247-0-5). V W Fredrickson.

Why Revival Tarries. Leonard Ravenhill. 176p. 1979. pap. 5.95 (ISBN 0-87123-607-9, 210607). Bethany Hse.

Why S. A.? Ernst Rohm. 1982. lib. bdg. 59.95 (ISBN 0-87700-368-8). Revisionist Pr.

Why Salt the Peanuts? Sayings of the Five Cents Psychiatrist. Ben Weininger & Henry Rabin. 1982. pap. 5.95 (ISBN 0-686-34451-0). Ross Erikson.

Why School Health. Kristen Amundson. 16p. 1987. pap. text ed. write for info. (ISBN 0-87652-121-9, 021-00211). Am Assn Sch Admin.

Why Sermon Outlines. Russell E. Spray. (Sermon Outline Ser.). 48p. (Orig.). 1980. pap. 2.50 (ISBN 0-8010-8188-2). Baker Bk.

Why Shoot a Butler. Georgette Heyer. Repr. lib. bdg. 19.95 (ISBN 0-89190-649-5, Pub. by River City Pr). Amereon Ltd.

Why Shoot a Butler? Georgette Heyer. 100p. 1987. pap. 2.95 (ISBN 0-425-09323-9). Berkley Pub.

Why Should I? Pamela R. Venti. LC 83-7360. (Illus.). 32p. (gr. 1-2). 1983. PLB 4.95 (ISBN 0-89693-213-3). Dandelion Hse.

Why Should I Care? Honest Answers to the Questions That Trouble Teens. William R. Grimbol. 144p. (Orig.). (YA) (gr. 8 up). Date not set. pap. 7.95 (ISBN 0-8066-2363-2, 10-7176). Augsburg.

Why Should "I" Speak in Tongues. Charles Hunter & Frances Hunter. 1976. pap. 5.95 (ISBN 0-917726-02-2). Hunter Bks.

Why Should I Speak in Tongues? 1984. pap. 0.95 (ISBN 0-930756-85-1, 541012). Aglow Pubns.

Why Should We Change Our Form of Government: Studies in Practical Politics. Nicholas M. Butler. LC 73-167321. (Essay Index Reprint Ser.). Repr. of 1912 ed. 17.00 (ISBN 0-8369-2758-3). Ayer Co Pubs.

Why Shouldn't I. Christopher Howell. LC 77-94479. 63p. 1977. perfect bound in wrappers 3.75 (ISBN 0-934332-02-9). L'Epervier Pr.

Why Sing? Toward a Theology of Catholic Church Music. Miriam T. Winter. 346p. (Orig.). 1984. pap. 11.95 (ISBN 0-912405-07-4). Pastoral Pr.

Why Small Businesses Fail: Don't Make the Same Mistake Once. William A. Delaney. 204p. 1984. 16.95 (ISBN 0-13-959016-1, Busn); pap. 9.95 (ISBN 0-13-959008-0). P-H.

Why So Many Bosses Fail in Their Jobs. Abraham C. Redquist. (Management & Inventiveness Science Library Bk.). (Illus.). 123p. 1983. 117.75 (ISBN 0-86654-093-8). Inst Econ Finan.

Why So Many Churches. Victor H. Prange. 1985. pap. 2.95 (ISBN 0-8100-0188-8, 15N0413). Northwest Pub.

Why S.O.B's Succeed & Nice Guys Fail in a Small Business. Ed. by Robert H. Morrison. 360p. 1976. 29.95 (ISBN 0-930566-01-7). Morrison Peterson Pub.

Why Sociology Does Not Apply: A Study of the Use of Sociology in Public Policy. R. A. Scott & A. Shore. 266p. 1979. pap. 19.50 (ISBN 0-444-99063-1). Elsevier.

Why Some Are Not Healed. Gordon Lindsay. (Divine Healing & Health Ser.). 1.25 (ISBN 0-89985-033-2). Christ Nations.

Why Some Positive Thinkers Get Powerful Results. Norman V. Peale. LC 86-5145. 224p. 1986. 15.95 (ISBN 0-8407-9053-8). Oliver-Nelson.

Why Some Positive Thinkers Get Powerful Results. Norman V. Peale. 224p. 1987. pap. 3.50 (ISBN 0-449-21359-5, Crest). Fawcett.

Why South Africa Will Survive. L. H. Gann & Peter Duignan. 320p. 1980. 26.00. St Martin.

Why South Africa Will Survive. L. H. Gann & Peter Duignan. 329p. 1981. 27.50 (ISBN 0-312-87878-8). St Martin.

Why Squander Illness? Charles M. Carty. 1974. pap. 1.50 (ISBN 0-89555-051-2). TAN Bks Pubs.

Why Stay Married? Jane Sawyer. (Outreach Ser.). 1982. pap. 1.25 (ISBN 0-8163-0443-2). Pacific Pr Pub Assn.

Why Stocks Go up (& Down) A Guide to Sound Investing. William H. Pike. LC 82-71875. 298p. 1983. 19.95 (ISBN 0-87094-314-6). Dow Jones-Irwin.

Why Stop? 2nd ed. Claude Dooley & Betty Dooley. LC 85-17663. 600p. (Orig.). 1985. pap. 14.95x (ISBN 0-88415-922-1, Lone Star Bks). Gulf Pub.

Why Stories. Edward W. Dolch & M. P. Dolch. (Dolch Basic Vocabulary Ser.). 176p. (gr. 1-6). 1958. PLB 6.57 (ISBN 0-8116-2502-8). Garrard.

Why Study Christian Science as a Science? Max Kappeler. 30p. 1973. pap. 3.50 (ISBN 0-85241-040-9). Kappeler Inst Pub.

Why Study Sociology? Elliott Krause. 187p. (Orig.). 1980. pap. text ed. write for info (ISBN 0-394-32200-2, RanC). Random.

Why Suffer? 2nd ed. Ann Wigmore. 120p. 1985. pap. 5.95 (ISBN 0-89529-192-4). Avery Pub.

Why Suicide? Jerry Johnston. LC 86-31165. 192p. 1987. 12.95 (ISBN 0-8407-9089-9). Oliver-Nelson.

Why Survive? Being Old in America. Robert N. Butler. 510p. 1985. pap. 10.95x (ISBN 0-06-131997-X, TB 1997, Torch). Har-Row.

Why Suya Sing: A Musical Anthropology of an Amazonian People. Anthony Seeger. (Cambridge Studies in Ethnomusicology). (Illus.). 176p. 1987. 49.50 (ISBN 0-521-34173-6); cassette 14.95 (ISBN 0-521-34174-4). Cambridge U Pr.

Why Switzerland? J. Steinberg. LC 75-36024. (Illus.). 225p. 1981. pap. 12.95 (ISBN 0-521-28144-X). Cambridge U Pr.

Why T'ang? Herbert Ingram. 1946. pap. 12.50x (ISBN 0-317-44247-3, Pub. by Han-Shan Tang Ltd). State Mutual Bk.

Why Tax Employee Benefits? Dallas L. Salisbury. LC 84-1683. 120p. (Orig.). 1984. pap. 14.00 (ISBN 0-86643-036-9). Employee Benefit.

Why Tax Employee Benefits? An EBRI-ERF Poicy Forum. Ed. by Dallas L. Salisbury. (Illus.). 122p. 1986. pap. 14.75 (ISBN 0-8191-5539-X, Pub. by Employee Benefit Rsch Inst). U Pr of Amer.

Why Teach? A First Look at Working with Young Children. Joanne Hendrick. LC 87-60267. 32p. 1987. 3.00 (ISBN 0-935989-05-6, NAEYC #220). Natl Assn Child Ed.

Why Teachers Organized. Wayne J. Urban. LC 82-11160. 203p. 1982. 22.50x (ISBN 0-8143-1714-6). Wayne St U Pr.

Why Teenagers Act the Way They Do. G. Keith Olson. 432p. (Orig.). 1987. pap. 15.95 (ISBN 0-931529-17-4). Group Bks.

Why Ten Million Low Income Americans Do Not Receive Food Stamps: A Review of the Research Literature. Robert Greenstein. 10p. 1984. 1.50 (37,274). NCLS Inc.

Why Test? 1983. 0.50 (ISBN 0-939418-52-5). Ferguson Florissant.

Why the Best Laid Business Plans Usually Go Wrong. Harry Browne. 1989. 12.95 (ISBN 0-671-67292-4, Fireside). S&S.

Why the Best-Laid Investment Plans Usually Go Wrong: And How You Can Find Safety & Profit in an Uncertain World. Harry Brown. Ed. by Howard Cady. LC 87-16593. 480p. 1987. 19.95 (ISBN 0-688-05995-3). Morrow.

Why the Bible Is Number One: The World's Sacred Writing in the Light of Science. Kenny Barfield. 304p. 1988. pap. 13.95 (ISBN 0-8010-0950-2). Baker Bk.

Why the Chicken Crossed the Road. David Macaulay. (Illus.). 32p. (gr. 4-6). 1987. 13.95 (ISBN 0-395-44241-9, Clarion). HM.

Why the Church Must Teach. Lucien E. Coleman, Jr. LC 84-4966. 1984. pap. 6.95 (ISBN 0-8054-3234-5). Broadman.

Why the Cookie Crumbles. Margories Lewis-Lloyd. (Outreach Ser.). 64p. pap. 1.25 (ISBN 0-317-66146-9). Pacific Pr Pub Assn.

Why the Cookie Crumbles. Marjorie L. Lloyd. (Outreach Ser.). pap. 1.25 (ISBN 0-8163-0400-9). Pacific Pr Pub Assn.

Why the Courts Don't Work. Richard Neely. 1983. text ed. 15.95 (ISBN 0-07-046152-X); pap. text ed. 7.95 (ISBN 0-07-046151-1). McGraw.

Why the Crab Has No Head. Barbara Knutson. (ps-4). 1988. 4.95. Lerner Pubns.

Why the Crab Has No Head: An African Folktale. Barbara Knutson. (ps-3). 1987. lib. bdg. 9.95 (ISBN 0-87614-322-2). Carolrhoda Bks.

Why the Crimean War? A Cautionary Tale. Norman Rich. LC 84-40593. (Illus.). 280p. 1985. 25.00 (ISBN 0-87451-328-6). U Pr of New Eng.

Why the Emperor's New Clothes Are Not Made in Colombia: A Case Study in Latin American & East Asian Manufactured Exports. David Morawetz. (World Bank Research Publications Ser.). (Illus.). 1981. 24.95x (ISBN 0-19-520283-X). Oxford U Pr.

Why the Green Nigger? Re-Mything Genesis. Elizabeth Dodson Gray. LC 79-89193. x, 166p. 1979. 12.95 (ISBN 0-934512-01-9). Roundtable Pr.

Why the Jews? Dennis Prager & Joseph Telushkin. 1985. pap. 6.95 (ISBN 0-671-55624-X, Touchstone Bks). S&S.

Why the Jews? The Reason for Anti-Semitism. Dennis Prager & Joseph Telushkin. 224p. 1983. 14.95 (ISBN 0-671-45270-3). S&S.

Why the King James Version. J. Reuben Clark, Jr. LC 79-15008. (Classics in Mormon Literature Ser.). 535p. 1979. 7.95 (ISBN 0-87747-773-6). Deseret Bk.

Why the Loon Calls. Retold by Ellen M. Dolan & Janet L. Bolinske. (Children's Classics Ser.). (Illus.). 30p. (Orig.). (gr. 1-3). 1987. text ed. 9.95 (ISBN 0-88335-565-5); pap. text ed. 4.95 (ISBN 0-88335-585-X). Milliken Pub Co.

Why the Lyrical Ballads? John E. Jordan. LC 75-27926. 1976. 33.00x (ISBN 0-520-03124-5). U of Cal Pr.

Why the March Hare Went Mad & Other Stories. Minnie T. Miller. 55p. (gr. k-4). 1972. 5.00 (ISBN 0-87881-002-1). Mojave Bks.

Why the North Star Stands Still. William R. Palmer. LC 57-11627. (Illus.). 118p. 1978. pap. 2.95 (ISBN 0-915630-12-5). Zion.

Why the North Won the Civil War. Ed. by David Donald. 1962. pap. 4.95 (ISBN 0-02-031660-7, Collier). Macmillan.

Why the Poor Get Richer & the Rich Slow Down: Essays in the Marshallian Long Period. W. W. Rostow. 394p. 1980. text ed. 25.00 (ISBN 0-292-73012-8). U of Tex Pr.

Why the Possum's Tail Is Bare: And Other North American Indian Nature Tales. Ed. by James E. Connolly. LC 84-26871. (Illus.). 56p. (gr. 3 up). 1985. PLB 12.95 (ISBN 0-88045-069-X). Stemmer Hse.

Why the Robin Has a Red Breast. M. Cleophas. (Illus.). (ps-3). 1.75 (ISBN 0-8198-0204-2); pap. 1.00 (ISBN 0-8198-0205-0). Dghtrs St Paul.

Why the Roman, the British, the French & the German Empires Fell & the Historical Future of the United States & Soviet Russia. Thomas G. Ludwig. (Illus.). 1980. 127.75 (ISBN 0-89266-215-8). Am Classical Coll Pr.

Why the South Lost the Civil War. Richard E. Beringer et al. LC 85-8638. (History Book Club Selection). (Illus.). 608p. 1986. 29.95 (ISBN 0-8203-0815-3). U of GA Pr.

Why the South Will Survive. Fifteen Southerners. LC 81-1313. 240p. 1981. pap. 12.00x (ISBN 0-8203-0566-9). U of Ga Pr.

Why the Soviet Union Wants SALT II. 1979. write for info. Comm Present Danger.

Why the Soviets Violate Arms Control Treaties. J. D. Douglass, Jr. 196p. 1988. text ed. 32.00 (ISBN 0-08-035960-4). Pergamon.

Why the Tides Ebb & Flow. Joan Bowden. (gr. k-3). 1979. PLB 12.95 (ISBN 0-395-28378-7). HM.

Why the Tooth Fairy Didn't Arrive Last Night. Carl E. Miner. (Illus.). 24p. 1986. write for info. Child Ventures.

Why the Vietcong Fought: A Study of Motivation & Control in a Modern Army in Combat. William D. Henderson. LC 79-7062. (Contributions in Political Science Ser.: No. 31). 1980. lib. bdg. 29.95 (ISBN 0-313-20708-9, HVC/). Greenwood.

Why the Whales Came. Michael Morpurgo. 140p. 1987. 17.95 (ISBN 0-7182-3982-2, Pub. by W Heinemann Ltd). David & Charles.

Why the Wilderness Is Called Adirondack: The Earliest Account of Founding of the MacIntyre Mine. Henry Dornburgh. LC 79-25055. 1980. pap. 3.95 (ISBN 0-916346-39-0). Harbor Hill Bks.

Why? There Is More to You Than Meets the Eye. Jean E. Beckman. (Illus.). 50p. (Orig.). (gr. 9-12). 1981. pap. 3.95 (ISBN 0-941992-00-4). Los Arboles Pub.

Why There Is No Heaven on Earth. Ephraim Sevela. Tr. by Richard Lourie. LC 81-47736. 224p. (Rus.). (YA) (gr. 7 up). 1982. PLB 10.89 (ISBN 0-06-025503-X). HarpJ.

Why They Buy: American Consumers Inside & Out. Robert Settle & Pamela Allreck. LC 86-13303. 351p. 1986. 22.95 (ISBN 0-471-84457-8); cassette 9.95 (ISBN 0-471-63123-X). Wiley.

Why They Call It Politics: A Guide to America's Government. 4th ed. Robert Sherrill & James D. Barber. 419p. 1984. pap. text ed. 13.00 net (ISBN 0-15-596003-2, HC). HarBraceJ.

Why They Did It: Stories of Eight Convicted Child Molesters. Shirley J. O'Brien. 204p. 1986. 24.00 (ISBN 0-398-05265-4). C C Thomas.

Why They Did Not Starve: Biocultural Adaptation in a South Indian Village. Morgan D. Maclachlan. LC 81-20203. (Illus.). 350p. 1983. text ed. 30.00 (ISBN 0-89727-001-0). ISHI PA.

Why They're Away: The Purpose of Death. Ellert L. Anderson. 1988. 10.95 (ISBN 0-533-08005-3). Vantage.

Why Things Are. Neil Ardley. (Illus.). 128p. 1984. lib. bdg. 11.79 (ISBN 0-671-49993-9). Messner.

Why Things Are. (Illus.). (gr. 1 up). Date not set. 10.95 (ISBN 0-671-49897-5, Little Simon). S&S.

Why Things Are: A Guide to Understanding the World Around Us. Simon & Schuster Staff. (Illus.). 128p. (gr. 3-7). 1988. pap. 7.95 (ISBN 0-671-67031-X). S&S.

Why Things Don't Work: The Anthropology of Daily Life. Marvin Harris. 208p. 1987. pap. 7.95 (ISBN 0-671-63577-8, Touchstone Bks). S&S.

Why This Skeptic Is a Christian. Claud C. Crawford. 100p. (Orig.). 1988. pap. 6.95 (ISBN 0-933697-06-6). Claud Crawford.

Why Tikopia Has Four Clans. Hooper & Firth. (Occasional Papers Ser.: No. 38). 60p. 1981. pap. text ed. 12.50x (Pub. by Royal Anthropological UK). Humanities.

Why Time Begins on Opening Days. (Sports Library). 304p. 1985. pap. 6.95 (ISBN 0-14-007661-1). Penguin.

Why Tomorrow? Li Shufen. (Illus.). 49p. (Orig.). (gr. 3-5). 1983. pap. 3.95 (ISBN 0-8351-1094-X). China Bks.

Why Tongues? Kenneth E. Hagin. 1975. pap. 0.50 mini bk (ISBN 0-89276-051-6). Hagin Ministries.

Why Trade It In? How to Keep Your Car Running Almost Indefinitely. 2nd ed. George Fremon & Suzanne Fremon. LC 76-42603. (Illus.). 176p. 1982. pap. 5.95 (ISBN 0-89709-039-X). Liberty Pub.

Why Tragedy Happens to Christians. Charles Capps. 187p. (Orig.). 1980. pap. 3.75 (ISBN 0-89274-175-9, HH-175). Harrison Hse.

TITLE INDEX
WICLIF & HUS.

Why Us? When Bad Things Happen to God's People. Warren Wiersbe. 160p. 1985. pap. 5.95 (ISBN 0-8007-5208-2, Power Bks). Revell.
Why Vegetarianism? write for info. (ISBN 0-938924-19-2). Sri Shirdi Sai.
Why Video Works: New Applications for Management. John A. Bunyan. LC 86-21106. (Illus.). 200p. 1986. 37.95 (ISBN 0-86729-079-X). Knowledge Indus.
Why Vietnam? Prelude to America's Albatross. Archimedes L. Patti. LC 80-51242. (Illus.). 700p. 1981. 25.00x (ISBN 0-520-04156-9); pap. 11.95x (ISBN 0-520-04783-4). U of Cal Pr.
Why Violence? A Philosophical Interpretation. Sergio Cotta. Tr. by Giovanni Gullace from Ital. LC 84-25779. Orig. Title: Perche la violenza? Una Interpretazione Filosofica. xiv, 150p. 1985. pap. 12.00 (ISBN 0-8130-0804-2). U Presses Fla.
Why Wait 'Til I'm Dead? Buy This Book Now. M. Agrelius. 64p. (Orig.). 1986. pap. 4.95 (ISBN 0-936805-00-5). Happy Val Whittier.
Why Wait till Marriage? see Por Que Esperar Hasta el Matrimonio?.
Why Wait? What You Need to Know About the Teen Sexuality Crisis. Josh McDowell & Dick Day. write for info. Heres Life.
Why War? Nicholas M. Butler. (Essay & General Literature Index Reprint Ser). 1969. Repr. of 1941 ed. 26.00 (ISBN 0-8046-0058-9, Pub. by Kennikat). Assoc Faculty Pr.
Why War? Frederic C. Howe. LC 73-125179. (Americana Library Ser.: No. 16). 394p. 1970. Repr. of 1916 ed. 20.00x (ISBN 0-295-95091-9). U of Wash Pr.
Why War? Frederick Howe. LC 70-147497. (Library of War & Peace; the Political Economy of War). 1972. lib. bdg. 46.00 (ISBN 0-8240-0291-1). Garland Pub.
Why War? Ideology, Theory, & History. Keith L. Nelson & Spencer C. Olin. LC 78-51746. 1980. 17.95x (ISBN 0-520-03672-7); pap. 10.95x (ISBN 0-520-04279-4). U of Cal Pr.
Why Was I Adopted? Carole Livingston. (Illus.). (gr. 1 up). 1978. text ed. 12.00 (ISBN 0-8184-0257-1). Lyle Stuart.
Why Was I Adopted? Carole Livingston. (Illus.). 48p. 1986. pap. 6.95 (ISBN 0-8184-0400-0). Lyle Stuart.
Why Watergate? Ed. by Paul J. Halpern. LC 74-21037. 1975. pap. 5.50x (ISBN 0-913530-03-4). Palisades Pub.
Why We Act That Way. John H. Miller. LC 47-354. pap. 56.00 (ISBN 0-317-10045-9, 2001338). Bks Demand UMI.
Why We Are Baptized. Kathleen England. LC 78-19180. (Illus.). (gr. 2-5). 1978. pap. 5.95 (ISBN 0-87747-893-7). Deseret Bk.
Why We Are Happily Married. Compiled by Harold Critcher & June Critcher. 1979. pap. 3.95 (ISBN 0-89265-054-0). Randall Hse.
Why We Are Not What We Think We Are: A New Approach to the Nature of Personal Identity & of Time. Andreas Trupp. (Studia Philosophica et Historica: Vol. 6). 113p. 1987. pap. 19.30 (ISBN 3-8204-0984-X). P Lang Pubs.
Why We Can't Wait. Martin Luther King, Jr. (Illus.). 159p. (RL 7). 1987. pap. 2.95 (ISBN 0-451-62181-6, ME2181, Ment). NAL.
Why We Do It. facs. ed. Edwin D. Wolff. LC 68-16990. (Essay Index Reprint Ser). 1929. 17.00 (ISBN 0-8369-1006-0). Ayer Co Pubs.
Why We Do Not Speak in Tongues. Don R. Pegram. 1982. pap. 1.25 (ISBN 0-89265-086-9). Randall Hse.
Why We Fought. C. H. Grattan. Ed. by Keith Nelson. LC 70-84163. 1969. 37.50x (ISBN 0-8290-1392-X). Irvington.
Why We Have Thanksgiving. Margaret Hillert. (Just Beginning-to-Read Ser.). (Illus.). 32p. (gr. 1-6). 1981. PLB 4.39 (ISBN 0-8136-5104-2, Dist. by Caroline Hse); pap. 1.95 (ISBN 0-8136-5604-4). Modern Curr.
Why We Laugh. 2nd & enl. ed. Samuel S. Cox. LC 67-13325. 1969. Repr. of 1880 ed. 26.50 (ISBN 0-405-08379-3, Blom Pubns). Ayer Co Pubs.
Why We Learn the Arabic Language. S. Inayatulla. pap. 2.00 (ISBN 0-686-18327-4). Kazi Pubns.
Why We Live in Community. Eberhard Arnold. 1976. pap. 1.50 (ISBN 0-87486-168-3). Plough.
Why We Lost the E. R. A. Jane J. Mansbridge. LC 86-6954. (Illus.). xii, 328p. 1986. lib. bdg. 35.00x (ISBN 0-226-50357-7); pap. 9.95 (ISBN 0-226-50358-5). U of Chicago Pr.
Why We Need a 'Third World Theology' CIIR Staff. 20p. 1984. 3.00x (ISBN 0-946848-05-X, Pub. by CIIR). State Mutual Bk.
Why We Need Confession. Russell Shaw. LC 85-63153. 125p. (Orig.). 1986. pap. 4.95 (ISBN 0-87973-537-6, 537). Our Sunday Visitor.
Why We Never Danced the Charleston. Harlan Greene. 176p. 1984. 12.95 (ISBN 0-312-87881-8, Pub. by Marek). St Martin.
Why We Never Danced the Charleston. Harlan Greene. (Contemporary American Fiction Ser.). 160p. 1985. pap. 5.95 (ISBN 0-14-008218-2). Penguin.
Why We Punctuate or Reason Versus Rule in the Use of Marks. Willaim L. Klein. 1978. Repr. of 1916 ed. lib. bdg. 20.00 (ISBN 0-8492-1463-7). R West.
Why We Serve: Personal Stories of Catholic Lay Ministers. Ed. by Doug Fisher. 176p. (Orig.). 1984. pap. 6.95 (ISBN 0-8091-2640-0). Paulist Pr.
Why We Should Read. facs. ed. Stuart P. Mais. LC 67-26760. (Essay Index Reprint Ser). 1921. 17.50 (ISBN 0-8369-0669-1). Ayer Co Pubs.
Why We Should Read. Stuart P. Mais. 1973. Repr. of 1921 ed. 20.00 (ISBN 0-8274-0116-7). R West.
Why We Sleep: The Functions of Sleep in Human & Other Mammals. James Horne. 360p. 1988. 47.50 (ISBN 0-19-261682-X). Oxford U Pr.
Why We Still Need the United Nations: The Collective Management of International Conflict, 1945-1984. Ernst B. Haas. LC 86-84126. (Policy Papers in International Affairs: No. 26). (Illus.). x, 115p. 1986. pap. 8.95x (ISBN 0-87725-526-1). U of Cal Intl St.
Why We Went to War. Newton D. Baker. LC 72-1278. (Select Bibliographies Reprint Ser). 1972. Repr. of 1936 ed. 12.00 (ISBN 0-8369-6820-4). Ayer Co Pubs.
Why We Were in Vietnam. Norman Podorhetz. 250p. 1983. pap. 7.95 (ISBN 0-671-47061-2, Touchstone). S&S.
Why We Write. Robert Atwan & Bruce Forer. 1986. pap. text ed. 13.50 scp (ISBN 0-06-040361-6, HarpC). Har-Row.
Why We're Here. Robert G. Krebs. 1987. 7.95 (ISBN 0-533-07098-8). Vantage.
Why Were We Born? Eric S. Dillett. 1980. 6.00 (ISBN 0-682-49534-4). Exposition-Phoenix.
Why Were You Created. Jim McKeever. 1980. 1.00 (ISBN 0-86694-083-9). Omega Pubns OR.
Why, What & How of Interest Development Centers. Berdine Stoltz & Pamela Saloom. 1978. pap. text ed. 7.95 (ISBN 0-936386-02-9). Creative Learning.
Why, Who & How of the Editorial Page. Kenneth Rystrom. 352p. 1983. text ed. write for info (ISBN 0-394-32985-6, RanC). Random.
Why Winners Win. Art Garner. 128p. 1981. 8.95 (ISBN 0-88289-267-3). Pelican.
Why Winners Win! John Torquato. 256p. 1983. 15.95 (ISBN 0-8144-5770-3). AMACOM.
Why Winners Win! Techniques of Advocate Selling. John Torquato. LC 82-73831. 240p. 1985. pap. 7.95 (ISBN 0-8144-7629-5). AMACOM.
Why Women Are So. Mary R. Coolidge. LC 72-2595. (American Women Ser: Images & Realities). 376p. 1972. Repr. of 1912 ed. 23.50 (ISBN 0-405-04452-6). Ayer Co Pubs.
Why Women Don't Have Wives: Professional Success & Motherhood. Terri Apter. LC 84-23658. 1985. 21.00 (ISBN 0-8052-3958-8). Schocken.
Why Women Kill Themselves. Ed. by David Lester. 168p. 1988. text ed. 28.75x (ISBN 0-398-05508-4). C C Thomas.
Why Women Lose at Bridge. Joyce Nicholson. (Master Bridge Ser.). 96p. 1985. 18.95 (ISBN 0-575-03709-1, Pub. by Gollancz England); pap. 9.95 (ISBN 0-575-03721-0, Pub. by Gollancz England). David & Charles.
Why Women Shouldn't Marry: A Guidebook for Women of the 80's. Cynthia S. Smith. 224p. 1988. 15.95 (ISBN 0-8184-0467-1). Lyle Stuart.
Why Women Wear Clothes. C. W. Cunnington. 1979. lib. bdg. 75.00 (ISBN 0-8490-2821-3). Gordon Pr.
Why Won't the Dragon Roar? Rosalyn Rosenbluth. LC 76-30610. (Imagination Ser.). (Illus.). (gr. k-4). 1977. PLB 6.69 (ISBN 0-8116-4407-3). Garrard.
Why Work? Arguments for the Leisure Society. Ed. by Vernon Richards. (Illus.). 210p. (Orig.). 1983. pap. 8.00 (ISBN 0-900384-25-5). Left Bank.
Why Work? Arguments for the Leisure Society. B. Russell et al. 1984. lib. bdg. 79.95 (ISBN 0-87700-644-X). Revisionist Pr.
Why Work? Careers & Employment in Biblical Perspective. John A. Bernbaum & Simon M. Steer. 1987. pap. 4.95 (ISBN 0-8010-0933-2). Baker Bk.
Why Work: Motivating the New Generation. Michael Maccoby. LC 87-31432. (Illus.). 272p. 1988. 18.95 (ISBN 0-671-47281-X). S&S.
Why Workers Behave the Way They Do. Duane Beeler et al. 240p. (Orig.). 1983. pap. 7.95 (ISBN 0-317-12241-X). Union Rep.
Why World Evangelism. David Howard. pap. 0.75 (ISBN 0-87784-141-1). Inter-Varsity.
Why You Act the Way You Do. Tim LaHaye. 342p. 1988. pap. 4.95 (ISBN 0-8423-8212-7). Tyndale.
Why You Are Who You Are: A Psychic Conversation. Graham Bernard. 208p. (Orig.). 1985. pap. 8.95 (ISBN 0-89281-100-5, Destiny Bks). Inner Tradit.
Why You Cannot Die! The Continuity of Life-Reincarnation Explaine. Lao Russell. (Illus.). 253p. 1972. text ed. 22.00x. U Sci & Philos.
Why You Cannot Know If You Are Saved! Mark D. Ladish. 1988. 8.95 (ISBN 0-533-07718-4). Vantage.
Why You Feel Down & What You Can Do About It. Irma Myers & Arthur Myers. LC 82-3271. 144p. (gr. 7 up). 1982. 11.95 (ISBN 0-684-17442-1, Pub. by Scribner). Macmillan.
Why You Should: The Pragmatics of Deontic Speech. James W. Forrester. LC 88-40111. 272p. 1988. 30.00x (ISBN 0-87451-453-3). U Pr of New Eng.
Why You Win or Lose. Fred C. Kelly. LC 62-22236. 1962. Repr. of 1930 ed. flexible cover 8.00 (ISBN 0-87034-002-6). Fraser Pub Co.
Why Your Child Can Read! Lea-Ruth Wilkens. LC 80-51610. 104p. (Orig.). 1980. pap. 3.95 (ISBN 0-9604638-0-1). Readon Pub.
Why Your Child is Afraid: Understanding the Normal Fears of Childhood from Birth to Adolescence & Helping Overcome Them. Robert Schacter & Carole S. McCauley. 256p. 1988. 17.95 (ISBN 0-671-62683-3). S&S.
Why Your Child Is Hyperactive. Ben F. Feingold. 1985. 7.95 (ISBN 0-394-73426-2). Random.
Why Your House May Endanger Your Health. Alfred V. Zam & Robert Gannon. 1982. pap. 7.95 (ISBN 0-671-44757-2, Touchstone Bks). S&S.
Why You're Richer Than You Think. Emyl Jenkins. (Illus.). 1982. 6.95 (ISBN 0-89256-186-6). Rawson Assocs.
Whys & Hows of Oil & Gas Investment. Lewis G. Mosburg, Jr. (Illus.). 176p. (Orig.). 1986. pap. text ed. 15.95 (ISBN 0-910649-22-7). Energy Textbks.
Whys Behind Testing Standards for Solid Fuel Burning Appliances. Ben A. Zimmer. 1981. 3.50 (ISBN 0-686-31891-9, TR 81-4). Society Fire Protect.
Whys of a Philosophical Scrivener. Martin Gardner. LC 83-4474. 484p. 1983. 22.50 (ISBN 0-688-02063-1, Quill NY); pap. 12.95 (ISBN 0-688-02064-X). Morrow.
Whyte Harte. P. C. Doherty. 256p. 1988. 16.95 (ISBN 0-312-02318-9). St Martin.
Wi-Ne-Ma the Woman-Chief & Her People. Alfred B. Meacham. LC 76-43773. Repr. of 1876 ed. 17.50 (ISBN 0-404-15628-2). AMS Pr.
WIBC Championship Tournament Program. Women's International Bowling Congress Staff. Ed. by Karen L. Sytsma. (Illus.). 80p. 1987. 1.00 (ISBN 0-318-21985-9). WIBC.
WICCA: A Solitary Guide for the Practitioner. Scott Cunningham. Ed. by Phyllis Galde. LC 88-45279. (Practical Magick Ser.). (Illus.). 240p. 1988. pap. 9.95 (ISBN 0-87542-118-0). Llewellyn Pubns.
Wichita: A Pictorial History. Kay Kirkman. Ed. by Donna R. Friedman. LC 81-15301. (Illus.). 208p. 1981. pap. 13.95 (ISBN 0-89865-147-6). Donning Co.
Wichita County Beginnings. Louise Kelly. 39.95 (ISBN 0-89015-347-7). Eakin Pr.
Wichita Experience: Mobilizing Corporate Resources to Meet Community Needs. Kerry K. Allen. 51p. 1978. pap. 3.65 (ISBN 0-318-17141-4, C12). VTNC Arlington.
Wichita Grammar. David S. Rood. LC 75-25122. (American Indian Linguistics Ser.). 1977. lib. bdg. 51.00 (ISBN 0-8240-1972-5). Garland Pub.
Wichita Gunman. Paul Ledd. (Shelter Ser.: No. 16). 1983. pap. 2.25 (ISBN 0-8217-1299-3). Zebra.
Wichita Poems: Poems. Michael Van Walleghen. LC 75-19257. 66p. 1975. 11.95 (ISBN 0-252-00447-7); pap. 8.95 (ISBN 0-252-00570-8). U of Ill Pr.
Wichita: The Early Years, 1865-80. H. Craig Miner. LC 81-23138. (Illus.). xiv, 201p. 1982. 17.50 (ISBN 0-8032-3077-X). U of Nebr Pr.
Wichtige Standards, Normen und Gesetzliche Bestimmungen Fuer Den Konsumgueterexport in die U. S. A. Griessbach. 185p. 1984. 15.00 (ISBN 0-86640-015-X). German Am Chamber.
Wichtigsten Konsonantischen Erscheinungen Des Vorgriechischen Mit Einem Appendix Uber Den Vokalismus. Edzard J. Furnee. (Janua Linguarum Ser: No. 150). 1972. pap. 51.20x (ISBN 90-2791-997-6). Mouton.
Wicked Angel. Taylor Caldwell. 224p. Repr. of 1965 ed. lib. bdg. 16.95x (ISBN 0-88411-167-9, Pub. by Aeonian Pr). Amereon Ltd.
Wicked Angel. Taylor Caldwell. 1980. pap. 1.95 (ISBN 0-449-23950-0, Crest). Fawcett.
Wicked City. Isaac Bashevis Singer. LC 72-175144. (Illus.). 40p. (gr. 3 up). 1972. o.s.i. 8.95 (ISBN 0-374-38426-6). FS&G.
Wicked Day. Mary Stewart. 384p. 1984. pap. 4.50 (ISBN 0-449-20519-3, Crest). Fawcett.
Wicked Designs. Lillian O'Donnell. 224p. 1987. pap. 2.95 (ISBN 0-449-21532-6, Crest). Fawcett.
Wicked Enchantment. Margot Benary-Isbert. 160p. 1986. pap. 2.75 (ISBN 0-441-88669-8, Pub. by Ace Science Fiction). Ace Bks.
Wicked French. Howard Tomb. 1988. pap. 3.95. Workman Pub.
Wicked Godmother. Marion Chesney. 1987. pap. 2.95 (ISBN 0-317-64610-9). St Martin.
Wicked Godmother. Marion Chesney. 1987. pap. 2.95 (ISBN 0-312-90885-7). St Martin.
Wicked Godmother. Marion Chesney. (Nightingale Ser.). 260p. 1988. pap. 12.95x (ISBN 0-8161-4400-1). G K Hall.
Wicked Good Book. Wicked Good Band & Steve Bither. (Illus.). 96p. (Orig.). 1985. pap. 7.95 (ISBN 0-912769-04-1). L Tapley.
Wicked Grandmother. Marion Chesney. 156p. 1987. 12.95 (ISBN 0-312-00206-8). St Martin.
Wicked Italian. Howard Tomb. 1988. pap. 3.95. Workman Pub.
Wicked Lady. Inglis Fletcher. (Albemarle Ser.). 245p. 1976. Repr. of 1962 ed. lib. bdg. 21.95x (ISBN 0-89244-009-0). Queens Hse-Focus Serv.
Wicked Loving Lies. Rosemary Rogers. 1976. pap. 3.95 (ISBN 0-380-00776-2, 60081-1). Avon.
Wicked Loving Murder. Orania Papazoglou. 192p. 1986. pap. 3.50 (ISBN 0-14-008548-3). Penguin.
Wicked Mate: The Antarctic Diary of Victor Campbell. Victor Campbell. Ed. by Harry G. King. (Antarctic Classics Ser.). (Illus.). 192p. 1988. 35.00 (ISBN 1-85297-030-8). Archival Facsimiles.
Wicked One. Mollie Hunter. LC 76-41515. (Story of Suspense Ser.). (gr. 5 up). 1977. PLB 12.89 (ISBN 0-06-022648-X). HarpJ.
Wicked One: A Story of Suspense. Mollie Hunter. LC 76-41515. (Trophy I Can Read Bks.). 136p. (gr. 5-8). 1980. pap. 1.95 (ISBN 0-06-440117-0, Trophy). HarpJ.
Wicked Pigeon Ladies in the Garden. Mary Chase. 15.75 (ISBN 0-8446-6192-9). Peter Smith.
Wicked Stepdog. Carol L. Benjamin. 128p. (gr. 5 up). 1986. pap. 2.50 (ISBN 0-380-70089-1, Flare). Avon.
Wicked Stepdog. Carole L. Benjamin. LC 81-43322. (Illus.). 128p. (gr. 3-7). 1982. (Crowell Jr Bks); PLB 11.89 (ISBN 0-690-04171-3). HarpJ.
Wicked Uncle. Patricia Wentworth. 17.95 (ISBN 0-88411-724-3, Pub. by Aeonian Pr). Amereon Ltd.
Wicked Uncle. Patricia Wentworth. 272p. 1986. pap. 3.50 (ISBN 0-446-30083-7). Warner Bks.
Wicked Uncles: The Father of Queen Victoria - His Brothers. facs. ed. Roger Fulford. LC 68-8461. (Essay Index Reprint Ser). 1968. Repr. of 1933 ed. 19.00 (ISBN 0-8369-0466-4). Ayer Co Pubs.
Wicked Wager. Margaret Summerville. (Regency Romance Ser.). 224p. 1987. pap. 2.50 (ISBN 0-451-14705-7, Sig). NAL.
Wicked Ways of Malcolm Mclaren: Sex Pistols, Boy George, Adam Ant, Butterfly, Bow Wow Wow, Buffalo Gals, Too Fast to Live, Too Young to Die. Craig Bromberg. LC 87-45599. (Illus.). 256p. (Orig.). 1988. pap. 11.95 (ISBN 0-06-096204-6, PL-6204, PL). Har-Row.
Wicked Widow. Carter Brown. (Orig.). 1981. pap. 1.75 (ISBN 0-505-51610-1, Pub. by Tower Bks). Leisure NY.
Wicked Willie's Guide to Women: A Worm's-Eye View of the Fair Sex. Peter Mayle. (Illus.). 64p. 1988. pap. 8.95 (ISBN 0-517-56652-4, Harmony). Crown.
Wicked Witch of Troll Cave. Don A. Torgersen. LC 80-12043. (Troll Stories Ser.). (Illus.). 32p. (gr. k-4). 1980. pap. 3.50 (ISBN 0-516-43672-4). Childrens.
Wicked Women of the Screen. David Quinlan. (Illus.). 160p. 1988. 18.95 (ISBN 0-312-02048-1). St Martin.
Wicked Wynsleys. Alanna Knight. 1977. pap. 1.50 (ISBN 0-8439-0472-0, Leisure Bks). Leisure NY.
Wickedest Woman in New York: Madame Restell, the Abortionist. Clifford Browder. LC 87-29013. (Illus.). 217p. 1988. 25.00 (ISBN 0-208-02183-3, Archon Bks). Shoe String.
Wickedness. Mary Midgley. 232p. 1986. pap. 8.95 (ISBN 0-7448-0053-6, 0053W). Routledge Chapman & Hall.
Wickedness: A Philosophical Essay. Mary Midgley. 208p. 1984. 29.95x (ISBN 0-7100-9759-X). Routledge Chapman & Hall.
Wicker Furniture. 2nd ed. Robert W. Swedberg & Harriett Swedberg. LC 88-50966. (New Ser.). 160p. 1988. pap. 13.95 (ISBN 0-87069-520-7). Wallace-Homestead.
Wicker Furniture Styles & Prices. Robert Swedberg & Harriet Swedberg. 160p. 1983. pap. 12.95 (ISBN 0-87069-409-X). Wallace-Homestead.
Wicker's Wishes. Carol B. Kaplan. Ed. by Janet L. Bolinske. (Animal Tales Ser.). (Illus.). 24p. (Orig.). (ps-k). Date not set. 17.95 (ISBN 0-88335-757-7). Milliken Pub Co.
Wickersham Commission, National Commission on Law Observance & Enforcement: Complete Reports, Including the Mooney-Billings Report, 14 Vols. Wickersham Commission - National Commission On Law Observance And Enforcement. LC 68-55277. (Criminology, Law Enforcement, & Social Problems Ser.: No. 6). (Illus.). 1968. Repr. of 1931 ed. 250.00x (ISBN 0-87585-006-5). Patterson Smith.
Wicket & the Dandelion Warriors: A Ewok Adventure. Larry Weinberg. LC 85-8183. (Illus.). 32p. (gr. 5-9). 1985. 4.95 (ISBN 0-394-87734-9, BYR). Random.
Wicket Finds a Way: An Ewok Adventure. Melinda Luke. LC 83-62252. (Ewok Mini-Storybooks). (Illus.). 32p. (ps-3). 1984. pap. 1.25 (ISBN 0-394-86356-9, BYR). Random.
Wickford Anthology. Ed. by Peter C. Crolius. LC 85-7265. (Illus.). 160p. (Orig.). 1985. pap. 6.95 (ISBN 0-934881-00-6). Dutch Island.
Wickford Point. John P. Marquand. 11.25 (ISBN 0-8446-2666-X). Peter Smith.
Wickford Point. John P. Marquand. 458p. 1988. pap. 11.95 (ISBN 0-89733-317-9). Academy Chi Pubs.
Wickham Claim: Being an Inquiry into the Attainder of Parker Wickham. Dwight Holbrook. LC 86-6040. 1986. lib. bdg. 21.50 (ISBN 0-938769-00-6, KEN5078.W52H65 1986). Suffolk Cnty Hist Soc.
Wickizer Annals. Mary A. Burgess. LC 80-11075. (Borgo Family Histories Ser.: No. 2). 125p. 1983. lib. bdg. 19.95x (ISBN 0-89370-802-X); pap. 9.95x (ISBN 0-89370-902-6). Borgo Pr.
Wicks & the Wacks. Louis Reed. LC 85-70443. (ps-2). 1985. pap. 5.00 (ISBN 0-916383-00-8, Univ Edtns). Aegina Pr.
Wiclif & Hus. Johann Loserth. Tr. by M. J. Evans. LC 78-63198. (Heresies of the Early Christian & Medieval Era: Second Ser.). 1979. Repr. of 1884 ed. 48.00 (ISBN 0-404-16236-3). AMS Pr.

Widdershins. George Oliver. Ed. by R. Reginald & Douglas Manville. LC 75-46297. (Supernatural & Occult Fiction Ser.). 1976. Repr. of 1911 ed. lib. bdg. 23.50x (ISBN 0-405-08157-X). Ayer Co Pubs.
Wide Angle Photography. Kalton C. Lahue. LC 77-74100. (Photography How-to Ser.). (Illus.). 1977. pap. 3.95 (ISBN 0-8227-4014-1). Petersen Pub.
Wide Awake at Three A. M. By Choice or by Chance. Richard Coleman. LC 86-7665. (Psychology Ser.). (Illus.). 192p. 1986. text ed. 21.95 (ISBN 0-7167-1795-6); pap. text ed. 12.95 (ISBN 0-7167-1796-4). W H Freeman.
Wide Components in Double & Multiple Stars. Ed. by J. Dommanget et al. 1988. lib. bdg. 74.00 (ISBN 90-277-2737-6). Kluwer Academic.
Wide Eyes in Burma & Thailand: Finding Your Way. Wayne Stier & Mars Cavers. (Illus.). 218p. (Orig.). 1983. 10.50 (ISBN 0-911447-01-6); pap. 10.00 (ISBN 0-911447-00-8). Meru Pub.
Wide Fields. Paul Green. LC 79-101911. Repr. of 1928 ed. 14.50 (ISBN 0-404-00625-6). AMS Pr.
Wide Horizon. Anna Brinton. 1947. pap. 2.50x (ISBN 0-87574-038-3, 038). Pendle Hill.
Wide House. Taylor Caldwell. 1974. Repr. of 1945 ed. lib. bdg. 27.95 (ISBN 0-88411-156-3, Pub. by Aeonian Pr). Amereon Ltd.
Wide Hybridization in Plants. N. V. Tsitsin. 368p. 1960. text ed. 76.00x (Pub. by Keter Pub Jerusalem). Coronet Bks.
Wide Is the Water. Jane A. Hodge. 288p. 1982. pap. 2.75 (ISBN 0-449-24563-2, Crest). Fawcett.
Wide Margin New Testament. Compiled by Windell Gann. 1976. 8.95 (ISBN 0-88428-042-X). Parchment Pr.
Wide-Mouthed Frog. Rex Schneider. LC 80-13449. (Illus.). 32p. (gr. k up). 1980. 9.95 (ISBN 0-916144-58-5). Stemmer Hse.
Wide My World, Narrow My Bed: Living & Loving the Single Life. Luci Swindoll. LC 82-7890. 220p. (Orig.). 1982. pap. 7.95 (ISBN 0-930014-89-8). Multnomah.
Wide Neighborhoods: A Story of the Frontier Nursing Service. Mary Breckinridge. LC 81-50181. (Illus.). 400p. 1981. 28.00 (ISBN 0-8131-1453-5); pap. 10.00 (ISBN 0-8131-0149-2). U Pr of Ky.
Wide Net & Other Stories. Eudora Welty. LC 73-12880. 214p. 1974. pap. 6.95 (ISBN 0-15-696610-7, Harv). HarBraceJ.
Wide-Ons. Diane Christian. LC 81-8979. 64p. 1981. 9.00 (ISBN 0-912184-00-0); pap. 4.00 (ISBN 0-912184-01-9). Synergistic Pr.
Wide Sargasso Sea. Jean Rhys. 192p. 1982. pap. 3.95 (ISBN 0-393-00056-7). Norton.
Wide Screen Movies: A History & Filmography of Wide Gauge Filmmaking. Robert E. Carr & R. M. Hayes. LC 86-43093. 516p. 1988. lib. bdg. 39.95x (ISBN 0-89950-242-3). McFarland & Co.
Wide Sleeve of Kwannon. Bruce Lancaster. (Illus.). 307p. 1975. Repr. of 1938 ed. lib. bdg. 19.95 (ISBN 0-89190-884-6, Pub. by River City Pr). Amereon Ltd.
Wide Was His Parish. Edward Elson. 320p. 1986. 12.95 (ISBN 0-8423-8205-4). Tyndale.
Wide, Wide World. Susan Warner. LC 72-78850. 1851. Repr. 69.00x (ISBN 0-403-01989-3). Somerset Pub.
Wide, Wide World. Susan Warner. 448p. 1986. text ed. 29.95 (ISBN 0-935312-65-X); pap. text ed. 11.95 (ISBN 0-935312-66-8). Feminist Pr.
Wide World All Around. Francelia Butler et al. (English & Humanities Ser.). (Illus.). 398p. 1987. pap. text ed. 25.95 (ISBN 0-582-28601-8). Longman.
Wide World of Arbitration: An Anthology. Ed. by Charlotte Gold & Susan Mackenzie. 236p. 15.00 (ISBN 0-943001-22-6). Am Arbitration.
Wide World of Clothing: Economics, Social Significance, Selection. Alpha Latzke & Helen P. Hostetter. LC 68-21650. (Illus.). pap. 80.50 (ISBN 0-8357-9999-9, 2012554). Bks Demand UMI.
Wide World of Girl Guiding & Girl Scouting. Girl Scouts of the U. S. A. Staff. (Illus.). 88p. (gr. 1-6). 1980. pap. text ed. 5.50 (ISBN 0-88441-143-5, 19-713). Girl Scouts USA.
Wide World of Girl Guiding & Girl Scouting: Leaders' Guide. Girl Scouts of the U. S. A. Staff. 24p. 1980. pap. text ed. 2.25 (ISBN 0-88441-144-3, 19-714). Girl Scouts USA.
Wide World of John Steinbeck. Peter Lisca. 338p. 1981. 30.00x (ISBN 0-87752-217-0). Gordian.
Wide World of Words. Joan D. Berbrich. (Orig.). (gr. 7-10). 1975. 11.58 (ISBN 0-87720-340-7). AMSCO Sch.
Wideacre. Philippa Gregory. 464p. 1987. 18.95 (ISBN 0-671-63462-3). S&S.
Wideacre. Philippa Gregory. 640p. 1988. pap. 4.95 (ISBN 0-671-64903-5). PB.
Wideband Communications Services & Equipment Markets. Int'l. Resource Development, Inc. Staff. 140p. 1986. 2100.00x (ISBN 0-88694-712-X). Intl Res Dev.
Widecombe Fair. Eden Phillpotts. 352p. 1983. pap. 7.50 (ISBN 0-907746-21-7, Pub. by A Mott Ltd). Longwood Pub Group.
Wideness of God's Mercy: Litanies to Enlarge Our Prayer, 2 vols. Jeffrey W. Rowthorn. Set. pap. 29.95 (ISBN 0-86683-789-2, HarpR). Har-Row.
Widening Atlantic? Domestic Change & Foreign Policy. Ed. by Andrew J. Pierre. 119p. 1984. pap. 5.95 (ISBN 0-87609-011-0). Coun Foreign.
Widening Atlantic: Domestic Changes & Foreign Policy. Ed. by Andrew J. Pierre. 144p. 1986. 20.00x (ISBN 0-8147-6597-1, Pub. by Columbia U Pr). NYU Pr.
Widening Circle: Essays on the Circulation of Literature in Eighteenth-Century Europe. Ed. by Paul J. Korshin et al. 1976. 27.95x (ISBN 0-8122-7717-1). U of Pa Pr.
Widening Circle: Sermons in Acts. W. E. McCumber. 80p. (Orig.). 1983. pap. 2.95 (ISBN 0-8341-0838-0). Beacon Hill.
Widening Gulf: Northern Attitudes to the Independent Irish State. Dennis Kennedy. 248p. 1988. 26.95 (ISBN 0-85640-396-2, Pub. by Blackstaff Ireland). Irish Bks Media.
Widening Gyre. Robert B. Parker. 1984. pap. 3.95 (ISBN 0-440-19535-7). Dell.
Widening Horizons. Zdenek Kopal. LC 73-99307. (Illus.). (gr. 9 up). 6.95 (ISBN 0-8008-8320-9). Taplinger.
Widening Light: Poems of the Incarnation. Ed. by Luci Shaw. (Wheaton Literary Ser.). 144p. 1984. pap. 6.95 (ISBN 0-87788-930-9). Shaw Pubs.
Widening the Circle: The Humanities in American Education. 16p. 1981. pap. 2.00 (ISBN 0-911696-11-3). Assn Am Coll.
Widening the Field: Continuing Education in Higher Education. Ed. by Colin Titmus. 121p. 1985. pap. 36.00x (ISBN 1-85059-012-5, Open Univ Pr). Taylor & Francis.
Widening the Horizons: Pastoral Responses to a Fragmented Society. Charles V. Gerkin. LC 86-7832. 154p. (Orig.). 1986. pap. 11.95 (ISBN 0-664-24037-2). Westminster John Knox.
Wider Circle. Roger Hutson & Patsy Hutson. 112p. 1985. pap. 3.95 (ISBN 0-310-29421-5, 6895P). Zondervan.
Wider Giving: Women Writing after a Long Silence. Intro. by Sondra Zeidenstein. LC 87-72314. 344p. (Orig.). 1988. pap. 14.95 (ISBN 0-9619111-0-7). Chicory Blue.
Wider Horizons. Dorothy Martin. (Peggy Ser.: No. 7). (gr. 7). 1985. pap. 3.50 (ISBN 0-8024-8307-0). Moody.
Wider Horizons in Christian Adult Education. Lawrence C. Little. LC 62-14381. pap. 87.00 (ISBN 0-8357-9763-5, 2017871). Bks Demand UMI.
Wider Horizons of American History. Herbert E. Bolton. 1967. pap. 5.95x (ISBN 0-268-00301-7). U of Notre Dame Pr.
Wider Uses for Foreign Languages see Language Teaching: Broader Contexts.
Wider World: Portraits in Adolescence. Kate Simon. LC 85-45233. 192p. 1986. 14.45i (ISBN 0-06-015526-4, HarpT). Har-Row.
Wider World: Portraits in an Adolescence. Kate Simon. LC 85-45233. 186p. 1987. pap. 6.95 (ISBN 0-06-091379-7, PL 1379, PL). Har-Row.
Widerrechtlicher Streik und Abwehraussperrung. Paul B. Schaeuble. (European University Studies: No. 2, Vol. 336). 262p. (Ger.). 1983. 35.80 (ISBN 3-8204-7780-2). P Lang Pubs.
Widerspruchsprinzip in der neueren sowjetischen Philosophie. N. Lobkowicz. (Sovietica Ser.: No. 4). 89p. (Ger.). 1960. lib. bdg. 16.00 (Pub. by Reidel Holland). Kluwer Academic.
Widor: The Life & Times of Charles-Marie Widor, 1844-1937. Andrew Thomson. (Illus.). 128p. 1988. 39.00 (ISBN 0-19-316417-5). Oxford U Pr.
Widow. Charity Blackstock. 1978. pap. 1.95 (ISBN 0-505-51219-X, Pub. by Tower Bks). Leisure NY.
Widow. Lynn Caine. 192p. 1987. pap. 3.95 (ISBN 0-553-26422-2). Bantam.
Widow. Nicolas Freeling. LC 80-10634. 256p. 1980. pap. 3.95 (ISBN 0-394-74467-5, Vin). Random.
Widow & the Parrot. Virginia Woolf. (Illus.). 32p. (gr. 2-7). 1988. 12.95 (ISBN 0-15-296783-4). HarBraceJ.
Widow & the Wildcatter. Fran Baker. (Loveswept Ser.: No. 246). 192p. (Orig.). 1988. pap. 2.50 (ISBN 0-553-21863-8). Bantam.
Widow Barnaby, 3 vols. in 2. Frances Trollope. LC 79-8208. Repr. of 1839 ed. Set. 84.50 (ISBN 0-404-62141-4). Vol. 1 (ISBN 0-404-62142-2). Vol. 2 (ISBN 0-404-62143-0). AMS Pr.
Widow LeRouge. Emile Gaboriau. Tr. by Fred Williams & George A. Ernst. LC 75-32746. (Literature of Mystery & Detection). 1976. Repr. of 1873 ed. 17.00x (ISBN 0-405-07872-2). Ayer Co Pubs.
Widow LeRouge. Emile Gaboriau. 293p. 1980. Repr. of 1900 ed. lib. bdg. 12.50x (ISBN 0-89968-184-0). Lightyear.
Widow Maker. Dean McElwain. (Preachers Law Ser.: No. 1). 224p. (Orig.). 1987. pap. 2.50 (ISBN 0-8439-2508-6, Leisure Bks). Leisure NY.
Widow, Nun & Courtesan: Three Novelettes from the Chinese. Lin Yu-T'ang. LC 75-112328. vi, 266p. 1971. Repr. of 1951 ed. lib. bdg. 35.00x (ISBN 0-8371-4716-6, LIWN). Greenwood.
Widow of Ratchets. Owen Brookes. 1980. pap. 2.75 (ISBN 0-441-88769-4). Ace Bks.
Widow to Widow. Phyllis R. Silverman. 240p. 1986. text ed. 19.95 (ISBN 0-8261-5030-6). Springer Pub.
Widowed. Philip Jebb. LC 83-11160. 1984. pap. 3.95 (ISBN 0-932506-30-5). St Bedes Pubns.
Widowed. Frances H. Mulliken. 1983. pap. 4.50 (ISBN 0-8309-0361-5). Herald Hse.
Widowed Beaver. Michael P. Jones. (Illus.). 150p. (Orig.). 1986. ltd. ed. 25.00 (ISBN 0-89904-203-1); text ed. 14.95 (ISBN 0-89904-201-5); pap. 9.95 (ISBN 0-317-67925-2). Crumb Elbow Pub.
Widower. Scott Campbell & Phyllis Silverman. 1987. 17.95 (ISBN 0-13-959503-1). P-H.
Widower. Elin Schoen. 224p. 1987. pap. 4.50 (ISBN 0-553-26908-9). Bantam.
Widower & Some Spinsters: Short Stories. Maria L. Pool. LC 78-101288. (Short Story Index Reprint Ser). 1899. 19.00 (ISBN 0-8369-3225-0). Ayer Co Pubs.
Widowers' Houses. George Bernard Shaw. Ed. by Jerald Bringle. LC 79-56699. (Bernard Shaw Early Texts: Play Manuscripts in Facsimile). 1981. lib. bdg. 67.00 (ISBN 0-8240-4575-0). Garland Pub.
Widows. Ariel Dorfman. LC 84-40224. 160p. 1984. pap. 6.95 (ISBN 0-394-71108-4, Vin). Random.
Widows. Ariel Dorfman. 1989. 7.95 (ISBN 0-14-011659-1). Penguin.
Widows: A Women's Ministry in the Early Church. Bonnie B. Thurston. LC 88-45249. 96p. (Orig.). 1989. pap. 8.95 (ISBN 0-8006-2317-7). Fortress.
Widows Are Not for Burning. A. K. Ray. 1985. 24.95. Asia Bk Corp.
Widow's Benefits: Retirement Pension see Adjudication Officers' Guide.
Widow's Children. Paula Fox. LC 86-61001. pap. 9.95 (ISBN 0-86547-251-3). N Point Pr.
Widows' Club. Dorothy Cannell. 320p. 1988. 16.95 (ISBN 0-553-05259-4). Bantam.
Widow's Dilemma. Helen Leszczynski. 80p. 1986. cancelled (ISBN 0-8062-2828-8). Carlton.
Widow's Gambit. Anthea Malcolm. 256p. 1988. pap. 2.95 (ISBN 0-8217-2357-X). Zebra.
Widow's Handbook: A Guide for Living. Charlotte Foehner & Carol Cozart. 225p. 1987. 18.95 (ISBN 1-55591-014-9); pap. 14.95 (ISBN 1-55591-023-8). Fulcrum Inc.
Widows in African Societies: Choices & Constraints. Ed. by Betty Potash. 336p. 1986. 35.00x (ISBN 0-8047-1299-9). Stanford U Pr.
Widows in the Dark. Elizabeth S. Gatov. 176p. 1986. pap. 3.95 (ISBN 0-446-30021-7). Warner Bks.
Widows in the Dark: Rescuing Your Financial Position. Elisabeth S. Gatov. LC 84-73372. 127p. 1985. pap. 8.95 (ISBN 0-943004-02-0). Common Knowledge.
Widow's Mite. Connie R. Crick. LC 86-91460. 163p. 1987. 11.95 (ISBN 0-533-07283-2). Vantage.
Widow's Mite & Other Stories. Ferrol Sams. LC 87-80971. 222p. 1987. 14.95 (ISBN 0-934601-26-7). Peachtree Pubs.
Widow's Mite & Other Stories. Ferrol Sams. 1989. 6.95. Penguin.
Widows of Broome: An Inspector Napoleon Bonaparte Mystery. Arthur W. Upfield. 1985. pap. 3.95 (ISBN 0-684-18389-7). Scribner.
Widows of Russia, Nabokov's Style & Other Essays. Carl R. Proffer. (Illus.). 325p. 1987. 25.00 (ISBN 0-88233-947-8). Ardis Pubs.
Widow's Son. Robert A. Wilson. (Historical Illuminatus Chronicles Ser.: Vol. 2). 352p. (Orig.). 1985. pap. 9.95 (ISBN 0-312-94457-8). Bluejay Bks.
Widow's Son. Robert A. Wilson. (Illuminatus: No. 2). 400p. 1989. pap. 4.95 mass mrkt. (ISBN 1-55802-177-9). Lynx Bks.
Widow's Taboo. A. Poulin, Jr. (Illus.). 1977. 20.00 (ISBN 0-685-50402-6, Pub by Mushinsha Bks); sewn in wrappers 5.95 (ISBN 0-685-50403-4). Small Pr Dist.
Widow's Tears. George Chapman. Ed. by Ethel M. Smeak. LC 65-24305. (Regents Renaissance Drama Ser). xxvi, 119p. 1966. 13.95x (ISBN 0-8032-0257-1); pap. 3.50x (ISBN 0-8032-5258-7, BB 217, Bison). U of Nebr Pr.
Widow's Tears. George Chapman. Ed. by Akihiro Yamada. (Revels Plays Ser.). 152p. 1975. 50.00 (ISBN 0-7190-1510-3, Pub. by Manchester Univ Pr). St Martin.
Widows, Vol. I: The Middle East, Asia, & the Pacific. Ed. by Helena Z. Lopata. LC 87-5410. xiii, 258p. 1987. 37.95 (ISBN 0-8223-0680-8); pap. 15.95 (ISBN 0-8223-0768-5). Duke.
Widows, Vol. II: North America. Ed. by Helena Z. Lopata. LC 87-5410. xii, 313p. 1987. lib. bdg. 40.00 (ISBN 0-8223-0724-3); pap. text ed. 16.95 (ISBN 0-8223-0770-7). Duke.
Wid's Year Book 1918. 1971. 49.50 (ISBN 0-405-02562-9, 58). Ayer Co Pubs.
Wid's Year Book 1918-1922. 1971. 198.00 (ISBN 0-405-02557-2, 128). Ayer Co Pubs.
Wid's Year Book: 1919-20. 1971. 49.50 (ISBN 0-405-02563-7, 57). Ayer Co Pubs.
Wid's Year Book 1920-1921. 1971. 49.50 (ISBN 0-405-02564-5, 56). Ayer Co Pubs.
Wid's Year Book 1921-1922. 1971. 49.50 (ISBN 0-405-02565-3, 55). Ayer Co Pubs.
Wie Alles Anfing see How It All Began: A Personal Account of a West German Urban Guerilla.
Wie geht's? 3rd ed. Dieter Sevin et al. LC 87-11934. 496p. 1988. text ed. price not set (ISBN 0-03-008632-9); price not set (ISBN 0-03-008633-7); price not set wkbk (ISBN 0-03-008634-5); price not set; price not set cassettes (ISBN 0-03-008637-X). HR&W.
Wie Geht's: An Introductory German Course. 2nd ed. Dieter Sevin et al. 478p. 1984. text ed. 31.95 (ISBN 0-03-063972-7). HR&W.
Wie Kam und Wie Kommt Es Zum Osterglauben? Hans-Willi Winden. (Disputationes Theologicae: Vol. 12). 352p. (Ger.). 1982. 39.45 (ISBN 3-8204-5820-4). P Lang Pubs.
Wieland & "Memoirs of Carwin". Charles B. Brown. Ed. by Sydney J. Krause & S. W. Reid. LC 78-15330. 310p. 1978. pap. text ed. 7.50x (ISBN 0-87338-220-X). Kent St U Pr.
Wieland & Shaftesbury. Charles Elson. LC 79-166024. (Columbia University. Germanic Studies, Old Ser.: No. 16). Repr. of 1913 ed. 22.50 (ISBN 0-404-50416-7). AMS Pr.
Wieland: Or, the Transformation. Charles B. Brown. 1969. pap. 5.95 (ISBN 0-385-03100-9, Anch). Doubleday.
Wieland: Or, the Transformation. Charles B. Brown. Ed. by F. L. Pattee. LC 58-13328. 351p. 1969. pap. 7.95 (ISBN 0-15-696680-8, Harv). HarBraceJ.
Wieland or the Transformation. Charles B. Brown. 279p. Repr. of 1984 ed. lib. bdg. 45.00 (ISBN 0-918377-98-6). Russell Pr.
Wieland und Bodmer. Fritz Budde. 1910. 27.00 (ISBN 0-384-06206-7); pap. 22.00 (ISBN 0-384-06205-9). Johnson Repr.
Wieland's Attitude Toward Woman & Her Cultural & Social Relations. Matthew G. Bach. LC 71-159988. (Columbia University. Germanic Studies, Old Ser.: No. 26). Repr. of 1922 ed. 11.50 (ISBN 0-404-50426-4). AMS Pr.
Wielding a Red Sword. Piers Anthony. (Incarnations of Immortality Ser.: Bk. 4). 1986. pap. 16.95 (ISBN 0-345-32220-7, Del Rey). Ballantine.
Wielding a Red Sword. Piers Anthony. (Incarnations of Immortality Ser.). 320p. 1987. pap. 4.50 (ISBN 0-345-32221-5, Del Rey). Ballantine.
Wielki Slownik Polsko-Rosyski (Polish-Russian Dictionary) Mirowicz. 1331p. (Pol. & Rus.). 1980. 125.00 (ISBN 0-686-87195-2, M-9131). French & Eur.
Wielopole-Wielopole. Tadeusz Kantor. Tr. by Mariusz Tchorek & George Hyde. (Illus.). 192p. 1988. 17.95 (ISBN 0-7145-2782-3, Dist. by Kampmann & Co). M Boyars Pubs.
Wiener Jugendstilsilber, Original, Fake or Composite: Vienna 20th Century Silver. Waltraud Neuwirth. (Illus.). 88p. (Orig., Eng. & Ger.). 1980. pap. 24.00 (ISBN 3-900282-14-5, Pub. by Waltraud Neuwirth). Seven Hills Bks.
Wiener Werkstaette. (Illus.). 1966. pap. 7.00 (ISBN 0-910810-10-9). Johannes.
Wiener Werkstatte. Wanda Quoika-Stanka. (Architecture Ser.: A 1801). 5p. 1987. 3.00 (ISBN 1-55590-271-5). Vance Biblios.
Wiener Werkstatte Avantgarde, Art Deco & Industrial Design. Waltraud Neuwirth. (Illus.). 240p. (Ger. & Eng.). 1984. 45.00 (ISBN 3-900282-22-6, Pub. by Waltraud Neuwirth). Seven Hills Bks.
Wiener Werkstatte Keramik: Original Ceramics, 1920-1931, Vol. I. Waltraud Neuwirth. (Illus.). 352p. (Eng. & Ger.). 1981. 79.00 (ISBN 3-900282-17-X, Pub. by Waltraud Neuwirth). Seven Hills Bks.
Wieniawski: Life & Times Ser. Wladyslaw Duleba. Tr. by Grazyna Czerny from Pol. (Illus.). 175p. 19.95 (ISBN 0-86622-017-8). Paganiniana Pubns.
Wier & Pouce. Steve Katz. LC 83-40578. (New American Fiction Ser.: No. 1). 367p. 1984. 17.95 (ISBN 0-940650-33-9); signed ed 30.00 (ISBN 0-940650-35-5); pap. 10.95 (ISBN 0-940650-47-9). Sun & Moon CA.
Wierd Soccer Match. Jerry Jenkins. (Dallas O'Neil & the Baker Street Sports Club Ser.). (Orig.). (YA) (gr. 9-12). 1986. pap. text ed. 3.95 (ISBN 0-8024-8237-6). Moody.
Wiesenberger Investment Companies Service. 42nd ed. Ed. by Paul A. Johnston. LC 43-14373. 345.00 (ISBN 0-686-46798-1). Warren Gorham & Lamont.
Wife. Stephen Emerson. 96p. 1985. 6.00 (ISBN 0-942986-02-4). LongRiver Bks.
Wife. Bharati Mukherjee. 224p. 1987. pap. 6.95 (ISBN 0-14-009300-1). Penguin.
Wife: A Libretto (For an Opera in Three Acts) 2nd ed. Janet Lewis. 64p. 1988. pap. 8.95 (ISBN 0-936784-63-6). J Daniel.
Wife & Other Stories. Anton Chekhov. Tr. by Constance Garnett from Rus. (Tales of Chekhov Ser.: Vol. 5). 200p. 1985. pap. 8.50 (ISBN 0-88001-052-5). Ecco Pr.
Wife Battering: A Systems Theory Approach. Jean Giles-Sims. LC 82-15555. (Guilford Perspectives on Marriage & the Family Ser.). 193p. 1983. lib. bdg. 30.00 (ISBN 0-89862-075-9, 2075). Guilford Pr.
Wife Battering: A Systems Theory Approach. Giles G. Sims. (Guilford Perspectives on Marriage & the Family Ser.). 193p. 1986. pap. 16.95 (ISBN 0-89862-910-1). Guilford Pr.
Wife Battering in Canada: The Vicious Circle. 72p. 1980. pap. 7.50 (ISBN 0-660-10483-0, SSC162, SSC). UNIPUB.
Wife for Mr. Watts. David Coe. 1982. 15.00x (ISBN 0-906660-39-4, Pub. by New Playwrights Network). State Mutual Bk.
Wife for My Son. Ali Ghalem. Tr. by G. Kazolias. LC 84-20414. Orig. Title: Une Femme Pour Mon Fils. 211p. (Orig.). 1984. pap. 6.95 (ISBN 0-916650-17-0). Banner Pr.

Wild Bird's Nest: Poems from the Irish. Frank O'Connor. 56p. 1971. Repr. of 1932 ed. 15.00x (ISBN 0-7165-1374-9, BBA 02075, Pub. by Cuala Press Ireland). Biblio Dist.
Wild Birds: Six Stories of the Port William Membership. Wendell Berry. LC 85-72988. 146p. 1986. 13.95 (ISBN 0-86547-216-5). N Point Pr.
Wild Blue. Walter J. Boyne & Steven L. Thompson. 1987. pap. 4.95 (ISBN 0-8041-0149-3, Pub. by Ivy). Ballantine.
Wild, Blue Berries: A Mystery Novel. Edna Hong. LC 87-9190. 144p. (Orig.). 1987. pap. 7.95 (ISBN 0-8066-2274-1, 10-7190). Augsburg.
Wild Blue: The Novel of the U. S. Air Force. Stephen L. Thompson & Walter J. Boyne. 1986. 19.95 (ISBN 0-517-56285-5). Crown.
Wild Blue Water. Jean Niemeier. LC 62-22127. (Illus.). 1962. 8.95 (ISBN 0-8323-0196-5). Binford-Metropolitan.
Wild Blue Yonder: Money, Politics, & the B-1 Bomber. Nick Kotz. LC 87-43057. 320p. 1987. 19.95 (ISBN 0-394-55700-X). Pantheon.
Wild Blue Yonder: Songs of the Air Force, 2 vols, Vol. 1. Ed. by C. W. Getz. LC 81-52998. (Illus.). 312p. 1981. 15.95x (ISBN 0-941196-00-3). Redwood Pr.
Wild Blue Yonder: Songs of the Air Force, Vol. II, The Stag Bar Edition. Ed. by C. W. Getz. LC 81-52998. (Illus.). 226p. 1986. 17.95 (ISBN 0-941196-49-6). Redwood Pr.
Wild Boar & Bear of Appalachin. 308p. (Orig.). 1986. pap. 8.95 (ISBN 0-317-44005-5). Atlantic Pub Co.
Wild Boars. Darrel Nicholson. (Nature Watch Bks.). (Illus.). 48p. (gr. 2-5). 1987. PLB 12.95 (ISBN 0-87614-308-7). Carolrhoda Bks.
Wild Body. Wyndham Lewis. LC 70-137666. (Studies in Poetry, No. 38). 1971. Repr. of 1927 ed. lib. bdg. 49.95x (ISBN 0-8383-1225-X). Haskell.
Wild Border Guns see Outlaw Breed.
Wild Bouquet: Nature Poems. Harry Martinson. Tr. by William J. Smith & Leif Sjoberg. LC 84-73437. (International Ser.). (Illus.). 80p. 1985. 10.95 (ISBN 0-933532-48-2). BkMk.
Wild Boy. Joan Tate. LC 73-5495. (Illus.). 112p. (gr. 5 up). 1973. PLB 11.89 (ISBN 0-06-026097-1). HarpJ.
Wild Boy of Aveyron. Jean-Marc-Gaspard Itard. Tr. by George Humphrey & Muriel Humphrey. 1962. pap. 15.00x (ISBN 0-13-959494-9). P-H.
Wild Boy of Aveyron. Harlan Lane. (Illus.). 384p. 1976. 24.50x (ISBN 0-674-95282-0); pap. 8.95 (ISBN 0-674-95300-2). Harvard U Pr.
Wild Boys: Three Novels see Soft Machine.
Wild Britain. Douglas Botting. (Illus.). 224p. Date not set. leatherette 22.50 (ISBN 0-89659-807-1). Abbeville Pr.
Wild Brothers: Maine Animal Tales. Jack Aley. (Illus.). 192p. (Orig.). 1987. pap. 8.95 (ISBN 0-912769-21-1). L Tapley.
Wild Brothers of the Indians: As Pictured by the Ancient Americans. Alice Wesche. LC 77-79064. (Illus.). (gr. 3-8). 1977. pap. 4.95 (ISBN 0-918080-21-5). Treasure Chest.
Wild Bunch. Rick Walters. (Orig.). 1980. pap. 1.75 (ISBN 0-505-51601-2, Pub. by Tower Bks). Leisure NY.
Wild Bunch see Border Trumpet.
Wild Bush Tribes of Tropical Africa. G. Cyril Claridge. LC 74-90111. (Illus.). 1969. Repr. of 1922 ed. 35.00 (ISBN 0-8371-2029-2, CLB&). Greenwood.
Wild California: Vanishing Lands, Vanishing Wildlife. A. Starker Leopold et al. Ed. by Raymond F Dasmann. 150p. 1985. 40.00x (ISBN 0-520-05293-5). U of Cal Pr.
Wild California: Vanishing Lands, Vanishing Wildlife. Leopold A. Starker. (Illus.). Date not set. pap. cancelled (ISBN 0-520-06024-5). U of Cal Pr.
Wild Canids: Their Systematics, Behavioral Ecology & Evolution. Ed. by M. W. Fox. LC 83-268. 526p. 1983. Repr. of 1975 ed. text ed. 37.50 (ISBN 0-89874-619-1). Krieger.
Wild Card. Margaret Hobbs. 224p. 1985. pap. 2.75 (ISBN 0-345-32002-6). Ballantine.
Wild Card Run. Sara Stamey. 240p. (Orig.). 1987. pap. 2.95 (ISBN 0-425-09705-6). Berkley Pub.
Wild Cards, No. 1. George R. Martin. 288p. (Orig.). 1987. pap. 3.95 (ISBN 0-553-26190-8, Spectra). Bantam.
Wild Cat. Mary Hoffman. LC 86-10007. (Animals in the Wild Ser.). (Illus.). 24p. (gr. k-5). 1986. PLB 11.33 (ISBN 0-8172-2399-1). Raintree Pubs.
Wild Cat. Robert N. Peck. (Illus.). (gr. 6-12). 1977. pap. 0.95 (ISBN 0-380-01728-8, 34173, Camelot). Avon.
Wild Cats. Mark Carwardine. (Illus.). 48p. (YA) (gr. 7 up). 1987. pap. 3.95 (ISBN 0-590-40741-4). Scholastic Inc.
Wild Cats. Jerolyn Nentl. Ed. by Howard Schroeder. LC 83-22506. (Wildlife (Habits & Habitat) Ser.). (Illus.). 48p. (gr. 4-5). 1984. PLB 10.95 (ISBN 0-89686-249-6). Crestwood Hse.
Wild Cats. Peggy D. Winston. Ed. by Donald J. Crump. LC 81-47742. (Books for Young Explorers: Series 8). 32p. (ps-3). 1981. lib. bdg. 12.95 (ISBN 0-87044-401-8). Natl Geog.
Wild Cats see Books for Young Explorers.
Wild Cats of the World Coloring Book. John Green. (ps up). 1988. pap. 2.75 (ISBN 0-486-25638-3). Dover.

Wild Cherries. Dale Herd. 100p. (Orig.). 1980. pap. 5.00 (ISBN 0-939180-16-2). Tombouctou.
Wild Child. John Shirley. 1988. 25.00 (ISBN 0-910489-26-2). Scream Pr.
Wild Children. Felice Holman. LC 83-8974. 160p. (gr. 5-7). 1983. PLB 12.95 (ISBN 0-684-17970-9, Pub. by Scribner). Macmillan.
Wild Children. Felice Holman. LC 85-3541. 152p. (gr. 5-9). 1985. pap. 4.95 (ISBN 0-14-031930-1). Penguin.
Wild Civility: Interactions in the Poetry & Thought of Robert Graves. Patrick J. Keane. LC 79-5428. 128p. 1980. pap. 8.95 (ISBN 0-8262-0296-9). U of Mo Pr.
Wild Coast. Jan Carew. 1958. 29.00 (ISBN 0-8115-3029-9). Kraus Repr.
Wild Coast: An Account of Politics in West Indies. Reynold A. Burrowes. 350p. 1984. text ed. 18.95 (ISBN 0-87073-037-1); pap. 11.95 (ISBN 0-87073-127-0). Schenkman Bks Inc.
Wild Coffee & Tea Substitutes of Canada. Nancy J. Turner & Adam F. Szczawinski. (Illus.). 1978. pap. 12.95 (ISBN 0-660-00090-3, 56558-0, Pub. by Natl Mus Canada). U of Chicago Pr.
Wild Colonial Boy: Bushranger Jack Donahoe, 1806-1830. John Meredith. (Studies in Australian Folklore: No. 3). (Illus.). 102p. (Orig.). 1985. pap. 12.95x (ISBN 0-908247-04-4). Legacy Bks.
Wild Concerto. Anne Mather. (Bestsellers Ser.). 384p. 1983. pap. 4.95 U. S. (ISBN 0-373-97006-4, Pub. by Worldwide). Harlequin Bks.
Wild Country. Louis Bromfield. 274p. Repr. of 1948 ed. lib. bdg. 18.95x (ISBN 0-88411-542-9, Pub. by Aeonian Pr). Amereon Ltd.
Wild Country. Dean Ing. 320p. (Orig.). 1985. pap. 2.95 (ISBN 0-8125-4102-2, Dist. by Warner Pub Services & St. Martin's Press). Tor Bks.
Wild Country All Game & Fish Recipes. Jay Jaxson. (Illus.). 81p. (Orig.). 1982. pap. text ed. 7.95 (ISBN 0-686-40837-3). Jackson G B.
Wild Cow Tales. Ben K. Green. (Illus.). 1969. 17.95 (ISBN 0-394-45188-0). Knopf.
Wild, Crazy & Crude Jokes. Don Brossard. 60p. 1987. 7.95 (ISBN 0-533-07169-0). Vantage.
Wild Dawn Fever. Melanie Davis. (Orig.). 1987. pap. 3.50 (ISBN 0-449-21416-8, Crest). Fawcett.
Wild Desires. Kathleen Drymon. 1982. pap. 3.50 (ISBN 0-8217-1103-2). Zebra.
Wild Dogs. Steve Maurer. 24p. (Orig.). 1981. pap. 3.50 (ISBN 0-940846-01-2). Hastings Bks.
Wild Dogs. Peter Skrzynecki. LC 85-15888. 202p. 1988. 9.96 (ISBN 0-7022-2014-0). U of Queensland Pr.
Wild Dogs. Wildlife Education, Limited, Staff. (Illus.). 20p. (Orig.). 1985. pap. 1.95 (ISBN 0-937934-40-2). Wildlife Educ.
Wild Dreams of a New Beginning: Including Landscapes of Living & Dying & Who Are We Now? Lawrence Ferlinghetti. LC 88-5304. 144p. 1988. 18.95 (ISBN 0-8112-1074-X); pap. 6.95 (ISBN 0-8112-1075-8, NDP663). New Directions.
Wild Duck. Henrik Ibsen. Ed. by Kai Jurgensen & Robert Schenkkan. Tr. by Kai Jurgensen & Robert Schenkkan. LC 66-21588. 1966. pap. text ed. 4.25x (ISBN 0-88295-046-0). Harlan Davidson.
Wild Duck. Henrik Ibsen. Ed. by Dounia B. Christiani. (Critcal Editions). (gr. 9-12). 1969. (NortonC); pap. text ed. 7.95x (ISBN 0-393-09825-7). Norton.
Wild Duck see Four Major Plays.
Wild Duck see Ibsen's Plays Notes.
Wild Duck & Hedda Gabler. new ed. Henrik Ibsen. Tr. by Michael Meyer. 1977. pap. 7.95 (ISBN 0-393-00843-6, Norton Lib). Norton.
Wild Ducks & Geese of North America. Sandra D. Romashko. LC 77-81167. (Illus.). 1978. pap. 2.95 (ISBN 0-89317-018-6). Windward Pub.
Wild Edible Fruits & Berries. Marjorie Furlong & Virginia Pill. LC 74-32015. (Illus.). 64p. 1974. 12.95 (ISBN 0-87961-033-6); pap. 6.95 (ISBN 0-87961-032-8). Naturegraph.
Wild Edible Plants of Western North America. color ed. Donald R. Kirk. LC 75-5998. (Illus.). 343p. 1975. 12.95 (ISBN 0-87961-037-9); pap. 6.95 (ISBN 0-87961-036-0). Naturegraph.
Wild Edibles, Identification for Living off the Land. rev. ed. Marian Van Atta. LC 84-62805. (Living off the Land Ser.). (Illus.). 64p. 1985. pap. text ed. 4.95 (ISBN 0-938524-01-1, Div. of Pine & Palm Press). Geraventure.
Wild Elephants in Captivity. Jack Adams. LC 81-69851. (Illus.). 206p. 1981. pap. 20.00x (ISBN 0-942074-00-9). Ctr Study Elephants.
Wild Flavor. Marilyn Kluger. LC 84-2760. 288p. 1984. 8.95 (ISBN 0-87477-338-5). J P Tarcher.
Wild Flower. Rosemarie Santini. (Orig.). 1986. pap. write for info. (ISBN 0-449-70069-0, Juniper). Fawcett.
Wild Flower Gardening: The National Trust Book Of. John Stevens. (Illus.). 192p. 1988. 25.95 (ISBN 0-87106-886-9). Globe Pequot.
Wild Flowers: A Portfolio of Frameable Prints. LC 84-45700. (Louise Lindsey Merrick Texas Environment Ser.: No. 8). (Illus.). 1985. 25.00 (ISBN 0-89096-232-4). Tex A&M Univ Pr.
Wild Flowers: Along Mt. McKinley Park Road. Louise Potter & Jerryne Cole. LC 79-52424. (Illus., Orig.). 1979. pap. 5.95 (ISBN 0-9602792-0-2). Camp Denali.

Wild Flowers in Britian & Northern Europe. Blamery & Fitter. 1987. pap. 13.95 (ISBN 0-00-219715-4). Greene.
Wild Flowers in Danger. John Fisher. (Illus.). 194p. 1988. 29.95 (ISBN 0-575-03893-4, Pub. by Gollancz England). David & charles.
Wild Flowers: Joel Meyerowitz Photographs. Joel Meyerowitz. LC 82-62725. (Illus.). 109p. 1986. pap. 16.45 (ISBN 0-8212-1627-9, 940658). NYGS.
Wild Flowers of Britain. Roger Phillips. (Illus.). 192p. (Orig.). 1977. pap. text ed. 19.95x (ISBN 0-916422-39-9, Pub. by Pan Bks England). Mad River.
Wild Flowers of Britain & Europe. Blamey & Fitter. pap. 13.95 (ISBN 0-00-219550-X, Pub. by Collins Pub England). Greene.
Wild Flowers of Britain & Northern Europe. Fitter & Blamey. 1978. pap. 14.95 (ISBN 0-00-219069-9, Collins Pub England). Greene.
Wild Flowers of California. Mary E. Parsons. (Illus.). 423p. Repr. of 1897 ed. 10.00 (ISBN 0-940228-06-8). Calif Acad Sci.
Wild Flowers of California. Mary E. Parsons. (Illus.). 14.50 (ISBN 0-8446-2708-9). Peter Smith.
Wild Flowers of Central Saudi Arabia. B. A. Vincett. 114p. 1977. 60.00x (ISBN 0-317-07184-X, Pub. by FW Classey UK). State Mutual Bk.
Wild Flowers of Eastern Canada. Katherine MacKenzie. (Illus.). 1973. pap. 2.95 (ISBN 0-02-119511-0). Tundra Bks.
Wild Flowers of Florida. Glenn Fleming et al. LC 76-43050. (Illus.). 1976. pap. 6.95 (ISBN 0-916224-08-2). Banyan Bks.
Wild Flowers of Kenya. Blundell. 1982. 29.95 (ISBN 0-00-219317-5, Collins Pub England). Greene.
Wild Flowers of Majorca, Minorca & Ibiza: With Keys to the Flora of the Balearic Islands. Elspeth Beckett. (Illus.). 224p. 1987. text ed. 55.00 (ISBN 90-6191-634-8, Pub. A A Balkema). Brookfield Pub Co.
Wild Flowers of Marin: A Layman's Handbook. Lilian McHoul. LC 79-51455. (Illus.). 1979. pap. 4.95 (ISBN 0-912908-08-4). Tamal Land.
Wild Flowers of North Alabama. Bonnie P. Tondera et al. 250p. 1987. 12.00 (ISBN 0-9619472-0-9). I H Paul.
Wild Flowers of North Carolina. William S. Justice & C. Ritchie Bell. LC 68-18051. (Illus.). xxviii, 217p. 1987. pap. 14.95 (ISBN 0-8078-4192-7). U of NC Pr.
Wild Flowers of Southern Africa. Sima Eliovson. (Illus.). 310p. 1982. 32.50 (ISBN 0-86954-088-2, Pub. by Macmillan S Africa). Intl Spec Bk.
Wild Flowers of Table Mountain. W. P. Jackson. 120p. 1981. 37.50x (ISBN 0-86978-146-4, Pub. by Timmins Africa). Intl Spec Bk.
Wild Flowers of the Big Thicket, East Texas, & Western Louisiana. Geyata Ajilvsgi. LC 78-21781. (W. L. Moody, Jr., Natural History Ser.: NO. 4). (Illus.). 448p. 1979. 22.50x (ISBN 0-89096-064-X); pap. 9.95 (ISBN 0-89096-065-8). Tex A&M Univ Pr.
Wild Flowers of the Great Lakes Region. Roberta L. Simonds & Henrietta Tweedie. (Illus.). 96p. 1984. pap. 5.95 (ISBN 0-914091-45-X). Chicago Review.
Wild Flowers of the Midwest. Katherine Mackenzie. LC 75-44840. (Illus.). 1976. pap. 2.95 (ISBN 0-912766-33-6). Tundra Bks.
Wild Flowers of the North York Moors National Park. Sylvia Arnold. 120p. 1986. 36.00 (ISBN 0-907033-42-3, Hutton Pr). State Mutual Bk.
Wild Flowers of the Northeast. Katherine Mackenzie. LC 75-44841. (Illus.). 1976. pap. 2.95 (ISBN 0-912766-32-8). Tundra Bks.
Wild Flowers of the South. Katherine MacKenzie. (Illus.). 1977. pap. 2.95 (ISBN 0-912766-56-5). Tundra Bks.
Wild Food. Roger Phillips. 1986. pap. 19.95 (ISBN 0-316-70611-6). Little.
Wild Food. Roger Phillips. 24.50 (ISBN 0-8446-6262-3). Peter Smith.
Wild Food: A Unique Photographic Guide to Finding, Cooking & Eating Wild Plants, Mushrooms & Seaweed. Roger Phillips. (Illus.). 159p. 1986. pap. 19.95x (ISBN 0-317-05062-1). Mad River.
Wild Food Cookbook. Frances Hamerston. (Illus.). 144p. 1988. 15.95 (ISBN 0-8138-0116-8). Iowa St U Pr.
Wild Foods: A Beginner's Guide to Identifying, Harvesting & Preparing Safe & Tasty Plants from the Outdoors. Laurence Pringle. LC 78-1910. (Illus.). 192p. (gr. 7 up). 1978. 12.95 (ISBN 0-02-775450-2, Four Winds). Macmillan.
Wild Foods & Animals: Coloring Book. 2nd ed. Lindia Runyon. (Illus.). 16p. (gr. 1 up). 1986. pap. 1.99 (ISBN 0-936699-01-9). Runyon Pub.
Wild Foods Cookery. John Tomikel. LC 78-57184. 1978. pap. 3.00 (ISBN 0-910042-34-9). Allegheny.
Wild Foods Field Guide & Cookbook. 2nd ed. Billy J. Tatum. LC 75-8909. (Illus.). 276p. 1985. pap. 6.95 (ISBN 0-911104-77-1). Workman Pub.
Wild Foods of Appalachia. rev. ed. William H. Gillespie. (Illus.). 200p. 1988. pap. 9.50 (ISBN 0-89092-020-6). Seneca Bks.
Wild Foods of the Desert. Darcy Williamson. (Illus.). 200p. (Orig.). 1985. pap. 7.95 (ISBN 0-89288-116-X). Maverick.
Wild Foods, What's Worth Eating? Phil King. 50p. 1987. write for info. (ISBN 0-9601900-4-X). Phil King.

Wild Fowl Decoys. Joel Barber. (Illus.). pap. 8.95 (ISBN 0-486-20011-6). Dover.
Wild Fowl Decoys. Joel Barber. (Illus.). 15.25 (ISBN 0-8446-1590-0). Peter Smith.
Wild Freedom. Max Brand. 240p. 1983. pap. 2.50 (ISBN 0-446-32769-7). Warner Bks.
Wild Fury. Gina Delaney. 496p. 1987. pap. 3.95 (ISBN 0-8217-1987-4). Zebra.
Wild Game & Country Cooking. Timothy E. Manion. 200p. 1983. spiral 9.95 (ISBN 0-9612936-0-8). Manion Outdoors Co.
Wild Game Cook Book. Martin Rywell. 74p. 1952. pap. 6.75 (ISBN 0-917420-05-5). Buck Hill.
Wild Game Cookbook. Compiled by Jim Dempsey. LC 87-16225. (Illus.). 156p. (Orig.). 1987. pap. 8.95 (ISBN 0-943247-01-2). UCS Press.
Wild Game Cookbook. John A. Smith. 64p. (Orig.). 1986. pap. 4.95 (ISBN 0-486-25127-6). Dover.
Wild Game Cookbook: A Remington Sportsmen's Library Bk. Ed. by L. W. Johnson. LC 70-114972. pap. 3.95 (ISBN 0-87502-907-8). Benjamin Co.
Wild Game Cookbook for Beginner & Expert: Outdoor Cook's Almanac. Joseph Lamagna. (Illus.). spiral bdg. 6.95x (ISBN 0-9610464-0-6). J Lamagna.
Wild Game Cookery: The Hunter's Home Companion. rev. ed. Carol V. Wary. 180p. 1988. pap. 12.95 (ISBN 0-88150-111-5). Countryman.
Wild Garden. Lys De Bray. (Illus.). 1978. 19.95 (ISBN 0-8317-9430-5, Mayflower Bks). Smith Pubs.
Wild Garden. William Robinson. (National Trust Classics Ser.). (Illus.). 304p. 13.95 (ISBN 0-317-62655-8, Pub. by Century Hutchinson). David & Charles.
Wild Garden. Violet Stevenson. (Gardening Ser.). 168p. 1985. 27.50 (ISBN 0-670-80566-1). Viking.
Wild Garden. Violet Stevenson. (Home Gardening Bookshelf Ser.). 168p. (Orig.). 1985. pap. 14.95 (ISBN 0-14-046710-6). Penguin.
Wild Garden: The Monterey Peninsula. Ron Mackie. (Illus.). 1985. pap. 7.95 (ISBN 0-910286-99-X). Boxwood.
Wild Gardening. Richard Austin. 1986. pap. 12.95 (ISBN 0-671-60241-1, Fireside). S&S.
Wild Garlic Islands: A Genealogical Account of the Ramsey Family. Robert H. Stone. LC 82-90342. (Illus.). 191p. (Orig.). 1982. 22.50 (ISBN 0-9609192-0-1). R H Stone.
Wild Garlic Islands: A Genealogical Account of the Ramsey Family--Updated Version. 158p. 1986. 24.95 (ISBN 0-9609192-3-6). R H Stone.
Wild Geese. Theodore H. Banks. LC 73-144741. (Yale Ser. of Younger Poets: No. 7). Repr. of 1921 ed. 18.00 (ISBN 0-404-53807-X). AMS Pr.
Wild Geese. Ogai Mori. Tr. by Sanford Goldstein & Kingo Ochiai. LC 59-14087. 1974. pap. 5.25 (ISBN 0-8048-1070-2). C E Tuttle.
Wild Geese. M. A. Ogilvie. LC 77-94181. (Illus.). 1978. 30.00 (ISBN 0-931130-00-X). Buteo.
Wild Geese & the Water. Bhagwan Shree Rajneesh. Ed. by Swami Krishna Prabhu. LC 85-43053. (Responses to Questions Ser.). 416p. (Orig.). 1985. pap. 4.95 (ISBN 0-88050-673-3). Chidvilas Inc.
Wild Geese, Pen Portraits of Famous Irish Exiles. Gerald Griffin. LC 77-2922. 1938. lib. bdg. 35.00 (ISBN 0-8414-4405-6). Folcroft.
Wild Geese: The Irish Soldier in Exile. Maurice N. Hennessy. LC 74-13747. (Illus.). 228p. Date not set. 16.95 (ISBN 0-8159-7215-6). Devin.
Wild Goose Chase. Anne George. (Illus.). 48p. (Orig.). Date not set. pap. 5.00 (ISBN 0-945301-00-6). Druid Pr.
Wild-Goose Chase: A Modern Critical Edition with Commentary and Notes Based on the 1652 Folio. John Fletcher. Ed. by Rota H. Lister & Stephen Orgel. LC 79-54349. (Renaissance Drama Second Ser.). 200p. 1980. lib. bdg. 26.00 (ISBN 0-8240-4466-5). Garland Pub.
Wild Goose Prints, No. 1. 1987. 20.00x (ISBN 0-947988-06-8, Pub. by Wild Goose Pubns Scotland). State Mutual Bk.
Wild Goose Prints, No. 2. 1987. 20.00x (ISBN 0-947988-10-6, Pub. by Wild Goose Pubns Scotland). State Mutual Bk.
Wild Gratitude. Edward Hirsch. LC 85-40348. (Poetry Ser.). 1986. 14.45 (ISBN 0-394-54848-5); pap. 8.95 (ISBN 0-394-74153-6). Knopf.
Wild Green Vegetables of Canada. Nancy J. Turner & Adam F. Szczawinski. (Edible Wild Plants of Canada). (Illus.). 150p. 1980. pap. 12.95 spiral bdg. (ISBN 0-660-10342-7, 56325-1, Pub. by Natl Mus Canada). U of Chicago Pr.
Wild Hamster. Alain Vaes. (Illus.). (ps-3). 1985. 14.95 (ISBN 0-316-89504-0). Little.
Wild Harp. Jacqueline La Tourrette. 576p. (Orig.). 1981. pap. 2.95 (ISBN 0-449-14408-9, GM). Fawcett.
Wild Harvest. Eleanor Gustafson. 288p. (Orig.). 1987. pap. 8.95 (ISBN 0-310-37391-3, 11657P). Zondervan.
Wild Harvest. Leonard Wiley. LC 66-13394. (Illus.). 1966. 15.00 (ISBN 0-911742-01-8). L Wiley.
Wild Heart Tamed. Colleen Shannon. 368p. (Orig.). 1986. pap. 3.95 (ISBN 0-441-88813-5, Pub. by Charter Bks). Ace Bks.
Wild Heritage. Allison Mitchell. 1984. pap. 3.75 (ISBN 0-451-13158-4, Sig). NAL.

Wild Shore. Kim S. Robinson. Ed. by Terry Carr. (New Ace Science Fiction Specials Ser.). (Orig.). 1984. pap. 3.50 (ISBN 0-441-88874-7, Pub. by Ace Science Fiction). Ace Bks.
Wild Shrubs & Vines. Don Stokes. (Illus.). Date not set. Repr. price not set (ISBN 0-87106-638-6). Globe Pequot.
Wild Southern Rose. Caroline Bourne. 1985. pap. 3.75 (ISBN 0-8217-1603-4). Zebra.
Wild Spain. Frederic Grunfeld. (Illus.). 224p. Date not set. leatherette 22.50 (ISBN 0-89659-805-5). Abbeville Pr.
Wild Spenders. Diana Davenport. 288p. 1984. 14.95 (ISBN 0-02-529810-0). Macmillan.
Wild Splendid Love. Eleanor Hodgson. pap. 3.50 (ISBN 0-8217-1354-X). Zebra.
Wild Splendor. Leta Tegler. 384p. (Orig.). 1988. pap. 3.95 (ISBN 0-380-75615-3). Avon.
Wild Sports in the Far West: The Narratives of a German Wanderer beyond the Mississippi, 1837-1843. Friedrich Gerstacker. LC 68-16624. pap. 102.30 (ISBN 0-317-26743-4, 2023381). Bks Demand UMI.
Wild Stallions. John Benteen. (Sundance Ser.: No. 7). 160p. 1981. pap. 1.75 (ISBN 0-8439-1046-1, Leisure Bks). Leisure NY.
Wild Star. Catherine Coutler. 1986. pap. 3.95 (ISBN 0-451-40013-5, Onyx). NAL.
Wild Storms of Heaven. June Lund Shiplett. (Orig.). 1980. pap. 3.95 (ISBN 0-451-12644-0, AE2640, Sig). NAL.
Wild Strawberries at 3000 Feet. Robert W. Olmsted. LC 86-60424. 64p. (Orig.). 1986. 19.95x (ISBN 0-89002-245-3); pap. 6.95x (ISBN 0-89002-244-5). Am Hist Pr.
Wild Streak. facsimile ed. Margaret E. Bailey. LC 72-106245. (Short Story Index Reprint Ser.). 1932. 18.00 (ISBN 0-8369-3281-1). Ayer Co Pubs.
Wild Streets. Western Writers Of America. LC 73-113693. (Short Story Index Reprint Ser). 1958. 20.00 (ISBN 0-8369-3422-9). Ayer Co Pubs.
Wild Style: The Next Wave. Cyn Zarco & Robert Hofler. 1985. pap. 7.95 (ISBN 0-671-55470-0, Pub. by Fireside). S&S.
Wild Surrender. Gina Delaney. (Zebra Romance Ser.). 496p. 1986. pap. 3.95 (ISBN 0-8217-1841-X). Zebra.
Wild Swan. Celeste De Blasis. 752p. (Orig.). 1985. pap. 4.95 (ISBN 0-553-26884-8). Bantam.
Wild Swans. Hans Christian Andersen. LC 81-65843. (Illus.). 40p. (gr. k up). 1981. 12.95 (ISBN 0-8037-9381-2); PLB 12.89 (ISBN 0-8037-9391-X). Dial Bks Young.
Wild Swans. Hans Christian Andersen. LC 80-27685. (Illus.). 32p. (gr. k-4). 1981. PLB 9.79 (ISBN 0-89375-480-3); pap. text ed. 1.95 (ISBN 0-89375-481-1). Troll Assocs.
Wild Swans. Hans Christian Andersen. Tr. by Naomi Lewis. LC 83-15805. (Illus.). 32p. (gr. 2-4). 11.95 (ISBN 0-911745-36-X). P Bedrick Bks.
Wild Swans. Hans Christian Andersen. (Illus.). 44p. (gr. 1-4). 1986. 7.95 (ISBN 0-8120-5711-2); Creative Character Building ed. 7.95 (ISBN 0-8120-5719-8). Barron.
Wild Swans, 6 bks. Ed. by Alma Gilleo. LC 76-730152. (Hans Christian Andersen Book Cassettes). (Illus.). 1976. Set. 24.95 (ISBN 0-89290-000-8); cassette incl. (ISBN 0-685-70090-9). Soc for Visual.
Wild Swans. Illus. by Susan Jeffers. LC 81-65843. (Pied Piper Bk.). (Illus.). 40p. (gr. k up). 1987. pap. 4.95 (ISBN 0-8037-0451-8, 0481-140). Dial Bks Young.
Wild Swans & Other Tales Based on the Ancient Irish. Ethel Mannin. 159p. 1983. Repr. of 1952 ed. lib. bdg. 30.00 (ISBN 0-8495-3944-7). Arden Lib.
Wild Swans at Coole. William B. Yeats. 64p. 1970. Repr. of 1917 ed. 15.00x (ISBN 0-7165-1352-8, BBA 02118, Pub. by Cuala Press Ireland). Biblio Dist.
Wild, Sweet Madness. Elizabeth Fritch. 432p. (Orig.). 1987. pap. 3.95 (ISBN 0-8439-2489-6, Leisure Bks). Leisure NY.
Wild Sweet Wilderness. Dorothy Garlock. 400p. (Orig.). 1985. pap. 3.95 (ISBN 0-445-20011-1, Pub. by Popular Lib). Warner Bks.
Wild Talents. Charles Fort. Ed. by Lester Del Ray. LC 75-409. (Library of Science Fiction). 1975. lib. bdg. 21.00 (ISBN 0-8240-1414-6). Garland Pub.
Wild Talents see Complete Books of Charles Fort.
Wild Teas, Coffees, & Cordials. Hilary Stewart. (Illus.). 128p. 1981. pap. 8.95 (ISBN 0-295-95804-9). U of Wash Pr.
Wild Texas Winds. Kit Prate. 480p. 1988. pap. 3.95 (ISBN 1-55817-082-0). Windsor NY.
Wild Things. Dion Henderson. LC 78-9687. (Illus.). 1979. 7.95 (ISBN 0-915024-18-7). Tamarack Pr.
Wild Things in the Yard. Wendy Anderson. 64p. (Orig.). 1986. 9.95 (ISBN 0-939395-00-2); pap. 5.95 (ISBN 0-939395-01-0). Thorntree Pr.
Wild Things to Cook. Dale Neutrelle. 1974. pap. 2.00 (ISBN 0-916552-00-4). Acoma Bks.
Wild Thorns. american ed. Sahar Khalifeh. Tr. by Trevor LeGassick & Elizabeth Fernea. 207p. 1988. pap. 9.95 (ISBN 0-940793-25-3, Olive Branch Pr). Interlink Pub.
Wild Thyme, Winter Lightning: The Symbolic Novels of L. P. Hartley. Anne Mulkeen. LC 73-18047. 210p. 1974. text ed. 22.50x (ISBN 0-8143-1494-5). Wayne St U Pr.
Wild Timothy. Gary Blackwood. LC 87-937. 160p. (gr. 4-8). 1987. 12.95 (ISBN 0-689-31352-7, Atheneum Childrens Bks). Macmillan.
Wild to the Heart. Rick Bass. 144p. 1988. 11.95 (ISBN 0-8117-1876-X). Stackpole.
Wild Town. Jim Thompson. LC 85-62249. 160p. 1986. pap. 3.95 (ISBN 0-916870-95-2, Pub. by Black Lizard Bks.). Creative Arts Bk.
Wild Towns of Nebraska. Wayne C. Lee. (Illus.). 147p. (Orig.). 1988. pap. 14.95 (ISBN 0-87004-325-0). Caxton.
Wild Trek. Jim Kjelgaard. (Skylark Ser.). 272p. 1981. pap. 2.75 (ISBN 0-553-15466-4). Bantam.
Wild Turkey: A Moses Wine Mystery. Roger L. Simon. 240p. 1986. pap. 3.50 (ISBN 0-446-30044-6), Warner Bks.
Wild Turkey Management: Current Problems & Programs. Ed. by Glen C. Sanderson & Helen C. Schultz. LC 72-87838. (Illus.). 366p. 1973. text ed. 37.00x (ISBN 0-8262-0133-4). U of Mo Pr.
Wild Type. Jeff Victoroff. 1989. 17.95 (ISBN 0-517-57127-7). Crown.
Wild "Uns. Caroline Andrew. 1985. 15.00x (Pub. by Pentland Pr UK). State Mutual Bk.
Wild Variations of the Theme of the Garden of Eden & Other Poems from Those Troubled Times. Rivka Kashtan. (Illus.). 160p. 1986. 14.95 (ISBN 0-933503-29-6). Shapolsky Pubs.
Wild Violets. Ruth B. Field. 368p. (Orig.). 1980. pap. 2.50 (ISBN 0-89083-635-3). Zebra.
Wild Violets. Ruth B. Field. 368p. 1987. pap. 3.95 (ISBN 0-8217-1973-4). Zebra.
Wild Washerwomen: A New Folk Tale. John Yeoman. (Illus.). 32p. (ps-2). 1986. pap. 3.95 (ISBN 0-517-56255-3). Crown.
Wild Water Canoeing. Robert Steidle. Tr. by Gertrude Menzel-Collin. (Illus.). 1976. 5.95 (ISBN 0-89149-026-4). Jolex.
Wild Waters. Ed. by James Raffan. (Illus.). 168p. 1987. 29.95 (ISBN 0-919493-99-8, Pub. by Key Porter Canada). U of Toronto Pr.
Wild Weasel. (Illus.). 74p. 1986. pap. 8.95 (ISBN 0-89747-178-4, 6042). Squad Sig Pubns.
Wild West: A History of the Wild West Shows. Don Russell. LC 77-102755. (Illus.). 150p. 1970. 9.95 (ISBN 0-88360-017-X, Dist. by Univ. of Texas Pr). Amon Carter.
Wild West Bartenders' Bible. Byron A. Johnson & Sharon Peregrine Johnson. LC 86-5971. (Illus.). 356p. 1986. 19.95 (ISBN 0-87719-050-X). Texas Month Pr.
Wild West Bears, Bk. 24. (ps-1). write for info. (ISBN 0-931363-22-5). Celia Totus Enter.
Wild West Riddles & Jokes. Joseph Rosenbloom. LC 85-2632. (Illus.). 128p. (gr. 3). 1985. 10.95 (ISBN 0-8069-4704-7); lib. bdg. 12.49 (ISBN 0-8069-4705-5); pap. 3.50 (ISBN 0-8069-7996-8). Sterling.
Wild West Rider. Stephen Overholser. (Time Machine Ser.: No. 9). 144p. (Orig.). 1985. pap. 2.25 (ISBN 0-553-25180-5). Bantam.
Wild Western Scenes: A Narrative in the Western Wilderness. facsimile ed. John B. Jones. LC 71-104501. (Illus.). 263p. Repr. of 1841 ed. lib. bdg. 28.00 (ISBN 0-8398-0958-1). Irvington.
Wild Western Scenes: A Narrative in the Western Wilderness. John B. Jones. (Illus.). 263p. 1986. pap. text ed. 6.95x (ISBN 0-8290-1954-5). Irvington.
Wild Westerns. Ed. by Bill Pronzini. 192p. 1986. 14.95 (ISBN 0-8027-4066-9). Walker & Co.
Wild, White Goose, Vol. I. Roshi Jiyu-Kennett. 1977. pap. 7.95 (ISBN 0-930066-02-2). Shasta Abbey.
Wild, White Goose, Vol. II. Roshi Jiyu-Kennett. 1978. pap. 8.95 (ISBN 0-930066-03-0). Shasta Abbey.
Wild, Wild Cookbook: A Guide for Young Wild-Food Foragers. Jean C. George. LC 82-45187. (Illus.). 192p. (gr. 5 up). 1982. (Crowell Jr Bks); PLB 12.89g (ISBN 0-690-04315-5). HarpJ.
Wild Wild Sunflower Child Anna. Nancy W. Carlstrom. LC 86-18226. (Illus.). 32p. (ps-1). 1987. PLB 13.95 (ISBN 0-02-717360-7). Macmillan.
Wild, Wild Women. Gene Curry. (Saddler Ser.: No. 5). (Orig.). 1980. pap. 1.75 (ISBN 0-686-86792-0, Pub. by Tower Bks). Leisure NY.
Wild Wildflowers of the West. Edith S. Kinucan & Penney R. Brons. (Illus.). 135p. (Orig.). (gr. 7 up). pap. 8.95 (ISBN 0-9615444-0-6). Kinucan & Brons.
Wild, Wildwood Flower & Other Deep South Tales. Olivia P. Solomon. LC 78-70631. 1979. 7.50 (ISBN 0-916620-23-9). Portals Pr.
Wild Willful Love. Valerie Sherwood. 576p. 1983. pap. 4.95 (ISBN 0-446-30368-2). Warner Bks.
Wild Willie, Wide Receiver. William C. Gault. LC 74-5006. 160p. (gr. 5-7). 1974. 7.95 (ISBN 0-525-42788-0). Dutton.
Wild Wind. Marjorie Sinclair. 272p. 1987. pap. 3.95 (ISBN 0-935180-30-3). Mutual Pub HI.
Wild Winds. Leslie O'Grady. 256p. 1987. pap. 2.95 (ISBN 0-451-14956-4, Sig). NAL.
Wild Winds Calling. June L. Shiplett. (Wind Ser.: Vol. 6). 1984. pap. 3.50 (ISBN 0-451-12953-9, Sig). NAL.
Wild Winds of Mayaland. Lucy Fuchs. (YA) (gr. 7 up). 1978. 9.95 (ISBN 0-685-85784-0, Avalon). Bouregy.
Wild Wines. Darcy Williamson. 96p. (Orig.). 1980. pap. 4.95 (ISBN 0-89288-034-1). Maverick.
Wild Wines, Colas, & Whiskeys. Phil King. LC 85-91054. 40p. (Orig.). 1986. pap. 5.00 (ISBN 0-9601900-6-6). Phil King.
Wild Wing: Great Hunting Eagle. Justin F. Denzel. LC 75-6829. (Famous Animal Stories Ser.). (Illus.). 48p. (gr. 2-5). 1975. PLB 6.89 (ISBN 0-8116-4856-7). Garrard.
Wild with All Regret. Natalie L. Petesch. LC 86-60697. (Illus.). 144p. (Orig.). 1986. lib. bdg. 15.95 (ISBN 0-930501-06-3); pap. 10.95 (ISBN 0-930501-07-1). Swallows Tale Pr.
Wild Woman: Amazon, Virgin & Matriarch in Anthropological Perspective. Kathleen Adams & Sharon Tiffany. 160p. 1985. 18.95 (ISBN 0-87073-213-7); pap. 11.95 (ISBN 0-87073-243-9). Schenkman Bks Inc.
Wild Women Don't Get the Blues. Barbara Emrys. 52p. 1977. 4.00 (ISBN 0-934816-00-X). Metis Pr Inc.
Wild Women of the West. Carl W. Breihan. 1982. pap. 2.50 (ISBN 0-451-11951-7, AE1951, Sig). NAL.
Wild Wyoming Heart. Sylvie F. Sommerfield. 512p. 1988. pap. 3.95 (ISBN 0-8217-2398-7). Zebra.
Wild Yam: Birth Control without Fear. Willa Shaffer. 8p. Date not set. pap. 2.95 (ISBN 0-913923-10-9). Woodland UT.
Wildcat Legacy: A Pictorial History of Kentucky Basketball. Russell Rice. LC 82-80433. (Illus.). 184p. 1982. 19.95 (ISBN 0-938694-09-X). JCP Corp VA.
Wildcat Round-up, No. 29. J. R. Roberts. (Gunsmith Ser.). 192p. 1985. pap. 2.50 (ISBN 0-441-30902-X) (ISBN 0-317-31901-9). Ace Bks.
Wildcat Summer. Mary Riskind. LC 84-22573. 174p. (gr. 5 up). 1985. 11.95 (ISBN 0-395-36217-2). HM.
Wildcat Tinker. Diane Misk. 136p. (Orig.). 1985. pap. 2.95 (ISBN 0-88120-737-3). SRA.
Wildcat Widow. Buck Gentry. (Scout Ser.: No. 21). 224p. 1987. pap. 2.50 (ISBN 0-8217-1851-7). Zebra.
Wildcat Woman. Gene Curry. (Saddler Ser.: No. 2). 1979. pap. 1.75 (ISBN 0-505-51407-9, Pub. by Tower Bks). Leisure NY.
Wildcats: Kentucky Football. Russ Rice. LC 75-26071. (College Sports Ser.). 1980. 11.95 (ISBN 0-87397-075-6). Strode.
Wildcatter. Desmond Meiring. 416p. 1988. 18.95x (ISBN 0-312-01533-X). St Martin.
Wildcatter: A Portrait of Robert O. Anderson. Kenneth Harris. LC 87-8183. (Illus.). 224p. 1987. 18.95 (ISBN 1-55584-048-5). Weidenfeld.
Wildcatter: The Story of Michel T. Halbouty & the Search for Oil. Jack Donahue. LC 83-10781. 270p. 1983. Repr. of 1979 ed. 24.00x (ISBN 0-87201-915-2). Gulf Pub.
Wildcatters. John Benteen. (Fargo Ser.: No. 5). (Orig.). 1980. pap. 1.50 (ISBN 0-505-51542-3, Pub. by Tower Bks). Leisure NY.
Wildcatters: Texas Independent Oilmen. Roger M. Olien & Diana D. Olien. Ed. by Scott Lubeck. (Illus.). 256p. 1984. 16.95 (ISBN 0-932012-85-X). Texas Month Pr.
Wildcliffe Bird. Constance Heaven. 288p. 1985. pap. 2.95 (ISBN 0-345-32119-7). Ballantine.
Wilde & the Nineties. Ed. by Charles Ryskamp. LC 66-26625. (Illus.). 75p. 1966. pap. 3.50 (ISBN 0-87811-010-0). Princeton Lib.
Wilde: Three Plays. Oscar Wilde. (Master Playwright Ser.). 320p. 1981. pap. 3.95 (ISBN 0-413-48530-7, NO. 3501). Heinemann Ed.
Wilder Domain of Evolutionary Thought. David R. Oldroyd & Ian G. Langham. 1983. lib. bdg. 54.50 (ISBN 90-277-1477-0, Pub. by Reidel Holland). Kluwer Academic.
Wilder in the West: Eliza Jane's Story of a Lady Homesteader. William T. Anderson. (Laura Ingalls Wilder Family Ser.). (Illus.). 44p. (YA) (gr. 8 up). 1985. pap. 3.95 (ISBN 0-9610088-4-9). Anderson MI.
Wilder Letters. John R. Wilder. (Political & Social Affairs Ser.: No. 1). (Orig.). 1986. pap. 7.95 (ISBN 0-916843-06-8, 103, Pub. by Writers Hse Pr). Inst Human Soc.
Wilder Shores of Love. Lesley Blanch. 368p. 1983. pap. 8.95 (ISBN 0-88184-055-6). Carroll & Graf.
Wilder Shores of Love. Sandra DuBay. 448p. (Orig.). 1988. pap. 4.50 (ISBN 0-8439-2654-6, Pub. by Leisure Bks CT). Leisure NY.
Wilder Summer. Stephen Krensky. LC 83-2664. 168p. (gr. 5-9). 1983. 12.95 (ISBN 0-689-30990-2, Atheneum Childrens Bks). Macmillan.
Wildering. Claire Lorrimer. 320p. 1983. pap. 3.95 (ISBN 0-345-30917-0). Ballantine.
Wilderness. Tony Dawson. 350p. 1987. 19.95. Papyrus Pubs.
Wilderness. Liam O'Flaherty. 212p. 1978. (Pub. by Wolfhound Pr Ireland); pap. 7.95. Irish Bks Media.
Wilderness. Liam O'Flaherty. 208p. 1987. 16.95 (ISBN 0-396-09130-X). Dodd.
Wilderness. Robert B. Parker. 256p. 1980. pap. 4.50 (ISBN 0-440-19328-1). Dell.
Wilderness. Anthony Smith. (Illus.). 1978. 14.95 (ISBN 0-8317-9450-X, Mayflower Bks). Smith Pubs.
Wilderness: A Journal of Quiet Adventure in Alaska. Rockwell Kent. (Illus.). 260p. 1983. pap. 8.95 (ISBN 0-918172-12-8). Leetes Isl.
Wilderness: A New Mexico Legacy. Corry McDonald. LC 84-26691. (Illus.). 128p. (Orig.). 1985. pap. 15.95 (ISBN 0-86534-056-0). Sunstone Pr.
Wilderness above the Sound: The Story of Mount Rainer National Park. Arthur Martinson. LC 85-63418. (Western Horizons Bk.). (Illus.). 96p. (Orig.). 1986. pap. 11.95 (ISBN 0-87358-398-1). Northland.
Wilderness & Gardens: An American Lady's Prospect. Margaret L. Been. (Illus.). 1974. pap. 5.00 (ISBN 0-87423-011-X). Westburg.
Wilderness & Natural Areas in the Eastern United States: A Management Challenge. Ed. by David L. Kulhavy & Richard N. Conner. 272p. 1986. 25.00 (ISBN 0-938361-00-7). Austin Univ Forestry.
Wilderness, & Other Poems. Louis O. Coxe. LC 58-59912. pap. 20.00 (ISBN 0-317-27943-2, 2055852). Bks Demand UMI.
Wilderness & the American Mind. rev., 3rd ed. Roderick Nash. LC 82-4874. 380p. 1982. text ed. 37.50t (ISBN 0-300-02905-5); pap. 12.95x (ISBN 0-300-02910-1, Y-440). Yale U Pr.
Wilderness & the City: American Classical Philosophy As a Moral Quest. Michael A. Weinstein. LC 82-4769. 176p. 1982. lib. bdg. 17.50x (ISBN 0-87023-375-0). U of Mass Pr.
Wilderness & the War-Path. James Hall. 1972. Repr. of 1846 ed. lib. bdg. 24.00 (ISBN 0-8422-8069-3). Irvington.
Wilderness Britain. Anthony Burton. (Illus.). 192p. 1985. 35.95 (ISBN 0-233-97640-X, Pub. by A Deutsch England). David & Charles.
Wilderness Britain. Anthony Burton. (Illus.). 196p. 1988. pap. 14.95 (ISBN 0-233-98162-4, Pub. by A Deutsch England). David & Charles.
Wilderness Byways see California.
Wilderness Cabin. rev. ed. Calvin Rutstrum. 192p. 1972. pap. 4.95 (ISBN 0-02-098500-2, Collier). Macmillan.
Wilderness Called Peace. Edmund Keeley. 1985. 16.95 (ISBN 0-671-47416-2). S&S.
Wilderness Called Peace. Edmund Kelley. 1987. pap. 4.95 (ISBN 0-440-39376-0, LE). Dell.
Wilderness Calling: The Hardeman Family in the American Westward Movement, 1750-1900. Nicholas P. Hardeman. LC 76-980. (Illus.). 1977. 32.50x (ISBN 0-87049-194-6). U of Tenn Pr.
Wilderness Challenge. LC 79-3241. (Books for World Explorers Series 2: No. 1). (Illus.). 104p. (gr. 3-8). 1980. 6.95 (ISBN 0-87044-333-X); PLB 8.50 (ISBN 0-87044-338-0). Natl Geog.
Wilderness Champion: The Story of a Great Hound. Joseph W. Lippincott. (Illus.). (YA) (gr. 7-9). 1944. 11.70i (ISBN 0-397-30099-9, Lipp Jr Bks); PLB 11.89 (ISBN 0-397-31320-9). HarpJ.
Wilderness Christians: The Moravian Mission to the Delaware Indians. Elma E. Gray & Leslie R. Gray. LC 72-84988. (Illus.). xiv, 354p. 1973. Repr. of 1956 ed. 22.00x (ISBN 0-8462-1701-5). Russell.
Wilderness Coast. Leila Garnsey. 64p. 1984. 7.50 (ISBN 0-317-16204-7). Ye Galleon.
Wilderness Coast. Jack Rudloe. (Illus.). 1988. 22.50 (ISBN 0-525-24607-X, Pub. by Truman Talley Bk). Dutton.
Wilderness Defender: Horace M. Albright & Conservation. Donald C. Swain. LC 70-93057. (Illus.). 1970. 20.00x (ISBN 0-226-78292-1). U of Chicago Pr.
Wilderness Dreams. 2nd ed. Wayne D. Thompson. (Illus.). 1982. pap. 4.95 (ISBN 0-914598-10-4). Padre Prods.
Wilderness Empire. Allan W. Eckert. LC 69-16974. (Winning of America Ser.). (Illus.). 1969. 25.00 (ISBN 0-316-20864-7). Little.
Wilderness Empire Seventeen Fifty-Five. Allan W. Eckert. 768p. 1985. pap. 4.95 (ISBN 0-553-26488-5). Bantam.
Wilderness Essays. John Muir. Ed. by Frank Buske. (Literature of the American Wilderness Ser.). 288p. 1980. pap. 4.95 (ISBN 0-87905-072-1, Peregrine Smith). Gibbs Smith Pub.
Wilderness Experience Program Final Evaluation Report. Richard Owen Kimball. 91p. 1979. cancelled (ISBN 0-318-13442-X). Assn Exper Ed.
Wilderness Family Pt. 2. Crome. (gr. 3-5). pap. 1.50 (ISBN 0-590-12113-8, Schol Pap). Scholastic Inc.
Wilderness Gourmet. Herschel L. Scott, Jr. & Herschel L. Scott, III. LC 83-61503. (Western Backpacking Ser.). (Illus.). 60p. 1983. pap. 3.95 (ISBN 0-88083-006-9). Poverty Hill Pr.
Wilderness Habitat: The Great Plains. Robert D. Bullock. (Illus., Orig.). (gr. 2-6). 1984. pap. 2.90 wkbk. (ISBN 0-915881-01-2). Inglewood Dis.
Wilderness Habitat: The Great Plains - A Young Reader's Journal. Robert Bullock. LC 86-81461. (Wilderness Habitat Ser.). (Illus.). 64p. (Orig.). (gr. k-8). 1987. pap. 5.95 (ISBN 0-943972-10-8). Homestead WY.
Wilderness Habitat: The Ozarks. Robert D. Bullock. (Illus.). 4p. (Orig.). (gr. 2-6). 1983. pap. 2.90 wkbk. (ISBN 0-915881-00-4). Inglewood Dis.
Wilderness Handbook. rev. & updated ed. Paul Petzoldt. (Illus.). 1984. pap. 9.95 (ISBN 0-393-30171-0). Norton.

Wildflowers of the Wallum. Elizabeth McDonald. 71p. 1985. 9.50 (ISBN 0-908175-16-7, Pub. by Boolarong Pubn Australia). Intl Spec Bk.
Wildflowers of the Wasatch & Uinta Mountains: Utah. (Nature & Scenic Bks.). pap. 3.95 (ISBN 0-937512-04-4). Wheelwright UT.
Wildflowers of the Western Cascades. Robert A. Ross & Henrietta L. Chambers. LC 87-29648. (Illus.). 141p. (Orig.). 1988. pap. 19.95 (ISBN 0-88192-078-9). Timber.
Wildflowers of Tidewater Virginia. Oscar W. Gupton & Fred C. Swope. LC 81-16247. (Illus.). 207p. 1982. 12.95 (ISBN 0-8139-0922-8). U Pr of Va.
Wildflowers of Yellowstone & Grand Teton National Parks. (Nature & Scenic Bks.). pap. 3.95 (ISBN 0-937512-05-2). Wheelwright UT.
Wildflowers of Yosemite. Lynn Wilson et al. (Illus.). 144p. (Orig.). 1987. pap. 7.95 (ISBN 0-9617651-0-0). Sunrise Prodns.
Wildflowers South Florida Natives: Indentification & Habitat of Indigenous Tropical Flora. 2nd ed. Arlene A. Schuyler. Ed. by Charlotte Hall & Richard Oppenheimer. LC 82-90756. (Illus.). 112p. (Orig.). 1982. pap. 5.95 (ISBN 0-910991-00-6). Facts FL.
Wildflowers Three, the Sierra Nevada. Elizabeth L. Horn. (Illus.). 1976. pap. 10.95 (ISBN 0-911518-40-1). Touchstone Pr Ore.
Wildflowers to Color. Ruth F. Brin & Mary K. Stalland. (Illus.). 36p. 1982. pap. 1.00 (ISBN 0-686-83871-8). Nodin Pr.
Wildflowers Two: Sagebrush Country. Ronald Taylor & Rolf Valum. (Illus.). pap. 12.95 (ISBN 0-911518-26-6). Touchstone Pr Ore.
Wildfoods Cookbook. Joy Spoczynska. 224p. 1985. 24.95x (ISBN 0-7090-1748-0, Pub. by R Hale Ltd UK); pap. 19.00x (ISBN 0-7090-1867-3, Pub. by R Hale Ltd UK). State Mutual Bk.
Wildfowl. Eric Hosking & Janet Kear. (Illus.). 160p. 1986. 24.95 (ISBN 0-8160-1152-4). Facts on File.
Wildfowl in Great Britain. 2nd ed. Myrfyn Owen et al. (Illus.). 450p. 1986. 62.50 (ISBN 0-521-30986-7). Cambridge U Pr.
Wildfowl of Britain & Europe. M. A. Ogilvie. 1982. 16.50x (ISBN 0-19-217723-0). Oxford U Pr.
Wildfowl Painting: The Art of Featherstroke Painting. Beebe Hopper. (Fine Arts Library). (Illus.). 64p. (Orig.). 1986. pap. 10.95 (ISBN 0-917121-04-X, 40-101). M F Weber Co.
Wildfowler: A Tale of the Shannon Estuary. Roger Moran. (Illus.). 128p. 1982. 10.50 (ISBN 0-85640-277-X, Pub. by Blackstaff Pr); pap. 5.25 (ISBN 0-85640-278-8). Longwood Pub Group.
Wildfowler's Heritage. Ed. by James M. Jordan & George T. Alcorn. LC 80-85153. (Illus.). 120p. 1984. 46.50 (ISBN 0-938694-03-0); deluxe ed. 125.00 (ISBN 0-686-70001-5); deluxe ed. with remarque 175.00 (ISBN 0-686-70002-3). JCP Corp VA.
Wilding Graft. Jack Clemo. 304p. 1983. pap. 7.50 (ISBN 0-907746-17-9, Pub. by A Mott Ltd). Longwood Pub Group.
Wildland Fire Management Terminology. (FAO Forestry Paper Ser.: No. 70). 255p. (Orig.). 1986. pap. text ed. 22.50 (ISBN 92-5-002420-7, F2970, FAO). UNIPUB.
Wildland Recreation: Ecology & Management. William E. Hammitt & David N. Cole. LC 86-23403. 304p. 1987. 37.50 (ISBN 0-471-87291-1). Wiley.
Wildlands & Woodlots: The Story of New England's Forests. Lloyd C. Irland. LC 81-69943. (Futures of New England Ser.). (Illus.). 233p. 1982. 20.00x (ISBN 0-87451-227-1). U Pr of New Eng.
Wildlands & Woodlots: The Story of New England's Forests. Lloyd C. Irland. LC 81-69943. (Futures of New England Ser.). (Illus.). 233p. 1985. pap. 10.95 (ISBN 0-87451-351-0). U Pr of New Eng.
Wildlife. Todd Strasser. LC 86-19861. 192p. (YA) (gr. 7 up). 1987. pap. 14.95 (ISBN 0-385-29560-X). Delacorte.
Wildlife. Todd Strasser. (gr. k-12). 1988. pap. 2.95 (ISBN 0-440-20151-9). Dell.
Wildlife Activity & Coloring Book. rev. ed. K. D. McKowen. (Illus.). 32p. (gr. 2-6). 1987. workbook 1.50 (ISBN 0-913635-02-2). Aspen Prods.
Wildlife: Activity Book. K. D. McKowen. (Illus.). 32p. (gr. 2-6). 1985. pap. 1.25 (ISBN 0-913635-00-6). Aspen Prods.
Wildlife Alert. Gene S. Stuart. LC 79-1792. (Books for World Explorers Series 1: No. 3). (Illus.). 104p. (gr. 3-8). 1980. 6.95 (ISBN 0-87044-318-6); PLB 8.50 (ISBN 0-87044-323-2). Natl Geog.
Wildlife & Fisheries: Career Opportunities. Ed. by Bert Kempers. (Illus.). 146p. 1986. pap. 39.95 (ISBN 0-935969-00-4). West Wind Prod.
Wildlife & Fisheries Research Needs. 83p. 1979. single copy 1.50 (ISBN 0-318-16866-9). Wildlife Mgmt.
Wildlife & Man in Texas: Environmental Change & Conservation. Robin W. Doughty. LC 83-45103. (Illus.). 256p. 1983. 16.95 (ISBN 0-89096-154-9). Tex A&M Univ Pr.
Wildlife & Plants of the Cascades. Vinson Brown & Charles Yocom. LC 75-29118. (American Wildlife Region Ser.: Vol. 8). (Illus.). 296p. 1971. 14.95 (ISBN 0-911010-81-5); pap. 8.95 (ISBN 0-911010-80-7). Naturegraph.
Wildlife & Plants of the Southern Rocky Mountains. Charles Yocom et al. (American Wildlife Region Ser.: Vol. 7). (Illus.). 138p. (gr. 4 up). 1969. 11.95 (ISBN 0-911010-13-0); pap. 5.95 (ISBN 0-911010-12-2). Naturegraph.
Wildlife & Wilderness: An Artist's World. Keith Shackleton. (Illus.). 120p. 1986. 29.95 (ISBN 0-88162-217-6). Salem Hse Pubs.
Wildlife Artists at Work. Pat Van Gelder. (Illus.). 176p. 1982. 27.95 (ISBN 0-8230-5749-6). Watson-Guptill.
Wildlife at Kennedy Space Center. Intro. by Mitch Varnes & Dorn Whitmore. (Space Center Bks.). (Illus.). 32p. (Orig.). 1988. pap. 7.95x (ISBN 0-317-68210-5). Graphic Hse.
Wildlife Biology. 2nd ed. Raymond F. Dasmann. LC 80-19006. 212p. 1981. write for info. (ISBN 0-471-08042-X). Wiley.
Wildlife Biotelemetry. Ed. by H. P. Kimmich. (Journal: Biotelemetry & Patient Monitoring: Vol. 7, No. 3-4). (Illus.). 116p. 1981. pap. 22.00 (ISBN 3-8055-2093-X). S Karger.
Wildlife: Cases, Law & Policy. David S. Favre. LC 82-71698. 277p. (Orig.). 1983. 17.50 (ISBN 0-86733-023-6, #5023). Assoc Faculty Pr.
Wildlife Chef. 2nd., rev. ed. Michigan United Conservation Clubs. 1986. pap. 3.95 (ISBN 0-933112-02-5). Mich United Conserv.
Wildlife Conference: Proceedings of the 7th Annual Wildlife Conference, 1983, San Francisco, California. San Francisco Zoological Gardens & California Academy of Sciences. Ed. by Nancy Venizelos & Celeste Grijalava. LC 85-1879. 1983. write for info. (ISBN 0-933155-00-X). SF Zoological.
Wildlife Conservation Evaluation. Ed. by Michael B. Usher. 400p. 1986. text ed. 66.00 (ISBN 0-412-26750-0, 9898, Pub. by Chapman & Hall England); pap. text ed. 33.00 (ISBN 0-412-26760-8, 9917, Pub. by Chapman & Hall England). Routledge Chapman & Hall.
Wildlife Conservation Principles & Practices. rev. ed. Ed. by Richard D. Teague & Eugene Decker. LC 79-2960. (Illus.). 280p. 1979. pap. 9.00 (ISBN 0-933564-06-6). Wildlife Soc.
Wildlife Country--How to Enjoy It. Ed. by Alma D. MacConomy. LC 77-75113. (Illus.). 208p. 1977. 12.95 (ISBN 0-912186-23-2). Natl Wildlife.
Wildlife Diseases Research & Economic Development: Proceedings of a Workshop held in Kabete, Kenya, 8-9 Sept. 1980. Ed. by L. Karstad & B. Nestel. 80p. 1981. pap. 5.00 (ISBN 0-88936-307-2, IDRC179, IDRC). UNIPUB.
Wildlife Ecology: A Guide to the Ecological Approach of Studying the Wildlife of the Central United States. 4th ed. Gary Twesten. Ed. by Urban Baum. (Illus.). 710p. 1988. 25.00 (ISBN 0-9602428-8-0). G Twesten.
Wildlife Ecology & Management. William L. Robinson & Eric G. Bolen. 608p. 1984. text ed. write for info. (ISBN 0-02-402250-0). Macmillan.
Wildlife Ecology & Management. 2nd ed. William L. Robinson & Eric G. Bolen. 1192p. 1989. write for info. (ISBN 0-02-402251-9). Macmillan.
Wildlife Family Album. David F. Robinson. Ed. by Alma D. MacConomy & Barbara Peters. LC 81-81904. (Illus.). 208p. 1981. 16.95 (ISBN 0-912186-41-0). Natl Wildlife.
Wildlife Feeding & Nutrition. Charles T. Robbins. LC 82-13720. 1983. 45.00 (ISBN 0-12-589380-9). Acad Pr.
Wildlife Feeding & Nutrition. Charles T. Robbins. (Animal Feeding & Nutrition Ser.). 464p. 1986. pap. 22.95 (ISBN 0-12-589381-7). Acad Pr.
Wildlife Gardener. John V. Dennis. LC 84-48653. (Illus.). 288p. 1985. 17.95 (ISBN 0-394-53582-0). Knopf.
Wildlife Gardener. John V. Dennis. 352p. 1988. pap. 4.95 (ISBN 0-345-34860-5). Ballantine.
Wildlife Habitat Conservation Teacher's Pac Series: An Environmental Education Teaching Aid, 9 vols. National Institute for Urban Wildlife. per pac 5.00 (ISBN 0-318-04278-9). Natl Inst Urban Wildlife.
Wildlife Identification Pocket Guide. (Illus.). 1986. pap. 1.95 (ISBN 0-916682-49-8). Outdoor Empire.
Wildlife Images: A Complete Guide to Outdoor Photography. John Wootters & Jerry T. Smith. (Illus.). 200p. 1981. 17.95 (ISBN 0-8227-3020-0). Petersen Pub.
Wildlife Images by Terra. Terra Parma. Ed. by Stained Glass Images Inc. Staff. (Illus.). 64p. 1987. 8.95 (ISBN 0-936459-01-8). Stained Glass.
Wildlife in America. Peter Matthiessen. LC 87-40057. (Illus.). 336p. 1987. 29.95 (ISBN 0-670-81906-9). Viking.
Wildlife in Danger. Robert Burton. LC 83-50393. (Silver Burdett Color Library). 48p. (gr. 4 up). 1983. 14.96 (ISBN 0-382-06730-4). Silver.
Wildlife in North Carolina. Ed. by Jim Dean & Lawrence S. Earley. LC 87-5858. (Illus.). xiii, 201p. 1987. 24.95 (ISBN 0-8078-1751-1). U of NC Pr.
Wildlife in Peril: The Threatened & Endangered Mammals of Colorado. John Murray. 1987. 29.50 (ISBN 0-911797-27-0); pap. 12.50 (ISBN 0-911797-28-9). R Rinehart Inc.
Wildlife in Transition: Man & Nature on Yellowstone's Northern Range. Paul Schullery et al. 1986. 17.50 (ISBN 0-911797-16-5). R Rinehart Inc.
Wildlife in Wood. Richard Le Master. (Illus.). 1979. 37.50 (ISBN 0-8092-7336-5). Contemp Bks.
Wildlife Law Enforcement. 3rd ed. William F. Sigler. 432p. 1980. pap. text ed. write for info. (ISBN 0-697-08208-3). Wm C Brown.
Wildlife Laws of Oklahoma: Oklahoma Statutes: Title 29, Game & Fish, & Title 22, Double Section Symbol 1111 Through 1113 As Amended Through Laws of the 1984 Regular Session of the Legislature. Oklahoma West Publishing Company Staff. LC 84-233658. 1984. write for info. West Pub.
Wildlife Laws of Oklahoma: Oklahoma Statutes, Title 29, Game & Fish , & Title 22, Double Section Symbol 1111 Through 1113 As Amended Through Laws of the 1986 Regular Session of the Legislature. LC 87-124022. Date not set. price not set. West Pub.
Wildlife: Making a Comeback. Ed. by Donald J. Crump. (Books for World Explorers Series Nine: No. 1). 104p. (gr. 3-8). 1987. 6.95 (ISBN 0-87044-656-8); PLB 8.50 (ISBN 0-87044-661-4). Natl Geog.
Wildlife Management. Robert H. Giles, Jr. LC 78-15700. (Animal Science Ser.). (Illus.). 416p. 1978. text ed. 29.95 (ISBN 0-7167-0082-4). W H Freeman.
Wildlife Management in Wilderness. Clay Schoenfeld & John C. Hendee. 1978. pap. 4.95 (ISBN 0-910286-60-4). Boxwood.
Wildlife Management on Your Land: The Practical Owner's Manual on How, What, When & Why. Charles L. Cadieux. (Illus.). 320p. 1985. 29.95 (ISBN 0-8117-1877-8). Stackpole.
Wildlife Management Techniques Manual. 4th ed. The Wildlife Society. Ed. by Sanford D. Schemnitz. LC 80-19970. (Illus.). 686p. 1980. 20.00 (ISBN 0-933564-08-2). Wildlife Soc.
Wildlife Observer's Guide Book. Charles E. Roth. LC 82-389. (Phalarope Bks.). (Illus.). 239p. 1982. 15.95 (ISBN 0-13-959536-8); pap. 9.95 (ISBN 0-13-959528-7). P-H.
Wildlife of Arabia. Ed. by Wilhelm Buttiker et al. (Illus.). 96p. 1981. text ed. 27.50 (ISBN 0-905743-27-X, Pub. by Stacey Intl UK). Humanities.
Wildlife of Cactus & Canyon Country. Marj Dunmire. 48p. (gr. 2-6). 1988. pap. 3.95 (ISBN 0-942559-05-3). Pegasus Graphics.
Wildlife of China. Ed. by Tang Guang You & Li Wei. (Illus.). 134p. 1986. text ed. 39.95 (ISBN 0-8351-1785-5). China Bks.
Wildlife of Eastern Australia. Stanley Breeden & Kay Breeden. (Illus.). 260p. 1974. 12.95 (ISBN 0-8008-8332-2). Taplinger.
Wildlife of the Deserts. Frederic H. Wagner. (Wildlife Habitat Ser.). (Illus.). 232p. 1980. 19.95 (ISBN 0-8109-1764-5, 1764-5). Abrams.
Wildlife of the Forests. Ann Sutton & Myron Sutton. (Wildlife Habitat Ser.). (Illus.). 1979. 19.95 (ISBN 0-8109-1759-9). Abrams.
Wildlife of the Intermountain West. Vinson Brown et al. (American Wildlife Region Ser.: Vol. 4). (Illus.). 144p. (gr. 4 up). 1968. 11.95 (ISBN 0-911010-15-7); pap. 5.95 (ISBN 0-911010-14-9). Naturegraph.
Wildlife of the Islands. William H. Amos. (Wildlife Habitat Ser.). (Illus.). 1980. 19.95 (ISBN 0-8109-1763-7). Abrams.
Wildlife of the Mountain West. Tony Elliott & Ray Fetzer, Jr. (This Is America Ser.). (Illus.). 62p. (Orig.). (gr. 1-6). 1984. pap. 2.50 (ISBN 0-914565-07-9, 07-9). Capstan Pubns.
Wildlife of the Mountains. Edward R. Ricciuti. (Wildlife Habitat Ser.). (Illus.). 1979. 19.95 (ISBN 0-8109-1757-2). Abrams.
Wildlife of the North American Deserts. 2nd ed. Jim Cornett. (Illus.). 214p. 1987. pap. 8.95 (ISBN 0-937794-06-6). Nature Trails.
Wildlife of the Northern Rocky Mountains. William Baker et al. (American Wildlife Region Ser.: Vol. 6). (Illus.). 112p. (gr. 4 up). 1961. 11.95 (ISBN 0-911010-11-4); pap. 5.95 (ISBN 0-911010-10-6). Naturegraph.
Wildlife of the Oceans. Albert C. Jensen. (Wldlife Habitat Ser.). (Illus.). 1979. 19.95 (ISBN 0-8109-1758-0). Abrams.
Wildlife of the Polar Regions. G. Carleton Ray & M. G. McCormick-Ray. (Wildlife Habitat Ser.). (Illus.). 232p. 1981. 19.95 (ISBN 0-8109-1768-8). Abrams.
Wildlife of the Prairie. Wilford L. Miller. 1976. 8.95 (ISBN 0-686-18906-X); soft cover 5.95 (ISBN 0-686-18907-8). Assoc Print.
Wildlife of the Prairies & Plains. Kai Curry-Lindahl. LC 80-27927. (Wildlife Habitat Ser.). (Illus.). 232p. 1981. 19.95 (ISBN 0-8109-1766-1). Abrams.
Wildlife of the Rivers. William H. Amos. LC 80-21928. (Wildlife Habitat Ser.). (Illus.). 232p. 1981. 19.95 (ISBN 0-8109-1767-X). Abrams.
Wildlife of the Royal Estates. Robin Page. (Illus.). 240p. 1985. 35.95 (ISBN 0-340-32352-3, Pub. by Hodder & Stoughton UK). David & Charles.
Wildlife of the Western Mountains. Jim Cornett. (Illus.). 244p. (Orig.). 1982. pap. 8.95 (ISBN 0-937794-03-1). Nature Trails.
Wildlife of Yellowstone & Grand Teton National Parks. (Nature & Scenic Bks.). pap. 3.50 (ISBN 0-937512-06-0). Wheelwright UT.
Wildlife on the Farm. Miriam Druist. (gr. 2 up). 1977. 6.35 (ISBN 0-686-23334-4). Rod & Staff.
Wildlife on the Watch. Mary Adrian. (Illus.). 64p. (gr. 2-6). 1974. PLB 6.95 (ISBN 0-8038-1553-0). Hastings.
Wildlife Painting. Joy Parsons. (Illus.). 144p. 1985. 25.95 (ISBN 0-7134-4106-2, Pub. by Batsford England). David & Charles.
Wildlife Painting Techniques of Modern Masters. Susan Rayfield. (Illus.). 144p. 1985. 27.50 (ISBN 0-8230-5750-X). Watson-Guptill.
Wildlife Pest Control Around Gardens & Homes. Terrell P. Salmon & Robert E. Lickliter. LC 84-50732. (Illus.). 128p. 1984. pap. 8.00x (ISBN 0-931876-66-4, 21385). ANR Pubns CA.
Wildlife Photographer. Bob Gibbons & Peter Wilson. (Illus.). 160p. 1988. pap. 17.95 (ISBN 0-7137-2044-1, Pub. by Blandford Pr England). Sterling.
Wildlife Population Ecology. Ed. by James S. Wakeley. LC 81-83148. 450p. 1982. lib. bdg. 20.00x (ISBN 0-271-00303-0); pap. text ed. 12.50x (ISBN 0-271-00304-9). Pa St U Pr.
Wildlife Production Systems: Economic Utilisation of Wild Ungulates. Ed. by R. J. Hudson et al. (Cambridge Studies in Applied Ecology & Resource Management). (Illus.). 400p. Date not set. price not set (ISBN 0-521-34099-3). Cambridge U Pr.
Wildlife Radio Tagging: Equipment, Field Techniques & Data Analysis. R. E. Kenward. (Biological Techniques Ser.). 1987. 37.00 (ISBN 0-12-404240-6). Acad Pr.
Wildlife Requiem. James Balog. 1984. 30.00 (ISBN 0-933642-06-7); pap. 20.00 (ISBN 0-933642-07-5). Intl Ctr Photo.
Wildlife Rescue. Barbara Ford. Ed. by Kathleen Tucker. LC 87-6133. (Illus.). 47p. (gr. 3-7). 1987. PLB 9.75 (ISBN 0-8075-9099-1). A Whitman.
Wildlife Signatures: A Guide to the Identification of Tracks & Scat. Abridged ed. DeLorme Publishing Company Staff. (Maine Geographic Ser.). (Illus.). 48p. 1983. pap. 2.95 (ISBN 0-89933-064-9). DeLorme Map.
Wildlife Sketching: Pen, pencil, Crayon & Charcoal Techniques. Frank J. Lohan. (Illus.). 128p. (Orig.). 1986. pap. 14.95 (ISBN 0-8092-5048-9). Contemp Bks.
Wildlife Specialist. Jack Rudman. (Career Examination Ser.: C-896). (Cloth bdg. avail. on request). 1988. pap. 14.00 (ISBN 0-8373-0896-8). Natl Learning.
Wildlife Three-D Coloring Books. Illus. by Steve Pileggi. (Illus., Orig.). (gr. k-5). Date not set. Incl. crayons. pap. 2.99 (ISBN 0-86679-071-3). Oak Tree Pubns.
Wildlife Through the Camera. Peter Bale. (Illus.). 224p. 1985. 24.95 (ISBN 0-88186-452-8). Parkwest Pubns.
Wildlife Two Thousand: Modeling Habitat Relationships of Terrestrial Vertebrates. Ed. by Jared Verner et al. LC 85-40769. (Illus.). 480p. 1986. text ed. 17.50x (ISBN 0-299-10520-2). U of Wis Pr.
Wildlife, Wild Death: Land Use & Survival in Eastern Africa. Rodger Yeager & Norman N. Miller. LC 86-5791. (Environmental Public Policy Ser.). 173p. 1986. 52.50 (ISBN 0-88706-168-0); pap. 17.95 (ISBN 0-88706-169-9). State U NY Pr.
Wildlife Woodcarvers: A Complete Book for Carving, Burning, & Painting Wildfowl. Carl Chapell & Clark Sullivan. (Illus.). 216p. 1986. 39.95 (ISBN 0-8117-1882-4). Stackpole.
Wildlife Woodcraft. Lois B. Phillips. LC 78-5267. (Illus.). 64p. 1978. 10.95 (ISBN 0-87961-067-0); pap. 4.95 (ISBN 0-87961-066-2). Naturegraph.
Wildlife's December Treasury. Ed. by Cecilia I. Parker & Howard F. Robinson. 192p. 1985. 20.95 (ISBN 0-912186-67-4). Natl Wildlife.
Wildlife's Holiday Album. Ed. by Alma D. MacConomy. LC 78-56861. (Illus.). 160p. 1978. 11.95 (ISBN 0-912186-27-5). Natl Wildlife.
Wildlings. Mary Leister. LC 76-2063. (Illus.). 192p. 1976. 10.95 (ISBN 0-916144-06-2). Stemmer Hse.
Wildly Speaking. May B. Grant. LC 75-122574. (Popular Ser.: No. 10). 1972. pap. 2.95 (ISBN 0-87768-005-1). Denver Mus Natl Hist.
Wildman. Martin Steingesser. (Illus.). 16p. 1985. deluxe ed. 75.00 (ISBN 0-913341-06-1); pap. 10.00 (ISBN 0-913341-05-3). Coyote Love.
Wildness Is All Around Us. Eugene Kinkead. (Illus.). 178p. 1978. 12.00 (ISBN 0-87690-277-8, QH541.5.C6K56). E Kinkead.
Wildness Pleases: The Origins of Romanticism. Christopher Thacker. LC 82-10769. 288p. 1983. 27.50x (ISBN 0-312-87960-1). St Martin.
Wildon Affair. Roland DeForrest. 256p. 1983. pap. 2.75 (ISBN 0-446-30207-4). Warner Bks.
Wildraith's Last Battle. Phyllis A. Karr. 50p. 1987. pap. 2.95 (ISBN 0-425-08026-9). Berkley Pub.
Wild's Magical Book of Cranial Effusions. Peter Wild. LC 70-150786. (Illus., Orig.). 1971. 4.00 (ISBN 0-912284-17-X); pap. 1.50 (ISBN 0-912284-18-8). New Rivers Pr.
Wilds of London. James Greenwood. LC 84-48268. (Rise of Urban Britain Ser.). 364p. 1985. 66.00 (ISBN 0-8240-6270-1). Garland Pub.
Wildstar. Linda Ladd. 272p. 1984. pap. 3.95 (ISBN 0-380-87171-8). Avon.
Wildtiere -in Gefaengschaft: ein Grundriss -Des Tiergartenbiologie see Wild Animals in Captivity: An Outline of the Biology of Zoological Gardens.

TITLE INDEX

WILL CAMPBELL & THE

Wildtrack. Bernard Cornwell. 320p. 1988. 17.95 (ISBN 0-399-13375-5, Putnam). Putnam Pub Group.
Wildwater: The Sierra Club Guide to Kayaking & Whitewater Boating. Lito Tejada-Flores. LC 77-28189. (Outdoor Activities Guides Ser.). (Illus.). 334p. 1978. pap. 9.95 (ISBN 0-87156-209-X). Sierra.
Wildwater West Virginia: The Northern Streams, Vol. 1. rev., exp. ed. P. Davidson et al. LC 85-7126. (Illus.). 192p. (Orig.). 1985. pap. 9.95 (ISBN 0-89732-021-2). Menasha Ridge.
Wildwater West Virginia: The Southern Streams, Vol. 2. P. Davidson et al. LC 85-7126. (Illus.). 158p. (Orig.). 1985. pap. 9.95 (ISBN 0-89732-029-8). Menasha Ridge.
Wildwood. John Farris. 448p. (Orig.). 1986. pap. 4.50 (ISBN 0-8125-8270-5, Dist. by Warner Pub. Services & St. Martin's Press). Tor Bks.
Wildwood. John Farris. 448p. 1986. 16.95 (ISBN 0-312-93919-1, Dist. by St. Martin's Press). Tor Bks.
Wildwoods Dad. Don Oakland. (Illus.). 220p. (Orig.). (gr. 5 up). 1987. pap. 6.95 (ISBN 0-9615242-1-9). Oak Pr.
Wildwoods Weekly Reader. Don Oakland. (Illus.). 255p. (Orig.). 1985. pap. 5.95 (ISBN 0-9615242-0-0). Oak Pr.
Wildwraith's Last Battle. Phyllis A. Karr. 288p. 1982. pap. 2.95 (ISBN 0-441-88969-7). Ace Bks.
Wiley & the Hairy-Man. Jack Stokes. (gr. k-12). 1970. pap. 2.00x (ISBN 0-88020-004-9). Coach Hse.
Wiley & the Hairy-Man. Suzan Zeder. (gr. k up). 1978. 3.00 (ISBN 0-87602-219-0). Anchorage.
Wiley & the Hairy-Man: Adapted from an American Folk Tale. Molly G. Bang. LC 75-38581. (Ready-to-Read Ser.). (Illus.). 64p. (gr. 1-4). 1976. 9.95 (ISBN 0-02-708370-5). Macmillan.
Wiley & the Hairy Man: Adapted from an American Folk Tale. Molly G. Bang. LC 87-2540. (Ready-to-Read Ser.). (Illus.). 64p. (gr. 1-4). 1987. pap. 3.95 (ISBN 0-689-71162-X, Aladdin Bks). Macmillan.
Wiley Business Math Handbook. Vec. 1988. pap. write for info. (ISBN 0-471-84340-7); wkbk. avail. (ISBN 0-471-84339-3). Wiley.
Wiley College Typewriting: A Competency Based Approach, Comprehensive Volume. Simcoe et al. (College Typewriting Ser.). 1986. pap. write for info. (ISBN 0-471-09402-1). Wiley.
Wiley Encyclopedia of Artificial Intelligence. Ed. by Stuart C. Shapiro. LC 86-26739. 679p. 1987. 175.00 (ISBN 0-471-80748-6, Wiley-Interscience). Wiley.
Wiley Encyclopedia of Packaging Technology. Marilyn Bakker. LC 86-4041. 746p. 1986. 95.00 (ISBN 0-471-80940-3, Pub. by Wiley-Interscience). Wiley.
Wiley Engineer's Desk Reference: A Concise Guide for the Professional Engineer. Sanford I. Heisler. LC 83-21690. 449p. 1984. 43.95 (ISBN 0-471-86632-6, Pub. by Wiley-Interscience). Wiley.
Wiley Medical Research Directory. Wiley Medical Publication Staff. LC 82-8627. 737p. 1984. 174.00 (ISBN 0-471-10335-7, Pub. by Wiley Med). Wiley.
Wiley Medical Research Directory Thesaurus to the Online Database. Ed. by J. E. Levy. 1985. pap. 48.00 (ISBN 0-471-90829-0). Wiley.
Wiley Office Handbook: Reference Guide, Word Finder, Word Processing Guide. 2nd ed. Rita Kutie & Virginia Huffman. LC 83-16707. (Word Processing Ser.). 465p. 1984. pap. write for info. (ISBN 0-471-87055-2). Wiley.
Wiley: One Hundred Seventy-Five Years of Publishing. Wiley. 279p. 1982. 35.95 (ISBN 0-471-86082-4). Wiley.
Wiley Reader: Designs for Writing. Caroline D. Eckhardt et al. LC 75-29499. 1976. pap. write for info. (ISBN 0-673-15668-0). Scott F.
Wiley-Ronald Federal Tax Desk Reference. Goran. 1986. write for info. (ISBN 0-471-87647-X); Supplement. pap. write for info. (ISBN 0-471-87554-6). Wiley.
Wiley's Federal Income Taxation, 1987. Dennis J. Gaffney et al. LC 86-13133. 1986. 34.95 (ISBN 0-471-84253-2). Wiley.
Wilford Woodruff. Francis M. Gibbons. LC 88-398. 400p. 1988. 14.95 (ISBN 0-87579-115-8). Deseret Bk.
Wilfred Grenfell, His Life & Work. James L. Kerr. LC 73-21177. 1977. lib. bdg. 35.00x (ISBN 0-8371-6068-5, KEWG). Greenwood.
Wilfred Owen. Wilfred Owen. Ed. by Jennifer Breen. (Routledge English Texts Ser.). 244p. (Orig.). 1988. pap. text ed. 12.95 (ISBN 0-415-00733-X, Pub. by Routledge UK). Routledge Chapman & Hall.
Wilfred Owen. Jon Stallworthy. 1975. 29.95x (ISBN 0-19-211719-X). Oxford U Pr.
Wilfred Owen: Anthem for a Doomed Youth. Kenneth Simcox. 166p. 1988. 27.50 (ISBN 0-7130-0179-8, Pub. by Woburn Pr England). Biblio Dist.
Wilfred Owen: The Complete Poems & Fragments. Ed. by Jon Stallworthy. 1984. 2vols slipcased 65.00 (ISBN 0-393-01830-X). Norton.
Wilfred Owen, 1893-1918: A Bibliography. William White. LC 66-28409. (Serif Ser.: No. 1). 1967. 10.00x (ISBN 0-87338-017-7). Kent St U Pr.
Wilfred Slept Here. Don Carroll. 1982. 15.00x (ISBN 0-903653-78-8, Pub. by New Playwrights Network). State Mutual Bk.
Wilfred the Rat. James Stevenson. LC 77-1091. (Illus.). 32p. (ps-3). 1977. PLB 11.88 (ISBN 0-688-84103-1). Greenwillow.
Wilfrid Gordon McDonald Partridge. Mem Fox. LC 85-14720. (Illus.). 32p. (gr. k-4). 1985. 11.95 (ISBN 0-916291-04-9). Kane Miller Bk.
Wilful Heiress. Victoria Thorne. 1985. 24.95x (ISBN 0-7090-2189-5, Pub. by R Hale Ltd UK). State Mutual Bk.
Wilful Woman: A Novel. Michael Talbot. LC 88-45316. 384p. 1989. 18.95 (ISBN 0-394-55296-2). Knopf.
Wilhelem Reich in Hell. Robert A. Wilson. LC 8-1290. 192p. (Orig.). 1987. pap. 9.95 (ISBN 0-941404-47-1). Falcon Pr AZ.
Wilhelm Dilthey: A Hermeneutic Approach to the Study of History & Culture. Ilse N. Bulhof. (Martinus Nijhoff Philosophy Library: No. 2). 225p. 1980. lib. bdg. 37.00 (ISBN 90-247-2360-4, Pub. by Martinus Nijhoff). Kluwer Academic.
Wilhelm Dilthey: An Introduction. Herbert A. Hodges. 1969. Repr. of 1944 ed. 23.50x (ISBN 0-86527-211-5). Fertig.
Wilhelm Dilthey: Pioneer of the Human Sciences. H. P. Rickman. LC 78-68828. 1979. 35.00x (ISBN 0-520-03879-7). U of Cal Pr.
Wilhelm Dilthey: The Critique of Historical Reason. Michael Ermarth. 11.00x (ISBN 0-226-21743-4). U of Chicago Pr.
Wilhelm Heinrich Wackenroder's Confessions & Fantasies. W. H. Wackenroder. Tr. by Mary H. Schubert. LC 73-136958. (Illus.). 1972. 22.50x (ISBN 0-271-01150-5). Pa St U Pr.
Wilhelm Hohenzollern: The Last of the Kaisers. Emil Ludwig. LC 74-100815. (Illus.). Repr. of 1927 ed. 31.25 (ISBN 0-404-04067-5). AMS Pr.
Wilhelm Hohenzollern: The Last of the Kaisers. Emil Ludwig. 1927. 45.00 (ISBN 0-8495-6261-9). Arden Lib.
Wilhelm Jordaens's "Avellana" A Fourteenth Century Virtue-Vice Debate. Lawrence J. Johnson. (Speculum Anniversary Monographs: No. 9). xi, 101p. (Orig.). 1986. 12.50x (ISBN 0-910956-89-8); pap. 6.50x (ISBN 0-910956-90-1). Medieval Acad.
Wilhelm Lehmann: A Critical Biography. David Scrase. LC 81-69880. (Studies in German Literature, Linguistics, & Culture: Vol. 13). (Illus.). 1983. Set. 33.00x (ISBN 0-938100-14-9); Pt. I, 191 Pp. 27.00 (ISBN 0-938100-15-7); Pt. II, 200 p.,1989. 29.00x (ISBN 0-938100-16-5). Camden Hse.
Wilhelm Lehmbruck: The Complete Graphic Work. Erwin Petermann. (Illus.). 428p. (Ger.). 1985. 240.00 (ISBN 1-55660-005-4). A Wofsy Fine Arts.
Wilhelm Liebknecht & the Founding of the German Social Democratic Party. Raymond H. Dominick, III. LC 81-16329. xiv, 551p. 1982. 30.00x (ISBN 0-8078-1510-1). U of NC Pr.
Wilhelm Liebknecht: Letters to the Chicago Workingmen's Advocate (1870-1871) Ed. by Philip S. Foner. 190p. 1983. 35.00 (ISBN 0-8419-0743-9). Holmes & Meier.
Wilhelm Liebknechts Briefwechsel Mit Karl Marx & Friedrich Engels. Ed. by Georg Eckert. (Quellen & Untersuchungen Zur Geschichte der Deutschen & Oesterreichischen Arbeiterbewegung: No. 5). (Illus.). 1963. 51.20x (ISBN 90-2790-154-6). Mouton.
Wilhelm Marr: The Patriarch of Anti-Semitism. Moshe Zimmerman. (Studies in Jewish History). 192p. 1986. 19.95x (ISBN 0-19-504005-8). Oxford U Pr.
Wilhelm Meister & His English Kinsmen. Susanne Howe. LC 30-1541. Repr. of 1930 ed. 17.00 (ISBN 0-404-03367-9). AMS Pr.
Wilhelm Meister, Vol. 1: The Years of Apprenticeship, Bks. 1-3. Johann Wolfgang Von Goethe. Tr. by H. M. Waidson from Ger. 1982. 7.95 (ISBN 0-7145-3675-X). Riverrun NY.
Wilhelm Meister, Vol. 2: The Years of Apprenticeship, Bks. 4-6. Johann Wolfgang Von Goethe. Tr. by H. M. Waidson from Ger. 1982. 7.95 (ISBN 0-7145-3699-7). Riverrun NY.
Wilhelm Meister, Vol. 3: The Years of Apprenticeship, Bks. 7 & 8. Johann Wolfgang Von Goethe. Tr. by H. M. Waidson from Ger. 1982. pap. 7.95 (ISBN 0-7145-3928-7); 11.95 (ISBN 0-7145-3702-0). Riverrun NY.
Wilhelm Meister, Vol. 4: The Years of Travel, Bk. 1. Johann Wolfgang Von Goethe. Tr. by H. M. Waidson from Ger. 1982. 11.95 (ISBN 0-7145-3827-2). Riverrun NY.
Wilhelm Meister, Vol. 5: The Years of Travel, Bk. 2. Johann Wolfgang Von Goethe. Tr. by H. M. Waidson from Ger. 1982. 11.95 (ISBN 0-7145-3838-8); pap. 7.95 (ISBN 0-7145-3932-5). Riverrun NY.
Wilhelm Meister, Vol. 6: The Years of Travel, Bk. 3. Johann Wolfgang Von Goethe. Tr. by H. M. Waidson from Ger. 1982. 11.95 (ISBN 0-7145-3840-X); pap. 7.95 (ISBN 0-7145-3934-1). Riverrun NY.
Wilhelm Meister's Apprenticeship & Travels see Goethe's Popular Works.
Wilhelm Muller: The Poet of the Schubert Song Cycles. Cecilia C. Baumann. LC 80-12806. (Studies in German Literature). (Illus.). 208p. 1981. 24.95x (ISBN 0-271-00266-2). Pa St U Pr.
Wilhelm Raabe: The Fiction of the Alternative Community. Ed. by Jeffrey L. Sammons. 435p. 1987. text ed. 45.00 (ISBN 0-691-06709-0). Princeton U Pr.
Wilhelm Raabes Roman Die Akten Des Vogelsangs. M. Boenneken. pap. 19.00 (ISBN 0-384-04905-2). Johnson Repr.
Wilhelm Reich: His Theory & Therapy. Regardie. Date not set. price not set. Falcon Pr Az.
Wilhelm Reich: The Evolution of His Work. David Boadella. 400p. (Orig.). 1986. pap. 9.95 (ISBN 1-85063-034-8). Routledge Chapman & Hall.
Wilhelm Schmidt & the Origin of the Idea of God. Ernest Brandewie. 352p. (Orig.). 1983. lib. bdg. 31.50 (ISBN 0-8191-3363-9); pap. text ed. 16.50 (ISBN 0-8191-3364-7). U Pr of Amer.
Wilhelm Tell. Friedrich von Schiller. Ed. by Kenneth J. Northcott. Tr. by William F. Mainland from Ger. LC 70-187835. (German Literary Classics in Translation Ser). 196p. 1972. 12.50x (ISBN 0-226-73800-0); pap. 8.95X (ISBN 0-226-73801-9, Phoen). U of Chicago Pr.
Wilhelm von Humboldt: A Biography, 2 vols. Paul R. Sweet. LC 77-26654. (Illus.). 1978. Vol. 1: 1767-1808, 323p. 25.00 (ISBN 0-8142-0278-0); Vol. 2: 1808-1835, 584p. 32.50 (ISBN 0-8142-0279-9). Ohio St U Pr.
Wilhelm von Humboldt as a Literary Critic. Richey A. Novak. (Germanic Studies in America: Vol. 9). 142p. 1972. 20.90 (ISBN 3-261-00318-9). P Lang Pubs.
Wilhelm Von Humboldt's Conception of Linguistic Relativity. Roger L. Brown. LC 67-30542. (Janua Linguarum, Ser. Minor: No. 65). (Orig.). 1967. pap. text ed. 13.60x (ISBN 90-2790-593-2). Mouton.
Wilhelm Waiblinger in Italy. Lawrence S. Thompson. (North Carolina. University. Studies in the Germanic Languages & Literatures: No. 9). Repr. of 1953 ed. 27.00 (ISBN 0-404-50909-6). AMS Pr.
Wilhelm Wundt & the Making of a Scientific Psychology. Ed. by Robert W. Rieber. LC 80-15877. 264p. 1980. 39.50x (ISBN 0-306-40483-4, Plenum Pr). Plenum Pub.
Wilhelmi Malmesbiriensis Monachi de Gestis Pontificum Anglorum Libri Quinque: From William of Malmsbury's Autograph. N. E. Hamilton. (Rolls Ser.: No. 52). Repr. of 1870 ed. 60.00 (ISBN 0-8115-1111-1). Kraus Repr.
Wilhelmina's Inheritance. Mimi D. Bolton & George W. Bolton. LC 84-51420. (Illus.). 147p. 1984. 10.95 (ISBN 0-9614274-0-X). Wisla Pubs.
Wilhite-Dew Debate. J. Porter Wilhite & James F. Dew. pap. 2.50 (ISBN 0-89315-355-9). Lambert Bk.
Wilkes & Liberty. G. Rude. 240p. 1983. pap. text ed. 9.95x (ISBN 0-85315-579-8, Lawrence & Wishart Pubs UK). Humanities.
Wilkes-Barre & Hazelton RY. E. J. Quinby. LC 72-87786. 1972. pap. 3.95 (ISBN 0-911868-01-1). Carstens Pubns.
Wilkes-Barre Variation, Two Knights Defense. Yakov Estrin. (Illus.). 114p. 1978. pap. 4.00 (ISBN 0-931462-00-2). Chess Ent Inc.
Wilkes County Papers, Seventeen Seventy-Seven to Eighteen Thirty-Three. Robert S. Davis, Jr. 338p. 1979. pap. 28.50 softcover (ISBN 0-89308-410-7). Southern Hist Pr.
Wilkes Expedition: The First United Ststes Exploring Expedition, 1838-1842. David B. Tyler. LC 68-25931. (American Philosophical Society, Memoirs: Vol. 73). pap. 113.30 (ISBN 0-317-28297-2, 2019713). Bks Demand UMI.
Wilkeson's Notes on Puget Sound. facs. ed. Wilkeson. 47p. pap. 4.95 (ISBN 0-8466-0045-5, S45). Shorey.
Wilkie Collins. R. Ashley. LC 75-30887. (Studies in Fiction, No. 34). 1975. lib. bdg. 75.00x (ISBN 0-8383-2095-3). Haskell.
Wilkie Collins. Robert Ashley. LC 74-6031. Repr. of 1952 ed. lib. bdg. 15.00 (ISBN 0-8414-2975-8). Folcroft.
Wilkie Collins. Norman Page. (Critical Heritage Ser.). 304p. 1985. pap. 15.00 (ISBN 0-7102-0589-9). Routledge Chapman & Hall.
Wilkie Collins, a Critical & Biographical Study. Dorothy L. Sayers. Ed. by E. R. Gregory. LC 76-53108. (Illus., Limited ed). 1977. pap. 12.50x (ISBN 0-918160-01-4). Friends Univ Toledo.
Wilkie Collins: An Annotated Bibliography 1889-1976. Kirk H. Beetz. LC 77-26609. (Author Bibliographies Ser.: No. 35). 175p. 1978. 17.50 (ISBN 0-8108-1103-0). Scarecrow.
Wilkie Collins & Charles Reade. M. L. Parish et al. 355p. 1983. Repr. of 1940 ed. lib. bdg. 250.00 (ISBN 0-89984-838-9). Century Bookbindery.
Wilkie Collins & Charles Reade, First Editions in the Library at Dormy House. Morris L. Parrish. (Illus.). 1940. 24.50 (ISBN 0-8337-2675-7). B Franklin.
Wilkie Collins & His Victorian Readers: A Study in the Rhetoric of Authorship. Sue Lonoff. LC 79-8835. (Studies in the Nineteenth Century: No. 2). (Illus.). 1982. 34.50 (ISBN 0-404-18044-2). AMS Pr.
Wilkie Collins, le Fann & Others. Stewart M. Ellis. 1973. Repr. of 1931 ed. 25.00 (ISBN 0-8274-1416-1). R West.
Wilkie Collins, le Fanu, & Others. facs. ed. Stewart M. Ellis. LC 68-29203. (Essay Index Reprint Ser). 1968. Repr. of 1931 ed. 19.00 (ISBN 0-8369-0413-3). Ayer Co Pubs.
Wilkie Collins: The Critical Heritage. Ed. by Norman Page. (Critical Heritage Ser.). 1974. 32.50x (ISBN 0-7100-7843-9). Routledge Chapman & Hall.
Wilkie Collins: Women, Property & Propriety. Philip O'Neill. 1988. 28.50 (ISBN 0-389-20771-3). Rowman.
Wilkin's Ghost. Robert Burch. LC 78-6293. (Illus.). (gr. 5-9). 1978. 9.95 (ISBN 0-670-76897-9). Viking.
Will, 2 vols. Brian O'Shaughnessy. LC 79-13524. 1980. Vol. 1, 240 P. 62.50 (ISBN 0-521-22679-1); Vol. 2, 360 P. 69.50 (ISBN 0-521-22680-5). Cambridge U Pr.
Will. Patricia Werner. Ed. by Jennifer Weis. 256p. (Orig.). 1988. pap. 3.95 (ISBN 0-7701-0898-9). PaperJacks US.
Will: A Dual Aspect Theory. Brian O'Shaughnessy. LC 79-13524. 1983. Vol. 2, 380 pgs. pap. 17.95 (ISBN 0-521-27254-8). Cambridge U Pr.
Will a Man Rob God? C. Phillip Johnson. 1981. pap. 3.00 (ISBN 0-933184-29-8). Flame Intl.
Will, a Modern Day Treasure Hunt. 2nd ed. Ronald Franks & Thomas Dowd. 1981. pap. text ed. 6.95 (ISBN 0-9607132-0-4). Tricore Assoc.
Will: A Modern Day Treasure Hunt. Tod Normot. 62p. 1982. 6.95 (ISBN 0-686-35968-2). Tricore Assoc.
Will Abstracts of Brooke County, (West) Virginia 1797-1850. K. T. McFarland. 88p. pap. text ed. 9.50 perfect binding (ISBN 0-933227-26-4). Closson Pr.
Will America Accept Love at Halftime? or How to Survive Pro-Football Sunday. Jim Klobuchar. pap. 2.95 (ISBN 0-87018-066-5). Ross.
Will America Surrender? Slobodan Draskovich. 480p. 1972. 12.95 (ISBN 0-8159-7211-3). Devin.
Will America Surrender? Slobodan Draskovich. 1976. pap. 9.95 (ISBN 0-8159-7217-2). Devin.
Will & a Way: What the U. S. Can Learn from Canada about Caring for the Elderly. Robert L. Kane & Rosalie A. Kane. 311p. 1988. pap. 15.00 (ISBN 0-231-06137-4). Columbia U Pr.
Will & a Way: What the United States Can Learn from Canada about Caring for the Elderly. Robert L. Kane & Rosalie S. Kane. LC 85-16616. (Columbia Studies of Social Gerontology & Aging). 275p. 1985. 37.50x (ISBN 0-231-06136-6). Columbia U Pr.
Will & Circumstance: Montesquieu, Rousseau, & the French Revolution. Norman Hampson. LC 82-40455. 294p. 1983. 19.50x (ISBN 0-8061-1843-1). U of Okla Pr.
Will & Coincidence: Conversations & Celestin Deliege & Hans Mayer. Pierre Boulez. (Illus.). 1977. 15.00 (ISBN 3-7630-9024-X). Kraus Repr.
Will & Estate Records in the Virginia State Library: A Researcher's Guide. John Vogt & T. William Kethley, Jr. iv, 186p. (Orig.). 1987. pap. 10.00 (ISBN 0-935931-27-9). Iberian Pub.
Will & Estate Records in the Virginia State Library: A Researcher's Guide. John Vogt & T. William Kethley, Jr. 186p. 1988. Repr. lib. bdg. 24.95x (ISBN 0-8095-8202-3). Borgo Pr.
Will & Political Legitimacy: A Critical Exposition of Social Contract Theory in Hobbes, Locke, Rousseau, Kant, & Hegel. Patrick Riley. 320p. 1982. text ed. 27.00x (ISBN 0-674-95316-9). Harvard U Pr.
Will & Spirit. Gerald G. May. LC 82-47751. (Illus.). 368p. 1987. pap. 15.95 (ISBN 0-06-250582-3, HarpR). Har-Row.
Will & Spirit: A Comtemplative Psychology. Gerald G. May. LC 82-47751. 384p. 1982. 25.45 (ISBN 0-06-065534-8, HarpR). Har-Row.
Will & the Grace. Diane Westlake. (Illus.). 80p. (Orig.). 1985. pap. 6.95 (ISBN 0-9614438-0-4). Fen Winnie.
Will & Trust Drafting & Estate Planning. Randy Spiro. 363p. (Orig.). 1985. pap. text ed. 39.50 (ISBN 0-89074-074-7). Lega Bks.
Will Anyone, Anywhere, Survive the American Century? Ruby Riddle. 1987. 13.95 (ISBN 0-533-06812-6). Vantage.
Will at the Crossroads: A Reconstruction of Kant's Moral Philosophy. J. Gray Cox. 220p. (Orig.). 1984. lib. bdg. 25.75 (ISBN 0-8191-3710-3). U Pr of Amer.
Will Barnet. Robert M. Doty. LC 84-396. (Illus.). 172p. 1984. 49.50 (ISBN 0-8109-0731-3). Abrams.
Will Barnet: Paintings & Prints, 1932-1982. Howard E. Wooden. LC 82-63132. (Illus.). 24p. 1983. pap. 5.00 (ISBN 0-939324-08-3). Wichita Art Mus.
Will Barnet: Twenty-Seven Master Prints. (Illus.). 1979. pap. 12.50 (ISBN 0-8109-2216-9). Abrams.
Will Be My Friend? Roy Nichols & Doris Nichols. LC 87-42783. (Illus.). 32p. (ps-7). 1987. 5.95 (ISBN 0-8344-0155-X, 155). Worthy TX.
Will Bradley: His Graphic Art. Will Bradley. Ed. by Clarence Hornung & Roberta W. Wong. (Illus.). pap. 6.50 (ISBN 0-486-20701-3). Dover.
Will Campbell & the Soul of the South. Thomas L. Connelly. 176p. 1982. 10.95 (ISBN 0-8264-0182-1). Continuum.

Will Capitalism Survive? A Challenge by Paul Johnson with Twelve Responses. Ed. by Ernest W. Lefever. LC 79-55316. 79p. 1979. pap. 6.75 (ISBN 0-89633-026-5). Ethics & Public Policy.
Will China Go Capitalist? 2nd ed. Steven N. Cheung. (Institute of Economic Affairs, Hobart Papers Ser.: No. 94). pap. 9.25 technical (ISBN 0-255-36152-1). Transatl Arts.
Will Christians Go Through the Great Tribulation? Gordon Lindsay. (Prophecy Ser.). 1.50 (ISBN 0-89985-065-0). Christ Nations.
Will Clauses: Annotations & Forms with Tax Effects, 4 vols. Joseph H. Murphy et al. 1960. Set, updates avail. looseleaf 355.00 (441); Updates 1985 252.00; Updates 1986 276.50. Bender.
Will Clayton: A Short Biography. facsimile ed. Ellen C. Garwood. LC 73-157335. (Select Bibliographies Reprint Ser). Repr. of 1958 ed. 17.00 (ISBN 0-8369-5795-4). Ayer Co Pubs.
Will County Circuit Clerk's Study: Recordkeeping, Administration, Management, Vol. II. National Center for State Courts Staff. 120p. 1977. manuscript 7.20 (MAB-141). Natl Ctr St Courts.
Will Dad Ever Move Back Home? Paula Z. Hogan. LC 79-24058. (Life & Living from a Child's Point of View Ser.). (Illus.). (gr. k-5). 1980. PLB 15.33 (ISBN 0-8172-1356-2). Raintree Pubs.
Will Drafting. Dana Shilling. LC 86-30265. 160p. 1987. 27.50 (ISBN 0-13-959727-1). P-H.
Will Drafting: Avoiding Pitfalls & Problems: ALI-ABA Video Law Review Study Materials. LC 86-218450. 222p. 1986. 40.00. Am Law Inst.
Will Drafting Explained. H. Eugene Netherton. 84p. 1987. 9.95 (ISBN 0-318-21767-8). Netherton.
Will Eisner Color Treasury. Will Eisner. Ed. by Jens P. Agger. (Illus.). 1982. 5.95 (ISBN 0-87816-006-X). Kitchen Sink.
Will Europe Fight for Oil: Energy Relations in the Atlantic Area. Ed. by Robert J. Lieber. 240p. 1983. 35.00 (ISBN 0-275-91035-0, C1035). Praeger.
Will Europe Reconquer the Leadership of the World? Meaningful Changes in a World of Distressing Confusion. Edward L. Tankersley. (Illus.). 1980. deluxe ed. 69.75x (ISBN 0-930008-46-4). Inst Econ Pol.
Will for Peace: Peace Action in the United Methodist Church: A History. Herman Will, Jr. 300p. 9.95 (CS1007). General Board.
Will God Run. Charles B. Hodge. LC 70-187827. (Illus.). 1965. 6.95 (ISBN 0-89112-053-X). Abilene Christ U.
Will Henry-Clay Fisher. Robert L. Gale. LC 82-71032. (Western Writer's Ser.: No. 52). (Illus., Orig.). 1982. pap. 2.95x (ISBN 0-88430-026-9). Boise St Univ.
Will Henry's West. Dale L. Walker. LC 83-51163. (Illus.). 240p. 1984. 18.00 (ISBN 0-87404-077-9). Tex Western.
Will Herberg: A Bio-Bibliography. Harry J. Ausmus. LC 85-21955. (Bio-Bibliographies in Law & Political Science Ser.: No. 2). 120p. 1986. lib. bdg. 36.95 (ISBN 0-313-25067-7, AWH/). Greenwood.
Will Herberg: From Right to Right. Harry J. Ausmus. LC 86-19357. (Studies in Religion). xx, 276p. 1987. 29.95x (ISBN 0-8078-1724-4). U of NC Pr.
Will Hinds: Artist of the Deep South. Norton (R. W.) Art Gallery. LC 79-187911. (Contemporary Realists Ser.). (Illus.). 1972. pap. 2.00x (ISBN 0-9600182-6-3). Norton Art.
Will I Cry Tomorrow? Susan Stanford. 1987. 9.95 (ISBN 0-8007-1512-8). Revell.
Will I Ever Be Older? Eva Grant. LC 80-24782. (Life & Living from a Child's Point of View Ser.). (Illus.). (gr. k-5). 1981. PLB 15.33 (ISBN 0-8172-1363-5). Raintree Pubs.
Will I Ever Be Older? Eva H. Grant. (Good Days-Bad Days Ser.). 32p. (gr. 1-3). 1986. 4.95 (ISBN 0-89191-206-1). Cook.
Will I Have a Friend? Miriam Cohen. LC 67-10127. (Illus.). 32p. (gr. k-1). 1967. pap. 11.95 (ISBN 0-02-722790-1). Macmillan.
Will I Have a Friend? Miriam Cohen. LC 86-17454. (Illus.). (gr. k-1). 1986. pap. 4.95 (ISBN 0-689-71141-7, Aladdin Bks). Macmillan.
Will I Live Another Day Before I Die? Thoughts on Suicide & Life. Ed. by Gallagher. (Reflections of Art Ser.). 95p. 1988. pap. 7.95 (ISBN 0-930194-44-6). Ctr Thanatology.
Will I See You Next Summer? Judith Enderle. (Caprice Romance Ser.: No. 45). 160p. 1984. pap. 2.25 (ISBN 0-441-88987-5, Pub by Tempo). Ace Bks.
Will, Imagination, & Reason. Claes G. Ryn. 392p. (Orig.). 1986. pap. 7.95 (ISBN 0-89526-807-8); 12.95 (ISBN 0-89526-579-6). Regnery Gateway.
Will Inflation Destroy America? Arthur Milton. 1977. 7.95 (ISBN 0-8065-0608-3, Pub. by Citadel Pr). Lyle Stuart.
Will Insley: The Opaque Civilization. Will Lnsley & Linda Shearer. LC 84-10701. (Illus.). 88p. 1984. pap. 15.00 (ISBN 0-295-96446-4). U of Wash Pr.
Will Insley: The Opaque Civilization. The Solomon R. Guggenheim Foundation. (Illus.). 88p. (Orig.). 1984. pap. 12.00 (ISBN 0-89207-047-1). S R Guggenheim.
Will Is Not the Way - the Living Trust Alternative. Vickie Schumacher et al. Ed. by Louis Austin. LC 88-90578. 64p. 1988. pap. write for info. (ISBN 0-945811-00-4). Schumacher Co.
Will It Be Okay? Crescent Dragonwagon. LC 76-48859. (Illus.). (gr. k-3). 1977. PLB 12.89 (ISBN 0-06-021738-3). HarpJ.
Will It Ever Be My Birthday? Dorothy Corey. Ed. by Ann Fay. LC 86-1565. (Illus.). 32p. (ps-1). 1986. PLB 11.95 (ISBN 0-8075-9106-8). A Whitman.
Will It Liberate: Questions about Liberation Theology. Michael Novak. 320p. (Orig.). 1987. 14.95 (ISBN 0-8091-0385-0). Paulist Pr.
Will It Rain? Holly Keller. LC 83-25423. (Illus.). 24p. (ps-1). 1984. 11.50 (ISBN 0-688-03839-5); PLB 10.88 (ISBN 0-688-03840-9). Greenwillow.
Will James Book of Cowboy Stories. Will James. lib. rep. ed. 19.50 (ISBN 0-684-15156-1, ScribT). Scribner.
Will James: The Life & Work of a Lone Cowboy. William G. Bell. LC 86-46365. (Illus.). 150p. 1987. 39.95 (ISBN 0-87358-439-2). Northland.
Will James: The Spirit of the Cowboy. William G. Bell et al. (Illus.). 96p. (Orig.). 1985. ltd. ed. 50.00 (ISBN 0-9614971-0-6). Nicolaysen Art Mus.
Will James: The Spirit of the Cowboy. William G. Bell et al. Pref. by J. M. Neil. (Illus.). 96p. (Orig.). 1985. pap. 12.95. Nicolaysen Art Mus.
Will James: The Spirit of the Cowboy. Ed. by J. M. Neil. LC 85-194446. (Illus.). x, 85p. 1985. pap. 12.95 (ISBN 0-9614971-1-4). U of Nebr Pr.
Will Many Be Saved? Ralph C. Martin. 48p. (Orig.). 1988. pap. text ed. 1.95 (ISBN 0-89283-392-0). Servant.
Will My Rabbit Go to Heaven? And Other Questions Children Ask. Jeremie Hughes. (Illus.). 128p. (gr. k up). 1988. pap. 4.95 (ISBN 0-7459-1221-4). Lion USA.
Will, My Son. Sarah Boston. 121p. 1981. pap. 4.50 (ISBN 0-86104-346-4, Pub. by Pluto Pr). Longwood Pub Group.
Will O' the Mill. Robert Louis Stevenson. 5.00 (ISBN 0-87482-064-2). Wake-Brook.
Will of God. Morris Ashcraft. LC 80-65714. 1980. pap. 4.95 (ISBN 0-8054-1620-X). Broadman.
Will of God. Paul Walkowski. 300p. 1988. 15.95 (ISBN 0-8283-1917-0). Branden Pub Co.
Will of God. Leslie D. Weatherhead. (Festival Books). 1976. pap. 2.95 (ISBN 0-687-45600-2). Abingdon.
Will of the Gods, Bk. IV. Sharon Green. (Jalar-Amazon Warrior Ser.). 384p. 1986. pap. 3.50 (ISBN 0-88677-039-4). DAW Bks.
Will of the People: Original Democracy in Non-Western Societies. Raul S. Manglapus. LC 86-29594. (Studies in Freedom: No. 4). 200p. 1987. lib. bdg. 29.95 (ISBN 0-313-25837-6, MWG/). Greenwood.
Will of the Tribe. Arthur W. Upfield. 216p. 1984. rack-size 4.50 (ISBN 0-684-18141-X, ScribT). Scribner.
Will Our Children Have Faith? John H. Westerhoff, III. 144p. 1983. pap. 6.95 (ISBN 0-8164-2435-7, AY7452, HarpR). Har-Row.
Will Our President Die in Office? Gordon Lindsay. (Prophecy Ser.). 1980. 2.25 (ISBN 0-89985-984-4). Christ Nations.
Will Our Tears Never Dry? Japanese Outcastes. John R. Terry. 200p. 1988. pap. 9.95 (ISBN 0-933704-72-0). Dawn Pr.
Will Power: Drafting Effective Wills. Linda R. Getzen & Edward F. Koren. LC 87-23900. 135p. (Orig.). 1987. pap. 19.95 (ISBN 0-8366-0003-7). Callaghan.
Will Requirements of Various States. George G. Coughlin. LC 84-231653. 40p. 1984. write for info. Am Coll Probate.
Will Rogers. Betty Rogers. (Illus.). 312p. (YA) (gr. 8 up). 1982. 18.95 (ISBN 0-8061-1526-2); pap. 9.95 (ISBN 0-8061-1600-5). U of Okla Pr.
Will Rogers: A Bio-Bibliography. Peter C. Rollins. LC 83-10696. (Popular Culture Bio-Bibliographies). xiii, 282p. 1984. lib. bdg. 36.95 (ISBN 0-313-22633-4, RWR/). Greenwood.
Will Rogers: America's Cowboy Philosopher. Louis Musso. Ed. by D. Steve Rahmas. LC 74-14622. (Outstanding Personalities Ser.: No. 74). 32p. 1974. lib. bdg. 3.75 incl. catalog cards (ISBN 0-87157-574-4); pap. 2.50 vinyl laminated covers (ISBN 0-87157-074-2). SamHar Pr.
Will Rogers: An Appreciation. David R. Milsten. 1976. lib. bdg. 59.95 (ISBN 0-8490-2826-4). Gordon Pr.
Will Rogers Book. Paula M. Love. 1972. 10.00 (ISBN 0-87244-030-3); soft cover o. p. 7.95 (ISBN 0-87244-031-1). Texian.
Will Rogers Cookbook, Birthday Centennial, 1879-1979. Ed. by Will Rogers Cooperative Association. LC 79-88115. 1979. 8.95 (ISBN 0-913530-19-0). Palisades Pub.
Will Rogers' Daily Telegrams: The Coolidge Years, 1926-1929, Vol. 1. Will Rogers. Ed. by James M. Smallwood & Steven K. Gragert. LC 77-91791. (The Writings of Will Rogers Ser., Series III: Vol. 1). (Illus.). 453p. 1978. 19.95 (ISBN 0-914956-10-8). Okla State Univ Pr.
Will Rogers' Daily Telegrams: The Hoover Years, 1929-1931, Vol. 2. Will Rogers. Ed. by James M. Smallwood & Steven K. Gragert. LC 78-70066. (The Writings of Will Rogers Ser., Series III: Vol. 2). (Illus.). 390p. 1978. 19.95 (ISBN 0-914956-11-6). Okla State Univ Pr.
Will Rogers' Daily Telegrams: The Hoover Years, 1931-1933, Vol. 3. Will Rogers. Ed. by James M. Smallwood & Steven K. Gragert. LC 78-78290. (The Writings of Will Rogers Ser., Series III: Vol. 3). (Illus.). 389p. 1979. 19.95 (ISBN 0-914956-12-4). Okla State Univ Pr.
Will Rogers' Daily Telegrams: The Roosevelt Years, 1933-1935, Vol. 4. Will Rogers. Ed. by James M. Smallwood & Steven K. Gragert. LC 77-91791. (The Writings of Will Rogers Ser., Series III: Vol. 4). (Illus.). 457p. 1979. 19.95 (ISBN 0-914956-13-2). Okla State Univ Pr.
Will Rogers: The Cowboy Who Walked with Kings. Cathereen L. Bennett. 11.95 (ISBN 0-88411-848-7, Pub. by Aeonian Pr). Amereon Ltd.
Will Rogers Treasury. 1986. 6.98 (62544X). Outlet Bk Co.
Will Rogers' Weekly Articles: The Coolidge Years, 1925-1927, Vol. 2. Will Rogers. Ed. by James M. Smallwood & Steven K. Gragert. LC 79-57650. (The Writings of Will Rogers Ser., Series IV: Vol. 2). (Illus.). 368p. 1980. 19.95 (ISBN 0-914956-16-7). Okla State Univ Pr.
Will Rogers' Weekly Articles: The Coolidge Years, 1927-1929, Vol. 3. Will Rogers. Ed. by James M. Smallwood & Steven K. Gragert. LC 79-57650. (The Writings of Will Rogers Ser., Series IV: Vol. 3). (Illus.). 304p. 1981. 19.95 (ISBN 0-914956-17-5). Okla State Univ Pr.
Will Rogers' Weekly Articles: The Harding-Coolidge Years, 1922-1925, Vol. 1. Will Rogers. Ed. by James M. Smallwood & Steven K. Gragert. LC 79-57650. (The Writings of Will Rogers Ser., Series IV: Vol. 1). (Illus.). 431p. 1980. 19.95 (ISBN 0-914956-15-9). Okla State Univ Pr.
Will Rogers' Weekly Articles: The Hoover Years: 1929-1931, Vol. 4. Will Rogers. Ed. by Steven K. Gragert. LC 79-57650. (Writings of Will Rogers Ser.: Series IV, Vol. 4). (Illus.). 278p. 1981. 17.95 (ISBN 0-914956-18-3). Okla State Univ Pr.
Will Roger's Weekly Articles: The Hoover Years 1931-1933, Vol. 5. Will Rogers. Ed. by Steven K. Gragert. LC 79-57650. (Writings of Will Rogers Ser.: Ser.IV, Vol 5). (Illus.). 280p. 1982. 17.95 (ISBN 0-914956-19-1). Okla State Univ Pr.
Will Rogers' Weekly Articles: The Roosevelt Years: 1933-1935, Vol. 6. Will Rogers. Ed. by Steven K. Gragert. LC 79-57650. (Writings of Will Rogers Ser.: Ser. IV, Vol. 6). (Illus.). 309p. 1982. 17.95 (ISBN 0-914956-21-3). Okla State Univ Pr.
Will Roosevelt Succeed? A Study of Fascist Tendencies in America. Archibald F. Brockway. LC 75-180392. Repr. of 1934 ed. 25.00 (ISBN 0-404-56108-X). AMS Pr.
Will Shakespeare: A Factotum & Agent. Alden Brooks. LC 77-39536. Repr. of 1937 ed. 25.00 (ISBN 0-404-01117-9). AMS Pr.
Will She Understand? New Short Stories. Fielding Dawson. LC 88-2450. (Illus.). 158p. 1988. 20.00 (ISBN 0-87685-730-6); deluxe ed. 30.00 (ISBN 0-87685-731-4); pap. 10.00 (ISBN 0-87685-729-2). Black Sparrow.
Will Somebody Please Listen to Me for a Change? John T. Robertson. LC 84-52712. (Illus.). 525p. (Orig.). 1985. pap. 13.95 (ISBN 0-9614557-0-5). Vu-Point Pubs.
Will Spring Be Early or Will Spring Be Late? Crockett Johnson. LC 59-9424. (Illus.). (gr. k-3). 1959. PLB 12.89 (ISBN 0-690-89423-6, Crowell Jr Bks). HarpJ.
Will Stark & Boobear: Ranger Scouts, Vol. 2. 2nd ed. Dorothea M. Thompson. (New Hampshire Heroes Ser.). (Illus.). 150p. (gr. 5-10). Date not set. pap. text ed. 9.95 (ISBN 0-931947-52-9). Thompson Pr.
Will That Be on the Final? Ohmer Milton. (Illus.). 100p. 1982. spiral bdg. 10.50 (ISBN 0-398-04676-X). C C Thomas.
Will the Antichrist Come Out of Russia? Gordon Lindsay. (Prophecy Ser.). 1.25 (ISBN 0-89985-066-9). Christ Nations.
Will the Defense Please Rest? A Guide to Marital Harmony. Les Carter. (Life Enrichment Ser.). 1986. pap. 7.95 (ISBN 0-8010-2513-3). Baker Bk.
Will the East Wind Blow? Hansi Reports on the Middle East. Maria A. Hirschmann. LC 78-71319. (Illus.). 160p. (Orig.). 1979. pap. text ed. 2.50 (ISBN 0-932878-04-0, HB-04). Hansi.
Will the Faculty Please Come to Order. John E. Longhurst. 68p. 1969. pap. 2.50x (ISBN 0-87291-003-2). Coronado Pr.
Will the Gentleman Yield? The Congressional Record Humor Book. Bill Hogan & Mike Hill. LC 87-10203. 128p. (Orig.). 1987. pap. 7.95 (ISBN 0-89815-215-1). Ten Speed Pr.
Will the Non-Russians Rebel? State, Ethnicity, & Stability in the U. S. S. R. Alexander J. Motyl. LC 86-24386. (Cornell Studies in Soviet History & Society). 224p. 1987. 24.95x (ISBN 0-8014-1947-6). Cornell U Pr.
Will the Psychologists Cure Us? Laurance Labadie. (Men & Movements in the History & Philosophy of Anarchism Ser.). 1979. lib. bdg. 59.95 (ISBN 0-685-96422-1). Revisionist Pr.
Will the Real Cal Cameron Please Stand Up? A. E. Cannon. (YA) (gr. 7 up). 1988. price not set. Delacorte.
Will the Real Gertrude Hollings Please Stand Up? Sheila Greenwald. LC 84-974. 168p. (gr. 3-7). 1983. 12.95 (ISBN 0-316-32707-7, Joy St Bks). Little.
Will the Real Gertrude Hollings Please Stand Up? Sheila Greenwald. 176p. (gr. k-6). 1985. pap. 2.95 (ISBN 0-440-49553-9, YB). Dell.
Will the Real Gertrude Hollings Please Stand Up? Sheila Greenwald. (gr. k-9). 1988. pap. 2.95. Scholastic Inc.
Will the Real Guru Please Stand up? Mariel Strauss. LC 78-61589. 1980. 7.95 (ISBN 0-87212-111-9). Libra.
Will the Real Jesus Christ & Christians Please Stand? (Orig.). 1983. pap. 2.75 (ISBN 0-914335-00-6). Highland.
Will the Real Me Please Stand Up? So We Can All Get to Know You! John S. Powell & Loretta Brady. 234p. 1985. pap. 6.95 (ISBN 0-89505-347-0). Tabor Pub.
Will the Real Me? Searchbook. John Powell. (Illus.). 72p. 1987. pap. 5.95 (ISBN 0-89505-405-1). Tabor Pub.
Will the Real Norman Mailer Please Stand up. Ed. by Laura Adams. LC 73-83259. 288p. 1974. 26.00 (ISBN 0-8046-9066-9, Pub. by Kennikat). Assoc Faculty Pr.
Will the Real Phony Please Stand up? rev. ed. Ethel Barrett & Peggy Parker. LC 84-17777. 224p. 1984. pap. 6.95 (ISBN 0-8307-1001-9, 5418383); Leader's Guide 3.95 (ISBN 0-8307-1009-4, 6101966). Regal.
Will the Real Teacher Please Stand Up? 2nd ed. Mary Greer & Bonnie Rubenstein. 1977. pap. 12.95 (ISBN 0-673-16153-6). Scott F.
Will the Real Winner Please Stand Up. Dallas Groten. 160p. 1985. pap. 4.95 (ISBN 0-87123-819-5, 210819). Bethany Hse.
Will the Real You Please Remain Standing! John A. Lynn. 204p. 1981. pap. 2.95 (ISBN 0-910068-38-0). Am Christian.
Will the Real You Please Stand Up! John A. Lynn. 113p. 1980. pap. 2.95 (ISBN 0-910068-28-3). Am Christian.
Will Therapy. Otto Rank. 1978. pap. 8.95 (ISBN 0-393-00898-3, Norton Lib). Norton.
Will There Really Be a Morning? Frances Farmer. 1973. pap. 3.50 (ISBN 0-440-19292-7). Dell.
Will They Ever Finish Brucker Boulevard. Ada L. Huxtable. 1988. pap. 10.95x (ISBN 0-520-06205-1). U of Cal Pr.
Will They Love Me When I Leave? A Weekend Father's Struggle to Stay Close to His Kids. C. W. Smith. 224p. 1987. 17.95 (ISBN 0-399-13249-X, Putnam). Putnam Pub Group.
Will They Still Be Dancing? Integration & Ethnic Tranformation among Yugoslav Immigrants in Scandinavia. (Illus.). 270p. 1987. 52.50x (ISBN 91-22-00836-5, Pub by Almqvist & Wiksell). Coronet Bks.
Will to Action, 2 vols. Friederich Nietzsche. (Illus.). 227p. 1986. Repr. of 1908 ed. Set. 179.85 (ISBN 0-89266-559-9). Am Classical Coll Pr.
Will to Be Well: The Real Alternative Medicine. Neville Hodgkinson. LC 85-26472. 240p. 1986. pap. 9.95 (ISBN 0-87728-659-0). Weiser.
Will to Believe. Marcus Bach. 186p. 1973. pap. 7.50 (ISBN 0-911336-46-X). Sci of Mind.
Will to Believe. William James. LC 78-5315. (Works of William James Ser.). 1979. 32.00x (ISBN 0-674-95281-2). Harvard U Pr.
Will to Believe & Human Immortality. William James. pap. 7.50 (ISBN 0-486-20291-7). Dover.
Will to Believe & Other Essays in Popular Philosophy & Human Immortality. William James. 15.75 (ISBN 0-8446-2313-X). Peter Smith.
Will to Believe: Novelists of the Nineteen Thirties. Richard Johnstone. 1982. pap. 5.95x (ISBN 0-19-281480-X). Oxford U Pr.
Will to Change: Poems. Adrienne Rich. LC 78-146842. 1971. pap. 5.95 (ISBN 0-393-04361-4). Norton.
Will to Civilization: An Inquiry into the Principles of Historic Change. John Katz. LC 74-25761. (European Sociology Ser.). 358p. 1975. Repr. 40.00x (ISBN 0-405-06515-9). Ayer Co Pubs.
Will to Die. Can Themba. (African Writers Ser.). 1972. pap. text ed. 6.00 (ISBN 0-435-90104-4). Heinemann Ed.
Will to Doubt. Bertrand Russell. (Philosophical Paperbook Series). 126p. 1983. pap. 4.95 (ISBN 0-8022-2436-9). Philos Lib.
Will to Freedom. John N. Figgis. LC 68-8236. 1969. Repr. of 1917 ed. 24.50 (ISBN 0-8046-0147-X, Pub. by Kennikat). Assoc Faculty Pr.
Will to Go on. Bernard Brodsky. 64p. (Orig.). 1981. pap. 3.75 (ISBN 0-931896-01-0). Cove View.
Will to Live. Hugh Franks. 1979. 15.00x (ISBN 0-7100-0181-9). Routledge Chapman & Hall.
Will to Live: Five Steps to Officer Survival. G. W. Boyd. (Illus.). 144p. 1980. photocopy ed. 17.50x (ISBN 0-398-04020-6). C C Thomas.
Will to Live: Selected Writings of Arthur Schopenhauer. Arthur Schopenhauer. Ed. by Richard Taylor. LC 67-17822. pap. 5.95x (ISBN 0-8044-6847-8). Ungar.
Will to Meaning. Viktor Frankl. 204p. 1988. pap. 7.95 (ISBN 0-452-00946-4, Z5472, Plume). NAL.
Will to Power, 2 vols. Friedrich Nietzsche. 1974. Set. lib. bdg. 200.00 (ISBN 0-87968-209-4). Gordon Pr.
Will to Power. Friedrich Nietzsche. Tr. by Walter Kaufmann. 1968. pap. 10.95 (ISBN 0-394-70437-1, Vin). Random.

William Baziotes: A Commemorative Exhibition. David S. Rubin. Ed. by Louise S. Bross & Lys Martin. LC 87-80348. (Illus.). 24p. (Orig.). 1987. pap. text ed. 9.00 (ISBN 0-941972-05-4). Freedman.
William Beaumont: Frontier Doctor. Virginia Burns. LC 78-72566. (Illus.). 1978. lib. bdg. 8.50 (ISBN 0-9604726-0-6). Enterprise Pr.
William Beckford. Robert J. Gemmett. LC 76-43256. (Twayne's English Authors Ser.). 189p. 1977. lib. bdg. 17.95 (ISBN 0-8057-6674-X). Irvington.
William Becknell: Father of the Santa Fe Trade. (Southwestern Studies Ser.: No. 68). 96p. 1982. 10.00 (ISBN 0-87404-128-7); pap. 5.00 (ISBN 0-87404-127-9). Tex Western.
William Beebe: An Annotated Bibliography. Tim M. Berra. LC 76-30857. (Illus.). 157p. 1977. 27.50 (ISBN 0-208-01608-2, Archon). Shoe String.
William Beebe: Underwater Explorer. Wyatt Blassingame. LC 75-29069. (Americans All Ser.). (Illus.). 96p. (gr. 3-6). 1976. PLB 7.12 (ISBN 0-8116-4584-3). Garrard.
William Beltz. Ellen Wolfe. LC 75-17744. (Story of an American Indian Ser.). (Illus.). 60p. (gr. 5 up). 1975. PLB 7.95 (ISBN 0-87518-044-2). Dillon.
William Bentinck & William Third. Marion E. Grew. LC 77-118473. 1971. Repr. of 1924 ed. 27.50 (ISBN 0-8046-1222-6, Pub. by Kennikat). Assoc Faculty Pr.
William Berry Hartsfield: Mayor of Atlanta. Harold H. Martin. LC 78-1550. (Illus.). 248p. 1978. 10.00 (ISBN 0-87797-115-3). Cherokee.
William Beveridge: A Biography. Jose Harris. 1977. 44.00x (ISBN 0-19-822459-1). Oxford U Pr.
William Billing's Anthem for Easter: The Persistence of an Early American Hit. Karl Kroger. (Illus.). 19p. 1987. pap. 4.50 (ISBN 0-944026-00-1, Dist. by Univ. Pr of Va). Am Antiquarian.
William Billings: Data & Documents. Hans Nathan. LC 75-33593. (Bibliographies in American Music: No. 2). 1976. 10.00 (ISBN 0-911772-67-7). Harmonie Pk Pr.
William Billings of Boston: Eighteenth-Century Composer. David McKay & Richard Crawford. LC 74-2971. (Illus.). 320p. 1975. 41.00x (ISBN 0-691-09118-8). Princeton U Pr.
William Black, Novelist: A Biography. Wemyss Reid. 1978. Repr. of 1902 ed. lib. bdg. 22.50 (ISBN 0-8495-4558-7). Arden Lib.
William Blake. Intro. by Harold Bloom. (Modern Critical Views Ser.). 201p. 1985. 24.50 (ISBN 0-87754-610-X). Chelsea Hse.
William Blake. O. Burdett. LC 74-1127. (Studies in Blake, No. 3). 1974. lib. bdg. 42.95x (ISBN 0-8383-2021-X). Haskell.
William Blake. Osbert Burdett. LC 74-3371. 1926. lib. bdg. 20.00 (ISBN 0-8414-3132-9). Folcroft.
William Blake. Martin Butlin. (Illus.). 80p. 1985. pap. 6.95 (ISBN 0-900874-23-6). Salem Hse Pubs.
William Blake. G. K. Chesterton. 1973. Repr. of 1910 ed. 35.00 (ISBN 0-8274-0715-7). R West.
William Blake. Gilbert K. Chesterton. LC 76-7995. 1976. Repr. of 1910 ed. lib. bdg. 27.00 (ISBN 0-8414-3383-6). Folcroft.
William Blake. Basil De Selincourt. LC 72-162018. (Illus.). 1972. Repr. of 1909 ed. 28.50x (ISBN 0-8154-0389-5). Cooper Sq.
William Blake. Basil De Selincourt. LC 70-173850. (Studies in Blake, No. 3). (Illus.). 1971. Repr. of 1909 ed. lib. bdg. 59.95x (ISBN 0-8383-1357-4). Haskell.
William Blake. Charles Gardner. LC 76-118001. (Studies in Blake, No. 3). 1970. Repr. of 1919 ed. lib. bdg. 49.95x (ISBN 0-8383-1056-7). Haskell.
William Blake. Herbert Jenkins. LC 73-3386. 1925. Repr. lib. bdg. 25.00 (ISBN 0-8414-2153-6). Folcroft.
William Blake. Edward Larrissy. 192p. 1985. 24.95x (ISBN 0-631-13485-9); pap. 8.95x (ISBN 0-631-13504-9). Basil Blackwell.
William Blake. H. M. Margoliouth. LC 67-26654. (Illus.). 184p. 1967. Repr. of 1961 ed. 21.50 (ISBN 0-208-00177-8, Archon). Shoe String.
William Blake. Ed. by Michael Mason. (Authors Ser.). 600p. 1988. 34.95 (ISBN 0-19-254196-X); pap. 14.95 (ISBN 0-19-282001-X). Oxford U Pr.
William Blake. John M. Murry. LC 74-9888. 1933. lib. bdg. 25.50 (ISBN 0-8414-6142-2). Folcroft.
William Blake. John M. Murry. LC 71-173845. (Studies in Blake, No. 3). 1971. Repr. of 1933 ed. lib. bdg. 75.00x (ISBN 0-8383-1344-2). Haskell.
William Blake. Martin K. Nurmi. LC 76-25476. (Illus.). 175p. 1976. text ed. 15.00x (ISBN 0-87338-191-2); pap. 8.50x (ISBN 0-87338-192-0). Kent St U Pr.
William Blake. Victor Paananen. (English Authors Ser.). 1977. lib. bdg. 15.95 (ISBN 0-8057-6672-3, Twayne). G K Hall.
William Blake. Intro. by Peter Porter. (Great Poets Ser.). (Illus.). 1986. 6.95 (ISBN 0-517-56291-X, C N Potter Bks). Crown.
William Blake. Kathleen Raine. (World of Art Ser.). (Illus.). 216p. 1985. pap. 11.95 (ISBN 0-500-20107-2). Thames Hudson.
William Blake. Alfred Story. LC 77-115183. (Studies in Blake, No. 3). 1970. Repr. of 1893 ed. lib. bdg. 39.95x (ISBN 0-8383-1009-5). Haskell.
William Blake. Algernon C. Swinburne. LC 67-12468. (Illus.). Repr. of 1868 ed. 25.50 (ISBN 0-405-09018-8). Ayer Co Pubs.
William Blake - Poet & Painter: An Introduction to the Illuminated Verse. Jean H. Hagstrum. LC 64-13950. (Illus.). 1964. pap. 6.95x (ISBN 0-226-31297-6, P795, Phoen). U of Chicago Pr.
William Blake: A Critical Essay. Algernon C. Swinburne. LC 74-3015. 1973. lib. bdg. 49.00 (ISBN 0-8414-7741-8). Folcroft.
William Blake: A Critical Essay. Algernon C. Swinburne. Ed. by Hugh J. Luke. LC 70-81397. xxiv, 319p. 1970. pap. 4.75x (ISBN 0-8032-5707-4, BB 504, Bison). U of Nebr Pr.
William Blake: A Man Without a Mask. J. Bronowski. LC 67-30809. (Studies in Blake, No. 3). 1969. Repr. of 1947 ed. lib. bdg. 75.00x (ISBN 0-8383-0709-4). Haskell.
William Blake: A Man Without a Mask. Jacob Bronowski. 1976. lib. bdg. 59.95 (ISBN 0-8490-1300-3). Gordon Pr.
William Blake: A New Kind of Man. Michael Davis. LC 77-71059. (Illus.). 1977. 30.00x (ISBN 0-520-03443-0); pap. 10.95x (ISBN 0-520-03456-2). U of Cal Pr.
William Blake & His Contempories & Followers: Selected Works from the Collection of Robert N. Essick. Robert N. Essick. LC 87-29349. (Illus.). 78p. 1987. 5.95 (ISBN 0-87328-093-8). Huntington Lib.
William Blake & His Poetry. Allardyce Nicoll. LC 71-120970. (Poetry & Life Ser.). Repr. of 1922 ed. 7.25 (ISBN 0-404-52527-X). AMS Pr.
William Blake & His Poetry. Allardyee Nicoll. LC 74-23588. 1974. Repr. of 1922 ed. lib. bdg. 33.50 (ISBN 0-8414-6276-3). Folcroft.
William Blake & the Moderns. Ed. by Robert J. Bertholf & Annette S. Levitt. LC 82-656. 294p. 1982. 59.50 (ISBN 0-87395-615-X); pap. 19.95 (ISBN 0-87395-616-8). State U NY Pr.
William Blake: Creative Will & the Poetic Image. Jack Lindsay. LC 76-40312. 1929. Repr. lib. bdg. 30.50 (ISBN 0-8414-5811-1). Folcroft.
William Blake: Creative Will & the Poetic Image. Jack Lindsay. LC 70-118005. (Studies in Blake, No. 3). 1970. Repr. of 1929 ed. lib. bdg. 49.95x (ISBN 0-8383-1061-3). Haskell.
William Blake: Engraver. Charles Ryskamp. LC 72-108006. (Illus.). 61p. 1969. pap. 3.50 (ISBN 0-87811-014-3). Princeton Lib.
William Blake: His Mysticism. Maung Ba Han. 1978. Repr. of 1924 ed. lib. bdg. 37.50 (ISBN 0-8495-0377-9). Arden Lib.
William Blake: His Mysticism. Maung Ba Han. LC 72-13650. 1974. Repr. of 1924 ed. lib. bdg. 30.00 (ISBN 0-8414-1234-0). Folcroft.
William Blake: His Philosophy & Symbols. S. Foster Damon. 20.25 (ISBN 0-8446-1145-X). Peter Smith.
William Blake in the Art of His Time. Corlette R. Walker et al. LC 75-620115. (Illus.). 104p. (Orig.). 1976. pap. 17.50 (ISBN 0-295-96182-1, Pub. by Univ. Art Museum UC Santa Barbara). U of Wash Pr.
William Blake in This World. Harold L. Bruce. 1978. Repr. of 1925 ed. lib. bdg. 35.50 (ISBN 0-8495-0440-6). Arden Lib.
William Blake in This World. Harold L. Bruce. LC 73-3184. Repr. of 1925 ed. lib. bdg. 30.00 (ISBN 0-8414-1779-2). Folcroft.
William Blake in This World. Harold L. Bruce. LC 73-18085. (Studies in Blake, No. 3). 1974. Repr. of 1925 ed. lib. bdg. 49.95x (ISBN 0-8383-1732-4). Haskell.
William Blake in This World. Harold L. Bruce. 15.75 (ISBN 0-8369-6924-3, 7805). Ayer co Pubs.
William Blake: Jerusalem. Ed. by William R. Hughes. 235p. 1983. Repr. of 1964 ed. lib. bdg. 40.00. Darby Bks.
William Blake: Mystic. Adeline M. Butterworth. LC 74-8017. 1911. lib. bdg. 17.50 (ISBN 0-8414-3186-8). Folcroft.
William Blake on the Lord's Prayer: 1757-1827. John H. Clarke. LC 70-95421. (Studies in Blake, No. 3). 1971. Repr. of 1927 ed. lib. bdg. 48.95x (ISBN 0-8383-0967-4). Haskell.
William Blake; or, the English Farmer, 1848. William E. Heygate. Ed. by Robert L. Wolff. LC 75-473. (Victorian Fiction Ser.). 1975. lib. bdg. 73.00 (ISBN 0-8240-1551-7). Garland Pub.
William Blake: Painter & Poet. Richard Garnett. 1973. lib. bdg. 27.00 (ISBN 0-8414-2012-2). Folcroft.
William Blake: Painter & Poet. Richard Garnett. LC 77-115857. (Studies in Blake, No. 3). 1970. Repr. of 1895 ed. lib. bdg. 27.95x (ISBN 0-8383-1074-5). Haskell.
William Blake: Poet & Mystic. P. Berger. LC 67-31287. (Studies in Blake, No. 3). 1969. Repr. of 1914 ed. lib. bdg. 75.00x (ISBN 0-8383-0778-7). Haskell.
William Blake: Printmaker. Robert N. Essick. LC 79-3205. (Illus.). 1980. 76.00x (ISBN 0-691-03954-2). Princeton U Pr.
William Blake: Prophet of Universal Brotherhood. Bernard Nesfield-Cookson. 480p. (Orig.). 1988. pap. 14.95 (ISBN 0-85030-562-4, Pub. by Aquarian Pr England). Sterling.
William Blake: Selected Poetry & Prose. Ed. by David Punter. (English Texts Ser.). 256p. 1988. pap. 8.95 (ISBN 0-415-00666-X). Routledge Chapman & Hall.
William Blake: The Critical Heritage. Ed. by G. E. Bentley. (Critical Heritage Ser.). (Illus.). 320p. 1975. 29.00x (ISBN 0-7100-8234-7). Routledge Chapman & Hall.
William Blake: The Man. Charles Gardner. LC 79-153324. Repr. of 1919 ed. 9.00 (ISBN 0-404-07906-7). AMS Pr.
William Blake: The Man. Charles Gardner. 1919. lib. bdg. 15.00 (ISBN 0-8414-4634-2). Folcroft.
William Blake: The Politics of Vision. Mark Schorer. 11.50 (ISBN 0-8446-2886-7). Peter Smith.
William Blake's Anticipation of the Individualistic Revolution. Kate L. Dickenson. LC 72-193732. 1974. Repr. of 1915 ed. lib. bdg. 15.00 (ISBN 0-8414-3789-0). Folcroft.
William Blake's Anticipation of the Individualistic Revolution. Kate L. Dickinson. 56p. 1980. Repr. of 1915 ed. lib. bdg. 17.50 (ISBN 0-8495-1055-4). Arden Lib.
William Blake's Circle of Destiny. Milton O. Percival. 1964. lib. bdg. 27.50x (ISBN 0-374-96384-3, Octagon). Hippocrene Bks.
William Blake's Design for Edward Young's Night Thoughts: Complete, Vols. 1 & 2. William Blake. Ed. by John E. Grant & Edward J. Rose. (Illus.). 1980. Set. 385.00x (ISBN 0-19-817312-1). Oxford U Pr.
William Blake's Engravings. Ed. by Geoffrey Keynes. LC 72-76491. (Illus.). 157p. 1972. Repr. of 1950 ed. lib. bdg. 25.00x (ISBN 0-8154-0417-4). Cooper Sq.
William Blake's Epic: Imagination Unbound. Joanne Witke. LC 85-30326. (Illus.). 335p. 1986. 27.50x (ISBN 0-312-88024-3). St Martin.
William Blake's Fourfold Man. Cecil A. Abrahams. (Studien zur Germanistik, Anglistik und Komparatistik: Vol. 72). 387p. (Orig.). 1978. pap. 34.00x (ISBN 3-416-01418-9, Pub. by Bouvier Verlag W Germany). Benjamins North Am.
William Blake's Illustrations to the Poetry of Milton. Pamela Dunbar. (Illus.). 1980. 59.00x (ISBN 0-19-817345-8). Oxford U Pr.
William Blake's Jerusalem. Minna Doskow. LC 81-65463. (Illus.). 388p. 1982. 37.50 (ISBN 0-8386-3090-1). Fairleigh Dickinson.
William Blake's Marriage of Heaven and Hell. Intro. by Harold Bloom. (Modern Critical Interpretations Ser.). 132p. 1987. 19.95 (ISBN 0-87754-729-7). Chelsea Hse.
William Blake's Poetry & Designs. Ed. by Mary L. Johnson & John F. Grant. (Norton Critical Edition). (Illus.). 661p. 1979. pap. text ed. 14.95x (ISBN 0-393-09083-3). Norton.
William Blake's Songs of Innocence & of Experience. Intro. by Harold Bloom. (Modern Critical Interpretations Ser.). 149p. 1987. 19.95 (ISBN 0-87754-730-0). Chelsea Hse.
William Blake's Theory of Art. Morris Eaves. LC 81-47914. (Illus.). 216p. 1982. 26.50x (ISBN 0-691-03990-9). Princeton U Pr.
William Blake's Works in Conventional Typography. William Blake. LC 82-10815. 1984. 55.00x (ISBN 0-8201-1388-3). Schol Facsimiles.
William Blake's Writings, 2 vols. William Blake. Ed. by G. E. Bentley. (Oxford English Texts Ser.). (Illus.). 1979. Set. 195.00x (ISBN 0-19-811885-6). Oxford U Pr.
William Blathwayt. Gertrude A. Jacobsen. (Yale Historical Studies, Miscellany: No. XXI). 1932. 75.00x (ISBN 0-685-69829-7). Elliots Bks.
William Blount. William H. Masterson. Repr. of 1954 ed. lib. bdg. 35.00x (ISBN 0-8371-2308-9, MABL). Greenwood.
William Bostwick: Connecticut Yankee in Antebellum Georgia. Marilyn A. Lavin. LC 77-14787. (Dissertations in American Economic History Ser.). 1978. 34.50 (ISBN 0-405-11044-8). Ayer Co Pubs.
William Branch Giles: A Study in the Politics of Virginia & the Nation from 1790 to 1830. Dice R. Anderson. 1966. 13.25 (ISBN 0-8446-1028-3). Peter Smith.
William Brice: A Selection of Painting & Drawing, 1947-1986. Richard Armstrong. Ed. by Howard Singerman & Ann Goldstein. LC 86-80091. (Illus.). 244p. (Orig.). pap. write for info. (ISBN 0-911291-12-1). Fellows Cont Art.
William Brice: Notations Nineteen Eighty-Two. (Illus.). 120p. 1984. 35.00 (ISBN 0-942642-06-6). Twelvetrees Pr.
William Bronk: An Essay. Cid Corman. 112p. 1976. 4.00 (ISBN 0-916562-06-9). Truck Pr.
William Browne (Fifteen Ninety to Sixteen Forty-Five) His Britannia's Pastorals & the Pastoral Poetry of the Elizabethan Age. Frederic W. Moorman. LC 71-102862. (Research & Source Works Ser.: No. 396). 1970. Repr. of 1897 ed. lib. bdg. 19.50 (ISBN 0-8337-2453-3). B Franklin.
William Burges & the High Victorian Dream. J. Mordaunt Crook. LC 81-1592. (Illus.). 632p. 1981. 60.00x (ISBN 0-226-12117-8). U of Chicago Pr.
William Burroughs: An Essay. Alan Ansen. LC 86-50577. (Illus.). 75p. 1986. pap. 12.98 (ISBN 0-934953-09-0); signed, ltd. ed. 35.00 (ISBN 0-934953-10-4). Water Row Pr.
William Burroughs: The Algebra of Need. Eric Mottram. 256p. 1978. pap. 7.95 (ISBN 0-7145-2563-4, Dist by Scribner). M Boyars Pubs.
William Butler Yeats. Anthony Bradley. LC 77-6953. (Literature and Life Ser.). 306p. 1980. 24.50x (ISBN 0-8044-2068-8). Ungar.
William Butler Yeats. Denis Donoghue. 1989. pap. 8.95. Ecco Pr.
William Butler Yeats. J. M. Hone. LC 72-3620. (English Literature Ser., No. 33). 1972. lib. bdg. 39.95x (ISBN 0-8383-1577-1). Haskell.
William Butler Yeats. J. H. Pollack. 1978. 42.50 (ISBN 0-685-24031-2). Bern Porter.
William Butler Yeats. J. H. Pollock. LC 75-43781. 1935. lib. bdg. 17.00 (ISBN 0-8414-6709-9). Folcroft.
William Butler Yeats. W. H. Pollock. LC 75-22355. (W. B. Yeats Ser., No. 72). 1975. lib. bdg. 39.95x (ISBN 0-8383-2104-6). Haskell.
William Butler Yeats: A Catalogue of an Exhibition from P. S. O'Hegarty Collection in the University of Kansas Library. Hester M. Black. Repr. of 1958 ed. lib. bdg. 10.00 (ISBN 0-8414-1647-8). Folcroft.
William Butler Yeats: The Lyric of Tragedy. Benjamin L. Reid. LC 77-13607. (Illus.). 1977. Repr. of 1961 ed. lib. bdg. 35.00x (ISBN 0-8371-9855-0, REYE). Greenwood.
William Butler Yeats: The Poet As a Mythmaker. Morton I. Seiden. LC 74-79395. 397p. 1974. Repr. of 1962 ed. lib. bdg. 25.00x (ISBN 0-8154-0491-3). Cooper Sq.
William Butler Yeats: The Poet in Contemporary Ireland. J. M. Hone. LC 73-21999. 1973. Repr. of 1916 ed. lib. bdg. 25.00 (ISBN 0-8414-4803-5). Folcroft.
William Byrd. Frank S. Howes. LC 77-27081. (Illus.). 1978. Repr. of 1928 ed. lib. bdg. 27.50x (ISBN 0-313-20182-X, HOWI). Greenwood.
William Byrd: A Guide to Research. Richard Turbet. Ed. by Guy A. Marco. LC 87-8644. (Composer Resource Manuals, Reference Library of the Humanities: Vol. 7). 450p. 1987. lib. bdg. 60.00 (ISBN 0-8240-8388-1). Garland Pub.
William Byrd of Westover. 2nd ed. Richmond C. Beatty. Pref. by M. Thomas Inge. xxxix, 243p. 1970. Repr. of 1932 ed. 26.00 (ISBN 0-208-00944-2, Archon). Shoe String.
William Byrd of Westover, 1674-1744. Pierre Marambaud. LC 70-151251. pap. 76.80 (2027069). Bks Demand UMI.
William Byrd's Histories of the Dividing Line Betwixt Virginia & North Carolina. William Byrd. (Illus.). xi, 340p. 1987. pap. 7.95 (ISBN 0-486-25553-0). Dover.
William C. A. Frerichs, Eighteen Twenty-Nine to Nineteen Hundred Five: A Retrospective Exhibition. Ed. by North Carolina Museum of Art. (Illus.). 1974. pap. 3.00x (ISBN 0-88259-075-8). NCMA.
William C. Norris: Portrait of a Maverick. James C. Worthy. LC 87-1808. 280p. 1987. 22.00 (ISBN 0-88730-087-1). Ballinger Pub.
William C. Whitney, Modern Warwick. Mark D. Hirsch. LC 69-19214. (Illus.). xiii, 622p. 1969. Repr. of 1948 ed. 47.50 (ISBN 0-208-00722-9, Archon). Shoe String.
William Camden & the Britannia. S. Piggott. (Albert Reckitt Archaeological Lectures). 1951. pap. 2.25 (ISBN 0-902732-83-8, Pub. by British Acad). Longwood Pub Group.
William Card Seventeen Ten to Seventeen Eighty-Five with Ancestors & Some Descendants. Grayce H. Alsterda. LC 86-174208. (Illus.). 66p. 1986. pap. text ed. 11.00 (ISBN 0-9617035-0-4). G H Alsterda.
William Carey. Basil Miller. 154p. 1985. pap. 3.50 (ISBN 0-87123-850-0, 200850). Bethany Hse.
William Carey-Missionary Pioneer. Kellsye Finnie. 1986. pap. 2.95 (ISBN 0-87508-187-8). CHR Lit.
William Carlos Williams. Intro. by Harold Bloom. (Modern Critical Views Ser.). 183p. 1986. 19.95 (ISBN 0-87754-637-1). Chelsea Hse.
William Carlos Williams. John M. Brinnin. (Pamphlets on American Writers Ser: No. 24). (Orig.). 1963. pap. 1.25x (ISBN 0-8166-0287-5, MPAW24). U of Minn Pr.
William Carlos Williams. Vivienne Koch. LC 73-9670. 292p. 1973. Repr. of 1950 ed. 30.00 (ISBN 0-527-52000-4). Kraus Repr.
William Carlos Williams. Emily M. Wallace & Kenneth Burke. Ed. by Charles Angoff. LC 73-10757. (Leverton Lecture Ser.: No. 1). (Illus.). 46p. 1974. 9.50 (ISBN 0-8386-1441-8). Fairleigh Dickinson.
William Carlos Williams: A New World Naked. Paul Mariani. (Illus.). 1981. text ed. 24.95 (ISBN 0-07-040362-7). McGraw.
William Carlos Williams: A New World Naked. Paul Mariani. 912p. 1982. pap. text ed. 12.95 (ISBN 0-07-040363-5). McGraw.
William Carlos Williams: A Poet in the American Theatre. David A. Fedo. Ed. by A. Walton Litz. LC 83-1132. (Studies in Modern Literature: No. 7). 214p. 1983. 42.95 (ISBN 0-8357-1410-1). UMI Res Pr.
William Carlos Williams: An American Artist. James E. Breslin. LC 85-16343. xvi, 246p. 1985. pap. 9.95 (ISBN 0-226-07407-2). U of Chicago Pr.
William Carlos Williams & John Sanford: A Correspondence. Frwd. by Paul Mariani. 55p. 1984. signed 25.00 (ISBN 0-933114-06-0); 17.00 (ISBN 0-933114-05-2); pap. 8.00 (ISBN 0-933114-04-4). Capra Pr.

William Ernest Henley. L. C. Cornford. 59.95 (ISBN 0-8490-1302-X). Gordon Pr.
William Ernest Henley. L. C. Cornford. LC 72-3679. (English Biography Ser., No. 31). 1972. Repr. of 1913 ed. lib. bdg. 35.95x (ISBN 0-8383-1580-1). Haskell.
William Ernest Henley. L. C. Cornford. 1973. Repr. of 1913 ed. 19.45 (ISBN 0-8274-1358-0). R West.
William Ernest Henley. Joseph M. Flora. LC 72-120015. (Twayne's English Authors Ser.). 1970. lib. bdg. 17.95 (ISBN 0-89197-977-8); pap. text ed. 4.95x (ISBN 0-89197-994-8). Irvington.
William Ernest Henley. John H. Robertson. 59.95 (ISBN 0-8490-1303-8). Gordon Pr.
William Ernest Henley: A Study in the Counter-Decadence of the Nineties. Jerome H. Buckley. LC 74-120238. 1971. Repr. lib. bdg. 18.50x (ISBN 0-374-91087-1, Octagon). Hippocrene Bks.
William Everson. Lee Bartlett. LC 85-70127. (Western Writers Ser.: No. 67). (Illus.). 50p. (Orig.). 1985. pap. 2.95x (ISBN 0-88430-041-2). Boise St Univ.
William Everson - On Writing the Waterbirds & Other Presentations: Collected Forewords & Afterwords 1935-1981. Ed. by Lee Bartlett. LC 83-3123. 288p. 1983. 18.50 (ISBN 0-8108-1617-2). Scarecrow.
William Everson: A Descriptive Bibliography, 1934-1976. Lee Bartlett & Allan Campo. LC 77-5397. (Author Bibliographies Ser.: No. 33). 119p. 1977. 17.50 (ISBN 0-8108-1037-9). Scarecrow.
William Everson: Poet from the San Joaquin. Campo & Carpenter. 1978. 10.00 (ISBN 0-912950-43-9); pap. 5.00 (ISBN 0-912950-44-7). Blue Oak.
William Everson: The Life of Brother Antoninus. Lee Bartlett. LC 87-11034. (Illus.). 288p. 1988. 25.95 (ISBN 0-8112-1060-X). New Directions.
William F. Buckley, Jr. Mark R. Winchell. (United States Author Ser.: No. 452). 180p. 1984. lib. bdg. 16.95 (ISBN 0-8057-7392-4, Twayne); pap. 6.95 (ISBN 0-8057-7431-9). G K Hall.
William F. Buckley Jr. Patron Saint of the Conservatives. John Judis. 1988. 22.95 (ISBN 0-671-45494-3). S&S.
William F. Ogburn on Culture & Social Change, Selected Papers. William F. Ogburn. Ed. by Otis D. Duncan. LC 64-23418. (History of Sociology Ser). 1964. pap. 2.95X (ISBN 0-226-62061-1, P171, Phoen). U of Chicago Pr.
William F. Reese. Mary N. Balcomb. LC 83-72443. (Illus.). 176p. 1984. 60.00 (ISBN 0-916029-00-X); Ltd. Ed. 250.00 (ISBN 0-916029-01-8). Blue Raven Pub Co.
William Falconer's the Shipwreck. Johann Friedrich. pap. 12.00 (ISBN 0-384-16940-6). Johnson Repr.
William Farel & the Story of the Swiss Reform. William M. Blackburn. Repr. of 1865 ed. 40.00 (ISBN 0-404-19870-8). AMS Pr.
William Faulkner. Intro. by Harold Bloom. (Modern Critical Views Ser.). 287p. 1986. 27.50 (ISBN 0-87754-652-5). Chelsea Hse.
William Faulkner. David Dowling. LC 88-4456. (Modern Novelists Ser.). 184p. 1988. 24.95 (ISBN 0-312-02058-9). St Martin.
William Faulkner. Alan W. Friedman. LC 82-40274. 240p. 1985. 16.95x (ISBN 0-8044-2218-4). Ungar.
William Faulkner. Frederick J. Hoffman. (Twayne's United States Authors Ser). 1966. pap. 8.95x (ISBN 0-8084-0326-5, T1, Twayne). New Coll U Pr.
William Faulkner. Frederick J. Hoffman. (United States Authors Ser.). 1966. lib. bdg. 16.95 (ISBN 0-8057-0244-X, Twayne). G K Hall.
William Faulkner. rev. ed. Frederick J. Hoffman. (United States Authors Ser.). 1985. pap. 6.95 (ISBN 0-8057-7444-0, Twayne). G K Hall.
William Faulkner. William V. O'Connor. LC 59-63269. (University of Minnesota Pamphlets on American Writers Ser.: No. 3). pap. 20.00 (ISBN 0-317-29465-2, 2055928). Bks Demand UMI.
William Faulkner: A Bibliography of Secondary Works. Compiled by Beatrice Ricks. LC 80-15251. (Scarecrow Author Bibliographies: No. 49). 684p. 1981. lib. bdg. 45.00 (ISBN 0-8108-1323-8). Scarecrow.
William Faulkner: A Critical Study. 3rd ed. Irving Howe. 320p. 1975. pap. 8.00x (ISBN 0-226-35484-9, P650, Phoen). U of Chicago Pr.
William Faulkner: American Writer. Frederick R. Karl. (Illus.). 1989. 35.00 (ISBN 1-55584-088-4). Weidenfeld.
William Faulkner: An Interpretation. Irving Malin. LC 76-165664. 109p. 1972. Repr. of 1957 ed. 15.00x (ISBN 0-87752-154-9). Gordian.
William Faulkner: Art in Theological Tension. John W. Hunt. LC 72-6942. (Studies in Fiction, No. 34). 1972. Repr. of 1965 ed. lib. bdg. 75.00x (ISBN 0-8383-1658-1). Haskell.
William Faulkner: First Encounters. Cleanth Brooks. LC 83-3634. 224p. 1983. 25.00x (ISBN 0-300-02995-0). Yale U Pr.
William Faulkner: First Encounters. Cleanth Brooks. LC 83-3634. 224p. 1985. pap. 9.95 (ISBN 0-300-03399-0, Y-523). Yale U Pr.
William Faulkner; Four Decades of Criticism. Ed. by Linda W. Wagner. 374p. 1973. 10.00 (ISBN 0-87013-176-1). Mich St U Pr.
William Faulkner: His Life & Work. David Minter. LC 80-13089. 344p. 1982. text ed. 30.00x (ISBN 0-8018-2347-1); pap. 9.95 (ISBN 0-8018-2463-X). Johns Hopkins.
William Faulkner: His Tippah County Heritage. Jane I. Haynes. 1985. ltd. ed. 29.50 (ISBN 0-935239-03-0). Seajay Society.
William Faulkner, Letters & Fictions. James G. Watson. 232p. 1987. text ed. 25.00x (ISBN 0-292-76503-7). U of Tex Pr.
William Faulkner, "Man Working," 1919-1962: A Catalogue of the William Faulkner Collections at the University of Virginia. University of Virginia Library & Linton R. Massey. LC 68-19477. pap. 67.00 (ISBN 0-317-30465-8, 2024829). Bks Demand UMI.
William Faulkner: Modern American Novelist & Nobel Prize Winner. James Barger. Ed. by D. Steve Rahmas. (Outstanding Personalities Ser.: No. 63). 32p. (Orig.). (YA) (gr. 7-12). 1973. lib. bdg. 3.75 incl. catalog cards (ISBN 0-87157-563-9); pap. 2.50 vinyl laminated covers (ISBN 0-87157-063-7). SamHar Pr.
William Faulkner of Oxford. Ed. by James W. Webb & A. Wigfall Green. LC 65-23763. (Illus.). Repr. of 1965 ed. 50.20 (ISBN 0-8357-9395-8, 2051671). Bks Demand UMI.
William Faulkner: Storyteller of the Heart. Stephen B. Oates. LC 86-46266. (Illus.). 416p. 1987. 22.50i (ISBN 0-06-015771-2, HarpT). Har-Row.
William Faulkner: The Abstract & the Actual. Panthea R. Broughton. LC 74-77324. xviii, 222p. 1974. 27.50 (ISBN 0-8071-0083-8). La State U Pr.
William Faulkner: The Art of Stylization. Lothar Honnighausen. (Cambridge Studies in American Literature & Culture). 240p. 1987. 34.50 (ISBN 0-521-33280-X). Cambridge U Pr.
William Faulkner: The Critical Heritage. Ed. by John Bassett. (Critical Heritage Ser.). 1975. 36.00x (ISBN 0-7100-8124-3). Routledge Chapman & Hall.
William Faulkner: The Making of a Novelist. Martin Kreiswirth. LC 83-1354. 208p. 1984. 18.00x (ISBN 0-8203-0672-X). U of Ga Pr.
William Faulkner: The Man & the Artist. Stephen B. Oates. 1987. 22.00 (ISBN 0-318-22576-X). Har Row.
William Faulkner: The Man & the Artist. Stephen B. Oates. LC 86-46266. (Illus.). 384p. 1988. pap. 9.95 (ISBN 0-06-091501-3, PL-1501, PL). Har-Row.
William Faulkner: The Novelist As Short Story Writer. Hans H. Skei. 296p. 1985. 32.00x (ISBN 82-00-07303-3); pap. 16.00x (ISBN 82-00-07302-5). Oxford U Pr.
William Faulkner, the William B. Wisdom Collection: A Descriptive Catalog. Thomas Bonner, Jr. & Guillermo N. Falcon. LC 79-26556. (Illus.). 1980. pap. 13.00 (ISBN 0-9603212-2-5). Tulane Univ.
William Faulkner: The Yoknapatawpha Country. Cleanth Brooks. LC 63-17023. (Illus.). 1963. 47.50x (ISBN 0-300-00329-3); pap. 15.95x (ISBN 0-300-00028-6, Y170). Yale U Pr.
William Faulkner: The Yoknapatawpha Fiction. Ed. by A. Robert Lee. LC 84-6274. (Critical Studies). 224p. 1986. 28.50x (ISBN 0-389-20489-7, BNB-08051). B&N Imports.
William Faulkner: Toward Yoknapatawpha & Beyond. Cleanth Brooks. LC 77-10898. 1978. 42.00x (ISBN 0-300-02204-2); pap. 11.95 (ISBN 0-300-02493-2). Yale U Pr.
William Faulkner's Absalom, Absalom! Intro. by Harold Bloom. (Modern Critical Interpretations Ser.). 160p. 1987. 19.95 (ISBN 1-55546-039-9). Chelsea Hse.
William Faulkner's "Absalom, Absalom!": A Critical Casebook. Elizabeth Muhlenfeld. Ed. by Noel Polk. LC 82-48497. (Faulkner Casebooks). 400p. 1984. lib. bdg. 45.00 (ISBN 0-8240-9227-9). Garland Pub.
William Faulkner's "Absalom, Absalom" A Critical Study. David P. Ragan. Ed. by A. Walton Litz. LC 87-23300. (Studies in Modern Literature: No. 85). 244p. 1987. 44.95 (ISBN 0-8357-1840-9). UMI Res Pr.
William Faulkner's Characters: An Index to the Published & Unpublished Fiction. Thomas E. Dasher. LC 80-9033. 450p. 1981. lib. bdg. 73.00 (ISBN 0-8240-9305-4). Garland Pub.
William Faulkner's Craft of Revision: The Snopes Trilogy, The Unvanquished, & Go Down, Moses. Joanne V. Creighton. LC 76-51441. pap. 47.60 (2032040). Bks Demand UMI.
William Faulkner's First Book: The Marble Faun Fifty Years Later. William Boozer. LC 75-6916. (Illus.). 1975. 7.50 (ISBN 0-686-12125-2). Pigeon Roost Pr.
William Faulkner's Gothic Domain. Elizabeth M. Kerr. LC 78-27795. (National University Pubns., Literary Criticism Ser.). 1979. 24.95 (ISBN 0-8046-9228-9, Pub. by Kennikat). Assoc Faculty Pr.
William Faulkner's Light in August. Intro. by Harold Bloom. (Modern Critical Interpretations Ser.). 184p. 1988. lib. bdg. 24.50 (ISBN 1-55546-040-2). Chelsea Hse.
William Faulkner's Light in August: A Critical Casebook. Francois Pitavy. LC 81-48416. 300p. 1982. lib. bdg. 48.00 (ISBN 0-8240-9385-2). Garland Pub.
William Faulkner's Sanctuary. Intro. by Harold Bloom. (Modern Critical Interpretations Ser.). 160p. 1988. lib. bdg. 19.95 (ISBN 1-55546-041-0). Chelsea Hse.
William Faulkner's Short Stories. James B. Carothers. Ed. by A. Walton Litz. LC 85-8523. (Studies in Modern Literature: No. 34). 166p. 1985. 39.95 (ISBN 0-8357-1500-0). UMI Res Pr.
William Faulkner's Soldier's Pay: A Bibliographical Study. Ed. by Francis J. Bosha. LC 80-54205. 542p. 1982. 42.50x (ISBN 0-87875-211-0). Whitston Pub.
William Faulkner's Women Characters: An Annotated Bibliography of Criticism, 1930-1983. Patricia E. Sweeney. LC 84-24572. 497p. 1985. lib. bdg. 52.00 (ISBN 0-87436-411-6). ABC-Clio.
William Faulkner's Yoknapatawpha: "A Kind of Keystone in the Universe". rev. ed. Elizabeth M. Kerr. LC 82-83490. 1985. 40.00 (ISBN 0-8232-1134-7); pap. 20.00 (ISBN 0-8232-1135-5). Fordham.
William Foxwell Albright. Leona Running & David Freedman. LC 75-11180. 1975. 15.00 (ISBN 0-8467-0071-9). Palos Verdes.
William Fulbright & the Vietnam War: The Dissent of a Political Realist. William C. Berman. LC 87-22600. 237p. 1988. 24.00x (ISBN 0-87338-351-6). Kent St U Pr.
William G. Brownlow: Fighting Parson of the Southern Highlands. E. Merton Coulter. LC 71-136309. (Tennesseana Editions Ser.). (Illus.). pap. 114.50 (ISBN 0-8357-9767-8, 2016173). Bks Demand UMI.
William G. McAdoo & the Development to National Economic Policy, 1913-1918. Dale N. Shook. Ed. by Stuart Bruchey. (Foreign Economic Policy of the United States Ser.). 429p. 1987. lib. bdg. 65.00 (ISBN 0-8240-8092-0). Garland Pub.
William G. R. Hind. J. Russell Harper. (Canadian Artists Ser.: No. 2). write for info. (Pub. by Natl Gallery Canada). U of Chicago Pr.
William Gardner's Book of Calligraphy. William Gardner. 170p. 1988. text ed. 72.00 (ISBN 0-7045-3101-1, Pub. by Wildwood Hse Bks.). Gower Pub Co.
William George Ward & the Catholic Revival. Wilfrid P. Ward. LC 75-29626. Repr. of 1893 ed. 41.75 (ISBN 0-404-14042-4). AMS Pr.
William George Ward & the Oxford Movement. Wilfrid P. Ward. LC 75-29625. Repr. of 1889 ed. 41.75 (ISBN 0-404-14043-2). AMS Pr.
William Gibbs McAdoo: A Passion for Change, 1863-1917. John J. Broesamle. LC 73-83261. 320p. 1974. 26.50 (ISBN 0-8046-9043-X, Pub. by Kennikat). Assoc Faculty Pr.
William Giddings Farrington, a Man of Vision. Patrick J. Nicholson. (Illus.). 320p. Date not set. 18.95x (ISBN 0-87201-292-1). Gulf Pub.
William Gillette: His Life & Works. H. Dennis Sherk. LC 81-85166. (Illus.). 250p. 1986. write for info. (ISBN 0-934468-12-5). Gaslight.
William Gilmore Simms. Joseph V. Ridgely. (Twayne's United States Authors Ser.). 1962. pap. 8.95x (ISBN 0-8084-0327-3, T28, Twayne). New Coll U Pr.
William Gilmore Simms. William Trent. LC 68-24944. (American Biography Ser., No. 32). 1969. Repr. of 1899 ed. lib. bdg. 75.00x (ISBN 0-8383-0249-1). Haskell.
William Gilmore Simms: A Reference Guide. Keen Butterworth & James E. Kibler, Jr. 1980. lib. bdg. 31.50 (ISBN 0-8161-1059-X, Hall Reference). G K Hall.
William Gilpin: Western Nationalist. Thomas L. Karnes. (Illus.). 393p. 1970. 22.50x (ISBN 0-292-70003-2). U of Tex Pr.
William Glackens & "The Eight" The Artist Who Freed American Art. Ira Glackens. LC 57-8771. (Illus.). 320p. 1983. 20.00 (ISBN 0-8180-0139-9); pap. text ed. 9.95 (ISBN 0-8180-0138-0). Horizon.
William Gladstone. Eric Brand. (World Leaders--Past & Present Ser.). (Illus.). 112p. 1986. lib. bdg. 16.95 (ISBN 0-87754-528-6). Chelsea Hse.
William Godwin. D. Fleisher. 69.95 (ISBN 0-87968-276-0). Gordon Pr.
William Godwin: A Chronology. V. Munoz. Tr. by W. Scott Johnson. (Libertarian & Anarchist Chronology Ser.). 1979. lib. bdg. 59.95 (ISBN 0-8490-3026-9). Gordon Pr.
William Godwin & His Work. Rosalie G. Grylls. LC 74-13753. 1974. Repr. of 1953 ed. lib. bdg. 38.00 (ISBN 0-8414-4525-7). Folcroft.
William Godwin & His World. Rosalie G. Grylls. 1978. Repr. of 1953 ed. lib. bdg. 35.00 (ISBN 0-8495-1930-6). Arden Lib.
William Godwin & Mary Wollstonecraft. Victor Robinson. 59.95 (ISBN 0-8490-1304-6). Gordon Pr.
William Godwin & Mary Wollstonecraft: Lives of Great Altrurians. Victor Robinson. LC 78-31579. 1978. lib. bdg. 39.50 (ISBN 0-8414-7361-7). Folcroft.
William Godwin: His Friends & Contemporaries, 2 Vols. C. Kegan Paul. LC 73-115359. Repr. of 1876 ed. Set. 19.50 (ISBN 0-404-04941-9). Vol. 1 (ISBN 0-404-04942-7). Vol. 2 (ISBN 0-404-04943-5). AMS Pr.
William Godwin: Philospher, Novelist, Revolutionary. Peter H. Marshall. LC 83-19823. (Illus.). 352p. 1984. text ed. 35.00 (ISBN 0-300-03175-0). Yale U Pr.
William Goebel: The Politics of Wrath. James C. Klotter. LC 77-76335. (Kentucky Bicentennial Bookshelf Ser.). (Illus.). 152p. 1977. 6.95 (ISBN 0-8131-0240-5). U Pr of Ky.
William Golding. rev. ed. Bernard F. Dick. (Twayne's English Authors Ser.: No. 57). 184p. 1987. lib. bdg. 18.95x (ISBN 0-8057-6925-0, Twayne). G K Hall.
William Golding. James Gindin. LC 87-26110. (Modern Novelists Ser.). 144p. 1988. 19.95 (ISBN 0-312-01617-4). St Martin.
William Golding: A Critical Study. 2nd ed. Mark Kinkead-Weeks & Ian Gregor. 282p. 1984. pap. 7.95 (ISBN 0-571-13259-6). Faber & Faber.
William Golding: A Critical Study. V. V. Subbarao. LC 87-80664. 1987. text ed. 22.50x (ISBN 0-938719-21-1). Envoy Press.
William Golding: A Structural Reading of His Fiction. Philip Redpath. LC 86-10710. 224p. 1986. 28.50x (ISBN 0-389-20647-4). B&N Imports.
William Golding: Some Critical Considerations. Ed. by Jack I. Biles & Robert O. Evans. LC 77-73705. pap. 73.80 (ISBN 0-317-26707-8, 2024357). Bks Demand UMI.
William Golding: The Man & His Books. Ed. by John Carey. 191p. 1987. 22.50 (ISBN 0-374-29023-7). FS&G.
William Goyen: A Descriptive Bibliography, 1938-1985. Stuart Wright. 1987. lib. bdg. 29.50x (ISBN 0-88736-057-2). Meckler Corp.
William Goyens: The Texan Who Said No to Failure. Jan Seale. (Texas History Biography Ser.). (Illus.). 29p. (gr. k-3). 1987. PLB 6.95 (ISBN 0-936927-09-7); pap. 2.95 (ISBN 0-936927-17-8). Knowing Pr.
William Green: Biography of a Labor Leader. Craig Phelan. (American Labor History Ser.). 256p. (Orig.). 1988. text ed. 39.50x (ISBN 0-88706-870-7); pap. 12.95x (ISBN 0-88706-871-5). State U NY Pr.
William Grenville: A Bibliography. Arnold Harvey. (Bibliographies of British Statesmen Ser.: No. 2). 1989. lib. bdg. 45.00 (ISBN 0-88736-313-X). Meckler Corp.
William Gropper. Louis Lozowick. (Illus.). 200p. 1981. 40.00 (ISBN 0-87982-033-0). Art Alliance.
William Gropper. Louis Lozowick. LC 80-67118. (Illus.). 240p. 1982. 40.00 (ISBN 0-8453-4730-6, Cornwall Bks). Assoc Univ Prs.
William H. Ashley: Enterprise & Politics in the Trans-Mississippi West. Richard M. Clokey. LC 78-21396. (Illus.). 320p. 1980. 24.95 (ISBN 0-8061-1525-4). U of Okla Pr.
William H. Crawford, Seventeen Seventy-Two to Eighteen Thirty-Four. Chase Mooney. LC 70-190534. pap. 96.50 (ISBN 0-317-26727-2, 2024361). Bks Demand UMI.
William H. Harrison, 1773-1841; John Tyler 1790-1862: Chronology, Documents, Bibliographical Aids. Ed. by D. A. Durfee. LC 76-116058. (Oceana Presidential Chronology Ser.). 160p. 1970. 8.00 (ISBN 0-379-12081-X). Oceana.
William H. Jackson. Beaumont Newhall & Diana E. Edkins. LC 73-89076. (Illus.). 158p. 15.95 (ISBN 0-88360-039-0, Dist. by Univ. of Texas Pr). Amon Carter.
William H. Sylvis & the National Labor Union. Charlotte Todes. LC 75-347. (Radical Tradition in America Ser.). 128p. 1975. Repr. of 1942 ed. 15.40 (ISBN 0-88355-251-5). Hyperion Conn.
William H. Taft. Paolo E. Coletta. Ed. by Carol B. Fitzgerald. (Meckler's Bibliographies of the Presidents of the United States, 1789-1989 Ser: No. 26). (Illus.). 1988. lib. bdg. 45.00x (ISBN 0-88736-140-4). Meckler Corp.
William H. Welch & the Rise of Modern Medicine. Donald Fleming. LC 86-46273. 240p. 1987. pap. text ed. 8.95x (ISBN 0-8018-3389-2). Johns Hopkins.
William Hale White (Mark Rutherford) A Critical Study. facs. ed. Irvin Stock. LC 72-126260. (Select Bibliographies Reprint Ser). 1956. 19.00 (ISBN 0-8369-5487-4). Ayer Co Pubs.
William Harborne & the Trade with Turkey, 1578-1581. Ed. by Susan Skilliter. (Oriental Documents: Vol. I). (Illus.). 300p. 1977. 40.00 (ISBN 0-85672-745-8, Pub. by British Acad). Longwood Pub Group.
William Hastie: Educator & Politician. Ed. by Nathan I. Huggins. (Black Americans of Achievement Ser.). (Illus.). 1989. 16.95 (ISBN 1-55546-589-7). Chelsea Hse.
William Hastie: Grace under Pressure. Gilbert Ware. LC 84-5657. (Illus.). 1984. 35.00 (ISBN 0-19-503298-5). Oxford U Pr.
William Hayes, Eighteen Seventy-One to Nineteen Forty: York Photographic Artist. Terry Buchanan. 82p. 1986. 43.00x (ISBN 0-907033-39-3, Hutton Pr). State Mutual Bk.
William Hazlitt. Augustine Birrell. 230p. 1983. Repr. of 1902 ed. text ed. 20.00 (ISBN 0-89984-134-1). Century Bookbindery.
William Hazlitt. Intro. by Harold Bloom. (Modern Critical Views Ser.). 192p. 1986. lib. bdg. 19.95x (ISBN 0-87754-685-1). Chelsea Hse.
William Hazlitt. A. Ireland. lib. bdg. 69.95 (ISBN 0-8490-1305-4). Gordon Pr.
William Hazlitt. Robert W. Uphaus. (Twayne's English Authors Ser.: No. 413). 130p. 1985. lib. bdg. 17.95 (ISBN 0-8057-6904-8, Twayne). G K Hall.

William Makepeace Thackeray see Benjamin Disraeli.
William Makepeace Thackeray: A Biography Including Hitherto Uncollected Letters & Speeches & a Bibliography of 1300 Items, 2 Vols. Lewis S. Benjamin. LC 15-5841. 1968. Repr. of 1910 ed. Set. 59.00x (ISBN 0-403-00112-9). Scholarly.
William Makepeace Thackeray: Contributions to the Morning Chronicle. Gordon N. Ray. LC 55-6945. 232p. 1966. pap. 8.95 (ISBN 0-252-72736-3). U of Ill Pr.
William Makepeace Thackeray in Great Victorians. F. Swinnerton. Ed. by H. J. Massingham & H. Massingham. 1932. 35.00 (ISBN 0-8274-3718-8). R West.
William Makepeace Thackeray's Vanity Fair. Intro. by Harold Bloom. (Modern Critical Interpretations Ser.). 168p. 1987. 19.95 (ISBN 0-87754-747-5). Chelsea Hse.
William March: An Annotated Checklist. Roy S. Simmonds. LC 86-30786. 215p. 1988. 16.95 (ISBN 0-8173-0361-8). U of Ala Pr.
William Marples & Sons Price List of American Tools & Hardware, Nineteen Hundred Nine. 1980. pap. 5.00 (ISBN 0-913602-41-8). K Roberts.
William Marsh Rice & His Institute: A Biographical Study. Ed. by Sylvia S. Morris. LC 72-87103. (Rice University Studies: Vol. 58, No. 2). 171p. 1972. pap. 12.95x (ISBN 0-89263-212-7). Rice Univ.
William Marshal: The Flower of Chivalry. Georges Duby. Tr. by Richard Howard from Fr. 136p. 1985. 15.45 (ISBN 0-394-54309-2). Pantheon.
William Marshal: The Flower of Chivalry. Georges Duby. LC 85-42837. 160p. 1987. pap. 6.95 (ISBN 0-394-75154-X). Pantheon.
William Marshall: Knight-Errant, Baron, & Regent of England. Sidney Painter. (Medieval Academy Reprints for Teaching Ser.). 318p. 1982. pap. 10.95c (ISBN 0-8020-6498-1). U of Toronto Pr.
William Meeker & Family. Kathleen K. Saffell. LC 87-60173. (Descendants of Timothy Meeker Ser.: Vol. 2). (Orig.). 1987. pap. 35.00 (ISBN 0-9617467-2-6). K K Saffell.
William Melrose in China 1845-1855. Ho-Cheung Mui & Lorna H. Mui. 301p. 1973. 60.00x (ISBN 0-317-69468-5, Pub. by Han-Shan Tang Ltd). State Mutual Bk.
William Mendenhall & Terry Sincich, a Second Course in Business Statistics: Regression Analysis. 2nd ed. Terry Sincich. 1986. pap. text ed. write for info. solns. manual (ISBN 0-02-380500-5). Macmillan.
William Merritt Chase. New ed. Ronald G. Pisano. (Illus.). 88p. (Orig.). 1982. pap. 16.95 (ISBN 0-8230-5738-0). Watson-Guptill.
William Merritt Chase in the Company of Friends. Ronald G. Pisano. LC 79-87491. (Illus.). 70p. 1979. catalogue 4.00 (ISBN 0-943526-06-X). Parrish Art.
William Merritt Chase: Summers at Shinnecock 1891-1902. D. Scott Atkinson & Nicolai Cikovsky, Jr. (Illus.). 95p. 1988. pap. 12.95 (ISBN 0-87663-539-7). Universe.
William Meyerowitz: The Artist Speaks. Theresa B. Meyerowitz. LC 84-45010. (Illus.). 192p. 1986. 40.00 (ISBN 0-8453-4768-3, Cornwall Bks). Assoc Univ Prs.
William Meyerowitz: The Artist Speaks. Theresa B. Meyerowitz. LC 84-45010. (Illus.). 192p. 1986. 40.00x (ISBN 0-87982-513-8). Art Alliance.
William Miller: Selected Works see Millennium in America: From the Puritan Migration to the Civil War.
William Molyneux of Dublin: 1656-1698. Ed. by J. G. Simms. (Illus.). 176p. 1982. 30.00x (ISBN 0-7165-0096-5, BBA 01004, Pub. by Irish Academic Pr Ireland). Biblio Dist.
William Morgan: Bibliography & Building List. Edward H. Teague. (Architecture Ser.: A 1436). 6p. 1985. 2.00 (ISBN 0-89028-486-5). Vance Biblios.
William Morris. Paul Bloomfield. LC 73-15902. 1934. lib. bdg. 25.00 (ISBN 0-8414-3322-4). Folcroft.
William Morris. Holbrook Jackson. LC 74-18287. 1974. Repr. of 1934 ed. lib. bdg. 27.00 (ISBN 0-8414-5318-7). Folcroft.
William Morris. Holbrook Jackson. LC 79-110848. 1971. Repr. of 1926 ed. lib. bdg. 35.00x (ISBN 0-8371-4515-5, JAWM). Greenwood.
William Morris. John W. Mackail. LC 74-20657. 1942. Repr. of 1901 ed. lib. bdg. 18.50 (ISBN 0-8414-5936-3). Folcroft.
William Morris. Alfred Noyes. LC 72-39201. (Select Bibliographies Reprint Ser.). Repr. of 1908 ed. 16.00 (ISBN 0-8369-6803-4). Ayer Co Pubs.
William Morris. Alfred Noyes. LC 70-173176. Repr. of 1908 ed. 14.00 (ISBN 0-405-08822-1, Pub. by Blom). Ayer Co Pubs.
William Morris. Alfred Noyes. 1973. lib. bdg. 20.00 (ISBN 0-8414-6662-9). Folcroft.
William Morris. Peter Stansky. LC 83-4185. (Past Mast Ser.). 1983. 13.95x (ISBN 0-19-287572-8); pap. 4.95 (ISBN 0-19-287571-X). Oxford U Pr.
William Morris. R. Tames. (Clarendon Biography Ser.). (Illus.). pap. 3.50 (ISBN 0-912728-55-8). Newbury Bks.
William Morris. Edward P. Thompson. LC 76-62712. 1977. Pantheon.
William Morris. Montague Weekley. LC 73-908. 1934. lib. bdg. 17.00 (ISBN 0-8414-2800-X). Folcroft.
William Morris: A Reference Guide. Gary L. Aho. (Reference Guides to Literature Ser.). 420p. 1985. lib. bdg. 53.00 (ISBN 0-8161-8449-6). G K Hall.
William Morris: A Study in Personality. Arthur Compton-Rickett. 1978. Repr. of 1913 ed. lib. bdg. 37.50 (ISBN 0-8495-0801-0). Arden Lib.
William Morris: A Study in Personality. Arthur Compton-Rickett. LC 73-160749. 1971. Repr. of 1913 ed. 27.00 (ISBN 0-8046-1563-2, Pub. by Kennikat). Assoc Faculty Pr.
William Morris: A Study in Personality. R. Compton-Rickett. LC 72-195148. 1973. lib. bdg. 22.00 (ISBN 0-8414-2374-1). Folcroft.
William Morris: An Address Delivered at Kelmscott House. John W. Mackail. LC 74-20765. 1974. Repr. of 1902 ed. lib. bdg. 17.50 (ISBN 0-8414-5938-X). Folcroft.
William Morris: An Address Delivered at the Annual Meeting of the National Home Reading Union, 28th Oct., 1910. John W. Mackail. LC 74-20768. 1974. Repr. of 1910 ed. lib. bdg. 17.50 (ISBN 0-8414-5942-8). Folcroft.
William Morris & His Circle. J. W. Mackail. 1907. lib. bdg. 20.50 (ISBN 0-8414-5999-1). Folcroft.
William Morris & His Circle. John W. Mackail. LC 79-117585. (English Literature Ser., No. 33). 1970. Repr. of 1907 ed. lib. bdg. 40.95 (ISBN 0-8383-1018-4). Haskell.
William Morris & His Circle. John W. Mackail. 65p. 1983. Repr. of 1907 ed. lib. bdg. 20.50 (ISBN 0-8492-1687-7). R West.
William Morris & His Earthly Paradises. Roderick Marshall. (Illus.). 317p. 1979. 32.50x (ISBN 0-389-20085-9). B&N Imports.
William Morris & His Earthly Paradises. Roderick Marshall. LC 80-70411. (Illus.). 317p. 1981. 22.50 (ISBN 0-8076-1012-7). Braziller.
William Morris & His Poetry. B. I. Evans. LC 74-23889. 1925. lib. bdg. 25.00 (ISBN 0-8414-3947-8). Folcroft.
William Morris & His Poetry. Benjamin I. Evans. LC 74-120987. (Poetry & Life Ser.). Repr. of 1925 ed. 7.25 (ISBN 0-404-52512-1). AMS Pr.
William Morris & His Work. Walter Crane. 1911. lib. bdg. 15.00 (ISBN 0-8414-3544-8). Folcroft.
William Morris & Kelmscott. Design Council Editors. 192p. 1987. pap. 50.00x (ISBN 0-85072-121-0, Design Council Bks). State Mutual Bk.
William Morris & the Arts & Crafts. Holbrook Jackson. 59.95 (ISBN 0-8490-1306-2). Gordon Pr.
William Morris & the Arts & Crafts. Kenneth Jackson. LC 74-9574. 1973. lib. bdg. 27.00 (ISBN 0-8414-5297-0). Folcroft.
William Morris & the Communist Ideal. Emily C. Townsend. LC 74-18411. 1974. Repr. of 1934 ed. lib. bdg. 17.00 (ISBN 0-8414-8602-6). Folcroft.
William Morris & the Middle Ages. Ed. by Joanna Banham & Jennifer Harris. LC 84-15494. (Illus.). 240p. 1984. (Pub. by Manchester Univ Pr); pap. 26.00 (ISBN 0-7190-1721-1). St Martin.
William Morris As a Socialist. G. D. Cole. LC 73-17131. 1960. lib. bdg. 15.00 (ISBN 0-8414-3508-1). Folcroft.
William Morris As Designer. Ray Witkinson. (Illus.). 148p. 1980. 22.50 (ISBN 0-289-70673-4). Eastview.
William Morris: As Seen by His Contemporaries. Robert D. MacLeod. LC 74-20769. 1974. Repr. of 1956 ed. lib. bdg. 17.50 (ISBN 0-8414-5935-5). Folcroft.
William Morris by Himself: Designs & Writings. Ed. by Gillian Naylor. (Illus.). 1988. 50.00 (ISBN 0-8212-1710-0). NYGS.
William Morris: Craftsman-Socialist. Holbrook Jackson. 59p. 1980. Repr. of 1908 ed. lib. bdg. 18.50 (ISBN 0-8495-2756-2). Arden Lib.
William Morris, Designer. Gerald H. Crow. LC 75-28168. 1975. Repr. of 1934 ed. lib. bdg. 37.00 (ISBN 0-8414-3469-7). Folcroft.
William Morris: Designer. Gerald H. Crow. 120p. 1980. Repr. of 1934 ed. lib. bdg. 35.00 (ISBN 0-8492-3970-2). R West.
William Morris, Edward Burne-Jones & the Kelmscott Chaucer. Duncan Robinson. 116p. 1982. 125.00x (ISBN 0-86092-038-0, Pub. by Fraser Bks). State Mutual Bk.
William Morris, Edward Burne-Jones, & The Kelmscott Chaucer. Duncan Robinson. (Illus.). 116p. 1987. 40.00 (ISBN 0-918825-17-2, Dist. by Kampmann & Co.). Moyer Bell Limited.
William Morris Full-Color Patterns & Design. William Morris. (Illus.). 48p. 1988. pap. 7.95t (ISBN 0-486-25645-6). Dover.
William Morris: His Art, His Writings & His Public Life. Aymer Vallance. LC 77-6968. 1977. Repr. of 1898 ed. lib. bdg. 55.00 (ISBN 0-89341-208-2). Longwood Pub Group.
William Morris: His Homes & Haunts. Countess Of Warwick. LC 73-13851. 1912. lib. bdg. 30.00 (ISBN 0-8414-3462-X). Folcroft.
William Morris: His Life & Work. Jack Lindsay. LC 79-13075. (Illus.). 1979. 14.95 (ISBN 0-8008-8339-X). Taplinger.
William Morris: His Life, Work & Friends. Philip Henderson. 388p. 1988. pap. 17.95 (ISBN 0-233-97855-0, Pub. by A Deutsch England). David & Charles.
William Morris: His Work & Influence. A. Clutton-Brock. 1978. Repr. of 1914 ed. lib. bdg. 29.50 (ISBN 0-8495-0849-5). Arden Lib.
William Morris: His Work & Influence. A. Clutton-Brock. 1978. Repr. of 1919 ed. lib. bdg. 29.00 (ISBN 0-8492-3900-1). R West.
William Morris in Private Press & Limited Editions: A Descriptive Bibliography of Books by & about William Morris 1891-1981. John J. Walsdorf. LC 82-42923. (Illus.). 632p. 1983. slipcased 95.00 (ISBN 0-89774-041-6). Oryx Pr.
William Morris in the Great Victorians. J. Middleton Murry. Ed. by H. J. Massingham. 1973. Repr. of 1932 ed. 45.00 (ISBN 0-8274-0131-0). R West.
William Morris Lieserson: A Biography. Michael J. Eisner. LC 67-13557. pap. 38.50 (ISBN 0-317-39679-X, 2023717). Bks Demand UMI.
William Morris: Medievalist & Revolutionary. Margaret R. Grennan. LC 76-102500. 1970. Repr. of 1945 ed. 10.00x (ISBN 0-8462-1459-8). Russell.
William Morris: Poet, Craftsmen, Socialist. Elizabeth L. Cary. LC 74-18124. 74. Repr. of 1902 ed. lib. bdg. 35.00 (ISBN 0-8414-3545-6). Folcroft.
William Morris: Romantic to Revolutionary. E. P. Thompson. LC 88-60490. 831p. 1988. pap. 19.95 (ISBN 0-8047-1509-2). Stanford U Pr.
William Morris Textiles. Linda Parry. LC 82-70184. (Illus.). 192p. 1983. 46.95 (ISBN 0-670-77075-2, Studio); pap. 24.95 (ISBN 0-670-77074-4). Viking.
William Morris: The Critical Heritage. Ed. by Peter Faulkner. (Critical Heritage Ser.). 480p. 1973. 38.50x (ISBN 0-7100-7520-0). Routledge Chapman & Hall.
William Morris: The Critical Heritage. Ed. by Peter Faulkner. (Critical Heritage Ser.). 1984. pap. 15.00 (ISBN 0-7102-0393-4). Routledge Chapman & Hall.
William Morris, the Man & the Myth. Robert P. Arnot. LC 76-107. 131p. 1976. Repr. of 1964 ed. lib. bdg. 35.00x (ISBN 0-8371-8652-8, ARWM). Greenwood.
William Morris to Whistler. Walter Crane. 1978. Repr. lib. bdg. 32.50 (ISBN 0-8495-0836-3). Arden Lib.
William Morris to Whistler. Walter Crane. LC 73-19972. 1911. lib. bdg. 30.50 (ISBN 0-8414-3534-0). Folcroft.
William Morris's "The Defence of Guenevere", & Other Poems. Ed. by Margaret A. Lourie. LC 80-83223. 275p. 1981. lib. bdg. 36.00 (ISBN 0-8240-9452-2). Garland Pub.
William Morton Wheeler, Biologist. Mary A. Evans & Howard E. Evans. LC 76-129117. (Illus.). 1970. 27.00x (ISBN 0-674-95330-4). Harvard U Pr.
William Mulready. Kathryn M. Heleniak. LC 79-21775. (Illus.). 1980. 75.00x (ISBN 0-300-02311-1). Yale U Pr.
William Nassington: Canon, Mystic, & Poet of the Speculum Vitae. Ingrid J. Peterson. (American University Studies VII-Theology & Religion: Vol. 19). 209p. 1987. text ed. 34.00 (ISBN 0-8204-0322-9). P Lang Pubs.
William O. Douglas: A Biography. Edwin P. Hoyt. LC 78-19868. (Illus.). 1979. 8.95 (ISBN 0-8397-8598-4). Eriksson.
William O'Brien & the Course of Irish Politics, 1881-1918. Joseph V. O'Brien. LC 74-22970. 350p. 1976. 38.50x (ISBN 0-520-02886-4). U of Cal Pr.
William Ockham, 2 vols. Marilyn McCord Adams. LC 86-40337. (Publications in Medieval Studies: No. 26). 1216p. 1987. text ed. 90.00x (ISBN 0-268-01940-1). U of Notre Dame Pr.
William of Malmesbury. R. M. Thomson. 196p. 1987. 45.00 (ISBN 0-85115-451-4, Pub. by Boydell & Brewer). Longwood Pub Group.
William of Malmesbury: Gesta Regum Anglorum, Atque Historia Novella, 2 vols. Ed. by T. D. Hardy. (English Historical Society Publications Ser.: Vol. 14). Repr. of 1840 ed. 96.00 (ISBN 0-8115-1544-3). Kraus Repr.
William of Newburgh: Historia Rerum Anglicarum Willelmi Parvi, Ordinis Sancti Augustini Canonici Regularis in Coenobio Beatae Mariae de Newburgh in Argo Eboracensi, 2 vols. in 1. Ed. by H. C. Hamilton. (English Historical Society Publications Ser.: Vol. 15). Repr. of 1856 ed. 61.00 (ISBN 0-8115-1547-8). Kraus Repr.
William of Newburgh, History I. Ed. by P. G. Walsh. (BC-AP Classical Texts). 250p. (Lat. & Eng.). 1986. text ed. 49.00x (ISBN 0-86516-152-6); pap. 16.50x (ISBN 0-86516-153-4). Bolchazy-Carducci.
William of Newburgh: The History of English Affairs I. Ed. by P. G. Walsh & M. Kennedy. (Classical Texts-Medieval Latin Texts). 200p. 1986. text ed. 37.50 (ISBN 0-85668-304-3, Pub. by Aris & Phillips); pap. text ed. 16.50 (ISBN 0-85668-305-1, Pub. by Aris & Phillips). Humanities.
William of Orange & the English Opposition, 1672-4. K. H. Haley. LC 74-30846. 231p. 1975. Repr. of 1953 ed. lib. bdg. 22.50x (ISBN 0-8371-7934-3, HAWO). Greenwood.
William of Orange: Personal Portrait, 2 vols. N. A. Robb. Incl. Vol. 1. Early Years, 1650-1673. 318p. 1969. 6.50 (ISBN 0-312-88165-7); Vol. 2. Later Years, 1674-1702. 580p. 1966 (ISBN 0-685-23146-1). LC 73-89359. (Illus.). St Martin.
William of Palerne. Norman T. Simms. LC 75-37599. 1975. lib. bdg. 55.00 (ISBN 0-8414-7549-0). Folcroft.
William of Palerne: An Alliterative Romance. G. H. Bunt. xii, 488p. 1985. 67.00x (ISBN 90-6088-094-3, Pub. by Boumas Boekhuis Netherlands). Benjamins North Am.
William of St. Thierry: Exposition on the Epistle to the Romans. William of St. Thierry. Ed. by John D. Anderson. (Cistercian Fathers Ser.: No. 27). 1980. 17.95 (ISBN 0-87907-327-6). Cistercian Pubns.
William of St. Thierry, Golden Epistle. LC 72-152482. (Cistercian Fathers Ser.: No. 12). 1971. pap. 4.00 (ISBN 0-87907-712-3). Cistercian Pubns.
William of St. Thierry: On Contemplating God, Prayer, Meditations. Tr. by Sr. Penelope. (Cistercian Fathers Ser.: No. 3). 1970. pap. 5.00 (ISBN 0-87907-903-7). Cistercian Pubns.
William of St. Thierry: The Enigma of Faith, Vol. 3. LC 74-4465. (Cistercian Fathers Ser.: No. 9). 1974. 7.95 (ISBN 0-87907-309-8). Cistercian Pubns.
William of St. Thierry: The Man & His Work. Jean M. Dechanet. Tr. by Richard Strachen from Fr. LC 73-152485. (Cistercian Studies: No. 10). 192p. 1972. 10.95 (ISBN 0-87907-810-3). Cistercian Pubns.
William of Sherwood's Introduction to Logic. William Shirwood. LC 66-16468. pap. 50.00 (ISBN 0-317-08266-3, 2000830). Bks Demand UMI.
William of Tyre: Historian of the Latin East. Peter W. Edbury & John G. Rowe. (Cambridge Studies in Medieval Life & Thought Ser.: No. 8). (Illus.). 192p. 1988. 39.50 (ISBN 0-521-26766-8). Cambridge U Pr.
William Orlando Darby: A Military Biography. Michael J. King. LC 80-21162. (Illus.). 219p. 1981. 23.50 (ISBN 0-208-01867-0, Archon). Shoe String.
William P. Letchworth: A Man for Others. Irene A. Beale. LC 1-90673. 214p. (Orig.). 1982. pap. 9.00 (ISBN 0-9608132-0-9). Chestnut Hill Pr.
William Paca: A Biography. Gregory A. Stiverson & Phebe R. Jacobsen. LC 76-17519. (Illus.). 1976. 7.95 (ISBN 0-938420-18-6); pap. 4.95 (ISBN 0-686-23680-7). Md Hist.
William Palmer: A Retrospective. Howard DaLee Spencer. LC 86-50124. (Illus.). 20p. 1986. pap. 3.00 (ISBN 0-939324-24-5). Wichita Art Mus.
William Paterson: Lawyer & Statesman, 1745-1806. John E. O'Connor. 1979. 37.00x (ISBN 0-8135-0880-0). Rutgers U Pr.
William Penhallow Henderson: Master Colorist of Santa Fe. David Bell & Daphne A. Deeds. LC 84-61888. (Illus.). 108p. (Orig.). 1984. pap. 13.00x (ISBN 0-910407-12-6). Phoenix Art.
William Penn. Hildegarde Dolson. (Landmark Ser.: No. 98). (Illus.). (gr. 3-7). 1963. Random.
William Penn. facsimile ed. William I. Hull. LC 78-179525. (Select Bibliographies Reprint Ser). Repr. of 1937 ed. 32.00 (ISBN 0-8369-6654-6). Ayer Co Pubs.
William Penn & Our Liberties. William W. Comfort. (Illus.). 146p. 1976. pap. 3.00 (ISBN 0-941308-02-2). Religious Soc Friends.
William Penn & the Founding of Pennsylvania, 1680-1684: A Documentary History. Ed. by Jean R. Soderlund & Richard S. Dunn. (Illus.). 380p. 1983. 30.95x (ISBN 0-8122-7862-3); pap. 12.95x (ISBN 0-8122-1131-6). U of Pa Pr.
William Penn, Architect of a Nation. John B. Trussell, Jr. LC 81-622575. (Illus.). 77p. (Orig.). 1980. pap. 2.75 (ISBN 0-89271-008-X). Pa Hist & Mus.
William Penn As Social Philosopher. Edward C. Beatty. 1972. lib. bdg. 24.50x (ISBN 0-374-90506-1, Octagon). Hippocrene Bks.
William Penn. Horticulturist. R. McM. Hunt. (Illus.). 39p. 1953. 5.00 (ISBN 0-913196-38-X). Hunt Inst Botanical.
William Penn: Mystic. Elizabeth G. Vining. LC 74-95891. (Orig.). 1969. pap. 2.50x (ISBN 0-87574-167-3, 167). Pendle Hill.
William Penn, Quaker & Pioneer. Bonamy Dobree. LC 78-15258. 1978. Repr. of 1932 ed. lib. bdg. 35.00 (ISBN 0-8414-3790-4). Folcroft.
William Penn, Quaker & Pioneer. Bonamy Dobree. 346p. 1983. Repr. of 1932 ed. lib. bdg. 45.50 (ISBN 0-8492-4227-4). R West.
William Penn, Thomas Gray & an Account of the Historical Associations of Stoke Poges. F. McDermott. 1973. Repr. of 1930 ed. lib. bdg. 30.00 (ISBN 0-8414-6026-4). Folcroft.
William Penn: 17th Century Founding Father. Edwin B. Bronner. LC 75-32728. (Illus.). 36p. (Orig.). 1975. pap. 2.50x (ISBN 0-87574-204-1). Pendle Hill.
William Penn's Legacy: Politics & Social Structure in Provincial Pennsylvania, 1726-1755. Alan Tully. LC 77-4548. (Studies in Historical & Political Science: 95 Ser., No- 2). (Illus.). 1978. text ed. 28.50x (ISBN 0-8018-1932-6). Johns Hopkins.
William Penn's Own Account of Lenni Lenape or Delaware Indians. Ed. by Albert C. Myers. (Illus.). 96p. (gr. 7 up). Date not set. pap. 4.95 (ISBN 0-912608-13-7). Mid Atlantic.
William Perkins' Commentary on Galatians. (Classic Commentaries Ser.). 1988. price not set (ISBN 0-8298-0786-1). Pilgrim NY.

TITLE INDEX WILLIAM STERNDALE BENNETT (EIGHTEEN

William Perkins 1558-1602, English Puritanist--His Pioneer Works on Casuistry: Discourse on Conscience & the Whole Treatise of Cases of Conscience. Thomas F. Merrill. xx, 242p. 1966. text ed. 49.50x (ISBN 0-317-55885-4, Pub. by B De Graaf Netherlands). Coronet Bks.
William Perry: The Refrigerator. Andre Roberts. LC 86-4184. (Sports Stars Ser.). (Illus.). 48p. (gr. 2-8). 1986. PLB 11.27 (ISBN 0-516-04358-7); pap. 2.95 (ISBN 0-516-44358-5). Childrens.
William Pickering, Publisher: A Memoir & Checklist of His Publications. Geoffrey L. Keynes. (Illus.). 1924. 22.50 (ISBN 0-8337-1917-3). B Franklin.
William Pitt. Walford D. Green. LC 73-14445. (Heroes of the Nation Ser.). Repr. of 1901 ed. 30.00 (ISBN 0-404-58263-X). AMS Pr.
William Pitt: A Bibliography. Arnold Harvey. (Bibliographies of British Statesmen Ser.: No. 1). 1988. lib. bdg. 45.00 (ISBN 0-88736-314-8). Meckler Corp.
William Pitt & the Great War. John H. Rose. LC 71-110862. (Illus.). xiv, 596p. 1971. Repr. of 1911 ed. lib. bdg. 35.00x (ISBN 0-8371-4533-3, ROWP). Greenwood.
William Plumer of New Hampshire. Lynn W. Turner. (Institute of Early American History & Culture Ser.). xiv, 366p. 1962. 30.00x (ISBN 0-8078-0845-8). U of NC Pr.
William Plumer's Memorandum of Proceedings in the United States Senate 1803-1807. Ed. by Everett S. Brown. LC 74-94626. (Law, Politics & History Ser). 1969. Repr. of 1923 ed. 85.00 (ISBN 0-306-71823-5). Da Capo.
William Poel & the Elizabethan Stage Society. Marion O'Connor. (Theatre in Focus Ser.). 120p. 1987. pap. 70.00 (ISBN 0-85964-164-3). Chadwyck-Healey.
William Poel's Hamlets: The Director as Critic. Rinda F. Lundstrom. Ed. by Bernard Beckerman. LC 84-22. (Theater & Dramatic Studies: No. 20). 204p. 1984. 42.95 (ISBN 0-8357-1547-7). UMI Res Pr.
William Porcher DuBose: Selected Writings. Ed. by Jon Alexander. (Sources of American Spirituality Ser.). 1988. 19.95 (ISBN 0-8091-0402-4). Paulist Pr.
William Preston & the Allegheny Patriots. Patricia G. Johnson. LC 76-9446. (Illus.). 1976. 15.00. Pat G Johnson.
William Randolph Hearst, American. Mrs. Fremont Older. LC 72-7195. (Select Bibliographies Reprints Ser.). 1972. Repr. of 1936 ed. 38.50 (ISBN 0-8369-6951-0). Ayer Co Pubs.
William Rice of Frederick County, Maryland, & Some of His Descendants. Millard M. Rice. (Illus.). 1979. pap. 4.00 (ISBN 0-913186-09-0). Monocacy.
William Richard Lethaby. Rebens. 1987. 45.95 (ISBN 0-85139-350-0). Van Nos Reinhold.
William Rimmer: A Yankee Michelangelo. Jeffrey Weidman et al. LC 85-70907. (Illus.). 135p. 1985. pap. 20.00x (ISBN 0-934358-14-1). Brockton Art Fuller.
William Rimmer: A Yankee Michelangelo: Brockton Art Museum-Fuller Memorial. William Rimmer et al. LC 85-70907. (Illus.). xvi, 119p. 1985. pap. 20.00 (ISBN 0-317-60227-6). U Pr of New Eng.
William Robinson: Eighteen Thirty-Eight to Nineteen Thirty-Five. Mea Allan. (Illus.). 288p. 1983. 23.95 (ISBN 0-571-11865-8). Faber & Faber.
William Robinson Leigh: Western Artist. D. Duane Cummins. LC 79-6707. (Gilcrease-Oklahoma Series on Western Art & Artists: Vol. 2). (Illus.). 200p. 1980. 32.50 (ISBN 0-8061-1628-5). U of Okla Pr.
William Rothenstein: The Portrait of an Artist in His Time. Robert Speaight. LC 79-8080. Repr. of 1962 ed. 39.50 (ISBN 0-404-18389-1). AMS Pr.
William Roy, Seventeen Twenty-Six to Seventeen Ninety: Pioneer of the Ordnance Survey. Yolande O'Donoghue. (Illus.). 56p. (Orig.). 1977. pap. 3.75 (ISBN 0-7141-0387-X, Pub. by British Lib). Longwood Pub Group.
William Rufus. Frank Barlow. LC 82-45902. (English Monarchs Ser.: No. 8). (Illus.). 464p. 1983. 30.00x (ISBN 0-520-04936-5). U of Cal Pr.
William Rufus Day, Supreme Court Justice from Ohio. Joseph E. McLean. LC 78-64202. (Johns Hopkins University. Studies in the Social Sciences. Sixty-Fourth Ser. 1946: 3). Repr. of 1946 ed. 18.00 (ISBN 0-404-61308-X). AMS Pr.
William Rush: American Sculptor. Ed. by Linda Bantel. LC 82-80636. (Illus.). 211p. (Orig.). 1982. 21.95x (ISBN 0-943836-00-X, Pub. by Penn Acad Fine Arts). U Pr of Va.
William S. Burroughs. Jennie Skerl. (United States Author Ser.). 1985. lib. bdg. 17.95 (ISBN 0-8057-7438-6, Twayne); pap. 7.95 (ISBN 0-8057-7456-4, Twayne). G K Hall.
William S. Burroughs: An Annotated Bibliography of His Works & Criticism. Michael B. Goodman. LC 75-23007. (Reference Library of the Humanities: Vol. 24). 100p. 1975. lib. bdg. 25.00 (ISBN 0-8240-9989-3). Garland Pub.
William S. Burroughs, Nineteen Fifty-Three to Nineteen Seventy-Three: A Bibliography. Ed. by Joe Maynard & Barry Miles. LC 77-2663. (Illus.). 243p. 1978. 20.00x (ISBN 0-8139-0710-1); signed ed. o.p. 50.00x (ISBN 0-8139-0930-9). U Pr of Va.
William S. Gray: Teacher, Scholar, Leader. Ed. by Jennifer A. Stevenson. 80p. 1985. pap. 5.00 (ISBN 0-87207-967-8). Intl Reading.
William Samuel Johnson: A Maker of the Constitution. George C. Groce, Jr. LC 37-33132. Repr. of 1937 ed. 14.50 (ISBN 0-404-02936-1). AMS Pr.
William Saroyan. Edward H. Foster. LC 84-70249. (Western Writers Ser.: No. 61). (Orig.). 1984. pap. 2.95x (ISBN 0-88430-035-8). Boise St Univ.
William Saroyan. Aram Saroyan. LC 83-21313. (Illus.). 224p. 1983. pap. 8.95 (ISBN 0-15-696780-4, Harv). HarBraceJ.
William Saroyan. Aram Saroyan. (Illus.). 170p. 1987. pap. 8.95 (ISBN 0-317-67226-6). Blackberry Bks.
William Saroyan: A Reference Guide. Elisabeth C. Foard. 1988. 35.00 (ISBN 0-8161-8943-9). G K Hall.
William Saroyan: My Real Work Is Being. David S. Calonne. LC 83-1184. (Illus.). xii, 185p. 1983. 19.95x (ISBN 0-8078-1565-9). U of NC Pr.
William Saroyan: The Man & the Writer Remembered. Ed. by Leo Hamalian. LC 86-45936. (Illus.). 264p. 1987. 35.00x (ISBN 0-8386-3308-0). Fairleigh Dickinson.
William Schuman. Flora R. Schreiber. 139p. Repr. of 1954 ed. lib. bdg. 39.00 (Pub. by Am Repr Serv). Am Biog Serv.
William Scott: Drawings. Lou Klepec. LC 75-684. 1975. 12.00 (ISBN 0-685-56530-0, Dist. by David Anderson Gallery). D Anderson.
William Shakespeare. George Brandes. 709p. 1916. lib. bdg. 65.00 (ISBN 0-8414-1688-5). Folcroft.
William Shakespeare. David W. Clarke. LC 70-179330. (Illus.). Repr. of 1950 ed. 12.50 (ISBN 0-404-01568-9). AMS Pr.
William Shakespeare. Terry Eagleton. (Rereading Literature Ser.). 110p. 1986. 14.95 (ISBN 0-631-14553-2). Basil Blackwell.
William Shakespeare. Terry Eagleton. 110p. 1987. pap. 7.95 (ISBN 0-631-14554-0). Basil Blackwell.
William Shakespeare. Victor Hugo. Tr. by M. B. Anderson. LC 70-169455. Repr. of 1906 ed. 42.50 (ISBN 0-404-03382-2). AMS Pr.
William Shakespeare. facsimile ed. Victor Hugo. Tr. by Melville B. Anderson. LC 77-128888. (Select Bibliographies Reprint Ser). Repr. of 1886 ed. 23.50 (ISBN 0-8369-5508-0). Ayer Co Pubs.
William Shakespeare. Victor Hugo. Tr. by Melville B. Anderson. 424p. 1983. Repr. of 1887 ed. lib. bdg. 65.00 (ISBN 0-89984-922-9). Century Bookbindery.
William Shakespeare. John Masefield. 1977. Repr. of 1911 ed. lib. bdg. 20.50 (ISBN 0-8414-6234-8). Folcroft.
William Shakespeare. Dorothy Turner. (Great Lives Ser.). (Illus.). 32p. (gr. 7-9). 1985. 11.90 (ISBN 0-531-00923-8, Pub. by Bookwright Pr). Watts.
William Shakespeare: A Biography. Frederick J. Pohl. Ed. by Stephen Butterfield & Bruce A. Burton. 256p. 1983. 16.75 (ISBN 0-9611422-1-9). Security Dupont.
William Shakespeare: A Commentary. Maurice R. Ridley. LC 83-45465. Repr. of 1936 ed. 25.00 (ISBN 0-404-20217-9). AMS Pr.
William Shakespeare: A Compact Documentary Life. S. Schoenbaum. LC 76-47436. (Illus.). 1977. 22.50x (ISBN 0-19-502211-4). Oxford U Pr.
William Shakespeare: A Compact Documentary Life. rev. ed. S. Schoenbaum. (Illus.). 405p. 1987. pap. 13.95 (ISBN 0-19-505161-0). Oxford U Pr.
William Shakespeare: A Documentary Life. S. Schoenbaum. (Illus.). 1975. 85.00x (ISBN 0-19-812046-X). Oxford U Pr.
William Shakespeare: A Handbook. 266p. Repr. of 1934 ed. lib. bdg. 35.00 (ISBN 0-918377-55-2). Russell Pr.
William Shakespeare: A Literary Biography. Karl Elze. LC 73-166028. Repr. of 1888 ed. 49.50 (ISBN 0-404-02328-2). AMS Pr.
William Shakespeare: A Reader's Guide. Alfred Harbage. 498p. 1963. pap. 3.95 (ISBN 0-374-50288-9). FS&G.
William Shakespeare: A Reader's Guide. Alfred Harbage. 1985. lib. bdg. 30.00x (ISBN 0-88254-837-9, Octagon). Hippocrene Bks.
William Shakespeare: A Study in Elizabethan Literature. Barrett Wendell. LC 72-159972. (Studies in Shakespeare, No. 24). 1971. Repr. of 1894 ed. lib. bdg. 49.95x (ISBN 0-8383-1254-3). Haskell.
William Shakespeare: A Textual Companion. Stanley Wells & Gary Taylor. 682p. 1988. 125.00 (ISBN 0-19-812914-9). Oxford U Pr.
William Shakespeare & Alleged Spanish Prototypes. Albert R. Frey. LC 70-169262. (Shakespeare Society of New York. Publications Ser.: No. 3). Repr. of 1886 ed. 16.00 (ISBN 0-404-54203-4). AMS Pr.
William Shakespeare & Robert Greene: The Evidence. W. Chapman. LC 73-18209. (Studies in Shakespeare, No. 24). 1974. lib. bdg. 75.00x (ISBN 0-8383-1731-6). Haskell.
William Shakespeare & the Birth of Merlin. Mark Dominik. LC 84-20694. 213p. 1985. 19.95 (ISBN 0-8022-2469-5). Philos Lib.
William Shakespeare: Comedies & Romances. Intro. by Harold Bloom. (Modern Critical Views Ser.). 298p. 1986. 29.50 (ISBN 0-87754-664-9). Chelsea Hse.
William Shakespeare, Eighteen Sixty-Four. Victor Hugo. Ed. by B. Levillot. 18.95 (ISBN 0-686-54050-6). French & Eur.
William Shakespeare: His Family & Friends. Charles I. Elton. Ed. by A. Hamilton Thompson. LC 72-166025. Repr. of 1904 ed. 57.50 (ISBN 0-404-02324-X). AMS Pr.
William Shakespeare: His Homes & Haunts. S. L. Bensusan. 87p. 1981. lib. bdg. 32.50 (ISBN 0-8495-0478-3). Arden Lib.
William Shakespeare: His World, His Work, His Influence, 3 vols. Ed. by John F. Andrews. LC 85-8305. 1985. lib. bdg. 180.00 (ISBN 0-684-17851-6, ScribR). Scribner.
William Shakespeare: Histories & Poems. Intro. by Harold Bloom. (Modern Critical Views Ser.). 203p. 1986. 29.50 (ISBN 0-87754-658-4). Chelsea Hse.
William Shakespeare, Player, Playmaker & Poet. Henry C. Beeching. LC 77-168571. (Illus.). Repr. of 1909 ed. 21.00 (ISBN 0-404-00724-4). AMS Pr.
William Shakespeare: Player, Playmaker & Poet. Henry C. Beeching. 1973. Repr. of 1909 ed. 15.00 (ISBN 0-8274-1670-9). R West.
William Shakespeare: Poet, Dramatist & Man. Hamilton W. Mabie. 345p. 1985. Repr. of 1900 ed. lib. bdg. 45.00 (ISBN 0-8495-3912-9). Arden Lib.
William Shakespeare: Prosody & Text. Bastiaan A. Van Dam & Cornelius O. Stoffel. LC 75-177557. Repr. of 1900 ed. 15.00 (ISBN 0-404-06752-2). AMS Pr.
William Shakespeare: Prosody & Text. Bastiaan A. Van Dam & Cornelius O. Stoffel. 1900. Repr. 10.00 (ISBN 0-8274-3715-3). R West.
William Shakespeare: Records & Images. S. Schoenbaum. (Illus.). 1981. 98.00x (ISBN 0-19-520234-1). Oxford U Pr.
William Shakespeare: Shakespeare l'Ancien. Victor Hugo. (Illus.). 83p. 1976. 1500.00 (ISBN 0-686-54049-2). French & Eur.
William Shakespeare: The Complete Works. William Shakespeare. Ed. by Stanley Wells et al. 448p. 1987. 45.00 (ISBN 0-19-812926-2); Original Spelling Edition, 1250 pp. 125.00 (ISBN 0-19-812919-X). Oxford U Pr.
William Shakespeare: The Complete Works. compact ed. William Shakespeare et al. Ed. by Stanley Wells & Gary Taylor. (Shakespeare Ser.). (Illus.). 1344p. 1989. 19.95 (ISBN 0-19-811747-7). Oxford U Pr.
William Shakespeare: The Tragedies. Intro. by Harold Bloom. (Modern Critical Views Ser.). 209p. 1986. 24.50 (ISBN 0-87754-617-7). Chelsea Hse.
William Shakespeare: The Tragedies. Paul A. Jorgensen. (Twayne's English Author Ser.: No. 415). 184p. 1985. lib. bdg. 16.95 (ISBN 0-8057-6906-4, Twayne). G K Hall.
William Shakespeare: Welt-Werk-Wirkung. Gerhard Mueller-Schwefe. (Sammlung Goschen 2208). 1978. 7.90x (ISBN 3-11-007545-8). De Gruyter.
William Shakespeare's Antony & Cleopatra. Intro. by Harold Bloom. (Modern Critical Interpretations Ser.). 1987. 24.50 (ISBN 0-87754-921-4). Chelsea Hse.
William Shakespeare's Coriolanus. Intro. by Harold Bloom. (Modern Critical Interpretations Ser.). 1987. 19.95 (ISBN 0-87754-923-0). Chelsea Hse.
William Shakespeare's Hamlet. Intro. by Harold Bloom. (Modern Critical Interpretations Ser.kespeare Ser.). 160p. 1986. 24.50 (ISBN 0-87754-924-9). Chelsea Hse.
William Shakespeare's Henry IV, Part II. Intro. by Harold Bloom. (Modern Critical Interpretations Ser.). 1987. 24.50 (ISBN 0-87754-926-5). Chelsea Hse.
William Shakespeare's Henry IV, Pt. 1. Intro. by Harold Bloom. (Modern Critical Interpretations Ser.). 160p. 1986. lib. bdg. 19.95x (ISBN 0-87754-925-7). Chelsea Hse.
William Shakespeare's Henry V. Intro. by Harold Bloom. (Modern Critical Interpretations Ser.). 1987. 19.95 (ISBN 0-87754-927-3). Chelsea Hse.
William Shakespeare's King Lear. Intro. by Harold Bloom. (Modern Critical Interpretations Ser.). 160p. 1987. 24.50 (ISBN 0-87754-929-X). Chelsea Hse.
William Shakespeare's Macbeth. Intro. by Harold Bloom. (Modern Critical Interpretations Ser.). 184p. 1987. 24.50 (ISBN 0-87754-930-3). Chelsea Hse.
William Shakespeare's Measure for Measure. Intro. by Harold Bloom. (Modern Critical Interpretations Ser.). 1987. 24.50 (ISBN 0-87754-931-1). Chelsea Hse.
William Shakespeare's Merchant of Venice. Intro. by Harold Bloom. (Modern Critical Interpretations Ser.). 142p. 1986. 19.50 (ISBN 0-87754-932-X). Chelsea Hse.
William Shakespeare's Midsummer Night's Dream. Intro. by Harold Bloom. (Modern Critical Interpretations Ser.). 160p. 1987. 19.95 (ISBN 0-87754-933-8). Chelsea Hse.
William Shakespeare's Othello. Intro. by Harold Bloom. (Modern Critical Interpretations Ser.). 160p. 1987. 19.50 (ISBN 0-87754-935-4). Chelsea Hse.
William Shakespeare's Richard II. Intro. by Harold Bloom. (Modern Critical Interpretations Ser.). 152p. 1988. lib. bdg. 19.95 (ISBN 0-87754-936-2). Chelsea Hse.
William Shakespeare's Sonnets. Intro. by Harold Bloom. (Modern Critical Interpretations Ser.). 1987. 24.50 (ISBN 0-87754-938-9). Chelsea Hse.
William Shakespeare's Taming of the Shrew. Intro. by Harold Bloom. (Modern Critical Interpretations Ser.). 136p. 1988. lib. bdg. 24.50 (ISBN 0-87754-939-7). Chelsea Hse.
William Shakespeare's: The Merchant of Venice. Intro. by Harold Bloom. (Modern Critical Interpretations Ser.). 142p. 1986. lib. bdg. 24.50x (ISBN 0-317-63002-4). Chelsea Hse.
William Shakespeare's The Tragedy of Hamlet: Translated into Modern English Verse. Tr. by Frank P. Zeidler. 1979. pap. 5.00 (ISBN 0-87423-025-X). Westburg.
William Shakespeare's The Winter's Tale. Intro. by Harold Bloom. (Modern Critical Interpretations Ser.). 168p. 1987. 24.50 (ISBN 0-87754-942-7). Chelsea Hse.
William Shakespeare's Twelfth Night. Intro. by Harold Bloom. (Modern Critical Interpretations). 168p. 1987. 24.50 (ISBN 0-87754-941-9). Chelsea Hse.
William Shakspere: A Biography. Charles Knight. LC 73-168057. Repr. of 1843 ed. 49.50 (ISBN 0-404-03734-8). AMS Pr.
William Shakspere: A Study in Elizabethan Literature. Barrett Wendell. LC 79-127906. Repr. of 1894 ed. 10.95 (ISBN 0-404-06905-3). AMS Pr.
William Sharp - "Fiona MacLeod", 1855-1905. Flavia Alaya. LC 75-113183. (Illus.). 1970. 20.00x (ISBN 0-674-95345-2). Harvard U Pr.
William Shenstone: An Eighteenth-Century Portrait. Arthur R. Humphreys. LC 75-41146. Repr. of 1937 ed. 12.50 (ISBN 0-404-14673-2). AMS Pr.
William Sheppard: Cromwell's Law Reformer. Nancy L. Matthews. (Studies in English Legal History). 320p. 1985. 57.50 (ISBN 0-521-26483-9). Cambridge U Pr.
William Shipley: Founder of the Royal Society of Arts. D. G. Allan. 1979. 22.50 (ISBN 0-85967-483-5); pap. 9.95 (ISBN 0-85967-484-3). Scolar.
William Shirley, Governor of Massachusetts, 1741-1756. George A. Wood. LC 72-78001. (Columbia University. Studies in the Social Sciences: No. 209). Repr. of 1920 ed. 17.50 (ISBN 0-404-51209-7). AMS Pr.
William Sidney Mount: Annotated Bibliography & Listings of Archival Holdings of the Museums at Stony Brook. David Cassedy & Gail Shrott. (Illus., Orig.). 1983. pap. 7.00 (ISBN 0-943924-05-7). Mus Stony Brook.
William Sidney Mount: Works in the Collection of the Museums at Stony Brook. David Cassedy & Gail Schrott. LC 83-23646. (Illus.). 96p. 1983. pap. 13.00 (ISBN 0-295-96324-7, Pub. by Museums at Stony Brook). U of Wash Pr.
William Sidney Mount: Works in the Collection of the Museums at Stony Brook. David Cassedy & Gail Shrott. (Illus.). 96p. (Orig.). 1983. pap. 13.50 (ISBN 0-943924-06-5, Dist. by University of Washington Press). Mus Stony Brook.
William Smith O'Brien & His Irish Revolutionary Companions in Penal Exlie. Blanche M. Touhill. LC 81-1899. (Illus.). 288p. 1981. text ed. 32.00x (ISBN 0-8262-0339-6). U of Mo Pr.
William Smith, Potter & Farmer: 1790-1858. George Sturt. (Illus.). 230p. 1978. 16.50 (ISBN 0-904573-08-7, Pub. by Caliban Bks); pap. 8.50 (ISBN 0-904573-44-3). Longwood Pub Group.
William Somerset Maugham. Richard H. Ward. Repr. of 1937 ed. lib. bdg. 35.50 (ISBN 0-8414-9520-3). Folcroft.
William Somerset Maugham: A Study of Technique & Literary Sources. Claude S. McIver. LC 73-3463. 1936. lib. bdg. 29.00 (ISBN 0-8414-2346-6). Folcroft.
William Somerset Maugham: An Appreciation. Desmond MacCarthy. LC 73-3462. 1933. lib. bdg. 17.00 (ISBN 0-8414-2331-8). Folcroft.
William Somerset Maugham: Some Aspects of the Man & His Work. Sven A. Jensen. LC 72-194425. 1957. lib. bdg. 25.00 (ISBN 0-8414-5380-2). Folcroft.
William Stafford. David A. Carpenter. LC 86-70651. (Western Writers Ser.: No. 72). 51p. (Orig.). 1986. pap. 2.95x (ISBN 0-88430-046-3). Boise St Univ.
William Stafford: You Must Revise Your Life. William Stafford. 1986. 24.95; pap. 8.95. U of Mich Pr.
William Stanley Jevons: Critical Assessments, 3 vols. Ed. by John C. Wood. (Critical Assessments of Leading Economists Ser.). 1988. Set. lib. bdg. 595.00 (ISBN 0-415-00387-3). Routledge Chapman & Hall.
William Steinitz Selected Chess Games. enl. ed. William Steinitz. Ed. by Charles Devide. LC 73-84915. 126p. 1974. Repr. of 1901 ed. 3.95 (ISBN 0-486-23025-2). Dover.
William Sterndale Bennett (Eighteen Fifteen to Eighteen Seventy-Three) Complete Works for Piano Solo, Vol. 17. (London Pianoforte School 1770-1860 Ser.). 190p. 1985. lib. bdg. 65.00 (ISBN 0-8240-6166-7). Garland Pub.
William Sterndale Bennett (Eighteen Fifteen to Eighteen Seventy-Three) Complete Works for Piano Solo, Vol. 18. Ed. by Nicholas Temperley. (London Pianoforte School 1770-1860 Ser.). 240p. 1985. lib. bdg. 70.00 (ISBN 0-8240-6167-5). Garland Pub.

William Sterndale Bennett, Three Symphonies (3,4,5) Ed. by Nocholas Temperley. (Symphony 1720-1840 Series E: Vol. 7). 1982. lib. bdg. 90.00 (ISBN 0-8240-3813-4). Garland Pub.

William Sterndale Bennett (1815-1873) The London Pianoforte School 1770-1860, Vol. 17-18. Ed. by Nicholas Temperly. 50.00. Garland Pub.

William Stewart Halsted, Surgeon. William G. MacCallum. LC 30-31890. pap. 65.80 (ISBN 0-317-28138-0, 2055744). Bks Demand UMI.

William Strickland. Lamia Doumato. (Architecture Ser.: A 1513). 8p. 1985. 2.00 (ISBN 0-89028-663-9). Vance Biblios.

William Strickland-Architect & Engineer 1788-1854. enl. ed. Agnes A. Gilchrist. LC 69-13714. (Architecture & Decorative Art Ser.). (Illus.). 1969. Repr. of 1950 ed. lib. bdg. 35.00 (ISBN 0-306-71235-0). Da Capo.

William Stroudley, Craftsman of Steam. H. Campbell Cornwell. LC 68-23836. (Illus.). 1968. 27.95x (ISBN 0-678-05591-2). Kelley.

William Stukeley: An Eighteenth Century Antiquary. rev. ed. Stuart Piggott. LC 84-51643. (Illus.). 1985. 19.95 (ISBN 0-500-01360-8). Thames Hudson.

William Styron. Melvin J. Friedman. LC 74-16889. 82p. 1974. 2.50 (ISBN 0-87972-071-9). Bowling Green Univ.

William Styron. Richard Pearce. (Pamphlets on American Writers Ser.: No. 98). (Orig.). 1971. pap. 1.25x (ISBN 0-8166-0616-1, MPAW98). U of Minn Pr.

William Styron. Judith Ruderman. (Literature & Life Ser.). 192p. 1987. 19.95x (ISBN 0-8044-2781-X). Ungar.

William Styron: An Annotated Bibliography of Criticism. Compiled by Philip W. Leon. LC 78-60256. 1978. lib. bdg. 35.00 (ISBN 0-313-20558-2, LWS/). Greenwood.

William Styron's Lie Down in Darkness: A Screenplay. Richard Yates. LC 85-60434. 208p. 1985. 15.95 (ISBN 0-933277-00-8); pap. 8.95 (ISBN 0-933277-01-6). Ploughshares Bks.

William Styron's Nat Turner: Ten Black Writers Respond. Ed. by John H. Clarke. LC 87-8695. 128p. 1987. Repr. of 1968 ed. lib. bdg. 29.75x (ISBN 0-313-25957-7, CLNT). Greenwood.

William Swaim, Fighting Editor: The Story of O. Henry's Grandfather. Ethel S. Arnett. LC 63-11676. (Illus.). 1963. 6.95x (ISBN 0-911452-02-8). Straughan.

William Sylvis, Pioneer of American Labor. Jonathan P. Grossman. 1972. lib. bdg. 22.00x (ISBN 0-374-93314-6, Octagon). Hippocrene Bks.

William T. Porter & the Spirit of the Times: Study of the Bear School of Humor. Norris W. Yates. Ed. by Richard M. Dorson. LC 77-70630. (International Folklore Ser.). 1977. Repr. of 1957 ed. lib. bdg. 19.00x (ISBN 0-405-10134-1). Ayer Co Pubs.

William T. Wiley. Jeff Kelley. (Illus.). 1983. pap. text ed. 12.00 (ISBN 0-9607452-3-8). Fuller Golden Gal.

William Tell. W. Vosco Call. (Children's Theatre Playscript Ser.). (gr. k-12). 1963. pap. 2.00x (ISBN 0-88020-063-4). Coach Hse.

William Tell. Friedrich von Schiller. LC 84-50434. (Silver Burdett Classics for Kids Ser.). (Illus.). 32p. (gr. 3 up). 1984. 5.96 (ISBN 0-382-06806-8). Silver.

William Tell. Harold G. Shane. Ed. by William Clark. (Hero Legends Bks.). (Illus.). 16p. (gr. 3-5). pap. 24.95 (ISBN 0-89290-078-4, BC15-1); 6 bks. & one cassette incl. Soc for Visual.

William Tell. Freidrich Von Schiller. LC 84-50438. (Silver Burdett Classics for Kids Ser.). 32p. (gr. 3 up). pap. 3.60 (ISBN 0-382-06947-1). Silver.

William Tell see Bride of Messina.

William Temple: An Archbishop for All Seasons. Charles W. Lowry. LC 81-43869. 170p. (Orig.). 1982. lib. bdg. 23.50 (ISBN 0-8191-2355-2); pap. text ed. 8.25 (ISBN 0-8191-2356-0). U Pr of Amer.

William Temple & Christian Social Ethics Today. Alan M. Suggate. 308p. 1987. 35.95 (ISBN 0-567-09455-3, Pub. by T & T Clark Ltd UK). Fortress.

William Temple, Twentieth-Century Christian. Joseph F. Fletcher. LC 63-12587. 1963. text ed. 15.00x (ISBN 0-8401-0741-2). A R Allenson.

William Temple's "Analysis" of Sir Philip Sidney's "Apology for Poetry". William Temple. Ed. & tr. by John Webster. LC 83-22060. (Medieval & Renaissance Texts & Studies: Vol. 32). 192p. 1984. 16.00 (ISBN 0-86698-066-0). Medieval & Renaissance NY.

William Temple's Philosophy of Religion. Owen C. Thomas. LC 61-4400. 1961. 10.00x (ISBN 0-8401-2330-2). A R Allenson.

William the Backwards Skunk. Chuck Jones. (Illus.). (ps up). 1987. 10.95 (ISBN 0-517-56063-1). Crown.

William the Conquerer & the Normans. Robin May. (Life & Times Ser.). (Illus.). 64p. (gr. 7-9). 1985. 12.40 (ISBN 0-531-18010-7, Pub. by Bookwright Pr). Watts.

William the Conqueror. Hilaire Belloc. 153p. 1983. Repr. of 1938 ed. lib. bdg. 35.00. Darby Bks.

William the Conqueror. E. A. Freeman. 59.95 (ISBN 0-8490-1307-0). Gordon Pr.

William the Conqueror: The Norman Impact upon England. David C. Douglas. (English Monarchs Ser.: No. 1). 1964. pap. 10.95 (ISBN 0-520-00350-0). U of Cal Pr.

William the Silent. Frederik Harrison. LC 70-112805. 1970. Repr. of 1897 ed. 26.50 (ISBN 0-8046-1072-X, Pub. by Kennikat). Assoc Faculty Pr.

William the Silent. Ruth Putnam. LC 73-14466. (Heroes of the Nation Ser.). Repr. of 1911 ed. 30.00 (ISBN 0-404-58284-2). AMS Pr.

William the Vehicle King. Laura P. Newton. LC 86-33412. (Illus.). 32p. (ps-2). 1987. 12.95 (ISBN 0-02-768230-7). Bradbury Pr.

William Third & the Defense of European Liberty, 1650-1702. Stephen B. Baxter. LC 75-8476. (Illus.). 1976. Repr. of 1966 ed. lib. bdg. 35.00x (ISBN 0-8371-8161-5, BAWI). Greenwood.

William Troy: Selected Essays. Ed. by Stanley Hyman. 1967. 35.00 (ISBN 0-8135-0553-4). Rutgers U Pr.

William Turnbull: Sculpture & Painting. Richard Morphet. (Illus.). 76p. pap. 6.95 (ISBN 0-900874-65-1). Salem Hse Pubs.

William Turner, Libellus de re Herbaria 1538, the Names of Herbes 1548. Intro. by James Britten et al. ix, 275p. 1965. Repr. of 1548 ed. 22.50x (ISBN 0-318-02524-8, Pub by Brit Mus Nat Hist England). Sabbot-Natural Hist Bks.

William Turner: Tudor Naturalist, Physician & Divine. Whitney R. Jones. 240p. 1988. text ed. 39.95 (ISBN 0-415-00359-8). Routledge Chapman & Hall.

William Tyndale. James F. Mozley. LC 70-109801. (Illus.). 1971. Repr. of 1937 ed. lib. bdg. 35.00x (ISBN 0-8371-4292-X, MOWT). Greenwood.

William Tyndale & the Translation of the English Bible. G. Barnett Smith. 20.00 (ISBN 0-8274-3719-6). R West.

William Vans Murray, Federalist Diplomat: The Shaping of Peace with France, 1797-1801. Peter P. Hill. LC 71-150347. 1971. 24.95x (ISBN 0-8156-0078-X). Syracuse U Pr.

William Vaughn Moody. Martin Halpern. (Twayne's United States Authors Ser). 1964. pap. 8.95x (ISBN 0-8084-0330-3, T64, Twayne). New Coll U Pr.

William Vaughn Moody. David D. Henry. LC 73-14578. 1934. Repr. lib. bdg. 35.00 (ISBN 0-8414-4768-3). Folcroft.

William Vaughn Moody: A Study. David D. Henry. 1978. Repr. of 1934 ed. lib. bdg. 42.50 (ISBN 0-8495-2378-8). Arden Lib.

William W. Holden: North Carolina's Political Enigma. Horace W. Raper. LC 84-2353. (James Sprunt Studies in History & Political Science: Vol. 59). xvi, 376p. 1985. 32.50x (ISBN 0-8078-5060-8). U of NC Pr.

William Wake's Gallican Correspondance & Related Documents, 1716-1731, 2 vols. Leonard Adams. (American University Studies: Series VII: Theology & Religion, Vol. 26). 810p. 1988. Set. text ed. 114.00 (ISBN 0-8204-0436-5). P Lang Pubs.

William Wallace. Andrew Fisher. 160p. 1986. pap. text ed. 12.50 (ISBN 0-85976-154-1, Pub. by John Donald UK). Humanities.

William Wallace Gilchrist, Eighteen Forty-Six to Nineteen Sixteen: A Moving Force in the Musical Life of Philadelphia. Martha F. Schleifer. LC 84-27717. (Composers of North America Ser.: No. 1). 203p. 1985. 17.50 (ISBN 0-8108-1784-5). Scarecrow.

William Walton: Behind the Facade. Susana Walton. (Illus.). 270p. 1988. 22.95 (ISBN 0-19-315156-1). Oxford U Pr.

William Walton: His Life & Music. Neil Tierney. (Illus.). 281p. 1985. 22.50 (ISBN 0-89341-533-2). Longwood Pub Group.

William Wantling: A Biography & Selected Writings. John Pryos. 80p. (Orig.). 1981. pap. 4.50 (ISBN 0-933180-09-8). Spoon Riv Poetry.

William Warren Scranton: Pennsylvania Statesman. George D. Wolf. LC 80-21736. (Keystone Bks.). (Illus.). 220p. 1981. 22.00x (ISBN 0-271-00278-6). Pa St U Pr.

William Wells & Maconaquah, White Rose of the Miamis. Julia M. Gilman. LC 85-60341. 327p. (Orig.). 1985. pap. 10.95 (ISBN 0-9614890-2-2). Jewel Pub Co.

William Wells Brown & Clotelle: A Portrait of the Artist in the First Negro Novel. J. Noel Heermance. LC 75-75450. (Illus.). ix, 203p. 1969. 22.00 (ISBN 0-208-00693-1, Archon); pap. 16.50 (ISBN 0-208-00942-6). Shoe String.

William Wells Brown: Author & Reformer. William E. Farrison. LC 69-19275. (Negro American Biographies & Autobiographies Ser.). 1969. 25.00x (ISBN 0-226-23897-0). U of Chicago Pr.

William Wetmore Story & His Friends, 2 vols. in one. Henry James. LC 69-18460. (Library of American Art Ser.). 1969. Repr. of 1903 ed. lib. bdg. 85.00 (ISBN 0-306-71249-0). Da Capo.

William, Where Are You? Mordicai Gerstein. LC 84-21479. (Fold-Out Bks.). (Illus.). 32p. (ps-1). 1985. 7.95 (ISBN 0-517-55644-8). Crown.

William Whiston. Ed. by Maureen Farrell & I. Bernard Cohen. LC 80-2088. (Development of Science Ser.). (Illus.). 1981. lib. bdg. 32.00x (ISBN 0-405-13854-7). Ayer Co Pubs.

William Whiston: Honest Newtonian. James E. Force. (Illus.). 240p. 1985. 42.50 (ISBN 0-521-26590-8). Cambridge U Pr.

William Wilfred Campbell: Selected Poetry & Essays. Ed. by Laurel Boone. 272p. 1987. text ed. 28.50 (ISBN 0-88920-960-X, Pub. by Wilfrid Laurier U Pr). Humanities.

William Wilkins, Seventeen Seventy-Eight to Eighteen Thirty-Nine. R. W. Liscombe. LC 78-73247. 320p. 1980. 54.50 (ISBN 0-521-22528-0). Cambridge U Pr.

William Winston Seaton on the National Intelligencer. Josephine Seaton. LC 70-125714. (American Journalists Ser.). 1970. Repr. of 1871 ed. 22.00 (ISBN 0-405-01695-6). Ayer Co Pubs.

William Withering & the Foxglove. R. D. Mann et al. 1986. lib. bdg. 135.75 (ISBN 0-85200-950-X, Pub. by MTP Pr England). Kluwer Academic.

William Woods Holden, Firebrand of North Carolina Politics. William C. Harris. LC 87-2699. (Southern Biography Ser.). 328p. 1987. text ed. 35.00 (ISBN 0-8071-1325-5). La State U Pr.

William Wordsworth. Andreas Baumgartner. LC 72-219784. (Ger.). 1897. lib. bdg. 16.00 (ISBN 0-8414-3177-9). Folcroft.

William Wordsworth. Intro. by Harold Bloom. (Modern Critical Views Ser.). 198p. 1985. 24.50 (ISBN 0-87754-613-4). Chelsea Hse.

William Wordsworth. Geoffrey H. Durrant. (British Authors Ser.). 32.50 (ISBN 0-521-07608-0); pap. 10.95 (ISBN 0-521-09584-0). Cambridge U Pr.

William Wordsworth. Ed. by Stephen Gill & Frank Kermode. LC 83-17278. (Oxford Authors Ser.). 1984. 29.95x (ISBN 0-19-254175-7); pap. 10.95x (ISBN 0-19-281333-1). Oxford U Pr.

William Wordsworth. Russell Noyes. (English Authors Ser.). 1972. lib. bdg. 15.95 (ISBN 0-8057-1580-0, Twayne). G K Hall.

William Wordsworth. E. Wordsworth. 1974. Repr. of 1974 ed. 17.45 (ISBN 0-8414-9600-5). Folcroft.

William Wordsworth. Elizabeth Wordsworth. LC 74-16289. (Studies in Wordsworth, No. 29). 1974. lib. bdg. 49.95x (ISBN 0-8383-1800-2). Haskell.

William Wordsworth: A Biographical Sketch. Andrew J. Symington. LC 77-14115. 1974. lib. bdg. 35.00 (ISBN 0-8414-7877-5). Folcroft.

William Wordsworth: A Reference Guide to British Criticism, 1793-1899. Ed. by N. S. Bauer. 1978. lib. bdg. 46.00 (ISBN 0-8161-7828-3, Hall Reference). G K Hall.

William Wordsworth & Annette Vallon. rev. ed. Emile Legouis. Ed. by Pierre Legouis. LC 67-16448. xviii, 176p. 1967. 25.00 (ISBN 0-208-00603-6, Archon). Shoe String.

William Wordsworth & the Age of English Romanticism. William Wordsworth et al. (Illus.). 285p. 1987. text ed. 65.00 (ISBN 0-8135-1273-5); pap. 29.95 (ISBN 0-8135-1274-3). Rutgers U Pr.

William Wordsworth, His Doctrine & Art in Their Historical Relations. 2nd ed. Arthur Beatty. LC 75-28992. Repr. of 1927 ed. 32.50 (ISBN 0-404-14003-3). AMS Pr.

William Wordsworth: His Homes & Haunts. Samuel L. Bensusan. LC 77-10639. 1977. Repr. lib. bdg. 12.50 (ISBN 0-8414-0502-6). Folcroft.

William Wordsworth: How to Know Him. Caleb T. Winchester. LC 76-51362. 1976. lib. bdg. 37.00 (ISBN 0-8414-9610-2). Folcroft.

William Wordsworth of Rydal Mount. Frederika Beatty. LC 74-161730. (Illus.). Repr. of 1939 ed. 24.50 (ISBN 0-404-07927-X). AMS Pr.

William Wordsworth, Seventeen Seventy to Eighteen Fifty. John D. Gordon. LC 73-12439. 1950. lib. bdg. 17.00 (ISBN 0-8414-4406-4). Folcroft.

William Wordsworth, Seventeen Seventy to Nineteen Sixty-Nine. J. Wordsworth. (Chatterton Lectures on an English Poet). 1969. pap. 5.50 (ISBN 0-85672-261-8, Pub. by British Acad). Longwood Pub Group.

William Wordsworth: The Borders of Vision. Jonathan Wordsworth. 1982. pap. 23.95x (ISBN 0-19-812831-2). Oxford U Pr.

William Wordsworth: The Poems, Vol. I. Ed. by William Wordsworth & John Hayden. LC 81-2994. 1072p. 1981. text ed. 57.00t (ISBN 0-300-02751-6); pap. 17.50x (ISBN 0-300-02754-0, YEP-7). Yale U Pr.

William Wordsworth: The Poems, Vol. II. Ed. by William Wordsworth & John Hayden. LC 81-2994. 1104p. 1981. text ed. 57.00t (ISBN 0-300-02752-4); pap. 18.50x (ISBN 0-300-02755-9, YEP-8). Yale U Pr.

William Wordsworth: The Poetry of Grandeur & of Tenderness. David Pirie. 320p. 1982. 35.00x (ISBN 0-416-31300-0, NO. 3651). Routledge Chapman & Hall.

William Wordsworth: The Prelude: a Parallel Text. Ed. by William Wordsworth & J. C. Maxwell. LC 81-3016. 576p. 1981. text ed. 42.00t (ISBN 0-300-02753-2); pap. 13.95x (ISBN 0-300-02756-7). Yale U Pr.

William Wordsworth und die Romantische Paradiese Konzeption. Dorothea Steiner. Ed. by James Hogg. (Romantic Reassessment Ser.). 283p. (Orig., Ger.). 1973. pap. 15.00 (ISBN 0-317-40112-2, Pub. by Salzburg Studies). Longwood Pub Group.

William Wordsworth's Prelude. Intro. by Harold Bloom. (Modern Critical Interpretations Ser.). 172p. 1986. 24.50 (ISBN 0-87754-749-1). Chelsea Hse.

William Wycherly: A Reference Guide. B. Eugene McCarthy. (Reference Guides to Literature Ser.). 1985. lib. bdg. 52.50 (ISBN 0-8161-8184-5, Hall Reference). G K Hall.

William Wyler: A Guide to References & Resources. Sharon Kern. 1984. lib. bdg. 50.00 (ISBN 0-8161-7920-4, Hall Reference). G K Hall.

Williams Collection of East Asian Ceramics. Kamer Aga-Oglu. (Illus.). 152p. 1985. pap. 7.00 (ISBN 0-89558-109-4). Detroit Inst Arts.

Williams Collection of Far Eastern Ceramics, Chinese, Siamese, & Annamese Ceramic Wares: Selected from the Collection of Justice & Mrs. G. M. Williams in the U. of Mich. Museum of Anthropology. Kamer Aga-Oglu. (Special Publications Ser.). (Illus.). 1972. pap. 4.00x. U Mich Mus Anthro.

Williams Collection of Far Eastern Ceramics: Tonnancour Section. Kamer Aga-Oglu. (Special Publications Ser.). (Illus.). 1975. pap. 8.00x (ISBN 0-932206-75-1). U Mich Mus Anthro.

William's Doll. Charlotte Zolotow. LC 70-183173. (Illus.). (ps-3). 1972. 11.95i (ISBN 0-06-027047-0); PLB 11.89 (ISBN 0-06-027048-9). HarpJ.

William's Doll. Charlotte Zolotow. LC 70-183173. (Trophy Picture Bks.). (Illus.). 32p. (ps-3). 1985. pap. 3.95 (ISBN 0-06-443067-7, Trophy). HarpJ.

Williams Introduction to the Profession of Medical Technology. 4th ed. David S. Lindberg et al. LC 84-912. (Illus.). 114p. 1984. pap. 9.50 (ISBN 0-8121-0937-6). Lea & Febiger.

Williams Manuscript of George Herbert's Poems. George Herbert. Ed. by Amy Charles. LC 76-54153. 1977. 50.00x (ISBN 0-8201-1286-0). Schol Facsimilies.

Williams Obstetrics. 17th ed. Jack A. Pritchard et al. (Illus.). 992p. 1984. 69.95 (ISBN 0-8385-9733-5). Appleton & Lange.

Williams Obstetrics: Study Guide. Charles R. Beckmann et al. 326p. 1985. pap. 29.95 (ISBN 0-8385-9735-1). Appleton & Lange.

Williams Pantycelyn. Glyn T. Hughes. (Writer of Wales Ser.). 180p. 1983. pap. text ed. 8.50x (ISBN 0-7083-0840-6, Pub. by U of Wales). Humanities.

Williams-Siegel Documentary: Including Williams' Poetry Talked About by Eli Siegel & William Carlos Williams Present & Talking: 1952. Eli Siegel. Ed. by Martha Baird & Ellen Reiss. LC 70-100610. 1970. 6.95 (ISBN 0-910492-12-3); pap. 4.95 (ISBN 0-910492-25-5). Definition.

Williams Site: A Frontier Mogollon Village in West-Central New Mexico. Watson Smith. LC 73-86928. (Peabody Museum Papers: Vol. 39, No. 2). 1973. pap. 10.00x (ISBN 0-87365-190-1). Peabody Harvard.

Williams-Sonoma Cookbook & Guide to Kitchenware. Chuck Williams. LC 85-18366. (Illus.). 304p. 1986. 19.95 (ISBN 0-394-54411-0). Random.

William's Vision of Piers the Plowman: Text A. Ed. by W. W. Skeat. (EETS OS Ser.: Vol. 28). Repr. of 1867 ed. 15.00 (ISBN 0-8115-3348-4). Kraus Repr.

William's Vision of Piers the Plowman: Text B, Pt. II. Ed. by W. W. Skeat. (EETS OS Ser.: Vol. 38). Repr. of 1869 ed. 17.00 (ISBN 0-8115-3349-2). Kraus Repr.

William's Window: An Introduction to Shakespeare's Plays for Young People. Marina Stockdale. 36p. (gr. 3-8). 1983. pap. 2.00 (ISBN 0-88680-209-1). I E Clark.

Williamsburg. 1982. 17.50 (ISBN 0-686-76279-7). Feldheim.

Williamsburg Art of Cookery. Helen Bullock. LC 43-6700. (Illus.). 276p. (Orig.). 1938. leather 20.00 (ISBN 0-910412-31-6); hardcover 7.95 (ISBN 0-910412-30-8). Williamsburg.

Williamsburg Blank Book Assortment: A New Universe Product Published with Colonial Williamsburg. 128p. Date not set. 3-piece bdg., leatherette spine 4.95 (ISBN 1-55550-765-4). Universe.

Williamsburg Christmas. Donna Sheppard. LC 80-7487. (Illus.). 84p. 1980. 11.95 (ISBN 0-03-057639-3). H Holt & Co.

Williamsburg Christmas. Donna C. Sheppard. LC 80-17179. (World of Williamsburg Ser.). (Illus.). 78p. (Orig.). 1980. pap. 4.95 (ISBN 0-87935-054-7). Williamsburg.

Williamsburg Collection of Antique Furnishings. Colonial Williamsburg Foundation Staff. LC 73-86811. (Decorative Art Ser). (Illus.). 120p. (Orig.). 1973. pap. 6.95 (ISBN 0-87935-017-2). Williamsburg.

Williamsburg Cookbook. rev. ed. Letha Booth & Joan P. Dutton. (Illus.). 1976. 13.50 (ISBN 0-03-086704-5, Pub by Williamsburg). H Holt & Co.

Williamsburg Cookbook. enl. & rev. ed. Letha Booth & Joan P. Dutton. LC 75-2328. (Illus.). 172p. (Orig.). 1975. pap. 8.95 (ISBN 0-910412-92-8). Williamsburg.

Williamsburg Hornbook. Felicity Wise. LC 73-16301. (Illus.). 128p. 1973. pap. 9.95 (ISBN 0-8117-1203-6). Stackpole.

Williamsburg Household. Joan Anderson. LC 87-33803. 48p. (gr. 3-6). 1988. 15.95 (ISBN 0-89919-516-4, Pub. by Clarion). Ticknor & Fields.

Williamsburg Songbook. John A. Edmunds. LC 64-20095. (Colonial Williamsburg). (Illus.). pap. 28.90 (ISBN 0-8357-9820-8, 2016516). Bks Demand UMI.

Williamson Reports: A Study. Sarah K. Vann. LC 75-149992. 212p. 1971. 17.50 (ISBN 0-8108-0375-5). Scarecrow.

Williamson Reports of Nineteen Twenty-One & Nineteen Twenty-Three: Including Training for Library Work & Training for Library Service. Charles C. Williamson. LC 78-25204. 276p. 1971. 21.00 (ISBN 0-8108-0417-4). Scarecrow.

Williamsport: Frontier Village to Regional Center. Robert H. Larson et al. LC 84-21930. (Illus.). 208p. 1984. 22.95 (ISBN 0-89781-110-0). Windsor Pubns Inc.

Willick O'Pirliebraes. David Sinclair. 1983. 30.00x (ISBN 0-907618-00-6, Pub. by Macdonald Pub UK). State Mutual Bk.

Willie. Willie Nelson. 1988. 18.95. S&S.

Willie: A Girl from a Town Called Dallas. Willie N. Lewis. LC 83-18081. (Illus.). 152p. 1984. 12.95 (ISBN 0-89096-175-1). Tex A&M Univ Pr.

Willie & Dwike: An American Profile. William Zinsser. LC 83-48843. 176p. 1984. 13.45i (ISBN 0-06-015275-3, HarpT). Har-Row.

Willie & Varaz: Memories of My Friend William Saroyan. Varaz Samuelian. LC 85-60101. (Illus.). 72p. 1985. 10.95. Panorama West.

Willie Bea & the Time the Martians Landed. Virginia Hamilton. LC 83-1659. 224p. (gr. 5-9). 1983. reinforced 13.00 (ISBN 0-688-02390-8). Greenwillow.

Willie Blows a Mean Horn. Ianthe Thomas. LC 74-2637. (Illus.). 24p. (gr. k-3). 1981. 8.70i (ISBN 0-06-026106-4); PLB 10.89 (ISBN 0-06-026107-2). HarpJ.

Willie Boy: A Desert Manhunt. Harry W. Lawton. 1976. pap. 8.50 (ISBN 0-939046-28-8). Malki Mus Pr.

Willie Geary "Bunk" Johnson: The New Iberia Years. Austin M. Sonnier, Jr. LC 76-16330. 1977. pap. 5.00 (ISBN 0-8008-1122-4, Crescendo). Taplinger.

Willie in the Big World: An Adventure with Numbers. Sven Nordqvist. LC 85-15307. (Illus.). 32p. (ps-3). 1986. 11.75 (ISBN 0-688-06142-7); lib. bdg. 11.88 (ISBN 0-688-06143-5). Morrow.

Willie Mays: Baseball Superstar. Sam Epstein & Beryl Epstein. LC 74-20954. (Garrard Sports Library). (Illus.). 96p. (gr. 3-6). 1975. PLB 7.12 (ISBN 0-8116-6671-9). Garrard.

Willie Mosconi on Pocket Billiards. Willie Mosconi. (Illus.). 1954. pap. 4.95 (ISBN 0-517-50779-X). Crown.

Willie Munzenberg: A Political Biography. Babette Gross. Tr. by Marian Jackson. 337p. 1974. 12.50 (ISBN 0-87013-173-7). Mich St U Pr.

Willie Nelson: Country Outlaw. Lola Scobey. (Orig.). 1982. pap. 2.95 (ISBN 0-89083-936-0). Zebra.

Willie the Plain Pint. O'Heithur. 127p. (Orig.). 1977. pap. 7.95 (ISBN 0-85342-507-8, Pub. by Mercier Pr Ireland). Irish Bks Media.

Willie the Slowpoke. Rose Greydanus. (Illus.). 32p. (gr. k-2). 1980. PLB 5.41 (ISBN 0-89375-394-7); pap. 1.50 (ISBN 0-89375-294-0); cassette 8.95. Troll Assocs.

Willie the Squowse. Ted Allan. (Illus.). (gr. 2 up). 1978. 8.95 (ISBN 0-8038-8086-3). Hastings.

Willie the Weenie Whiner. George C. Anderheggen. (Illus.). 20p. (Orig.). (gr. 5 up). 1983. 3.95 (ISBN 0-910717-01-X). Bookling Pubs.

Willie Visits Tulip Time. Lory Bertsch. (Illus.). 40p. (gr. k up). 1983. 4.50 (ISBN 0-682-49980-3). Exposition-Phoenix.

Willie Weirdie Zaps Al Jaffee. Al Jaffee. 1983. pap. 2.25 (ISBN 0-451-12279-8, Sig). NAL.

Willie's Whizmobile. Irwin Shapiro. LC 72-10559. (Garrard Venture Ser.). (Illus.). 40p. (gr. k-3). 1973. PLB 6.69 (ISBN 0-8116-6726-X); pap. 1.19 (9030). Garrard.

Willing & Unwilling: A Study in the Philosophy of Arthur Schopenhauer. Julian Young. 1987. lib. bdg. 39.50 (ISBN 90-247-3556-4, Pub. by Martinus Nijhoff Netherlands). Kluwer Academic.

Willing Dead. Patricia A. Stewart & Edna H. Maples. (Murder Mystery Parties Ser.). (Illus.). 52p. 1984. 8.00 (ISBN 0-317-31549-8). Univ Games.

Willing to Die, 3 vols. Joseph S. Le Fanu. Ed. by Devendra P. Varma. LC 76-5280. (Collected Works Ser.). 1977. Repr. of 1873 ed. Set. 79.50x (ISBN 0-405-09242-3); Vol. 1. 26.50x (ISBN 0-405-09243-1); Vol. 2. 26.50x (ISBN 0-405-09244-X); Vol. 3. 26.50x (ISBN 0-405-09245-8). Ayer Co Pubs.

Willing to Live, Ready to Die. Georgetta Bidwell-Voit. LC 87-90158. 159p. 1988. 13.95 (ISBN 0-533-07575-0). Vantage.

Willing Workers: The Work Ethics in Japan, England, & the United States. Tamotsu Sengoku. Tr. by Koichi Ezaki & Yuko Ezaki. LC 85-9552. (Illus.). xv, 152p. 1985. lib. bdg. 35.00 (ISBN 0-89930-137-1, SWK/, Quorum). Greenwood.

Willis. James Marshall. LC 74-5259. (Illus.). (gr. k-3). 1974. PLB 12.95 (ISBN 0-395-19494-6). HM.

Willis E. Lamb, Jr. A Festschrift on the Occasion of His 65th Birthday. Ed. by D. Ter Haar & M. O. Scully. (Physics Reports Reprint Book: Vol. 3). 518p. 1979. 100.00 (ISBN 0-444-85253-0, North Holland). Elsevier.

Willis Haviland Carrier, Father of Air-Conditioning. Margaret Ingels. LC 72-5056. (Technology & Society Ser.). (Illus.). 178p. 1972. Repr. of 1952 ed. 15.00 (ISBN 0-405-04708-8). Ayer Co Pubs.

Willis M. Tate: Views & Interviews. Ed. by Johnnie M. Grimes. LC 77-25103. (Illus.). 212p. 1978. 12.50 (ISBN 0-87074-163-2). SMU Press.

Willis R. Whitney, General Electric & the Origins of U. S. Industrial Research. George Wise. LC 84-27484. (Illus.). 400p. 1985. 29.00x (ISBN 0-231-06044-0). Columbia U Pr.

Williston on Contracts: 1957-1977, 22 vols. 3rd ed. Walter H. Jaeger. LC 59-558. 1957. Vols. 1-18. 1320.00 (ISBN 0-686-14488-0). Lawyers Co-Op.

Williston on Sales: 1973-74, 3 vols. 4th ed. Alphonse M. Squillante & John R. Fonseca. LC 73-88236. 1973-74. 199.50 (ISBN 0-686-14489-9); Suppl. 1987. 45.00; Suppl. 1988. 49.00. Lawyers Co-Op.

Willits Scrapbook: The Way it Was 1958-1974. Lois Mahan. LC 78-108189. 1975. 4.00 (ISBN 0-932820-00-X). Marco Polo.

Williwaw. Gore Vidal. LC 83-45855. Repr. of 1946 ed. 23.50 (ISBN 0-404-20276-4, PS3543). AMS Pr.

Williwaw. Gore Vidal. 176p. 1986. pap. 4.95 (ISBN 0-345-33233-4). Ballantine.

Willkommen in Washington. Eugenia M. Horstman. (Illus.). 36p. (Orig., Ger.). 1980. pap. 4.95 (ISBN 0-936478-02-0). Interpretive Pubns.

Willmaker. 2nd ed. Legisoft. LC 84-63151. (Illus.). 202p. (Orig.). 1986. pap. 49.95 incl. diskette (ISBN 0-87337-026-0). Nolo Pr.

Willmaker Commodore: Use Your Computer to Prepare & Update Your Own Valid Will. 202p. incl. disk 39.95 (ISBN 0-917316-98-3). Nolo Pr.

Willmaker: Use Your Computer to Prepare & Update Your Own Valid Will. 200p. 1988. Macintosh. 59.95 (ISBN 0-87337-065-1); IBM & Compatibles. 59.95 (ISBN 0-87337-063-5); Apple II. 59.95 (ISBN 0-87337-064-3); Commodore. 49.95 (ISBN 0-87337-066-X). Nolo Pr.

WILLMASTER: California Will Drafting System Manual. Philip C. Stork. 595p. 1985. looseleaf 120.00 (ES-37710). Cal Cont Ed Bar.

Willmington's Book of Bible Lists. H. L. Willmington. 240p. (Orig.). 1987. pap. text ed. 6.95 (ISBN 0-8423-8803-6). Tyndale.

Willmington's Guide to the Bible. H. L. Willmington. 1009p. 1981. 29.95 (ISBN 0-8423-8804-4). Tyndale.

Willmington's Survey of the Old Testament. Harold L. Willmington. 624p. 1987. 21.95 (ISBN 0-88207-824-0). Victor Bks.

Willo Mancifoot (and the Mugga Killa Whomps) Valerie H. Damon. Ed. by Dave Damon. LC 83-50739. (Illus.). (gr. 2-6). 1985. 14.95 (ISBN 0-932356-07-9); ltd. art ed. 100.00 (ISBN 0-932356-08-7). Star Pubns Mo.

Willobie His Avisa: The True Picture of a Modest Maide, and of a Chaste and Constant Wife. 1966. Repr. of 1635 ed. 30.50 (ISBN 0-8337-3809-7). B Franklin.

Willoughby Lake: Legends & Legacies. Harriet F. Fisher. Ed. by James Hayford. (Illus.). 114p. (Orig.). 1988. pap. 12.50 (ISBN 0-9610860-3-3). Orleans.

Willoughby Wallaby. (Sing-a-Story Ser.). 24p. 1987. pap. 2.95 (ISBN 0-553-15576-8). Bantam.

Willoughby Wallaby: Sing-A-Story. 24p. 1987. pap. 5.95 (ISBN 0-553-45903-1). Bantam.

Willow. Wayland Drew. 1988. pap. 4.95 (ISBN 0-345-35195-9, Del Rey). Ballantine.

Willow. Linda L. Miller. (Tapestry Ser.: No. 51). (Orig.). 1984. pap. 2.95 (ISBN 0-671-52357-0). PB.

Willow. Joan D. Vinge. 128p. (gr. 5-9). 1988. lib. bdg. 5.99 (ISBN 0-394-99573-2, BYR); pap. 2.95 (ISBN 0-394-89573-8, BYR). Random.

Willow & the Brownies. Emily James. LC 87-62953. (Willow Mini-Storybooks). (Illus.). 24p. (ps-3). 1988. pap. 1.25 (ISBN 0-394-89801-X, BYR). Random.

Willow Basketry of the Amana Colonies: History of Folk Art, Six Willow Basket Patterns. Joanna E. Schanz. Ed. by John Zug & Scott Elledge. LC 86-61010. 105p. (Orig.). 1986. pap. 8.95 (ISBN 0-941016-36-6). Penfield.

Willow Creek Home. Janice Shefelman. (Stories for Young Americans Ser.). (Illus.). 128p. (gr. 5-7). 1985. 8.95 (ISBN 0-89015-535-6). Eakin Pr.

Willow Farm Pickle Book. John McKinney. LC 73-89793. 1973. avail.; pap. 3.95 (ISBN 0-89016-000-7). Lightning Tree.

Willow Finds a Baby. Gail Herman. LC 87-63034. (Willow Mini-Storybooks Ser.). (Illus.). 24p. (ps-3). 1988. pap. 1.25 (ISBN 0-394-89865-6, BYR). Random.

Willow Game. Designed by Greg Costikyan. 1988. 29.95 (ISBN 0-312-93082-8). Tor Bks.

Willow Hill. Phyllis A. Whitney. 200p. (YA) (RL 7). 1975. pap. 1.50 (ISBN 0-451-09535-9, W9535, Sig). NAL.

Willow Maiden. Meghan Collins. LC 85-1533. (Illus.). 40p. (gr. k up). 1985. 11.95 (ISBN 0-8037-0217-5, 01160-350); PLB 11.89 (ISBN 0-8037-0218-3). Dial Bks Young.

Willow Maiden. Meghan Collins. LC 85-1533. (Pied Piper Paperback Ser.). (Illus.). 40p. (gr. k up). 1988. pap. 4.95 (ISBN 0-8037-0558-1, 0481-140). Dial Bks Young.

Willow, Oak & Rye: Basket Traditions in Pennsylvania. Jeannette Lasansky. LC 79-2709. (Illus.). 1979. pap. 12.50 (ISBN 0-271-00229-8, Keystone Bks). Pa St U Pr.

Willow Pattern: A Judge Dee Mystery. Robert Van Gulik. 176p. 1981. pap. 2.95 rack-size (ISBN 0-684-17317-4, ScribT). Scribner.

Willow Pattern China: Collectors Guide. rev. ed. Veryl M. Worth & Louise M. Loehr. Ed. by Randel Westley. (Illus.). 120p. (Orig.). 1986. pap. 11.95. H S Worth.

Willow Pattern China: Price Guide. 3rd rev. ed. Veryl M. Worth & Louise M. Loehr. 20p. (Orig.). 1986. pap. 3.50. H S Worth.

Willow Pool. Catherine Bradbury & Octavia Williams. (Applebury Tales: Stories for Young Nature Lovers Ser.). (Illus.). 30p. (gr. 4). 1988. 6.95 (Pub. by Dinosaur UK). Parkwest Pubns.

Willow Run. Glendon F. Swarthout. LC 74-26210. 248p. 1983. Repr. of 1943 ed. 27.50 (ISBN 0-404-58478-0). AMS Pr.

Willow Run: Study of Industrialization & Cultural Inadequacy. Carl L. Julliard & Edson Stermer. Ed. by Leon Stein. LC 77-70486. (Work Ser.). (Illus.). 1977. Repr. of 1952 ed. lib. bdg. 36.50x (ISBN 0-405-10158-9). Ayer Co Pubs.

Willow Source Book. Allan Varney & Eric Goldberg. 1988. pap. 10.95 (ISBN 0-8125-5802-2, Dist. by St Martin's Pr & Warner Pub Servs). Tor Bks.

Willow Sourcebook. Allen Varney. 1988. 24.95. Tor Bks.

Willow Sourcebook. Allen Varney & Eric Goldberg. (Illus.). 104p. Date not set. 10.95 (ISBN 0-312-93083-6). Tor Bks.

Willow: The Picture Storybook. Cathy West. (Illus.). 32p. (ps-3). 1988. lib. bdg. 5.99 (ISBN 0-394-99750-6, BYR); pap. 1.95 (ISBN 0-394-89750-1, BYR). Random.

Willow: The Storybook Based on the Movie. Adapted by Cathy E. Dubowski. (Illus.). 64p. (gr. k-5). 1988. lib. bdg. 8.99 (ISBN 0-394-99574-0, BYR); pap. 7.95 (ISBN 0-394-89574-6, BYR). Random.

Willow Water. Erika Mumford. 120p. (Orig.). 1988. pap. 7.95 (ISBN 0-9619960-1-3). Every Other Thursday.

Willow Wind. Arthur Sze. (Illus.). 72p. 1981. pap. 6.00 (ISBN 0-940510-00-6). Tooth of Time.

Willow Wind. Lynda Trent. (Tapestry Romance Ser.: No. 28). 320p. (Orig.). 1983. pap. 2.95 (ISBN 0-671-47574-6). PB.

Willow Wind Farm: Betsy's Story. Anne Pellowski. (Illus.). 176p. (gr. 9-12). 1981. 8.95 (ISBN 0-399-20781-3, Philomel). Putnam Pub Group.

Willow Work. Mary Butcher. (Illus.). 64p. 1987. 16.95 (ISBN 0-85219-610-5, Pub. by Batsford England). David & Charles.

Willowbrook Wars: A Decade of Struggle for Social Justice. Sheila M. Rothman & David J. Rothman. LC 84-47623. 480p. 1984. 27.45i (ISBN 0-06-015234-6, HarpT). Har-Row.

Willowby's World of Fluffits. Cloud Ten Creations Staff. 1984. incl. stickers 8.95 (ISBN 0-317-47377-8). Trillium Pr.

Willowby's World of Fluffits. Christine W. Vrooman. (Willowby's World Ser.). (Illus.). 56p. (Orig.). (gr. 2-6). 1984. pap. 8.95 with stickers incl. (ISBN 0-910349-02-9). Cloud Ten.

Willowby's World of Unicorns. Cloud Ten Creations Staff. 1982. incl. stickers 8.95; tchr's manual 4.00 (ISBN 0-89824-169-3). Trillium Pr.

Willowby's World of Unicorns. Christine W. Vrooman. Ed. by Sandy Kane & Peggy Ogden. (Willowby's World Ser.). (Illus.). 56p. (gr. 2-6). 1982. pap. 8.95 with stickers incl. Cloud Ten.

Willowby's World of Unicorns "Activity Book". Greg Gibbs. (Willowby's World Ser.). 14p. (Orig.). (gr. 2-6). 1984. pap. 4.00x (ISBN 0-910349-03-7). Cloud Ten.

Willowcat & the Chimney Sweep. Sara G. Harrell. LC 80-81702. (Illus.). 28p. (gr. k-3). 1980. 6.95 (ISBN 0-931948-07-X). Peachtree Pubs.

Willowhole Cemetery Madison County Texas. Allie M. Whitley & Mary Collie-Cooper. (Illus.). 61p. (Orig.). 1981. pap. 6.50 sprial binding (ISBN 0-943553-00-8). Collie-Cooper Ent.

Willowood. Mollie Hardwick. 288p. 1981. pap. 2.95 (ISBN 0-445-04680-5). Fawcett.

Willow's End. Dale R. Todd. LC 84-91321. 144p. 1985. 10.95 (ISBN 0-533-06414-7). Vantage.

Willpower Guide: Never Give Up. William Eddy. LC 88-6486. 100p. (Orig.). (YA) (gr. 12). 1988. pap. 7.95 (ISBN 0-945649-17-7). Rise Personal Dev.

Willpower: How to Gain It & Maintain It--A Simple Building Block Approach. Sandy S. Anderson & Robert G. Anderson. LC 87-70328. (Illus.). 96p. (Orig.). 1987. pap. 7.95 (ISBN 0-9617964-0-5, 964A). Calif Dream Pubns.

Willpower Is Not Enough: Understanding & Overcoming Addictions & Obsessive Behavior. Arnold Washton & Donna Boundy. 1988. 17.95 (ISBN 0-06-015996-0). Har-Row.

Wills. 2nd ed. Thomas E. Atkinson. (Hornbook Ser.). 975p. 1953. 23.95. West Pub.

Wills: Adaptable to Courses Utilizing Mechem & Atkinson's Casebook on Wills & Administration. Casenotes Publishing Co., Inc. Staff. Ed. by Norman S. Goldenberg et al. (Legal Briefs Ser.). 1980. pap. write for info. (ISBN 0-87457-144-8, 1220). Casenotes Pub.

Wills: Adaptable to Courses Utilizing Mennell's Casebook on California Decedents' Estates. Casenotes Publishing Co., Inc. Staff. Ed. by Norman S. Goldenberg et al. (Legal Briefs Ser.). 1976. pap. write for info. (ISBN 0-87457-145-6, 1221). Casenotes Pub.

Wills among the Norwich Enrolled Deeds: 1286-1508 see **Scotland's Border Country.**

Wills & Administrations of Elizabeth City County, Virginia, 1688-1800. Blanche A. Chapman. LC 80-68127. 198p. 1980. Repr. of 1941 ed. 15.00 (ISBN 0-8063-0909-1). Genealog Pub.

Wills & Administrations of Southampton County, Virginia, 1749-1800. Blanche A. Chapman. LC 80-68126. 208p. 1980. Repr. of 1947 ed. 15.00 (ISBN 0-8063-0907-5). Genealog Pub.

Wills & Administrations of Surry County, Virginia, 1671-1750. Eliza T. Davis. LC 80-67936. 184p. 1980. Repr. of 1955 ed. 15.00 (ISBN 0-8063-0899-0). Genealog Pub.

Wills & Estate Planning for Oregon. 3nd ed. Rees Johnson. (Illus.). 178p. 1987. pap. 5.95 (ISBN 0-88908-820-9). ISC Pr.

Wills & Estate Records of McMinn Co. Tennessee, 1820-1870. Reba B. Boyer. 202p. 1983. pap. 25.00 (ISBN 0-89308-328-3). Southern Hist Pr.

Wills & Intestacies. J. Comyn & R. Johnson. LC 78-92109. 1970. pap. text ed. 8.50 (ISBN 0-08-006690-9). Pergamon.

Wills & Inventories, from the Register of the Commissary of Bury St. Edmund's & the Archdeacon of Sudbury. Bury St. Edmund's Commissary Court Staff. Ed. by Samuel Tymms. (Camden Society, London. Publications. First Ser.: No. 49). Repr. of 1850 ed. 37.00 (ISBN 0-404-50149-4). AMS Pr.

Wills & Inventories from the Registers of the Commissary of Bury St. Edmunds. Ed. by Samuel Tymms. Repr. of 1850 ed. 37.00 (ISBN 0-384-62225-9). Johnson Repr.

Wills & Trusts Attorney's Record. 32p. 1983. 1.85x (95966-8). P-H.

Wills & Trusts in a Nutshell. Robert L. Mennell. LC 79-11590. (Nutshell Ser.). 392p. 1979. pap. text ed. 9.95 (ISBN 0-8299-2042-0). West Pub.

Wills & Wealth in Medieval Genoa, 1150-1250. Steven Epstein. (Harvard Historical Studies: No. 103). (Illus.). 288p. 1985. text ed. 22.50x (ISBN 0-674-95356-8). Harvard U Pr.

Wills & Where to Find Them (in Great Britain) Jeremy S. Gibson. LC 74-2775. (Illus.). 210p. 1974. 15.00 (ISBN 0-8063-0619-X). Genealog Pub.

Wills Before Eighteen Fifty-Eight. 1987. 30.00x (Pub. by Birmingham Midland Soc UK). State Mutual Bk.

Wills Book of Excellence: The Olympics. Ed. by M. J. Akbar. (Illus.). 250p. 1984. text ed. 40.00x (ISBN 0-86131-521-9, Pub. by Orient Longman Ltd India). Apt Bks.

Will's Boy: A Memoir. Wright Morris. 208p. 1982. pap. 6.95 (ISBN 0-14-006201-7). Penguin.

Wills, Death & Taxes: Basic Principles for Protecting Estates. Lawrence W. Dixon. LC 77-21380. (Quality Paperback: No. 228). 184p. (Orig.). 1977. pap. 1.00 (ISBN 0-8226-0228-8). Littlefield.

Wills, Estates & Trusts. (Information Services Ser.). Date not set. price not set ring bounc l'leaf. P-H.

Wills for Alberta. 7th ed. Cheryl Gottselig. 128p. 1987. 6.50 (ISBN 0-88908-246-4). ISC Pr.

Wills for British Columbia. 12th ed. Steven G. Wong. 112p. 1987. 6.50 (ISBN 0-88908-194-8). ISC Pr.

Wills for Ontario. 9th ed. Laurence C. Caroe. 100p. 1986. 5.95 (ISBN 0-88908-366-5). ISC Pr.

Wills for Washington. 4th ed. D. Van Fredenberg. 96p. 1987. pap. 6.95 (ISBN 0-88908-728-8). ISC Pr.

Wills from Doctors' Commons. Ed. by John G. Nichols & John Bruce. (Camden Society, London. Publications, First Ser.: No. 83). Repr. of 1863 ed. 19.00 (ISBN 0-404-50183-4). AMS Pr.

Wills from Doctors' Commons, 1495-1695. Canterbury England Prerogative Court Staff. 1863. 19.00 (ISBN 0-384-07345-X). Johnson Repr.

Wills (NY) Louis A Kass. 125p. 1979. 6.00 (ISBN 0-87526-247-3). Gould.

Wills of Early New York Jews, Seventeen Hundred Four to Seventeen Ninety-Nine. Ed. by Leo Hershkowitz. (Studies in American Jewish History: No. 4). (Illus.). 1967. 20.00 (ISBN 0-911934-17-0). Am Jewish Hist Soc.

Wills of Richmond County, Virginia, 1699-1800. Robert K. Headley, Jr. LC 83-80081. 220p. 1983. 20.00 (ISBN 0-8063-1021-9). Genealog Pub.

Wills of the Archdeaconry of Sudbury, 1630-35. Nesta Evans. (Suffolk Record Society Ser.: No. 30). 1987. 32.00 (ISBN 0-317-66637-1, Pub. by Boy & Brew). Longwood Pub Group.

Wills of the Archdeaconry of Suffolk, 1620-24. Marion Allen. (Suffolk Records Society Ser.: No. 29). 1987. 36.00 (ISBN 0-85115-492-1, Pub. by Boydell & Brewer). Longwood Pub Group.

Wills of the County of Essex, England, 1558-1565, Vol. 1. F. G. Emmison. LC 82-80974. (Illus.). 369p. lib. bdg. 43.75 (ISBN 0-915156-51-2). Natl Genealogical.

Wills of the U. S. Presidents. Herbert R. Collins & David B. Weaver. LC 75-32100. (Illus.). 1976. 29.95 (ISBN 0-916164-01-2). Stravon.

Wills of Westmoreland County, Virginia, 1654-1800. Augusta B. Fothergill. 238p. (Orig.). 1982. pap. 25.00 (ISBN 0-89308-323-2). Southern Hist Pr.
Wills Probate Procedure for Manitoba & Saskatchewan. 3rd ed. Ron Kruzeniski & Jane Gordon. 81p. 5.95 (ISBN 0-88908-510-2). ISC Pr.
Wills, Probate, Trusts & Decendents Estates: Text & Worksheet. David Crump. (Paralegal Studies Ser.). 60p. (Orig.). 1987. pap. text ed. 7.50 (ISBN 0-916081-12-5). J Marshall Pub Co.
Wills, Trust & Gifts, Vol. 7. Charles A. DeGrandpre. (New Hampshire Practice Ser.). 1987. 39.50. Equity Pub NH.
Wills, Trusts & Estate Administration for the Paralegal. 2nd ed. Dennis R. Hower. 853p. 1984. text ed. 43.25 (ISBN 0-314-85314-6). West Pub.
Wills, Trusts & Estate Planning - Law & Taxation, Cases & Materials. Joseph M. Dodge. (American Casebook Ser.). 707p. 1988. text ed. 34.95 (ISBN 0-314-37038-2). West Pub.
Wills, Trusts & Estates. 3rd ed. Jesse Dukeminier & Stanley M. Johanson. LC 83-82694. 1140p. 1984. text ed. 37.00 (ISBN 0-316-19514-6). Little.
Wills, Trusts & Estates, Including Taxation & Future Interests: Student Edition. William M. McGovern, Jr. et al. (Hornbook Ser.). 924p. 1988. text ed. write for info. (ISBN 0-314-36114-6). West Pub.
Wills, Trusts, & Future Interests: An Introduction to Estate Planning Cases & Materials. William M. McGovern, Jr. LC 82-20034. (American Casebook Ser.). 680p. 1982. text ed. 28.95 (ISBN 0-314-68828-5). West Pub.
Wills, Trusts & Gifts, Vol. 7. Charles A. DeGrandpre. (New Hampshire Practice Ser.). 500p. 1986. 41.00; 1987 supp. 10.00. Equity Pub NH.
Wills, Trusts Forms. (Information Services Ser.). Date not set. price not set ring bound l'leaf. P-H.
Will's Wonder Book see Louisa's Wonder Book: An Unknown Alcott Juvenile.
Willy, a Story of Water. J. Spar. LC 68-56819. (Illus.). 32p. (gr. 2-3). 1968. PLB 9.95 (ISBN 0-87783-051-7); pap. 3.94 deluxe ed (ISBN 0-87783-117-3); cassette o.s.i. 7.94x (ISBN 0-87783-233-1). Oddo.
Willy Bear. Mildred Kantrowitz. LC 80-15295. (Illus.). 40p. (ps-1). 1980. Repr. of 1976 ed. 7.95 (ISBN 0-02-749790-9, Four Winds). Macmillan.
Willy Brandt. Tom Viola. (World Leaders--Past & Present Ser.). (Illus.). 112p. (gr. 5 up). 1988. lib. bdg. 16.95 (ISBN 0-87754-512-X). Chelsea Hse.
Willy on Wheels. Sherry Howell. (Illus.). 63p. (Orig.). (gr. k-4). 1986. pap. 2.95 (ISBN 0-931563-05-4). Wishing Rm.
Willy Remembers. Irvin Faust. 256p. 1977. pap. 1.25 (ISBN 0-685-25025-3, 10405, Bard). Avon.
Willy the Champ. Anthony Browne. LC 85-10053. (Illus.). 32p. (ps-3). 1986. 7.95 (ISBN 0-394-87907-4); lib. bdg. 9.99 (ISBN 0-394-97907-9). Knopf.
Willy the Wimp. Anthony Browne. LC 84-14320. (Illus.). 32p. (ps-3). 1985. 7.95 (ISBN 0-394-87061-1); lib. bdg. 9.99 (ISBN 0-394-97061-6). Knopf.
Willys Dream Kit. Jan Novak. LC 84-25321. 320p. 1985. 19.95 (ISBN 0-15-196766-0). HarBraceJ.
Willys Model MA Prototype Jeep: TM-10-1103. Willys-Overland Motors, Inc. Ed. by Dan R. Post. LC 79-185933. (Illus.). 128p. 1971. pap. 12.95 (ISBN 0-911160-45-0). Post-Era.
Willy's Story. John C. Biardo. LC 85-80436. (Illus.). 32p. (gr. 3-6). 1986. cancelled 9.95 (ISBN 0-933181-01-9). Elmwood Park Pub.
Wilma Rudolph. Tom Biracree. (American Women of Achievement Ser.). (Illus.). 112p. (gr. 5 up). 1988. lib. bdg. 16.95x (ISBN 1-55546-675-3). Chelsea Hse.
Wilma Rudolph. Tom Biracree. (American Women of Achievement Ser.). (Illus.). 112p. (Orig.). (YA) (gr. 7-12). 1989. pap. 9.95 (ISBN 0-7910-0217-9). Chelsea Hse.
Wilma Rudolph on Track. Wilma Rudolph. (gr. 4-9). pap. cancelled (ISBN 0-671-33064-0). Wanderer Bks.
Wilma the Elephant. Erwin Moser. Tr. by Joel Agee. LC 86-1145. (gr. 3-8). 1986. 9.95 (ISBN 0-915361-45-0, Dist. by Watts). Adama Pubs Inc.
Wilmer Atkinson: An Autobiography. (American Newspapermen Ser.: 1790-1933). 1976. 21.50x. Beekman Pubs.
Wilmer, Cutler & Pickering Manual on Litigation Support Databases. Deanne C. Siemer & Douglas S. Land. LC 86-34020. 416p. 1987. 95.00 (ISBN 0-471-85977-X, Pub. by Wiley Law Pub.). Wiley.
Wilmer, Cutler & Pickering's Emergency Babysitting Facility. (National Report on Work & Family Ser.: No. 1). 32p. 1988. 35.00 (ISBN 0-87179-957-X). BNA.
Wilmington, North Carolina: A Historical & Architectural Portrait. Tony P. Wrenn. (Illus.). 341p. 1984. 30.00 (ISBN 0-8139-0959-7). U Pr of Va.
Wilmore Fitness Program. Jack H. Wilmore. 288p. 1981. pap. 8.95 (ISBN 0-671-79143-5, Wallaby). S&S.
Wilms' Tumor. C. Pochedly & E. S. Baum. 1984. 78.00 (ISBN 0-444-00857-8). Elsevier.
Wilms' Tumor (Nephroblastoma) & Related Renal Neoplasms of Childhood. Ed. by F. Gonzalez-Crussi. 304p. 1983. 125.00 (ISBN 0-8493-5670-9). CRC Pr.
Wilsford Site 22-Co-516, Coahoma County Mississippi. John M. Connaway. LC 84-620008. (Mississippi Department of Archives & History Archaeological Reports Ser.: No. 14). 222p. (Orig.). pap. 15.00. Mississippi Archives.
Wilson & Gisvold's Textbook of Organic Medicinal & Pharmaceutical Chemistry. 9th ed. Jaime N. Delgado & William Remers. LC 65-10424. (Illus.). 860p. 1989. price not set (ISBN 0-397-50877-8, Lippincott Medical). Lippincott.
Wilson & Gisvold's Textbook of Organic Medicinal & Pharmaceutical Chemistry. 8th ed. Ed. by Robert F. Doerge. (Illus.). 960p. 1982. text ed. 55.00 (ISBN 0-397-52092-1, 65-05903, Lippincott Medical). Lippincott.
Wilson & His Peacemakers: The Paris Peace Conference, 1919. Arthur Walworth. 1986. 35.00 (ISBN 0-393-01867-9). Norton.
Wilson & Poland: Four Essays Commemoration the Woodrow Wilson Centennial 1856-1956. 45p. 1.00 (ISBN 0-940962-45-4). Polish Inst Art & Sci.
Wilson & Revolutions: 1913-1921. Lloyd C. Gardner. LC 82-45089. 160p. (Orig.). 1982. pap. text ed. 11.25 (ISBN 0-8191-2416-8). U Pr of Amer.
Wilson & the League of Nations: Why America's Rejection? Ed. by Ralph A. Stone. LC 78-8323. (American Problem Ser.). 128p. 1978. pap. 6.50 (ISBN 0-88275-679-6). Krieger.
Wilson & Wilson's Comprehensive Analytical Chemistry: Thermal Analysis, Part B - Biochemical & Clinical Applications of Thermometric & Thermal Analysis, Vol. 12B. Ed. by N. D. Jespersen et al. 254p. 1982. 102.75 (ISBN 0-444-42062-2). Elsevier.
Wilson & Wilson's Comprehensive Analytical Chemistry, Vol. XX: Photometric Methods in Inorganic Trace Analysis. E. Upor et al. Ed. by G. Svehla. 208p. 1985. 158.00 (ISBN 0-444-99588-9). Elsevier.
Wilson & Wilson's Comprehensive Analytical Chemistry, Vol. XXII: Titrimetric Analysis in Organic Solvents. L. Safarik & Z. Stransky. Ed. by G. Svehla. 532p. 1987. 221.00 (ISBN 0-444-98984-6). Elsevier.
Wilson County, No. 95. G. Frank Burns. Ed. by Robert E. Corlew. (Tennessee County History Ser.). (Illus.). 144p. 1983. 12.50x (ISBN 0-87870-190-7). Memphis St Univ.
Wilson County, Tennessee, Deed Books C-M, 1793-1829. Thomas E. Partlow. 248p. 1984. 25.00 (ISBN 0-89308-540-5). Southern Hist Pr.
Wilson County, Tennessee, Deed Books N-Z, 1829-1853. Thomas E. Partlow. 464p. 1984. 35.00 (ISBN 0-89308-541-3). Southern Hist Pr.
Wilson County, Tennessee, Miscellaneous Records, 1800-1875. Thomas E. Partlow. 270p. 1982. 25.00 (ISBN 0-89308-283-X, TN 60). Southern Hist Pr.
Wilson, Edward Meryon, Nineteen Six to Nineteen Seventy-Seven. Alexander P. Cruikshank. (Memoirs of the Fellows of the British Academy). (Illus.). 24p. 1984. pap. 5.50 (ISBN 0-85672-476-9, Pub. by British Acad). Longwood Pub Group.
Wilson Farm Country Cookbook: Recipes from New England's Favorite Farm Stand. Lynne C. Wilson. LC 84-24408. (Illus.). 256p. 1985. write for info. (ISBN 0-201-09676-5); pap. 9.95 (ISBN 0-201-09677-3). Addison-Wesley.
Wilson Harris & the Modern Tradition: A New Architecture of the World. Sandra E. Drake. LC 85-9874. (Contributions in Afro-American & African Studies Ser.: No. 93). (Illus.). 240p. 1986. lib. bdg. 35.00 (ISBN 0-313-24783-8, DWI/). Greenwood.
Wilson Hurley: A Retrospective Exhibition. LC 85-45017. (Illus.). 88p. 1985. 25.00 (ISBN 0-913504-99-8); pap. 18.50 (ISBN 0-913504-96-3). Lowell Pr.
Wilson: Metaphorical Objects. Ellen H. Johnson et al. (Illus.). 12p. (Orig.). 1986. pap. 3.00 (ISBN 0-940665-01-8). Akron Art Mus.
Wilson Place. Brendan O'Byrne. 304p. 1984. pap. 10.95 (ISBN 0-907085-66-0, Pub. by Ward River Pr Ireland). Irish Bks Media.
Wilson Plot. David Leigh. 288p. 1988. 16.95 (ISBN 0-394-57241-6). Pantheon.
Wilson RV: An in-Basket Simulation. B. Reece & G. Manning. 1976. text ed. 13.40 (ISBN 0-07-051485-2). McGraw.
Wilson Sisters: A Biographical Study of Upper Middle-Class Victorian Life. Martha Westwater. LC 83-8173. (Illus.). xii, 250p. 1984. 29.95x (ISBN 0-8214-0727-9). Ohio U Pr.
Wilsonian Diplomacy. Edward B. Parsons. LC 77-80967. 1978. lib. bdg. 12.95 (ISBN 0-88273-006-1). Forum Pr IL.
Wilsonian Maritime Diplomacy: 1913-1921. Jeffrey J. Safford. 1978. 40.00x (ISBN 0-8135-0850-9). Rutgers U Pr.
Wilson's American Ornithology with Additions Including the Birds Described by Audubon, Bonaparte, Nutall, & Richardson. Alexander Wilson. LC 78-125767. (American Environmental Studies). 1970. Repr. of 1840 ed. 46.50 (ISBN 0-405-02693-5). Ayer Co Pubs.
Wilson's & Wilson's Comprehensive Analytical Chemistry: Volume XXI - New Developments in Conductimetric & Oscillometric Analysis. Ed. by G. Svehla et al. 330p. 1988. 147.50 (ISBN 0-444-42637-X). Elsevier.
Wilson's Dictionary of Bible Types. Walter L. Wilson. 1957. pap. 14.95 (ISBN 0-8028-1453-0). Eerdmans.
Wilson's Disease. Ed. by D. Bergsma et al. (Birth Defects: Original Article Ser.: Vol. IV, No 2). 140p. 1968. 25.00 (ISBN 0-317-60463-5, 0900). A R Liss.
Wilson's Disease. Charles A. Owen, Jr. LC 81-16805. (Copper in Biology & Medicine Ser.). 215p. 1982. 28.00 (ISBN 0-8155-0879-4). Noyes.
Wilson's Disease. I. Herbert Scheinberg & Irmin Sternlieb. (Major Problems in Internal Medicine Ser.: Vol. 23). (Illus.). 192p. 1984. write for info. (ISBN 0-7216-7953-6). Saunders.
Wilson's Foreign Policy in Perspective. Edward Buehrig. 11.25 (ISBN 0-8446-0521-2). Peter Smith.
Wilson's Photographics. Edward L. Wilson. LC 72-9247. (Literature of Photography Ser.). Repr. of 1881 ed. 23.00 (ISBN 0-405-04951-X). Ayer Co Pubs.
Wilt. Tom Sharpe. 224p. 1976. 25.95 (ISBN 0-436-45804-7, Pub. by Secker & Warburg UK). David & Charles.
Wilt. Tom Sharpe. 1984. pap. 3.95 (ISBN 0-394-72418-6, Vin). Random.
Wilt Alternative. Tom Sharpe. 224p. 1979. 24.95 (ISBN 0-436-45808-X, Pub. by Secker & Warburg UK). David & Charles.
Wilt Alternative. Tom Sharpe. LC 84-40055. 224p. 1984. pap. 3.95 (ISBN 0-394-72621-9, Vin). Random.
Wilt on High. Tom Sharpe. 1985. 13.45 (ISBN 0-394-54480-3). Random.
Wilt on High: Being the Further Misadventures of One Henry Wilt. Tom Sharpe. LC 85-40691. 224p. 1986. pap. 4.95 (ISBN 0-394-74321-0, Vin). Random.
Wilt Thou Torchy. Sewell Ford. LC 77-122703. (Short Story Index Reprint Ser.). (Illus.). 1917. 18.00 (ISBN 0-8369-3536-5). Ayer Co Pubs.
Wilton Book of Wedding Cakes. Ed. by Eugene T. Sullivan & Marilynn C. Sullivan. LC 75-175098. 1971. 10.99 (ISBN 0-912696-03-6). Wilton.
Wilton Celebrates the Rose in Cake & Food Decorating. Eugene T. Sullivan & Marilynn C. Sullivan. 1984. pap. 6.99 (ISBN 0-912696-33-8). Wilton.
Wilton Gardens: New & Rare Inventions of Water-Works. Isaac Caus. Ed. by John D. Hunt. LC 79-57005. (English Landscape Garden Ser.). (Illus.). 91p. 1982. lib. bdg. 19.00 (ISBN 0-8240-0178-8). Garland Pub.
Wilton Shows You How to Create Dramatic Tier Cakes. Eugene T. Sullivan & Marilynn C. Sullivan. 80p. 1985. 6.99 (ISBN 0-912696-34-6). Wilton.
Wilton Way of Cake Decorating, Vol. 1. Ed. by Eugene T. Sullivan & Marilynn C. Sullivan. LC 74-13330. 1974. 29.99 (ISBN 0-912696-04-4). Wilton.
Wilton Way of Cake Decorating, Vol. 2. Ed. by Eugene T. Sullivan & Marilynn C. Sullivan. LC 74-13330. 1977. 29.99 (ISBN 0-912696-11-7). Wilton.
Wilton Way of Cake Decorating: Vol. 3, Uses of Tubes. Ed. by Marilynn C. Sullivan & Eugene T. Sullivan. LC 74-13330. 1979. 29.99 (ISBN 0-912696-16-8). Wilton.
Wilton Way to Decorate for Christmas. LC 76-16083. 1976. 6.99 (ISBN 0-912696-07-9). Wilton.
Wilton's Music Hall. Jacqueline S. Bratton. (Theatre in Focus Ser.). (Illus.). 44p. (Orig.). 1980. pap. text ed. 70.00x incl. 50 slides (ISBN 0-85964-061-2). Chadwyck-Healey.
Wiltshire Essays. Maurice H. Hewlett. LC 78-99702. (Essay Index Reprint Ser.). 1921. 18.00 (ISBN 0-8369-1355-8). Ayer Co Pubs.
Wiltshire Folk Songs & Carols. Geoffry Hill. LC 77-26755. 29.50 (ISBN 0-8414-4859-0). Folcroft.
Wiltshire Landscape: Scenes from the Countryside 1920-40. 96p. 1987. 30.00x (ISBN 0-905392-36-1, Countryside Bks). State Mutual Bk.
Wiltshire Parson & His Friends: The Correspondence of William Lisle Bowles Together with Four Hitherto Unidentified Reviews by Coleridge. Garland Greever. 1926. 25.00 (ISBN 0-8274-3720-X). R West.
Wiltshire Rambles. Roger Jones. 72p. 1987. 30.00x (ISBN 0-905392-17-5, Countryside Bks). State Mutual Bk.
Wiltshire Woollen Industry in the Sixteenth & Seventeenth Centuries. 2nd rev. ed. G. D. Ramsay. 165p. 1965. Repr. of 1943 ed. 29.50x (ISBN 0-7146-1355-X, F Cass Co). Biblio Dist.
Wily Beguiled. Ed. by W. W. Greg. LC 82-45765. (Malone Society Reprints Ser.: No. 33). Repr. of 1912 ed. 40.00 (ISBN 0-404-63033-2). AMS Pr.
Wily Beguiled. LC 75-133769. (Tudor Facsimile Texts. Old English Plays Ser.: No. 115). Repr. of 1912 ed. 49.50 (ISBN 0-404-53415-5). AMS Pr.
WIM Poetry Test & Checklist. rev. ed. Ed. by SDiane Bogus. 20p. 1988. pap. 10.00 (ISBN 0-934172-20-X). WIM Pubns.
Wim Wenders. Jan Dawson & Wim Wenders. (Illus., Orig.). 1977. pap. 5.00 (ISBN 0-918432-04-9). NY Zoetrope.
Wimbledon. Rider McDowell. 400p. (Orig.). 1987. pap. 3.95 (ISBN 0-7701-0633-1). PaperJacks US.
Wimbledon: Centre Court of the Game. Max Robertson. LC 83-61263. (Illus.). 308p. 1984. 16.95 (ISBN 0-88186-450-1). Parkwest Pubns.
Wimbledon Fortnight. Patricia A. May. 1984. 15.00x (ISBN 0-317-59318-8, Pub. by New Playwrights Network). State Mutual Bk.
Wimp. John Ibbitson. (EMC Encounters Ser.). 96p. 1986. pap. text ed. 3.95 (ISBN 0-8219-0237-7, 35358); wkbk. 1.20 (ISBN 0-8219-0238-5, 35721). EMC.
Wimp & the Jock. John Ibbitson. LC 88-14078. (Fast Fiction Ser.). (Illus.). 96p. (Orig.). (gr. 5 up). Date not set. pap. 2.95 (ISBN 0-02-041792-6, Collier). Macmillan.
Wimp Factory: Our "Liberal" Congress. Nancy A. Smith. Ed. by Thomas B. Smith. (Illus.). iii, 66p. (Orig.). 1987. pap. 9.95 (ISBN 0-929184-00-9). Integrity.
Win! H. J. Ariston. LC 83-80422. 80p. (Orig.). 1983. pap. 5.95 (ISBN 0-935344-02-0). Jupiter Bks.
Win - Win Outcomes: A Physician's Negotiating Guide. Seymour J. Burrows. LC 84-60125. 200p. 1984. text ed. 26.95 (ISBN 0-931028-46-9). Pluribus Pr.
WIN Advocates Manual. Massachusetts Law Reform Institute. 91p. 1980. 7.00 (30,836). NCLS Inc.
Win at Backgammon. Millard Hopper. LC 72-86224. Orig. Title: Backgammon. (Illus.). 111p. 1972. pap. 2.75 (ISBN 0-486-22894-0). Dover.
Win at Backgammon. Millard Hopper. LC 72-86224. 1972. lib. bdg. 9.50x (ISBN 0-88307-549-0). Gannon.
Win at Cards with ESP: Develop Your ESP & Win at Cards. Donald Fair. LC 88-70978. (Illus.). 176p. (Orig.). 1988. price not set (ISBN 0-945060-14-9); pap. price not set (ISBN 0-945060-15-7). Bounty Pub.
Win at Checkers. Millard Hopper. xi, 109p. 1956. pap. 3.50 (ISBN 0-486-20363-8). Dover.
Win at Chess. Fred Reinfeld. 1945. pap. 3.50 (ISBN 0-486-20438-3). Dover.
Win at Hearts. Joseph Andrews & George Coffin. (Bridge & Other Card Games Ser.). (Illus.). 96p. (Orig.). pap. 3.50 (ISBN 0-486-24406-7). Dover.
Win at Poker. Jeff Rubens. 218p. 1984. pap. 4.95 (ISBN 0-486-24626-4). Dover.
Win at the Casino. Dennis R. Harrison. LC 82-71742. 128p. 1982. 12.95 (ISBN 0-8119-0450-4); pap. 7.95 (ISBN 0-8119-0451-2). Fell.
Win at the Casino. Dennis R. Harrison. pap. 3.50 (ISBN 0-345-31207-4). Ballantine.
Win, Lose, Draw. Sara Stamey. 1988. pap. 3.50 (ISBN 0-441-71428-5). Ace Bks.
Win: Lotto & Daily Numbers Playing Techniques. Steve Player. LC 88-81912. (Lomar Ser.: Vol. 7). (Illus.). 108p. 1988. pap. 9.95. Intergalactic NJ.
Win Me & You Lose. Phyllis A. Wood. (YA) (gr. 7 up). 1978. pap. 2.25 (ISBN 0-451-13540-7, Sig Vista). NAL.
Win Me & You Lose. Phyllis A. Wood. LC 76-44299. (Hiway Bk.: A High Interest-Low Reading Level Book). 136p. (gr. 7 up). 1977. 8.95 (ISBN 0-664-32605-6). Westminster John Knox.
Win, Place & Pro's. Tex Sheanan. (Illus., Orig.). 1984. pap. text ed. 6.95 (ISBN 0-89746-008-1). Gambling Times.
Win the Battle for Your Mind. Richard L. Strauss. 132p. 1986. pap. 5.95 (ISBN 0-87213-835-6). Loizeaux.
Win the Happiness Game. William G. Nickels. LC 80-29884. 1981. 11.95 (ISBN 0-87491-070-6); pap. 6.95 (ISBN 0-87491-528-7). Acropolis.
Win the Lottery! How to Pick Your Personal Lucky Numbers. Ellin Dodge. Date not set. pap. 2.95 (ISBN 0-671-62085-1). PB.
Win Trots & Flats. E. L. Digirolamo. 2.00 (ISBN 0-931138-00-0). Maiden Bks.
Win-Win Administration. Stephen K. Blumberg. 1983. pap. 10.95 (ISBN 0-913878-26-X). T Horton & Dghts.
Win-Win: Approaches to Conflict Resolution at Home, in Business, Between Groups & Across Cultures. Arnold Gerstein & James Reagan. (Illus.). 128p. 1986. 14.95 (ISBN 0-87905-215-5). Gibbs Smith Pub.
Win-Win Negotiating: Turning Conflict into Agreement. Fred E. Jandt. LC 84-25673. (Wiley Sound Business Cassettebooks). 300p. 1987. pap. 12.95 (ISBN 0-471-85877-3); incl. tape 34.95 (ISBN 0-471-61228-6). Wiley.
Win-Win Negotiating: Turning Conflict into Agreement. Fred E. Jandt & Paul Gillette. LC 84-25673. 300p. 1985. 19.95 (ISBN 0-471-88207-0). Wiley.
Win-Win Negotiations for Couples. Charlotte Whitney. Ed. by Camilla Ayers & Emily McKeigue. (Illus.). 208p. 1986. pap. 12.95 (ISBN 0-914918-66-4). Para Res.
Win-Win Negotiator. Ross Reck & Brian Long. 1988. 8.95 (ISBN 1-55525-233-8). Nightingale-Conant.
Win-Win Negotiator: How to Negotiate Favorable Agreements That Last. Ross R. Reck & Brian G. Long. LC 87-61727. (Illus.). 1987. 15.00 (ISBN 0-9616722-1-8, RR-1). Spartan MI.
Win-Win Performance Management-Appraisal: A Problem Solving Approach. Erwin Rausch. LC 85-12201. 344p. 1985. 24.95 (ISBN 0-471-86777-2). Wiley.
Win-Win Telemarketing for Wholesaler-Distributors. S. Michael Zibrun. 1988. 3-ring binder incl. 3 modules & audiocassette 185.00. Natl Assn Wholesale Dists.

Wind in the Rose-bush: And Other Stories of the Supernatural. Mary E. Wilkins Freeman. (Illus.). 237p. 1986. 15.95 (ISBN 0-89733-233-4); pap. 5.95 (ISBN 0-89733-232-6). Academy Chi Pubs.
Wind in the Sage. Christine Bennett. (Contemporary Teens Ser.). 224p. (Orig.). 1981. pap. 2.25 (ISBN 0-89531-144-5, 0146-96). Sharon Pubns.
Wind in the Sahara. R. V. Bodley. 1944. 25.00 (ISBN 0-686-17222-1). Scholars Ref Lib.
Wind in the Willows. Carpenter. Date not set. price not set. HM.
Wind in the Willows. Kenneth Grahame. (Airmont Classics Ser.). (gr. 4 up). pap. 1.75 (ISBN 0-8049-0105-8, CL-105). Airmont.
Wind in the Willows. Kenneth Grahame. 253p. (gr. 5-6). Repr. of 1908 ed. lib. bdg. 17.95x (ISBN 0-88411-877-0, Pub. by Aeonian Pr). Amereon Ltd.
Wind in the Willows. Kenneth Grahame. 234p. 1981. Repr. lib. bdg. 14.95x (ISBN 0-89966-305-2). Buccaneer Bks.
Wind in the Willows. Kenneth Grahame. (Illus.). (gr. 3-9). deluxe ed. 11.95 (ISBN 0-448-06028-0, G&D); Companion lib. ed. o.p. 2.95 (ISBN 0-448-05481-7). Putnam Pub Group.
Wind in the Willows. Kenneth Grahame. LC 80-12509. (Illus.). 216p. (gr. 4-6). 1980. 17.95. H Holt & Co.
Wind in the Willows. Kenneth Grahame. (Illus.). 224p. (Orig.). (RL 4). 1969. pap. 2.50 (ISBN 0-451-52164-1, Sig Classics). NAL.
Wind in the Willows. Kenneth Grahame. (Illus.). 256p. (gr. 4-12). 1983. pap. 1.95 (ISBN 0-553-21129-3, Bantam Classics). Bantam.
Wind in the Willows. Kenneth Grahame. (Illus.). 240p. (gr. 1 up). 1983. 15.75 (ISBN 0-670-77120-1). Viking.
Wind in the Willows. Kenneth Grahame. Ed. by Peter Green. (World's Classics Ser.). (YA) (gr. 5 up). 1983. pap. 2.95 (ISBN 0-19-281640-3). Oxford U Pr.
Wind in the Willows. Kenneth Grahame. LC 83-11573. (Illus.). 256p. (gr. 5 up). 1983. 18.95 (ISBN 0-684-17957-1, Pub. by Scribner). Macmillan.
Wind in the Willows. Kenneth Grahame. (Illus.). 240p. (gr. 4-6). 1984. pap. 2.95 (ISBN 0-14-031544-6, Puffin). Penguin.
Wind in the Willows. Kenneth Grahame. LC 85-13538. (Illus.). 224p. (gr. 2 up). 1985. 12.95 (ISBN 0-915361-32-9, Dist. by Watts). Adama Pubs Inc.
Wind in the Willows. Kenneth Grahame. (Illus.). 256p. (gr. 1 up). 1969. pap. 3.50 (ISBN 0-440-49555-5, YB). Dell.
Wind in the Willows. Kenneth Grahame. 1985. 15.95 (ISBN 0-670-80764-8). Viking.
Wind in the Willows. Kenneth Grahame. 1984. pap. 3.95 (ISBN 0-684-18025-1, Collier). Macmillan.
Wind in the Willows. Kenneth Grahame. (Apple Classics Ser.). (Illus.). 208p. (Orig.). (gr. 4-6). 1988. pap. 2.50 (ISBN 0-590-41294-9, Apple Classics). Scholastic Inc.
Wind in the Willows. Kenneth Grahame. (Illus.). 196p. (Orig.). (YA) 1988. pap. 7.95 (ISBN 0-8092-4489-6). Contemp Bks.
Wind in the Willows. Liz Peterson. 40p. 1984. pap. 2.50x (ISBN 0-88020-111-8). Coach Hse.
Wind in the Willows. (Illustrated Junior Library). (Illus.). 224p. (gr. 3-9). 1985. 15.95 (ISBN 0-399-20944-1, G&D); pap. 6.95 (ISBN 0-448-11028-8). Putnam Pub Group.
Wind in the Willows. (Classics Ser.). (gr. 4 up). 1988. pap. 3.95. Longman.
Wind in the Willows see New Method Supplementary Readers.
Wind in the Willows: A Musical Adaptation. Don Trifiletti. LC 76-27775. 1977. 10.00 (ISBN 0-682-48648-5, Banner). Exposition-Phoenix.
Wind in the Willows Activity Book. Illus. by Judy Brook. (Illus.). 1985. pap. 3.95 (ISBN 0-14-031871-2, Puffin). Penguin.
Wind in the Willows Coloring Book. Kenneth Grahame. 64p. 1976. pap. 2.75 (ISBN 0-486-23292-1). Dover.
Wind in the Willows: The Open Road. Kenneth Grahame. (Illus.). 48p. (ps-3). 1986. bds. 7.95 (ISBN 0-671-61095-3, Little Simon). S&S.
Wind in the Wires. Duncan Grinnell-Milne et al. Ed. by Stanley M. Ulanoff & James Gilbert. LC 79-7264. (Flight: Its First Seventy-Five Years Ser.). (Illus.). 1979. Repr. of 1968 ed. lib. bdg. 25.50x (ISBN 0-405-12174-1). Ayer Co Pubs.
Wind Is Not a River. Arnold Griese. LC 77-5082. (Illus.). (gr. 4-7). 1978. (Crowell Jr Bks); PLB 12.89 (ISBN 0-690-03842-9). HarpJ.
Wind Is Rising. Viola Wendt. LC 79-53723. 1979. pap. 4.50 (ISBN 0-916120-05-8). Carroll Coll.
Wind Leans West. August Derleth. LC 70-76506. (Wisconsin Saga Ser.). 323p. 1969. 8.95 (ISBN 0-88361-077-9). Stanton & Lee.
Wind Leaves No Shadow. Ruth Laughlin. LC 48-10425. 1948. pap. 6.95 (ISBN 0-87004-083-9). Caxton.
Wind Loading & Wind-Induced Structural Response. 216p. 1987. 20.00x (ISBN 0-87262-625-3). Am Soc Civil Eng.
Wind Loading on Buildings. Argus J. Macdonald. (Illus.). ix, 219p. 1975. 45.00 (ISBN 0-85334-626-7, Pub. by Elsevier Applied Sci England). Elsevier.
Wind Measurement Systems & Wind Tunnel Evaluation of Selected Instruments. J. V. Ramsdell & J. S. Wetzel. 70p. 1983. pap. 12.00 (ISBN 0-88016-006-3). Windbks.
Wind Mountain: Poems. Fred Chappell. LC 79-12332. 45p. 1979. text ed. 13.95x (ISBN 0-8071-0566-X); pap. 6.95 (ISBN 0-8071-0567-8). La State U Pr.
Wind of Chance. Rene Guillot. Tr. by Norman Dale. (Illus.). (gr. 6-9). 1958. 14.95 (ISBN 0-87599-048-7). S G Phillips.
Wind of Change. Judith Hagar. (Private Library Collection). 267p. 1986. mini-bound 6.95 (ISBN 0-938422-16-2). SOS Pubns CA.
Wind of Change. Harold Klemp. LC 80-50516. (Illus.). 194p. 1982. pap. 3.95 (ISBN 0-914766-75-9, 0188). Illum Way Pub.
Wind of Our Going. Patricia Goedicke. LC 84-73336. 120p. (Orig.). 1985. pap. 8.00 (ISBN 0-914742-84-1). Copper Canyon.
Wind of Promise. Dorothy Garlock. 1987. pap. 3.95 (ISBN 0-317-56922-8, Pub. by Popular Lib). Warner Bks.
Wind of the Land. Eugene P. Nassar. (Monograph Ser.: No. 11). 148p. (Orig.). 1979. 12.00 (ISBN 0-937694-06-1); pap. 5.00 (ISBN 0-937694-05-3). Assn Arab-Amer U Grads.
Wind of the Spirit. abr. ed. G. De Purucker. Ed. by W. Emmett Small & Helen Todd. 282p. 1971. pap. 3.25 (ISBN 0-913004-00-6). Point Loma Pub.
Wind of the Spirit. 2nd, rev. ed. G. De Purucker. LC 84-50118. 328p. 1984. 11.00 (ISBN 0-911500-67-7); pap. 6.00 (ISBN 0-911500-68-5). Theos U Pr.
Wind of the Spirit. James S. Stewart. 192p. 1984. pap. 6.95 (ISBN 0-8010-8250-1). Baker Bk.
Wind off the Island. Ernle Bradford. (Mariner's Library). 192p. 1988. pap. 12.95 (ISBN 0-246-13276-0, Pub. by Grafton Bks UK). Sheridan.
Wind on the Prairies: How the West Was Really Won. Helen P. French. (Illus.). 240p. 1982. 10.50 (Lochnivar). Exposition-Phoenix.
Wind on Your Cheek. William J. Schaldach. (Illus.). 160p. 1973. 17.50 (ISBN 0-88395-015-4); partial lea. bdg. boxed 75.00 (ISBN 0-685-32727-2). Freshet Pr.
Wind Over Ashes: Selected Poems. Leonard Randolph. (Illus.). 174p. (Orig.). 1982. pap. 7.00 (ISBN 0-932112-15-3). Carolina Wren.
Wind over Sand: The Diplomacy of Franklin Roosevelt. Frederick W. Marks, III. LC 86-24976. (Illus.). 472p. 1987. 29.95 (ISBN 0-8203-0929-X). U of Ga Pr.
Wind Power. Mike Cross. LC 85-70600. (Energy Today Ser.). (Illus.). 31p. (gr. 4-8). 1985. PLB 11.90 (ISBN 0-531-17007-1, Gloucester Pr). Watts.
Wind Power. Norman F. Smith. (Science Is What & Why Ser.). (gr. 3-7). 1981. PLB 6.99 (ISBN 0-698-30732-1, Coward). Putnam Pub Group.
Wind Power. LC 81-86271. (Fun with Science Ser.). 12.68 (ISBN 0-382-06628-6). Silver.
Wind Power: A Turning Point. Christopher Flavin. LC 81-52516. (Worldwatch Papers). 1981. pap. 4.00 (ISBN 0-916468-44-5). Worldwatch Inst.
Wind Power & Other Energy Options. David R. Inglis. LC 78-9102. (Illus.). 1978. 16.00 (ISBN 0-472-09303-7); pap. 9.95 (ISBN 0-472-06303-0). U of Mich Pr.
Wind Power Book. Jack Park. LC 81-128. (Illus.). 1981. 21.95 (ISBN 0-917352-05-X); pap. 14.95 (ISBN 0-917352-06-8). Cheshire.
Wind Power Equipment. D. F. Warne. (Illus.). 220p. 1983. 55.00 (ISBN 0-419-11410-6, NO. 6684, E & FN Spon). Routledge Chapman & Hall.
Wind Power Plants: Theory & Design. D. Le Gourieres. 300p. 1982. pap. 36.00 (ISBN 0-08-029967-9). Pergamon.
Wind Powered Electricity Generation Package. Ed. by Commonwealth Regional Renewable Energy Resources Information Systems Staff. 139p. 1985. pap. 20.00 (ISBN 0-643-03717-9, Pub. by CSIRO Australia). Intl Spec Bk.
Wind Pressure: A Revision of A 498. Mary Vance. (Architecture Ser.: A 1588). 30p. 1986. 7.50 (ISBN 0-89028-858-5). Vance Biblios.
Wind-Profile Measurements - Above a Maize. (Agricultural Research Reports: No. 882). 1978. pap. 16.00 (ISBN 90-220-0684-0, PDC134, PUDOC). UNIPUB.
Wind River. Gary McCarthy. 480p. (Orig.). 1984. pap. 3.95 (ISBN 0-345-30431-4). Ballantine.
Wind River Kill. Robert Kammen. 1987. pap. 2.50 (ISBN 0-8217-2213-1). Zebra.
Wind River Trails. Finis Mitchell. Ed. by Mel Davis. (Illus.). 144p. 1975. pap. 4.00 (ISBN 0-915272-03-2). Wasatch Pubs.
Wind River Winter: How the World Dies. Virginia S. Owens. 288p. 1987. pap. 10.95 (ISBN 0-310-45861-7, 12469P). Zondervan.
Wind Rose. Crescent Dragonwagon. LC 75-25414. (Illus.). 32p. (ps-3). 1976. 12.70i (ISBN 0-06-021741-3). HarpJ.
Wind, Sand & Stars. Antoine De Saint-Exupery. LC 65-35872. 243p. 1967. pap. 3.95 (ISBN 0-15-697090-2, Harv). HarBraceJ.
Wind Scales. Keith Waldrop. (Treacle Story Ser.: No. 4). (Illus.). 36p. 1976. signed ed. 8.00 (ISBN 0-914232-13-4). McPherson & Co.
Wind Shear. 1986. 25.00 (ISBN 0-89883-952-1, SP681). Soc Auto Engineers.
Wind, Snow & Temperature Effects on Structures Based on Probability. D. Ghiocel & D. Lungu. 411p. 1975. 48.00 (ISBN 0-85626-026-6). Abacus Pr.
Wind Song. Carl Sandburg. LC 60-10248. (Illus.). (gr. 5 up). 1960. 5.95 (ISBN 0-15-297497-0, HJ). HarBraceJ.
Wind Spirit: An Autobiography. Michel Tournier. Tr. by Arthur Goldhammer from Fr. LC 88-47660. 292p. 1988. 19.95 (ISBN 0-8070-7040-8). Beacon Pr.
Wind Sports. Anabel Dean. LC 82-13460. (Illus.). 170p. (gr. 5-9). 1982. 12.95 (ISBN 0-664-32696-X). Westminster John Knox.
Wind Star: The Building of a Sailship. Joseph Novitski. Date not set. 19.95. Macmillan.
Wind Strategy. David Houghton. (Sail to Win Ser.). (Illus.). 64p. 1987. pap. text ed. 9.95 (ISBN 0-87742-230-3). Intl Marine.
Wind Sweeps Away the Plum Blossoms: The Principles & Techniques of Yang Style T'ai Chi Spear & Staff. Stuart A. Olson. Tr. by Stuart A. Olson from Chinese. (Illus.). 150p. (Orig.). 1986. pap. 14.95 (ISBN 0-938045-00-8). Bubbling Well.
Wind Systems Life Cycle Cost Analysis: A Description & Users Manual. J. M. Sherman et al. 88p. (Orig.). 1984. pap. 19.95 (ISBN 0-88016-019-5). Windbks.
Wind That Round the Fastnet Sweeps. John M. Feehan. 160p. 1979. pap. 7.95 (ISBN 0-85342-550-7, Pub. by Mercier Pr Ireland). Irish Bks Media.
Wind That Shakes the Barley: A Novel of the Life & Loves of Robert Burns. James Barke. 384p. 1982. Repr. of 1945 ed. lib. bdg. 30.00. Darby Bks.
Wind That Swept Mexico: The History of the Mexican Revolution of 1910-1942. Anita Brenner & George R. Leighton. LC 77-149021. (Texas Pan American Ser.). (Illus.). 320p. 1971. pap. 14.95 (ISBN 0-292-79024-4). U of Tex Pr.
Wind That Tramps the World: Splashes of Chinese Color, Vol. 1. Frank Owen. LC 72-4426. (Short Story Index Reprint Ser). Repr. of 1929 ed. 14.50 (ISBN 0-8369-4186-1). Ayer Co Pubs.
Wind the Clock by Bittersweet. Bill Pauly. 32p. 1977. 10.00 (ISBN 0-913719-03-X); pap. 3.50 (ISBN 0-913719-02-1). High-Coo Pr.
Wind, the Sea & I. Kent Ramsing. LC 87-1212. 160p. 1987. 10.95 (ISBN 0-86534-112-5). Sunstone Pr.
Wind Through the Valleys. Donald Zelle. (Orig.). 1987. pap. 6.25 (ISBN 0-89536-876-5, 7862). CSS of Ohio.
Wind to Shake the World: The Story of the 1938 Hurricane. Everett S. Allen. (Illus.). 1976. 17.95 (ISBN 0-316-03426-6). Little.
Wind Tunnel Model Studies of Buildings & Structures. Ed. by Nicholas Isyumov. 48p. 1987. 10.00x (ISBN 0-87262-620-2). Am Soc Civil Eng.
Wind Tunnel Modeling for Civil Engineering Applications: Proceedings of the International Workshop on Wind Tunnell Modeling Criterian & Techniques in Civil Engineering Applications, Gaithersburg, Maryland, April 1982. International Workshop on Wind Tunnel Modeling Criteria & Techniques in Civil Engineering Applications (1982: Gaithersburg, MD) Ed. by Timothy A. Reinhold. LC 82-14594. pap. 160.00 (2027249). Bks Demand UMI.
Wind Turbine Engineering Design. David M. Eggleston. Ed. by Forrest S. Stoddard. LC 86-23331. 420p. 1987. 55.95 (ISBN 0-442-22195-9). Van Nos Reinhold.
Wind Turbines. Peacock. (Energy & Engineering Science Ser.). 1984. cancelled 0.00 (Pub. by Abacus England). IPS.
Wind-Ups: Japanese Wind-Up & Other Tin Toys from 1880 to 1950. Teruhisa Kitahara. LC 85-12811. (Illus.). 128p. 1985. pap. 12.95 (ISBN 0-87701-367-5). Chronicle Bks.
Wind, Water, Fire & Earth: Energy Lessons for the Physical Sciences. (Illus.). 1986. pap. 9.00 (ISBN 0-317-65976-6). Natl Sci Tchrs.
Wind Waves. Blair Kinsman. LC 83-20616. (Earth Sciences Ser.). 676p. 1984. pap. 14.95 (ISBN 0-486-64652-1). Dover.
Wind, Waves, & Weather. Ed. by Vivian Carmona-Agosto. Tr. by Marcela Rossman from Eng. (Rotary Drilling Series, Unit V: Lesson 1). (Illus.). 49p. (Orig., Span.). 1982. pap. text ed. 5.95 (ISBN 0-88698-046-1, 2.50112). PETEX.
Wind, Waves, & Weather. 2nd, rev. ed. Ed. by Nora Sheppard. (Rotary Drilling Ser., Unit V: Lesson 1). (Illus.). 70p. 1984. pap. text ed. 6.95 (ISBN 0-88698-069-0, 2.50110). PETEX.
Wind Will Not Forget. Carolyn Muentner. 68p. 1983. 8.95 (ISBN 0-9606240-3-1). Pearl-Win.
Wind Will Not Subside: Years in Revolutionary China,1964-1969. David Milton & Nancy D. Milton. LC 75-10370. 1976. pap. 7.95 (ISBN 0-394-70936-5). Pantheon.
Wind Without Rain see Krause Trio.
Wind Workshop VI: Sixth Biennial Wind Energy Conference & Workshop. Ed. by Barbara Glenn. 1983. Set. pap. text ed. 150.00x (ISBN 0-89553-125-9). Am Solar Energy.
Windbird. D. M. Murray. 1980. 4.95 (ISBN 0-89962-012-4). Todd & Honeywell.
WindBlown. Paul Hutchens. 1968. 2.95 (ISBN 0-87148-913-9). Pathway Pr.
Windbourne Pests & Diseases: Meteorology of Airborne Organisms. David E. Pedgley. LC 82-9197. 250p. 1982. 68.95x (ISBN 0-470-27516-2). Halsted Pr.
Windbreak: A Woman Rancher on the Northern Plains. Linda Hasselstrom. LC 87-11428. (Illus.). 256p. (Orig.). 1987. pap. 12.95 (ISBN 0-9609626-3-8). Barn Owl Bks.
Windfall: A Collection of Modern Poetry. Ed. by Louisa Persing. 1975. 5.95 (ISBN 0-686-10961-9). Palomar.
Windfall & Other Stories. Winifred M. Sanford. LC 87-43105. (Southwest Life & Letters Ser.). 160p. 1988. 17.95x (ISBN 0-87074-267-1); pap. 8.95 (ISBN 0-87074-268-X). SMU Press.
Windfall Journal. Robert Richter. (Illus.). 83p. 1980. pap. 4.00 (ISBN 0-936204-10-9). Jelm Mtn.
Windfall of Inherited Treasures. Betty C. Taussig. (Illus.). 109p. (Orig.). 1984. pap. 19.95 (ISBN 0-9613604-0-2). Windfall Pub.
Windfall Poems Nineteen Seventy-Seven: A Special Original Collection. R. Buckminster Fuller et al. Ed. by George Bush. 1977. text ed. 5.00. Mainespring.
Windfall Profits Tax: The Price for Decontrol. Oil Daily Editors. 248p. 1980. write for info. Oil Daily.
Windfalls. Alfred G. Gardiner. LC 70-105014. (Essay Index Reprint Ser.). 1920. 19.00 (ISBN 0-8369-1467-8). Ayer Co Pubs.
Windfalls for Wipeouts: Land Value Capture & Compensation. Donald G. Hagman & Dean J. Misczynski. 704p. 1978. pap. 25.95 (ISBN 0-318-13107-2); pap. 23.95 members (ISBN 0-318-13108-0). Am Plan Assn.
Windfalls for Wipeouts: Land Value Capture & Compensation. Ed. by Donald G. Hagman & Dean J. Misczynski. LC 77-82573. 660p. (Orig.). 1977. pap. 25.95 (ISBN 0-918286-11-5). Planners Pr.
Windfire. Arlene Fitzgerald. (Orig.). 1983. pap. 3.50 (ISBN 0-8217-1216-0). Zebra.
Windflower. Laura London. 464p. (Orig.). 1984. pap. 3.95 (ISBN 0-440-19534-9). Dell.
Windham. Richard C. Wiles. 20p. 1987. pap. 3.00 (ISBN 0-317-58826-5). Hope Farm.
Windhaven. George R. Martin & Lisa Tuttle. 1985. pap. 3.95 (ISBN 0-671-49616-6). PB.
Windhaven. George R. Martin & Lisa Tuttle. 1980. 17.50 (ISBN 0-671-25277-1). Ultramarine Pub.
Windhorse. Elaine Brook & Julie Donnelly. (Illus.). 1987. 17.95 (ISBN 0-396-09006-0). Dodd.
Windigo Psychosis: American Ethnological Society Proceedings, 1960. Morton I. Teicher. Ed. by Verne F. Ray. LC 84-45547. 1988. pap. 27.50 (ISBN 0-404-62654-8). AMS Pr.
Winding Alternating Current Machines: A Book for Winders, Repairmen, & Designers of Electric Machines. Michael Liwschitz-Garik & Celso Gentilini. 1950. 59.00 (ISBN 0-911740-03-1). Datarule.
Winding Down a Psychiatric Private Practice. Joe Deacon. LC 85-7341. (Private Practice Monograph). 112p. 1985. pap. text ed. 15.00x (ISBN 0-88048-103-X, 48-103-X). Am Psychiatric.
Winding Down: The Price of Defense. (Illus.). 359p. 1982. pap. 11.95 (ISBN 0-7167-1498-1); pap. text ed. 7.95. W H Freeman.
Winding Engine Calculations for the Mining. P. K. Chatterjee & P. J. Wetherall. 1982. 39.95 (ISBN 0-419-12650-3, NO. 6693, Pub. by E & FN Spon). Routledge Chapman & Hall.
Winding Passage: Essays & Sociological Journeys, 1960-1980. Daniel Bell. LC 79-57350. (Illus.). 394p. 1980. 34.25 (ISBN 0-89011-545-1). Abt Bks.
Winding Passage: Essays & Sociological Journeys, 1960-1980. Daniel Bell. LC 81-66858. 372p. 1981. pap. 8.00 (ISBN 0-465-09193-8, CN-5075). Basic.
Winding Passage: Essays & Sociological Journeys, 1960-1980. Daniel Bell. 394p. 1984. Repr. of 1980 ed. lib. bdg. 36.00 (ISBN 0-8191-4142-9). U Pr of Amer.
Winding Quest. Alan T. Dale. (Illus.). 432p. (Orig.). 1973. pap. 9.95 (ISBN 0-8192-1150-8). Morehouse.
Winding Stair. Jane A. Hodge. 1980. pap. 2.25 (ISBN 0-449-23590-4, Crest). Fawcett.
Winding Stair. Douglas C. Jones. LC 79-4195. 288p. 1979. pap. 5.95 (ISBN 0-03-000098-X). H Holt & Co.
Winding Stair: Sir Francis Bacon, His Rise & Fall. Daphne Du Maurier. 16.95 (ISBN 0-88411-545-3, Pub. by Aeonian Pr). Amereon Ltd.
Winding Trail: The Alabama-Coushatta Indians. Vivian Fox. (Illus.). 1983. 7.95 (ISBN 0-89015-397-3). Eakin Pr.
Winding up of Insolvent Companies in England & France. Christopher Livadas. 380p. 1983. 70.00 (ISBN 90-654-4087-9, Pub. by Kluwer Law Netherlands). Kluwer Academic.
Winding Valley Farm: Annie's Story. Anne Pellowski. (Illus.). 192p. 1982. 9.95 (ISBN 0-399-20863-1, Philomel). Putnam Pub Group.
Windjammer World. Carstarphen. 1979. pap. 6.95 (ISBN 0-89272-066-2). Down East.
Windjammers. Oliver E. Allen. LC 78-10819. (Seafarers Ser.). (Illus.). (gr. 7 up). 1979. lib. bdg. 21.27 (ISBN 0-8094-2704-4, Pub. by Time-Life). Silver.

Winds of Change: And Other Stories. Isaac Asimov. 1984. pap. 2.95 (Del Rey). Ballantine.
Winds of Change in China. Lesley Francis. 1985. pap. 1.25 (ISBN 9971-972-30-1). OMF Bks.
Winds of Change: The New Economic Challenges, India. D. N. Patodia. 150p. 1987. 21.00x (ISBN 0-8364-2060-8, Pub. by Allied India). South Asia Bks.
Winds of Change: Women Challenge the Church. Joan Chittister. LC 86-62124. 156p. (Orig.). 1986. pap. 6.95 (ISBN 0-934134-92-8). Sheed & Ward MO.
Winds of Darkover. Marion Zimmer Bradley. 192p. 1985. pap. 3.50 (ISBN 0-441-89261-2, Pub. by Ace Science Fiction). Ace Bks.
Winds of Desire. Jocelyn Haley. (Superromances Ser.). 384p. 1982. pap. 2.50 (ISBN 0-373-70031-8, Pub. by Worldwide). Harlequin Bks.
Winds of Enchantment. Jan McGowan. 352p. (Orig.). pap. 3.95 (ISBN 0-671-63407-0). Archway.
Winds of Evil. Arthur Upfield. (Napolean Bonaparte Mystery Ser.). 15.95 (ISBN 0-89190-563-4, Pub. by Am Repr). Amereon Ltd.
Winds of Evil. Arthur W. Upfield. 256p. 1987. pap. 3.95 (ISBN 0-02-025910-7, Collier). Macmillan.
Winds of Fire. Robin Dietierie. 1987. pap. 4.50 (ISBN 0-425-10413-3). Berkley Pub.
Winds of Fire. Vyankatesh Madgulkar. Tr. by Pramod Kale from Marathi. 113p. 1975. pap. 2.50 (ISBN 0-88253-693-1). Ind-US Inc.
Winds of Glory. Susan Wiggs. 400p. 1988. pap. 3.95 (ISBN 0-380-75482-7). Avon.
Winds of God. 2nd ed. Ethel E. Goss. (Illus.). 288p. 1958. pap. 5.95 (ISBN 0-912315-26-1). Word Aflame.
Winds of God. Norvel Hayes. 90p. (Orig.). 1985. pap. 4.95 (ISBN 0-89274-375-1). Harrison Hse.
Winds of Imagination. Petie W. Baldwin. LC 76-17537. 1976. pap. 5.00 (ISBN 0-917166-01-9). Creative Vent.
Winds of Ixtepeji: World View & Society in a Zapotec Town. Michael Kearney. (Illus.). 140p. 1986. pap. text ed. 7.95x (ISBN 0-88133-210-0). Waveland Pr.
Winds of Love. Rae Barelli. (YA) (gr. 7 up). 1984. 9.95 (ISBN 0-8034-8457-7, Avalon). Bouregy.
Winds of Love. Hollister Noble. (Orig.). 1981. pap. 2.95 (ISBN 0-89083-899-2). Zebra.
Winds of Love. Agnes S. Turnbull. 1978. pap. 1.75 (ISBN 0-449-23575-0, Crest). Fawcett.
Winds of Morning. Harold L. Davis. LC 77-138586. 344p. 1972. Repr. of 1952 ed. lib. bdg. 35.00x (ISBN 0-8371-5785-4, DAWM). Greenwood.
Winds of My Mind. Louise F. Underhill. (Illus.). 60p. (Orig.). 1986. pap. 5.00 (ISBN 0-936204-55-9). Jelm Mtn.
Winds of Passion. Barbara A. Cooper. 1981. pap. 2.75 (ISBN 0-89083-778-3). Zebra.
Winds of Retribution. Nick Nixon. LC 85-3858. 1987. 12.95 (ISBN 0-87949-250-3). Ashley Bks.
Winds of Rome. Leigh McAllister. LC 87-42908. 200p. 1988. pap. 9.95 (ISBN 1-55523-119-5). Winston-Derek.
Winds of Time. Jeanne Sanders. LC 86-70863. (Illus.). 50p. (Orig.). 1986. pap. 5.95 (ISBN 0-9617109-2-6). Armagh Press.
Winds of Time-Winds of Chance. 1987. pap. 4.00 (ISBN 0-934805-07-5). Gray Pubns WV.
Winds of Tomorrow: Social Change in a Maya Town. Richard A. Thompson. LC 73-90940. x, 182p. 1974. text ed. 12.50x (ISBN 0-226-79757-0). U of Chicago Pr.
Winds of War. Herman Wouk. 1971. 24.95 (ISBN 0-316-95500-0). Little.
Winds of War. Herman Wouk. pap. 5.95 (ISBN 0-671-63472-0). PB.
Winds of War & War & Remembrance. Herman Wouk. 1978. boxed set 39.90 (ISBN 0-316-95502-7). Little.
Winds of War: T. V. tie-in edition. Herman Wouk. LC 77-70195. 1983. pap. 4.95 (ISBN 0-671-46319-5). PB.
Wind's Song. Marjorie K. Lawrence. 6.95 (ISBN 0-317-53543-9). Vantage.
Wind's Twelve Quarters. Ursula K. Le Guin. LC 75-6372. 320p. 1987. pap. 6.95 (ISBN 0-06-091434-3, PL/1434, PL). Har-Row.
Wind's Will. Gerald W. Brace. 1964. 4.50 (ISBN 0-393-08435-3). Norton.
Windship Technology: Proceedings of the International Symposium on Windship Technology Southampton, U. K. April 23-25, 1985, 2 vols. Ed. by C. J. Satchwell. (Studies in Wind Engineering & Industrial Aerodynamics: Pt. 4A & B). 752p. 1985. Repr. Set. 302.75 (ISBN 0-444-42533-0). Elsevier.
Windshopping Maui: A Serious Sailor's Guide to the Valley Isle. Arleone Dibben-Young. (Illus.). 176p. (Orig.). 1987. pap. 12.95 (ISBN 0-9617864-0-X). A Dibben-Young.
Windsinger. Gary M. Smith. (Illus.). 176p. 1976. 7.95 (ISBN 0-87156-192-1). Windsinger.
Windsingers. Ed. by Charlotte M. Babcock et al. 125p. (Orig.). 1984. pap. text ed. write for info. (ISBN 0-917557-01-8). Wyo Writers.
Windsong. Judith E. French. 368p. (Orig.). 1988. pap. 3.95 (ISBN 0-380-75551-3). Avon.
Windsong. Valerie Sherwood. 1986. pap. 4.50 (ISBN 0-317-41571-9). PB.
Windsong: Texas Cherokee Princess. Raven Hail. LC 86-90672. (Illus.). 141p. (Orig.). 1986. pap. 7.95 (ISBN 0-9617696-1-0). Raven Hail Bks.
Windsor & Eton Step by Step. Christopher Turner. 72p. 1986. pap. 4.95 (ISBN 0-571-14529-9). Faber & Faber.
Windsor Handbook. Wallace Nutting. LC 73-77579. (Illus.). 1973. pap. 4.95 (ISBN 0-8048-1105-9). C E Tuttle.
Windsor McKay's Dream Days: An Original Compilation. First Collection of Comic Strip Features by the Creator of Little Nemo from the Years 1903 to 1914. Winsor McKay. Ed. by Bill Blackbeard. LC 76-53048. (Classic American Comic Strips Ser.). (Illus.). 1986. 31.00 (ISBN 0-88355-651-0). Hyperion Conn.
Windsor Plot. Pauline G. Winslow. 1986. pap. 4.95 (ISBN 0-312-90389-8). St Martin.
Windsor Red. Jennie Melville. LC 87-38245. 256p. 1988. 16.95 (ISBN 0-312-01846-0, Pub. by Thomas Dunne Bks). St Martin.
Windsor Style. Suzy Menkes. (Illus.). 224p. 1988. 34.95 (ISBN 0-88162-321-0). Salem Hse Pubs.
Windsor Style in America: A Continuing Study of the History & Regional Characteristics of the Most Popular Furniture Form of Eighteenth Century America, 1730-1840, Vol. 2. Charles Santore. (Illus.). 240p. 1987. 45.00 (ISBN 0-89471-551-8). Running Pr.
Windsor Style in America: A Pictorial Study of the History & Regional Characteristics of the Most Popular Furniture Form of 18th Century America, 1730-1830. Charles Santore. LC 81-10682. (Illus.). 215p. 45.00 (ISBN 0-89471-136-9). Running Pr.
Windstar: The Building of a Sailship. Joseph Novitski. (Illus.). 256p. 1988. 19.95 (ISBN 0-02-590830-8). Macmillan.
Windstorm. Katherine Sutcliffe. (Avon Romance Ser.). 368p. 1987. pap. 3.95 (ISBN 0-380-75264-6). Avon.
Windsurfing. Norman Barrett. Ed. by Franklin Watts Ltd. (Picture Library). (Illus.). 32p. (ps-9). 1988. 9.90 (ISBN 0-531-10354-4). Watts.
Windsurfing. Diana C. Gleasner. LC 85-14275. (Illus.). 64p. (Orig.). 1985. pap. 7.95 (ISBN 0-934802-24-6). ICS Bks.
Windsurfing: Basic & Funboard Techniques. Rev ed. Roger Jones. LC 84-47975. (Illus.). 128p. 1985. pap. 15.95 (ISBN 0-06-250429-0). Har-Row.
Windsurfing Funboard Handbook. Clive Boden & Angus Charter. (Illus.). 176p. 1984. 13.95 (ISBN 0-8120-5582-9). Barron.
Windsurfing: The Complete Guide. Glen Taylor. 1983. 15.75 (ISBN 0-8446-6057-4). Peter Smith.
Windsurfing: The Complete Guide. Rev. ed. Glenn Taylor. 304p. 1982. pap. text ed. 9.95 (ISBN 0-07-063158-1). McGraw.
Windsurfing the Fermi Sea, 2 pts. T. T. Kuo & J. Speth. 1987. Set. 95.25 (ISBN 0-444-87064-4); Pt. 1. 46.50 (ISBN 0-444-87065-2); Pt. 2. 61.00 (ISBN 0-444-87066-0). Elsevier.
Windsurfing (Wind Surf Ing) to Boardsail. Frank Fox. (Illus.). 96p. (Orig.). 1987. pap. 6.95 (ISBN 0-934965-03-X). Amber Co Pr.
Windswept. Ann F. Barron. 464p. 1985. pap. 3.95 (ISBN 0-380-89589-7). Avon.
Windswept Passion. Sonya T. Pelton. 1984. pap. 3.75 (ISBN 0-8217-1484-8). Zebra.
Windthorst: A Political Biography. Margaret L. Anderson. 1981. 78.00x (ISBN 0-19-822578-4). Oxford U Pr.
Windwagon Smith. Edna Shapiro. LC 69-12924. (American Folktales Ser.). (Illus.). 46p. (gr. 2-5). 1969. PLB 6.69 (ISBN 0-8116-4016-7). Garrard.
Windwalker. Blaine M. Yorgason. 112p. 1979. 5.95 (ISBN 0-88494-362-3). Bookcraft Inc.
Windward Crest. Anne Hampson. (Harlequin Presents Ser.). 192p. 1982. pap. 1.75 (ISBN 0-373-10494-4). Harlequin Bks.
Windward Road: Adventures of a Naturalist on Remote Caribbean Shores. Archie Carr. LC 79-23624. (Illus.). xl, 266p. 1979. pap. 12.00 (ISBN 0-8130-0639-2). U Presses Fla.
Windward West. Matt Braun. (Brannocks Ser.: No. 2). 336p. 1987. pap. 3.50 (ISBN 0-451-14701-4, Sig). NAL.
Windwood. Cynthia A. Kreke. 240p. (Orig.). 1981. pap. 2.25 (ISBN 0-8439-1003-8, Leisure Bks). Leisure NY.
Windwords: The First Two Years. Ed. by Beverly Dittrich. 360p. (Orig.). 1988. pap. 19.95 (ISBN 0-9620553-0-1). Windwords.
Windy Day. Janet Craig. LC 87-10909. (Illus.). 32p. (gr. k-2). 1987. PLB 5.41 (ISBN 0-8167-0982-3); pap. text ed. 1.50 (ISBN 0-8167-0983-1). Troll Assocs.
Windy Day Puppy. Linda Hayward. (Happy Day Shape Bks.). (Illus.). 12p. (ps-1). 1985. 5.95 (ISBN 0-448-10453-9, G&D). Putnam Pub Group.
Windy Day: Stories & Poems. Caroline F. Bauer. 1988. price not set. Lippincott.
Windy Day: Stories & Poems. Ed. by Caroline F. Bauer. LC 86-42994. (Illus.). 96p. (gr. 2-5). 1988. 11.95i (ISBN 0-397-32207-0, Lipp Jr Bks); PLB 11.89 (ISBN 0-397-32208-9). HarpJ.
Windy Day: Teddy Horsley Celebrates Pentecost on Whit Sunday. Leslie J. Francis & Nicola M. Slee. (Teddy Horsley Books for Young Christians). (Illus.). 24p. (ps-2). 1986. pap. 1.25 (ISBN 0-00-599748-8, Collins Liturgical). HarpR.
Windy Passage from Nostalgia. Richard Grossinger. 256p. (Orig.). 1974. pap. 5.00 (ISBN 0-913028-30-4). North Atlantic.
Windy Place. Henry Blakely. 1974. pap. 2.50. Broadside Pr.
Windy Rode. 106p. 1981. 2.25x (ISBN 0-686-46971-2, TXU 78-202). Rebel Mont Tem.
Windy: The Snow Goose. Robert Hunt. LC 74-735894. (Wildlife Stories Ser.). (Illus.). (gr. 2-5). 1978. 24.95 (ISBN 0-89290-035-0); 6 bks. & One cassette incl. Soc for Visual.
Windy Times: Poems & Prose. Gunter Kunert. Tr. by Agnes Stein. (Illus.). 227p. 1984. 14.95 (ISBN 0-87376-042-5). Red Dust.
Windy Tuesday Nights. Ralph Burns & Roger Pfingston. Ed. by Emilie Buchwald. LC 84-60939. (Mountains in Minnesota Ser.). 48p. 1984. pap. 6.00 (ISBN 0-915943-03-4). Milkweed Ed.
Wine. rev. ed. Hugh Johnson. 288p. 1986. 17.95 (ISBN 0-671-21997-9). S&S.
Wine. rev. ed. Hugh Johnson. 1987. pap. 10.95 (ISBN 0-671-63834-3, Fireside). S&S.
Wine. (Good Cook Ser.). (Illus.). 176p. 1983. 14.95 (ISBN 0-8094-2967-5). Time Life.
Wine. (Commodity Projections: 1985). 1979. pap. 7.50 (ISBN 0-686-59434-7, F1615, FAO). UNIPUB.
Wine-A Gentleman's Game: The Adventures of an Amateur Winemaker Turned Professional. Mark Miller. LC 83-47539. (Illus.). 224p. 1984. 17.45 (ISBN 0-06-015263-X, HarpT). Har-Row.
Wine: A Geographic Appreciation. Harm Jan DeBlij. LC 82-20648. (Illus.). 254p. 1983. text ed. 26.50x (ISBN 0-86598-091-8, Rowman & Allanheld). Rowman.
Wine Album. (Illus.). 160p. 1982. gift boxed 15.95 (ISBN 0-698-11206-7, Coward). Putnam Pub Group.
Wine: An Introduction. rev. ed. Maynard A. Amerine & Vernon L. Singleton. LC 75-46031. 1978. pap. 10.95x (ISBN 0-520-03202-0). U of Cal Pr.
Wine Analysis. Zoecklein. write for info. (ISBN 0-442-23463-5). Van Nos Reinhold.
Wine & Beer Making. Derek Watkins. (Leisure & Travel Ser.). 1978. 9.95 (ISBN 0-7153-7503-2). David & Charles.
Wine & Beermaking at Home. Kenneth Hill. LC 75-40968. (Illus.). 116p. 1976. 11.95 (ISBN 0-87523-185-3). Emerson.
Wine & Bitters. Isabelle K. Savell. (Illus.). 1975. pap. 2.95 (ISBN 0-911183-06-X). Rockland County Hist.
Wine & Conversation. Adrienne Lehrer. LC 82-48538. (Midland Bks: No. 308). 256p. 1983. 25.00x (ISBN 0-253-36550-3); pap. 17.50x (ISBN 0-253-20308-2). Ind U Pr.
Wine & Food of Spain. Jan Read et al. 1987. 19.95 (ISBN 0-316-73584-1). Little.
Wine & Food Society Menu Book: Recipes for Celebration. Alice W. Salmon & Hugo Dunn-Meynell. (Illus.). 256p. 1984. 25.95 (ISBN 0-442-28051-3). Van Nos Reinhold.
Wine & the Bottom Line. Edmund Osterland. 80p. 1980. pap. 9.95 (ISBN 0-317-57846-4, WL913). Natl Restaurant Assn.
Wine & the Music. William E. Barrett. 1977. pap. 1.25 (ISBN 0-380-01470-X, 09027). Avon.
Wine & the Will: Rabelais's Bacchic Christianity. Florence M. Weinberg. LC 78-181450. Repr. of 1972 ed. 47.30 (2027593). Bks Demand UMI.
Wine & Wine Service. Gino Nardella & Keith Doughterty. (Catering Ser.). (Illus.). 160p. 1987. pap. 18.95 (ISBN 0-7134-4825-3, Pub. by Batsford England). David & Charles.
Wine & Your Well Being. Salvatore P. Lucia. 160p. 1980. Repr. of 1971 ed. 9.95 (ISBN 0-932664-08-3). Wine Appreciation.
Wine Appreciation. Richard P. Vine. (Illus.). 544p. 1988. 60.00 (ISBN 0-8160-1148-6). Facts on File.
Wine Atlas of France: And Traveler's Guide to the Vineyards. Hugh Johnson & Hubrecht Duijker. (Illus.). 280p. 1987. 35.00 (ISBN 0-671-64232-4). S&S.
Wine Book. Rosalind Cooper. LC 81-83534. (Illus.). 1981. pap. 9.95 (ISBN 0-89586-131-3). Price Stern.
Wine Book. (Illus.). 64p. 1986. 16.95 (ISBN 0-88363-087-7). H L Levin.
Wine Cellar Book: A Practical Guide to Creating & Maintaining Your Own Personal Cellar. Steven Spurrier. (Illus.). 192p. 1986. 19.95 (ISBN 0-88162-197-8). Salem Hse Pubs.
Wine Cellar Record. Ernest Mittelberger. Ed. by Maurice Sullivan & Henry Roux. (Illus.). 1979. 32.50 (ISBN 0-932664-06-7). Wine Appreciation.
Wine Cookbook of Dinner Menus. Emily Chase. (Illus.). 1978. 6.95 (ISBN 0-932664-04-0). Wine Appreciation.
Wine Cookbook of Dinner Menus. Wine Advisory Board. Compiled by Chase Emily. LC 70-156348. 1971. 5.95 (ISBN 0-87832-038-5, WAB-6). Piper.
Wine Cooler Market. Ed. by Peter Allen. 200p. 1985. pap. text ed. 295.00 (ISBN 0-931634-18-0). FIND SVP.
Wine Country: A Pictorial History & Tour Guide. Phyllis Zauner. LC 83-50237. (Western Mini-Histories Ser.). (Illus.). 64p. (Orig.). 1983. pap. 4.50 (ISBN 0-936914-19-X). Zanel Pubns.
Wine Country Bed & Breakfast Almanac of the World Renowned Napa Valley. Ed. by Janet K. Stront. 1981. pap. 3.50 (ISBN 0-9614578-1-3). B & B Prod.
Wine Country-California. LC 87-80952. 176p. 1987. pap. 9.95 (ISBN 0-376-06946-5); pap. text ed. 14.95 (ISBN 0-376-06957-0). Sunset-Lane.
Wine Dark Sea. Robert Aickman. 1988. 18.95 (ISBN 1-557-10035-7, Arbor Hse). Morrow.
Wine-Dark Sea. Leonardo Sciascia. Tr. by Avril Bardoni from Ital. 142p. 1985. 14.95 (ISBN 0-85635-556-9). Carcanet.
Wine-Dark Sea. Leonardo Sciascia. Tr. by Avril Bardoni from Ital. 142p. 1988. pap. 6.95 (ISBN 0-85635-783-9). Carcanet.
Wine Drinker's Notebook. Compiled by James MacEwen & Jane Thatcher. LC 84-62091. 64p. 1985. 4.95 (ISBN 0-688-04713-0, Pub. by Beech Tree Bks). Morrow.
Wine Family in America, Section 3. Jacob D. Wine & J. Floyd Wine. LC 53-4352. (Illus.). 1971. 17.50 (ISBN 0-9604350-0-X). J F Wine.
Wine, Food & the Good Life. Arlene Mueller & Dorothy Indelicato. (Wine Cookbook). (Illus.). 144p. (Orig.). 1985. pap. 7.95 (ISBN 0-932664-47-4). Wine Appreciation.
Wine for Game & Fish: The Sporting Wife's Wine Companion. Jon Hurley. (Illus.). 128p. 1988. 22.95 (ISBN 0-85493-149-X, Pub. by Gollancz England). David & Charles.
Wine for Sale: Victoria Wine & the Liquor Trade, 1860-1984. Asa Briggs. LC 85-20877. (Illus.). x, 208p. 1986. 25.00 (ISBN 0-226-07485-4). U of Chicago Pr.
Wine Graffiti Book. Four Muscateers Staff. 98p. 1986. pap. 3.95 (ISBN 0-907621-15-5, Pub. by Quiller Pr England). Intl Spec Bk.
Wine Grape Varieties in the North Coast Counties of California. A. N. Kasimatis et al. 1977. pap. 3.00 (ISBN 0-931876-22-2, 4069). ANR Pubns CA.
Wine-Grower's Guide. rev ed. Philip M. Wagner. (Illus.). 1965. 14.95 (ISBN 0-394-40183-2). Knopf.
Wine Handbook. Serena Sutcliffe. 240p. 1982. pap. 14.95 (ISBN 0-671-45537-0, Fireside). S&S.
Wine Handbook. Serena Sutcliffe. (Illus.). 224p. 1987. pap. 10.95 (ISBN 0-671-63516-6, Fireside). S&S.
Wine in Everyday Cooking: Cooking with Wine for Family & Friends. Patricia Ballare. 128p. pap. 5.95 (ISBN 0-932664-45-8). Wine Appreciation.
Wine in the Bible & the Church. G. I. Williamson. 1976. pap. 3.95 (ISBN 0-87552-547-4). Presby & Reformed.
Wine into Words: A History & Bibliography of Wine Books in the English Language. James M. Gabler. LC 84-70446. (Illus.). 403p. 1985. 38.00 (ISBN 0-9613525-0-7). Bacchus Pr Ltd.
Wine Log. Irene J. Kleinsinger. (Illus.). 96p. 1982. leather cover 19.95 (ISBN 0-9605146-4-3); suede cover o.s.i. 11.75 (ISBN 0-9605146-3-5); vinyl cover 5.50 (ISBN 0-9605146-2-7). IJK Intl.
Wine Lover's Cookbook. Malcolm Herbert & Brian St. Pierre. (Wine Cookbook). (Illus.). 128p. (Orig.). 1983. pap. 7.95 (ISBN 0-932664-29-6). Wine Appreciation.
Wine Lover's Drink Book. John Poister. 160p. 1983. 7.95 (ISBN 0-02-010090-6, Collier). Macmillan.
Wine Lover's Guide to France. Michael Busselle. 1986. 24.95 (ISBN 0-316-11839-7). Little.
Wine Lover's Quiz Book: Challenging Questions & Answers for Wine Buffs & Bluffers. Peter Adams. 144p. 1987. pap. 9.95 (ISBN 0-89586-633-1). Price Stern.
Wine, Murder & Blueberry Sundaes. C. C. Risenhoover. Ed. by Shirley D. Ratisseau. LC 86-62064. 252p. 1986. 15.95 (ISBN 0-918865-04-2). McLennan Hse.
Wine Notebook: A Personal Journal with Quotes. (Illus.). 96p. (Orig.). 1986. lib. bdg. 15.90 (ISBN 0-89471-465-1); pap. 5.95 (ISBN 0-89471-464-3). Running Pr.
Wine of Astonishment. Earl Lovelace. (Caribbean Writers Ser.: No. 28). xiv, 146p. 1983. pap. text ed. 7.00 (ISBN 0-435-98880-8). Heinemann Ed.
Wine of Astonishment. Earl Lovelace. LC 84-48005. 160p. 1984. pap. 6.95 (ISBN 0-394-72795-9, Vin). Random.
Wine of Astonishment. William Sears. 192p. 1963. pap. 4.75 (ISBN 0-85398-009-8). G Ronald Pub.
Wine of Endless Life: Taoists Drinking Songs. Tr. by Jerome Seaton. 1985. 6.00 (ISBN 0-934834-59-8). White Pine.
Wine of Life: And Other Essays on Societies, Energy & Living Things. Harold J. Morowitz. LC 79-16404. 1979. 14.00 (ISBN 0-312-88227-0). Ox Bow.
Wine of Morning. Bob Jones. 252p. 1976. pap. 4.23 (ISBN 0-89084-056-3). Bob Jones Univ Pr.
Wine of Passion. Clarissa Ross. 1979. pap. 2.25 (ISBN 0-505-51390-0, Pub. by Tower Bks). Leisure NY.
Wine of the Dreamers. John D. MacDonald. 1981. pap. 3.50 (ISBN 0-449-14193-4, GM). Fawcett.
Wine of the Dreamers. John D. MacDonald. 15.95 (ISBN 0-89190-777-7, Pub. by Am Repr). Amereon Ltd.
Wine of the Puritans: A Study of Present Day America. Van Wyck Brooks. 1978. Repr. of 1908 ed. lib. bdg. 35.50 (ISBN 0-8495-0446-5). Arden Lib.

Wine of the Spirit: Prayer. Lilian P. Long. LC 87-91322. 208p. (Orig.). 1988. pap. 9.95 (ISBN 0-9619722-1-1). L P Long Pub.

Wine of Youth: Selected Stories of John Fante. John Fante. LC 84-20454. 269p. (Orig.). 1985. 20.00 (ISBN 0-87685-583-4); pap. 12.50 (ISBN 0-87685-582-6). Black Sparrow.

Wine on the Desert. Max Brand. 1976. Repr. of 1940 ed. lib. bdg. 18.95x (ISBN 0-88411-511-9, Pub. by Aeonian Pr). Amereon Ltd.

Wine Production Technology in the United States. Ed. by Maynard A. Amerine. LC 80-28041. (Symposium Ser.: No. 145). 1981. 34.95 (ISBN 0-8412-0596-5); pap. 19.95 (ISBN 0-8412-0602-3). Am Chemical.

Wine Regions of the Southern Hemisphere. Harm J. De Blij. LC 84-17949. (Illus.). 269p. 1985. 32.95x (ISBN 0-8476-7390-1, Rowman & Allanheld). Rowman.

Wine Roads of Europe. Marc Millon & Kim Millon. (Illus.). 288p. 1984. pap. 10.95 (ISBN 0-671-50408-8, Fireside). S&S.

Wine Routes of America: The Complete Travel Guide to Vineyards & Wineries. Jan Aaron & Leslie Jay. Ed. by Sandra Soule. (Illus.). 416p. Date not set. pap. 12.95 (ISBN 0-525-48436-1). Dutton.

Wine Scandal. Fritz Hallgarten. 184p. 1986. 18.95 (ISBN 0-932664-52-0). Wine Appreciation.

Wine Spectator Guide to Selected Wines, 1985. Ed. by Marvin Shanken. 96p. 1985. pap. 3.95 (ISBN 0-671-54247-8, Pub. by Fireside). S&S.

Wine Spectator Wine Maps see Wine Spectator's Wine Country Guide to California, 1988 Edition.

Wine Spectator Wine Maps: The Complete Guide to Wineries, Restaurants & Lodging in California Wine Country. rev. & exp. ed. Marvin R. Shanken. (Illus.). 46p. 1984. pap. 3.00 (ISBN 0-918076-26-9). M Shanken Comm.

Wine Spectator Wine Maps: The Complete Guide to Wineries, Restaurants & Lodging in California Wine Country, 1985. rev. ed. Marvin R. Shanken. (Illus.). 110p. 1985. pap. text ed. 5.20 (ISBN 0-918076-36-6). M Shanken Comm.

Wine Spectator Wine Maps, 1986: The Complete Guide to Wineries, Restaurants & Lodging in California Wine Country. 3rd, rev. ed. Marvin R. Shanken. (Illus.). 1986. pap. text ed. 5.20 (ISBN 0-918076-39-0). M Shanken Comm.

Wine Spectator's Wine Country Guide to California, 1988 Edition. 5th, rev. & enl. ed. Marvin R. Shanken. Orig. Title: Wine Spectator Wine Maps. (Illus.). 90p. 1988. pap. text ed. 6.20 (ISBN 0-918076-56-0). M Shanken Comm.

Wine Talk. Frank Prial. LC 78-58165. 1978. write for info. (ISBN 0-8129-0793-0). Times Bks.

Wine Tasting Handbook. Paul Gillette. (Illus.). 1988. pap. 7.95 (ISBN 0-913290-88-2). Camaro Pub.

Wine Tasting in California. LC 73-85632. (Illus.). 1985. 4.95 (ISBN 0-913290-05-X). Camaro Pub.

Wine Trivia. E. M. Quinlan et al. LC 85-70068. (Illus.). 197p. (Orig.). 1985. pap. 7.95 (ISBN 0-9611268-9-2). Quinlan Pr.

Wine Vintages of the West Coast. 2nd ed. Robin Bradley. (Illus.). 114p. 1986. pap. 12.95 (ISBN 0-9590183-1-X). Aris Bks Harris.

Wine, Women & Death: Medieval Hebrew Poems on the Good Life. Raymond P. Scheindlin. Tr. by Raymond P. Scheindlin from Hebrew. (Illus.). 218p. 1986. 15.95. JPS Phila.

Wine, Women, & Song. Ed. & tr. by John A. Symonds. LC 74-112944. Repr. of 1884 ed. 9.00 (ISBN 0-404-06319-5). AMS Pr.

Wine, Women, & Song: Medieval Latin Students' Songs. Ed. by John A. Symonds. LC 66-26826. (Medieval Library Ser.). Repr. of 1883 ed. 18.50x (ISBN 0-8154-0228-7). Cooper Sq.

Winegold: Short Stories. Joe Nigg. LC 85-51697. 71p. 1985. 15.00 (ISBN 0-933573-04-9); pap. 7.00 (ISBN 0-933573-05-7). Wayland Pr.

Winegrowers of France & the Government Since 1875. Charles K. Warner. LC 74-14029. 303p. 1975. Repr. of 1960 ed. lib. bdg. 35.00x (ISBN 0-8371-7779-0, WAWF). Greenwood.

Winegrowing in Eastern America: An Illustrated Guide to Viniculture East of the Rockies. Lucie T. Morton. LC 85-47696. (Illus.). 208p. 1985. 24.95 (ISBN 0-8014-1290-0). Cornell U Pr.

Winemakers Cookbook: Culinary Adventures with America's Premier Vintners. Lou S. Pappas. LC 86-17603. (Illus.). 108p. (Orig.). 1986. pap. 14.95 (ISBN 0-87701-373-X). Chronicle Bks.

Winemaker's Guide: Essential Information for Making Wine & Champagne. 2nd ed. F. S. Nury & K. C. Fugelsang. LC 78-65264. (Illus.). 141p. 1982. pap. 7.95 (ISBN 0-934136-27-0, Valley Calif). Western Tanager.

Winemaker's Reference Book. Jennifer Curry. (Illus.). 224p. 1985. 25.95 (ISBN 0-7153-8308-6). David & Charles.

Winequest: The Wine Dictionary. Ted Grudzinski. 469p. 1985. 28.00 (ISBN 0-9615063-0-X). Winequest.

Wineries of the Finger Lakes. James M. Morris. Ed. by Jack Sherman. (Illus.). 144p. 1985. pap. 4.95 (ISBN 0-9615964-8-1). I Stephanus Pub.

Wineries of the Mid-Atlantic. Jon Palmer. 220p. (Orig.). 1988. text ed. 30.00 (ISBN 0-8135-1346-4); pap. 12.95 (ISBN 0-8135-1351-0). Rutgers U Pr.

Wineries of the Northeast. James M. Morris. Ed. by Andrea Chesman. (Yankee Magazine Guidebook Ser.). (Illus.). 256p. pap. cancelled (ISBN 0-89909-151-2). Yankee Bks.

Wineries of the Northeast: A Comprehensive Guide to Touring & Tasting across New York & New England. James M. Morris. 208p. 1988. pap. 10.95 (ISBN 0-9615964-7-3). I Stephanus Pub.

Winery, Defenses, & Soundings at Gibeon. James B. Pritchard. (University Museum Monographs: No. 26). (Illus.). viii, 85p. 1964. pap. 15.00 (ISBN 0-934718-18-0). Univ Mus of U PA.

Wines. LC 83-4952. (Good Cook Ser.). (gr. 7 up). 1983. lib. bdg. 22.60 (ISBN 0-8094-2968-3, Pub. by Time-Life). Silver.

Wines & Beers of Old New England: A How-to-Do-It History. Sanborn C. Brown. LC 77-72519. (Illus.). 187p. 1978. pap. 7.95 (ISBN 0-87451-148-8). U Pr of New Eng.

Wines & Brandies of Spain & Mexico. Stan Jones. (Illus.). 1985. pap. 14.95 (ISBN 0-317-12908-2). Bar Guide.

Wines & Vineyards of Spain. Miguel Torres. 200p. 1982. 19.95 (ISBN 0-932664-27-X). Wine Appreciation.

Wines & Wine Gardens of Austria. S. F. Hallgarten & F. L. Hargaten. (Illus.). 340p. 1979. 19.95x (ISBN 0-932664-26-1). Wine Appreciation.

Wines & Wineries of America's Northwest. Ted J. Meredith. (Illus.). 224p. (Orig.). 1986. pap. 12.95 (ISBN 0-936666-03-X). Nexus WA.

Wines & Wineries of New South Wales. James Halliday. 165p. 1981. text ed. 14.50x (ISBN 0-7022-1570-8). U of Queensland Pr.

Wines & Wineries of Santa Barbara County. Cork Millner. (Illus.). 184p. 1985. pap. 8.50 (ISBN 0-87461-061-3). McNally & Loftin.

Wines & Wineries of South Australia. James Halliday. (Illus.). 144p. 1981. text ed. 14.50 boards (ISBN 0-7022-1571-6). U of Queensland Pr.

Wines & Wineries of Victoria. James Halliday. (Illus.). 152p. 1982. bds. 14.50 (ISBN 0-7022-1740-9). U of Queensland Pr.

Wines & Wineries of Western Australia. James Halliday. (Illus.). 119p. 1983. text ed. 14.50x (ISBN 0-7022-1673-9). U of Queensland Pr.

Wines, Beers, & Spirits: A Consumer's Sourcebook. Dean Tudor. 236p. 1985. lib. bdg. 25.00 (ISBN 0-87287-455-9). Libs Unl.

Wines Brewing Distillation. Gerald F. Steinlage. LC 72-189987. 91p. 1972. pap. 3.95 (ISBN 0-914754-01-7). Steinlage.

Wines of America. 3rd, rev. ed. Leon D. Adams. 640p. 1985. text ed. 22.95 (ISBN 0-07-000319-X). McGraw.

Wines of Australia. Oliver Mayo. 200p. 1986. 25.00 (ISBN 0-571-13868-3); pap. 13.95 (ISBN 0-571-13869-1). Faber & Faber.

Wines of Bordeaux. Edmund Penning-Roswell. 704p. (Orig.). 1983. pap. 12.95 (ISBN 0-932664-51-2). Wine Appreciation.

Wines of Bordeaux. Edmond Penning-Rowsell. 1981. 27.50 (ISBN 0-684-16982-7, ScribT). Scribner.

Wines of Bordeaux & Western France. John J. Baxevanis. 288p. 1987. 32.95 (ISBN 0-8476-7490-8). Rowman.

Wines of Chablis & the Yonne. Rosemary George. LC 84-50544. (Illus.). 216p. 1984. 29.95 (ISBN 0-85667-179-7, Pub. by P Wilson Pubs). Sotheby Pubns.

Wines of Champagne, Burgundy, & Eastern & Southern France. John J. Baxevanis. 224p. 1987. 32.95 (ISBN 0-8476-7534-3). Rowman.

Wines of Germany. Frank Schoonmaker. Rev. by Peter Sichel. 222p. 1986. 22.95 (ISBN 0-571-18076-0); pap. 11.95 (ISBN 0-571-13056-9). Faber & Faber.

Wines of Germany: Completely Revised Edition of Frank Schoonmaker's Classic. new ed. Peter Sichel. (Illus.). 224p. 1980. 12.95 (ISBN 0-8038-8100-2). Hastings.

Wines of Italy. Charles G. Bode. (Illus.). 135p. 1974. pap. 2.50 (ISBN 0-486-23003-1). Dover.

Wines of Italy. Charles G. Bode. 8.25 (ISBN 0-8446-5007-2). Peter Smith.

Wines of Pentagoet. John Gould. 1986. 14.95 (ISBN 0-393-02303-6). Norton.

Wines of Portugal. Jan Read. (Books on Wine). 192p. 1983. 12.95 (ISBN 0-571-11951-4); pap. 6.95 (ISBN 0-571-11952-2). Faber & Faber.

Wines of Saint-Emilion & Pomerol. Jeffrey Benson & Alastair Mackenzie. (Illus.). 300p. 39.95 (ISBN 0-85667-169-X). Sotheby Pubns.

Wines of Spain. Jan Read. (Books on Wine). (Illus.). 272p. 1983. pap. 6.95 (ISBN 0-571-11938-7). Faber & Faber.

Wines of Spain. 2nd ed. Jan Read. 272p. (Orig.). 1986. pap. 13.95 (ISBN 0-571-14621-X). Faber & Faber.

Wines of Texas. Sarah J. English. (Illus.). 160p. 1986. 12.95 (ISBN 0-89015-566-6). Eakin Pr.

Wines of the Graves. Pamela V. Price. LC 88-60435. (Illus.). 232p. 1988. 45.00 (ISBN 0-85667-334-X, Pub. by P Wilson Pubs). Sotheby Pubns.

Wines of the Midwest. Ruth E. Church. LC 77-83753. (Illus.). vii, 248p. 1982. cloth 21.95 (ISBN 0-8040-0779-9, Pub by Swallow); pap. 9.95 (ISBN 0-8040-0426-9, Pub by Swallow). Ohio U Pr.

Wines of the Rhone. 2nd ed. John Livingstone-Learmonth & Melvyn C. Master. LC 82-24207. (Books on Wine). 255p. 1983. 26.95 (ISBN 0-571-18075-2); pap. 10.95 (ISBN 0-571-13055-0). Faber & Faber.

Wines of the Rhone Valley: A Guide to Origins. Robert W. Mayberry. LC 87-16516. 224p. 1987. 29.95 (ISBN 0-8476-7430-4). Rowman.

Wines of the Rhone Valley & Provence: The Definitive Guide. Robert M. Parker, Jr. (Illus.). 480p. 1987. 22.95 (ISBN 0-671-63379-1). S&S.

Wines of the Rioja. Jan Read. LC 84-50546. (Illus.). 184p. 1984. 29.95 (ISBN 0-85667-186-X, Pub. by P Wilson Pubs). Sotheby Pubns.

Wines of the United States & Canada. John J. Baxevanis. 208p. 1988. 24.95 (ISBN 0-8476-7431-2). Rowman.

Wines, Spirits & Fermentations. Richard Hunderfund. (Illus.). 192p. (Orig.). 1983. pap. 10.95. Star Pub CA.

Wines: Their Sensory Evaluation. rev., Enl. ed. Maynard A. Amerine & Edward B. Roessler. LC 83-1539. (Illus.). 320p. 1983. text ed. 27.95 (ISBN 0-7167-1479-5). W H Freeman.

Winesburg by the Sea: Poems. Harold Witt. 1979. lib. bdg. 10.00x (ISBN 0-914476-70-X); pap. 5.00x (ISBN 0-914476-71-8). Thorp Springs.

Winesburg, Ohio. Sherwood Anderson. 1976. pap. 3.95 (ISBN 0-14-000609-5). Penguin.

Winesburg, Ohio. Sherwood Anderson. 256p. 1988. pap. 3.95 (ISBN 0-14-043304-X). Penguin.

Winesburg Ohio. Sherwood Anderson. Date not set. 17.95 (ISBN 0-8488-0417-1). Amereon Ltd.

Winesburg, Ohio Notes. Ann R. Morris. 61p. (Orig.). 1974. pap. text ed. 3.25 (ISBN 0-8220-1382-7). Cliffs.

Winesburg, Ohio: Text & Criticism. Sherwood Anderson. Ed. by John Ferres. (Viking Critical Library: No. 1). 1977. pap. 8.95 (ISBN 0-14-015501-5). Penguin.

Winewrights Register: And Marketplace for Small California Wineries. 4th ed. Bruce Cass. 240p. 1988. pap. 14.95 (ISBN 0-9619304-0-3). Winewrights Reg.

Winewrights Register: California's Best Micro-Wineries & How to Get Them. Bruce Cass. (Illus.). 256p. (Orig.). 1988. pap. 14.95 (ISBN 0-9619304-1-1). Winewrights Reg.

Winfield: A Player's Life. Dave Winfield & Tom Parker. LC 87-35313. 310p. 1988. 16.95 (ISBN 0-393-02467-9). Norton.

Winfield Scott Hancock: A Soldier's Life. 384p. 1988. 29.95 (ISBN 0-253-36580-5). Ind U Pr.

Winfield Scott: The Soldier & the Man. Charles W. Elliot. Ed. by Richard H. Kohn. LC 78-22379. (American Military Experience Ser.). (Illus.). 1979. Repr. of 1937 ed. lib. bdg. 57.50x (ISBN 0-405-11856-2). Ayer Co Pubs.

Wing & a Prayer. Guy Kingston. 192p. 1986. 15.95 (ISBN 0-8027-0887-0). Walker & Co.

Wing & Shot. Robert G. Wehle. 1964. 25.00 (ISBN 0-686-65297-5). Country Pr NY.

Wing Beat: A Collection of Eagle Woodcuts. G. E. Pogony. Tr. by Douglas J. Graham from Hungarian. LC 76-22176. (Illus.). 1976. 15.00x (ISBN 0-933652-10-0). Domjan Studio.

Wing-Brush. Ellis Ovesen. (Illus.). 80p. 1986. 6.50 (ISBN 0-8233-0420-5). Golden Quill.

Wing Chun Bil Jee: The Deadly Art of Thrusting Fingers. William Cheung. LC 83-50021. (Illus.). 160p. (Orig.). 1983. pap. 8.95 (ISBN 0-86568-045-0, 214). Unique Pubns.

Wing Chun Kung-Fu. J. Yimm Lee. LC 72-87863. (Chinese Arts Ser.). (Illus.). 1972. pap. 8.50x (ISBN 0-89750-037-7, 309, Dist. by Wehman). Ohara Pubns.

Wing Chun Kung-Fu. G. Wong. 8.95x (ISBN 0-685-63793-X). Wehman.

Wing Chun: The Art of Unarmed Defence & Attack. rev. ed. Joseph Cheng. (Illus.). 176p. 1986. pap. text ed. 12.00 (ISBN 0-87364-377-1). Paladin Pr.

Wing Chun, the Deceptive Hands. Douglas Wong. 1977. 5.95x (ISBN 0-685-83178-7). Wehman.

Wing Field: Edwardian Gentleman. George E. Alexander. (Illus.). 325p. 1986. 17.95 (ISBN 0-914339-14-1). P E Randall Pub.

Wing-Footed Wanderer: Conscience & Transcendence. Donald E. Miller. LC 77-1503. Repr. of 1977 ed. 45.60 (ISBN 0-8357-9032-0, 2016421). Bks Demand UMI.

Wing Leader. J. E. Johnson. Date not set. pap. 1.95 (ISBN 0-345-30472-1). Ballantine.

Wing of Love. Irma H. Cervantes. (Illus.). 72p. 1984. pap. 4.75x (ISBN 0-9609600-1-5). Five Windmills.

Wing on a Flea: A Book about Shapes. Ed Emberley. (Illus.). (ps-3). Date not set. 14.95. Little.

Wing Songs. Jean S. Duling. 80p. 1986. 6.50 (ISBN 0-8233-0412-4). Golden Quill.

Wing Theory. Abraham Robinson & J. A. Laurmann. LC 57-601. (Cambridge Aeronautical Ser.: No. 2). pap. 144.80 (ISBN 0-317-10805-0, 2051692). Bks Demand UMI.

Wingate of the Sudan. Ronald Wingate. LC 74-22507. (Illus.). 274p. 1975. Repr. of 1955 ed. lib. bdg. 35.00 (ISBN 0-8371-7862-2, WIWS). Greenwood.

Wingbone: Poetry from Colorado. Ed. by Janice Hays & Pamela Haines. LC 86-60199. 160p. (Orig.). 1986. pap. 9.95 (ISBN 0-937567-03-5). Sudden Jungle Pr.

Winged Assassin. Catherine Cooke. 288p. Date not set. pap. 2.95 (ISBN 0-441-89425-9, Pub. by Ace Science Fiction). Ace Bks.

Winged Bean Production in the Tropics. T. N. Kahn. (Plant Production & Protection Papers: No. 38). 223p. 1982. pap. 15.00 (ISBN 92-5-101230-X, F2366, FAO). UNIPUB.

Winged Bull. Dion Fortune. 328p. (Orig.). 1980. pap. 9.95 (ISBN 0-87728-501-2). Weiser.

Winged Colt of Casa Mia. Betsy Byars. (Illus.). 132p. (gr. 3-7). 1988. pap. 2.50 (ISBN 0-380-00201-9, Camelot). Avon.

Winged Dancer. Camarin Grae. 288p. 1986. pap. 8.95 (ISBN 0-930044-88-6). Naiad Pr.

Winged Darkness & Other Stories by William Heinesen. William Heinesen. Ed. by Hedin Bronner. Tr. by William Heinesen & Hedin Bronner. 200p. 1983. 26.50 (ISBN 0-8290-0990-6). Irvington.

Winged Darkness & Other Stories by William Heinesen. William Heinesen. Ed. by Hedin Bronner. 200p. 1985. pap. 14.95x (ISBN 0-8290-1669-4). Irvington.

Winged Defense. William Mitchell. LC 75-137977. (American History & Culture in the Twentieth Century Ser.). 1971. Repr. of 1925 ed. 28.50 (ISBN 0-8046-1432-6, Pub. by Kennikat). Assoc Faculty Pr.

Winged Defense: The Development & Possibilites of Modern Air Power - Economic & Military. William Mitchell. 320p. 1988. pap. 7.95 (ISBN 0-486-25771-1). Dover.

Winged Gospel: America's Romance with Aviation, Nineteen Hundred to Nineteen Fifty. Joseph J. Corn. 177p. 1987. pap. 9.95 (ISBN 0-19-504158-5). Oxford U Pr.

Winged Gospel: America's Romance with Aviation, 1900-1950. Joseph J. Corn. (Illus.). 1983. 24.95 (ISBN 0-19-503356-6). Oxford U Pr.

Winged Horse: The Story of the Poets & Their Poetry. J. Auslander & F. E. Hill. LC 68-24959. (Studies in Poetry, No. 38). 1968. Repr. of 1928 ed. lib. bdg. 75.00x (ISBN 0-8383-0328-5). Haskell.

Winged Life. Hannah Hurnard. 1975. pap. 3.95 (ISBN 0-8423-8225-9). Tyndale.

Winged Life: The Poetic Voice of Henry David Thoreau. Ed. by Robert Bly. LC 86-60603. (Illus.). 160p. 1986. 18.95 (ISBN 0-87156-762-8). Sierra.

Winged Majesty: The Boeing B-17 Flying Fortress in War & Peace. Steve Birdsall et al. (Illus.). 1980. pap. 3.95 (ISBN 0-686-71808-9, Pub. by Bomber). Aviation.

Winged Pharaoh. Joan Grant. 324p. 1985. pap. 7.95 (ISBN 0-89804-140-6). Ariel OH.

Winged Pharaoh. Joan M. Grant. 30.50 (ISBN 0-405-11794-9). Ayer Co Pubs.

Winged Samurai: Saburo Sakai & the Zero Fighter Aces. Henry Sakaida. 160p. 1985. pap. 14.95 (ISBN 0-912173-05-X). Champlin Museum.

Winged Stallion: Fighting & Training with the First Airborne. Michael Packe. (Illus.). 256p. 1988. 24.95 (ISBN 0-7137-2037-9, Pub. by Blandford Pr England). Sterling.

Winged Victory. Dan Brennan. 1978. pap. 1.50 (ISBN 0-505-51254-8, Pub. by Tower Bks). Leisure NY.

Winged Victory. V. M. Yeats. (Echoes of War Ser.). 1987. pap. 10.95 (ISBN 0-907675-45-X, Pub. by Buchan & Enright England). Seven Hills Bks.

Winged Watchman. Hilda Van Stockum. LC 62-16280. (Illus.). 228p. (gr. 4 up). 1963. 6.95 (ISBN 0-374-38448-7). FS&G.

Winged Wonders: The Story of the Flying Wings. E. T. Wooldridge. LC 83-600296. (Illus.). 230p. 1983. pap. 19.95 (ISBN 0-87474-967-0, WOWWP). Smithsonian.

Winged Word. Berkley Peabody. LC 72-91200. 562p. 1975. 59.50 (ISBN 0-87395-059-3). State U NY Pr.

Winged Words. Philip Howard. 288p. 1988. 24.95 (ISBN 0-19-520770-X). Oxford U Pr.

Winging It. Shirley Aycock. 24p. 1979. stapled chapbook 1.25 (ISBN 0-942432-01-0). M O P Pr.

Wingless Pegasus: A Handbook for Critics. George Boas. 1979. 21.00 (ISBN 0-405-10584-3). Ayer Co Pubs.

Wingless Victory: A Biography of Gabriele d'Annunzio & Eleonore Duse. Frances Winwar. LC 74-10363. 374p. 1974. Repr. of 1956 ed. lib. bdg. 35.00 (ISBN 0-8371-7671-9, WIWV). Greenwood.

Wingman. Mark Maloney. 464p. 1987. pap. 3.95 (ISBN 0-8217-2015-5). Zebra.

Wingman, No. 3: The Lucifer Crusade. Mack Maloney. 432p. 1987. pap. 3.95 (ISBN 0-8217-2232-8). Zebra.

Wingman, No. 4: Thunder in the East. Mack Maloney. 432p. 1988. pap. 3.95 (ISBN 0-8217-2453-3). Zebra.

Wingmaster: Gods in a Vortex, Pt. II. David Houston. 1981. pap. 2.25 (ISBN 0-8439-0945-5, Leisure Bks). Leisure NY.

Wings. Jeannette Angell. 448p. (Orig.). 1988. pap. 4.95 (ISBN 1-55802-020-9). Lynx Bks.

Wings. Arthur Kopit. (Mermaid Dramabook Ser.). 78p. 1978. 8.95 (ISBN 0-8090-1239-1); pap. 5.25 (ISBN 0-8090-9756-7). Hill & Wang.

Wings. Gene S. Porter. 1986. Repr. lib. bdg. 16.95x (ISBN 0-89966-531-4). Buccaneer Bks.

Wings. Neal Travis. 336p. 1985. pap. 3.95 (ISBN 0-380-89802-0). Avon.
Wings. LC 83-51813. (Illus.). 144p. 1984. 37.00 (ISBN 0-934738-05-X). Thomasson Grant.
Wings: A Tale of Two Chickens. James Marshall. LC 85-40953. (Viking Kestrel Picture Bks.). (Illus.). 32p. (ps-3). 1986. 11.95 (ISBN 0-670-80961-6, Viking Kestrel). Viking.
Wings: A Tale of Two Chickens. James Marshall. (ps up). 1988. pap. 3.95 (ISBN 0-14-050579-2, Puffin Bks). Penguin.
Wings above the Diamantina. Arthur W. Upfield. 320p. 1986. pap. 3.95 (ISBN 0-02-025970-0, Collier). Macmillan.
Wings & Roots. Susan Terris. LC 82-2553. 186p. (gr. 7 up). 1982. 10.95 (ISBN 0-374-38451-7). FS&G.
Wings & Saddles. (Southwestern Studies Ser.: No. 19). 1967. pap. 5.00 (ISBN 0-87404-133-3). Tex Western.
Wings & Things. Marc Brown. LC 81-12095. (Bright & Early Ser.: No. 26). (Illus.). 36p. (ps-1). 1982. 5.95 (ISBN 0-394-85130-7, XBYR); lib. bdg. 6.99 (ISBN 0-394-95130-1). Random.
Wings & Things: Origami That Flies. Stephen Weiss. (Illus.). 128p. 1984. pap. 8.95 (ISBN 0-312-88228-9). St Martin.
Wings at War Series, 6 vols. in one, No. 1-6. U. S. Air Force. Ed. by James Gilbert. LC 79-7301. (Flight: Its First Seventy-Five Years Ser.). (Illus.). 1979. Repr. of 1945 ed. lib. bdg. 34.50x (ISBN 0-405-12207-1). Ayer Co Pubs.
Wings Complete. Paul McCartney. (MPL Communications, Inc. Bks.). (Illus.). 1977. pap. 9.95 (ISBN 0-394-73503-X). Random.
Wings for Independent Thinking. Belinda Cochran & Carol Reid. (Illus.). 56p. (Orig.). (gr. 3-8). 1984. 5.95 (ISBN 0-88047-038-0, 8403). DOK Pubs.
Wings for Lai Ho. Genny Lim. Tr. by Gordon Lew. (Illus.). 48p. (Orig.). (gr. 5-8). 1982. pap. 5.95 (ISBN 0-934788-01-4). E-W Pub Co.
Wings for My Flight: The Peregrine Falcons at Chimney Rock. Marcy Houle. (Illus.). 160p. (Orig.). 1988. 15.95 (ISBN 0-935704-48-5); pap. 9.95 (ISBN 0-935704-49-3). Howe Brothers.
Wings for the Mad Flight: In Pursuit of Understanding the Brain. John F. Avedon. 1989. 18.95 (ISBN 0-385-24060-0). Doubleday.
Wings from Above. Anne Frost. (Illus.). 72p. (Orig.). 1987. pap. 9.95 (ISBN 0-9614624-4-2). Frost Pub.
Wings from Burma to the Himalayas. John W. Gordon. (Illus.). 265p. Date not set. 17.95x (ISBN 0-9615206-5-5). Marshall Pubs.
Wings in the Sea: The Humpback Whale. Lois K. Winn & Howard E. Winn. LC 84-40598. (Illus.). 163p. 1985. 25.00 (ISBN 0-87451-335-9); pap. 10.95 (ISBN 0-87451-336-7). U Pr of New Eng.
Wings Like Eagles: The Story of Soaring in the U. S. A. Paul A. Schweizer. LC 87-28850. (Illus.). 388p. 1988. 39.95 (ISBN 0-87474-828-3). Smithsonian.
Wings O'er the Sea. Grace Blakeslee. 1980. 5.50 (ISBN 0-8233-0323-3). Golden Quill.
Wings of Adrian. Jan Seabaugh. 224p. 1986. pap. 5.95 (ISBN 0-310-47341-1, 15580P). Zondervan.
Wings of Anger. Alfred V. Beaumont. LC 84-90259. 163p. 1985. 10.95 (ISBN 0-533-06298-5). Vantage.
Wings of Cessna: Model 120 to the Citation III. Edward H. Phillips. (Illus.). 128p. (Orig.). 1986. pap. 12.95 (ISBN 0-911139-05-2). Flying Bks.
Wings of Charity. Elouise B. Jackson. 1986. 6.75 (ISBN 0-8062-2311-1). Carlton.
Wings of Courage. Robert L. Gray. LC 84-61223. 154p. (Orig.). pap. 4.95. Omenana.
Wings of Death. Christopher Sloane. (Orig.). 1983. pap. 2.50 (ISBN 0-8217-1210-1). Zebra.
Wings of Eagles Feet of Clay. Leonard Garrett. 48p. 1987. 6.95 (ISBN 0-8062-2829-6). Carlton.
Wings of Fear. Carolyn Keene. (Nancy Drew Files Ser.: No. 13). 160p. (Orig.). (YA) (gr. 7 up). 1987. pap. 2.95 (ISBN 0-671-64137-9). Archway.
Wings of Fire. Henry Zeybel. 304p. (Orig.). 1988. pap. 3.95 (ISBN 0-671-64082-8). PB.
Wings of Flame. Nancy Springer. 256p. 1985. 13.95 (ISBN 0-312-93932-9, Dist. by St. Martin's Press). Tor Bks.
Wings of Flame. Nancy Springer. 256p. 1986. pap. 2.95 (ISBN 0-8125-5484-1, Dist. by Warner Pub Services & St. Martin's Press). Tor Bks.
Wings of Gold: An Account of Naval Aviation Training in World War II. Ed. by Wesley P. Newton & Robert R. Rea. LC 86-7013. 490p. 1987. 34.95 (ISBN 0-8173-0319-7). U of Ala Pr.
Wings of Gold II: The Fly Boys. T. E. Cruise. 1988. pap. 3.95. PB.
Wings of Gold No. 1: The Aces. T. E. Cruise. 384p. (Orig.). 1988. pap. 3.95 (ISBN 0-445-20628-4, Pub. by Popular Lib). Warner Bks.
Wings of Gold: The Flyboys, Bk. 2. T. E. Cruise. 352p. (Orig.). Date not set. pap. 3.95 (ISBN 0-445-20630-6, Pub. by Popular Lib). Warner Bks.
Wings of History: The Air Museums of Europe. Louis Divone. LC 88-5158. (Illus.). 320p. (Orig.). 1988. pap. 21.95 (ISBN 0-939047-21-7). Oakton Hills Pubns.
Wings of Judgment: American Bombing in World War II. Ronald Schaffer. (Illus.). 272p. 1985. 12.95 (ISBN 0-19-503629-8). Oxford U Pr.
Wings of Judgment: American Bombing in World War Two. Ronald Schaffer. 286p. 1988. pap. 8.95 (ISBN 0-19-505640-X). Oxford U Pr.
Wings of Life: Whole Vegetarian Cookery. Julie Jordan. LC 76-43075. (Cookbook Ser.). (Illus.). 256p. 1976. 20.95 (ISBN 0-912278-82-X); pap. 8.95 (ISBN 0-912278-77-3). Crossing Pr.
Wings of Love. Alexandra Lang-Carlin. 400p. (Orig.). 1987. pap. 3.95 (ISBN 0-8439-2501-9, Leisure Bks). Leisure NY.
Wings of Love & Random Thought. Bhagwan S. Rajneesh. 1979. pap. 4.50 (ISBN 0-89684-031-X, Pub. by Motilal Barnarsidass India). Orient Bk Dist.
Wings of Madness: A Novel of Charles Baudelaire. Geoffrey Wagner. LC 78-1039. 224p. 1978. lib. bdg. 17.95x (ISBN 0-89370-120-3); pap. 7.95x (ISBN 0-89370-220-X). Borgo Pr.
Wings of Man: The Legend of Captain H.T. Dick Merrill. Jack L. King. (Illus.). 416p. 1981. 5.95x (ISBN 0-911721-91-6). Aviation.
Wings of Night. Kathryn Collins. (Superromances Ser.). 384p. 1984. pap. 2.95 (ISBN 0-373-70097-0, Pub. by Worldwide). Harlequin Bks.
Wings of Oppression. facs. ed. Leslie P. Hill. LC 76-152921. (Black Heritage Library Collection Ser.). 1921. 15.25 (ISBN 0-8369-8765-9). Ayer Co Pubs.
Wings of Pegasus. Brigadier G. Chatterton. (Airborne Ser.: No. 14). (Illus.). 282p. 1982. 18.95 (ISBN 0-89839-060-5). Battery Pr.
Wings of Silver. Compiled by Jo Petty. LC 67-21924. (Illus.). 1968. 7.95 (ISBN 0-8378-1773-0). Gibson.
Wings of Song. Georgiana L. Lahr. 3.75 (ISBN 0-533-00625-2). Vantage.
Wings of Song. 544p. 1984. 6.95 (ISBN 0-87159-176-6). Unity School.
Wings of Stone. Linda Ty-Casper. (Readers International Ser.). 170p. 1986. 16.95 (ISBN 0-930523-26-1, Dist. by Consortium); pap. 8.95 (ISBN 0-930523-27-X). Readers Intl.
Wings of the Dove. Henry James. 1964. pap. 3.95 (ISBN 0-451-51872-1, CE1872, Sig Classics). NAL.
Wings of the Dove. Henry James. Ed. by J. Donald Crowley & Richard A. Hocks. (Norton Critical Edition Ser.). 1978. 17.50x (ISBN 0-393-04478-5); pap. 9.95x (ISBN 0-393-09088-4). Norton.
Wings of the Dove. Henry James. Ed. by Peter Brooks. (World's Classics Ser.). 1984. pap. 3.95 (ISBN 0-19-281631-4). Oxford U Pr.
Wings of the Dove. Henry James. Ed. by John Bayley. (Penguin Classics Ser.). 528p. 1986. pap. 3.95 (ISBN 0-14-043263-9). Penguin.
Wings of the Dove. Henry James. Date not set. pap. 4.50 (ISBN 0-452-00858-1, Mer). NAL.
Wings of the Dove, Vol. 1. Henry James. LC 79-158798. (Novels & Tales of Henry James Ser.: Vol. 19). Repr. of 1909 ed. lib. bdg. 27.50x (ISBN 0-678-02819-2). Kelley.
Wings of the Dove, Vol. 2. Henry James. LC 79-158798. (Novels & Tales of Henry James Ser.: Vol. 20). Repr. of 1909 ed. lib. bdg. 27.50x (ISBN 0-678-02820-6). Kelley.
Wings of the Falcon. Barbara Michaels. 1978. pap. 1.95 (ISBN 0-449-23750-8, Crest). Fawcett.
Wings of the Falcon. Barbara Michaels. 1988. pap. 3.95 (ISBN 0-425-11045-1). Berkley Pub.
Wings of the Luftwaffe. Eric Brown. (Illus.). 176p. 1987. 20.00 (ISBN 0-89141-297-2). Presidio Pr.
Wings of the Morning. David Beaty & Betty Beaty. 1984. pap. 3.95 (ISBN 0-8217-1369-8). Zebra.
Wings of the Navy: Flying Allied Carrier Aircraft of World War II. Eric Brown. (Illus.). 176p. 1987. 19.95 (ISBN 0-87021-995-2). Naval Inst Pr.
Wings of the North. Dick Turner. (Illus.). 288p. pap. 9.95 (ISBN 0-88839-060-2). Hancock House.
Wings of the Phoenix. Florine De Veer. 175p. (Orig.). 1987. pap. 6.95 (ISBN 1-55583-100-1). Alyson Pubns.
Wings of the Robin. Anthony E. Pryor. 35p. 1988. 5.95 (ISBN 0-533-07104-6). Vantage.
Wings of the Weird & Wonderful. Eric Brown. (Illus.). 160p. 1987. 19.95 (ISBN 0-8306-9404-8, 2404); pap. 12.95 (ISBN 0-8306-2404-X). TAB Bks.
Wings of the Wind. Ronald Hardy. 416p. 1987. 19.95 (ISBN 0-399-12986-3, Putnam). Putnam Pub Group.
Wings of Thought. Antonia B. Laird. LC 85-80429. 80p. 1985. 6.50 (ISBN 0-8233-0409-4). Golden Quill.
Wings on My Heels: A Newspaper Woman's Story. Ellen Taussig. (Illus.). 384p. (Orig.). 1987. pap. 12.50 (ISBN 0-914339-18-4). P E Randall Pub.
Wings on the Cross. P. Hamilton Pollock. 1978. 8.50 (ISBN 0-682-48999-9). Exposition-Phoenix.
Wings on the Screen. Bertil Skogsberg. Tr. by George Bisset from Swedish. LC 81-4790. (Illus.). 192p. cancelled (ISBN 0-498-02495-4). A S Barnes.
Wings on the Southwind: Birds & Creatures of the Southern Wetlands. Franklin Russell. LC 84-60286. (Illus.). 176p. 1984. 29.95 (ISBN 0-8487-0546-7). Oxmoor Hse.
Wings Over America: The Inside Story of American Aviation. Harry Bruno. 1942. 30.00 (ISBN 0-932062-21-0). Sharon Hill.
Wings Over Eastern England. G. M. Dixon & J. Rippon. 1984. 20.00x (ISBN 0-906791-09-X, Pub. by Minimax Bks UK). State Mutual Bk.
Wings over the Mexican Border: Pioneer Military Aviation in the Big Bend. Kenneth B. Ragsdale. (Illus.). 294p. 1984. 24.50 (ISBN 0-292-79025-2). U of Tex Pr.
Wings, Seventy-Eight. (Wings Anthologies Ser.). 2.00 (ISBN 0-939736-02-0). Wings ME.
Wings, Seventy-Seven. (Wings Anthologies Ser.). 2.00 (ISBN 0-939736-01-2). Wings ME.
Wings, Seventy-Six. (Wings Anthologies Ser.). 2.00 (ISBN 0-939736-00-4). Wings ME.
Wings: The Early Years of Aviation. Richard Rosenblum. LC 79-26363. (Illus.). 64p. (gr. 3-7). 1980. 8.95 (ISBN 0-02-777380-9, Four Winds). Macmillan.
Wings, the Vines. Katharyn M. Aal & Alice Fulton. LC 82-24978. 96p. 1983. pap. 6.50 (ISBN 0-935526-07-2). McBooks Pr.
Wings to Fly. Azura. (Illus.). 180p. 1987. pap. 11.95 (ISBN 0-930421-02-7). Hermes Pub Co.
Wings to Fly. Marguerite Smith. 1973. text ed. 1.75 (ISBN 0-686-09413-1). Expression.
Wings to the Lord. St. Jane Frances de Chantal. 1988. pap. 2.50 (ISBN 0-317-67465-X, SP0660). Dghtrs St Paul.
Wings to the Orient: Pan American Clipper Planes 1935-1945. Stan Cohen. LC 85-60319. (Illus.). 1985. pap. 12.95 (ISBN 0-933126-61-1). Pictorial Hist.
Wings Unfolding. Wesley LaViolette. LC 70-140225. 1971. 4.95 (ISBN 0-87516-040-9). DeVorss.
Wings Will Not Be Broken. Darryl Holmes. (Orig.). 1988. pap. 8.00 (ISBN 0-88378-137-9). Third World.
Wingshooter's Autumn. Willow Creek Press Editors. (Illus.). 256p. 1986. 65.00x (ISBN 0-932558-31-3). Willow Creek Pr.
Wingspread. Aiden W. Tozer. pap. 4.95 (ISBN 0-87509-218-7). Chr Pubns.
Wingwomen of Hera. Sandi Hall. LC 87-60779. 196p. (Orig.). 1987. pap. 8.95 (ISBN 0-933216-26-2). Spinsters Aunt Lute.
Winifred Holtby As I Knew Her. Evelyne White. 1973. Repr. of 1938 ed. 25.00 (ISBN 0-8274-0682-7). R West.
Winifred Holtby As I Knew Her: A Study of the Author & Her Works. Evelyne White. 1977. Repr. of 1938 ed. lib. bdg. 25.00 (ISBN 0-8495-5609-0). Arden Lib.
Winifred Nicholson. Judy Collins. (Illus.). 128p. 1987. pap. 12.95 (ISBN 0-946590-64-8, Pub. by Tate Gall Pubns). Salem Hse Pubs.
Winifred Nicholson: Paintings 1900-1978. 44p. 1979. 24.00x (ISBN 0-906474-09-4, Pub. by Third Eye Centre). State Mutual Bk.
Winifred's New Bed. Richard Howell & Lynn Howell. LC 85-5237. (Illus.). 32p. (ps-1). 1985. 8.95 (ISBN 0-394-87772-1). Knopf.
Wining & Dining with John Grisanti. John Grisanti. Ed. by Marianne Streich & Jane Coward. (Illus.). 192p. 1984. deluxe edition 25.00 (ISBN 0-939114-88-7); pap. 11.95 (ISBN 0-939114-84-4). Wimmer Bks.
Wink. Evelyn Harter. 240p. 1986. 14.95 (ISBN 0-312-88233-5). St Martin.
Winkie & Me. (gr. k up). pap. cancelled (ISBN 0-916816-03-6). Ryder Pr.
Winkie, the Cross-Eyed Witch. Bridget Fitzgerald. LC 71-189878. (Story & Its Verse Ser.). (Illus.). (gr. 1-2). 1973. 2.50 (ISBN 0-87884-020-6). Unicorn Ent.
Winking Owl: Art in the People's Republic of China. Ellen J. Laing. 250p. 1988. 45.00x (ISBN 0-520-06097-0). U of Cal Pr.
Winking Ruby Mystery. Carolyn Keene. (Dana Girls Ser.: Vol. 12). (Illus.). 192p. (gr. 4-7). 1974. 2.95 (ISBN 0-448-09092-9, G&D). Putnam Pub Group.
Winnebago Mysteries. Moira Crone. LC 81-71642. 128p. 1982. 12.95 (ISBN 0-914590-68-5); pap. 6.95 (ISBN 0-914590-69-3). Fiction Coll.
Winneconne, History's Crossing Place. Michael J. Goc. Ed. by Geraldine Driscoll. Ed. by Monty Giffin. (Illus.). 152p. 1987. 19.95x (ISBN 0-938627-01-5). New Past Pr.
Winner. Maureen O'Donoghue. 1988. 19.95 (ISBN 0-671-53198-0). S&S.
Winner All the Way. Eileen Goudge. (Senior Ser.: No. 3). 160p. (Orig.). (gr. 7-12). 1984. pap. 2.25 (ISBN 0-440-99480-2, LFL). Dell.
Winner at Sixty Plus. Earle G. Harris. (Illus., Orig.). 1987. pap. 4.50 (ISBN 0-9618822-0-4). Winners Plus.
Winner Names the Age: A Collection of Writings. Lillian Smith. Ed. by Michelle Cliff. 224p. 1978. 10.95 (ISBN 0-393-08826-X). Norton.
Winner Names the Age: A Collection of Writings. Lillian Smith. Ed. by Michelle Cliff. 224p. 1982. pap. 4.95 (ISBN 0-393-30044-7). Norton.
Winner on the Court. H. R. Sheffer. Ed. by Howard Schroeder. LC 80-28451. (Teamates Ser.). (Illus.). 48p. (gr. 3 up). 1981. PLB 7.95 (ISBN 0-89686-107-4). Crestwood Hse.
Winner Take All. Laurien Berenson. (American Romance Ser.: No. 210). 245p. Date not set. pap. 2.50 (ISBN 0-317-63700-2). Harlequin Bks.
Winner Take All. Kate Denton. (Romances Ser.: No. 2870). 192p. Date not set. pap. 1.95 (ISBN 0-317-63927-7). Harlequin Bks.
Winner Take All! John Gollehon. 176p. 1986. 6.95 (ISBN 0-914839-09-8). Gollehon Pr.
Winner Take All: A History of the Trans-Canada Canoe Trail. David Lavender. LC 77-4864. 350p. (Orig.). 1985. pap. 11.95 (ISBN 0-89301-104-5). U of Idaho Pr.
Winner Take All: Report of the Twentieth Century Fund Task Force on Reform of the Presidential Election Process. Ed. by William R. Keech. LC 78-9666. 82p. 1978. 22.50 (ISBN 0-8419-0399-9); pap. 12.50 (ISBN 0-8419-0400-6). Holmes & Meier.
Winner Take Nothing. Ernest Hemingway. 1933. pap. 4.95 (ISBN 0-684-71810-3, ScribT). Scribner.
Winner Take Nothing. Ernest Hemingway. 176p. 1982. pap. 4.95 rack size (ISBN 0-684-17426-X, ScribT). Scribner.
Winner Take Nothing. Ernest Hemingway. 14.95 (ISBN 0-89190-664-9, Pub. by Am Repr). Amereon Ltd.
Winner Take Nothing. Ernest Hemingway. 176p. 1988. pap. 5.95 (ISBN 0-02-051820-X, Collier). Macmillan.
Winner Take Nothing. Pierce McKenzie. 1987. pap. 2.50 (ISBN 0-451-14784-7, Sig). NAL.
Winner Takes All. Laurie Likken. (Sweet Dreams Ser.: 132). 192p. (YA) 1987. pap. 2.50 (ISBN 0-317-65474-8, Sweet Dreams). Bantam.
Winner Takes All. Dieter Wellershoff. Tr. by Paul Knight from Ger. 388p. 1986. 16.95 (ISBN 0-85635-679-4). Carcanet.
Winner Takes All, No. 132. (Sweet Dreams Ser.). 192p. (Orig.). (YA) (gr. 7-12). 1987. pap. 2.50 (ISBN 0-553-26790-6). Bantam.
Winner Takes All: Valuable Lessons from 21 Top Managers Who Faced Seemingly Insurmountable Odds - & Beat Them! Bryce Webster. 240p. 1987. pap. 12.95 (ISBN 0-8144-7689-9). AMACOM.
Winners. Mary-Ellen L. Collura. LC 86-6286. 136p. (YA) (gr. 6 up). 1986. 10.95 (ISBN 0-8037-0011-3, 01063-320). Dial Bks Young.
Winners. Julio Cortazar. Tr. by Elaine Kerrigan. (Modern Writers Ser.). 1984. pap. 8.95 (ISBN 0-394-72301-5). Pantheon.
Winners. 1987. pap. 7.95 (ISBN 0-8050-0367-3). H Holt & Co.
Winners: A Love Story. Donna Ball. 294p. 1982. 13.95 (ISBN 0-312-88229-7). St Martin.
Winners: A Who's Who of Motor Racing Champions. Ed. by Brian Laban. (Illus.). 192p. 1983. 14.95 (ISBN 0-85613-042-7). Beaufort Bks NY.
Winners & Champions: United's 1948 FA Cup & 1952 Championship Winning Teams. Alec Shorrocks. (Illus.). 272p. 1986. 17.95x (ISBN 0-213-16920-7, Pub. by Weidenfeld & Nicolson England). Biblio Dist.
Winners & Losers. Brian Blandford. LC 84-26709. 1985. pap. 4.95 (ISBN 0-8307-1012-4, S181422). Regal.
Winners & Losers. Gloria Emerson. 432p. 1985. pap. 7.95 (ISBN 0-14-008216-6). Penguin.
Winners & Losers. Sydney Harris. (Illus.). 370p. 1968. pap. 4.95 (ISBN 0-317-60038-9). Tabor Pub.
Winners & Losers at the Bridge Table. Bobby Goldman. 103p. 1979. pap. 3.95 (ISBN 0-939460-05-X). M Hardy.
Winners & Losers: How Elections Work in America. Jules Archer. LC 83-18368. (Illus.). 240p. (gr. 7-12). 1984. 14.95 (ISBN 0-15-297945-X, HJ). HarBraceJ.
Winners & Losers in Colombia's Economic Growth of the 1970's. Miguel Urrutia. (World Bank Publication Ser.). 1985. 19.95x (ISBN 0-19-520468-9). Oxford U Pr.
Winners & Losers in East-West Trade: A Behavioral Analysis of U. S.; Soviet Detente, 1970-1983. Ronald E. Hoyt. 256p. 1983. 36.95 (ISBN 0-275-91011-3, C1011). Praeger.
Winners & Losers: Social & Political Polarities in America. Irving L. Horowitz. (Duke Press Policy Studies). xv, 329p. 1984. text ed. 37.50 (ISBN 0-8223-0495-3); pap. 14.95 (ISBN 0-8223-0602-6). Duke.
Winners & Losers: The Race for the Presidency, 1988. Paul Simon. 1989. price not set. Continuum.
Winner's Circle. Charles P. Conn. 160p. 1983. pap. 2.95 (ISBN 0-425-06306-2). Berkley Pub.
Winner's Circle: Triumph of Jesus Christ. Kenneth R. Jones. 1987. 16.95 (ISBN 0-533-07092-9). Vantage.
Winner's Cut. Preston Pairo. 16.95 (ISBN 0-317-58116-3). Richardson & Steirman.
Winner's Cut. Preston Pairo. 256p. Date not set. pap. 3.95 (ISBN 0-373-97069-2, Pub. by Worldwide). Harlequin Bks.
Winner's Daily Word. Mike Murdock. (Orig.). mini bk. 0.75 (ISBN 0-89274-419-7). Harrison Hse.
Winner's Edge. Bob Oates, Jr. 1980. 12.95 (ISBN 0-686-68762-0, Mayflower Bks). Smith Pubs.
Winner's Edge. Denis Waitley. 192p. 1984. pap. 3.50 (ISBN 0-425-10000-6). Berkley Pub.
Winner's Edge: The Inside Guide to Betting Pro Football. Richard Raihall. (Guides to Sports Betting). 180p. (Orig.). 1984. pap. 9.95 (ISBN 0-915643-07-3); 10 copy display avail. (ISBN 0-915643-09-X). Santa Barb Pr.
Winner's Guide on Retail Selling. Peter R. Bol. LC 84-72669. 128p. (Orig.). 1985. pap. text ed. 6.95 (ISBN 0-9613917-0-7). Dynamic Comm.
Winner's Guide to Casino Gambling. Edwin Silberstang. 320p. 1981. pap. 7.95 (ISBN 0-452-25555-4, Z5555, Plume). NAL.
Winner's Guide to Casino Gambling. Edwin Silberstang. 368p. 1985. pap. 4.95 (ISBN 0-451-14844-4, Sig). NAL.

Winning Football with the Forward Pass. LaVell Edwards & Norman Chow. 126p. 1985. text ed. write for info. (ISBN 0-205-08205-X, Pub. by Longwood Div). Wm C Brown.
Winning Football with the Option Package Offense. Bob Petrino & Marty Mouat. 202p. 1985. 19.95 (ISBN 0-13-960931-8, Busn). P-H.
Winning for Peace: The Great Victory--Its World Impact. Boris Ponomarev. 136p. 1985. 20.00x (ISBN 0-317-42824-1, Pub by Collets (UK)). State Mutual BK.
Winning Golf. Peter Chamberlain. (Illus.). 160p. 1988. pap. 12.95. Sterling.
Winning Government Contracts: A Complete 27 Step Guide for Small Businesses. Eli Chappe. LC 83-22954. 266p. 1984. Repr. 69.95 (ISBN 0-13-960998-9, Busn). P-H.
Winning Grants: Leader's Guide. David Bauer. 86p. (Orig.). 1985. pap. text ed. 9.95 (ISBN 0-9614949-4-8). Great Plains.
Winning Heart... Tender & Courageous. Elizabeth S. Floyd. (Illus.). 80p. (Orig.). 1983. pap. 6.95 (ISBN 0-9613238-0-9). Impex Pub Co.
Winning Hitter: How to Play Championship Baseball. Charley Lau & Alfred Glassbrenner. (Illus.). 190p. 1984. pap. 7.95 (ISBN 0-688-03634-1, Quill NY). Morrow.
Winning Hitter: How to Play Championship Baseball. Charley Lau & Alfred Glossbrenner. (Illus.). 192p. 1984. 14.95 (ISBN 0-688-03391-1, Hearst Bks). Morrow.
Winning Horseplayer. Andrew Beyer. LC 83-142. 192p. 1983. 12.95 (ISBN 0-395-34392-5). HM.
Winning Horseplayer: A Revolutionary Approach to Thoroughbred Handicapping & Betting. Andrew Beyer. 208p. 1985. pap. 8.95 (ISBN 0-395-37761-7). HM.
Winning Ideas from Winning Schools: Recognizing Excellence. Dawn Heller. 200p. 1988. 25.00 (ISBN 0-87436-527-9). ABC-Clio.
Winning Ideas in the Social Studies. Steven L. Jantzen. LC 77-9530. (Illus.). 1977. pap. text ed. 5.95x (ISBN 0-8077-2541-2). Tchrs Coll.
Winning Image. James Gray. LC 81-69372. pap. 48.00 (ISBN 0-317-19832-7, 2023074). Bks Demand UMI.
Winning Image. James Gray, Jr. 192p. 1982. 13.95 (ISBN 0-8144-5667-7). AMACOM.
Winning Image. James Gray, Jr. LC 81-69372. 192p. 1984. pap. 8.95 (ISBN 0-8144-7611-2). AMACOM.
Winning in Labor Arbitration. Walt Baer. LC 82-70973. 192p. 1982. 29.95 (ISBN 0-8442-3071-5, Crain Bks). Natl Textbk.
Winning in the Futures Market. George Angell. LC 86-6280. (Illus.). 336p. 1987. pap. 19.95 (ISBN 0-385-19949-X). Doubleday.
Winning Investment Strategies: The Inflation-Beater's Investment Guide. New ed. Burton G. Malkiel. 192p. 1982. pap. 3.95 (ISBN 0-393-30031-5). Norton.
Winning Is Everything. David Marlow. 352p. 1983. 17.95 (ISBN 0-399-12801-8, Putnam). Putnam Pub Group.
Winning Isn't Always First Place. Dallas Groten. LC 83-14930. 160p. (Orig.). 1983. pap. 4.95 (ISBN 0-87123-613-3, 210613). Bethany Hse.
Winning Japan for Jesus. James Norton. 200p. 1988. pap. 9.95 (ISBN 0-933704-66-6). Dawn Pr.
Winning Karate. Joseph Jennings. (Winning Ser.). (Illus.). 224p. 1982. pap. 9.95 (ISBN 0-8092-5800-5). Contemp Bks.
Winning Life's Toughest Battles: Roots of Human Resilience. Julius Segal. 176p. 1986. text ed. 15.95 (ISBN 0-07-056034-X). McGraw.
Winning Life's Toughest Battles: Roots of Human Resilience. Julius Segal. 1987. pap. 2.95 (ISBN 0-8041-0145-0, Pub. by Ivy). Ballantine.
Winning Local & State Elections: The Guide to Organizing, Financing, & Targeting Your Campaign. Ann Beaudry & Bob Schaeffer. 208p. 1986. 17.95 (ISBN 0-02-902490-0). Free Pr.
Winning Low Energy Building Designs. Canadian Government Staff. 651p. 1980. text ed. 35.00x (Pub. by Inst Engeering Australia). Brookfield Pub Co.
Winning Low Energy Building Designs. 651p. 1980. 37.00 (ISBN 0-660-50675-0, SSC156, SSC). UNIPUB.
Winning Market Systems: Eighty Three Ways to Beat the Market. Gerald Appel. 232p. 1986. Repr. of 1974 ed. 29.95 (ISBN 0-934380-12-0). Traders Pr.
Winning Men of Tennis. Nathan Aaseng. LC 80-28598. (Sports Heroes Library). (Illus.). (gr. 4 up). 1981. PLB 7.95 (ISBN 0-8225-1068-5). Lerner Pubns.
Winning Moment: Paintings of the America's Cup. Ranulf Rayner. (Illus.). 1986. 45.00 (ISBN 0-393-02413-X). Norton.
Winning Money for College: The High School Student's Guide to Scholarship Contests. 2nd ed. Alan Deutschman. LC 86-30340. 217p. (Orig.). 1987. pap. 8.95 (ISBN 0-87866-555-2). Petersons Guides.
Winning Monologs for Young Actors. Peg Kehret. Ed. by Arthur Zapel & Kathy Pijanowski. LC 86-61109. 160p. (Orig.). (YA) (gr. 6-12). 1986. pap. text ed. 7.95 (ISBN 0-916260-38-0, B-127). Meriwether Pub.
Winning Monopoly. Kaz Darzinskis. LC 86-46054. (Illus.). 256p. 1987. pap. 6.95 (ISBN 0-06-096127-9, PL 6127, PL). Har-Row.
Winning Motor Vehicle Accident Cases. Joseph W. Moch. 1986. text ed. 75.00 (ISBN 0-934547-01-7, 5080). CRI-Comm Res.
Winning Moves: How to Survive (& Manage) a Business Shakeup. Jane Ciabattari. 256p. 1988. 17.95 (ISBN 0-89256-332-X). Rawson Assocs.
Winning Moves: The Body Language of Selling. Ken Delmar. LC 84-40088. 304p. 1985. 17.50 (ISBN 0-446-51301-6). Warner Bks.
Winning Moves: The Body Language of Selling. Ken Delmar. 320p. 1986. pap. 3.95 (ISBN 0-446-32997-5). Warner Bks.
Winning Negotiation Strategies for Bankers. Linda Richardson. 150p. 1987. 29.95 (ISBN 0-87094-990-X). Dow Jones-Irwin.
Winning Negotiation Strategies for Bankers. 147p. 1987. 27.50 (ISBN 0-317-66112-4, 251). Bank Admin Inst.
Winning Negotiations Strategies for Bankers. 147p. 1987. 54.00 (ISBN 0-317-66461-1, 645). Bank Admin Inst.
Winning of Andromache. Richard M. Byers. LC 87-80719. (Illus.). 190p. 1987. 10.00 (ISBN 0-9602048-2-2). Fairfield Hse.
Winning of Barbara Worth. Harold B. Wright. 1975. lib. bdg. 20.60x (ISBN 0-89966-208-0). Buccaneer Bks.
Winning of Barbara Worth. Harold B. Wright. (Illus.). 512p. 1987. Repr. of 1911 ed. 14.95 (ISBN 0-9618473-0-1). Holtville Tribune.
Winning of Freedom. William Wood. 1927. 49.50x (ISBN 0-686-83858-0). Elliots Bks.
Winning of Freedom see Pageant of America.
Winning of Independence. Marshall Smelser. LC 73-3104. 415p. 1973. pap. text ed. 6.95x (ISBN 0-531-06490-5). Wiener Pub Inc.
Winning of Independence. 428p. pap. 6.95 (ISBN 0-8160-1494-9). Facts on File.
Winning of Miss Lynn Ryan. Ilene Cooper. LC 87-15233. (Illus.). 128p. (gr. 3-6). 1987. 10.95 (ISBN 0-688-07231-3, Morrow Junior Books). Morrow.
Winning of the Midwest: Social & Political Conflict, 1888-1896. Richard Jensen. LC 71-149802. 1971. 12.50x (ISBN 0-226-39825-0). U of Chicago Pr.
Winning of the West. Theodore Roosevelt. Ed. & intro. by Harvey Wish. 12.00 (ISBN 0-8446-2827-1). Peter Smith.
Winning of the West, 4 vols. Theodore Roosevelt. 1900. Repr. 175.00x (ISBN 0-403-04339-5). Somerset Pub.
Winning of the World. Ben Hansen. 176p. (Orig.). 1980. pap. 5.95 (ISBN 0-931590-04-3). Antietam Pr.
Winning on the Marketing Front: The Corporate Manager's Game Plan. William A. Cohen. LC 85-12200. (Sound Business Cassettebooks Ser.). 381p. 1986. 19.95 (ISBN 0-471-81935-2). Wiley.
Winning on the Telephone. Donald H. Weiss. (Successful Office Skills Ser.). 54p. 1988. 3.50 (ISBN 0-8144-7699-6). AMACOM.
Winning Option. Ralph T. Dames. LC 79-23369. 128p. 1980. 18.95 (ISBN 0-88229-527-6). Nelson-Hall.
Winning over Sinning. Patricia Maxwell. (Lifeline Ser.). 95p. (Orig.). 1987. pap. 6.95 (ISBN 0-8163-0666-4). Pacific Pr Pub Assn.
Winning Performance: How America's High-Growth Midsize Companies Succeed. Donald K. Clifford, Jr. & Richard E. Cavanaugh. LC 85-47651. 1985. 19.95 (ISBN 0-553-05103-2). Bantam.
Winning Performance: How America's Midsize High-Growth Companies Succeed. rev. ed. Donald K. Clifford, Jr. & Richard C. Cavanagh. LC 87-47586. 320p. (Orig.). 1988. pap. 9.95 (ISBN 0-553-34463-3). Bantam.
Winning Pitcher: Baseball's Top Pitchers Demonstrate What It Takes to Be an Ace. Tom House. (Illus.). 160p. (Orig.). 1988. pap. 10.95 (ISBN 0-8092-4878-6). Contemp Bks.
Winning Platform Tennis. Doug Russell & Ernest Chu. LC 77-75848. (Winning Ser.). (Illus.). 1977. pap. 4.95 (ISBN 0-8092-7930-4). Contemp Bks.
Winning Play in Tournament & Duplicate Bridge: How the Experts Triumph. Fred L. Karpin. 242p. 1976. pap. 5.95 (ISBN 0-486-23333-2). Dover.
Winning Pocket Billiards. Willie Mosconi. (Illus.). 1965. pap. 5.95 (ISBN 0-517-50454-5). Crown.
Winning Poker Systems. Norman Zadeh. 1977. pap. 3.00 (ISBN 0-87980-332-0). Wilshire.
Winning Position. Mark McCrackin. 96p. (gr. 7 up). 1982. pap. 1.50 (ISBN 0-440-99483-7, LFL). Dell.
Winning Power of Stock Market Charts, 2 vols. C. M. Flumiani. (Illus.). 1985. Set. 198.75 (ISBN 0-86654-176-4). Inst Econ Finan.
Winning Power of Stock Market Charts, 2 Vols. Carlo M. Flumiani. (New Stock Market Library). (Illus.). 1977. 287.75 (ISBN 0-89266-071-6). Am Classical Coll Pr.
Winning Programs. 192p. 1984. 19.95 (ISBN 0-13-961368-4); pap. 10.95 (ISBN 0-13-961350-1). P-H.
Winning Psychology of Karate & Kung Fu. Curtis L. Faust. 33p. 1988. 7.95 (ISBN 0-533-07579-3). Vantage.
Winning Raquetball. Arthur Shay & Chuck Leve. LC 75-32992. (Winning Ser). 176p. 1976. pap. 7.95 (ISBN 0-8092-8062-0). Contemp Bks.
Winning Repeat Sales. Jard DeVille. LC 86-3902. 176p. 1986. 14.95 (ISBN 0-934395-23-3). Rutledge Hill Pr.
Winning Roller Skating: Figure & Freestyle. Randy Dayney & Joel H. Cohen. LC 76-6260. (Winning Ser.). (Illus.). 1977. pap. 5.95 (ISBN 0-8092-8153-8). Contemp Bks.
Winning Season for the Braves. Nate Aaseng. LC 82-72711. 1988. pap. 3.95 (ISBN 1-55513-950-7, Chariot Bks). Cook.
Winning Secrets of a Poker Master. J. D. McEvoy. 32p. 1986. pap. 5.95 (ISBN 0-934650-11-X). Sunnyside.
Winning Soccer. Al Miller & Norm Wingert. (Illus.). 149p. 1975. pap. 6.95 (ISBN 0-8092-8307-7). Contemp Bks.
Winning Soccer Drills. James P. McGettigan. LC 80-15783. 1983. pap. 5.95 (ISBN 0-13-961086-3, Reward). P-H.
Winning Softball. Joan Joyce & John Anquillare. (Illus.). 1975. pap. 6.95 (ISBN 0-8092-8429-4). Contemp Bks.
Winning Spiritual Warfare in the Family. Earl Paulk. 21p. 1987. pap. 1.50 (ISBN 0-917595-20-3). K-Dimension.
Winning Squash. Jahangir Khan et al. (Illus.). 96p. 1986. pap. 8.95 (ISBN 0-13-961103-7). P-H.
Winning Strategies for Business under 1986 Tax Reform. Kess & Westlin. 120p. (Orig.). 1986. pap. 8.00 (5385). Commerce.
Winning Strategies for Business Under 1986 Tax Reform. Sidney Kess & Bertil Westlin. LC 87-129299. 115p. Date not set. price not set. Commerce.
Winning Strategies for Individuals under 1986 Tax Reform Act. Kess & Westlin. 152p. (Orig.). 1986. pap. 8.00 (5386). Commerce.
Winning Strategies for Managing People. Robert Irwin & Rita Wolenik. 224p. 1985. 16.95 (ISBN 0-531-09595-9). Watts.
Winning Strategies for Nursing Managers. Joan O'Leary et al. (Illus.). 188p. 1986. text ed. 12.95 (ISBN 0-397-54541-X, Lippincott Nursing). Lippincott.
Winning Strategies in Selling. Jack Kinder, Jr. et al. LC 81-10518. 258p. 1981. 18.95 (ISBN 0-13-961128-2, Busn); 5.95. P-H.
Winning Strategy Games on the Commodore 64. Toby Matthews et al. 1985. 39.95 (ISBN 0-471-82521-2); disk 24.95 (ISBN 0-471-82519-0). Wiley.
Winning Streak. Walter Goldsmith & David Clutterbuck. 1985. 19.45 (ISBN 0-394-54485-4). Random.
Winning Streak. Arnold Grisman. 308p. 1985. 15.95 (ISBN 0-312-88231-9, J Kahn). St Martin.
Winning Streak. Arnold Grisman. 272p. 1987. pap. 3.50 (ISBN 0-14-009369-9). Penguin.
Winning Streak Workout Book. Walter Goldsmith & David Clutterbuck. 176p. 1986. 18.95x (ISBN 0-297-78704-7, Pub. by Weidenfeld & Nicolson England). Biblio Dist.
Winning Swiss Team Tactics in Bridge. Harold Feldheim. 1976. pap. 7.95 (ISBN 0-87643-027-2). Barclay Bridge.
Winning Tactics for Women over Forty: How to Take Charge of Your Life & Have Fun Doing It. Anne De Sola Cardoza & Mavis B. Sutton. LC 87-34768. 240p. (Orig.). 1988. 16.95; pap. 9.95 (ISBN 0-938179-09-8). Mills Sanderson.
Winning Tales from Scottish Houses. Euan MacPherson et al. LC 87-70812. (Illus.). 179p. 1987. 19.95 (ISBN 0-86241-133-5, Pub. by Canongate Pub Ltd); pap. 10.95 (ISBN 0-86241-117-3, Pub. by Canongate Pub Ltd). Dufour.
Winning Techniques for Athletic Fund Raising. Ed. by Particia L. Alberger. 97p. 1981. 14.50 (ISBN 0-89964-188-1). Coun Adv & Supp Ed.
Winning Tennis My Way. Jimmy Connors & Robert J. LaMarche. Date not set. price not set. S&S.
Winning the Battle for Sex Education. Irving R. Dickman. LC 82-61000. 64p. (Orig.). 1982. pap. 6.00 (ISBN 0-9609212-0-6). SIECUS.
Winning the Battle of the Experts: An Expert Witness' Point of View. Steven C. Bank. LC 83-151861. Date not set. manual 10.00 (989); audiotapes 95.00. Natl Prac Inst.
Winning the Battles of Life: This Land Is Your Land. Paul E. Toms. LC 86-15417. 1977. pap. 4.95 (ISBN 0-8307-1161-9, S413129). Regal.
Winning the Brain Race: A Bold Plan to Make Our Schools Competitive. David T. Kearns & Denis Doyle. 147p. 1988. 16.95 (ISBN 1-55815-002-1). ICS Pr.
Winning the Career Game. Patricia J. Sumner et al. 136p. (gr. 12). 1983. pap. 17.95 (ISBN 0-8403-3167-3). Kendall-Hunt.
Winning the Change Game: How to Implement Information Systems with Fewer Headaches & Bigger Paybacks. Kathy Farrell & Craig Broude. (Illus.). 1987. pap. 15.00 (ISBN 0-944532-00-4). Breakthroughs Ents.
Winning the Chemo Battle. Joyce S. Mitchell. LC 87-24055. 213p. 1988. 16.95 (ISBN 0-393-02532-2). Norton.
Winning the Confidence Game: How to Increase Your Self-Confidence. Cynthia Schubert. (Illus.). 112p. 1985. pap. 9.95 (ISBN 0-9614631-0-4). Arrow P.
Winning the Countertrade War. Schaffer. 1988. write for info. (ISBN 0-471-63252-X). Wiley.
Winning the Fire Service Leadership Game. H. Caulfield. Ed. by Diana Benzaia. LC 85-70551. 292p. 1985. 24.95 (ISBN 0-912212-09-8). Fire Eng.
Winning the Future: How to Succeed in an Economic Revolution. Robert A. Russel. 260p. (Orig.). 1986. 18.95 (ISBN 0-88184-191-9). Carroll & Graf.
Winning the Game. Pauline Reich. LC 87-82858. 216p. 1988. 24.95 (ISBN 0-87011-859-5). Kodansha.
Winning the Games People Play: How to Master the Art of Changing People's Behavior. Nathan B. Miron. LC 76-52149. (Illus.). 1977. 12.95 (ISBN 0-918418-01-1); pap. 7.95 (ISBN 0-918418-02-X). Mission Pr CA.
Winning the Games Scientists Play. Carl J. Sindermann. LC 82-12225. (Illus.). 304p. 1982. 15.95 (ISBN 0-306-41075-3, Plenum Pr). Plenum Pub.
Winning the High Technology Sales Game. James T. Healy. 1984. text ed. 25.95 (ISBN 0-8359-8700-0, Reston). P-H.
Winning the High Technology Sales Game. James T. Healy. 373p. 1985. 30.95 (ISBN 0-317-39391-X). Robot Inst Am.
Winning the Homework War. Frederic M. Levine & Kathleen M. Anesko. (Illus.). 224p. 1987. pap. 9.95 (ISBN 0-13-960956-3). P-H.
Winning the Information Systems Game: A Manager's Survival Guide. Nelson Dinerstein. LC 85-70191. 225p. 1985. 27.50 (ISBN 0-87094-642-0). Dow Jones-Irwin.
Winning the Interest Rate Game: A Guide to Debt Options. Frank J. Fabozzi. 324p. 1984. 35.00 (ISBN 0-917253-01-9). Probus Pub Co.
Winning the Investment Game. James Gipson. 192p. 1984. text ed. 21.50 (ISBN 0-07-023292-X). McGraw.
Winning the Investment Game: A Guide for All Seasons. James Gipson. 192p. 1987. pap. text ed. 10.95 (ISBN 0-07-023296-2). McGraw.
Winning the Invisible War. E. M. Bounds. 160p. 1984. pap. 2.95 (ISBN 0-88368-145-5). Whitaker Hse.
Winning the Job Interview Game: Tips for the High-Tech Era. Jo Danna. LC 85-61451. (Illus.). 223p. (Orig.). 1986. pap. 9.95.. (ISBN 0-9610036-2-6). Palomino Pr.
Winning the Land Use Game: A Guide for Developers & Citizen Protesters. Carolyn J. Logan. LC 81-15710. 208p. 1982. 35.00 (ISBN 0-275-90849-6, C0849). Praeger.
Winning the Marketing War: A Field Manual for Business Leaders. Gerald A. Michaelson. LC 86-11115. 320p. 1987. 22.95 (ISBN 0-8191-5781-3, Pub. by Madison Bks). U Pr of Amer.
Winning the Million Dollar Lawsuit. Pat Maloney, Sr. & Jack Pasqual. LC 82-21175. 258p. 1982. text ed. 99.50 (ISBN 0-87624-848-2, Inst Busn Plan). P-H.
Winning the Ph.D. Game: How to Get into & out of Graduate School with a Ph.D & a Job. Richard W. Moore. 288p. 1985. pap. 13.95 (ISBN 0-396-08403-6). Dodd.
Winning the Productivity Race. Bernard N. Slade & Raj Mohindra. 160p. 1985. 24.95 (ISBN 0-669-10799-9). Lexington Bks.
Winning: The Psychology of Competition. Stuart H. Walker. 1986. pap. 7.95 (ISBN 0-393-30267-9). Norton.
Winning the Radar war. Jack Nissen & A. W. Cockerill. LC 87-27123. (Illus.). 256p. 1988. 19.95x (ISBN 0-312-01535-6). St Martin.
Winning the Real Estate Game. Harvey Sherman & Patricia J. Sherman. (Illus.). 1977. pap. 4.95 (ISBN 0-686-20328-3). Sherman.
Winning the Restaurant Game. Jay Jacobs. 1979. text ed. 8.95 (ISBN 0-07-032154-X). McGraw.
Winning the Right to Know: A Handbook for Toxics Activists. Caron Chess. 100p. 1983. 8.95 (ISBN 0-89788-073-0). NCPA Washington.
Winning the Salary Game: Salary Negotiation for Women. Sherry Chastain. LC 80-20622. (General Trade Bks.). 170p. 1980. text ed. 12.95 (ISBN 0-471-08433-6, Pub. by Wiley Pr). Wiley.
Winning the Second American Revolution, Plus Winning your Personal Battle For Financial Success. Donald L. Krumm. (Illus.). 331p. (Orig.). 1985. pap. text ed. 14.95x (ISBN 0-917209-00-1). Am Liberty.
Winning the Second Battle: Canadian Veterans & the Return to Civilian Life, 1915-1930. Desmond Morton & Glenn Wright. 328p. 1987. 40.00x (ISBN 0-8020-5705-5); pap. 17.95 (ISBN 0-8020-6634-8). U of Toronto Pr.
Winning the War Within: Fighting Disease, Protecting Yourself. Mark P. Friedlander, Jr. & Terry M. Phillips. 256p. 1986. 18.95 (ISBN 0-87857-648-7); pap. 10.95 (ISBN 0-87857-649-5). Rodale Pr Inc.
Winning the West, No. 1: Rio Grande. Donald C. Porter. 304p. (Orig.). 1986. pap. 3.50 (ISBN 0-553-24535-X). Bantam.
Winning the White House: An Insider's Guide to American Presidential Elections. Aram Bakshian. 160p. 1984. 20.00x (ISBN 0-86360-015-8, Pub. by R Anderson Pubns Ltd). State Mutual Bk.

Winter. Richard L. Allington. Kathleen Krull. LC 80-25115. (E. G. Beginning to Learn about... Ser.). (Illus.). 32p. (ps-2). 1985. pap. 9.27 (ISBN 0-8172-2497-1). Raintree Pubs.
Winter. Richard L. Allington & Kathleen Krull. LC 80-25115. (Beginning to Learn About Ser.). (Illus.). 32p. (ps-2). 1981. PLB 15.33 (ISBN 0-8172-1340-6). Raintree Pubs.
Winter. Nancy M. Davis et al. (Davis Teaching Units Ser.: Vol. 1, No. 5). (Illus.). 29p. (ps-2). 1986. pap. 4.95 (ISBN 0-937103-05-5). DaNa Pubns.
Winter. Len Deighton. 1989. pap. 4.95. Ballantine.
Winter. Lynn Deighton. 1988. write for info. Random.
Winter. Donald Hall & Clifton C. Olds. LC 85-15767. (Illus.). 152p. (Orig.). 1986. 40.00x (ISBN 0-87451-354-5); pap. 19.95 (ISBN 0-87451-355-3). U Pr of New Eng.
Winter. Robert Highsmith. (Illus.). 26p. (ps). 1986. 2.95 (ISBN 0-02-747950-1). Macmillan.
Winter. Bela Liscsinszky. (Foods for All Seasons Ser.). (Illus.). 103p. 1987. 9.95 (ISBN 963-13-1893-1, Pub. by Corvina Kiado Hungary). Intl Spec Bk.
Winter. Colin McNaughton. LC 83-45236. (Very First Bks.). (Illus.). 10p. (ps-k). 1983. 4.95 (ISBN 0-8037-0040-7). Dial Bks Young.
Winter. Louis Santrey. LC 82-19353. (Discovering the Seasons Ser.). (Illus.). 32p. (gr. 4-7). 1982. lib. bdg. 10.79 (ISBN 0-89375-907-4); pap. text ed. 2.50 (ISBN 0-89375-908-2). Troll Assocs.
Winter. C. S. Vendrell & J. M. Parramon. (Exploring the Seasons Ser.). (Illus.). 32p. (ps-3). 1981. 11.93 (ISBN 0-516-02384-5). Childrens.
Winter. Ralph Whitlock. (Seasons Ser.). (Illus.). 48p. (gr. 1-6). 1987. lib. bdg. 11.90 (ISBN 0-531-18141-3, Pub. by Bookwright Pr). Watts.
Winter: A Novel of a Berlin Family. Len Deighton. LC 87-45842. 592p. 1988. 19.95 (ISBN 0-394-55177-X). Knopf.
Winter Activity Book. Elaine R. Cohen. (Stick-Out-Your-Neck Ser.). (Illus.). 32p. (gr. 4-7). 1984. pap. 1.98 (ISBN 0-88724-064-X, CD-8044). Carson-Dellos.
Winter: An Arms Race Protest. rev. ed. Edwin Ritchie. LC 83-70727. 56p. 1983. 5.25 (ISBN 0-9611008-0-X). Centralia Pr.
Winter: An Ecological Handbook. James Halfpenny & Roy Ozanne. (Illus.). 280p. 1988. pap. 14.95 (ISBN 1-55566-036-3). Johnson Bks.
Winter at Morristown Seventeen Seventy-Nine to Seventeen Eighty: The Darkest Hour. Samuel S. Smith. LC 79-52313. (Revolutionary War Bicentennial Ser.). (Illus.). 1979. pap. 9.95. Freneau.
Winter at Noon. M. B. Thornton. LC 77-86610. (Illus.). 1977. pap. 4.95 (ISBN 0-930830-02-4). Great Basin.
Winter at Valley Forge, Survival & Victory. James E. Knight. LC 81-23151. (Illus.). 32p. (gr. 5-9). 1982. PLB 9.79 (ISBN 0-89375-738-1); pap. text ed. 1.95 (ISBN 0-89375-739-X). Troll Assocs.
Winter Barn. Peter Parnall. LC 85-23898. (Illus.). 32p. (gr. k-3). 1986. 12.95 (ISBN 0-02-770170-0). Macmillan.
Winter Bear. Ruth Craft. LC 74-18178. (Illus.). 32p. (ps-2). 1975. 12.95 (ISBN 0-689-50017-3, M K McElderry). Macmillan.
Winter Bear. Ruth Craft. LC 74-18178. (Illus.). 32p. (ps-2). 1979. pap. 2.50 (ISBN 0-689-70456-9, Aladdin). Macmillan.
Winter Bells. W. D. Ehrhart. 20p. (Orig.). 1988. pap. 7.00 limited ed. (ISBN 0-938566-38-5). Adastra Pr.
Winter Blossom. Cynthia Sinclair. (Tapestry Romance Ser.: No. 27). 320p. (Orig.). 1983. pap. 2.95 (ISBN 0-671-49513-5). PB.
Winter Book. Harriet Webster. LC 88-1662. (Illus.). 128p. (Orig.). (gr. 3-7). Date not set. pap. 4.95 (ISBN 0-689-71235-9, Aladdin Bks). Macmillan.
Winter Book. Harriet Webster. LC 88-4371. (Illus.). 128p. (gr. 3-7). 1988. 12.95 (ISBN 0-684-18891-0). Scribner.
Winter Book of Switzerland. Ed. by Dore Ogrizek. (Illus.). 383p. 1957. 3.00 (ISBN 0-686-75372-0). Bookfinger.
Winter Botany. 3rd ed. William Trelease. (Illus.). 14.50 (ISBN 0-8446-3086-1). Peter Smith.
Winter Botany: An Identification Guide to Native & Cultivated Trees & Shrubs. William Trelease. (Illus.). 396p. 1967. pap. 8.95 (ISBN 0-486-21800-7). Dover.
Winter Break. Margaret Garland. (Caprice Romance Ser.: No. 56). 160p. 1985. pap. 2.25 (ISBN 0-441-89434-8, Pub by Tempo). Ace Bks.
Winter Bride. Carola Salisbury. 1979. pap. 1.95 (ISBN 0-449-23838-5, Crest). Fawcett.
Winter Brothers: A Season at the Edge of America. Ivan Doig. LC 80-7933. (Illus.). 246p. 1982. pap. 5.95 (ISBN --15-697215-8, Harv). HarBraceJ.
Winter Bulletin Boards. Imogene Forte. (Easy-To-Make-&-Use Ser.). (Illus.). 64p. (gr. k-6). 1985. pap. text ed. 5.95 (ISBN 0-86530-168-9, IP 112-9). Incentive Pubns.
Winter by Degrees. John Smolens. 224p. 1988. 16.95 (ISBN 0-525-24724-6). Dutton.
Winter Caboose. Dorothy Hamilton. LC 83-10816. (Illus.). 104p. (Orig.). (gr. 4-8). 1983. pap. 3.95 (ISBN 0-8361-3341-2). Herald Pr.
Winter Camp Kid & Will. Dusty Richards. 172p. 7.00. Intl Univ Pr.
Winter-Christmas. Sean O'Leary. (Busy Fingers Ser.). (Illus.). 16p. (gr. 1-4). 1987. pap. 3.95 (ISBN 0-86278-127-2, Pub. by O'Brien Pr Ireland). Irish Bks Media.
Winter College on Fundamental Nuclear Physics: Proceedings of the Winter College on Fundamental Nuclear Physics, Trieste, Italy, March 1984, 3 vols. Ed. by K. Dietrich et al. 1985. Set. 202.00 (ISBN 9971-978-25-3). Vol. 1, 732p. Vol. 2, 600p. Vol. 3, 652p. World Scientific Pub.
Winter Concert. Margaret H. Freydberg. LC 85-10955. 336p. 1985. 15.95 (ISBN 0-88150-050-X). Countryman.
Winter Constellations. 2nd. ed. Richard Blessing. Ed. by Dale Boyer. LC 77-72388. (Modern & Contemporary Poets of the West Ser.). (Orig.). 1977. pap. 4.50 (ISBN 0-916272-05-2). Ahsahta Pr.
Winter Count. Barry H. Lopez. 128p. 1982. pap. 3.95 (ISBN 0-380-58107-8, Bard). Avon.
Winter Count. Frederick Manfred. 1966. ltd. signed ed. 40.00 (ISBN 0-911506-05-5). Thueson.
Winter Count: Poems. Frederick Manfred. 1978. pap. 3.50 (ISBN 0-914476-78-5). Thorp Springs.
Winter Day. Douglas Florian. LC 86-33524. (Illus.). 24p. (ps-1). 1987. 11.75 (ISBN 0-688-07351-4); lib. bdg. 11.88 (ISBN 0-688-07352-2). Greenwillow.
Winter Day in Yosemite. Carl Sharsmith. Ed. by Ardeth Huntington. (Illus.). 39p. 1981. pap. 2.95 (ISBN 0-939666-20-0). Yosemite Assn.
Winter Days Holiday Lingo. Stella V. Alexandre. (gr. 3-6). 1987. pap. 7.95 (ISBN 0-8224-3886-0). D S Lake Pubs.
Winter Doves. David Cook. 224p. 1988. pap. 8.95 (ISBN 0-87951-225-3). Overlook Pr.
Winter Doves: A Love Story. David Cook. LC 84-22678. 225p. 1985. 15.95 (ISBN 0-87951-994-0). Overlook Pr.
Winter Dreams. H. R. Coursen. Ed. by Napoleon St. Cyr. LC 82-4152. (Illus., Orig.). 1982. pap. 4.00 (ISBN 0-910380-04-X). Cider Mill.
Winter Dreams. Stefanie Curtis. (Sweet Dreams Ser.: No. 141). 176p. (Orig.). 1988. pap. 2.50 (ISBN 0-553-27062-1). Bantam.
Winter Dreams & Other Such Friendly Dragons. Joseph J. Juknialis. LC 79-64821. (Illus.). 1979. pap. 7.95 (ISBN 0-89390-010-9). Resource Pubns.
Winter Ecology of Small Mammals. Ed. by Joseph F. Merritt. LC 84-72213. (Special Publications: No. 10, CMNH). (Illus.). 390p. 1984. 45.00 (ISBN 0-935868-10-0). Carnegie Mus.
Winter Eel. Norman Hindley. 1984. pap. 6.00 (ISBN 0-932136-06-0). Petronium Pr.
Winter Evening. Shrikant Varma. Tr. by Jai Ratan & K. B. Vaid. 100p. (Eng.). 1975. cancelled (ISBN 0-88253-674-5); pap. 4.80 (ISBN 0-88253-673-7). Ind-US Inc.
Winter Exploitation Systems of Bay-Breasted & Chestnut-Sided Warblers in Panama. Russell Greenberg. LC 83-17412. (UC Publications in Zoology: Vol. 116). 1984. pap. 10.00x (ISBN 0-520-09670-3). U of Cal Pr.
Winter Festivals. Contributors to Family Festivals Magazine Staff. LC 86-60893. 123p. (Orig.). 1986. pap. 7.95 (ISBN 0-89390-077-X). Resource Pubns.
Winter Festivals. Nigel Wells. 80p. 1980. pap. 7.50 (ISBN 0-906427-18-5, Pub. by Bloodaxe Bks). Dufour.
Winter Five Seasonal Cookbook. John W. Garvy, Jr. Ed. by Jeremiah Liebermann. (Five Phase Cookbook Ser.: No. 1). (Illus.). 1985. pap. 6.00 (ISBN 0-943450-19-5). Wellbeing Bks.
Winter Folk. G. Walton. (Illus.). 88p. 1987. pap. 3.95 (ISBN 0-87797-120-X). Cherokee.
Winter from the Journal of Henry Thoreau. Henry David Thoreau. Ed. by J. G. Blake. 439p. 1973. Repr. of 1887 ed. 22.50 (ISBN 0-87928-046-8). Corner Hse.
Winter Fun. Rita Schlachter. LC 85-14008. (Illus.). 48p. (Orig.). (gr. 1-3). 1986. PLB 9.49 (ISBN 0-8167-0584-4); pap. text ed. 1.95 (ISBN 0-8167-0585-2). Troll Assocs.
Winter Fun Book. Janet Dellosa & Patti Carson. (Stick-Out-Your-Neck Ser.). (Illus.). 32p. (ps-2). 1984. pap. 1.59 (ISBN 0-88724-060-7, CD-8048). Carson-Dellos.
Winter Garden. Pablo Neruda. Tr. by William O'Daly from Span. LC 86-71837. 80p. (Orig., Eng.). 1986. 15.00 (ISBN 0-914742-99-X); pap. 8.00 (ISBN 0-914742-93-0). Copper Canyon.
Winter Gardening in the Maritime Northwest: Cool Season Crops for the Year-Round Gardener. 2nd rev. ed. Binda Colebrook. (Illus.). 170p. (Orig.). 1984. pap. 10.95 (ISBN 0-916239-00-4). Maritime Pubns.
Winter Girl. Dorothy Hamilton. LC 75-40344. (Illus.). 120p. (gr. 3-7). 1976. o. p. 4.95 (ISBN 0-8361-1787-5); pap. 3.95 (ISBN 0-8361-1788-3). Herald Pr.
Winter Grace, Spirituality for the Later Years. Kathleen R. Fischer. LC 84-61975. 1985. pap. 7.95 (ISBN 0-8091-2675-3). Paulist Pr.
Winter Grass. Richard S. Wheeler. 224p. 1986. pap. 2.50 (ISBN 0-345-33166-4). Ballantine.
Winter Harvest. Jane C. Aragon. (Illus.). (ps-3). 1989. 14.95i (ISBN 0-316-04937-9). Little.
Winter Hawk. Craig Thomas. LC 86-33219. 372p. 1987. 18.95 (ISBN 0-688-07091-4). Morrow.
Winter Hawk. Craig Thomas. 905p. Date not set. Repr. of 1986 ed. lib. bdg. price not set (ISBN 0-89621-837-6). Thorndike Pr.
Winter Hawk. Craig Thomas. 1988. pap. 4.95 (ISBN 0-380-70389-0). Avon.
Winter Heart. Victoria Glenn. (Silhouette Romance Ser.). pap. 1.95 (ISBN 0-373-08534-6). Harlequin Bks.
Winter Hero. James L. Collier & Christopher Collier. LC 78-7609. 160p. (gr. 7 up). 1978. 9.95 (ISBN 0-02-722990-4, Four Winds). Macmillan.
Winter Hero. James L. Collier & Christopher Collier. 208p. (YA) (gr. 7 up). 1985. pap. 2.25 (ISBN 0-590-33696-7, Point); tchr's. guide 1.25 (ISBN 0-590-40680-9). Scholastic Inc.
Winter Hiking & Camping. rev. ed. John A. Danielsen. (Illus.). 220p. 1986. pap. 8.95 (ISBN 0-935272-37-2). ADK Mtn Club.
Winter Holiday. Arthur Ransome. (Swallows & Amazons Ser.: No. 4). (gr. 4-6). Date not set. pap. 9.95. Godine.
Winter Holiday Poems: Source Materials for Programs. Nona K. Duffy. LC 86-71209. (Illus., Orig.). 1986. pap. 4.95 (ISBN 1-55618-003-9). Brunswick Pub.
Winter House: Poems. Robert Gibb. LC 83-16841. (Breakthrough Ser.: No. 43). 80p. 1984. pap. 6.95 (ISBN 0-8262-0437-6). U of MO Pr.
Winter Hunger. Cliff Schimmels. 180p. 1985. pap. 4.95 (ISBN 0-89693-333-4). Victor Bks.
Winter Hunt. Henry Tall Bull & Tom Weist. (Indian Culture Ser.). (gr. 3-9). 1971. 1.95 (ISBN 0-89992-006-3). Coun India Ed.
Winter in Arabia. Freya Stark. LC 86-31222. 336p. 1987. 18.95 (ISBN 0-87951-278-4). Overlook Pr.
Winter in Arabia. Freya Stark & John Murray. 1972. 28.50 (ISBN 0-7195-2727-9). Transatl Arts.
Winter in Eden. Harry Harrison. (Spectra Ser.: Vol. 2). 416p. (Orig.). 1986. pap. 18.95 (ISBN 0-553-05163-6, Spectra). Bantam.
Winter in Eden. Harry Harrison. 448p. 1987. pap. 4.50 (ISBN 0-553-26628-4, Spectra). Bantam.
Winter in Jerusalem. Blanche D'Alpuget. LC 86-1758. 270p. 1986. 16.95 (ISBN 0-671-49808-8). S&S.
Winter in Jerusalem. Blanche D'Alpuget. 1987. pap. 6.95 (ISBN 0-671-64000-3, Touchstone Bks). S&S.
Winter in Majorca. George Sand. Tr. by Robert Graves from Fr. (Illus.). 1978. lib. bdg. 12.95 (ISBN 0-915864-69-X); pap. 8.95 (ISBN 0-915864-68-1). Academy Chi Pubs.
Winter in Moscow. 2nd ed. Malcolm Muggeridge. 268p. 1987. pap. 8.95 (ISBN 0-8028-0263-X). Eerdmans.
Winter in Prague: Documents on Czechoslovak Communism in Crisis. Ed. by Robin A. Remington. (Studies in Communism, Revisionism & Revolution Ser.). 1969. pap. 6.95x (ISBN 0-262-68014-9). MIT Pr.
Winter in Russia. Theophile Gautier. Tr. by M. M. Ripley. 1977. lib. bdg. 59.95 (ISBN 0-8490-2827-2). Gordon Pr.
Winter in Taos. Mabel D. Luhan. (Illus.). 264p. Repr. of 1935 ed. 14.95 (ISBN 0-686-38775-9). Las Palomas.
Winter in the Blood. James Welch. (Contemporary American Fiction Ser.). 192p. 1986. pap. 5.95 (ISBN 0-14-008644-7). Penguin.
Winter in the Enchanted Forest. (Enchanted Forest Ser.). (Illus.). (ps-1). 1985. 2.98 (ISBN 0-517-46982-0). Outlet Bk Co.
Winter in the Morning: A Young Girl's Life in the Warsaw Ghetto, 1939-1945. Janina Bauman. 256p. 1986. 18.95 (ISBN 0-02-902530-3). Free Pr.
Winter in the West, 2 Vols. Charles F. Hoffman. LC 70-108493. 1970. Repr. of 1835 ed. Set. 49.00x (ISBN 0-403-00215-X). Scholarly.
Winter in the West Indies, Described in Familiar Letters to Henry Clay, of Kentucky. 2nd ed. Joseph J. Gurney. LC 69-19356. (Illus.). 1969. Repr. of 1840 ed. 35.00 (ISBN 0-8371-1022-X, GUW&). Greenwood.
Winter in the Woods. W. S. Doxey. (Illus.). pap. 3.00 (ISBN 0-686-12232-1). Doxey.
Winter in the Woods. W. S. Doxey. 1975. 1.00 (ISBN 0-685-67936-5). Windless Orchard.
Winter in Thrush Green. Miss Read. 1982. Repr. lib. bdg. 17.95 (ISBN 0-89966-436-9). Buccaneer Bks.
Winter in Thrush Green. Miss Read. 226p. 1987. pap. 7.95 (ISBN 0-89733-264-4). Academy Chi Pubs.
Winter Is Here! Jane B. Moncure. LC 75-14201. (Illus.). (ps-2). 1975. 7.95 (ISBN 0-913778-10-9). Childs World.
Winter Is Here! Jane B. Moncure. LC 75-14201. (Seasons Awareness Bks.). (Illus.). 24p. (ps-2). 1975. PLB 11.93 (ISBN 0-516-05856-8). Childrens.
Winter Is Not Forever. Janette Oke. 224p. (Orig.). 1988. Large type. pap. 5.95 (ISBN 1-55661-002-5); pap. 7.95. Bethany Hse.
Winter Journey. T. Alan Broughton. 320p. 1981. pap. 2.95 (ISBN 0-449-24369-9, Crest). Fawcett.
Winter Journey. Ronald Frame. 176p. 1986. 13.95 (ISBN 0-317-39741-9). Beaufort Bks NY.
Winter Journey. Halvard Johnson. (Illus.). 1979. pap. 3.00. New Rivers Pr.
Winter Journeys. John Greening. 19.00x (ISBN 0-904524-52-3, Pub. by Rivelin Grapheme Pr). State Mutual Bk.
Winter Keys to Woody Plants of Maine. Fay Hyland & Christopher S. Campbell. (Illus.). 1977. pap. 6.95x (ISBN 0-89101-034-3). U Maine Orono.
Winter Kill. William Harrison. 1979. pap. 1.50 (ISBN 0-505-51441-9, Pub. by Tower Bks). Leisure NY.
Winter Kills. Richard Condon. 336p. 1975. pap. 2.25 (ISBN 0-440-16007-3). Dell.
Winter King. Lillian S. Cal. 288p. 1986. pap. 2.95x (ISBN 0-441-89443-7, Pub. by Ace Science Fiction). Ace Bks.
Winter King. Paul Hazel. (Spectra Ser.). 288p. 1987. pap. 3.50 (ISBN 0-553-26945-3, Spectra). Bantam.
Winter Light. Maria M. Gillan. LC 85-22364. 72p. (Orig.). 1985. pap. 5.95 (ISBN 0-941608-05-0). Chantry Pr.
Winter Light. Snyder Kirtland. (Illus.). 44p. (Orig.). 1987. pap. 14.75 (ISBN 0-911623-05-1). I Klang.
Winter Magic. Eveline Hasler. LC 85-2944. (Illus.). (ps-3). 1985. 11.75 (ISBN 0-688-05257-6, Morrow Junior Books); lib. bdg. 11.88 (ISBN 0-688-05258-4). Morrow.
Winter Magic. Jennifer Hyde. 1985. 24.95x (ISBN 0-7090-1649-2, Pub. by R Hale Ltd UK). State Mutual Bk.
Winter Man: Poems. Ken McKeon. (Orig.). 1975. Thorp Springs.
Winter Marines. Allen Glick. 352p. 1987. pap. 4.50 (ISBN 0-553-26799-X). Bantam.
Winter Miscellany. Humbert Wolfe. 1930. Repr. 20.00 (ISBN 0-8274-3722-6). R West.
Winter Mittens. Tim Arnold. LC 88-2736. (Illus.). 32p. (gr. 3-6). 1988. PLB 12.95 (ISBN 0-689-50449-7, M K McElderry). Macmillan.
Winter Moon. Mildred R. Trivers. 48p. (Orig.). 1984. pap. 3.95 (ISBN 0-935306-30-7). Barnwood Pr.
Winter Motivators: Positive Reinforcement Activities & Awards for December, January, & February. Ed. by Carol Provisor et al. (Illus.). 32p. 1987. wkbk. 4.95 (ISBN 0-939007-09-6). Canter & Assoc.
Winter Nest: A Poetry Anthology of Midwestern Women Poets of Color. Ed. by Angela Lobo-Cobb. (Poetics of Colors Ser.). 110p. (Orig.). 1987. pap. text ed. 5.00 (ISBN 0-916783-05-7). Blue Reed.
Winter News. John Haines. LC 66-14660. (Wesleyan Poetry Program: Vol. 29). 1966. pap. 8.95 (ISBN 0-8195-1029-7). Wesleyan U Pr.
Winter Nights Entertainments see **Easy-to-Do Entertainments & Diversions with Cards, String, Coins, Paper & Matches.**
Winter Notes on Summer Impressions. Fyodor Dostoyevsky. Tr. by Kyril Fitzlyon. 94p. 1986. 13.95 (ISBN 0-7043-2542-X, Pub. by Quartet Bks). Salem Hse Pubs.
Winter Notes on Summer Impressions. Fyodor Dostoyevsky. Tr. by Davie Patterson. 125p. 1988. 22.95 (ISBN 0-8101-0813-5); pap. 8.95 (ISBN 0-8101-0814-3). Northwestern U Pr.
Winter of Artifice. Anais Nin. LC 61-17530. 175p. (Orig.). 1961. pap. 5.95 (ISBN 0-8040-0322-X, Pub by Swallow). Ohio U Pr.
Winter of Magic's Return. Pamela Service. 1987. pap. 2.50 (ISBN 0-317-57106-0, Juniper). Fawcett.
Winter of Magic's Return. Pamela F. Service. LC 85-7952. 224p. (gr. 4-8). 1985. 14.95 (ISBN 0-689-31130-3, Atheneum Childrens Bks). Macmillan.
Winter of Magic's Return. Pamela F. Service. (gr. 5 up). 1988. pap. 2.50 (ISBN 0-449-70202-2, Juniper). Fawcett.
Winter of the Blue Snow. Robert Kammen. 288p. 1988. pap. 3.50 (ISBN 0-8217-2432-0). Zebra.
Winter of the Fisher. Cameron Langford. (Illus.). 224p. 1985. pap. 5.95 (ISBN 0-393-30283-0). Norton.
Winter of the Heart. Linda J. LaRosa. 1984. 19.95 (ISBN 0-399-12900-6, Putnam). Putnam Pub Group.
Winter of the Heart. Linda J. LaRosa. 656p. 1985. pap. 3.95 (ISBN 0-445-20104-5, Popular Lib). Warner Bks.
Winter of the Owl. June A. Hanson. 176p. (gr. 4-6). 1983. pap. 2.25 (ISBN 0-590-33783-1, Apple Paperbacks). Scholastic Inc.
Winter of the Wolf. Jory Sherman. 1987. 15.95 (ISBN 0-8027-4071-5). Walker & Co.
Winter of the Wolf. Jory Sherman. 320p. 1989. pap. 3.50. Tor Bks.
Winter of the Wolf. G. Clifton Wisler. (gr. 6 up). 1980. 9.95 (ISBN 0-525-66716-4, 0966-290). Lodestar Bks.
Winter of the World. Poul Anderson. 192p. 1988. pap. 3.50 (ISBN 0-451-15233-6, Sig). NAL.
Winter Olympics. Caroline Arnold. (Easy-Read Sports Bks.). (Illus.). 48p. (gr. 2-4). 1983. PLB 10.40 (ISBN 0-531-04623-0). Watts.
Winter Oysters. Brendan Galvin. LC 82-13367. (Contemporary Poetry Ser.). 88p. 1983. 9.95x (ISBN 0-8203-0643-6); pap. 5.95 (ISBN 0-8203-0644-4). U of Ga Pr.
Winter Palace. Dennis Jones. 352p. 1988. 17.95 (ISBN 0-316-47295-6). Little.
Winter Park Portrait: The Story of Winter Park & Rollins College. Richard N. Campen. (Illus.). 112p. 1987. 22.50 (ISBN 0-9601356-5-0). West Summit.
Winter Park's Old Alabama Hotel. Noella L. Schenck. (Illus., Orig.). 1982. pap. 6.95 (ISBN 0-89305-043-1). Anna Pub.

WIPO Model Law for Developing Countries on Inventions: Patents, Vol. 1. 146p. 1979. pap. 8.25 (ISBN 0-686-60249-8, WIPO61, WIPO). UNIPUB.
WIPO Model Law for Developing Countries on Inventions: Vol. 2: Know-How, Examination and Registration of Contracts, Inventors' Certificates, Technovations, and Transfer of Technology Patents, Vol.2. 102p. 1980. pap. 8.25 (ISBN 0-686-94217-5, WIPO65, WIPO). UNIPUB.
WIPO Worldwide Forum on the Piracy of Broadcasts & of the Printed Word: Geneva March 16-18, 1983. (No. 646 (E)). (Fr.). 1983. pap. text ed. 11.00 (ISBN 92-805-0102-X, WIPO77, WIPO). UNIPUB.
Wir, das Volk. 2nd ed. Lonnelle Aikman. Tr. by Paul Vidal. (Illus.). 144p. (Ger.). 1983. pap. 4.50 (ISBN 0-916200-02-7). US Capitol Hist.
Wir Wollen Deutsche Bleiben: The Story of the Volga Germans. George J. Walters & Charles Walters, Jr. LC 82-80798. (Illus.). 426p. 1982. 18.75 (ISBN 0-911311-00-9). Halcyon Hse.
Wira Textile Data Book. 2nd ed. Ed. by Rae Wira & Bruce Wira. 1983. 90.00x (ISBN 0-317-43606-6, Pub. by Wira Tech Group). State Mutual Bk.
Wirds An' Wark E' Seasons Roon: On an Aberdeenshire Farm. Alexander Fenton. (Illus.). 96p. 1987. pap. text ed. 8.00 (ISBN 0-08-035074-7, AUP). Pergamon.
Wire Association International Proceedings. Incl. 50th Annual Meeting (7680); 51st Annual Meeting (7681); 52nd Annual Meeting (7682); 53rd Annual Meeting (7683). 50.00 ea. (ISBN 0-318-03210-4). Wire Assn Intl.
Wire Association International: Proceedings, 54th Annual Conference. 50.00 (ISBN 0-318-04236-3). Wire Assn Intl.
Wire, Cable, & Fiber Optics. Business Communications Staff. 1988. pap. 1750.00 (ISBN 0-89336-514-9, G-070R). BCC.
Wire Flow Photography As a Papermaking Diagnostic Tool. C. W. Howe et al. (Pulp & Paper Technology Ser.: No. 3). pap. 20.00 (2031007). Bks Demand UMI.
Wire Index. 150.00 (ISBN 0-318-03229-5, 8540). Wire Assn Intl.
Wire Sculpture & Other Three Dimensional Construction. Gerald F. Brommer. LC 68-19999. (Illus.). (gr. 5-12). 1968. 12.95 (ISBN 0-87192-025-5). Davis Mass.
Wire Splicing. 2nd ed. R. Scot Skirving. 49p. 1980. pap. 6.50x (ISBN 0-85174-154-1). Sheridan.
Wire Tappers. Arthur Stringer. 1976. lib. bdg. 15.30x (ISBN 0-89968-121-2). Lightyear.
Wire Taps & Surveillance, Bk. 1. abr. ed. Michael P. Jones. (Illus.). 84p. 1984. pap. text ed. 12.00 (ISBN 0-89904-078-0). Crumb Elbow Pub.
Wire Taps & Surveillance, Bk. 2. abr. ed. Michael P. Jones. (Illus.). 31p. 1984. pap. text ed. 6.00 (ISBN 0-89904-079-9). Crumb Elbow Pub.
Wire That Fenced the West. Henry D. McCallum & Frances T. McCallum. (Illus.). 1985. pap. 9.95 (ISBN 0-8061-1559-9). U of Okla Pr.
Wire Transfer Security & Control Primer. 60p. 1980. 24.00 (656). Bank Admin Inst.
Wire Window. Frank J. Kenmore. 400p. 1988. pap. 3.95 (ISBN 1-55817-084-7). Windsor NY.
Wire Womb: Life in a Girls' Penal Institution. Henry P. Lampman. LC 72-90555. 191p. 1973. 18.95x (ISBN 0-911012-23-0). Nelson-Hall.
Wirecutter. John Brizzolara. LC 86-19757. 240p. 1987. 16.95 (ISBN 0-385-23437-6). Doubleday.
Wired. Bob Woodward. 1985. pap. 4.50 (ISBN 0-317-54722-4). PB.
Wired Cities: Shaping the Future of Communications. Intro. by William H. Dutton et al. 492p. 1987. 45.00 (ISBN 0-8161-1851-5, Hall Library); pap. 29.95 (ISBN 0-8161-1853-1, Hall Library). G K Hall.
Wired for Sound: An Advanced Student Workbook on Hearing & Hearing Aids. Carole B. Simko. (Illus.). vi, 156p. 1986. wkbk. 4.95x (ISBN 0-930323-16-5, Clerc Bks). Gallaudet Univ Pr.
Wired: The Short Life & Fast Times of John Belushi. Bob Woodward. LC 84-5334. (Illus.). 461p. 1984. 17.95 (ISBN 0-671-47320-4). S&S.
Wiregrass: A Mythical Australian Town. Garrie Hutchinson. (Illus.). 80p. 1986. pap. 12.95 (ISBN 0-85091-249-0, Pub. by Lothian). Intl Spec Bk.
Wireless at Sea: The First Fifty Years. Harry E. Hancock. LC 74-7683. (Telecommunications Ser). (Illus.). 233p. 1974. Repr. of 1950 ed. 25.50x (ISBN 0-405-06048-3). Ayer Co Pubs.
Wireline Logging Tool Catalog. LC 83-82854. 176p. 1984. 40.00x (ISBN 0-87201-907-1). Gulf Pub.
Wireline Logging Tool Catalog. 2nd ed. (Illus.). 450p. 1986. 79.00x (ISBN 0-87201-916-0). Gulf Pub.
Wireline Operations. Nancy Gore. LC 83-62077. (Oil & Gas Production Ser.). (Illus.). 80p. (Orig.). 1984. pap. text ed. 8.00 (ISBN 0-88698-043-7, 3.31010). PETEX.
Wires & Watts: Understanding & Using Electricity. Irwin Math. LC 81-2255. (Illus.). 96p. (gr. 7 up). 1981. 13.95 (ISBN 0-684-16854-5, Pub. by Scribner). Macmillan.
Wiretap: Listening in on America's Mafia. James Goode. (Illus.). 240p. 1988. pap. 6.95 (ISBN 0-671-66797-1, Fireside). S&S.
Wiretapping & Eavesdropping, Vol. 1. Clifford Fishman. LC 78-18629. 1978. 79.50 (ISBN 0-686-29234-0); Suppl. 1986. 28.50; Suppl. 1987. 31.00. Lawyers Co-Op.
Wiretapping & Electronic Eavesdropping, the Law & Its Implications: A Comparative Study. Juris Cederbaums. (New York University Criminal Law Education & Research Center Monograph: No. 2). 77p. (Orig.). 1969. pap. text ed. 8.50x (ISBN 0-8377-0402-2). Rothman.
Wiretapping & Electronic Surveillance. Studies Commission. (Illus.). 1983. pap. 10.95 (ISBN 0-317-03315-8). Loompanics.
Wiretapping & Electronic Surveillance. 1986. lib. bdg. 79.95 (ISBN 0-8490-3530-9). Gordon Pr.
Wiretapping in New York City. Ed. by Robert M. Fogelson. LC 74-3843. (Criminal Justice in America Ser.). 1974. Repr. 12.00x (ISBN 0-405-06180-3). Ayer Co Pubs.
Wiring a Continent: The History of the Telegraph Industry in the United States, 1832-1866. Robert L. Thompson. LC 72-5078. (Technology & Society Ser.). (Illus.). 590p. 1972. Repr. of 1947 ed. 34.00 (ISBN 0-405-04727-4). Ayer Co Pubs.
Wiring & Cable Designer's Handbook. Bernard S. Matisoff. (Illus.). 448p. 1986. 32.50 (ISBN 0-8306-2720-0, NO. 2720, TAB-TPR). TAB Bks.
Wiring Simplified: Based on 1984 Code. 34th ed. H. P. Richter & W. Creighton Schwan. LC 33-7980. 160p. 1983. 4.45 (ISBN 0-9603294-2-0). Park Pub.
Wiring Simplified: Based on 1987 Code. 35th ed. H. P. Richter & W. Creighton Schwan. LC 33-7980. 160p. 1986. 5.25 (ISBN 0-9603294-3-9). Park Pub.
Wiring up the Workplace: A Practical Guide for Management. Roger Camrass & Ken Smith. (Illus.). 167p. (Orig.). 1987. pap. 59.00 (ISBN 0-941723-00-3). BCR Enterprises.
Wirklichkeit: Interpretation eines Kapitels aus Hegels "Wissenschaft der Logik". Tomoyuki Yamane. (European University Studies: No. 20, Vol. 118). 85p. (Ger.). 1983. 14.20 (ISBN 3-8204-7418-8). P Lang Pubs.
Wirkung der Dosierten Distraktion auf das Ellenbogengelenk des Kaninchens. M. H. Hackenbroch. (Journal: Acta Anatomica: Vol. 96, Suppl. 63-1). (Illus.). 1977. 27.50 (ISBN 3-8055-2643-1). S Karger.
Wirkung und Nebenwirkungen Von Bleomycin. Ed. by D. K. Hossfeld & P. Engel. (Beitraege zur Onkologie - Contributions to Oncology Ser.: Vol. 12). x, 220p. 1982. pap. 36.00 (ISBN 3-8055-3504-X). S Karger.
Wiros & Deiwos; He Who Would be God: The Story of the Indo-Europeans. James L. Oswald. (Illus.). 210p. (Orig.). 1986. pap. 11.11 (ISBN 0-9613882-0-X). Waldos Pr.
Wirriyamu. Williams Sassine. Tr. by John Reed & Clive Wake. (African Writers Ser.). 148p. 1980. pap. 7.00 (ISBN 0-435-90199-0). Heinemann Ed.
Wirtschaft, Recht und Staat Im Nationalsozialismus: Analysen des Instituts Fur Sozialforschung, 1939-1942. Max Horkheimer et al. 320p. (Ger.). 1982. pap. cancelled (ISBN 3-434-00469-6). Irvington.
Wirtschaftgeschichte. H. Bauer. 304p. 1982. 45.95 (ISBN 0-8176-1225-4). Birkhauser.
Wirtschaftliche Schwankungen der zeit von Alexander bis Augustus. Fritz M. Heichelheim. Ed. by Moses Finley. LC 79-4981. (Ancient Economic History Ser.). (Illus., Ger.). 1980. Repr. of 1930 ed. lib. bdg. 16.00x (ISBN 0-405-12367-1). Ayer Co Pubs.
Wirtschaftliche Zusammenbruch Osterreich-Ungarns: Die Tragodie der Erschopfung. Gustav Gratz & Richard Schuller. (Wirtschafts-Und Sozialgeschichte des Weltkrieges (Osterreichische Und Ungarische Serie)). (Ger.). 1930. 95.00x (ISBN 0-317-27658-1). Elliots Bks.
Wirtschafts-Woerterbuch. 4th ed. R. Eichborn. 2169p. (Ger. & Eng., Dictionary of Economics). write for info (M-7687, Pub. by Econ Vlg.). French & Eur.
Wirtschafts-Woerterbuch. 2nd ed. R. Eichborn & A. Fuentes. 2174p. (Ger. & Span.). 250.00 (ISBN 3-430-12388-7, M-7686, Pub. by Econ Vlg.). French & Eur.
Wirtschaftssprache Franzoesisch-Deutsch. G. Haensch & R. Renner. 54p. (Fr. & Ger.). 1975. 32.00 (ISBN 3-19-006202-1, M-7683, Pub. by M. Hueber). French & Eur.
Wirtschaftssprache German-English. 2nd ed. Renner et al. (Ger. & Eng.). 1970. 43.50x (ISBN 3-19-006201-3). Adlers Foreign Bks.
Wirtschaftssprache Spanisch-Deutsch. G. Haensch & F. Casero. (Span. & Ger.). 1971. 85.00 (ISBN 3-19-006203-X, M-7684, Pub. by M. Hueber). French & Eur.
Wirtschaftswoerterbuch Spanisch-Deutsch. Eichborn & Fuentes. (Span. & Ger.). 1974. 250.00 (ISBN 3-430-12390-9, M-7685, Pub. by Econ). French & Eur.
Wirtshaftswachstum und Bevolke Rungsentwicklung in Preussen 1816 Bis 1914: Zur Frage demo-Okonomischer Entwicklungszusammenhange. Gerd Hohorst. Ed. by Stuart Bruchey. LC 77-77193. (Dissertations in European Economic History Ser.). (Illus., Ger.). 1977. lib. bdg. 43.00x (ISBN 0-405-10805-2). Ayer Co Pubs.
WISC-R Administration & Scoring: Handbook of Training Exercises. Shavaun M. Wall & Paula Hixenbaugh. (Professional Handbook Ser.). 220p. 1983. 36.50x (ISBN 0-87424-178-2). Western Psych.
WISC-R Compilation. Dorothy Sutton & John R. Whitworth. 1978. 3-ring binder program 35.00x (ISBN 0-87879-202-3). Acad Therapy.
WISC-R Prescriptions. Norma Banas & I. H. Wills. LC 78-12881. 1978. pap. 6.00x (ISBN 0-87879-206-6). Acad Therapy.
Wisconsin. new ed. Allan Carpenter. LC 77-13666. (New Enchantment of America State Bks.). (Illus.). 96p. (gr. 4 up). 1978. PLB 15.93 (ISBN 0-516-04149-5). Childrens.
Wisconsin. Martin Hintz. (Off the Beaten Path Ser.). (Illus.). 1989. pap. price not set (ISBN 0-87106-625-4). Globe Pequot.
Wisconsin. Dana F. Ross. (Wagons West Ser.: No. 19). 1987. pap. 4.50 (ISBN 0-317-56863-9). Bantam.
Wisconsin! Dana F. Ross. 420p. 1988. lib. bdg. 17.95x (ISBN 0-8161-4384-6, Large Print Bks). G K Hall.
Wisconsin. R. Conrad Stein. LC 87-9376. (America the Beautiful Ser.). (Illus.). 144p. (gr. 4 up). 1987. PLB 23.93 (ISBN 0-516-00495-6). Childrens.
Wisconsin. Turner Program Services, Inc. Staff & James I. Clark. (Portrait of America Library). 48p. (gr. 4 up). 1985. PLB 15.33 (ISBN 0-86514-448-6); pap. text ed. 9.27 (ISBN 0-86514-523-7); Beta video 113.33 (ISBN 0-86514-073-1); VHS video 113.33 (ISBN 0-86514-148-7); 3/4" video 136.00 (ISBN 0-86514-223-8); tchr's guide 13.27 (ISBN 0-86514-298-X); student activity bk. 6.60; index 13.27. Raintree Pubs.
Wisconsin. Michael Weimer & Clay Schoenfeld. (Illus.). 1985. 16.95 (ISBN 0-19-540629-X). Skyline Press.
Wisconsin: A Geography. Ingolf Vogeler et al. 256p. 1986. 47.00 (ISBN 0-86531-186-2); pap. 26.00. Westview.
Wisconsin: A History. Richard N. Current. LC 77-2176. (States & the Nation Ser.). (Illus.). 1977. 14.95 (ISBN 0-393-05624-4, Co-Pub by AASLH). Norton.
Wisconsin: A State Guide. Federal Writers' Project. 69.00x (ISBN 0-403-02198-7). Somerset Pub.
Wisconsin & the Mentally Ill. Dale W. Robison. Ed. by Gerald N. Grob. LC 78-22588. (Historical Issues in Mental Health Ser.). 1979. lib. bdg. 25.50x (ISBN 0-405-11939-9). Ayer Co Pubs.
Wisconsin Appellate Practice & Procedure Study: Final Report. National Center for State Courts Staff. 189p. 1975. pap. 2.50 (R-021). Natl Ctr St Courts.
Wisconsin Appellate Process Study: Preliminary Report. National Center for State Courts Staff. Ed. by John E. Mueller et al. 67p. (On loan through the NCSC Library). 1975. pap. write for info. (NCRO-066). Natl Ctr St Courts.
Wisconsin Atlas & Gazetteer. DeLorme Mapping Company Staff. 104p. (Orig.). 1989. pap. 12.95 (ISBN 0-89933-247-1). DeLorme Map.
Wisconsin Attorney's-Secretary's Handbook. Mariposa Publishing Inc. Staff. 1988. looseleaf 40.00 (ISBN 0-86678-737-2). Butterworth MN.
Wisconsin Automotive Directory. Ed. by T. L. Spelman. 1985. 24.95 (ISBN 1-55527-034-4). Auto Contact Inc.
Wisconsin Biennial, 1982. Jane Livingston. 36p. 1982. pap. 3.95 (ISBN 0-913883-02-6). Madison Art.
Wisconsin Biennial, 1984. George Neubert. (Illus.). 36p. (Orig.). 1985. 4.95 (ISBN 0-913883-12-3). Madison Art.
Wisconsin Birds: A Seasonal & Geographic Guide. Stanley A. Temple. LC 86-40487. 280p. 1987. text ed. 27.50x (ISBN 0-299-11430-9); pap. 9.95 (ISBN 0-299-11434-1). U of Wis Pr.
Wisconsin Business Directory, 1987-88. rev. ed. American Directory Publishing Co., Inc. Staff. 1550p. 1987. pap. 95.00 (ISBN 0-944316-13-1). Amer Directory.
Wisconsin Census Index 1836. Ronald V. Jackson. LC 77-86057. (Illus.). lib. bdg. 11.00 (ISBN 0-89593-152-4). Accelerated Index.
Wisconsin Census Index 1836. Ronald V. Jackson. (Illus.). lib. bdg. 18.00 (ISBN 0-317-16976-9). Accelerated Index.
Wisconsin Census Index 1837. Ronald V. Jackson. lib. bdg. 30.00 (ISBN 0-317-16977-7). Accelerated Index.
Wisconsin Census Index 1838. Ronald V. Jackson. (Illus.). lib. bdg. 30.00 (ISBN 0-317-16978-5). Accelerated Index.
Wisconsin Census Index 1840. Ronald V. Jackson. LC 77-86058. (Illus.). lib. bdg. 25.00 (ISBN 0-89593-153-2). Accelerated Index.
Wisconsin Census Index 1842. Ronald V. Jackson. (Illus.). lib. bdg. 30.00 (ISBN 0-317-16979-3). Accelerated Index.
Wisconsin Census Index 1850. Ronald V. Jackson. LC 77-86059. (Illus.). lib. bdg. 50.00 (ISBN 0-89593-154-0). Accelerated Index.
Wisconsin Census Index 1855. Ronald V. Jackson. (Illus.). lib. bdg. 70.00 (ISBN 0-317-16980-7). Accelerated Index.
Wisconsin Chippewa Myths & Tales & Their Relation to Chippewa Life. Victor Barnouw. LC 76-53647. 304p. 1977. 25.00x (ISBN 0-299-07310-6). U of Wis Pr.
Wisconsin Chronology & Factbook, Vol. 49. Robert I. Vexler. (Chronologies & Documentary Handbook of the States). 1978. 8.50 (ISBN 0-379-16174-5). Oceana.
Wisconsin Circuit Court Survey: Final Report. 110p. 1982. manuscript 6.60 (ISBN 0-317-59226-2, NCRO-049). Natl Ctr St Courts.
Wisconsin Civil Practice Forms, 1970-1983, 4 vols. LC 79-102900. 290.00. Callaghan.
Wisconsin Collections I see Wisconsin Collections: Wisconsin Practice Systems Library Selection.
Wisconsin Collections II see Wisconsin Collections: Wisconsin Practice Systems Library Selection.
Wisconsin Collections: Wisconsin Practice Systems Library Selection, 2 Vols. Robert W. Kohn & Alice K. Shiffert. Incl. Wisconsin Collections I; Wisconsin Collections II. LC 79-91165. 199.00. Lawyers Co-Op.
Wisconsin: Conflict of Laws. 8.50 (ISBN 0-686-90972-0); suppl. 6.00 (ISBN 0-686-90973-9). Am Law Inst.
Wisconsin: Contracts. 8.50 (ISBN 0-686-90448-6). Am Law Inst.
Wisconsin Corporations: Wisconsin Practice Systems. Jack A. Postlewaite. LC 79-91166. loosleaf bdg. 94.50; Suppl. 1986. 41.50; Suppl. 1988. 49.00. Lawyers Co-Op.
Wisconsin Criminal Code Annotated. Thomas Hammer & Robert Donohoo. Date not set. pap. price not set (ISBN 0-941161-21-8). PES Inc WI.
Wisconsin Death Trip. Michael Lesy. LC 72-12383. 1973. pap. 12.95 (ISBN 0-394-72139-X). Pantheon.
Wisconsin Divorce: Wisconsin Practice Systems Library Selection. Richard K. Olson. LC 79-91167. 94.50; Suppl. 1982. 22.00. Lawyers Co-Op.
Wisconsin Folklore. Walker B. Wyman. (Illus.). 1981. pap. 4.95 (ISBN 0-686-27304-4). U Pr Wisc River Falls.
Wisconsin Funeral Service: A Consumer's Guide. 3rd ed. pap. 2.95 (ISBN 0-318-23655-9). UWIM CCA.
Wisconsin Garden Guide. rev. & enl. ed. Jerry A. Minnich. LC 82-3388. (Illus.). 321p. 1982. pap. 9.95 (ISBN 0-88361-086-8). Stanton & Lee.
Wisconsin Historical & Biographical Index, Vol. 1. Ronald Vern Jackson. LC 78-53723. (Illus.). 1984. lib. bdg. 30.00 (ISBN 0-89593-205-9). Accelerated Index.
Wisconsin Hunting Encyclopedia. 1976. pap. 2.95 (ISBN 0-932558-06-2). Wisconsin Sptmn.
Wisconsin Ice Trade. Lee E. Lawrence. (Wisconsin Stories Ser.). 12p. pap. 1.25 (ISBN 0-686-76155-3). State Hist Soc Wis.
Wisconsin in Their Bones. August Derleth. LC 61-6918. (SAC Prairie Saga Ser.). 265p. 1961. cancelled (ISBN 0-88361-081-7). Stanton & Lee.
Wisconsin: In Words & Pictures. Dennis Fradin. LC 77-5330. (Young People's Stories of Our States). (Illus.). 48p. (gr. 2-5). 1977. PLB 13.27 (ISBN 0-516-03948-2). Childrens.
Wisconsin Insurance Law. 2nd ed. Anderson. 308p. 1986. pap. 45.00 (ISBN 0-941161-00-5). Pes Inc WI.
Wisconsin: Its Geography & Topography, History, Geology & Mineralogy. facsimile ed. Increase A. Lapham. LC 74-107. (Mid-American Frontier Ser.). 1975. Repr. of 1846 ed. 19.00x (ISBN 0-405-06874-3). Ayer Co Pubs.
Wisconsin Juvenile Court Practice & Procedure: In Protection of Children. Henry J. Plum & Frank J. Crisafi. 1986. 65.00 (ISBN 0-86678-364-4). Butterworth MN.
Wisconsin Law Clerk Evaluation. National Center for State Courts Staff. 74p. 1978. manuscript 4.44 (NCRO-006). Natl Ctr St Courts.
Wisconsin Library Media Skills Guide. rev. ed. 142p. 1987. 13.00 (ISBN 0-318-23791-1). Wisc Lib Assn.
Wisconsin Life Trip. Dave Wood. 1982. 5.95 (ISBN 0-934860-21-1). Adventure Pubns.
Wisconsin Logging Book Eighteen Thirty-Nine to Nineteen Thirty-Nine. 4rd, rev. ed. Malcolm Rosholt. LC 80-53389. (Illus.). 304p. 1985. lib. bdg. 29.95 (ISBN 0-910417-05-9). Rosholt Hse.
Wisconsin Lore. Robert E. Gard & L. G. Sorden. LC 62-12168. 335p. 1971. 9.95 (ISBN 0-88361-083-3). Stanton & Lee.
Wisconsin Magazine of History: Cumulative Index, 3 vols. Incl. Vols. 26-35 (1942-1952) 1955. 3.00 (ISBN 0-87020-025-9); Vols. 36-45 (1952-1962) 1962. 3.00 (ISBN 0-87020-026-7); Vols. 46-55 (1962-1972) 9.50 (ISBN 0-87020-139-5). State Hist Soc Wis.
Wisconsin Manufacturers Register, 1988. 568p. 1987. 87.00 (ISBN 0-318-02840-9). Manufacturers.
Wisconsin Map Studies Program: Activity Manual. V. Charles & Adelina Hartung. Ed. by J. L. Irvine. (Illus.). 82p. (gr. 4). 1981. Duplication Masters 49.00 (ISBN 0-943068-04-5); Teacher's Guide 5.00 (ISBN 0-943068-03-7). Graphic learning.
Wisconsin Medicine: Historical Perspectives. Ronald L. Numbers & Judith W. Leavitt. LC 80-52297. (Illus.). 224p. 1981. 19.95x (ISBN 0-299-08430-2). U of Wis Pr.
Wisconsin Misdemeanors & Moving Traffic Violations. Clifford Steele. 1988. looseleaf 85.00 (ISBN 0-86678-653-8). Butterworth Mn.
Wisconsin Municipal Court Study: Executive Summary. National Center for State Courts Staff. 70p. (On loan through the NCSC Library). 1982. write for info. (NCRO-052). Natl Ctr St Courts.
Wisconsin Municipal Court Study: Final Report. National Center for State Courts Staff. 76p. 1982. manuscript 4.56 (NCRO-053). Natl Ctr St Courts.

Wisdom of Laotse. Iverson L. Harris. 36p. 1972. pap. 0.75 (ISBN 0-913004-05-7). Point Loma Pub.

Wisdom of Laotse. Laotse. Ed. by Lin Yutang. LC 83-5481. 1948. 6.95 (ISBN 0-394-60476-8). Modern Lib.

Wisdom of Life. Arthur Schopenhauer. (Illus.). 147p. 1985. 117.75 (ISBN 0-89266-503-3). Am Classical Coll Pr.

Wisdom of Life: Being the First Part of Aphorismen Zur Lebensweisheit. Arthur Schopenhauer. Tr. & pref. by T. Bailey Saunders. LC 72-487. (Essay Index Reprint Ser.). Repr. of 1890 ed. 12.00 (ISBN 0-8369-2821-0). Ayer Co Pubs.

Wisdom of Love. Edward Riccardo. 192p. (Orig.). 1985. pap. 9.95 (ISBN 0-911541-06-3). Gregory Pub.

Wisdom of Man: Selected Discourses. M. R. Bawa Muhaiyaddeen. LC 80-20541. (Illus.). 168p. 1980. 7.95 (ISBN 0-914390-16-3). Fellowship Pr PA.

Wisdom of Many: Essays on the Proverb. Wolfgang Mieder & Alan Dundes. 1981. lib. bdg. 48.00 (ISBN 0-8240-9472-7). Garland Pub.

Wisdom of Marcus Aurelius. Nathan H. Dole. (Illus.). 145p. Repr. of 1903 ed. 127.75 (ISBN 0-89901-374-0). Found Class Reprints.

Wisdom of Mboto. Marguerite C. Mboto. 107p. 1987. write for info. Adir Enterprises.

Wisdom of Milton H. Erickson. Milton H. Erickson. Ed. by Ronald A. Havens. 350p. 1985. 39.50x (ISBN 0-8290-0963-9). Irvington.

Wisdom of Nyaaya. K. P. Bahadur. LC 78-670087. (Wisdom of India Ser.: Vol. 3). 246p. 1978. 9.25 (ISBN 0-89684-468-4). Orient Bk Dist.

Wisdom of Omar Khayyan. 1967. 5.00 (ISBN 0-8022-0849-5). Philos Lib.

Wisdom of Plato: An Attempt at an Outline, 2 vols. Nehemiah Jordan. LC 80-1409. (Orig.). 1981. Set. lib. bdg. 63.50 (ISBN 0-8191-1408-1); Set. pap. 40.75 (ISBN 0-8191-1409-X). Vol. I, 544p. Vol. 2, 536p. U Pr of Amer.

Wisdom of Poetry: Essays in Early English Literature in Honor of Morton W. Bloomfield. Intro. by Larry D. Benson & Siegfried Wenzel. viii, 315p. 1982. 22.95x (ISBN 0-918720-15-X); pap. 13.95x (ISBN 0-918720-16-8). Medieval Inst.

Wisdom of Proverbs, Job & Ecclesiastes. Derek Kidner. LC 85-11826. 176p. 1985. pap. 8.95 (ISBN 0-87784-405-4). Inter-Varsity.

Wisdom of Royal Glory (Kutadgu Bilig) A Turko-Islamic Mirror for Princes. Khass H. Yusuf. Tr. by Robert Dankoff. LC 82-20159. (Publications of The Center for Middle Eastern Studies: No. 16). 320p. 1983. 22.00x (ISBN 0-226-97179-1). U of Chicago Pr.

Wisdom of Saankhya. K. P. Bahadur. LC 78-901698. (Wisdom of India Ser.: Vol. 2). 222p. 1977. 9.25 (ISBN 0-89684-469-2). Orient Bk Dist.

Wisdom of St. Francis & His Companions. Compiled by Stephen Clissold. LC 78-27504. (Wisdom Books). 1979. pap. 4.95 (ISBN 0-8112-0721-8, NDP477). New Directions.

Wisdom of St. John. Bo Yin Ra. Tr. by Bodo A. Reichenbach from Ger. LC 74-15272. 112p. 1975. 8.00 (ISBN 0-915034-01-8). Kober Pr.

Wisdom of Science. Robert Hanbury Brown. (Illus.). 200p. 1986. 34.50 (ISBN 0-521-30726-0); pap. 14.95 (ISBN 0-521-31448-8). Cambridge U Pr.

Wisdom of Sidereal Astrology KMH9, No. 9. Andres Takra. (Illus.). 520p. 1983. pap. 18.00 (ISBN 0-89540-127-4, SB-127). Sun Pub.

Wisdom of Sir Walter Scott. Owen Redfern. LC 73-14592. 1907. Repr. lib. bdg. 35.00 (ISBN 0-8414-7244-0). Folcroft.

Wisdom of Sir Walter Scott: Criticisms & Opinions Collected from the Waverly Novels & Lockhart's Life of Sir Walter Scott. Walter Scott. LC 73-159707. (Research & Source Works Ser.: No. 752). 1971. Repr. of 1907 ed. lib. bdg. 22.50 (ISBN 0-8337-2917-9). B Franklin.

Wisdom of Solomon. E. G. Clarke. (Cambridge Bible Commentary on the New English Bible, Old Testament Ser.). 148p. 1973. pap. 8.95 (ISBN 0-521-09756-8). Cambridge U Pr.

Wisdom of Solomon. David Winston. LC 78-18150. (Anchor Bible Ser.: Vol. 43). 1979. pap. 20.00 (ISBN 0-385-01644-1, Anchor Pr). Doubleday.

Wisdom of Solomon Schechter. Bernard Mandelbaum. 1963. pap. 2.50 (ISBN 0-8381-3103-4). United Syn Bk.

Wisdom of Solomon the King: A Seventy-Two Card Deck & Book for Divination & Ritual. Llewellyn. 1988. 14.95 (ISBN 0-87542-701-4). Llewellyn Pubns.

Wisdom of Southern California. Lance Jencks. 68p. (Orig.). 1982. pap. 5.95 (ISBN 0-9609678-1-8). Lindenhof Pr.

Wisdom of Statecraft: Sir Herbert Butterfield & the Philosophy of International Politics. Alberto R. Coll. LC 85-1535. xvii, 173p. 1985. 27.50 (ISBN 0-8223-0607-7). Duke.

Wisdom of the Adepts: Esoteric Science in Human History. Thomas L. Harris. LC 72-2957. Repr. of 1884 ed. 55.00 (ISBN 0-404-10721-4). AMS Pr.

Wisdom of the Ages. Silvia Silk. (Illus.). 28p. (Orig.). 1982. pap. 5.00 (ISBN 0-938861-01-8). Jasmine Texts.

Wisdom of the Ancients. B-C Publishers Staff. 1983. 2.00x (ISBN 0-86516-022-8). Bolchazy-Carducci.

Wisdom of the Body. Yogi A. Desai. Ed. by Lisa Sarasohn. (Illus.). 40p. (Orig.). 1984. pap. 2.00 (ISBN 0-940258-13-7). Kripalu Pubns.

Wisdom of the Chinese: Their Philosophy in Sayings & Proverbs. Brian Brown. lib. bdg. 79.95 (ISBN 0-87968-138-1). Krishna Pr.

Wisdom of the Chinese: Their Philosophy in Saying & Proverbs. Ed. by Brian Brown. (Illus.). 207p. 1983. 40.00 (ISBN 0-89984-129-5). Century Bookbindery.

Wisdom of the Desert. Thomas Merton. LC 59-15021. 1970. 6.50 (ISBN 0-8112-0313-1); pap. 4.95 (ISBN 0-8112-0102-3, NDP295). New Directions.

Wisdom of the Desert Fathers. 1979. pap. 3.95 (ISBN 0-686-25228-4). Eastern Orthodox.

Wisdom of the Early Buddhists. Geoffrey Parrinder. LC 77-7945. (New Directions Wisdon Ser.). 1977. pap. 4.95 (ISBN 0-8112-0667-X, NDP444). New Directions.

Wisdom of the Far East: A Dictionary of Proverbs, Maxims, & Famous Classical Phrases of the Chinese, Japanese, & Korean. Young H. Yoo. LC 70-168691. (Dictionary Ser., No. 5). 1972. 13.50 (ISBN 0-912580-00-3). Far Eastern Res.

Wisdom of the Forest: Selections from the Hindu Upanishads. Tr. & intro. by Geoffrey Parrinder. LC 75-42114. (Wisdom Bks). 96p. 1976. pap. 1.95 (ISBN 0-8112-0607-6, NDP414). New Directions.

Wisdom of the Heart. Henry Miller. LC 41-28118. 1942. pap. 6.95 (ISBN 0-8112-0116-3, NDP94). New Directions.

Wisdom of the Heart: A Study of the Works of Mulk Raj Anand. Marlene Fisher. xiv, 207p. 1985. text ed. 27.50x (ISBN 0-86590-724-2, Pub. by Sterling Pubs India). APT Bks.

Wisdom of the Heart: Katherine Tingley Speaks. Katherine Tingley. Ed. by W. Emmett Small. LC 78-65338. 1978. pap. 5.75 (ISBN 0-913004-33-2). Point Loma Pub.

Wisdom of the Hindus. Brian Brown. 320p. 1981. pap. 18.00 (ISBN 0-89540-093-6, SB-093). Sun Pub.

Wisdom of the Jewish People. Lewis Browne. LC 87-24101. 773p. 1988. 40.00 (ISBN 0-87668-985-3). Aronson.

Wisdom of the Land. Solon Robinson. (Illus.). 1977. pap. 7.95 (ISBN 0-89328-012-7). Lorenz Corp.

Wisdom of the Lord: Homilies for Weekdays & Feast Days. Rev. Gene Ulses. LC 86-60910. 254p. (Orig.). 1986. 12.95 (ISBN 0-87973-512-0, 512). Our Sunday Visitor.

Wisdom of the Master. Abdu'l-Baha. 1988. pap. 11.95 (ISBN 0-933770-35-9). Kalimat.

Wisdom of the Mystic Masters. John K. Weed. 1968. 10.95 (ISBN 0-13-961516-4, Reward); pap. 5.95 (ISBN 0-13-961532-6). P-H.

Wisdom of the Novel: A Dictionary of Quotations. David Powell. LC 81-48423. (Reference Library of the Humanities). 624p. 1985. lib. bdg. 50.00 (ISBN 0-8240-9017-9); pap. 17.95 (ISBN 0-8240-8920-0). Garland Pub.

Wisdom of the Outlaw: The Boyhood Deeds of Finn in Gaelic Narrative Tradition. Joseph F. Nagy. LC 84-8826. 1985. 35.00x (ISBN 0-520-05284-6). U of Cal Pr.

Wisdom of the Overself. rev ed. Paul Brunton. LC 83-60833. 464p. (Orig.). 1984. pap. 8.95 (ISBN 0-87728-591-8). Weiser.

Wisdom of the Psyche. Ann B. Ulanov. LC 88-15964. 142p. (Orig.). 1988. pap. 8.95. Cowley Pubns.

Wisdom of the Saints: An Anthology of Voices. Jill H. Adels. 288p. 1987. 18.95 (ISBN 0-19-504152-6). Oxford U Pr.

Wisdom of the Sands. Saint Antoine De Saint-Exupery. Tr. by Stuart Gilbert from Fr. LC 79-15938. 1979. pap. 10.95 (ISBN 0-226-73372-6, P826). U of Chicago Pr.

Wisdom of the Sasanian Sages: Denkard Book VI. Tr. by Shaul Shaked. LC 79-2957. (Persian Heritage Ser.). 400p. 1983. 35.00x (ISBN 0-89158-376-9). Caravan Bks.

Wisdom of the Spanish Mystics. Stephen Clissold. (Wisdom Bks.). 3.95 (ISBN 0-8112-0663-7). New Directions.

Wisdom of the Stoics: Selections from Seneca, Epictetus & Marcus Aurelius. Ed. by Frances Hazlitt & Henry Hazlitt. LC 84-3493. 186p. (Orig.). 1984. lib. bdg. 25.25 (ISBN 0-8191-3870-3); pap. text ed. 11.00 (ISBN 0-8191-3871-1). U Pr of Amer.

Wisdom of the Taoists. D. Howard Smith. LC 80-15629. (Wisdom Ser.). 96p. 1980. 5.95 (ISBN 0-8112-0777-3, NDP509). New Directions.

Wisdom of the Tarot. Elisabeth Haich. 1983. pap. 12.50 (ISBN 0-943358-01-9). Aurora Press.

Wisdom of the Throne: An Introduction to the Philosophy of Mulla Sadra. Mulla Sadra. Tr. by James W. Morris from Arabic. LC 81-47153. (Princeton Library of Asian Translations). 300p. 1981. 38.50x (ISBN 0-691-06493-8). Princeton U Pr.

Wisdom of the Torah. Ed. by Dagobert D. Runes. 1966. pap. 2.25 (ISBN 0-8065-0015-8, 236, Pub. by Citadel Pr). Lyle Stuart.

Wisdom of the Upanishads. Besant. 5.50 (ISBN 0-8356-7092-9). Theos Pub Hse.

Wisdom of the Vedas. J. C. Chatterji. LC 80-51550. 100p. 1980. pap. 3.95 (ISBN 0-8356-0538-8, Quest). Theos Pub Hse.

Wisdom of the Zen Masters. Ed. by Irmgard Schloegl. LC 75-42115. (Wisdom Bks.). 96p. 1976. pap. 5.95 (ISBN 0-8112-0610-6, NDP415). New Directions.

Wisdom of the Zohar, 3 vols. Ed. by Isaiah Tishby. Tr. by David Goldstein. (Litman Library of Jewish Civilization). 1568p. 1988. Set. 198.00 (ISBN 0-19-710043-0). Oxford U Pr.

Wisdom of Thoreau. LC 67-29205. 1967. 5.00 (ISBN 0-8022-1719-2). Philos Lib.

Wisdom of Tolstoi. 128p. 1968. 5.00 (ISBN 0-317-37940-2). Philos Lib.

Wisdom of Vaisheshika. K. P. Bahadur. (Wisdom of India Ser.: Vol. 4). 207p. 1979. 10.50 (ISBN 0-89684-470-6). Orient Bk Dist.

Wisdom of Vedanta. K. P. Bahadur. (Wisdom of India Ser.: No. 6). 412p. 1985. text ed. 40.00x (ISBN 0-86590-725-0, Pub. by Sterling Pubs India). APT Bks.

Wisdom of Vedanta. H. L. Sharma. 140p. 1981. 15.95. Asia Bk Corp.

Wisdom of Walt Whitman. Laurens Maynard. 1979. Repr. of 1926 ed. lib. bdg. 29.00. Folcroft.

Wisdom of Words: Language, Theology & Literature in the New England Renaissance. Philip F. Gura. LC 80-25041. 203p. 1981. 35.00x (ISBN 0-8195-5053-1). Wesleyan U Pr.

Wisdom of Words: Language, Theology & Literature in the New England Renaissance. Philip F. Gura. x, 203p. 1985. pap. 10.95 (ISBN 0-8195-6120-7). Wesleyan U Pr.

Wisdom of Yoga. K. P. Bahadur. LC 77-985594. (Wisdom of India Ser.: Vol. 1). 116p. 1977. 9.25 (ISBN 0-89684-471-4). Orient Bk Dist.

Wisdom, or Mind, Will, & Understanding. LC 70-133770. (Tudor Facsimile Texts. Old English Plays Ser.: No. 2). Repr. of 1907 ed. 49.50 (ISBN 0-404-53302-7). AMS Pr.

Wisdom Revisited: Athena Speaks & Other Owl-Songs. Louise Jaffe. LC 87-91517. 48p. (Orig.). 1987. pap. 5.00. L Jaffe.

Wisdom Symposium: Papers from the Trinty College Medieval Festival. Ed. by Milla Cozart Riggio. LC 85-48070. (Studies in the Middle Ages: No. 11). (Illus.). 1986. 32.50 (ISBN 0-404-61441-8). AMS Pr.

Wisdom, the Principal Thing. Kenneth L. Jensen. 1971. pap. 2.95 (ISBN 0-685-24806-2). Pacific Mer.

Wisdom Tree. Gary D. Gurthrie. (Illus., Orig.). 1984. pap. 6.95 (ISBN 0-942494-87-3). Coleman Pub.

Wisdom Tree. Emma Hawkridge. LC 72-128257. (Essay Index Reprint Ser.). 1945. 33.00 (ISBN 0-8369-1881-9). Ayer Co Pubs.

Wisdom-Waves in New York, 2 pts. Sri Chinmoy. (Orig.). 1979. pap. 2.00 ea. Pt. 1, 53p (ISBN 0-88497-487-1). Pt. 2, 50p (ISBN 0-88497-488-X). Aum Pubns.

Wisdom Without Answers: A Guide to the Experience of Philosophy. Daniel Kolak & Raymond Martin. Date not set. pap. text ed. write for info. (ISBN 0-534-10236-0). Wadsworth Pub.

Wisdom's Call. facs. ed. Sutton E. Griggs. LC 75-89411. (Black Heritage Library Collection Ser). 1911. 15.50 (ISBN 0-8369-8587-7). Ayer Co Pubs.

Wisdom's Children: Home Education & the Roots of Restored Biblical Culture. Blair Adams & Joel Stein. 540p. (Orig.). 1988. pap. 12.95 (ISBN 0-916387-10-0). Truth Forum.

Wisdom's Daughter. H. Rider Haggard. 19.95 (ISBN 0-89190-714-9, Pub. by Am Repr). Amereon Ltd.

Wisdom's Daughter: The Life & Love Story of She-Who-Must-Be-Obeyed. H. Rider Haggard. Ed. by R. Reginald & Douglas Melville. LC 77-84230. (Lost Race & Adult Fantasy Ser.). 1978. Repr. of 1923 ed. lib. bdg. 33.00x (ISBN 0-405-10983-0). Ayer Co Pubs.

Wisdom's Fool. Eddie Doherty. 5.95 (ISBN 0-910984-08-5); pap. 3.95 (ISBN 0-910984-09-3). Montfort Pubns.

Wise & Healthy Living: A Mature Focus. Richard D. Underwood & Brenda B. Underwood. 240p. 1988. pap. 9.95 (ISBN 0-88908-686-9, 9565). ISC Pr.

Wise & Otherwise. Jack B. Scott. (Orig.). 1985. pap. text ed. 4.95 (ISBN 0-934688-21-4); leader's guide 3.95 (ISBN 0-934688-23-0). Great Comm Pubns.

Wise As Serpents; Harmless As Doves: Chinese Christian Tell Their Story. Ed. by Richard L. Van Houten. 288p. 1988. pap. 10.95. William Carey Lib.

Wise Blood. Flannery O'Connor. 232p. 1962. 10.95 (ISBN 0-374-29128-4); pap. 6.95 (ISBN 0-374-50584-5). FS&G.

Wise Blood see Collected Works.

Wise Child. Monica Furlong. LC 87-3063. 192p. (gr. 5 up). 1987. 11.95 (ISBN 0-394-89105-8); lib. bdg. 12.99 (ISBN 0-394-99105-2). Knopf.

Wise County, Virginia. Charles A. Johnson. 430p. 1988. Repr. of 1938 ed. 27.95 (ISBN 0-932807-29-1). Overmountain Pr.

Wise Fools. Plumb Willie. 94p. 1986. 19.00X (ISBN 0-7223-2007-8, Pub. by A H Stockwell England). State Mutual Bk.

Wise King: Studies in Royal Wisdom As Divine Revelation in the Old Testament & Its Environment. Leonidas Kaluglia. (Conciectanea Biblica. Old Testament Ser.: No. 15). 160p. (Orig.). 1980. pap. 25.00x (ISBN 0-317-65799-2). Coronet Bks.

Wise Man & the Star. Gordon Stowell. (Sticker Bks.). (Orig.). (ps-3). 1987. pap. 6.95 (ISBN 0-8024-8476-X). Moody.

Wise Man Stories. Friends Anonymous Staff. Ed. by Harold Smith & Alma Smith. (Orig.). 1979. pap. 2.95 (ISBN 0-87516-371-8). DeVorss.

Wise Men: Architects of the American Century. Walter Isaacson & Evan Thomas. 816p. 1986. 22.95 (ISBN 0-671-50465-7). S&S.

Wise Men Know What Wicked Things Are Written on the Sky. Russell Kirk. 240p. (Orig.). 17.95 (ISBN 0-89526-574-5); pap. 9.95 (ISBN 0-89526-787-X). Regnery Gateway.

Wise Men of Chelm. Douglas L. Lieberman. LC 81-69267. (Illus.). 64p. 1981. 3.50 (ISBN 0-88020-102-9); piano accompaniment 9.00 (ISBN 0-88020-105-3). Coach Hse.

Wise Men of Foreign Affairs: The History of the Council on Foreign Relations. Robert D. Schulzinger. LC 83-27321. 326p. 1984. 31.50 (ISBN 0-231-05528-5). Columbia U Pr.

Wise Men of Helm. Solomon Simon. (gr. 3-7). 1942. pap. 6.50 (ISBN 0-87441-125-4). Behrman.

Wise Men: Six Friends & the World They Made. Walter Isaacson & Evan Thomas. 1987. pap. 12.95 (ISBN 0-671-65712-7, Touchstone Bks). S&S.

Wise Old Owl. Louis M. Barrella. (Illus.). 48p. (gr. 4-6). 1988. 6.95 (ISBN 0-89962-669-6). Todd & Honeywell.

Wise Owl Books. Bill Martin, Jr. Incl. The Electric Eel (ISBN 0-03-085800-3); The Frightened Hare (ISBN 0-03-085801-1); Giant Fishes of the Open Sea (ISBN 0-03-085802-X); The Life of a Star (ISBN 0-03-085803-8); Hawk in the Sky (ISBN 0-03-085804-6). (Holt Science Ser.). (gr. 4-6). 1971. PLB 8.08 ea. (HoltE). H Holt & Co.

Wise Owl's ABC Book. Dorothy F. Richards. LC 81-6187. (Wise Owl Plus Ser.). (Illus.). 32p. (ps-2). 1981. 11.93 (ISBN 0-516-06561-0). Childrens.

Wise Owl's Birthday Colors. Dorothy F. Richards. LC 81-10144. (Wise Owl Plus Ser.). (Illus.). 32p. (ps-2). 1981. PLB 11.93 (ISBN 0-516-06562-9). Childrens.

Wise Owl's Book of Sounds, No. 35. Jane B. Moncure. LC 81-18094. (Wise Owl Plus Ser.). (Illus.). 32p. (ps-2). 1982. lib. bdg. 11.93 (ISBN 0-516-06564-5). Childrens.

Wise Owl's Counting Book. Dorothy F. Richards. LC 81-2399. (Wise Owl Plus Ser.). (Illus.). 32p. (ps-2). 1981. 11.93 (ISBN 0-516-06565-3). Childrens.

Wise Owl's Days of the Week. Jane B. Moncure. LC 81-9971. (Wise Owl Ser.). (Illus.). 32p. (ps-2). 1981. PLB 11.93 (ISBN 0-516-06563-7). Childrens.

Wise Owl's Time Book, No. 36. Jane B. Moncure. LC 81-38546. (Wise Owl Plus Ser.). (Illus.). 32p. (ps-2). 1982. lib. bdg. 11.93 (ISBN 0-516-06566-1). Childrens.

Wise Queen. Retold by Anthea Bell. LC 85-29845. (Illus.). 28p. (ps up). 1986. 13.95 (ISBN 0-88708-014-6). Picture Bk Studio.

Wise Queen. Kia Simon. (Shameless Hussy Children's Poetry Ser.). (Illus.). (gr. 2-8). 1979. pap. 1.95 (ISBN 0-915288-31-1). Shameless Hussy.

Wise Robin. (Ladybird Stories Ser.). (Illus., Arabic.). (gr. 1-4). 3.50x (ISBN 0-86685-243-3). Intl Bk Ctr.

Wise Rockshelter: A Multicomponent Site in Jackson County, Ohio. Jon Oplinger. LC 81-13750. (Research Papers in Archaeology Ser.). (Illus.). 62p. (Orig.). 1981. pap. 5.50x (ISBN 0-87338-262-5). Kent St U Pr.

Wise Sayings & Favorite Passages from the Works of Henry Fielding, Including His Essay on Conversation. Chas. W. Bingham. LC 74-12102. 1974. Repr. of 1909 ed. lib. bdg. 17.00 (ISBN 0-8414-3211-2). Folcroft.

Wise Silence: Photographs by Paul Caponigro. Marianne Fulton. LC 83-81480. (Illus.). 208p. 1983. 74.00 (ISBN 0-8212-1548-5, 948624). NYGS.

Wise Virgin. A. N. Wilson. 224p. 1983. 13.95 (ISBN 0-670-77528-2). Viking.

Wise Virgin. A. N. Wilson. 208p. 1984. pap. 4.95 (ISBN 0-14-006661-6). Penguin.

Wise Virgins. Leonard Woolf. LC 79-1861. 276p. 1979. 9.95 (ISBN 0-15-197511-6). HarBraceJ.

Wise, Witty & Tender Sayings. Alexander Main. 1973. Repr. of 1893 ed. 25.00 (ISBN 0-8274-1030-1). R West.

Wise Woman. Joyce Rogers. LC 80-68538. 1981. 8.95 (ISBN 0-8054-5289-3). Broadman.

Wise Woman. Naomi Strichartz. (Illus.). 43p. (Orig.). (gr. 2-6). 1986. pap. 3.50 (ISBN 0-9618182-0-4). Cranehill Pr.

Wise Woman & Other Fantasy Stories. George MacDonald. Ed. by Glenn G. Sadler. (Fantasy Stories of George MacDonald Ser.). 176p. 1980. pap. 5.95 (ISBN 0-8028-1860-9). Eerdmans.

Wise Woman Builds Her House. Bessie Patterson. 1979. pap. 4.95 (ISBN 0-89137-413-2). Quality Pubns.

Wise Woman Herbal for the Childbearing Year. Susun S. Weed. LC 85-71064. (Wise Woman Herbals Ser.: No. 1). (Illus.). 192p. (Orig.). 1985. 12.95 (ISBN 0-9614620-1-9); pap. 6.95 (ISBN 0-9614620-0-0). Ash Tree.

Wise Woman Knows. Bessie Patterson. 4.95 (ISBN 0-89137-422-1). Quality Pubns.

Wit & Wisdom of Yogi Berra. 2nd, rev. ed. Phil Pepe. 150p. 1988. 16.95 (ISBN 0-88736-318-0). Meckler Corp.
Wit, Humor & Shakespeare. John Weiss. LC 73-4187. 1973. Repr. of 1889 ed. lib. bdg. 49.50 (ISBN 0-8414-2846-8). Folcroft.
Wit, Humor & Shakespeare. John Weiss. 59.95 (ISBN 0-8490-1308-9). Gordon Pr.
Wit of a Woman. Ed. by W. W. Greg. LC 82-45772. (Malone Society Reprint Ser.: No. 40). Repr. of 1913 ed. 40.00 (ISBN 0-404-63040-5). AMS PR.
Wit of a Woman. LC 77-133770. (Tudor Facsimile Texts, No. 103. Old English Plays Ser.). Repr. of 1912 ed. 49.50 (ISBN 0-404-53403-1). AMS Pr.
Wit, Wisdom & Foibles of the Great. Charles A. Shriner. LC 68-30617. 704p. 1969. Repr. of 1918 ed. 46.00x (ISBN 0-8103-3297-3). Gale.
Wit, Wisdom & Foibles of the Great. Charles A. Shriner. 35.00 (ISBN 0-8490-1309-7). Gordon Pr.
Wit, Wisdom & Foibles of the Great Together with Numerous Anecdotes Illustrative of the Characters of People & Their Rules. Compiled by Charles A. Shriner. 685p. Repr. of 1918 ed. lib. bdg. 150.00 (ISBN 0-8414-8195-4). Folcroft.
Wit, Wisdom, & Pathos, from the Prose of Heinrich Heine: With a Few Pieces from the "Book of Songs". Ed. by J. Snodgrass. 1978. Repr. of 1888 ed. lib. bdg. 30.00 (ISBN 0-8492-8034-6). R West.
Wit Without Money: A Comedy. Francis Beaumont & John Fletcher. LC 73-25968. (English Experience Ser.: No. 264). 66p. Repr. of 1639 ed. 11.50 (ISBN 90-221-0264-5). Walter J Johnson.
Witch. Mary Johnston. 1914. Repr. lib. bdg. 49.00 (ISBN 0-8414-5425-6). Folcroft.
Witch. Thomas Middleton. LC 82-45692. (Malone Society Reprint Ser.: No. 89). Repr. of 1948 ed. 40.00 (ISBN 0-404-63089-8). AMS Pr.
Witch Amongst Us. Lois Bourne. 208p. 1986. 13.95 (ISBN 0-312-88425-7). St Martin.
Witch Amongst Us. Lois Bourne. 208p. 1988. 40.00x (ISBN 0-7090-2368-5, Pub. by R Hale Ltd UK). State Mutual Bk.
Witch & Other Stories. Anton Chekhov. Tr. by Constance Garnett from Rus. (Tales of Chekhov Ser.: Vol. 6). 200p. 1985. pap. 8.50 (ISBN 0-88001-053-3). Ecco Pr.
Witch & the Clown: Two Archetypes of Human Sexuality. Ann Ulanov & Barry Ulanov. LC 86-21628. 270p. 1987. pap. 14.95 (ISBN 0-933029-07-1). Chiron Pubns.
Witch & the Goddess in the Stories of Isak Dinesen: A Feminist Reading. Sara Stambaugh. LC 88-5393. (Challenging the Literary Cannon Ser.). 150p. 1988. 39.95 (ISBN 0-8357-1884-0). UMI Res Pr.
Witch & the Weather Report. Susan F. Schaeffer. LC 72-81233. 1972. pap. 2.75 (ISBN 0-913282-00-6). Seven Woods Pr.
Witch at the Window. Ruth Chew. (Illus.). 128p. (Orig.). (gr. 2-4). 1985. pap. 2.50 (ISBN 0-590-41219-1, Lucky Star). Scholastic Inc.
Witch Baby. Wendy Smith. LC 85-40590. (Viking Kestrel Picture Bks.). (Illus.). 32p. (ps-3). 1986. 7.95 (ISBN 0-670-80953-5, Viking Kestrel). Viking.
Witch Baby. Wendy Smith. (ps-3). 1988. pap. 3.50 (ISBN 0-317-69625-4, Puffin Bks). Penguin.
Witch-Cat. Joan Carris. LC 83-48448. (Illus.). 160p. (gr. 5 up). 1984. 11.70i (ISBN 0-397-32067-1, Lipp Jr Bks); PLB 11.89g (ISBN 0-397-32068-X). HarpJ.
Witch Cat. Joan Carris. (gr. 5 up). 1986. pap. 2.95 (ISBN 0-440-49477-X, YB). Dell.
Witch Child. Elizabeth Lloyd. 352p. 1987. pap. 3.95 (ISBN 0-8217-2230-1). Zebra.
Witch Daughter. Elizabeth Lloyd. 384p. 1988. pap. 3.95 (ISBN 0-8217-2353-7). Zebra.
Witch Doctor: Memoirs of a Partisan. Michael Temchin. (Illus.). 192p. (Orig.). 1983. 16.95 (ISBN 0-8052-5046-8); pap. 10.95 (ISBN 0-8052-5047-6). Holocaust Pubns.
Witch Doctor's Cookbook. Peggy Cochrane. LC 84-52022. (Illus.). 173p. (Orig.). 1984. pap. 7.95 (ISBN 0-9614031-0-1). Sherman Pr.
Witch Door. Elizabeth Ogilvie. 1976. Repr. of 1959 ed. lib. bdg. 14.95x (ISBN 0-88411-182-2, Pub. by Aeonian Pr). Amereon Ltd.
Witch down the Street. Stephanie Morgan. (Care Bears Ser.). (Illus.). 40p. (ps-3). 1983. cancelled 5.95 (ISBN 0-910313-02-4, 7003). Parker Bros.
Witch Family. Eleanor Estes. LC 60-11250. (Illus.). (gr. 3-7). 1960. 11.95 (ISBN 0-15-298571-9, HJ). HarBraceJ.
Witch Family. Eleanor Estes. LC 60-11250. (Illus.). (gr. 4-6). 1965. pap. 3.95 (ISBN 0-15-697645-5, VoyB). HarBraceJ.
Witch (From Bodeian Ms Malone 12) From Bodeian Manuscript Malone 12. Thomas Middleton. Ed. by L. Drees & H. De Vocht. (Material for the Study of the Old English Drama Ser.: No. 2, Vol. 18). pap. 11.00 (ISBN 0-8115-0311-9). Kraus Repr.
Witch, Goblin, & Ghost Are Back. Sue Alexander. LC 83-22157. (Illus.). 62p. (gr. 1-4). 1985. 6.95 (ISBN 0-394-86296-1, Pant Bks Young); lib. bdg. 7.99 (ISBN 0-394-96296-6). Pantheon.
Witch Goddess. Robert Adams. (Horseclans Ser.: No. 9). 1983. pap. 2.95 (ISBN 0-451-14027-3, AE1792, Sig). NAL.
Witch Got on at Paddington Station. Dyan Sheldon. (Illus.). 32p. (ps-3). 1988. 11.95 (ISBN 0-525-44352-5, 01160-350). Dutton.
Witch Grows Up. Norman Bridwell. (Illus.). 32p. (Orig.). (gr. k-3). 1987. pap. 1.95 (ISBN 0-590-40559-4). Scholastic Inc.
Witch Hazel, Four: The Best of Witch Hazel see Witch Hazel's Whackola Adventures.
Witch Hazel: Poems of a Lifetime. George C. Homans. 160p. 1987. 24.95 (ISBN 0-88738-200-2). Transaction Bks.
Witch Hazel's Crazy Adventures. Jonathon Thompson, Jr. (Illus.). 80p. (gr. 3-6). 1985. 4.50 (ISBN 0-933479-05-0). Thompson.
Witch Hazel's Whackey Adventures. Jonathon Thompson, Jr. (Illus.). 104p. (gr. 3-6). 1985. 5.50 (ISBN 0-933479-01-8). Thompson.
Witch Hazel's Whackola Adventures. Jonathon Thompson, Jr. Orig. Title: Witch Hazel, Four: The Best of Witch Hazel. (Illus.). 143p. (gr. 4-8). 1986. 6.50 (ISBN 0-933479-03-4). Thompson.
Witch-Herbalist of the Remote Town. Amos Tutuola. 205p. 1982. pap. 7.95 (ISBN 0-571-11704-X). Faber & Faber.
Witch Herself. Phyllis R. Naylor. LC 78-5437. (Illus.). 176p. (gr. 3-7). 1978. 7.95 (ISBN 0-689-30664-4, Atheneum Childrens Bk). Macmillan.
Witch Herself. Phyllis Naylor-Reynolds. (gr. k-6). 1988. pap. 2.95 (ISBN 0-440-40044-9, TB). Dell.
Witch Hill Murder. Pauline G. Winslow. 256p. 1983. pap. 5.95 (ISBN 0-312-88428-1). St Martin.
Witch Hunt. Scott Corbett. 144p. (gr. 5 up). 1985. 13.95 (ISBN 0-316-15750-3, Joy St Bks). Little.
Witch Hunt Activity Book. 32p. 1989. pap. 1.95. Tor Bks.
Witch Hunt: Biblical Solutions in the Search for Heretics. Bob Passantino & Gretchen Passantino. (Orig.). 1988. pap. 9.95. Lawson-Cook Pub.
Witch-Hunt in Early Modern Europe. Brian P. Levack. 1987. text ed. 24.95 (ISBN 0-582-49122-3); pap. text ed. 12.95 (ISBN 0-582-49123-1). Longman.
Witch Hunting in Southwestern Germany, 1562-1684: The Social & Intellectual Foundations. H. Erik Midelfort. LC 75-183891. 320p. 1972. 26.50x (ISBN 0-8047-0805-3). Stanford U Pr.
Witch in Room Six. Edith Battles. LC 86-45785. 160p. (gr. 3-7). 1987. 10.70i (ISBN 0-06-020412-5); PLB 10.89 (ISBN 0-06-020413-3). HarpJ.
Witch in the Cherry Tree. Margaret Mahy. (Illus.). 32p. (ps-2). 1985. Repr. of 1974 ed. 8.50x (ISBN 0-460-05884-3, BKA 05280, Pub. by J M Dent England). Biblio Dist.
Witch in the House. Ruth Chew. (Illus.). (gr. 2-3). 1976. pap. 1.95 (ISBN 0-590-00093-4). Scholastic Inc.
Witch King. Maeve Henry. LC 87-20370. 128p. (gr. 4-7). 1988. 12.95 (ISBN 0-531-05738-0); PLB 12.99 (ISBN 0-531-08338-1). Orchard Bks Watts.
Witch Lady. Nancy Carlson. LC 85-3756. (Illus.). 32p. (ps-3). 1985. PLB 9.95 (ISBN 0-87614-283-8). Carolrhoda Bks.
Witch Lady Mystery. Carol B. York. (gr. 4-6). 1977. pap. 2.50 (ISBN 0-590-40513-6, Apple Paperbacks). Scholastic Inc.
Witch Miss Seeton. Heron Carvic. 192p. 1988. pap. 2.95 (ISBN 0-425-10713-2). Berkley Pub.
Witch Next Door. Norman Bridwell. (Illus.). 32p. (gr. k-3). 1986. pap. 1.95 (ISBN 0-590-40433-4). Scholastic Inc.
Witch of Belsen & Other Stories. L. C. Wheeler. 1981. 15.00x (ISBN 0-7223-1389-6, Pub. by A H Stockwell England). State Mutual Bk.
Witch of Blackbird Pond. Elizabeth G. Speare. 256p. (gr. k-6). 1972. pap. 3.50 (ISBN 0-440-49596-2, YB). Dell.
Witch of Blackbird Pond. Elizabeth G. Speare. (Illus.). 256p. (gr. 7 up). 1958. 12.95 (ISBN 0-395-07114-3). HM.
Witch of Blackbird Pond. Elizabeth G. Speare. 256p. (gr. 5 up). 1978. pap. 3.25 (ISBN 0-440-99577-9, LFL). Dell.
Witch of Blackbird Pond see Newberry Library Award.
Witch of Blackbird Pond see Newbery Awards Collection.
Witch of Cumberland Gap. Bernard Stallard. (Illus.). 76p. 1981. pap. 5.95 (ISBN 0-9606908-0-8). B Stallard.
Witch of Edmonton. Thomas Dekker et al. (Methuen Student Editions). (Illus.). 128p. 1983. pap. 3.95 (ISBN 0-413-53260-7, NO. 3969). Heinemann Ed.
Witch of Edmonton by Thomas Dekker: A Critical Edition. Ed. by Etta S. Onat & Stephen Orgel. LC 79-54355. (Renaissance Drama Second Ser.). 400p. 1980. lib. bdg. 53.00 (ISBN 0-8240-4472-X). Garland Pub.
Witch of Fourth Street & Other Stories. Myron Levoy. LC 74-183174. (Illus.). 128p. (gr. 4-7). 1972. pap. 2.95i (ISBN 0-06-440059-X). HarpJ.
Witch of Goingsnake & Other Stories. Robert J. Conley. LC 88-4762. 184p. 1988. 17.95 (ISBN 0-8061-2148-3). U of Okla Pr.
Witch of Hissing Hill. Mary Calhoun. (Illus.). (gr. k-3). 1964. PLB 11.88 (ISBN 0-688-31762-6). Morrow.
Witch of Lagg. Ann Cheatham. (Orig.). (gr. k-12). 1987. pap. 2.50 (ISBN 0-440-99412-8, LFL). Dell.
Witch of Turner's Bald. Edna C. Pierson. (Illus.). 1971. 5.00 (ISBN 0-686-05889-5). Puddingstone.
Witch on a Motorcycle. new ed. Marian Frances. (Illus.). (gr. 3-4). 1972. pap. 1.50 (ISBN 0-89375-047-6). Troll Assocs.
Witch Poems. Ed. by Daisy Wallace. LC 76-9036. (Illus.). 32p. (gr. 1-4). 1976. reinforced bdg. 11.95 (ISBN 0-8234-0281-9). Holiday.
Witch Switch. Anne Harler. (Sappling Ser.). (Illus.). 64p. (Orig.). (gr. k-2). 1987. pap. 1.95 (ISBN 0-87406-245-4). Willowisp Pr.
Witch Tales. new ed. Corinne Denan. LC 79-66328. (Illus.). 48p. (gr. 3-6). 1980. lib. bdg. 9.59 (ISBN 0-89375-324-6); pap. 1.95 (ISBN 0-89375-323-8). Troll Assocs.
Witch, They Cried. Joanne Suter. 120p. (Orig.). 1985. pap. 2.95 (ISBN 0-88120-733-0). SRA.
Witch Tree Symbol. rev. ed. Carolyn Keene. LC 75-1580. (Nancy Drew Ser.: Vol. 33). (Illus.). 196p. (gr. 4-7). 1975. 4.50 (ISBN 0-448-09533-5, G&D); PLB 3.29 (ISBN 0-448-19533-X). Putnam Pub Group.
Witch, Warlock & Magician. W. H. Adams. 59.95 (ISBN 0-8490-1310-0). Gordon Pr.
Witch Watch. Betty Higgins. Ed. by Sun Star Publications Staff. (Jellybean Collection: Vol. 1). (Illus.). 24p. (Orig.). (gr. 3-8). 1986. pap. 2.95 (ISBN 0-937787-05-1). Sun Star Pubns.
Witch Water. Phyllis R. Naylor. LC 77-1057. (Illus.). 192p. (gr. 4-7). 1977. 9.95 (ISBN 0-689-30595-8, Childrens Bk). Atheneum.
Witch Water. Phyllis Naylor-Reynolds. (gr. k-6). 1988. pap. 2.95 (ISBN 0-440-40038-4, YB). Dell.
Witch Week. Diana W. Jones. LC 82-6074. 256p. (gr. 3-7). 1988. pap. 2.95 (ISBN 0-394-80600-X). Knopf.
Witch Week. Diane W. Jones. LC 82-6074. 224p. (gr. 5-9). 1982. reinforced bdg. 11.75 (ISBN 0-688-01534-4). Greenwillow.
Witch Who Became Someone Else. Anne C. Masland. (Illus.). 32p. (gr. k up). 1983. 6.95 (ISBN 0-682-40133-1). Exposition-Phoenix.
Witch Who Couldn't Tell Time. Pamela G. Spare. (Illus.). 64p. (Orig.). 1985. tchr's. ed. 19.95 (ISBN 0-9615515-0-X). B Collins.
Witch Who Lives down the Hall. Donna Guthrie. LC 85-887. (Illus.). 32p. (ps-3). 1985. pap. 12.95 (ISBN 0-15-298610-3, Pub. by HJ). HarBraceJ.
Witch Who Lost Her Shadow. Mary Calhoun. (Illus.). (gr. k-3). 1979. PLB 12.89 (ISBN 0-06-020947-X). HarpJ.
Witch Who Saved Halloween. Marian T. Place. (Illus.). (gr. 2-5). 1974. pap. 2.50 (ISBN 0-380-00097-0, Camelot). Avon.
Witch Who Went for a Walk. Margaret Hillert. (Illus.). (gr. 1-6). 1981. PLB 4.39 (Dist. by Caroline Hse); pap. 1.95 (ISBN 0-8136-5605-2). Modern Curr.
Witch Woman. Elizabeth E. Allen. 512p. 1987. pap. 3.95 (ISBN 0-446-34549-0). Warner Bks.
Witch Woman. James Cabell. 12.95 (ISBN 0-89190-273-2, Pub. by Am Repr). Amereon Ltd.
Witch Words: Poems of Magic & Mystery. Ed. by Robert Fisher. (Illus.). 80p. (gr. 3-6). 1987. laminated boards 9.95 (ISBN 0-571-14559-0). Faber & Faber.
Witch World: Trey of Swords, No. 7. (The Witch World Ser.). 1987. pap. 2.75 (ISBN 0-441-82346-7, Pub. by Ace Science Fiction). Ace Bks.
Witchcraft. Charles A. Hoyt. LC 80-24731. 160p. 1981. pap. 14.95 (ISBN 0-8093-1015-5). S Ill U Pr.
Witchcraft. Bernard Sleigh. 69.95 (ISBN 0-8490-1311-9). Gordon Pr.
Witchcraft & Black Magic. Montague Summers. LC 70-174114. (Illus.). 232p. 1971. Repr. of 1916 ed. 50.00x (ISBN 0-685-02995-6). Gale.
Witchcraft & Demonianism. Cecil H. Ewen. LC 79-8631. (Illus.). Repr. of 1933 ed. 48.50 (ISBN 0-404-18410-3). AMS Pr.
Witchcraft & Magic in Sixteenth & Seventeenth Century Europe. Geoffrey Scarre. LC 86-27399. (Studies in European History). 80p. 1987. pap. text ed. 8.50 (ISBN 0-391-03505-3). Humanities.
Witchcraft & Murder in Zimbabwe. Henry A. Clark. (Illus.). 163p. 1986. pap. 6.50 (ISBN 0-317-53265-0). Noontide.
Witchcraft & Religion: The Politics of Popular Belief. Christina Larner. 256p. 1984. 29.95x (ISBN 0-631-13447-6). Basil Blackwell.
Witchcraft & Religion: The Politics of Popular Belief. Christina Larner. Ed. by Alan Macfarlane. 184p. 1986. pap. text ed. 12.95x (ISBN 0-631-14779-9). Basil Blackwell.
Witchcraft & Second Sight in the Highlands & Islands of Scotland. John G. Campbell. 1976. Repr. 20.00x (ISBN 0-85409-978-6). Charles River Bks.
Witchcraft & Sorcery. Ed. by Max G. Marwick. 494p. 1987. pap. 6.95 (ISBN 0-14-022678-8, Pelican). Penguin.
Witchcraft & Sorcery in Ovambo. M. Hiltunen. (Finnish Anthropological Society Ser.: No. 17). 178p. (Orig.). 1986. pap. 27.50 (ISBN 951-95434-9-X). Coronet Bks.
Witchcraft & Sorcery of the North American Native Peoples. rev. ed. Ed. by Deward E. Walker. 1988. pap. 23.95 (ISBN 0-89301-127-4). U of Idaho Pr.
Witchcraft & Superstitious Record in the Southwestern District of Scotland. J. Maxwell Wood. (Illus.). 1976. 25.00x (ISBN 0-7158-1139-8). Charles River Bks.
Witchcraft & Superstitious Record in the Southwestern District of Scotland. John M. Wood. LC 76-25108. 1976. 55.00 (ISBN 0-8414-9530-0). Folcroft.
Witchcraft & the Nature of Man. Mark Graubard. 326p. (Orig.). 1985. pap. text ed. 15.50 (ISBN 0-8191-4314-6). U Pr of Amer.
Witchcraft at Salem. Chadwick Hansen. LC 69-15825. (Illus.). 1969. 12.95 (ISBN 0-8076-0492-5). Braziller.
Witchcraft at Salem. Chadwick Hansen. LC 99-943950. 252p. (YA) (RL 10). pap. 3.95 (ISBN 0-451-62214-6, ME2214, Ment). NAL.
Witchcraft at Salem. Chadwick Hansen. (Illus.). 252p. 1985. pap. 7.95 (ISBN 0-8076-1137-9). Braziller.
Witchcraft Delusion in Colonial Connecticut, 1647-1747. John Taylor. 172p. 1974. 17.50 (ISBN 0-87928-053-0). Corner Hse.
Witchcraft Delusion in Colonial Connecticut, 1647-97. John M. Taylor. LC 73-165414. (American Classics in History & Social Science Ser.: No. 196). 1971. Repr. of 1908 ed. lib. bdg. 21.00 (ISBN 0-8337-4445-3). B Franklin.
Witchcraft Delusion in New England, 3 vols. Samuel G. Drake. LC 79-120720. (Research & Source Works Ser.: No. 471). 1970. Repr. of 1866 ed. lib. bdg. 62.00 (ISBN 0-8337-0908-9). B Franklin.
Witchcraft Fact Book. Edmund M. Buczyski. (Illus.). 24p. 1984. pap. 4.00 (ISBN 0-939708-04-3). Magickal Childe.
Witchcraft for Tomorrow. Doreen Valiente. (Illus.). 205p. 1983. 14.95 (ISBN 0-919345-35-2); pap. 8.95 (ISBN 0-919345-83-2). Phoenix WA.
Witchcraft for Tomorrow. Doreen Valiente. 208p. 1988. 42.00x (ISBN 0-7091-6412-2, Pub. by R Hale Ltd UK). State Mutual Bk.
Witchcraft in Europe & America: Guide to the Microfilm Collection. Ed. by Diane M. Del Cervo. 112p. 1983. 50.00 (ISBN 0-89235-074-1). Res Pubns CT.
Witchcraft in Europe, 1100-1700: A Documentary History. Ed. by Alan C. Kors & Edward Peters. LC 71-170267. (Illus.). 1972. pap. 15.95x (ISBN 0-8122-1063-8, Pa Paperbks). U of Pa pr.
Witchcraft in History. Ronald Holmes. 1977. pap. 5.95 (ISBN 0-8065-0575-3, Pub. by Citadel Pr). Lyle Stuart.
Witchcraft in Ireland. Patrick Byrne. 80p. 1979. pap. 7.95 (ISBN 0-85342-038-6, Pub. by Mercier Pr Ireland). Irish Bks Media.
Witchcraft in North Carolina. Tom P. Cross. 70p. 1980. Repr. of 1919 ed. lib. bdg. 22.00 (ISBN 0-8414-9992-6). Folcroft.
Witchcraft in the Middle Ages. Jeffrey B. Russel. (Illus.). 1976. pap. 5.95 (ISBN 0-8065-0504-4, Pub. by Citadel Pr). Lyle Stuart.
Witchcraft in the Middle Ages. Jeffrey B. Russell. LC 72-37755. (Paperback Ser.). 394p. 1984. 38.50x (ISBN 0-8014-0697-8); pap. 10.95 (ISBN 0-8014-9289-0). Cornell U Pr.
Witchcraft in the Southwest: Spanish & Indian Supernaturalism on the Rio Grande. Marc Simmons. LC 79-18928. (Illus.). xiv, 184p. 1980. pap. 5.95 (ISBN 0-8032-9116-7, Bison). U of Nebr Pr.
Witchcraft in Western India. Sohaila Kapur. 176p. 1983. text ed. 15.95x (ISBN 0-86131-402-6, Pub. by Orient Longman Ltd. India). Apt Bks.
Witchcraft, Magic & Alchemy. Grillot De Givry. Tr. by J. Courtney Locke from Fr. (Illus.). 395p. 1971. pap. 9.95 (ISBN 0-486-22493-7). Dover.
Witchcraft, Magic & Alchemy. Grillot De Givry. lib. bdg. 95.00 (ISBN 0-87968-515-8). Krishna Pr.
Witchcraft, Magic & Alchemy. Grillot De Givry. (Illus.). 15.75 (ISBN 0-8446-0113-6). Peter Smith.
Witchcraft, Magic & Occultism. W. B. Crow. pap. 7.00 (ISBN 0-87980-173-5). Wilshire.
Witchcraft, Magic & Religion in Seventeenth Century Massachusetts. Richard Weisman. LC 83-15542. 288p. 1985. pap. text ed. 11.95x (ISBN 0-87023-494-3). U of MAss Pr.
Witchcraft of Salem Village. Shirley Jackson. (Landmark Ser.: No. 69). (Illus.). (gr. 4-6). 1963. lib. bdg. 8.99 (ISBN 0-394-90369-2, BYR). Random.
Witchcraft Papers. Peter Haining. 1974. 7.95 (ISBN 0-8216-0223-3, Pub. by Univ Bks). Lyle Stuart.
Witchcraft Poems: Salem, Sixteen Ninety-Two. Constance Carrier. (Chapbooks: No. 4). 1988. 30.00 (ISBN 0-937035-11-4). Stone Hse NY.
Witchcraft: The Gay Counterculture. Arthur Evans. 1977. pap. 5.95 (ISBN 0-915480-01-8). Fag Rag.
Witchcraft: The Heritage of a Heresy. H. Sebald. 262p. 1978. pap. 19.50 (ISBN 0-444-99059-3). Elsevier.
Witchcraft: The Old Religion. Leo L. Martello. 1987. pap. 6.95 (ISBN 0-8065-1028-5, Pub. by Citadel Pr). Lyle Stuart.
Witchcraft-the Sixth Sense. Justine Glass. pap. 7.00 (ISBN 0-87980-174-3). Wilshire.
Witchcraft Today. Gerald B. Gardner. 1970. pap. 2.45 (ISBN 0-8065-0002-6, Pub. by Citadel Pr). Lyle Stuart.
Witchcraft Today. Gerard B. Gardner. (Illus.). 184p. pap. 9.95 (ISBN 0-939708-03-5). Magickal Childe.
Witchdame. Kathleen Sky. 352p. 1985. pap. 2.95 (ISBN 0-425-07449-8). Berkley Pub.

With Both Eyes Open: Seeing Beyond Gender. Ed. by Patricia A. Johnson & Janet Kalven. 232p. 1988. pap. 10.95 (ISBN 0-8298-0777-2). Pilgrim NY.

With British Snipers to the Reich. C. Shore. (Illus.). 408p. 1988. Repr. of 1948 ed. 24.95 (ISBN 0-935856-02-1). Lancer.

With Byron in Italy: A Selection of the Poems & Letters of Lord Byron. Anna B. McMahan. 1973. Repr. of 1907 ed. 25.00 (ISBN 0-8274-0111-6). R West.

With Caesar's Legions. Reuben F. Wells. LC 60-16709. (Illus.). (gr. 7-11). 1951. 15.00x (ISBN 0-8196-0110-1). Biblo.

With Charity for All: Welfare & Society, Ancient Times to the Present. Meritt Ierley. 236p. 1984. 40.95 (ISBN 0-275-91194-2). Praeger.

With Charity Toward None: An Analysis of Ayn Rand's Philosophy. William F. O'Neill. (Quality Paperback: No. 179). 233p. 1977. pap. 6.95 (ISBN 0-8226-0179-6). Littlefield.

With Child. Phyllis Chesler. 1981. pap. 2.95 (ISBN 0-425-04834-9). Berkley Pub.

With Child: Birth Through the Ages. Jenny Carter & Therese Durietz. 288p. 1986. 75.00x (ISBN 0-906391-90-3, Pub. by Mainstream Scotland). State Mutual Bk.

With Child: Birth Through the Ages. Jenny Carter & Therese Duriez. (Illus.). 287p. 1988. 24.95 (ISBN 0-317-68288-1, Pub. by Mnstream Scotland). David & Charles.

With Child: One Couple's Journey to Their Adopted Children. Susan T. Viguers. LC 85-17742. 224p. 1986. 15.95 (ISBN 0-15-197514-0). HarBraceJ.

With Child: One Couple's Journey to Their Adopted Children. Susan T. Viguers. 240p. 1988. pap. 9.95 (ISBN 0-8093-1498-3). S Ill U Pr.

With Christ after the Lost. rev. ed. Lee R. Scarborough. Ed. by E. D. Head. 1953. 12.95 (ISBN 0-8054-6203-1). Broadman.

With Christ in Heavenly Realms: A Study of Ephesians. Phyllis Mitchell. (Enrichment Bible Studies). 60p. 1986. pap. 2.95 (ISBN 0-932305-22-9, 522007). Aglow Pubns.

With Christ in the School of Disciple Building: A Study of Christ's Method of Building Disciples. Carl Wilson. 1976. pap. 7.95 (ISBN 0-310-34591-X, 12312P). Zondervan.

With Christ in the School of Obedience. Andrew Murray. 108p. 1986. pap. 4.95 (ISBN 0-89693-281-8). Victor Bks.

With Christ in the School of Prayer. Andrew Murray. 288p. 1981. pap. 3.50 (ISBN 0-88368-106-4). Whitaker Hse.

With Christ in the School of Prayer. Andrew Murray. 288p. 1983. pap. 6.95 (ISBN 0-310-29771-0, 10527P). Zondervan.

With Christ in the School of Prayer. Andrew Murray. (Christian Library). 274p. 1986. Repr. 6.95 (ISBN 0-916441-57-1). Barbour & Co.

With Compass & Chain. Joseph W. Ernst. Ed. by Stuart Bruchey. LC 78-56727. (Management of Public Lands in the U. S. Ser.). 1979. lib. bdg. 28.50x (ISBN 0-405-11331-5). Ayer Co Pubs.

With Compassion Toward Some: Homosexuality & Social Work in America. Ed. by Robert Schoenberg & Richard Goldberg. LC 85-5838. 156p. 1985. pap. 8.95 (ISBN 0-918393-14-0). Harrington Pk.

With Consequences for All. ASCD Task Force on Increased High School Graduation Requirements. 31p. 1985. 3.50 (611-85418). Assn Supervision.

With Courage to Spare. John B. Toews. 185p. (Orig.). 1978. pap. 4.95 (ISBN 0-919797-26-1); 7.95 (ISBN 0-919797-25-3). Kindred Pr.

With Crook at the Rosebud. J. W. Vaughn. LC 87-27968. xvi, 253p. 1988. 21.95x (ISBN 0-8032-4657-9, Bison); pap. 8.95 (ISBN 0-8032-9554-5, Bison). U of Nebr Pr.

With Crook in the Black Hills: Stanley J. Morrow's 1876 Photographic Legacy. Paul L. Hedren. LC 85-501. (Illus.). 90p. (Orig.). 1986. pap. 9.95 (ISBN 0-87108-681-6). Pruett.

With Custer's Cavalry. Katherine G. Fougera. LC 86-4307. (Illus.). 319p. 1986. 25.95x (ISBN 0-8032-1973-3); pap. 7.95 (ISBN 0-8032-6860-2, Bison). U of Nebr Pr.

With Daring Faith. Rebecca H. Davis. (Orig.). 1987. pap. write for info. (ISBN 0-89084-414-3). Bob Jones Univ Pr.

With Death at My Back. Donna Huyck. (Uplook Ser.). pap. 0.99 (ISBN 0-8163-0427-0). Pacific Pr Pub Assn.

With Deep Respect. A. Kuznetsova. 195p. 1983. 6.95 (ISBN 0-8285-2390-8, Pub. by Raduga Pubs USSR). Imported Pubns.

With Dickens in Yorkshire. T. P. Cooper. 1973. 15.00 (ISBN 0-8274-0054-3). R West.

With Dignity: The Search for Medicare & Medicaid. Sheri I. David. LC 84-27941. (Contributions in Political Science Ser.: No. 12). xiv, 194p. 1985. lib. bdg. 35.00 (ISBN 0-313-24720-X, DWD/). Greenwood.

With Domingo Leal in San Antonio, 1734. Marian L. Martinello & Samuel P. Nesmith. Ed. by The Institute of Texan Cultures. (University of Texas Institute of Texan Culture Young Readers Ser.). (Illus.). 78p. (Orig.). (gr. 5-8). 1980. pap. 6.95 (ISBN 0-933164-40-8). U of Tex Inst Tex Culture.

With Due Care & Attention: A Review of Research on Informal Care. Gillian Parker. 1985. 20.00x (ISBN 0-317-57685-2, Pub. by FPSC UK). State Mutual Bk.

With Dusk. Octavio Armand. Tr. by Carol Maier from Span. 48p. (Orig.). 1984. ltd. ed. 24.00 (ISBN 0-937406-31-7); pap. 3.50 (ISBN 0-937406-30-9). Logbridge-Rhodes.

With Each Passing Moment. Mary Higginbotham. pap. 1.25 (ISBN 0-686-12748-X). Grace Pub Co.

With Ears Opening Like Morning Glories: Eudora Welty & the Love of Storytelling. Carol S. Manning. LC 85-921. (Contributions in Women's Studies: No. 58). xv, 221p. 1985. lib. bdg. 35.00 (ISBN 0-313-24776-5, MWE/). Greenwood.

With Eisenstein in Hollywood. Ivor Montagu. 356p. 1969. pap. 1.95 (ISBN 0-7178-0220-5). Intl Pubs Co.

With Elia & His Friends. J. R. Rees. 1903. Repr. 29.50 (ISBN 0-8274-3730-7). R West.

With Elia & His Friends in Books & Dreams. John Rogers. LC 74-8662. 1902. lib. bdg. 27.00 (ISBN 0-8414-7305-6). Folcroft.

With Emphasis on Intangibles. Howard E. Seals. 1968. pap. 2.00 (ISBN 0-9600232-0-8). H E Seals.

With Every Beat of Your Heart: An Ideabook for Community Heart Health Programs. (DHHS Publication NIH Ser.: No. 86-2641). (Illus.). 67p. (Orig.). 1987. pap. 3.75 (017-043-00116-8). USGPO.

With Eyes Toward Zion: Scholars Colloquium on America-Holy Land Studies. Ed. by Moshe Davis. LC 77-2493. (America & the Holy Land Ser.). (Illus.). 1977. lib. bdg. 24.50x (ISBN 0-405-10312-3). Ayer Co Pubs.

With Face to the Wall. Miltos Sahtouris. Tr. by Kimon Friar. 1980. 7.50 (ISBN 0-910350-10-8). Charioteer.

With Faith & Fury. Delos B. McKown. LC 84-43180. 440p. 1985. 19.95 (ISBN 0-87975-280-7). Prometheus Bks.

With Fate Conspire. Mike Shupp. (Destiny Makers Ser.: Bk. 1). 320p. (Orig.). 1985. pap. 2.95 (ISBN 0-345-32549-4, Pub. by Del Rey). Ballantine.

With Fire & Sword. Samuel H. M. Byers. 1983. Repr. of 1911 ed. 19.95 (ISBN 0-89201-110-6). Zenger Pub.

With Firmness in the Right: American Diplomatic Action Affecting Jews, 1840-1945. Cyrus Adler & Aaron M. Margalith. Ed. by Moshe Davis. LC 77-70651. (America & the Holy Land Ser.). 1977. Repr. of 1946 ed. lib. bdg. 40.00x (ISBN 0-405-10222-4). Ayer Co Pubs.

With Flowers from Israel. Jakob Rosenthal. LC 77-87941. (Illus.). 333p. 1978. 8.95 (ISBN 0-8022-2221-8). Philos Lib.

With Flying Colors. Lorena McCourtney. (Temptation Ser.: No. 158). 224p. Date not set. pap. 2.25 (ISBN 0-317-63848-3). Harlequin Bks.

With Flying Colors. L. J. Setright et al. (Pirelli Album of Motor Sport Ser.). 1987. 50.00 (ISBN 0-671-64459-9). Summit Bks.

With Forked Tongue. Ed. by Florian Coulmas. 210p. 1987. pap. 19.95 (ISBN 0-89720-084-5). Karoma.

With Freedom Fired: The Story of Robert Robinson, Cambridge Nonconformist. G. W. Hughes. 123p. 1955. Repr. 4.50 (ISBN 0-87921-018-4). Attic Pr.

With Freedom to Singapore. Oswald W. Gilmour. LC 70-79200. Repr. of 1950 ed. 27.50 (ISBN 0-404-54829-6). AMS Pr.

With Friend & Book in the Study & the Fields. J. Rogers Rees. 1973. Repr. of 1892 ed. 25.00 (ISBN 0-8274-0966-4). R West.

With Friends Like That. Emily Chase. (Girls of Canby Hall Ser.: No. 11). 192p. (Orig.). (gr. 7 up). 1985. pap. 2.25 (ISBN 0-590-40869-0). Scholastic Inc.

With Friends Like That. Michael Fairley. LC 80-22068. 1988. 19.95 (ISBN 0-87949-194-9). Ashley Bks.

With Friends Like These... Liza Fosburgh. (Orig.). 1983. pap. text ed. 3.50 (ISBN 0-671-45258-4). PB.

With Friends Like These... Alan D. Foster. (Del Rey Bk). 1977. pap. 2.95. Ballantine.

With Friends Like These... Alan D. Foster. pap. 2.95 (ISBN 0-345-32390-4). Ballantine.

With Friends Possessed. Holmes Alexander. LC 75-92683. 1970. 5.95 (ISBN 0-87004-196-7). Caxton.

With Fur Traders in Colorado, 1839-1840: The Journal of E. Willard Smith. E. Willard Smith. Intro. by LeRoy R. Hafen. (Illus.). 32p. 1989. pap. 4.50 (ISBN 0-944275-01-X). Territ Pr TN.

With Fury Poured Out: A Torah Perspective on the Holocaust. 300p. 1987. 16.95 (ISBN 0-88125-107-0). KTAV.

With General Chennault: The Story of the Flying Tigers in World War II. Robert Hotz. Repr. of 1943 ed. 19.95 (ISBN 0-89201-095-9). Zenger Pub.

With Gentleness, Humor & Love. Kathleen W & Jewell E. 1988. pap. 9.95 (ISBN 0-932194-77-X). Health Comm.

With Glad & Generous Hearts. William H. Willimon. 176p. 1986. pap. 7.95 (ISBN 0-8358-0536-0, ICN 613183, Dist. by Abingdon Press). Upper Room.

With God All Things Are Possible. Life-Study Fellowship. 1984. pap. 3.95 (ISBN 0-553-26249-1). Bantam.

With God in Hell: Judaism in the Ghettos & Deathcamps. Eliezer Berkovits. 1979. 9.95 (ISBN 0-88482-937-5, Sanhedrin Pr). Hebrew Pub.

With God in Russia. Walter J. Ciszek & Daniel L. Flaherty. 1966. pap. 5.50 (ISBN 0-385-03954-9, Im). Doubleday.

With God in Solitary Confinement. Richard Wurmbrand. 1979. pap. 4.95 (ISBN 0-88264-002-X). Living Sacrifice Bks.

With God on Our Side. Anthony Tuttle. 1978. pap. 2.25 (ISBN 0-89083-324-9). Zebra.

With God's Help Flowers Bloom. Elaine Anderson. 1978. pap. 4.95 (ISBN 0-89137-411-6); study guide 2.85 (ISBN 0-89137-412-4). Quality Pubns.

With Good Heart: Yaqui Beliefs & Ceremonies in Pascua, Village. Muriel T. Painter. Ed. by Edward H. Spicer & Wilma Kaemlein. LC 86-893. (Illus.). 533p. 1986. 35.00x (ISBN 0-8165-0875-5). U of Ariz Pr.

With Good Intentions: Quaker Work among the Pawnees, Otos, & Omahas in the 1870's. Clyde A. Milner, II. LC 81-16238. (Illus.). xvi, 246p. 1982. 21.50x (ISBN 0-8032-3066-4). U of Nebr Pr.

With Good Reason: An Introduction to Informal Fallacies. 3rd ed. S. Morris Engel. LC 85-61244. 256p. 1985. pap. text ed. write for info. (ISBN 0-312-88519-9); instr's. manual avail. (ISBN 0-312-88518-0). St Martin.

With Hammer in Hand: The Dominy Craftsmen of East Hampton, New York. Charles F. Hummel. LC 67-27362. (Illus.). 424p. 1976. Repr. 25.00 (ISBN 0-8139-0124-3, Pub. by Winterthur Museum). U Pr of Va.

With Head & Heart: The Story of Howard Thurman. Howard Thurman. LC 79-1848. (Illus.). 296p. 1981. pap. 9.95 (ISBN 0-15-697648-X, Harv). HarBraceJ.

With Hemingway: A Year in Key West & Cuba. Arnold Samuelson. LC 84-42632. (Illus.). 256p. 1984. 16.45 (ISBN 0-394-53983-4). Random.

With Heritage So Rich. Rev. ed. Ed. by Albert Rains & Laurance G. Henderson. LC 82-21536. (Landmark Reprint Ser.). 232p. 1983. 18.95 (ISBN 0-89133-104-2). Preservation Pr.

With Him in the Struggle: A Woman's Workshop on II Samuel. Myrna Alexander. (Woman's Workshop Ser.). 128p. 1986. pap. 4.50 (ISBN 0-310-37211-9, 10918P). Zondervan.

With His Hand in Yours. Phyllis Hobe. (Illus.). 48p. 1985. 6.95 (ISBN 0-8378-5074-6). Gibson.

With His Pistol in His Hand: A Border Ballad & Its Hero. Americo Paredes. (Illus.). 275p. 1958. pap. 9.95 (ISBN 0-292-70128-4). U of Tex Pr.

With History Around Me: Spokane Nostalgia. Lois Ryker. 76p. 1979. pap. 4.95 (ISBN 0-87770-229-2). Ye Galleon.

With Hitler in New York. Richard A. Grayson. LC 78-20695. 1979. 7.95 (ISBN 0-8008-8406-X). Taplinger.

With House in Hand: Organize Your Decorating. A Step-by-Step Planner for Home or Office. Marcia McAlister. 28p. 1984. pap. 9.95 (ISBN 0-9615587-1-7). M M Enter.

With Intent. Laurence Henderson. 187p. 1988. pap. 4.95 (ISBN 0-89733-321-7). Academy Chi Pubs.

With Interest: How to Profit from Interest Rate Fluctuations. Joseph E. Murphy. 150p. 1986. 25.00 (ISBN 0-87094-927-6). Dow Jones-Irwin.

With Ironside in North Russia. Andrew Soutar. LC 77-115585. (Russia Observed, Series I). 1970. Repr. of 1940 ed. 15.00 (ISBN 0-405-03062-2). Ayer Co Pubs.

With Jesus on the Scout Trail. Walter D. Cavert. (Orig.). 1970. pap. 3.75 (ISBN 0-687-45849-8). Abingdon.

With Joy & Gladness. (Illus.). 128p. 1988. 7.98. Dovetree Pr.

With Joy: Poems for Children. rev. ed. Ed. by T. E. Wade, Jr. LC 85-70788. (Illus.). 48p. 1985. 1.95 (ISBN 0-930192-13-3). Gazelle Pubns.

With Justice for All. John Perkins. LC 80-50262. 216p. 1982. text ed. 12.95 (ISBN 0-8307-0754-9, 5108802); pap. 5.95 (ISBN 0-8307-0934-7, 5418181). Regal.

With Justice for None: Destroying an American Myth. Gerry Spence. (Illus.). 320p. 1989. 18.95 (ISBN 0-8129-1696-4). Times Bks.

With Kitchener to Khartum. G. W. Steevens. 368p. 1987. 320.00x (ISBN 1-85077-161-8, Pub. by Darf Pubs Ltd). State Mutual Bk.

With Liberty & Justice Today: The Meaning of the Bill of Rights Today. H. V. Knight. LC 66-26725. 318p. (gr. 9 up). 1967. 10.00 (ISBN 0-379-00306-6). Oceana.

With Liberty & Justice for All: The Political Philosophy of George C. Wallace. Jerald R. Burke. LC 75-37228. 1976. 7.76 (ISBN 0-916620-02-6). Portals Pr.

With Light Reflected. Theodore Enslin. (Orig.). 1973. 7.50 (ISBN 0-912090-39-1); pap. 2.45 (ISBN 0-912090-38-3). Sumac Mich.

With Lord Byron in the Sandwich Islands. James Macrae. 90p. pap. 3.95 (ISBN 0-912180-14-5). Petroglyph.

With Louis & Duke: The Autobiography of a Jazz Clarinetist. Barney Bigard. Ed. by Barry Martyn. 176p. 1986. 38.95 (ISBN 0-317-66741-6). Oxford U Pr.

With Louis & the Duke: The/Autobiography of a Jazz Clarinetist. Barney Bigard. (Illus.). 1986. 24.95 (ISBN 0-19-520494-8). Oxford U Pr.

With Louis & the Duke: The Autobiography of a Jazz Clarinetist. Barney Bigard. Ed. by Barry Martyn. 176p. 1988. pap. 8.95 (ISBN 0-19-520637-1). Oxford U Pr.

With Love. Marilyn Moller. 32p. 1985. 5.95 (ISBN 0-89962-463-4). Todd & Honeywell.

With Love, at Christmas. Mem Fox. (Illus.). (gr. 2 up). 1988. 12.95 (ISBN 0-687-45863-3). Abingdon.

With Love, Edith: The L'Abri Family Letters, 1948-1960. Edith Schaefer. LC 87-45722. (Illus.). 448p. 1988. 17.95 (ISBN 0-06-067092-4, HarpR). Har-Row.

With Love: Forever Yours, Bk. 4. Marian J. Yoest. 98p. 1988. spiral bdg. 6.50 (ISBN 0-945105-04-5). Yoest Expressions.

With Love from Darling's Kitchen. Darling. 1982. pap. 11.95 (ISBN 0-930440-17-X). Royal Hse.

With Love, from Jo. Jossy Ann Bolivar. Ed. by Josefa V. Bolivar. LC 80-13999. (Illus.). 120p. (Orig.). 1980. pap. 5.95 (ISBN 0-914598-01-5). Padre Prods.

With Love from Karen. Marie Killilea. 320p. (gr. 5 up). 1980. pap. 3.25 (ISBN 0-440-99615-5, LFL). Dell.

With Love from Your Kitchen. Diana Von Welanetz & Paul Von Welanetz. LC 75-32855. (Illus.). 240p. 1976. pap. 8.95 (ISBN 0-87477-326-1). J P Tarcher.

With Love: Gratefully Yours, Bk. 2. Marian J. Yoest. 86p. 1987. spiral bdg. 6.50 (ISBN 0-945105-02-9). Yoest Expressions.

With Love: Joyfully Yours, Bk. 1. Marian J. Yoest. (Illus.). 90p. 1987. spiral bdg. 6.50 (ISBN 0-945105-01-0). Yoest Expressions.

With Love Series. Marian J. Yoest. 365p. (Orig.). 1988. spiral 19.95 (ISBN 0-945105-00-2). Yoest Expressions.

With Love: Sincerely Yours, Bk. 3. Marian J. Yoest. 88p. 1987. spiral bdg. 6.50. Yoest Expressions.

With Luck Lasting. Bernard Spencer. LC 64-21520. 1965. 11.95 (ISBN 0-8023-1096-6). Dufour.

With Lute & Lyre: History of Instruments. Grizelle Steel. 1977. lib. bdg. 34.95 (ISBN 0-8490-2829-9). Gordon Pr.

With Magical Horses to Ride. Winifred Morris. LC 84-21633. 156p. (gr. 4-8). 1985. 11.95 (ISBN 0-689-31108-7, Atheneum Childrens Bks). Macmillan.

With Malice Toward None: A War Diary by Cecil King. Cecil King. Ed. by William Armstrong. LC 70-175619. 343p. 1971. 28.50 (ISBN 0-8386-1067-6). Fairleigh Dickinson.

With Malice Toward None: The Life of Abraham Lincoln. Stephen B. Oates. (Illus.). 1978. pap. 4.95 (ISBN 0-451-62314-2, ME2314, Ment). NAL.

With Malice Toward None: The Musings of a Retired Politician. James M. Hare. 196p. 1972. 7.50 (ISBN 0-87013-168-0). Mich St U Pr.

With Malice Toward Some: A Documented Sampling of U. S. Government Conspiracy-Infiltration-Manipulation 1950-1979. pap. cancelled (ISBN 0-686-74642-2). Church of Scient Info.

With Merrill's Cavalry. Samuel E. Baird. Ed. by Charles Annegan. LC 80-69601. (Illus.). 51p. 1981. 10.00 (ISBN 0-9605200-0-7). C Annegan.

With Milton & the Cavaliers. Mrs. Frederick Boas. 1904. Repr. 20.00 (ISBN 0-8274-3732-3). R West.

With Mind & Heart. Howard Singer. (gr. 8 up). 3.95x (ISBN 0-8381-0203-4, 10-203). United Syn Bk.

With Mortal Voice: The Creation of Paradise Lost. John T. Shawcross. LC 80-51944. 208p. 1982. 16.00 (ISBN 0-8131-1450-0). U Pr of Ky.

With Murder in Mind. Freda Bream. 1985. 25.00x (ISBN 0-7090-1686-7, Pub. by R Hale Ltd UK). State Mutual Bk.

With Mustard on My Back. John N. Merrill. 76p. (Orig.). 1985. pap. 11.95 (ISBN 0-907496-27-X). State Mutual Bk.

With My Friends: Tales Told in Partnership; with an Introductory Essay on the Art & Mystery of Collaboration, Vol. 1. Brander Matthews. LC 72-3372. (Short Story Index Reprint Ser). Repr. of 1891 ed. 20.00 (ISBN 0-8369-4155-1). Ayer Co Pubs.

With My Legs. Harry Bornstein. (Signed English Ser.). 16p. (ps). 1975. pap. 3.50 (ISBN 0-913580-42-2, Clerc Bks). Gallaudet Univ Pr.

With My Whole Heart: Disciplines for Strengthening the Inner Life. Karen B. Mains. Ed. by Liz Heaney. LC 87-11297. 1987. 8.95 (ISBN 0-88070-197-8). Multnomah.

With Nehru in the Foreign Office. Subimal Dutt. 1977. 14.00x (ISBN 0-88386-905-5). South Asia Bks.

With No Answer. Ralph J. Mills, Jr. (W.N.J. Ser.: No. 13). 1980. pap. 6.00 (ISBN 1-55780-062-6). Juniper Pr WI.

With No Reservations, No. 203. Joan Bramsch. (Loveswept Ser.). 192p. (Orig.). 1987. pap. 2.50 (ISBN 0-553-21808-5). Bantam.

With O'Leary in the Grave. Kevin FitzGerald. (Illus.). 178p. 1987. pap. 8.95 (ISBN 0-19-282066-4). Oxford U Pr.

With One Accord in One Place. Armin R. Gesswein. 93p. (Orig.). 1978. pap. 2.45 (ISBN 0-87509-161-X). Chr Pubns.

With One Foot in the Furrow. Wiseview Plant Pathol. Staff & Paul Will. 480p. 1985. pap. 32.95 (ISBN 0-8403-3790-6). Kendall-Hunt.

With One Heart Bowing to the City of Ten Thousand Buddhas, Vol. IV. Heng Sure & Heng Chau. (Illus.). 136p. (Orig.). 1980. pap. 4.80 (ISBN 0-917512-90-1). Buddhist Text.

With One Heart Bowing to the City of Ten Thousand Buddhas, Vol. VI. Heng Sure & Heng Chau. (Illus.). 200p. (Orig.). 1981. pap. 7.20 (ISBN 0-917512-92-8). Buddhist Text.

With One Heart Bowing to the City of Ten Thousand Buddhas, Vol. I. Heng Sure & Heng Chau. (Illus.). 180p. (Orig.). 1977. pap. 7.20 (ISBN 0-917512-21-9). Buddhist Text.

With One Heart Bowing to the City of Ten Thousand Buddhas, Vol. II. Heng Sure & Heng Chau. (Illus.). 322p. (Orig.). 1979. pap. 8.40 (ISBN 0-917512-23-5). Buddhist Text.

With One Heart Bowing to the City of Ten Thousand Buddhas, Vol. IX. Heng Sure & Heng Chau. 220p. (Orig.). 1983. pap. 9.00. Buddhist Text.

With One Heart Bowing to the City of Ten Thousand Buddhas, Vol. III. Heng Sure & Heng Chau. (Illus.). 154p. (Orig.). 1980. pap. 6.00 (ISBN 0-917512-89-8). Buddhist Text.

With One Heart Bowing to the City of Ten Thousand Buddhas, Vol. VII. Heng Sure & Heng Chau. (Illus.). 160p. (Orig.). 1982. pap. 6.00 (ISBN 0-917512-99-5). Buddhist Text.

With One Heart Bowing to the City of Ten Thousand Buddhas, Vol. VIII. Heng Sure & Heng Chau. (Illus.). 232p. (Orig.). 1982. pap. 9.00 (ISBN 0-917512-53-7). Buddhist Text.

With One Heart Bowing to the City of Ten Thousand Buddhas, Vol. V. Heng Sure & Heng Chau. (Illus.). 127p. (Orig.). 1981. pap. 4.80. Buddhist Text.

With One Sky above Us: Life on an American Indian Reservation at the Turn of the Century. M. Gidley. LC 84-22088. (Illus.). 160p. (Orig.). pap. 9.95 (ISBN 0-295-96164-3). U of Wash Pr.

With One Voice: A Hymn Book for all the Churches. Harmony ed. 788p. Repr. of 1979 ed. 12.95 (ISBN 0-00-599582-5, Collins Liturgical). HarpR.

With One Voice: Melody: A Hymn Book for all the Churches. 714p. 1986. Repr. of 1977 ed. 4.95 (ISBN 0-00-599645-7, Collins Liturgical). HarpR.

With One Voice, Word Only Edition: Hymn Book for all the Churches. 592p. 1986. 3.50 (ISBN 0-318-23287-1, Collins Liturgical). HarpR.

With Only One Ear. 41p. 1977. 1.00 (ISBN 0-914389-17-3). Common Cause.

With Open Arms: Cuban Migration to the United States. Felix Masud-Piloto. LC 87-12809. 168p. 1988. 27.50 (ISBN 0-8476-7566-1). Rowman.

With Open Eyes. Ulrich Schaffer. LC 81-48213. (Illus., Orig.). 1982. 8.95 (ISBN 0-06-067074-6, RD 395, HarpR). Har-Row.

With Open Eyes: Conversations with Matthieu Galey. Marguerite Yourcenar. Tr. by Arthur Goldhammer from Fr. LC 85-45074. 291p. 1986. pap. 10.95 (ISBN 0-8070-6355-X, BP707). Beacon Pr.

With Open Hands. Henri Nouwen. 96p. 1985. pap. 4.95 large print ed. (ISBN 0-8027-2475-2). Walker & Co.

With Open Hands. Henri J. Nouwen. LC 71-177600. (Illus.). 160p. 1972. pap. 3.95 (ISBN 0-87793-040-6). Ave Maria.

With Open Hands. Henri J. Nouwen. 1985. pap. 2.50 (ISBN 0-345-35299-8). Ballantine.

With Open Heart. Michel Quoist. 264p. (Orig.). 1983. pap. 8.95 (ISBN 0-8245-0569-7). Crossroad NY.

With or Without. Charles Dickinson. 1987. 15.45 (ISBN 0-394-55492-2). Knopf.

With or Without. Charles Dickinson. 1988. pap. 7.95 (ISBN 0-02-019560-5, Collier). Macmillan.

With Our Hands: The Story of Carpenters in Massachusetts. Mark Erlich & David Goldberg. (Illus.). 256p. 1986. 29.95 (ISBN 0-87722-433-1). Temple U Pr.

With Our Own Hands: A Guide To Nuclear Awareness. Ed. by Cindy Courtier. (Illus.). 1985. pap. cancelled (ISBN 0-932727-04-2). Hope Pub Hse.

With Paper, About Paper. Ed. by Charlotta Kotik. LC 80-69318. (Illus.). 1980. pap. 7.50 (ISBN 0-914782-35-5). Buffalo Acad.

With Passion & Compassion: Third World Women Doing Theology. Ed. by Virginia Fabella & Mercy A. Oduyoye. Tr. by Phillip Berryman et al from Span., Port. & Fr. 282p. 1988. pap. 11.95 (ISBN 0-88344-628-6). Orbis Bks.

With Pen & Pencil on the Frontier in 1851: The Diary & Sketches of Frank Blackwell Mayer. facsimile ed. Frank B. Mayer. LC 75-103. (Mid-American Frontier Ser.). (Illus.). 1975. Repr. of 1932 ed. 18.00x (ISBN 0-405-06871-9). Ayer Co Pubs.

With Pen & Pencil on the Frontier in 1851: The Diary & Sketches of Frank Blackwell Mayer. Frank B. Mayer. Ed. by Bertha L. Heilbron. LC 86-717. (Borealis Books Reprint). xvii, 256p. 1986. pap. 9.95 (ISBN 0-87351-195-6). Minn Hist.

With Pen & Tongue. Ursula M. Bygott. 444p. 1980. 40.00x (ISBN 0-522-84150-3, Pub. by Melbourne U Pr Australia). Intl Spec Bk.

With Pen of Truth: A Reading of Walden. Raymond P. Tripp. 1972. pap. 10.00 (ISBN 0-9502699-0-5). Soc New Lang Study.

With Perfect Faith. David Bleich. 1982. 25.00x (ISBN 0-87068-891-X); pap. 14.95. Ktav.

With Pleated Eye & Garnet Wing: Symmetries of Italo Galvino. Ilene T. Olken. 168p. 1984. text ed. 16.95x (ISBN 0-472-10044-0). U of Mich Pr.

With Plunkett in Ireland: The Co-Op Organiser's Story. R. A. Anderson. (Co-Operative Studies). 308p. 1983. pap. 12.50x (ISBN 0-7165-0513-4, Pub. by Irish Academic Pr Ireland). Biblio Dist.

With Poor Immigrants to America. Stephen Graham. LC 73-13133. (Foreign Travelers in America, 1810-1935 Ser.). 366p. 1974. Repr. 26.50x (ISBN 0-405-05455-6). Ayer Co Pubs.

With Prayer & Psalm: The History of Wilmot, New Hampshire Churches. Florence Langley. LC 81-5116. 80p. 1981. 7.95x (ISBN 0-914016-77-6). Phoenix Pub.

With R. Wallenberg in Budapest. Per Anger. LC 80-84245. (Illus.). 191p. 1981. pap. 10.95 (ISBN 0-89604-047-X). Holocaust Pubns.

With Raoul Wallenberg in Budapest: Memories of the War Years in Hungary. Per Anger. LC 80-84245. (Illus.). 1981. 12.95 (ISBN 0-8052-5027-1, Pub. by Holocaust Library); pap. 10.95 (ISBN 0-8052-5026-3, Pub. by Holocaust Library). Schocken.

With Raoul Wallenberg in Budapest: Memories of the War Years in Hungary. Per Anger. Tr. by David M. Paul & Margareta Paul. (Illus.). 192p. 8.95 (ISBN 0-686-95103-4); pap. 4.95 (ISBN 0-686-99464-7). ADL.

With Reference to Reference. Catherine Z. Elgin. LC 82-15488. 208p. 1982. lib. bdg. 27.50 (ISBN 0-915145-52-9); pap. text ed. 12.75 (ISBN 0-915145-53-7). Hackett Pub.

With Respect to Readers: Dimensions of Literary Response. Walter J. Slatoff. LC 77-123995. 224p. 1970. 22.50x (ISBN 0-8014-0580-7). Cornell U Pr.

With Respect... to RFD: An Appreciation of Raymond Franklin DaBoll & His Contribution to the Letter Arts. Raymond DaBoll. Compiled by Rick Cusick. LC 77-77376. (Illus.). xvi, 142p. 1978. 25.00 (ISBN 0-931474-00-0). TBW Bks.

With Respect to the Japanese. John C. Condon. LC 81-85730. (Country Orientation Ser.). 96p. (Orig.). 1984. pap. text ed. 10.00 (ISBN 0-933662-49-1). Intercult Pr.

With Rifle & Plow. J. E. Wright et al. LC 79-124998. (Keystone State Historical Publications Ser). 1970. Repr. of 1938 ed. 18.00 (ISBN 0-8046-8514-2, Ira J Friedman). Assoc Faculty Pr.

With Ruth in Mind. Anselm Hollo. LC 79-28147. 50p. 1980. pap. 4.45 (ISBN 0-930794-18-4). Station Hill Pr.

With Santa Anna in Texas: A Personal Narrative of the Revolution. Jose E. De La Pena. Tr. by Carmen Perry. LC 75-16269. (Illus.). 240p. 1975. 16.95 (ISBN 0-89096-001-1). Tex A&M Univ Pr.

With Secret Friends. Cooper Edens. LC 84-149490. (Illus.). 48p. (YA) (gr. 7-12). 1981. pap. 8.95 (ISBN 0-914676-57-1). Green Tiger Pr.

With Shelley in Italy: A Selection of the Poems & Letters of Percy Bysshe Shelley Relating to His Life in Italy. Anna B. McMahan. 1977. Repr. of 1907 ed. lib. bdg. 40.00 (ISBN 0-8492-1714-8). R West.

With Sherman to the Sea: Civil War Letters, Diaries, & Reminiscences. Theodore F. Upson. Ed. by Oscar O. Winther. LC 58-12211. (Indiana University Civil War Centennial Ser.). (Illus.). 1968. Repr. of 1958 ed. 20.00 (ISBN 0-527-92300-1). Kraus Repr.

With Shield & Sword: American Military Affairs, Colonial Times to the Present. Warren W. Hassler, Jr. (Illus.). 462p. 1982. text ed. 32.95x (ISBN 0-8138-1627-0). Iowa St U Pr.

With Shuddering Fall. Joyce Carol Oates. LC 64-23317. 1964. 17.95 (ISBN 0-8149-0173-5). Vanguard.

With Signs Following. Stanley H. Frodsham. 288p. 1946. pap. 5.95 (ISBN 0-88243-635-X, 02-0635). Gospel Pub.

With Silence My Companion. Shuntaro Tanikawa. Tr. by William I. Elliott & Kazuo Kawamura. LC 75-21399. 55p. 1975. pap. 5.00 (ISBN 0-915986-02-7). Prescott St Pr.

With Sleepless Eye: The Daily Cycle of Services of the Orthodox Church. 2nd, rev. ed. Bessarion Agioantonodes. 1988. pap. text ed. price not set (ISBN 0-936649-18-6). St Anthony Orthodox.

With Slow & Halting Tongue. Lon L. Emerick. 1983. pap. 1.00x (ISBN 0-8134-2311-2). Inter Print Pubs.

With Sound & Color: An Intermediate Chinese-English Reader. Florence C. Chang. LC 80-68257. (Chinese Can Be Fun Bks.: Level 4). (Illus.). 71p. (Orig.). (gr. 7-9). 1980. pap. 6.00x (wkbk. incl.) (ISBN 0-936620-01-3). Ginkgo Hut.

With Special Section: A Sense of the Past & a Sense of Guilt. Ed. by Walter Goldschmidt & Douglas Price-Williams. (Ethos Ser.: Vol. 5, No. 4). 1977. 10.00 (ISBN 0-317-66361-5). Am Anthro Assn.

With Stalin Against Tito: Cominformist Splits in Yugoslav Communism. Ivo Banac. LC 88-47717. 320p. 1988. 32.50x (ISBN 0-8014-2186-1). Cornell U Pr.

With Stalin-memoirs. Enver Hoxha. (Illus.). 67p. 1980. pap. 2.00 (ISBN 0-86714-008-9). Marxist Leninist.

With Stethoscope in Asia: Korea. Sherwood Hall. LC 77-81765. 1981. Repr. of 1978 ed. 19.95 (ISBN 0-930696-01-8). MCL Assocs.

With Stevenson in Samoa. H. J. Moors. 1973. 35.00 (ISBN 0-8274-1022-0). R West.

With Strings Attached: Reminiscences & Reflections. Joseph Szigeti. LC 79-11318. (Music Reprint Ser.). 1979. Repr. of 1947 ed. lib. bdg. 42.50 (ISBN 0-306-79567-1). Da Capo.

With Tails We Win. Crowe & Bowen. (Illus.). 1954. pap. 2.00 (ISBN 0-9600102-5-4). Shields.

With Tennyson at the Keyboard: A Victorian Songbook. Joan H. Bouchelle. (Reference Library of the Humanities). 256p. 1985. lib. bdg. 40.00 (ISBN 0-8240-8872-7). Garland Pub.

With Thackeray in America. Lewis Melville. 25.00 (ISBN 0-8274-3733-1). R West.

With Thanks & Appreciation: The Sweet Nellie Book of Thoughts, Sentiments, Tokens & Traditions of the Past. Pat Ross. 1989. 8.95 (ISBN 0-670-82521-2). Viking.

With the Admiral of the Ocean Sea: A Narrative of the First Voyage to the Western World, Drawn Mainly from the Diary of Christopher Columbus. Charles P. MacKie. 371p. 1983. Repr. of 1891 ed. lib. bdg. 50.00 (ISBN 0-89984-949-0). Century Bookbindery.

With the Battlecruisers. Filson Young. (Classics of Naval Literature Ser.). 296p. 1986. 21.95 (ISBN 0-87021-795-X). Naval Inst Pr.

With the Begging Bowl. Ediriwira Sarachchandra. v, 250p. 1987. text ed. 27.50x (ISBN 81-7018-383-9, Pub. by B R Pub Corp Delhi). Apt Bks.

With the Border Ruffians: Memories of the Far West, 1852-1868. R. H. Williams. Ed. by E. W. Williams. LC 82-8400. (Illus.). xxii, 490p. 1982. 34.50x (ISBN 0-8032-4721-4); pap. 9.95 (ISBN 0-8032-9704-1, BB 799, Bison). U of Nebr Pr.

With the Boys: Little League Baseball & Preadolescent Culture. Gary A. Fine. LC 86-16056. 304p. 1987. text ed. 37.50x (ISBN 0-226-24936-0); pap. text ed. 12.95 (ISBN 0-226-24937-9). U of Chicago Pr.

With the Camel Corps up the Nile. Count Gleichen. (Illus.). 1976. Repr. 25.00 (ISBN 0-7158-1108-8). Charles River Bks.

With the Church. Ed. by Mathias Goossens. 6.95 (ISBN 0-8199-0148-2, L39000). Franciscan Herald.

With the Contras: A Reporter in the Wilds of Nicaragua. Christopher Dickey. 1986. 18.95 (ISBN 0-671-53298-7). S&S.

With the Contras: A Reporter in the Wilds of Nicaragua. Christopher Dickey. 336p. 1987. pap. 6.95 (ISBN 0-671-63313-9, Touchstone Bks). S&S.

With the Dutch in the East: An Outline of the Military Operations in Lombock, 1894. Wouter Cool. Tr. by E. J. Taylor from Dutch. LC 77-86968. (Illus.). Repr. of 1897 ed. 32.00 (ISBN 0-404-16702-0). AMS Pr.

With the Eagles. Paul L. Anderson. LC 57-9447. (Illus.). (gr. 7-11). 1929. 15.00 (ISBN 0-8196-0100-4). Biblo.

With the Eyes of the Mind: An Empirical Analysis of Out-of-Body States. Glen O. Gabbard & Stuart W. Twemlow. LC 84-15914. 286p. 1984. 35.00 (ISBN 0-275-91160-8, C1160). Praeger.

With the Fathers: Studies in the History of the United States. John B. McMaster. LC 75-173113. Repr. of 1896 ed. 18.00 (ISBN 0-405-08771-3, Pub. by Blom). Ayer Co Pubs.

With the Five Year Olds. Joan Gallagher. 44p. 1969. pap. 1.95 (ISBN 0-685-46931-X). Ed Solutions.

With the Good Shepherd. Leroy Brownlow. 1969. gift ed. 6.95 (ISBN 0-915720-12-4). Brownlow Pub Co.

With the Huckleberry Christ: A Spiritual Journey. Kristen J. Ingram. 96p. (Orig.). 1985. pap. 5.95 (ISBN 0-86683-798-1, HarpR). Har-Row.

With the Hungarian Independence Movement, 1943-1947: An Eyewitness Account. Istvan Szent-Miklosy. LC 87-2371. 280p. 1988. lib. bdg. 45.95 (ISBN 0-275-92574-9, C2574). Praeger.

With the Immortals. Francis M. Crawford. Ed. by R. Reginald & Douglas Menville. LC 75-46264. (Supernatural & Occult Fiction Ser.). 1976. Repr. of 1888 ed. lib. bdg. 23.50x (ISBN 0-405-08122-7). Ayer Co Pubs.

With the Immortals. Alfred Tennyson. 15.00 (ISBN 0-8274-3734-X). R West.

With the Indians in the Rockies. James W. Schultz. (James Willard Schultz Reprint Ser.). 144p. (gr. 6 up). 1985. 15.95 (ISBN 0-8253-0324-9); pap. 7.95 (ISBN 0-8253-0319-2). Beaufort Bks NY.

With the Indians in the Rockies. James W. Schultz. (J. W. Schultz Reprint Ser.). 15.95 (ISBN 0-317-65098-X); pap. 7.95 (ISBN 0-317-65099-8). Confluence Pr.

With the Irish Against Rommel: A Diary of 1943. Strome Galloway. 176p. 1987. 91.00x (Pub. by Picton UK). State Mutual Bk.

With the Lord Today, 4 vols. Hal M. Helms. (Orig.). 1985. Set. 14.95 set (ISBN 0-941478-39-4). Paraclete Pr.

With the Mission to Menelik, 1897. A. E. Gleichen. 376p. Repr. of 1898 ed. text ed. 82.80x (ISBN 0-576-17109-3, Pub. by Gregg Intl Pubs England). Gregg Intl.

With the Nez Perces: Alice Fletcher in the Field, 1889-92. E. Jane Gay. Ed. by Frederick E. Hoxie & Joan T. Mark. LC 80-23045. (Illus.). xxxviii, 228p. 1987. pap. 7.95 (ISBN 0-8032-7024-0, Bison). U of Nebr Pr.

With the Northwest Wind. R. B. Cunningham Graham & Edward Carpenter. 59.95 (ISBN 0-8490-1312-7). Gordon Pr.

With the Offal Eaters. Douglas Houston. 1986. pap. 9.95 (ISBN 0-906427-70-3, Pub. by Bloodaxe Bks). Dufour.

With the Old Breed at Peleliu & Okinawa. Eugene B. Sledge. LC 81-12122. (Illus.). 344p. 1981. 15.95 (ISBN 0-89141-119-4). Presidio Pr.

With the One Hundred Second Infantry Division Through Germany. (Divisional Ser.: No. 19). (Illus.). 296p. 1981. Repr. of 1947 ed. 25.00 (ISBN 0-89839-045-1). Battery Pr.

With the Peasants of Aragon: Libertarian Communism in the Liberated Areas. Agustin Souchy-Bauer. Tr. by Abe Bluestien from Span. 145p. (Orig.). 1982. pap. 4.50 (ISBN 0-317-14869-9). Left Bank.

With the Pilgrims to Canterbury: And the History of the Hospital of St. Thomas. Stanley G. Wilson. LC 70-178306. Repr. of 1934 ed. 14.50 (ISBN 0-404-06997-5). AMS Pr.

With the Pilgrims to Mecca: The Great Pilgrimage of A.H. 1319, A.D. 1902. Gazanfar A. Khan & Wilfred Sparroy. LC 77-876447. Repr. of 1905 ed. 24.50 (ISBN 0-404-16417-X). AMS Pr.

With the Power of Each Breath: A Disabled Women's Anthology. Ed. by Susan E. Browne et al. 360p. 1985. pap. 9.95 (ISBN 0-939416-06-9); 24.95 (ISBN 0-939416-09-3). Cleis Pr.

With the Precision of Bats. Atanas Slavov. 309p. 1986. 17.95 (ISBN 0-911050-59-0). Occidental.

With the Procession. Henry B. Fuller. 1983. Repr. of 1895 ed. deluxe ed. 39.00 (ISBN 0-403-04585-1). Scholarly.

With the Procession. Henry B. Fuller. LC 65-17288. (Chicago in Fiction Ser.). pap. 72.00 (2026773). Bks Demand UMI.

With the Procession. Henry B. Fuller. (Collected Works of Henry B. Fuller). 1988. Repr. of 1895 ed. lib. bdg. 59.00x. Am Biog Serv.

With the Riff Kabyles. Bernd Terhorst. LC 69-18998. (Illus.). 1969. Repr. of 1926 ed. 25.00x (ISBN 0-8371-4948-7, TER&). Greenwood.

With the Royal Headquarters in Eighteen Seventy to Seventy-One. Julius A. Von Verdy Du Vernois. LC 79-142243. Repr. of 1897 ed. 21.50 (ISBN 0-404-06757-3). AMS Pr.

With the Russian Army, 1914-1917. Alfred W. Knox. 1977. lib. bdg. 59.95 (ISBN 0-8490-2830-2). Gordon Pr.

With the Russian Army, 1914-1917: Being Chiefly Extracts from the Diary of a Military Attache - 2 Vols. in 1. Alfred W. Knox. LC 74-115552. (Russia Observed Ser.). (Illus.). 1971. Repr. of 1921 ed. 48.00 (ISBN 0-405-03084-3). Ayer Co Pubs.

With the Ups Comes the Downs. Connie Crawford. (Illus.). 104p. (Orig.). 1986. pap. 2.95 (ISBN 0-936369-01-9). Son-Rise Pubns.

With the Wind, Kevin Dolan. Bryce Milligan. LC 86-70018. (Illus.). 130p. (YA) (gr. 7 up). 1987. 15.95 (ISBN 0-931722-44-6). Corona Pub.

With the Wits. Paul E. More. 1919. 15.00 (ISBN 0-8274-3735-8). R West.

With Their Ears Pricked Forward: Tales of Mules I've Known. Joshua A. Lee. LC 80-19667. 144p. 1980. 3.98 (ISBN 0-89587-018-5). Blair.

With Their Ears Pricked Forward, Tales of Mules I've Known. Joshua A. Lee. 138p. 10.00 (ISBN 0-318-12513-7). Am Donkey.

With Their Islands Around Them. Kenneth Brower. LC 74-4455. (Illus.). 1974. 8.95 (ISBN 0-03-013121-9). Friends of Earth.

With These Hands. Photos by Ken Light. (Illus., Orig.). 1986. pap. 9.95 (ISBN 0-8298-0576-1). Pilgrim NY.

With These Hands: Women Working on the Land. Ed. by Joan M. Jensen. (Women's Lives-Women's Work Ser.). (Illus.). 318p. (gr. 11 up). 1981. pap. 9.95 (ISBN 0-912670-71-1); teaching guide, 64p o.p. 5.00 (ISBN 0-912670-81-9). Feminist Pr.

With Thine Adversary in the Way: A Quaker Witness for Reconciliation. Margarethe Lachmund. Tr. by Florence Kite. LC 79-91957. (Orig.). 1979. pap. 2.50x (ISBN 0-87574-228-9). Pendle Hill.

With This Ring. Leona Blair. 1985. pap. 4.50 (ISBN 0-440-19709-0). Dell.

With This Ring. Marian Wells. LC 84-9301. 200p. (Orig.). 1984. pap. 5.95 (ISBN 0-87123-615-X, 210615). Bethany Hse.

With Tongue in Cheek. Sandra Pittman. LC 86-72589. (Illus.). 128p. (Orig.). 1986. pap. 6.95 (ISBN 0-940873-86-9). AKG.

With Trotsky in Exile: From Prinkipo to Coyoacan. Jean Van Heijenoort. (Illus.). 1978. 15.00x (ISBN 0-674-80255-1). Harvard U Pr.

With Trumpet & Drum. Eugene Field. LC 70-116402. (Granger Index Reprint Ser.). 1892. 12.00 (ISBN 0-8369-6143-9). Ayer Co Pubs.

With Two Wheels & a Camera. Bert Kopperl. 1979. 12.50 (ISBN 0-682-49352-X, Banner). Exposition-Phoenix.

With Walker in Nicaragua & Other Early Poems. Ernesto Cardenal. Tr. by Jonathan Cohen. 1985. 17.00x (ISBN 0-8195-5123-6); pap. 9.95 (ISBN 0-8195-6118-5). Wesleyan U Pr.

With Walt Whitman in Camden, 3 Vols. Horace Traubel. 1961. Repr. of 1905 ed. 37.50x, boxed set (ISBN 0-87471-003-0). Rowman.

With Wanda: Town & Country Poems. Paul Zimmer. 1980. pap. 5.95 (ISBN 0-931848-32-6). Dryad Pr.

With Wandering Steps & Slow. Joy Hoffman. LC 81-18566. 140p. (Orig.). 1982. pap. 4.95 (ISBN 0-87784-804-1). Inter-Varsity.

With Warm Regards. William H. Fetridge. LC 75-35055. 1976. 7.95 (ISBN 0-85013-039-5). Dartnell Corp.

With West Bengal Chief Ministers: Memoirs, 1962-1977. Saroj Chakrabarty. cancelled (ISBN 0-86131-117-5, Orient Longman). South Asia Bks.

With William Burroughs. Bockris. pap. 7.95 (ISBN 0-8050-0186-7). Seaver Bks.

With William Burroughs: A Report from the Bunker. Victor Bockris. LC 80-24905. (Illus.). 256p. 1981. 14.95; pap. 7.95. Seaver Bks.

With Wings: An Anthology of Literature by & about Women with Disabilities. Ed. by Marsha Saxton & Florence Howe. 350p. 1987. text ed. 29.95 (ISBN 0-935312-61-7); pap. 12.95 (ISBN 0-935312-62-5). Feminist Pr.

With Wings As Eagles. Perry D. Gresham. LC 80-66183. 1980. 10.95 (ISBN 0-89305-025-3). Anna Pub.

With Wings As Eagles. William S. Pinkston, Jr. (Illus.). 127p. (gr. 2). 1983. pap. 6.28 (ISBN 0-89084-231-0). Bob Jones Univ Pr.

With Wings As Eagles. John R. Price. 112p. (Orig.). 1987. pap. 6.95 (ISBN 0-942082-07-9). Quartus Bks.

With Wings As Eagles: Toward Personal Christian Maturity. William B. Oglesby, Jr. LC 87-51654. 194p. 1987. text ed. 14.95x (ISBN 1-55605-035-6); pap. text ed. 9.95x (ISBN 1-55605-036-4). Wyndham Hall.

With Wings of an Eagle. James H. Goodman. Ed. by Helen Graves. LC 86-51084. (Rusty Charm Ser.). 280p. 1986. 12.95 (ISBN 1-55523-017-2). Winston-Derek.

With Wings of Eagles. Richard C. Hoefler. 1983. 5.35 (ISBN 0-89536-624-X, 2352). CSS of Ohio.

With Wolfe in Canada: The Winning of a Continent. G. A. Henty. 1978. lib. bdg. 30.00 (ISBN 0-8495-2322-2). Arden Lib.

With Wooden Sword: A Portrait of Francis Sheehy-Skeffington, Militant Pacifist. Leah Levenson. LC 82-22560. (Illus.). 282p. 1983. text ed. 22.95X (ISBN 0-930350-42-1). NE U Pr.

With Wordsworth in England: A Selection of Poems & Letters. Anna B. McMahan. (Illus.). 1907. Repr. 25.00 (ISBN 0-8274-3736-6). R West.

With You & Without You. Ann M. Martin. LC 85-21990. 192p. (gr. 4-8). 1986. 11.95 (ISBN 0-8234-0601-6). Holiday.

With You & Without You. Ann M. Martin. 192p. (YA) (gr. 7 up). 1987. pap. 2.50 (ISBN 0-590-40589-6, Apple Paperbacks). Scholastic Inc.

With You, Dear Child, in Mind. Lynn Groth. (Cradle Roll Program Ser.). 16p. (Orig.). (ps). 1985. pap. 1.25 (ISBN 0-938272-77-2). Wels Board.

With You I Want to Climb a Mountain. Theresa H. Baruksen. (Earth Poetry Ser.). 1987. pap. 6.00 (ISBN 0-933494-35-1). Earthwise Pubns.

With Your Own Two Hands. Seymour Bernstein. 312p. 1986. 19.95 (ISBN 0-911320-08-3, 50530530). Schirmer Bks.

With Your Own Two Hands: Self-Discovery Through Music. Seymour Bernstein. (Illus.). 320p. 1981. 18.95 (ISBN 0-02-870310-3). Schirmer Bks.

With Your Promises: Planning Your Marriage Service. 40p. (Orig.). 1980. pap. 3.95 (ISBN 0-8066-1872-8, 10-7212). Augsburg.

With Zola in England: A Story of Exile. Ernest Vizetelly. 1977. lib. bdg. 59.95 (ISBN 0-8490-2831-0). Gordon Pr.

With Zola in England: A Story of Exile. Ernest A. Vizetelly. 1904. 25.00 (ISBN 0-8274-3737-4). R West.

Withcline. Noah Webster. (Crime Club Ser.). 1989. 12.95 (ISBN 0-385-24610-2). Doubleday.

Withdrawal from Empire: A Military View. William Jackson. LC 86-29855. (Illus.). 289p. 1987. 29.95 (ISBN 0-312-00552-0). St Martin.

Withdrawal, Retirement, & Disputes: What You & Your Firm Need to Know. Lowell E. Rothschild & Edward B. Berger. LC 86-71286. 99p. 1986. 39.95 (ISBN 0-89707-242-1). Amer Bar Assn.

Wither the State? Politics & Public Enterprise in Three Countries. Ira Sharkansky. LC 79-18780. 1979. 20.00 (ISBN 0-934540-01-2); pap. text ed. 11.95x (ISBN 0-934540-00-4). Chatham Hse Pubs.

Wither the Welfare State. Arthur Seldon. (Institute of Economic Affairs, Occasional Papers Ser.: No. 60). pap. 5.95 technical (ISBN 0-255-36146-7). Transatl Arts.

Witherby's Insurance Dictionary. Hugh Cockerell. 235p. 1980. 113.00x (ISBN 0-900886-50-1, Pub. by Witherby & Co England). State Mutual Bk.

Withered Branch. Derek S. Savage. LC 75-42377. (Studies in Fiction, No. 34). 1974. lib. bdg. 49.95x (ISBN 0-8383-1947-5). Haskell.

Withered Branch: Six Studies in the Modern Novel. D. S. Savage. LC 74-11463. 1950. lib. bdg. 37.00 (ISBN 0-8414-7778-7). Folcroft.

Withered Branch: Six Studies in the Modern Novel. Derek S. Savage. LC 78-58270. (Essay Index in Reprint Ser.). 1978. Repr. 18.75x (ISBN 0-8486-3031-9). Roth Pub Inc.

Withered Nosegay. Noel Coward. 266p. 1987. pap. 8.95 (ISBN 0-88184-316-4). Carroll & Graf.

Withering Days of the Nguyen Dynasty. 33p. (Orig.). 1978. pap. text ed. 7.50x (ISBN 0-566-04014-X, Pub. by Inst Southeast Asian Stud). Gower Pub Co.

Withering into Truth. Margery Cavanaugh. (Juniper Bk.: No. 41). 1983. pap. 5.00 (ISBN 1-55780-040-5). Juniper Pr WI.

Wither's Emblems. George Wither. Bd. with Foundations Unearthed. Marie B. Hall. Date not set. pap. 19.95 (ISBN 0-938760-11-4). Veritat Found.

Withhold Not Correction. Bruce Ray. pap. 3.95 (ISBN 0-8010-7687-0). Baker Bk.

Withhold Not Correction. Bruce Ray. 1978. pap. 4.95 (ISBN 0-87552-400-1). Presby & Reformed.

Within a Delirium. M. A. Lanahan. 23p. 1986. pap. 8.00x (ISBN 0-7223-2046-9, Pub. by A H Stockwell England). State Mutual Bk.

Within a Miraculous Realm. Richard J. Oddo. (Illus.). 320p. (Orig.). 1988. pap. 9.95 (ISBN 0-945637-00-4). Spirit Warrior Pr.

Within a Rainbowed Sea. Chris Newbert. 1987. 75.00 (ISBN 0-941831-09-4); author's ed. 95.00; collector's ed. 2250.00. Beyond Words Pub.

Within a Rainbowed Sea. Christopher Newbert. Ed. by Paul Berry. LC 84-72023. (Illus.). 208p. 1984. 75.00 (ISBN 0-681-29908-8); author's edition 95.00 (ISBN 0-317-43389-X); ltd. collector's ed. 2000.00 (ISBN 0-317-43390-3). Island Heritage.

Within a Yard of Hell. Don Wilkerson. 161p. (Orig.). 1987. pap. 7.95 (ISBN 0-941478-81-5). Paraclete Pr.

Within & Without: Anthology of Prison Literature. 1978. pap. 2.00 (ISBN 0-931350-04-2). Moonlight Pubns.

Within-&-Without Wears His Coat Wrong-Side-Out. 16p. 1975. pap. 0.99 (ISBN 0-8285-1274-4, Pub. by Progress Pubs USSR). Imported Pubns.

Within Doors: Poems Written by Residents of a Nursing Home. Ed. by William Barber. 1977. pap. 2.35 (ISBN 0-686-22748-4). Printed Word.

Within Each Jew. Cieplinski. cancelled. Rossel Bks.

Within Heaven's Gates. Rebecca Springer. 128p. 1984. pap. 3.50 (ISBN 0-88368-125-0). Whitaker Hse.

Within Human Experience: The Philosophy of William Ernest Hocking. Leroy S. Rouner. LC 71-75433. (Illus.). 1969. text ed. 20.00x (ISBN 0-674-95380-0). Harvard U Pr.

Within Me, Without You... Donita Simpson. 1973. pap. 6.50 (ISBN 0-685-99410-4). Peace Ways.

Within My Heart. Shirley Sealy. 168p. 1983. 7.95 (ISBN 0-934126-37-2). Randall Bk Co.

Within My Sacred Lodge. M. Irving Chriswell. (Illus.). 28p. 1981. pap. 2.50 (ISBN 0-88053-006-5, M-012). Macoy Pub.

Within Normal Limits. Todd Grimson. (Vintage Contemporaries Ser.). 1987. 5.95 (ISBN 0-394-74617-1, Vin). Random.

Within Our Reach. David M. Call. LC 83-26162. 68p. 1984. 5.95 (ISBN 0-87747-975-5). Deseret Bk.

Within Our Reach: Breaking the Cycle of Disadvantage & Despair. Lisbeth B. Schorr & Daniel Schorr. LC 87-27886. 384p. 1988. pap. 19.95 (ISBN 0-385-24243-3, Anch). Doubleday.

Within Ourselves. Ellen O'Connor. 91p. 1982. 7.95 (ISBN 0-9613897-0-2). VALEN PUB.

Within Prison Walls, Being a Narrative of Personal Experience During a Week of Voluntary Confinement in the State Prison at Auburn, New York. Thomas M. Osborne. LC 69-14940. (Criminology, Law Enforcement, & Social Problems Ser.: No. 72). 1969. Repr. of 1914 ed. 15.00x (ISBN 0-87585-072-3). Patterson Smith.

Within Range. Gil Ott. (Poetry Chapbooks Ser.). 28p. (Orig.). 1986. pap. 4.00 (ISBN 0-930901-38-X). Burning Deck.

Within Reach. Barbara Delinsky. 400p. 1986. pap. 3.95 (ISBN 0-373-97018-8, Pub. by Worldwide). Harlequin Bks.

Within the Barbed Wire Fence: A Japanese Man's Account of His Internment in Canada. Takeo U. Nakano & Leatrice Nakano. (Illus.). 136p. 1981. 15.00x (ISBN 0-295-95789-1). U of Wash Pr.

Within the Bones of Memory. Kay Gould-Caskey. 168p. 1984. 10.95 (ISBN 0-932229-00-X). Falling Water.

Within the Castle. Madeline, Sr. & Teresa Avila. 1983. 9.50 (ISBN 0-8199-0820-7). Franciscan Herald.

Within the Dramatic Spectrum: The University of Florida, Department of Classics Comparative Drama Conference Papers. Ed. by Karelisa V. Hartigan. (Vol. VI). 236p. (Orig.). 1986. lib. bdg. 28.50 (ISBN 0-8191-5185-8, Pub by Univ of Florida Dept of Classics Comparative Drama Conference); pap. text ed. 14.50 (ISBN 0-8191-5186-6). U Pr of Amer.

Within the Earth, a Mountain. LC 88-70296. 150p. 1988. write for info. (ISBN 0-933294-03-4). Backroads.

Within the Four Seas. B. A. Garside. 150p. 1985. 15.00 (ISBN 0-913720-58-5). Beil.

Within the Four Seas: The Dialogue of East & West. Joseph Needham. 1979. pap. 7.50 (ISBN 0-8020-6360-8). U of Toronto Pr.

Within the Gates. Gordon Lindsay. (Sorcery & Spirit World Ser.). 1.75 (ISBN 0-89985-095-2). Christ Nations.

Within the Halls of Pilate. David T. Lusk. 4.50 (ISBN 0-89137-538-4). Quality Pubns.

Within the Labyrinth. Norman Lewis. 258p. 1986. Repr. 16.95 (ISBN 0-88184-253-2). Carroll & Graf.

Within the Pale: The True Story of Anti-Semitic Persecutions in Russia. facsimile ed. Michael Davitt. LC 74-27976. (Modern Jewish Experience Ser.). 1975. Repr. of 1903 ed. 25.50x (ISBN 0-405-06705-4). Ayer Co Pubs.

Within the Plantation Household: Black & White Women of the Old South. Elizabeth Fox-Genovese. LC 88-40139. (Gender & American Culture Ser.). (Illus.). 500p. 1988. 34.95x (ISBN 0-8078-1808-9); pap. 12.95 (ISBN 0-8078-4232-X). U of NC Pr.

Within the Rim, & Other Essays, 1914-15. facs. ed. Henry James. LC 68-22102. (Essay Index Reprint Ser). 1918. 15.00 (ISBN 0-8369-0567-9). Ayer Co Pubs.

Within the Rock of Ages: Life & Work of Augustus Moretague Toplady. George Lawton. 249p. 1983. 35.00 (ISBN 0-227-67836-2). Attic Pr.

Within the Rose. Hunce Voelcker. (Illus.). 60p. 1976. 6.00 (ISBN 0-915572-19-2). Panjandrum.

Within the Sound of These Waves: The Story of the Kings of Hawaii Island, Containing a Full Account of the Death of Captain Cook, Together with the Hawaiian Adventures of George Vancouver & Sundry Other Mariners. William H. Chickering. LC 70-138584. (Illus.). 1971. Repr. of 1941 ed. lib. bdg. 35.00x (ISBN 0-8371-5783-8, CHSW). Greenwood.

Within the Underworld Sky: Mimbres Art in Context. Barbara L. Moulard. 190p. 1984. 50.00 (ISBN 0-942642-11-2). Twelvetrees Pr.

Within the Whirlwind. Eugenia Ginzburg. Tr. by Ian Boland. LC 80-8748. (Helen & Kurt Wolff Bk.). 448p. 1981. 17.50 (ISBN 0-15-197517-5). HarBraceJ.

Within the Whirlwind. Eugenias Ginzburg. Tr. by Ian Boland. LC 80-8748. (Helen & Kurt Wolff Book Ser.). 448p. 1982. pap. 9.95 (ISBN 0-15-697649-8, Harv). HarBraceJ.

Within This Wilderness. Feenie Ziner. 1978. 8.95 (ISBN 0-393-07516-8). Norton.

Within You Is the Power. Joseph Murphy. LC 77-86026. 1978. pap. 6.00 (ISBN 0-87516-247-9). DeVorss.

Without a Brush. Peggy Caldwell. (Illus.). 76p. (Orig.). 1978. pap. 6.95 (ISBN 0-917119-38-X, 45-1209). Priscillas Pubns.

Without a Dowry & Other Plays. Alexander Ostrovsky. Ed. & tr. by Norman Henley. 340p. 1988. 32.50 (ISBN 0-88233-933-8). Ardis Pubs.

Without a Man in the House. Wilma Burton. LC 78-68403. pap. 5.95 (ISBN 0-89107-158-X). Good News.

Without a Man of Her Own. Linda Dubreuil. (Orig.). 1975. pap. 1.50 (ISBN 0-685-53906-7, LB282DK, Leisure Bks). Leisure NY.

Without a Trace. K. K. Beck. 1988. pap. 3.95 (ISBN 0-515-09700-4). Jove Pubns.

Without a Trace. Charles Berlitz. 1985. pap. 3.50 (ISBN 0-345-32517-6). Ballantine.

Without Armor. J. Hilton. 19.95 (ISBN 0-88411-844-4, Pub. by Aeonian Pr). Amereon Ltd.

Without Bias: A Guidebook for Nondiscriminatory Communication. 200p. 15.95. Intl Assn Busn Comm.

Without Blemish: Today's Problem. Jeanette H. Walworth. LC 72-3104. (Black Heritage Collection Ser.). Repr. of 1886 ed. 18.75 (ISBN 0-8369-9089-7). Ayer Co Pubs.

Without Bombast & Blunders: An Executive's Guide to Effective Writing. Frances D. Naczi. LC 80-17857. 1980. pap. 5.95 (ISBN 0-87863-007-4, Farnsworth Pub Co). Longman Finan.

Without Cherry Blossom. facs. ed. Panteleimon S. Romanov. Ed. by Stephen Graham. Tr. by L. Zarine. LC 78-142275. (Short Story Index Reprint Ser.). 1932. 15.25 (ISBN 0-8369-3759-7). Ayer Co Pubs.

Without Cherry Blossom. Panteleimon S. Romanov. Ed. by Stephen Graham. Tr. by L. Zarine from Rus. LC 72-90310. (Soviet Literature in English Translation Ser.). 287p. 1973. Repr. of 1930 ed. 21.25 (ISBN 0-88355-020-2). Hyperion Conn.

Without Child: Experiencing & Resolving Infertility. Ellen S. Glazer & Susan L. Cooper. 288p. 1988. 17.95 (ISBN 0-669-16889-0). Lexington Bks.

Without Christ in Their Hearts: Religion in the Soviet Union. George Moshinsky. 250p. 1988. write for info. (ISBN 0-938103-01-6). ZZYZX Pub.

Without Consent: Mass-Elite Linkages in Presidential Politics. Warren E. Miller. LC 88-3217. 200p. 1988. 20.00 (ISBN 0-8131-0550-1). U Pr of Ky.

Without Consent or Contract. Robert Fogel. 1988. write for info. (ISBN 0-393-01887-3). Norton.

Without Controversy Great Is the Mystery of Godliness. rev. ed. Clarence Harris. Ed. by Althea Haris. (Illus.). 185p. 1982. pap. 4.95 (ISBN 0-686-39817-3). Gospel Place.

Without Dentures: The Miracle of Dental Implants. Leonard Linkow. Ed. by Bryce Webster. 212p. 1987. 9.95 (ISBN 0-8119-0713-9). Fell.

Without Falling. Leslie Dick. 160p. (Orig.). 1988. 14.95 (ISBN 0-87286-232-1); pap. 6.95 (ISBN 0-87286-224-0). City Lights.

Without Fear or Favor. H. F. Keplinger. LC 82-11883. 164p. 1982. 20.00x (ISBN 0-87201-917-9). Gulf Pub.

Without Feathers. Woody Allen. LC 74-29597. 1975. PLB 8.95 (ISBN 0-394-49743-0). Random.

Without Feathers. Woody Allen. 224p. 1983. pap. 3.50 (ISBN 0-345-33697-6). Ballantine.

Without Foundations: Justification in Political Theory. Don Herzog. LC 84-21492. 264p. 1985. 26.50x (ISBN 0-8014-1723-6). Cornell U Pr.

Without God, Without Creed: The Origins of Unbelief in America. James Turner. LC 84-15397. (New Studies in American Intellectual & Cultural History). 336p. 1985. text ed. 34.50x (ISBN 0-8018-2494-X). Johns Hopkins.

Without God, Without Creed: The Origins of Unbelief in America. James Turner. LC 84-15397. (New Studies in American Intellectual & Cultural History). 336p. 1986. pap. text ed. 12.95x (ISBN 0-8018-3407-4). Johns Hopkins.

Without Help or Hindrance: Religious Identity in American Culture. 2nd ed. Eldon G. Ernst. 244p. 1987. pap. text ed. 12.75 (ISBN 0-8191-5565-9). U Pr of Amer.

Without Honor. David Hagberg. 448p. 1989. pap. 4.95 (ISBN 0-8125-0413-5). Tor Bks.

Without Honor: Defeat in Vietnam & Cambodia. Arnold R. Isaacs. LC 83-48054. (Illus.). 576p. 1983. 35.00x (ISBN 0-8018-3060-5). Johns Hopkins.

Without Honor: Defeat in Vietnam & Cambodia. Arnold R. Isaacs. LC 84-40027. 576p. 1984. pap. 9.95 (ISBN 0-394-72595-6, Vin). Random.

Without Justice for All: The Constitutional Rights of Aliens. Elizabeth Hull. LC 84-19798. (Contributions in Political Science Ser.: No. 129). xiii, 244p. 1985. lib. bdg. 36.95 (ISBN 0-313-23670-4, HAP/). Greenwood.

Without Lawful Authority. Manning Coles. (Spies and Intrigues Ser.: No. 4). 246p. 1984. pap. 5.95 (ISBN 0-918172-16-0). Leetes Isl.

Without Mercy. Leonard Jordan. (Orig.). 1981. pap. 2.95 (ISBN 0-89083-847-X). Zebra.

Without Music. Michael Palmer. LC 77-22452. 100p. (Orig.). 1977. pap. 5.00 (ISBN 0-87685-288-6). Black Sparrow.

Without My Cloak. Kate O'Brien. (Virago Modern Classics Ser.). 490p. 1987. pap. 7.95 (ISBN 0-14-016155-4). Penguin.

Without Noise of Arms. Walter Briggs. LC 75-11163. (Illus.). 222p. 1987. pap. 19.95 (ISBN 0-87358-418-X, Entrada Bks). Northland.

Without Our Past: A Handbook for the Preservation of Canada's Architectural Heritage. Ann Falkner. (Illus.). 1976. pap. 9.95 (ISBN 0-8020-6298-9). U of Toronto Pr.

Without Passport: The Life & Work of Paul Richard. Michel P. Richard. (American University Studies IX: History: Vol. 28). 281p. 1987. text ed. 44.95 (ISBN 0-8204-0444-6). P Lang Pubs.

Without Precedent: The Life & Career of Eleanor Roosevelt. Ed. by Joan Hoff-Wilson & Marjorie Lightman. 1987. 17.50x (ISBN 0-253-19100-9); pap. 8.95 (ISBN 0-253-20327-9, MB-327). Ind U Pr.

Without Prejudice. I. Zangwill. LC 72-13302. (Essay Index Reprint Ser.). Repr. of 1896 ed. 19.25 (ISBN 0-8369-8183-9). Ayer Co Pubs.

Without Proof or Evidence: Essays of O. K. Bouwsma. O. K. Bouwsma. Ed. by J. L. Craft & Ronald E. Hustwit. LC 83-10269. xvi, 161p. 1984. 19.50X (ISBN 0-8032-1174-0). U of Nebr Pr.

Without Rhetoric: An Architectural Aesthetic 1955-1972. Alison Smithson & Peter Smithson. 1974. 17.50x (ISBN 0-262-19119-9). MIT Pr.

Without Roof. Kinereth Gensler. LC 80-70829. 64p. 1981. pap. 7.95 (ISBN 0-914086-32-4). Alicejamesbooks.

Without Shelter: The Career of Ellen Glasgow. J. R. Raper. LC 82-15863. (Southern Literary Studies). xii, 273p. 1982. Repr. of 1971 ed. lib. bdg. 45.50x (ISBN 0-313-23742-5, RAWS). Greenwood.

Without Shoes. David Chorlton. LC 87-70069. 40p. (Orig.). 1987. pap. 5.00 (ISBN 0-934996-44-X). American Studies Pr.

Without Sin among You. Katherine Stapleton. (Orig.). 1979. pap. 2.50 (ISBN 0-89083-506-3). Zebra.

Without Spanking or Spoiling: A Practical Approach to Toddler & Preschool Guidance. Elizabeth Crary. LC 79-18253. (Illus.): 104p. (Orig.). 1979. pap. 8.95 (ISBN 0-9602862-0-9); write for info leaders' guide (ISBN 0-9602862-1-7). Parenting Pr.

Without Stopping. Paul Bowles. LC 72-175258. (Illus.). 380p. 1985. pap. 9.50 (ISBN 0-88001-061-4). Ecco Pr.

Without Sympathy or Enthusiasm: The Problem of Administrative Compassion. Victor A. Thompson. LC 74-3999. 137p. 1975. pap. 6.95 (ISBN 0-8173-4826-3). U of Ala Pr.

Without the Bomb: The Politics of Nuclear Non-Proliferation. Mitchell Reiss. 368p. 1988. 35.00 (ISBN 0-231-06438-1). Columbia U Pr.

Without the Chrysanthemum & the Sword. Jean Stoetzel. LC 76-7582. (Illus.). 1976. Repr. of 1955 ed. lib. bdg. 27.50x (ISBN 0-8371-8856-3, STWCS). Greenwood.

Without the Law: Administrative Justice & Legal Pluralism in 19th-Century England. H. W. Arthurs. 328p. 1985. 32.50x (ISBN 0-8020-5654-7). U of Toronto Pr.

Wittgenstein - Aesthetics & Transcendental Philosophy. Ed. by Kjell S. Johannessen & Tore Nordenstam. 193p. 1981. pap. 29.50 (ISBN 0-686-34398-0, Pub. by Reidel Holland). Kluwer Academic.

Wittgenstein: A Critique. J. N. Findlay. (International Library of Philosophy). 240p. 1985. 29.95x (ISBN 0-7102-0330-6). Routledge Chapman & Hall.

Wittgenstein: A Life, Young Ludwig, 1889-1921. Brian McGuinness. (Illus.). Date not set. 22.50 (ISBN 0-520-06496-8). U of Cal Pr.

Wittgenstein & Derrida. Henry Staten. LC 84-3525. xx, 182p. 1984. 19.95x (ISBN 0-8032-4138-0). U of Nebr Pr.

Wittgenstein & Derrida. Henry Staten. LC 84-3225. xx, 182p. 1986. pap. 7.95 (ISBN 0-8032-9169-8, Bison). U of Nebr Pr.

Wittgenstein & His Times. Ed. by Brian McGuinness. LC 81-52670. 1982. lib. bdg. 15.00x (ISBN 0-226-55881-9). U of Chicago Pr.

Wittgenstein & Historical Understanding. Aryeh Botwinick. LC 80-5968. 65p. (Orig.). 1981. pap. text ed. 7.00 (ISBN 0-8191-1431-6). U Pr of Amer.

Wittgenstein & Justice: The Significance of Ludwig Wittgenstein for Social & Political Thoughts. Hanna R. Pitkin. 1985. Repr. of 1972 ed. 37.50x (ISBN 0-520-05471-7). U of Cal Pr.

Wittgenstein & Modern Philosophy. Justus Hartnack. Tr. by Maurice Cranston. LC 67-17743. pap. 38.00 (ISBN 0-317-09087-9, 2050334). Bks Demand UMI.

Wittgenstein & Modern Philosophy. 2nd ed. Justus Hartnack. Tr. by Maurice Cranston from Danish. LC 85-40604. 176p. (Orig.). 1985. text ed. 11.95x (ISBN 0-268-01936-3); pap. text ed. 5.95x (ISBN 0-268-01937-1). U of Notre Dame Pr.

Wittgenstein & Phenomenology. Nicholas F. Gier. LC 80-26980. (Ser. in Philosphy). 260p. 1981. 59.50 (ISBN 0-87395-518-8); pap. 19.95 (ISBN 0-87395-519-6). State U NY Pr.

Wittgenstein & Political Philosophy: A Re-Examination of the Foundation of Social Science. John W. Danford. LC 78-6716. 1978. lib. bdg. 20.00x (ISBN 0-226-13593-4). U of Chicago Pr.

Wittgenstein & Political Philosophy: A Re-Examination of the Foundations of Social Science. John W. Danford. LC 78-6716. xiv, 166p. 1981. pap. 6.95x (ISBN 0-226-13594-2). U of Chicago Pr.

Wittgenstein & Political Philosophy: A Reexamination of the Foundations of Social Science. John W. Danford. 280p. 1988. pap. 17.95x (ISBN 0-226-13595-0, Midway Reprint). U of Chicago Pr.

Wittgenstein & Social Theory. David Bloor. LC 83-7183. 250p. 1983. 30.00x (ISBN 0-231-05800-4); pap. 14.50x. Columbia U Pr.

Wittgenstein Bibliography. Compiled by V. A. Shanker & S. G. Shanker. (Critical Assessment & Bibliography Ser.). 352p. 1986. 69.00 (Pub. by Croom Helm UK). Routledge Chapman & Hall.

Wittgenstein Bibliography. Compiled by V. A. Shanker & S. G. Shanker. (Critical Assessment & Bibliography Ser.). 1987. 95.00x (ISBN 0-7099-4431-4, Pub. by Croom Helm UK). Routledge Chapman & Hall.

Wittgenstein: Conversations, 1949-1951. O. K. Bouwsma. Ed. by J. L. Craft & Ronald E. Hustwit. LC 85-27222. 62p. 1986. lib. bdg. 16.50 (ISBN 0-87220-009-4); pap. 5.95 (ISBN 0-87220-008-6). Hackett Pub.

Wittgenstein, Frege & the Vienna Circle. G. P. Baker & P. M. Hacker. Date not set. text ed. 40.00 (ISBN 0-631-14704-7). Basil Blackwell.

Wittgenstein: From Mysticism to Ordinary Language: A Study of Viennese Positivism & the Thought of Ludwig Wittgenstein. Russell Nieli. LC 86-23144. (Philosophy Ser.). 261p. 1987. 44.50 (ISBN 0-88706-397-7); pap. 14.95 (ISBN 0-88706-398-5). State U NY Pr.

Wittgenstein: Language & World. John V. Canfield. LC 81-4522. 240p. 1981. lib. bdg. 20.00x (ISBN 0-87023-318-1). U of Mass Pr.

Wittgenstein: Lectures & Conversations on Aesthetics, Psychology, & Religious Belief. Ludwig Wittgenstein. Ed. by Cyril Barrett. 1967. pap. 7.95x (ISBN 0-520-01354-9). U of Cal Pr.

Wittgenstein: Meaning & Understanding: Essays on the Philosophical Investigations. G. P. Baker & P. M. Hacker. LC 85-20838. xxvi, 374p. 1986. pap. 14.95x (ISBN 0-226-03540-9). U of Chicago Pr.

Wittgenstein on Foundations. Gertrude D. Conway. LC 88-676. 1989. text ed. 45.00 (ISBN 0-391-03585-1). Humanities.

Wittgenstein on Meaning. Colin McGinn. 160p. 1985. 29.95x (ISBN 0-631-13764-5). Basil Blackwell.

Wittgenstein on Meaning. Colin McGinn. 216p. (Orig.). Date not set. pap. text ed. 15.95 (ISBN 0-631-15681-X). Basil Blackwell.

Wittgenstein on Rules & Private Language. Saul Kripke. LC 79-26088. 128p. 1982. text ed. 16.00x (ISBN 0-674-95400-9). Harvard U Pr.

Wittgenstein on Rules & Private Language. Saul A. Kripke. 160p. 1984. pap. 7.95x (ISBN 0-674-95401-7). Harvard U Pr.

Wittgenstein on the Foundations of Mathematics. Crispin Wright. 500p. 1980. text ed. 37.00x (ISBN 0-674-95385-1). Harvard U Pr.

Wittgenstein Rules, Grammar & Necessity: An Analytical Commentary on the Philosophical Investigations, Vol. 2. G. P. Baker & P. M. Hacker. 360p. 1985. 49.95 (ISBN 0-631-13024-1). Basil Blackwell.

Wittgenstein, Skepticism & Political Participation: An Essay in the Epistemology of Democratic Theory. Aryeh Botwinick. 52p. (Orig.). 1985. pap. text ed. 6.00 (ISBN 0-8191-4816-4). U Pr of Amer.

Wittgenstein: Sources & Perspectives. Ed. by C. Grant Luckhardt. LC 78-58633. 368p. 1978. 38.50x (ISBN 0-8014-1122-X). Cornell U Pr.

Wittgenstein, the Early Philosophy: An Exposition of the Tractatus. Henry L. Finch. LC 73-135985. 1982. text ed. 19.95x (ISBN 0-391-00123-X). Humanities.

Wittgenstein: The Man & His Philosophy. A. J. Ayer. 1985. 17.45 (ISBN 0-394-54347-5). Random.

Wittgenstein: To Follow a Rule. Ed. by Steven H. Holtzman & Christopher M. Leich. (International Library of Philosophy). 250p. 1981. 30.00x (ISBN 0-7100-0760-4). Routledge Chapman & Hall.

Wittgenstein-Understanding & Meaning: An Analytical Commentary on the Philosophical Investigations, Vol. 1. G. P. Baker & P. M. Hacker. LC 79-15740. 1980. lib. bdg. 60.00x (ISBN 0-226-03526-3). U of Chicago Pr.

Wittgenstein Workbook. Christopher Coope et al. LC 79-135161. 1970. pap. 8.95x (ISBN 0-520-01840-0). U of Cal Pr.

Wittgenstein's City. Robert J. Ackermann. LC 87-10895. 288p. (Orig.). 1988. lib. bdg. 25.00x (ISBN 0-87023-589-3); pap. text ed. 12.95x (ISBN 0-87023-590-7). U of Mass Pr.

Wittgenstein's Conception of Philosophy. K. T. Fann. LC 65-24178. 1969. pap. 11.95x (ISBN 0-520-01837-0). U of Cal Pr.

Wittgenstein's Lectures, Cambridge Nineteen Thirty to Nineteen Thirty-Two: From the Notes of John King & Desmond Lee. Ed. by Desmond Lee. 124p. 1980. 18.50x (ISBN 0-8476-6201-2). Rowman.

Wittgenstein's Lectures, Cambridge 1932-1935: From the Notes of Alice Ambrose & Margaret Macdonald. Ed. by Alice Ambrose. 225p. 1979. 25.00x (ISBN 0-8476-6151-2). Rowman.

Wittgenstein's Lectures, Cambridge 1930-1932: From the Notes of John King & Desmond Lee. Ludwig Wittgenstein. Ed. by Desmond Lee. LC 81-19823. (Phoenix Ser.). 136p. 1982. pap. 5.50X (ISBN 0-226-90438-5). U of Chicago Pr.

Wittgenstein's Lectures, Cambridge 1932-1935. Ludwig Wittgenstein. Ed. by Margaret Macdonald & Alice Ambrose. LC 81-19818. (Phoenix Ser.). xii, 226p. 1982. pap. 6.95X (ISBN 0-226-90439-3). U of Chicago Pr.

Wittgenstein's Mistress. David Markson. LC 87-73068. 240p. 1988. 20.00 (ISBN 0-916583-25-2). Dalkey Arch.

Wittgenstein's Nephew: A Novel. Thomas Bernhard. Tr. by David McLintock from Ger. LC 88-45317. 112p. 1989. 17.95 (ISBN 0-394-56376-X). Knopf.

Wittgenstein's Philosophy of Mathematics. Klenk. 1976. pap. 24.00 (ISBN 90-247-1842-2, Pub. by Martinus Nijhoff Netherlands). Kluwer Academic.

Wittgenstein's Philosophy of Mind. Ashok Vohra. LC 85-31983. 225p. 1986. 26.95 (ISBN 0-8126-9031-1). Open Court.

Wittgenstein's Relevance for Theology. Ignace D'hert. (European University Studies: Ser. 23, Vol. 44). 237p. 1978. pap. 27.15 (ISBN 3-261-03092-5). P Lang Pubs.

Wittgenstein's Tractatus: A Critical Exposition of Its Main Lines on Thought. Erik Stenius. LC 81-13222. xi, 241p. 1982. Repr. of 1964 ed. lib. bdg. 35.00x (ISBN 0-313-23246-6, STWI). Greenwood.

Wittgenstein's Tractatus: An Introduction. H. O. Mounce. LC 81-40474. viii, 136p. 1981. lib. bdg. 19.00x (ISBN 0-226-54318-8); pap. text ed. 7.95x (ISBN 0-226-54319-6). U of Chicago Pr.

Wittgenstein's Tractatus & the Modern Arts. Jorn K. Bramann. LC 85-1270. (Illus.). 224p. (Orig.). 1985. pap. 15.95 (ISBN 0-913623-05-9, T146). Adler Pub Co.

Wittgenstein's Vienna. Allan Janik & Stephen Towlmin. (Illus.). 1974. pap. 10.95 (ISBN 0-671-21725-9, Touchstone Bks). S&S.

Wittgenstein's Vision. Charles H. Cox & Jean W. Cox. LC 84-337. 1984. 10.95 (ISBN 0-87212-178-X). Libra.

Wittig Chemistry: Dedicated to Professor Dr. G. Wittig. Ed. by M. J. Dewar et al. (Topics in Current Chemistry Ser.: Vol. 109). (Illus.). 220p. 1983. 54.00 (ISBN 0-387-11907-8). Springer-Verlag.

Wittrings--Aspects of Mathematics, Vol. 2. Ed. by M. Knebusch & M. Kolster. 1982. 16.50 (ISBN 3-528-08512-6, Pub. by Vieweg & Sohn Germany). IPS.

Witty & Witless, or a Dialogue on Wit & Folly. John Heywood. LC 74-133679. (Tudor Facsimile Texts. Old English Plays Ser.: No. 9). Repr. of 1909 ed. 49.50 (ISBN 0-404-53309-4). AMS Pr.

Witty Ditties & Cassette Tapes 1 Through 6. Joyce M. Burkes. LC 84-52873. (Illus.). 24p. (ps-5). 1986. incl. cassette 4.95 ea. (ISBN 0-931218-25-X, 4112). Joybug.

Witty Ditties with Cassette 1. Joyce M. Burkes. LC 84-52873. (Illus.). 24p. (ps-1). 1986. incl. cassette 4.95 (ISBN 0-931218-28-4, 4101). Joybug.

Witty Ditties with Cassette 2. Joyce M. Burkes. LC 84-52873. (Illus.). 24p. (ps-1). 1986. 4.95, incl. cassette (ISBN 0-931218-29-2, 4102). Joybug.

Witty Ditties with Cassette 3. Joyce M. Burkes. LC 84-52873. (Illus.). 24p. (ps-2). 1986. 4.95, incl. cassette (ISBN 0-931218-30-6, 4103). Joybug.

Witty Ditties with Cassette 4. Joyce M. Burkes. LC 84-52873. (Illus.). 24p. (ps-1). 1986. 4.95, incl. cassette (ISBN 0-931218-31-4, 4104). Joybug.

Witty Ditties with Cassette 5. Joyce M. Burkes. LC 84-52873. (Illus.). 24p. (gr. 2-4). 1986. 4.95, incl. cassette (ISBN 0-931218-32-2, 4105). Joybug.

Witty Ditties with Cassette 6. Joyce M. Burkes & Debi Ade. LC 84-52873. (Illus.). 24p. (gr. 1-5). 1986. 4.95, incl. cassette (ISBN 0-931218-33-0, 4106). Joybug.

Witty Sayings by Witty People. William H. Browne. LC 74-15727. (Popular Culture in America Ser.). 304p. 1975. Repr. 25.50x (ISBN 0-405-06363-6). Ayer Co Pubs.

Wivenhoe & Brightlingsea Railway. Paul Brown. 1984. 20.00x (ISBN 0-86025-889-0, Pub. by Ian Henry Pubns England). State Mutual Bk.

Wivenhoe & Brightlingsea Railway. Paul Brown. 1988. 30.00x (Pub. by Ian Henry Pubns England). State Mutual Bk.

Wives. Gamaliel Bradford. LC 72-2591. (American Women Ser.: Images & Realities). 328p. 1972. Repr. of 1925 ed. 22.00 (ISBN 0-405-04448-8). Ayer Co Pubs.

Wives. Parley J. Cooper. 384p. 1987. pap. 3.95 (ISBN 0-671-81627-6). PB.

Wives & Daughters. Elizabeth Gaskell. 1982. pap. 4.75x (ISBN 0-460-01110-3, Evman). Biblio Dist.

Wives & Daughters. Elizabeth Gaskell. Ed. by Frank G. Smith. (English Library Ser.). 720p. 1969. pap. 5.95 (ISBN 0-14-043046-6). Penguin.

Wives & Daughters. Elizabeth Gaskell. Ed. by Angus Easson. (World's Classics Ser.). 784p. 1988. pap. 5.95 (ISBN 0-19-281702-7). Oxford U Pr.

Wives & Daughters: The Women of Sixteenth Century England. Kathy L. Emerson. LC 82-50408. 407p. 1984. 30.00x (ISBN 0-87875-246-3). Whitston Pub.

Wives & Lovers. T. A. Gabriel. 400p. (Orig.). 1986. pap. 3.95 (ISBN 0-8439-2380-6, Leisure Bks). Leisure NY.

Wives & Midwives: Childbirth & Nutrition in Rural Malaysia. Carol Laderman. LC 83-47664. (Comparative Studies of Health Systems & Medical Care: Vol. 7). (Illus.). 267p. 1984. lib. bdg. 38.00x (ISBN 0-520-04924-1); pap. 9.95x (ISBN 0-520-06036-9). U of Cal Pr.

Wives & Property: Reform of the Married Women's Property Law in Nineteenth-Century England. Lee Holcombe. 368p. 1982. 13.95c (ISBN 0-8020-5573-7); pap. 13.95 (ISBN 0-8020-6476-0). U of Toronto Pr.

Wives at War & Other Stories. Flora Nwapa. pap. 7.00 (ISBN 978-2272-00-0, Pub. by Tana Pr Nigeria). Three Continents.

Wives Excuse, or, Cuckolds Make Themselves. new, critical ed. Thomas Southerne. Ed. by Ralph R. Thornton. (Illus.). 1974. 7.50x (ISBN 0-915180-19-7); pap. 3.50x (ISBN 0-915180-20-0). Harrowood Bks.

Wives for Sale: An Ethnographic Study of British Popular Divorce. Samuel P. Menefee. 1981. 26.00x (ISBN 0-312-88629-2). St Martin.

Wives, Husbands & Alcohol: A Study of Informal Drinking Control Within the Family. M. Holmila. (Finnish Foundation for Alcohol Studies: Vol. 36). 1988. pap. 20.00 (ISBN 951-9192-37-9). Rutgers Ctr Alcohol.

Wives of the God-King: The Rituals of the Devadasis of Puri. Frederique A. Marglin. (Illus.). 1985. 29.95x (ISBN 0-19-561731-2). Oxford U Pr.

Wives of the Presidents. Arden D. Melick. Ed. by Ernest Dupuy. LC 77-141. (Hammond Profile Ser.). (Illus.). 96p. (gr. 7 up). 1985. 8.95 (ISBN 0-8437-3813-8). Hammond Inc.

Wives of the Prophet. F. Hussain. 9.50 (ISBN 0-686-18463-7). Kazi Pubns.

Wives Play. John Reason. 1982. 15.00x (ISBN 0-903653-45-1, Pub. by New Playwrights Network). State Mutual Bk.

Wizard. Ozzie Smith & Rob Rains. LC 88-1832. 224p. 1988. 16.95 (ISBN 0-8092-4594-9). Contemp Bks.

Wizard. John Varley. 384p. 1985. pap. 3.95 (ISBN 0-425-09841-9). Berkley Pub.

Wizard. John Varley. 1987. pap. 3.95 (ISBN 0-441-90067-4, Pub. by Ace Science Fiction). Ace Bks.

Wizard & the War Machine. Lawrence Watt-Evans. 304p. (Orig.). 1987. pap. text ed. 3.50 (ISBN 0-345-33459-0, Del Rey). Ballantine.

Wizard at Large. Terry Brooks. LC 88-77805. 304p. 1988. 17.95 (ISBN 0-345-34773-0, Del Rey Bks). Ballantine.

Wizard Children of Finn. Tannen. LC 80-20955. (Illus.). 256p. (gr. 3 up). 1981. Knopf.

Wizard Children of Finn. Mary Tannen. 216p. (YA) (gr. 3-7). 1982. pap. 2.25 (ISBN 0-380-57661-9, 65607-8, Camelot). Avon.

Wizard Exposed: Magic Tricks by & Interviews with Harry Houdini, Howard Thurston & Other Past Masters of Magic. Ed. by David Meyer. (Illus.). 200p. (Orig.). 1987. pap. 18.95 (ISBN 0-916638-39-1). Meyerbooks.

Wizard, From Durham & London MSS. Simon Baylie. Ed. by H. De Vocht. (Material for the Study of the Old English Drama Ser.: No. 2, Vol. 4). pap. 24.00 (ISBN 0-8115-0297-X). Kraus Repr.

Wizard in Bedlam. Christopher Stasheff. 192p. 1986. pap. 2.95 (ISBN 0-441-90215-4, Pub. by Ace Science Fiction). Ace Bks.

Wizard in the Tree. Lloyd Alexander. 144p. (gr. 5 up). 1981. pap. 3.25 (ISBN 0-440-49556-3, YB). Dell.

Wizard in the Tree. Lloyd Alexander. (Illus.). 144p. (gr. 4-7). 1974. 9.95 (ISBN 0-525-43128-4). Dutton.

Wizard in Waiting. Robert D. Hughes. 208p. (Orig.). 1982. pap. 2.95 (ISBN 0-345-34602-5, Del Rey). Ballantine.

Wizard of Bergen. Robert B. Benson. (Wolfgang Brandt Ser.). 100p. (Orig.). (YA) (gr. 7-12). 1987. pap. 7.50 (ISBN 0-9616327-1-2). Brandt Bks.

Wizard of Earthsea. Ursula K. Le Guin. 192p. (gr. 9-12). 1984. pap. 3.50 (ISBN 0-553-26250-5). Bantam.

Wizard of Earthsea. Ursula K. Le Guin. LC 68-21992. (Illus.). (gr. 5 up). 1968. 12.95 (ISBN 0-395-27653-5, Pub. by Parnassus). HM.

Wizard of Fourth Street. Simon Hawke. Date not set. pap. 3.95 (ISBN 0-445-20842-2, Pub. by Popular Lib). Warner Bks.

Wizard of Id-Charge! Johnny Hart & Brant Parker. 1984. pap. 1.95 (ISBN 0-449-12737-0, GM). Fawcett.

Wizard of Id: No. 8. Johnny Hart & Brant Parker. (Wizard of Id Ser.). (Illus.). 1984. pap. 1.95 (ISBN 0-449-12764-8, GM). Fawcett.

Wizard of Id: Pick a Card, Any Card. Johnny Hart & Brant Parker. (Illus., Orig.). 1986. pap. 2.25 (ISBN 0-449-12923-3, GM). Fawcett.

Wizard of Id-Yield! Johnny Hart & Brant Parker. (Illus.). 1982. pap. 1.95 (ISBN 0-449-13653-1, GM). Fawcett.

Wizard of Linn. A. E. Van Vogt. 1976. Repr. of 1962 ed. lib. bdg. 16.95x (ISBN 0-88411-976-9, Pub. by Aeonian Pr). Amereon Ltd.

Wizard of Loneliness. John Nichols. 1987. pap. 7.95 (ISBN 0-393-30473-6, Shoreline Bks). Norton.

Wizard of Oz. L. Frank Baum. LC 79-52644. 1985. 2.25 (ISBN 0-345-31363-1, Del Rey); pap. 2.95 (ISBN 0-345-33590-2). Ballantine.

Wizard of Oz. L. Frank Baum. (Illus.). (gr. 4-6). 1956. il. jr. lib. o.p. 5.95 (ISBN 0-448-05826-X, G&D); deluxe ed. 11.95 (ISBN 0-448-06026-4); Companion Lib. Ed. 2.95 (ISBN 0-448-05470-1). Putnam Pub Group.

Wizard of Oz. L. Frank Baum. (Oz Fantasy Library). (Illus.). (gr. 2 up). pap. 3.95 (ISBN 0-528-87187-0). Macmillan.

Wizard of Oz. L. Frank Baum. (Illus.). (gr. 2-4). 1984. pap. 2.25 (ISBN 0-590-40442-3). Scholastic Inc.

Wizard of Oz. L. Frank Baum. (Bambi Classics Ser.). (Illus.). 224p. (Orig.). (YA) (gr. 9-12). 1981. pap. 3.95 (ISBN 0-89531-060-0, 0221-48). Sharon Pubns.

Wizard of Oz. L. Frank Baum. LC 82-1109. (Illus.). 232p. (gr. 2-4). 1982. 18.95 (ISBN 0-03-061661-1). H Holt & Co.

Wizard of Oz. L. Frank Baum. (Puffin Classics Ser.). (gr. 3-7). 1983. pap. 2.25 (ISBN 0-14-035001-2, Puffin). Penguin.

Wizard of Oz. L. Frank Baum. LC 83-13792. (Looking Glass Library). (Illus.). 64p. (ps-3). 1984. 6.95 (ISBN 0-394-85331-8, BYR); lib. bdg. 8.99 (ISBN 0-394-95331-2). Random.

Wizard of Oz. L. Frank Baum. Ed. by Jean L. Scrocco. LC 85-8479. (Illus.). 192p. (ps up). 1985. 16.95 (ISBN 0-88101-018-9). Unicorn Pub.

Wizard of Oz. L. Frank Baum. LC 84-82589. (Golden Classics Ser.). (Illus.). 176p. (gr. k-12). 1986. 8.95 (ISBN 0-307-17115-9, Pub. by Golden Bks). Western Pub.

Wizard of Oz. Abridged ed. L. Frank Baum. Ed. by Heidi K. Corso. (Illus.). 80p. (ps up). 1988. 5.95 (ISBN 0-88101-076-6). Unicorn Pub.

Wizard of Oz. L. Frank Baum. (Children's Classics Ser.). 32p. (gr. k-3). 1988. 5.95 (ISBN 0-8249-8264-9). Ideals.

Wizard of Oz. Ed. by Michael P. Hearn. (Critical Heritage Ser.). (Illus.). 320p. 1983. 19.95. Schocken.

Wizard of Oz. R. Eugene Jackson. 72p. 1977. pap. 2.50 (ISBN 0-88680-205-9); royalty 35.25 (ISBN 0-317-03609-2). I E Clark.

Wizard of Oz. rev. ed. William-Alan Landes & Marilyn Standish. (Wondrawhopper Ser.). (gr. 3-12). 1985. pap. text ed. 6.00 (ISBN 0-88734-105-5); tchr's ed 26.00 (ISBN 0-88734-011-3). Players Pr.

Wizard of Oz. (Illustrated Junior Library). (Illus.). 224p. (gr. 3-9). 1981. pap. 6.95 (ISBN 0-448-11026-1, G&D). Putnam Pub Group.

Wizard of Oz: A Limerick Version. Inge U. Lostdamsel. (Odd Books for Odd Moments). (Illus.). ii, 117p. 1986. pap. 4.95 (ISBN 0-317-65963-4). Winds World Pr.

Wizard of Oz: A Story to Color. (Illus.). 64p. (ps-3). 1985. pap. 2.95 (ISBN 0-394-87211-8, BYR). Random.

Wizard of Oz: Music & Lyrics. rev. ed. (Wondrawhopper Ser.). (gr. 3-12). 1985. pap. text ed. 12.00 (ISBN 0-88734-010-5). Players Pr.

Woerterbuch der Psychiatrie und Medizinischen Psychologie. 2nd ed. Uwe H. Peters. (Ger., Eng. & Fr., Dictionary of Psychiatry & Medical Psychology). 1977. pap. 65.00 (ISBN 3-541-06552-4, M-6972). French & Eur.
Woerterbuch der Psychologie. 11th ed. Wilhelm Hehlmann. (Ger.). 1974. pap. 45.00 (ISBN 3-520-26911-2, M-6964). French & Eur.
Woerterbuch der Psychologie. Guenther V. Clauss. (Ger.). 1976. 35.00 (ISBN 3-7609-0256-1, M-6963). French & Eur.
Woerterbuch der Reinen und Angewandten Physik, Vol. 1. L. De Vries. (Ger. & Eng., Dictionary of Physics & Applied Physics). 1964. 38.00 (ISBN 3-486-30942-0, M-6954). French & Eur.
Woerterbuch der Reinen und Angewandten Physik, Vol. 2. L. De Vries. (Eng. & Ger., Dictionary of Physics & Applied Physics). 1964. 38.00 (ISBN 0-686-56615-7, M-6962). French & Eur.
Woerterbuch der Reprographie: Begriffe und Definitionen. 3rd rev. ed. Deutsches Komittee fuer Reprographie. 273p. (Ger., Eng. & Fr., Dictionary of Reprography: Terms & Definitions). 1976. pap. 85.00 (ISBN 0-686-56614-9, M-6961). French & Eur.
Woerterbuch der Schulpaedagogik. 4th ed. Arnold Schwendtke. (Ger.). 1976. pap. 17.95 (ISBN 3-451-09001-5, M-6960). French & Eur.
Woerterbuch der Schweisstechnik. A. Kleiber. (Eng. & Ger., Dictionary of Welding). 1970. 110.00 (ISBN 3-87097-024-3, M-6959). French & Eur.
Woerterbuch der Seeschiffahrt, Vol. 1. 2nd ed. Hans Rinke. (Eng. & Ger., Dictionary of Merchant Shipping). 1975. 59.95 (ISBN 3-19-006294-3, M-6958). French & Eur.
Woerterbuch der Seeschiffahrt, Vol. 2. 2nd ed. Hans Rinke. (Ger. & Eng., Dictionary of Merchant Shipping). 59.95 (ISBN 3-19-006295-1, M-6957). French & Eur.
Woerterbuch der Sozialarbeit und der Sozialpaedagogik. Arnold Schwendtke. (Ger.). 1977. pap. 16.95 (ISBN 3-494-02072-8, M-6955). French & Eur.
Woerterbuch der Spanischen und Deutschen Rechts und Wirtschaftssprache, Vol. 1. H. Becher. (Span. & Ger.). 1971. 225.00 (ISBN 3-406-00469-5, M-6956). French & Eur.
Woerterbuch der Technik. Rudolf Walther. (Eng. & Ger., Dictionary of Technology). 1974. 88.00 (ISBN 3-7736-5100-7, M-6952). French & Eur.
Woerterbuch der Technik, Vol. 1. Karl H. Radde. (Span. & Ger.). 1977. 86.00 (ISBN 3-7736-5530-4, M-6949). French & Eur.
Woerterbuch der Technik, Vol. 2. Karl H. Radde. (Span. & Ger.). 1977. 86.00 (ISBN 3-7736-5531-2, M-6950). French & Eur.
Woerterbuch der Textilindustrie, Vol. 2. Louis de Vries. (Eng. & Ger., Dictionary of Textile Industry). pap. 65.00 (ISBN 0-686-56612-2, M-6948). French & Eur.
Woerterbuch der Ungarischen Rechts und Verwaltungssprache, Vol. 1. 2nd ed. Sandor Karcsay. (Ger. & Hungarian.). 1969. 38.00 (ISBN 3-406-03325-3, M-6947). French & Eur.
Woerterbuch der Ungarischen Rechts und Verwaltungssprache, Vol. 2. 2nd ed. (Ger. & Hungarian.). 1972. 38.00 (ISBN 3-406-03326-1, M-6946). French & Eur.
Woerterbuch der Vorschulerziehung. (Ger.). 1976. pap. 24.95 (ISBN 0-686-56611-4, M-6944). French & Eur.
Woerterbuch der Weidmannssprache. Franz Kehrein. (Ger.). 1969. 110.00 (ISBN 3-500-26250-3, M-6943). French & Eur.
Woerterbuch der Werbung und des Marketing. Clemens Gruber. (Eng. & Ger.). 1977. pap. 35.95 (ISBN 3-19-006312-5, M-6942). French & Eur.
Woerterbuch der Wirtschaft. 7th ed. Horst C. Recktenwald. (Ger.). 1975. 59.95 (ISBN 3-520-11407-0, M-6941). French & Eur.
Woerterbuch des Arbeits und Sozialrechtd. Alexandre Bonnefoi. (Ger. & Fr.). 1975. 85.00 (ISBN 3-19-006293-5, M-6938). French & Eur.
Woerterbuch Des Bibliothekars in 22 Sprachen. 6th rev. ed. Z. Pipics. 385p. (Librarian's Practical Dictionary in 22 Languages). 1974. 295.00 (ISBN 3-7940-4109-7, M-7540, Pub. by Vlg. Dokumentation). French & Eur.
Woerterbuch des Buches. H. Helmut. (Ger.). 1976. pap. 59.95 (ISBN 3-465-00186-9, M-6937). French & Eur.
Woerterbuch des Juedischen Rechts. M. Cohn. (Illus.). xii, 196p. (Ger.). 1981. 65.50 (ISBN 3-8055-2062-X). S Karger.
Woerterbuch des Kraftfahrzeugwesens. Otto Vollnhals. (Ger. & Ital.). 1975. 125.00 (ISBN 3-7736-5120-1, M-6936). French & Eur.
Woerterbuch des Pantentwesens in 5 Sprachen. Gyorgy L. Szendy. (Ger., Eng., Fr., Span. & Rus., Dictionary of Patents in Five Languages). 1974. 125.00 (ISBN 3-18-400269-1, M-6935). French & Eur.
Woerterbuch des Steuerrechts. Rudolf Roessler. (Ger.). 1971. 75.00 (ISBN 3-448-00204-6, M-6934). French & Eur.
Woerterbuch des Verlagswesens in 20 Sprachen. 2nd ed. Imre Mora. (Ger., The Publisher's Practical Dictionary in 20 Languages). 1977. 195.00 (ISBN 3-7940-4112-7, M-6933). French & Eur.
Woerterbuch des Wirtschafts, Rechts und Handelssprache. C. Dietl. (Eng. & Ger., Dictionary of Economic, Legal & Commercial Terms). 1970. 125.00 (ISBN 3-87527-003-7, M-6939). French & Eur.
Woerterbuch Elektrotechnik und Elektronik. 2nd ed. H. Schwenkhagen. (Ger. & Eng., Dictionary of Electrical Engineering and Electronics). 1967. 128.00 (ISBN 0-686-56610-6, M-6927). French & Eur.
Woerterbuch Elektrotechnik und Elektronik. H. F. Schwenkhagen & H. Meinhhold. (Ger. & Eng., Dictionary of Electrical Engineering and Electronics). 1978. 250.00 (ISBN 3-7736-5072-8, M-6928). French & Eur.
Woerterbuch Erdoelverarbeitung-Petrolchemie. W. Leipnitz. (Eng., Ger., Fr. & Rus., Dictionary of Petroleum-processing). 1977. 125.00 (ISBN 0-686-56609-2, M-6925). French & Eur.
Woerterbuch fuer Aerzte. 2nd ed. Lejeune & Bunjes. (Ger., Dictionary for Physicians). 1968. pap. 55.00 (ISBN 3-13-370502-4, M-6924). French & Eur.
Woerterbuch fuer Architektur: Hochbau und Baustoffe. (Fr. & Ger.). 1979. 232.00 (ISBN 0-686-56608-4, M-6923). French & Eur.
Woerterbuch fuer Bautechnik und Baumaschinen. 5th, rev. ed. H. Bucksch. 875p. (Ger. & Fr.). 1982. pap. 195.00 (ISBN 0-686-56607-6, M-6922). French & Eur.
Woerterbuch fuer das Wasser und Abwasserfach. 2nd ed. Fritz Meinck. (Ger., Eng., Fr. & Ital., Dictionary of Water and Sewage Disposal Plants). 1977. 128.00 (ISBN 3-486-35352-7, M-6920). French & Eur.
Woerterbuch fuer Metallurgie, Mineralogie, Geologie, Bergbau und die Oelindustrie. (Eng., Fr., Ger. & Ital., Dictionary of Metallurgy, Mineralogy, Geology, Mining and Oil Industry). 1970. 88.00 (ISBN 3-7625-0751-1, M-6912). French & Eur.
Woerterbuch fuer Strassenbau und Strassenverkehe. Karl Steinig. (Fr. & Ger.). 1970. 175.00 (ISBN 3-7812-0560-6, M-6921). French & Eur.
Woerterbuch fuer Wirtschaft: Recht und Handel, Vol. 1. Georges Potonnier. (Ger. & Fr.). 1970. 175.00 (ISBN 3-87097-030-8, M-6919). French & Eur.
Woerterbuch fuer Wirtschaft: Recht und Handel, Vol. 2. Georges Potonnier. (Fr. & Ger.). 1970. 125.00 (ISBN 3-87097-031-6, M-6918). French & Eur.
Woerterbuch Geowissenschaften, Vol. 1. A. Watznauer. (Eng. & Ger., English-German Dictionary of Geo-Sciences). 1973. 95.00 (ISBN 3-87144-139-2, M-6917). French & Eur.
Woerterbuch Geowissenschaften, Vol. 2. A. Watznauer. (Ger. & Eng., German-English Dictionary of Geo-Sciences). 1973. 95.00 (ISBN 3-87144-140-6, M-6916). French & Eur.
Woerterbuch Kybernetik. Alfred Oppermann. (Ger. & Eng., Dictionary of Cybernetics). 1969. pap. 22.50 (ISBN 3-7940-3258-6, M-6915). French & Eur.
Woerterbuch Medizinischer Fachausdruecke. 2nd ed. Fachredaktion. (Ger.). 1973. 59.95 (ISBN 3-13-437802-7, M-6913). French & Eur.
Woerterbuch Musik. Horst Leuchtmann. (Ger. & Eng., Dictionary of Terms in Music). 1977. 125.00 (ISBN 3-7940-3186-5, M-6911). French & Eur.
Woerterbuch Pferd und Reiter. Zdzislaw Baranowski. (Eng., Fr. & Ger., Dictionary of Horses and Horsemanship). 1977. 24.95 (ISBN 0-273-00937-0, M-6910). French & Eur.
Woerterbuch Physik, 3 vols. Ralf Sube & Gunther Eisenreich. (Eng., Ger., Fr. & Rus., Dictionary of Physics). 1970. Set. 495.00 (ISBN 3-87144-143-0, M-6909). French & Eur.
Woerterbuch Werkzeuge. 2nd ed. Henry G. Freeman. (Ger. & Eng., Dictionary of Tools). 1960. leatherette 165.00 (ISBN 3-7736-5052-3, M-6908). French & Eur.
Woerterbuch Werkzeuge und Werkzeugmaschinen. Kurt Stellhorn. (Ger. & Fr.). 1969. leatherette 115.00 (ISBN 3-7736-5260-7, M-6907). French & Eur.
Woerterbuch zum Religionsunterricht. (Ger.). 1976. 17.95 (ISBN 0-686-56606-8, M-6906). French & Eur.
Woerterbuch zur Geschichte. 3rd ed. Erich Bayer. (Ger.). 1974. pap. 39.95 (ISBN 3-520-28903-2, M-6905). French & Eur.
Woerterbuch zur Politik und Wirtschaftpolitik. Hans E. Zahn. (Ger., Eng. & Fr.). 1976. 125.00 (ISBN 3-7819-2011-9, M-6904). French & Eur.
Woerterbuch zur Politischen Oekonomie. 2nd ed. Gert V. Eynern. (Ger.). 1977. pap. 35.00 (ISBN 3-531-21148-X, M-6902). French & Eur.
Woerterbuch zur Publizistik. K. Koszyk. (Ger.). 1970. 59.95 (ISBN 3-7940-4281-6, M-6901). French & Eur.
Woerterbuch zur Sexualpolitik und ihren Grenzgebieten. (Ger.). pap. 39.95 (ISBN 3-7615-0016-5, M-6900). French & Eur.
Woggle-Bug Book. L. Frank Baum. LC 78-6887. (gr. 1-6). 1978. Repr. of 1905 ed. 30.00x (ISBN 0-8201-1308-5). Schol Facsimiles.
Woggle of Witches. Adrienne Adams. LC 70-161536. (Illus.). 32p. (ps-1). 1971. 12.95 (ISBN 0-684-12506-4, Pub. by Scribner). Macmillan.
Woggle of Witches. Adrienne Adams. LC 87-18703. (Illus.). 32p. (Orig.). (gr. k-3). 1985. pap. 3.95 (ISBN 0-689-71050-X, Aladdin). Macmillan.
Wojciech Jaruzelski: Polish General. Ed. by Arthur M. Schlesinger, Jr. (World Leaders - Past & Present). (Illus.). (gr. 5-12). 1989. 16.95 (ISBN 1-55546-839-X). Chelsea Hse.
Wok: A Chinese Cookbook. Gary Lee. LC 79-19094. (Illus., Orig.). 1970. pap. 6.95 (ISBN 0-911954-06-6). Bristol Pub Ent CA.
Wok Appetizers & Light Snacks. Gary Lee. (Illus.). 182p. (Orig.). 1982. pap. 6.95 (ISBN 0-911954-67-8). Bristol Pub Ent CA.
Wok Cook Book. Sunset Editors. LC 78-53676. (Illus.). 80p. 1978. pap. 5.95 (ISBN 0-376-02963-3, Sunset Bks.). Sunset-Lane.
Wok Cookbook. Carol DeMasters. (Illus.). 1983. pap. 3.95 (ISBN 0-8249-3017-7). Ideals.
Wok Cookery. Ceil Dyer. 1981. pap. 4.95 (ISBN 0-440-19663-9). Dell.
Wok Cookery. Ceil Dyer. LC 77-83279. (Illus.). 1977. pap. 8.95 (ISBN 0-912656-75-1). Price Stern.
Wok Cooking. Weinstein. (Easy Cooking Ser.). 1983. 5.95 (ISBN 0-8120-5532-2). Barron.
Wok Cooking, Vol. 1. G. Godchaux Lefebvre. (Audio Cassette Cooking School Library). 16p. 1982. pap. text ed. 9.95x (ISBN 0-910327-01-7). Cuisine Prods.
Wok for All Seasons. Martin Yan. (Illus.). 236p. 1988. pap. 12.95 (ISBN 0-385-24386-3). Doubleday.
Wok Miracles. Cecilia J. Au-Yeung. (Chopsticks Wok Ser.). (Illus.). 128p. (Eng. & Chinese.). 1985. pap. 5.95 (ISBN 9-627-01851-1). Parkwest Pubns.
Wok Way. Tuan. LC 74-176166. (Illus.). 1974. pap. 2.95 (ISBN 0-915942-01-1). SF Design.
Wok Your Way Skinny. Annette Annechild. pap. 8.95 (ISBN 0-671-42691-5). PB.
Wokcraft. Charles Schafer & Violet Schafer. LC 73-183774. (Illus.). 1972. pap. 5.95 (ISBN 0-394-70788-5, Dist. by Random). Taylor & Ng.
Woking to Portsmouth. Vic Mitchell & Keith Smith. 1986. 34.75x (ISBN 0-906520-25-8, Pub. by Middleton Pr UK). State Mutual Bk.
Woldman's Engineering Alloys. 6th ed. Robert C. Gibbons. 1979. 112.00 (ISBN 0-87170-086-7). ASM.
Wole Soyinka. James Gibbs. LC 85-80890. 170p. 1986. 27.50 (ISBN 0-394-55137-0). Grove.
Wole Soyinka. James Gibbs. LC 85-80890. 170p. 1986. pap. 11.95 (ISBN 0-394-62111-5, Ever). Grove.
Wole Soyinka. Gerald Moore. LC 74-176321. 114p. 1972. 24.50 (ISBN 0-8419-0095-7, Africana); pap. 12.50 (ISBN 0-8419-0113-9, Africana). Holmes & Meier.
Wole Soyinka: A Bibliography of Primary & Secondary Sources. James Gibbs et al. LC 85-14671. (Bibliographies & Indexes in Afro-American & African Studies: No. 7). 117p. 1986. lib. bdg. 36.95 (ISBN 0-313-23937-1, GWS/). Greenwood.
Wole Soyinka: An Introduction to His Writing. Obi Maduakor. LC 86-29434. (Critical Studies in Black Life & Culture: Garland Reference Library of the Humanities). 250p. 1987. lib. bdg. 35.00 (ISBN 0-8240-9141-8). Garland Pub.
Wole Soyinka & Modern Tragedy: A Study of Dramatic Theory & Practice. Ketu H. Katrak. LC 85-27153. (Contributions in Afro-American & African Studies: No. 96). (Illus.). 204p. 1986. lib. bdg. 35.00 (ISBN 0-313-24074-4, KMT/). Greenwood.
Woleaian-English Dictionary. Ho-Min Sohn & Anthony F. Tawerilmang. (Pali Language Texts: Micronesia). 382p. (Pali & Eng.). 1976. pap. text ed. 14.00x (ISBN 0-8248-0415-5). UH Pr.
Woleaian Reference Grammar. Ho-Min Sohn. (PALI Language Texts: Micronesia). 328p. (Orig.). 1975. pap. text ed. 15.00x (ISBN 0-8248-0356-6). UH Pr.
Wolf. Max Davidson. 224p. 1984. 15.95 (ISBN 0-7043-2387-7, Pub. by Quartet Bks). Salem Hse Pubs.
Wolf. Paula Hogan. LC 79-13309. (Life Cycles Clippers Ser.). (Illus.). 32p. (gr. k-3). 1981. PLB 27.99 incl. cassette (ISBN 0-8172-1846-7); cassette 14.00. Raintree Pubs.
Wolf. Paula Z. Hogan. LC 79-13309. (Life Cycles Bks.). (Illus.). 32p. (gr. k-3). 1979. PLB 14.65 (ISBN 0-8172-1507-7). Raintree Pubs.
Wolf. Richard Rose. 1982. pap. 2.50 (ISBN 0-89083-961-1). Zebra.
Wolf. Richard Rose. 288p. (Orig.). 1980. pap. 2.50 (ISBN 0-89083-657-4). Zebra.
Wolf: A False Memoir. Jim Harrison. 1981. pap. 5.95 (ISBN 0-385-29160-4, Delta). Dell.
Wolf: A False Memoir. Jim Harrison. LC 74-159131. 1971. Ultramarine Pub.
Wolf: A False Memoir. Jim Harrison. 1989. pap. 8.95 (ISBN 0-440-55018-1, Delta). Dell.
Wolf! A Modern Look. Wolves in American Culture Committee. LC 86-63259. 64p. 1986. pap. 8.95 (ISBN 0-942802-15-2). Northword.
Wolf & Bear Stories. Walker Wyman. 63p. pap. 3.00 (ISBN 0-318-03969-9). U Pr Wisc River Falls.
Wolf & Coyote Trapping. A. R. Harding. (Illus.). 252p. pap. 3.50 (ISBN 0-936622-27-X). A R Harding Pub.
Wolf & Man: Evolution in Parallel. Roberta L. Hall & Henry S. Sharp. 210p. 1978. 60.50 (ISBN 0-12-319250-1). Acad Pr.
Wolf & the Buffalo. Elmer Kelton. LC 85-20814. (Texas Tradition Ser.: No. 5). 425p. 1986. 17.95 (ISBN 0-87565-058-9); pap. 10.95 (ISBN 0-87565-059-7). Tex Christian.
Wolf & the Dove. Kathleen E. Woodiwiss. 1983. pap. 3.95 (ISBN 0-380-00778-9, 81919-8). Avon.
Wolf & the Dove. Kathleen E. Woodiwiss. 704p. 1987. 19.95 (ISBN 0-8161-4312-9). G K Hall.
Wolf & the Raven: Totem Poles of Southeastern Alaska. 2nd ed. Viola E. Garfield & Linn A. Forrest. LC 49-8492. (Illus.). 161p. 1961. pap. 9.95 (ISBN 0-295-73998-3). U of Wash Pr.
Wolf & the Seven Kids. new ed. Jacob Grimm & Wilhelm K. Grimm. LC 78-18076. (Illus.). 32p. (gr. 1-4). 1979. PLB 9.79 (ISBN 0-89375-138-3); pap. 1.95 (ISBN 0-89375-116-2). Troll Assocs.
Wolf & the Seven Little Kids. Linda M. Jennings. LC 86-6629. (Illus.). (ps-2). 1986. PLB 8.95 (ISBN 0-382-09306-2). Silver.
Wolf & the Winds. Frank B. Linderman. LC 86-40075. 224p. 1986. 16.95 (ISBN 0-8061-2007-X). U of Okla Pr.
Wolf at the Door. Victoria Gordon. (Harlequin Romances Ser.). 192p. 1981. pap. 1.50 (ISBN 0-373-02433-9). Harlequin Bks.
Wolf Bell. Shirley R. Murphy. 176p. 1980. pap. 2.25 (ISBN 0-380-50666-1, 62216-5, Flare). Avon.
Wolf by the Ears: Thomas Jefferson & Slavery. John C. Miller. LC 76-51590. 1977. 17.95 (ISBN 0-02-921500-5). Free Pr.
Wolf by the Ears: Thomas Jefferson & Slavery. John C. Miller. 1980. pap. 7.95 (ISBN 0-452-00629-5, F629, Mer). NAL.
Wolf-Children & Feral Man. Joseph A. Singh & Robert M. Zingg. LC 66-23445. (Illus.). xli, 379p. 1966. Repr. of 1942 ed. 32.50 (ISBN 0-208-00599-4, Archon). Shoe String.
Wolf Children & the Problem of Human Nature: With the Complete Text of the Wild Boy of Aveyron. Lucien Malson & Jean-Marc-Gaspard Itard. LC 72-81769. 192p. 1972. pap. 7.00 (ISBN 0-85345-264-4). Monthly Rev.
Wolf Country. Will Brennan. (Lythway Ser.). 168p. 1988. lib. bdg. 17.50x (ISBN 0-7451-0712-5, Pub. by Chivers Pr UK). G K Hall.
Wolf Courts Girl: The Equivalence of Hunting & Mating in Bushman Thought. Daniel F. McCall. LC 79-631803. (Papers in International Studies: Africa Ser.: No. 7). 1970. pap. 3.25x (ISBN 0-89680-040-7, Ohio U Ctr Intl). Ohio U Pr.
Wolf Cub Scout Action Book. 64p. 1980. pap. 1.15x (ISBN 0-8395-3902-9, 3902). BSA.
Wolf Cub Scout Book. rev. ed. (Illus.). 224p. (gr. 2). 1986. pap. 2.75x (ISBN 0-8395-3234-2, 3234). BSA.
Wolf Dog of the Woodland Indians. Margaret Z. Searcy. LC 81-19763. (Illus.). 114p. (gr. 4-8). 1982. 9.95 (ISBN 0-8173-0091-0). U of Ala Pr.
Wolf Dog Range. Lee Floren. 1978. pap. 1.25 (ISBN 0-8439-0530-1, Leisure Bks). Leisure NY.
Wolf-Dreams. Michael D. Weaver. 192p. 1987. pap. 2.95 (ISBN 0-380-75198-4). Avon.
Wolf Driving Sled: Sel Poems 1970-1980. Gary Lawless. 1981. pap. 3.50 (ISBN 0-942396-28-6). Blackberry ME.
Wolf Huber Studies: Aspects of Renaissance Thought & Practice in Danube School Painting. Patricia Rose. LC 76-23711. (Outstanding Dissertations in the Fine Arts - 16th Century). (Illus.). 1977. Repr. of 1973 ed. lib. bdg. 76.00 (ISBN 0-8240-2725-6). Garland Pub.
Wolf Hunter. Joel Kauffmann. 112p. (Orig.). (gr. 1-7). 1986. pap. 7.95 (ISBN 0-687-45890-0). Abingdon.
Wolf in Man's Clothing. Mignon G. Eberhart. 224p. 1983. pap. 3.50 (ISBN 0-446-31207-X). Warner Bks.
Wolf in Sheep's Clothing: The Search for a Child Killer. Tommy McIntyre. LC 88-5738. (Great Lakes Bks.). 432p. 1988. 34.95x (ISBN 0-8143-1966-1); pap. 14.95x (ISBN 0-8143-1989-0). Wayne St U Pr.
Wolf in the Garden. Alfred H. Bill. 144p. 1972. pap. 0.75 (ISBN 0-87818-008-7). Centaur.
Wolf in the Southwest: The Making of an Endangered Species. Ed. by David E. Brown. LC 82-17399. 195p. 1983. pap. 12.95 (ISBN 0-8165-0796-1). U of Ariz Pr.
Wolf in Winter: A Story of Francis Assisi. John Sack. LC 85-60296. 128p. (Orig.). 1985. pap. 4.95 (ISBN 0-8091-6556-2). Paulist Pr.
Wolf Kahn: Landscape Painter. Martica Sawin. LC 81-51081. (Illus.). 96p. 1981. pap. 19.95. Taplinger.
Wolf Kahn, New Landscapes. Lawrence Campbell. Ed. by Gayle Maxon & Diana Hancock. LC 88-80230. (Illus.). 22p. 1988. 12.00 (ISBN 0-935037-19-5). Peters Corp NM.
Wolf Man. Sandra Clark. (Harlequin Presents Ser.). 192p. 1982. pap. 1.75 (ISBN 0-373-10514-2). Harlequin Bks.
Wolf Man. Ian Thorne. Ed. by Howard Schroeder. LC 76-51146. (Monsters Ser.). (Illus.). 48p. (gr. 3 up). 1977. PLB 9.95 (ISBN 0-913940-71-2); pap. 4.95 (ISBN 0-913940-78-X). Crestwood Hse.
Wolf-Man. Ed. by Muriel Gardiner. LC 70-151227. (Illus.). 400p. 1986. pap. 8.95 (ISBN 0-465-09196-2, PL 1571). Basic.

Woman Abuse: Facts Replacing Myths. Lewis Okun. LC 84-26912. 298p. 1985. 49.50 (ISBN 0-88706-077-3); pap. 16.95x (ISBN 0-88706-079-X). State U NY Pr.

Woman Activist Fund. Virginia General Assembly Voting Record. 1979. pap. 2.00 (ISBN 0-917560-14-0). Woman Activist.

Woman Activist Guide for Women Candidates. rev. ed. Flora Crater. 1978. pap. 1.00 (ISBN 0-917560-11-6). Woman Activist.

Woman Activist Guide to Precinct Politics. 2nd ed. Flora Crater. 1979. pap. 2.00. Woman Activist.

Woman Activists. Anne W. Garland. Date not set. price not set. Feminist Pr.

Woman Against the World. Evelyn Hanna. 480p. (Orig.). 1983. pap. 3.50 (ISBN 0-345-28931-5). Ballantine.

Woman Against Women in Victorian England: A Life of Eliza Lynn Linton. Nancy F. Anderson. LC 86-45798. (Illus.). 272p. 1987. 29.50 (ISBN 0-253-36600-3). Ind U Pr.

Woman Alcoholic & Her Total Recovery Program. Bonnie-Jean Kimball. 24p. (Orig.). 1976. pap. 0.95 (ISBN 0-89486-061-5). Hazelden.

Woman Alive! Nelle McFather. 304p. 1984. pap. 3.25 (ISBN 0-8439-2146-3, Leisure Bks). Leisure NY.

Woman Alone. Norma G. Bie. 53p. 1988. 6.95 (ISBN 0-533-07519-X). Vantage.

Woman Alone. Patricia O'Brien. LC 72-94650. 288p. 1974. write for info. (ISBN 0-8129-0344-7). Times Bks.

Woman: An Affirmation. Alice Fannin et al. 1979. pap. text ed. 15.50 (ISBN 0-669-01991-7); answer key 2.00 (ISBN 0-669-01992-5). Heath.

Woman & Catholicism: My Break with the Roman Catholic Church. Sheelagh Conway. Ed. by Colleen Dimson. 272p. (Orig.). 1987. pap. 4.50 (ISBN 0-7701-0745-1). Paperjacks US.

Woman & Certain Women. Philip Garrison. 15p. (Orig.). 1971. pap. 3.00 (ISBN 0-932264-16-6). Trask Hse Bks.

Woman & Child: The Legacy of Baby M. Phyllis Chesler. 256p. 16.95. Times Bks.

Woman & Fatigue. Holly Atkinson. pap. 4.50 (ISBN 0-671-63179-9). PB.

Woman & Her Master, 2 vols. Sydney Morgan. LC 75-21813. (Pioneers of the Woman's Movement: an International Perspective Ser.). viii, 429p. 1976. Repr. of 1840 ed. 30.25 (ISBN 0-88355-267-1). Hyperion Conn.

Woman & Her Needs see Liberating the Home.

Woman & Labor. Olive Schreiner. 75.00 (ISBN 0-87968-349-X). Gordon Pr.

Woman & Man: Biblical Encounter Ser. Erhard S. Gerstenberger & Wolfgang Schrage. Tr. by Douglas W. Stott from Ger. LC 81-10898. 256p. (Orig.). 1982. pap. 10.95 (ISBN 0-687-45920-6). Abingdon.

Woman & Nature: The Roaring Inside Her. Susan Griffin. LC 77-11812. 1979. pap. 7.95 (ISBN 0-06-090744-4, CN 744, PL). Har-Row.

Woman & Society. Rudolf Steiner. 24p. 1986. pap. 4.50 (ISBN 0-85440-444-9, Pub. by Steinerbooks). Anthroposophic.

Woman & Society in Eighteenth-Century France: Essays in Honour of John Stephenson Spink. Ed. by Eva Jacobs et al. 285p. 1979. 49.50 (ISBN 0-485-11184-5, Pub. by Athlone Pr UK). Humanities.

Woman & Temperance; or, the Work & Workers of the Woman's Christian Temperance Union. Frances E. Willard. LC 74-38443. (Religion in America, Ser. 2). 654p. 1972. Repr. of 1883 ed. 38.00 (ISBN 0-405-04093-8). Ayer Co Pubs.

Woman & the Demon: The Life of a Victorian Myth. Nina Auerbach. (Illus.). 256p. 1982. text ed. 22.50x (ISBN 0-674-95406-8). Harvard U Pr.

Woman & the Demon: The Life of a Victorian Myth. Nina Auerbach. 272p. 1984. pap. 7.95 (ISBN 0-674-95407-6). Harvard U Pr.

Woman & the Haunted Mansion. Herlet E. Wakefield. LC 83-91498. 127p. 1984. 10.00 (ISBN 0-533-06088-5). Vantage.

Woman & the Lyre: Women Writers in Classical Greece & Rome. Jane M. Snyder. LC 88-10114. (Illus.). 208p. 1989. text ed. 24.95x (ISBN 0-8093-1455-X). S Ill U Pr.

Woman & the Myth: Margaret Fuller's Life & Writings. Bell G. Chevigny. LC 76-19030. (Midland Bks.: No. 243). 528p. 1976. 20.00x (ISBN 0-253-16574-1); pap. 8.95x (ISBN 0-253-20243-4). Ind U Pr.

Woman & the Myth: Margaret Fuller's Life & Writings. Ed. by Bell G. Chevigny. 528p. (Orig.). 1977. pap. 8.95 (ISBN 0-912670-43-6). Feminist Pr.

Woman & the Sea. Richard Tregaskis. (Illus.). 6.50 (ISBN 0-910550-17-4). Elysium.

Woman & Womanhood in America. Ronald W. Hogeland. (Problems in American Civilization Ser.). 1974. pap. text ed. 7.50 (ISBN 0-669-85597-9). Heath.

Woman Appeared to Me. Renee Vivien. Tr. by Jeannette H. Foster from Fr. LC 76-45689. 1979. 5.00 (ISBN 0-930044-06-1). Naiad Pr.

Woman As Chameleon: Or How to Be an Ideal Woman. Melissa Sadoff. (Illus.). 164p. 1988. 15.95 (ISBN 0-7043-2616-7, Pub. by Quartet Bks). Salem Hse Pubs.

Woman As Divine: Tales of the Goddess. Mariam Baker. (Illus., Orig.). 1982. pap. 8.95 (ISBN 0-9609916-0-3). Crescent Heart.

Woman As Force in History. Mary R. Beard. 1985. Repr. of 1946 ed. lib. bdg. 27.50x (ISBN 0-374-90503-7, Octagon). Hippocrene Bks.

Woman As Force in History: A Study in Traditions & Realities. Mary R. Beard. 365p. 1987. pap. 12.95 (ISBN 0-89255-113-5). Persea Bks.

Woman As Good As the Man: Or the Equality of Both Sexes. Poullain de la Barre. Intro. by Gerald MacLean. LC 88-10808. 160p. 1988. 26.00x (ISBN 0-8143-1953-X); pap. 12.95x (ISBN 0-8143-1954-8). Wayne St U Pr.

Woman As Hero in Old English Literature. Jane Chance. (Illus.). 192p. 1986. pap. text ed. 12.50x (ISBN 0-8156-2346-1). Syracuse U Pr.

Woman As Image in Medieval Literature from the Twelfth Century to Dante. Joan M. Ferrante. 176p. 1985. pap. 8.95 (ISBN 0-939464-43-8). Labyrinth Pr.

Woman As Mediatrix: Essays on Nineteenth-Century European Women Writers-Prepared under the Auspices of Hofstra University. Ed. by Avriel H. Goldberger. LC 86-14236. (Contributions in Women's Studies: No. 73). 210p. 1987. lib. bdg. 29.95 (ISBN 0-313-25515-6, GWX/). Greenwood.

Woman As Myth & Metaphor in Latin American Narrative. Carmelo Virgillo & Naomi E. Lindstrom. LC 85-1019. 214p. 1986. text ed. 20.00x (ISBN 0-8262-0460-0). U of Mo Pr.

Woman As Priest, Bishop & Laity in the Early Catholic Church to 440 A.D. 2nd ed. Arthur F. Ide. LC 81-13464. (Woman in History Ser.: Vol. 9B). (Illus.). viii, 125p. 1983. 20.95 (ISBN 0-86663-037-6); pap. 5.95 (ISBN 0-86663-038-4). Ide Hse.

Woman As Writer. Jeanette Webber & Joan Grumman. (Illus., LC 77-074379). 1978. pap. text ed. 21.50 (ISBN 0-395-26438-3). HM.

Woman at Apocalypse. Frederick W. Ayer. 1981. pap. 5.00 (ISBN 0-682-49809-2). Exposition-Phoenix.

Woman at Mid-Life: Moving Beyond Stereotypes. Vernie Dale. LC 84-52884. 80p. 1985. pap. text ed. 2.95 (ISBN 0-89243-230-6). Liguori Pubns.

Woman at Otowi Crossing. rev. ed. Frank Waters. 332p. 1987. pap. text ed. 9.95 (ISBN 0-8040-0893-0, Pub by Swallow). Ohio U Pr.

Woman at Otowi Crossing: A Novel. rev. ed. Frank Waters. LC 66-25961. 314p. 1987. pap. 9.95 (Swallow). Ohio U Pr.

Woman at Point Sur. reissue 1987 ed. Robinson Jeffers. 1987. pap. 7.70 (ISBN 0-87140-115-0). Liveright.

Woman at Point Zero. Nawal El Saadawi. Tr. by Sherif Hetata. 1983. 13.95 (ISBN 0-86232-517-X, Pub. by Zed Pr England); pap. 7.95 (ISBN 0-86232-110-7, Pub. by Zed Pr England). Humanities.

Woman at the End of the Mattress. Michael Knoll. Ed. by Joan H. Lee. 332p. 1981. pap. 3.50 (ISBN 0-932220-12-6). Broken Whisker.

Woman at the Well. Adrian Van Kaam. 6.95 (ISBN 0-87193-092-7). Dimension Bks.

Woman at War. Dacia Maraini. Tr. by Mara Benetti & Elspeth Spottiswood. LC 88-81204. 300p. (Orig.). 1988. pap. 13.95 (ISBN 0-934977-12-7). Italica Pr.

Woman at War. Dacia Mariani. Tr. by Mara Benetti & Elspeth Spottiswood. 282p. 1985. cancelled (ISBN 0-86316-075-1); pap. cancelled (ISBN 0-907637-03-5). Writers & Readers.

Woman at Work. Mary Anderson. LC 73-13451. (Illus.). 266p. 1973. Repr. of 1951 ed. lib. bdg. 35.00 (ISBN 0-8371-7133-4, ANWW). Greenwood.

Woman-Aware & Choosing. new ed. Betty J. Coble. LC 75-7943. 156p. 1975. 9.95 (ISBN 0-8054-5613-9). Broadman.

Woman Be Free: The Clear Message of Scripture. Patricia Gundry. 1988. pap. 6.95 (ISBN 0-310-25361-6, 10500P). Zondervan.

Woman Before History Was Written. Date not set. lib. bdg. cancelled (ISBN 0-86663-025-2); pap. text ed. cancelled (ISBN 0-86663-026-0). Ide Hse.

Woman Bowler. 5.00 (ISBN 0-686-30134-X). WIBC.

Woman by Design. Frances Kennett. LC 88-42654. 512p. 1988. 18.95 (ISBN 0-394-56544-4). Random.

Woman Called En. Tomie O'Hara. 160p. 1986. 17.50 (ISBN 0-86358-079-3, Pandora Pr); pap. 6.95 (ISBN 0-86358-082-3). Routledge Chapman & Hall.

Woman Called Golda. Michael Avallone. 272p. 1982. pap. 2.95 (ISBN 0-8439-1114-X, Leisure Bks). Leisure NY.

Woman-Centered Pregnancy & Birth. Federation of Feminist Women's Health Centers Staff & Ginny Cassidy-Brinn. LC 83-70352. (Illus.). 204p. 1984. pap. 11.95 (ISBN 0-939416-03-4). Cleis Pr.

Woman: Charm & Power. Robert P. Downes. 1974. lib. bdg. 69.95 (ISBN 0-685-51378-5). Revisionist Pr.

Woman Chief. Rose Sobol. 112p. (YA) (gr. 5-9). 1979. pap. 1.25 (ISBN 0-440-99657-0, LFL). Dell.

Woman, Church, & State: A Historical Account of the Status of Woman Through the Christian Ages, with Reminiscenses of the Matriarchate. 2nd ed. Matilda J. Gage. LC 72-2602. (American Women Ser.: Images & Realities). 558p. 1972. Repr. of 1900 ed. 32.00 (ISBN 0-405-04458-5). Ayer Co Pubs.

Woman Clothed with the Sun. Ed. by John J. Delaney. LC 60-5922. 1961. pap. 4.95 (ISBN 0-385-08019-0, Im). Doubleday.

Woman Clothed with the Sun, & Other Stories. Frank L. Lucas. LC 71-122731. (Short Story Index Reprint Ser). 1938. 18.00 (ISBN 0-8369-3564-0). Ayer Co Pubs.

Woman Composers. Carol Plantamura. (Illus.). 48p. pap. 3.50 (ISBN 0-88388-110-1). Bellerophon Bks.

Woman, Culture, & Society. Ed. by Michelle Z. Rosaldo & Louise Lamphere. LC 73-89861. 360p. 1974. 35.00x (ISBN 0-8047-0850-9); pap. 9.95 (ISBN 0-8047-0851-7, SP133). Stanford U Pr.

Woman Cyclist: Training & Racing Techniques. Elaine Mariolle & Michael Shermer. (Illus.). 224p. (Orig.). Date not set. pap. 8.95 (ISBN 0-8092-4941-3). Contemp Bks.

Woman: Dependent or Independent Variable? Rhoda K. Unger & Florence L. Denmark. LC 75-765161. 848p. 1975. 39.95x (ISBN 0-88437-000-3). Psych Dimensions.

Woman Destroyed. Simone De Beauvoir. Tr. by Patrick O'Brian. LC 84-1846. 256p. 1987. 7.95 (ISBN 0-394-71103-3). Pantheon.

Woman Detective: Gender & Genre. Kathleen G. Klein. 272p. 1988. 24.95 (ISBN 0-252-01522-3). U of Ill Pr.

Woman Doctor. Florence Haseltine & Yvonne Yaw. 384p. 1980. pap. 2.95 (ISBN 0-345-30150-1). Ballantine.

Woman-Doctor: The Education of Jane Patterson, M.D. Jane Patterson & Lynda Madaras. 224p. 1983. pap. 3.95 (ISBN 0-380-83063-9, 83063-9). Avon.

Woman Doctor's Civil War: Esther Hill Hawks' Diary. Ed. by Gerald Schwartz. LC 84-11998. (Illus.). 325p. 1986. 21.95 (ISBN 0-87249-435-7). U of SC Pr.

Woman Doctor's Diet for Teenage Girls. Barbara Edelstein. 288p. 1985. pap. 3.50 (ISBN 0-345-34601-7). Ballantine.

Woman Doctor's Guide to Overcoming Cystitis. Kathryn Schrotenboer & Sue Berckman. LC 87-7723. 224p. 1987. pap. 8.95 (ISBN 0-452-25947-9, Plume). NAL.

Woman Doctor's Medical Guide for Women. Edelstein. 1987. pap. 4.95 (ISBN 0-553-26318-8). Bantam.

Woman Driver. Jean Thompson. 272p. 1985. 15.95 (ISBN 0-531-09789-7). Watts.

Woman, Earth, Spirit. Helen Luke. 112p. 1984. pap. 7.95 (ISBN 0-8245-0633-2). Crossroad NY.

Woman Entrepreneur: Starting, Financing, & Managing a Successful Business. Robert D. Hisrich & Candida G. Brush. 240p. 1985. 21.95 (ISBN 0-669-09189-8). Lexington Bks.

Woman Evangelist: The Life & Times of Charismatic Evangelist Maria B. Woodworth-Etter. Wayne E. Warner & Wayne E. Warner. LC 86-11854. (Studies in Evangelicalism: No. 8). (Illus.). 354p. 1986. 32.50 (ISBN 0-8108-1912-0). Scarecrow.

Woman Executive. Evelyn Park. Ed. by Sylvia Ashton. LC 77-80278. 1979. 14.95 (ISBN 0-87949-086-1). Ashley Bks.

Woman Feels Different from a Man. Pat Vornkahl. 100p. Date not set. 6.95 (ISBN 1-55523-168-3). Winston-Derek.

Woman: First among the Faithful. Francis J. Moloney. LC 85-73197. 128p. 1986. pap. 4.95 (ISBN 0-87793-333-2). Ave Maria.

Woman for Our Time. Spartaco Lucarini. LC 74-77253. 1974. 3.95 (ISBN 0-8198-0324-3). Dghtrs St Paul.

Woman for President, Foundation of the Federation of the Goths, Stretching from Iran to Norway. H. Winky-Lotz. (Historical Novel, Europe About 175 B. C. to 95 B. C. Ser.: Vol. I). (Illus.). 312p. 1980. 14.55 (ISBN 0-936112-02-6); pap. 11.25 (ISBN 0-936112-09-3). Willyshe Pub.

Woman for President, the Roots of "Cinderella" of Our Fairy Tale. H. Winky-Lotz. (Historical Novel, Europe About 95 B. C. to 57 B. C. Ser.: Vol. II). (Illus.). 245p. 1980. 14.55 (ISBN 0-936112-08-5); pap. 11.25 (ISBN 0-936112-03-4). Willyshe Pub.

Woman-from Head to Toes. Patricia Norimatsu. LC 82-90058. 277p. 1983. pap. 9.95x (ISBN 0-9606890-2-8). Morris Pub.

Woman from Memphis. 2nd ed. Robert Sargent. LC 78-64527. (Illus.). 1979. perfect bdg. 7.00 (ISBN 0-915380-07-2). Word Works.

Woman God Can Use. Pamela Heim. LC 85-73070. 176p. 1986. pap. 6.95 (ISBN 0-89636-190-X). Accent Bks.

Woman Hater. Diana Palmer. (Silhouette Romance Ser.). pap. 1.95 (ISBN 0-373-08532-X). Harlequin Bks.

Woman Hating: A Radical Look at Sexuality. Andrea Dworkin. Date not set. pap. 9.95 (ISBN 0-525-48397-7). Dutton.

Woman: Her Position & Influence in Ancient Greece & Rome & Among the Early Christians. James Donaldson. 69.95 (ISBN 0-87968-065-2). Gordon Pr.

Woman: Her Rights, Wrongs, Privileges, & Responsibilities. facs. ed. L. P. Brockett. LC 70-114869. (Select Bibliographies Reprint Ser.). 1869. 32.00 (ISBN 0-8369-5274-X). Ayer Co Pubs.

Woman in a Lampshade. Elizabeth Jolley. 232p. 1986. pap. 6.95 (ISBN 0-14-008418-5). Penguin.

Woman in a World of Men: An Autobiography of a Farmer's Daughter. Mary L. Little. LC 85-90285. 49p. 1986. 7.95 (ISBN 0-533-06782-0). Vantage.

Woman in All Ages & All Nations. Thomas L. Nichols. 75.00 (ISBN 0-8490-1314-3). Gordon Pr.

Woman in All Ages & in All Countries: Women of the Romance Countries. John R. Effinger. 1981. Repr. of 1907 ed. lib. bdg. 45.00. Century Bookbindery.

Woman in America. Ed. by Robert J. Lifton. LC 77-11064. 1977. Repr. of 1965 ed. lib. bdg. 35.00x (ISBN 0-8371-9810-0, LIWO). Greenwood.

Woman in America: A Guide to Information Sources. Ed. by Virginia R. Terris. LC 73-17564. (American Studies Information Guide Ser.: Vol. 7). 544p. 1980. 68.00x (ISBN 0-8103-1268-9). Gale.

Woman in American Society: A Selected Bibliography, Nos. 810-811. 2nd ed. Ed. by Lenwood G. Davis. 1975. 10.00 (ISBN 0-686-20355-0). CPL Biblios.

Woman in Ancient Africa. Heinrich Loth. Tr. by Sheila Marnie from Ger. (Illus.). 192p. 1988. 35.00 (ISBN 0-88208-218-3). Chicago Review.

Woman in Ancient Israel under the Torah & Talmud. Arthur F. Ide. LC 82-9184. (Women in History Ser.: Vol. 5B). (Illus.). 86p. (Orig.). 1982. 10.95 (ISBN 0-86663-080-5); pap. text ed. 2.95 (ISBN 0-86663-081-3). Ide Hse.

Woman in Apartment. Cynthia Pickard. LC 72-179817. (New Poetry Ser.). Repr. of 1957 ed. 16.00 (ISBN 0-404-56017-2). AMS Pr.

Woman in Art Nouveau Decoration: One Hundred Forty-One Designs. Julius Klinger. (Pictorial Archive Ser.). 32p. 1985. pap. 5.95 (ISBN 0-486-24797-X). Dover.

Woman in Athletic Administration. Jackie Lapin & Bonnie L. Parkhouse. 1980. text ed. write for info. (ISBN 0-673-16213-3). Scott F.

Woman in Battle: A Narrative of the Exploits, Adventures, & Travels of Madame Loreta Janeta Valazquez, Otherwise Known As Lieutenant Harry T. Buford, Confederate States Army. Loreta J. Velazquez. Ed. by C. J. Worthington. LC 72-2632. (American Women Ser.: Images & Realities). 680p. 1972. Repr. of 1876 ed. 38.50 (ISBN 0-405-04485-2). Ayer Co Pubs.

Woman in Black. E. C. Bentley. 1976. lib. bdg. 13.95x (ISBN 0-89968-166-2). Lightyear.

Woman in Black. Susan Hill. LC 85-70145. 176p. 1986. 15.95 (ISBN 0-87923-576-4). Godine.

Woman in Black: A Ghost Story. Susan Hill. LC 87-70145. (Illus.). 176p. 1987. pap. 9.95 (ISBN 0-87923-706-6). Godine.

Woman in Christian Tradition. George H. Tavard. LC 72-12637. pap. 67.30 (ISBN 0-317-26144-4, 2024373). Bks Demand UMI.

Woman in Contemporary Business. 2nd ed. Callie F. Struggs. LC 82-3126. (Woman in History Ser.: Vol. 56B). (Illus.). 60p. 1982. unbound 2.00. Ide Hse.

Woman in Greek Civilization before 100 B.C. 2nd ed. Arthur F. Ide. LC 81-13468. (Woman in History Ser.: Vol. 7B). (Illus.). 83p. 1983. lib. bdg. 10.95 (ISBN 0-86663-031-7); pap. text ed. 2.95 (ISBN 0-86663-032-5). Ide Hse.

Woman in Her Prime. A. Konadu. (African Writers Ser.). 1967. pap. text ed. 6.00 (ISBN 0-435-90040-4). Heinemann Ed.

Woman in History. Date not set. lib. bdg. price not set; pap. text ed. price not set (ISBN 0-86663-005-8). Ide Hse.

Woman in Irish Legend, Life & Literature. Ed. by S. F. Gallagher. LC 82-22792. (Irish Literary Studies: No. 14). 158p. 1983. text ed. 28.50x (ISBN 0-389-20361-0). B&N Imports.

Woman in Islam. Wiebke Walther. (Image of Women Ser.). (Illus.). 192p. 1982. 35.00 (ISBN 0-8390-0256-4, Allanheld & Schram). Abner Schram Ltd.

Woman in Islam: A Manual with Special Reference to Conditions in India. Violet R. Jones. LC 79-2942. (Illus.). 455p. 1987. Repr. of 1941 ed. 35.00 (ISBN 0-8305-0107-X). Hyperion Conn.

Woman in Judaism. Denese B. Mann. 1979. pap. 6.50 (ISBN 0-9603348-0-7). Jonathan Pubns.

Woman in Levi's. Eulalia Bourne. LC 66-27382. pap. 56.00 (ISBN 0-317-28054-6, 2025552). Bks Demand UMI.

Woman in Management: Career & Family Issues. Ed. by Jennie Farley. LC 83-2338. 112p. (Orig.). 1983. pap. 8.95 (ISBN 0-87546-100-X). ILR Pr.

Woman in Medicine. Maria Steward. 1977. lib. bdg. 59.95 (ISBN 0-8490-2832-9). Gordon Pr.

Woman in Mind. Alan Ayckbourn. 96p. (Orig.). 1986. pap. 7.95 (ISBN 0-571-14520-5). Faber & Faber.

Woman in Modern Life. Ed. by William C. Bier. LC 68-20626. (Pastoral Psychology Ser.: No. 5). x, 278p. 1968. 25.00 (ISBN 0-8232-0800-1). Fordham.

Woman in Music. Louis Elson. 69.95 (ISBN 0-87968-459-3). Gordon Pr.

Woman in Red. Paula Gosling. 240p. 1985. pap. 2.95 (ISBN 0-445-20019-7, Pub. by Popular Lib). Warner Bks.

Woman in Residence. Michelle Harrison. 272p. 1983. pap. 6.95 (ISBN 0-14-006723-X). Penguin.

Woman in Residence: A Physician's Account of Her Training in Obstetrics & Gynecology. Michelle Harrison. 1982. 13.45 (ISBN 0-394-51885-3). Random.

Woman, Poet, Scientist: Essays in New World Anthropology Honoring Dr. Emma Louise Davis. Ed. by Great Basin Foundation Staff & Thomas C. Blackburn. LC 85-6075. (Anthropological Papers: No. 29). (Illus.). 256p. (Orig.). 1985. pap. 21.50 (ISBN 0-87919-106-6). Ballena Pr.
Woman Poet: The East. Ed. by Elaine Dallman et al. LC 81-69793. (Woman Poet Ser.). (Illus.). 123p. 1982. casebound 19.95 (ISBN 0-935634-03-7); pap. 12.50 (ISBN 0-935634-02-9). Women-in-Lit.
Woman Poet: The Midwest. Ed. by Elaine Dallman et al. LC 81-69793. (Woman Poet Ser.). (Illus.). 115p. 1985. casebound 19.95 (ISBN 0-935634-05-3); pap. 12.50 (ISBN 0-935634-04-5). Women-in-Lit.
Woman Poet: The South. Ed. by Elaine Dallman et al. LC 81-69793. (Woman Poet Ser.). (Illus.). 1988. casebound 19.95 (ISBN 0-935634-07-X); pap. 12.50 (ISBN 0-935634-06-1). Women-in-Lit.
Woman Poet: The West. Ed. by Elaine Dallman et al. LC 79-55988. (Woman Poet Ser.). (Illus.). 100p. (Orig.). 1980. casebound 19.95 (ISBN 0-935634-01-0). Women-in-Lit.
Woman Power in Textile & Apparel Sales. Eric Hertz & Jerry Sherman. LC 78-61155. 1979. 8.95 (ISBN 0-87005-199-7). Fairchild.
Woman Question. 2nd ed. Kenneth E. Hagin. 1983. pap. 2.50 (ISBN 0-89276-405-8). Hagin Ministries.
Woman Question. Ed. by Thomas R. Smith. LC 79-2951. 229p. 1982. Repr. of 1919 ed. 24.75 (ISBN 0-8305-0114-2). Hyperion Conn.
Woman Question see Thoughts on Women & Society.
Woman Question in Classical Sociological Theory. Terry R. Kandal. 192p. (Orig.). 1988. pap. text ed. 19.50 (ISBN 0-8130-0796-8). U Presses Fla.
Woman Question in Mrs. Gaskell's Life & Works. A. Rubenius. (Essays & Studies on English Language Literature: Vol. 5). pap. 37.00 (ISBN 0-8115-0203-1). Kraus Repr.
Woman Question: Society & Literature in Britain & America, 1837-1883, 3 Vols. Elizabeth Helsinger & Robin Sheets. Incl. Vol. 1. Defining Voices. 1983. lib. bdg. 22.00 (ISBN 0-8240-9301-1); Vol. 2. Social Issues. 1983. lib. bdg. 33.00 (ISBN 0-8240-9232-5); Vol. 3. Literary Issues. 1983. lib. bdg. 33.00 (ISBN 0-8240-9233-3). LC 80-9040. 1983. Garland Pub.
Woman Rebel. Ed. by Margaret Sanger & Alex Baskin. LC 75-3728. 1976. 31.95 (ISBN 0-914924-02-8). Archives Soc Hist.
Woman Run Mad. John L'Heureux. 1988. 17.95 (ISBN 0-670-81752-X). Viking.
Woman Said Yes: Encounters with Life & Death. Jessamyn West. 192p. 1986. pap. 6.95 (ISBN 0-15-698290-0, Harv). HarBraceJ.
Woman Sealed in the Tower: A Psychological Approach to Feminine Spirituality. Betsy Caprio. 1983. pap. 5.95 (ISBN 0-8091-2486-6). Paulist Pr.
Woman, Sex & Religion. Arthur F. Ide. 1984. lib. bdg. cancelled (ISBN 0-86663-067-8); pap. text ed. cancelled (ISBN 0-86663-068-6). Ide Hse.
Woman Shall Conquer. rev. ed. Don Sharkey. 258p. 1976. pap. 4.95 (ISBN 0-913382-01-9, 101-1). Prow Bks-Franciscan.
Woman Sitting at the Machine, Thinking: Poems. Karen Brodine. LC 87-83121. 100p. (Orig.). 1988. pap. write for info. (ISBN 0-932323-01-4). Freedom Soc.
Woman Song II. Ed. by Stephanie Schmidts et al. (Illus.). 115p. (Orig.). 1987. text ed. 7.95 (ISBN 0-934821-02-X). NRVC.
Woman Songs. Ruth de Menezes. (Illus.). 94p. 1982. pap. 6.00 (ISBN 0-941358-02-X). Claremont CA.
Woman Space: Future & Fantasy Stories by Women. Ed. by Claudia M. Lamperti. LC 80-83471. 96p. (Orig.). 1981. pap. 4.95 (ISBN 0-934678-04-9). New Victoria Pubs.
Woman Speaks: The Lectures, Seminars, & Interviews of Anais Nin. Ed. by Evelyn Hinz. LC 75-15111. 270p. 1975. 13.95x (ISBN 0-8040-0693-8, Pub by Swallow); pap. 8.95x (ISBN 0-8040-0694-6, Pub by Swallow). Ohio U Pr.
Woman Suffrage, Arguments & Results. National American Woman Suffrage Association. LC 19-13099. Repr. of 1910 ed. 42.00 (ISBN 0-527-66300-X). Kraus Repr.
Woman Suffrage in Mexico. Ward M. Morton. LC 62-20735. (Illus.). 1962. 10.00x (ISBN 0-8130-0165-X). U Presses Fla.
Woman Suffrage Movement in Canada: The Start of Liberation. Catherine L. Cleverdon. LC 73-82587. (Social History of Canada Ser.). 1974. pap. 9.95c (ISBN 0-8020-6218-0). U of Toronto Pr.
Woman Suffrage Movement in Tennessee. A. Elizabeth Taylor. 1978. Repr. of 1957 ed. lib. bdg. 16.00x (ISBN 0-374-97850-6, Octagon). Hippocrene Bks.
Woman: Survivor in the Church. Joan Ohanneson. (Orig.). 1980. pap. 6.95 (ISBN 0-86683-607-1, HarpR). Har-Row.
Woman Take Two. Telcine Turner. 1987. 7.95 (ISBN 0-533-06426-0). Vantage.
Woman Talk. Sandra Royster. 1974. pap. 1.50 (ISBN 0-88378-033-X). Third World.
Woman Tenderfoot. Grace G. Seton-Thompson. (Illus.). 362p. 1987. pap. 9.95 (ISBN 0-941130-47-9). N Lyons Bks.
Woman That Never Evolved. Sarah B. Hrdy. 276p. 1983. pap. 6.95 (ISBN 0-674-95541-2); 20.00 (ISBN 0-674-95540-4). Harvard U Pr.
Woman: The Eternal Primitive. W. J. Fielding. 59.95 (ISBN 0-8490-1317-8). Gordon Pr.
Woman the Gatherer. Ed. by Frances Dahlberg. LC 80-25262. 1983. text ed. 30.00x (ISBN 0-300-02572-6); pap. 10.95x (ISBN 0-300-02989-6, Y-476). Yale U Pr.
Woman, the Second Coming. Rose B. Green. 5.95 (ISBN 0-8453-2173-0, Cornwall Bks). Assoc Univ Prs.
Woman Thing. Harriet Daimler. LC 83-84628. 192p. 1984. pap. 3.50 (ISBN 0-394-62459-9, B491, BC). Grove.
Woman to Deliver Her People: Joanna Southcott & English Millenarianism in an Era of Revolution. James K. Hopkins. 326p. 1982. text ed. 30.00x (ISBN 0-292-79017-1). U of Tex Pr.
Woman to Mother: A Transformation. Vangie Bergum. 160p. 1988. 34.95 (ISBN 0-89789-183-X); pap. 12.95 (ISBN 0-89789-182-1). Bergin & Garvey.
Woman to Woman. Marguerite Duras & Xaviere Gauthier. Tr. by Katharine A. Jensen from Fr. LC 86-30796. (European Women Writers Ser.). xii, 200p. 1987. 16.95 (ISBN 0-8032-1672-6). U of Nebr Pr.
Woman to Woman: Conversations with Mary. Jeannette Cooper. LC 88-71021. 104p. (Orig.). 1988. pap. 4.95 (ISBN 0-87793-383-9). Ave Maria.
Woman to Woman: European Feminists. Bonnie C. Bluh. LC 74-20184. 1974. pap. 6.00 (ISBN 0-9603234-0-6). Starogubski.
Woman to Woman: Female Friendship in Victorian Fiction. Tess Cosslett. LC 88-8856. 1988. text ed. 45.00 (ISBN 0-391-03591-6, Co-Pub. by Harvester Pr UK). Humanities.
Woman to Woman: From Sabotage to Support. Judith Briles. 1987. 18.95 (ISBN 0-317-55897-8). New Horizon NJ.
Woman to Woman: Selected Talks from the BYU Women's Conferences. LC 86-2048. 223p. 1986. 9.95 (ISBN 0-87579-035-6). Deseret Bk.
Woman to Women. Ye Hudit. (Illus.). 128p. 1982. 8.95 (ISBN 0-89962-241-0). Todd & Honeywell.
Woman Trap. Enki Bilal. Ed. by Bernd Metz. Tr. by Tom Leighton from Fr. (Illus.). 64p. (Orig.). 1988. pap. 12.95 (ISBN 0-87416-050-2). Catalan Communs.
Woman Triumphant: Feminism in French Literature 1610-1652. Ian MacLean. (Illus.). 1977. 49.00x (ISBN 0-19-815741-X). Oxford U Pr.
Woman under Monasticism. Lina Eckenstein. 59.95 (ISBN 0-8490-1318-6). Gordon Pr.
Woman under Monasticism: Chapters on Saint-Lore & Convent Life Between A. D. 500 & A. D. 1500. Lina Eckenstein. LC 63-11028. 1963. Repr. of 1896 ed. 10.00x (ISBN 0-8462-0363-4). Russell.
Woman under the English Law: From the Landing of the Saxons to the Present Time. Arthur R. Cleveland. (Illus.). xvi, 315p. 1987. Repr. of 1896 ed. lib. bdg. 32.50x (ISBN 0-8377-2012-5). Rothman.
Woman under the Surface: Poems & Prose Poems. Alicia Ostriker. LC 81-47938. (Princeton Series of Contemporary Poets). 77p. 1982. 16.00x (ISBN 0-691-06512-8); pap. 10.95 (ISBN 0-691-01390-X). Princeton U Pr.
Woman Unliberated: Difficulties & Limitations in Changing Self. C. M. Hall. LC 78-21874. 170p. 1979. pap. 24.25 (ISBN 0-89116-097-3). Hemisphere Pub.
Woman Vanishes. Caroline Crane. (Nightingale Ser.). 288p. 1988. pap. 15.95 (ISBN 0-8161-4478-8). G K Hall.
Woman Ventures. facsimile ed. David G. Phillips. LC 78-104543. (Illus.). 337p. Repr. of 1902 ed. lib. bdg. 27.50 (ISBN 0-8398-1569-7). Irvington.
Woman Ventures. David G. Phillips. (American Author Ser.). 1981. Repr. lib. bdg. 29.00 (ISBN 0-686-71947-6). Scholarly.
Woman Ventures. David G. Phillips. (Illus.). 337p. 1986. pap. text ed. 6.95x (ISBN 0-8290-1958-8). Irvington.
Woman Versus Woman: The Extra Marital Affair. Shirley Eskapa. 212p. 1984. 13.95 (ISBN 0-531-09845-1). Watts.
Woman Wanted. Joanna M. Glass. 256p. 1985. 13.95 (ISBN 0-312-88644-6). St Martin.
Woman Warrior. Maxine H. Kingston. 1976. 15.95 (ISBN 0-394-40067-4). Knopf.
Woman Warrior: Memoirs of a Girlhood Among Ghosts. Maxine H. Kingston. LC 77-3246. 1977. pap. 3.95 (ISBN 0-394-72392-9, Vin). Random.
Woman Who Changed & Other Stories. Pearl S. Buck. 14.95 (ISBN 0-8488-0436-8). Amereon Ltd.
Woman Who Could Not Read, & Other Tales. Mikhail Zoshchenko. Tr. by E. Fen from Rus. LC 72-90319. (Soviet Literature in English Translation Ser.). 153p. 1973. Repr. of 1940 ed. 15.00 (ISBN 0-88355-028-8). Hyperion Conn.
Woman Who Couldn't Be Stopped. S. Delphine Wedmore. LC 86-61680. (Illus.). 515p. (Orig.). 1986. pap. 10.50 (ISBN 0-9616887-0-X). Sisters Christ Charity.
Woman Who Disappeared see Heinemann Guided Readers.
Woman Who Drinks Too Much. Jean Kirkpatrick. 9p. 1976. pap. 1.50 (ISBN 0-318-19528-3). WFS.
Woman Who Escaped from Shame. Toby Olson. LC 85-18389. 352p. 1986. 16.45 (ISBN 0-394-54715-2). Random.
Woman Who Escaped from Shame. Toby Olson. 320p. 1987. pap. 7.95 (ISBN 0-02-023231-4, Collier). Macmillan.
Woman Who Had Everything. Davidyne S. Mayleas. 1987. pap. 4.50 (ISBN 0-380-75327-8). Avon.
Woman Who Had Imagination & Other Stories. facs. ed. Herbert E. Bates. LC 77-103239. (Short Story Index Reprint Ser.). 1934. 18.00 (ISBN 0-8369-3276-5). Ayer Co Pubs.
Woman Who Knew Too Much. Dana Clarins. 224p. 1986. pap. 3.95 (ISBN 0-553-26100-2). Bantam.
Woman Who Knocked out Sugar Ray. Ralph Dranow. Ed. by Sandy Darlington & Julie Reynolds. LC 81-70081. (Illus.). 192p. (Orig.). 1982. pap. 4.95 (ISBN 0-9604152-5-4). Arrowhead Pr.
Woman Who Laughed. Mildred Cable & Francesca French. 1984. pap. 3.95 (ISBN 0-7208-0568-6). OMF Bks.
Woman Who Lived in a Prologue. Nina Schneider. 384p. 1985. pap. 3.95 (ISBN 0-380-59881-7, 59881-7, Bard). Avon.
Woman Who Lost Her Names: Selected Writings by American Jewish Women. Ed. by Julia W. Mazow. LC 79-2986. 240p. 1981. pap. text ed. 10.00 (ISBN 0-06-250567-X, CN 4017, HarpR). Har-Row.
Woman Who Loved. Daughters of St. Paul. (Encounter Ser.). (gr. 3-7). 3.00 (ISBN 0-8198-0240-9); pap. 2.00 (ISBN 0-8198-4708-9). Dghtrs St Paul.
Woman Who Loved Reindeer. Meredith A. Pierce. 242p. (gr. 5 up). 1985. 14.95 (ISBN 0-316-70742-2, 707422, Joy St Bks). Little.
Woman Who Murdered Black Satin: The Bermondsey Horror. Albert Borowitz. LC 80-39756. (Illus.). 347p. 1981. 21.50 (ISBN 0-8142-0320-5). Ohio St U Pr.
Woman Who Owned the Shadows. Paula G. Allen. LC 83-50233. 217p. (Orig.). 1983. pap. 8.95 (ISBN 0-933216-07-6). Spinsters Aunt Lute.
Woman Who Rides Like a Man. Tamora Pierce. LC 85-20054. 288p. (gr. 7-9). 1986. 14.95 (ISBN 0-689-31117-6, Atheneum Childrens Bks). Macmillan.
Woman Who Slept with Men to Take the War Out of Them. Deena Metzger. LC 81-17750. 220p. 1983. pap. 7.95 (ISBN 0-914728-47-4, PS3563.E864W6). Wingbow Pr.
Woman Who Stole Everything & Other Stories. Arnold Bennett. LC 74-17057. (Collected Works of Arnold Bennett: Vol. 89). 1976. Repr. of 1927 ed. 28.00 (ISBN 0-518-19170-2). Ayer Co Pubs.
Woman Who Toils. John Van Vorst & Marie Van Vorst. 163p. 1974. Repr. of 1903 ed. 4.00 (ISBN 0-89215-000-9). U Cal LA Indus Rel.
Woman Who Waits. facsimile ed. Frances R. Donovan. LC 74-3941. (Women in America Ser.: From Colonial Times to the 20th Century). 228p. 1974. Repr. of 1920 ed. 18.00x (ISBN 0-405-06089-0). Ayer Co Pubs.
Woman Who Was Changed & Other Stories. Pearl S. Buck. LC 78-69522. 1979. o.s.i 11.45i (ISBN 0-690-01789-8). T Y Crowell.
Woman Who Was God. Francis King. 1988. 17.95 (ISBN 1-55584-248-8). Weidenfeld.
Woman Who Was Not All There. Paula Sharp. 1988. 16.95 (ISBN 0-06-015989-8). Har-Row.
Woman Who Works, the Parent Who Cares: A Revolutionary Program for Raising Your Child. Sirgay Sanger & John Kelly. 1987. 17.95 (ISBN 0-316-77049-3). Little.
Woman Who Works, the Parent Who Cares: A Revolutionary Program for Raising Your Child. Sirgay Sanger & John Kelly. LC 87-46170. 288p. 1988. pap. 7.95 (ISBN 0-06-097159-2, PL-7159, PL). Har-Row.
Woman, Why Do You Weep? Circumcision & Its Consequences. Asma El Dareer. (Illus.). 144p. 1983. 18.75x (ISBN 0-86232-098-4, Pub. by Zed Pr England); pap. 7.50x (ISBN 0-86232-099-2). Humanities.
Woman, Wife & Mother. Pat Harrison. 160p. 1984. pap. 3.50 (ISBN 0-89274-315-8). Harrison Hse.
Woman with a Purpose: The Diaries of Elizabeth Smith 1872-1884. Ed. by Veronica Strong-Boag. (Social History of Canada Ser.). 320p. 1980. 27.50x (ISBN 0-8020-2360-6); pap. 10.00 (ISBN 0-8020-6397-7). U of Toronto Pr.
Woman with the Eggs. Jon Erickson. LC 87-42583. (Andersen Fairy Tales Ser.). (Illus.). 32p. (gr. 2-4). 1987. PLB 9.95 (ISBN 1-55532-319-7). Stevens Inc.
Woman Without a Name. Romulus Linney. 57p. 1986. pap. 3.50 (ISBN 0-317-52991-9). Dramatists Play.
Woman Without Eden (Mujer Sin Eden) Carmen Conde. Tr. by Jose R. De Armas & Alexis Levitin. LC 85-80641. (Coleccion Alacran Azul Ser.). 175p. (Orig., Span.). 1986. pap. 12.00 (ISBN 0-89729-375-4). Ediciones.
Woman, Woman. Angela De Hoyos. LC 85-73350. 80p. (Orig.). 1986. pap. 7.00 (ISBN 0-934770-51-4). Arte Publico.
Woman, Work & Property in North-West India. Ursula Sharma. 1980. 25.00x (ISBN 0-422-77120-1, NO.2018, Pub. by Tavistock); pap. 13.95 (ISBN 0-422-78640-3, NO. 3926). Routledge Chapman & Hall.
Woman-Work: Women & the Party in Revolutionary China. Delia Davin. (Illus.). 1979. pap. 5.95 (ISBN 0-19-285080-6). Oxford U Pr.
Woman Wrapped in Silence. John W. Lynch. 288p. 1976. pap. 5.95 (ISBN 0-8091-1905-6). Paulist Pr.
Woman Writer: Occasions & Opportunities. Joyce Carol Oates. 320p. 1988. 18.95 (ISBN 0-525-24652-5, Pub. by W Abrahams Bk). Dutton.
Womancare: A Gynecological Guide to Your Body. Lynda Madaras & Jane Patterson. 960p. 1984. pap. 12.95 (ISBN 0-380-87643-4). Avon.
Womanchange! Louise McCants. 160p. 1986. text ed. 12.50 (ISBN 0-682-40293-1). Exposition-Phoenix.
Womanclature: The Queen Bee Syndrome. Normjean Macleod. LC 83-73517. (Herland Ser.: No. 6). (Illus.). 52p. pap. 5.00 (ISBN 0-934996-26-1). American Studies Pr.
Womanguides: Readings Toward a Feminist Theology. Rosemary R. Ruether. LC 84-14508. 286p. 1986. 24.95 (ISBN 0-8070-1202-5); pap. 10.95 (ISBN 0-8070-1203-3, BP 726). Beacon Pr.
Womanhood & Other Misfortunes: Bi-Lingual Edition. Lourdes Espinola. 1985. pap. 7.00 (ISBN 0-317-60615-8). Latitudes Pr.
Womanhood in Radical Protestantism: 1525-1675. Joyce L. Irwin. LC 79-66370. (Studies in Women & Religion: Vol. 1). xxx, 296p. 1979. lib. bdg. 49.95x (ISBN 0-88946-547-9). E Mellen.
Womanhood Media: Current Resources About Women. Helen Wheeler. LC 72-7396. 355p. 1972. 22.50 (ISBN 0-8108-0549-9). Scarecrow.
Womanhood Media Supplement: Additional Current Resources About Women. Helen Wheeler. LC 72-7396. 489p. 1975. 27.50 (ISBN 0-8108-0858-7). Scarecrow.
Womanhood: The Feminine in Ancient Hellenism, Gnosticism, Christianity, & Islam. Raoul Mortley. 119p. 1983. (Pub. by Aris & Phillips UK); pap. text ed. 15.00x (ISBN 0-85668-913-0). Humanities.
Womaning: Overcoming Male Dominance of Executive Row. Dean B. Peskin. Ed. by Sylvia Ashton. LC 80-13060. 1981. 18.95 (ISBN 0-87949-165-5). Ashley Bks.
Womankind. June Stephenson. 355p. (Orig.). 1988. pap. 14.00 (ISBN 0-941138-05-4). Diemer-Smith.
Womankind: Beyond the Stereotypes. 2nd ed. Nancy Reeves. LC 81-71348. 199p. 1982. lib. bdg. 29.95x (ISBN 0-202-30299-7); pap. text ed. 14.95x (ISBN 0-202-30300-4). Aldine de Gruyter.
Womankind in Western Europe. Thomas Wright. LC 87-23497. 1987. 60.00x (ISBN 0-8201-1425-1). Schol Facsimiles.
Womankind in Western Europe: From the Earliest Times to the 17th Century. Thomas Wright. LC 77-81655. 1977. Repr. of 1869 ed. lib. bdg. 40.00 (ISBN 0-89341-175-2). Longwood Pub Group.
Womanly Art of Breastfeeding. 4th, rev. ed. La Leche League International Staff. Ed. by Judy Torgus. LC 87-82123. (Illus.). 422p. 1987. pap. 8.95 (ISBN 0-912500-34-4). La Leche.
Womanly Art of Breastfeeding. 4th, rev. ed. La Leche League International Staff. LC 87-15355. (Illus.). 384p. 1988. pap. 8.95 (ISBN 0-452-26000-0, Plume). NAL.
Womanly Art of Breastfeeding. La Leche League International Staff. LC 83-61753. (Illus.). 384p. 1983. pap. 8.95 (ISBN 0-452-25973-8, Plume). NAL.
Womanly Art of Breastfeeding. La Leche League International Staff. LC 83-13414. 384p. 1983. 12.95 (ISBN 0-453-00453-9). NAL.
Womanpower: A Manual for Workshops in Personal Effectiveness. Laura G. Manis. LC 76-54156. 1977. pap. text ed. 6.75x (ISBN 0-910328-10-2). Carroll Pr.
Womanpower & Health Care. Marlene Grissum & Carol Spengler. LC 75-41571. 1976. pap. 14.00 (ISBN 0-316-32895-2). Little.
Womanpower: The Arab Debate on Women at Work. Nadia Hijab. (Illus.). 200p. 1988. 42.50 (ISBN 0-521-26443-X); pap. 11.95 (ISBN 0-521-26992-X). Cambridge U Pr.
Womanprayer, Spiritjourney: 56 Meditations on Scripture. Judy Esway. LC 86-51538. 80p. (Orig.). 1987. pap. 4.95 (ISBN 0-89622-326-4). Twenty-Third.
WomanPrayer, WomanSong: Resources for Ritual. Miriam T. Winter. (Illus.). 264p. 1987. pap. 14.95 (ISBN 0-940989-00-X). Meyer Stone Bks.
Womanpriest: A Personal Odyssey. rev. ed. Alla R. Bozarth. Ed. by Lura J. Geiger. (Illus.). 217p. 1988. pap. 11.95 (ISBN 0-931055-51-2). LuraMedia.
Womanpriest: A Personal Odyssey. Alla Bozarth-Campbell. 229p. 1978. 9.95 (ISBN 0-8091-0243-9). Wisdom House.
Womanrise (Anthology) Rashidah Ismaili et al. Ed. by Louis R. Rivera. (Illus.). 128p. (Orig.). 1978. pap. 4.25 (ISBN 0-917886-05-4). Shamal Bks.
Woman's Bible, 2 vols. in 1. Elizabeth C. Stanton. LC 72-2626. (American Women Ser: Images & Realities). 380p. 1972. Repr. of 1895 ed. 25.50 (ISBN 0-405-04481-X). Ayer Co Pubs.
Woman's Bible. Elizabeth C. Stanton. 1974. Repr. 12.95 (ISBN 0-9603042-1-5). Coalition Women-Relig.
Woman's Bible Study. Ruth Spradley. (Illus.). 80p. 1988. pap. 4.95 (ISBN 0-87403-480-9). Standard Pub.
Woman's Body: An Owner's Manual. Diagram Group. 1978. pap. 4.95 (ISBN 0-553-25486-3). Bantam.

Woman's Revenge: The Chronology of Dispossession in Maupassant's Fiction. Mary E. Donaldson. LC 86-80314. (French Forum Monographs: No. 64). 156p. 1986. pap. 12.95x (ISBN 0-917058-65-8). French Forum.
Woman's Right, 1867 - Woman's Wrongs, a Counter-Irritant, 1868. John Todd & Mary A. Dodge. LC 72-2628. (American Women Ser.: Images & Realities). 246p. 1972. 16.00 (ISBN 0-405-04455-0). Ayer Co Pubs.
Woman's Ritual Headwear (Romania) Cella Neamtu. Tr. by Eugenia Popescu-Judetz from Fr. (Illus.). 110p. (Orig.). 1981. pap. 10.00 (ISBN 0-936922-03-6). Tamburitza.
Woman's Role in Economic Development. Ester Boserup. 290p. 1986. text ed. 41.95 (ISBN 0-566-05139-7, Pub. by Gower Pub England). Gower Pub Co.
Woman's Role in the Church. John M. Jicks & Bruce L. Morton. pap. 2.95 (ISBN 0-89315-362-1). Lambert Bk.
Woman's Self-Defense. Michael G. Pickering. LC 78-22054. (Illus.). 144p. 1979. pap. 5.95 (ISBN 0-89037-166-0). Anderson World.
Woman's Selling Game: How to Sell Yourself & Anything Else. Carole Hyatt. LC 79-11166. 252p. 1979. 8.95 (ISBN 0-87131-289-1). M Evans.
Woman's Selling Game: How to Sell Yourself & Anything Else. Carole Hyatt. 1988. pap. 9.95 (ISBN 0-446-38244-2). Warner Bks.
Woman's Share in Primitive Culture. Otis T. Mason. 75.00 (ISBN 0-87968-460-7). Gordon Pr.
Woman's Share in Social Culture. Anna G. Spencer. LC 72-2623. (American Women Ser.: Images & Realities). 342p. 1972. Repr. of 1913 ed. 23.50 (ISBN 0-405-04479-8). Ayer Co Pubs.
Woman's Softball Book. Connie P. Johnson & Margie Wright. (Illus.). 208p. 1984. pap. 10.95 (ISBN 0-88011-209-3, PJOH0209). Leisure Pr.
Woman's Song. Joy M. Davis. LC 83-70376. (Orig.). 1984. pap. 5.95 (ISBN 0-8054-5243-5). Broadman.
Woman's Stretching Book. Susan L. Peterson. LC 82-83927. (Illus.). 112p. (Orig.). 1983. pap. 8.95 (ISBN 0-88011-095-3, PPET0095). Leisure Pr.
Woman's Tale: A Journal of Inner Exploration. Ronda Chervin & Mary Neill. 160p. (Orig.). 1980. pap. 7.95 (ISBN 0-8164-2016-5, HarpR). Har-Row.
Woman's Touch. Isabelle Anscombe. (Nonfiction Ser.). 216p. 1986. pap. 12.95 (ISBN 0-14-008100-3). Penguin.
Woman's Touch: Women in Design from 1860 to the Present Day. Isabelle Anscombe. (Illus.). 210p. 1984. 20.00 (ISBN 0-670-77825-7, Elizabeth Sifton Bks). Viking.
Woman's Transformations: A Psychological Theology. Jenny Hammett. LC 82-14287. (Symposium Ser.: Vol. 8). 112p. 1982. lib. bdg. 19.95x (ISBN 0-88946-918-0). E Mellen.
Woman's "True" Profession: Voices from the History of Teaching. Ed. by Nancy Hoffman. (Women's Lives - Women's Work Ser.). (Illus.). 352p. (Orig.). (gr. 11 up). 1981. 9.95 (ISBN 0-912670-93-2); teaching guide, 64p. o.p. 5.00 (ISBN 0-912670-82-7). Feminist Pr.
Woman's Voice in Latin American Literature. Naomi Lindstrom. LC 86-51313. 200p. (Orig.). 1989. 26.00 (ISBN 0-89410-295-8); pap. 16.00 (ISBN 0-89410-296-6). Three Continents.
Woman's Voices in American Poetry: "The Beauty of Inflections or the Beauty of Innuendoes. Ed. by Susan Van Dyne. 54p. 1981. pap. 3.50 (ISBN 0-87391-024-9). Smith Coll.
Woman's Walden. Ruthe T. Spinnanger. LC 84-71120. 176p. 1985. pap. 4.95 (ISBN 0-88270-554-7). Bridge Pub.
Woman's Way: The Memoirs of Flora Solomon. Flora Solomon & Barry Litvinoff. 240p. 1984. 16.95 (ISBN 0-671-46002-1). S&S.
Woman's Who's Who of America: A Biographical Dictionary of Contemporary Women of the United States & Canada, 1914-1915. LC 74-6280. 946p. 1976. Repr. of 1914 ed. 95.00x (ISBN 0-8103-4018-6). Gale.
Woman's Work & Woman's Culture. Josephine Butler. 69.95 (ISBN 0-8490-1319-4). Gordon Pr.
Woman's Work for Jesus. Annie T. Wittenmyer. Ed. by Carolyn D. Gifford & Donald Dayton. (Women in American Protestant Religion 1800-1930 Ser.). 240p. 1987. lib. bdg. 35.00 (ISBN 0-8240-0685-2). Garland Pub.
Woman's Work in America. Ed. by Annie N. Meyer. LC 72-2615. (American Women Ser: Images & Realities). 462p. 1972. Repr. of 1891 ed. 24.50 (ISBN 0-405-04469-0). Ayer Co Pubs.
Woman's Work in Municipalities. Mary R. Beard. LC 72-2588. (American Women Ser). Repr. of 1915 ed. 20.00 (ISBN 0-405-04446-1). Ayer Co Pubs.
Woman's Work in Music. Arthur Elson. LC 76-22330. (Illus.). 1976. Repr. of 1904 ed. lib. bdg. 30.00 (ISBN 0-89341-013-6). Longwood Pub Group.
Woman's Work in the Church. John M. Ludlow. LC 75-33300. 1976. Repr. of 1866 ed. 24.95 (ISBN 0-89201-007-X). Zenger Pub.
Woman's Work: The Housewife, Past & Present. Ann Oakley. 1976. pap. 3.95 (ISBN 0-394-71960-3, Vin). Random.
Woman's Workshop on David & His Psalms. Carolyn Nystrom. (Woman's Workshop Ser.). 144p. 1982. pap. 2.95 (ISBN 0-310-41931-X, 11276P). Zondervan.
Woman's Workshop on Faith. Martha Hook. (A Woman's Workshop Ser.). 1977. leaders 3.95 (ISBN 0-310-26231-3, 11681P); students 4.50 (ISBN 0-310-26241-0, 11682P). Zondervan.
Woman's Workshop on Forgiveness. Kirkie Morrissey. (Woman's Workshop Ser.). 160p. 1982. pap. 4.95 (ISBN 0-310-44931-6, 16245P). Zondervan.
Woman's Workshop on James. Carolyn Nystrom & Margaret Fromer. (Woman's Workshop Ser.). 144p. (Orig.). 1980. pap. 2.95 (ISBN 0-310-41901-8, 11273P). Zondervan.
Woman's Workshop on Mastering Motherhood. Barbara Bush. (Women's Workshop Ser.). 144p. 1981. pap. 2.95 (ISBN 0-310-43031-3, 12013P). Zondervan.
Woman's Workshop on Philippians. Margaret Fromer & Paul Fromer. (Woman's Workshop Ser.). 128p. 1982. pap. 4.50 (ISBN 0-310-44771-2, 11312P). Zondervan.
Womans Workshop on Proverbs. Diane Bloem. 1978. leader's manual 5.95 (ISBN 0-310-21371-1, 10684P); student manual 4.50 (ISBN 0-310-21361-4, 10683P). Zondervan.
Woman's Workshop on Romans-Leader's Manual. Carolyn Nystrom. 112p. (Orig.). 1981. pap. 3.95 (ISBN 0-310-41911-5, 11274P). Zondervan.
Woman's Workshop on Romans-Student's Manual. Carolyn Nystrom. 144p. (Orig.). 1981. pap. 2.95 (ISBN 0-310-41921-2, 11275P). Zondervan.
Woman's Workshop on the Beautitudes. Diane Bloem. (Orig.). 1981. Student's Manual, 96 Pages. pap. 4.50 (ISBN 0-310-42651-0, 11217P). Zondervan.
Woman's Workshop on the Sermon on the Mount. Diane Bloem. 1987. pap. 4.50 (ISBN 0-310-42701-0, 10739P). Zondervan.
Woman's Worth: Sexual Economics & the World of Women. Lisa Leghorn & Katherine Parker. 352p. 1981. 22.95x (ISBN 0-7100-0836-8); pap. 10.50 (ISBN 0-7100-0855-4). Routledge Chapman & Hall.
Womansafe. E. Stephanie. 28p. (Orig.). 1985. pap. 1.50 (ISBN 0-89486-313-4). Hazelden.
Womanscripts: Writing about Women by Women. Gayle A. Gray. (Orig.). 1987. pap. 7.95 (ISBN 0-935941-04-5). One-Horse Pr.
Womanspirit: A Guide to Woman's Wisdom. Hallie Iglehart. LC 83-47724. (Illus.). 192p. (Orig.). 1983. pap. 7.95 (ISBN 0-06-064089-8, CN 4076, HarpR). Har-Row.
Womanspirit Rising: A Feminist Reader in Religion. Carol P. Christ & Judith Plaskow. LC 78-3363. (Orig.). 1979. pap. 9.95 (ISBN 0-06-061385-8, RD 275, HarpR). Har-Row.
Womansword: What Japanese Words Say about Women. Kittredge Cherry. LC 86-45726. (Illus.). 144p. 1987. pap. 13.95 (ISBN 0-87011-794-7). Kodansha.
Womanwrit: The Poems & Photographs of Sandra Lake Miller. Sandra L. Miller. LC 82-90847. (Illus.). 64p. (Orig.). 1982. pap. 5.00 (ISBN 0-9609448-0-X). S L Miller.
Womb of Space: The Cross-Cultural Imagination. Wilson Harris. LC 83-1639. (Contributions in Afro-American & African Studies: No. 73). xx, 151p. 1983. lib. bdg. 35.00 (ISBN 0-313-23774-3, HWO/). Greenwood.
Wombalong. Judith Pugh. (Illus.). 32p. (gr. 2-5). 1986. 9.95 (ISBN 0-915391-20-1, Pub. by Mad Hatter Bks); pap. 6.95 (ISBN 0-915391-19-8, Pub. by Mad Hatter Bks). Slawson Comm.
Wombat Duet. Ed. by Ray G. Cook. (Illus.). 22p. 1984. pap. 10.00 (ISBN 0-9602002-6-6). Ray Cook.
Wombat Stew. Marcia K. Vaughan. LC 85-63492. (Illus.). 32p. (ps-3). 1986. 8.75 (ISBN 0-382-09211-2). Silver.
Women. Charles Bukowski. LC 78-21998. 296p. 1982. 20.00 (ISBN 0-87685-391-2); pap. 10.00 (ISBN 0-87685-390-4). Black Sparrow.
Women. Joan Reiter. LC 78-1346. (Old West Ser.). (Illus.). 1978. 19.94 (ISBN 0-8094-1514-3, Pub. by Time-Life). Silver.
Women. Joan Reiter & Time-Life Books Editors. (Old West Ser.). (Illus.). 1978. 14.95 (ISBN 0-8094-1512-7). Time-Life.
Women. facsimile ed. Booth Tarkington. LC 74-178464. (Short Story Index Reprint Ser.). Repr. of 1925 ed. 20.00 (ISBN 0-8369-4064-4). Ayer Co Pubs.
Women, Vol. 1 (incl. 1976-1978 Supplements) Ed. by Eleanor C. Goldstein. (Social Issues Resources Ser.). 1979. 75.00 (ISBN 0-89777-012-9). Soc Issues.
Women, Vol. 2 (incl. 1979-1983 Supplements) Ed. by Eleanor C. Goldstein. (Social Issues Resources Ser.). 1984. 75.00 (ISBN 0-89777-044-7). Soc Issues.
Women see Jewish Library.
Women - From Witch-hunt to Politics. Birgitta Leander. 251p. 1986. pap. 14.25 (ISBN 92-3-102333-0, U1477 6011, UNESCO). UNIPUB.
Women: A Bibliography of Bibliographies. Patricia K. Ballou. 1980. lib. bdg. 22.00 (ISBN 0-8161-8292-2, Hall Reference). G K Hall.
Women: A Bibliography of Bibliographies. 2nd ed. Patricia K. Ballou. (Reference Bks - Women's Studies). 349p. 1986. lib. bdg. 30.00x (ISBN 0-8161-8729-0). G K Hall.
Women: A Feminist Perspective. 3rd ed. Jo Freeman. (Orig.). 1984. pap. text ed. 19.95 (ISBN 0-87484-568-8). Mayfield Pub.
Women: A PDI Reference Work, Vol. 1. Ed. by Florence L. Denmark et al. LC 75-5161. 626p. 1977. 39.95x (ISBN 0-88437-001-1). Psych Dimensions.
Women: A Pictorial Archive from Nineteenth-Century Sources. Jim Harter. 14.25 (ISBN 0-8446-5770-0). Peter Smith.
Women: A Pictorial Archive from Nineteeth Century Sources. Ed. by Jim Harter. (Pictorial Archive Ser.). 1978. pap. 5.95 (ISBN 0-486-23703-6). Dover.
Women: A World Report. Compiled by New Internationalist Publication Staff. LC 85-13573. (Illus.). 376p. 1986. 29.95 (ISBN 0-19-520490-5). Oxford U Pr.
Women, a World Report: A New Internationalist Book. 388p. 1987. pap. 8.95 (ISBN 0-19-505064-9). Oxford U Pr.
Women: A Worldwide View of Their Management Development Needs. Martha G. Burrow. LC 76-10796. pap. 20.00 (ISBN 0-317-09919-1, 2051525). Bks Demand UMI.
Women Activists: Challenging the Abuse of Power. Anne W. Garland. 150p. 1988. 29.95 (ISBN 0-935312-79-X); pap. 9.95 (ISBN 0-935312-80-3). Feminist Pr.
Women Administrators in Education: A Review of Research, 1960-1975. National Association of Women Deans, Administrators & Counselors. 1979. pap. 5.00 (ISBN 0-686-23291-7). Natl Assn Women.
Women Administrators in Higher Education: Their Geographic Mobility. Vicki M. Curby. 1980. 5.00 (ISBN 0-317-01239-8); members 4.00 (ISBN 0-317-01240-1). Natl Assn Women.
Women Adrift: Independent Wage Earners in Chicago, 1880-1930. Joanne J. Meyerowitz. (Women in Culture & Society Ser.). (Illus.). xxiv, 224p. 1988. 29.95x (ISBN 0-226-52197-4). U of Chicago Pr.
Women Afield. Lucille H. McConnaughey. 1987. 12.95 (ISBN 0-533-07168-2). Vantage.
Women After Treatment: A Study of Former Mental Patients & Their Normal Neighbors. Shirley S. Angrist et al. LC 68-20043. 1968. 28.00x (ISBN 0-89197-471-7). Irvington.
Women Against Apartheid: The Fight for Freedom in South Africa, 1920-1975. Nancy Van Vuuren. LC 78-62222. 1979. perfect bdg. 11.95 (ISBN 0-88247-575-4). R & E Pubs.
Women Against Censorship. Ed. by Varda Burstyn. 210p. 1985. pap. 8.95 (ISBN 0-88894-455-1). Salem Hse Pubs.
Women Against Men. Storm Jameson. (Virago Modern Classics Ser.). 304p. 1985. pap. 6.95 (ISBN 0-14-016121-X). Penguin.
Women Against War. Women's Division of Soka Gakkai Staff. LC 86-45068. 248p. 1986. 17.95 (ISBN 0-87011-777-7). Kodansha.
Women Ahead of Time: Bibliographic Checklists of 115 Female Authors of Science Fiction & Fantasy. Gordon Benson, Jr. 165p. (Orig.). Date not set. pap. 9.95 (ISBN 0-912613-02-5). Galactic Central.
Women Aloft. Valerie Moolman. LC 80-20475. (Epic of Flight Ser.). lib. bdg. 21.27 (ISBN 0-8094-3288-9, Pub. by Time-Life). Silver.
Women Aloft. Valerie Moolman & Time-Life Books Editors. (Epic of Flight Ser.). (Illus.). 176p. 1981. 14.95 (ISBN 0-8094-3287-0). Time-Life.
Women among the Brethren: Stories of Fifteen Mennonite Brethren & Krimmer Mennonite Brethren Women. Katie F. Wiebe. LC 79-54802. 197p. (Orig.). 1979. pap. 6.95 (ISBN 0-935196-00-5). Kindred Pr.
Women Analyze Women: The French, English, & American Scene. Elaine H. Baruch & Lucienne Serrano. 320p. 1988. 27.95 (ISBN 0-8147-1098-0). NYU Pr.
Women & a Changing Civilization. Winifred Holtby. LC 77-16373. 226p. 1977. lib. bdg. 11.95 o. p. (ISBN 0-915864-28-2); pap. 1.00 (ISBN 0-915864-27-4). Academy Chi Pubs.
Women & Aging: An Anthology by Women. Calyx Editorial Collective et al. Ed. by Lisa Dornitrovich & Cheryl McLean. (Illus.). 262p. (Orig.). 1986. pap. 12.00 (ISBN 0-934971-00-5); 24.95 (ISBN 0-934971-07-2). Calyx BKs.
Women & AIDS. Diane Richardson. 160p. 1987. 29.95 (ISBN 0-416-01741-X, A0762); pap. 9.95 (ISBN 0-416-01751-7, A0766). Routledge Chapman & Hall.
Women & Alcohol: A Dangerous Pleasure. Geraldine Youcha. 1986. pap. 7.95 (ISBN 0-517-55978-1). Crown.
Women & Ambition: A Bibliography. Patricia S. Faunce. LC 79-18347. 724p. 1980. lib. bdg. 40.00 (ISBN 0-8108-1242-8). Scarecrow.
Women & American Foreign Policy: Lobbyists, Critics, & Insiders. Ed. by Edward P. Crapol. LC 86-22798. (Contributions in Women's Studies: No. 76). 213p. 1987. lib. bdg. 32.95 (ISBN 0-313-24636-X, CWF/). Greenwood.
Women & American Socialism, 1870-1920. Mari J. Buhle. LC 81-719. (Working Class in American History Ser.). (Illus.). 370p. 1981. 24.95 (ISBN 0-252-00873-1); pap. 10.95 1983 (ISBN 0-252-01045-0). U of Ill Pr.
Women & American Trade Unions. 2nd ed. James J. Kenneally. 256p. 1981. pap. 8.95 (ISBN 0-920792-10-3). Eden Pr.
Women & Analysis: Dialogues on Psychoamalytic Views of Femininity. Ed. by Jean Strouse. (Non-Fiction Ser.). 375p. 1985. pap. 8.95 (ISBN 0-8398-2878-0, Gregg). G K Hall.
Women & Angels. Harold Brodkey. (Author's Workshop Ser.). 157p. 1985. boxed 30.00. JPS Phila.
Women & Anxiety. Helen DeRosis. 1981. pap. 9.95 (ISBN 0-385-29121-3, Delta). Dell.
Women & Appletrees. Moa Martinson. Tr. by Margaret S. Lacy. 224p. 1985. pap. 8.95 (ISBN 0-935312-38-2). Feminist Pr.
Women & Art: A History of Women Painters & Sculpters from the Renaissance to the 20th Century. Elsa H. Fine. (Illus.). 242p. 1978. 38.50 (ISBN 0-8390-0187-8, Allanheld & Schram); pap. 15.95 (ISBN 0-8390-0212-2). Abner Schram Ltd.
Women & Atheism: The Ultimate Liberation. Madalyn M. O'Hair. 23p. 1979. 2.50 (ISBN 0-911826-17-3). Am Atheist.
Women & British Periodicals, 1832-1867: A Bibliography. E. M. Palmegiano. LC 76-24734. (Reference Library of the Humanities Ser.: Vol. 55). 1977. lib. bdg. 25.00 (ISBN 0-8240-9943-5). Garland Pub.
Women & Business Ownership: A Bibliography. Marcia LaSota. 180p. 1987. lib. bdg. 37.50 (ISBN 0-933474-45-8). Media Mktg Group.
Women & Business Ownership: An Annotated Bibliography. 180p. 1986. pap. 9.00 (ISBN 0-318-21376-1, S/N 003-000-00646-8). USGPO.
Women & Cancer. Ed. by Steven D. Stellman. LC 86-26943. (Women & Health Ser.: Vol. 11(3/4)). 384p. 1987. pap. text ed. 17.95 (ISBN 0-918393-31-0). Harrington PK.
Women & Cancer. Ed. by Steven D. Stellman. LC 86-26943. (Women & Health Ser.: Vol. 11, No. 3/4). 384p. (Orig.). 1987. text ed. 39.95 (ISBN 0-86656-613-9). Haworth Pr.
Women & Change in Latin America: New Directions in Sex & Class. Ed. by June Nash & Helen Safa. (Illus.). 384p. 1985. text ed. 39.95 (ISBN 0-89789-069-8); pap. text ed. 16.95 (ISBN 0-89789-070-1). Bergin & Garvey.
Women & Child Development: Some Contemporary Issues. G. Narayana Reddy. 1987. 22.00x (ISBN 0-317-68214-8, Pub. by Chugh Pubns India). South Asia BKs.
Women & Children First. Sally Benson. 1976. Repr. of 1943 ed. lib. bdg. 8.95 (ISBN 0-89190-872-2, Pub. by River City Pr). Amereon Ltd.
Women & Children First: And Other Stories. Francine Prose. LC 87-46051. 224p. 1988. 16.95 (ISBN 0-394-56573-8). Pantheon.
Women & Children in a Bengali Village. Ronald P. Rohner & Manjusri Chaki-Sircar. LC 87-25463. (Illus.). 231p. 1988. 25.00x (ISBN 0-87451-431-2). U Pr of New Eng.
Women & Children Last: The Plight of Poor Women in Affluent America. Ruth Sidel. 243p. 1986. 16.95 (ISBN 0-670-80973-X). Viking.
Women & Children Last: The Plight of Poor Women in Affluent America. Ruth Sidel. 256p. 1987. pap. 6.95 (ISBN 0-14-010013-X). Penguin.
Women & Choice: A New Beginning. Mary R. Joyce. LC 85-81556. 208p. (Orig.). 1986. pap. 7.95 (ISBN 0-9615722-0-5). LifeCom.
Women & Class in Africa. Ed. by Claire Robertson & Iris Berger. 300p. 1986. 55.00 (ISBN 0-8419-0979-2); pap. 19.95 (ISBN 0-8419-1187-8). Holmes & Meier.
Women & Colonization: Anthropological Perspectives. Ed. by Mona Etienne & Eleanor Leacock. (Illus.). 352p. 1980. 34.95x (ISBN 0-03-052586-1); pap. 16.95 (ISBN 0-03-052581-0). Bergin & Garvey.
Women & Colonization: Anthropological Perspectives. Ed. by Mona Etienne & Eleanor Leacock. LC 79-15318. 352p. 1980. Praeger.
Women & Community in Oman. Christine Eickelman. (Illus.). 240p. 1984. 35.00x (ISBN 0-8147-2165-6); pap. 15.00x (ISBN 0-8147-2166-4). NYU Pr.
Women & Consequence. Jane Bown. (Illus.). 112p. 1987. 22.50 (ISBN 0-87663-652-0). Universe.
Women & Counter-Power. Ed. by Yolande Cohen. 244p. 1988. 39.95 (ISBN 0-921689-11-X, Dist. by U of Toronto Pr); pap. 19.95 (ISBN 0-921689-10-1, Dist. by U of Toronto Pr). Black Rose Bks.
Women & Crime. Rita J. Simon. LC 74-25067. 144p. 1978. pap. text ed. 11.50 (ISBN 0-669-01646-2). Heath.
Women & Crime: The Life of the Female Offender. Frances M. Heidensohn. 240p. 1986. 35.00x (ISBN 0-8147-3433-2). NYU Pr.
Women & Crime: The Life of the Female Offender. Frances M. Heidensohn. 240p. (Orig.). 1986. 15.00x (ISBN 0-8147-3434-0). NYU Pr.
Women & Criminality: The Woman as Victim, Offender & Practitioner. Ronald B. Flowers. LC 86-33646. (Contributions in Criminology & Penology Ser.: No. 18). 234p. 1987. lib. bdg. 37.95 (ISBN 0-313-25365-X, FWL/). Greenwood.
Women & Death: Linkages in Western Thought & Literature. Beth A. Bassein. LC 83-8544. (Contributions in Women's Studies: No. 44). xii, 236p. 1984. lib. bdg. 35.00 (ISBN 0-313-23924-X, BWD/). Greenwood.

Women & Party Politics in Peninsular Malaysia. Virginia H. Dancz. (East Asian Social Science Monographs). (Illus.). 292p. 1987. 32.50 (ISBN 0-19-582689-2). Oxford U Pr.

Women & Peace: Theoretical, Historical & Practical Perspectives. Ed. by Ruth R. Pierson et al. LC 87-6778. 249p. 1987. 45.00 (ISBN 0-7099-4068-8, Pub. by Croom Helm UK). Routledge Chapman & Hall.

Women & Philanthropy in Nineteenth-Century England. F. K. Prochaska. (Illus.). 1980. pap. 21.00x (ISBN 0-19-822628-4). Oxford U Pr.

Women & Political Conflict: Portraits of Struggle in Times of Crisis. Ed. by Rosemary Ridd & Helen Callaway. 246p. 1987. 38.00 (ISBN 0-8147-7398-2); pap. 15.00x (ISBN 0-8147-7399-0). NYU Pr.

Women & Politics. Vicky Randall. LC 82-10657. 237p. 1984. pap. 11.95 (ISBN 0-312-88728-0). St Martin.

Women & Politics: Activism, Attitudes & Office-Holding, Vol. 2. Gwen Moore. (Research in Politics & Society Ser.). 1986. 54.50 (ISBN 0-89232-556-9). Jai Pr.

Women & Politics: An International Perspective. 2nd ed. Vicky Randall. xii, 362p. 1988. 32.50x (ISBN 0-226-70391-6); pap. 12.95x (ISBN 0-226-70392-4). U of Chicago Pr.

Women & Politics in the USSR: Consciousness Raising & Soviet Women's Groups. Genia K. Browning. LC 87-9604. 188p. 1987. 29.95 (ISBN 0-312-00953-4). St Martin.

Women & Politics in Western Europe. Ed. by Sylvia Bashevkin. 128p. 1986. 29.50x (ISBN 0-7146-3275-9, F Cass Co). Biblio Dist.

Women & Politics: The Visible Majority. Rev. ed. Sandra Baxter & Marjorie Lansing. (Women & Culture Ser.). 1983. text ed. 22.95 (ISBN 0-472-10043-2); pap. text ed. 12.95 (ISBN 0-472-08043-1). U of Mich Pr.

Women & Population Growth: Choice Beyond Childbearing. Kathleen Newland. LC 77-91827. (Worldwatch Papers). 1977. pap. 4.00 (ISBN 0-916468-15-1). Worldwatch Inst.

Women & Poverty. Ed. by Barbara C. Gelpi et al. LC 86-6907. 275p. 1986. text ed. 25.00x (ISBN 0-226-28726-2). U of Chicago Pr.

Women & Poverty in the Third World. Ed. by Mayra Buvinic & Margaret A. Lycette. LC 82-8992. 344p. 1983. 39.50x (ISBN 0-8018-2681-0). Johns Hopkins.

Women & Power in the Middle Ages. Ed. by Mary Erler & Maryanne Kowaleski. LC 87-5840. 320p. 1988. 30.00x (ISBN 0-8203-0957-5); pap. 15.00x (ISBN 0-8203-0958-3). U of Ga Pr.

Women & Property in Colonial New York: The Transition from Dutch to English Law, 1643-1727. Linda B. Biemer. LC 82-23701. (Studies in American History & Culture: No. 38). pap. 44.00 (2070036). Bks Demand UMI.

Women & Prophetic Leadership: Female Prophecy in the Judeo-Christian Tradition. Deborah L. Menken. (Illus.). 250p. (Orig.). 1989. 12.95; pap. 9.95. Phrontisterion.

Women & Prostitution: A Social History. Vern Bullough & Bonnie Bullough. 1987. pap. 15.95 (ISBN 0-87975-372-2). Prometheus Bks.

Women & Psychotherapy: An Assessment of Research & Practice. Ed. by Annette M. Brodsky & Rachel Hare-Mustin. LC 80-14842. 428p. 1980. lib. bdg. 40.00 (ISBN 0-89862-605-6, 2605). Guilford Pr.

Women & Psychotherapy: An Assessment Research & Practice. Ed. by Annette M. Brodster & Rachel Hare-Mustin. 428p. 1986. pap. 19.95 (ISBN 0-89862-909-8). Guilford Pr.

Women & Public Policies. rev, exp. ed. Joyce Gelb & Marian L. Palley. 288p. 1986. text ed. 27.50x (ISBN 0-691-07710-X); pap. text ed. 8.95x (ISBN 0-691-02251-8). Princeton U Pr.

Women & Quakerism. Hope E. Luder. LC 74-82914. 36p. (Orig.). 1974. pap. 2.50x (ISBN 0-87574-196-7). Pendle Hill.

Women & Racial Discrimination in Rhodesia. A. K. Weinrich. (Illus.). 143p. 1979. pap. 5.25 (ISBN 92-3-101621-0, U960, UNESCO). UNIPUB.

Women & Recession. Ed. by Jill Rubery. (International Library of Economics). 288p. 1988. text ed. 49.95 (ISBN 0-7102-0701-8, Pub. by Routledge UK); pap. text ed. 19.95 (ISBN 0-7102-1337-9, Pub. by Routledge UK). Routledge Chapman & Hall.

Women & Relapse. Suzanne B. Cusack. 36p. (Orig.). 1984. pap. 1.50 (ISBN 0-89486-237-5). Hazelden.

Women & Religion. Judith Plaskow. Ed. by Joan Arnold & Joan A. Romero. LC 74-83126. (American Academy of Religion. Aids for the Study of Religion). Repr. of 1974 ed. 54.00 (ISBN 0-8357-9581-0, 2017557). Bks Demand UMI.

Women & Religion: A Reader for the Clergy. Regina Coll. 128p. 1982. pap. 5.95 (ISBN 0-8091-2461-0). Paulist Pr.

Women & Religion in America: Nineteen Hundred to Nineteen Sixty-Eight, Vol. 3. Ed. by Rosemary R. Ruether & Rosemary S. Keller. (Illus.). 452p. 1986. 26.45 (ISBN 0-06-066833-4, HarpT). Har-Row.

Women & Religion in America: The Colonial & Revolutionary Period, Vol. II. Ed. by Rosemary R. Ruether & Rosemary S. Keller. LC 80-8346. (Illus.). 448p. 1988. 25.45 (ISBN 0-06-066832-6, HarpR); pap. 15.95 (ISBN 0-06-064303-X, RD-634). Har-Row.

Women & Religion in America, Vol. I: The 19th Century. Rosemary R. Ruether & Rosemary S. Keller. LC 80-8346. (Illus.). 368p. 1982. pap. 12.95 (ISBN 0-06-066828-8, RD 344, HarpR). Har-Row.

Women & Religion: Readings in the Western Tradition from Aeschylus to Mary Daly. Ed. by Elizabeth Clark & Herbert W. Richardson. LC 76-9975. 1976. pap. 11.95 (ISBN 0-06-061398-X, RD-178, HarpR). Har-Row.

Women & Revolution: A Discussion of the Unhappy Marriage of Marxism & Feminism. Ed. by Lydia Sargent. LC 80-54829. (Political Controversies Ser.). 400p. 1981. 20.00 (ISBN 0-89608-062-5); pap. 10.00 (ISBN 0-89608-061-7). South End Pr.

Women & Revolution in Iran. Guity Nashat. (Replica Edition Ser.). 250p. 1983. softcover 25.00x (ISBN 0-86531-931-6). Westview.

Women & Revolution in Viet Nam. Arlene Eisen. (Asia Ser.). (Illus.). 310p. 1984. 29.95x (ISBN 0-86232-175-1, Pub. by Zed Pr); pap. 11.50 (ISBN 0-86232-176-X, Pub. by Zed Pr). Humanities.

Women & Revolution in Yugoslavia. Barbara Jancar. (Illus.). 250p. (Orig.). 1988. price not set (ISBN 0-912869-09-7); pap. price not set (ISBN 0-912869-10-0). Arden Pr.

Women & Rural Development in China: Production & Reproduction. Elizabeth Croll. (Women, Work, & Development: No. 11). vii, 172p. (Orig.). 1985. pap. 14.00 (ISBN 92-2-105217-6). Intl Labour Office.

Women & Rural Transformation. R. Mehra. 176p. 1983. text ed. 19.95x (ISBN 0-391-02944-4, Pub. by Concept Pubs India). Humanities.

Women & Russia: Feminist Writings from the Soviet Union. Ed. by Tatyana Mamonova. LC 82-73963. 224p. 1984. 23.95x (ISBN 0-8070-6708-3); pap. 10.95x (ISBN 0-8070-6709-1, BP 670). Beacon Pr.

Women & Schooling. Rosemary Deem. (Education Bks). 1980. pap. 8.95 (ISBN 0-7100-8958-9). Routledge Chapman & Hall.

Women & Science. Valjean McLenighan. LC 79-13659. (Movers & Shapers Ser.). (Illus.). (gr. 4-8). 1979. PLB 13.31 (ISBN 0-8172-1379-1). Raintree Pubs.

Women & Self-Confidence: How to Take Charge of Your Life. Carol V. Havey. LC 86-63909. (Women & Success Ser.: No. I). (Illus.). 304p. (Orig.). 1987. pap. 9.95 (ISBN 0-9617887-0-4). Positive Pr.

Women & Self-Esteem. Linda T. Sanford & Mary E. Donovan. (Nonfiction Ser.). 480p. 1985. pap. 7.95 (ISBN 0-14-008225-5). Penguin.

Women & Self-Reliance in India: The SEWA Story. Jennefer Sebstad. 368p. 1988. 35.00x (ISBN 0-86232-353-3, Pub. by Zed Pr England); pap. 12.50 (ISBN 0-86232-354-1, Pub. by Zed Pr England). Humanities.

Women & Sex Roles. 2nd ed. Irene Frieze et al. (Illus.). pap. write for info. (ISBN 0-393-95382-3); instr's manual avail. Norton.

Women & Sex Roles: Social Psychological Perspective. Irene H. Frieze et al. (Illus.). 1978. 19.95 (ISBN 0-393-01163-1); pap. 14.95x (ISBN 0-393-09063-9); instr's. manual, 1981 avail. (ISBN 0-393-95168-5). Norton.

Women & Sex Therapy. Ed. by Ellen Cole & Esther D. Rothblum. (Women & Therapy Ser.: Vol. 7, Nos. 2 & 3). (Illus.). 314p. 1988. text ed. 29.95 (ISBN 0-86656-808-5). Haworth Pr.

Women & Sex Therapy: Closing the Circle of Sexual Knowledge. Intro. by Ellen Cole & Esther D. Rothblum. (Women & Therapy Ser.: Vol. 7). (Illus.). 314p. 1988. pap. text ed. 16.95 (ISBN 0-918393-54-X). Harrington PK.

Women & Sexuality in America: A Bibliography. Nancy Sahli. 424p. 1984. lib. bdg. 54.95 (ISBN 0-8161-8099-7, Hall Reference). G K Hall.

Women & Sexuality in the Novels of Thomas Hardy. Rosemarie Morgan. 224p. 1988. text ed. 45.00 (ISBN 0-415-00268-0, Pub. by Routledge UK). Routledge Chapman & Hall.

Women & Slavery in Africa. Ed. by Claire C. Robertson & Martin A. Klein. LC 83-47769. (Illus.). 352p. 1983. text ed. 23.50x (ISBN 0-299-09460-X). U of Wis Pr.

Women & Social Change in India. J. M. Everett. 232p. 1979. 15.95. Asia Bk Corp.

Women & Social Change in India. Jana M. Everett. 1979. 19.95 (ISBN 0-312-88731-0). St Martin.

Women & Social Class. Pamela Abbott & Roger Sapsford. 240p. 1988. text ed. 49.95 (ISBN 0-422-60990-0, Pub. by Tavistock England); pap. text ed. write for info. (ISBN 0-422-61000-3, Pub. by Tavistock England). Routledge Chapman & Hall.

Women & Social Security: An Institutional Dilemma. Marilyn R. Flowers. LC 77-23075. 41p. 1977. pap. 5.00 (ISBN 0-8447-3259-1). Am Enterprise.

Women & Socialization: A Study of Their Status & Role in the Lower Castes of India. Usha Kanhere. 177p. 1987. 25.00x (Pub. by Mittal). South Asia Bks.

Women & Society. Neera Desai. 1987. 42.50x (ISBN 81-202-0188-4, Pub. by Ajanta). South Asia Bks.

Women & Society: A Critical Review of the Literature with a Selected Annotated Bibliography. Ed. by Marie B. Rosenberg & Len V. Bergstrom. LC 73-77874. pap. 90.00 (ISBN 0-317-10619-8, 2021948). Bks Demand UMI.

Women & Society, Citations 3601 to 6000: An Annotated Bibliography. Ed. by JoAnn D. Een et al. LC 77-18985. pap. 69.50 (ISBN 0-317-10699-6, 2021890). Bks Demand UMI.

Women & Society in India. Neera Desai & M. Krishnaraj. 1987. 41.00x (ISBN 81-202-0188-4, Pub. by Ajanta). South Asia Bks.

Women & Society: Northern India in the Eleventh & Twelfth Centuries. Saroj Gulati. 1985. 35.00x (ISBN 0-8364-1413-6, Pub. by Chanakya India). South Asia Bks.

Women & Spirituality. Carol Ochs. LC 83-3397. (New Feminist Perspectives Ser.). 166p. 1983. 18.95x (ISBN 0-8476-7232-8, Rowman & Allanheld); pap. 9.95x (ISBN 0-8476-7233-6). Rowman.

Women & Sport. Ed. by J. Borms et al. (Medicine & Sport Science Ser.: Vol. 14). (Illus.). xiv, 234p. 1981. 82.75 (ISBN 3-8055-2725-X). S Karger.

Women & Sport: From Myth to Reality. Ed. by Carole A. Oglesby. LC 77-19255. (Illus.). 256p. 1978. pap. 11.00 (ISBN 0-8121-0618-0). Lea & Febiger.

Women & Sports. Janice Kaplan. 208p. 1980. pap. 2.50 (ISBN 0-380-50260-7, 50260-7, Discus). Avon.

Women & Spouse Abuse: Index of Modern Information. Willard T. Brainard. LC 88-47635. 150p. 1988. 34.50 (ISBN 0-88164-784-5); pap. 26.50 (ISBN 0-88164-785-3). ABBE Pubs Assn.

Women & State Socialism: Sex Inequality in the Soviet Union & Czechoslovakia. Alena Heitlinger. 1979. 32.95x (ISBN 0-7735-0504-0). McGill-Queens U Pr.

Women & Stepfamilies: Voices of Anger & Love. Ed. by Nan B. Maglin & Nancy Schniedewind. (Women in the Political Economy Ser.). 448p. 1988. 29.95 (ISBN 0-87722-586-9). Temple U Pr.

Women & Success in American Society in the Works of Edna Ferber. Mary R. Shaughnessy. 1975. lib. bdg. 75.00 (ISBN 0-87968-454-2). Gordon Pr.

Women & Symbolic Interaction. Ed. by Mary J. Deegan & Michael Hill. 265p. 1987. pap. text ed. 14.95x (ISBN 0-04-497006-4). Unwin Hyman.

Women & Teaching: Themes for a Spirituality of Pedagogy. Maria Harris. 1988. pap. 3.95 (ISBN 0-8091-2991-4). Paulist Pr.

Women & Technology. S. C. Jain. 1985. 21.00x (ISBN 0-8364-1427-6, Pub. by Rawat). South Asia Bks.

Women & the Alphabet: A Series of Essays. Thomas W. Higginson. LC 72-2607. (American Women Ser.: Images & Realities). 374p. 1972. Repr. of 1900 ed. 23.50 (ISBN 0-405-04462-3). Ayer Co Pubs.

Women & the American City. Ed. by Catherine Stimpson et al. LC 80-53136. 280p. 1981. lib. bdg. 8.95x (ISBN 0-226-77478-3); pap. 5.95x o.s.i (ISBN 0-226-77479-1). U of Chicago Pr.

Women & the American Economy: A Look to the 1980's. Ed. by Juanita M. Kreps. LC 76-4105. (American Assembly Guides Ser.). (Illus.). 192p. 1976. 10.00 (ISBN 0-13-962324-8); pap. 4.00 (ISBN 0-13-962316-7). Am Assembly.

Women & the American Experience. Nancy Woloch. 480p. 1984. pap. text ed. 17.00 (ISBN 0-394-32319-X, KnopfC). Knopf.

Women & the American Labor Movement: From Colonial Times to the Eve of World War I. Philip S. Foner. LC 79-63035. 29.95 (ISBN 0-02-910370-3); pap. 17.95 1982. Free Pr.

Women & the American Labor Movement: From the First Trade Unions to the Present. Philip S. Foner. 1982. pap. 15.95x (ISBN 0-317-30519-0). Free Pr.

Women & the American Labor Movement: From World War I to the Present. Philip S. Foner. LC 80-753. (Illus.). 1980. 29.95 (ISBN 0-02-910380-0); pap. 15.95 2 vol. abbreviated edition (ISBN 0-02-910470-X). Free Pr.

Women & the American Left: A Guide to Sources. Mari J. Buhle. 290p. 1983. lib. bdg. 41.50 (ISBN 0-8161-8195-0, Hall Reference). G K Hall.

Women & the Ancestors: Black Carib Kinship & Ritual. Virginia Kerns. LC 82-2601. (Illus.). 246p. 1983. 14.95 (ISBN 0-252-00982-7). U of Ill Pr.

Women & the Arizona Political Process. Ed. by Rita M. Kelly. LC 88-2632. (Illus.). 202p. (Orig.). 1988. lib. bdg. 27.50 (ISBN 0-8191-6891-2); pap. text ed. 14.50 (ISBN 0-8191-6892-0). U Pr of Amer.

Women & the Art of Negotiating. Gerard I. Nierenberg. Date not set. 16.95 (ISBN 0-671-60391-4, Fireside); pap. 8.95 (ISBN 0-671-55555-3, Fireside). S&S.

Women & the Authority of Inspiration: A Reexamination of Two Prophetic Movements from a Contemporary Feminist Perspective. Elaine C. Huber. LC 85-15823. 262p. (Orig.). 1985. lib. bdg. 29.25 (ISBN 0-8191-4903-9); pap. text ed. 14.50 (ISBN 0-8191-4904-7). U Pr of Amer.

Women & the Blues: Discovering the Passion Within When Life Seems Less Than You Had Hoped For. Jennifer James. LC 87-45708. 240p. 1988. 16.95 (ISBN 0-06-254063-7, HarpR). Har-Row.

Women & the British Empire: An Annotated Guide to Sources. Susan F. Bailey. LC 82-49161. 200p. 1983. lib. bdg. 46.00 (ISBN 0-8240-9162-0). Garland Pub.

Women & the Business Game: Strategies for Successful Ownership. rev. ed. Charlotte Taylor. 258p. 1983. pap. 11.95 (ISBN 0-9611214-0-8). Venture Con Pr.

Women & the Career Game: Play to Win! Ronald E. Petit. (Illus.). 147p. (Orig.). 1982. pap. 7.95. Prof Dev Serv.

Women & the Career Game: Play to Win!!! Ronald E. Petit. 147p. 1984. pap. 7.95. Petit Indust.

Women & the Chinese Poets. T. B. Partington. 59.95 (ISBN 0-8490-1320-8). Gordon Pr.

Women & the Chip. Heather Menzies. 98p. 1981. pap. text ed. 9.95x (ISBN 0-920380-88-3, Pub. by Inst Res Pub Canada). Brookfield Pub Co.

Women & the Church. Ed. by Christopher Nichol. 102p. (Orig.). 1984. pap. 6.95 (ISBN 0-318-20037-6, Pub. by Tertiary Christian Studies). ANZ Religious Pubns.

Women & the Comics. Trina Robbins & Catherine Yronwode. 19.95 (ISBN 0-913035-01-7); pap. 11.95 (ISBN 0-913035-02-5). Eclipse Bks.

Women & the Cuban Revolution. Elizabeth Stone. 160p. 1982. lib. bdg. 15.00 (ISBN 0-87348-607-2); pap. 4.95 (ISBN 0-87348-608-0). Path Pr NY.

Women & the Economy: A Comparative Study of Britain & the United States. A. T. Mallier & M. J. Rosser. LC 86-4011. 1986. 29.95 (ISBN 0-312-88732-9). St Martin.

Women & the English Renaissance: Literature & the Nature of Womankind, 1540-1620. Linda Woodbridge. LC 82-24792. 376p. 1984. 21.95 (ISBN 0-252-01027-2). U of Ill Pr.

Women & the English Renaissance: Literature & the Nature of Womankind 1540-1620. Linda Woodbridge. LC 82-24792. 376p. 1986. pap. 10.95x (ISBN 0-252-01390-5). U of Ill Pr.

Women & the Enlightenment. Ed. by Margaret Hunt & Margaret Jacob. LC 84-590. (Women & History: No. 9). 93p. 1984. text ed. 24.95 (ISBN 0-86656-190-0). Haworth Pr.

Women & the Family. rev. ed. Leon Trotsky. Tr. by Max Eastman et al from Rus. LC 72-92457. 80p. 1973. pap. 3.95 (ISBN 0-87348-218-2). Path Pr NY.

Women & the Family in Rural Taiwan. Margery Wolf. LC 70-183895. (Illus.). 1972. 20.00x (ISBN 0-8047-0808-8); pap. 8.95x (ISBN 0-8047-0849-5). Stanford U Pr.

Women & the Family in the Middle East: New Voices of Change. Ed. by Elizabeth W. Fernea. (Illus.). 368p. 1985. 24.50x (ISBN 0-292-75528-7); pap. 11.95 (ISBN 0-292-75529-5). U of Tex Pr.

Women & the Family: Two Decades of Change. Ed. by Beth B. Hess & Marvin B. Sussman. LC 84-12967. (Marriage & Family Review Ser.: Vol. 7, No. 3/4). 252p. 1984. text ed. 34.95 (ISBN 0-86656-291-5, B291). Haworth Pr.

Women & the Future: Changing Sex Roles in Modern America. Janet Z. Giele. LC 77-2472. 1979. pap. text ed. 14.95 (ISBN 0-02-911690-2). Free Pr.

Women & the Future: Changing Sex Roles in Modern America. Janet Z. Giele. LC 77-2472. 1978. 14.95 (ISBN 0-02-911700-3). Free Pr.

Women & the Ideal Society: Plato's "Republic" & Modern Myths of Gender. Natalie H. Bluestone. LC 87-6002. 248p. (Orig.). 1987. lib. bdg. 25.00x (ISBN 0-87023-580-X); pap. text ed. 11.95x (ISBN 0-87023-581-8). U of Mass Pr.

Women & the Italian Resistance, 1943-45. Jane Slaughter. (Illus.). 220p. (Orig.). 1989. price not set (ISBN 0-912869-13-5); pap. price not set (ISBN 0-912869-14-3). Arden Pr.

Women & the Knife. Clay Sheringham. 96p. 1982. 8.95 (ISBN 0-89962-258-5). Todd & Honeywell.

Women & the Knife. Clay Sheringham. 118p. 1983. 12.95 (ISBN 0-913171-00-X). AMB Pr.

Women & the Labor Movement. Alice Henry. LC 70-156416. (American Labor Ser., No. 2). 1971. Repr. of 1923 ed. 16.00 (ISBN 0-405-02924-1). Ayer Co Pubs.

Women & the Law. Susan Atkins & Brenda Hoggett. 224p. 1985. 24.95x (ISBN 0-85520-181-9); pap. 11.95x (ISBN 0-85520-180-0). Basil Blackwell.

Women & the Law. Eve Cary & Kathleen W. Peratis. 12.95 (ISBN 0-8442-6005-3). Natl Textbk.

Women & the Law. Shirley M. Hufstedler. 20p. (Orig.). 1977. pap. text ed. 5.00 (ISBN 0-8191-5865-8, Pub. by Aspen Inst for Humanistic Studies). U Pr of Amer.

Women & the Law. Carol H. Lefcourt. LC 84-11150. 1984. 75.00 (ISBN 0-87632-441-3). Clark Boardman.

Women & the Law in Washington State. Ed. by Northwest Women's Law Center. 128p. 1982. pap. 5.95 (ISBN 0-914842-84-6). Madrona Pubs.

Women & the Law, India. T. N. Srivastava. 1985. 22.50x (ISBN 0-8364-1419-5, Pub. by Intellectual India). South Asia Bks.

Women & the Law of Property in Early America. Marylynn Salmon. LC 85-20865. (Studies in Legal History). xviii, 267p. 1986. 26.00x (ISBN 0-8078-1687-6). U of NC Pr.

Women & the Law: The Social Historical Perspective. Ed. by D. Kelly Weisberg. 328p. 1982. Vol. I: Woman & the Criminal Law. 18.95 (ISBN 0-87073-586-1); pap. 11.95, 320p. (ISBN 0-87073-587-X); Vol. II: Property, Family, & the Legal Profession. 18.95 (ISBN 0-87073-592-6); pap. 11.95 (ISBN 0-87073-593-4). Schenkman Bks Inc.

Women at the Well: Feminist Perspectives on Spiritual Direction. Kathleen Fischer. 1988. pap. 9.95. Paulist Pr.

Women at Their Work. Betty L. English. LC 76-42924. (Pied Piper Bk.). 48p. (gr. k-4). 1988. pap. 4.95 (ISBN 0-8037-0496-8, 0481-140). Dial Bks Young.

Women at War with America: Private Lives in a Patriotic Era. D'Ann Campbell. (Illus.). 320p. 1984. text ed. 20.00x (ISBN 0-674-95475-0). Harvard U Pr.

Women at Work. Mary F. Fox & Sharlene Hesse-Biber. LC 83-61533. (Illus.). 276p. (Orig.). 1983. 12.95 (ISBN 0-87484-525-4, 525). Mayfield Pub.

Women at Work. William L. O'Neill. LC 72-182506. 384p. 1972. pap. 4.95 (ISBN 0-8129-6237-0). Times Bks.

Women at Work. Ed. by Rosalind M. Schwartz. (Monograph & Research Ser.: No. 48). (Orig.). 1988. pap. price not set (ISBN 0-89215-145-5). U Cal La Indus Rel.

Women at Work. Sylvia Senter et al. 304p. 1983. pap. 6.95 (ISBN 0-399-50701-9, Perigee). Putnam Pub Group.

Women at Work. (Massachusetts Historical Society Picture Book Ser.). (Illus.). 16p. 1983. pap. 3.50 (ISBN 0-934909-20-2). Mass Hist Soc.

Women at Work: An International Survey. Ed. by M. J. Davidson & C. L. Cooper. LC 84-3645. 300p. 1984. 51.95 (ISBN 0-471-90459-7). Wiley.

Women at Work: Annotated Bibliography. Mei L. Bickner & Marlene Shaughnessey. 420p. 1977. Vol. II. 12.00 (ISBN 0-89215-064-5). U Cal LA Indus Rel.

Women at Work in India: A Bibliography. Ed. by Suchitra Anant et al. 240p. 1987. text ed. 22.50 (ISBN 0-8039-9512-1). Sage.

Women at Work in Uraguay. (Women in a World Perspective Ser.). pap. 6.50 (ISBN 92-3-102110-9, U1341, UNESCO). UNIPUB.

Women at Work: One Hundred Fifty Photographs by Lewis Hine. Lewis Hine. (Illus.). 128p. (Orig.). 1981. pap. 7.95 (ISBN 0-486-24154-8). Dover.

Women at Work: The Transformation of Work & Community in Lowell, Massachusetts, 1826-1860. Thomas Dublin. LC 79-10701. 360p. 1981. 29.50x (ISBN 0-231-04166-7); pap. 13.00x (ISBN 0-231-04167-5). Columbia U Pr.

Women Attached: The Daily Lives of Women with Young Children. Jacqueline Tivers. LC 85-18439. 334p. 1985. 32.50 (ISBN 0-312-88726-4). St Martin.

Women, Authority & the Bible. Alvera Mickelsen. LC 86-7158. 252p. (Orig.). 1986. pap. 11.95 (ISBN 0-87784-608-1). Inter-Varsity.

Women Authors of Our Day in Their Homes. Francis W. Halsey. 1903. Repr. 25.00 (ISBN 0-8274-3739-0). R West.

Women-Battering: Victims & Their Experiences. Mildred D. Pagelow. (Sage Library of Social Research: Vol. 129). 256p. 1981. 35.00 (ISBN 0-8039-1681-7); pap. 16.95 (ISBN 0-8039-1682-5). Sage.

Women Before God: Our Own Spirituality. Lavinia Byrne. LC 88-50331. 144p. (Orig.). 1988. pap. 7.95 (ISBN 0-89622-365-5). Twenty-Third.

Women Between Cultures: The Lives of Kinnaird College Alumnae in British India. Michelle Maskiell. (Foreign & Comparative Studies Program, South Asian Ser.: No. 9). (Illus.). 1984. pap. text ed. 10.00x (ISBN 0-915984-86-5). Syracuse U Foreign Comp.

Women Beware Women. Thomas Middleton. Ed. by Roma Gill. (New Mermaids Ser.). 1980. pap. 5.95x (ISBN 0-393-90047-9). Norton.

Women Beware Women. Thomas Middleton. Ed. by J. R. Mulryne. (Revels Plays Ser.). 201p. 1975. 45.00 (ISBN 0-7190-1509-X, Pub. by Manchester Univ Pr); pap. 11.00 (ISBN 0-7190-1614-2). St Martin.

Women Beware Women & Pity in History: Two Plays. Howard Barker. 128p. (Orig.). 1988. pap. 6.95. Riverrun NY.

Women: Beyond Equal Rights. Dee Jepsen. 1986. pap. 7.95 (ISBN 0-8499-3051-0). Word Bks.

Women, Biology & Public Policy. Virginia Sapiro. (Yearbooks in Women's Policy Studies: Vol. 10). 320p. (Orig.). 1985. text ed. 35.00 (ISBN 0-8039-2452-6); pap. text ed. 16.95 (ISBN 0-8039-2453-4). Sage.

Women, Branch Stories, & Religious Rhetoric in a Tamil Buddhist Text. Paula Richman. (Foreign & Comparative Studies-South Asian: No. 12). (Orig.). 1988. write for info. (ISBN 0-915984-90-3). Syracuse U Foreign Comp.

Women Brave in the Face of Danger: Photographs of Latin & North American Women. Margaret Randall. LC 85-2634. (Illus.). 128p. (Orig.). 1985. 25.95 (ISBN 0-89594-162-7); pap. 10.95 (ISBN 0-89594-161-9). Crossing Pr.

Women Business Owners: Selling to the Government. (Illus.). 74p. 1987. 9.50 (S/N 045-000-00247-1). USGPO.

Women Called to Witness: Evangelical Feminism in the Nineteenth Century. Nancy A. Hardesty. LC 83-45959. 176p. (Orig.). 1984. pap. 8.95 (ISBN 0-687-45959-1). Abingdon.

Women Camp Followers of the American Revolution. Walter H. Blumenthal. LC 74-3931. (Women in America Ser). 104p. 1974. Repr. of 1952 ed. 13.00 (ISBN 0-405-06077-7). Ayer Co Pubs.

Women Carpet Weavers in Rural Turkey: Patterns of Employment, Earnings & Status. Gunseli Berik. (Women, Work & Development: No. 15). v, 112p. (Orig.). 1987. pap. 14.00 (ISBN 92-2-106004-7). Intl Labour Office.

Women Centered Training: Responding to Issues & Ideas for Women in Development. Janis Droegkamp & Fredi Munger. (Illus.). 51p. (Orig.). 1980. pap. 4.00 (ISBN 0-932288-56-1). Ctr Intl Ed U of MA.

Women, Change, & the Church. Nancy Van Scoyoc. LC 80-15739. (Into Our Third Century Ser.). 96p. (Orig.). 1980. pap. 3.95 (ISBN 0-687-45958-3). Abingdon.

Women Changing Therapy. Ed. by Joan H. Robbins & Rachel J. Siegel. LC 84-19276. 240p. 1985. pap. text ed. 9.95 (ISBN 0-918393-07-8). Harrington Pk.

Women Changing Therapy: New Assessments, Values, & Strategies in Feminist Therapy. Ed. by Joan H. Robbins & Rachel J. Siegel. LC 83-12643. (Women & Therapy Ser.: Vol. 2, Nos. 2 & 3). 240p. 1983. text ed. 29.95 (ISBN 0-86656-239-7, B239); pap. text ed. 19.95 (ISBN 0-86656-240-0, B240). Haworth Pr.

Women Chefs: A Collection of Portraits & Recipes from California's Culinary Pioneers. Jim Burns & Betty A. Brown. 220p. 1987. pap. 16.95 (ISBN 0-943186-37-4). Aris Bks Harris.

Women Choose Women. Women in the Arts. (Illus.). 126p. 1973. pap. 3.00 (ISBN 0-318-16869-3). Women Arts Found.

Women Christian: New Vision. Mary T. Malone. 176p. 1985. pap. 7.25 (ISBN 0-697-02064-9). Wm C Brown.

Women-Church. Rosemary R. Ruether. 1986. 18.95 (ISBN 0-06-066834-2). Har-Row.

Women, Class & History: Feminist Perspectives on Australia 1788-1978. Elizabeth Windschuttle. 604p. 1982. pap. 10.95 (ISBN 0-00-635722-9, Pub. by W Collins Australia). Intl Spec Bk.

Women Clergy: Breaking Through Gender Barriers. Edward C. Lehman, Jr. 300p. 1985. 26.95 (ISBN 0-88738-071-9). Transaction Bks.

Women Clergy in England: Sexism, Modern Conciousness, & Church Viability. Edward C. Lehman, Jr. LC 86-28547. (Studies in Religion & Society: Vol. 16). 224p. 1987. lib. bdg. 49.95x (ISBN 0-88946-858-3). E Mellen.

Women Clergy in the Episcopal Church. Mary Donovan. (Orig.). 1988. pap. 4.50 (ISBN 0-88028-081-6). Forward Movement.

Women Coming of Age. Jane Fonda & Mignon McCarthy. 1986. pap. 10.95 (ISBN 0-671-62102-5, Fireside). S&S.

Women Communicating: Studies of Women's Talk. Barbara Bate & Anita Taylor. Ed. by Brenda Dervin. (Communication & Information Science Ser.). 352p. 1988. text ed. 45.00 (ISBN 0-89391-475-4); pap. text ed. 27.50 (ISBN 0-89391-476-2). Ablex Pub.

Women Composers: A Checklist of Works for the Solo Voice. Miriam Stewart-Green. 1980. lib. bdg. 52.00 (ISBN 0-8161-8498-4, Hall Reference). G K Hall.

Women Composers: A Discography. Jane Frasier. LC 83-22563. (Detroit Studies in Music Bibliography: No. 50). 1983. 25.00 (ISBN 0-89990-018-6). Harmonie Pk Pr.

Women Composers & Hymnists: A Concise Biographical Dictionary. Gene Claghorn. LC 83-20429. 288p. 1984. 24.00 (ISBN 0-8108-1680-6). Scarecrow.

Women Composers, Conductors & Musicians of the Twentieth Century: Selected Biographies, Vol. I. Jane W. LePage. LC 80-12162. 388p. 1980. 27.50 (ISBN 0-8108-1298-3). Scarecrow.

Women Composers, Conductors & Musicians of the Twenieth Century: Selected Biographies, Vol. II. Jane W. Le Page. LC 80-12162. (Illus.). 388p. 1983. lib. bdg. 29.00 (ISBN 0-8108-1597-4). Scarecrow.

Women Composers, Conductors, & Musicians of the Twentieth Century: Seclected Biographies, Vol. III. Jane W. LePage. LC 80-12162. (Illus.). 333p. 1988. 32.50 (ISBN 0-8108-2082-X). Scarecrow.

Women Composers: The Lost Tradition Found. Diane P. Jezic. 180p. (Orig.). 1988. 29.95 (ISBN 0-935312-94-3); pap. 12.95 (ISBN 0-935312-95-1). Feminist Pr.

Women Construction Workers. G. P. Sinha. (Illus.). 78p. 1975. 5.95. Asia Bk Corp.

Women Crime & Criminal Justice. Allison Morris. 256p. (Orig.). Date not set. text ed. 39.95 (ISBN 0-631-15444-2); pap. text ed. 14.95 (ISBN 0-631-15445-0). Basil Blackwell.

Women, Crime, & Criminology: A Feminist Critique. Carol Smart. 1976. 18.95x (ISBN 0-7100-8449-8). Routledge Chapman & Hall.

Women, Crime, & Criminology: A Feminist Critique. Carol Smart. 1978. pap. 9.95x (ISBN 0-7100-8833-7). Routledge Chapman & Hall.

Women, Crime, & Justice. Ed. by Susan K. Datesman. Frank R. Scarpitti. (Illus., Orig.). 1980. pap. text ed. 9.95x (ISBN 0-19-502676-4). Oxford U Pr.

Women Cross-Culturally: Change & Challenge. Ed. by Ruby Rohrlich-Leavitt. (World Anthropology Ser.). (Illus.). xiv, 670p. 1975. 49.25 (ISBN 90-279-7649-X). Mouton.

Women, Culture & Morality: Selected Essays. Ed. by Joseph L. DeVitis. (American University Studies XI: Anthropology & Sociology: Vol. 10). 418p. 1987. text ed. 49.50 (ISBN 0-8204-0447-0). P Lang Pubs.

Women, Culture & Politics. Angela Y. Davis. LC 88-42674. (Illus.). 256p. 1989. 17.95 (ISBN 0-394-56976-8). Random.

Women, Decision Making, & the Future. Barbara B. Clowse. LC 85-19091. 180p. 1986. pap. 8.95 (ISBN 0-8042-1137-X, John Knox). Westminster John Knox.

Women, Design, & the Cambridge School. Dorothy M. Anderson. LC 80-81341. (Illus.). 246p. 1980. 15.95 (ISBN 0-914886-10-X). PDA Pubs.

Women Directors: The Emergence of a New Cinema. Barbara K. Quart. LC 87-1141. 290p. 1988. lib. bdg. 39.95 (ISBN 0-275-92962-0, C2962). Praeger.

Women Discover Orgasm: A Therapist's Guide to a New Treatment Approach. Lonnie G. Barbach. LC 79-7847. (Illus.). 1980. 24.95 (ISBN 0-02-901800-5). Free Pr.

Women Doctors in Gilded-Age Washington: Race, Gender, & Professionalization. Gloria Moldow. LC 86-19251. (Women in American History Ser.). (Illus.). 262p. 1987. 24.95 (ISBN 0-252-01379-4). U of Ill Pr.

Women Draw Nineteen Eighty-Four. Paula Youens & Suzanne Perkins. (Illus.). 1984. pap. 5.95 (ISBN 0-7043-3919-6, Pub. by The Women's Press). Salem Hse Pubs.

Women, Drinking & Pregnancy. Moira Plant. 208p. 1985. 36.00 (ISBN 0-422-78610-1, 9483, Pub. by Tavistock England). Routledge Chapman & Hall.

Women, Drinking, & Pregnancy. Moira Plant. 184p. 1987. pap. 16.95 (ISBN 0-422-61750-4, Pub. by Routledge UK). Routledge Chapman & Hall.

Women, Education, & Employment: A Bibliography of Periodical Citations, Pamphlets, Newspapers, & Government Documents, 1970-1980. Renee Feinberg. LC 82-7816. 274p. 1982. 29.50 (ISBN 0-208-01967-7, Lib Prof Pubns). Shoe String.

Women, Education, Employment: Family Living (A Study of Emerging Hindu Wives in Urban India) Mondira Devi. 224p. 1987. 32.00x (ISBN 81-212-0104-7, Pub. by Gian Pub Hse India). South Asia Bks.

Women, Education, Equality: A Decade of Experiment. 109p. 1975. pap. 5.00 (ISBN 92-3-101300-9, U718, UNESCO). UNIPUB.

Women Educators: Employees of Schools in Western World Countries. Ed. by Patricia A. Schmuck. LC 86-14532. 251p. 1987. 44.50 (ISBN 0-88706-442-6); pap. 18.95x (ISBN 0-88706-443-4). State U NY Pr.

Women Eighteen Seventy to Nineteen Twenty-Eight: A Select Guide to Printed & Archival Sources in the United Kingdom. Margaret Borrow. 1981. lib. bdg. 73.00 (ISBN 0-8240-9450-6). Garland Pub.

Women, Elections & Representation. R. Darcy et al. 181p. (Orig.). 1987. pap. text ed. 13.95 (ISBN 0-582-28536-4). Longman.

Women, Employment & Development in the Arab World. Ed. by Julinda A. Nasr et al. LC 84-9935. (New Babylon - Studies in the Social Sciences: No. 41). xi, 146p. 1985. 32.50 (ISBN 90-279-3380-4). Mouton.

Women Encouraging Women: Who Will Disciple Me? Lucibel Van Atta. Ed. by Liz Heaney. LC 87-28264. (Orig.). 1988. pap. 7.95 (ISBN 0-88070-214-1). Multnomah.

Women Entrepreneurs in India: Socio-Economic Study of Delhi 1975-85. Medha D. Vinze. 238p. 1987. 22.00x (ISBN 0-8364-2094-2, Pub. by Mittal). South Asia Bks.

Women Entrepreneurs, Networking & Sweet Potato Pie. Corita Communications Editors. 1987. 13.99 (ISBN 0-933016-03-4). Corita Comm.

Women, Ethnics, & Exotics: Images of Power in Mid-Nineteenth-Century American Fiction. Kristin Herzog. LC 82-15881. 280p. 1983. text ed. 24.95x (ISBN 0-87049-372-8). U of Tenn Pr.

Women Expressionists. Shulamith Behr. LC 88-5902. (Illus.). 80p. 1988. pap. text ed. 19.95 (ISBN 0-8478-0963-3). Rizzoli Intl.

Women, Faith, & Economic Justice. Jackie M. Smith. (Illus.). 80p. (Orig.). 1985. pap. 5.95 (ISBN 0-664-24600-1). Westminster John Knox.

Women Faithful for the Future. Maria Riley. (Illus.). 32p. (Orig.). 1987. pap. 2.00 (ISBN 1-55612-103-2). Sheed & Ward MO.

Women, Family, & Community in Colonial America: Two Perspectives. Linda E. Speth & Alison D. Hirsch. LC 82-23326. (Women & History Ser.: No. 4). 79p. 1983. text ed. 29.95 (ISBN 0-86656-191-9, B191). Haworth Pr.

Women, Family, & Ritual in Renaissance Italy. Christiane Klapisch-Zuber. Tr. by Lydia G. Cochrane. LC 84-28061. (Illus.). xvi, 338p. 1985. 13.95x (ISBN 0-226-43926-7). U of Chicago Pr.

Women Farmers in Africa: Rural Development in Mali & the Sahel. Ed. by Lucy E. Creevey. LC 85-27771. (Illus.). 232p. 1986. text ed. 29.95x (ISBN 0-8156-2358-5); pap. text ed. 14.95x (ISBN 0-8156-2359-3). Syracuse U Pr.

Women Farmers of Malawi: Food Production in the Zomba District. David Hirschmann & Megan Vaughan. LC 84-19264. (Research Ser.: No. 58). (Illus.). x, 143p. 1984. pap. 8.95x (ISBN 0-87725-158-4). U of Cal Intl St.

Women, Feminism & Biology. Lynda Birke. 232p. 1986. text ed. 25.00 (ISBN 0-416-01221-3, 9810); pap. text ed. 11.95 (ISBN 0-416-01231-0, 9828). Routledge Chapman & Hall.

Women, Feminism & Family Therapy. Ed. by Lois Braverman. LC 87-36664. (Journal of Psychothrapy & the Family Ser.: Vol. 3, No. 4). 180p. 1988. text ed. 22.95 (ISBN 0-86656-696-1). Haworth Pr.

Women, Feminist Identity & Society in the 1980's: Selected Papers. Ed. by Myriam Diaz-Diocaretz & Iris Zavala. LC 84-28286. (Critical Theory Ser.: No. 1). v, 138p. 1985. 32.00x (ISBN 0-915027-50-X); pap. 19.95x (ISBN 0-915027-51-8). Benjamins North Am.

Women Filmmakers: A Critical Reception. Louise Heck-Rabi. LC 83-20070. 408p. 1984. 29.50 (ISBN 0-8108-1660-1). Scarecrow.

Women, Fire, & Dangerous Things: What Categories Reveal about the Mind. George Lakoff. LC 86-19136. (Illus.). xviii, 614p. 1987. 29.95 (ISBN 0-226-46803-8). U of Chicago Pr.

Women First: The Female Tradition in English Physical Education, 1880-1980. Sheila Fletcher. LC 84-70367. (Illus.). 194p. 1984. 36.50 (ISBN 0-485-11248-5, Pub. by Athlone Pr UK); pap. 14.00 (ISBN 0-485-12046-1). Humanities.

Women, Food & Sex. Soledad De Montalvo-Mielche. 400p. (Orig.). 1986. pap. 8.00 (ISBN 0-910309-22-1). Am Atheist.

Women for All Seasons: Poetry & Prose about the Transitions in Women's Lives. Intros. by Joanne Leedom-Ackerman & Wanda Coleman. 76p. (Orig.). 1988. pap. 8.00 (ISBN 0-944587-00-3). Womans Bldg.

Women for Hire: A Study of the Female Office Worker. Fiona McNally. LC 79-12793. 1979. 22.50x (ISBN 0-312-88735-3). St Martin.

Women for Human Rights. Marcia M. Conta. LC 79-13331. (Movers & Shapers Ser.). (Illus.). 48p. (gr. 4-8). 1979. PLB 13.31 (ISBN 0-8172-1378-3). Raintree Pubs.

Women, Foreign Assistance, & Advocacy Administration. Kathleen Staudt. LC 84-15935. 188p. 1985. 35.00 (ISBN 0-275-90168-8, C0168). Praeger.

Women, Freedom, & Calvin. Jane D. Douglass. LC 85-8778. 156p. 1985. pap. 11.95 (ISBN 0-664-24663-X). Westminster John Knox.

Women Freedom Fighters in Karnataka. S. Shintri & K. Raghavendra Rao. 1985. pap. 6.00x (ISBN 0-8364-1485-3, Pub. by Karnataka Univ). South Asia Bks.

Women From Birth to Death: The Female Life Cycle in Britain 1830-1914. Ed. by P. Jalland & J. Hooper. LC 85-27070. 348p. 1986. text ed. 37.50x (ISBN 0-391-03382-4). Humanities.

Women! from Mars. Christopher Langley. LC 76-15099. 1976. 15.00 (ISBN 0-87832-018-0). Piper.

Women: From the Greeks to the French Revolution. Ed. by Susan G. Bell. LC 80-51750. xiv, 313p. 1973. 29.50x (ISBN 0-8047-1094-5); pap. 10.95x (ISBN 0-8047-1082-1). Stanford U Pr.

Women, Gender & Social Psychology. Ed. by Virginia O'Leary et al. 400p. 1985. text ed. 39.95 (ISBN 0-89859-447-2). L Erlbaum Assocs.

Women Guarding Men. Lynn E. Zimmer. LC 85-28857. (Studies in Crime & Justice). xiv, 264p. 1986. 25.00x (ISBN 0-226-98339-0). U of Chicago Pr.

Women Have Always Worked: A Historical Overview. Alice Kessler-Harris. (Women's Lives - Women's Work Ser.). (Illus.). 208p. (Orig.). (gr. 11 up). 1980. o. p. 14.95 (ISBN 0-912670-86-X); pap. 9.95 (ISBN 0-912670-67-3); teaching guide, 80p. 5.00 (ISBN 0-912670-77-0). Feminist Pr.

Women-Headed Households in Rural India. Ranjana Kumari. 125p. 1988. text ed. 22.50x (Pub. by Radiant Pubs India). Advent NY.

Women Healers in Medieval Life & Literature. facs. ed. Muriel J. Hughes. LC 68-57322. (Essay Index Reprint Ser). 1943. 15.00 (ISBN 0-8369-0552-0). Ayer Co Pubs.

Women, Health & Culture. Ed. by Phyllis N. Stern. (Health Care for Women International Publication Ser.). 170p. 1985. text ed. 29.95 (ISBN 0-89116-372-7). Hemisphere Pub.

Women, Health & Development: A Report by the Director-General. (WHO Offset Publication Ser.: No. 90). 41p. 1985. pap. 4.20 (ISBN 92-4-170090-4). World Health.

Women, Health & Healing. 12.95 (ISBN 0-317-31490-4, 9329). Routledge Chapman & Hall.

Women, Health & Healing: Toward a New Perspective. Ed. by Ellen Lewin. Virginia Olesen. (Contemporary Issues in Health, Medicine, & Social Policy). 300p. (Orig.). 1985. 33.00x (9263, Pub. by Tavistock England); pap. 12.95 (ISBN 0-422-78030-8, 9264). Routledge Chapman & Hall.

Women, Health, & Poverty. Ed. by Cesar A. Perales. Lauren S. Young. LC 87-26274. (Women & Health Ser.). 270p. 1988. text ed. 34.95 (ISBN 0-86656-684-8). Haworth Pr.

Women, Health, & Reproduction. Helen Roberts. 208p. (Orig.). 1981. pap. 11.95x (ISBN 0-7100-0703-5). Routledge Chapman & Hall.

Women Helping Women: A Guide to Organizing a Post-Mastectomy Program in Your Community. pap. 2.50 (ISBN 0-686-81725-7). NCJW.

Women in Frankish Society: Marriage & the Cloister, 500-900. Suzanne F. Wemple. LC 80-54051. (Illus.). 352p. 1985. pap. text ed. 21.95 (ISBN 0-8122-1209-6). U of Pa Pr.

Women in French Literature. Ed. by Michel Guggenheim. (Stanford French & Italian Studies: Vol. 58). 224p. 1988. pap. 34.50 (ISBN 0-915838-74-5). Anma Libri.

Women in Gainful Occupations, Eighteen Seventy to Nineteen Twenty. United States Bureau of the Census. LC 78-12048. (Illus.). 1979. Repr. of 1929 ed. lib. bdg. 35.00x (ISBN 0-313-20679-1, DCWG). Greenwood.

Women in Geology: Proceedings. Northeastern Women's Geoscientists Conference, First. Ed. by S. D. Halsey et al. LC 76-21580. (Illus.). 1976. pap. 2.00 (ISBN 0-915492-02-4). Ash Lad Pr.

Women in German Yearbook Four: Feminist Studies & German Culture. Ed. by Marianne Burkhard & Jeanette Clausen. (Illus.). 234p. (Orig.). 1988. lib. bdg. 26.75 (ISBN 0-8191-6703-7, Pub. by Coalition of Women in German); pap. text ed. 14.50 (ISBN 0-8191-6704-5, Pub. by Coalition of Women in German). U Pr of Amer.

Women in German Yearbook Three. Ed. by Marianne Burkhard & Edith Waldstein. (Feminist Studies in German Culture). (Illus.). 148p. (Orig.). 1987. lib. bdg. 24.50 (ISBN 0-8191-5771-6, Pub. by Coalition of Women in German); pap. text ed. 11.75 (ISBN 0-8191-5772-4). U Pr of Amer.

Women in German Yearbook Two. Ed. by Marianne Burkhard & Edith Waldstein. (Feminist Studies in German Culture). 158p. (Orig.). 1986. lib. bdg. 24.75 (ISBN 0-8191-5375-3, Pub. by Coalition of Women in German); pap. text ed. 12.25 (ISBN 0-8191-5376-1). U Pr of Amer.

Women in German Yearbook 1: Feminist Studies & German Culture. Ed. by Marianne Burkhard & Edith Waldstein. 168p. (Orig.). 1985. lib. bdg. 26.25 (ISBN 0-8191-4600-5); pap. text ed. 11.50 (ISBN 0-8191-4601-3). U Pr of Amer.

Women in God's Presence. Compiled by Delores Taylor. LC 87-71311. 375p. (Orig.). 1988. pap. 14.95 (ISBN 0-87509-395-7). Chr Pubns.

Women in Government. Suzanne E. Sheldon & Roger A. Sheldon. (Illus.). 160p. 1983. (VGM Career Horzns); pap. 7.95 (ISBN 0-8442-6284-6, VGM Career Horzns). Natl Textbk.

Women in Greek Myth. Mary R. Lefkowitz. LC 86-7146. 164p. 1986. text ed. 22.50x (ISBN 0-8018-3367-1). Johns Hopkins.

Women in Health & Development in South-East Asia. Rekha Dayal. (SEARO Regional Health Papers: No. 8). 133p. 1985. pap. 4.20 (ISBN 92-9022-177-1). World Health.

Women in Health & Illness: Life Experiences & Crises. Diane K. Kjervik & Ida M. Martinson. (Illus.). 261p. 1986. 27.95 (ISBN 0-7216-2086-8). Saunders.

Women in Hellenistic Egypt: From Alexander to Cleopatra. Sarah B. Pomeroy. LC 84-3122. 266p. 1984. 16.95 (ISBN 0-8052-3911-1). Schocken.

Women in Her Dreams. Candace Denning. LC 87-82588. 224p. 1988. 16.95 (ISBN 0-86547-319-6). N Point Pr.

Women in Higher Education: A Contemporary Bibliography. Kathryn M. Moore & Peter A. Wollitzer. 114p. 1979. 7.00 (ISBN 0-686-27999-9). Natl Assn Women.

Women in Higher Education Administration. Ed. by Adrian Tinsley et al. LC 83-82747. (Higher Education Ser.: No. 45). 1984. pap. text ed. 12.95x (ISBN 0-87589-995-1). Jossey-Bass.

Women in Hispanic Literature: Icons & Fallen Idols. Ed. by Beth Miller. LC 81-14663. 480p. 1984. text ed. 35.00x (ISBN 0-520-04291-3); pap. text ed. 11.95x (ISBN 0-520-04367-7). U of Cal Pr.

Women in History. Jerry Aten. 144p. (gr. 4-8). 1986. wkbk. 9.95 (ISBN 0-86653-344-3). Good Apple.

Women in History. Ed. by Donald L. Shepherd. (Great Adventures of History Ser.). 1973. pap. 1.50 (ISBN 0-87687-011-6, BM011). Mankind Pub.

Women in India. Albertine Gaur. (Illus.). 28p. (Orig.). 1980. pap. 2.95 (ISBN 0-904654-52-4, Pub. by British Lib). Longwood Pub Group.

Women in India. Susan H. Gross. (Women in World Area Studies). (Illus.). 111p. 1980. pap. 7.95 (ISBN 0-86596-004-6). Glenhurst Pubns.

Women in India & Nepal. Michael Allen & Sal Mokherjee. 1982. pap. 24.00x (ISBN 0-908070-07-1, Pub. by Australia Nat Univ). South Asia Bks.

Women in India: Two Perspectives. Susan W. Jacobson. 1986. Repr. of 1982 ed. 10.00x (ISBN 0-8364-1617-1, Pub. by Manohar India). South Asia Bks.

Women in Indian History: A Biographical Dictionary. T. P. Saxena. 114p. 1979. 14.95. Asia Bk Corp.

Women in Indian Industry. A. Ramanamma. 232p. 1987. 27.50x (ISBN 0-8364-2085-3, Pub. by Mittal). South ASia Bks.

Women in Indian Society: A Book of Readings. Ed. by Rehana Ghadially. 380p. Date not set. text ed. 30.00 (ISBN 0-8039-9564-4); pap. text ed. 14.95 (ISBN 0-8039-9565-2). Sage.

Women in India's Freedom Struggle. Manmohan Kaur. 1985. text ed. 35.00x (ISBN 0-86590-617-3, Pub. by Sterling Pubs India). Apt Bks.

Women in Industry. Louis D. Brandeis & Josephine Goldmark. LC 73-89720. (American Labor, from Conspiracy to Collective Bargaining Ser., No. 1). 121p. 1969. Repr. of 1907 ed. 12.00 (ISBN 0-405-02106-2). Ayer Co Pubs.

Women in Industry: A Study in American Economic History. Edith Abbott. LC 70-89714. (American Labor, from Conspiracy to Collective Bargaining Ser.: No. 1). 408p. 1969. Repr. of 1910 ed. lib. bdg. 25.50 (ISBN 0-405-02101-1). Ayer Co Pubs.

Women in Industry: Their Health & Efficiency. Anna M. Baetjer. Ed. by Leon Stein. LC 77-70480. (Work Ser.). (Illus.). 1977. Repr. of 1946 ed. lib. bdg. 32.00x (ISBN 0-405-10154-6). Ayer Co Pubs.

Women in Ireland: An Annotated Bibliography. Compiled by Anna Brady. LC 87-25043. (Bibliographies & Indexes in Women's Studies: No. 6). 520p. 1988. lib. bdg. 45.00 (ISBN 0-313-24486-3, BWR/). Greenwood.

Women in Ireland: Voices of Change. Jenny Beale. 1987. 29.95x (ISBN 0-253-36461-2); pap. 10.95x (ISBN 0-253-20413-5). Ind U Pr.

Women in Irish Society: The Historical Dimension. Ed. by Margaret Mac Curtain & Donncha O'Corrain. LC 79-964. (Contributions in Women's Studies: No. 11). 1979. lib. bdg. 35.00 (ISBN 0-313-21254-6, MWI/). Greenwood.

Women in Islam. Marjorie W. Bingham & Susan H. Gross. (Illus.). 130p. 1980. pap. 7.95 (ISBN 0-86596-000-3). Glenhurst Pubns.

Women in Islam. Aisha Lemu & Fatima Heeren. 51p. (Orig.). 1978. pap. 3.50 (ISBN 0-86037-004-6, Pub. by Islamic Found UK). New Era Pubns MI.

Women in Islam. M. M. Siddiqui. 10.50 (ISBN 0-686-18462-9). Kazi Pubns.

Women in Islam. M. M. Siddiqui. 1969. 10.50 (ISBN 0-87902-069-5). Orientalia.

Women in Islam. Bo Utas. 10.00x (ISBN 0-317-20252-9). Intl Bk Ctr.

Women in Islam: Social Attitudes & Historical Perspectives. Ed. by V. Boutas. 224p. 1983. 30.00x (ISBN 0-7007-0154-0, Pub. by Curzon England). State Mutual Bk.

Women in Islamic Societies: Social Attitudes & Historical Perspectives. Ed. by Bo Utas. LC 88-1615. 260p. 1988. pap. 13.95 (ISBN 0-940793-12-1, Olive Branch Pr). Interlink Pub.

Women in Israel. Susan H. Gross & Marjorie W. Bingham. (Women in World Area Studies). (Illus.). 88p. 1980. pap. 7.95 (ISBN 0-86596-001-1). Glenhurst Pubns.

Women in Japan: from Ancient Times to the Present. Marjorie W. Bingham & Susan H. Gross. Ed. by Janet M. Donaldson. (Women in World Area Studies). (Illus.). 317p. (Orig.). 1987. pap. 11.95 (ISBN 0-914227-08-4). Glenhurst Pubns.

Women in Jazz: A Discography of Instrumental Music, Nineteen Thirteen to Nineteen Sixty-eight. Jan Leder. LC 85-17657. (Discographies Ser.: No. 19). xv, 311p. 1985. lib. bdg. 36.95 (ISBN 0-313-24790-0, LMI/). Greenwood.

Women in Joyce. Ed. by Suzette Henke & Elaine Unkeless. LC 81-4663. 240p. 1982. 22.95 (ISBN 0-252-00891-X). U of Ill Pr.

Women in Kentucky. Helen D. Irvin. LC 77-92924. (Kentucky Bicentennial Bookshelf Ser.). (Illus.). 144p. 1979. 6.95 (ISBN 0-8131-0239-1). U Pr of Ky.

Women in Khaki: The American Enlisted Woman. Michael Rustad. LC 82-9025. 304p. 1982. 35.00 (ISBN 0-275-90892-5, C0892). Praeger.

Women in Latin America: From Pre-Columbian Times to the 20th Century, Vol. I. Marjorie W. Bingham & Susan H. Gross. Ed. by Janet M. Donaldson. LC 84-73429. (Women in World Area Studies). (Illus.). 210p. (Orig.). 1985. pap. 8.95. (ISBN 0-914227-04-1). Glenhurst Pubns.

Women in Latin America: The 20th Century, Vol. II. Susan H. Gross & Marjorie W. Bingham. Ed. by Janet M. Donaldson. LC 84-73429. (Women in World Area Studies). (Illus.). 176p. (Orig.). 1985. pap. 8.95 (ISBN 0-914227-07-6). Glenhurst Pubns.

Women in Law Enforcement. 2nd ed. P. Horne. (Illus.). 288p. 1980. 32.50 (ISBN 0-398-04029-X). C C Thomas.

Women in Law: Explorations in Law, Family & Sexuality. Ed. by Julia Brophy & Carol Smart. 192p. 1985. 26.95x (ISBN 0-7102-0607-0); pap. 12.95 (ISBN 0-7102-0259-8). Routledge Chapman & Hall.

Women in LC's Terms: A Thesaurus of Library of Congress Subject Headings Relating to Women. Ellen J. Waite et al. 112p. 1988. 28.50 (ISBN 0-89774-444-6). Oryx Pr.

Women in Librarianship: Melvil's Rib Symposium. Ed. by Margaret Myers & Mayra Scarborough. (Issues in Library & Information Sciences Ser.: No. 2). 1975. pap. text ed. 15.00 (ISBN 0-8135-0807-X). Rutgers U SICLS.

Women in Literature: Criticism of the Seventies. Carol F. Myers. LC 75-35757. 263p. 1976. 18.50 (ISBN 0-8108-0885-4). Scarecrow.

Women in Local Politics. Ed. by Debra W. Stewart. LC 80-14526. vi, 232p. 1980. 18.50 (ISBN 0-8108-1312-2). Scarecrow.

Women in Love. Sandy Dempsey. LC 84-72756. (Herland Ser.: No. 7). 52p. (Orig.). 1985. pap. 5.00 (ISBN 0-934996-30-X). American Studies Pr.

Women in Love. Graham Holderness. LC 86-768. 160p. 1986. 42.00x (ISBN 0-335-15254-6, Pub. by Open Univ Pr); pap. 13.00x (ISBN 0-335-15253-8, Pub. by Open Univ Pr). Taylor & Francis.

Women in Love. D. H. Lawrence. 1976. pap. 3.95 (ISBN 0-14-004260-1). Penguin.

Women in Love. D. H. Lawrence. Ed. by Charles Ross. (English Library). 512p. 1982. pap. 4.95 (ISBN 0-14-043156-X). Penguin.

Women in Love. D. H. Lawrence. 421p. 1984. Repr. lib. bdg. 25.95x (ISBN 0-89966-496-2). Buccaneer Bks.

Women in Love. D. H. Lawrence. 25.95 (ISBN 0-89190-612-6, Pub. by Am Repr). Amereon ltd.

Women in Love. D. H. Lawrence. Ed. by David Farmer et al. (Cambridge Edition of the Works of D. H. Lawrence). (Illus.). 700p. 1987. 79.50 (ISBN 0-521-23565-0); pap. 24.95 (ISBN 0-521-28041-9). Cambridge U Pr.

Women in Management. Ed. by Nancy J. Adler & Dafna N. Izraeli. LC 88-4520. 232p. 1988. text ed. 27.50 (ISBN 0-87332-417-X). M E Sharpe.

Women in Management. Douglas C. Basil & Edna Traver. 140p. 1972. 14.50 (ISBN 0-8290-1568-X). Irvington.

Women in Management. Carol S. Greenwald. (Studies in Productivity: Highlights of the Literature Ser.: Vol. 12). 49p. 1980. pap. 39.00 (ISBN 0-89361-019-4). Work in Amer.

Women in Management. Harvey Lieberman. (Simulation Game Ser.). 1975. pap. 24.90 (ISBN 0-89401-095-6); pap. 21.50 two or more (ISBN 0-685-78132-1). Didactic Syst.

Women in Management. Irene Place. (Illus.). 160p. 1983. 9.95 (ISBN 0-8442-6649-3, VGM Career Horzns); pap. 7.95 (ISBN 0-8442-6650-7, VGM Career Horzns). Natl Textbk.

Women in Management. 2nd ed. Bette A. Stead. (Illus.). 432p. 1985. text ed. 29.00 (ISBN 0-13-961871-6); pap. text ed. write for info. (ISBN 0-13-961863-5). P-H.

Women in Management. Betty A. Stead. (Illus.). 1978. P-H.

Women in Management, Vol. 12. Carol Greenwald. LC 80-20757. (Work in America Institute Studies in Productivity). (Orig.). 1982. pap. 35.00. Pergamon.

Women in Management: An Annotated Bibliography & Sourcelist. Compiled by Judith A. Leavitt. LC 82-2190. 216p. 1982. lib. bdg. 33.00 (ISBN 0-89774-026-2). Oryx Pr.

Women in Management: Environment & Role. Milton L. Shuch. (ITT Key Issues Lecture Ser.). 93p. 1981. pap. text ed. 7.87 scp (ISBN 0-672-97919-5). Bobbs.

Women in Mathematics. Lynn M. Osen. 224p. 1974. pap. 6.95 (ISBN 0-262-65009-6). MIT Pr.

Women in Media: A Documentary Source Book. Maurine Beasley & Sheila Gibbons. 198p. 1977. 5.95 (ISBN 0-930470-00-1); pap. 5.00 tchrs. ed. Womens Inst Free Press.

Women in Medicine. Carol Lopate. LC 68-19526. (Josiah Macy Foundation Ser.). (Illus.). 204p. 1968. 22.50x (ISBN 0-8018-0391-8). Johns Hopkins.

Women in Medieval History & Historiography. Ed. by Susan Mosher Stuard. (Middle Ages Ser.). 229p. 1987. text ed. 28.95x (ISBN 0-8122-8048-2). U of Pa Pr.

Women in Medieval-Renaissance Europe. Susan H. Gross & Marjorie W. Bingham. LC 83-20787. (Women in World Area Studies). 180p. (Orig.). 1984. 13.95; pap. 10.95 (ISBN 0-914227-02-5). Glenhurst Pubns.

Women in Medieval Society. Ed. by Susan M. Stuard. LC 75-41617. (Middle Ages Ser). 220p. 1976. pap. 10.95x (ISBN 0-8122-1088-3). U of Pa Pr.

Women in Medieval Times: An Annotated Bibliography. Anne Echols & Marty Williams. 450p. 1988. text ed. 49.00x. Wiener Pub Inc.

Women in Mid-Life Crisis. Jim Conway & Sally Conway. 391p. 1983. pap. 8.95 (ISBN 0-8423-8379-4). Tyndale.

Women in Midlife. Ed. by Grace Baruch & Jeanne Brooks-Gunn. (Women in Context Ser.). 416p. 1984. 39.50x (ISBN 0-306-41444-9, Plenum Pr). Plenum Pub.

Women in Ministry. Anne A. Jackson & Cleola I. Spears. (Illus.). 350p. (Orig.). pap. write for info. (ISBN 0-9605892-3-6). Dawn Ministries.

Women in Ministry. L. E. Maxwell. 156p. 1987. pap. 5.95 (ISBN 0-89693-337-7). Victor Bks.

Women in Modern America: A Brief History. 2nd ed. Lois W. Banner. 294p. 1984. pap. text ed. 12.00 net (ISBN 0-15-596196-9, HC). HarBraceJ.

Women in Modern China. Marjorie W. Bingham & Susan H. Gross. (Women in World Area Studies). (Illus.). 107p. 1980. pap. 7.95 (ISBN 0-86596-003-8). Glenhurst Pubns.

Women in Modern India. Neera Desai. 334p. 1977. 12.95. Asia Bk Corp.

Women in Modern India. E. C. Gedge & Mithan Choksi. LC 74-33940. (Pioneer's of the Woman's Movement Ser.). x, 161p. 1975. Repr. of 1929 ed. 17.60 (ISBN 0-88355-262-0). Hyperion-Conn.

Women in Modern Industry. B. L. Hutchins. LC 79-56959. (English Working Class Ser.). 1980. lib. bdg. 37.00 (ISBN 0-8240-0112-5). Garland Pub.

Women in Motion. Alexa L. Foreman. LC 83-72435. 248p. 1983. 19.95 (ISBN 0-87972-266-5). Bowling Green Univ.

Women in Music. Carol Neuls-Bates. LC 81-48045. (Illus.). 288p. 1982. pap. 8.95x (ISBN 0-06-132060-9, TB 2060, Torch). Har-Row.

Women in Muslim Family Law. John L. Esposito. LC 81-18273. (Contemporary Issues in the Middle East Ser.). 172p. 1982. pap. text ed. 10.95X (ISBN 0-8156-2278-3). Syracuse U Pr.

Women in Muslim Rural Society. Joseph Ginat. LC 79-66432. 259p. 1981. 34.95 (ISBN 0-87855-342-8). Transaction Bk.

Women in Navajo Society. Ruth Roessel. LC 81-1293. (Illus.). 184p. 1981. 15.00x (ISBN 0-936008-01-6). Navajo Curr.

Women in Nazi Germany. Katherine Thomas. LC 78-63726. (Studies in Fascism: Ideology & Practice). 104p. Repr. of 1943 ed. 18.50 (ISBN 0-404-16998-8). AMS Pr.

Women in Neighborhood Evangelism. Marjorie Stewart. LC 77-93410. 128p. 1978. pap. 1.50 (ISBN 0-88243-723-2, 02-0723). Gospel Pub.

Women in New Worlds, Vol. 2. Ed. by Rosemary S. Keller & Louise L. Queen. 448p. (Orig.). 1982. pap. 13.95 (ISBN 0-687-45969-9). Abingdon.

Women in New Worlds: Vol. 1. Ed. by Hilah F. Thomas & Rosemary S. Keller. LC 81-7984. (Historical Perspectives on the Wesleyan Tradition Ser.). 448p. (Orig.). 1981. pap. 13.95 (ISBN 0-687-45968-0). Abingdon.

Women in Nigeria Today. S. Bappa et al. 272p. 1985. 29.95x (ISBN 0-86232-447-5, Pub. by Zed Pr); pap. 9.95 (ISBN 0-86232-448-3, Pub. by Zed Pr). Humanities.

Women in Nineteenth Century Egypt. Judith E. Tucker. (Cambridge Middle East Library). 264p. 1985. 39.50 (ISBN 0-521-30338-9). Cambridge U Pr.

Women in North America: Summaries of Biographical Articles in History Journals. Pamela R. Byrne & Susan Kinnell. (People in History Ser.). 146p. (YA) (gr. 9-12). 1988. pap. text ed. 18.00 (ISBN 0-87436-537-6). ABC Clio.

Women in Organizations: Barriers & Breakthroughs. Joseph J. Pilotta. 101p. (Orig.). 1983. pap. text ed. 6.50x (ISBN 0-88133-008-6). Waveland Pr.

Women in Particular: An Index to American Women. Kali Herman. LC 83-43251. 760p. 1984. lib. bdg. 95.00 (ISBN 0-89774-088-2). Oryx Pr.

Women in Perspective: A Guide for Cross Cultural Studies. Sue-Ellen Jacobs. LC 72-93987. 312p. 1974. pap. 9.95 (ISBN 0-252-00345-4). U of Ill Pr.

Women in Political Theory. Diana Coole. LC 87-22883. 256p. 1988. lib. bdg. 32.00x (ISBN 1-55587-075-9); pap. text ed. 14.95x (ISBN 1-55587-076-7). Lynne Rienner.

Women in Politics. Ed. by Jane S. Jaquette. LC 74-1037. pap. 101.50 (ISBN 0-317-07771-6, 2021502). Bks Demand UMI.

Women in Politics. Sharon Whitney & Tom Raynor. 144p. (gr. 7-12). 1986. PLB 12.40 (ISBN 0-531-10243-2). Watts.

Women in Politics: A Bibliography. Ina J. Weis. (Public Administration Ser.: P 2187). 23p. 1987. 6.25 (ISBN 1-55590-367-3). Vance Biblios.

Women in Popular Culture: A Reference Guide. Katherine Fishburn. LC 81-13421. (American Popular Culture Ser.). ix, 267p. 1982. lib. bdg. 36.95 (ISBN 0-313-22152-9, FWC/). Greenwood.

Women in Power. Ginny McReynolds. LC 79-13301. (Movers & Shapers Ser.). (Illus.). (gr. 4-8). 1979. PLB 13.31 (ISBN 0-8172-1376-7). Raintree Pubs.

Women in Print-One: Opportunities for Women's Studies Research in Language & Literature. Ed. by Ellen Messer-Davidow & Joan E. Hartman. LC 82-3596. (MLA Commission on the Status of Women in the Profession Ser.). 198p. 1982. 30.00x (ISBN 0-87352-336-9); pap. 16.50x (ISBN 0-87352-337-7). Modern Lang.

Women in Print-Two: Opportunities for Women's Studies Publication in Language & Literature. Ed. by Ellen Messer-Davidow & Joan E. Hartman. (MLA Commission on the Status of Women in the Profession Ser.). 173p. 1982. 30.00x (ISBN 0-87352-338-5); pap. 16.50x (ISBN 0-87352-339-3). Modern Lang.

Women in Prison (Eighteen Thirty-Four - Nineteen Twenty-Eight) Ed. by Sheila M. Rothman & David J. Rothman. (Women & Children First Ser.). 500p. 1986. lib. bdg. 60.00 (ISBN 0-8240-7692-3). Garland Pub.

Women in Protest Eighteen Hundred to Eighteen Fifty. Malcolm Thomis & Jennifer Grimmett. LC 81-21290. 166p. 1982. 25.00x (ISBN 0-312-88746-9). St Martin.

Women in Public Life. Ed. by Beryl A. Radin & Hoyt Purvis. 56p. 1976. pap. 3.50 (ISBN 0-89940-404-9). LBJ Sch Pub Aff.

Women in Public Office: A Biographical Directory & Statistical Analysis. 2nd ed. Compiled by Center for the American Woman & Politics Staff. LC 78-7463. 600p. 1978. 47.50 (ISBN 0-8108-1142-1). Scarecrow.

Women in Public: The Women's Movement 1850 to 1900. Patricia Hollis. 336p. 1980. pap. text ed. 17.95x (ISBN 0-04-900034-9). Unwin Hyman.

Women in the West: The Woman Suffrage Movement, 1869-1896. Beverly Beeton. Ed. by Harold Hyman & Stuart Bruchey. LC 86-4716. (American Legal & Constitutional History Ser.). 200p. 1986. lib. bdg. 30.00 (ISBN 0-8240-8251-6). Garland Pub.
Women in the White House: Four First Ladies. Bennett Wayne. LC 75-20388. (Garrard Target Ser.). (Illus.). 168p. (gr. 5 up). 1976. PLB 7.99 (ISBN 0-8116-4915-6). Garrard.
Women in the Wind. Margaret Ritter. 685p. 1985. 18.95 (ISBN 0-671-54327-X). S&S.
Women in the Wind. Margaret Ritter. 1986. pap. text ed. 4.95 (ISBN 0-07-052982-5). McGraw.
Women in the Work Force. John H. Bernardin. LC 82-13170. 256p. 1982. 35.00 (ISBN 0-275-90761-9, C0761). Praeger.
Women in the Workplace. Ed. by Kathryn Borman et al. LC 84-2941. (Modern Sociology Ser.). 268p. 1984. text ed. 37.50 (ISBN 0-89391-166-6). Ablex Pub.
Women in the Workplace. Phyllis A. Wallace. LC 81-12775. 240p. 1982. 24.95 (ISBN 0-86569-069-3); pap. 15.00 (ISBN 0-86569-096-0). Auburn Hse.
Women in the Workplace: A Man's Perspective. Lloyd S. Lewan & Ronald G. Billingsley. LC 88-90731. (Illus.). 125p. (Orig.). 1988. pap. 7.50 (ISBN 0-9620360-0-5). Remington Pr.
Women in the World: An International Atlas. Ann Olson & Joni Seager. (Illus.). 128p. 1986. 19.45 (ISBN 0-671-60297-7, Touchstone); pap. 12.95 (ISBN 0-671-63070-9). S&S.
Women in the World: Annotated History Resources for the Secondary Student. Lyn Reese & Jean Wilkinson. LC 87-16436. (Illus.). 228p. 1987. 19.50 (ISBN 0-8108-2050-1). Scarecrow.
Women in the World Economy: An INSTRAW Study. Susan Joekes. 176p. 1987. 21.00 (ISBN 0-19-504947-0). Oxford U Pr.
Women in the World Religions, Past & Present. Ed. by Ursula King. LC 86-21213. (God Ser.). 261p. (Orig.). 1987. 22.95 (ISBN 0-913757-32-2, Pub. by New Era Bks.); pap. 12.95 (ISBN 0-913757-33-0, Pub. by New Era Bks). Paragon Hse.
Women in the World, 1975-1985: The Women's Decade. 2nd rev. ed. Lynne B. Iglitzin & Ruth Ross. LC 85-6158. (Studies in International & Comparative Politics: No. 16). 484p. 1986. lib. bdg. 37.50 (ISBN 0-87436-409-4); pap. 18.50 (ISBN 0-87436-473-6). ABC-Clio.
Women in Theatre: Compassion & Hope. Karen Malpede. LC 84-26138. 304p. 1985. 12.95 (ISBN 0-87910-035-4). Limelight Edns.
Women in Theatre: Compassion & Hope. Ed. by Karen Malpede. LC 81-12488. 304p. 1983. pap. 10.00x (ISBN 0-89676-054-5). Drama Bk.
Women in Their Own Business. Katherine Oana. (Illus.). 160p. 1983. pap. 7.95 (ISBN 0-8442-6297-8, VGM Career Horzns). Natl Textbk.
Women in their Speech Communities. Ed. by Jennifer Coates & Deborah Cameron. (Illus.). 208p. (Orig.). 1989. pap. text ed. 14.95 (ISBN 0-582-00969-3). Longman.
Women in Therapy. Harriet G. Lerner. LC 87-19326. 296p. 1988. 27.50x (ISBN 0-87668-978-0). Aronson.
Women in Third World Development. Sue E. Charlton. 250p. 1984. lib. bdg. 31.50x (ISBN 0-86531-734-8); pap. text ed. 13.95x (ISBN 0-86531-735-6). Westview.
Women in Today's Church. George Watkins. 56p. 1984. pap. 2.25 (ISBN 0-88144-025-6). Christian Pub.
Women in Tolstoy: The Ideal & the Erotic. Ruth C. Benson. LC 72-92631. pap. 38.30 (ISBN 0-317-09648-6, 2020225). Bks Demand UMI.
Women in Top Jobs, 1968 to 1979. Michael Fogarty et al. (Policy Studies Institute Ser.). vii, 273p. 1981. text ed. 30.50x (ISBN 0-435-83806-7). Gower Pub Co.
Women in Traditional China. Susan H. Gross. (Illus.). 120p. 1980. pap. 7.95 (ISBN 0-86596-002-X). Glenhurst Pubns.
Women in Transition: Career, Family, & Life Satisfaction in Three Cohorts. Catherine A. Faver. 192p. 1984. 35.00 (ISBN 0-275-91152-7, C1152). Praeger.
Women in Treatment: Creating a New Self-Image. Ed. by Barbara McFarland. 80p. 1984. pap. 5.95 (ISBN 0-89486-196-4). Hazelden.
Women in Trollope's Palliser Novels. Deborah D. Morse. Ed. by Juliet McMaster. LC 87-21497. (Nineteenth-Century Studies). 174p. 1987. 39.95 (ISBN 0-8357-1847-6). UMI Res Pr.
Women in Tune: Getting in Tune with God, Yourself & Others. Betty Malz. 192p. 1987. 9.95 (ISBN 0-8007-9112-6). Revell.
Women in Turkey (1976) T. Taskiran. (Illus.). pap. 7.00. Heinman.
Women in Twentieth-Century Literature: A Jungian View. Bettina L. Knapp. LC 86-43033. (Illus.). 256p. 1987. 24.95x (ISBN 0-271-00493-2). Pa St U Pr.
Women in U. S. History: An Annotated Bibliography. Common Women Collective Staff. LC 77-350179. (Illus.). 2.60 (ISBN 0-9601122-1-9). Common Women.
Women in War. Shelley Saywell. (Illus.). 352p. 1987. pap. 6.95 (ISBN 0-14-007623-9). Penguin.
Women in War: First Hand Accounts from World War II. Shelley Saywell. LC 85-50420. 320p. 1985. 17.95 (ISBN 0-670-80348-0). Viking.
Women in Washington: Advocates for Public Policy. Irene Tinker. LC 83-7761. (Sage Yearbooks in Women's Policy Studies: Vol. 7). 1983. 35.00 (ISBN 0-8039-2069-5); pap. 16.95 (ISBN 0-8039-2070-9). Sage.
Women in Western Civilization. Elizabeth Walsh. 320p. 1982. 18.95 (ISBN 0-87073-386-9); pap. 11.95 (ISBN 0-87073-387-7). Schenkman Bks Inc.
Women in Western European History: A Select Chronological, Geographical, & Topical Bibliography from Antiquity to the French Revolution. Ed. by Linda Frey et al. LC 81-20300. iv, 760p. 1982. lib. bdg. 50.95 (ISBN 0-313-22858-2, FEW/). Greenwood.
Women in Western European History: A Select Chronological, Geographical, & Topical Bibliography: The Nineteen & Twentieth Centuries. Ed. by Linda Frey et al. LC 81-20300. lxvi, 1088p. 1984. lib. bdg. 56.95 (ISBN 0-313-22859-0, FRW/). Greenwood.
Women in Western European History, First Supplement: A Select Chronological, Geographical, & Topical Bibliography. Ed. by Linda Frey et al. LC 86-22777. 764p. 1986. 67.95 (ISBN 0-313-25109-6, FYS/). Greenwood.
Women in Western Political Philosophy: Kant to Nietzsche. Ed. by Ellen Kennedy & Susan Mendus. LC 86-26066. 224p. 1987. 32.50 (ISBN 0-312-00425-7); pap. 12.95 (ISBN 0-312-00426-5). St Martin.
Women in Western Political Thought. Susan M. Okin. LC 79-84004. 1979. 41.00x (ISBN 0-691-07613-8); pap. 10.50x (ISBN 0-691-02191-0). Princeton U Pr.
Women in World Religions. Ed. by Arvind Sharma. LC 87-6475. (McGill Studies in the History of Religions). 302p. (Orig.). 1987. 39.50x (ISBN 0-88706-374-8); pap. 12.95x (ISBN 0-88706-375-6). State U NY Pr.
Women into the Unknown: A Sourcebook on Women Explorers & Travelers. Marion Tingling. 1989. 55.85 (ISBN 0-313-25328-5, TWU/). Greenwood.
Women: Invisible In Church & Theology. Ed. by Elisabeth S. Fiorenza & Mary Collins. (Concilium Ser.: Vol. 182). 128p. 1985. pap. 14.95 (Pub. by T & T Clark Ltd UK). Fortress.
Women, Law, & the Genesis Tradition. C. Carmichael. 112p. 1979. 16.50x (ISBN 0-85224-364-2, Pub. by Edinburgh U Pr Scotland). Columbia U Pr.
Women Lawyers Journal: 1911-1986, 72 vols. Bound set. 1040.75x (ISBN 0-686-90099-5). Rothman.
Women Lawyers: Supplementary Data to the 1971 Lawyer Statistical Report. Ed. by Martha Grossblat & Bette H. Sikes. LC 52-1123. pap. 26.00 (ISBN 0-317-29201-3, 2022253). Bks Demand UMI.
Women Leaders in African History. David Sweetman. (African Historical Biographies Ser.). (Illus.). xii, 100p. (Orig.). 1984. pap. text ed. 8.50x (ISBN 0-435-94480-0). Heinemann Ed.
Women Leaders in Contemporary U. S. Politics. Ed. by Frank P. LeVeness & Jane P. Sweeney. LC 86-24825. 164p. (Orig.). 1987. PLB 25.00x (ISBN 0-931477-87-5); pap. text ed. 12.95x (ISBN 0-931477-88-3). Lynne Rienner.
Women Leaders in the Ancient Synagogue: Inscriptional Evidence & Background Issues. Bernadette J. Brooten. LC 82-10658. (Brown Judaic Studies). 292p. 1982. pap. 20.00 (14 00 36). Scholars Pr GA.
Women Leading: Making Tough Choices on the Fast Track. Nancy Collins et al. LC 87-25130. 208p. 1988. 17.95 (ISBN 0-8289-0567-3). Greene.
Women, Letters & the Novel. Ruth Perry. LC 79-8637. (Studies in the Eighteenth Century: No. 4). (Illus.). 1980. 39.50 (ISBN 0-404-18025-6). AMS Pr.
Women, Literature, Criticism. Ed. by Harry R. Garvin. LC 77-95051. (Bucknell Review Ser.: Vol. 24, No. 1). 177p. 1978. 16.50 (ISBN 0-8387-2230-X). Bucknell U Pr.
Women Living Change. Susan C. Bourque & Donna R. Divine. LC 84-25277. (Women in the Political Economy Ser.). 288p. 1985. 29.95 (ISBN 0-87722-369-6). Temple U Pr.
Women Living Longer & Better: Ideas & Ideals from Swedish Health Care. Ed. by Gunnela Westlander. LC 88-2927. (Women & Health Ser.: Vol. 13, Nos. 3-4). (Illus.). 190p. 1988. pap. text ed. 9.95 (ISBN 0-918393-46-9). Harrington Pk.
Women Making History: Conversations with Fifteen New Yorkers. Helen Benedict et al. Ed. by Maxine Gold. LC 85-2976. 160p. (Orig.). 1985. pap. 4.95 (ISBN 0-9610688-1-7). NYC Comm Women.
Women Making It. Ruth Halcomb. 288p. 1981. pap. 2.95 (ISBN 0-345-29348-7). Ballantine.
Women Making Music: The Western Art Tradition, 1150-1950. Ed. by Jane Bowers & Judith Tick. LC 85-8642. (Illus.). 422p. 1986. pap. 14.95 (ISBN 0-252-01470-7). U of Ill Pr.
Women Managers: Changing Organizational Cultures. Asplund. LC 88-10801. 150p. 1988. write for info. (ISBN 0-471-91292-1). Wiley.
Women Managers: Travellers in a Male World. Judi Marshall. LC 83-23579. 260p. 1984. pap. 29.95 (ISBN 0-471-90419-8). Wiley.
Women, Marriage, & Politics, 1860-1914. Pat Jalland. (Illus.). 380p. 1987. 37.00x (ISBN 0-19-822668-3). Oxford U Pr.
Women, Marriage, & Politics, 1860-1914. Pat Jalland. (Illus.). 384p. 1988. pap. 13.95 (ISBN 0-19-282087-7). Oxford U Pr.
Women MBAs: A Foot in the Door. Mary D. Fillmore. (Illus.). 245p. 1987. 25.00 (ISBN 0-8161-8728-2). G K Hall.
Women Mean Business: Successful Strategies for Starting Your Own Business. Moneca Litton. 208p. 1987. pap. 16.95 (ISBN 1-55013-017-X, Pub. by Key Porter Canada). U of Toronto Pr.
Women-Men. Paul Verlaine. Tr. by Allistair Elliot. 151p. 1984. 13.95 (ISBN 0-935296-44-1); pap. 8.95 (ISBN 0-935296-45-X). Sheep Meadow.
Women, Men & Language. Jennifer Coates. (Studies in Language & Linguistics). 200p. 1986. pap. text ed. 12.95 (ISBN 0-582-29133-X). Longman.
Women, Men & the Bible. Virginia Mollencott. 160p. 1988. pap. 7.95 (ISBN 0-8245-0893-9). Crossroad NY.
Women, Men, & the Bible. Virginia R. Mollenkott. LC 76-40446. 1977. pap. 8.95 (ISBN 0-687-45970-2) (ISBN 0-687-81914-8). Abingdon.
Women, Men, & the International Division of Labor. Ed. by June Nash & Maria P. Fernandez-Kelly. LC 82-10447. (SUNY Series in the Anthropology of Work). (Illus.). 463p. 1984. 49.50x (ISBN 0-87395-683-4); pap. 14.95x (ISBN 0-87395-684-2). State U NY Pr.
Women Men Love - Women Men Leave. Connell Cowan & Melvyn Kinder. 1988. pap. 4.95 (ISBN 0-451-15306-5, Sig). NAL.
Women Men Love - Women Men Leave: Why Men Are Drawn to Women - What Makes Them Want to Stay. Connell Cowan & Melvyn Kinder. 1987. 18.95 (ISBN 0-517-56248-0, C N Potter Bks). Crown.
Women Men Love--Women Men Leave: Understanding Passion & Commitment. Melvyn I. Kinder & Connell Cowan. 1987. 18.95 (C N Potter Bks). Crown.
Women-Men-Management. Ann Harriman. 336p. 1985. pap. 13.95 (ISBN 0-275-91810-6, B1810). Praeger.
Women: Menopause & Middle Age. Vidals Clay. 1977. perfect bdg. 5.00 (ISBN 0-912786-37-X). Know Inc.
Women Ministers: A Quaker Contribution. Robert J. Leach. Ed. by Ruth Blattenberger. LC 79-84922. 1979. pap. 2.50x (ISBN 0-87574-227-0). Pendle Hill.
Women Ministers: How Women Are Re-defining Traditional Roles. Ed. by Judith L. Weidman. LC 80-8345. 192p. (Orig.). 1981. pap. 7.95 (ISBN 0-06-069291-X, RD 528, HarpR). Har-Row.
Women Ministers?! Women in Paul & Adventchristendom. Craig R. Dunham. 98p. (Orig.). 1986. pap. 4.95 (ISBN 0-913439-04-5). Henceforth.
Women, Ministry, & the Church. Joan Chittister. LC 82-62418. 1983. pap. 5.95 (ISBN 0-8091-2528-5). Paulist Pr.
Women, Nazis, & Universities: Female University Students in the Third Reich, 1933-1945. Jacques R. Pauwels. LC 83-20161. (Contributions in Women's Studies: No. 50). (Illus.). 288p. 1984. lib. bdg. 35.00 (ISBN 0-313-24203-8, PWU/). Greenwood.
Women, Nineteen Eighty. 43p. 1987. 5.00 (ISBN 92-1-130099-1, E.85.IV.4). UN.
Women Nineteen Fifty-Seven to Nineteen Seventy-Five. Photos by Joan Liffring-Zug. LC 81-80099. (Illus.). 72p. 1981. pap. 12.50 (ISBN 0-9603858-4-3). Penfield.
Women Novelists. Reginald Johnson. LC 72-3467. (Studies in Fiction, No. 34). 1972. Repr. of 1918 ed. lib. bdg. 49.95x (ISBN 0-8383-1496-1). Haskell.
Women Novelists. facs. ed. Reginald B. Johnson. LC 67-23235. (Essay Index Reprint Ser). 1967. Repr. of 1919 ed. 18.00 (ISBN 0-8369-0576-8). Ayer Co Pubs.
Women Novelists. M. Masefield. 59.95 (ISBN 0-8490-1323-2). Gordon Pr.
Women Novelists from Fanny Burney to George Eliot. facs. ed. Muriel A. Masefield. LC 67-23244. (Essay Index Reprint Ser.). 1934. 17.00 (ISBN 0-8369-0689-6). Ayer Co Pubs.
Women Novelists in Spain & Spanish America. Lucia Fox-Lockert. LC 79-23727. 356p. 1979. 24.00 (ISBN 0-8108-1270-3). Scarecrow.
Women Novelists of Queen Victoria's Reign. Mrs. Oliphant et al. LC 74-34124. 1897. lib. bdg. 45.00 (ISBN 0-8414-6521-5). Folcroft.
Women Novelists: Their Contribution to the Proletarian Novel in the Victorian Age. K. C. Shrivastava. Ed. by James Hogg. (Romantic Reassessment Ser.). (Orig.). 1984. pap. 15.00 (ISBN 3-7052-0526-9, Pub. by Salzburg Studies). Longwood Pub Group.
Women Novelists Today: A Survey of English Writers in the Seventies & Eighties. Olga Kenyon. LC 87-35602. 208p. 1988. 29.95 (ISBN 0-312-01344-2). St Martin.
Women of a Certain Age: The Midlife Search for Self. Lillian Rubin. LC 79-1681. 320p. 1981. pap. 7.95 (ISBN 0-06-090833-5, CN 833, PL). Har-Row.
Women of Academe: Outsiders in the Sacred Grove. Mona Harrington & Nadya Aisenberg. LC 87-30067. 224p. 1988. lib. bdg. 30.00x (ISBN 0-87023-606-7); pap. 10.95 (ISBN 0-87023-607-5). U of Mass Pr.
Women of Action in Tudor England. Pearl Hogrefe. (Illus.). 1977. 11.50x (ISBN 0-8138-0910-X). Iowa St U Pr.
Women of Africa: Roots of Oppression. Maria R. Cutrufelli. Tr. by Nicolas Romano from Ital. LC 83-225772. (Illus.). 192p. 1983. 25.00x (ISBN 0-86232-083-6, 1-102, Pub. by Zed Pr); pap. 9.25 (ISBN 0-86232-084-4). Humanities.
Women of America: A History. Carol Berkin & Mary B. Norton. LC 78-69589. (Illus.). 1979. pap. text ed. 26.76 (ISBN 0-395-27067-7). HM.
Women of America: Clara Barton. rev. ed. Cindy Klingel. (We the People Ser.). (gr. 2-4). 1987. 11.65 (ISBN 0-88682-168-1). Creative Ed.
Women of America: Dolly Madison. Cindy Klingel. (We the People Ser.). (gr. 2-4). 1987. 11.65 (ISBN 0-88682-167-3). Creative Ed.
Women of America: Elizabeth Blackwell. rev. ed. Cindy Klingel. (We the People Ser.). (gr. 2-4). 1987. 11.65 (ISBN 0-88682-169-X). Creative Ed.
Women of America: Harriet Tubman. Cindy Klingel. (We the People Ser.). (gr. 2-4). 1987. 11.65 (ISBN 0-88682-166-5). Creative Ed.
Women of America: Jane Addams. Cindy Klingel. (We the People Ser.). (gr. 2-4). 1987. 11.65 (ISBN 0-88682-165-7). Creative Ed.
Women of America: Susan B. Anthony. rev. ed. Cindy Klingel. (We the People Ser.). (gr. 2-4). 1987. 11.65 (ISBN 0-88682-164-9). Creative Ed.
Women of Amran: A Middle Eastern Ethnographic Study. Susan Dorsky. (Illus.). 216p. 1986. 22.50x (ISBN 0-87480-250-4). U of Utah Pr.
Women of Asia: Yesterday & Today. Soon Man Rhim. 140p. (Orig.). 1982. pap. 7.95 (ISBN 0-377-00134-1). Friendship Pr.
Women of Bengal. M. M. Urquhart. 165p. 1987. Repr. of 1925 ed. 24.50x (ISBN 0-8364-2159-0, Pub. by Gian Pubs Hse). South Asia Bks.
Women of Brewster Place. Gloria Naylor. (Contemporary American Fiction Ser.). 208p. 1983. pap. 6.95 (ISBN 0-14-006690-X). Penguin.
Women of Brewster Place: A Novel in Seven Stories. Gloria Naylor. (Illus.). 208p. 1988. pap. 4.50 (ISBN 0-451-82202-1). NAL.
Women of Brewster Place: A Novel in Seven Stories. Gloria Naylor. 1988. pap. 4.50. Penguin.
Women of Cairo: Scenes of Life on the Orient, 2 Vols. Gerard de Nerval. LC 77-87652. 720p. Repr. of 1929 ed. Set. 67.50 (ISBN 0-404-16420-X). AMS Pr.
Women of Calvary. Marguerite D. Brown. 1982. pap. 5.25 ea. (ISBN 0-89536-526-X, 2331). CSS of Ohio.
Women of China: Imperialism & Women's Resistance, 1900-1949. Bobby Siu. 210p. 1982. text ed. 20.25x (ISBN 0-905762-58-4, Pub. by Zed Pr); pap. text ed. 9.25 (ISBN 0-905762-63-0). Humanities.
Women of Color: A Filmography of Minority & Third World Women. Maryann Oshana. LC 82-49143. (Reference Library of Social Science). 350p. 1984. 30.00 (ISBN 0-8240-9140-X). Garland Pub.
Women of Crisis. Robert Coles & Jane H. Coles. 304p. 1979. pap. 8.95 (ISBN 0-385-29169-8, Delta). Dell.
Women of Cuba. Inger Holt-Seeland. LC 82-2889. (Illus.). 128p. 1982. 14.95 (ISBN 0-88208-142-X); pap. 7.95 (ISBN 0-88208-143-8). Chicago Review.
Women of Darkness. Kathryn Ptacek. 400p. 1989. pap. price not set. Tor Bks.
Women of Darkness: Original Horror & Dark Fantasy by Contemporary Women Writers. Ed. by Kathryn Ptacek. 320p. 1988. 17.95. Tor Bks.
Women of Early Christianity. Alexander Carroll. 75.00 (ISBN 0-87968-268-X). Gordon Pr.
Women of Eden. Marilyn Harris. 608p. 1982. pap. 3.50 (ISBN 0-345-30970-7). Ballantine.
Women of Egypt. Elizabeth Cooper. LC 79-2934. (Illus.). 380p. 1988. Repr. of 1914 ed. 33.00 (ISBN 0-8305-0102-9). Hyperion Conn.
Women of El Salvador: The Price of Freedom. Marilyn Thomson. LC 86-7364. (Illus.). 176p. 1986. text ed. 27.50 (ISBN 0-89727-071-1); pap. text ed. 9.95 (ISBN 0-89727-073-8). ISHI PA.
Women of England from Anglo-Saxon Times to the Present: Interpretive Bibliographical Essays. Ed. by Barbara Kanner. LC 78-32166. 429p. 1979. 37.50 (ISBN 0-208-01639-2, Archon). Shoe String.
Women of Europe: Women Members of the European Parliament & Equality Policy. Elizabeth Vallance & Elizabeth Davies. 200p. 1986. 37.50 (ISBN 0-521-26562-2). Cambridge U Pr.
Women of Exile: German-Jewish Autobiographies Since Nineteen Thirty-Three. Ed. by Andreas Lixl-Purcell. LC 87-24952. (Contributions in Women's Studies: No. 91). 241p. 1988. lib. bdg. 35.00 (ISBN 0-313-25921-6, LXP/). Greenwood.
Women of Fair Hope. Paul M. Gaston. LC 84-103. (Mercer University Lamar Memorial Lecture Ser.: No. 25). 160p. 1984. 15.00x (ISBN 0-8203-0718-1). U of Ga Pr.

TITLE INDEX WOMEN OF TRACHIS

Women of Fair Hope. Paul M. Gaston. LC 84-103. (Mercer University Lamar Memorial Lecture: No. 25). 160p. 1986. pap. 9.95x (ISBN 0-8203-0840-4). U of GA Pr.

Women of Faith. Gladys Seashore. 1983. pap. 2.50 (ISBN 0-911802-55-X). Free Church Pubns.

Women of Faith & Spirit: Profiles of Fifteen Biblical Witnesses. Margaret Wold. LC 86-28770. 144p. (Orig.). 1987. pap. 6.95 (ISBN 0-8066-2251-2, 10-7236). Augsburg.

Women of Faith & Spirit: Their Words & Thoughts. Ed. by Mary A. Warner & Dayna Beilenson. LC 87-60949. (Illus.). 64p. 1987. 5.95 (ISBN 0-88088-583-1). Peter Pauper.

Women of Faith in Dialogue. Virginia R. Mollencott. 144p. (Orig.). 1987. pap. 9.95 (ISBN 0-8245-0823-8). Crossroad NY.

Women of Gion. Akahige Namban. 1988. pap. 4.50 (ISBN 0-8216-5036-X). Blue Moon Bks.

Women of Grace. Betty J. Grams. LC 77-93409. 128p. 1978. pap. 2.50 (ISBN 0-88243-751-8, 02-0751); leader's guide 3.95 (ISBN 0-88243-336-9, 02-0336). Gospel Pub.

Women of Grace: A Biographical Dictionary of British Women Saints, Martyrs & Reformers. Kathleen Parbury. 224p. 1985. 25.00x (ISBN 0-85362-213-2, Oriel). Routledge Chapman & Hall.

Women of Grace: James's Plays & the Comedy of Manners. Susan Carlson. Ed. by A. Walton Litz. LC 84-23932. (Studies in Modern Literature Ser.: No. 48). 200p. 1984. 37.95 (ISBN 0-8357-1617-1). UMI Res Pr.

Women of Guinea Lane. Gabriel Fielding. 288p. 1988. 18.95 (ISBN 0-09-163980-8, Pub. by Century Hutchinson). David & Charles.

Women of Hawaii. Don Berry. (Illus.). 84p. (Orig.). 1986. pap. 17.95 (ISBN 0-916947-04-1). Winn Bks.

Women of Her Word: Hispanic Women Write. Ed. by Evangelina Vigil-Pinon. Date not set. price not set. Arte Publico.

Women of Ideas: And What Men Have Done to Them. Dale Spender. 800p. (Orig.). 1984. pap. 9.95 (ISBN 0-7448-0003-X, Ark Paperbks). Routledge Chapman & Hall.

Women of India: An Annotated Bibliography. Harshida Pandit. LC 82-49172. 1985. 52.00 (ISBN 0-8240-9175-2). Garland Pub.

Women of Iran. Ed. by Farah Azari. 225p. (Orig.). 1984. pap. 8.00 (ISBN 0-903729-95-4). Evergreen Dist.

Women of Iron & Velvet & the Books They Wrote in France. Margaret Crosland. LC 77-359824. pap. 63.80 (ISBN 0-317-29891-7, 2019384). Bks Demand UMI.

Women of Iron & Velvet: French Women Writers After George Sand. Margaret Crosland. LC 75-8202. 192p. 1976. 10.95 (ISBN 0-8008-8436-1). Taplinger.

Women of Letters, 2 vols. Gertrude T. Mayer. LC 73-1197. (Essay Index Reprint Ser.). Repr. of 1894 ed. 48.75 (ISBN 0-518-10059-6). Ayer Co Pubs.

Women of Letters, 96 vols. (AMS Press Reprint Ser.). Repr. Set. write for info. (ISBN 0-404-56700-2). AMS Pr.

Women of Letters: Selected Letters of Elizabeth Barrett Browning & Mary Russell Mitford. Ed. by Meredith B. Raymond & Mary R. Sullivan. 312p. 1987. 29.95 (ISBN 0-8057-9023-3, Twayne). G K Hall.

Women of Lowell: An Original Anthology. Ed. by Leon Stein & Annette K. Baxter. LC 74-3989. (Women in America Ser). 362p. 1974. Repr. of 1974 ed. 29.00x (ISBN 0-405-06127-7). Ayer Co Pubs.

Women of Magdalena: An Epic Poem. S. Diane Bogus. (Illus.). 40p. 1988. write for info. (ISBN 0-934172-15-3); pap. write for info. (ISBN 0-934172-16-1). WIM Pubns.

Women of Maine. Lee Agger. (Illus.). 250p. 1982. pap. 10.95 (ISBN 0-930096-21-5). G Gannett.

Women of Marrakech. Leonora Peets. Tr. by Rein Taagepera from Estonian. LC 87-26536. 240p. 1988. lib. bdg. 27.95 (ISBN 0-8223-0812-6). Duke.

Women of Mathematics: A Bibliographic Sourcebook. Ed. by Louise S. Grinstein & Paul J. Campbell. LC 86-25711. 312p. 1987. lib. bdg. 45.00 (ISBN 0-313-24849-4, GWM/). Greenwood.

Women of Medieval France. Pierce Butler. 75.00 (ISBN 0-87968-269-8). Gordon Pr.

Women of Messina. Elio Vittorini. Tr. by Frances Frenaye & Frances Keene. LC 73-78787. 320p. 1973. 9.50 (ISBN 0-8112-0496-0); pap. 3.75 (ISBN 0-8112-0497-9, NDP365). New Directions.

Women of Methodism: Its Three Foundresses, Susanna Wesley, the Countess of Huntingdon, & Barbara Heck. Abel Stevens. Ed. by Carolyn D. Gifford & Donald Dayton. (Women in American Protestant Religion 1800-1930 Ser.). 304p. 1987. lib. bdg. 45.00 (ISBN 0-8240-0676-3). Garland Pub.

Women of Mexico City, 1790-1857. Silvia M. Arrom. LC 83-51324. (Illus.). 400p. 1985. 42.50x (ISBN 0-8047-1233-6). Stanford U Pr.

Women of Minnesota: Selected Biographical Essays. Ed. by Barbara Stuhler & Gretchen Kreuter. LC 77-3361. (Illus.). 402p. 1977. 12.95 (ISBN 0-87351-112-3). Minn Hist.

Women of Mr. Wesley's Methodism. Earl K. Brown. LC 83-22010. (Studies in Women & Religion: Vol. 11). 273p. 1984. lib. bdg. 49.95x (ISBN 0-88946-538-X). E Mellen.

Women of Modern Science. Edna Yost. LC 84-12981. (Illus.). xiv, 176p. 1984. Repr. of 1959 ed. lib. bdg. 38.50 (ISBN 0-313-23115-X, YOWS). Greenwood.

Women of Montparnasse. Morrill Cody & Hugh Ford. LC 81-71638. (Illus.). 192p. 1984. 16.95 (ISBN 0-8453-4747-0, Cornwall Bks). Assoc Univ Prs.

Women of My Other Worlds. Olivia Casberg. LC 84-27221. 100p. (Orig.). 1985. pap. 5.95 (ISBN 0-933380-30-5). Olive Pr Pubns.

Women of New England, Vol. I. Lee Agger. 1985. pap. 9.95 (ISBN 0-930096-68-1). G Gannett.

Women of New England, Vol. II. Lee Agger. 1986. pap. 10.95 (ISBN 0-317-19633-2). G Gannett.

Women of New York: The Underworld of the Great City. George Ellington. LC 72-2600. (American Women Ser.: Images & Realities). 770p. 1972. Repr. of 1869 ed. 40.00 (ISBN 0-405-04456-9). Ayer Co Pubs.

Women of Old Hawaii. Maxine Mrantz. LC 87-125364. (Hawaiiana Ser.). (Illus.). 38p. (Orig.). pap. 3.95 (ISBN 0-941351-01-7). Aloha Pub.

Women of Omdurman: Life, Love & the Cult of Virginity. Anne Cloudsley. LC 83-40625. 181p. 1985. 22.50 (ISBN 0-312-88755-8). St Martin.

Women of Pakistan, Two Steps Forward; One Step Back? Khawar Mumtaz & Farida Shaheed. LC 87-13319. (Illus.). 256p. 1987. 37.50 (ISBN 0-86232-280-4, Pub. by Zed Pr England); pap. 11.50 (ISBN 0-86232-281-2, Pub. by Zed Pr England). Humanities.

Women of Psychology. Gwendolyn Stevens & Sheldon Gardner. 300p. 1982. Set. text ed. 15.25. Vol. I (ISBN 0-87073-443-1). Vol. II (ISBN 0-87073-445-8). Set. pap. text ed. 9.95. Vol. I (ISBN 0-87073-444-X). Vol. II (ISBN 0-87073-446-6). Schenkman Bks Inc.

Women of Rural Asia. Robert O. Whyte & Pauline Whyte. (Women in Contemporary Society Ser.). 285p. (Orig.). 1982. lib. bdg. 26.50x (ISBN 0-86531-278-8); pap. text ed. 11.50x (ISBN 0-86531-337-7). Westview.

Women of Skid Row: A Pen & Ink Sketchbook with Commentary. Ann A. Wolken. (Illus., Orig.). 1982. pap. 10.00 (ISBN 0-943756-00-6). Shadyside.

Women of Smoke. Marjorie Agosin. Tr. by Naomi Lindstrom. 112p. 1988. pap. 10.95 (ISBN 0-935480-34-X). Lat Am Lit Rev Pr.

Women of Some Importance: Mary Wollstonecraft. Ralph Nevill. 304p. 1981. Repr. of 1929 ed. lib. bdg. 40.00 (ISBN 0-8495-4025-9). Arden Lib.

Women of South Asia: A Guide to Resources. Carol Sakala. LC 79-28191. 1980. lib. bdg. 40.00 (ISBN 0-527-78574-1). Kraus Intl.

Women of Southeast Asia: Illinois University Center for SEAsian Studies. Penny Van Esterik. (Occasional Paper Ser.: No. 9). viii, 274p. (Orig.). 1982. pap. 14.00 (ISBN 0-686-38779-1). North Ill U Ctr SE Asian.

Women of Spirit. Rosemary Ruether & Eleanor McLaughlin. 1979. pap. 11.95 (ISBN 0-671-24805-7, Touchstone Bks). S&S.

Women of Steel: Female Blue-Collar Workers in the Basic Steel Industry. Kay Deaux & Joseph C. Ullman. 208p. 1983. 35.00 (ISBN 0-275-90969-7, C0969). Praeger.

Women of Suye Mura. Robert J. Smith & Ella L. Wiswell. LC 82-2708. (Illus.). 320p. 1983. pap. 11.00x (ISBN 0-226-76345-5). U of Chicago Pr.

Women of the Air. Judy Lomax. LC 86-24206. (Illus.). 1987. 15.95 (ISBN 0-396-08980-1). Dodd.

Women of the Air. Judy Lomax. 1988. pap. 3.95 (ISBN 0-8041-0311-9, Pub. by Ivy). Ballantine.

Women of the Air. David Mondey. LC 81-86277. (In Profile Ser.). 1982. PLB 13.96 (ISBN 0-382-06634-0). Silver.

Women of the American Revolution. Elizabeth Ellet. LC 68-31269. (American History & Americana Ser., No. 47). 1969. lib. bdg. 175.00x (ISBN 0-8383-0197-5). Haskell.

Women of the American Revolution, Vol. I. Elizabeth Ellet. 348p. 1980. Repr. of 1848 ed. 20.00 (ISBN 0-87928-106-5). Corner Hse.

Women of the American Revolution, Vol. II. Elizabeth Ellet. 312p. 1980. Repr. of 1848 ed. 20.00 (ISBN 0-87928-107-3). Corner Hse.

Women of the American Revolution, Vol. III. Elizabeth Ellet. 396p. 1980. Repr. of 1850 ed. 20.00 (ISBN 0-87928-108-1). Corner Hse.

Women of the Andes. Susan C. Bourque & Kay B. Warren. (Women & Culture Ser.; Patriarchy & Social Change in Two Peruvian Towns). 320p. 1981. text ed. 18.50x (ISBN 0-472-06330-8); pap. text ed. 11.95x (ISBN 0-472-09330-4). U of Mich Pr.

Women of the Barrio: Class & Gender in a Colombian City. Kristina Bohman. (Stockholm Studies in Social Anthropology: No. 13). (Illus.). 374p. 1984. pap. text ed. 45.00x (ISBN 91-7146-423-9, Pub. by Almqvist & Wiksell). Humanities.

Women of the Bible. Daughters of St. Paul. LC 71-145574. (Illus.). 5.95 (ISBN 0-8198-0322-7); pap. 4.95 (ISBN 0-8198-0323-5). Dghtrs St Paul.

Women of the Bible. rev. ed. Frances VanderVelde. LC 83-19894. (Illus.). 260p. 1973. pap. 7.95 (ISBN 0-8254-3951-5). Kregel.

Women of the Bible: Sculpture. Edwina Sandys & James P. Morton. Ed. by Thomas Piche, Jr. LC 86-83188. (Illus.). 24p. (Orig.). 1986. pap. text ed. write for info. (ISBN 0-914407-07-4). Everson Mus.

Women of the Bible Speak to Women of Today. Dorothy Elder. LC 86-70873. (Illus.). 288p. (Orig.). 1986. pap. 12.00 (ISBN 0-87516-574-5). DeVorss.

Women of the Bible Tell Their Stories. Mary E. Jensen. LC 78-52193. 1978. pap. 7.95 (ISBN 0-8066-1663-6, 10-7235). Augsburg.

Women of the Caesars. Guglielmo Ferrero. (Illus.). 1977. 117.75 (ISBN 0-89266-632-3). Am Classical Coll Pr.

Women of the Caesars. Guglielmo Ferrero. Tr. by Christian Gause. 337p. 1978. Repr. of 1911 ed. 21.00 (ISBN 0-87928-093-X). Corner Hse.

Women of the Caesars: Their Lives & Portraits on Coins. Giorgio Giacosa. 55.00 (ISBN 0-318-19612-3). Numismatic Fine Arts.

Women of the Caribbean. Ed. by Pat Ellis. 176p. 1987. 29.95 (ISBN 0-86232-596-X, Pub. by Zed Pr UK); pap. 9.95 (ISBN 0-86232-597-8, Pub. by Zed Pr UK). Humanities.

Women of the Celts. Jean Markale. 315p. 1986. pap. 12.95 (ISBN 0-89281-150-1). Inner Tradit.

Women of the Celts. Jean Markale. 315p. 1986. 24.95 (ISBN 0-89281-201-X). Inner Tradit.

Women of the Cloth: New Opportunity for the Churches. Jackson W. Carroll & Barbara J. Hargrove. LC 82-47740. 288p. 1983. 14.45 (ISBN 0-06-061321-1, HarpR). Har-Row.

Women of the Confederacy. Francis B. Simkins & James W. Patton. LC 70-145300. (Illus.). 1971. Repr. of 1936 ed. 39.00 (ISBN 0-403-01212-0). Scholarly.

Women of the Depression: Caste & Culture in San Antonio, 1929-1939. Julia K. Blackwelder. LC 83-40496. (Texas A&M Southwestern Studies: No. 2). (Illus.). 1984. 22.50x (ISBN 0-89096-177-8). Tex A&M Univ Pr.

Women of the English Renaissance & Reformation. Retha M. Warnicke. LC 82-12180. (Contributions in Women's Studies: No. 38). viii, 228p. 1983. lib. bdg. 35.00 (ISBN 0-313-23611-9, WTW/). Greenwood.

Women of the Fertile Crescent: An Anthology of Arab Women's Poems. Ed. & tr. by Kamal Boullata. LC 77-3834. (Illus., Orig.). 1978. pap. 10.00 (ISBN 0-914478-42-7). Three Continents.

Women of the Forest. Robert Murphy et al. LC 74-9912. (Illus.). 256p. 1974. pap. 11.00 (ISBN 0-231-03881-X). Columbia U Pr.

Women of the Forest. 2nd ed. Yolanda Murphy & Robert F. Murphy. LC 85-14969. 275p. 1985. 25.00x (ISBN 0-231-06088-2); pap. 11.00x (ISBN 0-231-06089-0). Columbia U Pr.

Women of the Four Winds. Dual ed. Elizabeth F. Olds. (Illus.). 263p. 1985. 17.95 (ISBN 0-395-36199-0); pap. 9.95 (ISBN 0-395-39584-4). HM.

Women of the French Revolution. Linda Kelly. (Illus.). 170p. 1988. 29.95 (ISBN 0-241-12112-4, Pub. by Hamish Hamilton). David & Charles.

Women of the French Revolution. R. McNair Wilson. 75.00 (ISBN 0-8490-1324-0). Gordon Pr.

Women of the French Revolution. R. McNair Wilson. LC 72-110928. 1970. Repr. of 1936 ed. 24.50 (ISBN 0-8046-0910-1, Pub. by Kennikat). Assoc Faculty Pr.

Women of the Future: The Female Main Character in Science Fiction. Betty King. LC 83-21030. 295p. 1984. 20.00 (ISBN 0-8108-1664-4). Scarecrow.

Women of the Golden Horn. LC 76-3077. 1976. pap. 3.00 (ISBN 0-916816-01-X). Ryder Pr.

Women of the Gospel. Daughters of St. Paul. LC 74-32122. 1975. 5.95 (ISBN 0-8198-0495-9). Dghtrs St Paul.

Women of the Left Bank: Paris, 1900-1940. Shari Benstock. (Illus.). 566p. (Orig.). 1986. 26.95 (ISBN 0-292-79029-5); pap. 12.95 (ISBN 0-292-79040-6). U of Tex Pr.

Women of the Louisiana Legislature. Louise B. Johnson. LC 86-81866. (Illus.). 101p. (Orig.). 1986. 18.50 (ISBN 0-9617394-0-1). Greenbay Pub.

Women of the Mayflower & Women of Plymouth Colony. Ethel J. Noyes. LC 73-12780. 197p. Repr. of 1921 ed. 36.00x (ISBN 0-8103-3668-5). Gale.

Women of the Medieval World. Julius Kirshner & Suzanne F. Wemple. 390p. (Orig.). Date not set. pap. text ed. 15.95 (ISBN 0-631-15492-2). Basil Blackwell.

Women of the Medieval World: Essays in Honor of John H. Mundy. Ed. by Julius Kirshner & Suzanne F. Wemple. 352p. 1985. 45.00x (ISBN 0-631-13872-2). Basil Blackwell.

Women of the Mediterranean. Ed. by Monique Gadant. Tr. by A. M. Berrett from Fr. 208p. 1986. 32.50 (ISBN 0-86232-527-7, Pub. by Zed Pr UK); pap. 11.50 (ISBN 0-86232-528-5, Pub. by Zed Pr UK). Humanities.

Women of the New Right. Rebecca E. Klatch. (Women in the Political Economy Ser.). 288p. 1987. 24.95 (ISBN 0-87722-470-6). Temple U Pr.

Women of the New Right. Rebecca E. Klatch. (Women in the Political Economy Ser.). 264p. 1988. pap. text ed. 14.95 (ISBN 0-87722-590-7). Temple U Pr.

Women of the New Testament. Abraham Kuyper. pap. 5.95 (ISBN 0-310-36751-4, 9996P). Zondervan.

Women of the North. Jane Wordsworth. (Illus.). 207p. 1983. Repr. of 1981 ed. 15.95 (ISBN 0-00-216977-0, Pub. by W Collins New Zealand). Intl Spec Bk.

Women of the Old Testament. Rebecca Daniel. (Our Greatest Heritage Ser.). (Illus.). 32p. (gr. 7-12). 1983. wkbk. 3.95 (ISBN 0-86653-142-4, SS 811). Good Apple.

Women of the Old Testament. Abraham Kuyper. pap. 5.95 (ISBN 0-310-36761-1, 9997P). Zondervan.

Women of the Orient. 2nd ed. Boye De Mente. LC 84-42989. 1985. pap. 4.95 (ISBN 0-914778-57-9). Phoenix Bks.

Women of the Raj. Margaret Macmillan. LC 87-50183. (Illus.). 256p. 1988. 17.95 (ISBN 0-500-01420-5). Thames Hudson.

Women of the Regent Hotel: The Unheard Voices of the Homeless in Poems, With Portraits by Elliot Schneider. The Women of the Regent Hotel. 32p. (Orig.). 1988. pap. text ed. 10.00 (ISBN 0-9619403-0-1). Jewish Bd Family.

Women of the Regiment: Marriage & the Victorian Army. Myna Trustram. (Illus.). 280p. 1984. 44.50 (ISBN 0-521-26294-1). Cambridge U Pr.

Women of the Renaissance: A Study of Feminism. L. De Maulde & R. LaClaviere. 1976. lib. bdg. 69.95 (ISBN 0-8490-2835-3). Gordon Pr.

Women of the Renaissance: A Study of Feminism. R. De Maulde. LC 78-15352. 1978. Repr. of 1905 ed. lib. bdg. 65.00 (ISBN 0-8414-3665-7). Folcroft.

Women of the Republic: Intellect & Ideology in Revolutionary America. Linda K. Kerber. LC 79-28683. (Institute of Early American History & Culture Ser.). xiv, 304p. 1980. 27.50x (ISBN 0-8078-1440-7). U of NC Pr.

Women of the Republic: Intellect & Ideology in Revolutionary America. Linda K. Kerber. (Illus.). 320p. 1986. pap. 8.95 (ISBN 0-393-30345-4). Norton.

Women of the Roman Aristocracy As Christian Monastics. Anne E. Hickey. Ed. by Margaret R. Miles. LC 86-19242. (Studies in Religion: No. 1). 159p. 1986. 39.95 (ISBN 0-8357-1757-7). UMI Res Pr.

Women of the Salons. Evelyn B. Hall. LC 73-90640. (Essay Index Reprint Ser). 1926. 19.00 (ISBN 0-8369-1262-4). Ayer Co Pubs.

Women of the Shadows. Ann Cornelisen. 1977. pap. 6.95 (ISBN 0-394-72345-7, Vin). Random.

Women of the Shtetl: Through the Eye of Y. L. Peretz. Ruth Adler. LC 78-69895. (Illus.). 152p. 1979. 17.50 (ISBN 0-8386-2336-0). Fairleigh Dickinson.

Women of the South Distinguished in Literature. Mary Forrest, pseud. 1972. Repr. of 1861 ed. lib. bdg. 28.00 (ISBN 0-8422-8047-2). Irvington.

Women of the Third World. Jeanne Bisilliat et al. Tr. by Enne Amann & Peter Amann. LC 86-46328. 104p. 1987. 19.50x (ISBN 0-8386-3311-0). Fairleigh Dickinson.

Women of the Twenties. George H. Douglas. LC 86-1848. (Illus.). 230p. 1986. 16.95 (ISBN 0-933071-06-X, Dist. by W. W. Norton). Saybrook Pub Co.

Women of the United Arab Emirates. Linda Soffan. LC 80-492966. 127p. 1980. 26.50x (ISBN 0-389-20001-8, 06690). B&N Imports.

Women of the Upper Class. Susan A. Ostrander. LC 83-18214. (Women in the Political Economy Ser.). 256p. 1984. 16.95 (ISBN 0-87722-334-3). Temple U Pr.

Women of the Upper Class. Susan A. Ostrander. (Women in the Political Economy Ser.). 256p. 1986. pap. 9.95 (ISBN 0-87722-475-7). Temple U Pr.

Women of the War: Their Heroism & Self-Sacrifice. Frank Moore. xvi, 596p. Repr. of 1866 ed. 69.00 (ISBN 0-932051-34-0, Pub. by Am Repr Serv). Am Biog Serv.

Women of the West. Cathy Luchetti & Carol Olwell. LC 81-13035. (Illus.). 240p. 1982. pap. 17.00 (ISBN 0-917946-03-0). Antelope Island.

Women of the West. Rick Steber. (Old Oregon Country Ser.: Vol. 5). (Illus.). 60p. (Orig.). 1988. pap. 4.95 (ISBN 0-945134-05-3). Bonanza Pub Ltd.

Women of the Word: Contemporary Sermons by Women Clergy. Bracken et al. Ed. by Charles Hackett. LC 84-52656. (Illus.). 144p. (Orig.). 1985. pap. 8.95 (ISBN 0-932419-00-3). Susan Hunter.

Women of the World: Illusion & Reality. U. Phadnis & I. Malani. 285p. 1979. 18.95. Asia Bk Corp.

Women of the World: The Great Foreign Correspondents. Julia Edwards. (Illus.). 304p. 1988. 17.95 (ISBN 0-395-44486-1). HM.

Women of Theresienstadt: Voices from a Concentration Camp. Ed. by Ruth Schwertfeger. 200p. 1988. 22.00 (ISBN 0-85496-192-5, Pub. by Manchester Univ Pr). St Martin.

Women of To-Day. facs. ed. Margaret I. Cole. LC 68-16920. (Essay Index Reprint Ser). 1938. 20.00 (ISBN 0-8369-0325-0). Ayer Co Pubs.

Women of Trachis. Sophocles. Tr. by C. K. Williams & Gregory W. Dickerson. (Greek Texts in New Translations Ser.). 1978. text ed. 19.95x (ISBN 0-19-502050-2). Oxford U Pr.

Women of Trachis. Sophokles. Tr. by Ezra Pound from Gr. LC 56-6530. 96p. 1985. pap. 6.95 (ISBN 0-8112-0948-2, NDP597). New Directions.

Women of Trachis see Sophocles Two.

Women of Turkey & Their Folk-Lore, 2 vols. Lucy M. Garnett. LC 77-87539. Repr. of 1891 ed. 73.50 set (ISBN 0-404-16590-7). AMS Pr.
Women of Valor. Samuel Kostman. (MS Ser.). (YA) (gr. 7-12). 1978. PLB 8.97 (ISBN 0-8239-0425-3). Rosen Group.
Women of Valor: The Trials & Triumphs of Seven Saints. Alicia Von Stamwitz. 64p. 1986. pap. 1.95 (ISBN 0-89243-258-6). Liguori Pubns.
Women of Value, Men of Renown: New Perspectives in Trobriand Exchange. Annette B. Weiner. (Illus.). 321p. 1976. pap. 20.00x (ISBN 0-292-79004-X). U of Tex Pr.
Women of Value, Men of Renown: New Perspectives in Trobriand Exchange. Annette B. Weiner. (Texas Press Sourcebooks in Anthropology: No. 11). (Illus.). 321p. 1976. pap. text ed. 8.95 (ISBN 0-292-79019-8). U of Tex Pr.
Women of Vision. Ed. by Denise Du Pont. 176p. 1988. 14.95 (ISBN 0-312-02321-9). St Martin.
Women of Wisdom. Tsultrim Allione. (Illus.). 224p. (Orig.). 1985. pap. 12.95 (ISBN 0-7102-0240-7). Routledge Chapman & Hall.
Women of Wisdom. Tsultrim Allione. (Illus.). 320p. 1986. pap. 11.95 (ISBN 1-85063-044-5). Routledge Chapman & Hall.
Women of Wonder: Science Fiction Stories by Women About Women. Ed. by Pamela Sargent. LC 74-8583. (gr. 9 up). 1975. pap. 4.95 (ISBN 0-394-71041-X, Vin). Random.
Women on Campus. Ed. by Elizabeth Janeway. LC 74-32507. 256p. 1975. 21.95x (Pub. by Change Mag); pap. 10.95x (ISBN 0-915390-03-5). Transaction Bks.
Women on College & University Faculties: A Historical Survey & a Study of Their Present Academic Status. Lucille A. Pollard. Ed. by Walter P. Metzger. LC 76-55186. (Academic Profession Ser.). (Illus.). 1977. Repr. lib. bdg. 30.00x (ISBN 0-405-10019-1). Ayer Co Pubs.
Women on Film: The Critical Eye. Marsha McCreadie. LC 82-13221. 176p. 1983. 35.00 (ISBN 0-275-91042-3, C1042). Praeger.
Women on Heroin. Marsha Rosenbaum. (Crime, Law & Deviance Ser.). 205p. (Orig.). 1981. 25.00x (ISBN 0-8135-0921-1); pap. 10.00 (ISBN 0-8135-0946-7). Rutgers U Pr.
Women on Menopause: A Change for the Better. Anne Dickson & Nikki Henriques. 160p. (Orig.). 1988. pap. 9.95 (ISBN 0-89281-237-0). Inner Tradit.
Women on the American Frontier. William W. Fowler. 527p. 1976. Repr. of 1876 ed. 22.50 (ISBN 0-87928-074-3). Corner Hse.
Women on the Breadlines. Meridel Le Sueur. LC 78-108080. (Worker Writer Ser.). (Illus.). 1978. pap. text ed. 2.00 (ISBN 0-931122-34-1). West End.
Women on the Color Line: Evolving Stereotypes & the Writings of George Washington Cable, Grace King, Kate Chopin. Anna S. Elfenbein. LC 87-37192. 325p. 1988. 27.50x (ISBN 0-8139-1169-9). U Pr of VA.
Women on the Couch. Claudia B. Pacheco. Tr. by Margareth P. Kowarick & Carlos G. De Freitas, II. 187p. 1988. pap. 9.00 (ISBN 0-939019-02-7). Proton Pub Hse.
Women on the Ice. Elizabeth Chipman. (Illus.). 242p. 1987. 28.50 (ISBN 0-522-84324-7, Pub. by Melbourne U Pr). Intl Spec Bk.
Women on the Job: The Communist View. new ed. Judy Edelman. 56p. 1973. pap. 0.70 (ISBN 0-87898-101-2). New Outlook.
Women on the Line. Ruth Cavendish. 166p. 1982. pap. 12.50x (ISBN 0-7100-0987-9). Routledge Chapman & Hall.
Women on the Move: A Feminist Perspective. Ed. by Jean Ramage Leppaluoto. 306p. 1972. pap. 6.00 (ISBN 0-317-34800-0, X050). Know Inc.
Women on the Outside Looking In. Linda P. McIlwain. LC 84-90611. 96p. (Orig.). 1985. pap. 5.95 (ISBN 0-930555-03-1). Wings Faith Pub.
Women on the Texas Frontier. Ann Malone. (Southwestern Studies: No. 70). 92p. 1983. pap. 5.00 (ISBN 0-87404-130-9). Tex Western.
Women on the U. S. Mexico Border: Responses to Change. Vicki Ruiz & Susan Tiano. LC 86-22305. (Thematic Studies in Latin America). 256p. 1987. text ed. 39.95x (ISBN 0-04-497038-2); pap. text ed. 14.95x (ISBN 0-04-497039-0). Unwin Hyman.
Women on the Wall. Wallace Stegner. LC 80-22461. x, 277p. 1980. 23.50x (ISBN 0-8032-4111-9); pap. 8.95 (ISBN 0-8032-9110-8, BB 710, Bison). U of Nebr Pr.
Women on War. Ed. by Daniela Gioseffi. (Illus.). 400p. (Orig.). 1988. 19.95 (Touchstone Bks); pap. 9.95 (ISBN 0-671-66781-5, Touchstone Bks). S&S.
Women, or Pour et Contre, 3 vols. in 2. Charles R. Maturin. LC 79-8173. Repr. of 1818 ed. Set. 84.50 (ISBN 0-404-62043-4). AMS Pr.
Women Organizing: An Anthology. Bernice Cummings & Victoria Schuck. LC 79-18956. 422p. 1979. 27.50 (ISBN 0-8108-1245-2). Scarecrow.
Women over Forty: Visions & Realities. Marilyn Block et al. (Focus on Women Ser.: No. 4). 172p. 1981. text ed. 21.95 (ISBN 0-8261-3000-3); pap. text ed. 15.95 (ISBN 0-8261-3001-1). Springer Pub.
Women Paraprofessionals in Upper Volta's Rural Development. Ellen Taylor. (Special Series on Paraprofessionals). 56p. (Orig.). 1981. pap. text ed. 6.60 (ISBN 0-86731-049-9). Cornell CIS RDC.
Women Participation in Rural Environment. G. P. Swarnkar. 1987. 23.00x (ISBN 81-85076-37-5, Pub. by Chugh Pubns India). South Asia Bks.
Women, Philosophy & Sport: A Collection of New Essays. Ed. by Betsy C. Postow. LC 83-10146. 331p. 1983. 24.00 (ISBN 0-8108-1638-5). Scarecrow.
Women Physicians: Careers, Status & Power. Judith Lorber. 250p. 1985. 25.00 (ISBN 0-422-79040-0, NO. 9071); pap. 10.95 (ISBN 0-422-79050-8, NO. 9103). Routledge Chapman & Hall.
Women Physicians in Leadership Roles. Leah J. Dickstein & Carol C. Nadelson. LC 86-3574. (Issues in Psychiatry Ser.). 352p. 1986. text ed. 18.50x (ISBN 0-88048-203-6, 48-203-6). Am Psychiatric.
Women Pilots with the AAF, Nineteen Forty-One - Nineteen Forty-Four. J. Merton England & Joseph Reither. (USAF Historical Studies: No. 55). 122p. 1946. pap. text ed. 17.00x (ISBN 0-89126-138-9). MA-AH Pub.
Women Pioneers of Science. rev. ed. Louis Haber. LC 79-87517. (gr. 5-9). 1979. 12.95 (ISBN 0-15-299202-2, HJ). HarBraceJ.
Women Playwrights in England: 1363-1750. Nancy Cotton. LC 78-73155. 256p. 1980. 25.00 (ISBN 0-8387-2381-0). Bucknell U Pr.
Women Poem. Tim Reynolds. 1973. 10.00 (ISBN 0-916228-01-0); pap. 2.50 (ISBN 0-916228-02-9). Phoenix Bk Shop.
Women Poets of China. Tr. by Kenneth Rexroth & Chung Ling. LC 72-6791. Orig. Title: Orchid Boat. 160p. 1982. pap. 5.95 (ISBN 0-8112-0821-4, NDP528). New Directions.
Women Poets of Japan. Tr. by Kenneth Rexroth & Ikuko Atsumi. LC 77-1833. 192p. 1982. pap. 7.95 (ISBN 0-8112-0820-6, NDP527). New Directions.
Women Poets of Science Fiction. (Illus.). 1987. looseleaf 12.95 (ISBN 0-938075-07-1). Ocean View Bks.
Women Poets of the West: An Anthology, 1850-1950. 4th ed. Ed. by Tom Trusky. LC 77-83227. (Modern & Contemporary Poets of the West Ser). (Orig.). 1978. pap. 6.50 (ISBN 0-916272-08-7). Ahsahta Pr.
Women Police, a Study of the Development & Status of the Women Police Movement. Chloe Owings. LC 69-14941. (Criminology, Law Enforcement, & Social Problems Ser.: No. 28). 1969. Repr. of 1925 ed. 19.00x (ISBN 0-87585-028-6). Patterson Smith.
Women, Policing & Male Violence: An Internation Perspective. Ed. by Jalna Hanmer et al. 240p. 1988. text ed. 52.50 (ISBN 0-415-00692-9); pap. text ed. 15.95 (ISBN 0-415-00693-7). Routledge Chapman & Hall.
Women Political Leaders. Linda Healy. (Illus.). 1987. pap. 5.95 (ISBN 0-913290-56-4). Camaro Pub.
Women, Politics, & Change: The Kaum Ibu UMNO Malaysia, 1945-1972. Lenore Manderson. (East Asian Social Science Monographs). (Illus.). 1980. 45.00x (ISBN 0-19-580437-6). Oxford U Pr.
Women: Portraits. James B. Hall et al. (Patterns in Literary Art Ser.). 1976. pap. 13.80 (ISBN 0-07-025575-X). McGraw.
Women, Poverty, & Child Support. Paula Roberts. (Illus.). 166p. (Orig.). 1986. pap. 15.00 (ISBN 0-941077-15-2, 41,980). NCLS Inc.
Women, Power, & Change. Ed. by Ann Weick & Susan T. Vandiver. (Orig.). 1981. pap. text ed. 14.95x (ISBN 0-87101-092-5). Natl Assn Soc Wkrs.
Women, Power & Economic Change: The Nandi of Kenya. Regina S. Oboler. LC 83-45345. (Illus.). 368p. 1985. 38.50x (ISBN 0-8047-1224-7). Stanford U Pr.
Women, Power & Policy: Toward the Year 2000. 2nd ed. Ed. by Ellen Boneparth & Emily Stoper. (Government & Politics Ser.). 320p. 1988. text ed. 38.50 (ISBN 0-08-034486-0); pap. text ed. 17.50 (ISBN 0-08-034485-2). Pergamon.
Women, Power & Political Systems. Margherita Rendel. 1981. 25.00x (ISBN 0-312-88769-8). St Martin.
Women, Power & Politics. M. Stacey & M. Price. 1981. pap. 10.50 (ISBN 0-422-76150-8, NO.3452). Routledge Chapman & Hall.
Women, Power, & Subversion: Social Strategies in British Fiction, 1778-1860. Judith L. Newton. LC 81-1068. 200p. 1981. 20.00x (ISBN 0-8203-0564-2). U of Ga Pr.
Women, Power & Subversion: Social Strategies in British Fiction, 1778-1860. Judith L. Newton. 224p. 1985. pap. text ed. 11.95 (ISBN 0-416-41200-9, 9761). Routledge Chapman & Hall.
Women, Power & Therapy: Issues for Women. Ed. by Marjorie Braude. LC 87-14873. (Women & Therapy Ser.). 340p. 1987. text ed. 34.95 (ISBN 0-86656-653-8). Haworth Pr.
Women Pray. Ed. by Karen L. Roller. 96p. (Orig.). 1986. pap. 3.95 (ISBN 0-8298-0737-3). Pilgrim NY.
Women Priests: An Emerging Ministry in the Episcopal Church (1960 to 1980) John H. Morgan. 185p. (Orig.). 1985. pap. 12.95x (ISBN 0-932269-48-6). Wyndham Hall.
Women Priests & Other Fantasies. Vincent P. Miceli. LC 80-66294. 1985. 19.95 (ISBN 0-8158-0423-7). Chris Mass.
Women Priests in Australia: The Anglican Crisis. David Wetherell. 156p. (Orig.). 1987. pap. 9.95 (ISBN 0-86786-113-4, Pub. by Spectrum Pub). ANZ Religious Pubns.
Women, Production, & Patriarchy in Late Medieval Cities. Martha C. Howell. LC 85-31816. (Women in Culture & Society Ser.). xvi, 286p. 1986. lib. bdg. 25.00x (ISBN 0-226-35503-9). U of Chicago Pr.
Women, Production, & Patriarchy in Late Medieval Cities. Martha C. Howell. (Women in Culture & Society Ser.). (Illus.). xvi, 285p. 1989. pap. 12.95 (ISBN 0-226-35504-7). U of Chicago Pr.
Women: Psychology's Puzzle. Joanna B. Rohrbaugh. LC 79-7345. 1981. pap. 12.95x (ISBN 0-465-09209-8, TB-5090). Basic.
Women, Race & Class. Angela Y. Davis. LC 82-40414. 288p. 1983. pap. 5.95 (ISBN 0-394-71351-6, Vin). Random.
Women Reading Women's Writing. Sue Roe. LC 87-9494. 304p. 1987. 32.50 (ISBN 0-312-00952-6). St Martin.
Women, Reason & Nature: Some Philosophical Problems with Feminism. LC 82-12207. 165p. 1982. 22.00x (ISBN 0-691-07274-4). Princeton U Pr.
Women, Religion, & Development in the Third World. Theodora C. Foster. LC 83-13670. 288p. 1984. 35.00 (ISBN 0-275-90957-3, C0957). Praeger.
Women, Religion, & Social Change. Ed. by Yvonne Y. Haddad & Ellison B. Findly. LC 85-4747. (Illus.). 508p. 1985. 59.50 (ISBN 0-88706-068-4); pap. 19.50x (ISBN 0-88706-069-2). State U NY Pr.
Women Remembered: A Guide to Landmarks of Women's History in the United States. Marion Tinling. LC 85-17639. 810p. 1986. 76.95 (ISBN 0-313-23984-3, TWR/). Greenwood.
Women, Resistance & Revolution: A History of Women & Revolution in the Modern World. Sheila Rowbotham. 1973. pap. 3.50 (ISBN 0-394-71954-9, Vin). Random.
Women Saints of East & West. Ed. by Swami Ghanananda & John Steward-Wallace. LC 79-65731. 1979. pap. 7.95 (ISBN 0-87481-036-1). Vedanta Pr.
Women Say, the Men Say. Evelyn Shapiro & Barry Shapiro. 1979. pap. 14.95 (ISBN 0-440-09626-X). Delacorte.
Women Scientists from Antiquity to the Present: An Index. Caroline L. Herzenberg. LC 85-23985. 1986. lib. bdg. 30.00 (ISBN 0-933951-01-9). Locust Hill Pr.
Women Scientists in America: Struggles & Strategies to 1940. Margaret W. Rossiter. LC 81-20902. (Illus.). 464p. 1982. text ed. 45.00x (ISBN 0-8018-2443-5). Johns Hopkins.
Women Scientists in America: Struggles & Strategies to 1940. Margaret W. Rossiter. 1984. pap. 10.95x (ISBN 0-8018-2509-1). Johns Hopkins.
Women See Men. I. Kalmus & R. Ripp. 1977. text ed. 12.95 (ISBN 0-07-033248-7). McGraw.
Women-Sex & Sexuality. Ed. by Catherine Stimpson & Ethel S. Person. 384p. 1981. 20.00x (ISBN 0-226-77476-7); pap. 8.95 (ISBN 0-226-77477-5, P 914, Phoen). U of Chicago Pr.
Women, Sex & the Law. Rosemarie Tong. LC 83-16001. (New Feminist Perspectives Ser.). 224p. 1984. 24.50x (ISBN 0-8476-7230-1, Rowman & Allanheld); pap. 8.95x (ISBN 0-8476-7231-X). Rowman.
Women, Sexuality & Social Control. Carol Smart & Barry Smart. (Orig.). 1978. pap. 8.95x (ISBN 0-7100-8723-3). Routledge Chapman & Hall.
Women Shaping History. Denise DeClue. LC 79-13734. (Movers & Shapers Ser.). (Illus.). (gr. 4-8). 1979. PLB 13.31 (ISBN 0-8172-1380-5). Raintree Pubs.
Women, Social Science & Public Policy. Ed. by Jacqueline Goodnow & Carole Pateman. 162p. 1985. text ed. 27.95x (ISBN 0-86861-693-1). Unwin Hyman.
Women Social Scientists: Asia-Pacific. (Social & Human Sciences in Asia & the Pacific, Rushsap Directories Ser.: No. 2). 319p. 1987. pap. 7.00 (UB370, UB). UNIPUB.
Women, Society & Sex. Ed. by Johnson E. Fairchild. 255p. 1952. 11.50x (ISBN 0-911378-28-6). Sheridan.
Women, Society, the State & Abortion: A Structural Analysis. Patrick J. Sheehan. LC 87-14615. 1987. lib. bdg. 32.95 (ISBN 0-275-92744-X, C2744). Praeger.
Women Speak to God: The Prayers & Poems of Jewish Women. Ed. by Marcia C. Spiegel & Deborah L. Kremsdorf. LC 86-51498. 100p. (Orig.). 1987. pap. 9.98 (ISBN 0-9608054-6-X). Womans Inst-Cont Jewish Ed.
Women Speaking: An Annotated Bibliography of Verbal & Nonverbal Communication, 1970-1980. Mary E. Jarrard & Phyllis R. Randall. LC 82-15737. (Garland Reference Library of Social Science). 478p. 1982. 73.00 (ISBN 0-8240-9281-3). Garland Pub.
Women, Sport & Performance: A Physiological Perspective. Christine L. Wells. LC 84-25255. 345p. 1985. text ed. 26.00x (ISBN 0-931250-87-0, BWEL0087). Human Kinetics.
Women, Sports, & the Law: A Comprehensive Research Guide to Sex Discrimination in Sports. Karen Tokarz. LC 86-27039. (Legal Research Guides Ser.: Vol. 3). v, 135p. 1986. lib. bdg. 29.50 (ISBN 0-89941-528-8). W S Hein.
Women, State, & Ideology: Studies from Africa & Asia. Ed. by Haleh Afshar. LC 86-14432. 245p. 1987. 44.50X (ISBN 0-88706-393-4); pap. 14.95X (ISBN 0-88706-394-2). State U NY Pr.
Women, State, & Party in Eastern Europe. Ed. by Sharon L. Wolchik & Alfred G. Meyer. (Policy Studies). (Illus.). xiv, 454p. 1985. 45.00 (ISBN 0-8223-0660-3); pap. 16.95 (ISBN 0-8223-0659-X). Duke.
Women, State, & Revolution: Essays on Power & Gender in Europe Since 1789. Ed. by Sian Reynolds. LC 86-16074. (Illus.). 208p. 1987. lib. bdg. 25.00x (ISBN 0-87023-552-4); pap. text ed. 9.95x (ISBN 0-87023-553-2). U of Mass Pr.
Women Still Weep: A Sequel to Women Must Weep. Mary Orr. 1980. pap. 1.95x (ISBN 0-686-68851-1). Dramatists Play.
Women Students in India. S. Sharma. 171p. 1979. 14.95. Asia Bk Corp.
Women Studies: A Bibliography of Dissertations 1870-1982. Compiled by V. F. Gilbert & D. S. Tatla. 650p. 1985. 85.00x (ISBN 0-631-13714-9). Basil Blackwell.
Women Surviving: The Holocaust-Proceedings of the Conference. Esther Katz & Joan M. Ringelheim. (Occasional Papers: No. 1). 100p. (Orig.). 1983. pap. write for info. (ISBN 0-913865-00-1). Inst Res Hist.
Women Take Care. Tish Sommers & Laurie Shields. Ed. by Judy MacLean. 224p. 1987. 16.95 (ISBN 0-937404-28-4); pap. 9.95 (ISBN 0-937404-27-6). Triad Pub FL.
Women Take Charge: Asserting Your Rights in the Marketplace. Nina Easton. 202p. 1983. pap. 6.50 (ISBN 0-318-04129-4). Ctr Responsive Law.
Women Taken in Adultery & The Poggenpuhl Family. Tr. by Theodor Fontane. LC 78-31371. 1979. lib. bdg. 15.00x (ISBN 0-226-25680-4). U of Chicago Pr.
Women Talking. Ed. by Justine Hill. (Illus.). 256p. 1976. 12.95 (ISBN 0-8184-0235-0). Lyle Stuart.
Women Teachers on the Frontier. Polly W. Kaufman. LC 83-14699. 296p. 1984. 32.00x (ISBN 0-300-03043-6). Yale U Pr.
Women Teachers on the Frontier. Polly W. Kaufman. LC 83-14699. 296p. 1985. pap. text ed. 9.95x (ISBN 0-300-03402-4, Y-525). Yale U Pr.
Women Teaching for Change: Gender, Class & Power. Kathleen Weiler. (Critical Studies in Education Ser.). 192p. 1987. text ed. 29.95 (ISBN 0-89789-127-9); pap. text ed. 12.95 (ISBN 0-89789-128-7). Bergin & Garvey.
Women, Technology & Innovation. Ed. by Joan Rothschild. (Journal of Women's Studies International Quarterly 4(Si)). 88p. 1982. 23.00 (ISBN 0-08-028943-6). Pergamon.
Women, Technology, & Power: Ten Stars & the History They Made. Marguerite Y. Zientara. LC 85-47670. 248p. 1987. 18.95 (ISBN 0-8144-5820-3). AMACOM.
Women, the Arts, & the Nineteen Twenties in Paris & New York. Ed. by Kenneth W. Wheeler & Virginia L. Lussier. LC 81-7510. 250p. 1982. 24.95 (ISBN 0-87855-908-6). Transaction Bks.
Women, the Challenge & the Call: An Agenda for Christian Women in Today's World. Dee Jepsen. (Christian Essentials Ser.). 48p. (Orig.). 1987. pap. 1.95 (ISBN 0-89283-323-8). Servant.
Women, the Courts & Equality. Laura L. Crites & Winifred L. Hepperle. LC 86-15515. (Sage Yearbooks in Women's Policy Studies: Vol. 11). 1987. 35.00 (ISBN 0-8039-2811-4); pap. 16.95 (ISBN 0-8039-2812-2). Sage.
Women, the Family, & Freedom: The Debate in Documents, Vol.II, 1880-1950. Ed. by Susan G. Bell. Karen M. Offen. LC 82-61081. xvi, 474p. 1983. 32.50x (ISBN 0-8047-1172-0); pap. 14.95x (ISBN 0-8047-1173-9). Stanford U Pr.
Women, the Family, & Freedom. The Debate in Documents Vol.1,1750-1880. Ed. by Susan G. Bell & Karen M. Offen. LC 82-61081. xvi, 561p. 1983. 35.00x (ISBN 0-8047-1170-4); pap. 15.95x (ISBN 0-8047-1171-2). Stanford U Pr.
Women, the Family & Peasant Revolution in China. Kay A. Johnson. LC 82-24748. x, 282p. 1985. lib. bdg. 25.00x (ISBN 0-226-40187-1); pap. 11.95 (ISBN 0-226-40189-8). U of Chicago Pr.
Women, the Family & Social Work. Ed. by Eve Brook & Ann Davis. (Tavistock Library of Social Work Practice Ser.). 192p. (Orig.). 1985. 27.50 (ISBN 0-422-77940-7, 9484, Pub. by Tavistock England); pap. text ed. 12.95 (ISBN 0-422-77950-4, 9485, Pub. by Tavistock England). Routledge Chapman & Hall.
Women: The Fifth World. Elise Boulding. LC 80-65602. (Headline Ser.: No. 248). (Illus.). 64p. (Orig.). 1980. pap. 4.00 (ISBN 0-87124-059-9). Foreign Policy.

Women: The Last Colony. Maria Mies. 1988. text ed. 45.00 (ISBN 0-86232-455-6, Pub. by Zed Pr UK); pap. text ed. 15.00 (ISBN 0-86232-456-4, Pub. by Zed Pr UK). Humanities.

Women, the Law, & the Constitution. Ed. by Kermit L. Hall. (United States Constitutional & Legal History Ser.). 531p. 1987. lib. bdg. 70.00 (ISBN 0-8240-0138-9). Garland Pub.

Women, the Law, & the Economy. E. Diane Pask et al. 1985. 35.50 (ISBN 0-409-98865-0). Butterworth Legal Pubs.

Women: The Longest Revolution. Juliet Mitchell. LC 83-43144. 336p. 1984. pap. 9.95 (ISBN 0-394-72574-3). Pantheon.

Women: The Recruiter's Last Resort. Dina Portnoy. 40p. 1974. 2.00 (ISBN 0-686-43095-6). Recon Pubns.

Women, the Unions & Work or What is Not to Be Done. Selma James. 1972. pap. 2.50 (ISBN 0-912786-33-7). Know Inc.

Women... The World's Greatest Salesmen! Jean R. Nave. 96p. (Orig.). 1984. pap. 6.95 (ISBN 0-930115-00-7). Windemere Pr.

Women: Their Changing Roles. Ed. by Elizabeth Janeway. LC 72-5020. (Great Contemporary Issues Ser.). (Illus.). 1973. 35.00 (ISBN 0-405-04164-0); 30.00subscribers (ISBN 0-685-41644-5). Ayer Co Pubs.

Women Therapists Working with Women: New Theory & Process of Feminist Therapy. Ed. by Claire Brody. (Focus on Women: Vol. 7). 192p. 1984. text ed. 20.95 (ISBN 0-8261-4550-7). Springer Pub.

Women Through the Bible: Devotions for Women's Groups. Marlys Taege. 160p. 1987. pap. 6.50 (ISBN 0-570-04460-X, 12-3064). Concordia.

Women Towards Modernization. K. N. Jha. 1985. 12.50x (ISBN 0-8364-1431-4, Pub. by Jayaprint India). South Asia Bks.

Women Towards Modernization. K. N. Jha. 1986. 14.00x (ISBN 0-8364-1542-6, Pub. by Janaki). South Asia Bks.

Women, Tradition & Culture. Malladi Subbamma. 1985. text ed. 22.50x (ISBN 0-86590-616-5, Pub. by Sterling Pubs India). Apt Bks.

Women Treating Women: Case Material from Women Treated by Female Psychoanalysts. Anne E. Bernstein & Gloria M. Warner. LC 84-8996. xv, 310p. 1985. text ed. 35.00x (ISBN 0-8236-6863-0, 06863). Intl Univs Pr.

Women Trial Lawyers: How They Succeed in Practice & in the Courtroom. Janine Warsaw. 304p. 1986. 29.95 (ISBN 0-13-962374-4). P-H.

Women Troubadours. Meg Bogin. (Illus.). 192p. 1980. pap. 5.95 (ISBN 0-393-00965-3). Norton.

Women under Apartheid. (Illus.). 120p. 1982. pap. 7.50 (ISBN 0-88208-200-0, Pub. by Intl Defence England). Chicago Review.

Women under Apartheid. 119p. 1981. 7.00 (ISBN 0-317-36678-5). Africa Fund.

Women under Communism: Family in Russia & China. Paul Chao. LC 77-89932. 231p. 1977. lib. bdg. 27.95x (ISBN 0-930390-01-6); pap. text ed. 14.95x (ISBN 0-930390-00-8). Gen Hall.

Women under Polygamy. Walter M. Gallichan. LC 72-9639. (Illus.). Repr. of 1914 ed. 47.50 (ISBN 0-404-57443-2). AMS Pr.

Women under Primitive Buddhism: Laywomen & Almswomen. I. B. Horner. 391p. 1975. 15.95. Asia Bk Corp.

Women under Stress. Randy Alcorn & Nancy Alcorn. LC 86-18213. (Touch of Grace Ser.). (Orig.). 1986. pap. 7.95 (ISBN 0-88070-157-9). Multnomah.

Women under Stress. Donald R. Morse & M. Lawrence Furst. 400p. 1981. 26.95 (ISBN 0-442-26648-0). Van Nos Reinhold.

Women under the English Law, from the Landing of the Saxons to the Present Time. Arthur R. Cleveland. LC 87-9602. Date not set. price not set. Rothman.

Women under the Influence: Alcohol & Its Impact. Brigid McConville. 160p. 1985. 15.00 (ISBN 0-8052-3977-4); pap. 6.95 (ISBN 0-8052-0776-7). Schocken.

Women under the Knife. Herbert Keyser. LC 83-61171. 160p. 1984. 9.95 (ISBN 0-89313-036-2). G F Stickley Co.

Women under the Knife. Herbert H. Keyser. 176p. 1986. pap. 3.95 (ISBN 0-446-32911-8). Warner Bks.

Women versus Men: A Conflict of Navajo Emergence. Berard Haile. Ed. by Karl W. Luckert. LC 81-7433. (American Tribal Religions Ser.: Vol. 6). viii, 119p. 1981. 14.95x (ISBN 0-8032-2319-6); pap. 9.95x (ISBN 0-8032-7211-1, BB 785, Bison). U of Nebr Pr.

Women Veterans: America's Forgotten Heroines. June A. Willenz. 272p. 1984. 19.50 (ISBN 0-8264-0241-0). Continuum.

Women View Librarianship: Nine Perspectives. Kathryn R. Lundy. LC 80-23611. (ACRL Publications in Librarianship: No. 41). 108p. 1980. pap. 8.00x (ISBN 0-8389-3251-7). ALA.

Women, Violence & Social Control. Ed. by Jalna Hanmer & Mary Maynard. LC 86-27294. 260p. 1987. 29.95 (ISBN 0-391-03514-2); pap. text ed. 12.50 (ISBN 0-391-03515-0). Humanities.

Women, Vol. 3 (incl. 1984-1987 Supplements, Vol. 3. Ed. by Eleanor C. Goldstein. (Social Issues Resources Ser.). 1988. 60.00 (ISBN 0-89777-076-5). Soc Issues.

Women vs. Women: The Uncivil Business War. Tara R. Madden. 224p. 1987. 17.95 (ISBN 0-8144-5900-5). AMACOM.

Women Wage-Earners: Their Past, Their Present, & Their Future. Helen Campbell. LC 72-2594. (American Women Ser: Images & Realities). 324p. 1972. Repr. of 1893 ed. 20.000 (ISBN 0-405-04451-8). Ayer Co Pubs.

Women Walking. Lisa Grenelle. LC 77-99152. 77p. 1978. 5.00 (ISBN 0-8233-0271-7). Golden Quill.

Women, War & Revolution. Ed. by Carol R. Berkin & Clara M. Lovett. LC 79-26450. 310p. 1980. 35.00 (ISBN 0-8419-0502-9); pap. 14.75 (ISBN 0-8419-0545-2). Holmes & Meier.

Women War Correspondents in the Vietnam War, 1961-1975. Virginia Elwood-Akers. LC 87-23313. (Illus.). 294p. 1988. 29.50 (ISBN 0-8108-2033-1). Scarecrow.

Women Who Achieved for God. Winnie Christensen. (Fisherman Bible Studyguide). 80p. 1984. pap. 2.95 (ISBN 0-87788-937-6). Shaw Pubs.

Women Who Believed God. Winnie Christensen. (Fisherman Bible Studyguide Ser.). 77p. 1983. saddle-stiched 2.95 (ISBN 0-87788-936-8). Shaw Pubs.

Women Who Changed Things. Linda Peavy & Ursula Smith. LC 82-21612. (Illus.). 208p. (gr. 7 up). 1983. 12.95 (ISBN 0-684-17849-4, Pub. by Scribner). Macmillan.

Women Who Compete. Nancy T. Marshall & Pam Vredevelt. (Illus.). 192p. (Orig.). 1988. pap. 7.95 (ISBN 0-8007-5277-5). Revell.

Women Who Dared. Valjean McLenighan. LC 79-13718. (Movers & Shapers Ser.). (Illus.). (gr. 4-8). 1979. PLB 13.31 (ISBN 0-8172-1375-9). Raintree Pubs.

Women Who Dared: The History of Finnish American Women. Marsha Penti et al. Ed. by Carl Ross & K. Marianne Brown. LC 86-80998. (Illus.). xi, 164p. (Orig.). 1986. pap. text ed. 10.00 (ISBN 0-932833-05-5). Immig His Res.

Women Who Dared to Be Different. Ed. & commentaries by Bennett Wayne. LC 72-6802. (Garrard Target Ser.). (Illus.). 168p. (gr. 5 up). 1973. PLB 7.99 (ISBN 0-8116-4902-4). Garrard.

Women Who Date Too Much: (And Those Who Should Be So Lucky) Linda Sunshine. LC 87-24841. 160p. 1988. 10.95 (ISBN 0-453-00608-6). NAL.

Women Who Do & Women Who Don't: Join the Women's Movement. Robyn Rowland. (Illus.). 224p. (Orig.). 1984. pap. 8.95 (ISBN 0-7102-0296-2). Routledge Chapman & Hall.

Women Who Drink: Alcoholic Experience & Psychotherapy. Vasanti Burtle. (Illus.). 304p. 1979. 32.50x (ISBN 0-398-03854-6). C C Thomas.

Women Who Embezzle or Defraud: A Study of Convicted Felons. Dorothy Zietz. LC 81-8638. 172p. 1981. 35.00 (ISBN 0-275-90748-1, C0748). Praeger.

Women Who Fought: An American History. Gail Reifert & Eugene M. Dermody. 1978. pap. 4.95 (ISBN 0-9603636-0-2). Dermody.

Women Who Hate Me. Dorothy Allison. LC 84-121194. 60p. 1983. pap. 5.95 (ISBN 0-9602284-2-X). Firebrand Bks.

Women Who Kill. Ann Jones. 1988. pap. 4.95 (ISBN 0-449-21609-8, Crest). Fawcett.

Women Who Knew Too Much. Tania Modleski. 200p. 1987. 25.00 (ISBN 0-416-01701-0, A0412); pap. 10.95 (ISBN 0-416-01711-8). Routledge Chapman & Hall.

Women Who Lived, Cities That Died. Geraldine Daesch. (Riverstone International Poetry Chapbook Ser.). 21p. (Orig.). 1985. write for info. (ISBN 0-936600-05-5). Riverstone Foothills.

Women Who Love Too Much. Robin Norwood. 320p. 1986. pap. 4.95 (ISBN 0-671-64541-2). PB.

Women Who Love Too Much: When You Keep Wishing & Hoping He'll Change. Robin Norwood. LC 85-4654. 266p. 1985. 14.95 (ISBN 0-87477-355-5, Dist. by St Martin). J P Tarcher.

Women Who Made the West. Western Writers of America. 1981. pap. 2.95 (ISBN 0-380-56507-2, 56507-2, Discus). Avon.

Women Who Make Our Novels. Grant Overton. Repr. lib. bdg. 19.95x (ISBN 0-89190-689-4, Pub. by River City Pr). Amereon Ltd.

Women Who Make Our Novels. facsimile, rev. ed. Grant M. Overton. LC 67-23257. (Essay Index Reprint Ser.). 1928. 21.50 (ISBN 0-8369-0758-2). Ayer Co Pubs.

Women Who Marry Houses: Panic & Protest in Agoraphobia. Robert Seidenberg & Karen DeCrow. LC 82-14934. 204p. 1983. pap. text ed. 7.95 (ISBN 0-07-016283-2). McGraw.

Women Who Use Organized Family Planning Services: United States, 1979. Eugenia Eckard. Ed. by Mary Olmstead. 55p. 1981. pap. text ed. 1.75 (ISBN 0-8406-0239-1). Natl Ctr Health Stats.

Women Who Want to Be Boss: Business Revelations & Success Strategies from America's Top Female Executives. Marlene Jensen. LC 86-16707. 192p. 1987. 15.95 (ISBN 0-385-23375-2). Doubleday.

Women Who Win. Mary C. Crowley. (Illus.). 160p. 1979. 9.95 (ISBN 0-8007-0993-4). Revell.

Women Who Win. Francene Sabin. 160p. (gr. 5 up). 1977. pap. 1.50 (ISBN 0-440-99643-0, LFL). Dell.

Women Who Win. Francene Sabin. LC 74-20835. (Illus.). 192p. (gr. 7 up). 1975. Random.

Women Whose Lives Are Food, Men Whose Lives Are Money, Poems. Joyce Carol Oates. LC 77-17220. (Illus.). 80p. 1978. 13.95 (ISBN 0-8071-0391-8). La State U Pr.

Women Winning: A Handbook for Action Against Sex Discrimination. Ed. by Virginia E. Pendergrass. LC 78-27379. 196p. 1979. 19.95x (ISBN 0-88229-450-4); pap. 9.95x (ISBN 0-88229-699-X). Nelson-Hall.

Women Winning: How to Run for Office. Barbara M. Trafton. LC 83-22875. 160p. 1984. 14.95 (ISBN 0-916782-45-X); pap. 9.95 (ISBN 0-916782-44-1). Harvard Common Pr.

Women with a Cause. Ed. by Bennett Wayne. LC 75-4971. (Garrard Target Ser.). (Illus.). 168p. (gr. 5 up). 1975. PLB 7.99 (ISBN 0-8116-4914-8). Garrard.

Women with & Without. Carol Murray. (American Dust Ser.: No. 14). 200p. 1984. 10.95 (ISBN 0-913218-81-2). Dustbooks.

Women with Cancer. Ed. by B. L. Andersen. (Contributions to Psychology & Medicine Ser.). (Illus.). 330p. 1986. 50.00 (ISBN 0-387-96360-X). Springer-Verlag.

Women with Disabilities: Essays in Psychology, Culture, & Politics. Ed. by Michelle Fine & Adrienne Asch. 1988. 34.95 (ISBN 0-87722-474-9). Temple U Pr.

Women with Long Hair. Ed. by Green Tiger Press Staff. (Envelope Library). (Illus.). 12p. (Orig.). (YA) (gr. 7-9). 1982. pap. 2.50 (ISBN 0-88138-006-7). Green Tiger Pr.

Women with Vision: The Presentation Sisters of South Dakota, 1880-1985. Susan C. Peterson & Courtney A. Vaughn-Roberson. LC 87-20451. 334p. 1988. 24.95 (ISBN 0-252-01493-6). U of Ill Pr.

Women Without Men: Gender & Morality in an Algerian Town. Willy Jansen. (Illus.). xvi, 303p. 1986. pap. 38.25 (ISBN 90-04-08345-6, Pub. by E J Brill). Heinman.

Women, Wives, Mothers: Values & Options. Jessie Bernard. LC 74-18210. 294p. 1975. pap. text ed. 17.95x (ISBN 0-202-30281-4). Aldine de Gruyter.

Women, Women Writers & the West. Ed. by Lawrence L. Lee & Merrill E. Lewis. LC 78-69805. 252p. 1978. 15.00x (ISBN 0-87875-146-7). Whitston Pub.

Women, Work & Computerization: Opportunities & Disadvantages: Proceedings of the IFIP WG9.1 First Working Conference on Women, Work & Computerization, Riva del Sole, Tuscany, Italy, Sept. 17-21, 1984. Ed. by A. Olerup et al. 372p. 1986. 68.50 (ISBN 0-444-87864-5, North Holland). Elsevier.

Women, Work & Demographic Issues. 159p. (Orig.). 1984. pap. 11.40 (ISBN 92-2-103886-6). Intl Labour Office.

Women, Work & Demographic Issues: Report of an ILO-UNITAR Seminar, Tashkent, U. S. S. R., October 11-19, 1983. 159p. 1986. pap. 11.40 (ISBN 92-2-103886-6, ILO407, ILO). UNIPUB.

Women, Work, & Divorce. Richard R. Peterson. (Sociology of Work Ser.). 192p. 1988. 39.50x (ISBN 0-88706-858-8); pap. 12.95x (ISBN 0-88706-859-6). State U NY Pr.

Women, Work & Family. Ed. by T. Scarlett Epstein et al. LC 86-3778. 240p. 1986. 27.50x (ISBN 0-312-88786-8). St Martin.

Women, Work & Family. Louise A. Tilly & Joan W. Scott. 274p. 1987. pap. 11.95 (ISBN 0-416-01681-2). Routledge Chapman & Hall.

Women, Work & Family in the British, Canadian & Norwegian Offshore Oilfields. Ed. by Jane Lewis et al. LC 86-31393. 200p. 1987. 39.95 (ISBN 0-312-00528-8). St Martin.

Women, Work & Family in the Soviet Union. Ed. by Gail W. Lapidus. Tr. by Vladimir Talmy from Rus. LC 81-9281. 352p. 1982. pap. 15.95 (ISBN 0-87332-255-X). M E Sharpe.

Women, Work, & Fertility, Nineteen Hundred to Nineteen Eighty-Six. Susan H. Van Horn. (American Social Experience Ser.: No. 8). 232p. 1989. pap. 15.00x (ISBN 0-8147-8760-6). NYU Pr.

Women, Work, & Fertility 1900-1987. Susan H. Van Horn. (American Social Experience Ser.: No. 8). 256p. 1988. 35.00x (ISBN 0-8147-8759-2). NYU Pr.

Women, Work, & Ideology in the Third World. Ed. by Haleh Afshar. 280p. 1986. 15.95 (ISBN 0-422-79700-6, 9606, Pub. by Tavistock England); pap. write for info. (ISBN 0-422-79710-3, 9607, Pub. by Tavistock England). Routledge Chapman & Hall.

Women, Work, & National Policy: The Kennedy-Johnson Years. Patricia G. Zelman. LC 81-16351. (Studies in American History & Culture: No. 33). pap. 44.80 (2070095). Bks Demand UMI.

Women, Work & Poverty. E. Fiorenza & A. Carr. (Concilium Ser.). Date not set. pap. 14.95 (ISBN 0-567-30074-9, Pub. by T & T Clark Ltd UK). Fortress.

Women, Work & Protest: A Century of U. S. Women's History. Ed. by Ruth Milkman. 320p. (Orig.). 1985. pap. 14.95x (ISBN 0-7100-9940-1). Routledge Chapman & Hall.

Women, Work, & Technology: Transformations. Ed. by Barbara D. Wright. (Women & Culture Ser.). 350p. 1987. text ed. 32.00x (ISBN 0-472-09373-8); pap. text ed. 13.50x (ISBN 0-472-06373-1). U of Mich Pr.

Women, Work & Wages. Gilda Berger. LC 85-15379. (Illus.). 128p. (gr. 7-12). 1986. lib. bdg. 12.90 (ISBN 0-531-10074-X). Watts.

Women, Work, & Wages. National Research Council Committee on Occupational Classification & Analysis. 148p. 1981. pap. 13.50x (ISBN 0-309-03177-X). Natl Acad Pr.

Women Workers & the Industrial Revolution, 1750-1850. 2nd & rev. ed. Ivy Pinchbeck. 342p. 1969. 32.50x (ISBN 0-7146-1351-7, F Cass Co). Biblio Dist.

Women Workers & the Sweated Trades: The Origins of Minimum Wage Legislation. Jenny Morris. 256p. 1986. text ed. 47.50 (ISBN 0-566-05188-5, Pub. by Gower Pub England). Gower Pub Co.

Women Workers in Fifteen Countries: Essays in Honor of Alice Hanson Cook. Ed. by Jennie Farley. LC 85-2375. (Cornell International Industrial & Labor Relations Reports Ser.: No. 11). 224p. 1985. pap. 9.95 (ISBN 0-87546-114-X). ILR Pr.

Women Workers in Multinational Enterprises in Developing Countries. Linda Kim. 119p. 1985. pap. 10.50 (ISBN 92-2-100532-1, ILO432, ILO). UNIPUB.

Women Workers in Multinational Enterprises in Developing Countries. viii, 119p. (Orig.). 1985. pap. 10.50 (ISBN 92-2-100532-1). Intl Labour Office.

Women Workers in the Japanese Cotton Mills: 1880-1920. Yasue A. Kidd. LC 78-108068. (East Asia Papers: No. 20). 81p. 1978. 3.00 (ISBN 0-939657-20-1). Cornell East Asia Pgm.

Women Workers in the Second World War. Penny Summerfield. 214p. 1984. 28.00 (ISBN 0-7099-2317-1, Pub. by Croom Helm Ltd). Routledge Chapman & Hall.

Women Workers in the Sri Lanka Plantation Sector. Rachel Kurian. (Women, Work & Development Ser.: No. 5). 138p. 1983. pap. 14.00 (ISBN 92-2-102992-1, ILO206, ILO). UNIPUB.

Women Workers in the Sri Lanka Plantation Sector: An Historical & Contemporary Analysis. Rachel Kurian. (Women, Work & Development Ser.: No. 5). xiv, 138p. (Orig.). 1982. pap. 14.00 (ISBN 92-2-102992-1). Intl Labour Office.

Women Workers in the Unorganized Sector: The Calcutta Experience. Nixmala Banerjee. 208p. 1985. pap. text ed. 10.00x (ISBN 0-86131-492-1, Pub. by Sangam Bks India). Apt Bks.

Women Workers View: Their Learning. Jean M. Golaszewski & Joyce L. Kornbluh. (Program on Women & Work Ser.). 82p. 1983. pap. 4.00 (ISBN 0-87736-347-1). U of Mich Inst Labor.

Women Working: An Anthology of Stories & Poems. Ed. by Nancy Hoffman & Florence Howe. (Women's Lives-Women's Work Ser.). (Illus.). 309p. 1979. pap. 9.95 (ISBN 0-912670-57-6); teaching guide, 80p. o.p. 5.00 (ISBN 0-912670-63-0). Feminist Pr.

Women Working: Comparative Perspectives in Developing Areas. Alma T. Junsay & Tim B. Heaton. (Contributions in Women's Studies: No. 99). 1989. price not set (ISBN 0-313-26368-X, JWK/). Greenwood.

Women Working Home: The Homebased Business Guide & Directory. Marion Behr & Wendy Lazar. (Illus.). 176p. (Orig.). 1981. pap. 12.95 (ISBN 0-939240-00-9). WWH Pr.

Women Working: Prostitution Now. Eileen McLeod. (Illus.). 180p. 1982. pap. 15.00 (ISBN 0-7099-1717-1, Pub. by Croom Helm Ltd). Routledge Chapman & Hall.

Women Working: Theories & Facts in Perspective. 2nd ed. Ed. by Ann H. Stromberg & Shirley Harkess. LC 77-89921. 431p. 1987. pap. 17.95 (ISBN 0-87484-301-4). Mayfield Pub.

Women Working: Theories & Facts in Perspective. 2nd ed. Ed. by Ann H. Stromberg & Shirley Harkess. 448p. 1987. pap. 18.95 (ISBN 0-87484-744-3, Dist. by Kampmann). Mayfield Pub.

Women Working Together for Personal, Economic & Community Development. Suzanne Kindervatter. LC 83-61079. (Illus.). 103p. (Orig.). 1983. pap. text ed. 10.00 (ISBN 0-912917-01-6). OEF Intl.

Women Working Together for Personal, Economic & Community Development. 2nd ed. Suzanne Kindervatter. LC 87-31276. (Illus.). 105p. 1987. pap. 10.00 (ISBN 0-912917-18-0). OEF Intl.

Women, World War & Permanent Peace. May W. Sewall. LC 75-743. (Pioneers of the Woman's Movement: an International Perspective Ser.). (Illus.). xxx, 206p. 1976. Repr. of 1915 ed. 20.35 (ISBN 0-88355-274-4). Hyperion Conn.

Women Worldwalkers: New Dimensions of Science Fiction & Fantasy. Ed. by Jane B. Weedman. (Proceedings of the Comparative Literature Symposium Ser.: Vol. 16). 250p. 1985. 50.00 (ISBN 0-89672-133-7). Tex Tech Univ Pr.

Women Write Murder. Ed. by Martin H. Greenberg & Edward D. Hoch. (Academy Mystery Novellas Ser.: No. 5). 224p. 1987. pap. 5.95. Academy Chi Pubs.

Women Writers. B. G. MacCarthy. 1946. Repr. lib. bdg. 35.50 (ISBN 0-8414-6230-5). Folcroft.

Women Writers & Poetic Identity: Dorothy Wordsworth, Emily Bronte & Emily Dickinson. Margaret Homans. LC 80-7527. 272p. 1987. 31.00x (ISBN 0-691-06440-7); pap. text ed. 13.50x (ISBN 0-691-10218-X). Princeton U Pr.

Women Writers & the City: Essays in Feminist Literary Criticism. Ed. by Susan M. Squier. LC 83-17109. 336p. 1984. pap. 12.95x (ISBN 0-87049-416-3). U of Tenn Pr.

Women Writers in Black Africa. Lloyd W. Brown. LC 80-1710. (Contributions in Women's Studies: No. 21). vii, 204p. 1981. lib. bdg. 35.00 (ISBN 0-313-22540-0, BRW/). Greenwood.

Women Writers in Russian Modernism: An Anthology. Ed. by Temira Pachmuss. LC 78-8957. 376p. 1978. 29.95 (ISBN 0-252-00224-5); pap. 10.95 (ISBN 0-252-00700-X). U of Ill Pr.

Women Writers in Translation: An Annotated Bibliography, 1945-1981. Isabelle de Courtivron & Margery Resnick. LC 80-9039. (Reference Library of the Humanities). 200p. 1984. lib. bdg. 50.00 (ISBN 0-8240-9332-1). Garland Pub.

Women Writers of Spain: An Annotated Bio-Bibliographical Guide. Ed. by Carolyn L. Galerstein & Kathleen McNerney. LC 86-379. (Bibliographies & Indexes in Women's Studies: No. 2). 410p. 1986. lib. bdg. 46.95 (ISBN 0-313-24965-2, GWO/). Greenwood.

Women Writers of Spanish America: An Annotated Bio-Bibliographical Guide. Ed. by Diane E. Marting. LC 86-33552. (Bibliographies & Indexes in Women's Studies: No. 5). 468p. 1987. lib. bdg. 49.95 (ISBN 0-313-24969-5, MWN/). Greenwood.

Women Writers of the Contemporary South. Ed. by Peggy W. Prenshaw. LC 84-5165. (Southern Quarterly Ser.). (Illus.). 235p. 1984. 22.50x (ISBN 0-87805-222-4). U Pr of Miss.

Women Writers of the Middle Ages: A Critical Study of Texts from Perpetua (203) to Marguerite Porete (1310) Peter Dronke. LC 83-7456. 1984. o. p. 57.50 (ISBN 0-521-25580-5); pap. 16.95 (ISBN 0-521-27573-3). Cambridge U Pr.

Women-Writers of the Nineteenth Century. Marjory A. Bald. LC 63-8356. 1963. Repr. of 1923 ed. 17.00x (ISBN 0-8462-0342-1). Russell.

Women Writers of the Renaissance & Reformation. Ed. by Katharina M. Wilson. 678p. 1987. 40.00x (ISBN 0-8203-0865-X); pap. 19.95 (ISBN 0-8203-0866-8). U of Ga Pr.

Women Writers of the West Coast: Speaking of Their Lives & Careers. Ed. by Marilyn Yalom. LC 83-15005. (Illus.). 141p. (Orig.). 1983. pap. 10.00 (ISBN 0-88496-204-0). Capra Pr.

Women Writers of the West Coast: Speaking of Their Lives & Careers. Ed. by Marilyn Yalom. 160p. 1988. Repr. lib. bdg. 24.95x (ISBN 0-8095-4053-3). Borgo Pr.

Women Writers Talking. Ed. by Janet Todd. 200p. 1983. 37.50 (ISBN 0-8419-0756-0); pap. 14.95 (ISBN 0-8419-0757-9). Holmes & Meier.

Women Writing about Men. Jane Miller. 303p. (Orig.). 1986. pap. 8.95 (ISBN 0-394-74425-X). Pantheon.

Women Writing & Writing about Women. Ed. by Mary Jacobus. LC 79-53439. 201p. 1979. text ed. 28.50x (ISBN 0-06-493268-0). B&N Imports.

Women Writing in America: Voices in Collage. Blanche H. Gelfant. LC 84-40298. (Illus.). 290p. 1985. 24.00x (ISBN 0-87451-307-3); pap. 10.95 (ISBN 0-87451-308-1). U Pr of New Eng.

Women...a World Survey. Ruth L. Sivard. (Illus.). 44p. 1985. pap. 5.00 (ISBN 0-918281-00-8). World Prior.

Women...A World Survey. 1987. pap. 6.00 (ISBN 0-317-61845-8). World Prior.

Womenfolk & Fairy Tales. Ed. by Rosemary Minard. LC 74-26555. (Illus.). 176p. (gr. 2-5). 1975. 13.95 (ISBN 0-395-20276-0). HM.

Womenfolks: Growing Up Down South. Shirley Abbott. LC 82-16880. 224p. 1983. 13.95 (ISBN 0-89919-156-8). Ticknor & Fields.

Womenfolks: Growing Up Down South. Shirley Abbott. LC 82-16880. 210p. 1984. pap. 8.95 (ISBN 0-89919-283-1). Ticknor & Fields.

Women's Activism & Social Change: Rochester, New York, 1822-1872. Nancy A. Hewitt. LC 83-45940. (Paperback Ser.). 281p. 1984. 32.50x (ISBN 0-8014-1616-7); pap. 9.95x. Cornell U Pr.

Women's Adornment: What Does the Bible Really Say? Ralph Woodrow. LC 76-17711. (Illus.). 1976. pap. 3.00 (ISBN 0-916938-01-8). R Woodrow.

Women's America: Refocusing the Past. 2nd ed. Ed. by Linda K. Kerber & Jane De Hart-Mathews. 528p. 1987. 29.95x (ISBN 0-19-504202-6); pap. 16.95 (ISBN 0-19-504203-4). Oxford U Pr.

Women's Annotated Legal Bibliography. Benjamin N. Cardozo. 1984. 50.00 (ISBN 0-87632-349-2). Clark Boardman.

Women's Annotated Legal Bibliography. Cardozo, Benjamin N., School of Law Staff. LC 83-15219. xviii, 331p. 1984. Repr. of 1984 ed. lib. bdg. 45.00. W S Hein.

Women's Annual, No. 1: 1980--The Year in Review. Ed. by Barbara Haber. 343p. 1981. 39.00 (ISBN 0-8161-8530-1, Hall Reference). G K Hall.

Women's Annual, No. 2: 1981--The Year in Review. Ed. by Barbara Haber. 344p. 1982. lib. bdg. 39.00 (ISBN 0-8161-8614-6, Hall Reference). G K Hall.

Women's Annual, No. 3: 1982-1983. Ed. by Barbara Haber. 452p. 1983. lib. bdg. 39.00 (ISBN 0-8161-8641-3, Hall Reference). G K Hall.

Women's Annual, No. 4: 1983-1984. Ed. by Sarah M. Pritchard. 248p. 1984. 39.00 (ISBN 0-8161-8703-7, Hall Reference); pap. 14.95 (ISBN 0-8161-8725-8). G K Hall.

Women's Annual: 1984-1985, No. 5. Ed. by Mary McFeely. (Reference Publications, Women's Studies Annual). 184p. 1985. lib. bdg. 39.00 (ISBN 0-8161-8717-7); pap. text ed. 16.95 (ISBN 0-8161-8741-X). G K Hall.

Women's Associations & Organizations Based in England: A Directory. Data Notes Publishing Staff. Date not set. pap. text ed. 6.95 (ISBN 0-911569-39-1, Pub. by Data Notes). Prosperity & Profits.

Women's Associations & Organizations: Midwest Region Directory. Data Notes Publishing Staff. Date not set. pap. text ed. 6.95 (ISBN 0-911569-27-8, Pub. by Data Notes). Prosperity & Profits.

Women's Associations & Organizations: Mountain Region Directory. Data Notes Publishing Staff. Date not set. pap. text ed. 6.95 (ISBN 0-911569-28-6, Pub. by Data Notes). Prosperity & Profits.

Women's Associations & Organizations: Northeast Region Directory. Data Notes Publishing Staff. Date not set. pap. text ed. 6.95 (ISBN 0-911569-32-4, Pub. by Data Notes). Prosperity & Profits.

Women's Associations & Organizations: Pacific Coast, Hawaii & Alaska Directory. Data Notes Publishing Staff. Date not set. pap. text ed. 6.95 (ISBN 0-911569-31-6, Pub. by Data Notes). Prosperity & Profits.

Women's Associations & Organizations: Southwest Regional Directory. Data Notes Publishing Staff. Date not set. pap. text ed. 6.95 (ISBN 0-911569-37-5, Pub. by Data Notes). Prosperity & Profits.

Women's Atlas of the United States. Anne Gibson & Timothy Fast. (Illus.). 256p. 1987. 35.00 (ISBN 0-8160-1170-2). Facts on File.

Women's Attitudes Towards Work. Shirley Dex. LC 87-32365. 224p. 1988. 39.95 (ISBN 0-312-01611-5). St Martin.

Women's Autobiography: Essays in Criticism. Estelle C. Jelinek. LC 79-2600. 286p. pap. 74.40 (AU00356). Bks Demand UMI.

Women's Best: The Art & Life of Mary Ellen Best, 1809-1891. Carolyn Davidson. 1985. 19.98 (ISBN 0-517-56086-0). Crown.

Women's Bible Studies--Colossians. Ruth Spradley. (Women's Bible Studies Ser.). (Illus.). 144p. 1987. pap. 4.95 (ISBN 0-87403-232-6, 39932). Standard Pub.

Women's Bible Studies--Philippians. Ruth Spradley. (Women's Bible Studies Ser.). (Illus.). 144p. 1987. pap. 4.95 (ISBN 0-87403-231-8, 39931). Standard Pub.

Women's Bible: Study Guide. Coalition on Women & Religion Staff. 1975. 5.95 (ISBN 0-9603042-2-3). Coalition Women-Relig.

Women's Bible Study 2 Corinthians. Ruth Spradley. (Illus.). 176p. 1988. pap. 4.95 (ISBN 0-87403-479-5). Standard Pub.

Women's Bodies, Women's Dreams. Patricia Garfield. 1988. pap. 9.95 (ISBN 0-345-33905-3). Ballantine.

Women's Bodybuilding Illustrated. (Illus.). Date not set. pap. 11.45 (ISBN 0-317-53435-1). Anderson World.

Womens Bodybuilding Photo Book. (Illus.). 160p. (Orig.). 1983. pap. 11.95 (ISBN 0-89037-267-5). Anderson World.

Women's Book of Healing. Diane Stein. Ed. by Phyllis Galde. LC 87-45748. (New Age Ser.). (Illus.). 300p. 1987. 12.95 (ISBN 0-87542-759-6). Llewellyn Pubns.

Women's Book of World Records & Achievements. Ed. by Lois D. O'Neill. (Quality Paperbacks Ser.). (Illus.). xiii, 800p. 1983. pap. 14.95 (ISBN 0-306-80206-6). Da Capo.

Women's Budget. Jane Midgley. (Illus.). 1987. 3.00 (ISBN 0-9506968-0-3, Co-pub. by Addams Peace). WILPF.

Women's Bureau: Its History, Activities & Organization. Gustavus A. Weber. LC 72-3030. (No. 22). Repr. of 1923 ed. 21.50 (ISBN 0-404-57122-0). AMS Pr.

Women's Burnout: How to Spot it, How to Reverse It, & How to Prevent It. Herbert J. Freudenberger & Gail North. 260p. 1986. pap. 6.95 (ISBN 0-14-009414-8). Penguin.

Women's Career Development. Ed. by Barbara A. Gutek & Laurie Larwood. (Illus.). 240p. 1987. text ed. 27.95 (ISBN 0-8039-2717-7). Sage.

Women's Careers: Pathways & Pitfalls. Ed. by Suzanna Rose & Laurie Larwood. LC 88-2344. 240p. 1988. lib. bdg. 39.95 (ISBN 0-275-92724-5, C2724). Praeger.

Women's Challenge: Ministry in the Flesh. M. Timothy Prokes. 2.95 (ISBN 0-87193-006-4). Dimension Bks.

Women's Changing Role. rev. ed. Carol Foster. (Information Aids Ser.). 96p. 1988. pap. text ed. 16.95 (ISBN 0-936474-79-3). Info Plus TX.

Women's Choices: The Philosophical Problems of Feminism. Mary Midgley & Judith Hughes. LC 83-16049. 256p. 1984. 22.50 (ISBN 0-312-88791-4). St Martin.

Women's Claims: A Study in Political Economy. Lisa Peattie & Martin Rein. 152p. 1983. 29.95x (ISBN 0-19-877179-7); pap. 10.95x (ISBN 0-19-877180-0). Oxford U Pr.

Women's Coats, Suits, Rainwear & Furs. 6th ed. (Fact File Ser.). 50p. 1987. pap. 17.50 (ISBN 0-87005-591-7). Fairchild.

Women's Collections: Libraries, Archives, & Consciousness. Ed. by Suzanne Hildenbrand. LC 84-22529. (Special Collections Ser.: Vol. 3, No. 3 & 4). 194p. 1986. 32.95 (ISBN 0-86656-273-7). Haworth Pr.

Women's Computer Literacy Handbook. Deborah L. Brecher. (Illus.). 1985. pap. 9.95 (ISBN 0-452-25565-1, Plume). NAL.

Women's Concerns & Planning: A Methodological Approach for Their Integration into Local, Regional & National Planning. (Socio-Economic Studies: No. 13). (Illus.). 166p. (Orig.). 1987. pap. text ed. 11.50 (ISBN 92-3-102392-6, U1566, UNESCO). UNIPUB.

Women's Consciousness, Women's Conscience: A Reader in Feminist Ethics. Ed. by Barbara H. Andolsen et al. 340p. 1985. 24.95 (ISBN 0-86683-958-5, AY8540, HarpR). Har-Row.

Women's Consciousness, Women's Conscience. Ed. by Barbara H. Andolsen et al. LC 85-50124. 336p. 1987. pap. 12.95 (ISBN 0-06-254102-1, HarpR). Har-Row.

Women's Cookbook. Lis Bensley & Colleen Sullivan. 240p. 1986. 16.95 (ISBN 0-670-80738-9). Viking.

Women's Costume in French Texts of the 11th & 12th Centuries. E. R. Goddard. 1973. Repr. of 1927 ed. 24.00 (ISBN 0-384-19040-5). Johnson Repr.

Women's Culture: The Women's Renaissance of the Seventies. Ed. by Gayle Kimball. LC 81-9004. 1981. write for info.; pap. 10.00 (ISBN 0-8108-1496-X). Scarecrow.

Women's Day Complete Guide to Entertaining. Carol Cutler. pap. 5.95 (ISBN 0-317-56853-1). PB.

Women's Decameron. Julia Voznesenskaya. LC 86-10896. 304p. 1986. 18.95 (ISBN 0-87113-101-3). Atlantic Monthly.

Women's Decameron. Julia Voznesenskaya. Tr. by W. B. Linton. 320p. 1987. pap. 9.95 (ISBN 0-8050-0601-X). H Holt & Co.

Women's Development: Some Critical Issues. Government of India Staff & UNICEF Staff. 92p. 1978. 10.95. Asia Bk Corp.

Women's Diaries of the Westward Journey. Lillian Schlissel. LC 80-54143. (Illus.). 272p. 1982. 16.95 (ISBN 0-8052-3774-7). Schocken.

Women's Diaries of the Westward Journey. Lillian Schlissel. (Illus.). 262p. (Orig.). 1983. pap. 10.95 (ISBN 0-8052-0747-3). Schocken.

Women's Dionysian Initiation: The Villa of Mysteries in Pompeii. Linda Fierz-David & Gladys Phelan. LC 88-4893. (Jungian Classics Ser.: Vol. 11). 160p. 1988. pap. 17.50 (ISBN 0-88214-510-X). Spring Pubns.

Women's Directory. Date not set. 2.20. Coun Soc Wk Ed.

Women's Economic Justice Agenda for the States: Issues of the 1990's. Ed. by Linda Tarr-Whelan & Lynne Isensee. 1987. 12.95 (ISBN 0-89788-098-6). NCPA Washington.

Women's Education, A World View: Annotated Bibliography of Doctoral Dissertations, Vol. 1. Compiled by Franklin Parker & Betty J. Parker. LC 78-73791. xii, 470p. 1979. 39.95 (ISBN 0-313-20891-3, PEW/). Greenwood.

Women's Education, A World View: Vol. 2-Annotated Bibliography of Books & Reports. Ed. by Franklin Parker & Betty J. Parker. LC 78-73791. xv, 689p. 1981. lib. bdg. 49.95 (ISBN 0-313-23206-7, PEY/). Greenwood.

Women's Education in Developing Countries: Opportunities & Outcomes. Audrey C. Smock. LC 81-8560. 304p. 1981. 38.95 (ISBN 0-275-90720-1, C0720). Praeger.

Women's Education in the Third World: Comparative Perspectives. Ed. by Gail P. Kelly & Carolyn M. Elliot. LC 82-789. 406p. 1983. 59.50 (ISBN 0-87395-619-2); pap. 19.95 (ISBN 0-87395-620-6). State U NY Pr.

Women's Education in the United States: A Guide to Information Sources. Ed. by Kay S. Wilkins. LC 79-54691. (Education Information Guide Ser.: Vol. 4). 232p. 1979. 68.00x (ISBN 0-8103-1410-X). Gale.

Women's Employment & Fertility: A Comparative Analysis of World Fertility Survey Results for 38 Developing Countries. 96p. 1986. 15.00 (ISBN 92-1-151152-6, E.85.XIII.5). UN.

Women's Encampment for a Future of Peace & Justice: Images & Writings. Mima Cataldo et al. (Illus.). 120p. 1986. 19.95 (ISBN 0-87722-422-6). Temple U Pr.

Women's Exchange Cook Book: Blue Book, Vol. II. Compiled by Woman's Exchange of Memphis, Tennessee. 5.95 (ISBN 0-918544-98-X). Wimmer Bks.

Women's Experience & Education. Ed. by Sharon L. Rich & Ariel Phillips. (Reprint Ser.: No. 17). 312p. 1985. pap. 15.95x (ISBN 0-916690-19-9). Harvard Educ Rev.

Women's Experience in America. Esther Katz & Anita Rapone. LC 79-64179. 414p. 1980. pap. text ed. 14.95x (ISBN 0-87855-668-0). Transaction Bks.

Women's Fiction from Latin America: Selections from Twelve Contemporary Authors. Ed. & tr. by Evelyn P. Garfield. LC 88-3670. (Latin American Literature & Culture Ser.). (Illus.). 384p. 1988. 32.00x (ISBN 0-8143-1858-4); pap. 15.95x (ISBN 0-8143-1859-2). Wayne St U Pr.

Women's Fight for Liberation. Gail Shaffer. (Topics of Our Times Ser.: No. 11). 32p. lib. bdg. 3.75 incl. catalog cards (ISBN 0-87157-812-3); pap. 2.50 vinyl laminated covers (ISBN 0-87157-312-1). SamHar Pr.

Women's Film & Female Experience 1940-1950. Andrea S Walsh. LC 83-24486. 268p. 1986. pap. 12.95 (ISBN 0-275-92599-4, B2599). Praeger.

Women's Films in Print: An Annotated Guide to Eight Hundred Films Made by Women. Bonnie Dawson. LC 74-80642. 1975. pap. 10.00x (ISBN 0-912932-02-3). Booklegger Pr.

Women's Folklore, Women's Culture. Ed. by Rosan A. Jordan & Susan J. Kalcik. LC 84-12019. (American Folklore Society New Ser.). (Illus.). 288p. (Orig.). 1985. pap. text ed. 18.95 (ISBN 0-8122-1206-1). U of Pa Pr.

Women's Foreign Policy Council Directory: A Guide to Women Foreign Policy Specialists & Listings of Women & Organizations Working on International Affairs. Ed. & intro. by Mim Kelber. LC 87-10496. 336p. (Orig.). 1987. pap. 35.00 (ISBN 0-317-58738-2). WFPC.

Women's Foreign Policy Directory. Ed. by Mim Kelber. 318p. 1987. pap. 35.00 (ISBN 0-9617596-0-7). WFPC.

Women's Friendship in Literature. Janet Todd. LC 79-20175. 1980. 40.00x (ISBN 0-231-04562-X); pap. 18.00x (ISBN 0-231-04563-8). Columbia U Pr.

Women's Garment Workers. Louis Levine, pseud. LC 72-89752. (American Labor, from Conspiracy to Collective Bargaining Ser., No. 1). 608p. 1969. Repr. of 1924 ed. 20.00 (ISBN 0-405-02139-9). Ayer Co Pubs.

Women's Groups in Rural Development. (Programmes for Better Family Living Reports: No. 15). 76p. 1976. pap. 7.50 (ISBN 0-685-68968-9, F1081, FAO). UNIPUB.

Women's Guide to Philadelphia. Christina Long & Dorel Shannon. (Illus.). 297p. 1983. pap. 8.95x (ISBN 0-912751-00-2). Prestegord Pubs.

Women's Guide to Re-Entry Employment. Mary Zimmeth. 170p. (Orig.). 1981. pap. 2.50 (ISBN 0-684-17164-3, ScribT). Scribner.

Women's Guild of Saint John's Evangelical & Reformed Church of Richmond, Virginia. Women's Guild of Saint John's Evangelical & Reformed Church of Richmond. 1951. spiral bdg 2.00 (ISBN 0-87517-007-2). Dietz.

Women's Gymnastics. Jill Coulton. (Sports Ser.). (Illus.). 1977. 7.95 (ISBN 0-7158-0592-4). Charles River Bks.

Women's Gymnastics. Elizabeth Danskin. (Hancock House Physical Education Ser.). (Illus.). 120p. (Orig.). (gr. 12). 1983. pap. 14.95 (ISBN 0-88839-045-9). Hancock House.

Women's Gymnastics. Jack Wiley. LC 79-64732. (Illus.). 176p. (Orig.). 1980. pap. 7.95 (ISBN 0-89037-223-3). Anderson World.

Women's Gymnastics: Coach, Participant, Spectator. Mimi Murray. 1979. text ed. 30.00 (ISBN 0-205-06162-1, 6261620). Allyn.

Women's Health: Ambulatory Care, Vol. 1. Ed. by Lois Sonstegard. 361p. 1982. 42.50 (ISBN 0-8089-1501-0, 794184). Grune.

Women's Health Book. Loretta Kurban. LC 86-91266. 90p. (Orig.). 1987. pap. 8.00 (ISBN 0-938863-24-X). Libra Press Chi.

Women's Health Care: A Guide to Alternatives. Kay Weiss. LC 83-3167. 426p. 1984. pap. 17.95 (ISBN 0-8359-8780-9). Appleton & Lange.

Women's Health: Childbearing, Vol. 2. Ed. by Lois Sonstegard. 385p. 1982. 42.50 (ISBN 0-8089-1508-8, 794185). Grune.

Women's Health Cookbook. Lis Bensley & Colleen Sullivan. 288p. 1988. pap. 7.95 (ISBN 0-14-046833-1). Penguin.

Women's Health in the Community. J. Orr. 1987. 8.30 (ISBN 0-471-91105-4). Wiley.

Women's Health Nursing. Fields. (Nursing Examination Review Ser.: Vol. 2). 1984. 14.50 (ISBN 0-87488-497-7). Med Exam.

Women's Health Perspectives: An Annual Review, Vol. 1. Ed. by Carol J. Leppa & Connie Miller. 256p. 1988. 45.00 (ISBN 0-89774-452-7). Oryx Pr.

Women's Health: Readings on Social, Economic & Political Issues. Worcester & Whatley. 304p. 1987. pap. text ed. 19.95 (ISBN 0-8403-4581-X). Kendall-Hunt.

Women's Health, Vol. 3: Crisis & Illness in Childbearing. Sonstegard et al. 1987. write for info. (ISBN 0-8089-1792-7). Grune.

Women's History - American History. 2nd ed. Annette K. Baxter. Louise Stevenson. LC 83-61357. (Selected Syllabi from American Colleges & Universities in History Ser.). 1987. pap. text ed. 14.50x (ISBN 0-910129-12-6). Wiener Pub Inc.

Women's History as Women's Education: Essays by Natalie Zemon Davis & Joan Wallach Scott. Natalie Z. Davis & Joan W. Scott. (Illus.). 40p. (Orig.). 1985. pap. 4.00 (ISBN 0-87391-038-9). Smith Coll.

Women's Studies in Western Europe: A Resource Guide. Ed. by Stephen Lehmann & Eva Sartori. 129p. pap. text ed. 18.00x (ISBN 0-8389-7037-0). ALA.

Women's Suffrage: A Record of the Women's Sufferage Movement in the British Isles. H. Blackburn. Repr. of 1902 ed. 28.00 (ISBN 0-527-08680-0). Kraus Repr.

Women's Suffrage & Progressive Reform: The Fight for the Nineteenth Amendment. Richard C. Keller. Ed. by Robert E. Burke & Frank Freidel. (Modern American History Ser.). 99.00 (ISBN 0-8240-5657-4). Garland Pub.

Women's Suffrage & Social Politics in the French Third Republic. Steven C. Hause & Anne R. Kenney. LC 84-42579. (Illus.). 376p. 1984. 47.50x (ISBN 0-691-05427-4); pap. 16.50x (ISBN 0-691-10167-1). Princeton U Pr.

Women's Suffrage & the Police: Three Senate Documents. U. S. Senate Committee On The District Of Columbia. LC 73-154569. (Police in America Ser). 1971. Repr. of 1913 ed. 54.00 (ISBN 0-405-03389-3). Ayer Co Pubs.

Women's Suffrage in New Zealand. rev. ed. Patricia Grimshaw. (Illus.). 176p. 1988. pap. 22.50 (ISBN 1-86940-021-6). Oxford U Pr.

Women's Suffrage: The Reform Against Nature. Horace Bushnell. LC 75-33280. 1976. Repr. of 1869 ed. 10.50 (ISBN 0-89201-000-2). Zenger Pub.

Women's Tennis: A Historical Documentary. Angela Lumpkin. LC 79-57328. 200p. 1981. 15.00x (ISBN 0-87875-189-0). Whitston Pub.

Women's Therapy Groups: Paradigms of Feminist Treatment. Claire Brody. (Women's Ser.). 288p. 1987. text ed. 28.95 (ISBN 0-8261-5570-7). Springer Pub.

Women's Thesaurus: An Index of Language Used to Describe & Locate Information by & about Women. Ed. by Mary E. Capek. LC 86-46231. 640p. 1987. 37.50i (ISBN 0-06-181171-8, HarpT). Har-Row.

Women's Trade Union Leagues in Great Britain & United States of America. Gladys Boone. LC 68-58549. (Columbia University Studies in the Social Sciences: No. 489). Repr. of 1942 ed. 21.00 (ISBN 0-404-51489-8). AMS Pr.

Women's Travel Guide: Twenty-Five American Cities. Jane E. Lasky & Brenda Fine. 500p. 1986. 24.95 (ISBN 0-8161-8735-5); pap. 12.95 (ISBN 0-8161-9053-4). G K Hall.

Women's Utopias in Nineteenth & Twentieth Century Fiction. Nan B. Albinski. 224p. 1988. lib. bdg. 45.00 (ISBN 0-415-00330-X). Routledge Chapman & Hall.

Women's Views of the Political World of Men. Ed. by Judith H. Stiehm. LC 83-18041. 220p. 1984. lib. bdg. 29.95 (ISBN 0-941320-13-8); pap. text ed. 12.95 (ISBN 0-941320-22-7). Transnatl Pubs.

Women's Views on Guns & Self-Defense. William L. Garrison. 114p. (Orig.). 1983. pap. 5.50 (ISBN 0-911475-23-0). Second Amend.

Women's Voices. Ed. by Pat C. Hoy, II et al. 960p. 1989. pap. text ed. price not set (ISBN 0-394-38097-5). Random.

Women's Voices from Latin America: Interviews with Six Contemporary Authors. Evelyn P. Garfield. LC 85-20231. (Illus.). 189p. 1985. 21.50x (ISBN 0-8143-1782-0). Wayne St U Pr.

Women's Voices from Latin America: Interviews with Six Contemporary Authors. Evelyn P. Garfield. LC 87-25354. (Illus.). 189p. 1987. pap. 9.95x (ISBN 0-8143-1962-9). Wayne St U Pr.

Women's Vote: Beyond the Nineteenth Amendment. League of Women Voters Education Fund. 24p. 1983. pap. text ed. 1.75 (ISBN 0-89959-344-5, 425). LWV US.

Women's Wages. Emilie J. Hutchinson. LC 68-56661. (Columbia University. Studies in the Social Sciences: No. 202). Repr. of 1919 ed. 16.50 (ISBN 0-404-51202-X). AMS Pr.

Women's Ways of Knowing: The Development of Self, Voice, & Mind. Mary F. Belenky et al. 1986. 19.95 (ISBN 0-465-09212-8). Basic.

Women's Ways of Knowing: The Development of Self, Voice, & Mind. Mary F. Belenky et al. LC 85-74881. 272p. 1988. pap. 10.95 (ISBN 0-465-09213-6, PL 5209). Basic.

Women's Welfare-Women's Rights. Ed. by Jane Lewis. (Illus.). 240p. 1982. (Pub. by Croom Helm); pap. 13.50 (ISBN 0-7099-4100-5). Routledge Chapman & Hall.

Women's West. Ed. by Susan Armitage & Elizabeth Jameson. LC 86-14672. (Illus.). 336p. 1987. 24.95 (ISBN 0-8061-2043-6); pap. 12.95 (ISBN 0-8061-2067-3). U of Okla Pr.

Women's Winning Doubles. Pat Baskower & Joanne Williams. Ed. by George Erikson. (Illus.). 176p. (Orig.). 1985. pap. 8.95 (ISBN 0-915643-10-3). Santa Barb Pr.

Women's Words from Lona Abbey. Kathy Galloway. 1987. 10.00x (ISBN 0-947988-08-4, Pub. by Wild Goose Pubns Scotland). State Mutual Bk.

Women's Work. Marion McLeod & Lydia Wevers. 240p. 1986. pap. 9.95 (ISBN 0-19-558136-9). Oxford U Pr.

Women's Work. Anne T. Wallach. 368p. 1987. pap. 3.95 (ISBN 0-451-11610-0, Sig). NAL.

Women's Work & Chicano Families: Cannery Workers of the Santa Clara Valley. Patricia Zavella. LC 87-5245. (Anthropology of Contemporary Issues Ser.). 216p. 1987. 35.00x (ISBN 0-8014-1730-9); pap. 10.95x (ISBN 0-8014-9410-9). Cornell U Pr.

Women's Work & Family Values, 1920-1940. Winifred D. Wandersee. LC 80-21100. 192p. 1981. text ed. 21.00x (ISBN 0-674-95535-8). Harvard U Pr.

Women's Work & Wages. Edward Cadbury et al. LC 79-56954. (English Working Class Ser.). 1980. lib. bdg. 40.00 (ISBN 0-8240-0108-7). Garland Pub.

Women's Work & Wages. Matheson S. Cadbury. 1976. lib. bdg. 59.95 (ISBN 0-8490-2836-1). Gordon Pr.

Women's Work & Women's Studies 1972. Dicki L. Ellis et al. pap. 6.00 (ISBN 0-912786-24-8). Know Inc.

Women's Work-at-Home Handbook: Income & Independence. Patricia McConnel. LC 86-47573. 320p. (Orig.). 1986. pap. 9.95 (ISBN 0-553-34324-6). Bantam.

Women's Work, Class & the Urban Household. Ursula Sharma. 240p. 1986. text ed. 37.00 (ISBN 0-422-79320-5, 1003, Pub. by Tavistock England); pap. text ed. 16.95 (ISBN 0-422-79330-2, 1012, Pub. by Tavistock England). Routledge Chapman & Hall.

Women's Work, Collective Bargaining, Comparable Worth-Pay Equity, Job Evaluation...& All That: An Annotated Bibliography. Helene S. Tanimoto & Gail T. Inaba. (Occasional Publication: No. 152). 52p. 1985. 4.00 (ISBN 0-318-19012-5). U Hawaii.

Women's Work, Collective Bargaining, Comparable Worth-Pay Equity, Job Evaluation... & All That: An Annotated Bibliography. 2nd ed. Helene S. Tanimoto & Gail T. Inaba. (Occasional Publication: No. 159). 76p. 1987. 7.00 (ISBN 0-318-23504-8). U Hawaii.

Women's Work: Development & the Division of Labor by Gender. Eleanor Leacock & Helen I. Safa. 320p. 1986. 39.95 (ISBN 0-89789-035-3); pap. 16.95 (ISBN 0-89789-036-1). Bergin & Garvey.

Women's Work in Britain & America from the Nineties to World War I: An Annotated Bibliography. Mary D. McFeely. 158p. 1982. lib. bdg. 29.00 (ISBN 0-8161-8504-2, Hall Reference). G K Hall.

Women's Work in the Third World Agriculture: Concepts & Indicators. Ruth Dixon-Mueller. (Women, Work & Development: No. 9). v, 151p. (Orig.). 1985. pap. 14.00 (ISBN 92-2-105107-2). Intl Labour Office.

Women's Work, Markets, & Economic Development in Nineteenth-Century Ontario. Marjorie G. Cohen. 286p. 1988. 35.00x (ISBN 0-8020-2651-6); pap. 14.95 (ISBN 0-8020-6677-1). U of Toronto Pr.

Women's Work, Men's Work: Sex Segregation on the Job. National Research Council. 173p. (Orig.). 1985. pap. text ed. 16.50x (ISBN 0-309-03429-9). Natl Acad Pr.

Women's Work, Men's Work: The Ambivalence of Equality. Virginia Novarra. LC 79-67452. (Ideas in Progress Ser.). 160p. 1980. 12.00 (ISBN 0-7145-2680-0, Dist by Scribner); pap. 6.95 (ISBN 0-7145-2681-9, Dist by Scribner). M Boyars Pubs.

Women's Work, Women's Health: Myths & Realities. Jeanne M. Stellman. LC 77-5200. 1978. pap. 5.95 (ISBN 0-394-73452-1). Pantheon.

Women's Work, 1840-1940. Elizabeth Roberts. (Studies in Economic & Social History). 96p. 1988. pap. text ed. 9.95 (ISBN 0-333-36610-7, Pub. by Macmillan UK). Humanities.

Women's Working Lives: Patterns & Strategies. Susan Yeandle. 272p. 15.95 (ISBN 0-422-78960-7, 9277, Pub. by Tavistock England). Routledge Chapman & Hall.

Women's Workshop on Bible Marriages. Diane B. Bloem & Robert C. Bloem. (Woman's Workshop Series of Study Books). 128p. (Orig.). 1980. pap. 4.50 student's manual (ISBN 0-310-21391-6, 10687P); pap. 5.95 leader's manual (ISBN 0-310-21401-7, 10688P). Zondervan.

Women's Workshop on Time Management. Ann Roecker. 96p. 1988. pap. 4.95 (ISBN 0-310-37931-8, Pub. by Lamplighter). Zondervan.

Women's World: A Holistic Approach to Dealing with Stress. (Stress in Modern Society Ser.: No. 16). 1987. 32.50 (ISBN 0-404-63267-X). AMS Pr.

Women's World: From the New Scholarship. Ed. by Marilyn Safir et al. LC 84-26327. 336p. 1985. 38.95 (ISBN 0-275-90158-0, C0158). Praeger.

Women's World Handbook. Dorothy VanderKaay. LC 74-79541. 1974. 3.95 (ISBN 0-87227-063-7); pap. 2.25 (ISBN 0-87227-048-3). Reg Baptist.

Women's Writing: A Challenge to Theory. Ed. by Moira Monteith. LC 86-10056. 192p. 1986. 29.95 (ISBN 0-312-88798-1). St Martin.

Women's Yellow Pages: 1985 Edition. 7th ed. Ed. by Leslie Stone. (Illus.). 192p. 1985. pap. 4.95 (ISBN 0-9610748-7-6). Womens Yellow Pgs.

Women's Yellow Pages: 1986 Edition. 8th ed. Ed. by Leslie Stone. (Illus.). 192p. 1986. pap. 4.95 (ISBN 0-9610748-8-4). Womens Yellow Pgs.

Women's Yellow Pages, 1987. 9th ed. Ed. & intro. by Leslie Stone. 192p. (Orig.). 1986. pap. 4.95 (ISBN 0-9610748-9-2). Womens Yellow Pgs.

Women's Yellow Pages, 1988: Tenth Anniversary Edition. Ed. & intro. by Leslie Stone. (Illus.). 192p. (Orig.). 1987. pap. 4.95 (ISBN 0-9610748-0-9). Womens Yellow Pgs.

Women's Yellow Pages, 1989. 11th ed. Ed. & intro. by Leslie Stone. (Illus.). 192p. 1988. pap. 4.95 (ISBN 0-9610748-1-7). Womens Yellow Pgs.

Womensleuth Anthology: Contemporary Mystery Stories by Women. Ed. by Irene Zahava. LC 88-443. 150p. (Orig.). 1988. 22.95 (ISBN 0-89594-272-0); pap. 6.95 (ISBN 0-89594-271-2). Crossing Pr.

Womonseed. Sunlight Staff. 240p. (Orig.). 1986. pap. 8.95 (ISBN 0-9615129-5-4). Tough Dove.

Womunafu's Bunafu: A Study of Authority in a Nineteenth-Century African Community. David W. Cohen. LC 77-71976. (Illus.). 1977. 28.00x (ISBN 0-691-03093-6). Princeton U Pr.

Won by One: Helping Your Friends & Those Closest to You Enjoy a Relationship with Jesus Christ. Ron Rand. Ed. by Ed Stewart. 252p. (Orig.). 1988. pap. 6.95 (ISBN 0-8307-1238-0, 5419235). Regal.

Won Gil's Secret Diary. Ruth C. Burkholder. LC 83-16529. (Illus.). 14p. (Orig.). (gr. 1-3). 1984. pap. 4.95 (ISBN 0-377-00138-4). Friendship Pr.

Won-Hyo & Yul-Kok of Tae Kwon Do Hyung. Jhoon Rhee. LC 70-157046. (Korean Arts Ser.). (Illus.). 1971. pap. text ed. 9.95x (ISBN 0-89750-002-4, 107, Dist. by Wehman). Ohara Pubns.

Wonder. Edythe Draper. 448p. (gr. 1-4). 1984. 5.95 (ISBN 0-8423-8385-9). Tyndale.

Wonder Album of Filmland. Ed. by C. Winchester. 1976. lib. bdg. 150.00 (ISBN 0-8490-2837-X). Gordon Pr.

Wonder & Other Essays: Eight Studies in Aesthetics & Neighboring Fields. R. W. Hepburn. 176p. 1984. 15.00x (ISBN 0-85224-488-6, Pub. by Edinburgh U Pr Scotland). Columbia U Pr.

Wonder & Whimsy: The Fantastic World of Christina Rossetti. Thomas B. Swann. LC 60-10130. 112p. 1960. 5.00 (ISBN 0-685-31680-7). M Jones.

Wonder Book. Nathaniel Hawthorne. (Airmont Classics Ser.). (gr. 5 up). pap. 1.25 (ISBN 0-8049-0118-X, CL-118). Airmont.

Wonder Book. Nathaniel Hawthorne. (Bambi Classics Ser.). (Illus.). 204p. (Orig.). (YA) (gr. 9-12). 1981. pap. 3.95 (ISBN 0-89531-058-9, 0221-48). Sharon Pubns.

Wonder Book & Tanglewood Tales. Nathaniel Hawthorne. Ed. by William Charvat et al. LC 77-150221. (Centenary Edition of the Works of Nathaniel Hawthorne Ser.: Vol. 7). (Illus.). 476p. (gr. 5 up). 1972. 35.00x (ISBN 0-8142-0158-X). Ohio St U Pr.

Wonder Book for Girls & Boys. Nathaniel Hawthorne. LC 87-50436. 362p. (gr. 3-7). 1987. pap. 7.95 (ISBN 0-940561-07-7). White Rose Pr.

Wonder Book for Girls & Boys see Tales & Sketches.

Wonder Book of Trains. (gr. k-3). 1980. 0.79 (ISBN 0-8431-4158-1). Wonder.

Wonder Book of Travellers' Tales. Henry C. Adams. (Black & Gold Lib). (Illus.). 1942. 6.95 (ISBN 0-87140-998-4). Liveright.

Wonder Circus. E. J. Hall. 64p. 1984. text ed. 2.60 (ISBN 0-07-025753-1). McGraw.

Wonder Clock. Howard Pyle. (Illus.). (gr. 5 up). 15.50 (ISBN 0-8446-2767-4). Peter Smith.

Wonder Clock or, Four & Twenty Marvelous Tales, Being One for Each Hour of the Day. Howard Pyle. (Illus.). xiv, 319p. (gr. 3-6). pap. 5.95 (ISBN 0-486-21446-X). Dover.

Wonder Drugs: How They Work. Mark S. Gold. 224p. 1987. pap. 7.95 (ISBN 0-671-52344-9). PB.

Wonder-Full World of Numbers. Stanley Bezuszka & Margaret Kenney. (Contemporary Motivated Mathematics Ser.). 97p. (Orig.). (gr. 3-6). 1971. pap. text ed. 1.50 (ISBN 0-917916-05-0). Boston Coll Math.

Wonder in a Technical World: An Introduction to the Method & Writers of Philosophy. Vincent P. Branick. LC 80-67205. 256p. 1980. lib. bdg. 13.25 (ISBN 0-8191-1248-8). U Pr of Amer.

Wonder in Aliceland. Caroling. (Illus.). 130p. 1982. pap. 4.95 (ISBN 0-942488-01-6). Wholeo Bks.

Wonder Kid Meets the Evil Lunch Snatcher. Lois Duncan. LC 87-26490. (Illus.). 76p. (gr. 7-10). 1988. 9.95 (ISBN 0-316-19558-8). Little.

Wonder O' the Wind. Phillip Keller. 1986. 7.95 (ISBN 0-8499-3061-8). Word Bks.

Wonder O' the Wind. W. Phillip Keller. 1982. 9.95 (ISBN 0-8499-0337-8). Word Bks.

Wonder of Barbie. Paris Manos & Susan Manos. (Illus.). 136p. 1987. pap. 9.95 (ISBN 0-89145-336-9, 1808). Collector Bks.

Wonder of Becoming You: How a Jewish Girl Grows Up. Miriam Grossman. (gr. 6-8). 1988. 7.95 (ISBN 0-87306-438-0). Feldheim.

Wonder of Being Human: Our Brain & Our Mind. John Eccles & Daniel N. Robinson. LC 83-49044. 192p. 1984. 16.95 (ISBN 0-02-908860-7). Free Pr.

Wonder of Being Human: Our Brain & Our Mind. John Eccles & Daniel N. Robinson. LC 84-25562. (New Science Library). 182p. 1985. pap. 8.95 (ISBN 0-87773-312-0, 73521-8). Shambhala Pubns.

Wonder of Birds. Ed. by Robert M. Poole. (Illus.). 280p. 1983. deluxe ed. 39.95 (ISBN 0-87044-471-9); Includes Field Guide to the Birds of North America & 4 record album of bird sounds. 29.95 (ISBN 0-87044-470-0). Natl Geog.

Wonder of Comfort. Ed. by Phyllis Hobe. LC 82-8322. (Small Wonders Ser.). (Illus.). 108p. (Orig.). 1982. pap. 4.95 (ISBN 0-664-26003-9, A Bridgebooks Publication). Westminster John Knox.

Wonder of God. Russell Shull. 1975. pap. 0.25, 5 for 1.00. Macalester.

Wonder of Guadalupe. Francis Johnston. LC 81-53041. 143p. 1981. pap. 5.00 (ISBN 0-89555-168-3). TAN Bks Pubs.

Wonder of His Love. Palmer T. Ellard. 26p. 1985. 5.95 (ISBN 0-533-06379-5). Vantage.

Wonder of Love. Ed. by Phyllis Hobe. LC 82-8376. (Small Wonders Ser.). (Illus.). 112p. 1982. pap. 4.95 (ISBN 0-664-26001-2, A Bridgebooks Publication). Westminster John Knox.

Wonder of Miracles: Bible Stories That Live. Margaret Graham. LC 87-45702. 160p. 1988. 13.45 (ISBN 0-06-063381-6, HarpR). Har-Row.

Wonder of Prayer. Ed. by Phyllis Hobe. LC 82-8317. (Small Wonders Ser.). (Illus.). 112p. (Orig.). 1982. pap. 4.95 (ISBN 0-664-26002-0, A Bridgebooks Publication). Westminster John Knox.

Wonder of Seeing Double: Poems. Robert B. Shaw. LC 88-1072. 88p. (Orig.). 1988. lib. bdg. 17.50 (ISBN 0-87023-637-7); pap. 7.95 (ISBN 0-87023-638-5). U of Mass Pr.

Wonder of Sex, How to Teach Children. J. C. Willke & Mrs. Willke. 1983. pap. 4.95 (ISBN 0-910728-17-8). Hayes.

Wonder of the Real: A Sketch in Basic Philosophy. rev., enlarged ed. Francis J. Klauder. LC 72-94706. (Illus.). 116p. 1973. 9.95 (ISBN 0-8158-0300-1). Chris Mass.

Wonder of the Word of God. Robert L. Sumner. 1969. pap. 1.95 (ISBN 0-87398-933-3). Sword of Lord.

Wonder of Words, Bk. II. Edward Chinn. Ed. by Michael L. Sherer. LC 86-28366. (Orig.). 1987. pap. 7.50 (ISBN 0-89536-867-6, 7826, Co. Pub. by Forward Movement). CSS of Ohio.

Wonder of Words, Bk. 2. Edward Chinn. (Orig.). 1987. pap. 7.50 (ISBN 0-88028-059-X, Co-Pub. by CSS of OH). Forward Movement.

Wonder of Words: An Introduction to Language for Every Man. Isaac Goldberg. LC 74-164294. 502p. 1971. Repr. of 1938 ed. 48.00x (ISBN 0-8103-3777-0). Gale.

Wonder of Words: One Hundred Words & Phrases Shaping How Christians Think & Live. Edward Chinn. (Orig.). 1985. pap. 5.75 (ISBN 0-89536-737-8, 5822). CSS of Ohio.

Wonder Square. Stanley Bezuszka et al. (Motivated Math Project Activity Booklets). 30p. (Orig.). (gr. 6-12). 1976. pap. text ed. 1.25 (ISBN 0-917916-15-8). Boston Coll Math.

Wonder Tales. K. Chukovsky. 50p. 1973. 2.95 (ISBN 0-8285-1276-0, Pub. by Progress Pubs USSR). Imported Pubns.

Wonder Tales of Alsace-Lorraine. Bernard Henderson & C. Clavert. 1976. lib. bdg. 59.95 (ISBN 0-8490-2838-8). Gordon Pr.

Wonder That Is Hindu Dharma. Ram C. Gupta. 240p. 1987. text ed. 27.95x (ISBN 81-7018-426-6, Pub. by B R Pub Corp Delhi). Apt Bks.

Wonder: The Book of We. (Infinity Ser.: No. 9). 1972. text ed. 2.50 (ISBN 0-03-004011-6, 243, HarpR); tchr's. guide 1.15 (ISBN 0-03-004016-7, 244). Har-Row.

Wonder Voyages upon Unmoving Clouds. Steven G. Farrell. LC 84-90410. 64p. 1984. 6.50 (ISBN 0-8233-0391-8). Golden Quill.

Wonder Wheels. Lee B. Hopkins. LC 78-11774. (Illus.). (YA) 1979. Knopf.

Wonder Women of Sports. Betty M. Jones. LC 80-20232. (Step-up Book Ser.: No. 33). (Illus.). 72p. (gr. 2-5). 1981. pap. 3.95 boards o.s.i. (ISBN 0-394-84475-0). Random.

Wonder-Working Lawyers of Talmudic Bablonia: The Theory & Practice of Judaism in Its Formative Age. Jacob Neusner. LC 87-6161. (Studies in Judaism). (Illus.). 372p. (Orig.). 1987. lib. bdg. 28.50 (ISBN 0-8191-6287-6, Pub. by Studies in Judaism); pap. text ed. 16.75 (ISBN 0-8191-6288-4, Pub. by Studies in Judaism). U Pr of Amer.

Wonder-Working Power of God. Cornelia Addington. LC 87-70231. 152p. 1987. pap. 5.95 (ISBN 0-87516-589-3). DeVorss.

Wonder-Working Providence of Sions Saviour in New England (1654) Edward Johnson. LC 74-5118. 256p. 1974. lib. bdg. 35.00x (ISBN 0-8201-1130-9). Schol Facsimiles.

Wonderful Adventure of Captain Priest. Samuel A. Hammett. LC 76-166740. 1971. Repr. 49.00x (ISBN 0-403-01374-7). Scholarly.

Wonderful Adventures of Mrs. Seacole in Many Lands. Ed. by William Andrews. Mary Seacole. (Schomburg Library of Nineteenth-Century Black Women Writers). 256p. 1988. 16.95 (ISBN 0-19-505249-8). Oxford U Pr.

Wonderful Adventures of Phra the Phoenician. Edwin L. Arnold. Ed. by R. Reginald & Douglas Menville. LC 80-19173. (Newcastle Forgotten Fantasy Library Ser.: Vol. 11). 329p. 1980. Repr. of 1977 ed. lib. bdg. 19.95x (ISBN 0-89370-510-1). Borgo Pr.

Wonderful Apparition: The Story of Halley's Comet. Richard B. Peterson. (Illus.). 195p. 1985. 18.95x (ISBN 0-935125-00-0). Lighthouse Writers.

Wonderful Bicycle Parade. Susan Borges. (Illus.). 36p. (Orig.). Date not set. 10.95 (ISBN 0-941526-05-4). Prospect Hill.

TITLE INDEX

WONDROUS CREST-JEWEL IN PERFORMANCE

Wonderful Century, Its Successes & Its Failures. Alfred R. Wallace. 412p. Repr. of 1898 ed. text ed. 49.68x (ISBN 0-576-29130-7, Pub. by Gregg Intl Pubs England). Gregg Intl.
Wonderful Country. Tom Lea. LC 83-40498. (Illus.). 400p. 1984. Repr. of 1952 ed. 15.95 (ISBN 0-89096-185-9). Tex A&M Univ Pr.
Wonderful Crisis of Middle Age. Eda LeShan. 320p. 1985. pap. 4.50 (ISBN 0-446-34064-2). Warner Bks.
Wonderful Cut-outs of Oz: Thirty-Five Stand-up Figures to Please the Young & the Young at Heart. Rob R. MacVeigh. (Illus.). 32p. 1985. pap. 4.95 (ISBN 0-517-55916-1). Crown.
Wonderful Discoveries of the Witchcrafts of M. & P. Flower. Margaret Flower. LC 72-5992. (English Experience Ser.: No. 517). 50p. 1972. Repr. of 1619 ed. 6.00 (ISBN 90-221-0517-2). Walter J Johnson.
Wonderful Dog & Other Tales. Mikhail Zoshchenko. Tr. by E. Fen from Rus. LC 72-90320. (Soviet Literature in English Translation Ser.). 179p. 1973. Repr. of 1942 ed. 15.95 (ISBN 0-88355-029-6). Hyperion Conn.
Wonderful Ethiopians of the Ancient Cushite Empire. Drusilla D. Houston. 280p. 1985. 20.00 (ISBN 0-933121-00-8); pap. 11.95 (ISBN 0-933121-01-6). Black Classic.
Wonderful Father Book. Richard Mann. (Illus., Orig.). 1985. pap. 5.95. Turnbull & Willoughby.
Wonderful Flight to the Mushroom Planet. Eleanor Cameron. (Illus.). (gr. 4-6). 1954. 14.95 (ISBN 0-316-12537-7, Joy St Bks). Little.
Wonderful Flight to the Mushroom Planet. Eleanor Cameron. 214p. (gr. 3-7). 1988. pap. 4.95 (ISBN 0-316-12540-7, Joy St Bks). Little.
Wonderful Focus of You. Joanne Kyger. (Orig.). 1980. pap. 5.00 (ISBN 0-915990-22-9). Z Pr.
Wonderful Food of Provence. Jean-Noel Escudier & Peta J. Fuller. LC 87-45612. (Illus.). 256p. 1988. pap. 12.95 (ISBN 0-06-097131-2, PL-7131, PL). Har-Row.
Wonderful Fool. Shusako Endo. Tr. by Francis Mathy from Japanese. LC 83-47553. 224p. 1983. 13.45 (ISBN 0-06-859853-X, HarpT). Har-Row.
Wonderful Good Cooking. Ed. by Johnny Schrock et al. LC 75-1726. 136p. 1975. pap. 7.95 (ISBN 0-8361-1765-4). Herald Pr.
Wonderful Hay Tumble. Kathleen M. Harris. LC 87-12305. (Illus.). 32p. (ps-2). 1988. 11.95 (ISBN 0-688-07151-1); PLB 11.88 (ISBN 0-688-07152-X). Morrow.
Wonderful Inventions: Motion Pictures, Broadcasting, & Recorded Sound at the Library of Congress. Ed. by Iris Newsom. LC 83-600369. (Illus.). 384p. 1985. 40.00 (ISBN 0-317-59971-2). Lib Congress.
Wonderful Journey. Gill McBarnet. (Illus.). 32p. (gr. k-2). 1986. 6.95 (ISBN 0-9615102-2-6). Ruwanga Trad.
Wonderful Life: The Films & Career of James Stewart. Tony Thomas. (Illus.). 256p. 1988. pap. 15.95 (ISBN 0-8065-1081-1, Pub. by Citadel Pr). Lyle Stuart.
Wonderful Love. Jack Bemporad & Stephen Bindman. 175p. Date not set. pap. 9.95 (ISBN 0-932385-15-X). Human Futures.
Wonderful Money Making Opportunity for Everyone: Roadside Marketing for Maximal Profits. Lawrence Watts. (Illus.). 1980. 137.45 (ISBN 0-89266-214-X). Am Classical Coll Pr.
Wonderful Mrs. Trumbly. Sally Wittman. LC 81-47737. (Illus.). 40p. (gr. k-3). 1982. 10.70i (ISBN 0-06-026511-6). HarpJ.
Wonderful Private World of Liberace. Liberace. (Illus.). 224p. 1986. 29.45i (ISBN 0-06-015481-0, HarpT). Har-Row.
Wonderful Story of God's Creation. Terrie K. Tomoko. (ps-3). 1978. plastic bdg. 2.50 (ISBN 0-8198-0375-8); pap. 1.75 (ISBN 0-8198-0376-6). Dghtrs St Paul.
Wonderful Story of Henry Sugar & Six More. Roald Dahl. (gr. 4-8). 1979. pap. 2.95 (ISBN 0-553-15445-1, Skylark Bk). Bantam.
Wonderful Story of Henry Sugar & Six More. Roald Dahl. 224p. 1988. pap. 3.95 (ISBN 0-14-032874-2, Puffin Bks). Penguin.
Wonderful Story of Zaal & How He Was Saved by the Magnificent Magical Bird Seemorgh. M. Batmanglij & N Batmanglij. LC 86-12665. (Illus.). 48p. (gr. 4 up). 1986. 18.50 (ISBN 0-934211-01-9). Mage Pubs Inc.
Wonderful Surprise. Martha Marshall. LC 83-7343. (Illus.). 32p. (gr. 1-2). 1983. PLB 4.95 (ISBN 0-89693-214-1). Dandelion Hse.
Wonderful, Sweet & Wild. Date not set. 4.95x (ISBN 0-89741-024-6). Roadrunner Tech.
Wonderful Terrible Time. Mary Stolz. (Illus.). (ps-7). PLB 11.89 (ISBN 0-06-026064-5). HarpJ.
Wonderful Visit. H. G. Wells. Ed. by R. Reginald & Douglas Melville. LC 77-84274. (Lost Race & Adult Fantasy Ser.). 1978. Repr. of 1895 ed. lib. bdg. 24.50x (ISBN 0-405-11013-8). Ayer Co Pubs.
Wonderful Way That Babies Are Made. Larry Christenson. LC 82-12813. 48p. (Orig.). (ps up). 1982. 8.95 (ISBN 0-87123-627-3, 230627). Bethany Hse.
Wonderful Webbers. June Lange. (Illus.). 1967. 12.95 (ISBN 0-910550-19-0). Elysium.
Wonderful Wedding. George Fitzmaurice & John Guinan. (Lost Play Ser.). 1978. pap. 1.95x (ISBN 0-912262-52-4). Proscenium.
Wonderful Wisdom. Valerie Owen. 137p. (Orig.). 1984. pap. text ed. 4.95 (ISBN 0-914307-24-X). Word Faith.
Wonderful Wizard of Oz. L. Frank Baum. (Airmont Classics Ser.). (Illus.). (gr. 4 up). pap. 1.75 (ISBN 0-8049-0069-8, CL-69). Airmont.
Wonderful Wizard of Oz. L. Frank Baum. 139p. 1981. Repr. PLB 15.95x (ISBN 0-89966-347-8). Buccaneer Bks.
Wonderful Wizard of Oz. L. Frank Baum. (Illus.). vii, 268p. (gr. k-6). 1960. pap. 5.95 (ISBN 0-486-20691-2). Dover.
Wonderful Wizard of Oz. L. Frank Baum. 193p. 1981. Repr. PLB 11.95x (ISBN 0-89967-021-0). Harmony Raine.
Wonderful Wizard of Oz. L. Frank Baum. (Illus.). (gr. 4 up). 15.00 (ISBN 0-8446-1610-9). Peter Smith.
Wonderful Wizard of Oz. L. Frank Baum. (gr. 5-6). 17.95 (ISBN 0-88411-772-3, Pub. by Aeonian Pr). Amereon Ltd.
Wonderful Wizard of Oz. L. Frank Baum. LC 86-62556. (Illus.). 316p. (ps up). 1987. 17.00 (ISBN 0-688-06944-4, Morrow Junior Books). Morrow.
Wonderful Wizard of Oz. L. Frank Baum. (Illus.). 1986. 25.00 (ISBN 0-520-05822-4). U of Cal Pr.
Wonderful Wizard of Oz. L. Frank Baum. (Illus.). 188p. (gr. 2-6). 1987. lib. bdg. 12.95 (ISBN 1-55736-013-8). ABC-Clio.
Wonderful Wizard of Oz. L. Frank Baun. 256p. 1984. pap. 2.25 (ISBN 0-451-51864-0, Sig Classics). NAL.
Wonderful Wizard of Oz. Virginia Koste. (Children's Theatre Playscript Ser.). 60p. (gr. 3-7). 1982. saddle stitch 2.50x (ISBN 0-88020-106-1). Coach Hse.
Wonderful World of Gift Giving. Linda P. Silbert & Alvin J. Silbert. (Little Twirps Preschool Ser.). (gr. 3-7). 1983. workbook 2.98 (ISBN 0-89544-024-5). Silbert Bress.
Wonderful World of Ginkel Bugs. Helen Lowry. 32p. 1987. 6.50 (ISBN 0-8062-2928-4). Carlton.
Wonderful World of Honey: The Only Nutrition-Wise Sugarless Cookbook, Beauty Aids & Preventive Medicine. Joe M. Parkhill. 160p. 1978. spiral bdg. 6.95 (ISBN 0-936744-01-4). Country Bazaar.
Wonderful World of Horses Coloring Album. Rita Warner. (Illus.). 32p. (Orig.). (gr. 3 up). 1976. pap. 3.95 (ISBN 0-8431-1709-5, 69-8). Troubador Pr.
Wonderful World of Magic & Witchcraft. Leonard R. Ashley. LC 85-25310. (Illus.). 1986. 17.50 (ISBN 0-934878-71-4); pap. 10.95 (ISBN 0-934878-72-2). Dembner Bks.
Wonderful World of Maps. James F. Madden. Ed. by Hammond Incorporated Staff. LC 77-23410. (Illus.). 64p. (Orig.). (gr. 7-11). 1986. 8.95 (ISBN 0-8437-3411-6). Hammond Inc.
Wonderful World of Natural-Food Cookery see Natural Food Cookery.
Wonderful World of Netsuke. Raymond Bushell. LC 64-24948. (Illus.). 1964. 11.00 (ISBN 0-8048-0631-4). C E Tuttle.
Wonderful World of Oprah. J. Dooley. 128p. (Orig.). 1988. pap. 2.95 (ISBN 1-55547-238-9). Critics Choice Paper.
Wonderful World of Penthouse Sex. Ed. by Marco Vassi. 368p. 1976. pap. 3.95 (ISBN 0-446-32025-0). Warner Bks.
Wonderful World of Pollen. Joe M. Parkhill. 160p. (Orig.). 1982. pap. text ed. 6.95 (ISBN 0-936744-06-5). Country Bazaar.
Wonderful World of San Diego. 2nd ed. Anne Gray. LC 74-76733. (Illus.). (gr. 4 up). 1975. pap. 3.95 (ISBN 0-88289-081-6). Pelican.
Wonderful World of Stochastics: A Tribute to Elliott W. Montroll. Ed. by M. F. Shlesinger & G. H. Weiss. (Studies in Statistical Mechanics: Vol. 12). 250p. 1985. 47.75 (ISBN 0-444-86937-9, North-Holland). Elsevier.
Wonderful World of Succulents: Cultivation & Description of Selected Succulent Plants Other Than Cacti. Werner Rauh. Tr. by Harvey L. Kendall from Ger. LC 83-20148. (Illus.). 164p. 1984. 49.50x (ISBN 0-87474-780-5, RAWW). Smithsonian.
Wonderful World of Superstition, Prophecy & Luck. Leonard R. Ashley. LC 83-23182. (Illus.). 192p. (Orig.). 1984. pap. 8.95 (ISBN 0-934878-33-1). Dembner Bks.
Wonderful World of Walking. Bill Gale. 320p. 1988. pap. 9.95 (ISBN 0-440-50032-X, Dell Trade). Dell.
Wonderful World of "Whey Lovers". Christina Dillane & Susan Dusharme. Rev. by Joe M. Parkhill. 160p. (Orig.). 1983. pap. text ed. 6.95 (ISBN 0-936744-08-1). Country Bazaar.
Wonderful World Within You: Your Inner Nutritional Environment. Rev. ed. Roger J. Williams. (Illus.). 278p. 1987. pap. 14.95 (ISBN 0-942333-00-4). Bio-Comns Pr.
Wonderful Years, Wonderful Years. George V. Higgins. 1988. 18.950- (ISBN 0-8050-0694-X). H Holt & Co.
Wonderfully Made for This Life & the Next. Russell Shull. 1980. pap. 0.50. Macalester.
Wondering about Physics: Using Spreadsheets to Find Out. Dykstra. 1988. pap. write for info. (ISBN 0-471-63174-4). Wiley.
Wondering at the World: Instructional Manual to Accompany KIO & GUS. Matthew Lipman & Ann M. Sharp. (Philosophy for Children Ser.). 500p. 1986. 37.50x (ISBN 0-916834-20-4). Inst Advncmnt Philos Child.
Wondering at the World: Instructional Manual to Accompany KIO & GUS. Matthew Lipman & Ann M. Sharp. 526p. 1986. 39.50 (ISBN 0-8191-5471-7, Pub. by Inst for Advancement of Philosophy for Children). U Pr of Amer.
Wondering: Invitations to Think about the Future for Primary Grades. R. E. Myers & E. P. Torrance. (Orig.). 1984. pap. 2.95 (ISBN 0-936386-22-3). Creative Learning.
Wonderings. Gerald T. Bouressa. 38p. 1986. 5.95 (ISBN 0-533-06855-X). Vantage.
Wonderings. Kenneth Patchen. LC 79-148535. (Illus., Orig.). 1971. 5.95 (ISBN 0-8112-0346-8); pap. 1.75 (ISBN 0-8112-0149-X, NDP320). New Directions.
Wonderlamp. Don Stevenson & Hugh F. Blyth. (Illus.). 48p. 1983. Kalimat.
Wonderlijke Problemen Leerzaam Tijoverdrijf Door Puzzle En Spel see Master Book of Mathematical Puzzles & Recreations.
Wonderous Mushroom: Mycolatry in Mesoamerica. R. Gordon Wasson. LC 79-26895. (Illus.). 178p. 1988. text ed. 29.95 (ISBN 0-07-068441-3). McGraw.
Wonderous Power, Wonderous Love. 250p. 1983. pap. 5.95 (ISBN 0-89066-052-2). World Wide Pubs.
Wonders! Dick Hilliard & Beverly Valenti-Hilliard. (Center Celebration Ser.). (Illus.). 48p. (Orig.). (gr. 1 up). 1981. pap. text ed. 4.95 (ISBN 0-89390-032-X). Resource Pubns.
Wonders Around the Sun. Mary G. Bonner. (Illus.). (gr. 4-7). PLB 6.19 (ISBN 0-8313-0010-8). Lantern.
Wonder's Child: My Life in Science Fiction. Jack Williamson. (Illus.). 288p. 1984. 15.95 (ISBN 0-312-94454-3); ltd. ed. cancelled 40.00 (ISBN 0-312-94455-1). Bluejay Bks.
Wonder's Child: My Life in Science Fiction. Jack Williamson. 288p. 1985. pap. 8.95 (ISBN 0-312-94456-X). Bluejay Bks.
Wonders from the Earth. Date not set. 15.95 (ISBN 0-8351-2047-3). China Bks.
Wonders have been Found. Sylvia J. Michaelson & Holly J. Michaelson. (Illus.). 224p. 10.00 (ISBN 0-9617005-0-5). Ministering Angel.
Wonders Hidden see Visionary.
Wonders Hidden: Audubon's Early Years see Visionary: The Life Story of Flicker of the Serpentine.
Wonders in the Midst. Ward Patterson. LC 78-62709. 96p. (Orig.). 1979. pap. 2.25 (ISBN 0-87239-237-6, 40076). Standard Pub.
Wonders in Weeds. William Smith. 187p. 1977. 13.00x (ISBN 0-8464-1062-1). Beekman Pubs.
Wonders in Weeds. William Smith. 1980. 19.50 (ISBN 0-85032-151-4, Pub. by Daniel Co England). State Mutual Bk.
Wonders, Inc. Crawford Kilian. (Illus.). (gr. 1 up). 1968. 6.95 (ISBN 0-87466-058-0, Pub. by Parnassus). HM.
Wonders of Bible Chronology. Philip Mauro. 1974. pap. 5.95 (ISBN 0-685-52825-1). Reiner.
Wonders of Creation see Maravillas De la Creacion.
Wonders of Creation & the World Hereafter. Elizabeth Walton. 110p. 1986. 30.00 (ISBN 0-7212-0746-4, Pub. by Regency Pr). State Mutual Bk.
Wonders of Creation: Natural History Drawings in the British Library. Desmond Ray. (Illus.). 252p. 1986. 39.95 (ISBN 0-7123-0071-6, Pub. by British Lib). Longwood Pub Group.
Wonders of Earth. Gary Webster. LC 67-13770. 1967. 3.50 (ISBN 0-685-42654-8, Pub. by Sheed). Guild Bks.
Wonders of Energy. David Adler. LC 82-20042. (Troll Question & Answer Bks.). (Illus.). 32p. (gr. 3-6). 1983. PLB 9.59 (ISBN 0-89375-884-1); pap. text ed. 1.95 (ISBN 0-89375-885-X). Troll Assocs.
Wonders of India. Tr. by G. S. Freeman-Grenville. 124p. 1982. 35.00x (ISBN 0-85692-063-0, Pub. by E-W Pubns England). State Mutual Bk.
Wonders of Inventions. Mary G. Bonner. (Illus.). (gr. 4-9). 1961. PLB 6.19 (ISBN 0-8313-0007-8). Lantern.
Wonders of Ireland. facsimile ed. P. W. Joyce. Intro. by Hank Harrison. (P. W. Joyce, Irish History Ser.). 242p. (Orig.). Date not set. pap. 24.95 (ISBN 0-918501-57-1). Archives Pr.
Wonders of Light & Shadow. Society for Promoting Christian Knowledge. LC 72-9236. (Literature of Photography Ser.). Repr. of 1851 ed. 14.00 (ISBN 0-405-04941-2). Ayer Co Pubs.
Wonders of Magic. John Booth. LC 86-60002. (Illus.). xiv, 301p. 1986. text ed. 39.50 (ISBN 0-943230-03-9). Ridgeway Pr.
Wonders of Man. Gary Webster. LC 57-6055. 1957. 3.50 (ISBN 0-685-42655-6, Pub. by Sheed). Guild Bks.
Wonders of Mules. Lavine & Scuro. (Illus.). 64p. 8.00 (ISBN 0-318-01794-6). Am Donkey.
Wonders of Nature. Walter Linsenmaier. LC 78-62133. (Picturebacks Ser.). (Illus.). 32p. (ps-3). 1980. (BYR); pap. 1.95 (ISBN 0-394-84091-7). Random.
Wonders of Nature Take-Along Library, 5 bks. (Illus.). 160p. (ps-3). 1987. pap. 9.95 boxed set (ISBN 0-394-89106-6, BYR). Animal Babies, by Harry McNaught. Dinosaurs & Prehistoric Animals, by Peter Zallinger. Wild Animals from Alligator to Zebra, by Arthur Singer. Wonders of Nature, by Walter LinsenMaier. Random.
Wonders of Qigong: A Chinese Exercise for Fitness, Health, & Longevity. China Sports Magazine Staff. Ed. by Wayfarer Publications Staff. LC 85-51522. 112p. 1985. pap. 10.95 (ISBN 0-935099-07-7). Wayfarer Pubns.
Wonders of Rivers. Rae Bains. LC 81-7423. (Illus.). 32p. (gr. 2-4). 1982. PLB 9.89 (ISBN 0-89375-570-2); pap. text ed. 1.95 (ISBN 0-89375-571-0). Troll Assocs.
Wonders of Salvage: Deep Sea Diving for Sunken Ships & Treasures. David Masters. 1977. lib. bdg. 75.00 (ISBN 0-8490-2839-6). Gordon Pr.
Wonders of Salvation. John L. Shuler. 1985. pap. 6.95 (ISBN 0-8163-0591-9). Pacific Pr Pub Assn.
Wonders of Science. John House. (Science Ser.). 24p. (gr. 3-5). 1977. wkbk. 5.00 (ISBN 0-8209-0155-5, S-17). ESP.
Wonders of Skiing. H. Schneider & A. Fanck. 1976. lib. bdg. 69.95 (ISBN 0-8490-2840-X). Gordon Pr.
Wonders of Speech. Alvin Silverstein & Virginia Silverstein. LC 87-31370. (Illus.). 192p. (gr. 7 up). 1988. 11.95 (ISBN 0-688-06534-1). Morrow.
Wonders of the Age: Masterpieces of Early Safavid Painting, 1501-1576. Stuart C. Welch. LC 79-2480. 223p. 1979. pap. 12.95 (ISBN 0-916724-38-7). Harvard Art Mus.
Wonders of the Desert. Louis Sabin. LC 81-7397. (Illus.). 32p. (gr. 2-4). 1982. PLB 9.89 (ISBN 0-89375-574-5); pap. text ed. 1.95 (ISBN 0-89375-575-3); cassette 9.95. Troll Assocs.
Wonders of the Desert. Nikolai Sladkov. Tr. by Eugene Yankovsky. 26p. 1983. pap. 1.99 (ISBN 0-8285-2954-X, Pub. by Malysh Pubs USSR). Imported Pubns.
Wonders of the Forest. Francene Sabin. LC 81-7401. (Illus.). 32p. (gr. 2-4). 1982. PLB 9.89 (ISBN 0-89375-572-9); pap. text ed. 1.95 (ISBN 0-89375-573-7). Troll Assocs.
Wonders of the Human Brain. Margaret Keeler. LC 83-60111. (Strange but True Ser.). (Illus.). 64p. (gr. 6 up). 1983. 10.96 (ISBN 0-382-06690-1). Silver.
Wonders of the Invisible World. large type ed. Cotton Mather. pap. 6.95 (ISBN 0-910122-46-6). Amherst Pr.
Wonders of the Jungle. National Wildlife Staff. Ed. by Victor Waldrop. 96p. (gr. 1-7). 1986. 12.95 (ISBN 0-912186-72-0); PLB 14.95. Natl Wildlife.
Wonders of the Night Sky. F. Zigel. Tr. by George Yankovsky from Rus. (Illus.). 208p. 1968. 12.00x (ISBN 0-8464-0975-5). Beekman Pubs.
Wonders of the Past, 2 vols. J. A. Hammerton. (Illus.). 1986. Repr. Set. text ed. 500.00x (ISBN 81-7018-269-7, Pub. by B R Pub Corp Delhi). Vol. I: X, 1-628pgs. Vol. II: viii, 629-1252pgs. Apt Bks.
Wonders of the Pond. Francene Sabin. LC 81-7407. (Illus.). 32p. (gr. 2-4). 1982. PLB 9.89 (ISBN 0-89375-576-1); pap. text ed. 1.95 (ISBN 0-89375-577-X); cassette 9.95. Troll Assocs.
Wonders of the Sea. Louis Sabin. LC 81-3334. (Illus.). 32p. (gr. 2-4). 1982. PLB 9.89 (ISBN 0-89375-578-8); pap. text ed. 1.95 (ISBN 0-89375-579-6); cassette 9.95. Troll Assocs.
Wonders of the Seasons. Keith Brandt. LC 81-7411. (Illus.). 32p. (gr. 2-4). 1982. PLB 9.89 (ISBN 0-89375-580-X); pap. text ed. 1.95 (ISBN 0-89375-581-8). Troll Assocs.
Wonders of the Sky. Fred Schaaf. 1984. 16.00 (ISBN 0-8446-6099-X). Peter Smith.
Wonders of the Sky: Observing Rainbows, Comets, Eclipses, the Stars, & Other Phenomena. Fred Schaaf. (Illus.). 224p. (Orig.). 1983. pap. 7.95 (ISBN 0-486-24402-4). Dover.
Wonders of the World, Ordeals of the Soul, Revelations of the Spirit. Rudolf Steiner. Tr. by Dorothy Lenn et al from Ger. 190p. 1983. pap. 13.00 (ISBN 0-85440-363-9, Pub by Steinerbooks). Anthroposophic.
Wonders of Water. Jane Dickinson. LC 82-17388. (Troll Question & Answer Bks.). (Illus.). 32p. (gr. 3-6). 1983. PLB 9.59 (ISBN 0-89375-874-4); pap. text ed. 1.95 (ISBN 0-89375-875-2). Troll Assocs.
Wonders She Performs. Louis Kaczmarek. 192p. (Orig.). 1986. 10.95 (ISBN 0-937495-22-0); pap. 6.95 (ISBN 0-317-65645-7). Trinity Comns.
Wonders with Wire. Michelle Minett. 1985. 13.00x (ISBN 0-86025-863-7, Pub. by Ian Henry Pubns England). State Mutual Bk.
Wondersmith & Other Macabre Stories. Intro. by Peter Tremayne. (Illus.). 220p. 1987. pap. 10.95 (ISBN 0-86327-152-9, Pub. by Wolfhound Pr Ireland). Irish Bks Media.
Wonderworks: Science Fiction & Fantasy Art. Michael Whelan. Ed. by Polly Freas & Kelly Freas. LC 79-12575. (Illus.). 1979. (Starblaze); pap. 11.95 (ISBN 0-915442-74-4, Starblaze); collector's edition 30.00 (ISBN 0-915442-83-3). Donning Co.
Wondrous Apple. L. Kuzmin. 87p. 1985. 6.95 (ISBN 0-8285-3199-4, Pub. by Raduga Pubs USSR). Imported Pubns.
Wondrous Crest-Jewel in Performance: Text & Translation of the Ascaryacudamani of Saktibhadra. Tr. by V. Ragahavan et al. 1985. 16.95x (ISBN 0-19-561714-2). Oxford U Pr.

Wond'rous Fare. Lyn Stallworth. (Illus.). 48p. (YA) 1988. 14.95 (ISBN 0-8092-4481-0). Contemp Bks.
Wondrous Gift: A Christmas Story. Daisy Newman. (Orig.). 1982. pap. text ed. write for info. (ISBN 0-941308-01-4). Religious Soc Friends.
Wondrous Is God in His Saints. Ed. by Father Benedict. LC 85-63506. (Illus.). 190p. (Orig.). 1985. pap. 6.95 (ISBN 0-936649-00-3). St Anthony Orthodox.
Wondrous Ships. S. Sakharnov. 16p. 1975. pap. 0.99 (ISBN 0-8285-1277-9, Pub. by Progress Pubs USSR). Imported Pubns.
Wonnltatigkeit und Armenpflege Im Vorchristlichen Altertum. Hendrik Bolkestein. Ed. by Gregory Vlastos. LC 78-15858. (Morals & Law in Ancient Greece Ser.). 1979. Repr. of 1939 ed. lib. bdg. 37.00x (ISBN 0-405-11531-8). Ayer Co Pubs.
Won't Know Till I Get There. Walter D. Myers. LC 81-71128. 192p. (gr. 7 up). 1982. 11.95 (ISBN 0-670-77862-1). Viking.
Won't Know Till I Get There. Walter D. Myers. (gr. 5-9). 1988. pap. 3.95 (ISBN 0-317-69636-X, Puffin Bks). Penguin.
Won't Somebody Play with Me? Steven Kellogg. LC 72-708. (Pied Piper Bk.). (Illus.). (gr. k-3). 1976. pap. 3.95 (ISBN 0-8037-9612-9). Dial Bks Young.
Won't Somebody Play with Me? Steven Kellogg. (Illus.). 32p. (ps-3). 1972. 9.95 (ISBN 0-8037-9739-7). Dial Bks Young.
Won't You Come Home Billy Bob Bailey? Lewis Grizzard. LC 80-23407. 240p. 1980. 11.95 (ISBN 0-931948-10-X). Peachtree Pubs.
Won't You Come Home, Billy Bob Bailey? Lewis Grizzard. 304p. 1987. pap. 3.95 (ISBN 0-446-32606-2). Warner Bks.
Won't You Join the Dance. Bhagwan Shree Rajneesh. Ed. by Ma Prem Maneesha. LC 83-43217. (Initiation Talks Ser.). 320p. (Orig.). 1983. pap. 4.95 (ISBN 0-88050-676-8). Chidvilas Inc.
Wood. Guy N. Smith. 1987. pap. 3.50 (ISBN 0-440-19753-8). Dell.
Wood. Robert Summitt & Alan Sliker. (Vol. IV). 472p. 1980. 87.50 (ISBN 0-8493-0234-X). CRC Pr.
Wood. Kathryn Whyman. (Resources Today Ser.). (Illus.). 32p. (gr. 1-6). 1987. lib. bdg. 10.90 (ISBN 0-531-17058-6, Gloucester Pr). Watts.
Wood: A Manual for Its Use As a Shipbuilding Material. Ed. by U. S. Navy, Bureau of Ships. LC 82-74415. (Illus.). 418p. 1983. 25.00 (ISBN 0-9610602-0-4). Teaparty Bks.
Wood Adhesives Chemistry & Technology. Pizzi. 304p. 1983. 79.75 (ISBN 0-8247-1579-9). Dekker.
Wood Adhesives in Nineteen Eighty-Five: Status & Needs. 328p. 1986. 30.00 (ISBN 0-935018-32-8). Forest Prod.
Wood Adhesives: Present & Future: Journal of Applied Polymer Science, Applied Polymer Symposium, No. 40. Ed. by A. Pizzi. 1985. pap. write for info. (ISBN 0-471-81334-6). Wiley.
Wood: American Gothic. (Let's Get Lost in a Painting Ser.). 1983. write for info. Garrard.
Wood: An Ancient Fuel with a New Future. Nigel Smith. LC 80-54881. (Worldwatch Papers). 1981. pap. 4.00 (ISBN 0-916468-41-0). Worldwatch Inst.
Wood & Agricultural Residues: Research on Use for Feed, Fuels, & Chemicals. Ed J. Soltes. 1983. 71.00 (ISBN 0-12-654560-X). Acad Pr.
Wood & Canvas Canoe: A Complete Guide to its History, Construction, Restoration & Maintenance. Jerry Stelmok & Rollin Thurlow. LC 87-80698. 253p. (Orig.). 1988. pap. 15.95 (ISBN 0-88448-046-1). Harpswell Pr.
Wood & Celluosics: Industrial Utilization Biotechnology Structure & Properties. Ed. by J. F. Kennedy et al. (Polymer Science & Technology Ser.). 664p. 1987. 100.00 (ISBN 0-470-20884-8). Halsted Pr.
Wood & Fiber Science. Ed. by Bruce Cutter. (Orig.). pap. text ed. 55.00 (ISBN 0-686-40829-2). Soc Wood.
Wood & Garden. Gertrude Jekyll. (Illus.). 380p. 1981. 29.50 (ISBN 0-907462-11-1). Antique Collect.
Wood & Garden. rev. ed. Gertrude Jekyll. LC 82-16364. (Jekyll Garden Bks.). (Illus.). 345p. 1984. 24.50 (ISBN 0-88143-004-8); pap. 11.95 (ISBN 0-88143-058-7). Ayer Co Pubs.
Wood & Lacquer Art of Korea. Lee Jongseok. 287p. 1986. 140.00x (ISBN 0-317-68527-9, Pub. by Han-Shan Tang Ltd). State Mutual Bk.
Wood & Paper. Jacqueline Dineen. (World's Harvest Ser.). 32p. (gr. 4-8). 1988. lib. bdg. 9.95 (ISBN 0-89490-226-1). Enslow Pubs.
Wood & Water: The Story of Seaboard Lumber & Marine. E. G. Perrault. (Illus.). 256p. 1986. 24.95 (ISBN 0-295-96307-7, Pub. by Douglas & McIntyre Canada). U of Wash Pr.
Wood & Wood Grains: A Photographic Album for Artists & Designers. Phil Brodatz. 1972. 6.95 (ISBN 0-486-22424-4). Dover.
Wood & Wood Grains: A Photographic Album for Artists & Designers. Phil Brodatz. (Illus.). 15.50 (ISBN 0-8446-0040-7). Peter Smith.
Wood As an Energy Resource. David A. Tillman. 1978. 22.50 (ISBN 0-12-691260-2). Acad Pr.
Wood As an Industrial Arts Material. Wayne K. Murphey & Richard Jorgensen. 1974. 31.00 (ISBN 0-08-017906-1); pap. 17.00 (ISBN 0-08-017907-X). Pergamon.
Wood As Fuel: Energy for Developing Countries. Susan V. Bogach. LC 84-26640. 176p. 1985. 35.00 (ISBN 0-275-90062-2, C0062). Praeger.
Wood Beyond the World. William Morris. 261p. 1972. pap. 5.95 (ISBN 0-486-22791-X). Dover.
Wood, Birds, Water, Stone. Nick Bozanic. 8p. (Orig.). 1983. pap. 2.95 (ISBN 0-935306-20-X). Barnwood Pr.
Wood, Brick, & Stone: The North American Settlement Landscape Barns & Farm Structures, Vol. 2. Allen G. Noble. LC 83-24110. (Illus.). 192p. 1986. pap. 14.95 (ISBN 0-87023-518-4). U of Mass Pr.
Wood, Brick, & Stone: The North American Settlement Landscape Houses, Vol. 1. Allen G. Noble. LC 83-24110. (Illus.). 168p. 1986. pap. 14.95 (ISBN 0-87023-517-6). U of Mass Pr.
Wood, Brick, & Stone: The North American Settlement Landscape; Vol. I, Houses. Allen G. Noble. LC 83-24110. (Illus.). 160p. 1984. 30.00x (ISBN 0-87023-410-2). U of Mass Pr.
Wood, Brick, & Stone: The North American Settlement Landscape: Vol. 2, Barns & Farm Structures. Allen G. Noble. LC 83-24110. (Illus.). 186p. 1984. 30.00x (ISBN 0-87023-411-0). U of Mass Pr.
Wood Burns Red. Roberta B. Goldstein. 1966. 3.00 (ISBN 0-8233-0031-5). Golden Quill.
Wood Carver of Salem: Samuel McIntire, His Life & Work. Frank Cousins & Phil M. Riley. LC 74-119649. (BCL Ser. II). Repr. of 1916 ed. 20.00 (ISBN 0-404-01786-X). AMS Pr.
Wood Carvers of Cordova, New Mexico: Social Dimensions of an Artistic "Revival". Charles L. Briggs. LC 79-20883. 272p. 1980. 26.95x (ISBN 0-87049-275-6). U of Tenn Pr.
Wood-Carvers of Hong Kong: Craft Production in the World Capitalist Periphery. Eugene Cooper. (Illus.). 153p. 1988. pap. text ed. 7.95x (ISBN 0-88133-341-7). Waveland Pr.
Wood Carving. George Jack. 1978. pap. 9.95 (ISBN 0-8008-8462-0, Pentalic). Taplinger.
Wood Carving. (Illus.). 48p. (gr. 6-12). 1966. pap. 1.25x (ISBN 0-8395-3315-2, 3315). BSA.
Wood Carving & Whittling for Everyone. Franklin H. Gottshall. LC 77-23224. (Illus.). 1980. pap. 11.95 (ISBN 0-684-16742-5, SL 921, ScribT). Scribner.
Wood Carving & Whittling for Everyone. Franklin H. Gottshall. LC 77-23224. (Illus.). 1977. 12.95 (ISBN 0-684-14886-2, ScribT). Scribner.
Wood Carving: Twenty-Three Traditional Decorative Projects. Alan Bridgewater & Gill Bridgewater. (Illus.). 272p. 1988. 22.95 (ISBN 0-8306-0979-2); pap. 14.95 (ISBN 0-8306-2979-3). TAB Bks.
Wood Chair in America. Brickel Assoc., Inc. Staff & Green. LC 82-90454. (Illus.). 120p. 1982. pap. 19.95 (ISBN 0-9609844-0-2). E & S Brickel.
Wood Chemistry: Fundamentals & Applications. Eero Sjostrom. LC 81-3614. 1981. 35.00 (ISBN 0-12-647480-X). Acad Pr.
Wood: Chemistry, Ultrastructure, Reactions. Dietrich Fengel & Gert Wegener. (Illus.). xii, 613p. 1984. 159.00 (ISBN 3-11-008481-3). De Gruyter.
Wood Combustion: Principles, Processes & Economics. David Tillman et al. LC 81-10907. 1981. 26.00 (ISBN 0-12-691240-8). Acad Pr.
Wood Conserving Cook Stoves: A Design Guide. 114p. (Eng., Fr., Span. & Arabic.). 1980. perfect bdg. 9.95 (ISBN 0-317-36131-7); In French. 6.55 (ISBN 0-86619-197-6, 19063); In Spanish. 6.55 (ISBN 0-86619-198-4, 18063); In Arabic. 6.55 (ISBN 0-86619-199-2, 17063). Vols Tech Asst.
Wood Construction Materials: Bibliography. 62p. 1981. 20.00 (ISBN 0-317-34179-0, 683B4); members 15.00 (ISBN 0-317-34180-4). Forest Prod.
Wood Density Variation in Plantation-Grown Pinus Patula from the Viphya Plateau, Malawi. P. G. Adlard et al. 1978. 40.00x (ISBN 0-85074-045-2, Pub. by For Lib Comm England). State Mutual Bk.
Wood Deterioration & Its Prevention by Preservative Treatments. Darrel D. Nicholas. Incl. Vol. 1. Degradation & Protection of Wood. 416p. 1982. pap. text ed. 35.00x (ISBN 0-8156-2285-6); Vol. 2. Preservatives & Preservative Systems. 448p. 1984. text ed. 37.00x o. p. (ISBN 0-8156-5038-8). LC 73-4640. (Wood Science Ser.: No. 5). (Illus.). 1973. pap. text ed. 37.00x (ISBN 0-8156-2303-8). Syracuse U Pr.
Wood Duck Baby. Berniece Freschet. (Illus.). 48p. (gr. 1-3). 1983. pap. 6.99 (ISBN 0-399-61191-6, Putnam). Putnam Pub Group.
Wood Effect: Unaccounted Contributor to Error & Confusion in Acoustics & Audio. R. C. Johnsen. (Illus.). 112p. (Orig.). 1988. pap. 7.95 (ISBN 0-929383-00-1). Modern Audio Assn.
Wood Energy: A Practical Guide to Heating with Wood. Mary Twitchell. (Illus.). 172p. 1978. pap. 7.95 (ISBN 0-88266-145-0). World Wide OR.
Wood, Energy & Households, Vol. 6: Perspectives on Rural Kenya. (Energy, Environment & Development Ser.: Vol. 6). 223p. Date not set. 24.50 (ISBN 0-8419-9774-8, Africana). Holmes & Meier.
Wood Engineering. German Gurfinkel. 560p. text ed. 20.95 (ISBN 0-8403-2476-6). Kendall-Hunt.
Wood Engineering & Construction Handbook. Keith F. Faherty & Thomas G. Williamson. 764p. 1989. 64.50 (ISBN 0-07-019895-0). McGraw.
Wood Engineering Handbook. U. S. Forest Products Laboratory. LC 82-7610. 1982. 49.95 (ISBN 0-13-962449-X, Busn). P-H.
Wood Engraving. George E. Mackley. 128p. 1984. 90.00x (ISBN 0-905418-84-0, Pub. by Gresham England). State Mutual Bk.
Wood Engraving. George E. Mackley. 144p. 1985. 39.00x (ISBN 0-946095-18-3, Pub. by Gresham England). State Mutual Bk.
Wood Engraving of Tizah Ravillous. Anne Ullman et al. 48p. 1987. 105.00x (ISBN 0-86092-099-2, Pub. by Gordon Fraser). State Mutual Bk.
Wood Engravings by Lucien Pissarro. Ashmolean Museum Staff. (Illus.). 29p. 1981. 250.00 (ISBN 0-907849-35-0, Pub. by Ashmolean Mus). Longwood Pub Group.
Wood Engravings by Lucien Pissarro. 1981. 250.00x (ISBN 0-317-20348-7, Pub. by Ashmolean Museum). State Mutual Bk.
Wood Engravings of John Farleigh. Monica Poole. (Illus.). 128p. 1985. 125.00x (ISBN 0-946095-09-4, Pub. by Gresham England); deluxe ed. 500.00x (ISBN 0-946095-15-9). State Mutual Bk.
Wood Extraction with Oxen & Agricultural Tractors. E. Otavo Rodriguez. (FAO Forestry Paper: No. 49). (Illus.). 92p. (Orig.). 1987. pap. text ed. 8.25 (ISBN 92-5-102129-5, F3006, FAO). UNIPUB.
Wood Finisher's Handbook. Sam Allen. LC 84-8557. (Illus.). 160p. (Orig.). 1985. pap. 10.95 (ISBN 0-8069-7914-3). Sterling.
Wood Finishing. Harry R. Jeffrey. (gr. 9-12). 1957. pap. text ed. 11.40 (ISBN 0-02-666200-0). Bennett IL.
Wood Finishing. D. Newell. 1986. cancelled (ISBN 0-442-26835-1). Van Nos Reinhold.
Wood Finishing & Refinishing. Alan Hall & James Heard. LC 81-4708. (Illus.). 216p. 1982. (Owl Bks); pap. 9.95 (ISBN 0-03-018861-X). H Holt & Co.
Wood Finishing & Refinishing. Tom Philbin. Ed. by Marilyn M. Auer. LC 81-69641. (Illus.). 144p. (Orig.). 1982. pap. 7.95 (ISBN 0-932944-54-X). Creative Homeowner.
Wood Finishing with George Frank. George Frank. LC 87-26758. (Illus.). 144p. 1988. 19.95 (ISBN 0-8069-6562-2). Sterling.
Wood Fire in Number Three. facsimile ed. Francis H. Smith. LC 76-94743. (Short Story Index Reprint Ser.). 1905. 19.00 (ISBN 0-8369-3123-8). Ayer Co Pubs.
Wood-Frame House Construction. rev. ed. Illus. by L. O. Anderson & Taylor F. Winslow. (Illus.). 1976. pap. 11.25 (ISBN 0-910460-20-5). Craftsman.
Wood-Frame House Construction see How to Build a Wood-Frame House.
Wood Frame Housebuilding: An Illustrated Guide. Bette G. Wahlfeldt. (Illus.). 288p. 1988. 21.95 (ISBN 0-8306-0405-7, 3005); pap. 14.95 (ISBN 0-8306-9305-X). TAB Bks.
Wood from the Scholar's Table. Rebecca R. Jones. 176p. 1984. 125.00x (ISBN 0-317-43713-5, Pub. by Han-Shan Tang Ltd). State Mutual Bk.
Wood Furniture: Finishing, Refinishing, Repairing. 2nd ed. James E. Brumbaugh. LC 73-91640. (Illus.). 352p. 1974. 12.95 (ISBN 0-672-23409-2, Pub. by Audel). Macmillan.
Wood Gas As Engine Fuel. (FAO Forestry Paper: No. 72). (Illus.). 173p. (Orig.). 1987. pap. text ed. 18.00 (ISBN 92-5-102436-7, F3013, FAO). UNIPUB.
Wood Handbook: Wood as an Engineering Material. Forest Products Laboratory Staff & Forest Service Staff. 340p. 1988. 68.00 (ISBN 0-89116-124-4). Hemisphere Pub.
Wood Heat. Allan A. Swenson. 1980. pap. 2.95 (ISBN 0-449-14248-5, GM). Fawcett.
Wood Heat Safety. Jay W. Shelton. LC 79-17951. (Illus.). 165p. 1979. pap. 9.95 (ISBN 0-88266-160-4, Garden Way Pub). Storey Comm Inc.
Wood Houses. Werner Blaser. (Illus.). 1985. 38.00 (ISBN 3-85977-079-9, Pub. by Wepf & Co.). Interbk Inc.
Wood Houses: Form in Rural Architecture. 2nd ed. Werner Blaser. (Illus.). 216p. (Eng., Fr & Ger.). 1985. pap. 19.00 (ISBN 0-89192-300-4, Pub. by Wepf & Co). Interbk Inc.
Wood in American Life 1776-2076. Wally G. Youngquist & Herbert O. Fleischer. LC 77-85427. 192p. 1977. 11.00 (ISBN 0-935018-00-X); members 9.00. Forest Prod.
Wood Laminating. rev. ed. J. Hugh Capron. (gr. 11-12). 1963. 23.20 (ISBN 0-02-671510-4). Glencoe Bennett & McKnight.
Wood Machining Processes. Peter Koch. LC 64-20120. (Wood Processing Ser.). (Illus.). pap. 135.50 (ISBN 0-317-10867-0, 2012599). Bks Demand UMI.
Wood Markets: Alternatives to Residential Construction. 105p. 1987. 22.00 (ISBN 0-935018-34-4). Forest Prod.
Wood: Materials & Processes. John L. Feirer. 587p. (gr. 7-12). 1975. text ed. 15.96 o.p (ISBN 0-02-666210-8); wkbk. 6.64 (ISBN 0-02-666220-5). Bennett IL.
Wood: Materials & Processes. rev. ed. John L. Feirer. (gr. 7-12). 1980. text ed. 22.20 (ISBN 0-02-666240-X). tchr's. ed. 5.28 (ISBN 0-02-666250-7). Bennett IL.
Wood Motifs in American Domestic Architecture see Ornamental Carpentry of Nineteenth-Century American Houses: One Hundred Sixty-Five Photographs.
Wood: Nature's Cellular, Polymeric, Fibre Composite. J. M. Dinwoodie. 140p. 1988. pap. text ed. 40.00 (ISBN 0-901462-35-7, Pub. by Inst Metals). Brookfield Pub Co.
Wood Notes: A Companion & Guide for Birdwatchers. Richard H. Wood. (Illus.). 192p. 1984. O.P. 15.95 (ISBN 0-13-962580-1); pap. 6.95 (ISBN 0-13-962572-0). P-H.
Wood Ornaments & Creche. U-Bild Enterprises. 24p. 1982. pap. 3.50 (ISBN 0-910495-01-7). U-Bild.
Wood Package. Ed. by Rikuyo-Sha Staff. 176p. 1986. 65.00 (ISBN 4-897-37060-4, Pub. by Rikuyo-Sha Japan). Bks Nippan.
Wood, Paper, Textiles, Plastics & Photographic Materials see Chemical Technology: An Encyclopedic Treatment.
Wood Path. Foster Robertson. LC 75-1439. 40p. (Orig.). 1975. pap. 2.00 (ISBN 0-914476-36-X). Thorp Springs.
Wood Polishing & Finishing Techniques. Aidan Walker. 1986. 9.95 (ISBN 0-316-91847-4). Little.
Wood Preservation Manual. (FAO Forestry Report: No. 76). 152p. 1986. pap. text ed. 15.75 (ISBN 92-5-102470-7, F3089, FAO). UNIPUB.
Wood Primer: The Sculpture of David Nash. (Illus.). 76p. 1987. 24.95 (ISBN 0-938491-07-5); pap. 15.95 (ISBN 0-938491-08-3). Bedford Arts Pubs.
Wood Project, Book I. Sibley. 1985. 6.60 (ISBN 0-87006-545-9). Goodheart.
Wood Projects for the Garden. rev. ed. Ron Hildebrand et al. LC 87-70189. (Illus.). 96p. (Orig.). 1987. pap. 6.95 (ISBN 0-89721-102-2). Ortho.
Wood Projects for the Home. Ortho Books Editorial Staff & Ron Hildebrand. LC 80-66343. (Illus.). 96p. (Orig.). 1981. pap. 6.95 (ISBN 0-917102-85-1). Ortho.
Wood Quay: The Clash over Dublin's Viking Past. Thomas F. Heffernan. (Illus.). 200p. 1988. 19.95 (ISBN 0-292-79042-2). U of Tex Pr.
Wood Rats of Colorado: Distribution & Ecology. Robert B. Finley, Jr. (Museum Ser.: Vol. 10, No. 6). 340p. 1958. 17.00 (ISBN 0-686-80280-2). U of KS Mus Nat Hist.
Wood Recycling: Info Mapping Index. Data Notes Publishing Staff. LC 83-90734. 30p. 1983. pap. text ed. 3.95 (ISBN 0-911569-47-2, Pub. by Data Notes). Prosperity & Profits.
Wood Residue as an Energy Source. 118p. 1975. 18.00 (ISBN 0-935018-10-7). Forest Prod.
Wood Residue as an Energy Source. 118p. 1975. 18.00 (603P7513). Forest Prod.
Wood Rot: Repair & Prevention. George T. Demaree. (Orig.). Date not set. pap. 15.95 (ISBN 0-935831-37-1). Tradesman Pub.
Wood-rotting Aphyllophorales of the Southern Appalachian Spruce-fir Forest. Hack S. Jung. (Bibliotheca Mycologica Ser.: Vol. 119). (Illus.). 260p. 1987. pap. text ed. 80.00x (ISBN 3-443-59020-9). Lubrecht & Cramer.
Wood Smoke & Pigeon Pie. Joan Kent. 192p. 1981. 20.00x (ISBN 0-561-00297-5, Pub. by Bailey Bros & Swinfen Ltd). State Mutual Bk.
Wood Stove Cookery. Pamela G. Wubben. 50p. 1981. pap. 3.75 (ISBN 0-935442-05-7). One Percent.
Wood-Stove Dissemination: Proceedings of the Conference Held at Wolfheze, the Netherlands. Ed. by Robin Clarke. (Illus.). 202p. (Orig.). 1985. pap. 19.75x (ISBN 0-946688-55-9, Pub. by Intermediate Tech England). Intermediate Tech.
Wood Stoves. Sunset Editors. LC 79-88160. (Illus.). 96p. 1979. pap. 6.95 (ISBN 0-376-01882-8, Sunset Bks). Sunset-Lane.
Wood Structure & Identification. 2nd ed. Harold Core et al. 1979. pap. 14.95x (ISBN 0-8156-5043-4). Syracuse U Pr.
Wood Structures: Design Guide & Commentary. 426p. 1975. pap. 16.00x (ISBN 0-87262-109-X). Am Soc Civil Eng.
Wood Technology. Glenn E. Baker & L. Dayle Yeager. LC 72-83817. 1974. scp 30.85 (ISBN 0-672-97507-6); scp students manual 10.28 (ISBN 0-672-97107-0). Bobbs.
Wood Technology: Chemical Aspects. Ed. by Irving S. Goldstein. LC 77-2368. (ACS Symposium Ser.: No. 43). 1977. 34.95 (ISBN 0-8412-0373-3). Am Chemical.
Wood Technology in the Design of Structures. 5th, rev. ed. Robert J. Hoyle & Frank E. Woeste. (Illus.). 360p. 1989. text ed. 49.95x (ISBN 0-8138-1975-X). Iowa St U Pr.
Wood Two. 156p. pap. 14.95 (2204). Morgan.
Wood Type Alphabets. Ed. by Rob R. Kelly. LC 77-78607. (Pictorial Archive Ser.). (Illus.). 1977. pap. 4.50 (ISBN 0-486-23533-5). Dover.
Wood Type Alphabets: 100 Fonts. Ed. by Rob R. Kelly. 11.25 (ISBN 0-8446-5590-2). Peter Smith.
Wood Type & Printing Collectibles. Robert P. Long. (Illus.). 1980. pap. 7.95 (ISBN 0-9600064-0-0). R P Long.
Wood Ultrastructure: An Atlas of Electron Micrographs. Wilfred A. Cote, Jr. LC 67-21204. (Illus.). 64p. 1967. pap. 20.00x (ISBN 0-295-97868-6). U of Wash Pr.

Woodrow Wilson. Perry Leavell. (World Leaders: Past & Present Ser.). (Illus.). 112p. 1987. lib. bdg. 16.95x (ISBN 0-87754-557-X). Chelsea Hse.
Woodrow Wilson, 2 vols. John M. Mulder & Ernest M. White. Ed. by Carol B. Fitzgerald. (Meckler's Bibliographies of the Presidents of the United States, 1789-1989 Ser.: No. 27). (Illus.). 1989. lib. bdg. 90.00x (ISBN 0-88736-141-2). Meckler Corp.
Woodrow Wilson. 3rd ed. Arthur Walworth. 1979. pap. 10.95x (ISBN 0-393-09012-4). Norton.
Woodrow Wilson: A Great Life in Brief. John A. Garraty. LC 76-54860. 1977. Repr. of 1956 ed. lib. bdg. 22.50x (ISBN 0-8371-9371-0, GAWW). Greenwood.
Woodrow Wilson: A Medical & Psychological Biography. Edwin A. Weinstein. LC 81-47162. (Papers of Woodrow Wilson-Supplementary Volume). (Illus.). 440p. 1981. 31.00x (ISBN 0-691-04683-2). Princeton U Pr.
Woodrow Wilson: A Selected Bibliography. Laura S. Turnbull. LC 70-159106. 1971. Repr. of 1948 ed. 18.50 (ISBN 0-8046-1650-7, Pub. by Kennikat). Assoc Faculty Pr.
Woodrow Wilson: An Intimate Memoir. new ed. Cary T. Grayson. LC 60-10998. (Illus.). 154p. 1977. Repr. of 1960 ed. 7.50 (ISBN 0-87107-038-3). Potomac.
Woodrow Wilson & a Revolutionary World, 1913-1921. Ed. by Arthur S. Link. LC 82-2565. (Supplementary Volumes to The Papers of Woodrow Wilson Ser.). viii, 244p. 1982. 25.00x (ISBN 0-8078-1529-2). U of NC Pr.
Woodrow Wilson & Colonel House: A Personality Study. Alexander L. George & Juliette L. George. 1956. pap. 6.95 (ISBN 0-486-21144-4). Dover.
Woodrow Wilson & His Work. William E. Dodd. 1958. 11.25 (ISBN 0-8446-1156-5). Peter Smith.
Woodrow Wilson & the American Diplomatic Tradition: The Treaty Fight in Perspective. Lloyd E. Ambrosius. 325p. 1987. 34.50 (ISBN 0-521-33453-5). Cambridge U Pr.
Woodrow Wilson & the Balance of Power. Edward H. Buehrig. 13.25 (ISBN 0-8446-0522-0). Peter Smith.
Woodrow Wilson & the Politics of Morality. John M. Blum. (Library of American Biography). 1962. pap. write for info. (ISBN 0-316-10052-8). Scott F.
Woodrow Wilson & the Progressive Era: 1910-1917. Arthur S. Link. (New American Nation Ser.). (Illus.). pap. 9.95x (ISBN 0-06-133023-X, TB3023, Torch). Har-Row.
Woodrow Wilson & the Rebirth of Poland, 1914-1920: A Study in the Influence on American Policy of Minority Groups of Foreign Origin. Louis L. Gerson. LC 74-179575. xi, 166p. 1972. Repr. of 1953 ed. 22.50 (ISBN 0-208-01229-X, Archon). Shoe String.
Woodrow Wilson & the War Congress, 1916-18. Seward W. Livermore. LC 66-14666. Orig. Title: Politics Is Adjourned. 335p. 1968. pap. 5.95x (ISBN 0-295-78564-0, WP42). U of Wash Pr.
Woodrow Wilson & the World Settlement, Vols. 1 & 2. R. S. Baker. (Illus.). 1958. 13.25 ea. (ISBN 0-8446-1039-9). Peter Smith.
Woodrow Wilson & the World War see No Break Here.
Woodrow Wilson & World Politics: America's Response to War & Revolution. N. Gordon Levin, Jr. LC 68-15893. 1968. pap. 9.95x (ISBN 0-19-500803-0). Oxford U Pr.
Woodrow Wilson & World War I: Nineteen Seventeen to Nineteen Twenty-One. Robert H. Ferrell. LC 84-48160. (New American Nation Ser.). (Illus.). 336p. 1986. pap. 8.95 (ISBN 0-06-091216-2, PL 1216, PL). Har-Row.
Woodrow Wilson & World War I: 1917-1921. Robert H. Ferrell. LC 84-48160. (Illus.). 312p. 1985. 19.45i (ISBN 0-06-011229-8, HarpT). Har-Row.
Woodrow Wilson As a Military & Diplomatic Leader, 2 vols. Eugene Brooks. (Illus.). 258p. 1987. Set. 189.75 (ISBN 0-86722-157-7). Inst Econ Finan.
Woodrow Wilson As I Know Him. Joseph P. Tumulty. LC 71-127912. Repr. of 1921 ed. 29.50 (ISBN 0-404-06527-9). AMS Pr.
Woodrow Wilson As I Know Him. Joseph P. Tumulty. LC 79-145332. 1971. Repr. of 1921 ed. 27.00 (ISBN 0-403-01243-0). Scholarly.
Woodrow Wilson: Disciple of Revolution. J. C. Wise. 59.95 (ISBN 0-8490-1325-9). Gordon Pr.
Woodrow Wilson: Mini-Play. (President's Choice Ser.). (gr. 8 up). 1978. 6.50 (ISBN 0-89550-315-8). Stevens & Shea.
Woodrow Wilson: Revolution, War, & Peace. Arthur S. Link. LC 79-50909. 1979. pap. text ed. 8.95x (ISBN 0-88295-798-8). Harlan Davidson.
Woodrow Wilson, Revolutionary Germany, & Peacemaking, 1918-1919: Missionary Diplomacy & the Realities of Power. Klaus Schwabe. LC 84-13073. x, 566p. 1985. 40.00x (ISBN 0-8078-1618-3). U of NC Pr.
Woodrow Wilson: Some Princeton Memories. Ed. by W. S. Myers. 1946. 22.50x (ISBN 0-691-04580-1). Princeton U Pr.
Woodrow Wilson: The Academic Years. H. W. Bragdon. LC 67-27081. (Illus.). 1967. 34.50x (ISBN 0-674-95595-1, Belknap Pr). Harvard U Pr.
Woodrow Wilson: The Early Years. George C. Osborn. LC 68-13451. (Illus.). xiii, 346p. 1968. 35.00 (ISBN 0-8071-0636-4). La State U Pr.
Woodrow Wilson: The Years of Preparation. John M. Mulder. LC 77-72128. (Illus.). 1978. 38.50x (ISBN 0-691-04647-6). Princeton U Pr.
Woodrow Wilson: World Statesman. Kendrick A. Clements. (Twentieth Century American Biography Ser.). 288p. 1987. 24.95 (ISBN 0-8057-7756-3, Twayne); pap. 10.95 (ISBN 0-8057-7779-2, Twayne). G K Hall.
Woodrow Wilson, 1856-1924: Chronology, Documents, Bibliographical Aids. Robert I. Vexler. LC 78-83747. (Presidential Chronology Ser.: No. 11). 123p. (gr. 9 up). 1969. PLB 8.00 (ISBN 0-379-12061-5). Oceana.
Woodrow Wilson's Case for the League of Nations. Woodrow Wilson. Ed. by Hamilton Foley. LC 23-17370. (Illus.). 1969. Repr. of 1923 ed. 20.00 (ISBN 0-527-97180-4). Kraus Repr.
Woodrow Wilson's China Policy. Tien-Yi Li. LC 79-96186. 1970. Repr. of 1953 ed. lib. bdg. 19.00x (ISBN 0-374-94997-2, Octagon). Hippocrene Bks.
Woods. Shrikrishna Alanahally. Tr. by Rajeeve Taranath from Kannada. Orig. Title: Kaadu. 112p. 1979. pap. 2.95 (ISBN 0-86578-091-9). Ind-US Inc.
Woods. David Mamet. LC 78-73033. 1979. 10.00 (ISBN 0-394-50519-0, GP819). Grove.
Woods. David Mamet. LC 78-73033. 1979. pap. 3.95 (ISBN 0-394-17078-4, E725, Ever). Grove.
Woods. David Plante. LC 81-70071. 160p. 1982. 8.95 (ISBN 0-689-11289-0). Atheneum.
Woods & Forests. Michel Cuisin. LC 80-53902. (Nature's Hidden World Ser.). 48p. (gr. 2 up). 13.96 (ISBN 0-382-06451-8). Silver.
Woods Dual Power: Manual on Woods Automobile. (Illus.). 24p. pap. 2.95 (ISBN 0-8466-6019-9, U19). Shorey.
Woods Hole Cantata: Essays on Science & Society. Gerald Weissman. 1986. pap. 8.95 (ISBN 0-395-42113-6). HM.
Woods Hole Cantata: Essays on Science & Society. Gerald Weissmann. 252p. 1985. text ed. 16.50 (ISBN 0-88167-181-9). Raven.
Woods Hole Reflections. Ed. by Mary L. Smith. LC 82-62234. (Illus.). 300p. 1983. 22.95 (ISBN 0-9611374-0-1). Woods Hole Hist.
Woods Home. R. M. Schneider. 64p. 1984. text ed. 2.80 (ISBN 0-07-055475-7). McGraw.
Woods Injurious to Human Health. Bjorn M. Hausen. (Illus.). 189p. 1981. 31.50x (ISBN 3-11-008485-6). De Gruyter.
Woods, Lakeboat, Edmond: Three Plays. David Mamet. 288p. 1987. 9.95 (ISBN 0-394-62362-2). Grove.
Wood's New England Prospect. William Wood. Ed. by Jeremiah Colburn. 1966. 19.00 (ISBN 0-8337-3864-X). B Franklin.
Woods, Shore, Desert: A Notebook, May 1968. Thomas Merton. (Illus.). 16.95 (ISBN 0-89013-140-6); pap. 6.95 (ISBN 0-89013-139-2). Museum NM Pr.
Woods We Live with. Herbert F. Schiffer & Nancy N. Schiffer. LC 77-92332. (Illus.). 202p. 1977. 24.95 (ISBN 0-916838-10-2). Schiffer.
Woods Words. Walter F. McCulloch. 219p. 1958. pap. 19.95 (Pub. by Oregon Historical Society & Champorg Press). Miller Freeman.
Woods Words. Walter F. McCulloch. 1977. pap. 9.95x (ISBN 0-88246-082-X). Oreg St U Bkstrs.
Woods-Working Women: Sexual Integration in the U. S. Forest Service. Elaine P. Enarson. LC 83-6725. 182p. 1984. text ed. 18.95x (ISBN 0-8173-0188-7). U of Ala Pr.
Woodsedge. Barbara Knight. 192p. 1987. 15.95 (ISBN 0-8027-0956-7). Walker & Co.
Woodsey Log Library, 4 bks. Marci Ridlon. (Illus.). 128p. (ps-1). 1981. Boxed Set. 6.95 (ISBN 0-394-84911-6). Random.
Woodshed Mystery. Gertrude C. Warner. LC 62-19726. (Boxcar Children Mysteries Ser.). (Illus.). 128p. (gr. 3-7). PLB 8.95 (ISBN 0-8075-9206-4). A Whitman.
Woodshop Tool Maintenance. rev. ed. Beryl M. Cunningham & Wm. Holtrop. (Illus.). 296p. 1974. pap. text ed. 23.96 (ISBN 0-02-666280-9). Bennett IL.
Woodside of Yesterday. Brenda L. Gillie. (Illus.). 138p. Date not set. price not set; pap. price not set. B Gillie.
Woodsman. Don Wright. 416p. 1986. pap. 3.95 (ISBN 0-8125-8989-0, Dist. by Warner Pub Service & St. Martin's Press). Tor Bks.
Woodsman. Donald K. Wright. LC 85-149596. (Frontier Library). 418p. 1985. 13.95 (ISBN 0-915463-07-5, Pub. by Jameson Bks, Dist. by Kampmann). Green Hill.
Woodsman, Mountaineers. Ralph Session. (Illus.). 48p. 1985. pap. 3.50 (ISBN 0-911183-22-1). Rockland County Hist.
Woodsmen of the West. Martin A. Grainger. (Western Writers Ser.: No. 2). 216p. 1988. lib. bdg. 17.95 (ISBN 0-940242-35-4); pap. 8.95 (ISBN 0-940242-34-6). Fjord Pr.
Woodstock. Walter Scott. 1969. Repr. of 1906 ed. 13.95x (ISBN 0-460-00072-1, Evman). Biblio Dist.
Woodstock. write for info (Weedy Rail Bks). Railhead Pubns.
Woodstock & Sycamore Traction Company. William E. Robertson. LC 85-4886. (Illus.). 56p. 1985. pap. 10.00 (ISBN 0-933449-00-3). Transport Trails.
Woodstock Art Heritage. Ed. by The Woodstock Artists Association Staff. 1988. pap. 24.95 (ISBN 0-317-67053-0). Overlook Pr.
Woodstock Craftsman's Manual. Jean Young. LC 76-185655. (Illus.). 488p. (Orig.). pap. 9.95 (ISBN 0-14-046340-2). J Young Bks.
Woodstock Festival Remembered. Jean Young & Michael Lang. (Illus.). 128p. (Orig.). 1985. pap. 15.00 (ISBN 0-345-28003-2). J Young Bks.
Woodstock Handmade Houses. Robert Haney & David Ballantine. 96p. (Orig.). 1976. pap. 6.95 (ISBN 0-345-25592-5). Ballantine.
Woodstock: History of an American Town. Alf Evers. LC 86-16461. (Illus.). 750p. 1987. 37.50 (ISBN 0-87951-983-5); signed, leatherbound 125.00 (ISBN 0-87951-313-6). Overlook Pr.
Woodstock Magic. Fran Lantz & Eileen Goudge. (Swept Away Ser.: No. 2). 1986. pap. 2.50 (Flare). Avon.
Woodstock Railroad. Date not set. price not set (Weedy Rail Bks). Railhead Pubns.
Woodstock's Art Heritage: The Permanent Collection of the Woodstock Artist's Association. Ed. by Lillian Fortess. LC 87-11071. (Illus.). 180p. 1988. pap. 24.50 (ISBN 0-87951-294-6). Overlook Pr.
Woodstove Cookery: At Home on the Range. Jane Cooper. LC 77-10640. (Illus.). 208p. 1977. pap. 6.95 (ISBN 0-88266-108-6, Garden Way Pub). Storey Comm Inc.
Woodstove Cookerybook. Tom Lippert & Laurel H. Lippert. LC 82-102151. (Illus.). 60p. (Orig.). 1981. pap. 3.95 (ISBN 0-941800-00-8). Tulip Pr.
Woodsum Family. G. T. Ridlon. LC 72-146531. (Saco Valley Settlements Ser). 1970. pap. 3.00 (ISBN 0-8048-0356-2). C E Tuttle.
Woodswoman. Anne LaBastille. pap. 8.95 (ISBN 0-525-48367-5). Dutton.
Woodturner's Art: Fundamentals & Projects. Ronald Roszkiewicz & Phyllis Straw. (Practical Arts Library). (Illus.). 288p. 1987. 35.00 (ISBN 0-02-605250-4). Macmillan.
Woodturner's Bible. 2nd, rev. & enl. ed. Percy W. Blandford. (Illus.). 1986. 24.95 (ISBN 0-8306-0954-7, 1954); pap. 16.95 (ISBN 0-8306-1954-2). TAB Bks.
Woodturner's Companion. Ron Roszkiewicz. LC 84-8557. (Illus.). 256p. (Orig.). 1985. pap. 14.95 (ISBN 0-8069-7940-2). Sterling.
Woodturner's Handbook. Frank W. Coggins. (Illus.). 224p. 21.95 (ISBN 0-8306-0769-2, 1769); pap. 12.95 (ISBN 0-8306-1769-8, 1769P). TAB Bks.
Woodturner's Project Book. Phil Jones & Charles Mercer. LC 86-23077. (Illus.). 224p. (Orig.). 1987. pap. 12.95 (ISBN 0-8069-6478-2). Sterling.
Woodturning. Eldon Rebhorn. (gr. 9-12). 1970. text ed. 21.10 (ISBN 0-02-671520-1). Glencoe Bennett & McKnight.
Woodturning - the Purpose of the Object: The Purpose of the Object. Stephen Hogbin. (Illus.). 83p. 1986. 24.95 (ISBN 0-909134-14-6, Pub. by J Ferguson Australia). Intl Spec Bk.
Woodturning: A Designer's Notebook. Ray Key. (Illus.). 144p. (Orig.). 1987. pap. 12.95 (ISBN 0-8069-6566-5). Sterling.
Woodturning in Pictures. Bruce Boulter. (Illus.). 144p. (Orig.). 1983. pap. 12.95 (ISBN 0-8069-7742-6). Sterling.
Woodturning Projects & Techniques. Bruce Boulter. (Illus.). 224p. (Orig.). 1987. pap. 14.95 (ISBN 0-8069-6480-4). Sterling.
Woodville Long Ago. Martha Lutz & Arthur Lutz. 68p. (gr. 3-7). 1986. pap. write for info. Vimach Assocs.
Woodward Collection of Jades & Other Hard Stones. John Getz. 107p. 1913. 1750.00x (ISBN 0-317-69206-2, Pub. by Han-Shan Tang Ltd). State Mutual Bk.
Woodwards Historical Series, 10 Vols. (Illus.). 1864-69. Set. 185.00 (ISBN 0-8337-3883-6). B Franklin.
Woodward's Reminiscences of the Creek or Muscogee Indians: Alabama, Georgia & Mississippi. rev. ed. Thomas W. Woodward. 1970. pap. 12.50 (ISBN 0-87651-010-1). Southern U Pr.
Woodwind Anthology. (Illus.). 1986. 65.00 (ISBN 0-686-15891-1). Instrumental Co.
Woodwind, Brass & Percussion Instruments of the Orchestra: A Bibliographic Guide. Allen B. Skei. LC 83-49079. (Reference Library of the Humanities). 286p. 1984. lib. bdg. 39.00 (ISBN 0-8240-9021-7). Garland Pub.
Woodwind Care & Maintenance. R. G. Pellerin. (Illus.). 107p. (Orig.). 1979. 6.00. Intro Musicaids.
Woodwind Concertos: Five Solo Concertos for Woodwind Instruments. Ed. by Richard Maunder. (Johann Christian Bach Ser., 1735-1782). 1986. lib. bdg. 75.00 (ISBN 0-8240-6085-7). Garland Pub.
Woodwind Ensemble. Himie Voxman & Lyle Merriman. 21.00 (ISBN 0-686-15887-3). Instrumental Co.
Woodwind Solo. Himie Voxman & Lyle Merriman. 21.00 (ISBN 0-686-15888-1). Instrumental Co.
Woodwinds: Fundamental Performance Techniques. Gene A. Saucier. LC 80-5223. (Illus.). 300p. 1981. pap. text ed. 16.50 (ISBN 0-02-872300-7). Schirmer Bks.
Woodwork. Boy Scouts of America. (Illus.). 48p. (gr. 6-12). 1970. pap. 1.25x (ISBN 0-8395-3316-0, 3316). BSA.
Woodwork. Lawler. (Beginner's Guides Ser.). (gr. 4-9). 1980. PLB 11.95 (ISBN 0-88110-034-X); pap. 2.95 (ISBN 0-86020-309-3). EDC.
Woodwork Joints: Kinds of Joints., How They Are Cut, & Where Used. Charles H. Hayward. LC 75-16454. (Home Craftsman Bk.). (Illus.). 176p. 1974. pap. 8.95 (ISBN 0-8069-8806-1). Sterling.
Woodwork of Greek Roofs. A. Trevor Hodge. LC 60-51252. (Cambridge Classical Studies). pap. 47.50 (ISBN 0-317-26411-7, 2024467). Bks Demand UMI.
Woodwork Technology for Schools & Colleges. John Strefford & Guy McMurdo. 128p. 1982. 30.00x (ISBN 0-7217-4008-1, Pub. by Schofield & Sims UK). State Mutual Bk.
Woodworker's Bible. Alf Martensson. 1982. pap. 11.95 (ISBN 0-672-52717-0). Bobbs.
Woodworker's Guide to Master Craftsman Techniques. Woodworkers Magazine Editors. (Illus.). 288p. 1988. 24.95 (ISBN 0-8306-9061-1, 3061); pap. 15.95 (ISBN 0-8306-9361-0, 3061). TAB Bks.
Woodworker's Handbook: A Complete Course for Craftsmen, Do-It-Yourselfers & Hobbyists. The London College of Furniture & Victor Hutchins. (Illus.). 216p. 1984. 27.95 (ISBN 0-668-06162-6, 6162-6). Arco.
Woodworker's Thirty Best Projects. Woodworker Magazine Editors. (Illus.). 1988. 23.95 (ISBN 0-8306-0421-9, 3021); pap. 14.95 (ISBN 0-8306-9321-1). TAB Bks.
Woodworker's Thirty-Nine Sure-Fire Projects. Woodworker Magazine Editors. (Illus.). 224p. 1988. 23.95 (ISBN 0-8306-9051-4, 3051); pap. 14.95 (ISBN 0-8306-9351-3, 3051). TAB Bks.
Woodworking. Los Angeles Unified School District. LC 77-73286. 96p. (gr. 7-9). 1978. pap. text ed. 4.40 (ISBN 0-02-820400-X). Glencoe.
Woodworking. McKnight Staff Members & Wilbur R. Miller. LC 78-53386. (Basic Industrial Arts Ser.). (Illus.). 1978. softbound 6.60 (ISBN 0-02-672800-1). Glencoe Bennett & McKnight.
Woodworking. rev. ed. Willis H. Wagner. LC 80-27505. (Build-a-Course Ser.). (Illus.). 120p. 1984. text ed. 7.20 (ISBN 0-87006-503-3). Goodheart.
Woodworking & Cabinetmaking. F. Richard Boller. 400p. 16.95 (ISBN 0-02-512800-0, Pub. by Audel). Macmillan.
Woodworking & Places Nearby. Carol Cox. 1979. pap. 5.00 (ISBN 0-914610-13-9). Hanging Loose.
Woodworking Factbook: Basic Information on Wood for Wood Carvers, Home Woodshop Craftsmen, Tradesmen & Instructors. Donald G. Coleman. (Illus.). 18.95 (ISBN 0-8315-0024-7). Speller.
Woodworking for Industry. Feirer. 1979. text ed. 23.72 (ISBN 0-02-666350-3); student guide 7.96 (ISBN 0-02-666360-0); tchr's. ed. 4.60 (ISBN 0-02-666380-5). Bennett IL.
Woodworking for Industry. Feirer. 1983. text ed. 27.96 (ISBN 0-02-666390-2). Bennett IL.
Woodworking for Young Children. Patsy Skeen & Anita P. Garner. LC 84-61512. 104p. 1984. pap. text ed. 5.00 (ISBN 0-912674-85-7, NAEYC #122). Natl Assn Child Ed.
Woodworking Hand Tools Explained. John Nagle. LC 78-730852. 1979. wkbk. 6.00 (ISBN 0-8064-0263-6, 703); audio visual pkg. 279.00 (ISBN 0-8064-0264-4). Bergwall.
Woodworking in the Rockies. Colorado Springs Fine Arts Center Staff. LC 82-71534. (Illus.). 52p. (Orig.). 1982. pap. 6.00 (ISBN 0-686-35850-3). CO Springs Fine Arts.
Woodworking Industry Machinery. (UNIDO Guides to Information Sources: No. 31). pap. 4.00 (ISBN 92-1-106159-8, 1D/214). UN.
Woodworking Machine Operator. William Weiss. LC 76-732033. 1977. wkbk. 7.00 (ISBN 0-8064-0261-X, 702); audio visual pkg. 349.00 (ISBN 0-8064-0262-8). Bergwall.
Woodworking Planes: A Descriptive Register of Wooden Planes. Alvin Sellens. LC 78-52687. (Illus.). 1978. 13.50 (ISBN 0-9612068-1-0). Sellens.
Woodworking Principles & Practices. R. Cliffe. (Illus.). 486p. 1981. 24.96 (ISBN 0-8269-4820-0). Am Technical.
Woodworking Projects, No. II. Sunset Editors. LC 83-82502. 96p. (Orig.). 1984. pap. text ed. 6.95 (ISBN 0-376-04888-3). Sunset-Lane.
Woodworking Projects. LC 84-22194. (Illus.). 96p. (Orig.). 1984. pap. 8.95 (ISBN 0-937558-12-5). Shopsmith.
Woodworking Projects for the Home Workshop. Rosario Capotosto. LC 88-16013. (Popular Science Ser.). (Illus.). 416p. (Orig.). 1988. pap. 16.95 (ISBN 0-8069-6888-5). Sterling.
Woodworking Projects I. Sunset Editors. LC 75-6222. (Illus.). 96p. 1975. pap. 5.95 (Sunset BKs). Sunset-Lane.
Woodworking Projects I. (Illus.). 96p. 1986. 14.95 (ISBN 0-87857-618-5); pap. 9.95 (ISBN 0-87857-615-0). Rodale Pr Inc.
Woodworking Projects II: Sixty Easy-To-Make Projects From Hands On Magazine. (Illus.). 96p. 1986. 14.95 (ISBN 0-87857-619-3); pap. 8.95 (ISBN 0-87857-616-9). Rodale Pr Inc.
Woodworking Projects III. Hands on Magazine Editors. 96p. 1988. 14.95 (ISBN 0-87857-784-X); pap. 9.95 (ISBN 0-87857-780-7). Rodale Pr Inc.

Word Bird's Christmas Words. Jane B. Moncure. LC 86-31666. (Word Bird's Word House Words Ser.). (Illus.). 32p. (gr. k-2). 1987. PLB 7.95 (ISBN 0-89565-361-3). Childs World.
Word Bird's Circus Surprise. Jane B. Moncure. LC 80-29528. (Word House Words for Early Birds Ser.). (Illus.). 32p. (gr. k-2). 1981. PLB 7.95 (ISBN 0-89565-162-9). Childs World.
Word Bird's Circus Surprise. Jane B. Moncure. LC 80-29528. (Word Birds for Early Birds Ser.). (Illus.). 32p. (ps-1). 1983. 11.93 (ISBN 0-516-06554-8). Childrens.
Word Bird's Easter Words. Jane B. Moncure. (Word Bird's Word House Words Ser.). (Illus.). 32p. (gr. k-2). 1987. PLB 7.95 (ISBN 0-89565-363-X). Childs World.
Word Bird's Fall Words. Jane B. Moncure. LC 85-5935. (Word House Words for Early Birds Ser.). (Illus.). 32p. (gr. k-2). 1985. lib. bdg. 7.95 (ISBN 0-89565-308-7). Childs World.
Word Bird's Halloween Words. Jane B. Moncure. LC 86-31024. (Word Bird's Word House Words Ser.). (Illus.). 32p. (gr. k-2). 1987. PLB 7.95 (ISBN 0-89565-359-1). Childs World.
Word Bird's Hats. Jane B. Moncure. LC 81-18065. (Word House Words for Early Birds Ser.). (Illus.). (ps-2). 1982. lib. bdg. 7.95 (ISBN 0-89565-221-8). Childs World.
Word Bird's Hats. Jane B. Moncure. LC 81-18065. (Word Birds for Early Birds Ser.). (ps-2). 1982. 11.93 (ISBN 0-516-06558-0). Childrens.
Word Bird's Shapes. Jane B. Moncure. LC 83-15255. (Word House Words for Early Birds Ser.). (Illus.). 32p. (gr. k-2). 1983. PLB 7.95 (ISBN 0-89565-255-2). Childs World.
Word Birds Shapes. Jane B. Moncure. LC 83-15255. (Word Birds for Early Birds Ser.). (Illus.). 32p. (ps-1). 1983. 11.93 (ISBN 0-516-06573-4). Childrens.
Word Bird's Spring Words. Jane B. Moncure. LC 85-5902. (Word House Words for Early Birds Ser.). (Illus.). 32p. (gr. k-2). 1985. lib. bdg. 7.95 (ISBN 0-89565-310-9). Childs World.
Word Bird's Summer Words. Jane B. Moncure. LC 85-5930. (Word House Words for Early Birds Ser.). (Illus.). 32p. (gr. k-2). 1985. lib. bdg. 7.95 (ISBN 0-89565-311-7). Childs World.
Word Bird's Thanksgiving Words. Jane B. Moncure. LC 86-32639. (Word Bird's Word House Words Ser.). (Illus.). 32p. (gr. k-2). 1987. PLB 7.95 (ISBN 0-89565-360-5). Childs World.
Word Bird's Valentine Day Words. Jane B. Moncure. (Word Bird's Word House Words Ser.). (Illus.). 32p. (gr. k-2). 1987. PLB 7.95 (ISBN 0-89565-362-1). Childs World.
Word Bird's Winter Words. Jane B. Moncure. LC 85-5942. (Word House Words for Early Birds Ser.). (Illus.). 32p. (gr. k-2). 1985. lib. bdg. 7.95 (ISBN 0-89565-309-5). Childs World.
Word Book. American Heritage Dictionary Editors. LC 76-698. 1976. 3.95 (ISBN 0-395-24521-4). HM.
WORD Book. David Bolocan. LC 85-2528. (Illus.). 240p. (Orig.). 1985. 24.95 (ISBN 0-8306-0958-X, 1958). TAB Bks.
Word Book II. 2nd ed. Ed. by Houghton Mifflin Company Staff. LC 83-8501. (Word Desk II). 384p. 1983. 3.95. HM.
Word Book in Pathology & Laboratory Medicine. Sheila B. Sloane & John Dusseau. 610p. 1984. pap. 23.95 (ISBN 0-7216-1099-4). Saunders.
Word-Bringer. Edward Llewellyn. 1986. pap. 2.95 (ISBN 0-88677-142-0). DAW Bks.
Word, Brother. Will Inman & Chuck Taylor. 40p. (Orig.). 1986. PLB 8.95 (ISBN 0-941720-38-1); pap. 3.95 (ISBN 0-941720-37-3). Slough Pr TX.
Word Building. Dale McMasters. (Language Arts Ser.). 24p. (gr. 4-7). 1976. wkbk. 5.00 (ISBN 0-8209-0305-1, WB-1). ESP.
Word Building. 2nd ed. Samuel C. Monson. (Illus., Orig.). 1968. pap. text ed. write for info. (ISBN 0-02-382210-4). Macmillan.
Word Building One. Nora Doyle. Ed. by Jean Fischer. (Golden Step Ahead Workbooks). (Illus.). 36p. (gr. 1). 1984. 1.95 (ISBN 0-307-23542-4, Golden Bks). Western Pub.
Word Building Two. Nora Doyle. Ed. by Jean Fischer. (Golden Step Ahead Workbooks). (Illus.). 36p. (gr. 2). 1984. 1.95 (ISBN 0-307-23550-5, Golden Bks). Western Pub.
Word by Microsoft. Robert Williams. Date not set. price not set. P-H.
Word-by-Word Translations of Songs & Arias, Pt. 1: German & French. Berton Coffin et al. LC 66-13746. 620p. 1966. 32.50 (ISBN 0-8108-0149-3). Scarecrow.
Word-by-Word Translations of Songs & Arias, Pt. 2: Italian. Arthur Schoep & Daniel Harris. LC 66-13746. 575p. (A Companion to The Singer's Repertoire). 1972. 32.50 (ISBN 0-8108-0463-8). Scarecrow.
Word-Carrying Giant: The Growth of the American Bible Society. Creighton B. Lacy. LC 77-22655. 311p. 1977. pap. 6.95 (ISBN 0-87808-425-8). William Carey Lib.
Word Child. Iris Murdoch. LC 75-1418. 400p. 1975. 12.95 (ISBN 0-670-78236-X). Viking.
Word Child. Iris Murdoch. 392p. 1987. pap. 6.95 (ISBN 0-14-008153-4). Penguin.
Word Companion: The Definitive Guide to Using Microsoft Word 3 for the Macintosh. Judy Mynhier & Gena Cobb. Ed. by Marjorie Maddox et al. LC 87-70443. (Illus.). 500p. (Orig.). 1987. pap. 19.95 (ISBN 0-936767-05-7). Cobb Group.
Word Comprehension & Paragraph Exercises C. (gr. 1-3). 1972. pap. text ed. 1.50 (ISBN 0-8449-1972-1); tchrs' manual 2.00. Learning Line.
Word Comprehension & Paragraph Exercises F. (gr. 4-6). 1972. pap. text ed. 1.50 (ISBN 0-8449-1974-8); 2.00. Learning Line.
Word Controlled Humans. John Harland. LC 80-52563. 120p. 1981. 8.95 (ISBN 0-914752-13-8); pap. 5.00 (ISBN 0-914752-12-X). Sovereign Pr.
Word Controlled Humans. John Harland. 111p. 1986. pap. 5.00 (ISBN 0-317-53297-9). Noontide.
Word Controlled Humans: Who Is Responsible for the Destruction of the American Dream? John Harland. 1982. lib. bdg. 69.00 (ISBN 0-87700-444-7). Revisionist Pr.
Word Count of Modern Arabic Prose. Jacob M. Landau. LC 59-8208. 485p. 1971. pap. 10.00x (ISBN 0-87950-275-4). Spoken Lang Serv.
Word Crafting. Robert Coulson. 64p. 1988. 6.95 (ISBN 0-8062-3270-6). Carlton.
Word Cultures: Radical Theory & Practice in William S. Burroughs' Fiction. Robin Lydenberg. LC 86-30719. 256p. 1987. 24.95 (ISBN 0-252-01413-8). U of Ill Pr.
Word Desk Set II, 3 vols. (Illus.). 1983. Set. pap. 12.95; pap. 3.95 ea. (ISBN 0-395-34028-4). HM.
Word Detective in French. Heather Amery. (Word Detective Ser.). (Illus.). 50p. (gr. 3-7). 1983. 10.95 (ISBN 0-86020-663-7). EDC.
Word Detective in German: Word Detective Ser. Heather Amery. (Illus.). 50p. (gr. 3-7). 1983. 10.95 (ISBN 0-86020-664-5). EDC.
Word Detective Picture Word Book. King & Emery. (Word Detective Picture Word Bks.). (gr. k-3). 1982. 10.95 (ISBN 0-86020-662-9, Usborne-Hayes). EDC.
Word Directory: Spelling-Division. Adele Christoffers. 1957. 5.50 (ISBN 0-682-40023-8). Exposition-Phoenix.
Word Disclosed. Gail R. O'Day. LC 86-24510. 112p. (Orig.). 1987. pap. 7.95 (ISBN 0-8272-4219-0). CBP.
Word Discrimination. John W. Black. 64p. 1985. pap. text ed. 8.95x (ISBN 0-8134-2465-8, 2465). Inter Print Pubs.
Word Distribution in the Interior South. Gordon R. Wood. (Publications of the American Dialect Society: No. 35). 24p. 1961. pap. 1.10 (ISBN 0-8173-0635-8). U of Ala Pr.
Word Division Manual. 3rd ed. J. E. Silverthorn & Devern J. Perry. 168p. 1984. pap. text ed. write for info. (ISBN 0-538-11981-0, K98U). SW Pub.
Word Expert Semantics: An Interlingual Knowledge-Based Approach. B. C. Papegaay. (Distributed Language Translation Ser.). x, 254p. 1986. write for info.; pap. write for info. (ISBN 90-6765-261-X). Foris Pubns.
Word Express: The First Twenty-Five Hundred Words of Spoken English. Jerry Stemach & William B. Williams. Ed. by Rick Brownell. 288p. 1988. tchr's. ed. (3-ring binder) 35.00 (ISBN 0-87879-592-8); pkg. of 25 8-pg. protocols 10.00 (ISBN 0-87879-614-2). Acad Therapy.
Word Find Puzzles, No. 1. Linda Doherty. 96p. 1988. pap. 1.95 (ISBN 0-8125-7875-9, Dist. by St Martin's Pr & Warner Pub Servs). Tor Bks.
Word Find Puzzles, No. 4. Linda Doherty. 1987. pap. 1.50 (ISBN 0-8125-7881-3). Tor Bks.
Word Finder. 4th ed. Ruth I. Anderson et al. (gr. 9-12). 1974. pap. 3.95 (ISBN 0-8224-3355-9). D S Lake Pubs.
Word Finder. Rodale Press, Inc. Staff & J. I. Rodale. 1317p. 1987. 21.95 (ISBN 0-87857-138-8). Rodale Pr Inc.
Word Finder in German. Anne Civardi. (Picture Word Bks.). (Illus.). 48p. (gr. k-3). 1984. 10.95 (ISBN 0-86020-771-4). EDC.
Word-Finder List for Whiz Mob see Some Expressions from Herman Melville.
Word Finder: The Phonic Key to the Dictionary. rev. ed. Marvin L. Morrison. LC 86-61846. 408p. 1987. pap. 11.95 (ISBN 0-9608376-1-2). Pilot Light.
Word Finders in English. Anne Civardi. (Picture Word Finders Bks.). 48p. (gr. k-3). 1984. 10.95 (ISBN 0-86020-767-6). EDC.
Word Finding: A Language Rehabilitation Manual for Aphasic Adults. Daniel J. Carlson. Ed. by Cindy Drolet. LC 87-82069. 107p. (Orig.). 1987. pap. 34.50 incl. card set (ISBN 0-9609464-1-1). Imaginart Pr.
Word Finds Three. Linda Doherty. 96p. 1988. pap. 1.95 (ISBN 0-8125-7879-1). Tor Bks.
Word Finds Two. Linda Doherty. 96p. 1988. pap. 1.95 (ISBN 0-8125-7877-5). Tor Bks.
Word Fitly Spoken. Kenneth G. Mills. (Illus.). 211p. 1980. 24.95 (ISBN 0-686-64679-7); pap. 17.95 (ISBN 0-919842-05-4). Sun-Scape Pubns.
Word for Every Day. Jimmy Swaggart. 768p. Date not set. 20.00 (ISBN 0-935113-09-6). Swaggart Ministries.
Word for Every Day: Three Hundred & Sixty-Five Devotional Reading. Alvin N. Rogness. LC 81-65650. 376p. 1981. kivar 13.95 (ISBN 0-8066-1886-8, 10-7284). Augsburg.
Word for Teaching Is Learning: Essays for James Britton. Ed. by Martin Lightfoot & Nancy Martin. LC 88-5069. xvii, 300p. 1988. pap. text ed. 17.50x (ISBN 0-86709-237-8). Boynton Cook Pubs.
Word for Us, Gospels of John & Mark, Epistles to the Romans, & the Galations. Joann Haugerud. LC 77-83418. 1977. 7.95 (ISBN 0-9603042-3-1). Coalition Women-Relig.
Word for Word. Edward C. Pinkerton. LC 77-20391. xxxii, 432p. 1982. 39.95. Verbatim Bks.
Word for Word. Andrew A. Rooney. 288p. 1986. 16.95 (ISBN 0-399-13200-7, Perigee Bks). Putnam Pub Group.
Word for Word. Andrew A. Rooney. 400p. 1987. lib. bdg. 17.95 (ISBN 0-8161-4315-3, Large Print Bks). G K Hall.
Word for Word. Andrew A. Rooney. 1987. pap. 3.95 (ISBN 0-425-10526-1). Berkley Pub.
Word for Word: A Dictionary of Etymological Cognates. Edward C. Pinkerton. 454p. 1982. 60.00x (ISBN 0-930454-06-5). Gale.
Word for Word: Essays on the Arts of Language, Vol.I. Cid Corman. LC 76-48282. 180p. (Orig.). 1977. 14.00 (ISBN 0-87685-276-2); pap. 5.00 (ISBN 0-87685-275-4); ltd. signed o.p. 17.50 (ISBN 0-87685-277-0). Black Sparrow.
Word Formation in Generative Grammar. Mark Aronoff. (Linguistic Inquiry Monographs). 134p. 1976. pap. text ed. 15.95x (ISBN 0-262-51017-0). MIT Pr.
Word-Formation in Provencal. Edward L. Adams. 37.00 (ISBN 0-384-38802-7). Johnson Repr.
Word Formation in the Noun & Adjective. J. K. Norbury. LC 67-10258. (Studies in the Modern Russian Language: No. 13). pap. 33.80 (ISBN 0-317-27313-2, 2024503). Bks Demand UMI.
Word Formation in the Roman Sermo Plebius. Frederic T. Cooper. 365p. Repr. of 1895 ed. lib. bdg. 55.00x (ISBN 0-317-46448-5, Pub. by G Olms BRD). Coronet Bks.
Word Frequencies of Spoken American English. Hartvig Dahl. LC 80-116646. xii, 348p. 1980. 60.00. Verbatim Bks.
Word Frequencies of Spoken American English. Hartvig. 300p. 1980. 95.00x (ISBN 0-930454-07-3, Pub. by Verbatim). Gale.
Word Frequency in Newspaper Bengali. Jack A. Dabbs. LC 66-64723. 1966. 3.00 (ISBN 0-911494-04-9). Dabbs.
Word from Below: Essays on Modern Literature & Culture. Robert Langbaum. LC 87-40140. 288p. 1987. text ed. 35.00x (ISBN 0-299-11180-6); pap. text ed. 12.95x (ISBN 0-299-11184-9). U of Wis Pr.
Word Fun. (Baby's First Bks.). (Illus.). 14p. (ps). 1979. bds. 2.25 (ISBN 0-448-16274-1, G&D). Putnam Pub Group.
Word Fun. (Questron Electronic Workbook Library Ser.). (Illus.). 32p. (gr. 2-5). 1985. 3.95 (ISBN 0-394-87693-8). Random.
Word Game. Wilbert J. Levy. (YA) (gr. 6-10). pap. 8.33 (ISBN 0-87720-671-6). AMSCO Sch.
Word Game: Improving Communications. Edgar Dale. LC 75-19957. (Fastback Ser.: No. 60). (Orig.). 1975. pap. 0.90 (ISBN 0-87367-060-4). Phi Delta Kappa.
Word Game Winning Dictionary. Ed. by Bruce Wetterau. (Orig.). 1980. pap. 2.95 (ISBN 0-451-09214-7, E9214, Sig). NAL.
Word Games. Gyles Brandreth. LC 86-46047. (Illus.). 128p. 1987. 13.45i (ISBN 0-06-055069-4, HarpT). Har-Row.
Word Games for Health Professionals, 2 vols. Susan M. Sparks & Joyce L. Hayman. Incl. Vol. 1. 1974 (ISBN 0-937126-80-2); 77p. 1979 (ISBN 0-937126-82-9). 3.95 ea. Am Journal Nurse.
Word Games in English. Spencer. (gr. 7 up). 1976. pap. text ed. 4.75 (ISBN 0-88345-252-9, 18446). Prentice ESL.
Word Geography of England. Harold Orton & Nathalia Wright. 1975. 76.00 (ISBN 0-12-785608-0). Acad Pr.
Word: God's Manual for Maturity. Agnes Lawless & Eadie Goodboy. (Bible Study Enrichment Ser.). 64p. (Orig.). 1980. pap. 2.95 (ISBN 0-930756-59-2, 522004). Aglow Pubns.
Word Grammar. Richard Hudson. 300p. 1984. 45.00x (ISBN 0-631-13186-8). Basil Blackwell.
Word Grammar. Richard Hudson. 272p. 1986. pap. text ed. 17.95x (ISBN 0-631-14757-8). Basil Blackwell.
Word-Hoard: An Introduction to Old English Vocabulary. 2nd ed. Stephen A. Barney. LC 76-47003. (Yale Language Ser.). 96p. 1985. pap. 7.95. Yale U Pr.
Word Hunt, No. 1. Ed. by Ann Mitchell. 128p. 1982. pap. 1.50 (ISBN 0-505-51791-4, Pub. by Tower Bks). Leisure NY.
Word Hunt, No. 2. Ed. by Ann Mitchell. 128p. 1982. pap. 1.50 (ISBN 0-505-51793-0, Pub. by Tower Bks). Leisure NY.
Word Hunt No. 3. 128p. 1982. pap. 1.50 (ISBN 0-505-51821-X, Pub. by Tower Bks). Leisure NY.
Word Identification Techniques. Josephine Ives & Laura Z. Bursak. LC 85-60930. 261p. (Orig.). 1979. pap. 21.16 (ISBN 0-395-30638-8). HM.
Word-Image-Psyche. Bettina L. Knapp. LC 83-17856. (Illus.). ix, 247p. 1985. 23.50 (ISBN 0-8173-0206-9). U of Ala Pr.
Word in Edgewise. Irene Warsaw. 1964. 5.00 (ISBN 0-8233-0111-7). Golden Quill.
Word in Season. William F. Maestri. LC 84-11026. 153p. (Orig.). 1983. pap. 6.95 (ISBN 0-8189-0459-3). Alba.
Word in Season, Vol. II. Dick Mills. 192p. (Orig.). 1987. pap. 6.95 (ISBN 0-89274-427-8). Harrison Hse.
Word in Season, 3 vols. Ed. by John E. Rotelle. Tr. by Edith Barnecut. (Word In Season Ser.). (Orig.). 1987. pap. 12.50 ea. Vol. I, 230 pg (ISBN 0-941491-14-5). Vol. II, 230 pg (ISBN 0-941491-12-9). Vol. III, 230 pg (ISBN 0-941491-13-7). Augustinian Pr.
Word in Season, Vol. 1. Dick Mills. (Orig.). 1986. pap. 6.95 (ISBN 0-89274-418-9). Harrison Hse.
Word in Stone: The Role of Architecture in the Nationalist Socialist Ideology. Robert R. Taylor. (Illus.). 1974. 42.50x (ISBN 0-520-02193-2). U of Cal Pr.
Word in Time. Arthur J. Dewey. 204p. (Orig.). 1986. pap. 14.95 (ISBN 0-941850-18-8). Liturgical Pubns.
Word in Worship. William Skudlarek. LC 80-25525. (Abingdon Preacher's Library). 128p. (Orig.). 1981. pap. 7.95 (ISBN 0-687-46131-6). Abingdon.
Word in Your Ear. Philip Howard. 1983. 17.95 (ISBN 0-19-520437-9). Oxford U Pr.
Word-Index to a Week on the Concord & Merrimack Rivers. James Karabatsos. LC 80-2510. Repr. of 1971 ed. 18.50 (ISBN 0-404-19058-8). AMS Pr.
Word-Index to James Joyce's Dubliners. Ed. by Gary Lane. LC 71-183760. (Reference Ser., No. 44). 270p. 1972. lib. bdg. 75.00x (ISBN 0-8383-1384-1). Haskell.
Word Index to James Joyce's "Portrait of the Artist". Leslie Hancock. LC 67-13937. 160p. 1967. 6.00x (ISBN 0-8093-0253-5). S Ill U Pr.
Word Index to James Joyce's Stephen Hero. Chester G. Anderson. 185p. 1980. Repr. of 1958 ed. lib. bdg. 35.00 (ISBN 0-8495-0220-9). Arden Lib.
Word Index to Poe's Fiction. Ed. by Burton R. Pollin. 512p. 1982. 40.00x (ISBN 0-87752-225-1). Gordian.
Word-Index to the Poems of Walther von der Vogelweide. 2nd ed. Ed. by Roe-Merrill S. Heffner & W. P. Lehmann. 82p. 1950. pap. 11.50x (ISBN 0-299-00663-8). U of Wis Pr.
Word Index to the Poetry of C.S. Lewis. Sara P. McLaughlin & Mark O. Webb. LC 88-17562. 1988. lib. bdg. 30.00 (ISBN 0-933951-21-3). Locust Hill Pr.
Word-Index to the Texts of Steinmeyer: "Die kleineren althochdeutschen Sprachdenkmaler". Ed. by Roe-Merrill S. Heffner. 184p. 1961. pap. 17.50x (ISBN 0-299-02393-1). U of Wis Pr.
Word Index to Walden, With Textual Notes. J. Stephen Sherwin. LC 80-2517. (Thoreau Ser.). 176p. 1981. Repr. of 1960 ed. 27.00 (ISBN 0-404-19065-0). AMS Pr.
Word-Indices to Old English Non-Poetic Texts. Intro. by Fred C. Robinson. Incl. No. 6. Mattie A. Harris. Repr. of 1899 ed; No. 24. Harvey W. Chapman. Repr. of 1905 ed; No. 35. Loring H. Dodd. Repr. of 1908 ed. (Yale Studies in English Ser.). vii, 458p. 1974. 37.50 (ISBN 0-208-01388-1, Archon). Shoe String.
Word-Information Processing: A System Approach. Mona J. Casady & Dorothy Sandburg. 1985. text ed. write for info. (ISBN 0-538-23850-X, W85). SW Pub.
Word Information Processing: Administration & Office Automation. 2nd ed. Walter Kleinschrod & Leonard Kruk. 288p. 1983. text ed. 28.99 scp (ISBN 0-672-98442-3); scp instr's guide 7.33 (ISBN 0-672-98443-1). Bobbs.
Word-Information Processing: Applications, Skills & Procedures. L. Joyce Arntson. LC 82-18009. 434p. 1983. 21.50 (ISBN 0-534-01345-7). PWS Kent Pub.
Word-Information Processing Concepts. 3rd ed. Mona J. Casdy. 218p. 1988. pap. text ed. write for info. (ISBN 0-538-23611-6, W62U). SW Pub.
Word-Information Processing: Concepts & Applications. Lina G. Baber. (Illus.). 352p. 1984. text ed. 30.95 (ISBN 0-675-20095-4); practice set 16.95 (ISBN 0-675-20181-0). Merrill.
Word-Information Processing: Concepts & Procedures. L. Joyce Arnston. LC 82-18020. 1983. 19.75 (ISBN 0-534-01346-5). PWS Kent Pub.
Word-Information Processing Concepts: A Systems Approach. 2nd ed. Mona Casady. 1989. text ed. price not set (ISBN 0-538-70030-0, WP40BA). SW Pub.
Word-Information Processing: Concepts of Office Automation. 2nd ed. Marly Bergerud & Jean Gonzalez. LC 83-19815. (Word Processing Ser.: 1-388). 528p. 1984. text ed. write for info. (ISBN 0-471-87056-0). Wiley.
Word Information Processing: Concepts, Procedures, & Systems. 2nd ed. L. Joyce Arntson. 368p. 1987. pap. text ed. 21.75 (ISBN 0-534-06228-8). PWS Kent Pub.
Word-Information Processing: Essentials Concepts. 2nd ed. Marilyn K. Popyk. 240p. 1986. text ed. 22.25 (ISBN 0-07-050593-4). McGraw.
Word Information Processing: Exercises Applications, & Procedures. L. Joyce Arntson & Lora B. Todesco. 256p. (gr. 11-12). 1987. pap. text ed. 21.25 (ISBN 0-534-06234-2). PWS Kent Pub.

Word Processing & Information Systems: A Practical Approach to Concepts. Marilyn K. Popyk. LC 82-25902. 352p. 1983. text ed. 33.70 (ISBN 0-07-050574-8). McGraw.
Word Processing & Information Systems: A Practical Approach to Concepts. 2nd ed. Marilyn K. Popyk. 372p. 1986. text ed. 28.95 (ISBN 0-07-050594-2). McGraw.
Word Processing & Office Automation: A Supervisory Perspective. Gilbert J. Konkel & Phyllis J. Peck. LC 82-80637. (Illus.). 168p. 1982. pap. 12.95x (ISBN 0-911054-05-7). Office Pubns.
Word Processing & Other Automated Publication Systems, Vol. 6. Shirley G. Carter. Ed. by Robert J. Zabielski. (Anthology). 250p. 1981. pap. 25.00x (ISBN 0-914548-35-2, Pub. by Soc Tech Comm). Univelt Inc.
Word Processing & Publishing: Some Guidelines for Authors. Peter Denley. 24p. (Orig.). 1985. pap. 3.00 (ISBN 0-85672-509-9, Pub. by British Acad). Longwood Pub Group.
Word Processing & Text Editing. John Zarrella. LC 80-114189. (Microprocessor Software Engineering Concepts Ser.). (Illus.). 156p. 1980. pap. 12.00 (ISBN 0-935230-01-7). Microcomputer Appns.
Word Processing & the Automated Office. Alan Paterson. (Engineering Management Ser.). 150p. 1985. 26.95 (ISBN 0-470-20147-9). Halsted Pr.
Word Processing Applications. Helen W. Taylor et al. 1985. pap. text ed. write for info. (ISBN 0-8359-8832-5, Reston). P-H.
Word Processing Applications: Accounting. Velma Jesser & Brenda Jennings. LC 85-6578. 104p. 1986. write for info. (ISBN 0-471-82442-9); tchr's. manual avail. Wiley.
Word Processing Applications for Microcomputers. Ralph Ruby, Jr. & Robert W. Mooney. Ed. by Molly Gardiner & Robert Horan. (Illus.). 187p. 1987. pap. text ed. write for info. (ISBN 0-574-20895-X, 13-3895). SRA.
Word Processing Applications for Office Professionals. Mckay. 1988. pap. price not set (ISBN 0-471-61249-9). Wiley.
Word Processing Applications: Insurance. Velma Jesser & Brenda Jennings. LC 85-6602. 136p. 1986. write for info. (ISBN 0-471-82998-6). Wiley.
Word Processing Applications: Legal. Velma Jesser & Brenda Jennings. LC 85-9246. 152p. 1986. write for info. (ISBN 0-471-82999-4). Wiley.
Word Processing Applications: Medical. Velma Jesser & Brenda Jennings. LC 85-9274. 56p. 1986. write for info. (ISBN 0-471-82997-8). Wiley.
Word Processing Basics: An Introduction for Young People. Art Dudley. LC 84-22315. (Illus.). 48p. (gr. 4-9). 1985. PLB 9.95 (ISBN 0-13-963513-0). P-H.
Word Processing Buyer's Guide. Arthur Naiman. LC 82-17898. (Illus.). 304p. 1983. pap. text ed. 16.95 (ISBN 0-07-045869-3, BYTE Bks). McGraw.
Word Processing Communication Skills. Cheryl M. Luke & Ann J. Swafford. 136p. 1988. pap. text ed. 7.50 (ISBN 0-15-596660-X, HC); instr's manual 1.00 (ISBN 0-15-596661-8). HarBraceJ.
Word Processing: Concepts & Applications. Bettie H. Ellis. (Illus.). 48p. 1980. text ed. 16.44 (ISBN 0-07-019242-1). McGraw.
Word Processing: Concepts & Applications. 2nd ed. Bettie H. Ellis. 232p. 1986. pap. text ed. 14.08 (ISBN 0-07-019278-2). McGraw.
Word Processing: Concepts & Careers. 4th ed. Marly Bergerud & Jean Gonzales. 336p. 1988. pap. write for info. (ISBN 0-471-84503-5). Wiley.
Word Processing: Concepts & Careers. 3rd ed. Marly Bergerud & Jean Gonzalez. LC 83-10242. (Word Processing Ser.: 1-388). 313p. 1984. write for info. (ISBN 0-471-87057-9). Wiley.
Word Processing Cookbook. Glenn Stuart. 34.00 (ISBN 0-13-963398-7); pap. 19.95 (ISBN 0-13-963380-4); 21.33 (ISBN 0-13-963421-5). P-H.
Word Processing Curriculum Guide. 128p. 1980. 7.50 (ISBN 0-318-15257-6). Natl Busn Ed Assoc.
Word Processing Equipment. Kline D. Strong. 80p. 1979. pap. 20.00. Amer Bar Assn.
Word Processing Equipment. Kline D. Strong. 80p. pap. 20.00. Chicago Review.
Word Processing: Essential Concepts. Marilyn K. Popyk. LC 83-768. (Illus.). 240p. 1983. text ed. 27.05 (ISBN 0-07-048472-4). McGraw.
Word Processing Exercises for Word Processors, Microcomputers, & Electronic Typewriters. N. Kathryn Layman & Adrienne G. Renner. (Working Papers). 224p. 1984. write for info. working paper (ISBN 0-13-967514-0). P-H.
Word Processing Exercises for Word Processors, Microcomputers, & Electronic Typewriters. 2nd ed. N. Kathryn Layman & Adrienne G. Renner. (Illus.). 272p. 1988. pap. text ed. write for info. (ISBN 0-13-963588-2). P-H.
Word Processing Explosion. Gilbert J. Konkel & Phyllis J. Peck. LC 76-21172. (Illus.). 1976. pap. 8.50 (ISBN 0-911054-03-0). Office Pubns.
Word Processing: First Step to the Office of the Future. Kathleen F. Curley. 174p. 1983. 35.00 (ISBN 0-275-91717-7, C1717). Praeger.
Word Processing for Business Publications: How to Produce Proposals, Manuals, Catalogs, Newsletters & More. Herman R. Holtz. (BYTE Book). 256p. 1984. pap. text ed. 9.95 (ISBN 0-07-029657-X). McGraw.
Word Processing for Solicitors. Kevin Townsend & Kate Taphouse. 186p. 1983. text ed. 37.00 (ISBN 0-566-03450-6). Gower Pub Co.
Word Processing for Technical Writers. Robert Krull. (Technical Communication Ser.: Vol. 3). 190p. (Orig.). 1988. pap. text ed. 18.50 (ISBN 0-89503-049-7). Baywood Pub.
Word Processing for the IBM PC & PCjr & Compatible Computers. Carol B. Matthews & Martin S. Matthews. (Illus.). 428p. 1985. pap. text ed. 20.95 (ISBN 0-07-040952-8, Byte Bks). McGraw.
Word Processing Glossary. Harold C. Durbin. LC 84-70288. 364p. 1984. pap. 15.00 (ISBN 0-936786-07-8). Durbin Assoc.
Word Processing Handbook. Katherine Aschner. pap. 8.95 (ISBN 0-88908-913-2, 9530). TAB Bks.
Word Processing Handbook. Ivan Flores. 512p. 1982. 42.95 (ISBN 0-442-22526-1). Van Nos Reinhold.
Word Processing Handbook: A Step-by-Step Guide to Automating Your Office. 2nd ed. Katherine Aschner. 273p. 1983. pap. 8.95. ISC Pr.
Word Processing: Hands-on Exercises. Patricia A. Custer. (Illus.). 240p. 1984. pap. text ed. write for info. (ISBN 0-13-963463-0). P-H.
Word Processing in the Courts. National Center for State Courts Staff. Ed. by Bureau of Justice Statistics. LC 84-14860. 60p. (Orig.). 1984. pap. 10.00 (ISBN 0-89656-077-5, R-091). Natl Ctr St Courts.
Word Processing in the Transitional Office. Joseph L Kish, Jr. (Illus.). 208p. 1985. 31.95 (ISBN 0-442-24713-3). Van Nos Reinhold.
Word Processing Input. Dorinda Clippinger. 1983. pap. text ed. write for info. (ISBN 0-8359-8802-3, Reston). P-H.
Word Processing Made Simple. Ronald W. Hadley et al. 512p. 1984. spiral bound 40.00x (ISBN 0-669-07410-1). Lexington Bks.
Word Processing Made Simple. Betty Hutchinson & Warner A. Hutchinson. LC 82-46019. (Made Simple Ser.). (Illus.). 128p. 1984. pap. 4.95 (ISBN 0-385-18835-8). Doubleday.
Word Processing Management. Waterhouse. 1988. price not set (ISBN 0-471-60782-7). Wiley.
Word Processing Manual. M. Sanderson & M. K. Rawlinson. 200p. 1982. pap. text ed. 23.00x (ISBN 0-7121-2323-7). Trans-Atl Phila.
Word Processing Needs in the Domestic Relations Division & Bureau of Support, Cuyahoga County (Ohio) Court of Common Pleas: A Technical Assistance Report. National Center for State Courts Staff. 8p. 1985. manuscript 1.00 (NERO, T/A-527). Natl Ctr St Courts.
Word Processing on the BBC Micro: Wordwise & Epson. Michael Wood. 100p. 1984. pap. text ed. 9.05 (ISBN 0-471-81046-0). Wiley.
Word Processing on the IBM Personal Computer. Danny Goodman. 1983. pap. 19.95. Bobbs.
Word Processing on the UNIX System. Morris Krieger. (BYTE Book). (Illus.). 1985. pap. text ed. 19.95 (ISBN 0-07-035498-7). McGraw.
Word Processing on the Wang Professional Computer. Terry L. Fucci. 158p. 1988. pap. 15.00 net (ISBN 0-15-596685-5, HC). HarBraceJ.
Word Processing: Operations, Applications, & Administration. Walter Kleinschrod et al. LC 79-13613. 1980. scp 28.44 (ISBN 0-672-97270-0); scp tchr's. manual 3.67 (ISBN 0-672-97271-9). Bobbs.
Word Processing Operations: Document Preparation. 2nd ed. Jane E. Varner. 416p. (Orig.). 1986. pap. text ed. write for info. (ISBN 0-574-20785-6, 13-3785); write for info. working papers (ISBN 0-574-20787-2, 13-3787); write for info. instr's guide (ISBN 0-574-20786-4, 13-3786). Sci Res Assoc Coll.
Word Processing Power with Microsoft Word. 2nd ed. Peter Rinearson. 432p. (Orig.). 1986. pap. 19.95 (ISBN 0-914845-89-6). Microsoft.
Word Processing Power with Microsoft Word. 3rd ed. Peter Rinearson & Joanne Woodcock. 512p. 1988. softcover 19.95 (ISBN 1-55615-126-8). Microsoft.
Word Processing Primer. Mitch Waite & Julie Arca. 188p. 1982. pap. text ed. 18.95 (ISBN 0-07-067761-1, BYTE Bks). McGraw.
Word Processing Procedures for Today's Office. Mary J. Forbes. 232p. 1983. pap. 22.00 (EY-00027-DP) (ISBN 0-932376-42-8). Digital Pr.
Word Processing Profits at Home. rev. ed. Peggy Glenn. LC 87-25188. 220p. 1987. pap. 15.95 (ISBN 0-936930-86-1). Aames-Allen.
Word Processing Security. R. Doswell. 150p. 1982. pap. 20.75 (ISBN 0-471-89432-X). Wiley.
Word Processing Simplified & Self-Taught. Joseph Coleman. LC 82-24501. (Simplified & Self-Taught Ser.). (Illus.). 128p. 1983. pap. 4.95 (ISBN 0-668-05601-0). Arco.
Word Processing Simplified for Superscript: TRS 80 Models III IV & IVP. Rosemary K. Bekaert. (Illus.). 208p. (Orig.). 1985. pap. 25.00 (ISBN 0-9615582-0-2). Kelly Ent.
Word Processing Simulations for Electronic Typewriters & Text Editors. Carol A. Wheeler & Marie Dalton. LC 81-11630. (Word Processing Ser.). 224p. 1982. pap. write for info. (ISBN 0-471-08158-2). Wiley.
Word Processing Skills & Applications. Elizabeth Walls & Mary A. Flynn. 1984. pap. text ed. write for info. (ISBN 0-8359-8812-0, Reston). P-H.
Word Processing Skills & Applications Using the Wang Systems. 2nd ed. Agnes Cecela. 1985. pap. text ed. 23.95 (ISBN 0-8359-8824-4, Reston); instr's. manual avail. (ISBN 0-8359-8825-2). P-H.
Word Processing Skills & Simulations. Jennie Mason. LC 78-15761. 1979. pap. 15.12scp (ISBN 0-672-97197-6); scp tchr's manual 7.33 (ISBN 0-672-97135-6). Bobbs.
Word Processing Software for the IBM PC. P. B. Seybold & R. T. Marshak. (Illus.). 201p. 1985. pap. text ed. 16.95 (ISBN 0-07-056322-5, Byte Bks). McGraw.
Word Processing Supervision. Reba B. Davis & John L. Balderson. 320p. 1984. text ed. 26.35 scp (ISBN 0-672-98448-2); scp instr's. guide 7.33 (ISBN 0-672-98449-0). Bobbs.
Word Processing: The Applications Specialist. Patricia A. Custer. (Illus.). 352p. 1986. text ed. write for info. (ISBN 0-13-963562-9). P-H.
Word Processing: The Corresponding Secretary. 1985. pap. 6.35 (ISBN 0-87350-321-X); tchr's. manual 17.55 (ISBN 0-87350-327-9); forms wkbk. 9.90 (ISBN 0-87350-326-0). Milady Pub.
Word Processing: The Useable Portable Guide. Jon Haber & Herbert R. Haber. (Illus.). 254p. (Orig.). 1988. pap. 11.95 (ISBN 0-945765-00-2). Useable Portable Pubns.
Word Processing Training on the Wang. Jean M. Conlin & Robert G. Conlin. 400p. 1985. pap. write for info. (ISBN 0-13-963406-1). P-H.
Word Processing Users' Manual. Thomas J. Anderson & William R. Trotter. LC 73-94097. 1976. pap. 12.95 (ISBN 0-8144-5424-0). AMACOM.
Word Processing Using IBM Displaywriter. Rebecca C. Latif. 1984. pap. text ed. write for info. (ISBN 0-8359-8814-7, Reston). P-H.
Word Processing Using the Wang Processor. Bert Dumpe. 1984. write for info. (ISBN 0-471-60642-1). Wiley.
Word Processing Using WANG Systems. Rebecca C. Latif-Pembry. 288p. 1987. pap. text ed. 18.00 net (ISBN 0-15-596668-5, WANG, HC). HarBraceJ.
Word Processing with DisplayWrite III. Jacklyn M. Williford. LC 85-22600. 156p. 1986. pap. 16.95 (ISBN 0-471-83070-4). Wiley.
Word Processing with IBM's Displaywrite Series. Judy Crondahl. 256p. 1985. pap. 17.95 not set (ISBN 0-317-37789-2). S&S.
Word Processing with Superscripsit & the TRS-80: Models III & 4. Lewis M. Elia & Joseph A. Fall. Ed. by Harry R. Moon. (Illus.). 161p. pap. text ed. 16.75 (ISBN 0-87350-345-7); 95.00 (ISBN 0-87350-346-5). Milady Pub.
Word Processor. Jack Rudman. (Career Examination Ser.: C-3184). (Cloth bdg. avail. on request). 1988. pap. 12.00 (ISBN 0-8373-3184-6). Natl Learning.
Word Processor & Calculator Development System MVP-Forth. 06/1987 ed. Thomas E. Wempe. (MVP-Forth Bks.: Vol. 9). 173p. pap. text ed. 20.00 (ISBN 0-914699-32-6). Mntn View Pr.
Word Processor & Calculator Development System Source. Thomas E. Wempe. (MVP-Forth Ser.: Vol. 10). 220p. (Orig.). 1987. pap. text ed. 20.00 (ISBN 0-914699-56-3). Mntn View Pr.
Word Processor & the Writing Teacher. Linda R. Knapp. 1985. pap. text ed. 23.00 (ISBN 0-8359-8831-7, Reston). P-H.
Word Processor Comparison Tables. 1985. 39.95 (ISBN 0-910085-10-2). IGA Rsch.
Word Processors: A Programmed Training Guide with Practical Applications. N. Kathryn Layman & Adrienne G. Renner. (Illus.). 352p. 1981. text ed. write for info. (ISBN 0-13-963520-3). P-H.
Word Processors & Information Processing: What They Are & How to Buy. 2nd ed. Dan Poynter. LC 81-11128. (Illus.). 172p. (Orig.). 1982. 11.95 (ISBN 0-915516-31-4). Para Pub.
Word Processors & the Writing Process: An Annotated Bibliography. Compiled by Paula R. Nancarrow et al. LC 83-22749. xi, 146p. 1984. lib. bdg. 36.95 (ISBN 0-313-23995-9, NAW/). Greenwood.
Word Processors & Typewriters Worldwide: Opportunities & Pitfalls. Villy Diernisse. (Illus.). 270p. 1984. 1200.00x (ISBN 0-910211-01-9). Laal Co.
Word Pursuit: Based on the Original Hinky Pinky Word Game. Charles E. Kohlhase. 112p. 1985. pap. 7.95 (ISBN 0-671-52512-3, Pub. by Monarch Pr). S&S.
Word Puzzles. Patricia Muncy. (gr. 4-6). 1974. pap. 5.95 (ISBN 0-8224-7488-3). D S Lake Pubs.
Word Recognition in Foreign & Native Language. C. J. Koster. (Netherlands Phonetic Archives Ser.). x, 171p. 1987. write for info. (ISBN 90-6765-327-6); pap. write for info. (ISBN 90-6765-326-8). Foris Pubns.
Word Recognition Program. (Readiness Level-3 bks. Auditory, Visual & Motor Visual). 1981. Classroom Set. 294.30 (ISBN 0-8484-0924-8). B Loft.
Word Recognition: The Why & the How. Patrick Groff & Dorothy Z. Seymour. 220p. 1987. 26.75x (ISBN 0-398-05322-7). C C Thomas.
Word Recreations: Games & Diversions from Word Ways. A. Ross Eckler. LC 79-51884. (Orig.). 1980. pap. 4.95 (ISBN 0-486-23854-7). Dover.
Word Remains: A Life of Oscar Romero. James R. Brockman. LC 82-3607. (Illus.). 256p. (Orig.). 1982. pap. 12.95 (ISBN 0-88344-364-3). Orbis Bks.
Word Resources. 3rd ed. Freida Radke. LC 78-16414. 1979. pap. 13.24 scp. Odyssey Pr.
Word Resources. 3rd ed. Thomas E. Walker. LC 78-16414. 1979. pap. 13.24 scp; pap. 3.67 scp answer key (ISBN 0-672-61440-5). Bobbs.
Word Resources. 3rd ed. Thomas E. Walker. 276p. 1979. pap. text ed. write for info. (ISBN 0-02-423840-6). Macmillan.
Word Scan Puzzles. Fred Justus. (Puzzles Ser.). 24p. (gr. 3). 1980. wkbk. 5.00 (ISBN 0-8209-0297-7, PU-11). ESP.
Word Search: Favorite Bible Stories from Genesis. John H. Tiner. pap. 2.70 (ISBN 0-89137-615-1). Quality Pubns.
Word Search Puzzles for Earth Science Classrooms. Chad Johnson. 40p. (Orig.). (YA) (gr. 7-12). 1987. pap. 2.00 (ISBN 0-9617324-1-5). Bog Butter.
Word Search Puzzles: Fun with Bible Words & Themes. Edward M. Seagrist. (Bible Puzzle & Quiz Bks.). 79p. 1985. pap. 3.95 (ISBN 0-8010-8257-9). Baker Bk.
Word Shadows of the Great: The Lure of Autograph Collecting. Thomas F. Madigan. LC 70-145705. (Illus.). 318p. 1971. Repr. of 1930 ed. 43.00x (ISBN 0-8103-3378-3). Gale.
Word Signals. Sally Strohm. (English Ser.). 24p. (gr. 4-7). 1979. wkbk. 5.00 (ISBN 0-8209-0185-7, E-13). ESP.
Word Singers. Ed. by Norman Simms. (Pacific Quarterly Moana Special Issue: Vol. 8, No. 4). 80p. 1984. pap. 12.00 (ISBN 0-317-20181-6, Pub. by Outrigger Pubs New Zealand). Three Continents.
Word Skills. Mary F. Pecci. (Super Seatwork). (Illus.). 238p. 1980. 12.95 (ISBN 0-943220-04-1). Pecci Educ Pubs.
Word Structure. Lillian Lieberman. (Reading Superstar Ser.). 64p. (gr. k-3). 1987. 6.95 (ISBN 0-912107-67-7). Monday Morning Bks.
Word Structure & Comprehension. Nicholas Criscuolo. (gr. 3-6). 1987. pap. 5.95 (ISBN 0-8224-2729-X). D S Lake Pubs.
Word-Studies in French & English, 1st Ser. Thomas A. Jenkins. (LM). 1933. pap. 16.00 (ISBN 0-527-00818-4). Kraus Repr.
Word Studies in the Greek New Testament, for the English Reader, 16 bks. Kenneth S. Wuest. Incl. Bk. 1. Golden Nuggets; Bk. 2. Bypaths; Bk. 3. Treasures; Bk. 4. Untranslatable Riches; Bk. 5. Studies in Vocabulary; Bk. 6. Great Truths to Live by; Bk. 7. Mark; Bk. 8. Romans. pap. 9.95 (ISBN 0-8028-1231-7); Bk. 9. Galatians; Bk. 10. Ephesians & Colossians; Bk. 11. Philippians; Bk. 12. Pastoral Epistles. pap. 6.95 (ISBN 0-8028-1236-8); Bk. 13. Hebrews. pap. 6.95 (ISBN 0-8028-1235-X); Bk. 14. First Peter. pap. 5.95 o. p. (ISBN 0-8028-1237-6); Bk. 15. In These Last Days; Bk. 16. Prophetic Light in the Present Darkness. Set. pap. 85.20 (ISBN 0-8028-1248-1); Current 4 vols. 79.95 (ISBN 0-8028-2280-0). Eerdmans.
Word Studies in the New Testament, 2 Vols. Marvin Vincent. 1957. 49.95 (ISBN 0-8028-8083-5). Eerdmans.
Word Studies on the Holy Spirit. Ethelbert W. Bullinger. LC 85-7631. 232p. 1985. pap. 7.95 (ISBN 0-8254-2246-9). Kregel.
Word Study New Testament & Concordance. Ralph Winter. 1990p. 1978. text ed. 39.95 (ISBN 0-8423-8390-5). Tyndale.
Word Sublime & Its Context, 1650-1760. Theodore E. Wood. LC 77-165151. (De Proprietatibus Litterarum, Ser. Major: No. 7). 231p. 1972. text ed. 24.00x (ISBN 90-2792-073-7). Mouton.
Word System. Happy Caldwell. 60p. 1981. pap. 1.50 (ISBN 0-89274-176-7). Harrison Hse.
Word: The English from Hebrew Dictionary. Isaac E. Mozeson. 1988. 29.95 (ISBN 0-933503-44-X). Shapolsky Pubs.
Word: The Greater Mysteries of Welsh Witchcraft. Rhuddlwm Gawr. LC 85-73758. (Illus.). 224p. (Orig.). 1988. 20.95 (ISBN 0-931760-48-8, CP 101277); pap. 16.95 (ISBN 0-931760-27-5). Camelot GA.
Word, The New Century Version: New Testament. LC 84-51094. (Illus.). 556p. 1984. 13.95 (ISBN 0-8344-0123-1, 123). Worthy TX.
Word Thinkercises. Becky Daniel. 64p. (gr. 4-8). 1988. wkbk. 6.95 (ISBN 0-86653-394-X, GA1034). Good Apple.
Word Three-Point-Zero on the MAC: A Guide to Power & Performance. Tim Knight. (Illus.). 400p. 1988. 19.95. Prentice Hall Pr.
Word to the Wise. rev. ed. Donald Gee. Orig. Title: Proverbs for Pentecost. 80p. 1975. pap. 0.95 (ISBN 0-88243-632-5, 02-0632). Gospel Pub.
Word Trip Games for the (l), (r), & (s) Sounds. Patrick Carr. 1974. text ed. 11.75x (ISBN 0-8134-1603-5). Inter Print Pubs.
Word Wagon. Barbara Gregorich. Ed. by Joan Hoffman. (Fast Forward Enrichment Ser.). 32p. (Orig.). (ps-1). wkbk 1.95 (ISBN 0-88743-129-1). Sch Zone Pub Co.
Word Warps: A Glossary of Unfamiliar Terms. David Diefendorf. (Illus.). 128p. (Orig., Includes index). 1984. pap. 4.95 (ISBN 0-913589-02-0). Williamson Pub Co.

Words & Their Meaning. H. Jackson. (Learning about Language Ser.). 320p. pap. text ed. 15.95 (ISBN 0-582-29154-2). Longman.
Words & Their Ways in English Speech. James B. Greenough & George L. Kittredge. 1980. Repr. of 1901 ed. lib. bdg. 50.00 (ISBN 0-89341-482-4). Longwood Pub Group.
Words & Things. Roger Brown. LC 58-9395. 1968. 18.95 (ISBN 0-02-904800-1); pap. text ed. 10.95 (ISBN 0-02-904810-9). Free Pr.
Words & Things: An Examination of, & an Attack on, Linguistic Philosophy. Ernest Gellner. 1979. pap. 10.95 (ISBN 0-7100-0285-8). Routledge Chapman & Hall.
Words & Values: Some Leading Words & Where They Lead Us. Peggy Rosenthal. 1983. 24.95 (ISBN 0-19-503364-7); pap. 8.95 (ISBN 0-19-503584-4). Oxford U Pr.
Words & What They Do to You: Beginning Lessons in General Semantics for Junior & Senior High School. Catherine Minteer. 128p. (gr. 7-12). 1971. text ed. 6.00x (ISBN 0-910780-06-4). Inst Gen Seman.
Words & Women. Casey Miller & Kate Swift. LC 75-36601. 200p. 1977. pap. 2.95 (ISBN 0-385-04858-0, Anchor Pr). Doubleday.
Words & Wonders: A Collection of Proverbs, Poems & Song Lyrics. Arthur C. Ford. 96p. 1984. 6.50 (ISBN 0-682-40187-0). Exposition-Phoenix.
Words & Works of Jesus Christ. J. Dwight Pentecost. 576p. 1981. 20.95 (ISBN 0-310-30940-9, 17015). Zondervan.
Words Apart: Losing Your Hearing As an Adult. Lesley Jones et al. 250p. 1988. lib. bdg. 79.95. Routledge Chapman & Hall.
Words Are Important: Primary Level (Tan) Bk. E. H. Schuster. (gr. 4). 1985. pap. 2.60x (ISBN 0-8437-7983-7). Hammond Inc.
Words Are Important Series. E. H. Schuster. Incl. Level A (Blue) Bk. (gr. 5) (ISBN 0-8437-7985-3); Level B (Red) Bk. (gr. 6) (ISBN 0-8437-7991-8); Level C (Green) Bk. (gr. 7) (ISBN 0-8437-7980-2); Level D (Orange) Bk. (gr. 8) (ISBN 0-8437-7950-0); Level E (Purple) Bk. (gr. 9) (ISBN 0-8437-7955-1); Level F (Brown) Bk. (gr. 10) (ISBN 0-8437-7960-8); Level G (Pink) Bk. (gr. 11) (ISBN 0-8437-7965-9); Level H (Grey) Bk. (gr. 12) (ISBN 0-8437-7970-5). 1985. pap. 2.60x ea. Hammond Inc.
Words Around Us. Tim O'Halloran. (Illus.). 48p. (ps-k). 1985. PLB 11.66 (ISBN 0-87617-030-0, Pub. by C Hayes Pr). Penworthy Pub.
Words Around Us. Tim O'Halloran. (Illus.). 48p. (ps-k). 1985. 9.95 (ISBN 0-88625-124-9). C Hayes Pr.
Words Around Us in French. Tim O'Halloran. (Illus.). 48p. (Fr.). (ps-k). 1985. 9.95 (ISBN 0-88625-125-7). C Hayes Pr.
Words Around Us in Spanish. Tim O'Halloran. (Illus.). 48p. (Span.). (ps-k). 1985. 9.95 (ISBN 0-88625-126-5). C Hayes Pr.
Words As Eggs: Psyche in Language & Clinic. Russell A. Lockhart. LC 83-18233. 233p. (Orig.). 1983. pap. 15.00 (ISBN 0-88214-323-9). Spring Pubns.
Words at War, Words at Peace: Essays on Language in General & Particular Words. facsimile ed. Eric Partridge. LC 76-117911. (Select Bibliographies Reprint Ser). Repr. of 1948 ed. 18.00 (ISBN 0-8369-5364-9). Ayer Co Pubs.
Words at Work. 2nd ed. Joseph Bellafiore. (gr. 10-12). 1968. pap. text ed. 8.25 (ISBN 0-87720-320-2). AMSCO Sch.
Words at Work: Lectures on Textual Structure. Randolph Quirk. 137p. 1987. pap. text ed. 9.95x (ISBN 9971-69-102-7, Pub. by Singapore U Pr). Ohio U Pr.
Words Before Midnight. Richard Poole. 60p. 1981. pap. 8.95 (ISBN 0-907476-03-1). Dufour.
Word's Body: An Incarnational Aesthetic of Interpretation. Alla Bozarth-Campbell. LC 79-111. 189p. 1980. 18.75 (ISBN 0-8173-0009-0). U of Ala Pr.
Words by Heart. Ouida Sebestyen. 144p. (gr. 4-8). 1983. pap. 2.95 (ISBN 0-553-27179-2, Starfire). Bantam.
Words by Heart. Ouida Sebestyen. LC 78-27847. (gr. 5 up). 1979. 13.95 (ISBN 0-316-77931-8, Joy St Bks). Little.
Words Can Hurt. Paula Bussard. (Critter County Ser.). (Illus.). 28p. (gr. k-3). 1985. 1.29 (ISBN 0-87239-965-6, 3385). Standard Pub.
Words Can Kill. Kenn Davis. (Orig.). 1984. pap. 2.50 (ISBN 0-317-05464-3, Crest). Fawcett.
Words Can Tell: A Book about Our Language. Christina Ashton. LC 87-20333. (Illus.). 128p. (YA) (gr. 6 up). 1988. 9.79 (ISBN 0-671-65223-0). Messner.
Words Chiseled from Rock. Eddie B. Pittman, Jr. LC 87-61254. (Illus.). 80p. (Orig.). 1987. pap. 5.00 (ISBN 0-9618791-0-6). Pub Press.
Words, Conversation & Poetry: From the Musical, "Omar, Man of Fire". Omar Maximillian. 64p. (Orig.). 1983. pap. 5.50 (ISBN 0-682-40120-X). Exposition-Phoenix.
Words Every College Student Should Know. 2nd, Rev. ed. Kenneth A. Oliver. LC 81-81919. 500p. (Orig.). 1982. pap. 13.95 (ISBN 0-913244-57-0). Hapi Pr.
Words, Facts & Phrases. Eliezer E. Edwards. 59.95 (ISBN 0-8490-1327-5). Gordon Pr.
Words, Facts & Phrases: A Dictionary of Curious, Quaint, & Out-of-the-Way Matters. Eliezer E. Edwards. LC 68-21768. 640p. 1968. Repr. of 1881 ed. 42.00x (ISBN 0-8103-3087-3). Gale.
Words Fail Me. Philip Howard. 1981. 21.95x (ISBN 0-19-520237-6). Oxford U Pr.
Words Fitly Spoken: Reflections & Prayers. Robert H. Klenck. LC 79-13449. 1979. 10.95 (ISBN 0-934878-35-8, 07764-1, Dist. by W.W. Norton). Dembner Bks.
Words for All Seasons. Arthur Lerner. (Illus.). 104p. (Orig.). 1983. pap. 6.95 (ISBN 0-938292-06-4). Being Bks.
Words for All Seasons: Selected Poems. 2nd ed. Jacques Prevert. Tr. by Teo Savory from Fr. LC 79-1179. (Illus.). 1979. 20.00 (ISBN 0-87775-121-8); pap. 8.00 (ISBN 0-87775-122-6). Unicorn Pr.
Words for Carla. Barbara B. Robinson. (Illus.). 72p. (Orig.). pap. 4.95 (ISBN 0-916630-48-X). Pr Pacifica.
Words for Clothing in the Principal Indo-European Languages. G. S. Lane. (LD Ser.). 1931. pap. 13.00 (ISBN 0-527-00755-2). Kraus Repr.
Words for "Horse" in French & Provencal. Clement M. Woodard. (Language Dissertation Ser.: No. 29). 1939. pap. 16.00 (ISBN 0-527-00775-7). Kraus Repr.
Words for Murder Perhaps. Edward Candy. 192p. 1985. pap. 2.75 (ISBN 0-345-31952-4). Ballantine.
Words for Music Perhaps. William B. Yeats. 60p. 1970. Repr. of 1932 ed. 15.00x (ISBN 0-7165-1375-7, BBA 02119, Pub. by Cuala Press Ireland). Biblio Dist.
Words for Puzzle Solvers. Dolores Holmquist. 144p. 1987. 9.95 (ISBN 0-8062-3133-5). Carlton.
Words for Reading: Reading for Words. Elton F. Henly. 1980. pap. text ed. write for info. (ISBN 0-13-964171-8). P-H.
Words: For Robert Burchfield's Sixty-Fifth Birthday. Ed. by E. G. Stanley & T. E. Hoad. 1988. 39.50 (ISBN 0-85991-259-0, Pub. by Boydell & Brewer). Longwood Pub Group.
Words for School Administrators: Examples of Commendations & Constructive Suggestions for Thorough Teacher Evaluation. rev. ed. Donald R. Wilson. LC 80-71091. 170p. 1983. 11.95x (ISBN 0-939136-00-7). Schl Admin Bkst.
Words for Students of English, Vol. 1. Ed. by Holly D. Rogerson & Lionel Menasche. (Pitt Series in English As a Second Language). (Illus.). 176p. (Orig.). 1988. pap. 12.95x (ISBN 0-8229-8218-8). U of Pittsburgh Pr.
Words for Students of English, Vol. 2. Ed. by Holly D. Rogerson & Lional Menasche. (Pitt Series in English As a Second Language). (Illus.). 200p. (Orig.). 1988. pap. 12.95x (ISBN 0-8229-8219-6). U of Pittsburgh Pr.
Words for Students of English, Vol. 3. Ed. by Holly D. Rogerson & Lionel Menasche. (Pitt Series in English As a Second Language). (Illus.). 216p. (Orig.). 1988. pap. 12.95x (ISBN 0-8229-8220-X). U of Pittsburgh Pr.
Words for Students of English, Vol. 4. Ed. by Holly D. Rogerson & Lionel Menasche. (Pitt Series in English As a Second Language). (Illus.). 232p. (Orig.). 1988. pap. 12.95x (ISBN 0-8229-8221-8). U of Pittsburgh Pr.
Words for Students of English, Vol. 5: A Vocabulary Series for ESL. Holly D. Rogerson et al. (Pitt Series in English as a Second Language). (Illus.). 272p. (Orig.). 1989. pap. text ed. 12.95x (ISBN 0-8229-8222-6). U of Pittsburgh Pr.
Words for Students of English, Vol. 6: A Vocabulary Series for ESL. Holly D. Rogerson et al. (Pitt Series in English As a Second Language). (Illus.). 272p. (Orig.). 1989. pap. text ed. 12.95x (ISBN 0-8229-8223-4). U of Pittsburgh Pr.
Words for Telemarketing. Steven Isaac. Date not set. 39.95 (ISBN 0-87280-158-6). Asher-Gallant.
Words for the Quiet Moments. Reva Mendes. 35p. 1973. pap. 1.00 (ISBN 0-87516-185-5). DeVorss.
Words for the Weary. Allen Puffenberger. (Orig.). 1987. pap. 7.25 (ISBN 0-89536-875-7, 7861). CSS of Ohio.
Words for the Wild: The Sierra Club Trailside Reader. Ed. by Ann Ronald. LC 86-22097. (Sierra Club Totebook Ser.). 384p. (Orig.). 1987. pap. 10.95 (ISBN 0-87156-709-1). Sierra.
Words for the Wind. T. K. Doraiswamy. (Greenbird Book). 76p. 1975. 14.00 (ISBN 0-88253-676-1); pap. cancelled (ISBN 0-88253-675-3). Ind-US Inc.
Words for Your Wedding: The Wedding Service Book. David Glusker & Peter Misner. LC 85-45353. 1986. pap. 7.95 (ISBN 0-06-063131-7, PL 4126, PL). Har-Row.
Words from a Deaf Child & Other Verses. Mervin D. Garretson. LC 84-81182. 128p. (Orig.). 1984. pap. 7.95 (ISBN 0-930805-00-3). Fragonard Pr.
Words from the Cross. Stephen C. Rowan. LC 87-51281. (Illus.). 64p. (Orig.). 1988. pap. 3.95 (ISBN 0-89622-354-X). Twenty-Third.
Words from the Heart. Rosemary Pavlina. 1987. 6.95 (ISBN 0-533-07252-2). Vantage.
Words from the Heart. Lisa Roose-Church. (Illus.). 24p. (Orig.). 1989. saddle stapled 2.50. Poetry Magic.
Words from the Land: Encounters with Natural History Writing. Ed. by Stephen Trimble. (Illus.). 352p. 1988. 17.95 (ISBN 0-87905-242-2). Gibbs Smith Pub.
Words from the Myths. Isaac Asimov. (Illus.). 224p. (gr. 5-10). 1961. 13.95 (ISBN 0-395-06568-2). HM.
Words from the Myths. Isaac Asimov. (Illus.). 144p. (RL 6). 1969. pap. 2.50 (ISBN 0-451-14097-4, Sig). NAL.
Words from the Source II. Starr Farish. (Illus.). 300p. 1987. 15.95 (ISBN 0-9605492-5-0). Touch Heart.
Words from Within. Marty Irwin. LC 85-4103. 62p. 1985. pap. 5.95 (ISBN 0-938232-94-0, Dist. by Baker & Taylor Co.). Winston-Derek.
Words God Gave Me. Hattie M. McDonald. 1986. cancelled (ISBN 0-8062-2303-0). Carlton.
Words in a Corner: Studies in Montaigne's Latin Quotations. Mary B. McKinley. LC 80-70810. (French Forum Monographs: No. 26). 129p. (Orig.). 1981. pap. 10.95x (ISBN 0-917058-25-9). French Forum.
Words in Action see Words That Make a Difference.
Words in Action: The Five C's Approach to Good Writing. John F. McGuire. LC 84-5182. 226p. (Orig.). 1984. lib. bdg. 27.50 (ISBN 0-8191-3951-3); pap. text ed. 11.25 (ISBN 0-8191-3952-1). U Pr of Amer.
Words in Color. rev. ed. Caleb Gattegno. (Orig.). (gr. k-12). 1977. Mini-charts 7.50 (ISBN 0-87825-143-X); Word Charts. 100.00 (ISBN 0-87825-131-6); Phonic Code Charts. 40.00 (ISBN 0-87825-132-4); Book R-0. 0.25 (ISBN 0-87825-127-8); Book R-1. 0.65 (ISBN 0-87825-128-6); Book R-2. 1.50 (ISBN 0-87825-129-4); Book R-3. 1.50 (ISBN 0-87825-130-8); Worksheets 1-7. 3.65 (ISBN 0-87825-178-2); Worksheets 8-14. 1.65 (ISBN 0-87825-059-X). Ed Solutions.
Words in Commotion. Tommaso Landolfi. Ed. by Kathrine Jason. LC 85-41063. 1986. 17.95 (ISBN 0-670-80518-1). Viking.
Words in Commotion: And Other Stories. Tommaso Landolfi. Ed. by Kathrine Jason. 324p. 1988. pap. 7.95 (ISBN 0-14-009477-6). Penguin.
Words in Everyday Life. G. L. Brook. 207p. 1981. 28.50x (ISBN 0-389-20218-5, 07000). B&N Imports.
Words in Flight: An Introduction to Poetry. Richard Abcarian. LC 79-181898. 267p. 1972. pap. 12.50 (ISBN 0-534-00147-5, WA). Krieger.
Words in Hock. Anne Atik. 1974. wrappers 3.50 (ISBN 0-685-46792-9, Pub. by Enitharmon Pr); 4.75 (ISBN 0-685-46793-7); special edition 150.00 (ISBN 0-685-46794-5). Small Pr Dist.
Words in Motion: Modern Japanese Calligraphy. Yomiuri Shimbun. (Illus.). 188p. (Orig.). 1984. 30.00 (ISBN 0-295-96238-0). U of Wash Pr.
Words in Our Hands. Ada B. Litchfield. Ed. by Kathleen Tucker. LC 79-28402. (Albert Whitman Concept Bks.: Level 2). (Illus.). (gr. 2-6). 1980. PLB 11.25 (ISBN 0-8075-9212-9). A Whitman.
Words in Our Pockets: The Feminist Writers Guild Handbook. Ed. by Celeste West. 368p. 15.95 (ISBN 0-913218-02-2); pap. 9.95 (ISBN 0-913218-01-4). Dustbooks.
Words in Our Pockets: The Feminist Writers' Guild Handbook on How to Get Published & Get Paid. Ed. by Celeste West. LC 81-2106. (Illus.). 368p. 1985. 15.95x (ISBN 0-912932-09-0); pap. 9.95x (ISBN 0-912932-10-4). Booklegger Pr.
Words in Pain. John J. Wright. LC 85-60470. (Illus.). 147p. 1986. 11.95 (ISBN 0-89870-070-1); pap. 7.95 (ISBN 0-89870-076-0). Ignatius Pr.
Words in Reflection: Modern Language Theory & Postmodern Fiction. Allen Thiher. LC 84-65. 256p. 1984. lib. bdg. 22.50x (ISBN 0-226-79491-1). U of Chicago Pr.
Words in Reflection: Modern Language Theory & Postmodern Fiction. Allen Thiher. LC 84-65. viii, 248p. 1987. pap. 10.95 (ISBN 0-226-79493-8). U of Chicago Pr.
Words in Reverse. Laurie Anderson. 16p. (Orig.). 1979. pap. 3.00 (ISBN 0-917061-02-0). Top Stories.
Words in Search of Victims: The Achievement of Jerzy Kosinski. Paul R. Lilly, Jr. LC 88-3021. 260p. 1988. 24.00x (ISBN 0-87338-366-4). Kent St U Pr.
Words in Season. Ivor Brown. LC 74-4839. 159p. 1974. Repr. of 1961 ed. lib. bdg. 35.00x (ISBN 0-8371-7489-9, BRWS). Greenwood.
Words in Stone: Pierre Ecrite. Yves Bonnefoy. Tr. by Susanna Lang. LC 75-32481. 160p. (Eng. & Fr.). 1976. lib. bdg. 14.00x (ISBN 0-87023-203-7). U of Mass Pr.
Words in Swedenborg & Their Meanings in Modern English. 54p. 1985. pap. 2.75 (ISBN 0-910557-13-6). Acad New Church.
Words in the Blood: Contemporary Indian Writers of North & South America. Ed. by Jamake Highwater. LC 84-4905. 416p. 1984. pap. 8.95 (ISBN 0-452-00680-5, Mer). NAL.
Words in the Mind: An Introduction to the Mental Lexicon. Jean Aitchison. 288p. Date not set. text ed. 39.95 (ISBN 0-631-14441-2); pap. text ed. 15.95 (ISBN 0-631-14442-0). Basil Blackwell.
Words in the Mind: Exploring Some Effects of Poetry, English & French. Charles Davy. 178p. 1983. Repr. of 1965 ed. lib. bdg. 30.00. Darby Bks.
Words in the Mourning Time: Poems. Robert Hayden. (Orig.). 1970. 7.95 (ISBN 0-8079-0161-X). October.
Words Index to James Joyce's Stephen Hero. Chester G. Anderson. LC 76-49592. 1977. lib. bdg. 27.50 (ISBN 0-8414-2961-8). Folcroft.
Words, Inspiration & Lovers. Susan A. Montelius. 6.95 (ISBN 0-317-53544-7). Vantage.
Words into Rhythm. D. W. Harding. LC 76-7805. 1976. 29.95 (ISBN 0-521-21267-7). Cambridge U Pr.
Words into Type. 3rd ed. M. Skillin & R. Gay. 1974. 35.95 (ISBN 0-13-964262-5). P-H.
Words Like Angels Come. Valiska Gregory. (William N. Judson Ser.: No. 24). 40p. (Orig.). (YA) (gr. 7 up). 1987. 15.00 (ISBN 1-55780-094-4); o. p. 25.00 (ISBN 1-55780-093-6); pap. 6.00 (ISBN 1-55780-095-2). Juniper Pr WI.
Words Like Arrows: A Treasure of Yiddish Folk Sayings. Compiled by Shirley Kumove. 288p. 1986. pap. 9.95 (ISBN 0-446-38193-4). Warner Bks.
Words Like These. Bruce Wetteroth. (Ohio Review Bks Ser.). 72p. 1986. 10.95 (ISBN 0-942148-07-X); pap. 5.95 (ISBN 0-942148-06-1). Ohio Review.
Words Made Easy. Visual Education Corporation Staff. LC 83-9816. (Illus.). 296p. (gr. 9 up). 1984. wkbk. 13.16 (ISBN 0-07-039664-7). McGraw.
Words Made Flesh: God Speaks to Us in the Ordinary Things of Life. Harry Blamires. 173p. (Orig.). 1985. pap. 6.95 (ISBN 0-89283-235-5). Servant.
Words Made Flesh: Scripture, Psychology & Human Communication. Fran Ferder. LC 85-73255. 184p. (Orig.). 1986. pap. 5.95 (ISBN 0-87793-331-6). Ave Maria.
Words, Meaning & People. Sanford Berman. LC 82-84221. 102p. 1982. pap. text ed. 7.00x (ISBN 0-918970-31-8). Intl Gen Semantics.
Words Most Often Misspelled & Mispronounced. Gleeson & Colvin. 1984. pap. 3.95 (ISBN 0-671-53154-9). PB.
Words of a Woman Who Breathes Fire. Kitty Tsui. LC 83-60254. 80p. 1983. pap. 5.95 (ISBN 0-933216-06-8). Spinsters Aunt Lute.
Words of Albert Schweitzer. Albert Schweitzer. Intro. by Norman Cousins. LC 84-18890. (Newmarket Words Ser.). (Illus.). 112p. 1984. 9.95 (ISBN 0-937858-41-2). Newmarket.
Words of Certitude. Pope John Paul II. 266p. 1985. pap. 7.95 large print ed. (ISBN 0-8027-2477-9). Walker & Co.
Words of Certitude: Excerpts from His Talks & Writings As Bishop & Pope. Pope John Paul II. Tr. by Anthon Buono from Ital. LC 80-81440. 136p. 1980. pap. 3.95 (ISBN 0-8091-2302-9). Paulist Pr.
Words of Cheer for Daily Life. C. H. Spurgeon. 1978. pap. 3.25 (ISBN 0-686-09101-9). Pilgrim Pubns.
Words of Christ. Illus. by Judy Pelikan. Ed. by Pat Golbitz. LC 86-60824. (Illus.). 64p. 1986. 15.95 (ISBN 0-688-06240-7). Morrow.
Words of Christ: Forty Meditations. Frank Topping. 126p. pap. 6.95 (ISBN 0-7188-2563-2, Pub. by Lutterwrth). Attic Pr.
Words of Comfort. J. R. Miller. (Illus.). 1976. 6.95 (ISBN 0-89957-518-8); pap. 4.95 (ISBN 0-89957-517-X). AMG Pubs.
Words of Comfort. (Words of ... Ser.). (Illus.). 48p. 1983. 3.95 (ISBN 0-8407-5331-4). Nelson.
Words of Comfort & Cheer. Charles E. Cowman. 1988. price not set (ISBN 0-310-35400-5). Zondervan.
Words of Comfort & Inspiration. Rodeney D. Roberts. 112p. 1989. 9.95 (ISBN 0-89962-788-9). Todd & Honeywell.
Words of Comfort: Consolation & Hope in Scripture. Mary H. Valentine. 1988. 10.95 (ISBN 0-88347-218-X). Thomas More.
Words of Conscience: Religious Statements on Conscientious Objection. 220p. 1983. 5.00 (ISBN 0-318-15981-3); 10 copies 45.00 (ISBN 0-318-15982-1). NISBCO.
Words of Counsel for Christian Workers. C. H. Spurgeon. 160p. 1985. pap. 3.29. Pilgrim Pubns.
Words of Delight: A Literary Introduction to the Bible. Leland Ryken. 372p. 1988. pap. 15.95 (ISBN 0-8010-7743-5). Baker Bk.
Words of Desmond Tutu. Selected by Naomi Tutu. (Illus.). 128p. 1989. 10.95 (ISBN 1-55704-038-9). Newmarket.
Words of Ecstasy in Sufism. Carl W. Ernst. LC 84-113. (SUNY Series in Islam). 184p. 1985. 49.50 (ISBN 0-87395-917-5); pap. 17.95 (ISBN 0-87395-918-3). State U NY Pr.
Words of Encouragement. (Words of ... Ser.). (Illus.). 48p. 1983. 3.95 (ISBN 0-8407-5332-2). Nelson.
Words of Eternal Life. (Illus.). 1988. 8.50 (ISBN 0-8198-8210-0, SC0475). Dghtrs St Paul.
Words of Faith. Karl Rahner. 96p. 1986. pap. 5.95 (ISBN 0-8245-0788-6). Crossroad NY.
Words of Faith. (Words of ... Ser.). (Illus.). 48p. 1983. 3.95 (ISBN 0-8407-5333-0). Nelson.
Words of Faith: A Devotional Dictionary. Charles S. Mueller. 160p. (Orig.). 1985. pap. 6.50 (ISBN 0-570-03968-1, 12-3003). Concordia.
Words of Friendship. (Words of ... Ser.). (Illus.). 48p. 1983. 3.95 (ISBN 0-8407-5334-9). Nelson.
Words of Gandhi. Intro. by Richard Attenborough. LC 82-14403. (Newmarket Words Ser.). (Illus.). 112p. 1982. 10.95 (ISBN 0-937858-14-5). Newmarket.

Wordstar, Lotus 1-2-3 & dBase III Plus: Student Software Manual. Ernest S. Colantonio. 219p. 1987. pap. text ed. 16.00 (ISBN 0-669-14114-3); Buttonware software kit IBM PC 21.50 (ISBN 0-669-11229-1); Buttonware software manual IBM PC 13.50 (ISBN 0-669-11231-3). Heath.
WordStar Made Easy. 2nd ed. Walter A. Ettlin. 164p. (Orig.). 1982. pap. text ed. 15.95 (ISBN 0-07-931090-7). Osborne-McGraw.
Wordstar, Mailmerge, Spellstar, Correctstar Step by Step. Raylene Dill. Ed. by Sherry Robson. handbook-workbook 24.50x (ISBN 0-89262-117-6); exercise disk Apple CPM avail. (ISBN 0-89262-119-2); IBM PC compatibles avail. (ISBN 0-89262-120-6); guide 50.00 (ISBN 0-89262-118-4). Career Pub.
WordStar on the IBM PC. Richard Curtis. (BYTE Bk.). 208p. 1985. pap. text ed. 11.95 (ISBN 0-07-014978-X). McGraw.
WordStar on the IBM PC. Rebecca C. Latif. 1985. pap. text ed. write for info. (ISBN 0-8359-8818-X, Reston). P-H.
Wordstar Procedures Manual. Dennis P. Curtin. (Illus.). 176p. 1988. manual 15.00 (ISBN 0-13-964321-4). P-H.
WordStar Professional: An Advanced Book. Ruth Ashley & Judi N. Fernandez. 1988. pap. 19.95 (ISBN 0-471-63619-3). Wiley.
WordStar Professional Made Easy. Walter A. Ettlin. 300p. 1988. pap. text ed. 17.95 (ISBN 0-07-881354-9). Osborne-McGraw.
WordStar Professional: The Complete Reference. Carole B. Matthews & Martin S. Matthews. 850p. 1988. cancelled (ISBN 0-07-881372-7); pap. text ed. 24.95 (ISBN 0-07-881332-8). Osborne-McGraw.
WordStar Professional: The Pocket Reference. Chris Gilbert. 128p. 1988. pap. text ed. 5.95 (ISBN 0-07-881402-2). Osborne-McGraw.
WordStar: Program Reference Guide. Kamphausen & Wiesa. 120p. 1987. text ed. 9.95 (ISBN 1-557550-08-5). Abacus Soft.
WordStar Quick & Dirty. Carol H. Ham. (Illus.). 162p. (Orig.). 1988. pap. 13.95 (ISBN 0-935920-43-9). Natl Pub Black Hills.
WordStar Quick Reference Handbook. Center for Professional Computer Education Staff. LC 86-15932. 192p. 1987. pap. 19.95 (ISBN 0-471-85375-5). Wiley.
WordStar Simplified for the IBM Personal Computer. Don Cassel. (Illus.). 160p. 1984. pap. text ed. 12.95 (ISBN 0-13-963612-9). P-H.
WordStar Simplified: Mastering the Essentials. Maureen A. Culleeney. (Illus.). 256p. 1985. pap. 17.95 (ISBN 0-13-963596-3). P-H.
WordStar Simplified with WordStar 3.3: MailMerge, Spellstar & StarIndex. Don Cassel. 176p. 1985. text ed. 24.33 (ISBN 0-13-963646-3); 14.95 (ISBN 0-13-963638-2). P-H.
WordStar Survivor's Guide to WordPerfect. WordPerfect Corporation Staff. 161p. (Orig.). 1987. pap. 12.95 (ISBN 1-55692-024-5). WordPerfect.
WordStar: The Second Phase. Emil Flock et al. 1988. pap. 21.95 (ISBN 0-673-38146-3). Scott F.
WordStar Tips & Techniques. Robert Wolenik. 1986. pap. 15.95 (ISBN 0-673-18601-6). Scott F.
WordStar Tips & Traps. Dick Andersen et al. 239p. (Orig.). 1986. pap. 17.95 (ISBN 0-89588-261-2). Sybex.
WordStar Training Manual: Word Processing on the Microcomputer. 3rd ed. Hannawell & Sorenson. (Illus.). 109p. (Orig.). 1985. pap. 11.95 spiral bound (ISBN 0-942728-09-2). Custom Pub Co.
Wordstar Without Tears: A Self-Teaching Guide. Ruth Ashley et al. LC 84-17314. 218p. 1985. pap. 16.95 (ISBN 0-471-80540-8). Wiley.
WordStar 2000 Plus Handbook. Greg M. Perry. 400p. 1988. pap. text ed. 21.95 (ISBN 0-07-881334-4). Osborne-McGraw.
WordStar 2000 Plus, Rel. 3.0 Step by Step Survival Text. Richard C. Bonen & Darla S. Babcock. Ed. by Sherry Robson. Date not set. handbook-wkbk. 24.50x (ISBN 0-89262-170-2); guide 50.00 (ISBN 0-89262-172-9); price not set exercise disk (ISBN 0-89262-171-0). Career Pub.
Wordstar 4.D Made Easy. Walter A. Ettlin. 300p. 1987. pap. text ed. 16.95 (ISBN 0-07-881011-6). Osborne-McGraw.
WordStrength. Joan Robinson. (Roots of Language Ser.). (gr. 4-8). 1989. pap. 7.95 (ISBN 0-8224-7451-4). D S Lake Pubs.
Wordsworth. Peter Burra. LC 73-10495. 1974. Repr. of 1936 ed. lib. bdg. 17.50 (ISBN 0-8414-3191-4). Folcroft.
Wordsworth. Peter Burra. LC 72-2096. (Studies in Wordsworth, No. 29). 1972. Repr. of 1935 ed. lib. bdg. 35.95x (ISBN 0-8383-1486-4). Haskell.
Wordsworth. Oliver Elton. LC 74-12494. 1924. lib. bdg. 15.00 (ISBN 0-8414-3962-1). Folcroft.
Wordsworth. Oliver Elton. 96p. 1980. Repr. of 1924 ed. 20.50 (ISBN 0-8492-0788-6). R West.
Wordsworth. Solomon F. Gingerich. LC 72-196436. 1908. lib. bdg. 20.00 (ISBN 0-8414-4651-2). Folcroft.
Wordsworth. William C. Hall. LC 75-15825. 1928. Repr. lib. bdg. 15.00 (ISBN 0-8414-4925-2). Folcroft.
Wordsworth. Charles H. Herford. LC 75-28999. Repr. of 1930 ed. 18.50 (ISBN 0-404-14010-6). AMS Pr.
Wordsworth. Charles H. Herford. LC 72-187481. 1930. lib. bdg. 25.00 (ISBN 0-685-10922-4). Folcroft.
Wordsworth. Andrew Lang. 1897. Repr. 25.00 (ISBN 0-8274-3742-0). R West.
Wordsworth. Compiled by & illus. by Patricia Machin. (Pocket Poets Ser.). (Illus.). 52p. 1987. 4.95 (ISBN 0-88162-298-2). Salem Hse Pubs.
Wordsworth. George Mallaby. LC 74-8475. 1950. Repr. lib. bdg. 25.50 (ISBN 0-8414-6132-5). Folcroft.
Wordsworth. Rosaline Masson. 1979. Repr. lib. bdg. 10.00 (ISBN 0-8495-3844-0). Arden Lib.
Wordsworth. F. W. Myers. Ed. by John Morley. LC 68-58389. (English Men of Letters Ser.). Repr. of 1888 ed. lib. bdg. 12.50 (ISBN 0-404-51721-8). AMS Pr.
Wordsworth. F. W. Myers. (English Men of Letters Ser.). 1979. Repr. of 1919 ed. lib. bdg. 15.00 (ISBN 0-8495-3829-7). Arden Lib.
Wordsworth. F. W. Myers. 1919. Repr. lib. bdg. 16.50 (ISBN 0-8414-6696-3). Folcroft.
Wordsworth. Walter A. Raleigh. LC 76-131811. 1970. Repr. of 1903 ed. 29.00x (ISBN 0-403-00698-8). Scholarly.
Wordsworth. Herbert E. Read. LC 83-1723. 194p. 1983. Repr. of 1958 ed. lib. bdg. 35.00x (ISBN 0-313-23321-7, REWO). Greenwood.
Wordsworth. Herbert E. Read. LC 83-45460. Repr. of 1949 ed. 25.00 (ISBN 0-404-20209-8). AMS Pr.
Wordsworth. F. W. Robertson. LC 76-21751. 1853. lib. bdg. 22.00 (ISBN 0-8414-7245-9). Folcroft.
Wordsworth. Elizabeth Wordsworth. 1891. 20.00 (ISBN 0-8274-3747-1). R West.
Wordsworth. William Wordsworth. (Plain Texts of the Poets Ser.). 1968. pap. 2.50x (ISBN 0-7022-0629-6). U of Queensland Pr.
Wordsworth: A Biographic Aesthetic Study. George H. Calvert. 1878. lib. bdg. 25.00 (ISBN 0-8414-1551-X). Folcroft.
Wordsworth: A Biographic Aesthetic Study. 1978. Repr. of 1878 ed. lib. bdg. 25.00 (ISBN 0-8495-0810-X). Arden Lib.
Wordsworth: A Collection of Critical Essays. Ed. by Meyer H. Abrams. 1972. 12.95 (Spec). P-H.
Wordsworth: A Critical Introduction. Paul Hamilton. LC 86-326. (Harvester New Readings Ser.). 172p. 1986. text ed. 29.95x (ISBN 0-391-03417-0). Humanities.
Wordsworth: A Lecture. George T. Smart. LC 77-24240. 1902. lib. bdg. 15.50 (ISBN 0-8414-7931-3). Folcroft.
Wordsworth: A Re-Interpretation. Frederick W. Bateson. LC 83-45410. Repr. of 1954 ed. 27.50 (ISBN 0-404-20020-6). AMS Pr.
Wordsworth: A Sense of History. Alan Liu. (Illus.). 650p. 1988. 39.50x (ISBN 0-8047-1373-1). Stanford U Pr.
Wordsworth: An Introduction & a Selection. Norman Nicholson. 1978. Repr. of 1949 ed. 25.00 (ISBN 0-8492-1964-7). R West.
Wordsworth & Coleridge. Guy Boas. 1925. 19.00 (ISBN 0-8274-3748-X). R West.
Wordsworth & Coleridge: Selected Critical Essays. William Wordsworth & Samuel Taylor Coleridge. Ed. by Thomas M. Raysor. LC 58-12022. (Crofts Classics Ser.). 1958. pap. text ed. 1.25x (ISBN 0-88295-104-1). Harlan Davidson.
Wordsworth & Coleridge: The Radical Years. Nicholas Roe. (Oxford English Monographs Ser.). (Illus.). 324p. 1988. 45.00 (ISBN 0-19-812868-1). Oxford U Pr.
Wordsworth & Coleridge 1795-1834. H. M. Margoliouth. LC 66-20231. vii, 206p. 1966. Repr. of 1953 ed. 21.50 (ISBN 0-208-00604-4, Archon). Shoe String.
Wordsworth & His Circle. David W. Rannie. LC 72-3432. (Studies in Wordsworth, No. 29). (Illus.). 1972. Repr. of 1907 ed. lib. bdg. 59.95x (ISBN 0-8383-1537-2). Haskell.
Wordsworth & His Message in Quest & Vision. W. J. Dawson. 1892. Repr. 15.00 (ISBN 0-8274-3749-8). R West.
Wordsworth & His Poetry. William H. Hudson. LC 73-120984. (Poetry & Life Ser.). Repr. of 1914 ed. 7.25 (ISBN 0-404-52520-2). AMS Pr.
Wordsworth & His Poetry. William H. Hudson. LC 72-191803. 1914. lib. bdg. 30.00 (ISBN 0-8414-5227-X). Folcroft.
Wordsworth & His Poetry. William H. Hudson. LC 70-103193. 1970. Repr. of 1914 ed. 24.00 (ISBN 0-8046-0830-X, Pub. by Kennikat). Assoc Faculty Pr.
Wordsworth & Jeffrey in Controversy. Russell Noyes. 1979. Repr. of 1939 ed. lib. bdg. 12.50 (ISBN 0-8274-4271-8). R West.
Wordsworth & Kipling in Collected Essays, Papers, Etc, Vol. 11. Robert Bridges. Repr. 10.00 (ISBN 0-8274-3750-1). R West.
Wordsworth & Literary Criticism. John A. Chapman. LC 76-30784. 1977. Repr. of 1932 ed. lib. bdg. 12.50 (ISBN 0-8414-3463-8). Folcroft.
Wordsworth & Philosophy. Newton P. Stallknecht. (Studies in Wordsworth, No. 29). 1970. Repr. of 1929 ed. lib. bdg. 50.00x (ISBN 0-8383-0345-5). Haskell.
Wordsworth & Philosophy: Empiricism & Transcendentalism in the Poetry. Keith G. Thomas. Ed. by Juliet McMaster. (Nineteenth-Century Studies). 1988. price not set (ISBN 0-8357-1880-8). UMI Res Pr.
Wordsworth & Pope. J. R. Sutherland. LC 75-33997. Repr. of 1944 ed. lib. bdg. 17.00 (ISBN 0-8414-7545-8). Folcroft.
Wordsworth & Schelling: A Typological Study of Romanticism. E. D. Hirsch, Jr. LC 71-163004. (Yale Studies in English Ser.: No. 145). xiii, 214p. 1971. Repr. of 1960 ed. 25.00 (ISBN 0-208-01128-5, Archon). Shoe String.
Wordsworth & Tennyson. David G. James. LC 74-28390. 1974. Repr. lib. bdg. 40.50 (ISBN 0-8414-5345-4). Folcroft.
Wordsworth & Tennyson. David G. James. LC 71-39860. (Studies in Comparative Literature, No. 35). 1970. pap. 12.95x (ISBN 0-8383-0046-4). Haskell.
Wordsworth & the Art of Landscape. Russell Noyes. LC 72-6864. (Studies in Wordsworth, No. 29). 1972. Repr. of 1968 ed. lib. bdg. 49.95x (ISBN 0-8383-1660-3). Haskell.
Wordsworth & the Beginnings of Modern Poetry. Robert Rehder. 246p. 1981. 27.50x (ISBN 0-389-20209-6). B&N Imports.
Wordsworth & the Coleridges. Ellis Yarnall. LC 77-21005. 1977. Repr. of 1909 ed. lib. bdg. 42.00 (ISBN 0-8414-9950-0). Folcroft.
Wordsworth & the Coleridges. Ellis Yarnell. 331p. 1980. Repr. of 1909 ed. lib. bdg. 45.00 (ISBN 0-8492-3120-5). R West.
Wordsworth & the Human Heart. John Beer. LC 78-15767. 277p. 1979. 32.00x (ISBN 0-231-04646-4). Columbia U Pr.
Wordsworth & the Lake District: A Guide to the Poems & Their Places. David McCracken. (Illus.). 320p. 1985. 24.00x (ISBN 0-19-212240-1); pap. 7.95 (ISBN 0-19-281396-X). Oxford U Pr.
Wordsworth & the Literature of Travel. Charles N. Coe. 1979. Repr. of 1953 ed. lib. bdg. 16.00x (ISBN 0-374-91791-4, Octagon). Hippocrene Bks.
Wordsworth & the Poetry of Encounter. Frederick Garber. LC 71-157888. 207p. 1971. 19.95 (ISBN 0-252-00184-2). U of Ill Pr.
Wordsworth & the Poetry of Epitaphs. D. D. Devlin. 143p. 1980. 28.50x (ISBN 0-389-20040-9). B&N Imports.
Wordsworth & the Poetry of Human Suffering. James H. Averill. LC 79-21783. 318p. 1980. 31.50x (ISBN 0-8014-1249-8). Cornell U Pr.
Wordsworth & the Poetry of Self-Sufficiency: A Study of the Poetic Development 1796-1814. Brian Cosgrove. Ed. by James Hogg. (Romantic Reassessment ser.). 327p. (Orig.). 1982. pap. 15.00 (ISBN 3-7052-0565-X, Pub. by Salzburg Studies). Longwood Pub Group.
Wordsworth & the Poetry of Sincerity. David D. Perkins. LC 64-10443. 1964. 20.00x (ISBN 0-674-95820-9, Belknap Pr). Harvard U Pr.
Wordsworth & "The Recluse". Kenneth R. Johnston. LC 83-19713. 397p. 1984. 35.00x (ISBN 0-300-03108-4). Yale U Pr.
Wordsworth & the Seventeenth Century. I. Crofts. LC 74-28470. lib. bdg. 15.00 (ISBN 0-8414-3501-4). Folcroft.
Wordsworth & the Vocabulary of Emotion. Josephine Miles. 1965. lib. bdg. 18.00x (ISBN 0-374-95681-2, Octagon). Hippocrene Bks.
Wordsworth & the Worth of Words. Hugh S. Davies. Ed. by John Kerrigan & Jonathan Wordsworth. 336p. 1987. 49.50 (ISBN 0-521-30909-3). Cambridge U Pr.
Wordsworth & Tolstoi & Other Papers. Anna M. Guthrie. LC 74-7283. 1922. Repr. lib. bdg. 20.50 (ISBN 0-8414-4507-9). Folcroft.
Wordsworth as Critic. Warwick J. Owen. LC 73-398699. pap. 63.50 (2026371). Bks Demand UMI.
Wordsworth Chronology. F. B. Pinion. 160p. 1988. lib. bdg. 35.00x (ISBN 0-8161-8950-1, Hall Reference). G K Hall.
Wordsworth Country: As Interpreted by His Poetry. Easton S. Valentine. 25.00 (ISBN 0-8274-3752-8). R West.
Wordsworth Criticism since Nineteen Fifty-Two: A Bibliography. Ronald B. Hearn. Ed. by James Hogg. (Romantic Reassessment Ser.). 93p. (Orig.). 1978. pap. 15.00 (ISBN 3-7052-0545-5, Pub. by Salzburg Studies). Longwood Pub Group.
Wordsworth Dictionary of Persons & Places with Familiar Quotations from His Works. John R. Tutin. LC 79-76128. (Bibliography & Reference Ser.: No. 267). 1969. Repr. of 1891 ed. 16.00 (ISBN 0-8337-3582-9). B Franklin.
Wordsworth Dictionary of Persons & Places with the Familiar Quotations from His Works Including Index & a Chronologically Arranged List of His Best Poems, 2 vols in 1. John R. Tutin. LC 1-12935. Repr. of 1891 ed. 17.00 (ISBN 0-384-62050-7). Johnson Repr.
Wordsworth, Freud & the Spots of Time: Interpretation in 'The Prelude' David Ellis. 200p. 1985. 37.50 (ISBN 0-521-26555-X). Cambridge U Pr.
Wordsworth: How to Know Him. C. T. Winchester. 1916. 30.00 (ISBN 0-8274-3746-3). R West.
Wordsworth in a New Light. Emile Legouis. LC 75-43580. 1923. lib. bdg. 15.00 (ISBN 0-8414-5651-8). Folcroft.
Wordsworth in among My Books. James R. Lowell. (Nd Series). Repr. 20.00 (ISBN 0-8274-3753-6). R West.
Wordsworth in Democracy & Other Addresses. James R. Lowell. Repr. 20.00 (ISBN 0-8274-3754-4). R West.
Wordsworth in Early American Criticism. Annabel Newton. LC 74-23675. 1974. Repr. lib. bdg. 35.00 (ISBN 0-8414-6281-X). Folcroft.
Wordsworth in England. Katherine Peek. LC 74-86283. 1969. Repr. of 1943 ed. lib. bdg. 20.00x (ISBN 0-374-96346-0, Octagon). Hippocrene Bks.
Wordsworth in Literature & Life. Edwin P. Whipple. 1873. 40.00 (ISBN 0-8274-3755-2). R West.
Wordsworth in "Science & Literary Criticism". Herbert Dingle. 1949. Repr. 20.00 (ISBN 0-8274-3756-0). R West.
Wordsworth: Lectures & Essays. Heathcote W. Garrod. LC 75-28997. Repr. of 1923 ed. 20.00 (ISBN 0-404-14008-4). AMS Pr.
Wordsworth: Play & Politics, a Study of Wordsworth's Poetry, 1787-1800. John Turner. LC 85-14535. 192p. 1986. 25.00 (ISBN 0-312-88940-2). St Martin.
Wordsworth: Poems. William Wordsworth. Selected by W. E. Williams. (Poetry Library). 192p. 1985. pap. 4.95 (ISBN 0-14-058506-0). Penguin.
Wordsworth: Poetical Works. rev. ed. William Wordsworth. Ed. by Thomas Hutchinson & Ernest De Selincourt. (Oxford Standard Author Ser.). (Illus.). 1950. Repr. of 1936 ed. leatherbound 60.00. Oxford U Pr.
Wordsworth: Poetry & Prose with Essays by Coleridge, Hazlitt & Dequincey. David N. Smith. 1921. 20.00 (ISBN 0-8274-3744-7). R West.
Wordsworth: Selected Poems. William Wordsworth. Ed. by George W. Meyer. LC 50-8748. (Crofts Classics Ser.). 1950. pap. text ed. 3.95x (ISBN 0-88295-103-3). Harlan Davidson.
Wordsworth, Shelley, Keats, & Other Essays. new ed. David Masson. LC 72-13205. (Essay Index Reprint Ser.). Repr. of 1875 ed. 18.75 (ISBN 0-8369-8168-5). Ayer Co Pubs.
Wordsworth, Shelley, Keats, & Other Essays. David Masson. LC 68-58239. (Research & Source Ser.: No. 489). 1970. Repr. of 1875 ed. lib. bdg. 18.50 (ISBN 0-8337-2292-1). B Franklin.
Wordsworth, Shelley, Keats, & Other Essays. David Masson. LC 72-196538. 1874. lib. bdg. 25.50 (ISBN 0-8414-6496-0). Folcroft.
Wordsworth since Nineteen Sixteen. Richard A. Rice. LC 76-43095. 1924. lib. bdg. 17.00 (ISBN 0-8414-7336-6). Folcroft.
Wordsworth: The Chronology of the Middle Years, 1800-1815. Mark L. Reed. LC 74-77179. 768p. 1975. text ed. 37.00x (ISBN 0-674-95777-6). Harvard U Pr.
Wordsworth Treasury. William Wordsworth. (Illus.). 48p. 1978. 5.95 (ISBN 0-85683-043-7). Dufour.
Wordsworth, Turner, & Romantic Landscape: A Study of the Traditions of the Picturesque & the Sublime. Matthew C. Brennan. LC 87-70973. (Studies in English & American Literature, Linguistics & Culture: Vol. 5). (Illus.). 165p. 1987. 28.00x (ISBN 0-938100-51-3). Camden Hse.
Wordsworthian Criticism. James V. Logan. LC 74-7025. 304p. 1974. Repr. of 1961 ed. 35.00x (ISBN 0-87752-171-9). Gordian.
Wordsworthian Criticism 1964-1973: An Annotated Bibliography. David H. Stam. LC 72-81870. 120p. 1974. 15.00 (ISBN 0-87104-237-1). NY Pub Lib.
Wordsworthiana. William Knight. LC 77-22726. 1977. Repr. of 1889 ed. lib. bdg. 49.50 (ISBN 0-8414-5548-1). Folcroft.
Wordsworth's Art of Allusion. Edwin Stein. LC 86-43026. 256p. 1988. 23.50x (ISBN 0-271-00483-5). Pa St U Pr.
Wordsworth's Formative Years. George W. Meyer. LC 74-3373. 1943. Repr. lib. bdg. 30.00 (ISBN 0-8414-6119-8). Folcroft.
Wordsworth's French Daughter. George M. Harper. LC 78-3810. 1921. lib. bdg. 16.00 (ISBN 0-8414-4960-0). Folcroft.
Wordsworth's Great Period Poems: Four Essays. Marjorie Levinson. 176p. 1986. 32.50 (ISBN 0-521-30829-1). Cambridge U Pr.
Wordsworth's Heroes. Willard Spiegelman. LC 84-28015. 1985. 35.00x (ISBN 0-520-05365-6). U of Cal Pr.
Wordsworth's Informed Reader: Structures of Experience in His Poetry. Susan E. Meisenhelder. LC 86-28169. 256p. Date not set. 22.95x (ISBN 0-8265-1218-6). Vanderbilt U Pr.
Wordsworth's Interest in Painters & Pictures. Martha H. Shackford. LC 75-30013. Repr. of 1945 ed. 16.00 (ISBN 0-404-14019-X). AMS Pr.
Wordsworth's Interest in Painters & Pictures. Martha H. Shackford. 1979. Repr. of 1945 ed. lib. bdg. 15.00 (ISBN 0-8495-4916-7). Arden Lib.
Wordsworth's Interest in Painters & Pictures. Martha H. Shackford. LC 78-1082. 1973. Repr. of 1945 ed. 15.00 (ISBN 0-8492-2460-8). R West.
Wordsworth's Language of Men. J. P. Ward. LC 84-11076. 256p. 1984. 28.50x (ISBN 0-389-20500-1). B&N Imports.
Wordsworth's Literary Criticism. Nowell C. Smith. 1905. lib. bdg. 40.50 (ISBN 0-8414-7854-6). Folcroft.

Work Capacity Restraints in Tropical Agricultural Development. Hartmut Brandt. (Medical Care in Developing Countries Ser.: Vol. 8). 278p. 1980. 28.90 (ISBN 3-8204-6900-1). P Lang Pubs.
Work Center Management Training Aid. LC 85-70229. 42p. 1985. 28.00 (ISBN 0-935406-63-8). Am Prod & Inventory.
Work, Community & Power: The Experience of Labor in Europe & America, 1900-1925. Ed. by James E. Cronin & Carmen Sirianni. 306p. 1983. 29.95 (ISBN 0-87722-308-4); pap. text ed. 12.95 (ISBN 0-87722-309-2). Temple U Pr.
Work Concerning the Trewnesse of the Christian Religion. Philippe de Mornay. Tr. by Philip Sidney from Fr. LC 75-45384. 680p. 1976. Repr. of 1587 ed. lib. bdg. 90.00x (ISBN 0-8201-1166-X). Schol Facsimiles.
Work Control. Intro. by David R. Howard. 143p. 1988. pap. 25.00 (ISBN 0-913359-44-0). Assn Phys Plant Admin.
Work Creation. M. P. Jackson & V. Hanby. 168p. 1979. text ed. 35.50x (ISBN 0-566-00287-6). Gower Pub Co.
Work Culture & Society in Industrializing America: Essays in America's Working Class & Social History. Herbert G. Gutman. 1977. pap. 6.36 (ISBN 0-394-72251-5, Vin). Random.
Work, Culture & Society: Issues & Debates in the Sociology of Work. Ed. by Rosemary Deem & Graeme Salaman. LC 85-11542. 256p. 1985. 65.00x (ISBN 0-335-15136-1, Open Univ Pr); pap. 24.00x (ISBN 0-335-15135-3, Open Univ Pr). Taylor & Francis.
Work Decisions in the Nineteen Eighties. Eli Ginzberg et al. 137p. 1982. 24.95 (ISBN 0-86569-094-4). Auburn Hse.
Work Disincentive Effects of Unemployment Insurance. Raymond Munts & Irwin Garfinkel. 65p. 1974. pap. 1.00 (ISBN 0-911558-24-1). W E Upjohn.
Work, Distances: Poems. Ken Smith. LC 75-189189. 98p. 1972. 7.95 (ISBN 0-8040-0588-5, Pub by Swallow); (Pub by Swallow). Ohio U Pr.
Work-Education Council: Profiles of Collaborative Efforts. Ed. by Lois Rudick. 180p. 1979. 10.00. Natl Inst Work.
Work-Education Councils: Profiles of Collaborative Efforts. Ed. by Lois Rudick. 180p. 1979. 10.00. Nat'l Inst Work.
Work-Education Exchange, Vol. 4 No. 4. 12p. 2.00. Natl Inst Work.
Work, Employment & Unemployment: Perspectives on Work & Society. Ed. by Kenneth Thompson. 1985. pap. 26.00x (ISBN 0-335-10594-7, Open Univ Pr). Taylor & Francis.
Work Ethic: An Analytical View, 1983. 15.00 (ISBN 0-913447-24-2). Indus Relations Res.
Work Ethic in Business: Proceedings of the Third National Conference on Business Ethics. Ed. by W. Michael Hoffman & Thomas J. Wyly. LC 80-22708. (Ethics Resource Center Ser.). 384p. 1981. text ed. 30.00 (ISBN 0-89946-068-2). Oelgeschlager.
Work Ethic in Industrial America Eighteen Fifty to Nineteen Twenty. Daniel T. Rodgers. LC 77-81737. 1980. pap. 9.00X (ISBN 0-226-72352-6, 9-860, Phoen). U of Chicago Pr.
Work Ethic in Industrial America: 1850-1920. Daniel T. Rodgers. LC 77-81737. 1978. lib. bdg. 26.00x (ISBN 0-226-72351-8). U of Chicago Pr.
Work Ethic: Pride, or Mental Illness. E. Jordan Blakely. Ed. by M. Sarah Ross. 1985. pap. 7.95 (ISBN 0-9614582-0-8). Blakely.
Work Ethic: Working Values & Values That Work. David J. Cherrington. LC 80-65871. pap. 75.50 (ISBN 0-317-26705-1, 2023512). Bks Demand UMI.
Work Evaluation & Adjustment: An Annotated Bibliography 1984. rev. ed. Ronald Fry. 252p. 1985. pap. 21.50x (ISBN 0-916671-62-3). Material Dev.
Work Experience & Psychological Development Through the Lifespan. Ed. by Jeylan Mortimer & Kathryn M. Borman. (AAAS Selected Symposium Ser.: No. 107). 320p. 1987. pap. 29.95 (ISBN 0-8133-7467-7). Westview.
Work Experience in Secondary Schools. Ed. by John Eggleston. (Routledge Education Bks.). 192p. 1983. 21.50x (ISBN 0-7100-9219-9). Routledge Chapman & Hall.
Work Experiment: Six Americans in a Swedish Plant. Robert B. Goldmann. LC 75-45049. 48p. 1976. pap. 3.50 (ISBN 0-916584-00-3). Ford Found.
Work, Family & Personality. Jeylan Mortimer et al. Ed. by Gerald Platt. LC 85-20951. (Modern Sociology Ser.). 272p. 1986. text ed. 37.50 (ISBN 0-89391-293-X). Ablex Pub.
Work Family Sex Roles Language. Ed. by Mario Barrera. LC 80-53691. 1980. pap. 6.00 (ISBN 0-89229-007-2). Tonatiuh-Quinto Sol Intl.
Work for Being in the Machine Age. Donald Petacchi. LC 80-82646. 174p. 1980. 13.95 (ISBN 0-8022-2376-1). Philos Lib.
Work for Profit: Fun, Health, Happiness, Security. O. A. Battista. LC 75-8351. 1975. pap. 4.95 (ISBN 0-915074-02-8). Knowledge TX.
Work (Four Issues) Ed. by John Sinclair & Ron Caplan. Bd. with Whe're (One Issue. (Avant-Garde Magazines Ser.). 716p. 1972. Repr. of 1965 ed. 44.00 (ISBN 0-405-01754-5). Ayer Co Pubs.
Work from Waste: Recycling Wastes to Create Employment. Jon Vogler. (Illus.). 396p. (Orig.). 1981. pap. 15.25x (ISBN 0-903031-79-5, Pub. by Intermediate Tech England). Intermediate Tech.
Work Furlough & the County Jail. Alvin Rudoff. 212p. 1975. 19.00 (ISBN 0-398-03437-0). C C Thomas.
Work-Game Sheets for Magnet Magic Etc. Marie A. Hoyt. (Illus.). 28p. (Orig.). (gr. 2-8). 1984. pap. text ed. 2.50 (ISBN 0-914911-03-1). Educ Serv Pr.
Work Groups: A Bibliography. Marian Dworaczek. (Public Administration Ser.: P 2142). 16p. 1987. 5.00 (ISBN 1-55590-282-0). Vance Biblios.
Work Hard & You Shall Be Rewarded: Urban Folklore from the Paperwork Empire. Alan Dundes & Carl R. Pagter. LC 77-74429. (Midland Bks: No. 207). (Illus.). 248p. 1978. pap. 6.95 (ISBN 0-253-20207-8). Ind U Pr.
Work Hardening. Ed. by J. P. Hirth & J. Weertman. LC 67-29669. (Metallurgical Society Conference Ser.: No. 46). pap. 98.50 (ISBN 0-317-11258-9, 2001534). Bks Demand UMI.
Work Hardening in Tension & Fatigue: Proceedings of a Symposium, Cincinnati, Ohio, Nov. 11, 1975. Ed. by Anthony W. Thompson. LC 77-76058. pap. 66.30 (ISBN 0-317-08184-5, 2015014). Bks Demand UMI.
Work Hazards & Industrial Conflict. Carl Gersuny. LC 80-51506. (Illus.). 178p. 1981. 20.00x (ISBN 0-87451-189-5). U Pr of New Eng.
Work, Health, & Income among the Elderly. Ed. by Gary Burtless. LC 86-26892. (Studies in Social Economics). 276p. 1987. pap. 26.95 (ISBN 0-8157-1176-X). Brookings.
Work in America: Report of a Special Task Force to the Secretary of Health, Education, & Welfare. U. S. Department of Health, Education, & Welfare. 262p. 1973. pap. 8.95x (ISBN 0-262-58023-3). MIT Pr.
Work in America: The Decade Ahead. Ed. by Clark Kerr & Jerome M. Rosow. (Work in America Ser.). 1979. 22.95 (ISBN 0-442-20372-1). Van Nos Reinhold.
Work in France: Representations, Meaning, Organization, & Practice. Ed. by Steven L. Kaplan & Cynthia J. Koepp. LC 85-22352. (Illus.). 576p. 1986. 44.50x (ISBN 0-8014-1697-3). Cornell U Pr.
Work in Intergovernmental Organizations on Transnational Companies. International Fiscal Association. (Congress Seminar Series of the International Fiscal Association: No. 1). 1979. pap. 16.00 (ISBN 90-200-0491-3, Pub. by Kluwer Law Netherlands). Kluwer Academic.
Work in Market & Industrial Societies. Ed. by Herbert Applebaum. LC 83-9267. (Anthropology of Work Ser.). 316p. 1984. 44.50x (ISBN 0-87395-810-1); pap. 12.95 (ISBN 0-87395-811-X). State U NY Pr.
Work in Modern Society: A Sociology Reader. Lauri Perman. 304p. 1985. pap. text ed. 22.95 (ISBN 0-8403-3846-5). Kendall-Hunt.
Work in Mound Exploration of the Bureau of Ethnology. Cyrus Thomas. Repr. of 1887 ed. 25.00x (ISBN 0-403-03727-1). Scholarly.
Work in Non-Market & Transitional Societies. Ed. by Herbert Applebaum. LC 83-4970. (Anthropology of Work Ser.). 398p. 1984. 44.50 (ISBN 0-87395-774-1); pap. 12.95 o.s.i (ISBN 0-87395-775-X). State U NY Pr.
Work in Progress. Kevin Power & Ian Tyson. 1977. 1.75 (ISBN 0-685-04202-2, Pub. by Trigram Pr). Small Pr Dist.
Work in Progress: Joyce Centenary Essays. Ed. by Richard F. Peterson et al. LC 82-16943. 192p. 1983. 18.95x (ISBN 0-8093-1094-5). S Ill U Pr.
Work-in-Progress Notebook for Writers. Kimberly Coale. 52p. (Orig.). 1987. pap. 7.00 (ISBN 0-936993-10-3, 87-9-X). Europa Media.
Work in Progress on Alcoholism, Vol. 273. Ed. by Frank A. Seixas & Suzie Eggleston. (Annals of the New York Academy of Sciences). 664p. 1976. 43.00x (ISBN 0-89072-052-5). NY Acad Sci.
Work in the English Novel: The Myth of Vocation. Ruth Danon. LC 83-22890. 222p. 1986. 29.95x (ISBN 0-389-20599-0). B&N Imports.
Work in the Hood: The First Entertaining Organic Chemistry Laboratory Guide. James W. Zubrick. LC 80-69113. (Illus.). 120p. (Orig.). 1980. pap. 4.50 (ISBN 0-937926-00-0). Scienspot.
Work in the Nineteen Eighties: Emancipation & Derogation. Bengtove Gustavsson & Jan Karlsson. 220p. 1985. text ed. 34.50 (ISBN 0-566-00862-9). Gower Pub Co.
Work in the Soviet Union: Attitudes & Issues. Murray Yanowitch. LC 84-27651. 216p. 1985. 35.00 (ISBN 0-87332-307-6). M E Sharpe.
Work in the Twenty-First Century. American Society for Personnel Administration Staff. (Orig.). 1984. pap. text ed. 6.50. Am Soc Personnel.
Work in the Twenty-First Century: An Anthology of Writings. Isaac Asimov et al. 132p. (Orig.). 1984. 14.95 (ISBN 0-88254-939-1); pap. 5.95. Hippocrene Bks.
Work Incentive Experience. Ed. by Charles Garvin et al. LC 77-83926. 256p. 1978. text ed. 23.50x (ISBN 0-916672-99-9, Pub. by Allanheld). Rowman.
Work Incentives & Income Guarantees: The New Jersey Negative Income Tax Experiment. Ed. by Joseph A. Pechman & P. Michael Timpane. LC 75-2321. (Studies in Social Experimentation). 232p. 1975. 28.95 (ISBN 0-8157-6976-8); pap. 10.95 (ISBN 0-8157-6975-X). Brookings.
Work Incentives for the Disabled & Blind Under the Social Security & Supplemental Income Programs: A Training Aid for Vocational Rehabilitation Counselors. 36p. 1985. 4.00 (39,890). NCLS Inc.
Work, Income & Inequality. Frances Stewart. LC 81-24065. 304p. 1982. 32.50x (ISBN 0-312-88943-7). St Martin.
Work Independence & the Severely Disabled: A Bibliography. Gerardo Bilotto & Veronica Washam. LC 79-91351. 108p. 1980. 7.50 (ISBN 0-686-38821-6). Human Res Ctr.
Work Is Dangerous to Your Health: A Handbook of Health Hazards in the Workplace & What You Can Do about Them. Susan M. Daum & Jeanne M. Stellman. 1973. pap. 7.95 (ISBN 0-394-71918-2, V-918, Vin). Random.
Work Is Dangerous to Your Health: A Handbook of Health Hazards in the Workplace & What You Can Do about Them. Jeanne M. Stellman & Susan M. Daum. LC 72-12386. 1973. pap. 5.95. Pantheon.
Work Is Hell: A Cartoon Book. Matt Groening. LC 86-42637. 48p. pap. 5.95 (ISBN 0-394-74864-6). Pantheon.
Work, Its Rewards & Discontents Series, 65 vols. Ed. by Leon Stein. (Illus.). 1977. lib. bdg. 1784.00 (ISBN 0-405-10150-3). Ayer Co Pubs.
Work, Jobs, & Occupations: A Critical Review of the Dictionary of Occupational Titles. 431p. 1980. pap. 14.95x (ISBN 0-309-03093-5). Natl Acad Pr.
Work, Learning, & the American Future. James O'Toole. LC 76-50726. (Higher Education Ser.). 256p. 1977. text ed. 27.95x (ISBN 0-87589-304-X). Jossey-Bass.
Work-Leisure Trade Off: Reduced Work Time for Managers & Professionals. Ann Harriman. LC 81-17782. 200p. 1982. 35.00 (ISBN 0-275-90814-3, C0814). Praeger.
Work-Life Book: Managing Your Life. Richard Gillespie. Ed. & illus. by Dan Youra. (Illus.). 186p. (Orig.). 1988. pap. 9.95 (ISBN 0-317-69959-8). Olympic Pub.
Work Lights. David Young. LC 77-75642. (CSU Poetry Ser.: No. 4). 45p. 1977. pap. 4.75 (ISBN 0-914946-06-4). Cleveland St Univ Poetry Ctr.
Work, Marriage & Motherhood: The Career Persistence of Female Physicians. Dorothy Mandelbaum. LC 81-1420. 320p. 1981. 40.95 (ISBN 0-275-90676-0, C0676). Praeger.
Work Measurement: A Guidebook to Word Processing Management. 2nd ed. Arthur L. Thursland. 1981. text ed. 45.00 (ISBN 0-935220-01-1). Assn Info Sys.
Work Measurement: A Systems Approach. George L. Smith. LC 77-89953. (Illus.). pap. 25.30 (ISBN 0-317-10683-X, 2015250). Bks Demand UMI.
Work Measurement in Banking. 2nd ed. Donald L. Caruth. LC 84-2872. 250p. 1984. text ed. 47.00 (ISBN 0-87267-045-7). Bank Admin Inst.
Work Measurement: Principles & Practice. Ed. by Richard L. Shell. 1986. 39.95 (ISBN 0-89806-085-0). Inst Indus Eng.
Work, Mobility, & Participation: A Comparative Study of American & Japanese Industry. Robert E. Cole. LC 77-80468. 304p. 1979. 35.00x (ISBN 0-520-03542-9); pap. 12.95x (ISBN 0-520-04204-2). U of Cal Pr.
Work Motivation Attitudes of Apparel Workers: Methodology Used in the Study. Emma W. Bragg. LC 83-61829. (Illus.). 186p. 1983. pap. 24.75 (ISBN 0-9611930-0-X). E W Bragg.
Work Motivation: Theory, Issues, & Applications. Craig C. Pinder. (Scott, Foresman Series in Organizational Behavior & Human Resources). 1984. pap. write for info. (ISBN 0-673-15799-7). Scott F.
Work Nineteen Sixty-One to Nineteen Seventy-Three. Yvonne Rainer. LC 73-87480. (Nova Scotia Ser.). (Illus.). 338p. 1974. o.s.i 40.00x (ISBN 0-8147-7360-5). NYU Pr.
Work of a Common Woman: Collected Poetry (1964-1977) Judy Grahn. LC 79-27318. (Feminist Ser.). 158p. 1984. 19.95 (ISBN 0-89594-156-2, C1978); pap. 7.95 (ISBN 0-89594-155-4). Crossing Pr.
Work of Adalbert Johann Volck, 1828-1912: Who Chose for His Name the Anagram, V. Blada, 1861-1865. George M. Anderson. (Illus.). 222p. 1970. 20.00 (ISBN 0-938420-19-4). Md Hist.
Work of an Evangelist. Karl G. Wilks. 45p. (Orig.). 1987. pap. 5.00 (ISBN 0-9616912-1-2). K G Wilks.
Work of an Evangelist. 888p. 1984. 19.95 (ISBN 0-89066-049-2). World Wide Pubs.
Work of Atget, 4 vols. John Szarkowoski & Maria M. Hambourg. (Illus.). 1985. Set. 700.00 (ISBN 0-317-68572-4, Pub. by Gordon Fraser). State Mutual Bk.
Work of Atget: Modern Times, Vol. IV. John Szarkowski & Maria M. Hambourg. (Illus.). 192p. 1985. 45.00 (ISBN 0-87070-218-1, 954187, Pub. by Museum Mod Art). NYGS.
Work of Atget: Old France, Vol. I. John Szarkowski & Maria M. Hambourg. LC 81-80130. (Illus.). 180p. 1981. 40.00 (ISBN 0-87070-204-1, 056502, Pub. by Museum Mod Art). NYGS.
Work of Atget: The Ancien Regime, Vol. III. John Szarkowski & Maria M. Hambourg. LC 81-80130. (Illus.). 192p. 1983. 40.00 (ISBN 0-87070-217-3, 954179, Pub. by Museum Mod Art). NYGS.
Work of Atget: The Art of Old Paris, Vol. II. John Szarkowski & Maria M. Hambourg. 192p. 1982. 40.00 (ISBN 0-87070-212-2, 954160, Pub. by Museum Mod Art). NYGS.
Work of Augustus Saint-Gaudens. John H. Dryfhout. LC 82-7095. (Illus.). 368p. 1985. 60.00x (ISBN 0-87451-243-3); pap. 29.95 (ISBN 0-87451-287-5). U Pr of New Eng.
Work of Ben Jonson. Ben Jonson. Ed. by C. H. Herford et al. Incl. Vol. 1. 54.00x (ISBN 0-19-811352-8); Vol. 2. 54.00x (ISBN 0-19-811353-6); Vol. 5. 54.00x (ISBN 0-19-811356-0); Vol. 7. 54.00x (ISBN 0-19-811358-7); Vol. 8. 54.00x (ISBN 0-19-811359-5); Vol. 10. 54.00x (ISBN 0-19-811361-7); Vol. 11. 54.00x (ISBN 0-19-811362-5). 1925-52. Oxford U Pr.
Work of Bernardino de Sahagun: Pioneer Ethnographer of Sixteenth-Century Aztec Mexico. Ed. by J. Jorge Klor de Alva et al. LC 87-83484. (Institute for Mesoamerican Studies on Culture and Society Ser.: No. 2). (Illus.). 372p. (Orig.). 1988. pap. text ed. 25.00x (ISBN 0-942041-11-9). U of Tex Pr.
Work of Boards of Education. Hans C. Olsen. LC 77-177134. (Columbia University. Teachers College. Contributions to Education: No. 213). Repr. of 1926 ed. 22.50 (ISBN 0-404-55213-7). AMS Pr.
Work of Brian W. Aldiss: An Annotated Bibiography & Guide. Margaret Aldiss. LC 87-746. (Bibliographies of Modern Authors Ser.: No. 9). 200p. 1988. lib. bdg. 22.95x (ISBN 0-89370-388-5); pap. text ed. 12.95x (ISBN 0-89370-488-1). Borgo Pr.
Work of Bruce McAllister: An Annotated Bibliography & Guide. rev. ed. David R. Bourquin. LC 85-22400. (Bibliographies of Modern Authors Ser.: No. 10). 32p. 1986. lib. bdg. 19.95x (ISBN 0-89370-389-3); pap. text ed. 9.95x (ISBN 0-89370-489-X). Borgo Pr.
Work of Chad Oliver: An Annotated Bibliography & Guide. H. W. Hall. LC 86-2288. (Bibliographies of Modern Authors Ser.: No. 12). 60p. 1988. lib. bdg. 19.95x (ISBN 0-89370-391-5); pap. text ed. 9.95x (ISBN 0-89370-491-1). Borgo Pr.
Work of Charles Abrams: Housing & Urban Renewal in the U. S. A. & the Third World. Ed. by O. H. Koenigsberger et al. (Illus.). 264p. 1981. 94.00 (ISBN 0-08-026111-6). Pergamon.
Work of Charles Beaumont: An Annotated Bibliography & Guide. William F. Nolan. LC 85-460. (Bibliographies of Modern Authors Ser.: No. 6). 48p. 1986. lib. bdg. 19.95x (ISBN 0-89370-385-0); pap. text ed. 9.95x (ISBN 0-89370-485-7). Borgo Pr.
Work of Christ see Studies in Dogmatics: Theology.
Work of Colin Wilson: An Annotated Bibliography & Guide. Colin Stanley. LC 84-11181. (Bibliographies of Modern Authors Ser.: No. 1). 200p. (Orig.). 1988. lib. bdg. 24.95x (ISBN 0-89370-817-8); pap. text ed. 14.95x (ISBN 0-89370-917-4). Borgo Pr.
Work of Craft. Carla Needleman. 160p. 1981. pap. 2.95 (ISBN 0-380-55871-8, 55871-8, Discus). Avon.
Work of Craft. Carla Needleman. 160p. 1987. pap. 8.95 (ISBN 1-85063-061-5, 30615, Ark Paperbks). Routledge Chapman & Hall.
Work of David H. Keller: An Annotated Bibiography & Guide. Mike Ashley. (Bibliographies of Modern Authors Ser.). 64p. 1989. lib. bdg. 19.95x (ISBN 0-8095-0502-9); pap. text ed. 9.95x (ISBN 0-8095-1502-4). Borgo Pr.
Work of Dean Ing: An Annotated Bibliography & Guide. Scott A. Burgess. LC 87-827. (Bibliographies of Modern Authors Ser.: No. 11). 60p. 1988. lib. bdg. 19.95x (ISBN 0-89370-395-8); pap. text ed. 9.95x (ISBN 0-89370-495-4). Borgo PR.
Work of Donald A. Wollheim: An Annotated Bibliography & Guide. Mike Ashley. (Bibliographies 0f Modern Authors Ser.). 64p. 1989. lib. bdg. 19.95x (ISBN 0-89370-392-3); pap. text ed. 9.95x (ISBN 0-89370-492-X). Borgo Pr.
Work of Faith. Spiros Zodhiates. (Trilogy Ser.: Vol. 2). (Illus.). pap. 6.95 (ISBN 0-89957-545-5). AMG Pubs.
Work of FAO & Related Organizations Concerning Marine Science & Its Applications. (Fisheries Technical Papers: No. 74). 21p. 1968. pap. 7.50 (ISBN 0-686-93076-2, F1735, FAO). UNIPUB.
Work of Frank Lloyd Wright. Frank Lloyd Wright. (Illus.). 25.00 (ISBN 0-8180-0001-5). Horizon.
Work of George Eliot, 10 vols. George Eliot. 1987. Repr. Set. lib. bdg. 750.00 (ISBN 0-89987-227-1). Darby Bks.
Work of George Zebrowski: An Annotated Bibliography & Guide. Jeffrey M. Elliot & R. Reginald. LC 84-24239. (Bibliographies of Modern Authors Ser.: No. 4). 54p. 1985. lib. bdg. 19.95x (ISBN 0-89370-383-4); pap. 9.95x (ISBN 0-89370-483-0). Borgo Pr.

Work Stress: Health Care Systems in the Workplace. Ed. by James C. Quick et al. LC 86-30636. 346p. 1987. lib. bdg. 39.95 (ISBN 0-275-92329-0, C2329). Praeger.

Work Study & Related Management Services. Dennis A. Whitmore. 1976. pap. 17.95 (ISBN 0-434-92255-2, Pub. by W Heinemann Ltd). David & Charles.

Work, Study, Travel Abroad 1986-1987. 8th ed. Council on International Educational Exchange Staff. 368p. 1985. pap. 7.95 (ISBN 0-312-88952-6). St Martin.

Work, Study, Travel Abroad 1988-1989. 9th ed. Council on International Educational Exchange. 416p. 1988. pap. 8.95x (ISBN 0-312-01539-9). St Martin.

Work-Team Guide for the People: Performance Profile. Bob Crosby & Gil Crosby. 29p. 1985. pap. write for info. (ISBN 0-88390-186-2). Univ Assocs.

Work Teams & Team Building. R. H. Guest. (Work in America Productivity Studies: No. 44). 54p. 1986. pap. 39.00 (ISBN 0-08-034240-X, L120, Pub. by PPI). Pergamon.

Work, Technology, & Education: Dissenting Essays in the Intellectual Foundations of American Education. Ed. by Walter Feinberg & Henry Rosemont, Jr. LC 75-4854. (Illus.). 222p. 1975. 22.95 (ISBN 0-252-00252-0); pap. 8.95 (ISBN 0-252-00649-6). U of Ill Pr.

Work, the Joy & the Triumph of the Will. Armand Schwerner. 1977. signed o.p. 10.00 (ISBN 0-685-89004-X); perfect bound in wrappers 3.00. New Rivers Pr.

Work Touching the Good Ordering of a Common Weal. Joannes Ferrarius Montanus. Tr. by William Bauande. 430p. Repr. of 1559 ed. 45.00 (ISBN 0-384-15509-X). Johnson Repr.

Work Transformed: Automation & Labor in the Computer Age. Harley Shaiken. 320p. (Orig.). 1986. pap. text ed. 14.95x (ISBN 0-669-13214-4). Lexington Bks.

Work Trap. 2nd ed. Martin C. Helldorfer. LC 80-52059. 96p. 1983. pap. 5.95 (ISBN 0-89571-017-X). Affirmation.

Work, Unemployment, & Mental Health. Peter Warr. 384p. 1987. 55.00 (ISBN 0-19-852158-8); pap. 32.50 (ISBN 0-19-852159-6). Oxford U Pr.

Work, Unemployment & the New Technology. Colin Gill. 220p. 1985. 24.95x (ISBN 0-7456-0022-0); pap. 9.95x (ISBN 0-7456-0023-9). Basil Blackwell.

Work, Union & Community: Industrial Man in South India. Uma Ramaswami. 1983. 14.95x (ISBN 0-19-561503-4). Oxford U Pr.

Work Values & Background Factors As Predictors of Women's Desire to Work. Lorraine Dittrich Eyde. 1962. pap. 3.00 (ISBN 0-87776-108-6, R108). Ohio St U Admin Sci.

Work Values Inventory: MRC Machine-Scorable Test Booklets. Donald E. Super. 56.94 (ISBN 0-395-09529-8); directions manual 3.42 (ISBN 0-395-09530-1); examination set pap. 1.62 (ISBN 0-395-09531-X). HM.

Work, Wages & Profits. 2nd ed. H. L. Gantt. LC 72-9509. (Management History Ser.: No. 41). (Illus.). 312p. 1973. Repr. of 1919 ed. 23.00 (ISBN 0-87960-048-9). Hive Pub.

Work, Wages & Welfare in a Developing Metropolis: Consequences of Growth in Bogota, Columbia. Rakesh Mohan. (World Bank Publication Papers). 400p. 1987. 29.95x (ISBN 0-19-520540-5). Oxford U Pr.

Work, Wages, & Welfare in a Developing Metropolis: Consequences of Growth in Bogota, Columbia see Trabajo, Ingreso y Bienestar en una Metropolis en Desarrollo: Consecuencias del Crecimiento en Bogota.

Work, Welfare & Economic Theory. Ugo Pagano. 264p. 1985. 29.95x (ISBN 0-631-13728-9). Basil Blackwell.

Work, Welfare & Taxation: A Study of Labour Supply Incentives in the U. K. Michael Beenstock. 220p. 1987. text ed. 39.95x (ISBN 0-04-331104-0); pap. text ed. 14.95x (ISBN 0-04-331105-9). Unwin Hyman.

Work: What It Has Meant to Men Through the Ages. Adriano Tilgher. Ed. by Leon Stein. Tr. by Dorothy C. Fisher from Ital. LC 77-70538. (Work Ser.). 1977. Repr. of 1930 ed. lib. bdg. 21.00x (ISBN 0-405-10208-9). Ayer Co Pubs.

Work When You Want to Work. John Fanning & George Sullivan. 1985. pap. 3.50 (ISBN 0-671-52561-1). PB.

Work-Wise: Learning about the World of Work from Books--Critical Guide to Book Selection & Usage. Diane Gersoni-Edelman. LC 79-11920. (Selection Guide Ser.: No. 3). 258p. 1980. 27.95 (ISBN 0-87436-264-4). Neal-Schuman.

Work with Display Units 86: Selected Papers from the International Conference, Stockholm, Sweden, May 12-15, 1986. Ed. by B. Knave & P. G. Wideback. 880p. 1987. 85.00 (ISBN 0-444-70171-0, North-Holland). Elsevier.

Work with Knowledge of Results see Quantitative Aspects of the Evolution of Concepts.

Work with Passion: How to Do What You Love for a Living. Nancy Anderson. 308p. 1984. (Co-published with Carroll & Graf); pap. 8.95. New Wrld Lib.

Work with Passion: How to Do What You Love for a Living. Nancy Anderson. 224p. 1984. 15.95 (ISBN 0-88184-099-8). Carroll & Graf.

Work with Passion: How to Do What You Love for a Living. Nancy Anderson. 310p. (Orig.). 1986. pap. 8.95 (ISBN 0-88184-212-5, Co-Pub. with Whatever Pub). Carroll & Graf.

Work Without End: Abandoning Shorter Hours for the Right to Work. Benjamin K. Hunnicutt. LC 87-13966. (Illus.). 352p. 1988. 39.95 (ISBN 0-87722-520-6). Temple U Pr.

Work Without Salvation: America's Intellectual & Industrial Alienation, 1880-1910. James B. Gilbert. LC 74-2249. 256p. 1977. 29.50x (ISBN 0-8018-1954-7). Johns Hopkins.

Work, Women, & the Labour Market. Ed. by Jackie West. 192p. 1982. pap. 11.50x (ISBN 0-7100-0970-4). Routledge Chapman & Hall.

Work, Women & the Stuggle for Self-Sufficiency: The Win Experience. Aliki Coudroglou. LC 82-13679. 214p. 1982. lib. bdg. 29.75 (ISBN 0-8191-2654-3); pap. text ed. 13.25 (ISBN 0-8191-2655-1). U Pr of Amer.

Work You Give Us to Do: A Mission Study. Episcopal Church Center Staff. 179p. (Orig.). 1982. pap. 4.95 (ISBN 0-8164-7116-9, HarpR); study guide 1.25 (ISBN 0-8164-7117-7). Har-Row.

Work Your Way Around the World. 2nd ed. Susan Griffith. (Illus.). 320p. 1987. pap. 10.95 (ISBN 0-907638-72-4, Pub. by Vacation-Work England). Writers Digest.

Work, Youth, & Schooling: Historical Perspectives on Vocationalism in American Education. Ed. by Harvey Kantor & David B. Tyack. LC 81-50788. 384p. 1982. 32.50x (ISBN 0-8047-1121-6). Stanford U Pr.

Work Zone Traffic Control: Standards & Guidelines see Manual on Uniform Traffic Control Devices for Streets & Highways: Traffic Controls for Street & Highway Construction & Maintenance Operations.

Workability of Concrete. G. H. Tattersall. (Illus.). 1976. pap. 12.75x (ISBN 0-7210-1032-6, Pub. by C & CA London). Scholium Intl.

Workability Testing Techniques. Ed. by G. E. Dieter. 1984. 80.00 (ISBN 0-87170-174-X). ASM.

Workable Competition in the Radio Broadcasting Industry. new ed. Peter O. Steiner. Ed. by Christopher H. Sterling. LC 78-21741. (Dissertations in Broadcasting Ser.). (Illus.). 1979. lib. bdg. 32.50x (ISBN 0-405-11777-9). Ayer Co Pubs.

Workable Faith. June S. Wood. 1975. 6.95 (ISBN 0-8022-2152-1). Philos Lib.

Workable Government: The Constitution after 200 Years. Ed. by Burke Marshall. (An American Assembly Bk.). (Orig.). 1987. 19.95 (ISBN 0-393-02480-6); pap. 9.95 (ISBN 0-393-30431-0). Norton.

Workable Plan for Sensible Government. Frank W. McKay. 116p. (Orig.). 1984. pap. 2.95 (ISBN 0-930333-00-4). Switz Pr.

Workable Workplace: Excellence at Work for You. Melvin J. LeBaron. LC 87-83597. 200p. 1988. text ed. 18.95 (ISBN 0-944329-01-2). Et Cetera.

Workaday Schooners, the Edward W. Smith Photographs Taken on Narragansett Bay, 1895-1905, Together with Writings & Plans Describing the Designs & Use of Schooners of the Period. Edward W. Smith. LC 77-189815. pap. 49.00 (ISBN 0-317-29741-4, 2015662). Bks Demand UMI.

Workaholic & His Family: An Inside Look. Frank B. Minirth et al. 144p. (Orig.). 1981. pap. 5.95 (ISBN 0-8010-6191-1). Baker Bk.

Workaholic Syndrome. Judith K. Sprankle & Henry Ebel. 192p. 1987. 16.95 (ISBN 0-8027-0917-6). Walker & Co.

Workaholics: Living with Them, Working with Them. Marilyn Machlowitz. 1981. pap. 3.50 (ISBN 0-451-62224-3, ME2224, Ment). NAL.

Workbench Book. Scott Landis. LC 86-51321. (Illus.). 256p. 1987. 24.95 (ISBN 0-918804-76-0, W.W. Norton). Taunton.

Workbench Guide to Electronic Projects You Can Build in Your Spare Time. Carl G. Grolle & Michael B. Girosky. LC 81-2169. 256p. 1981. 17.95 (ISBN 0-13-965269-8, Parker). P-H.

Workbench Guide to Electronic Troubleshooting. Robert C. Genn, Jr. 216p. 1977. 17.95. P-H.

Workbench Guide to Semiconductor Circuits & Projects. Michael Gannon. 256p. 1982. 18.95 (ISBN 0-13-965277-9). P-H.

Workbench Treasury of Coffee, Tea & Serving Table Projects. Workbench Magazine Staff. LC 81-80204. (Illus.). 56p. (Orig.). 1981. pap. 4.95 (ISBN 0-86675-002-9, 29). Mod Handcraft.

Workbench Treasury of Decks, Patios, Gazebos & More. Workbench Magazine Staff. LC 83-17250. (Illus.). 56p. (Orig.). 1984. pap. 4.95 (ISBN 0-86675-009-6, 96). Mod Handcraft.

Workbench Treasury of Infant's & Children's Furniture. Workbench Magazine Staff. LC 83-25093. (Illus.). 56p. 1984. pap. 4.95 (ISBN 0-86675-011-8, 118). Mod Handcraft.

Workbench Treasury of Occasional & End Table Projects. Workbench Magazine Staff. LC 82-18769. (Illus.). 56p. (Orig.). 1983. pap. 4.95 (ISBN 0-86675-006-1, 61). Mod Handcraft.

Workbench Treasury of Outdoor Toys & Playhouses. Workbench Magazine Staff. LC 83-9374. (Illus.). 56p. (Orig.). 1983. pap. 4.95 (ISBN 0-86675-008-8, 88). Mod Handcraft.

Workbench Treasury of Shelves, Racks, & Built-Ins. Workbench Magazine Staff. LC 82-60699. (Illus.). 56p. (Orig.). 1982. pap. 4.95 (ISBN 0-86675-005-3, 53). Mod Handcraft.

Workbench Treasury of Weekend Wood Projects. Workbench Magazine Staff. LC 84-29592. (Illus.). 56p. (Orig.). 1985. pap. 4.95 (ISBN 0-86675-012-6, 126). Mod Handcraft.

Workbench Treasury of Wooden Toy Projects. Workbench Magazine Staff. LC 81-83667. (Illus.). 56p. 1982. pap. 4.95 (ISBN 0-86675-003-7, 37). Mod Handcraft.

Workboat Engineer & Oiler. rev. "B" ed. Robert J. Ward. Ed. by Richard A. Block. (Illus.). 850p. (Orig.). 1986. pap. 62.00 (ISBN 0-934114-80-3, BK-107). Marine Educ.

Workboats. Jan Adkins. LC 85-14288. (Illus.). 48p. (gr. 5 up). 1985. 12.95 (ISBN 0-684-18228-9, Pub. by Scribners). Macmillan.

Workboats. K. D. Troup. 1980. write for info. (ISBN 0-85501-212-9). Wiley.

Workboats. K. D. Troup. 288p. 1982. text ed. 100.00x (ISBN 0-471-26067-3, Pub. by Wiley Heyden). Wiley.

Workbook. 8th ed. Tom M. Hendricks. 200p. 1988. 20.00x. T M H Pub Co.

Workbook & Laboratory Manual in Chemistry. rev. ed. Walter L. Ahner. (Illus.). (gr. 11-12). 1964. pap. 12.50 (ISBN 0-87720-125-0). AMSCO Sch.

Workbook & Laboratory Manual in Physics. 2nd ed. Walter L. Ahner & Sheldon R. Diamond. (Illus., Orig.). (gr. 11-12). 1967. 12.50 (ISBN 0-87720-176-5). AMSCO Sch.

Workbook & Manual Introduction to Horticulture. 3rd ed. T. Richard Fisher. 1982. pap. text ed. 13.95x (ISBN 0-89917-366-7). TIS Inc.

Workbook & Study Guide for Disciplined Creative Innovation. Richard H. Montgomery. (Illus.). 1987. loose-leaf 13.95 (ISBN 0-915991-07-1). R H Mont Assocs.

Workbook & Study Guide for First Care. Sheryle L. Wills & Sharyn F. Tremblay. (Illus.). 184p. (Orig.). 1983. pap. 4.95x (ISBN 0-940122-08-1). Mosby Multi-Media.

Workbook & Tape Manual for En Route: Introduction au Francais et au Monde Francophone. Albert Valdman et al. 522p. 1986. pap. write for info. (ISBN 0-02-422290-9). Macmillan.

Workbook Exercises in Alphabetic Filing. 3rd. rev. ed. R. J. Stewart et al. 48p. 1980. pap. text ed. 7.48 (ISBN 0-07-061451-2). McGraw.

Workbook for a Beginning-Intermediate Grammar of Hellenistic Greek. Lane C. McGaughy. LC 76-44351. (Society of Biblical Literature. Sources for Biblical Study). 1976. pap. text ed. 7.95 (ISBN 0-89130-093-7, 060306). Scholars Pr GA.

Workbook for Achieving Competence in Mathematics. Mandery & Schneider. (YA) (gr. 7-9). 1987. pap. 6.67 (ISBN 0-87720-209-5). AMSCO Sch.

Workbook for Aesop's Fables Reader. H. Dorizas. 1976. 2.50 (ISBN 0-685-73008-5). Divry.

Workbook for Aphasia: Exercises for the Redevelopment of Higher Level Language Functioning. rev. ed. Susan H. Brubaker. LC 85-91276. 381p. 1985. Repr. of 1978 ed. spiral bound 28.00x (ISBN 0-8143-1803-7). Wayne St U Pr.

Workbook for Astronomy. Jerry Waxman. LC 83-7526. 1984. 24.95 (ISBN 0-521-25312-8). Cambridge U Pr.

Workbook for Basic Human Anatomy & Physiology: Traditional & Innovative Exercises. Kathryn E. Malone & Jane M. Schneider. 363p. 1983. pap. text ed. 15.95 (ISBN 0-471-09244-4). Wiley.

Workbook for Beauty Culture Theory. Milady Editors. (Illus.). 1981. Repr. of 1981 ed. 11.30 (ISBN 0-87350-121-7). Milady Pub.

Workbook for Cognitive Skills: Exercises for Thought Processes & Word Retrieval. Susan Howell-Brubaker. LC 87-7352. 250p. 1987. spiral bdg. 35.00x (ISBN 0-8143-1903-3). Wayne St U Pr.

Workbook for Composing for the Jazz Orchestra. William Russo & Reid Hyams. LC 61-8642. 1979. Spiral bdg. 6.95X (ISBN 0-226-73214-2). U of Chicago Pr.

Workbook for Creating Excellence. Hickman & Michael A. Silva. 1986. pap. 9.95 (ISBN 0-452-25749-2, Plume). NAL.

Workbook for Creative Problem Solving: The Basic Course. Scott G. Isaksen & Donald J. Treffinger. 28p. (Orig.). 1985. pap. 5.25 (ISBN 0-943456-11-8). Bearly Ltd.

Workbook for Demotic Greek I: Providing Supplementary Exercises in Writing & Spelling, Complementing the Oral-Aural Emphasis of the Text. Peter Bien et al. 104p. 1973. pap. text ed. 7.00x (ISBN 0-87451-090-2). U Pr of New Eng.

Workbook for Emergency Care in the Streets. 3rd ed. James C. McClintock & Nancy L. Caroline. 1987. pap. text ed. 14.50 (ISBN 0-316-55437-5). Little.

Workbook for Engineering Graphics. Herbert W. Yankee. 1985. pap. text ed. 16.00 (ISBN 0-534-04168-X, 23R2051, Pub. by PWS Engineering). PWS Kent Pub.

Workbook for Financial Self-Assessment in Independent Schools. Sorrel R. Paskin. 1983. pap. 20.00 (ISBN 0-934338-61-2). NAIS.

Workbook for Freedom & Crisis, 2 vols. 2nd ed. Jane Herndon & Sylvia Krebs. 1979. 4.95x ea.; Vol. 1. (ISBN 0-394-32294-0); Vol. 2. (ISBN 0-394-32295-9). Random.

Workbook for Fundamentals of Speech Communication. 2nd ed. Bert E. Bradley et al. 144p. 1981. spiral bdg. 9.95 (ISBN 0-8403-2383-2). Kendall-Hunt.

Workbook for Greek Children Reader. H. Dorizas. 1976. 2.50 (ISBN 0-685-79097-5). Divry.

Workbook for Head Writing & News Editing. 5th ed. Arthur C. Wimer & Dale Brix. 416p. 1983. write for info wire coil (ISBN 0-697-04351-7). Wm C Brown.

Workbook for Human Factors in Engineering & Design. Mark S. Sanders & Ernest J. McCormick. 1982. pap. text ed. 11.95 (ISBN 0-8403-2716-1). Kendall-Hunt.

Workbook for Intercultural Encounters: The Fundamentals of Intercultural Communication. Donald W. Klopf. (Orig.). 1987. pap. 10.95 wkbk. (ISBN 0-89582-172-9). Morton Pub.

Workbook for Introductory Human Anatomy & Physiology. Margaret Kehoe et al. 144p. 1983. wkbk. 8.95 (ISBN 0-8403-3634-9). Kendall-Hunt.

Workbook for Language Skills: Exercises for Written & Verbal Expression. Susan H. Brubaker. LC 84-11893. 288p. 1984. spiral bound 28.00x (ISBN 0-8143-1778-2). Wayne St U Pr.

Workbook for Life-Span Psychology. Mimi L. La Driere & Justin Pikunis. 178p. (Orig.). 1983. pap. text ed. 15.00 (ISBN 0-8191-3266-7). U Pr of Amer.

Workbook for Mass Communication & Society. 4th ed. Val E. Limburg. 144p. 1987. pap. text ed. 13.50 (ISBN 0-8403-4472-4). Kendall-Hunt.

Workbook for MRI & CT of the Head & Neck. 2nd ed. Anthony A. Mancuso. 250p. 1988. 43.00 (ISBN 0-683-05478-3). Williams & Wilkins.

Workbook for Nonverbal Communication. John J. Trombetta. 112p. 1985. pap. text ed. 13.50 (ISBN 0-8403-3697-7). Kendall-Hunt.

Workbook for Oklahoma: The Story of Its Past & Present. rev. ed. Estelle Faulconer. (Illus.). 105p. 1968. pap. 3.95 (ISBN 0-8061-0579-8). U of Okla Pr.

Workbook for Papier-Mache Dolls & Furniture. Marie L. Sitton. (Illus.). 34p. 1984. pap. 3.95 (ISBN 0-87588-211-0, 2643). Hobby Hse.

Workbook for Planning Christian Education. Kenneth D. Blazier. 48p. 1983. pap. 3.95 (ISBN 0-8170-0996-5). Judson.

Workbook for Practical Nurses. 3rd ed. Audrey L. Sutton. 1969. pap. text ed. 14.95 (ISBN 0-7216-8682-6). Saunders.

Workbook for Professional Barber Styling. Milady Staff. 1984. 12.78 (ISBN 0-87350-144-6). Milady Pub.

Workbook for Program Evaluation in the Human Services. Walter E. Riddick & Eva M. Stewart. 196p. (Orig.). 1981. pap. text ed. 12.25 (ISBN 0-8191-1783-8). U Pr of Amer.

Workbook for Radio & TV News Editing & Writing. 5th ed. Arthur Wimer & Dale Brix. 320p. 1980. write for info. wire coil (ISBN 0-697-04334-7). Wm C Brown.

Workbook for Reasoning Skills: Exercises for Cognitive Facilitation. Susan H. Brubaker. LC 83-50961. 304p. 1983. spiral bound 28.00x (ISBN 0-8143-1760-X). Wayne St U Pr.

Workbook for Software Entrepreneurs. A. L. Frank. (Illus.). 128p. 1985. text ed. 40.00 (ISBN 0-13-965302-3). P-H.

Workbook for Speech Fundamentals. David H. Dobkins & Richard Kneller. 128p. 1980. pap. text ed. 8.95 (ISBN 0-8403-2257-7). Kendall-Hunt.

Workbook for "Statistical Methods in Education & Psychology". A. K. Kurtz & S. Mayo. 1978. pap. 12.50 (ISBN 0-387-90324-0). Springer-Verlag.

Workbook for the Life Sciences. Elmo A. Law. 1979. pap. text ed. 12.95 (ISBN 0-8403-2122-8). Kendall-Hunt.

Workbook for the Numbers Game: Statistics in Psychology. Gail E. Levy & Joan G. Snodgrass. 1977. 8.95x (ISBN 0-19-502300-5). Oxford U Pr.

Workbook for the Original Doll Artist. Marie L. Sitton. (Illus.). 24p. 1988. write for info. Hobby Hse.

Workbook for the Restoration Ideal. Marshall Leggett. 96p. 1986. pap. 2.95 wkbk. (ISBN 0-87403-068-4, 3176). Standard Pub.

Workbook for the Verbally Apraxic Adult. Karen B. Richards & Maureen O'Brien Fallon. 144p. 1987. wkbk. 18.95 (ISBN 0-317-64735-0, 7367). Communication Skill.

Workbook for Total Patient Care. 6th ed. Hood & Dincher. 1984. pap. 13.95 (ISBN 0-8016-2244-1). Mosby.

Workbook for Trainees in General Practice. P. Freeling. (Illus.). 1983. pap. 17.00 (ISBN 0-7236-0681-1). PSG Pub Co.

Workbook for Voice Improvement. 2nd ed. Virginia L. Agnello & Cindy Garcia. 1983. pap. 7.95x (ISBN 0-8134-2284-1, 2284). Inter Print Pubs.

Workbook for Writers. 2nd ed. Celia Millward. 1983. pap. text ed. 14.95 (ISBN 0-03-062322-7). HR&W.

Workers & Dissent in the Redwood Empire. Daniel Cornford. 267p. 1987. 34.95 (ISBN 0-87722-499-4). Temple U Pr.

Workers & Employers: Documents on Trade Union & Industrial Relations in Britain since the Nineteenth Century. Ed. by J. T. Ward & Hamish Fraser. LC 80-50398. xxxii, 374p. 1981. 39.50 (ISBN 0-208-01878-6, Archon). Shoe String.

Workers & Incentives. M. R. Sertel. (Contributions to Economic Analysis: Vol. 140). 240p. 1982. 94.75 (ISBN 0-444-86360-5, I-124-82, North-Holland). Elsevier.

Workers & Production Politics on a Nicaraguan State Farm. Gary Ruchwarger. (Development, Conflict, & Social Change Ser.). 135p. 1988. pap. 17.95 (ISBN 0-8133-7407-3). Westview.

Workers & Revolution in Iran: A Third World Experience of Workers' Control. Assef Bayat. 244p. 1987. 37.50 (ISBN 0-86232-389-4, Pub. by Zed Pr); pap. 12.50 (ISBN 0-86232-390-8, Pub. by Zed Pr). Humanities.

Workers & the Right in Spain, 1900-1936. Colin M. Winston. LC 84-42553. (Illus.). 344p. 1984. text ed. 39.00x (ISBN 0-691-05433-9). Princeton U Pr.

Workers & Their Tools: A Guide to the Ergonomic Design of Hand Tools & Small Presses. Leo Greenberg & Don B. Chaffin. (Illus.). 130p. 1978. 19.25 (ISBN 0-87812-161-7). Pendell Pub.

Workers & Unions in Bombay, Nineteen Eighteen to Nineteen Twenty-Nine: A Study of Organisation in the Cotton Mills. Richard Newman. 1982. pap. 22.00x (ISBN 0-686-91580-1, Pub. by Australian Nat Univ). South Asia Bks.

Workers & Wages in an Urban Labor Market. Albert Rees & George P. Shultz. LC 75-110114. (Studies in Business & Society Ser). 1970. 15.00x (ISBN 0-226-70705-9). U of Chicago Pr.

Workers & Workplaces in Revolutionary China. Ed. by Stephen Andors. Tr. by Jay Mathews et al. LC 76-53710. (China Book Project Ser.). 440p. 1977. 40.00 (ISBN 0-87332-094-8). M E Sharpe.

Workers at Risk: Voices from the Workplace. Dorothy Nelkin & Michael S. Brown. LC 83-9319. (Illus.). xviii, 220p. 1984. 20.00 (ISBN 0-226-57127-0). U of Chicago Pr.

Workers at Risk: Voices from the Workplace. Dorothy Nelkin & Michael S. Brown. LC 83-9319. xviii, 220p. 1986. pap. 9.95 (ISBN 0-226-57128-9). U of Chicago Pr.

Workers at War. Frank J. Warne. LC 74-22762. (Labor Movement in Fiction & Non-Fiction). Repr. of 1920 ed. 25.00 (ISBN 0-404-58515-9). AMS Pr.

Workers Before & After Lenin. Manya Gordon. LC 74-22743. Repr. of 1941 ed. 31.50 (ISBN 0-404-58495-0). AMS Pr.

Workers, Bosses, & Bureaucrats: A Socialist View of the Labor Movement in the 1930's. Tom Kerry. 300p. 1980. lib. bdg. 23.00 (ISBN 0-87348-604-8); pap. 7.95 (ISBN 0-87348-603-X). Path Pr NY.

Worker's Capitalism. Herbert Mertz, Jr. 1979. pap. 3.95 (ISBN 0-934340-00-5). New Visions Pr.

Workers' Co-Operative Handbook. Peter Cockerton & Anna Whyatt. 128p. 1984. 20.75x (ISBN 0-317-54698-8, Pub. by Plunkett Foundation). State Mutual Bk.

Workers Co-Operatives: Jobs & Dreams. Jenny Thornley. 1981. text ed. 45.00x (ISBN 0-435-83890-3). Gower Pub Co.

Workers' Co-Operatives: Jobs & Dreams. Jenny Thornley. 218p. 1982. 30.00x (ISBN 0-317-54786-0, Pub. by Plunkett Foundation). State Mutual Bk.

Workers Co-Operatives Past, Present & Future. The Co-Operative Bank Staff & PA Management Consultants Staff. 148p. 1985. 123.00x (ISBN 0-902453-11-4, Pub. by Plunkett Foundation). State Mutual Bk.

Workers' Co-Operatives: Potential & Problems. Mary Linehan & Vincent Tucker. 256p. 1983. 22.00x (ISBN 0-317-54787-9, Pub. by Plunkett Foundation). State Mutual Bk.

Workers' (Communist) Party & American Trade Unions. David M. Schneider. LC 78-64128. (Johns Hopkins University. Studies in the Social Sciences. Forty-Sixth Ser. 1928: 2). Repr. of 1928 ed. 24.50. AMS Pr.

Worker's Compensation. Hamline University, Advanced Legal Education Staff. LC 83-216835. 324p. 1984. 37.10. Hamline Law.

Worker's Compensation, 2 vols. Hamline University Advanced Legal Education Staff. LC 84-241371. 782p. 1984. 42.40 (ISBN 0-317-18283-8). Hamline Law.

Workers' Compensation, 2 vols. Hamline University, Advanced Legal Eduction Staff. 798p. 1985. Set. 3-ring binder 58.30 (ISBN 0-317-42515-3). Hamline Law.

Workers' Compensation. New Jersey Institute for Continuing Legal Education Staff. (Illus.). 137p. 1983. pap. 20.00. NJ Inst CLE.

Workers' Compensation. 184p. 1982. 7.00 (ISBN 0-318-02487-X). ICLE Georgia.

Workers' Compensation. 312p. 1983. 7.50 (ISBN 0-318-02489-6). ICLE Georgia.

Workers' Compensation. 398p. 1984. 17.50 (ISBN 0-318-02490-X). ICLE Georgia.

Workers' Compensation. 1980. 20.00 (ISBN 0-317-57854-5). NJ Inst CLE.

Workers' Compensation: A Bibliography. Marian Dworaczek. (Public Administration Ser.: P 1974). 38p. 1986. 10.00 (ISBN 0-89028-934-4). Vance Biblios.

Workers' Compensation & Employee Protection Laws in a Nutshell. Jack B. Hood & Benjamin A. Hardy, Jr. LC 83-21658. (Nutshell Ser.). 274p. 1983. pap. text ed. 9.95 (ISBN 0-314-78064-5). West Pub.

Workers' Compensation & Employment Rights Cases & Materials. 2nd ed. Wex S. Malone et al. LC 80-11963. (American Casebook Ser.). 993p. 1980. text ed. 33.95 (ISBN 0-8299-2088-9). West Pub.

Workers' Compensation & Work-Related Illnesses & Diseases. Peter S. Barth & H. Allan Hunt. 391p. 1980. pap. 13.95x (ISBN 0-262-52080-X). MIT Pr.

Workers' Compensation & Work-Related Illnesses & Diseases. Peter S. Barth & H. Allen Hunt. 1980. text ed. 52.50x (ISBN 0-262-02141-2). MIT Pr.

Workers' Compensation & Workplace Safety: Some Lessons from Economic Theory. Richard B Victor & Linda Cohen. LC 83-3145. 1982. 7.50 (ISBN 0-8330-0487-5, R-2918-1CJ). Rand Corp.

Workers' Compensation Benefits: Adequacy, Equity, & Efficiency. Ed. by John D. Worrall & David Appel. LC 85-8208. 208p. 1985. cloth 26.00 (ISBN 0-87546-115-8). ILR Pr.

Workers' Compensation in Michigan: Problems & Prospects. H. Allan Hunt. 24p. 1979. pap. 1.95 (ISBN 0-911558-62-4). W E Upjohn.

Worker's Compensation Law, 2 Vols. 3rd ed. Sheldon St. Clair. 715p. 1985. pap. text ed. 57.50 (ISBN 0-89074-079-8). Lega Bks.

Worker's Compensation Law & Insurance. 2nd ed. Albert J. Millus et al. Ed. by Emanuel Levy. 1980. 27.50 (ISBN 0-686-26810-5). Roberts Pub.

Workers' Compensation Law Institute. 204p. 1982. 8.00 (ISBN 0-318-02488-8). ICLE Georgia.

Workers' Compensation Law Institute. 75p. 1983. 7.00 (ISBN 0-318-02491-8). ICLE Georgia.

Workers' Compensation Law of Ohio. 2nd ed. James L. Young. 395p. 1972. Suppl. 1984. 47.50. Anderson Pub Co.

Workers' Compensation Law of the State of Alaska: Including Digest & Supplementary Laws. rev. ed. LC 85-213689. Date not set. price not set. Am Ins NY.

Workers' Compensation Law of the State of Arizona: Including Digest & Supplementary Law with Annotations Through January 1981. rev. ed. LC 85-213725. Date not set. price not set. Am Ins NY.

Workers' Compensation Law of the State of Delaware: Including Digest & Laws. rev. ed. LC 85-165644. Date not set. price not set. Am Ins NY.

Workers' Compensation Law of the State of South Dakota: Containing Workers' Compensation Law, Occupational Disease Disability Law, Including Digests & Supplementary Laws. rev. ed. LC 85-214133. Date not set. price not set. Am Ins NY.

Workers' Compensation Law of the State of Utah: Containing the Workers' Compenstion Law, the Occupational Disease Disability Law, Including Digests & Supplementary Laws with Annotations Through July 1979. rev. ed. LC 85-165647. Date not set. price not set. Am Ins NY.

Workers' Compensation Law Reports. write for info. (90). Commerce.

Workers' Compensation Laws of California. Warren L. Hanna. 1985. Updates annually. pap. 29.00 (840); 1985 27.00,. Bender.

Workers' Compensation Manual: Injury to Persons & Property Section. 20.00 (ISBN 0-317-62693-0). DC Bar Assn.

Workers Compensation: Perspective for the Eighties. 133p. 1981. 24.50 (ISBN 0-318-16893-6). Soc Charter Prop Underwriters.

Workers' Compensation Practice Manual. Paul A. Gargano. 1988. price not set looseleaf (ISBN 0-88063-222-4). Butterworth Legal Pubs.

Workers' Compensation Practice (Seminar Materials) New Jersey Institute for Continuing Legal Education Staff. (Illus.). 140p. 1985. amfile 25.00. NJ Inst CLE.

Workers' Compensation Practice: Seminar Materials. 140p. 1985. 25.00 (ISBN 0-317-57862-6). NJ Inst CLE.

Worker's Compensation Review Analyst. Jack Rudman. (Career Examination Ser.: C-308). (Cloth bdg. avail. on request). pap. 14.00 (ISBN 0-8373-0308-7). Natl Learning.

Workers' Compensation Social Worker I. Jack Rudman. (Career Examination Ser.: C-1319). 1988. pap. 14.00 (ISBN 0-8373-1319-8). Natl Learning.

Workers' Compensation Social Worker II. Jack Rudman. (Career Examination Ser.: C-1320). 1988. pap. 16.00 (ISBN 0-8373-1320-1). Natl Learning.

Workers' Compensation System in Michigan: A Closed Case Survey. H. Allan Hunt. LC 82-20250. 225p. (Orig.). 1982. pap. text ed. 13.95 (ISBN 0-88099-005-8). W E Upjohn.

Workers' Compensation, 1986, 2 vols. Hamline University, School of Law Staff & Advanced Legal Education Staff. LC 86-224045. 1206p. 1986. 68.90 (ISBN 0-317-59036-7). Hamline Law.

Workers' Compensation 1987. Hamline University School of Law Advanced Legal Education Staff. 1600p. 1987. 132.50. Hamline Law.

Workers' Control in America: Studies in the History of Work, Technology, & Labor Struggles. David Montgomery. LC 78-32001. (Illus.). 1979. 32.50 (ISBN 0-521-22580-9). Cambridge U Pr.

Workers' Control in America: Studies in the History of Work, Technology, & Labor Struggles. David Montgomery. 1980. 7.95 (ISBN 0-521-28006-0). Cambridge U Pr.

Worker's Control under Plan & Market. Comisso. 1979. text ed. 35.00t (ISBN 0-300-02334-0). Yale U Pr.

Workers' Councils in Czechoslovakia. Vladimir Fisera. LC 78-25995. 1979. 25.00x (ISBN 0-312-88959-3). St Martin.

Worker's Earnings & Corporate Economic Structure. Randy Hodson. (Monograph). 1983. 32.50 (ISBN 0-12-351780-X). Acad Pr.

Worker's Education. Philip Hopkins. LC 85-338. 208p. 1985. 65.00x (ISBN 0-335-15030-6, Open Univ Pr); pap. 29.00x (ISBN 0-335-15029-2). Taylor & Francis.

Worker's Education & Its Techniques: A Worker's Education Manual. 1983. 12.25 (ISBN 92-2-100195-4). Intl Labour Office.

Workers' Education for International Understanding. (Education Studies & Documents: No. 8). pap. 16.00 (UNESCO). UNIPUB.

Workers' Educational Association: Aims & Achievements 1903-1977. Roger Fieldhouse. (Landmarks & New Horizons Ser.: No. 4). 1977. pap. 3.50 (ISBN 0-87060-072-9, LHN 4). Syracuse U Cont Ed.

Workers' Emotions in Shop & Home: Study of Individual Workers from the Psychological & Physiological Standpoint. Rexford B. Hersey. Ed. by Leon Stein. LC 77-70503. (Work Ser.). (Illus.). 1977. Repr. of 1932 ed. lib. bdg. 37.50x (ISBN 0-405-10175-9). Ayer Co Pubs.

Workers from the North: Plantations, Bolivian Labor, & the City in Northwest Argentina. Scott Whiteford. (Latin American Monographs: No. 54). 201p. 1981. text ed. 25.00x (ISBN 0-292-79015-5). U of Tex Pr.

Worker's Guide to Direct Action. 1983. pap. 0.50 (ISBN 0-317-02256-3). Indus Workers World.

Worker's Guide to Right to Know about Hazards in the Workplace. Marianne P. Brown. 33p. 1987. 7.00 (ISBN 0-89215-140-4). U Cal LA Indus Rel.

Workers' Health, Workers' Democracy: The Western Miners' Struggle, 1891-1925. Alan Derickson. LC 88-47722. 264p. 1989. 26.95x (ISBN 0-8014-2060-1). Cornell U Pr.

Workers in American History. 32nd ed. James Oneal. LC 78-156437. (American Labor Ser., No. 2). 1971. Repr. of 1912 ed. 17.00 (ISBN 0-405-02935-7). Ayer Co Pubs.

Workers in Arms: The Austrian Schutzbund & the Civil War of 1934. Ilona Duczynska. LC 77-70970. 1978. 15.00 (ISBN 0-85345-410-8). Monthly Rev.

Workers in Bondage: The Origins & Bases of Unfree Labour in Queensland 1824-1916. Kay Saunders. LC 81-11386. (Scholar's Library). (Illus.). 213p. 1982. text ed. 37.50x (ISBN 0-7022-1283-0). U of Queensland Pr.

Workers in Fire. M. Mansfield. 1937. Repr. 35.00 (ISBN 0-8274-3759-5). R West.

Workers in Imperial Germany: The Miners at the Ruhr. S. H. Hickey. (Oxford Historical Monographs). (Illus.). 340p. 1985. 44.00x (ISBN 0-19-822935-6). Oxford U Pr.

Workers in Industrial America: Essays on the 20th Century Struggle. David Brody. 1980. pap. text ed. 8.95x (ISBN 0-19-502491-5). Oxford U Pr.

Workers in Society. T. Timofeyev. 320p. 1981. 8.00 (ISBN 0-8285-2050-X, Pub. by Progress Pubs USSR). Imported Pubns.

Workers in the Dawn, 3 Vols. in 1. George Gissing. LC 68-59358. Repr. of 1880 ed. 55.00 (ISBN 0-404-02777-6). AMS Pr.

Workers in the Dawn. George Gissing. Ed. by Pierre Coustillas. 920p. (Orig.). 1985. pap. 8.95 (ISBN 0-416-01101-2, NO. 9283). Routledge Chapman & Hall.

Workers, Jobs, & Inflation. Ed. by Martin N. Baily. LC 82-70891. 365p. 1982. 31.95 (ISBN 0-8157-0764-9); pap. 12.95 (ISBN 0-8157-0763-0). Brookings.

Worker's Lament. Gordon Lester-Massman. 16p. 1982. pap. 1.00 (ISBN 0-686-37940-3). Samisdat.

Workers' Management in Yugoslavia: Recent Developments & Trends. Ed. by N. Pasic & S. Grozdanic. viii, 198p. 1982. 24.50 (ISBN 92-2-103034-2); pap. 17.50 (ISBN 92-2-103035-0). Intl Labour Office.

Workers' Management in Yugoslavia: Recent Development & Trends. N. Pasic et al. 1982. 42.00x (ISBN 0-317-54715-1, Pub. by Plunkett Foundation). State Mutual Bk.

Workers Management in Yugoslavia, 1982. 1983. pap. 17.50 (ILO268, ILO). UNIPUB.

Workers, Managers & Technological Change: Emerging Patterns of Labor Relations. Daniel B. Cornfield. (Studies in Work & Industry). 366p. 1987. 37.50x (ISBN 0-306-42450-9, Plenum Pr). Plenum Pub.

Workers, Managers, & Welfare Capitalism: The Shoeworkers & Tanners of Endicott Johnson, 1890-1950. Gerald Zahavi. LC 87-6035. (Working Class in American History Ser.). 312p. 1988. 24.95 (ISBN 0-252-01444-8). U of Ill Pr.

Workers' Movement. Alain Touraine et al. Tr. by Ian Patterson. (Illus.). 322p. 1987. 49.50 (ISBN 0-521-30852-6). Cambridge U pr.

Workers of African Trade. Ed. by Catherine Coquery-Vidrovitch & Paul E. Lovejoy. LC 85-2259. (African Modernization & Development Ser.: Vol. 11). (Illus.). 304p. 1985. text ed. 29.95 (ISBN 0-8039-2472-0). Sage.

Workers of Tianjin, 1900-1949. Gail Hershatter. LC 86-1270. 328p. 1986. 37.50x (ISBN 0-8047-1318-9). Stanford U Pr.

Workers on Relief. Grace Adams. LC 74-137154. (Poverty U. S. A. Historical Record Ser.). 1971. Repr. of 1939 ed. 23.50 (ISBN 0-405-03091-6). Ayer Co Pubs.

Workers on the Edge: Work, Leisure, & Politics in Industrializing Cincinnati, 1788-1890. Steven J. Ross. (Columbia History of Urban Life Ser.). 464p. 1985. 37.50x (ISBN 0-231-05520-X). Columbia U Pr.

Workers on the Edge: Work, Leisure & Politics in Industrializing Cincinnati, 1788-1890. Steven J. Ross. (Columbia History of Urban Life Ser.). 406p. 1987. pap. text ed. 17.50 (ISBN 0-231-05521-8, Kings Crown Paperbacks). Columbia U Pr.

Workers on the Nile. Joel Beinin & Zachary Lockman. (Studies on the Near East). 520p. 1988. text ed. 75.00 (ISBN 0-691-05506-8). Princeton U Pr.

Workers on the Rand: Factories, Townships & Popular Culture, 1886-1942. Luli Callinicos. (People's History of South Africa Ser.: Vol. II). 160p. 1985. pap. 8.95 (Pub. by Ravan Pr). Ohio U Pr.

Workers on the Waterfront: Seamen, Longshoremen, & Unionism in the 1930s. Bruce Nelson. LC 87-28749. 432p. 1988. 29.95 (ISBN 0-252-01487-1). U of Ill Pr.

Workers Opposition. Alexandra Kollontai. (Illus.). 36p. Date not set. pap. 1.95 (ISBN 0-939306-45-X). Left Bank.

Workers, Participation, & Democracy: Internal Politics in the British Union Movement. Joel D. Wolfe. LC 85-5413. (Contributions in Political Science Ser.: No. 136). (Illus.). xii, 258p. 1985. lib. bdg. 46.95 (ISBN 0-313-24692-0, WOW/). Greenwood.

Workers' Participation in an Internationalized Economy. Ed. by Bernhard Wilpert et al. LC 78-1388. 300p. 1978. 17.50x (ISBN 0-87338-214-5). Kent St U Pr.

Workers' Participation in Decisions Within Undertakings. International Labour Office Staff. xi, 224p. (Orig.). 1983. pap. 21.00 (ISBN 92-2-101988-8). Intl Labour Office.

Worker's Participation in Decisions Within Undertakings. 224p. 1981. pap. 21.00 (ISBN 92-2-101988-8, ILO182, ILO). UNIPUB.

Workers Participation in Europe. Walter Kolvenbach & Alfred Metzner Verlag GmbH, Frankfurt. 80p. 1977. 20.00 (ISBN 90-312-0043-3, Pub. by Kluwer Law, Netherlands). Kluwer Academic.

Workers' Participation in Industry. rev ed. Michael Poole. 1978. pap. 7.95x (ISBN 0-7100-8824-8). Routledge Chapman & Hall.

Workers' Participation in Managerial Decision Making: A Study in a Developing Economy. M. A. Mannan. x, 208p. 1987. text ed. 35.00x (ISBN 81-7035-031-X, Pub. by Daya Pub Hse India). Apt Bks.

Workers' Participation in the European Community. Ed. by R. Blanpain. 1984. pap. text ed. 30.00 (ISBN 90-6544-187-5, Pub. by Kluwer Law Netherlands). Kluwer Academic.

Workers' Particpation: A Voice in Decisions, 1981-1985. Ed. by Jacques Monat & Hedva Sarfati. 284p. 1986. pap. 21.00 (ISBN 92-2-105232-X). Intl Labour Office.

Workers, Producers, Transportation & Services Cooperatives see History of the Cooperative Movement in Israel.

Workers Profit Sharing: The Riddle of History Solved. 2nd ed. Shirley Telford. 1973. pap. 2.00 (ISBN 0-9600202-6-8). William & Rich.

Workers' Revolution in Russia, 1917: The View from Below. Ed. by Daniel H. Kaiser. (Illus.). 176p. 1987. 32.50 (ISBN 0-521-34166-3); pap. 8.95 (ISBN 0-521-34971-0). Cambridge U Pr.

Workers' Rights. Mary Gibson. LC 83-17788. (Philosophy & Society Ser.). 176p. 1983. 25.00x (ISBN 0-8476-6756-1, Rowman & Allanheld); pap. 8.95x (ISBN 0-8476-7351-0). Rowman.

Workers Rights, East & West. Adrian Karatnycky & Alexander Motyl. 130p. 1980. pap. 12.95 (ISBN 0-87855-867-5). Transaction Bks.

Worker's Rights, East, & West. Adrian Karatnycky & Alexander J. Motyl. 150p. 4.95 (ISBN 0-318-14690-8). League Indus Demo.

Worker's Self-Management & Organizational Power in Yugoslavia. Ed. by William N. Dunn & Joseph Obradovic. LC 78-16307. 1978. pap. text ed. 21.95x (ISBN 0-8229-8261-7, Pub. by U Ctr Intl St). U of Pittsburgh Pr.

Working Dress. Diana De Marly. 191p. 1987. 44.50 (ISBN 0-8419-1111-8). Holmes & Meier.

Working Dress in Colonial & Revolutionary America. Peter F. Copeland. LC 76-15309. (Contributions in American History Ser.: No. 58). (Illus.). 1977. lib. bdg. 46.95 (ISBN 0-8371-9033-9, COD/). Greenwood.

Working Effectively with Administrative Groups. Ed. by Ronald W. Toseland & Paul H. Ephros. LC 87-23809. (Social Work with Groups Ser.). 120p. 1987. text ed. 19.95 (ISBN 0-86656-746-1). Haworth Pr.

Working Effectively with Task Force Oriented Groups. Donald Seaman. Ed. by Alan Pardoen. (Adult Education Association Professional Development Ser.). (Illus.). 144p. 1981. text ed. 24.95 (ISBN 0-07-000554-0). McGraw.

Working Effectively with Trustees: Building Cooperative Campus Leadership. Barbara E. Taylor. Ed. & frwd. by Jonathan D. Fife. LC 87-1598. (ASHE-ERIC Higher Education Report Series 1987: No.2). 143p. (Orig.). 1987. pap. text ed. 10.00x (ISBN 0-913317-38-1). Assn Study Higher Ed.

Working Environment & Safety & Health: Joint Committee for Postal & Telecommunications Services, Report III. 36p. 1985. pap. 5.70 (ISBN 92-2-103917-X, ILO365, ILO). UNIPUB.

Working Environment in the Construction Industry: National Policies & Legislation in ECE Countries. LC 85-46985. 139p. 1986. 15.00 (ISBN 92-1-116341-2, E.85.II.E.27). UN.

Working Family's Kitchen Guide. Sheila Kennedy & Susan Seidman. LC 79-22643. (Illus.). 168p. (Orig.). 1980. pap. 5.95 (ISBN 0-89286-157-6). One Hund One Prods.

Working Fire. George Hall & John Burks. LC 84-23254. (Illus.). 96p. 1985. pap. 8.95 (ISBN 0-87701-352-7). Chronicle Bks.

Working Fire: The San Francisco Fire Department. George Hall & John Burks. (Illus.). 96p. 1982. 14.95 (ISBN 0-916290-14-X). Squarebooks.

Working for a Wholesaler. Faye Gold & Raymond J. Grandfield. (Distributive Career Ser., Bk. 4). (Illus.). 128p. (gr. 7 up). 1973. text ed. 3.50 (ISBN 0-87005-119-9). Fairchild.

Working for Boroko: The Origins of a Coercive Labour System in South Africa. Marian Lacey. 422p. 1981. pap. text ed. 18.50x (ISBN 0-86975-190-5, Pub. by Ravan Pr). Ohio U Pr.

Working for Capitalism. Richard Pfeffer. LC 78-23345. 1979. 39.50x (ISBN 0-231-04426-7); pap. 16.00x (ISBN 0-231-04427-5). Columbia U Pr.

Working for Children. Judith S. Mearing. LC 78-1148. (Jossey-Bass Social & Behavorial Science Ser.). pap. 92.00 (ISBN 0-317-09508-0, 2021731). Bks Demand UMI.

Working for Democracy: American Workers from the Revolution to the Present. Ed. by Paul Buhle & Alan Dawley. LC 85-5845. (Illus.). 168p. 1985. 19.95 (ISBN 0-252-01220-8); pap. 6.95 (ISBN 0-252-01221-6). U of Ill Pr.

Working for Equality. Fiona Macdonald. Ed. by Ed MacDonald. (Women History Makers Ser.). (Illus.). 48p. (gr. 4 up). 1988. 11.90 (ISBN 0-531-19500-7, Hampstead Pr). Watts.

Working for God. Andrew Murray. (Orig.). 1980. pap. 2.95 (ISBN 0-87508-404-4). Chr Lit.

Working for Life: Careers in Biology. Thomas A. Easton. 118p. 1984. 12.95. Learned Info.

Working for Life: Careers in Biology. 2nd ed. Thomas A. Easton. (Illus.). 140p. 1988. 14.95 (ISBN 0-938734-21-0). Plexus Pub.

Working for Love. Tessa Dahl. 1989. 16.95 (ISBN 0-440-50114-8). Delacorte.

Working for Peace: A Handbook of Practical Psychology & Other Tools. Ed. by Neil Wollman. LC 85-19706. 288p. (Orig.). 1985. pap. 9.95 (ISBN 0-915166-37-2). Impact Pubs Cal.

Working for Success. Larry Anderson. LC 88-70593. 125p. (Orig.). 1988. pap. 7.95 (ISBN 0-9620270-0-6). Anderson OH.

Working for the Railroad: The Organization of Work in the Nineteenth-Century. Walter Licht. LC 82-61372. (Illus.). 352p. 1987. 32.00x (ISBN 0-691-04700-6); pap. text ed. 14.50x (ISBN 0-691-10221-X). Princeton U Pr.

Working for the Reader: Culture, Literature, War & Politics in Books from the 1950's to the Present. Herbert Mitgang. 1970. 7.50 (ISBN 0-8180-1124-6); pap. 3.95 (ISBN 0-8180-1155-6). Horizon.

Working for the Sovereign: Employee Relations in the Federal Government. Sar A. Levitan & Alexandra B. Noden. LC 82-49064. (Policy Studies in Employment & Welfare). 160p. 1983. text ed. 20.00x (ISBN 0-8018-3028-1). Johns Hopkins.

Working for the United Nations: 1948-1968. Sze Szeming. (Illus.). 66p. 1986. pap. 8.00 (ISBN 0-9611428-4-7). LISZ Pubns.

Working for Victory? Images of Women in the First World War, 1914-18. Diana Condell & Jean Liddiard. (Illus.). 192p. 1987. 35.00 (ISBN 0-7102-0974-6, A0747, Pub. by Routledge UK). Routledge Chapman & Hall.

Working for Wildlife: The Beginning of Preservation in Canada. Janet Foster. LC 78-315369. pap. 73.80 (2026455). Bks Demand UMI.

Working for You: A Guide to Employing Women in Nontraditional Jobs. rev. ed. 1979. 5.00 (ISBN 0-934966-04-4). WOW Inc.

Working for Yourself. Maurice Ainsworth. 128p. 1987. 21.00x (ISBN 0-7063-6613-1, Pub. by Ward Lock Educ Co Ltd). State Mutual Bk.

Working for Yourself: A Guide to Success for People Who Work Outside the 9 to 5 World. P. Namanworth & G. Busnar. 288p. 1985. text ed. 18.95 (ISBN 0-07-009347-4); pap. text ed. 10.95 (ISBN 0-07-009346-6). McGraw.

Working Forces in Japanese Politics, 1867-1920. Uichi Iwasaki. LC 21-7669. (Columbia University. Studies in the Social Sciences: No. 220). Repr. of 1921 ed. 15.00 (ISBN 0-404-51220-8). AMS Pr.

Working Free: Practical Alternatives to the Nine to Five Job. John Applegath. 192p. 1982. 13.95 (ISBN 0-8144-5658-8); pap. 6.95. AMACOM.

Working Free: Practical Alternatives to the 9 to 5 Job. John Applegath. pap. 2.95 (ISBN 0-345-31075-6). Ballantine.

Working Friendship: The Correspondence Between Richard Strauss & Hugo Von Hofmannsthal. Tr. by Hanns Hammelmann & Ewald Osers. LC 61-13839. 580p. 1974. pap. 17.50x (ISBN 0-8443-0050-0). Vienna Hse.

Working from Home: Everything You Need to Know about Living & Working under the Same Roof. Paul Edwards & Sarah Edwards. LC 84-23992. (Illus.). 432p. 1985. pap. 11.95 (ISBN 0-87477-240-0). J P Tarcher.

Working from Home: Everything You Need to Know about Living & Working under the Same Roof. rev. ed. Paul Edwards & Sarah Edwards. 448p. 1987. 12.95 (ISBN 0-87477-457-8). J P Tarcher.

Working Girl in a Man's World. Jan Manette. LC 66-22896. 223p. 1966. 4.95 (ISBN 0-915988-01-1, Pub. by Hawthorne Books). Reading Gems.

Working Girls of Boston. Carroll D. Wright. LC 73-89711. (American Labor, from Conspiracy to Collective Bargaining Ser., No. 1). 133p. 1969. Repr. of 1889 ed. 13.00 (ISBN 0-405-02158-5). Ayer Co Pubs.

Working Girls of Cincinnati: An Original Anthology. Ed. by Leon Stein & Annette K. Baxter. LC 74-3981. (Women in America Ser). (Illus.). 182p. 1974. Repr. 18.00x (ISBN 0-405-06129-3). Ayer Co Pubs.

Working Green Wood with Peg. Patrick Spielman. LC 79-91406. (Illus.). 160p. 1980. pap. 12.95 (ISBN 0-8069-8924-6). Sterling.

Working Group Meeting on Efficiency & Conservation in the Use of Energy: Proceedings. (Energy Resources Development Ser.: No. 22). 131p. 1981. pap. 11.00 (ISBN 92-1-119173-4, E.80.11.F.12). UN.

Working Guide for Directors of Not-For-Profit Organizations. Charles Waldo. LC 85-24396. 160p. 1986. 35.00 (ISBN 0-89930-091-X, WHD/). Greenwood.

Working High Magic. Rev. ed. Nelson White & Anne White. LC 81-51402. (Illus.). 125p. (Orig.). 1981. pap. 30.00 (ISBN 0-939856-27-1). Tech Group.

Working Horse. Geoffrey Patterson. (Illus.). 32p. (gr. 2-5). 1986. 10.95 (ISBN 0-233-97786-4). Andre Deutsch.

Working Hours: Assessing the Potential for Reduction. Michael White. v, 104p. (Orig.). 1987. pap. 14.00 (ISBN 92-2-106151-5). Intl Labour Office.

Working in a Service Industry. Faye Gold & Raymond J. Grandfield. (Distributive Career Ser., Bk. 3). (Illus.). 128p. (gr. 10-12). 1973. pap. text ed. 3.50 (ISBN 0-87005-117-2). Fairchild.

Working in a Service Station. Peter Novellino. (Series 971). (Orig.). 1980. pap. 6.00 wkbk. (ISBN 0-8064-0439-6); audio-visual pkg. 169.00 (ISBN 0-8064-0440-X). Bergwall.

Working in a Store. Faye Gold & Raymond J. Grandfield. (Distributive Career Ser., Bk. 2). (Illus.). 96p. (gr. 9-12). 1972. pap. 3.50 (ISBN 0-87005-114-8). Fairchild.

Working in Agricultural Industry. Jasper S. Lee. (Illus.). (gr. 9-10). 1978. pap. 16.96 (ISBN 0-07-000831-0). McGraw.

Working in Agricultural Mechanics. Glen C. Shinn & Curtis Weston. Ed. by Max L. Amberson. (Illus.). 1978. pap. 19.96 (ISBN 0-07-000843-4). McGraw.

Working in Animal Science. Paul Peterson et al. Ed. by Max L. Amberson. (Illus.). (gr. 9-10). 1978. pap. 19.96 (ISBN 0-07-000839-6). McGraw.

Working in Canada. Ed. by Walter Johnson. 160p. 1983. 29.95 (ISBN 0-920057-14-4, Dist. by U of Toronto Pr); pap. 12.95 (ISBN 0-920057-13-6, Dist. by the U of Toronto). Black Rose Bks.

Working in Canvas. 2nd ed. P. W. Blandford. (Illus.). 74p. 1981. pap. 6.50x (ISBN 0-85174-416-8). Sheridan.

Working in Foundations: Career Patterns of Women & Men. Teresa J. Odendahl et al. LC 84-60649. 125p. (Orig.). 1985. pap. text ed. 12.95 (ISBN 0-87954-134-2). Foundation Ctr.

Working in Hawaii: A Labor History. Edward D. Beechert. LC 85-8640. 448p. 1985. text ed. 30.00x (ISBN 0-8248-0890-8). UH Pr.

Working in Horticulture. William B. Richardson & Gary Moore. (Career Preparations for Agricultural-Agribusiness Ser.). (Illus.). 1980. text ed. 29.96 (ISBN 0-07-052285-5). McGraw.

Working in Metal: Management & Labor in the Metal Industries of Europe & the U. S. A., 1890 to 1914. Chris McGuffie. 302p. (Orig.). 1985. 29.95 (ISBN 0-85036-312-8, Pub. by Merlin Pr UK). Longwood Pub Group.

Working In Miniature: A Machine Piecing Approach to Minature Quilts. Becky Schaefer. LC 86-71881. (Illus.). 84p. (Orig.). 1987. pap. 14.95 (ISBN 0-914881-06-X). C & T Pub.

Working in Organisations. Andrew Kakabadse et al. 400p. 1987. text ed. 47.50 (ISBN 0-566-02432-2, Pub. by Gower Pub England). Gower Pub Co.

Working in Organizations. Don Davidson. 304p. 1987. pap. text ed. 24.95x (ISBN 0-273-02761-1). Trans-Atl Phila.

Working in Plant Science. Douglas D. Bishop. Ed. by Max L. Amberson & Stephen R. Chapman. (Illus.). (gr. 9-10). 1978. pap. 18.96 (ISBN 0-07-000835-3). McGraw.

Working in Plant Science: Activity Guide. Lark P. Carter et al. Ed. by Max Aaberson. (Illus.). (gr. 9-10). 1978. pap. text ed. 12.96 (ISBN 0-07-000836-1). McGraw.

Working in Precious Metals. Ernest A. Smith. 414p. 1987. 60.00x (ISBN 0-7198-0032-3, Pub. by E Bruton Assocs Ltd UK). State Mutual Bk.

Working in Social Work: Growing & Thriving in Human Services. Armand Lauffer. LC 86-29700. (Sourcebooks in the Human Services Ser.: Vol. 6). 400p. 1987. text ed. 29.95 (ISBN 0-8039-2041-5). Sage.

Working in South Africa. Ed. by Ken Dovey et al. 397p. 1985. pap. 15.95 (ISBN 0-86975-263-4, Pub. by Ravan Pr). Ohio U Pr.

Working in Space, AAS5. Ed. by George V. Butler et al. LC 81-20528. (Illus.). 138p. 1981. 20.00 (ISBN 0-915928-57-4). AIAA.

Working in Teams: A Practical Manual for Improving Work Groups. James H. Shonk. 128p. 1982. 14.95 (ISBN 0-8144-5718-5). AMACOM.

Working in the Arts: A Guide for Enterprise, Employment & Assistance. Keith Windschuttle. 92p. 1988. pap. text ed. 12.95x (ISBN 0-7022-2090-6). U of Queensland Pr.

Working in the European Communities. Ajraban. 84p. 1984. 40.00x (ISBN 0-86021-742-6, Pub. by Hobsons Ltd UK). State Mutual Bk.

Working in the Transportation Industry. Faye Gold & Raymond J. Grandfield. (Distributive Career Ser., Bk. 5). (Illus.). 128p. (gr. 9-12. 1974. wkbk 3.50 (ISBN 0-87005-121-0). Fairchild.

Working in the Twenty-First Century. Ed. by C. Stewart Sheppard. Donald C. Carroll. LC 79-24775. 235p. 1980. 34.95 (ISBN 0-471-07755-0, Pub. by Wiley-Interscience). Wiley.

Working in Wood: An Illustrated Encyclopedia. Ernest Scott. (Illus.). 272p. 1980. 25.00 (ISBN 0-399-12550-7, Putnam). Putnam Pub Group.

Working in Wood: Boxes & Small Chests. John Trussell. (Illus.). 96p. 1986. 18.95 (ISBN 0-85219-608-3, Pub. by Batsford England). David & Charles.

Working Inside Out: Tools for Change. Margo Adair. LC 84-22912 (Illus.). 414p. (Orig.). 1985. pap. 9.95 (ISBN 0-914728-50-4). Wingbow Pr.

Working It Out: Sanity & Success in the Workplace. Stephen Strasser. 256p. 1988. 16.95 (ISBN 0-13-965112-8). P-H.

Working it Out: The Domestic Double Standard. Judith K. Sprankle. 224p. 1986. 16.95 (ISBN 0-8027-0883-8). WAlker & Co.

Working It Out Together: A Guide for Dual Career Couples. Jack Loughary & Theresa Ripley. 167p. 1987. pap. 12.95. United Learn.

Working It Out: 23 Women Writers, Artists, Scientists, & Scholars Talk About Their Lives & Work. Ed. by Sara Ruddick & Pamela Daniels. LC 76-54624. 1978. pap. 9.95 (ISBN 0-394-73557-9). Pantheon.

Working It Through. Elisabeth Kubler-Ross. (Illus.). 176p. 1987. pap. 5.95 (ISBN 0-02-022000-6, Collier). Macmillan.

Working Knowledge: Skill & Community in a Small Shop. Douglas Harper. LC 86-30708. (Illus.). x, 214p. 1987. 29.95x (ISBN 0-226-31688-2). U of Chicago Pr.

Working Life: A Social Science Contribution to Work Reform. Ed. by Bertil Gardell & Gunn Johansson. LC 80-40289. 347p. 1981. 73.95x (ISBN 0-471-27801-7, Pub. by Wiley-Interscience). Wiley.

Working Life: A Social Science Contribution to Work Reform. Ed. by Bertil Gardell & Gunn Johansson. LC 80-40289. (Illus.). 361p. pap. 93.90 (2030476). Bks Demand UMI.

Working Life of Women in the Seventeenth Century. Alice Clark. 328p. 1968. Repr. of 1919 ed. 29.50x (ISBN 0-7146-1291-X, BHA-01291, F Cass Co). Biblio Dist.

Working Life of Women in the Seventeenth Century. Alice Clark. LC 67-31558. 1968. Repr. of 1919 ed. 35.00x (ISBN 0-678-05039-2). Kelley.

Working Life of Women in the Seventeenth Century. Alice Clark. 368p. 1982. pap. 9.95 (ISBN 0-7100-9045-5). Routledge Chapman & Hall.

Working Lives: An Oral History of Rhode Island Labor. Ed. by Paul M Buhle. (American Places Ser.). (Illus.). 79p. 1987. pap. text ed. 12.00 (ISBN 0-932840-05-1, Dist. by University Publishing Associates). RI Pubns Soc.

Working Lives: The American Workforce since 1920. John D. Owen. LC 85-45166. 240p. 1985. 33.00x (ISBN 0-669-11265-8). Lexington Bks.

Working Lives: The "Southern Exposure" History of Labor in the South. Ed. by Marc S. Miller. (Illus.). 1981. 17.95 (ISBN 0-394-50912-9); pap. 7.95 (ISBN 0-394-73965-5). Pantheon.

Working Man's Political Economy, Founded upon the Principle of Immutable Justice & the Inalienable Rights of Man: Designed for the Promotion of National Reform. John Pickering. LC 79-156421. (American Labor Ser., No. 2). 1971. Repr. of 1847 ed. 19.00 (ISBN 0-405-02940-3). Ayer Co Pubs.

Working Manual for Altar Guilds. rev. ed. Dorothy C. Diggs. (Orig.). 1957. pap. 6.95 (ISBN 0-8192-1028-5). Morehouse.

Working Memory. Alan Baddeley. (OXford Psychology Ser.: No. 11). (Illus.). 300p. 1986. 45.00 (ISBN 0-19-852116-2). Oxford U Pr.

Working Memory. Alan Baddeley. (Psychology Ser.: No. 11). 304p. 1987. pap. 26.95 (ISBN 0-19-852133-2). Oxford U Pr.

Working Men & Ganja: Marijuana Use in Rural Jamaica. Melanie C. Dreher. LC 81-6872. (Illus.). 232p. 1982. text ed. 21.00 (ISBN 0-89727-025-8). ISHI PA.

Working Men's Association, the First Convention & the National Association. Working Men's Association Staff et al. Ed. by Dorothy Thompson. (Chartism, Working-Class Politics in the Industrial Revolution Ser.). 132p. 1987. lib. bdg. 25.00 (ISBN 0-8240-5586-1). Garland Pub.

Working Men's College, 1854-1904. Ed. by John L. Davies. LC 75-144594. Repr. of 1904 ed. 21.50 (ISBN 0-404-01978-1). AMS Pr.

Working Men's Social Clubs & Educational Institutes. Henry Solly. LC 79-56943. (English Working Class Ser.). 1980. lib. bdg. 29.00 (ISBN 0-8240-0124-9). Garland Pub.

Working Methods in Neuropsychopharmacology: The Team Approach. Michael H. Joseph & John L. Waddington. (Studies in Neuroscience). 288p. 1987. 65.00 (ISBN 0-7190-2245-2, Pub. by Manchester Univ Pr). St Martin.

Working Miracles of Love: A Collection of Teachings. Yogi A. Desai. LC 85-50126. (Illus.). 184p. 1985. pap. text ed. 5.95 (ISBN 0-940258-15-3). Kripalu Pubns.

Working Mom. Bee L. Wang & Richard Stellway. 1987. pap. 6.95 (ISBN 1-55513-322-3, LifeJourney). Cook.

Working Mom's Survival Guide. Jayne Garrison. 96p. 1988. pap. 2.25 (ISBN 0-8423-8397-2). Tyndale.

Working Mother: A Survey of Problems & Programs in Nine Countries. 2nd rev. ed. Alice H. Cook. LC 78-620004. 84p. 1978. pap. 4.75 (ISBN 0-87546-067-4). ILR Pr.

Working Mothers: An Evaluative Review of the Consequences for Wife, Husband, & Child. Lois W. Hoffman & F. Ivan Nye. LC 74-6744. (Social & Behavioral Science Ser.). 1974. 29.95x (ISBN 0-87589-243-4). Jossey-Bass.

Working Mothers & Guilt. Kay Kuzma. (Lifestyle Ser.). 30p. 1987. pap. 0.75 (ISBN 0-8163-0717-2). Pacific Pr Pub Assn.

Working Mother's Complete Handbook. rev. ed. Gloria Norris & JoAnn Miller. LC 84-2062. 352p. 1984. pap. 9.95 (ISBN 0-452-25523-6, Plume). NAL.

Working of Econometric Models. M. Morishima et al. LC 79-184901. (Illus.). 300p. 1972. 49.50 (ISBN 0-521-08502-0). Cambridge U Pr.

Working of Mineral Deposits. Georgi Popov. 616p. 1983. text ed. cancelled (ISBN 0-8290-1477-2). Irvington.

Working of State Trading in India. Kulwant R. Gupta. 349p. Repr. of 1970 ed. text ed. 24.00X. Coronet Bks.

Working on a New Play: A Play Development Handbook for Actors, Directors, Designers, & Playwrights. Edward M. Cohen. 256p. 1988. 16.95 (ISBN 0-13-441502-7). Prentice Hall Pr.

Working on It. Joan Oppenheimer. LC 79-3763. (gr. 7 up). 1980. 7.95 (ISBN 0-15-299629-X, HJ). HarBraceJ.

Working on It. Joan Oppenheimer. 144p. (YA) (gr. 7 up). 1986. pap. 2.25 (ISBN 0-440-99514-0, LFL). Dell.

Working on the Quality of Working Life. International Council for the Quality of Working Life. (International Series on the Quality of Working Life: Vol. 8). 1979. lib. bdg. 36.75 (ISBN 0-89838-001-4, Pub. by Martinus Nijhoff Netherlands). Kluwer Academic.

Working on Words. John Canney et al. viii, 260p. (Orig.). 1981. pap. text ed. 17.95x (ISBN 0-913580-72-4, Clerc Bks). Gallaudet Univ Pr.

Working on Working. Office of Radio & Television for Learning, WGBH Educational Foundation. 84p. 1979. 5.50 (ISBN 0-318-15602-4, SN24). Natl Ctr Res Voc Ed.

Working Order. Eric Batstone. 376p. 1985. 39.95x (ISBN 0-631-13751-3). Basil Blackwell.

Working Out a Painting. Colleen Browning. (Illus.). 144p. 1988. 27.50 (ISBN 0-8230-2994-8). Watson-Guptill.

Working Out: The Total Shape-Up Guide for Men. Charles Hix. LC 82-19208. (Illus.). 224p. 1983. 17.95 (ISBN 0-671-45793-4). S&S.

Working with Communication Skill. Rose M. O'Donnell. 112p. (Orig.). 1987. wkbk. 24.95 (ISBN 0-88450-218-X, 7385). Communication Skill.

Working with Computers. Robert H. Blissmer & Roland Alden. LC 88-81324. 1989. pap. text ed. price not set (ISBN 0-395-43301-0); instr's. manual, test bank avail. HM.

Working with Computers. National Computing Centre. 86p. 1982. pap. 7.65 (ISBN 0-471-89433-8, DP00, Pub. by Wiley-Interscience). Wiley.

Working with Computers. Keith Wicks. (World of Science Ser.). (Illus.). 64p. (YA) (gr. 4-7). 12.95 (ISBN 0-8160-1071-4). Facts on File.

Working with Computers: Computer Orientation for Foreign Students. Michael Barlow. LC 86-83418. (Illus.). 320p. (Orig.). 1987. 23.95 (ISBN 0-940753-07-3); pap. 15.95 (ISBN 0-940753-08-1). Athelstan Pubns.

Working with Computers: Theory versus Outcome. Ed. by G. C. Van der Veer et al. (Computers & People Ser.). 268p. 1988. price not set (ISBN 0-12-711705-9). ACad Pr.

Working with Couples for Marriage Enrichment: A Guide to Developing, Conducting, & Evaluating Programs. Diana S. Richmond Garland. LC 83-48158. (Social & Behavioral Science Ser.). 1983. text ed. 31.95x (ISBN 0-87589-573-5). Jossey-Bass.

Working with dBase II. M. De Pace. 174p. 1985. pap. text ed. 15.95x (ISBN 0-00-383251-1, Pub. by Collins England). Sheridan.

Working with dBASE MAC: A User's Guide & Reference. Rusel DeMaria & George Fontaine. 400p. (Orig.). 1988. pap. 19.95. Prentice Hall Pr.

Working with dBase Mac: Pushing Productivity to the Limit. Rusel Demaria & George Fontaine. (Illus.). 500p. 1988. pap. 24.95 (ISBN 0-13-939760-4). Brady Comp Bks.

Working with dBASE on the Macintosh. Kent Blankenbaker & Brad Vavra. 250p. (Orig.). pap. cancelled (ISBN 0-938862-67-7). Weber Systems.

Working with Depressed Women: A Feminist Approach. Alison Corob. (Community Care Practice Handbook Ser.). Orig. Title: Social Work with Depressed Women. 200p. 1986. text ed. 11.00 (ISBN 0-566-05100-1). Gower Pub Co.

Working with Difficult Customers. David El Fattal. 59p. (Orig.). 1988. pap. 6.00. El Fattal Enterprises.

Working with Disadvantaged Parents & Their Children: Methods & Outcome in a Service-Centered Study. Sally Provence & Audrey Naylor. LC 82-48906. 192p. 1983. text ed. 25.00x (ISBN 0-300-02854-7). Yale U Pr.

Working with DisplayWrite Three. Rob Krumm. 320p. 1986. 24.95 (ISBN 0-8306-9564-8, 2664); pap. 17.95 (ISBN 0-8306-9664-4, 2664P). Tab Bks.

Working with DisplayWrite 4. Stephen T. Cobb. 1988. pap. 21.95 (ISBN 0-673-38020-3). Scott F.

Working with Dreams: Expand, Heal, & Transform Your Life Through Your Dreams. Montague Ullman & Nan Zimmerman. LC 79-12866. (Illus.). 352p. 1985. pap. 8.95 (ISBN 0-87477-356-3). J P Tarcher.

Working with Drug Users. Ronno Griffiths & Brian Pearson. (Community Care Practice Handbook Ser.: Vol. 25). 117p. 1988. pap. text ed. 10.00x (ISBN 0-7045-0582-7, Pub. by Gower Pub England). Gower Pub Co.

Working with Easy Script. Randall McMullan. (Illus.). 160p. 1984. pap. 11.95 (ISBN 0-246-12565-9, Pub. by Granada England). Sheridan.

Working with Families of the Mentally Ill. Kayla Bernheim & Anthony Lehman. LC 85-18754. 1985. 22.95 (ISBN 0-393-70009-7). Norton.

Working with Fiberglass: Techniques & Projects. Jack Wiley. (Illus.). 220p. 1986. 19.95 (ISBN 0-8306-0739-0); pap. 11.95 (ISBN 0-8306-2739-1, NO. 2739). TAB Bks.

Working with Focus: An Introduction to Database Management. Clifford A. Schaffer. (Illus.). 256p. 1987. pap. 22.95 (ISBN 0-8306-2810-X, 2810, TAB-TPR). TAB Bks.

Working with God. Gardner Hunting. 1934. 5.95 (ISBN 0-87159-174-X). Unity School.

Working with Health Care Consultants. John G. Nackel et al. (Illus.). 64p. (Orig.). 1986. pap. 18.75 (ISBN 0-939450-88-7, AHA CATALOG NO. 001114). AHPI.

Working with History: The Historical Records Survey in Louisiana & the Nation, 1936-1942. Burl Noggle. LC 81-5789. xii, 148p. 1981. text ed. 20.00x (ISBN 0-8071-0881-2). La State U Pr.

Working with Ion-Selective Electrodes. Karl Camman. Tr. by A. H. Schroeder from Ger. (Chemical Laboratory Practice Ser.). (Illus.). 1979. 49.00 (ISBN 0-387-09320-6). Springer-Verlag.

Working with Legal Assistants: A Team Approach for Lawyers & Legal Assistants - 1, 2 vols. LC 80-69532. 793p. (Orig.). pap. 55.00 set (ISBN 0-89707-030-5, 511-0065); Vol. 1 1980. pap. 25.00 (511-0060); Vol. 2 1981. pap. 40.00 (511-0064). Amer Bar Assn.

Working with Library Consultants. Beverly A. Rawles & Michael B. Wessels. LC 84-7942. x, 238p. 1984. 27.50 (ISBN 0-208-02018-7, Lib Prof Pubns); pap. 21.50x (ISBN 0-208-02019-5, Lib Prof Pubns). Shoe String.

Working with Lotus Agenda. John R. Ottensmann & Jan Neuenschwander. (Illus.). 256p. 1988. pap. 17.95 (ISBN 0-8306-3161-5, 3161). TAB Bks.

Working with Lotus HAL: A 1-2-3 User's Guide. Douglas J. Wolf. (Illus.). 176p. 1988. 24.95 (ISBN 0-8306-0273-9, 2973); pap. 15.95 (ISBN 0-8306-2973-4). TAB Bks.

Working with Manuscript. Walton Beacham. (Business Productivity Library). 1987. pap. 21.95 (ISBN 0-553-34435-8). Bantam.

Working with Men's Groups. Roger Karsk & Bill Thomas. LC 87-50080. 126p. Repr. of 1979 ed. plastic spiral bound 19.95 (ISBN 0-938586-05-X). Whole Person.

Working with Metal. (Home Repair & Improvement Ser.). (Illus.). 128p. 1981. 11.95 (ISBN 0-8094-3470-9). Time-Life.

Working with Metal. LC 82-14339. (Home Repair & Improvement Ser.). (gr. 7 up). 1981. lib. bdg. 15.94 (ISBN 0-8094-3471-7, Pub. by Time-Life). Silver.

Working with Microsoft Word 3.0 for the Macintosh. Ezra Shapiro. 300p. 1987. cancelled (ISBN 0-672-48407-2). Sams.

Working with Microsoft Works. John Campbell. 320p. 1987. cancelled (ISBN 0-672-46426-8). Sams.

Working with Microsoft Works. John L. Campbell. (Illus.). 256p. 1988. pap. 21.95 (ISBN 0-8306-3119-4, 3119). TAB Bks.

Working with MS-DOS V3.2. Weber Systems Inc. Staff. 300p. 1986. pap. 19.95 (ISBN 0-938862-16-2). Weber Systems.

Working with MSX BASIC. Ian Sinclair. (Illus.). 160p. 1984. pap. 19.95 (ISBN 0-00-383103-5, Pub. by Collins England). Sheridan.

Working with Multimate. Richard Rose. 288p. (Orig.). 1986. pap. 17.95 (ISBN 0-938862-55-3). Weber Systems.

Working with Multiproblem Families. Lisa Kaplan. LC 85-45010. 192p. 1986. 29.00x (ISBN 0-669-13210-1); pap. 14.95x (ISBN 0-669-11097-3). Lexington Bks.

Working with No Data: Semitic & Egyptian Studies Presented to Thomas O. Lambdin. Ed. by David M. Golomb & Susan T. Hollis. LC 87-30571. (Illus.). xvi, 264p. 1988. text ed. 28.50x (ISBN 0-931464-35-8). Eisenbrauns.

Working with Older Adults. J. Stanley Rendahl. LC 84-80708. (Equipping Ser.). (Illus.). 130p. (Orig.). 1984. pap. 5.95 (ISBN 0-935797-08-4). Harvest IL.

Working with Older People. U. S. Department of Health, Education & Welfare-Public Health Service. Ed. by Leon Stein. LC 79-8669. (Growing Old Ser.). 1980. Repr. of 1970 ed. lib. bdg. 14.00x (ISBN 0-405-12784-7). Ayer Co Pubs.

Working with Older Persons: Cognitive & Phenomenological Methods. Edmund Sherman. LC 84-5746. 1984. lib. bdg. 37.00 (ISBN 0-89838-144-4, Pub. by Kluwer-Nijhoff (Netherlands)). Kluwer Academic.

Working with ORACLE: An Introduction to Database Management. Jack L. Hursch & Carolyn Hurrsch. (Illus.). 240p. 1987. pap. 19.95 (ISBN 0-8306-2916-5, 2916, TAB-TPR). TAB Bks.

Working With Parents. Cliff Cunningham & Hilton Davis. LC 85-13777. (Children with Special Needs Ser.). 160p. 1985. 59.00x (ISBN 0-335-15036-5, Open Univ Pr); pap. text ed. 21.00x (ISBN 0-335-15035-7). Taylor & Francis.

Working with Parents: A Practical Guide for Teachers & Therapists. Roy McConkey. 325p. 1985. text ed. 27.95 (ISBN 0-914797-13-1, Co-Pub. by Croom Helm Ltd); pap. text ed. 17.95 (ISBN 0-914797-14-X, Co-Pub. by Croom Helm Ltd). Brookline Bks.

Working with Parents & Infants. Rose Bromwich. LC 80-16141. 384p. 1978. pap. text ed. 21.00x (ISBN 0-936104-41-4, 1216). Pro Ed.

Working with Parents of College Students. Ed. by Robert D. Cohen. LC 85-60839. (Student Services Ser.: No. 32). (Orig.). 1985. pap. text ed. 12.95x (ISBN 0-87589-770-3). Jossey-Bass.

Working with Parents of Exceptional Children: A Guide for Professionals. Richard Gargiulo. LC 84-81345. 240p. 1985. pap. text ed. 22.36 (ISBN 0-395-35767-5). HM.

Working with Parents of Exceptional Children. Stewart Ehly et al. 286p. 1985. text ed. 29.95 case (ISBN 0-675-20586-7). Merrill.

Working with Parents of Handicapped Children: A Book of Readings for School Personnel. Ed. by Michael L. Henniger & Elizabeth M. Nesselroad. LC 84-13169. 556p. (Orig.). 1984. lib. bdg. 39.50 (ISBN 0-8191-4181-X); pap. text ed. 24.00 (ISBN 0-8191-4182-8). U Pr of Amer.

Working with Parents of Handicapped Children. William L. Heward et al. LC 78-61269. (Illus.). pap. 82.50 (ISBN 0-317-58111-2, AU00347). Bks Demand UMI.

Working with Patients: Introductory Guidelines for Psychotherapists. Helen A. De Rosis. LC 77-896. 208p. 1977. 15.00x (ISBN 0-87586-057-5). Agathon.

Working with PC Works. Michael L. Sloan. 1988. pap. 19.95 (ISBN 0-673-38192-7). Scott F.

Working with People. John L. Beckley. 158p. 1985. 14.95 (ISBN 0-910187-03-7). Economics Pr.

Working with People. Doran C. McCarty. (Broadman Leadership Ser.). (Orig.). 1987. pap. 5.95 (ISBN 0-8054-3241-8). Broadman.

Working with People, Bugs, & Apples: An Old Fashioned Family, L. M. & Grace Smith, Parents of Ten. Malcolm L. Smith. LC 78-73543. (Illus.). 1979. 11.50 (ISBN 0-686-28585-9). M L Smith.

Working with People Called Patients. Milton M. Berger. LC 76-46483. 1977. pap. 14.95 (ISBN 0-87630-126-X). Brunner-Mazel.

Working with People: Clinical Uses of Personal Construct Psychology. Ed. by Gavin Dunnett. 224p. 1988. lib. bdg. 49.50 (ISBN 0-415-00262-1). Routledge Chapman & Hall.

Working with People in Crisis: Theory & Practice. Samuel L. Dixon. 203p. 1979. pap. text ed. 19.95 (ISBN 0-675-20594-8). Merrill.

Working with People in Crisis: Theory & Practice. 2nd ed. Samuel L. Dixon. 224p. 1987. pap. text ed. 19.95 (ISBN 0-675-20701-0). Merrill.

Working with People: The Helping Process. 3rd ed. Naomi I. Brill. LC 84-941. (Orig.). 1984. pap. 15.95 (ISBN 0-582-28460-0). Longman.

Working with Physicians in Health Promotion: A Key to Successful Programs. Salvinija G. Kernaghan & Barbara E. Giloth. LC 84-2925. 120p. (Orig.). 1983. pap. 18.75 (ISBN 0-939450-21-6, 070124). AHPI.

Working with PICK. (Walter Stagner). 330p. (Orig.). 1987. pap. 19.95 (ISBN 0-938862-22-7). Weber Systems.

Working with Plant Supplies & Services. William Farrington et al. (Illus.). 144p. 1980. pap. 13.96 (ISBN 0-07-019965-5). McGraw.

Working with Plastics. Time-Life Books Editors. LC 81-18459. (Home Repair & Improvement Ser.: No. 31). (Illus.). 128p. 1982. 11.95 (ISBN 0-8094-3506-3). Time-Life.

Working with Plastics. LC 81-18459. (Home Repair & Improvement Ser.). (gr. 7 up). 1982. lib. bdg. 15.94 (ISBN 0-8094-3507-1, Pub. by Time-Life). Silver.

Working with Pysarthric Clients. Sandra J. Roberson & Fay Thomson. 108p. 1987. pap. text ed. 16.95 (ISBN 0-88450-211-2). Communication Skill.

Working with Q & A. Ken Knecht. 352p. 1986. pap. 19.95 (ISBN 0-938862-71-5). Weber Systems.

Working with Q & A: Practical Techniques in Database Design. Neil Dunlop. 304p. 1987. pap. 19.95 (ISBN 0-673-18729-2). Scott F.

Working with Reflex. Walter Stagner. 300p. 1987. pap. 19.95 (ISBN 0-938862-75-8). Weber Systems.

Working with Refugees. Ed. by Peter Rose. (CMS Migration & Ethnicity Ser.). 175p. 1986. 17.50 (ISBN 0-913256-77-3); pap. 12.95 (ISBN 0-913256-97-8). Ctr Migration.

Working with Religious Issues in Therapy. Robert J. Lovinger. LC 84-6198. 328p. 1984. 30.00x (ISBN 0-87668-727-3). Aronson.

Working with Roosevelt. Samuel I. Rosenman. LC 75-168391. (FDR & the Era of the New Deal Ser.). (Illus.). 1972. Repr. of 1952 ed. lib. bdg. 55.00 (ISBN 0-306-70328-9). Da Capo.

Working with RT-11. David Beaumont et al. (DEC Books). (Illus.). 150p. 1984. pap. 25.00 (ISBN 0-932376-31-2, EY-00021-DP). Digital Pr.

Working with Rural Youth. facsimile ed. Edmund D. Brunner. LC 74-1669. (Children & Youth Ser.). 132p. 1974. Repr. of 1942 ed. 14.00 (ISBN 0-405-05949-3). Ayer Co Pubs.

Working with Sidekick. Ronald D. Lee. 150p. (Orig.). 1988. pap. 9.95 (ISBN 0-938862-82-0). Weber Systems.

Working with Sounds see Specific Skill Reading Series: 1982.

Working with Stained Glass: Fundamental Techniques & Applications. Jean-Jacques Duval. LC 74-184975. (Funk & W Bk.). (Illus.). 144p. 1974. pap. 5.95i o.s.i (ISBN 0-308-10153-7, F112). T Y Crowell.

Working with Statistics. Stuart Reid. 183p. 1987. pap. 14.95 (ISBN 0-8476-7590-4, Rowman & Allanhead). Rowman.

Working with Structuralism: Essays & Reviews on Nineteenth & Twentieth-Century Literature. David Lodge. 240p. 1981. pap. 8.95x (ISBN 0-7100-9330-6). Routledge Chapman & Hall.

Working with Structuralism: Essays & Reviews on Nineteenth & Twentieth Century Literature. David Lodge. 224p. 1986. pap. 5.95 (ISBN 0-7448-0043-9). Routledge Chapman & Hall.

Working with Student Teachers. Florence B. Stratemeyer & M. Lindsey. LC 58-8555. 502p. 1958. pap. text ed. 13.95x (ISBN 0-8077-2222-7). Tchrs Coll.

Working with SuperCalc Four. Jerry Willis & William Pasewark. 300p. 1987. 24.95 (ISBN 0-8306-0214-3, 2814). TAB Bks.

Working with the Aged. 2nd. ed. Marcella B. Weiner et al. 256p. 1986. 19.95 (ISBN 0-8385-9833-1). Appleton & Lange.

Working with the Atom: Careers for You. (Public Affairs & Information Program: General). 41p. 1982. pap. 1.75 (ISBN 0-318-02236-2). US Coun Energy Awareness.

Working with the Bilingual Community. LC 79-84372. 90p. (Orig.). 1979. pap. 6.75 (ISBN 0-89763-013-0). Natl Clearinghse Bilingual Ed.

Working with the Community: A Developer's Guide. Douglas R. Porter et al. (Community Builders Handbook Supplement Ser.). 200p. 1985. pap. 44.00 (ISBN 0-87420-646-4). Urban Land.

Working with the Computer. Gilbert Mansell. 156p. 1971. pap. 13.00 (ISBN 0-08-016014-X). Pergamon.

Working with the Dreaming Body. Arnold Mindell. 128p. 1985. 19.95x (ISBN 0-7102-0609-7); pap. 8.95 (ISBN 0-7102-0465-5). Routledge Chapman & Hall.

Working with the Elderly. Eunice Mortimer. Ed. by Martin Davies. (Community Care Practice Handbook Ser.: No. 9). vi, 91p. (Orig.). 1982. pap. text ed. 6.50x (ISBN 0-435-82607-7). Gower Pub Co.

Working with the Elderly: Group Process & Techniques. 2nd ed. Irene M. Burnside. LC 83-19774. 700p. 1986. pap. text ed. 25.00 (ISBN 0-86720-379-X). Jones & Bartlett.

Working with the Elderly in Their Residence. Dean Tjosvold & Mary M. Tjosvold. 240p. 1983. 38.95 (ISBN 0-275-91090-3, C1090). Praeger.

Working with the Family in Primary Care: A Systems Approach to Health & Illness. Janet Christie-Seely. 576p. 1983. 30.95 (ISBN 0-275-91424-0, C1424). Praeger.

Working with the Family in Primary Care: A Systems Approach to Health & Illness. Ed. by Janet Christie-Seely. 584p. 1984. 27.95 (ISBN 0-03-063899-2). Soc Tchrs Fam Med.

Working with the FAR: Course Manual. LC 86-187522. Date not set. price not set. Fed Pubns Inc.

Working with the Hands: Being a Sequel to "Up from Slavery"Covering the Author's Experiences in Industrial Training at Tuskegee. Booker T. Washington. LC 76-92241. (American Negro: His History & Literature Ser., No. 3). 1970. Repr. of 1904 ed. 18.00 (ISBN 0-405-01941-6). Ayer Co Pubs.

Working with the Hands, Being a Sequel to "Up from Slavery". Booker T. Washington. LC 73-77216. (Illus.). 1969. Repr. of 1904 ed. 35.00x (ISBN 0-8371-1314-8, WWH&). Greenwood.

Working with the IBM Assistant Series. Mary Johnson. 304p. 1987. pap. 19.95 (ISBN 0-673-18734-9). Scott F.

Working with the Impulsive Person. Ed. by H. A. Wishnie & J. Nevis-Olesen. LC 79-13899. 202p. 1979. 27.50x (ISBN 0-306-40184-3, Plenum Pr). Plenum Pub.

Working with the Intermarried: A Practical Guide for Workshop Leaders. Andrew Baker & Lori Goodman. LC 85-71160. 36p. (Orig.). 1985. pap. 4.00 (ISBN 0-87495-071-6). Am Jewish Comm.

Working with the Mentally Handicapped in Their Residences. Dean Tjosvold & Mary Tjosvold. (Illus.). 256p. 1981. text ed. 24.95 (ISBN 0-02-932490-4). Free Pr.

Working with the Unix System. pap. 23.95 (ISBN 0-318-23491-2). UNISYS Corp.

Working with the Wool: How to Weave a Navajo Rug. Noel Bennett. Bd. with Designing with the Wool. slipcased 14.95 (ISBN 0-87358-422-8). Northland.

Working with the Wool: How to Weave a Navajo Rug. Noel Bennett & Tiana Bighorse. LC 73-174994. (Illus.). 1971. pap. 8.95 (ISBN 0-87358-084-2). Northland.

Working with Troubled Adolescents. John Coleman. 1987. 40.00 (ISBN 0-12-179720-1). Acad Pr.

Working with Troubled Children. Victor Savicki & Rosemary S. Brown. LC 80-15953. 408p. 1981. text ed. 44.95 (ISBN 0-87705-087-2); pap. text ed. 19.95 (ISBN 0-89885-243-9). Human Sci Pr.

Working with Truman: A Personal Memoir of the White House Years. Ken Hechler. (Illus.). 320p. 1982. 16.95 (ISBN 0-399-12762-3, Putnam). Putnam Pub Group.

Working with Ventura Publisher. Nathan Goldenthal. 290p. (Orig.). 1988. pap. 19.95. Weber Systems.

Working With Video. Brian Winston. (Illus.). 260p. 1986. 27.50 (ISBN 0-8174-6433-6, Amphoto); pap. 19.95 (ISBN 0-8174-6434-4, Amphoto). Watson-Guptill.

Working with Violent Families. Frank G. Bolton & Susan R. Bolton. 400p. 1987. text ed. 35.00 (ISBN 0-8039-2586-7); pap. text ed. 17.95 (ISBN 0-8039-2587-5). Sage.

Working with Volunteer Leaders in the Church. Reginald M. McDonough. LC 75-16579. 140p. 1976. pap. 6.50 (ISBN 0-8054-3214-0). Broadman.

Working with Water. Neil Ardley. (Action Science Ser.). 32p. (gr. 4-6). 1983. PLB 11.90 (ISBN 0-531-04519-6). Watts.

Working with Windscreen Glass. Michelle Minett. 1985. 13.00x (ISBN 0-86025-861-0, Pub. by Ian Henry Pubns England). State Mutual Bk.

Working with Women's Group, Vol. 2. Louise Y. Eberhardt. LC 87-50081. 144p. 1987. Repr. of 1978 ed. plastic spiral bdg 19.95x (ISBN 0-938586-11-4). Whole Person.

Working with Women's Groups, Vol. 1. Louise Y. Eberhardt. LC 87-50081. 172p. 1987. Repr. of 1976 ed. plastic spiral bdg 19.95x (ISBN 0-938586-10-6). Whole Person.

Working with Wood. Time-Life Books Editors. (Home Repair & Improvement Ser.). (Illus.). 1979. 11.95 (ISBN 0-8094-2426-6). Time-Life.

Working with Wood. LC 81-9279. (Home Repair & Improvement Ser.). (Illus.). (gr. 7 up). 1979. lib. bdg. 15.94 (ISBN 0-8094-2427-4, Pub. by Time-Life); 14.60 (ISBN 0-686-66219-9). Silver.

TITLE INDEX WORKS

Working with Word. Chris Kinata & Gordon McComb. 592p. 1988. pap. 21.95 (ISBN 1-55615-032-6). Microsoft.
Working with WordPerfect: A Complete Guide. 2nd ed. S. Scott Zimmerman & Beverly B. Zimmerman. 1987. pap. 18.95 (ISBN 0-673-38018-1). Scott F.
Working with WordPerfect on the Apple IIGS. S. Scott Zimmerman & Beverly B. Zimmerman. 1988. pap. 17.95 (ISBN 0-317-66974-5). Scott F.
Working with WordPerfect Version 4.1. S. Garth True. 400p. (Orig.). pap. cancelled (ISBN 0-317-67787-X). Weber Systems.
Working with Wordperfect 5.0. Richard P. Wilkes & Bruce E. Rodgers. 352p. 1988. pap. 19.95 (ISBN 0-553-34491-9). Bantam.
Working with Words: A Guide to Teaching & Learning Vocabulary. Ruth Gairns & Stuart Redman. (Handbooks for Language Teachers Ser.). (Illus.). 208p. 1986. 27.95 (ISBN 0-521-26889-3); pap. 10.95 (ISBN 0-521-31709-6). Cambridge U Pr.
Working with Words: Literacy Beyond School. Jane Mace. (Chameleon Education Ser.). 144p. 1981. pap. 4.95 (ISBN 0-906495-15-6). Writers & Readers.
Working with Words One. Carol Jordens. Ed. by Patti Reynolds. (Golden Step Ahead Workbooks). (Illus.). 36p. (gr. 1). 1984. 1.95 (ISBN 0-307-23543-2, Golden Bks). Western Pub.
Working with Words Two. Donna Hahn. Ed. by Patti Reynolds. (Golden Step Ahead Workbks.). (Illus.). 36p. 1984. 1.95 (ISBN 0-307-23551-3, Golden Bks). Western Pub.
Working with Wordstar Professional: Release 4.0. Walton Beacham. (Computers Ser.). 352p. 1988. pap. 21.95 (ISBN 0-553-34493-5). Bantam.
Working with Works: A Guide to Microsoft Works. Michael L. Sloan. 320p. 1987. pap. 18.95 (ISBN 0-673-18359-9). Scott F.
Working with Xenix System V. Martin L. Moore. 1986. pap. 19.95 (ISBN 0-673-18080-8). Scott F.
Working with Young Children. Lavisa C. Wilson & Neith Headley. 8p. 1983. pap. 1.95 (ISBN 0-87173-101-0). ACEI.
Working with Your Bank. Richard E. Petersen. 164p. 40.00 (ISBN 0-318-15161-8); comm line assn. 36.00 (ISBN 0-318-15162-6); NAW members 32.00 (ISBN 0-318-15163-4). Natl Assn Wholesale Dists.
Working with Your Woodland: A Landowner's Guide. Mollie Beattie et al. LC 83-40016. (Futures of New England Ser.). (Illus.). 334p. 1983. 27.50x (ISBN 0-87451-265-4); pap. 12.95 (ISBN 0-87451-266-2). U Pr of New Eng.
Working Woman. Anne R. Clifton et al. 300p. 1987. text ed. write for info. (ISBN 0-88048-252-4). Am Psychiatric.
Working Woman: A Guide to Fitness & Health. Anita Shreve & Patricia Lone. 1986. 16.95 (ISBN 0-8016-4606-5). Mosby.
Working Woman: A Male Manager's View. Ray A. Killian. LC 76-138567. pap. 56.00 (ISBN 0-317-09731-8, 2051532). Bks Demand UMI.
Working Woman Book. Barbara Dale & Jim Dale. (Illus.). 128p. (Orig.). 1985. pap. 6.95 (ISBN 0-8362-1254-1). Andrews & McMeel.
Working Woman Financial Advisor: What to Do with the Money You Make. Bonnie Siverd. (Illus.). 336p. 1987. pap. 9.95 (ISBN 0-446-38169-1). Warner Bks.
Working Woman Report: Succeeding in Business in the Eighties. Working Woman Editors & Gay Bryant. 355p. 1984. 16.95 (ISBN 0-671-47454-5). S&S.
Working Woman's Cookbook & Entertainment Guide. Pat McMillen. LC 83-3814. 252p. 1983. 15.95 (ISBN 0-672-52708-1). Bobbs.
Working Woman's Guide to Breastfeeding. Nancy Dana & Anne Price. Orig. Title: Breastfeeding for the Working Woman. (Illus.). 144p. (Orig.). 1987. pap. 6.95 (ISBN 0-88166-095-7). Meadowbrook.
Working Woman's Guide to Breastfeeding. Anne Price & Nancy B. Dana. 146p. Date not set. pap. 6.95 (ISBN 0-671-63624-3). S&S.
Working Woman's Stress First Aid Handbook. Bee Epstein. 64p. (Orig.). 1985. pap. 5.95 (ISBN 0-9616204-0-4). Becoming Pr.
Working Woman's Wedding Planner. Susan T. D'Arcy. 160p. 1986. pap. 12.95 (ISBN 0-13-966383-5). P-H.
Working Women. Ed. by Tobi Lippin. (Southern Exposure Ser.). (Illus.). 128p. (Orig.). 1982. pap. 4.00 (ISBN 0-943810-12-4). Inst Southern Studies.
Working Women: A Portrait of South Africa's Women Workers. Lesley Lawson. 144p. 1986. pap. 12.95 (ISBN 0-86975-276-6, Pub. by Ravan Pr). Ohio U Pr.
Working Women & Childbearing: United States. (Series 23: No. 9). 53p. 4.25. Natl Ctr Health Stats.
Working Women & Divorce: An Account of Evidence Given on Behalf of the Women's Co-operative Guild Before the Royal Commission on Divorce, London, 1911. Women's Co-operative Guild & Anna Martin. Bd. with Married Working Woman: A Study, London, 1911. 1980. lib. bdg. 15.00 (ISBN 0-8240-0128-1). Garland Pub.
Working Women & Popular Movements in Bengal. Sunil Sen. 1986. 12.50x (ISBN 0-8364-1603-1, Pub. by KP Bagchi India). South Asia Bks.
Working Women & Socialist Politics in France, 1880-1914: A Regional Study. Patricia Hilden. 320p. 1986. text ed. 34.50x (ISBN 0-19-821935-0). Oxford U Pr.
Working Women for Freedom. Angela Terrano et al. (Illus.). 56p. (Orig.). 1976. pap. 1.00x (ISBN 0-914441-18-3). News & Letters.
Working Women in Japan: Discrimination, Resistance, & Reform. Alice H. Cook & Hiroko Hayashi. LC 80-17706. (Cornell International Industrial & Labor Relations Reports: No. 10). 128p. 1980. pap. 7.95 (ISBN 0-87546-079-8). ILR Pr.
Working Women in Mexico During the Porfiriato, 1880-1910. Vivian M. Vallens. LC 77-91452. 1978. pap. 10.95 perfect bdg. (ISBN 0-88247-526-6). R & E Pubs.
Working Women in Recession. Roderick Martin & Judith Wallace. (Illus.). 1984. 42.00x (ISBN 0-19-878006-0); pap. 16.95x (ISBN 0-19-878005-2). Oxford U Pr.
Working Women in Renaissance Germany. Merry F. Wiesner. (Douglass Series on Women's Lives & the Meaning of Gender). (Illus.). 250p. 1986. text ed. 28.00 (ISBN 0-8135-1138-0). Rutgers U Pr.
Working Women in Socialist Countries: The Fertility Connection. Ed. by Valentina Bodrova & Richard Anker. xvi, 234p. (Orig.). 1985. pap. 119.25 (ISBN 92-2-103910-2). Intl Labour Office.
Working Women in Socialist Countries: The Fertility Connection. Ed. by Valentina Bodrova & Richard Anker. (World Employment Programme Study). 234p. 1985. pap. 19.25 (ISBN 92-2-103910-2, ILO409, ILO). UNIPUB.
Working Women in South Africa. Lesley Lawson. Ed. by Richard Kuper. (Illus.). 144p. (Orig.). 1986. pap. 11.25 (ISBN 0-7453-0206-8, Pub. by Pluto Pr). Longwood Pub Group.
Working Women in South-East Asia: Development, Subordination & Emancipation. Noeleen Heyzer. 192p. 1986. 65.00x (ISBN 0-335-15384-4, Open Univ Pr); pap. 24.00x (ISBN 0-335-15383-6, Open Univ Pr). Taylor & Francis.
Working Women in the Economic Future: A Selected Bibliography with Emphasis on Canada. Ontario Ministry of Treasury & Economics, Library Services Staff. (Public Administration Ser.: P 1999). 39p. 1986. 10.00 (ISBN 0-89028-999-9). Vance Biblios.
Working Women: Past, Present, Future. Ed. by Karen S. Koziara et al. 441p. 1987. text ed. 35.00 (ISBN 0-87179-547-7, 0547). BNA.
Working Women: The Subterranean World of Street Prostitution. Arlene Carmen & Howard Moody. LC 84-48585. 256p. 1985. 16.00 (ISBN 0-06-039040-9, C&M Bessie Bk). Har-Row.
Working Womenroots: An Oral History Primer. 2nd ed. Debra Bernhardt & M. Brady Mikusko. 33p. 1980. pap. 3.50 (ISBN 0-87736-342-0). U of Mich Inst Labor.
Working Wooden Toys. Marion Millett. (Illus.). 128p. (Orig.). 1985. (Pub. by Blandford Pr England); pap. 9.95 (ISBN 0-7137-1688-6, Pub. by Blandford Pr England). Sterling.
Working World. Baskin & Morton. 236p. 1986. pap. text ed. 9.95 (ISBN 0-15-596710-X). HarBraceJ.
Working Writing. Greg Larkin. 480p. 1985. pap. text ed. 24.95 (ISBN 0-675-20237-X). Merrill.
Working: Your Rights & Responsibilities. Herbert L. Beskin. 62p. 1983. 12.75 (33,844). NCLS Inc.
Working Your Way Through WordStar. Sally Graham. 125p. 1985. write for info. (ISBN 0-538-23102-5, W10U). SW Pub.
Working Your Way to the Bottom: The Feminization of Poverty. Hilda Scott. 180p. 1985. pap. 8.95 (ISBN 0-86358-011-4, Pandora Pr). Routledge Chapman & Hall.
Workingclass Giant: The Life of William Z. Foster. Arthur Zipser. LC 81-2503. 228p. (Orig.). 1981. 11.00 (ISBN 0-7178-0590-5); pap. 4.25 (ISBN 0-7178-0582-4). Intl Pubs Co.
Workingman's Wife: Her Personality, World & Life Style. Lee Rainwater et al. Ed. by Lewis A. Coser & Walter W. Powell. LC 79-7014. (Perennial Works in Sociology Ser.). 1979. Repr. of 1959 ed. lib. bdg. 19.00x (ISBN 0-405-12113-X). Ayer Co Pubs.
Workingmen of Waltham: Mobility in American Urban Industrial Development, 1850-1890. Howard M. Gitelman. LC 74-6822. (Illus.). 208p. 1974. 24.50x (ISBN 0-8018-1570-3). Johns Hopkins.
Workingmen's Democracy: The Knights of Labor & American Politics. Leon Fink. LC 82-6902. (Working Class in American History Ser.). 272p. 1985. pap. 10.95 (ISBN 0-252-01256-9). U of Ill Pr.
Workingmen's Party of the United States. Philip S. Foner. LC 83-26553. (Studies in Marxism: Vol. 14). 148p. 1984. 19.95x (ISBN 0-930656-35-0); pap. 6.95 (ISBN 0-930656-36-9). MEP Pubns.
Workings. Robert Walton. 61p. 1985. 15.00x (ISBN 0-85088-940-5, Pub. by Gomer Pr). State Mutual Bk.
Workings of Old Testament Narrative. Peter D. Miscall. LC 82-5993. (SBL Semeia Studies). 158p. 1983. pap. 10.50 (ISBN 0-89130-584-X, 06-06-12). Scholars Pr GA.
Workings of the Indeterminate-Sentence Law & the Parole System in Illinois. Andrew A. Bruce et al. LC 68-19466. (Criminology, Law Enforcement, & Social Problems Ser.: No. 5). 1968. Repr. of 1928 ed. 15.00x (ISBN 0-87585-005-7). Patterson Smith.
Workings of the Picaresque in the British Novel. Lars Hartveit. LC 86-20840. 176p. 1987. 39.95 (ISBN 0-391-03477-4, Pub. by Humanities Press & Solum Forlag). Humanities.
Workless: An Exploration of the Social Contract Between Society & the Worker. 2nd, rev. & enl. ed. Dennis Marsden. (Illus.). 275p. 1982. pap. 14.95 (ISBN 0-7099-1723-6, Pub. by Croom Helm Ltd). Routledge Chapman & Hall.
Worklife Education & Training & the Ordeal of Change. Charles Stewart. 79p. 1980. 10.00 (ISBN 0-86510-032-2). Natl Inst Work.
Worklife Transitions: Adult Learning. Paul E. Barton. 1982. text ed. 19.95 (ISBN 0-07-003974-7). McGraw.
Workload Characterization of Computer Systems & Computer Networks. Ed. by G. Serazzi. 176p. 1986. 73.75 (ISBN 0-444-70051-X, North-Holland). Elsevier.
Workload Measures in the Court. Harry O. Lawson & Barbara J. Gletne. 202p. 1980. pap. 10.00 (ISBN 0-89656-043-0, R-051). Natl Ctr St Courts.
Workload of the Supreme Court. Gerhard Caspar & Richard A. Posner. xiii, 131p. 1976. pap. 5.00 (ISBN 0-910058-78-4). Amer Bar Assn.
Workload of the Supreme Court. Gerhard Casper & Richard A. Posner. LC 76-49801. pap. 33.50 (2027140). Bks Demand UMI.
Workman & the Franchise. Frederick D. Maurice. LC 68-18601. 1970. Repr. of 1866 ed. 29.50x (ISBN 0-678-00592-3). Kelley.
Workmen of God. Oswald Chambers. 1965. pap. 3.95 (ISBN 0-87508-131-2). Chr Lit.
Workmen of God. William S. Deal. 1975. pap. 0.95 (ISBN 0-686-11025-0). Crusade Pubs.
Workmen's Compensation Examiner. Jack Rudman. (Career Examination Ser.: C-1644). (Cloth bd. avail. on request). 1988. pap. 14.00 (ISBN 0-8373-1644-8). Natl Learning.
Workmen's Compensation for Occupational Injuries & Death: Desk Edition, 2 vols. Arthur Larson. 1972. looseleaf set 220.00 (347); Updates. 1985 159.50; 1986 184.00. Bender.
Workmen's Compensation in Maryland. Evelyn E. Singleton. LC 78-64158. (Johns Hopkins University. Studies in the Social Sciences. Fifty-Third Ser. 1935: 2). Repr. of 1935 ed. 24.50 (ISBN 0-404-61268-7). AMS Pr.
Workmen's Compensation in Twentieth Century Britain: Law, History & Social Policy. P. W. Bartrip. 180p. 1987. text ed. 37.00x (ISBN 0-566-05485-X, Pub. by Gower Pub England). Gower Pub Co.
Workmen's Compensation Law Review. Kay Flynn & David Lloyd. LC 73-93978. 1986. Set 1-9. lib. bdg. 410.00 (108550); per vol. 47.50. W S Hein.
Workmen's Earnings, Strikes & Savings. Samuel Smiles. LC 83-48497. (World of Labour-English Workers 1850-1890 Ser.). 168p. 1984. lib. bdg. 20.00 (ISBN 0-8240-5724-4). Garland Pub.
Workout Game: Managing Non-Performing Real Estate Assets. Ed. by Stuart M. Bloch. LC 86-81722. 358p. 1987. 59.95 (ISBN 0-88057-611-1). Land Dev Inst.
Workout Magic. Cashman. 1988. write for info. Wiley.
Workouts & Bankruptcy Reorganization Workshop. Michael L. Cook & Wilbur L. Ross. LC 86-202062. 265p. Date not set. price not set. HarBraceJ.
Workouts That Work for Women Who Work. Barbara Pearlman. LC 87-20166. (Illus.). 192p. 1988. pap. 12.95 (ISBN 0-385-24276-X, Dolp). Doubleday.
Workplace Democracy. Daniel Zwerdling. LC 79-2025. 1979. pap. 9.95x (ISBN 0-06-131990-2, TB 1990, Torch). Har-Row.
Workplace Democracy. Daniel Zwerdling. 17.75 (ISBN 0-8446-5869-3). Peter Smith.
Workplace Democracy. Daniel Zwerdling. 188p. 1978. 9.95 (ISBN 0-318-15078-6, Pub. by Harper & Row). NASCO.
Workplace Democracy: An Inquiry into Employee Participation in Canadian Work Organizations. Donald V. Nightingale. 336p. 1982. 35.00x (ISBN 0-8020-5574-5); pap. 15.95 (ISBN 0-8020-6470-1). U of Toronto Pr.
Workplace Democracy & Social Change. Ed. by Frank Lindenfeld & Joyce Rothschild-Whitt. LC 82-80137. 456p. 1982. 20.00 (ISBN 0-87558-101-3, Pub. by Extending Hor Bks); pap. 12.00 (ISBN 0-87558-102-1). Porter Sargent.
Workplace Democracy: The Political Effects of Participation. Edward S. Greenberg. LC 86-47641. (Paperback Ser.). 272p. 1986. 29.95x (ISBN 0-8014-1921-2); pap. 11.95x. Cornell U Pr.
Workplace Democracy: The Political Effects of Participation. Edward S. Greenberg. LC 86-47641. 272p. 1988. pap. 10.95x (ISBN 0-8014-9530-X). Cornell U Pr.
Workplace Democratization. Paul Bernstein. LC 79-66569. 127p. 1980. pap. text ed. 12.95x (ISBN 0-87855-711-3). Transaction Bks.
Workplace Environmental Exposure Level (WEEL) Guides. FRAmerican Industrial Hygiene Association Staff. 5.00 ea.; Full set 125.00. Am Indus Hygiene.
Workplace Industrial Relations & Technical Change. W. W. Daniel. 352p. 1987. 35.00 (ISBN 0-86187-917-1, Pub. by Pinter Pubs UK). Columbia U Pr.
Workplace Industrial Relations in Britain. W. W. Daniel & Neil Millward. (Policy Studies Institute Ser.). xx, 333p. 1983. text ed. 38.50x (ISBN 0-566-05152-4); pap. text ed. 21.00x (ISBN 0-435-83191-7). Gower Pub Co.
Workplace Management. Taiichi Ohno. Ed. by Cheryl Rosen. LC 87-43173. (Japanese Management Ser.). (Illus.). 176p. 1988. 34.95 (ISBN 0-317-66859-5). Prod Press.
Workplace Privacy: Employee Testing, Surveillance, Wrongful Discharge, & Other Areas of Vulnerability. Michael Shepard & Robert L. Duston. 188p. 1987. 95.00 (ISBN 0-87179-941-3). BNA.
Workplace Safety & Health. James R. Chelius. 1977. pap. 7.00 (ISBN 0-8447-3274-5). Am Enterprise.
Workplace Within: Psychodynamics of Organizational Life. Larry Hirschhorn. (MIT Press Series on Organization Studies). 280p. 1988. 16.95 (ISBN 0-262-08169-5). MIT Pr.
Workrights. Robert E. Smith. 1983. 15.95; pap. 8.95. Privacy Journal.
Works. Aristophanes. Incl. Acharnians, Clouds, Knights, Wasps (ISBN 0-674-99197-4); Peace, Birds, Frogs (ISBN 0-674-99198-2); Lysistrata, Thesmophoriazusae, Ecclesiazusae, Plutus (ISBN 0-674-99199-0). (Loeb Classical Library: No. 178-180). 13.95x ea. Harvard U Pr.
Works, 14 Vols. Francis Bacon. Ed. by J. Spedding et al. 1858-74. Set. 2289.00x (ISBN 3-7728-0023-8). Adlers Foreign Bks.
Works, 10 Vols. Francis Beaumont & John Fletcher. Ed. by A. R. Waller & A. Glover. LC 76-83295. 1969. Repr. of 1912 ed. lib. bdg. 230.00 (ISBN 0-374-90513-4, Octagon). Hippocrene Bks.
Works, 3 vols. Richard Bentley. Ed. by Alexander Dyce. LC 66-6448. Repr. of 1838 ed. Set. 105.00 (ISBN 0-404-00760-0). AMS Pr.
Works, 4 vols. Lord Bolingbroke. 1967. Repr. of 1844 ed. Set. 185.00x (ISBN 0-7146-1011-9, F Cass Co). Biblio Dist.
Works, 16 vols. George Borrow. Ed. by Clement Shorter. LC 24-5080. Repr. of 1924 ed. Set. 300.00 (ISBN 0-404-00970-0); 20.00 ea. AMS Pr.
Works, 12 vols. Edmund Burke. Repr. of 1899 ed. 895.00x (ISBN 0-403-04342-5). Somerset Pub.
Works, 2 vols. Callimachus. Ed. by Rudolph Pfeiffer. 316p. 1985-1986. Vol. 1: Fragmenta. 89.00x (ISBN 0-19-814115-7); Vol. 2: Hymni et Epigrammata. 69.00x (ISBN 0-19-814116-5). Oxford U Pr.
Works, 4 vols. Samuel Clarke. LC 75-11207. (British Philosophers & Theologians of the 17th & 18th Century Ser.: Vol. 12). 3274p. 1976. Repr. of 1742 ed. Set. lib. bdg. 204.00 (ISBN 0-8240-1762-5). Garland Pub.
Works. James Fenimore Cooper. Incl; Vol. 2. 45.00 (ISBN 0-8371-2674-6, COWB); Vol. 3. 45.00 (ISBN 0-8371-2675-4, COWC); Vol. 4. 45.00 (ISBN 0-8371-2676-2, COWD); Vol. 5. 45.00 (ISBN 0-8371-2677-0, COWE); Vol. 6. 45.00 (ISBN 0-8371-2678-9, COWF); Vol. 7. 45.00 (ISBN 0-8371-2679-7, COWG); Vol. 8. 45.00 (ISBN 0-8371-2680-0, COWH); Vol. 9. 45.00 (ISBN 0-8371-2681-9, COWI); Vol. 10. 45.00 (ISBN 0-8371-2682-7, COWJ). LC 69-13864. 1970. Repr. Greenwood.
Works, 18 Vols. Charles Darwin. LC 73-147085. Repr. of 1897 ed. Set. 765.00 (ISBN 0-404-08400-1); 42.50 ea. AMS Pr.
Works, 3 vols. Benjamin De Casseres. 300.00 (ISBN 0-87968-467-4). Gordon Pr.
Works, 17 vols. Guy De Maupassant. 1975. Repr. of 1903 ed. deluxe ed. 375.00 (ISBN 0-8274-4056-1). R West.
Works, 10 vols. John Galt. Ed. by David S. Meldrum & William Roughead. LC 37-3805. Repr. of 1936 ed. Set. 325.00 (ISBN 0-404-02700-8); 32.50 ea. AMS Pr.
Works, 8 Vols. Elizabeth C. Gaskell. Ed. by A. W. Ward. LC 70-148782. Repr. of 1906 ed. Set. 380.00 (ISBN 0-404-07250-X); 47.50 ea. AMS Pr.
Works. Stefan George. LC 79-168108. (North Carolina. University. Studies in the Germanic Languages & Literature: No. 2). Repr. of 1949 ed. 34.00 (ISBN 0-404-50902-9). AMS Pr.
Works, 21 vols. William Hazlitt. Ed. by Percival P. Howe. LC 71-37649. Repr. of 1934 ed. Set. 630.00 (ISBN 0-404-03210-9); 30.00 ea. AMS Pr.
Works, 8 vols. Richard Hurd. Repr. of 1811 ed. Set. 195.00 (ISBN 0-404-03470-5). AMS Pr.
Works. Roger Hutchinson. 1842. 31.00 (ISBN 0-384-25120-X). Johnson Repr.
Works, 14 vols. Washington Irving. 1850-1851. Set. 695.00 (ISBN 0-403-00384-9). Scholarly.
Works, 14 vols. Washington Irving. 1988. Repr. of 1851 ed. Set. lib. bdg. 425.00x. Am Biog Serv.
Works. Soame Jenyns. 1202p. Repr. of 1790 ed. text ed. 132.48x (ISBN 0-576-02103-2, Pub. by Gregg Intl Pubs England). Gregg Intl.
Works, 4 Vols. John Jewel. 1845-1850. Set. 204.00 (ISBN 0-384-27217-7). Johnson Repr.

Works, 9 vols. in 3. William Law. 2080p. Repr. of 1893 ed. Set. cancelled (ISBN 3-4870-5100-1). Adlers Foreign Bks.
Works, Pts. I-IV, Pt. V. David Lindsay. Ed. by J. Small & F. Hall. (EETS, OS Ser.: Nos. 11, 19, 35, 37). Repr. of 1871 ed. Pts. I-iV. 45.00 (ISBN 0-527-00013-2). Kraus Repr.
Works, 10 Vols. John Locke. 1963. Repr. of 1823 ed. Set. half leather 686.00x (ISBN 3-511-02600-8). Adlers Foreign Bks.
Works, 14 Vols. Henry Wadsworth Longfellow. Repr. of 1891 ed. Set. 525.00 (ISBN 0-404-04040-3); 37.50 ea. AMS Pr.
Works. Kung-Sun Lung. Tr. by Max Perleberg from Chinese. LC 73-884. (China Studies: from Confucius to Mao Ser.). xxiii, 160p. 1973. Repr. of 1952 ed. 17.50 (ISBN 0-88355-077-6). Hyperion Conn.
Works. Randy McClave. 1987. 5.95 (ISBN 0-8062-2421-5). Carlton.
Works. Christopher Marlowe. Ed. by C. F. Brooke. 1910. 59.00x (ISBN 0-19-811372-2). Oxford U Pr.
Works, 3 Vols. John Marston. Ed. by A. H. Bullen. 1970. Repr. of 1887 ed. Set. cancelled (ISBN 3-4870-2962-6). Adlers Foreign Bks.
Works, 2 vols. in 4 pts. John Milton. Ed. by Frank A. Patterson. LC 31-10596. 1940. 35.00. Vol. 2 Pt. 2 (ISBN 0-231-08709-8). Columbia U Pr.
Works, 20 vols. Francis Parkman. LC 69-19160. (Illus.). Repr. of 1902 ed. Set. 770.00 (ISBN 0-404-04920-6); 38.50 ea. AMS Pr.
Works, 10 vols. Thomas L. Peacock. Ed. by H. B. Brett-Smith & C. E. Jones. LC 71-181967. Repr. of 1924 ed. Set. 450.00 (ISBN 0-404-04970-2); o.p. 28.00 ea. AMS Pr.
Works. Sandor Petofi. LC 73-77696. (Literature Ser.). (Illus.). 453p. 1973. 14.90 (ISBN 0-914648-04-7). Hungarian Cultural.
Works, 3 Vols. Plotinus. (Loeb Classical Library: No. 440-442). 13.95x ea. Vol. 1 (ISBN 0-674-99484-1). Vol. 2 (ISBN 0-674-99486-8). Vol. 3 (ISBN 0-674-99487-6). Harvard U Pr.
Works, 22 vols. William H. Prescott. Ed. by Wilfred H. Munro et al. LC 69-16761. Repr. of 1904 ed. Set. 825.00 (ISBN 0-404-05150-2); 37.50 ea. AMS Pr.
Works, 2 Vols. Prudentius. (Loeb Classical Library: No. 387, 398). 13.95x ea. Vol. 1 (ISBN 0-674-99426-4). Vol. 2 (ISBN 0-674-99438-8). Harvard U Pr.
Works. Dante G. Rossetti. Ed. by William M. Rossetti. 1972. Repr. of 1911 ed. cancelled (ISBN 3-4870-4360-2). Adlers Foreign Bks.
Works. Globe ed. William Shakespeare. Ed. by William G. Clark & William A. Wright. LC 69-18315. Repr. of 1864 ed. 95.00 (ISBN 0-404-05950-3). AMS Pr.
Works. William Shakespeare. Ed. by John P. Collier. LC 78-175849. Repr. of 1844 ed. 12.50 (ISBN 0-404-01618-9). AMS Pr.
Works, 7 Vols. William Shakespeare. Ed. by Lewis Theobald. LC 68-58620. Repr. of 1733 ed. 350.00 (ISBN 0-404-05790-X). AMS Pr.
Works, 9 Vols. Old Cambridge ed. William Shakespeare. Ed. by William A. Wright et al. LC 68-59035. Repr. of 1893 ed. Set. 425.00 (ISBN 0-404-05940-6). AMS Pr.
Works, 3 vols. Thomas Shepard. Ed. by John A. Albro. LC 49-1393. Repr. of 1853 ed. Set. 85.00 (ISBN 0-404-05990-2). Vol. 1 (ISBN 0-404-05991-0). Vol. 2 (ISBN 0-404-05992-9). Vol. 3 (ISBN 0-404-05993-7). AMS Pr.
Works, 5 Vols. Adam Smith. Ed. by D. Stewart. 1963. Repr. of 1811 ed. Set. cancelled (ISBN 3-5350-0478-0). Adlers Foreign Bks.
Works, 21 Vols. Herbert Spencer. 1966. Repr. of 1884 ed. Set. 3500.00x (ISBN 3-535-00480-2). Adlers Foreign Bks.
Works. C. H. Spurgeon. 1976. pap. 1.50 (ISBN 0-686-16845-3). Pilgrim Pubns.
Works, 4 vols. William Temple. LC 68-31006. (Illus.). 1968. Repr. of 1814 ed. Set. lib. bdg. 88.75x (ISBN 0-8371-0679-6, TEWO); Vol. 1. lib. bdg. 24.50 (ISBN 0-8371-1775-5, TEWA); Vol. 2. lib. bdg. 24.50 (ISBN 0-8371-0851-9, TEWB); Vol. 3. lib. bdg. 24.50 (ISBN 0-8371-0852-7, TEWC); Vol. 4. lib. bdg. 24.50 (ISBN 0-8371-0853-5, TEWD). Greenwood.
Works, 4 vols. Benjamin Whichcote. LC 75-11265. (British Philosophers & Theologians of the 17th & 18th Centuries: Vol. 64). 1977. Repr. of 1751 ed. lib. bdg. 204.00 ea. (ISBN 0-8240-1814-1). Garland Pub.
Works, 14 Vols. Israel Zangwill. LC 73-99252. Repr. of 1925 ed. Set. 525.00 (ISBN 0-404-07080-9); 37.50 ea. AMS Pr.
Works, Vol. 1. Euripides. Incl. Rhesus; Hecuba; Daughters of Troy; Helen; Iphigeneia at Aulis. (Loeb Classical Library: No. 9). 13.95x (ISBN 0-674-99010-2). Harvard U Pr.
Works, Vol. 2. Euripides. Incl. Orestes; Iphigeneia in Taurica; Andromache; Cyclops; Ion; Electra. (Loeb Classical Library: No. 10). 13.95x (ISBN 0-674-99011-0). Harvard U Pr.
Works, Vol. 3. Euripides. Incl. Madness of Hercules; Children of Hercules; Phoenician Maidens; Suppliants; Bacchanals. (Loeb Classical Library: No. 11). 13.95x (ISBN 0-674-99012-9). Harvard U Pr.
Works, Vol. 4. Euripides. Incl. Hippolytus; Medea; Alcestis; Ion. (Loeb Classical Library: No. 12). 13.95x (ISBN 0-674-99013-7). Harvard U Pr.
Works - Centenary Edition, 15 vols. Theodore Parker. LC 75-3307. Repr. of 1911 ed. 595.00 set (ISBN 0-404-59300-3). AMS Pr.
Works: A Quarterly of Writing, Vol. 1-4, No. 3. Repr. of 1974 ed. unbound, lacks vol. 3, no. 1 87.00 (ISBN 0-404-19564-4). AMS Pr.
Works & Correspondence of David Ricardo: Index, Vol. 11. David Ricardo. Ed. by P. Sraffa & Maurice Dobb. 1973. 62.50 (ISBN 0-521-20039-3). Cambridge U Pr.
Works & Correspondence of David Ricardo: Principles of Political Economy, Vol. 1. David Ricardo. Ed. by P. Sraffa. 437p. 1981. pap. 19.95 (ISBN 0-521-28505-4). Cambridge U Pr.
Works & Criticism of Gerard Manley Hopkins: A Comprehensive Bibliography. Edward H. Cohen. LC 68-31683. pap. 58.50 (ISBN 0-317-10563-9, 2022585). Bks Demand UMI.
Works & Criticism of Gerard Manley Hopkins: A Comprehensive Bibliography. Edward H. Cohen. LC 68-31683. pap. 58.30 (2029517). Bks Demand UMI.
Works & Days. Hesiod. Ed. by W. R. Connor. LC 78-18606. (Greek Texts & Commentaries Ser.). 1979. Repr. of 1932 ed. lib. bdg. 17.00x (ISBN 0-405-11446-X). Ayer Co Pubs.
Works & Days. Hesiod. Tr. by Richmond Lattimore. Bd. with Theogony; Shield of Herakles. LC 59-6027. 250p. 1959. 10.95 (ISBN 0-472-43903-0). U of Mich Pr.
Works & Doctrine of Jacques Hittorff (1792-1867, 2 vols. Donald D. Schmeider. LC 76-23721. (Outstanding Dissertations in the Fine Arts Ser.). (Illus.). 1264p. 1977. lib. bdg. 161.00 (ISBN 0-8240-2727-2). Garland Pub.
Works & Life of Christopher Marlowe, 6 Vols. Christopher Marlowe. Ed. by R. H. Case. 1644p. 1966. Repr. of 1933 ed. Set. 125.00x (ISBN 0-87752-067-4). Gordian.
Works & Life of Thomas Browne, 4 Vols. Thomas Browne. Ed. by Simon Wilkin. LC 68-57225. Repr. of 1836 ed. Set. 190.00 (ISBN 0-404-01150-0); 47.50 ea. Vol. 1 (ISBN 0-404-01151-9). Vol. 2 (ISBN 0-404-01152-7). Vol. 3 (ISBN 0-404-01153-5). Vol. 4 (ISBN 0-404-01154-3). AMS Pr.
Works & Lives: The Anthropologist As Author. Clifford Geertz. LC 87-20310. 168p. 1988. 19.95 (ISBN 0-8047-1428-2). Stanford U Pr.
Works & More. Max Beerbohm. LC 12-30603. 1896. 39.00 (ISBN 0-403-00144-7). Scholarly.
Works & More. Max Beerbohm. 1988. Repr. of 1896 ed. lib. bdg. 59.00x. Am Biog Serv.
Works & Worlds of Art. Nicholas Wolterstorff. (CLLP Ser.). (Illus.). 1980. 55.00x (ISBN 0-19-824419-3); pap. 17.95x (ISBN 0-19-824426-6). Oxford U Pr.
Works by Arthur B. Davies: From the Collection of Mr. & Mrs. Herbert Brill. John P. Driscoll. (Illus.). 36p. 1979. pap. 3.00 exhibition catalogue (ISBN 0-911209-15-8). Penn St Art.
Works by Felix Morisseau-Leroy: Recolte, Natif-Natal, Antigone en Creole, Diacoute. Felix Morisseau-Leroy. 1954. Four works in one unit. 24.00 (ISBN 0-8115-2963-0). Kraus Repr.
Works Companion. Steven Cobb et al. Ed. by Linda Baughman. (Illus.). 704p. (Orig.). 1987. pap. 22.95 (ISBN 0-936767-06-5). Cobb Group.
Works, Examined, Corrected & Published: By H. Holland. Richard Greenham. LC 72-5999. (English Experience Ser.: No. 524). 496p. 1973. Repr. of 1599 ed. 70.00 (ISBN 90-221-0524-5). Walter J Johnson.
Works for Solo Voice of Johann Adolf Hasse, 1699-1783. Sven H. Hansell. (Detroit Studies in Music Bibliography Ser.: No. 12). 1968. pap. 6.00 (ISBN 0-911772-32-4). Harmonie Pk Pr.
Works for Violin: The Complete Sonatas & Partitas for Unaccompanied Violin & the Six Sonatas for Violin & Clavier. Johann Sebastian Bach. 1978. pap. 6.95 (ISBN 0-486-23683-8). Dover.
Works, Fourteen Sixty to Fourteen Ninety. Peter Schott. Ed. by Murray A. Cowie & Marian L. Cowie. LC 63-63888. (North Carolina. University. Studies in the Germanic Languages & Literatures: No. 41). Repr. of 1963 ed. 39.00 (ISBN 0-404-50941-X). AMS Pr.
Works from the Collection of Dorothy & Herbert Vogel. Bret Waller. (Illus.). 59p. 1977. pap. 3.00 (ISBN 0-912303-14-X). Michigan Mus.
Works in African History. Ed. by David Henige. Incl. 1960-1974. 7.00 (ISBN 0-918456-14-2); 1975-1977. 10.00 (ISBN 0-918456-15-0). (Archival & Bibliographic Ser.). 1978. African Studies Assn.
Works in Architecture of Robert & James Adam, 3 vols. in 1. Robert Adam. LC 78-67644. (Scottish Enlightenment Ser.). Repr. of 1788 ed. 135.00 (ISBN 0-404-17233-4). AMS Pr.
Works in Five Volumes. Mykola Khvylovy. Ed. by H. Kostiuk. Incl. Vol. 1. 438p. 15.00; Vol. 2. 409p. 15.00; Vol. 3. 505p. 1982. 20.00; Vol. 4. 662p. 25.00; Vol. 5. 834p. 1985. 30.00. LC 77-66383 (ISBN 0-914834-20-7). Smoloskyp.
Works in Progress, Vol. 1. Michael P. Jones. (Works in Progress Ser.). (Illus.). 16p. 1984. pap. text ed. 1.60 (ISBN 0-89904-075-6). Crumb Elbow Pub.
Works in Prose & Verse. Anne Bradstreet. Ed. by Ellis. 18.00 (ISBN 0-8446-1087-9). Peter Smith.
Works in Verse & Prose, 2 Vols. Nicholas Breton. 1967. Repr. of 1879 ed. Set. cancelled (ISBN 3-4870-2378-4). Adlers Foreign Bks.
Works in Verse & Prose Complete of Henry Vaughan, Silurist, 4 vols. Henry Vaughan. LC 73-21067. (Fuller Worthies' Library). Repr. of 1871 ed. Set. 200.00 (ISBN 0-404-11493-8); Vol. 1. (ISBN 0-404-11494-6); Vol. 2. (ISBN 0-404-11495-4); Vol. 3. (ISBN 0-404-11496-2); Vol. 4. (ISBN 0-404-11497-0). AMS Pr.
Works in Verse & Prose Complete of the Right Honourable Fulke Greville, 4 vols. Fulke G. Brooke. Ed. by Alexander B. Grosart. LC 79-181918. (Fuller Worthies Library). Repr. of 1870 ed. Set. 200.00 (ISBN 0-404-02940-X). AMS Pr.
Works in Verse & Prose of Nicholas Breton, 2 Vols. Nicholas Breton. Ed. by Alexander B. Grosart. LC 75-181917. (BCL Ser. II). Repr. of 1879 ed. Set. 57.50 (ISBN 0-404-50294-6). Vol. 1 (ISBN 0-404-50383-7). Vol. 2 (ISBN 0-404-50384-5). AMS Pr.
Works in Verse & Prose of Nicholas Breton see **Chertsey Worthies Library.**
Works: Including Hermes, or a Philosophical Inquiry & Philological Inquiries, 3 vols. James Harris. LC 72-147973. Repr. of 1786 ed. Set. 105.00 (ISBN 0-404-08240-8); Vol. 1. 35.00 (ISBN 0-404-08241-6); Vol. 2. 35.00 (ISBN 0-404-08242-4); Vol. 3. 35.00 (ISBN 0-404-08243-2). AMS Pr.
Work's Indiana Practice with Forms, 1971-1981, 7 vols. Arch N. Bobbitt & Frederic C. Sipe. Set. 315.00; Suppl. 1985. 75.00. Anderson Pub Co.
Works Manager to-Day. facsimile ed. Sidney Webb. LC 73-148906. (Select Bibliographies Reprint Ser). Repr. of 1917 ed. 17.00 (ISBN 0-8369-5669-9). Ayer Co Pubs.
Works of Abigail (Smith) Adams, 1744-1818. Abigail Smith Adams. Date not set. Repr. of 1840 ed. price not set. Am Biog Serv.
Works of Alan Hovhaness: A Catalog Opus 1-Opus 360. Richard Howard. (Am American Music Ser.: Ams-1). (Illus.). 28p. (Orig.). 1983. pap. 4.00x (ISBN 0-912483-00-8, Pub. by Kahn & Averill UK). Pro-Am Music.
Works of Alexander Agassiz, 1837-1910. Alexander Agassiz. 1987. Repr. of 1877 ed. lib. bdg. price not set. Am Biog Serv.
Works of Alexander Hamilton, 12 Vols. Alexander Hamilton. Ed. by Henry C. Lodge. LC 68-24980. (American History & Americana Ser., No. 47). 1969. Repr. of 1904 ed. lib. bdg. 450.00x (ISBN 0-8383-0160-6). Haskell.
Works of Alexander Hamilton, 12 vols. Alexander Hamilton. 1987. Repr. of 1904 ed. Set. lib. bdg. 795.00 (ISBN 0-317-60364-7). Am Biog Serv.
Works of Alexander Pope, 10 Vols. Alexander Pope. Ed. by John W. Croker et al. LC 66-29708. 5462p. 1967. Repr. of 1886 ed. Set. 300.00x (ISBN 0-87752-087-9). Gordian.
Works of Alexander Viets Griswold, 1841-1908. Alexande V. Allen. 1987. Repr. of 1907 ed. Set. lib. bdg. price not set. Am Biog Serv.
Works of Alfred Lord Tennyson, 12 vols. 1981. Repr. of 1892 ed. Set. lib. bdg. 475.00 (ISBN 0-8495-5210-9). Arden Lib.
Works of Alfred Lord Tennyson: Annotated, 9 Vols. Alfred Tennyson. Ed. by Hallam Tennyson. LC 76-120197. Repr. of 1908 ed. Set. 202.50 (ISBN 0-404-06370-5); 22.50 ea. AMS Pr.
Works of Alfred the Great, 2 vols. Alfred the Great. 1977. Set. lib. bdg. 250.00 (ISBN 0-8490-2843-4). Gordon Pr.
Works of Alfred W. Arrington, 1810-1867. Alfred W. Arrington. Date not set. Repr. of 1869 ed. Set. lib. bdg. price not set. Am Biog Serv.
Works of Alice Dunbar-Nelson, Vol. 1. Alice Dunbar-Nelson. Ed. by Gloria T. Hull. (Schomburg Library of Nineteenth-Century Black Women Writers). 480p. 1988. 22.50 (ISBN 0-19-505250-1). Oxford U Pr.
Works of Alice Dunbar-Nelson, Vol. 2. Alice Dunbar-Nelson. Ed. by Gloria T. Hull. (Schomburg Library of Nineteenth-Century Black Women Writers). 384p. 1988. 22.50 (ISBN 0-19-505251-X). Oxford U Pr.
Works of Alice Dunbar-Nelson, Vol. 3. Alice Dunbar-Nelson. Ed. by Gloria T. Hull. (Schomburg Library of Nineteenth-Century Black Women Writers). 352p. 1988. 22.50 (ISBN 0-19-505252-8). Oxford U Pr.
Works of Allan Ramsay, 3 vols. Allan Ramsay. Incl. Vols 1 & 2. Ed. by Burns Martin & John W. Oliver; Vol. 3. Ed. by Alexander M. Kinghorn & Alexander Law. 1961. Repr. of 1951 ed. Set. 92.00 (ISBN 0-384-49543-5). Johnson Repr.
Works of Amos Bronson Alcott, 1799-1888. Amos B. Alcott. 1987. Repr. of 1882 ed. lib. bdg. price not set. Am Biog Serv.
Works of Anatole France, 40 vols. Anatole France. 1975. 2700.00 (ISBN 0-8490-1329-1). Gordon Pr.
Works of Anatole France in An English Translation, 34 Vols. Frederic Chapman. 1983. Repr. of 1909 ed. lib. bdg. 800.00 set (ISBN 0-89987-280-8). Darby Bks.
Works of Anne Bradstreet. Anne Bradstreet & Jeannie Hensley. LC 67-17312. (The John Harvard Library Ser.). 368p. 1981. pap. 8.95x (ISBN 0-674-95999-X, Belknap Pr). Harvard U Pr.
Works of Anne Bradstreet in Prose and Verse. Anne D. Bradstreet. 1976. Repr. 59.00x (ISBN 0-403-08995-6, Regency). Scholarly.
Works of Anne Brastreet, 1612-1672, 3 vols. Anne Bradstreet. 1987. Set. lib. bdg. 189.00 (ISBN 0-317-59761-2). Am Biog Serv.
Works of Aphra Behn, 6 Vols. Aphra Behn. Ed. by Montague Summers. LC 67-22243. 1967. Repr. of 1915 ed. Set. 164.00 (ISBN 0-405-08253-3, Blom Pubns); 27.50 ea. Vol. 1 (ISBN 0-405-08254-1). Vol. 2 (ISBN 0-405-08255-X). Vol. 3 (ISBN 0-405-08256-8). Vol. 4 (ISBN 0-405-08257-6). Vol. 5 (ISBN 0-405-08258-4). Vol. 6 (ISBN 0-405-08259-2). Ayer Co Pubs.
Works of Aphra Behn, 6 vols. Aphra Behn. Ed. by Montague Summers. LC 67-24964. 2916p. 1967. Repr. of 1916 ed. Set. 200.00x (ISBN 0-87753-004-1). Phaeton.
Works of Apostolic Fathers, 2 vols. Apostolic Fathers. Incl. Vol. 1. Clement, Ignatius, Polycarp, Didache, Barnabas (ISBN 0-674-99027-7); Vol. 2. Shepherd of Hermas, Martyrdom of Polycarp, Epistle to Diognetus (ISBN 0-674-99028-5). (Loeb Classical Library: No. 24-25). 13.95x ea. Harvard U Pr.
Works of Archibald Alexander, 1772-1851. Archibald Alexander. 1987. Repr. of 1852 ed. Set. lib. bdg. price not set. Am Biog Serv.
Works of Aristotle: The Famous Philosopher. LC 73-20613. (Sex, Marriage & Society Ser.). (Illus.). 268p. 1974. Repr. 14.00x (ISBN 0-405-05792-X). Ayer Co Pubs.
Works of Art from the Collection of Paul J. Sachs see **Exhibition Catalogues from the Fogg Art Museum.**
Works of Art of the Corporation of London: A Catalogue of Paintings, Watercolours, Drawings, Prints & Sculpture. Vivien Knight. (Illus.). 368p. 1987. 74.25 (ISBN 0-85941-379-9, Pub. by Woodhead-Faulkner). Longwood Pub Group.
Works of Arthur B. Davies. Joseph S. Czestochowski. LC 79-11546. (Illus.). 1979. 75.00 (ISBN 0-226-68946-8, Chicago Visual Lib); 5 colorfiches & 2 b & w fiches incl. U of Chicago Pr.
Works of Arthur Symons: An Appreciation. W. G. Murdock. LC 72-187957. 1973. Repr. of 1907 ed. lib. bdg. 20.00 (ISBN 0-8414-0591-3). Folcroft.
Works of Asher Benjamin: Boston, 1806-1843, 7 vols. Asher Benjamin. Incl. Country Builder's Assistant: 1797. 84p. 45.00 (ISBN 0-306-71027-7); American Builder's Companion: 1806. 158p. 45.00 (ISBN 0-306-71026-9); Rudiments of Architecture: 1814. 162p. 45.00 (ISBN 0-306-71031-5); Practical House Carpenter: 1830. 248p. 45.00 (ISBN 0-306-71029-3); Practice of Architecture: 1833. 236p. 45.00 (ISBN 0-306-71030-7); Builder's Guide: 1839. 174p. 47.50 (ISBN 0-306-70971-6); Elements of Architecture: 1843. 290p. 47.50 (ISBN 0-306-71028-5). (Architecture & Decorative Art Ser.). 1974. Set. 285.00 (ISBN 0-306-71032-3). Da Capo.
Works of Attila Jozsef. Attila Jozsef. LC 76-150131. (Literature Ser.). (Illus.). 224p. 1973. 12.00 (ISBN 0-914648-01-2). Hungarian Cultural.
Works of Beaumont & Fletcher, 11 Vols. facs. ed. Francis Beaumont & John Fletcher. LC 74-119953. (Select Bibliographies Reprint Ser). 1843-1846. Set. 325.00 (ISBN 0-8369-5396-7). Ayer Co Pubs.
Works of Ben Jonson, 9 vols. W. Gifford. 1979. Repr. of 1875 ed. Set. lib. bdg. 300.00 (ISBN 0-8495-2004-5). Arden Lib.
Works of Benjamin B. Warfield, 10 vols. B. B. Warfield. 1981. Repr. of 1932 ed. 149.50 (ISBN 0-8010-9645-6). Baker Bk.
Works of Benjamin Disraeli, Earl of Beaconsfield, 20 vols. Benjamin Disraeli. Incl. Vols. 1-2. Vivian Grey: A Romance of Youth. LC 76-12451; Vols. 3-4. Young Duke, etc. LC 76-12450; Vols. 5-6. Contarini Fleming: A Psychological Romance, etc. LC 76-12449; Vol. 7. Alroy: Or, the Prince of the Captivity. LC 76-12448; Vols. 8-9. Henrietta Temple: A Love Story, etc. LC 76-12447; Vols. 10-11. Venetia, etc. LC 76-12445; Vols. 12-13. Coningsby: Or, the New Generation & Selected Speeches. LC 76-12444; Vols. 17-18. Lothair & Letters to His Sister. LC 76-12443; Vols. 19-20. Endymion, Miscellania. LC 76-12442; Vols. 14-16. Sybil; Tancred. LC 76-148746. (Illus.). Repr. of 1904 ed. Set. 800.00 (ISBN 0-404-08800-7); 40.00 ea. AMS Pr.
Works of Benjamin Parke Avery, 1828-1875. Benjamin A. Avery. Bd. with California in Prose & Verse. 1987. Repr. of 1887 ed. 79.00. Am Biog Serv.
Works of Bishop Joseph Hall, 10 Vols. Joseph Hall. Ed. by P. Wynter. LC 76-86830. Repr. of 1863 ed. Set. 375.00 (ISBN 0-404-03070-X); 37.50 ea. AMS Pr.
Works of Bret Harte, 18 vols. 1981. Repr. of 1899 ed. Set. lib. bdg. 350.00 (ISBN 0-8495-2356-7). Arden Lib.
Works of Brooks, 6 vols. Thomas Brooks. 1980. Set. 118.95 (ISBN 0-85151-302-6). Banner of Truth.
Works of Bulgarian Emigrants: An Annotated Bibliography. George I. Paprikoff. 693p. 1985. 34.00 (ISBN 0-937785-05-9). Sliabhair.
Works of C. B. McClellan: Special Collector's Edition. Ed. by Dave Basso. (Illus.). 48p. 1987. 169.00 (ISBN 0-936332-24-7). Falcon Hill Pr.
Works of Captain Alexander Radcliffe. Alexander Radcliffe. LC 81-9003. 1981. Repr. of 1696 ed. 45.00x (ISBN 0-8201-1365-4). Schol Facsimiles.

TITLE INDEX WORKS OF HORATIO ALGER

Works of Captain Marryat, 20 vols. (Illus.). 1981. Repr. Set. lib. bdg. 600.00 (ISBN 0-89984-310-7). Century Bookbindery.

Works of Catherine Esther Beecher, 1800-1878. Catherine Beecher. 1987. Repr. of 1871 ed. Set. lib. bdg. price not set. Am Biog Serv.

Works of Charles & Mary Lamb, 7 vols. Charles Lamb & Mary Lamb. Ed. by E. V. Lucas. LC 70-115252. 1903-05. Repr. 350.00x (ISBN 0-403-00366-0). Scholarly.

Works of Charles & Mary Lamb, Vols. 1-5. Charles Lamb & Mary Lamb. Ed. by E. V. Lucas. LC 68-59332. (Illus.). Repr. of 1904 ed. Set. 122.50 (ISBN 0-404-03830-1); 24.50 ea. AMS Pr.

Works of Charles Anthon, 1797-1867. Charles Anthon. 1987. Repr. of 1850 ed. Set. lib. bdg. price not set. Am Biog Serv.

Works of Charles Babbage, 11 vols. Ed. by Martin Campbell-Kelly. 2160p. 1988. Set. 995.00 (ISBN 0-8147-1428-5). NYU Pr.

Works of Charles Darwin, Vols. I-X. Ed. by Paul H. Barrett & R. B. Freeman. 1987. Set. 730.00 (ISBN 0-8147-1799-3). NYU Pr.

Works of Charles Darwin: A Bibliography. Ed. by R. B. Freeman. 235p. 1977. 17.95 (ISBN 0-8464-1152-0). Beekman Pubs.

Works of Charles Darwin: Charles Darwin's Diary of the Voyage of H. M. S. Beagle, Vol. I. Ed. by Paul H. Barrett & R. B. Freeman. (Illus.). 464p. 1987. 75.00 (ISBN 0-8147-1796-9). NYU Pr.

Works of Charles Darwin: Geological Observations on South America, Vol. IX. Ed. by Paul H. Barrett & R. B. Freeman. (Illus.). 360p. 1987. 75.00 (ISBN 0-8147-1794-2). NYU Pr.

Works of Charles Darwin: Geological Observations on the Volcanic Island Visited During the Voyage of H. M. S. Beagle, Vol. VIII. Ed. by Paul H. Barrett & R. B. Freeman. (Illus.). 168p. 1987. 75.00 (ISBN 0-8147-1793-4). NYU Pr.

Works of Charles Darwin: Journal of Researches into the Geology & Natural History of the Various Countries Visitied by H. M. S. Beagle, Vol. II, Pt. I. Ed. by Paul H. Barrett & R. B. Freeman. (Illus.). 256p. 1987. 75.00 (ISBN 0-8147-1787-X). NYU Pr.

Works of Charles Darwin: Journal of Researches into the Geology & Natural History of the Various Countries Visited by H. M. S. Beagle, Vol. III, Pt. 2. Ed. by Paul H. Barrett & R. B. Freeman. (Illus.). 264p. 1987. 75.00 (ISBN 0-8147-1788-8). NYU Pr.

Works of Charles Darwin: The Foundations of the Orgin of the Species, Two Essays Written in 1842 & 1844, Vol. X. Ed. by Frances Darwin et al. 240p. 1987. 75.00 (ISBN 0-8147-1795-0). NYU Pr.

Works of Charles Darwin: The Zoology of the Voyage of H. M. S. Beagle, under the Command of Captain Fitzroy, During the Years 1832-1836, Vol. IV, Pts. I & II. Ed. by Paul H. Barrett & R. B. Freeman. (Illus.). 264p. 1987. 95.00 (ISBN 0-8147-1789-6). NYU Pr.

Works of Charles Darwin: The Zoology of the Voyage of H. M. S. Beagle, under the Command of Captain Fitzroy, During the Years 1832-1836, Vol. V, Pt. III. Ed. by Paul H. Barrett & R. B. Freeman. (Illus.). 264p. 1987. 95.00 (ISBN 0-8147-1790-X). NYU Pr.

Works of Charles Darwin: The Zoology of the Voyage of H. M. S. Beagle, under the Command of Captain Fitzroy, During the Years 1832-1836, Vol. VI, Pt. IV & V. Ed. by Paul H. Barrett & R. B. Freeman. (Illus.). 376p. 1987. 95.00 (ISBN 0-8147-1791-8). NYU Pr.

Works of Charles Dickens: With Introductions, General Essay, & Notes by Andrew Lang, 34 vols. 1984. Repr. of 1905 ed. Set. lib. bdg. 1200.00 (ISBN 0-89984-933-4). Century Bookbindery.

Works of Charles Follen Adams, 1842-1918. Charles F. Adams. Date not set. Repr. of 1888 ed. Set. lib. bdg. price not set. Am Biog Serv.

Works of Charles Francis Adams Jr., 1835-1915. Charles F. Adams, Jr. 1987. Repr. of 1916 ed. Set. lib. bdg. price not set. Am Biog Serv.

Works of Charles Kendall Adams, 1835-1902. Charles K. Adams. 1987. Repr. of 1903 ed. Set. lib. bdg. price not set. Am Biog Serv.

Works of Charles Kingsley, 3 vols. Charles Kingsley. 1981. Repr. of 1857 ed. Set. lib. bdg. 97.50 (ISBN 0-89984-925-3). Century Bookbindery.

Works of Charles Kingsley, 28 vols. Charles Kingsley. 10200p. 1880. Repr. of 1885 ed. Set. lib. bdg. 1395.00x (Pub. by G Olms BRD). Coronet Bks.

Works of Charles Kingsley, 7 vols. Charles Kingsley. 2261p. 1987. Repr. of 1898 ed. Set. lib. bdg. 500.00 (ISBN 0-89987-462-2). Darby Bks.

Works of Charles Kingsley, 6 vols. (Illus.). 1981. Set. lib. bdg. 295.00 (ISBN 0-89984-306-9). Century Bookbindery.

Works of Charles Reade, 17 Vols. Charles Reade. LC 73-118070. Repr. of 1896 ed. Set. 637.50 (ISBN 0-404-05260-6); 37.50 ea. AMS Pr.

Works of Charles T. Griffes: A Descriptive Catalogue. Donna K. Anderson. Ed. by George Buelow. LC 83-4983. (Studies in Musicology: No. 68). 588p. 1983. 64.95 (ISBN 0-8357-1419-5). UMI Res Pr.

Works of Christoph Nichelmann: A Thematic Index. Douglas A. Lee. LC 71-151301. (Detroit Studies in Music Bibliography Ser.: No. 19). 1971. pap. 6.00 (ISBN 0-911772-41-3). Harmonie Pk Pr.

Works of Christopher Marlowe, 3 vols. Ed. by A. H. Bullen. 1979. Repr. of 1885 ed. Set. lib. bdg. 300.00 (ISBN 0-8492-3731-9). R West.

Works of Christopher Marlowe, 3 vols. Ed. by A H. Bullen. 1063p. Repr. of 1835 ed. Set. lib. bdg. 400.00 (ISBN 0-8414-2824-7). Folcroft.

Works of Colonel John Trumbull: Artist of the American Revolution. rev. ed. Theodore Sizer. LC 67-20337. (Illus.). pap. 95.30 (ISBN 0-317-10479-9, 2016795). Bks Demand UMI.

Works of Daniel Waterland, 11 Vols. Daniel Waterland. Ed. by William Von Mildert. Repr. of 1828 ed. Set. 215.00 (ISBN 0-404-06860-X); 20.00 ea. AMS Pr.

Works of David Everett. David Everett. LC 82-3390. 1983. 60.00x (ISBN 0-8201-1378-6). Schol Facsimiles.

Works of David Mallet, 3 Vols. new corr. ed. David Mallet. LC 74-144567. Repr. of 1759 ed. Set. 57.50 (ISBN 0-404-08580-6). AMS Pr.

Works of E. L. Henry: Recollections of a Time Gone by. Norton, R. W., Art Gallery Staff. (Illus.). 56p. 1987. pap. 12.00x (ISBN 0-913060-26-7). Norton Art.

Works of Edgar Allan Poe, 10 vols. facsimile ed. Edgar Allan Poe. Ed. by Edmund C. Stedman & George E. Woodberry. LC 71-169773. (Select Bibliographies Reprint Ser). Repr. of 1895 ed. Set. 250.00 (ISBN 0-8369-5993-0). Ayer Co Pubs.

Works of Edgar Allan Poe: With a Study of His Life & Writings by Charles Baudelaire. Edgar Allan Poe. Tr. by H. Curwen. LC 77-11472. Repr. of 1872 ed. 42.50 (ISBN 0-404-16334-3). AMS Pr.

Works of Edmund Burke, 12 vols. Edmund Burke. 1987. Repr. of 1899 ed. Set. lib. bdg. 895.00 (ISBN 0-317-59640-3). Am Biog Serv.

Works of Edmund Spencer. R. Morris. 1988. Repr. lib. bdg. 99.00x. Am Biog Serv.

Works of Edmund Spenser, 6 Vols. Edmund Spenser. Ed. by John Hughes. LC 79-175998. Repr. of 1715 ed. Set. 195.00 (ISBN 0-404-06200-8); 32.50 ea. Vol. 1 (ISBN 0-404-06201-6). Vol. 2 (ISBN 0-404-06202-4). Vol. 3 (ISBN 0-404-06203-2). Vol. 4 (ISBN 0-404-06204-0). Vol. 5 (ISBN 0-404-06205-9). Vol. 6 (ISBN 0-404-06206-7). AMS Pr.

Works of Edmund Spenser: A Variorum Edition, 11 vols. Edmund Spenser et al. Ed. by Edwin Greenlaw & Charles Grosvenor Osgood. Incl. Vol. 1. Faerie Queene: Book One. Ed. by Frederick Morgan Padelford. 568p. 1932. 45.00x (ISBN 0-8018-0234-2); Vol. 2. Faerie Queene: Book Two. Ed. by Edwin Greenlaw. 529p. 1933. 45.00x (ISBN 0-8018-0235-0); Vol. 3. Faerie Queene: Book Three. Ed. by Frederick Morgan Padelford. 442p. 1934. 45.00x (ISBN 0-8018-0236-9); Vol. 4. Faerie Queene: Book Four. Ed. by Ray Heffner. 371p. 1935. 45.00x (ISBN 0-8018-0237-7); Vol. 5. Faerie Queene: Book Five. Ed. by Ray Heffner. 387p. 1936. 45.00x (ISBN 0-8018-0238-5); Vol. 6. Faerie Queene: Books Six & Seven. Ed. by James G. McManaway et al. 518p. 1938. 45.00x (ISBN 0-8018-0239-3); Vol. 7. The Minor Poems, Part One. Ed. by Charles Grosvenor Osgood et al. 746p. 1943. 45.00x (ISBN 0-8018-0240-7); Vol. 8. The Minor Poems, Part Two. Ed. by Charles G. Osgood et al. 757p. 1947. 45.00x (ISBN 0-8018-0241-5); Vol. 9. Index to the Poetry. Ed. by Charles G. Osgood. 135p. 1957. 25.00x (ISBN 0-8018-0242-3); Vol. 10. Prose Works. Letters, Axiochus, A View of the Present State of Ireland, A Brief Note of I. Ed. by Rudolf Gottfried. 586p. 1949. 45.00x (ISBN 0-8018-0243-1); Vol. 11. Life of Edmund Spenser. Alexander C. Judson. (Illus.). 250p. 1945. 30.00x (ISBN 0-8018-0244-X). Set. 425.00x (ISBN 0-8018-2131-2). Johns Hopkins.

Works of Edmund Spenser with the Principal Illustrations of the Various Commentators, 8 Vols. Edmund Spenser. Ed. by H. J. Todd. LC 72-175999. Repr. of 1805 ed. Set. 320.00 (ISBN 0-404-06210-5); 40.00 ea. AMS Pr.

Works of Edward Atkinson, 1827-1905. Edward Atkinson. 1987. Repr. of 1904 ed. Set. lib. bdg. price not set. Am Biog Serv.

Works of Edward Bellamy, 1850-1898. Edward Bellamy. 1987. Repr. of 1900 ed. Set. lib. bdg. price not set. Am Biog Serv.

Works of Edward Ruscha. Dave Hickey & Peter Plagens. LC 81-20242. (Illus.). 182p. 1982. 35.00 (ISBN 0-933920-21-0, Dist. by Rizzoli); pap. 20.00 (ISBN 0-933920-22-9). Hudson Hills.

Works of Edward Stillingfleet with a Life by Richard Bentley, 6 Vols. Edward Stillingfleet. LC 78-176444. Repr. of 1710 ed. Set. lib. bdg. 400.00 (ISBN 0-404-06270-9). Vol. 1 (ISBN 0-404-06271-7). Vol. 2 (ISBN 0-404-06272-5). Vol. 3 (ISBN 0-404-06273-3). Vol. 4 (ISBN 0-404-06274-1). Vol. 5 (ISBN 0-404-06275-X). Vol. 6 (ISBN 0-404-06276-8). AMS Pr.

Works of Edwin Hunter Pendleton Arden, 1864-1918. Edwin H. Arden. 1987. Repr. Set. lib. bdg. price not set. Am Biog Serv.

Works of Elisha Benjamin Andrews, 1844-1917. Elisha B. Andrews. 1987. Repr. of 1913 ed. Set. lib. bdg. price not set. Am Biog Serv.

Works of Elizabeth (Chase) Akers, 1832-1911. Elizabeth Ankers. 1987. Repr. of 1902 ed. Set. lib. bdg. price not set. Am Biog Serv.

Works of English Poets, from Chaucer to Cowper, 21 Vols. Alexander Chalmers. 1971. Repr. of 1810 ed. Set. 2016.00x (ISBN 3-487-02603-1). Adlers Foreign Bks.

Works of Fenimore Cooper, 16 vols. James Fenimore Cooper. 475.00 (ISBN 0-8274-3762-5). R West.

Works of Fielding: Amelia, Joseph Andrews, History of Tom Jones, Jacobites Journal, Miscellanies, True Patriot, 7 vols. Henry Fielding. Set. 250.00x (ISBN 0-8195-5146-5). Wesleyan U Pr.

Works of Fisher Ames, 2 vols. Fisher Ames. Ed. by Seth Ames. LC 73-146132. (Research & Source Works Ser.: No. 711). 1971. Repr. of 1854 ed. Set. lib. bdg. 48.50 (ISBN 0-8337-0063-4). B Franklin.

Works of Fisher Ames, 2 vol. set. Seth Ames. Ed. by William Allen. LC 81-13568. 1984. 30.00 set (ISBN 0-86597-013-0, Liberty Clas); pap. 15.00 set (ISBN 0-86597-016-5). Liberty Fund.

Works of Fisher Ames, 2 Vols. Ed. by Seth Ames. LC 69-14409. (American Public Figures Ser.). 1969. Repr. of 1854 ed. Set. lib. bdg. 89.50 (ISBN 0-306-71122-2). Da Capo.

Works of Fisher Ames, 1758-1808. Fisher Ames. 1987. Repr. of 1835 ed. Set. lib. bdg. price not set. Am Biog Serv.

Works of Francesco Landini. Francesco Landino. Ed. by L. Ellinwood. (Med Acad Amer Pubns). 1939. 42.00 (ISBN 0-527-01703-5). Kraus Repr.

Works of Francesco Soriano: Vol. I, "Motets for Eight Voices," 1597. Francesco Soriano. Ed. by S. Philip Kniseley. LC 79-25222. (Illus.). 130p. 1980. pap. 12.00x (ISBN 0-8130-0668-6). U Presses Fla.

Works of Francis Bacon, 15 vols. Francis Bacon. Repr. Set. lib. bdg. 695.00x (ISBN 0-403-00003-3). Scholarly.

Works of Francis Beaumont & John Fletcher, 4 vols. Francis Beaumont. Ed. by A. H. Bullen. LC 75-41306. (BCL Ser. II). 1976. Repr. of 1912 ed. Varorium Edition. 105.00 set (ISBN 0-404-14820-4). AMS Pr.

Works of Francis Beaumont & John Fletcher: Variorum Edition, 4 vols. 1978. Repr. of 1904 ed. lib. bdg. 250.00 set (ISBN 0-8495-0122-9). Arden Lib.

Works of Francis Thompson, 3 Vols. Francis Thompson. Ed. by W. Meynell. LC 70-118947. Repr. of 1913 ed. Set. 87.50 (ISBN 0-404-06460-4); Vol. 1 (ISBN 0-404-06461-2). Vol. 2 (ISBN 0-404-06462-0). Vol. 3 (ISBN 0-404-06463-9). AMS Pr.

Works of Francis Thompson: Poems, 2 Vols. 228p. Repr. of 1913 ed. Set. lib. bdg. 75.00 (ISBN 0-317-19016-4). R West.

Works of Francis Thompson: Prose. 291p. Repr. of 1913 ed. lib. bdg. 50.00 (ISBN 0-317-19014-8). R West.

Works of Fulke Greville. Morris W. Croll. LC 70-100743. (English Literature Ser.). 1979. pap. 39.95x (ISBN 0-8383-0019-7). Haskell.

Works of Gabriel Harvey, 3 Vols. Gabriel Harvey. Ed. by Alexander B. Grosart. LC 20-2123. Repr. of 1885 ed. Set. 90.00 (ISBN 0-404-03200-1); 30.00 ea. Vol. 1 (ISBN 0-404-03201-X). Vol. 2 (ISBN 0-404-03202-8). Vol. 3 (ISBN 0-404-03203-6). AMS Pr.

Works of Geber. Ibn H. Jabir. LC 79-8615. Repr. of 1928 ed. 32.50 (ISBN 0-404-18479-0). AMS Pr.

Works of Genius. Richard Marek. LC 86-47951. 320p. 1987. 17.95 (ISBN 0-689-11889-9). Atheneum.

Works of Genius. Richard Marek. 1988. pap. 4.50 (ISBN 0-451-15497-5, Sig). NAL.

Works of Genius: A Catalogue & a Commentary, Pt. 1, A-c. John H. Jenkins. (Illus.). 9.50 (ISBN 0-8363-0151-X). Jenkins.

Works of Geoffrey Chaucer. Geoffrey Chaucer. Ed. by Alfred W. Pollard. LC 73-399393. (Select Bibliographies Reprint Ser.). 1972. Repr. of 1898 ed. 33.00 (ISBN 0-8369-9903-7). Ayer Co Pubs.

Works of Geoffrey Chaucer. 2nd ed. Geoffrey Chaucer. Ed. by F. N. Robinson. (New Cambridge Editions). xliv, 1002p. 1957. text ed. 32.95 (ISBN 0-395-05568-7). HM.

Works of George Arnold, 1834-1865. George Arnold. 1987. Repr. of 1867 ed. Set. lib. bdg. price not set. Am Biog Serv.

Works of George Dalgarno of Aberdeen. George Dalgarno. Ed. by Thomas Maitland. LC 74-165338. (Maitland Club, Glasgow. Publications: No. 29). Repr. of 1834 ed. 16.75 (ISBN 0-404-52987-9). AMS Pr.

Works of George Dalgarno of Aberdeen. George Dalgarno. Repr. of 1834 ed. 22.00 (ISBN 0-384-10697-8). Johnson Repr.

Works of George Farquhar, Vols. I & II. George Farquhar. Ed. by Shirley S. Kenny. (English Texts Ser.). (Illus.). 1988. Vol. 1 688p. 105.00x (ISBN 0-19-811858-9); Vol. 2 656p. 105.00 (ISBN 0-19-812342-6). Oxford U Pr.

Works of George Fox, Vols. 1-8. George Fox. Incl. Vols. 1 & 2. Journal or Historical Account of the Life, Travels, Sufferings, Christian Experiences & Labour of Love in the Work of the Ministry, of That Ancient, Eminent, & Faithful Servant of Jesus Christ, George Fox. LC 75-16194. Vol. 1 (ISBN 0-404-09351-5). Vol. 2 (ISBN 0-404-09352-3); Vol. 3. Great Mystery of the Great Whore Unfolded. LC 75-16195. 616p (ISBN 0-404-09353-1); Vols. 4-6. Gospel Truth Demonstrated, in a Collection of Doctrinal Books, Given Forth by That Faithful Minister of Jesus Christ, George Fox. LC 75-16199. Vol. 4 (ISBN 0-404-09354-X). Vol. 5 (ISBN 0-404-09355-8). Vol. 6 (ISBN 0-404-09356-6); Vols. 7 & 8. Collection of Many Select & Christian Epistles, Letters & Testimonies. LC 75-16207. Vol. 7 (ISBN 0-404-09357-4). Vol. 8 (ISBN 0-404-09358-2). Repr. of 1831 ed. Set. 320.00 (ISBN 0-404-09350-7); 40.00 ea. AMS Pr.

Works of George Gissing. Incl. In the Year of the Jubilee. Ed. by P. F. Kropholler. LC 75-29849. 453p (ISBN 0-8386-1886-3); Our Friend the Charlatan. Ed. & intro. by Pierre Coustillas. LC 75-29850. 327p (ISBN 0-8386-1884-7); Unclassed. Ed. & intro. by Jacob Korg. LC 75-29850. 457p. 1976. 24.50 ea. Fairleigh Dickinson.

Works of George L. Aiken, 1830-1876. George L. Aiken. 1987. Repr. Set. lib. bdg. price not set. Am Biog Serv.

Works of George Savile, Marquis of Halifax, Vol. II. George Savile. Ed. by Mark N. Brown. (English Texts Ser.). (Illus.). 500p. 1988. 96.00 (ISBN 0-19-812337-X). Oxford U Pr.

Works of George Savile, Marquis of Halifax, Vol. III. George Savile. Ed. by Mark N. Brown. (English Texts Ser.). (Illus.). 500p. 1988. 96.00 (ISBN 0-19-812338-8). Oxford U Pr.

Works of George Savile, Marquis of Halifax, Vol. I. George Savile. Ed. by Mark N. Brown. (English Texts Ser.). (Illus.). 500p. 1988. 96.00 (ISBN 0-19-812752-9). Oxford U Pr.

Works of George Tyrrell, 18 titles in 20 vols. George Tyrrell. Repr. Set. 265.00 (ISBN 0-404-07850-8); Ea. vol. write for info. AMS Pr.

Works of Gilbert Crispin. Gilbert Crispin. Ed. by G. R. Evans & Anna S. Abulafia. (Auctores Britannici Medii Aevi: Vol. VIII). (Illus.). 288p. 1986. 88.00x (ISBN 0-19-726035-7). Oxford U Pr.

Works of Girolamo Savoldo: The 1955 Dissertation, with a Review of Research, 1955-1985. Creighton E. Gilbert. Ed. by S. J. Freedberg. (Outstanding Dissertations in Fine Arts Ser.). (Illus.). 690p. 1985. Repr. of 1955 ed. 70.00 (ISBN 0-8240-6856-4). Garland Pub.

Works of H. G. Wells, 1887-1925. Geoffrey H. Wells. LC 68-5207. 274p. 1926. Repr. 15.00 (ISBN 0-8337-3728-7). B Franklin.

Works of H. G. Wells 1887-1925: A Bibliography, Dictionary, & Subject-Index. Geoffrey H. Wells. 274p. 1983. 87.00 (ISBN 0-89984-532-0). Century Bookbindery.

Works of Hannah Adams, 1755-1831. Hannah Adams. 1987. Repr. of 1826 ed. Set. lib. bdg. price not set. Am Biog Serv.

Works of Heinrich Heine, 20 vols. Heinrich Heine. Tr. by Charles G. Leland. LC 76-13343. Repr. of 1906 ed. 20.00 ea.; 400.00 set (ISBN 0-404-15250-3). AMS Pr.

Works of Henry Abbey, 1842-1911. Henry Abbey. Date not set. Repr. of 1910 ed. Set. lib. bdg. price not set. Am Biog Serv.

Works of Henry Adams, 1838-1918. Henry Adams. 1987. Repr. of 1930 ed. Set. lib. bdg. price not set. Am Biog Serv.

Works of Henry Barnard, 1811-1900. Henry Barnard. 1987. Repr. of 1854 ed. Set. lib. bdg. price not set. Am Biog Serv.

Works of Henry Howard & of Sir Thomas Wyatt the Elder, 2 Vols. Henry Howard & Thomas Wyatt. Ed. by George F. Nott. 1815-16. Set. 97.50 (ISBN 0-404-04803-X). AMS Pr.

Works of Henry Mills Alden, 1839-1919. Henry M. Alden. 1987. Repr. of 1910 ed. Set. lib. bdg. price not set. Am Biog Serv.

Works of Henry Ward Beecher, 1813-1887. Henry W. Beecher. 1987. Repr. of 1885 ed. Set. price not set. Am Biog Serv.

Works of Herbert Baxter Adams, 1850-1901. Herbert B. Adams. 1987. Repr. of 1900 ed. Set. lib. bdg. price not set. Am Biog Serv.

Works of Herman Melville. Herman Melville. LC 87-14445. 736p. 1987. 9.98 (ISBN 0-517-65084-3). Outlet Bk Co.

Works of Herodian, 2 vols. Herodian. (Loeb Classical Library: No. 454-455). (Gr. & Eng.). 13.95x ea. Vol. 1 (ISBN 0-674-99500-7). Vol. 2 (ISBN 0-674-99501-5). Harvard U Pr.

Works of Hesiod, 2 vols. in one. Hesiodus. Tr. by Thomas Cooke. LC 79-158284. Repr. of 1728 ed. 40.00 (ISBN 0-404-54170-4). AMS Pr.

Works of Hew Ainslie, 1792-1878. Hew Ainslie. 1987. Repr. of 1855 ed. Set. lib. bdg. price not set. Am Biog Serv.

Works of Horace, 2 vols. Horace. LC 70-179303. (Eng. & Lat.). 1976. Repr. of 1792 ed. 87.50 set (ISBN 0-404-54150-X). AMS Pr.

Works of Horatio Alger Jr., 1834-1899. Horatio Alger. 1987. Repr. of 1883 ed. Set. lib. bdg. price not set. Am Biog Serv.

Works of Hsuntze. Hsun-Tzu. Tr. by Homer H. Dubs from Chinese. LC 75-41145. Repr. of 1928 ed. 23.50 (ISBN 0-685-70791-1). AMS Pr.

Works of Hugh Latimer, Sometime Bishop of Worcester, Martyr, 1555, 2 Vols. Hugh Latimer. Repr. of 1845 ed. Set. 80.00 (ISBN 0-384-31480-5). Johnson Repr.

Works of Isaac Disraeli, 6 vols. Isaac Disraeli. Ed. by Benjamin Disraeli. 3333p. Repr. of 1881 ed. Set. lib. bdg. 357.50x (Pub. by G Olms BRD). Coronet Bks.

Works of Isaac Newton Arnold, 1815-1884. Issac N. Arnold. 1987. Repr. of 1884 ed. Set. lib. bdg. price not set. Am Biog Serv.

Works of Isaac Watts, 6 Vols. Isaac Watts. Ed. by G. Burder. LC 70-131027. Repr. of 1811 ed. Set. lib. bdg. 650.00 (ISBN 0-404-06890-1). Vol. 1 (ISBN 0-404-06891-X). Vol. 2 (ISBN 0-404-06892-8). Vol. 3 (ISBN 0-404-06893-6). Vol. 4 (ISBN 0-404-06894-4). Vol. 5 (ISBN 0-404-06895-2). Vol. 6 (ISBN 0-404-06896-0). AMS Pr.

Works of J. Fenimore Cooper: The Deerslayer, the Pathfinder, the Pioneers, 10 vols. 1984. Repr. of 1891 ed. lib. bdg. 500.00 set. Century Bookbindery.

Works of J. M. Barrie, 18 vols. James M. Barrie. Incl. Vol. 1. Auld Licht Idylls, etc. Repr. of 1929 ed (ISBN 0-404-08781-7); Vol. 2. My Lady Nicotine, etc. Repr. of 1929 ed (ISBN 0-404-08782-5); Vol. 3. When a Man's Single. Repr. of 1929 ed (ISBN 0-404-08783-3); Vol. 4. Little Minister. Repr. of 1929 ed (ISBN 0-404-08784-1); Vol. 5. Sentimental Tommy. Repr. of 1929 ed (ISBN 0-404-08785-X); Vol. 6. Tommy & Grizel. Repr. of 1929 ed (ISBN 0-404-08786-8); Vol. 7. Little White Bird. Repr. of 1930 ed (ISBN 0-404-08787-6); Vol. 8. Margaret Ogilvy & Others. Repr. of 1930 ed (ISBN 0-404-08788-4); Vol. 9. Courage, etc. Repr. of 1930 ed (ISBN 0-404-08789-2); Vol. 10. Peter Pan & Other Plays. Repr. of 1930 ed (ISBN 0-404-08790-6); Vol. 11. Admirable Crichton etc. Repr. of 1930 ed (ISBN 0-404-08791-4); Vol. 12. What Every Woman Knows & Other Plays. Repr. of 1930 ed (ISBN 0-404-08792-2); Vol. 13. Dear Brutus & Other Plays. Repr. of 1931 ed (ISBN 0-404-08793-0); Vol. 14. Mary Rose & Other Plays. Repr. of 1931 ed (ISBN 0-404-08794-9); Vol. 15. M'Connachie & J. M. B., etc. Repr. of 1940 ed (ISBN 0-404-08795-7); Vol. 16. Greenwood Hat, etc. Repr. of 1940 ed (ISBN 0-404-08796-5); Vol. 17. Boy David, etc. Repr. of 1941 ed (ISBN 0-404-08797-3); Vol. 18. Professor's Love-Story, etc. Repr. of 1941 ed (ISBN 0-404-08798-1). LC 79-146660. 32.50 ea.; 585.00 set (ISBN 0-404-08780-9). AMS Pr.

Works of Jacob Abbott, 1803-1879. Jacob Abbott. Date not set. Repr. of 1879 ed. Set. lib. bdg. price not set. Am Biog Serv.

Works of Jacques Lacan: An Introduction. Bice Benvenuto & Roger Kennedy. LC 86-3847. 237p. 1986. 27.50; pap. 12.95. St Martin.

Works of Jakob Boehme, 4 vols. Jakob Boehme. 1974. lib. bdg. 1500.00 (ISBN 0-87968-465-8). Gordon Pr.

Works of James Abram Garfield, 2 Vols. facs. ed. James A. Garfield. Ed. by Burke A. Hinsdale. LC 73-117877. (Select Bibliographies Reprint Ser). 1882. Set. 82.50 (ISBN 0-8369-5330-4). Ayer Co Pubs.

Works of James Adair, 1709-1783. James Adair. Date not set. Repr. of 1700 ed. Set. lib. bdg. price not set. Am Biog Serv.

Works of James Allen, 1849-1925. James L. Allen. 1987. Repr. of 1925 ed. Set. lib. bdg. price not set. Am Biog Serv.

Works of James Arminius, 3 vols. James Arminius. Tr. by William Nicoles from Dutch. Repr. of 1875 ed. Set. text ed. 75.00 (ISBN 0-8010-0206-0). Baker Bk.

Works of James Fenimore Cooper: Red Rover Edition, 32 vols. 1984. Repr. Set. lib. bdg. 1200.00. Century Bookbindery.

Works of James Gillray. James Gillray. LC 68-21201. (Illus.). 1968. Repr. of 1851 ed. 50.00 (ISBN 0-405-08562-1, Blom Pubns). Ayer Co Pubs.

Works of James McNeill Whistler. facsimile ed. Elisabeth L. Cary. LC 77-157328. (Select Bibliographies Reprint Ser). Repr. of 1907 ed. 24.50 (ISBN 0-8369-5788-1). Ayer Co Pubs.

Works of James McNeill Whistler. Elisabeth L. Cary. LC 77-6969. 1977. Repr. of 1913 ed. lib. bdg. 35.00 (ISBN 0-89341-217-1). Longwood Pub Group.

Works of James O'Connor, the Deaf Poet, with a Biography Sketch of the Author. James O'Connor. 59.95 (ISBN 0-8490-1330-5). Gordon Pr.

Works of James Pilkington, Lord Bishop of Durham. James Pilkington. 1842. Repr. of 1842 ed. 55.00 (ISBN 0-384-46530-7). Johnson Repr.

Works of James Ussher, 17 Vols. James Ussher. Ed. by C. R. Elrington & J. H. Todd. LC 70-177553. Repr. of 1864 ed. Set. lib. bdg. 360.00 (ISBN 0-404-06730-1). AMS Pr.

Works of Jane (Goodwin) Austin, 1831-1894. Jane Austin. 1987. Repr. of 1892 ed. Set. lib. bdg. price not set. Am Biog Serv.

Works of Jean Fernand Brierre: Chansons Secretes; Nous Garderons le Dieu; Black Soul; Belle; Les Aieules; Dessalines Nous Parle; Petion y Bolivar; La Source; La Nuit; Or, Uranium, Cuivre, Radium. Jean F. Brierre. 1961. Ten works in one unit. 51.00 (ISBN 0-8115-3043-4). Kraus Repr.

Works of Jean Louis Rodolphe Agassiz, 1807-1873. Jean L. Agassiz. 1987. Repr. of 1868 ed. Set. lib. bdg. price not set. Am Biog Serv.

Works of Jeremy Belknap, 1744-1798. Jeremy Belknap. 1987. Repr. of 1796 ed. Set. lib. bdg. price not set. Am Biog Serv.

Works of John Adams, 10 vols. John Adams. LC 78-128978. Repr. of 1856 ed. Set. 325.00 (ISBN 0-404-00310-9); 32.50 ea. AMS Pr.

Works of John Adams, Second President of the United States, 10 Vols. facs. ed. John Adams. LC 77-80620. (Select Bibliographies Reprint Ser.). Repr. of 1856 ed. Set. 410.00 (ISBN 0-8369-5020-8). Ayer Co Pubs.

Works of John Adams, 1704-1740. John Adams. 1987. Repr. of 1709 ed. Set. lib. bdg. price not set. Am Biog Serv.

Works of John & Charles Wesley. 2nd rev. ed. Richard Green. LC 74-26049. Repr. of 1906 ed. 23.00 (ISBN 0-404-12924-2). AMS Pr.

Works of John Andrews, 1746-1813. John Andrews. 1987. Repr. of 1813 ed. Set. lib. bdg. price not set. Am Biog Serv.

Works of John Bachman, 1790-1874. John Bachman. 1987. Set. lib. bdg. price not set. Am Biog Serv.

Works of John Bascom, 1827-1911. John Bascom. 1987. Repr. of 1913 ed. Set. lib. bdg. price not set. Am Biog Serv.

Works of John Bramhall, 5 Vols. John Bramhall. LC 73-39519. Repr. of 1845 ed. Set. 145.00 (ISBN 0-404-52060-X). AMS Pr.

Works of John Bunyan, 3 Vols. John Bunyan. Ed. by George Offor. LC 78-154136. Repr. of 1856 ed. Set. lib. bdg. 225.00 (ISBN 0-404-09250-0). AMS Pr.

Works of John Day. John Day. Ed. by A. H. Bullen. 35.00x (ISBN 0-87556-044-X). Saifer.

Works of John Dryden. John Dryden. Incl. Vol. I, Poems, 1649-1680. Ed. by Edward N. Hooker & H. T. Swedenberg. 1956. 55.00x (ISBN 0-520-00358-6); Vol. II, Poems, 1681-1684. Ed. by H. T. Swedenberg. 1973; Vol. III, Poems, 1685-1692. Ed. by Earl Miner & Vinton A. Dearing. 1970. 55.00x (ISBN 0-520-01625-4); Vol. IV, Poems, 1693-1699. Ed. by A. B. Chambers et al. 1974. 55.00x (ISBN 0-520-02120-7); Vol. VIII, Plays, The Wild Gallant, The Rival Ladies, The Indian Queen. Ed. by John H. Smith et al. 1962. 55.00x (ISBN 0-520-00359-4); Vol. IX, Plays; The Indian Emperour, Secret Love, Sir Martin Mar-All. Ed. by John Loftis & Vinton A. Dearing. 1966. 55.00x (ISBN 0-520-00360-8); Vol. X, Plays; The Tempest, Tyrannick Love, An Evening's Love. Ed. by Maximillan E. Novak & George R. Guffey. 1970. 55.00x (ISBN 0-520-01589-4); Vol. XI, Plays; The Conquest of Granada, Part I & II, Marriage-a-la Mode, & The Assignation: Or, Love in a Nunnery. Ed. by John Loftis et al. 1978. 55.00x (ISBN 0-520-02125-8); Vol. XIII, Plays: All for Love Oedipus, Troilus & Cressida. Ed. by Maximillian E. Novak et al. 1984. 55.00x (ISBN 0-520-02127-4); Vol. XV, Plays: Albion & Albanius, Don Sebastian, Amphitryon. Ed. by Earl Miner. 1976. 55.00x (ISBN 0-520-02129-0); Vol. XVII, Prose, 1668-1691, an Essay of Dramatic Poesie & Shorter Works. Ed. by Samuel A. Monk & E. A. Maurer. 1972. 55.00x (ISBN 0-520-01814-1); Vol. XVIII, Prose: The History of the League, 1684. Ed. by Alan Roper & Dearing Vinton. 1974. 55.00x (ISBN 0-520-02131-2); Vol. XIX, Prose, The Life of St. Francis Xavier. Ed. by Alan Roper & Dearing A. Vinton. 1979. 55.00x (ISBN 0-520-02132-0). U of Cal Pr.

Works of John Flavel, 6 vols. Set. 118.95 (ISBN 0-85151-060-4). Banner of Truth.

Works of John Henry Alexander, 1812-1867. John H. Alexander. 1987. Repr. of 1852 ed. Set. lib. bdg. price not set. Am Biog Serv.

Works of John Henry Newman: Essay & Sketches, 3 vols. Ed. by Charles F. Harrold. 1131p. Repr. of 1948 ed. Set. lib. bdg. 100.00 (ISBN 0-89984-537-1). Century Bookbindery.

Works of John Knox, 6 Vols. John Knox. Ed. by David Laing. LC 67-35016. Repr. of 1864 ed. Set. 345.00 (ISBN 0-404-52880-5). AMS Pr.

Works of John Locke, 2 Vols. John Locke. LC 74-94275. (Select Bibliographies Reprint Ser.). 1877. Set. 56.00 (ISBN 0-8369-5049-6); Vol. 1. 28.00 (ISBN 0-8369-9980-0); Vol. 2. 28.00 (ISBN 0-8369-9981-9). Ayer Co Pubs.

Works of John Locke: A Comprehensive Bibliography from the Seventeenth Century to the Present. John C. Attig. LC 85-14670. (Bibliographies & Indexes in Philosophy Ser.: No. 1). xx, 185p. 1985. lib. bdg. 40.95 (ISBN 0-313-24359-X, AJL/). Greenwood.

Works of John Marston, 3 vols. Ed. by A. H. Bullen. 1979. Repr. of 1887 ed. Set. lib. bdg. 400.00 (ISBN 0-8495-0502-X). Arden Lib.

Works of John Metham. John Metham. Ed. by H. Craig. (EETS, OS Ser.: No. 132). 44.00 (ISBN 0-527-00129-5). Kraus Repr.

Works of John Newton, 6 vols. John Newton. 1985. Repr. of 1820 ed. Set. 132.95 (ISBN 0-85151-460-X). Banner of Truth.

Works of John Owen, Vol. I. John Owen. 1980. 19.95 (ISBN 0-85151-123-6). Banner of Truth.

Works of John Owen, Vol. II. John Owen. 1980. 19.95 (ISBN 0-85151-124-4). Banner of Truth.

Works of John Owen, Vol. III. John Owen. 1980. 19.95 (ISBN 0-85151-125-2). Banner of Truth.

Works of John Owen, Vol. IV. John Owen. 1980. 19.95 (ISBN 0-85151-068-X). Banner of Truth.

Works of John Owen, Vol. V. John Owen. 1980. 19.95 (ISBN 0-85151-067-1). Banner of Truth.

Works of John Owen, Vol. VI. John Owen. 1980. 19.95 (ISBN 0-85151-126-0). Banner of Truth.

Works of John Owen, Vol. VII. John Owen. 1980. 19.95 (ISBN 0-85151-127-9). Banner of Truth.

Works of John Owen, Vol. VIII. John Owen. 1980. 19.95 (ISBN 0-85151-066-3). Banner of Truth.

Works of John Owen, Vol. IX. John Owen. 1980. 16.95 (ISBN 0-85151-065-5). Banner of Truth.

Works of John Owen, Vol. X. John Owen. 1980. 19.95 (ISBN 0-85151-064-7). Banner of Truth.

Works of John Owen, Vol. XI. John Owen. 1980. 19.95 (ISBN 0-85151-128-7). Banner of Truth.

Works of John Owen, Vol. XII. John Owen. 1980. 19.95 (ISBN 0-85151-129-5). Banner of Truth.

Works of John Owen, Vol. XIII. John Owen. 1980. 19.95 (ISBN 0-85151-063-9). Banner of Truth.

Works of John Owen, Vol. XIV. John Owen. 1980. 19.95 (ISBN 0-85151-062-0). Banner of Truth.

Works of John Owen, Vol. XV. John Owen. 1980. 19.95 (ISBN 0-85151-130-9). Banner of Truth.

Works of John Owen, Vol. XVI. John Owen. 1980. 19.95 (ISBN 0-85151-061-2). Banner of Truth.

Works of John Owen, 16 vols. John Owen. 1980. Set. 279.95 (ISBN 0-85151-392-1). Banner of Truth.

Works of John Philip Sousa. Paul E. Bierley. LC 84-80665. 1984. 28.50 (ISBN 0-918048-04-4). Integrity.

Works of John Stevens Cabot Abbott, 1805-1877. John S. Abbott. Date not set. Repr. of 1873 ed. Set. price not set. Am Biog Serv.

Works of John Taylor the Water Poet, 3 vols. John Taylor. LC 14-20890. 630p. 1869. Repr. 86.50 (ISBN 0-8337-3484-9). B Franklin.

Works of John Taylor the Water Poet Not Included in the Folio Edition of 1630, 5 vols in 4. John Taylor. Vols. 1-3. 142.50 set (ISBN 0-685-23107-0); Vol. 1. 29.50 ea. (ISBN 0-8337-3485-7). Vol. 2 (ISBN 0-8337-3486-5). Vol. 3 (ISBN 0-8337-3487-3). Vol. 4. 54.00 (ISBN 0-8337-3488-1). B Franklin.

Works of John Wesley. Ed. by Albert C. Outler. (Wesley Works Ser.). 608p. 1987. 49.95 (ISBN 0-687-46213-4). Abingdon.

Works of John Wesley, 14 vols. John Wesley. Set. 249.50 (ISBN 0-8010-9616-2). Baker Bk.

Works of John Wesley. John Wesley. Ed. by W. Reginald Ward & Richard P. Heitzenrater. Incl. Volume 18: Journals & Diaries (1735-1739) 400p. 49.95 (ISBN 0-687-46221-5); Volume 1: Sermons I, 1-33. 49.95; Volume 2: Sermons II, 34-70. 49.95; Volume 3: Sermons III, 71-114. 49.50 (ISBN 0-687-46212-6); Volume 4: Sermons IV, 115-151. 49.95. 1988. Abingdon.

Works of John Wesley: A Collection of Hymns for the Use of the People Called Methodists, Vol. 7. John Wesley. Ed. by Franz Hildebrandt & Oliver A. Beckerlegge. (Oxford Edition of the Works of John Wesley Ser.). (Illus.). 1984. 86.00x (ISBN 0-19-812529-1). Oxford U Pr.

Works of John Wesley: Letters I, 1721-1739, Vol. 25. John Wesley. Ed. by Frank Baker. (Oxford Edition of the Works of John Wesley Ser.). 1980. 45.00x (ISBN 0-19-812545-3). Oxford U Pr.

Works of John Wesley: (Letters II), 1740-1755, Vol. 26. John Wesley. Ed. by Frank Baker. (Oxford Edition of the Works of John Wesley Ser.). (Illus.). 1982. 45.00x (ISBN 0-19-812546-1). Oxford U Pr.

Works of John Wesley: Sermons 1-33, Vol. 1. 1008p. 1984. 49.95 (ISBN 0-687-46210-X). Abingdon.

Works of John Wesley, Volume 2: Sermons II, 34-70. Albert C. Outler. 600p. 1985. 49.95 (ISBN 0-687-46211-8). Abingdon.

Works of John Whitgift, Archbishop of Canterbury, 3 Vols. John Whitgift. Set. 147.00; Vol. 1. 41.00; Vol. 2. 51.00; Vol. 3. 55.00. Johnson Repr.

Works of John Woolman, 2 Pts. facs. ed. John Woolman. LC 78-83893. (Black Heritage Library Collection Ser.). 1885. 19.75 (ISBN 0-8369-8694-6). Ayer Co Pubs.

Works of Jonathan Edwards, 2 vols. Jonathan Edwards. 1979. Set. 88.95 (ISBN 0-85151-397-2); Vol. 1. 46.95 (ISBN 0-85151-216-X); Vol. 2. 46.95 (ISBN 0-85151-217-8). Banner of Truth.

Works of Jonathan Swift. D. Laing Purves. 1979. Repr. of 1872 ed. lib. bdg. 45.00 (ISBN 0-8492-2159-5). R West.

Works of Joseph Alden, 1807-1885. Joseph Alden. 1987. Repr. of 1880 ed. Set. lib. bdg. price not set. Am Biog Serv.

Works of Joseph Butler. Joseph Bulter. Ed. by W. E. Gladstone. 1986. Repr. of 1897 ed. lib. bdg. 40.00X (ISBN 0-935005-38-2). Ibis Pub VA.

Works of Joseph Conrad. Joseph Conrad. 3900.00 (ISBN 0-384-55125-4). Johnson Repr.

Works of Joseph Henry Allen, 1820-1980. Joseph H. Allen. 1987. Repr. of 1984 ed. Set. lib. bdg. price not set. Am Biog Serv.

Works of Josephus, 9 vols. Josephus. Ed. by E. H. Warmington. Incl. Vol. 1. Life; Against Apion (ISBN 0-674-99205-9); Vols 2-3. Jewish War. Vol. 2, Bks 1-3. (ISBN 0-674-99223-7); Vol. 3, Bks. 4-7, Index To Vols. 2 & 3. (ISBN 0-674-99232-6); Vols 4-9. Antiquities. Vol. 4, Bks 1-4. (ISBN 0-674-99267-9); Vol. 5, Bks 5-8. (ISBN 0-674-99310-1); Vol. 6, Bks 9-11. (ISBN 0-674-99360-8); Vol. 7, Bks 12-14. (ISBN 0-674-99402-7); Vol. 8, Bks 15-17. (ISBN 0-674-99451-5); Vol. 9, Bks 18-20, General Index. (ISBN 0-674-99477-9). (Loeb Classical Library: No. 186, 203, 210, 242, 281, 326, 365, 410, 433). 13.95x ea. Harvard U Pr.

Works of Josephus. Flavius Josephus. 800p. 1980. 19.95 (ISBN 0-913573-86-8). Hendrickson MA.

Works of Jules Verne. Jules Verne. (YA) (gr. 2-7). cancelled (ISBN 0-517-41372-8). Outlet Bk Co.

Works of Julian, 3 Vols. Julian. (Loeb Classical Library: No. 13, 29, 157). 13.95x ea.; Vol. 1. (ISBN 0-674-99014-5); Vol. 2. lib. bdg. (ISBN 0-674-99032-3); Vol. 3. (ISBN 0-674-99173-7). Harvard U Pr.

Works of Kalidasa: Dramas, Vol. I. Ed. by C. R. Devadhar. 959p. 1985. Repr. of 1966 ed. 35.00x (ISBN 81-208-0023-0, Pub. by Motilal Banarsidass India). Orient Bk Dist.

Works of Kalidasa: Kavya, Vol. 11. Ed. by C. R. Devadhar. 1093p. 1984. Repr. 42.00x (ISBN 0-317-60584-4, Pub. by Motilal Banarsidass India). Orient Bk Dist.

Works of Kalidasa: Kayva, Vol. II. Ed. by C. R. Devadhar. 1093p. 1984. Repr. 46.00x (ISBN 81-208-0024-9, Pub. by Motilal Banarsidass India). South Asia Bks.

Works of Lady Blessington. Marguerite P. Blessington. LC 71-37681. (Women of Letters Ser.). Repr. of 1838 ed. 47.50 (ISBN 0-404-56717-7). AMS Pr.

Works of Laurence Sterne, 6 Vols. Laurence Sterne. Ed. by George Saintsbury. LC 73-129387. Repr. of 1894 ed. Set. 60.00 (ISBN 0-404-08080-4); 10.00 ea. AMS Pr.

Works of Lord Bolingbroke, 4 vols. Henry S. Bolingbroke. LC 67-16351. 1967. Repr. of 1844 ed. 195.00x (ISBN 0-678-05028-7). Kelley.

Works of Lord Macaulay Complete: The Albany Edition, 12 vols. Thomas B. Macaulay. LC 76-42708. Repr. of 1898 ed. Set. 540.00 (ISBN 0-404-59480-8); 45.00 ea. AMS Pr.

Works of Louisa May Alcott. Louisa May Alcott. (gr. 5-6). 35.95 (ISBN 0-88411-173-3, Pub. by Aeonian Pr). Amereon Ltd.

Works of Louisa May Alcott. Ed. by C. Booss. (Avenel Readers Library). (Illus.). 800p. 1982. 7.98 (ISBN 0-517-37167-7, Avenel); jacketed ed. 7.98 (ISBN 0-517-37146-4). Outlet Bk Co.

Works of Louisa May Alcott, 1832-1888. Louisa May Alcott. 1987. Repr. of 1886 ed. Set. lib. bdg. price not set. Am Biog Serv.

Works of Love. Wright Morris. LC 51-11978. x, 269p. 1972. pap. 6.95x (ISBN 0-8032-5767-8, BB 558, Bison). U of Nebr Pr.

Works of Love: Selected Poems of Ivan V. Lalic. Ivan V. Lalic. Tr. by Francis R. Jones from Yugoslavian. (Poetry in Translation Ser.). 80p. (Orig.). 1981. pap. 8.95 (ISBN 0-85646-078-8, Pub. by Anvil Pr Poetry). Longwood Pub Group.

Works of Love: Some Christian Reflections in the Form of Discourse. Soren Kierkegaard. pap. 7.95x (ISBN 0-06-130122-1, TB122, Torch). Har-Row.

Works of Love: Some Christian Reflections in the Form of Discourses. Soren Kierkegaard. Tr. by Long. LC 64-7445. 1962. 18.25 (ISBN 0-8446-2373-3). Peter Smith.

Works of M. P. Shiel. Ed. by A. Reynolds Morse. Incl. Vol. 1. Writings. (Illus.). 426p. 45.00 (ISBN 0-934236-00-3); pap. 25.00 ring-bound (ISBN 0-317-39296-4); pap. 32.50 (ISBN 0-317-39297-2); Vol. II, pg. 1-414. The Shielography Updated. 45.00 (ISBN 0-317-39299-9); ring bound 37.50; pap. 32.50 (ISBN 0-317-39300-6); Vol. III, Pt. I. The Shielography Updated. 45.00 (ISBN 0-317-39301-4); ring bound 37.50 (ISBN 0-317-39302-2); pap. 32.50 (ISBN 0-317-39303-0); Vol. IV. Shiel in Diverse Hands: A Collection of Essays in M. P. Shiel. 501p. 1983. 32.50x. 1986. Reynolds Morse.

Works of M. P. Shiel, 2 vols, Vol. 2, Pts. 1 & 2. rev. ed. A. Reynolds Morse. Orig. Title: Works of M. P. Shiel, a Study in Bibliography 1948. (Illus.). 864p. 1980. 90.00x (ISBN 0-686-62335-5); pap. 65.00x (ISBN 0-686-62336-3); 22 ring binder with tabbed sections 75.00x. Reynolds Morse.

Works of M. P. Shiel, a Study in Bibliography 1948 see Works of M. P. Shiel.

Works of Man. Ronald Clark. 352p. 1985. 29.95 (ISBN 0-670-80483-5). Viking.

Works of Man. Ronald W. Clark. 352p. 1985. 29.95 (ISBN 0-317-59772-8, VPO1). Am Soc Civil Eng.

Works of Mark Twain, 25 vols. Samuel Clemens. 1987. Repr. Set. lib. bdg. 1250.00 (ISBN 0-317-59639-X). Am Biog Serv.

Works of Mather Byles. Mather Byles. LC 78-6439. 1978. 70.00x (ISBN 0-8201-1309-3). Schol Facsimiles.

Works of Matthew Arnold, 15 vols. Matthew Arnold. LC 72-113544. (BCL Ser.: No. 1). Repr. of 1904 ed. deluxe ed. 425.00. Set (ISBN 0-404-00450-4). AMS Pr.

Works of Matthew Arnold, 15 Vols. Matthew Arnold. LC 70-107157. 1970. Repr. of 1903 ed. Set. 395.00x (ISBN 0-403-00201-X); 40.00 ea. Scholarly.

Works of Max Beerbohm. Max Beerbohm. 192p. 1985. Repr. of 1896 ed. lib. bdg. 39.00 (ISBN 0-932051-90-1, Pub. by Am Repr Serv). Am Biog Serv.

Works of Mencius see Four Books of Chinese Classics.

Works of Mercy. John B. Martin & Catherine Martin. 1.17 (ISBN 0-8091-9337-X). Paulist Pr.

Works of Miss Thackeray, 15 vols. Anne I. Ritchie. LC 70-37717. Repr. 525.00 set (ISBN 0-404-56810-6); 35.00 ea. AMS Pr.

Works of Mr. John Oldham. John Oldham. LC 79-26304. 1980. Repr. of 1686 ed. 90.00x (ISBN 0-8201-1337-9). Schol Facsimiles.

Works of Mr. William Shakespear, 6 vols. rev. ed. William Shakespeare. Ed. by Thomas Hanmer. LC 69-16818. (Illus.). Repr. of 1744 ed. Set. lib. bdg. 595.00 (ISBN 0-404-01970-6). AMS Pr.

Works of Mister William Shakespear, 7 Vols. William Shakespeare. Ed. by Nicholas Rowe. LC 82-74393. Repr. of 1710 ed. Set. 375.00 (ISBN 0-404-05770-5). AMS Pr.

Works of Monsieur Noverre, Translated from the French, 3 vols. Jean G. Noverre. LC 76-43930. Repr. of 1783 ed. Set. 87.50 (ISBN 0-404-60110-3). AMS Pr.

Works of Morris & of Yeats: In Relation to Early Saga Literature. Dorothy M. Hoare. 1978. Repr. of 1937 ed. lib. bdg. 32.50 (ISBN 0-8495-2317-6). Arden Lib.

Works of Morris & Yeats in Relation to Early Saga Literature. Dorothy M. Hoare. LC 72-193501. 1973. lib. bdg. 20.00 (ISBN 0-8414-5087-0). Folcroft.

Works of Mrs. Amelia Opie, 3 vols. Amelia A. Opie. LC 70-37706. (Women of Letters Ser.). Repr. of 1843 ed. 47.50 ea.; Set. 142.50 (ISBN 0-404-56796-7). AMS Pr.

Works of Nathaniel Ames, 1708-1764: The First American Almanac, 1725. Nathaniel Ames. 1987. Repr. of 1725 ed. lib. bdg. 79.00 (ISBN 0-317-59731-0). Am Biog Serv.

Works of Nathaniel Hawthorne, 12 vols. Nathaniel Hawthorne. Repr. Set. lib. bdg. 595.00 (ISBN 0-403-00022-X). Scholarly.

Works of Nathaniel Hawthorne, 12 vols. Nathaniel Hawthorne. 1987. Set. lib. bdg. 795.00 (ISBN 0-317-59642-X). Am Biog Serv.

Works of Nehemiah Adams, 1806-1878. Nehemiah Adams. 1987. Repr. of 1873 ed. Set. lib. bdg. price not set. Am Biog Serv.

Works of Nicholas Ridley, D.D., Sometime Lord Bishop of London, Martyr, 1555. Nicholas Ridley. Repr. of 1841 ed. 41.00 (ISBN 0-384-50840-5). Johnson Repr.

Works of Orestes A. Brownson, 20 Vols. Orestes A. Brownson. Ed. by Henry F. Brownson. LC 12-30124. Repr. of 1907 ed. Set. 900.00 (ISBN 0-404-01180-2); 45.00 ea. AMS Pr.

Works of Oscar Wilde, 15 Vols. Oscar Wilde. LC 75-148333. Repr. of 1909 ed. Set. 412.50 (ISBN 0-404-59610-X); 27.50 ea. AMS Pr.

Works of Paul Allen, 1775-1826. Paul Allen. 1987. Repr. of 1821 ed. Set. lib. bdg. price not set. Am Biog Serv.

Works of Pere Torroella: A Catalan Writer of the Fifteenth Century. Pedro Bach & Rita Bach. 332p. 2.80 (ISBN 0-318-14319-4); pap. text ed. 2.00 (ISBN 0-318-14320-8). Hispanic Inst.

Works of Petronius Arbiter, in Prose & Verse. Petronius Arbiter. LC 73-158324. Repr. of 1736 ed. 34.50 (ISBN 0-404-54129-1). AMS Pr.

Works of Plato, 5 Vols. Plato. LC 78-16080. Repr. of 1804 ed. Set. 290.00 (ISBN 0-404-16360-2). AMS Pr.

Works of Plato. Plato. Ed. by Irwin Edman. Tr. by Benjamin Jowett. 1965. pap. write for info (ISBN 0-394-30971-5, T71, RanC). Random.

Works of Plato. Plato. Ed. & intro. by Irwin Edman. LC 31-2780. 1931. 11.95 (ISBN 0-394-60420-2). Modern Lib.

Works of Plato, 5 vols. Thomas Taylor. Ed. by Burton Feldman & Robert Richardson. LC 78-60899. (Myth & Romanticism Ser.: Vol. 24). (Illus.). 1983. Set. lib. bdg. 400.00 (ISBN 0-8240-3573-9). Garland Pub.

Works of President Edwards, 10 Vols. Jonathan Edwards. Ed. by Edward Williams & Edward Parsons. LC 68-56782. (Research & Source Works Ser.: No. 271). 1968. Repr. of 1847 ed. 245.00 (ISBN 0-8337-1019-2). B Franklin.

Works of Ralph Green. Ralph Green. LC 81-51378. 112p. 1981. Repr. of 1955 ed. 24.95 (ISBN 0-932606-02-4). Ye Olde Print.

Works of Ralph Vaughan Williams. 2nd ed. Michael Kennedy. 1980. 39.95x (ISBN 0-19-315453-6); pap. 15.95x (ISBN 0-19-315454-4). Oxford U Pr.

Works of Ralph Waldo Emerson, 5 vols. Ralph Waldo Emerson. Set. 125.00 (ISBN 0-8274-3763-3). R West.

Works of Reverend G. W, 6 vols. George Whitefield. LC 75-31107. Repr. of 1772 ed. 230.00 set (ISBN 0-404-13530-7). AMS Pr.

Works of Richard Alsop, 1761-1815. Richard Alsop. 1987. Repr. of 1856 ed. Set. lib. bdg. price not set. Am Biog Serv.

Works of Richard Sibbes, Vol. VI. Richard Sibbes. 560p. 1983. Repr. 18.95 (ISBN 0-85151-372-7). Banner of Truth.

Works of Richard Sibbes, Vol. IV. Richard Sibbes. 527p. 1983. Repr. 18.95 (ISBN 0-85151-371-9). Banner of Truth.

Works of Richard Sibbes, Vol. 1. Richard Sibbes. 1979. 18.95 (ISBN 0-85151-169-4). Banner of Truth.

Works of Richard Sibbes, Vol. 3. Richard Sibbes. 543p. 1981. 18.95 (ISBN 0-85151-329-8). Banner of Truth.

Works of Richard Sibbes, Vol. 7. Richard Sibbes. Ed. by Alexander B. Grosart. 604p. 1982. 18.95 (ISBN 0-85151-341-7). Banner of Truth.

Works of Richard Wagner, 10 Vols. in 7. Richard Wagner. Ed. by Michael Balling. LC 72-75306. (Music Ser). (Ger). 1971. Repr. of 1912 ed. Set. lib. bdg. 550.00 (ISBN 0-306-77250-7); lib. bdg. 89.50 ea. Da Capo.

Works of Robert Boyle, 6 vols. Robert Boyle. Ed. by Thomas Birch. 4769p. Set. lib. bdg. 950.00x (Pub. by G Olms BRD). Coronet Bks.

Works of Robert Davenport. Robert Davenport. Ed. by A. H. Bullen. LC 68-24819. 27.50 (ISBN 0-405-08436-6, Pub. by Blom). Ayer Co Pubs.

Works of Robert Fergusson. Robert Fergusson. Ed. by A. B. Grosart. LC 75-144464. Repr. of 1851 ed. 22.50 (ISBN 0-404-08555-5). AMS Pr.

Works of Robert G. Ingersoll, 12 Vols. Robert G. Ingersoll. LC 70-170063. Repr. of 1929 ed. Set. 782.00 (ISBN 0-404-03490-X); 60.00 ea. AMS Pr.

Works of Robert Louis Stevenson, 26 vols. Robert Louis Stevenson. LC 70-143897. Repr. of 1923 ed. Set. 1040.00 (ISBN 0-404-08750-7). AMS Pr.

Works of Robert Louis Stevenson, 10 vols. Robert Louis Stevenson. Repr. 475.00 (ISBN 0-8274-3764-1). R West.

Works of Robert Louis Stevenson, 10 vols. Robert Louis Stevenson. 1987. Repr. of 1906 ed. Set. lib. bdg. 750.00 (ISBN 0-89987-835-0). Darby Bks.

Works of Robert Sanderson, 6 Vols. Robert Sanderson. Ed. by W. Jacobson. LC 76-175433. Repr. of 1854 ed. Set. lib. bdg. 210.00 (ISBN 0-404-05570-2); 35.00 ea. AMS Pr.

Works of Robert Whytt. Robert Whytt. Bd. with Memoirs on the Nervous System. Marshall Hall; Memoirs. Pierre J. Cabanis; Two Essays. G. S. Hall & E. DuBois-Reymond. LC 77-72191. (Contributions to the History of Psychology Ser., Vol. I, Pt. E: Physiological Psychology). 508p. 1978. Repr. of 1768 ed. 30.00 (ISBN 0-89093-174-7). U Pubns Amer.

Works of Rufus Choate, 2 Vols. Rufus Choate. Ed. by Samuel G. Brown. LC 72-70. Repr. of 1862 ed. Set. 82.00 (ISBN 0-404-01526-3). AMS Pr.

Works of Saint Patrick: Saint Secundius Hymn on St. Patrick. (Ancient Christian Writers Ser.: No. 17). 10.95. Paulist Pr.

Works of Samuel Austin Allibone, 1816-1889. Samuel A. Allibone. 1987. Repr. of 1880 ed. Set. lib. bdg. price not set. Am Biog Serv.

Works of Samuel Butler, 20 Vols. Samuel Butler. Ed. by Henry F. Jones & A. T. Bartholomew. LC 77-181920. (BCL Ser. II). Repr. of 1926 ed. Set. 800.00 (ISBN 0-404-01320-1); 40.00 ea. AMS Pr.

Works of Samuel Johnson, 11 Vols. Samuel Johnson. Ed. by Francis P. Walesby. LC 79-126085. Repr. of 1825 ed. Set. 357.50 (ISBN 0-404-03610-4); 32.50 ea. AMS Pr.

Works of Shakespear, 6 Vols. William Shakespeare. Ed. by Alexander Pope. LC 68-55096. Repr. of 1725 ed. Set. lib. bdg. 945.00 (ISBN 0-404-05780-2). AMS Pr.

Works of Shakespear, 8 Vols. William Shakespeare. Ed. by William Warburton. LC 68-55097. Repr. of 1747 ed. Set. lib. bdg. 420.00 (ISBN 0-404-05800-0). AMS Pr.

Works of Sir David Lindsay of the Mount, 1490-1555, 4 vols. Ed. by Douglas Hamer. 1931-1936. 150.00 (ISBN 0-384-32819-9). Johnson Repr.

Works of Sir Francis Bacon, 15 vols. Francis Bacon. 1987. Repr. Set. lib. bdg. 1074.00 (ISBN 0-317-59636-5). Am Biog Serv.

Works of Sir George Etheredge. A. W. Verity. LC 72-6131. 1974. lib. bdg. 57.50 (ISBN 0-8414-0100-4). Folcroft.

Works of Sir Philip Sidney. Edith J. Morley. LC 77-7979. 1901. lib. bdg. 17.50 (ISBN 0-8414-6163-5). Folcroft.

Works of Sir Thomas Browne, 3 Vols. Ed. by Charles Sayle. 351p. 1983. Repr. of 1927 ed. lib. bdg. 350.00 set (ISBN 0-89987-963-2). Darby Bks.

Works of Sir Thomas Urquhart of Cromarty, Knight. Thomas Urquhart. LC 76-165339. (Maitland Club. Glasgow. Publications: No. 30). Repr. of 1834 ed. 35.00 (ISBN 0-404-52989-5). AMS Pr.

Works of Sir Thomas Urquhart of Cromarty, Knight. Thomas Urquhart. Repr. of 1834 ed. 46.00 (ISBN 0-384-63365-X). Johnson Repr.

Works of Sir Walter Raleigh, 8 Vols. Walter Raleigh. Ed. by Thomas Birch. 1965. Repr. of 1829 ed. 297.00 (ISBN 0-8337-2895-4). B Franklin.

Works of Sir William Davenant, 2 Vols. William Davenant. LC 67-31454. 1968. Set. 55.00 (ISBN 0-405-08433-1, Blom Pubns); 27.50 ea. Vol. 1 (ISBN 0-405-08434-X). Vol. 2 (ISBN 0-405-08435-8). Ayer Co Pubs.

Works of Sir William Jones. William Jones. Ed. by Burton Feldman & Robert D. Richardson. LC 78-60883. (Myth & Romanticism Ser.). 1984. lib. bdg. 160.00 (ISBN 0-8240-3563-1). Garland Pub.

Works of Spinoza, 2 Vols. Benedict D. Spinoza. Tr. by Elwes. Set. 29.50 (ISBN 0-8446-2986-3). Peter Smith.

Works of Spiritualism & Healing, 6 vols. Maurice Barbanell. 800.00 (ISBN 0-8490-1331-3). Gordon Pr.

Works of Stefan George. 2nd ed. Stefan George. Tr. by Olga Marx & Ernst Morwitz. (Studies in the Germanic Languages & Literatures Ser.: No. 78). xxvi, 427p. 1974. 30.00x (ISBN 0-8078-8078-7). U of NC Pr.

Works of Stephen Crane: Vol. 1. Bowery Tales. Stephen Crane. Ed. by Fredson Bowers. Incl. Maggie; George's Mother. LC 68-8536. (Illus.). 184p. 1969. 27.50x (ISBN 0-8139-0258-4). U Pr of Va.

Works of Stephen Crane: Vol. 10: Poems & Literary Remains. Stephen Crane. Ed. by Fredson Bowers. LC 68-8536. 1975. 27.50x (ISBN 0-8139-0610-5). U Pr of Va.

Works of Stephen Crane, Vol. 2: The Red Badge of Courage. Stephen Crane. Ed. by Fredson Bowers. LC 68-8536. 1975. 27.50x (ISBN 0-8139-0514-1). U Pr of Va.

Works of Stephen Crane, Vol. 3. Stephen Crane. Ed. by Fredson Bowers. Bd. with The Third Violet; Active Service. LC 68-8536. 492p. 1976. 27.50x (ISBN 0-8139-0666-0). U Pr of Va.

Works of Stephen Crane: Vol. 4, The O'Ruddy. Stephen Crane. Ed. by Fredson Bowers. LC 68-8536. (Illus.). 362p. 1971. 27.50x (ISBN 0-8139-0341-6). U Pr of Va.

Works of Stephen Crane: Vol. 5, Tales of Adventure. Stephen Crane. Ed. by Fredson Bowers. LC 68-8536. (Illus.). 242p. 1970. 27.50x (ISBN 0-8139-0302-5). U Pr of Va.

Works of Stephen Crane: Vol. 6, Tales of War. Stephen Crane. Ed. by Fredson Bowers. LC 68-8536. (Illus.). 400p. 1970. 32.50x (ISBN 0-8139-0294-0). U Pr of Va.

Works of Stephen Crane: Vol. 7, Tales of Whilomville. Stephen Crane. Ed. by Fredson Bowers. Incl. The Monster; His New Mittens. LC 68-8536. (Illus.). 277p. 1969. 27.50x (ISBN 0-8139-0259-2). U Pr of Va.

Works of Stephen Crane, Vol. 8: Tales, Sketches, & Reports. Stephen Crane. Ed. by Fredson Bowers. LC 68-8536. (Illus.). 1183p. 1973. 47.50x (ISBN 0-8139-0405-6). U Pr of Va.

Works of Stephen Crane, Vol. 9: Reports of War. Stephen Crane. Ed. by Fredson Bowers. LC 68-8536. (Illus.). 678p. 1971. 37.50x (ISBN 0-8139-0342-4). U Pr of Va.

Works of Stephen Hawes. Stephen Hawes. LC 75-14304. 400p. 1975. Repr. lib. bdg. 50.00x (ISBN 0-8201-1148-1). Schol Facsimiles.

Works of Stephen Pearl Andrews, 1812-1886. Stephen P. Andrews. 1987. Repr. of 1877 ed. Set. lib. bdg. price not set. Am Biog Serv.

Works of Susan Ferrier, 4 Vols. Susan Ferrier. LC 74-118948. Repr. of 1929 ed. Set. 200.00 (ISBN 0-404-02380-0). Vol. 1 (ISBN 0-404-02381-9). Vol. 2 (ISBN 0-404-02382-7). Vol. 3 (ISBN 0-404-02383-5). Vol. 4 (ISBN 0-404-02384-3). AMS Pr.

Works of Tennyson, 9 vols. Alfred Tennyson. Ed. by Hallam Tennyson. Incl. Vol. 1; Vol. 2; Vol. 3; Vol. 4; Vol. 5. lib. bdg. 19.75 (ISBN 0-8371-4575-9, TEWQ); Vol. 6; Vol. 7; Vol. 8; Vol. 9. (Illus.). 1970. Repr. Greenwood.

Works of That Learned & Judicious Divine Mr. Richard Hooker with an Account of His Life & Death by Isaac Walton, 3 vols. 7th ed. Richard Hooker. LC 76-125020. (Research & Source Works Ser.: No. 546). 1970. Repr. of 1888 ed. 103.00 (ISBN 0-8337-1731-6). B Franklin.

Works of the English Poets from Chaucer to Cowper, 21 vols. Ed. by Alexander Chalmers. Incl. Vol. 1. lib. bdg. 32.50 (CHEA); Vol. 2. lib. bdg. 32.50 (ISBN 0-8371-0790-3, CHEB); Vol. 3. lib. bdg. 32.50 (ISBN 0-8371-0791-1, CHEC); Vol. 4. lib. bdg. 32.50 (ISBN 0-8371-0792-X, CHED); Vol. 5. lib. bdg. 32.50 (ISBN 0-8371-0793-8, CHEE); Vol. 6. lib. bdg. 32.50 (ISBN 0-8371-0794-6, CHEF); Vol. 7. lib. bdg. 32.50 (ISBN 0-8371-0795-4, CHEG); Vol. 8. lib. bdg. 32.50 (ISBN 0-8371-0796-2, CHEH); Vol. 9. lib. bdg. 32.50 (ISBN 0-8371-0797-0, CHEI); Vol. 10. lib. bdg. 32.50 (ISBN 0-8371-0798-9, CHEJ); Vol. 11. lib. bdg. 32.50 (ISBN 0-8371-0799-7, CHEK); Vol. 12. lib. bdg. 32.50 (ISBN 0-8371-0800-4, CHEL); Vol. 13. lib. bdg. 32.50 (ISBN 0-8371-0801-2, CHEM); Vol. 14. lib. bdg. 32.50 (ISBN 0-8371-0802-0, CHEN); Vol. 15. lib. bdg. 32.50 (ISBN 0-8371-0803-9, CHEO); Vol. 16. lib. bdg. 32.50 (ISBN 0-8371-0804-7, CHEQ); Vol. 17. lib. bdg. 32.50 (ISBN 0-8371-0805-5, CHER); Vol. 18. lib. bdg. 32.50 (ISBN 0-8371-0806-3, CHES); Vol. 19. lib. bdg. 32.50 (ISBN 0-8371-0807-1, CHEU); Vol. 20. lib. bdg. 32.50 (ISBN 0-8371-0808-X, CHEV); Vol. 21. lib. bdg. 32.50 (ISBN 0-8371-0809-8). LC 69-13853. 1969. Repr. of 1810 ed. Set. lib. bdg. 605.00x (ISBN 0-8371-0344-4, CHEP). Greenwood.

Works of the English Poets from Chaucer to Cowper: Including the Series Ed., with Prefaces Biographical & Critical, by Dr. S. Johnson & the Most Approved Translations, 21 Vols. Alexander Chalmers. Ed. by S. Johnson. (English Literary Reference Ser.). 1969. Repr. of 1810 ed. Set. 825.00 (ISBN 0-384-08322-6). Johnson Repr.

Works of the Ettrick Shepherd, 2 Vols. James Hogg. LC 72-144466. Repr. of 1866 ed. Set. 124.50 (ISBN 0-404-08558-X); Vol. 1 (ISBN 0-404-08559-8). Vol. 2 (ISBN 0-404-08560-1). AMS Pr.

Works of the Ever Memorable Mr. John Hales of Eaton, 3 vols. in 2. John Hales. Ed. by D. Dalrymple. LC 77-131037. Repr. of 1765 ed. 82.50 (ISBN 0-404-03050-5). AMS Pr.

Works of the Mind. Ed. by Robert H. Heywood. LC 47-11892. 1966. pap. 2.45x (ISBN 0-226-33267-5, P239, Phoen). U of Chicago Pr.

Works of the Most Reverend Father in God, William Laud, D. D, 7 vols. William Laud. LC 74-5373. (Library of Anglo-Catholic Theology: No. 11). Repr. of 1860 ed. Set of 9 pts. 350.00 (ISBN 0-404-52120-7). AMS Pr.

Works of the People of Old: Na Hana A Ka Po'e Kahiko. S. M. Kamakau. Ed. by Dorothy B. Barrere. Tr. by Mary K. Pukui. LC 75-21315. (Special Publication Ser.: No. 61). (Illus.). 178p. 1987. pap. 16.50 (ISBN 0-910240-18-3). Bishop Mus.

Works of the Reverend Sydney Smith, 3 Vols. 1984. Repr. of 1845 ed. Set. lib. bdg. 200.00 (ISBN 0-8492-8121-0). Vol. 1, 474 pp. Vol. 2, 495 pp. Vol. 3, 479 pp. R West.

Works of the Right Rev. John England, First Bishop of Charleston. John England & Iqnatius A. Reynolds. 191.00 (ISBN 0-405-10822-2). Ayer Co Pubs.

Works of the Seraphic Father St. Francis of Assisi: Translated by a Religious of the Order. 269p. 1982. Repr. of 1890 ed. lib. bdg. 40.00. Century Bookbindery.

Works of Thomas Adams, 3 vols. Thomas Adams. LC 72-158226. Repr. of 1862 ed. Set. 65.00 (ISBN 0-404-00350-8); 22.50 ea. Vol. 1 (ISBN 0-404-00351-6). Vol. 2 (ISBN 0-404-00352-4). Vol. 3 (ISBN 0-404-00353-2). AMS Pr.

Works of Thomas Bailey Aldrich, 1836-1907. Thomas B. Aldrich. 1987. Repr. of 1903 ed. Set. lib. bdg. price not set. Am Biog Serv.

Works of Thomas Campion. Thomas Campion. Ed. by Walter R. Davis. (Seventeenth Century Ser.). 1970. pap. 2.95x (ISBN 0-393-00439-2, Norton Lib). Norton.

Works of Thomas Carlyle, 30 Vols. Thomas Carlyle. Ed. by H. D. Traill. LC 79-22238. (BCL Ser. II). Repr. of 1899 ed. Set. 1200.00 (ISBN 0-404-09800-2); 40.00 ea. AMS Pr.

Works of Thomas Chatterton, 3 Vols. Thomas Chatterton. Ed. by Robert Southey & Joseph Cottle. LC 71-80892. 1968. Repr. of 1803 ed. Set. 125.00 (ISBN 0-404-01540-9). Vol. 1 (ISBN 0-404-01541-7). Vol. 2 (ISBN 0-404-01542-5). Vol. 3 (ISBN 0-404-01543-3). AMS Pr.

Works of Thomas Gold Appleton, 1812-1884. Thomas G. Appleton. 1987. Repr. of 1879 ed. Set. lib. bdg. price not set. Am Biog Serv.

Works of Thomas Goodwin, 12 Vols. Thomas Goodwin. LC 74-168155. Repr. of 1866 ed. Set. lib. bdg. 450.00 (ISBN 0-404-02870-5); 37.50 ea. AMS Pr.

Works of Thomas Gray, 4 vols. Thomas Gray. Ed. by Edmund Gosse. 1884. Repr. lib. bdg. 135.00 (ISBN 0-8414-4675-X). Folcroft.

Works of Thomas Gray in Verse & Prose, 4 Vols. Thomas Gray. Ed. by Edmund Gosse. LC 76-168185. Repr. of 1884 ed. Set. 70.00 (ISBN 0-404-02900-0). Vol. 1 (ISBN 0-404-02901-9). Vol. 2 (ISBN 0-404-02902-7). Vol. 3 (ISBN 0-404-02903-5). Vol. 4 (ISBN 0-404-02904-3). AMS Pr.

Works of Thomas Hardy in Prose & Verse. Thomas Hardy. 3000.00 (ISBN 0-384-21360-X). Johnson Repr.

Works of Thomas Hardy in Prose: With Prefaces & Notes, 18 vols. Thomas Hardy. LC 83-45547. (Wessex Edition Ser.). 7000p. 1984. Set. 684.00 (ISBN 0-404-60730-6); 38.00. AMS Pr.

Works of Thomas Hill Green, 3 Vols. 3rd ed. Thomas H. Green. Ed. by R. L. Nettleship. Repr. of 1894 ed. Set. 135.00 (ISBN 0-404-02910-8). AMS Pr.

Works of Thomas Hill Green, 3 Vols. 2nd ed. Thomas H. Green. Ed. by R. L. Nettleship. LC 1-18259. 1968. Repr. of 1889 ed. Set. 156.00 (ISBN 0-527-35820-7). Kraus Repr.

Works of Thomas Hood, 8 vols. Thomas Hood. Ed. by Thomas Hood, Jr. LC 70-170044. Repr. of 1869 ed. Set. 320.00 (ISBN 0-404-03340-7); 40.00 ea. AMS Pr.

Works of Thomas Lovell Beddoes. Thomas L. Beddoes. Ed. by H. W. Donner. LC 75-41023. (BCL Ser. II). 1976. Repr. of 1935 ed. 49.50 (ISBN 0-404-14507-8). AMS Pr.

Works of Thomas Manton, 22 Vols. Thomas Manton. LC 76-172841. Repr. of 1875 ed. Set. 465.00 (ISBN 0-404-04200-7); 21.50 ea. AMS Pr.

Works of Thomas Middleton, 8 Vols. Thomas Middleton. Ed. by A. H. Bullen. LC 78-181958. Repr. of 1886 ed. Set. 360.00 (ISBN 0-404-04330-5). AMS Pr.

Works of Thomas Nabbes, 2 Vols. in 1. Thomas Nabbes. Ed. by A. H. Bullen. LC 68-24818. 1968. Repr. 33.00 (ISBN 0-405-08812-4). Ayer Co Pubs.

Works of Thomas Southerne, Vol. II. Ed. by Robert Jordan & Harold Love. (Oxford English Texts Ser.). (Illus.). 512p. 1988. 91.00 (ISBN 0-19-812798-7). Oxford U Pr.

Works of Thomas Southerne, Vol. I. Ed. by Robert Jordan & Harold Love. (Oxford English Texts Ser.). (Illus.). 560p. 1988. 98.00 (ISBN 0-19-811859-7). Oxford U Pr.

Works of Thomas Vaughan, 2 vols. Thomas Vaughan. Ed. by Alan Rudram & Jennifer D. Brockman. (Illus.). 1984. Set. 98.00x (ISBN 0-19-812473-2). Oxford U Pr.

Works of Timothy Shay Arthur, 1809-1885. Timothy S. Arthur. 1987. Repr. of 1879 ed. Set. lib. bdg. price not set. Am Biog Serv.

Works of Tobias Smollett, Vol. I: The Adventures of Ferdinand Count Fathom. Tobias Smollett. Ed. by Jerry C. Beasley. LC 87-26368. 504p. 1988. 40.00 (ISBN 0-8203-1010-7). U of GA Pr.

Works of Tomioka Tessai. Ed. by James Cahill. (Illus.). 152p. (Orig.). 1968. pap. 5.00 (ISBN 0-88397-015-5, Pub. by Intl Exhibit Foun). C E Tuttle.

Works of Tomioka Tessai. Kokusai Bunka Shinkokai Staff. (Illus.). 115p. 1966. pap. 70.00x (ISBN 0-317-69292-5, Pub. by Han-Shan Tang Ltd). State Mutual Bk.

Works of Tomioka Tessai from the Museum Yamato Bunkakan Collection. Yamato Bunkakan. 109p. 1976. pap. 100.00x (Pub. by Han-Shan Tang Ltd). State Mutual Bk.

Works of Virgil, 3 Vols. Virgil. Repr. of 1883 ed. Set. cancelled (ISBN 3-4870-0545-X). Adlers Foreign Bks.

Works of Voltaire: A Contemporary Version, 2 vols. Voltaire. lib. bdg. 500.00 (ISBN 0-87968-228-0). Gordon Pr.

Works of W. Somerset Maugham, 47 bks. W. Somerset Maugham. 1977. Set. 940.00x (ISBN 0-405-07804-8). Ayer Co Pubs.

Works of Washington Allston, 1779-1843. Washington Allston. 1987. Repr. of 1841 ed. Set. lib. bdg. price not set. Am Biog Serv.

Works of Washington Irving, 27 vols. Washington Irving. LC 70-170808. Repr. of 1889 ed. Set. 877.50 (ISBN 0-404-03510-8); 32.50 ea. AMS Pr.

Works of Washington Irving, 3 vols. Richard H. Stoddard. 1885. Repr. 125.00 set (ISBN 0-8274-3767-6). R West.

Works of Wesley, Vol. 3 & 4: The Journal of John Wesley. John Wesley. 1986. Vol. 3, 496p. 25.95 (ISBN 0-310-51290-5, 17172); Vol. 4, 544p. 25.95 (ISBN 0-310-51300-6, 17173). Zondervan.

Works of Wesley: Wesley's Standard Sermons, 2 vols. John Wesley. Ed. by E. H. Sugden & Joseph Allison. 544p. 1986. Vol. 1. 25.95 (ISBN 0-310-51270-0, 17170); Vol. 2. 25.95 (ISBN 0-310-51280-8, 17171). Zondervan.

Works of Wilkie Collins, 30 Vols. Wilkie Collins. Repr. of 1900 ed. Set. 1200.00 (ISBN 0-404-01750-9); 40.00 ea. AMS Pr.

Works of William Allen, 1784-1868. William Allen. 1987. Repr. of 1866 ed. Set. lib. bdg. price not set. Am Biog Serv.

Works of William Andrus Alcott, 1798-1859. William A. Alcott. 1987. Repr. of 1859 ed. Set. lib. bdg. price not set. Am Biog Serv.

Works of William Apes. William Apes. 1987. Repr. of 1836 ed. Set. lib. bdg. price not set. Am Biog Serv.

Works of William Austin 1778-1841. William Austin. Date not set. Repr. lib. bdg. price not set. Am Biog Serv.

Works of William Blake in the Huntington Collections: A Complete Catalogue. Robert N. Essick. LC 85-10689. (Illus.). 256p. 1985. 20.00 (ISBN 0-87328-084-9). Huntington Lib.

Works of William Blake, Poetic, Symbolic, & Critical, 3 Vols. William Blake. LC 79-13496. (Illus.). Repr. of 1893 ed. Set. 145.50 (ISBN 0-404-08990-9); 48.50 ea. Vol. 1 (ISBN 0-404-08961-5). Vol. 2 (ISBN 0-404-08999-2). Vol. 3 (ISBN 0-404-08993-3). AMS Pr.

Works of William Carleton, 2 Vols. facsimile ed. William Carleton. LC 77-106257. (Short Story Index Reprint Ser.). 1881. Set. 88.00 (ISBN 0-8369-3294-3). Ayer Co Pubs.

Works of William Chillingworth, 3 Vols. William Chillingworth. Repr. of 1838 ed. Set. lib. bdg. 95.00 (ISBN 0-404-01570-0). Vol. 1 (ISBN 0-404-01571-9). Vol. 3 (ISBN 0-404-01572-7). Vol. 4 (ISBN 0-404-01573-5). AMS Pr.

Works of William Collins. William Collins. Ed. by Richard Wendorf & Charles Ryskamp. (English Texts Ser.). (Illus.). 1979. text ed. 75.00x (ISBN 0-19-812749-9). Oxford U Pr.

Works of William Cowper, 15 Vols. William Cowper. Ed. by Robert Southey. LC 71-18097. Repr. of 1837 ed. Set. 525.00 (ISBN 0-404-01840-8); 35.00 ea. AMS Pr.

Works of William E. Channing, D.D. 1060p. 1982. Repr. of 1889 ed. lib. bdg. 150.00 (ISBN 0-8495-0959-9). Arden Lib.

Works of William Ellery Channing, 2 vols. in 1. William E. Channing. LC 70-114815. (Research & Source Works Ser.: No. 626). 1971. Repr. of 1882 ed. lib. bdg. 46.50 (ISBN 0-8337-0530-X). B Franklin.

Works of William Ernest Henley, 7 Vols. William E. Henley. Repr. of 1908 ed. Set. 192.50 (ISBN 0-404-03290-7); 27.50 ea. AMS Pr.

Works of William Ernest Henley, 7 vols. Repr. of 1908 ed. Set. lib. bdg. 400.00 (ISBN 0-89987-396-0). Darby Bks.

Works of William Foster Apthorp, 1848-1913. William F. Apthrop. 1987. Repr. of 1901 ed. Set. lib. bdg. price not set. Am Biog Serv.

Works of William Francis Allen, 1830-1889. William F. Allen. 1987. Repr. of 1890 ed. Set. lib. bdg. price not set. Am Biog Serv.

Works of William Hogarth. 1978. Repr. of 1825 ed. lib. bdg. 35.00 luxury ed. (ISBN 0-932106-03-X, Pub. by Marathon Pr). S J Durst.

Works of William Livingstone Alden, 1837-1908. William L. Alden. 1987. Repr. of 1908 ed. Set. lib. bdg. price not set. Am Biog Serv.

Works of William Loring Andrews, 1837-1920. William L. Andrews. 1987. Repr. of 1906 ed. Set. lib. bdg. price not set. Am Biog Serv.

Works of William Morris (Bibliography) William Morris. Ed. by R. C. Briggs. LC 76-29610. Repr. of 1962 ed. lib. bdg. 25.00 (ISBN 0-8414-6104-X). Folcroft.

Works of William Perkins, 3 Vols. William Perkins. LC 74-144670. Repr. of 1613 ed. Set. lib. bdg. 285.00 (ISBN 0-404-05050-6). Vol. 1 (ISBN 0-404-05051-4). Vol. 2 (ISBN 0-404-05052-2). Vol. 3 (ISBN 0-404-05053-0). AMS Pr.

Works of William Shakespeare, 16 Vols. William Shakespeare. Ed. by James O. Halliwell-Phillipps. LC 69-18314. (Illus.). Repr. of 1865 ed. Set. 1920.00 (ISBN 0-404-05920-1). AMS Pr.

Works of William Waldorf Astor, 1848-1919. William A. Astor. 1987. Repr. of 1900 ed. Set. lib. bdg. price not set. Am Biog Serv.

Works of William Wells Brown. William W. Brown. 1858. Three works in one unit. 39.00 (ISBN 0-8115-3024-8). Kraus Repr.

Works of Zbigniew Kazimierz Brzezinski. Christine E. Thompson. (Public Administration Ser.: P 1666). 7p. 1985. 2.00 (ISBN 0-89028-376-1). Vance Biblios.

Works on Facility Management: A Bibliography. John B. Evans. (Architecture Ser.: A 1414). 13p. 1985. 2.00 (ISBN 0-89028-444-X). Vance Biblios.

Works on Horses & Equitation: A Bibliographical Record of Hippology. Frederik H. Huth. 439p. Repr. of 1887 ed. lib. bdg. 63.50x (ISBN 3-487-08211-X, Pub. by G Olms BRD). Coronet Bks.

Works on Paper. Eliot Weinberger. LC 86-8763. 160p. 1986. 22.95 (ISBN 0-8112-1000-6); pap. 9.95 (ISBN 0-8112-1001-4, NDP627). New Directions.

Works on Paper 1900-1960 from Southern California Collections. David W. Steadman. LC 77-82659. (Illus.). 132p. 1977. 7.95 (ISBN 0-915478-10-2). Galleries Coll.

Works on Subud, 3 vols. J. G. Bennett. 300.00 (ISBN 0-8490-1332-1). Gordon Pr.

Works on the Foundations of Statistical Physics. Nikolai S. Krylov. Tr. by A. B. Migdal et al from Rus. LC 78-70611. (Princeton Series in Physics). 1979. 33.00x (ISBN 0-691-08230-8). Princeton U Pr.

Works on Vision. George Berkeley. Ed. by Colin M. Turbayne. LC 81-7160. (Library of Liberal Arts: No. 83). iii, 158p. 1981. Repr. of 1963 ed. lib. bdg. 35.00x (ISBN 0-313-23186-9, BEWV). Greenwood.

Works Progress Administration in New York City. J. D. Millett. LC 77-74950. (American Federalism-the Urban Dimension Ser.). 1978. Repr. of 1938 ed. lib. bdg. 20.00x (ISBN 0-405-10496-0). Ayer Co Pubs.

Works Progress Administration of Virginia Historical Inventory: Blandford Cemetery, Petersburg, Virginia. 444p. 1980. Repr. of 1937 ed. 35.00 (ISBN 0-88490-089-4). VA State Lib.

Works: Vol. 1. Prose, 2 vols, Vol. 2. Poetry. Joel Barlow. LC 68-17012. 1970. Set. 130.00x (ISBN 0-8201-1062-0). Schol Facsimiles.

Works, Vol. 7: Problems - Problemata. Aristotle. Ed. by David Ross. Tr. by J. I. Beare. 1927. text ed. 32.00x (ISBN 0-19-824207-7); Vol. 9: Ethics. Ethica Nicomachea. Magna Moralia. Ethica Eudemia. pap. 34.95x. Oxford U Pr.

Works with English Texts. Ed. by Warburton. (Johann Christian Bach Ser.). 1985. lib. bdg. 75.00 (ISBN 0-8240-6074-1). Garland Pub.

Works: With Introductions by George Saintsbury, 18 vols. facsimile ed. Honore De Balzac. LC 78-150468. (Short Story Index Reprint Ser.). Repr. of 1901 ed. Set. 550.00 (ISBN 0-8369-3791-0). Ayer Co Pubs.

Worksheet & Instructor's Guide to Accompany Your Massachusetts Government. 10th ed. Harold M. Gay. 1985. write for info. Gov Res Pubns.

Worksheet Book: Building Skills for 1-2-3 & Symphony. Ed. by Steven E. Miller. (Best of Lotus Magazine Ser.). 400p. 1988. pap. 21.95 (ISBN 0-201-15039-5). Addison-Wesley.

Worksheets for the Abacus, Vol 1. Joan A. Cotter. (Illus.). 192p. 1988. pap. 16.95 (ISBN 0-9609636-2-6). Activities Learning.

Worksheets for the Abacus, Vol. 2. Joan A. Cotter. (Illus.). 122p. 1988. 16.95 (ISBN 0-9609636-5-0). Activities Learning.

Workshirts & Silk Suits. Gary Class. 4.00 (ISBN 0-318-11914-5). Great Raven Pr.

Workshoes for Christ. A. D. Wright. 1979. pap. 3.75 (ISBN 0-89225-185-9). Gospel Advocate.

Workshop Leader's Guide. (Instructor Training- II). 50p. 1980. 37.50 (ISBN 0-317-32430-6, 625701); members 30.00 (ISBN 0-317-32431-4). Am Bankers.

Workshop Leaders Handbook. NASSP staff. (Orig.). 1985. pap. text ed. 24.95 (ISBN 0-88210-169-2). Natl Assn Principals.

Workshop of Democracy: The American Experiment from the Emancipation Proclamation to the Eve of the New Deal. James M. Burns. LC 85-40697. 683p. 1986. pap. 12.95 (ISBN 0-394-74320-2, Vin). Random.

Workshop of Democracy: The American Experiment, Vol. II. James M. Burns. LC 85-40231. 672p. 1985. 24.45 (ISBN 0-394-51275-8). Knopf.

Workshop of the British Empire: Engineering & Shipbuilding in the West of Scotland. Michael S. Moss & John R. Hume. LC 77-2429. (Illus.). 192p. 1978. 50.00 (ISBN 0-8386-2170-8). Fairleigh Dickinson.

Workshop on Biotechnology of Antibiotics, Alkaloids & Steroids of Medicinal Importance. R. Vlahov. 1987. pap. text ed. write for info. (ISBN 0-89573-653-5). VCH Pubs.

Workshop on Calculation of Crystal Packing & Non-Bonded Forces. American Crystallographic Association Staff. 1984. 15.00x (ISBN 0-317-12233-9). Polycrystal Bk Serv.

Workshop on Ceramics of East & Southeast Asia: Seameo Project in Archaeology & Fine Arts: Final Report. 150p. 1981. 45.00x (ISBN 0-317-45332-7, Pub. by Han-Shan Tang Ltd). State Mutual Bk.

Workshop on Computer Architecture for Pattern Analysis & Machine Intelligence (CAPAMI '87) Proceedings. 238p. 1987. 50.00 (ISBN 0-8186-0804-8, EZ804). IEEE Comp Soc.

Workshop on Computer Vision: Proceedings. 382p. 1987. 66.00 (ISBN 0-8186-0779-3, EZ779). IEEE Comp Soc.

Workshop on Farming Systems Research: Proceedings. 153p. (Orig.). 1987. pap. 24.00 (ISBN 92-9066-119-4, Pub. by ICRISAT (India)). Agribookstore.

Workshop on Fertility Control. Ed. by J. R. Newton et al. (International Congress & Symposium Ser.: No. 31). 80p. 1980. pap. 18.00 (ISBN 1-85315-051-7, Pub. by Royal Society of Medicine Services Ltd). Longwood Pub Group.

Workshop on Interactive Computing, CAD-CAM, Electrical Engineering Education, 2nd, George Washington Univ., Nov. 30 - Dec. 2, 1983: Proceedings. LC 83-82758. vi, 163p. 1984. 30.00; pap. 30.00 (ISBN 0-8186-0521-9); microfiche 30.00 (ISBN 0-8186-4521-0). IEEE Comp Soc.

Workshop on New Directions in Mossbauer Spectroscopy, Argonne National Lab, June 1977. Ed. by Gilbert J. Perlow. LC 77-90635. (AIP Conference Proceedings: No. 38). (Illus.). 1977. lib. bdg. 15.00 (ISBN 0-88318-137-1). Am Inst Physics.

Workshop on Non-Perturbative Quantum Chromodynamics: Oklahoma State University March, 1983. Ed. by K. Milton & M. Samuel. (Progress in Physics Ser.: Vol. 7). 400p. 1983. 32.50 (ISBN 0-8176-3127-5). Birkhauser.

Workshop on Numerical Treatment of Inverse Problems in Differential & Integral Equations. Peter Deuflhard & Ernst Hairer. (Progress in Scientific Computing: Vol. 2). 372p. 1983. 37.50x (ISBN 0-8176-3125-9). Birkhauser.

Workshop on Oral Retinoids in Dermatology Held on the 15th International Congress of Dermatology, Mexico City, October 1977. Ed. by C. E. Orfanos & R. Schuppli. 1978. pap. 17.50 (ISBN 3-8055-2950-3). S Karger.

Workshop on Photonic Logic & Information Processing: (Advanced Institute) Ed. by Bowden & Duthie. 114p. 1986. 29.00 (ISBN 0-89252-804-4, 769). SPIE.

Workshop on Polarized 3He Beams & Targets (Princeton, NJ 1984) Ed. by R. W. Dunford & F. P. Calaprice. LC 85-48026. (AIP Conference Proceedings Ser.: No. 131). 224p. 1985. lib. bdg. 39.25 (ISBN 0-88318-330-7). Am Inst Physics.

Workshop on Prepaid Legal Services for Practicing Attorneys. 200p. 1985. 30.00 (ISBN 0-317-40256-0, 2-008). Am Prepaid.

Workshop on Probability & Statistics: Proceedings, 3 vols. Ed. by W. L. Harper & C. A. Hooker. (Western Ontario Ser.: No. 6). 1975. Set. 147.50 (ISBN 90-277-0614-X); Set. pap. 79.00 (ISBN 90-277-0615-8); Vol. 1. 55.00 (ISBN 90-277-0616-6); Vol. 1. pap. 29.00 (ISBN 90-277-0617-4); Vol. 2. 68.50 (ISBN 90-277-0618-2); Vol. 2. pap. 37.00 (ISBN 90-277-0619-0); Vol. 3. 39.50 (ISBN 90-277-0620-4); Vol. 3. pap. 24.00 (ISBN 90-277-0621-2, Pub. by Reidel Holland). Kluwer Academic.

Workshop on Teaching Techniques for Art Teachers in Schools. Seameo Project in Arahaelogy & Fine Arts Staff. 150p. 1980. pap. 60.00x (Pub. by Han-Shan Tang Ltd). State Mutual Bk.

Workshop on the Conservation of the Orangutan. Ed. by Leobert E. De Boer. LC 82-7722. (Illus.). 353p. 1982. 76.00 (ISBN 90-6193-702-7, Pub. by Junk Pubs Netherlands). Kluwer Academic.

Workshop on the Phenomenon Known as "El Nino" Proceedings, Guayaquil, Ecuador 4-12 Dec. 1974. (Illus.). 284p. 1980. pap. 12.75 (ISBN 92-3-101509-5, U1019, UNESCO). UNIPUB.

Workshop on the Preservation of Traditional Performing Arts. Seameo Project in Archaeology & Fine Arts Staff. 75p. 1979. pap. 53.00x (Pub. by Han-Shan Tang Ltd). State Mutual Bk.

Workshop on the Role of Earthworms in the Stabilization of Organic Residues: Proceedings, Vol. I. Mary Appelhof. LC 81-65289. 340p. 1981. pap. 25.00x (ISBN 0-939294-07-9, TD-772-W6-1981, Dist. by Flower Pr). Beech Leaf.

Workshop on the Role of Earthworms in the Stabilization of Organic Residues: Volume 2, Bibliography. Compiled by Diane Worden. LC 81-65289. 490p. (Orig.). 1981. pap. 50.00 (ISBN 0-939294-08-7, TD-772-W6-1981). Beech Leaf.

Workshop on the Role of Earthworms in the Stabilization of Organic Residues, 2 vols. 1981. 70.00 set (ISBN 0-939294-09-5, TD-772-W6-1981). Beech Leaf.

Workshop Planning. Rev., 2nd ed. Ruth S. Smith. LC 78-24240. (Guide Ser.: No. 3). (Illus.). 65p. 1979. pap. 6.50 (ISBN 0-915324-15-6); pap. 5.25 members. CSLA.

Workshop Proceedings: On Non-Economic Factors in Energy Supply & Demand, Virginia, 1979, Institute for the Future. Electric Power Research Institute Staff. 64p. 1980. 4.00 (ISBN 0-318-14428-X). Inst Future.

Workshop Processes, Practices & Materials. Bruce J. Black. (Illus.). 282p. 1979. pap. 22.50x (ISBN 0-7131-3409-7). Trans-Atl Phila.

Workshop Production Management: Motion & Time Study. David A. Hietala. (Illus.). 67p. (Orig.). 1979. pap. 4.75x (ISBN 0-916671-16-X). Material Dev.

Workshop Technology, Pt. 1. 5th ed. W. A. Chapman. (Illus.). 1976. pap. 24.00x (ISBN 0-7131-3269-8). Trans-Atl Phila.

Workshop Technology, Pt. 2. 4th ed. W. A. Chapman. (Illus.). 1972. 24.00x (ISBN 0-7131-3272-8). Trans-Atl Phila.

Workshop Technology, Part 3. 3rd ed. W. A. Chapman. (Illus.). 675p. 1975. pap. 33.50x (ISBN 0-7131-3351-1). Trans-Atl Phila.

Workshop Wage Determination. S. W. Lerner et al. 1969. flexi-cover 15.25 (ISBN 0-08-006578-3). Pergamon.

Workshops & Seminars: Planning, Producing & Profiting. Pat R. Materka. Date not set. price not set. S&S.

Workshops & Seminars: Planning, Promoting, Producing, Profiting. Pat R. Materka. 224p. 1985. 15.95 (ISBN 0-13-967795-X); pap. 10.95 (ISBN 0-13-967787-9). P-H.

Workshops for Jail Library Service: A Planning Manual. Linda Schexnaydre & Kaylyn Robbins. 116p. 1981. pap. 17.00x (ISBN 0-8389-3259-2). ALA.

Workshops in Bile Acid Research: Serum Bile Acids in Health & Disease-Pathophysiology of the Enterohepatic Circulation. E. Roda et al. 144p. 1983. lib. bdg. 35.00 (ISBN 0-85200-749-3, Pub. by MTP Pr Netherlands). Kluwer Academic.

Workshops in Cognitive Processes. 2nd. ed. A. Bennett et al. 136p. 1982. pap. 9.95x (ISBN 0-7100-0932-1). Routledge Chapman & Hall.

Workshops in Organizing. Roger Hayes et al. Ed. by Tim Ledwith. LC 87-146206. (Orig.). 1985. Part 1: Introduction to Organizing, 18p. 2.00 (ISBN 0-88156-056-1); Part 2: Research & Power, 18p. 2.00 (ISBN 0-88156-057-X); Part 3: Issues & Strategy, 18p. 2.00 (ISBN 0-88156-058-8); Part 4: Leadership, 18p. 2.00 (ISBN 0-88156-059-6). Comm Serv Soc NY.

Workshops in Perception. Roderick P. Power et al. 244p. 1981. pap. 9.95x (ISBN 0-7100-0931-3). Routledge Chapman & Hall.

Workshops: Laboratories for Student Leaders. NASSP Staff. 1974. pap. 6.00 (ISBN 0-88210-057-2). Natl Assn Principals.

Workshops Notebook. Ragan Report Workshop. Ed. by Lawrence Ragan & Catherine Lange. (Communications Library). 88p. 1982. three-ring binder 60.00 (ISBN 0-931368-11-1). Ragan Comm.

Workshops on Chromosomal Aspects of the Male Sterility in Mammals: Abstracts. Ed. by A. G. Searle & P. De Boer. (Journal; Cytogenetics & Cell Genetics: Vol. 27; No. 4). (Illus.). 84p. 1980. pap. 7.50 (ISBN 3-8055-1610-X). S Karger.

Worksource Nineteen Eighty-Eight. John E. Fogle. 500p. 1987. write for info. Turnbull & Co.

Workspace: Creating Environments in Organizations. Franklin D. Becker. LC 81-10671. 238p. 1981. 31.95 (ISBN 0-03-059137-6). Praeger.

Workstation Design for Current Office Environments. 1986. 20.00 (ISBN 0-939874-73-3). ASSE.

Workstations & Publication Systems. Ed. by R. A. Earnshaw. (Illus.). 230p. 1987. 29.50 (ISBN 0-387-96527-0). Springer-Verlag.

Worktext in Introductory Algebra. Wright & New. pap. write for info. (ISBN 0-205-10268-9). Wm C Brown.

World Ate Suppliers Directory. Network Staff. 1983. 175.00x (ISBN 0-317-43574-4, Pub. by Network Events Ltd). State Mutual Bk.
World Atlas. Hammond Incorporated Staff. LC 82-675036. (Random House Library of Knowledge). (Illus.). 112p. (gr. 5 up). 1982. lib. bdg. 11.99 (ISBN 0-394-94663-4); pap. 10.95 smyth-sewn (ISBN 0-394-84663-X). Random.
World Atlas. Date not set. price not set. Am Map.
World Atlas for Students. Hammond Incorporated Editors. LC 80-81916. 56p. (YA) (gr. 8-12). 1986. pap. text ed. 5.53x (ISBN 0-8437-7820-2). Hammond Inc.
World Atlas of Archaeology. Ed. by Michael Wood. LC 85-675137. (Illus.). 413p. 1985. lib. bdg. 83.00 (ISBN 0-8161-8747-9). G K Hall.
World Atlas of Architecture. Frwd. by John J. Norwich. (Illus.). 408p. 1984. lib. bdg. 83.00 (ISBN 0-8161-8716-9, Hall Reference). G K Hall.
World Atlas of Architecture. (Illus.). 408p. 75.00 (ISBN 0-317-54967-7). Apollo.
World Atlas of Geomorphic Features. R. Snead. 1980. 52.95 (ISBN 0-442-28973-1). Van Nos Reinhold.
World Atlas of Geomorphic Features. Rodman E. Snead. LC 77-28009. 320p. 1980. 39.50 (ISBN 0-88275-272-3). Krieger.
World Atlas of Golf. Pat Ward-Thomas et al. (Illus.). 280p. 14.98 (ISBN 0-8317-9501-8). Smith Pubs.
World Atlas of Military History: 1860-1945. Arthur Banks. LC 73-90857. (Illus.). 200p. 1978. 22.50 (ISBN 0-88254-454-3). Hippocrene Bks.
World Atlas of Military History 1861-1945. Arthur Banks. (Quality Paperbacks Ser.). (Illus.). 180p. 1988. pap. 12.95 (ISBN 0-306-80332-1). Da Capo.
World Atlas of Military History 1945-1984, Vol. III. Tom Hartman & John Mitchell. (World Atlas of Military History Ser.). (Illus.). 108p. 1985. 24.95 (ISBN 0-87052-000-8). Hippocrene Bks.
World Atlas of Military History 1945-1984. Tom Hartman & John Mitchell. (Quality Paperbacks Ser.). (Illus.). 120p. 1988. pap. 14.95 (ISBN 0-306-80316-X). Da Capo.
World Atlas of Railways. Ed. by O. S. Nock. (Illus.). 1978. 10.95 (ISBN 0-8317-9500-X, Mayflower Bks). Smith Pubs.
World Atlas of Revolution. Andrew Wheatcroft. LC 83-675888. (Illus.). 208p. 1983. 19.95 (ISBN 0-671-46286-5); pap. 10.95 (ISBN 0-671-47207-0). S&S.
World Atlas of Satellites. Ed. by Donald M. Jansky. LC 83-71123. (Telecommunications Ser.). (Illus.). 252p. 1983. 19.00 (ISBN 0-89006-117-3). Artech Hse.
World Atlas of Warfare: Military Innovations That Changed the Course of History. Richard Holmes. 1988. 40.00 (ISBN 0-670-81967-0). Viking.
World Atlas of Wine. Hugh Johnson. 304p. 1986. 45.00 (ISBN 0-671-50893-8). S&S.
World Authors, Nineteen Fifty to Nineteen Seventy: A Companion Volume to Twentieth Century Authors. Ed. by John Wakeman. LC 75-172140. (Wilson Authors Ser.). 1593p. 1975. 88.00 (ISBN 0-8242-0419-0). Wilson.
World Authors, Nineteen Seventy to Nineteen Seventy-Five: A Biographical Dictionary. Ed. by John Wakeman & Stanley J. Kunitz. LC 79-21874. (Wilson Authors Ser.). 893p. 1980. 68.00 (ISBN 0-8242-0641-X). Wilson.
World Authors 1975-1980. Ed. by Vineta Colby. LC 85-10045. 831p. 1985. 68.00 (ISBN 0-8242-0715-7). Wilson.
World Backwards: Russian Futurist Books, 1912-16. Susan P. Compton. (Illus.). 136p. 1978. 14.25 (ISBN 0-7141-0397-7, Pub. by British Lib); pap. 8.95 (ISBN 0-7141-0396-9). Longwood Pub Group.
World Banana Economy: Statistical Compendium. (Economic & Social Development Papers: No. 31). 36p. (Eng., Fr. & Span.). 1983. pap. 7.50 (ISBN 92-5-001395-7, F2487, FAO). UNIPUB.
World Banana Economy 1970-1984. (FAO Economic & Social Development Ser.: No. 57). (Illus.). 81p. (Orig.). 1986. pap. text ed. 7.50 (ISBN 92-5-102376-X, F2918, FAO). UNIPUB.
World Bank: A Critical Analysis. Cheryl Payer. LC 81-84738. 316p. 1982. pap. 12.00 (ISBN 0-85345-602-X). Monthly Rev.
World Bank & Agricultural Development: An Insider's View. Montague Yudelman. 44p. (Orig.). 1985. pap. text ed. 10.00 (ISBN 0-915825-11-2). World Resources Inst.
World Bank & Structural Transformation in Developing Countries: The Case of Zaire. Winsome J. Leslie. LC 87-3358. 200p. 1987. lib. bdg. 30.00x (ISBN 1-55587-036-8). Lynne Rienner.
World Bank & the Poor. Aart Van De Laar. (Institute for Social Studies Series on the Development of Societies: Vol. 6). 271p. 1980. lib. bdg. 15.00 (ISBN 0-89838-042-1, Pub. by Martinus Nijhoff Netherlands). Kluwer Academic.
World Bank Annual Report. 216p. (Orig.). 1987. pap. text ed. 5.00 (ISBN 0-317-66938-9, WB208, Pub. by Wrld Bank). UNIPUB.
World Bank Atlas. 16th ed. 24p. 1981. pap. 5.00 (ISBN 0-686-39723-1). World Bank.
World Bank Atlas 1986. (Eng., Fr. & Span.). 1986. Eng. Ed. 5.00 (BK-0684); Fr. Ed. 5.00 (BK-0685); Span. Ed. 5.00 (BK0686). World Bank.
World Bank Atlas 1987. 20th ed. (Illus.). 29p. (Eng., Fr. & Span.). 1987. Incl. 1988 update. 6.50 (ISBN 0-8213-0863-7, BK0863). World Bank.
World Bank: Borrowers Perspective. Y. Venugopal Reddy. 143p. 1986. text ed. 20.00x (ISBN 81-207-0032-5, Pub. by Sterling Pubs India). Apt Bks.
World Bank Commodity Models, 2 vols. Ed. by Shamsher Singh. (Working Paper: No. 6). ii, 545p. 1981. Set. 20.00 (ISBN 0-686-39662-6, BK9048). World Bank.
World Bank Glossary, 2 vols. (Eng., Fr. & Span.). 1986. Vol. I, Eng. - Fr., Fr. - Eng. 35.00 (BK0819); Vol. II, Eng.- Span., Span. - Eng. 30.00 (BK0820). World Bank.
World Bank: How It Can Serve U. S. Interests. E. Dwight Phaup. 57p. 1984. pap. 4.00 (ISBN 0-89195-213-6). Heritage Found.
World Bank in Rwanda: The Case of the Office de Valorisation Agricole et Pastorale du Mutara. Rene Lemarchand. LC 82-70681. 78p. 1982. pap. text ed. 5.00 (ISBN 0-941934-39-X). Indiana Africa.
World Bank Lending to Small Enterprises. Jacob Levitsky. (Industry & Finance Paper: No. 16). 62p. 1986. 5.00 (BK0814). World Bank.
World Bank Research Program 1986. (Abstracts of Current Studies Ser.). 260p. 1987. 12.00 (ISBN 0-8213-0898-X, BK-0898). World Bank.
World Bank Research Program, 1987: Abstracts of Current Studies. 80p. 1988. 12.00 (ISBN 0-8213-1037-2, BK1037). World Bank.
World Bank Since Bretton Woods. Edward S. Mason & Robert E. Asher. LC 73-1089. 915p. 1973. 31.95 (ISBN 0-8157-5492-2). Brookings.
World Banking & Finance: Cooperation Versus Conflict. George Macesich. LC 84-17908. 192p. 1984. 40.95 (ISBN 0-275-91220-5, C1220). Praeger.
World Bank's Support for the Alleviation of Poverty, Appendix 1 & 2. 64p. 1988. 5.00 (ISBN 0-8213-1087-9, BK1087). World Bank.
World Bayonets: Eighteen Hundred to Present. Anthony Carter. (Illus.). 72p. 1987. 14.95 (ISBN 0-85368-855-9, Pub. by Arms & Armour). Sterling.
World Before. Ruth Montgomery. 1985. pap. 3.95 (ISBN 0-449-20923-7, Crest). Fawcett.
World Before Man. David Lambert & Andrew Current. (World of Science Ser.). (Illus.). 64p. (YA) (gr. 7 up). 12.95 (ISBN 0-8160-1067-6). Facts on File.
World Before the Deluge. Louis Figuier. 1977. lib. bdg. 69.95 (ISBN 0-8490-2844-2). Gordon Pr.
World Behind the Scenes. Percy H. Fitzgerald. 1972. 22.00 (ISBN 0-405-09133-8, 1718). Ayer Co Pubs.
World Below. Sydney F. Wright. LC 75-10672. (Classics of Science Fiction Ser.). viii, 344p. 1976. 15.40 (ISBN 0-88355-350-3); pap. 10.00 (ISBN 0-88355-466-6). Hyperion Conn.
World Beneath Us. Anita McConnell. (World of Science Ser.). (Illus.). 64p. (YA) (gr. 7 up). 12.95 (ISBN 0-8160-1068-4). Facts on File.
World Beneath Your Feet see Books for Young Explorers.
World Between the Eyes: Poems. Fred Chappell. LC 73-152706. 1971. 13.95 (ISBN 0-8071-0942-8). La State U Pr.
World Between the Ox & the Swine: Dada Drawings by Hans Richter. Hans Richter. (Illus.). 1971. 2.00 (ISBN 0-911517-43-X). Mus of Art RI.
World Between Women. Ed. by Irene Reti et al. (Illus.). 126p. (Orig.). 1987. pap. 7.95 (ISBN 0-939821-27-3). HerBooks.
World Bewitch'd; or, an Examination of the Common Opinions Concerning Spirits. Balthasar Bekker. LC 79-8093. Repr. of 1695 ed. 30.00 (ISBN 0-404-18404-9). AMS Pr.
World Beyond & You: A Guide to Developing Your Own Spiritual Potential. Eva Billand. 174p. 1984. 14.95 (ISBN 0-930267-02-8). Bergh Pub.
World Beyond Healing. Nicholas Wade. 1987. 15.95 (ISBN 0-393-02335-4). Norton.
World Beyond the Hill: The Story of Science Fiction As the Quest for Transcendence. Alexei Panshin & Cory Panshin. 384p. Date not set. 17.95 (ISBN 0-87477-384-9). J P Tarcher.
World Bibliography of African Bibliographies. Theodore Besterman. Rev. by J. D. Pearson. 105p. 1975. 27.50x (ISBN 0-87471-749-3). Rowman.
World Bibliography of Armed Land Conflict: From Waterloo to World War I, 2 vols. Dale E. Floyd. LC 79-54082. 800p. 1980. Set. 65.00 (ISBN 0-89453-147-6). M Glazier.
World Bibliography of Bibliographies, 5 Vols. 4th ed. Theodore Besterman. 1963. Set. 275.00x (ISBN 0-87471-294-7). Rowman.
World Bibliography of Bibliographies 1964-1974, 2 vols. Compiled by Alice F. Toomey. 1166p. 1977. Set. 95.00x (ISBN 0-87471-999-2). Rowman.
World Bibliography of Translations of the Meanings of the Holy Qur'an: Printed Translations 1515-1980. Ed. by Ekmeleddin Ihsanoglu et al. 600p. 1988. lib. bdg. 125.00 (ISBN 0-7103-0229-0, Kegan Paul). Routledge Chapman & Hall.
World Bibliography on International Documentation, 2 vols. Th. Dimitrov. LC 80-5653. 846p. 1981. Set. 95.00 (ISBN 0-89111-010-0). UNIFO Pubs.
World Biotech Report 1986, 7 pts, Vol. 2. Incl. Pt. 1. Food Processing. 140p. pap. text ed. 50.00 (ISBN 0-86353-057-5); Pt. 2. Diagnostics & Health Care. 100p. pap. text ed. 50.00 (ISBN 0-86353-062-1); Pt. 3. Bioprocessing. 180p. pap. text ed. 50.00 (ISBN 0-86353-069-9); Pt. 4. Business, Legal & Regulatory Issues. 200p. pap. text ed. 50.00 (ISBN 0-86353-078-8); Pt. 5. Molecular Electronics. 88p. pap. text ed. 50.00 (ISBN 0-86353-079-6); Pt. 6. Pharmaceuticals. 100p. pap. text ed. 50.00; Pt. 7. Agriculture. 108p. pap. text ed. 50.00 (ISBN 0-86353-081-8). 916p. 1986. pap. text ed. 300.00 (ISBN 0-86353-076-1). Online.
World Biotech Report 1988: Proceedings of Biotech 88 held in London, May 1988. 500p. 1988. pap. text ed. 180.00 (ISBN 0-86353-145-8, Online Pubns). Online.
World Birds. Brian Martin. (Illus.). 208p. 1987. 19.95 (ISBN 0-85112-891-2, Pub. by Guinness Superlatives). Sterling.
World Blacks: Self Help & Achievement. James H. Boykin. LC 79-53631. ix, 193p. 1979. pap. 10.00x (ISBN 0-9603342-0-3). Boykin.
World Blindness & Its Prevention, Vol. I. John Wilson & International Agency for the Prevention of Blindness. 1980. text ed. 27.50x (ISBN 0-19-261249-2). Oxford U Pr.
World Blindness & Its Prevention, Vol. 2. John Wilson. 1984. 16.95x (ISBN 0-19-261480-0). Oxford U Pr.
World Blindness & Its Prevention, Vol. 3. International Agency for the Prevention of Blindness Staff. Ed. by Carl Kupfer. (Illus.). 160p. 1989. 39.95t (ISBN 0-19-261755-9). Oxford U Pr.
World Book Atlas. rev. ed. Ed. by World Book, Inc. Staff. LC 86-50621. 432p. (YA) (gr. 7-12). 1988. write for info. (ISBN 0-7166-3181-4). World Bk.
World Book Complete Word Power Library, 2 vols, Vol. 1 & 2. Ed. by World Book, Inc. Staff. LC 80-53648. (gr. 7-12). 1981. Vol. 1, 404pgs. write for info. (ISBN 0-7166-3110-5); Vol. 2, 437 Pgs. write for info. (ISBN 0-7166-3111-3). World Bk.
World Book Desk Reference Set, 4 vols. World Book Editors. LC 87-50569. (Illus.). 936p. 1987. Set. lib. bdg. write for info. (ISBN 0-7166-3193-8). The World Book of Instant Facts. The World Book Grammar & Style Guide. The World Book of Nations. The World Book of Home Facts. World Bk.
World Book Desk Reference Set. World Book Staff. Incl. Grammar & Style Guide. LC 83-60800 (ISBN 0-7166-3167-9); Instant Facts. LC 83-60801 (ISBN 0-7166-3168-7); Book of Nations. LC 83-60799 (ISBN 0-7166-3166-0); Tables & Formulas. LC 83-60798 (ISBN 0-7166-3165-2). (Illus.). 928p. (YA) (gr. 4 up). 1983. lib. bdg. write for info (ISBN 0-7166-3164-4). World Bk.
World Book Dictionary, 2 vols. Ed. by Clarence L. Barnhart & Robert K. Barnhart. LC 86-71197. (Illus.). 2554p. (gr. 4-12). 1987. write for info. (ISBN 0-7166-0287-3). World Bk.
World Book Dictionary: 1988, 2 vols. Ed. by Clarence L. Barnhart & Robert K. Barnhart. LC 87-50782. (Illus.). 2554p. 1988. lib. bdg. write for info. (ISBN 0-7166-0288-1). World Bk.
World Book Encyclopedia of Science: The Heavens, the Planet Earth, Physics Today, Chemistry Today, the Animal World, the Plant World, the Human Body, 7 vols. Ed. by World Book, Inc. Staff. LC 86-50622. (Illus.). 1000p. 1986. lib. bdg. write for info. (ISBN 0-7166-3192-X). World Bk.
World Book Encyclopedia: 1988 Edition, 22 vols. Ed. by World Book Editors. LC 87-50087. (Illus.). 14000p. 1987. PLB write for info. (ISBN 0-7166-0088-9). World Bk.
World Book Encyclopedia: 1988 Edition, 22 vols. Ed. by World Book, Inc. Staff. LC 87-51239. 1988. PLB write for info. (ISBN 0-7166-0089-7). World Bk.
World Book Health & Medical Annual. Ed. by World Book Staff. (Illus.). (gr. 6-12). 1986. write for info. (ISBN 0-7166-1187-2). World Bk.
World Book Health & Medical Annual. Ed. by World Book Staff. LC 87-648075. (Illus.). 1987. lib. bdg. write for info. (ISBN 0-7166-1188-0). World Bk.
World Book Industry: The Future of International Publishing. Peter Curwen. (Illus.). 298p. 1986. 50.00x (ISBN 0-8160-1405-1). Facts On File.
World Book Learning Library, 7 vols. Ed. by World Book Staff. LC 86-50558. (Illus.). 896p. (gr. 6-9). 1986. write for info. (ISBN 0-7166-3184-9). World Bk.
World Book Medical Encyclopedia: Your Guide to 600D Health. World Book Editors. LC 87-50666. (Illus.). 1024p. 1987. write for info. (ISBN 0-7166-3195-4). World Bk.
World Book of America's Presidents, 2 vols. rev. ed. Ed. by World Book, Inc. Staff. LC 87-51146. (Illus.). 448p. (YA) (gr. 4 up). 1988. Set. PLB write for info. (ISBN 0-7166-3196-2). World Bk.
World Book of Diabetes in Practice, Vol. 2. Ed. by L. Krall et al. 320p. 1986. pap. 55.25 (ISBN 0-444-80824-8). Elsevier.
World Book of Practical Diabetes. Krall. 1984. 147.00 (ISBN 0-444-90286-4). Elsevier.
World Book of Sport Psychology. John Salmela. 1981. text ed. 22.95 (ISBN 0-932392-08-3); pap. 15.95. Mouvement Pubns.
World Book of Test Taking. World Book, Inc. Staff. LC 81-69689. (Illus.). 736p. (gr. 4-12). 1982. write for info. (ISBN 0-7166-3151-2). World Bk.
World Book Year, 1987. Ed. by World Book Staff. LC 62-4818. (Illus.). (gr. 6-12). 1987. write for info. (ISBN 0-7166-0487-6). World Bk.
World Brain. facs. ed. H. G. Wells. LC 78-128332. (Essay Index Reprint Ser.). 1938. 19.00 (ISBN 0-8369-2033-3). Ayer Co Pubs.
World Broadcast Advertising: Four Reports. U. S. Bureau of Foreign & Domestic Commerce Staff. LC 84-27466. (History of Broadcasting: Radio to Television Ser.). 1977. 20.00 (ISBN 0-405-03586-1, 11253). Ayer Co Pubs.
World Broadcasting in the Age of the Satellite. W. J. Howell, Jr. Ed. by Melvin J. Voigt. LC 86-3380. (Communication & Information Science Ser.). 340p. 1986. text ed. 45.00 (ISBN 0-89391-340-5); pap. 29.50. Ablex Pub.
World Broadcasting Systems: A Comparative Analysis. Sydney W. Head. 457p. 1985. text ed. write for info. (ISBN 0-534-04734-3). Wadsworth Pub.
World Brotherhood of the Rosycross. Catharose De Petri & Jan Van Rijckenborg. (De Wereldbroederschap van het Rozekruis). (Orig.). pap. 10.00 (ISBN 0-317-62502-0). Rozekruis Pr.
World Business Cycles. 1st ed. Ed. by Economist Staff. 191p. 1982. 95.00x (ISBN 0-85058-057-9, Pub. by Economist). Gale.
World Business Travel Guide. Uniglobe Travel International Incorporated Staff. (Illus.). 400p. (Orig.). 1987. pap. 9.95 (ISBN 0-920197-39-6, Pub. by Summerhill CN). Sterling.
World by Itself: The Pastoral Moment in Cooper's Fiction. Daniel H. Peck. LC 76-25868. 1977. 25.00x (ISBN 0-300-02027-9). Yale U Pr.
World by Sevens: A Kid's Book of Lists. Louis Phillips. (Illus.). 96p. (gr. 4 up). 1981. lib. bdg. 8.90 (ISBN 0-531-02883-6). Watts.
World Calendar: Addresses & Occasional Papers Chronologically Arranged on the Progress of Calendar Reform Since 1930. Elisabeth Achelis. LC 73-102214. 194p. Repr. of 1937 ed. 40.00x (ISBN 0-8103-3784-3). Gale.
World Came to St. Louis: A Visit to the 1904 World's Fair. Dorothy D. Birk. LC 79-10396. (Illus.). 1979. 10.95 (ISBN 0-8272-4213-1). CBP.
World Can Break Your Heart. Daniel Curzon. LC 84-19409. 256p. (Orig.). 1985. pap. 6.95 (ISBN 0-915175-07-X). Knights Pr.
World Canals. Charles Hadfield. (Illus.). 432p. 1986. 29.95x (ISBN 0-8160-1376-4). Facts On File.
World Capital Shortage. Alan Heslop. (Key Issues Lecture Ser). 1978. scp 12.71 (ISBN 0-672-97208-5); pap. 7.87 scp (ISBN 0-672-97170-4). Bobbs.
World Capitalist Economy. V. V. Rymalov. 327p. 1982. 8.95 (ISBN 0-8285-2404-1, Pub. by Progress Pubs USSR). Imported Pubns.
World Car Catalogue, 1971. Compiled by Automobile Club of Italy Staff. (Illus.). 1971. 45.95 (ISBN 0-910714-03-7). Herald Bks.
World Cars 1974. Ed. by Automobile Club of Italy Staff. LC 74-3055. (Illus.). 440p. 1974. 75.00 (ISBN 0-910714-06-1). Herald Bks.
World Cars 1978. Ed. by Automobile Club of Italy Staff. LC 74-643381. (Illus.). 1978. 50.00 (ISBN 0-910714-10-X). Herald Bks.
World Cars 1979. Ed. by Automobile Club of Italy Staff. LC 7-643381. (Illus.). 1979. 50.00 (ISBN 0-910714-11-8). Herald Bks.
World Cars 1982. Automobile Club of Italy Staff. LC 74-643381. (Illus.). 440p. 1982. 50.00 (ISBN 0-910714-14-2). Herald Bks.
World Cartography. Incl. Vol. 12. pap. 3.50 (ISBN 0-686-94358-9, UN72/1/9); Vol. 13. pap. 5.00 (ISBN 0-686-99353-5, UN75/1/6); Vol. 15. (Illus.). 89p. 1979. pap. 7.00 (E.78.1.14); Vol. 16. 97p. 1980. pap. 9.00 (ISBN 0-686-72721-5, E.80.1.12); Vol. XIX. 68p. 1987. pap. 9.00 (ISBN 92-1-100317-2, E.87.I.15). UN.
World Cartography, Vol. XVIII. 67p. 1986. 8.50 (ISBN 92-1-100284-2, E.85.I.23). UN.
World Catalogue of Genetic Stocks: Barley. Supplement No. 1. pap. 5.75 ea. (F486, FAO). Supplement No. 2 (F487). UNIPUB.
World Catalogue of Genetic Stocks: Rice. Supplement No. 8. pap. 5.75 ea. (F499, FAO); Supplement No. 9. pap. 5.75 (F498); Supplement No. 10. pap. 5.75 (F497); Supplement No. 7. pap. 5.75; Supplement No. 6. pap. 5.75 (F496, F500). UNIPUB.
World Catalogue of Genetic Stocks: Wheat. Supplement No. 3. pap. 5.75 (F501, FAO); Supplement No. 7. pap. 5.75 (F502); Supplement No. 8. pap. 5.75 (F503); Supplement No. 9. pap. 5.75 (F504, F496). UNIPUB.
World Catastrophe: Behold He Cometh. Rhodalee M Hailey. 128p. 1986. 7.75 (ISBN 0-8062-2704-4). Carlton.
World Cattle, 2 Vols. John E. Rouse. LC 69-10620. (Illus.). 1972. Set. 50.00x (ISBN 0-8061-0864-9). U of Okla Pr.
World Celebrities in Ninety Photographic Portraits. Fred Stein. 96p. 1989. pap. 9.95 (ISBN 0-486-25843-2). Dover.
World Census of Agriculture, 1970: Analysis & International Comparison of Data. (Statistics Ser.: No. 37). 300p. 1981. pap. 25.00 (ISBN 92-5-101037-4, F2290, FAO). UNIPUB.

World Debt: Who Is to Pay? Jacobo Schatan. LC 87-13330. 144p. 1987. 35.00 (ISBN 0-86232-688-5, Pub. by Zed); pap. 9.95 (ISBN 0-86232-689-3, Pub. by Zed). Humanities.
World Decision. Robert Herrick. (Collected Works of Robert Herrick). 1988. Repr. of 1916 ed. lib. bdg. 59.00x. Am Biog Serv.
World Decision see Collected Works.
World Deep-Sea Container Shipping. Roy Pearson & John Fossey. 258p. 1983. text ed. 69.95x (ISBN 0-566-00582-4). Gower Pub Co.
World Defense Forces: A Compendium of Current Military Information for All Countries of the World. Ed. by Barbara H. Pope. 137p. 1987. lib. bdg. 24.50 (ISBN 0-87436-486-8). ABC-Clio.
World Deforestation in the Twentieth Century. Ed. by John F. Richards & Richard P. Tucker. (Policy Studies). 304p. 1988. lib. bdg. 47.50 (ISBN 0-8223-0784-7). Duke.
World Demand Prospects for Jute. M. Elton Thigpen et al. (Commodity Working Paper Ser.: No. 16). 186p. 1987. 10.00 (ISBN 0-8213-0867-X, BK0867). World Bank.
World Design Sources Directory 1980: An ICOGRADA ICSID Publication. Ed. by Centre De Creation Industrielle, Paris, France Staff. LC 79-41455. 192p. 1980. 46.00 (ISBN 0-08-025676-7). Pergamon.
World Destroyed: Hiroshima & the Origins of the Arms Race. Martin J. Sherwin. LC 86-40523. 1977. pap. 9.95 (ISBN 0-394-75204-X, Vin). Random.
World Destroyed: Hiroshima & the Origins of the Arms Race. Martin J. Sherwin. pap. write for info. (Vin). Random.
World Development Report Nineteen Eighty-Six. The World Bank. (World Bank Publication Ser.). (Illus.). 250p. 1986. 26.00x (ISBN 0-19-520517-0); pap. text ed. 9.95x (ISBN 0-19-520518-9). Oxford U Pr.
World Development Report, 1978. World Bank. 1978. pap. text ed. 9.95x (ISBN 0-19-502500-8). Oxford U Pr.
World Development Report 1980. World Bank. (Illus.). 1980. text ed. 26.00x (ISBN 0-19-502833-3); pap. text ed. 9.95x (ISBN 0-19-502834-1). Oxford U Pr.
World Development Report 1981. World Bank. (Illus.). 1981. text ed. 26.00 (ISBN 0-19-502997-6); pap. text ed. 9.95x (ISBN 0-19-502998-4); Spanish Ed. pap. text ed. 6.95x (ISBN 0-19-503098-2). Oxford U Pr.
World Development Report, 1982. World Bank. (Illus., Orig.). 1982. 26.00x (ISBN 0-19-503224-1); pap. 9.95x (ISBN 0-19-503225-X). Oxford U Pr.
World Development Report 1983. The World Bank. (Illus.). 1983. 26.00x (ISBN 0-19-520431-X); pap. 9.95x (ISBN 0-19-520432-8). Oxford U Pr.
World Development Report 1984. World Bank. (Illus.). 1984. 26.00x (ISBN 0-19-520459-X); pap. 9.95x (ISBN 0-19-520460-3). Oxford U Pr.
World Development Report, 1985. (Illus.). 256p. 1985. text ed. 20.00x (ISBN 0-19-520481-6); pap. text ed. 9.95x (ISBN 0-19-520482-4). Oxford U Pr.
World Development Report 1986: The Hesitant Recovery & Prospects for Sustained Growth. (Trade & Pricing Policies in World Agriculture Ser.). 266p. 1986. 26.00 (X0517); Eng. pap. text ed. 9.95 ea. (X0518). Arabic (IB 0856). Chinese (IB 0857). French (IB 0855). German (IB 0858). Japanese (IB 0859). Portugese (IB 0860). Spanish (IB 0861). World Bank.
World Development Report, 1987. The World Bank Staff. (World Bank Publication). 298p. 1987. text ed. 26.00 (ISBN 0-19-520562-6); pap. text ed. 12.95 (ISBN 0-19-520563-4). Oxford U Pr.
World Development Report, 1988. The World Bank Staff. (World Bank Publications). (Illus.). 285p. 1988. text ed. 26.00 (ISBN 0-19-520649-5); pap. text ed. 12.95 (ISBN 0-19-520650-9). Oxford U Pr.
World Diagnostic Imaging Markets: Long-Term Affects of DRGs & Emerging Technologies. 200p. 1985. 995.00 (ISBN 0-317-41584-0). Market Res Co.
World Dictionaries in Print, 1983: A Guide to General & Subject Dictionaries in World Languages. 579p. 1983. 99.50 (ISBN 0-8352-1615-2). Bowker.
World Directory of Biological & Medical Sciences Libraries. Ed. by Ursula Poland. (IFLA Publication Ser.: Vol. 42). xii, 203p. 1988. lib. bdg. 430.00 (ISBN 3-598-21772-2). K G Saur.
World Directory of Crystallographers: & of Other Scientists Employing Crystallographic Methods. 6th ed. Ed. by A. L. Bednowitz. 1981. pap. 10.00 (ISBN 90-277-1310-3, Pub. by Reidel Holland). Kluwer Academic.
World Directory of Crystallographers & of Other Scientists Employing Crystallographic Methods, 1986. 7th ed. Ed. by Allan L. Bednowitz & Armin P. Segmuller. 1986. lib. bdg. 14.00 (ISBN 90-277-2094-0, Pub. by Reidel Netherlands). Kluwer Academic.
World Directory of Dental Schools: 1963. 282p. (Eng. & Fr.). 1967. 9.20 (ISBN 92-4-150003-4). World Health.
World Directory of Energy Information. Compiled by Cambridge Information & Research Services Limited & Christopher Swain. LC 81-754. Vol. 1. pap. 84.00 (2027221); Vol. 2. pap. 107.50. Bks Demand UMI.
World Directory of Engineering Schools. 2nd ed. Geographics Editors. LC 80-66864. 1980. pap. 28.95 (ISBN 0-930722-02-7). Geographics.
World Directory of Human Rights Institutions, 1988. UNESCO. LC 87-23188. 232p. 1988. 49.95 (ISBN 0-85496-229-8, Pub. by Berg Pubs). St Martin.
World Directory of Human Rights Teaching & Research Institutions, 1988. (World Social Science Information Directories Ser.: No. 5). 216p. 1988. pap. 29.00 (ISBN 92-3-102504-X, U1650, UNESCO). UNIPUB.
World Directory of Landscape Architects. Ed. by Donald M. Roberts. (Orig.). 1988. pap. 24.95. WDOLA.
World Directory of Map Collections. Ed. by John A. Wolter & Ronald E. Grimm. (IFLA Publication Ser.: vol. 31). 405p. 1986. lib. bdg. 36.50 (ISBN 3-598-20374-8). K G Saur.
World Directory of Mathematicians, 1986. 8th ed. (Vol. 8). 976p. 1986. pap. text ed. 30.00 (ISBN 0-317-52075-X). Am Math.
World Directory of Medical Schools. 4th ed. 348p. (Eng. & Fr.). 1970. 8.00 (ISBN 92-4-050000-6). World Health.
World Directory of Multinational Enterprises, 3 Vols. 2nd ed. Ed. by John M. Stopford & John H. Dunning. 1700p. 1983. Set. 385.00x (ISBN 0-8103-0521-6, Pub. by Macmillan England). Gale.
World Directory of Nuclear Utility Management. 1987. 200.00 (ISBN 0-89448-510-5, 250009). Am Nuclear Soc.
World Directory of Peace Research & Training Institutions, 1988. 6th ed. UNESCO. 300p. 1987. 49.95 (ISBN 0-85496-156-9, Pub. by Berg Pubs). St Martin.
World Directory of Peace Research & Training Institutions, 1988. 6th ed. (World Social Science Information Directories Ser.). 271p. 1988. pap. 35.00 (ISBN 92-3-102486-8, U1655, UB). UNIPUB.
World Directory of Pharmaceutical Manufacturers. 6th ed. 1985. 340.00 (ISBN 0-8002-3890-7). Intl Pubns Serv.
World Directory of Post-Basic & Post-Graduate Schools of Nursing. 223p. (Eng., Fr. & Rus.). 1965. 7.20 (ISBN 92-4-150000-X). World Health.
World Directory of School of Pharmacy: 1963. 301p. (Eng., Fr & Rus.). 1966. 9.20 (ISBN 92-4-150001-8). World Health.
World Directory of Schools for Animal Health Assistants. (Also avail. in French). 1974. pap. 9.60 (ISBN 92-4-150005-0). World Health.
World Directory of Schools of Public Health: 1971. 277p. 16.00 (ISBN 92-4-150003-4, 1322). World Health.
World Directory of Schools of Public Health & Postgraduate Training Programmes in Public Health. 3rd ed. 189p. 1986. pap. 17.40 (ISBN 92-4-150007-7). World Health.
World Directory of Scottish Associations. M. Brander & I. Macleod. 242p. 1986. 70.00x (Pub. by S P A Bks Ltd). State Mutual Bk.
World Directory of Social Science Institutions: Research, Advanced Training, Documentation, Professional Bodies. 4th ed. (World Social Science Information Services: No. II). 905p. 1986. pap. text ed. 24.00 (ISBN 92-3-002358-2, U1501, Pub. by Unesco). UNIPUB.
World Directory of Venereal-Disease Treatment Centres at Ports: Application of the International Agreement of Brussels, 1924 Respecting Facilities to Be Given to Merchant Seamen for the Treatment of Venereal Diseases. 3rd ed. 196p. 1972. 9.60 (ISBN 92-4-050001-4, 1442). World Health.
World Directory of Veterinary Schools: 1971. 1972. 14.40 (ISBN 92-4-150004-2). World Health.
World Disarmament. Ed. by Ron Huzzard & Christopher Meredith. LC 85-71752. 238p. 1985. 35.00 (ISBN 0-85124-412-2, Pub. by Spokesman UK); pap. 12.95 (ISBN 0-85124-413-0, Pub. by Spokesman UK). Dufour.
World Disarmament: An Idea Whose Time Has Come. Ed. by Ron Huzzard & Christopher Meredith. 240p. 60.00x (Pub. by Bertrand Russell Hse); pap. 40.00x. State Mutual Bk.
World Divided. Ed. by G. K. Helleiner. LC 75-16606. (Perspectives on Development Ser.: No. 5). 1976. 54.50 (ISBN 0-521-20948-X); pap. 16.95x (ISBN 0-521-29006-6). Cambridge U Pr.
World Does Move. Booth Tarkington. LC 76-8903. 1976. Repr. of 1928 ed. lib. bdg. 35.00x (ISBN 0-8371-8876-8, TAWD). Greenwood.
World Drama. Oscar G. Brockett & Mark Pape. 1984. pap. text ed. 18.95 (ISBN 0-03-057668-7). HR&W.
World Drama, Vol. 1: Ancient Greece, Rome, India, China, Japan, Medieval Europe, England. Ed. by Barrett H. Clark. pap. 10.95 (ISBN 0-486-20057-4). Dover.
World Drama, Vol. 2: Italy, Spain, France, Germany, Denmark, Russia, Norway. Ed. by Barrett H. Clark. 1933. pap. 10.95 (ISBN 0-486-20059-0). Dover.
World Dynamics. 2nd ed. W. Forrester. 1973. 22.50x (ISBN 0-262-06066-3); pap. 8.95x (ISBN 0-262-56018-6). MIT Pr.
World Eco-Crisis: International Organizations in Response. Ed. by David A. Kay & Eugene B. Skolnikoff. LC 79-178153. 332p. 1972. 20.00x (ISBN 0-299-06151-5, 615); pap. 5.95x (ISBN 0-299-06154-X). U of Wis Pr.
World Economic Crisis. Ed. & intro. by William P. Bundy. 256p. 1975. 8.95x (ISBN 0-393-05545-0). Norton.
World Economic Data: A Compendium of Current Economic Information for All Countries of the World. Ed. by Cecelia A. Albert. (Illus.). 231p. 1987. lib. bdg. 28.50 (ISBN 0-87436-485-X). ABC-Clio.
World Economic Development. Herman Kahn. 1979. lib. bdg. 48.50 (ISBN 0-89158-392-0). Westview.
World Economic Environment & Prospects for India. M. Narasimham. 190p. 1988. text ed. 30.00x (ISBN 81-207-0769-9, Pub. by Sterling Pubs India). Apt Bks.
World Economic Growth. Ed. by Arnold C. Harberger. 508p. 1985. text ed. 22.95 (ISBN 0-917616-63-4); pap. text ed. 9.95 (ISBN 0-917616-62-6). ICS Pr.
World Economic Interdependence & the Evolving North-South Relationship. OECD Staff. 84p. (Orig.). 1983. pap. 9.00x (ISBN 92-64-12446-2). OECD.
World Economic Order: Past & Prospects. Ed. by Sven Grassman & Erik Lundberg. LC 79-18803. 1981. 42.50x (ISBN 0-312-89046-X). St Martin.
World Economic Outlook, April 1985, No. 4: A Survey. International Monetary Fund Staff. ix, 283p. 1985. pap. 12.00 (ISBN 0-939934-45-0). Intl Monetary.
World Economic Outlook, April 1986, No. 6. International Monetary Fund Staff. (World Economic & Financial Surveys Ser.). x, 270p. 1986. 15.00 (ISBN 0-939934-66-3). Intl Monetary.
World Economic Outlook, April 1987. IMF Staff. 1987. 17.00 (IB0978). World Bank.
World Economic Outlook, April 1987, No. 8: A Survey by the Staff of the International Monetary Fund. International Monetary Fund Staff. (World Economic & Financial Surveys Ser.). iv, 194p. 1987. pap. 15.00 (ISBN 0-939934-85-X). Intl Monetary.
World Economic Outlook, April 1988: A Survey by the Staff of the International Monetary Fund. (World Economic & Financial Surveys Ser.). 200p. 1988. write for info. (ISBN 1-55775-011-4). Intl Monetary.
World Economic Outlook, No. 1: A Survey by the Staff of the International Monetary Fund. International Monetary Fund Staff. (Occasional Papers: No. 9). 210p. 1982. 8.00 (ISBN 0-686-97773-4). Intl Monetary.
World Economic Outlook, No. 10: A Survey. International Monetary Fund Staff. (World Economic & Financial Surveys Ser.). 189p. 1988. 15.00. Intl Monetary.
World Economic Outlook, No.2: A Survey. International Monetary Fund Staff. (Occasional Papers: No. 27). 222p. 1984. pap. 12.00 (ISBN 0-317-05980-7). Intl Monetary.
World Economic Outlook, October 1985, No. 5: Revised Projections. International Monetary Fund Staff. 109p. 1985. pap. 10.00 (ISBN 0-939934-54-X). Intl Monetary.
World Economic Outlook, October 1986, No. 7: Revised Projections by the Staff of the International Monetary Fund. International Monetary Fund Staff. (World Economic & Financial Surveys Ser.). 112p. 1986. pap. 12.00 (ISBN 0-939934-78-7). Intl Monetary.
World Economic Outlook, October 1987, No. 9: Revised Projections by the Staff of the International Monetary Fund. (World Economic & Financial Surveys Ser.). 100p. 1987. pap. 12.00 (ISBN 0-939934-88-4). Intl Monetary.
World Economic Outlook, September 1984, No. 3: Revised Projections. International Monetary Fund Staff. (Occasional Papers: No. 32). 73p. 1984. pap. 7.50 (ISBN 0-317-13490-6). Intl Monetary.
World Economic Outlook 1987: Revised Projections by the Staff of the International Monetary Fund. (World Economic & Financial Surveys Ser.). 118p. 1987. pap. text ed. 12.00 (ISBN 0-317-68045-5, IMF87, Pub. by Internat Monet Fund). UNIPUB.
World Economic Problems. Ed. by Kimberly A. Elliott & John Williamson. LC 88-2787. (Special Reports Ser.: No. 7). 293p. (Orig.). 1988. pap. 15.95 (ISBN 0-88132-055-2). Inst Intl Eco.
World Economic Recovery: The Priority of International Monetary & Financial Cooperation. 25p. 1983. pap. 5.00 (ISBN 92-1-109033-4, E.82.II.C.3). UN.
World Economic Survey. 1987. 22.00 (ISBN 92-1-109113-6, E.87.II.C.1). UN.
World Economic Survey, 1986. 1986. 15.00 (ISBN 92-1-109110-1, E.86.11.C.1). UN.
World Economy. Christopher Hutton-Williams. 1984. 3.95 (ISBN 0-521-27791-4). Cambridge U Pr.
World Economy. David Killingray. Ed. by Malcolm Yapp et al. (World History Ser.). (Illus.). 32p. (gr. 6-11). 1980. lib. bdg. 6.95 (ISBN 0-89908-143-6); pap. text ed. 2.45 (ISBN 0-89908-118-5). Greenhaven.
World Economy. Rudolf Steiner. pap. 4.95 (ISBN 0-85440-266-7). Anthroposophic.
World Economy & East-West Trade, Vol. 1. Ed. by F. Nemschak. 1976. soft cover 29.00 (ISBN 0-387-81390-X). Springer-Verlag.
World Economy & Its Main Developmental Tendencies. Jozsef Nyilas. 1982. lib. bdg. 49.50 (ISBN 0-686-38405-9, Pub. by Martinus Nijhoff Netherlands). Kluwer Academic.
World Economy & World Hunger: The Response of the Churches. Robert L. McCan. 119p. 1982. 16.00 (ISBN 0-89093-497-5); pap. 5.00. U Pubns Amer.
World Economy: Changes & Challenges. Research Reports Editors. LC 83-7333. 196p. 1983. 9.95 (ISBN 0-87187-266-8). Congr Quarterly.
World Economy: History & Prospect. W. W. Rostow. LC 77-24053. 877p. 1978. 40.00x (ISBN 0-292-79008-2); pap. 25.00x (ISBN 0-292-79016-3). U of Tex Pr.
World Economy in Transition. Michael Beenstock. 240p. 1983. text ed. 34.95x (ISBN 0-04-339033-1). Unwin Hyman.
World Economy in Transition. 2nd ed. Michael Beenstock. 250p. 1984. pap. text ed. 15.95x (ISBN 0-04-339035-8). Unwin Hyman.
World Economy in Transition. Eugene Staley. LC 76-137961. (Economic Thought, History & Challenge Ser.). 1971. Repr. of 1939 ed. 26.50 (ISBN 0-8046-1463-6, Pub. by Kennikat). Assoc Faculty Pr.
World Economy in Transition: Essays Presented to Surendra Patel on his Sixtieth Birthday. Ed. by K. Ahooja-Patel. 314p. 1986. text ed. 41.00 (ISBN 0-08-031285-3). Pergamon.
World Economy, Money, & the Great Depression, 1919-1939. Gottfried Haberler. LC 75-42762. 1976. pap. 5.00 (ISBN 0-8447-3198-6). Am Enterprise.
World Economy Series, 37 bks. Ed. by Mira Wilkins. 1982. write for info. Ayer Co Pubs.
World Economy since the War: The Politics of Uneven Development. E. A. Brett. 1985. 35.00 (ISBN 0-275-90197-1, C0197); pap. 14.95 (ISBN 0-275-91668-5, B1668). Praeger.
World Economy: Trade & Finance. Beth V. Yarbrough & Robert M. Yarbrough. (Illus.). 688p. 1988. text ed. price not set (ISBN 0-03-003474-4). Dryden Pr.
World Education Encyclopedia, 3 vols. George Kurian. (Illus.). 1800p. 1988. Set. 175.00x (ISBN 0-87196-748-0). Facts On File.
World Elsewhere. Nirmal Verma. (Readers International Ser.). 238p. 1988. Repr. of 1986 ed. 16.95 (ISBN 0-930523-46-6, Dist. by Consortium). Readers Intl.
World Elsewhere: The Place of Style in American Literature. Richard Poirier. 1966. pap. 4.95 (ISBN 0-19-500778-6). Oxford U Pr.
World Elsewhere: The Place of Style in American Literature. Richard Poirier. LC 85-40376. 272p. 1985. pap. 9.95 (ISBN 0-299-09934-2). U of Wis Pr.
World Encompassed & Analagous Contemporary Documents Concerning Sir Francis Drake's Circumnavigation of the World. Francis Drake. LC 78-75030. (Illus.). 28.50x (ISBN 0-8154-0307-0). Cooper Sq.
World Encompassed by Sir F. Drake, Being His Next Voyage to That to Nombre De Dios. Francis Drake. LC 78-26252. (English Experience Ser.: No. 103). 108p. 1969. Repr. of 1628 ed. 16.00 (ISBN 90-221-0103-7). Walter J Johnson.
World Encompassed by Sir Francis Drake. Francis Drake. Ed. by W. S. Vaux. (Hakluyt Soc., First Ser.: No. 16). Repr. of 1854 ed. 32.00 (ISBN 0-8337-0909-7). B Franklin.
World Encompassed: The First European Maritime Empires, c. 800-1650. G. V. Scammell. LC 80-6319. (Illus.). 536p. 1981. 45.00x (ISBN 0-520-04422-3). U of Cal Pr.
World Encyclopedia. H. G. Wells. 1978. Repr. of 1936 ed. lib. bdg. 25.00 (ISBN 0-8495-5801-8). Arden Lib.
World Encyclopedia. H. G. Wells. LC 73-18411. lib. bdg. 17.00 (ISBN 0-8414-9509-2). Folcroft.
World Encyclopedia of Aero Engines. Bill Gunston. (Illus.). 192p. 1987. 24.95 (ISBN 0-85059-717-X, Pub. by PSL P Stephens England). Sterling.
World Encyclopedia of Black Peoples, Vol. 1. Ed. by Harry Waldman. LC 74-28076. 1974-81. lib. bdg. 59.00 ea. (ISBN 0-403-01796-3). Scholarly.
World Encyclopedia of Cartoons. Ed. by M. Horn. LC 79-3186. (Illus.). 752p. 1980. 100.00 (ISBN 0-87754-088-8). Chelsea Hse.
World Encyclopedia of Cartoons, 2 vols. Ed. by Maurice Horn. 787p. 1980. 125.00x. Gale.
World Encyclopedia of Cartoons, 6 vols. Ed. by Maurice Horn. (Illus.). 900p. Set. 100.00 (ISBN 0-87754-399-2). Chelsea Hse.
World Encyclopedia of Cartoons, 2 vols. Ed. by Maurice Horn & Richard E. Marschall. LC 79-21953. (Illus.). 872p. 1980. 60.00 (ISBN 0-87754-097-7). Chelsea Hse.
World Encyclopedia of Civil Aircraft, from Leonardo da Vinci to the Present. Enzo Angelucci. LC 82-4642. (Illus.). 414p. 1982. 29.95 (ISBN 0-517-54724-4). Crown.
World Encyclopedia of Comics, 1 vol. ed. Ed. by M. Horn. LC 75-22322. (Illus.). 785p. 1976. text ed. 39.50 (ISBN 0-87754-030-6). Chelsea Hse.

World Futures: A Critical Analysis of Alternatives. Barry B. Hughes. LC 84-47964. 256p. 1985. text ed. 28.50x (ISBN 0-8018-3236-5); pap. text ed. 10.95x (ISBN 0-8018-3237-3). Johns Hopkins.

World Games & Recipes. 56p. 1979. pap. 3.00 (ISBN 0-686-88516-3, 23-105). Girl Scouts USA.

World Games: The Tradition of Anti-realist Revolt. Christopher Nash. 440p. 1988. text ed. 42.50 (ISBN 0-416-34710-X). Routledge Chapman & Hall.

World Gas Option Symposium March 1980. (Fuel Applications). 189p. 25.00 (ISBN 0-910091-46-3). Inst Gas Tech.

World Gas Trade: A Resource for the Future. Ed. by Melvin A. Conant. 350p. 1986. 55.00 (ISBN 0-8133-7185-6). Westview.

World Gazetteer of Boundaries. George Kurian. 900p. 1988. 120.00 (ISBN 0-87436-504-X). ABC-Clio.

World Geography of Human Diseases. Ed. by G. Melvyn Howe. 1978. 137.50 (ISBN 0-12-357150-2). Acad Pr.

World Geography Study Aid. Herbert O. Kruger et al. 1986. pap. 1.95 (ISBN 0-87738-044-9). Youth Ed.

World Gold Coin Value Guide. Lorraine S. Durst & Sanford J. Durst. LC 80-51832. 1981. softcover 9.00 (ISBN 0-686-64442-5); lib. bdg. 12.00 (ISBN 0-915262-54-1). S J Durst.

World Gold Deposits. J. J. Bache. 160p. 1986. 47.75 (ISBN 0-444-01077-7). Elsevier.

World Government, Ready or Not! Garry Davis. LC 84-23362. (Illus.). 400p. 1984. pap. 14.95 (ISBN 0-931545-00-5). Juniper Ledge Pub.

World Grain Trade Statistics: Exports by Source & Destination. annual Incl. 1960. pap. 5.75 (ISBN 0-685-48253-7, F510). UNIPUB; 1960-61. 1961. pap. 5.75 (F511). UNIPUB; 1961-62. 1962. pap. 5.75 (ISBN 0-685-48254-5, F512). UNIPUB; 1963-64. 1964. pap. 5.75 (ISBN 0-685-48255-3, F513). UNIPUB; 1964-65. 1966. pap. 6.00 (ISBN 0-685-48256-1, F514). UNIPUB; 1965-1966. 1967. pap. 5.75 (ISBN 0-685-48257-X, F515). UNIPUB; 1966-67. 1968. pap. 5.75 (F516). UNIPUB; 1967-68. 1968. pap. 6.00 (ISBN 0-685-48258-8, F517). UNIPUB; 1968-69. 1970. pap. 5.75 (ISBN 0-685-48259-6, F518). UNIPUB; 1969-70. 1971. pap. 6.25 (ISBN 0-685-48260-X, F519). UNIPUB; 1970-71. 1972. pap. 6.25 (ISBN 0-685-48261-8, F520). UNIPUB; 1971-72. 1973. pap. 6.25 (F521). UNIPUB; 1972-73. 1974. pap. 8.75 (F522). UNIPUB; 1973-74. 1975. pap. 8.75 (F523). UNIPUB. (Orig., FAO). UNIPUB.

World Grain Trade Statistics 1958-59. pap. 5.75 (F509, FAO). UNIPUB.

World Graphic Design Now. Yasuku Kamura et al. (Design Now Ser.: Vol. 1). (Illus.). 234p. 1988. 79.95 (ISBN 4-0618-9411-0, Pub. by Kodansha Ltd Tokyo). Bks Nippan.

World Guide to Abbreviations of Associations & Institutions, 1972. cancelled (ISBN 3-7940-1398-0). Intl Pubns Serv.

World Guide to Abbreviations of Organizations. 8th ed. Ed. by F. A. Buttress. 750p. 1987. 115.00x (Pub. by Grand River). Gale.

World Guide to Abbreviations of Organizations, 1974. cancelled (ISBN 0-8103-2015-0). Intl Pubns Serv.

World Guide to Automobile Manufactures. Brian Laban et al. LC 87-81834. (Illus.). 544p. 1987. 50.00 (ISBN 0-8160-1844-8). Facts on File.

World Guide to Battery-Powered Road Transportation. Electric Vehicle Council Staff. 393p. 1980. 50.00 (ISBN 0-317-34116-2, 0479202). Edison Electric.

World Guide to Beer. rev. ed. Michael Jackson. (Illus.). 256p. 1988. 29.95 (ISBN 0-89471-649-2). Running Pr.

World Guide to Beer. Ed. by Michael Jackson. (Illus.). 255p. 1984. Repr. of 1977 ed. 14.98 (ISBN 0-89471-292-6, Pub. by Courage Bks). Running Pr.

World Guide to Exchange Control Regulations. Ed. by Philip Bentley. (Euromoney Ser.). 420p. (Orig.). 1986. spiral-bound 150.00 (ISBN 0-903121-69-7, Pub. by Woodhead-Faulkner). Longwood Pub Group.

World Guide to Foreign Services. Ed. by Michael Jackisch. 838p. 1986. 155.00 (ISBN 3-926393-00-9). Gale.

World Guide to Higher Education: A Comparative Survey of Systems, Degrees & Qualifications. 1976. 20.00 (ISBN 92-3-101251-7, U723, UNESCO). UNIPUB.

World Guide to Higher Education: A Comparative Survey of Systems, Degrees and Qualifications. 2nd ed. (Studies on the Evaluation of Qualifications at the Higher Education Level). (Illus.). 369p. (Co-published with Bowker Publishing Co., Epping, and Unipub, New York). 1982. pap. 41.00 (ISBN 92-3-101914-7, U1232, UNESCO). UNIPUB.

World Guide to Libraries. 8th ed. Ed. by Helga Legenfelder et al. (Handbook of International Documentation & Information Ser.). 1340p. 1987. lib. bdg. 220.00 (ISBN 3-598-20536-8). K G Saur.

World Guide to Mountains & Mountaineering. John Cleare. LC 78-25727. (Illus.). 1979. 19.95 (ISBN 0-8317-9546-8, Mayflower Bks). Smith Pubs.

World Guide to Nude Beaches & Recreation. rev. ed. Lee Baxandall. (Illus.). 240p. pap. 17.95 (ISBN 0-517-56921-3, Harmony). Crown.

World Guide to Scientific Associations & Learned Societies. 4th ed. Ed. by Barbara Verrel & Helmut Opitz. 947p. 1984. lib. bdg. 135.00 (ISBN 3-598-20522-8). K G Saur.

World Guide to Social Work Education. 2nd ed. Compiled by Vijaya Rao & Katherine A. Kendall. LC 83-78853. 288p. 1984. pap. text ed. 22.00 (ISBN 0-87293-001-7). Coun Soc Wk Ed.

World Guide to Special Libraries. Ed. by Helga Lengenfelder. 990p. 1983. lib. bdg. 150.00 (ISBN 3-598-20528-7). K G Saur.

World Guide to Terminological Activities: Organizations, Commissions, Terminology Banks. 2nd ed. Compiled by Magdalena Krommer-Benz. (Infoterm Ser.: Vol. 4). 158p. 1985. lib. bdg. 56.00 (ISBN 3-598-21368-9). K G Saur.

World Guide to Trade Associations. 3rd ed. Ed. by Barbara Verrel & Helmut Opitz. (Handbook of International Documentation & Information: Vol. 12). 1200p. 1985. lib. bdg. 200.00 (ISBN 3-598-20527-9). K G Saur.

World Guide to Whisky: A Comprehensive Taste-Guide to Single Malts & the World's Best-known Blends. Michael Jackson. LC 87-9429. (Illus.). 224p. 1988. 24.95 (ISBN 0-88162-284-2). Salem Hse Pubs.

World, Guilt & Self-Conflict: The Guilt Chapter. Eli Siegel. 26p. 1966. pap. write for info. (ISBN 0-911492-15-1). Aesthetic Realism.

World Gym Musclebuilding System. Joe Gold & Robert Kennedy. (Illus.). 224p. 1987. pap. 12.95 (ISBN 0-8092-4713-5). Contemp Bks.

World Ham Net Directory. Mike Witkouski. 28p. (Orig.). 1987. pap. 7.96 (ISBN 0-936653-07-8). Tiare Pubns.

World Handbook of Political & Social Indicators. Bruce M. Russett et al. LC 77-13514. (Tools & Methods of Comparative Research: No. 1). (Illus.). 1977. Repr. of 1964 ed. lib. bdg. 35.00x (ISBN 0-8371-9857-7, RUWH). Greenwood.

World Handbook of Political & Social Indicators. 2nd ed. Charles L. Taylor & Michael C. Hudson. LC 70-179479. (Illus.). 464p. 1972. pap. 13.95x (ISBN 0-300-01871-1). Yale U Pr.

World Handbook of Political & Social Indicators, 2 Vols. 3rd ed. Charles L. Taylor & David Jodice. LC 82-40447. 352p. 1983. Vol. 1. 30.00x (ISBN 0-300-03027-4); Vol. 2. 24.50x (ISBN 0-300-03028-2). Yale U Pr.

World Handbook of Political & Social Indicators II: Cross-National Aggregate Data, 1950-1965. 2nd ed. Charles Lewis Taylor & Michael C. Hudson. 1973. write for info., codebk (ISBN 0-89138-059-0). ICPSR.

World Handbook of Political & Social Indicators II: Sections 2-5, 1948-1967. 2nd ed. Charles Lewis Taylor & Michael C. Hudson. LC 75-40942. 1975. write for info., codebk (ISBN 0-89138-123-6). ICPSR.

World Has Definitely Changed: New Economic Forces & Their Implications for the Next Decade. A. Gary Shilling. (Illus.). 179p. 1987. pap. 8.00 (ISBN 0-9618562-1-1). LESP.

World Has Definitely Changed: New Economic Forces & Their Implications for the Next Decade. A. Gary Shilling. (Illus.). 250p. 1988. Repr. of 1986 ed. text ed. 19.95 (ISBN 0-9618562-0-3). Weiss Pubns.

World Health. J. Hampton. (World Issues Ser.). (Illus.). 48p. (gr. 5 up). Date not set. PLB 15.93 (ISBN 0-86592-281-0). Rourke Corp.

World Health & Population. Nance Fyson. (Today's World 20th Century Ser.). (Illus.). 72p. (gr. 7-12). 1987. 17.95 (ISBN 0-7134-5204-8, Pub. by Batsford England). David & Charles.

World Health & the World Health Organization: A Medical Subject Analysis & Research Index with Bibliography. John C. Bartone. LC 83-71663. 152p. 1985. 34.50 (ISBN 0-88164-020-4); pap. 26.50 (ISBN 0-88164-021-2). ABBE Pubs Assn.

World Health Organization. John M. Starrels. 44p. 1985. pap. 5.00 (ISBN 0-89195-214-4). Heritage Found.

World Health Statistics Annual. Incl. Vol. 1. 1968. 1971. pap. 29.60 (ISBN 92-4-067681-3); Vols. 2 & 3. 1969, 2 vols. 1972-73. Vol. 2. pap. 9.60 (ISBN 92-4-067692-9); Vol. 3. pap. 12.00 (ISBN 92-4-067693-7); Vols. 2 & 3. 1970, 2 vols. 1973-74. Vol. 2. pap. 9.60 (ISBN 92-4-067702-X); Vol. 3. pap. 12.00 (ISBN 92-4-067703-8); Vols. 1-3. 1971, 3 vols. 1975. Vol. 1. pap. 40.00 (ISBN 92-4-067711-9); Vol. 2. pap. 22.40 (ISBN 92-4-067712-7); Vol. 3. pap. 12.80 (ISBN 0-686-16945-X); Vols. 1-3. 1972, 3 vols. 1975-76. Vol. 1. pap. 51.20 (ISBN 92-4-067721-6); Vol. 2. pap. 12.80 (ISBN 92-4-067722-4); Vol. 3. pap. 12.80 (ISBN 92-4-067723-2). pap. World Health.

World Health Statistics Annual: 1973-76, Vol. 1. 1976. pap. 54.40 (ISBN 92-4-067761-5). World Health.

World Health Statistics Annual 1985: Global Overview, Vital Statistics & Life Tables, Environmental Health, Causes of Death. 531p. 1985. pap. 51.00 (ISBN 92-4-067851-4). World Health.

World Health Statistics Annual 1987: Global Review, Evaluation of the Global Strategy for Health for All Vital Statistics & Life Tables, Causes of Death. 692p. 1986. pap. 54.00 (ISBN 92-4-067861-1). World Health.

World Held Hostage: The War Waged by International Terrorism. Desmond McForan. LC 87-4776. 278p. 1987. 29.95 (ISBN 0-312-00835-X). St Martin.

World Historical Plays. August Strindberg. Tr. by Arvid Paulson from Swedish. LC 75-120537. (Library of Scandinavian Literature: Vol. 6). 1970. 8.50x (ISBN 0-89067-017-X). Am Scandinavian.

World History. 3rd ed. William H. McNeill. (Illus.). 1979. 29.95x (ISBN 0-19-502554-7); pap. text ed. 18.95x (ISBN 0-19-502555-5). Oxford U Pr.

World History. B. V. Rao. 466p. 1984. text ed. 30.00x (ISBN 0-86590-808-7, Sterling Pubs India); pap. 15.95x (ISBN 0-86590-315-8). Apt Bks.

World History. Ed. by Kevin Reilly. LC 84-50565. (Selected Syllabi from American College & Universities in History Ser.). 260p. (Orig.). 1985. pap. text ed. 14.50 (ISBN 0-910129-23-1). Wiener Pub Inc.

World History: A Brief Introduction. Joseph Reither. LC 65-17275. Orig. Title: World History at a Glance. (Illus.). 512p. 1973. pap. text ed. 12.95 (ISBN 0-07-051875-6). McGraw.

World History at a Glance see World History: A Brief Introduction.

World History Dates: All the Facts You Need to Know at a Glance. J. Chisholm. (History Handbooks Ser.). (Illus.). 128p. (gr. 6 up). 1987. PLB 14.96 (ISBN 0-88110-232-6); pap. 9.95 (ISBN 0-86020-954-7). EDC.

World History, Eighteen Fifteen to Nineteen Twenty. Eduard Fueter. Tr. by Sidney B. Fay from Ger. LC 79-17754. (Illus.). 1980. Repr. of 1924 ed. lib. bdg. 42.50x (ISBN 0-313-22088-3, FUWH). Greenwood.

World History in Juvenile Books: A Geographical & Chronological Guide. Seymour Metzner. LC 72-11598. 356p. 1973. 22.00 (ISBN 0-8242-0441-7). Wilson.

World History in the Light of Anthroposophy: And As a Foundation for Knowledge of the Human Spirit. new ed. Rudolf Steiner. Tr. by George Adams & Mary Adams. 159p. 1977. 20.00 (ISBN 0-85440-315-9); pap. 11.95 (ISBN 0-85440-316-7). Anthroposophic.

World History in the Twentieth Century. 2nd ed. R. D. Cornwell. (Illus.). 1981. pap. text ed. 14.50x (ISBN 0-582-33075-0). Longman.

World History Made in the Present. Ilija Poplasen. (Illus.). 325p. 1986. 20.00 (ISBN 0-935352-20-1). MIR PA.

World History: Nineteen Hundred to the Present Day. Christopher Leeds. 256p. (Orig.). 1986. pap. text ed. 18.95x (ISBN 0-7121-2002-5). Trans-Atl Phila.

World History of Photography. Naomi Rosenblum. Ed. by Walton Rawls. LC 83-73417. (Illus.). 673p. 1984. 45.00 (ISBN 0-89659-438-6). Abbeville Pr.

World History of Physical Education: Cultural, Philosophical & Comparative. 2nd ed. Deobold B. Van Dalen & Bruce Bennett. 1971. write for info. ref. ed. (ISBN 0-13-967919-7). P-H.

World History of the Twentieth Century Vol. 1: Western Dominance 1900-45. J. A. Grenville. (Illus.). 605p. 1980. 35.00x (ISBN 0-389-20171-5, 06947). B&N Imports.

World History of the Twentieth Century: Vol. 1, Western Dominance, 1900-1945. J. A. Grenville. LC 84-40300. (Illus.). 605p. 1984. pap. text ed. 15.00x (ISBN 0-87451-315-4). U Pr of New Eng.

World History: Patterns of Change & Continuity. Peter N. Stearns. 1986. pap. text ed. 28.95 scp (ISBN 0-06-046386-4, HarpC). Har-Row.

World History Review Text. 2nd ed. Irving Gordon. (gr. 10-12). 1979. text ed. 18.33 (ISBN 0-87720-625-2); pap. text ed. 13.25 (ISBN 0-87720-624-4). AMSCO Sch.

World History: The Destiny-Idea & the Causality-Principle. Oswald Spengler. (Illus.). 167p. 1984. 137.55 (ISBN 0-89901-176-4). Found Class Reprints.

World History 1988-89, Vol. 1. Ed. by David McComb. (Annual Editions Ser.). (Illus.). 256p. 1988. pap. text ed. 9.95 (ISBN 0-87967-708-2). Dushkin Pub.

World History 1988-89, Vol. 2. Ed. by David McComb. (Annual Editions Ser.). (Illus.). 256p. 1988. pap. text ed. 9.95 (ISBN 0-87967-736-8). Dushkin Pub.

World Hoax. Ernest F. Elmhurst. 233p. 1976. pap. 4.50x (ISBN 0-911038-81-7). Noontide.

World Hoax: The Jew. Ernest Elmhurst. 1982. lib. bdg. 69.95 (ISBN 0-87700-328-9). Revisionist Pr.

World Hotel Directory. Ed. by Financial Times Staff. 1986. 95.00 (ISBN 0-912289-65-1); Standing Order. 85.50. St James Pr.

World Housing Survey, 1974. pap. 11.00 (ISBN 92-1-130005-3, E.75.IV.8). UN.

World Human Rights Guide. Charles Humana. LC 85-27584. (Illus.). 354p. 1986. 35.00 (ISBN 0-8160-1404-3). Facts On File.

World Hunger: A Challenge to American Policy. Sol M. Linowitz. LC 80-85486. (Headline Ser.: No. 252). (Illus.). 64p. 1980. pap. 4.00 (ISBN 0-87124-065-3). Foreign Policy.

World Hunger: A Neo-Malthusian Perspective. Mitchell H. Kellman. LC 86-21221. 261p. 1987. lib. bdg. 38.95 (ISBN 0-275-92247-2, C2247). Praeger.

World Hunger & Moral Obligation. William Aiken & Hugh LaFollette. 224p. 1977. pap. text ed. write for info. (ISBN 0-13-967950-2). P-H.

World Hunger and Social Justice. Ed. by Gary E. McCuen. (Ideas In Conflict Ser.). (Illus.). 176p. 1986. lib. bdg. 11.95 (ISBN 0-86596-055-0). G E McCuen Pubns.

World Hunger & the World Economy: And Other Essays in Development Economics. Keith B. Griffin. 525p. 1987. 49.50 (ISBN 0-8419-1128-2); pap. 19.95 (ISBN 0-8419-1129-0). Holmes & Meier.

World Hunger: The Responsibility of Christian Education. Suzanne C. Toton. LC 81-16906. 224p. (Orig.). 1982. pap. 7.95 (ISBN 0-88344-716-9). Orbis Bks.

World Hunger: Twelve Myths. Frances M. Lappe & Joseph Collins. (Food First Ser.). 192p. 1986. pap. 17.95 (ISBN 0-394-55626-7). Grove.

World Hunger: Twelve Myths. Frances M. Lappe & Joseph Collins. (Food First Ser.). 192p. pap. 8.95 (ISBN 0-394-62297-9, Ever). Grove.

World Hunger: Twelve Myths. Frances M. Lappe & Joseph Collins. 208p. 1986. 17.95 (ISBN 0-317-66242-2); pap. 8.95 (ISBN 0-317-66243-0). Inst Food & Develop.

World Hydrocarbon Markets-Current Status, Projected Prospects & Future Trends: Proceedings of the International Workshop, Mexico City, April 1982. International Workshop, World Hydrocarbon Markets & M. S. Wionczek. (Illus.). 225p. 1982. 48.00 (ISBN 0-08-029962-8). Pergamon.

World Hypotheses: A Study in Evidence. Stephen C. Pepper. 1970. pap. 11.95x (ISBN 0-520-00994-0). U of Cal Pr.

World Illiteracy at Mid-Century, a Statistical Study. UNESCO. 1970. Repr. of 1957 ed. lib. bdg. 35.00x (ISBN 0-8371-3405-6, UNWI). Greenwood.

World Immigration. Maurice R. Davie. LC 82-48299. (World Economy Ser.). 588p. 1983. lib. bdg. 72.00 (ISBN 0-8240-5354-0). Garland Pub.

World in a Classroom. Chris Searle. (Education Ser.). 288p. 1980. 16.00 (ISBN 0-904613-45-3); pap. 4.45 (ISBN 0-904613-46-1). Writers & Readrs.

World in a Frame: What We See in Films. Leo Braudy. LC 84-225. xii, 274p. 1984. pap. 9.95x (ISBN 0-226-07155-3). U of Chicago Pr.

World in Amber. A. Orr. 1985. 14.95 (ISBN 0-312-94459-4, Dist. by St. Martin). Bluejay Bks.

World in Amber. A. Orr. 224p. 1986. pap. 2.95 (ISBN 0-8125-4800-0, Dist. by Warner Pub. Services & St. Martin's Press). Tor Bks.

World in an Olive Leaf. Cynthia Pickard. 48p. (Orig.). 1985. 25.00 (ISBN 0-931757-26-6); pap. 15.00 (ISBN 0-931757-27-4). Pterodactyl Pr.

World in Between: Christian Healing & the Struggle for Spiritual Survival. Emmanuel Milingo. Ed. by Mona Macmillan. 144p. (Orig.). 1985. pap. 5.95 (ISBN 0-88344-354-6). Orbis Bks.

World in Crisis? Geographical Perspectives. Ed. by R. J. Johnston & P. J. Taylor. 304p. 1986. text ed. 45.00x (ISBN 0-631-13466-2); pap. text ed. 15.95x (ISBN 0-631-13524-3). Basil Blackwell.

World in Crucible: Nineteen Fourteen to Nineteen Nineteen. Bernadotte E. Schmitt & Harold C. Bedeler. LC 83-48384. (Rise of Modern Europe Ser.). (Illus.). 553p. 1984. 19.50i (ISBN 0-06-015268-0, HarpT). Har-Row.

World in Crucible, Nineteen Fourteen to Nineteen Nineteen. Bernadotte E. Schmitt & Harold C. Vedeler. LC 84-48384. (Rise of Modern Europe Ser.). (Illus.). 608p. 1985. pap. 9.95 (ISBN 0-06-091197-2, CN1197, PL). Har-Row.

World in Depression, Nineteen Twenty-Nine to Nineteen Thirty-Nine. rev. & enl. ed. Charles P. Kindleberger. (History of the World Economy in the Twentieth Century: Vol. 4). 1986. 45.00 (ISBN 0-520-05591-8); pap. 10.95 (ISBN 0-520-05592-6). U of Cal Pr.

World in Falseface. George J. Nathan. LC 75-120099. 326p. 1972. 22.50 (ISBN 0-8386-7963-3). Fairleigh Dickinson.

World in Figures. Ed. by Economist Staff. (Illus.). 296p. 1985. 69.95 (ISBN 0-528-81049-9). Rand McNally.

World in Figures. 3rd ed. 294p. 1981. 72.00x (ISBN 0-85058-046-3, Pub. by Economist). Gale.

World in Figures. (Reference Bks.). 1750p. 1988. lib. bdg. 65.00 (ISBN 0-8161-8954-4). G K Hall.

World in Literature, 2 vols. rev. ed. George K. Anderson & Robert Warnock. 1967. text ed. write for info. Vol. 1 (ISBN 0-673-05636-8). Vol. 2 (ISBN 0-673-05637-6). Scott F.

World in March Nineteen Thirty Nine. Ed. by Arnold J. Toynbee & Frank T. Ashton-Gwatkin. 60.00 (ISBN 0-685-13639-6); pap. 54.00 (ISBN 0-384-61134-6). Johnson Repr.

World in Miniature: Engravings of the German Little Masters, 1500-1550. Ed. by Stephen H. Goddard. (Illus.). 256p. (Orig.). 1988. pap. 19.95 (ISBN 0-913689-26-2). Spencer Muse Art.

World in Morning. Lewis Banci. 1978. pap. 1.95 (ISBN 0-505-51229-7, Pub. by Tower Bks). Leisure NY.

World in My Garden. Polly Park. (Illus.). 120p. 1988. 24.95 (ISBN 0-86417-180-3, Pub. by Kangaroo Pr). Intl Spec Bk.

World Mineral Exploration: Trends & Economic Issues. Ed. by John E. Tilton et al. 500p. 1988. 60.00 (ISBN 0-915707-28-4). Resources Future.

World Mineral Trends & U. S. Supply Problems. Leonard L. Fischman. 535p. 1981. 30.00 (ISBN 0-317-60312-4). RFF Assocs.

World Mineral Trends & U. S. Supply Problems. Leonard L. Fischman. xxxiv, 535p. 1981. 30.00 (ISBN 0-8018-2491-5). Resources Future.

World Minerals & World Politics. Charles K. Leith. LC 74-113286. 1970. Repr. of 1931 ed. 23.50 (ISBN 0-8046-1322-2, Pub. by Kennikat). Assoc Faculty Pr.

World Mining & Metals Technology. Ed. by Alfred Weiss. LC 76-19748. (Illus.). 1976. text ed. 10.00x (ISBN 0-89520-036-8). Soc Mining Eng.

World Mission: An Analysis of the World Christian Movement (Part I, the Biblical--Historical Foundation) Ed. by Jonathan Lewis. (Illus.). 144p. (Orig.). 1987. wkbk. 6.95 (ISBN 0-87808-208-5). William Carey Lib.

World Mission: An Analysis of the World Christian Movement (Part II, the Strategic Dimension) Ed. by Jonathan Lewis. (Illus.). 186p. (Orig.). 1987. mannual 6.95 (ISBN 0-87808-209-3). William Carey Lib.

World Mission: An Analysis of the World Christian Movement (Part III, Cross Cultural Considerations) Ed. by Jonathan Lewis. (Illus.). 170p. (Orig.). 1987. mannual 6.95 (ISBN 0-87808-210-7). William Carey Lib.

World Mission & World Survival. E. Luther Copeland. LC 84-14963. 1985. pap. 5.95 (ISBN 0-8054-6335-6). Broadman.

World Missions: Building Bridges or Barriers. Ed. by Theodore Williams. 101p. (Orig.). 1979. pap. 2.00 (ISBN 0-936444-02-9). World Evang Fellow.

World Missions Today. Terry C. Hulbert. LC 78-68233. 96p. 1979. pap. text ed. 5.95 (ISBN 0-910566-16-X); looseleaf instr's guide with binder 9.95 (ISBN 0-910566-28-3). Evang Tchr.

World Modeling: A Dialogue. Ed. by C. W. Churchman & R. O. Mason. (North-Holland - TIMS Studies in the Management Sciences: Vol. 2). 164p. 1976. pap. 32.50 (ISBN 0-7204-0388-X, North-Holland). Elsevier.

World Modeling: A Dialogue, Vol. 2. Ed. by Churchman & Mason. (TIMS Studies in the Management Sciences). 179p. 24.50 (ISBN 0-318-14464-6). Inst Mgmt Sci.

World Modernization: The Limits of Convergence. W. E. Moore. LC 79-14769. 1979. 27.95 (ISBN 0-444-99062-3, MWM/, Pub. by Elsevier). Greenwood.

World Monetary & Financial System: Issues for Reforms. N. A. Sarma & V. K. Bhalla. 1987. 17.50x (ISBN 81-7017-227-6, Pub. by Abhinav India). South Asia Bks.

World Monetary Crisis. Peter Coffey. LC 74-14711. 128p. 1974. 25.00 (ISBN 0-312-89180-6). St Martin.

World Monetary Equilibrium: International Monetary Theory in an Historical-Institutional Context. John E. Floyd. (Illus.). 224p. 1985. text ed. 28.95 (ISBN 0-8122-7983-2). U of Pa Pr.

World Monetary Reform: Plans & Issues. Ed. by Herbert G. Grubel. 1963. 40.00x (ISBN 0-8047-0169-5). Stanford U Pr.

World Money & Securities Market. Lynette J. Kemp. (Euromoney Ser.). 486p. (Orig.). 1984. pap. 115.00 (ISBN 0-903121-66-2, Pub. by Woodhead-Faulkner). Longwood Pub Group.

World Money & Securities Markets. 450p. 1984. pap. 120.00 (ISBN 0-8002-4071-5). Intl Pubns Serv.

World More Attractive. Irving Howe. LC 70-134096. (Essay Index Reprint Ser). 1963. 18.00 (ISBN 0-8369-1958-0). Ayer Co Pubs.

World More Human: A Church More Christian. Ed. by George Devine. 204p. 1984. pap. text ed. 10.00 (ISBN 0-8191-3851-7, College Theo Soc). U Pr of Amer.

World Motor Vehicle Data Book. 1986. 35.00 (ISBN 0-317-05087-7). Motor Veh Man.

World Museum Publications 1982: A Directory of Art & Cultural Museums, Their Publications & Audio-Visual Materials. 711p. 1982. 125.00x (ISBN 0-8352-1444-3). Bowker.

World Music: A Sourcebook for Teachers. Lynne Jessup. (Illus.). 64p. (Orig.). 1988. pap. price not set (ISBN 0-937203-19-X). World Music Pr.

World Mythology. Donna Rosenberg. 552p. pap. 14.95 (ISBN 0-8442-5548-3, NTC Busn Bks). Natl Textbk.

World Natural Gas-Two Thousand. 232p. 1978. 180.00 (ISBN 0-686-76143-X). Barrows Co.

World Naval History of the Late Eighteenth Century, 2 vols. Admiram A Mahan. (Illus.). 366p. 1986. Set. 267.75 (ISBN 0-86722-133-X). Inst Econ Pol.

World News Prism: Changing Media, Clashing Ideologies. 2nd ed. William A. Hachten. 162p. 1987. pap. text ed. 12.95x (ISBN 0-8138-1579-7). Iowa St U Pr.

World Newspaper Industry. Peter Dunnett. 288p. 1988. text ed. 45.00 (ISBN 0-7099-0834-2, Pub. by Croom Helm UK). Routledge Chapman & Hall.

World Next Door. Brad Ferguson. 320p. 1989. pap. price not set (ISBN 0-8125-3795-5). Tor Bks.

World Nitrogen Survey. William F. Sheldrick. (Technical Paper: No. 59). 254p. 1987. 12.00 (ISBN 0-8213-0895-5, BK0895). World Bank.

World Non-Ferrous Metal Production & Prices, 1700-1976. Christopher J. Schmitz. 432p. 1979. 35.00x (ISBN 0-7146-3109-4, F Cass Co). Biblio Dist.

World Nuclear Directory. 7th ed. C. W. Wilson. 100p. 1985. 220.00x (ISBN 0-582-90025-5, Pub. by Longman). Gale.

World Nuclear Directory. 8th ed. 1988. 250.00 (Pub. by Longman). Gale.

World Nuclear Energy International Conference: Proceedings. 266p. 44.00 (ISBN 0-317-33042-X, 140001). Am Nuclear Soc.

World Nuclear Energy: Toward a Bargain of Confidence. Ed. by Ian Smart. LC 82-179. 416p. 1982. text ed. 42.50x (ISBN 0-8018-2652-7). Johns Hopkins.

World Nutrition & Nutrition Education. H. M. Sinclair & G. R. Howat. (Illus.). 272p. (Co-published with Oxford University Press, Oxford). 1980. 28.50 (ISBN 92-3-101736-5, U1057, UNESCO). UNIPUB.

World Nutritional Determinants. Ed. by G. H. Bourne. (World Review of Nutrition & Dietetics Ser.: Vol. 45). (Illus.). x, 226p. 1984. 132.00 (ISBN 3-8055-3948-7). S Karger.

World Ocean. 2nd ed. William Anikouchine & Richard Sternberg. (Illus.). 512p. 1981. write for info. (ISBN 0-13-967778-X). P-H.

World Ocean Atlas: Arctic Ocean, Vol. 3. Ed. by Sergei G. Gorshkov. LC 78-40616. 184p. 1983. 485.00 (ISBN 0-08-028735-2). Pergamon.

World Ocean Atlas, Vol. 2: Atlantic & Indian Oceans. S. G. Gorshkov. 3504p. 1979. 475.00 (ISBN 0-08-021953-5). Pergamon.

World Oceans: An Introduction. Alun C. Duxbury & Alison Duxbury. (Illus.). 475p. 1984. write for info. (ISBN 0-201-11348-1); write for info. instr's manual (ISBN 0-201-11364-3). Addison-Wesley.

World Oestridae (Diptera), Mammals & Continental Drift. N. Papavero. (Series Entomologica: No. 14). 1977. lib. bdg. 45.00 (ISBN 90-6193-124-X, Pub. by Junk Pubs Netherlands). Kluwer Academic.

World of a Falcon. Virginia Harrison. LC 87-42611. (Where Animals Live Ser.). (Illus.). 32p. (gr. 2-3). 1988. PLB 9.95 (ISBN 1-55532-308-1). Stevens Inc.

World of a Hasidic Master: Levi Yitzhak of Berditchev. Samuel H. Dresner. 264p. 1986. pap. 8.95 (ISBN 0-933503-59-8). Shapolsky Pubs.

World of a Jellyfish. David Shale & Jennifer Coldrey. LC 86-5704. (Where Animals Live Ser.). (Illus.). 32p. (gr. 2-3). 1986. 9.95 (ISBN 1-55532-073-2). Stevens Inc.

World of a Market. Mark Tobey. LC 81-11524. (Illus.). 80p. 1981. pap. 12.50 (ISBN 0-295-95843-X). U of Wash Pr.

World of a Renaissance Jew: The Life & Thought of Abraham Ben Mordecai Farissol. David Ruderman. 1981. 20.00x (ISBN 0-87820-405-9). Ktav.

World of Aldus Manutius: Business & Scholarship in Renaissance Venice. M. J. Lowry. LC 78-58631. (Illus.). 304p. 1979. 49.50x (ISBN 0-8014-1214-5). Cornell U Pr.

World of Alexander Kins. Smith. 192p. 1985. 19.95 (ISBN 0-317-64864-0). Collector Bks.

World of Alexander-Kins. Patricia Smith. (Illus.). 208p. 1985. 19.95 (ISBN 0-89145-304-0). Collector Bks.

World of Allah. David Duncan. 30.00x (ISBN 0-86685-370-7). Intl Bk Ctr.

World of Allah. David D. Duncan. 1982. 40.00 (ISBN 0-395-32504-8). HM.

World of Amish Quilts. Rachel Pellman & Kenneth Pellman. LC 84-80651. (Illus.). 128p. 1984. pap. 15.95 deluxe ed. (ISBN 0-934672-22-9). Good Bks PA.

World of Amish Quilts. Rachel Pellman & Kenneth Pellman. LC 84-80651. (Illus.). 128p. Repr. of 1984 ed. 24.95 (ISBN 0-934672-48-2). Good Bks PA.

World of Amphibians. B. F. Sergeev. 188p. 1986. pap. 3.95 (ISBN 0-8285-3252-4, Pub. by Mir Pubs USSR). Imported Pubns.

World of Amphibians & Reptiles. Milli U. Tanara. Tr. by Simon Pleasance. LC 79-1441. (Abbeville Press Encyclopedia of Natural Science). (Illus.). 256p. 1979. 13.95 (ISBN 0-89659-037-2). Abbeville Pr.

World of Ancient Times. Carl Roebuck. (Illus.). 758p. 1974. pap. text ed. write for info. (ISBN 0-02-402700-6, Pub. by Scribner). Macmillan.

World of Animals: The San Diego Zoo & the Wild Animal Park. Bill Bruns. LC 83-7289. 288p. 1983. 35.00 (ISBN 0-8109-1601-0). Abrams.

World of Armand Hammer. John Bryson. LC 85-15115. (Illus.). 1985. 35.00 (ISBN 0-8109-1093-4). Abrams.

World of Art. Paul Weiss. LC 61-5168. (Arcturus Books Paperbacks). 204p. 1964. pap. 6.95x (ISBN 0-8093-0112-1). S Ill U Pr.

World of Art & Museums. Carl Zigrosser. 309p. 1975. 20.00 (ISBN 0-87982-014-4). Art Alliance.

World of Art Deco. Bevis Hillier. (Illus.). 224p. 1981. pap. 14.50 (ISBN 0-525-47680-6). Dutton.

World of Arthur Boyd Houghton. Paul Hogarth. 144p. 1982. 95.00x (ISBN 0-900406-75-5, Pub. by Fraser Bks). State Mutual Bk.

World of Asia. new ed. Akira Iriye et al. LC 78-67277. (Orig.). 1979. pap. text ed. 17.95x (ISBN 0-88273-500-4). Forum Pr IL.

World of Asif Currimbhoy. Faubion Bowers. 4.80 (ISBN 0-89253-664-0); flexible cloth 3.00 (ISBN 0-89253-665-9). Ind-US Inc.

World of Atget. Berenice Abbott. (Illus.). 256p. 1980. 27.50 (ISBN 0-8180-1415-6). Horizon.

World of Athens: An Introduction to Classical Athenian Culture. Joint Association of Classical Teachers. (Joint Association of Classical Teachers' Greek Course Background Bks.). (Illus.). 416p. 1984. 54.50 (ISBN 0-521-26789-7); pap. 14.95 (ISBN 0-521-27389-7). Cambridge U Pr.

World of Baking. Dolores Casella. 1968. 12.95 (ISBN 0-87250-027-6); pap. 9.95 (ISBN 0-87250-040-3). D White.

World of Ballet. Robin May. Ed. by Wendy Barish. 96p. (gr. 3-7). 1984. 10.95 (ISBN 0-671-50072-4). Wanderer Bks.

World of Bamboo. Shinji Takama. Tr. by D. T. Ooka from Japanese. (Illus.). 237p. (Orig.). 1983. 75.00 (ISBN 0-89346-203-9). Heian Intl.

World of Barbara Pym. Janice Rossen. LC 86-24810. 208p. 1987. 19.95 (ISBN 0-312-00090-1). St Martin.

World of Barbie Dolls. Paris Manos & Susan Manos. (Illus.). 144p. 1986. pap. 9.95 (ISBN 0-89145-229-X). Collector Bks.

World of Baroque & Classical Musical Instruments. Jeremy Montagu. LC 78-65227. (Illus.). 136p. 1979. 39.95 (ISBN 0-87951-089-7). Overlook Pr.

World of Bats. Alvin Novick. (Illus.). 70.00. Brown Bk.

World of Bells, No.1. Dorothy M. Anthony. (Illus.). 50p. 1980. Repr. of 1971 ed. mechanical bdg. 8.95 (ISBN 0-9607944-1-7). Anthony D M.

World of Bells, No. 2. Dorothy M. Anthony. (Illus.). 50p. 1980. Repr. of 1974 ed. mechanical bdg. 8.95 (ISBN 0-9607944-2-5). Anthony D M.

World of Bells, No.4. Dorothy M. Anthony. (Illus.). 50p. 1980. mechanical bdg. 7.95 (ISBN 0-9607944-0-9). Anthony D M.

World of Bells, Vol. 5. Dorothy M. Anthony. (Illus.). 50p. 1984. mechanical bdg. 8.95 (ISBN 0-9607944-3-3). Anthony D M.

World of Biology. P. William Davis & Eldra P. Solomon. 872p. 1986. text ed. 42.75 (ISBN 0-03-059997-0); student guide 16.00 (ISBN 0-03-059998-9). SCP.

World of Biology. Thomas G. Overmire. LC 84-14998. 579p. 1986. write for info. (ISBN 0-471-88000-0); write for info. study guide 204p. (ISBN 0-471-81511-X). Wiley.

World of Bionics. Alvin Silverstein & Virginia B. Silverstein. (Illus.). (gr. 5 up). 1979. 8.95 (ISBN 0-416-30221-1, NO. 0140). Routledge Chapman & Hall.

World of Birds. Gianfranco Bologna. Tr. by Simon Pleasance. LC 79-1190. (Abbeville Press Encyclopedia of Natural Science). (Illus.). 256p. 1979. 13.95 (ISBN 0-89659-034-8). Abbeville Pr.

World of Black Singles: Changing Patterns of Male-Female Relations. Robert Staples. LC 80-1025. (Contributions in Afro-American & African Studies: No. 57). xxi, 259p. 1981. lib. bdg. 35.00 (ISBN 0-313-22478-1, SBS/). Greenwood.

World of Black Singles: Changing Patterns of Male-Female Relations. Robert Staples. LC 80-1025. (Contributions in Afro-American & African Studies: No. 57). (Illus.). xxi, 259p. 1982. pap. 12.95 (ISBN 0-313-23609-7, SBSPB). Greenwood.

World of Books. 2nd. rev. ed. Dorothy S. Brown. 70p. 1988. 7.50 (ISBN 0-939791-32-3). Tchrs Eng Spkrs.

World of Books & Information: Essays in Honor of Lord Dainton. Ed. by Maurice Line. 1987. 37.50 (ISBN 0-7123-0125-9, Pub. by British Lib). Longwood Pub Group.

World of Breads. Dolores Casella. (Illus.). 1966. D White.

World of Bu-Di. Cecilia J. Au-Yeung. (Illus.). 208p. (Chinese & Eng.). 1988. 40.00 (ISBN 962-7018-12-0, Pub. by Chpsticks HK). Seven Hills Bks.

World of Buddhism: Buddhist Monks & Nuns in Society & Culture. Ed. by Heinz Bechert & Richard Gombrich. LC 84-8125. (Illus.). 308p. 1984. 49.95 (ISBN 0-87196-982-3). Facts on File.

World of Buddhist Awakening. Takamaro Shigaraki. 96p. 1983. pap. 6.95. Buddhist Study.

World of Burmese Women. Mi Mi Khaing. (Third World Studies). (Illus.). 208p. 1984. 32.50x (ISBN 0-86232-179-4, Pub. by Zed Pr England); pap. 12.50 (ISBN 0-86232-180-8, Pub. by Zed Pr England). Humanities.

World of Business. 2nd ed. T. Murphy. 593p. 1988. 31.50 (ISBN 0-471-79708-1). Wiley.

World of Business. Dan Steinhoff. (Illus.). 1979. text ed. 39.95 (ISBN 0-07-061134-3). McGraw.

World of Business. Wichita State University Staff & Gerald H. Graham. 1985. text ed. write for info. (ISBN 0-201-11440-2, 150A13); write for info. instr's. manual (ISBN 0-201-11441-0); write for info. student activity guide (ISBN 0-201-11442-9). Addison Wesley.

World of Butterflies. David Saintsing. LC 86-5706. (Where Animals Live Ser.). (Illus.). 32p. (gr. 2-3). 1986. 9.95 (ISBN 1-55532-072-4). Stevens Inc.

World of C. Wright Mills. Herbert Aptheker. LC 60-50975. 1976. Repr. of 1960 ed. 24.00 (ISBN 0-527-03003-1). Kraus Repr.

World of Cactus & Succulents. Ed. by Ortho Books Staff. LC 77-89689. (Illus.). 1978. pap. 6.95 (ISBN 0-917102-59-2). Ortho.

World of Can Themba: Selected Writings. Essop Patel. (Staffrider Ser.: No. 18). 224p. 1985. pap. 12.95 (ISBN 0-86975-145-X, Pub. by Ravan Pr). Ohio U Pr.

World of Canadian Wine. John Schreiner. (Illus.). 286p. 12.95 (ISBN 0-295-96301-8). U of Wash Pr.

World of Canadian Writing: Critiques & Recollections. George Woodcock. 304p. 1980. 20.00x (ISBN 0-295-95721-2). U of Wash Pr.

World of Captain John Smith. Genevieve Foster. LC 59-11853. (Hudson River Editon Ser.). (Illus.). (gr. 5-11). 1978. Repr. of 1959 ed. lib. rep. ed. 25.00 (ISBN 0-684-15726-8, ScribJ). Scribner.

World of Carl Larsson. Bo Lindwall & Hans-Curt Koster. LC 84-152789. (Illus.). 196p. (Orig.). 1982. 39.95 (ISBN 0-914676-93-8). Green Tiger Pr.

World of Cartooning: A Complete Guide. Bill Barry. Ed. by Joan Harryman. (Illus.). 128p. (Orig.). 1988. pap. 19.95 (ISBN 0-944099-02-5). CB Pubns.

World of Cartooning: How Caricatures Develop. Mike Peters. Ed. by Marilyn Jarvis. (Illus.). 128p. (Orig.). 1985. pap. 9.95 (ISBN 0-913428-55-8). Landfall Pr.

World of CB Radio. rev ed. Long et al. LC 87-70878. (Illus.). 240p. 1987. pap. 9.95 (ISBN 0-913990-53-1). Book Pub Co.

World of Ceramics: Masterpieces from the Cleveland Museum of Art. Jenifer Neils. LC 82-1308. (Illus.). 176p. (Orig.). 1982. 3.95x (ISBN 0-910386-68-4, Pub. by Cleveland Mus of Art). Ind U Pr.

World of Ceramics: Masterpieces from the Cleveland Museum of Art. Jenifer Neils. 166p. 1982. 60.00x (ISBN 0-317-45331-9, Pub. by Han-Shan Tang Ltd). State Mutual Bk.

World of Chaim Potok see Studies in American Jewish Literature: Isaac Bashevis Singer.

World of Change: Britain in the Early Modern Age 1450-1700. Rosemary Kelly. LC 87-50950. (Illus.). 220p. (YA) (gr. 11 up). 1988. pap. 12.95 (ISBN 0-85950-249-X, Pub. by S Thornes); tchr's. guide 45.00 (ISBN 0-85950-617-7). Dufour.

World of Charles Dickens. Angus Wilson. (Illus.). 302p. 1985. pap. 10.95 (ISBN 0-89733-172-9). Academy Chi Pubs.

World of Cheese. Evan Jones. LC 76-13697. (Illus.). 1978. pap. 7.95 (ISBN 0-394-73622-2). Knopf.

World of Cheese. Evan Jones. 1976. 12.50 (ISBN 0-394-49755-4). Knopf.

World of Chickens. Jennifer Coldrey. LC 86-5718. (Where Animals Live Ser.). (Illus.). 32p. (gr. 2-3). 1986. 9.95 (ISBN 1-55532-071-6). Stevens Inc.

World of Chiyogami: Hand-Printed Patterned Papers of Japan. Ann Herring. LC 86-40438. (Illus.). 96p. 1987. 19.95 (ISBN 0-87011-813-7). Kodansha.

World of Choice: Careers & You - Student Workbook. Ralp Ressler. LC 77-4182. (Illus.). (YA) (gr. 9-12). 1978. pap. 9.95 (ISBN 0-88280-050-7); tchr's guide 14.95 (ISBN 0-88280-051-5). ETC Pubns.

World of Christopher Robin. A. A. Milne. (gr. 1-4). 1958. boxed with "World of Pooh" 29.95 (ISBN 0-525-43348-1). Dutton.

World of Christopher Robin. A. A. Milne. (Illus.). (ps up). 1988. 14.95 (ISBN 0-525-44448-3, 01451-440). Dutton.

World of Christy, 4 bks. Maud Johnson. Incl. I'm Christy; Christy's Choice; Christy's Love; Christy's Senior Year. (Orig.). (gr. 11 up). 1984. Boxed Set. pap. 9.00 (ISBN 0-590-00661-4, Wildfire). Scholastic Inc.

World of Cockatoos. Karl Diefenbach. (Illus.). 208p. 1985. text ed. 24.95 (ISBN 0-86622-034-8, H-1072). TFH Pubns.

World of Coins & Coin Collecting. David L. Ganz. (Illus.). 288p. 1985. 22.50 (ISBN 0-684-18238-6, ScribT). Scribner.

World of Col. John W. Thomason, USMC. Martha A. Turner. 400p. 1984. 19.95 (ISBN 0-89015-439-2). Eakin Pr.

World of Color. Sylvia R. Tester. LC 76-13629. (Illus.). (ps-3). 1976. 7.45 (ISBN 0-913778-55-9). Childs World.

World of Computers. Marilyn Schnake. (Illus.). 579p. 1985. text ed. 37.25 (ISBN 0-314-85295-6). West Pub.

World of Computing. Ronald Anderson & David R. Sullivan. 1988. 38.50 (ISBN 0-395-43554-4). HM.

World of Construction. Donald G. Lux et al. (gr. 7-9). 1982. text ed. 23.20 (ISBN 0-02-668500-0); tchrs' guide 44.64 (ISBN 0-02-668530-2); lab. manual no. 1 8.80 (ISBN 0-02-668510-8); lab. manual no. 2 8.80 (ISBN 0-02-668520-5); filmstrip set 667.80 (ISBN 0-02-668540-X); transparency set o.p. 160.00 (ISBN 0-686-36900-9). Glencoe Bennett & McKnight.

World of Cosmetology: A Professional Text. Sylvia Franco et al. LC 79-20678. (Illus.). 512p. 1980. text ed. 33.96 (ISBN 0-07-021791-2). McGraw.

World of Count Basie. Stanley Dance. (Quality Paperbacks Ser.). (Illus.). xxii, 399p. 1985. pap. 10.95 (ISBN 0-306-80245-7). Da Capo.

World of Countertrade. 250p. 1983. 1250.00 (ISBN 0-318-00537-9). Busn Trend.

World of Courtesans. Moti Chandra. 1974. 15.00x (ISBN 0-7069-0082-0). Intl Bk Dist.

World of Crabs. Jennifer Coldrey. LC 85-30294. (Where Animals Live Ser.). (Illus.). 32p. (gr. 2-3). 1986. 9.95 (ISBN 1-55532-063-5). Stevens Inc.

World of Credit. David B. Triemert. 312p. 1988. 19.95 (ISBN 0-942731-00-X). Papermate Pub.

World of Cross Stitch. Masano Onoue. (Illus.). 100p. (Orig.). 1983. pap. 6.95 (ISBN 0-87040-558-6). Japan Pubns USA.

World of Dance. Melvin Berger. LC 78-14498. (Illus.). (YA) (gr. 7 up). 1978. 16.95 (ISBN 0-87599-221-8). S G Phillips.

World of Daniel O'Connell. Ed. by Donal McCartney. (Illus.). 240p. 1980. pap. 8.95 (ISBN 0-85342-589-2, Pub. by Mercier Pr Ireland). Irish Bks Media.

World of Dante: Essays on Dante & His Times. Cecil Grayson. (Illus.). 1980. text ed. 42.00x (ISBN 0-19-815760-6). Oxford U Pr.

World of Dante: Six Studies in Language & Thought. Ed. by Stanley B. Chandler & J. A. Molinaro. LC 66-7811. 1966. pap. 35.80 (ISBN 0-317-09697-4, 2020466). Bks Demand UMI.

World of De Grazia: An Artist of the American Southwest. Harry Redl & Buck Saunders. LC 81-67693. (Illus.). 200p. 1981. 49.50 (ISBN 0-940402-00-9). Chrysalis.

World of Deer. David Saintsing. LC 87-6539. (Where Animals Live Ser.). (Illus.). 32p. (gr. 2-3). 1987. PLB 9.95 (ISBN 1-55532-302-2). Stevens Inc.

World of Desserts & Delicacies from Solo. LC 76-5972. 1976. pap. 1.95 (ISBN 0-87502-049-6). Benjamin Co.

World of Difference. Barbara Johnson. LC 86-46286. 256p. 1987. text ed. 24.50x (ISBN 0-8018-2651-9). Johns Hopkins.

World of Difference. Barbara Johnson. LC 86-46286. 240p. 1988. pap. 9.95x (ISBN 0-8018-3745-6). Johns Hopkins.

World of Difference. Heather McHugh. 1981. 9.95 (ISBN 0-395-30231-5); pap. 5.95 (ISBN 0-395-30232-3). HM.

World of Difference: Following Christ Beyond Your Cultural Walls. Thom Hopler. LC 81-57818. 192p. (Orig.). 1981. pap. 7.95 (ISBN 0-87784-747-9); pap. 1.95 study guide (ISBN 0-87784-802-5). Inter-Varsity.

World of Difference: Gender Roles in Perspective. Esther R. Greenglass. 350p. 1982. pap. write for info. (ISBN 0-471-79949-1). Wiley.

World of Dinosaurs. Richard Moody. LC 77-73208. (Illus.). (gr. 4-8). 1977. (G&D); PLB 3.99 (ISBN 0-448-13438-1). Putnam Pub Group.

World of Doberman Pinschers. Anna K. Nicholas. (Illus.). 640p. 1986. 49.95 (ISBN 0-86622-123-9, H-1082). TFH Pubns.

World of Don Camillo. Giovanni Guareschi. 576p. 1982. 20.95 (ISBN 0-575-02933-1, Pub. by Gollancz England). David & Charles.

World of Don Quixote. Richard L. Predmore. LC 67-20879. pap. 36.80 (ISBN 0-317-29791-0, 2017010). Bks Demand UMI.

World of Dragonflies. Virginia Harrison. LC 87-42610. (Where Animals Live Ser.). (Illus.). 32p. (gr. 2-3). 1988. PLB 9.95 (ISBN 1-55532-310-3). Stevens Inc.

World of Dreams. Havelock Ellis. 288p. 1981. Repr. of 1922 ed. lib. bdg. 40.00 (ISBN 0-89987-208-5). Darby Bks.

World of Dreams. Havelock Ellis. LC 75-43879. (Illus.). 300p. 1976. Repr. of 1922 ed. 42.00x (ISBN 0-8103-3780-0). Gale.

World of Dreams. Lu Wenfu. Tr. by Yu Fanqin & Ralph Lake. 248p. (Orig.). 1986. pap. 5.95x (ISBN 0-8351-1601-8). China Bks.

World of Duke Ellington. Stanley Dance. LC 80-29358. (Quality Paperbacks Ser.). xii, 311p. 1980. pap. 9.95 (ISBN 0-306-80136-1). Da Capo.

World of Dunnet Landing: A Sarah Orne Jewett Collection. Sarah O. Jewett. Ed. by David Green. 12.00 (ISBN 0-8446-2159-5). Peter Smith.

World of Dylan Thomas. Clark Emery. LC 61-21742. 1962. pap. 15.95x (ISBN 0-87024-308-X). U of Miami Pr.

World of Earl Hines. Stanley Dance. LC 82-25252. (Quality Paperbacks Ser.). (Illus.). 334p. 1983. pap. 10.95 (ISBN 0-306-80182-5). Da Capo.

World of Electronic Switching. J. G. Pearce. (Illus.). 140p. 8.00 (ISBN 0-317-06294-8). Intertec IL.

World of Electronics, 4 Bks. Griffin & Beale. (Electronic World Ser.). (gr. 4-8). 12.95 (ISBN 0-86020-643-2). EDC.

World of Elia: Charles Lamb's Essayistic Romanticism. Fred V. Randel. (National University Publications Literary Criticism Ser.). 1975. 21.95 (ISBN 0-8046-9118-5, Pub. by Kennikat). Assoc Faculty Pr.

World of Ellen G. White. Ed. by Gary Land et al. 288p. 1987. 16.95 (ISBN 0-8280-0395-5). Review & Herald.

World of Emotions: Clinical Studies of Affects & Their Expression. Ed. by Charles W. Socarides. LC 77-12735. 638p. 1977. text ed. 47.50x (ISBN 0-8236-6867-3). Intl Univs Pr.

World of Eric Lim. C. Ray Wylie. (Illus.). 128p. 1987. 8.95 (ISBN 0-682-40356-3). Exposition-Phoenix.

World of Europe, 2 vols. Neil J. Hackett et al. 1973. pap. text ed. 11.95x ea.; Vol. 1. (ISBN 0-88334-060-7); Vol. 2. (ISBN 0-88334-061-5). Ind Sch Pr.

World of Europe Since Eighteen Fifteen, Vol. 3. David H. Pinkney. LC 78-67276. 1979. pap. text ed. 12.95x (ISBN 0-88273-332-X). Forum Pr IL.

World of Europe Since Seventeen Fifteen, Vol. II. rev. ed. Ralph Greenlaw et al. LC 78-67276. 1979. pap. text ed. 13.95x (ISBN 0-88273-329-X). Forum Pr IL.

World of Europe to Eighteen Fifteen, Vol. 2. DeLamar Jensen et al. LC 78-67276. 1979. pap. text ed. 12.95x (ISBN 0-88273-331-1). Forum Pr IL.

World of Europe to Fifteen Hundred, Vol. 1. Neil J. Hackett et al. LC 78-67276. 1979. pap. text ed. 12.95x (ISBN 0-88273-330-3). Forum Pr IL.

World of Europe to Seventeen Fifteen, Vol. I. rev. ed. Neil Hackett et al. LC 78-67276. pap. text ed. 13.95x (ISBN 0-88273-328-1). Forum Pr IL.

World of Faces: Masks of the Northwest Coast Indians. Edward Malin. LC 77-26786. (Illus.). 158p. 1978. 19.95 (ISBN 0-917304-05-5). Timber.

World of Falconry. H. Schlegel & J. A. Verster De Wulverhorst. Tr. by Timothy Chilvers. LC 80-51189. Orig. Title: Chasse Au Vol. (Illus.). 184p. (Fr.). 1980. 60.00 (ISBN 0-86565-004-7). Vendome.

World of Fantasy. (Shorewood Art Programs for Education Ser.). 8p. 1974. tchr's. ed. 86.00 (ISBN 0-88185-006-3); mounted prints 119.00. Shorewood Fine Art.

World of Fashion Jewelry. Barbara Ellman. LC 86-70569. (Illus.). 212p. (Orig.). 1986. pap. 13.95 (ISBN 0-9616652-0-3). Aunt Louise Pub.

World of Feelings. Nancy H. Dean. 64p. 1986. cancelled (ISBN 0-8062-2610-2). Carlton.

World of Fighting Dogs. Carl Semencic. (Illus.). 288p. 1984. 16.95 (ISBN 0-87666-566-0, H-1069). TFH Pubns.

World of Fish. Franco De Carli. Tr. by Jean Richardson. LC 79-1436. (Abbeville Press Encyclopedia of Natural Science). (Illus.). 1979. 13.95 (ISBN 0-89659-035-6); pap. 7.95 (ISBN 0-89659-029-1). Abbeville Pr.

World of Fishes. Hiroshi Takeuchi. Ed. by Kathy Pohl. LC 85-28212. (Nature Close-Ups Ser.). (Illus.). 32p. (gr. 4). 1986. PLB 15.33 (ISBN 0-8172-2548-X); pap. text ed. 9.27 (ISBN 0-8172-2573-0). Raintree Pubs.

World of Flannery O'Connor. Josephine Hendin. LC 76-108208. pap. 47.00 (ISBN 0-317-28709-5, 2055500). Bks Demand UMI.

World of Flat Racing. Brough Scott & Gerry Cranham. (Illus.). 280p. 1984. 55.00 (ISBN 0-437-15600-1, Pub. by Worlds Work). David & Charles.

World of Frogs. Jennifer Coldrey. LC 85-30297. (Where Animals Live Ser.). (Illus.). 32p. (gr. 2-3). 1987. 9.95 (ISBN 1-55532-024-4). Stevens Inc.

World of Furs. David G. Kaplan. Ed. by Ed Kleinman. LC 75-153567. pap. 61.80 (ISBN 0-317-30062-8, 2025035). Bks Demand UMI.

World of G Scale, 1989: A Walthers Catalog & Reference Manual. (Illus.). 208p. (YA) 1988. pap. price not set (ISBN 0-941952-24-X). W K Walthers.

World of GEM. Joe Byrd & Joe Guzaitis. (Illus.). 225p. 1987. pap. 20.00 (ISBN 0-13-967696-1). P-H.

World of General Haushofer: Geopolitics in Action. Andreas Dorpalen. LC 66-21393. 1942. Repr. 28.00 (ISBN 0-8046-0112-7, Pub. by Kennikat). Assoc Faculty Pr.

World of George Perkins Marsh. Jane Curtis et al. LC 82-7394. (Illus.). 128p. 1982. 14.95 (ISBN 0-914378-89-9); pap. 9.95 (ISBN 0-914378-90-2). Countryman.

World of George Price: A Fifty-Five Year Retrospective. George Price. 1987. 24.95 (ISBN 0-8253-0449-0); signed boxed ed. 50.00 (ISBN 0-8253-0450-4). Beaufort Bks NY.

World of George Washington. Richard M. Ketchum. (Power & Personality Ser.). (Illus.). 1984. 15.95 (ISBN 0-517-55349-X, Harmony). Crown.

World of Gilbert & Sullivan. William A. Darlington. 21.00 (ISBN 0-8369-5573-0, 6637). Ayer Co Pubs.

World of Ginger Fox. Mike Baron. (Illus.). 64p. (Orig.). 1986. pap. 6.95 (ISBN 0-938965-02-6). Comico Comic Co.

World of Ginger Fox. Mike Baron. (Illus.). 66p. 1987. 27.95 (ISBN 0-938965-03-4). Comico Comic Co.

World of Golf. Ed. by Gordon Menzies. LC 83-61260. (Illus.). 224p. 1984. 19.95 (ISBN 0-88186-451-X). Parkwest Pubns.

World of Golf. Ed. by Gordon Menzies. 224p. 16.95 (ISBN 0-318-17830-3). Nineteenth Hole.

World of Grace. L. J. O'Donovan. 1980. pap. 14.95x (ISBN 0-8245-0406-2). Crossroad NY.

World of Graft. facs. ed. Josiah Flynt. LC 72-150181. (Select Bibliographies Reprint Ser.). 1901. 18.00 (ISBN 0-8369-5694-X). Ayer Co Pubs.

World of Grandma Moses. Jane Kallir. LC 84-81943. pap. 20.00 (ISBN 0-317-41848-3, 2025898). Bks Demand UMI.

World of Grown Ups: Children's Conceptions of Society. H. G. Furth. 29.95 (ISBN 0-444-99065-8, FWO/, Pub. by Elsevier). Greenwood.

World of Gurus. Vishal Mangalwadi. 1987. 12.00x (ISBN 0-8364-2046-2, Pub. by Usha). South Asia Bks.

World of H. G. Wells. Van-Wyck Brooks. 190p. 1973. Repr. of 1915 ed. lib. bdg. 59.95 (ISBN 0-8490-1334-8). Gordon Pr.

World of H. G. Wells. Van-Wyck Brooks. LC 72-92949. (English Literature Ser., No. 33). Repr. of 1915 ed. lib. bdg. 49.95x (ISBN 0-8383-0962-3). Haskell.

World of H. G. Wells. Van-Wyck Brooks. LC 70-131649. 1970. Repr. of 1915 ed. 15.00 (ISBN 0-403-00536-1). Scholarly.

World of Haldeman-Julius. Albert Mordell. 18.95x (ISBN 0-317-18412-1). New Coll U Pr.

World of Harlequin: A Critical Study of the Commedia dell'Arte. Allardyce Nicoll. LC 76-18411. (Illus.). 258p. 1987. 59.50 (ISBN 0-521-05834-1); pap. 19.95 (ISBN 0-521-29132-1). Cambridge U Pr.

World of Harlequin: A Critical Study of the Commedia Dell'arte. Allardyce Nicoll. LC 76-18411. pap. 64.80 (ISBN 0-317-27311-6, 2024501). Bks Demand UMI.

World of Henri Wallon. Ed. by Gilbert Voyat. LC 81-66757. 312p. 1984. 30.00x (ISBN 0-87668-434-7). Aronson.

World of Herbs & Spices. Ortho Books Editorial Staff. LC 78-57892. (Illus.). 1979. pap. 6.95 (ISBN 0-917102-72-X). Ortho.

World of Herodotus. Aubrey De Selincourt. LC 81-83969. 400p. 1982. pap. 12.00 (ISBN 0-86547-070-7). N Point Pr.

World of Heroes: Selections from Homer, Herodotus & Sophocles. Joint Association of Classical Teachers' Greek Course. LC 79-10740. (Illus.). 1979. pap. 11.95x (ISBN 0-521-22462-4). Cambridge U Pr.

World of Hesiod. Andrew R. Burn. LC 66-29859. 1966. Repr. of 1936 ed. 15.00 (ISBN 0-405-08332-7, Blom Pubns). Ayer Co Pubs.

World of Higher Education: An Annotated Guide to the Major Literature. Paul L. Dressel & Sally R. Pratt. LC 71-158562. (Jossey-Bass Series in Higher Education). pap. 64.00 (ISBN 0-317-10873-5, 2013934). Bks Demand UMI.

World of His Own: The Artwork of Warren A. Van Ess. Warren A. Van Ess. LC 74-4372. (Illus.). pap. 20.00 (ISBN 0-317-10400-4, 2012826). Bks Demand UMI.

World of His Own: The Double Life of George Borrow. David Williams. (Illus.). 1982. 19.95x (ISBN 0-19-211762-9). Oxford U Pr.

World of History. Ed. by Courtland Canby et al. LC 83-49178. (History & Historiography Ser.). 224p. 1985. lib. bdg. 25.00 (ISBN 0-8240-6353-8). Garland Pub.

World of HO Scale - 1989: A Walthers Catalog & Reference Manual. (Illus.). 760p. (Orig.). 1988. pap. price not set (ISBN 0-941952-23-1, 913-638). W K Walthers.

World of HO Scale, 1988: A Walthers Catalog & Reference Manual. (Illus.). 720p. 1987. pap. 13.98 (913-634). W K Walthers.

World of Homer. Andrew Lang. LC 68-54281. Repr. of 1910 ed. 10.00 (ISBN 0-404-03870-0). AMS Pr.

World of Hope: Progressives & the Struggle for an Ethical Life. David B. Danbom. 320p. 1986. 24.95 (ISBN 0-87722-453-6). Temple U Pr.

World of Horses. Jan Burgess. Ed. by Wendy Barish. (Illus.). 96p. (gr. 3 up). 1984. 9.95 (ISBN 0-671-52528-X). Wanderer Bks.

World of Horses. James Reynolds. 1979. Repr. of 1947 ed. lib. bdg. 35.00 (ISBN 0-8492-2397-0). R West.

World of Humanism, Fourteen Fifty-Three to Fifteen Seventeen. Myron P. Gilmore. LC 83-10718. (Rise of Modern Europe Ser.). (Illus.). xv, 326p. 1983. Repr. of 1952 ed. lib. bdg. 48.50x (ISBN 0-313-24081-7, GIWO). Greenwood.

World of Hunger: A Strategy for Survival. Jonathan Power & Anne-Marie Holenstein. 1977. 18.75 (ISBN 0-85117-097-8). Transatl Arts.

World of Hurt. Bo Hathaway. (Vietnam Ser.). 304p. (Orig.). 1984. pap. 3.50 (ISBN 0-380-69567-7). Avon.

World of Hurt: A Novel. Bo Hathaway. LC 80-18147. 272p. 1981. 11.95 (ISBN 0-8008-8586-4). Taplinger.

World of Ideas: Essays on the Past & Future. The World of Ideas. LC 68-15678. pap. 40.30 (ISBN 0-317-09763-6, 2005010). Bks Demand UMI.

World of Ideas: Essential Readings for College Writers. 2nd ed. Lee A. Jacobus. Date not set. price not set (ISBN 0-312-89221-7); instr's. manual avail. (ISBN 0-312-89222-5). St Martin.

World of Imagination. Janet L. Ainge. 64p. 1987. 7.00 (ISBN 0-8062-3121-1). Carlton.

World of Indonesian Textiles. Wanda Warming & Michael E. Gaworski. LC 80-82526. (Illus.). 200p. 1981. 50.00 (ISBN 0-87011-432-8). Kodansha.

World of Inflation. Geoffrey Maynard & W. Van Ryckeghem. LC 75-26030. 272p. 1975. text ed. 27.50x (ISBN 0-06-494673-8). B&N Imports.

World of Insects. Adriano Zanetti. Tr. by Catherine Athill. LC 79-1424. (Abbeville Press Encyclopedia of Natural Science). (Illus.). 256p. 1979. 13.95 (ISBN 0-89659-036-4); pap. 7.95 (ISBN 0-89659-030-5). Abbeville Pr.

World of International Tax Planning. Milton Grundy. LC 83-15078. 1984. 44.50 (ISBN 0-521-25955-X). Cambridge U Pr.

World of Irises. Ed. by Bee Warburton. LC 77-73698. (Illus.). 1978. 15.00 (ISBN 0-9601242-1-7). Am Iris.

World of Islam. Thomas B. Irving. Orig. Title: Tide of Islam. (Illus.). 200p. 1985. 17.50 (ISBN 0-915597-20-9); pap. 9.95 (ISBN 0-915597-18-7). Amana Bks.

World of Islam. Ed. by James Kritzeck. LC 79-52558. (Islam Ser.). (Illus.). 1980. Repr. of 1959 ed. lib. bdg. 32.00x (ISBN 0-8369-9265-2). Ayer Co Pubs.

World of Islam. Xavier de Planhol. 153p. 1959. pap. 8.95x (ISBN 0-8014-9830-9). Cornell U Pr.

World of Islam. John B. Taylor. (Orig.). 1979. pap. 3.95 (ISBN 0-377-00086-8). Friendship Pr.

World of James McNeill Whistler. facs. ed. Horace Gregory. LC 70-80621. (Select Bibliographies Reprint Ser). 1959. 23.00 (ISBN 0-8369-5033-X). Ayer Co Pubs.

World of Jan Saudek. Jan Saudek. LC 82-73758. (Illus.). 144p. 1983. 35.00 (ISBN 0-89381-116-5). Aperture.

World of Japanese Ceramics. Herbert H. Sanders & Kenkichi Tomimoto. LC 67-16771. (Illus.). 267p. 1983. pap. 18.95 (ISBN 0-87011-557-X). Kodansha.

World of Japanese Prints. Sarah Thompson. 44p. 1986. 56.00x (ISBN 0-317-69748-X, Pub. by Han-Shan Tang Ltd). State Mutual Bk.

World of Jeeves. P. G. Wodehouse. LC 88-45072. 576p. 1988. 19.95 (ISBN 0-06-015968-5, HarpT). Har-Row.

World of Jennie G. E. Ogilvie. 372p. 1987. pap. text ed. 5.95 (ISBN 0-07-047789-2). McGraw.

World of Jennie G. Elisabeth Ogilvie. 368p. 1986. text ed. 16.95 (ISBN 0-07-047783-3). McGraw.

World of Jimmy Connors. Jim Burke. (Illus., Orig.). 1976. pap. 1.50 (ISBN 0-685-64019-1, LB330DK, Leisure Bks). Leisure NY.

World of John Cleaveland: Family & Community in Eighteenth Century New England. Christopher M. Jedrey. 256p. 1981. pap. text ed. 6.95x (ISBN 0-393-95199-5). Norton.

World of John of Salisbury. Ed. by Michael J. Wilks. (Studies in Church History: Subsidia 3). 400p. 1985. text ed. 45.00x (ISBN 0-631-13122-1). Basil Blackwell.

World of Kameda Bosai. Stephen Addiss. LC 84-2004. (Illus.). 127p. 1984. pap. 16.95 (ISBN 0-89494-019-8). New Orleans Mus Art.

World of Kameda Bosai: The Calligraphy, Poetry, Painting & Artistic Circle of a Japanese Literatus. Stephen Addiss. LC 84-2004. (Illus.). 128p. 1984. 35.00x (ISBN 0-7006-0251-8). U Pr of KS.

World of Korean Ceramics. Jon C. Covell. (Illus.). 128p. 1986. 19.95 (ISBN 0-87296-022-6, Pub. by Si-Sa-Yong-o-SA Korea). Si-Sa-Yong-o-Sa.

World of Krypton. 160p. 1987. pap. 2.50 (ISBN 0-8125-7738-8). Tor Bks.

World of Krypton: The Home of Superman. 160p. 1982. pap. 1.95 (ISBN 0-523-49017-8, Dist. by Warner Pub Services & Saint Martin's Press). Tor Bks.

World of K'ung Shang-Jen: A Man of Letters in Early Ch'ing China. Richard E. Strassberg. LC 83-1838. 520p. 1983. 37.50x. Columbia U Pr.

World of Lady Addle: The Memoirs of Mipsie & Lady Addle at Home. Mary Dunn. (Illus.). 256p. 1986. 12.95 (ISBN 0-86072-085-3, Pub. by Quartet Bks). Salem Hse Pubs.

World of Language for Deaf Children: Basic Principles, a Maternal Reflective Method, Pt. 1. 3rd ed. A. Van Uden. (Modern Approaches to the Diagnosis & Instruction of Multi-Handicapped Children: Vol. 4). 348p. 1977. text ed. 27.25 (ISBN 90-265-0253-2, Pub. by Swets & Zeitlinger Netherlands). Hogrefe Intl.

World of Large Scale Systems. J. D. Palmer & R. Saeks. LC 82-6169. 360p. 1982. 38.10 (ISBN 0-87942-162-2, PC01560). Inst Electrical.

World of Learning 1988. 1900p. 1988. 220.00x (ISBN 0-946653-31-3, Pub. by Europa Pubns). Taylor & Francis.

World of Learning 1988. 38th ed. 1896p. 1988. 190.00x (Pub. by Europa England). Gale.

World of Lego Toys. Henry Wiencek. (Illus.). 176p. 1987. 27.50 (ISBN 0-8109-1790-4); pap. 17.95 (ISBN 0-8109-2362-9). Abrams.

World of Light: Portraits & Celebrations. May Sarton. (Illus.). 1976. 17.95 (ISBN 0-393-07506-0). Norton.

World of Light: Portraits & Celebrations. May Sarton. (Illus.). 1988. pap. 4.95 (ISBN 0-393-30500-7). Norton.

World of Lizards. Virginia Harrison. LC 87-42608. (Where Animals Live Ser.). (Illus.). 32p. (gr. 2-3). 1988. PLB 9.95 (ISBN 1-55532-307-3). Stevens Inc.

World of Logotypes, Vol. 1. Al Cooper. LC 75-29774. 1976. 28.50 (ISBN 0-910158-20-7). Art Dir.

World of Logotypes, Vol. 2. Al Cooper. LC 75-29774. (Illus.). 1978. 28.50 (ISBN 0-910158-34-7). Art Dir.

World of Logotypes, Vol. 3. Al Cooper. LC 75-29774. (Illus.). 356p. 1982. 28.50 (ISBN 0-910158-82-7). Art Dir.

World of Lone Wolf: Beyond the Nightmare Gate. Ian Page & Joe Dever. 224p. 1987. 2.50 (ISBN 0-317-60333-7, 09892-3). Berkley Pub.

World of Lone Wolf: Grey Star the Wizard. Ian Page & Joe Dever. 240p. 1987. pap. 2.95 (ISBN 0-425-09590-8, Pub. by Berkley-Pacer). Berkley Pub.

World of Lone Wolf: The Forbidden City. Joe Dever & Ian Page. 128p. 1987. pap. 2.50 (ISBN 0-425-10103-7, Pub. by Berkley-Pacer). Berkley Pub.
World of Lone Wolf: War of the Wizards. Joe Dever & Ian Page. 1987. pap. 2.50 (ISBN 0-425-10539-3). Berkley Pub.
World of Love. Elizabeth Bowen. 160p. 1988. pap. 5.95 (ISBN 0-14-008541-6). Penguin.
World of Love. Barbara Cartland. (Camfield Ser.: No. 42). 176p. (Orig.). 1987. pap. 2.75 (ISBN 0-515-08882-X). Jove Pubns.
World of Love: Eleanor Roosevelt & Her Friends, 1943-1962. Joseph P. Lash. (Paperbacks Ser.). 656p. 1985. pap. text ed. 9.95 (ISBN 0-07-036487-7). McGraw.
World of Luis Bunuel: Essays in Criticism. Ed. by Joan Mellen. (Illus.). 1978. pap. 9.95 (ISBN 0-19-502399-4). Oxford U Pr.
World of M. C. Escher. M. C. Escher & J. C. Locher. pap. 9.95 (ISBN 0-451-79961-5, G9961, Abrams Art Bks). NAL.
World of M. C. Escher. Ed. by J. L. Locher. H. S. Coxeter. (Illus.). 252p. 1988. 19.95 (ISBN 0-8109-8084-3). Abrams.
World of Macaws. Dieter Hoppe. Tr. by Arthur Freud & R. Edward Ugarte. (Illus.). 144p. 1985. Repr. of 1983 ed. 29.95 (ISBN 0-86622-125-5, H-1079). TFH Pubns.
World of Man: Prose Passages Chiefly from the Works of the Great Historians, Classical & English. L. J. Cheney. 1979. Repr. of 1933 ed. lib. bdg. 30.00 (ISBN 0-8492-3966-4). R West.
World of Man: Prose Passages from the Works of the Great Historians, Classical & English. L. J. Cheney. 1933. 15.00 (ISBN 0-686-17674-X). Quaker City.
World of Marathons. Sandy Treadwell. LC 86-23067. (Illus.). 192p. 1986. 24.95 (ISBN 0-941434-98-2). Stewart Tabori & Chang.
World of Marcus Garvey: Race & Class in Modern Society. Judith Stein. LC 85-7084. (Illus.). xii, 294p. 1985. text ed. 25.00 (ISBN 0-8071-1236-4). La State U Pr.
World of Mathematics, 4 vols. Ed. by James R. Newman. 2784p. 1988. Boxed Set. (79.95 pre-pub) 99.95 (ISBN 1-55615-149-7); Boxed Set. pap. 50.00 (ISBN 1-55615-148-9). Microsoft.
World of Mazes. Robert E. Vardeman. (Cenothaph Road Ser.: No. 3). 224p. 1984. pap. 2.75 (ISBN 0-441-91031-9, Pub. by Ace Science Fiction). Ace Bks.
World of Medieval & Renaissance Musical Instruments. Jeremy Montagu. LC 76-5987. (Illus.). 136p. 1976. 39.95 (ISBN 0-87951-045-5). Overlook Pr.
World of Medieval Learning. Anders Piltz. Tr. by David Jones. (Illus.). 310p. 1981. 30.00x (ISBN 0-389-20206-1). B&N Imports.
World of Medieval Women. Ed. by Constance H. Berman & Charles W. Connell. 163p. (Orig.). 1985. pap. 9.50 (ISBN 0-937058-22-X). West Va U Pr.
World of Melodrama. Frank Rahill. LC 66-25466. 1967. 24.95x (ISBN 0-271-73113-3). Pa St U Pr.
World of "Mestre" Tamoda: Angolan Stories. Uanhenga Xitu. Tr. by Annella McDermott from Port. 200p. (Orig.). 1988. 16.95 (ISBN 0-930523-42-3, Dist. by Consortium); pap. 8.95 (ISBN 0-930523-43-1). Readers Intl.
World of Mexican Cooking. Mary Margaret Curry. LC 79-143007. 1987. pap. 4.95 (ISBN 0-931722-46-2). Corona Pub.
World of Mice. Virginia Harrison. LC 87-42609. (Where Animals Live Ser.). (Illus.). 32p. (gr. 2-3). 1988. PLB 9.95 (ISBN 1-55532-309-X). Stevens Inc.
World of Microbes. Howard Gest. LC 87-12664. (Illus.). 264p. 1987. 18.95 (ISBN 0-910239-10-X). Sci Tech Pubs.
World of Microbes. Howard Gest. (Illus.). 250p. text ed. 19.95 (ISBN 0-8053-2820-3). Benjamin-Cummings.
World of Mirth. Michael G. Michaud. 31p. (Orig.). 1988. pap. write for info (ISBN 0-9620574-0-1). MGM Pr.
World of Miss Universe. Ana M. Cumba. LC 75-26269. (Illus.). 270p. 1976. 9.95 (ISBN 0-87141-053-2). Manyland.
World of Mr. Mulliner. P. G. Wodehouse. LC 74-5813. 622p. 1985. pap. 11.95 (ISBN 0-8008-8581-3). Taplinger.
World of Model Airplanes. William J. Winter. Ed. by Model Aviation Editors. (Illus.). 1983. 22.95 (ISBN 0-684-17877-X, ScribT). Scribner.
World of Model Airplanes: Building & Flying Free, Control-line, & Radio-Controlled Models. The Model Aviation Editors & William J. Winter. (Illus.). 288p. 1986. pap. 10.95 (ISBN 0-684-18665-9). Scribner.
World of Model Cars. Guy R. Williams. (Illus.). 156p. 1976. 24.95 (ISBN 0-233-96287-5, Pub. by A Deutsch England). David & Charles.
World of Moses. Paul F. Bork. LC 78-5022. (Horizon Ser.). 1978. pap. 5.95 (ISBN 0-8127-0166-6). Review & Herald.
World of Musical Comedy. 4th ed. Stanley Green. LC 83-26340. (Quality Paperbacks Ser.). (Illus.). 494p. 1984. pap. 18.95 (ISBN 0-306-80207-4). Da Capo.
World of Musical Sound. Roderick D. Gordon. 1982. pap. text ed. 13.95 (ISBN 0-8403-2922-9). Kendall-Hunt.
World of Myths: A Dictionary of Universal Mythology. F. C. Bray. 75.00 (ISBN 0-8490-1335-6). Gordon Pr.
World of N & Z, 1988: A Walthers Catalog & Reference Manual. (Illus.). 368p. 1987. pap. 9.98 (ISBN 0-941952-22-3, 913-628). W K Walthers.
World of Nat Nakasa: Selected Writings of the Late Nat Nakasa. Ed. by Essop Patel. (Staffrider Ser.: No. 27). 150p. 1985. pap. 12.95 (ISBN 0-86975-050-X, Pub. by Ravan Pr). Ohio U Pr.
World of Nations: A Study of the National Implications in the Work of Karl Marx. Solomon F. Bloom. Repr. of 1941 ed. 16.50 (ISBN 0-404-00899-2). AMS Pr.
World of Natural Sciences & Its Phenomenology. 2nd ed. H. Kuhlenbeck. Ed. by J. Gerlach. (Human Brain & Its Universe Ser.: Vol. 1). (Illus.). xiv, 282p. 1981. 110.00 (ISBN 3-8055-1817-X). S Karger.
World of Nature. Robin Dunbar. (Illus.). 240p. 15.98 (ISBN 0-8317-9619-7). Smith Pubs.
World of Nature in the Works of Federico Garcia Lorca. Ed. by Joseph W. Zdenek. (Winthrop College: Studies on Major Modern Writers). 150p. 1980. pap. 8.00x (ISBN 0-933040-01-6). Spanish Lit Pubns.
World of Northern Evergreens. E. C. Pielou. (Paperback Ser.). 200p. 1988. 36.50x (ISBN 0-8014-2116-0); pap. 10.95 (ISBN 0-8014-9424-9). Cornell U Pr.
World of Nothing. Ronald L. Fair. LC 71-105237. 1970. 15.00 (ISBN 0-89366-096-5). Ultramarine Pub.
World of Nothing: Two Novellas. Ronald L. Fair. 133p. 1970. 5.95x (ISBN 0-911860-44-4). Chatham Bkseller.
World of Nudes. Roy Dean. (Illus.). 1975. 7.95 (ISBN 0-685-53563-0). Rho-Delta Pr.
World of O. Henry - Five One Act Plays. Jesse F. Knight. LC 77-15687. (Lion Theatrical Ser.: No. 1). 1980. pap. 3.50 (ISBN 0-930962-03-6). Lion Ent.
World of Odysseus. rev. ed. M. I. Finley. 1979. pap. 6.95 (ISBN 0-14-020570-5, Pelican). Penguin.
World of Odysseus. M. I. Finley. 1988. 15.75 (ISBN 0-8446-6298-4). Peter Smith.
World of Oil. A. F. Fox. 1964. pap. 10.50 (ISBN 0-08-010686-2). Pergamon.
World of Opera. Robert Lawrence. LC 77-2268. (Illus.). 1977. Repr. of 1956 ed. lib. bdg. 35.00x (ISBN 0-8371-9551-9, LAWO). Greenwood.
World of Order & Light: The Fiction of John Gardner. Gregory L. Morris. LC 83-9195. 259p. 1984. 25.00x (ISBN 0-8203-0696-7). U of Ga Pr.
World of Orderic Vitalis. Oderic Vitalis. Ed. by Marjorie Chibnall. (Illus.). 264p. 1984. 58.00x (ISBN 0-19-821937-7). Oxford U Pr.
World of Origami. abr. ed. Isao Honda. LC 65-27101. (Illus.). 200p. 1976. pap. 14.95 (ISBN 0-87040-383-4). Japan Pubns USA.
World of Our Fathers. Irving Howe. LC 75-16342. (Illus.). 714p. 1976. 14.95 (ISBN 0-15-146353-0). HarBraceJ.
World of Our Fathers. Irving Howe. 560p. 1983. pap. 12.95 (ISBN 0-671-49252-7, Touchstone). S&S.
World of Our Fathers: The Jews of Eastern Europe. Milton Meltzer. LC 74-14755. (Illus.). 256p. (gr. 7 up). 1974. 11.95 (ISBN 0-374-38530-0). FS&G.
World of Our Mothers: Lives of Jewish Immigrant Women. Sydney S. Weinberg. LC 87-13233. (Illus.). xxvi, 326p. 1988. 22.95 (ISBN 0-8078-1762-7). U of NC Pr.
World of Ovid's Metamorphoses. Joseph B. Solodow. LC 87-24159. (Illus.). x, 278p. 1988. 32.50x (ISBN 0-8078-1771-6). U of NC Pr.
World of Owen Gromme. Michael Mentzer & Judith R. Coopey. LC 83-51148. (Illus.). 240p. 1983. 65.00 (ISBN 0-88361-088-4); deluxe ed. 175.00 (ISBN 0-88361-089-2); limited ed 950.00 (ISBN 0-88361-090-6). Stanton & Lee.
World of Owls. David Saintsing. LC 87-6537. (Where Animals Live Ser.). (Illus.). 32p. (gr. 2-3). 1987. PLB 9.95 (ISBN 1-55532-301-4). Stevens Inc.
World of Patience Gromes: Making & Unmaking a Black Community. Scott C. Davis. LC 88-98. 232p. 1988. 20.00 (ISBN 0-8131-1644-9). U Pr of Ky.
World of Paul Crume. Ed. by Marion Crume. LC 80-14072. 312p. 1980. 15.00 (ISBN 0-87074-176-4). SMU Press.
World of PC-DOS. Peter H. Mackie. 125p. 1984. pap. 9.95 (ISBN 0-88056-145-9); IBM-PC, IBM-PC XT, Compaq. incl. disk 29.95 (ISBN 0-88056-198-X). Weber Systems.
World of PC-DOS. Peter H. Mackie. 125p. pap. 9.95 (ISBN 0-517-56389-4); pap. 29.95 (ISBN 0-517-56390-8); software pkg. incl. Crown.
World of Penguins. David Saintsing. LC 87-6536. (Where Animals Live Ser.). (Illus.). 32p. (gr. 2-3). 1987. PLB 9.95 (ISBN 1-55532-274-3). Stevens Inc.
World of Percy French. Brendan O'Dowda. (Illus.). 192p. 1981. pap. 10.50 (ISBN 0-85640-255-9, Pub. by Blackstaff Pr). Longwood Pub Group.
World of Philip Potter. William H. Gentz. 1974. pap. 2.95 (ISBN 0-377-00006-X). Friendship Pr.
World of Philosophy. H. Kuhlenbeck. Ed. by J. Gerlach. (Limited Volume Series: The Human Brain & Its Universe: Vol. 3). xiv, 508p. 1982. 198.00 (ISBN 3-8055-3419-1). S Karger.
World of Philosophy: An Introduction. Robert B. McLaren. LC 82-14214. (Illus.). 272p. 1983. text ed. 23.95x (ISBN 0-8304-1000-7); pap. text ed. 11.95x (ISBN 0-88229-815-1). Nelson-Hall.
World of Phyllis Haylor & Ballroom Dancing. Bryan Allen. (Ballroom Dance Ser.). 1986. lib. bdg. 79.95 (ISBN 0-8490-3366-7). Gordon Pr.
World of Phyllis Haylor & Ballroom Dancing. Ed. by Bryan Allen. (Ballroom Dance Ser.). 1985. lib. bdg. 79.95 (ISBN 0-87700-660-1). Revisionist Pr.
World of Physics: A Small Library of the Literature of Physics from Antiquity to the Present, 3 vols. Jefferson H. Weaver. LC 86-1903. (Illus.). 1120p. 1987. Vol. I. 29.95 (ISBN 0-671-49926-2); Vol. II. 29.95 (ISBN 0-671-49930-0); Vol. III. 29.95 (ISBN 0-671-49931-9); Set. 75.00 (ISBN 0-671-64216-2). S&S.
World of Piers Plowman. Ed. by Jeanne Krochalis & Edward Peters. LC 75-11167. (Middle Ages Ser). 1975. pap. 13.95 (ISBN 0-8122-1085-9, Pa Paperbks). U of Pa Pr.
World of Placido Domingo. Daniel Snowman. 448p. 1987. Repr. of 1985 ed. lib. bdg. 19.95 (ISBN 1-55736-009-X). ABC-Clio.
World of Play. Ed. by Frank E. Manning. LC 82-83395. (Association for the Anthropological Studies of Play: Vol. 7). 229p. (Orig.). 1983. pap. text ed. 18.00x (ISBN 0-88011-059-7, PMAN0059). Leisure Pr.
World of Politics: A Concise Introduction. 2nd ed. James F. Barnes et al. LC 83-61601. 220p. 1984. pap. text ed. write for info. (ISBN 0-312-89228-4). St Martin.
World of Polo: Past & Present. J. N. Watson. (Illus.). 192p. 1986. 36.95 (ISBN 0-88162-203-6). Salem Hse Pubs.
World of Pooh. A. A. Milne. (gr. 1-4). 1957. boxed with "World of Christopher Robin" 29.95. Dutton.
World of Pooh. A. A. Milne. (Illus.). (ps up). 1988. 14.95 (ISBN 0-525-44447-5, 01451-440). Dutton.
World of Prayer, 2 vols. Elie Munk. 24.95 set (ISBN 0-87306-080-6). Feldheim.
World of Prayer. Elie Munk. Tr. by Henry Biberfeld & Leonard Oschry. Orig. Title: Welt der Gebete. 1978. pap. 14.95 (ISBN 0-87306-170-5). Feldheim.
World of Prayer. Adrienne Von Speyr. Tr. by Graham Harrison from Ger. LC 84-80904. 311p. (Orig.). 1985. pap. 10.95 (ISBN 0-89870-033-7). Ignatius Pr.
World of Professional Golf 1986. Mark McCormack. 1986. 22.50 (ISBN 0-936557-00-1). Golf Shop Collect.
World of Programming Languages. M. W. Marcotty & H. Ledgard. (Springer Books in Professional Computing). (Illus.). 385p. 1986. pap. 29.95 (ISBN 0-387-96440-1). Springer-Verlag.
World of Psychic Research. Hereward Carrington. pap. 2.00 (ISBN 0-87980-254-5). Wilshire.
World of Ptavvs. Larry Niven. 192p. pap. 2.95 (ISBN 0-345-34508-8). Ballantine.
World of Quantum Chemistry: Proceedings. First International Congress of Quantum Chemistry, Menton, France, July 4-10, 1973. Ed. by R. Daudel & B. Pullman. LC 73-91429. 1974. lib. bdg. 58.00 (ISBN 90-277-0421-X, Pub. by Reidel Holland). Kluwer Academic.
World of Quino. Quino. (Illus.). 128p. 1986. pap. 8.95 (ISBN 0-8050-0092-5). H Holt & Co.
World of Rabbits. Jennifer Coldrey. LC 85-28988. (Where Animals Live Ser.). (Illus.). 32p. (gr. 2-3). 1986. 9.95 (ISBN 1-55532-064-3). Stevens Inc.
World of Rashid Hussein: A Palestinian Poet in Exile. Ed. by Kamal Boullata & Mirene Ghossein. LC 78-62611. (Monograph: No. 12). (Illus.). 208p. (Orig.). 1979. pap. 6.50 (ISBN 0-937694-07-X). Assn Arab-Amer U Grads.
World of Richard Wright. Michel Fabre. LC 85-6230. (Center for the Study of Southern Culture Ser.). 1985. 27.50x (ISBN 0-87805-258-5). U Pr of Miss.
World of Robert Bateman. Illus. by Robert Bateman. Ramsay Derry. LC 84-29837. (Illus.). 180p. 1985. 50.00 (ISBN 0-394-54654-7). Random.
World of Robert Flaherty. Richard Griffith. LC 72-166104. 1972. Repr. of 1953 ed. lib. bdg. 32.50 (ISBN 0-306-70296-7). Da Capo.
World of Robert Flaherty. Richard Griffith. 1970. Repr. of 1953 ed. lib. bdg. 35.00x (ISBN 0-8371-3400-5, GRRF). Greenwood.
World of Romanian Theater. Ruth S. Lamb. (Illus.). 136p. 1976. pap. 8.95 (ISBN 0-912434-20-1). Ocelot Pr.
World of Romantic & Modern Musical Instruments. Jeremy Montagu. LC 80-26106. (Illus.). 136p. 1981. 39.95 (ISBN 0-87951-126-5). Overlook Pr.
World of Rome. Michael Grant. 1987. pap. 7.95 (ISBN 0-452-00849-2, Mer). NAL.
World of Rosaphrenia: The Sexual Psychology of the Female. Major J. Baisden, Jr. LC 72-178852. 224p. 1971. 6.95 (ISBN 0-912984-01-5). Allied Res Soc.
World of Rottweilers. Anna K. Nicholas. (Illus.). 336p. 1986. 34.95 (ISBN 0-86622-124-7, H-1083). TFH Pubns.
World of Russo. Illus. by Michele Russo. (Illus.). 110p. (Orig.). 1981. pap. 12.95 (ISBN 0-938996-00-2). Bigoni Bks.
World of Satellite Television. 5th, rev. ed. Mark Long & Jeffrey Keating. (Illus.). 224p. (YA) (gr. 12). 1988. pap. 18.95. MLE Inc.
World of Scarcities: Critical Issues in Public Policy. David Novick. LC 75-42278. 194p. 1976. 48.95x (ISBN 0-470-15002-5). Halsted Pr.
World of Science: An Anthology for Writers. Gladys G. Leithauser & Marilyn P. Bell. 560p. 1987. pap. text ed. write for info. HR&W.
World of Science & the Rule of Law: A Study of the Observance & Violations of the Human Rights of Scientists in the Participating States of the Helsinki Accords. John Ziman et al. LC 85-24662. 352p. 1986. 37.00x (ISBN 0-19-825516-0). Oxford U Pr.
World of Seals. David Saintsing & Douglas Allan. LC 87-6524. (Where Animals Live Ser.). (Illus.). 32p. (gr. 2-3). 1987. PLB 9.95 (ISBN 1-55532-300-6). Stevens Inc.
World of Secrets: The Uses & Limits of Intelligence. Walter Laqueur. LC 85-47567. (Twentieth Century Fund Bks.). 368p. 1985. 21.95 (ISBN 0-465-09237-3). Basic.
World of Secrets: The Uses & Limits of Intelligence. Walter Laqueur. LC 85-45313. 416p. 1987. pap. 11.95 (ISBN 0-465-09236-5, PL 5184). Basic.
World of Serendipity. Marcus Bach. 167p. 1980. pap. 5.95 (ISBN 0-87516-398-X). DeVorss.
World of Sex Perspectives on Japan & the West, Vol. 1: Sexual Equality. Iwao Hoshii. 180p. 1987. 60.00x (ISBN 0-904404-54-4, Pub. by P Norbury Pubns Ltd). State Mutual Bk.
World of Sex Perspectives on Japan & the West, Vol. 2: Sex & Marriage. Iwao Hoshii. 332p. 1987. 65.00x (ISBN 0-904404-55-2, Pub. by P Norbury Pubns Ltd). State Mutual Bk.
World of Sex Perspectives on Japan & the West, Vol. 3: Responsible Parenthood. Iwao Hoshii. 256p. 1987. 59.00x (ISBN 0-904404-56-0, Pub. by P Norbury Pubns Ltd). State Mutual Bk.
World of Sex Perspectives on Japan & the West, Vol. 4: Sex in Ethics & Law. Iwao Hoshii. 300p. 1987. 65.00x (ISBN 0-904404-57-9, Pub. by P Norbury Pubns Ltd). State Mutual Bk.
World of Shakespeare. Alan Dent. LC 78-20691. 1979. pap. 7.95 (ISBN 0-8008-8597-X). Taplinger.
World of Sharks. Andrew Langley. Ed. by Janet Caulkins. (Topics Ser.). (Illus.). 32p. (gr. 1-6). 1988. 10.40 (ISBN 0-531-18211-8, Pub. by Bookwright Pr). Watts.
World of Shining Prince. Ivan Morris. 1985. pap. 7.95 (ISBN 0-14-055083-6). Penguin.
World of Sholom Aleichem. Maurice Samuel. LC 86-47697. 344p. 1986. pap. 9.95 (ISBN 0-689-70709-6, 343). Atheneum.
World of Short Fiction. Ed. by Robert C. Albrecht. LC 69-11841. 1970. pap. text ed. 10.95 (ISBN 0-02-900350-4). Free Pr.
World of Show Jumping. Neil F. Blake. 1973. Repr. 14.95 (ISBN 0-912830-29-8). Printed Horse.
World of Silence. Max Picard. LC 53-5808. 232p. pap. 8.95 (ISBN 0-89526-939-2). Regnery Gateway.
World of Sled Dogs. Lorna Coppinger. LC 76-7131. (Illus.). 303p. 1977. 19.95 (ISBN 0-87605-671-0). Howell Bk.
World of Somerset Maugham: An Anthology. Ed. by Klaus W. Jonas. LC 73-156196. 200p. 1972. Repr. of 1959 ed. lib. bdg. 35.00x (ISBN 0-8371-6147-9, JOSM). Greenwood.
World of Sorrow: The African Slave Trade to Brazil. Robert E. Conrad. LC 85-23160. (Illus.). 215p. 1986. text ed. 25.00 (ISBN 0-8071-1245-3). LA State U Pr.
World of Space. Cass R. Sandak. Ed. by Frank Sloan. (New Frontiers Ser.). (Illus.). 32p. (YA) (gr. 7-9). 1988. 11.90 (ISBN 0-531-10459-1). Watts.
World of Sports for Girls. Gail A. Myers. LC 81-10440. (Illus.). 160p. (gr. 5-9). 1981. 10.95 (ISBN 0-664-32683-8). Westminster John Knox.
World of Squirrels. Jennifer Coldrey. LC 85-30296. (Where Animals Live Ser.). (Illus.). 32p. (gr. 2-3). 1987. 9.95 (ISBN 1-55532-065-1). Stevens Inc.
World of Star Trek. rev. & updated ed. David Gerrold. (Illus.). 288p. 1984. pap. 9.95 (ISBN 0-312-94463-2). Bluejay Bks.
World of States: Connected Essays. J. D. Miller. 1981. 27.50x (ISBN 0-312-89240-3). St Martin.
World of Stereographs. William C. Darrah. LC 77-92123. 246p. 1977. 22.50 (ISBN 0-913116-04-1). W C Darrah.
World of Stone: The Aran Islands. Ed. by Curriculum Development Unit. (Illus.). 80p. (Orig.). 1982. pap. 7.95 (ISBN 0-905140-12-5, Pub. by O'Brien Pr Ireland). Irish Bks Media.
World of Stories. Retold by & narrated by Katharine Hepburn. (Illus.). 128p. (ps up). 1988. Incl. cassette. 19.95 (ISBN 0-06-022296-4). HarpJ.
World of Story: Short Fiction of the Twentieth Century. Selected by Clifton Fadiman. 1985. pap. write for info. HM.
World of Strangers. Nadine Gordimer. 272p. 1984. pap. 7.95 (ISBN 0-14-001704-6). Penguin.
World of Strangers: Order & Action in Urban Public Space. Lyn H. Lofland. 223p. 1985. pap. text ed. 9.95x (ISBN 0-88133-136-8). Waveland Pr.
World of Surgery, Nineteen Forty Five to Nineteen Eighty Five: Memoirs of One Participant. James D. Hardy. (Illus.). 385p. 1986. 39.95 (ISBN 0-8122-8000-8). U of PA Pr.

World of Yesterday's Humanist Today: Proceedings of the 1981 Stefan Zweig Symposium. Ed. by Marion Sonnenfeld. LC 83-541. 357p. 1983. 59.50x (ISBN 0-87395-599-4). State U NY Pr.
World of Young Andrew Jackson. Suzanne Hilton. (Young Presidents Ser.). (Illus.). (gr. 5-8). Date not set. 12.95. Walker & Co.
World of Young George Washington. Suzanne Hilton. LC 86-13296. (Illus.). 112p. (gr. 5-9). 1987. 12.95 (ISBN 0-8027-6657-9); PLB 12.85 (ISBN 0-8027-6658-7). Walker & Co.
World of Young Herbert Hoover. Suzanne Hilton. (gr. 5-8). 1987. 12.95 (ISBN 0-8027-6708-7); PLB 13.85 (ISBN 0-8027-6709-5). Walker & Co.
World of Young Tom Jefferson. Suzanne Hilton. (Illus.). 96p. (gr. 3-6). 1986. 12.95 (ISBN 0-8027-6621-8); lib. bdg. 12.85 (ISBN 0-8027-6622-6). Walker & Co.
World of Zen. Ed. by Nancy W. Ross. (Illus.). 1960. pap. 9.95 (ISBN 0-394-70301-4, Vin). Random.
World Oil Co. vs. Northeast Shipbuilding, Inc. & Toiler Salvage Co. Defective Designs, Negligence. Thomas F. Geraghty. 230p. 1983. 17.95 (ISBN 1-55681-099-7); tchr's. manual 5.00 (ISBN 1-55681-074-1). Natl Inst Trial Ad.
World Oil: Coping With the Dangers of Success. Christopher Flavin. LC 85-51495. (Worldwatch Papers). 1985. pap. 4.00 (ISBN 0-916468-66-6). Worldwatch Inst.
World Oil's Cementing Oil & Gas Wells: Including Casing Handling Procedures. George O. Suman & Richard C. Ellis. (World Oil Handbook Ser.: Vol. 3). pap. 20.00 (ISBN 0-317-26814-7, 2024313). Bks Demand UMI.
World on Paper: Studies on the Second Scientific Revolution. Enrico Bellone. Tr. by Mirella Giaconni & Ricardo Giaconni. 220p. 1980. pap. 9.95x (ISBN 0-262-52081-8). MIT Pr.
World on Wheels: Or, Carriages, with Their Historical Associations from the Earliest to the Present Time. Ezra Stratton. LC 72-83800. (Illus.). Repr. of 1878 ed. 29.00 (ISBN 0-405-09006-4). Ayer Co Pubs.
World One. Date not set. price not set (ISBN 0-9619914-0-2). Americus Pr.
World Order: Its Intellectual & Cultural Foundations. Ed. by F. Ernest Johnson. LC 68-26188. (Religion & Civilization Ser.). 1969. Repr. of 1945 ed. 26.50 (ISBN 0-8046-0223-9, Pub. by Kennikat). Assoc Faculty Pr.
World Order of Baha'u'llah. 2nd rev. ed. Shoghi Effendi. LC 56-17685. 1974. 16.95 (ISBN 0-87743-031-4, 108-020). Baha'i.
World Order Perspective on Authoritarian Tendencies. Richard A. Falk. (Working Papers: No. 10). (Illus.). 67p. (Orig.). 1980. pap. text ed. 2.00 (ISBN 0-911646-17-5). World Policy.
World Order Perspective on Authoritarian Tendencies. Richard A. Falk. 67p. 1980. pap. 5.95x. Transaction Bks.
World Order: Socialist Perspectives. Ed. by Ray Bush et al. 288p. Date not set. text ed. 49.95 (ISBN 0-7456-0028-X); pap. text ed. 19.95 (ISBN 0-7456-0029-8). Basil Blackwell.
World Orders. B. P. Menon. (Writers Workshop Blackbird Ser.). 32p. 1978. flexible cloth 6.00 (ISBN 0-86578-056-0). Ind-US Inc.
World Organization. Raymond Bridgman. LC 77-147575. (Library of War & Peace; Int'l. Organization, Arbitration & Law). 1972. 46.00 (ISBN 0-8240-0341-1). Garland Pub.
World Out of Time. Larry Niven. pap. 2.95 (ISBN 0-345-33696-8). Ballantine.
World Outreach Intercessory Prayer Warriors. Dee Deason & Velma Deason. 1983. pap. 2.50 (ISBN 0-910709-40-8). PTL Repro.
World Outside: The Fiction of Paul Bowles. Richard F. Patteson. 167p. 1987. text ed. 18.95x (ISBN 0-292-79034-1); pap. 7.95 (ISBN 0-292-79035-X). U of Tex Pr.
World Outside the Window: The Selected Essays of Kenneth Rexroth. Kenneth Rexroth. Ed. by Bradford Morrow. LC 86-28610. 352p. 1987. 24.95 (ISBN 0-8112-1024-3); pap. 12.95 (ISBN 0-8112-1025-1, NDP639). New Directions.
World Painting Index, 2 vols. Patricia P. Havlice. Incl. Vol. 1. Bibliography, Paintings by Unknown Artists, Painters & Their Works; Vol. 2. Titles of Works & Their Painters. LC 76-52407. 2136p. 1977. Set. 92.50 (ISBN 0-8108-1016-6). Scarecrow.
World Painting Index: First Supplement 1973-1980, 2 vols. Patricia P. Havlice. Incl. Vol. I. Bibliography, Paintings by Unknown Artists, Painters & Their Works; Vol. II. Titles of Works & Their Painters. LC 82-3355. 1233p. 1982. Set. 69.50 (ISBN 0-8108-1531-1). Scarecrow.
World Patent Law: Patent Statutes, Regulations & Treaties, 11 vols. John P. Sinnott. (Patent Law & Practice Ser.: Vols. 2B-2L). 1974. looseleaf set 400.00 (622); Updates avail. 1985 245.00; 1986 260.00. Bender.
World Peace? A Work Based on Interviews with Foreign Diplomats. Anthony J. Donovan. LC 86-71893. 128p. (Orig.). 1986. pap. write for info. (ISBN 0-9617258-0-X). A J Donovan.
World Peace: A Written Debate. William H. Taft & William J. Bryan. Repr. of 1917 ed. 20.00 (ISBN 0-527-88632-7). Kraus Repr.
World Peace: A Written Debate Between William Howard Taft & William Jennings Bryan. William H. Taft. LC 73-137553. (Peace Movement in America Ser). 156p. 1972. Repr. of 1917 ed. lib. bdg. 13.95x (ISBN 0-89198-083-0). Ozer.
World Peace & the Developing Countries: Annals of Pugwash 1985. Ed. by Joseph Rotblat & Ubiratan D'Ambrosio. 264p. 1986. text ed. 39.50x (ISBN 0-333-43636-9, Pub. by Macmillan London); pap. text ed. 19.50x (ISBN 0-333-43637-7). Sheridan.
World Peace & World Government: From Vision to Reality a Baha'i Approach. J. Tyson. 96p. (Orig.). 1986. pap. 3.25 (ISBN 0-85398-235-X). G Ronald Pub.
World Peace Council & Soviet Active Measures. Herbert Romerstein. pap. 5.00 (ISBN 0-935067-01-9). Nathan Hale Inst.
World Peace Gathering. Dharma Realm Buddhist Association Staff. (Illus.). 128p. (Orig.). pap. 5.00 (ISBN 0-917512-05-7). Buddhist Text.
World Peace Through World Law. 2nd, rev. ed. Grenville Clark & Louis B. Solon. 388p. 1960. 34.95 (ISBN 0-87855-358-4). Transaction Bks.
World Peace Through World Law: Two Alternative Plans. 3rd ed. Grenville Clark. LC 66-21198. pap. 147.30 (ISBN 0-317-09601-X, 2003006). Bks Demand UMI.
World-Peacemaker. Joe Lewis. pap. 2.95 (ISBN 0-87505-329-7). Borden.
World Perspectives: A European Assessment. Jacques F. Lesourne. Tr. by Sharon L. Romeo. 3000p. (Fr.). 1986. 45.00 (ISBN 2-88124-179-4). Gordon & Breach.
World Perspectives: Aspects of Education for International Understanding. Derek Heater. 1986. 32.00x (ISBN 0-905777-53-0, Pub. by Hesketh UK). State Mutual Bk.
World Perspectives in the Sociology of the Military. Ed. by George A. Kourvetaris & Betty A. Dobratz. LC 76-45941. 294p. 1977. text ed. 32.95 (ISBN 0-87855-207-3). Transaction Bks.
World Petroleum Arrangements, 1987. Gordon H. Barrows. Ed. by D. Jeune & M. Guerra. (Basic Oil Laws & Concession Contracts Ser.). 589p. 1987. 385.00 (ISBN 0-89069-001-4). Barrows Co.
World Petroleum Market. M. A. Adelmam. 458p. 1973. 37.00 (ISBN 0-8018-1422-7). Resources Future.
World Petroleum Market. M. A. Adelman. LC 72-4029. (Resources for the Future Ser.). (Illus.). 456p. 1973. 37.00x. Johns Hopkins.
World Petroleum Market: The Market for Petroleum & Petroleum Products in the 1980's. Stuart Sinclair. 250p. 60.00x (ISBN 0-87196-914-9). Facts on File.
World Petroleum Resources & Reserves. Joseph P. Riva, Jr. (Special Study). (Illus.). 250p. 1983. lib. bdg. 48.00x (ISBN 0-86531-446-2). Westview.
World Philosophy, 5 vols. LC 82-60268. 2572p. 1982. Set. 250.00x (ISBN 0-89356-325-0). Salem Pr.
World Photography Sources. Ed. by David N. Bradshaw & Catherine Hahn. 515p. 40.00 (ISBN 0-9607992-1-4). Directories.
World Pipelines. Ed. by J. N. Tiratsoo. LC 83-81452. 128p. 1983. 59.00x (ISBN 0-87201-925-X). Gulf Pub.
World Place Location Learning System. 4th ed. Richard M. MacKinnon. LC 87-71469. 91p. 1988. wkbk. 3.70 (ISBN 0-9618558-0-0). A Hancock Coll.
World Point-World Line. Kathleen M. Podolsky. LC 82-15164. (Illus.). 72p. (Orig.). 1982. pap. 14.95 (ISBN 0-942714-00-8). LIM Press CA.
World Police & Paramilitary Forces. John M. Andrade. LC 85-17247. 245p. 1986. 100.00x (ISBN 0-943818-14-1, Stockton Pr). Groves Dict Music.
World Politics. James N. Rosenau et al. LC 75-22766. (Illus.). 1976. text ed. 17.95 (ISBN 0-02-927040-5). Free Pr.
World Politics. 2nd ed. Starr. LC 84-24673. (Illus.). 617p. 1985. 23.95 (ISBN 0-7167-1701-8). W H Freeman.
World Politics & International Economics. Ed. by C. Fred Bergsten & Lawrence B. Krause. LC 75-15684. pap. 93.30 (ISBN 0-317-20637-0, 2024128). Bks Demand UMI.
World Politics & International Law. Francis A. Boyle. (Policy Studies). xii, 366p. 1985. 35.00 (ISBN 0-8223-0609-3); pap. 14.95 (ISBN 0-8223-0655-7). Duke.
World Politics & the Cause of War Since 1914. Amos Yoder. LC 85-22759. (Illus.). 254p. (Orig.). 1986. lib. bdg. 26.25 (ISBN 0-8191-5045-2); pap. text ed. 12.00 (ISBN 0-8191-5046-0). U Pr of Amer.
World Politics & Western Reason: Universalism, Pluralism, Hegemony. R. J. Walker. (Working Papers: No. 19). 32p. 1982. pap. 2.00 (ISBN 0-911646-25-6). World Policy.
World Politics Debated. Herbert M. Levine. 384p. 1983. pap. 19.95 (ISBN 0-07-037433-3). McGraw.
World Politics Debated. 2nd ed. Herbert M. Levine. 480p. 1985. text ed. 19.95 (ISBN 0-07-037450-3). McGraw.
World Politics Debated. 3rd ed. Herbert M. Levine. 512p. 1988. 19.95 (ISBN 0-07-037479-1). McGraw.
World Politics in Modern Civilization, 2 vols. Harry E. Barnes. Set. 150.00 (ISBN 0-87700-038-7). Revisionist Pr.
World Politics in the General Asssembly. Hayward R. Alker & Bruce M. Russett. LC 65-22313. (Yale Studies in Political Science: No. 15). pap. 88.00 (ISBN 0-317-09370-3, 2021974). Bks Demand UMI.
World Politics in the Twentieth Century. Peter R. Beckman. (Illus.). 400p. 1984. pap. write for info. (ISBN 0-13-968768-8). P-H.
World Politics since Nineteen Forty-Five. 4th ed. Peter Calvocoressi. LC 81-6055. 516p. 1982. pap. 19.95 5th ed (ISBN 0-582-29713-3). Longman.
World Politics: Trend & Transformation. 2nd ed. Charles W. Kegley, Jr. & Eugene R. Wittkopf. LC 84-51146. 600p. 1985. pap. text ed. write for info. (ISBN 0-312-89248-9); instr's. manual avail. St Martin.
World Pollen & Spore Flora, 9 vols. Ed. by Siwert Nilsson. 260p. (Orig.). 1980. Set. pap. text ed. 135.00x (Pub. by Almqvist & Wiksell). Coronet Bks.
World Pollen Flora, 4 vols. G. Erdtman. Incl. Vol. 1. Coriariaceae. 1970. pap.; Vol. 2. Gyrostemonaceae. B. Prijanto. 1970. pap.; Vol. 3. Batidacene. B. Prijanto. 1970. pap.; Vol. 4. Globularioceae. J. Praglowski & K. Gyllander. 1971. pap.. (Illus.). Set. pap. 39.95x (ISBN 0-02-844210-5). Hafner.
World Population: An Analysis of Vital Data. Nathan Keyfitz & Wilhelm Flieger. LC 68-14010. xvi, 672p. 1968. 50.00x (ISBN 0-226-43234-3). U of Chicago Pr.
World Population & Development: Challenges & Prospects. Ed. by Philip M. Hauser. (Illus.). 708p. 1979. 18.00x (ISBN 0-8156-2216-3); pap. 9.95x (ISBN 0-8156-2219-8). Syracuse U Pr.
World Population & Resources: A Report. Political & Economic Planning. LC 78-14136. (Illus.). 1980. Repr. of 1955 ed. 30.25 (ISBN 0-88355-810-6). Hyperion Conn.
World Population & the United Nations: Challenge & Response. Stanley P. Johnson. (Illus.). 300p. 1988. 59.50 (ISBN 0-521-32207-3); pap. 22.95 (ISBN 0-521-31104-7). Cambridge U pr.
World Population & U. S. Policy: The Choices Ahead. Ed. by Jane Menken. (American Assembly Bk.). 255p. 1986. 18.95 (ISBN 0-317-60287-X); pap. 8.95 (ISBN 0-393-30399-3). Norton.
World Population: Basic Documents, 4 vols. James A. Joyce. LC 75-6869. 1976. text ed. 180.00 set (ISBN 0-379-10062-2). Oceana.
World Population Crisis: Policy Implications & the Role of Law: Proceedings of the American Society of International Law Regional Meeting & the John Bassett Moore Society of International Law Symposium. Ed. by John M. Paxman. LC 80-19753. vi, 179p. 1980. Repr. of 1971 ed. lib. bdg. 35.00x (ISBN 0-313-22619-9, PAWO). Greenwood.
World Population Growth & Living Standards. Kuan-I Chen. 12.95x (ISBN 0-317-18410-5). New Coll U Pr.
World Population Growth & Response 1965-1975: A Decade of Global Action. Population Reference Bureau Editors. (Illus.). 271p. 1976. pap. text ed. 4.00 (ISBN 0-917136-00-4). Population Ref.
World Population Policies. Jyoti S. Singh. LC 78-19756. 1979. 42.95 (ISBN 0-275-90424-5, C0424). Praeger.
World Population Policies, Vol. I: Population Studies No. 102, Afghanistan to France. 247p. 1988. pap. 28.00 (ISBN 92-1-151165-8, E.87.XIII.4). UN.
World Population Problems: An Introduction to Population Geography. D. Gordon Bennett. LC 83-62691. 250p. 1984. pap. text ed. 12.95 (ISBN 0-941226-04-2). Park Pr Co.
World Population Projections 1984: Short & Long Term Estimates by Age & Sex with Related Demographic Statistics. My T. Vu. 480p. 35.00 (ISBN 0-8213-0431-3, BK 0431). World Bank.
World Population Projections 1985: Short & Long-Term Estimates by Age & Sex with Related Demographic Statistics. My T. Vu. LC 85-23083. 480p. 1986. text ed. 50.00x (ISBN 0-8018-3322-1). Johns Hopkins.
World Population Projections, 1987-88 Edition: Short & Long-Term Estimates. K. C. Zachariah & My T. Vu. LC 87-35248. 500p. 1988. text ed. 52.95x (ISBN 0-8018-3673-5). Johns Hopkins.
World Population Prospects: Estimates & Projections As Assessed in 1984. (Population Studies: No. 98). 330p. 1986. pap. 35.00 (ISBN 92-1-151159-3, E.86.XIII.3). UN.
World Population: The Present & Future Crisis. Phyllis T. Piotrow. LC 80-69582. (Headline Ser.: No. 251). (Illus.). 80p. (Orig.). 1980. pap. 4.00 (ISBN 0-87124-064-5). Foreign Policy.
World Population Trends & Their Impact on Economic Development. Ed. by Dominick Salvatore. (Contributions in Economics & Economic History Ser.: No. 82). 1988. price not set (ISBN 0-313-25765-5, SVE/). Greenwood.
World Population Trends, Population & Development Interrelations & Population Policies: 1983 Monitoring Report, Vol. II. (Population & Development Interrelations & Population Policies Ser.). 279p. 1985. pap. text ed. 29.00 (ISBN 92-1-151155-0, E.85.XIII.2). UN.
World Population Trends, Population & Development, Interrelations & Population Policies, Vol. 1. 235p. 25.00 (ISBN 92-1-151156-9, E.84.XIII.10). UN.
World Population Trends, Population & Development Interrelations & Population Policies: 1983 Monitoring Report, Vol. 1. (Population Studies: No. 93). 235p. 1986. pap. text ed. 25.00 (ISBN 92-1-151156-9, E.84.XIII.10). UN.
World Poverty & Development: A Survey of American Opinion. Paul A. Laudicina. LC 73-89873. (Monographs: No. 8). 126p. 1973. 2.50 (ISBN 0-686-28687-1). Overseas Dev Council.
World Poverty & Development: A Survey of American Opinion. Paul A. Laudicina. (Monograph Ser.: No. 8). 126p. 1973. 2.50 (ISBN 0-318-16163-X). Overseas Dev Council.
World-Power & Evolution. Ellsworth Huntington. LC 73-14157. (Perspectives in Social Inquiry Ser.). 292p. 1974. Repr. 17.00x (ISBN 0-405-05503-X). Ayer Co Pubs.
World Power & Evolution. Ellsworth Huntington. 1919. 15.50x (ISBN 0-686-83862-9). Elliots Bks.
World Power Assessment: A Calculus of Strategic Drift. new ed. Ray S. Cline. LC 75-21986. (Illus.). 250p. 1975. pap. text ed. 12.95 (ISBN 0-89206-000-X). CSI Studies.
World Power Foundation: Its Goals & Platform. Harold Thomas. 1980. pap. 6.95 (ISBN 0-686-29511-0). Loompanics.
World Powers in South & Southeast Asia: The Politics of Super Nationalism. Imam Zafar. 200p. 1972. 9.50x (ISBN 0-89684-513-3). Orient Bk Dist.
World Powers in the Twentieth Century. 2nd ed. Harriet Ward. 1985. pap. text ed. 13.00x (ISBN 0-435-31911-6). Heinemann Ed.
World Prehistory: A Brief Introduction. Brian M. Fagan. 1979. pap. text ed. write for info. (ISBN 0-673-39005-5). Scott F.
World Prehistory in New Perspective. 3rd ed. John G. Clark. LC 76-51318. (Illus.). 1977. 67.50 (ISBN 0-521-21506-4); pap. 21.95 (ISBN 0-521-29178-X). Cambridge U Pr.
World Premiere Performance of "Gold". Jack London et al. 32p. 1973. pap. 3.00 (ISBN 0-918466-03-2). Quintessence.
World Premiere Performance of "Scorn of Women". Jack London et al. 1979. pap. 3.00 (ISBN 0-918466-04-0). Quintessence.
World Prices & Development. Ed. by Stephany Griffith-Jones et al. 380p. 1985. text ed. 39.50 (ISBN 0-566-00890-4). Gower Pub Co.
World Print Competition 77: 1977. 53p. 9.00 (ISBN 0-317-36172-4); members 7.00 (ISBN 0-317-36173-2). World Print Coun.
World Print Four. World Print Council. 108p. 1983. 14.00 (ISBN 0-9602496-2-1); members 11.00. World Print Coun.
World Print Three: 1980. 120p. 12.00 (ISBN 0-317-36170-8); members 10.00 (ISBN 0-317-36171-6). World Print Coun.
World Priorities. Ed. by Boris Pregel et al. LC 75-29389. 277p. 1977. pap. text ed. 14.95x (ISBN 0-87855-633-8). Transaction Bks.
World Problems. Brian Ferris & Peter Toyne. 236p. 1979. pap. 12.95 (ISBN 0-7175-0509-X). Dufour.
World Problems in the Classroom. Herbert J. Abraham. LC 73-76702. 223p. (Orig.). 1973. pap. 5.00 (ISBN 92-3-101048-4, U729, UNESCO). UNIPUB.
World Problems in the Classroom. Rev. ed. (Educational Studies & Documents: No. 4). (Illus.). 59p. 1981. pap. 5.00 (ISBN 92-3-101817-5, U1108, UNESCO). UNIPUB.
World Problems-Two. S. T. Adian & C. Higman. (Studies in Logic: Vol. 95). x, 578p. 1980. 131.75 (ISBN 0-444-85343-X). Elsevier.
World Product & Income: International Comparisons of Real Gross Product Phase 3. Irving B. Kravis et al. LC 81-15569. (Illus.). 400p. 1982. text ed. 38.00x (ISBN 0-8018-2359-5); pap. text ed. 17.00x (ISBN 0-8018-2360-9). Johns Hopkins.
World Protein Resources. Symposium on Evaluation of World Resources, Atlantic City, 1965 & Aaron M. Altschul. LC 66-28666. (American Chemical Society, Advances in Chemistry Ser.: No. 57). pap. 75.80 (ISBN 0-317-09899-3, 2050185). Bks Demand UMI.
World Public Order of the Environment: Towards an International Ecological Law & Organization. Jan Schneider. LC 78-11712. pap. 87.10 (2031928). Bks Demand UMI.
World Pulp & Paper Demand, Supply & Trade: Selected Papers of an Expert Consultation held in Tunis, Sept. 1977, 2 Vols. (Forestry Papers: No. 4-1 & 4-2). (Illus., Eng., Fr. & Span.). 1977. Vol. 1. pap. 21.25 (ISBN 92-5-100505-2, F1434, FAO); Vol. 2. pap. 15.75 (ISBN 92-5-100532-X, F1432). UNIPUB.
World Quite Round: Two Stories & a Novella. Gordon Weaver. LC 85-23680. 130p. 1986. text ed. 15.95 (ISBN 0-8071-1291-7); pap. 9.95 (ISBN 0-8071-1326-3). LA State U Pr.
World Radio TV Handbook 1988. Andrew G. Sennitt. 600p. 1988. pap. 19.95 (ISBN 0-8230-5919-7, Billboard Bks). Watson-Guptill.
World Radio TV Handbook 1989. Andrew G. Sennitt. 576p. 1989. pap. 19.95 (ISBN 0-8230-5920-0, Billboard Bks). Watson-Guptill.
World Railway Systems. Bernard De Fontgalland. Tr. by V. Hoskins. 220p. 1984. 39.50 (ISBN 0-521-24541-9). Cambridge U Pr.

World Studies Program: Activity Manual. rev. ed. J. Fisher & R. Dryer. (Illus.). 126p. (gr. 6). 1981. duplication masters 49.00 (ISBN 0-943068-07-X); tchr's. guide 5.00 (ISBN 0-943068-05-3). Graphic Learning.

World Studies Program: Work-A-Text. rev. ed. J. Fisher & Rick Dryer. Ed. by J. L. Irvin & Elizabeth Yockstick. (Illus.). 126p. (gr. 6). 1981. wkbk. 3.50 (ISBN 0-943068-06-1). Graphic Learning.

World Sugar Economy: An Econometric Analysis of Long-Term Developments. Jose de Vries. (Working Paper: No. 5). vii, 124p. 1980. 8.00 (ISBN 0-686-36097-4, BK-9047). World Bank.

World Sugar Economy in War. Ed. by Bill Albert & Adrian Graves. 272p. 1988. lib. bdg. 59.95 (ISBN 0-415-00127-7). Routledge Chapman & Hall.

World Sulphur Survey. William F. Sheldrick. (Technical Paper: No. 24). 198p. 1984. 10.00 (ISBN 0-8213-0379-1, BK 0379). World Bank.

World Super Carriers: Naval Air Power Today. Tony Holmes & Jean P. Montbazt. (Osprey Color Library). (Illus.). 128p. 1988. pap. 14.95 (ISBN 0-85045-848-X, Pub. by Osprey England). Motorbooks Intl.

World Supermicro Computer Market. Market Intelligence Research Company Staff. 210p. 1985. pap. text ed. 495.00 (ISBN 0-317-19664-2). Market Res Co.

World Survey. Neil Dalgleish. (Illus.). 128p. 1976. pap. 7.95 (ISBN 0-7175-0750-5). Dufour.

World Survey of CAM. J. Hatvany et al. (Illus.). 141p. 1983. pap. 69.95 (ISBN 0-408-01255-2). Butterworth.

World Survey of Drug & Narcotic Control: A Medical Subject Analysis & Research Index with Bibliography. Clarence A. Levy. LC 83-71739. 140p. 1985. 34.50 (ISBN 0-88164-014-X); pap. 26.50 (ISBN 0-88164-015-8). ABBE Pubs Assn.

World Survey of Education: Educational Policy, Legislation & Administration, Vol. 5. LC 59-1913. (Illus.). 418p. 1971. 50.50 (ISBN 92-3-100932-X, U732, UNESCO). UNIPUB.

World Survey of Major Activities in Controlled Fusion Research: Nuclear Fusion, 1986 (Special Supplement) International Atomic Energy Agency Staff. (Illus.). 563p. (Orig.). 1987. pap. text ed. 115.00 (ISBN 92-0-139086-6, ISP23 86, IAEA). UNIPUB.

World Survey of Nonferrous Smelters. Ed. by J. C. Taylor & H. R. Traulsen. LC 87-42883. (Illus.). 365p. 1987. 90.00 (ISBN 0-87339-026-1). Metal Soc.

World Survey on the Role of Women in Development. 238p. 1986. 11.00 (ISBN 92-1-130109-2, E.86.IV.3). UN.

World Survival: The Third World Struggle. Grainne O'Flynn. (Illus.). 128p. 1984. 17.95 (ISBN 0-86278-040-3, Pub. by O'Brien Pr Ireland); pap. 10.95 (ISBN 0-86278-041-1, Pub. by O'Brien Pr Ireland). Irish Bks Media.

World Symposium on the Importance of the Patent System to Developing Countries. 1978. pap. 13.75 (ISBN 0-685-65239-4, WIPO52, WIPO). UNIPUB.

World Symposium on Warm-Water Pond Fish Culture: Proceedings, Rome, 1966, 2 Vols. (Fisheries Reports: No. 44, Vols. 3-4). 1967-68. Vol. 3, 426p. pap. 27.50 (ISBN 0-686-92950-0, F1395, FAO); Vol. 4, 495p. pap. 27.55 (ISBN 0-686-98807-8, F1664). UNIPUB.

World System Critique of Freire's Philosophy of Education: Naming the World Capitalist Reality. (Project on Goals, Processes & Indicators of Development). 26p. 1981. pap. 5.00 (ISBN 92-808-0330-1, TUNU165, UNU). UNIPUB.

World System: Models, Norms, Variations. Ed. by Ervin Laszlo. (International Library of Systems Theory & Philosophy Ser). 224p. 1973. 7.95 (ISBN 0-8076-0695-2). Braziller.

World Tables, 2 vol. set. 3rd ed. World Bank Data Staff. LC 83-49368. pap. text ed. 25.00x (ISBN 0-8018-3201-2); Vol. 2, Social Data, 184, 1984. text ed. 25.00x; pap. text ed. 12.50x (ISBN 0-8018-3203-9); Set. pap. text ed. 35.50x (ISBN 0-8018-3264-0). Johns Hopkins.

World Tables, 1976: From the Data Files of the World Bank. World Bank. LC 76-41204. pap. 140.00 (ISBN 0-317-29213-7, 2022228). Bks Demand UMI.

World Tables 1987. 4th ed. 534p. 1988. 30.00 (ISBN 0-8213-1035-6, BK1035). World Bank.

World Tales. Idries Shah. 375.00 (ISBN 0-384-54958-6). Johnson Repr.

World Tanks & Reconnaissance Vehicles since 1945. Noel Ayliffe-Jones. (Illus.). 144p. 1984. 19.95 (ISBN 0-88254-978-2). Hippocrene Bks.

World Tapestry Today. Ed. by Jim Brown. Tr. by Trans-Laangg Co. Staff. LC 88-70295. (Illus.). 80p. (Orig., Fr., Eng. & Ger.). 1988. pap. 14.95 (ISBN 0-945858-01-9). Am Tapestry Alliance.

World Task of Pacifism. A. J. Muste. 1942. pap. 2.50x (ISBN 0-87574-013-8, 013). Pendle Hill.

World Tax Reform: A Progress Report. Ed. by Joseph A. Pechman. LC 88-70469. 294p. 1988. pap. 11.95x (ISBN 0-8157-6999-7). Brookings.

World Tea Trade: A Survey of the Production, Distribution & Consumption of Tea. Denys Forrest. 243p. 1985. 52.50 (ISBN 0-85941-259-8, Pub. by Woodhead-Faulkner). Longwood Pub Group.

World Textile Trade: An International Perspective. E. L. Love. 52p. 1978. 30.00x (ISBN 0-686-63809-3). State Mutual Bk.

World That Could Be. Robert C. North. (Portable Stanford Ser.). (Illus.). 1978. (Norton Lib); pap. 4.45 (ISBN 0-393-00882-7). Norton.

World That FDR Built: Vision & Reality. Edward Mortimer. (Illus.). 416p. 1988. 24.95 (ISBN 0-684-18687-X). Scribner.

World That God Destroyed & Other Poems. Frederick E. Pierce. 1911. 29.50x (ISBN 0-686-83865-3). Elliots Bks.

World That Perished. John C. Whitcomb. pap. 5.95 (ISBN 0-88469-059-8). BMH Bks.

World That Perished. rev. ed. John C. Whitcomb. (Illus.). 176p. 1988. pap. 8.95 (ISBN 0-8010-9690-1). Baker Bk.

World That Shaped the New Testament. Calvin J. Roetzel. LC 85-12492. 180p. 1985. pap. 11.95 (ISBN 0-8042-0455-1, John Knox). Westminster John Knox.

World That Works. Sara Ensor. Ed. by Vera Frampton. (Illus.). 182p. (Orig.). 1986. pap. text ed. 10.00x (ISBN 1-85239-500-1); Tchrs. Ed. 6.50x (ISBN 1-85239-501-X). Grosvenor USA.

World, the Flesh, & Angels. Mary Campbell. LC 88-47882. (Barnard New Women Poets Ser.). 80p. 1989. 17.95 (ISBN 0-8070-6806-3); pap. 7.95 (ISBN 0-8070-6807-1). Beacon Pr.

World, the Flesh, & Myself. Michael Davidson. (Gay Modern Classics Ser.). (Illus.). 368p. 1985. 10.95 (ISBN 0-907040-64-0, Pub. by GMP England); pap. write for info. (ISBN 0-907040-63-2, Pub. by GMP England). Alyson Pubns.

World, the Flesh & the Devil. Reay Tannahill. 448p. 1987. 17.95 (ISBN 0-517-56227-8). Crown.

World, the Flesh & the Devil. Reay Tannahill. 512p. 1988. pap. 4.95 (ISBN 0-8041-0227-9, Pub. by Ivy). Ballantine.

World the Slaveholders Made: Two Essays in Interpretation. Eugene D. Genovese. 1971. pap. 2.95 (ISBN 0-394-71676-0, Vin). Random.

World the Slaveholders Made: Two Essays in Interpretation. Eugene D. Genovese. xxiv, 280p. 1988. 35.00x (ISBN 0-8195-5198-8); pap. 12.95 (ISBN 0-8195-6204-1). Wesleyan U Pr.

World, the Text, & the Critic. Edward Said. 336p. 1984. pap. 8.95x (ISBN 0-674-96187-0). Harvard U Pr.

World, the Text, & the Critic. Edward W. Said. 352p. 1983. 21.00x (ISBN 0-674-96186-2). Harvard U Pr.

World, the Work, & the West of W. H. D. Koerner. William H. Hutchinson. LC 78-58125. (Illus.). 1979. 47.50 (ISBN 0-8061-1471-1). U of Okla Pr.

World, the Worldless. William Bronk. LC 64-16822. 1964. 6.00 (ISBN 0-685-79023-1); sewn in wrappers 1.50. Small Pr Dist.

World Theater of Wagner: A Celebration of 150 Years of Wagner Productions. Charles Osborne. LC 82-130. (Illus.). 224p. 1982. 36.50 (ISBN 0-02-594050-3). Macmillan.

World Theater: The Structure & Meaning of Drama. Seymour Reiter. 1973. 10.00 (ISBN 0-8180-0503-3). Horizon.

World Their Household: The American Women's Foreign Mission Movement & Cultural Transformation, 1870-1920. Patricia R. Hill. (Women & Culture Ser.). 300p. 1985. text ed. 19.50x (ISBN 0-472-10055-6). U of Mich Pr.

World They Made Together: Black & White Values in Eighteenth Century Virginia. Mechal Sobel. (Illus.). 374p. 1988. text ed. 25.00 (ISBN 0-691-04747-2). Princeton U Pr.

World Thought Police. T. Schuman. 62p. 1985. pap. 5.60 (ISBN 0-935090-14-2). Almanac Pr.

World Through Literature. Ed. by Charlton G. Laird. LC 77-99639. (Essay Index Reprint Ser.). 1951. 33.00 (ISBN 0-8369-1359-0). Ayer Co Pubs.

World Through My Window. Ruth Orkin. LC 78-2153. (Illus.). 1978. 20.25i (ISBN 0-06-013293-0, HarpT). Har-Row.

World Tin Market: Political Pricing & Economic Competition. William L. Baldwin. LC 83-8888. (Duke Press Policy Studies). xii, 273p. 1983. 45.00 (ISBN 0-8223-0505-4). Duke.

World to Fifteen Hundred. 3rd ed. Leften S. Stavrianos. (Illus.). 384p. 1982. pap. write for info. (ISBN 0-13-968263-5). P-H.

World to Fifteen Hundred: A Global History. 5th ed. Leften S. Stavrianos. (Illus.). 384p. 1987. pap. text ed. price not set (ISBN 0-13-965500-X). P-H.

World Today. Keith Lye. (World of Science Ser.). (Illus.). 64p. (YA) 1985. 12.95 (ISBN 0-8160-1072-2). Facts on File.

World too Wide. Gregory Mcdonald. 336p. (Orig.). 1987. 17.95 (ISBN 0-940595-07-9). Hill & Co Pubs.

World Too Wide. Gregory McDonald. 1987. write for info. Putnam Pub Group.

World Topics Yearbook. annual ed. Ed. by Marilyn R. Trier. (Illus.). 12.95 (ISBN 0-87566-011-8). United Ed.

World Trade. C. A. Hills. (Today's World Ser.). (Illus.). 72p. (gr. 7-10). 1981. 17.95 (ISBN 0-7134-3472-4, Pub. by Batsford England). David & Charles.

World Trade & Output of Manufactures: Structural Trends & Developing Countries' Exports. Donald B. Keesing. (Working Paper Ser.: No. 316). v, 69p. 1979. 5.00 (ISBN 0-686-36214-4, WP-0316). World Bank.

World Trade & Payments: An Introduction. 4th ed. Richard E. Caves & Ronald W. Jones. LC 84-19396. 1984. text ed. 34.00 (ISBN 0-673-39119-1). Scott F.

World Trade Annual Supplement, 1980, 5 vols. 190.00x ea.; Set. 950.00x. Vol. 1. Vol. 2. Vol. 3. Vol. 4. Vol. 5. Walker & Co.

World Trade Annual, 1980, 5 vols. 100.00x ea.; Set. 500.00x (ISBN 0-8027-4800-7). Vol. 1 (ISBN 0-8027-4801-5). Vol. 2 (ISBN 0-8027-4802-3). Vol. 3 (ISBN 0-8027-4803-1). Vol. 4 (ISBN 0-8027-4805-8). Vol. 5 (ISBN 0-8027-4806-6). Walker & Co.

World Trade Center. Anthony W. Robins. LC 87-2246. (Classics in American Architecture Ser.). (Illus.). 64p. (Orig.). 1987. 13.95 (ISBN 0-910923-37-X); pap. cancelled (ISBN 0-910923-36-1). Pineapple Pr.

World Trade Competition: Western Countries & Third World Markets. Ed. by Center for Strategic & International Studies Staff. LC 81-11930. 464p. 1981. 56.95 (ISBN 0-275-90600-0, C0600). Praeger.

World Trade: Constraints & Opportunities in the 80's. Bela Balassa. (Atlantic Papers: No. 36). 70p. 1979. pap. 6.50x (ISBN 0-916672-76-X, Pub. by Allanheld). Rowman.

World Trade in Forest Products. Ed. by James S. Bethel. LC 83-17012. (Geo. S. Long Publication Series). 551p. 40.00x (ISBN 0-295-96078-7). U of Wash Pr.

World Trade in Forest Products, 2: An International Symposium. Ed. by Gerard F. Schreuder. 564p. 1986. 40.00x (ISBN 0-317-39949-7). U of Wash Pr.

World Trade Index: 1988. 1984. 420.00x (ISBN 0-686-75402-6, Pub. by Eagle Pub England). State Mutual Bk.

World Trade Issues in the Mid-1980s. Sidney Golt. (British-North American Committee Ser.). 112p. 1982. pap. 7.00 (ISBN 0-902594-42-7, BN32-NPA198). Natl Planning.

World Trade Issues: Regime, Structure & Policy. James M. Lutz & Young W. Kihl. LC 84-15986. 288p. 1985. 42.95 (ISBN 0-275-90127-0, C0127). Praeger.

World Trade of the Law of GATT. Jackson. 948p. 1969. 40.00x (ISBN 0-672-81235-5, Bobbs-Merrill Law). Michie Co.

World Trade Rivalry: Trade Equity & Competing Industrial Policies. William A. Lovett. LC 85-40388. 304p. 1987. 35.00x (ISBN 0-669-11027-2). Lexington Bks.

World Trade System: Some Inquiries into Its Spatial Structure. Ron J. Johnston. LC 76-6744. 250p. 1976. 26.00x (ISBN 0-312-89250-0). St Martin.

World Trade War. Jon Woronoff. 320p. 1984. 35.00 (ISBN 0-275-91294-9, C1294). Praeger.

World-Traded Services: The Challenge for the Eighties. Raymond J. Krommenacker. 221p. 1984. text ed. 54.00 (ISBN 0-89006-153-X). Artech Hse.

World Trademark Law & Practice, 3 vols. Ethan Horwitz. (Illus.). 1982. Set, updates avail. looseleaf 240.00 (425); Updates 1985 96.50; 1986 174.00. Bender.

World Trademarks & Logotypes: A Collection of Symbols & Their Applications. Ed. by Takenbou Igarashi. (Reference Books - Graphic Arts). 368p. 1986. 95.00x (ISBN 0-8161-8808-4, Pub. by Graphic-Sha Pub Co Ltd Japan). G K Hall.

World Trademarks & Logotypes, No.2. Ed. by T. Igarashi. (Collection of Symbols & Their Applications Ser.). (Illus.). 400p. 1987. 75.00 (ISBN 4-766-10439-0, Pub. by Graphic Sha Japan). Bks Nippan.

World Transport of Energy: Prospects to 1995. D. Hawdon. (Illus.). 120p. 1985. pap. 220.00 (ISBN 0-86010-811-2). Graham & Trotman.

World Travel Market. Robert Senior. 266p. 1986. 310.00x (ISBN 0-686-92044-9, Euromonitor). State Mutual Bk.

World Travel Market. Robert Senior. (Illus.). 266p. 1983. 60.00x (ISBN 0-87196-124-5). Facts on File.

World Travels of Middle-Aged Native. Perle W. Briggs. 1988. 16.95 (ISBN 0-533-07636-6). Vantage.

World Treasure Atlas. Thomas P. Terry. (Illus.). 144p. (Orig.). 1978. pap. 7.50 (ISBN 0-939850-01-X). Spec Pub.

World Treasury of Children's Literature, 2 vols. Ed. by Clifton Fadiman. (Illus.). (ps-3). in slipcase 40.00 (ISBN 0-316-27302-3). Little.

World Treasury of Contemporary Science Fiction. Ed. by David G. Hartwell. 832p. 1989. 29.95 (ISBN 0-316-34941-0). Little.

World Treasury of Grand Opera: Its Triumphs, Trials & Great Personalities. Ed. by George R. Marek. LC 74-167383. (Essay Index Reprint Ser.). Repr. of 1957 ed. 32.00 (ISBN 0-8369-2463-0). Ayer Co Pubs.

World Treasury of Great Poems. Ed. by Eddie-Lou Cole. 39.95 (ISBN 0-317-29095-9). World Poetry Pr.

World Treaty Index, 5 vols. 2nd ed. Peter H. Rohn. LC 83-3872. 4271p. 1984. Set. lib. bdg. 850.00 (ISBN 0-87436-141-9). ABC-Clio.

World Trends in Medical Education: Faculty, Students, & Curriculum. Ed. by Elizabeth Purcell. LC 79-144335. (Josiah Macy Foundation Ser). Repr. of 1971 ed. 62.00 (ISBN 0-8357-9292-7, 2015693). Bks Demand UMI.

World Truck Handbook. 2nd ed. Nick Georgano. 336p. pap. 16.95 (ISBN 0-7106-0366-5). Janes Info Group.

World Turned Upside Down. Christopher Hill. 1984. pap. 6.95 (ISBN 0-14-055147-6, Pelican). Penguin.

World Turned Upside Down. Marcia Sewall. (Illus.). 32p. (ps-3). 1986. 13.95 (ISBN 0-316-78182-7, Joy St Bks). Little.

World Turned Upside Down: The Prose and Poetry of the American Revolution. Ed. by James H. Pickering. 1975. 26.00 (ISBN 0-8046-9082-0, Pub. by Kennikat). Assoc Faculty Pr.

World Two Thousand A.D. Gordon Lindsay. (Prophecy Ser.). 2.50 (ISBN 0-89985-064-2). Christ Nations.

World under God's Law. 5th ed. T. Robert Ingram. LC 62-16216. 1970. pap. text ed. 3.50 (ISBN 0-686-05040-1). St Thomas.

World Union Company: A Design for Planetary Evolution. John R. Stahl. (Illus.). 60p. (Orig.). 1980. pap. 5.00 (ISBN 0-945303-07-6). Evanescent Pr.

World University Insights: With Your Future in Mind. Howard J. Zitko. Orig. Title: New Age Perspectives in Questions & Answers. 208p. 1980. pap. 7.50 (ISBN 0-941902-01-3). World Univ AZ.

World Unmanned Aircraft. Kenneth Munson. (Illus.). 208p. 1988. 40.00 (ISBN 0-7106-0401-7). Janes Info Group.

World Unsuspected: Portraits of Southern Childhood. Intro. by Alex Harris. LC 87-5085. (The Lyndhurst Series on the South, Published for the Duke University Center for Documentary Photography). (Illus.). xxii, 237p. 1987. 16.95 (ISBN 0-8078-1748-1). U of NC Pr.

World Uraniam Potential: An International Evaluation. 1979. 16.00 (ISBN 92-64-11883-7). OECD.

World Vegetables: Principles, Production & Nutritive Values. Masatoshi Yamaguchi. (Illus.). 1983. 39.95 (ISBN 0-87055-433-6). AVI.

World Vegetation. Denis R. Riley & Anthony Young. 1967. 9.95x (ISBN 0-521-06083-4). Cambridge U Pr.

World View. Michael Kearney. Ed. by L. L. Langness & Robert B. Edgerton. LC 83-20945. (Publications in Anthropology & Related Fields Ser.). (Illus.). 244p. (Orig.). 1984. pap. text ed. 9.95x (ISBN 0-88316-550-3). Chandler & Sharp.

World View of Art History: Selected Readings. Virgil H. Bird et al. 464p. 1985. pap. text ed. 39.95 (ISBN 0-8403-3503-2). Kendall-Hunt.

World View of Contemporary Physics: Does It Need a New Mataphysics? Richard F. Kitchener. 208p. 1988. 39.50 (ISBN 0-88706-741-7); pap. 12.95 (ISBN 0-88706-742-5). State U NY Pr.

World View 1982: An Economic & Geopolitical Yearbook. Rev. ed. Pluto-Maspero Project. Tr. by Patrick Camiller. (Illus.). 313p. (Orig.). 1982. pap. 10.00 (ISBN 0-89608-148-6). South End Pr.

World Viewed: Reflections on the Ontology of Film. enl. ed. Stanley Cavell. (Paperback Ser.: No. 151). 1980. 18.50x (ISBN 0-674-96197-8); pap. 6.95 (ISBN 0-674-96196-X). Harvard U Pr.

World War Debt Settlements. Harold G. Moulton & Leo Pasvolsky. LC 36-6779. 1971. Repr. of 1926 ed. 35.00 (ISBN 0-384-40243-7). Johnson Repr.

World War Debts & United States Foreign Policy, 1919-1929. William G. Pullen. Ed. by Stuart Bruchey. (Foreign Economic Policy of the United States Ser.). 157p. 1987. lib. bdg. 30.00 (ISBN 0-8240-8088-2). Garland Pub.

World War I. S. L. Marshall. LC 85-3968. (American Heritage Library). (Illus.). 384p. (Orig.). 1985. pap. 9.95 (ISBN 0-8281-0434-4). HM.

World War I. Pierre Miquel. LC 85-40207. (Silver Burdett Picture Histories Ser.). (Illus.). 64p. (gr. 5 up). 1986. PLB 14.96 (ISBN 0-382-06889-0). Silver.

World War I. (C. C. Publications Social Studies Ser.). (Illus.). 64p. 1985. pkg of 5 wkbk 21.25 (ISBN 0-574-51769-3). SRA.

World War I & the Growth of United States Predominance in Latin America. Emily S. Rosenberg. Ed. by Stuart Bruchey. (Foreign Economic Policy of the United States Ser.). 266p. 1987. lib. bdg. 40.00 (ISBN 0-8240-8089-0). Garland Pub.

World War I & the Weimar Artists: Dix, Grosz, Beckmann, Schlemmer. Matthias Eberle. LC 85-51723. 192p. 1986. 27.00x (ISBN 0-300-03557-8). Yale U Pr.

World War I Aviation Books in English: An Annotated Bibliography. James P. Noffsinger. LC 86-26109. (Illus.). 331p. 1987. 29.50 (ISBN 0-8108-1951-1). Scarecrow.

World War I Flying Ace. Richard Muller. (Time Machine Ser.: No. 24). (Illus.). 144p. (Orig.). 1988. pap. 2.50 (ISBN 0-553-27231-4). Bantam.

World War I: I Was There. William L. Hanson. Ed. by Gregory M. Franzwa. LC 82-8228. (Illus.). 126p. 1982. 11.95 (ISBN 0-935284-24-9). Patrice Pr.

Worldly Power: The Making of the Wall Street Journal. Edward E. Scharff. LC 85-26741. (Illus.). 315p. 1985. 18.95 (ISBN 0-8253-0359-1). Beaufort Bks NY.
Worldly Power: The Making of the Wall Street Journal. Edward E. Scharff. 1987. pap. 9.95 (ISBN 0-317-56711-X, Plume). NAL.
Worldly Theologians: The Persistence of Religion in Nineteenth Century American Thought. Michael D. Clark. LC 80-5840. 328p. (Orig.). 1982. lib. bdg. 30.75 (ISBN 0-8191-1778-1); pap. text ed. 15.25 (ISBN 0-8191-1779-X). U Pr of Amer.
Worldmaker. A. C. Ellis. 240p. 1985. pap. 2.95 (ISBN 0-441-91102-1). Ace Bks.
Worldmark Encyclopedia of the Nations, 5 vols. 6th ed. Ed. by M. Y. Sachs. LC 83-26073. 1750p. 1984. Set. 225.00x (ISBN 0-471-88622-X); Vol. 1. 50.00 (ISBN 0-471-83657-5); Vol. 3. 50.00 (ISBN 0-471-83658-3); Vol. 4. 50.00 (ISBN 0-471-83655-9); Vol. 5. 50.00 (ISBN 0-471-83656-7); Vol. 2. 50.00 (ISBN 0-471-84790-9). Wiley.
Worldmark Encyclopedia of the Nations, 5 vols. 7th ed. Ed. by Moshe Y. Sachs. (Illus.). 1800p. 1988. Set. 250.00 (ISBN 0-471-62406-3). Wiley.
Worldmark Encyclopedia of the States. 2nd ed. Ed. by Moshe Sachs. LC 85-26455. 690p. 1986. 99.95 (ISBN 0-471-83213-8). Wiley.
Worlds. Joe W. Haldeman. 1982. pap. 2.50 (ISBN 0-671-43594-9, Timescape). PB.
World's Aircraft Carriers Nineteen Fourteen to Nineteen Forty-Five. Roger Chesneau. (Warships Illustrated Ser.: No. 8). (Illus.). 68p. (Orig.). 1987. pap. 9.95 (ISBN 0-85368-768-4, Pub. Arms & Armour). Sterling.
Worlds & I. Ella W. Wilcox. Ed. by Annette K. Baxter. LC 79-8823. (Signal Lives Ser.). (Illus.). 1980. Repr. of 1896 ed. lib. bdg. 45.00x (ISBN 0-405-12867-3). Ayer Co Pubs.
Worlds & Lives: The Poetry of Randall Jarrell. Charlotte H. Beck. LC 81-19361. 108p. 1983. 16.00x (ISBN 0-8046-9300-5, Natl U). Assoc Faculty Pr.
Worlds Apart. Owen Barfield. LC 63-17798. 1964. pap. 10.95 (ISBN 0-8195-6017-0). Wesleyan U Pr.
Worlds Apart. Joe Haldeman. LC 83-47875. 227p. (YA) (gr. 7 up). 1983. 15.00. Ultramarine Pub.
Worlds Apart. Richard Jackson. LC 86-30718. (Alabama Poetry Ser.). 80p. 1987. 11.75 (ISBN 0-8173-0343-X); pap. 5.95 (ISBN 0-8173-0344-8). U of Ala Pr.
Worlds Apart. Jill Murphy. 144p. (gr. 3-7). 1989. 13.95 (ISBN 0-399-21566-2, Putnam). Putnam Pub Group.
Worlds Apart. Janet Rosenstock. 320p. 1987. pap. 3.95 (ISBN 0-671-61854-7). PB.
Worlds Apart: A Handbook on World Views. 2nd ed. Norman L. Geisler & William D. Watkins. 1989. price not set. Baker Bk.
Worlds Apart: A Novel of the Future. Joe Haldeman. LC 83-47875. 252p. 1983. 14.95. Viking.
Worlds Apart: An Anthology of Lesbian & Gay Science Fiction & Fantasy. Ed. by Camilla Decarnin et al. 288p. (Orig.). 1986. pap. 7.95 (ISBN 0-932870-87-2). Alyson Pubns.
Worlds Apart? Long-Term Care in Australia & the United States. Ed. by Sandra J. Newman. LC 87-29770. (Home Health Care Services Quarterly Ser.). (Illus.). 130p. 1988. text ed. 19.95 (ISBN 0-86656-703-8). Haworth Pr.
World's Apart: Readings for a Sociology of Education see Toward a Sociology of Education.
Worlds Apart: Structural Parallels in Poetry of Paul Valery, Saint-John Perse, Benjamin Peret & Rene Char. Elizabeth R. Jackson. (De Proprietatibus Litterarum Series Practica: No. 106). 256p. 1976. pap. text ed. 37.60x (ISBN 90-2793-394-4). Mouton.
Worlds Apart: Technology & North-South Relations in the Global Economy. Sam Cole & Ian Miles. 256p. 1984. 18.95x (ISBN 0-8476-7374-X). Rowman.
Worlds Apart: The Market & the Theater in Anglo-American Thought, 1550-1750. Jean-Christophe Agnew. 248p. 1986. 24.95 (ISBN 0-521-24322-X). Cambridge U Pr.
Worlds Apart: Women under Immigration Law. Ed. by Jacqueline Bhabha et al. 176p. (Orig.). 1985. pap. 7.50 (ISBN 0-7453-0021-9, Pub. by Pluto Pr). Longwood Pub Group.
World's Beef Business. James R. Simpson & Donald E. Farris. (Illus.). 334p. 1982. text ed. 23.95x (ISBN 0-8138-0960-6); pap. text ed. 14.50x (ISBN 0-8138-1924-5). Iowa St U Pr.
World's Best. 3rd ed. Ed. by Marian V. Cooper. 500p. 1988. 19.95 (ISBN 0-945332-08-4). Agora Inc MD.
World's Best Aussie Jokes. A. N. Ocker. (Illus.). 96p. (Orig.). 1987. pap. 4.95 (ISBN 0-207-15311-6, Pub. by Angus & Robertson). Salem Hse Pubs.
World's Best Business Hotels. Ed. by William Davis. 1985. 65.00 (ISBN 0-912289-54-6). St James Pr.
World's Best Christmas Carols. rev. ed. 64p. 1987. pap. 2.95 (ISBN 0-87403-212-1, 9848). Standard Pub.
World's Best Dirty Jokes. Mr. J. (Illus.). 1979. pap. 4.95 (ISBN 0-8065-0702-0, Pub. by Citadel Pr). Lyle Stuart.
World's Best Dirty Jokes. Mr. J. (Illus.). 160p. 1976. 7.95 (ISBN 0-8184-0223-7). Lyle Stuart.
World's Best Dirty Jokes. Mr. J. pap. 3.50 (ISBN 0-345-33106-0). Ballantine.
World's Best Dirty Limericks. David M. (Illus.). 192p. 1982. 8.95 (ISBN 0-8184-0324-1). Lyle Stuart.
World's Best Epigrams. Lawson J. Gilchrist. 231p. 1980. Repr. of 1924 ed. lib. bdg. 30.00 (ISBN 0-8495-3327-9). Arden Lib.
World's Best Essays From the Earliest Period to the Present Time, 10 vols. Ed. by David J. Brewer. 1982. Repr. of 1900 ed. lib. bdg. 500.00 (ISBN 0-8495-0230-6, SET). Arden Lib.
World's Best Fairy Tales, 2 vols. Ed. by Reader's Digest Editors. LC 79-89496. (Illus.). 832p. 1967. Set. 22.95 (ISBN 0-89577-078-4, Pub. by RD Assn). Random.
World's Best Fishing Holes: Over Seventy Great Destinations Where the Joy of Fishing Is Worth a Special Trip. E. L. Rogers. (Illus.). 256p. 1986. 16.95 (ISBN 0-13-968892-7). P-H.
World's Best Funny Songs. Esther Nelson. LC 87-753871. (Illus.). 128p. (gr. 2-8). 1988. 10.95 (ISBN 0-8069-6770-6); PLB 13.29 (ISBN 0-8069-6771-4). Sterling.
World's Best Home Study Mail Order Guide. 1987. lib. bdg. 59.00 (ISBN 0-317-55330-5). Gordon Pr.
World's Best Hope. Francis Biddle. (Midway Reprint Ser). xiv, 176p. 1974. pap. 8.50x (ISBN 0-226-04621-4). U of Chicago Pr.
World's Best Hymns. Louis K. Harlow. Ed. by J. W. Churchill. 1978. Repr. of 1893 ed. lib. bdg. 25.00 (ISBN 0-8495-2323-0). Arden Lib.
Worlds Best Indoor Games. Gyles Brandreth. LC 81-48342. (Illus.). 304p. 1982. pap. 7.95 (ISBN 0-394-71001-0). Pantheon.
World's Best Irish Jokes. 92p. 1982. pap. 3.95 (ISBN 0-8065-0861-2, Pub. by Citadel Pr). Lyle Stuart.
World's Best Loved Poems. James G. Lawson. Repr. of 1927 ed. lib. bdg. 30.00 (ISBN 0-8495-3430-5). Arden Lib.
World's Best Loved Poems. Ed. by James G. Lawson. 1927. 18.45 (ISBN 0-06-065210-1, HarpR). Har-Row.
World's Best Optical Illusions. Charles H. Paraquin. Tr. by Paul Kuttner. LC 87-13885. (Illus.). 96p. (Orig.). (YA) (gr. 4-12). 1987. pap. 4.95 (ISBN 0-8069-6644-0). Sterling.
World's Best Party Games. Sheila A. Barry. LC 86-30038. (Illus.). 128p. 1987. 10.95 (ISBN 0-8069-6482-0); pap. 13.29 (ISBN 0-8069-6484-7); 12.49 (ISBN 0-8069-6483-9). Sterling.
World's Best Picture Puzzles. Doug Anderson. LC 87-25261. (Illus.). 128p. 1988. pap. 4.95 (ISBN 0-8069-6778-1). Sterling.
World's Best Poetry, 10 vols. Ed. by Bliss Carman. 1975. Set. lib. bdg. 1200.00 (ISBN 0-87968-323-6). Gordon Pr.
World's Best Poetry, 10 Vols. Ed. by Bliss Carman. LC 81-83524. 4944p. 1982. Repr. of 1904 ed. lib. bdg. 459.99x (ISBN 0-89609-300-X). Roth Pub Inc.
World's Best Poetry: Critical Companion, Supplement III. Roth Publishing Inc. Editorial Board. LC 82-84763. 400p. 1986. 49.95x (ISBN 0-89609-242-9). Roth Pub Inc.
World's Best Poetry for Children, 2 vols. Roth Publishing Inc. Editoral Board. LC 85-81109. (Illus.). 1000p. (gr. k-8). 1986. Set. lib. bdg. 89.99x (ISBN 0-89609-260-7). Roth Pub Inc.
World's Best Poetry: Supplement IV, Minority Poetry of America; an Anthology of Asian, Black, Hispanic, & Native American Poetry. Ed. by Roth Publishing, Inc., Staff. LC 82-84763. 370p. 1987. 49.95x (ISBN 0-89609-265-8). Roth Pub Inc.
World's Best Poetry: Supplement One: Twentieth Century English & American Verse, 1900-1929. Granger Book Company Editorial Board. LC 82-84763. (No. I). 352p. 1983. 49.95x (ISBN 0-89609-236-4). Roth Pub Inc.
World's Best Poetry: Supplement Two: Twentieth Century English & American Verse, 1930-1950. Granger Book Company, Editorial Board Staff. LC 82-84763. 1984. 49.95x (ISBN 0-89609-239-9). Roth Pub Inc.
World's Best Puzzles. Charles B. Townsend. LC 85-30284. (Illus.). 128p. (Orig.). 1986. 10.95 (ISBN 0-8069-4732-2); lib. bdg. 13.29 (ISBN 0-8069-4733-0); pap. 4.95 (ISBN 0-8069-4734-9). Sterling.
World's Best Religious Quotations. James G. Lawson. 1979. Repr. lib. bdg. 35.00 (ISBN 0-8492-1610-9). R West.
World's Best Sailboats: A Survey. Ferenc Mate. 1986. 39.95 (ISBN 0-317-58092-2). Norton.
World's Best Science Fiction Annual, 1983. Ed. by Donald A. Wollheim. 1983. pap. 2.95 (ISBN 0-87997-822-8). DAW Bks.
World's Best Science Fiction Annual 1984. Ed. by Donald A. Wollheim & Arthur W. Saha. 1984. pap. 2.95 (ISBN 0-87997-934-8). DAW Bks.
World's Best Science Fiction Annual, 1985. Ed. by Donald A. Wollheim. 304p. 1985. pap. 2.95 (ISBN 0-88677-047-5). DAW Bks.
World's Best Science Fiction Annual 1987. Ed. by Donald A. Wolheim. 1987. pap. 3.50 (ISBN 0-317-61863-6). DAW Bks.
World's Best Science Fiction Annual 1987. Ed. by Donald A. Wollheim. 304p. 1987. pap. 3.95 (ISBN 0-88677-203-6). DAW Bks.
World's Best Science Fiction, 1988. Ed. by Donald A. Wollheim. 1988. pap. 3.50 (ISBN 0-88677-281-8). DAW Bks.
World's Best Sports Riddles & Jokes. Joseph Rosenbloom. LC 87-30434. (Illus.). 128p. (gr. 4-12). 1988. 10.95 (ISBN 0-8069-6772-2); PLB 13.29 (ISBN 0-8069-6773-0). Sterling.
World's Best Travel Games. Sheila A. Barry. LC 87-7065. (Illus.). 128p. (YA) (gr. 5 up). 1987. 10.95 (ISBN 0-8069-6550-9); PLB 13.29 (ISBN 0-8069-6551-7). Sterling.
World's Best Travel Games. Sheila A. Barry. LC 87-7065. (Illus.). 128p. (gr. 2-8). 1988. pap. 4.95. Sterling.
World's Best "True" Ghost Stories. C. B. Colby. LC 88-11703. (Illus.). 128p. (YA) (gr. 6-12). 1988. 10.95 (ISBN 0-8069-6876-1). Sterling.
World's Best Yiddish Dirty Jokes. Mr. P. (Illus.). 128p. 1984. pap. 4.95 (ISBN 0-8065-0887-6, Pub. by Citadel Pr). Lyle Stuart.
Worlds Between Two Rivers: Perspectives on American Indians in Iowa. Ed. by Gretchen M. Bataille et al. LC 77-16107. pap. cancelled (ISBN 0-317-42103-4, 2025949). Bks Demand UMI.
Worlds Between Two Rivers: Perspectives on American Indians in Iowa. Ed. by Gretchen M. Bataille et al. (Iowa Heritage Collection Ser.). (Illus.). 148p. 1987. pap. 4.95 (ISBN 0-8138-1794-3). Iowa St U Pr.
Worlds Beyond Dune: The Best of Frank Herbert, 5 bks. Frank Herbert. Incl. Jesus Incident; Whipping Star; Destination: Void; Godmakers; Dosadi Experiment. 1987. Boxed Set. pap. 17.85 (ISBN 0-425-09465-0). Berkley Pub.
Worlds Beyond: The Everlasting Frontier. Ed. by New Dimensions Foundation. LC 78-54345. 320p. 1978. pap. 6.95 (ISBN 0-915904-36-5). And-Or Pr.
Worlds Beyond the World: The Fantastic Vision of William Morris. Richard Mathews. LC 78-247. (Milford Ser: Popular Writers of Today Vol. 13). 63p. 1978. lib. bdg. 16.95x (ISBN 0-89370-118-1); pap. 7.95x (ISBN 0-89370-218-8). Borgo Pr.
Worlds Beyond Thought: Conversations on Now-Consciousness. Albert Blackburn. LC 87-82604. 218p. (Orig.). 1988. pap. 12.00 (ISBN 0-9613054-3-6). Idylwild Bks.
World's Biggest Motorcycle Race: The Daytona 200. Rusty Rae. LC 77-92297. (Superwheels & Thrill Sports Bks.). (Illus.). (gr. 4-9). 1978. PLB 8.95 (ISBN 0-8225-0422-7). Lerner Pubns.
World's Championship Matches: 1921 & 1927. Jose R. Capablanca. LC 76-28101. 1977. pap. 3.50 (ISBN 0-486-23189-5). Dover.
World's Chief Languages. Mario Pei. 1960. 25.00x (ISBN 0-913298-07-7). S F Vanni.
World's Coastline. Ed. by Eric C. Bird & Maurice L. Schwartz. (Illus.). 1184p. 1985. 105.95 (ISBN 0-442-21116-3). Van Nos Reinhold.
World's Debt to Pasteur. Hilary Koprowski & Stanley A. Plotkin. LC 85-10381. (Wistar Symposium Ser.: Vol. 3). 352p. 1985. 39.50 (ISBN 0-8451-2002-6). A R Liss.
World's Debt to the Irish. J. J. Walsh. 250.00 (ISBN 0-87968-360-0). Gordon Pr.
World's Design. Salvador De Madariaga. 1938. 12.50x (ISBN 0-686-17395-3). R S Barnes.
World's Discoverers: The Story of Bold Voyages by Brave Navigators During a Thousand Years. William H. Johnson. 1977. lib. bdg. 59.95 (ISBN 0-8490-2847-7). Gordon Pr.
World's Economic Crisis. Arthur Salter et al. LC 72-137960. (Economic Thought, History & Challenge Ser). 1971. Repr. of 1932 ed. 27.00 (ISBN 0-8046-1462-8, Pub. by Kennikat). Assoc Faculty Pr.
World's Economic Crisis, & the Way of Escape. facsimile ed. Arthur Salter et al. LC 79-152221. (Essay Index Reprints - Halley Stewart Lecture Ser., 1931). Repr. of 1932 ed. 18.00 (ISBN 0-8369-2340-5). Ayer Co Pubs.
World's Economic Plight & Community Responsibility. Community Service Editors. 1977. pap. 1.00 (ISBN 0-910420-24-6). Comm Serv OH.
World's Elite Forces. Bruce Quarrie. Ed. by Hillary Cige. 256p. 1988. pap. 3.95 (ISBN 0-425-10852-X). Berkley Pub.
World's End. T. Coraghessan Boyle. 414p. 1987. 19.95 (ISBN 0-670-81489-X). Viking.
World's End. T. Coraghessan Boyle. 480p. 1988. pap. 8.95 (ISBN 0-14-009760-0). Penguin.
World's End. Joan D. Vinge. 1984. pap. 2.95 (ISBN 0-8125-5711-5, Dist. by Warner Pub. Services & Saint Martin's Press). Tor Bks.
World's End. Joan D. Vinge. 230p. 1984. 15.00 (ISBN 0-89366-141-4). Ultramarine Pub.
World's End & Other Stories. Paul Theroux. 224p. 3.95 (ISBN 0-671-49762-6). WSP.
World's Eye. Albert M. Potts. LC 79-4009. (Illus.). 104p. 1982. 22.00 (ISBN 0-8131-1387-3). U Pr of Ky.
World's Fair. E. L. Doctorow. 1985. 17.45 (ISBN 0-394-52528-0). Random.
World's Fair. E. L. Doctorow. (Large print Books). 476p. 1986. lib. bdg. 19.95 (ISBN 0-8161-4085-5, Large Print Bks). G K Hall.
World's Fair. E. L. Doctorow. 1986. pap. 4.95 (ISBN 0-449-21237-8, Crest). Fawcett.
Worlds Fair, Eighteen Eighty-One: Catalogue Illustration. Theodore Reff. (Modern Art in Paris Ser.). 1981. lib. bdg. 53.00 (ISBN 0-8240-4705-2). Garland Pub.
World's Fair Fun Trivia Book. Carole Marsh. (Tomorrow's Books for Today's Children). (Illus.). 160p. (Orig.). (gr. 4 up). 1982. pap. 4.95 (ISBN 0-935326-06-5). Gallopade Pub Group.
Worlds Fair Kit S. P. A. R. K. Carole Marsh. (S. P. A. R. K. Ser.). (Illus.). 50p. (Orig.). (gr. 3-12). 1986. pap. 49.95 (ISBN 0-935326-85-5). Gallopade Pub Group.
World's Fair Midways: An Affectionate Account of American Amusement Areas from the Crystal Palace to the Crystal Ball. Edo McCullough. LC 75-22828. (America in Two Centuries Ser). (Illus.). 1976. Repr. of 1966 ed. 16.00x (ISBN 0-405-07700-9). Ayer Co Pubs.
World's Fair, New Orleans. Joshua M. Pailet. LC 85-81259. (Illus.). 120p. 1987. 39.95 (ISBN 0-9615647-0-9). Gallery Fine.
World's Fair New Orleans. Ed. by Jean W. Stastny. (Illus.). 48p. 1984. write for info. Picayune Pr.
World's Fair of Eighteen Eighty-Nine. Ed. by Theodore Reff. (Modern Art in Paris 1855 to 1900). 330p. 1981. lib. bdg. 53.00 (ISBN 0-8240-4704-4). Garland Pub.
World's Fair of Eighteen Fifty-Five: Modern Art in Paris 1855-1900. Ed. by Theodore Reff. 694p. 1981. lib. bdg. 53.00 (ISBN 0-8240-4701-X). Garland Pub.
World's Fair of Eighteen Seventy-Eight. Ed. by Theodore Reff. (Modern Art in Paris 1855 to 1900). 388p. 1981. lib. bdg. 53.00 (ISBN 0-8240-4703-6). Garland Pub.
World's Fair of Eighteen Sixty-Seven. Ed. by Theodore Reff. (Modern Art in Paris 1855 to 1900). 224p. 1981. lib. bdg. 53.00 (ISBN 0-8240-4702-8). Garland Pub.
World's Fair of Nineteen Hundred: General Catalogue. Ed. by Theodore Reff. (Modern Art in Part in Paris 1855 to 1900). 582p. 1981. lib. bdg. 53.00 (ISBN 0-8240-4706-0). Garland Pub.
World's Fair of Nineteen Hundred: Retrospective Exhibition of French Art, 1800 to 1889. Ed. by Theodore Reff. (Modern Art in Paris 1855 to 1900). (Illus.). 442p. 1981. lib. bdg. 53.00 (ISBN 0-8240-4707-9). Garland Pub.
World's Fair of Nineteen Hundred: Retrospective Exhibition of Fine Art, 1889 to 1900. Ed. by Theodore Reff. (Modern Art in Paris 1855 to 1900). 581p. 1981. lib. bdg. 53.00 (ISBN 0-8240-4708-7). Garland Pub.
World's Fair Spoons, Vol. I: The World's Columbian Exposition. Chris A. McGlothlin. LC 85-70480. (Illus.). 1985. 35.00 (ISBN 0-9614824-0-0). Fla Rare Coin.
World's Family. Ken Heyman. LC 83-4476. (Illus.). 192p. 1983. 19.95 (ISBN 0-399-12833-6, Putnam); pap. 9.95 (ISBN 0-399-50927-5, Perigee). Putnam Pub Group.
Worlds Fighting Shotguns. Thomas F. Swearengen. (World Weapons Ser.: Vol. IV). 1978. 29.95 (ISBN 0-686-73789-X). TBN Ent.
World's First Airline: The St. Peterburg-Tampa Airboat Line, 1914. 2nd ed. Gay B. White. 1982. pap. 6.95 (ISBN 0-912522-74-7). Aero-Medical.
Worlds First & Only Authentic-Authorized Interview with Jesus Christ Including the Venusian Connection. Ken Faro & Margie Faro. (Illus.). 210p. (Orig.). 1987. pap. 9.95 (ISBN 0-9618459-0-2). Astral Pr.
World's First Ever Pop-Up Games Book. Ron Van Der Meer. (Illus.). 8p. (gr. k-3). 1982. 9.95 (ISBN 0-440-06943-2). Delacorte.
World's First Love. Fulton J. Sheen. 240p. 1976. pap. 3.95 (ISBN 0-385-11559-8, Im). Doubleday.
World's Food. Ed. by Clyde L. King. LC 75-26307. (World Food Supply Ser). (Illus.). 1976. Repr. of 1917 ed. 24.50x (ISBN 0-405-07786-6). Ayer Co Pubs.
World's Food: A Study of the Interrelations of World Populations, National Diets & Food Potentials. M. K. Bennett. LC 75-26295. (World Food Supply Ser). (Illus.). 1976. Repr. of 1954 ed. 23.50x (ISBN 0-405-07768-8). Ayer Co Pubs.
Worlds from Words: A Theory of Language in Fiction. James Phelan. LC 80-25844. (Chicago Originals Paperback Ser.). 256p. 1981. pap. 20.00X (ISBN 0-226-66690-5). U of Chicago Pr.
World's Grasses: Their Differention, Distribution, Economics. John W. Bews. 1977. lib. bdg. 59.95 (ISBN 0-8490-2848-5). Gordon Pr.
World's Great Adventure Stories. facsimile ed. LC 79-163049. (Short Story Index Reprint Ser.). (YA) (gr. 7 up). Repr. of 1929 ed. 38.50 (ISBN 0-8369-3963-8). Ayer Co Pubs.
World's Great Age: The Story of a Century's Search for a Philosophy of Life. Philo M. Buck, Jr. 382p. 1983. Repr. of 1936 ed. lib. bdg. 45.00 (ISBN 0-89987-959-4). Darby Bks.
World's Great Chess Games. Ed. by Reuben Fine. (Chess Ser.). 397p. 1983. pap. 7.95 (ISBN 0-486-24512-8). Dover.
World's Great Contemporary Poems. Ed. by Eddie-Lou Cole. 39.95 (ISBN 0-317-29100-9). World Poetry Pr.
World's Great Dailies: Profiles of Fifty Newspapers. John C. Merrill & Hal Fisher. (Illus.). 416p. 1980. (Communication Arts); pap. text ed. 10.50x (ISBN 0-8038-8096-0, Communication Arts). Hastings.
World's Great Men of Color, Vol. 1. J. A. Rogers. 1972. 11.95 (ISBN 0-02-081300-7). Macmillan.

World's Wit & Humor: An Encyclopedia of the Classic Wit & Humor of All Nations, 15 vols. in 3 mini-print vols. Ed. by Joel C. Harris. 1973. Repr. of 1905 ed. 165.00 (ISBN 0-8108-0543-X). Scarecrow.

Worlds Within. John R. Fearn. LC 84-11035. 32p. 1984. Repr. of 1982 ed. lib. bdg. 19.95x (ISBN 0-89370-798-8). Borgo Pr.

Worlds Within Women: Myth & Mythmaking in Fantastic Literature by Women. Thelma J. Shinn. LC 86-7592. (Contributions to the Study of Science Fiction & Fantasy Ser.: No. 22). 229p. 1986. lib. bdg. 35.00 (ISBN 0-313-25101-0, SWN/). Greenwood.

Worlds Within Worlds: The Story of Nuclear Energy. Isaac Asimov. 1980. 10.95 (ISBN 0-89875-000-8, Pub. by U Pr Pacific); (Pub by U Pr Pacific). Intl Spec Bk.

World's Wonder & Other Essays. Gabrielle M. Long. (Essay Index Reprint Ser). 1938. 20.00 (ISBN 0-8369-1223-3). Ayer Co Pubs.

World's Worst Elephant Jokes. 1973. pap. 1.95 (ISBN 0-8431-0010-9). Price Stern.

World's Worst Golf Jokes. Martin A. Ragaway. 48p. 1972. pap. 1.95 (ISBN 0-8431-0200-4). Price Stern.

World's Worst Jokes. Price Stern Editors. 1969. pap. 1.75 (ISBN 0-8431-0068-0). Price Stern.

World's Worst Knock Knock Jokes. Kati Stern & Claudia Sloan. 1974. 1.95 (ISBN 0-8431-0204-7). Price Stern.

World's Worst Poet. William McGonagall. (Orig.). 1979. pap. 4.95 (ISBN 0-87243-088-X, Pub. by Octavo Pr). Templegate.

World's Worst Riddles. 1974. pap. 1.95 (ISBN 0-8431-0205-5). Price Stern.

World's Worst Weeds: Distribution & Biology. LeRoy G. Holm. LC 74-78866. pap. 155.30 (2027026). Bks Demand UMI.

Worldshakers. Milt Machlin. pap. 3.50 (ISBN 0-345-29676-1). Ballantine.

Worldstone. Victoria Strauss. LC 85-42802. (Illus.). 324p. (gr. 7 up). 1985. 14.95 (ISBN 0-02-788380-9, Four Winds). Macmillan.

Worldview & Communication of the Gospel. Marguerite G. Kraft. LC 78-10196. (Illus.). 220p. 1978. pap. 7.95 (ISBN 0-87808-324-3). William Carey Lib.

Worldviews. Ninian Smart. LC 82-16877. 190p. 1983. pap. 7.95x (ISBN 0-684-17812-5). Scribner.

Worldviews & Warrants: Plurality & Authority in Theology. Intro. by William Schweiker. LC 87-18987. 126p. (Orig.). 1987. lib. bdg. 18.25 (ISBN 0-8191-6613-8); pap. text ed. 9.75 (ISBN 0-8191-6614-6). U Pr of Amer.

Worldviews: Crosscultural Explorations of Human Beliefs. Ninian Smart. 192p. 1983. pap. text ed. write for info. (ISBN 0-02-412010-3, Pub. by Scribner). Macmillan.

Worldwide Braking Trends: Medium & Heavy Duty Trucks. 1985. 20.00 (ISBN 0-89883-915-7, SP 644). Soc Auto Engineers.

Worldwide Chamber of Commerce Directory, 1988. rev. ed. Jan Pierce. 250p. 1988. pap. 22.00. World Bank.

Worldwide Chamber of Commerce Directory, 1988. rev. ed. Ed. by Jan Pierce. 250p. 1988. pap. 22.00 (ISBN 0-943581-01-X). WWCCD.

WorldWide Chamber of Commerce Directory: 1987 Edition. Ed. by Jan Pierce. 228p. 1987. pap. 22.00 (ISBN 0-943581-00-1). WWCCD.

Worldwide Church of God. Bryce Pettitt. (Truthway Ser.). 26p. (Orig.). 1981. pap. text ed. 1.25 (ISBN 0-87148-916-3). Pathway Pr.

Worldwide Concession Contracts & Petroleum Legislation. Gordon H. Barrows. LC 83-2221. 320p. 1983. 64.95 (ISBN 0-87814-226-6, P-4323). Pennwell Bks.

Worldwide Creative Ojo Book. Diane Thomas. LC 79-88350. 1979. pap. 2.95 (ISBN 0-918126-06-1). Hunter Ariz.

Worldwide Dessert Contest. Dan Elish. LC 87-24694. (Illus.). 208p. (gr. 4-6). 1988. 13.95 (ISBN 0-531-05752-6); PLB 13.99 (ISBN 0-531-08352-7). Orchard Bks Watts.

Worldwide Directory Eighty-Five: AP-DJ Telerate-Euromoney. Ed. by Cheryl White. (Euromoney Ser.). 636p. (Orig.). 1986. pap. 115.00 (ISBN 0-903121-72-7, Pub. by Woodhead-Faulkner). Longwood Pub Group.

Worldwide Directory of Mineral Industries Education & Research. Ed. by H. Wohlbier et al. LC 68-9304. 1968. 37.50x (ISBN 0-87201-912-8). Gulf Pub.

Worldwide Emission Control: Automotive Catalysts. 1985. 26.00 (ISBN 0-89883-912-2, SP 641). Soc Auto Engineers.

Worldwide Encyclopedia of Study & Learning Opportunities Abroad. J. M. De La Croix & Carole Copeland. 136p. 1988. pap. 30.00. Elite Assocs.

Worldwide Family History. Noel Currer-Briggs. 200p. 1982. 19.95x (ISBN 0-7100-0934-8). Routledge Chapman & Hall.

Worldwide Financial Reporting & Audit Requirements: A Peat Marwick Inventory. Peat Marwick International Staff. LC 83-198100. 258p. Date not set. price not set. Peat Marwick.

Worldwide Geographic Location Codes. 400p. (Orig.). 1987. pap. 19.00 (S/N 022-003-01144-7). USGPO.

Worldwide Inflation: Theory & Recent Experience. Ed. by Lawrence B. Krause & Walter S. Salant. LC 76-51580. 686p. 1976. 34.95 (ISBN 0-8157-5030-7); pap. 16.95 (ISBN 0-8157-5029-3). Brookings.

Worldwide Interiors. Ed. by Rikuyo-sha. 240p. 1988. 55.00 (ISBN 0-317-67585-0). Bks Nippan.

Worldwide Investment Analysis: The Case of Aluminum. Martin S. Brown. (Working Paper: No. 603). 168p. 8.00 (ISBN 0-8213-0212-4, WP 0603). World Bank.

Worldwide Laser Markets. International Resource Development Inc Staff. 188p. 1987. 1850.00x (ISBN 0-88694-742-1). Intl Res Dev.

Worldwide Lubricant Trends. 1986. 35.00 (ISBN 0-89883-947-5, SP 676). Soc Auto Engineers.

Worldwide Photovoltaics. Business Communications Staff. 207p. 1988. pap. 1950.00 (ISBN 0-89336-512-2, E-038R). BCC.

Worldwide Practical Petroleum Reservoir Engineering Methods. H. C. Slider. LC 83-4067. 825p. 1983. 84.95 (ISBN 0-87814-234-7, P-4334). Pennwell Bks.

Worldwide Register of Adult Education: 1980. Alex Sandri-White. 1973. 8.95x (ISBN 0-685-22747-2); supplement incl. (ISBN 0-686-76917-1). Aurea.

Worldwide Restrictions on Advertising: An Outline of Principles, Problems & Solutions. Robert Bruce & Bruce P. Keller. 65p. 1985. non-members 50.00; members 25.00. Intl Advertising Assn.

Worldwide Riches Opportunites, 2 vols. 2nd ed. Tyler G. Hicks. 150p. 1983. pap. 25.00 ea. Vol. 1 (ISBN 0-914306-73-1). Vol. 2 (ISBN 0-914306-74-X). Intl Wealth.

Worldwide Riches Opportunities, 2 vols. 3rd ed. Tyler G. Hicks. 150p. 1987. pap. 25.00 ea. Vol. 1 (ISBN 0-934311-11-0). Vol. 2 (ISBN 0-934311-12-9). Intl Wealth.

Worldwide Riches Opportunities, 2 vols. 600p. 1987. Set. 60.00 (ISBN 0-317-55735-1). B Klein Pubns.

Worldwide Robotics Survey & Directory 1981. 40p. 1981. pap. 28.00 (ISBN 0-318-01087-9, RIA(02)). Robot Inst Am.

Worldwide Robotics Survey & Directory 1982. 40p. 1982. pap. 15.00; Set. pap. 20.00 1981 & 1982 (ISBN 0-318-01089-5, RIA(03A)). Robot Inst Am.

Worldwide Robotics Survey & Directory. 3rd ed. 79p. 1985. pap. 41.00 (ISBN 0-317-39394-4). Robot Inst Am.

Worldwide Secrets for Staying Young. Paavo Airola. 206p. 1982. pap. 6.95 (ISBN 0-932090-12-5). Health Plus.

Worldwide Secrets for Staying Young. Paavo Airola. (Health Plus Bk.). 208p. 6.95. Contemp Bks.

Worldwide Telecommunications Guide for the Business Manager. Walter L. Vignault. LC 87-2002. (Telecommunications Ser.). 417p. 1987. 49.95 (ISBN 0-471-85828-5, Pub. by Wiley-Interscience). Wiley.

Worldwide Theory Testing. Raoul Naroll et al. LC 76-48559. (HRAF Manuals Ser.). 139p. 1976. pap. 10.00 (ISBN 0-87536-662-7). HRAFP.

Worldwide Truck Electronic Systems: Trends for the '90's. 1986. 10.00 (ISBN 0-89883-960-2, SP689). Soc Auto Engineers.

Worldwide View of Diesel Combustion Emissions & Analysis. 1983. 55.00 (ISBN 0-89883-089-3, P130). Soc Auto Engineers.

Worm. Simon I. Childer. 192p. (Orig.). 1988. pap. 3.50 (ISBN 1-55785-060-7). Bart Books.

Worm Day. Harriet Ziefert. (Illus.). (gr. 2-4). 1987. 7.95 (ISBN 0-316-98767-0). Little.

Worm Day (Mr. Rose's Class) Harriet Ziefert. (Illus.). 64p. 1988. pap. 2.50 (ISBN 0-553-15619-5, Skylark). Bantam.

Worm Farm. Charlie Morgan. 1962. pap. 3.00 (ISBN 0-914116-00-2). Shields.

Worm of Consciousness & Other Essays. Nicola Chiaromonte. Ed. by J. Ferrone & D. Willen. LC 76-29695. 270p. 1977. 3.95 (ISBN 0-15-698370-2, Harv). HarBraceJ.

Worm of Doubt: A Lennox Kemp Mystery. M. R. Meek. 208p. 1988. 14.95 (ISBN 0-684-18939-9). Scribner.

Worm Ouroboros. E. R. Eddison. (Del Rey Bk). 1977. 3.95 (ISBN 0-345-30152-8). Ballantine.

Worm Plans a Great Escape. Rod Hunt. (Little Stories). (Illus.). 32p. (ps-2). 1987. 5.95 (ISBN 0-09-167230-9, Pub. by Century Hutchinson). David & Charles.

Worms Are Singing. Jerry Bumpus. 1979. 1.75 (ISBN 0-912824-22-0). Vagabond Pr.

Worms Eat My Garbage. Mary Appelhof. LC 82-242012. (Illus., Orig.). 1982. pap. 6.95 (ISBN 0-942256-03-4). Flower Pr.

Worms of Kukumlima. Daniel M. Pinkwater. LC 80-24713. (gr. 4-7). 1981. 9.95 (ISBN 0-525-43380-5). Dutton.

Worms of the Earth. Robert E. Howard. 1987. pap. 2.95 (ISBN 0-441-91771-2). Ace Bks.

Worm's Tale. Barbro Lindgren. Tr. by Dianne Jonasson from Swedish. (Illus.). 28p. (ps up). 1988. 11.95 (ISBN 91-29-59068-X, Pub. by R & S Bks). FS&G.

Wormwood. Marie Corelli. pap. 5.95 (ISBN 0-910122-38-5). Amherst Pr.

Wormwood. Ken Smith. LC 87-73049. 64p. (Orig.). 1988. pap. 11.95 (ISBN 1-85224-037-7, Pub. by Bloodaxe Bks). Dufour.

Wormwood Regulars. Marvin Malone. 40p. 1986. pap. 3.00 (ISBN 0-935390-11-1). Wormwood Rev.

Worn Earth. Paul Engle. LC 72-144738. (Yale Ser. of Younger Poets: No. 31). Repr. of 1932 ed. 18.00 (ISBN 0-404-53831-2). AMS Pr.

Woronin. (Phytopathological Classics Ser.). 32p. 1934. 7.00 (ISBN 0-89054-005-5). Am Phytopathol Soc.

Worrell New Testament. rev. ed. A. S. Worrell. 1980. 11.95 (ISBN 0-88243-392-X, 01-0392). Gospel Pub.

Worried about Crime. Kit Kuperstock. LC 84-25150. 176p. (Orig.). 1985. pap. 7.95 (ISBN 0-8361-3385-4). Herald Pr.

Worried Money: A Guide to Swiss Banking. Frank Wayne. LC 81-20213. 1982. pap. 4.50 (ISBN 0-86663-891-1). Ide Hse.

Worried Sick: Our Troubled Quest for Wellness. Arthur J. Barsky, III. LC 87-32508. 1988. 17.95 (ISBN 0-316-08255-4). Little.

Worried Widow. Gerald Hammond. 192p. 1988. 13.95x (ISBN 0-312-01541-0). St Martin.

Worry: A Maieutic Analysis. M. G. Campion. 350p. 1986. text ed. 47.50x (ISBN 0-566-05118-4). Gower Pub Co.

Worry Free Worry. Ben Leach. (Uplook Ser.). 32p. 1982. pap. 0.99 (ISBN 0-8163-0516-1). Pacific Pr Pub Assn.

Worry Pill & Other Stories Based on Proverbs. (gr. 2-6). 4.95 (ISBN 0-318-21964-6, 2850001). CEF Press.

Worry Week. Anne Lindberg. (gr. 3-7). 1988. pap. 2.50 (ISBN 0-380-70394-7, Camelot). Avon.

Worry Week. Anne Lindbergh. LC 84-19299. (Illus.). 131p. (gr. 3-6). 1985. 11.95 (ISBN 0-15-299675-3, HJ). HarBraceJ.

Worse Pills, Better Pills. Sidney M. Wolfe et al. Ed. by Public Citizen Litigation Group Staff. 562p. 1988. pap. 12.00 (ISBN 0-937188-51-4). Pub Citizen Inc.

Worse Than Rotten, Ralph. Jack Gantos. (Illus.). (gr. k-3). 1978. PLB 12.95 (ISBN 0-395-27106-1). HM.

Worse Than Rotten, Ralph. Jack Gantos. (Illus.). (gr. k-3). 1982. pap. 4.95 (ISBN 0-395-32919-1). HM.

Worse Than the Disease: Pitfalls of Medical Progress. Diana B. Dutton. 520p. 1988. 29.95 (ISBN 0-521-34023-3). Cambridge U Pr.

Worse Than Willy! James Stevenson. LC 83-14201. (Illus.). 32p. (gr. k-3). 1984. 10.25 (ISBN 0-688-02596-X); PLB 10.88 (ISBN 0-688-02597-8). Greenwillow.

Worship. John E. Burkhardt. LC 81-23116. 162p. 1982. pap. 8.95 (ISBN 0-664-24409-2). Westminster John Knox.

Worship. Siudy. 1980. 6.15 (ISBN 0-8298-0393-9). Pilgrim NY.

Worship. Evelyn Underhill. LC 78-20499. 1987. Repr. of 1937 ed. 32.00 (ISBN 0-88355-874-2). Hyperion Conn.

Worship. Evelyn Underhill. (Crossroad Paperback Ser.). (Illus.). 1982. pap. 14.95 (ISBN 0-8245-0466-6). Crossroad NY.

Worship. John Woolman. 1950. pap. 2.50x (ISBN 0-87574-051-0, 051). Pendle Hill.

Worship-A Close Encounter of the Best Kind. Hershel Rosser. (NYD Discovery Bks.). (Illus.). 32p. (gr. 8-12). 1983. 1.50 (ISBN 0-88243-825-5, 02-0825); leader's guide 3.95 (ISBN 0-88243-845-X, 02-0845). Gospel Pub.

Worship! A Mass Book for Africa. Ed. by Anthony Gittins. (Illus.). 64p. 1986. pap. 1.50 (ISBN 0-00-599686-4, Collins Liturgical). HarpR.

Worship & Conflict under Colonial Rule: A South Indian Case. Arjun Appadurai. LC 80-24508. (Cambridge South Asian Studies: No. 27). pap. 71.80 (2031614). Bks Demand UMI.

Worship & Ethics: A Study in Rabbinic Judaism. Max Kadushin. LC 63-10586. 350p. 1975. Bloch.

Worship & Freedom: A Black American Church in Zambia. Walton J. Johnson. LC 77-22388. 190p. 1978. 44.50 (ISBN 0-8419-0315-8, Africana). Holmes & Meier.

Worship & Hymnody. Gary R. Shiplett. (Illus.). 122p. (Orig.). 1980. pap. text ed. 8.95 (ISBN 0-916260-08-9). Meriwether Pub.

Worship & Politics. Rafael Avila. Tr. by Alan Neely. LC 81-38356. 127p. (Orig.). 1981. pap. 6.95 (ISBN 0-88344-714-2). Orbis Bks.

Worship & Reformed Theology: The Liturgical Lessons of Mercersburg. Jack M. Maxwell. LC 75-45492. (Pittsburgh Theological Monographs: No. 10). 1976. pap. 12.00 (ISBN 0-915138-12-3). Pickwick.

Worship & Secular Man: An Essay on the Liturgical Nature of Man. Raimundo Panikkar. LC 72-93339. pap. 29.80 (ISBN 0-317-26670-5, 2025123). Bks Demand UMI.

Worship & Spirituality. Don E. Saliers. LC 84-7211. (Spirituality & the Christian Life Ser.: Vol. 5). 114p. 1984. pap. 7.95 (ISBN 0-664-24634-6). Westminster John Knox.

Worship & Witness. (Faith & Life Ser.). 2.10 (ISBN 0-02-805110-6, 80511). Benziger Pub Co.

Worship & Work. Colman J. Barry. LC 80-10753. (Illus.). 526p. 1980. pap. text ed. 12.50 (ISBN 0-8146-1123-0). Liturgical Pr.

Worship as Jesus Taught It. Judson Cornwall. 1987. pap. 6.95 (ISBN 0-932081-16-9). Victory Hse.

Worship As Pastoral Care. rev. ed. William H. Willimon. LC 79-894. 1979. 11.95 (ISBN 0-687-46388-2). Abingdon.

Worship As Praise & Empowerment. David R. Newman. 160p. 1988. pap. 9.95 (ISBN 0-8298-0774-8). Pilgrim NY.

Worship Celebrations for Youth. John Brown. 1980. pap. 4.95 (ISBN 0-8170-0866-7). Judson.

Worship Explored. V. Talmadge. 1988. 12.95 (ISBN 0-86544-047-6). Salv Army suppl South.

Worship: Exploring the Sacred. James Empereur. 1987. pap. 11.95 (ISBN 0-912405-33-3). Pastoral Pr.

Worship Handbook: A Practical Guide to Reform & Renewal. Thomas A. Langford, III & Bonnie S. Jones. LC 84-70648. 88p. (Orig.). 1984. pap. 5.95 (ISBN 0-88177-011-6, DRO11B). Discipleship Res.

Worship His Majesty. Ed. by Larry Reftery. 32p. 1981. pap. 0.75 (ISBN 0-88144-056-6). Christian Pub.

Worship Hymnal. 671p. 1971. 6.95 (ISBN 0-318-18907-0); piano ed. 16.00 (ISBN 0-919797-30-X). Kindred Pr.

Worship in Action. John Maxwell. LC 81-50436. 139p. 1981. pap. 4.95 (ISBN 0-89622-143-1). Twenty-Third.

Worship in Islam. Al-Ghazzali. Ed. by Edwin E. Calverley. LC 79-2860. 242p. 1981. Repr. of 1925 ed. 23.00 (ISBN 0-8305-0032-4). Hyperion Conn.

Worship in the Early Church. rev. ed. Ralph P. Martin. 144p. 1975. pap. 7.95 (ISBN 0-8028-1613-4). Eerdmans.

Worship in the Name of Jesus. 376p. 1987. pap. 15.95 (ISBN 0-570-03804-9, 12HH2913). Concordia.

Worship in the Round: Patterns of Informative & Participative Worship. Ed. by Keith Pearson. (Illus.). 88p. (Orig.). 1983. pap. 6.95 (ISBN 0-85819-343-4, Pub. by JBCE). ANZ Religious Pubns.

Worship in the World's Religions. 2nd ed. Geoffrey Parrinder. (Quality Paperback: No. 316). 239p. 1976. pap. 6.95 (ISBN 0-8226-0316-0). Littlefield.

Worship Is a Verb. Robert E. Webber. 224p. 1985. 12.95 (ISBN 0-8499-0371-8, 0371-8). Word Bks.

Worship Is All of Life. Robert A. Morey. LC 83-73375. (Illus.). 115p. (Orig.). 1984. pap. 5.45 (ISBN 0-87509-336-1). Chr Pubns.

Worship Leader's Guide. Shari Iverson. (Illus.). 40p. 1986. pap. 4.50 (ISBN 0-914936-97-2). Bible Temple.

Worship of Augustus Caesar. Alexander Del Mar. Repr. of 1899 ed. 10.00 (ISBN 0-913022-19-5). Angriff Pr.

Worship of God: Some Theological, Pastoral & Practical Reflections. Ralph P. Martin. 237p. (Orig.). 1982. pap. 10.95 (ISBN 0-8028-1934-6). Eerdmans.

Worship of Nature. James G. Frazer. LC 73-21271. (Gifford Lectures: 1924-25). Repr. of 1926 ed. 41.50 (ISBN 0-404-11427-X). AMS Pr.

Worship of Priapus. Richard P. Knight. LC 73-76829. (Illus.). 300p. 1974. Repr. of 1786 ed. 25.00 (ISBN 0-8216-0207-1, Pub. by Univ Bks). Lyle Stuart.

Worship of the Dead: The Origin & Nature of Pagan Idolatry & Its Bearing Upon the Early History of Egypt & Babylonia. J. Garnier. LC 77-85617. 1977. Repr. of 1904 ed. lib. bdg. 50.00 (ISBN 0-89341-300-3). Longwood Pub Group.

Worship of the Scottish Reformed Church, 1550-1638: The Hastie Lectures in the University of Glasgow, 1930. William McMillan. LC 83-45585. Date not set. Repr. of 1931 ed. 35.00 (ISBN 0-404-19903-8). AMS Pr.

Worship of the Visible Spectrum. Judith Skillman. LC 87-23275. 80p. 1988. 14.95 (ISBN 0-932576-55-9); pap. 7.95 (ISBN 0-932576-56-7). Breitenbush Bks.

Worship Old & New. Robert E. Webber. 256p. 1982. pap. 12.95 (ISBN 0-310-36651-8, 12207P). Zondervan.

Worship: Our Gift to God. Cathi Trzeciak. (Concept Books for Children). (Illus.). 24p. (gr. k-4). 1986. pap. 3.95 saddlestitched (ISBN 0-570-08531-4, 56-1558). Concordia.

Worship Planbook. Paul E. Engle. (Orig.). 1981. pap. 3.95 (ISBN 0-934688-03-6). Great Comm Pubns.

Worship: Rediscovering the Missing Jewel. Ronald B. Allen & Gordon Borror. (Critical Concern Bks.). 1987. pap. 7.95 (ISBN 0-88070-140-4). Multnomah.

Worship: Renewal to Practice. Collins. 1987. 11.95 (ISBN 0-912405-32-5). Pastoral Pr.

Worship Resources for Youth. Jerry O. Cok. 133p. (Orig.). 1983. pap. 12.00 (ISBN 0-914527-25-8). C-Four Res.

Worship: The Christian's Highest Occupation. A. P. Gibbs. pap. 5.95 (ISBN 0-937396-57-5). Walterick Pubs.

Worship the Lord. James R. Esther & Donald J. Bruggink. 96p. (Orig.). 1987. pap. 3.95 (ISBN 0-8028-0330-X). Eerdmans.

Worship the Lord. Louis Pratt. 1983. 4.35 (ISBN 0-89536-580-4, 2332). CSS of Ohio.

Worship: The Missing Jewel of the Evangelical Church. A. W. Tozer. 30p. 1979. bklet 1.45 (ISBN 0-87509-219-5). Chr Pubns.

Worship the Night. Mary Vigliante. 288p. 1985. pap. 3.50 (ISBN 0-8439-2302-4, Leisure Bks). Leisure NY.

Worship: The Search for Liturgical Language. Gail Ramshaw-Schmitt. 1988. pap. 11.95 (ISBN 0-912405-49-X). Pastoral Pr.

Wounded Sky. Diane Duane. (Gregg Press Science Fiction - Star Trek Ser.). 256p. 1986. lib. bdg. 11.95x (ISBN 0-8398-2933-7, Gregg). G K Hall.
Wounded Soldiers of Industry: Industrial Compensation Policy, 1833-1897. P. W. Bartrip & S. B. Burman. LC 83-8229. (Oxford Socio-Legal Studies). (Illus.). 1983. 34.00x (ISBN 0-19-827509-9). Oxford U Pr.
Wounded Stag. William Johnston. 1986. pap. 8.95 (ISBN 0-06-064208-4, RD 558, HarpR). Har-Row.
Wounded Warriors. R. Loren Sandford. 1987. pap. 4.95 (ISBN 0-932081-17-7). Victory Hse.
Wounded Wolf. Jean C. George. LC 76-58711. (Illus.). (ps-3). 1978. PLB 12.89 (ISBN 0-06-021950-5). HarpJ.
Wounded Woman: Healing the Father-Daughter Relationship. Linda S. Leonard. LC 82-6289. xx, 186p. 1982. 20.00 (ISBN 0-8040-0397-1, Pub. by Swallow). Ohio U Pr.
Wounded Woman: Healing the Father-Daughter Relationship. Linda S. Leonard. LC 83-42801. 179p. (Orig.). 1982. pap. 8.95 (ISBN 0-394-72183-7). Shambhala Pubns.
Wounded Woman: Healing the Father-Daughter Relationship. Linda S. Leonard. xix, 179p. 1988. pap. 8.95 (245, Pub. by New Sci Lib-Shambhala). Shambhala Pubns.
Wounds Beneath the Flesh: Anthology of Native American Poetry. Ed. by Maurice Kenny. 1987. 6.00. White Pine.
Wounds in the Rain. Stephen Crane. LC 72-3294. (Short Story Index Reprint Ser). 1972. Repr. of 1900 ed. 24.50 (ISBN 0-8369-4145-4). Ayer Co Pubs.
Wounds in the Rain: A Collection of Stories Relating to the Spanish-American War of 1898. Stephen Crane. 347p. 1983. Repr. of 1905 ed. lib. bdg. 40.00 (ISBN 0-89987-146-1). Darby Bks.
Wounds of Civil War. Thomas Lodge. Ed. by J. W. Houppert. LC 68-63050. (Regents Renaissance Drama Ser). xxii, 115p. 1969. 12.95x (ISBN 0-8032-0269-5); pap. 2.95x (ISBN 0-8032-5268-4, BB 230, Bison). U of Nebr Pr.
Wounds of Civil War. Thomas Lodge. LC 82-45754. (Malone Society Reprint Ser.: No. 21). Repr. of 1910 ed. 40.00 (ISBN 0-404-63021-9). AMS Pr.
Wounds of War & the Process of Healing. Fred Wilcox & Jerold M. Starr. (Lessons of the Vietnam War Ser.). (Illus.). 32p. 1988. pap. text ed. 3.00 (ISBN 0-945919-10-7). Ctr Social Studies.
Wounds of War: The Psychological Aftermath of Combat in Vietnam. Herbert Hendin & Ann P. Haas. LC 83-46074. 267p. 1984. 16.95 (ISBN 0-465-09259-4). Basic.
Woven & Graphic Art of Anni Albers. Nicholas F. Weber et al. LC 85-600008. (Illus.). 140p. 1985. 39.95 (ISBN 0-87474-978-6, HEAA); pap. 19.95 (ISBN 0-87474-977-8, HEAAP). Smithsonian.
Woven Cloth Construction. S. Robinson & T. Marks. 178p. 1973. 60.00x (ISBN 0-686-63810-7, Pub. by Wira Tech Group). State Mutual Bk.
Woven Structure & Design, Pt. 1: Single Cloth Construction. Doris Goerner. 1986. 85.00x (ISBN 0-317-68394-2, Pub. by Wira Tech Group). State Mutual Bk.
Woven Structure & Design: Single Cloth Construction by Goerner, Wira, 1986, Pt. 1. Doris Goerner. 1986. 85.00x (ISBN 0-317-56739-X, Pub. by Wira Tech Group). State Mutual Bk.
Woven with the Ship. facs. ed. Cyrus T. Brady. LC 73-128722. (Short Story Index Reprint Ser). 1902. 20.00 (ISBN 0-8369-3613-2). Ayer Co Pubs.
Wovoka. Mel Boring. LC 80-24003. (Story of an American Indian Ser.). (Illus.). 64p. (gr. 5 up). 1981. PLB 7.95 (ISBN 0-87518-179-1). Dillon.
Wow see Auditioner's Handbook.
Wow God. Frances Clare. 189p. pap. 5.95 (ISBN 0-89221-131-8). New Leaf.
Wow God. Sr. Francis Clare. LC 75-32009. 192p. 1975. 5.95 (ISBN 0-89221-006-0); pap. 2.95 (ISBN 0-89221-057-5). New Leaf.
Wow! God Made Me. Ruth A. Noble. 1981. 5.75 (ISBN 0-89536-479-4, 2330). CSS of Ohio.
Wow-Ipits: Eight Asmat Woodcarvers of New Guinea. Adrianus A. Gerbrands. (Art in Its Context Field Reports: Vol. 3). (Photos). 1967. text ed. 20.80x (ISBN 0-686-22474-4). Mouton.
Wow! You Can Fly! R. G. Austin. (Which Way Secret Door Bks.: No. 1). (Illus.). (gr. 1-3). 1983. pap. 1.95 (ISBN 0-671-46979-7). Archway.
Woyzeck. Georg Buchner. Tr. by John Mackendrick. 39p. 1980. pap. 7.95 (ISBN 0-413-38820-4, NO. 3010). Heinemann Ed.
Woyzeck. Georg Buchner. (German Texts Ser.). 120p. Date not set. pap. text ed. 15.00 (ISBN 0-317-65495-0). Basil Blackwell.
Woyzeck see Leonce & Lena: Lenz; Woyzeck.
Woza Afrika! A Collection of South African Plays. Ed. by Duma Ndlovu. 1987. 16.95 (ISBN 0-8076-1169-7); pap. 8.95 (ISBN 0-8076-1170-0). Braziller.
Woza Albert! Percy Mtwa & Mbongeni Ngema. 80p. 1983. pap. 5.95 (ISBN 0-413-53000-0, NO. 3893). Heinemann Ed.
Wozu Philosophie? Stellungnahmen eines Arbeitskreises. Ed. by Herrmann Luebbe. 1978. 15.20 (ISBN 3-11-007513-X). De Gruyter.
WP Software Market for Microcomputers in W. Europe. 244p. 1984. 1550.00 (ISBN 0-86621-553-0, E629). Frost & Sullivan.
WPA & the Federal Relief Policy. Donald S. Howard. LC 72-2374. (FDR & the Era of the New Deal Ser). 888p. 1973. Repr. of 1943 ed. lib. bdg. 95.00 (ISBN 0-306-70489-7). Da Capo.
WPA Art in Michigan. Christine N. Ruby. (Illus.). 175p. 1988. 34.95x (ISBN 0-8143-2061-9, Great Lks Bks). Wayne St U Pr.
WPA Guide to America: The Best of 1930s America As Seen by the Federal Writers Project. Ed. by Bernard A. Weisberger. (Illus.). 512p. 1985. pap. 14.95 (ISBN 0-394-72959-5). Pantheon.
WPA Guide to California. Federal Writers Project Staff et al. (Illus.). 713p. 1984. pap. 11.95 (ISBN 0-394-72290-6). Pantheon.
WPA Guide to Cincinnati. Writers' Program of WPA, Ohio Staff. LC 87-72224. (Illus.). 611p. 1988. Repr. of 1943 ed. lib. bdg. 25.00; text ed. 29.95. Cinc Hist Soc.
WPA Guide to Illinios. Federal Writer's Project. 9.95 (ISBN 0-394-72195-0). Pantheon.
WPA Guide to Minnesota. Federal Writers' Project. LC 84-29475. (Borealis Books Reprint). xi, 539p. 1985. pap. 9.95 (ISBN 0-87351-185-9). Minn Hist.
WPA Guide to New Orleans. Federal Writer's Project. 8.95 (ISBN 0-394-71588-8). Pantheon.
WPA Guide to New York City. Federal Writers' Project. 1982. 19.50 (ISBN 0-394-52792-5); pap. 8.95 (ISBN 0-394-71215-3). Pantheon.
WPA Guide to Philadelphia. rev. ed. Pref. by E. Digby Baltzell. (Illus.). 736p. (Orig.). 1988. pap. 19.95 (ISBN 0-8122-1270-3). U of Pa Pr.
WPA Guide to Tennessee. Federal Writers' Project of the Work Projects Administration Staff. LC 85-31507. Orig. Title: Tennessee: A Guide to the State. (Illus.). 608p. 1986. lib. bdg. 29.95x (ISBN 0-87049-383-3); pap. 12.95 (ISBN 0-87049-384-1). U of Tenn Pr.
WPA Guide to Texas. Intro. by Don Graham. LC 85-28830. (Texas Classics Ser.). (Illus.). 718p. 1986. 24.95 (ISBN 0-87719-036-4); pap. 14.95 (ISBN 0-87719-040-2). Texas Month Pr.
WPA Guide to the Arrowhead Country. Workers of the WPA Writers Program Staff. LC 87-34923. (Illus.). 235p. 1988. pap. 9.95 (ISBN 0-87351-227-8). Minn Hist.
WPA Guide to Washington, D. C. Federal Writer's Project. 8.95 (ISBN 0-394-72192-6). Pantheon.
WPA Guide to 1930s. Arkansas Federal Writer's Project of the Works Progress Administration. (Illus.). xiv, 512p. 1987. pap. 12.95 (ISBN 0-7006-0341-7). U Pr of KS.
WPA Guide to 1930s Colorado. Federal Writer's Project of the Works Progress Administration. LC 87-40240. (Illus.). lxii, 576p. 1987. pap. 12.95 (ISBN 0-7006-0342-5). U Pr of KS.
WPA Guide to 1930's Iowa. Federal Writer's Project of the Works Progress Administration for the State of Iowa. Intro. by Joseph F. Wall. 584p. 1986. pap. 14.95 (ISBN 0-8138-0997-5). Iowa St U Pr.
WPA Guide to 1930s Kansas. The Federal Writers' Project of the Work Progress Administration. LC 84-51694. Orig. Title: Kansas: A Guide to the Sunflower State. (Illus.). xxxiv, 540p. 1984. pap. 12.95 (ISBN 0-7006-0249-6). U Pr of KS.
WPA Guide to 1930s Missouri. Compiled by Federal Writers' Project of the Works Progress Administration. LC 86-50110. (Illus.). lxviii, 656p. 1986. pap. 14.95 (ISBN 0-7006-0292-5). U Pr of KS.
WPA Guide to 1930's New Jersey. Federal Writers' Project of the Works Progress Administration for New Jersey. 750p. 1986. 19.95 (ISBN 0-8135-1152-6). Rutgers U Pr.
WPA Guide to 1930s Oklahoma. Compiled by Federal Writers' Project of the Works Progress Administration Staff. LC 86-50226. (Illus.). xxxviii, 442p. 1986. pap. 12.95 (ISBN 0-7006-0294-1). U Pr of KS.
WPPSS: Who Is to Blame for the WPPSS Disaster. James Leigland & Robert B. Lamb. LC 86-7924. 272p. 1986. prof. 34.95x (ISBN 0-88730-127-4). Ballinger Pub.
WPS Career Planning Program: Leader's Handbook. Jacqueline N. Buck et al. 53p. (Orig.). 1985. pap. text ed. 23.50 (ISBN 0-87424-201-0). Western Psych.
WPS Career Planning Program: Student Handbook. Jacqueline N. Buck et al. 1986. pap. text ed. 29.50x (ISBN 0-87424-200-2). Western Psych.
WQ-Ten Electro Acupuncture Machine. Jake Fratkin. Ed. by Robert L. Felt. 48p. (Orig.). pap. 7.95 (ISBN 0-912111-03-8). Paradigm Pubns.
WRA, a Story of Human Conservation see U. S. War Relocation Authority.
Wrack & Other Stories. Siegfried Lenz. Ed. by C. A. Russ. 168p. (Orig.). 1967. pap. text ed. 5.50x (ISBN 0-435-38536-4). Heinemann Ed.
Wrack & Roll. Bradley Denton. 416p. (Orig.). 1986. pap. 3.50 (ISBN 0-445-20306-4, Pub. by Popular Lib). Warner Bks.
Wrack & Rune. Charlotte MacLeod. 208p. 1988. pap. 3.50 (ISBN 0-380-61911-3). Avon.
Wraiths of Time. Andre Norton. 224p. 1988. pap. 2.95 (ISBN 0-345-35485-0, Del Rey). Ballantine.
Wrangell & the Gold of the Cassiar. Clarence L. Andrews. 61p. pap. 4.95 (ISBN 0-8466-0267-9, S267). Shorey.
Wrangell-Saint Elias: International Mountain Wilderness. Ed. by Alaska Geographic Staff. LC 80-26210. (Alaska Geographic Ser.: Vol. 8, No. 1). (Illus., Orig.). 1981. pap. 9.95 album style (ISBN 0-88240-149-1). Alaska Northwest.
Wranglers & Physicists: Studies on Cambridge Mathematical Physics in the Nineteenth Century. Ed. by P. M. Harman. LC 85-1485. 320p. 1985. 47.50 (ISBN 0-7190-1756-4, Pub. by Manchester Univ Pr). St Martin.
Wrap It in Flags. Robert Terrall. LC 85-12244. (Penguin Fiction Ser.). 320p. 1986. pap. 6.95 (ISBN 0-14-008045-7). Penguin.
Wrap It up, I'll Take It. Deborah C. Edwards. LC 79-55884. (Illus.). 62p. (Orig.). 1980. pap. 3.95 (ISBN 0-9603750-0-7). Teachers Load.
Wrapped in a Ribbon. Flavia Weedn. (Illus.). 96p. 1986. 9.95 (ISBN 0-913289-10-8). Roserich Ltd.
Wrappings. Harmony Hammond. LC 83-50232. (Illus.). 112p. (Orig.). 1983. pap. text ed. 9.50 (ISBN 0-939858-05-3). T S L Pr.
Wrath. David Robbins. 368p. (Orig.). 1988. pap. 3.95 (ISBN 0-8439-2629-5, Pub. by Leisure Bks CT). Leisure NY.
Wrath of Allah: Islamic Revolution & Reaction in Iran. Ramy Nima. 170p. (Orig.). 1983. pap. 9.50 (ISBN 0-86104-733-8, Pub by Pluto Pr). Longwood Pub Group.
Wrath of Athena. Jenny S. Clay. LC 83-2996. 240p. 1983. 32.00x (ISBN 0-691-06574-8). Princeton U Pr.
Wrath of Condo. Vico Confino. 171p. (Orig.). 1985. pap. 7.95 (ISBN 0-9615100-0-5). River Bend Club.
Wrath of Garde. Jerry LaPlante. (Chameleon Ser.: No. 1). 1979. pap. 1.95 (ISBN 0-89083-437-7). Zebra.
Wrath of God. David S. Cole. 1986. 11.95 (ISBN 0-533-06517-8). Vantage.
Wrath of God. Jack Higgins & James Graham. 224p. 1985. pap. 3.50 (ISBN 0-425-07748-9). Berkley Pub.
Wrath of God. John MacArthur, Jr. (John MacArthur's Bible Studies). (Orig.). 1986. pap. 3.95 (ISBN 0-8024-5096-2). Moody.
Wrath of God: South Africa, the Middle East, European Political Unification, Soviet Russia & the Ethical Degeneration of the American Society, 2 vols. Anselmo Cnecchi. (Illus.). 187p. 1986. Set. 227.50 (ISBN 0-86722-124-0). Inst Econ Pol.
Wrath of Grapes: Drinking & the Church Divided. Andre S. Bustanoby. 128p. (Orig.). 1987. pap. 5.95 (ISBN 0-8010-0944-8). Baker Bk.
Wrath of Heaven on Earth. Wim Malgo. 9.95 (ISBN 0-937422-30-4); pap. 6.95 (ISBN 0-937422-29-0). Midnight Call.
Wrath of John Steinbeck. Robert Bennett. LC 74-3126. 1973. lib. bdg. 18.50 (ISBN 0-685-33548-8). Folcroft.
Wrath of John Steinbeck. Robert Bennett. 59.95 (ISBN 0-8490-1337-2). Gordon Pr.
Wrath of John Steinbeck. Robert Bennett. LC 74-34402. (Studies in Fiction, No. 34). 1970. Repr. of 1939 ed. lib. bdg. 49.95x (ISBN 0-8383-0347-1). Haskell.
Wrath of the Ancestors. A. C. Jordan. Tr. by A. C. Jordan & Priscilla P. Jordan. Orig. Title: Ingqumbo Yeminyanya. 277p. 1980. pap. 9.00 (ISBN 0-89410-331-8, Pub. by Lovedale Pr South Africa). Three Continents.
Wrath of the King. Walter C. Utt. LC 66-29028. (Dest ser.). 1984. pap. 2.99 (ISBN 0-317-28334-0). Pacific Pr Pub Assn.
Wrath of the Lion. Jack Higgins. 192p. 1981. pap. 1.95 (ISBN 0-449-13739-2, GM). Fawcett.
Wrath of the Seven Horsemen. Andrew Robinson. Ed. by George MacDonald & S. Coleman Charlton. 32p. (Orig.). (YA) (gr. 10-12). 1987. pap. 6.00 (ISBN 0-915795-86-8). Iron Crown Ent Inc.
Wray, CO Centennial. East Yuma County Historical Society. (Illus.). 264p. 1986. write for info. (ISBN 0-88107-053-X). Curtis Media.
Wreath Book. Rob Pulleyn. (Illus.). 144p. 1988. 19.95. Sterling.
Wreath for Jenny's Grave. Charlotte Hunt. (Black Dagger Crime Ser.). 304p. 1988. text ed. 14.95x (ISBN 0-86220-720-7, Pub. by Firecrest Pub Ltd). Prescott Pr NH.
Wreath for Rivera. Ngaio Marsh. 1976. Repr. of 1949 ed. lib. bdg. 20.95x (ISBN 0-88411-499-6, Pub. by Aeonian Pr). Amereon Ltd.
Wreath for Rivera. Ngaio Marsh. LC 75-44993. (Crime Fiction Ser). 1976. Repr. of 1949 ed. lib. bdg. 21.00 (ISBN 0-8240-2385-4). Garland Pub.
Wreath for the Enemy. Pamela Frankau. LC 86-33325. 320p. 1987. pap. 10.00 (ISBN 0-914232-84-3). McPherson & Co.
Wreath for the Maidens. John Munonye. (African Writers Ser.). 1973. pap. text ed. 7.00 (ISBN 0-435-90121-4). Heinemann Ed.
Wreath for Udomo. Peter Abrahams. LC 83-45608. Repr. of 1956 ed. 32.00 (ISBN 0-404-20001-X). AMS Pr.
Wreath of Christmas Poems. Ed. by Albert Hayes & J. Laughlin. LC 72-80975. 32p. 1972. pap. 1.95 (ISBN 0-8112-0459-6, NDP347). New Directions.
Wreath of Laurel, Being Speeches on Dramatic & Kindred Occasions. William Winter. LC 73-130098. (Drama Ser). 1970. Repr. of 1898 ed. lib. bdg. 15.00 (ISBN 0-8337-3828-3). B Franklin.
Wreath of Light: Devotions for Families Using the Advent Wreath. Nancy Vignec. 40p. pap. 3.50 (ISBN 0-8066-1727-6, 23-3008). Augsburg.
Wreath of Stars. Bob Shaw. 1987. pap. 2.95 (ISBN 0-671-65365-2). Baen Bks.
Wreath on the Crown. John Cule. 143p. 1985. 25.00x (ISBN 0-85088-395-4, Pub. by Gomer Pr). State Mutual Bk.
Wreathmaking from the State of Maine. Michele Maks. LC 87-72681. (Illus.). 52p. 1987. pap. 8.95 (ISBN 0-89272-244-4). Down East.
Wreaths for All Seasons. Steve Sherman. 1988. 18.00 (ISBN 0-8446-6299-2). Peter Smith.
Wreaths for All Seasons. Steven Sherman. (Illus.). 1986. pap. 10.95 (ISBN 0-8289-0586-X). Greene.
Wreaths: Techniques & Materials...Step-by-Step Projects...Creative Ideas for the Year Round. Richard Kollath. (Illus.). 144p. 1988. 18.95 (ISBN 0-8160-1863-4). Facts on File.
Wreck. Parley Cooper. 320p. 1987. pap. 3.95 (ISBN 0-7701-0652-8). Paperjacks US.
Wreck. Rabindranath Tagore. 414p. Date not set. 6.95. Asia Bk Corp.
Wreck Diving: A Guide for Sport Divers. Dick Geyer. LC 82-10575. (New Century Aquatics Ser.). (Illus.). 1982. pap. 8.95 (ISBN 0-8329-0131-8). New Century.
Wreck of the Chancellor. Jules Verne. Repr. lib. bdg. 18.95x (ISBN 0-88411-914-9, Pub. by Aeonian Pr). Amereon Ltd.
Wreck of the Deutschland. John E. Keating. 1979. Repr. of 1963 ed. lib. bdg. 29.50 (ISBN 0-8495-3125-X). Arden Lib.
Wreck of the Deutschland. John E. Keating. LC 74-13638. 1963. Repr. lib. bdg. 20.00 (ISBN 0-8414-5510-4). Folcroft.
Wreck of the Edmund Fitzgerald. 10th ed. Frederick Stonehouse. (Illus.). 1977. pap. 7.49 (ISBN 0-932212-05-0). Avery Color.
Wreck of the Mary Deare. Hammond Innes. 1977. pap. 0.75 (ISBN 0-380-01477-7, 03491). Avon.
Wreck of the Mary Deare. Hammond Innes. 296p. 1985. pap. 3.50 (ISBN 0-88184-152-8). Carroll & Graf.
Wreck of the Memphis. Edward L. Beach. 19.95 (ISBN 0-88411-774-X, Pub. by Aeonian Pr). Amereon Ltd.
Wreck of the Rusty Nail. G. B. Trudeau. LC 82-83139. 128p. 1983. pap. 5.25 (ISBN 0-03-061732-4). H Holt & Co.
Wreck of the SV. Nikolai. Tr. by Alton S. Donnelly from Rus. & Quileute. Intro. by Kenneth S. Owens. (North Pacific Studies: Vol. 8). (Illus.). 128p. 1985. 14.95x (ISBN 0-87595-124-4). Oregon Hist.
Wreck of the Titan. facs. ed. Morgan Robertson. LC 71-132125. (Short Story Index Reprint Ser). 1912. 13.00 (ISBN 0-8369-3682-5). Ayer Co Pubs.
Wreck of the Titanic Foretold? Ed. by Martin Gardner. LC 85-46045. 175p. 1986. 19.95 (ISBN 0-87975-321-8). Prometheus Bks.
Wreck of the Zephyr. Chris Van Allsburg. LC 82-23371. (Illus.). 32p. (ps up). 1983. PLB 15.95 (ISBN 0-395-33075-0). HM.
Wreckage of Agathon. John Gardner. 288p. 1985. pap. 8.95 (ISBN 0-525-48180-X, Obelisk). Dutton.
Wrecked Japanese Junks Adrift in the North Pacific Ocean. Bert Webber. (Illus.). 202p. 1984. 12.95 (ISBN 0-87770-290-X); pap. 8.95 (ISBN 0-87770-309-4). Ye Galleon.
Wrecked on the Feejees. William S. Cary. 106p. 1987. 14.95. Ye Galleon.
Wreckers. David Edgar. 1977. pap. 4.95 (ISBN 0-413-38510-8, NO. 2985). Heinemann Ed.
Wrecking Crew. Donald Hamilton. (Matt Helm Ser). 1979. pap. 1.75 (ISBN 0-449-14053-9, GM). Fawcett.
Wrecking Crew. Larry Levis. LC 78-181398. (Pitt. Poetry Ser.). 1972. 16.95x (ISBN 0-8229-3238-5). U of Pittsburgh Pr.
Wrecks, Rescues & Investigations: Selected Documents of the U. S. Coast Guard & Its Predecessors. new ed. Ed. by Bernard C. Nalty et al. LC 78-12312. (Illus.). 1978. lib. bdg. 60.00 (ISBN 0-8420-2130-2). Scholarly Res Inc.
Wren. Marie Killilea. (Illus.). (gr. 3-7). 1981. pap. 0.95 (ISBN 0-440-49704-3, YB). Dell.
Wrestlemania. Edward Ricciuti. Ed. by Tom Emanuel. (Illus.). 100p. (Orig.). 1986. pap. 5.95 (ISBN 0-9616263-2-1). WWF Bks.
Wrestlers & Other Poems. Toby Olson. LC 73-92344. 64p. 1974. 12.95 (ISBN 0-87929-028-5). Barlenmir.
Wrestlers with Christ. facs. ed. Karl Pfleger. Tr. by E. I. Watkin. LC 68-16968. (Essay Index Reprint Ser). 1936. 20.00 (ISBN 0-8369-0785-X). Ayer Co Pubs.
Wrestlin Jacob: A Portrait of Religion in the Old South. Erskine Clark. LC 78-52453. 1979. pap. 3.95 (ISBN 0-8042-1089-6, John Knox). Westminster John Knox.
Wrestling Basics. Ron Fox. (Illus.). 48p. (gr. 3-7). 1986. PLB 10.95 (ISBN 0-13-969320-3). P-H.
Wrestling Boys: An Exhibition of Chinese & Japanese Ceramics from the 16th-18th Centuries. Gordon Lang. 98p. 1983. 50.00x (ISBN 0-317-44248-1, Pub. by Han-Shan Tang Ltd). State Mutual Bk.
Wrestling: Coaching to Win. John K. Johnston et al. (Illus.). 1979. pap. 6.25 (ISBN 0-8015-8933-9, Hawthorn). Dutton.

Write to the Top. George Beahm. Ed. by Robert S. Friedman. 112p. 1988. pap. 5.95 (ISBN 0-89865-551-X). Donning Co.
Write to the Top: Writing for Corporate Success. Deborah Dumaine. LC 82-40145. Date not set. price not set (ISBN 0-394-52505-1); pap. 8.95 (ISBN 0-394-71226-9). Random.
Write True to Yourself So You Sell: 19 Lessons in Folios. Bert M. Anderson. write for info. 95.00 (ISBN 0-917628-02-0). Coraco.
Write up a Storm. Linda Polon & Aileen Cantwell. LC 78-18528. 1979. pap. 12.95 (ISBN 0-673-16154-4). Scott F.
Write Way to Spell, Vol. 2. Marcia Weinstein. 1984. 4.95 (ISBN 0-87594-278-4). Book-Lab.
Write Way to Spell Workbook, Vol. 1. Marcia Weinstein. 1984. pap. text ed. 4.95 (ISBN 0-87594-216-4); tchr's guide 3.50 (ISBN 0-87594-217-2). Book-Lab.
Write What You Mean: A Handbook of Business Communication. new ed. Allen Weiss. LC 77-11954. 1977. 9.95 (ISBN 0-8144-5453-4). AMACOM.
Write What You Mean: A Handbook of Business Communications. Allen Weiss. LC 77-11954. 192p. 1981. pap. 5.95 (ISBN 0-8144-7544-2). AMACOM.
Write with Style: A Technique Book for G.C.S.E. English. Colin Bowman. 1987. 30.00x (ISBN 0-7217-0625-8, Pub. by Schofield & Sims). State Mutual Bk.
Write with Your Ears. Mary Jo Roberts. (Illus.). 158p. 1983. pap. 19.95 (ISBN 0-913609-00-5); wkbk. 14.95 (ISBN 0-913609-01-3). Hse of Tomorrow.
Write, Wrote, Written. 2nd ed. Maureen S. Bogdanowicz. 160p. (Orig.). 1985. pap. text ed. 9.95 (ISBN 0-8403-3611-X, 40361101). Kendall-Hunt.
Write Your Congressman: Constituents Communications & Representation. Stephen E. Frantzich. LC 85-12275. 174p. 1985. 35.00 (ISBN 0-275-90204-8, C0204). Praeger.
Write Your Own Adventure Programs. J. Tyler & L. Hawarth. (Computer & Electronics Ser.). (Illus.). 48p. (gr. 6 up). 1983. lib. bdg. 9.96 (ISBN 0-88110-143-5); pap. 2.95 (ISBN 0-86020-741-2). EDC.
Write Your Own Contracts: Business. Robert Cottrell. 350p. (Orig.). 1987. pap. 14.95 (ISBN 0-937313-13-0). Ogden Shepard Pub.
Write Your Own Contracts: Family-Personal. Robert Cottrell. 256p. (Orig.). 1987. pap. 14.95 (ISBN 0-937313-17-3). Ogden Shepard Pub.
Write Your Own Contracts-Household, Tenant, Landlord. Robert Cottrell. (Write Your Own Contracts Ser.). 256p. (Orig.). 1987. pap. 14.95 (ISBN 0-937313-23-8). Ogden Shepard Pub.
Write Your Own Contracts: Real Estate & Leases. Robert Cottrell. 320p. (Orig.). 1987. pap. 14.95 (ISBN 0-937313-33-5). Ogden Shepard Pub.
Write Your Own Horoscope. 3rd, rev. ed. Joseph F. Goodavage. 1979. pap. 3.95 (ISBN 0-451-14991-2, Sig). NAL.
Write Your Own Sports Mystery Kit. Carole Marsh. (Carole Marsh Bks.). (Illus.). 48p. (Orig.). (gr. 3-12). 1986. pap. 24.00 (ISBN 0-935326-11-1). Gallopade Pub Group.
Write Your Own Story. Vivian Dubrovin. (First Bks.). 72p. (gr. 4-8). 1984. lib. bdg. 10.40 (ISBN 0-531-04739-3). Watts.
Write Your Own Wedding: A Personal Guide for Couples of All Faiths. rev. ed. Mordecai L. Brill et al. LC 85-7156. 120p. 1985. pap. 5.95 (ISBN 0-8329-0398-1). New Century.
Write Your Own Will. R. J. Schartz. 1961. pap. 4.95 (ISBN 0-02-081990-0, Collier). Macmillan.
Write Your Ticket to Success: A Do-It-Yourself Guide to Effective Resume Writing & Job Hunting. 2nd ed. I. Norman Johansen. (Illus.). 1976. 7.95 (ISBN 0-918350-00-X). Job Hunters Forum.
Write Your Way into College: A Successful College Essay. George Ehrenhaft. LC 87-13905. 128p. 1987. pap. 9.95 (ISBN 0-8120-2997-6). Barron.
Write Your Way to Success with the Paragraph System. Caulean Vesey. (Illus.). 206p. (Orig.). 1982. pap. 9.95. Excel Pr.
Write Your Way to Success: With the Paragraph System. Caulean Vesey. 188p. 1984. 10.00. Trillium Pr.
Writeful. Gary Hoffman. LC 82-52460. 211p. (Orig.). 1986. pap. 8.95 (ISBN 0-937363-00-6). Verve Pr.
Writer. M. B. Goffstein. LC 83-49488. (Charlotte Zolotow Bks.). (Illus.). 32p. (ps up). 1984. 12.95i (ISBN 0-06-022142-9); PLB 12.89g (ISBN 0-06-022143-7). HarpJ.
Writer & Commitment. John Mander. LC 75-18402. 215p. 1975. Repr. of 1961 ed. lib. bdg. 35.00x (ISBN 0-8371-8332-4, MAWCO). Greenwood.
Writer & Politics. Ed. by Peter Davison et al. LC 77-90620. (Literary Taste, Culture & Mass Communication Se.: Vol. 11). 285p. 1978. 65.00x (ISBN 0-85964-046-9). Chadwyck-Healey.
Writer & Politics. George Woodcock. LC 72-193760. 1948. lib. bdg. 37.00 (ISBN 0-8414-9796-6). Folcroft.
Writer & Psychoanalysis. Edmund Bergler. 320p. 1986. Repr. of 1954 ed. text ed. 30.00X (ISBN 0-8236-6869-X). Intl Univs Pr.
Writer & Public in France: From the Middle Ages to the Present Day. John Lough. 1978. text ed. 45.00x (ISBN 0-19-815749-5). Oxford U Pr.
Writer & Society: Studies in the Fiction of Guenter Grass & Heinrich Boll. Charlotte W. Ghurye. (European University Studies, German Language & Literature: Ser. 1, Vol. 139). 76p. 1976. pap. 11.75 (ISBN 3-261-01861-5). P Lang Pubs.
Writer & the Absolute. Wyndham Lewis. LC 75-7240. 202p. 1975. Repr. of 1952 ed. lib. bdg. 25.00x (ISBN 0-8371-8098-8, LEWR). Greenwood.
Writer As Celebrity: Intimate Interviews. Maralyn L. Polak. 24p. 1986. pap. 9.95 (ISBN 0-87131-477-0). M Evans.
Writer As Shaman: The Pilgrimages of Conrad Aiken & Walker Percy. Ted R. Spivey. LC 86-12433. 224p. 1986. 24.95 (ISBN 0-86554-199-X, MUP/H182). Mercer Univ Pr.
Writer at His Craft. Sherwood Anderson. Ed. by Jack Salzman et al. 1978. 22.50x (ISBN 0-911858-37-7). Appel.
Writer at War: Arnold Bennett, 1914-1918. Kinley E. Roby. LC 72-79335. 326p. 1972. 32.50 (ISBN 0-8071-0243-1). La State U Pr.
Writer, Audience, Subject: Bridging the Communication Gap. Mary S. Ply & Donna H. Winchell. 1988. pap. text ed. price not set (ISBN 0-673-18325-4). Scott F.
Writer in America. W. Stegner. LC 76-51266. (American Literature Ser, No. 49). 1977. lib. bdg. 49.95x (ISBN 0-8383-2127-5). Haskell.
Writer in America. Wallace Stegner. LC 76-25034. 1951. lib. bdg. 29.00 (ISBN 0-8414-7605-5). Folcroft.
Writer in Extremis: Expressionism in Twentieth-Century German Literature. Walter H. Sokel. 1959. 20.00x (ISBN 0-8047-0556-9). Stanford U Pr.
Writer in Pennsylvania, 1681-1981. John J. Burke. LC 81-85496. 93p. 1982. pap. 5.95 (ISBN 0-686-36440-6). St Joseph.
Writer in Performance. Jack Dodds. 737p. 1986. text ed. write for info. (ISBN 0-02-330380-8). Macmillan.
Writer in Philadelphia, 1682-1982. John J. Burke. LC 81-51298. 84p. 1981. pap. 5.95 (ISBN 0-686-36439-2). St Joseph.
Writer in the Room. Ray B. West, Jr. LC 67-30730. vi, 266p. 1968. 6.50 (ISBN 0-87013-120-6). Mich St U Pr.
Writer Is a State of Being: Your Personal Desktop Conference. Susan Henry. LC 87-51002. (Illus.). 144p. (Orig.). 1988. pap. 12.95 (ISBN 0-943149-05-3). Rickreall Creek Hse.
Writer of the Plains: The Biography of B. M. Bower. new ed. Orrin A. Engen. (Illus.). 56p. (Orig.). 1973. 6.00 (ISBN 0-686-05538-1); text ed. 3.60 (ISBN 0-686-05539-X). Pontine Pr.
Writer on Her Work. Ed. by Janet Sternburg. 228p. 1981. pap. 8.95 (ISBN 0-393-00071-0). Norton.
Writer on Her Work. Ed. by Janet Sternburg. 1980. 14.95 (ISBN 0-393-01361-8). Norton.
Writer Publisher. Charles N. Aronson. LC 75-36854. 1976. 10.00 (ISBN 0-915736-07-1); pap. 7.00 (ISBN 0-915736-08-X). C N Aronson.
Writer Teaches Writing. 2nd ed. Donald M. Murray. LC 84-81981. 304p. 1984. text ed. 25.16 (ISBN 0-395-35441-2). HM.
Writer to Writer. A. W. Biddle. 256p. 1985. text ed. 17.95 (ISBN 0-07-005213-1). McGraw.
Writer Written: The Artist & Creation in the New Literatures in English. Jean-Pierre Durix. LC 87-7518. (Contributions to the Study of World Literatures: No. 21). 192p. 1987. lib. bdg. 29.95 (ISBN 0-313-25894-5, DXA/). Greenwood.
Writers: A Sense of Ireland. Ed. by Andrew Carpenter & Peter Fallon. LC 80-12681. 1980. 20.00 (ISBN 0-8076-0970-6). Braziller.
Writer's Advisor. Ed. by Leland G. Alkire, Jr. & Cheryl I. Westerman. LC 84-24715. 478p. 1985. 65.00x (ISBN 0-8103-2093-2). Gale.
Writer's Agenda: The Wadsworth Writer's Guide. shorter ed. Hans P. Guth. Date not set. pap. text ed. write for info. (ISBN 0-534-09696-4). Wadsworth Pub.
Writer's Agenda: The Wadsworth Writer's Guide & Handbook. Hans P. Guth. Date not set. text ed. write for info. (ISBN 0-534-09636-0). Wadsworth Pub.
Writer's Almanac & Fact Book. Mary A. De Vries. 1986. pap. 3.95 (ISBN 0-317-38976-9, Sig). NAL.
Writer's America: Landscape in Literature. Alfred Kazin. LC 88-1299. (Illus.). 256p. 1988. 24.95 (ISBN 0-394-57142-8). Knopf.
Writers & Friends. Edward Weeks. 1982. 15.95 (ISBN 0-316-92791-0, Pub. by Atlantic Monthly Pr). Little.
Writers & Pilgrims: Medieval Pilgrimage Narratives & Their Posterity. Donald R. Howard. LC 79-64480. (Quantum Books: No. 17). 100p. 1980. 22.00x (ISBN 0-520-03926-2). U of Cal Pr.
Writers' & Poets' Yearbook 1982. (Orig.). 1982. pap. 25.00x (ISBN 0-901976-76-8, Pub. by United Writers Pubns England). State Mutual Bk.
Writers & Politics: A Partisan Review Reader. Ed. by Edith Kurzweil & William Phillips. 352p. 1983. pap. 11.95 (ISBN 0-7100-9316-0). Routledge Chapman & Hall.
Writers & Politics in Modern Britain, France, & Germany. J. E. Flower et al. LC 77-7595. 280p. 1977. 34.50 (ISBN 0-8419-0320-4). Holmes & Meier.
Writers & Politics in Modern Italy. J. A. Gatt-Rutter. LC 78-18829. (Writers & Politics Ser.). 66p. 1978. 13.50 (ISBN 0-8419-0413-8); pap. 9.50 (ISBN 0-8419-0416-2). Holmes & Meier.
Writers & Politics in Modern Scandinavia. Janet Mawby. LC 78-18931. (Writers & Politics Ser.). 53p. 1979. 14.50 (ISBN 0-8419-0414-6); pap. text ed. 9.50 (ISBN 0-8419-0417-0). Holmes & Meier.
Writers & Politics in Modern Spain. John Butt. LC 78-18704. (Writers & Politics Ser.). 75p. 1978. 14.50 (ISBN 0-8419-0412-X); pap. 9.50 (ISBN 0-8419-0415-4). Holmes & Meier.
Writers & Politics in Nigeria. James Booth. LC 80-17670. (Writers & Politics Ser.). 128p. 1981. 29.50 (ISBN 0-8419-0650-5, Africana); pap. text ed. 16.50 (ISBN 0-8419-0651-3). Holmes & Meier.
Writers & Politics in West Germany. K. Stuart Parkes. LC 86-13900. 256p. 1986. 29.95 (ISBN 0-312-89347-7). St Martin.
Writers & Production Artists see International Dictionary of Films & Filmmakers.
Writers & Readers. George B. Hill. LC 72-8517. (Essay Index Reprint Ser.). 1972. Repr. of 1892 ed. 18.00 (ISBN 0-8369-7317-8). Ayer Co Pubs.
Writers & Readers. George B. Hill. 1973. Repr. of 1892 ed. 30.00 (ISBN 0-8274-0247-3). R West.
Writers & Society in Contemporary Italy: A Collection of Essays. Ed. by Michael Caesar & Peter R. Hainsworth. LC 83-40503. 302p. 1984. 27.50 (ISBN 0-312-89350-7); pap. 12.95 (ISBN 0-312-89351-5). St Martin.
Writers & Society in Modern Japan. Irena Powell. LC 82-48432. 165p. 1983. 14.95 (ISBN 0-87011-558-8). Kodansha.
Writers & Their Background: Geoffrey Chaucer. Ed. by Derek Brewer. LC 74-84295. xiv, 401p. 1975. pap. 10.00x (ISBN 0-8214-0184-X). Ohio U Pr.
Writers & Their Background: Matthew Arnold. Ed. by Kenneth Allott. LC 75-15339. xxxvi, 353p. 1976. 20.00x (ISBN 0-8214-0197-1); pap. 10.00x (ISBN 0-8214-0198-X). Ohio U Pr.
Writers & Their Background: Robert Browning. Ed. by Isobel Armstrong. LC 72-96846. xxvi, 365p. 1975. 20.00x (ISBN 0-8214-0131-9); pap. 10.00x (ISBN 0-8214-0132-7). Ohio U Pr.
Writer's Art. James J. Kilpatrick. 264p. 1985. pap. 8.95 (ISBN 0-8362-7925-5). Andrews & McMeel.
Writer's Art, A Collection of Short Stories. Wallace E. Stegner. LC 74-148645. 358p. 1972. Repr. of 1950 ed. lib. bdg. 25.00x (ISBN 0-8371-6009-X, STWA). Greenwood.
Writer's Art: A Practical Rhetoric & Handbook. Fred D. White. 534p. 1986. text ed. write for info. (ISBN 0-534-06084-6). Wadsworth Pub.
Writer's Art by Those Who Have Practiced It: Hazlitt, Emerson, Poe, Stevenson. Rollo W. Brown. 1921. Repr. 30.00 (ISBN 0-8274-3773-0). R West.
Writers at Home. Ed. by Gervase Jackson-Stops. LC 85-12900. (Illus.). 200p. 1986. 22.95 (ISBN 0-8160-1318-7). Facts on File.
Writers at Work. Ed. by George Plimpton. (Paris Review Interviews Ser.: No. 6). 384p. 1984. 22.50 (ISBN 0-670-79099-0). Viking.
Writer's at Work, Vol. VI. Ed. by George Plimpton. 416p. 1985. pap. 9.95 (ISBN 0-14-007736-7). Penguin.
Writers at Work. (Paris Review Interview Ser.: No. 7). 384p. 1986. 22.95 (ISBN 0-670-80888-1). Viking.
Writers at Work, Vol. 3. (Paris Review Interviews, Third Ser.). 1977. pap. 9.95 (ISBN 0-14-004542-2). Penguin.
Writers at Work, Vol. 5. Ed. by George Plimpton. (Paris Review Interviews, Fifth Ser.). 416p. 1981. pap. 9.95 (ISBN 0-14-005818-4). Penguin.
Writers at Work: The Paris Review Interviews. Ed. by George Plimpton. 352p. 1988. pap. 8.95 (ISBN 0-14-010761-4). Penguin.
Writers at Work: The Paris Review Interviews. Ed. by George Plimpton. 1988. 22.95 (ISBN 0-670-82101-2). Viking.
Writers at Work: The Paris Review Interviews, First Series, Vol. 1. Ed. by Malcolm Cowley. 1977. pap. 9.95 (ISBN 0-14-004540-6). Penguin.
Writers at Work: The Paris Review Interviews, Fourth Series, Vol. 4. Ed. by George Plimpton. 1977. pap. 9.95 (ISBN 0-14-004543-0). Penguin.
Writers at Work: The Paris Review Interviews, Second Series, Vol. 2. Ed. by George Plimpton. 1977. pap. 9.95 (ISBN 0-14-004541-4). Penguin.
Writers at Work VII: The Paris Review Interviews. Ed. by George Plimpton. 352p. 1988. pap. 7.95 (ISBN 0-14-008500-9). Penguin.
Writers at Work (W. B. Yeats, Richard Aldington, Sinclair Lewis, Wyndham Lewis, Somerset Maugham Etc.) Louise Morgan. LC 72-10206. Repr. of 1931 ed. lib. bdg. 30.00 (ISBN 0-8414-0625-1). Folcroft.
Writer's Block & How to Use It. Victoria Nelson. LC 84-29148. 204p. (Orig.). 1985. 14.95 (ISBN 0-89879-168-5). Writers Digest.
Writer's Block: The Cognitive Dimension. Mike Rose. LC 83-662. (Studies in Writing & Rhetoric). 142p. (Orig.). 1983. pap. 10.95x (ISBN 0-8093-1141-0). S Ill U Pr.
Writer's Block: The Cognitive Dimension. Mike Rose. 132p. 1984. 10.95 (ISBN 0-317-37083-9). NCTE.
Writer's Book of Synonyms. Evelyn Rothstein. (Illus.). 52p. (Orig.). (gr. 2-8). 1984. pap. text ed. 5.00 (ISBN 0-9606172-9-9). ERA-CCR.
Writer's Britain: Landscape in Literature. Margaret Drabble. LC 79-2117. (Illus.). 1979. 22.50 (ISBN 0-394-50819-X). Knopf.
Writer's Britain: Landscape in Literature. Margaret Drabble. LC 86-50921. (Illus.). 288p. 1987. pap. 15.95 (ISBN 0-500-27340-5). Thames Hudson.
Writer's Capital. Louis Auchincloss. 1979. pap. 4.95 (ISBN 0-395-28518-6). HM.
Writer's Choices. Leonora Woodman & Thomas P. Adler. 1985. text ed. write for info. (ISBN 0-673-15584-6). Scott F.
Writer's Choices. 2nd ed. Leonora Woodman & Thomas P. Adler. 1987. pap. text ed. write for info. (ISBN 0-673-18841-8). Scott F.
Writer's Choices with Handbook. 2nd ed. Leonora Woodman & Thomas P. Adler. 1987. text ed. write for info. (ISBN 0-673-18840-X). Scott F.
Writer's Circle: Reading, Thinking, Writing. Sarah Morgan & Michael Vivion. LC 86-60670. 416p. Date not set. pap. text ed. price not set (ISBN 0-312-89345-0); inst'rs. manual 00.23 (ISBN 0-312-89346-9). St Martin.
Writer's Companion. Marcella Frank. 144p. 1983. pap. text ed. 9.95 (ISBN 0-13-969790-X). P-H.
Writer's Companion. Richard Marius. 224p. 1984. pap. text ed. 9.00 (ISBN 0-394-32745-4). Knopf.
Writer's Companion: A Short Handbook. William H. Roberts. 1984. text ed. write for info. (ISBN 0-673-39291-0); tchr's. manual avail. Scott F.
Writer's Congress. LC 44-3435. 1944. 7.50. Pacific Bk Supply.
Writers' Congress: The Proceedings of the Conference Held in October 1943. 1982. lib. bdg. 85.00 (ISBN 0-89984-009-4). Century Bookbindery.
Writer's Craft. John Hersey. 1973. write for info (ISBN 0-394-31799-8, RanC). Random.
Writer's Craft: A Process Reader. Sheena Gillespie et al. 1986. pap. text ed. write for info. (ISBN 0-673-18173-1). Scott F.
Writer's Craft: A Process Reader. 2nd ed. Sheena Gillespie et al. 1988. pap. text ed. price not set (ISBN 0-673-38242-7). Scott F.
Writer's Craft: Hopwood Lectures, 1965-1981. Ed. by Robert A. Martin. 304p. 1982. pap. 9.95 (ISBN 0-472-06337-5). U of Mich Pr.
Writer's Desk Book. William D. Orcutt. 1978. Repr. of 1917 ed. lib. bdg. 20.00 (ISBN 0-8492-2026-2). R West.
Writer's Diary: Being Extracts from the Diary of Virginia Woolf. Virginia Woolf. Ed. by Leonard Woolf. LC 73-5737. 355p. 1973. pap. 6.95 (ISBN 0-15-698380-X, Harv). HarBraceJ.
Writer's Digest Guide to Manuscript Formats. Dian D. Buchman & Seli Grover. 192p. 1987. 16.95 (ISBN 0-89879-293-2). Writers Digest.
Writer's Digest Handbook of Magazine Article Writing. Ed. by Jean M. Fredette. 256p. 1988. 15.95 (ISBN 0-89879-328-9). Writers Digest.
Writer's Directory Nineteen Eighty-Eight to Nineteen Ninety. Ed. by Roland Turner. 1988. 95.00 (ISBN 0-912289-87-2); Standing Order. 85.00 (ISBN 0-317-62303-6). St James Pr.
Writers Directory: 1976-1978. 1500p. 1976. 35.00 (ISBN 0-312-89425-2). St Martin.
Writer's Directory: 1980-1982. 1979. 40.00 (ISBN 0-312-89426-0). St Martin.
Writers Directory, 1986-88. 1986. 85.00 (ISBN 0-912289-28-7); standing order 75.00. St James Pr.
Writers Directory 1988-90. 8th, rev. & enl. ed. LC 77-166289. 1100p. 1987. 85.00 (Pub. by St James). Gale.
Writer's Do's & Don'ts. Carol A. Osley. (Orig.). 1982. pap. 2.00 (ISBN 0-910119-03-1). SOCO Pubns.
Writer's Encyclopedia. Kirk Polking. 532p. 1987. pap. 16.95 (ISBN 0-89879-265-7). Writers Digest.
Writer's Eye: Field Notes & Watercolors. Paul Horgan. (Illus.). 96p. 1988. 24.95 (ISBN 0-8109-1792-0). Abrams.
Writers for Children. Ed. by Jane M. Bingman. (Illus.). 720p. 1987. 75.00 (ISBN 0-684-18165-7). Scribner.
Writers for Young Adults: Biographies Master Index. 2nd ed. Ed. by Adele Sarkissian. (Biographical Index Ser.: Vol. 6). 416p. 1984. 92.00x (ISBN 0-8103-1473-8). Gale.
Writers' Forum, Vol. 1, 1974; Vol. 11, 1985. Alex Blackburn. LC 78-649046. 231p. (Orig.). 1985. Set. pap. 8.95x (ISBN 0-9602992-5-4). Writers Forum.
Writers' Forum, Vol. 12. Ed. by Alex Blackburn. LC 78-649046. (Vol. 12). 240p. (Orig.). 1986. pap. text ed. 8.95 (ISBN 0-9602992-6-2). Writers Forum.
Writers' Forum, No. 13. Ed. by Alex Blackburn. LC 78-649046. 245p. (Orig.). 1987. pap. 8.95 (ISBN 0-9602992-7-0). Writers Forum.
Writers' Forum, No. 14. Ed. by Alex Blackburn. LC 78-649046. 1988. pap. 8.95 (ISBN 0-317-70092-8). Writers Forum.
Writers Forum 10, 1984. Ed. by Alex Blackburn. LC 78-649046. 1984. pap. 8.95 (ISBN 0-9602992-4-6). Writers Forum.
Writers Forum 7, 1981. Ed. by Alex Blackburn. LC 78-649046. pap. 8.95 (ISBN 0-686-87317-3). Writers Forum.

Writer's Workshop: Techniques in Creative Writing. Barry Maybury. 1979. 19.95 (ISBN 0-7134-1557-6, Pub. by Batsford England). David & Charles.

Writer's World: An Essay Anthology. Linda Woodson. 380p. 1986. pap. text ed. 12.00 net (ISBN 0-15-597683-4, Pub. by HC); instr's. manual 1.95 (ISBN 0-15-597684-2). HarBraceJ.

Writer's World: Gwyn Thomas 1913-1981. Ed. by Dai Smith. (Illus.). 83p. 1986. pap. 11.95 (ISBN 0-89955-468-7, Pub.by Welsh Wales). Intl Spec Bk.

Writer's World: T. Harri Jones 1921-1965. Ed. by Pat Power. (Illus.). 104p. 1987. pap. 11.95 (ISBN 0-89955-467-9, Pub. by Welsh Wales). Intl Spec Bk.

Writers, Wrecks & Whales see And Hereby Hangs the Tale Series: Little Known Facts about Well-Known People, Places or Things.

Writers Writing. Lil Brannon & Melinda Knight. LC 82-14587. 192p. (Orig.). 1982. pap. text ed. 12.50x (ISBN 0-86709-045-6). Boynton Cook Pubs.

Writer's Yellow Pages. Ed. by Steve Davis. 456p. (Orig.). 1988. 21.95 (ISBN 0-911061-16-9). S Davis Pub.

Writin' Is Fightin' Thirty-Seven Years of Boxing on Paper. Ishmael Reed. 192p. 1988. 18.95 (ISBN 0-689-11975-5). Atheneum.

Writing. Richard L. Allington. Kathleen Krull. LC 80-15334. (E. G. Beginning to Learn about... Ser.). (Illus.). 32p. (ps-2). 1985. pap. 9.27 (ISBN 0-8172-2499-8). Raintree Pubs.

Writing. Richard L. Allington & Kathleen Krull. LC 80-15334. (Beginning to Learn about Ser.). (Illus.). 32p. (ps-2). 1980. PLB 14.65 (ISBN 0-8172-1321-X). Raintree Pubs.

Writing. Gregory Cowan & Elizabeth Cowan. 1980. text ed. write for info. (ISBN 0-673-15665-6). Scott F.

Writing. 2nd ed. Elizabeth Cowan-Neeld. 1986. text ed. write for info. (ISBN 0-673-18150-2). Scott F.

Writing. Tom Raworth. 1982. 10.00 (ISBN 0-935724-12-5). Figures.

Writing. Kathy Sweeney et al. 64p. (gr. 2-4). 1985. 6.95 (ISBN 0-912107-39-1). Monday Morning Bks.

Writing. J Tyler & G. Round. (First Learning Ser.). (Illus.). 24p. (ps up). 1987. pap. 2.95 (ISBN 0-7460-0218-1). EDC.

Writing: A College Handbook. James A. Heffernan & John E. Lincoln. (Illus.). 1982. text ed. 12.95x (ISBN 0-393-95150-2). Norton.

Writing: A College Handbook. 2nd ed. James A. Heffernan & John E. Lincoln. 1986. text ed. 13.95x (ISBN 0-393-95499-4); tchr's. ed. avail. (ISBN 0-393-95507-9); diagnostic-achievement tests avail. (ISBN 0-393-95509-5); Manual & 5 1/4 Disk. 19.95x (ISBN 0-393-95692-X); Manual & 3 1/2 Disk. 19.95x (ISBN 0-393-95779-9). Norton.

Writing a College Handbook: Revision Chart. Heffernan & Lincoln. 1982. write for info (ISBN 0-393-95327-0). Norton.

Writing: A College Rhetoric. Laurie G. Kirszner & Stephen R. Mandell. 1984. text ed. 21.95 (ISBN 0-03-059151-1). HR&W.

Writing: A College Rhetoric. 2nd ed. Laurie G. Kirszner & Stephen R. Mandell. (Illus.). 652p. 1988. text ed. price not set (ISBN 0-03-012094-2). HR&W.

Writing: A College Rhetoric Brief. 2nd ed. Laurie G. Kirszner & Stephen R. Mandell. (Illus.). 512p. 1988. text ed. price not set (ISBN 0-03-012089-6). HR&W.

Writing: A College Rhetoric, Brief Edition. Laurie G. Kirszner & Stephen R. Mandell. 448p. 1985. pap. text ed. 16.95 (ISBN 0-03-001417-4, HoltC). HR&W.

Writing-A College Workbook: Ancillary for Writing a College Handbook. James A. Heffernan & John E. Lincoln. 300p. 1982. instr's. manual avail. (ISBN 0-393-95181-2); diagnostic tests avail.; write for info. answer pamphlet (ISBN 0-393-95229-0). Norton.

Writing: A College Workbook (Ancillary for Writing: A College Handbook) 2nd ed. James W. Heffernan & John E. Lincoln. 1986. pap. text ed. 9.95x (ISBN 0-393-95503-6). Norton.

Writing: A Content Approach to ESL Composition. Mark Jenkins. (Illus.). 240p. 1986. pap. text ed. write for info. (ISBN 0-13-969544-3). P H.

Writing: A Diagnostic Approach. Eva S. Weiner. 1987. pap. 7.00 (ISBN 0-13-969858-2). Prentice Hall Pr.

Writing: A Guide Business Professionals. C. W. Griffin. 419p. 1987. pap. text ed. 17.95 (ISBN 0-15-597676-1, HC). HarBraceJ.

Writing a Job-Winning Resume. John E. McLaughlin & Stephen K. Merman. (Illus.). 1980. (Spec); pap. 6.95 (ISBN 0-13-970228-8). P-H.

Writing a Living Will: Using a Durable Power-of-Attorney. George J. Alexander. LC 87-15816. 160p. 1987. lib. bdg. 29.95 (ISBN 0-275-92801-2, C2801); pap. 12.95 (ISBN 0-275-92939-6, B2939). Praeger.

Writing a Local History: A Practical Guide. David Dymond. 1981. 25.00X (ISBN 0-317-52178-0, Pub. by Pinhorns UK). State Mutual Bk.

Writing a Novel. John Braine. 224p. 1975. pap. text ed. 6.95 (ISBN 0-07-007112-8). McGraw.

Writing a Novel. Dorothy Bryant. LC 78-69766. 1978. pap. 6.95 (ISBN 0-931688-02-7). Ata Bks.

Writing a Practical Guide. Joseph P. Dagher. LC 74-11784. (Illus.). 1976. pap. text ed. 19.50 (ISBN 0-395-18621-8); instr's. manual 1.35 (ISBN 0-395-18803-2). HM.

Writing a Publishable Research Report: In Education, Psychology, & Related Disciplines. Ronald P. Carver. 156p. 1984. spiral bdg. 20.75x (ISBN 0-398-04986-6). C C Thomas.

Writing a Research Paper. rev. ed. Jonatha Ceely et al. 1983. pap. text ed. 3.50x (ISBN 0-88334-108-5). Ind Sch Pr.

Writing a Research Paper. Lionel Menasche. LC 83-12492. (Pitt Series in English As a Second Language). (Illus.). 144p. 1984. pap. 8.95x (ISBN 0-8229-8216-1). U of Pittsburgh Pr.

Writing: A Short Course. Elizabeth Cowan-Neeld. 1987. pap. text ed. write for info (ISBN 0-673-38027-0). Scott F.

Writing a Story: A Writer's Self-Report. Leif Fearn. 59p. 1983. 7.00 (ISBN 0-940444-21-6). Kabyn.

Writing a Successful Grant Application. Liane Reif-Lehrer. 100p. 1982. pap. 15.00 (ISBN 0-86720-009-X). Jones & Bartlett.

Writing a Successful Grant Application. 2nd, rev. ed. Liane Rief-Lehrer. 200p. 1988. 20.00 (ISBN 0-86720-104-5). Jones & Bartlett.

Writing a Technical Paper. Donald H. Menzel et al. 1961. pap. text ed. 3.95 (ISBN 0-07-041493-9). McGraw.

Writing a Television Play. 2nd; rev. ed. Michelle Cousin. xiii, 202p. (Orig.). 1986. pap. 14.95 (ISBN 0-931642-18-3) (ISBN 0-317-39310-3). Lintel.

Writing a Thriller. Andre Jute. 112p. 1987. pap. 10.95 (ISBN 0-312-01114-8). S: Martin.

Writing a UNIX Device Driver. Janet I. Egan & Thomas J. Teixeira. 357p. 1988. pap. 24.95 (ISBN 0-471-62859-X). Wiley.

Writing a Woman's Life. Carolyn G. Heilbrun. 1988. 14.95 (ISBN 0-393-02601-9). Norton.

Writing about Amusing Things. Joan D. Berbrich. (Orig.). (gr. 10-12). 1981. pap. 8.08 (ISBN 0-87720-427-6). AMSCO Sch.

Writing about Curious Things. Joan D. Berbrich. (Orig.). (gr. 8). 1981. pap. text ed. 10.42 (ISBN 0-87720-394-6). AMSCO Sch.

Writing about Fascinating Things. Joan D. Berbrich. (Orig.). (gr. 8-10). 1980. wkbk. 10.58 (ISBN 0-87720-391-1). AMSCO Sch.

Writing about Food & Families, Fashion & Furnishings. Ann Burkhardt. (Illus.). 126p. 1984. 10.95x (ISBN 0-8138-1941-5). Iowa St U Pr.

Writing about Imaginative Literature. Edward J. Gordon. 196p. 1973. pap. text ed. 9.00 net (ISBN 0-15-597850-0, HC). HarBraceJ.

Writing about Literature. rev ed. B. Bernard Cohen. 256p. 1973. pap. write for info. (ISBN 0-673-07653-9). Scott F.

Writing about Literature. Elizabeth Kahn et al. (Theory & Research into Practice Ser.). 54p. (Orig.). 1984. pap. 7.25 (ISBN 0-8141-5877-3). NCTE.

Writing about Literature. Lynn Klamkin & Margot Livesey. 1040p. 1986. pap. text ed. 21.95 (ISBN 0-03-001508-1, HoltC). HR&W.

Writing about Literature: Aims & Process. Joyce MacAllister. 320p. 1987. pap. text ed. write for info. (ISBN 0-02-373030-7). Macmillan.

Writing about Literature: Step by Step. 2nd ed. Patricia M. McKeague. 208p. 1986. pap. text ed. 15.95 (ISBN 0-8403-4044-3). Kendall-Hunt.

Writing about Music: A Style Book for Reports & Theses. rev. enl. ed. Demar Irvine. LC 56-13245. (Illus.). 220p. 1968. pap. 9.95x (ISBN 0-295-78558-6). U of Wash Pr.

Writing about My Feelings. Charlie Daniel & Becky Daniel. (gr. 1-4). 1978. 6.95 (ISBN 0-916456-18-8, GA80). Good Apple.

Writing about People. Joan D. Berbrich. (gr. 10-12). 1979. wkbk. 12.17 (ISBN 0-87720-382-2). AMSCO Sch.

Writing about Pictures: Using Pictures to Develop Language & Writing Skills, 6 bks. A. J. Evans & Marilyn Palmer. (gr. 1-3). 1982. Bk. 1: Completing Sentences. pap. text ed. 3.75x (ISBN 0-8077-5994-5); Bk. 2: Writing Sentences. pap. text ed. 3.75x (ISBN 0-8077-6031-5); Bk. 3: Getting At The Story. pap. text ed. 3.75x (ISBN 0-8077-6032-3); Bk. 4: Linking Story Ideas. pap. text ed. 3.75x (ISBN 0-8077-6033-1); Bk. 5: Writing Your Story, I. pap. text ed. 3.75x (ISBN 0-8077-6034-X); Bk. 6: Writing Your Story, II. pap. text ed. 3.75x (ISBN 0-8077-6035-8); tchrs. manual 2.95x (ISBN 0-8077-6036-6). Tchrs Coll.

Writing about Science. Ed. by Mary E. Bowen & J. A. Mazzeo. (Illus.). 1979. pap. text ed. 10.95x (ISBN 0-19-502476-1). Oxford U Pr.

Writing Academic English. A. Oshima & A. Hogue. 264p. (Orig.). 1982. pap. text ed. write for info. (ISBN 0-201-05479-5). Addison-Wesley.

Writing across Languages: Analysis of L2 Text. Teacher's ed. Ulla Connor & Robert Kaplan. (A-W Second Language Professional Library). 1986. pap. text ed. 18.95 (ISBN 0-201-11184-5). Addison-Wesley.

Writing Across Languages & Cultures: Issues in Contrastive Rhetoric. Ed. by Alan C. Purves. (Written Communication Annual Ser.: Vol. 2). 320p. 1988. text ed. 35.00 (ISBN 0-8039-2686-3); pap. text ed. 16.95 (ISBN 0-8039-2687-1). Sage.

Writing Across the Curriculum Pamphlets. Ed. by Nancy Martin. 144p. (Orig.). 1984. pap. text ed. 10.00x (ISBN 0-86709-101-0). Boynton Cook Pubs.

Writing Across the Curriculum Using Sociological Concepts. James A. Glynn. 64p. 1983. wkbk. 4.95 (ISBN 0-9603180-2-X). Fairway Hse.

Writing Across the Disciplines: Research into Practice. Ed. by Art Young & Toby Fulwiler. LC 85-24329. 320p. (Orig.). 1986. pap. text ed. 13.50x (ISBN 0-86709-131-2). Boynton Cook Pubs.

Writing Activites to Develop Mathematical Thinking. M. A. Dirkes. 116p. 12.95 (ISBN 0-89824-049-2). Trillium Pr.

Writing after Fifty. Leonard L. Knott. LC 85-12004. 218p. 1985. 12.95 (ISBN 0-89879-191-X, 2739). Writers Digest.

Writing Agricultural Information Bulletins: Reaching Developing Country Farmers. Cathy C. Carter. 1987. pap. text ed. 5.00 (ISBN 0-931901-06-5). NCSU Plant Pathol.

Writing Aids Through the Grades: One Hundred Eighty-Six Developmental Writing Activities. Ruth Carlson. LC 77-108775. 1970. pap. 8.95x (ISBN 0-8077-1141-1). Tchrs Coll.

Writing Air, Written Water. Roberta Gould. 102p. (Orig.). 1980. 5.95 (ISBN 0-936628-00-6). Waterside.

Writing All the Way. William J. McCleary. 350p. 1988. pap. text ed. write for info. (ISBN 0-534-08604-7). Wadsworth Pub.

Writing American English. Bernard Seward. Ed. by Roger E. Olsen. (Illus.). 90p. (gr. 3-12). 1982. pap. text ed. 4.95 (ISBN 0-88084-023-4). Alemany Pr.

Writing American History: Essays on Modern Scholarship. John Higham. LC 70-108209. pap. 54.30 (ISBN 0-317-27824-X, 2056038). Bks Demand UMI.

Writing an Expression see Language Learning: The Intermediate Phase.

Writing: An Introduction. Irwin H. Weiser. 1988. pap. text ed. price not set (ISBN 0-673-39986-9). Scott F.

Writing: Analysis & Application. Robert F. Willson, Jr. 1980. pap. text ed. write for info. (ISBN 0-02-428120-4). Macmillan.

Writing & Analyzing Effective Computer System Documentation. Ann Stuart. 288p. 1985. text ed. 21.95 (ISBN 0-03-063892-5). HR&W.

Writing & Art Go Hand in Hand. Diane Bonica. 80p. (gr. 2-6). 1988. pap. text ed. 6.95 (ISBN 0-86530-068-2, IP 13-2). Incentive Pubns.

Writing & Defending a Thesis or Dissertation in Psychology & Education. Roy Martin. 120p. 1980. lexotone 13.00 (ISBN 0-398-03947-X). C C Thomas.

Writing & Designing Operator Manual. Schoff. 1984. 25.95 (ISBN 0-534-03362-8). Van Nos Reinhold.

Writing & Difference. Jacques Derrida. Tr. by Alan Bass from Fr. LC 77-25933. 1978. lib. bdg. 25.00x (ISBN 0-226-14328-7). U of Chicago Pr.

Writing & Difference. Jacques Derrida. Tr. by Alan Bass from Fr. LC 77-25933. 1980. pap. 12.00x (ISBN 0-226-14329-5, P865, Phoen). U of Chicago Pr.

Writing & Editing: For High Reader Impact. Cortland G. Smith. 56p. spiral bdg. 10.00 (ISBN 0-686-16749-X). C G Smith.

Writing & Editing School News. 2nd & rev. ed. William N. Harwood. (Illus.). 364p. (gr. 10-12). 1983. pap. 10.57 (ISBN 0-931054-11-7). Clark Pub.

Writing & Fantasy in Proust: La Place de la Madeleine. Serge Doubrovsky. Tr. by Carol M. Bove & Paul Bove. LC 85-31823. xviii, 165p. 1986. 19.95x (ISBN 0-8032-1670-X). U of Nebr Pr.

Writing & Illuminating & Lettering. Edward Johnston. 1977. pap. 11.95 (ISBN 0-8008-8731-X, Pentalic). Taplinger.

Writing & Implementing an IEP. Thomas Lovitt. LC 79-52660. 1980. pap. 11.95 (ISBN 0-8224-7507-3). D S Lake Pubs.

Writing & Laterality Characteristics of Stuttering Children: A Comparative Study of 70 Grade School Stutterers & 70 Matched Non-Stutterers. Egbert J. Spadino. LC 70-177754. (Columbia University. Teachers College. Contributions to Education: No. 837). Repr. of 1941 ed. 22.50 (ISBN 0-404-55837-2). AMS Pr.

Writing & Learning. 2nd ed. Anne R. Gere. 786p. 1988. text ed. write for info. (ISBN 0-02-341460-X). Macmillan.

Writing & Learning Across the Curriculum 11-16. Nancy Martin et al. 176p. 1976. pap. text ed. 12.50x (ISBN 0-86709-095-2, 6063-7, Pub. by Ward Lock Educational England). Boynton Cook Pubs.

Writing & Life. Don Knefel. 464p. 1986. pap. text ed. 17.95 (ISBN 0-03-001503-0, HoltC). HR&W.

Writing & Logic. Gerald Levin. 276p. 1982. pap. text ed. 11.00 net (ISBN 0-15-597788-1, HC); instr's manual (ISBN 0-15-597789-X). HarBraceJ.

Writing & Madness: (Literature-Philosophy-Psychoanalysis) Shoshana Felman. Tr. by Martha N. Evans & Brian Massumi. LC 84-19845. 256p. 1985. 27.50x (ISBN 0-8014-1285-4). Cornell U Pr.

Writing & Madness: Literature-Philosophy-Psychoanalysis. Shoshana Felman. Tr. by Martha N. Evans & Brian Massumi. LC 84-19845. 256p. 1986. pap. 9.95x (ISBN 0-8014-9394-3). Cornell U Pr.

Writing & Managing Winning Technical Proposals. Timothy Whalen. 200p. 1987. text ed. 60.00 (ISBN 0-89006-236-6). Artech Hse.

Writing & Politics. Ed. by Harold Jaffe & Lawrence McCaffery. (Fiction International Ser.: No. 15). (Illus.). 224p. (Orig.). 1984. pap. 7.00 (ISBN 0-317-13345-4). SDSU Press.

Writing & Ratification of the U. S. Constitution: A Bibliography. Russell R. Wheeler. 44p. Date not set. write for info. Fed Judicial Ctr.

Writing & Reading Across the Curriculum. 2nd ed. Laurence Behrens & Leonard Rosen. 1985. write for info. (ISBN 0-673-39196-5). Scott F.

Writing & Reading Across the Curriculum. 3rd ed. Laurence Behrens & Leonard J. Rosen. 1988. pap. text ed. write for info. (ISBN 0-673-39765-3). Scott F.

Writing & Reading Across the Curriculum. Ed. & intro. by Malcolm P. Douglass. (Claremont Reading Conference Yearbook Ser.). 276p. (Orig.). 1985. pap. 15.00 (ISBN 0-941742-03-2). Claremont Grad.

Writing & Reading Differently: Deconstruction & the Teaching of Composition & Literature. Ed. by G. Douglas Atkins & Michael L. Johnson. LC 85-13464. x, 222p. 1985. pap. 12.95x (ISBN 0-7006-0283-6). U Pr of KS.

Writing & Reading in a Balanced Curriculum. Ed. by Malcolm P. Douglass. (Claremont Reading Conference Yearbook Ser.). 222p. (Orig.). 1982. pap. 11.00 (ISBN 0-941742-00-8). Claremont Grad.

Writing & Reading in Early Childhood: A Functional Approach. Roy Moxley. LC 81-9686. (Illus.). 290p. 1982. 34.95 (ISBN 0-87778-180-X). Educ Tech Pubns.

Writing & Reading in Henry James. Susanne Kappeler. LC 80-18181. 242p. 1980. 30.00x (ISBN 0-231-05198-0). Columbia U Pr.

Writing & Reading of Verse. C. E. Andrews. 1973. Repr. of 1934 ed. 35.00 (ISBN 0-8274-1667-9). R West.

Writing & Reading: The Vital Arts. Dorothy Rubin. 400p. 1983. pap. text ed. write for info. (ISBN 0-02-404250-1). Macmillan.

Writing & Reporting the News. Mitchell Stephens & Gerald Lanson. 448p. 1986. pap. text ed. 20.95 (ISBN 0-03-060483-4, HoltC). HR&W.

Writing & Researching Term Papers & Reports: A New Guide for Students. Eugene Ehrlich & Daniel Murphy. (Desk Editions). (gr. 10-12). 1968. pap. 3.50 (ISBN 0-553-26079-0). Bantam.

Writing & Revising: A Workbook. J. Karl Nicholas. 250p. 1981. pap. text ed. write for info. (ISBN 0-13-971499-5). P-H.

Writing & Rewriting. 2nd ed. Janet Mayes. 1981. pap. text ed. write for info. (ISBN 0-02-378200-5). Macmillan.

Writing & Rewriting the Holocaust: Narrative & the Consequences of Interpretation. James E. Young. LC 87-35791. 256p. 1988. 27.50 (ISBN 0-253-36716-6). Ind U Pr.

Writing & Selling Information the Mail Order Way. John Riddle. LC 84-20659. 35p. 1985. pap. 3.50 (ISBN 0-87576-115-1). Pilot Bks.

Writing & Selling Poetry, Fiction, Articles, Plays & Local History. Marcia Muth. LC 85-490. 96p. (Orig.). 1985. pap. 8.95 (ISBN 0-86534-048-X). Sunstone Pr.

Writing & Sexual Difference. Elizabeth Abel. LC 82-11131. (Phoenix Ser.). 312p. 1983. pap. 8.95 (ISBN 0-226-00076-1). U of Chicago Pr.

Writing & Speaking. Michael Gamble & Terri K. Gamble. 1983. text ed. write for info (ISBN 0-394-33254-7, RanC). Random.

Writing & the Body. Gabriel Josipovici. LC 82-9042. (Illus.). 160p. 1983. 23.00x (ISBN 0-691-06550-0). Princeton U Pr.

Writing & the Experience of Limits. Philippe Sollers. Ed. by David Hayman. Tr. by Phillip Barnard. LC 82-25258. (European Perspectives Ser.). 224p. 1983. 28.00x (ISBN 0-231-05292-8). Columbia U Pr.

Writing & the Holocaust. Ed. by Berel Lang. 1989. price not set (ISBN 0-8419-1184-3); pap. price not set (ISBN 0-8419-1185-1). Holmes & Meier.

Writing & the Writer. Frank Smith. 1982. pap. text ed. 17.95 (ISBN 0-03-058837-5). HR&W.

Writing & the Writer. Frank Smith. 272p. 1986. pap. 15.95 (ISBN 0-89859-856-7). L Erlbaum Assocs.

Writing & Understanding U. S. Patent Claims. Thomas J. Greer, Jr. 125p. 1979. pap. 20.00x (ISBN 0-87215-238-3). Michie Co.

Writing & Word Processing for Engineers & Scientists: How to Get Your Message Across in Today's High Technology World. P. Mail & R. W. Sykes. 1985. pap. text ed. 19.95 (ISBN 0-07-039776-7). McGraw.

Writing Arabic: A Practical Introduction to Ruq'ah Script. T. F. Mitchell. 1953. pap. 14.95x (ISBN 0-19-815150-0). Oxford U Pr.

Writing for Many Roles. Mimi Schwartz. 240p. (Orig.). 1985. pap. text ed. 12.50x (ISBN 0-86709-097-9). Boynton Cook Pubs.
Writing for Mass Communication. Earl R. Hutchison, Sr. (Illus.). 474p. 1986. pap. text ed. 21.95 (ISBN 0-582-29033-3). Longman.
Writing for Me. Roberta Mendel. (Scribbler Ser.). 22p. (Orig.). 1984. pap. 2.00 (ISBN 0-936424-11-7). Pin Prick.
Writing for Meaning: A Basic Worktext. Michael Shea. 361p. 1988. pap. text ed. 11.00 (ISBN 0-15-597870-5, HC); instr's manual 2.75 (ISBN 0-15-597871-3). HarBraceJ.
Writing for Newspapers. 2nd ed. John Wolcott. 54p. Date not set. pap. 5.95 (ISBN 0-931435-03-X). Features NW.
Writing for Nurse Managers. Kathleen Mastrian & Eric Birdsall. LC 85-18005. 157p. 1986. pap. 14.95 (ISBN 0-471-82174-8). Wiley.
Writing for Nursing & Allied Professions. Cormack. (Illus.). 192p. 1984. pap. 13.50 (ISBN 0-632-01129-7, B-1269-1). Mosby.
Writing for Pleasure & Profit in Retirement. David A. Phillips. (Self-Confidence, Self-Competence Ser.). 52p. (Orig.). 1985. pap. 6.95 (ISBN 0-932123-01-5). Stone Trail Pr.
Writing for Professional Publication. 2nd ed. Van Til. 36.95 (ISBN 0-205-08467-2, Pub. by Longwood Div). Allyn.
Writing for Public Relations. George A. Douglas. (Marketing & Management Ser.). 192p. 1980. pap. text ed. 20.50 (ISBN 0-675-08171-8). Merrill.
Writing for Readers. George R. Bramer & Dorothy Sedley. (Illus.). 500p. 1981. text ed. 21.95 (ISBN 0-675-08045-2). Merrill.
Writing for Religious & Other Specialty Markets. Dennis E. Hensley & Rose A. Adkins. (Orig.). 1987. pap. 8.95 (ISBN 0-8054-7911-2). Broadman.
Writing for Results in Business, Government, the Sciences & the Professions. 2nd ed. David W. Ewing. LC 79-11756. 448p. 1979. 33.95 (ISBN 0-471-05036-9). Wiley.
Writing for Results: Principles & Practice. Dugan Laird. LC 77-88052. 1978. pap. text ed. write for info. (ISBN 0-201-04114-6). Addison-Wesley.
Writing for Science, Industry, & Technology. Howard H. Hirschhorn. LC 79-63643. 282p. 1980. 18.50 (ISBN 0-442-21905-9, VN): Krieger.
Writing for Social Scientists: How to Start & Finish Your Thesis, Book, or Article. Howard S. Becker. LC 85-16504. (Chicago Guides to Writing, Editing, & Publishing). xii, 180p. 1986. lib. bdg. 20.00x (ISBN 0-226-04107-7); pap. text ed. 6.95 (ISBN 0-226-04108-5). U of Chicago Pr.
Writing for Story: Craft Secrets of Dramatic Nonfiction. Jon Franklin. 288p. 1987. pap. 4.95 (ISBN 0-451-62555-2, Ment). NAL.
Writing for Story: Craft Secrets of Dramatic Nonfiction by a Two-Time Pulitzer Prize Winner. Jon Franklin. LC 85-48132. 320p. 1986. 19.95 (ISBN 0-689-11785-X). Atheneum.
Writing for Success. Allan A. Glatthorn. 160p. 1985. pap. 7.95 (ISBN 0-673-15915-9). Scott F.
Writing for Technical & Business Magazines. Robert H. Dodds. LC 80-23843. (Illus.). 206p. 1982. Repr. of 1969 ed. text ed. 16.50 (ISBN 0-89874-237-4). Krieger.
Writing for Technical & Professional Journals. John H. Mitchell. LC 67-31374. (Wiley Series on Human Communication). (Illus.). pap. 78.90 (ISBN 0-317-10698-8, 2016469). Bks Demand UMI.
Writing for Technicians. 3rd ed. Marva T. Barnett. LC 86-19843. 358p. 1987. pap. text ed. 19.95 (ISBN 0-8273-2833-8); instr's. guide 10.00 (ISBN 0-8273-2834-6). Delmar.
Writing for Television. Stuart Kaminsky. (Orig.). 1988. pap. 8.95 (ISBN 0-440-50025-7, Dell Trade Pbks). Dell.
Writing for Television. Gilbert V. Seldes. LC 68-8743. (Illus.). 1968. Repr. of 1952 ed. lib. bdg. 45.00x (ISBN 0-8371-0217-0, SEWT). Greenwood.
Writing for Television & Radio. 4th ed. Robert L. Hilliard. 385p. 1984. pap. text ed. write for info. (ISBN 0-534-02782-2). Wadsworth Pub.
Writing for the Broadcast Media. Mayeux. 1985. 35.00 (ISBN 0-205-08343-9, 488343). Allyn.
Writing for the Fun of It: An Experience-Based Approach to Composition. Robert C. Hawley & Isabel L. Hawley. LC 73-83548. 110p. (Orig.). 1974. pap. 6.95 (ISBN 0-913636-02-9). Educ Res MA.
Writing for the Mass Media. James G. Stovall. 240p. 1985. pap. text ed. write for info. (ISBN 0-13-972035-9). P-H.
Writing for the Media. Martin J. Maloney & Paul M. Rubenstein. 1980. text ed. write for info. (ISBN 0-13-970558-9). P-H.
Writing for the Media. Sandy Pesmen. LC 82-72510. 160p. 1983. pap. 17.95 (ISBN 0-8442-3076-6, Crain Bks). Natl Textbk.
Writing for the Media. William L. Rivers & Alison R. Work. 288p. 1988. pap. 17.95 (ISBN 0-87484-829-6); wkbk. 7.95 (ISBN 0-87484-830-X). Mayfield Pub.
Writing for the Media: Film, Television, Video & Radio. 2nd ed. Paul M. Rubenstein & Martin J. Maloney. (Illus.). 320p. 1988. pap. text ed. price not set (ISBN 0-13-971508-8). P-H.
Writing for the Pedal Harp: A Standardized Manual for Composers & Harpists. Ruth K. Inglefield & Lou Anne Neill. LC 82-23896. (New Instrumentation: Vol. 6). (Illus.). 112p. 1983. text ed. 30.00x (ISBN 0-520-04832-6). U of Cal Pr.
Writing for the Real World see Writing on the Job.
Writing for the Religious Market. Marvin Ceynar. 1986. 2.25 (ISBN 0-89536-804-8, 6822). CSS of Ohio.
Writing for the Soaps. Jean Rouverol. LC 84-17410. 232p. 1984. 14.95 (ISBN 0-89879-146-4). Writers Digest.
Writing for the Technical Professions. Thomas N. Trzyna & Margaret W. Batschelet. 411p. 1987. text ed. write for info. (ISBN 0-534-07884-2). Wadsworth Pub.
Writing for the Twenty-First Century: Computers & Research Writing. William Wresch et al. 320p. 1988. pap. 11.95 spiral bdg. (ISBN 0-07-072051-7). McGraw.
Writing for the Twilight Zone. George C. Johnson. Ed. by Frederick J. Mayer. (Illus.). 130p. (Orig.). 1980. pap. 10.00 (ISBN 0-9605404-0-7); special limited edition, signed 50.00 (ISBN 0-686-36857-6). Outre House.
Writing for the Welfare Client: AFDC Forms & Their Messages. James S. Hanna, Jr. (Illus.). 186p. (Orig.). 1985. pap. text ed. 30.00 (ISBN 0-9607024-3-1). J S Hanna.
Writing for the Women's Market. Donna J. Epstein. 160p. (Orig.). pap. cancelled (ISBN 0-89471-285-3); lib. bdg. cancelled (ISBN 0-89471-286-1). Running Pr.
Writing for Your Peers: The Primary Journal Paper. Sylvester P. Carter. LC 87-2513. 137p. 1987. lib. bdg. 29.95 (ISBN 0-275-92630-3, C2630); pap. 9.95 (ISBN 0-275-92229-4, B2229). Praeger.
Writing for Your Reader. Dick Friedrich & Angela Harris. 256p. (Orig.). 1980. plastic comb. 9.95 (ISBN 0-8403-2157-0). Kendall Hunt.
Writing for Your Readers: Notes on the Writer's Craft from the Boston Globe. Donald Murray. LC 82-82588. (Illus.). 172p. 1983. pap. 8.95 (ISBN 0-87106-975-X). Globe Pequot.
Writing from a Legal Perspective. George D. Gopen. LC 80-27849. 225p. 1981. text ed. 17.95 (ISBN 0-8299-2123-0). West Pub.
Writing from Experience. Ed. by Richard A. Condon & Burton O. Kurth. LC 72-8541. (Essay Index Reprint Ser.). 1972. Repr. of 1960 ed. 19.00 (ISBN 0-8369-7310-0). Ayer Co Pubs.
Writing from Experience. Marcella Frank. 288p. 1983. pap. text ed. write for info. (ISBN 0-13-970285-7). P-H.
Writing, from Idea to Printed Page: Case Histories of Stories & Articles Published in the Saturday Evening Post. Ed. by Glen Gundell. LC 69-10104. Repr. of 1949 ed. lib. bdg. cancelled (ISBN 0-8371-0458-0, GUW). Greenwood.
Writing: From Inner World to Outer World. Barbara F. Clouse. (Illus.). 368p. 1983. pap. 19.95 (ISBN 0-07-011407-2). McGraw.
Writing from Scratch: The Essay. John C. Pratt. LC 87-12087. 120p. 1987. 19.95 (ISBN 0-8191-5444-X, Pub. by Hamilton Pr); pap. 8.95 (ISBN 0-8191-5445-8, Hamilton Pr). U Pr of Amer.
Writing from Scratch: The Play. Michael Stephens. Ed. by John C. Pratt. 136p. 1988. 19.95 (ISBN 0-8191-6801-7, Pub. Madison Bks); pap. 8.95 (ISBN 0-8191-6802-5). U Pr of Amer.
Writing from Sources. Brenda Spatt. LC 82-60459. 350p. 1983. text ed. 11.96 (ISBN 0-312-89468-6); instr's. manual avail. (ISBN 0-312-89469-4). St. Martin.
Writing from Sources. 2nd ed. Brenda Spatt. LC 86-60667. 475p. 1986. pap. text ed. write for info. (ISBN 0-312-89470-8); instr's. manual 00.21 (ISBN 0-312-89471-6). St Martin.
Writing from Start to Finish. John Schultz. LC 82-14595. 408p. 1982. 17.50x (ISBN 0-86709-039-1). Boynton Cook Pubs.
Writing from Start to Finish: A Rhetoric with Readings. Jeffrey L. Duncan. 474p. 1985. pap. text ed. 13.00 net (ISBN 0-15-598260-5, HC); instr's. manual avail. (ISBN 0-15-598261-3). HarBraceJ.
Writing from the Inside. George Core & Walter Sullivan. 1983. 8.95x (ISBN 0-393-95246-0); instr's. manual avail. (ISBN 0-393-95337-8). Norton.
Writing from Within: A Step-by-Step Guide to Telling Your Life's Stories. Bernard Selling. 240p. 1988. 15.95 (ISBN 0-89793-061-4); pap. 9.95 (ISBN 0-89793-054-1); Spiral binding (classroom ed.) 12.95 (ISBN 0-89793-052-5). Hunter Hse.
Writing Game: A Biography of WILL IRWIN. Robert V. Hudson. 200p. 1982. text ed. 14.75x (ISBN 0-8138-1931-8). Iowa St U Pr.
Writing Good Prose: A Simple Structural Approach. 4th ed. Alexander E. Jones & Claude W. Faulkner. 269p. 1979. pap. text ed. write for info. (ISBN 0-02-361290-8, Pub. by Scribner). Macmillan.
Writing Good Sentences. 3rd ed. Claude W. Faulkner. 320p. 1981. pap. text ed. 16.95 (ISBN 0-02-336470-X, Pub. by Scribner). Macmillan.
Writing Good Software in FORTRAN. Graham Smith. (Illus.). 384p. 1988. text ed. 30.00 (ISBN 0-13-969601-6). P-H.
Writing Groups: History, Theory & Implications. Anne R. Gere. (Studies in Writing & Rhetoric). 128p. 1987. pap. text ed. 10.95x (ISBN 0-8093-1354-5). S Ill U Pr.
Writing Guides. rev. ed. Sandra Panman & Richard Panman. 1986. text ed. 14.95 (ISBN 0-912813-06-7); pap. text ed. 11.95 (ISBN 0-912813-05-9); student management forms 1.95 (ISBN 0-912813-07-5); avail. instr's. manual (ISBN 0-912813-08-3). Active Lrn.
Writing Handbook. Michael P. Kammer et al. LC 52-13885. (gr. 9-12). 1953. pap. text ed. 6.60 (ISBN 0-8294-0110-5); tchrs' ed dictation exercises 2.00. Loyola.
Writing Handbook for Computer Professionals. William D. Skees. (Computer Technology Ser.). (Illus.). 296p. 1982. 27.50 (Lifetime Learn). Van Nos Reinhold.
Writing Handbook for Computer Professionals. William D. Skees. 296p. 1982. 35.95 (ISBN 0-534-97946-7). Van Nos Reinhold.
Writing Help. (Help for Home & School Ser.). (ps-1). 2.50 (ISBN 0-86653-248-X, GA 595). Good Apple.
Writing Help. (Help for Home & School Ser.). (gr. k-2). 2.50 (ISBN 0-86653-249-8, GA 598). Good Apple.
Writing Help. (Help for Home & School Ser.). (gr. 1-3). 2.50 (ISBN 0-86653-250-1, GA 597). Good Apple.
Writing Help. (Help for Home & School Ser.). (gr. 2-4). 2.50 (ISBN 0-86653-251-X, GA 596). Good Apple.
Writing Historical Fiction. Rhona Martin. 96p. 1988. 10.95 (ISBN 0-312-01848-7). St Martin.
Writing History. Paul Veyne. Tr. by Mina Moore-Rinvolucri from Fr. 342p. 1984. 30.00x (ISBN 0-8195-5067-1); pap. 14.95x (ISBN 0-8195-6076-6). Wesleyan U Pr.
Writing History & Making Policy, Vol. VI: The Cold War, Vietnam, & Revisionism. Richard A. Melanson. LC 83-10362. (Exxon Ser.). 260p. 1983. lib. bdg. 28.50 (ISBN 0-8191-3352-3); pap. text ed. 11.00 (ISBN 0-8191-3353-1). U Pr of Amer.
Writing History Papers. James D. Bennett & Lowell H. Harrison. LC 78-66987. (Orig.). 1979. pap. text ed. 4.50x (ISBN 0-88273-105-X). Forum Pr IL.
Writing Home. Katharyn Machan Aal & Barbara Crooker. LC 83-1715. (Orig.). 1983. pap. 4.50 (ISBN 0-935020-08-X). Gehry Pr.
Writing Home. Hugo Williams. 64p. 1986. pap. 6.95 (ISBN 0-19-211970-2). Oxford U Pr.
Writing Home: Immigrants in Brazil & the United States, 1890-1891. Witold Kula & Nina Assorodobraj-Kula. (East European Monographs: No. 210). 714p. 1986. 50.00 (ISBN 0-88033-107-0). East Eur Quarterly.
Writing How & Why: Instructional Manual to Accompany Suki. Ed. by Matthew Lipman & Ann M. Sharp. 384p. 1980. tchrs. ed. 37.50x (ISBN 0-916834-14-X, TX 726-631). Inst Advncmnt Philos Child.
Writing Ideas Ready to Use! Barbara Gruber. (Instant Idea Bks.). (Illus.). 64p. 1983. 5.95 (ISBN 0-86734-050-9, FS-8304). Schaffer Pubns.
Writing in a Bilingual Program: Habia Una Vez. Carole Edelsky. Ed. by Marcia Farr. LC 85-31569. (Writing Research Ser.: Vol. 5). 256p. 1986. text ed. 39.50 (ISBN 0-89391-304-9); pap. 22.50 (ISBN 0-89391-381-2). Ablex Pub.
Writing in a Modern Temper: Essays on French Literature & Thought, in Honor of Henri Peyre. Ed. by Mary A. Caws. (Stanford French & Italian Studies: Vol. 33). 286p. 1984. pap. 34.50 (ISBN 0-915838-04-4). Anma Libri.
Writing in a State of Siege. Andre Brink. 1986. pap. text ed. 8.95 (ISBN 0-671-62289-7). Summit Bks.
Writing in a State of Siege: Essays on Politics & Literature. Andre Brink. 256p. 1984. 15.95 (ISBN 0-671-47751-X). Summit Bks.
Writing in Action: A Collaborative Rhetoric for College Writers. Lea Masiello. viii, 199p. 1986. pap. text ed. write for info. (ISBN 0-02-377030-9). Macmillan.
Writing in College. William J. Kerrigan. 191p. (Orig.). 1976. pap. text ed. 10.00 net (ISBN 0-15-597881-0, HC). HarBraceJ.
Writing in College: Style & Substance. Patricia S. Taylor. 1988. pap. text ed. price not set (ISBN 0-673-39926-5). Scott F.
Writing in Earth Science. Robert L. Bates. 50p. (Orig.). 1988. pap. text ed. 3.95 (ISBN 0-913312-92-4). Am Geol.
Writing in Elementary School Social Studies. Ed. by Barry K. Beyer & Robert Gilstrap. LC 82-5480. 216p. (Orig.). 1982. pap. 10.95 (ISBN 0-89994-267-9). Soc Sci Ed.
Writing in England Today: The Last Fifteen Years. Karl Miller. 10.00 (ISBN 0-8446-2591-4). Peter Smith.
Writing in Focus. Ed. by Florian Coulmas & Konrad Ehlich. LC 83-13095. (Trends in Linguistics Studies & Monographs: No. 24). viii, 405p. 1983. 84.25x (ISBN 90-279-3359-6). Mouton.
Writing in General & the Short Story in Particular. Rust Hills. 1979. pap. 2.95 (ISBN 0-553-22695-9). Bantam.
Writing in General & the Short Story in Particular. Rust Hills. 1987. 16.95 (ISBN 0-395-44255-9); pap. 8.95 (ISBN 0-395-44268-0). HM.
Writing in Gold: Byzantine Society & Its Icons. Robin Cormack. (Illus.). 1985. 25.00x (ISBN 0-19-520486-7). Oxford U Pr.
Writing in Groups: New Techniques for Good Writing Without Drills. 4th ed. Goran G. Moberg. 208p. 1985. pap. 15.95 (ISBN 0-8403-3706-X, Co-Pub with the Writing Consultant). Kendall-Hunt.
Writing in Law Practice. Frank E. Cooper. 556p. 1963. text ed. 19.00x (ISBN 0-672-81021-2, Bobbs-Merrill Law). Michie Co.
Writing in Nonacademic Settings. Ed. by Lee Odell & Dixie Goswami. (Guilford Perspectives in Writing Research Ser.). 553p. 1986. text ed. 50.00 (ISBN 0-89862-252-2); pap. 24.95 (ISBN 0-89862-906-3). Guilford Pr.
Writing in Organizations: Purposes, Strategies & Processes. P. Maki & C. Schilling. 416p. 1987. pap. text ed. 18.95 (ISBN 0-07-030361-4). McGraw.
Writing in Real Time: Modelling Production Processes. Ann Matsuhashi. Ed. by Marcia Farr. LC 86-22214. (Writing Research Ser.: Vol. 16). 320p. 1987. text ed. 39.50 (ISBN 0-89391-400-2); pap. 24.50 (ISBN 0-89391-417-7). Ablex Pub.
Writing in Restaurants. David Mamet. 176p. 1987. pap. 6.95 (ISBN 0-14-008981-0). Penguin.
Writing in Restaurants: Essays & Prose. David Mamet. 192p. 1986. 15.95 (ISBN 0-670-81140-8). Viking.
Writing in Subject-Matter Fields: A Bibliographic Guide, with Annotations & Writing Assignments. Eva M. Burkett. LC 76-30397. 204p. 1977. 18.00 (ISBN 0-8108-1012-3). Scarecrow.
Writing in the Arts & Sciences. Elaine P. Maimon et al. 1981. text ed. write for info. (ISBN 0-673-39227-9). Scott F.
Writing in the Center: Teaching in a Writing Center Setting. Irene L. Clark. 96p. 1986. pap. text ed. 12.95 (ISBN 0-8403-3601-2). Kendall-Hunt.
Writing in the Content Areas: Research Implications. Joanne M. Yates. (What Research Says to the Teacher Ser.). 32p. 1983. 2.95 (ISBN 0-8106-1060-4). NEA.
Writing in the Disciplines. Diane Durkin. 480p. 1987. pap. text ed. write for info. (ISBN 0-394-35533-4, RanC). Random.
Writing in the Disciplines: A Reader for Writers. Mary L. Kennedy et al. (Illus.). 544p. 1987. pap. text ed. write for info. (ISBN 0-13-970450-7). P-H.
Writing in the Liberal Arts Tradition: A Rhetoric with Readings. James L. Kinneavy et al. 446p. 1985. text ed. 27.50 scp (ISBN 0-690-01522-4, HarpC). Har-Row.
Writing in the Margin: Spanish Literature of the Golden Age. Paul J. Smith. 240p. 1988. 55.00 (ISBN 0-19-815847-5). Oxford U Pr.
Writing in the Secondary School: English & the Content Areas. Arthur N. Applebee. LC 81-18799. (Research Report Ser.: No. 21). 130p. 1981. pap. 9.50 (ISBN 0-8141-5884-6). NCTE.
Writing in the Social Sciences. Joyce S. Steward & Majorie Smelstor. 1984. pap. text ed. write for info. (ISBN 0-673-15460-2). Scott F.
Writing in Two Parts see Beginning to Compose.
Writing in Winter. Constance Scheerer. LC 85-70736. (Target Midwest Poetry Ser.). 80p. (Orig.). 1985. pap. 5.25 (ISBN 0-933532-54-7). BKMK.
Writing "Independent" History: African Historiography, 1960-1980. Caroline Neale. LC 84-15756. (Contributions in Afro-American & African Studies: No. 85). ix, 208p. 1985. lib. bdg. 35.00 (ISBN 0-313-24652-1, NID/). Greenwood.
Writing Instruction in Nineteenth-Century American Colleges. James A. Berlin. LC 83-20116. (Studies in Writing & Rhetoric Ser.). 128p. (Orig.). 1984. pap. 8.50x (ISBN 0-8093-1166-6). S Ill U Pr.
Writing Instruction In Nineteenth-Century American Colleges. 114p. 1984. 10.95 (ISBN 0-317-37081-2). NCTE.
Writing Instruments. 150p. 1985. 595.00 (ISBN 0-318-00529-8). Busn Trend.
Writing Interactive Compilers & Interpreters. P. J. Brown. LC 79-40513. (Computing Ser.). 265p. 1981. pap. 24.95x (ISBN 0-471-10072-2). Wiley.
Writing Interestingly, Lesson 9. Michael Adelstein. Ed. by Betty Samuels. (Business of Better Writing Ser.). 19p. 1984. wkbk. 3.00 (ISBN 0-910475-17-2). KET.
Writing: Invention, Form & Style. Leonard A. Podis & Joanne M. Podis. 1984. text ed. write for info. (ISBN 0-673-15525-0). Scott F.
Writing Ireland: Colonialism, Nationalism & Culture. David Cairns & Shaun Richards. LC 88-1540. (Cultural Politics Ser.). 192p. 1988. 39.95 (ISBN 0-7190-2371-8, Pub. by Manchester Univ Pr); pap. 11.95 (ISBN 0-7190-2372-6, Pub. by Manchester Univ Pr). St Martin.
Writing Is a Social Disease. Gerald Kaminski. 86p. 1986. pap. 5.95 (ISBN 0-931896-06-1). Cove View.
Writing Is an Aid to Memory. Hejinian Lyn. 1978. 10.00 (ISBN 0-685-99356-6); pap. 4.00 (ISBN 0-685-99357-4). Figures.
Writing Is Childs Play. Donna Connell. (ITL Early Writing Program Ser.). 1985. pap. 8.50 (ISBN 0-88671-195-9). Am Guidance.
Writing Is Critical Action. Tilly Warnock. 1988. pap. text ed. price not set (ISBN 0-673-18934-1). Scott F.

Writing Research Papers Across the Curriculum. Susan M. Hubbuch. 256p. 1985. pap. text ed. 7.95 (ISBN 0-03-063193-9, HoltC). HR&W.
Writing Research Papers Across the Curriculum, 1984 MLA Version. Susan M. Hubbuch. 284p. 1987. pap. text ed. write for info. (ISBN 0-03-012014-4). HR&W.
Writing Resumes - A Self-Paced Workbook. Stephen D. Bruce. (The BLR Career Development & Outplacement Workshop Ser.). 1985. wkbk 21.95 (ISBN 1-55645-540-2). Busn Legal Reports.
Writing Right: Diagnosing, Remediating & Improving Handwriting. Betty Duvall. 148p. (Orig.). 1987. pap. text ed. 21.95 (ISBN 0-943024-02-1). Duvall.
Writing Road to Reading: A Modern Method of Phonics for Teaching Children to Read. 2 ed. Romalda B. Spalding & Walter T. Spalding. 272p. 1970. pap. 14.95 (ISBN 0-688-07818-4); phonograms 17.95 (ISBN 0-688-15001-2). Morrow.
Writing Road to Reading: The Spalding Method of Phonic for Teaching Speech, Writing & Reading. 3rd, rev. ed. Romalda B. Spalding & Walter T. Spalding. LC 86-647. 288p. 1986. pap. 14.95 (ISBN 0-688-06634-8, Quill). Morrow.
Writing Room: A Resource Book for Teachers of English. Harvey S. Wiener. 1981. pap. text ed. 10.95x (ISBN 0-19-502826-0). Oxford U Pr.
Writing School-Master. John Davies. LC 76-57376. (English Experience Ser.: No. 794). 1977. Repr. of 1636 ed. lib. bdg. 20.00 (ISBN 90-221-0794-9). Walter J Johnson.
Writing Science & Medicine for Communication. Lynn & Chapman. 26.95 (ISBN 0-317-64316-9). Van Nos Reinhold.
Writing Science Fiction. Christopher Evans. 96p. 1988. 10.95 (ISBN 0-312-01849-5). St Martin.
Writing Science News for the Mass Media. 2nd ed. David W. Burkett. LC 72-84334. 223p. 1973. 15.00x (ISBN 0-87201-924-1). Gulf Pub.
Writing Scientific Papers-Reports. 8th ed. Paul W. Jones & Michael L. Keene. 384p. 1981. pap. text ed. write for info. (ISBN 0-697-03773-8). Wm C Brown.
Writing Screenplays That Sell. Michael Hauge. 1988. pap. text ed. 9.95 (ISBN 0-07-027068-6). McGraw.
Writing Scripts for Television, Radio & Film. Edgar E. Willis & Camille D'Arienzo. LC 80-22260. 322p. 1981. pap. text ed. 20.95 (ISBN 0-03-052706-6). HR&W.
Writing: Self-Expression & Communication. Dietrich & Kaiser. 544p. 1986. pap. text ed. 14.00 net (ISBN 0-15-598250-8, Pub. by HC); instr's. manual net 2.00 (ISBN 0-15-598251-6). HarBraceJ.
Writing Sense: A Handbook of Composition. David R. Pichaske. LC 74-15134. 1975. pap. text ed. 9.95 (ISBN 0-02-925170-2). Free Pr.
Writing Sentences & Paragraphs. Doris Rikkers. Ed. by Joan Hoffman. (I Know It! Bks.). (Illus.). 32p. (gr. 5 up). 1980. wkbk. 1.95 (ISBN 0-938256-25-4). Sch Zone Pub Co.
Writing Sentences, Paragraphs, & Essays. Anthony Winkler & Jo Ray McCuen. 256p. 1981. pap. text ed. write for info. (ISBN 0-574-22060-7, 13-5060); instr's. guide avail. (ISBN 0-574-22061-5, 13-5061). SRA.
Writing Short Business Reports. N. Carr-Ruffino. 1980. pap. 18.95 (ISBN 0-07-010155-8). McGraw.
Writing Short Stories for Young People. George E. Stanley. LC 86-28928. 228p. 1987. 15.95 (ISBN 0-89879-256-8). Writers Digest.
Writing Skills. Ed. by NEBSS Staff & NRMC Staff. (Open Learning for Supervisory Management Ser.: 302). (Illus.). 106p. 1986. 17.50 (ISBN 0-08-070072-1, Pub. by PPL). Pergamon.
Writing Skills. Shew-Pincar. Ed. by Alton L. Raygor. (Basic Skills Ser.). (Illus.). 1979. pap. text ed. 21.95 (ISBN 0-07-056690-9). McGraw.
Writing Skills for Nurses. Gertrude Schneller & Christine Godwin. 1983. pap. text ed. 19.95 (ISBN 0-8359-8798-1). Appleton & Lange.
Writing Skills for Technical Students. Delaware Technical & Community College, English Department Staff. 400p. 1982. pap. text ed. write for info. (ISBN 0-13-970665-8). P-H.
Writing Skills for Technical Students. 2nd ed. Delaware Technical & Community College. 336p. 1988. pap. text ed. price not set (ISBN 0-13-970781-6). P-H.
Writing Skills Handbook. 2nd ed. Charles Bazerman & Harvey S. Wiener. 1988. pap. text ed. 9.56 (ISBN 0-395-35746-2); instr's. manual 2.36 (ISBN 0-395-46923-6). HM.
Writing Skills Handbook. Harvey S. Wiener & Charles Bazerman. LC 82-83202. 144p. 1983. pap. text ed. 11.95 (ISBN 0-395-33017-3). HM.
Writing Skills Test. rev. ed. Nancy Varness. (GED Ser.). 300p. 1985. pap. 7.65 (ISBN 0-8092-5589-8). Contemp Bks.
Writing Solutions: Beginnings, Middles & Endings. T. Fensch. (Communication Textbook Ser.). 184p. Date not set. 32.50 (ISBN 0-8058-0410-2); pap. 16.95 (ISBN 0-8058-0411-0). L Erlbaum Assocs.
Writing Southern History: Essays in Historiography in Honor of Fletcher M. Green. Ed. by Arthur S. Link & Rembert W. Patrick. LC 81-6585. x, 502p. 1981. Repr. of 1965 ed. lib. bdg. 45.00x (ISBN 0-313-22782-9, LIWS). Greenwood.
Writing Southern History: Essays in Historiography in Honor of Fletcher M. Green. Ed. by Arthur S. Link & Rembert W. Patrick. LC 65-23761. 1965. pap. text ed. 11.95 (ISBN 0-8071-0123-0). La State U Pr.
Writing! Step-by-Step. Incl. Book 3. 1985 (ISBN 0-8294-0484-8); Book 4. 1985 (ISBN 0-8294-0486-4); Book 5. 1985 (ISBN 0-8294-0488-0); Book 6. 1986 (ISBN 0-8294-0510-0); Book 7. 1986 (ISBN 0-8294-0512-7); Book 8. 1985 (ISBN 0-8294-0514-3). pap. 2.40 ea. Loyola.
Writing Step by Step: Easy Strategies for Writing & Revising. Robert de Beaugrande. 382p. 1985. pap. text ed. 13.00 net (ISBN 0-15-598258-3, HC); instr's. manual avail. (ISBN 0-15-598259-1). HarBraceJ.
Writing Stories for Little Children. pap. 1.50 (ISBN 0-686-32338-6). Rod & Staff.
Writing: Strategies for All Disciplines. Barbara F. Walvoord. (Illus.). 480p. 1985. text ed. 15.95 (ISBN 0-13-147349-2). P-H.
Writing Strategies for ESL Students. Judith A. Johnson. 352p. 1983. pap. write for info. (ISBN 0-02-361020-4). Macmillan.
Writing Structured COBOL Programs. David L. Johnson. 550p. 1986. pap. text ed. write for info. (ISBN 0-201-11591-3); write for info. instr's. manual (ISBN 0-201-11592-1); write for info. study guide (ISBN 0-201-11593-X); write for info. test item file (ISBN 0-201-11594-8); write for info. pseudocodepads (ISBN 0-201-11596-4). Addison-Wesley.
Writing Study Guides. Anita Morris. (Orig.). 1984. pap. text ed. 8.95x (ISBN 0-86184-127-1). Trans Atl Phila.
Writing Successful Proposals. Donald Duren & Jill Andreoni. (Illus.). 144p. 1979. pap. 7.98 (ISBN 0-9604056-0-7). Durand Intl.
Writing System for Engineers & Scientists. Edmond H. Weiss. LC 81-775. (Illus.). 288p. 1982. text ed. 32.00 (ISBN 0-13-971606-8). P-H.
Writing System of Modern Persian. Herbert H. Paper & Mohammad A. Jazayery. LC 76-40543. 40p. 1976. pap. 5.00x (ISBN 0-87950-284-3). Spoken Lang Serv.
Writing Systems: A Linguistic Introduction. Geoffrey Sampson. (Illus.). 288p. 1986. 35.00x (ISBN 0-8047-1254-9). Stanford U Pr.
Writing Systems of the World: Alphabets, Syllabaries, Pictograms. Akira Nakanishi. LC 79-64826. (Illus.). 1980. 19.50 (ISBN 0-8048-1293-4). C E Tuttle.
Writing Talks. Ed. by Bob Perelman. 305p. 1985. 14.95 (ISBN 0-8093-1180-1). S Ill U Pr.
Writing Talks: Views on Teaching Writing from Across the Professions. Ed. by Muffy E. Siegel & Toby Olson. 176p. 1983. pap. text ed. 12.50x (ISBN 0-86709-077-4). Boynton Cook Pubs.
Writing Tasks: An Authentic-Task Approach to Individual Writing Needs. David Jolly. 166p. 1984. text ed. 7.50 (ISBN 0-521-22924-3); 10.95 (ISBN 0-521-28972-6). Cambridge U Pr.
Writing: Teachers & Children at Work. Donald Graves. LC 82-21177. 312p. (Orig.). 1982. pap. text ed. 14.00x (ISBN 0-435-08203-5). Heinemann Ed.
Writing Teacher's Sourcebook. Ed. by Gary Tate & Edward P. Corbett. 1981. pap. text ed. 12.95x (ISBN 0-19-502878-3). Oxford U Pr.
Writing Teacher's Sourcebook. 2nd ed. Ed. by Gary Tate & Edward P. Corbett. (Illus.). 384p. 1988. pap. 16.95 (ISBN 0-19-505338-9). Oxford U Pr.
Writing Technical Articles, Speeches, & Manuals. Mark Forbes. LC 88-10157. 1988. write for info. (ISBN 0-471-60097-0); pap. 24.95 (ISBN 0-471-60096-2). Wiley.
Writing Television & Motion Picture Scripts That Sell. Evelyn Goodman. (Orig.). Date not set. pap. text ed. 9.95 (ISBN 0-9613885-8-7). Westbourne Ent.
Writing Term Papers. Alan Heineman & Hulon Willis. 165p. 1988. pap. text ed. 6.50 net (ISBN 0-15-598284-2, HC). HarBraceJ.
Writing Term Papers & Reports. 4th ed. George S. Hubbell. (Orig.). 1969. pap. 4.95 (ISBN 0-06-460037-8, CO 37, B&N Bks). Har-Row.
Writing That Means Business: How to Get Your Message Across Quickly & Effectively. Ellen Roddick. 198p. 1986. pap. 8.95 (ISBN 0-02-015380-5, Collier). Macmillan.
Writing That Means Business: The Manager's Guide; How to Get Your Message Across with Less Effort & Greater Impact. Ellen Roddick. 128p. 1984. 10.95 (ISBN 0-02-604400-5). Macmillan.
Writing That Sells. John C. Bancroft. (Illus.). 180p. 1975. pap. 10.95 (ISBN 0-686-11023-4). J C Bancroft.
Writing That Works. Kenneth Roman & Joel Raphaelson. LC 80-8695. 160p. 1981. 12.95i (ISBN 0-06-014843-8, HarpT). Har-Row.
Writing That Works. Kenneth Roman & Joel Raphaelson. 112p. (Orig.). 1985. pap. 6.95 (ISBN 0-06-463710-7, EH 710, B&N Bks). Har-Row.
Writing That Works: How to Write Effectively on the Job. 3rd ed. Walter E. Oliu et al. LC 87-60516. 608p. 1988. pap. text ed. write for info. (ISBN 0-312-00275-0); write for info. instr's. manual (ISBN 0-312-00276-9); write for info. instr's. ed. (ISBN 0-312-01286-1). St Martin.
Writing the Absence of the Father: Undoing Oedipal Structures in the Contemporary American Novel. Francesco A. Ancona. 172p. (Orig.). 1986. lib. bdg. 26.00 (ISBN 0-8191-5097-5); pap. text ed. 12.25 (ISBN 0-8191-5098-3). U Pr of Amer.
Writing the Academic Essay. John R. Wilson. 384p. 1988. pap. 18.95 (ISBN 0-675-20737-1). Merrill.
Writing the Advanced Short Story. Simone Bibeau. (Illus.). 32p. (gr. 1-12). 1983. pap. text ed. 1.95 (ISBN 0-940406-07-1). Perception Pubns.
Writing the Apocalypse: Ends & Endings in Contemporary U. S. & Latin American Fiction. Lois P. Zamora. 230p. Date not set. price not set (ISBN 0-521-36223-7). Cambridge U Pr.
Writing the Australian Crawl. William Stafford. Ed. by Donald Hall. LC 77-5711. (Poets on Poetry Ser.). pap. 8.95 (ISBN 0-472-87300-8). U of Mich Pr.
Writing the Beginning Short Story. Simone Bibeau. (Illus.). 32p. (Orig.). (gr. 1-9). 1983. pap. text ed. 1.95 (ISBN 0-940406-06-3). Perception Pubns.
Writing the Broadway Musical. Aaron Frankel. LC 76-58925. 1977. pap. 17.95x (ISBN 0-89676-044-8). Drama Bk.
Writing: The Business Letter. Albert G. Craz & Edward P. Mavragis. (Writing Ser.). 68p. 1981. wkbk. 3.95 (ISBN 0-9602800-1-4). Comp Pr.
Writing: The Composition. Albert G. Craz & Edward P. Mavragis. (Writing Ser.). 66p. 1981. wkbk. 3.95 (ISBN 0-9602800-3-0). Comp Pr.
Writing the Creative Article Today. Marjorie Holmes. LC 85-20212. 165p. 1986. 12.95 (ISBN 0-87116-146-X). Writer.
Writing the Doctoral Dissertation. Gordon B. Davis & Clyde A. Parker. LC 78-7598. 1979. pap. 6.95 (ISBN 0-8120-0997-5). Barron.
Writing the Easy Way. Phillis Dutwin & Harriet Diamond. (Easy Way Ser.). 224p. 1985. pap. text ed. 8.95 (ISBN 0-8120-2729-9). Barron.
Writing the Economics Paper. Lawrence Morse. 1981. pap. text ed. 6.95 (ISBN 0-8120-2113-4). Barron.
Writing the Family Narrative. Lawrence P. Gouldrup. LC 87-70106. 157p. (Orig.). 1987. pap. 10.95 (ISBN 0-916489-27-2, 141). Ancestry.
Writing the Fantasy Story. Simone Bibeau. (Illus.). 32p. (Orig.). (gr. 1-9). 1983. pap. text ed. 1.95 (ISBN 0-940406-08-X). Perception Pubns.
Writing the Margins: Edith Wharton, Ellen Glasgow, and the Literary Tradition of the Ruined Woman. Catherine E. Saunders. LC 86-73024. (The LeBaron Russell Briggs Prize Honors Essay in English, 1986). 92p. 1987. pap. text ed. 5.00x (ISBN 0-674-96235-4). Harvard U Pr.
Writing the Modern Mystery. Barbara Norville. LC 86-15795. 209p. 1986. 15.95 (ISBN 0-89879-235-5). Writers Digest.
Writing the Natural Way: Using Right-Brain Techniques to Release Your Expressive Powers. Gabriele L. Rico. LC 81-126. (Illus.). 288p. 1983. 15.95 (ISBN 0-87477-186-2); pap. 10.95 (ISBN 0-87477-236-2). J P Tarcher.
Writing: The Nature, Development, & Communication, Vol. 2. Ed. by C. H. Frederiksen & J. F. Dominic. 256p. 1982. 29.95x (ISBN 0-89859-158-9). L Erlbaum Assocs.
Writing the News. Douglas A. Anderson & Bruce Itule. 400p. 1988. pap. text ed. 21.00 (ISBN 0-394-37419-3, RanC); 13.00 (ISBN 0-394-37676-5). Random.
Writing the Novel: From Plot to Print. Lawrence Block. LC 79-1067. 197p. 1985. pap. 8.95 (ISBN 0-89879-208-8). Writers Digest.
Writing the Nursing Resume. Health Care Education Associates Staff. 80p. 1986. 19.95 (ISBN 0-8016-2119-4). Mosby.
Writing: The Process Essay. Carol Gladstone. 55p. 1986. wkbk. 3.25 (ISBN 0-910307-11-3). Comp Pr.
Writing the Psychology Paper. Robert Sternberg. LC 77-9250. 1977. pap. text ed. 6.95 (ISBN 0-8120-0772-7). Barron.
Writing: The Report. Albert G. Craz & Edward P. Mavragis. (Writing Ser.). 66p. 1981. wkbk. 3.95 (ISBN 0-9602800-2-2). Comp Pr.
Writing the Research Paper. Lotte Blustein & Rosemary J. Geary. (Illus.). 62p. (gr. 7 up). 1985. pap. text ed. 6.50 (ISBN 0-9605248-2-7). Blustein-Geary.
Writing the Research Paper. Marilyn S. Samuels. 1978. pap. text ed. 10.00 (ISBN 0-87720-965-0). AMSCO Sch.
Writing the Research Paper: A Guide & Sourcebook. Martha H. Cummins & Carole Slade. LC 78-69613. (Illus.). 1979. pap. text ed. 17.95 (ISBN 0-395-27259-9); instr's manual 0.50 (ISBN 0-395-27260-2). HM.
Writing the Research Paper: A Handbook. 2nd ed. Anthony C. Winkler & Jo R. McCuen. 284p. 1985. pap. text ed. 7.95 (ISBN 0-15-598291-5, HC). HarBraceJ.
Writing the Screenplay: TV & Film. Alan A. Armer. 272p. 1988. pap. text ed. write for info. (ISBN 0-534-08292-0). Wadsworth Pub.
Writing the Script: A Practical Guide for Films & Television. Wells Root. LC 79-1927. 252p. pap. 6.95 (ISBN 0-03-044221-4). H Holt & Co.
Writing the Short-Story: A Practical Handbook on the Rise, Structure, Writing, & Sale of the Modern Short Story. J. Berg Esenwein. 1979. Repr. of 1908 ed. lib. bdg. 25.00 (ISBN 0-8495-1330-8). Arden Lib.
Writing the South: Ideas of an American Region. Richard Gray. (Cambridge Studies in American Literature & Culture). (Illus.). 346p. 1986. 29.95 (ISBN 0-521-30687-6). Cambridge U Pr.
Writing the Winning Proposition. Herman R. Holtz & Terry D. Schmidt. (Business Communication Ser.). (Illus.). 384p. 1981. text ed. 35.95 (ISBN 0-07-029649-9). McGraw.
Writing Themes about Literature. 5th ed. Edgar V. Roberts. 352p. 1983. pap. 16.00 (ISBN 0-13-971655-6). P-H.
Writing Themes about Literature. 6th ed. Edgar V. Roberts. 368p. pap. text ed. 16.00 (ISBN 0-13-970757-3). P-H.
Writing Themes about Literature: A Guide to Accompany the Norton Introduction to Literature. 3rd ed. Ed. by Carl E. Bain et al. 1983. pap. 4.95x (ISBN 0-393-95350-5). Norton.
Writing Themes about Literature (Brief Edition) Edgar V. Roberts. (Illus.). 224p. 1982. pap. 12.00 ref. ed. (ISBN 0-13-970566-X). P-H.
Writing Through Experience: A Process Approach. Charles R. Duke. 1983. write for info. (ISBN 0-673-39208-2). Scott F.
Writing Through Music. Ursula O. Ronnholm. Tr. by Miguel Montero. (Illus.). 74p. (gr. k-3). 1986. pap. text ed. 4.00 (ISBN 0-941911-04-7). Two Way Bilingual.
Writing Through Reading. Stephen C. Lewis & M. Cecile Forte. (Illus.). 372p. 1983. pap. text ed. write for info. (ISBN 0-13-971630-0). P-H.
Writing Tips. American Physical Therapy Association Staff. (Orig.). 1985. pap. 2.50 (ISBN 0-912452-52-8). Am Phys Therapy Assn.
Writing to Be Published. Gene Boone. 1984. pap. 4.95x (ISBN 0-317-11581-2, Pub. by Exploits Pub Ltd Canada). RSVP Press.
Writing to Be Published. 2nd ed. Gene Boone. 40p. (Orig.). 1986. pap. 4.00 saddle-stitched (ISBN 0-930865-00-6). RSVP Press.
Writing to Be Read. 3rd, rev. ed. Ken Macrorie. LC 84-14922. 304p. (gr. 9-12). 1984. pap. 12.50x (ISBN 0-86709-133-9). Boynton Cook Pubs.
Writing to Create Ourselves: New Approaches for Teachers, Students, & Writers. T. D. Allen. LC 82-1878. 255p. 1982. 17.95x (ISBN 0-8061-1768-0). U of Okla Pr.
Writing to Eat. Madelon Chambliss. 88p. 1983. 6.95x (ISBN 0-9612420-0-0). Madelon Chamb.
Writing to Explain. Kathleen A. Rogers. (gr. 3-6). 1987. pap. 6.95 (ISBN 0-8224-7537-5). D S Lake Pubs.
Writing: To Finish a Story. Carol Gladstone. 54p. 1988. wkbk. 3.25 (ISBN 0-910307-10-5). Comp Pr.
Writing to Inform. Kathleen A. Rogers. (gr. 3-6). 1987. pap. 6.95 (ISBN 0-8224-7536-7). D S Lake Pubs.
Writing to Inspire: A Guide to Writing & Publishing for the Expanding Religious Market. William Gentz et al. 319p. 1988. pap. 14.95 (ISBN 0-89879-302-5). Writers Digest.
Writing to Learn. James Howard. 53p. (Orig.). 1983. pap. 7.95 (ISBN 0-931989-10-8). Coun Basic Educ.
Writing to Learn. William K. Zinsser. 256p. 1988. pap. text ed. 11.50 (ISBN 0-06-047398-3, HarpC). Har-Row.
Writing to Learn Across the Curriculum. John W. Myers. LC 84-61203. (Fastback Ser.: No. 209). 50p. (Orig.). 1984. pap. 0.90 (ISBN 0-87367-209-7). Phi Delta Kappa.
Writing to Learn: Essays & Reflections on Writing Across the Curriculum. Christopher Thaiss. 160p. 1983. pap. 17.95 (ISBN 0-8403-3123-1). Kendall-Hunt.
Writing to Learn: How to Write & Think Clearly about Any Subject at All. William Zinsser. LC 87-45825. 224p. 1988. 15.95 (ISBN 0-06-015884-0). Har-Row.
Writing to Persuade. Kathleen A. Rogers. (gr. 3-6). 1987. pap. 6.95 (ISBN 0-8224-7538-3). D S Lake Pubs.
Writing to Read: A Parent's Guide to the New, Early Learning Program for Children. John H. Martin & Ardy Friedberg. (Illus.). 211p. 1986. 17.95 (ISBN 0-446-51341-5). Warner Bks.
Writing to Sell. rev. ed. Scott Meredith. LC 74-1837. 256p. (YA) 1974. 15.00 (ISBN 0-06-012929-8, HarpT). Har-Row.
Writing to Sell. Scott Meredith. LC 86-45128. 256p. 1987. 15.95i (ISBN 0-06-015637-6, HarpT). Har-Row.
Writing to Survive: The Private Notebooks of Conrad Richter. Harvena Richter. LC 87-34237. (Illus.). 264p. 1988. 22.50 (ISBN 0-8263-1034-6); pap. 12.95 (ISBN 0-8263-1035-4). U of NM Pr.
Writing to the Point. 4th ed. William J. Kerrigan & Allan A. Metcalf. 206p. 1987. pap. 12.95 (ISBN 0-15-598313-X). HarBraceJ.
Writing to Win. Mel Lewis. 160p. 1988. pap. price not set (ISBN 0-07-084942-0). McGraw.
Writing Today: A Rhetoric & Handbook. Patricia Moody. (Illus.). 512p. 1981. pap. text ed. write for info. (ISBN 0-13-971556-8); write for info. wkbk.& key (ISBN 0-13-971572-X). P-H.
Writing Tom Sawyer: The Adventures of a Classic. Charles A. Norton. LC 82-17164. 168p. 1983. lib. bdg. 18.95x (ISBN 0-89950-067-6). McFarland & Co.

Writings of Bret Harte, 20 Vols. Bret Harte. Repr. of 1903 ed. Set. 750.00 (ISBN 0-404-03170-6); 37.50 ea. AMS Pr.

Writings of Camilla Eyring Kimball. Ed. by Edward L. Kimball. LC 88-70095. 155p. 1988. 10.95 (ISBN 0-87579-143-3). Deseret Bk.

Writings of Camra Laye. Adele King. (Studies in African Literature). 1981. text ed. 21.00x (ISBN 0-435-91680-7); pap. text ed. 12.50x (ISBN 0-435-91681-5). Heinemann Ed.

Writings of Cassius Marcellus Clay: Including Speeches & Addresses. Cassius M. Clay. Ed. by Horace Greeley. LC 70-82185. (Anti-Slavery Crusade in America Ser). 1969. Repr. of 1848 ed. 24.50 (ISBN 0-405-00634-9). Ayer Co Pubs.

Writings of Catherine Booth, 6 Vols. Catherine Booth. 1986. Repr. of 1880 ed. Set. deluxe ed. 19.95 (ISBN 0-86544-038-7). Salvation Army.

Writings of Catherine Booth, 6 vols. Catherine Booth. 1101p. 1986. deluxe 19.95. Salv Army Suppl South.

Writings of Charles Dickens: First Edition. Charles Dickens. 1978. Repr. of 1913 ed. lib. bdg. 37.00 (ISBN 0-8495-1132-1). Arden Lib.

Writings of Charles Jencks, Apostle, by Post-Modernism. Carole Cable. (Architecture Ser.: A 1455). 9p. 1985. 2.00 (ISBN 0-89028-545-4). Vance Biblios.

Writings of Charles S. Peirce: A Chronological Edition: Vol. 1, 1857-1866. Charles S. Peirce. Ed. by Edward C. Moore et al. LC 79-1993. 738p. 1982. 37.50x (ISBN 0-253-37201-1). Ind U Pr.

Writings of Charles S. Peirce: A Chronological Edition: Vol. 2, 1867-1871. Charles S. Peirce. Ed. by Edward C. Moore et al. LC 79-1993. 704p. 1984. 35.00x (ISBN 0-253-37202-X). Ind U Pr.

Writings of Charles S. Peirce: A Chronological Edition: Vol. 3, 1872-1878. Charles S. Peirce. Ed. by Christian J. Kloesel & Max H. Fisch. LC 79-1993. 672p. 1986. 40.00x (ISBN 0-253-37203-8). Ind U Pr.

Writings of Christopher Gadsden, 1746-1805. Ed. by Richard Walsh. 1967. 21.95x (ISBN 0-87249-104-8). U of SC Pr.

Writings of Colonel William Byrd. William Byrd. Ed. by J. S. Bassett. LC 76-125631. (Research & Source Ser.: No. 518). (Illus.). 1970. Repr. of 1901 ed. lib. bdg. 32.00 (ISBN 0-8337-0442-7). B Franklin.

Writings of E. M. Forster. Dame Rose Macaulay. LC 73-12868. 1974. Repr. of 1938 ed. lib. bdg. 45.00 (ISBN 0-8414-6014-0). Folcroft.

Writings of Edward Fitzgerald, 7 Vols. variorum ed. Edward Fitzgerald. LC 67-18645. 2068p. Repr. of 1903 ed. Set. 200.00x (ISBN 0-87753-015-7). Phaeton.

Writings of Edward Hutton. Dennis E. Rhodes. 1975. Repr. of 1955 ed. 20.00 (ISBN 0-8274-4089-8). R West.

Writings of Elliott Carter: An American Composer Looks at Modern Music. Ed. by Else Stone & Kurt Stone. LC 76-48539. (Illus.). 416p. 1977. 20.00x (ISBN 0-253-36720-4). Ind U Pr.

Writings of Evelyn Waugh. Ian Littlewood. LC 82-18513. 256p. 1983. text ed. 28.50x (ISBN 0-389-20350-5, 07208). B&N Imports.

Writings of F. A. Harper, 2 vols. F. A. Harper. (Humane Studies Ser.). 1048p. 1980. Set. text ed. 25.00x (ISBN 0-89617-000-4). Humanities.

Writings of Fermin Francisco Lasuen, 2 vols. Ed. by Finbar Kenneally. (Documentary Ser.). (Illus.). 1965. Set. 35.00 (ISBN 0-88382-008-0). AAFH.

Writings of Florence Scovel Shinn. Florence S. Shinn. 368p. (Orig.). 1988. pap. 10.95 sewn bdg. (ISBN 0-87516-610-5). DeVorss.

Writings of General John Forbes Relating to His Service in North America. John Forbes. LC 78-106091. (First American Frontier Ser). 1971. Repr. of 1938 ed. 22.00 (ISBN 0-405-02849-0). Ayer Co Pubs.

Writings of George Eliot with the Life by J. W. Cross, 25 vols. George Eliot. LC 74-114748. (Illus.). Repr. of 1908 ed. Set. 862.50 (ISBN 0-404-02280-4); 34.50 ea. AMS Pr.

Writings of German Composers: Bach, Brahms, Mozart. Ed. by James Steakley & Jost Hermand. (German Library: Vol. 51). 303p. 1985. 27.50x (ISBN 0-8264-0292-5); pap. 10.95 (ISBN 0-8264-0293-3). Continuum.

Writings of Havelock Ellis, 12 vols. Havelock Ellis. 1975. lib. bdg. 50.00 ea. (ISBN 0-8490-1338-0). Gordon Pr.

Writings of Henry Cowell: A Descriptive Bibliography. Bruce Saylor. LC 77-81276. (I. S. A. M. Monographs: No. 7). 44p. 1977. pap. 4.00 (ISBN 0-914678-07-8). Inst Am Music.

Writings of Henry Cu Kim. Henry C. Kim. Ed. & tr. by Dae-Sook Suh. (Papers from the Center for Korean Studies: No. 13). 306p. 1987. text ed. 32.00 (ISBN 0-8248-1159-3). Uh Manoa Cks.

Writings of Henry D. Thoreau. Henry David Thoreau. Incl. Walden. Ed. by J. Lyndon Shanley. 404p. 1971. 35.50x (ISBN 0-691-06194-7); Maine Woods. Ed. by Joseph J. Moldenhauer. 468p. 1972. 38.50x (ISBN 0-691-06224-2); pap. 12.95 (ISBN 0-691-01404-3); Reform Papers. Ed. by Wendell Glick. 436p. 1973. 38.50x (ISBN 0-691-06241-2); Illustrated Maine Wood: With Photographs from the Gleason Collection. Ed. by Joseph J. Moldenhauer. 1974. 25.00x (ISBN 0-691-06278-1); pap. 8.95 (ISBN 0-691-01338-1); Illustrated Walden with Photographs from the Gleason Collection. Ed. by J. Lyndon Shanley. 385p. 1973. 39.50x (ISBN 0-691-06266-8); pap. 9.50 (ISBN 0-691-01309-8); Early Essays & Miscellanies. Ed. by Joseph J. Moldenhauer & Edwin Moser. 1975. 47.00x (ISBN 0-691-06286-2); Journal, 1837-1844, Vol. 1. Ed. by John C. Broderick. LC 78-70325. 1980. 38.50x (ISBN 0-691-06361-3); Week on the Concord & Merrimack Rivers. Ed. by Carl Hoyde. LC 78-51201. 1980. 44.50x (ISBN 0-691-06376-1). Princeton U Pr.

Writings of Henry Wadsworth Longfellow: The Riverside Edition, 11 vols. Henry Wadsworth Longfellow. 1886. 300.00 (ISBN 0-8274-3775-7). R West.

Writings of Hippocrates on the Human Body, Its Diseases & Their Cure, 2 vols. Hippocrates. Tr. by Francis Adams. (Illus.). 417p. 1988. Set. 237.45 (ISBN 0-89266-612-9). Am Classical Coll Pr.

Writings of Hugh Swinton Legare. H. S. Legare. Ed. by Mary S. L. Bullen. LC 70-107413. (American Public Figures Ser). 1970. Repr. of 1846 ed. lib. bdg. 145.00 (ISBN 0-306-71885-5). Da Capo.

Writings of J. Frank Dobie: A Bibliography. Mary L. McVicker. LC 68-23421. 1968. ltd. ed. boxed, signed 25.00 (ISBN 0-685-85504-X); 13.95 (ISBN 0-685-85505-8). Mus Great Plains.

Writings of James M. Nack: The Deaf & Dumb Poet. James M. Nack. 59.95 (ISBN 0-8490-1339-9). Gordon Pr.

Writings of James Stephens: Variations on a Theme of Love. Patricia McFate. LC 78-13287. 1979. 20.00x (ISBN 0-312-89509-7). St Martin.

Writings of Jean-Paul Sarte, 2 vols. Tr. by Richard C. McCleary from Fr. Incl. Vol. 1. A Bibliographical Life. 763p. text ed. 39.95x (ISBN 0-8101-0430-X); Vol. 2. Selected Prose. text ed. 21.95x (ISBN 0-8101-0431-8). (Studies in Phenomenology & Existential Philosophy). 1974 (73-85750). Northwestern U Pr.

Writings of John Bradford...Martyr, 1555, 2 Vols. John Bradford. Repr. of 1853 ed. Set. 92.00 (ISBN 0-384-05440-4). Johnson Repr.

Writings of John Lothrop Motley, 17 vols. John L. Motley. Ed. by George W. Curtis. Incl. Vols. 1-5. Rise of the Dutch Republic. Vol. 1 (ISBN 0-404-04521-9). Vol. 2 (ISBN 0-404-04522-7). Vol. 3 (ISBN 0-404-04523-5). Vol. 4 (ISBN 0-404-04524-3). Vol. 5 (ISBN 0-404-04525-1); Vol. 6-11. History of the United Netherlands. Vol. 6 (ISBN 0-404-04526-X). Vol. 7 (ISBN 0-404-04527-8). Vol. 8 (ISBN 0-404-04528-6). Vol. 9 (ISBN 0-404-04529-4). Vol. 10 (ISBN 0-404-04530-8). Vol. 11 (ISBN 0-404-04531-6); Vols. 12-14. Life & Death of John of Barneveld, Advocate of Holland, with a View of the Primary Causes & Movements of the Thirty Years' War. Vol. 12 (ISBN 0-404-04532-4). Vol. 13 (ISBN 0-404-04533-2). Vol. 14 (ISBN 0-404-04534-0); Vols. 15-17. Correspondence. Vol. 15 (ISBN 0-404-04535-9). Vol. 16 (ISBN 0-404-04536-7). Vol. 17 (ISBN 0-404-04537-5). Repr. of 1900 ed. Set. 552.50; 32.50 ea. (ISBN 0-404-04520-0). AMS Pr.

Writings of John Marshall, Late Chief Justice of the United States, upon the Federal Constitution. xvii, 725p. 1987. Repr. of 1890 ed. lib. bdg. 65.00x (ISBN 0-8377-2735-9). Rothman.

Writings of John Quincy Adams, 7 vols. John Q. Adams. Ed. by Worthington C. Ford. LC 68-30993. (Illus.). 1969. Repr. of 1917 ed. Set. lib. bdg. 180.00x (ISBN 0-8371-9937-9, ADWR); Vol. 2. lib. bdg. 26.75 (ISBN 0-8371-0775-X, ADWB); Vol. 3. lib. bdg. 30.00 (ISBN 0-8371-0776-8, ADWC); Vol. 4. lib. bdg. 28.00 (ISBN 0-8371-0777-6, ADWD); Vol. 5. lib. bdg. 30.00 (ISBN 0-8371-0778-4, ADWE); Vol. 6. lib. bdg. 33.50 (ISBN 0-8371-0779-2, AWDF); Vol. 7. lib. bdg. 25.75 (ISBN 0-8371-0780-6, ADWG). Greenwood.

Writings of Jonathan Edwards: Theme, Motif, & Style. William J. Scheick. LC 75-18689. 192p. 1975. 19.50x (ISBN 0-89096-004-6). Tex A&M Univ Pr.

Writings of Jonathan Swift. Jonathan Swift. Ed. by Robert Greenberg & William Piper. (Critical Editions Ser.). 500p. 1973. pap. text ed. 14.95x (ISBN 0-393-09415-4). Norton.

Writings of Jonathan Swift. Jonathan Swift. Ed. by Henry Morley. 1889. Repr. 40.00 (ISBN 0-8274-3776-5). R West.

Writings of Junipero Serra, 4 vols. Ed. by Antonine Tibesar. (Documentary Ser.). (Illus.). 1966. 60.00 (ISBN 0-88382-003-X). AAFH.

Writings of King Alfred. Frederick Harrison. (Beowulf & the Literature of the Anglo-Saxons Ser., No. 2). 1970. pap. 39.95x (ISBN 0-8383-0042-1). Haskell.

Writings of Leon Trotsky Nineteen Thirty-Four to Nineteen Thirty-Five. Leon Trotsky. Ed. by George Breitman & Beverly Scott. LC 73-80226. 1972. lib. bdg. 30.00 (ISBN 0-87348-194-1). Path Pr NY.

Writings of Leon Trotsky: Supplement I, (1929-33) Leon Trotsky. Ed. by George Breitman. LC 73-88120. 1979. lib. bdg. 30.00 (ISBN 0-87348-562-9); pap. 10.95 (ISBN 0-87348-563-7). Path Pr NY.

Writings of Leon Trotsky: Supplement II, (1934-40) Leon Trotsky. Ed. by George Breitman. 1979. lib. bdg. 30.00 (ISBN 0-87348-564-5); pap. 10.95 (ISBN 0-87348-565-3). Path Pr NY.

Writings of Leon Trotsky, 1929. Leon Trotsky. Ed. by George Breitman et al. LC 73-88120. (Illus.). 464p. 1975. 30.00 (ISBN 0-87348-458-4); pap. 10.95 (ISBN 0-87348-459-2). Path Pr NY.

Writings of Leon Trotsky, 1930. Leon Trotsky. Ed. by George Breitman & Sarah Lovell. Tr. by Russell Block et al from Rus., Fr. & Chinese. LC 73-88120. (Illus.). 444p. 1975. 30.00 (ISBN 0-87348-412-6); pap. 10.95 (ISBN 0-87348-413-4). Path Pr NY.

Writings of Leon Trotsky, 1930-31. Leon Trotsky. Ed. by George Breitman & Sarah Lovell. Tr. by George Saunders et al. LC 73-88120. 448p. 1974. 30.00 (ISBN 0-87348-324-3); pap. 10.95 (ISBN 0-87348-350-2). Path Pr NY.

Writings of Leon Trotsky, 1932. Leon Trotsky. Ed. by George Breitman & Sarah Lovell. Tr. by Iain Fraser et al from Rus., Fr., Ger., Bulgarian, Gr. & Danish. LC 73-88120. 1973. 30.00 (ISBN 0-87348-310-3); pap. 10.95 (ISBN 0-87348-311-1). Path Pr NY.

Writings of Leon Trotsky: 1932-33. Leon Trotsky. Ed. by George Breitman & Sarah Lovell. Tr. by George Saunders et al from Rus. & Fr. LC 73-88120. (Illus.). 1973. 30.00 (ISBN 0-87348-227-1); pap. 10.95 (ISBN 0-87348-228-X). Path Pr NY.

Writings of Leon Trotsky, 1933-34. Leon Trotsky. Ed. by George Breitman & Beverly Scott. Tr. by John G. Wright et al from Rus. & Fr. LC 73-80226. 356p. 1972. cloth 30.00 (ISBN 0-87348-213-1). Path Pr NY.

Writings of Leon Trotsky, 1933-34. 2nd ed. Leon Trotsky et al. Ed. by George Breitman et al. Tr. by John G. Wright et al LC 73-80226. 1975. pap. 10.95 (ISBN 0-87348-418-5). Path Pr NY.

Writings of Leon Trotsky, 1934-35. 2nd ed. Leon Trotsky. Ed. by George Breitman & Beverly Scott. Tr. by John G. Wright et al from Rus. LC 73-80226. (Illus.). 416p. (Orig.). 1974. pap. 10.95 (ISBN 0-87348-403-7). Path Pr NY.

Writings of Leon Trotsky, 1935-36. Leon Trotsky. Ed. by Naomi Allen & George Breitman. LC 73-80226. (Illus.). 1977. 30.00 (ISBN 0-87348-501-7); pap. 10.95 (ISBN 0-87348-502-5). Path Pr NY.

Writings of Leon Trotsky, 1936-37. Leon Trotsky. Ed. by Naomi Allen & George Breitman. LC 73-80226. 1978. lib. bdg. 30.00 (ISBN 0-87348-511-4); pap. 10.95 (ISBN 0-87348-512-2). Path Pr NY.

Writings of Leon Trotsky 1937-38. Leon Trotsky. Ed. by Naomi Allen & George Breitman. LC 73-80226. (Writings of Leon Trotsky (1929-40)). 432p. 1976. 30.00 (ISBN 0-87348-468-1); pap. 10.95 (ISBN 0-87348-469-X). Path Pr NY.

Writings of Leon Trotsky, 1938-39. Leon Trotsky. Ed. by Naomi Allen & George Breitman. LC 73-80226. (Illus.). 432p. 1974. 30.00 (ISBN 0-87348-365-0); pap. 10.95 (ISBN 0-87348-366-9). Path Pr NY.

Writings of Leon Trotsky, 1939-1940. new ed. Leon Trotsky. Ed. by George Breitman & Naomi Allen. LC 73-80226. (Illus.). 464p. 1973. 30.00 (ISBN 0-87348-312-X); pap. 10.95 (ISBN 0-87348-313-8). Path Pr NY.

Writings of Mao: Sept. 1949-Dec. 1955, Vol. 1. Mao Zedong. Ed. by Michael Y. M. Kau & John Leung. 814p. 1986. text ed. 90.00 (ISBN 0-87332-391-2). M E Sharpe.

Writings of Mao Zedong, Vol, 2. Kau. Date not set. write for info. (ISBN 0-87332-392-0). M E Sharpe.

Writings of Margaret Fuller. Sarah M. Ossoli. Ed. by Mason Wade. LC 72-122079. Repr. of 1941 ed. lib. bdg. 45.00x (ISBN 0-678-03177-0). Kelley.

Writings of Marie Corelli, 28 vols. Marie Corelli. 1976. lib. bdg. 34.95 ea. Gordon Pr.

Writings of Mark Twain, 25 vols. Samuel L. Clemens. Incl. Vols. 1 & 2. Innocents Abroad, Pts. 1 & 2. Set. 75.00 (ISBN 0-686-66711-5); (ISBN 0-403-02325-4); (ISBN 0-403-02326-2); Vols. 3 & 4. Gilded Age, Pts. 1 & 2. Set. 75.00 (ISBN 0-686-66712-3); (ISBN 0-403-02327-0); (ISBN 0-403-02328-9); Vols. 5 & 6. Tramp Abroad, Pts. 1 & 2. Set. 50.00x (ISBN 0-686-66713-1); (ISBN 0-403-02329-7); (ISBN 0-403-02330-0); Vols. 7 & 8. Following the Equator, Pts. 1 & 2. Set. 75.00x (ISBN 0-686-66714-X); (ISBN 0-403-02331-9); (ISBN 0-403-02332-7); Vols. 9 & 10. Roughing It, Pts. 1 & 2. Set. 75.00x (ISBN 0-686-66715-8); (ISBN 0-403-02333-5); (ISBN 0-403-02334-3); Vol. 11. Life on the Mississippi. 69.00x (ISBN 0-403-02341-6); Vol. 12. Adventures of Tom Sawyer. 39.00x (ISBN 0-403-02342-4); Vol. 13. Huckleberry Finn. 39.00x (ISBN 0-403-02335-1); Vol. 14. Pudd'nhead Wilson. 39.00x (ISBN 0-403-02336-X); Vol. 15. Prince & the Pauper. 39.00x (ISBN 0-403-02337-8); Vol. 16. Connecticut Yankee in King Arthur's Court. 39.00x (ISBN 0-403-02338-6); Vols. 17 & 18. Joan of Arc, Pts. 1 & 2. Set. 75.00x (ISBN 0-685-27293-1); (ISBN 0-403-02240-1); (ISBN 0-403-02239-8); Vol. 19. Connecticut Yankee in King Arthur's Court. 39.00x (ISBN 0-685-27294-X); Vol. 20. Tom Sawyer Abroad. 39.00x (ISBN 0-403-02343-2); Vol. 24. Thirty Thousand Bequest. 39.00x (ISBN 0-403-02348-3); Vol. 25. Christian Science. 39.00x (ISBN 0-403-02349-1). LC 79-7769. 1869-1909. Set. 1495.00 (ISBN 0-403-03736-0). Scholarly.

Writings of Martin Buber. Martin Buber. Ed. by Will Herberg. (Orig.). pap. 8.95 (ISBN 0-452-00616-3, F616, Mer). NAL.

Writings of Medieval Women. Ed. by Marcelle Thiebaux. LC 83-49069. (Library of Medieval Texts). 200p. 1986. lib. bdg. 30.00 (ISBN 0-8240-9417-4). Garland Pub.

Writings of Paul Rolland: An Annotated Bibliography. Mark Joseph Eisele. 4.00 (ISBN 0-318-18119-3). Am String Tchrs.

Writings of Paul Rosenfeld: An Annotated Bibliography. Charles L. Silet. LC 79-7931. 250p. 1980. lib. bdg. 43.00 (ISBN 0-8240-9532-4). Garland Pub.

Writings of Pedro Albizu Campos. Pedro A. Campos. (Puerto Rico Ser.). 1979. lib. bdg. 69.95 (ISBN 0-8490-3016-1). Gordon Pr.

Writings of Pilgrim Marpeck. Ed. by William Klassen & Walter Klaassen. LC 77-87419. (Classics of the Radical Reformation Ser.: No. 2). (Illus.). 608p. 1978. 24.95x (ISBN 0-8361-1205-9). Herald Pr.

Writings of President Frederick M. Smith, Vol. 1. Ed. by Norman D. Ruoff. LC 78-6428. 1978. pap. 10.00 (ISBN 0-8309-0215-5). Herald Hse.

Writings of President Frederick M. Smith, Vol. 2. Ed. by Norman D. Ruoff. LC 78-6428. 1979. pap. 10.00 (ISBN 0-8309-0239-2). Herald Hse.

Writings of President Frederick M. Smith, Vol. III: The Zionic Enterprise. Ed. by Norman D. Ruoff. 1981. pap. 10.00 (ISBN 0-8309-0300-3). Herald Hse.

Writings of Rafael Sabatini, 21 vols. Rafael Sabatini. 1981. Repr. of 1924 ed. Set. lib. bdg. 500.00 (ISBN 0-89987-766-4). Darby Bks.

Writings of Ramon Betances, 9 vols. Ramon Betances. (Puerto Rico Ser.). 1979. Set. lib. bdg. 1500.00 (ISBN 0-8490-3017-X). Gordon Pr.

Writings of Robert Grosseteste, Bishop of Lincoln: 1235-1253. S. H. Thomson. Repr. of 1940 ed. 29.00 (ISBN 0-527-89820-1). Kraus Repr.

Writings of Robert Smithson: Essays with Illustrations. Ed. by Nancy Holt. LC 78-58536. 1979. 35.00x (ISBN 0-8147-3394-8); pap. 19.95 (ISBN 0-8147-3395-6). NYU Pr.

Writings of Saint Francis of Assisi. Saint Frances D'Assisi. Tr. by Paschal Robinson. 1977. lib. bdg. 59.95 (ISBN 0-8490-2822-1). Gordon Pr.

Writings of St. Patrick, with the Metrical Life of St. Patrick. Saint Patrick & Saint Fiacc. pap. 2.95 (ISBN 0-686-25558-5). Eastern Orthodox.

Writings of St. Paul. St. Paul. Ed. by Wayne Meeks. (Critical Edition Ser). 1972. 12.95x (ISBN 0-393-04338-X); pap. 10.95x (ISBN 0-393-09979-2). Norton.

Writings of Sam Houston, Eighteen Thirteen to Eighteen Thirty-Six, 8 Vols. Ed. by Amelia W. Williams & Eugene C. Barker. Set. 185.00 (ISBN 0-685-13280-3). Jenkins.

Writings of the Ante-Nicene Fathers, 10 vols. Ante-Nicene Fathers. Ed. by A. Roberts & J. Donaldson. 1951. Set. 179.50 (ISBN 0-8028-8097-5); 22.95 ea. Eerdmans.

Writings of the Late Elder John Leland, Including Some Events of His Life. John Leland. Ed. by L. F. Greene. LC 73-83420. (Religion in America, Ser. 1). 1969. Repr. of 1845 ed. 38.50 (ISBN 0-405-00245-9). Ayer Co Pubs.

Writings of the Late Elder John Leland, by Leland. Ed. by L. F. Greene. 1986. Repr. of 1845 ed. 35.00 (ISBN 0-317-47642-4). Church History.

Writings of the New Testament: An Interpretation. Luke T. Johnson. LC 85-16202. 640p. 1986. pap. 18.95 (ISBN 0-8006-1886-6, 1-1886). Fortress.

Wrongful Death. Hamline University, Advanced Legal Education Staff. LC 84-211003. 155p. 1984. pap. 21.20. Hamline Law.
Wrongful Death in Ohio, with Forms. John W. McCormac. LC 82-244891. (Illus.). 209p. 1982. 37.50. Anderson Pub Co.
Wrongful Death Litigation. LC 83-71583. (Civil Practice Ser.: No. 5). 147p. (Orig.). 1983. pap. 30.00 (ISBN 0-941916-10-3). Assn Trial Ed.
Wrongful Discharge & the Derogation of the At-Will Employment Doctrine. Andrew D. Hill. LC 86-83224. (Labor Relations & Public Policy Ser.). (Orig.). 1987. pap. 27.50 (ISBN 0-89546-066-1). Indus Res Unit-Wharton.
Wrongful Discharge Claims: A Preventive Approach. Paul I. Weiner et al. 476p. 1986. text ed. 75.00 (ISBN 0-317-64522-6, H1-2985). PLI.
Wrongful Employment Termination Practice. 923p. 1987. 95.00 (ISBN 0-88124-155-5, CP-30900). Cal Cont Ed Bar.
Wrongly Dividing the Word of Truth. H. A. Ironside. pap. 1.25 (ISBN 0-87213-392-3). Loizeaux.
Wrongs of Indian Womanhood. Marcus Fuller. 1984. Repr. of 1900 ed. 32.50x (ISBN 0-8364-1160-9, Pub. by Inter-India Pubns). South Asia Bks.
Wrongs of Indian Womanhood. Marcus B. Fuller. 290p. 1984. Repr. of 1900 ed. text ed. 37.50x (ISBN 0-86590-297-6, Pub. by Inter India Pubns India). Apt Bks.
Wrongway Applebaum. Marjorie Lewis. LC 84-3242. (Illus.). 64p. (gr. 3-6). 1984. 9.95 (ISBN 0-698-20610-X, Coward). Putnam Pub Group.
Wros-tonne & Other Stories of Science Fantasy. Mary Ann Schuller. LC 87-90482. (Illus.). 134p. (Orig.). (gr. 3-8). 1987. pap. 4.95 (ISBN 0-9617889-0-9). Sweet Koala Pr.
Wrought Covenant: Source Material for the Study of Craftsmen & Community in Southeastern New England 1620-1700. Robert B. St. George. LC 79-52349. (Illus.). 132p. (Orig.). 1979. pap. 7.86 (ISBN 0-934358-06-0). Brockton Art Fuller.
Wrought Iron. F. Kuhn. 1986. 44.75X (ISBN 0-245-53800-3, Pub. by Harrap Ltd England). State Mutual Bk.
Wrought Iron. Fritz Kuhn. Tr. by Charles B. Johnson. (Illus.). 120p. 1983. Repr. 21.95 (ISBN 0-318-19603-4). Larson Pub.
Wrought Iron in Architecture. Gerald K. Geerlings. 1984. 18.50 (ISBN 0-8446-6103-1). Peter Smith.
Wrought Iron in Architecture: An Illustrated Survey. Gerald K. Geerlings. (Antiques Ser.). 202p. 1984. pap. 9.95 (ISBN 0-486-24535-7). Dover.
Wrought Iron Work. (Illus.). 109p. 1960. pap. 6.00 (ISBN 0-89192-340-3, Pub. by Wepf & Co). Interbk Inc.
Wrought Ironwork. CoSIRA Staff. (Illus.). 104p. 1986. 15.95 (ISBN 0-02-528480-0). Macmillan.
Wrought Ironwork. Ed. by CoSIRA Staff. 39.00x (ISBN 0-317-44798-X, Pub. by CoSIRA UK). State Mutual Bk.
WSLCN & WSLPR: Water-Surface Computation in Prismatic Channel for Micro-Computer. Edward Chew. 187p. 1988. spiral bdg. 24.95 (ISBN 0-533-07716-8). Vantage.
Wu Han: Attacking the Present Through the Past. James R. Pusey. (East Asian Monographs Ser: No. 33). 1969. pap. 11.00x (ISBN 0-674-96275-3). Harvard U Pr.
Wu Style of Tai Chi Chuan. T. C. Lee. LC 81-50511. (Illus.). 120p. (Orig.). 1981. pap. 6.95 (ISBN 0-86568-022-1, 211). Unique Pubns.
Wu Tse-t'ien & the Politics of Legitimation in T'ang China. R. W. Guisso. LC 78-4840. (Occasional Papers: Vol. 11). (Illus.). 335p. 1978. 9.00 (ISBN 0-914584-11-1). WWUCEAS.
Wu Wenying & the Art of Southern Song Ci Poetry. Grace S. Fong. 192p. 1987. text ed. 27.50 (ISBN 0-691-06703-1). Princeton U Pr.
Wuerttemberg Emigration Index, Vol. III. Trudy Schenk & Ruth Froelke. LC 85-52453. (Illus.). 264p. 1987. 16.95 (ISBN 0-916489-25-6, 395). Ancestry.
Wuerttemberg Emigration Index, Vol. IV. Trudy Schenk & Ruth Froelke. LC 85-52453. (Illus.). 264p. 1988. 16.95 (ISBN 0-916489-26-4, 396). Ancestry.
Wuerttemberg Emigration Index, Vol. II. Compiled by Trudy Schenk & Ruth Frolke. LC 85-52453. (Illus.). 256p. 1986. 16.95 (ISBN 0-916489-15-9); pap. 12.95 (ISBN 0-916489-20-5). Ancestry.
Wuerttemberg Emigration Index, Vol. I. Compiled by Trudy Schenk et al. LC 85-52453. 230p. Date not set. 15.95 (ISBN 0-916489-08-6). Ancestry.
Wuggie Norple Story. Daniel Pinkwater. LC 88-878. (Illus.). 40p. (gr. k-4). Date not set. pap. 4.50 (ISBN 0-689-71257-X, Aladdin Bks). Macmillan.
Wuggie Norple Story. Daniel M. Pinkwater. LC 79-19014. (Illus.). 40p. (gr. k-3). 1980. 9.95 (ISBN 0-02-774670-4, Four Winds). Macmillan.
Wuggly Ump. Edward Gorey. LC 86-11273. (Illus.). (ps up). 1986. 6.95 (ISBN 0-915361-56-6, Dist. by Watts). Adama Pubs Inc.
Wujing Well. Date not set. 1.95 (ISBN 0-8351-0938-0). China Bks.
Wulfheim. Sax Rohmer. 1972. 8.50 (ISBN 0-685-33438-4). Bookfinger.
Wulfstans Prose. Angus McIntosh. LC 74-20541. 1973. lib. bdg. 20.00 (ISBN 0-8414-5902-9). Folcroft.
Wulfstanstudien. Karl Jost. 1978. Repr. of 1950 ed. lib. bdg. 50.00 (ISBN 0-8495-2708-2). Arden Lib.
Wulfstantudien. Karl Jost. 1979. Repr. of 1950 ed. lib. bdg. 50.00 (ISBN 0-8492-1273-1). R West.
Wulfston's Odyssey. Jean Lorrah & Winston A. Howlett. (Savage Empire Ser.: No. 6). 208p. 1987. pap. 2.95 (ISBN 0-451-15056-2, Sig). NAL.
Wump World. Bill Peet. (Illus.). (gr. k-3). 1981. pap. 3.95 (ISBN 0-395-31129-2). HM.
Wump World. Bill Peet. LC 72-124999. (Illus.). (gr. 3-5). 1970. PLB 10.95 (ISBN 0-395-19841-0). HM.
Wunderlich's Salute: The Interrelationship of the German-American Bund, Camp Siegfried, Yaphank, Long Island, & the Young Siegfrieds & Their Relationship with American & Nazi Institutions. Marvin D. Miller. LC 82-62515. (Illus.). 336p. 1983. pap. 10.95 (ISBN 0-9610466-0-0). Malamud-Rose.
Wunderwelt Film. H. W. Siska. 1976. lib. bdg. 105.95 (ISBN 0-8490-2823-X). Gordon Pr.
Wundt Studies. Ed. by Wolfgang G. Bringmann & Ryan D. Tweney. 445p. (Orig.). 1980. pap. text ed. 28.00 (ISBN 0-88937-001-X). Hogrefe Intl.
Wurlitzer Jukebox Installation Instructions for Remote Control Equipment 24 Record Models 1938-45. 56p. 1983. Repr. of 1941 ed. 10 mil. lam. covers, spiral bound 12.50 (ISBN 0-913698-44-X, R-191). AMR Pub Co.
Wurlitzer Jukebox Model 1017 Service Manual & Parts Catalog, Plus Service Manual & Parts Catalog for Wall Box Models 3025, 3031 & 3045. 152p. 1983. Repr. of 1946 ed. 10 mil. lam. covers, sp. bound 15.00 (ISBN 0-913698-13-X, R-173). AMR Pub Co.
Wurlitzer Jukebox Model 1080 Parts Catalog & Brochure. 78p. 1983. Repr. of 1947 ed. 10 mil. laminated spiral bdg. 21.50 (ISBN 0-913698-14-8, R-156). AMR Pub Co.
Wurlitzer Jukebox Model 1100 Service Manual & Parts Catalog 1948-49. 134p. 1983. Repr. of 1948 ed. 10 mil. laminated spiral bdg. 27.50 (ISBN 0-913698-15-6, R-182). AMR PUb Co.
Wurlitzer Jukebox Model 1250 Service Manual & Parts Catalog. 94p. 1983. Repr. of 1950 ed. 10 mil. laminated spiral bdg. 24.50 (ISBN 0-913698-16-4, R-184). AMR Pub Co.
Wurlitzer Jukebox Model 1400 & 1450 Service Manual, Parts Catalog & Brochure. 135p. 1983. Repr. of 1951 ed. 10 mil. lam. covers, sp. bound 29.50 (ISBN 0-913698-17-2, R-187). AMR Pub Co.
Wurlitzer Jukebox Model 1500A & 1550A Service Manual, Parts Catalog & Brochure. 118p. 1983. Repr. of 1953 ed. 10 mil. lam. covers, sp. bound 32.50 (ISBN 0-913698-18-0, R-219). AMR Pub Co.
Wurlitzer Jukebox Model 1800 Service Manual, Parts Catalog & Brochure. 166p. 1983. Repr. of 1955 ed. 10 mil. lam. covers, sp. bound 35.00 (ISBN 0-913698-22-9, R-209). AMR Pub Co.
Wurlitzer Jukebox Model 1900 Service Manual, Parts Catalog & Brochure. 112p. 1983. Repr. of 1956 ed. 10 mil. laminated spiral bdg. 32.50 (ISBN 0-913698-23-7, R-230). AMR Pub Co.
Wurlitzer Jukebox Model 2000 Service Manual, Parts Catalog & Brochure. 100p. 1983. Repr. of 1956 ed. 10 mil. laminated spiral bdg. 29.50 (ISBN 0-913698-24-5, R-234). AMR Pub Co.
Wurlitzer Jukebox Model 2100 Service Manual, Parts Catalog & Brochure. 119p. 1983. Repr. of 1957 ed. 10 mil. laminated spiral bdg. 32.50 (ISBN 0-913698-25-3, R-218). AMR Pub Co.
Wurlitzer Jukebox Model 2104 Service Manual, Parts Catalog & Brochure. 102p. 1983. Repr. of 1957 ed. 10 mil. laminated spiral bdg. 29.50 (ISBN 0-913698-26-1, R-236). AMR Pub Co.
Wurlitzer Jukebox Model 2150 Service Manual & Parts Catalog. 115p. 1983. Repr. of 1957 ed. 10 mil. laminated spiral bdg. 32.50 (ISBN 0-913698-27-X, R-238). AMR Pub Co.
Wurlitzer Jukebox Model 2200 Service Manual & Parts Catalog. 93p. 1983. Repr. of 1958 ed. 10 mil. laminated spiral bdg. 29.50 (ISBN 0-913698-28-8, R-235). AMR Pub Co.
Wurlitzer Jukebox Model 2204 Service Manual & Parts Catalog. 102p. 1983. Repr. of 1958 ed. 10 mil. laminated spiral bdg. 29.50 (ISBN 0-913698-29-6, R-237). AMR Pub Co.
Wurlitzer Jukebox Model 2250 Service Manual & Parts Catalog. 131p. 1983. Repr. of 1958 ed. 10 mil. lam. covers, spiral bnd. 32.50 (ISBN 0-913698-30-X, R-239). AMR Pub Co.
Wurlitzer Jukebox Model 2304 & 2304S Service Manual, Parts Catalog & Brochure. 98p. 1983. Repr. of 1959 ed. 10 mil. laminated spiral bdg. 29.50 (ISBN 0-913698-32-6, R-213). AMR Pub Co.
Wurlitzer Jukebox Model 2400 Series Service Manual, Parts Catalog & Brochure. 150p. 1983. Repr. of 1960 ed. 10 mil. lam. covers, spiral bnd. 32.50 (ISBN 0-913698-33-4, R-198). AMR Pub Co.
Wurlitzer Jukebox Model 2500 Series Service Manual, Parts Catalog & Brochure. 128p. 1983. Repr. of 1961 ed. 10 mil. lam. covers, spiral bnd. 32.50 (ISBN 0-913698-34-2, R-199). AMR Pub Co.
Wurlitzer Jukebox Model 2600 Series Service Manual, Parts Catalog & Brochure. 121p. 1983. Repr. of 1962 ed. 10 mil. lam. covers, spiral bnd. 32.50 (ISBN 0-913698-35-0, R-203). AMR Pub Co.
Wurlitzer Jukebox Model 2700 Series Service Manual, Parts Catalog & Brochure. 124p. 1983. Repr. of 1962 ed. 10 mil. lam. covers, spiral bnd 32.50 (ISBN 0-913698-36-9, R-207). AMR Pub Co.
Wurlitzer Jukebox Model 2800 Series Service Manual, Parts Catalog & Brochure. 141p. 1983. Repr. of 1964 ed. 10 mil. lam. covers, spiral bnd. 35.00 (ISBN 0-913698-37-7, R-208). AMR Pub Co.
Wurlitzer Jukebox Model 2900 Series Service Manual, Parts Catalog & Brochure. 144p. 1983. Repr. of 1965 ed. 10 mil. laminated spiral bdg. 35.00 (ISBN 0-913698-38-5, R-205). AMR Pub Co.
Wurlitzer Jukebox Model 3000 Series Service Manual, Parts Catalog & Brochure. 62p. 1983. Repr. of 1966 ed. 10 mil. lam. covers, spiral bnd. 26.50 (ISBN 0-913698-39-3, R-204). AMR Pub Co.
Wurlitzer Jukebox Model 3100 Series Service Manual, Parts Catalog & Brochure. 120p. 1983. Repr. of 1967 ed. 10 mil. lam. covers, spiral bnd. 32.50 (ISBN 0-913698-40-7, R-206). AMR Pub Co.
Wurlitzer Jukebox Model 3300 Series Service Manual: Parts Manual & Trouble Shooting Charts of 1969. Wurlitzer Company Staff. 138p. 1984. 10 mil laminated covers 32.50 (ISBN 0-913599-04-2, R-247). AMR Pub Co.
Wurlitzer Jukebox Model 950 Instructions. 18p. 1983. Repr. of 1942 ed. 5 mil. laminated spiral bdg. 9.50 (ISBN 0-913698-12-1, R-179). AMR Pub Co.
Wurlitzer Jukebox Models of the 3200 Series Service: Parts Manual & Trouble Shooting Charts of 1968. Wurlitzer Company Staff. 124p. 1984. Repr. of 1968 ed. 10 mil laminated covers, spiral bdg. 32.50 (ISBN 0-913599-06-9, R-252). AMR Pub Co.
Wurlitzer Jukebox Models of the 3400 Series: Service Parts Manual & Brochure of 1970. Wurlitzer Company Staff. 150p. 1983. Repr. of 1970 ed. 10 mil laminated spiral bdg. 35.00 (ISBN 0-913599-07-7, R-256). AMR Pub Co.
Wurlitzer Jukebox Models of the 3700 Series: Service & Parts Manual "Americana" of 1973. Compiled by Frank Adams. 136p. 1984. Repr. of 1973 ed. 10 mil laminated covers, spiral bdg. 35.00 (ISBN 0-913599-09-3, R-251). AMR Pub Co.
Wurlitzer Jukebox Models of the 3800 Series: Service & Parts Manual of 1974, "Americana". Wurlitzer Company Staff. 133p. 1983. Repr. of 1974 ed. 10 laminated covers, spiral bdg. 32.50 (ISBN 0-913599-11-5, R-257). AMR Pub Co.
Wurlitzer Jukebox Models 1600, 1650, 1600A & 1650A Service Manual & Parts Catalog & Two Brochures. 142p. 1983. Repr. of 1954 ed. 10 mil. laminated spiral bdg. 35.00 (ISBN 0-913698-19-9, R-220). AMR Pub Co.
Wurlitzer Jukebox Models 1700 & 1700HF Installation Instructions & Technical Data. 46p. 1983. Repr. of 1954 ed. 10 mil. laminated spiral bdg. 16.50 (ISBN 0-913698-21-0, R-193). AMR Pub Co.
Wurlitzer Jukebox Models 1700 & 1700HF Service Manual, Parts Catalog & Brochure. 166p. 1983. Repr. of 1954 ed. 10 mil. laminated spiral bdg. 35.00 (ISBN 0-913698-20-2, R-211). AMR Pub Co.
Wurlitzer Jukebox Models 700 & 800 Parts Catalog. 98p. 1983. Repr. of 1940 ed. 10 mil. lam. covers, sp. bound 24.50 (ISBN 0-913698-11-3, R-202). AMR Pub Co.
Wurlitzer Jukebox Parts Catalog for Models P-500, G-500, P-500-A, G-500-A, 600, 600-A. 123p. 1983. Repr. of 1938 ed. 10 mil. laminated spiral bdg. 26.50 (ISBN 0-913698-09-1, R-189). AMR Pub Co.
Wurlitzer Jukebox Parts Catalog for Models 24 & 24-A. 70p. 1983. Repr. of 1938 ed. 10 mil. laminated spiral bdg. 22.50 (ISBN 0-913698-08-3, R-200). AMR Pub Co.
Wurlitzer Jukebox Parts Catalogue for Models P-10, P-12, P-30, P-400, 312, 412, 35, 400 & Limited on 316, 416, & 716. 74p. 1983. Repr. of 1937 ed. 10 mil. laminated spiral bdg. 24.50 (ISBN 0-913698-05-9, R-196). AMR Pub Co.
Wurlitzer Jukebox Remote Control & Auxiliary Equipment Catalog for 24 Record Models 1938-43. 58p. 1983. Repr. of 1942 ed. 10 mil. lam. covers, spiral bnd. 15.00 (ISBN 0-913698-42-3, R-201). AMR Pub Co.
Wurlitzer Jukebox Remote Control & Auxiliary Equipment Catalog for All 24 Record Wurlitzer Jukeboxes. 58p. 1983. Repr. of 1948 ed. 10 mil. laminated spiral bdg. 15.00 (ISBN 0-913698-45-8, R-159). AMR Pub Co.
Wurlitzer Jukebox Remote Control Equipment of 1940 Catalog: For the 24 Record Models 24 & 24A, 500, 600, 700, 800. Including Counter Model Stands for the Models 41, 71, & 61. Wurlitzer Co. Ed. by Frank Adams. 42p. 1984. Repr. of 1940 ed. 10 mil laminated spiral bdg. 15.00 (ISBN 0-913599-40-9, R-285). AMR Pub Co.
Wurlitzer Jukebox Remote Control Parts Catalog for Wall Box Models 100-115-120-123-125-320, Adapter Model 130 & 300. 66p. 1983. Repr. of 1938 ed. 10 mil. laminated spiral bdg. 12.50 (ISBN 0-913698-41-5, R-157). AMR Pub Co.
Wurlitzer Jukebox Series of the 3500: Service & Parts Manual for 1971 "Zodiac". Wurlitzer Company Staff. 160p. 1983. Repr. of 1970 ed. 10 mil laminated spiral bdg. 35.00 (ISBN 0-913599-13-1, R-262). AMR Pub Co.
Wurlitzer Jukebox Service & Parts Manual: Model 5220 Wall Box & Steppers, (Includes Schematics & Brochure on the 5220 Series Wall Boxes. Compiled by Frank Adams. 36p. 1984. Repr. 10 mil laminated covers 15.00 (ISBN 0-913599-01-8, R-245). AMR Pub Co.
Wurlitzer Jukebox Service & Parts Manual: Model 5250 Wall Box & 2100 Stepper, Produced for the Models 2200 & 2250. Wurlitzer Company Staff. 58p. 1984. Repr. of 1959 ed. 10 mil laminated spiral bdg. 17.50 (ISBN 0-913599-10-7, R-246). AMR Pub Co.
Wurlitzer Jukebox Service Instructions & Parts Catalog for Wall Box Model 3020; Impulse Stepper Model 219; Impulse Transmitter Model 215 & Impulse Receiver Model 216. 66p. 1983. Repr. of 1948 ed. 10 mil. lam. covers, spiral bound 12.50 (ISBN 0-913698-46-6, R-163). AMR Pub Co.
Wurlitzer Jukebox Service Manual & Brochure for Models 24 & 24A. 125p. 1983. Repr. of 1938 ed. 10 mil. laminated spiral bdg. 24.50 (R-167). AMR Pub Co.
Wurlitzer Jukebox Service Manual & Parts Catalog for Model 2140 Bar Box & Model 212 Master Unit: For 24 Record Models. 84p. 1983. Repr. of 1949 ed. 10 mil. lam. covers, spiral bound 22.50 (ISBN 0-913698-47-4, R-240). AMR Pub Co.
Wurlitzer Jukebox Service Manual & Parts Catalog for Model 5210 Wall Box & Model 2000 Stepper Unit: 200 Selection. 44p. 1983. Repr. of 1956 ed. 10 mil. laminated spiral bdg. 15.00 (ISBN 0-913698-48-2, R-243). AMR Pub Co.
Wurlitzer Jukebox Service Manual for Models P-10 & P-12, 1934-35. 90p. 1983. 10 mil. laminated spiral bdg. 24.50 (ISBN 0-913698-04-0, R-161). AMR Pub Co.
Wurlitzer Jukebox Service Manual for Models 312, 412, 35. 114p. 1983. Repr. of 1936 ed. 10 mil. lam. covers, sp. bound 29.50 (ISBN 0-913698-06-7, R-192). AMR Pub Co.
Wurlitzer Jukebox Service Manual for Models 750, 750-E, 780, 780-E, 700, 800, 500, 500-A, 600, 600-A, 600 Keyboard, 600-A Keyboard. 174p. 1983. Repr. of 1938 ed. 10 mil. lam. covers, sp. bound 27.50 (ISBN 0-913698-10-5, R-181). AMR Pub Co.
Wurlitzer Jukebox Service Manual for Remote Control Systems 1938-1945. 136p. 1983. Repr. of 1945 ed. 10 mil. lam. covers, spiral bnd. 19.50 (ISBN 0-913698-43-1, R-197). AMR Pub Co.
Wurlitzer Jukebox Service Parts Manual & Brochure: Models of the 3600 Series of 1972. Wurlitzer Company Staff. 124p. 1984. Repr. of 1972 ed. 10 mil laminated covers, spiral bdg. 32.50 (ISBN 0-913599-08-5, R-253). AMR Pub Co.
Wurlitzer Jukeboxes, Vol. II. Ed. by Frank Adams. 168p. 1984. deluxe ed. 19.50 spiral bound (ISBN 0-913599-50-6, R-295). AMR Pub Co.
Wurlitzer Jukeboxes, 1934-74. Compiled by Frank Adams. 242p. (Orig.). 1984. pap. 14.50 Spiral bdg. (ISBN 0-913599-43-3, R-232E). AMR Pub Co.
Wurlitzer Model 1050: The Jukebox Service Manual Supplement & Brochure of 1973. Wurlitzer Company Staff. Ed. by Frank Adams. 76p. 1984. Repr. of 1973 ed. 10 mil laminated covers, spiral bdg 29.50 (ISBN 0-913599-14-X, R-254). AMR Pub Co.
Wurlitzer Parts Catalogue for Jukebox Models 41 & 71. 52p. 1983. Repr. of 1940 ed. 10 mil. laminated covers, spiral bound 15.00 (R-170). AMR Pub Co.
Wurlitzer Service Instructions & Parts Catalog for Model 1015 Commercial Phonograph. rev. ed. Rudolph Wurlitzer Co. Staff. Ed. by Ricky J. Botts. (Illus.). 106p. 1984. pap. 13.00 (ISBN 0-912789-02-6). Jukebox Coll New.
Wurlitzer Service Manual & Parts Catalogue 1937-39: For Models 50, 51 & 61. 192p. 1983. 10 mil. laminated spiral bdg. 32.50 (ISBN 0-913698-02-4, R-180). AMR Pub Co.
Wurzelatlas Mitteleuropaeischer Gruenlandpflanzen, Vol 1: Monocotyledoneae. L. Kutschera & E. Lichtenegger. (Illus.). 516p. (Ger.). 1982. lib. bdg. 120.00x (ISBN 3-437-30359-7). Lubrecht & Cramer.
Wuthering Heights. Emily Bronte. (Airmont Classics Ser.). (gr. 9 up). 1964. pap. 2.95 (ISBN 0-8049-0011-6, CL-11). Airmont.
Wuthering Heights. Emily Bronte. (Literature Ser.). (gr. 9-12). 1969. pap. text ed. 7.42 (ISBN 0-87720-720-8). AMSCO Sch.
Wuthering Heights. Emily Bronte. 320p. (gr. 7-12). 1983. pap. 2.25 (ISBN 0-553-21258-3, Bantam Classics). Bantam.
Wuthering Heights. Emily Bronte. Ed. by Walter Kendrick. (Classics Ser.). 400p. 1980. deluxe ed. 14.95 (ISBN 0-8464-1072-9). Beekman Pubs.
Wuthering Heights. Emily Bronte. 1961. pap. 2.25 (ISBN 0-440-39728-6, LE). Dell.

Wyoming Statutes, Annotated, 11 vols. with indexes & rules. 1979. write for info. (ISBN 0-87215-139-5). Michie Co.

Wyoming Stories; City Tales. Gretel Ehrlich & Edward Hoagland. (Capra Back-to-Back Ser.). 128p. 1988. Repr. lib. bdg. 19.95x (ISBN 0-8095-4105-X). Borgo Pr.

Wyoming Sun. Edward Bryant. (Illus.). 132p. 1980. pap. 6.00 (ISBN 0-936204-12-5). Jelm Mtn.

Wyoming: Trusts. 8.50 (ISBN 0-686-90977-1); suppl. 6.00 (ISBN 0-686-90978-X). Am Law Inst.

Wyoming U. S. Marshal: A Fictional Novel about the Escapades of a U. S. Marshall in & about Lanamie, Wyoming. Gary Twesten. 1984. write for info. (ISBN 0-9602428-0-5). G Twesten.

Wyoming University: The First 100 Years. Deborah Hardy et al. Ed. by N. Roberts & D. Beck. (Illus.). 320p. 1986. lib. bdg. 19.95 (ISBN 0-941570-01-0). U of Wyoming.

Wyoming Way. Roe Richmond. (Orig.). 1981. pap. 1.95 (ISBN 0-8439-0926-9, Leisure Bks). Leisure NY.

Wyoming Wench. Dirk Fletcher. (Spur Ser.: No. 5). 240p. (Orig.). 1984. pap. 2.75 (ISBN 0-8439-2135-8, Leisure Bks). Leisure NY.

Wyoming: Wild & Wooly. William F. Bragg. LC 83-9603. (Illus.). 168p. 1983. 14.95 (ISBN 0-87108-628-X); pap. 7.95 (ISBN 0-87108-631-X). Pruett.

Wyoming Wildfire. Leigh Greenwood. (Heartfire Romance Ser.). 1987. pap. 3.75 (ISBN 0-8217-2107-0). Zebra.

Wyoming Windsong. Mary L. Smith. LC 86-70150. (Frontier Romance Ser.). 196p. 1986. pap. 6.95 (ISBN 0-89636-211-6). Accent Bks.

Wyoming's People. 2nd ed. Clarice Whittenburg & Carol Stinneford. 213p. 1978. pap. 7.95x (ISBN 0-933472-12-9); activity bk. 5.00x (ISBN 0-933472-37-4). Johnson Bks.

Wyoming's Wind River Range. Joe Kelsey. (Wyoming Geographic Ser.: No. 2). (Illus., Orig.). 1988. pap. 15.95 (ISBN 0-938314-54-8). Am Geog Pub.

Wyrldmaker. Terry Bisson. 176p. 1988. pap. 2.95 (ISBN 0-380-75359-6). Avon.

Wyrms. Orson S. Card. 263p. 1987. 16.95 (ISBN 0-87795-894-7, Arbor Hse). Morrow.

Wyrms. Orson S. Card. 352p. 1988. pap. 3.95 (ISBN 0-8125-3357-7). Tor Bks.

Wyst: Alastor Seventeen Sixteen. Jack Vance. (Alastor Ser.: Bk. 3). 272p. 1984. Repr. of 1978 ed. lib. bdg. 15.00 (ISBN 0-934438-97-8). Underwood-Miller.

Wythe County Marriages, Seventeen Ninety to Eighteen Fifty. John Vogt & T. William Kethley, Jr. (Virginia Historic Marriage Register Ser.). (Illus.). ix, 224p. (Orig.). 1985. pap. 9.50 (ISBN 0-935931-21-X). Iberian Pub.

Wythe County Marriages, Seventeen Ninety to Eighteen Fifty. John Vogt & T. William Kethley, Jr. (Virginia Historic Marriage Register Ser.). 224p. 1988. Repr. lib. bdg. 24.95x (ISBN 0-8095-8235-X). Borgo Pr.

Wyvern. A. A. Attanasio. 480p. 1988. 19.95 (ISBN 0-89919-409-5). Ticknor & Fields.

Wyvern Mystery: A Novel, 3 vols. Joseph Le Fanu. Ed. by Devendra P. Varma. LC 76-5282. (Collected Works Ser.). 1977. Repr. of 1869 ed. Set. 69.50x (ISBN 0-405-09250-4); Vol. 1. 23.50x (ISBN 0-405-09251-2); Vol. 2. 23.50x (ISBN 0-405-09252-0); Vol. 3. 23.50x (ISBN 0-405-09253-9). Ayer Co Pubs.

WYXIE Wonderland: An Unauthorized Fifty Year Diary of WXYZ Detroit. Dick Osgood. LC 81-82501. 1981. 19.95 (ISBN 0-87972-186-3); pap. 9.95 (ISBN 0-87972-187-1). Bowling Green.

Wyznania Niechrzescijanskie na Drugim Soborze Watykanskim. Jan Lichten. 24p. 1965. 2.50 (ISBN 0-940962-46-2). Polish Inst Arts.

X

X. Sue Coe & Judith Moore. (Raw One-Shot Ser.: No. 6). (Illus.). 32p. 1986. 9.95 (ISBN 0-915043-06-8). Raw Bks & Graph.

X..; see Oeuvres.

X.. see Oeuvres.

X- & Gamma-Ray Astronomy: Proceedings. International Astronomical Union Symposium, 55, Madrid, May 11-13, 1972. Ed. by H. Bradt & R. Giaconni. LC 72-92526. (Illus.). 323p. 1973. lib. bdg. 50.00 (ISBN 90-277-0303-5, Pub. by Reidel Holland); pap. 26.00 (ISBN 90-277-0337-X). Kluwer Academic.

X-Bar Grammar: Attribution & Prediction in Dutch. F. C. Van Gestel. xii, 189p. 1986. pap. write for info. (ISBN 90-6765-251-2). Foris Pubns.

X-Efficiency: Theory, Evidence & Applications. Rodger S. Frantz. 1988. lib. bdg. 46.50 (ISBN 0-89838-242-4). Kluwer Academic.

X-Factor. Andre Norton. 224p. 1984. pap. 2.50 (ISBN 0-345-31557-X, Del Rey). Ballantine.

X Factor: An American Cultural Dilemma. Neil M. Fleishman. LC 84-91375. 204p. 1986. 14.95 (ISBN 0-533-06460-0). Vantage.

X in Paris. Michael Brodsky. 180p. (Orig.). 1988. pap. 9.95 (ISBN 0-941423-13-1). FWEW.

X-Ing Warm. Ronald Bayes. 34p. (Orig.). 1968. pap. 2.00 (ISBN 0-932264-06-9). Trask Hse Bks.

X-Linked Mental Retardation. John M. Opitz. LC 84-3858. 390p. 1984. 43.00 (ISBN 0-8451-0234-6). A R Liss.

X-Linked Mental Retardation & Verbal Disability. Ed. by Daniel Bergsma. (March of Dimes Ser.: Vol. 10, No. 1). 11.50 (ISBN 0-686-10022-0). March of Dimes.

X-Linked Mental Retardation, 2. John M. Opitz. LC 86-36. 758p. 1986. 64.00 (ISBN 0-8451-4211-9, 4211). A R Liss.

X-Log: A Sex Diary. Gordon Usticke. 1978. loose-leaf version 7.95 (ISBN 0-686-15719-2); softcover 4.95 (ISBN 0-686-15720-6). X-Log.

X-Men. Christopher Claremont & Brent E. Anderson. (Marvel Graphic Novel: No. 5). 5.95. Marvel Comics.

X-Men in an X-Cellent Death. Kate Novak. LC 86-91772. (Marvel Super Heroes Adventure Gamebook Ser.: No. 6). 192p. (Orig.). 1987. pap. 2.95 (ISBN 0-88038-437-9). TSR Inc.

X-One: Experimental Fiction Project. Alvin Greenberg et al. Ed. by Harry Smith. LC 76-20256. (Illus.). 232p. 1976. pap. 5.00 (ISBN 0-912292-41-5). The Smith.

X-OPEN Portability Guide. Ed. by The X-OPEN Group. 702p. 1985. 75.00 (ISBN 0-444-87839-4, North Holland). Elsevier.

X-Open Portability Guide. 2nd rev. ed. Ed. by X-Open Group. 1826p. 1987. wire-bound in 5 pts. 125.00 (ISBN 0-444-70179-6, North Holland). Elsevier.

X-Planes: X-1 to X-31. rev. ed. Jay Miller. LC 87-23991. (Illus.). 192p. 1988. 29.95 (ISBN 0-517-56749-0, Or Press). Crown.

X-R Chart & Beyond. (Illus.). 362p. 1987. pap. 50.00 (ISBN 0-317-59809-0, GM8501). Am Foundrymen.

X-Rated Bible: An Irreverent Survey of Sex in the Scriptures. Ben E. Akerley. (Illus.). 428p. (Orig.). 1985. pap. 8.00 (ISBN 0-910309-19-1). Am Atheist.

X-Rated Riddles. Matt Phillips. 1981. pap. 1.95. Price Stern.

X-Rated Romance. Tina Sunshine. 144p. 1982. pap. 2.50 (ISBN 0-380-79905-7, Flare). Avon.

X-Rated Romance. Tina Sunshine. 142p. (YA) (gr. 7 up). 1988. pap. 2.50 (ISBN 0-380-87817-8, Flare). Avon.

X-Rated Romance Classics. Jonathan Thompson, Jr. (Illus.). 60p. Date not set. price not set (ISBN 0-933479-20-4). Thompson.

X-Rated Romance, No. 1 - Sexercise. Jonathan Thompson, Jr. (Illus.). 175p. 1987. 7.00 (ISBN 0-933479-14-X). Thompson.

X-Rated Romance, No. 2 - Condom-Miniums. Jonathan Thompson, Jr. (Illus.). 70p. Date not set. 5.50 (ISBN 0-933479-16-6). Thompson.

X-Rated Romance, No. 3 - Operation: Sex. Jonathan Thompson, Jr. (Illus.). 60p. Date not set. 4.50 (ISBN 0-933479-18-2). Thompson.

X-Rated Super Romances. Jonathan Thompson, Jr. (Illus.). 50p. Date not set. price not set (ISBN 0-933479-00-X). Thompson.

X-Rated Video Directory. Ed. by Film World Editors. (Orig.). 1985. pap. 4.95 (ISBN 0-87067-925-2, BH929). Holloway.

X-Rated Videotape Guide. rev. ed. Robert H. Rimmer. 1986. pap. 16.95 (ISBN 0-517-56058-5, Harmony). Crown.

X-Ray Absorption: Principles, Applications, Techniques of EXAFS, SEXAFS & XANES. Ed. by D. C. Koningsberger & R. Prins. LC 86-28991. (Chemical Analysis Ser.). 1988. 89.95 (ISBN 0-471-87547-3). Wiley.

X-Ray Analysis & the Structure of Organic Molecules. Jack D. Dunitz. LC 78-15588. (George Fisher Baker Non-Resident Lectureship in Chemistry Ser.). 528p. 1979. 79.50x (ISBN 0-8014-1115-7). Cornell U Pr.

X-Ray & Atomic Inner-Shell Physics, 1982. Ed. by Bernd Crasemann. LC 82-74075. (AIP Conf. Proc. Ser.: No. 94). 802p. 1982. lib. bdg. 44.50 (ISBN 0-88318-193-2). Am Inst Physics.

X Ray & Extreme Ultraviolet Optics. Underwood. (Pure & Applied Optics Ser.). 1988. write for info. (ISBN 0-471-06491-2). Wiley.

X-Ray & Neutron Diffraction. G. E. Bacon. 1966. pap. 28.00 (ISBN 0-08-011998-0). Pergamon.

X-Ray & Optical Emission Analysis of High-Temperature Alloys: A Symposium. American Society for Testing & Materials Staff. LC 65-18213. (American Society for Testing & Materials Special Technical Publication Ser.: No. 376). pap. 20.00 (ISBN 0-317-09803-9, 2000851). Bks Demand UMI.

X-Ray & VUV Interaction Data Bases, Calculations, & Measurements. Ed. by Del Grande et al. 1988. 43.00 (ISBN 0-89252-946-6, 911). SPIE.

X-Ray Astronomy. Ed. by R. Giacconi & H. Gursky. LC 74-79569. (Astrophysics & Space Science Library: No. 43). 450p. 1974. lib. bdg. 76.00 (ISBN 90-277-0295-0, Pub. by Reidel Holland); pap. 34.00 (ISBN 90-277-0387-6). Kluwer Academic.

X-Ray Astronomy. Riccardo Giacconi. 1981. 44.50 (ISBN 90-277-1261-1, Pub. by Reidel Holland). Kluwer Academic.

X-Ray Astronomy. Ed. by Richard Giacconi & Giancarlo Setti. (NATO Advanced Study Institutes Series, C. Mathematical & Physical Sciences: No. 60). 400p. 1980. lib. bdg. 47.50 (ISBN 90-277-1156-9, Pub. by Reidel Holland). Kluwer Academic.

X-Ray Astronomy in the Exosat Era. Ed. by A. Peacock. 1985. lib. bdg. 94.00 (ISBN 90-277-2099-1, Pub. by Reidel Holland). Kluwer Academic.

X-Ray Astronomy, Including a Catalogue & Bibliography of Galactic X-Ray Sources: Proceedings of the 21st Plenary Meeting, Innsbruck, Austria, 1978. Ray Armstong. Ed. by W. A. Baity & L. E. Peterson. (Illus.). 1979. 76.00 (ISBN 0-08-023418-6). Pergamon.

X-Ray Atlas of the Royal Mummies. Ed. by James E. Harris & Edward F. Wente. LC 79-23704. (Illus.). 1980. lib. bdg. 75.00x (ISBN 0-226-31745-5). U of Chicago Pr.

X-Ray Calibration: Techniques-Sources-Detectors. Ed. by Rockett & Lee. 260p. 1986. 50.00 (ISBN 0-89252-724-2, 689). SPIE.

X-Ray Coordinator. Jack Rudman. (Career Examination Ser.: C-1536). (Cloth bdg. avail. on request). pap. 16.00 (ISBN 0-8373-1536-0). Natl Learning.

X-Ray Crystallography. Martin J. Buerger. LC 80-12459. 564p. 1980. Repr. of 1942 ed. lib. bdg. 39.50 (ISBN 0-89874-176-9). Krieger.

X-Ray Determination of Electron Distribution. R. J. Weiss. Ed. by E. P. Wohlforth. (Selected Topics in Solid State Physics: Vol. 6). 1966. 26.50 (ISBN 0-444-10305-8, North-Holland). Elsevier.

X-Ray Diagnosis in Neonates. Koteles. 1983. cancelled 22.00 (ISBN 963-05-3061-9, Pub. by Akademiai Kaido Hungary). IPS.

X-Ray Diagnosis in Neonates. G. Koteles. 174p. 1982. 116.00x (ISBN 0-569-08747-3, Pub. by Collets (UK)). State Mutual Bk.

X-Ray Diagnosis of Congenital Heart Disease in Infants, Children & Adults: Pathologic, Hemodynamic, & Clinical Correlations As Related to Chest Film. 2nd ed. Larry P. Elliott & Gerold L. Schiebler. (Illus.). 424p. 1979. photocopy ed. 50.50x (ISBN 0-398-03857-0). C C Thomas.

X-Ray Diagnosis of the Alimentary Tract in Infants & Children. Edward B. Singleton. LC 58-14433. pap. 88.00 (ISBN 0-317-19894-7, 2011940). Bks Demand UMI.

X-ray Differential Diagnosis in Small Bowel Disease: A Practical Approach. J. L. Sellink. (Series in Radiology). 1988. lib. bdg. 99.50 (ISBN 0-89838-351-X, Pub. by Martinus Nijhoff Netherlands). Kluwer Academic.

X-Ray Diffraction. Bertram E. Warren. LC 68-25928. (Addison-Wesley Metallurgy & Materials Ser.). (Illus.). pap. 101.70 (ISBN 0-317-58234-8, 2056385). Bks Demand UMI.

X-Ray Diffraction by Disordered & Ordered Systems: Covering X-Ray Diffraction by Gases, Liquids & Solids & Indicating How the Theory of Diffraction by These Different States of Matter Is Related & How It Can Be Used to Solve Structural Problems. David W. Hukins. (Illus.). 173p. 1981. text ed. 37.00 (ISBN 0-08-023976-5). Pergamon.

X-Ray Diffraction Methods in Polymer Science. Leroy E. Alexander. Ed. by James Krumhansl. LC 78-23488. 600p. 1979. Repr. of 1969 ed. lib. bdg. 42.00 (ISBN 0-88275-801-2). Krieger.

X-Ray Diffraction of Ions in Aqueous Solutions: Hydration & Complex Formation. Ed. by Mauro Magini. 288p. 1988. 150.00 (ISBN 0-8493-6945-2, 6945). CRC Pr.

X-Ray Diffraction Procedures: For Polycrystalline & Amorphous Materials. 2nd ed. Harold P. Klug & Leroy E. Alexander. LC 73-21936. (Illus.). 966p. 1974. 103.00x (ISBN 0-471-49369-4, Pub. by Wiley-Interscience). Wiley.

X-Ray Diffraction Study to Assess the Potential Economic-Pharmaceutical Uses for Nigerian Clays. Paul Anaejionu. (Science & Development in Africa Ser.). 1979. pap. 10.00x (ISBN 0-914970-22-4). Conch Mag.

X-Ray Diffraction Topography. B. K. Tanner. LC 75-45196. 1976. 50.00 (ISBN 0-08-019692-6). Pergamon.

X-Ray Emission from Clusters of Galaxies. C. Sarazin. (Illus.). 250p. 1988. 49.50 (ISBN 0-521-32957-4). Cambridge U Pr.

X-Ray Emission Line & Absorption Wave Lengths & Two-Theta Tables - DS37-A. 306p. 1970. 54.00 (ISBN 0-8031-0825-7, 05-037010-39). ASTM.

X-Ray Emission of Auroral Electrons & Magnetospheric Dynamics. L. L. Lazutin. (Physics & Chemistry in Space Ser.: Vol. 14). (Illus.). 220p. 1986. 79.00 (ISBN 0-387-15335-7). Springer-Verlag.

X-Ray Emission Spectrography in Geology. Isidore Adler. (Methods in Geochemistry & Geophysics: Vol. 4). xii, 258p. 1966. 68.00 (ISBN 0-444-40004-4). Elsevier.

X-Ray Emission Wavelength & DEU Tables for Nondiffractive Analysis - DS 46. 40p. 1970. pap. 5.00 (ISBN 0-8031-0826-5, 05-046000-39). ASTM.

X-Ray Examination of the Stomach: A Description of the Roentgenologic Anatomy, Physiology, & Pathology of the Esophagus & Duodenum. rev. ed. Frederic E. Templeton. LC 64-23426. pap. 154.00 (ISBN 0-317-42269-3, 2025792). Bks Demand UMI.

X-Ray Fluorescence Spectrometry. Ron Jenkins. LC 88-10797. (Chemical Analysis Ser.). 1988. 65.00 (ISBN 0-471-83675-3). Wiley.

X-Ray Fluorescent Scanning of the Thyroid. Ed. by M. H. Jonckheer & F. Deconinck. 1983. lib. bdg. 39.50 (ISBN 0-89838-561-X, Pub. by Martinus Nijhoff Netherlands). Kluwer Academic.

X-Ray Imaging, No. II. Ed. by Knight & Bowen. 155p. 1986. 43.00 (ISBN 0-89252-726-9, 691). SPIE.

X-Ray Imaging Equipment: An Introduction. Euclid Seeram. (Illus.). 610p. 1985. 49.00 (ISBN 0-398-05078-3). C C Thomas.

X-Ray Information Book: A Consumers' Guide to Avoiding Unnecessary Medical & Dental X-Rays. Priscilla W. Laws & The Public Citizen Health Research Group. 154p. 1983. 14.50 (ISBN 0-374-29342-2); pap. 5.95 (ISBN 0-374-51730-4). FS&G.

X-Ray Instrumentation for the Photon Factory. Ed. by S. Hosoya et al. 1986. lib. bdg. 94.50 (ISBN 90-277-2243-9, Pub. by Reidel Holland). Kluwer Academic.

X-Ray Instrumentation in Astronomy. Ed. by Culhane. 417p. 1985. 57.00 (ISBN 0-89252-632-7, 597). SPIE.

X-Ray Methods. Clive Whiston. Ed. by F. Elizabeth Prichard. (Analytical Chemistry by Open Learning Ser.). 300p. 1987. write for info. (ISBN 0-471-91387-1). Wiley.

X-Ray Microanalysis in Electron Microscopy for Biologists. A. John Morgan. (Royal Microscopical Society Microscopy Handbooks Ser.). (Illus.). 1985. pap. 8.95x (ISBN 0-19-856409-0). Oxford U Pr.

X-Ray Microanalysis in the Electron Microscope. J. A. Chandler. (Practical Methods in Electron Microscopy: Vol. 5, Pt. II). 1977. 20.50 (ISBN 0-7204-0607-2, North-Holland). Elsevier.

X-Ray Microscopy. P. Cheng & G. Jan. (Illus.). 430p. 1987. 89.50 (ISBN 0-387-18148-2). Springer-Verlag.

X-Ray Microscopy: Proceedings of the International Symposium in Gottingen, West Germany, September 14-16, 1983. Ed. by G. Schmahl & D. Rudolph. (Springer Series in Optical Sciences: Vol. 43). (Illus.). 350p. 1984. 36.00 (ISBN 0-387-13271-6). Springer-Verlag.

X-Ray Optics & Microanalysis: Proceedings of the Sixth International Conference. Ed. by Gunji K. Shinoda et al. 908p. 1972. 100.00x (ISBN 0-86008-077-3, Pub. by U of Tokyo Japan). Columbia U Pr.

X-Ray Optics: Applications to Solids. Ed. by H. J. Queisser. (Topics in Applied Physics: Vol. 22). (Illus.). 1977. 51.00 (ISBN 0-387-08462-2). Springer-Verlag.

X-Ray Photoelectron Spectroscopy: Application to Metals & Alloys see Photoelectron Spectrometry.

X-Ray Photoelectron Spectroscopy of Solid Surfaces. V. I. Nefedov. viii, 200p. 1987. lib. bdg. 113.00 (ISBN 90-6764-080-8). Coronet Bks.

X-Ray Photogrammetry. Bertil Hallert. 1970. 42.00 (ISBN 0-444-40805-3). Elsevier.

X-Ray Physics for Radiologic Technologists. Richard H. Schmidt. LC 72-75592. (Illus.). 224p. 1973. 12.50x (ISBN 0-87527-131-6). Green.

X-Ray Plasma Spectroscopy & the Properties of Multiply-Charged Ions. Ed. by I. I. Sobel'man. (Proceedings of the Lebedev Physics Institute of the Academy of the U. S. S. R. Ser.: Vol. 179). 263p. 1988. text ed. 87.00 (ISBN 0-941743-23-3). Nova Sci Pubs.

X-Ray Spectrometry. Ed. by H. K. Herglotz & L. S. Birk. (Practical Spectrometry Ser.: Vol. 2). 1978. soft cover 95.00 (ISBN 0-8247-7036-6). Dekker.

X-Ray Spectrometry. 1987. write for info. Wiley.

X-Ray Spectroscopy. B. K. Agarwal. (Springer Series in Optical Sciences: Vol. 15). (Illus.). 1979. 48.00 (ISBN 0-387-09268-4). Springer-Verlag.

X-Ray Symposium 1981. Ed. by A. G. Davis Philip. 76p. 1981. pap. 12.00 (ISBN 0-9607902-0-9). L Davis Pr.

X-Ray Technician. Jack Rudman. (Career Examination Ser.: C-910). (Cloth bdg. avail. on request). pap. 14.00 (ISBN 0-8373-0910-7). Natl Learning.

X-Ray Technician I. Jack Rudman. (Career Examination Ser.: C-1840). (Cloth bdg. avail. on request). pap. 14.00 (ISBN 0-8373-1840-8). Natl Learning.

X-Ray Technician II. Jack Rudman. (Career Examination Ser.: C-1841). (Cloth bdg. avail. on request). pap. 14.00 (ISBN 0-8373-1841-6). Natl Learning.

X-Ray Technician III. Jack Rudman. (Career Examination Ser.: C-1842). (Cloth bdg. avail. on request). pap. 16.00 (ISBN 0-8373-1842-4). Natl Learning.

X-Ray Techniques in Art Galleries & Museums. D. Graham & T. Eddie. 136p. 1985. 48.00x (ISBN 0-85274-782-9, Pub. by A Hilger UK). Taylor & Francis.

Y Chromosome Pt. B: Clinical Aspects of Y Chromosome Abnormalities. Avery A. Sandberg. (Progress & Topics in Cytogenetics: Vol. 6B). 420p. 1985. 98.00 (ISBN 0-8451-2407-2). A R Liss.

Y Despues de la Muerte, Que? Edgar Contreras. Orig. Title: After Death, What. (Span.). 1988. pap. 4.95 (ISBN 0-8254-1130-0). Kregel.

y Direct Marketer's Workbook. Herman Holtz. LC 86-13340. 348p. 1987. 37.95 (ISBN 0-471-83066-6); pap. 14.95 (ISBN 0-471-85032-2). Wiley.

Y. E. S.: Shapedown Youth Evaluation Scale. 2nd., rev. ed. Laurel M. Mellin. LC 86-71116. (Illus.). 269p. 1986. write for info. (ISBN 0-935902-10-4). Balboa Pub.

Y Fidel Creo el Punto X. Reinol Gonzalez. (Illus.). 320p. (Orig., Span.). 1987. pap. 15.95 (ISBN 0-917049-13-6). Saeta.

Y-Fourteen Report: Digital Representation of Physical Object Shapes, No. 1. 1976. 4.00 (ISBN 0-317-31366-5, N00007). ASME.

Y-Fourteen Report, No. 2: Guideline for Documenting of Computer Systems Used in Computer - Aided Preparation of Product Definition Data - User Instructions Book No. N00078. 1977. pap. text ed. 2.50 (ISBN 0-685-81929-9). ASME.

Y Geiriadur Mawr: The Complete Welsh-English-English-Welsh Dictionary. Ed. by Gomer Press Staff. 367p. 1986. 58.50x (ISBN 0-85088-462-4, Pub. by Gomer Pr). State Mutual Bk.

Y Geiriadur Mawr: The Complete Welsh-English, English-Welsh Dictionary. H. Meurig & W. O. Thomas. Ed. by S. J. Williams. 859p. (Welsh & Eng.). 1981. 75.00 (ISBN 0-686-97426-3, M-9434). French & Eur.

Y Hoc Cham Cuu Trung Hoa. Hang-Thanh. LC 87-51531. (Illus.). 142p. 1988. pap. 8.00 (ISBN 0-944211-01-1). Vo Lam Pub.

Y. I. G. Filters. J. Helszajin. LC 84-17308. 1986. 54.95 (ISBN 0-471-90516-X). Wiley.

Y-Indian Guide Programs: Leaders Manual. YMCA of the U. S. A. Staff. 40p. 1984. pap. text ed. 8.00x (ISBN 0-931250-78-1, Pub. by YMCA USA). Human Kinetics.

Y las Naranjas Azules. Herge. (Illus.). 62p. (Span.). 15.95. French & Eur.

Y Luego el Fin. David Ewert. 204p. 1987. pap. 6.95 (ISBN 0-8361-1294-6). Herald Pr.

Y. M. C. A. & Y. W. C. A. Architecture: A Bibliography. Mary E. Huls. (Architecture Ser.: A 1586). 7p. 1986. 3.00 (ISBN 0-89028-816-X). Vance Biblios.

Y No Se lo Trago la Tierra - And the Earth Did Not Devour Him. Tomas Rivera. Tr. by Evangelina Vigil. LC 87-70275. 180p. (Span. & Eng.). 1987. 8.50 (ISBN 0-934770-72-7). Arte Publico.

Y No Se Lo Trago la Tierra (Spanish-English) Tomas Rivera. LC 76-479. 175p. 1976. pap. 6.00 (ISBN 0-915808-09-9). Editorial Justa.

Y. O. L. (Your Own Law) A Complete Guide for the Layman. Walter E. Hempstead, Jr. 240p. 1980. 3.95 (ISBN 0-940094-01-0). Hempstead House.

Y-Our Greater Self. Peter D. Marritt. (Illus.). 76p. (Orig.). 1984. pap. 5.00 (ISBN 0-932009-07-7). Moonowl Creat.

Y Skippers: An Aquatics Program for Children Five & Under. Orig. ed. YMCA of the U. S. A. Staff. LC 86-32399. (Illus.). 240p. 1987. spiral bdg. 20.00x (ISBN 0-87322-100-1, Pub. by YMCA USA). Human Kinetics.

Y Soccer Coaches Manual. Ed. by Steven D. Houseworth & Stephen Jeffries. (Illus.). 40p. (Orig.). 1986. pap. text ed. 4.00x (ISBN 0-87322-027-7, Pub. by YMCA USA). Human Kinetics.

Y-Trail Blazers Manual. Ed. by Charles C. Kujawa. 59p. 1973. pap. text ed. 4.00x (ISBN 0-88035-061-X, Pub. by YMCA USA). Human Kinetics.

Y-Trail Maidens & Mates Manual. Ed. by Charles C. Kujawa. 63p. 1979. pap. 5.25x (ISBN 0-88035-062-8, Pub. by YMCA USA). Human Kinetics.

Y-Trail Programs Manual. Ed. by YMCA of the U. S. A. Staff. (Illus.). 64p. 1987. saddle stitch 7.00x (ISBN 0-87322-117-6, Pub. by YMCA USA). Human Kinetics.

Y tu que dices? 2nd ed. Gene S. Kupferschmid. LC 85-82128. 253p. 1986. pap. text ed. 14.50. Heath.

Y Twelve M: Solution of Large & Sparse Systems of Linear Algebraic Equations. Z. Zlatev et al. (Lecture Notes in Computer Science Ser.: Vol. 121). 128p. 1981. pap. 12.00 (ISBN 0-387-10874-2). Springer-Verlag.

Ya! & John-Juan. Douglas Woolf. LC 79-123990. 1975. 7.95 (ISBN 0-685-79056-8). Small Pr Dist.

Ya! & John-Juan. Douglas Woolf. LC 79-123990. 7.95 (ISBN 0-942296-03-6). Wolf Run Bks.

Ya Gotta to Be Jokin. H. B. Waldegrave. 1986. 42.00x (ISBN 0-86332-085-6, Pub. by Book Guild Ltd). State Mutual Bk.

Ya Gotta Wanna. Warren M. Hoffman. (Illus.). 110p. (Orig.). 1981. pap. 2.95 (ISBN 0-940916-00-2). Daybreak Pr.

Y'a Qu'un Woodstock. Charles M. Schulz. pap. 5.95 (ISBN 0-03-061654-9). H Holt & Co.

Ya, Sure, Ya Betcha! Charlene Power. (Illus.). 63p. 1981. 2.95 (ISBN 0-88498-050-2). Brevet Pr.

Yachas Harav V'hatalmid. (Hebrew.). 1.00 (ISBN 0-914131-75-3, E05). Torah Umesorah.

Yacht Cruising. Patrick Ellam. (Illus.). 1983. 19.50 (ISBN 0-393-03280-9). Norton.

Yacht Designer's Sketch Book. Jan Nicolson. (Illus.). 160p. 1982. 24.95 (ISBN 0-333-33070-6, Pub by Macmillan London). Sheridan.

Yacht Designing & Planning. rev. ed. Howard I. Chapelle. (Illus.). 1971. 27.95 (ISBN 0-393-03169-1). Norton.

Yacht Designs. William Garden. LC 76-8772. pap. 57.80 (ISBN 0-317-42194-8, 2026095). Bks Demand UMI.

Yacht Joinery & Fitting: Practical Guidance on the Planning & Building of Cabin Accommodation in Sailing & Power Craft. Mike Saunders. LC 80-84457. pap. 48.30 (2026804). Bks Demand UMI.

Yacht Navigation - My Way. John Coote. (Illus.). 1989. 19.95 (ISBN 0-393-03326-0). Norton.

Yacht Owners Register, 1984. (Illus.). 1152p. 1984. 85.00 (ISBN 0-915953-00-5). Yacht Owners.

Yacht Portraits: The Best of Contemporary Marine art. Ed. by Fabio Ratti. (Illus.). 165p. 1987. 65.00 (ISBN 0-911378-76-6). Sheridan.

Yacht Racing for Beginners. Jeff Toghill's Sailing School Staff. 1986. pap. 6.95 (ISBN 0-393-30297-0). Norton.

Yacht Racing Protests & Appeals. J. Feller. 7.95 (ISBN 0-393-60008-4). Norton.

Yacht Racing Rules: A Complete Guide, 1985-1988. Mary Pera. (Illus.). 1985. 13.95 (ISBN 0-393-03308-2). Norton.

Yachting Dictionary. A. Tetsmann & H. Lind. 192p. 1980. 50.00x (ISBN 0-686-82331-1, Pub. by Collets (UK)). State Mutual Bk.

Yachting Guide to Bermuda. Ed. by Jane Harris & Edward Harris. (Illus.). 144p. 1988. 14.95. Bluewater Bks.

Yachting Signal Book. James R. Collier. LC 84-45262. (Illus.). 128p. 1985. 17.50 (ISBN 0-87033-324-0). Cornell Maritime.

Yachting Trivia. Jon B. Johansen. 64p. 1986. pap. 2.00 (ISBN 0-941216-31-4). Cay-Bel.

Yachtman's Emergency Handbook. rev. ed. Neil Hollander & Harald Mertes. Ed. by John R. Whiting. LC 86-12070. (Illus.). 288p. 1986. 19.95 (ISBN 0-688-06610-0, Pub. by Hearst Marine Bks). Morrow.

Yachtmaster: An Examination Handbook with Exercises. Pat Langley-Price & Philip Ouvry. (Illus.). 224p. 1987. 27.50 (ISBN 0-229-11662-0). Sheridan.

Yachtmaster Exercises. Pat Langley-Price & Philip Ouvry. (Illus.). 128p. 1984. pap. 14.50 (ISBN 0-229-11715-5, Adlard Coles). Sheridan.

Yachts & Yachting. Vanderdecken. Repr. of 1873 ed. 60.00 (ISBN 0-85967-568-8). Scolar.

Yachtsman's Guide to the Atlantic Coasts of Spain & Portugal. D. M. Sloma et al. 140p. 1983. 75.00x (ISBN 0-85288-087-1, Pub. by Imray Laurie Norie & Wilson UK). State Mutual Bk.

Yachtsman's Guide to the Bahamas, 1987. Tropic Isle Publishers, Inc. Ed. by Meredith H. Fields. (No. 37). (Illus.). 410p. 1986. 14.95 (ISBN 0-937379-01-8). Tropic Isle Pub.

Yachtsman's Guide to the Bahamas, 1988, No. 38. rev. ed. Tropic Isle Publishers Inc. Staff. Ed. by Meredith Fields. (Illus.). 410p. 1987. 16.95 (ISBN 0-937379-02-6). Tropic Isle Pub.

Yachtsman's Guide to the Virgin Island & Puerto Rico: 1987. 4th ed. Ed. by Meredith H. Fields. (Illus.). 240p. 1986. 12.95 (ISBN 0-937379-00-X). Tropic Isle Pub.

Yachtsman's Guide to the Windward Islands. 2nd, rev. ed. Julius M. Wilensky. Ed. by John R. Van Ost. LC 78-65702. (Illus.). 1978. 19.95 (ISBN 0-918752-01-9). Wescott Cove.

Yachtsman's Legal Guide to Co-Ownership. Paula Odin & Dexter Odin. LC 80-71020. 1981. 12.50 (ISBN 0-8286-0087-2). J De Graff.

Yachtsman's Navigation Manual. Jeff E. Toghill. LC 76-24492. 1977. 5.95 (ISBN 0-8286-0099-6). J De Graff.

Yachtsman's Pilots, Vol. V: The Scilly Isles. Robin Brandon. 40p. 1983. 40.00x (ISBN 0-85288-090-1, Pub. by Imray Laurie Norie & Wilson UK). State Mutual Bk.

Yachtsman's Pocket Almanac. Gary Jobson. 1986. pap. 6.95 (ISBN 0-671-62376-1, Fireside). S&S.

Yad B'Yad Bowl-A-Thon see Kadima Kesher Series.

Yadava Sculpture. S. R. Deshpande. (Illus.). 107p. 1985. text ed. 60.00x (ISBN 0-86590-715-3, Pub. by B R Pub Corp India). Apt Bks.

Yag Laser Bronchoscopy. Jean-Francois Dumon et al. LC 84-26310. 128p. 1985. 35.00 (ISBN 0-275-91311-2, C1311). Praeger.

Yage Letters. William Burroughs & Allen Ginsberg. LC 63-12222. (Orig.). 1963. pap. 3.00 (ISBN 0-87286-004-3). City Lights.

Yagi Antenna Design. Lawson. 1986. 15.00 (ISBN 0-87259-041-0). Am Radio.

Yagna (The Eternal Energy) Panduranga Malyala. (Illus.). 36p. (Orig.). 1984. pap. text ed. 4.00x (ISBN 0-938924-23-0). Sri Shirdi Sai.

Yagua Days. Cruz Martel. LC 75-27601. (Pied Piper Bk.). (Illus.). 40p. (ps-3). 1987. PLB 11.89 (ISBN 0-8037-9766-4); pap. 3.95 (ISBN 0-8037-0457-7, 0383-120). Dial Bks Young.

Yagua Mythology: Epic Tendencies in a New World Mythology. Paul S. Powlison. Ed. by William R. Merrifield. LC 84-63152. (International Museum of Cultures Publications: No. 16). (Illus.). 132p. (Orig.). 1985. pap. 14.00x (ISBN 0-88312-172-7); microfiche (2) 4.00 (ISBN 0-88312-254-5). Summer Inst Ling.

Yahweh & Son: A Teenager's Guide to the Bible. Anthony J. Marinelli. 160p. (Orig.). 1986. pap. 7.95 (ISBN 0-8091-9568-2). Paulist Pr.

Yahweh & the Gods of Canaan: An Historical Analysis of Two Contrasting Faiths. William F. Albright. 1978. Repr. of 1968 ed. 12.00x (ISBN 0-931464-01-3). Eisenbrauns.

Yahweh Is a Warrior. Millard C. Lind. LC 80-16038. (Christian Peace Shelf Ser.). 240p. 1980. pap. 11.95x (ISBN 0-8361-1233-4). Herald Pr.

Yahweh: The Divine Name in the Bible. G. H. Parke-Taylor. 134p. 1975. text ed. 14.95x (ISBN 0-88920-014-9, Pub. by Wilfrid Laurier Canada). Humanities.

Yajnavalkya Smriti: With the Commentary of Vijnanesvara, Called the Mitaksara, & Notes from the Gloss of Balambhatta. Yajnavalkya. Tr. by Srisa Chandra Vidyarnava. LC 73-3813. (Sacred Books of the Hindus: No. 21). Repr. of 1918 ed. 48.00 (ISBN 0-404-57821-7). AMS Pr.

Yajnavalkya's Smriti: With the Commentary of Vijnanesvara, Called the Mitaksara, & the Gloss of Balambhatta. Yajnavalkya. Tr. by Srisa Chandra Vasu. LC 73-3787. (Sacred Books of the Hindus: No. 2). Repr. of 1909 ed. 19.00 (ISBN 0-404-57802-0). AMS Pr.

Yajurveda (Summary) Date not set. 5.00 (ISBN 0-938924-30-3). Sri Shirdi Sai.

Yakety-Yak-Yak Yak. Richard Hefter & Jacquelyn Reinach. LC 77-7250. (Sweet Pickles Ser.). (gr. k-2). 1977. 2.95 (ISBN 0-03-021436-X). HR&W.

Yakima: Northwest. Ed. by Frank W. Porter, III. (Indians of North America Ser.). (Illus.). (gr. 5 up). 1989. 16.95 (ISBN 1-55546-735-0). Chelsea Hse.

Yakima Valley see Trolley Trails Through the West.

Yakimas: A Critical Bibliography. Helen H. Schuster. LC 81-48089. (Newberry Library D'Arcy McNickle Center for the History of the American Indian Bibliographical Ser.). (Illus.). 168p. 1982. pap. 5.95x (ISBN 0-253-36800-6). Ind U Pr.

Yako s Nami Bog. S. Lavroff. 73p. 1980. pap. 3.00 (ISBN 0-317-29142-4). Holy Trinity.

Yakshagana: A Dance Drama of India. Martha B. Ashton. 1977. 35.00x (ISBN 0-88386-972-1). South Asia Bks.

Yakshi from Didarganj. P. Lal. 42p. 1973. 8.00 (ISBN 0-88253-267-7); flexible bdg. 4.00 (ISBN 0-89253-518-0). Ind-US Inc.

Yakubu Gowon: Faith in a United Nigeria. J. D. Clarke. (Illus.). 150p. 1986. 29.50x (ISBN 0-7146-3286-4, F Cass Co). Biblio Dist.

Yakusa Tattoo. Jerry Ahern & Sharon Ahern. 320p. (Orig.). Date not set. pap. 3.95 (ISBN 0-671-62668-X). PB.

Yakuza: The Explosive Account of Japan's Criminal Underworld. David Kaplan & Alec Dubro. (Illus.). 352p. 1987. pap. 8.95 (ISBN 0-02-033990-9, Collier). Macmillan.

Yale: A History. Brooks M. Kelley. LC 73-86902. (University Ser.: No. 3). (Illus.). 592p. 1974. 37.50x (ISBN 0-300-01636-0). Yale U Pr.

Yale Critics: Deconstruction in America. Ed. by Johnathan Arac et al. LC 83-1127. (Theory & History of Literature Ser.: Vol. 6). 259p. 1983. 29.50x (ISBN 0-8166-1201-3); pap. 13.95 (ISBN 0-8166-1206-4). U of Minn Pr.

Yale Edition of Horace Walpole's Correspondence, Vol. 43. Horace Walpole. Ed. by Edwine M. Martz & Ruth K. McClure. LC 65-11182. 408p. 1983. text ed. 70.00t (ISBN 0-300-02711-7). Yale U Pr.

Yale Edition of Horace Walpole's Correspondence, Vols. 44-48. Horace Walpole. Ed. by Warren H. Smith & Edwine M. Martz. LC 65-11182. 424p. 1983. text ed. 345.00t (ISBN 0-300-02718-4). Yale U Pr.

Yale Edition of the George Eliot Letters. George Eliot. Ed. by Gordon S. Haight. Incl. Vol. 1. 1836-1851. 377p. 1954; Vol. 2. 1852-1858. 513p. 1954. text ed. 60.00 (ISBN 0-300-01088-5); Vol. 3. 1859-1861. 475p. 1954. text ed. 60.00 (ISBN 0-300-01089-3); Vol. 4. 1862-1868. 502p. 1955; Vol. 5. 1869-1873. 475p. 1955; Vol. 6. 1874-1877. 440p. 1955; Vol. 7. 1878-1880. 535p. 1955. LC 52-12063. 1975. text ed. 60.00 ea. Yale U Pr.

Yale French Studies: Everyday Life, No. 73. Yale French Studies Staff. 272p. 1987. pap. 13.95x (ISBN 0-300-04047-4). Yale U Pr.

Yale French Studies: The Anxiety of Anticipation. Sima Godfrey. (No. 66). 1984. pap. 13.95 (ISBN 0-300-03180-7). Yale U Pr.

Yale French Studies: The Language of Difference Writing in Quebec(ois) Ralph Sarkonak. (Yale French Studies: No. 65). 256p. 1983. pap. 12.95 (ISBN 0-300-03025-8). Yale U Pr.

Yale French Studies: The Lesson of Paul de Man, No. 69. Ed. by Peter Brooks et al. 288p. (Orig.). 1985. pap. 12.95x (ISBN 0-300-03409-1). Yale U Pr.

Yale French Studies, 71: Men Women of Letters. Ed. by Charles A. Porter. 200p. 1986. pap. 13.95x (ISBN 0-300-03697-3). Yale U Pr.

Yale Gertrude Stein. Gertrude Stein. LC 80-5398. 480p. 1980. text ed. 10.95 (ISBN 0-300-02574-2); pap. 10.95 (ISBN 0-300-02609-9). Yale U Pr.

Yale in the Civil War. Ellsworth Eliot, Jr. (Illus.). 1932. 95.00x (ISBN 0-685-69817-3). Elliots Bks.

Yale in the World War, 2 vols. George H. Nettleton. 1925. 150.00x (ISBN 0-685-40002-6). Elliots Bks.

Yale Law Journal: 1891-1986, 95 vols. Bound set. 3848.00x (ISBN 0-686-90101-0). Rothman.

Yale Lectures on Preaching. Henry W. Beecher. 1976. Repr. of 1872 ed. 39.00x (ISBN 0-403-06546-1, Regency). Scholarly.

Yale Lectures on Preaching. Henry W. Beecher. (Works of Henry Ward Beecher). vii, 359p. Repr. of 1873 ed. lib. bdg. 39.00 (ISBN 0-932051-02-2, Pub. by Am Repr Serv). Am Biog Serv.

Yale Manuscript. Matthew Arnold. Commentary by S. O. Ullmann. 1988. text ed. 45.00 (ISBN 0-472-10105-6). U of Mich Pr.

Yale Mathematics Building Competition: Architecture for a Time of Questioning. Ed. by Charles W. Moore & Nicholas Pyle. LC 73-77162. (Illus.). 128p. 1974. 35.00x (ISBN 0-300-01621-2). Yale U Pr.

Yale Men Who Died in the Second World War: A Memorial Volume of Biographical Sketches. Ed. by Eugene E. Kone. 1951. 75.00x (ISBN 0-685-89794-X). Elliots Bks.

Yale Near Eastern Researches, Vols. 1-3. Repr. of 1968 ed. Set. 82.50 (ISBN 0-404-60260-6); 27.50 ea. AMS Pr.

Yale Oriental Series: Babylonian Texts, Vols. 1-10. Repr. of 1966 ed. Set. 385.00 (ISBN 0-404-60250-9). AMS Pr.

Yale Oriental Series Researches, Vols. 1-24. (Yale Babylonian Collection). Repr. of 1949 ed. Set. 884.00 (ISBN 0-404-60270-3). AMS Pr.

Yale Papryi in the Beinecte Rare Book & Manuscript Library 1. John F. Oates & Alan E. Samuel. (American Society of Papyrology Ser.). 1974. 30.00 (ISBN 0-89130-696-X, 31-00-02). Scholars Pr GA.

Yale Papyri in the Beinecke Rare Book & Manuscript Library II. Susan A. Stephens. (American Studies in Papyrology: No. 24). 1985. 67.00 (ISBN 0-89130-513-0, 31 00 24). Scholars Pr GA.

Yale Psychological Studies see Experimental Study of Decision Types & Their Mental Correlates.

Yale Psychological Studies, N.S, Vol. 1, No. 1. Ed. by Charles H. Judd. Bd. with Theory of Psychological Dispositions. Charles A. Dubray. Repr. of 1905 ed; Psychological Studies from the Catholic University of America. Ed. by E. A. Pace. Repr. of 1905 ed; Visual Illusion of Motion During Eye Closure. Harvey Carr. Repr. of 1906 ed. (Psychology Monographs General & Applied: Vol. 7). pap. 36.00 (ISBN 0-8115-1406-4). Kraus Repr.

Yale Psychology Studies see Scientific Study of the College Student.

Yale Psychology Studies N. S. see Psychological Experiences Connected with Different Parts of Speech.

Yale Review Anthology. facs. ed. Yale Review. Ed. by Wilbur Cross & Helen MacAfee. LC 72-128336. (Essay Index Reprint Ser). 1942. 20.00 (ISBN 0-8369-2098-8). Ayer Co Pubs.

Yale Review of Law & Social Action: 1970-1973, Vols. 1-3. Bound set. 90.00x (ISBN 0-686-90102-9). Rothman.

Yale Review: Old Series, 19 Vols. & Index. LC 71-85769. 1969. Repr. of 1892 ed. 695.00x (ISBN 0-678-00532-X). Kelley.

Yale Romanic Studies, Vols 2-16, 18-21, & 23 in 20 vols. Repr. of 1944 ed. Set. 606.00 (ISBN 0-404-53200-4). AMS Pr.

Yale Series of Younger Poets, Vols. 1-64. Repr. of 1919 ed. 18.00 ea.; 1134.00 set (ISBN 0-404-53800-2). AMS Pr.

Yale Talks. Charles R. Brown. 1919. 29.50x (ISBN 0-686-51327-4). Elliots Bks.

Yale to Wade-Giles Exercise Book. Gerard P. Kok. 1.00 (ISBN 0-88710-124-0). Yale Far Eastern Pubns.

Yale Trivia. Christopher Harding. LC 85-73128. (Illus.). 221p. 1986. pap. 7.95 (ISBN 0-933341-24-5). Quinlan Pr.

Yale University Art Gallery Selections. Alan Shestack. Ed. by Alan Shestack. (Illus.). 112p. (Orig.). 1984. pap. 7.50x (ISBN 0-89467-027-1). Yale Art Gallery.

Yale University Publications in Anthropology, Nos. 1-7. LC 78-118240. 145p. 1970. pap. 15.00x (ISBN 0-87536-518-3). HRAFP.

Yale University Publications in Anthropology, NoS. 8-13. LC 70-118246. 163p. 1970. pap. 15.00x (ISBN 0-87536-520-5). HRAFP.

Yale Yesterdays. Clarence Deming. 254p. 1984. Repr. of 1915 ed. lib. bdg. 50.00 (ISBN 0-8492-4224-X). R West.

Yale's Podiatric Medicine. 3rd ed. Jeffrey Yale. (Illus.). 560p. 1986. 59.95 (ISBN 0-683-09319-3). Williams & Wilkins.

Ya'll Come. Arlie Duff. 200p. 1983. pap. 9.95 (ISBN 0-89015-404-X). Eakin Pr.

Yalta. Pierre De Senarclens. Tr. by Jasmer Singh from Fr. 224p. 1987. 24.95 (ISBN 0-88738-152-9). Transaction Bks.

Yalta Myths: An Issue in U. S. Politics, 1945-1955. Athan Theoharis. LC 70-105269. 280p. 1970. 28.00x (ISBN 0-8262-0088-5). U of Mo Pr.

Yankee Shoes: A Light Verse Saunter Through Our Second Hundred Years. Mollee Kruger. LC 75-21446. 100p. 1975. pap. 2.50 (ISBN 0-913184-03-9). Maryben Bks.

Yankee Skippers to the Rescue. Felix Riesenberg. LC 78-93374. (Essay Index Reprint Ser). 1940. 21.50 (ISBN 0-8369-1313-2). Ayer Co Pubs.

Yankee Stepfather: General O. O. Howard & the Freedmen. William S. McFeely. 368p. 1983. pap. 6.50 (ISBN 0-393-00537-2). Norton.

Yankee Stonecutters. facs. ed. Albert T. Gardner. LC 68-58790. (Essay Index Reprint Ser). 1945. 21.00 (ISBN 0-8369-0114-2). Ayer Co Pubs.

Yankee Stranger. Ed Figueroa & Dorothy Harshman. (Illus.). 231p. 1982. 11.00 (ISBN 0-682-49902-1). Exposition-Phoenix.

Yankee Stranger. Elswyth Thane. 1976. Repr. of 1954 ed. lib. bdg. 20.95x (ISBN 0-88411-963-7, Pub. by Aeonian Pr). Amereon Ltd.

Yankee, Swedish & Italian Acculturation & Economic Mobility in Jamestown, New York from 1860 to 1920. Paul A. Spengler. Ed. by Francesco Cordasco. LC 80-897. (American Ethnic Groups Ser.). 1981. lib. bdg. 38.50x (ISBN 0-405-13457-6). Ayer Co Pubs.

Yankee Teacher: The Life of William Torrey Harris. K. F. Leidecker. Repr. of 1946 ed. 39.00 (ISBN 0-527-56000-6). Kraus Repr.

Yankee Theatre; the Image of America on the Stage. Francis Hodge. text ed. 19.25 (ISBN 0-8369-8198-7, 8336). Ayer Co Pubs.

Yankee Traders, Old Coasters, & African Middlemen: A History of American Legitimate Trade with West Africa in the Nineteenth Century. George E. Brooks. LC 79-129253. (Pub. by Boston U Pr). 1970. 35.00 (ISBN 0-8419-8707-6, Africana). Holmes & Meier.

Yankee Trivia Book. Peter Farrow. (Illus.). 125p. (Orig.). 1985. pap. 5.95 (ISBN 0-912769-03-3). L Tapley.

Yankee Whalers in the South Seas. A. B. Whipple. LC 72-77517. (Illus.). 1972. pap. 6.75. C E Tuttle.

Yankee Wildlife. Hilbert R. Siegler. (Illus.). 1987. 9.95. Equity Pub NH.

Yankee Witches. Ed. by Frank McSherry et al. (Illus.). 315p. (Orig.). 1988. pap. 10.95 (ISBN 0-912769-32-7). L Tapley.

Yankees: An Illustrated History. George Sullivan & John Powers. (Illus.). 312p. 1982. pap. 12.95 (ISBN 0-13-971812-5). P-H.

Yankees at the Court. Susan M. Alsop. 1985. pap. 4.95. WSP.

Yankees at the Court. Susan M. Alsop. pap. 4.95. PB.

Yankee's Book of Whatsits. Ed. by Clarissa M. Silitch. LC 75-17109. (Illus.). 64p. (Orig.). 1975. pap. 4.95 (ISBN 0-911658-67-X). Yankee Bks.

Yankees by the Number: Complete History of the Uniform Number Assignments on the N. Y. Yankees Baseball Club, 1929 to the Present. George D. Wolf. 46p. (Orig.). 1986. pap. text ed. 9.95 (ISBN 0-9616503-0-3). G Wolf.

Yankees in Santo Domingo: Data & Official Documents. Max H. Urena. (Santo Domingo Ser.). 1979. lib. bdg. 69.95 (ISBN 0-8490-3018-8). Gordon Pr.

Yankees in the Republic of Texas: Their Origin & Impact. Arthur C. Burnett. 1952. 7.50 (ISBN 0-685-05007-6). A Jones.

Yankee's Lady. Kay McMahon. pap. 3.95 (ISBN 0-317-43142-0). Zebra.

Yankees Made Simple-The South Made Simple. Michael Hicks. (Illus.). 175p. (Orig.). 1982. pap. 7.95 (ISBN 0-932012-44-2). Texas Month Pr.

Yankees Trivia. Mike Getz. (Illus.). 183p. 1986. pap. 7.95 (ISBN 0-933341-82-2). Quinlan Pr.

Yanks Are Coming: American Immigration to Australia. Dennis L. Cuddy. LC 77-79060. 1977. 11.95 (ISBN 0-88247-459-6). R & E Pubs.

Yanks Are Coming: The United States in the First World War. Albert Marrin. LC 86-3585. (Illus.). 256p. (gr. 5 up). 1986. PLB 15.95 (ISBN 0-689-31209-1, Atheneum Childrens Bks). Macmillan.

Yanks Down Under, Nineteen Forty-One to Forty-Five: The American Impact on Australia. E. Daniel Potts & Annette Potts. (Illus.). 1986. 29.95 (ISBN 0-19-554500-1). Oxford U Pr.

Yanks from the South! The First Land Campaign of the Civil War; Rich Mountain, West Virginia. Francis E. Haselberger. LC 87-91999. (Illus.). 323p. (YA) (gr. 12). 1987. 18.00 (ISBN 0-9619953-0-0). Past Glories.

Yanks meet Reds: Recollections of U. S. & Soviet Vets from the Linkup in W. W. II. Intro. by & Mark C. Scott. (Illus.). 300p. 1988. pap. 9.95 (ISBN 0-88496-276-8). Capra Pr.

Yankton Sioux. Herbert T. Hoover. (Indians of North America Ser.). (Illus.). 104p. (gr. 5 up). 1988. lib. bdg. 16.95x (ISBN 1-55546-736-9). Chelsea Hse.

Yannis. John Giannaris. (Illus.). 200p. Date not set. price not set (ISBN 0-935819-04-5). Pilgrimage Pub.

Yannis Manglis. Harry T. Hionides. LC 74-31009. (Twayne's World Authors Ser.). 162p. 1975. 17.95 (ISBN 0-8057-2578-4). Irvington.

Yanomamo: The Fierce People. 3rd ed. Napolean Chagnon. LC 83-313. 224p. 1984. pap. text ed. 10.95 (ISBN 0-03-062328-6). HR&W.

Yanosh's Island. Yossi Abolafia. LC 86-19462. 32p. (gr. k-3). 1987. 11.75 (ISBN 0-688-06816-2); PLB 11.88 (ISBN 0-688-06817-0). Greenwillow.

Yanov Torah. Erwin Herman & Agnes Herman. LC 85-5269. (Illus.). 48p. (gr. 5 up). 1985. 10.95 (ISBN 0-930494-45-8); pap. 5.95 (ISBN 0-930494-46-6). Kar Ben.

Yanqui. Douglas Unger. LC 86-45159. 320p. 1986. 16.45i (ISBN 0-06-015645-7, HarpT). Har-Row.

Yanqui. Douglas Unger. 352p. 1988. pap. 3.95 (ISBN 0-345-34940-7). Ballantine.

Yanqui Dollar: The Contribution of U. S. Private Investment to Underdevelopment in Latin America. Susanne Bodenheimer & Dave Danning. (Illus.). 64p. 1971. pap. 3.00 (ISBN 0-916024-03-2). NA Cong Lat Am.

Yanqui Politics & the Isthmian Canal. Lawrence O. Ealy. LC 74-127385. 1971. 22.50x (ISBN 0-271-01126-2). Pa St U Pr.

Yantra Kosha. Sourindro M. Tagore. LC 74-24227. 1976. Repr. of 1875 ed. 27.50 (ISBN 0-404-12839-4). AMS Pr.

Yantras of Womanlove. Tee Corinne. 100p. (Orig.). 1982. pap. 6.95 (ISBN 0-930044-30-4). Naiad Pr.

Yao Ceremonial Paintings. Jacques Lemoine. 168p. 1982. 208.00x (ISBN 0-317-68732-8, Pub. by Han-Shan Tang Ltd). State Mutual Bk.

Yao-English Dictionary. Sylvia J. Lombard. Ed. by Herbert C. Purnell, Jr. LC 76-29799. (Cornell University Southeast Asia Program Ser.: No. 69). pap. 98.00 (ISBN 0-317-10129-3, 2010474). Bks Demand UMI.

Yao: The Chiikala Cha Wayao. new ed. Yohanna Barnaba Abdallah. Tr. by M. Sanderson. 132p. 1973. 26.00x (ISBN 0-7146-2462-4, BHA 02462, F Cass Co). Biblio Dist.

Yaoci Tulu: Catalogue of Yao Wares. Shaanxi Provincial Museum Staff. 10p. 1957. 175.00x (ISBN 0-317-45334-3, Pub. by Han-Shan Tang Ltd). State Mutual Bk.

YAP: Political Leadership & Culture Change in an Island Society. Sherwood G. Lingenfelter. 282p. 1975. text ed. 16.00x (ISBN 0-8248-0301-9). UH Pr.

Yapese-English Dictionary. John T. Jensen. LC 76-47495. (Pali Language Texts Micronesia Ser.). pap. 50.50 (ISBN 0-317-55704-1, 2029582). Bks Demand UMI.

Yapese Reference Grammar. John T. Jensen et al. LC 76-40952. (PALI Language Texts: Micronesia). 360p. (Orig.). 1977. pap. text ed. 17.50x (ISBN 0-8248-0476-7). UH Pr.

Yaquai Terror. Buck Gentry. (Scout Ser.: No. 11). (Orig.). 1983. pap. 2.50 (ISBN 0-317-00700-9). Zebra.

Yaqui Deer Songs Maso Bwikam: A Native American Poetry. Larry Evers & Felipe S. Molina. LC 86-19313. (Sun Tracks Ser.: No. 14). 239p. 1986. pap. 29.95x (ISBN 0-8165-0991-3); pap. 15.95 (ISBN 0-8165-0995-6). U of Ariz Pr.

Yaqui Easter. Muriel T. Painter. LC 74-153706. 40p. 1971. pap. 3.95 (ISBN 0-8165-0168-8). U of Ariz Pr.

Yaqui Life: The Personal Chronicle of a Yaqui Indian. Rosalio Moises et al. LC 76-56789. Orig. Title: Tall Candle: the Personal Chronicle of a Yaqui Indian. (Illus.). lx, 251p. 1977. 23.95x (ISBN 0-8032-0944-4); pap. 5.95 (ISBN 0-8032-5857-7, BB 637, Bison). U of Nebr Pr.

Yaqui Myths & Legends. Ruth W. Giddings. LC 60-63129. (Illus.). 180p. 1968. pap. 6.50 (ISBN 0-8165-0467-9). U of Ariz Pr.

Yaqui Resistance & Survival: The Struggle for Land & Autonomy, 1821-1910. Evelyn Hu-DeHart. LC 83-40265. (Illus.). 400p. 1984. text ed. 27.50x (ISBN 0-299-09660-2). U of Wis Pr.

Yaqui Women: Contemporary Life Histories. Jane Holden Kelley. LC 77-14063. (Illus.). vi, 263p. 1978. 32.50x (ISBN 0-8032-0912-6). U of Nebr Pr.

Yaquis: A Cultural History. Edward H. Spicer. LC 79-27660. 393p. 1980. 35.00x (ISBN 0-8165-0589-6). U of Ariz Pr.

Yarb & Cretine; or, Rising from Bonds. George B. Swayze. LC 72-4644. (Black Heritage Library Collection Ser.). Repr. of 1906 ed. 26.25 (ISBN 0-8369-9128-1). Ayer Co Pubs.

Yarborough of Texas. William G. Phillips. LC 74-107544. (Congressional Leadership Ser., Vol. 4). 1969. 4.95 (ISBN 0-87491-124-9); pap. 2.95 (ISBN 0-87491-125-7). Acropolis.

Yard of Sun. Christopher Fry. LC 76-121048. 1970. 9.95x (ISBN 0-19-501245-3). Oxford U Pr.

Yard of Tame Birds. K. Kirshina. (Illus.). 20p. 1978. pap. 1.99 (ISBN 0-8285-0003-7, Pub. by Progress Pubs USSR). Imported Pubns.

Yardbird Lives! Ed. by Ishmael Reed & Al Young. LC 77-18321. 1978. pap. 5.95 (ISBN 0-394-17041-5, E710, Ever). Grove.

Yardbird Suite: A Compendium of the Music & Life of Charlie Parker. Lawrence O. Koch. (Illus.). 300p. 1983. write for info. Bowling Green Univ.

Yardstick. Russell Epprecht. (New York Quarter Ser.: Vol. II). 208p. (Orig.). 1984. pap. 8.95 (ISBN 0-912195-11-8). Domesday Bks.

Yardsticks for Assessing Displacement & Neighborhood Change. 100p. 1982. 20.00 (ISBN 0-318-17710-2, DG 82-902). Pub Tech Inc.

Yardsticks of the Universe. Owen Bishop. LC 83-15782. (Illus.). 130p. 1984. pap. 5.95 (ISBN 0-911745-42-4). P Bedrick Bks.

Yareba Language. H. Weimer & N. Weimer. (Dictionaries of Papua New Guinea Ser.: No. 2). 525p. 1974. pap. 4.95 (ISBN 0-7263-0283-X); microfiche (6) 10.00 (ISBN 0-88312-726-1). Summer Inst Ling.

Yaril's Children. Marcia J. Bennett. 288p. 1988. pap. 3.50 (ISBN 0-345-34844-3, Del Rey). Ballantine.

Yarn: A Resource Guide for Handweavers. Celia Quinn. LC 85-60953. (Illus.). 112p. 1985. 3-ring binder 15.00 (ISBN 0-934026-17-3). Interweave.

Yarn Production & Properties. E. Dyson et al. 96p. 1974. 70.00x (ISBN 0-686-63811-5). State Mutual Bk.

Yarn Production & Properties. W. Nutter. 110p. 1971. 70.00x (ISBN 0-686-63812-3). State Mutual Bk.

Yarn Production & Properties. P. A. Smith. 123p. 1969. 70.00x (ISBN 0-686-63813-1). State Mutual Bk.

Yarn Revolution. P. W. Harrison. 162p. 1976. 60.00x (ISBN 0-686-63814-X). State Mutual Bk.

Yarn Winding: Some Technical Considerations & a Review of Yarn Tension Meters. Ed. by Wira Staff. 30.00x (ISBN 0-317-43585-X, Pub. by Wira Tech Group). State Mutual Bk.

Yaroshenko in St. Petersburg. I. V. Polenova. 222p. (Rus.). 1983. 18.00x (ISBN 0-317-57378-0, Pub. by Collets UK). State Mutual Bk.

Yaroslav the Wise. Ivan Kocherha. Tr. by Walter May. 129p. 1984. 4.95 (ISBN 0-8285-2699-0). Imported Pubns.

Yarrow. Charles De Lint. 256p. 1986. pap. 2.95 (ISBN 0-441-94000-5, Pub. by Ace Science Fiction). Ace Bks.

Yarrow: Its Poets & Poetry. R. Borland. 1890. Repr. 25.00 (ISBN 0-8274-3779-X). R West.

Yasavarman of Kanauj: Study of Political History, Society & Cultural Life of Northern India. Shyam M. Mishra. 1978. 15.00x (ISBN 0-8364-0105-0). South Asia Bks.

Yashima: An Ashura Noh by Zeami. Will Petersen. (Illus.). 1977. 20.00 (ISBN 0-685-50399-2, Pub by Mushinsha Bks); sewn in wrappers 5.95 (ISBN 0-685-50400-X). Small Pr Dist.

Yashimoto's Last Dive. Antony Trew. 288p. 1987. 16.95 (ISBN 0-312-01116-4). St Martin.

Yashpal Looks Back: Selections from an Autobiography. Yashpal. Ed. by Corinne Friend. 200p. 1981. text ed. 27.50x (ISBN 0-7069-1350-7, Pub. by Vikas India). Advent NY.

Yasir Arafat. Rebecca Stefoff. LC 87-32564. (World Leaders Ser.). (Illus.). 112p. (YA) (gr. 7 up). 1988. 16.95 (ISBN 1-55546-826-8). Chelsea Hse.

Yasir Arafat. Rebecca Stefoff. (World Leaders Ser.). (Illus.). 112p. (gr. 5 up). 1989. PLB 15.95. Chelsea Hse.

Yasmina's Daughter. Corinne Childs. 320p. 1984. pap. 3.25 (ISBN 0-8439-2125-0, Leisure Bks). Leisure NY.

Yassi Ada, Volume I: A Seventh-Century Byzantine Shipwreck. George F. Bass et al. LC 81-40401. (Nautical Archaeology Ser.: No. 1). (Illus.). 368p. 1982. 89.50x (ISBN 0-89096-063-1). Tex A&M Univ Pr.

Yasuo Kuniyoshi: Artist As Photographer. Bruce Weber. (Illus.). 80p. 1983. pap. 10.00 (ISBN 0-941276-02-3). Norton Gal Art.

Yates Garden Guide. 36th, rev. & enl. ed. Ed. by Yates Seeds Ltd. Staff. (Illus.). 310p. 1986. pap. 7.95 (ISBN 0-00-636721-6, Pub. by W Collins Australia). Intl Spec Bk.

Yatindramatadipika. Srinivasadasa. Tr. by Swami Adidevananda. (Sanskrit & Eng.). 2.95 (ISBN 0-87481-428-6). Vedanta Pr.

Yavanajataka of Sphujidhvaja, 2 vols. Tr. by David Pingree. (Harvard Oriental Ser: No. 48). 1978. Set. 90.00x (ISBN 0-674-96373-3). Harvard U Pr.

Yawar Fiesta. Jose M. Arguedas. Tr. by Frances H. Barraclough from Span. (Texas Pan American Ser.). 224p. 1985. 19.95x (ISBN 0-292-79601-3); pap. 8.95 (ISBN 0-292-79602-1). U of Tex Pr.

Yawara Stick & Police Baton. photocopy ed. J. McCauslin Moynahan, Jr. (Illus.). 88p. 1963. 10.75 (ISBN 0-398-04369-8). C C Thomas.

Yawn, et Al: A Key to Reserve Buoyancy for Human Flight. Millicent Linden. LC 78-64375. (Evolutionary New Material from Tension in Repose Ser.). (Illus.). 1978. saddle stitch 7.00 (ISBN 0-912628-06-5). M Linden NY.

Yazoo: Law & Politics in the New Republic: The Case of Fletcher v. Peck. C. Peter Magrath. LC 66-19584. 259p. pap. 67.40 (2030026). Bks Demand UMI.

Yazoo River. Frank E. Smith. LC 88-1123. (Illus.). 1988. 30.00 (ISBN 0-87805-353-0); pap. 14.95 (ISBN 0-87805-355-7). U Pr of Miss.

Y'bird, Vol. 1 No. 1. Ishmael Reed. (Illus.). 1977. pap. 4.95 (ISBN 0-931676-00-2). Reed & Youngs Quilt.

Ye Are Gods. Annalee Skarin. 343p. 1973. pap. 5.95 (ISBN 0-87516-344-0). DeVorss.

Ye Are My Friends. Marvin J. Ashton. 151p. 1982. 9.95 (ISBN 0-87747-934-8). Deseret Bk.

Ye Countie of Albemarle in Carolina: A Collection of Documents, 1664-1675. Ed. by William S. Powell. (Illus.). xxxii, 101p. 1958. 5.00 (ISBN 0-86526-000-1). NC Archives.

Ye Giglampz: A Weekly Illustrated Journal Devoted to Art, Literature & Satire. Jon C. Hughes. Ed. by Lafcadio Hearn & Henry Farny. (Illus.). 100p. 1973. 95.00 (ISBN 0-686-47721-9). Crossroad Bks Public.

Ye Gods! Anne S. Baumgartner. 192p. 1984. 14.95 (ISBN 0-8184-0349-7). Lyle Stuart.

Ye Historie of Ye Town of Greenwich, County of Fairfield & State of Connecticut. Spencer P. Mead. LC 79-15402. (Illus.). 1979. Repr. of 1911 ed. 37.50 (ISBN 0-916346-35-8). Harbor Hill Bks.

Ye Kingdome of Accawmacke: or The Eastern Shore of Virginia in the Seventeenth Century. Jennings C. Wise. x, 406p. 1988. pap. 20.00 (ISBN 1-55613-117-8). Heritage Bk.

Ye Olde Bards Inn. Thomas L. Hakes. (Illus.). 20p. 1985. pap. 4.00x (ISBN 0-915020-45-9). Bardic.

Ye Olde Dream Book. Fra. Zarathustra. LC 86-51388. 56p. (Orig.). 1987. pap. 15.00x (ISBN 0-939856-69-7). Tech Group.

Ye Olde Middlesex Courts. George J. Miller. 76p. (Orig.). pap. 7.00 (ISBN 1-55613-010-4). Heritage BK.

Ye Olden Blue Laws. Gustavus Myers. 274p. 1980. Repr. of 1921 ed. lib. bdg. 25.00 (ISBN 0-8495-3795-9). Arden Lib.

Ye Olden Time: English Customs in the Middle Ages. Emily S. Holt. LC 72-164343. 226p. 1971. Repr. of 1884 ed. 35.00x (ISBN 0-8103-3798-3). Gale.

Ye Search the Scriptures. Watchman Nee. Tr. by Stephen Kaung. 1974. 4.75 (ISBN 0-935008-46-2); pap. 3.75 (ISBN 0-935008-47-0). Christian Fellow Pubs.

Ye Shall Receive Power: The Amazing Miracle of Holy Spirit Baptism. Peter Popoff. Ed. by Don Tanner. LC 82-71629. (Illus.). 96p. 1982. pap. 2.00 (ISBN 0-938544-14-4). Faith Messenger.

Ye Solace of Pilgrimes. John Capgrave. Ed. by C. A. Mills. LC 78-63453. (Crusades & Military Orders: Second Ser.). Repr. of 1911 ed. 25.00 (ISBN 0-404-16375-0). AMS Pr.

Yeager: An Autobiography. Chuck Yeager & Leo Janos. LC 85-3959. (Illus.). 352p. 1985. 17.95 (ISBN 0-553-05093-1). Bantam.

Yeager: An Autobiography. Chuck Yeager & Leo Janos. 1986. 18.95 (ISBN 0-8161-4023-5, Large Print Bks). G K Hall.

Yeager: An Autobiography. Chuck Yeager & Leo Janos. 448p. (Orig.). 1986. pap. 4.95 (ISBN 0-553-25674-2). Bantam.

Yeah, But. Fanny Howe. 128p. (YA) (gr. 7 up). 1982. pap. 1.95 (ISBN 0-380-79186-2, 79186-2, Flare). Avon.

Yeah but, Children Need... Karen L. Rancourt. 144p. 1978. 18.95x (ISBN 0-87073-959-X). Schenkman Bks Inc.

Year. Suzanne Lange. LC 78-120787. (gr. 8 up). 1970. 14.95 (ISBN 0-87599-173-4). S G Phillips.

Year: A Celebration. Tom Tolnay. (Illus.). 32p. (Orig.). 1988. pap. 14.00. Birch Brook Pr.

Year after the Armada. Martin A. Hume. LC 71-110909. 1970. Repr. of 1896 ed. 25.50 (ISBN 0-8046-0891-1, Pub. by Kennikat). Assoc Faculty Pr.

Year after the Riots: American Responses to the Palestinian Crisis of 1929-30. Naomi W. Cohen. 200p. 1988. 24.95x (ISBN 0-8143-1914-9). Wayne St U Pr.

Year After Year: A Tale. Mrs. Caroline A. Clive. LC 79-8252. Repr. of 1858 ed. 44.50 (ISBN 0-404-61822-7). AMS Pr.

Year Ahead: Nineteen Eighty-Seven. Naisbitt Group & John Naisbitt. (Orig.). 1986. pap. 6.95 (ISBN 0-446-38342-2). Warner Bks.

Year Ahead: 1985. Naisbitt Group & John Naisbitt. 64p. 1985. pap. 6.95. AMACOM.

Year Ahead-1986: Ten Powerful Trends Shaping Your Future. The Naisbitt Group & John Naisbitt. 112p. (Orig.). 1985. pap. 5.95 (ISBN 0-446-38330-9). Warner Bks.

Year America Discovered Texas: Centennial '36. Kenneth B. Ragsdale. LC 86-30041. (Centennial Series of the Association of Former Students: No. 23). (Illus.). 352p. 1987. 18.95 (ISBN 0-89096-299-5). Tex A&M Univ Pr.

Year Amongst the Persians. Granville & Brown. (Century Classic Ser.). 1987. pap. 15.95 (ISBN 0-7126-0453-7, Pub. by Century Hutchinson). David & Charles.

Year Amongst the Persians: Impressions As to the Life, Character, & Thought of the People of Persia. 3rd ed. Edward G. Browne. LC 83-45722. Repr. of 1950 ed. 61.50 (ISBN 0-404-20046-X). AMS Pr.

Year & a Day: Poems. Carlos Baker. LC 63-14645. 1963. 7.95 (ISBN 0-8265-1064-7). Vanderbilt U Pr.

Year Around Conditioning for Army Football. Timothy Kearin. LC 80-82965. (Illus.). 128p. (Orig.). 1980. pap. 8.95 (ISBN 0-918438-60-8, PKEA0060). Leisure Pr.

Year Around: Poems for Children. Compiled by Alice I. Hazeltine. LC 72-11921. (Granger Index Reprint Ser.). (Decorations by Paula Hutchison). (YA) (gr. 7 up). 1973. Repr. of 1956 ed. 15.00 (ISBN 0-8369-6403-9). Ayer Co Pubs.

Year at Elk Meadow. Jackie Gilmore. (ps-3). 1986. pap. 3.95 (ISBN 0-911797-24-6). R Rinehart Inc.

Year at Great Dixter. Christopher Lloyd. LC 86-51644. (Illus.). 192p. 1987. 24.95 (ISBN 0-670-80982-9). Viking.

Year of the Gopher. Phyllis R. Naylor. LC 86-17317. 224p. (YA) (gr. 7 up). 1987. 13.95 (ISBN 0-689-31333-0, Atheneum Childrens Bks). Macmillan.
Year of the Gopher. Phyllis R. Naylor. 208p. (YA) (gr. 7 up). 1988. pap. 2.95 (ISBN 0-553-27131-8, Starfire). Bantam.
Year of the Gorilla. George B. Schaller. LC 64-13946. (Illus.). 1964. pap. 5.50 (ISBN 0-226-73638-5, P209, Phoen). U of Chicago Pr.
Year of the Gorilla. George B. Schaller. (Illus.). 304p. 1988. pap. 12.95 (ISBN 0-226-73648-2). U of Chicago Pr.
Year of the Handicapped. J. C. Poole. 118p. 1983. 8.00 (ISBN 0-682-49990-0). Exposition-Phoenix.
Year of the Hare. Helen Luster. pap. 2.95 (ISBN 0-686-18860-8). Man-Root.
Year of the Hiker. J. B. Keane. 94p. 1969. pap. 7.95 (ISBN 0-85342-090-4, Pub. by Mercier Pr Ireland). Irish Bks Media.
Year of the Hopi. Tyrone Stewart et al. LC 79-18865. (Illus.). 96p. 1982. pap. 14.95 (ISBN 0-8478-0427-5). Rizzoli Intl.
Year of the Horse. Alfred Koehn. 45p. 1942. 350.00x (ISBN 0-317-68530-9, Pub. by Han-Shan Tang Ltd). State Mutual bk.
Year of the Hot Jock & Other Stories. Irvin Faust. 228p. 1985. 15.95 (ISBN 0-525-24343-7, 01549-460, Pub. by W Abrahams Bk). Dutton.
Year of the Indians. Gerald N. Hill. (Illus.). 54p. (Orig.). (gr. 4-7). 1985. pap. 4.95 (ISBN 0-912133-06-6). Hilltop Pub Co.
Year of the Intern. Robin Cook. pap. 2.95 (ISBN 0-451-14981-5, Sig). NAL.
Year of the King: An Actor's Diary & Sketchbook. Antony Sher. LC 86-88. (Illus.). 256p. 1987. Repr. of 1985 ed. 17.95 (ISBN 0-87910-064-8). Limelight Edns.
Year of the Locust. David Nixon. 138p. (Orig.). 1980. pap. 3.95 (ISBN 0-8341-0675-2). Beacon Hill.
Year of the Longley. Willis Johnson. LC 78-70046. (Illus.). 1978. pap. 4.75 (ISBN 0-941238-01-6). Penobscot Bay.
Year of the Lord. Herbert O'Driscoll. 143p. (Orig.). 1987. pap. 8.95 (ISBN 0-8192-1400-0). Morehouse.
Year of the Lord: Reflections on the Sunday Readings. Alfred McBride. 240p. cycle A 7.25 (ISBN 0-697-01847-4); cycle B 7.25 (ISBN 0-697-01848-2); cycle C 7.25 (ISBN 0-697-01849-0). Wm C Brown.
Year of the Lord's Favor: Preaching the Three-Year Lectionary. Sherman E. Johnson. 300p. 1983. pap. 13.95 (ISBN 0-8164-2359-8, HarpR). Har-Row.
Year of the Lucy. Anne McCaffrey. 320p. 1986. 15.95 (ISBN 0-312-93981-7, Dist. by St. Martin's Press). Tor Bks.
Year of the Lucy. Anne McCaffrey. 320p. 1987. pap. 3.95 (ISBN 0-8125-8565-8). Tor Bks.
Year of the Monkey. Carole Berry. 288p. 1988. 16.95 (ISBN 0-312-01850-9). St Martin.
Year of the Monkey: Revolt on Campus, 1968-69. William McGill. 304p. 1982. text ed. 19.95 (ISBN 0-07-044997-X). McGraw.
Year of the Oath. George R. Stewart. LC 77-150422. (Civil Liberties in American History Ser.). 1971. Repr. of 1950 ed. lib. bdg. 22.50 (ISBN 0-306-70103-0). Da Capo.
Year of the Perfect Christmas Tree: An Appalachian Tale. Gloria M. Houston. LC 87-24551. (Illus.). 32p. (ps-3). 1988. 12.95 (ISBN 0-8037-0299-X, 01258-370); PLB 12.89 (ISBN 0-8037-0300-7). Dial Bks Young.
Year of the Phoenix, Gandhi's Pivotal Year: 1893-94. T. K. Mahadovan. 196p. 1985. 5.00 (ISBN 0-317-60741-3). World Without War Pubns.
Year of the Prince. Right On Editors. 64p. 1984. 5.95. Sharon Pubns.
Year of the Prince. Sharon Starbooks. (Star Bk.). (Illus.). 64p. (Orig.). 1984. pap. 4.95 (ISBN 0-451-82108-4, Sig). NAL.
Year of the Ransom. Poul Anderson. 1988. 15.95 (ISBN 0-8027-6800-8). Walker & Co.
Year of the Silence. Madge Reinhardt. LC 78-59573. 177p. 1978. pap. 5.50 (ISBN 0-917162-08-0). Back Row Pr.
Year of the Sword. Avner Gold. Ed. by Y. Y. Reinman. (Ruach Ami Ser.: No. 3). (Illus.). 112p. (gr. 5 up). 1984. pap. 4.95 (ISBN 0-935063-02-1). CIS Comm.
Year of the Three Kaisers: Bismarck & the German Succession, 1887-1888. J. Alden Nichols. LC 86-7028. 432p. 1987. 34.95 (ISBN 0-252-01307-7). U of Ill Pr.
Year of the Tiger. Bernard Wolf. LC 87-22007. (Illus.). 128p. (gr. 5 up). 1988. PLB 14.95 (ISBN 0-02-793390-3). Macmillan.
Year of the Trout. Steve Raymond. LC 85-6155. (Illus.). 208p. 1985. 19.95 (ISBN 0-8329-0384-1, Pub. by Winchester Pr). New Century.
Year of the Trout. Steve Raymond. 1988. 7.95 (ISBN 0-671-66173-6, Fireside). S&S.
Year of the Uprising. Stanlake Samkange. (African Writers Ser.). 1978. pap. text ed. 7.00 (ISBN 0-435-90190-7). Heinemann Ed.
Year of the Vulture. Amita Malik. 1972. 16.00 (ISBN 0-8046-8817-6, Pub. by Kennikat). Assoc Faculty Pr.
Year of the Whale. Victor B. Scheffer. LC 68-57084. (Illus.). 224p. 1969. pap. 8.95 (ISBN 0-684-71886-3, ScribT). Scribner.
Year of the Wild Boar. Helen Mears. LC 73-7457. 346p. 1973. Repr. of 1942 ed. lib. bdg. 35.00x (ISBN 0-8371-6936-4, MEWB). Greenwood.
Year of the World. William B. Scott. LC 72-148299. Repr. of 1846 ed. 12.00 (ISBN 0-404-05649-0). AMS Pr.
Year of Victory. Ivan Konev. Tr. by David Mishne. (Illus.). 248p. 1984. 7.95 (ISBN 0-8285-2826-8, Pub. by Progress Pubs USSR). Imported Pubns.
Year of Victory. Ivan Konev. 248p. 1984. 22.00x (ISBN 0-317-54529-9, Pub. by Collets (UK)). State Mutual Bk.
Year of Wreck. facsimile ed. George C. Benham. LC 75-38639. (Black Heritage Library Collection). Repr. of 1880 ed. 26.00 (ISBN 0-8369-8997-X). Ayer Co Pubs.
Year on a Monitor & the Destruction of Fort Sumter. Alvah F. Hunter. Ed. by Craig L. Symonds & William N. Still, Jr. (Classics in Maritime History Ser.). (Illus.). 184p. 1987. 21.95 (ISBN 0-87249-531-0). U of SC Pr.
Year One: A Lesson of Hope from Personal Tragedy. John Tittensor. 107p. 1987. pap. 4.95 (ISBN 0-14-007299-3). Penguin.
Year Participated. Rudolf Steiner. Tr. by Owen Barfield from Ger. 52p. 1986. pap. 9.95 (ISBN 0-85440-790-1, Pub. by Steinerbooks). Anthroposophic.
Year 'Round Activities for Four-Year-Old Children. Anthony Coletta & Kathleen Coletta. LC 85-30934. 248p. 1986. pap. 17.50x (ISBN 0-87628-983-9). Ctr Appl Res.
Year 'Round Activities for Three-Year-Old Children. Anthony Coletta & Kathleen Coletta. LC 85-26998. 244p. 1986. pap. 17.50x (ISBN 0-87628-982-0). Ctr Appl Res.
Year 'Round Activities for Two-Year-Old Children. Anthony Coletta & Kathleen Coletta. LC 85-24264. 254p. 1986. pap. 17.50x (ISBN 0-87628-981-2). Ctr Appl Res.
Year-Round, All-Occasion Make Your Own Greeting Card Book. Charles Bennett et al. LC 84-8459. (Illus.). 1984. pap. 7.95 (ISBN 0-87477-321-0). J P Tarcher.
Year-Round Business Tax Planning: One Hundred Fifty-Three Ways to Win After Tax Reform. Irving L. Blackman. (Special Report Ser.: No. 1401630315x). 55p. (Orig.). 1987. pap. 24.00 (ISBN 0-916181-28-6). Blackman Kallick Bartelstein.
Year-Round Crafts for Kids. Barbara L. Dondiego. (Illus.). 256p. 1987. 19.95 (ISBN 0-8306-0904-0); pap. 12.95 (ISBN 0-8306-2904-1). TAB Bks.
Year Round Flower Gardener. Anne Halpin. 1989. 22.95 (ISBN 0-671-64950-7); pap. 15.95 (ISBN 0-671-67711-X). S&S.
Year Round Hobbycraft. Willard Waltner & Elma Waltner. (Illus.). (gr. 4 up). 6.70 (ISBN 0-8313-0100-7). Lantern.
Year Round Holidays. Janet Dellosa & Patti Carson. (Stick-Out-Your-Neck Ser.). (Illus.). 32p. (ps-2). 1984. pap. 1.59 (ISBN 0-88724-058-5, CD-8043). Carson-Dellos.
Year-Round Personal Tax Planning: One Hundred Ninety-One Ways to Win after Tax Reform. Irving L. Blackman. (Special Report Ser.: No. 13). 59p. 1987. pap. 24.00 (ISBN 0-916181-27-8). Blackman Kallick Bartelstein.
Year-Round Preschool Activity Patterns. Cathy Falk. 48p. (Orig.). (ps-k). 1983. pap. 4.95 (ISBN 0-87239-680-0, 2141). Standard Pub.
Year-Round Programs for Young Players. Aileen Fisher. LC 85-8153. 334p. (Orig.). (gr. 3-7). 1985. 13.95 (ISBN 0-8238-0266-3). Plays.
Year 'Round Quotebook. E. C. McKenzie. 1985. pap. 4.95 (ISBN 0-8010-6184-9). Baker Bk.
Year 'Round Sermon Outlines. C. W. Keiningham. (Pulpit Library). 96p. 1987. pap. 3.95 (ISBN 0-8010-5483-4). Baker Bk.
Year-Round Turkey Cookbook: A Guide to Delicious, Nutritious Dining with Today's Versatile Turkey. Barbara Gibbons. (Illus., Orig.). 1979. pap. text ed. 6.95 (ISBN 0-07-023261-X). McGraw.
Year Santa Overslept. E. Maurine Rathje. (Illus.). 32p. (gr. 1-2). 1987. 6.95 (ISBN 0-89962-610-6). Todd & Honeywell.
Year the Lights Came On. Terry Kay. LC 76-15170. 1976. 8.95 (ISBN 0-395-24403-X). HM.
Year the Summer Died. Patricia L. Gauch. 160p. (gr. 7 up). 1985. 12.95 (ISBN 0-399-21114-4, Putnam). Putnam Pub Group.
Year the World Was Out of Step with Jancy Fried. Jean Fiedler. LC 81-47530. 156p. 1981. 9.95 (ISBN 0-15-299818-7, HJ). HarBraceJ.
Year They Sold Wall Street. Tim Carrington. 256p. 1987. pap. 6.95 (ISBN 0-14-009794-5). Penguin.
Year They Sold Wall Street: The Inside Story of the Shearson-American Express Merger, and How it Changed Wall Street Forever. Timothy Carrington. (Illus.). 235p. 1985. 17.95 (ISBN 0-395-34394-1); pap. 7.95. HM.
Year Three. Foster H. Shannon. (Green Leaf Bible Ser.). 170p. (gr. 3 up). 1986. pap. 15.00 (ISBN 0-938462-07-5). Green Leaf CA.
Year to Remember. Bruce Van Blair. 280p. (Orig.). 1988. pap. 9.95 (ISBN 0-934125-05-8). Glen Abbey Bks.
Year Two Thousand. Ed. by John R. Stott. LC 83-12871. 179p. 1983. pap. 7.95 (ISBN 0-87784-845-9). Inter-Varsity.
Year Two Thousand. Raymond Williams. LC 83-21966. 269p. 1984. 16.45 (ISBN 0-394-53552-9); pap. 7.16 (ISBN 0-394-72259-0). Pantheon.
Year Two Thousand: A Critical Biography of Edward Bellamy. Sylvia Bowman. 1979. Repr. of 1958 ed. lib. bdg. 29.00x (ISBN 0-374-90879-6, Octagon). Hippocrene Bks.
Year Two Thousand & Mental Retardation. Ed. by Stanley C. Plog & M. B. Santamour. (Current Topics In Mental Health Ser.). (Illus.). 240p. 1980. 35.00x (ISBN 0-306-40252-1, Plenum Pr). Plenum Pub.
Year with Mary. John Paul, II. Tr. by Anthony M. Buono from Ital. 320p. (Orig.). 1986. pap. 7.00 (ISBN 0-89942-370-1, 370/22). Catholic Bk Pub.
Year with New England's Birds: A Guide to Twenty-Five Field Trips. Sandy Mallett. LC 77-26352. (Illus.). 120p. 1978. pap. 5.95 (ISBN 0-912274-87-5). Backcountry Pubns.
Year with the Baha'is of India & Burma. Sidney Sprague. (Historical Reprint Ser.). (Illus.). 1986. 8.95 (ISBN 0-933770-57-X). Kalimat.
Year with the Ladies of Llangollen. Ed. by Elizabeth Mavor. 240p. 1987. pap. 5.95 (ISBN 0-14-006976-3). Penguin.
Year with Two Winters. Martin Robbins. 65p. (Orig.). 1984. pap. 8.95 (ISBN 0-932662-55-2). St Andrews NC.
Year Without a Santa Claus. Phyllis McGinley. (Illus.). (gr. k-3). 1957. 12.70i (ISBN 0-397-30399-8, Lipp Jr Bks); PLB 12.89 (ISBN 0-397-31969-X). HarpJ.
Year Without Michael. Susan B. Pfeffer. 176p. (Orig.). (YA) (gr. 7-12). 1987. 13.95 (ISBN 0-553-05430-9, Starfire). Bantam.
Year Without Michael. Susan B. Pfeffer. 176p. (YA) 1988. pap. 2.95 (ISBN 0-553-27373-6, Starfire). Bantam.
Yearbook. Melissa Davis. 224p. (Orig.). (YA) (gr. 7 up). 1987. pap. 2.50 (ISBN 0-590-40205-6, Point). Scholastic Inc.
Yearbook. David Marlow. Date not set. pap. 1.95 (ISBN 0-449-23551-3, Crest). Fawcett.
Yearbook. David Marlowe. 228p. 1982. pap. 2.50 (ISBN 0-449-70029-1, Juniper). Fawcett.
Yearbook, No. 46. Ed. by James W. Scott. LC 37-13376. (Association of Pacific Coast Geographers Ser.). (Illus.). 160p. 1985. pap. text ed. 7.00x (ISBN 0-87071-246-2). Oreg St U Pr.
Yearbook Commercial Arbitration, No. V. Ed. by P. Sanders. 350p. 1980. pap. 24.00 (ISBN 90-268-1152-7, Pub. by Kluwer Law Netherlands). Kluwer Academic.
Yearbook Commercial Arbitration, Vol. I. Ed. by P. Sanders. 266p. 1976. pap. 14.00 (ISBN 0-686-40945-0, Pub. by Kluwer Law Netherlands). Kluwer Academic.
Yearbook Commercial Arbitration, Vol. II. Ed. by P. Sanders. 294p. 1977. 17.00 (ISBN 90-26-8092-39, Pub. by Kluwer Law Netherlands). Kluwer Academic.
Yearbook Commercial Arbitration, Vol. VI. Ed. by P. Sanders. 465p. 1982. 30.00 (ISBN 90-654-4046-1, Pub. by Kluwer Law Netherlands). Kluwer Academic.
Yearbook Commercial Arbitration, Vol. VIII. Ed. by P. Sanders. 432p. 1983. pap. 30.00 (ISBN 90-654-4118-2, Pub. by Kluwer Law Netherlands); Avail. Vols. I-V, 1976-1980. 75.00 (ISBN 90-654-4129-8). Kluwer Academic.
Yearbook Commercial Arbitration, Vol. III. Ed. by P. Sanders. 334p. 1978. pap. 20.00 (ISBN 90-26-8096-97). Kluwer Academic.
Yearbook Commercial Arbitration, Vol. IV. Ed. by P. Sanders. 420p. 1979. pap. 24.00 (ISBN 90-26-8106-87). Kluwer Academic.
Yearbook Commercial Arbitration: A Publication under the Auspices of the International Council for Commercial Arbitration (ICCA, Vol. 3. Ed. & compiled by Pieter Sanders. 1978. pap. 24.00 (ISBN 90-207-0729-9, Pub. by Martinus Nijhoff Netherlands). Kluwer Academic.
Yearbook Commercial Arbitration 1981, Vol. VI. Ed. by P. Sanders. 352p. 24.00 (ISBN 0-686-40989-2, Pub. by Kluwer Law Netherlands). Kluwer Academic.
Yearbook Commercial Arbitration 1982, Vol. VII. Ed. by P. Sanders. 465p. 30.00 (ISBN 90-65440-46-1, Pub. by Kluwer Law Netherlands). Kluwer Academic.
Yearbook for Traditional Music. Ed. by D. Christensen. Orig. Title: International Folk Music Council Journal. 230p. (Eng., Fr. & Ger.). 28.00 (ISBN 0-318-14547-2). Intl Coun Trad.
Yearbook II: Best All-Round Couple. Melissa Davis. 208p. (gr. 7 up). 1988. pap. 2.50 (ISBN 0-590-41546-8, Point). Scholastic Inc.
Yearbook Killer. Tom Philbin. (Orig.). 1981. pap. 1.95 (ISBN 0-449-14400-3, GM). Fawcett.
Yearbook Nineteen Eighty Mit deutschem Registerschluessel. Ed. by W. Theilheimer. (Synthetic Methods of Organic Chemistry Ser.: Vol. 34). xx, 524p. 1980. 332.00 (ISBN 3-8055-0327-X). S Karger.
Yearbook Nineteen Eighty-Seven. A. F. Finch. (Theilheimer's Synthetic Methods of Organic Chemistry Ser.: Vol. 41). xx, 520p. 1987. 393.50 (ISBN 3-8055-4496-0). S Karger.
Yearbook Nineteen, 1983. Ed. by A. F. Finch. (Theilheimer's Synthetic Methods of Organic Chemistry Ser.: Vol. 37). xxiv, 576p. 1983. 356.00 (ISBN 3-8055-3600-3). S Karger.
Yearbook of Agriculture, 1939: Food & Life; Part 1: Human Nutrition. U.S. Department of Agriculture. LC 75-26321. (World Food Supply Ser). (Illus.). 1976. Repr. of 1939 ed. 32.00x (ISBN 0-405-07797-1). Ayer Co Pubs.
Yearbook of Agriculture, 1940: Farmers in a Changing World. U.S. Department of Agriculture. LC 75-26320. (Illus.). 1976. Repr. of 1940 ed. 92.50x (ISBN 0-405-07796-3). Ayer Co Pubs.
Yearbook of American & Canadian Churches, 1988. Ed. by Constant H. Jacquet. 304p. 1988. pap. 18.95 (ISBN 0-687-46643-1). Abingdon.
Yearbook of American & Canadian Church 1986. Ed. by Constant H. Jacquet, Jr. 304p. (Orig.). 1986. pap. 17.95 (ISBN 0-687-46641-5). Abingdon.
Yearbook of American & Canadian Churches, 1987. Ed. by H. Constant Jacquet. 304p. 1987. pap. 18.95 (ISBN 0-687-46642-3). Abingdon.
Yearbook of American Universities & College. George Kurian. (Garland Reference Library of Social Science). c, 1637p. 1987. lib. bdg. 60.00 (ISBN 0-8240-7942-6). Garland Pub.
Yearbook of Astronomy, 1985. Ed. by Patrick Moore. (Illus.). 1984. pap. 9.95 (ISBN 0-393-30203-2). Norton.
Yearbook of Astronomy, 1986. 1985. 15.95 (ISBN 0-393-30254-7). Norton.
Yearbook of Astronomy, 1987. Ed. by Patrick Moore. 1986. 16.95 (ISBN 0-393-02391-5). Norton.
Yearbook of Astronomy, 1988. Ed. by Patrick Moore. (Illus.). 1987. 18.95 (ISBN 0-393-02526-8). Norton.
Yearbook of Astronomy, 1989. 27th ed. Patrick Moore. (Illus.). 1989. 19.95 (ISBN 0-393-02633-7). Norton.
Yearbook of Comparative & General Literature, No. 32, 1983. National Council of Teachers of English, Comparative Literature Committee. pap. 40.00 (ISBN 0-317-30475-5, 2024821). Bks Demand UMI.
Yearbook of Comparative & General Literature: No. 31, 1982. National Council of Teachers of English, Comparative Literature Committee. pap. 41.80 (ISBN 0-317-29731-7, 2022204). Bks Demand UMI.
Yearbook of Comparative & General Literature, 1984, No. 33. National Council of Teachers of English, Comparative Literature Committee. pap. 32.00 (2026243). Bks Demand UMI.
Yearbook of Construction Articles, 3 vols. 145.00 ea. Vol. 1, 1982. Vol. 2, 1983. Vol. 3, 1984. Fed Pubns Inc.
Yearbook of Construction Statistics. Incl. 1963-1972. pap. 19.00 (E.74.XVII.9); 1964-1973. pap. 22.00 (E.75.XVII.10); 1965-1974. pap. 22.00 (E.76.XVII.8); 1966-1975. pap. 26.00 (E.77.XVII.13); 1967-1976. pap. 21.00 (E.78XVII.12); 1969-1978. (International Statistics). pap. 25.00 (E.80.XVII.12). UN.
Yearbook of Drug Abuse, Vol. I. Ed. by Leon Brill & Ernest Harms. LC 70-174271. (Illus.). 386p. 1973. text ed. 44.95 (ISBN 0-87705-060-0). Human Sci Pr.
Yearbook of Drug Therapy, 1988. Hollister. 1988. 45.00 (ISBN 0-8151-4615-9). Year Bk Med.
Yearbook of Education, Nineteen Fifty-Eight: The Secondary School Curriculum. facsimile ed. Ed. by George Z. Bereday & Joseph A. Lauwerys. LC 73-38704. (Essay Index Reprint Ser). Repr. of 1958 ed. 32.00 (ISBN 0-8369-2680-3). Ayer Co Pubs.
Yearbook of Education, Nineteen Fifty-Nine: Higher Education. facsimile ed. Ed. by George Z. Bereday & Joseph A. Lauwerys. LC 73-38704. (Essay Index Reprint Ser). Repr. of 1959 ed. 29.00 (ISBN 0-8369-2681-1). Ayer Co Pubs.
Yearbook of Education, Nineteen Fifty-Seven: Education & Philosophy. facsimile ed. Ed. by George Z. Bereday & Joseph A. Lauwerys. LC 73-38704. (Essay Index Reprint Ser). Repr. of 1957 ed. 22.00 (ISBN 0-8369-2679-X). Ayer Co Pubs.
Yearbook of Emergency Medicine, 1985. Wagner. 1985. 44.95 (ISBN 0-8151-9056-5). Year Bk Med.
Yearbook of Emergency Medicine, 1988. Wagner. 1988. 47.00 (ISBN 0-8151-9059-X). Year Bk Med.
Yearbook of European Law, Vol. 5: 1985. Ed. by F. G. Jacobs. 492p. 1987. 85.00 (ISBN 0-19-825546-2). Oxford U Pr.
Yearbook of European Law, 1981, Vol. 1. Ed. by F. G. Jacobs. 1982. 89.00x (ISBN 0-19-825384-2). Oxford U Pr.
Yearbook of European Law, 1982, Vol. 2. Ed. by F. G. Jacobs. 1983. 105.00x (ISBN 0-19-825490-3). Oxford U Pr.
Yearbook of European Law, 1983, 3 vols. Ed. by F. G. Jacobs. 1984. 85.00x (ISBN 0-19-825504-7). Oxford U Pr.
Yearbook of European Law, 1984. Ed. by F. G. Jacobs. 480p. 1986. 85.00x (ISBN 0-19-825521-7). Oxford U Pr.
Yearbook of European Law, 1986, Vol. 6. Ed. by F. G. Jacobs. 504p. 1987. 98.00 (ISBN 0-19-825605-1). Oxford U Pr.
Yearbook of European Law, 1987, Vol. 7. Ed. by Francis Jacobs. 500p. 1988. 110.00 (ISBN 0-19-825625-6). Oxford U Pr.

Yearbook of the International Law Commission, Vol. I. 1982. 35.00 (ISBN 92-1-133257-5, E.83.V.2). UN.
Yearbook of the International Law Commission, Vol. I. 1983. 33.00 (ISBN 92-1-133264-8, E.84.V.6). UN.
Yearbook of the International Law Commission: 1985, Vol. II/Pt. I. 1986. write for info. (ISBN 92-1-133279-6, E.86.V.5). UN.
Yearbook of the International Law Commission, 1984, Vol. II, Pt. 2. 232p. 1985. 13.50 (E.85.V.7). UN.
Yearbook of the International Law Commission 1982: Documents of the Thirty-Fourth Session, Vol. II, Pt. I. 282p. 1986. pap. text ed. 33.00 (ISBN 92-1-133334-2, E.83.V.3). UN.
Yearbook of the International Law Commission 1983: Documents of the Thirty-Fifth Session, Vol. II, Pt. I. 232p. 1986. pap. text ed. 23.00 (E.84.V.7/PT. 1). UN.
Yearbook of the International Law Commission 1984: Documents of the 36th Session, Vol. I, Pt. I. 176p. 1986. 17.50 (ISBN 92-1-133340-7, E.85.V.7). UN.
Yearbook of the International Law Commission 1982: Report of the Commission to the General Assembly on the Work of the 34th Session, Vol. II, Pt. 2. 148p. 1985. pap. 16.50 (E.83.V.3/PT. 2). UN.
Yearbook of the International Law Commission 1983: Report of the Commission to the General Assembly on the Work of Its Thirty-fifth Session, Vol. II, Pt. 2. 94p. 1985. pap. 12.50 (ISBN 92-1-133331-8, E.84.V.7/PT. 2). UN.
Yearbook of the International Law Commission 1984: Report of the Commission to the General Assembly on the Work of Its 36th Session, Vol. II pt. 2. 112p. 1986. 13.50 (ISBN 92-1-133337-7, E.85.V.7). UN.
Yearbook of the International Law Commission 1984: Summary Records of the Meetings of the 36th Session, 7 May-27 July 1984, Vol. I. 356p. 1986. 35.00 (ISBN 92-1-133336-9, E.85.V.6). UN.
Yearbook of the International Law Commission 1985: Summary Records of the Meetins of the 37th Session 6 May - 26 July 1985, Vol. I. 352p. 1987. 35.00 (ISBN 92-1-133341-5, E.86.V.4). UN.
Yearbook of the International Law Commission 1986, Vol. 2, Pt. 2: Report of the Commission to the General Assembly on the Work of its 38th Session. 68p. 1988. pap. 9.00 (ISBN 92-1-133298-2, E.87.V.8 (PART II)). UN.
Yearbook of the United Nations. 1981. 75.00 (ISBN 92-1-100038-6, E.84.I.1). UN.
Yearbook of the United Nations, Vol. 11. 604p. 1957. Repr. 58.00 (E.58.I.1). UN.
Yearbook of the United Nations, Vol. 12. 622p. 1958. 35.00 (E.59.I.1). UN.
Yearbook of the United Nations, Vol. 13. 660p. 1959. Repr. 58.00 (E.60.I.1). UN.
Yearbook of the United Nations, Vol. 14. 840p. 1960. 35.00 (E.61.I.1). UN.
Yearbook of the United Nations, Vol. 15. 813p. 1961. 35.00 (E.62.I.1). UN.
Yearbook of the United Nations, Vol. 16. 783p. 1962. 35.00 (E.63.I.1). UN.
Yearbook of the United Nations, Vol. 18. 710p. 1964. Repr. 58.00 (E.65.I.1). UN.
Yearbook of the United Nations, Vol. 24. 1177p. 1970. 35.00 (E.72.I.1). UN.
Yearbook of the United Nations, Vol. 25. 861p. 1971. 35.00 (E.73.I.1). UN.
Yearbook of the United Nations, Vol. 26. 861p. 1972. 35.00 (E.74.I.1). UN.
Yearbook of the United Nations, Vol. 27. 1048p. 1973. 35.00 (E.75.I.1). UN.
Yearbook of the United Nations, Vol. 28. 1170p. 1974. 35.00 (E.76.I.1). UN.
Yearbook of the United Nations, Vol. 29. 1975. 35.00x (E.77.I.1). UN.
Yearbook of the United Nations, Vol. 30. 1153p. 1976. 42.00 (E.78.I.1). UN.
Yearbook of the United Nations, Vol. 32. 1978. 60.00 (E.80.I.1). UN.
Yearbook of the United Nations, Vol. 33. 1450p. 1979. 72.00 (E.82.I.1). UN.
Yearbook of the United Nations, Vol. 34. 1450p. 1980. 72.00 (E.83.I.1). UN.
Yearbook of the United Nations, Vol. 36. 1716p. 1982. 75.00 (ISBN 92-1-100295-8, E.85.I.1). UN.
Yearbook of the United Nations: 1946-1977. Incl. Vol. 3. 1948-49. 1171p. Repr. 75.00 (UN50/1/11); Vols. 4 & 5. 1950-1951. Repr. Vol. 4, 1068 pgs. 75.00 (UN51/1/24); Vol. 5, 1030 pgs. 50.00 (UN52/1/30). Repr. UN.
Yearbook of the United Nations: 1978 & Beyond. Incl. Vol. 32. 1978. 1312p. 60.00 (UN80/1/1). UNIPUB; Vol. 33. 1979. 1450p. 1980. 72.00 (ISBN 0-686-43291-6). UNIPUB. UN). UNIPUB.
Yearbook of the United Nations, 1982, Vol. 36. 1607p. 1985. 75.00 (ISBN 92-1-100038-6, E.84.I.1). UN.
Yearbook of the United Nations, 1983, Vol. 37. 1431p. 1987. 85.00 (ISBN 92-1-100312-1, E.86.I.1). UN.
Yearbook of Wines, Alcohol & Spirits of the Common Market. 213p. 1980. pap. 76.25 (ISBN 2-8029-0012-9, ED10, ED). UNIPUB.
Yearbook of World Armaments & Disarmaments, 1987. Stockholm International Peace Research Institute. (SIPRI Yearbook Ser.). (Illus.). 536p. 1987. 65.00 (ISBN 0-19-829114-0). Oxford U Pr.
Yearbook on India's Foreign Policy, 1982-1983. Ed. by Satish Kumar. 266p. 1985. text ed. 49.95 (ISBN 0-8039-9488-5, Pub. by Sage India). Sage.
Yearbook on India's Foreign Policy 1984-85. Ed. by Satish Kumar. 286p. 1988. text ed. 49.95 (ISBN 0-8039-9533-4). Sage.
Yearbook on International Affairs. Richard F. Staar. Incl. 1970. (No. 100). 1971. 25.00x (ISBN 0-8179-6001-5); 1971. (No. 105). 900p. 1971. 25.00x (ISBN 0-8179-6051-1); 1972. (No. 105). 700p. 1972. 25.00 (ISBN 0-8179-6181-X); 1974. (No. 140). 600p. 1974. 25.00x (ISBN 0-8179-6401-0); 1975. (No. 146). 650p. 1975. 25.00x (ISBN 0-8179-6461-4); 1976. (No. 160). 1976. 25.00x (ISBN 0-8179-6601-3); 1978. 1978. 35.00x (ISBN 0-8179-6951-9); 1979. (No. 215). 1979. 35.00x (ISBN 0-8179-7151-3); 1982. (No. 272). 576p. 1982. 39.95x (ISBN 0-8179-7721-X); 1983. (No.286). 534p. 1983; 1985. (No. 327). 600p. 1985. 49.95x (ISBN 0-8179-8271-X). (Publications Ser.). Hoover Inst Pr.
Yearbook on International Communist Affairs, 1969. Ed. by Richard V. Allen. LC 67-31024. (Publications Ser.: No. 92). 1970. 25.00x (ISBN 0-8179-1921-X). Hoover Inst Pr.
Yearbook on International Communist Affairs: 1986. Ed. by Richard F. Staar. xxxiv, 600p. 1986. 49.95x (ISBN 0-8179-8321-X). Hoover Inst Pr.
Yearbook on International Communist Affairs, 1987. Ed. by Richard F. Staar & Margit N. Grigory. (Yearbook Ser.). 1987. 49.95 (ISBN 0-8179-8651-0); PLB 49.95 (ISBN 0-317-57947-9, P-365). Hoover Inst Pr.
Yearbook on International Communist Affairs, 1988: Parties & Revolutionary Movements. Ed. by Richard F. Staar. (P-380 Ser.). 640p. 1988. text ed. 49.95 (ISBN 0-8179-8801-7). Hoover Inst Pr.
Yearbook on Latin American Communist Affairs, 1971. William E. Ratliff. LC 73-177413. (Publications Ser.: No. 112). 194p. 1971. pap. 7.95x (ISBN 0-8179-6121-6). Hoover Inst Pr.
Yearbook on Socialist Legal Systems. Ed. by William E. Butler. (Yearbook Ser.). 240p. 1986. text ed. 67.00 (ISBN 0-941320-48-0). Transnatl Pubs.
Yearbook on Socialist Legal Systems, 1987. Ed. by William E. Butler. (Yearbook Ser.). 1987. text ed. 67.00 (ISBN 0-941320-49-9). Transnatl Pubs.
Yearbook, 1979. Facts on File Digest Staff. 1980. lib. bdg. 85.00 (ISBN 0-87196-038-9). Facts on File.
Yearbook, 1981: With Reaction Titles Vol. 31 to 35 & Cumulative Index; Mit Deutschem Registerschluessel. (Synthetic Methods of Organic Chemistry Ser.: Vol. 35). xviii, 838p. 1981. 465.50 (ISBN 3-8055-1607-X). S Karger.
Yearbook, 1982. Ed. by A. F. Finch. (Theilheimer's Synthetic Methods of Organic Chemistry Ser.: Vol. 36). xxiv, 532p. 1982. 332.00 (ISBN 3-8055-3446-9). S Karger.
Yearbook, 1984. Ed. by Alan Finch. (Theilheimer's Synthetic Methods of Organic Chemistry Ser.: Vol. 38). (Illus.). xxiv, 624p. 1984. 385.50 (ISBN 3-8055-3817-0). S Karger.
Yearbook, 1985. Ed. by A. F. Finch. (Theilheimer's Synthetic Methods of Organic Chemistry Ser.: Vol. 39). xxiv, 548p. 1985. 381.50 (ISBN 3-8055-3987-8). S Karger.
Yearbook 1986 with Reaction Titles & Cumulative Index of Vols. 36-40. Ed. by A. F. Finch. (Theilheimer's Synthetic Methods of Organic Chemistry Ser.: Vol. 40). xxiv, 1016p. 1986. bound 593.50 (ISBN 3-8055-4241-0). S Karger.
Yearbook 1988. Ed. by A. F. Finch. (Theilheimer's Synthetic Methods of Organic Chemistry Ser.: Vol. 42). (Illus.). xx, 596p. 1988. 447.50 (ISBN 3-8055-4698-X). S Karger.
Yearbook 47. Ed. by James W. Scott. LC 37-13376. (Association of Pacific Coast Geographers Yearbooks Ser.). (Illus.). 136p. 1987. pap. text ed. 7.00 (ISBN 0-87071-247-0). Oreg St U Pr.
Yearbooks of the Association of Pacific Coast Geographers, 1935-1985, Vols. 1-47. Association of Pacific Coast Geographers. LC 37-13376. One Copy. pap. 2.00; Two-Four Copies. pap. 1.50; Five or More Copies. pap. 1.00. Oreg St U Pr.
Yearling. Marjorie K. Rawlings. LC 85-40301. (Scribner's Illustrated Classics). (Illus.). 416p. (gr. 3 up). 1985. 24.95 (ISBN 0-684-18461-3); deluxe, ltd. ed. 75.00 (ISBN 0-684-18508-3). Macmillan.
Yearling. Marjorie K. Rawlings. (Illus.). 448p. (YA) (gr. 5 up). 1988. pap. 4.95 (ISBN 0-02-044931-3, Collier). Macmillan.
Yearly Digest of Supreme Court Criminal Cases. Surendra Malik. 45.00x (ISBN 0-317-54840-9, Pub. by Eastern Bk India). State Mutual Bk.
Yearly Planning Guide for the Church Usher. Thomas L. Clark. 1986. pap. 3.95 (ISBN 0-8054-9407-3). Broadman.
Yearly Supreme Court & Full Bench Cases Digest 1986. 1986. 150.00x (ISBN 0-317-62648-5, Pub. by Capital Law Hse). State Mutual Bk.
Yearning for the Holy Land: Hasidic Tales of Israel. Ed. by Yoel Rappel. Tr. by Shmuel Himmelstein. LC 85-18604. 1985. 11.95 (ISBN 0-915361-27-2, 09730-7, Dist. by Watts); pap. 9.95. Adama Pubs Inc.
Yearning for the Holy Land: Hasidic Tales of Israel. Ed. by Yoel Rappel. (Illus.). 176p. 1987. pap. 9.95 (ISBN 0-915361-86-8, Dist. by Watts); 11.95 (ISBN 0-317-56162-6, Dist. by Watts). Adama Pubs Inc.
Yearning for Yesterday: A Sociology of Nostalgia. Fred Davis. LC 78-19838. 1979. 12.95 (ISBN 0-02-906950-5). Free Pr.
Yearning, Learning, Earning & Returning: a Community-Adult Teacher's Handbook. David W. Cochran. 32p. 1981. pap. text ed. 4.00 (ISBN 0-939926-03-2). Fruition Pubns.
Yearning to Breathe Free. Ed. by Barbara Fisher & Richard Spiegel. 32p. (Orig.). (gr. 4-9). 1984. pap. 2.00 (ISBN 0-934830-33-9). Ten Penny.
Yearning to Understand: Why Our Quest to Live in Space Must Never End. Douglas Kirk. Ed. by Valerie Matthews. LC 86-60530. (Illus.). 166p. (Orig.). 1986. pap. 6.95 (ISBN 0-934279-03-9). Morton Falls Pub.
Yearnings. Gary Metras. 16p. 1979. pap. 1.00 (ISBN 0-686-27504-7). Samisdat.
Years. LaVyrle Spencer. 480p. 1986. pap. 4.50 (ISBN 0-515-08489-1). Jove Pubns.
Years. Virginia Woolf. LC 37-27268. 435p. 1969. pap. 7.95 (ISBN 0-15-699701-0, Harv). HarBraceJ.
Years after Fifty. Wingate M. Johnson. 14.00 (ISBN 0-405-18502-2). Ayer Co Pubs.
Years & Me. George Collier. LC 85-90847. 144p. (Orig.). 1985. pap. 6.95 (ISBN 0-934318-61-1). Falcon Pr MT.
Years As Catches. Robert Duncan. 1977. sewn in wrappers 3.00 (ISBN 0-685-80007-5). Oyez.
Years at the Ending. Joseph Leftwich. LC 83-45131. 72p. 1984. 11.95 (ISBN 0-8453-4767-5, Cornwall Bks). Assoc Univ Prs.
Year's Best Fantasy: First Annual Collection. Ed. by Ellen Datlow & Terri Windling. 512p. 1988. 19.95 (ISBN 0-312-01851-7); pap. 12.95 (ISBN 0-312-01852-5). St Martin.
Years Best Fantasy Stories, No. 12. Ed. by Arthur W. Saha. 240p. 1986. pap. 2.95 (ISBN 0-88677-163-3). DAW Bks.
Year's Best Fantasy Stories, No. 13. Ed. by Arthur W. Saha. 240p. 1987. pap. 2.95 (ISBN 0-88677-233-8). DAW Bks.
Year's Best Fantasy Stories, No. 11. Ed. by Arthur W. Saha. (Science Fiction Ser.). 1986. pap. 2.95 (ISBN 0-88677-097-1). DAW Bks.
Year's Best Fantasy Stys, No. 14. Ed. by Arthur W. Saha. 1988. pap. 3.50 (ISBN 0-88677-307-5). DAW Bks.
Year's Best Horror, No. 16. Ed. by Karl E. Wagner. 1988. pap. 3.95. DAW Bks.
Year's Best Horror Stories. Ed. by Karl W. Edward. (Science Fiction Ser.: X). 240p. pap. 2.95 (ISBN 0-88677-160-9). DAW Bks.
Year's Best Horror Stories. Ed. by Karl W. Edward. (Science Fiction Ser.: XI). 240p. pap. 2.95 (ISBN 0-88677-161-7). DAW Bks.
Year's Best Horror Stories. Ed. by Karl W. Edward. (Science Fiction Ser.: VIII). 224p. pap. 2.95 (ISBN 0-88677-158-7). DAW Bks.
Year's Best Horror Stories. Ed. by Karl W. Edward. (Science Fiction Ser.: IX). 224p. pap. 2.95 (ISBN 0-88677-159-5). DAW Bks.
Year's Best Horror Stories, No. XV. Ed. by Karl E. Wagner. 304p. 1987. pap. 3.50 (ISBN 0-88677-226-5). DAW Bks.
Year's Best Horror Stories XV. Karl E. Wagner. 1987. pap. 3.50. DAW Bks.
Years Best Horror XIV. Ed. by Karl E. Wagner. 1986. pap. 3.50 (ISBN 0-88677-156-0). DAW Bks.
Year's Best Mystery & Suspense Stories 1983. Edward D. Hoch. 264p. 1983. 13.95 (ISBN 0-8027-0747-5); pap. 6.95 (ISBN 0-8027-7235-8). Walker & Co.
Years Best Mystery & Suspense Stories, 1984. Edward D. Hoch. 252p. 1984. 14.95 (ISBN 0-8027-5597-6). Walker & Co.
Year's Best Mystery & Suspense Stories, 1985. Ed. by Edward D. Hoch. 256p. 1985. 15.95 (ISBN 0-8027-5634-4); pap. 8.95 (ISBN 0-8027-7286-2). Walker & Co.
Year's Best Mystery & Suspense Stories, 1986. Ed. by Edward D. Hoch. 228p. 1986. 16.95 (ISBN 0-8027-0919-2); pap. 9.95 (ISBN 0-8027-7292-7). Walker & Co.
Year's Best Mystery & Suspense Stories. Edward J. Hoch. 1987. 17.95 (ISBN 0-8027-0983-4); pap. cancelled (ISBN 0-8027-7309-5). Walker & Co.
Year's Best Science Fiction. 4th ed. Ed. by Gardner Dozois. 608p. 1987. 19.95 (ISBN 0-312-00709-4); pap. 11.95 (ISBN 0-312-00710-8). St Martin.
Year's Best Science Fiction: Fifth Annual Collection. Ed. by Gardner Dozois. 624p. 1988. 19.95 (ISBN 0-312-01853-3); pap. 12.95 (ISBN 0-312-01854-1). St Martin.
Year's Best Science Fiction: First Annual Collection. Ed. by Gardner Dozois. (Year's Best Science Fiction Ser.: No. 1). 576p. 1984. lib. bdg. 17.95 (ISBN 0-312-94482-9); pap. 9.95 (ISBN 0-312-94483-7). Bluejay Bks.
Year's Best Science Fiction: Second Annual Collection. Ed. by Gardner Dozois. 576p. 1985. 19.95 (ISBN 0-312-94484-5, Dist. by St. Martin); pap. 10.95 (ISBN 0-312-94485-3, Dist. by St. Martin). Bluejay Bks.
Years Best Science Fiction: Third Annual Collection. Ed. & intro. by Gardner Dozois. 624p. 1986. 19.95 (ISBN 0-312-94486-1); pap. 10.95 (ISBN 0-312-94487-X). Bluejay Bks.
Years Eighteen Eighty-One to Eighteen Ninety-Four in Russia: A Memorandum Found in the Papers of N. Kh. Bunge. George E. Snow. (Transactions Ser.: Vol. 71, Pt. 6). 1981. pap. 8.00 (ISBN 0-87169-716-5). Am Philos.
Years from Now. Gary Glickman. LC 86-46320. (Illus.). 1987. 16.95 (ISBN 0-394-55513-9). Knopf.
Years from Now. Gary Glickman. 276p. 1988. pap. 7.95 (ISBN 0-452-26142-2, Plume). NAL.
Years in Passing: St. Ignatius High School. Nelson Callahan & Jim Toman. LC 86-71069. (Illus.). 183p. (Orig.). 1986. pap. 15.00 (ISBN 0-936760-04-4). Cleveland Landmarks.
Years: Memoirs of a Member of the Duma, 1906-1917. V. V. Shulgin. 425p. 1984. 24.95 (ISBN 0-88254-855-7). Hippocrene Bks.
Years of Adventure 1858-1898 see Lugard.
Years of Authority 1898-1945 see Lugard.
Years of Awakening. Mary Luyters. 1976. pap. 5.95 (ISBN 0-380-00734-7, 69492-1, Discus). Avon.
Years of Challenge: Selected Speeches of Indira Gandhi 1966-1969. rev. ed. Indira Gandhi. LC 74-168325. 498p. 1973. 7.50x (ISBN 0-89684-473-0). Orient Bk Dist.
Years of Childhood. Sergei Aksakov. Tr. by J. D. Duff from Rus. (World's Classics-Paperback Ser.). 1983. pap. 7.95 (ISBN 0-19-281574-1). Oxford U Pr.
Years of Childhood see Memoirs of the Aksakov Family.
Years of Crisis: Collected Essays, 1970-1983. James Hitchcock. LC 84-80758. 285p. 1984. 12.95 (ISBN 0-89870-049-3); pap. 10.95 (ISBN 0-89870-069-8). Ignatius Pr.
Years of Decision: American Politics in the 1890's. R. Hal Williams. 219p. 1978. pap. text ed. write for info (ISBN 0-394-34204-6, RanC). Random.
Years of Endeavour. Indira Gandhi. 826p. 34.95 (ISBN 0-940500-97-3, Pub. by Pubns Div India). Asia Bk Corp.
Years of Endeavour: Selected Speeches, 1969-1972. Indira Gandhi. 826p. 1983. Repr. 34.95. Asia Bk Corp.
Years of Estrangement: American Relations with the Soviet Union, 1933 to 1941. Thomas R. Maddux. LC 79-26489. ix, 238p. 1980. 19.50x (ISBN 0-8130-0653-8). U Presses Fla.
Years of Experience. Georgiana Kirby. LC 79-134373. Repr. of 1887 ed. 37.50 (ISBN 0-404-08421-4). AMS Pr.
Years of Fighting Exile. Milton V. Williams. 85p. 1986. pap. 8.00 (ISBN 0-948833-01-7, Peepal Tree UK). Three Continents.
Years of Grace. Margaret A. Barnes. 29.95 (ISBN 0-317-28525-4, Pub. by Am Repr). Amereon Ltd.
Years of High Purpose: From Trusteeship to Nationhood. Mason Sears. LC 80-5161. (Illus.). 205p. 1980. text ed. 24.25 (ISBN 0-8191-1052-3); pap. text ed. 11.00 (ISBN 0-8191-1053-1). U Pr of Amer.
Years of High Theory: Invention & Tradition in Economic Thought 1962 to 1939. George L. Shackle. LC 67-12320. 336p. 1983. pap. 18.95 (ISBN 0-521-27478-8). Cambridge U Pr.
Years of High Theory: Invention & Tradition on Economic Thought, 1926-1939. George L. Shackle. 1967. 57.50 (ISBN 0-521-06279-9). Cambridge U Pr.
Years of Hope: Australian Art & Criticism 1959-1968. Gary Catalano. (Illus.). 1981. 45.00x (ISBN 0-19-554220-7). Oxford U Pr.
Years of Infamy: The Untold Story of America's Concentration Camps. Michi Weglyn. LC 75-34397. (Illus.). 1976. pap. 10.95 (ISBN 0-688-07996-2). Morrow.
Years of John. Ed. by Hugh McGinlay. (Years of Ser.). 96p. 1985. pap. 8.95 (ISBN 0-85819-521-6, Pub. by JBCE). ANZ Religious Pubns.
Years of Lyndon Johnson: The Path to Power. Robert A. Caro. LC 83-47823. (Illus.). 960p. 1984. pap. 9.95 (ISBN 0-394-71654-X, Vin). Random.
Years of MacArthur: Triumph & Disaster, 1945-1964, Vol. III. D. Clayton James. (Illus.). 864p. 1985. 35.00 (ISBN 0-395-36004-8). HM.
Years of MacArthur: Vol. 1. 1880-1941. D. Clayton James. 1970. 19.95 (ISBN 0-395-10948-5). HM.
Years of MacArthur Vol. 2: Nineteen Forty-One to Nineteen Forty-Five. D. Clayton James. LC 76-108685. 960p. 1975. 19.95 (ISBN 0-395-20446-1). HM.
Years of Madness. W. E. Woodward. 312p. (Orig.). 1967. pap. 3.25 (ISBN 0-686-05062-2). Frontier Press Calif.
Years of My Youth. facsimile ed. William D. Howells. LC 70-146859. (Select Bibliographies Reprint Ser). Repr. of 1916 ed. 16.00 (ISBN 0-8369-5626-5). Ayer Co Pubs.
Years of My Youth & Three Essays. William D. Howells. LC 78-166119. (Selected Edition of W. D. Howells: Center for Editions of American Authors: Vol. 29). 448p. 1975. 20.00x (ISBN 0-253-36850-2). Ind U Pr.
Years of No Decision. Muhammad El Farra. 350p. 1987. 37.50 (ISBN 0-7103-0215-0, Kegan Paul). Routledge Chapman & Hall.

Yellow Butter Purple Jelly Red Jam Black Bread. Mary Ann Hoberman. (Illus.). 64p. (ps-3). 1981. 9.50 (ISBN 0-670-79382-5). Viking.
Yellow Cars of Los Angeles. Jim Walker. LC 77-71538. (Interurbans Special Ser.: No. 43). (Illus.). 320p. 1977. 36.95 (ISBN 0-916374-25-4). Interurban.
Yellow Claw. Sax Rohmer. 1976. lib. bdg. 13.95x (ISBN 0-89968-142-5). Lightyear.
Yellow Dog. Gary Lawless. 1986. pap. 3.00 (ISBN 0-942396-40-5). Blackberry ME.
Yellow Dog Contract. Joel I. Seldman. LC 78-64146. (Johns Hopkins University. Studies in the Social Sciences. Fiftieth Ser. 1932: 4). Repr. of 1932 ed. 24.50 (ISBN 0-404-61257-1). AMS Pr.
Yellow-Dog Contract. Ross Thomas. LC 83-48959. 272p. 1987. pap. 3.50 (ISBN 0-06-080847-0, P 847, PL). Har-Row.
Yellow Dogs. Donald Zochert. 1989. 16.95 (ISBN 0-87113-254-0). Atlantic Monthly.
Yellow Dogs & Dark Horses. John R. Starr. LC 87-951. 240p. 1987. 14.95 (ISBN 0-87483-030-3). August Hse.
Yellow Dress. Ursula V. Williams. 190p. 1984. 34.00x (ISBN 0-946041-24-5, Pub. by Kensal Pr UK). State Mutual Bk.
Yellow Earth. Ralph P. Gates. 1983. pap. 3.00 (ISBN 0-686-40181-6). Basin Pub.
Yellow Earth, Green Jade: Constants in Chinese Political Mores. Simon De Beaufort. (Harvard Studies in International Affairs: No. 41). 90p. 1984. pap. text ed. 8.00 (ISBN 0-8191-4059-7). U Pr of Amer.
Yellow Emperor's Classic of Internal Medicine. Tr. by Ilza Veith. 1966. pap. 10.95 (ISBN 0-520-02158-4). U of Cal Pr.
Yellow Fairy Book. Andrew Lang. (Illus.). (gr. 2 up). 15.00 (ISBN 0-8446-0758-4). Peter Smith.
Yellow Fairy Book. Andrew Lang. (gr. 5 up). 1988. pap. 2.25 (ISBN 0-14-035089-6, Puffin Bks). Penguin.
Yellow Fairy Book. Ed. by Andrew Lang. (Illus.). 321p. (gr. 4-6). pap. 5.95 (ISBN 0-486-21674-8). Dover.
Yellow Feather Mystery. Franklin W. Dixon. (Hardy Boys Ser: Vol. 33). (gr. 5-9). 1954. 4.50 (ISBN 0-448-08933-5, G&D); PLB 3.29 (ISBN 0-448-18933-X). Putnam Pub Group.
Yellow Fever in the North: The Methods of Epidemiology. William Coleman. LC 86-40456. (Wisconsin Publications in the History of Science & Medicine). 304p. 1987. text ed. 49.50x (ISBN 0-299-11110-5); pap. text ed. 17.50x (ISBN 0-299-11114-8). U of Wis Pr.
Yellow Fever Studies: An Original Anthology. Ed. by Barbara G. Rosenkrantz. LC 76-40355. (Public Health in America Ser.). 1977. Repr. of 1977 ed. lib. bdg. 24.50x (ISBN 0-405-09882-0). Ayer Co Pubs.
Yellow Flowers. Andrew Wylie. 1972. pap. 4.95 (ISBN 0-934450-04-8). Unmuzzled Ox.
Yellow Fog. Les Daniels. 304p. 1988. pap. 3.95 (ISBN 0-8125-1675-3). Tor Bks.
Yellow for Peril, Black for Beautiful. Turner Cassity. LC 74-21627. 80p. 1975. pap. 3.95 (ISBN 0-8076-0776-2). Braziller.
Yellow-Fronted Amazon Parrots. Edward J. Mulawka. (Illus.). 160p. 9.95 (ISBN 0-87666-835-X, PS-781). TFH Pubns.
Yellow Glove. Naomi S. Nye. LC 86-21534. 86p. 1986. 13.95 (ISBN 0-932576-41-9); pap. 7.95 (ISBN 0-932576-42-7). Breitenbush Bks.
Yellow Hat. J. M. Espelt & M. Ginesta. (Hat Wkbks.). (Illus.). 48p. (ps-2). Date not set. pap. 2.95 (ISBN 0-8431-2205-6). Price Stern.
Yellow Horde, Being a Short & Truthful History of the Taking of California & Oregon by the Chinese in the Year A. D. 1899. Robert Wolter. (Imaginary Wars & Battle Ser.: No. 5). 144p. 1989. lib. bdg. 19.95x (ISBN 0-89370-357-5); pap. 9.95x (ISBN 0-89370-457-1). Borgo Pr.
Yellow Horse. Dee Brown. (YA) 1989. pap. price not set (ISBN 0-440-20246-9). Dell.
Yellow House. Blake Morrison. (Illus.). 32p. (ps-3). 1987. 12.95 (ISBN 0-15-299820-9, HJ). HarBraceJ.
Yellow House Mystery. Gertrude C. Warner. LC 53-13243. (Boxcar Children Mysteries). (Illus.). 128p. (gr. 3-7). PLB 8.95 (ISBN 0-8075-9365-6). A Whitman.
Yellow House on the Corner. Rita Dove. LC 80-65700. (Poetry Ser.). 1980. 9.95 (ISBN 0-915604-39-6); pap. 4.95 (ISBN 0-915604-40-X). Carnegie-Mellon.
Yellow Jacket: A Four Corners Anasazi Ceremonial Center. Frederic Lange et al. LC 86-82465. (Illus.). 72p. (Orig.). 1986. pap. 5.95 (ISBN 1-55566-005-3). Johnson Bks.
Yellow Light. Garret Hongo. LC 81-16050. (Wesleyan Poetry Program Ser.: Vol. 104). 78p. 1982. 17.00x (ISBN 0-8195-2104-3); pap. 8.95 (ISBN 0-8195-1104-8). Wesleyan U Pr.
Yellow Lola. Edward Dorn. LC 80-68260. 132p. 1981. o. p. signed ltd. ed. 20.00 (ISBN 0-932274-14-5); pap. 6.00 (ISBN 0-932274-13-7). Cadmus Eds.
Yellow Magic: The Story of Penicillin. J. D. Ratcliff. 1945. 25.00 (ISBN 0-8274-4256-4). R West.
Yellow Napoleon: A Romance of West Africa. Arthur E Southon. LC 72-4613. (Black Heritage Library Collection Ser.). Repr. of 1928 ed. 17.00 (ISBN 0-8369-9127-3). Ayer Co Pubs.
Yellow Pages for Students & Teachers. Imogene Forte & Joy Mackenzie. LC 79-93126. 96p. (gr. 2-6). 1980. pap. text ed. 7.95 (ISBN 0-913916-88-9, IP 88-9). Incentive Pubns.
Yellow Pages Handbook of Objections & Responses. Jeffrey Price. (Illus.). 128p. (Orig.). (YA) 1988. pap. 12.95 (ISBN 0-945909-00-4). Idlewood Pub.
Yellow Pages Industry Sourcebook, 1987-88. Ed. by Frederica Evan. 368p. 1987. 295.00x (ISBN 0-88709-013-3). Comm Trends Inc.
Yellow Pages of Undergraduate Innovations: A Guide to Innovations in Higher Education. Ed. by Douglas A. Kleiber. 243p. 1974. pap. 12.95x (Pub. by Change Mag). Transaction Bks.
Yellow Pages Report: Advertising in the Yellow Pages. rev. ed. W. F. Wagner. (Information for Action Ser.). (Illus.). 174p. 1988. pap. 20.00 (ISBN 0-937769-05-3). Mark Inc CA.
Yellow Peephole Book. Dorothy Savage. (Peephole Bks.). (Illus.). 10p. (ps). 1986. pap. 1.95 (ISBN 0-525-44248-0). Dutton.
Yellow Peril: Chinese Americans in American Fiction, 1850-1940. William F. Wu. LC 81-12701. (Illus.). 241p. 1981. 25.00 (ISBN 0-208-01915-4, Archon). Shoe String.
Yellow Peril, Eighteen Ninety to Nineteen Twenty-Four, 2 vols. in one. Richard A. Thompson. Ed. by Roger Daniels. LC 78-54833. (Asian Experience in North America Ser.). 1979. lib. bdg. 39.00x (ISBN 0-405-11290-4). Ayer Co Pubs.
Yellow Peril in Action: A Possible Chapter in History. Marsden Manson. (Imaginary Wars & Battles Ser.: No. 2). 144p. 1989. lib. bdg. 19.95x (ISBN 0-89370-356-7); pap. 9.95x (ISBN 0-89370-456-3). Borgo Pr.
Yellow Raft in Blue Water. Michael Dorris. LC 86-26947. 1987. 16.95 (ISBN 0-8050-0045-3). H Holt & Co.
Yellow Raft in Blue Water. Michael Dorris. 646p. Date not set. Repr. lib. bdg. price not set (ISBN 0-89621-115-0). Thorndike Pr.
Yellow Raft in Blue Water. Michael Dorris. 384p. 1988. pap. 7.95 (ISBN 0-446-38787-8). Warner Bks.
Yellow Rain. Peter McCurtin. (Soldier of Fortune Ser.). 224p. 1984. pap. 2.50 (ISBN 0-8439-2089-0, Leisure Bks). Leisure NY.
Yellow River. Robert S. Anson. LC 80-52503. (Rivers of the World Ser.). 68p. (gr. 4 up). PLB 14.96 (ISBN 0-382-06371-6). Silver.
Yellow River: A Five Thousand Year Journey Through China. Kevin Sinclair. (Illus.). 206p. 1987. 35.00 (ISBN 0-89535-192-7). Knapp Pr.
Yellow River Valley: A Geopolitical Appraisal. Joseph D. Lowe. (Illus.). vii, 40p. 1982. pap. 7.00 (ISBN 0-9605506-4-X). Lowe Pub.
Yellow Robe Monster. Ed. by Zhang Wen. (Monkey Ser.: No. 8). (Illus.). 74p. (gr. 4 up). 1985. pap. 7.95 (ISBN 0-8351-1368-X). China Bks.
Yellow Rolls Royce. Jack Pearl. 14.95 (ISBN 0-88411-443-0, Pub. by Aeonian Pr). Amereon Ltd.
Yellow Room. Mary R. Rinehart. 352p. 1988. pap. 3.50 (ISBN 0-8217-2262-X). Zebra.
Yellow Star. Simcha B. Unsdorfer. LC 61-6930. 1983. 9.95 (ISBN 0-87306-336-8); pap. 6.95 (ISBN 0-87306-337-6). Feldheim.
Yellow Star Sticker. P. Stanton. (Learn-a-Lot Ser.). (gr. k-3). Bk. & cassette 4.95 (ISBN 0-932715-08-7). Evans FL.
Yellow Stars & Ice. Susan Stewart. LC 80-8587. (Princeton Ser. of Contemporary Poets). 78p. 1981. 13.00x (ISBN 0-691-06468-7); pap. 7.50 (ISBN 0-691-01379-9). Princeton U Pr.
Yellow Sun, Bright Sky: The Indian Country Stories of Oliver La Farge. Ed. by David L. Caffey. (Illus.). 208p. (Orig.). 1988. 22.50 (ISBN 0-8263-1101-6); pap. 12.95 (ISBN 0-8263-1033-8). U of NM Pr.
Yellow Thread Cat. Mary A. Tien. LC 84-4793. (Illus.). 20p. (Orig.). (gr. 1-6). 1984. pap. 3.25 (ISBN 0-9603840-8-1). Andrew Mtn Pr.
Yellow Umbrella. Henrik Drescher. LC 87-70157. (Illus.). 40p. (ps-2). 1987. 9.95 (ISBN 0-02-733240-3). Bradbury Pr.
Yellow Wallpaper. Charlotte P. Gilman. 64p. 1973. pap. 4.50 (ISBN 0-912670-09-6). Feminist Pr.
Yellow Ware. Joan Liebowitz. (Illus.). 124p. 1985. pap. 19.95 (ISBN 0-88740-041-8). Schiffer.
Yellow Wind. David Grossman. Tr. by Haim Watzman from Hebrew. 188p. 1988. 17.95 (ISBN 0-374-29345-7). FS&G.
Yellow Wolf: His Own Story. Lucullus V. McWhorter. (Illus.). 324p. 1984. 19.95 (ISBN 0-87004-317-X); pap. 14.95 (ISBN 0-87004-315-3). Caxton.
Yellowcake & Crocodiles. John Lea & Robert Zehner. 200p. 1987. text ed. 34.95 (ISBN 0-86861-875-6). Unwin Hyman.
Yellowcake: The International Uranium Cartel. June Taylor & Michael Yokell. (Pergamon Policy Studies). 1980. text ed. 54.00 (ISBN 0-08-022473-3). Pergamon.
Yellowfish. John Keeble. LC 79-2651. 320p. 1987. pap. 8.95 (ISBN 0-06-091443-2, PL/1443, PL). Har-Row.
Yellowhair. Charles G. Taylor & Jason Kane. (Custer Monograph: No. 6). 1979. Repr. of 1977 ed. limited ed. 10.00x (ISBN 0-940696-08-8). Monroe County Lib.
Yellowstone. Photos by Fred Hirschmann. LC 81-86038. (Illus.). 88p. (Orig.). 1982. pap. 9.95 (ISBN 0-912856-75-0). Gr Arts Ctr Pub.
Yellowstone: A Wilderness Beseiged. Richard A. Bartlett. LC 85-988. 437p. 1985. 24.95 (ISBN 0-8165-0890-9). U of Ariz Pr.
Yellowstone Explorers Guide. Carl Schreier. LC 82-84287. (Explorers Guide Ser.). (Illus.). 52p. (Orig.). 1983. pap. 4.95 (ISBN 0-943972-02-7); PLB 12.95 (ISBN 0-943972-03-5). Homestead WY.
Yellowstone Fishing Guide. Robert E. Charlton. (Illus.). 51p. (Orig.). 1982. pap. 4.50 (ISBN 0-943390-00-1). Tri-County.
Yellowstone Is... Mike Logan. (Illus.). 90p. 1987. pap. 9.95 (ISBN 0-937959-20-0). Falcon Pr MT.
Yellowstone Jewel. Dorothy Dixon. (Leather & Lace Ser.: Vol. 9). 1983. pap. 2.50 (ISBN 0-8217-1237-3). Zebra.
Yellowstone Kelly. Peter Bowen. LC 86-27193. 260p. 1988. 17.95 (ISBN 0-915463-40-7, Pub. by Jameson Bks). Green Hill.
Yellowstone Kelly: The Memoirs of Luther S. Kelly. Luther S. Kelly. Ed. by M. M. Quaife. LC 26-9001. (Illus.). xiv, 300p. 1973. pap. 8.95 (ISBN 0-8032-5784-8, Bison). U of Nebr Pr.
Yellowstone Kill. Buck Gentry. (Scout Ser.: No. 12). 1983. pap. 2.50 (ISBN 0-8217-1254-3). Zebra.
Yellowstone National Park. Hiram M. Chittenden. LC 64-11334. (Illus.). 208p. 1964. pap. 5.95 (ISBN 0-8061-0937-8). U of Okla Pr.
Yellowstone National Park. John Muir. Ed. by William R. Jones. (Illus.). 1978. pap. 3.95 (ISBN 0-89646-043-6). Outbooks.
Yellowstone National Park. John Muir. (Illus.). 1979. pap. 3.95 (ISBN 0-89646-076-7). Outbooks.
Yellowstone National Park. updated ed. Ruth S. Radlauer. LC 75-2159. (Parks for People Ser). (Illus.). 48p. (gr. 3-12). 1975. PLB 13.27 (ISBN 0-516-07487-3); pap. 4.50 (ISBN 0-516-47487-1). Childrens.
Yellowstone National Park: Land of Fire & Falling Water. Tim McNulty. (Illus.). 72p. 1986. 30.00 (ISBN 0-917627-13-X); pap. 16.95 (ISBN 0-917627-12-1). Woodlands Pr.
Yellowstone Park: Absaroka Range see Field Book.
Yellowstone Pioneers: The Story of Hamilton Stores & Yellowstone National Park. Gwen Petersen. Ed. by Linda S. Davis. LC 85-50965. (Illus.). 120p. Date not set. pap. 9.95 (ISBN 0-917859-23-5). Sunrise SBCA.
Yellowstone Place Names. Lee H. Whittlesey. 250p. 1988. 11.95 (ISBN 0-295-96706-4, Dist. for Montana Historical Society). U of Wash Pr.
Yellowstone Savage: Life in Nature's Wonderland. Joyce B. Lohse. LC 87-34212. (Illus.). 144p. (Orig.). 1988. pap. 7.95 (ISBN 0-944915-00-0). J D Charles.
Yellowstone: Selected Photographs, 1870-1960. Carl Schreier. LC 88-80159. (Illus.). 160p. (Orig.). 1988. 24.95 (ISBN 0-943972-12-4); pap. 17.95 (ISBN 0-943972-11-6). Homestead WY.
Yellowstone Sketches. Marj Dunmire. (Illus.). 24p. 1979. pap. 4.95 (ISBN 0-942559-01-0). Pegasus Graphics.
Yellowstone Stage Holdups. Jack E. Haynes. (Illus.). 30p. 1988. Repr. lib. bdg. 19.95x (ISBN 0-8095-6109-3). Borgo Pr.
Yellowstone Story, 2 vols. Aubrey L. Haines. LC 76-56546. (Illus.). 1977. Vol. I. pap. 8.95 (ISBN 0-87081-104-5); Vol. II. pap. 9.95 (ISBN 0-87081-116-9). Colo Assoc.
Yellowstone Teton Wit. William Gibson. (Illus.). 216p. 1986. 6.98 (ISBN 0-936023-03-1). Interp Mktg Prods.
Yellowstone: The Grand Old Park. Randy Collings. (Illus.). 80p. 1982. pap. 8.95 (ISBN 0-933692-21-8). A R Collings.
Yellowstone: The Story Behind the Scenery. Hugh Crandall. LC 76-57453. (Illus.). 48p. 1977. pap. 4.50 (ISBN 0-916122-21-2). KC Pubns.
Yellowstone to Yosemite: Early Adventures in the Mountain West. Illus. by Thomas Moran et al. Ed. by Lito Tejada-Flores. (Illus.). 144p. 1988. pap. 12.95 (ISBN 0-941283-01-1). Western Eye Pr.
Yellowstone's Geysers, Hot Springs & Fumaroles. Carl Schreier. LC 84-63019. (Illus.). 96p. (Orig.). 1987. pap. 9.95 (ISBN 0-943972-09-4). Homestead WY.
Yellowthread Street. William Marshall. 144p. pap. 3.50 (ISBN 0-445-40548-1). Mysterious Pr.
Yellowthroat. Penny Hayes. 304p. 1988. pap. 8.95 (ISBN 0-941483-10-X). Naiad Pr.
Yemassee. William G. Simms. Ed. by Joseph V. Ridgely. (Masterworks of Literature Ser). 1964. pap. 10.95x (ISBN 0-8084-0337-0). New Coll U Pr.
Yemen. (Let's Visit Places & Peoples - - Nations, Dependencies, & Sovereignties of the World Ser.). (Illus.). (gr. 5 up). 1989. 12.95 (ISBN 0-7910-0156-3). Chelsea Hse.
Yemen: A Travel Survival Kit. Pertti Hamalainen. (Illus.). 184p. (Orig.). 1988. pap. 8.95 (ISBN 0-86442-006-4). Lonely Planet.
Yemen Arab Republic: Development of a Traditional Economy. Otto Maiss. xxviii, 303p. 1979. pap. 20.00 (ISBN 0-686-36125-3, BK-9109). World Bank.
Yemen Arab Republic: The Politics of Development, 1962-1986. Robert D. Burrowes. (Special Studies on the Middle East). 168p. 1987. 28.00 (ISBN 0-8133-0435-0). Westview.
Yemen Enters the Modern World: Secret U. S. Documents on the Rise of the Second Power on the Arabian Peninsula. Ed. by Ibrahim Al-Rashid. (Documents on the History of Arabia Ser.: Vol. 6). 1984. ltd. ed. 500 copies 34.95x (ISBN 0-89712-058-2). Documentary Pubns.
Yemen in Early Islam: A Political History. Abd A. Al-Mad'aj. LC 88-617. (Durham Middle East Monographs). 248p. 1988. text ed. 40.00 (ISBN 0-86372-102-8, Pub. by Ithaca Pr UK). Humanities.
Yemen: The Search for a Modern State. John E. Peterson. LC 81-48187. 224p. 1982. 25.00x (ISBN 0-8018-2784-1). Johns Hopkins.
Yemen: Traditionalism vs. Modernity. Mohammed A. Zabarah. LC 81-20982. 176p. 1982. 35.00 (ISBN 0-275-90929-8, C0929). Praeger.
Yemen: Transformation of a Society. Ziad Abu-Amr. (Special Studies on the Middle East). 200p. 1989. pap. 26.50 (ISBN 0-8133-7602-5). Westview.
Yemen under the Rule of Iman Ahmad. Ibrahim Al-Rashid. (Documents on the History of Arabia Ser.: Vol. VII). 289p. 1985. text ed. 39.95x (ISBN 0-89712-059-0). Documentary Pubns.
Yemenite Cookbook. Zion Levi & Hani Agabria. LC 87-4584. (Illus.). 240p. 1988. 22.95 (ISBN 0-8050-0394-0, Pub. by Seaver Bks). Seaver Bks.
Yemenite Jewry: Origins, Culture, & Literature. Reuben Ahroni. LC 84-48649. (Jewish Literature and Culture Ser.). (Illus.). 288p. 1986. 27.50x (ISBN 0-253-36807-3). Ind U Pr.
Yemenite Jews: A Photographic Essay. Zion M. Ozeri. LC 84-23600. (Illus.). 96p. 1985. 19.95 (ISBN 0-8052-3980-4). Schocken.
Yemenites of Israel. Herbert S. Lewis. (Illus.). 260p. 1987. lib. bdg. 37.50 (ISBN 0-89727-080-0). ISHI PA.
Yemens. Compiled by G. Rex Smith. (World Bibliographical Ser.: No. 50). 161p. 1984. lib. bdg. 33.00 (ISBN 0-903450-87-9). ABC-Clio.
Yemens: Country Studies. Richard F. Nyrop. LC 86-1164. (DA Pam 550-183. Area Handbook Ser.). (Illus.). 408p. 1986. 16.50 (ISBN 0-318-22481-X, S/N 008-020-01090-1). USGPO.
Yemin Moshe: The Story of a Jerusalem Neighborhood. Eliezer D. Jaffe. LC 87-21819. 88p. 1988. lib. bdg. 37.95 (ISBN 0-275-92690-7, C2690). Praeger.
Yen-Dollar Agreement: Liberalizing Japanese Capital Markets. Jeffrey A. Frankel. LC 84-27842. (Policy Analyses in International Economics Ser.: No. 9). 86p. (Orig.). 1984. pap. 10.00 (ISBN 0-88132-035-8). Inst Intl Eco.
Yen for a Yacht. Robert S. Woodbury. LC 79-26932. 208p. 1980. 9.95 (ISBN 0-914440-30-6). EPM Pubns.
Yen! Japan's New Financial Empire & Its Threat to America. Daniel Burstein. 352p. 1988. 19.95 (ISBN 0-671-64763-6). S&S.
Yenan & the Great Powers. James Reardon-Anderson. LC 79-23343. 1979. 27.50x (ISBN 0-231-04784-3). Columbia U Pr.
Yenan: Colonel Peterkin's Dixie Mission to China. William Head. 1986. write for info. (ISBN 0-89712-175-9). Documentary Pubns.
Yenan in June 1937: Talks with the Communist Leaders. T. A. Bisson. LC 73-620023. (China Research Monographs: No. 11). 71p. 1973. pap. 2.50x (ISBN 0-912966-12-2). IEAS.
Yenan Way in Revolutionary China. Mark Selden. LC 79-152272. (East Asian Ser: No. 62). 1971. 21.00x (ISBN 0-674-96560-4); pap. 9.95x (ISBN 0-674-96561-2, HP40). Harvard U Pr.
Yenching Journal of Chinese Studies: 1927-1949, 20 vols. Harvard-Yenching Institute, Staff. (Chinese.). 600.00x (ISBN 0-89986-260-8). Oriental Bk Store.
Yenching University & Sino-Western Relations, 1916-1952. Philip West. (East Asian Ser.: No. 85). 1976. 20.00x (ISBN 0-674-96569-8). Harvard U Pr.
Yendi. Steven Brust. 3.50 (ISBN 0-441-94460-4, Pub. by Ace Science Fiction). Ace Bks.
Yendi: Jhereg, No. 2. Steven Brust. 224p. 1987. pap. 2.95 (ISBN 0-441-94459-0, Pub. by Charter Bks). Ace Bks.
Yengema Cave Report. Carleton S. Coon et al. (University Museum Monographs: No. 31). (Illus.). 77p. 1968. pap. 15.00 (ISBN 0-934718-23-7). Univ Mus of U PA.
Yentl the Yeshiva Boy. Isaac Bashevis Singer. Tr. by Marion Magid & Elizabeth Pollet. (Illus.). 58p. 1983. 10.95 (ISBN 0-374-29347-3); limited ed. 50.00 (ISBN 0-374-29348-1). FS&G.
Yeoman Farmer & Westward Expansion of U. S. Cotton Production. facsimile ed. James D. Foust. LC 75-2581. (Dissertations in American Economic History). (Illus.). 1975. 23.00x (ISBN 0-405-07201-5). Ayer Co Pubs.
Yeoman in Tudor & Stuart England. Albert J. Schmidt. (Folger Guides to the Age of Shakespeare). 1961. 3.95 (ISBN 0-918016-20-7). Folger Bks.
Yeomanry Regiments: A Pictorial History. P. J. Mileham. (Illus.). 136p. 1985. 19.95 (ISBN 0-87052-214-0). Hippocrene Bks.

Yeomen of the Guard. W. S. Gilbert. (Facsimile Classics Ser.). (Illus.). 1979. Repr. of 1929 ed. 5.95 (ISBN 0-8317-9940-4, Mayflower Bks). Smith Pubs.

Yerbamente Suyo. 3rd ed. Penny C. Royal. 130p. 1987. 5.95 (ISBN 0-9609226-3-6). Sound Nutri.

Yerbas de la Gente: A Study of Hispano-American Medicinal Plants. Karen C. Ford. (Anthropological Papers: No. 60). (Illus.). 1975. pap. 5.00x (ISBN 0-932206-58-1). U Mich Mus Anthro.

Yerma see Three Tragedies.

Yerma: A Tragic Poem in Threee Acts & Six Scenes. Federico Garcia Lorca. Ed. by Ian Macpherson et al. (Hispanic Classics--Modern Ser.). 144p. (Eng. & Span.). 1987. text ed. 49.95 (ISBN 0-85668-337-X, Pub. by Aris & Phillips); pap. text ed. 16.50 (ISBN 0-85668-338-8, Pub. by Aris & Phillips). Humanities.

Yersinia Enterocolitica. Ed. by Edward J. Bottone. 240p. 1981. 95.00 (ISBN 0-8493-5545-1). CRC Pr.

Yersinia Enterocolitica. International Symposium on Yersinia, 3rd, Montreal, September 1977. Ed. by Philip B. Carter et al. (Contributions to Microbiology & Immunology Ser.: Vol. 5). (Illus.). 1979. 103.50 (ISBN 3-8055-2927-9). S Karger.

Yersinia, Pasteurella & Francisella: Proceedings. International Symposium on Yersinia, Pasteurella & Francisella, Malmoe, April 1972. Ed. by Winblad. (Contributions to Microbiology & Immunology Ser.: Vol. 2). 1973. 50.00 (ISBN 3-8055-1636-3). S Karger.

Yertle the Turtle & Other Stories. Dr. Seuss. (Illus.). (gr. k-3). 1958. 9.95 (ISBN 0-394-80087-7, BYR); lib. bdg. 9.99 (ISBN 0-394-90087-1). Random.

Yes! Ann Kiemel. LC 83-51214. 128p. 1984. pap. 2.95 (ISBN 0-8423-8563-0). Tyndale.

Yes. Kim Kulp. 144p. (Orig.). 1987. pap. 5.95 (ISBN 0-937947-03-2). Publius Pub.

Yes - Natalie There Is a Santa Claus Because Grandpa Kelly Told Me So. Richard E. Kendall. LC 87-81722. 155p. (Orig.). 1987. pap. 4.95 (ISBN 0-944288-00-6). Kendall Pub.

Yes & No: A Book of Opposites. Richard Hefter. 1980. text ed. 4.50 (ISBN 0-07-027809-1). McGraw.

Yes & No of the Psyche. E. Gwen Mountford. 1985. 10.00x (ISBN 0-317-62267-6, Guild of Pastoral Psych). State Mutual Bk.

Yes & No: The Intimate Folklore of Africa. Alta Jablow. LC 72-13867. 223p. 1973. Repr. of 1961 ed. lib. bdg. 35.00x (ISBN 0-8371-6757-4, JAYN). Greenwood.

Yes Book. Jose D. Vinck. 1976. pap. 3.75 (ISBN 0-685-77499-6). Franciscan Herald.

Yes Book: An Answer to Life (a Manual of Christian Existentialism) Jose de Vinck. LC 77-190621. 200p. 1972. 15.75 (ISBN 0-911726-12-8); pap. 12.75 (ISBN 0-911726-11-X). Alleluia Pr.

"Yes" Book of Sex for Men. Ted Mcilvenna. (Illus.). 128p. 1986. 20.00 (ISBN 0-8184-0367-5). Lyle Stuart.

Yes, Boss. Scott Seldin. LC 82-72103. (Illus.). 128p. 1982. 10.95 (ISBN 0-943778-01-8); pap. 5.95 (ISBN 0-943778-02-6). Blythe-Pennington.

Yes, Dog, That's Right! Warren Eckstein & Fay Eckstein. LC 79-54766. (Illus.). 1980. 2.98 (ISBN 0-931866-03-0). Alpine Pubns.

Yes Girl. Kathryn Makris. 192p. (Orig.). (gr. 7 up). 1985. pap. 2.25 (ISBN 0-590-33263-5, Wildfire). Scholastic Inc.

Yes, God Can. Jerry Hayner. LC 84-4153. 1985. 7.50 (ISBN 0-8054-2258-7). Broadman.

Yes, God...I Am a Creative Woman. Anne Ortlund et al. LC 83-80610. 225p. (Orig.). 1983. pap. 4.50 (ISBN 0-935797-02-5). Harvest IL.

Yes, Helen, There Were Dinosaurs. Lewis S. Brown. Ed. by Lena M. Brown. (Illus.). 152p. (Orig.). 1982. pap. 7.95 (ISBN 0-9608542-0-7). L S Brown Pub.

Yes, I Am. Norman P. Grubb. 1982. pap. text ed. 4.95 (ISBN 0-87508-206-8). Chr Lit.

Yes, I Am a Mother Who Happens to Be Single: I Can Survive Anything! Janice J. Drummer. (Illus.). 44p. 1988. pap. write for info. Vantage.

Yes-I-Can Guide to Mastering Real Estate. Stephen J. Fogel & Mark B. Rosin. 1987. 19.95 (ISBN 0-8129-1637-9). Times Bks.

Yes, I Do Mind If You Smoke. Rhoda Nichter. LC 77-83110. 1978. 15.95 (ISBN 0-87949-114-0). Ashley Bks.

Yes, I Remember. Jessie Ivey. 21p. Date not set. pap. 2.00 (ISBN 0-686-97738-6). Ivey Pubns.

Yes, I'll Teach--Now What? Ruth Ward. LC 81-70171. (Illus.). 95p. (Orig.). 1982. pap. 3.95 (ISBN 0-87509-313-2); Leader's guide. 2.95 (ISBN 0-87509-315-9). Chr Pubns.

Yes Is Forever. Jane W. Abbott. (Superromance Ser.: No. 263). 308p. Date not set. pap. 2.75 (ISBN 0-317-63881-5). Harlequin Bks.

Yes Is Forever. Daughters of St. Paul. (Encounter Ser.). (Illus.). 109p. 1982. 3.00 (ISBN 0-8198-8700-5, EN0260); pap. 2.00 (ISBN 0-8198-8702-1). Dghtrs St Paul.

Yes! Jesus Loves Me. Ed. by Judy Sparks. (Happy Day Bks.). (Illus.). 24p. (ps-2). 1985. 1.59 (ISBN 0-87239-882-X, 3682). Standard Pub.

Yes, Johnny Can Read. Judith B. Sowell & Ruth G. May. 120p. 1982. pap. text ed. 17.95 (ISBN 0-8403-2874-5). Kendall-Hunt.

Yes, Lord. Harald Bredesen. (Orig.). 1987. pap. 6.95 (ISBN 0-89274-455-3). Harrison Hse.

Yes Minister, Vol. 2. Jonathan Lynn & Antony Jay. 188p. pap. cancelled (ISBN 0-88186-976-7). Parkwest Pubns.

Yes, Mrs. Williams: A Personal Record of My Mother. William Carlos Williams. 1959. 19.95 (ISBN 0-8392-1136-8). Astor-Honor.

Yes, Mrs. Williams: A Personal Record of My Mother. 2nd ed. William Carlos Williams. LC 59-9887. 160p. (Orig.). 1982. pap. 5.95 (ISBN 0-8112-0832-X, NDP534). New Directions.

Yes My Son, There Is a God! Don J. Black. 36p. (Orig.). (YA) (gr. 11 up). 1978. pap. 2.00 (ISBN 0-942241-24-X, 8815). Pubs Bk Sales.

Yes, No, Little Hippo. Jane B. Moncure. (Magic Castle Readers Ser.). (Illus.). 32p. (ps-2). 1987. 11.93 (ISBN 0-516-05724-3). Childrens.

Yes, No, Little Hippo. Jane B. Moncure. LC 87-21211. (Magic Castle Readers Ser.). (Illus.). 32p. (ps-2). 1987. PLB 7.75 (ISBN 0-89565-411-3). Childs World.

Yes, No or Maybe. Ya I. Khurgin. 220p. 1985. pap. 15.00x (ISBN 0-317-52970-6, Pub. by Collets (UK)). State Mutual Bk.

Yes-No, Stop-Go: Some Patterns in Mathematic Logic. Judith L. Gersting & Kuczkowski. LC 76-46376. (Young Math Ser.). (Illus.). (gr. k-3). 1977. PLB 12.89 (ISBN 0-690-01130-X, Crowell Jr Bks). HarpJ.

Yes, Nor or Maybe. Ya. Khurgin. 251p. 1985. pap. 3.95 (ISBN 0-8285-3106-4, Pub. by Mir Pubs USSR). Imported Pubns.

Yes or No? Straight Answers to Tough Questions about Christianity. Peter Kreeft. 168p. (Orig.). 1984. 5.95 (ISBN 0-89283-217-7). Servant.

Yes Prime Minister: The Diaries of the Right Hon. James Hacker. Barbara Vine et al. 1988. 19.95 (ISBN 0-88162-335-0). Salem Hse Pubs.

Yes Review Workbook, High School Entrance. Leonard Bennet et al. 1986. pap. 8.95 (ISBN 0-87738-026-0). Youth Ed.

Yes, the Lord Has Also Gone. CIIR Staff. 8p. 1984. 10.00x (ISBN 0-946848-12-2, Pub. by CIIR). State Mutual Bk.

Yes They Can! A Handbook for Effectively Parenting the Handicapped. Renee Mollan. LC 81-84681. (Illus.). 104p. 1981. Repr. 11.95. Reality Prods.

Yes to Life: Memoirs of Corliss Lamont. Corliss Lamont. (Illus.). 1981. 14.95 (ISBN 0-8180-0232-8). Horizon.

Yes to Mission. Douglas Webster. LC 66-72166. 1966. text ed. 6.00x (ISBN 0-8401-2703-0). A R Allenson.

Yes, Today's Mortgages Make Home Buying Easier. National Association of Home Builders. 126p. 1986. pap. 16.00 (ISBN 0-86718-254-7). Nat Assn H Build.

Yes, Virginia. Illus. by Suzanne Hausman. (Illus.). 6.95 (ISBN 0-685-86235-6). Pubns Devl Co TX.

Yes with Variations. Ken McLaren. (Orig.). 1983. pap. 3.50 (ISBN 0-939196-00-X). The Smith.

Yes You Can. Carolyn Bashlor. Ed. by Darryl Hicks. (Testimony Ser.: No. 16). 144p. Date not set. pap. 4.00 (ISBN 0-9616966-1-3). Designer Bks.

Yes You Can! An Innovative Approach to Happiness. Raymond L. Lemke. LC 88-61002. (Illus.). 192p. (Orig.). 1988. pap. 6.95 (ISBN 0-929099-00-1). Omaha Pr Pub.

Yes!, You Can Learn a Foreign Language. Marjorie Brown-Azarowicz et al. 128p. 1986. pap. 6.95 (ISBN 0-8442-9340-7, Passport Bks). Natl Textbk.

Yes! You Can Own a Piece of the Block. George E. Hill. (Illus.). 91p. (Orig.). 1986. pap. 16.59 (ISBN 0-9617555-0-4); cassette tape 12.95 (ISBN 0-9617555-1-2). Fawncrest Assocs.

Yes, You Can Sign! American Sign Language Phrase Book. William A. Angelbeck. (Illus.). 88p. (Orig.). pap. 5.95 (ISBN 0-317-18912-3). Century Pub.

Yes You Can Teach. Florence Nelson. LC 77-73639. (Illus.). 56p. 1977. pap. 5.00 spiral (ISBN 0-918328-00-4). Carma.

Yes, Your Excellency. V. E. Stevenson-Hamilton. 229p. 1985. 39.00x (ISBN 0-9506012-9-2, Pub. by T Harmsworth Pub). State Mutual Bk.

Yeshiva, Vols. 1 & 2. Chaim Grade. Tr. by Curt Leviant from Yiddish. 1979. pap. 11.95 (ISBN 0-932232-05-1). Menorah Pub.

Yeshiva Children Write Poetry: From the Heart We Sing. Ed. by Manfred Gans. 6.95 (ISBN 0-914131-76-1, D43). Torah Umesorah.

Yeshiva in America. William B. Helmreich. 384p. 1981. text ed. 19.95 (914640). Free Pr.

Yeshiva University Haggada. Brander. Date not set. pap. 9.95. Ktav.

Yeshua Buddha. Jay G. Williams. LC 78-8789. (Orig.). 1978. pap. 3.95 (ISBN 0-8356-0515-9, Quest). Theos Pub Hse.

Yeshua: The Hidden Years. Joan R. Sheldon. 79p. 1988. 8.95 (ISBN 0-533-07479-7). Vantage.

Yesod. David Meltzer. 1969. 5.00 (ISBN 0-685-01059-7, Pub. by Trigram Pr). pap. 2.50 (ISBN 0-686-66274-1). Small Pr Dist.

Yesterday see History of the English Novel.

Yesterday: A Collection of Thoughts. Marcia S. Ivans. LC 81-90596. 96p. (Orig.). 1981. pap. 4.95 (ISBN 0-686-32555-9). Ivans Pub NY.

Yesterday: A Study of Hebrews in the Light of Chapter 13. Floyd V. Filson. LC 67-7015. (Studies in Biblical Theology: 2nd Ser., No. 4). 1967. pap. text ed. 10.00x (ISBN 0-8401-3054-6). A R Allenson.

Yesterday & After see History of the English Novel.

Yesterday & Today. Larbi Layachi. LC 85-3912. 189p. 1985. 14.00 (ISBN 0-87685-632-6); signed cloth 25.00 (ISBN 0-87685-633-4); pap. 8.50 (ISBN 0-87685-631-8). Black Sparrow.

Yesterday & Today from the Kitchens of Stokely-Van Camp. LC 79-54945. (Orig.). 1981. 5.95 (ISBN 0-87502-071-2). Benjamin Co.

Yesterday & Today in the U. S. A. Intermediate ESL Reader. Anna H. Live. 1977. pap. text ed. write for info. (ISBN 0-13-972273-4). P-H.

Yesterday & Today in the U. S. A. Intermediate ESL Reader. 2nd ed. Anna H. Live. (Illus.). 288p. 1988. pap. text ed. write for info. P-H.

Yesterday & Tomorrow. Jules Vernes. 4.95 (ISBN 0-8470-7018-2). Assoc Bk.

Yesterday & Tomorrow. Erin Yorke. 384p. 1987. pap. 3.95 (ISBN 0-373-97034-X, Pub. by Worldwide). Harlequin Bks.

Yesterday & Tomorrow: Roots of the National Revolution. 96p. 1986. pap. 6.50 (ISBN 0-317-53270-7). Noontide.

Yesterday: Book One of a Trilogy see Yesterday, Today, & Tomomorrow.

Yesterday I Was a Crying Dream. Sri Chinmoy. 50p. (Orig.). 1975. pap. 2.00 (ISBN 0-88497-225-9). Aum Pubns.

Yesterday I Was Leaving. Tr. by Rich Ives from Ger. (Orig.). 1986. pap. 7.00 (ISBN 0-937669-25-3). Owl Creek Pr.

Yesterday in Salem: A Collection of Nostalgic Articles. Dale E. Shaffer. (Illus.). 90p. (Orig.). 1986. pap. 4.25 (ISBN 0-915060-23-X). D E Shaffer.

Yesterday in Santa Fe. Marc Simmons. LC 87-6449. (Illus.). 96p. (Orig.). pap. 8.95 (ISBN 0-86534-108-7). Sunstone Pr.

Yesterday in the Hills. Floyd C. Watkins & Charles H. Watkins. LC 82-2642. (Brown Thrasher Bks.). 200p. 1982. pap. 6.95 (ISBN 0-8203-0623-1). U of Ga Pr.

Yesterday in the Nineteen Twenties. Bob Naylor. LC 83-61988. (Illus.). 62p. (Orig.). 1983. pap. 6.95 (ISBN 0-914275-00-3). Piquet Pr.

Yesterday in the Texas Hill Country. Gilbert J. Jordan. LC 78-21774. (Illus.). 192p. 1979. 12.95 (ISBN 0-89096-067-4). Tex A&M Univ Pr.

Yesterday Man. David Stringer. 1986. 45.00x (ISBN 0-86332-114-3, Pub. by Book Guild Ltd). State Mutual Bk.

Yesterday: Memoirs of a Russian-Jewish Lawyer. O. O. Gruzenberg. Ed. & tr. by Don C. Rawson. LC 80-39850. 288p. 1981. 35.00x (ISBN 0-520-04264-6). U of Cal Pr.

Yesterday or Tomorrow? Aspects of the Work of Robert A. Heinlein. Ed. by R. Reginald & George Slusser. (Studies in Literary Criticism: Vol. 5). 1988. 19.95x (ISBN 0-916732-76-2); pap. 9.95x (ISBN 0-916732-75-4). Starmont Hse.

Yesterday or Tomorrow? The Work of Robert A. Heinlein. R. Reginald & George E. Slusser. (Starmont Studies in Literary Criticism: No. 5). 160p. Date not set. Repr. of 1984 ed. lib. bdg. 19.95x (ISBN 0-89370-977-8). Borgo Pr.

Yesterday: The Biography of a Beatle. Chet Flippo. LC 88-6951. 1988. pap. 18.95 (ISBN 0-385-23482-1). Doubleday.

Yesterday, Today & Forever. Edythe E. Bregnard. (Illus.). 96p. (Orig.). 1978. 6.50 (ISBN 0-9616565-1-4, TX 641-587); pap. 3.50 (ISBN 0-9616565-0-6). Pisces Pr AZ.

Yesterday, Today & Forever. Jeane Dixon. 440p. 1987. pap. 8.95 (ISBN 0-8362-7941-7). Andrews & McMeel.

Yesterday, Today, & Forever. Kathi Mills. 216p. 1989. pap. 6.95 (ISBN 0-8361-3488-5). Herald Pr.

Yesterday Today & Forever. Maria Von Trapp. LC 75-32010. 174p. 1975. pap. 3.50 (ISBN 0-89221-035-4). New Leaf.

Yesterday, Today, & Tomomorrow. new ed. Leydel J. Willis. Incl. Yesterday: Book One of a Trilogy. 4.95. 1976. Harlo Pr.

Yesterday, Today & Tomorrow. Elizabeth M. Trotter. 1980. 5.00 (ISBN 0-682-49478-X). Exposition-Phoenix.

Yesterday, Today, & Tomorrow, Bk. 2: Today. new ed. Leydel J. Willis. (gr. 8-12). 1977. 4.95 (ISBN 0-8187-0030-0). Harlo Pr.

Yesterday, Today & Tomorrow: Book Three of a Trilogy. Leydel J. Willis. LC 80-65230. 1980. 4.95 (ISBN 0-930416-06-6). Clodele.

Yesterday, Today & Tomorrow: The Farmer Takes a Hand. rev. ed. Marquis W. Childs. LC 52-5629. 178p. 1980. pap. 2.25 (ISBN 0-686-28113-6). Natl Rural.

Yesterday, Today & Tomorrow (Today) Book Two of a Trilogy. Leydel J. Willis. 1978. 4.95 (ISBN 0-930416-04-X). Clodele.

Yesterday, Today, & Tomorrow: Yesterday, Book One of a Trilogy. new ed. Leydel J. Willis. 1976. 4.95 (ISBN 0-8187-0021-1). Clodele.

Yesterday, Today, Tomorrow. Margret T. Lewis. LC 85-51320. (Illus.). 41p. 1985. 5.95 (ISBN 0-938232-73-8). Winston-Derek.

Yesterdays. Harold S. Ladoo. LC 74-75919. (Anansi Fiction Ser.: No. 29). 110p. 1974. 4.95 (ISBN 0-88784-431-6, Pub. by Hse Anansi Pr Canada); pap. 4.95 (ISBN 0-88784-329-8). U of Toronto Pr.

Yesterdays - & All Our Yesterdays: Feminist Statements, Historical Introductions, & Primary Sources for Metro-East IL Feminism 1970-79. Beatrice A. Stegeman. (Illus.). 600p. 1988. 95.00 (ISBN 0-935772-05-7). Diotima Bks.

Yesterday's Addicts: American Society & Drug Abuse, 1865-1920. H. Wayne Morgan. LC 73-7421. 220p. 1974. 16.95x (ISBN 0-8061-1135-6); pap. 8.95x (ISBN 0-8061-1636-6). U of Okla Pr.

Yesterday's Airplanes. Don Berliner. LC 80-10915. (Superwheels & Thrill Sports Bks.). (Illus.). (gr. 4-9). 1980. PLB 8.95 (ISBN 0-8225-0444-8). Lerner Pubns.

Yesterday's Akron. Kenneth Nichols. LC 75-2162. (Historic Cities Ser.: No. 14). (Illus.). 1975. 9.95 (ISBN 0-912458-51-8). E A Seemann.

Yesterday's Asheville. Joan Langley & Wright Langley. LC 75-14380. (Historic Cities Ser.: No. 17). (Illus.). 128p. 1975. 9.95 (ISBN 0-912458-56-9). E A Seemann.

Yesterday's Atlanta. Franklin M. Garrett. LC 74-75291. (Historic Cities Ser.: No. 8). (Illus.). 176p. 1974. 9.95 (ISBN 0-912458-35-6). E A Seemann.

Yesterday's Atlanta. Franklin M. Garrett. LC 74-75291. (Illus.). 1977. pap. 5.95 (ISBN 0-912458-90-9). E A Seemann.

Yesterday's Augusta. A. Ray Rowland & Helen Callahan. LC 76-10699. (Historic Cities Ser.: No. 27). (Illus.). 128p. 1976. 7.95 (ISBN 0-912458-66-6). E A Seemann.

Yesterday's Authors of Books for Children: Facts & Pictures about Authors & Illustrators of Books for Young People, 2 vols. Ed. by Anne Commire. LC 76-17501. (Yesterday's Authors of Books for Children Ser.). (Illus.). (YA) (gr. 7-12). 70.00x ea.; Vol. 1, 1977. (ISBN 0-8103-0073-7); Vol. 2 1978. (ISBN 0-8103-0090-7). Gale.

Yesterday's Birmingham. Malcolm C. McMillan. LC 75-14471. (Historic Cities Ser.: No. 18). (Illus.). 208p. 1975. 12.95 (ISBN 0-912458-40-2). E A Seemann.

Yesterday's Burdens: A Novel. Robert M. Coates. LC 74-23583. (Lost American Fiction Ser.). 275p. 1975. 7.95 (ISBN 0-8093-0717-0). S Ill U Pr.

Yesterday's California. Russ Leadabrand et al. LC 75-14450. (Historic States Ser.: No. 3). (Illus.). 272p. 1975. 14.95 (ISBN 0-912458-41-0). E A Seemann.

Yesterday's Cars. Paul R. Dexler. LC 79-1462. (Superwheels & Thrill Sports Bks.). (Illus.). (gr. 4 up). 1979. PLB 8.95 (ISBN 0-8225-0420-0). Lerner Pubns.

Yesterday's Chicago. Herman Kogan & Rick Kogan. LC 76-10381. (Historic Cities Ser.: No. 22). (Illus.). 1976. 12.95 (ISBN 0-912458-65-8). E A Seemann.

Yesterday's Children. David Gerrold. 1976. Repr. of 1972 ed. lib. bdg. 17.95x (ISBN 0-88411-193-8, Pub. by Aeonian Pr). Amereon Ltd.

Yesterday's Children. Linda Moore. 1986. 12.00 (ISBN 0-916620-60-3). Portals Pr.

Yesterday's Cincinnati. Luke Feck. LC 75-14411. (Illus.). 1977. pap. 5.95 (ISBN 0-912458-91-7). E A Seemann.

Yesterday's Cincinnati. 2nd ed. Luke Feck. (Illus.). 240p. 1987. 15.95 (ISBN 0-89879-291-6). Writers Digest.

Yesterday's Cleveland. George E. Condon. LC 76-21243. (Historic Cities Ser: No. 30). (Illus.). 160p. 1976. 9.95 (ISBN 0-912458-73-9). E A Seemann.

Yesterday's Columbus: A Pictorial History of Ohio's Capital. George E. Condon. (Seemann's Historic Cities Ser.: No. 31). (Illus.). 1977. 9.95 (ISBN 0-912458-94-1). E A Seemann.

Yesterday's Connecticut. Malcolm L. Johnson. LC 76-10391. (Historic States Ser.: No. 6). (Illus.). 144p. 1976. 9.95 (ISBN 0-912458-74-7). E A Seemann.

Yesterday's Daughter. Patricia Calvert. LC 86-13753. 144p. (YA) (gr. 7 up). 1986. 11.95 (ISBN 0-684-18746-9, Pub. by Scribner). Macmillan.

Yesterday's Daughter. Patricia Calvert. (YA) 1988. pap. 2.50 (ISBN 0-380-70470-6, Flare). Avon.

Yesterday's Detroit. Frank Angelo. LC 74-75292. (Illus.). 1977. pap. 5.95 (ISBN 0-912458-89-5). E A Seemann.

Yesterday's Dreams Become Tommorrow's Memories. James A. Logue. 1988. 5.95 (ISBN 0-533-07706-0). Vantage.

Yesterday's Echoes Today & Tomorrow. Addie H. Yeager. 40p. 1988. 7.00 (ISBN 0-8062-3204-8). Carlton.

Yesterday's Enemy. William Haggard. 15.95 (ISBN 0-88411-665-4, Pub. by Aeonian Pr). Amereon Ltd.

Yesterday's Faces, Vol. 2. Robert Sampson. LC 82-73597. 1984. 24.95 (ISBN 0-87972-262-2); pap. 12.95 (ISBN 0-87972-263-0). Bowling Green Univ.

Yesterday's Faces: A Study of Series Characters in the Early Pulp Magazines, Vol. 1. Robert Sampson. LC 82-73597. 1983. 20.95 (ISBN 0-87972-217-7); pap. 10.95 (ISBN 0-87972-218-5). Bowling Green Univ.

Yesterday's Faces, a Study of Series Characters in the Early Pulp Magazines: The Solvers, Vol. 4. Robert Sampson. LC 82-73597. (Illus.). 320p. 1987. 35.95 (ISBN 0-87972-414-5); pap. 17.95 (ISBN 0-87972-415-3). Bowling Green Univ.

Yesterday's Faces: From the Dark Side, Vol. 3. Robert Sampson. LC 82-73597. (Illus.). 266p. 1897. 25.95 (ISBN 0-87972-362-9); pap. 11.95 (ISBN 0-87972-363-7). Bowling Green Univ.
Yesterday's Fire Engines. Paul W. Hatmon. LC 80-11158. (Superwheels & Thrill Sports Bks.). (Illus.). (gr. 4-9). 1980. PLB 8.95 (ISBN 0-8225-0430-8). Lerner Pubns.
Yesterday's Florida. Nixon Smiley. LC 74-75296. (Historic States Ser.: No. 1). (Illus.). 256p. 1974. 12.95 (ISBN 0-912458-39-9). E A Seemann.
Yesterday's Florida Keys. Stan Windhorn & Wright Langley. LC 74-7669. (Illus.). pap. 5.95 (ISBN 0-912458-93-3). E A Seemann.
Yesterday's Florida Keys. Stan Windhorn & Wright Langley. LC 74-76691. (Seemann's Historic Cities Ser.: No. 12). (Illus.). 128p. 1985. Repr. of 1974 ed. 11.95 (ISBN 0-911607-00-5). Langley Pr.
Yesterday's Ft. Myers. Marian Godown & Alberta Rawchuck. LC 75-559. (Historic Cities Ser.: No. 15). (Illus.). 1975. 7.95 (ISBN 0-912458-49-6). E A Seemann.
Yesterday's Girl. Madeline Sunshine. 208p. (Orig.). (gr. 7 up). 1982. pap. 1.95 (ISBN 0-590-32446-2, Windswept). Scholastic Inc.
Yesterday's Gone. N. J. Crisp. LC 83-47879. 324p. 1983. 16.95 (ISBN 0-670-79389-2). Viking.
Yesterday's Gone. N. J. Crisp. 320p. 1988. pap. 3.95 (ISBN 0-14-010817-3). Penguin.
Yesterday's Gower. J. Mansel Thomas. 234p. 1982. 23.70x (ISBN 0-85088-747-X, Pub. by Gomer Pr). State Mutual Bk.
Yesterday's Heroes: Revisiting the Old-Time Baseball Stars. Marty Appel. LC 88-3516. (Illus.). 288p. 1988. 16.95 (ISBN 0-688-07516-9). Morrow.
Yesterday's Horses. Jean S. Doty. LC 84-42981. 120p. (gr. 5-9). 1985. 10.95 (ISBN 0-02-733040-0). Macmillan.
Yesterday's Indiana. Byron L. Troyer. LC 75-14381. (Illus.). 1977. pap. 7.95 (ISBN 0-912458-84-4). E A Seemann.
Yesterday's Island. Anne Weale. (Harlequin Presents Ser.). 192p. 1983. pap. 1.95 (ISBN 0-373-10622-X). Harlequin Bks.
Yesterday's Key West. Stan Windhorn & Wright Langley. LC 73-80596. (Historic Cities Ser: No. 4). (Illus.). 144p. 1973. 8.95 (ISBN 0-912458-25-9). E A Seemann.
Yesterday's Key West. Stan Windhorn & Wright Langley. LC 73-80596. (Seemann's Historic Cities Ser.). (Illus.). 144p. 1983. Repr. of 1973 ed. 11.95 (ISBN 0-911607-01-3). Langley Pr.
Yesterday's Lifestyle-Today's Survival: The Life of a Real Ozark Mountain Hillbilly. Dee-Dee McWilliams. (Illus.). 80p. (Orig.). 1983. pap. 4.95 (ISBN 0-943962-01-3). Viewpoint Pr.
Yesterday's Los Angeles. Norman Dash. LC 76-21249. (Historic Cities Ser.: No. 26). (Illus.). 208p. 1976. 12.95 (ISBN 0-912458-70-4). E A Seemann.
Yesterday's Love. Alice M. Johnson. 112p. 1988. 8.95 (ISBN 0-8062-3316-8). Carlton.
Yesterday's Massachusetts. Ivan Sandrof. (Seamann's Historic States Ser.: No. 7). (Illus.). 9.95 (ISBN 0-89530-000-1). E A Seemann.
Yesterday's Memphis. Charles W. Crawford. LC 76-10384. (Historic Cities Ser: No. 25). (Illus.). 160p. 1976. 9.95 (ISBN 0-912458-69-0). E A Seemann.
Yesterday's Miami. Nixon Smiley. LC 73-80590. (Illus.). 1977. pap. 5.95 (ISBN 0-912458-78-X). E A Seemann.
Yesterday's Michigan. Frank Angelo. LC 75-45219. (Historic States Ser.: No. 5). (Illus.). 1976. 13.95 (ISBN 0-912458-62-3). E A Seemann.
Yesterday's Milwaukee. Robert W. Wells. LC 76-10377. (Historic Cities Ser: No. 23). (Illus.). 144p. 1976. 9.95 (ISBN 0-912458-67-4). E A Seemann.
Yesterday's Motorcycles. Bob Karolevitz. LC 85-81540. (Illus.). 136p. 1986. text ed. 11.95 (ISBN 0-940161-05-2); pap. text ed. 7.95 (ISBN 0-940161-02-8). Dakota Homestead Pub.
Yesterday's Music. Megan Hughes. 288p. 1984. pap. 2.95 (ISBN 0-8439-2085-8, Leisure Bks). Leisure NY.
Yesterday's Nashville. Carl Zibart. LC 75-44475. (Historic Cities Ser.: No. 16). (Illus.). 1976. 9.95 (ISBN 0-912458-57-7). E A Seemann.
Yesterday's Palm Beach. Stuart B. McIver. LC 76-15394. (Historic Cities Ser: No. 29). (Illus.). 144p. 1976. 9.95 (ISBN 0-912458-72-0). E A Seemann.
Yesterday's Papers: The Rolling Stones in Print, 1963-1984. Jessica MacPhail. (Rock & Roll Reference Ser.: No. 19). (Illus.). 236p. 1986. 29.50 (ISBN 0-87650-209-5, 3450); 39.50. Pierian.
Yesterday's People: Life in Contemporary Appalachia. Jack E. Weller. LC 65-27012. 184p. 1965. pap. 5.00 (ISBN 0-8131-0109-3). U Pr of Ky.
Yesterday's Philadelphia. George Wilson. LC 75-2161. (Historic Cities Ser.: No. 13). (Illus.). 1974. 9.95 (ISBN 0-912458-50-X). E a Seemann.
Yesterday's Polk County. Louise K. Frisbie. LC 75-44454. (Illus.). 1976. 8.95 (ISBN 0-912458-64-X, Pub-by E A Seemann). Imperial Pub Co.
Yesterdays: Popular Song in America. Charles Hamm. (Illus.). 560p. 1983. pap. 11.95 (ISBN 0-393-30062-5). Norton.
Yesterday's Radicals: A Study of the Affinity Between Unitarianism & Broad Church Anglicanism in the Nineteenth Century. Dennis G. Wigmore-Beddoes. 182p. 1971. 19.95 (ISBN 0-227-67751-X). Attic Pr.
Yesterday's Rochdale. Hendon Publishing Co., Ltd. Staff. 1986. 22.40x (ISBN 0-317-54198-6, Pub. by Hendon Pub UK). State Mutual Bk.
Yesterday's Roses. Lynda Trent. 1988. pap. 4.50 (ISBN 0-451-40077-1, Onyx). NAL.
Yesterday's Rulers: The Making of the British Colonial Service. Robert Heussler. LC 63-8326. (Illus.). 1963. 24.95x (ISBN 0-8156-0029-1). Syracuse U Pr.
Yesterday's San Diego. Neil Morgan & Tom Blair. LC 74-44455. (Historic Cities Ser.: No. 21). 1976. 9.95 (ISBN 0-912458-63-1). E A Seemann.
Yesterday's Sarasota. Del Marth. LC 73-80594. (Illus.). 1977. pap. 5.95 (ISBN 0-912458-77-1). E A Seemann.
Yesterday's School & Yesterday's School Books, 2 Vols. Ruth Freeman & Larry G. Freeman. LC 62-16427. 1962. Set. 15.00 (ISBN 0-686-66391-8). Vol. 1 (ISBN 0-87282-068-8). Vol. 2 (ISBN 0-87282-069-6). Am Life Foun.
Yesterday's Snowman. Gail Mack. LC 78-6090. (Illus.). (ps-2). 1979. 6.95 (ISBN 0-394-83662-6). Pantheon.
Yesterday's Soldiers: European Military Professionalism in South America, 1890-1940. Frederick M. Nunn. LC 82-6961. xiv, 365p. 1983. 28.50x (ISBN 0-8032-3305-1). U of Nebr Pr.
Yesterday's Son. A. C. Crispin. (Star Trek Ser.). (Orig.). 1983. pap. 2.95 (ISBN 0-671-47315-8, Timescape). PB.
Yesterday's Son, No. 11. 192p. 1987. pap. 3.50 (ISBN 0-671-60550-X). PB.
Yesterday's Spy. Len Deighton. 224p. 1976. pap. 2.95 (ISBN 0-446-30882-X). Warner Bks.
Yesterday's Streets. Silvia Tennenbaum. LC 81-1119. 544p. 1981. 15.95 (ISBN 0-394-51478-5). Random.
Yesterday's Streets. Silvia Tennenbaum. 576p. 1982. pap. 3.95 (ISBN 0-345-30030-0). Ballantine.
Yesterday's Summer. Leydel J. Willis. 24p. 1984. pap. 3.00 (ISBN 0-930416-09-0). Clodele.
Yesterday's Tampa. Hampton Dunn. LC 72-82937. (Illus.). 1977. pap. 5.95 (ISBN 0-912458-92-5). E A Seemann.
Yesterdays, Today & Smiles, Vol. II. Mary E. Pitney. 32p. 1987. 6.95 (ISBN 0-8062-3151-3). Carlton.
Yesterday's Tomorrows: Favorite Stories from Forty Years As a Science Fiction Writer. Ed. by Frederik Pohl. 1982. pap. 9.95 (ISBN 0-425-05648-1). Berkley Pub.
Yesterday's Tomorrows: Past Visions of the American Future. Ed. by Joseph J. Corn & Brian Horrigan. (Illus.). 208p. (Orig.). 1984. 29.95 (ISBN 0-671-54276-1); pap. 17.95 (ISBN 0-671-54133-1). Summit Bks.
Yesterday's Toys. Larry Freeman & Ruth Freeman. LC 61-15922. (Illus., Orig.). 1962. 5.00 (ISBN 0-87282-057-2). Am Life Foun.
Yesterday's Toys with Today's Prices. Fred Fintel & Marilyn Fintel. LC 84-52273. 200p. 1985. pap. text ed. 14.95 (ISBN 0-87069-438-3). Wallace-Homestead.
Yesterday's Trains. Patrick C. Dorin. LC 81-3696. (Superwheels & Thrill Sports Bks.). (Illus.). (gr. 4-9). 1981. PLB 8.95 (ISBN 0-8225-0439-1, ASTERISKS). Lerner Pubns.
Yesterday's Trucks. Patrick C. Dorin. LC 81-20717. (Superwheels & Thrill Sports Bks.). (Illus.). (gr. 4-9). 1982. PLB 8.95 (ISBN 0-8225-0502-9). Lerner Pubns.
Yesterday's Washington, D. C. Charles Ewing. LC 76-10376. (Historic Cities Ser: No. 24). (Illus.). 160p. 1976. 9.95 (ISBN 0-912458-68-2). E A Seemann.
Yesterdays with Actors. Catherine M. Reignolds Winslow. LC 72-1481. (Essay Index Reprint Ser.). Repr. of 1887 ed. 18.00 (ISBN 0-8369-2879-2). Ayer Co Pubs.
Yesterdays with Authors. James T. Fields. (Illus.). 1970. Repr. of 1900 ed. 16.50 (ISBN 0-404-00603-5). AMS Pr.
Yesterdays with Authors. James T. Fields. LC 75-108481. (Illus.). 1970. Repr. of 1900 ed. 14.00x (ISBN 0-403-00209-5). Scholarly.
Yesterday's Word Today. John F. Craghan. LC 82-12648. 496p. 1982. pap. 14.95 (ISBN 0-8146-1273-3). Liturgical Pr.
Yesterdays Yesteryears: The Lesney "Matchbox" Models. Robert Carter & Eddy Rubinstein. (Illus.). 128p. 1987. 29.95 (ISBN 0-85429-578-X, Pub. by G T Foulis Ltd). Haynes Pubns.
Yesteryear in Annapolis. Harold N. Burdett. LC 74-26773. (Illus.). 102p. 1974. pap. 4.00 (ISBN 0-87033-197-3). Tidewater.
Yesteryear in Clark County, Ohio, 2 vols. in one. Ed. by Mary A. Skardon. (Annual Monograph Ser.). 76p. (Repr. of 1947 & 1948 eds.). 1978. pap. 4.00 (ISBN 0-686-29091-7). Clark County Hist Soc.
Yesteryears. Lee T. Rector. Compiled by Kathleen Tibbetts & Laurene J. Tibbetts. 117p. 1982. write for info. Rector Pub.
Yesteryears of Green Oak, Eighteen Thirty to Nineteen Thirty. Green Oak Township Historical Society Staff. LC 81-2270. (Illus.). xii, 338p. 1981. 22.50 (ISBN 0-936792-00-0). Green Oak Township.
Yet. Cid Corman. 1974. pap. 6.00 (ISBN 0-685-40886-8); pap. 8.00 signed ed. (ISBN 0-685-40887-6). Elizabeth Pr.
Yet Another Voice. Norman McDaniel. 1978. pap. 1.50 (ISBN 0-8439-0516-6, Leisure Bks). Leisure NY.
Yet I Weep, Yet I Joy. Salvatore Cipparone. 4.95 (ISBN 0-686-20578-2). Ivory Scroll.
Yet More Wandering Thoughts. Thomas Smyth. 80p. 1982. 6.00 (ISBN 0-682-49884-X). Exposition-Phoenix.
Yet Not I. David Campbell. 88p. (Orig.). 1978. pap. 1.95 (ISBN 0-912315-39-3). Word Aflame.
Yet Once More: Verbal & Psychological Pattern in Milton. Edward S. Le Comte. Repr. of 1953 ed. 12.50 (ISBN 0-404-03918-9). AMS Pr.
Yet Will I Praise Him. Terry Law & Shirley Law. (Illus.). 256p. (Orig.). 1987. pap. 7.95 (ISBN 0-8007-9106-1). Revell.
Yet Will I Serve Him. Hoyt E. Stone. 1976. pap. 3.95 (ISBN 0-87148-931-7). Pathway Pr.
Yet Will I Trust Him. Rob Burkhart. LC 79-91705. (Study & Grow Electives). 64p. 1985. pap. 3.95 (ISBN 0-8307-1016-7, 6102002). Regal.
Yet Will I Trust Him: Accepting the Sovereignty of God in Times of Need. rev. ed. Peg Rankin. Ed. by Mary Beckwith. 180p. 1988. pap. 6.95 (ISBN 0-8307-1279-8, 5419458). Regal.
Yeux et la Lumiere. Vercors. 256p. 1950. 4.95 (ISBN 0-686-55145-1). French & Eur.
Yevgeny Yevtushenko: Selected Poetry. Ed. by R. R. Milner-Gulland. 1963. 6.70 (ISBN 0-08-009808-8); pap. 5.15 (ISBN 0-08-009807-X). Pergamon.
Yezidis: A Study in Survival. John S. Guest. (Illus.). 220p. 1986. 59.95 (ISBN 0-7103-0115-4, 01154). Routledge Chapman & Hall.
Ygnacio Valley Eighteen Thirty-Four to Nineteen Seventy. George Emanuels. (Illus.). 1985. 20.00. Diablo Bks.
Ygnacio Valley, 1834-1970. 3rd ed. George Emanuels. (Illus.). 128p. 1982. casebound 20.00 (ISBN 0-317-44755-6). Panorama West.
YHWH...Is Not a Radio Station in Minneapolis: And Other Things Everyone Should Know. Craig M. Wilson. LC 82-48405. (Illus.). 96p. (Orig.). 1983. pap. 5.95 (ISBN 0-06-069432-7, RD422, HarpR). Har-Row.
YHWH's Combat with the Sea: A Canaanite Tradition in the Religion of Ancient Israel. Carola Kloos. 243p. 1986. pap. 38.25 (ISBN 90-04-08096-1, Pub. by E J Brill). Heinman.
Yiddish: A Survey & a Grammar. S. A. Birnbaum. 1979. 42.50x (ISBN 0-8020-5382-3). U of Toronto Pr.
Yiddish Alphabet Book. Frederica Postman. (Illus.). 1988. 12.95 (ISBN 1-55774-029-1, Dist. by Watts). Adama Pubs Inc.
Yiddish & English: A Century of Yiddish in America. Sol Steinmetz. LC 84-16201. 152p. 1986. 20.50. U of Ala Pr.
Yiddish As a Language of the People. Moshe Perlman. 17.85 (ISBN 0-317-58555-X). P-H.
Yiddish Dictionary Sourcebook. Herman Galvin. 1983. 20.00x (ISBN 0-87068-715-8). Ktav.
Yiddish-English Dictionary. 24.50 (ISBN 0-87559-193-0). Shalom.
Yiddish-English-Hebrew Dictionary. Ed. by Alexander Harkavy. LC 86-31414. 624p. 1988. Repr. 29.95 (ISBN 0-8052-4027-6). Schocken.
Yiddish Film. R. Gordon. 1977. lib. bdg. 59.95 (ISBN 0-8490-2851-5). Gordon Pr.
Yiddish Folktales. Ed. by Beatrice S. Weinreich & Leonard Wolf. LC 88-42594. 1988. 19.95 (ISBN 0-394-54618-0). Pantheon.
Yiddish in America: Social & Cultural Foundations. Milton Doroshkin. LC 72-78612. (Illus.). 281p. 1970. 26.50 (ISBN 0-8386-7453-4). Fairleigh Dickinson.
Yiddish in America: Socio-Linguistic Description & Analysis. Joshua A. Fishman. LC 65-63395. (General Publications Ser: Vol. 36). (Orig.). 1965. pap. text ed. 9.95x (ISBN 0-87750-110-6). Res Ctr Lang Semiotic.
Yiddish Language & Dialect: An Historical Study, 2 vols. Mathias Mieses. 1978. Set. lib. bdg. 95.00 (ISBN 0-685-62307-6). Revisionist Pr.
Yiddish Linguistics: A Classified Bilingual Index of Yiddish Serials & Collections, 1913-1958. David M. Bunis. 1984. lib. bdg. 25.00 (ISBN 0-8240-9758-0). Garland Pub.
Yiddish Linguistics: A Multilingual Bibliography, 1959-1973. Joan G. Bratkowsky. 1984. lib. bdg. 50.00 (ISBN 0-8240-9804-8). Garland Pub.
Yiddish Literature, 10 Vols, No. IV. Ed. by R. Gordon 1986. lib. bdg. 975.00 (ISBN 0-8490-3859-6). Gordon Pr.
Yiddish Literature, 10 Vols, No. III. Ed. by R. Gordon. 1986. lib. bdg. 950.95 (ISBN 0-8490-3858-8). Gordon Pr.
Yiddish Literature, 10 Vols, No. II. Ed. by R. Gordon. 1986. lib. bdg. 975.00 (ISBN 0-8490-3857-X). Gordon Pr.
Yiddish Literature, 10 Vols, No. I. Ed. by R. Grodon. 1986. lib. bdg. 975.95 (ISBN 0-8490-3856-1). Gordon Pr.
Yiddish Literature in English Translation; Books Published 1945-1967. 2nd ed. Dina Abramowicz. LC 71-5971. 39p. 1968. pap. 3.00 (ISBN 0-914512-11-0). Yivo Inst.
Yiddish Literature in English Translation: List of Books in Print. Compiled by Dina Abramowicz. 1976. pap. text ed. 7.50 (ISBN 0-914512-36-6). Yivo Inst.
Yiddish Press: An Americanizing Agency. Mordecai Soltes. LC 75-89237. (American Education: Its Men, Institutions & Ideas Ser). 1969. Repr. of 1925 ed. 15.00 (ISBN 0-405-01474-0). Ayer Co Pubs.
Yiddish Proverbs. Ed. by Hanan J. Ayalti. LC 49-11135. (Illus., Bilingual). 1963. pap. 4.75 (ISBN 0-8052-0050-9). Schocken.
Yiddish Proverbs: A Collection. Malachi McCormick. (Proverbs of the World Ser.). (Illus.). 60p. (Orig.). 1982. pap. text ed. 12.50 (ISBN 0-943984-02-5). Stone St Pr.
Yiddish Scientific Institute Historishe Shriftn. Ed. by Yiddish Scientific Institute, Warsaw. 1977. lib. bdg. 132.95 (ISBN 0-8490-2852-3). Gordon Pr.
Yiddish Stories Old & New. Ed. by Irving Howe & Eliezer Greenberg. (YA) (gr. 7 up). 1977. pap. 2.50 (ISBN 0-380-00887-4, 47803, Bard). Avon.
Yiddish Stories Old & New. Ed. by Irving Howe & Eliezer Greenberg. LC 74-8116. 128p. (gr. 7 up). 1974. 5.95 (ISBN 0-8234-0246-0). Holiday.
Yiddish Tales. facsimile ed. Ed. by Moses Rischin. Tr. by Helena Frank from Yiddish. LC 74-29531. (Modern Jewish Experience Ser.). (Eng.). 1975. Repr. of 1912 ed. 47.50x (ISBN 0-405-06755-0). Ayer Co Pubs.
Yiddish Teacher. rev. ed. Hyman Goldin. 144p. 1977. pap. 5.95 (ISBN 0-88482-687-2). Hebrew Pub.
Yiddish Two: A Textbook for Intermediate Courses. Mordkhe Schaechter. LC 85-14187. (Illus.). 524p. 1986. text ed. 30.00 (ISBN 0-89727-052-5). ISHI PA.
Yiddish Writers' Almanac: Year After Year, 1987. Ed. by A. Vergelis. 228p. 1987. pap. 9.95 (ISBN 0-8285-3494-2, Pub. by Raduga Pubs USSR). Imported Pubns.
Yiddishe Kinder Alef. 3rd ed. Joseph Mlotek. 128p. 1985. pap. 5.00 (ISBN 0-318-22116-0). Workmen's Circle.
Yiddishe Kinder Beyz. Joseph Mlotek & Matis Olitsky. 120p. 1975. pap. 5.00 (ISBN 0-318-22117-9). Workmen's Circle.
Yiddishe Kinder Giml. S. Efron & Yudel Mark. 271p. 1985. pap. 6.00 (ISBN 0-318-22118-7). Workmen's Circle.
Yield Curve Analysis: The Fundamentals of Risk & Return. Livingston G. Douglas. 1988. 39.95 (ISBN 0-13-972456-7). Prentice Hall Pr.
Yield, Flow & Fracture of Polycrystals. T. N. Baker. (Illus.). 380p. 1984. 93.75 (ISBN 0-85334-225-3, Pub. by Elsevier Applied Sci England). Elsevier.
Yield Formation in the Main Field Crops. J. Petr et al. (Developments in Crop Science Ser.: No. 13). 336p. 1988. 105.25 (ISBN 0-444-98954-4). Elsevier.
Yield Improvement in Wheat. write for info. (ISBN 0-89118-523-2). Crop Sci Soc Am.
Yield Modeling & Defect Tolerance in VLSI. Ed. by W. R. Moore et al. 304p. 1988. 75.00 (ISBN 0-85274-398-X, Pub. by A Hilger UK). Taylor & Francis.
Yield Response to Water. C. L. Bentvelsen & V. Branscheid. (Irrigation & Drainage Papers: No. 33). (Illus.). 201p. (Eng., Fr. & Span.). 1979. pap. 20.25 (ISBN 92-5-100744-6, F1843, FAO). UNIPUB.
Yield Simulation for Integrated Circuits. Duncan Moore & Henry Walker. 1987. lib. bdg. 39.95 (ISBN 0-89838-244-0). Kluwer Academic.
Yield Table for Wrap-Around Mortgage No. 707. rev. ed. 27.50 (ISBN 0-685-59991-4). Finan Pub.
Yield Table for Wraparound Loans. Financial Publishing Co. Staff. 258p. 1980. pap. 27.50 (ISBN 0-87600-707-8). Finan Pub.
Yielding to Courage: The Spiritual Path to Overcoming Fear. Judith C. Lechman. LC 87-46215. 160p. 1988. 14.95 (ISBN 0-06-065222-5, HarpR). Har-Row.
Yielding to the Power of God: The Importance of Surrender, Abandonment, & Obedience to God's Will. Ann Shields. 48p. (Orig.). 1987. pap. 1.95 (ISBN 0-89283-348-3). Servant.
Yields If Prepaid, Seventy-Eight's Method No. 841. Financial Publishing Company Staff. cancelled (ISBN 0-685-02561-6). Finan Pub.
Yin & Yang: Two Hands Clapping. Jim W. Garvy, Jr. Ed. by Jeremiah Liebermann. (Five Phase Energetics Ser.: No. 2). (Illus.). 1985. pap. 3.00 (ISBN 0-943450-01-2). Wellbeing Bks.
Yin Chih Wen: The Tract of the Quiet Way. Yin Chih Wen. Tr. by Teitaro Suzuki & Paul Carus. LC 78-70142. Repr. of 1906 ed. 16.50 (ISBN 0-404-17415-9). AMS Pr.
Yin: New Poems. Carolyn Kizer. 1984. 12.95 (ISBN 0-918526-44-2); pap. 6.95 (ISBN 0-918526-45-0). Boa Edns.
Yin Soon. (Sharazad Stories Ser.). (Illus., Arabic.). (gr. 5-12). pap. 3.50x (ISBN 0-86685-246-8). Intl Bk Ctr.
Yin Zhou Qingtong Qi Tonglun. Ed. by Rong Geng & Zhang Weichi. 151p. 315.00x (ISBN 0-317-69225-9, Pub. by Han-Shan Tang Ltd). State Mutual Bk.
Yindala: An Original Australian Story. Barbara McNab. 42p. (gr. 3-5). 1986. 4.95 (ISBN 0-533-06398-1). Vantage.
Ying-Ling Does Mitzvot. Neva Goldstein-Alpern. (Illus.). 12p. (ps). 1987. 4.95 (ISBN 0-910818-72-X). Judaica Pr.
Ying Yang: The Chinese Way of Love. Charles Humana & Wang Wu. 256p. 1980. pap. 1.50 (ISBN 0-380-01478-5, 11585). Avon.

Ying-Ying: Pieces of a Childhood. Jeanne Joe. (Illus.). 112p. (Orig.). (gr. 4 up). 1982. pap. 4.95 (ISBN 0-934788-02-2). E-W Pub Co.

Yingl Tsingl Khvat. Mani Leib. (Illus.). 32p. (ps-5). 11.95 (ISBN 0-918825-52-0, Dist. by Kampmann & Co.); lib. bdg. 11.75x (ISBN 0-918825-54-7). Moyer Bell Limited.

Yingzao Fashi. Li Jie. 1925. 3150.00x (ISBN 0-317-68532-5, Pub. by Han-Shan Tang Ltd). State Mutual Bk.

Yinkyo Shutsuda Hakushoku Doki No Kenkyu. Suiji Umehara. 1932. 375.00x (ISBN 0-317-45335-1, Pub. by Han-Shan Tang Ltd). State Mutual Bk.

Yinxu Wenzi Zhuihe. Guo Reyu. 9p. 1955. 595.00x (ISBN 0-317-69230-5, Pub. by Han-Shan Tang Ltd). State Mutual Bk.

Yira Yira Tango for Advanced Dancers. (Ballroom Dance Ser.). 1985. lib. bdg. 60.00 (ISBN 0-87700-751-9). Revisionist Pr.

Yira Yira Tango for Advanced Dancers. (Ballroom Dance Ser.). 1986. lib. bdg. 59.95 (ISBN 0-8490-3297-0). GOrdon PR.

Yitzchak, Son of Abraham. Zev Paamoni. (Shulsinger Biblical Ser.). (Illus.). (gr. 5-10). 1970. 4.00 (ISBN 0-914080-25-3). Shulsinger Sales.

Yivo Biblyografye 1942-1950: Bibliography of the Publications of the Yiddish Scientific Institute, Vol. 2. LC 47-36672. (Yivo Institute for Jewish Research, Organizatsye Fun der Yidisher Visnshaft: No. 38). 158p. (Yiddish.). 1955. 5.00 (ISBN 0-914512-30-7). Yivo Inst.

Y'Know What? M. Mildred Valeska. 1985. 6.50 (ISBN 0-8062-2455-X). Carlton.

Ylla's Cats: Eighty-Five Photographs. Ylla, pseud. 80p. 1988. pap. 5.95 (ISBN 0-486-25615-4). Dover.

YMCA Camping Centennial Series, 2 vols. Incl. Personnel. (No. 1). (Illus.). 37p. 1982. 4.95x (ISBN 0-88035-003-2); Program. (No. 2). (Illus.). 48p. 1983. 6.95x (ISBN 0-88035-007-5). YMCA USA). Human Kinetics.

YMCA Camping Centennial Series. YMCA of the U. S. A. Staff. 1984. 3-ring notebook 12.50x (ISBN 0-931250-81-1, Pub. by YMCA USA). Human Kinetics.

YMCA Cardiac Therapy Participant's Handbook. YMCA of the U. S. A. Staff. 40p. 1979. pap. 3.00x (ISBN 0-88035-066-0, Pub. by YMCA USA). Human Kinetics.

YMCA Competitive Swimming & Diving Coaches Manual. Ed. by John M. Ferrell et al. 1981. 3 ring binder 18.00x (ISBN 0-88035-028-8, Pub. by YMCA USA). Human Kinetics.

YMCA Day Camp Manual, 7 pts. (Illus.). 172p. 1982. 3-ring notebook 20.00 (ISBN 0-88035-004-0, Pub. by YMCA USA). Human Kinetics.

YMCA Home Team Family Handbook. YMCA of the U. S. A. Staff. 16p. 1984. Ten for 10.00x. pap. text ed. 1.00x (ISBN 0-931250-89-7, Pub. by YMCA USA). Human Kinetics.

YMCA Home Team Leaders Guide. YMCA of the U. S. A. Staff. 49p. 1984. pap. text ed. 8.00x (ISBN 0-931250-90-0, Pub. by YMCA USA). Human Kinetics.

YMCA Membership Retention: A Project of the Urban Group Marketing Task Force. YMCA of the U. S. A. Staff. 1988. 3 ring notebook 55.00 (ISBN 0-87322-184-2, YMCA USA). Human Kinetics.

YMCA Personnel & Salary Administration Plan, 8 sections. National Board of YMCA. Ed. by Earl Armstrong. (Illus.). 185p. 1983. 3 ring notebook 50.00x (ISBN 0-88035-008-3, YMCA USA). Human Kinetics.

YMCA Preschool Age Child Care Manual. 1987. 3-ring ntbk. 40.00x (ISBN 0-87322-093-5, Pub. by YMCA USA). Human Kinetics.

YMCA Programs for New Families. 1987. 3-ring ntbk. 35.00x (ISBN 0-87322-116-8, Pub. by YMCA USA). Human Kinetics.

YMCA Progressive Swimming Instructor's Guide. Ed. by YMCA of the U. S. A. Staff. 102p. (Orig.). pap. text ed. 12.00x (ISBN 0-87322-057-9, Pub. by YMCA USA). Human Kinetics.

YMCA Risk Management Program. YMCA of the U. S. A. Staff. 84p. 1983. pap. text ed. 10.00x (ISBN 0-88035-059-8, Pub. by YMCA USA). Human Kinetics.

YMCA School Age Child Care. 165p. 1982. pap. 50.00x 3 ring notebook (ISBN 0-88035-006-7, YMCA USA). Human Kinetics.

YMCA Wellness Notebook. (Illus.). 1983. 3-ring notebook 20.00x (ISBN 0-88035-043-1, YMCA USA). Human Kinetics.

YMCArdiac Therapy. Gary Fry & Kathy Berra. (Illus.). 400p. 1981. text ed. 10.00x (ISBN 0-88035-000-8, YMCA USA). Human Kinetics.

Ymecto Ilbeta.... ("In Lieu of Flowers)...". Emilia Resanovich. 320p. 1984. 12.00 (ISBN 0-915887-05-3). Kosovo Pub Co.

Yngling. John Dalmas. 256p. (Orig.). 1987. pap. 2.95 (ISBN 0-8125-3473-5, Dist. by Warner Pub Services & St. Martin's Press). Tor Bks.

Yo el Supremo. Agusto R. Bastos. (Ayacucho Library Collection Ser.: Vol. 123). (Span.). 1986. 29.95 (ISBN 0-317-56874-4, Pub. by Biblioteca Ayacucho); pap. 15.00 (ISBN 0-317-56875-2, Pub. by Biblioteca Ayacucho). Humanities.

Yo, en Cristo Resucitado see I, in Christ Arisen.

Yo en una Nube Volaba. M. Pliatskovski. (Illus.). 21p. (Span.). 1979. pap. 1.99 (ISBN 0-8285-1310-4, Pub. by Progress Pubs USSR). Imported Pubns.

Yo Ho & Kim. Ruth Jaynes. (gr. 1-4). 2.33 (ISBN 0-87505-319-X, Pub. by Lawrence). Borden.

Yo Ho & Kim at Sea. Ruth Jaynes. (gr. 1-4). 2.33 (ISBN 0-87505-320-3, Pub. by Lawrence). Borden.

Yo? Obedecer a Mi Marido? Elisabeth R. Handford. Orig. Title: Me? Obey Him? 128p. (Span.). 1984. pap. 3.50 (ISBN 0-8254-1302-8). Kregel.

Yo, Poe. Frank Gannon. 112p. 1987. 14.95 (ISBN 0-670-81481-4). Viking.

Yo, Poe. Frank Gannon. 160p. 1988. pap. 5.95 (ISBN 0-14-009743-0). Penguin.

Yo Puedo: Bilingual Leadership Program for Junior & Senior High. Uvaldo Palomares & Gerry Ball. 1980. 89.95 (ISBN 0-86584-036-9). Palomares & Assoc.

Yo Soy Cereza, Vuela Conmigo. new ed. Glen Chase. Tr. by J. De Torres from Eng. (Pimienta Collection, Cereza Delicias Ser: No. 6). (Illus.). 160p. (Span.). 1975. pap. 1.25 (ISBN 0-88473-236-3). Fiesta Pub.

Yo Vengo de los Arabos. Esteban J. Palacios & Jose A. Madrigal. LC 86-82605. (Coleccion Caniqui Ser.). 131p. (Orig.). 1987. pap. 9.95 (ISBN 0-89729-420-3). Ediciones.

Yobbo Nowt. John McGrath. 72p. (Orig.). 1981. pap. 5.95 (ISBN 0-904383-76-8, NO. 4135). Routledge Chapman & Hall.

Yobgorgle: Mystery Monster of Lake Ontario. Daniel M. Pinkwater. LC 79-11364. 156p. (gr. 3-6). 1979. 8.95 (ISBN 0-395-28970-X, Clarion). HM.

Yobo: A Novel of Korea. Whalen M. Wehry. LC 83-82585. 458p. 1984. 17.50x (ISBN 0-930878-38-8). Hollym Intl.

Yobri: Etude Geographique Du Terroir D'un Village Gourmantche De Haute-Volta. Gerard Remy. (Atlas Des Structurews Agraires Au Sud Du Sahara: No. 1). (Illus.). 1967. pap. 14.00x (ISBN 90-2796-056-9). Mouton.

Yochib: The River Cave. C. William Steele. LC 85-5894. (Illus.). 176p. (Orig.). 1985. 15.95 (ISBN 0-939748-09-6); pap. 10.95 (ISBN 0-939748-10-X). Cave Bks MO.

Yod, Your Special Life Purpose. Miss Dee. LC 83-70271. 72p. 1983. 7.95 (ISBN 0-86690-234-1, 2287-01). Am Fed Astrologers.

Yoda's Activity Book. James Razzi. (Illus.). 96p. (gr. 1-6). 1981. pap. 4.95 (ISBN 0-394-84689-3). Random.

Yoga. J. F. C. Fuller. 180p. 1975. 7.00 (ISBN 0-911662-55-3). Yoga.

Yoga. James Hewitt. (Teach Yourself Ser.). (Illus.). 209p. 1988. pap. 7.95 (ISBN 0-679-72118-5). Random.

Yoga: A Gem for Women. Geeta Iyengar. (Illus.). 307p. 1986. 16.94 (ISBN 0-317-62743-0, Allied Pubs Pvt). Timeless Bks.

Yoga & Depth Psychology. I. P. Sachdeva. 1978. 10.95 (ISBN 0-89684-049-2, Pub. by Motilal Banarsidass India). Orient Bk Dist.

Yoga & Depth Psychology. I. P. Sachdeva. 1979. 16.00x (ISBN 0-8364-0454-8). South Asia Bks.

Yoga & Depth Psychology. I. P. Sachdeva. 269p. 1978. 19.95 (ISBN 0-317-12334-3, Pub. by Motilal Banarsi). Asia Bk Corp.

Yoga & Education. Ed. by Norman C. Dowsett & Sitaram Jayaswal. (Integral Educaion Ser.: No. 6). 95p. 1977. pap. 2.25 (ISBN 0-89071-273-5). Aurobindo Assn.

Yoga & Health. Selvarajan Yesudian & Elisabeth Haich. (Unwin Paperbacks). (Illus.). 1978. pap. 8.95 (ISBN 0-04-149033-9). Unwin Hyman.

Yoga & Indian Philosophy. Karel Werner. 1977. 11.50x (ISBN 0-8426-0900-8, Pub. by Motilal Banarsidass India). Orient Bk Dist.

Yoga & Indian Philosophy. Karel Werner. 1979. 12.50x (ISBN 0-8364-0479-3). South Asia Bks.

Yoga & Its Objects. Sri Aurobindo. 33p. 1984. pap. 0.75 (ISBN 0-89071-314-6, Pub. by Sri Aurobindo Ashram India). Aurobindo Assn.

Yoga & Long Life. 5th ed. Yogi Gupta. LC 58-9502. (Illus.). 1983. 15.00 (ISBN 0-911664-01-7). Yogi Gupta.

Yoga & Mysticism: An Introduction to Vedanta. Swami Prabhavananda. 53p. 1984. pap. 3.95 (ISBN 0-87481-020-5). Vedanta Pr.

Yoga & Prayer. Michaelle. Tr. by Diane Cumming. pap. 6.50 (ISBN 0-87061-059-7). Chr Classics.

Yoga & Psychotherapy: The Evolution of Consciousness. Swami Rama et al. 332p. 13.95 (ISBN 0-89389-000-6); pap. 9.95 (ISBN 0-89389-036-7). Himalayan Pubs.

Yoga & Spiritual Life. rev. ed. Sri Chinmoy. LC 74-81309. 160p. 1974. pap. 4.95 (ISBN 0-88497-040-X). Aum Pubns.

Yoga & the Bhagavad-Gita: An Introduction to the Philosophy of Yoga. Tom McArthur. LC 87-29808. 112p. 1987. Repr. lib. bdg. 22.95x (ISBN 0-8095-7037-8). Borgo Pr.

Yoga & the Hindu Tradition. Jean Varenne. Tr. by Derek Coltman from Fr. LC 75-19506. 1976. pap. 4.95X (ISBN 0-226-85116-8, P744, Phoen). U of Chicago Pr.

Yoga & the Jesus Prayer Tradition: An Experiment in Faith. Thomas Matus. 200p. (Orig.). 1984. pap. 8.95 (ISBN 0-8091-2638-9). Paulist Pr.

Yoga & Yogic Powers. Yogi Gupta. LC 63-14948. (Illus.). 1963. 20.00 (ISBN 0-911664-02-5). Yogi Gupta.

Yoga Aphorisms. W. Q. Judge. 59.95 (ISBN 0-8490-1343-7). Gordon Pr.

Yoga Aphorisms of Patanjali. Tr. & pref. by William Q. Judge. xxi, 74p. 1930. Repr. of 1889 ed. 3.00 (ISBN 0-938998-11-0). Theosophy.

Yoga As Philosophy & Religion. S. Dasgupta. lib. bdg. 79.95 (ISBN 0-87968-104-7). Krishna Pr.

Yoga As Philosophy & Religion. S. Dasgupta. 200p. 1978. 14.95. Asia Bk Corp.

Yoga As Philosophy & Religion. Surendranath Dasgupta. 1987. Repr. of 1924 ed. 12.50x (ISBN 81-208-0217-9, Pub. by Motilal Banarsidass). South Asia Bks.

Yoga Can Change Your Life. Swami Jyotir Maya Nanda. (Illus.). 1975. pap. 4.99 (ISBN 0-934664-14-5). Yoga Res Foun.

Yoga During Pregnancy. Vibeke Berg. 1983. 6.95 (ISBN 0-686-44925-8, Fireside). S&S.

Yoga During Pregnancy. Sandra Jordan. (Illus.). 132p. (Orig.). 1987. pap. 12.00 (ISBN 0-9619374-0-8). Sun Moon HI.

Yoga Essays for Self-Improvement. Jyotir Swami & Maya Nanda. LC 81-65248. 248p. 1981. pap. 4.99 (ISBN 0-934664-39-0, 030). Yoga Res Foun.

Yoga Exercises for Every Body. Ruth Bender. 1975. spiral bdg. 9.95 (ISBN 0-917434-00-5). Ruben Pub.

Yoga Exercises for Health & Happiness. Swami Jyotir Maya Nanda. (Illus.). 1973. pap. 4.99 (ISBN 0-934664-15-3). Yoga Res Foun.

Yoga Exercises for More Flexible Bodies. Ruth Bender. 1977. spiral bdg. 9.95 (ISBN 0-917434-02-1). Ruben Pub.

Yoga, Facts & Fancies. K. Raghavan. 1983. 7.50x (ISBN 0-8364-0950-7, Pub. by Mukhopadhyay India). South Asia Bks.

Yoga Food Book: A Guide to Vegetarian Eating & Cooking. Larry M. Buxbaum. (Illus.). 115p. 1975. spiral bdg. 4.00 (ISBN 0-915594-01-3). Univ Great Brother.

Yoga for a Better Life. David Schonfeld. LC 79-6548. (Illus.). 1980. pap. 6.50 (ISBN 0-8356-0536-1, Quest). Theos Pub Hse.

Yoga for a New Age: A Modern Approach to Hatha Yoga. rev. ed. Bob Smith & Linda B. Smith. Ed. by Helen P. Smith. LC 86-90391. (Illus.). 260p. 1986. pap. 11.95 (ISBN 0-9616545-0-3). Smith Prod.

Yoga for All Ages. Rachel Carr. (Illus.). 160p. 1975. pap. 4.95 (ISBN 0-671-22151-5, Fireside). S&S.

Yoga for Americans. Indra Devi. 1971. pap. 2.25 (ISBN 0-451-09869-2, E9869, Sig). NAL.

Yoga for Beginners. Swami Gnaneswarananda. Ed. by Mallika C. Gupta. LC 74-29557. 200p. 1975. pap. 4.95 (ISBN 0-9600826-1-1). Vivekananda.

Yoga for Handicapped People. Barbara Brosnan. (Human Horizon Ser.). (Illus.). 208p. 1982. pap. 17.95 (ISBN 0-285-64952-3, Pub. by Souvenir Pr England). Brookline Bks.

Yoga for Health. Richard Hittleman. LC 82-90825. 256p. (Orig.). 1983. pap. 8.95 (ISBN 0-345-32798-5). Ballantine.

Yoga for Musicians & Other Special People. Eleanor Winding. (Illus.). 68p. (Orig.). 1982. pap. 7.95 (ISBN 0-88284-193-9). Alfred Pub.

Yoga for People over Fifty: Exercise Without Exhaustion. Suza Norton. LC 76-18445. 1977. 9.95 (ISBN 0-8159-7404-3). Devin.

Yoga for Physical & Mental Fitness. Sachindra K. Majumdar. LC 68-31613. (Illus.). 1968. 7.95 (ISBN 0-87396-013-0); pap. 3.95 (ISBN 0-87396-014-9). Stravon.

Yoga for Physical Fitness. R. Hittleman. 255p. 1978. 8.95. Asia Bk Corp.

Yoga for Pregnancy: Ninety-Two Safe, Gentle Stretches Appropriate for Pregnant Women & New Mothers. Sandra Jordan. (Illus.). 144p. 1988. pap. 9.95 (ISBN 0-312-02322-7). St Martin.

Yoga for the Eighties. (Illus.). 36p. 6.95. Arcline Pubns.

Yoga for the Fun of It! Hatha Yoga for Preschool Children. 3rd ed. Suzanne L. Schreiber. (Illus.). 54p. (Orig.). (ps). 1981. pap. 6.00 (ISBN 0-9608320-0-9). Sugar Marbel Pr.

Yoga for the Modern Man. M. P. Pandit. 115p. 1979. 4.00 (ISBN 0-941524-13-2). Lotus Light.

Yoga for the Modern Man. M. P. Pandit. 128p. 1988. text ed. 12.95x (ISBN 81-207-0759-1, Pub by Sterling pubs India). Apt Bks.

Yoga for the Nineties. Harbhajan Singh Khalsa. (Illus.). 36p. 1988. Repr. lib. bdg. 22.95x (ISBN 0-8095-6502-1). Borgo Pr.

Yoga for the West: A Manual for Designing Your Own Practice. Ian Rawlinson. Ed. by Alastair McNeilage. (Illus.). 200p. (Orig.). 1988. lib. bdg. 15.95 (ISBN 0-916360-26-1). CRCS Pubns CA.

Yoga for You. I. Devi. 184p. 1978. 6.95. Asia Bk Corp.

Yoga Guide. Swami Jyotir Maya Nanda. (Illus.). 1972. pap. 2.99 (ISBN 0-934664-16-1). Yoga Res Foun.

Yoga Hygiene Simplified. S. Yogendra. 155p. 1980. 8.95. Asia Bk Corp.

Yoga Illustrated Dictionary. H. Day. (Illus.). 186p. 1971. 8.95. Asia Bk Corp.

Yoga Illustrated Dictionary. Harvey Day. (Illus.). 1970. 12.95 (ISBN 0-87523-177-2). Emerson.

Yoga: Immortality & Freedom. 2nd ed. Mircea Eliade. Tr. by Willard R. Trask. LC 58-8986. (Bollingen Ser.: Vol. 56). 1970. 50.00x (ISBN 0-691-09848-4); pap. 12.50x (ISBN 0-691-01764-6). Princeton U Pr.

Yoga in Daily Life. K. S. Joshi. 163p. 1971. pap. 2.00 (ISBN 0-88253-044-5). Ind-US Inc.

Yoga in Life. Swami Lalitananda. (Illus.). 1972. pap. 2.99 - (ISBN 0-934664-17-X). Yoga Res Foun.

Yoga in Practice. Swami Jyotir Maya Nanda. (Illus.). 1974. pap. 0.99 (ISBN 0-934664-18-8). Yoga Res Foun.

Yoga in Pregnancy. Vibeke Berg. 135p. 1977. 12.95 (ISBN 0-940500-24-8, Pub. by D B Taraporwala India). Asia Bk Corp.

Yoga in Sri Aurobindo's Epic Savitri. Sri M. Pandit. 236p. 1979. 10.95 (ISBN 0-941524-15-9). Lotus Light.

Yoga Integral. Swami Jyotir Maya Nanda. (Illus.). 112p. (Span.). 1984. pap. 2.85 (ISBN 0-934664-51-X). Yoga Res Foun.

Yoga Is for Me. Susan N. Terkel. LC 81-18623. (Sports for Me Bks.). (Illus.). 48p. (gr. 2-5). 1982. PLB 7.95 (ISBN 0-8225-1098-7). Lerner Pubns.

Yoga Lessons for Developing Spiritual Consciousness. A. P. Mukerji. 7.00 (ISBN 0-911662-24-3). Yoga.

Yoga: Meaning, Values & Practice. Phulgenda Sinha. 1973. pap. 2.50 (ISBN 0-88253-259-6). Ind-US Inc.

Yoga Moves with Alan Finger. Alan Finger & Lynda Guber. (Illus.). 160p. (Orig.). 1984. pap. 9.95 (ISBN 0-671-50064-3, Wallaby). S&S.

Yoga Mystic Songs for Meditation, 6 Vols. Swami Lalitananda. 1975. pap. 2.99 ea. (ISBN 0-934664-19-6). Yoga Res Foun.

Yoga Mystic Stories & Parables. Swami Jyotir Maya Nanda. (Illus.). 1974. pap. 3.99 (ISBN 0-934664-24-2). Yoga Res Foun.

Yoga of Divine Love: A Commentary on Narada Bhakti Sutras. Swami Jyotir Maya Nanda. 1982. pap. 4.99 (ISBN 0-934664-42-0). Yoga Res Foun.

Yoga of Divine Works. 2nd ed. Sri Aurobindo. (Life Companion Library). (Illus.). 270p. Date not set. pap. 8.95 (ISBN 0-89744-015-3). Auromere.

Yoga of Herbs: (An Ayurvedic Guide to Herbal Medicine) Vasant Lad & David Frawley. LC 86-81538. (Illus.). 254p. (Orig.). 1986. pap. 11.95 (ISBN 0-941524-24-8). Lotus Light.

Yoga of Knowledge: Talks at Centre, Vol. II. M. P. Pandit. LC 86-80692. 282p. (Orig.). 1986. pap. 7.95 (ISBN 0-941524-23-X). Lotus Light.

Yoga of Light: The Classic Esoteric Handbook of Kundalini Yoga. Rieker Hans-Ulrich. Tr. by Elsy Becherer. LC 79-167868. (Illus.). 1974. pap. 7.95 (ISBN 0-913922-07-2). Dawn Horse Pr.

Yoga of Love. Madhav P. Pandit. LC 81-86373. (Talks at Center Ser.: Vol. III). 112p. (Orig.). 1982. pap. 3.95 (ISBN 0-941524-16-7). Lotus Light.

Yoga of Nutrition. Omraam M. Aivanhov. (Izvor Collection Ser.: Vol. 204). 130p. pap. 5.95 (ISBN 0-911857-03-6). Prosveta USA.

Yoga of Perfect Sight. 3rd ed. R. S. Agarwal. 1979. pap. 14.00 (ISBN 0-89744-948-7). Auromere.

Yoga of Perfect Sight: With Letters of Sri Aurobindo. R. S. Agarwal. (Illus.). 223p. 1979. pap. 5.50 (ISBN 0-89071-261-1). Aurobindo Assn.

Yoga of Perfection (Srimad Bhagavad Gita) Swami Jyotir Maya Nanda. (Illus.). 1973. pap. 3.99 (ISBN 0-934664-25-0). Yoga Res Foun.

Yoga of Self-Perfection. Madhav P. Pandit. LC 83-81299. (Talks at Centre Ser.: Vol. IV). 312p. (Orig.). 1983. pap. 7.95 (ISBN 0-941524-20-5). Lotus Light.

Yoga of Sex-Sublimation, Truth & Non-Violence. Swami Jyotir Maya Nanda. (Illus.). 1974. pap. 3.99 (ISBN 0-934664-26-9). Yoga Res Foun.

Yoga of the Bhagavad Gita. Sri-Krishna Prem. 256p. 1988. pap. 12.95 (ISBN 1-85230-023-X, Pub. by Element Bks UK). Tempest Brookline.

Yoga of the Guhyasamajatantra. Alex Wayman. 1977. 18.50 (ISBN 0-89684-003-4, Pub. by Motilal Banarsidass India). Orient Bk Dist.

Yoga of the Inward Path. Ronald P. Beesley. 1978. pap. 5.95 (ISBN 0-87516-269-X). DeVorss.

Yoga of Works: Talks at Centre I. M. P. Pandit. LC 85-50695. 192p. 1985. pap. 7.95 (ISBN 0-941524-21-3). Lotus Light.

Yoga of Yama. W. Cornold. 64p. 1970. pap. 4.95 (ISBN 0-88697-041-5). Life Science.

Yoga Philosophy in Relation to Other Systems of Indian Thought. S. N. Gupta. 1974. 13.50 (ISBN 0-89684-343-2). Orient Bk Dist.

Yoga Philosophy of Patanjali: Containing His Yoga Aphorisms with Vyasa's Commentary in Sanskrit & a Translation with Annotations Containing Many Suggestions for the Practice of Yoga. S. Hariharananda Aranya. Tr. by P. N. Mukerji from Sanskrit. LC 83-4944. 510p. 1984. 39.50x (ISBN 0-87395-728-8); pap. 10.95x (ISBN 0-87395-729-6). State U NY Pr.

Yoga Postures for Higher Awareness. 2nd, enl. ed. Sri Kriyananda. (Illus.). 140p. 1971. pap. 8.95 (ISBN 0-916124-25-8). Crystal Clarity.

Yoga Practice. S. Sivannda. 66p. 1977. 5.95. Asia Bk Corp.

Yoga Psychology. Swami Abhedananda. 8.95 (ISBN 0-87481-614-9). Vedanta Pr.

Yoga Psychology: A Practical Guide to Meditation. rev. ed. Swami Ajaya. LC 76-374539. 115p. 1976. pap. 5.95 (ISBN 0-89389-052-9). Himalayan Pubs.

Yoga Quotations from the Wisdom of Swami Jyotir Maya Nanda. Ed. by Swami Lalitananda. (Illus.). 1974. pap. 3.99 (ISBN 0-934664-27-7). Yoga Res Foun.

Yoga, Sadhana & Samadhi. Pranab Bandyopadhyay. 1987. 16.00x (ISBN 0-8364-2132-9, Pub. by KL Mukhopadhyay). South Asia Bks.

Yoga, Science of the Self. rev. ed. Marcia Moore & Mark Douglas. LC 67-19602. (Illus.). 1979. 10.00 (ISBN 0-912240-01-6). Arcane Pubns.

Yoga Secrets of Psychic Powers. Swami Jyotir Maya Nanda. (Illus.). 1974. pap. 4.99 (ISBN 0-934664-28-5). Yoga Res Foun.

Yoga Self-Taught. Andre Van Lysebeth. Tr. by Carola Congreve from Fr. Orig. Title: J'Apprends le Yoga. (Illus.). 264p. 1973. pap. 6.95 (ISBN 0-06-463360-8, EH 360, B&N Bks). Har-Row.

Yoga Stories & Parables. Swami Jyotir Manda. (Illus.). 1976. pap. 3.99 (ISBN 0-934664-41-2). Yoga Res Foun.

Yoga-Sutras of Patanjali. Ballantyne & Shastri. Ed. by S. B. Tailang. Repr. of 1983 ed. 8.50 (ISBN 0-89684-474-9). Orient Bk Dist.

Yoga Sutras of Patanjali. 8th ed. Patanjali. Tr. by Charles Johnston from Sanskrit. 1987. pap. 6.50 (ISBN 0-914732-08-0). Bro Life Inc.

Yoga-Sutras of Patanjali with the Exposition of Vyasa: A Translation & Commentary Volume I. Pandit U. Arya. xxi, 493p. 1986. pap. 16.95 (ISBN 0-89389-092-8). Himalayan Pubs.

Yoga System. rev. ed. Mithrapuram K. Alexander. LC 77-140373. (Illus.). 1971. 8.95 (ISBN 0-8158-0257-9); pap. 6.95 (ISBN 0-686-66311-X). Chris Mass.

Yoga-System of Patanjali. James H. Woods. 1977. Repr. 14.50 (ISBN 0-89684-272-X, Pub. by Motilal Banarsidass India). Orient Bk Dist.

Yoga-Systems of Patanjali: The Doctrine of the Concentration of the Mind. James Woods. lib. bdg. 90.00 (ISBN 0-87968-083-0). Krishna Pr.

Yoga: The Alpha & the Omega, 10 vols, Vols. 1-5. Bhagwan Shree Rajneesh. Ed. by Ma Ananda Prem & Ma Yoga Sudha. LC 76-902396. (Yoga Ser.). (Illus., Orig.). 1976. Vol I, 272 pgs. o.p. 9.95 ea. (ISBN 0-88050-177-4). Vol II, 266 pgs. 1976 (ISBN 0-88050-178-2). Vol. III, 298 pgs. 1976 o.p (ISBN 0-88050-179-0). Vol. IV, 280 pgs. 1976 (ISBN 0-88050-180-4). Vol. V, 266 pgs. 1976 (ISBN 0-88050-181-2). Chidvilas Inc.

Yoga: The Alpha & the Omega, 10 vols, Vols. 6-10. Bhagwan Shree Rajneesh. Ed. by Swami Prem Chinmaya & Ma Yoga Sudha. LC 76-902396. (Yoga Ser.). (Illus., Orig.). 1977. Vol. VI, 270 pgs. 9.95 ea. (ISBN 0-88050-182-0). Vol. VII250p 1977 (ISBN 0-88050-183-9). Vol. VIII, 298 pgs. 1977 (ISBN 0-88050-184-7). Vol. IX, 346 pgs. 1978 (ISBN 0-88050-185-5). Vol. X, 270 pgs. 1978 (ISBN 0-88050-186-3). Chidvilas Inc.

Yoga: The Art of Integration. Mehta. 15.95 (ISBN 0-8356-7513-0). Theos Pub Hse.

Yoga... The Art of Living: The Hunza-Yoga Way to Better Living. Renee Taylor. LC 78-75329. (Illus.). 224p. 1975. pap. 4.50 (ISBN 0-87983-112-X). Keats.

Yoga: The Hatha Yoga & Raja Yoga of India. Annie Besant. 73p. 1974. pap. 7.95 (ISBN 0-88697-035-0). Life Science.

Yoga: The Science of the Soul, Vol. 1. 2nd ed. Bhagwan Shree Rajneesh. Ed. by Swami Krishna Mahasattva. LC 84-42812. (Yoga Ser.). 304p. 1984. pap. 4.95 (ISBN 0-88050-677-6). Chidvilas Inc.

Yoga: The Spirit of Union. Lar Caughlan. 96p. 1981. pap. text ed. 14.00 (ISBN 0-8403-2487-1). Kendall-Hunt.

Yoga: The Technique of Health & Happiness. I. Devi. 76p. 1979. 5.50. Asia Bk Corp.

Yoga the Technique of Liberation. Virendra Shekhavat. 80p. 1980. 10.95x (ISBN 0-317-07708-2, Sterling India). Asia Bk Corp.

Yoga: The Technique of Liberation. Virenda Shekhawat. 90p. 1979. text ed. 7.50 (ISBN 0-89684-264-9, Pub. by Sterling India). Orient Bk Dist.

Yoga Twenty-Eight Day Exercise Plan. Richard Hittleman. 320p. 1973. pap. 4.50 (ISBN 0-553-25775-7). Bantam.

Yoga Twenty-Eight Day Exercise Plan. Richard Hittleman. LC 74-87903. (Illus.). 224p. 1969. 9.95 (ISBN 0-911104-00-3, 145); pap. 7.95 (ISBN 0-911104-21-6, 194). Workman Pub.

Yoga Unveiled, Part 1. 1977. 16.50 (ISBN 0-8426-1031-6, Pub. by Motilal Banarsidass India). Orient Bk Dist.

Yoga Vasistha, Vol. III. Swami Jyotirmayananda. 304p. (Orig.). 1986. pap. 4.99 (ISBN 0-934664-33-1). Yoga Res Foun.

Yoga Vasistha, 2 vols. Jyotir Maya Nanda. Incl. Vol. 1. 1977. 4.99 (ISBN 0-934664-30-7). Yoga Res Foun.

Yoga Vasistha Ramayana. rev. ed. D. N. Bose. 1984. Repr. of 1954 ed. 12.50x (ISBN 0-8364-1181-1, Pub. by Mukhopadhyaya India). South Asia Bks.

Yoga Way Cookbook: Natural Vegetarian Recipes. rev. ed. Himalayan International Institute Staff. LC 80-81994. (Illus.). 249p. 1980. spiral bdg. 9.95 (ISBN 0-89389-067-7). Himalayan Pubs.

Yoga Wisdom of the Upanishads: Kena..Mundaka..Prashna..Ishavasya. Jyotir M. Nanda. (Illus.). 1974. pap. 4.99 (ISBN 0-934664-36-6). Yoga Res Foun.

Yoga: Yogic Suksma Vyayama. Dhirenda Brahmachari. (Illus.). 232p. 1975. 8.95 (ISBN 0-88253-802-0). Ind-US Inc.

Yoga, You, Your New Life. K. Japananda. (Illus.). 208p. pap. 5.95 spiral bdg. (ISBN 0-9613099-0-3). Temple Kriya Yoga.

Yoga, Youth & Reincarnation. Jess Stearn. (Illus.). 352p. 1983. pap. 3.95 (ISBN 0-553-26057-X). Bantam.

Yogacara Idealism. 2nd rev. ed. A. K. Chatterjee. 1976. 13.95 (ISBN 0-8426-0742-0). Orient Bk Dist.

Yogacara Idealism. Ashok K. Chatterjee. 1987. Repr. of 1968 ed. 12.75x (ISBN 81-208-0315-9, Pub. by Motilal Banarsidass). South Asia Bks.

Yogananda Returns. Robert R. Leichtman. (From Heaven to Earth Ser.). 104p. (Orig.). 1981. pap. 3.50 (ISBN 0-89804-066-3). Ariel OH.

Yogasutra of Patanjali on Concentration of Mind. Fernanda Tola & Carmen Dragonetti. Tr. by K. D. Prithipaul. 268p. 1986. 21.00x (Pub. by Motilal Banarsidass); pap. 15.00 (ISBN 81-208-0259-4). South Asia Bks.

Yogasutra of Patanjali: On Concentration of Mind. Ed. by Fernando Tola & Carmen Dragonetti. Tr. by K. D. Prithipaul. 200p. 1987. 19.95 (ISBN 81-208-0258-6, Pub. by Motilal Banarsidass India); pap. 15.00 (Pub. by Motilal Banarsidass India). Orient Bk Dist.

Yogasutra of Patanjali: With Commentary of Vyasa. Bangali Baba. 115p. 1982. 10.50 (ISBN 81-208-0154-7, Pub. by Motilal Banarsidass India); pap. 7.95 (ISBN 81-208-0155-5, Pub. by Motilal Banarsidass India). Orient Bk Dist.

Yogasutras of Patanjali. 2nd ed. Tr. by M. N. Dwivedi from Sanskrit. 159p. 1983. Repr. of 1980 ed. 9.50 (ISBN 81-7030-091-6, Pub. by Motilal Banarsidass India). Orient Bk Dist.

Yogavarttika of Vijnanabhiksu, Vol. 3: Vibhutipada. Tr. by T. S. Rukmani. 1988. 26.00x (ISBN 81-215-0057-5, Munshiram Manoharial India). South Asia Bks.

Yoghurt: Science & Technology. A. Y. Tamime. LC 83-24940. (Illus.). 444p. 1985. (PBL); pap. text ed. 32.00 (ISBN 0-08-025502-7, PBL). Pergamon.

Yogi & the Bear: Story of Indo-Soviet Relations. S. Nihal Singh. LC 85-62583. 324p. 1986. 29.00 (ISBN 0-913215-12-0). Riverdale Co.

Yogi of Cockroach Court. Frank Waters. LC 72-91922. 277p. 1947. pap. 6.95 (ISBN 0-8040-0613-X, Swallow). Ohio U Pr.

Yogi Philosophy. Lillian Covan. Ed. by Frederick H. Clauss. (Orig.). 1987. pap. text ed. 5.95 (ISBN 0-9618370-0-4). Halcyon Days Pr.

Yogi, the Commissar & the Third World Church. Paul D. Clasper. 92p. (Orig.). 1982. pap. 5.00 (ISBN 0-686-37580-7, Pub. by New Day Philippines). Cellar.

Yogic Cure for Common Diseases. rev., enl. ed. Phulgenda Sinha. (Orient Paperbacks Ser.). 204p. 1981. pap. 4.95 (ISBN 0-86578-076-5); 9.50 (ISBN 0-86578-227-X). Ind-US Inc.

Yogic Management of Asthma & Diabetes. S. Saraswati. 1979. 9.95. Asia Bk Corp.

Yogic Pranayama: Breathing for Long, Long Life. K. S. Joshi. 180p. 1983. pap. 9.00 (ISBN 0-86578-222-9). Ind-US Inc.

Yogic Psalter. Henry Compton. 64p. 1984. 29.00x (ISBN 0-7212-0679-4, Pub. by Regency Pr). State Mutual Bk.

Yogo: The Great American Sapphire. rev. ed. Stephen Voynick. (Illus.). 262p. 1987. pap. 9.95 (ISBN 0-87842-217-X). Mountain Pr.

Yogurt Six or Eight Ounce Container Cookbook: Ingredient Substitution Editon. Alpha Pyramis Research Division Staff. 18p. 1986. pap. 4.95 (ISBN 0-913597-84-8, Pub. by Alpha Pyramis). Prosperity & Profits.

Yojokun: Japanese Secret of Good Health. Ekiken Kaibara. 1974. 9.95 (ISBN 0-89346-101-6); pap. 2.95 (ISBN 0-89346-047-8). Heian Intl.

Yoke & the Arrows. rev. ed. Herbert L. Matthews. LC 61-9963. 1969. pap. 2.95 (ISBN 0-8076-0560-3); 5.00 (ISBN 0-8076-0145-4). Braziller.

Yoke & the Star. Tana de Gamez. 1977. pap. 1.95 (ISBN 0-8439-0475-5, Leisure Bks). Leisure NY.

Yoke Made Easy. Alfred Doerffler. LC 75-2344. 128p. 1974. pap. 5.95 (ISBN 0-570-03027-7, 6-1155). Concordia.

Yoke of Magic. Robert E. Vardeman & Geo W. Proctor. (Swords of Raemllyn Ser.: No. 2). 208p. 1985. pap. 2.95 (ISBN 0-441-94841-3). Ace Bks.

Yoke of Marriage. Fely Ramos. 64p. 1984. 7.95 (ISBN 0-89962-369-7). Todd & Honeywell.

Yoke of the Thorah. Henry Harland. LC 75-104474. 320p. Repr. of 1887 ed. lib. bdg. 21.50 (ISBN 0-8398-0759-7). Irvington.

Yoke of the Thorah. Henry Harland. 320p. 1986. pap. text ed. 8.95x (ISBN 0-8290-1962-6). Irvington.

Yoke of the Thorah, by Sidney Luska. Henry Harland. Repr. of 1887 ed. 23.00 (ISBN 0-384-21370-7). Johnson Repr.

Yoked by Violence. John Pauker. LC 77-179802. (New Poetry Ser.). Repr. of 1949 ed. 16.00 (ISBN 0-404-56002-4). AMS Pr.

Yoked with a Lamb, & Other Stories. facsimile ed. Helen R. Martin. LC 76-152948. (Short Story Index Reprint Ser.). Repr. of 1930 ed. 19.00 (ISBN 0-8369-3807-0). Ayer Co Pubs.

Yokley's Law of Subdivisions. 2nd ed. Michie Co's Editorial Staff. 790p. 1981. 60.00x (ISBN 0-87215-401-7). Michie Co.

Yoknapatawpha Chronicle of Gavin Stevens. John K. Crane. LC 87-42809. 312p. 1988. 37.50x (ISBN 0-941664-90-2). Susquehanna U Pr.

Yoko Ono. Jerry Hopkins. (Illus.). 320p. 1987. 17.95 (ISBN 0-02-553950-7). Macmillan.

Yokogawa Collection: Chinese Ceramics in the Tokyo National Museum. Tokyo National Museum Staff. 82p. 1982. 925.00x (ISBN 0-317-45336-X, Pub. by Han-Shan Tang Ltd). State Mutual Bk.

Yokohama, California. Toshio Mori. LC 84-21987. 176p. (Orig.). 1985. pap. 8.95 (ISBN 0-295-96167-8). U of Wash Pr.

Yokohama Ukiyoe. Tamba Tsuneo. 29p. 1962. 2450.00x (ISBN 0-317-69459-6, Pub. by Han-Shan Tang Ltd). State Mutual Bk.

Yokohama Ukiyoe-Shutaisei. Kankawa Prefectural Museum Staff. 553p. 1980. 3150.00x (ISBN 0-317-68531-7, Pub. by Han-Shan Tang Ltd). State Mutual Bk.

Yokomitsu Riichi, Modernist. Dennis Keene. LC 79-28532. (Modern Asia Literature Ser.). 1980. 29.50x (ISBN 0-231-04938-2). Columbia U Pr.

Yokuts Language of California. Stanley S. Newman. pap. 19.00 (ISBN 0-384-41210-6). Johnson Repr.

Yolanda & the Strange Objects. Lezley Saar. LC 78-64740. (Illus.). 1978. pap. 6.95 (ISBN 0-918408-10-5). Reed & Cannon.

Yolande. Ellen Noone. 1985. 24.95x (ISBN 0-7090-1704-9, Pub. by R Hale Ltd UK). State Mutual Bk.

Yolande's Atlanta: From the Historical to the Hysterical. Yolande Gwin. LC 83-61918. 270p. 1983. 9.95 (ISBN 0-931948-43-6). Peachtree Pubs.

Yolngu & Their Land: A System of Land Tenure & the Fight for Its Recognition. Nancy M. Williams. LC 85-61474. (Illus.). 328p. 1986. 35.00x (ISBN 0-8047-1306-5). Stanford U Pr.

Yolo County: Land of Changing Patterns. Joanne Larkey & Shipley Walters. Ed. by Marilyn Horn. (Illus.). 136p. 1987. 25.95 (ISBN 0-89781-223-9). Windsor Pubns Inc.

Yom Kippur. Norma Simon. (Festival Series of Picture Storybooks). (Illus.). (ps-k). 1959. plastic cover 4.50 (ISBN 0-8381-0702-8). United Syn Bk.

Yom Kippur Anthology. Ed. by Philip Goodman. LC 72-151312. (Illus.). 399p. 1971. 9.95 (ISBN 0-8276-0026-7, 245). JPS Phila.

Yom Kippur - Ashkenaz: Zichron Yosef see Machzor.

Yom Kippur-Sefard: Zichron Zev see Machzor.

Yom Kippur War. Avram Adan. 479p. pap. 10.95 (ISBN 0-931933-34-X). Richardson & Steirman.

Yom Kippur War: Israel & the Jewish People. Ed. by Moshe Davis. LC 74-10466. 381p. 1974. 11.00 (ISBN 0-405-06192-7). Ayer Co Pubs.

Yoma: Or, Yom Kippur, 2 vols. (Hebrew & Eng.). 30.00 (ISBN 0-910218-57-9). Bennet Pub.

Yomtevdike Teg. Compiled by Chane Mlotek & Malke Gottlieb. (Songbook for the Holidays Ser.). (Illus.). 105p. pap. 6.00 (ISBN 0-318-20363-4). Workmen's Circle.

Yomtovdike Teg: Yiddish Songbook. 120p. pap. 4.50 (ISBN 0-318-13641-4). Board Jewish Educ.

Yon Mountain: A Doctor of Faith Walks with God. Alta W. Eitel. LC 85-90286. 101p. 1986. 10.95 (ISBN 0-533-06783-9). Vantage.

Yonadab: A Play. Peter Shaffer. LC 86-45315. (Cornelia & Michael Bessie Book Ser.). 80p. 1988. 14.95 (ISBN 0-06-039060-3); pap. 7.95 (ISBN 0-06-039061-1, PL). Har-Row.

Yonah-Jonah. Meir Zlotowitz. (Art Scroll Tanach Ser.). 160p. 1978. 13.95 (ISBN 0-89906-081-1); pap. 10.95 (ISBN 0-89906-082-X). Mesorah Pubns.

Yonder. Tony Johnston. LC 86-11549. (ps-3). 1988. 12.95 (ISBN 0-8037-0277-9, 012358-320); PLB 12.89 (ISBN 0-8037-0278-7). Dial Bks Young.

Yonder Comes the Other Side of Time. Suzette H. Elgin. 1986. pap. 2.95 (ISBN 0-88677-110-2). DAW Bks.

Yondering. Louis L'Amour. (Western Ser.). 208p. (Orig.). 1982. pap. 2.95 (ISBN 0-553-26039-1). Bantam.

Yongle Palace Murals. Ed. by Liao Ping. 109p. 1985. 245.00x (ISBN 0-317-69262-3, Pub. by Han-Shan Tang Ltd). State Mutual Bk.

Yoni. Howard Bogot. (ps). 1982. pap. 4.00 (ISBN 0-686-82564-0). UAHC.

Yonitantra. Ed. by J. A. Schoterman. 1985. 11.00x (ISBN 0-8364-1326-1, Pub. by Manohar India). South Asia Bks.

Yonnondio. Tillie Olsen. 1984. 16.25 (ISBN 0-8446-6089-2). Peter Smith.

Yonnondio. Tillie Olsen. 16.25. Peter Smith.

Yonnondio. Tillie Olsen. 1989. pap. 7.95 (ISBN 0-440-55012-2, Delta). Dell.

Yonnondio: From the Thirties. Tillie Olsen. 144p. (YA) (gr. 9 up). 1975. pap. 1.95 (ISBN 0-440-39881-9, LE). Dell.

Yoo-Hoo Little Rabbit. J. P. Miller. LC 85-61529. (ps). 1986. 2.95 (ISBN 0-394-87884-1, BYR). Random.

Yordan Yovkov. Edward Mozejko. 117p. 1984. pap. 9.95 (ISBN 0-89357-117-2). Slavica.

Yordim. Micha Lev. LC 85-52008. 300p. 1986. 14.95 (ISBN 0-933149-03-4). Woodbine House.

Yorick & the Critics: Sterne's Reputation in England, 1760-1868. Alan B. Howes. LC 75-163005. (Yale Studies in English Ser.: No. 139). x, 186p. 1971. Repr. of 1958 ed. 24.50 (ISBN 0-208-01129-3, Archon). Shoe String.

York, 2 vols. Ed. by Alexandra F. Johnston & Margaret Rogerson. LC 78-14756. (Records of Early English Drama Ser.). 1979. Set. 87.50x (ISBN 0-8020-2304-5). U of Toronto Pr.

York. (AA City Guides). (Illus.). 120p. 1988. pap. 18.95 (ISBN 0-86145-510-X, Pub. by British Tour). Salem Hse Pubs.

York Art: A Subject List of Extant & Lost Art Including Items Relevant to Early Drama. Clifford Davidson & David E. O'Connor. (Early Drama, Art, & Music Ser.). (Illus.). 1978. 14.95x (ISBN 0-918720-05-2); pap. 8.95x (ISBN 0-918720-04-4). Medieval Inst.

York As It Was: Fifth Impression. Hendon Publishing Co., Ltd. Staff. 1986. 9.10x (ISBN 0-317-54199-4, Pub. by Hendon Pub UK). State Mutual BK.

York Ballad Operas & Yorkshiremen. Ed. by Walter H. Rubsamen. (Ballad Opera Ser.). 1975. lib. bdg. 61.00 (ISBN 0-8240-0926-6). Garland Pub.

York County Marriage Returns, 1771-1794. George W. Chamberlain. 14p. 1986. pap. 2.50 (ISBN 0-935207-34-1). DanBury Hse Bks.

York County Marriages Seventeen Seventy to Eighteen Sixty-Nine: Implied in York County, S. C. Probate Records. rev. ed. Barbara R. Langdon. 100p. (Orig.). 1986. pap. text ed. 15.00 (ISBN 0-938741-00-4). Langdon & Langdon.

York County (ME) Juvenile Intake Service Evaluation. National Center for State Courts Staff. 74p. 1975. manuscript 4.44 (NERO-044). Natl Ctr St Courts.

York County, South Carolina Minutes of the County Court 1786-1797. Laurence K. Wells. 199p. 1981. 25.00 (ISBN 0-913363-00-6). SCMAR.

York County, Virginia Wills, Deeds, Orders, 1657-1659, Vol. 5. Lindsay O. Duvall. (Virginia Colonial Abstracts, Series II). 1978. Repr. of 1961 ed. 17.50 (ISBN 0-89308-066-7). Southern Hist Pr.

York, Maine, Marriages, 1697-1760. Michael J. Denis. 25p. 1985. pap. 3.75 (ISBN 0-935207-15-5). Danbury Hse Bks.

York Minster. Lucy Beckett & Angelo Hornak. (Illus.). 96p. pap. 13.95 (ISBN 0-935748-29-6). Scala Books.

York Mystery Plays. Richard Beadle & Pamela M. King. 1984. 34.00x (ISBN 0-19-811189-4); pap. 12.95x (ISBN 0-19-811197-5). Oxford U Pr.

York Plays: The Plays Performed on the Day of Corpus Christi in the 14th, 15th, & 16th Centuries. Ed. by Lucy T. Smith. LC 63-15180. (Illus.). 1963. Repr. of 1885 ed. 21.00x (ISBN 0-8462-0313-8). Russell.

Yorke the Adventurer, & Other Stories. facsimile ed. Louis Becke. LC 71-37535. (Short Story Index Reprint Ser.). Repr. of 1925 ed. 18.00 (ISBN 0-8369-4094-6). Ayer Co Pubs.

Yorkshire. G. Bernard Wood. (Batsford Britain Ser.). 1979. 8.95 (ISBN 0-8038-8591-1). Hastings.

Yorkshire & North Lincolnshire. 3rd ed. H. Tolley & K. Orrell. LC 77-87393. (Geography of the British Isles Ser.). (Illus.). 1978. limp bdg. 7.95x (ISBN 0-521-21918-3). Cambridge U Pr.

Yorkshire Anthology. Joseph H. Turner. 433p. 1980. Repr. of 1901 ed. lib. bdg. 55.00 (ISBN 0-8414-8425-2). Folcroft.

Yorkshire Boyhood. Roy Hattersley. (Illus.). 224p. 1984. pap. 9.95x (ISBN 0-19-281481-8). Oxford U Pr.

Yorkshire Cistercian Heritage: Introduction. James Hogg. (Orig.). 1985. pap. 16.00 (ISBN 3-7052-0260-X, Pub. by Salzburg Studies). Longwood Pub Group.

Yorkshire Cistercian Heritage, Vol. 2: Rievaulx, Jervaulx, Byland. James Hogg. (Orig.). 1978. pap. 16.00 (ISBN 3-7052-0261-8, Pub. by Salzburg Studies). Longwood Pub Group.

Yorkshire Cistercian Heritage, Vol. 3: Fountains, Kirstall, Meaux. James Hogg. (Orig.). 1978. pap. 16.00 (ISBN 3-7052-0262-6, Pub. by Salzburg Studies). Longwood Pub Group.

Yorkshire Coast Lines. Hendon Publishing Co., Ltd. Staff. 1986. 22.40x (ISBN 0-317-54172-2, Pub. by Hendon Pub UK). State Mutual Bk.

Yorkshire Dales. Brian Spencer. (Visitor's Guides Ser.). (Illus.). 160p. (Orig.). 1986. pap. 8.95 (ISBN 0-935161-49-X). Hunter Pub NY.

Yorkshire Dales. (AA Ordinance Survey-Leisure Guides Ser.). (Illus.). 120p. 1986. 22.95 (ISBN 0-86145-234-8, Pub. by Automobile Assn Brit); pap. 15.95 (ISBN 0-86145-233-X, Pub. by Automobile Assn Brit). Salem Hse Pubs.

Yorkshire Families: Directory 1987. 1987. 30.00x (Pub. by Birmingham Midland Soc UK). State Mutual Bk.

Yorkshire from AD One Thousand. David Hey. (Regional History of England Ser.). 340p. 1986. 39.95 (ISBN 0-582-49211-4); pap. text ed. 31.95 (ISBN 0-582-49212-2). Longman.

Yorkshire Gyspy Fairs, Customs & Caravans 1885-1985. Alan E. Jones. 125p. 1986. 45.00x (ISBN 0-907033-43-1, Hutton Pr). State Mutual Bk.

Yorkshire Jurassic Flora: Vol. I, Thallophyta-Pteridophyta. Thomas Maxwell Harris. (Illus.). 1961. 33.00x (ISBN 0-565-00148-5, Pub. by Brit Mus Nat Hist). Sabbot-Natural Hist Bks.

You & Your Estate: A Simple Legal Guide for Iowa Residents in Understanding & Protecting Their Estate. Theodore L. Kubicek. LC 87-92113. 148p. 1988. 14.00 (ISBN 0-9619787-0-8). T L Kubicek.

You & Your Family. Ed. by John Robson. (Illus.). 30p. (Orig.). (gr. 2-4). 1981. pap. 2.50 (ISBN 0-936098-30-9). Intl Marriage.

You & Your Feelings: Understanding the Ups & Downs of Adolescence. Eda LeShan. LC 74-22254. 128p. (gr. 6 up). 1975. 9.95 (ISBN 0-02-757330-3). Macmillan.

You & Your Fitness & Health. K. Fraser & J. Tatchell. (Body Books). (Illus.). 48p. (YA) (gr. 6-10). 1987. PLB 12.96 (ISBN 0-88110-234-2); pap. 5.95 (ISBN 0-7460-0004-9). EDC.

You & Your Food: Understanding Nutrition, Calories, Vitamins & the Things You Eat. J. Tatchell & D. Wells. (Body Books). (Illus.). 48p. (YA) (gr. 6-10). 1986. PLB 12.96 (ISBN 0-88110-222-9); pap. 5.95 (ISBN 0-86020-939-3). EDC.

You & Your Hair. Elaine Budd. (Illus.). 144p. (gr. 7 up). 1984. pap. 1.95 (ISBN 0-590-03861-3, Wildfire Bks). Scholastic Inc.

You & Your Hand: A Textbook of Modern Hand Analysis. rev. ed. Beverly C. Jaegers. (Illus.). 176p. 1984. pap. text ed. 6.00x. Aries Prod.

You & Your Hearing: How to Protect It, Preserve It, & Restore It. Arthur S. Freese. 1980. 3.95 (ISBN 0-684-16240-7, ScribT). Scribner.

You & Your Hormones. Max D. Rubenstein. 1960. 13.95x (ISBN 0-8084-0387-7). New Coll U Pr.

You & Your Husband's Mid-Life Crisis. Sally Conway. (Orig.). 1980. pap. 6.95 (ISBN 0-89191-318-1). Cook.

You & Your Husband's Mid-Life Crisis. Sally Conway. 1987. pap. 6.95 study guide (ISBN 1-55513-228-6, Life Journey). Cook.

You & Your Irish Wolfhound. John A. Donovan. LC 76-20960. (Breed Bks.). (Illus.). 1977. 24.95 (ISBN 0-87714-053-7). Denlingers.

You & Your Life Style. Charles F. Kemp. LC 79-24531. (Orig.). 1980. pap. 5.95 (ISBN 0-8272-4402-9). CBP.

You & Your National Government. League of Women Voters Education Fund Staff. (Illus.). 32p. 1977. pap. 1.00 (ISBN 0-89959-027-6, 273); pap. 3.75, 5 copies, 12.50 25 copies (ISBN 0-686-77308-X). LWV US.

You & Your National Government. rev. ed. League of Women Voters Education Fund Staff. (Illus.). 31p. 1985. pap. 1.75 (273). LWV US.

You & Your Network. Fred Smith. 1984. 9.95 (ISBN 0-8499-0373-4). Word Bks.

You & Your Parents: Strategies for Building an Adult Relationship. Harold I. Smith. LC 87-17555. 160p. (Orig.). 1987. pap. 8.95 (ISBN 0-8066-2267-9, 10-7407). Augsburg.

You & Your Pension. Ralph Nader & Kate Blackwell. 215p. 1973. pap. 1.65 (ISBN 0-686-36546-1). Ctr Responsive Law.

You & Your Pet: Aquarium Pets. Phil Steinberg. LC 78-54359. (You & Your Pet Bks.). (Illus.). (gr. 4 up). 1978. PLB 5.95 (ISBN 0-8225-1255-6). Lerner Pubns.

You & Your Pet: Birds. Phil Steinberg. LC 78-54352. (You & Your Pet Bks.). (Illus.). (gr. 4 up). 1978. PLB 5.95 (ISBN 0-8225-1251-3). Lerner Pubns.

You & Your Pet: Cats. Phil Steinberg. LC 78-54353. (You & Your Pet Bks.). (Illus.). (gr. 4 up). 1978. PLB 5.95 (ISBN 0-8225-1252-1). Lerner Pubns.

You & Your Pet: Dogs. Phil Steinberg. LC 78-54354. (You & Your Pet Bks.). (Illus.). (gr. 4 up). 1978. PLB 5.95 (ISBN 0-8225-1253-X). Lerner Pubns.

You & Your Pet: Rodents & Rabbits. Phil Steinberg. LC 78-54365. (You & Your Pet Bks.). (Illus.). (gr. 4 up). 1978. PLB 5.95 (ISBN 0-8225-1256-4). Lerner Pubns.

You & Your Pet: Terrarium Pets. Phil Steinberg. LC 78-54360. (You & Your Pet Bks.). (Illus.). (gr. 4 up). 1978. PLB 5.95 (ISBN 0-8225-1254-8). Lerner Pubns.

You & Your Pony. Pepper M. Healey. 1978. pap. 6.00 (ISBN 0-87980-360-6). Wilshire.

You & Your Poodle. Mollie Skelton. 7.95 (ISBN 0-87666-362-5, PS-641). TFH Pubns.

You & Your Prostate. F. P. Twinem. (Illus.). 120p. 1980. 10.75 (ISBN 0-398-04012-5). C C Thomas.

You & Your Retarded Child: A Manual for Parents of Retarded Children. 2nd ed. Samuel A. Kirk et al. LC 67-20824. (Pacific Books Paperbounds, PB-2). (Orig.). 1968. pap. 4.95 (ISBN 0-87015-161-4). Pacific Bks.

You & Your Rights. Reader's Digest Editors. LC 81-84665. 448p. 1982. 17.97 (ISBN 0-89577-137-3). RD Assn.

You & Your Small Wonder: Activities for Busy Parents & Babies, Book 1. Merle B. Karnes. LC 82-71049. (Illus.). 163p. (Orig.). 1982. pap. 9.95 ea. 1 copy (ISBN 0-913476-58-7); pap. 7.95 ea. 5 or more copies. Am Guidance.

You & Your Small Wonder: 18-36 Months, Bk. 2. Merle B. Karnes. 1984. pap. 6.95 (ISBN 0-394-72414-3). Random.

You & Your Teen. Charles Bradshaw. (Family Ministry Ser.). (Illus.). 84p. 1985. pap. text ed. 19.95 (ISBN 0-89191-950-3). Cook.

You & Your Wedding. Winifred Gray. 368p. (Orig.). 1986. pap. 3.95 (ISBN 0-553-25293-3). Bantam.

You & Your Will. Paul Ashley. 240p. 1985. pap. 3.95 (ISBN 0-451-62569-2, Ment). NAL.

You & Yourself. Lothar G. Vollweiler. 112p. 1985. pap. text ed. 16.95 (ISBN 0-8403-3735-3). Kendall-Hunt.

You Are a Money Brain. William C. Drollinger & William C. Drollinger, Sr. LC 81-67503. 1981. write for info. (ISBN 0-914244-07-8). Epic Pubns.

You Are a Monster. Edward Packard. (Choose Your Own Adventure Ser.: No. 84). 128p. (gr. 4). 1988. pap. 2.50 (ISBN 0-553-27474-0). Bantam.

You Are a Person of Worth. Jefferson Breen. LC 86-91860. 1988. 12.00 (ISBN 0-87212-202-6). Libra.

You Are a Rainbow. Ed. by Norah Hills. LC 79-13393. (Illus.). 128p. (Orig.). 1979. pap. 4.95 (ISBN 0-916438-25-2). Univ of Trees.

You Are a Shark. Edward Packard. (Choose Your Own Adventure Ser.: No. 45). (gr. 5-12). 1985. pap. 2.25 (ISBN 0-553-26386-2). Bantam.

You Are a Special Person. Bob Bird. 16p. (Orig.). 1974. pap. 1.50 (ISBN 0-934804-06-0). Inspiration MI.

You Are A Winner. Marjorie Burns Sherratt. LC 85-91150. 71p. (Orig.). 1985. pap. 5.25 (ISBN 0-9615778-0-0, 01). You Are Winner.

You Are All Sanpaku. Sakurazawa Nyoiti, pseud. 1980. pap. 5.95 (ISBN 0-8065-0728-4, Pub. by Citadel Pr). Lyle Stuart.

You Are Always My Friend. Ed. by Susan P. Schutz. (Illus.). 96p. 1981. 13.95 (ISBN 0-88396-150-4). Blue Mtn Pr CO.

You Are Always Your Own Experience! 4th ed. Tom Johnson. 269p. 1982. pap. 7.95 (ISBN 0-941992-01-2). Los Arboles Pub.

You Are an Acolyte: A Manual for Acolytes. (Illus.). (gr. 6-9). 1977. pap. 3.50 (ISBN 0-8066-1552-4, 10-7409). Augsburg.

You Are Barbara Jordan: An In-Basket Exercise on Nursing Service Administration. 1970. participant's kit 7.50 (ISBN 0-87914-015-1, 654630); instructor's guide 7.50 (ISBN 0-87914-016-X, 654631). Hosp Res & Educ.

You Are Beautiful: You Really Are. Joyce P. Beaman. LC 81-52869. 240p. 1981. 7.95 (ISBN 0-935054-06-5). Webb-Newcomb.

You Are Born to Victory. John Glossinger. 115p. 1981. pap. 3.95 (ISBN 0-87516-445-5). DeVorss.

You Are Forever see Creation Trilogy.

You Are Gifted. R. B. Thomas. (International Correspondence Program Ser.). (Orig.). 1985. pap. text ed. 6.95 (ISBN 0-87148-935-X). Pathway Pr.

You Are God. Mary. 1955. pap. 5.95 (ISBN 0-87516-057-3). DeVorss.

You Are Greater Than You Know. Lou Austin. 7.50 (ISBN 0-934538-16-6); pap. 4.50 (ISBN 0-934538-11-5). Partnership Foundation.

You Are Here, Dainty Dinosaur. (Beginning to Read Ser.). (gr. 2 up). 1988. PLB 5.95 (ISBN 0-8136-5214-6); pap. 2.95 (ISBN 0-8136-5714-8). Modern Curr.

You Are Invisible. 2nd, enl. ed. Raymond C. Barker. LC 73-1654. 160p. 1986. pap. 5.95 (ISBN 0-87516-576-1). DeVorss.

You Are Involved in a Fable. Barry Goodman. 64p. (Orig.). 1986. 9.95 (ISBN 0-939395-04-5); pap. 5.95 (ISBN 0-939395-05-3). Thorntree Pr.

You Are Loved. Alma Kern. (Illus.). 144p. 1991. pap. 5.00 (ISBN 0-9614955-1-0). Lutheran Womens.

You Are Loved. (Four Very Special Gift Bks.). 48p. 1985. 2.25 (ISBN 0-8407-6680-7). Nelson.

You Are Loved & Forgiven. rev. ed. Lloyd J. Ogilvie. LC 86-10186. 192p. 1986. text ed. 12.95 (ISBN 0-8307-1168-6, 5111616); pap. text ed. 7.95 (ISBN 0-8307-1110-4, S412117). Regal.

You Are Mountain. Mary Donahoe. 32p. 1984. chapbook 6.00 (ISBN 0-911051-11-2). Plain View.

You Are My Beloved Sermon Book. Frederick Kemper & George M. Bass. 1980. pap. 7.50 (ISBN 0-570-03821-9, 12-2761). Concordia.

You Are My Favorites. Pope John Paul II. 1980. 6.95 (ISBN 0-8198-8701-3). Dghtrs St Paul.

You Are My Friends. Ron Wormser et al. 36p. 1988. pap. price not set (ISBN 0-934396-42-6). Churches Alive.

You Are My God: A Pioneer of Renewal Recounts His Pilgramage in Faith. David Watson. 196p. 1984. pap. 5.95 (ISBN 0-87788-972-4). Shaw Pubs.

You Are My Sunshine: The Jimmie Davis Story. Gus Weill. (Illus.). 200p. 1987. pap. 6.95 (ISBN 0-88289-660-1). Pelican.

You Are My Witness: A Self-Study Guide to Personal Witnessing. Joyce Martin. (Illus.). 48p. (Orig.). 1986. pap. 2.50 (ISBN 0-936625-05-8). Womans Mission Union.

You Are Never Alone. Charles L. Allen. 160p. 1984. pap. 6.95 (ISBN 0-8007-5145-0, Power Bks). Revell.

You Are Not Alone. Martin Grossack. 1975. pap. 2.25 (ISBN 0-685-81630-3). Inst Rat Liv.

You Are Not Alone: A Guide for Battered Women. Linda P. Rouse. LC 83-83182. 136p. 1986. pap. 11.95 unabridged (ISBN 0-918452-73-2); pap. 11.50 abridged ed. pkg. of 4 (ISBN 0-918452-70-8). Learning Pubns.

You Are Not Alone: Understanding & Dealing with Mental Illness. Clara C. Park & Leon N. Shapiro. 1976. pap. 8.95 (ISBN 0-316-69075-9). Little.

You Are Not the Target. Laura Huxley. 289p. 1963. 8.95 (ISBN 0-374-29380-5). FS&G.

You Are Not the Target: Transforming Negative Feelings into Creative Action Harmonious Relationships. Laura A. Huxley. 304p. 1986. Repr. of 1963 ed. 8.95 (ISBN 0-87477-381-4). J P Tarcher.

You Are Number One! Beverly Amstutz. (Illus.). 30p. (gr. k-9). 1982. pap. 2.50x (ISBN 0-937836-08-7). Precious Res.

You Are Psychic! Pete Sanders, Jr. (Illus.). 256p. 1989. 14.95 (ISBN 0-89256-336-2). Rawson Assocs.

You Are Psychic: How to Discover & Develop Your Hidden Psychic Abilities. The Directors of the Institute for Psychic Development Staff. 225p. (Orig.). 1986. pap. 14.95 (ISBN 0-938707-01-9). Savadove Prod.

You Are Responsible. George King. 173p. 1961. 9.25 (ISBN 0-937249-03-3). Aetherius Soc.

You Are Somebody Special. 2nd ed. C. W. Shedd. 1982. text ed. 12.95 (ISBN 0-07-056511-2). McGraw.

You Are Special. Alma Kern. (Illus.). 144p. (Orig.). 1985. pap. 5.00 (ISBN 0-9614955-0-2, 2050). Lutheran Womens.

You Are Special. (Four Very Special Gift Bks.). 48p. 1985. 2.25 (ISBN 0-8407-6678-5). Nelson.

You Are Special! (Wellinworld Tapes & Books for Children: 2-9). 36p. (ps-4). 1985. 8.95 (ISBN 0-88684-176-3); cassette tape avail. Listen USA.

You Are Special to Jesus. Annetta Dellinger. 1984. pap. 4.95 (ISBN 0-570-04089-2, 56-1457). Concordia.

You Are the Answer: A Journey of Awakening. Paul N. Tuttle. 275p. (Orig.). 1985. pap. 12.50x (ISBN 0-934501-00-9). Kairos Inc.

You Are the Coach: College Football. Nathan Aaseng. (gr. 6-12). 1985. pap. 2.25 (ISBN 0-440-99840-9, LFL). Dell.

You Are the Coach: Football. Nathan Aaseng. 112p. (gr. 5 up). 1983. pap. 2.50 (ISBN 0-440-99136-6, LFL). Dell.

You Are the Editor: Sixty-One Editing Lessons That Improve Writing Skills. Eric Johnson. (Makemaster Bks.). (gr. 5-12). 1981. pap. 11.95 (ISBN 0-8224-7696-7); wkbk 3.95 (ISBN 0-8224-7697-5). D S Lake Pubs.

You Are the Flag. 1985. 1.00 (ISBN 0-934021-04-X). Natl Flag Foun.

You Are the Future - You Are My Hope. Pope John Paul II. 1979. pap. 3.95 (ISBN 0-8198-0633-1). Dghtrs St Paul.

You Are the Gift. Anna Cook. (Illus.). 80p. (Orig.). 1987. pap. 5.95 (ISBN 0-936029-04-8). Western Bk Journ.

You Are the Manager: Baseball. Nathan Aaseng. 112p. (gr. 5 up). 1984. pap. 2.50 (ISBN 0-440-99829-8, LFL). Dell.

You Are the Message: Secrets of the Master Communicators. Roger Ailes & John Kraushar. 240p. 1987. 19.95 (ISBN 0-87094-976-4). Dow Jones-Irwin.

You Are the Message: Secrets of the Master Communicators. Roger Ailes & Jon Kraushar. 1988. 8.95 (ISBN 0-671-66224-4). S&S.

You Are the Rain. R. R. Knudson. LC 73-15397. 160p. (gr. 7 up). 1974. 5.95 (ISBN 0-440-08759-7). Delacorte.

You Are the World. Jiddu Krishnamurti. 160p. 1973. pap. 4.95 (ISBN 0-06-080303-7, P303, PL). Har-Row.

You Are There Activity Books: Old Testament - New Testament. Bev Gundersen. (Illus.). 96p. (gr. 3-7). 1988. Old Testament. price not set (ISBN 0-87403-460-4, 13-02356); New Testament. price not set (ISBN 0-87403-461-2, 12-02357). Standard Pub.

You Are This Nation. Harold Norris. LC 75-27812. 160p. 1976. 7.50 (ISBN 0-8187-0020-3). Harlo Pr.

You Are Very Special: A Biblical Guide to Self-Worth. Verna Birkey. 160p. 1977. pap. 5.95 (ISBN 0-8007-5032-2, Power Bks). Revell.

You Are Welcome. 2nd rev. ed. Keith H. Parks. 32p. 1981. pap. 2.49 (ISBN 0-88151-013-0). Lay Leadership.

You Are What You Are. Valjean McLenighan. (Beginning-to-Read Ser.). (Illus.). (gr. 1-3). 1977. PLB 4.39 (ISBN 0-8136-5081-X, Dist. by Caroline Hse); pap. 1.95 (ISBN 0-8136-5581-1). Modern Curr.

You Are What You Ate. Sherry A. Rogers. 225p. (Orig.). 1988. pap. text ed. 7.95 (ISBN 0-9618821-1-5). Prestige NY.

You Are What You Breathe: The Negative Ion Story. Robert Massy. 32p. 1980. 1.50 (ISBN 0-916438-41-4, Dist. by New Era Pr). Univ of Trees.

You Are What You Choose. Maralene Wesner & E. Miles. LC 84-3110. (Orig.). 1984. pap. 4.95 (ISBN 0-8054-5247-8). Broadman.

You Are What You Eat. Victor H. Lindlahr. LC 80-19722. 128p. 1980. Repr. of 1971 ed. lib. bdg. 19.95x (ISBN 0-89370-604-3). Borgo Pr.

You Are What You Eat. Victor H. Lindlahr. LC 80-19722. 1971. pap. 4.95 (ISBN 0-87877-004-6, H-4). Newcastle Pub.

You Are What You Say: Diagnosis & Cure for the Troublesome Tongue. Karen B. Mains. 256p. 1988. pap. 7.95 (ISBN 0-310-34211-2, 12767P). Zondervan.

You Are What You Swallow. Elaine Rossignol. LC 86-83406. 220p. (Orig.). 1988. pap. 9.95 (ISBN 0-89896-240-4). Larksdale.

You Are What You Think, 2 vols. Doug Hooper. 1980. Vol. I. pap. write for info. (ISBN 0-9604702-0-4); Vol. II. pap. write for info. (ISBN 0-9604702-1-2). D Hooper.

You Are What You Think. Doug Hooper. 157p. 1981. pap. 6.95 (ISBN 0-13-972976-3). P-H.

You Are What You Think: Basic Issues in Pastoral Counseling. Robert C. Brien. 182p. (Orig.). 1986. pap. 5.95 (ISBN 0-87227-102-1). Reg Baptist.

You Are Witnesses This Day. Brian Entwistle. 1987. pap. 5.00 (ISBN 0-8309-0480-8). Herald Hse.

You Are Wonderful. Robert Schuller. 72p. 1987. 7.95 (ISBN 0-8378-1827-3). Gibson.

You Are Worth a Fortune. Arthur Milton. 1977. 6.95 (ISBN 0-8065-0589-3, Pub. by Citadel Pr). Lyle Stuart.

You Are Your Birthday. Ellen Dodge. 1986. pap. 8.95 (ISBN 0-671-61091-0, Fireside). S&S.

You Are Your Blood Type. Toshitaka Nomi & Alexander Besher. 208p. 1988. pap. 6.95 (ISBN 0-671-63342-2). PB.

You Are Your First Name. Ellen Dodge. 436p. pap. 6.95 (ISBN 0-671-61763-X, Fireside). S&S.

You Are Your First Name. Ellin D. Young. (Orig.). 1983. pap. 6.95 (ISBN 0-671-44832-3, Long Shadow Bks). PB.

You As a Law Enforcement Officer. Eve P. Steinberg. LC 84-14578. 160p. 1985. pap. 8.00 (ISBN 0-668-06205-3). Arco.

You Asked about Rheumatoid Arthritis: Reassuring Advice from a Distinguished Medical Team for All Who Suffer from North America's No. 1 Crippling Disease. Ed. by Harold S. Robinson. LC 81-17048. (Illus.). 128p. 1982. 9.95 (ISBN 0-8253-0088-6). Beaufort Bks NY.

You Asked for It, Charlie Brown. Charles Schulz. 1985. pap. 2.95 (ISBN 0-449-20967-9, Crest). Fawcett.

You be Good & I'll be Night: Jump on the Bed Poems. Eve Merriam. LC 87-24859. (Illus.). 40p. (ps-2). 1988. 12.95 (ISBN 0-688-06742-5); PLB 12.88 (ISBN 0-688-06743-3). Morrow.

You Be the Judge. Don Stewart. 96p. (Orig.). 1983. 2.95 (ISBN 0-89840-055-4). Heres Life.

You Be the Jury. Ed. by Marvin Miller. (Minute Mystery Ser.). (Illus.). 80p. (Orig.). (gr. 4-6). 1987. pap. 2.50 (ISBN 0-590-40193-9). Scholastic Inc.

You: Become a Full Person. Edward A. Maziarz. (Illus.). 132p. (Orig.). 1983. pap. text ed. 6.95 (ISBN 0-9611274-0-6). Shaman Bks.

You Believe. James Bales. pap. 2.95 (ISBN 0-89315-425-3). Lambert Bk.

You Belong. Allen H. Marheine. LC 79-21954. (Orig.). 1980. pap. 3.45 (ISBN 0-8298-0380-7). Pilgrim NY.

You Better Believe It. Kenneth J. Roberts. LC 77-84944. (Illus.). 1977. pap. 5.95 (ISBN 0-87973-750-6). Our Sunday Visitor.

You Brew It Yourself: The Complete Guide to Home Brewing. Leigh P. Beadle. 99p. 1981. 5.95. FS&G.

You Bright & Risen Angels. William T. Vollman. LC 86-47693. (Illus.). 512p. 1987. 22.95 (ISBN 0-689-11852-X). Atheneum.

You Bright & Risen Angels. William T. Vollmann. 640p. 1988. pap. 9.95 (ISBN 0-14-011087-9). Penguin.

You Bring Out the Music in Me: Music in Nursing Homes. Ed. & intro. by Beckie Karras. LC 87-22931. (Activities, Adaptation & Aging Ser.). (Illus.). 140p. 1988. text ed. 14.95 (ISBN 0-86656-699-6). Haworth Pr.

You Bring the Confetti. Luci Swindoll. 160p. 1986. 9.95 (ISBN 0-8499-0527-3). Word Bks.

You Call This a Family? Ed. by Gregg Lewis & Tim Stafford. (Campus Life Ser.). 160p. 1986. pap. 5.95 (ISBN 0-8423-8574-6). Tyndale.

You Can! Robert H. Shindler. Ed. by Sara Schreiner. 23p. 1985. pap. text ed. 2.95 (ISBN 0-914985-01-9). S M S Pub.

You Can Almost Take It with You: Commonsense Investing & Estate Planning. Edwin C. Anderson. 192p. 1987. pap. 12.95 (ISBN 0-8224-9893-6). D S Lake Pubs.

You Can Analyze Your Own Handwriting. Robert Holder. pap. 4.50 (ISBN 0-451-13721-3, Sig). NAL.

You Can Anything. Peter Seymour. (Surprise Bks.). 22p. (ps-1). 1986. 5.95 (ISBN 0-8431-1462-2). Price Stern.

You Can Be a Better Parent. Joseph F. Nielson. (Christian Counseling Aids Ser.). 1977. pap. 0.95 (ISBN 0-8010-6691-3). Baker Bk.

You Can Be a Chalk Artist. Art Barr. LC 77-93247. (Illus.). 1978. pap. 4.95 spiral bdg. (ISBN 0-89636-001-6). Accent Bks.

You Can Be A Country Music Songwriter. Johnny Robbins. (Illus.). 84p. 1982. pap. 4.95 (ISBN 0-9609748-0-6). Green Block.

You Can Be a Doctor in Thirty Minutes. Jim Becker et al. LC 84-3638. 12p. (Orig.). 1984. pap. text ed. 6.95 (ISBN 0-446-38101-2). Warner Bks.

You Can Be a Great Parent. Charlie W. Shedd. LC 76-128353. 1982. pap. 2.25 (ISBN 0-8499-4166-0, 98070). Word Bks.

You Can Never Go Wrong by Lying: And Other Solutions to the Moral Dilemas of Our Times. Patricia Marx. 1986. pap. 5.95 (ISBN 0-395-38465-6). HM.

You Can Never Tell. Ellen Conford. (gr. 4-9). 1988. pap. 2.50. Scholastic Inc.

You Can Only Slide so Long. Donzell Thomas. 1982. pap. 2.75 (ISBN 0-87067-012-3). Holloway.

You Can Overcome. Jim McKeever. 1981. 10.95 (ISBN 0-86694-091-X); pap. 6.95 (ISBN 0-86694-092-8). Omega Pubns Or.

You Can Overcome Fear. J. E. Adams. pap. 1.25 (ISBN 0-8010-0093-9). Baker Bk.

You Can Overcome Fear! Joy Berry. Ed. by Orly Kelly et al. LC 84-52423. (You Can! Ser.). (Illus.). 48p. (gr. 1-7). 1985. 4.98 (ISBN 0-941510-34-4). Living Skills.

You Can Overcome Your Fears, Phobias, & Worries. Louis O. Caldwell. 1985. pap. 1.25 (ISBN 0-8010-2506-0). Baker Bk.

You Can Paint Anything in Oils or Acrylics. Sherry Nelson & Jackie Shaw. (Illus.). 32p. (Orig.). 1987. pap. 7.95 (ISBN 0-941284-38-7). Deco Design Studio.

You Can Paint Flowers, Plants & Nature. Patricia Monahan. (Studio Ser.: Vol. 2). (Illus.). 64p. (Orig.). 1986. pap. 6.95 (ISBN 0-89134-137-4). North Light Bks.

You Can Paint Landscapes. Jenny Rodwell. (Studio Ser.: Vol. 3). (Illus.). 64p. (Orig.). 1986. pap. 7.95 (ISBN 0-89134-139-0). North Light Bks.

You Can Paint Outdoors in Watercolor. Alwyn Cranshaw. (Studio Ser.: Vol. 6). (Illus.). 64p. (Orig.). 1987. pap. 7.95 (ISBN 0-89134-217-6). North Light Bks.

You Can Paint Portraits. Patricia Monahan. (Studio Ser.: Vol. 4). (Illus.). 64p. (Orig.). 1986. pap. 6.95 (ISBN 0-89134-136-6). North Light Bks.

You Can Paint Still Lifes. Alwyn Cranshaw. (Studio Ser.: Vol. 7). (Illus.). 64p. (Orig.). 1987. pap. 7.95 (ISBN 0-89134-218-4). North Light Bks.

You Can Paint Wildlife. Martin Knowelden. (Studio Ser.: Vol. 8). (Illus.). 64p. (Orig.). 1987. pap. 7.95 (ISBN 0-89134-219-2). North Light Bks.

You Can Plan a Good Marriage. John M. Drescher. pap. 1.25 (ISBN 0-8010-2907-4). Baker Bk.

You Can Plan & Select Music: Discover & Shape Your Music Ministry-A-Step-by-Step Guide for Church Leaders. Robert C. Bennett. 48p. 1988. pap. 4.95. Abingdon.

You Can Postpone Anything But Love: Expanding Our Potential As Parents. Randy Rolfe. 174p. (Orig.). 1985. pap. 9.95 (ISBN 0-935019-07-3). Ambassador Pr.

You Can Prevent Cancer. Ernest H. Rosenbaum. Ed. by Sheila Mahoney & Nancy Wiltsek. (Illus.). 29p. 1984. pap. 2.50 (ISBN 0-933161-00-X). Better H Prog.

You Can Prevent or Overcome a Nervous Breakdown. Louis O. Caldwell. (Christian Counseling Aids Ser.). 1978. pap. 1.25 (ISBN 0-8010-2415-3). Baker Bk.

You Can Protect Yourself & Your Family from AIDS. Clif Cartland. 192p. 1987. pap. 8.95 (ISBN 0-8007-5262-7). Revell.

You Can Reach Families Through Their Babies. Elizabeth Gangel & Elsiebeth McDaniel. 64p. 1976. pap. 3.95 (ISBN 0-88207-140-8). Victor Bks.

You Can Receive the Holy Ghost Today. Bob Buess. 1967. pap. 2.50 (ISBN 0-934244-14-6). Sweeter Than Honey.

You Can Remember, 12 vols. Bruno Furst & Lotte Furst. 352p. 1978. pap. 36.95 boxed (ISBN 0-911744-50-9). Career Pub IL.

You Can Repair Your Own Sewing Machine. Rev. ed. Grover J. Tharp. (Illus.). 35p. wkbk. 4.00x (ISBN 0-9614713-0-1). Sewing Machine Man.

You Can Save a Bundle on Your Car Insurance. Paul Majka. 96p. 1982. pap. 3.95 (ISBN 0-312-89679-4); prepack 39.50 (ISBN 0-312-89680-8). St Martin.

You Can Save Your Marriage. Paul D. Meier. 15p. 1988. pap. 1.95 (ISBN 0-8010-6237-3). Baker Bk.

You Can Say No! Joy W. Berry. Ed. by Nancy Cochran & Susan Motycka. LC 84-52442. (You Can! Ser.). (Illus.). 48p. (gr. 1-7). 1985. 4.98 (ISBN 0-941510-75-1). Living Skills.

You Can Say "No" A Book about Protecting Yourself. Betty Boegehold. (Golden Learn about Living Bks.). (Illus.). 32p. (gr. k-3). 1985. 3.95 (ISBN 0-307-12483-5, 12483, Pub. by Golden Bks). Western Pub.

You Can Say No to a Drink or a Drug: What Every Kid Should Know. Susan Newman. (Illus.). 1986. pap. 8.95 (ISBN 0-399-51228-4, Perigee). Putnam Pub Group.

You Can Sketch & Draw in Color. Jenny Rodwell. (Studio Ser.: Vol. 1). (Illus.). 64p. (Orig.). 1986. pap. 7.95 (ISBN 0-89134-138-2). North Light Bks.

You Can So Get There from Here. 9th ed. LC 79-92914. 52p. pap. 5.95 (ISBN 0-912552-19-0). Missions Adv Res Com Ctr.

You Can Spend Less & Sell More: The Advertising Book. rev. ed. William K. Witcher. (Information for Action Ser.). (Illus.). 208p. 1988. pap. 19.95 (ISBN 0-937769-03-7). Mark Inc CA.

You Can Start a Bible Study Group: Making Friends, Changing Lives. rev. ed. Gladys Hunt. (Resource for Fisherman Bible Studyguides). 96p. 1984. Repr. of 1971 ed. lib. bdg. 2.95 (ISBN 0-87788-974-0). Shaw Pubs.

You Can Stay Alive: Wilderness Living & Emergency Survival. Larry Wells & Robert Giles. LC 81-80952. 100p. (Orig.). 1981. pap. 6.95 (ISBN 0-88290-181-8, 4028). Horizon Utah.

You Can Still Change the World. 3.50 (ISBN 0-318-02218-4). Chrstphrs NY.

You Can Stop Arthritis. 48p. 1980. pap. 2.50 (ISBN 0-9605680-0-X). Vita Pr TN.

You Can Stop Feeling Guilty. Louis O. Caldwell. (Christian Counseling Aids Ser.). 1978. pap. 1.25 (ISBN 0-8010-2414-5). Baker Bk.

You Can Stop Smoking. Jacquelyn Roger. pap. 3.95 (ISBN 0-671-63204-3). PB.

You Can Stop: The Smokenders Guide on How to Give up Cigarettes. Jacqueline Rogers. 1983. pap. 3.95 (ISBN 0-671-62691-4). PB.

You Can Succeed! Eric P. Jensen. LC 79-13489. (gr. 10-12). 1979. pap. 6.95 (ISBN 0-8120-2084-7). Barron.

You Can Survive. H. Smith. 1982. text ed. 9.95 (ISBN 0-07-058960-7). McGraw.

You Can Survive Trauma! Joy Berry. Ed. by Nancy Cochran & Susan Motycka. LC 84-52426. (You Can! Ser.). (Illus.). 48p. (gr. 1-7). 1985. 4.98 (ISBN 0-941510-33-6). Living Skills.

You Can Take It With You. Sheldon Rappaport. 198p. pap. 8.95 (ISBN 0-942494-38-5). Coleman Pub.

You Can Talk to (Almost) Anyone about (Almost) Anything: A Speaking Guide for Business & Professional People. Elaine Cogan & Ben Padrow. LC 84-15531. (Illus.). 116p. (Orig.). 1984. lib. bdg. 14.95 (ISBN 0-87678-021-4); pap. 7.95 (ISBN 0-87678-022-2). Continuing Ed Pubns.

You Can Teach Adults. Jacobsen. 1981. 3.95 (ISBN 0-88207-148-3). Victor Bks.

You Can Teach Adults Successfully. Ron Davis et al. (Training Successful Teachers Ser.). 48p. (Orig.). 1984. pap. 2.95 (ISBN 0-87239-808-0, 3208). Standard Pub.

You Can Teach Children Successfully. Twila Sias. (Training Successful Teachers Ser.). 48p. (Orig.). 1984. pap. 2.95 (ISBN 0-87239-806-4, 3206). Standard Pub.

You Can Teach Four's & Five's. Lebar & Riley. 1981. 3.95 (ISBN 0-88207-142-4). Victor Bks.

You Can Teach High Schoolers. Hooton & Heidubrocht. 64p. 1981. 3.95 (ISBN 0-88207-147-5). Victor Bks.

You Can Teach Juniors & Middlers. Joyce Gibson & Eleanor Hance. 64p. 1981. pap. 3.95 (ISBN 0-88207-145-9). Victor Bks.

You Can Teach Old Type New Tricks. Phillip R. Baldus & Harold L. Baldus. (Illus.). 24p. 1985. pap. 10.00 (ISBN 0-933107-01-3). Phils Photo.

You Can Teach Preschoolers Successfully. Betty Aldridge. (Training Successful Teachers Ser.). 48p. (Orig.). 1984. pap. 2.95 (ISBN 0-87239-805-6, 3205). Standard Pub.

You Can Teach Primaries. Elsiebeth McDaniel. 64p. 1981. pap. 3.95 (ISBN 0-88207-143-2). Victor Bks.

You Can Teach Teens Successfully. Roy Reiswig. (Training Successful Teachers Ser.). 48p. (Orig.). 1984. pap. 2.95 (ISBN 0-87239-807-2, 3207). Standard Pub.

You Can Teach Two's & Three's. Mary E. Barbour. 64p. 1981. pap. 3.95 (ISBN 0-88207-149-1). Victor Bks.

You Can Teach Young Teens. Norma Felske. 1981. 3.95 (ISBN 0-88207-146-7). Victor Bks.

You Can Teach Your Child Successfully: Grades 4-8. Ruth Beechick. (Illus.). 396p. 1988. 18.95 (ISBN 0-940319-05-5); pap. 13.70 (ISBN 0-940319-04-7). Arrow Connection.

You Can Teach Your Dog to Eliminate on Command. M. L. Smith. Tr. by Syd Stibbard. (Illus.). 83p. (Orig.). 1984. pap. 5.95 (ISBN 0-9617649-0-2). Smith Sager Pubns.

You Can Too. Mary C. Crowley. 176p. 1980. pap. 5.95 (ISBN 0-8007-5028-4, Power Bks). Revell.

You Can Train Your Cat. Jo Loeb & Paul Loeb. 1979. pap. 3.95 (ISBN 0-671-25147-3, Fireside). S&S.

You Can Travel Free. Robert W. Kirk. LC 84-1166. 192p. (Orig.). 1985. pap. 7.95 (ISBN 0-88289-437-4). Pelican.

You Can Trust the Bible. John MacArthur, Jr. 1988. pap. 1.95 (ISBN 0-8024-7199-4). Moody.

You Can Trust Your Bible. Neale Pryor. 3.95 (ISBN 0-89137-524-4). Quality Pubns.

You Can Type for Doctors at Home! Ruth de Menezes. 72p. 1981. pap. 10.00 (ISBN 0-941358-00-3). Claremont CA.

You Can Understand the Bible. Fernon Retzer. 1984. pap. 1.95 (ISBN 0-317-28295-6). Pacific Pr Pub Assn.

You Can Win. Roger Campbell. 132p. 1985. pap. 5.50 (ISBN 0-89693-317-2). Victor Bks.

You Can Win at the Polls: A Finance Campaign Kit. 325.00 (ISBN 0-87545-034-2). Natl Sch Pr.

You Can Win with Love. Dale Galloway. LC 76-15129. 176p. 1980. pap. 2.95 (ISBN 0-89081-233-0). Harvest Hse.

You Can Write. Mary E. Grasso & Margaret S. Maney. 416p. 1986. pap. text ed. 12.95 (ISBN 0-8403-3866-X). Kendall-Hunt.

You Can Write a Novel. Geoffrey Bocca. LC 83-13990. 133p. 1983. 14.95 (ISBN 0-13-976845-9); pap. 5.95 (ISBN 0-13-976837-8). P-H.

You Can Write! Practical Writing Skills for Hawaii. Victor C. Pellegrino. LC 81-71307. (Illus.). 296p. 1982. text ed. 12.95 (ISBN 0-935848-05-3); pap. text ed. 9.95 (ISBN 0-935848-04-5); wkbk, Feb. 1985 4.95 (ISBN 0-935848-28-2); Tchr's manual 3.00. Bess Pr.

You Can, You Can. Belk Clothilde. 12p. (Orig.). 1988. write for info. Babe Co.

You Cannot Hold Back the Dawn. John C. Dowd. LC 74-75619. 1974. 4.95 (ISBN 0-8198-0320-0); pap. 3.95 (ISBN 0-8198-0321-9). Dghtrs St Paul.

You Can't Be Serious. Steve Race. 112p. 1986. 14.95x (ISBN 0-297-78756-X, Pub. by Weidenfeld & Nicolson England). Biblio Dist.

You Can't Beat the Beatitudes. George O. Wood & William J. Krutza. LC 78-58721. 96p. 1978. pap. 1.25 (ISBN 0-88243-719-4, 02-0719). Gospel Pub.

You Can't Beat the Enemy While Raising His Flag see Strategic Outlook & Alliances.

You Can't Borrow from Tomorrow. Betty Carmichael. 1984. 8.95 (ISBN 0-8062-2410-X). Carlton.

You Can't Catch Diabetes from a Friend. Lynne Kipnis & Susan Adler. LC 79-1165. (Illus.). 1979. 9.95 (ISBN 0-9600472-3-9). Triad Pub FL.

You Can't Catch Me! Joanne Oppenheim. LC 86-7211. (Illus.). 32p. (gr. k). 1986. 12.95 (ISBN 0-395-41452-0). HM.

You Can't Count on Dying. Natalie H. Cabot. Ed. by Leon Stein. LC 79-8662. (Growing Old Ser.). 1980. Repr. of 1961 ed. lib. bdg. 25.50x (ISBN 0-405-12779-0). Ayer Co Pubs.

You Can't Do It All. Irvina S. Lew. 288p. 1987. 3.95 (ISBN 0-425-10114-2). Berkley Pub.

You Can't Do It All: Ideas That Work for Mothers Who Work. Irvina S. Lew. LC 85-48125. (Illus.). 320p. 1986. 16.95 (ISBN 0-689-11556-3). Atheneum.

You Can't Do That. G. Seldes. LC 70-37287. (Civil Liberties in American History Ser). 308p. 1972. Repr. of 1938 ed. lib. bdg. 27.50 (ISBN 0-306-70201-0). Da Capo.

You Can't Do That: Beatles Bootlegs & Novelty Records, 1963-1980. Charles Reinhart. LC 80-83515. (Rock & Roll Reference Ser.: No. 5). (Illus.). 450p. 1981. 19.50 (ISBN 0-87650-128-5). Pierian.

You Can't Drown the Fire: Latin American Women Writing in Exile. Ed. by Alicia Partnoy. 260p. (Orig.). 1988. 21.95 (ISBN 0-939416-16-6); pap. 9.95 (ISBN 0-939416-17-4). Cleis Pr.

You Can't Escape. Faith Baldwin. 1976. Repr. of 1943 ed. lib. bdg. 17.95x (ISBN 0-88411-625-5, Pub. by Aeonian Pr). Amereon Ltd.

You Can't Fly Home Again. Ron Rendleman. LC 79-89581. 1980. pap. 2.95 (ISBN 0-89221-066-4). New Leaf.

You Can't Get Lost in Cape Town. Zoe Wicomb. 11.95 (ISBN 0-317-64912-4); pap. 6.95. Pantheon.

You Can't Get the Coons All up One Tree: True Life Story of John N. Jones. Ed. by Leona P. Carver. 244p. (Orig.). 1980. pap. 7.95x (ISBN 0-686-36932-7). Coltharp Pub.

You Can't Get There from Here. Mary Anderson. 208p. 1983. pap. 2.25 (ISBN 0-441-94981-9). Ace Bks.

You Can't Get There from Here. Ogden Nash. (Illus.). 208p. 1984. pap. 6.95 (ISBN 0-316-59854-2). Little.

You Can't Go Home Again. Thomas Wolfe. 390p. 1981. Repr. lib. bdg. 16.95x (ISBN 0-89966-294-3). Buccaneer Bks.

You Can't Go Home Again. Thomas Wolfe. 576p. 1973. pap. 5.95 (ISBN 0-06-080314-2, P314, PL). Har-Row.

You Can't Have Your Cake & Eat It Too: A Program for Controlling Bulimia. Lillie Weiss et al. 130p. (Orig.). 1986. pap. 6.95 (ISBN 0-88247-750-1). R & E Pubs.

You Can't Keep a Good Woman Down: Stories. Alice Walker. LC 80-8761. 180p. 1982. pap. 4.95 (ISBN 0-15-699778-9, Harv). HarBraceJ.

You Can't Kill a Dead Man. Daniel Panger. 208p. (Orig.). 1982. pap. 2.25 (ISBN 0-8439-1057-7, Leisure Bks). Leisure NY.

You Can't Kill the Spirit. Pam McAllister. (Barbara Deming Memorial Series: Stories of Women & Nonviolence: Pt. 1). 240p. (Orig.). 1988. 34.95 (ISBN 0-86571-130-5); pap. 10.95 (ISBN 0-86571-131-3). New Soc Pubs.

You Can't Lose. James A. Aderman. Ed. by William E. Fischer. (Bible Class for Young Adults Ser.). (Illus.). 36p. (Orig.). 1987. pap. 2.95 tch'rs. ed.; tch'rs. ed. 2.95. Wels Board.

You Can't Make a Move Without Your Muscles. Paul Showers. LC 81-43323. (Let's-Read-&-Find-Out Science Bks.). (Illus.). 40p. (gr. k-3). 1982. (Crowell Jr Bks); PLB 12.89 (ISBN 0-690-04185-3). HarpJ.

You Can't Make Me! A Behavior Management Handbook. Judith K. Schneider et al. (Competent Caregiver Ser.). (Illus.). 62p. 1986. pap. text ed. 6.95 (ISBN 0-944454-03-8); wkbk. 3.95 (ISBN 0-944454-13-5); 2.95 (ISBN 0-944454-14-3). CAPE Center.

You Can't Manage Alone. John S. Morgan & J. R. Philp. 256p. (Orig.). 1985. pap. 6.95 (ISBN 0-310-33602-3, 12766P). Zondervan.

You Can't Manage Alone: Practical Prayers for Conscientious Managers. John Morgan & J. R. Philp. 272p. 1986. gift ed. 12.95 (ISBN 0-310-33608-2, 12766G). Zondervan.

You Can't Sneeze with Your Eyes Open: And Other Freaky Facts about the Human Body. Barbara Seuling. (Freaky Facts Ser.). (Illus.). 80p. (gr. 4 up). 1986. 10.95 (ISBN 0-525-67185-4, 01063-320). Lodestar Bks.

You Can't Start a Car with a Cross. Ron Lavin. 1984. 5.95 (ISBN 0-89536-648-7, 2507). CSS of Ohio.

You Can't Steal First Base. Charles G. Hamilton. LC 74-164909. 1972. 6.95 (ISBN 0-8022-2057-6). Philos Lib.

You Can't Take It with You. John J. Farley. Ed. by R. Reed. LC 81-83622. 1982. pap. 7.95 (ISBN 0-88247-616-5). R & E Pubs.

You Can't Take It with You see Three Comedies of American Family Life.

You Can't Take It with You: A Step-by-Step, Personalized Approach to Your Will to Avoid Probate & Taxes. David C. Larsen. Ed. by Robert Loomis. LC 87-45910. (Illus.). 144p. 1988. pap. 6.95 (ISBN 0-394-75543-X, Vin). Random.

You Can't Take Twenty Dogs on a Date. Betty Cavanna. (YA) (gr. 7-12). 1979. pap. 1.95 (ISBN 0-590-05784-7). Scholastic Inc.

You Can't Tell the Players. Barton R. Friedman. (Cleveland Poets Ser.: No. 21). 46p. (Orig.). 1979. pap. 3.50 (ISBN 0-914946-17-X). Cleveland St Univ Poetry Ctr.

You Can't Turn Back. Darwin Gross. 98p. (Orig.). 1985. pap. 4.95 (ISBN 0-931689-02-3). SOS Pub OR.

You Can't Win: The Autobiography of Jack Black. 2nd ed. Jack Black. 406p. 1988. pap. 9.95 (ISBN 0-941693-07-4). Amok Press.

You Come Too. Robert Frost. LC 59-12940. (Illus.). 96p. (YA) (gr. 4 up). 1959. 9.95 (ISBN 0-8050-0299-5); pap. 3.95 (ISBN 0-8050-0316-9). H Holt & Co.

You Come with Naked Hands: The Story of the San Francisco to Moscow March for Peace. Bradford Lyttle. LC 66-1279. (Illus.). 289p. 1966. 17.00 (ISBN 0-934676-08-9). Greenlf Bks.

You Could - Feel Good. Suzanne Harrill. Ed. by Jim Gross. 96p. (Orig.). 1988. pap. 6.95 (ISBN 0-912949-17-1). Uni-Sun.

You Could Argue but You'd Be Wrong. Pete Franklin & Terry Pluto. 256p. 1988. 17.95 (ISBN 0-8092-4674-0). Contemp Bks.

You Could Call It Murder. Lawrence Block. 140p. 1987. pap. 4.95 (ISBN 0-88150-086-0, Foul Play). Countryman.

You Could Look It Up: More on Language. William Safire. (Illus.). 368p. 1988. 22.50 (ISBN 0-8129-1324-8). Times Bks.

You Count-You Really Do! William A. Miller. LC 76-27078. 1977. pap. 6.95 (ISBN 0-8066-1569-9, 10-7420). Augsburg.

You Cry for Worse than Nothing. Joe D. Johnson. 55p. 1975. pap. 3.50 (ISBN 0-915564-07-6). Joe D Johnson.

You Die, Du Ma! Jonathan Cain. (Saigon Commandos Ser.: No. 8). 1985. pap. 2.50 (ISBN 0-8217-1629-8). Zebra.

You Dirty Dog. Stephen Caitlin. LC 87-19182. (Giant First-Start Readers Ser.). (Illus.). (gr. k-2). 1987. PLB 9.89 (ISBN 0-8167-1103-8); pap. 2.95 (ISBN 0-8167-1104-6). Troll Assocs.

You Do It Too. (Tiny Tots World Ser.). 2.95 (Brimax Bks). Borden.

You Do Not Have to Wait. Tom Johnson. 1987. pap. 3.00 (ISBN 0-941992-11-X). Los Arboles Pub.

You Don't Have to Ache: Orthotherapy. Arthur A. Michelle. LC 73-150795. 224p. 1983. pap. 5.95 (ISBN 0-87131-411-8). M Evans.

You Don't Have to Act Your Age: Physical Fitness for the Retired. Win McFadden. (Illus.). x, 116p. (Orig.). 1985. pap. 5.95 (ISBN 0-9614494-0-3). Bryan-Lee Pub.

You Don't Have to Be a Computer Genius to Land a Computer Job: How to Find a Career in the World's Fastest Growing Field. Jack L. Stone & Stephen S. Roberts. LC 83-17910. 252p. 1984. pap. 9.95 (ISBN 0-672-52790-1). Bobbs.

You Don't Have to Be a Perfect Girl. Patricia Aks. 192p. (Orig.). (gr. 7-12). 1981. pap. 1.95 (ISBN 0-590-31397-5). Scholastic Inc.

You Don't Have to Be Beautiful to Be a Model. Ron Millkie & Ray Carlson. LC 77-26794. 38p. 1986. pap. 3.50 (ISBN 0-87576-064-3). Pilot Bks.

You Don't Have to Be British to Do Shakespeare: ABC's for the Bard. Judy Magee. LC 84-90250. 92p. 1985. 8.95 (ISBN 0-533-06287-X). Vantage.

You Don't Have to Be Chinese to Cook Great Chinese Food. Rita Edelman. 1975. 4.95 (ISBN 0-913806-57-9). Laddin Pr.

You Don't Have to Be Crazy to Work Here... But it Sure Helps. Wayne B. Norris. (Illus.). 196p. (Orig.). 1986. pap. 7.95 (ISBN 0-8431-1496-7). Price Stern.

You Don't Have to Be Gay: Hope & Freedom for Males Struggling with Homosexuality or for Those Who Know of Someone Who Is. J. A. Konrad. 288p. (Orig.). 1987. pap. 14.95 (ISBN 0-942817-07-9). Pacific Hse.

You Don't Have to Be in Who's Who to Know What's What. Sam Levenson. 1982. pap. 2.95 (ISBN 0-671-45428-5). PB.

You Don't Have to Be Next. Dr. Jochen Aumiller. 1980. pap. 5.95 (ISBN 0-8065-0683-0, Pub. by Citadel Pr). Lyle Stuart.

You Don't Have to Be Sick, 4 bks. in 1. Lady P. Cilento. 336p. 1984. pap. 3.50 (ISBN 0-87983-403-X). Keats.

You Don't Have to be Sick Anymore! John D. Woolston. 112p. (Orig.). 1988. pap. text ed. 2.25. J D Woolston.

You Don't Have to Count Your Birthdays Until... Martin Ragaway. (Laughter Library). (Illus.). 1979. pap. 1.95 (ISBN 0-8431-0534-8). Price Stern.

You Don't Have to Go It Alone. Leslie B. Flynn. LC 80-66722. 160p. (Orig.). 1981. pap. 4.95 (ISBN 0-89636-058-X). Accent Bks.

You Don't Have to Live with Cystitis: A Woman Urologist Tells How to Avoid It- What to Do about It. Larrian Gillespie. LC 85-43087. 256p. 1986. 18.95 (ISBN 0-89256-302-8). Rawson Assocs.

You Don't Have to Live with Cystitis! How to Avoid It - What to Do about It. Larrian Gillespie. 304p. 1988. pap. 7.95 (ISBN 0-380-70486-2). Avon.

You Don't Have to Quit. Anne Ortlund & Ray Ortlund. 1988. pap. 7.95 (ISBN 0-8407-9561-0). Oliver-Nelson.

You Don't Have to Slay a Dragon. John M. Stuart & Marjorie L. Stuart. LC 75-14540. (Illus.). 313p. 1976. 8.95 (ISBN 0-915730-01-4). Marburger.

You Don't Know Me but... A Collection of Prize-Winning Recipes. Getschmann. pap. 8.95 (ISBN 0-87505-081-6). Borden.

You Don't Know My God. Peter A. Duro & Carol J. Duro. LC 85-81388. 238p. (Orig.). 1985. pap. 5.95 (ISBN 0-9615955-0-7). Emmanuel Christian.

You Don't Know What Love Is: Contemporary American Stories. Ed. by Ron Hansen. LC 87-15219. 312p. (Orig.). 1987. pap. 13.95 (ISBN 0-86538-060-0). Ontario Rev NJ.

You Don't Look Like a Musician. Bud Freeman. LC 73-89352. 135p. 1974. 5.95 (ISBN 0-913642-05-3). Balamp Pub.

You Don't Look Thirty-Five, Charlie Brown! Charles M. Schulz. 224p. 1985. 17.95 (ISBN 0-03-005859-7, Owl Bks.); pap. 9.95 (ISBN 0-03-005624-1). H Holt & Co.

You Don't Need That Damn Broker: A Complete Guide to Selling Your Own Home. Kam Kavanaugh. LC 81-90038. 96p. 1981. pap. 5.95 (ISBN 0-9605742-0-4). Kambrina.

You Don't Need to Have a Repeat Cesarean. Nicki Royall. LC 82-83775. 204p. 1983. 14.95 (ISBN 0-8119-0487-3). Fell.

You Don't See Me. Schultz K. Miller. (Children's Theatre Playscript Ser.). 1985. pap. 2.50x (ISBN 0-88020-120-7). Coach Hse.

You Dropped It, You Pick It up! Jim Paul. Ed. by Joe Planas. LC 83-82572. (Illus.). 222p. 1984. 14.95 (ISBN 0-9612822-0-7). Eds Pub Co.

You Gentiles. Maurice Samuels. 1979. lib. bdg. 59.95 (ISBN 0-8490-3019-6). Gordon Pr.

You Gentiles. Maurice Samuels. pap. 3.00x (ISBN 0-911038-08-6). Noontide.

You Get So Alone at Times That It Just Makes Sense. Charles Bukowski. LC 86-13662. 318p. 1986. 20.00 (ISBN 0-87685-684-9); signed ltd. ed. o.p. 30.00 (ISBN 0-87685-685-7); pap. 12.50 (ISBN 0-87685-683-0). Black Sparrow.

You Get What You Pay For. Larry Beinhart. 356p. 1988. 18.95 (ISBN 0-688-06613-5). Morrow.

You Give Great Meeting, Sid. G. B. Trudeau. 128p. 1983. pap. 5.25 (ISBN 0-03-061733-2). H Holt & Co.

You Go Away. Dorothy Corey. LC 75-33015. (Self Starter Bks.). (Illus.). 32p. (ps). 1975. PLB 9.75 (ISBN 0-8075-9441-5). A Whitman.

You Gotta Deal with It: Black Family Relations in a Southern Community. Theodore Kennedy. (Illus.). 1980. 24.95x (ISBN 0-19-502591-1); pap. text ed. 9.95x (ISBN 0-19-502592-X). Oxford U Pr.

You Gotta Have Heart: Dallas Green's Rebuilding of the Cubs. Ned Colletti. LC 85-4405. (Illus.). 272p. 1985. 15.95 (ISBN 0-912083-11-5). Diamond Communications.

You Gotta Keep Dancin' Tim Hansel. LC 85-11298. 150p. 1985. pap. 6.95 (ISBN 0-89191-722-5, 57224). Cook.

You Gotta Lose to Win. Franklin Greenwald & Maigen Elske. (Aphorisms Trilogy Ser.: Vol. 2). (Illus.). 25p. 1985. pap. 4.95 (ISBN 0-936779-01-2). No Secrets Pr.

You Gotta Want It! Coach Woit's Progressive Program for Total Fitness. Dick Woit & Steve Fiffer. (Orig.). 1986. pap. 9.95 (ISBN 0-933893-17-5). Bonus Books.

You Have a Friend, Dainty Dinosaur. (Beginning to Read Ser.). (gr. 2 up). 1988. PLB 5.95 (ISBN 0-8136-5212-X); pap. 2.95 (ISBN 0-8136-5712-1). Modern Curr.

You Have a Girlfriend, Alfie Atkins? Gunilla Bergstrom. Tr. by Joan Sandin from Swedish. (Illus.). 28p. (ps up). 1988. 6.95 (ISBN 91-29-59062-0, Pub. by R & S Bks). FS&G.

You Have a Pacemaker. rev. ed. Barbara L. Johnston & Julia A. Purcell. Ed. by Nancy R. Hull. LC 81-23461. 28p. 1988. pap. text ed. 3.25 (ISBN 0-939838-12-5). Pritchett & Hull.

You Have a Point There: A New & Complete Guide to Punctuation. Eric Partridge. (Orig.). 1978. pap. 7.95 (ISBN 0-7100-8753-5). Routledge Chapman & Hall.

You Have a Right: A Guide for Minors. Leland S. Englebardt. LC 79-4678. (gr. 6 up). 1979. PLB 11.88 (ISBN 0-688-51893-1). Lothrop.

You Have a Right to Be Free. Wayne E. Anderson. 40p. 1986. pap. 1.95 (ISBN 0-913748-08-0). Orovan Bks.

You Have Been Here Before: A Psychologist Looks at Past Lives. Edith Fiore. 256p. 1986. pap. 3.50 (ISBN 0-345-33822-7). Ballantine.

You Have No Country! Workers' Struggle Against War. Mary E. Marcy. Ed. by Franklin Rosemont. 80p. lib. bdg. 17.95 (ISBN 0-88286-059-3); pap. 4.50 (ISBN 0-88286-058-5). C H Kerr.

You Have Seen Their Faces. facsimile ed. Erskine Caldwell & Margaret Bourke-White. Ed. by Dan C. McCurry & Richard E. Rubenstein. LC 74-30622. (American Farmers & the Rise of Agribusiness Ser.). (Illus., With a new introductory note by Erskine Caldwell). 1975. Repr. of 1937 ed. 20.00x (ISBN 0-405-06769-0). Ayer Co Pubs.

You Have to Treat Your Heart. C. Aitmatov et al. 271p. 1986. 9.95 (ISBN 0-8285-3453-5, Pub. by Raduga Pubs USSR). Imported Pubns.

You Hear the Ice Talking: The Ways of People & Ice on Lake Champlain. I. Sheldon Posen. LC 86-29914. (Illus.). 70p. (Orig.). 1986. pap. 11.00 (ISBN 0-9617701-1-2). C E F Lib Syst.

You, I, & the Others. Paul Weiss. LC 79-13375. 428p. 1980. 25.95x (ISBN 0-8093-0923-8). S Ill U Pr.

You! Jonah! Thomas J. Carlisle. LC 68-20587. (Illus.). pap. 20.00 (ISBN 0-8357-9134-3, 2012750). Bks Demand UMI.

You Keep Waiting for Geese. Viola Wendt. LC 75-29746. (Illus.). 1975. text ed. 6.75 (ISBN 0-916120-01-5); pap. text ed. 3.95x (ISBN 0-916120-02-3). Carroll Coll.

You Know: A Discourse-Functional Study. Jan-Ola Ostman. (Pragmatics & Beyond Ser.: II: 7). ix, 91p. (Orig.). 1981. pap. 20.00x (ISBN 90-272-2516-8). Benjamins North Am.

You Know I Can't Hear You When the Water's Running. Robert Anderson. LC 67-22664. 92p. 1967. 16.95 (ISBN 0-910278-11-3). Boulevard.

You Know It's a Fantasy When... Julie Castiglia. 1987. pap. 1.95 (ISBN 0-8431-1814-8). Price Stern.

You Know Me. W. A. Rocker. 1972. 7.50 (ISBN 0-912090-24-3); pap. 2.45 (ISBN 0-912090-23-5). Sumac Mich.

You Know Me Al. Ring Lardner. 218p. Repr. of 1914 ed. lib. bdg. 17.95x (ISBN 0-88411-584-4). Amereon Ltd.

You Know Me Al: A Busher's Letters. Ring Lardner. LC 84-40077. 224p. 1984. pap. 5.95 (ISBN 0-394-72634-0, Vin). Random.

You Know These Lines: A Bibliography of the Most Quoted Verses in American Poetry. Merle Johnson. 1973. Repr. of 1935 ed. 30.00 (ISBN 0-8274-0264-3). R West.

You Know What Is Right. Jim Heynen. LC 84-62303. 208p. 1985. 13.50 (ISBN 0-86547-194-0). N Point Pr.

You Know When You're over Fifty When... Herbert I. Kavet. (Illus.). 96p. (Orig.). 1984. pap. 3.95 (ISBN 0-8092-5342-9). Contemp Bks.

You Know When You're over Forty When... Herbert I. Kavet. (Illus.). 96p. 1984. pap. 3.95 (ISBN 0-8092-5363-1). Contemp Bks.

You Know You Are a College Student When... Paul Barlow, Jr. (Illus.). 96p. 1986. pap. 3.95 (ISBN 0-8431-1571-8). Price Stern.

You Know You're a Mother When... Melodie M. Davis. 112p. 1987. pap. 4.95 (ISBN 0-310-44811-5, 12478P). Zondervan.

You Know You're Fat When... Once Upon a Planet, Inc. (Illus.). 32p. (Orig.). 1982. pap. 1.25 (ISBN 0-88009-016-2). Planet Bks.

You Know You're Really in Love When....You Know It's Time to Break up When. Margaret Howard. (Illus.). 80p. (Orig.). (gr. 7 up). 1981. pap. 1.95 (ISBN 0-590-31786-5, Schol Pap). Scholastic Inc.

You Know You're Really Pregnant When... Lisa E. Arnold. (Illus.). 64p. 1987. 9.95 (ISBN 0-8431-1916-0). Price Stern.

You Learn by Living. Eleanor Roosevelt. LC 83-6838. 224p. 1983. pap. 9.95 (ISBN 0-664-24494-7). Westminster John Knox.

You Learn to Type. Alan C. Lloyd & R. Krevolin. 1966. text ed. 24.08 (ISBN 0-07-038160-7). McGraw.

You Live after Death. Harold Sherman. 176p. 1987. pap. 2.95 (GM). Fawcett.

You Live & Love. Valentine Rasputin. Tr. by Alan G. Myers. Date not set. 16.95 (ISBN 0-8149-0916-7). Vanguard.

You Live Once. John D. MacDonald. 1981. pap. 1.95 (ISBN 0-449-14050-4, GM). Fawcett.

You Look Funny! Joy Kim. LC 86-30839. (Illus.). 32p. (gr. k-2). 1987. PLB 5.41 (ISBN 0-8167-0976-9); pap. text ed. 1.50 (ISBN 0-8167-0977-7). Troll Assocs.

You Look Ridiculous Said the Rhinoceros to the Hippopotamus. Bernard Waber. (Illus.). (gr. k-3). 1966. reinforced bdg. 13.95 (ISBN 0-395-07156-9). HM.

You Look Ridiculous Said the Rhinoceros to the Hippopotamus. Bernard Waber. (Illus.). (gr. k-3). 1979. pap. 3.95 (ISBN 0-395-28007-9). HM.

You Lucky Duck! Emily A. McCully. LC 87-81764. (Golden Storytime Bks.). (Illus.). 24p. (ps-1). 1988. 2.95 (ISBN 0-307-10970-4, Pub. by Golden Bks). Western Pub.

You Make the Angels Cry. Denys Cazet. LC 82-9581. (Illus.). 32p. (ps-k). 12.95 (ISBN 0-02-717830-7). Bradbury Pr.

You Make the Difference. Eric Butterworth. LC 76-9959. 160p. 1984. 12.45 (ISBN 0-06-061271-1, HarpR). Har-Row.

You Make the Difference: Cadette & Senior Girl Scout Leaders' Guide. Girl Scouts of the U. S. A. Staff. 40p. (Orig.). 1980. pap. text ed. 3.00 (ISBN 0-88441-330-6, 20-705). Girl Scouts USA.

You Make the Difference: The Handbook for Cadette & Senior Girl Scouts. Girl Scouts of the U. S. A. Staff. (Illus.). 72p. (Orig.). (YA) (gr. 7-12). 1980. pap. text ed. 3.75 (ISBN 0-88441-329-2, 20-704). Girl Scouts USA.

You May Plow Here: The Narrative of Sara Brooks. Ed. by Thordis Simonsen. LC 85-11534. 1986. 12.95 (ISBN 0-393-02257-9). Norton.

You May Plow Here: The Narrative of Sara Brooks. Ed. by Thordis Simonsen. 1987. pap. 6.95 (ISBN 0-671-63848-3, Touchstone Bks). S&S.

You Mean I Can't Do This? 2nd ed. Catholic Health Association Division of Legal Services Staff. LC 81-15457. (Illus.). 40p. 1981. pap. text ed. 0.50 (ISBN 0-87125-067-5). Cath Health.

You Mean I Have to Stand Up & Say Something? Joan Detz. LC 86-3611. (Illus.). 86p. (gr. 7-12). 1986. PLB 12.95 (ISBN 0-689-31221-0, Atheneum Childrens Bks). Macmillan.

You Mean So Much to Me. Ed. by Susan P. Schutz. LC 82-74103. (Illus.). 64p. (Orig.). 1983. pap. 4.95 (ISBN 0-88396-184-9). Blue Mtn Pr CO.

You Mean the Bible Teaches That. Charles C. Ryrie. 1974. pap. 5.95 (ISBN 0-8024-9828-0). Moody.

You Mean to Say You Still Don't Know Who We Are? Seven Kabuki Plays. Ed. by Cellin Gluck & Yasushi Takeda. Tr. by Mitsuko Unno from Japanese. 260p. 1976. pap. 7.95 (ISBN 4-89360-033-8, Pub. by Personally Oriented Ltd. SoPA). C E Tuttle.

You Might As Well Live: The Life & Times of Dorothy Parker. John Keats. LC 86-18691. (Illus.). 320p. 1986. pap. 8.95 (ISBN 0-913729-49-3). Paragon Hse.

You Might Have Asked. Stuart Olyott. pap. 9.95 (ISBN 0-87552-951-8, Evangel Pr UK). Presby & Reformed.

You Must Break Out Sometimes & Other Stories. facsimile ed. Thomas O. Beachcroft. LC 75-113648. (Short Story Index Reprint Ser.). 1937. 18.00 (ISBN 0-8369-3377-X). Ayer Co Pubs.

You Must Know Everything. Isaac Babel. Ed. by Nathalie Babel. Tr. by Max Hayward from Rus. 283p. 1969. 10.95 (ISBN 0-374-29408-9); pap. 6.95 (ISBN 0-374-51580-8). FS&G.

You Must Know Everything. Isaac Babel. Tr. by Max Hayward. 304p. 1984. pap. 8.95 (ISBN 0-88184-027-0). Carroll & Graf.

You Must Relax. 5th, rev. ed. Edmund Jacobson. LC 75-33112. (Illus.). 256p. 1976. text ed. 8.95 (ISBN 0-07-032182-5). McGraw.

You Must Relax. 5th ed. Edmund Jacobson. 1978. pap. text ed. 5.95 (ISBN 0-07-032184-1). McGraw.

You Must Remember This. Joyce Carol Oates. 480p. 1987. 19.95 (ISBN 0-525-24545-6, Pub. by W Abrahams Bk). Dutton.

You Must Remember This. Joyce Carol Oates. LC 87-46320. 450p. 1988. pap. 8.95 (ISBN 0-06-097169-X, PL-7169, PL). Har-Row.

You Must Revise Your Life. William Stafford. (Poets on Poetry Ser.). 176p. 1986. text ed. 22.00 (ISBN 0-472-09371-1); pap. 8.95 (ISBN 0-472-06371-5). U of Mich Pr.

You Must Tell Your Children. Joan Thiry et al. Ed. by Joan Thiry. LC 79-84288. (Illus.). 64p. 1981. pap. 9.95 (ISBN 0-935046-01-1); incl. oral history cassette 7.95 (ISBN 0-935046-00-3); text & cassette 14.95. Chateau Thierry.

You Need Never Lose at Bridge: Winning Techniques from Victor Mollo's Bridge Club. Victor Mollo. (Illus.). 176p. 1987. pap. 6.95 (ISBN 0-671-64236-7, Fireside). S&S.

You Never Can Tell. Ellen Conford. (Illus.). 156p. (gr. 7 up). 1984. 14.95 (ISBN 0-316-15267-6). Little.

You Never Can Tell. Ellen Conford. 160p. (YA) (gr. 7 up). pap. 2.75 (ISBN 0-671-66182-5). Archway.

You Never Can Tell. George Bernard Shaw. Ed. by Daniel J. Leary. LC 79-56704. (Bernard Shaw Early Texts: Play Manuscripts in Facsimile). 1981. lib. bdg. 94.00 (ISBN 0-8240-4580-7). Garland Pub.

You Never Can Tell When You May Meet a Leopard. Goldie Down. Ed. by Tom Davis. 128p. (gr. 1 up). 1980. pap. 6.95 (ISBN 0-8280-0026-3). Review & Herald.

You Never Knew Her As I Did! Mollie Hunter. LC 81-47114. 224p. (YA) (gr. 7 up). 1981. 12.70i (ISBN 0-06-022678-1); PLB 12.89 (ISBN 0-06-022679-X). HarpJ.

You Never Lose. Barbara Stretton. 256p. (gr. 5-9). 1982. 9.95 (ISBN 0-394-85230-3); lib. bdg. 9.99 (ISBN 0-394-95230-8). Knopf.

You Never Miss the Water till... The Ogallalla Story. Morton N. Bittinger & Elizabeth B. Green. LC 80-50167. 1981. 7.00 (ISBN 0-918334-33-0). WRP.

You Never Stop Being a Parent. Helen K. Hosier. 192p. 1986. pap. 6.95 (ISBN 0-8007-5248-1, Power Bks). Revell.

You Now Have Custody of You (In Favor of the Divorced) Richard M Cromie. 25p. (Orig.). 1987. pap. 1.50 (ISBN 0-914733-10-9). Desert Min.

You Only Get Married for the First Time Once. Judy Markey. 1988. 17.95 (ISBN 0-385-24739-7). Doubleday.

You Only Have One Life--Give It Your Best Shot: Five Steps to Health, Wealth, Happiness. Richard S. Clarke. 1979. 8.99 (ISBN 0-682-49280-9, Banner). Exposition-Phoenix.

You Only Live Once: Memories of Ian Fleming. Ivar Bryce. (Foreign Intelligence Bk.). 152p. 1984. Repr. 12.00 (ISBN 0-89093-446-X). U Pubns Amer.

You Only Live Twice. Ian Fleming. pap. 9.95 Fr. ed (ISBN 0-685-11630-1); pap. 9.95 Span. ed (ISBN 0-685-11631-X). French & Eur.

You Only Live Twice. Ian Fleming. pap. 2.95 (ISBN 0-451-13708-6, AE2108, Sig). NAL.

You Owe Yourself a Drunk: An Ethnography of Urban Nomads. James P. Spradley. 314p. 1988. pap. text ed. 14.75 (ISBN 0-8191-6856-4). U Pr of Amer.

You Play the Black & the Red Comes Up. Richard Hallas, pseud. LC 85-72931. (Hardboiled Fiction Ser.). 1986. 14.95 (ISBN 0-88748-058-6). Carnegie-Mellon.

You Play the Black & the Red Comes Up. Richard Hallas, pseud. LC 86-70458. 144p. 1986. pap. 3.95 (ISBN 0-88739-006-4, Pub. by Black Lizard). Creative Arts Bk.

You: Prayer for Beginners & Those Who Have Forgotten How. Mark Link. LC 76-41584. 1976. pap. 4.95 (ISBN 0-913592-78-1). Tabor Pub.

You Promised, Lord: Prayers for Boys. Ron Klug. LC 83-70502. (Augsburg Young Readers Ser.). 80p. (Orig.). (gr. 3-7). 1983. pap. 4.50 (ISBN 0-8066-2008-0, 10-7417). Augsburg.

You Promised Me God. Donald Deffner. LC 12-2792. (Illus.). 1981. pap. 3.50 (ISBN 0-570-03827-8). Concordia.

You Push, I Ride. Abby Levine. Ed. by Kathleen Tucker. (Illus.). 32p. (ps). 1988. PLB 11.95 (ISBN 0-8075-9444-X). A Whitman.

You Put up with Me, I'll Put up with You. Barbara Corcoran. LC 86-17217. 176p. (gr. 6-8). 1987. PLB 12.95 (ISBN 0-689-31305-5, Atheneum Childrens Bks). Macmillan.

You Put up with Me, I'll Put up with You. Barbara Corcoran. 176p. (gr. 3-7). 1989. pap. 2.50 (ISBN 0-380-70558-3, Camelot). Avon.

You Read to Me, I'll Read to You. John Ciardi. LC 62-16296. (Illus.). (gr. k-6). 1961. (Lipp Jr Bks); PLB 10.89 (ISBN 0-397-30646-6). HarpJ.

You Read to Me, I'll Read to You. John Ciardi. LC 62-16296. (Trophy Nonfiction Bks.). (Illus.). 64p. (ps up). 1987. pap. 4.95 (ISBN 0-06-446060-6, Trophy). HarpJ.

You Really Don't Have To! Natural Therapy Updated. Herald Maleske. LC 80-52427. 200p. 1980. 12.95 (ISBN 0-937792-00-4). Nat Therapy.

You Said, Why This Interest in Goddessess. Susan Lee & Susanaha Libana. (Fastbook 1985 Ser.). 20p. 1985. 6.00 (ISBN 0-911051-17-1). Plain View.

You Say You Want a Revolution: Rock Music in American Culture. Robert G. Pielke. LC 85-25940. 270p. 1986. 24.95 (ISBN 0-8304-1005-8). Nelson-Hall.

You See I Don't Forget, Selected Poems & Stories. Ernest Tedlock. Ed. by Gary Elder. LC 80-12807. 1980. pap. 4.95 (ISBN 0-914974-22-X). Holmgangers.

You See the Future, No. 44. Deborah L. Goodman. 64p. (Orig.). 1988. pap. 2.50 (ISBN 0-553-15565-2, Skylark). Bantam.

You See 3-D Coloring Book. Illus. by Bob Roper. 32p. (gr. 1-5). 1988. pap. 3.95 (ISBN 0-590-41857-2). Scholastic Inc.

You Shall Be My Witnesses: How to Reach Your City for Christ. Larry Rosenbaum. LC 86-90426. 144p. (Orig.). 1986. pap. 5.00 (ISBN 0-938573-00-4). SOS Minist Pr.

You Shall Have No Other Gods: Israelite Religion in the Light of Hebrew Inscriptions. Jeffrey H. Tigay. LC 86-20442. (Harvard Semitic Studies). 130p. 1987. 16.95 (ISBN 1-55540-063-9, 04-04-31). Scholars Pr GA.

You Shall Not Steal: Community & Property in the Biblical Tradition. Robert Gnuse. LC 85-4810. 176p. (Orig.). 1985. pap. 9.95 (ISBN 0-88344-799-1). Orbis Bks.

You Should Meet Them. Elizabeth W. Davis. 1983. write for info. E W H Davis.

You Should Not Get a Home Equity Line of Credit: Thirteen Reasons - the Answer Book. Larry Oxenham. (Answer Book Ser.: Vol. II). (Illus.). 40p. 1987. 4.75 (ISBN 0-943813-01-8). Page One Pub.

You Should Write a Book! Walter E. Owen. 256p. 1988. 12.95 (ISBN 0-944957-27-7). Rivercross Pub.

You Shouldn't Have to Say Good-Bye. Patricia Hermes. LC 82-47933. 120p. (gr. 4-6). 1982. 10.95 (ISBN 0-15-299944-2, HJ). HarBraceJ.

You Shouldn't Have to Say Good-Bye. Patricia Hermes. 128p. (gr. 4-6). 1984. pap. 2.50 (ISBN 0-590-41359-7, Apple Paperbacks). Scholastic Inc.

You Shouldn't Have to Say Goodbye. Patricia Hermes. 128p. (gr. 4-6). pap. 2.50 (ISBN 0-590-41355-4, Apple Paperbacks). Scholastic Inc.

You Sign the Little Cheque & We Sign the Big One. T. P. Halloran. 72p. 1978. 41.00 (ISBN 0-900886-28-5, Pub. by Witherby & Co England). State Mutual Bk.

You Slept Where Last Night? Tim Conway. 96p. 1985. pap. 2.95 (ISBN 0-8431-1239-5). Price Stern.

You Take Jesus, I'll Take God. Samuel Levine. LC 80-82731. 134p. (Orig.). 1980. pap. 4.95 (ISBN 0-9604754-1-9). Hamoroh Pr.

You Take the High Node & I'll Take the Low Node: Proceedings - Papers from the Comparative Syntax Festival. Ed. by Claudia Corum & Cedrik Smith-Stark. 422p. 1973. pap. 6.00 (ISBN 0-914203-03-7). Chicago Ling.

You Tell 'Em, Andy Capp. Reginald Smythe. 1979. pap. 2.95 (ISBN 0-449-13594-2, GM). Fawcett.

You... the Doctor: A Basic Guide to a Rewarding Career. American Medical Association Staff. (Illus., Orig.). 1987. pap. 8.50 (ISBN 0-89970-310-0, OP-422). AMA.

You... the Doctor: Challenges & Opportunities. American Medical Association Staff. (Illus.). 35p. (Orig.). 1987. pap. 2.50 (ISBN 0-89970-311-9, OP-416). AMA.

You The Mayor? Barbara Ackerman. 200p. 1988. 24.95 (ISBN 0-86569-178-9); pap. 17.95 (ISBN 0-86569-179-7). Auburn Hse.

You the Singer. Barbara Harlow. 158p. 1985. pap. 18.95 (ISBN 0-937276-06-5). Hinshaw Mus.

You Think You Got Troubles. Janice Potulny. (Illus.). 64p. (ps-2). 1984. 5.50 (ISBN 0-682-40189-7). Exposition-Phoenix.

You Think You Have Troubles? Janice C. Potulny. (Illus.). 33p. 1985. 5.50 (ISBN 0-8059-2969-X). Dorrance.

You Too Can Be Prosperous. Robert A. Russell. 162p. 1975. pap. 3.95 (ISBN 0-87516-205-3). DeVorss.

You, Too, Can Canoe. John Foshee. LC 76-58244. 1977. 12.95 (ISBN 0-87397-116-7). Strode.

You, Too, Can Find Peace. Madge Haines. Ed. by Raymond H. Woolsey. (Banner Ser.). 128p. (Orig.). 1987. pap. 6.95 (ISBN 0-8280-0366-1). Review & Herald.

You Too Can Heal. George King. (Illus.). 133p. 1976. pap. 9.25 (ISBN 0-937249-09-2). Aetherius Soc.

You, Too, Can Stop Drinking. G. Z. Patten. LC 76-57471. (Illus.). 1977. 10.00 (ISBN 0-682-48733-3). Exposition-Phoenix.

You Too Can Work Wonders. Harry Mier & Joan Mier. (Illus.). 1968. 4.50 (ISBN 0-910962-05-7); pap. 2.25 (ISBN 0-910962-06-5). Merit Calif.

You Touched Me. D. H. Lawrence. (Creative's Classics Ser.). 48p. (gr. 6 up). 1982. PLB 8.95 (ISBN 0-87191-894-3). Creative Ed.

You Try It. Robert A. Russell. 1953. pap. 5.95 (ISBN 0-87516-326-2). DeVorss.

You-Two. Jean Ure. LC 84-8947. (Illus.). (gr. 4-7). 1984. 10.25 (ISBN 0-688-03857-3, Morrow Junior Books). Morrow.

You Two Can Be a Kahuna see Huna: A Beginner's Guide.

You Unlimited. Norman Lunde. LC 65-23608. 1985. pap. 5.95 (ISBN 0-87516-249-5). DeVorss.

You Unlimited. Patricia Turner. LC 87-40265. 197p. 1987. 12.95 (ISBN 1-55523-105-5). Winston-Derek.

You Want Me to Know What? 2nd ed. Terry Powell. (Foundation Ser.). (Illus.). 142p. (Orig.). 1986. pap. 2.95 (ISBN 0-935797-04-1). Harvest IL.

You Want to Be a What? William N. McKeen. 1987. 5.95 (ISBN 0-533-07313-8). Vantage.

You Want to Be My Friends? Eric Carle. Date not set. price not set (Philomel Bks). Putnam Pub Group.

You Wanted to Know...What a Waldorf School Is... & What It Is Not. Alan Howard. 1984. pap. 3.50 (ISBN 0-916786-72-2). St George Bk Serv.

You Were Born Again to Be Together. Dick Sutphen. 1986. pap. 3.95 (ISBN 0-671-61759-1). PB.

You Were Born on Your Very First Birthday. Linda Girard. Ed. by Kathy Tucker. LC 84-17220. (Albert Whitman Concept Bks.). (Illus.). 32p. (ps-3). 1983. PLB 11.95 (ISBN 0-8075-9455-5). A Whitman.

You Were Designed to Live for One Hundred & Forty Years. Arnold Perrin. 1.00 (ISBN 0-939736-06-3). Wings ME.

You Were Smaller than a Dot. Glen C. Griffin. LC 72-90685. 31p. (gr. k-6). 1980. pap. 4.95 (ISBN 0-87747-817-1). Deseret Bk.

You Who Have Dreams. Maxwell Anderson. 1978. Repr. lib. bdg. 32.50 (ISBN 0-8495-0102-4). Arden Lib.

You Who Have Dreams. Maxwell Anderson. LC 76-39796. 1976. Repr. of 1925 ed. lib. bdg. 29.50 (ISBN 0-8414-2996-0). Folcroft.

You Who Have Dreams. Maxwell Anderson. 1985. 42.50 (ISBN 0-317-39610-2). Bern Porter.

You Will Hear Thunder: Akhmatova: Poems. Anna Akhmatova. Tr. by D. M. Thomas. LC 84-62245. 140p. 1985. text ed. 22.00x (ISBN 0-8214-0805-4); pap. text ed. 11.00x (ISBN 0-8214-0806-2). Ohio U Pr.

You Will Never Be the Same. Basilea Schlink. 192p. 1972. pap. 3.50 (ISBN 0-87123-661-3, 200661). Bethany Hse.

You Will Never Be the Same. Cordwainer Smith. Ed. by Lester Del Ray. LC 75-429. (Library of Science Fiction). 1975. lib. bdg. 21.00 (ISBN 0-8240-1429-4). Garland Pub.

You Will Plant Your Vineyards Once More. Georgia B. Houle. (Illus.). 60p. (Orig.). 1986. pap. 8.40 (ISBN 0-940139-08-1). Tot Lot Child Care.

You Win Some, You Loose Some. Jean Ure. (gr. k-12). 1988. pap. 2.95 (ISBN 0-440-99845-X, LFL). Dell.

You Win Some, You Lose Some. Jean Ure. LC 85-16134. 182p. (YA) (gr. 7 up). 1986. pap. 14.95 (ISBN 0-385-29434-4). Delacorte.

You Win Some, You Lose Some. Jean Ure. (gr. 7 up). 1988. pap. 2.95 (ISBN 0-440-20037-7, LFL). Dell.

You Won't Believe Your Eyes. Ed. by Donald J. Crump. LC 86-7637. (Books for World Explorers Series 8: No. 3). (Illus.). 104p. (gr. 3-8). 1987. 6.95 (ISBN 0-87044-611-8); PLB 8.50 (ISBN 0-87044-616-9). Natl Geog.

You Would If You Loved Me. Nora Stirling. 176p. (gr. 7-10). 1982. pap. 2.50 (ISBN 0-380-01631-1, 60113-3, Flare). Avon.

You Write the Ticket, Lord. Dorothy Galde. 144p. 1983. pap. 5.95 (ISBN 0-89840-047-3). Heres Life.

You, Your Child & Drugs. CSAA. 1971. pap. 1.75 (ISBN 0-87183-238-0). Jewish Bd Family.

You, Your Parents, & the Nursing Home. Nancy Fox. LC 86-83887. 175p. 1986. pap. 10.95 (ISBN 0-87975-317-X). Prometheus Bks.

You, Your Stars & Your Partner. Diana Hunt. LC 79-107016. 1970. 6.95 (ISBN 0-8008-8763-8). Taplinger.

You, Yours & Crime Resistance: How You, Your Family, & Your Community Can Work to Reduce Crime. (FBI Ser.). 1986. lib. bdg. 79.95 (ISBN 0-8490-3810-3). Gordon Pr.

You...& Being a Teenager. Feryl J. Bergin. (Illus.). 112p. 4.95 (ISBN 0-936955-00-7). Eminent Pubns.

You'd Better Believe It! Kenneth D. Barney. LC 75-22608. (Radiant Life Ser.). 128p. 1976. pap. 2.50 (ISBN 0-88243-887-5, 02-0887); teacher's guide 3.95 (ISBN 0-88243-161-7, 32-0161). Gospel Pub.

You'd Better Believe It! Martin Goldwyn. (Illus.). 256p. 1982. pap. 5.95 (ISBN 0-8065-0792-6, Pub. by Citadel Pr). Lyle Stuart.

You'd Better Believe It. Martin M. Goldwyn. (Illus.). 1979. 10.00 (ISBN 0-8065-0672-5, Pub. by Citadel Pr). Lyle Stuart.

You'd Better Believe It. Bill James. 192p. 1985. 12.95 (ISBN 0-312-89683-2). St Martin.

You'd Better Come Quietly. Leonard Feeney. LC 79-105011. (Essay Index Reprint Ser.). 1939. 36.50 (ISBN 0-8369-1569-0). Ayer Co Pubs.

Yougga Finds Mother Teresa: Adventures of a Beggar Boy in India. Kirsten Bang. Tr. by Kathryn Spink from Fr. LC 83-4267. (Illus.). 176p. (Orig.). 1983. pap. 3.95 (ISBN 0-8164-2469-1, HarpR). Har-Row.

Youghiogheny: Appalachian River. Tim Palmer. LC 84-2301. (Illus.). 352p. 1984. 24.95x (ISBN 0-8229-3495-7); pap. 9.95 (ISBN 0-8229-5361-7). U of Pittsburgh Pr.

Youghiogheny River Flip Map. Ron Rathnow. LC 86-12654. (Great American Rivers Flip Map Ser.). (Illus.). 40p. 1987. pap. text ed. 3.95 (ISBN 0-89732-056-5). Menasha Ridge.

You'll Be Old Someday, Too. Richard Worth. LC 85-29419. 128p. (gr. 7-12). 1986. lib. bdg. 11.90 (ISBN 0-531-10158-4). Watts.

You'll Die Laughing. Marjorie J. Grove. (Mystery Puzzler Ser.: No. 5). (Illus., Orig.). 1978. pap. 1.95 (ISBN 0-89083-408-3). Zebra.

You'll Die Today. Marjorie J. Grove. (Mystery Puzzlers Ser.: No. 22). (Illus., Orig.). 1979. pap. 1.95 (ISBN 0-685-94562-6). Zebra.

You'll Die Tomorrow. Marjorie J. Grove. (Mystery Puzzler Ser.: No. 9). (Illus., Orig.). 1978. pap. 1.95 (ISBN 0-89083-421-0). Zebra.

You'll Die When You Hear This. Marjorie J. Grove. (Mystery Puzzlers Ser.: No. 1). (Illus., Orig.). 1978. pap. 1.95 (ISBN 0-89083-395-8). Zebra.

You'll Die Yesterday. Marjorie J. Grove. (Mystery Puzzlers Ser.: No. 18). (Illus., Orig.). 1979. pap. 1.95 (ISBN 0-89083-453-9). Zebra.

You'll Get a Bang Out of This Beetle Bailey, No. 27. Mort Walker. 128p. 1984. pap. 1.95 (ISBN 0-441-05254-1). Ace Bks.

You'll Miss Me When I'm Gone. Stephan Roos. LC 87-25961. 168p. (YA) (gr. 7 up). 1988. pap. 13.95 (ISBN 0-385-29633-9). Delacorte.

You'll Never Come Back. Elizabeth W. Freeman. LC 79-66735. 1979. pap. write for info. (ISBN 0-87930-124-4). Miller Freeman.

You'll Never Get No for an Answer: Positional Selling. Jack Carew. (Illus.). 240p. 1987. 17.95 (ISBN 0-671-62495-4). S&S.

You'll Never Guess What We Did in Gym Today! Kenneth G. Tillman & Patricia R. Toner. LC 83-22071. 228p. 1984. 18.95 (ISBN 0-13-977075-5, Busn). P-H.

You'll Never Hang Me. Lee Deighton. 160p. 1981. pap. 1.75 (ISBN 0-345-29119-0). Ballantine.

You'll Pay for This...All of You! Bill Rechin et al. 1979. pap. 1.95 (ISBN 0-449-14121-7, GM). Fawcett.

You'll Soon Grow into Them, Titch. Pat Hutchins. LC 82-11755. (Illus.). 32p. (gr. k-3). 1983. 11.75 (ISBN 0-688-01770-3); PLB 11.88 (ISBN 0-688-01771-1). Greenwillow.

You'll Soon Grow into Them, Titch. Pat Hutchins. LC 84-22251. (Illus.). 32p. (ps-3). 1985. pap. 3.95 (ISBN 0-14-050434-6, Puffin). Penguin.

You'll Survive: Late Blooming, Early Blooming, Loneliness, Klutziness, & Other Problems of Adolescence, & How to Live Through Them. Fred Powledge. LC 85-43351. 144p. (gr. 6-8). 1986. 11.95 (ISBN 0-684-18632-2, Pub. by Scribner). Macmillan.

Youma: The Story of a West Indian Slave. Lafcadio Hearn. LC 74-80890. Repr. of 1890 ed. 14.50 (ISBN 0-404-03208-7). AMS Pr.

Young Abolitionists: Or, Conversations on Slavery. facs. ed. J. Elizabeth Jones. LC 75-138339. (Black Heritage Library Collection Ser.). 1848. 12.00 (ISBN 0-8369-8731-4). Ayer Co Pubs.

Young Actor's Workbook. Judith R. Seto. LC 83-49383. 368p. 1984. pap. 9.95 (ISBN 0-394-62040-2, E923, Ever). Grove.

Young Adam. Alexander Trocchi. 256p. (Orig.). 1982. pap. 5.95 (ISBN 0-7145-3925-2). Riverrun NY.

Young Adolescent. Peter Blos. LC 73-125597. 1974. pap. 12.95x (ISBN 0-02-904300-X). Free Pr.

Young Adult & Intellectual Freedom: Proceedings. University of Wisconsin, Madison, Wisconsin, June 14-18, 1976. Ed. by Mary L. Woodworth. 228p. 1977. pap. 4.00 (ISBN 0-936442-05-0). U Wis Sch Lib.

Young Adult Book Review Index, 1987. Ed. by Barbara Beach. 1988. 85.00 (ISBN 0-8103-4373-8). Gale.

Young Adult Chronic Patient. Ed. by Bert Pepper & Hilary Ryglewicz. LC 81-48483. (Mental Health Services Ser.: No. 14). 1982. pap. 14.95x (ISBN 0-87589-908-0). Jossey-Bass.

Young Adult: Development After Adolescence. Gene Bocknek. 232p. 1986. pap. 15.95 (ISBN 0-89876-129-8). Gardner Pr.

Young Adult Literature: Background & Criticism. Ed. by Millicent Lenz & Ramona Mahood. LC 80-23489. 524p. 1980. 30.00x (ISBN 0-8389-0302-9). ALA.

Young Adult Literature in the Seventies: A Selection of Readings. Ed. by Jana Varlejs. LC 78-6562. 462p. 1978. lib. bdg. 17.50 (ISBN 0-8108-1134-0). Scarecrow.

Young Adult Literature: Issues & Perspectives. Mary E. Gallagher. (Studies in Librarianship). (Orig.). 1988. pap. 20.00 (ISBN 0-87507-038-8). Cath Lib Assn.

Young Adult Living Handbook. Ed. by Jean M. Hiesberger. LC 79-92005. (Paths of Life Ser.). 126p. 1980. 2.95 (ISBN 0-8091-2259-6). Paulist Pr.

Young Adult Ministry. Terry Hershey. LC 86-3103. 276p. (Orig.). 1986. pap. 12.95 (ISBN 0-931529-08-5). Group Bks.

Young Adult Ministry Resources. rev. ed. Thomas Lynch et al. 96p. 1988. pap. 5.95 (ISBN 1-55586-171-7). US Catholic.

Young Adult Novel. Daniel Pinkwater. LC 81-43391. 128p. (YA) (gr. 7 up). 1982. 11.70 (ISBN 0-690-04188-6, Crowell Jr Bks); PLB 11.89 (ISBN 0-690-04189-6). HarpJ.

Young Adult Piano Course, Bk. 1. John Brimhall. (Piano Course Ser.). 32p. (Orig.). 1985. pap. text ed. 4.50 (ISBN 0-8494-1356-7, T561). Hansen Ed Mus.

Young Adult Piano Course, Bk. 2. John Brimhall. (Piano Course Ser.). 32p. (Orig.). 1984. pap. text ed. 4.50 (ISBN 0-8494-1357-5, T562). Hansen ED Mus.

Young Adults. Daniel M. Pinkwater. (Illus.). 192p. (Orig.). 1985. pap. 5.95 (ISBN 0-8125-8710-3, Dist. by Warner Pub Services & St. Martin's Press). Tor Bks.

Young Adults: A Call to Dialogue. L. June Montgomery. LC 79-92088. 1980. 7.95 (ISBN 0-87212-112-7). Libra.

Young Alaskans. Emerson Hough. 1976. lib. bdg. 14.25x (ISBN 0-89968-049-6). Lightyear.

Young Alaskans in the Rockies. Emerson Hough. 1976. lib. bdg. 15.25x (ISBN 0-89968-050-X). Lightyear.

Young Alcoholics. Tom Alibrandi. LC 77-87741. 219p. 1978. pap. 7.95 (ISBN 0-89638-014-9). CompCare.

Young Alcoholics: A Book for Parents. Jack Mumey. 208p. 1986. pap. 8.95 (ISBN 0-8092-4852-2). Contemp Bks.

Young Alec & the Magic Voice. Robert G. French. (Children's Theatre Playscript Ser.). (gr. k-12). 1969. pap. 2.00x (ISBN 0-88020-066-9). Coach Hse.

Young Amanda, the Truant Bride & Beggars May Sing. Sara Seale. (Harlequin Romances (3-in-1) Ser.). 576p. 1983. pap. 3.95 (ISBN 0-373-20070-6). Harlequin Bks.

Young America: A Folk-Art History. Jean Lipman & Elizabeth V. Warren. LC 86-10248. (Illus.). 200p. 1986. 45.00 (ISBN 0-933920-75-X, Dist. by Rizzoli); pap. 25.00 museum distribution only (ISBN 0-933920-76-8). Hudson Hills.

Young America: A Newspaper Published at Delafield Waukesha County, Wisconsin 1859-1860. Ed. by Nelson C. Hawks. 43p. 1984. pap. 5.00 (ISBN 0-9613121-0-6). Hawks Inn Hist Soc.

Young American Award Winners. (Illus.). 40p. 1982. 4.70 (ISBN 0-686-47651-4); 4.20. Am Craft.

Young American Photography. Ed. by Gary Wolfson. LC 74-13172. (Illus.). 108p. 1976. pap. 9.95 (ISBN 0-912810-17-3). Lustrum Pr.

Young American Writers. Ed. by Richard Kostelanetz. LC 67-28160. 1978. 70.00 (ISBN 0-932360-05-X); pap. 15.00 (ISBN 0-932360-04-1). RK Edns.

Young & Evil: Homosexuality. Charles Ford & Parker Tyler. LC 75-12351. 1975. Repr. of 1933 ed. 14.00x (ISBN 0-405-07392-5). Ayer Co Pubs.

Young & Famous: Hollywood's Newest Superstars. Daniel Cohen & Susan Cohen. (gr. 4 up). 1987. pap. 2.50 (ISBN 0-671-63493-3). Archway.

Young & Famous: Sports Newest Superstars. Daniel Cohen & Susan Cohen. (gr. 4 up). 1987. pap. 2.50 (ISBN 0-671-64597-8). Archway.

Young & Female: Turning Points in the Lives of Eight American Women. Compiled by Pat Ross. (Illus.). (gr. 6 up). 1972. (BYR). Random.

Young Anger. Rose Lesniak. LC 79-20880. (Illus.). 1979. pap. 3.00 (ISBN 0-915124-34-3, Pub. by Toothpaste). Coffee Hse.

Young Astronomer. S. Snowden. (Hobby Guides Ser.). (Illus.). 32p. (YA) (gr. 5-10). 1983. PLB 12.96 (ISBN 0-88110-028-5); pap. 5.95 (ISBN 0-86020-651-3). EDC.

Young Astronomer's Handbook. Ian Ridpath. LC 83-15701. (Illus.). 224p. (gr. 7 up). 1984. 9.95 (ISBN 0-668-06046-8). Arco.

Young at Art: An Anti-Coloring Book for Pre-Schoolers. Susan Striker. (Illus., Orig.). (ps). 1985. pap. 6.95 (ISBN 0-671-49649-2, Fireside). S&S.

Young at Heart. Jackie Leigh. 192p. 1987. 2.25 (ISBN 0-425-10516-4). Berkley Pub.

Young Athletes: Biological, Psychological, & Educational Perspectives. Ed. by Robert M. Malina. (Illus.). 312p. 1988. text ed. 32.00 (ISBN 0-87322-173-7). Human Kinetics.

Young Athlete's Guide to Kickboxing Questions & Answers. 2nd, rev. ed. Ed. by Robert Ostovich. (Illus.). 91p. 1987. pap. 12.95 (ISBN 0-318-22771-1). Eau Gallie.

Young Athlete's Manual. Robert Gardner. LC 85-8864. (Illus.). 160p. (gr. 5 up). 1985. 9.97 (ISBN 0-671-49369-8). Messner.

Young Atom Detective. Charles Coombs. (Illus.). (gr. 4-7). PLB 6.19 (ISBN 0-8313-0021-3). Lantern.

Young Authors of America, Vol. 1. Ed. by Ellen Rudin. (Illus.). 102p. (gr. 5-8). 1988. pap. 0.60 (ISBN 0-440-84003-1). Dell.

Young Bear: The Legend of Bear Bryant's Boyhood. S. C. Lee. LC 77-14848. (Strode Superstar Ser.). (gr. 7-12). 1983. pap. 6.95 (ISBN 0-87397-250-3). Strode.

Young Beginner. Nathan Bergenfeld. (Acorn Basic Lessons for Piano Ser.). 1977. pap. 2.95 (ISBN 0-8256-2684-6). Music Sales.

Young Ben Franklin. Laurence Santrey. LC 81-23067. (Illus.). 48p. (gr. 4-6). 1982. PLB 9.79 (ISBN 0-89375-768-3); pap. text ed. 1.95 (ISBN 0-89375-769-1). Troll Assocs.

Young Ben: Franklin's Fight for Freedom. Faye Parker. (Children's Theatre Playscript Ser.). (gr. k-12). 1958. pap. 2.00x (ISBN 0-88020-065-0). Coach Hse.

Young Black Adults: Liberation & Family Attitudes. George B. Thomas. 1974. pap. 1.95 (ISBN 0-377-00002-7). Friendship Pr.

Young, Black & Male in America: An Endangered Species. Ed. by Jewelle T. Gibbs. 1988. 28.95 (ISBN 0-86569-169-X); pap. 17.95 (ISBN 0-86569-180-0). Auburn Hse.

Young Blades of Grass. Hazel Bremm. 1983. 9.50 (ISBN 0-8233-0364-0). Golden Quill.

Young Boswell. Chauncey B. Tinker. LC 71-131850. 1970. Repr. of 1922 ed. 13.00x (ISBN 0-403-00737-2). Scholarly.

Young Brer Rabbit & Other Trickster Tales from the Americas. Jaqueline S. Weiss. (Illus.). 80p. (gr. 3-7). 1985. 14.95 (ISBN 0-88045-037-1). Stemmer Hse.

Young Brer Rabbit: And other Trickster Tales of the Americas. 2nd ed. Jacqueline S. Weiss. (Illus.). 72p. 1987. pap. 9.95 (ISBN 0-88045-138-6); cassette & book 21.90 (ISBN 0-88045-105-X); cassette only 8.95 (ISBN 0-88045-104-1). Stemmer Hse.

Young, British & Black: A Monograph on the Work of Sankofa Film-Video Collective & Black Audio Film Collective. Coco Fusco. (Illus.). 64p. (Orig.). 1988. pap. 4.00 (ISBN 0-936739-15-0). Hallwalls Inc.

Young Brothers Massacre. Paul W. Barrett & Mary H. Barrett. LC 87-19156. (Illus.). 160p. (Orig.). 1988. pap. 9.95 (ISBN 0-8262-0650-6). U of Mo Pr.

Young Calvin. Alexandre Ganoczy. Tr. by David Foxgrover & Wade Provo. LC 87-10516. (Illus.). 408p. 1987. 24.95 (ISBN 0-664-21840-7). Westminster John Knox.

Young Calvin in Paris: Or, the Scholar & the Cripple. William W. Blackburn. LC 83-45602. Date not set. Repr. of 1868 ed. 30.00 (ISBN 0-404-19869-4). AMS Pr.

Young Captain Jack; or, Son of a Soldier. Horatio Alger. 267p. 1974. Repr. of 1901 ed. lib. bdg. 18.95x (ISBN 0-88411-808-8, Pub. by Aeonian Pr). Amereon Ltd.

Young Cartoonist. Syd Hoff. (Illus.). 192p. 1983. 16.95 (ISBN 0-87396-094-7). Stravon.

Young Internationalists. Ed. by Thomas A. Hiatt & Mark F. Gerzon. LC 70-188981. 278p. 1973. 14.00x (ISBN 0-8248-0218-7, Eastwest Ctr). UH Pr.

Young Ireland: A Fragment of Irish History, 1840-1850. Charles G. Duffy. LC 71-127257. (Europe 1815-1945 Ser.). 796p. 1973. Repr. of 1881 ed. lib. bdg. 79.50 (ISBN 0-306-71119-2). Da Capo.

Young Ireland Movement. Richard Davis. 1987. 29.95 (ISBN 0-389-20773-X). Rowman.

Young Islanders. Elizabeth Ogilvie. Repr. lib. bdg. 13.95x (ISBN 0-88411-341-8, Pub. by Aeonian Pr). Amereon Ltd.

Young Jefferson Davis, 1808-1846. William A. Shelton. 32.00 (ISBN 0-405-14108-4). Ayer Co Pubs.

Young Jesus in the Temple. Alyce Bergey. (Arch Bks.). (Illus.). 24p. (gr. k-4). 1986. pap. 1.29 saddlestitched (ISBN 0-570-06203-9, 59-1426). Concordia.

Young Joe. Jan Ormerod. LC 85-17128. (Illus.). 24p. (ps). 1985. 4.95 (ISBN 0-688-04210-4). Lothrop.

Young John Dewey: An Essay in American Intellectual History. Neil Coughlan. LC 74-33519. 200p. 1975. 13.00x (ISBN 0-226-11604-2). U of Chicago Pr.

Young John Tyler. Katherine T. Ellett. (Illus.). 1976. 4.75 (ISBN 0-87517-016-1). Dietz.

Young Kate: The Remarkable Hepburns & the Childhood That Shaped an American Legend. Christopher Andersen. (Illus.). 1988. 18.95 (ISBN 0-8050-0709-1). H Holt & Co.

Young King. (Classics Ser.). (gr. 4 up). Date not set. pap. 3.95 (ISBN 0-582-54158-1). Longman.

Young Krishna. Francis G. Hutchins. LC 80-66834. (Illus.). 132p. 1980. 29.50 (ISBN 0-935100-01-6); pap. 14.00 (ISBN 0-935100-05-9). Amarta Pr.

Young La Fontaine. Philip A. Wadsworth. LC 78-128943. (Northwestern Humanities Ser.: No. 29). 1970. Repr. of 1952 ed. 28.00 (ISBN 0-404-50729-8). AMS Pr.

Young Lady's Accidence. Caleb Bingham. LC 81-5663. (Amer. Linguistics Ser.). 1981. Repr. of 1785 ed. 40.00x (ISBN 0-8201-1360-3). Schol Facsimilies.

Young Lady's Friend, by a Lady. Eliza W. Farrar. LC 74-3947. (Women in America Ser). 452p. 1974. Repr. of 1836 ed. 32.00x (ISBN 0-405-06093-9). Ayer Co Pubs.

Young Landlords. Walter D. Meyers. 1980. pap. 2.25 (ISBN 0-380-52191-1, 67561-7, Flare). Avon.

Young Landlords. Walter D. Myers. LC 79-13264. (gr. 7 up). 1979. 11.50 (ISBN 0-670-79454-6). Viking.

Young Learners & the Microcomputer. Daniel Chandler. 128p. 1984. 42.00x (ISBN 0-335-10579-3, Pub. by Open Univ Pr); pap. 21.00x (ISBN 0-335-10578-5, Open Univ Pr). Taylor & Francis.

Young Learner's Handbook. Stephen Tchudi. LC 87-4523. 192p. (YA) (gr. 7 up). 1987. 14.95 (ISBN 0-684-18676-4, Pub. by Scribner). Macmillan.

Young Legionary. Douglas Hill. (gr. k-12). 1987. pap. 2.50 (ISBN 0-440-99910-3, LFL). Dell.

Young Lieutenant. Martin Weik. LC 87-31922. 1988. 22.95 (ISBN 0-87949-275-9). Ashley Bks.

Young Lions. Irwin Shaw. LC 58-6365. 1958. 7.95 (ISBN 0-394-60809-7). Modern Lib.

Young Lives at Stake: The Education of Adolescents. Charity James. LC 77-166550. 272p. 1972. 15.00 (ISBN 0-87586-035-4). Agathon.

Young Living. rev. ed. Nanalee Clayton. (Illus.). (gr. 7-8). 1983. text ed. 21.00 (ISBN 0-02-666440-2); tchr's. guide 13.00 (ISBN 0-02-666450-X); student ed. 5.60 (ISBN 0-02-666460-7). Bennett IL.

Young Lloyd George. John Grigg. 1978. Repr. of 1973 ed. 42.00x (ISBN 0-520-02677-2). U of Cal Pr.

Young Longfellow, 1807-1843. Lawrance Thompson. 1969. lib. bdg. 27.50x (ISBN 0-374-97885-9, Octagon). Hippocrene Bks.

Young Lonigan see Studs Lonigan.

Young Look. Eloise Franco. (Illus.). (gr. 3-7). 1979. pap. 4.95 (ISBN 0-87516-294-0). DeVorss.

Young Love & Other Infidelities. Stepas Zobarskas. 1971. 4.95 (ISBN 0-87141-035-4). Manyland.

Young Lucretia & Other Stories by Mary E. Wilkins Freeman. Mary E. Wilkins Freeman. LC 79-106287. (Short Story Index Reprint Ser.). 1892. 18.00 (ISBN 0-8369-3324-9). Ayer Co Pubs.

Young Lukacs. Lee Congdon. LC 82-11162. xiii, 235p. 1983. 25.00x (ISBN 0-8078-1538-1). U of NC Pr.

Young Luther. Robert H. Fife. LC 79-131040. 1970. Repr. of 1928 ed. 19.50 (ISBN 0-404-02385-1). AMS Pr.

Young Male Salvadoran Asylum Case - Transcript. 160.00. Natl Lawyers Guild.

Young Male Salvadoran Asylum Documentation Materials. Complete collection. 100.00; Basic Packet. 55.00. Natl Lawyers Guild.

Young Man: A Novel. Botho Strauss. Tr. by Edna McCown from Ger. LC 88-45319. 416p. 1989. 19.95 (ISBN 0-394-54648-2). Knopf.

Young Man from Home: James Balfour Eighteen Thirty to Nineteen Thirteen. Andrew Lemon. (Illus.). 194p. 1983. 24.95x (ISBN 0-522-84238-0, Pub. by Melbourne U Pr Australia). Intl Spec Bk.

Young Man in a Hurry & Other Short Stories. facsimile ed. Robert W. Chambers. LC 71-103504. (Short Story Index Reprint Ser). 1904. 19.00 (ISBN 0-8369-3246-3). Ayer Co Pubs.

Young Man in a Hurry (William Carey) Iris Clinton. 1961. pap. 3.50 (ISBN 0-87508-630-6). Chr Lit.

Young Man in Paris: 1927-1932. John Weld. (Illus.). 208p. 1985. 14.95 (ISBN 0-89733-111-7). Academy Chi Pubs.

Young Man Luther. Erik H. Erikson. 1962. pap. 5.95 (ISBN 0-393-00170-9). Norton.

Young Man Shinran. Takamichi Takahatake. (SR Supplements Ser.: Vol. 18). 244p. 1987. pap. text ed. 17.50 (ISBN 0-88920-169-2, Pub. by Wilfrid Laurier U Pr). Humanities.

Young Man with a Horn. Dorothy Baker. 1977. Repr. of 1938 ed. lib. bdg. 15.95x (ISBN 0-89244-025-2, Pub. by Queens Ltd). Amereon Ltd.

Young Manhood of Studs Lonigan see Studs Lonigan.

Young Man's Guide to Sex. Jay Gale. 1984. 14.95 (ISBN 0-03-069396-9). H Holt & Co.

Young Man's Guide to Sex. Jay Gale. (Illus.). 1988. pap. 7.95 (ISBN 0-89586-691-9, Body Pr). Price Stern.

Young Mariners. Carse Robert. 5.95 (ISBN 0-911660-20-8). Yankee Peddler.

Young Mark Twain & the Mississippi. Harnett T. Kane. LC 87-4531. (Landmark Bks.: No. 113). (Illus.). 176p. (gr. 5-9). 1966. PLB 8.99 (ISBN 0-394-90413-3, BYR); pap. 2.95 (ISBN 0-394-89182-1). Random.

Young Marooners. Francis R. Goulding. 1973. Repr. of 1852 ed. lib. bdg. 59.95 (ISBN 0-8490-1344-5). Gordon Pr.

Young Masters & Misses. Telfer Stokes. LC 84-61206. (Artist's Bks.). (Illus.). 116p. (Orig.). 1984. pap. 5.00 (ISBN 0-87070-674-8). Museum Mod Art.

Young Maude Adams. Phyllis Robbins. (Illus.). 1959. 4.00 (ISBN 0-8338-0058-2). M Jones.

Young Men & Military Service see Youth in Transition.

Young Men Are Coming. Ed. by Centaur Books Staff. 1985. 35.00x (ISBN 0-900001-19-4, Pub. by Centaur Bks). State Mutual Bk.

Young Men Look at Military Service: A Preliminary Report. Jerome Johnston & Jerald C. Bachman. LC 79-633213. (University of Michigan Survey Research Center, Youth in Transition Document Ser.: No. 193). pap. 31.80 (ISBN 0-317-09335-5, 2004633). Bks Demand UMI.

Young Men's Gold. Daniel M. Epstein. LC 77-20739. 72p. 1978. 14.95 (ISBN 0-87951-071-4); pap. 8.95 (ISBN 0-87951-076-5). Overlook Pr.

Young Mexicans. Jacqueline Barnitz. (Illus.). 1971. pap. 2.00 (ISBN 0-913456-13-6, Pub. by Ctr Inter-Am Rel). Interbk Inc.

Young Mill-Wright & Miller's Guide. Oliver Evans. LC 72-5047. (Technology & Society Ser.). (Illus.). 438p. 1972. Repr. of 1850 ed. 32.00 (ISBN 0-405-04699-5). Ayer Co Pubs.

Young Mr. Dickens. Marjorie Beech. 1982. 15.00x (ISBN 0-903653-42-7, Pub. by New Playwrights Network). State Mutual Bk.

Young Mistley. Henry S. Merriman. Ed. by Herbert Van Thal. 1888-1966. 8.95 (ISBN 0-685-09212-7); pap. 5.95 (ISBN 0-304-93090-3). Dufour.

Young Monsters. Ed. by Isaac Asimov et al. LC 84-48352. 224p. (YA) (gr. 6-9). 1985. PLB 12.89g (ISBN 0-06-020170-3); pap. 7.95 (ISBN 0-06-020169-X). HarpJ.

Young Moses. Diana Craig. LC 84-50449. (Silver Burdett Bible Stories Ser.). (Illus.). 24p. (gr. 3 up). 1984. PLB 6.96; pap. 5.45 (ISBN 0-382-06946-3). Silver.

Young Moses, Crown Prince of Egypt. Asher Lehmann. Ed. by Bonnie Goldman & Neva Goldstein-Alpern. Tr. by Gertrude Hirschler. 150p. (gr. 9-12). 1987. 6.95 (ISBN 0-910818-64-9). Judaica Pr.

Young Mountaineers. facsimile ed. Mary N. Murfree. LC 70-98588. (Short Story Index Reprint Ser). 1897. 18.00 (ISBN 0-8369-3162-9). Ayer Co Pubs.

Young Mrs. Burton. Margaret Penn. 256p. 1981. pap. 10.95 (ISBN 0-521-28298-5). Cambridge U Pr.

Young Mrs. Burton. Margaret Penn. 260p. 1980. 16.50 (ISBN 0-904573-35-4, Pub. by Caliban Bks). Longwood Pub Group.

Young Mrs. Cavendish. K. K. Beck. 1987. 16.95 (ISBN 0-8027-0979-6). Walker & Co.

Young Mussolini & the Intellectual Origins of Fascism. A. James Gregor. LC 78-64470. (Institute of International Studies, UC Berkeley). 1979. 37.50x (ISBN 0-520-03799-5). U of Cal Pr.

Young Mutants. Ed. by Isaac Asimov et al. LC 83-48444. 224p. (YA) (gr. 6-9). 1984. pap. 7.95 (ISBN 0-06-020156-8). HarpJ.

Young Naturalist. A. Mitchell. (Hobby Guides Ser.). (Illus.). 32p. (gr. 5-10). 1984. PLB 12.96 (ISBN 0-88110-235-0); pap. 5.95 (ISBN 0-86020-653-X). EDC.

Young Naturalist: From Texas Parks & Wildlife Magazine. Ilo Hiller. LC 83-45107. (Louise Lindsey Merrick Texas Environment Ser.: No. 6). (Illus.). 170p. (gr. 2-8). 1983. 15.95 (ISBN 0-89096-163-8). Tex A&M Univ Pr.

Young Nietzsche & the Wagnerian Experience. Frederick R. Love. LC 63-63585. (North Carolina. University. Studies in the Germanic Languages & Literatures: No. 39). Repr. of 1963 ed. 27.00 (ISBN 0-404-50939-8). AMS Pr.

Young Nixon: An Oral Inquiry. Ed. by Renee K. Schulte. 1978. 13.95 (ISBN 0-930046-02-1); pap. 7.95 (ISBN 0-930046-01-3). CSUF Oral Hist.

Young Offender. Donald J. West. 334p. 1967. text ed. 37.50x (ISBN 0-8236-7020-1). Intl Univs Pr.

Young Offenders & the Law. Lionel Rose. (History in Focus Ser.). (Illus.). 72p. (gr. 7-12). 1984. 17.95 (ISBN 0-7134-1299-2, Pub. by Batsford England). David & Charles.

Young Ole Devil. J. T. Edson. 192p. 1988. pap. 2.75 (ISBN 0-441-94991-6, Charter Bks). Ace Bks.

Young Parents. Jane C. Miner. LC 85-4851. (Illus.). 160p. (gr. 7 up). 1985. 9.79 (ISBN 0-671-49848-7). Messner.

Young Patient with Degenerative Hip Disease. Ed. by John Sevastik & Ian Goldie. (Illus.). 322p. (Orig.). 1986. pap. text ed. 100.00x (ISBN 91-22-00784-9, Pub. by Almqvist & Wiksell). Coronet Bks.

Young Patriots: Six Brave Boys in the Civil War. Horatio Alger, Jr. (Gold Signature Ser.). (Illus.). 154p. 1987. 24.00. G K Westgard.

Young Pattullo. J. I. Stewart. 320p. 1976. 7.95 (ISBN 0-393-08367-5). Norton.

Young Peacemakers' Project Book. Kathleen Fry-Miller & Judith Myers-Walls. 208p. (Orig.). 1988. pap. 9.95 (ISBN 0-87178-976-0). Brethren.

Young People & Cultural Institutions: A UNESCO Survey: Eight Young People Give Their Views on the Cultural Institutions in Their Countries. 87p. 1980. pap. 5.00 (ISBN 92-3-101698-9, U1001, UNESCO). UNIPUB.

Young People & Heroin: An Examination of Heroin Use in the North of England. Geoffrey Pearson et al. 72p. 1987. pap. text ed. 27.95 (ISBN 0-566-05388-8, Pub. by Gower Pub England). Gower Pub Co.

Young People & Society. Ted Tapper. 176p. 1972. 22.00 (ISBN 0-208-01249-4, Archon). Shoe String.

Young People at Risk: Is Prevention Possible? Eli Ginzberg et al. (Studies in Health Policy). 160p. 1988. 29.50 (ISBN 0-8133-0525-X). Westview.

Young People Learning to Care: Making a Difference through Youth Participation. Mary C. Kohler. 160p. 1983. pap. 7.95 (ISBN 0-8164-2429-2, HarpR). Har-Row.

Young People of Leningrad: School & Work Options & Attitudes. Evelina Vasil'eva. LC 75-46109. pap. 52.30 (ISBN 0-317-41982-X, 2026126). Bks Demand UMI.

Young People Reading. Ed. by R. J. Selleck. (Second Century in Australian Education Ser.: Vol. 8). 1973. pap. 8.50x (ISBN 0-522-84040-X, Pub. by Melbourne U Pr). Intl Spec Bk.

Young People Talk about Death. McHugh. (gr. 7 up). 1980. PLB 9.90 (ISBN 0-531-02884-4, C10). Watts.

Young People with Handicaps: The Road to Adulthood. OECD & CERI. 66p. (Orig.). 1987. pap. 13.00 (ISBN 92-64-12903-0). OECD.

Young People with Problems: A Guide to Bibliotherapy. Jean A. Pardeck & John T. Pardeck. LC 83-18601. xv, 176p. 1984. lib. bdg. 36.95 (ISBN 0-313-23836-7, PYP/). Greenwood.

Young People's Dyirbal: An Example of Language Death from Australia. Annette Schmidt. (Cambridge Studies in Linguistics: Supplementary Volumes). 300p. 1985. 37.50 (ISBN 0-521-30510-1). Cambridge U Pr.

Young People's Guide to Yellowstone Park. Robin Tawney. LC 83-60358. (Illus.). 136p. (Orig.). (gr. 7-12). 1985. 11.95 (ISBN 0-912299-24-X); pap. 7.95 (ISBN 0-912299-04-5). Stoneydale Pr Pub.

Young People's Health: A Challenge for Society. (Technical Report Ser.: No. 731). 117p. 1986. pap. 9.60 (ISBN 92-4-120731-0). World Health.

Young People's Introduction to the World of Wall Street. C. M. Flumiani. 88p. 1987. pap. text ed. 87.75 (ISBN 0-86654-230-2). Inst Econ Finan.

Young People's Mass Book. Ed. by Tony Castle. (Illus.). 64p. (gr. 4-6). 1986. pap. 29.95 (ISBN 0-00-599743-7, Collins Liturgical). HarpR.

Young People's Medicine. Euteline Johnson. 32p. 1986. 5.95 (ISBN 0-89962-522-3). Todd & Honeywell.

Young People's Nature Guide. Allen H. Benton & Richard L. Bunting. (Illus.). 177p. (gr. 2-4). 1978. pap. text ed. 3.00 (ISBN 0-942788-05-2). Marginal Med.

Young People's Parables: The Malcolm Muggeridge & Children's Society Award for Young Authors. Ed. by Geoffrey Barlow. 108p. (Orig.). 1984. pap. 4.95 (ISBN 0-7043-3457-7, Pub. by Quartet Bks). Salem Hse Pubs.

Young People's Science Dictionary, 2 vols. Young People's Science Encyclopedia Editors. LC 67-17925. (Illus.). (gr. 4 up). 1979. lib. bdg. 22.60 (ISBN 0-516-00274-0). Childrens.

Young People's Speaker: Designed for Young People of Twelve Years. facsimile ed. Ed. by E. C. Rook & L. J. Rook. LC 70-37019. (Granger Index Reprint Ser.). (YA) (gr. 7 up). Repr. of 1892 ed. 14.00 (ISBN 0-8369-6318-0). Ayer Co Pubs.

Young People's Story of DuPage County. Jean Moore & Richard Crabb. (Illus.). 120p. 1981. 8.95 (ISBN 0-916445-03-8). Crossroads Comm.

Young People's Yellow Pages: A National Sourcebook for Youth. Alvin Rosenbaum. (Illus.). 320p. (Orig.). 1983. 14.95 (ISBN 0-399-50970-4, GD Perigee); pap. 8.95 (ISBN 0-399-50846-5). Putnam Pub Group.

Young Person with Down's Syndrome: Transition from Adolescence to Adulthood. Siegfried M. Pueschel. LC 87-26830. 260p. (Orig.). 1988. pap. text ed. 21.00 (ISBN 0-933716-90-7, 907). P H Brookes.

Young Person's First Book of Wealth. A. David Silver. (Illus.). 300p. (YA) (gr. 7-12). 1987. wkbk. 15.95x (ISBN 0-945214-00-6). Silver Prescrip Pr.

Young Persons Guide to BBC BASIC. National Computer Centre Staff & Michael Milan. 110p. 1983. pap. 7.75x (ISBN 0-471-87935-5). Wiley.

Young Person's Guide to Love. Morton Hunt. LC 75-28371. 181p. (gr. 5 up). 1975. 10.95 (ISBN 0-374-38757-5). FS&G.

Young Person's Guide to Military Service. rev. ed. Jeff Bradley. LC 86-33719. (Illus.). 207p. 1987. 16.95 (ISBN 0-916782-82-4, Dist. by Kampmann); pap. 9.95 (ISBN 0-916782-83-2). Harvard Common Pr.

Young Person's Guide to Playing the Piano. Sidney Harrison. (Illus.). 104p. (Orig.). 1982. pap. 5.95 (ISBN 0-571-11864-X). Faber & Faber.

Young Person's History of Israel. David Bamberger. Ed. by Nicholas Mandelkern. (Illus.). 150p. (Orig.). (gr. 5-7). 1985. pap. 6.95 (ISBN 0-87441-393-1); By Sara M. Schacheer & Priscilla Fishman. tchr's guide 12.50x (ISBN 0-87441-419-9); student's activity bk. 3.50x (ISBN 0-87441-429-6). Behrman.

Young Person's Philosophical Dictionary. Florence G. Goodman. (gr. 5-12). 1978. pap. 9.95x (ISBN 0-917232-06-2). Gee Tee Bee.

Young Petrella: Stories. Michael Gilbert. LC 87-46138. 224p. 1988. 15.95 (ISBN 0-06-015934-0, HarpT). Har-Row.

Young Phenomenon: Paperbacks in Our Schools. John Gillespie & Diana L. Spirt. LC 72-2653. (ALA Studies in Librarianship: No. 3). pap. 38.00 (ISBN 0-317-26350-1, 2024228). Bks Demand UMI.

Young Philip Sidney, Fifteen Seventy-Two to Fifteen Seventy-Seven. James M. Osborn. LC 77-151584. (Elizabethan Club Ser.: No. 5). pap. 147.80 (ISBN 0-317-29286-2, 2022026). Bks Demand UMI.

Young Photographer's Handbook. George Haines. LC 83-19656. (Illus.). 224p. (YA) (gr. 7 up). 1984. 9.95 (ISBN 0-668-06048-4). Arco.

Young Pianist: An Approach for Teachers & Students. 2nd ed. Joan Last. (Illus.). 1972. pap. 12.95x (ISBN 0-19-322287-6). Oxford U Pr.

Young Playwrights Festival Collection. Dramatists Guild Foundation Editors. 256p. 1983. pap. 3.95 (ISBN 0-380-83642-4, 83642-4, Bard). Avon.

Young Reader's Book of Church History. Frederick A. Norwood & Jo Carr. LC 81-20505. (Illus.). 176p. (gr. 4 up). 1982. 11.95 (ISBN 0-687-46827-2). Abingdon.

Young Reader's Encyclopedia of Jewish History. Ed. by Ilana Shamir & Shlomo Shavit. LC 87-10599. (YA) (gr. 7 up). 1987. 15.95 (ISBN 0-670-81738-4, Viking Kestrel). Viking.

Young Readers' Picturebook of Tar Heel Authors. 5th & rev. ed. Richard Walser & Mary Reynolds Peacock. (Illus.). vi, 74p. 1981. pap. 3.00 (ISBN 0-86526-184-9). NC Archives.

Young Rebel. Samellyn J. Wood. 112p. (Orig.). 1985. pap. 2.95 (ISBN 0-88120-736-5). SRA.

Young Reinhold Niebuhr: The Early Writings - 1911 to 1931. rev. ed. Ed. by William G. Chrystal. 256p. 1982. pap. 8.95 (ISBN 0-8298-0607-5). Pilgrim NY.

Young Richelieu: A Psychoanalytic Approach to Leadership. Elizabeth W. Marvick. LC 82-24754. (Orig.). 1983. 32.00x (ISBN 0-226-50904-4); pap. 14.00x (ISBN 0-226-50905-2). U of Chicago Pr.

Young Rider's Companion. George Wheatley. LC 81-27509. (Books for Adult & Young Adults). (Illus.). 120p. (gr. 4 up). 1981. PLB 15.95 (ISBN 0-8225-0767-6, AACR1). Lerner Pubns.

Young Rider's Guide to Horse & Pony Care. rev. ed. Jane Kidd. (Illus.). 200p. 1988. 12.95 (ISBN 0-87605-870-5). Howell Bk.

Young Rider's Handbook. Angela Sayer. LC 83-19734. (Illus.). 224p. (gr. 5 up). 1984. 9.95 (ISBN 0-668-06044-1). Arco.

Young Rissa. F. M. Busby. 192p. 1984. pap. 2.95 (ISBN 0-425-08505-8). Berkley Pub.

Young Robert Duncan: Portrait of the Poet as Homosexual in Society. Ekbert Faas. LC 83-15541. 400p. (Orig.). 1983. 20.00 (ISBN 0-87685-489-7); pap. 12.50 (ISBN 0-87685-488-9). Black Sparrow.

Young Rocky: A True Story of Attilio Rocky Castellani. Joseph Kinney & Adolph Caso. 1985. pap. 5.95 (ISBN 0-8283-1902-2). Branden Pub Co.

Young Run Away. Anthony Washington. (Illus., Orig.). (gr. 3-6). 1984. pap. 2.98 (ISBN 0-9613078-2-X). Detroit Black.

Young Runaways. K. M. Kapadia. 212p. 1971. 8.50. Asia Bk Corp.

Young Runner's Handbook. Elizabeth G. Barley & Mark Bloom. 128p. 1981. pap. 1.95 (ISBN 0-446-90999-8). Warner Bks.

Young Russia: The Genesis of Russian Radicalism in the 1860s. Abbott Gleason. LC 82-23875. xiv, 438p. 1983. pap. 12.00x (ISBN 0-226-29961-9). U of Chicago Pr.

Young Sam Clemens. Cyril Clemens. LC 76-49929. 1977. lib. bdg. 32.50 (ISBN 0-8414-3473-5). Folcroft.

Young Sam Johnson. James L. Clifford. (McGraw-Hill Paperbacks Ser.). (Illus.). 400p. 1981. pap. text ed. 6.95 (ISBN 0-07-011381-5). McGraw.

Young Samson. Israel I. Taslitt. 192p. 1968. 4.95 (ISBN 0-88482-749-6). Hebrew Pub.

Young Scarron. Thomas Mozeen. (Flowering of the Novel, 1740-1775 Ser: Vol. 37). 1975. Repr. of 1752 ed. lib. bdg. 55.00 (ISBN 0-8240-1136-8). Garland Pub.

Young Scientist Book of Evolution: Discoveries & Theories of the Origins of Life. Cork. (Young Scientist Ser.). (Illus.). 32p. (gr. 4-8). 1985. PLB 12.96 (ISBN 0-88110-219-9); pap. 5.95 (ISBN 0-86020-867-2). EDC.

Young Scientist Book of Medicine Doctors & Health: How Illness Can Be Prevented & Cured. Beasant. (Young Scientist Ser.). (Illus.). 32p. (gr. 4-8). 1986. PLB 12.96 (ISBN 0-88110-221-0); pap. 5.95 (ISBN 0-86020-948-2). EDC.

Young Scientist Book of Stars & Planets: Discovering the Secrets of the Sky at Night. Maynard. (Young Scientist Ser.). (Illus.). 32p. (gr. 4-8). 1976. PLB 12.96 (ISBN 0-88110-313-6); pap. 5.95 (ISBN 0-86020-094-9). EDC.

Young Scientist Explore: An Encyclopedia of Energy Activities. Jerry DeBruin. (Illus.). 32p. (gr. 4-8). 1985. wkbk. 4.95 (ISBN 0-86653-270-6). Good Apple.

Young Scientist Explore: Dinosaurs. Linda Penn. (Illus.). 32p. (gr. 1-3). 1985. wkbk. 4.95 (ISBN 0-86653-313-3). Good Apple.

Young Scientist Explore: Electricity & Magnetism. Jerry DeBruin. (Illus.). 32p. (gr. 4-8). 1985. wkbk. 4.95 (ISBN 0-86653-269-2). Good Apple.

Young Scientist Explore: The Kingdom of Plants. Linda Penn. (Illus.). 32p. (gr. 1-3). 1985. wkbk. 4.95 (ISBN 0-86653-315-X). Good Apple.

Young Scientist Explore: The Sun, Moon & Stars. Linda Penn. (Illus.). 32p. (gr. 1-3). 1985. wkbk. 4.95 (ISBN 0-86653-314-1). Good Apple.

Young Scientist: The World of Water. Jerry DeBruin. (Illus.). 32p. (gr. 4-8). 1985. wkbk 4.95 (ISBN 0-86653-288-9). Good Apple.

Young Scientists Explore Air, Land & Water Life, Bk. 3. Linda Penn. (gr. 1-3). 1982. 4.95 (ISBN 0-86653-071-1, GA 404). Good Apple.

Young Scientists Explore Animal Friends. Linda Penn. (Superific Science Ser.). (Illus.). 32p. (gr. 1-3). 1983. wkbk. 4.95 (ISBN 0-86653-124-6, GA 454). Good Apple.

Young Scientists Explore Animals, Bk. 2. Jerry DeBruin. (gr. 4-7). 1982. 4.95 (ISBN 0-86653-073-8, GA 406). Good Apple.

Young Scientists Explore Butterflies & Moths. Linda Penn. (Superific Science Ser.). (Illus.). 32p. (gr. 1-3). 1983. wkbk. 4.95 (ISBN 0-86653-111-4, GA 452). Good Apple.

Young Scientists Explore Inner & Outer Space. Jerry DeBruin. (Superific Science Ser.). (Illus.). 32p. (gr. 4-7). 1983. wkbk. 4.95 (ISBN 0-86653-152-1, GA 457). Good Apple.

Young Scientists Explore Insects, Bk. 1. Linda Penn. (gr. 1-3). 1982. 4.95 (ISBN 0-86653-070-3, GA 403). Good Apple.

Young Scientists Explore the Five Senses. Jerry DeBruin. (Superific Science Ser.). (Illus.). 32p. (gr. 4-7). 1983. wkbk. 4.95 (ISBN 0-86653-114-9, GA 455). Good Apple.

Young Scientists Explore the Moon, Bk. 3. Jerry DeBruin. (gr. 4-7). 1982. 4.95 (ISBN 0-86653-074-6, GA 407). Good Apple.

Young Scientists Explore the Seasons. Linda Penn. (Superific Science Ser.). (Illus.). 32p. (gr. 1-3). 1983. wkbk. 4.95 (ISBN 0-86653-123-8, GA 453). Good Apple.

Young Scientists Explore the Weather. Jerry DeBruin. (Superific Science Ser.). (Illus.). 32p. (gr. 4-7). 1983. wkbk. 4.95 (ISBN 0-86653-129-7, GA 456). Good Apple.

Young Scientists Explore the World Around Them, Bk. 1. Jerry DeBruin. (gr. 4-7). 1982. 4.95 (ISBN 0-86653-072-X, GA 405). Good Apple.

Young Scientists Explore the World of Nature, Bk. 1. Linda Penn. (gr. 1-3). 1982. 4.95 (ISBN 0-86653-069-X, GA 402). Good Apple.

Young Sea Officers Sheet Anchor. Lever. 17.95x (ISBN 0-685-70714-8). Wehman.

Young Server's Book of the Mass. Kenneth Guentert. LC 86-60894. 73p. 1987. pap. 4.95 (ISBN 0-89390-078-8). Resource Pubns.

Young Shakespeare. Russell Fraser. (Illus.). 224p. 1988. 29.00x (ISBN 0-231-06764-X). Columbia U Pr.

Young Shelley: Genesis of a Radical. Kenneth N. Cameron. 437p. 1980. Repr. of 1951 ed. lib. bdg. 49.50. Century Bookbindery.

Young Sherlock Holmes. Alan Arnold. pap. 2.95 (ISBN 0-671-61443-6). PB.

Young Sioux Warrior. Francis L. Kroll. (Illus.). (gr. 4-7). PLB 6.19 (ISBN 0-8313-0074-4). Lantern.

Young, Sober, & Free. Ed. by Shelly Marshall. 137p. 1978. 6.95 (ISBN 0-89486-055-0). Hazelden.

Young Spartacus, 4 vols, No. 6. Young Communist League of America. 1970. Repr. of 1935 ed. Greenwood.

Young Stages: A Guide to Theatre & Dance for Youth in the San Francisco Bay Area. Ed. by Debra J. Crane & Misha Berson. LC 82-51320. (Illus.). 72p. (Orig.). 1982. pap. 5.00 (ISBN 0-9605896-1-9). Theatre Bay Area.

Young Stamp-Collectors. Rosamond Praeger. (Illus.). 56p. 1985. 15.95 (ISBN 0-9508551-1-1, Pub. by Portmoon Pr UK). R Clark.

Young Star Travelers. Ed. by Isaac Asimov et al. LC 85-45276. 240p. (YA) (gr. 7 up). 1986. 13.25 (ISBN 0-06-020178-9); PLB 12.89 (ISBN 0-06-020179-7). HarpJ.

Young Stephen Foster. Faye Parker. (Children's Theatre Playscript Ser.). (gr. k-12). 1968. pap. 2.00x (ISBN 0-88020-067-7). Coach Hse.

Young-Stirs: The Pittsburgh Children's Cookbook. (Illus.). 200p. (Orig.). (ps-12). 1985. pap. 7.95 (ISBN 0-9615457-0-4). Genesis Inc.

Young Students' Book of Child Care. 4th ed. Leonora Pitcairn. LC 76-58076. 1978. 8.95x (ISBN 0-521-21671-0). Cambridge U Pr.

Young Swimmer. Bill Libby. LC 82-17289. (Illus.). 160p. (gr. 4 up). 1983. 10.25 (ISBN 0-688-01992-7). Lothrop.

Young Tableaux in Combinatorics, Invariant Theory, & Algebra: An Anthology of Recent Work. Ed. by Joseph P. Kung. LC 82-11330. 347p. 1982. 38.50 (ISBN 0-12-428780-8). Acad Pr.

Young Teenage Reading Habits: A Study of the Bookmaster Scheme. Jean Bird. LC 82-233284. (BNB RF Report: No. 9). (Illus.). 129p. (Orig.). 1983. pap. 14.25 (ISBN 0-7123-3007-0, Pub. by British Lib). Longwood Pub Group.

Young Think: A Pre-School Thinking Skills Program. Sydney B. Tyler. (Just Think Program Ser.). 74p. (Orig.). (ps-1). 1982. pap. text ed. 15.00 report cover (ISBN 0-912781-01-7). Thomas Geale.

Young Thomas Jefferson. Francene Sabin. LC 85-1093. (Illus.). 48p. (gr. 4-6). 1985. lib. bdg. 9.79 (ISBN 0-8167-0561-5); pap. text ed. 1.95 (ISBN 0-8167-0562-3). Troll Assocs.

Young Titan. F. Van Wyck Mason. 1976. Repr. of 1959 ed. lib. bdg. 29.20x (ISBN 0-89190-355-0, Pub. by River City Pr). Amereon Ltd.

Young Tom or Very Mixed Company. Forrest Reid. 169p. 1987. pap. 7.95 (ISBN 0-85449-055-8, Pub. by GMP England). Alyson Pubns.

Young Torless. Robert Musil. (Modern Classics Ser.). 1982. pap. 7.95 (ISBN 0-394-71015-0). Pantheon.

Young Towns of Lima. P. Lloyd. LC 79-51826. (Urbanization in Developing Countries Ser.). (Orig.). 1980. 42.50 (ISBN 0-521-22871-9); pap. 13.95 (ISBN 0-521-29688-9). Cambridge U Pr.

Young Trailers. Joseph Altsheler. 1976. lib. bdg. 20.95x (ISBN 0-89968-005-4). Lightyear.

Young Trailers. Joseph Altsheler. (Young Trailer Ser.). Repr. lib. bdg. 20.95x (ISBN 0-89966-479-2). Buccaneer Bks.

Young Trailers. Joseph Altsheler. 21.95 (ISBN 0-89190-824-2, Pub. by Am Repr). Amereon ltd.

Young Turks. Stephen Seemayer. LC 81-68126. (Illus.). 160p. (Orig.). 1981. pap. 10.00 (ISBN 0-937122-06-8). Astro Artz.

Young Turks Before the Dawn of History. John F. Kirakossian. 1989. price not set (ISBN 0-943071-12-7). Sphinx Pr.

Young Unicorns. Madeleine L'Engle. 224p. (YA) (gr. 8 up). 1980. pap. 3.25 (ISBN 0-440-99919-7, LFL). Dell.

Young Unicorns. Madeleine L'Engle. LC 68-13682. 256p. (gr. 7 up). 1968. 12.95 (ISBN 0-374-38778-8). FS&G.

Young United States, Seventeen Eighty-Three to Eighteen Thirty. Edwin Tunis. LC 75-29613. (Illus.). 160p. (YA) (gr. 7 up). 1976. 19.70 (ISBN 0-690-01065-6, Crowell Jr Bks). HarpJ.

Young Van Dyck. Alan McNairn. (Illus.). 1980. 29.95osi (ISBN 0-88884-456-5, 56579-3, Pub. by Natl Mus Canada); pap. 19.95 (ISBN 0-88884-468-9, 56578-5). U of Chicago Pr.

Young Victoria Reigns. 1982. 15.00x (ISBN 0-906660-00-9, Pub. by New Playwrights Network). State Mutual Bk.

Young Vincent Massey. Claude Bissell. 272p. 1981. 24.95 (ISBN 0-8020-2398-3). U of Toronto Pr.

Young Visitor to Mars. Richard M. Elam. (Illus.). (gr. 4-7). PLB 6.19 (ISBN 0-8313-0031-0). Lantern.

Young Voice. Ed. by Robert McGovern & Richard Snyder. 24p. 1972. pap. 1.00 (ISBN 0-912592-16-8). Ashland Poetry.

Young Voice Three. Ed. by Robert McGovern & Richard Snyder. 27p. 1974. pap. 1.95 (ISBN 0-912592-20-6). Ashland Poetry.

Young Voice Two. Ed. by Robert McGovern & Richard Snyder. 24p. 1973. pap. 1.00 (ISBN 0-912592-18-4). Ashland Poetry.

Young Voltaire. Cleveland B. Chase. 253p. 1980. Repr. of 1926 ed. lib. bdg. 35.00 (ISBN 0-8495-0799-5). Arden Lib.

Young Voltaire. facsimile ed. Cleveland B. Chase. LC 79-160962. (Select Bibliographies Reprint Ser). Repr. of 1926 ed. 22.00 (ISBN 0-8369-5830-6). Ayer Co Pubs.

Young Voter's Manual: A Topical Dictionary of American Government & Politics. Leon W. Blevins. (Quality Paperback: No. 260). 366p. (Orig.). 1975. pap. 9.50 (ISBN 0-8226-0260-1). Littlefield.

Young Voyageur: Trade & Treachery at Michilimackinac. rev. ed. Dirk Gringhuis. (Illus.). 202p. (gr. 9 up). 1969. pap. 2.50 (ISBN 0-911872-34-5). Mackinac Island.

Young West: A Sequel to Edward Bellamy's Celebrated Novel Looking Backward. Solomon Schindler. LC 70-154462. (Utopian Literature Ser). 1971. Repr. of 1894 ed. 19.00 (ISBN 0-405-03544-6). Ayer Co Pubs.

Young Widow. Ferguson. 12.00 (ISBN 0-405-13935-7). Ayer Co Pubs.

Young Wife, or Duties of Woman in the Marriage Relation. William A. Alcott. LC 73-169369. (Family in America Ser). (Illus.). 382p. 1972. Repr. of 1837 ed. 23.00 (ISBN 0-405-03845-3). Ayer Co Pubs.

Young Wife's Tale. Renee Shann. (Lythway). 1988. lib. bdg. 19.50 (ISBN 0-7451-0670-6, Pub. by Chivers Pr UK). G K HAll.

Young Witches & Warlocks. Ed. by Isaac Asimov et al. LC 85-45849. 224p. (YA) (gr. 7 up). 1987. 12.70i (ISBN 0-06-020183-5); PLB 12.89 (ISBN 0-06-020184-3). HarpJ.

Young Witness: Evangelism to & by Children & Youth. Jane Hagstrom. 56p. (Orig.). 1986. pap. 4.95 (ISBN 0-8066-2233-4, 23-3036). Augsburg.

Young Wolf: Early Adventure Stories of Jack London. Jack London. 258p. 1988. Repr. lib. bdg. 22.95x (ISBN 0-8095-4054-1). Borgo Pr.

Young Wolf: The Early Adventure Stories of Jack London. Jack London. Ed. & intro. by Howard Lachtman. LC 83-25185. 258p. 1984. pap. 8.95 (ISBN 0-88496-210-5). Capra Pr.

Young Woman & Her Self-Esteem. Anita Canfield. 93p. 1983. 9.95 (ISBN 0-934126-41-0). Randall Bk Co.

Young Woman Citizen. Mary Austin. LC 18-21835. 1976. pap. 8.95x. Designs Three.

Young Woman: Psychosomatic Aspects of Obstetrics & Gynaecology. L. Dennerstein & M. De Senarclens. (International Congress Ser.: Vol. 618). 1983. 146.50 (ISBN 0-444-90316-X). Elsevier.

Young Woman's Guide to Sex. Jacqueline Voss & Jay Gale. LC 86-4786. (Illus.). 256p. 1987. 16.95 (ISBN 0-8050-0082-8). H Holt & Co.

Young Woman's Guide to Sex. Jacqueline Voss & Jay Gale. (Illus.). 1988. pap. 7.95 (ISBN 0-89586-692-7, Body Pr). Price Stern.

Young Woman's Journal: A Place to Keep Dreams & Memories. (Illus.). 96p. (Orig.). (YA) (gr. 6 up). 1988. lib. bdg. 15.90 (ISBN 0-89471-644-1); pap. 5.95 (ISBN 0-89471-643-3). Running Pr.

Young Worker, Vols. 1-14, No. 17. Young Communist League of America. 1972. Repr. of 1936 ed. Vols. 1 & 2. lib. bdg. 72.00 (ISBN 0-313-21964-8, YW01); Vols. 3-5. lib. bdg. 105.00 (ISBN 0-313-21965-6, YW02); Vols. 6 & 7. lib. bdg. 99.00 (ISBN 0-313-21966-4, YW03); Vols. 8 & 9. lib. bdg. 125.00 (ISBN 0-313-21967-2, YW04); Vols. 10 & 11. lib. bdg. 99.00 (ISBN 0-313-21968-0, YW05); Vol. 12. lib. bdg. 88.00 (ISBN 0-313-21969-9, YW06); Vol. 13. lib. bdg. 105.00 (ISBN 0-313-21970-2, YW07); Vols. 13 & 14. lib. bdg. 83.00 (ISBN 0-313-21971-0, YW08). Greenwood.

Young Writer. J. A. Christensen. LC 74-88375. (Illus.). (gr. 8-12). 1970. text ed. 14.95x (ISBN 0-87015-180-0). Pacific Bks.

Young Writer at Work. Ed. by Jessie Rehder. LC 62-11938. 1962. 13.24x (ISBN 0-672-63148-2). Odyssey Pr.

Young Writer's Handbook. Susan Tchudi. LC 84-5312. 176p. (gr. 7 up). 1984. 12.95 (ISBN 0-684-18090-1, Pub. by Scribner). Macmillan.

Young Writer's Handbook: A Practical Guide for the Beginner Who Is Serious about Writing. Susan Tchudi & Stephen Tchudi. LC 87-1463. (Illus.). 176p. (gr. 7 up). 1987. pap. 4.95 (ISBN 0-689-71170-0, Aladdin Bks). Macmillan.

Young Years. June Pomerinke. LC 85-90524. (Illus.). 300p. (Orig.). 1986. pap. 8.50 prepaid (ISBN 0-9616273-0-1). Young Pr Idaho.

Youngblood. John O. Killens. LC 81-16156. (Brown Thrasher Bks.). 512p. 1982. pap. 8.95 (ISBN 0-8203-0602-9). U of Ga Pr.

Youngblood Hawke. Herman Wouk. LC 62-7698. 1988. 21.95 (ISBN 0-385-02974-8). Doubleday.

Youngblood Hawke. Herman Wouk. 1982. pap. 5.95 (ISBN 0-671-45472-2). PB.

Younge Site: An Archaeological Record from Michigan. Emerson F. Greenman. (Occasional Contributions Ser.: No. 6). (Illus.). 1937. pap. 3.00x (ISBN 0-932206-01-8). U Mich Mus Anthro.

Younger American Poets. facs. ed. Jessie B. Rittenhouse. LC 68-16971. (Essay Index Reprint Ser). 1904. 20.00 (ISBN 0-8369-0826-0). Ayer Co Pubs.

Younger American Poets. Ed. by Douglas Sladen. 1979. Repr. of 1891 ed. lib. bdg. 45.00 (ISBN 0-8492-8090-7). R West.

Younger American Poets Eighteen-Thirty to Eighteen-Ninety, with an Appendix of Younger Canadian Poets. Ed. by Goodridge B. Roberts & Douglas Sladen. 666p. 1981. Repr. of 1891 ed. lib. bdg. 75.00 (ISBN 0-8495-4959-0). Arden Lib.

Younger Brother, Don Yod: A Tibetan Play, Being the Secret Biography from the Words of the Glorious Lama, the Holy Reverend Blo Bzang Ye Shes. Ye Shes Blo Bzang. Tr. by Thubten J. Norbu & Robert B. Ekvall. LC 74-19623. pap. 39.50 (ISBN 0-317-10095-5, 2050129). Bks Demand UMI.

Younger Church in Search of Maturity: Presbyterianism in Brazil from 1910-1959. Paul E. Pierson. LC 73-89596. 306p. 1974. 8.00 (ISBN 0-911536-49-3). Trinity U Pr.

Younger Churchmen Look at the Church. facsimile ed. Ed. by Ralph H. Read. LC 74-156708. (Essay Index Reprint Ser). Repr. of 1935 ed. 21.50 (ISBN 0-8369-2330-8). Ayer Co Pubs.

Younger Critics in North America. Ed. by Richard Kostelanetz. 205p. (Orig.). 1984. pap. text ed. 20.00 (ISBN 0-317-17971-3). RK Edns.

Younger Earth. Alex Stella. LC 85-73469. 220p. 1986. 7.00 (ISBN 0-9602044-3-1). A Stella.

Younger French Poets see Some Modern French Poets.

Younger Generation. Rudolf Steiner. LC 67-29493. 179p. 1984. pap. 9.95 (ISBN 0-910142-42-4). Anthroposophic.

Younger Goethe & the Visual Arts. W. D. Robson-Scott. (Angelica Germanica Ser.). 200p. 52.50 (ISBN 0-521-23321-6). Cambridge U Pr.

Younger Irish Poets. Ed. by Gerald Dawe. 184p. (Orig.). 1982. pap. 8.95 (Pub. by Blackstaff Pr). Longwood Pub Group.

Younger Man Guns. Lewis B. Patten. 1986. pap. 2.75 (ISBN 0-451-14266-7, Sig). NAL.

Younger Pitt: The Reluctant Transition. John Ehrman. LC 82-42859. (Illus.). 704p. 1983. 41.00x (ISBN 0-8047-1184-4). Stanford U Pr.

Younger Pitt: The Years of Acclaim. John Ehrman. (Illus.). 726p. 1969. 47.50x (ISBN 0-8047-1186-0). Stanford U Pr.

Younger Son: Poet: An Autobiography in Three Parts. Karl J. Shapiro. LC 88-6204. 1988. 16.95 (ISBN 0-912697-86-5). Algonquin Bks.

Youngest Day: Nature & Grace on Shelter Island. Robert F. Capon. LC 82-48414. (Illus.). 160p. 1983. 11.45 (ISBN 0-06-061309-2, HarpR). Har-Row.

Youngest Drama. Ashley Dukes. LC 77-646. 1924. lib. bdg. 30.00 (ISBN 0-8414-3804-8). Folcroft.

Youngest Minority: Lawyers in Defense of Children, 2 Vols. 350p. 1977. pap. 8.50 (ISBN 0-686-47930-0, 513-0007). Amer Bar Assn.

Youngest Prophet: The Life of Jacinta Marto, Fatima Visionary. Christopher Rengers. LC 85-30789. 144p. (Orig.). 1986. pap. 5.95 (ISBN 0-8189-0496-8). Alba.

Youngest Science. Lewis Thomas. (New Age Bk.). 1984. pap. 6.95 (ISBN 0-553-34066-2). Bantam.

Youngest Science: Notes of a Medicine Watcher. Lewis Thomas. (Alfred P. Sloan Foundation Ser.). 300p. 1983. 14.75 (ISBN 0-670-79533-X). Viking.

Youngest Voyageur. Duane R. Lund. 1985. 7.95 (ISBN 0-934860-41-6). Adventure Pubns.

Young's Analytical Concordance to the Bible. Young. cancelled (ISBN 0-686-12407-3); cancelled (ISBN 0-686-12408-1). Church History.

Young's Analytical Concordance to the Bible. Robert Young. 1955. 21.95 (ISBN 0-8028-8084-3); indexed 22.95 (ISBN 0-8028-8085-1). Eerdmans.

Young's Analytical Concordance to the Bible. rev. ed. Robert Young. LC 82-14203. 1220p. 1986. 24.95 (ISBN 0-8407-4945-7). Nelson.

Young's Analytical Concordance to the Bible. Robert Young. 1216p. Date not set. 18.95 (ISBN 0-917006-29-1). Hendrickson MA.

Young's Learning Medical Terminology: A Worktext. 6th ed. Austrin & Young. 1986. 24.95 (ISBN 0-8016-0407-9). Mosby.

Young's Literal Translation of the Bible. Robert Young. 24.95 (ISBN 0-8010-9921-8). Baker Bk.

Young's Night Thoughts. J. W. Mackail. 1918. 25.50 (ISBN 0-8274-3781-1). R West.

Youniverse: Gestalt Therapy, Non-Western Religions & the Present Age. Jesse J. Thomas. LC 77-89164. (Illus.). 1978. 8.95 (ISBN 0-930626-00-1); pap. 4.95 (ISBN 0-930626-01-X). Psych & Consul Assocs.

Yount on Agency Management. Lewis C. Yount. 158p. 1986. 14.95 (ISBN 0-87863-190-9, 2403-06, Longman Fin Serv Pub). Longman Finan.

Your Aching Back: A Doctor's Guide to Relief. Augustus A. White, III. 288p. 1984. pap. 3.95 (ISBN 0-553-24304-7). Bantam.

Your Ads Advisor. Jacinth I. Baublitz. 72p. 1987. cancelled (ISBN 0-9610316-2-X). J I Baublitz.

Your Advertising's Great...How's Business? The Revolution in Sales Promotion. Bud Frankel & Hal W. Phillips. 250p. 1985. 19.95 (ISBN 0-87094-543-2). Dow Jones-Irwin.

Your Affordable Solar Home. Dan Hibshman. LC 82-10747. (Tools for Today Ser.). (Illus.). 128p. (Orig.). 1983. pap. 7.95 (ISBN 0-87156-327-4). Sierra.

Your Afghan Hound. Sue A. Kauffman. LC 69-19735. (Your Dog Bk.). (Illus.). 1969. 13.95 (ISBN 0-87714-018-9). Denlingers.

Your Aging Parents. John Deedy. 192p. (Orig.). 1984. pap. 7.95 (ISBN 0-88347-160-4). Thomas More.

Your Airedale Terrier. Barbara Strebeigh & Pauline I. McCready. LC 76-45234. (Your Dog Bk.). (Illus.). 1977. 13.95 (ISBN 0-87714-040-5). Denlingers.

Your Aladdin's Lamp. William H. Hornaday & Harlan Ware. 288p. 1979. pap. 8.50 (ISBN 0-911336-75-3). Sci of Mind.

Your Alaskan Flight Plan. 2nd ed. Don Downie & Julia Downie. (Illus.). 256p. 1989. pap. 18.95 (ISBN 0-8306-2452-X, 2452). TAB Bks.

Your Alaskan Malamute. Dianne Ross. LC 76-45235. (Your Dog Bk.). (Illus.). 1977. 13.95 (ISBN 0-87714-047-2). Denlingers.

Your Allergy-What to Do about It. Allan Knight. 1975. pap. 3.00 (ISBN 0-87980-304-5). Wilshire.

Your Amazing Senses: Thirty-Six Games, Puzzles & Tricks to Show How Your Senses Work. Ron Van Der Meer & Atie Van Der Meer. (Illus.). 12p. (gr. 4-7). 1987. pap. 9.95 (ISBN 0-689-71184-0, Aladdin Bks). Macmillan.

Your Ancients Revisited: A History of Child Development see Review of Child Development Research.

Your Apple II Needs You: Thirty Programming Projects for the Apple II. Frank Wattenberg. (Illus.). 352p. 1984. pap. text ed. 15.95 (ISBN 0-13-977975-2). P-H.

Your Ass is Grass. Carole Marsh. (Of All the Gaul Ser.). (Illus.). 125p. 1987. pap. 7.95 (ISBN 1-55609-203-2). Gallopade Pub Group.

Your Astrological Guide to Fitness. Eva Shaw. LC 87-14287. (Illus.). 208p. (Orig.). 1988. pap. text ed. 9.95 (ISBN 0-938179-10-1). Mills Sanderson.

Your Atari Computer: A Guide to the Atari 400 & 800 Personal Computers. Lon Poole et al. 548p. (Orig.). 1982. pap. text ed. 17.95 (ISBN 0-07-047856-2). Osborne-McGraw.

Your Attitude Is Showing. 5th, rev. ed. Elwood N. Chapman. Ed. by W. Philip Gerould & Byron Riggan. (Illus.). 194p. 1987. pap. text ed. write for info. (ISBN 0-574-20905-0, 13-3905). SRA.

Your Attitude: Key to Success. John Maxwell. 160p. 1984. pap. 5.95. Heres Life.

Your Attitude: Key to Success. John Maxwell. 156p. 1985. pap. 5.95 (ISBN 0-89840-102-X). Heres Life.

Your Automatic Camera. Dennis Curtin. (Your Automatic Camera Ser.). (Illus.). 128p. (Orig.). 1980. pap. 6.95 (ISBN 0-930764-17-X). Curtin & London.

Your Baby & Child: From Birth to Age Five. Penelope Leach. pap. 16.95 (ISBN 0-394-73509-9). Knopf.

Your Baby & Child: From Birth to Age Five. Penelope Leach. LC 77-75010. 1978. 24.45 (ISBN 0-394-40755-5). Knopf.

Your Baby: Basic Care & First Aid. Pamela Zuckerman. (Illus.). 20p. 1987. with hanging chain & index tabs 9.95 (ISBN 0-8120-5837-2). Barron.

Your Baby Boy. Barty Phillips. (Illus.). 64p. 1987. Laminated boards. pap. 4.95 (ISBN 0-88162-291-5). Salem Hse Pubs.

Your Baby Comes Home. Better Homes & Gardens Editors. 1987. pap. 2.95 (ISBN 0-696-01721-0). BH&G.

Your Baby... Gift of God. Elizabeth A. Hambrick-Stowe. (Looking Up Ser.). (Orig.). 1985. pap. 1.25 (ISBN 0-8298-0549-4). Pilgrim NY.

Your Baby Girl. Barty Phillips. (Illus.). 64p. 1987. Laminated. pap. 4.95 (ISBN 0-88162-290-7). Salem Hse Pubs.

Your Baby Grows Up. Better Homes & Gardens Editors. 1987. pap. 2.95 (ISBN 0-696-01723-7). BH&G.

Your Baby: Healthy Eating. Better Homes & Gardens Editors. (Illus.). 48p. 1988. pap. 2.95 (ISBN 0-696-01728-8). BH&G.

Your Baby Needs Music. Barbara Cass-Beggs. (Illus.). 144p. 1980. pap. 5.95 (ISBN 0-312-89768-5). St Martin.

Your Baby: Questions Parents Ask. Better Homes & Gardens Editors. (Illus.). 48p. 1988. pap. 2.95 (ISBN 0-696-01729-6). BH&G.

Your Baby: The Beginning. Better Homes & Gardens Editors. 1987. pap. 2.95 (ISBN 0-696-01720-2). BH&G.

Your Baby: The First Wondrous Year. Ed. by Richard A. Chase et al. (Illus.). 416p. 1984. 14.95 (ISBN 0-02-075810-3, Collier). Macmillan.

Your Baby, Your Birth: A Guide to Alternatives. Kathleen Anderson. 300p. Date not set. price not set (ISBN 0-917982-14-2). Cougar Bks.

Your Baby, Your Body. Carol Dilfer. (Illus.). 1977. o. p. 8.95 (ISBN 0-517-52855-X); pap. 5.95 (ISBN 0-517-52856-8). Crown.

Your Baby, Your Way. Sheila Kitzinger. LC 86-42983. 288p. 1987. 19.45 (ISBN 0-394-54573-7). Pantheon.

Your Baby's First Steps. Better Homes & Gardens Editors. 1987. pap. 2.95 (ISBN 0-696-01722-9). BH&G.

Your Baby's First Thirty Months. Lucie W. Barber & Herman Williams. LC 81-80307. (Illus.). 160p. 1981. pap. 7.95 (ISBN 0-89586-062-7). Price Stern.

Your Baby's Secret World: Four Phases for Effective Parenting (A Professional & Practical Guide) Larry V. Cheldelin. Ed. by J. Brown. (Illus., Orig.). 1983. pap. 4.95 (ISBN 0-8283-1850-6). Branden Pub Co.

Your Bad Back. Leon Marshall. 1985. 22.00x (ISBN 0-86025-857-2, Pub. by Ian Henry Pubns England). State Mutual Bk.

Your Balancing Act: Five Steps to Wellness. Carolyn Taylor. (Skill Builder Ser.). (Illus.). 184p. (Orig.). 1988. pap. 15.95 (ISBN 0-943920-75-2). Metamorphous Pr.

Your Basenji. Evelyn M. Green. LC 76-20959. (Your Dog Bk.). (Illus.). 1976. 13.95 (ISBN 0-87714-041-3). Denlingers.

Your Basic Guide to Nutrition. F. J. Stare & V. Aronson. LC 82-61762. 194p. 1983. 11.95 (ISBN 0-89313-026-5). G F Stickley Co.

Your Basic Love Story. Jack Blumner. (Illus.). 1984. pap. 4.95 (ISBN 0-03-069581-3). H Holt & Co.

Your Beagle. Robert J. Berndt. LC 75-41979. (Your Dog Bk.). (Illus.). 1976. 13.95 (ISBN 0-87714-034-0). Denlingers.

Your Beginning with God. Ed. by Dwayne Norman. 31p. 1982. pap. 1.95 (ISBN 0-88144-063-9). Christian Pub.

Your Best Helper. John L. Shuler. (Anchor Ser.). 1984. pap. 6.95 (ISBN 0-8163-0544-7). Pacific Pr Pub Assn.

Your Best Interest: A Money Book for the Computer Age. Tom Weishaar. LC 85-81877. (Illus.). 172p. (Orig.). 1985. pap. 9.95 (ISBN 0-931137-00-4). Infobooks.

Your Best Wishes Can Come True. Phyllis F. Cowell. (Care Bear Ser.). (Illus.). 40p. (ps-3). 1984. 5.95 (ISBN 0-910313-18-0). Parker Bros.

Your Better Self: Christianity, Psychology, & Self-Esteem. Ed. by Craig W. Ellison. LC 82-47742. 224p. (Orig.). 1982. pap. 8.95 (ISBN 0-686-97230-9, RD/408, HarpR). Har-Row.

Your Bible: An Introduction to the Word. rev. ed. R. Laird Harris. 96p. 1976. pap. text ed. 5.95 (ISBN 0-910566-12-7); looseleaf instr's guide with binder 9.95 (ISBN 0-910566-29-1). Evang Tchr.

Your Boat's Electrical System. rev. ed. Conrad Miller & E. S. Maloney. (Illus.). 512p. 1988. 16.95 (ISBN 0-688-08132-0, Pub. by Beech Tree Bks). Morrow.

Your Boat's Electrical System, 1981-1982. Conrad Miller & Elbert S. Maloney. 1984. 16.95 (ISBN 0-87851-805-3, Hearst Marine Bk). Morrow.

Your Body. Irene Fekete & Peter D. Ward. (World of Science Ser.). (Illus.). 64p. (YA) (gr. 7 up). 12.95 (ISBN 0-87196-989-0). Facts on File.

Your Body - Biofeedback at Its Best. Beata Jencks. LC 77-24618. (Illus.). 304p. 1978. 24.95x (ISBN 0-88229-351-6); pap. 12.95x (ISBN 0-88229-508-X). Nelson-Hall.

Your Body & How It Works. Patricia Lauber. (Gateway Ser.: No. 25). (Illus.). (gr. 3-5). 1966. (BYR); lib. bdg. 8.99 (ISBN 0-394-90125-8). Random.

Your Body & How It Works. Ovid Wong. LC 86-9686. (Science Activities Ser.). (Illus.). 128p. (gr. 5 up). 1986. PLB 14.60 (ISBN 0-516-00534-0). Childrens.

Your Body Doesn't Lie. John Diamond. 208p. 1980. pap. 3.50 (ISBN 0-446-30859-5). Warner Bks.

Your Body Is Your Best Doctor. Melvin E. Page & H. Leon Abrams, Jr. (Pivot Health Book). Orig. Title: Health Versus Disease. 256p. 1972. pap. 1.95 (ISBN 0-87983-021-2). Keats.

Your Body Is Your Own. Amy C. Bahr. LC 85-80575. (It's OK to Say No Picture Bks.). (Illus.). 32p. (ps-2). 1986. 4.95 (ISBN 0-448-15326-2, G&D). Putnam Pub Group.

Your Body Speaks Its Mind. Stanley Keleman. 188p. 1981. 10.95 (ISBN 0-934320-03-9); pap. 7.95 (ISBN 0-934320-01-2). Center Pr.

Your Body: The Ultimate Lethal Weapon. Keith Yates. (Illus.). 104p. (Orig.). 1987. pap. text ed. 12.00 (ISBN 0-87364-438-7). Paladin Pr.

Your Body, Your Baby, Your Life. Angela Phillips. (Illus.). 192p. (Orig.). 1983. pap. 5.95 (ISBN 0-86358-006-8, Pandora Pr). Routledge Chapman & Hall.

Your Body's Response. Edgar Brown & Kaye Behrens. LC 82-90165. (Illus.). 192p. (Orig.). 1985. 22.95 (ISBN 0-9613697-1-X); pap. 16.95 (ISBN 0-9613697-0-1). Madison Ave Pub.

Your Book of Financial Planning. Ed. by Loren Dunton. 1983. text ed. 29.95 (ISBN 0-8359-9505-4, Reston). P-H.

Your Book of Heraldry. Richard Slade. 7.95 (ISBN 0-685-91533-6). Transatl Arts.

Your Book of Knitted Toys. Brenda Morton. LC 72-11090. 1973. 5.95 (ISBN 0-8008-8757-3). Taplinger.

Your Book of Magic. Alexander Van Rensselaer. (gr. 9 up). 1968. 7.95 (ISBN 0-571-06939-8). Transatl Arts.

Your Book of Modelling. Richard Slade. (gr. 4 up). 1968. 5.95 (ISBN 0-571-08387-0). Transatl Arts.

Your Book of Money. David Jones. (gr. 7 up). 1971. 6.50 (ISBN 0-571-09341-8). Transatl Arts.

Your Book of Music. Michael Short & Imogen Holst. LC 82-9377. (Your Book of... Ser.). (Illus.). 96p. (gr. 3-6). 1983. 11.95 (ISBN 0-571-18031-0). Faber & Faber.

Your Book of Patchwork. Priscilla Lobley. LC 74-6048. 6.50 (ISBN 0-8008-8760-3). Taplinger.

Your Book of Veteran & Edwardian Cars. John Coleman. (gr. 7 up). 1972. 5.95 (ISBN 0-571-09375-2). Transatl Arts.

Your Book of Vintage Cars. John Coleman. (Illus.). (gr. 7 up). 1969. 4.50 (ISBN 0-571-08276-9). Transatl Arts.

Your Book of Watching Wildlife. Michael Blackmore. (gr. 7 up). 1972. 5.25 (ISBN 0-571-08347-1). Transatl Arts.

Your Borzoi. Alfred W. Edlin. LC 75-41983. (Your Dog Bk.). 1976. 13.95 (ISBN 0-87714-042-1). Denlingers.

Your Boxer. Lorraine C. Meyer. LC 78-187777. (Your Dog Bk.). (Illus.). 128p. 1973. 13.95 (ISBN 0-87714-004-9). Denlingers.

Your Brain & Nervous System. Leslie J. LeMaster. LC 84-7635. (New True Bks.). (Illus.). 48p. (gr. k-4). 1984. PLB 12.60 (ISBN 0-516-01931-7); pap. 3.95 (ISBN 0-516-41931-5). Childrens.

Your Brain & the Mind of Christ. William G. Rorick. LC 84-50081. 140p. 1984. 6.95 (ISBN 0-938232-43-6). Winston-Derek.

Your Brain at Work: A New View of Personality & Behavior. Margaret A. Golton. 114p. (Orig.). 1983. pap. 7.95. Frank Pubns.

Your Brain-Image Power: How to Selfsex & Imagize Your Way to Super-Successful Living. George E. Corder. LC 82-90505. 200p. 1983. lib. bdg. 25.00 (ISBN 0-9609246-0-4). Brain-Image.

Your Brain Is Younger Than You Think: A Guide to Mental Aging. Richard M. Torack. LC 80-21237. 164p. 1981. text ed. 18.95x (ISBN 0-88229-538-1); pap. 9.95 (ISBN 0-88229-761-9). Nelson-Hall.

Your Breast & You: What Every Woman Needs to Know about Breast Diseases, Breast Cancer & Cosmetic Breast Surgery Before She Has a Breast Problem. D. S. Halbert. Ed. by Delno Roberts. LC 84-72983. (Illus.). 238p. 1986. 14.95 (ISBN 0-931609-00-3). Askon Pub.

Your Brother's Keeper: A Guide for Families Confronting Psychiatric Illness. James R. Morrison. LC 79-27810. 352p. 1981. 21.95 (ISBN 0-88229-563-2). Nelson-Hall.

Your Bull Terrier. Marilyn Drewes. LC 77-92121. (Your Dog Bk.). (Illus.). 1978. 13.95 (ISBN 0-87714-043-X). Denlingers.

Your Bulldog. Robert J. Berndt. LC 75-41980. (Your Dog Bk.). (Illus.). 1976. 13.95 (ISBN 0-87714-036-7). Denlingers.

Your Burro is No Jackass: And over 100 Other Things No One Ever Told You. Jim Aylward. (Illus.). 64p. (gr. 3-7). pap. 2.25 (ISBN 0-380-63453-8, 63453-8, Camelot). Avon.

Your Business-America's Best Tax Shelter. Irving L. Blackman. LC 84-102848. (Special Report Ser.: No. 1). 51p. 1987. pap. 21.00 (ISBN 0-916181-00-6). Blackman Kallick Bartelstein.

Your Business & the Law. Adams. 1985. 45.00. Butterworth Legal Pubs.

Your Business Phone Guide. Alan H. Jordan. 201p. 1984. Three Ring Bdg. 100.00 (ISBN 0-916257-02-9). Special Project.

Your Business Phone Guide, Vol. 1. Alan H. Jordan. 201p. 120.00 (ISBN 0-318-04113-8). Add-Effect Assoc.

Your Business Records. 32p. 1982. 3.25x (97818-0). P-H.

Your Business, Your Son & You. Jack H. McQuaig. 192p. 20.00 (ISBN 0-686-62444-0). B Klein Pubns.

Your Cairn Terrier. Girard A. Jacobi. LC 75-41982. (Your Dog Bk.). (Illus.). 1976. 13.95 (ISBN 0-87714-039-1). Denlingers.

Your Can Have a Church Library: Start, Enhance, & Expand Your Religious Learning Center-A-Step-by-Step Guide for Church Leaders. Maryann J. Dotts. 48p. 1988. pap. 4.95. Abingdon.

Your Caprice Horoscopes, 1985: Aries. 96p. 1984. pap. 1.95 (ISBN 0-441-09460-0). Ace Bks.

Your Caprice Horoscopes, 1985: Cancer. 96p. 1984. pap. 1.95 (ISBN 0-441-09469-4). Ace Bks.

Your Caprice Horoscopes, 1985: Capricorn. 96p. 1984. pap. 1.95. Ace Bks.

Your Caprice Horoscopes, 1985: Gemini. 96p. 1984. pap. 1.95 (ISBN 0-441-09462-7). Ace Bks.

Your Caprice Horoscopes, 1985: Leo. 96p. 1984. pap. 1.95 (ISBN 0-441-09464-3). Ace Bks.

Your Caprice Horoscopes, 1985: Libra. 96p. 1984. pap. 1.95 (ISBN 0-441-09466-X). Ace Bks.

Your Caprice Horoscopes, 1985: Pisces. 96p. 1984. pap. 1.95 (ISBN 0-441-09471-6). Ace Bks.

Your Caprice Horoscopes, 1985: Sagittarius. 96p. 1984. pap. 1.95 (ISBN 0-441-09468-6). Ace Bks.

Your Caprice Horoscopes, 1985: Scorpio. 96p. 1984. pap. 1.95 (ISBN 0-441-09467-8). Ace Bks.

Your Caprice Horoscopes, 1985: Taurus. 96p. 1984. pap. 1.95 (ISBN 0-441-09461-9). Ace Bks.

Your Caprice Horoscopes, 1985: Virgo. 96p. 1984. pap. 1.95 (ISBN 0-441-09465-1). Ace Bks.

Your Career: A Contemporary Approach to Self-Development. 368p. 1975. scp 19.31 (ISBN 0-672-96833-9); scp tchr's manual 7.33 (ISBN 0-672-96869-X). Bobbs.

Your Career As a Medical Secretary Transcriber. Selma G. Berkeley & Barbara E. Jackson. LC 74-34233. (Wiley Biomedical-Health Publication Ser.). pap. 39.60 (ISBN 0-317-28655-2, 2055088). Bks Demand UMI.

Your Career: Choices, Chances, Changes. 4th ed. David C. Borchard et al. 256p. 1988. pap. text ed. 16.95 (ISBN 0-8403-4618-2, 40334301). Kendall-Hunt.

Your Career: How to Make It Happen. Julie G. Levitt. 1985. write for info. wkbk. (ISBN 0-538-07650-X, G65). SW Pub.

Your Career: How to Plan It, How to Manage It, How to Change It. Richard H. Buskirk. 192p. 1977. pap. 3.50 (ISBN 0-451-62559-5, Ment). NAL.

Your Career in Archaeology. George E. Stuart. 30p. 1986. pap. 1.50 (ISBN 0-932839-08-8). Soc Am Arch.

Your Career in Federal Civil Service. Flint O. DuPre. 288p. 1981. pap. 5.95 (ISBN 0-06-463529-5, EH529, B&N Bks). Har-Row.

Your Career in Health Care. Beverly J. Rambo & Diane Watson. 1976. text ed. 29.95 (ISBN 0-07-051166-7). McGraw.

Your Career in Marketing. 2nd ed. John A. Beaumont et al. 1976. text ed. 25.08 (ISBN 0-07-004245-4). McGraw.

Your Career in Nursing. Lila Anastas. (Illus.). 210p. 1984. pap. text ed. 10.95 (ISBN 0-88737-074-8, 41-1952). Natl League Nurse.

Your Career in the World of Work. Milton Berlye. LC 75-12236. 1975. pap. 19.96 scp (ISBN 0-672-97534-3). Bobbs.

Your Career in Travel & Tourism. Laurence Stevens. LC 85-62185. (Illus.). 190p. 1985. pap. text ed. 10.00 (ISBN 0-916032-25-6). Delmar.

Your Catholic Wedding: A Complete Plan-Book. Christopher Aridas. LC 81-43250. (Illus.). 192p. 1982. pap. 3.95 (ISBN 0-385-17731-3, Im). Doubleday.

Your Cat's First Year. Jane Burton & Kim Taylor. 1985. 12.95. S&S.

Your Check Is in the Mail. rev. ed. Bruce Goldman et al. 432p. 1984. pap. 7.95 (ISBN 0-446-37926-3). Warner Bks.

Your Chevrolet-Pontiac. Mort Schultz & Consumer Reports Books Editors. (Illus.). 432p. 1989. pap. 8.00 (ISBN 0-89043-221-X). Consumer Reports.

Your Chihuahua. Ruth L. Murray. LC 66-22308. (Your Dog Bk.). (Illus.). 1966. 8.95 (ISBN 0-87714-019-7); pap. 4.95 (ISBN 0-87714-020-0). Denlingers.

Your Child & Vitamin E. Wilfrid E. Shute. LC 79-88120. 1979. pap. 2.25 (ISBN 0-87983-202-9). Keats.

Your Child & X-Rays: A Parents' Guide to Radiation, X-Rays & Other Imaging Procedures. Avice M. O'Connell et al. (Illus.). 128p. (Orig.). 1988. pap. 8.95 (ISBN 0-936635-05-3). Lion Pr NY.

Your Child at Play: Birth to One Year. Marilyn Segal. LC 85-325. (Your Child at Play Ser.). (Illus.). 288p. 1985. 16.95 (ISBN 0-937858-50-1); pap. 9.95 (ISBN 0-937858-51-X). Newmarket.

Your Child at Play: One to Two Years. Marilyn Segal & Don Adcock. LC 84-14318. (Your Child at Play Ser.). (Illus.). 224p. 1985. 16.95 (ISBN 0-937858-52-8); pap. 9.95 (ISBN 0-937858-53-6). Newmarket.

Your Child at Play Starter Set, 3 vols. Marilyn Segal & Don Adcock. (Illus.). 720p. 1986. Set. slipcased 29.85 (ISBN 0-937858-77-3); 9.95 ea. Birth to One Year. One to Two Years. Two to Three Years. Newmarket.

Your Child at Play: Three to Five Years. Marilyn Segal & Don Adcock. LC 86-60294. (Your Child at Play Ser.: Vol. 4). (Illus.). 224p. 1986. 16.95 (ISBN 0-937858-72-2); pap. 9.95 (ISBN 0-937858-73-0). Newmarket.

Your Child at Play: Two to Three Years. Marilyn Segal & Don Adcock. LC 84-12598. (Your Child at Play Ser.). (Illus.). 208p. 1985. 16.95 (ISBN 0-937858-54-4); pap. 9.95 (ISBN 0-937858-55-2). Newmarket.

Your Child Can Be a Super Reader. Leonard Kusnetz. 144p. (gr. 2-10). 1985. pap. 5.95 (ISBN 0-317-60232-2). Liberty Pub.

Your Child Can Read Better: Handbook for Parents. Donna Hartmann & Arlyss Stump. LC 79-84490. (Orig.). 1980. pap. text ed. 19.95 (ISBN 0-918452-19-8); with instr's manual 0.00. Learning Pubns.

Your Child from One to Six. (DHEW Publication OHDS Ser.: No. 78-30026). (Illus.). 92p. 1978. pap. 2.00 (ISBN 0-318-21900-X, S/N 017-091-00219-3). USGPO.

Your Child from Six to Twelve: Saf Lerman Answers Questions about Those Middle Years. Saf Lerman. (Winston Family Handbook Ser.). 96p. (Orig.). 1985. pap. 9.95 (ISBN 0-86683-825-2, HarpR). Har-Row.

Your Child in School. Thomas Sobol & Harriet Sobol. 300p. (gr. k-2). 1987. 17.95 (ISBN 0-87795-867-X). Morrow.

Your Child in School: Kindergarten Through Second Grade. Tom Sobol & Harriet Sobol. 1988. 8.70 (ISBN 0-688-08247-5, Quill). Morrow.

Your Child in School: The Intermediate Years. Tom Sobol & Harriet Sobol. 336p. (gr. 3-5). 1987. 18.95 (ISBN 0-87795-924-2, Arbor Hse). Morrow.

Your Child in Sports: A Complete Guide. Lawrence Galton. 288p. 1980. pap. 7.95 (ISBN 0-531-09952-0). Watts.

Your Child Is a Person: A Psychological Approach to Parenthood Without Guilt. Stella Chess et al. 224p. 1977. pap. 5.95 (ISBN 0-14-004439-6). Penguin.

Your Child Is Bright. Bernard Green. 192p. 1982. 11.95 (ISBN 0-312-89771-5). St Martin.

Your Child Is Crying! Derwin J. Jeffries. 1970. 6.95x (ISBN 0-910742-03-0). Home & Sch.

Your Child Makes Sense: A Guidebook for Parents. Edith Buxbaum. 204p. (Orig.). 1961. text ed. 25.00x (ISBN 0-8236-7040-6). Intl Univs Pr.

Your Child: Pregnancy Through Preschool. Fitzhugh Dodson & Ann Alexander. (Illus.). 416p. 1986. pap. 14.95 (ISBN 0-671-45894-9, Fireside). S&S.

Your Children Should Know: Personal Safety Strategies for Parents to Teach Their Children. Flora Colao & Tamar Hosansky. LC 86-46215. (Illus.). 208p. 1987. pap. 6.95 (ISBN 0-06-097104-5, PL 7104, PL). Har-Row.

Your Children Should Know: Teach Your Children the Strategies That Will Keep Them Safe from Assault & Crime. Flora Colao & Tamar Hosansky. LC 83-5981. (Illus.). 192p. 1983. 16.95 (ISBN 0-672-52777-4). Bobbs.

Your Child's Birth: A Comprehensive Guide for Pregnancy, Birth, & Postpartum. Ed. by Sheila T. Woerth et al. (Avery's Childbirth Education Ser.). (Illus.). 96p. (Orig.). 1982. pap. 5.95 (ISBN 0-89529-182-7). Avery Pub.

Your Child's Career: A Guide to Home-Based Career Education. Garth L. Mangum et al. LC 77-22791. 1977. text ed. 6.95 (ISBN 0-913420-75-1). Olympus Pub Co.

Your Child's Confirmation: Reflections for Parents on the Sacrament of Christian Identity. Carol Luebering. 1987. pap. 1.95 (ISBN 0-317-57176-1). St Anthony Mess Pr.

Your Child's Dreams. Patricia Garfield. LC 84-91042. 356p. (Orig.). 1984. pap. 3.95 (ISBN 0-345-31047-0). Ballantine.

Your Child's Education: A School Guide for Parents. Mark Wolraich et al. (Illus.). 176p. 1984. pap. 19.75 (ISBN 0-398-04921-1). C C Thomas.

Your Child's Experience in Speech Correction. James D. Bryden. (Illus.). 1966. pap. text ed. 0.75 (ISBN 0-8134-0851-2, 851). Inter Print Pubs.

Your Child's First Communion: A Look at Your Dreams. Carol Luebering. 32p. (Orig.). 1984. pap. 1.35 (ISBN 0-86716-035-7). St Anthony Mess Pr.

Your Child's First Journey: A Guide to Prepared Birth from Pregnancy to Parenthood. 2nd ed. Ginny Brinkley et al. 1988. pap. 10.95 (ISBN 0-89529-372-2). Avery Pub.

Your Child's First Journey: A Guide to Prepared Birth from Pregnancy to Parenthood. Childbirth Education Association of Jacksonville, Fla., Inc. Staff & Ginny Brinkley. (Avery's Childbirth Education Ser.). (Illus.). 256p. (Orig.). 1982. pap. 9.95 (ISBN 0-89529-150-9). Avery Pub.

Your Child's First Year. Parents Magazine Editors. 176p. (Orig.). 1986. pap. 5.95 (ISBN 0-345-32171-5). Ballantine.

Your Child's Growing Mind: A Guide to Learning & Brain Development from Birth to Adolescence. Jane M. Healey. 1989. pap. 7.95 (ISBN 0-385-23150-4). Doubleday.

Your Child's Growing Mind: A Parent's Guide to Learning from Birth to Adolescence. Jane M. Healy. LC 86-2058. 336p. 1987. pap. 17.95 (ISBN 0-385-23149-0). Doubleday.

Your Child's Health: A Pediatric Guide for Parents. Barton D. Schmitt. LC 87-47687. 304p. (Orig.). 1987. pap. 12.95 (ISBN 0-553-34400-5). Bantam.

Your Child's Mind: Making the Most of Public Schools. Helen P. Barnette. LC 83-26109. (Potentials: Guides for Productive Living Ser.: Vol. 2). 112p. (Orig.). 1984. pap. 7.95 (ISBN 0-664-24519-6). Westminster John Knox.

Your Child's Mind: The Complete Book of Infant & Child Mental Health Care. Anne Roiphe & Herman Roiphe. 480p. 1985. 19.95 (ISBN 0-312-89783-9, Pub. by Marek). St Martin.

Your Child's Mind: The Complete Guide to Infant & Child Emotional Well-Being. Herman Roiphe & Anne Roiphe. 448p. 1986. pap. 10.95 (ISBN 0-312-89784-7). St Martin.

Your Child's Numerology. Robin Stein. 1987. pap. 3.50 (ISBN 0-449-13288-9, GM). Fawcett.

Your Child's School Records: Questions & Answers about a Set of Rights for Parents & Students. Children's Defense Fund Staff. 20p. (Orig.). 1986. pap. 2.75 (ISBN 0-938008-54-4). Children's Defense.

Your Child's Self-Esteem: The Key to His Life. Dorothy C. Briggs. LC 70-121948. 360p. 1975. pap. 9.95 (ISBN 0-385-04020-2, Dolp). Doubleday.

Your Child's Speech & Language. Brooks et al. 52p. 1978. pap. text ed. 9.00x (ISBN 0-89079-039-6, 1070). Pro Ed.

Your Child's Teachable Moments: Making the Most Of. Wanda B. Pelfrey. 1988. pap. 5.95 (ISBN 0-8024-5206-X). Moody.

Your Child's Teeth: A Parent's Guide to Making & Keeping Them Perfect. Stephen J. Moss. 1977. 8.95 (ISBN 0-395-25344-6); pap. 7.95 (ISBN 0-395-27592-X). HM.

Your Child's Vision: A Parent's Guide to Seeing, Growing, & Developing. Richard S. Kavner. LC 85-1859. (Illus.). 250p. 1985. 16.95 (ISBN 0-317-38194-6, Fireside). S&S.

Your Child's Vision: The Complete Guide to Growth & Development. Richard S. Kavner. LC 85-1859. (Illus.). 320p. 1985. pap. 9.95 (ISBN 0-671-46176-1, Fireside); pap. text ed. 9.95 (ISBN 0-671-55449-2, Fireside). S&S.

Your Chinese Horoscope for Nineteen Eighty-Nine. Neil Somerville. (Illus.). 144p. (Orig.). 1988. pap. 4.99 (ISBN 0-85030-649-3, Pub. by Aquarian Pr England). Sterling.

Your Chinese Roots. Thomas Tsu-wee Tan. (Illus.). 262p. 1987. pap. 9.95 (ISBN 0-89346-285-3). Heian Intl.

Your Choice: A Young Woman's Guide to Making Decisions about Unmarried Pregnancy. Caryl Hansen. 176p. (Orig.). 1980. pap. 2.25 (ISBN 0-380-75853-9, Flare). Avon.

Your Choice: Allowing Your Emotions to Empower You. Nick Berar & Judy Huston. (Orig.). 1985. wkbk 50.00 (ISBN 0-934685-00-2). Choice Pubns.

Your Choice, Snoopy. Charles M. Schulz. (Peanuts Ser.). 1987. pap. 2.25 (ISBN 0-317-57102-8, Juniper). Fawcett.

Your Christian Wedding. Elizabeth Swadley. LC 66-15149. 1966. 8.95 (ISBN 0-8054-7902-3). Broadman.

Your Church & You: History & Images of Catholicism. Michael Pennock. LC 83-70053. (High School Religion Text Program Ser.). (Illus., Orig.). (YA) (gr. 9-12). 1983. pap. text ed. 5.50 student text, 288p (ISBN 0-87793-268-9); tchr's. manual, 120p 3.50 (ISBN 0-87793-269-7). Ave Maria.

Your Church Can Be Healthy. C. Peter Wagner. LC 79-974. (Creative Leadership Ser.). 1979. pap. 7.95 (ISBN 0-687-46870-1). Abingdon.

Your Church Can Grow. rev. ed. C. Peter Wagner. LC 84-8314. 1984. pap. 7.95 (ISBN 0-8307-0978-9, 5418284). Regal.

Your Church Has a Fantastic Future! A Possibility Thinker's Guide to a Successful Church. rev. ed. Robert H. Schuller. LC 86-11906. (Illus.). 336p. 1986. 14.95 (ISBN 0-8307-1180-5, 5111659). Regal.

Your Church Has Personality. Kent R. Hunter. Ed. by Lyle E. Schaller. (Creative Leadership Ser.). 129p. (Orig.). 1985. pap. 7.95 (ISBN 0-687-46875-2). Abingdon.

Your Church's Ministry of Prayer. Robert V. Dodd. 1981. 3.00 (ISBN 0-89536-476-X, 2501). CSS of Ohio.

Your City. Edward L. Thorndike. LC 75-22842. (America in Two Centuries Ser). 1976. Repr. of 1939 ed. 16.00x (ISBN 0-405-07713-0). Ayer Co Pubs.

Your City's 1040: Federal Tax Reform & Municipalities. 110p. 1987. 15.00 (ISBN 0-933729-17-0). Natl League Cities.

Your Classroom Corporation. Nina Crosby. 51p. (Orig.). 1979. pap. text ed. 6.95 (ISBN 0-914634-72-0, 7910). DOK Pubs.

Your Code Name Is Jonah. Edward Packard. (Choose Your Own Adventure Ser.). 114p. (gr. 2-7). 1987. Repr. of 1979 ed. 8.95 (ISBN 0-942545-15-X); lib. bdg. 9.95 (ISBN 0-942545-20-6). Grey Castle.

Your College Application. Scott Gelband et al. 132p. 1986. pap. 9.95 (ISBN 0-87447-247-4). College Bd.

Your Colon - Learn about It for a Better Life. John E. Cogan. 1988. 10.95 (ISBN 0-533-07817-2). Vantage.

Your Colon, Its Character, Care & Therapy. Stan Malstrom. (Tree of Knowledge Ser.: No. 3). Date not set. pap. 2.95 (ISBN 0-913923-36-2). Woodland UT.

Your Colors at Home: Decorating Made Easy with Your Seasonal Colors. Lauren Smith & Rose B. Gilbert. (Illus.). 200p. 1986. 18.95 (ISBN 0-87491-748-4); pap. 11.95 (ISBN 0-87491-822-7). Acropolis.

Your Commodore 128: A Guide to the Commodore 128 Computer. John Heilborn. (Illus.). 480p. (Orig.). 1986. pap. text ed. 16.95 (ISBN 0-07-881227-5). Osborne-McGraw.

Your Commodore 64: A Guide to the Commodore 64 Computer. John Heilborn & Ran Talbott. 464p. (Orig.). 1984. pap. text ed. 16.95 (ISBN 0-07-047853-8). Osborne-McGraw.

Your Complete Guide to Estate Planning. rev. ed. P. J. Callahan. LC 70-150939. (Legal Almanac Giant: No. 1). 399p. 1971. 8.50 (ISBN 0-379-10976-X). Oceana.

Your Complete Wedding Planner. Marjabelle Y. Stewart. (Illus.). 1980. gift edition 13.95 (ISBN 0-679-50744-2). McKay.

Your Completeness in Christ. John MacArthur, Jr. (John MacArthur's Bible Studies). 1985. pap. 4.95 (ISBN 0-8024-5114-4). Moody.

Your Computer Can Kill You. Dick Whitson. 1984. looseleaf 74.95 (ISBN 0-917194-15-2). Prog Studies.

Your Computer Can Kill You: Startling Report. Dick Whitson. 1984. 9.95 (ISBN 0-917194-17-9). Prog Studies.

Your Condo-Co-Op: Tips for Living Comfortably in a Small Space. Jean E. Laird. 1983. pap. write for info. (ISBN 0-8289-0515-0). Greene.

Your Conscience As Your Guide. Peter Toon. LC 83-62870. 102p. (Orig.). 1984. pap. 5.95 (ISBN 0-8192-1339-X). Morehouse.

Your Creative Power. Alex F. Osborn. (Lib. Rep. Ed.). 1972. 25.00x (ISBN 0-684-15314-9, ScribT). Scribner.

Your Creative Self. 2nd ed. Tom Johnson. 1987. pap. 3.25 (ISBN 0-941992-15-2). Los Arboles Pub.

Your Creative Workshop. Rose Oster. 1977. pap. 0.75 (ISBN 0-87516-236-3). DeVorss.

Your Crocodile Is Ready. Wayne Haas. 1984. 6.25 (ISBN 0-89536-620-7, 4888). CSS of Ohio.

Your Dachshund. Herman G. Cox. LC 66-22305. (Your Dog Bk.). (Illus.). 1966. 8.95 (ISBN 0-87714-021-9); pap. 4.95 (ISBN 0-87714-022-7). Denlingers.

Your Daily Numerology: A Lifetime Guide for Success. Sandra K. Stein & Carol A. Schuler. LC 88-4279. 223p. 1988. lib. bdg. 24.95x (ISBN 0-8095-6125-5). Borgo Pr.

Your Daily Numerology: A Lifetime Guide for Success. Sandra K. Stein & Carol A. Schuler. 160p. (Orig.). 1987. pap. 9.95 (ISBN 0-87877-125-5). Newcastle Pub.

Your Daughters Shall Prophesy: Feminist Alternatives in Theological Education. Cornwall Collective Staff. LC 80-14891. 155p. 1980. pap. 6.95 (ISBN 0-8298-0404-8). Pilgrim NY.

Your Day & Night. Walter Russell. (Divine Iliad Ser.). 1946. pap. 1.50. U Sci & Philos.

Your Day in Court. rev. ed. Joseph M. Sindell. 1979. pap. 1.10 (ISBN 0-88450-050-0, 6112). Lawyers & Judges.

Your Days Are Numbered. 21st ed. Florence Campbell. 246p. 1980. pap. 7.95 (ISBN 0-87516-422-6). DeVorss.

Your Deaf Child: A Guide for Parents. Helmer R. Myklebust. (Illus.). 150p. 1979. spiral bdg. 17.50x (ISBN 0-398-03127-4). C C Thomas.

Your DEC Rainbow 100: Use, Applications & BASIC. Eric Kiebler. 1984. pap. text ed. 18.95 (ISBN 0-03-064178-0). HR&W.

Your Desert & Mine. Nina P. Shumway. 1979. 12.95 (ISBN 0-88280-072-8). ETC Pubns.

Your Desert & Mine. Nina P. Shumway. (Illus.). 336p. 1979. 10.00 (ISBN 0-937794-12-0). Nature Trails.

Your Desire or God's Will? Jerry O. Nwonye. 64p. 1987. 7.75 (ISBN 0-8062-3162-9). Carlton.

Your Diabetic Child. Felicia M. Saunders. 176p. (Orig.). 1986. pap. 3.95 (ISBN 0-553-25948-2). Bantam.

Your Diamond Dreams Cut Open My Arteries. Else Lasker-Schuler. Tr. by Robert P. Newton. LC 82-2656. (Studies in the Germanic Languages & Literatures: No. 100). ix, 317p. 1983. 22.50x (ISBN 0-8078-8100-7). U of NC Pr.

Your Dinner's Poured Out. Paddy Crosbie. (Illus.). 224p. 1982. (Pub. by O'Brien Pr Ireland); pap. 8.95 (ISBN 0-86278-032-2). Irish Bks Media.

Your Doctor, My Doctor. Joan Drescher. 32p. (gr. 1-3). 1987. 10.95 (ISBN 0-8027-6668-4); PLB 11.85 (ISBN 0-8027-6669-2). Walker & Co.

Your Dog & Astrology. (Illus.). 1976. pap. 1.00 (ISBN 0-685-77475-9). Jay Pub.

Your Dog & the Law. Murray Loring. 252p. (Orig.). 1983. pap. 9.98 (ISBN 0-931866-13-8). Alpine Pubns.

Your Dog: Companion & Helper. Milo D. Pearsall & Margaret E. Pearsall. LC 80-14115. (Illus.). 160p. 1980. 9.98 (ISBN 0-931866-07-3). Alpine Pubns.

Your Dog, His Health & Happiness: The Breeder's & Pet Owners Guide to Better Dog Care. Louis D. Vine. LC 72-88607. 446p. 1973. pap. 8.95 (ISBN 0-668-02876-9). Arco.

Your Dog: Its Development, Behaviour & Training. John Rogerson. (Illus.). 256p. 1988. 29.95 (ISBN 0-09-173473-8, Pub. by Century Hutchinson). David & Charles.

Your Dreams & What They Mean. Nerys Dee. pap. 7.99 (ISBN 0-85030-353-2, Pub. by Aquarian Pr England). Sterling.

Your Dreams & What They Mean: How to Understand the Secret Language of Sleep. Nerys Dee. LC 86-18797. 176p. 1986. lib. bdg. 19.95x (ISBN 0-8095-7002-5). Borgo Pr.

Your Dreams: God's Neglected Gift. Herman Riffel. pap. 2.95 (ISBN 0-345-33205-9). Ballantine.

Your Duties & Responsibilities. 2nd ed. Richard C. Ireland. LC 75-1403. (Professional Waitress Ser.). 75p. 1975. pap. text ed. 5.75 (ISBN 0-89103-009-3). Ireland Educ.

Your Education: Supplemental & Summer Study Workbooks. Fasenmyer et al. (gr. k-6). 1970. pap. text ed. 6.95 ea. Beatty.

Your Eight Year Old. Louise B. Ames & Carol C. Haber. 1989. 15.95 (ISBN 0-440-50116-4). Delacorte.

Your Emotional Life & What You Can Do about It. James Drane. 204p. 1984. 9.95 (ISBN 0-88347-157-4). Thomas More.

Your Employee Assistance Program: Check It Out for Yourself. Paula J. King. 16p. (Orig.). 1980. 1.50 (ISBN 0-89486-092-5, 1938B). Hazelden.

Your Encounter with Life, Death & Immortality. Ruth E. Norman. (Illus.). 1978. pap. 2.00 (ISBN 0-932642-43-8). Unarius Pubns.

Your English Springer Spaniel. Reed. F. Hankwitz. LC 72-80629. (Your Dog Bk.). (Illus.). 160p. 1973. 13.95 (ISBN 0-87714-007-3). Denlingers.

Your Environment & You: Understanding Ecology. E. H. Blaustein et al. 1978. write for info. (ISBN 0-379-00803-3). Oceana.

Your Environment & You: Understanding the Pollution Problem, Level 2. E. H. Blaustein et al. LC 74-5230. 1974. 8.75x (ISBN 0-379-00802-5). Oceana.

Your Erroneous Zones. Wayne W. Dyer. 1977. pap. 4.50 (ISBN 0-380-01669-9, 60088-9). Avon.

Your Eyes. 2nd ed. Thomas Chalkley. (Illus.). 144p. 1982. pap. 10.75x (ISBN 0-398-04629-8). C C Thomas.

Your Eyes. Joan Iveson-Iveson. (All about You Ser.). (Illus.). (gr. k-6). 1986. lib. bdg. 9.90 (ISBN 0-531-18014-X, Pub. by Bookwright Pr). Watts.

Your Eyes & You. (Eye Health & Safety Curriculum Guide Ser.). (Illus.). 37p. (gr. k-3). 1980. pap. 4.00 (ISBN 0-9612370-3-1). Minn Soc Prev Blind.

Your Eyes Hear for You. Irving S. Marcus. 80p. (Orig.). 1985. pap. 10.00 (ISBN 0-935473-00-9). SHHH.

Your Eyes Will Be Opened: A Study of the Greek (Ethiopic) Apocalypse of Peter. Dennis D. Buchholz. LC 86-27900. (SBL Dissertation Ser.). 500p. 1987. 19.95 (ISBN 1-55540-024-8, 06-01-97); pap. 12.95 (ISBN 1-55540-025-6). Scholars Pr GA.

Your Fabulous Volunteers: A History of the Washington Emergency Squad & Emergency Services in Warren County. rev. ed. Richard E. Harpster. Ed. by Larry K. Smith. (Illus.). 365p. 1985. 14.95 (ISBN 0-9604020-1-2). Wash Emerg Squad.

Your Face. Jack Winder. Ed. by Alton Jordan. (I Can Read Underwater Bks.). (Illus.). (gr. k-3). 1974. PLB 3.95 (ISBN 0-89868-008-5, Read Res); pap. text ed. 1.75 (ISBN 0-89868-041-7). ARO Pub.

Your Face Never Lies: An Introduction to Oriental Diagnosis. Michio Kushi. (Macrobiotic Home Library). 96p. 1983. pap. 5.95 (ISBN 0-89529-214-9). Avery Pub.

Your Faith: A Popular Presentation of Catholic Belief. LC 81-85557. (Redemptorist Pastoral Publication Ser.). 64p. 1982. pap. 3.95 (ISBN 0-89243-154-7). Liguori Pubns.

Your Faith Account. Dana Holmes. 48p. (Orig.). 1983. pap. 0.95 (ISBN 0-88144-019-1, CPS/019). Christian Pub.

Your Faith & You: A Synthesis of Catholic Belief. rev. ed. Michael Pennock. LC 86-70575. (High School Religion Text Program Ser.). (Illus.). 320p. 1986. pap. text ed. 6.95 student text, 312p (ISBN 0-87793-334-0); tchr's. manual, 224p 9.95 (ISBN 0-87793-335-9). Ave Maria.

Your Faith Can Heal You. Norvel Hayes. 80p. 1983. pap. 2.50 (ISBN 0-89274-273-9). Harrison Hse.

Your Faith Is Growing! N. R. Day. 51p. (Orig.). 1981. pap. 5.95 (ISBN 0-940754-10-X). Ed Ministries.

Your Faith Is Your Fortune. Neville. pap. 5.50 (ISBN 0-87516-078-6). DeVorss.

Your Faith: Leader's Guide. Louis J. Bamonte. 1978. tchr's ed 2.95 (ISBN 0-89243-085-0). Liguori Pubns.

Your Faith on Trial. Wallis C. Metts. 180p. (Orig.). 1979. pap. 4.20 (ISBN 0-89084-112-8). Bob Jones Univ Pr.

Your Family. rev. & expanded ed. John MacArthur, Jr. (Moody Press Electives Ser.). 1983. pap. 3.95 (ISBN 0-8024-0257-7). Moody.

Your Family: A Love & Maintenance Manual for People with Parents & Other Relatives. Jim Conway et al. LC 81-20809. 120p. (Orig.). 1982. pap. 3.95 (ISBN 0-87784-370-8). Inter-Varsity.

Your Family & Its Money. Helen M. Thal. (gr. 9-12). 1973. text ed. 14.64 (ISBN 0-395-14225-3). HM.

Your Family & You. (Benziger Family Life Program Ser.). (gr. 2). 1978. 2.00 (ISBN 0-02-651550-4); tchrs. ed. 4.00 (ISBN 0-02-651560-1); family handbook 1.00 (ISBN 0-02-651590-3). Benziger Pub Co.

Your Family Finances: Record for Expense & Savings. Dorothy Simmons & Herbert B. Howell. 1950. pap. 1.29x (ISBN 0-8138-1830-3). Iowa St U Pr.

Your Family Heritage: A Guide to Preserving Family History. Ronald D. Ross. LC 88-60501. 144p. 1988. 19.95 (ISBN 0-9620144-0-0). R D Ross.

Your Family History: A Handbook for Research & Writing. David Kyvig & Myron A. Marty. LC 77-86030. 1978. pap. text ed. 5.95x (ISBN 0-88295-774-0). Harlan Davidson.

Your Family History: How to Use Oral History Family Archives, & Public Documents to Discover Your Heritage. Allan J. Lichtman. LC 77-76582. 1978. pap. 5.95 (ISBN 0-394-72332-5, Vin). Random.

Your Family: Leader's Guide. (Electives Ser.). 1983. pap. 2.50 (ISBN 0-8024-0307-7). Moody.

Your Family, My Family. Joan Drescher. (Illus.). 32p. (gr. 2-5). 1980. PLB 8.85 (ISBN 0-8027-6383-9). Walker & Co.

Your Family Records. 2nd ed. Carol Pladsen & Denis Clifford. LC 84-60121. 215p. 1986. pap. 14.95 (ISBN 0-87337-036-8). Nolo Pr.

Your Family Tree. Garland E. Hopkins. 1949. pap. 2.50 (ISBN 0-87517-035-8). Dietz.

Your Family Tree, Being a Glance at Scientific Aspects of Genealogy. David S. Jordan & Sarah L. Kimball. LC 67-28625. 346p. 1979. Repr. of 1929 ed. 17.50 (ISBN 0-8063-0199-6). Genealog Pub.

Your Family Tree Connection. Chris M. Reading & Ross S. Meillon. Orig. Title: Relatively Speaking. (Illus.). 288p. (Orig.). 1988. pap. 9.95 (ISBN 0-87983-483-8). Keats.

Your Father. James L. Weil. 1973. pap. 8.00 (ISBN 0-685-36873-4). Elizabeth Pr.

Your Father Loves You: Daily Insights for Knowing God. James I. Packer. Ed. & compiled by Jean Watson. 392p. 1986. pap. 9.95 (ISBN 0-87788-975-9). Shaw Pubs.

Your Favorite Fairy Tale. Bridget Tomlinson. LC 85-23394. (Bright Idea Bks.). (Illus.). 48p. (gr. 2-3). 1986. PLB 10.95 (ISBN 1-55532-022-8). Stevens Inc.

Your Feet Are Killing Me! John D. Vose. 1985. 18.95x (ISBN 0-901976-46-6, Pub. by United Writers Pubns England). State Mutual Bk.

Your Fertile Hours. Emily Faugno. LC 85-71462. 248p. 1986. 16.95 (ISBN 0-86690-295-3, 2346-01). Am Fed Astrologers.

Your Fertility Signals: How to Read Them to Achieve or Avoid Pregnancy. Merryl Winstein. (Illus.). 184p. (Orig.). 1987. 14.95 (ISBN 0-9619401-1-5); pap. 9.95 (ISBN 0-9619401-0-7). Smooth Stone Pr.
Your Film Acting Career: How to Break into the Movies & TV & Survive in Hollywood. M. K. Lewis & Rosemary Lewis. (Illus.). 1983. o. p. 4.98 (ISBN 0-517-54911-5); pap. 8.95 (ISBN 0-517-54912-3). Crown.
Your Film & the Lab. 2nd ed. L. Bernard Happe. (Media Manuals Ser.). (Illus.). 208p. 1983. pap. 18.95 (ISBN 0-240-51212-X). Focal Pr.
Your Final PCS: Transition from Military to Civilian Life. Jason Leigh. (Illus.). 125p. (Orig.). 1986. pap. cancelled (ISBN 0-934145-87-3). Airborne Pr.
Your Finances in Changing Times. Larry Burkett. (Christian Financial Concepts Ser.). 1982. pap. 6.95 (ISBN 0-8024-2548-8). Moody.
Your Financial Security: Effective Strategies for Every Stage of life. Sylvia Porter. Ed. by Jennifer Williams. LC 87-34988. (Illus.). 256p. 1988. 16.95 (ISBN 0-688-08050-2). Morrow.
Your First Adventure: Little Fox & the Birthday Party, No. 11. Marcia Leonard. 24p. (Orig.). 1987. pap. 2.50 (ISBN 0-553-15502-4). Bantam.
Your First Adventure: Little Goat's Big Brother, No. 12. Marcia Leonard. 24p. (Orig.). 1987. pap. 2.50 (ISBN 0-553-15503-2). Bantam.
Your First Adventure: Little Kitten Sleeps Over, No. 9. Adapted by Marcia Leonard. 32p. (Orig.). 1987. pap. 2.50 (ISBN 0-553-15472-9). Bantam.
Your First Adventure: Little Puppy's Rainy Day, No. 10. Marcia Leonard. 32p. (Orig.). 1987. pap. 2.50 (ISBN 0-553-15473-7). Bantam.
Your First BASIC Program. Rodnay Zaks. LC 83-60488. (Illus.). 182p. 1983. pap. 14.95 (ISBN 0-89588-092-X). SYBEX.
Your First Budgie. Illus. by E. Videla. (Illus.). 32p. 1983. 3.95 (ISBN 0-87666-868-6, ST-003). TFH Pubns.
Your First Business Computer. Peter Luedtke & Rainer Luedtke. 224p. 1983. pap. 16.00 (ISBN 0-932376-27-4, EY-00008-DP). Digital Pr.
Your First Car. George Fremon & Suzanne Fremon. LC 81-80572. (Illus.). 176p. 1981. pap. 5.95 (ISBN 0-89709-024-1). Liberty Pub.
Your First Goldfish. E. Videla. (Illus.). 32p. 1982. 3.95 (ISBN 0-87666-574-1, ST-002). TFH Pubns.
Your First Hamster. Illus. by Juan-Carlos Villarroel. (Show & Tell Ser.). (Illus.). 32p. (gr. 2-4). 1983. 3.95 (ISBN 0-87666-939-9, ST-004). TFH Pubns.
Your First Horse. George C. Saunders. pap. 5.00 (ISBN 0-87980-251-0). Wilshire.
Your First Microprocessor: Organizing, Construction, Debugging. James W. Coffron. LC 83-62032. (Illus.). 352p. 1984. pap. 17.95 (ISBN 0-13-978446-2). P-H.
Your First Personal Computer: How to Buy & Use It. C. Buffington. 256p. 1983. pap. text ed. 8.95 (ISBN 0-07-008832-2, BYTE Bks). McGraw.
Your First Pet: & How to Take Care of It. Carla Stevens. LC 74-2267. (Ready-to-Read Ser.). 128p. (gr. 1-4). 1974. 8.95 (ISBN 0-02-788200-4). Macmillan.
Your First Point to Point Horse. Joe Hartigan. pap. 3.50 (ISBN 0-85131-212-8, NL51, Pub. by J A Allen U K). S R Smith Sporting Bks.
Your First Puppy. Illus. by O. Vega & M. Igor. (Show & Tell Ser.). (Illus.). 32p. (gr. 2-4). 1983. 3.95 (ISBN 0-87666-558-X, ST-005). TFH Pubns.
Your First Resume. Ronald W. Fry. 150p. (Orig.). 1988. pap. 9.95 (ISBN 0-934829-25-X). Career Pr Inc.
Your First Romance: Twenty Do-It-Yourself Novels You Can Complete & Sell. Jerry Biederman & Tom Silberkleit. 176p. 1984. pap. 8.95 (ISBN 0-312-89790-1). St Martin.
Your First Trip to Europe: Where, What & How, Vol. 1. Jordan Levenson. LC 84-82461. 110p. 1985. pap. 18.50x (ISBN 0-914442-11-2). Levenson Pr.
Your First Year of Marriage. Tom McGinnis. pap. 3.00 (ISBN 0-87980-256-1). Wilshire.
Your Fit Pregnancy. Date not set. pap. 8.95 (ISBN 0-02-499940-7). Anderson World.
Your Five Senses. Ray Broekel. LC 84-7603. (New True Bks.). (Illus.). 48p. (gr. k-4). 1984. lib. bdg. 12.60 (ISBN 0-516-01932-5); pap. 3.95 (ISBN 0-516-41932-3). Childrens.
Your Five Year Old: Sunny & Serene. Louise B. Ames & Frances L. Ilg. 1981. pap. 7.95 (ISBN 0-385-29145-0, Delta). Dell.
Your Flag. (Illus.). 64p. (gr. 6-12). 1986. pap. 3.00x (ISBN 0-8395-3188-5, 3188). BSA.
Your Florida Divorce: Working with the Law & Your Lawyer. Tann H. Hunt. 111p. (Orig.). 1985. pap. 4.95 (ISBN 0-931769-12-4). Equity.
Your Florida Garden. rev. & abridged ed. John V. Watkins & Herbert S. Wolfe. LC 68-23403. 368p. 1987. pap. 9.95 (ISBN 0-8130-0862-X). U Presses Fla.
Your Food-Allergic Child: A Parent's Guide. Janet E. Meizel. (Illus.). 200p. (Orig.). pap. 9.95 (ISBN 0-938179-16-0). Mills Sanderson.
Your Foot's on My Feet: And Other Tricky Nouns. Marvin Terban. LC 85-19561. (gr. 2-5). 1986. 11.95 (ISBN 0-89919-411-7, Pub. by Clarion); pap. 4.95 (ISBN 0-89919-413-3). Ticknor & Fields.
Your Ford. Schultz. 416p. 1988. pap. 8.00 (ISBN 0-89043-214-7). Consumer Reports.
Your Former Friend, Matthew. Louann Gaeddart. 80p. 1985. pap. 2.25 (ISBN 0-553-15345-5, Skylark). Bantam.
Your Former Friend, Matthew. LouAnn Gaeddert. (Illus.). 80p. (gr. 3-6). 1984. 11.95 (ISBN 0-525-44086-0). Dutton.
Your Fortune in Foreclosures: Fortune Businesses. Bruce Erb. 240p. 1987. 16.95 (ISBN 0-89586-572-6). Price Stern.
Your Fortune in the Microcomputer Business: Getting Started, Vol. I. Victor Wild. (Illus.). 304p. 1982. pap. 15.95 (ISBN 0-938444-04-2). Wildfire Pub.
Your Fortune in the Microcomputer Business: Growth, Survival, Success, Vol. II. Victor Wild. (Illus.). 256p. 1982. pap. 15.95 (ISBN 0-938444-05-0). Wildfire Pub.
Your Fortune in Your Name; or Kabalistic Astrology. Sepharial. LC 81-21658. 96p. 1981. Repr. of 1981 ed. lib. bdg. 19.95x (ISBN 0-89370-656-6). Borgo Pr.
Your Four Great Emotions. David Seabury. 108p. 1969. pap. 4.95 (ISBN 0-911336-22-2). Sci of Mind.
Your Four Year Old: Wild & Wonderful. Louise B. Ames & Frances L. Ilg. 1980. pap. 7.95 (ISBN 0-385-29143-4, Delta). Dell.
Your Fourteen Day Total Shape-up Plan. Annette Capone. 128p. (gr. 7 up). 1984. pap. 1.95 (ISBN 0-590-30913-7, Wildfire). Scholastic Inc.
Your Fragile Legacy: Cultural & Fossil Resources on the Public Lands. (Illus.). 24p. 1986. pap. 1.50 (ISBN 0-318-21596-9, S/N 024-011-00130-1). USGPO.
Your Freedom to Be. Jack H. Holland. LC 77-92780. 1977. pap. 4.50 deluxe (ISBN 0-87852-002-3). Inst Human Growth.
Your Freedom to Be Whole. Henlee Barnette. LC 84-2381. (Potentials: Guides to Productive Living Ser.: Vol. 7). 118p. 1984. pap. 7.95 (ISBN 0-664-24526-9). Westminster John Knox.
Your Friend the Holy Spirit. Morris Venden. (Anchor Ser.). 95p. (Orig.). 1987. pap. 6.95 (ISBN 0-8163-0682-6). Pacific Pr Pub Assn.
Your Friends & Mine. Kenny Rogers. 1987. 40.00 (ISBN 0-316-75421-8). Little.
Your Friends from Sesame Street. Sesame Street. (Cloth Bks). (Illus.). (ps). 1979. 2.95 (ISBN 0-394-84137-9, BYR). Random.
Your Friendship Potential. Ed. by Bill R. Swetmon & Linda Swetmon. 112p. (Orig.). Date not set. pap. 5.95 (ISBN 0-89225-319-3). Gospel Advocate.
Your Future: A Guide for the Handicapped Teenager. rev. ed. S. Norman Feingold & Norma Miller. (gr. 7-12). 1986. 9.97 (ISBN 0-8239-0424-5). Rosen Group.
Your Future As a Lawyer. rev. ed. Charles Z. Cohen. (gr. 7-12). 1983. 9.97. Rosen Group.
Your Future As a Secretary. Rev. ed. Nell B. Noyes. LC 73-88829. (Careers in Depth Ser.). (Illus.). (gr. 7 up). 1979. PLB 10.97 (ISBN 0-8239-0483-0). Rosen Group.
Your Future As a Shorthand Reporter. Edward Van Allen. LC 69-13005. (Careers in Depth Ser.). (gr. 7 up). 1977. PLB 9.97 (ISBN 0-8239-0401-6). Rosen Group.
Your Future As a Working Woman. Rev. ed. Gloria S. Pearlstein. (Careers in Depth Ser.). (Illus.). 144p. (gr. 7-12). 1981. PLB 9.97 (ISBN 0-8239-0307-9). Rosen Group.
Your Future As a Writer. Rick Mitz. (Careers in Depth Ser.). (Illus.). 128p. 1981. lib. bdg. 9.97 (ISBN 0-8239-0516-0). Rosen Group.
Your Future As an Airline Steward-Stewardess. Lyman K. Randall. 1979. 9.97. Rosen Group.
Your Future Career in the American Government. Rick Mitz. (gr. 7-12). 1978. PLB 9.97 (ISBN 0-8239-0452-0). Rosen Group.
Your Future: George Sweeting on Bible Prophecy. George Sweeting. 1984. 6.95 (ISBN 0-8024-0404-9). Moody.
Your Future Health Care. Tinsley R. Harrison. LC 73-13222. 164p. 1974. 10.50 (ISBN 0-87527-132-4). Green.
Your Future in a Dental Hygiene Career. 2nd rev. ed. Barbara E. Paige. LC 69-14464. (Careers in Depth Ser.). (Illus.). (gr. 9 up). 1980. PLB 9.97 (ISBN 0-8239-0434-2). Rosen Group.
Your Future in a Mental Health Career. Fenton Keyes. (Careers in Depth Ser.). (Illus.). 180p. (gr. 7-12). 1981. PLB 9.97 (ISBN 0-8239-0362-1). Rosen Group.
Your Future in a Public Relations Career. rev. ed. Edward L. Bernays. (Careers in Depth Ser.). 1983. PLB 9.97 (ISBN 0-8239-0443-1). Rosen Group.
Your Future in Agribusiness. Chester Hutchison. (Careers in Depth Ser.). (Illus.). (gr. 7-12). 1977. PLB 9.97 (ISBN 0-8239-0394-X). Rosen Group.
Your Future in Architecture. Richard Roth. LC 60-11116. (Careers in Depth Ser.). (gr. 7-12). 1979. PLB 9.97. Rosen Group.
Your Future in Art. The Design Schools. (Illus.). 32p. (gr. 10-12). 1981. pap. text ed. 1.25 (ISBN 0-9607016-0-5). Design Schools.
Your Future in Aviation Careers in the Air. rev. ed. Kimball Scribner. (Careers in Depth Ser.). (Illus.). (gr. 7-12). 1982. PLB 9.97 (ISBN 0-8239-0490-3). Rosen Group.
Your Future in Aviation Careers on the Ground. rev. ed. Kimball Scribner. (Careers in Depth Ser.). (Illus.). (gr. 7-12). 1983. PLB 9.97 (ISBN 0-8239-0491-1). Rosen Group.
Your Future in Big Business. Charles Heath. (Careers in Depth Ser.). 120p. 1980. lib. bdg. 9.97 (ISBN 0-8239-0498-9). Rosen Group.
Your Future in Broadcasting. Rev. ed. John R. Rider. LC 70-146047. (Careers in Depth Ser.). (Illus.). (gr. 7 up). 1979. PLB 9.97 (ISBN 0-8239-0454-7). Rosen Group.
Your Future in Credit Management. rev. ed. William F. Bryan. (Careers in Depth Ser.). 1984. lib. bdg. 9.97 (ISBN 0-8239-0514-4). Rosen Group.
Your Future in Exotic Occupations. Rev. ed. S. Norman Feingold & Dora Evers. LC 76-182515. (Careers in Depth Ser.). (Illus.). 160p. (gr. 7 up). 1980. PLB 9.97 (ISBN 0-8239-0260-9). Rosen Group.
Your Future in Fashion. The Design Schools. (Illus.). 32p. (gr. 10-12). 1983. pap. text ed. 1.25 (ISBN 0-9607016-1-3). Design Schools.
Your Future in Foreign Service Careers. James P. Duncan, Jr. (Careers in Depth Ser.). (gr. 7-12). 1979. PLB 9.97 (ISBN 0-8239-0460-1). Rosen Group.
Your Future in Insurance Careers. Barry Bloomgarden. (Careers in Depth Ser.). (gr. 7-12). 1978. PLB 9.97 (ISBN 0-8239-0455-5). Rosen Group.
Your Future in Medical Assisting. rev. ed. Norma B. Chernok. 1982. 9.97 (ISBN 0-8239-0359-1). Rosen Group.
Your Future in Medical Illustrating: Art & Photography. Julia Nakamura & Massy Nakamura. LC 78-140096. (Careers in Depth Ser.). (Illus.). (gr. 7 up). 1971. PLB 9.97 (ISBN 0-8239-0236-6). Rosen Group.
Your Future in Museums. William Burns. LC 67-15470. (Careers in Depth Ser.). (gr. 7-12). 1974. PLB 9.97 (ISBN 0-8239-0053-3). Rosen Group.
Your Future in New Optometric Careers. James R. Gregg. (Careers in Depth Ser.). (gr. 7 up). 1978. PLB 9.97 (ISBN 0-8239-0449-0). Rosen Group.
Your Future in Space: The U. S. Space Camp Training Program. Penelope McPhee & Raymond McPhee. LC 86-9003. (Illus.). 128p. (YA) (gr. 7 up). 1986. pap. 14.95 (ISBN 0-517-56418-1). Crown.
Your Future in the Beauty Business. Rev. ed. Fashion Group Inc., Friends & Staff. Ed. by Christine Le Vathes. LC 68-31559. (Careers in Depth Ser.). (Illus.). (gr. 9 up). 1979. PLB 9.97 (ISBN 0-8239-0482-2). Rosen Group.
Your Future in the Nursery Industry. Rev. ed. John J. Pinney. LC 67-10084. (Careers in Depth Ser). (Illus.). 144p. (gr. 7 up). 1982. PLB 9.97 (ISBN 0-8239-0331-1). Rosen Group.
Your Future in the Performing Arts. Glenn Loney & Laurence Epstein. (Careers in Depth Ser.). (Illus.). 1980. lib. bdg. 9.97 (ISBN 0-8239-0511-X). Rosen Group.
Your Future in the Science of Oceanography. Jonathan S. Wood. (Careers in Depth Ser.). (Illus.). (gr. 7-12). 1979. lib. bdg. 9.97 (ISBN 0-8239-0438-5). Rosen Group.
Your Future in Word Processing. rev. ed. Phyllis Peck & Gilbert Konkel. (Careers in Depth Ser.). (Illus.). 140p. (gr. 7-12). 1985. lib. bdg. 9.97 (ISBN 0-8239-0532-2). Rosen Group.
Your Future Is Your Friend: Let's Feel Good about Ourselves. Robert H. Schuller. 144p. 1987. pap. 3.50 (ISBN 0-553-26580-6). Bantam.
Your Future Lives. Brad Steiger et al. (Illus.). 200p. (Orig.). 1988. pap. 14.95 (ISBN 0-914918-82-6, Pub. by Whiteford Pr). Schiffer.
Your Future Mate. Nancy Van Pelt. (Outreach Ser.). 32p. 1983. pap. 1.25 (ISBN 0-8163-0531-5). Pacific Pr Pub Assn.
Your Future Together. J. Champlin. 32p. 1985. pap. 4.95 (ISBN 0-89505-502-3). Tabor Pub.
Your Future Working with Older Adults. Martin Murray. (Careers in Depth Ser.). 144p. 1982. lib. bdg. 9.97 (ISBN 0-8239-0540-3). Rosen Group.
Your German Shepherd Puppy. rev. ed. H. Ernest Hart. (Illus.). 127p. 1985. text ed. 9.95 (ISBN 0-86622-039-9, PS-643). TFH Pubns.
Your German Shorthaired Pointer. Gertrude Dapper. LC 74-29657. (Your Dog Bk.). (Illus.). 1975. 13.95 (ISBN 0-87714-030-8). Denlingers.
Your Gifted Child & You. rev ed. Felice Kaufmann. LC 76-21990. 1981. pap. text ed. 7.50 (ISBN 0-86586-096-3). Coun Exc Child.
Your God-Given Potential. Winifred W. Hausmann. LC 77-80458. 1978. 5.95 (ISBN 0-87159-182-0). Unity School.
Your God Is Alive & Well & Appearing in Popular Culture. John W. Nelson. LC 76-26092. 216p. 1976. softcover 5.95 (ISBN 0-664-24866-7). Westminster John Knox.
Your God Is Too Small. John B. Phillips. 1987. pap. 3.95 (ISBN 0-02-088510-5, Collier). Macmillan.
Your God, My God. Mike Creswell. Ed. by Celeste Pennington. (Human Touch-Photo Text Ser.). 172p. 1980. 7.95 (ISBN 0-937170-22-4). Home Mission.
Your God, My God: A Woman's Workshop on Ruth. Anne Wilcox. (Woman's Workshop Ser.). 1985. student's manual 4.50 (ISBN 0-310-44711-9, 12027P). Zondervan.
Your Golden Key to Success: A Self Help Odyssey. Al G. Manning. LC 82-60767. (Illus.). 1982. 12.95 (ISBN 0-941698-04-1); pap. 5.95 (ISBN 0-941698-05-X). Pan-Ishtar.
Your Good Health: How to Stay Well, & What to Do When You're Not. Harvard Medical School. Ed. by William I. Bennett & G. Timothy Johnson. LC 87-19671. (Illus.). 448p. 1987. 24.95 (ISBN 0-674-96631-7). Harvard U Pr.
Your Good Thoughts Have Power. J. David King. (Illus.). 128p. (Orig.). 1987. pap. 5.00 (ISBN 0-9617359-0-2). Friend Man Assn.
Your Government & You: Simplified American Government. John H. Hoek. (Illus.). 96p. 1987. pap. 4.00 (ISBN 0-88323-223-5, 212); tchr's. key 1.50 (ISBN 0-88323-125-5, 213). Richards Pub.
Your Great Dane. Lina Basquette. LC 70-187772. (Your Dog Bk.). (Illus.). 128p. 1972. 13.95 (ISBN 0-87714-000-6). Denlingers.
Your Greatest Power. J. Martin Kohe. 1977. 8.95 (ISBN 0-685-74305-5). Success Unltd.
Your Greatest Strength. Grant Lewi. LC 85-52191. 144p. 1986. pap. 6.95 (ISBN 0-87728-661-2). Weiser.
Your Growing Child. Time-Life Books Editors. (Successful Parenting Ser.). 144p. 1987. 12.95 (ISBN 0-8094-5916-7); lib. bdg. write for info. (ISBN 0-8094-5917-5). Time Life.
Your Growing Child: From Babyhood Through Adolescence. Penelope Leach. 1986. pap. 14.95 (ISBN 0-394-71066-5). Knopf.
Your Guide to a Financially Secure Retirement. rev. & updated ed. C. Colburn Hardy. 204p. 1984. pap. 8.95 (ISBN 0-452-25621-6, Plume). NAL.
Your Guide to Better Health, Greater Energy. Johnson. 1944. 2.95 (ISBN 0-910140-28-6). C & R Anthony.
Your Guide to Better Nutrition. Sarah S. Strawn. 65p. 1985. pap. text ed. 8.95x incl. wkbk. (ISBN 0-89892-060-4). Contemp Pub Co of Raleigh.
Your Guide to Care of the Heart. Albert Goldin. LC 83-61170. 128p. 1985. 10.95 (ISBN 0-89313-035-4). G F Stickley Co.
Your Guide to Consumer Credit & Bankruptcy. 36p. 1980. pap. 1.00 (ISBN 0-686-47826-6). Amer Bar Assn.
Your Guide to Direct Mail. John Fraser-Robinson. (Illus.). 256p. 1988. 24.95 (ISBN 0-07-707085-2). McGraw.
Your Guide to Foot Care. Marvin Sandler. LC 83-61169. 178p. 1984. 13.95 (ISBN 0-89313-034-6). G F Stickley Co.
Your Guide to Home Storage. Alan Briscoe. 21p. 1974. pap. 1.95 (ISBN 0-88290-041-2). Horizon Utah.
Your Guide to IRAs & Fourteen Other Retirement Plans. Harry J. Lister. 224p. 1985. pap. 15.95 (ISBN 0-673-15995-7). Scott F.
Your Guide to Job Promotion. John Mepham. 154p. 1987. 39.00x (ISBN 0-317-59252-1, Pub. by Mgmt Update UK). State Mutual Bk.
Your Guide to Job Promotion. John H. Mepham. 144p. 1986. 39.00x (ISBN 0-946679-19-3, Pub. by Mgmt Update UK). State Mutual Bk.
Your Guide to Mental Help. John P. Callan. LC 82-50528. 200p. 1982. 9.50 (ISBN 0-89313-059-1). G F Stickley Co.
Your Guide to Non-Prescription Drugs. American Pharmaceutical Association Staff. (Illus.). 500p. Date not set. price not set (ISBN 0-8290-1580-9). Irvington.
Your Guide to Physical Fitness. Ellington Darden. LC 82-60780. 136p. 1982. 10.95 (ISBN 0-89313-058-3). G F Stickley Co.
Your Guide to POSIX. USR Group Publication Staff. 10p. 1987. pap. 1.00 (ISBN 0-936593-04-0). USR Group.
Your Guide to Problems of the Ear, Nose & Throat. Michael Morelock & J. B. Vap. LC 85-50471. 160p. 1985. pap. 10.95 (ISBN 0-89313-046-X). G F Stickley Co.
Your Guide to Social Security Benefits, 1989-90. Leona G. Rubin. 208p. 1989. 17.95x (ISBN 0-8160-1999-1); pap. 9.95x (ISBN 0-8160-2000-0). Facts on File.
Your Guide to the Seventh Edition of James M. McCrimmon's: Writing with a Purpose. Sharon McConnell & Jolyne Daughtry. (Orig.). 1980. pap. text ed. 20.95 (ISBN 0-8403-2706-4, 40270601). Kendall-Hunt.
Your Guide to Urology. Charles D. Saunders. LC 82-60000781. (Illus.). 130p. 1982. 9.50 (ISBN 0-89313-057-5). G F Stickley.
Your Guide to Writing Research Papers. Ed. by Julie Hutchinson. 36p. 1985. Repr. wkbk. 3.95x (ISBN 0-89892-059-0). Contemp Pub Co of Raleigh.
Your Gut Feelings: A Complete Guide to Living Better with Intestinal Problems. Henry D. Janowitz. (Illus.). 224p. 1987. 17.95 (ISBN 0-19-504309-X). Oxford U Pr.
Your Handbook for Healing. Craig Carter. 64p. 1981. pap. 6.95 (ISBN 0-911336-86-9). Sci of Mind.
Your Handbook of Weaving. Marie H. Walling & Joyce Barnette. Bd. with Pride of Weaving. (Illus.). 16p. Date not set. pap. price not set. Turtle Lodge.
Your Handbook of Weaving see Pride of Weaving.

Your Million Dollar Recipe for Riches. Thomas C. Stender. (Illus.). 180p. 1984. pap. 14.95 (ISBN 0-916933-00-8). New World Pubns.
Your Mind & Breast Diseases. Sarah Splaver. LC 78-62152. 1978. pap. 9.95 (ISBN 0-932208-00-2). Veritas Pr.
Your Mind & Your Health. Ellen G. White. 31p. 1964. pap. 0.99 (ISBN 0-8163-0083-6, 24505-0). Pacific Pr Pub Assn.
Your Mind Can Drive You Crazy...Only If You Let It, No. 1. 3rd ed. James A. Takacs. LC 79-87577. 202p. (Orig.). Date not set. pap. 9.95 (ISBN 0-910673-00-4). J A Takacs.
Your Mind Can Heal You. Frederick Bailes. LC 78-128864. 206p. 1975. pap. 6.95 (ISBN 0-87516-201-0). DeVorss.
Your Mind Can Keep You Well see How Your Mind Can Keep You Well.
Your Mind Matters. John R. Stott. LC 72-94672. 64p. 1973. pap. 4.95 (ISBN 0-87784-441-0). Inter-Varsity.
Your Miniature Pinscher. Buris R. Boshell. LC 69-19733. (Your Dog Bk.). (Illus.). 1969. 13.95 (ISBN 0-87714-024-3). Denlingers.
Your Miniature Schnauzer. Mildred L. Doud. LC 73-84514. (Your Dog Bk.). (Illus.). 160p. 1974. 13.95 (ISBN 0-87714-015-4). Denlingers.
Your Ministry at Home. Robert L. Samms & Maryann E. Samms. LC 87-72831. (Lay Action Ministry Program Ser.). 112p. (Orig.). 1988. pap. 4.95 (ISBN 0-89191-487-0, 67389). Cook.
Your Money - Going or Growing? Bernard Schneider. (Illus.). (gr. 7 up). 1978. wkbk 3.75 (ISBN 0-912486-33-3). Finney Co.
Your Money & What to Do With It. Gilbert M. Tucker. 1960. 9.95 (ISBN 0-8159-7401-9). Devin.
Your Money & Your Life. C. Hardy. 1983. pap. 9.95 (ISBN 0-317-31404-1). AMACOM.
Your Money & Your Life: How to Plan Your Long-Range Financial Security. C. Colburn Hardy. (Illus.). 1979. 15.95 (ISBN 0-8144-5529-8). AMACOM.
Your Money & Your Life: Planning Your Financial Future. 2nd ed. C. Colburn Hardy. 352p. 1982. 19.95 (ISBN 0-8144-5574-3). AMACOM.
Your Money & Your Life: Planning Your Financial Future. 2nd ed. C. Colburn Hardy. LC 82-71317. pap. 79.30 (ISBN 0-317-27198-9, 2023933). Bks Demand UMI.
Your Money & Your Life: Practical Guidance for Earning, Managing & Giving Money. Ken Wilson. (Living as a Christian Ser.). 96p. (Orig.). 1983. pap. 3.50 (ISBN 0-89283-171-5). Servant.
Your Money & Your Wife. Ritchie Perry. (Orig.). 1981. pap. 2.25 (ISBN 0-345-29060-7). Ballantine.
Your Money: Frustration or Freedom? Howard Dayton. 1979. pap. 5.95 (ISBN 0-8423-8725-0). Tyndale.
Your Money Matters. Malcolm MacGregor & Stanley C. Baldwin. LC 75-56123. 176p. 1977. pap. 5.95 (ISBN 0-87123-662-1, 210662). Bethany Hse.
Your Money or Your Health: A Senior Citizen's Guide to Avoiding High Charging Medicare Doctors. Daniel W. Sigelman. 134p. 1980. 4.00. Pub Citizen Inc.
Your Money or Your Life: A New Look at Jesus' View of Wealth & Power. John Alexander. LC 86-45010. 256p. 1986. 14.45 (ISBN 0-06-060151-5, HarpR). Har-Row.
Your Money or Your Life: Economy & Religion in the Middle Ages. Jacques Le Goff. Tr. by Patricia Ranum. LC 87-25248. 116p. 1988. 18.95 (ISBN 0-942299-14-0). Zone Bks.
Your Money Personality: What It Is & How You Can Profit from It. Kathleen Gurney. LC 87-24449. 312p. 1988. 18.95 (ISBN 0-385-24254-9). Doubleday.
Your Motive Factor. Olson & Hanratty. 24p. 1981. 3.00 (ISBN 0-317-66044-6, 1361-01). Am Fed Astrologers.
Your Move: A New Approach to the Study of Movement & Dance. Ann H. Guest. 343p. 1983. 46.00 (ISBN 0-677-06350-4); pap. 28.00 (ISBN 0-677-06365-2); tchrs' guide 17.00 (ISBN 0-677-06395-4). Gordon & Breach.
Your Move Discussion Guide. Robert I. Ward. 19p. (Orig.). 1984. pap. 6.95 (ISBN 0-89486-228-6). Hazelden.
Your Move, God. Francis Clare. LC 82-81212. 144p. 1982. pap. 4.95 (ISBN 0-89221-102-4). New Leaf.
Your Movie Guide to Action-Adventure Video Tapes & Discs. Video Times Editors & Consumer Guide Editors. 1985. pap. 1.95 (ISBN 0-451-13934-8, Sig). NAL.
Your Movie Guide to Adult Video Tapes & Discs. Ed. by Video Times Editors. 1985. pap. 1.95 (ISBN 0-451-13935-6, Sig). NAL.
Your Movie Guide to Childrens Video Tapes & Discs. Video Times Consumer Guide Editors. 1985. pap. 1.95 (ISBN 0-451-13931-3, Sig). NAL.
Your Movie Guide to Classic Video Tapes & Discs. Video Times Consumer Guide Editors. 1985. pap. 1.95 (ISBN 0-451-13928-3, Sig). NAL.
Your Movie Guide to Comedy Video Tapes & Discs. Video Times Consumer Guide Editors. 1985. pap. 1.95 (ISBN 0-451-13932-1, Sig). NAL.
Your Movie Guide to Drama. Ed. by Video Times Editors. 1985. pap. 1.95 (ISBN 0-451-13940-2, Sig). NAL.
Your Movie Guide to Foreign Tapes & Discs. Ed. by Video Times Editors & Consumer Guide Editors. 1985. pap. 1.95 (ISBN 0-451-13937-2, Sig). NAL.
Your Movie Guide to Horror Video Tapes & Discs. Video Times Consumer Guide Editors. 1985. pap. 1.95 (ISBN 0-451-13929-1, Sig). NAL.
Your Movie Guide to Musicals Tapes & Discs. Ed. by Video Times Editors. 1985. pap. 1.95 (ISBN 0-451-13939-9, Sig). NAL.
Your Movie Guide to Mystery-Suspense Tapes & Discs. Ed. by Video Times Editors. 1985. pap. 1.95 (Sig). NAL.
Your Movie Guide to Science Fiction Video Tapes & Discs. Video Times Consumer Guide Editors. 1985. pap. 1.95 (ISBN 0-451-13930-5, Sig). NAL.
Your Movie Guide to Western Tapes & Discs. Ed. by Video Times Editors & Consumer Guide Editors. 1985. pap. 1.95 (ISBN 0-451-13936-4, Sig). NAL.
Your Movie Review Book. Harvey E. Levine & Jana Pantazelos. LC 87-90517. (Illus.). 90p. (Orig.). 1987. pap. 9.95 (ISBN 0-318-22841-6). Six Eighty Pr.
Your Mule Is Crowing. Callie B. Young. 112p. 1988. 8.95 (ISBN 0-8062-3034-7). Carlton.
Your Mysterious Powers of E.S.P. rev. & updated ed. Harold Sherman. 256p. 1988. pap. 4.50 (ISBN 0-451-15583-1, J9315, Sig). NAL.
Your Name-All About It. Mary P. Lee. LC 79-22145. (Illus.). 128p. (gr. 3-7). 1980. 9.95 (ISBN 0-664-32656-0). Westminster John Knox.
Your Name Company: Accounting Practice Set for the Computer. Thomas W. Charles & Frederic M. Stiner, Jr. 130p. 1985. pap. 17.50 (ISBN 0-534-04506-5). PWS Kent Pub.
Your Name, Your Number, Your Destiny. Juno Jordan & Helen Houston. 96p. 1982. pap. 5.95 (ISBN 0-87877-062-3). Newcastle Pub.
Your Name, Your Number, Your Destiny: Two Guides to Numerology. Juno Jordon & Helen Houston. LC 83-3901. 91p. 1983. Repr. of 1982 ed. lib. bdg. 19.95x (ISBN 0-89370-662-0). Borgo Pr.
Your Native Land, Your Life: Poems. Adrienne Rich. 1986. 14.95 (ISBN 0-393-02318-4); pap. 6.95 (ISBN 0-393-30325-X). Norton.
Your Native Shade Trees. 1972. 0.15 (ISBN 0-686-20734-3). SUNY Environ.
Your Natural Beauty Sampler. Linda Clark et al. LC 77-92810. 1978. pap. 1.95 (ISBN 0-87983-168-5). Keats.
Your Natural Gifts: How to Recognize & Develop Them for Success & Self-Fulfillment. rev. ed. Margaret E. Broadley. 160p. 1986. pap. 6.95 (ISBN 0-914440-90-X). EPM Pubns.
Your Needs Met. Jack Addington & Cornelia Addington. 156p. 1982. pap. 4.95 (ISBN 0-87516-490-0). DeVorss.
Your Neighbor Celebrates. Arthur Gilbert & Oscar Tarcov. 38p. 0.75 (ISBN 0-686-74967-7). ADL.
Your Neighbor Celebrates. Arthur Gilbert & Oscar Tarcov. 6.00x (ISBN 0-87068-364-0, Pub. by Friendly Hse). Ktav.
Your Neighbor Worships. Arthur Gilbert. 31p. 1.50 (ISBN 0-686-74968-5). ADL.
Your New Baby & Bowser. Stephen C. Rafe. (Other Dog Bks.). (Illus.). 1989. write for info. (ISBN 0-87714-138-X). Denlingers.
Your New Beginning: Step Two. Willie Malone. 64p. (Orig.). 1983. pap. 2.50 (ISBN 0-88144-008-6). Christian Pub.
Your New Birth. Robert Halverstadt. 1982. pap. 0.75 (ISBN 0-88144-001-9, CPS-001). Christian Pub.
Your New Home & How to Take Care of It. rev. ed. (Illus.). 64p. 1988. pap. text ed. 20.00 (ISBN 0-86718-318-7). Nat Assn H Build.
Your New Job: Tips for Career Success. 56p. 1986. pap. 3.50 (ISBN 0-912857-34-X). Inst Finan Educ.
Your New Lawyer. 1983. 35.00 (ISBN 0-318-02104-8). NALP.
Your New Lawyer: The Legal Employer's Complete Guide to Recruitment, Development & Management. Gary A. Munneke & American Bar Association, Committee on Selection, Training, & Utilization of Lawyers. LC 83-71229. xiii, 320p. 1983. 45.00 (ISBN 0-89707-101-8, 511-0075). Amer Bar Assn.
Your New Life in the Country: How to Plan & Manage It for Enjoyment & Profit. Gregory Wood. (Illus.). 288p. (Orig.). 1987. pap. 17.95 (ISBN 0-8117-2267-8). Stackpole.
Your New Life in the United States. LORC Staff. 215p. (Span., Chinese, Hmong, Khmer, Lao, Vietnamese.). 1984. pap. 5.00. Ctr Appl Ling.
Your Newborn Baby: Everything You Need To Know Featuring Joan Lunden. Michael Krauss & Sue Castle. LC 87-40410. 160p. 1988. 15.95 (ISBN 0-446-51374-1). Warner Bks.
Your Nineteen Eighty-Seven to Eighty-Eight Guide to Social Security Benefits. Leona R. Rubin. 208p. 1986. 16.95x (ISBN 0-8160-1567-8); pap. 9.95x (ISBN 0-8160-1568-6). Facts on File.
Your Nineteen Eighty-Six Money Saving Tax Guide. The J. K. Lasser Tax Institute. Date not set. write for info. S&S.
Your Norwegian Elkhound. Helen E. Franciose & Nancy C. Swanson. LC 73-84513. (Your Dog Bk.). (Illus.). 160p. 1974. 12.95 (ISBN 0-87714-014-6). Denlingers.
Your Nose & Ears. Joan Iveson-Iveson. LC 85-71729. (All about You Ser.). (Illus.). 24p. (gr. k-3). 1986. lib. bdg. 9.90 (ISBN 0-531-18042-5, Pub. by Bookwright Pr). Watts.
Your Number's Up: A Calculus Approach to Successful Math Study. C. A. Oxrieder. 1982. text ed. write for info. (ISBN 0-201-05526-0); instr's guide o.p. 1.50 (ISBN 0-201-05527-9). Addison-Wesley.
Your Nutritious Garden. 44p. 1984. pap. 3.95 (ISBN 0-915873-03-6, 1-1013). Natl Gardening Assn.
Your Old Balls. Hale Hawkins. (Illus.). 80p. (Orig.). 1980. pap. 4.95 (ISBN 0-938194-00-3). Lively Hills.
Your Old English Sheepdog. Alice J. Boyer. LC 75-41985. (Your Dog Bk.). (Illus.). 1978. 13.95 (ISBN 0-87714-048-0). Denlingers.
Your Old Pal, Al. Constance C. Greene. 160p. (gr. k-6). 1981. pap. 2.95 (ISBN 0-440-49862-7, YB). Dell.
Your Old Pal, Al. Constance C. Greene. LC 79-12350. (gr. 5-9). 1979. 13.95 (ISBN 0-670-79575-5). Viking.
Your One-Year-Old: The Fun-Loving, Fussy 12- to 24-Month-Old. Louise B. Ames et al. (Illus.). 1982. 11.95 (ISBN 0-385-29186-8). Delacorte.
Your One-Year-Old: The Fun-Loving, Fussy 12-to-24-Month Old. Louise B. Ames et al. (Illus.). 1983. pap. 7.95 (ISBN 0-385-29206-6, Delta). Dell.
Your Own Exercises. Ebbitt Cutler. (Illus.). 64p. 1988. pap. 4.95 (ISBN 0-88776-194-1). Tundra Bks.
Your Own Horse. Wolfgang Holzel. Tr. by Bill Charlton. (Poster Bks.). (Illus.). 64p. 1986. 4.95 (ISBN 0-86622-149-2). TFH Pubns.
Your Own Import-Export Business: Winning the Trade Game, Vol. 1. Carl A. Nelson. LC 87-83461. (Illus.). 215p. 1988. 22.95 (ISBN 0-945493-01-0); pap. 14.95 (ISBN 0-945493-00-2). Global Busn Comns.
Your Own Path. Elise N. Morgan. (Meditation Ser.). 1928. 4.50 (ISBN 0-87516-333-5). DeVorss.
Your Own Pigs You May Not Eat. Paula G. Rubel & Abraham Rosman. LC 78-7544. (Illus.). 1978. lib. bdg. 30.00x (ISBN 0-226-73082-4). U of Chicago Pr.
Your Own Risk. Philip Parisi. (Illus.). 28p. (Orig.). 1981. pap. 2.50 (ISBN 0-914278-34-7). Copper Beech.
Your Own Shortcut Shorthand. Lauren R. Geringer. LC 79-55059. (Orig.). 1980. pap. 5.95 (ISBN 0-935020-06-3). Gehry Pr.
Your Own Super Magic Show. Marvin Miller. (Illus.). 32p. (Orig.). (gr. 3-6). 1984. pap. 4.95 (ISBN 0-590-33044-6). Scholastic Inc.
Your Painful Neck & Back: A Complete Guide to Self-Help. James W. Fisk. (Illus.). 205p. 1988. pap. text ed. 9.95 (ISBN 0-09-952000-1, Pub. by Century Hutchinson). David & Charles.
Your Painting Questions Answered from A to Z. Helen Van Wyk. Ed. by Herbert Rogoff. (Illus.). 200p. (Orig.). 1988. pap. text ed. 16.50. Art Instr Assocs.
Your Parents & Your Self. David Klein & Marymae E. Klein. LC 86-20390. 176p. (gr. 7 up). 1986. 11.95 (ISBN 0-684-18684-5, Pub. by Scribner). Macmillan.
Your Particular Grief. Wayne E. Oates. LC 81-3328. 114p. 1981. pap. 7.95 (ISBN 0-664-24376-2). Westminster John Knox.
Your Passport to Making It Abroad. Mark Altschuler. 2.95 (ISBN 0-8315-0133-2). Speller.
Your Past Lives: A Reincarnation Handbook: Eight Techniques for Exploring When You Lived, Who You Loved, How You Died, & What Your Past Lives Means in Your Life Today. 1987. 16.95 (ISBN 0-517-56301-0). Crown.
Your Past Lives & the Healing Process. Adrian Finkelstein. 233p. (Orig.). 1985. pap. 9.95x (ISBN 0-87418-001-5). Coleman Pub.
Your Past Lives & the Healing Process. Adrian Finkelstein. 233p. (Orig.). 1985. pap. 11.95. A Finkelstein.
Your Paths in Ink: Graphoanalysis & the Personality. Johanna L. Wyland. (Illus.). 86p. 1980. 6.95 (ISBN 0-682-49604-9). Exposition-Phoenix.
Your Pekingese. Robert J. Berndt. LC 77-87761. (Your Dog Bk). (Illus.). 1978. 13.95 (ISBN 0-87714-049-9). Denlingers.
Your Pennsylvania. Lucille Wallower. Ed. by Daphne B. Brebner & S. K. Stevens. (gr. 4-6). 1959. 6.35 (ISBN 0-931992-07-9). Penns Valley.
Your Pension & Your Spouse: The Joint & Survivor Dilemma. R. George Martorana. 28p. (Orig.). 1985. pap. 7.95 (ISBN 0-89154-278-7). Intl Found Employ.
Your Pension Rights at Divorce: What Women Need to Know. Women's Legal Defense Fund Staff. 21p. 1983. 3.00 (ISBN 0-317-67863-9). Women's Legal Defense.
Your People, My People: The Meeting of Jews & Christians. Ed. by A. R. Eckardt. 212p. 7.95 (ISBN 0-686-95188-3). ADL.
Your Perfect Partnership. Lou Austin. 8.75 (ISBN 0-934538-17-4); pap. 4.50 (ISBN 0-934538-12-3). Partnership Foundation.
Your Perfect Right: A Guide to Assertive Living. 5th ed. Robert E. Alberti & Michael L. Emmons. LC 86-7267. 228p. 1986. 11.95 (ISBN 0-915166-08-9); pap. 7.95 (ISBN 0-915166-07-0). Impact Pubs Cal.
Your Perfect Write: The Manual for Self-Help Writers. Robert E. Alberti. LC 85-14188. 160p. (Orig.). 1985. pap. 9.95 (ISBN 0-915166-40-2). Impact Pubs Cal.
Your Personal Career Consultant: A Step-by-Step Guide to Finding a Successful & Satisfying Career. Michele Shapiro. Ed. by Gail Lehman. (ARCO Education & Guidance Ser.). 256p. (Orig.). 1988. pap. 8.95. Prentice Hall Pr.
Your Personal Colors & Numbers. Louise L. Hay. LC 86-82079. 56p. 1986. pap. 3.95 (ISBN 0-937611-16-6). Hay House.
Your Personal Computer Can Make You Rich in Stocks & Commodities. Curtis M. Arnold. LC 83-51498. (Illus.). 300p. 14.95 (ISBN 0-9613048-0-4). M D Weiss Pub.
Your Personal Computer Can Make You Rich in Stocks & Commodities. Curtis M. Arnold. 310p. 1985. 19.95 (ISBN 0-89526-596-6). Regnery Gateway.
Your Personal Computer Dictionary. N. Mazloum & M. Breskin. 160p. 1985. pap. text ed. 9.95 (ISBN 0-07-041196-4, BYTE Bks). McGraw.
Your Personal Financial Fitness Program: 1987-88 Edition. Elizabeth S. Lewin. (Illus.). 160p. 1987. pap. 9.95 (ISBN 0-8160-1580-5). Facts on File.
Your Personal Financial Planner. Richard J. Stillman. (Illus.). 176p. 1981. 15.95 (ISBN 0-13-980516-8, Spec). P-H.
Your Personal Fitness Advisor. Ed. by Peg Angsten. (Illus.). 240p. (Orig.). 1988. pap. 12.95 (ISBN 0-937359-23-8). HDL Pubs.
Your Personal Guide to Marketing a Nonprofit Organization. Robert S. Topor. 155p. 1988. 18.50 (ISBN 0-89964-254-3). Coun Adv & Supp Ed.
Your Personal Guide to Pre-Retirement Planning. Pilot Staff. LC 83-13275. 43p. 1983. pap. 5.00 (ISBN 0-87576-106-2). Pilot Bks.
Your Personal Handbook of Prayer. Phyllis Hobe. LC 83-3475. 256p. 1983. 11.95 (ISBN 0-664-27007-7). Westminster John Knox.
Your Personal Mark Twain. Mark Twain. 228p. 1969. pap. 1.95 (ISBN 0-7178-0223-X). Intl Pubs Co.
Your Personal Plumber. L. F. Greer. LC 79-54891. 1979. 24.95 (ISBN 0-686-26464-9). Plumbing Pubns.
Your Personal Record. Howard Wilson. 1964. pap. 1.50 (ISBN 0-910022-25-9). ARA.
Your Personal Vitamin Profile: A Medical Scientist Shows You How to Chart Your Individual Vitamin & Mineral Formala. Michael Colgan. 1982. 14.95 (ISBN 0-688-01505-0); pap. 8.95 (ISBN 0-688-01506-9). Morrow.
Your Personal Winning Lottery Numbers. Robert R. Hieronimus. 336p. (Orig.). 1986. pap. 3.95 (ISBN 0-446-30100-0). Warner Bks.
Your Personality Analysis in Addition to Poetry. Silvia Silk. (Illus.). 27p. (Orig.). 1979. pap. 5.00 (ISBN 0-938861-00-X). Jasmine Texts.
Your Personality Tree: Understanding Why You Do What You Do. Florence Littauer. 160p. 1986. 11.95 (ISBN 0-8499-0571-0). Word Bks.
Your Personalized Health Profile: Choosing the Diet That's Right for You. Myron Winick. LC 85-7293. (Illus.). 224p. 1985. 16.95 (ISBN 0-688-05114-6). Morrow.
Your Personalized Health Profile: Nutrition to Prevent Disease. 1987. pap. 3.50 (ISBN 0-345-34029-9). Ballantine.
Your Personally Tailored Diet. Stephan Lehane. (Illus.). 1984. 15.95 (ISBN 0-13-980541-9, Busn); pap. 5.95 (ISBN 0-13-980525-7, Busn). P-H.
Your Pet Parakeet: A Complete Care Guide. John C. Biardo. LC 87-83187. (Illus.). 130p. (Orig.). pap. 4.95 (ISBN 0-933181-04-3). Elmwood Park Pub.
Your Phobia: Understanding Your Fears Through Contextual Therapy. Manuel D. Zane & Harry Milt. LC 84-12454. 304p. 1984. 15.95x (ISBN 0-88048-008-4, 48-008-4). Am Psychiatric.
Your Phobia: Understanding Your Fears Through Contextual Therapy. Manuel D. Zane & Harry Milt. 304p. 1986. pap. 4.95 (ISBN 0-446-32720-4). Warner Bks.
Your Phone's Ringing! J. David Lang. (Illus.). 64p. (gr. 10-12). 1985. pap. 2.50 (ISBN 0-87239-897-8, 2827). Standard Pub.
Your Phone's Ringing, No. 2. J. David Lang. (Illus.). 64p. (gr. 10-12). 1985. pap. 2.50 (ISBN 0-87239-898-6, 2828). Standard Pub.
Your Piano & Your Piano Technician. Virgil E. Smith. LC 80-82009. 56p. 1981. pap. 3.45 (ISBN 0-8497-5078-4, WP71, Pub. by Kjos West). Kjos.
Your Pilot's License. 3rd ed. Joe Christy & Clay Johnson. (Illus.). 160p. 1983. pap. 9.95 (ISBN 0-8306-2367-1, 2367). TAB Bks.
Your Pony Book. Tineke Bartels-De Vries & Egbert Van Zon. (Illus.). 96p. 1982. pap. text ed. 7.95 (ISBN 0-8065-0794-2, Pub. by Citadel Pr). Lyle Stuart.
Your Pony Book. Hermann Wiederhold. pap. 2.00 (ISBN 0-87980-331-2). Wilshire.
Your Poodle, Standard, Miniature & Toy. Frank T. Sabella. LC 69-19732. (Your Dog Bk.). (Illus.). 1969. 13.95 (ISBN 0-87714-023-5). Denlingers.
Your Power of Encouragement. Jeanne Doering. (Moody Press Electives Ser.). (Orig.). 1985. leader's guide 2.50 (ISBN 0-8024-0688-2). Moody.
Your Power to Heal. Harold Sherman. 1978. pap. 2.50 (ISBN 0-449-14007-5, GM). Fawcett.

Your Vital Papers Logbook. AARP's Worker Equity Dept. 32p. 1985. pap. 4.95 (ISBN 0-673-24833-X). Am Assn Retire.
Your Vital Statistics. Gyles Brandreth. 128p. 1986. pap. 8.95 (ISBN 0-8065-0980-5). Lyle Stuart.
Your Vizsla. John X. Strauz & Joseph F. Cunningham. LC 70-187775. (Your Dog Bk.). (Illus.). 128p. 1973. 13.95 (ISBN 0-87714-006-5). Denlingers.
Your Voice & How to Use It Successfully. C. Berry. 1986. pap. 24.75X (ISBN 0-245-52886-5, Pub. by Harrap Ltd England); cassette 22.50X (ISBN 0-245-52901-2, Pub. by Harrap Ltd England). State Mutual Bk.
Your Voice at City Hall: The Politics, Procedures, & Policies of District Representation. Peggy Heilig & Robert J. Mundt. LC 83-24287. (SUNY Series in Urban Public Policy). 171p. 1985. 52.50 (ISBN 0-87395-821-7); pap. 19.95 (ISBN 0-87395-820-9). State U NY Pr.
Your Voice: Methods for Strengthening & Developing the Voice. Eugene Feuchtinger. Orig. Title: Voice Development Hints. Nelson-Hall.
Your Water & Your Health. Allan E. Banik & Carlson Wade. LC 81-81289. (Pivot Original Health Bks.). 128p. 1974. pap. 2.95 (ISBN 0-87983-254-1). Keats.
Your Way to Success in Money, Life & Friends. Joe Lewis. (Futurology in Investments Ser.). 14.95 (ISBN 0-87505-150-2). Borden.
Your Wealth-Building Years. Adriane G. Berg. LC 85-61813. 272p. 1987. pap. 9.95 (ISBN 0-937858-82-X). Newmarket.
Your Wealth in God's World. John J. Davis. LC 83-19286. 144p. 1984. pap. 4.95 (ISBN 0-87552-219-X). Presby & Reformed.
Your Wealth in God's World: Does the Bible Support the Free Market? John J. Davis. 134p. Date not set. pap. 4.95 (ISBN 0-8010-2965-1). Baker Bk.
Your Wedding. Bibi Winfield & Annette Spence. 144p. 1987. pap. 5.95 spiral bdg. (ISBN 0-671-63506-9, Fireside). S&S.
Your Wedding: A Complete Guide to Planning & Enjoying It. Nancy Piccione. 194p. 1982. pap. 5.95 (ISBN 0-13-981407-8). P-H.
Your Wedding: How to Plan & Enjoy It. Marjorie B. Woods. 208p. 1986. pap. 3.50 (ISBN 0-515-08543-X). Jove Pubns.
Your Wedding: Making it Perfect. Yetta F. Gruen. 384p. 1986. pap. 8.95 (ISBN 0-14-046755-6). Penguin.
Your Wedding Workbook. 5th ed. Natalia M. Belting & James R. Hine. (Illus.). 1986. pap. 9.95x (ISBN 0-8134-2481-X, 2481). Inter Print Pubs.
Your Weight. Douglas A. Eagles. (First Bks). (Illus.). 72p. (gr. 4 up). 1982. PLB 10.40 (ISBN 0-531-04395-9). Watts.
Your Welsh Corgi, Cardigan-Pembroke. Robert J. Berndt. LC 77-87762. (Your Dog Bk.). (Illus.). 1978. 13.95 (ISBN 0-87714-052-9). Denlingers.
Your Will & What to Do about It. Samuel G. Kling. pap. 5.00 (ISBN 0-87980-216-2). Wilshire.
Your Window Greenhouse. Leigh Seddon. (Illus.). 32p. 1986. pap. 4.95 (ISBN 0-88266-343-7, Garden Way Pub). Storey Comm Inc.
Your Wonderful Body. Ed. by Donald J. Crump. LC 81-47892. (Books for World Explorers: Series 4, No. 1). 104p. (gr. 4-8). 1982. 6.95 (ISBN 0-87044-423-9); PLB 8.50 (ISBN 0-87044-428-X). Natl Geog.
Your Word Is Fire: The Hasidic Masters on Contemplative Prayer. Ed. by Arthur Green & Barry W. Holtz. LC 87-9835. 144p. (Orig.). 1987. pap. 7.95 (ISBN 0-8052-0842-9). Schocken.
Your Word Is Near. Huub Oosterhuis. Tr. by N. D. Smith from Dutch. LC 68-20848. 192p. 1968. pap. 4.95 (ISBN 0-8091-1775-4, Deus). Paulist Pr.
Your Word Is Your Wand. F. Shinn. 4.95x. Wehman.
Your Word Is Your Wand. Florence S. Shinn. 1978. pap. 3.50 (ISBN 0-87516-259-2). DeVorss.
Your Word, O Lord. Cornelius M. Buckley. LC 87-80961. (Illus.). 300p. (Orig.). (YA) (gr. 7-12). 1987. pap. 9.95 (ISBN 0-89870-174-0). Ignatius Pr.
Your Words in Prayer in Time of Illness. Arnaldo Pangrazzi. 72p. (Orig.). 1982. pap. 1.25 (ISBN 0-8189-0417-8). Alba.
Your Words: Public & Private. 2nd ed. Anne Passel. LC 81-40773. (Illus.). 248p. 1982. pap. text ed. 13.25 (ISBN 0-8191-1867-2). U Pr of Amer.
Your Work Matters to God. Doug Sherman & William Hendricks. (Orig.). 1988. Handbook. pap. 14.95 (ISBN 0-89109-224-2). NavPress.
Your Work on the Pulpit Committee. Leonard E. Hill. LC 70-93916. 1970. pap. 3.25 (ISBN 0-8054-3502-6). Broadman.
Your Working Life: A Guide to Getting & Holding a Job. Edwin L. Herr & Roberta Moore. LC 79-28360. Orig. Title: Career Education. (Illus.). 464p. 1980. text ed. 28.96 (ISBN 0-07-028342-7). McGraw.
Your World & Mine. Halbert L. Dunn. 1970. 5.95 (ISBN 0-87948-001-7). Beatty.
Your World of Pets. Susan McGrath. Ed. by Donald J. Crump. LC 85-7288. (Books for World Explorers Series 6: No. 4). (Illus.). 104p. (gr. 3-8). 1985. 6.95 (ISBN 0-87044-517-0); PLB 8.50 (ISBN 0-87044-522-7). Natl Geog.
Your Year-Round Investment Planner: Keeping Track of Your Investments--Know What You Own, What's It's Worth & What to Do with It. Nancy Dunnan. 96p. (Orig.). 1988. pap. 5.95 (ISBN 0-06-096245-3, PL-6245, PL). Har-Row.
Your Yorkshire Terrier. 2nd, rev. ed. Morris Howard. LC 75-52421. (Your Dog Bk.). (Illus.). 1979. 13.95 (ISBN 0-87714-084-7). Denlingers.
Your Young Heart. Bryan Bearden. Frwd. by Wally Wilkerson. 157p. (Orig.). pap. text ed. 4.95 (ISBN 0-89225-310-X). Gospel Advocate.
Yourcenar Collection: A Descriptive Catalogue. Robert R. Nunn & Edward J. Geary. (Illus.). 1984. pap. 6.00 (ISBN 0-916606-07-4). Bowdoin Coll.
You're a Better Parent Than You Think! Raymond N. Guarendi. 252p. 1985. O.P. 15.95 (ISBN 0-13-981861-8); pap. 8.95 (ISBN 0-13-981853-7). P-H.
You're a Gent, Andy Capp. Reginald Smythe. (Andy Capp Ser.). 1979. pap. 1.25 (ISBN 0-449-13964-6, GM). Fawcett.
You're a Good Sport, Charlie Brown. Charles M. Schulz. LC 76-8128. (Illus.). (gr. 1 up). 1976. 4.95 (ISBN 0-394-83297-3, BYR); lib. bdg. 5.99 (ISBN 0-394-93297-8). Random.
You're a Good Sport, Charlie Brown. Charles M Schulz. (gr. 1 up). 1977. pap. 1.95 (ISBN 0-590-08502-6). Scholastic Inc.
You're a Hooker, Then: An Autobiography. Colin Deans. 216p. 1987. 50.00x (ISBN 1-85158-079-4, Pub. by Mainstream Scotland). State Mutual Bk.
You're a Knockout, Andy Capp. Reginald Smythe. (Orig.). 1985. pap. 2.25 (ISBN 0-449-12656-0, GM). Fawcett.
You're a Little Kid with a Big Heart. Bernard Waber. (Illus.). (gr. k-3). 1980. PLB 8.95 (ISBN 0-395-29163-1). HM.
You're a Mormon Now: A Handbook for New Members of the Church of Jesus Christ of Latter-day Saints. Dennis Lythgoe et al. 75p. (Orig.). 1983. pap. 6.95 (ISBN 0-913420-37-9). Olympus Pub Co.
You're a Real Hero, Amanda. Arvella Whitmore. (gr. 5-9). 1985. 12.95 (ISBN 0-395-38950-X). HM.
You're a Riot, Andy Capp. Smythe. 1979. pap. 1.25 (ISBN 0-449-13591-8, GM). Fawcett.
You're a Winner, Charlie Brown. Charles M. Schulz. 1987. pap. 2.25 (ISBN 0-449-21458-3, Crest). Fawcett.
You're All Grown up, Vancouver. Margaret Evans. Ed. by Diane Brown. 96p. (Orig.). 1987. pap. 9.95 (ISBN 0-317-58238-0). Hancock House.
You're an Ace, Snoopy! Charles M. Schulz. 1987. pap. 2.25 (ISBN 0-449-21402-8, Crest). Fawcett.
You're Beautiful: Quick Reference Self Help Program for All Situations. Al G. Manning & Rachel L. Manning. LC 87-62127. 1987. pap. 6.95 (ISBN 0-941698-16-5). Pan Ishtar.
You're Dumber in the Summer: And Over 100 Other Things No One Ever Told You. Jim Aylward. (Illus.). 64p. (gr. 3-7). pap. 2.25 (ISBN 0-380-57935-9, 57935-9, Camelot). Avon.
You're Fired. Byron A. Dickman. LC 76-73206. 1978. write for info. (ISBN 0-932984-00-2). Gracelaine.
You're God's Masterpiece. Wesley Runk. 1985. 4.50 (ISBN 0-89536-757-2, 5863). CSS of Ohio.
You're Going Out There a Kid, but You're Coming Back a Star. Linda Hirsch. (Illus.). 128p. (Orig.). (gr. 3-7). 1984. pap. 2.25 (ISBN 0-553-15272-6, Skylark). Bantam.
You're Gonna Love It. Chuck Lewis. LC 85-2574. 128p. (Orig.). 1985. pap. 7.95 (ISBN 0-89815-138-4). Ten Speed Pr.
You're Hired! rev. ed. Don R. Beeman & Richard G. Rump. 180p. 1984. pap. text ed. 7.50 (ISBN 0-914399-00-4). DBA Pr.
You're Hired! Albert C. Van Roden & Thomas D. Bachhuber. LC 81-80571. (Illus.). 80p. 1981. pap. 3.95 (ISBN 0-89709-025-X). Liberty Pub.
You're Hired! Insights for Christian Women Who Work Outside the Home. Millie Van Wyke. 120p. 1983. pap. 5.95 (ISBN 0-8010-9292-2). Baker Bk.
You're in Business: Building Business English Skills. John T. French. 1984. pap. text ed. 12.40 (ISBN 0-201-11498-4). Addison-Wesley.
You're in Charge: A Guide to Becoming Your Own Therapist. Janette Rainwater. LC 82-9104. 221p. 1985. pap. 9.00 (ISBN 0-87516-552-4). DeVorss.
You're in Charge: Nutrition for Preschool Children. Society for Nutrition Education. 16p. 1984. pap. 5.00 (ISBN 0-318-04037-9). Soc Nutrition Ed.
You're in Control: A Guide for Latter-day Saint Youth. Ron Woods. LC 86-16532. 115p. (YA) (gr. 5 up). 1986. 8.95 (ISBN 0-87579-046-1). Deseret Bk.
You're in Good Zodiac Company. Lois H. Sargent. 128p. 1972. 3.00 (ISBN 0-86690-154-X, 1447-01). Am Fed Astrologers.
You're in Love, Charlie Brown. Charles M. Schulz. (Illus.). (ps up). 1974. 1.95 (ISBN 0-394-83044-X). Random.
You're in the Driver's Seat. Gerald Howland. 1986. pap. 7.95 (ISBN 0-8289-0593-2). Greene.
You're in the Juniors Now. Margaret Joy. (Illus.). (gr. 3-6). 1988. 9.95 (ISBN 0-317-69547-9). Faber & Faber.
You're Invited. St. Anthony of Padua Mother's Guild Staff. Ed. by Judy Hein & Eileen Rathgaber. (Cookbook Ser.). (Illus.). 261p. (Orig.). 1986. spiral softcook 10.00 (ISBN 0-9616243-0-2). St Anthony Northport.
You're My Best Friend, Lord. Lois W. Johnson. LC 76-3866. 112p. (Orig.). (gr. 4-7). 1976. pap. 4.50 (ISBN 0-8066-1541-9, 10-7490). Augsburg.
You're Nearly There: Christian Sex Education for Ten-to-Teens. Mary Kehle. LC 73-85963. (Illus.). 80p. 1973. pap. 2.50 (ISBN 0-87788-969-4). Shaw Pubs.
You're Never Too Old for Nuts & Berries. G. B. Trudeau. LC 76-6751. 1976. 3.95 (ISBN 0-03-018216-6). H Holt & Co.
You're Next on the List. David O. Woodbury. LC 68-5154. 1968. pap. 1.00 pocketsize (ISBN 0-88279-025-0). Western Islands.
You're No Friend of Mine. Emily Chase. (Girls of Canby Hall Ser.). 192p. (Orig.). (gr. 7 up). 1984. pap. 2.25 (ISBN 0-590-40080-0). Scholastic Inc.
You're Not Elected, Charlie Brown. Charles M. Schulz. (Illus.). (ps up). 1973. 3.95 (ISBN 0-394-83045-8). Random.
You're Not Elected, Charlie Brown. Charles M. Schulz. (Illus.). 96p. (gr. 3-7). 1980. pap. 1.95 (ISBN 0-590-08820-3). Scholastic Inc.
You're Not for Real, Snoopy: Selected Cartoons from "Peanuts Every Sunday", Vol. II. Charles M. Schulz. (Peanuts Ser.). (Illus.). (gr. 3-7). 1981. pap. 1.75 (ISBN 0-449-23879-2, Crest). Fawcett.
You're Not the Maid: A Working Parents Survival Manual. (Illus.). 50p. (Orig.). 1985. pap. 4.50 (ISBN 0-9606722-2-2). J A Ent.
You're Not Too Old to Have a Baby. Jane Price. 1978. pap. 3.95 (ISBN 0-14-004910-X). Penguin.
You're Not Too Old to Win at Tennis. Edward B. Gellert. LC 84-71251. (Illus.). 64p. (Orig.). 1984. pap. 6.95 (ISBN 0-9613520-0-0). CIPRA.
You're OK-The World's All Wrong. C. W. Dalton. Ed. by Sara Herschler & L. D. Garland. LC 84-70707. 542p. 1985. 17.95 (ISBN 0-916969-00-2). Big Blue Bks.
You're on... Teaching Assertiveness & Communication Skills. Honey Loring & Jeremy Birch. (Illus.). 85p. (Orig.). 1984. pap. 8.95 (ISBN 0-9613102-0-0). StressPress.
You're on the Air with Mike Miller. new ed. Mike Miller. LC 74-78647. (Illus.). 155p. (Orig.). 1975. pap. 3.95 (ISBN 0-88435-001-0). Chateau Pub.
You're on the Wrong Foot Again, Charlie Brown. Charles M. Schulz. (Peanuts Collector Ser.: No. 2). (Illus.). 128p. (ps up). 1987. pap. 5.95 (ISBN 0-345-34872-9). Pharos Bks NY.
You're on Your Own, Snoopy: Selected Cartoons from "Ha, Ha, Herman, Charlie Brown", Vol. I. Charles M. Schulz. (Peanuts Ser.). (Illus.). 1985. pap. 1.95 (ISBN 0-449-20592-4, Crest). Fawcett.
You're Only Human Once. Grace Moore. Ed. by Andrew Farkas. LC 76-29958. (Opera Biographies). (Illus.). 1977. Repr. of 1944 ed. lib. bdg. 23.50 (ISBN 0-405-09698-4). Ayer Co Pubs.
You're Only Old Once! Dr. Seuss. LC 85-20495. (Illus.). 48p. 1986. 10.95 (ISBN 0-394-55190-7). Random.
You're Our Child: A Social-Psychological Approach to Adoption. Jerome Smith & Franklin I. Miroff. LC 80-5957. 110p. (Orig.). 1981. lib. bdg. 24.25 (ISBN 0-8191-1416-2); pap. text ed. 9.00 (ISBN 0-8191-1417-0). U Pr of Amer.
You're Our Child: The Adoption Experience. Jerome Smith & Franklin Miroff. 260p. (Orig.). 1987. pap. 9.95 (ISBN 0-8191-5036-3, Pub. by Madison Bks). U Pr of Amer.
You're Our Kind of Dog, Snoopy: Selected Cartoons from "And a Woodstock in a Birch Tree". Charles M. Schulz. 128p. 1983. pap. 1.95 (ISBN 0-449-20462-6, Crest). Fawcett.
You're Smarter Than You Think: At Least 500 Fun Ways to Expand Your Intelligence. Linda P. Moore. (Illus.). 254p. 1985. pap. 9.95 (ISBN 0-03-063858-5, Owl Bks). H Holt & Co.
You're So Smart, Snoopy: Selected Cartoons from "You're Out of Sight, Charlie Brown", Vol. I. Charles M. Schulz. (Peanuts Ser.). (Illus.). 1983. pap. 1.95 (ISBN 0-449-20408-1, Crest). Fawcett.
You're Someone Special. 2nd ed. Bruce S. Narramore. 176p. 1980. pap. 4.95 (ISBN 0-310-30331-1, 11038P). Zondervan.
You're Something Else, Andy Capp. Reginald Smythe. 128p. (Orig.). 1983. pap. 1.95 (ISBN 0-449-12629-3, GM). Fawcett.
You're Speaking-Who's Listening? Jeanne Ferguson & Maria B. Miller. 1980. pap. text ed. write for info. (ISBN 0-574-22560-9, 13-5560); instr's. guide avail. (ISBN 0-574-22561-7, 13-5561). SRA.
You're Standing on My Fingers. H. Warren Lewis. LC 78-98409. (Illus.). 1969. 8.95 (ISBN 0-8310-7076-5). Howell-North.
You're Supposed to Lead, Charlie Brown. Charles M. Shulz. 1988. pap. 2.95 (ISBN 0-449-21488-5, Crest). Fawcett.
You're Sure Silly, Billy. May Justus. LC 72-1077. (Garrard Venture Ser.). (Illus.). 64p. (gr. 1-3). 1972. PLB 6.89 (ISBN 0-8116-6958-0). Garrard.
You're the Boss. Edward J. Flynn. LC 82-24156. x, 244p. 1983. Repr. of 1947 ed. lib. bdg. 35.00x (ISBN 0-313-23627-5, FLYB). Greenwood.
You're the Boss. Joe Robinson. 352p. 1987. 17.95 (ISBN 0-312-01027-3). St Martin.
You're the Boss: A Guide to Managing People with Understanding & Effectiveness. Natasha Josefowitz. LC 84-15332. 272p. (Orig.). 1985. pap. 8.95 (ISBN 0-446-37744-9). Warner Bks.
You're the Detective! Twenty-Four Solve-Them-Yourself Picture Mysteries. Lawrence Treat. LC 82-49346. (Illus.). 80p. (Orig.). (gr. 3-6). 1983. pap. 6.95 (ISBN 0-87923-478-4). Godine.
You're the Greatest, Charlie Brown. Charles M. Schulz. LC 79-4622. (Illus.). (gr. 1 up). 1979. 4.95 (ISBN 0-394-84260-X, BYR); lib. bdg. 5.99 (ISBN 0-394-94260-4). Random.
You're the Greatest, Charlie Brown. Charles M. Schulz. (Illus.). 96p. (gr. 3-7). 1980. pap. 1.95 (ISBN 0-590-31215-4). Scholastic Inc.
You're the Scaredy-Cat. Mercer Mayer. LC 80-16859. (Illus.). 40p. (ps-3). 1980. Repr. of 1974 ed. 7.95 (ISBN 0-02-765250-5, Four Winds). Macmillan.
You're the Tutor. National Commission on Resources for Youth Staff. 66p. 1970. pap. 2.00 (ISBN 0-912041-03-X). Natl Comm Res Youth.
You're Too Sweet. John P. Connelly. (gr. 4-9). 1968. 9.95 (ISBN 0-8392-1173-2). Astor-Honor.
You're Weird, Sir! Charles M. Schulz. LC 82-18658. (Illus.). 192p. (gr. 2-4). 1982. pap. 4.95 (ISBN 0-03-062099-6). H Holt & Co.
You're What? Help for Pregnant Teens. Karen Sandvig. 150p. 1988. pap. 7.95 (ISBN 0-8307-1267-4, 5419371). Regal.
You're Worth It! But Do You Believe It? Brent D. Earles. 112p. 1985. pap. 5.95 (ISBN 0-8010-3427-2). Baker Bk.
You're You, Charlie Brown. Charles M. Schulz. 1968. 1.50 (ISBN 0-03-073000-7). H Holt & Co.
Your're Really a Model Now! Marcie Anderson. 96p. (gr. 5-8). 1985. 2.25 (ISBN 0-87406-042-7). Willowisp Pr.
Yours Affectionately, Peter Rabbit. Beatrix Potter. (Illus.). 96p. 1983. 6.95 (ISBN 0-7232-3178-8). Warne.
Yours, Brett. Barbara Samuels. 192p. (YA) (gr. 7 up). 1988. 13.95 (ISBN 0-525-67255-9, 01354-410). Lodestar Bks.
Yours by Choice: A Guide for Adoptive Parents. rev ed. Jane Rowe. 1982. pap. 7.95 (ISBN 0-7100-9035-8). Routledge Chapman & Hall.
Yours... Faithfully. Claudia Jameson. (Harlequin Romances Ser.). 192p. 1984. pap. 1.75 (ISBN 0-373-02594-7). Harlequin Bks.
Yours for the Asking: A Cornucopia of Free Information. Ed. by David Corn & Randi Vladimer. 102p. 1981. 5.00 (ISBN 0-936758-02-3). Ctr Responsive Law.
Yours If You Ask. Susan P. Schutz. LC 78-56321. (Illus.). 1978. 13.95 (ISBN 0-88396-028-1). Blue Mtn Pr CO.
Yours In Hell. Terrence L. Smith. 384p. 1987. 17.95 (ISBN 0-312-89828-2). St Martin.
Yours in Struggle: Three Feminist Perspectives on Anti-Semitism & Racism. Elly Bulkin et al. LC 84-80956. 240p. 1984. pap. 7.95 (ISBN 0-9602284-3-8). Firebrand Bks.
Yours Is a Share: The Call of Liturgical Ministry. Austin Fleming. 1985. pap. 4.95 (ISBN 0-912405-20-1). Pastoral Pr.
Yours Is the Earth: The Life & Times of Charles Mitchell. J. P. Gabbedy. 1972. 29.50 (ISBN 0-85564-052-9, Pub. by U of W Austral Pr). Intl Spec Bk.
Yours Is the Power. Florence Widutis. LC 57-9315. 1978. pap. 4.95 (ISBN 0-87516-245-2). DeVorss.
Yours, Mine, & Ours: How Families Change When Remarried Parents Have a Child Together. Anne C. Bernstein. 480p. 1989. 19.95 (ISBN 0-684-18700-0). Scribner.
Yours or Mine. Ezra H. Heywood. 59.95 (ISBN 0-8490-1345-3). Gordon Pr.
Yours Sincerely, Ann W. Shephard (Letters from a College Dean) Ed. by Ann Squires. 1978. pap. 6.00 (ISBN 0-911518-48-7). Touchstone Pr Ore.
Yours Till Niagara Falls. Ed. by Lillian Morrison. LC 50-6508. (Illus.). (gr. 4 up). 1950. 12.70 (ISBN 0-690-91268-4, Crowell Jr Bks). HarpJ.
Yours Till Niagara Falls, Abby. Jane O'Connor. (Illus.). 128p. (gr. 4-6). 1982. pap. 2.50 (ISBN 0-590-41119-5, Apple Paperbacks). Scholastic Inc.
Yours Till Niagara Falls, Abby see Best-Selling Apples.
Yours Truly: A Personal Guide to Self-Discovery. Deena Sackman & Zalman Magid. (Illus.). 138p. (Orig.). 1987. pap. 6.95 (ISBN 0-938711-02-4). Tecolote Pubns.
Yours Truly, from Hell. Terrance L. Smith. 384p. 1987. 17.95 (ISBN 0-317-53573-0). St Martin.
Yours Truly, Harvey Donaldson. Harvey Donaldson. Ed. by Dave Wolfe. 271p. 1981. text ed. 19.50 (ISBN 0-935632-01-8). Wolfe Pub Co.
Yours Truly, Jack the Ripper. Pamela West. 320p. 1987. 17.95 (ISBN 0-312-00868-6, J Kahn). St Martin.
Yours Truly, Jack the Ripper. Pamela West. (YA) 1989. pap. price not set (ISBN 0-440-20259-0). Dell.
Yours Truly, King Arthur: How Medieval People Wrote... & How You Can, Too. Marc Drogin. LC 79-66643. 1982. 10.95 (ISBN 0-8008-8765-4, Pentalic). Taplinger.
Yours Truly, King Arthur: How Medieval People Wrote... & How You Can, Too! Marc Drogin. LC 79-66643. (Illus.). 95p. 1983. pap. 9.95 (ISBN 0-8008-8766-2, Pentalic). Taplinger.
Yours Truly, Love, Janie. Ann Reit. 176p. (Orig.). (gr. 7 up). 1981. pap. 2.25 (ISBN 0-590-31849-7, Wildfire). Scholastic Inc.

Youth Leading Youth. Shane Barker. LC 87-22347. 121p. (YA) (gr. 7-12). 1987. 9.95 (ISBN 0-87579-111-5). Deseret Bk.

Youth League Baseball: Coaching & Playing. Tom Easton et al. (Illus.). 164p. (Orig.). (gr. 2 up). 1984. pap. 7.95 (ISBN 0-87670-082-2, Dist. by Sterling). Athletic Inst.

Youth League Basketball: Coaching & Playing. Ed. by Athletic Institute Staff. (Illus.). 128p. (Orig.). 1984. pap. 7.95. Athletic Inst.

Youth League Football: Coaching & Playing. Ed. by Athletic Institute Staff. (Illus.). 128p. (Orig.). (gr. 2 up). 1984. pap. 7.95 (ISBN 0-87670-081-4). Athletic Inst.

Youth Ministries Handbook. Barrie Smith & Ruth Smith. 120p. 1984. pap. text ed. 12.50 (ISBN 0-8309-0402-6). Herald Hse.

Youth Ministries Ideas III. Dale Jones. 1986. pap. 6.00 (ISBN 0-8309-0470-0). Herald Hse.

Youth Ministries Ideas Two. Lauren E. Say et al. (Orig.). 1985. pap. 6.00 (ISBN 0-8309-0427-1). Herald Hse.

Youth Ministries: Thinking Big With Small Groups. Carolyn C. Brown. 96p. 1984. pap. 7.95 (ISBN 0-687-47203-2). Abingdon.

Youth Ministry Activity Book. Rose T. Stupak. (Illus.). 100p. (Orig.). 1988. pap. 9.95. Resource Pubns.

Youth Ministry & Wilderness Camping. Erik C. Madsen. 160p. 1982. pap. 7.95 (ISBN 0-8170-0962-0). Judson.

Youth Ministry Cargo. Joani Schultz et al. LC 86-14836. (Illus.). 410p. (Orig.). 1986. 18.95 (ISBN 0-931529-14-X). Group Bks.

Youth Ministry Clip Art. Dave Adamson & Steve Hunt. (Illus., Orig.). 1987. pap. 14.95 (ISBN 0-931529-26-3). Group Bks.

Youth Ministry Clip Art Calendar, School Year '88-'89. (Illus.). 32p. (Orig.). 1988. pap. 5.95 (ISBN 0-931529-40-9). Group Bks.

Youth Ministry Drama & Comedy. Chuck Bolte & Paul McCusker. 230p. (Orig.). 1987. pap. 12.95 (ISBN 0-931529-21-2). Group Bks.

Youth Ministry from Start to Finish. Janet Litherland. Ed. by Arthur L. Zapel. LC 85-62467. (Illus.). 128p. (Orig.). 1985. pap. 7.95 (ISBN 0-916260-35-6, B-193). Meriwether Pub.

Youth Ministry Idea Book. Rose T. Stupak. (Illus.). 100p. (Orig.). 1988. pap. 9.95 (ISBN 0-89390-127-X). Resource Pubns.

Youth Ministry Ideabook. 1986. 5.95 (ISBN 0-89536-797-1, 6815). CSS of Ohio.

Youth Ministry in the Church. Stanley J. Watson. LC 78-73597. 1978. pap. 2.50 (ISBN 0-8054-3228-0, 4232-28). Broadman.

Youth Ministry: Its Renewal in the Local Church. rev. ed. Lawrence O. Richards. 1972. 22.95 (ISBN 0-310-32010-0, 18150). Zondervan.

Youth Ministry: Making & Shaping Disciples. Jeffrey D. Jones. 96p. 1986. pap. 5.95 (ISBN 0-8170-1091-2). Judson.

Youth Ministry Resource Book. Ed. by Gene Roehlkepartain. (Orig.). 1988. pap. price not set (ISBN 0-931529-22-0). Group Bks.

Youth Ministry: The New Team Approach. Ginny W. Holderness. LC 80-82186. (Illus.). 160p. (Orig.). 1981. pap. 12.95 (ISBN 0-8042-1410-7, John Knox). Westminster John Knox.

Youth Ministry...Finding Your Way: Catholic Youth Ministry, Youth Ministry Training. Sofia Berrones. (Illus.). 56p. (Orig.). 1987. pap. text ed. write for info. (ISBN 0-942417-00-3). Mission Catechists.

Youth Mobilization for Development in Asian Settings. (Regional Youth Meetings). 1979. pap. 5.00 (ISBN 92-3-101686-5, U923, UNESCO). UNIPUB.

Youth Movement in China. Tsi Chang Wang. lib. bdg. 79.95 (ISBN 0-87968-565-4). Krishna Pr.

Youth Movement to Bruderhof: Letters & Diaries of Annemarie Arnold (Nee Wachter) Annemarie Arnold. Ed. by Hutterian Brethren & Woodcrest Bruderhof. LC 85-12434. (Illus.). 220p. (Orig.). 1985. pap. 8.00 (ISBN 0-87486-183-7). Plough.

Youth Nights Made Easier. Leo Symmank & Karen Jurgensen. 96p. 1987. pap. 8.95 (ISBN 0-570-04501-0, 30-2775). Concordia.

Youth of Europe. Anthony J. Kerr. LC 64-25505. 1964. 10.00 (ISBN 0-8023-1068-0). Dufour.

Youth of Frederick the Great. Ernest Lavisse. LC 71-172308. Repr. of 1892 ed. 24.75 (ISBN 0-404-03891-3). AMS Pr.

Youth of Goethe. P. H. Brown. LC 77-133283. (Studies in German Literature, No. 13). Repr. of 1913 ed. lib. bdg. 54.95x (ISBN 0-8383-1182-2). Haskell.

Youth of Haouch el Harimi, a Lebanese Village. Judith R. Williams. LC 68-23032. (Middle Eastern Monographs Ser: No. 20). 1968. pap. 4.50x (ISBN 0-674-96675-9). Harvard U Pr.

Youth of James Whitcomb Riley. Marcus Dickey. 1973. Repr. of 1919 ed. 35.00 (ISBN 0-8274-1777-2). R West.

Youth of Vichy France. W. D. Halls. 1981. 63.00x (ISBN 0-19-822577-6). Oxford U Pr.

Youth: Open the Door. Eloise Mellor. 1969. pap. 3.00 (ISBN 0-87516-114-6). DeVorss.

Youth or Experience? Manning the Modern Military. Martin Binkin & Irene Kyriakopoulos. LC 79-12633. (Studies in Defense Policy). 84p. 1979. pap. 7.95 (ISBN 0-8157-0969-2). Brookings.

Youth Outreach & Evangelism: Youth Work Guides Ser. Ed. by John Mallison. (Illus.). 104p. (Orig.). 1975. pap. 5.95 (ISBN 0-85819-108-3, Pub. by JBCE). ANZ Religious Pubns.

Youth-Parent Socialization Panel Study, 1965 & 1973, 2 vols. M. Kent Jennings & Richard G. Niemi. LC 81-81765. 1981. Set. write for info., codebk (ISBN 0-89138-947-4); Vol. 1. (ISBN 0-89138-948-2); Vol. 2. (ISBN 0-89138-949-0). ICPSR.

Youth Participation: A Concept Paper. 85p. 1975. pap. 5.00 (ISBN 0-912041-08-0). Natl Comm Res Youth.

Youth Participation & Experiential Education: Theory, Research, & Programs. Ed. by Daniel Conrad & Diane Hedin. LC 81-20114. (Child & Youth Services Ser.: Vol. 4, Nos. 3 & 4). 156p. 1982. text ed. 29.95 (ISBN 0-917724-99-2, B99). Haworth Pr.

Youth Participation for Early Adolescents. Joan Schine & Diane Harrington. LC 81-86310. (Fastback Ser.: No. 174). 50p. (Orig.). 1982. pap. 0.90 (ISBN 0-87367-174-0). Phi Delta Kappa.

Youth Participation in Documenting CETA Youth Employment Programs. Bruce Dollar & Peter Kleinbard. 62p. 1981. pap. 5.00 (ISBN 0-912041-10-2). Natl Comm Res Youth.

Youth Participation in Youth Advocacy. Peter Kleinbard. 65p. 1982. pap. 5.00 (ISBN 0-912041-12-9). Natl Comm Res Youth.

Youth Pastor's Handbook. Ed. by E. S. Caldwell. 144p. 1987. 3 ring binder 25.00 (ISBN 0-930525-02-7, Creation Hse). Strang Comms Co.

Youth Plan Worship. Betty Jane & J. Martin Bailey. 256p. (Orig.). 1987. pap. 10.95 (ISBN 0-8298-0745-4). Pilgrim NY.

Youth Poems. Winsom Amos. (Illus.). 24p. (Orig.). (gr. 6-12). 1983. pap. 1.75x (ISBN 0-932510-00-0). Soma Pr.

Youth Problems. Research Reports Editors. LC 82-18222. 176p. 1982. pap. 10.95 (ISBN 0-87187-244-7). Congr Quarterly.

Youth: Problems & Approaches. Ed. by S. J. Shamsie. LC 72-79353. pap. 75.70 (ISBN 0-317-09751-2, 2014579). Bks Demand UMI.

Youth Profile: India. K. K. Siddh & S. K. Gupta. 79p. (Orig.). 1987. pap. text ed. 18.75 (ISBN 0-317-67236-3, UB356, UB). UNIPUB.

Youth Profile Thailand. Wilawan Kanjanapan. (RUSHSAP Series on Occasional Monographs & Papers: No. 16). (Illus.). 87p. (Orig.). 1986. pap. text ed. 7.50 (ISBN 0-318-21275-7, UB208, UNESCO). UNIPUB.

Youth Program Hour Idea Book. Compiled by Larry Leonard & Jack McCormick. 144p. 1985. pap. 6.95 (ISBN 0-8341-0949-2). Beacon Hill.

Youth Related Indicators. 141p. (Orig.). 1984. pap. 7.50 (UB149, UB). UNIPUB.

Youth Restored. Mikhail Zoshchenko. Tr. by Joel Stern. 210p. 1984. 20.00 (ISBN 0-88233-629-0). Ardis Pubs.

Youth Retreats: Creating Sacred Space for Young People. Aileen A. Doyle. (Illus.). 109p. 1986. spiral bdg. 12.95 (ISBN 0-88489-177-1). St Mary's.

Youth Review: Social Conditions of Young People in Wolverhampton. Paul Willis et al. 350p. 1988. text ed. 55.00 (ISBN 0-566-07001-4, Pub. by Gower Pub England). Gower Pub Co.

Youth Service: A Guidebook for Developing & Operating Effective Programs. 70p. Date not set. 12.50. Ind Sector.

Youth Service & Interprofessional Studies. I. Bulman et al. 1970. 31.00 (ISBN 0-08-015736-X). Pergamon.

Youth Services Coordinator. Jack Rudman. (Career Examination Ser.: C-2324). (Cloth bdg. avail. on request). pap. 16.00 (ISBN 0-8373-2324-X). Natl Learning.

Youth Services Specialist. Jack Rudman. (Career Examination Ser.: C-1641). (Cloth bdg. avail. on request). 1988. pap. 14.00 (ISBN 0-8373-1641-3). Natl Learning.

Youth-Serving Organizations Directory. 2nd ed. Ed. by Annie M. Brewer. 1185p. 1980. 80.00x (ISBN 0-8103-0238-1). Gale.

Youth Soccer: A Handbook for Coaches & Parents. Ed. by Eugene Brown & Vern Seefeldt. (Illus.). 400p. 1988. pap. text ed. 21.95 (ISBN 0-936157-28-3). Benchmark Pr.

Youth Soccer: Amateur Coach. Gerald O'Shea. 1986. 10.95 (ISBN 0-317-54063-7). Greene.

Youth, Socialization, & Mental Health. William P. Lebra. LC 73-85581. (Mental Health Research in Asia & the Pacific Ser: Vol. 3). 320p. 1974. text ed. 17.50x (ISBN 0-8248-0293-4, Eastwest Ctr). UH Pr.

Youth, Society & the Public Library. Miriam Braverman. LC 78-17267. 1979. 25.00x (ISBN 0-8389-0260-X). ALA.

Youth Specialties Clip Art Book. Wayne Rice. 240p. (Orig.). 1985. pap. 14.95 (ISBN 0-310-34911-7, 10824P). Zondervan.

Youth Specialties Clip Art Book, Vol. II. Compiled by Wayne Rice. 112p. 1987. pap. 14.95 (ISBN 0-310-39791-X, 10828P). Zondervan.

Youth Suicide. Michael Peck et al. (Series on Death & Suicide: Vol. 6). 224p. 1985. pap. text ed. 15.95 (ISBN 0-8261-4480-2). Springer Pub.

Youth Suicide: Depression & Loneliness. Brent Q. Hafen & Kathryn J. Frandsen. 200p. (Orig.). 1986. pap. 9.95 (ISBN 0-917895-11-8). Cordillera CO.

Youth Tell Their Story: A Study of the Conditions & Attitudes of Young People in Maryland Between the Ages of 16 & 24. facsimile ed. Howard M. Bell. LC 74-1665. (Children & Youth Ser.: Social Problems & Social Policy). 290p. 1974. Repr. of 1938 ed. 24.50x (ISBN 0-405-05946-9). Ayer Co Pubs.

Youth, Tradition & Development in Africa: Regional Meeting on Youth in Africa, Nairobi, Kenya, 17-22 December 1979. (Regional Youth Meetings: No. 3). (Illus.). 146p. 1981. pap. 6.00 (ISBN 92-3-101918-X, U1185, UNESCO). UNIPUB.

Youth Training. David Lee et al. 500p. 1988. text ed. 35.00 (ISBN 0-566-05325-X, Pub. by Gower Pub England). Gower Pub Co.

Youth Training & Employment: From New Deal to New Federalism. Paul Bullock. (Monograph & Research Ser.: No. 43). 350p. 1985. 15.00 (ISBN 0-89215-133-1). U Cal LA Indus Rel.

Youth Training & the Search for Work: A Study of Young People in Crisis. Ed. by Denis Gleeson. (Routledge Education Bks.). 200p. (Orig.). 1983. pap. 19.95x (ISBN 0-7100-9513-9). Routledge Chapman & Hall.

Youth Training Scheme: A New Curriculum; Episode 1. Terry A. Edwards. 1984. 25.00x (ISBN 0-905273-96-6, Falmer Pr); pap. 16.00x (ISBN 0-905273-95-8). Taylor & Francis.

Youth Training Scheme in the United Kingdom. Paul G. Chapman & Michael J. Tooze. 134p. 1987. text ed. 39.95 (ISBN 0-566-05360-8). Gower Pub Co.

Youth: Transition to Adulthood. James S. Coleman et al. LC 73-92757. viii, 194p. 1986. pap. text ed. 12.00x (ISBN 0-226-11343-4, Midway Reprint). U of Chicago Pr.

Youth: Transition to Adulthood-Report on Youth of the President's Advisory Committee. James S. Coleman et al. LC 73-92757. 1974. pap. 12.00x (P589, Midway). U of Chicago Pr.

Youth Try the Impossible. Donald J. Moore. 96p. 1983. pap. 3.95 (ISBN 0-942684-03-6). Camp Guidepts.

Youth Tutoring Youth: A Manual for Trainers. 120p. 1970. pap. 5.00 (ISBN 0-912041-05-6). Natl Comm Res Youth.

Youth Tutoring Youth: Supervisor's Manual. 64p. (Orig.). 1968. pap. 3.50 (ISBN 0-912041-00-5). Natl Comm Res Youth.

Youth Unemployment. Mark Casson. LC 79-11242. 141p. 1979. 27.75 (ISBN 0-8419-5050-4). Holmes & Meier.

Youth Unemployment. Michael D. Jackson. LC 84-29332. 180p. 1985. 29.00 (ISBN 0-7099-1453-9, Pub. by Croom Helm Ltd). Routledge Chapman & Hall.

Youth, Unemployment & Schooling. Ed. by Stephen Walker & Len Barton. 192p. 1986. 65.00x (ISBN 0-335-15228-7, Open Univ Pr); pap. 21.00x (ISBN 0-335-15227-9). Taylor & Francis.

Youth Unemployment & State Intervention. Teresa L. Rees & Paul Atkinson. 160p. 1983. pap. 12.50x (ISBN 0-7100-9263-6). Routledge Chapman & Hall.

Youth Unemployment & Training: A Collection of National Perspectives. Ed. by R. Fiddy. 234p. 1985. 33.00x (ISBN 0-905273-86-9, Falmer Pr); pap. 18.00x (ISBN 0-905273-85-0). Taylor & Francis.

Youth Unemployment in Great Britian. P. E. Hart. (National Institute of Economic & Social Research Occasional Paper Ser.: No. 43). (Illus.). 168p. 1988. 34.50 (ISBN 0-521-35348-3). Cambridge U Pr.

Youth Unemployment in the Federal Republic of Germany: Theory, Empirical Results & Policy Implications: An Economic Analysis. Wolfgang Franz. 265p. 1982. pap. text ed. 56.50x (Pub. by J C B Mohr BRD). Coronet Bks.

Youth Unemployment: The Causes & Consequences. Ed. by OECD Staff. (Illus.). 134p. (Orig.). 1980. pap. text ed. 9.50x (ISBN 92-64-12137-4, 81-80-05-1). OECD.

Youth Violence: Programs & Prospects. Ed. by Steven J. Apter & Arnold P. Goldstein. (Pergamon General Psychology Ser.). (Illus.). 304p. 1986. 43.00 (ISBN 0-08-031922-X, Pub. by P P I). Pergamon.

Youth, Vol 3 (Incl. 1986-1987 Supplements) Ed. by Eleanor C. Goldstein. 1987. 15.00 (ISBN 0-89777-086-2). Soc Issues.

Youth Volleyball Coaches Manual. John M. Ferrell & Clifford T. McPeak. 64p. 1983. pap. 3.00x (ISBN 0-88035-065-2, Pub. by YMCA USA). Human Kinetics.

Youth Without Work: Three Countries Approach to the Problem. Shirley Williams et al. 255p. (Orig., Avail. FREN. & ENG.). 1981. pap. text ed. 15.00x (ISBN 92-64-12240-0). OECD.

Youth Without Youth: Three Fantastic Novellas. Mircea Eliade. Intro. by Matei Calinescu. Tr. by Mac Linscott Ricketts from Romanian. 256p. 1988. 18.95 (ISBN 0-8142-0457-0). Ohio St U Pr.

Youth Work Programs: Problems & Policies, Vol. No. 3. Lewis L. Lorwin. LC 74-1694. (Children & Youth Ser.). 212p. 1974. Repr. of 1941 ed. 20.00x (ISBN 0-405-05970-1). Ayer Co Pubs.

Youth Workers' Handbook. Steve Clapp & Jerry O. Cook. 280p. 1981. pap. 11.00 (ISBN 0-914527-05-3). C-Four Res.

Youth Worker's Manual. Daryl Dale. 126p. 1987. wkbk. 9.95 (ISBN 0-87509-350-7). Chr Pubns.

Youth Worker's Personal Management Handbook. Ed. by Lee Sparks. LC 84-73152. 264p. 1985. 16.95 (ISBN 0-931529-03-4). Group Bks.

Youthful Haunts of Longfellow. George T. Edwards. 1907. Repr. 25.00 (ISBN 0-8274-3782-X). R West.

Youthful High School Noncompleters: Enhancing Opportunities for Employment & Education. Larry G. Martin. 59p. 1987. 7.00 (ISBN 0-318-23415-7, IN316). Natl Ctr Res Voc Ed.

Youthful Recreations. (Illus.). 1810. 1.50 (ISBN 0-911132-07-4). Phila Free Lib.

YOUTHJOBS: Toward a Private-Public Partnership. David Bresnick. LC 84-3343. 160p. 1984. lib. bdg. 35.00 (ISBN 0-89930-093-6, BYJ/, Quorum). Greenwood.

Youthjobs: Toward a Private-Public Partnership. David Bresnick. 151p. 1986. pap. text ed. 14.95 (ISBN 0-9610834-2-5). Human Serv Pr.

Youths' Guide to Job Hunting. Margaret Brownley. 32p. (Orig.). (YA) (gr. 8-12). 1988. pap. 2.95. Comm Intervention.

Youth's Noble Path see Tales of All Times.

Youth's P-Mess & Complete. Sarah Johnson. 32p. 1986. 6.50 (ISBN 0-8062-2848-2). Carlton.

Youthtrends: Capturing the One Hundred Sixty Billion Dollar Youth Market. Lawrence Graham & Lawrence Hamdan. 288p. 1987. 15.95 (ISBN 0-312-00704-3, Pub. by Thomas Dunne Bks). St Martin.

You've Been Away All Summer. Sheila Hayes. 160p. (gr. 4-7). 1986. 12.95 (ISBN 0-525-67182-X, 01258-370). Lodestar Bks.

You've Been Away All Summer. Sheila Hayes. 160p. (gr. 4-8). 1988. pap. 2.50 (ISBN 0-590-40791-0, Apple Paperbacks). Scholastic Inc.

You've Come a Long Way, Snoopy: Selected Cartoons from "Thompson Is in Trouble", Vol. I. Charles M. Schulz. (Peanuts Ser.). (Illus.). 1983. pap. 1.95 (ISBN 0-449-20358-1, Crest). Fawcett.

You've Got a Friend, Charlie Brown: Selected Cartoons from "You'll Flip, Charlie Brown", Vol. I. Charles M. Schulz. 1985. pap. 2.25 (ISBN 0-449-20698-X, Crest). Fawcett.

You've Got a Song. Donna Gading & Daniel Pokorny. (Illus.). pap. 3.00 (ISBN 0-317-62988-3, SL044). Natl Assn Deaf.

You've Got Charisma. Lloyd J. Ogilvie. 177p. 1983. pap. 4.35 (ISBN 0-687-47268-7). Abingdon.

You've Got It Made. Marian Burros. 1985. pap. 7.95 (ISBN 0-671-55239-2). PB.

You've Got to be Kid-ding! A Look at Adolescents. Helen Ryley et al. (Illus.). 185p. 1985. pap. text ed. 9.95 (ISBN 0-911023-01-1, PA 341 650). ATC Boulder.

You've Got to Be Kidding, Snoopy. Charles M. Schulz. (Peanuts Ser.). (Illus.). 1983. pap. 1.95 (ISBN 0-449-20440-5, Crest). Fawcett.

You've Got to Be You, Snoopy: Selected Cartoons from "You've Come a Long Way, Charlie Brown", Vol. II. Charles M. Schulz. (Peanuts Ser.). (Illus.). 1981. pap. 2.95 (ISBN 0-449-23774-5, Crest). Fawcett.

You've Got to Get Through the Outside Layer. Hilary Tupling et al. 144p. 1981. pap. text ed. 15.00 (ISBN 0-9593811-0-4). Am Assn Diabetes Ed.

You've Got to Learn, Because I've Got to Teach. Robert Sorgi. 224p. (Orig.). 15.95 (ISBN 0-944248-03-9). Court Hse Sq Pr.

You've Got to Ride the Subway. Madge Reinhardt. LC 76-4760. 278p. 1977. pap. 6.50 (ISBN 0-917162-02-1). Back Row Pr.

You've Gotta Hand It to God! Timothy M. Powell. LC 84-73557. (Radiant Life Ser.). 128p. 1985. 2.95 (ISBN 0-88243-859-X, 02-0859); tchr's. guide 3.95 (ISBN 0-88243-199-4, 32-0199). Gospel Pub.

You've Really Got Me, God! Alan Porter. (Direction Bks.). pap. 1.45 (ISBN 0-8010-7019-8). Baker Bk.

You've Taught Too Long If You Remember When... William C. Elwell & Ruth E. Elwell. (Illus.). 40p. (Orig.). 1988. pap. 4.00 (ISBN 1-55787-030-6). Heart of the Lakes.

Yovhannes Tclkurancci & the Mediaeval American Lyric Tradition. James R. Russell. LC 85-22066. (Armenian Texts & Studies). 260p. 1987. 16.95 (21-02-07); pap. 12.95 (ISBN 0-89130-930-6). Scholars Pr GA.

Yowsah! Yowsah! Yowsah! The Roaring Twenties. Kenneth R. Bruce. (Illus.). 160p. 1981. pap. 8.95 (ISBN 0-686-73518-8). Star Pub CA.

Ypsilanti-Perry Preschool Project: Preschool Years & Longitudinal Results Through Fourth Grade. D. P. Weikart et al. LC 77-92916. (Monographs of the High-Scope Educational Research Foundation: No. 3). 142p. (Orig.). 1978. pap. 12.00 (ISBN 0-931114-02-0). High-Scope.

Ypsilanti Preschool Curriculum Demonstration Project: Preschool Years & Longitudinal Results. D. P. Weikart et al. LC 77-92917. (Monographs of the High-Scope Educational Research Foundation: No. 4). 152p. 1978. pap. 12.00 (ISBN 0-931114-03-9). High-Scope.

Yum Yum. Janet Ahlburg & Allan Ahlburg. LC 84-40124. 20p. (ps-k). 1985. 7.95 (ISBN 0-670-79620-4). Viking.

Yum, Yum. Arthur Dorros. LC 87-47542. (Illus.). 12p. (ps-1). 1987. 2.95 (ISBN 0-694-00187-2, Crowell Jr Bks). HarpJ.

Yuma. Russell Smith. 176p. 1982. pap. 1.95 (ISBN 0-8439-1079-8, Leisure Bks). Leisure NY.

Yuma: California. Ed. by Frank W. Porter, III. (Indians of North America Ser.). (Illus.). (gr. 5 up). 1989. 16.95 (ISBN 1-55546-737-7). Chelsea Hse.

Yuma: Renegade Gold. Russell Smith. 1979. pap. 1.50 (ISBN 0-8439-0660-X, Leisure Bks). Leisure NY.

Yuma Roundup, No. 3. J. D. Hardin. 1987. pap. 2.75 (ISBN 0-425-10348-X). Berkley Pub.

Yuman & Yaqui Music. Frances Densmore. LC 72-1884. (Music Ser.). (Illus.). 272p. 1972. Repr. of 1932 ed. lib. bdg. 27.50 (ISBN 0-306-70512-5). Da Capo.

Yuman Tribes of the Gila River. Leslie Spier. LC 74-118641. (Illus.). 1970. Repr. of 1933 ed. lib. bdg. 25.00x (ISBN 0-8154-0333-X). Cooper Sq.

Yuman Tribes of the Gila River. Leslie Spier. LC 77-92480. (Illus.). 1978. pap. 7.95 (ISBN 0-486-23611-0). Dover.

Yummers! James Marshall. LC 72-5400. (Illus.). 32p. (gr. k-3). 1973. PLB 11.95 (ISBN 0-395-14757-3). HM.

Yummers! James Marshall. (Illus.). (gr. 4-8). 1986. pap. 3.95 (ISBN 0-395-39590-9, Sandpiper). HM.

Yummers Too. James Marshall. LC 86-10667. (Illus.). 32p. (gr. k-3). 1986. 12.95 (ISBN 0-395-38990-9). HM.

Yummies for Tummies. Sayre School. (Illus.). 96p. (gr. 4 up). 1977. pap. 4.95 (ISBN 0-918544-37-8). Wimmer Bks.

Yummy, Yummy. Judith Grey. LC 81-2360. (Illus.). 32p. (gr. k-2). 1981. PLB 9.89 (ISBN 0-89375-543-5); pap. 2.95 (ISBN 0-89375-544-3). Troll Assocs.

Yundong: Mass Campaigns in Chinese Communist Leadership. Gordon Bennett. LC 75-620060. (China Research Monographs: No. 12). 133p. 1976. pap. text ed. 2.25x (ISBN 0-912966-15-7). IEAS.

Yung-Ho-Kung. F. D. Lessing. 1942. 525.00x (ISBN 0-317-68533-3, Pub. by Han-Shan Tang Ltd). State Mutual Bk.

Yung Sung Ch'i-Kung: The Six Healing Sounds. Gin Foon Mark. (Illus., Orig.). Date not set. pap. price not set (ISBN 0-938045-06-7). Bubbling-Well.

Yung Wing: The First Chinese Student in the United States. Shao Yuen Carol. (Connecticut Educational History Ser.). 24p. 1987. pap. 2.50. I N Thut World Educ Ctr.

Yunini's Story of the Trail of Tears. Ada L. Barry. LC 74-7924. (Illus.). Repr. of 1932 ed. 34.50 (ISBN 0-404-11810-0). AMS Pr.

Yunnan. Paddy Booz. (Illus.). 208p. 1987. pap. 9.95 (ISBN 0-8442-9822-0, Passport Bks). Natl Textbk.

Yunnan Jinning Shizhaishan Gumu Qun Faju Baogao. Yunnan Provincial Museum Staff. 149p. 1959. 665.00x (ISBN 0-317-69264-X, Pub. by Han-Shan Tang Ltd). State Mutual Bk.

Yunnan Qing Tongqi. Yunnan Provincial Museum Staff. 216p. 1981. 420.00x (ISBN 0-317-69267-4, Pub. by Han-Shan Tang Ltd). State Mutual Bk.

Yunnan School: A Renaissance in Chinese Painting. Joan L. Cohen. LC 87-83744. (Illus.). 160p. 1988. 75.00 (ISBN 0-9619771-0-8). Fingerhut Group.

Yunus Emre & His Mystical Poetry. Ed. by Talat S. Halman. LC 81-81923. (Indiana University Turkish Studies Ser.). 208p. (Orig.). 1981. 29.95x (ISBN 0-253-39806-1); pap. 14.25x (ISBN 0-317-04023-5); pap. 14.25 (ISBN 0-253-39802-9). Ind U Pr.

Yunus Emre (Selected Poems) Ilhan Basgoz & Talat S. Halman. (Indiana University Turkish Studies Ser.). 1981. Record 8.95X (ISBN 0-253-39803-7). Ind U Pr.

Yup the Organization. James Wavada. 224p. 1986. 15.95 (ISBN 0-531-15503-X). Watts.

Yup'ik Eskimo Dictionary. Compiled by Steven A. Jacobson. (Illus.). viii, 757p. 1984. pap. 18.00 (ISBN 0-933769-21-0). Alaska Native.

Yup'ik Eskimo Grammar. Irene Reed et al. viii, 330p. 1977. pap. 7.50 (ISBN 0-933769-26-1). Alaska Native.

Yupik Eskimo Prosodic Systems: Descriptive & Comparative Studies. Michael Krauss et al. (Alaska Native Language Center Research Papers: No. 7). (Illus.). vi, 216p. 1985. pap. 15.00 (ISBN 0-933769-37-7). Alaska Native.

Yup...Nope, & Other Vermont Dialogues. Keith W. Jennison. (Illus.). 96p. (Orig.). 1976. pap. 7.95 (ISBN 0-914378-14-7). Countryman.

Yuppie Handbook. Marissa Piesman & Marilee Hartley. 128p. (Orig.). 1984. pap. 4.95 (ISBN 0-671-47684-X, Long Shadow Bks). PB.

Yuppies Invade My House at Dinnertime: A Tale of Brunch, Bombs, & Gentrification in an American City. Ed. by Joseph Barry & John Derevlany. LC 87-82140. (Illus.). 208p. (Orig.). 1987. pap. 7.95 (ISBN 0-944421-01-6). Big River NJ.

Yurak Chrestomathy. Gyula Decsy. LC 65-63391. (Uralic & Altaic Ser: Vol. 50). (Orig., Yurak). 1966. pap. text ed. 4.00x (ISBN 0-87750-004-5). Res Ctr Lang Semiotic.

Yuri Bondarev, Yuri Bondarev on Craftmanship. Yu Idashkin & Yu Bondarev. 285p. 1985. 7.95 (ISBN 0-8285-2821-7, Pub. by Raduga Pubs USSR). Imported Pubns.

Yuri Gagarin: First Man in Space. Mitchell R. Sharpe. LC 74-75841. (Heroes of Space Ser). (Illus.). (gr. 7 up). 1969. 4.95 (ISBN 0-87397-203-1). Strode.

Yuri Vasnetsov: Paintings, Drawings, Watercolours, Book Illustrations, Lithographs, Theatrical Designs, Porcelain. Ed. by Vsevolod Petrov. 196p. 1984. 165.00x (ISBN 0-317-57494-9, Pub. by Collets UK). State Mutual Bk.

Yurok Myths. Alfred L. Kroeber. LC 75-3772. 460p. 1976. 35.00x (ISBN 0-520-02977-1); pap. 9.95 (ISBN 0-520-03639-5). U of Cal Pr.

Yurth Burden. Andre Norton. (Science Fiction Ser.). 160p. 1987. pap. 2.95 (ISBN 0-88677-249-4). DAW Bks.

Yurtyet. Ed. by Charles J. Stanley. LC 79-84627. (Illus.). 52p. (Orig.). 1979. pap. 7.50 perfect bdg. (ISBN 0-934376-03-4). Pittore Euforico.

Yury Olesha: The Complete Short Stories & the Three Fat Men. Yury Olesha. Tr. by Aimee Fisher from Rus. 1979. 17.50 (ISBN 0-88233-213-9). Ardis Pubs.

Yury Trifonov: A Critical Study. Nina Kolesnikoff. 1988. 21.50 (ISBN 0-87501-051-2). Ardis Pubs.

Yusef: The Journey of the Frangi; a Crusade in the East. John R. Browne. Ed. by Moshe Davis. LC 77-70686. (America & the Holy Land Ser.). (Illus.). 1977. Repr. of 1853 ed. lib. bdg. 24.00x (ISBN 0-405-10232-1). Ayer Co Pubs.

Yushka. A. Kuprin. 26p. 1977. pap. 1.49 (ISBN 0-8285-1256-6, Pub. by Progress Pubs USSR). Imported Pubns.

Yussel's Prayer. Barbara Cohen. LC 80-25377. (Illus.). 32p. (gr. k-4). 1981. 11.75 (ISBN 0-688-00460-1); PLB 11.88 (ISBN 0-688-00461-X). Lothrop.

Yust for Fun. Eleonora Olson & Ethel Olson. (Illus.). 60p. 1979. pap. 2.50 (ISBN 0-9602914-1-5). Eggs Pr.

Yusuf Meherally: Quest for New Horizons. Madhu Dandavate. 1986. 19.00 (ISBN 0-86132-139-1, Pub. by Popular Prakashan). South Asia Bks.

Yuwipi: Vision & Experience in Oglala Ritual. William K. Powers. LC 81-10501. (Illus.). xiv, 113p. 1984. pap. 4.95 (ISBN 0-8032-8710-0, BB 877, Bison). U of Nebr Pr.

Yvain dans le Miroir: Une Poetique de la reflexion dans le "Chevalier au lion" de Chretien de Troyes. Joan T. Grimbert. (Purdue University Monographs in Romance Languages: Vol. 25). xii, 226p. 1988. pap. 17.95x (ISBN 1-55619-055-7); 40.95 (ISBN 1-55619-055-7). Benjamins North Am.

Yvain (Le Chevalier au Lion) Chrestien De Troyes. Intro. by T. B. Reid. (French Texts Ser.). 288p. (Orig., Fr.). 1984. pap. text ed. 10.00 (ISBN 0-7190-0134-X, Pub. by Manchester Univ Pr.). St Martin.

Yvain; or, the Knight with the Lion. Chretien De Troyes. Tr. by Ruth H. Cline from Fr. LC 73-85026. 222p. 1975. pap. 6.95x (ISBN 0-8203-0758-0). U of Ga Pr.

Yvain, Ou le Chevalier Au Lion. Chretien De Troyes. Ed. by Jan Nelson et al. LC 68-22800. (Medieval French Literature Ser). (Orig., Fr.). 1968. pap. 6.95x (ISBN 0-89197-477-6). Irvington.

Yvain, the Knight of the Lion. Chretien De Troyes. LC 86-23346. 224p. 1987. text ed. 22.50 (ISBN 0-300-03837-2, Y-640); pap. 7.95 (ISBN 0-300-03838-0). Yale U Pr.

Yvar, Prince of Rus. Richard Cloke. LC 80-80543. (Illus.). pap. 8.75 (ISBN 0-917458-08-7, Pub. by Cerulean Pr). Kent Pubns.

Yves Bonnefoy. Mary A. Caws. (World Authors Ser.: No. 702). 150p. 1984. lib. bdg. 20.95 (ISBN 0-8057-6549-2, Twayne). G K Hall.

Yves de Vallone: The Making of an Espirit-Fort. James O'Higgins. 1982. 35.00 (ISBN 90-247-2520-8, Pub. by Martinus Nijhoff Netherlands). Kluwer Academic.

Yves Klein. Pierre Restany. (Illus.). 1982. 75.00 (ISBN 0-8109-1205-8). Abrams.

Yves Klein Nineteen Twenty-Eight to Nineteen Sixty-Two: A Retrospective. Ed. by Institute for the Arts Staff. LC 81-86085. (Illus.). 1982. pap. 25.00 (ISBN 0-914412-27-2). Inst for the Arts.

Yves Saint Laurent & the Photography of Fashion. Yves S. Laurent. LC 88-45314. (Illus.). 224p. 1988. 100.00 (ISBN 0-394-57326-9). Knopf.

Yves Tanguy. James T. Soby. LC 75-169321. (Museum of Modern Art Publications in Reprint). 72p. 1972. Repr. of 1955 ed. 15.00 (ISBN 0-405-01579-8). Ayer Co Pubs.

Yvette-a Novelette, & Ten Other Stories. facsimile ed. Guy De Maupassant. Tr. by Mrs. John Galsworthy. LC 70-150550. (Short Story Index Reprint Ser.). Repr. of 1916 ed. 15.00 (ISBN 0-8369-3847-X). Ayer Co Pubs.

Yvon Delbos at the Quai D'Orsay: French Foreign Policy During the Popular Front, 1936-1938. John E. Dreifort. LC 72-85252. (Illus.). xiv, 274p. 1973. 29.95x (ISBN 0-7006-0094-9). U Pr of KS.

Yvonne: An Autobiography. Yvonne De Carlo & Doug Warren. 288p. 1987. 17.95 (ISBN 0-312-00217-3, Pub. by Thomas Dunne Bks). St Martin.

Yvonne Jacquette: Tokyo Nightviews. LC 86-60688. (Illus.). 10p. (Orig.). 1986. pap. 5.00 (ISBN 0-916606-11-2). Bowdoin Coll.

Yvonne Porcella: A Colorful Book. Yvonne Porcella. LC 85-90510. (Illus.). 120p. (Orig.). 1986. pap. 22.00 (ISBN 0-936589-00-0). Porcella Studios.

Yvor Winters: An Annotated Bibliography 1919-1982. Grosvenor Powell. LC 83-14466. (Scarecrow Author Bibliographies: No. 66). 214p. 1983. 19.00 (ISBN 0-8108-1653-9). Scarecrow.

Yvor Winters: The Uncollected Essays & Reviews. Ed. by Francis Murphy. LC 72-91915. 320p. 1972. 18.00x (ISBN 0-8040-0604-0, Pub by Swallow). Ohio U Pr.

Ywain: The Knight of the Lion. Chretien De Troyes. Tr. by Robert W. Ackerman & Frederick W. Locke. LC 77-10461. (Milestones of Thought Ser.). pap. 5.95x (ISBN 0-8044-6084-1). Ungar.

Z

Z. Vassilis Vassilikos. 1985. pap. 3.95 (ISBN 0-394-72990-0). Pantheon.

Z Comm. Kyle Maning. (Swastika). 288p. (Orig.). 1988. pap. 3.95 (ISBN 0-8439-2652-X, Pub. by Leisure Bks CT). Leisure NY.

Z-Cycle: Winning by a Force of a Fourth Type. Wilbur W. Bigelow. LC 78-56742. (Illus.). 281p. 1980. 14.95 (ISBN 0-936366-00-1); pap. 9.95 (ISBN 0-936366-01-X). Crown.

Z-D Generation. Ed Sanders. 32p. 1981. pap. 3.50 (ISBN 0-930794-35-4). Station Hill Pr.

Z for Zachariah. Robert C. O'Brien. LC 74-76736. 256p. (YA) (gr. 7 up). 1975. 13.95 (ISBN 0-689-30442-0, Atheneum Childrens Bks). Macmillan.

Z for Zachariah. Robert C. O'Brien. LC 86-23228. 256p. (gr. 7). 1987. pap. 3.95 (ISBN 0-02-044650-0, Collier). Macmillan.

Z Is for Zombie. Mel Gilden. (GLC Bk.). 96p. (gr. 3-7). 1988. pap. 2.50 (ISBN 0-380-75686-2, Camelot). Avon.

Z Is for Zombie. Theodore Roscoe. (Starmont Facsimile Fiction Ser.: No. 2). 128p. 1989. lib. bdg. 17.95x (ISBN 0-8095-5451-8). Borgo Pr.

Z Is for Zombie. Theodore Roscoe. (Facsimile Fiction Ser.: Vol. 2). 1988. 17.95x (ISBN 1-55742-043-2); pap. 8.95x (ISBN 1-55742-042-4). Starmont Hse.

Z moroku vikiv na svitlo nashykh dniv, lektsii dopovidi rozvidky. Wasyl O. Luciw. 200p. (Ukrainian.). 1986. pap. 20.00 (ISBN 0-317-47660-2). Slavia Lib.

Z R Wins. Fitzhugh Green. Ed. by R. Reginald & Douglas Melville. LC 77-84232. (Lost Race & Adult Fantasy Ser.). 1978. Repr. of 1924 ed. lib. bdg. 24.50x (ISBN 0-405-10980-6). Ayer Co Pubs.

Z-Series Datsun. Ray Hutton. (Collector's Guide Ser.). (Illus.). 1982. 29.95 (ISBN 0-947981-02-0, Pub. by Motor Racing England). Motorbooks Intl.

Z-Transform Electromagnetic Transient Analysis in High-Voltage Networks. W. Derek Humpage. (IEE Power Engineering Ser.: No. 3). 264p. 1982. pap. 75.00 (ISBN 0-906048-79-6, P0003). Inst Elect Eng.

Z Transform Theory & Applications. Robert Vich. 1987. lib. bdg. 69.00 (ISBN 90-277-1917-9, Pub. by Reidel Holland). Kluwer Academic.

Z Was Zapped: A Play in Twenty-Six Acts. Chris Van Allsburg. (Illus.). 56p. (ps up). 1987. 15.95 (ISBN 0-395-44612-0, Clarion). HM.

Z-80 Assembly Language Programming. Lance A. Levanthal et al. 640p. (Orig.). 1979. pap. text ed. 19.95 (ISBN 0-07-931021-4). Osborne-McGraw.

Z-80 Assembly Language Programming. Stelle & Tomek. LC 87-6616. 308p. 1987. 26.95 (ISBN 0-88175-146-4, Computer Sci Pr). W H Freeman.

Z-80 Microprocessor Technology: Hardware, Software & Interfacing. James W. Bignell & Robert Donovan. 416p. 1986. text ed. 34.95 (ISBN 0-8273-2492-8); instr's. guide 9.00 (ISBN 0-8273-2493-6). Delmar.

Za Chei Schet? Compiled by Yuri Felshtinsky. LC 86-4626. 188p. (Orig., Rus.). 1986. pap. 10.00 (ISBN 0-938920-69-3). Hermitage.

ZA VSE V Otvete. Feliks Kuznetsov. 588p. 1984. 52.00x (ISBN 0-317-40665-5, Pub. by Collets UK). State Mutual Bk.

Zabajaba Jungle. William Steig. LC 87-17690. (Michael di Capua Bks.). (Illus.). (ps-4). 1987. 13.95 (ISBN 0-374-38790-7). FS&G.

Zabern Nineteen Hundred Thirteen: Consensus Politics in Imperial Germany. David Schoenbaum. 208p. 1982. text ed. 29.95x (ISBN 0-04-943025-4). Unwin Hyman.

Zacchaeus Meets the Savior. Neal Boehlke. 1980. pap. 1.29 (ISBN 0-570-06132-6, 59-1250, Arch Bk). Concordia.

Zaccheus Meets Jesus. Diane Stortz. (Happy Day Bible Stories Bks.). (Illus.). 24p. (ps-2). 1984. 1.59 (ISBN 0-87239-766-1, 3726). Standard Pub.

Zachariah Chandler: A Political Biography. Mary K. George. 300p. 1969. 8.50 (ISBN 0-87013-139-7). Mich St U Pr.

Zacharias Ursinus: The Reluctant Reformer-His Life & Times. Derk Visser. 192p. 1983. pap. 7.95 (ISBN 0-8298-0691-1). Pilgrim NY.

Zachary Goes to the Zoo. Jill Krementz. LC 86-60109. (Tough Enough Bks.). (Illus.). 24p. (ps-1). 3.95 (ISBN 0-394-88236-9, BYR). Random.

Zachary Taylor. K. Jack Bauer. Ed. by Carol B. Fitzgerald. (Meckler's Bibliographies of the Presidents of the United States, 1789-1989 Ser.: No. 12). (Illus.). 1989. lib. bdg. 45.00x (ISBN 0-88736-126-9). Meckler Corp.

Zachary Taylor: Soldier, Planter, Statesman of the Old Southwest. K. Jack Bauer. LC 85-11028. (Southern Biography Ser.). (Illus.). 348p. 1985. text ed. 35.00 (ISBN 0-8071-1237-2). La State U Pr.

Zachary Taylor, 1784-1850 & Millard Fillmore, 1800-1874: Chronology, Documents, Bibliographical Aids. J. J. Farrell. LC 78-116061. (Presidential Chronology Ser). 1971. 8.00 (ISBN 0-379-12078-X). Oceana.

Zach's Law, No. 225. Kay Hooper. 192p. 1987. pap. 2.50 (ISBN 0-553-21852-2, Loveswept). Bantam.

Zack, Sam, & the Rich Fool. Joyce M. Smith. 64p. 1988. pap. 3.50 (ISBN 0-8423-8854-0). Tyndale.

Zacualpa: A Study of Ancient Quiche Artifacts. Samuel K. Lothrop. LC 77-11508. (Carnegie Institution of Washington. Publication: No. 472). 1977. Repr. of 1936 ed. 20.00 (ISBN 0-404-16269-X). AMS Pr.

Zacualpa, El Quiche, Guatemala: An Ancient Provincial Center of the Highland Maya. Robert Wauchope. (Illus.). xvi, 308p. 1975. 30.00 (ISBN 0-939238-44-6). Tulane MARI.

Zadar. Alexander Taylor. LC 76-28505. 1976. pap. 2.95 (ISBN 0-917488-00-8). Ziesing Bros.

Zaddick Christ: A Suite of Wood Engravings. Bernard A. Solomon. (Illus.). 84p. 1974. 16.95 (ISBN 0-87921-022-2). Attic Pr.

Zadie; or, the Book of Fate, 1749. Voltaire. Ed. by Michael F. Shugrue. Incl. Amours of Zeokinizal King of the Kofiranis, 1749. Claude Crebillon. (Flowering of the Novel, 1740-1775 Ser: Vol. 25). 1975. lib. bdg. 61.00 (ISBN 0-8240-1124-4). Garland Pub.

Zadig. Voltaire. (Classiques de la civilisation francaise). pap. 3.95 (ISBN 0-685-34065-1). French & Eur.

Zadig see Candide.

Zadig avec Memnon. Voltaire. Ed. by Jacques Spica. 128p. 1977. 3.95 (ISBN 0-686-55762-X). French & Eur.

Zadig l'Ingenu. Voltaire. Tr. by John Butt from Fr. (Classics Ser). 1978. pap. 5.95 (ISBN 0-14-044126-3). Penguin.

Zadig, Micromegas et Autres Contes. Voltaire. Ed. by Grimal. (Bibliotheque de Cluny). pap. 5.50 (ISBN 0-685-34064-3). French & Eur.

Zadoc Pine & Other Stories. facsimile ed. Henry C. Bunner. LC 70-94704. (Short Story Index Reprint Ser). 1891. 18.00 (ISBN 0-8369-3086-X). Ayer Co Pubs.

Zafloya; or the Moor: A Romance of the Fifteenth Century, 3 vols, Vol. 8. Charlotte Dacre. LC 73-22763. (Gothic Novels Ser.). 802p. 1974. Repr. of 1806 ed. Set. 86.00x (ISBN 0-405-06014-9). Ayer Co Pubs.

Zagadka Tolstogo. Mark A. Aldanov. LC 79-91652. (Brown University Slavic Reprint Ser.: No. 7). pap. 34.50 (ISBN 0-317-28393-6, 2022394). Bks Demand UMI.

Zagat Nineteen Eighty-Eight Boston Restaurant Survey. Eugene H. Zagat, Jr. & Nina S. Zagat. Ed. by Corby Kummer & Jane Lavine. (Orig.). 1988. pap. 8.95 (ISBN 0-943421-03-9). Zagat.

Zagat Nineteen Eighty-Eight Los Angeles Restaurant Survey. Eugene Zagat, Jr. & Nina S. Zagat. Ed. by Merrill Shindler & Karen Berk. 140p. (Orig.). 1987. pap. 8.95 (ISBN 0-943421-02-0). Zagat.

Zagat Nineteen Eighty-Eight New Orleans Restaurant Survey. Eugene H. Zagat, Jr. & Nina S. Zagat. Ed. by Pat Denechaud & Sharon Litwin. (Orig.). 1988. pap. 8.95 (ISBN 0-943421-04-7). Zagat.

Zagat Nineteen Eighty-Eight New York City Restaurant Survey. Eugene H. Zagat, Jr. & Nina S. Zagat. 145p. (Orig.). 1987. pap. 9.95 (ISBN 0-943421-00-4). Zagat.

Zagat Nineteen Eighty-Eight Washington, D. C. Restaurant Survey. Eugene H. Zagat, Jr. & Nina S. Zagat. Ed. by Olga Boikess. 110p. (Orig.). 1987. pap. 8.95 (ISBN 0-943421-01-2). Zagat.

Zagat Survey of New York City Food Sources. Eugene H. Zagat, Jr. & Nina S. Zagat. Ed. by Margo P. Ernst. 143p. (Orig.). 1986. pap. 8.95 (ISBN 0-9612574-3-1). Zagat.

Zagorsk Museum of History & Art: A Guide. Collet's Staff. (Rus.). 1983. 20.00x (ISBN 0-317-57311-X, Pub. by Collets UK). State Mutual Bk.

Zagreb-Croatian Spring. Ivo M. Omrcanin. 1976. pap. 5.95 (ISBN 0-8059-2240-7). Dorrance.

Zagros, Hindu Kush, Himalaya: Geodynamic Evolution. H. K. Gupta & F. M. Delany. (Geodynamics Series: Vol. 3). 323p. 1981. 36.00 (ISBN 0-87590-507-2). Am Geophysical.

Zaharias: The Sports Career of Mildred Didrickson Zaharias. James Hahn & Lynn Hahn. Ed. by Howard Schroeder. LC 80-28383. (Sports Legends Ser.). (Illus.). 48p. (Orig.). (gr. 3-5). 1981. PLB 8.95 (ISBN 0-89686-122-8). Crestwood Hse.

Zahlentheorie, 6 vols. Paul Bachmann. (Nos. 15-20). (Ger). Repr. Set. 175.00 (ISBN 0-384-02990-6). Johnson Repr.

Zahlentheorie. S. J. Borewicz & I. R. Safarewic. (Mathematische Reihe Ser.: No. 32). (Illus.). 468p. (Ger.). 1966. 57.95x (ISBN 0-8176-0039-6). Birkhauser.

Zahr-I-Ishq or Poison of Love: A Love Narrative from Awadh. Navvab M. Shawq. Tr. by Shah A. Salam & Jeffrey J. Donaghue. xiv, 140p. 1983. text ed. 18.95x (ISBN 0-86590-110-4). Apt Bks.

Zebra. Caroline Arnold. LC 87-1503. (Illus.). 48p. (gr. 2-5). 1987. 11.75 (ISBN 0-688-07067-1, Morrow Junior Books); lib. bdg. 11.88 (ISBN 0-688-07068-X, Morrow Junior Books). Morrow.

Zebra. Mary Hoffman. LC 84-24793. (Animals in the Wild Ser.). (Illus.). 24p. (gr. k-3). 1985. PLB 11.33 (ISBN 0-8172-2414-9). Raintree Pubs.

Zebra Finches. K. J. Lawrence. (South Group Colorguide Ser.). 1982. pap. 3.50 (ISBN 0-940842-12-2). South Group.

Zebra Finches. Mervin F. Roberts. (Illus.). 1981. 9.95 (ISBN 0-87666-882-1, KW-055). TFH Pubns.

Zebra Finches. Cyril Rogers. (Illus.). 94p. 1977. pap. 3.95 (ISBN 0-7028-1085-1). Avian Pubns.

Zebra Finches. (Pet Care Ser.). 80p. (Orig.). 1985. pap. 3.95 (ISBN 0-8120-3497-X). Barron.

Zebra-Striped Hearse. Ross Macdonald. 224p. 1984. pap. 3.95 (ISBN 0-553-27362-0). Bantam.

Zebra-Striped Hearse see Archer in Jeopardy.

Zebra Wall. Kevin Henkes. LC 87-18454. 160p. (gr. 3 up). 1988. 10.95 (ISBN 0-688-07568-1). Greenwillow.

Zebra Who Learned to Dance see Sidney Duck & the Blue Monster.

Zebulon Pike's Arkansas Journal. Zebulon M. Pike. Ed. by Stephen H. Hart & Archer B. Hulbert. LC 72-138172. (Illus.). 200p. 1972. Repr. of 1932 ed. lib. bdg. 35.00x (ISBN 0-8371-5629-7, PIAJ). Greenwood.

Zeby Polska...(Let Poland Be...) Aleksander Biedak. (Illus.). 60p. (Orig., Pol.). 1986. 6.00 (ISBN 0-930401-06-9). Artex Pr.

Zechariah. Homer Heater, Jr. (Bible Study Commentary Ser.). 128p. (Orig.). 1988. pap. 6.95 (ISBN 0-310-36911-8, 18287P). Zondervan.

Zechariah. J. Carl Laney. (Everyman's Bible Commentary Ser.). (Orig.). 1984. pap. 6.95 (ISBN 0-8024-0445-6). Moody.

Zechariah Chafee, Jr. Donald L. Smith. (Illus.). 386p. 1986. text ed. 27.00x (ISBN 0-674-96685-6). Harvard U Pr.

Zechstein Basin with Emphasis on Carbonate Sequences. Ed. by H. Feuchtbauer & T. Peryt. (Contributions to Sedimentology Monograph: No. 9). (Illus.). 328p. 1980. pap. text ed. 65.00x (ISBN 3-510-57009-X). Lubrecht & Cramer.

Zechstein Facies in Europe. Ed. by T. M. Peryt. (Lecture Notes in Earth Sciences Ser.: Vol. 10). x, 272p. 1987. pap. 49.50 (ISBN 0-387-17710-8). Springer-Verlag.

Zed. Rosemary Harris. 192p. (YA) (gr. 7 up). 1984. 12.95 (ISBN 0-571-11947-6). Faber & Faber.

Zed & Two Noughts. Peter Greenaway. 150p. (Orig.). 1986. pap. 11.95 (ISBN 0-571-13767-9). Faber & Faber.

Zed Pan African Diary Nineteen Seventy-Nine. Robert Molteno & Henry Freedman. 144p. 1979. pap. 1.00 (ISBN 0-905762-26-6, Pub. by Zed Pr England). Humanities.

Zeek Silver Moon. Amy Ehrlich. LC 70-181787. (Illus.). 32p. (ps-3). 1972. 7.95 (ISBN 0-8037-9825-3). Dial Bks Young.

Zeely. Virginia Hamilton. LC 67-10266. (Illus.). 128p. (gr. 5-7). 1967. 12.95 (ISBN 0-02-742470-7). Macmillan.

Zeely. Virginia Hamilton. LC 86-22197. (Illus.). 128p. (gr. 5-7). 1986. pap. 3.95 (ISBN 0-689-71110-7, Aladdin Bks). Macmillan.

Zeffirelli: An Autobiography. Franco Zeffirelli. (Illus.). 376p. 1986. 19.95 (ISBN 1-55584-022-1). Weidenfeld.

Zehn Bucher Frankischer Geschichte, 3 vols. 4th ed. Saint Gregorius. Ed. by S. Hellmann. Tr. by Wilhel M Von Geisebrecht. 1911-1913. 34.00 ea. (ISBN 0-384-19908-9). Johnson Repr.

Zehnte Bildungsjahr unter Bildungspolitischem Aspekt. Ludger Busshoff. (European University Studies: No. 11, Vol. 135). 234p. (Ger.). 1982. 27.90 (ISBN 3-8204-7044-1). P Lang Pubs.

Zeichen und Bezeichnetes: Sprachphilosophische Untersuchungen zum Problem der Referenz. Edmund Runnggaldier. (Grundlagen der Kommunikation - Bibliothekausgabe Ser.). xii, 363p. (Ger.). 1985. 43.20x (ISBN 3-11-010107-6). De Gruyter.

Zeis' Manual of Plastic Surgery. Eduard Zeis. Tr. by T. J. Patterson & Blair O. Rogers. (Illus.). 360p. 1988. 72.00 (ISBN 0-19-261746-X). Oxford U Pr.

Zeisberger's Indian Dictionary: English, German, Iroquois - the Onandaga & Algonquin - the Delaware. David Zeisberger. LC 76-43905. 248p. (Eng., Ger. & Iroquois.). Repr. of 1887 ed. 42.50 (ISBN 0-404-15802-1). AMS Pr.

Zeiss General Catalogue for 1936. (Illus.). 68p. 1980. pap. 7.95 (ISBN 0-906447-10-0, Pub. by Hove Foto Bks). Seven Hills Bks.

Zeiss Ikon Cameras, 1926-1939. D. B. Tubbs. (Illus.). 144p. 1980. 22.95 (ISBN 0-906447-21-6, Pub. by Hove Foto Bks). Seven Hills Bks.

Zeiss Microscopes for Microsurgery. W. H. Lang & F. Muchel. (Illus.). 144p. 1981. 31.00 (ISBN 0-387-10784-3). Springer-Verlag.

Zeit, Tod und Ewigkeit in der Renaissance Literatur, Vol. 3. Ed. by James Hogg. 1987. pap. 25.00 (ISBN 3-7052-0197-2, Pub. by Salzburg Studies). Longwood Pub Group.

Zeit und Ewigkeit: Studien zum Wortschatz der Geistlichen Texte des Alt-und Fruehmittelhochdeutschen. Harald Burger. LC 74-174177. (Studia Linguistica Germanica: Vol. 6). 1972. 34.00x (ISBN 3-11-003995-8). De Gruyter.

Zeit und Zeiterlebnis in den Werken Max Frischs: Bedeutung und Technische Darstellung. Erna M. Dahms. (Quellen und Forschungen zur Sprach und Kulturgeschichte der Germanischen Voelker). 1976. 30.40 (ISBN 3-11-006679-3). De Gruyter.

Zeit Von Den Leoniden see Time of the Leonids.

Zeitalter der Deutschen Erhebung see Age of German Liberation, 1795-1815.

Zeiten, Volker und Menschen, 7 vols. in four. Karl Hillebrad. LC 78-67356. (European Political Thought Ser.). (Ger.). 1979. Repr. of 1886 ed. lib. bdg. 184.00x (ISBN 0-405-11701-9); lib. bdg. 46.00x ea. Vol. 1 (ISBN 0-405-11702-7). Vol. 2 (ISBN 0-405-11703-5). Vol. 3 (ISBN 0-405-11704-3). Vol. 4 (ISBN 0-405-11705-1). Ayer Co Pubs.

Zeitgenoessische Deutsche Dialektgedicht. Josef Berlinger. (European University Studies: No. 1, Vol. 688). 392p. (Ger.). 1983. 28.40 (ISBN 3-8204-7813-2); 28.40 (ISBN 3-8204-7553-2). P Lang Pubs.

Zeitroman: The Novel & Society in Germany, 1830-1900. Roger Hillman. LC 83-5461. (Australian & New Zealand Studies in German Language & Literature: Vol. 12). 186p. 1983. pap. text ed. 19.45 (ISBN 0-8204-0010-6). P Lang Pubs.

Zeitschriften des Jungen Deutschland: Indices, 2 vols. Alfred Estermann. (Illus., Ger.). 1975. 166.00 (ISBN 0-318-23475-0). Kraus Repr.

Zeitschriftenerwerbung un Lieferantewahl in Wissenschaftlichen der Bundesrepublik Deutschland. Eike Schmuser. (Bibliotgekspraxis Ser.: Vol. 27). 130p. (Ger.). 1986. lib. bdg. 24.00 (ISBN 3-598-21128-7). K G Saur.

Zeitung fuer Die elegante Welt, 3 vols. Ed. by Heinrich Laube. 1973. Repr. of 1833 ed. 100.00 ea. (ISBN 0-384-70845-5). Johnson Repr.

Zeitungs-Innovationen. Lorenz Goslich. x, 198p. (Ger.). 1987. pap. text ed. 23.00 (ISBN 3-598-10695-5). K G Saur.

Zeitungswissenschaften in Koln. Hans-Georg Klose. 370p. (Ger.). 1988. pap. text ed. 25.00 (ISBN 3-598-21302-6). K G Saur.

Zeitungwissenschaft in Westfalen, 1914-1945: DasInstitut fur Zeitungwissenschaft in Munster und die Zeitungwissenschaft in Dortmund. Ed. by Bettina Maoro. 368p. (Ger.). 1987. lib. bdg. 25.00 (ISBN 3-598-21300-X). K G Saur.

Zejel. F. Sanchez. 62p. 1.25 (ISBN 0-318-14321-6). Hispanic Inst.

Zeke Hatfield & a Ghost Named Rocky. John Barrett. (Silver Dollar City Stories). (Illus.). (gr. k-10). 1978. 1.99 (ISBN 0-686-22892-8). Silver Dollar.

Zekmet the Stone Carver: A Tale of Ancient Egypt. Mary Stolz. LC 86-22931. (Illus.). 32p. (gr. 2-5). 1988. 13.95 (ISBN 0-15-299961-2). HarBraceJ.

Zelda. Nancy Milford. LC 83-47568. (Illus.). 464p. 1983. pap. 8.95 (ISBN 0-06-091069-0, CN 1069, PL). Har-Row.

Zelda; Frontier Life in America: A Fantasy in Three Acts. Kaye McDonough. LC 78-15332. 1978. pap. 3.50 (ISBN 0-87286-104-X). City Lights.

Zelda M'Tana. F. M. Busby. 320p. 1986. pap. 2.95 (ISBN 0-425-09296-8). Berkley Pub.

Zelda Strikes Again! Lynn Hall. 144p. (gr. 3 up). 1988. 13.95 (ISBN 0-15-299966-3). HarBraceJ.

Zelda the Zebra. (Zoo Babies Ser.). 16p. (gr. k-6). 1982. pap. 1.25 (ISBN 0-8249-8035-2). Ideals.

Zelenoe Okno - Stikhi - Russian: The Green Window - Poems. Vadim Kreyd. LC 87-15536. 72p. (Orig., Rus.). 1987. 10.00 (ISBN 0-911971-22-X). Effect Pub.

Zelerod's Doom. Jacqueline Lichtenberg & Jean Lorrah. 280p. 1986. pap. 3.50 (ISBN 0-88677-145-5). DAW Bks.

Zella, Zack & Zodiac. Bill Peet. (gr. k-3). 1985. 12.95 (ISBN 0-317-40567-5). HM.

Zelmira Rossini, 2 vols. Rossini. (Romantic Opera Ser.). 1979. lib. bdg. 198.00 (ISBN 0-8240-2911-9). Garland Pub.

Zemanim. Edgar Frank. 6.00 (ISBN 0-87306-063-6). Feldheim.

Zement Woerterbuch. C. Van Amerongen. 202p. (Ger. & Eng., Dictionary of Cement). 1967. 15.95 (ISBN 3-7625-1171-3, M-7691, Pub. by Bauverlag). French & Eur.

Zemindari Settlement of Bengal, 2 vols. 1985. Repr. of 1879 ed. Set. text ed. 200.00x (ISBN 0-86590-390-5, Pub. by B R Pub Corp Delhi). Vol. 1, 436 p. Vol. 2, 441 p. Apt Bks.

Zemiros Shabbos. 1982. pap. 1.50 large (ISBN 0-686-76284-3); pap. 1.25 medium; pap. 0.50 small. Feldheim.

Zemiroth - Sabbath Songs. Nosson Scherman. Ed. by Meir Zlotowitz. (Artscroll Mesorah Ser.). 1979. 15.95 (ISBN 0-89906-156-7); pap. 12.95 (ISBN 0-89906-157-5). Mesorah Pubns.

Zemlja Imjeninnitsa. V. Nikiforoff-Volgin. 182p. 1960. pap. 6.00 (ISBN 0-317-30418-6). Holy Trinity.

Zemlya za kholmom. Dora Shturman. 256p. (Rus.). 1983. pap. 7.00 (ISBN 0-938920-32-4). Hermitage.

Zemstvo in Russia: An Experiment in Local Self-Government. Ed. by Terence Emmons & Wayne S. Vucinich. LC 81-3897. 464p. 1982. 49.50 (ISBN 0-521-23416-6). Cambridge U Pr.

Zen: A Semantic Approach. C. N. Hu. (Illus.). 118p. (Orig.). 1988. pap. 7.95. Victory Press.

Zen: A Way of Life. Christmas Humphreys. LC 65-17332. 1971. pap. 7.95 (ISBN 0-316-38160-8). Little.

Zen Action-Zen Person. T. P. Kasulis. LC 80-27858. 192p. 1985. pap. text ed. 7.95x (ISBN 0-8248-1023-6). UH Pr.

Zen & American Thought. Van Meter Ames. 1978. Repr. of 1962 ed. lib. bdg. 35.00 (ISBN 0-313-20066-1, AMZA). Greenwood.

Zen & Christian: The Journey Between. John Eusden. 224p. 1981. 10.95 (ISBN 0-8245-0099-7). Crossroad NY.

Zen & Hasidism. Ed. by Harold Heifetz. LC 78-9073. 1978. 10.95 (ISBN 0-8356-0514-0). Theos Pub Hse.

Zen & Japanese Culture. D. T. Suzuki. (Bollingen Ser.: Vol. 64). (Illus.). 1959. pap. 10.95x (ISBN 0-691-01770-0). Princeton U Pr.

Zen & Japanese Culture. Daisetz T. Suzuki. 478p. 1973. 100.00x (ISBN 0-317-68510-4, Pub. by Han-Shan Tang Ltd). State Mutual Bk.

Zen & Modern Japanese Religions. Michael Pye. 1985. 13.00 (ISBN 0-7062-3148-1, Pub. by Ward Lock Educ Co Ltd). State Mutual Bk.

Zen & Reality see Great Awakening.

Zen & the Art of Calligraphy. Omori Sagen & Terayama Katsujo. 115p. 1983. pap. 63.00x (ISBN 0-317-69268-2, Pub. by Han-Shan Tang Ltd). State Mutual Bk.

Zen & the Art of Calligraphy. Omori Sogen & Terayama Katsujo. Tr. by John Stevens from Japanese. (Illus.). 128p. (Orig.). 1983. pap. 13.95 (ISBN 0-7100-9284-9). Routledge Chapman & Hall.

Zen & the Art of Medicaid. Rene Reixach. 42p. 1983. 3.75 (36,170). NCLS Inc.

Zen & the Art of Motorcycle Maintenance: An Inquiry into Values. Robert M. Pirsig. LC 73-12275. 1974. pap. 19.95 (ISBN 0-688-00230-7). Morrow.

Zen & the Art of Motorcycle Maintenance: An Inquiry into Values. Robert M. Pirsig. 1979. pap. 10.95 (ISBN 0-688-05230-4). Morrow.

Zen & the Art of Motorcycle Maintenance. Robert M. Pirsig. 416p. (gr. 10 up). 1976. pap. 4.95 (ISBN 0-553-25748-X). Bantam.

Zen & the Art of Pottery. Ken Beittel. (Illus.). 208p. 32.50 (ISBN 0-8348-0221-X). Weatherhill.

Zen & the Art of the Macintosh. Michael Green. 1986. lib. bdg. 33.80 (ISBN 0-89471-348-5); pap. 16.95 (ISBN 0-89471-347-7). Running Pr.

Zen & the Art of Writing. Manjushri J Vitale. 90p. (Orig.). 1984. pap. 10.95 (ISBN 0-932896-07-3). Westcliff Pubns.

Zen & the Bible: A Priest's Experience. J. K. Kadowaki. (Orig.). 1980. pap. 8.95 (ISBN 0-7100-0402-8). Routledge Chapman & Hall.

Zen & the Birds of Appetite. Thomas Merton. LC 68-25546. 1968. pap. 4.95 (ISBN 0-8112-0104-X, NDP261). New Directions.

Zen & the Fine Arts. Shinichi Hisamatsu. Tr. by Gishin Tokiwa. LC 76-136562. (Illus.). 400p. 1982. pap. 24.95 (ISBN 0-87011-519-7). Kodansha.

Zen & the Fine Arts. Hisamatsu Shin'ichi. 400p. 1971. 770.00x (ISBN 0-317-69269-0, Pub. by Han-Shan Tang Ltd). State Mutual Bk.

Zen & the Mind: A Scientific Approach to Zen Practice. Tomio Hirai. (Illus., Orig.). 1978. 10.50 (ISBN 0-87040-391-5). Japan Pubns USA.

Zen & the Taming of the Bull. Walpola Rahula. 160p. 1978. 33.00 (ISBN 0-317-68578-3, Pub. by Gordon Fraser). State Mutual Bk.

Zen & the Ways. Trevor Leggett. Ed. by Florence Sakade. LC 87-50165. (Illus.). 272p. (Orig.). 1987. pap. 8.95 (ISBN 0-8048-1524-0). C E Tuttle.

Zen & Us. Karlfried G. Durckheim. Tr. by Vincent Nash from Ger. 144p. 1987. pap. 8.95 (ISBN 0-525-48331-4). Dutton.

Zen & Western Thought. Masao Abe. Ed. by William R. LaFleur. LC 83-24153. 1985. text ed. 24.95x (ISBN 0-8248-0952-1). UH Pr.

Zen & Zen Classics: Selections from R. H. Blyth. Ed. by Frederick Franck. (Illus.). 1978. pap. 8.95 (ISBN 0-394-72489-5, Vin). Random.

Zen Approach to Bodytherapy: From Rolf to Feldenfrais to Tanouye Roshi. Dub Leigh. 1987. pap. 10.95x (ISBN 0-8248-1099-6, Pub. by Inst Zen Studies). UH Pr.

Zen Art for Meditation. Stewart W. Holmes & Chimyo Horioka. LC 73-78279. (Illus.). 1978. pap. 5.50 (ISBN 0-8048-1255-1). C E Tuttle.

Zen Buddhism. Christmas Humphreys. 256p. 1988. pap. 13.95 (ISBN 0-04-294095-8). Unwin Hyman.

Zen Buddhism - A History: India & China. Heinrich Dumoulin. 384p. 1988. pap. 14.95 (ISBN 0-02-908260-9). Macmillan.

Zen Buddhism & Psychoanalysis. Erich Fromm et al. LC 60-5293. 1970. pap. 7.95 (ISBN 0-06-090175-6, CN175, PL). Har-Row.

Zen Buddhism & Psychoanalysis. D. T. Suzuki et al. 180p. 1960. 200.00x (Pub. by Han-Shan Tang Ltd). State Mutual Bk.

Zen Comics. Ioanna Salajan. LC 74-35679. 88p. 1974. pap. 4.95 (ISBN 0-8048-1120-2). C E Tuttle.

Zen Comics, Vol. II. Ioanna Salajan. LC 82-50094. (Illus.). 88p. (Orig.). 1982. pap. 5.25 (ISBN 0-8048-1445-7). C E Tuttle.

Zen Comments on the Mumonkan. Zenkei Shibayama. LC 73-18692. (Illus.). 384p. 1984. pap. 10.95 (ISBN 0-06-067278-1, CN 4091, HarpR). Har-Row.

Zen Concrete & Etc. D. A. Levy et al. (Illus.). 100p. 1988. pap. 10.00 (ISBN 0-941160-04-1). Ghost Pony Pr.

Zen Dance Meditation in Movement. Sun O. Lee & Alan Heyman. (Illus.). 108p. 1985. 24.00 (ISBN 0-8048-1428-7, Pub. by Seoul Intl Tourist Korea). C E Tuttle.

Zen Dawn. Tr. by Jonathan C. Cleary from Chinese. LC 85-27904. 135p. (Orig.). 1986. pap. 8.95 (ISBN 0-87773-359-7, 74388-1). Shambhala Pubns.

Zen Dictionary. Ernest Wood. LC 72-77518. 1972. pap. 6.95 (ISBN 0-8048-1060-5). C E Tuttle.

Zen: Direct Pointing to Reality. Anne Bancroft. (Art & Imagination Ser.). (Illus.). 1987. pap. 11.95 (ISBN 0-500-81018-4). Thames Hudson.

Zen Doctrine of No Mind. D. T. Suzuki. 1981. pap. 9.95 (ISBN 0-87728-182-3). Weiser.

Zen Driving. K. T. Berger. 1988. pap. 6.95 (ISBN 0-345-35350-1). Ballantine.

Zen Effects: The Life of Alan Watts. Monica Furlong. 1986. 17.95 (ISBN 0-395-35344-0). HM.

Zen Effects: The Life of Alan Watts. Monica Furlong. (Illus.). 256p. 1987. pap. 7.95 (ISBN 0-395-45392-5). HM.

Zen Enlightenment: Origins & Meaning. Heinrich Dumoulin. LC 78-27310. 188p. 1979. pap. 7.95 (ISBN 0-8348-0141-8). Weatherhill.

Zen Experience. Thomas Hoover. (Illus., Orig.). 1980. pap. 5.95 (ISBN 0-452-25315-2, Z5315, Plume). NAL.

Zen Eye. Sokei-an Sasaki. Ed. by Mary Farkas. LC 84-48129. 136p. (Orig.). Date not set. pap. 10.95 (ISBN 0-87011-696-7). Kodansha.

Zen Flesh, Zen Bones. Paul Reps. LC 57-10199. (Illus.). 1957. 12.95 (ISBN 0-8048-0644-6). C E Tuttle.

Zen Flesh, Zen Bones: A Collection of Zen & Pre-Zen Writings. Ed. by Paul Reps. 1961. pap. 4.95 (ISBN 0-385-08130-8, A233, Anch). Doubleday.

Zen for Americans: Including the Sutra of Forty-Two Chapters. Soyen Shaku. Tr. by D. T. Suzuki. 220p. 1974. pap. 6.95 (ISBN 0-87548-273-2). Open Court.

Zen for Beginners. Judith Blackstone & Zoran Josipovic. (Writers & Readers Documentary Comic Bks.). (Illus.). 176p. (Orig.). 1986. pap. 6.95 (ISBN 0-86316-116-2). Writers & Readers.

Zen Forest: Sayings of the Masters. Soiku Shigematsu. LC 81-31. (Illus.). 200p. 1981. 19.95 (ISBN 0-8348-0159-0). Weatherhill.

Zen Guide: Where to Meditate in Japan. Martin Roth & John Stevens. (Illus.). 152p. pap. 7.50 (ISBN 0-8348-0202-3). Weatherhill.

Zen Haiku & Other Zen Poems of J. W. Hackett. rev. ed. James W. Hackett. (Illus.). 224p. 1983. 14.95 (ISBN 0-87040-533-0). Japan Pubns USA.

Zen Harvest: Japanese Zen Folk Sayings (Haiku, Dodoitsu & Waka) Ed. & tr. by Soiku Shigematsu. LC 87-82594. 208p. 1988. pap. 12.95 (ISBN 0-86547-328-5). N Point Pr.

Zen Imagery Exercises: Meridian Exercises for Wholesome Living. Shizuto Masunaga & Stephen Brown. LC 86-80220. (Illus.). 192p. (Orig.). 1986. pap. 13.95 (ISBN 0-87040-669-8). Japan Pubns USA.

Zen in American Life & Letters. Ed. by Robert S. Ellwood. LC 87-51198. (Interplay: Vol. 6). 200p. (Orig.). 1987. 25.00x (ISBN 0-89003-261-0); pap. 16.00x (ISBN 0-89003-260-2). Undena Pubns.

Zen in the Art of Archery. Eugen Herrigel. 1971. pap. 4.95 (ISBN 0-394-71663-9, V663, Vin). Random.

Zen in the Art of Flower Arrangement: An Introduction to the Spirit of the Japanese Art of Flower Arrangement. Gustie L. Herrigel. 1974. pap. 6.95 (ISBN 0-7100-7942-7). Routledge Chapman & Hall.

Zen in the Art of Helping. David Brandon. 1978. pap. 3.45 (ISBN 0-385-29193-0, Delta). Dell.

Zen in the Art of Painting. Helmut Brinker. 192p. 1988. pap. 14.95 (ISBN 1-85063-058-5, Arkana). Routledge Chapman & Hall.

Zen in the Art of the Tea Ceremony. Bo Gyllensvard. Tr. by Peter Lemesurier from Ger. 36p. 1979. 50.00x (Pub. by Han-Shan Tang Ltd). State Mutual Bk.

Zen in the Art of the Tea Ceremony. Horst Hammitzsch. 112p. 1982. pap. 2.95 (ISBN 0-380-59907-4, Discus). Avon.

Zen in the Art of the Tea Ceremony. Horst Hammitzsch. Tr. by Peter Lemesurier. 128p. 1988. pap. cancelled (ISBN 0-525-48421-3, Obelisk). Dutton.

Zen in the Martial Arts. Joe Hyams. LC 78-62884. 143p. 1979. 10.95 (ISBN 0-87477-114-5); pap. 6.95 (ISBN 0-87477-101-3). J P Tarcher.

Zen in the Martial Arts. Joe Hyams. 144p. 1982. pap. 3.95 (ISBN 0-553-26078-2). Bantam.

Zen Ink Paintings. Sylvan Barnet & William Burto. LC 82-80648. (Great Japanese Art Ser.). (Illus.). 96p. 1982. 24.95 (ISBN 0-87011-521-9). Kodansha.

Zen Inklings: Some Stories, Fables, Parables, Sermons & Prints with Notes & Commentaries. Donald Richie. LC 82-2561. (Illus.). 162p. 1982. 17.95 (ISBN 0-8348-0170-1). Weatherhill.

Zero Population Growth; Implications. Ed. by Joseph J. Spengler. (Illus.). 1975. pap. text ed. 5.00 (ISBN 0-89055-113-8). Carolina Pop Ctr.
Zero Quality Control: Source Inspection & Poka-Yoke System. Shigeo Shingo. Tr. by Andrew P. Dillon from Japanese. (Illus.). 303p. 1986. 65.00 (ISBN 0-915299-07-0). Prod Press.
Zero-Range Potentials & Their Applications in Atomic Physics. Yu. N. Demkov & V. N. Ostrovskii. Ed. by P. G. Burke. Tr. by S. M. Ermolaev from Rus. (Physics of Atoms & Molecules Ser.). (Illus.). 274p. 1988. 75.00x (ISBN 0-306-42779-6, Plenum Pr). Plenum Pub.
Zero Seven Fifty-Five: Pearl Harbor Heroes: Heroism of 250 Men & Women 7 December 1941. Don Ross & Helen Ross. 200p. 1941. pap. 11.95 (ISBN 0-930942-15-9). Rokalu Pr.
Zero Seven Five Five: The Heroes of Pearl Harbor. Donald K. Ross & Helen L. Ross. (Illus.). 158p. (Orig.). 1988. pap. 11.95 (ISBN 0-9620552-0-4). Rokalu Pr.
Zero Stone. Andre Norton. 224p. 1985. pap. 2.75 (ISBN 0-441-95966-0). Ace Bks.
Zero-Sum Society. Lester C. Thurow. 230p. 1981. pap. 6.95 (ISBN 0-14-005807-9). Penguin.
Zero-Sum Solution. Lester Thurow. 416p. 1986. pap. 9.95 (ISBN 0-671-62814-3, Touchstone Bks). S&S.
Zero-Sum Solution: Building a World Class American Economy. Lester Thurow. 1985. 18.95 (ISBN 0-671-55232-5). S&S.
Zero-Symmetric Graphs: Trivalent Graphical Regular Representations of Groups. H. S. Coxeter et al. LC 81-4604. 1981. 34.50 (ISBN 0-12-194580-4). Acad Pr.
Zero: The Air War in the Pacific in World War II, from the Japanese Viewpoint. Masatake Okumiya et al. LC 79-20670. Repr. of 1956 ed. 25.00 (ISBN 0-89201-082-7). Zenger Pub.
Zero Weather. Ramon S. Morningstar. Ed. by Una King & Delia Moon. LC 80-20072. 367p. (Orig.). 1980. pap. 3.95 (ISBN 0-937770-00-0). Family Pub CA.
Zeroglyphics. rev. & enl. ed. Adriano Spatola. Tr. by Guilia Niccolai & Paul Vangelisti. 1977. pap. 4.00 (ISBN 0-88031-045-6). Invisible-Red Hill.
Zeros of Bernoulli, Generalized Bernoulli, & Euler Polynomials. Karl Dilcher. (MEMO Ser.: No. 386). 104p. 1988. write for info. (ISBN 0-8218-2449-X). Am Math.
Zeros of Sections of Power Series. A. Edrei et al. (Lecture Notes in Mathematics Ser.: Vol. 1002). 115p. 1983. pap. 10.00 (ISBN 0-387-12318-0). Springer Verlag.
Zerstreut in alle Winde see Scattered to All the Winds (Sixteen Eighty-Five to Seventeen Twenty): Migrations of the Dauphine French Huguenots into Italy, Switzerland, & Germany.
Zerubbabel: R&SM, No. 49. 200p. 1970. fabricoid bdg. 13.50 (ISBN 0-88053-276-9). Macoy Pub.
Zerubu & Other Angels I Have Met. Lewis F. Shaffer. 213p. (Orig.). 1988. pap. write for info. (ISBN 0-929389-02-6). Son Shine Ministries.
Zest for Life: The Story of Mary Bagot Stack. Prunella Stack. 182p. 1988. 27.50 (ISBN 0-7206-0697-7, Pub. by P Owen Ltd). Dufour.
Zest for Quest. Beth Hitchock. 144p. 1977. pap. 2.00 (ISBN 0-9601556-1-9). Snyder Inc.
Zest Is Best: Poems. Harvey Jackins. 1973. 5.00 (ISBN 0-911214-06-2); pap. 3.50 (ISBN 0-911214-24-X). Rational Isl.
Zesty Pizzas. Bennett & Upton. (Easy Cooking Ser.). 1983. 5.95 (ISBN 0-8120-5536-5). Barron.
Zeta-Function of Riemann. E. C. Titchmarsh. (Cambridge Tracts in Mathematics & Mathematical Physics Ser: No. 26). 1964. Repr. of 1930 ed. 8.95x (ISBN 0-02-853600-2). Hafner.
Zeta Potential in Colloid Science. R. J. Hunter. LC 80-42268. 1981. 97.00 (ISBN 0-12-361960-2). Acad Pr.
Zettel. Ludwig Wittgenstein. Ed. by G. E. M. Anscombe & G. H. Von Wright. Tr. by G. E. M Anscombe. 1967. pap. 9.95x (ISBN 0-520-01635-1). U of Cal Pr.
Zeuge im Attischen Recht & die Griechische Asylie, 2 vols. in one. Ernst Leisi & Eilhard Schlesinger. Ed. by Gregory Vlastos. LC 78-14608. (Morals & Law in Ancient Greece Ser.). 1979. Repr. of 1933 ed. lib. bdg. 21.00x (ISBN 0-405-11584-9). Ayer Co Pubs.
Zeugnis & Zeichen see Summons & Sign.
Zeus: A Study of Ancient Religion, 2 vols. Arthur B. Cook. Incl. Vol. 1. Zeus, God of the Bright Sky. LC 64-25839. (Illus.). 885p. Repr. of 1914 ed; Vol. 2. Zeus, God of the Dark Sky: Thunder & Lightning, 2 pts. LC 64-25839. Repr. of 1925 ed. 200.00x set (ISBN 0-8196-0156-X); Vol. 2, Pt. 1. Text & Notes. xliii, 858p; Vol. 2, Pt. 2. Appendixes & Index. (Illus.). 539p. Biblo.
Zeus & Hera-Archetypal Image of Father, Husband & Wife see Archetypal Images in Greek Religion.
Zeus, God of the Bright Sky see Zeus: A Study of Ancient Religion.
Zeus, God of the Dark Sky: Thunder & Lightning see Zeus: A Study of Ancient Religion.
Zeus Has Two Urns. Charles E. Jarvis. LC 76-377748. (Illus., Orig.). 1976. pap. 4.95 (ISBN 0-915940-01-9). Ithaca Pr MA.
Zeven Stemmen Spreken see Seven Voices Speak.

Zhang Daqian Hua Ji. Meishujia Chubanshe. 1982. 70.00x (ISBN 0-317-68535-X, Pub. by Han-Shan Tang Ltd). State Mutual Bk.
Zhanguo Xi Mugong Sun X Jiehe Yi Yanjiu. Lin Shoujin. 169p. 1981. 100.00x (ISBN 0-317-69275-5, Pub. by Han-Shan Tang Ltd). State Mutual Bk.
Zhar-Ptitsa: Revue Russe d'Art et de Literature, No. 1. 45p. 1983. Repr. of 1921 ed. 20.00 (ISBN 0-88233-372-0). Ardis Pubs.
Zheleznaia Zhenshchina. Nina Berberova. LC 80-54020. 400p. (Orig., Rus.). 1981. pap. 18.50 (ISBN 0-89830-039-8). Russica Pubs.
Zheltyi d iavol see Gold: The Yellow Devil.
Zhen Zhen's Dream. Mei Ying. (Illus.). 45p. (Orig.). (ps-4). 1982. pap. 2.95 (ISBN 0-686-81669-2). China Bks.
Zhenia's Childhood. Boris Pasternak. 128p. 1982. 13.95 (ISBN 0-8052-8128-2, Pub. by Allison & Busby England); pap. 5.95 (ISBN 0-8052-8129-0, Pub. by Allison & Busby England). Schocken.
Zhenskie Rasskazy: Women's Stories. Ruth Zernova. LC 81-6677. 160p. (Rus.). 1981. pap. 7.50 (ISBN 0-938920-04-9). Hermitage.
Zhi Ma Funeral Ceremony of the Na-Khi of Southwest China. Joseph F. Rock. Repr. of 1955 ed. 28.00 (ISBN 0-384-51600-9). Johnson Repr.
Zhitie Prepodobnago Antonija Velikago. Saint Athanasius. 47p. pap. 2.00 (ISBN 0-317-29181-5). Holy Trinity.
Zhitie Prepodobnogo Evfrosina Pskovskogo: Pervonachal'naia Redaktsiia. Ed. by N. Serebrianskii. (Monuments of Early Russian Literature: Vol. 3). 118p. 1982. pap. 8.00 (ISBN 0-933884-21-4). Berkeley Slavic.
Zhitija Russkikh Svatikh, v 2 tom, 2 vols. Mother Thais. LC 82-81204. Vol. 1. pap. 10.00 (ISBN 0-88465-012-X); Vol. 2. pap. 13.00 (ISBN 0-88465-020-0). Holy Trinity.
Zhitija Svjatikh v 12 tomov, 12 vols. Saint Dimitri Rostov. 10000p. Repr. of 1968 ed. 360.00 (ISBN 0-317-29175-0). Holy Trinity.
Zhitije Prepodobnago Vasilia Novago i Videnije Grirorije, utchenika Ego. 125p. pap. 5.00 (ISBN 0-317-29188-2). Holy Trinity.
Zhitije Svjatago Pravednago Ioanna Kronshtatdskago Tchudotvortsa. 23p. 1964. pap. 1.00 (ISBN 0-317-29199-8). Holy Trinity.
Zhizn' dlja vsjekh i smert' za vsjekh. V. V. Kniazev. 1971. pap. 1.00 (ISBN 0-317-30338-4). Holy Trinity.
Zhizn' i Neobychainye Prikliucheniia Soldata Ivana Chonkina, Vol. 1: Litso Neprikosnovennoe. Vladimir Voinovich. 287p. (Rus.). 1985. pap. 12.50 (ISBN 0-87501-020-2). Ardis Pubs.
Zhizn' i Neobychainye Prikliucheniia Soldata Ivana Chonkina, Vol. 2: Pretendent na Prestol. Vladimir Voinovich. 357p. (Rus.). 1987. pap. 12.50 (ISBN 0-87501-044-X). Ardis Pubs.
Zhizn' Valaamskago Monakha Germana (Aljaskinskago)-Amerikanskago Missionjera. 24p. pap. 1.00 (ISBN 0-317-29192-0). Holy Trinity.
Zhizneopisanie i Tvorenije Blazhennejshago Antonia, Mitropolita Kievskago i Galitzkago, v 17 tomakh, 17 vols. Ed. by Archbishop Nikon Rklitsky. 6000p. 1971. pap. 200.00 (ISBN 0-317-29015-0). Holy Trinity.
Zhongguo Cigi De Faming: Shaoxing Chutu Gu Taoci Yanjiu. Jiang Xuantai & Oin Mingzhi. 1956. 300.00x (ISBN 0-317-44254-6, Pub. by Han-Shan Tang Ltd). State Mutual Bk.
Zhongguo Ciqi Shi Luncong: Collection of Articles on the History of Chinese Ceramics. Tong Shuye & Shi Xuetong. 138p. 1958. 70.00x (ISBN 0-317-45338-6, Pub. by Han-Shan Tang Ltd). State Mutual Bk.
Zhongguo de Ciqi (Chinese Porcelain) 284p. 1963. 100.00x (ISBN 0-317-46361-6, Pub. by Han-Shan Tang Ltd). State Mutual Bk.
Zhongguo Gu Taoci Lunwenji: Treatise on Archaic Chinese Pottery. 321p. 1982. 32.50x (ISBN 0-317-46362-4, Pub. byHan-Shan Tang Ltd). State Mutual Bk.
Zhongguo Gudai Duliang Shuwei Ji. 238p. 1981. 210.00x (ISBN 0-317-69278-X, Pub. by Han-Shan Tang Ltd). State Mutual Bk.
Zhongguo Gudai Muke Hua Zuanji. Compiled by Zheng Zhenduo. 1985. 3000.00x (ISBN 0-317-69279-8, Pub. by Han-Shan Tang Ltd). State Mutual Bk.
Zhongguo Gudai Taosu Yishu: Ancient Chinese Pottery Sculpture. 1955. 250.00x (ISBN 0-317-45339-4, Pub. by Han-Shan Tang Ltd). State Mutual Bk.
Zhongguo Lidaj Diaosu-Qin Shinhuang Ling Tongsu Qun: Ancient Chinese Sculptural Works-Clay Figures from Qin Shihuang's Tomb. 30p. 1983. 250.00x (ISBN 0-317-46363-2, Pub. by Han-Shan Tang Ltd). State Mutual Bk.
Zhongguo Qingci Shilue: History of Chinese Porclein. Chen Wanli. 60p. 1956. 60.00x (ISBN 0-317-43859-X, Pub. by Han-Shan Tang Ltd). State Mutual Bk.
Zhongguo Taoci Shi: History of Chinese Ceramics. Wu Renjing & Xin Anchao. 145p. 1954. 50.00x (ISBN 0-317-45340-8, Pub. by Han-Shan Tang Ltd). State Mutual Bk.
Zhongshan. Galeries Nationales du Grand Palais Staff. 93p. 1985. pap. 140.00x (ISBN 0-317-68613-5, Pub. by Han-Shan Tang Ltd). State Mutual Bk.

Zhonnguo Weidade Faming-Ciqi. Fu Zhenlun. 96p. 1955. 15.00x (ISBN 0-317-43770-4, Pub. by Han-Shan Tang Ltd). State Mutual Bk.
Zhostovo Painted Trays: Contemporary Masters. I. A. Romanova. 206p. 1986. 30.00 (ISBN 0-8285-3742-9, Pub. by Sovietskaya Rossia Pubs USSR). Imported Pubns.
Zhou Enlai. Merrilyn Fitzpatrick. (Leaders of Asia Ser.). 1984. pap. 4.95 (ISBN 0-7022-1884-7). U of Queensland Pr.
Zhou Enlai. Dorothy Hoobler & Thomas Hoobler. LC 85-26926. (World Leaders--Past & Present Ser.). (Illus.). 112p. (YA) (gr. 8 up). 1986. side sewn 16.95 (ISBN 0-87754-516-2). Chelsea Hse.
Zhou Enlai: A Biography. Dick Wilson. LC 83-47928. (Illus.). 356p. 1984. 17.95 (ISBN 0-670-22011-6). Viking.
Zhou Enlai: A Profile. Percy J. Fang & Lucy G. Fang. (Illus.). 238p. 1986. pap. 9.95 (ISBN 0-8351-1712-X). China Bks.
Zhou Enlai & Deng Xiaping in the Chinese Leadership Succession Crisis. David W. Chang. LC 83-16863. 410p. (Orig.). 1984. lib. bdg. 33.25 (ISBN 0-8191-3586-0); pap. text ed. 17.75 (ISBN 0-8191-3587-9). U Pr of Amer.
Zhuan Ke. Lin Suqing. 219p. 1986. 105.00x (ISBN 0-317-68536-8, Pub. by Han-Shan Tang Ltd). State Mutual Bk.
Zhurbins. V. Kochetov. 461p. 1980. 11.25 (ISBN 0-8285-1928-5, Pub. by Progress Pubs USSR). Imported Pubns.
Zhurnal "Sovremennik" Eighteen Forty-Seven to Eighteen Sixty-Six: Ukazatel' Soderzhaniia. V. Bograd. (Rus.). 1959. 90.00 (ISBN 0-8115-3815-X). Kraus Repr.
Zia. Scott O'Dell. 144p. (gr. 4 up). 1978. pap. 2.75 (ISBN 0-440-99904-9, LFL). Dell.
Zia. Scott O'Dell. LC 75-44156. (Illus.). 224p. (gr. 4-8). 1976. 14.95 (ISBN 0-395-24393-9). HM.
Zia's Law: Human Rights under Military Rule in Pakistan. 1985. 7.00 (ISBN 0-934143-04-8). Lawyers Comm Intl.
Zia's Pakistan. R. G. Sawhney. 200p. 1985. 19.95. Asia Bk Corp.
Zia's Pakistan: Politics & Stability in a Frontline State. Ed. by Craig Baxter. (Westview Special Studies on South & Southeast Asia). 160p. 1985. pap. 16.50x (ISBN 0-8133-7113-9). Westview.
Zickary Zan: Childhood Folklore. Compiled by Jack Solomon & Olivia Solomon. LC 79-1117. (Illus.). 208p. 1980. 14.95 (ISBN 0-8173-0012-0). U of Ala Pr.
Ziegler-Natta Catalysts & Polymerizations. John Boor, Jr. 1979. 95.00 (ISBN 0-12-115550-1). Acad Pr.
Zielsprache Deutsch: Deutsch. Ellen Feld. Ed. by Von Nardroff Feld. 1981. text ed. write for info. (ISBN 0-02-336810-1). Macmillan.
Zig-Zag. Richard Thornley. LC 88-70373. 172p. 1988. pap. 7.95 (ISBN 0-932274-45-5). Cadmus Eds.
Zig-Zag the Zebra. Heather Guttschuss. (Starburst Ser.). 91p. (Orig.). 1987. pap. 6.95 (ISBN 0-8163-0689-3). Pacific Pr Pub Assn.
Zig Ziglar's Secrets of Closing the Sale. Zig Ziglar. 416p. 1987. pap. 7.95 (ISBN 0-425-08102-8). Berkley Pub.
Zigarren des Pharaos. Herge. (Illus.). 62p. (Ger.). pap. 15.95 (ISBN 0-686-54307-6). French & Eur.
Ziggle Dance at the Zoo. Bevan Kllair. LC 79-91133. (Kreative Kapers for Kids Ser.). (ps-6). 1979. pap. 3.00 (ISBN 0-935712-01-1). B A Scott.
Ziggy & Friends. Tom Wilson. LC 81-72006. (Illus.). 128p. 1982. pap. text ed. 3.95 (ISBN 0-8362-1136-7). Andrews & McMeel.
Ziggy & Friends. Tom Wilson. 1983. pap. 1.95 (ISBN 0-451-12248-8, Sig). NAL.
Ziggy Faces Life. Tom Wilson. LC 81-65136. 128p. 1981. pap. 4.95 (ISBN 0-8362-1167-7). Andrews & McMeel.
Ziggy Faces Life...Again! Tom Wilson. 1982. pap. 1.75 (ISBN 0-451-11790-5, AJ1790, Sig). NAL.
Ziggy in the Fast Lane. Tom Wilson. (Illus.). 256p. (Orig.). 1987. pap. 4.95 (ISBN 0-8362-2089-7). Andrews & McMeel.
Ziggy in the Rough. Tom Wilson. 104p. (Orig.). 1985. pap. 5.95 (ISBN 0-8362-2076-5). Andrews & McMeel.
Ziggy Stardust: David Bowie, Nineteen Seventy-Two to Nineteen Seventy-Four. Mick Rock. (Illus.). 128p. 1984. pap. 12.95 (ISBN 0-312-89882-7). St Martin.
Ziggy Treasury. Tom Wilson. LC 77-10302. (Illus.). 1977. pap. 8.95 (ISBN 0-8362-0738-6). Andrews & McMeel.
Ziggy's Big Little Book. Tom Wilson. (Illus.). 256p. 1983. pap. 3.95 (ISBN 0-8362-1990-2). Andrews & McMeel.
Ziggy's Follies. Tom Wilson. 1988. pap. 5.95 (ISBN 0-8362-1827-2). Andrews & McMeel.
Ziggy's Place. Tom Wilson. 256p. pap. 4.95 (ISBN 0-8362-7961-1). Andrews & McMeel.
Ziggy's Ups & Downs. Tom Wilson. 1985. pap. 1.95 (ISBN 0-451-13875-9, Sig). NAL.
Ziggy's Ups & Downs. Tom Wilson. 256p. 1986. pap. 4.95 (ISBN 0-8362-2078-1). Andrews & McMeel.
Zigzag. Anthony Haden-Guest. (Illus.). 256p. 1988. 17.95 (ISBN 0-13-983958-5). Prentice Hall Pr.
Zihuatanejo & Ixtapa. Grover T. Tate. (Maverick Vagabond Ser.). (Illus.). 124p. 1983. pap. 5.95 (ISBN 0-89288-098-8). Maverick.

Zillah-Abidan. Edith Cutting. (Might Have Been Ser.). (Illus.). 48p. (gr. 2-7). 1985. wkbk. 2.48 (ISBN 0-86653-306-0). Good Apple.
ZIM: The Autobiography of Eugene Zimmerman. Eugene Zimmerman. Ed. by Walter S. Brasch. LC 85-63420. (Illus.). 144p. 1988. 40.00x (ISBN 0-941664-23-6). Susquehanna.
Zimbabwe. Patricia Barnes-Svarney. (Places & Peoples of the World Ser.). (Illus.). 96p. (gr. 5 up). 1989. PLB 11.95x. Chelsea Hse.
Zimbabwe. Colin Stoneman & Lionel Cliffe. (Marxist Regimes Ser.). 220p. 1988. 35.00x (ISBN 0-86187-454-4, Pub. by Pinter Pubs UK); pap. 12.50x (ISBN 0-86187-455-2, Pub. by Pinter Pubs UK). Columbia U Pr.
Zimbabwe see Commercial Business & Trade Laws.
Zimbabwe - Monomotapa Culture in Southeast Asia. Heinrich A. Wieschoff. LC 76-44801. Repr. of 1941 ed. 27.00 (ISBN 0-404-15981-8). AMS Pr.
Zimbabwe: A Country Study. 2nd ed. Ed. by Harold D. Nelson. LC 83-11946. (Area Handbook Ser.: DA Pam 550-171). 393p. 1983. 8.00 (ISBN 0-318-21902-6, S/N 008-020-00964-4). USGPO.
Zimbabwe: A Revolution That Lost Its Way? Andre Astrow. (Illus.). 270p. 1983. 29.95x (ISBN 0-86232-140-9, Pub. by Zed Pr England); pap. 9.95 (ISBN 0-86232-141-7). Humanities.
Zimbabwe: A Treasure of Africa. Al Stark. LC 85-6944. (Discovering Our Heritage Ser.). (Illus.). 160p. (gr. 5 up). 1986. PLB 12.95 (ISBN 0-87518-308-5). Dillon.
Zimbabwe & the CGIAR Centers: A Study of Their Collaboration in Agricultural Research. K. J. Billing. (CGIAR Study Paper: No. 6). 176p. 1985. 8.00 (ISBN 0-317-59192-4, BK 0643). World Bank.
Zimbabwe Controversy: A Case of Colonial Historiography. David Chanaiwa. (Foreign & Comparative Studies-Eastern African Ser.: No. 8). 142p. 1973. pap. 5.50x (ISBN 0-915984-05-9). Syracuse U Foreign Comp.
Zimbabwe Culture: Ruins & Reactions. Gertrude Caton-Thompson. LC 79-100283. Repr. 25.00x (ISBN 0-8371-2936-2). Greenwood.
Zimbabwe Culture: Ruins & Reactions. Gertrude C. Thompson. 299p. 1971. Repr. of 1931 ed. 37.50x (ISBN 0-7146-1886-1, BHA-01886, F Cass Co). Biblio Dist.
Zimbabwe: Energy Planning for National Development. Richard H. Hosier. (Energy, Environment & Development in Africa Ser.: Vol. 9). 206p. 1988. 27.50 (ISBN 0-8419-9780-2). Holmes & Meier.
Zimbabwe in Pictures. Department of Geography, Lerner Publications. (Visual Geography Ser.). (Illus.). (gr. 5 up). 1988. 9.95 (ISBN 0-8225-1825-2). Lerner Pubns.
Zimbabwe Independence Movements: Select Documents. Ed. by Christopher Nyangoni & Gideon Nyandoro. LC 79-51834. 456p. 1979. text ed. 30.00x (ISBN 0-06-495222-3). B&N Imports.
Zimbabwe: Prose & Poetry. rev. 2nd ed. Solomon M. Mutswairo. LC 74-7822. 1979. 18.00 (ISBN 0-914478-82-6); pap. 7.00 (ISBN 0-914478-83-4). Three Continents.
Zimbabwe: Wages of War. 1986. 10.00 (ISBN 0-934143-07-2). Lawyers Comm Intl.
Zimbabwe's Economic Prospects. Robert I. Rotberg & William H. Overholt. (Seven Springs Reports). 32p. 1980. pap. 3.00 (ISBN 0-943006-10-4). Seven Springs.
Zimbabwe's Inheritance. Ed. by Colin Stoneman. 1982. 27.50x (ISBN 0-312-89883-5). St Martin.
Zimmerfrei. Ulrike Cohen & Karl-Heinz Osterloh. Incl. Student Text. 81p. 9.95 (ISBN 3-468-49420-3); Workbook. 57p. 5.50 (ISBN 3-468-49421-1); Teacher's Suppplement. 32p. 3.95 (ISBN 3-468-49422-X); Text-Cassette. 12.95 (ISBN 3-468-84440-9). Langenscheidt.
Zimmerman Site. facsimile ed. Kenneth G. Orr et al. Ed. by James A. Brown. (Reports of Investigations Ser.: No. 9). (Illus.). 86p. 1974. pap. 2.10x (ISBN 0-89792-021-X). Ill St Museum.
Zimmerman Site: Further Excavations at the Grand Village of Kaskaskia. Margaret K. Brown. (Reports of Investigations Ser.: No. 32). (Illus.). 124p. 1975. pap. 3.00x (ISBN 0-89792-058-9). Ill St Museum.
Zimmerman Telegram. Barbara W. Tuchman. 1985. pap. 4.95 (ISBN 0-345-34240-2). Ballantine.
Zimmermann Telegram. Barbara W. Tuchman. 1966. 14.95 (ISBN 0-02-620320-0). Macmillan.
Zimmermann Telegram. Barbara W. Tuchman. 1988. pap. 7.95 (ISBN 0-345-32425-0). Ballantine.
Zimmermann Telegram of January 16, 1917 & Its Cryptographic Background. William F. Friedman & Charles J. Mendelsohn. LC 76-53121. (Cryptographic Ser.). 1976. lib. bdg. 16.20 (ISBN 0-89412-123-5); pap. 8.20 (ISBN 0-89412-009-3). Aegean Park Pr.
Zinaida Hippius: An Intellectual Profile. Temira Pachmuss. LC 70-86197. (Illus.). 512p. 1970. 12.50x (ISBN 0-8093-0409-0). S Ill U Pr.
Zinc & Copper in Medicine. Z. A. Karcioglu & R. M. Sarper. (Illus.). 696p. 1980. 65.75x (ISBN 0-398-03977-1). C C Thomas.
Zinc & Its Alloys & Compounds. S. W. Morgan. LC 85-5590. (Industrial Metals Ser.). 245p. 1985. 64.95 (ISBN 0-470-20213-0). Halsted Pr.

Zodiac Arch. Freya Stark. 1975. 16.95 (ISBN 0-7195-1784-2). Transatl Arts.

Zodiac Charted Designs for Cross-Stitch Needlepoint & Other Techniques. Ed. by Lindberg Press. 48p. 1985. pap. 2.95 (ISBN 0-486-24932-8). Dover.

Zodiac Designs Book. Caren Caraway. (International Design Library). (Illus.). 48p. 1980. pap. 5.95 (ISBN 0-916144-47-X). Stemmer Hse.

Zodiac: Exploring Human Qualities & Characteristics. Mary R. Moore. LC 84-17977. (Vocabureader Workbook: No. 1). (Illus.). 112p. (Orig.). (gr. 5 up). 1984. pap. 6.50x (ISBN 0-86647-009-3). Pro Lingua.

Zodiac, Key to Man & the Universe, Vol. 220. Omraam M. Aivanhov. (IZVOR Collection). 176p. (Orig.). 1986. pap. 5.95 (ISBN 2-85566-369-5). Prosveta USA.

Zodiac Pattern Book. Ed. by Diane Martin. (Orig.). 1986. pap. 14.95 (ISBN 0-931485-05-3). Scriptorium Pr.

Zodiac Poems. Robin K. Willoughby. 1978. 1.00 (ISBN 0-934834-19-9). White Pine.

Zodiac Symposium on Adaption: Proceedings. 1978. pap. 24.00 (ISBN 90-220-0680-8, PDC131, PUDOC). UNIPUB.

Zodiac: The Eco-Thriller. Neal Stephenson. 300p. 1988. pap. 7.95 (ISBN 0-87113-181-1). Atlantic Monthly.

Zodiacal Symbology & Its Power. Isidore Kozminsky. 192p. 5.50 (ISBN 0-86690-122-1, 1270-01). Am Fed Astrologers.

Zodiak Explorer's Handbook: A Unique Guide to Using Birth Chart for Inner Exploration. Helene Hess. (Illus.). 142p. (Orig.). 1987. pap. 8.99 (ISBN 0-85030-484-9, Pub. by Aquarian Pr England). Sterling.

Zodiake of Life. Marcellus Palingenius. Tr. by Barnabe Googe. LC 48-275. 1977. Repr. of 1576 ed. 60.00x (ISBN 0-8201-1214-3). Schol Facsimiles.

ZOE: The God-Kind of Life. Kenneth E. Hagin. 1981. pap. 2.50 (ISBN 0-89276-402-3). Hagin Ministries.

Zoe's Book. Gail Pass. 224p. 1987. pap. 7.95 (ISBN 0-930044-95-9). Naiad Pr.

Zoe's Cats. Zoe Stokes. LC 81-53055. (Illus.). 1982. 12.95 (ISBN 0-500-01273-3). Thames Hudson.

Zoetropes: Poems Nineteen Seventy to Nineteen Eighty-Two. Bill Manhire. 80p. (Orig.). 1987. pap. 9.50 (ISBN 0-85635-575-5). Carcanet.

Zofingia Lectures: The Collected Works of C. G. Jung. C. G. Jung. Ed. by William McGuire. Tr. by Jan van Heurck. LC 83-42592. (Bollingen Ser.: XX). (Illus.). 160p. 1983. 20.95 (ISBN 0-691-09899-9). Princeton U Pr.

Zohar. Tr. by Maurice Simon & Paul Levertoff. 1934. 75.00 (ISBN 0-900689-39-0); pap. 55.00. Soncino Pr.

Zohar, 5 Vols. Set. 75.00x (ISBN 0-685-01046-5); pap. 55.00x. Bloch.

Zohar: Bereshith. rev.,3rd ed. Nurho De Manhar. (Secret Doctrine Reference Ser.). 432p. 1985. 21.00 (ISBN 0-913510-53-X). Wizards.

Zohar-English Only, 5 vols. Set. 95.00 (ISBN 0-910218-91-9). Bennet Pub.

Zohar: Hebrew Text, 21 vols. Shimon Bar Yohai. 300.00 set (ISBN 0-943688-67-1); 18.00 ea. Res Ctr Kabbalah.

Zohar: Hebrew Text, 10 vols. condensed ed. Shimon Bar Yohai. 1981. 15.00 ea. (ISBN 0-943688-68-X); 150.00 set. Res Ctr Kabbalah.

Zohar: Parashat Pinhas, Vol. II. Tr. by Philip S. Berg from Hebrew & Aramaic. 256p. 1987. 15.95 (ISBN 0-943688-52-3); pap. 11.95 (ISBN 0-943688-53-1). Res Ctr Kabbalah.

Zohar: Parashat Pinhas, Vol. III. Tr. by Philip S. Berg. 256p. 1988. 15.95 (ISBN 0-943688-54-X); pap. 11.95 (ISBN 0-943688-55-8). Res Ctr Kabbalah.

Zohar: Parshat Pinhas, Vol. I. Tr. by Philip S. Berg. 288p. 1986. 15.95 (ISBN 0-943688-50-7); pap. 11.95 (ISBN 0-943688-51-5). Res Ctr Kabbalah.

Zohar, The Book of Enlightment. Daniel C. Matt. (Classics of Western Spirituality). 320p. 1982. 12.95 (ISBN 0-8091-0320-6); pap. 10.95 (ISBN 0-8091-2387-8). Paulist pr.

Zohar-The Book of Splendor: Basic Readings from the Kabbalah. Ed. by Gershom Scholem. LC 63-11040. 1963. pap. 3.95 (ISBN 0-8052-0045-2). Schocken.

Zohrab: An Introduction. Ed. & tr. by Ara Baliozian. 79p. 1985. pap. 3.95 (ISBN 0-920553-00-1). Natl Assn Arm.

Zola. Philip Walker. 288p. 1985. 32.50x (ISBN 0-7102-0518-X). Routledge Chapman & Hall.

Zola. Emile Zola. Ed. by Marc Bernard. Tr. by Jean M. Leblon. (Illus.). 1977. Repr. of 1960 ed. lib. bdg. 35.00x (ISBN 0-8371-9820-8, BEZO). Greenwood.

Zola & His Time: The History of His Martial Career in Letters, with His Circle of Friends, His Remarkable Enemies, Cyclopean Labours, Public Campaigns, Trials & Ultimate Glorification. Matthew Josephson. 573p. 1985. Repr. of 1929 ed. lib. bdg. 50.00 (ISBN 0-8492-5612-7). R West.

Zola & His Time: The History of His Martial Career in Letters. Matthew Josephson. 558p. 1985. Repr. of 1928 ed. lib. bdg. 50.00. Century Bookbindery.

Zola & the Bourgeoisie: A Study of Themes & Techniques in "Les Rougon Macquart". Brian Nelson. LC 81-10954. 240p. 1983. 28.50x (ISBN 0-389-20110-3, 06884). B&N Imports.

Zola & the Dreyfus Case. Lee M. Friedman. 59.95 (ISBN 0-87968-029-6). Gordon Pr.

Zola & the Dreyfus Case. Lee M. Friedman. (World History Ser., No. 48). (Illus.). 1970. pap. 39.95x (ISBN 0-8383-0092-8). Haskell.

Zola aux Etats-Unis. Albert J. Salvan. 1943. 20.00 (ISBN 0-527-78650-0). Kraus Repr.

Zola Dictionary. J. G. Patterson. LC 68-27179. 272p. 1969. Repr. of 1912 ed. 34.00x (ISBN 0-8103-3173-X). Gale.

Zola Dictionary. J. G. Patterson. 75.00 (ISBN 0-8490-1350-X). Gordon Pr.

Zola: La Terre. Ronnie Butler. (Critical Guides to French Texts Ser.: No. 36). 80p. 1984. pap. 4.50 (ISBN 0-7293-0180-X, Pub. by Grant & Cutler). Longwood Pub Group.

Zola: Photographer. Francois Emile-Zola & Massin. Tr. by Liliane E. Tuck from Fr. (Illus.). 192p. 1988. 26.95 (ISBN 0-8050-0747-4). Seaver Bks.

Zoladex: a New Treatment for Prostatic Cancer: Proceedings of a Conference, London, April 23, 1987, No. 125. G. D. Chisholm. (Orig.). 1988. pap. 12.50 (ISBN 0-905958-58-6, Pub. by Royal Society of Medicine Services Ltd). Longwood Pub Group.

Zolar's Book of Dreams, Numbers, & Lucky Days. Zolar. Date not set. write for info. S&S.

Zolar's Book of the Spirits. Zolar. (Illus.). 368p. (Orig.). 1987. pap. 9.95 (ISBN 0-13-984048-6). P-H.

Zolar's Compendium of Occult Theories & Practices. Zolar. (Illus.). 448p. 1987. pap. 9.95 (ISBN 0-13-983990-9). P-H.

Zolar's Encyclopedia & Dictionary of Dreams. Zolar. LC 63-21071. 417p. 1972. pap. 8.95 (ISBN 0-668-02540-9). Arco.

Zolar's Encyclopedia of Ancient & Forbidden Knowledge. Zolar. LC 83-15812. 488p. (Orig.). 1984. pap. 7.95 (ISBN 0-668-05894-3). Arco.

Zolar's Encyclopedia of Omens, Signs & Superstitions. Zolar. (Illus.). 352p. 1989. pap. 11.95 (ISBN 0-13-984006-0). Prentice Hall Pr.

Zola's Crowds. Naomi Schor. LC 78-1564. pap. 60.00 (ISBN 0-317-42338-X, 2025869). Bks Demand UMI.

Zola's Germinal: A Critical Study of Its Primary Sources. R. H. Zakarian. 200p. 1972. text ed. 47.50x (ISBN 0-317-55940-0, Pub. by Droz Switzerland). Coronet Bks.

Zola's Son Excellence Eugene Rougon. Richard B. Grant. LC 60-6649. pap. 38.50 (ISBN 0-317-26760-4, 2023392). Bks Demand UMI.

Zollverein. 2nd ed. W. O. Henderson. 375p. 1968. Repr. of 1959 ed. 32.50x (ISBN 0-7146-1322-3, F Cass Co). Biblio Dist.

Zollverein & British Industry. J. R. MacDonald. Repr. of 1903 ed. 16.00 (ISBN 0-527-59380-X). Kraus Repr.

Zolotaia Nasha Zhelezka. Vasily P. Aksenov. (Rus.). 1979. pap. 6.50 (ISBN 0-88233-480-8). Ardis Pubs.

Zolotoe Runo & Russian Modernism. William Richardson. 200p. 1986. 27.50 (ISBN 0-88233-795-5). Ardis Pubs.

Zolotyi Homin. Pavlo Hryhorovych Tychyna. LC 68-52067. (Shkil'na Biblioteka Ser.). 1967. pap. text ed. 8.00 (ISBN 0-918884-25-X). Slavia Lib.

Zolta Configuration. David Quammen. 352p. 1984. pap. 3.50 (ISBN 0-8125-0800-9, Dist. by Warner Pub Services & St. Martin's Press). Tor Bks.

Zoltan Bay. Francis S. Wagner. 118p. 1985. 88.00x (ISBN 0-569-08862-3, Pub. by Collets (UK)). State Mutual Bk.

Zoltan Kodaly, a Hungarian Musician. Percy M. Young. LC 75-45268. (Illus.). 231p. 1976. Repr. of 1964 ed. lib. bdg. 38.50 (ISBN 0-8371-8650-1, YOZK). Greenwood.

Zoltan Szabo Paints Landscapes: Advanced Techniques in Watercolor. Zoltan Szabo. (Illus.). 176p. 1977. 29.95 (ISBN 0-8230-5980-4). Watson-Guptill.

Zombie! Tremayne. 1987. pap. 2.95 (ISBN 0-312-90923-3). St Martin.

Zombie Jamboree. Robert Merkin. 336p. 1987. pap. text ed. 4.95 (ISBN 0-07-041519-6). McGraw.

Zombie Jamboree. Robert B. Merkin. LC 86-745. 320p. 1986. 16.95 (ISBN 0-688-01946-3). Morrow.

Zombies That Ate Pittsburgh: The Films of George A. Romero. Paul R. Gagne. (Illus.). 1987. pap. 14.95 (ISBN 0-396-08520-2). Dodd.

Zona. Sergei Dovlatov. LC 82-15486. 128p. (Rus.). 1982. pap. 6.00 (ISBN 0-938920-23-5). Hermitage.

Zona Gale. Harold P. Simonson. (Twayne's United States Authors Ser). 1962. pap. 8.95x (ISBN 0-8084-0338-9, T18, Twayne). New Coll U Pr.

Zona Libre. Samuel E. Bell & James M. Smallwood. (Southwestern Studies: No. 69). 100p. 1982. pap. 5.00 (ISBN 0-87404-129-5). Tex Western.

Zonal Polynomials. Akimichi Takemura. LC 84-47886. (IMS Lecture Notes-Monograph Ser.: Vol. 4). vi, 104p. 1984. pap. 15.00 (ISBN 0-940600-05-6). Inst Math.

Zondervan Family Cookbook. Patricia Gundry. 360p. 1988. 14.95 (Pub. by Zondervan Bks). Zondervan.

Zondervan Manual of Style for Authors, Editors & Proofreaders. rev. ed. 1977. pap. 3.95 (ISBN 0-310-35021-2, 6200P). Zondervan.

Zondervan Nineteen Eighty-Seven Pastor's Annual: A Planned Preaching Program for the Year. T. T. Crabtree. (Pastor's Annual Ser.). 384p. 1986. 12.95 (ISBN 0-310-22701-1, 11384P). Zondervan.

Zondervan Pictorial Bible Atlas. E. M. Blaiklock. (Illus.). 1969. 27.95 (ISBN 0-310-21240-5, 6763). Zondervan.

Zondervan Pictorial Encyclopedia of the Bible, 5 vols. new ed. Ed. by Merrill C. Tenney. (Illus.). 1974. Set. text ed. 149.95 (ISBN 0-310-33188-9, 6700). Zondervan.

Zondervan 1988: A Planned Preaching Program for the Year. rev. ed. T. T. Crabtree. (Zondervan Pastor's Annuals). 400p. 1987. Repr. of 1968 ed. 12.95 (ISBN 0-310-22711-9, 11385P). Zondervan.

Zondervan 1989 Pastor's Annual. T. T. Crabtree. 384p. 1988. pap. 12.95 (ISBN 0-310-61311-6, 11386P). Zondervan.

Zone: A Prison Camp Guard's Story. Sergei Dovlatov. Tr. by Anne Frydman from Rus. LC 85-40118. 192p. 1985. 14.45 (ISBN 0-394-53522-7). Knopf.

Zone: Blind Fire, No. 2. James Rouch. 1985. pap. 2.50 (ISBN 0-8217-1588-7). Zebra.

Zone du Jour. Dan Raphael. 28p. (Orig.). 1981. pap. 3.00 (ISBN 0-937013-00-5). Potes Poets.

Zone Four. Ed. by Michel Feher. (Illus.). 450p. 1989. 37.95 (ISBN 0-942299-24-8); pap. 18.95. Zone Bks.

Zone Journals. Charles Wright. 112p. 1988. 14.95 (ISBN 0-374-29753-3). FS&G.

Zone Journals. Charles Wright. 1989. pap. 8.95 (ISBN 0-374-52112-3, Noonday). FS&G.

Zone Melting. William G. Pfann & Donald T. Hawkins. LC 77-7238. 326p. 1978. Repr. of 1958 ed. lib. bdg. 21.50 (ISBN 0-88275-541-2). Krieger.

Zone, No. 4: Sky Strike. James Rouch. 224p. 1986. pap. 2.50 (ISBN 0-8217-1770-7). Zebra.

Zone, No. 6: Plague Bomb. James Rouch. 224p. 1986. pap. 2.50 (ISBN 0-8217-1911-4). Zebra.

Zone, No. 7: Killing Ground. James Rouch. 224p. 1988. pap. 2.50 (ISBN 0-8217-2494-0). Zebra.

Zone of Emergence: A Case Study of an Older Suburb. George S. Sternlieb & W. Patrick Beaton. LC 78-186710. 220p. 1972. 24.95x (ISBN 0-87855-035-6). Transaction Bks.

Zone of Emergence: Observations of Lower, Middle & Upper Working Class Communities of Boston, 1905-1914. 2nd ed. Robert A. Woods & Albert J. Kennedy. 1969. 25.00x (ISBN 0-262-23040-2). MIT Pr.

Zone of Fire. Conrad Detrez. Tr. by Lydia Davis. LC 86-4289. 320p. 1986. 17.95 (ISBN 0-15-199989-9). HarBraceJ.

Zone One & Two. (Illus.). 1987. pap. 20.00 (ISBN 0-942299-22-1). Zone Bks.

Zone Policeman 88: A Close Range Study of the Panama Canal & Its Workers. Harry A. Franck. LC 71-111713. (American Imperialism: Viewpoints of United States Foreign Policy, 1898-1941). 1970. Repr. of 1913 ed. 20.00 (ISBN 0-405-02019-8). Ayer Co Pubs.

Zone System for 35mm Photographers. Carson Graves. (Illus.). 112p. 1982. pap. text ed. 18.95x (ISBN 0-240-51773-3). Focal Pr.

Zone System for 35mm Photographers: A Basic Guide to Exposure Control. Carson Graves. (Illus.). 112p. 1982. pap. 13.95 (ISBN 0-930764-39-0). Curtin & London.

Zone Systemizer. John Dowdell, III & Richard Zakia. LC 73-87272. 63p. 1973. pap. 19.95 (ISBN 0-87100-040-7). Morgan.

Zone Three. Ed. by Michel Feher. (Illus.). 450p. 1989. 37.95 (ISBN 0-942299-23-X); pap. 18.95. Zone Bks.

Zone VI Workshop. Fred Picker. (Illus.). 128p. 1978. 13.95 (ISBN 0-8174-0574-7, Amphoto). Watson-Guptill.

Zones of Conflict: An Atlas of Future Wars. John Keegan & Andrew Wheatcroft. 1986. 18.95 (ISBN 0-671-60115-6); pap. 10.95 (ISBN 0-671-62411-3). S&S.

Zones of Pain. Marjorie Agosin. Tr. by cola Franzen. 1988. 9.00. White Pine.

Zones of the Spirit. August Strindberg. LC 73-21632. (Studies in Scandianvian Life & Literature, No. 18). 1974. lib. bdg. 53.95x (ISBN 0-8383-1758-8). Haskell.

Zoning & Development Rights: A Bibliography. Mary E. Huls. LC 85-233574. (Public Administration Series-Bibliography). 6p. 1985. 2.00 (ISBN 0-89028-564-0, P1764). Vance Biblios.

Zoning & Land Use Controls, 9 vols. Patrick J. Rohan. 1977. Set. looseleaf 420.00 (845); Updates 1985. 387.00; Supplement 1986. 383.50. Bender.

Zoning & Planning Deskbook. Douglas W. Kmiec. 1986. 85.00 (ISBN 0-87632-479-0). Clark Boardman.

Zoning & Planning Law Handbook 1987. Ed. by Noah J. Gordan. 1987. 65.00 (ISBN 0-87632-499-5). Clark Boardman.

Zoning & Property Rights. Robert H. Nelson. 1977. pap. 10.95x (ISBN 0-262-64019-8). MIT Pr.

Zoning & Subdivision Law in Virginia: A Handbook. 4.00 (ISBN 0-317-69892-3). U Va Ctr Pub Serv.

Zoning & Zoning Law: A Revision of A-481. Mary Vance. (Architecture Ser.: a 1507). 45p. 1985. 6.75 (ISBN 0-89028-657-4). Vance Biblios.

Zoning at Sixty: Mediating Public & Private Rights. Ed. by Charles M. Haar & Jerold S. Kayden. LC 88-71466. (Illus.). 400p. (Orig.). Date not set. lib. bdg. price not set (ISBN 0-918286-57-3); pap. price not set. Planners Pr.

Zoning Board Manual. Frederick H. Bair, Jr. LC 84-60300. 132p. 1984. 14.95 (ISBN 0-918286-32-8). Planners Pr.

Zoning Board of Adjustment in North Carolina. Michael B. Brough et al. 128p. 1984. 7.50 (ISBN 0-686-39447-X). U of NC Inst Gov.

Zoning Control of Sex Businesses. Frederic A. Strom. LC 77-26984. 1977. pap. 5.95 (ISBN 0-87632-239-9). Clark Boardman.

Zoning Game: Municipal Practices & Policies. Richard F. Babcock. 218p. 1988. 19.50; pap. 12.50. Lincoln Inst Land.

Zoning Game-Revisited. Richard F. Babcock & Charles L. Siemon. LC 85-21659. (Linclon Institute of Land Policy Bk.). 256p. 1985. text ed. 19.50x (ISBN 0-89946-199-9). Oelgeschlager.

Zoning Hawaii: An Analysis of the Passage & Implementation of Hawaii's Land Classification Law. Phyllis Myers. LC 76-5914. (Illus.). 128p. 1976. 8.95 (ISBN 0-89164-033-9); pap. 4.95 (ISBN 0-89164-032-0). Conservation Foun.

Zoning Inspector. Jack Rudman. (Career Examination Ser.: C-2340). (Cloth bdg. avail. on request). pap. 14.00 (ISBN 0-8373-2340-1). Natl Learning.

Zoning Inspector II. Jack Rudman. (Career Examination Ser.: C-3079). 1988. pap. 14.00 (ISBN 0-8373-3079-3). Natl Learning.

Zoning Law & Practice, 8 vols. 4th ed. E. C. Yokley. Set & 1987 cum. suppl. 300.00x (ISBN 0-87215-207-3, 69485); 1987 cum. suppl. 90.00x (ISBN 0-87215-855-1); Individual vols. 40.00. Michie Co.

Zoning Law Anthology, Vol. 1. Ed. by Philip A. Garon. LC 78-66283. (National Law Anthology Ser.). 1978. text ed. 66.63 (ISBN 0-914250-17-5). Intl Lib.

Zoning Law Anthology, (1979-1983) Ed. by Donald J. Hoyes. (National Law Anthology Ser.: Vol. II). 1000p. 1988. text ed. 99.95 (ISBN 0-914250-40-X). Intl Lib.

Zoning Law Anthology, (1984-1987) Ed. by Donald J. Hoyes. (Natinal Law Anthology Ser.: Vol. III). 1000p. 1988. text ed. 99.95 (ISBN 0-914250-45-0). Intl Lib.

Zoning: The Laws, Administration, & Court Decisions During the First Twenty Five Years. Edward M. Bassett. LC 73-11916. (Metropolitan America Ser.). 280p. 1974. Repr. of 1936 ed. 17.00x (ISBN 0-405-05385-1). Ayer Co Pubs.

Zonitid Snails from Pacific Islands, 4 pts. in 3 vols. H. B. Baker. (BMB). Repr. of 1941 ed. Pt. 1. 21.00 (ISBN 0-527-02266-7); Pt. 2. 15.00 (ISBN 0-527-02273-X); Pt. 3. 22.00 (ISBN 0-527-02274-8). Kraus Repr.

Zoo. Illus. by Pam Adams. (Pre-Reading Ser.). (Illus.). 24p. (ps-2). 1974. 4.50 (ISBN 0-85953-032-9, Pub. by Child's Play England). Playspaces.

Zoo. Gail Gibbons. LC 87-582. (Illus.). 32p. (ps-3). 1987. 12.95i (ISBN 0-690-04631-6, Crowell Jr Bks); PLB 12.89 (ISBN 0-690-04633-2). HarpJ.

Zoo. Tanya Maiboroda. (Hidden Picture Coloring Bks.). (Illus.). 48p. (gr. 4-7). 1987. pap. 2.95 (ISBN 0-8431-1879-2). Price Stern.

Zoo. Jan Pienkowski. (Illus.). 32p. (ps-1). 1985. 11.95 (ISBN 0-434-95652-X, Pub. by W Heinemann Ltd). David & Charles.

Zoo. Price, Stern & Sloan Staff. (Mini-Shape Folding Bks.). (Illus.). 18p. (ps). 1986. 2.95 (ISBN 0-8431-1836-9). Price Stern.

Zoo: A Behind-the-Scenes Look at the Animals & the People Who Care for Them. Don Gold. (Illus.). 368p. 1988. 18.95 (ISBN 0-8092-4617-1). Contemp Bks.

Zoo & Wild Animal Medicine. 2nd ed. Murray E. Fowler. (Illus.). 1127p. 1986. 89.00 (ISBN 0-7216-1013-7). Saunders.

Zoo Animals. Illus. by Valerie Greeley. LC 83-22513. (Illus.). 12p. (ps). 1984. bds. 3.95 (ISBN 0-911745-24-6, Bedrick Blackie). P Bedrick Bks.

Zoo Animals. Leonard Shortall. (Cloth Bks.). (Illus.). 8p. (ps). 1980. 2.50 (ISBN 0-394-84398-3, BYR). Random.

Zoo Animals. Zokeisha. (Chubby Board Bks.). (Illus.). 16p. (ps). 1982. board 2.95 (ISBN 0-671-44895-1, Little Simon). S&S.

Zoo Animals. (Animal Information Ser.). 32p. (Orig.). (ps-1). 1984. pap. 1.25 (ISBN 0-8431-1515-7). Price Stern.

Zoo Animals. (Press Out & Play Board Bks.). (Illus.). 12p. (ps). 1987. bds. 5.95 (ISBN 0-8431-1934-9). Price Stern.

Zoo: Avec: Le Fer et la Velours, Le Silence de la Mer, Vol. 1. Vercors. 197p. 1978. 20.00 (ISBN 0-686-55146-X). French & Eur.

Zoo Babies see Books for Young Explorers.

Zoo Doings: Animal Poems. Jack Prelutsky. LC 82-11996. (Illus.). 80p. (gr. 1-3). 1983. 10.95 (ISBN 0-688-01782-7); PLB 10.88 (ISBN 0-688-01784-3). Greenwillow.

Zoo for All Seasons: The Smithsonian Animal World. Smithsonian Institute. (Illus.). 1979. 19.95 (ISBN 0-393-80003-2). Norton.

Zoo for All Seasons: The Smithsonian Animal World. LC 79-52492. (Illus.). 192p. 1979. 19.95 (ISBN 0-89599-003-2, Dist. by Norton). Smithsonian Bks.

Zoo for Mister Muster. Arnold Lobel. LC 62-7313. (Illus.). (ps-3). PLB 11.89 (ISBN 0-06-023991-3). HarpJ.

Zthorg - God's Computer. Harry McKinzie. 170p. (Orig.). pap. 20.00 (ISBN 0-86626-017-X). McKinzie Pub.

Zu den aeltesten Beruehrungen zwischen Roemern und Germanen: Die Franken see Romania Germanica: Sprach-und Siedlungsgeschichte der Germanen auf dem Boden des alten Roemerreiches.

Zu den Kunstformen des Mittelalterlichen Epos. Rudolf Fischer. 1965. pap. 25.00 (ISBN 0-384-15765-3). Johnson Repr.

Zu Geschichte der Vereinigten Staaten von Amerika. rev. 2nd ed. Zu-Wernigerode Stolberg. (Sammlung Goeschen, 7005). 268p. 1973. pap. 6.70x (ISBN 3-11-004364-5). De Gruyter.

Zub the Tooth Fairy. Schulte Dewitt. 1982. 9.95 (ISBN 0-913730-06-8). Robinson Pr.

Zucchini. Barbara Dana. LC 80-8448. (Charlotte Zolotow Bks.). (Illus.). 128p. (gr. 3-5). 1982. 13.70i (ISBN 0-06-021394-9); PLB 13.89g (ISBN 0-06-021395-7). HarpJ.

Zucchini. Barbara Dana. (Illus.). 160p. (gr. 3-6). pap. 2.75 (ISBN 0-553-15437-0, Skylark). Bantam.

Zucchini & All That Squash. Rachel Bard & Caroline Kellogg. LC 84-52215. 96p. (Orig.). 1985. pap. 7.95 (ISBN 0-9603666-1-X). R & M Pr WA.

Zucchini Cookbook. 3rd, rev. ed. Paula Simmons. LC 74-77037. (Illus.). 132p. (YA) 1983. pap. 6.95 (ISBN 0-914718-81-9). Pacific Search.

Zucchini Cookery. Virg Lemley & Jo Lemley. 1976. pap. 3.75 (ISBN 0-931798-02-7). Wilderness Hse.

Zucchini Patch. Kathey L. Sherves & Bonnie Millhollin. Ed. by Ruth Blackett. (Illus.). 108p. 1980. spiral binding 5.95 (ISBN 0-940158-00-0). Zucchini Patch.

Zucchini Plague: And Other Tales of Suburbia. William Geist. 288p. 1987. pap. 7.95 (ISBN 0-671-63434-8, Fireside). S&S.

Zucchini Sampler. Jan Siegrist. (Illus.). 48p. (Orig.). 1986. pap. 2.50 (ISBN 0-933050-41-0). New Eng Pr VT.

Zucchini Warriors. Gordon Korman. 208p. (gr. 4-7). Date not set. 10.95 (ISBN 0-590-41335-X, Pub. by Scholastic Hardcover). Scholastic Inc.

Zuchinni Warriors. Gordon Korman. (gr. 4-6). 1988. 10.95 (Scholastic Hardcovers). Scholastic Inc.

Zucker-Bedurfnis, Zwang oder Sucht? 112p. (Ger.). 1981. pap. 5.95 (ISBN 0-89192-351-9, Pub. by Gottlieb Duttweiler Inst). Interbk Inc.

Zucker und Zuckeraustauschstoffe. Symposium, Muenchen, 1974. Ed. by N. Zoellner & P. Heuckenkamp. (Nutrition & Metabolism Ser.: Vol. 18, Suppl. 1). (Illus.). 200p. 1975. 31.50 (ISBN 3-8055-2173-1). S Karger.

Zuckerman Bound. 1986. pap. 5.95 (ISBN 0-449-21090-1, Crest). Fawcett.

Zuckerman Bound: A Trilogy & Epilogue. Philip Roth. LC 84-23265. 784p. 1985. 22.50 (ISBN 0-374-29943-9); pap. 9.95 (ISBN 0-374-51899-8). FS&G.

Zuckerman Unbound. Philip Roth. 288p. 1982. pap. 3.50 (ISBN 0-449-24521-7). Fawcett.

Zuckerman Unbound. Philip Roth. 225p. 1981. 10.95 (ISBN 0-374-29945-5). FS&G.

Zuercher Kunsthaus-ein Museumsbau Von Moser. Jehle. (Institut fuer Geschichte und Theorie der Architecture Ser.: Vol. 22). 158p. 1983. pap. text ed. 19.95x (ISBN 0-8176-1242-4). Birkhauser.

Zug the Bug: A Flip-the-Page Rhyming Book. Colin Hawkins & Jacqui Hawkins. (Illus.). 22p. (ps-3). 1988. 9.95 (ISBN 0-399-21556-5). Putnam Pub Group.

Zukofsky's "A" An Introduction. Barry Ahearn. LC 81-13000. 254p. 1983. 25.00x (ISBN 0-520-04378-2); pap. 9.95x (ISBN 0-520-04965-9). U of Cal Pr.

Zukunft der Mikroelektronik und Mikrotechnik in der Schweiz. Gottlieb Duttweiler Institut Staff. 281p. (Orig., Ger.). 1983. pap. 45.00 (ISBN 0-89192-362-4). Interbk Inc.

Zuleika Dobson. Max Beerbohm. 256p. 1983. pap. 6.95 (ISBN 0-14-006713-2). Penguin.

Zulliger Individual & Group Test. Hans Zulliger. Ed. by Fritz Salomon. LC 69-19369. 1969. text ed. 50.00x (ISBN 0-8236-7080-5). Intl Univs Pr.

Zulu Aftermath: A Nineteenth-Century Revolution in Bantu Africa. John D. Omer-Cooper. (Ibadan History Ser). 208p. 1966. pap. 11.95x (ISBN 0-8101-0588-8). Northwestern U Pr.

Zulu Bone Oracle. Brian Crowley. (Illus.). 120p. (Orig.). 1988. pap. 8.95 (ISBN 0-914728-65-2). Wingbow Pr.

Zulu-English Dictionary. J. W. Colenso. 742p. text ed. 99.36x (ISBN 0-576-11609-2, Pub. by Gregg Intl Pubs England). Gregg Intl.

Zulu-English, English-Zulu Dictionary. rev. ed. Ed. by C. M. Doke. (Zulu & Eng.). pap. 12.50. Heinman.

Zulu-English, English-Zulu Dictionary. pap. text ed. 32.50 (ISBN 0-87557-096-8). Saphrograph.

Zulu Family. Nancy D. Mckenna. (Families the World over Ser.). (Illus.). 32p. (gr. 2-5). 1986. PLB 8.95 (ISBN 0-8225-1666-7). Lerner Pubns.

Zulu-Kafir Dictionary. J. L. Dohne. 458p. 1857. Repr. text ed. 82.80x (ISBN 0-576-11610-6, Pub. by Gregg Intl Pubs England). Gregg Intl.

Zulu King Speaks: Statements Made by Cetshwayo Kampande on the History & Customs of His People. Ed. by Colin deB. Webb & John B. Wright. (Illus.). 150p. 1987. text ed. 17.95 (ISBN 0-86980-153-8, Pub. by Univ Natal Pr South Africa). Intl Spec Bk.

Zulu Poems. Mazisi Kunene. LC 70-136492. 95p. 1970. 12.50x (ISBN 0-8419-0061-2, Africana); (Africana). Holmes & Meier.

Zulu Proverbs. rev. ed. C. L. Nyembezi. 1963. 17.50 (ISBN 0-85494-051-0). Heinman.

Zulu War. David Clammer. (Battle Standards Ser.). (Illus.). 224p. (Orig.). 1988. pap. 7.95 (ISBN 0-7153-9246-8, Pub. by David & Charles Pub England). Sterling.

Zulu War: A Pictorial History. Michael Barthorp. (Illus.). 192p. 1984. pap. 12.95 (ISBN 0-7137-1469-7, Pub. by Blandford Pr England). Sterling.

Zulu War Journal of Henry Harford, C.B. Ed. by Daphne Child. LC 79-28593. (Illus.). 88p. 1980. 16.50 (ISBN 0-208-01858-1, Archon). Shoe String.

Zulu War, 1879: The Terrible Night at Rorke's Drift. James W. Bancroft. (Illus.). 168p. 1988. 40.00 (ISBN 0-87052-571-9). Hippocrene Bks.

Zululand. M. Reardon. Date not set. 32.00 (ISBN 0-87556-729-0). Saifer.

Zulus. John Mack. LC 80-50901. (Surviving Peoples Ser.). 64p. (gr. 6 up). PLB 13.96 (ISBN 0-382-06360-0). Silver.

Zulus & the British Frontiers. Thomas J. Lucas. LC 73-78579. 1969. Repr. of 1879 ed. 35.00x (ISBN 0-8371-1413-6, LUZ&). Greenwood.

Zulus of Southern Africa. Harriet Ngubane. (Original People Ser.). (Illus.). 48p. (gr. 4-8). 1987. PLB 75.96 6 bk. set (ISBN 0-317-60592-5); PLB 12.66 (ISBN 0-86625-261-4). Rourke Corp.

Zum Mineralstoffhaushalt Einiger Chenopodiaceae bei Hohen Boruns Salzangeboten: Freilandstudiens in den Suedwestlichen U. S. A. und Kulturversuche mit Atriplex Halimus L. und Hortensis L. U. Letschert. (Dissertationes Botanica Ser.: Vol. 96). (Illus.). 244p. (Ger.). 1986. pap. 55.00x (ISBN 3-443-64008-7). Lubrecht & Cramer.

Zum Mongolischen Tanjur. Friedrich Weller. 35p. 1949. 24.00x (ISBN 0-317-68614-3, Pub. by Han-Shan Tang Ltd). State Mutual Bk.

Zum Problem der Begabung und Intelligenz. Hans Werder. (Psychologische Praxis Ser.: Vol. 55). vi, 194p. 1980. pap. 18.75 (ISBN 3-8055-1123-X). S Karger.

Zum Problem des Pollenfluges in den Hochalpen. Maren Jochimsen. (Dissertationes Botanicae Ser.). (Illus.). 252p. (Ger.). 1986. pap. 60.00x (ISBN 3-443-64003-6). Lubrecht & Cramer.

Zum Rollenspieleinsatz in der Grundschule. Gesine Spiess. (European University Studies: No. 11, Vol. 137). 338p. (Ger.). 1982. 37.90 (ISBN 3-8204-5831-X). P Lang Pubs.

Zum Standort der Europaischen Literatur: Funktion, Soziale Bezuge und Weltbild im Mittelater. Joseph Szoverffy. (Medieval Classics: Texts & Studies: Vol. 22). viii, 72p. 1986. pap. 10.00 (ISBN 90-04-08425-8, Pub. by E J Brill). Heinman.

Zumarraga & His Family: Letters to Vizcaya 1536-1548. Ed. by Richard E. Greenleaf. Tr. by Neal Kaveny. (Documentary Ser.). 1979. pap. 25.00 (ISBN 0-88382-013-7). AAFH.

Zumarraga & the Mexican Inquisition: 1536-1543. Richard E. Greenleaf. (Monograph Ser.). (Illus.). 1962. 20.00 (ISBN 0-88382-053-6). AAFH.

Zumpin, More Poems for Two Children. John M. Shaw. 1969. 5.00 (ISBN 0-9607778-9-X). Friends Fla St.

Zumwalt's Fort: An Archaeological Study of Frontier Process in Missouri. Gregory A. Waselkov & Robert T. Bray. (Missouri Archaeologist Ser.: Vol. 40). (Illus.). 129p. (Orig.). 1979. pap. 5.00 (ISBN 0-943414-57-1). MO Arch Soc.

Zuni. Ruth L. Bunzel. pap. 5.00 (ISBN 0-685-71705-4). J J Augustin.

Zuni Atlas. T. J. Ferguson. LC 85-40474. (Civilization of the American Indian Ser.: Vol. 172). (Illus.). 154p. 1985. 24.95 (ISBN 0-8061-1945-4). U of Okla Pr.

Zuni Breadstuff. Frank H. Cushing. LC 74-7948. Repr. of 1920 ed. 48.50 (ISBN 0-404-11835-6). AMS Pr.

Zuni Contemporary Pottery. Marian Rodee & Jim Ostler. LC 87-655. (Illus.). 92p. 1987. pap. 9.95 (ISBN 0-317-60740-5). Max Mus.

Zuni Daily Life. John M. Roberts. Bd. with Zuni Kin Terms. David M. Schneider & John M. Roberts. 145p. LC 67-2866. (Monographs Ser.). 174p. 1965. pap. 12.00x (ISBN 0-87536-810-7). HRAFP.

Zuni Fetishes. Frank H. Cushing. LC 66-23329. (Illus.). 43p. 1966. pap. 3.00 (ISBN 0-916122-03-4). KC Pubns.

Zuni Fetishism. Ruth Kirk. (Illus.). 72p. 1988. pap. 4.75 (ISBN 0-936755-06-7). Avanyu Pub.

Zuni Folk Tales. Frank H. Cushing. LC 74-7949. Repr. of 1901 ed. 35.50 (ISBN 0-404-11836-4). AMS Pr.

Zuni Folk Tales. Frank H. Cushing. 1977. lib. bdg. 59.95 (ISBN 0-8490-2858-2). Gordon Pr.

Zuni Folk Tales. Frank H. Cushing. LC 85-28960. 474p. 1986. pap. 12.95 (ISBN 0-8165-0986-7). U of Ariz Pr.

Zuni Indians: Their Mythology, Esoteric Fraternities, & Ceremonies. Matilda C. Stevenson. LC 6-35065. (U. S. Bureau of American Ethnology, 23rd Annual Report 1901-02). Repr. of 1904 ed. 75.00 (ISBN 0-384-58130-7). Johnson Repr.

Zuni Indians: Their Mythology, Esoteric Fraternities & Ceremonies. 2nd ed. Matilda C. Stevenson. LC 74-124509. (Beautiful Rio Grande Classics Ser.). (Illus.). 784p. 1985. Repr. of 1904 ed. lib. bdg. 45.00 (ISBN 0-87380-068-0). Rio Grande.

Zuni Katcinas. Ruth L. Bunzel. LC 72-13917. (Beautiful Rio Grande Classics Ser.). (Illus.). 358p. 1984. lib. bdg. 30.00 (ISBN 0-87380-099-0). Rio Grande.

Zuni Kin & Clan. Alfred L. Kroeber. LC 76-43765. (AMNH. Anthropological Papers: Vol. 18, Pt. 2). 1984. Repr. of 1917 ed. 32.50 (ISBN 0-404-15618-5). AMS Pr.

Zuni Kin Terms see Zuni Daily Life.

Zuni Law: A Field of Values, with an Appendix. W. Smith & J. Roberts. Incl. Practical Zuni Orthography. Stanley Newman. (HU PMP). 1954. 32.00 (ISBN 0-527-01312-9). Kraus Repr.

Zuni Mythology, 2 Vols. Ruth Benedict. LC 75-82366. (Columbia Univ. Contributions to Anthropology Ser.: No. 21). 1969. Repr. of 1935 ed. Set. 70.00 (ISBN 0-404-50571-6); 35.00 ea. AMS Pr.

Zuni Pottery. Marian Rudee & James Ostler. (Illus.). 92p. 1987. pap. 9.95 (ISBN 0-88740-100-7, 100-7). Schiffer.

Zuni: Selected Writings of Frank Hamilton Cushing. Frank H. Cushing. Ed. by Jesse Green. LC 78-14295. (Illus.). xiv, 440p. 1979. 31.50x (ISBN 0-8032-2100-2); pap. 9.95 (ISBN 0-8032-7007-0, BB 779, Bison). U of Nebr Pr.

Zuni Texts. Ruth L. Bunzel. LC 73-3551. (American Ethnological Society. Publications: No. 15). Repr. of 1933 ed. 34.50 (ISBN 0-404-58165-X). AMS Pr.

Zuniga: An Album of His Sculpture. Carlos F. Echeverria. Commentary by Zuniga. (Illus.). 99.50 (ISBN 0-686-30118-8). Landmark NY.

Zur Archaologie Der Pei-Chi-(550-577) Und Sui-Zeit. Kate Finsterbusch. 147p. 1976. pap. 259.00x (ISBN 0-317-69283-6, Pub. by Han-Shan Tang Ltd). State Mutual Bk.

Zur Biologie des Phytopathogenen Pilzes: Gerlachia nivalis (Erreger des Schneeschimmels) Molekularbiologische Untersuchungen an verschiedenen Feldisolaten. Gabriele Leipoldt. (Bibliotheca Mycologica Ser.: Vol. 109). (Illus.). 164p. (Ger.). 1987. pap. text ed. write for info. (ISBN 3-443-59010-1). Lubrecht & Cramer.

Zur Biologie und Systematik der Flechtengattungen Heppia und Peltula im suedlichen Afrika. B. Budel. (Bibliotheca Lichenologica Ser.: Vol. 23). (Illus.). 150p. (Ger.). 1987. 60.00x (ISBN 3-443-58002-5). Lubrecht & Cramer.

Zur Chemotaxonomie Mariner Rhodophyceen am Beispiel einer Leucin-Decarboxylase. B. Aufermann. (Bibliotheca Phycologica Ser.: No. 43). (Illus.). 1978. pap. text ed. 24.00x (ISBN 3-7682-1206-8). Lubrecht & Cramer.

Zur Chronologie Mittelhellenistischer Muenzserien 220-160 vor Chr. Christof Boehringer. (Antike Muenzen und Geschnittene Steine Ser.: Vol. 5). (Illus.). 240p. 1972. 71.20 (ISBN 3-11-001763-6). De Gruyter.

Zur Deutschen Literatur und Philosophie Ausgewahlte Aufsatze. Hermann Boschenstein. Ed. by Rodney Symington. (Kanadische Studien zur Deutschen Sprache und Literatur: Vol. 35). 318p. 1986. text ed. 34.00 (ISBN 0-8204-0383-0). P Lang Pubs.

Zur Dialektik von Exposition und Darstellung: Ansatze zu einer Kritik der Arbeiten Martin Heideggers, Theodor W. Adornos & Jacques Derrida. Wilke Sabine. (Stanford German Studies: Vol. 24). 234p. 1988. text ed. 32.50 (ISBN 0-8204-0766-6). P Lang Pubs.

Zur Diskussion. 3rd ed. Dieter Sevin & Ingrid Sevin. 329p. 1987. pap. text ed. 22.95 scp (ISBN 0-06-045924-7, HarpC). Har-Row.

Zur Entstehung des Kapitalismus in Venedig. Reinhard Heynen. Ed. by L. Brentano. LC 70-171411. (Research & Source Works Ser: No. 822). 1971. Repr. of 1905 ed. lib. bdg. 21.00 (ISBN 0-8337-1688-3). B Franklin.

Zur Entstehungsgeschichte von Goethes Torquato Tasso. H. Rueff. pap. 9.00 (ISBN 0-384-52485-0). Johnson Repr.

Zur Entwicklung der Perfektumschreibung im Deutschen. A. J. Zieglschmid. (LD). pap. 16.00 (ISBN 0-527-00752-8). Kraus Repr.

Zur Fletchtenflora der Inneralpinen Trockentaeler unter Besonderer Beruecksichtinhung des Vinschgaus. A. Buschardt. (Bibliotheca Lichenologica 10). 1979. lib. bdg. 48.00x (ISBN 3-7682-1226-2). Lubrecht & Cramer.

Zur Genese des Selbstbewusstseins: Eine Studie ueber den Beitrag des phaenomenologischen Denkens zur Frage der Entwicklung des Selbstbewusstseins. Ursula Rohr-Dietschi. LC 72-81567. (Phaenomenologisch-psychologische Forschungen, Vol. 14). 197p. 1975. 31.60x (ISBN 3-11-004048-4). De Gruyter.

Zur Genesis des Modernen Kapitalismus. Jacob Strieder. LC 68-6086. (Ger). 1967. Repr. of 1935 ed. 23.50 (ISBN 0-8337-3436-9). B Franklin.

Zur Geographie des Mittelenglischen Wortschatzes. Rolf Kaiser. (Ger.). 36.00 (ISBN 0-384-28490-6); pap. 31.00. Johnson Repr.

Zur Geschichte der Gymnischen Agone an Griechischen Festen. Theophil Klee. 136p. 1980. 12.50 (ISBN 0-89005-336-7). Ares.

Zur Geschichte der Lateinischen Facetiensammlunge des XV. & XVI. Jahrhunderts. Konrad Vollert. (Ger). 13.00 (ISBN 0-384-64870-3); pap. 11.00 (ISBN 0-685-02161-0). Johnson Repr.

Zur Geschichte der Nationalen Protektorate der Kardinale. Josef Wodka. 14.00 (ISBN 0-384-68955-8). Johnson Repr.

Zur Gesellschaft & Religion der Nueer. J. P. Crazzolara. 1953. 46.00 (ISBN 0-384-10150-X). Johnson Repr.

Zur Grundlegung Christlicher Ethik Theologische Konzeptionen der Gegenwart im Lichte des Analogie-Problems. Kotaro Okayama. (Theologische Bibliothek Toepelmann: Vol. 30). 1977. 24.40x (ISBN 3-11-005812-X). De Gruyter.

Zur Heliandmetrik: Das Verhaeltnis Von Rhythmus und Satzgewicht Im Altsaechsischen. Ingeborg Hinderschiedt. (German Language & Literature Monographs: No. 8). vi, 143p. 1979. 22.00x (ISBN 90-272-4001-9). Benjamins North Am.

Zur Lehre vo Inhalt und Gegenstand der Vorstellungen: Eine Psycologische Untersuchung. Kasimir Twardowski. (Philosophia Resources Library). 144p. 1983. Repr. of 1894 ed. 40.00 (ISBN 3-88405-017-6). Philosophia Pr.

Zur Lehre vom Allgemeinen Bankvertrag. Hans-Ulrich Fuchs. (European University Studies: No. 2, Vol. 294). xxi, 212p. (Ger.). 1982. 27.90 (ISBN 3-8204-7120-0). P Lang Pubs.

Zur Literargeschichte der Staats und Sozialwissenschaften. Gustav F. Von Schmoller. 1967. Repr. of 1888 ed. 25.50 (ISBN 0-8337-3155-6). B Franklin.

Zur Logik Empirischer Theorien. Ed. & tr. by Wolfgang Balzer. 331p. 1983. 31.20 (ISBN 3-11-008236-5); pap. 16.80 (ISBN 3-11-009711-7). De Gruyter.

Zur Niederdeutschen Dietrichsage: Untersuchungen. Waldemar Haupt. 36.00 (ISBN 0-384-21795-8); pap. 31.00. Johnson Repr.

Zur Oekologie der Mykorrhiza Pilze. R. Agerer. (Bibliotheca Mycologica Ser.: vol. 97). (Illus.). 160p. 1985. pap. text ed. 35.00x (ISBN 3-7682-1423-0). Lubrecht & Cramer.

Zur Oekologie der Porlinge, II: Entwicklungsmorphologie der Fruchtkoerper und ihre Beeinflussung durch Klimatische und Andere Faktoren. Ingo Nuss. (Bibliotheca Mycologica: Vol. 105). (Illus.). 456p. (Ger.). 1986. pap. text ed. 99.00x (ISBN 3-443-59006-3). Lubrecht & Cramer.

Zur Okologie der Andinen Paramoregion. H. Sturm. (Biogeographica: No. 14). 1978. lib. bdg. 24.00 (ISBN 90-6193-215-7, Pub. by Junk Pubs Netherlands). Kluwer Academic.

Zur Permanenten "Ueberinvestition" in Sozialistischen Wirtschaftssystemen. Viktor Heese. (European University Studies: No. 5, Vol. 390). 338p. (Ger.). 1982. 38.40 (ISBN 3-8204-7241-X). P Lang Pubs.

Zur Phaenologie des aequatorialen Regenwaldes im Ost-Zaire (Kivu) nebst Planzenliste und Klimadaten. F. Dieterlen. (Dissertations Botanica: No. 47). (Illus.). 1979. pap. 17.50x (ISBN 3-7682-1215-7). Lubrecht & Cramer.

Zur Phanomenologie der Tauschungen. Herbert Leyendelker. LC 78-66735. (Phenomenology Ser.). 189p. 1980. lib. bdg. 26.00 (ISBN 0-8240-9563-4). Garland Pub.

Zur Phanomenologie des Inneren Zeitbewusstseins: (1893-1917) Husserl. (Husserliana Ser: No. 10). 1966. lib. bdg. 53.00 (ISBN 90-247-0227-5, Pub. by Martinus Nijhoff Netherlands). Kluwer Academic.

Zur Psychologie der Aufgabenschwierigkeit. Marion Kloep. (European University Studies: No. 11, Vol. 139). vi, 355p. (Ger.). 1982. 21.05 (ISBN 3-8204-5833-6). P Lang Pubs.

Zur Sprache und Literatur der Mandaer: Mit Beitraegen von Kurt Rudolph & Eric Segelberg. Rudolf Macuch. 1976. 76.00x (ISBN 3-11-004838-8). De Gruyter.

Zur Syntax von Einbettungsstrukturen im Klassischen Chinesisch. Robert H. Gassmann. (SAS-S Ser.: Vol. 6). 227p. (Ger.). 1982. 25.00 (ISBN 3-261-05002-0). P Lang Pubs.

Zur Textkonstitution Afro-Amerikanischer Initiationsliterature, Vol. 1. Heinz C. Lueffe. (Studien zur Englischen und Amerikanischen Literatur). 194p. (Ger.). 1982. 23.15 (ISBN 3-8204-5956-1). P Lang Pubs.

Zur Theorie der Vergleichenden Literaturwissenschaft. Ed. by Horst Ruediger et al. 87p. 1971. 6.70x (ISBN 3-11-003622-3). De Gruyter.

Zur Tonitat Nordchinesischer Mundarten. Franz Giet. Repr. of 1950 ed. 46.00 (ISBN 0-384-18465-0). Johnson Repr.

Zur Wesenslehre des Psychischen Lebens und Erlebens. (Phaenomenologica Ser: No. 27). 1968. 16.00 (ISBN 90-247-0260-7, Pub. Bu Martinus Nijhoff Netherlands). Kluwer Academic.

Zur Wirkung des Schleppereinsatzes in der Weltlandwirtschaft und der Schlepperindustrie im Laufe der Wirtschaftlichen Entwicklung. Manfred Sievers. (European University Studies: No. 5, Vol. 432). 200p. (Ger.). 1983. 24.20 (ISBN 3-8204-7711-X). P Lang Pubs.